COLLINS
DIZIONARIO
INGLESE▸ITALIANO
ITALIANO▸INGLESE

HarperCollins*Publishers*

COLLINS
ENGLISH▸ITALIAN
ITALIAN▸ENGLISH
DICTIONARY

HarperCollins*Publishers*

First published in this edition 1995

HarperCollins Publishers
P.O. Box, Glasgow G4 ONB, Great Britain
ISBN 0 00 470293-X

10 East 53rd Street, New York, NY 10022
ISBN 0-06-275517-X

First HarperCollins edition published 1995

Library of Congress Cataloguing-in-Publication Data

HarperCollins Italian-English, English-Italian dictionary /
   [contributors, Gabriella Bacchelli ... et al.].
      p.   cm.
   ISBN 0-06-275517-X :
      1. Italian language—Dictionaries—English. 2. English language—
Dictionaries—Italian.   I. Bacchelli, Gabriella.
PC1640.H325 1995
453' .21—dc20   94-42350
                                                     CIP

95 96 97 98 99   HCM 10 9 8 7 6 5 4 3 2 1

Corpus Acknowledgements
We would like to thank those authors and publishers who kindly gave
permission for copyright material to be used in the Bank of English. We
would also like to thank Times Newspapers Ltd and the BBC World Service
for providing valuable data.

A catalogue record for this book is available from the British Library

Typeset by Tradespools Ltd, Somerset, Great Britain
Printed in Great Britain by HarperCollins Manufacturing, Glasgow

general editors/a cura di
Michela Clari   Catherine E. Love

editors/redazione
Gabriella Bacchelli   Daphne Day
Loredana Riu   Mirella Alessio
Francesca Logi

with/con
Katherine Snell   Timothy Shaw   David Katan
Martin de Sa'Pinto   Judy Moss

project leader/caporedattore
Donald Watt

coordinating editor/coordinazione di redazione
Janice McNeillie

editorial staff/segreteria di redazione
Carmela Celino
Sandra Harper   Gail Norfolk
Anne Convery   Angela Jack   Anne-Marie Banks

computing/elaborazione automatica dei dati
André Gautier

with/con la collaborazione di
Carol Peters and Eugenio Picchi
Istituto di Linguistica Computazionale CNR Pisa

Our thanks also go to Prof. John M. Dodds of the Scuola Superiore per Interpreti e Traduttori of the University of Trieste

Si ringrazia il Prof. John M. Dodds della Scuola Superiore per Interpreti e Traduttori dell'Università degli Studi di Trieste

BASED ON COLLINS CONCISE ITALIAN DICTIONARY

general editor/a cura di
Catherine E. Love

coordinating editors/redazione
Michela Clari   R.M. Kochanowska   Roberta Martignon

general editor/a cura di
Michela Clari · Catherine E. Love

editors/redazione
Gabriella MacPhell · Daphne Day
Loredana Riu · Mirella Abriani
Francesca Logi

with/con
Katherine Snoh · Timothy Shaw · David Karas
Marie de Sa' Pinto · Judy Moss

project leader/caporedattore
Donald Watt

coordinating editor/coordinazione di redazione
Janice McNeillie

editorial staff/segreteria di redazione
Carol ie Celino
Sandra Harper · Gail Norfolk
Anne Convery · Angela Jack · Anne-Marie Banks

computing elaborazione informatica dei dati
Anne Gautier

with/con il collaborazione di
Carol Peters and Eugenio Picchi
Istituto di Linguistica Computazionale CNR Pisa

Our thanks also due to Prof. John M. Dodds of the
Scuola Superiore per Interpreti e Traduttori of
the University of Trieste
Siamo grati al Prof. John M. Dodds della Scuola
Superiore per Interpreti e Traduttori dell'Uni-
versità degli Studi di Trieste

BASED ON COLLINS CONCISE ITALIAN DICTIONARY

general editor/a cura di
Catherine E. Love

compiled by/a cura del lessione
Michela Clari · B.M. Kabanowska · Rhoda Maddigout

HOW TO USE THE DICTIONARY

The dictionary contains a great deal of information, in a condensed form. Some words are complicated – they have a large number of senses, or they have several different meanings.

Another problem is that one word may function as a verb, a noun, an adjective, an adverb etc. To avoid time-wasting and frustration, you should develop a strategy for approaching entries, and to do this you need to be aware of the pointers that are provided to guide you to the particular information you want.

These pointers are numbers, letters and typefaces: it is important to understand how they are used and to pay attention to them.

Numbers

These are used in two ways:

Numbers in boxes

When a word is not just a noun, or just a verb, (ie if it can be more than one part of speech), a number is given to each function it can perform. Thus, if you want to translate "he cleaned his teeth", and you need to look up **clean**, decide first of all what function the word has. Having decided that it is a verb with an object (ie a transitive verb) you can then run your eye down the numbered items in the entry until you get to VT (verb, transitive) – which is what you want. It is the fourth grammatical category, so preceded by the number [4].

clean [kliːn] [1] ADJ (*comp* **-er**, *superl* **-est**) (*gen*) pulito(-a); (*sheet of paper*) nuovo(-a); (*smooth, clear: outline, movement, break*) netto(-a); (*fair: fight, game*) leale, corretto(-a); **to wipe sth clean** pulire qc; **to make a clean sweep** fare piazza pulita; **the doctor gave me a clean bill of health** il medico ha garantito che godo di ottima salute; **to make a clean breast of sth** togliersi qc dalla coscienza; **a clean record** (*Police*) una fedina penale pulita; **to have a clean driving licence**, (*Am*) **to have a clean record** non aver mai preso contravvenzioni.

[2] ADV: **he clean forgot** si è completamente dimenticato; **he got clean away** se l'è svignata senza lasciare tracce; **the ball went clean through the window** la palla prese in pieno la finestra; **to come clean** (*fam: admit guilt*) confessare; (: *tell unpleasant truth*) dire veramente come stanno le cose; **I'm clean out of cigarettes** non ho neanche mezza sigaretta.

[3] N pulita, ripulitura.

[4] VT (*gen*) pulire; (*blackboard*) cancellare; (*shoes*) lucidare; **to clean one's teeth** (*Brit*) lavarsi i denti

Looking first at the numbered categories means you waste no time looking at irrelevant sections.

Numbers at the end of a word

When words are spelt the same, but are actually separate entities – eg **fine** in English (which could mean good, or a financial penalty) or **piano** in Italian (flat, a plan or a musical instrument) they are given as separate entries, with the headword followed by a number. If what you find at the first entry is obviously not what you want, go on to look at the following one(s).

Letters in shaded boxes

These are used to distinguish different senses of a word. Paying attention to them can save a lot of time when you are dealing with a word such as **get** that has all sorts of meanings: if, for example, you wanted to translate "I was starting to get tired" and were looking up **get**, you should first decide on the word's grammatical function (it's a verb without an object ie an intransitive verb) – that will take you to [2] VI. Next you need to decide what meaning the word has in your particular context. **a** (*go*) is the first possibility, but this doesn't fit – so you look next at **b** (*become, be*) – which takes you to the right translation.

When you look up an Italian word and find a number of different translations, scan the lettered sections for the one that fits your context.

Material appearing in italics

As we have just seen, material appearing in italics helps you pinpoint the sense of a word. It may be another way of saying the same thing, or an adjective, noun etc that often occurs with the word when it has a particular sense – eg when **get** means **receive**, letters and presents are typical examples of things you can get, so these appear in italics. When you are trying to track down the right translation, make sure you take note of these italic pointers, which are distinguishable at a glance from the bold roman type used for the source language, and normal roman used for translations.

Where to look for combinations of words

When faced by such combinations as **back wheel**, **back page** and **back number** you may be uncertain where to look. Is **back** an adjective, in which case you should look in the appropriate section under **back** or is it the first element in a compound word, which you should look for in its alphabetical place? (Compound words are marked by this symbol ♦.)

The important things to remember are:

1. You should look for such items under their first element – eg under **back**, not under **wheel**, **page**, or **number**.

2. You should bear in mind that the combination may appear as a separate entry, as does **back number**, or under the first element. If you don't find it at the first option, try the second.

Italian combinations of two words or more such as **pesce rosso** and **acqua di rose** always appear under their first element.

Where to find verb + adverb/preposition combinations

"She came into the room" and "she came into a large fortune" include the same verb + preposition, (**come + into**), but the second combination is a phrasal verb, with a special sense (**inherit**), and is treated in a separate entry, which is marked by this symbol ▶.

To find how to translate the first example you should look under **come**. If you are in doubt in such cases, the quickest thing is to look first for a phrasal verb entry. If that doesn't provide the information you need, look then at the entry for the verb on its own.

Where to look for phrases

Idioms and set phrases generally appear under their first important element, thus "filare dritto" appears under **filare** and "to burn one's boats" appears under **burn**. However, in the case of verbs that have a great many meanings, such as **prendere**, **fare**, **mettere**, or **set**, **do** and **get**, phrases appear under another key word in the expression – "to set a trap", for example comes under **trap**. This is to make things easier for the user, who will find the phrase quicker in the short entry **trap** than in the long and complicated entry **set**.

Alphabetical order

Entries appear in strict alphabetial order: **CV** comes between **cut-up** and **C & W**. Note that "&" does not affect the order. **Pet name** comes between **petition** and **Petrarch**, not immediately after **pet**. Only phrasal verbs break this rule: thus **give away** comes before **give-and-take** because all phrasal combinations are listed directly after the main verb.

At the top of each page of the dictionary you will find the first and last words treated on it – this is to help you find the entry you want as quickly as possible.

The design of the dictionary

The previous section is intended to help solve problems that may be encountered in using the dictionary. However, to exploit fully the information it offers, users will find it worthwhile to familiarize themselves in more detail with the way the dictionary is organized and how entries are structured.

How words are listed

Derived words such as **fortunately**, **delivery**, **deliverance**, and **installazione**, **utilità**, **utilmente** appear as headwords. (In some dictionaries such words are treated under the word they derive from.)

Compound words in English may consist of one word (eg **housewife**), two or more words (eg **news agency**, **state of the art**) or two or more words joined by a hyphen (eg **do-it-yourself**). All types can appear as headwords. Compounds consisting of two or more words are preceded by the symbol ♦.

In Italian, compounds proper consist of a single word, eg **accendisigari**, **capostazione**, and these appear as headwords. Combinations of two words or more, such as **strisce pedonali** or **acqua minerale** are to be found under their first element (ie **striscia** or **acqua**). They are preceded by this symbol ▶.

Phrasal verbs, for example **make up** or **put up with**, appear in bold type, under the main verb. They are marked by the symbol ▶.

Proper nouns, for example **Francia**, **Venezia**, **Alpi**, **Edinburgh**, **Thames**, **Adonis**, **Mosè**. Important place names and well-known Biblical and mythological names are included in the dictionary.

Acronyms and abbreviations: for example **I.V.A.**, **UNESCO**, **ad.** These appear in alphabetical order in the main body of the dictionary, not in a separate supplement.

The organization of entries

Syllable points: On the English-Italian side of the dictionary syllable points appear in headwords, to show how they may be hyphenated: **pae·di·at·ric**.

Phonetic transcription: Headwords are followed by their pronunciation in square brackets, in the International Phonetic Alphabet. On page xx   you will find a full list of the symbols used in this system.

Parts of speech

If the headword functions only as a noun, or verb etc the relevant part of speech appears in small capitals after the phonetics.

headword	pronunciation	part of speech category	translations

rissa ['rissa] SF fight, brawl

If it has more than one function, each part of speech is numbered and these numbers appear at the start of the line.

col·lar ['kɒlə^r] ⓵ N (*of shirt, blouse, coat*) colletto, collo;   **by the collar** afferrare qn per il bavero.
 (*for dog*) collare *m*; (*Tech*) anello, fascetta; **to grab sb**   ⓶ VT (*fam: person, object*) beccare.

Meaning categories

When a headword has more than one sense, the entry is divided into sections marked by a letter in a shaded box:
a b c
    Each meaning category can include a number of related senses. At the end of each category there may be phrases, in bold type, with translations in roman.

al·to·geth·er [ˌɔ:ltə'gɛðə^r] ADV **a** (*in all*) in tutto, comples-   è stato piuttosto spiacevole; **how much is that alto-**
sivamente; (*on the whole*) tutto considerato, tutto   **gether?** quant'è in tutto?
sommato, nel complesso, nell'insieme; **altogether it**   **b** (*entirely*) del tutto, completamente; **I'm not alto-**
was rather unpleasant tutto sommato *or* in complesso   **gether sure** non sono del tutto *or* proprio sicuro.

Indicators

The section above on ***Material appearing in italics*** gives a partial explanation of the pointers, or indicators, which are provided to help the user choose the most suitable translation for a particular context.

    Clear and effective indicators are of great importance since many words have several meanings or shades of meaning, while others, which seem to have only one meaning in one language, call for different translations, depending on context or the other words (collocates) used with them. The full range of indicators used in the dictionary can be listed as follows:

▷ substitutes for the headword
▷ contextual indicators
▷ subject field indicators
▷ style and register labels
▷ chronological labels
▷ literal/figurative labels
▷ regional labels

These labels relate to the source language and are in English on the English-Italian side of the dictionary, and in Italian on the other side. They appear in italics, within round brackets, and immediately precede the translation.

Substitutes for the headword: Synonyms or partial definitions of the headword often appear as indicators.

dis·trac·tion [dɪs'trækʃən] N **a** (*interruption*) distrazione *f*;
(*entertainment*) distrazione, diversivo **b** (*distress,*
madness): **to drive sb to distraction** far impazzire qn.

Contextual indicators: These provide typical contexts in which the user may find or wish to use the headword. They are of various types: some of the commonest are listed below:

▷ typical noun subjects of an intransitive verb: **fluc·tu·ate** ... (*cost*) ... (*person*)
▷ typical noun objects of a transitive verb: **ful·fil** ... (*duty*) ... (*promise*)
▷ typical noun complements of an adjective: **full-length** ... (*portrait*) ... (*dress*)
▷ typical noun complements of another noun: **full·ness** ... (*of detail*)
▷ typical adjective complements of an adverb: **in·tense·ly** ... (*moved*)
▷ typical verb complements of an adverb: **un·fair·ly** ... (*treat, criticize*)

Subject field indicators

Subject field indicators (eg *Med, Pol, Bot*) are used to distinguish meanings of the headword according to specific fields of application. They begin with capital letters and are often abbreviated. For the full list, and explanations of what the abbreviations stand for, see page xxii.

at·tack [ə'tæk] ⬚1 N **a** (*Mil, fig*) attacco; (*on individual*) aggressione *f*; **surprise attack** attacco di sorpresa; **attack on sb's life** attentato alla vita di qn; **to be under attack (from)** essere attaccato(-a) (da); **to launch an**

attack (on) (*Mil, Sport*: *fig*) sferrare un attacco (a) **b** (*Med*) attacco, accesso. ⬚2 VT (*Mil, Med, fig*) attaccare; (*person*) aggredire, assalire; (*tackle*: *job, problem*) affrontare.

They are also used when the meaning in the source language is clear, but possibly ambiguous in the target language. This is true in the case of **oratorio**, which in English has only a musical sense, while in Italian it can also be an oratory.

Style and register labels

These have been given to words that are not neutral language. On both sides of the dictionary you will find the labels (*frm*) = formal, (*fam*) = informal or colloquial and (*iro*) = ironic. Literary use is marked as (*liter*) on the English side and (*letter*) on the Italian. Humorous use is labelled (*hum*) or (*scherz*) on the Italian side. (*euph*) or (*euf*) indicates euphemistic use and (*pej*) or (*pegg*) pejorative language. The labels (*offensive*) or (*offensivo*) speak for themselves.

In all languages there are colloquial and vulgar expressions which are widely used, but which non-native speakers need to approach with caution. Such words are marked (*fam!*).

Chronological labels: When a word or expression would generally be regarded as old fashioned, we have the label (*old*), or (*ant*) on the Italian side.

Literal/figurative labels: (*lit*) and (*fig*) indicate literal and figurative senses.

Regional labels: These include (*Scot*) = Scottish, (*Ir*) = Irish and (*dial*) = dialect.

American English: (*Am*) is used to mark American spellings and pronunciations, and words and expressions that are more current in the US than in Britain – though they may be familiar to many speakers of British English. (*Brit*) labels words and phrases used mainly in Britain.

The use of punctuation in indicators

You will often find two or more words in italics (indicators) preceding a translation. In the entry for **passenger** (see below), the fact that there are commas between *boat, plane* and *car* shows that the translation **passeggero** works in relation to all three words. Similarly, when used as an adjective with *aircraft* or *liner* the word can be translated **di linea** or **passeggeri**.

pas·sen·ger ['pæsɪndʒəʳ] ⬚1 N (*in boat, plane, car*) passeggero(-a); (*on train*) viaggiatore(-trice), passeggero(-a).

⬚2 ADJ (*aircraft, liner*) di linea, passeggeri *inv*; (*train*) viaggiatori *inv*.

If, however, there is a colon between words in italics, as in the entry **refresh** (see below), a different reading is called for. In the case of refresh, if the subject of the verb is a drink, the appropriate translation is **rinfrescare**, while if the subject is sleep, or a bath, it is **ristorare**. *Subj* is not repeated a second time – the colon which appears at the beginning of the second set of brackets stands for it. Whenever a colon is the first element inside brackets it refers back to a word that has already appeared as an indicator.

re·fresh [rɪ'frɛʃ] VT (*subj*: *drink*) rinfrescare; (: *food, sleep, bath*) ristorare …

Use of "tu" and "lei"

Partly as a consequence of the dictionary's emphasis on colloquial language, and also to avoid confusion between the 2nd and 3rd person use of **lei**, the familiar form **tu** (you) occurs in examples somewhat more often that the formal **lei**. Numerous examples of the 2nd person use of **lei** are to be found in the LANGUAGE IN USE supplement.

Translations

It will often be found that a particular indicator is followed by two or more translations, separated by commas. These translations are interchangeable, each of them serving equally well to translate the sense in question. When a different sense calls for a different translation a further indicator appears.

Sometimes part of a translation is optional, and therefore appears in brackets, thus at **neo** (mole) the translation for the figurative use is "(slight) flaw".

neo ['nɛo] SM (gen) mole; (sul viso) beauty spot; (fig: imperfezione) (slight) flaw; (: di persona) slight defect.

In the case of some derived words, such as **absurdity** and **absurdly**, the user is referred to the entry for the root word (see adj). At **absurd** two translations are given, to match the different senses indicated. In the entries for **absurdity** and **absurdly** there is the same sense division, and appropriate translations, but the indicators are not repeated. The user chooses the appropriate translation by looking back at **absurd**. Here the translations are not interchangeable and they are therefore separated by semi-colons rather than commas.

ab·surd [əb'sɜːd] ADJ assurdo(-a); (appearance, hat) ridicolo(-a).

ab·surd·ity [əb'sɜːdɪtɪ] N **a** (no pl: see adj) assurdità, assurdo; ridicolaggine f **b** (thing etc) assurdità f inv; the

absurdities of life le assurdità della vita.

ab·surd·ly [əb'sɜːdlɪ] ADV (see adj) assurdamente; in modo ridicolo.

Explanatory glosses and cultural equivalents

It is not always possible to give a direct translation of words or phrases, given that there are British concepts and institutions that have no equivalents in Italian culture, and vice versa. Sometimes it is necessary to offer instead an explanatory gloss, which appears in italics – see for example **angel dust** or **ginnasio**. In other cases an approximate equivalent is given – see for example **ACI** or **Speaker**. Such equivalents are preceded by the symbol ≈.

Grammatical information given in the dictionary

Gender: Both sides of the dictionary give the feminine endings for Italian adjectives, and where appropriate the feminine form of nouns.

Plurals: Irregular plurals and those presenting any sort of difficulty appear after the headword on both sides of the dictionary.

Irregular forms: Irregular plurals of nouns, such as **mice** and **mila** (thousands) also appear alphabetically in the word list, with a cross reference to the singular. Similarly, irregular verb forms such as **went**, **gone**, **abbia** and **corso** are listed, and cross-referred to their infinitives.

The fact that an Italian verb is irregular is noted immediately after the part of speech number. English irregular verbs are followed immediately by their past tenses and past participles.

Auxiliary verbs: Information is given on whether Italian intransitive verbs take the auxiliary **essere** or **avere**. No such information is given for transitive verbs, since they always form compound tenses with **avere**.

Italian reflexive and pronominal verbs

Reflexive verbs such as **radersi** and **vestirsi** are distinguished from intransitive pronominal verbs such as **sbagliarsi** and **ricordarsi**. Reflexives are to be found under the part of speech headed VR (verbo riflessivo), pronominal verbs under VIP (verbo intransitivo pronominale). Some verbs can be used both ways: **ammazzarsi**, for example, used reflexively, means "to kill oneself", while used as a pronominal intransitive it means "to die"

ammazzare [ammat'tsare] **1** VT (uccidere) to kill; (fig: affaticare) to exhaust, wear out; **ammazzare il tempo** to kill time.

2 ammazzarsi VR (uso reciproco) to kill e.o.; (suicidarsi)

to kill o.s, commit suicide; **ammazzarsi di lavoro** to kill o.s. with work, work o.s. to death.

3 ammazzarsi VIP (rimanere ucciso) to die, be killed.

As can be seen from the above entry, reciprocal reflexives are treated under the VR heading: "ammazzarsi" can also translate as "to kill each other".

Indirect reflexives, such as "lavarsi le mani", given that they take a direct object, are to be found as examples under the transitive verb category.

Special entries

Words that are the nuts and bolts of the language, such as auxiliary and modal verbs, and the main prepositions and conjunctions, are given specially clear and detailed treatment, with a large number of examples. To help users scan the list of examples, a significant word accompanying the item is italicized – home and school under **at**, for example. These italicized words appear in the list in alphabetical order. Special entries have a grey background and thus stand out from the rest of the text.

COME USARE IL DIZIONARIO

Quando si consulta un dizionario bilingue lo si fa per capire il significato di una parola o di un'espressione che non si conoscono, oppure per scoprire come si dice qualcosa nella lingua straniera. È importante che ciò che l'utente trova consultando il dizionario sia strutturato in modo chiaro e gli consenta di accedere alle informazioni di cui ha bisogno nel minor tempo possibile, aiutandolo sia nella comprensione che nella produzione di lingua straniera. Nel compilare questo dizionario abbiamo cercato di presentare le informazioni nel modo più semplice e chiaro possibile, evidenziandole con numeri, lettere o caratteri tipografici diversi (neretto, corsivo, tondo ecc.). Al fine di sviluppare una strategia di consultazione che faciliti la ricerca delle informazioni è necessario capire quali siano e come siano state usate queste convenzioni.

Numeri

I numeri sono stati usati in due modi: racchiusi in un quadratino o in posizione esponenziale rispetto al lemma.

Numeri racchiusi in un quadratino

I numeri racchiusi in un quadratino precedono le diverse parti del discorso, come aggettivo, verbo transitivo, pronome ecc., quando una parola ha più di una funzione grammaticale. Se per esempio volete tradurre la parola **fondere** in frasi come "il metallo fonde a temperature elevate", stabilirete innanzitutto quale sia la funzione grammaticale del verbo nel vostro contesto. In questo caso il verbo **fondere** è usato intransitivamente e quindi la traduzione va cercata nella categoria [2] VI.

> **fondere** ['fondere] VB IRREG [1] VT **a** (*gen*) to melt; (*metallo*) to fuse, melt; (*fig: colori*) to blend, merge; (: *enti, classi, Inform*) to merge
> **b** (*statua, campana*) to cast.
> [2] VI (*aus* **avere**) to melt; **mi fonde il cervello** (*fig*) I can't think straight any more, my brain has seized up.
> [3] **fondersi** VR (*uso reciproco: unirsi: correnti, enti*) to merge, unite.
> [4] **fondersi** VIP (*sciogliersi*) to melt.

Numeri in posizione esponenziale

I numeri in posizione esponenziale rispetto al lemma sono usati per distinguere gli omografi, ossia parole che presentano la stessa grafia e spesso la stessa pronuncia ma che sono completamente diverse dal punto di vista del significato come in italiano **diritto**[1] (retto) e **diritto**[2] (prorogativa) e inglese **fine**[1] (bello) e **fine**[2] (multa).

Lettere in campo grigio

Le lettere introducono le diverse categorie di significato di una parola. Possono farvi risparmiare molto tempo, specialmente se avete a che fare con una parola come **attaccare**, che ha svariati significati. Se per esempio volete tradurre la frase "mi ha attaccato l'influenza" e cercate **attaccare**, dovete innanzitutto stabilire la funzione grammaticale della parola; dato che si tratta di un verbo transitivo, andrete a [1] VT. Dovete quindi stabilire che significato ha la parola nel vostro contesto. **a** (*far aderire*) è la prima possibilità, ma non si adatta al contesto; nemmeno **b** (*Mil, Sport, fig*) e **c** (*cominciare: discorso, lite*) coprono il significato del verbo nella vostra frase; passate quindi a **d** (*contagiare, anche fig*), che vi darà la traduzione appropriata.

> **attaccare** [attak'kare] [1] VT **a** (*far aderire*) to attach; (*incollare: manifesto*) to stick up; (: *francobollo*) to stick (on); (*cucire*) to sew (on); (*legare*) to tie (up); (*appendere: quadro*) to hang (up)
> **b** (*Mil, Sport, fig*) to attack
> **c** (*cominciare: discorso, lite*) to start, begin; **attaccare discorso con qn** to start a conversation with sb
> **d** (*contagiare, anche fig*) to affect; **ha attaccato il morbillo a sua cugina** he's given his cousin the measles.
> [2] VI (*aus* **avere**) **a** (*incollare*) to stick
> **b** (*aver successo*): **la nuova moda non attacca** the new fashion isn't catching on; **con me non attacca!** it doesn't work with me!, that won't work with me! ...

Quando cercate una parola inglese e trovate una serie di traduzioni diverse, scorrete velocemente le sezioni precedute dalle lettere per trovare quella che si adatta al vostro contesto.

Indicazioni in corsivo

Come abbiamo appena visto, il materiale in corsivo aiuta ad individuare i significati di una parola. Può essere un sinonimo, un aggettivo o un sostantivo che compaiono spesso assieme alla parola, quando essa ha un certo significato. Per esempio, quando **dare** significa **organizzare**, tra le cose che si possono organizzare ci sono una festa, un banchetto, oppure uno spettacolo: ebbene queste parole compaiono in corsivo. Quando si cerca di individuare la traduzione giusta va tenuto conto di queste indicazioni in corsivo, che si differenziano sia dal materiale nella lingua di partenza, in grassetto, che dalle traduzioni, in tondo.

Dove cercare i lemmi

I lemmi vanno ricercati al loro posto nell'ordine alfabetico. Si noti che sono stati trascurati nell'ordinamento alfabetico i trattini all'interno di parola ed il carettere &, usato in parole come **B&B**, **R&R** ecc.

L'ordine sarà pertanto come appare nel seguente esempio: **cut up**, **CV**, **C&W**.

Dove cercare i lemmi composti formati da più parole

In inglese sono stati considerati come lemmi a sé stanti anche alcuni composti formati da due o più parole aventi grafia separata, come **fast food** e **state of the art**, che sono elencati quindi in ordine alfabetico. Dovendo tradurre espressioni come **back wheel**, **back page** e **back number**, potreste essere incerti su dove cercarle e chiedervi se **back** vada considerato un aggettivo, nel qual caso bisognerebbe guardare nella sezione appropriata sotto **back**, oppure sia il primo elemento di una parola composta, che andrebbe cercata al suo posto nell'ordine alfabetico.

Sarà utile ricordare che se la combinazione non compare come lemma a sé stante, bisognerà cercarla sotto il primo elemento che la compone – cioè sotto **back** e non sotto **wheel**, **page** o **number**.

Dove cercare i verbi + avverbio/preposizione

Nelle frasi "she came into the room" e "she came into a large fortune" compaiono lo stesso verbo e la stessa preposizione ("come" e "into") ma solo nel secondo caso si tratta di un phrasal verb, cioè di una combinazione fissa con un significato particolare (**ereditare**), che compare come voce a sé stante, contrassegnata da una losanga. Per tradurre il secondo esempio, invece, bisogna guardare sotto il verbo **come**. In caso di dubbio, verificate innanzitutto se si tratta di un phrasal verb. Se la vostra ricerca non vi fornirà le indicazioni di cui avete bisogno, cercate sotto il verbo in questione. I phrasal verbs inglesi come **get off**, **get on**, **get out** ecc., seguono immediatamente, in ordine alfabetico, il verbo da cui dipendono.

Dove cercare le locuzioni

In genere locuzioni ed espressioni idiomatiche si trovano sotto il primo elemento fondamentale della locuzione. Per esempio "filare diritto" si trova sotto **filare** e "to burn one's boats", sotto **burn**. Tuttavia, nel caso di verbi con molti significati, come **fare**, **mettere**, **prendere** o **set**, **do** e **get**, le locuzioni compaiono generalmente sotto un'altra parola che compone l'espressione. Per esempio "to set a trap" è stata posta sotto **trap**, e non sotto **set**, allo scopo di facilitare l'utente, che troverà molto più rapidamente l'espressione nella breve voce **trap**, piuttosto che nella voce **set**, molto più complessa.

Lemmario e struttura delle voci

L'intento di questa parte è di fornire un elenco completo degli elementi che costituiscono il dizionario e delle informazioni che è possibile ricavarne. Una conoscenza approfondita di questi elementi insieme ad una corretta strategia di consultazione consentiranno all'utente di sfruttare quest'opera al meglio.

Il lemmario

I lemmi sono elencati naturalmente in ordine alfabetico e sono stampati in neretto. Nel margine superiore di ogni pagina compare una testatina che riporta il primo e l'ultimo lemma di quella pagina: ciò renderà più rapida la consultazione del dizionario.

Derivati: Per maggiore facilità di consultazione i lemmi che derivano dalla radice di un'altra parola, come ad esempio **fortunately**, **delivery**, **deliverance** e in italiano **installazione**, **utilità**, e **utilmente** compaiono tutti come lemmi principali.

Nomi composti: **nailbrush**, **word processor**, **accendisigari** e **capostazione** sono nomi composti e sono inseriti in ordine alfabetico. Nella parte inglese-italiano, anche molti nomi composti formati da due o più parole (es. **news agency**), o ancora da due o più parole unite da un trattino (es. **do-it-yourself**), compaiono come lemmi principali in ordine alfabetico.

♦ è il simbolo che precede i composti inglesi formati da più parole nella parte inglese-italiano.

Nella parte italiano-inglese, invece, solo i lemmi formati da un'unica parola compaiono come lemmi a sé stanti. Le collocazioni fisse costituite da due vocaboli come **pesce rosso** o **acqua di rose** andranno ricercate sotto il primo degli elementi che costituiscono l'espressione (cioè, rispettivamente, sotto **pesce** e sotto **acqua**).

► è il simbolo che precede le collocazioni fisse con funzione nominale nella parte italiano-inglese.

Phrasal verbs: I phrasal verbs inglesi come **make up** o **put up with** compaiono in forma di sottolemmi in ordine alfabetico, in neretto, dopo il lemma principale.

► è il simbolo che precede i phrasal verbs inglesi nella parte inglese-italiano.

Nomi propri: Nel lemmario sono stati inclusi i principali nomi geografici come **Francia**, **Venezia**, **Alpi**, **Edinburgh**, **Thames** e i nomi dei personaggi biblici e mitologici più importanti, come **Mosè** e **Adonais**.

Sigle e abbreviazioni: Per maggior facilità di consultazione le abbreviazioni e le sigle come **I.V.A.**, **UNESCO** ed **ab.** sono state inserite in ordine alfabetico nel testo, e non in tavole a parte.

La struttura delle voci

Suddivisione in sillabe: Date le difficoltà che può presentare la suddivisione in sillabe delle parole in lingua inglese, nella parte inglese-italiano è stata data indicazione, mediante l'introduzione di puntini, di come vadano suddivise le parole: **pae·di·at·ric**.

Trascrizione fonetica: Tutti i lemmi sono seguiti dalla pronuncia, che si trova tra parentesi quadre. Come in tutti i principali dizionari moderni è stato adottato il sistema noto come "alfabeto fonetico internazionale". Troverete qui di seguito a pag.xx un elenco completo dei caratteri utilizzati in questo sistema.

Nella parte inglese-italiano, per la pronuncia di nomi composti formati da due o più parole non unite dal trattino, si dovrà cercare la trascrizione di ciascuna di queste parole alla rispettiva posizione alfabetica.

Categorie grammaticali

Quando la parola ha una sola funzione grammaticale, la categoria grammaticale di appartenenza compare in maiuscoletto subito dopo la trascrizione fonetica.

lemma	pronuncia	categoria grammaticale	traduzioni
	rissa ['rissa] SF	fight, brawl	

Se la parola ha più di una funzione, ogni categoria grammaticale viene contrassegnata da un numero: [1] [2] [3] introducono la categoria grammaticale; compaiono sempre a capo riga.

> **col·lar** ['kɒlə⁰'] [1] N (of shirt, blouse, coat) colletto, collo; (for dog) collare m; (Tech) anello, fascetta; **to grab sb by the collar** afferrare qn per il bavero.
> [2] VT (fam: person, object) beccare.

Categorie di significato

Le voci più complesse sono suddivise in categorie di significato, ognuna preceduta da una lettera minuscola in neretto in campo grigio chiaro: **a b c** introducono le categorie di significato; nelle voci più lunghe e complesse compaiono a capo riga.

Ciascuna categoria di significato può riportare una o più accezioni seguite da una serie di frasi illustrative in grassetto, seguite a loro volta dalle relative traduzioni in tondo.

> **al·to·geth·er** [ˌɔːltə'gɛðə⁰'] ADV **a** (in all) in tutto, complessivamente; (on the whole) tutto considerato, tutto sommato, nel complesso, nell'insieme; **altogether it was rather unpleasant** tutto sommato or in complesso è stato piuttosto spiacevole; **how much is that altogether?** quant'è in tutto?
> **b** (entirely) del tutto, completamente; **I'm not altogether sure** non sono del tutto or proprio sicuro.

Indicatori

Si chiamano indicatori le informazioni in corsivo tra parentesi che introducono le diverse accezioni di un lemma. Come già accennato al paragrafo *Indicazioni in corsivo*, la funzione degli indicatori è di guidare l'utente nella scelta della traduzione più adatta ad un contesto specifico. A volte gli indicatori appaiono dopo una traduzione per segnalarne il registro o l'ambito.

Moltissime parole hanno più di un significato o diverse sfumature di significato; altre, pur mantenendo un significato relativamente unitario, si traducono in modo diverso a seconda del contesto in cui si trovano o dei loro collocatori, cioè delle parole assieme alle quali vengono usate. Nel dizionario sono stati usati diversi tipi di indicatori:

▷ indicatori che sostituiscono il lemma
▷ indicatori contestuali
▷ indicatori di campo semantico
▷ indicatori di stile o registro
▷ indicatori cronologici
▷ indicatori dell'uso figurato o letterale
▷ indicatori di uso regionale

Questi indicatori si referiscono alla lingua di partenza, e sono in italiano nella parte italiano-inglese e in inglese nella parte inglese-italiano; compaiono tra parentesi tonde e in corsivo subito prima della traduzione.

Indicatori che sostituiscono il lemma

Uno degli indicatori che troverete più di frequente consiste in un sinonimo o in una parziale definizione del lemma.

> **malizia** [ma'littsja] SF (*cattiveria*) malice, spite; (*furbizia*)
> mischievousness; (*astuzia*) clever trick; **con malizia**
> maliciously, spitefully; mischievously; cleverly.

Indicatori contestuali

Gli indicatori contestuali forniscono i contesti tipici in cui è possibile trovare il lemma. Possono essere di vario tipo: qui di seguito troverete gli indicatori contestuali più comuni.

▷ soggetto tipico di un verbo intransitivo: **fiorire** ... (*albero*) ... (*fig:sentimento*) ... (:*commercio, arte*) ...

▷ oggetto tipico di un verbo transitivo: **dissotterare** ... (*cadavere*) ... (*tesori, rovine*) ... (*fig:sentimento*) ...

▷ sostantivo che viene usato spesso in combinazione con l'aggettivo in questione: **collerico** ... (*persona*) ... (*parole*) ... (*temperamento*) ...

▷ sostantivo che viene usato spesso in combinazione con il sostantivo in questione: **groviglio** ... (*di fili, lana*) ... (*fig:di idee*) ...

▷ verbo che viene usato spesso in combinazione con l'avverbio in questione: **involontariamente** ... (*sorridere*) ... (*spingere*) ...

Indicatori di campo semantico

Gli indicatori di campo semantico (cioè *Med, Pol, Bot* ecc.) vengono usati per differenziare i vari significati del lemma secondo una specifica suddivisione in campi semantici. Questi indicatori, sempre tra parentesi e in corsivo, hanno l'iniziale maiuscola e sono spesso abbreviazioni (per l'elenco completo delle abbreviazioni vedere pag. xxii.

> **nervatura** [nerva'tura] SF (*Anat*) nerves *pl*, nervous
> system; (*Bot*) veining; (*Archit, Tecn*) rib.

Questi indicatori vengono anche usati quando il significato di una parola è chiaro nella lingua d'origine, ma possono insorgere ambiguità nella lingua di arrivo. Per esempio il sostantivo **oratorio** in inglese ha solo il significato musicale, mentre in italiano può indicare anche il luogo dove si prega.

Indicatori di stile e di registro

Gli indicatori di stile o registro sono stati usati per tutti i vocaboli che esulano dal linguaggio standard. Alcuni indicatori compaiono sia nella sezione inglese-italiano che in quella italiano-inglese; si tratta di (*frm*) per l'uso formale, (*fam*) per l'uso informale o colloquiale e (*iro*) per l'uso ironico. L'uso letterario è contrassegnato da (*liter*) nella parte inglese e da (*letter*) in quella italiana. Per quello scherzoso sono stati usati rispettivamente (*hum*) e (*scherz*), mentre (*euph*) ed (*euf*) sottolineano le espressioni eufemistiche e (*pej*) e (*pegg*) l'uso peggiorativo.

Vi sono espressioni informali e volgari in tutte le lingue che, pur essendo largamente diffuse, sono da usare con estrema cautela. Per aiutare il lettore ad identificare questi lemmi è stato inserito l'indicatore (*fam*) seguito da un punto esclamativo.

Da evitare anche quelle parole contrassegnate dagli indicatori (*offensive*) ed (*offensivo*)

Indicatori cronologici: Quando l'uso di una parola o di un'espressione è da considerarsi ormai sorpassato, compare l'indicatore (*old*) in inglese e (*ant*) in italiano.

Indicatori di uso letterale e figurato: Sono (*lit*) per l'uso letterale e (*fig*) per quello figurato.

Indicatori di uso regionale: Tra gli indicatori di uso regionale ricordiamo (*Scot*) per le parole o espressioni scozzesi, (*Ir*) per quelle irlandesi e (*dial*) per segnalare che una parola o espressione è di uso prevalentemente dialettale.

....

Americanismi: L'abbreviazione (*Am*) segnala le grafie e le pronunce americane e le parole ed espressioni che, sebbene generalmente conosciute sia dai parlanti americani che da quelli inglesi, sono usate con maggiore frequenza negli Stati Uniti. Quando una parola o un'espressione viene usata prevalentemente nell'inglese britannico, ciò è segnalato dall'indicatore (*Brit*).

Uso della punteggiatura negli indicatori

Prima di una traduzione troverete spesso due o più indicatori, in corsivo e nella stessa parentesi. Nella voce **marino**, riportata qui sotto, il fatto che *aria* e *fondali* siano separati tra loro da una virgola indica che la traduzione **sea** funziona sia dovendo tradurre "aria marina" che "fondale marino". Analogamente **seaside** può essere usata sia per tradurre "città marina" che "colonia marina".

> **marino, a** [ma'rino] AGG (*aria, fondali*) sea *attr*; (*fauna*) marine; (*città, colonia*) seaside *attr*.

Se invece gli indicatori sono separati da un punto doppio, come ad esempio in **refresh**, riportato qui sotto, ciò indica che essi si riferiscono insieme alla traduzione. Se il soggetto di **refresh** è **drink**, la traduzione adatta è **rinfrescare**, mentre se il soggetto del verbo è **sleep** oppure **bath**, la traduzione è **ristorare**. L'indicatore "subj" non viene ripetuto la seconda volta, ma viene richiamato dal punto doppio. Ogni volta che il punto doppio compare come primo elemento dell'indicatore ci si dovrà riferire all'indicatore precedente.

> **re·fresh** [rɪ'frɛʃ] VT (*subj: drink*) rinfrescare; (: *food, sleep, bath*) ristorare ...

Traduzioni

Tutte le traduzioni nel dizionario corrispondono il più possibile ai loro equivalenti nella lingua di partenza sia a livello semantico che a livello sintattico e di registro linguistico. Particolare attenzione è stata fatta alle costruzioni tipiche e ai loro equivalenti nella lingua di arrivo.

Spesso, dopo uno stesso indicatore, compaiono più traduzioni separate tra di loro da una virgola, come ad esempio in **ammonimento**.

> **ammonimento** [ammoni'mento] SM (*rimprovero*) reprimand, admonishment; (*lezione*) lesson, warning.

Va sottolineato che queste traduzioni sono sempre intercambiabili con riferimento al significato riportato dall'indicatore. Ogni volta che un contesto diverso ha richiesto una traduzione diversa, questo è stato segnalato inserendo un nuovo indicatore.

A volte parte della traduzione è opzionale, e quindi compare tra parentesi. Per esempio alla voce **neo** la traduzione per il senso figurato è (slight flaw).

> **neo** ['nɛo] SM (*gen*) mole; (*sul viso*) beauty spot; (*fig: imperfezione*) (slight) flaw; (: *di persona*) slight defect.

In alcuni casi all'interno della voce compare un rimando ad un'altra parola (per es. *vedi vt*) seguito da più traduzioni separate tra di loro da punti e virgola. Ciò succede, ad esempio, con alcuni derivati, come per esempio **appianamento**, che deriva da **appianare**. In questo caso le varianti di traduzione vanno riferite al sistema di indicatori della parola indicata dal rimando. Nel caso specifico, **levelling** va riferito a (*terreno*), **settlement** a (*fig: contesa, lite*) e **ironing out** a (*difficoltà*). L'introduzione dei punti e virgola invece delle virgole segnala quindi che le traduzioni non sono intercambiabili.

> **appianamento** [appjana'mento] SM (*vedi vt*) levelling; settlement; ironing out.

> **appianare** [appja'nare] [1] VT (*terreno*) to flatten, level; (*fig: contesa, lite*) to settle; (*difficoltà*) to iron out, smooth away.
> [2] **appianarsi** VIP (*divergenze*) to be ironed out.

Glosse esplicative ed equivalenti culturali

Non sempre è possibile fornire una traduzione assolutamente corrispondente al lemma di partenza, basti pensare al caso di istituzioni o di concetti che esistono nella cultura italiana ma non in quella inglese e viceversa, e quindi non hanno un traducente efficace nell'altra lingua. A volte è stato quindi necessario usare una glossa esplicativa, che compare in corsivo (vedere ad esempio le voci **angel dust** o **ginnasio**), altre volte è stato dato un equivalente approssimativo nell'altra lingua (vedere ad esempio **A.C.I** o **Speaker** (*Brit Parliament*). ≈ è il simbolo che precede gli equivalenti culturali.

Informazioni grammaticali presenti nel dizionario

Genere: Sia dal lato italiano-inglese che da quello inglese-italiano del dizionario sono state indicate le desinenze femminili degli aggettivi italiani e dei sostantivi riferiti a persona.

Plurali: I plurali irregolari e quelli la cui formazione può creare delle difficoltà compaiono dopo il lemma in entrambe le lingue.

Verbi irregolari: È stata data indicazione dell'irregolarità dei verbi italiani subito dopo la categoria grammaticale; per i verbi irregolari inglesi, invece, sono state introdotte, subito dopo il lemma, le forme irregolari del passato e del participio passato.

Verbi ausiliari: È stato indicato l'ausiliare **essere** o **avere** per tutti i verbi intransitivi italiani, mentre per i verbi transitivi non compare alcuna indicazione in quanto i tempi composti di tali verbi vengono formati sempre con l'ausiliare **avere**.

Verbi riflessivi e verbi pronominali italiani

I verbi riflessivi come **radersi** e **vestirsi** sono stati distinti dai verbi intransitivi pronominali come **sbagliarsi** e **ricordarsi** mediante la distinzione tra le categorie grammaticali vʀ (verbo riflessivo) e vɪᴘ (verbo intransitivo pronominale). Le forme riflessive reciproche (come "si amano") e le forme riflessive indirette (come "lavarsi le mani") sono state differenziate all'interno della voce principale. Le forme riflessive reciproche compaiono nella categoria grammaticale vʀ, precedute dall'indicatore (*uso reciproco*), mentre quelle riflessive indirette sono state inserite come esempi sotto la categoria del transitivo, dato che si tratta di forme pronominali transitive in quanto prendono l'oggetto diretto. In inglese non esiste la forma pronominale del verbo, e quando un verbo viene usato in connessione con **oneself** traduce in generale una forma riflessiva vera e propria. Si confrontino, ad esempio, le traduzioni di **ammazzarsi** nel senso di **suicidarsi** e quindi realmente riflessivo (**to kill o.s.**) e **ammazzarsi** nel senso di **trovare la morte** (**to die, be killed**).

Phrasal verbs inglesi

Verbi come **get off** e **make up**, i cosiddetti phrasal verbs, costituiscono spesso un problema per gli studenti stranieri che incontrano difficoltà nel distinguerli dalle normali costruzioni con avverbi o preposizioni (ad esempio "he came into the room", normale costruzione con preposizione, e il phrasal verb "he came into money"). I phrasal verbs sono suddivisi in base alla funzione grammaticale degli elementi che li costituiscono. Alla voce **get off**, come vediamo qui di seguito, le qualifiche grammaticali sono vᴛ + ᴀᴅᴠ, vɪ + ᴘʀᴇᴘ e vɪ + ᴀᴅᴠ. Alcuni phrasal verbs sono composti da tre elementi, come per esempio **get off with**.

▶**get off** ⬚1 vᴛ + ᴀᴅᴠ **a** (*remove: clothes, stain*) levare, togliere
  b (*send off*) spedire;
  she got the baby off to sleep ha fatto addormentare il bambino
  c (*save from punishment*) far assolvere, tirar fuori
  d (*have as holiday: day, time*) prendersi;
  we got 2 days off abbiamo avuto 2 giorni liberi.
  ⬚2 vɪ + ᴘʀᴇᴘ (*bus, train, plane, bike*) scendere da; (*fam: escape: chore, lessons*) evitare, sfuggire a.
  ⬚3 vɪ + ᴀᴅᴠ **a** (*from bus, train, plane, bike*) scendere;
  to tell sb where to get off (*fam*) dire a qn di andare a farsi benedire
  to get off to a good start (*fig*) cominciare bene
  b (*depart: person*) andare via
  c (*escape injury, punishment*) cavarsela;
  he got off with a fine se l'è cavata con una multa
  d (*from work*) staccare
▶**get off with** vɪ + ᴀᴅᴠ + ᴘʀᴇᴘ (*fam: start relationship with*) mettersi con

Forme irregolari

Per rendere più agevole la ricerca del lettore straniero abbiamo inserito in ordine alfabetico le principali forme irregolari di verbi e sostantivi con un rimando alla voce in cui il lemma viene trattato per esteso. Ad esempio participi passati quali l'inglese **gone** o l'italiano **corso**, e plurali irregolari quali **mice** e **mila** compaiono in ordine alfabetico con un rimando alla voce principale.

Voci complesse

Le parole che in qualche modo costituiscono i cardini della lingua, come i verbi ausiliari, le principali preposizioni, congiunzioni e così via, sono state privilegiate da una strutturazione più chiara e articolata e da una fraseologia molto ricca, e appaiono stampate su fondo grigio. Per semplificare ulteriormente la consultazione, una o più parole significative all'interno delle locuzioni illustrative appaiono in neretto corsivo. Le frasi sono disposte in ordine alfabetico in base ai termini evidenziati al loro interno.

PHONETIC TRANSCRIPTION

CONSONANTS

NB: The pairing of some vowel sounds only indicates approximate equivalence.

CONSONANTI

NB: La messa in equivalenza di certi suoni indica solo una rassomiglianza approssimativa.

_pupp_y	p	_p_adre
_ba_by	b	_bam_bino
_t_en_t_	t	_tut_to
_dadd_y	d	_dad_o
_c_or_k_ _k_iss _ch_ord	k	_c_ane _ch_e
_g_a_g_ _gu_ess	g	_g_ola _gh_iro
_s_o ri_ce_ ki_ss_	s	_s_ano
cou_s_in bu_zz_	z	_s_vago e_s_ame
_sh_eep _s_ugar	ʃ	_sc_ena
plea_s_ure bei_ge_	ʒ	
_ch_ur_ch_	tʃ	pe_c_e lan_ci_are
_j_ud_ge_ _g_eneral	dʒ	_gi_ro _gi_oco
_f_arm ra_ffl_e	f	a_f_a _f_aro
_v_ery re_v_	v	_v_ero bra_v_o
_th_in ma_ths_	θ	
_th_at o_th_er	ð	
litt_le_ ba_ll_	l	_l_etto a_l_a
	ʎ	_gl_i
_r_at b_r_at	r	_r_ete a_r_co
_m_u_mm_y co_mb_	m	ra_m_o _m_adre
_n_o ra_n_	n	_n_o fuma_n_te
	ɲ	_gn_omo
si_ng_i_ng_ ba_n_k	ŋ	
_h_at re_h_eat	h	
_y_et	j	bu_i_o p_i_acere
_w_all be_w_ail	w	_u_omo g_u_aio
lo_ch_	x	

TRASCRIZIONE FONETICA

VOWELS

NB: **p**, **b**, **t**, **d**, **k**, **g** are not aspirated in Italian.

VOCALI

NB: **p**, **b**, **t**, **d**, **k**, **g** sono seguiti da un'aspirazione in inglese.

h_ee_l b_ea_d	i: i	v_i_no _i_dea
h_i_t p_i_ty	ɪ	
	e	st_e_lla _ede_ra
s_e_t t_e_nt	ɛ	_e_poca ecc_e_tto
_a_pple b_a_t	æ a	m_a_mm_a a_more
_a_fter c_ar_ c_al_m	ɑ:	
f_u_n c_ou_sin	ʌ	
ov_er a_bove	ə	
_ur_n f_er_n w_or_k	ɜ:	
w_a_sh p_o_t	ɒ ɔ	r_o_sa _o_cchio
b_or_n c_or_k	ɔ:	
	o	p_o_nte ognun_o_
f_u_ll s_oo_t	ʊ u	_u_tile z_u_cca
b_oo_n l_ew_d	u:	

DIPHTHONGS

DITTONGHI

ɪə	b_ee_r t_ie_r
ɛə	t_ea_r f_ai_r th_ere_
eɪ	d_a_te pl_ai_ce d_ay_
aɪ	l_i_fe b_uy_ cry
aʊ	_ow_l f_ou_l n_ow_
əʊ	l_ow_ n_o_
ɔɪ	b_oi_l boy _oi_ly
ʊə	p_oo_r t_ou_r

MISCELLANEOUS

VARIE

ʳ per l'inglese: la 'r' finale viene pronunciata se seguita da una vocale.
ˈ primary or strong stress
ˌ secondary or weak stress

ABBREVIATIONS   ABBREVIAZIONI

abbreviations	*abbr*	abbreviazione
adjective	*adj*	aggettivo
administration	*Admin*	amministrazione
adverb	*adv*	avverbio
aviation, aeronautics	*Aer*	aeronautica, trasporti aerei
adjective	*agg*	aggettivo
agriculture	*Agr*	agricoltura
American	*Am*	americano
administration	*Amm*	amministrazione
anatomy	*Anat*	anatomia
old	*ant*	antico
archaeology	*Archeol*	archeologia
architecture	*Archit*	architettura
article	*art*	articolo
astrology	*Astrol*	astrologia
astronomy	*Astron*	astronomia
attributive	*attr*	attributivo
auxiliary	*aus*	ausiliare
cars and motoring	*Aut*	automobile, automobilismo
auxiliary	*aux*	ausiliare
adverb	*avv*	avverbio
biology	*Bio*	biologia
botany	*Bot*	botanica
British, Great Britain	*Brit*	britannico, Gran Bretagna
chemistry	*Chem, Chim*	chimica
cinema	*Cine*	cinema
commerce	*Comm*	commercio
comparative	*comp*	comparativo
computers	*Comput*	informatica, computers
conditional	*cond*	condizionale
conjunction	*cong*	congiunzione
subjunctive	*congiunt*	congiuntivo
conjunction	*conj*	congiunzione
building trade	*Constr*	edilizia
cooking	*Culin*	culinaria, cucina
before	*dav a*	davanti a
definite	*def*	definito
demonstrative	*dem*	dimostrativo
determining	*det*	determinativo
dialect	*dial*	dialetto
defective	*dif*	difettivo
demonstrative	*dimostr*	dimostrativo
law	*Dir*	diritto
direct	*dir*	diretto
et cetera	*ecc*	eccetera
economics	*Econ*	economia
building trade	*Edil*	edilizia
electricity, electronics	*Elec, Elettr*	elettricità, elettronica
exclamation	*escl*	esclamazione
especially	*esp*	specialmente
et cetera	*etc*	eccetera
euphemistic	*euph, euf*	eufemismo
exclamation	*excl*	esclamazione
feminine	*f*	femminile
informal, colloquial, familiar	*fam*	familiare, colloquiale
vulgar, offensive, taboo	*fam!*	volgare, tabù
railways	*Ferr*	ferrovia
figurative	*fig*	figurato
finance	*Fin*	finanza
physics	*Fis*	fisica
photography	*Fot*	fotografia
formal	*frm*	formale
football	*Ftbl*	calcio
generally, in most senses	*gen*	generale, nella maggior parte dei casi
geography	*Geog*	geografia
geology	*Geol*	geologia
geometry	*Geom*	geometria
grammar	*Gram, Gramm*	grammatica
humorous	*hum*	scherzoso
impersonal	*impers*	impersonale
indefinite	*indef*	indefinito
indefinite	*indet*	indeterminativo
indicative	*indic*	indicativo

indirect	*indir*	indiretto
infinitive	*infin*	infinito
computers	*Inform*	informatica, computers
interrogative	*interrog*	interrogativo
invariable	*inv*	invariabile
Irish	*Ir*	irlandese
ironical	*iro*	ironico
irregular	*irreg*	irregolare
literary	*letter*	letterario
linguistics	*Ling*	linguistica
literary	*lit*	letterario
masculine	*m*	maschile
mathematics	*Math, Mat*	matematica
medicine	*Med*	medicina
meteorology, weather	*Met, Meteor*	meteorologia
either masculine or feminine	*m/f*	maschile o femminile,
depending on sex		secondo il sesso
military	*Mil*	militare
mythology	*Mitol*	mitologia
music	*Mus*	musica
mythlogy	*Myth*	mitologia
noun	*n*	sostantivo
nautical, naval	*Naut*	nautica
negative	*neg*	negativo
no plural	*no pl*	niente plurale
object	*obj, ogg*	oggetto
oneself	*o.s.*	
passive	*pass*	passivo
past historic	*pass rem*	passato remoto
pejorative	*pej, pegg*	peggiorativo
personal	*pers*	personale
photography	*Phot*	fotografia
physics	*Phys*	fisica
plural	*pl*	plurale
poetic, literary	*poet*	poetico, letterario
politics	*Pol*	politica
possessive	*poss*	possessivo
past participle	*pp*	participio passato
predicative	*pred*	predicativo
prefix	*pref*	prefisso
preposition	*prep*	preposizione
present	*pres*	presente
pronoun	*pron*	pronome
present participle	*prp*	participio presente
psychology	*Psych, Psic*	psicologia
past tense	*pt*	passato
	qc	qualcosa
	qn	qualcuno
religion	*Rel*	religione
relative	*rel*	relativo
noun	*s*	sostantivo
somebody	*sb*	
humorous	*scherz*	scherzoso
school	*Scol*	sistema scolastico
Scottish	*Scot*	scozzese
singular	*sg*	singolare
sociology	*Sociol*	sociologia
subject	*sogg*	soggetto
especially	*spec*	specialmente
something	*sth*	
subjunctive	*sub*	congiuntivo
subject	*subj*	soggetto
suffix	*suff*	suffisso
superlative	*superl*	superlativo
technology, technical	*Tech, Tecn*	tecnica, tecnologia
specialist's term	*tech term*	termine da specialista
telecommunications	*Telec*	telecomunicazioni
specialist's term	*termine tecn*	termine da specialista
typography, printing	*Tip*	tipografia
television	*TV*	televisione
typography, printing	*Typ*	tipografia
university	*Univ*	università
usually	*usu*	di solito
verb	*vb*	verbo
intransitive verb	*vi*	verbo intransitivo
intransitive pronominal verb	*vip*	verbo intransitivo pronominale
transitive verb	*vt*	verbo transitivo
zoology	*Zool*	zoologia
registered trademark	®	marchio registrato
introduces a cultural equivalent	≈	introduce un'equivalenza culturale

VERBI INGLESI

present	pt	pp	present	pt	pp
arise	arose	arisen	fall	fell	fallen
awake	awoke	awaked	feed	fed	fed
be (am, is,	was,	been	feel	felt	felt
are; being)	were		fight	fought	fought
bear	bore	born(e)	find	found	found
beat	beat	beaten	flee	fled	fled
become	became	become	fling	flung	flung
begin	began	begun	fly (flies)	flew	flown
behold	beheld	beheld	forbid	forbade	forbidden
bend	bent	bent	forecast	forecast	forecast
beseech	besought	besought	forget	forgot	forgotten
beset	beset	beset	forgive	forgave	forgiven
bet	bet, betted	bet, betted	forsake	forsook	forsaken
bid	bid, bade	bid, bidden	freeze	froze	frozen
bind	bound	bound	get	got	got, (Am)
bite	bit	bitten			gotten
bleed	bled	bled	give	gave	given
blow	blew	blown	go (goes)	went	gone
break	broke	broken	grind	ground	ground
breed	bred	bred	grow	grew	grown
bring	brought	brought	hang	hung,	hung,
build	built	built		hanged	hanged
burn	burnt,	burnt,	have (has;	had	had
	burned	burned	having)		
burst	burst	burst	hear	heard	heard
buy	bought	bought	hide	hid	hidden
can	could	(been able)	hit	hit	hit
cast	cast	cast	hold	held	held
catch	caught	caught	hurt	hurt	hurt
choose	chose	chosen	keep	kept	kept
cling	clung	clung	kneel	knelt,	knelt,
come	came	come		kneeled	kneeled
cost	cost	cost	know	knew	known
creep	crept	crept	lay	laid	laid
cut	cut	cut	lead	led	led
deal	dealt	dealt	lean	leant, leaned	leant, leaned
dig	dug	dug	leap	leapt, leaped	leapt, leaped
do (3rd	did	done	learn	learnt,	learnt,
person: he/				learned	learned
she/it/does)			leave	left	left
draw	drew	drawn	lend	lent	lent
dream	dreamed,	dreamed,	let	let	let
	dreamt	dreamt	lie (lying)	lay	lain
drink	drank	drunk	light	lit, lighted	lit, lighted
drive	drove	driven	lose	lost	lost
dwell	dwelt	dwelt	make	made	made
eat	ate	eaten	may	might	—

present	pt	pp	present	pt	pp
mean	meant	meant	spell	spelt,	spelt,
meet	met	met		spelled	spelled
mistake	mistook	mistaken	spend	spent	spent
mow	mowed	mown,	spill	spilt, spilled	spilt, spilled
		mowed	spin	spun	spun
must	(had to)	(had to)	spit	spat	spat
pay	paid	paid	split	split	split
put	put	put	spoil	spoiled,	spoiled,
quit	quit, quitted	quit, quitted		spoilt	spoilt
read	read	read	spread	spread	spread
rid	rid	rid	spring	sprang	sprung
ride	rode	ridden	stand	stood	stood
ring	rang	rung	steal	stole	stolen
rise	rose	risen	stick	stuck	stuck
run	ran	run	sting	stung	stung
saw	sawed	sawn	stink	stank	stunk
say	said	said	stride	strode	stridden
see	saw	seen	strike	struck	struck,
seek	sought	sought			stricken
sell	sold	sold	strive	strove	striven
send	sent	sent	swear	swore	sworn
set	set	set	sweep	swept	swept
shake	shook	shaken	swell	swelled	swollen,
shall	should	—			swelled
shear	sheared	shorn,	swim	swam	swum
		sheared	swing	swung	swung
shed	shed	shed	take	took	taken
shine	shone	shone	teach	taught	taught
shoot	shot	shot	tear	tore	torn
show	showed	shown	tell	told	told
shrink	shrank	shrunk	think	thought	thought
shut	shut	shut	throw	threw	thrown
sing	sang	sung	thrust	thrust	thrust
sink	sank	sunk	tread	trod	trodden
sit	sat	sat	wake	woke,	woken,
slay	slew	slain		waked	waked
sleep	slept	slept	wear	wore	worn
slide	slid	slid	weave	wove,	woven,
sling	slung	slung		weaved	weaved
slit	slit	slit	wed	wedded,	wedded,
smell	smelt,	smelt,		wed	wed
	smelled	smelled	weep	wept	wept
sow	sowed	sown, sowed	win	won	won
speak	spoke	spoken	wind	wound	wound
speed	sped,	sped,	wring	wrung	wrung
	speeded	speeded	write	wrote	written

ITALIAN VERBS

	Gerund	Past Participle	Present	Imperfect	Past Historic
DORMIRE	dormendo	dormito	dormo	dormivo	dormii
			dormi	dormivi	dormisti
			dorme	dormiva	dormì
			dormiamo	dormivamo	dormimmo
			dormite	dormivate	dormiste
			dormono	dormivano	dormirono
PARLARE	parlando	parlato	parlo	parlavo	parlai
			parli	parlavi	parlasti
			parla	parlava	parlò
			parliamo	parlavamo	parlammo
			parlate	parlavate	parlaste
			parlano	parlavano	parlarono
VENDERE	vendendo	venduto	vendo	vendevo	vendei o vende
			vendi	vendevi	vendesti
			vende	vendeva	vendette
			vendiamo	vendevamo	vendemmo
			vendete	vendevate	vendeste
			vendono	vendevano	vendettero
FINIRE	finendo	finito	finisco	finivo	finii
			finisci	finivi	finisti
			finisce	finiva	finì
			finiamo	finivamo	finimmo
			finite	finivate	finiste
			finiscono	finivano	finirono
AVERE	avendo	avuto	ho	avevo	ebbi
			hai	avevi	avesti
			ha	aveva	ebbe
			abbiamo	avevamo	avemmo
			avete	avevate	aveste
			hanno	avevano	ebbero
ESSERE	essendo	stato	sono	ero	fui
			sei	eri	fosti
			è	era	fu
			siamo	eravamo	fummo
			siete	eravate	foste
			sono	erano	furono

zufolo ['tsufolo] sm (*Mus*) flageolet.
zumare [dzu'mare] vi (*aus* avere), vt (*Cine, Fot*) to zoom in;
zumare qn to zoom in on sb.
zuppa ['tsuppa] sf soup; **se non è zuppa è pan bagnato**
(*fig*) it's six of one and half a dozen of the other ► **zuppa**
inglese (*Culin*) *liqueur-soaked sponge with a filling of*
cream and chocolate.
zuppiera [tsup'pjɛra] sf (soup) tureen.
zuppo, a ['tsuppo] agg: **zuppo (di)** soaked (with),
drenched (with).
Zurigo [dzu'rigo] sf Zurich.

freezing point *o* above zero; **zero in condotta** (*Scol*) bad marks for behaviour (*Brit*); **ridursi a zero** (*fig*) to have nothing left, be at rock-bottom; **capelli tagliati a zero** close-cropped hair; **sparare a zero su qn/qc** (*fig*) to lay into sb/sth; **ricominciare da zero** to go back to square one; **partire da zero** to start from scratch

  b (*Calcio*) nil (*Brit*); (*Tennis*) love; **vincere per tre a zero** to win three-nil.

  2 AGG INV zero *attr*; **l'ora zero** zero hour.

zeta ['dzɛta] SM O F (*pl f inv* **zeta**, *pl f* **zete**, *pl m inv* **zeta**) (*lettera*) zed (*Brit*), zee (*Am*), (the letter) z.

Zeus ['dzɛus] SM Zeus.

zia ['tsia] SF aunt.

zibaldone [dzibal'done] SM (*Letteratura*) author's note-book.

zibellino [dzibel'lino] SM (*animale, pelliccia*) sable.

zibetto [dzi'betto] SM (*animale*) zibet; (*sostanza*) civet.

zibibbo [dzi'bibbo] SM *kind of muscat grape*.

zigano, a [tsi'gano] AGG, SM/F gypsy.

zigolo ['dzigolo] SM (*Zool*) bunting.

zigomo ['dzigomo] SM cheekbone; **zigomi sporgenti** high cheekbones.

zigote [dzi'gote] SM (*Bio*) zygote.

zigrinare [dzigri'nare] VT (*gen*) to knurl; (*pellame*) to grain; (*monete*) to mill.

zig zag [dʒig 'dʒag] SM INV zigzag; **camminare/andare a zig zag** to zigzag.

zigzagare [dzigdza'gare] VI (*aus* **avere**) to zigzag.

Zimbabwe [dzim'babwe] SM: **lo Zimbabwe** Zimbabwe.

zimbello [tsim'bɛllo] SM (*Caccia*) decoy (bird); (*fig*) laughing stock.

zincare [tsin'kare] VT to galvanize, coat with zinc.

zinco ['tsinko] SM zinc.

zingaresco, a, schi, sche [tsinga'resko] AGG gypsy *attr*.

zingaro, a ['tsingaro] AGG, SM/F gypsy.

zio, zii ['tsio] SM uncle; **i miei zii** (*zio e zia*) my uncle and aunt ▸ **zio d'America** (*fig*) rich uncle.

zipolo ['tsipolo] SM (*di botte*) bung.

zircone [dzir'kone] SM zircon.

zitella [tsi'tɛlla] SF (*pegg*) spinster, old maid.

zitellone [tsitel'lone] SM (elderly) bachelor.

zittire [tsit'tire] **1** VT to silence, hush *o* shut up.

  2 VI (*aus* **avere**) to hiss.

zitto, a ['tsitto] AGG quiet, silent; **zitto!** be quiet!, shut up! (*fam*); **stare zitto** to keep quiet, shut up (*fam*); **zitto zitto** (*di nascosto*) on the quiet.

zizzania [dzid'dzanja] SF (*pianta*) darnel; (*fig*) discord; **seminare zizzania** to sow discord.

zoccolo ['tsɔkkolo] SM **a** (*di cavallo*) hoof **b** (*calzatura*) clog **c** (*Archit*) plinth; (*di parete*) skirting (board) (*Brit*), baseboard (*Am*); (*di armadio*) base (support).

zodiacale [dzodia'kale] AGG of the zodiac, zodiac *attr*; **segno zodiacale** sign of the zodiac.

zodiaco [dzo'diako] SM zodiac.

zolfanello [tsolfa'nɛllo] SM (sulphur (*Brit*) *o* sulfur (*Am*)) match.

zolfatara [tsolfa'tara] SF sulphur (*Brit*) *o* sulfur (*Am*) mine.

zolfo ['tsolfo] SM sulphur (*Brit*), sulfur (*Am*).

zolla ['dzolla] SF (*di terra*) clod (of earth).

zolletta [dzol'letta] SF (*di zucchero*) (sugar) lump *o* cube.

zona ['dzɔna] SF (*gen*) area, zone; (*regione*) area, region; (*di città*) district ▸ **zona di depressione** (*Meteor*) trough of low pressure ▸ **zona disco** (*Aut*) ≈ meter zone ▸ **zona erogena** erogenous zone ▸ **zona giorno** (*di casa*) living

area ▸ **zona di guerra** war zone ▸ **zona industriale** industrial estate ▸ **zona notte** (*di casa*) sleeping area ▸ **zona pedonale** pedestrian precinct (*Brit*) *o* mall (*Am*) ▸ **zona verde** (*Aut*) restricted parking zone *o* area; (*Urbanistica*) green area.

zonale [dzo'nale] AGG district *attr*, area *attr*.

zonizzare [dzonid'dzare] VT to zone.

zonizzazione [dzoniddzat'tsjone] SF zoning.

zonzo ['dzondzo]: **a zonzo** AVV: **andare a zonzo** to wander about, stroll about.

zoo ['dzɔo] SM INV zoo.

zoologia [dzoolo'dʒia] SF zoology.

zoologico, a, ci, che [dzoo'lɔdʒiko] AGG zoological; **giardino zoologico** zoological garden(s), zoo.

zoologo, a, gi, ghe [dzo'ɔlogo] SM/F zoologist.

zoom [zu:m] SM INV (*Fot*) zoom (lens).

zoosafari [dzoosa'fari] SM INV safari park.

zootecnia [dzootek'nia] SF zootechnics *sg*.

zootecnico, a, ci, che [dzoo'tɛkniko] AGG zootechnical; **il patrimonio zootecnico di un paese** a country's livestock resources.

zoppia [tsop'pia] SF (*di cavallo*) lameness.

zoppicante [tsoppi'kante] AGG (*persona*) limping; (*fig*) shaky, weak.

zoppicare [tsoppi'kare] VI (*aus* **avere**) (*persona*) to have a limp, walk with a limp, limp; (: *essere zoppo*) to be lame; (*fig*: *mobile*) to be shaky; **zoppica in matematica** (*fig*) he's weak in maths (*Brit*) *o* math (*Am*), math(s) isn't his strong point.

zoppo, a ['tsɔppo] **1** AGG (*persona*) lame; (*mobile*) wobbly, shaky.

  2 SM/F lame person.

zoster ['dzɔster] AGG INV = **herpes zoster**.

zotico, a ['dzɔtiko] SM/F lout, boor.

zuava [dzu'ava] SF: **pantaloni alla zuava** knickerbockers.

zucca ['tsukka] SF (*Bot*) pumpkin; (: *di forma allungata*) marrow (*Brit*), vegetable marrow; (*scherz*) head; **avere sale in zucca** to be sensible, have sense; **non gli entra in zucca** it won't enter his thick skull.

zuccherare [tsukke'rare] VT to sugar, put sugar in, add sugar to.

zuccherato, a [tsukke'rato] AGG sweet, sweetened.

zuccheriera [tsukke'rjɛra] SF sugar bowl.

zuccherificio, ci [tsukkeri'fitʃo] SM sugar refinery.

zuccherino, a [tsukke'rino] **1** AGG sweet, sugary.

  2 SM piece of sugar, lump of sugar.

zucchero ['tsukkero] SM sugar ▸ **zucchero di canna** cane sugar ▸ **zucchero caramellato** caramel ▸ **zucchero filato** candy floss (*Brit*), cotton candy (*Am*) ▸ **zucchero in grani** crushed sugar lumps ▸ **zucchero in polvere** caster sugar ▸ **zucchero semolato** granulated sugar ▸ **zucchero a velo** icing sugar (*Brit*), confectioner's sugar (*Am*).

zuccheroso, a [tsukke'roso] AGG sweet, sugary.

zucchetto [tsuk'ketto] SM skullcap.

zucchina [tsuk'kina] SF, **zucchino** [tsuk'kino] SM courgette (*Brit*), zucchini (*Am*).

zuccone, a [tsuk'kone] **1** AGG dull, dense, slow(-witted).

  2 SM/F dunce, blockhead.

zuccotto [tsuk'kɔtto] SM (*Culin*) *dome-shaped dessert made of sponge, cream, chocolate and candied fruit*.

zuffa ['tsuffa] SF fight, brawl.

zufolare [tsufo'lare] VT, VI (*aus* **avere**) to whistle.

zufolio,lii [tsufo'lio] SM whistling.

ITALIAN VERBS

Future	Present Conditional	Present Subjunctive	Imperfect Subjunctive	Imperative
dormirò	dormirei	dorma	dormissi	dormi!
dormirai	dormiresti	dorma	dormissi	dorma!
dormirà	dormirebbe	dorma	dormisse	dormite!
dormiremo	dormiremmo	dormiamo	dormissimo	dormano!
dormirete	dormireste	dormiate	dormiste	
dormiranno	dormirebbero	dormano	dormissero	
parlerò	parlerei	parli	parlassi	parla!
parlerai	parleresti	parli	parlassi	parli!
parlerà	parlerebbe	parli	parlasse	parlate!
parleremo	parleremmo	parliamo	parlassimo	parlino!
parlerete	parlereste	parliate	parlaste	
parleranno	parlerebbero	parlino	parlassero	
venderò	venderei	venda	vendessi	vendi!
venderai	venderesti	venda	vendessi	venda!
venderà	venderebbe	venda	vendesse	vendete!
venderemo	venderemmo	vendiamo	vendessimo	vendano!
venderete	vendereste	vendiate	vendeste	
venderanno	venderebbero	vendano	vendessero	
finirò	finirei	finisca	finissi	finisci!
finirai	finiresti	finisca	finissi	finisca!
finirà	finirebbe	finisca	finisse	finite!
finiremo	finiremmo	finiamo	finissimo	finiscano!
finirete	finireste	finiate	finiste	
finiranno	finirebbero	finiscano	finissero	
avrò	avrei	abbia	avessi	abbi!
avrai	avresti	abbia	avessi	abbia!
avrà	avrebbe	abbia	avesse	abbiate!
avremo	avremmo	abbiamo	avessimo	abbiano!
avrete	avreste	abbiate	aveste	
avranno	avrebbero	abbiano	avessero	
sarò	sarei	sia	fossi,	sii!
sarai	saresti	sia	fossi	sia!
sarà	sarebbe	sia	fosse	siate!
saremo	saremmo	siamo	fossimo	siano!
sarete	sareste	siate	foste	
saranno	sarebbero	siano	fossero	

ITALIAN VERBS

1 Gerund 2 Past Participle 3 Present 4 Imperfect
5 Past Historic 6 Future 7 Conditional
8 Present Subjunctive 9 Imperfect Subjunctive
10 Imperative

accadere *like* cadere
accedere *like* concedere
accendere 2 acceso 5 accesi, accendesti
accingersi *like* cingere
accludere *like* alludere
accogliere *like* cogliere
accondiscendere *like* scendere
accorgersi *like* scorgere
accorrere *like* correre
accrescere *like* crescere
addirsi *like* dire
addurre *like* ridurre
affiggere 2 affisso 5 affissi, affiggesti
affliggere 2 afflitto 5 afflissi, affliggesti
aggiungere *like* giungere
alludere 2 alluso 5 allusi, alludesti
ammettere *like* mettere
andare 3 vado, vai, va, andiamo, andate, vanno
    6 andrò *etc* 8 vada 10 va'!, vada!, andate!, vadano!
annettere 2 annesso 5 annettei, annettesti
anteporre *like* porre
apparire 2 apparso 3 appaio, appari, appare,
appaiono 5 apparvi, apparisti, apparve, apparvero
    8 appaia
appartenere *like* tenere
appendere 2 appeso 5 appesi, appendesti
apporre *like* porre
apprendere *like* prendere
aprire 2 aperto 3 apro 5 aprii *o* apersi, apristi
    8 apra
ardere 2 arso 5 arsi, ardesti
arrendersi *like* rendere
arridere *like* ridere
ascendere *like* scendere
ascrivere *like* scrivere
aspergere 2 asperso 5 aspersi, aspergesti
assalire *like* salire
assistere 2 assistito 5 assistei *o* assistetti, assistesti
assolvere 2 assolto 5 assolvei *o* assolvetti *o* assolsi,
    assolvesti
assuefare *like* fare
assumere 2 assunto 5 assunsi, assumesti
astenersi *like* tenere
astrarre *like* trarre
attendere *like* tendere
attenersi *like* tenere
attingere *like* tingere
attrarre *like* trarre
AVERE *see page xxvi/xxvii*
avvedersi *like* vedere
avvenire *like* venire
avvincere *like* vincere
avvolgere *like* volgere
benedire *like* dire
bere 1 bevendo 2 bevuto 3 bevo *etc* 4 bevevo *etc*
    5 bevvi *o* bevetti, bevesti 6 berrò *etc* 8 beva *etc*
    9 bevessi *etc*

cadere 5 caddi, cadesti 6 cadrò *etc*
capovolgere *like* volgere
chiedere 2 chiesto 5 chiesi, chiedesti
chiudere 2 chiuso 5 chiusi, chiudesti
cingere 2 cinto 5 cinsi, cingesti
circoncidere *like* decidere
coesistere *like* esistere
cogliere 2 colto 3 colgo, colgono
    5 colsi, cogliesti 8 colga
coincidere 2 coinciso 5 coincisi, coincidesti
coinvolgere *like* volgere
commettere *like* mettere
commuovere *like* muovere
comparire *like* apparire
compiacere *like* piacere
compiangere *like* piangere
comporre *like* porre
comprendere *like* prendere
comprimere 2 compresso 5 compressi, comprimesti
compromettere *like* mettere
concedere 2 concesso 5 concessi *o* concedei *o*
    concedetti, concedesti
concludere *like* alludere
concorrere *like* correre
condiscendere *like* scendere
condividere *like* dividere
condurre *like* ridurre
confondere *like* fondere
congiungere *like* giungere
connettere *like* annettere
conoscere 2 conosciuto 5 conobbi, conoscesti
consistere *like* assistere
contendere *like* tendere
contenere *like* tenere
contorcere *like* torcere
contraddire *like* dire
contraddistinguere *like* distinguere
contraffare *like* fare
contrapporre *like* porre
contrarre *like* trarre
contravvenire *like* venire
convenire *like* venire
convergere 2 converso 5 conversi, convergesti
convincere *like* vincere
convivere *like* vivere
coprire *like* aprire
correggere *like* reggere
correre 2 corso 5 corsi, corresti
corrispondere *like* rispondere
corrodere *like* rodere
corrompere *like* rompere
cospargere *like* spargere
costringere *like* stringere
costruire 2 costruito 5 costruii, costruisti
crescere 2 cresciuto 5 crebbi, crescesti
crocifiggere *like* affliggere
cuocere 2 cotto 3 cuocio, cociamo, cuociono
    5 cossi, cocesti
dare 3 do, dai, dà, diamo, date, danno 5 diedi *o* detti,
    desti, diede *o* dette, demmo, deste, diedero *o* dettero 6
    darò *etc* 8 dia *etc* 9 dessi *etc* 10 da'!, dai!, date!, diano!

dattiloscrivere *like* scrivere
decadere *like* cadere
decidere ② deciso ⑤ decisi, decidesti
decomporre *like* porre
decorrere *like* correre
decrescere *like* crescere
dedurre *like* ridurre
deludere *like* alludere
demordere *like* mordere
deporre *like* porre
deprimere *like* comprimere
deridere *like* ridere
descrivere *like* scrivere
desistere *like* esistere
desumere *like* assumere
detenere *like* tenere
detergere *like* tergere
detrarre *like* trarre
devolvere ② devoluto
   ⑤ devolvei *o* devolvetti, devolvesti
difendere ② difeso ⑤ difesi, difendesti
diffondere *like* fondere
dimettere *like* mettere
dipendere *like* appendere
dipingere *like* tingere
dire ① dicendo ② detto ③ dico, dici, dice, diciamo, dite,
   dicono ④ dicevo *etc* ⑤ dissi, dicesti ⑥ dirò *etc*
   ⑧ dica, diciamo,diciate, dicano ⑨ dicessi *etc*
   ⑩ di'!, dica!, dite!, dicano!
dirigere ② diretto ⑤ diressi, dirigesti
discendere *like* scendere
dischiudere *like* chiudere
disciogliere *like* sciogliere
disconoscere *like* conoscere
discorrere *like* correre
discutere ② discusso ⑤ discussi, discutesti
disdire *like* dire
disfare *like* fare
disgiungere *like* giungere
disilludere *like* alludere
disperdere *like* perdere
dispiacere *like* piacere
disporre *like* porre
dissolvere ② dissolto *o* dissoluto ⑤ dissolsi *o*
   dissolvetti *o* dissolvei, dissolvesti
dissuadere *like* persuadere
distendere *like* tendere
distinguere ② distinto ⑤ distinsi, distinguesti
distogliere *like* togliere
distorcere *like* torcere
distrarre *like* trarre
distruggere *like* struggere
divenire *like* venire
divergere *like* convergere
dividere ② diviso ⑤ divisi, dividesti
dolere ③ dolgo, duoli, duole, dolgono ⑤ dolsi,
   dolesti ⑥ dorrò *etc* ⑧ dolga
DORMIRE *see page xxvi/xxvii*
dovere ③ devo *o* debbo, devi, deve, dobbiamo,
   dovete, devono *o* debbono ⑥ dovrò *etc* ⑧ deva *o*
   debba, dobbiamo, dobbiate, devano *o* debbano

eccellere ② eccelso ⑤ eccelsi, eccellesti
eleggere *like* leggere
elidere ② eliso ⑤ elisi, elidesti
eludere *like* alludere
emergere ② emerso ⑤ emersi, emergesti
emettere *like* mettere
equivalere *like* valere
erigere *like* dirigere
erodere *like* rodere
erompere *like* rompere
escludere *like* accludere
esigere ② esatto ⑤ esigei *o* esigetti, esigesti
esistere ② esistito ⑤ esistei *o* esistetti, esistesti
espandere *like* spandere
espellere ② espulso ⑤ espulsi, espellesti
esplodere ② esploso ⑤ esplosi, esplodesti
esporre *like* porre
esprimere *like* comprimere
ESSERE *see page xxvi/xxvii*
estendere *like* tendere
estinguere *like* distinguere
estorcere *like* torcere
estrarre *like* trarre
estromettere *like* mettere
evadere ② evaso ⑤ evasi, evadesti
evolversi ② evoluto ⑤ evolvetti *o* evolvei *o* evolsi,
   evolvesti
fare ① facendo ② fatto ③ faccio, fai, fa, facciamo, fate,
   fanno ④ facevo *etc* ⑤ feci, facesti ⑥ farò *etc* ⑧ faccia
   etc ⑨ facessi *etc* ⑩ fa'!, faccia!, fate!, facciano!
fendere ② fesso
fingere *like* cingere
FINIRE *see page xxvi/xxvii*
flettere ② flesso ⑤ flettei, flettesti
fondere ② fuso ⑤ fusi, fondesti
fotocomporre *like* porre
fraintendere *like* tendere
frammettere *like* mettere
frapporre *like* porre
friggere ② fritto ⑤ frissi, friggesti
fungere ⑤ funsi, fungesti
genuflettersi *like* flettere
giacere ③ giaccio, giaci, giace, giacciamo, giacete,
   giacciono ⑤ giacqui, giacesti ⑧ giaccia *etc* ⑩ giaci!,
   giaccia!, giacete!, giacciano!
giungere ② giunto ⑤ giunsi, giungesti
giustaporre *like* porre
godere ⑥ godrò *etc*
illudere *like* alludere
immergere *like* emergere
immettere *like* mettere
imporre *like* porre
imprimere *like* comprimere
incidere *like* decidere
includere *like* accludere
incorrere *like* correre
incutere *like* discutere
indire *like* dire
indisporre *like* porre
indulgere ② indulto ⑤ indulsi, indulgesti
indurre *like* ridurre

inferire¹ ② inferto ⑤ infersi, inferisti
inferire² ② inferito ⑤ inferii, inferisti
infiggere *like* affiggere
infliggere *like* affliggere
infrangere ② infranto ⑤ infransi, infrangesti
infondere *like* fondere
ingiungere *like* giungere
inscrivere *like* scrivere
insistere *like* assistere
insorgere *like* sorgere
intendere *like* tendere
intercorrere *like* correre
interdire *like* dire
interporre *like* porre
interrompere *like* rompere
intervenire *like* venire
intingere *like* tingere
intraprendere *like* prendere
intrattenere *like* tenere
intravedere *like* vedere
introdurre *like* ridurre
intromettersi *like* mettere
invadere *like* evadere
irrompere *like* rompere
iscrivere *like* scrivere
istruire *like* costruire
ledere ② leso ⑤ lesi, ledesti
leggere ② letto ⑤ lessi, leggesti
liquefare *like* fare
maledire *like* dire
manomettere *like* mettere
mantenere *like* tenere
mettere ② messo ⑤ misi, mettesti
misconoscere *like* conoscere
mordere ② morso ⑤ morsi, mordesti
morire ② morto ③ muoio, muori, muore, moriamo,
    morite, muoiono ⑥ morirò *o* morrò *etc* ⑧ muoia
mungere ② munto ⑤ munsi, mungesti
muovere ② mosso ⑤ mossi, movesti
nascere ② nato ⑤ nacqui, nascesti
nascondere ② nascosto ⑤ nascosi, nascondesti
nuocere ② nuociuto ③ noccio *o* nuoccio, nuoci, nuoce,
    nociamo *o* nuociamo, nocete *o* nuocete, nocciono *o*
    nuocciono, ④ nocevo *o* nuocevo *etc* ⑤ nocqui, nocesti
    ⑥ nocerò *o* nuocerò *etc* ⑦ noccia *o* nuoccia
occorrere *like* correre
occludere *like* accludere
offendere *like* difendere
offrire ② offerto ③ offro ⑤ offrii *o* offersi, offristi
    ⑧ offra
omettere *like* mettere
opporre *like* porre
opprimere *like* comprimere
ottenere *like* tenere
ottundere ② ottuso ⑤ ottusi, ottundesti
parere ② parso ③ paio, paiamo, paiono ⑤ parvi,
    paresti ⑥ parrò *etc* ⑧ paia, paiamo, paiate, paiano
PARLARE *see page xxvi/xxvii*
percorrere *like* correre
percuotere ② percosso ⑤ percossi, percuotesti
perdere ② perso *o* perduto ⑤ persi *o* perdei *o* perdetti,
    perdesti

permanere *like* rimanere
permettere *like* mettere
persistere *like* esistere
persuadere ② persuaso ⑤ persuasi, persuadesti
pervadere *like* invadere
pervenire *like* venire
piacere ② piaciuto ③ piaccio, piacciamo, piacciono
    ⑤ piacqui, piacesti ⑧ piaccia *etc*
piangere ② pianto ⑤ piansi, piangesti
piovere ⑤ piovve
porgere ② porto ⑤ porsi, porgesti
porre ① ponendo ② posto ③ pongo, poni, pone,
    poniamo, ponete, pongono ④ ponevo *etc* ⑤ posi,
    ponesti ⑥ porrò *etc* ⑧ ponga, poniamo, poniate,
    pongano ⑨ ponessi *etc*
posporre *like* porre
possedere *like* sedere
potere ③ posso, puoi, può, possiamo, potete, possono
    ⑥ potrò *etc* ⑧ possa, possiamo, possiate, possano
precludere *like* accludere
precorrere *like* correre
prediligere ② prediletto ⑤ predilessi, prediligesti
predire *like* dire
predisporre *like* porre
preesistere *like* esistere
prefiggersi *like* affiggere
preludere *like* alludere
prendere ② preso ⑤ presi, prendesti
premettere *like* mettere
preporre *like* porre
prescegliere *like* scegliere
prescindere *like* scindere
prescrivere *like* scrivere
presiedere *like* sedere
presumere *like* assumere
presupporre *like* porre
pretendere *like* tendere
prevalere *like* valere
prevedere *like* vedere
prevenire *like* venire
produrre *like* ridurre
proferire *like* inferire²
profondere *like* fondere
promettere *like* mettere
promuovere *like* muovere
propendere ② propenso
proporre *like* porre
prorompere *like* rompere
prosciogliere *like* sciogliere
proscrivere *like* scrivere
proteggere ② protetto ⑤ protessi, proteggesti
protendere *like* tendere
protrarre *like* trarre
provenire *like* venire
provvedere *like* vedere
pungere ② punto ⑤ punsi, pungesti
putrefare *like* fare
racchiudere *like* chiudere
raccogliere *like* cogliere
radere ② raso ⑤ rasi, radesti
radiotrasmettere *like* mettere

raggiungere *like* **giungere**
rapprendersi *like* **prendere**
rarefare *like* **fare**
ravvedersi *like* **vedere**
ravvolgere *like* **volgere**
recidere *like* **decidere**
redigere ② redatto ⑤ redassi, redigesti
redimere ② redento ⑤ redensi, redimesti
reggere ② retto ⑤ ressi, reggesti
rendere ② reso ⑤ resi, rendesti
reprimere *like* **comprimere**
rescindere *like* **scindere**
resistere *like* **esistere**
respingere *like* **spingere**
restringere *like* **stringere**
retrocedere *like* **concedere**
riaccendere *like* **accendere**
riammettere *like* **mettere**
riandare *like* **andare**
riapparire *like* **apparire**
riappendere *like* **appendere**
riaprire *like* **aprire**
riassumere *like* **assumere**
riavere *like* **avere**
ricadere *like* **cadere**
richiedere *like* **chiedere**
richiudere *like* **chiudere**
ricomparire *like* **apparire**
ricomporre *like* **porre**
ricondurre *like* **ridurre**
ricongiungere *like* **giungere**
ridere ② riso ⑤ risi, ridesti
ridire *like* **dire**
ridiscendere *like* **scendere**
ridurre ① riducendo ② ridotto ③ riduco *etc*
  ④ riducevo *etc* ⑤ ridussi, riducesti ⑥ ridurrò *etc*
  ⑧ riduca *etc* ⑨ riducessi *etc*
rieleggere *like* **leggere**
riemergere *like* **emergere**
riempire ① riempiendo ③ riempio, riempi, riempie,
  riempiono
rifare *like* **fare**
riflettere ② riflettuto o riflesso
rifondere *like* **fondere**
rifrangere *like* **infrangere**
rifulgere ② rifulso ⑤ rifulsi, rifulgesti
rileggere *like* **leggere**
rimanere ② rimasto ③ rimango, rimangono ⑤ rimasi,
  rimanesti ⑥ rimarrò *etc* ⑧ rimanga
rimettere *like* **mettere**
rimordere *like* **mordere**
rimpiangere *like* **piangere**
rimuovere *like* **muovere**
rinascere *like* **nascere**
rinchiudere *like* **chiudere**
rincorrere *like* **correre**
rincrescere *like* **crescere**
rinvenire *like* **venire**
ripercorrere *like* **correre**
ripercuotere *like* **percuotere**
riporre *like* **porre**

riprendere *like* **prendere**
riprodurre *like* **ridurre**
ripromettersi *like* **mettere**
riproporre *like* **porre**
riscoprire *like* **aprire**
riscrivere *like* **scrivere**
riscuotere *like* **scuotere**
risolvere *like* **assolvere**
risorgere *like* **sorgere**
rispondere ② risposto ⑤ risposi, rispondesti
ritenere *like* **tenere**
ritorcere *like* **torcere**
ritrarre *like* **trarre**
ritrasmettere *like* **mettere**
riuscire *like* **uscire**
rivedere *like* **vedere**
rivivere *like* **vivere**
rivolgere *like* **volgere**
rodere ② roso ⑤ rosi, rodesti
rompere ② rotto ⑤ ruppi, rompesti
salire ③ salgo, sali, salgono ⑧ salga
sapere ③ so, sai, sa, sappiamo, sapete, sanno ⑤ seppi,
  sapesti ⑥ saprò *etc* ⑧ sappia *etc* ⑩ sappi!, sappia!,
  sappiate!, sappiano!
scadere *like* **cadere**
scegliere ② scelto ③ scelgo, scegli, sceglie, scegliamo,
  scegliete, scelgono ⑤ scelsi, scegliesti ⑧ scelga,
  scegliamo, scegliate, scelgono ⑩ scegli!, scelga!,
  scegliamo!, scegliete!, scelgano!
scendere ② sceso ⑤ scesi, scendesti
schiudere *like* **chiudere**
scindere ② scisso ⑤ scissi, scindesti
sciogliere ② sciolto ③ sciolgo, sciogli, scioglie,
  sciogliamo, sciogliete, sciolgono ⑤ sciolsi, sciogliesti
  ⑧ sciolga, sciogliamo, sciogliate, sciolgano ⑩ sciogli!,
  sciolga!, sciogliamo!, sciogliete!, sciolgano!
scommettere *like* **mettere**
scomparire *like* **apparire**
scomporre *like* **porre**
sconfiggere ② sconfitto ⑤ sconfissi, sconfiggesti
sconvolgere *like* **volgere**
scoprire *like* **aprire**
scorgere ② scorto ⑤ scorsi, scorgesti
scorrere *like* **correre**
scrivere ② scritto ⑤ scrissi, scrivesti
scuotere ② scosso ③ scuoto, scuoti, scuote, scotiamo,
  scotete, scuotono ⑤ scossi, scotesti ⑥ scoterò *etc*
  ⑧ scuota, scotiamo, scotiate, scuotano ⑩ scuoti!,
  scuota!, scotiamo!, scotete!, scuotano!
sedere ③ siedo, siedi, siede, siedono ⑧ sieda
sedurre *like* **ridurre**
seppellire ② sepolto
sfare *like* **fare**
smettere *like* **mettere**
smuovere *like* **muovere**
socchiudere *like* **chiudere**
soccorrere *like* **correre**
soddisfare *like* **fare**
soffriggere *like* **frigere**
soffrire ② sofferto ⑤ soffrii o soffersi, soffristi
soggiacere *like* **giacere**

soggiungere *like* giungere

solere ② solito ③ soglio, suoli, suole, sogliamo, solete, sogliono ⑧ soglia, sogliamo, sogliate, sogliano

sommergere *like* emergere

sopprimere *like* comprimere

sopraffare *like* fare

sopraggiungere *like* giungere

soprassedere *like* sedere

sopravvenire *like* venire

sopravvivere *like* vivere

soprintendere *like* tendere

sorgere ② sorto ③ sorsi, sorgesti

soprendere *like* prendere

sorreggere *like* reggere

sorridere *like* ridere

sospendere *like* appendere

sospingere *like* spingere

sostenere *like* tenere

sottintendere *like* tendere

sottoesporre *like* porre

sottomettere *like* mettere

sottoporre *like* porre

sottoscrivere *like* scrivere

sottostare *like* stare

sottrarre *like* trarre

sovraesporre *like* porre

sovrapporre *like* porre

sovrastare *like* stare

sovvenire *like* venire

spandere ② spanto ⑤ spandei, spandesti

spargere ② sparso ⑤ sparsi, spargesti

sparire ⑤ sparii, sparisti

spegnere ② spento ③ spengo, spengono ⑤ spensi, spegnesti ⑧ spenga

spendere ② speso ⑤ spesi, spendesti

spingere ② spinto ⑤ spinsi, spingesti

spiovere *like* piovere

sporgere *like* porgere

stare ② stato ③ sto, stai, sta, stiamo, state, stanno ⑤ stetti, stesti ⑥ starò *etc* ⑧ stia *etc* ⑩ sta'!, stia!, state!, stiano!

stendere *like* tendere

stingere *like* tingere

storcere *like* torcere

stracuocere *like* cuocere

strafare *like* fare

stramaledire *like* dire

stravedere *like* vedere

stravincere *like* vincere

stravolgere *like* volgere

stringere ② stretto ⑤ strinsi, stringesti

struggere ② strutto ⑤ strussi, struggesti

stupefare *like* fare

succedere *like* concedere

suddividere *like* dividere

supporre *like* porre

svenire *like* venire

svolgere *like* volgere

tacere ② taciuto ③ taccio, tacciono ⑤ tacqui, tacesti ⑧ taccia

teletrasmettere *like* mettere

tendere ② teso ⑤ tesi, tendesti *etc*

tenere ③ tengo, tieni, tiene, tengono ⑤ tenni, tenesti ⑥ terrò *etc* ⑧ tenga

tergere ② terso ⑤ tersi, tergesti

tingere ② tinto ⑤ tinsi, tingesti

togliere ② tolto ③ tolgo, togli, toglie, togliamo, togliete, tolgono ⑤ tolsi, togliesti ⑧ tolga, togliamo, togliate, tolgano ⑩ togli!, tolga!, togliamo!, togliete!,tolgano!

torcere ② torto ⑤ torsi, torcesti

torrefare *like* fare

tradurre *like* ridurre

trafiggere *like* sconfiggere

transigere *like* esigere

trarre ① traendo ② tratto ③ traggo, trai, trae, traiamo, traete, traggono ④ traevo *etc* ⑤ trassi, traesti ⑥ trarrò *etc* ⑧ tragga ⑨ traessi *etc*

trascendere *like* scendere

trascorrere *like* correre

trascrivere *like* scrivere

trasfondere *like* fondere

trasmettere *like* mettere

trasparire *like* apparire

trasporre *like* porre

trattenere *like* tenere

travolgere *like* volgere

tumefarsi *like* fare

uccidere ② ucciso ⑤ uccisi, uccidesti

udire ③ odo, odi, ode, odono ⑧ oda

ungere ② unto ⑤ unsi, ungesti

uscire ③ esco, esci, esce, escono ⑧ esca

valere ② valso ③ valgo, valgono ⑤ valsi, valesti ⑥ varrò *etc* ⑧ valga

vedere ② visto *o* veduto ⑤ vidi, vedesti ⑥ vedrò *etc*

VENDERE *see page* xxvi/xxvii

venire ② venuto ③ vengo, vieni, viene, vengono ⑤ venni, venisti ⑥ verrò *etc* ⑧ venga

vilipendere *like* appendere

vincere ② vinto ⑤ vinsi, vincesti

vivere ② vissuto ⑤ vissi, vivesti

volere ③ voglio, vuoi, vuole, vogliamo, volete, vogliono ⑤ volli, volesti ⑥ vorrò *etc* ⑧voglia *etc* ⑩ vogli!, voglia!, vogliate!, vogliano!

volgere ② volto ⑤ volsi, volgesti

A

A, a [eɪ] N **a** (*letter*) A, a *form inv*; **A for Andrew**, (*Am*) **A for Able** ≈ A come Ancona; **to know sth from A to Z** sapere *or* conoscere qc dall'a alla zeta; **to get from A to B** spostarsi da un punto all'altro **b** : **A9** (*Brit*: *road*) ≈ SS 9 (= *strada statale*) **c** (*Mus*) la *m inv* **d** (*Scol*: *mark*) ≈ 10, ≈ ottimo.

---

a [eɪ, ə] INDEF ART (*before vowel or silent h* an [æn, ən, n])
a un *m* (uno + *s impure, gn, pn, ps, x, z*), una *f* (un' + *vowel*);
▷**an** *apple* una mela
▷**I haven't got a** *car* non ho la macchina
▷**a** *child* **is full of curiosity** i bambini sono molto curiosi
▷**he's a** *doctor* è medico, fa il medico
▷**a** *drink* **would be nice** berrei volentieri qualcosa
▷**half an** *hour* mezz'ora
▷**as a young** *man* da giovane
▷**a** *mirror* uno specchio
▷**a** *Mr Smith* **called to see you** l'ha cercata un certo signor Smith
▷**what a** *surprise*! che sorpresa!
b (*each*) a, per;
▷**2 apples a** *head* 2 mele a testa *or* (per) ciascuno
▷**50 kilometres an** *hour* 50 chilometri all'ora
▷**3 times a** *month* 3 volte al mese
▷**£4 a** *person* *or* **a** *head* 4 sterline per *or* a persona
▷**£4 a** *pound* 4 sterline alla libbra.

♦ **A-1** [ˌeɪˈwʌn] ADJ di prim'ordine, eccellente.
a. ABBR = **acre**.
AA [eɪˈeɪ] N ABBR **a** (*Brit*: = *Automobile Association*) ≈ A.C.I. *m* (= *Automobile Club d'Italia*) **b** (= *Alcoholics Anonymous*) A.A. *f* (= *Anonima Alcolisti*) **c** (*Am*: = *Associate in/of Arts*) ≈ laurea in lettere **d** (*Mil*) = **anti-aircraft**.
AAA [ˌeɪeɪˈeɪ] N ABBR **a** (= *American Automobile Association*) ≈ A.C.I. *m* (= *Automobile Club d'Italia*) **b** (*Brit*) = *Amateur Athletics Association*.
aard·vark [ˈɑːdˌvɑːk] N oritteropo.
AB [eɪˈbiː] ① N ABBR (*Am*) = **able-bodied seaman**.

② ABBR (*Canada*) = *Alberta*.
aback [əˈbæk] ADV: **to be taken aback** essere colto(-a) *or* preso(-a) alla sprovvista, rimanere sconcertato(-a).
aba·cus [ˈæbəkəs] N (*pl* **abacuses** *or* **abaci** [ˈæbəsaɪ]) abaco, pallottoliere *m*.
aban·don [əˈbændən] ① VT **a** (*desert*) abbandonare; **to abandon ship** abbandonare la nave **b** (*give up*: *plan, hope, game*) abbandonare, rinunciare a; **to abandon o.s. to sth** abbandonarsi a qc, lasciarsi andare a qc.
② N abbandono; **with gay abandon** sfrenatamente, spensieratamente.
aban·doned [əˈbændənd] ADJ (*unrestrained*: *manner*) disinvolto(-a), spontaneo(-a).
aban·don·ment [əˈbændənmənt] N abbandono.
abase [əˈbeɪs] VT (*frm*) umiliare, mortificare; **to abase o.s.** umiliarsi, abbassarsi.
abashed [əˈbæʃt] ADJ imbarazzato(-a).
abate [əˈbeɪt] VI (*frm*: *anger, enthusiasm, storm*) placarsi, calmarsi; (: *pain*) calmarsi; (: *fever*) abbassarsi, calare; (: *flood*) abbassarsi; (: *noise*) diminuire, affievolirsi.
abate·ment [əˈbeɪtmənt] N (*frm*: *of pollution, noise*) soppressione *f*, eliminazione *f*; **Noise Abatement Society** associazione *contro l'inquinamento acustico*.
ab·at·toir [ˈæbətwɑː] N (*Brit*) macello, mattatoio.
ab·bess [ˈæbɪs] N badessa.
ab·bey [ˈæbɪ] N abbazia, badia.
ab·bot [ˈæbət] N abate *m*.
ab·bre·vi·ate [əˈbriːvɪeɪt] VT abbreviare.
ab·bre·via·tion [əˌbriːvɪˈeɪʃən] N abbreviazione *f*.
ABC [ˌeɪbiːˈsiː] ① N (*Am*: *also*: **ABC's** *npl*) abbiccì *m inv*, alfabeto; **as easy as** ABC facile come bere un bicchiere d'acqua.
② N ABBR (= *American Broadcasting Company*) rete televisiva americana.
ab·di·cate [ˈæbdɪkeɪt] ① VI abdicare.
② VT (*throne*) abdicare a; (*responsibility*) rinunciare a.
ab·di·ca·tion [ˌæbdɪˈkeɪʃən] N (*of monarch*) abdicazione *f*.
ab·do·men [ˈæbdəmən] N addome *m*.
ab·domi·nal [æbˈdɒmɪnl] ADJ addominale.
ab·duct [æbˈdʌkt] VT rapire.

ab·duc·tion [æb'dʌkʃən] N rapimento, sequestro di persona.

ab·duc·tor [æb'dʌktəʳ] N rapitore(-trice).

abed [ə'bɛd] ADV (*liter*) a letto.

Abel ['eɪbəl] N Abele *m*.

Ab·er·do·nian [ˌæbə'dəʊnɪən] [1] ADJ di Aberdeen.
[2] N abitante *m/f* o originario(-a) di Aberdeen.

ab·er·rant [ə'bɛrənt] ADJ (*Bio, gen*) aberrante.

ab·er·ra·tion [ˌæbə'reɪʃən] N aberrazione *f*; **in a moment of mental aberration** in un momento di aberrazione mentale; **a youthful aberration** una follia *or* un errore giovanile.

abet [ə'bɛt] VT (*Law*); see **aid**.

abey·ance [ə'beɪəns] N (*frm*): **to be in abeyance** (*law, custom*) essere in disuso; (*matter, plan*) essere in sospeso.

ab·hor [əb'hɔ:ʳ] VT aborrire, provare orrore per.

ab·hor·rence [əb'hɒrəns] N avversione *f*, orrore *m*; **to have an abhorrence of sth** detestare qc.

ab·hor·rent [əb'hɒrənt] ADJ odioso(-a), detestabile, ripugnante; **to be abhorrent to sb** ripugnare a qn.

abide [ə'baɪd] (*pt, pp* **abided**) VT (*only neg*) sopportare, soffrire; **I can't abide him** non lo posso soffrire *or* sopportare

▶ **abide by** VI + PREP (*rules*) conformarsi a, attenersi a; (*consequences*) accettare; (*promise*) tener fede a, rispettare.

abid·ing [ə'baɪdɪŋ] ADJ (*memory etc*) duraturo(-a).

abil·ity [ə'bɪlɪtɪ] N capacità *f inv*, abilità *f inv*; **abilities** NPL capacità *fpl*, doti *fpl*; **to the best of my ability** con il massimo impegno; **a person of great abilities** una persona molto dotata.

ab·ject ['æbdʒɛkt] (*frm*) ADJ (*poverty*) abietto(-a); (*apology*) umiliante; (*coward*) indegno(-a), vile.

ab·ject·ly ['æbʒɛktlɪ] (*frm*) ADV (*behave, apologize*) bassamente, servilmente; (*lie, act*) indegnamente, vilmente.

ab·jure [əb'dʒʊəʳ] VT (*frm*) abiurare.

ablaze [ə'bleɪz] ADV, ADJ in fiamme; **the house was ablaze with light** (*fig*) la casa era tutta illuminata, la casa risplendeva di luci.

able ['eɪbl] ADJ (*person*) capace, bravo(-a); (*piece of work*) abile, intelligente; **to be able to do sth** poter fare qc, essere in grado di fare qc; **he's not able to walk** non può *or* non è in grado di *or* non è in condizione di camminare; **those who are able to pay** coloro che sono in condizione *or* che possono permettersi di pagare.

♦ **able-bodied** [ˌeɪbl'bɒdɪd] ADJ robusto(-a), valido(-a); **able-bodied citizen** cittadino idoneo *or* abile (al servizio militare).

♦ **able-bodied seaman** N (*Brit*) marinaio scelto.

ab·lutions [ə'blu:ʃənz] NPL (*Rel, also hum*) abluzioni *fpl*.

ably ['eɪblɪ] ADV abilmente.

ABM [ˌeɪbi:'ɛm] N ABBR (*Mil*: = *anti-ballistic missile*) ABM *m*.

ab·nor·mal [æb'nɔ:məl] ADJ anormale.

ab·nor·mal·ity [ˌæbnɔ:'mælɪtɪ] N (*condition*) anormalità *f inv*; (*instance*) anomalia *f*.

ab·nor·mal·ly [æb'nɔ:məlɪ] ADV in modo anormale; (*exceptionally*) insolitamente, stranamente.

aboard [ə'bɔ:d] [1] ADV (*Naut, Aer*) a bordo; **to go aboard** salire a bordo; **all aboard!** (*Rail*) (signori) in carrozza *or* in vettura!; (*Naut*) tutti a bordo!.
[2] PREP: **aboard the ship** a bordo (della nave), sulla nave; **aboard the train** in *or* sul treno.

abode [ə'bəʊd] N (*old*) dimora; (*Law*) domicilio, dimora; **of no fixed abode** senza fissa dimora.

abol·ish [ə'bɒlɪʃ] VT abolire.

abo·li·tion [æbəʊ'lɪʃən] N abolizione *f*.

♦ **A-bomb** ['eɪˌbɒm] N bomba A.

abomi·nable [ə'bɒmɪnəbl] ADJ (*detestable*) abominevole; (*unpleasant*) pessimo(-a), orrendo(-a), orribile.

abomi·nably [ə'bɒmɪnəblɪ] ADV disgustosamente; **to be abominably rude to sb** essere terribilmente maleducato(-a) con qn.

abomi·nate [ə'bɒmɪneɪt] VT (*frm*) aborrire.

abom·ina·tion [əˌbɒmɪ'neɪʃən] N (*feeling*) avversione *f*, disgusto; (*detestable act, thing*) azione *f* (*or* cosa) orrenda; **to hold sth in abomination** detestare qc.

Abo·rigi·nal [ˌæbə'rɪdʒɪnəl] [1] N aborigeno(-a) d'Australia.
[2] ADJ (*settlement, culture*) aborigeno(-a).

abo·rigi·nal [ˌæbə'rɪdʒɪnəl] ADJ (*indigenous*) aborigeno(-a), indigeno(-a).

Abo·rigi·ne [ˌæbə'rɪdʒɪnɪ] N aborigeno(-a) d'Australia.

abort [ə'bɔ:t] [1] VI (*Med*) abortire; (*fig: plans, space mission*) fallire (prematuramente).
[2] VT **a** (*Med*): **to abort a baby** *or* **a pregnancy** interrompere una gravidanza **b** (*fig*) sospendere, rinunciare a portare a termine; (*Comput*) interrompere l'esecuzione di.

abor·tion [ə'bɔ:ʃən] N (*Med*) aborto; **to have an abortion** (*termination*) abortire; (*miscarriage*) avere un aborto (spontaneo).

abor·tion·ist [ə'bɔ:ʃənɪst] N chi esegue aborti clandestini.

abor·tive [ə'bɔ:tɪv] ADJ (*Med*) abortivo(-a); (*fig: plan*) fallito(-a), mancato(-a); (: *attempt*) vano(-a), infruttuoso(-a).

abound [ə'baʊnd] VI (*frm: exist in great quantity*) abbondare; (: *have in great quantity*): **to abound in** *or* **with** abbondare di, essere ricco(-a) di.

---

about [ə'baʊt]
[1] ADV
a (*place: here and there*) qua e là, in giro;
▷ **to be about again** (*after illness*) essere di nuovo in piedi
▷ **we were about early** eravamo in piedi presto
▷ **is Paul about?** (*Brit*) hai visto Paul in giro?
▷ **to look about** guardarsi intorno
▷ **they left all their things lying about** hanno lasciato tutta la loro roba in giro
▷ **to run about** (*Brit*) correre qua e là
▷ **there's a lot of measles about** c'è molto morbillo in giro
▷ **to walk about** camminare
▷ **it's the other way about** (*Brit fig*) è il contrario, è viceversa
b (*approximately*) circa, quasi, pressappoco;
▷ **she's about the same age as you** ha pressappoco la tua età
▷ **it's just about finished** è quasi finito
▷ **it takes about 10 hours** ci vogliono circa 10 ore
▷ **(at) about 2 o'clock** verso le due
▷ **it is about 2 o'clock** sono circa le due
▷ **about 50 people** una cinquantina di persone
▷ **that's about right** è più o meno giusto
c: **to be about to do sth** stare per fare qc
▷ **he was about to cry** stava per piangere
▷ **I'm not about to do all that for nothing** non ho

intenzione di fare tutto questo per niente

▷**they were about to fire** when ... erano sul punto di sparare quando..., erano lì lì per sparare quando....

2 PREP

a (place) intorno a;

▷**somewhere about here** qui intorno da qualche parte

▷**he looked about him** si è guardato intorno

▷**to do jobs about the house** fare lavori in casa

▷**her clothes were scattered about the room** i suoi vestiti erano tutti sparsi or in giro per la stanza

▷**to wander about the town** andare in giro per la città

b (relating to) su, a proposito di, riguardo a;

▷**do something about it!** fai qualcosa!

▷**how about coming with us?** che ne dici or diresti di venire con noi?

▷**how about a drink?** beviamo qualcosa?, e se bevessimo qualcosa?

▷**there's something about a soldier which** ... c'è qualcosa nei soldati che...

▷**there's something interesting about her** ha qualcosa di interessante

▷**we talked about it** ne abbiamo parlato

▷**a book about travel** un libro sui viaggi

▷**what is it about** di che si tratta?

▷**what about me?** e io?

▷**what about it?** (what do you say) che te ne pare?, cosa ne pensi?; (what of it) e allora?

c (occupied with): **while you're about it** ... già che ci sei... .

♦ **about-face** [ə‚baʊt'feɪs], **about-turn** [ə‚baʊt'tɜ:n] N (Mil, fig) dietro front m inv.

above [ə'bʌv] **1** ADV di sopra, al di sopra; (in text) prima, sopra; **mentioned above** summenzionato(-a); **the flat above** l'appartamento di sopra or al piano di sopra; **from above** dall'alto; **the clouds above** le nuvole sovrastanti; **children of 7 years or above** ragazzi dai 7 anni in su or a partire dai 7 anni; **orders from above** ordini superiori or (che vengono) dall'alto; **the address above** l'indirizzo di cui sopra.

2 PREP sopra; **above all** soprattutto; **above the clouds** al di sopra delle nuvole; **the Thames above London** il Tamigi a monte di Londra; **2000 metres above sea level** 2000 metri sopra il livello del mare; **he is above me in rank** ha un grado superiore al mio; **I couldn't hear above the din** non riuscivo a sentire in mezzo a or attraverso tutto quel frastuono; **she's above that sort of thing** è superiore a queste cose; **he's not above a bit of blackmail** non rifuggirebbe dal ricatto; **it's above me** è troppo complicato per me, è al di sopra delle mie possibilità; **to get above o.s.** montarsi la testa; **children above 7 years of age** ragazzi al di sopra dei 7 anni (di età); **costing above £10** più caro di 10 sterline.

above·board [ə‚bʌv'bɔ:d] ADJ leale, onesto(-a); **are you sure this is aboveboard?** sei sicuro che sia una faccenda pulita?

♦ **above-mentioned** [ə'bʌv'mɛnʃənd] ADJ (frm) summenzionato(-a), di cui sopra.

♦ **above-named** [ə'bʌv'neɪmd] ADJ (frm) suddetto(-a).

abra·sion [ə'breɪʒən] N abrasione f; (injury) escoriazione f, abrasione f.

abra·sive [ə'breɪsɪv] **1** ADJ abrasivo(-a); (fig: person, personality) caustico(-a); (: voice) stridente; (: manner) brusco(-a).

2 N abrasivo.

abra·sive·ly [ə'breɪsɪvlɪ] ADV (fig) aspramente.

abreast [ə'brɛst] ADV di fianco, fianco a fianco; **to march 4 abreast** marciare in riga per 4; **to come abreast of** affiancarsi a; **to keep abreast of the news/times** tenersi aggiornato(-a).

abridge [ə'brɪdʒ] VT ridurre.

abridged [ə'brɪdʒd] ADJ ridotto(-a).

abridge·ment [ə'brɪdʒmənt] N (act of abridging) riduzione f; (shortened version) edizione f ridotta.

abroad [ə'brɔ:d] ADV (in foreign parts) all'estero; **to go abroad** andare all'estero; **there is a rumour abroad that** ... (fig frm) si sente dire in giro che..., circola la voce che...; **how did the news get abroad?** (fig frm) come si è sparsa or diffusa la notizia?

ab·ro·gate ['æbrəʊ‚geɪt] VT (law) abrogare; (agreement) revocare; (responsibility) venir meno a.

ab·rupt [ə'brʌpt] ADJ (halt, person) brusco(-a); (departure) improvviso(-a); (slope) ripido(-a), erto(-a); (style) discontinuo(-a), sconnesso(-a).

ab·rupt·ly [ə'brʌptlɪ] ADV bruscamente.

ab·rupt·ness [ə'brʌptnɪs] N (of person) rudezza; (of halt) repentinità; (of slope) ripidezza; (of style) discontinuità.

ab·scess ['æbsɛs] N (Med) ascesso.

ab·scond [əb'skɒnd] VI fuggire, scappare.

ab·seil ['æbseɪl] VI (Mountaineering) discendere a corda doppia.

ab·seil·ing ['æbseɪlɪŋ] N discesa a corda doppia.

ab·sence ['æbsəns] N (of person) assenza; (of thing) mancanza; **in the absence of** (person) in assenza di; (thing) in mancanza di; **in my absence** in mia assenza; **in the absence of any evidence** non essendoci prove; **absence of mind** distrazione f.

ab·sent [adj 'æbsənt; vb æb'sɛnt] **1** ADJ (person) assente; (thing) assente, mancante; (fig: also: **absent-minded**) distratto(-a); **to be absent without leave** (Mil) essere assente ingiustificato(-a).

2 VT: **to absent o.s. from sth** non presentarsi a qc.

ab·sen·tee [‚æbsən'ti:] N assente m/f.

ab·sen·tee·ism [‚æbsən'ti:ɪzəm] N assenteismo.

ab·sen·tia [‚æb'sɛntɪə] (frm): **he was condemned in absentia** fu condannato in contumacia.

ab·sent·ly ['æbsəntlɪ] ADV distrattamente.

♦ **absent-minded** [‚æbsənt'maɪndɪd] ADJ distratto(-a).

♦ **absent-mindedly** [‚æbsənt'maɪndɪdlɪ] ADV distrattamente.

♦ **absent-mindedness** [‚æbsənt'maɪndɪdnɪs] N distrazione f.

ab·sinthe, ab·sinth ['æbsɪnθ] N assenzio.

ab·so·lute ['æbsəlu:t] **1** ADJ (gen) assoluto(-a); (support) totale, completo(-a), senza riserve; (proof) inconfutabile; (denial) categorico(-a); (lie) bello(-a) e buono(-a); **he's an absolute idiot** è un perfetto idiota; **it's an absolute scandal** è un autentico scandalo.

2 N assoluto.

ab·so·lute·ly ['æbsəlu:tlɪ] ADV completamente, assolutamente; **oh yes, absolutely!** oh sì, altro che!

ab·so·lu·tion [‚æbsə'lu:ʃən] N (Rel) assoluzione f.

ab·so·lut·ism ['æbsəlu:‚tɪzm] N (Pol) assolutismo.

ab·solve [əb'zɒlv] VT: **to absolve sb (from or of)** (sin etc) assolvere qn (da); **to absolve sb from** (oath) sciogliere qn da; (obligation etc) liberare qn da.

ab·sorb [əb'sɔ:b] VT (also fig) assorbire; (costs) ammortizzare; (information) assimilare; **she was absorbed in a**

book era immersa *or* assorta nella lettura di un libro.

ab·sor·ben·cy [ab'sɔːbənsɪ] N capacità d'assorbimento.

ab·sor·bent [əb'sɔːbənt] ADJ assorbente.

♦ **absorbent cotton** N (*Am*) cotone *m* idrofilo.

ab·sorb·ing [əb'sɔːbɪŋ] ADJ avvincente, molto interessante.

ab·sorp·tion [əb'sɔːpʃən] N **a** (*Physiology*) assorbimento; (*Aut*) ammortizzamento; (*fig: of person into group*) integrazione *f* **b** (*fig*) concentrazione *f*; **his absorption in his work prevented him from noticing** ... era così assorbito nel suo lavoro che non ha notato... .

ab·stain [əb'steɪn] VI (*not vote*): **to abstain (from)** astenersi (da); **to abstain from drinking/smoking** astenersi dal bere/dal fumare.

ab·stain·er [əb'steɪnəʳ] N (*teetotaller*) astemio(-a).

ab·ste·mi·ous [əb'stiːmɪəs] ADJ (*person: in eating, drinking*) moderato(-a).

ab·ste·mi·ous·ness [əb'stiːmɪəsnɪs] N sobrietà, temperanza.

ab·sten·tion [əb'stɛnʃən] N astensione *f*.

ab·sti·nence ['æbstɪnəns] N astinenza.

ab·sti·nent ['æbstɪnənt] ADJ astinente.

ab·stract [*adj, n* 'æbstrækt; *vb* æb'strækt] 1 ADJ astratto (-a).
2 N (*summary*) riassunto, sommario; (*picture*) opera astratta; **in the abstract** in teoria, in astratto.
3 VT (*remove*) estrarre; (*summarize*) riassumere.

ab·stract·ed [æb'stræktɪd] ADJ (*expression, look*) distratto (-a).

ab·strac·tion [æb'strækʃən] N **a** (*absence of mind*) distrazione *f* **b** (*Philosophy etc*) astrazione *f*, concetto astratto.

ab·struse [əb'struːs] ADJ (*theory, concept*) astruso(-a).

ab·surd [əb'sɜːd] ADJ assurdo(-a); (*appearance, hat*) ridicolo(-a).

ab·surd·ity [əb'sɜːdɪtɪ] N **a** (*no pl: see adj*) assurdità, assurdo; ridicolaggine *f* **b** (*thing etc*) assurdità *f inv*; **the absurdities of life** le assurdità della vita.

ab·surd·ly [əb'sɜːdlɪ] ADV (*see adj*) assurdamente; in modo ridicolo.

ABTA ['æbtə] N ABBR = *Association of British Travel Agents*.

Abu Dha·bi [ˌæbuː'dɑːbɪ] N Abu Dhabi *f*.

abun·dance [ə'bʌndəns] N abbondanza, gran quantità; **in abundance** in abbondanza, in gran quantità.

abun·dant [ə'bʌndənt] ADJ (*crop, supply*) abbondante; (*proof*) ampio(-a).

abun·dant·ly [ə'bʌndəntlɪ] ADV in grande abbondanza; **he made it abundantly clear to me that ...** mi ha fatto chiaramente capire che... .

abuse [*n* ə'bjuːs; *vb* ə'bjuːz] 1 N **a** (*insults*) insulti *mpl*, ingiurie *fpl*, improperi *mpl*; **to heap abuse on sb** coprire qn di insulti
b (*cruel treatment: of children*) abuso; (: *of patients, prisoners*) maltrattamento
c (*misuse: of drugs, solvents*) abuso; **abuse of power** abuso di potere; **open to abuse** che si presta ad abusi.
2 VT **a** (*misuse: position, power*) abusare di; (: *drugs, solvents*) far abuso di
b (*revile*) insultare
c (*maltreat: children*) approfittare sessualmente di; (: *patients, prisoners*) maltrattare.

abu·sive [əb'juːsɪv] ADJ (*person*) villano(-a); (*language*) offensivo(-a), ingiurioso(-a).

abu·sive·ly [əb'juːsɪvlɪ] ADV offensivamente.

abut [ə'bʌt] VI: **to abut on sth** confinare con qc.

abys·mal [ə'bɪzməl] ADJ (*ignorance*) abissale, crasso(-a); (*result, food*) pessimo(-a); (*weather, job*) da cani; **abysmal poverty** la povertà più nera.

abys·mal·ly [ə'bɪzməlɪ] ADV in modo atroce; **abysmally ignorant** di un'ignoranza crassa; **to fail abysmally** fallire miseramente; **his work is abysmally bad** il suo lavoro è un disastro.

abyss [ə'bɪs] N (*liter*) abisso, baratro.

AC [ˌeɪ'siː] N ABBR **a** (*Elec*: = *alternating current*) c.a. (= *corrente alternata*) **b** (*Am*)= *athletic club*.

a/c ABBR (*Banking etc*: = *account, account current*) c.

aca·cia [ə'keɪʃə] N (*pl* **acacias** *or* **acacia**) acacia.

aca·dem·ic [ˌækə'dɛmɪk] 1 ADJ **a** (*Univ*) accademico(-a), universitario(-a); (*intellectual*) intellettuale; **academic life** vita universitaria; **academic subjects** materie *fpl* umanistiche e scientifiche
b (*irrelevant*) puramente formale; **that's rather academic now** ormai è un po' superfluo al lato pratico.
2 N docente *m/f* universitario(-a), universitario(-a).

acad·emi·cian [əˌkædɪ'mɪʃən] N accademico.

aca·demi·cism [ˌækə'dɛmɪˌsɪzəm], **aca·dem·ism** [ə'kædəˌmɪzəm] N (*Art*) accademismo.

♦ **academic year** N (*Brit*) anno accademico.

acad·emy [ə'kædəmɪ] N (*learned body*) accademia; (*school*) scuola privata; **academy of music** (*Brit*) conservatorio; **military/naval academy** accademia militare/navale.

ACAS ['eɪkæs] N ABBR (*Brit*: = *Advisory, Conciliation and Arbitration Service*) *comitato per il miglioramento della contrattazione collettiva.*

ac·cede [æk'siːd] (*frm*) VI: **to accede to** (*throne*) salire a, ascendere a; (*office, position*) accedere a; (*request*) aderire a, accedere a.

ac·cel·er·ate [æk'sɛləreɪt] 1 VT accelerare, affrettare.
2 VI (*Aut*) accelerare.

ac·cel·era·tion [ækˌsɛlə'reɪʃən] N (*Aut, Phys*) accelerazione *f*.

ac·cel·era·tor [ækˌsɛləreɪtəʳ] N (*Aut, Tech*) acceleratore *m*.

ac·cent ['æksənt] N (*all senses*) accento.

ac·cent·ed ['æksəntɪd] ADJ: **he speaks in heavily accented English** parla inglese con un forte accento straniero.

ac·cen·tu·ate [æk'sɛntjuˌeɪt] VT (*syllable*) accentuare; (*need, difference etc*) accentuare, mettere in risalto *or* in evidenza.

ac·cen·tua·tion [ækˌsɛntjuː'eɪʃən] N accentuazione *f*.

ac·cept [ək'sɛpt] VT (*gen*) accettare; (*acknowledge*) ammettere; **I can't accept that he's really in financial difficulties** mi rifiuto di credere che abbia davvero delle difficoltà economiche; **he refused to accept defeat** non ha voluto ammettere la sua sconfitta; **it's the accepted thing** è un'usanza comunemente accettata.

ac·cept·able [ək'sɛptəbl] ADJ (*satisfactory*) accettabile; (*welcome: gift, offer*) gradito(-a); **tea is always acceptable** un tè è sempre ben accetto, un tè lo si beve sempre volentieri.

ac·cept·ance [ək'sɛptəns] N accettazione *f*; (*of person: by others*) accoglienza (favorevole); (: *for job, membership*) accettazione; (*of proposal*) accoglimento; **I've received two acceptances** ho ricevuto due risposte positive; **to meet with general acceptance** incontrare il favore *or* il consenso generale.

ac·cess ['æksɛs] 1 N accesso; **to have/gain access to sb/sth** avere/ottenere libero accesso presso qn/a qc; **the burglars gained access through a window** i ladri

sono penetrati da or attraverso una finestra; **we don't have access to a good sports complex** non abbiamo l'opportunità di frequentare un buon centro sportivo. 2 VT (*Comput*) accedere a.

ac·ces·sibil·ity [æk,sɛsɪ'bɪlɪtɪ] N accessibilità.

ac·ces·sible [æk'sɛsəbl] ADJ (*place*) accessibile, che si può raggiungere facilmente; (*person, information*) facilmente reperibile.

ac·ces·sion [æk'sɛʃən] N (*addition*) aggiunta; (*to library*) accessione f, acquisto; (*of king*) ascesa or salita al trono.

ac·ces·so·ry [æk'sɛsərɪ] N **a** (*gen pl*: *Dress, Comm*) accessorio; **toilet accessories** (*Brit*) articoli mpl da toletta **b** (*Law*) complice m/f.

♦ **access road** N strada d'accesso; (*to motorway*) raccordo di entrata.

♦ **access time** N (*Comput*) tempo di accesso.

ac·ci·dent ['æksɪdənt] N (*harmful*) incidente m, disgrazia; (*unexpected*) (puro) caso; **road accident** incidente stradale; **to meet with** or **to have an accident** avere un incidente; **accidents at work** infortuni mpl sul lavoro; **by accident** (*by chance*) per caso; (*unintentionally*) senza volere, per sbaglio; **accidents will happen** sono cose che capitano or succedono.

ac·ci·den·tal [,æksɪ'dɛntl] ADJ (*by chance*) accidentale, fortuito(-a), casuale; (*unintentional*) involontario(-a); **accidental death** morte f accidentale.

ac·ci·den·tal·ly [,æksɪ'dɛntəlɪ] ADV (*by chance*) per caso; (*unintentionally*) senza volere, inavvertitamente; **accidentally on purpose** (*fam*) di proposito, ma senza darlo a vedere.

♦ **accident black spot** N luogo famigerato per gli incidenti.

♦ **accident insurance** N assicurazione f contro gli infortuni.

♦ **accident-prone** ['æksɪdənt,prəʊn] ADJ predisposto(-a) agli incidenti; **he's very accident-prone** è un vero passaguai.

acclaim [ə'kleɪm] 1 VT acclamare.
2 N (*approval*) consenso; (*applause*) applauso.

ac·cla·ma·tion [,æklə'meɪʃən] N (*approval*) acclamazione f; (*applause*) applauso; **by acclamation** per acclamazione.

ac·cli·ma·ti·za·tion [ə,klaɪmətaɪ'zeɪʃən], (*Am*) **ac·cli·ma·tion** [,æklaɪ'meɪʃən] N acclimatazione f.

ac·cli·ma·tize [ə'klaɪmətaɪz], (*Am*) **ac·cli·mate** ['æklɪmeɪt] VT acclimatare; **to acclimatize o.s. (to)** acclimatarsi (a), adattarsi (a); **to become acclimatized** acclimatarsi.

ac·co·lade ['ækəleɪd] N (*frm: praise*) elogio, encomio; (*: award, honour*) onorificenza.

ac·com·mo·date [ə'kɒmədeɪt] VT **a** (*lodge, have room for*: *person*) ospitare, alloggiare; (*: thing*) ospitare, accogliere; **this car accommodates 4 people comfortably** quest'auto può trasportare comodamente 4 persone **b** (*oblige, help*) favorire; (*satisfy*) venire incontro a **c** (*differences*) conciliare **d** (*adjust to*: *idea, situation*): **accommodate o.s. to** venire incontro a, adattarsi a.

ac·com·mo·dat·ing [ə'kɒmədeɪtɪŋ] ADJ (*easy to deal with*) accomodante, conciliante; (*willing to help*) gentile, premuroso(-a).

ac·com·mo·da·tion [ə,kɒmə'deɪʃən] N, (*Am*) **ac·com·mo·da·tions** NPL **a** (*place to live*) sistemazione f, alloggio; (*space*) posto; **"accommodation to let"** "camere in affitto"; **have you any accommodation (available)?** avete posto?; **seating accommodation** (*Brit*) posti a sedere

b (*frm: adjustment, adaptation*) adattamento **c** (*Anat*) accomodazione f.

♦ **accommodation address** N recapito.

♦ **accommodation bureau,** (*Brit*) **accommodation agency** N agenzia immobiliare.

ac·com·pa·ni·ment [ə'kʌmpənɪmənt] N (*also Mus*) accompagnamento.

ac·com·pa·nist [ə'kʌmpənɪst] N (*Mus*) accompagnatore(-trice).

ac·com·pa·ny [ə'kʌmpənɪ] VT (*gen*) accompagnare; (*Mus*): **to accompany (on)** accompagnare (a).

ac·com·plice [ə'kʌmplɪs] N: **accomplice (in)** complice m/f (di).

ac·com·plish [ə'kʌmplɪʃ] VT (*task, mission*) compiere, portare a termine; (*one's design*) realizzare; (*purpose*) ottenere.

ac·com·plished [ə'kʌmplɪʃt] ADJ (*pianist, cook*) esperto(-a).

ac·com·plish·ment [ə'kʌmplɪʃmənt] N (*completion*) realizzazione f, compimento, completamento; (*thing achieved*) risultato, impresa; **accomplishments** NPL (*skills*) doti fpl.

ac·cord [ə'kɔːd] 1 N (*harmony*) accordo; **of his own accord** spontaneamente, di sua iniziativa; **with one accord** all'unanimità, di comune accordo; **to be in accord with** essere d'accordo con.
2 VT accordare.
3 VI: **to accord (with)** andare d'accordo (con), accordarsi (con).

ac·cord·ance [ə'kɔːdəns] N: **in accordance with** secondo, in conformità di or a.

ac·cord·ing [ə'kɔːdɪŋ] PREP: **according to** secondo, stando a; **according to him** secondo lui; **according to what he says** stando a quanto dice; **they will be punished according to the seriousness of their crimes** saranno puniti a seconda della gravità dei loro delitti; **it went according to plan** è andata secondo quanto previsto.

ac·cord·ing·ly [ə'kɔːdɪŋlɪ] ADV (*all senses*) di conseguenza.

ac·cor·di·on [ə'kɔːdɪən] N (*Mus*) fisarmonica.

ac·cor·di·on·ist [ə'kɔːdɪənɪst] N (*Mus*) fisarmonicista m/f.

ac·cost [ə'kɒst] VT (*confront*) abbordare; (*approach*) avvicinare.

ac·count [ə'kaʊnt] N **a** (*report*) resoconto, relazione f; **to give an account of sth** fare un resoconto di or una relazione su qc; **to keep an account of** tenere nota di; **to bring** or **call sb to account for sth/for having done sth** chiedere a qn di render conto di qc/per aver fatto qc; **by all accounts** a detta di tutti, a quanto si dice; **to give a good account of o.s.** farsi onore, dare un'ottima prova di sé

b (*consideration*) considerazione f, conto; (*importance*) importanza, conto; **it's of no account** non importa; **of little account** di poca importanza; **on no account** per nessuna ragione, per nessun motivo, in nessun caso; **on account of** a causa di; **on his account** (*for his benefit*) per lui; **to take account of sth**, **take sth into account** tener conto di qc, prendere in considerazione qc; **to turn sth to good account** trarre profitto da qc

c (*at shop, bank, Comm*) conto; **to open an account (with)** aprire un conto (presso); **"account payee only"** (*Brit: on cheque*) "non trasferibile"; **they have the Pirelli account** la Pirelli è fra i loro clienti; **your account is still outstanding** il suo conto non è ancora stato saldato; **to get £50 on account** ricevere 50 sterline come or in or di acconto, ricevere un acconto di 50 sterline; **to put £50**

down on account versare un acconto di 50 sterline; **to buy sth on account** comprare qc a credito

d (*Comm*): **accounts** NPL conti *mpl*; **to keep/do the accounts** tenere/fare i conti; **accounts department** ufficio *m* contabilità *inv*

► **account for** VI + PREP **a** (*explain*) spiegare, giustificare; (*give reckoning of*: *actions, expenditure*) render conto di, rispondere di; **that accounts for it** questo spiega tutto; **all the children were accounted for** nessun ragazzo mancava all'appello; **there's no accounting for tastes** tutti i gusti son gusti

b (*represent*) rappresentare

c (*destroy, kill*) uccidere, distruggere.

ac·count·abil·ity [əˌkaʊntəˈbɪlɪtɪ] N responsabilità.

ac·count·able [əˈkaʊntəbl] ADJ: **to be accountable (for sth/to sb)** essere responsabile (di qc/verso qn).

ac·count·an·cy [əˈkaʊntənsɪ] N ragioneria.

ac·count·ant [əˈkaʊntənt] N ragioniere(-a), contabile *m/f*; (*for personal finances*) ≈ commercialista *m/f*.

ac·count·ing [əˈkaʊntɪŋ] N (*auditing*) contabilità; (*subject, field*) ragioneria.

♦ **accounting period** N esercizio finanziario, periodo contabile.

♦ **account number** N numero di conto.

♦ **account payable** N (*Am*) conto passivo.

♦ **account receivable** N (*Am*) conto da esigere.

ac·cou·tre·ments [əˈkuːtrəmənts] NPL (*frm, hum*) equipaggiamento *msg*.

ac·cred·it·ed [əˈkrɛdɪtɪd] ADJ (*authorized*) accreditato(-a).

ac·cre·tion [əˈkriːʃən] N (*frm: gen, Law*) accrescimento.

ac·crue [əˈkruː] VI (*mount up*) aumentare; (: *interest*) maturare; **to accrue to** derivare a; **the notoriety that accrued to him** la notorietà che gliene è derivata.

ac·crued [əˈkruːd] ADJ (*interest*) maturato(-a); **accrued charges** ratei *mpl* passivi.

ac·cu·mu·late [əˈkjuːmjʊleɪt] [1] VT accumulare.

[2] VI accumularsi.

ac·cu·mu·la·tion [əˌkjuːmjʊˈleɪʃən] N (*amassing*) accumulo, accumulazione *f*; (*mass, heap*) mucchio, cumulo.

ac·cu·mu·la·tor [əˈkjuːmjʊleɪtəʳ] N (*Elec*) accumulatore *m*.

ac·cu·ra·cy [ˈækjʊrəsɪ] N (*see adj*) accuratezza; esattezza; precisione *f*; fedeltà.

ac·cu·rate [ˈækjʊrɪt] ADJ (*description, report, assessment*) accurato(-a), esatto(-a), preciso(-a); (*observation, estimate*) accurato(-a); (*answer*) corretto(-a), esatto(-a); (*shot, instrument, worker*) preciso(-a); (*copy*) fedele.

ac·cu·rate·ly [ˈækjʊrɪtlɪ] ADV (*see adj*) accuratamente; con esattezza; correttamente; con precisione; fedelmente.

ac·cu·sa·tion [ˌækjʊˈzeɪʃən] N accusa.

ac·cu·sa·tive [əˈkjuːzətɪv] [1] ADJ (*Gram*) accusativo(-a).

[2] N (*Gram*) accusativo; **in the accusative** all'accusativo.

ac·cuse [əˈkjuːz] VT: **to accuse sb (of)** accusare qn (di).

ac·cused [əˈkjuːzd] N (*Law*): **the accused** l'accusato(-a), l'imputato(-a).

ac·cus·er [əˈkjuːzəʳ] N accusatore(-trice).

ac·cus·ing [əˈkjuːzɪŋ] ADJ (*look, tone*) accusatore(-trice), d'accusa.

ac·cus·ing·ly [əˈkjuːzɪŋlɪ] ADV con fare d'accusa.

ac·cus·tom [əˈkʌstəm] VT: **to accustom sb to sth/to doing sth** abituare qn a qc/a fare qc; **to accustom o.s. to sth** abituarsi a qc.

ac·cus·tomed [əˈkʌstəmd] ADJ (*usual*) abituale; **to be accustomed to sth** essere abituato(-a) a qc; **to get accustomed to sth/to doing sth** abituarsi *or* adattarsi a qc/a fare qc.

AC/DC [ˈeɪsiːˈdiːsiː] [1] N ABBR (= *alternating current/direct current*) c.a./c.c. (= *corrente alternata/corrente continua*).

[2] ADJ ABBR (*fam: bisexual*) bisessuale.

ACE [eɪs] N ABBR = *American Council on Education*.

ace [eɪs] [1] N (*Cards, fig: sportsman, driver*) asso; **to be within an ace of** (*Brit*) essere a un pelo da; **to keep an ace up one's sleeve** avere un asso nella manica; **to serve an ace** (*Tennis*) effettuare un servizio vincente.

[2] ADJ (*fam: excellent*) eccezionale; **to be ace at sth** essere bravissimo(-a) in *or* a qc; **sixty of his ace pilots** sessanta dei suoi piloti migliori.

acer·bic [əˈsɜːbɪk] ADJ (*frm: also fig*) acido(-a).

ac·etate [ˈæsɪteɪt] N acetato.

acetic [əˈsiːtɪk] ADJ acetico(-a).

♦ **acetic acid** N acido acetico.

ac·etone [ˈæsɪtəʊn] N acetone *m*.

acety·lene [əˈsɛtɪliːn] N acetilene *m*; **acetylene burner** becco ad acetilene; **acetylene welding** saldatura ad acetilene.

ache [eɪk] [1] N (*pain*) dolore *m*, male *m*; **stomach ache** mal *m* di stomaco; **I've got stomach ache** *or* (*Am*) **a stomach ache** ho mal di stomaco; **I'm full of aches and pains** mi fa male dappertutto, sono pieno di dolori.

[2] VI (*hurt*) far male, dolere; **it makes my head ache** mi fa venire *or* mi dà il mal di testa; **I'm aching all over** sono tutto indolenzito, mi duole dappertutto; **it made her heart ache to see …** (*fig*) le piangeva il cuore vedere….

[3] VT (*yearn*): **to ache to do sth** morire dalla voglia di fare qc.

achieve [əˈtʃiːv] [1] VT (*aim*) raggiungere; (*success, effect*) ottenere; (*victory*) riportare; (*result*) conseguire.

[2] VI (*be successful*) avere successo.

achieve·ment [əˈtʃiːvmənt] N (*act*) realizzazione *f*, raggiungimento, compimento; (*thing achieved*) risultato, successo; **that's quite an achievement** è una bella impresa, è un bel successo.

achiev·er [əˈtʃiːvəʳ] N (*Sociol*): **she is a high achiever** ha una personalità vincente.

Achilles [əˈkɪliːz] N Achille *m*.

♦ **Achilles heel** N tallone *m* di Achille.

♦ **Achilles tendon** N (*Anat*) tendine *m* di Achille.

ach·ing [ˈeɪkɪŋ] ADJ (*gen*) dolorante; (*sad*) afflitto(-a).

acid [ˈæsɪd] [1] N (*Chem, drug*) acido.

[2] ADJ (*Chem*) acido(-a); (*sour*) acido(-a), acidulo(-a); (*fig: wit, remark*) caustico(-a); **acid salts** (*Chem*) sali *mpl* acidi; **acid oxides** (*Chem*) ossiacidi *mpl*.

♦ **acid-base** [ˈæsɪdˌbeɪs] ADJ (*Chem*): **acid-base reactions** reazioni *fpl* acido-base *inv*.

acid·ic [əˈsɪdɪk] ADJ acido(-a).

acidi·fi·ca·tion [əˌsɪdɪfɪˈkeɪʃən] N acidificazione *f*.

acidi·fy [əˈsɪdɪˌfaɪ] VT, VI acidificare.

acid·ity [əˈsɪdɪtɪ] N acidità.

ac·id·ly [ˈæsɪdlɪ] ADV acidamente.

♦ **acid rain** N pioggia acida.

♦ **acid test** N prova del fuoco.

ac·knowl·edge [əkˈnɒlɪdʒ] VT (*mistake*) riconoscere, ammettere; (*truth*) riconoscere; (*claim*) prendere atto di; (*letter: also:* **acknowledge receipt of**) accusare ricevuta di; (*help, present*) manifestare la propria gratitudine per; (*greeting*) rispondere a, ricambiare; **I smiled at him but he didn't even acknowledge me** gli ho sorriso ma lui non ha nemmeno dato segno di accorgersi di me; **to acknowledge sb as leader** riconoscere qn come capo; **to acknowledge o.s. beaten** ammettere la propria sconfitta.

ac·knowl·edged [əkˈnɒlɪdʒd] ADJ (*leader, expert etc*) riconosciuto(-a).

ac·knowl·edge·ment [əkˈnɒlɪdʒmənt] **a** N (*admission*) ammissione *f*, riconoscimento; (*of letter*) conferma (di aver ricevuto); **in acknowledgement of** a riconoscimento di **b** : **acknowledgements** NPL (*in book*) ringraziamenti *mpl*.

ACLU [ˌeɪsiːɛlˈjuː] N ABBR (= *American Civil Liberties Union*) *unione americana per le libertà civili.*

acme [ˈækmɪ] N (*frm*) culmine *m*, acme *f*.

acne [ˈæknɪ] N acne *f*.

aco·lyte [ˈækəʊlaɪt] N (*Rel, liter*) accolito.

acorn [ˈeɪkɔːn] N (*Bot*) ghianda.

acous·tic [əˈkuːstɪk] ADJ acustico(-a).

acous·ti·cal·ly [əˈkuːstɪklɪ] ADV acusticamente.

♦ **acoustic coupler** [əˈkuːstɪkˈkʌpləʳ] N (*Comput*) accopiatore *m* acustico.

acous·tics [əˈkuːstɪks] ☐ NSG (*Phys*) acustica. ☐ NPL (*of room*) acustica *nsg*.

♦ **acoustic screen** N pannello acustico.

ac·quaint [əˈkweɪnt] VT **a** (*inform*): **to acquaint sb with sth** informare qn di qc, far sapere qc a qn, mettere qn al corrente di qc; **he's already acquainted with the facts** è già informato *or* a conoscenza dei fatti; **to acquaint o.s. with sth** familiarizzarsi con qc, impratichirsi su qc **b** (*with person*): **to be acquainted with sb** conoscere (personalmente) qn; **to become acquainted with sb** fare la conoscenza di qn; **we became acquainted in Paris** ci siamo conosciuti a Parigi.

ac·quaint·ance [əˈkweɪntəns] N **a** (*with person, subject etc*): **acquaintance (with)** conoscenza (di); **to make sb's acquaintance** fare la conoscenza di qn; **it improves on acquaintance** più lo si conosce e più lo si apprezza **b** (*person*) conoscente *m/f*, conoscenza; **a business acquaintance** una conoscenza di lavoro; **an acquaintance of mine** un mio conoscente.

ac·qui·esce [ˌækwɪˈɛs] VI (*frm: agree*): **to acquiesce (to)** acconsentire (a).

ac·qui·es·cence [ˌækwɪˈɛsns] N (*frm*) acquiescenza, consenso.

ac·qui·es·cent [ˌækwɪˈɛsnt] ADJ (*frm*) acquiescente.

ac·quire [əˈkwaɪəʳ] VT (*possessions, territory, knowledge*) acquisire; (*language*) apprendere; (*habit*) contrarre, prendere; (*reputation*) farsi; **to acquire a taste for** prender gusto a.

ac·quired [əˈkwaɪəd] ADJ acquisito(-a); **it's an acquired taste** è una cosa che si impara ad apprezzare.

ac·qui·si·tion [ˌækwɪˈzɪʃən] N acquisto.

ac·quisi·tive [əˈkwɪzɪtɪv] ADJ (*person*) a cui piace accumulare; (*: pej*) materialista.

ac·quisi·tive·ness [əˈkwɪzɪtɪvnɪs] N tendenza ad accumulare; (*pej*) materialismo.

ac·quit [əˈkwɪt] VT **a** (*Law*): **to acquit sb (of)** assolvere qn (da) **b** : **to acquit o.s. (well/badly)** (*frm*) comportarsi (bene/male).

ac·quit·tal [əˈkwɪtl] N (*Law*) assoluzione *f*.

acre [ˈeɪkəʳ] N acro (= *4047 m²*).

acre·age [ˈeɪkərɪdʒ] N superficie *f* in acri.

ac·rid [ˈækrɪd] ADJ (*smell*) acre, pungente; (*fig*) pungente.

Ac·ri·lan® [ˈækrɪlæn] N fibra acrilica.

ac·ri·mo·ni·ous [ˌækrɪˈməʊnɪəs] ADJ (*frm: remark*) astioso (-a), malevolo(-a); (*: argument*) aspro(-a).

ac·ri·mo·ny [ˈækrɪmənɪ] N (*frm*) acrimonia.

ac·ro·bat [ˈækrəˌbæt] N acrobata *m/f*.

ac·ro·bat·ic [ˌækrəʊˈbætɪk] ADJ acrobatico(-a).

ac·ro·bat·ics [ˌækrəʊˈbætɪks] NPL acrobazie *fpl*.

ac·ro·nym [ˈækrənɪm] N acronimo.

Acropo·lis [əˈkrɒpəlɪs] N: **the Acropolis** l'Acropoli *f*.

across [əˈkrɒs] ☐ PREP **a** (*from one side to other of*) attraverso; **to go across a bridge** attraversare un ponte; **to take sb across the road** far attraversare la strada a qn; **there was a motif printed across the front of his tee-shirt** c'era un disegno stampato sul davanti della sua maglietta; **he gave interviews across the country** ha concesso delle interviste in tutto il paese **b** (*on the other side of*) dall'altra parte di, al di là di; **the shop across the road** il negozio sull'altro lato *or* dall'altra parte della strada; **across from** di fronte a; **across the street from our house** di fronte *or* dirimpetto a casa nostra **c** (*crosswise over*) di traverso a.

☐ ADV **a** (*direction*) dall'altra parte; **to jump across** saltare dall'altra parte, attraversare con un salto; **I helped the old man across** ho aiutato il vecchio ad attraversare; **don't go round, go across** non fare il giro, attraversa *or* passa nel mezzo; **to cut sth across** tagliare qc per *or* di traverso; **3 across** (*in crosswords*) 3 orizzontale; **to get sth across to sb** (*fig*) far capire qc a qn **b** (*measurement*) in larghezza; **the lake is 12 km across** il lago ha una larghezza di 12 km *or* è largo 12 km.

♦ **across-the-board** [əˈkrɒsðəˈbɔːd] ADJ generale.

acryl·ic [əˈkrɪlɪk] ☐ ADJ acrilico(-a). ☐ N acrilico.

act [ækt] ☐ VI **a** (*take action*) agire; **he acted to stop it** è intervenuto per fermarlo **b** (*function: thing, person*): **to act as** fungere da, fare da; (*: drug*) agire; **he acts as my assistant** mi fa da assistente; **acting in my capacity as chairman, I ...** in qualità di presidente, io...; **it acts as a deterrent** serve da deterrente; **to act for sb** agire in nome *or* per conto di qn; **who is acting for the defendant?** chi è l'avvocato difensore? **c** (*behave*) comportarsi; **to act like a fool** fare lo(-a) stupido(-a), comportarsi come uno(-a) stupido(-a); **she acted as if she was upset** si era mostrata contrariata **d** (*Theatre, Cine*) recitare; **he's only acting** sta solo facendo finta *or* recitando.

☐ VT (*play*) rappresentare, mettere in scena; (*part*) recitare, interpretare; **to act Hamlet** recitare la parte di Amleto; **to act the fool** (*fig*) fare lo(-a) stupido(-a) *or* il/la cretino(-a).

☐ N **a** (*deed*) atto; **an act of kindness** un atto di gentilezza; **an act of folly** una pazzia, una follia; **I was in the act of writing to him** stavo (proprio) scrivendo a lui; **to catch sb in the act** cogliere qn in flagrante *or* sul fatto; **I caught him in the act of stealing** l'ho sorpreso a rubare **b** (*also:* **act of Parliament**) legge *f* **c** (*Theatre: of play*) atto; (*in circus, music-hall*) numero; (*fig: pretence*) scena, messinscena; **it's only an act** è tutta scena, è solo una messinscena

► **act on, act upon** VI + PREP (*advice*) seguire, agire in base a; (*order, instructions*) agire in base a, eseguire.

► **act out** VT (*event*) ricostruire; (*fantasies*) mettere in atto.

► **act up** VI + ADV (*fam: person*) fare i capricci; (*: injury*) farsi sentire; (*: machine*) fare degli scherzi.

act·ing [ˈæktɪŋ] ☐ ADJ che fa le funzioni di; **he is the acting manager** fa le veci del direttore. ☐ N recitazione *f*; **to do some acting** fare del teatro (*or* del cinema).

ac·tion [ˈækʃən] N **a** (*doing*) azione *f*; (*deed*) fatto, azione; (*movement: of horse, athlete*) stile *m*; (*effect: of acid, drug*

etc) azione, effetto; (*Mil*) azione, combattimento; (*Tech: of clock, machine*) meccanismo; **to take action** passare all'azione, agire; **to put a plan into action** realizzare un piano; **to be out of action** assere fuori combattimento; (*machine etc*) non funzionare, essere fuori uso; **killed in action** (*Mil*) ucciso(-a) in combattimento

  b (*Law*) azione *f* legale, processo; **to bring an action against sb** (*Law*) intentare causa contro qn.

♦ **action replay** N (*Brit TV*) replay *m inv*.

♦ **action stations** NPL (*Mil*): **action stations!** ai posti di combattimento!

ac·ti·vate ['æktɪveɪt] VT attivare; (*mechanism*) fare funzionare; (*Chem, Phys*) rendere attivo(-a).

ac·ti·va·tion [ækti'veɪʃən] N attivazione *f*.

ac·tive ['æktɪv] ADJ (*gen, Gram, volcano*) attivo(-a); **to play an active part in** partecipare attivamente a, prendere parte attiva in; **we are giving it active consideration** lo stiamo considerando attentamente.

ac·tive·ly ['æktɪvlɪ] ADV attivamente; **to be actively involved in** prendere parte attiva in.

♦ **active partner** N (*Comm*) socio effettivo *or* accomandatario.

♦ **active service,** (*Am*) **active duty** N (*Mil*): **to be on active service** prestar servizio in zona di operazioni.

ac·tiv·ist ['æktɪvɪst] N attivista *m/f*.

ac·tiv·ity [æk'tɪvɪtɪ] N (*gen*) attività *f inv*; (*of scene*) animazione *f*, movimento; **social activities** attività ricreative.

♦ **act of God** N calamità *f inv* naturale.

♦ **Act of Parliament** N legge *f*.

ac·tor ['æktə'] N attore *m*.

ac·tress ['æktrɪs] N attrice *f*.

♦ **Acts of the Apostles** N (*Bible*): **the Acts of the Apostles** gli Atti degli Apostoli.

ACTT [,eɪsi:ti:'ti:] N ABBR (*Brit*: = *Association of Cinematographic, Television and Allied Technicians*) sindacato dei tecnici cinematografici, televisivi e affini.

ac·tual ['æktjʊəl] ADJ (*amount, result*) reale, vero(-a), effettivo(-a); (*example*) concreto(-a); **in actual fact** in realtà; **what were his actual words?** cosa ha detto esattamente?

ac·tu·al·ity [ækt'ʃʊ'ælɪtɪ] N: **but in actuality** ... ma in realtà... .

ac·tu·al·ly ['æktjʊəlɪ] ADV (*really*) veramente, davvero; (*even*) addirittura, perfino; **he actually expected us to put him up for the whole holiday** si aspettava sul serio che lo ospitassimo per tutta la vacanza!; **that's not true, actually** questo non è affatto vero; **I wasn't actually there** a *or* per dire la verità io non c'ero.

ac·tu·ary ['æktjʊərɪ] N attuario(-a).

ac·tu·ate ['æktjʊeɪt] VT (*frm: person*) spingere; (*Tech: machine*) attivare; **actuated by** animato(-a) da.

acu·ity [ə'kju:ɪtɪ] N (*frm*) acutezza.

acu·men ['ækjʊmɛn] N acume *m*, perspicacia; **business acumen** fiuto negli affari.

acu·punc·ture ['ækjʊpʌŋktʃə'] N agopuntura.

acu·punc·tur·ist [,ækjʊ'pʌŋktʃərɪst] N agopuntore(-trice).

acute [ə'kju:t] ADJ (*eyesight, accent, angle*) acuto(-a); (*hearing, smell etc*) fine; (*pain, anxiety, joy*) intenso(-a); (*crisis, shortage*) grave; (*person, mind*) perspicace, dotato (-a) di acume.

acute·ly [ə'kju:tlɪ] ADV (*intensely*) intensamente; (*shrewdly*) con perspicacia.

AD [,eɪ'di:] □1□ ADV ABBR (= *Anno Domini*) d.C.
  □2□ N ABBR (*Am Mil*) = **active duty.**

ad [æd] N ABBR = **advertisement.**

ad·age ['ædɪdʒ] N (*old*) adagio, detto.

Adam ['ædəm] N Adamo; **I don't know him from Adam** non ho idea di chi sia.

ada·mant ['ædəmənt] ADJ inflessibile, irremovibile.

♦ **Adam's apple** N pomo d'Adamo.

a·dapt [ə'dæpt] □1□ VT (*machine*) modificare, fare delle modifiche a; (*building*) trasformare; (*text*) adattare; **to adapt o.s. to sth** adattarsi a qc.
  □2□ VI: **to adapt (to)** adattarsi (a).

adapt·abil·ity [ə,dæptə'bɪlɪtɪ] N adattabilità, capacità di adattamento.

adapt·able [ə'dæptəbl] ADJ (*person*) adattabile, che sa adattarsi; (*device*) adattabile; **he's very adaptable** si adatta facilmente.

ad·ap·ta·tion [,ædæp'teɪʃən] N adattamento.

adapt·er, adap·tor [ə'dæptə'] N **a** (*Elec: for several plugs*) presa multipla; (: *for 2-pin to 3-pin system*) adattatore *m*, riduttore *m* **b** (*of novel*) chi cura un adattamento.

ADC [,eɪdi:'si:] N ABBR (*Mil*) = **aide-de-camp.**

add [æd] □1□ VT: **to add (to)** aggiungere (a); (*Math*) sommare (a), addizionare (a); **he added that ...** ha aggiunto che...; **added to which ...** e per giunta..., e per di più...; **to add insult to injury** aggiungere al danno le beffe.
  □2□ VI (*count*) fare le addizioni *or* le somme, addizionare

▶ **add in** VT + ADV aggiungere, includere

▶ **add on** VT + ADV aggiungere

▶ **add to** VI + PREP aumentare, accrescere

▶ **add up** □1□ VT + ADV (*figures*) addizionare, sommare; (*advantages etc*) mettere insieme.
  □2□ VI + ADV: **it adds up to 25** la somma è 25; **it doesn't add up** (*fig fam*) non quadra, non ha senso; **it doesn't add up to much** (*fig*) non è un granché; **it's all beginning to add up** (*fig fam*) tutto comincia a diventare chiaro.

ad·den·dum [ə'dɛndəm] N (*pl* **addenda** [ə'dɛndə]) aggiunta; **addenda** NPL (*to book, report*) addenda *mpl*.

ad·der ['ædə'] N vipera.

ad·dict ['ædɪkt] N tossicomane *m/f*, drogato(-a); (*fig*) fanatico(-a); **drug addict** tossicodipendente *m/f*, tossicomane *m/f*; **heroin addict** eroinomane *m/f*; **television addict** teledipendente *m/f*.

ad·dicted [ə'dɪktɪd] ADJ: **addicted (to)** (*drugs etc*) dipendente (da); (*fig*) fanatico(-a) (di), maniaco(-a) (di); **to become addicted to cocaine** diventare cocainomane; **to be addicted to drink** essere dedito(-a) al bere; **to be addicted to chocolate** essere un(a) cioccolato-dipendente.

ad·dic·tion [ə'dɪkʃən] N assuefazione *f*; (*Med*) tossicomania; **drug addiction** tossicodipendenza; **to have an addiction to chocolate** essere cioccolato-dipendente.

ad·dic·tive [ə'dɪktɪv] ADJ che dà assuefazione.

ad·ding ma·chine ['ædɪŋmə'ʃi:n] N addizionatrice *f*.

Ad·dis Aba·ba ['ædɪs'æbəbə] N Addis Abeba *f*.

ad·di·tion [ə'dɪʃən] N aggiunta; (*Math*) addizione *f*; **if my addition is correct** se ho fatto bene i conti; **there has been an addition to the family** la famiglia si è accresciuta; **in addition to** oltre a, in aggiunta a; **in addition,** ... inoltre,... .

ad·di·tion·al [ə'dɪʃənl] ADJ supplementare.

ad·di·tion·al·ly [ə'dɪʃnəlɪ] ADV in più, per di più.

ad·di·tive ['ædɪtɪv] N additivo.

ad·dress [ə'drɛs] □1□ N **a** (*of house etc*) indirizzo, recapito; (*on envelope, Comput*) indirizzo; **absolute/relative**

address (*Comput*) indirizzo assoluto/relativo
b (*talk*) discorso, allocuzione *f*
c : **form of address** (*gen*) formula di cortesia; (*in letters*) formula d'indirizzo *or* di intestazione; **the correct form of address for a bishop** la maniera corretta di rivolgersi ad un vescovo.
2 VT **a** (*direct: letter*) indirizzare; (: *write name etc on envelope*) mettere *or* scrivere l'indirizzo su; (*remarks etc*) rivolgere; **this letter is wrongly addressed** l'indirizzo su questa lettera è sbagliato; **please address your complaints to the manager** (*frm*) per i reclami si rivolga al direttore; **to address o.s. to sth** (*frm*) indirizzare le proprie energie verso qc
b (*person*) rivolgersi a; (*meeting*) parlare a, fare un discorso a; **she addressed him as "Your Lordship"** si rivolse a lui chiamandolo "Sua Eccellenza"; **the judge addressed the jury** il giudice si è rivolto alla giuria.
♦ **address book** N rubrica.
ad·dressee [ˌædrɛˈsiː] N destinatario(-a).
ad·duce [əˈdjuːs] VT (*frm: fact, reason*) addurre.
Aden [ˈeɪdən] N Aden *f*; **the Gulf of Aden** il golfo di Aden.
ad·enoids [ˈædɪnɔɪdz] NPL adenoidi *fpl.*
adept [ˈædɛpt] 1 ADJ: **adept in** *or* **at sth/at doing sth** abile *or* esperto(-a) in qc/nel fare qc.
2 N: **adept (in, at)** esperto(-a) (in).
ad·equa·cy [ˈædɪkwəsɪ] N adeguatezza.
ad·equate [ˈædɪkwɪt] ADJ (*amount, supply*): **adequate (for/to do sth)** sufficiente (a/per fare qc); (*reward, description, explanation*): **adequate (for)** adeguato(-a) (a); (*tool*): **adequate (to)** adatto(-a) (a); (*essay, performance*) passabile; (*person*) all'altezza; **to feel adequate to a task** sentirsi all'altezza di un compito.
ad·equate·ly [ˈædɪkwɪtlɪ] ADV (*heated, paid*) adeguatamente, sufficientemente; (*perform, answer*) convenientemente; **will he do it adequately?** sarà all'altezza?
ad·here [ədˈhɪəʳ] VI: **to adhere to** (*surface, party, policy*) aderire a; (*belief*) rimanere fedele a; (*promise*) mantenere; (*rule, decision*) attenersi a, seguire.
ad·her·ence [ədˈhɪərəns] N: **adherence (to)** adesione *f* (a).
ad·her·ent [ədˈhɪərənt] N (*person*) aderente *m/f.*
ad·he·sion [ədˈhiːʒən] N (*Tech*) aderenza; (*fig: of supporters*) consenso.
ad·he·sive [ədˈhiːzɪv] 1 ADJ adesivo(-a); **adhesive tape** (*Brit: for parcels etc*) nastro adesivo; (*Am Med*) cerotto adesivo.
2 N adesivo.
ad·he·sive·ness [ədˈhiːzɪvnɪs] N adesività.
ad hoc [ˌædˈhɒk] ADJ (*decision*) ad hoc *inv*; (*committee*) apposito(-a).
adieu [əˈdjuː] N addio.
ad in·fi·ni·tum [ˌædɪnfɪˈnaɪtəm] ADV all'infinito.
adi·pose [ˈædɪˌpəʊs] ADJ adiposo(-a).
ad·ja·cen·cy [əˈdʒeɪsənsɪ] N attiguità.
ad·ja·cent [əˈdʒeɪsənt] ADJ: **adjacent (to)** adiacente (a).
ad·jec·ti·val [ˌædʒɛkˈtaɪvəl] ADJ aggettivale.
ad·jec·ti·val·ly [ˌædʒɛkˈtaɪvəlɪ] ADV con funzione di aggettivo.
ad·jec·tive [ˈædʒɛktɪv] N aggettivo.
ad·join [əˈdʒɔɪn] VT essere contiguo(-a) a *or* attiguo(-a) a; **the room adjoining mine** la stanza accanto alla mia.
ad·join·ing [əˈdʒɔɪnɪŋ] ADJ contiguo(-a), attiguo(-a), adiacente.
ad·journ [əˈdʒɜːn] 1 VT (*suspend*) aggiornare, rimandare, rinviare; **to adjourn a meeting till the following week**

aggiornare *or* rinviare un incontro alla settimana seguente; **to adjourn a meeting for a month** rinviare un incontro di un mese.
2 VI **a** sospendere la seduta; (*Parliament*) sospendere i lavori
b (*move*) spostarsi; **they adjourned to the pub** (*fam*) si sono trasferiti al pub.
ad·journ·ment [əˈdʒɜːnmənt] N (*of meeting*) rinvio, aggiornamento.
Adjt ABBR (*Mil*) = **adjutant.**
ad·ju·di·cate [əˈdʒuːdɪkeɪt] VT (*contest*) giudicare; (*claim*) decidere su.
ad·ju·di·ca·tion [əˈdʒuːdɪˈkeɪʃən] N (*of contest*) giudizio; (*of claim*) decisione *f.*
ad·ju·di·ca·tor [əˈdʒuːdɪˌkeɪtəʳ] N (*of dispute, competition*) arbitro.
ad·junct [ˈædʒʌŋkt] N (*gen*) aggiunta; (*Gram*) complemento.
ad·just [əˈdʒʌst] 1 VT (*instrument, tool, speed*) regolare; (*wages, prices*) modificare; (*aim, tie, dress*) aggiustare.
2 VI: **to adjust (to)** adattarsi (a).
ad·just·able [əˈdʒʌstəbl] ADJ regolabile; **adjustable pliers** pinza *fsg* regolabile.
ad·just·ed [əˈdʒʌstɪd] ADJ (*Psych*) integrato(-a).
ad·just·er [əˈdʒʌstəʳ] N = **loss adjuster.**
ad·just·ing en·try [əˈdʒʌstɪŋˈɛntrɪ] N (*Econ*) scrittura di conguaglio.
ad·just·ment [əˈdʒʌstmənt] N (*of instrument*) regolazione *f*; (*of wages, prices*) modifica, aggiustamento; (*of person*) adattamento; **to make an adjustment to one's plans** modificare i propri piani.
ad·ju·tant [ˈædʒətənt] N (*Mil*) aiutante *m/f.*
ad–lib [ædˈlɪb] 1 VT, VI improvvisare.
2 N improvvisazione *f.*
3 ADJ improvvisato(-a), estemporaneo(-a).
4 ADV (*speak*) a piacere.
ad·man [ˈædmæn] N (*fam*) pubblicitario.
ad·min [ˈædmɪn] N ABBR (*fam*) = **administration.**
ad·min·is·ter [ədˈmɪnɪstəʳ] VT **a** (*manage: company*) dirigere, gestire; (: *fund*) amministrare **b** (*dispense: medicine*) somministrare; (: *justice, laws*) amministrare; **to administer an oath to sb** far prestare giuramento a qn.
ad·min·is·tra·tion [ədˌmɪnɪsˈtreɪʃən] N **a** (*of company*) direzione *f*, gestione *f*; (*of fund, justice*) amministrazione *f*; (*of medicine*) somministrazione *f* **b** (*Am Pol*) governo.
ad·min·is·tra·tive [ədˈmɪnɪstrətɪv] ADJ amministrativo (-a).
ad·min·is·tra·tive·ly [ədˈmɪnɪstrətɪvlɪ] ADV amministrativamente.
ad·min·is·tra·tor [ədˈmɪnɪstreɪtəʳ] N amministratore(-trice); (*of will*) curatore(-trice).
ad·mi·rable [ˈædmərəbl] ADJ ammirevole.
ad·mi·rably [ˈædmərəblɪ] ADV ammirevolmente; **he is admirably suited to the job** è perfettamente adatto a quel lavoro.
ad·mi·ral [ˈædmərəl] N ammiraglio.
Ad·mi·ral·ty [ˈædmərəltɪ] N (*Brit*): **the Admiralty** l'Ammiragliato.
ad·mi·ral·ty [ˈædmərəltɪ] N ammiragliato.
♦ **Admiralty Board** N: **the Admiralty Board** (*Brit*) ≈ il Ministero della Marina Militare.
ad·mi·ra·tion [ˌædməˈreɪʃən] N ammirazione *f.*
ad·mire [ədˈmaɪəʳ] VT ammirare; **she was admiring herself in the mirror** si rimirava allo *or* davanti allo specchio.

ad·mir·er [əd'maɪərəʳ] N ammiratore(-trice).
ad·mir·ing [əd'maɪərɪŋ] ADJ (*person*) pieno(-a) di ammirazione; (*look*) di ammirazione.
ad·mir·ing·ly [əd'maɪərɪŋlɪ] ADV con ammirazione.
ad·mis·sible [əd'mɪsəbl] ADJ ammissibile.
ad·mis·sion [əd'mɪʃən] N **a** (*entry: to society, school etc*) ammissione *f*; (: *to exhibition, night club, building*) entrata, ingresso; (*price*) prezzo del biglietto (d'ingresso); **"admission free"** *or* **"free admission"** "ingresso gratuito"
  b (*confession*) ammissione *f*, confessione *f*; **it would be an admission of defeat** sarebbe come dichiararsi sconfitto; **by his own admission** per sua ammissione.
ad·mit [əd'mɪt] VT **a** (*allow to enter*) lasciar entrare, far entrare; (: *air, light*) lasciar passare; **children not admitted** vietato l'ingresso ai bambini; **this ticket admits two** questo biglietto è valido per due persone; **he was admitted to hospital** è stato ricoverato all'ospedale
  b (*acknowledge*) ammettere, riconoscere; (: *crime*) ammettere *or* confessare (di aver compiuto); **it is hard, I admit** è difficile, lo ammetto *or* devo ammetterlo; **I must admit that ...** devo ammettere *or* confessare che...
  ► **admit of** VI + PREP (*frm*) dare adito a
  ► **admit to** VI + PREP riconoscere.
ad·mit·tance [əd'mɪtəns] N ingresso; **they refused me admittance** mi hanno rifiutato il permesso di entrare; **to gain admittance** riuscire a entrare; **"no admittance"** "vietato l'ingresso".
ad·mit·ted·ly [əd'mɪtɪdlɪ] ADV bisogna ammettere *or* riconoscere (che), va detto (che).
ad·mon·ish [əd'mɒnɪʃ] VT (*frm: reprimand*) ammonire; **to admonish sb (for)** riprendere qn (per).
ad·moni·tion [æːdmə'nɪʃən] N (*frm*) ammonizione *f*.
ad nau·seam [ˌæd'nɔːsɪæm] ADV fino alla nausea, a non finire.
ado [ə'duː] N: **without (any) more ado** senza più indugi.
ado·les·cence [ˌædəʊ'lɛsns] N adolescenza.
ado·les·cent [ˌædəʊ'lɛsnt] ADJ, N adolescente *(m/f)*.
Adonis [ə'dəʊnɪs] N Adone *m*.
adopt [ə'dɒpt] VT (*child, method*) adottare; (*report, suggestion*) approvare; (*Pol: candidate*) scegliere.
adopt·ed [ə'dɒptɪd] ADJ adottivo(-a).
adop·tion [ə'dɒpʃən] N (*see vb*) adozione *f*; approvazione *f*; scelta.
adop·tive [ə'dɒptɪv] ADJ adottivo(-a).
ador·able [ə'dɔːrəbl] ADJ adorabile.
ador·ably [ə'dɔːrəblɪ] ADV adorabilmente.
ado·ra·tion [ˌædɔː'reɪʃən] N adorazione *f*.
adore [ə'dɔːʳ] VT adorare.
ador·ing [ə'dɔːrɪŋ] ADJ (*look, glance*) pieno(-a) di adorazione, adorante; **he has adoring parents** i suoi genitori lo adorano.
ador·ing·ly [ə'dɔːrɪŋlɪ] ADV con adorazione, con venerazione.
adorn [ə'dɔːn] VT (*liter*) abbellire, ornare.
adorn·ment [ə'dɔːnmənt] N (*liter*) ornamento, decorazione *f*.
ADP [ˌeɪdiː'piː] N ABBR = **automatic data processing**.
ad·re·nal [ə'driːnəl] ADJ surrenale; **adrenal (gland)** (ghiandola) surrenale *f*.
adrena·lin [ə'drɛnəlɪn] N adrenalina; **it gets the adrenalin going** ti dà una scarica di adrenalina.
Adri·at·ic [ˌeɪdrɪ'ætɪk] [1] ADJ adriatico(-a).
  [2] N: **the Adriatic (Sea)** l'Adriatico, il mare Adriatico.

adrift [ə'drɪft] ADV (*esp Naut*) alla deriva; **to come adrift** (*wire, rope etc*) essersi staccato(-a) *or* sciolto(-a).
adroit [ə'drɔɪt] ADJ abile, destro(-a).
adroit·ly [ə'drɔɪtlɪ] ADV abilmente.
adroit·ness [ə'drɔɪtnɪs] N abilità.
ADT [ˌeɪdiː'tiː] N ABBR (*Am: = Atlantic Daylight Time*) ora legale di New York.
adu·late ['ædjʊleɪt] VT (*frm*) adulare.
adu·la·tion [ˌædjʊ'leɪʃən] N adulazione *f*.
adult ['ædʌlt] [1] ADJ (*person, animal*) adulto(-a); (*behaviour*) da adulto; (*film, book*) per adulti.
  [2] N adulto(-a); **"adults only"** ≈ "vietato ai minori di 18 anni".
  ♦ **adult education** N scuola per adulti.
adul·ter·ate [ə'dʌltəreɪt] VT adulterare.
adul·tera·tion [ə'dʌltə,reɪʃən] N (*of food, drink*) adulterazione *f*.
adul·ter·er [ə'dʌltərəʳ] N adultero.
adul·ter·ess [ə'dʌltərɪs] N adultera.
adul·ter·ous [ə'dʌltərəs] ADJ (*relationship*) adulterino(-a); (*person*) adultero(-a).
adul·tery [ə'dʌltərɪ] N adulterio.
adult·hood [ə'dʌlthʊd] N età adulta.
ad·vance [əd'vɑːns] [1] VT **a** (*move forward: time, date*) anticipare; (*further: plan, knowledge*; *Mil: troops*) far avanzare; (*promote: interests*) favorire; (: *person: in career*) promuovere
  b (*idea, suggestion, claim*) avanzare
  c (*money*) anticipare; **she wants him to advance her a loan** vuole che lui le faccia un prestito.
  [2] VI (*move forward, also Mil*) avanzare; (*science, technology*) fare progressi, progredire; (*civilization, mankind*) migliorare, fare progressi; **to advance on sb** (*threateningly*) avanzare contro qn.
  [3] N **a** (*Mil*) avanzata; (*fig: progress*) passo (in) avanti, progresso; **the advance of old age** l'avanzare dell'età *or* degli anni; **recent advances in technology** i recenti progressi della tecnica; **to make advances to sb** (*gen*) tentare un approccio con qn; (*amorously*) fare delle avances a qn; **in advance** in anticipo; **to arrive in advance of sb** arrivare in anticipo su qn *or* prima di qn; **to send sth a week in advance** spedire qc con una settimana di anticipo
  b (*loan*): **advance (on)** anticipo (su); (: *from bank*) anticipazione *f* bancaria (su).
  [4] ADJ (*payment, booking*) anticipato(-a); (*copy of book*) distribuito(-a) in anticipo; **we weren't given any advance warning of his visit** non ci avevano dato nessun preavviso del suo arrivo.
ad·vanced [əd'vɑːnst] ADJ (*ideas, civilization etc*) progredito(-a), avanzato(-a); (*Scol: studies*) superiore; (: *class*) avanzato(-a); (: *student*) di livello più avanzato; **of advanced years** avanti negli anni.
ad·vance·ment [əd'vɑːnsmənt] N (*improvement*) miglioramento; (*promotion*) promozione *f*, avanzamento.
  ♦ **advance notice** N preavviso.
  ♦ **advance party** N (*Mil*) squadra di perlustrazione; (*of explorers*) gruppo che va in avanscoperta.
ad·van·tage [əd'vɑːntɪdʒ] N (*gen, Tennis*) vantaggio; **she has the advantage of youth** ha il vantaggio di essere giovane; **the plan has many advantages** il progetto presenta molti vantaggi; **it's to our advantage** è nel nostro interesse, torna a nostro vantaggio; **to have an advantage over sb** avere un vantaggio su qn; **to take advantage of** (*opportunity*) approfittare di, sfruttare; **to**

take **advantage of sb** (*unfairly, sexually etc*) approfittare *or* approfittarsi di qn.
ad·van·taged [əd'vɑːntɪdʒd] ADJ (*person, group*) privilegiato(-a).
ad·van·ta·geous [ˌædvən'teɪdʒəs] ADJ: **advantageous (to)** vantaggioso(-a) (per).
ad·van·ta·geous·ly [ˌædvən'teɪdʒəslɪ] ADV vantaggiosamente.
Ad·vent ['ædvənt] N (*Rel*) Avvento.
ad·vent ['ædvənt] N (*frm: arrival*) avvento.
♦ **Advent calendar** N calendario dell'Avvento.
ad·ven·ti·tious [ˌædvɛn'tɪʃəs] ADJ (*frm: event, situation*) fortuito(-a).
ad·ven·ture [əd'vɛntʃəʳ] ① N avventura.
  ② ADJ (*story, film*) di avventure.
♦ **adventure playground** N campo giochi attrezzato.
ad·ven·tur·er [əd'vɛntʃərəʳ] N avventuriero.
ad·ven·tur·ess [əd'vɛntʃərɪs] N avventuriera.
ad·ven·tur·ous [əd'vɛntʃərəs] ADJ avventuroso(-a).
ad·ven·tur·ous·ly [əd'vɛntʃərəslɪ] ADV avventurosamente.
ad·verb ['ædvɜːb] N avverbio.
ad·ver·bial [æd'vɜːbɪəl] ADJ avverbiale.
ad·ver·bial·ly [æd'vɜːbɪəlɪ] ADV avverbialmente.
ad·ver·sary ['ædvəsərɪ] N avversario(-a), antagonista *m/f*.
ad·verse ['ædvɜːs] ADJ (*criticism, decision, effect*) sfavorevole; (*wind*) contrario(-a); **adverse to** contrario(-a) a; **adverse weather conditions** condizioni atmosferiche avverse; **in adverse circumstances** nelle avversità.
ad·verse·ly [æd'vɜːslɪ] ADV sfavorevolmente.
ad·ver·sity [əd'vɜːsɪtɪ] N avversità *f inv*.
ad·vert ['ædvɜːt] N ABBR (*Brit fam*) = **advertisement**.
ad·ver·tise ['ædvətaɪz] ① VT (*Comm etc*) fare pubblicità *or* réclame a, reclamizzare; **to advertise a flat for sale** mettere un annuncio per vendere un appartamento.
  ② VI fare (della) pubblicità *or* (della) réclame; **to advertise for** (*staff*) cercare tramite annuncio; **to advertise on television** fare pubblicità in televisione.
ad·ver·tise·ment [əd'vɜːtɪsmənt] N (*Comm*) réclame *f inv*, pubblicità *f inv*; (*on TV*) spot *m inv*; (*in classified ads*) inserzione *f*, annuncio; **to put an advertisement in the paper** mettere un annuncio sul giornale; **an advertisement for soap** la réclame *or* la pubblicità di un sapone.
ad·ver·tis·er ['ædvətaɪzəʳ] N azienda che reclamizza un prodotto; (*in newspaper*) inserzionista *m/f*.
ad·ver·tis·ing ['ædvətaɪzɪŋ] N pubblicità (commerciale); (*advertisements collectively*) pubblicità, réclame *f inv*; **my brother's in advertising** mio fratello lavora nel settore pubblicitario.
♦ **advertising agency** N agenzia pubblicitaria *or* di pubblicità.
♦ **advertising campaign** N campagna pubblicitaria.
ad·vice [əd'vaɪs] N consiglio, consigli *mpl*; **a piece of advice** un consiglio; **legal advice** consulenza legale; **to ask (sb) for advice** chiedere il consiglio (di qn), chiedere un consiglio (a qn); **to take sb's advice** seguire il consiglio *or* i consigli di qn.
♦ **advice note** N (*Brit Comm*) avviso di spedizione.
ad·vis·able [əd'vaɪzəbl] ADJ consigliabile, raccomandabile; **I do not think it advisable for you to come** non le consiglierei di venire.
ad·vise [əd'vaɪz] VT **a** (*counsel*): **to advise sb (on sth)** consigliare qn (a proposito di qc); **to advise sb to do sth** consigliare a qn di fare qc; **to advise sb against sth** sconsigliare qc a qn; **to advise against doing sth**

sconsigliare a qn di fare qc; **he advises the President on foreign affairs** è il consigliere del Presidente in materia di affari esteri; **you would be well/ill advised to go** (*frm*) faresti bene/male ad andare
  b (*frm: inform*): **to advise sb of sth** avvisare qn di qc.
ad·vis·ed·ly [əd'vaɪzɪdlɪ] ADV (*deliberately*) deliberatamente.
ad·vis·er, **ad·vis·or** [əd'vaɪzəʳ] N (*in politics*) consigliere (-a); (*in business*) consulente *m/f*.
ad·vi·so·ry [əd'vaɪzərɪ] ADJ (*body*) consultivo(-a); **in an advisory capacity** in veste di consulente.
ad·vo·ca·cy ['ædvəkəsɪ] N: **the advocacy of** l'appoggio a.
ad·vo·cate [*n* 'ædvəkɪt; *vb* 'ædvəkeɪt] ① N (*Scot Law*) avvocato (difensore); (*fig*) sostenitore(-trice); **to be an advocate of** essere a favore di.
  ② VT sostenere la validità di, propugnare.
advt. ABBR = **advertisement**.
AEA [ˌeɪiː'eɪ] N ABBR (*Brit*: = *Atomic Energy Authority*) ≈ ENEA *m*.
AEC [ˌeɪiː'siː] N ABBR (*Am*: = *Atomic Energy Commission*) ≈ ENEA *m*.
Aegean [iː'dʒiːən] N: **the Aegean (Sea)** il mar *m* Egeo, l'Egeo.
aegis ['iːdʒɪs] N (*frm*): **under the aegis of** sotto l'egida di.
Aeneas [ɪ'niːəs] N Enea *m*.
aeo·lian [iː'əʊlɪən] ADJ (*Geol*) eolico(-a); **aeolian harp** arpa eolia.
Aeolus ['iːələs] N Eolo.
aeon, (*esp Am*) **eon** ['iːən] N eternità *f inv*.
aer·ate ['ɛəreɪt] VT (*water*) gassare; (*blood*) ossigenare; (*soil*) aerare.
aera·ted ['ɛəreɪtɪd] ADJ (*Chem*) aerato(-a); **aerated water** acqua gassata.
aer·ial ['ɛərɪəl] ① ADJ aereo(-a); **aerial photograph** fotografia aerea; **aerial railway** teleferica, funivia.
  ② N (*Brit: Radio, TV*) antenna.
aero... ['ɛərəʊ] PREF aero... .
aero·bat·ics ['ɛərəʊ'bætɪks] NPL (*stunts*) acrobazie *fpl* aeree.
aero·bic [ɛə'rəʊbɪk] ADJ aerobico(-a).
aero·bics [ɛə'rəʊbɪks] NSG aerobica.
aero·drome ['ɛərəˌdrəʊm] N (*esp Brit*) aerodromo.
aero·dy·nam·ic ['ɛərəʊdaɪ'næmɪk] ADJ aerodinamico(-a).
aero·dy·nam·ics ['ɛərəʊdaɪ'næmɪks] NSG aerodinamica.
aero·gramme ['ɛərəʊˌgræm] N aerogramma *m*.
aero·naut·ical [ˌɛərə'nɔːtɪkəl] ADJ aeronautico(-a).
aero·naut·ics [ˌɛərə'nɔːtɪks] NSG aeronautica.
aero·plane ['ɛərəˌpleɪn] N (*esp Brit*) aeroplano.
aero·sol ['ɛərəˌsɒl] N (*can*) aerosol *m inv*.
aero·space in·dus·try ['ɛərəʊspeɪs'ɪndəstrɪ] N **industria aerospaziale**.
Aeschylus ['iːskələs] N Eschilo.
Aesop ['iːsɒp] N Esopo.
aes·thete, (*Am*) **es·thete** ['iːsθiːt] N esteta *m/f*.
aes·thet·ic, (*Am*) **es·thet·ic** [iːs'θɛtɪk] ADJ estetico(-a).
aes·thet·i·cal·ly, (*Am*) **es·thet·i·cal·ly** [iːs'θɛtɪkəlɪ] ADV esteticamente.
aes·thet·ics, (*Am*) **es·thet·ics** [iːs'θɛtɪks] NSG estetica.
AEU [ˌeɪiː'juː] N ABBR (*Brit*: = *Amalgamated Engineering Union*) sindacato dei tecnici.
afar [ə'fɑːʳ] ADV (*old, liter*) lontano; **from afar** da lontano.
AFB [ˌeɪɛf'biː] N ABBR (*Am*)= *Air Force Base*.
AFDC [ˌeɪɛfdiː'siː] N ABBR (*Am*: = *Aid to Families with Dependent Children*) ≈ A.F. (= *assegni familiari*).
af·fabil·ity [ˌæfə'bɪlɪtɪ] N affabilità.

af·fa·ble ['æfəbl] ADJ affabile.

af·fa·bly ['æfəblɪ] ADV affabilmente.

af·fair [ə'fɛə'] N **a** (*event*) faccenda, affare *m*; (*love affair*) relazione *f* (amorosa); (: *brief*) avventura; **it will be a big affair** sarà un avvenimento; **the Watergate affair** il caso Watergate; **that's my affair** sono affari *or* fatti miei; **it's a bad state of affairs** è una brutta situazione
b : **affairs** NPL (*business*) affari; **foreign affairs** affari esteri; **affairs of state** affari di stato.

af·fect [ə'fɛkt] VT **a** (*have an effect on*) influire su, incidere su; (*concern*) riguardare, concernere; (*harm: health etc*) danneggiare; **it did not affect my decision** non ha influenzato la mia decisione, non ha influito sulla mia decisione
b (*move emotionally*) colpire, toccare; **he seemed much affected** sembrava molto colpito
c (*feign*) fingere.

af·fec·ta·tion [,æfɛk'teɪʃən] N affettazione *f*; **affectations** NPL modi *mpl* affettati, leziosaggini *fpl*.

af·fect·ed [ə'fɛktɪd] ADJ affettato(-a).

af·fect·ed·ly [ə'fɛktɪdlɪ] ADV affettatamente.

af·fect·ing [ə'fɛktɪŋ] ADJ (*liter: scene, story*) toccante.

af·fec·tion [ə'fɛkʃən] N affetto.

af·fec·tion·ate [ə'fɛkʃənɪt] ADJ affettuoso(-a).

af·fec·tion·ate·ly [ə'fɛkʃənɪtlɪ] ADV affettuosamente.

af·fi·da·vit [,æfɪ'deɪvɪt] N (*Law*) affidavit *m inv*.

af·fil·i·ate [ə'fɪlɪeɪt] [1] VT: **to affiliate to/with** associare a; **to affiliate o.s. to** associarsi a. [2] N affiliata.

af·fil·i·ated [ə'fɪlɪeɪtɪd] ADJ: **affiliated (to** *or* **with)** affiliato (-a) (a), associato(-a) (a); **affiliated company** filiale *f*.

af·fil·ia·tion [ə,fɪlɪ'eɪʃən] N affiliazione *f*; **to have affiliations with** essere affiliato(-a) a.

af·fine ['æfaɪn] ADJ (*Math*) affine.

af·fin·ity [ə'fɪnɪtɪ] N (*relationship*) affinità *f inv*; (*liking*) simpatia.

af·firm [ə'fɜ:m] VT affermare, asserire.

af·fir·ma·tion [æfə'meɪʃən] N affermazione *f*, asserzione *f*.

af·firma·tive [ə'fɜ:mətɪv] [1] ADJ affermativo(-a). [2] N: **to answer in the affirmative** rispondere affermativamente *or* di sì.

af·firma·tive·ly [ə'fɜ:mətɪvlɪ] ADV affermativamente.

af·fix¹ [ə'fɪks] VT (*signature etc*) apporre; (*stamp*) attaccare.

af·fix² ['æfɪks] N (*Gram*) affisso.

af·flict [ə'flɪkt] VT affliggere.

af·flic·tion [ə'flɪkʃən] N (*suffering*) afflizione *f*, sofferenza; (*bodily*) infermità *f inv*.

af·flu·ence ['æfluəns] N (*wealth*) ricchezza; (*plenty*) abbondanza.

af·flu·ent ['æfluənt] ADJ ricco(-a); **the affluent society** la società del benessere.

af·ford [ə'fɔ:d] VT **a** : **to afford sth/to do sth** permettersi qc/di fare qc; **can we afford a car?** possiamo permetterci un'automobile?; **I can't afford the time** non ho proprio il tempo, non ho veramente tempo; **I can't afford not to do it** non mi posso permettere di non farlo; **an opportunity you cannot afford to miss** un'occasione che non puoi lasciarti sfuggire
b (*frm: provide: opportunity*) offrire, fornire.

af·ford·able [ə'fɔ:dəbl] ADJ (*che ha un prezzo*) abbordabile.

af·for·esta·tion [æ,fɒrɪs'teɪʃən] N imboschimento.

af·fray [ə'freɪ] N (*Law*) rissa.

af·front [ə'frʌnt] [1] N affronto.
[2] VT fare un affronto a; **to be affronted (by)** offendersi

(per).

Af·ghan ['æfgæn] [1] N (*person*) afgano(-a); (*language*) afgano; (*dog: also:* **Afghan hound**) levriero afgano.
[2] ADJ afgano(-a).

Af·ghani·stan [æf'gænɪˌstɑ:n] N l'Afganistan *m*.

afield [ə'fi:ld] ADV: **far afield** lontano, distante.

AFL-CIO [,eɪɛf'ɛlˌsi:aɪ'əʊ] N ABBR (= *American Federation of Labor and Congress of Industrial Organisations*) *confederazione sindacale*.

afloat [ə'fləʊt] ADV, ADJ a galla; **to keep afloat** (*also fig*) rimanere a galla.

afoot [ə'fʊt] ADJ, ADV in preparazione, in corso; **there's trouble afoot** ci sono guai in vista; **there is something afoot** si sta preparando qualcosa.

afore·men·tioned [əˌfɔ:'mɛnʃənd], **afore·said** [ə'fɔ:sɛd] ADJ (*Law*) suddetto(-a), summenzionato(-a).

afraid [ə'freɪd] ADJ impaurito(-a); **to be afraid** aver paura; **to be afraid for sb** temere per qn, preoccuparsi per qn; **to be afraid of sb/sth** aver paura di qn/qc; **I was afraid to ask** avevo paura di *or* non osavo domandare; **I'm afraid of hurting her** temo di *or* ho paura di farle male; **I'm afraid he's out** (*regret*) mi rincresce *or* dispiace, ma è fuori; **I'm afraid I have to go now** mi dispiace, ma adesso devo proprio andare; **I'm afraid so!** ho paura di sì!, temo proprio di sì!; **I'm afraid not** no, mi dispiace, purtroppo no; **I am afraid that I'll be late** mi dispiace, ma farò tardi.

afresh [ə'frɛʃ] ADV da capo, di nuovo; **to start afresh** ricominciare (tutto) da capo.

Af·ri·ca ['æfrɪkə] N Africa.

Af·ri·can ['æfrɪkən] ADJ, N africano(-a).

Af·ri·kaans [,æfrɪ'kɑ:ns] N afrikaans *m*.

Af·ri·kan·er [,æfrɪ'kɑ:nə'] N africander *m/f inv*.

Afro ['æfrəʊ] N (*fam*) pettinatura *f* afro *inv*.

♦ **Afro-American** ['æfrəʊə'mɛrɪkən] ADJ, N afroamericano(-a).

AFT [,eɪɛf'ti:] N ABBR (= *American Federation of Teachers*) *sindacato degli insegnanti*.

aft [ɑ:ft] ADV (*Naut*) a *or* verso poppa; **to go aft** andare a poppa.

af·ter ['ɑ:ftə'] [1] ADV (*afterwards*) dopo; **the day after** il giorno dopo *or* seguente.
[2] PREP **a** (*time, order, place*) dopo; **day after day** giorno dopo giorno; **for kilometre after kilometre** per chilometri e chilometri; **you tell me lie after lie** mi stai dicendo una bugia dopo l'altra; **time after time** tantissime volte; **after dinner** dopo cena; **the day after tomorrow** dopodomani; **soon after eating it** poco dopo averlo mangiato; **after all** dopotutto, malgrado tutto; **half after two** (*Am*) le due e mezzo; **one after the other** uno(-a) dopo l'altro(-a); **shut the door after you** chiudi la porta dietro di te; **after you!** prima lei!, dopo di lei!
b (*in pursuit*) dietro; **he ran after me** mi è corso dietro, mi ha rincorso; **the police are after him** è ricercato dalla polizia; **what/who are you after?** (*fam*) (che) cosa/chi cerca?.
[3] CONJ dopo che; **after he had eaten he went out** dopo aver mangiato *or* che ebbe mangiato uscì.
[4] ADJ (*Naut*) poppiero(-a).

after·birth ['ɑ:ftəˌbɜ:θ] N placenta (e membrane fetali).

after·care ['ɑ:ftəˌkɛə'] N (*Brit: of patients*) assistenza medica post-degenza; (: *of prisoners*) servizio di assistenza per ex-detenuti.

♦ **after-dinner** ['ɑ:ftəˌdɪnə'] ADJ: **after-dinner drink** digestivo; **after-dinner speaker** *oratore che viene invitato a*

parlare alla fine di un pranzo o ricevimento.

♦ **after-effect** [ˈɑːtərɪfɛkt] N (*of events*) ripercussione *f*, conseguenza; (*of drug*) reazione *f*; (*of illness, experience*) postumi *mpl*.

after·life [ˈɑːftəˌlaɪf] N vita dell'al di là.

after·math [ˈɑːftəˌmæθ] N conseguenze *fpl*, strascichi *mpl*; **in the aftermath of** nel periodo dopo.

after·noon [ˈɑːftəˈnuːn] N pomeriggio; **in the afternoon** nel *or* di pomeriggio; **at 3 o'clock in the afternoon** alle 3 del pomeriggio; **good afternoon!** buon giorno!

♦ **afternoon performance** N matinée *f inv*.

♦ **afternoon tea** N tè *m inv*.

af·ters [ˈɑːftəz] N (*Brit fam: dessert*) dessert *m inv*.

♦ **after-sales service** [ˌɑːftəˈseɪlzˌsɜːvɪs] N servizio assistenza clienti.

♦ **after-shave (lotion)** [ˈɑːftəˌʃeɪv (ləʊʃən)] N (lozione *f*) dopobarba *m inv*.

after·shock [ˈɑːftəˌʃɒk] N scossa di assestamento.

after·taste [ˈɑːftəˌteɪst] N retrogusto.

after·thought [ˈɑːftəˌθɔːt] N ripensamento; **it was very much an afterthought** è stata una cosa completamente improvvisata; **we added it as an afterthought** l'abbiamo aggiunto solo più tardi.

after·wards [ˈɑːftəwədz] ADV dopo, più tardi, in seguito; **soon afterwards** poco dopo.

again [əˈgɛn] ADV ancora, di nuovo, un'altra volta; **to begin/see again** ricominciare/rivedere; **he opened it again** l'ha aperto di nuovo, l'ha riaperto; **come again soon!** torna presto!; **again and again** ripetutamente, tante volte; **I've told him again and again** gliel'ho detto e ripetuto; **never again!** mai più!; **not ...again** non... più; **now and again** di tanto in tanto, a volte; **as much again** due volte tanto; **then again** (*on the other hand*) d'altra parte; (*moreover*) inoltre.

against [əˈgɛnst] PREP **a** (*in contact with*) a, contro; **I was leaning against the desk** ero appoggiato alla scrivania; **he leaned the ladder against the wall** appoggiò la scala al *or* contro il muro

b (*in opposition to*) contro; **he was against going** era contrario ad andare; **what have you got against me?** cos'hai contro di me?; **it's against the law** è contrario alla *or* contro la legge; **to run against sb** (*Pol*) contrapporre la propria candidatura a quella di qn

c (*in contrast to*): **against the light** controluce; **against a blue background** su uno sfondo azzurro

d (*Brit: in comparisons*): **(as) against** in confronto a, contro.

Agamemnon [ˈægəˈmɛmnɒn] N Agamennone *m*.

agape [əˈgeɪp] ADJ (*person: surprised*) a bocca aperta; (*mouth*) spalancato(-a).

agar [ˈeɪgəʳ], **agar-agar** [ˌeɪgəˈeɪgəʳ] N agar-agar *m inv*.

age [eɪdʒ] ①︎ N **a** età *f inv*; (*of thing*) anni *mpl*; **old age** vecchiaia; **what's his age?** *or* **what age is he?** quanti anni ha?; **when I was your age** quando avevo la tua età; **he doesn't look his age** non dimostra la sua età *or* i suoi anni; **at the age of** all'età di; **to come of age** diventare maggiorenne, raggiungere la maggiore età

b (*period*) epoca, era; **the Iron Age** l'età del ferro

c (*fam: long time*): **we waited (for) ages** abbiamo aspettato per ore; **it's an age** *or* **ages since I saw him** sono secoli che non lo vedo.

②︎ VT fare invecchiare, invecchiare.

③︎ VI invecchiare.

aged [ˈeɪdʒɪd; *sense b* eɪdʒd] ①︎ ADJ **a** (*old*) anziano(-a), attempato(-a) **b** dell'età di; **a boy aged 10** un ragazzo di 10 anni.

②︎ NPL: **the aged** (*elderly*) gli anziani, i vecchi.

♦ **age group** N generazione *f*; **the 40 to 50 age group** le persone fra i 40 e i 50 anni.

age·ing [ˈeɪdʒɪŋ] ADJ che diventa vecchio(-a); **an ageing filmstar** una diva stagionata.

age·less [ˈeɪdʒlɪs] ADJ (*eternal*) eterno(-a); (*always young*) senza età.

♦ **age limit** N limite *m* di età.

agen·cy [ˈeɪdʒənsɪ] N **a** (*office*) agenzia; (*distributorship*) rappresentanza **b** (*instrumentality*): **through** *or* **by the agency of** grazie a, per mezzo *or* per opera di.

agen·da [əˈdʒɛndə] N ordine *m* del giorno, agenda; **on the agenda** all'ordine del giorno.

agent [ˈeɪdʒənt] N **a** (*Comm, Police, Theatre etc*) agente *m/f*; (*representative*) rappresentante *m/f*; **to be sole agent for** avere la rappresentanza esclusiva per; **agent's commission** provvigione *f*; **he is not a free agent** (*fig*) non è padrone di fare quel che vuole **b** (*Chem*) agente *m*.

agent pro·vo·ca·teur [aʒɑ̃ prɔvɔkatœr] N agente *m* provocatore.

♦ **age of consent** N see **consent**.

♦ **age-old** [ˈeɪdʒˌəʊld] ADJ secolare.

ag·glom·er·ate [əˈglɒmərɪt] N (*Geol*) agglomerato.

ag·glom·era·tion [əglɒməˈreɪʃən] N agglomerazione *f*.

ag·gran·dize·ment, **ag·gran·dise·ment** [əˈgrændɪzmənt] N: **for aggrandizement** per aumentare il proprio prestigio.

ag·gra·vate [ˈægrəveɪt] VT aggravare, peggiorare; (*annoy*) esasperare, irritare.

ag·gra·vat·ing [ˈægrəveɪtɪŋ] ADJ esasperante, irritante.

ag·gra·va·tion [ˌægrəˈveɪʃən] N (*of situation etc*) aggravamento, peggioramento; (*annoyance*) esasperazione *f*, irritazione *f*.

ag·gre·gate [ˈægrɪgɪt] ①︎ N **a** (*total*) insieme *m*; **in the aggregate** nel complesso; **on aggregate** (*Sport*) con punteggio complessivo **b** (*Geol*) aggregato; (*Constr*) materiali *mpl* inerti.

②︎ ADJ complessivo(-a).

ag·gres·sion [əˈgrɛʃən] N aggressione *f*; (*aggressiveness*) aggressività.

ag·gres·sive [əˈgrɛsɪv] ADJ aggressivo(-a); (*salesman, approach etc*) intraprendente.

ag·gres·sive·ly [əˈgrɛsɪvlɪ] ADV aggressivamente.

ag·gres·sive·ness [əˈgrɛsɪvnɪs] N aggressività.

ag·gres·sor [əˈgrɛsəʳ] N aggressore/aggreditrice.

ag·grieved [əˈgriːvd] ADJ: **aggrieved (at, by)** offeso(-a) (da), addolorato(-a) (da).

ag·gro [ˈægrəʊ] N ABBR (*Brit fam: aggression*) aggressività; (: *problems*) grane *fpl*.

aghast [əˈgɑːst] ADJ: **aghast (at)** (*shocked*) sbigottito(-a) (a); (*terrified*) inorridito(-a) (a), atterrito(-a) (a); **to be aghast at the idea of doing sth** essere atterrito(-a) all'idea di fare qc.

ag·ile [ˈædʒaɪl] ADJ agile, svelto(-a).

agil·ity [əˈdʒɪlɪtɪ] N agilità *f inv*.

agin [əˈgɪn] PREP (*esp Scot*): **to be agin sth** essere contro qc.

agi·tate [ˈædʒɪteɪt] ①︎ VT (*perturb*) turbare, mettere in (uno stato di) agitazione; (*shake*) agitare.

②︎ VI (*Pol*): **to agitate (for/against)** fare un'agitazione (per/contro).

agi·tat·ed [ˈædʒɪteɪtɪd] ADJ agitato(-a), inquieto(-a).

agi·ta·tion [ˌædʒɪˈteɪʃən] N agitazione *f*.

agi·ta·tor [ˈædʒɪteɪtəʳ] N (*Pol: usu pej*) agitatore(-trice).

aglow [əˈgləʊ] ADJ (*liter: sky, mountains*) splendente; (: *fig*:

person) raggiante.

AGM [ˌeidʒiːˈɛm] N ABBR = **annual general meeting**.

ag·nos·tic [ægˈnɒstɪk] ADJ, N agnostico(-a).

ag·nos·ti·cism [ægˈnɒstɪsɪzəm] N agnosticismo.

ago [əˈgəʊ] ADV: **a week ago** una settimana fa; **long ago** molto tempo fa; **not long ago** poco tempo fa; **as long ago as 1960** già nel 1960; **how long ago?** quanto tempo fa?; **how long ago was it?** quanto tempo fa è successo?, da quanto tempo è successo?

agog [əˈgɒg] ADJ: **(all) agog (to hear sth)** ansioso(-a) *or* impaziente (di sentire qc); **agog with excitement** emozionato(-a), eccitato(-a).

ago·nize [ˈægənaɪz] VI: **to agonize (over)** angosciarsi (per).

ago·nized [ˈægəˌnaɪzd] ADJ (*moan, indecision*) angoscioso(-a).

ago·niz·ing [ˈægənaɪzɪŋ] ADJ (*cry, decision*) penoso(-a), angoscioso(-a); (*pain, death*) straziante.

ago·ny [ˈægənɪ] N (*pain*) dolore *m* atroce; (: *mental*) angoscia, tormento; **I was in agony** avevo dei dolori atroci, soffrivo atrocemente; **to suffer agonies of doubt** avere dei dubbi atroci.

♦ **agony aunt** N (*Brit fam*) *chi tiene la rubrica della posta del cuore.*

♦ **agony column** N posta del cuore.

ago·ra·pho·bia [ˌægərəˈfəʊbɪə] N (*Psych*) agorafobia.

ago·ra·pho·bic [ˌægərəˈfəʊbɪk] N (*Psych*) agorafobo(-a).

agrar·ian [əˈgrɛərɪən] ADJ agrario(-a).

agree [əˈgriː] **1** VI **a** (*be in agreement*): **to agree (with sb/sth)** essere *or* trovarsi d'accordo (con qn/qc); **to agree on/about sth** essere d'accordo su/riguardo a qc; **I quite agree** sono perfettamente d'accordo; **don't you agree?** non sei d'accordo?

b (*come to terms*): **to agree (on sth)** mettersi d'accordo (su qc), accordarsi (su qc)

c (*consent*): **to agree to sth** accettare qc, acconsentire a qc

d (*be in harmony: things*) andare d'accordo, concordare; (: *persons: get on together*) andare d'accordo; (*Gram*) concordare

e (*food*): **garlic doesn't agree with me** non riesco a digerire l'aglio, l'aglio mi rimane sullo stomaco.

2 VT **a** (*come to agreement*): **to agree (that)** essere d'accordo (sul fatto che); (*admit*) ammettere (che); **it was agreed that ...** è stato deciso (di comune accordo) che...; **are we all agreed?** siamo tutti d'accordo?; **is that agreed?** (siamo) d'accordo?; **to agree to differ** rimanere ognuno della propria idea; **to agree a price** pattuire un prezzo

b (*consent*): **to agree to do sth** accettare di fare qc, acconsentire a fare qc.

agree·able [əˈgriːəbl] ADJ (*pleasing*) piacevole, gradevole; (*willing*) disposto(-a); **to be agreeable to sth/to doing sth** essere ben disposto(-a) a qc/a fare qc; **if you are agreeable** se sei d'accordo; **are you agreeable to this?** è d'accordo con questo?

agree·ably [əˈgriːəblɪ] ADV piacevolmente.

agreed [əˈgriːd] ADJ (*time, place*) stabilito(-a).

agree·ment [əˈgriːmənt] N (*gen*) accordo; (*consent*) consenso; **by mutual agreement** di comune accordo; **to come to an agreement** venire a un accordo, accordarsi; **in agreement** d'accordo; **to be in agreement with sb** essere *or* trovarsi d'accordo con qn.

ag·ri·cul·tur·al [ˌægrɪˈkʌltʃərəl] ADJ (*gen*) agricolo(-a); (*college, studies*) agrario(-a); **agricultural expert** agro-

nomo(-a).

ag·ri·cul·tur·al·ist [ˌægrɪˈkʌltʃərəlɪst], **ag·ri·cul·tur·ist** [ˌægrɪˈkʌltʃərɪst] N (*agricultural scientist*) agronomo(-a).

ag·ri·cul·ture [ˈægrɪkʌltʃəʳ] N agricoltura; **commercial agriculture** agricoltura di mercato.

aground [əˈgraʊnd] ADV (*Naut*) in secca; **to run aground** arenarsi, incagliarsi.

ahead [əˈhɛd] ADV **a** (*in space*) avanti, davanti; **ahead of** davanti a; **they were (right) ahead of us** erano (proprio) davanti a noi; **to go ahead** andare avanti; **go ahead!** avanti!; (*fig*) fai pure!, prego!; **to get ahead of sb** superare qn; **go right** *or* **straight ahead!** vada diritto!

b (*in time: book, plan*) in anticipo; **ahead of time** in anticipo; **Italy is one hour ahead of Britain at the moment** attualmente l'Italia è un'ora avanti *or* avanti di un'ora rispetto all'Inghilterra; **he finished half an hour ahead of the others** ha finito con mezz'ora di anticipo sugli *or* rispetto agli altri, ha finito mezz'ora prima degli altri; **to look ahead** (*fig*) guardare avanti, pensare all'avvenire; **to be ahead of one's time** precorrere i propri tempi.

ahoy [əˈhɔɪ] EXCL ehi!; **ship ahoy!** ehi della nave!

AI [ˈeɪˈaɪ] N ABBR **a** = Amnesty International **b** (*Comput*) = **artificial intelligence c** = **artificial insemination**.

AID [ˌeɪaɪˈdiː] N ABBR **a** = *artificial insemination by donor* **b** (*Am*: = *Agency for International Development*) A.I.D. *f*.

aid [eɪd] **1** N aiuto, assistenza; **economic aid** aiuti *mpl* economici, assistenza economica; **with the aid of** con l'aiuto di; **in aid of** a favore di; **what's all this in aid of?** (*fam*) a cosa serve tutto questo?; **to come to the aid of** venire in aiuto a.

2 VT (*person*) aiutare; (*progress, recovery*) contribuire a; **to aid sb to do sth** aiutare qn a fare qc; **to aid and abet sb** (*Law*) essere complice di qn.

aide [eɪd] N (*person*) aiutante *m/f*; (*Mil*) aiutante *m* di campo, addetto; (*militare*); (*Pol*) consigliere(-a), addetto(-a).

♦ **aide-de-camp** [ˌeɪddəˈkɒŋ] N (*Mil*) aiutante *m* di campo.

AIDS [eɪdz] N ABBR (= *acquired immune deficiency syndrome*) AIDS *m or f*.

AIH [ˌeɪaɪˈeɪtʃ] N ABBR = *artificial insemination by husband*.

ail [eɪl] VI (*old*) essere sofferente.

ailer·on [ˈeɪlərɒn] N (*Aer*) alettone *m*.

ail·ing [ˈeɪlɪŋ] ADJ infermo(-a), sofferente; (*fig: economy, industry etc*) in difficoltà.

ail·ment [ˈeɪlmənt] N malanno.

aim [eɪm] **1** N (*of weapon*) mira; (*fig: purpose, object*) scopo, proposito; **his aim is bad** non ha una buona mira; **to take aim** prendere la mira; **to take aim at sth/sb** mirare a qc/qn; **to have no aim in life** non avere un preciso scopo nella vita.

2 VT: **to aim (at)** (*gun*) puntare (su *or* contro); (*missile*) lanciare (contro); (*blow etc*) tirare (a); (*remark, criticism*) rivolgere (a); (*camera*) dirigere (verso); **to aim to do sth** aspirare a fare qc; (*less formal*) avere l'intenzione di fare qc.

3 VI (*also*: **to take aim**) prendere la mira, mirare; **to aim at sth** (*also fig*) mirare a qc; **to aim for the goal** (*Ftbl*) tirare in porta.

aim·less [ˈeɪmlɪs] ADJ senza scopo.

aim·less·ly [ˈeɪmlɪslɪ] ADV senza scopo.

ain't [eɪnt] ABBR (*fam!: incorrect use*) = **am not, is not, are not, has not, have not**.

air [ɛəʳ] **1** N **a** aria; **in the open air** all'aria aperta,

all'aperto; **by air** (*travel*) in aereo; (*Post*) per via *or* posta aerea; **to get some fresh air** andare a prendere una boccata d'aria (fresca); **to clear the air** (*fig*) chiarire la situazione; **there's something in the air** (*fig*) c'è qualcosa nell'aria; **our plans are up in the air** (*fig*) i nostri progetti non sono ancora ben definiti

b (*Radio, TV*): **to be on the air** (*programme*) essere in onda; (*station*) trasmettere; (*person*) parlare alla radio (*or* alla televisione); **we're now going off the air** la trasmissione si conclude qui

c (*appearance*) aria, aspetto; **with a guilty air** con aria colpevole; **she had an air of mystery about her** aveva una certa aria di mistero; **to give o.s. airs** darsi delle arie.

2 VT (*room, bed*) arieggiare; (*clothes*) far prendere aria a; (*idea, grievance*) esprimere pubblicamente, manifestare; (*views*) far conoscere.

3 ADJ (*current, bubble*) d'aria; (*pressure*) atmosferico (-a); (*Mil: base, attack etc*) aereo(-a).

♦ **air bag** N airbag *m inv*.

♦ **air base** N base *f* aerea.

♦ **air bed** N (*Brit*) materassino gonfiabile.

air·borne ['ɛəˌbɔːn] ADJ (*troops*) aerotrasportato(-a), aviotrasportato(-a); (*plane*) in volo; **as soon as the plane was airborne** appena l'aereo ebbe decollato; **suddenly we were airborne** in un attimo avevamo già preso quota.

♦ **air brake** N (*Aut*) freno pneumatico.

air·bus ['ɛəˌbʌs] N aerobus *m inv*, airbus *m inv*.

♦ **air cargo** N carico trasportato per via aerea.

♦ **air cleaner** N (*Aut*) filtro dell'aria.

♦ **air-conditioned** ['ɛəkənˌdɪʃnd] ADJ con *or* ad aria condizionata.

♦ **air-conditioner** ['ɛəˌkənˈdɪʃənə'] N climatizzatore *m*, condizionatore *m* (d'aria).

♦ **air conditioning** N aria condizionata, condizionamento d'aria.

♦ **air-cooled** ['ɛəˌkuːld] ADJ raffreddato(-a) ad aria.

♦ **air corridor** N corridoio aereo.

air·craft ['ɛəˌkrɑːft] N INV aeromobile *m*, apparecchio, velivolo.

♦ **aircraft carrier** N portaerei *f inv*.

air·crew ['ɛəˌkruː] N equipaggio (*di un aereo*).

♦ **air cushion** N cuscino gonfiabile; (*Tech*) cuscino d'aria.

air·drome ['ɛəˌdrəʊm] N (*Am*) = **aerodrome**.

air·field ['ɛəˌfiːld] N campo d'aviazione.

♦ **air force** N aviazione *f* militare.

♦ **air freight** **1** N (*mode of transport*) spedizione *f* merci per via aerea; (*goods*) carico spedito per via aerea.
2 ADV (*send*) per via aerea.

air·gun ['ɛəˌgʌn] N fucile *m* ad aria compressa.

♦ **air hostess** N hostess *f inv*.

air·i·ly ['ɛərɪlɪ] ADV con disinvoltura.

air·ing ['ɛərɪŋ] N: **to give an airing to** (*linen*) arieggiare, far prendere aria a; (*room*) arieggiare; (*fig: ideas etc*) ventilare.

♦ **airing cupboard** N *armadio riscaldato per asciugare panni*.

♦ **air lane** N corridoio aereo.

air·less ['ɛəlɪs] ADJ (*room*) senz'aria; (*day*) senza un filo di vento.

♦ **air letter** N aerogramma *m*.

air·lift ['ɛəˌlɪft] N ponte *m* aereo.

air·line ['ɛəˌlaɪn] N linea *or* compagnia aerea, avioli-

nea.

air·lin·er [ɛəˈlaɪnə'] N aereo di linea.

air·lock ['ɛəˌlɒk] N (*in pipe*) bolla d'aria; (*in spacecraft etc*) camera d'equilibrio.

air·mail ['ɛəˌmeɪl] N posta aerea; **by airmail** per via *or* posta aerea.

air·man ['ɛəmən] N (*pl* **-men**) aviere *m*.

♦ **air mattress** N materassino gonfiabile.

♦ **air navigation** N navigazione *f* aerea.

air·plane ['ɛəˌpleɪn] N (*Am*) aeroplano.

♦ **air pocket** N vuoto d'aria.

air·port ['ɛəˌpɔːt] **1** N aeroporto.
2 ADJ (*staff*) aeroportuale; (*manager, security etc*) dell'aeroporto.

♦ **air pump** N pompa per l'aria.

♦ **air raid** N incursione *f* aerea.

♦ **air rifle** N fucile *m* ad aria compressa.

♦ **air-sea rescue** [ˌɛəsiːˈrɛskjuː] N salvataggio aereo in mare.

air·ship ['ɛəˌʃɪp] N dirigibile *m*, aeronave *f*.

♦ **air show** N (*trade exhibition*) salone *m* dell'aviazione; (*flying display*) manifestazione *f* aerea.

♦ **air·sick** ['ɛəˌsɪk] ADJ: **to be airsick** soffrire di mal d'aria *or* d'aereo.

♦ **air sickness** N mal *m* d'aria.

air·space ['ɛəˌspeɪs] N spazio aereo.

air·speed ['ɛəˌspiːd] N velocità *f inv* di crociera (*Aer*).

♦ **air·strike** ['ɛəˌstraɪk] N attacco aereo.

air·strip ['ɛəˌstrɪp] N pista d'atterraggio.

air·taxi ['ɛəˌtæksɪ] N aereotaxi *m inv*.

♦ **air terminal** N air-terminal *m inv*.

air·tight ['ɛəˌtaɪt] ADJ (*container*) a chiusura ermetica; (*seal, cap*) ermetico(-a).

♦ **air time** N (*Radio*) spazio radiofonico; (*TV*) spazio televisivo.

♦ **air-to-air** ['ɛətʊˈɛə'] ADJ (*Mil*) aria-aria *inv*.

♦ **air-to-ground** ['ɛətəˈgraʊnd], **air-to-surface** ['ɛətəˈsɜːfɪs] ADJ (*Mil*) aria-terra *inv*.

♦ **air traffic control** N controllo del traffico aereo.

♦ **air traffic controller** N controllore *m* del traffico aereo.

air·waves ['ɛəˌweɪvz] NPL onde *f pl* radio *inv*.

air·way ['ɛəˌweɪ] N **a** (*Aer*) rotta aerea **b** : **the airways** NPL le vie *f pl* respiratorie.

♦ **air waybill** N (*Comm*) bolletta di trasporto aereo.

air·worthi·ness ['ɛəˌwɜːðɪnɪs] N idoneità al volo.

air·worthy ['ɛəˌwɜːðɪ] ADJ idoneo(-a) al volo, in condizione di poter volare.

airy ['ɛərɪ] ADJ (*comp* **-ier**, *superl* **-iest**) (*place*) arieggiato (-a); (*room*) arioso(-a); (*remark etc*) superficiale; (*manner*) spensierato(-a), noncurante.

♦ **airy-fairy** ['ɛərɪˈfɛərɪ] ADJ (*fam*) vago(-a).

aisle [aɪl] N (*of church: lateral*) navata laterale; (: *central*) navata centrale; (*of theatre, train, coach, plane*) corridoio; (*in supermarket*) passaggio; **it had them rolling in the aisles** li ha fatti rotolare (per terra) dalle risate.

aitch [eɪtʃ] N acca; **to drop one's aitches** (*Brit*) non pronunciare l'acca (iniziale).

ajar [əˈdʒɑː'] ADV, ADJ socchiuso(-a).

Ajax ['eɪdʒæks] N Aiace *m*.

AK ABBR (*Am Post*)= *Alaska*.

aka [ˌeɪkeɪˈeɪ] ABBR (= *also known as*) alias.

akim·bo [əˈkɪmbəʊ] ADV: **with arms akimbo** con le mani sui fianchi.

akin [əˈkɪn] ADJ: **akin to** (*similar to*) equivalente a, simile a;

(*of same family as*) imparentato(-a) a.

AL ABBR (*Am Post*)= *Alabama*.

ala·bas·ter ['æləbɑːstə'] N alabastro.

à la carte [ɑːlɑː'kɑt] ADJ, ADV alla carta.

alac·rity [ə'lækrɪtɪ] N: **with alacrity** prontamente.

à la mode [ɑːlɑː'məʊd] [1] ADJ di moda.

[2] ADV alla moda.

alarm [ə'lɑːm] [1] N (*warning, signal*) allarme *m*; **to raise the alarm** dare l'allarme; **there's no need for any alarm** non c'è bisogno di allarmarsi.

[2] VT allarmare, spaventare; **to be alarmed (at)** essere preoccupato(-a) (per) *or* allarmato(-a) (da).

♦ **alarm clock** N sveglia.

alarmed [ə'lɑːmd] ADJ (*person*) allarmato(-a); (*house, car etc*) dotato(-a) di allarme.

alarm·ing [ə'lɑːmɪŋ] ADJ allarmante, preoccupante.

alarm·ing·ly [ə'lɑːmɪŋlɪ] ADV in modo allarmante; **alarmingly close** pericolosamente vicino(-a).

alarm·ist [ə'lɑːmɪst] N allarmista *m/f*.

alas [ə'læs] EXCL (*frm*) ohimè!, ahimè!

Alas·ka [ə'læskə] N l'Alasca.

Al·ba·nia [æl'beɪnɪə] N l'Albania.

Al·ba·nian [æl'beɪnɪən] [1] ADJ albanese.

[2] N (*person*) albanese *m/f*; (*language*) albanese *m*.

al·ba·tross ['ælbətrɒs] N albatro.

al·be·it [ɔːl'biːɪt] CONJ (*frm*) sebbene + *sub*, benché + *sub*.

al·bi·no [æl'biːnəʊ] ADJ, N albino(-a).

al·bum ['ælbəm] N album *m inv*; (*L.P.*) 33 giri *m inv*, L.P. *m inv*; **photograph album** (*containing photos*) album di *or* delle fotografie; (*new*) album per fotografie.

al·bu·men ['ælbjʊmɪn] N albume *m*.

al·che·mist ['ælkɪmɪst] N alchimista *m/f*.

al·che·my ['ælkɪmɪ] N alchimia.

al·co·hol ['ælkəhɒl] N alcool *m inv*; **I never touch alcohol** non bevo (mai) alcolici.

♦ **alcohol-free** ['ælkəhɒl'friː] ADJ analcolico(-a).

al·co·hol·ic [ˌælkə'hɒlɪk] [1] ADJ alcolico(-a).

[2] N alcolizzato(-a).

al·co·hol·ism ['ælkəhɒlɪzəm] N alcolismo.

al·cove ['ælkəʊv] N alcova.

Ald. ABBR = **alderman**.

al·der ['ɔːldə'] N ontano.

alderman ['ɔːldəmən] N (*pl* **-men**) consigliere *m* comunale.

ale [eɪl] N birra.

alert [ə'lɜːt] [1] ADJ (*acute, wide-awake*) sveglio(-a); (*watchful*) vigile; (*mind*) pronto(-a), agile, vivace; (*expression*) intelligente.

[2] N allarme *m*; **to be on the alert** (*person*) stare all'erta; (*troops*) essere in stato di allarme.

[3] VT: **to alert sb (to sth)** avvisare qn (di qc), avvertire qn (di qc); **to alert sb to the dangers of sth** mettere qn in guardia contro qc.

alert·ness [ə'lɜːtnɪs] N prontezza.

Aleu·tian Is·lands [ə'luːʃən 'aɪləndz] NPL: **the Aleutian Islands** le isole *fpl* Aleutine.

♦ **A-level** ['eɪˌlɛvl] N (*Brit*) diploma di studi superiori.

Al·ex·an·dria [ˌælɪg'zændrɪə] N Alessandria (d'Egitto).

al·fal·fa [æl'fælfə] N erba medica.

al·fres·co [æl'freskəʊ] ADJ, ADV all'aperto.

al·gae ['ældʒiː] NPL alghe *fpl*.

al·ge·bra ['ældʒɪbrə] N algebra.

al·ge·bra·ic [ˌældʒɪ'breɪɪk] ADJ algebrico(-a).

Al·ge·ria [æl'dʒɪərɪə] N Algeria.

Al·ge·rian [æl'dʒɪərɪən] ADJ, N algerino(-a).

Al·giers [æl'dʒɪəz] N Algeri *fsg*.

al·go·rithm ['ælgəˌrɪðəm] N (*Comput*) algoritmo.

ali·as ['eɪlɪəs] [1] N falso nome *m*, pseudonimo.

[2] ADV alias, altrimenti detto(-a).

ali·bi ['ælɪbaɪ] N alibi *m inv*.

al·ien ['eɪlɪən] [1] ADJ (*very different*): **alien to** estraneo(-a) (a), alieno(-a) (da); (*of foreign country*) straniero(-a), forestiero(-a).

[2] N (*foreigner*) straniero(-a), forestiero(-a); (*extra-terrestrial*) extraterrestre *m/f*, alieno(-a).

al·ien·ate ['eɪlɪəneɪt] VT alienare; **her behaviour has alienated her friends** il suo comportamento ha fatto allontanare gli amici.

al·iena·tion [ˌeɪlɪə'neɪʃən] N alienazione *f*.

alight[1] [ə'laɪt] ADJ: **to be alight** (*building*) essere in fiamme; (*fire*) essere acceso(-a).

alight[2] [ə'laɪt] VI (*from vehicle*): **to alight (from)** scendere (da); (*bird*): **to alight (on)** posarsi (su).

align [ə'laɪn] VT allineare; **to align o.s. with** allinearsi con, schierarsi dalla parte di.

align·ment [ə'laɪnmənt] N (*Tech, Pol*) allineamento; (*Aut: also:* **wheel alignment**) assetto; **out of alignment (with)** non allineato(-a) (con); **a new alignment of political forces** un nuovo schieramento delle forze politiche.

alike [ə'laɪk] [1] ADJ PRED simile, uguale; **to be alike** OR **to look alike** assomigliarsi; **you're all alike!** siete tutti uguali!.

[2] ADV allo stesso modo; **winter and summer alike** sia d'estate che d'inverno.

ali·men·ta·ry [ˌælɪ'mɛntərɪ] ADJ alimentare.

♦ **alimentary canal** N tubo digerente.

ali·mo·ny ['ælɪmənɪ] N (*Law: payment*) alimenti *mpl*.

alive [ə'laɪv] ADJ (*living*) vivo(-a), in vita, vivente; (*fig: lively*) vivace, sveglio(-a); (: *active*) attivo(-a); **to stay alive** sopravvivere; **he was buried alive** è stato sepolto vivo; **it's good to be alive** essere vivi è una bella cosa; **he's the best footballer alive** è il miglior calciatore vivente *or* esistente; **to keep a tradition alive** mantener viva *or* in vita una tradizione; **to come alive** (*fig*) risvegliarsi, rianimarsi; **to be alive with** (*insects etc*) brulicare *or* pullulare di; **alive to** (*danger, honour*) conscio(-a) di.

al·ka·li ['ælkəlaɪ] N alcali *m inv*.

al·ka·line ['ælkəlaɪn] ADJ alcalino(-a).

al·kane ['ælkeɪn] N alcano.

al·kene ['ælkiːn] N alcheno.

al·kyne ['ælkaɪn] N alchino.

all [ɔːl]

[1] ADJ tutto(-a), tutti(-e) *pl*;

▷ **all** *day* tutto il giorno

▷ **all** *his* **life** tutta la sua vita

▷ **all** *men* tutti gli uomini

▷ **it's not as hard/bad as all** *that* non è mica così duro/cattivo

▷ **all** *the* **books** tutti i libri

▷ **all** *the* **country** tutto il paese

▷ **all** *the* **time** tutto il tempo

▷ **for all** *their* **efforts** nonostante tutti i loro sforzi

▷ **all** *three* tutti(-e) e tre

▷ **all** *three* **books** tutti e tre i libri.

[2] PRON

[a] tutto(-a);

▷ **he ate** *it* **all** l'ha mangiato tutto

▷ **all is** *lost* tutto è perduto

▷**all** *of* it tutto(-a)

▷**is** *that* **all**? non c'è altro?; (*in shop*) basta così?

▷**if** *that's* **all then it's not important** se è tutto lì allora non ha importanza

b (*plural*) tutti(-e);

▷**all** *of* **the girls** tutte le ragazze

▷**all** *of* **them** tutti(-e) (loro)

▷**all** *of* **us went** ci siamo andati tutti

▷**we all sat down** ci sedemmo tutti quanti, noi tutti ci sedemmo

c (*in phrases*)

▷*above* **all** soprattutto, più di tutto

▷*after* **all** dopotutto

▷**not** *at* **all** (*in answer to question*) niente affatto, per niente; (*in response to thanks*) prego!, s'immagini!, si figuri!

▷**I'm not** *at* **all tired** non sono affatto *or* per niente stanco

▷**anything** *at* **all will do** andrà bene qualsiasi cosa

▷*for* **all I know** per quel che ne so io, per quanto ne so

▷**all** *in* **all** tutto sommato

▷**50 men** *in* **all** 50 uomini in tutto

▷**most** *of* **all** (*more than anybody*) più di chiunque altro, soprattutto; (*more than anything*) più di qualsiasi altra cosa, soprattutto.

3 ADV tutto;

▷**all** *alone* tutto (-a) solo (-a)

▷**all** *but* quasi

▷**it's all** *dirty* è tutto sporco

▷**dressed all** *in* **black** vestito(-a) tutto(-a) di nero

▷**to be/feel all** *in* (*fam*) essere/sentirsi sfinito(-a) *or* distrutto(-a)

▷**to go all** *out* mettercela tutta

▷**she was going all** *out* **down the motorway** stava andando a tutto gas sull'autostrada

▷**things aren't all** *that* **good/bad** le cose non vanno poi così bene/male

▷**the score is** *two* **all** il punteggio è di due a due

▷**all** *wrong* tutto sbagliato(-a); see also **over, right, alone.**

Allah ['ælə] N Allah *m*.

al·lay [ə'leɪ] VT (*frm: fears*) dissipare.

♦ **all clear** N (*Mil*) cessato allarme *m inv*; (*fig*) okay *m*.

♦ **all-comers** [ɔ:l'kʌmə's] N tutti(-e); **the competition is open to all-comers** la gara è aperta a tutti.

♦ **all-day** ['ɔ:l'deɪ] ADJ che dura tutto il giorno.

al·le·ga·tion [,ælɪ'geɪʃən] N accusa, asserzione *f*.

al·lege [ə'lɛdʒ] VT asserire, dichiarare; **he is alleged to have said ...** avrebbe detto che... .

al·leged [ə'lɛdʒd] ADJ presunto(-a); **the alleged crime** il presunto delitto.

al·leg·ed·ly [ə'lɛdʒɪdlɪ] ADV da quel che si dice, secondo quanto si asserisce.

al·le·giance [ə'li:dʒəns] N fedeltà, lealtà; **to swear allegiance to** fare giuramento di fedeltà a.

al·le·gor·ical [,ælɪ'gɒrɪkəl], **al·le·gor·ic** [,ælɪ'gɒrɪk] ADJ allegorico(-a).

al·le·gori·cal·ly [,ælɪ'gɒrɪklɪ] ADV allegoricamente.

al·le·go·ry ['ælɪgərɪ] N allegoria.

♦ **all-embracing** [,ɔ:lɪm'breɪsɪŋ] ADJ che abbraccia tutto, universale.

al·ler·gic [ə'lɜ:dʒɪk] ADJ: **allergic to** allergico(-a) a.

al·ler·gy ['ælədʒɪ] N allergia.

al·le·vi·ate [ə'li:vɪeɪt] VT alleviare.

al·le·via·tion [əli:vɪ'eɪʃən] N alleviamento.

al·ley ['ælɪ] N (*between buildings*) vicolo; (*in garden, park*) vialetto; (*Am Tennis*) corridoio; **blind alley** vicolo cieco.

alley·way ['ælɪˌweɪ] N vicolo.

al·li·ance [ə'laɪəns] N (*Pol*) alleanza.

allied ['ælaɪd] ADJ alleato(-a).

al·li·ga·tor ['ælɪgeɪtə'] N alligatore *m*.

♦ **all-important** [,ɔ:lɪm'pɔ:tənt] ADJ cruciale, fondamentale, importantissimo(-a).

♦ **all-in** [,ɔ:l'ɪn] ADJ, ADV (*Brit: price, charge*) tutto compreso *inv*; **I'll let you have them at an all-in price** te li farò avere ad un prezzo forfettario.

♦ **all-in wrestling** N lotta americana.

al·lit·era·tion [ə,lɪtə'reɪʃən] N allitterazione *f*.

♦ **all-night** [,ɔ:l'naɪt] ADJ (*café, garage*) aperto(-a) tutta la notte; (*vigil, party*) che dura (*or* è durato(-a) *etc*) tutta la notte.

al·lo·cate ['æləʊkeɪt] VT (*allot*): **to allocate (to)** (*duties, sum, time*) assegnare (a); (: *in budget: money*) stanziare (per); (*distribute*): **to allocate (among)** ripartire (fra), distribuire (fra).

al·lo·ca·tion [æləʊ'keɪʃən] N (*see vb*) assegnazione *f*, stanziamento; distribuzione *f*; **allocation of overheads** imputazione *f* delle spese generali.

al·lot [ə'lɒt] VT **a** (*assign: task, share, time*): **to allot (to)** dare (a), assegnare (a) **b** (*share among group*) spartire (tra); **in the allotted time** nel tempo fissato *or* prestabilito.

al·lot·ment [ə'lɒtmənt] N (*Brit: land*) piccolo lotto di terreno (*dato in affitto per coltivazioni ad uso familiare*); (*share*) spartizione *f*.

al·lo·trope ['æləˌtrəʊp] N allotropo.

♦ **all-out** [,ɔ:l'aʊt] ADJ (*attack*) con tutti i mezzi a disposizione; (*effort etc*) totale; **to make an all-out effort to do sth** impegnare tutte le proprie energie per fare qc.

♦ **all-over** [,ɔ:l'əʊvə'] ADJ (*gen*) totale; **all-over tan** abbronzatura integrale.

al·low [ə'laʊ] VT **a** (*permit*): **to allow sb to do sth** permettere a qn di fare qc, autorizzare qn a fare qc; **smoking is not allowed** è vietato fumare, non è permesso fumare; **he is allowed to do it** lo può fare; **he's not allowed alcohol** gli hanno proibito l'alcol; **to allow sb in/out** *etc* lasciare entrare/uscire *etc* qn; **allow me!** mi permetta!, se mi permette!, prego!

b (*make provision for*) tener conto di, calcolare; **we must allow 3 days for the journey** dobbiamo calcolare 3 giorni per il viaggio; **allow 5 cm for the hem** lasciare 5 cm in più per il bordo

c (*grant: money, rations*) concedere, accordare; (*Law: claim, appeal*) riconoscere, ammettere; (*Sport: goal*) convalidare; **to allow that** (*frm: concede*) ammettere che

▶ **allow for** VI + PREP tener conto di, calcolare.

al·low·able [ə'laʊəbəl] ADJ **a** (*Fin: expenses, costs*) deducibile **b** (*behaviour*) lecito(-a).

al·low·ance [ə'laʊəns] N (*payment*) assegno; (*for travelling, accommodation*) indennità *f inv*; (*ration*) razione *f*; (*Tax*) detrazione *f* d'imposta; (*discount*) riduzione *f*, sconto; **monthly clothing allowance** cifra mensile per il vestiario; **family allowance** (*old: child benefit*) assegni *mpl* familiari; **to make allowance(s) for** (*person*) scusare; (*allow for: shrinkage etc*) tener conto di.

al·loy ['ælɔɪ] **1** N lega; (*fig*) ombra.

2 ADJ: **alloy wheels** (*Aut*) cerchi *mpl* in lega.

♦ **all-party** ['ɔ:l'pɑ:tɪ] ADJ (*Pol*) di tutti i partiti.

♦ **all-powerful** [ˈɔːlˈpaʊəfʊl] ADJ onnipotente.

♦ **all-purpose** [ˈɔːlˈpɜːpəs] ADJ per tutti gli usi.

♦ **all right** ADV (*feel, work*) bene; (*as answer*) va bene.

♦ **all-round** [ˈɔːlˈraʊnd] ADJ (*athlete etc*) completo(-a), versatile; (*education*) ampio(-a), completo(-a).

♦ **all-rounder** [ˌɔːlˈraʊndəʳ] N: **to be a good all-rounder** (*Brit esp Sport*) essere bravo(-a) in tutto.

♦ **All Saints' Day** N Ognissanti *m inv*.

♦ **All Souls' Day** N il Giorno dei Morti.

all·spice [ˈɔːlˌspaɪs] N pepe *m* della Giamaica.

♦ **all-star** [ˈɔːlˈstaːʳ] ADJ (*film, play*) recitato(-a) da attori famosi; **an all-star cast** un cast di attori famosi.

♦ **all-time** [ˈɔːlˈtaɪm] ADJ (*record*) senza precedenti, assoluto(-a).

al·lude [əˈluːd] VI: **to allude to** alludere a, fare allusione a.

al·lure [əˈljʊəʳ] ① N fascino.
② VT allettare, affascinare.

al·lur·ing [əˈljʊərɪŋ] ADJ allettante, seducente.

al·lu·sion [əˈluːʒən] N accenno, allusione *f*; (*Literature*) riferimento.

al·lu·sive [əˈluːsɪv] ADJ allusivo(-a), pieno(-a) di allusioni; (*Literature*) pieno(-a) di riferimenti.

al·lu·sive·ly [əˈluːsɪvlɪ] ADV allusivamente.

al·lu·vial [əˈluːvɪəl] ADJ alluvionale.

al·lu·vium [əˈluːvɪəm] N materiale *m* alluvionale.

♦ **all-weather** [ˈɔːlˈwɛðəʳ] ADJ per tutte le stagioni.

ally [*n* ˈælaɪ; *vb* əˈlaɪ] ① N alleato(-a).
② VT: **to ally o.s. with** allearsi con.

al·ma·nac [ˈɔːlmənæk] N almanacco.

al·mighty [ɔːlˈmaɪtɪ] ① ADJ onnipotente; (*fam*) enorme, colossale.
② N: **the Almighty** l'Onnipotente.

al·mond [ˈɑːmənd] N (*nut*) mandorla; (*also:* **almond tree**) mandorlo.

♦ **almond paste** N (*Culin*) pasta di mandorle.

al·most [ˈɔːlməʊst] ADV quasi; **he almost fell** per poco non è caduto.

alms [ɑːmz] NPL (*old*) elemosina *sg*; **to give alms** fare l'elemosina.

♦ **alms·house** [ˈɑːmzˌhaʊs] N ospizio.

aloft [əˈlɒft] ADV in alto; (*Naut*) sull'alberatura.

alone [əˈləʊn] ADJ, ADV (da) solo(-a); **all alone** tutto(-a) solo(-a); **am I alone in thinking so?** sono il solo a pensarla così?; **leave me alone!** lasciami in pace!, lasciami stare!; **to let** *or* **leave sth alone** (*object*) lasciar stare qc; (*business, scheme*) non immischiarsi in qc; **let alone** ... figuriamoci poi..., tanto meno...; **he can't read, let alone write** non sa leggere, figuriamoci scrivere; **you can't do it alone** non puoi farlo da solo; **the flight alone cost £600** il volo da solo è costato 600 sterline.

along [əˈlɒŋ] ① ADV: **to move along** (*person, car*) andare avanti; **he was hopping/limping along** veniva saltellando/zoppicando; **come along with me** vieni con me; **are you coming along?** vieni anche tu?; **move along there!** muovetevi, avanti!; (*said by policeman*) circolare!; **along with the others** con gli altri, insieme agli altri; **take it along** prendilo con te; **I knew all along** sapevo fin dall'inizio.
② PREP lungo; **to walk along the street** camminare lungo la strada; **the trees along the path** gli alberi lungo il sentiero; **along here** per di qua; **somewhere along the way** (*also fig*) da qualche parte lungo la strada.

along·side [əˈlɒŋˈsaɪd] ① ADV (*Naut*) sottobordo; **we brought our boat alongside** (*of a pier/shore etc*) abbiamo accostato la barca (al molo/alla riva *etc*).
② PREP (*along*) lungo; (*beside*) accanto a; **the railway runs alongside the beach** la ferrovia costeggia la spiaggia; **to come alongside the quay** accostare al molo; **to work alongside other people** lavorare assieme ad altre persone.

aloof [əˈluːf] ① ADJ riservato(-a), distaccato(-a).
② ADV a distanza, in disparte; **to stand aloof (from)** tenersi a distanza (da) *or* in disparte (da).

aloof·ness [əˈluːfnɪs] N riserbo, distacco.

aloud [əˈlaʊd] ADV ad alta voce, a voce alta.

al·paca [ælˈpækə] N (*animal, wool*) alpaca *m inv*.

al·pha [ˈælfə] ① N alfa *m or f inv*.
② ADJ (*Phys*): **alpha particle** particella *f* alfa *inv*.

al·pha·bet [ˈælfəbɛt] N alfabeto.

al·pha·beti·cal [ˌælfəˈbɛtɪkəl] ADJ alfabetico(-a); **in alphabetical order** in ordine alfabetico.

al·pha·beti·cal·ly [ˌælfəˈbɛtɪkəlɪ] ADV alfabeticamente.

al·pha·bet·ize [ˈælfəbətaɪz] VT mettere in ordine alfabetico.

al·pha·nu·mer·ic [ˌælfənjuːˈmɛrɪk] ADJ alfanumerico(-a).

al·pine [ˈælpaɪn] ADJ alpino(-a); (*plant, pasture*) alpestre; **alpine skiing** sci *m* alpino.

♦ **alpine hut** N rifugio alpino.

al·pin·ism [ˈælpɪnɪzəm] N alpinismo.

al·pin·ist [ˈælpɪnɪst] N alpinista *m/f*.

Alps [ælps] NPL: **the Alps** le Alpi.

al·ready [ɔːlˈrɛdɪ] ADV già.

al·right [ɔːlˈraɪt] ADJ = **all right**.

Al·sace [ælˈsæs] N l'Alsazia.

Al·sa·tian [ælˈseɪʃən] ① N a (*Brit: dog*) pastore *m* tedesco, (cane *m*) lupo b (*person*) alsaziano(-a).
② ADJ alsaziano(-a).

also [ˈɔːlsəʊ] ADV a (*too*) anche, pure; **her cousin also came** è venuto anche suo cugino b (*moreover*) inoltre, anche; **also, I must explain** ... (e) inoltre devo spiegare..., devo anche spiegare... .

♦ **also-ran** [ˈɔːlsəʊˌræn] N (*Sport*) (cavallo) non piazzato; (*fam: person*) perdente *m/f*.

al·tar [ˈɒltəʳ] N altare *m*; **high altar** altar maggiore.

al·ter [ˈɒltəʳ] ① VT (*gen*) modificare, cambiare, alterare; (*opinion: one's own*) cambiare, mutare; (: *sb else's*) far cambiare *or* mutare; (*garment, building*) fare una modifica (*or* delle modifiche) a.
② VI cambiare.

al·tera·tion [ˌɒltəˈreɪʃən] N (*act: see vb*) modifica, cambiamento; (*in appearance*) cambiamento, trasformazione *f*; **alterations** NPL (*to garment, building*) modifiche *fpl*; **timetable subject to alteration** orario soggetto a variazioni; **to make alterations in sth** apportare delle modifiche a qc.

al·ter·ca·tion [ˌɒltəˈkeɪʃən] N (*frm*) alterco, litigio.

al·ter·nate [*adj* ɒlˈtɜːnɪt; *vb* ˈɒltəneɪt] ① ADJ (*alternating: layers*) alternato(-a); (*every other: days*) alterni(-e) *pl*, uno(-a) sì e uno(-a) no; **on alternate days** ogni due giorni; **alternate angles** angoli alterni.
② VI: **to alternate (with/between)** alternarsi (a/fra), avvicendarsi (a/fra).
③ VT (*crops*) alternare, avvicendare.

al·ter·nate·ly [ɒlˈtɜːnɪtlɪ] ADV alternatamente.

al·ter·nat·ing cur·rent [ˈɒltəneɪtɪŋˈkʌrənt] N corrente *f* alternata.

al·ter·na·tive [ɒlˈtɜːnətɪv] ① ADJ (*solutions*) alternativo(-a), altro(-a); (*medicine, energy*) alternativo(-a).
② N (*choice*) alternativa; **you have no alternative but to go** non hai altra alternativa che andare; **there are**

several alternatives ci sono diverse alternative *or* possibilità; **there is no alternative** non c'è altra alternativa *or* scelta.

al·ter·na·tive·ly [ɒl'tɜːnətɪvlɪ] ADV in alternativa, altrimenti.

♦ **alternative medicine** N medicina alternativa.

al·ter·na·tor ['ɒltəneɪtəʳ] N (*Elec, Aut*) alternatore *m*.

al·though [ɔːl'ðəʊ] CONJ benché + *sub*, sebbene + *sub*.

al·time·ter ['æltɪmiːtəʳ] N altimetro.

al·ti·tude ['æltɪtjuːd] N altitudine *f*, altezza, quota; (*Geom*) altezza; **at these altitudes** a questa altezza; **to gain/lose altitude** (*Aer*) prendere/perdere quota.

alto ['æltəʊ] N (*instrument*) contralto; (*male*) contraltino; (*female*) contralto.

al·to·geth·er [ˌɔːltə'gɛðəʳ] ADV **a** (*in all*) in tutto, complessivamente; (*on the whole*) tutto considerato, tutto sommato, nel complesso, nell'insieme; **altogether it was rather unpleasant** tutto sommato *or* in complesso è stato piuttosto spiacevole; **how much is that altogether?** quant'è in tutto?
b (*entirely*) del tutto, completamente; **I'm not altogether sure** non sono del tutto *or* proprio sicuro.

al·tru·ism ['æltrʊɪzəm] N altruismo.

al·tru·is·tic [ˌæltrʊ'ɪstɪk] ADJ altruistico(-a).

al·tru·is·ti·cal·ly [ˌæltrʊ'ɪstɪklɪ] ADV altruisticamente.

alu·min·ium [ˌæljʊ'mɪnɪəm], (*Am*) **alu·mi·num** [ə'luːmɪnəm] N alluminio.

alum·na [ə'lʌmnə] N (*Am Univ*) ex allieva.

alum·nus [ə'lʌmnəs] N (*Am Univ*) ex allievo.

al·veo·lar [æl'vɪələʳ] ADJ alveolare.

al·veo·lus [æl'vɪələs] N alveolo.

al·ways ['ɔːlweɪz] ADV sempre; **as always** come sempre; **you can always go by train** puoi sempre prendere il treno.

Alzheimer's ['æltshaɪməz] N (*also:* **Alzheimer's disease**) morbo di Alzheimer.

AM [ˌeɪ'ɛm] ABBR (= *amplitude modulation*) AM.

am [æm] 1ST PERS SG PRESENT of **be**.

a.m. [ˌeɪ'ɛm] ADV ABBR (= *ante meridiem*) del mattino.

AMA [ˌeɪɛm'eɪ] N ABBR = *American Medical Association*.

amalgam [ə'mælgəm] N amalgama *m*.

amal·gam·ate [ə'mælgəmeɪt] ☐1 VT (*metals, also fig*) amalgamare; (*Comm*) fondere.
☐2 VI (*metals, also fig*) amalgamarsi; (*Comm*) fondersi.

amal·gama·tion [əˌmælgə'meɪʃən] N (*see vb*) amalgamazione *f*; fusione *f*.

amanu·en·sis [əˌmænjʊ'ɛnsɪs] N (*pl* **amanuenses** [əˌmænjʊ'ɛnsiːz]) (*frm*) amanuense *m*.

amass [ə'mæs] VT accumulare, ammassare.

ama·teur ['æmətəʳ] ☐1 N dilettante *m/f*.
☐2 ADJ (*player, painter*) dilettante; (*activity*) dilettantistico(-a), per dilettanti; **amateur dramatics** filodrammatica.

ama·teur·ish ['æmətərɪʃ] ADJ (*pej*) dilettantesco(-a), da dilettanti.

ama·teur·ism ['æmətərɪzm] N dilettantismo.

amaze [ə'meɪz] VT stupire, sbalordire; **to be amazed (at)** essere sbalordito(-a) (da).

amaze·ment [ə'meɪzmənt] N stupore *m*, meraviglia; **to my amazement ...** con mia gran sorpresa...; **he looked at me in amazement** mi guardò stupito.

amaz·ing [ə'meɪzɪŋ] ADJ sorprendente, sbalorditivo(-a); (*bargain, offer*) sensazionale.

amaz·ing·ly [ə'meɪzɪŋlɪ] ADV incredibilmente.

Ama·zon ['æməzən] ☐1 N **a**: **the Amazon** (*river*) il Rio

delle Amazzoni **b** (*Myth*) Amazzone *f*.
☐2 ADJ (*basin*) amazzonico(-a); **the Amazon rainforest** la foresta amazzonica.

Ama·zo·nian [ˌæmə'zəʊnɪən] ADJ amazzonico(-a).

am·bas·sa·dor [æm'bæsədəʳ] N ambasciatore(-trice).

♦ **ambassador-at-large** [æm'bæsədərət'lɑːdʒ] N (*Am*) ambasciatore(-trice) a disposizione.

am·bas·sa·dor·ial [æmˌbæsə'dɔːrɪəl] ADJ di ambasciatore.

am·ber ['æmbəʳ] ☐1 N ambra.
☐2 ADJ (*colour*) ambra *inv*, ambrato(-a); (*Brit: traffic light*) giallo(-a).

am·ber·gris ['æmbəˌgriːs] N ambra grigia.

am·bi·dex·trous [ˌæmbɪ'dɛkstrəs] ADJ ambidestro(-a).

am·bi·ence ['æmbɪəns] N (*liter: atmosphere*) ambiente *m*; **the restaurant has a pleasant ambience** il ristorante ha un'atmosfera piacevole.

am·bi·ent ['æmbɪənt] ADJ ambiente *inv*; **ambient temperature** temperatura ambiente.

am·bi·gu·ity [ˌæmbɪ'gjuːɪtɪ] N ambiguità *f inv*.

am·bigu·ous [æm'bɪgjʊəs] ADJ ambiguo(-a).

am·bigu·ous·ly [æm'bɪgjʊəslɪ] ADV ambiguamente.

am·bit ['æmbɪt] N (*frm*) ambito.

am·bi·tion [æm'bɪʃən] N ambizione *f*, aspirazione *f*; **he has no ambition** non ha nessuna ambizione; **to achieve one's ambition** realizzare le proprie aspirazioni *or* ambizioni.

am·bi·tious [æm'bɪʃəs] ADJ ambizioso(-a); **to be ambitious for one's children** avere delle ambizioni per i propri figli.

am·bi·tious·ly [æm'bɪʃəslɪ] ADV ambiziosamente.

am·biva·lence [æm'bɪvələns] N ambivalenza.

am·biva·lent [æm'bɪvələnt] ADJ ambivalente.

am·ble ['æmbl] ☐1 VI (*also:* **to amble along** *or* **about:** *person*) camminare tranquillamente *or* senza fretta; **he ambled up to me** mi è venuto incontro senza fretta.
☐2 N (*of horse*) ambio.

am·bro·sia [æm'brəʊzɪə] N (*liter*) ambrosia.

am·bu·lance ['æmbjʊləns] ☐1 N ambulanza, autoambulanza.
☐2 ADJ: **ambulance driver** guidatore(-trice) d'ambulanza.

am·bush ['æmbʊʃ] ☐1 N (*attack*) imboscata, agguato; (*place*) agguato; **to lie in ambush** stare in agguato; **to lie in ambush for sb** tendere un'imboscata a qn.
☐2 VT tendere un'imboscata a qn.

ame·ba [ə'miːbə] N (*Am*) = **amoeba**.

ame·lio·rate [ə'miːlɪəˌreɪt] VT (*frm*) migliorare.

ame·lio·ra·tion [əˌmiːlɪə'reɪʃən] N (*frm*) miglioramento.

amen ['ɑː'mɛn] EXCL così sia, amen.

ame·nable [ə'miːnəbl] ADJ: **amenable to** (*advice*) ben disposto(-a) verso; **amenable to flattery** sensibile alle lusinghe; **amenable to reason** ragionevole.

amend [ə'mɛnd] VT (*law etc*) emendare; (*text*) correggere.

amend·ment [ə'mɛndmənt] N (*see vb*) emendamento; correzione *f*.

amends [ə'mɛndz] NPL: **to make amends (to sb) for sth** (*apologize*) farsi perdonare (da qn) per qc; (*compensate*) risarcire *or* indennizzare (qn) per qc.

amen·ity [ə'miːnɪtɪ] N (*facility*) *struttura ricreativa o commerciale*; **a house with all amenities** una casa con tutte le comodità.

Ameri·ca [ə'mɛrɪkə] N America.

Ameri·can [ə'mɛrɪkən] ☐1 ADJ americano(-a).
☐2 N (*person*) americano(-a); (*language: also:* **American**

English) americano.

ameri·can·ism [ə'mɛrɪkənɪzəm] N americanismo.

ameri·can·ize [ə'mɛrɪkənaɪz] VT americanizzare.

am·ethyst ['æmɪθɪst] N ametista.

Amex ['æmɛks] N ABBR = *American Stock Exchange*.

Am·har·ic [æm'hærɪk] 1 ADJ amarico(-a).

　2 N (*language*) amarico.

ami·abil·ity [ˌeɪmɪə'bɪlɪtɪ] N amabilità, affabilità.

ami·able ['eɪmɪəbl] ADJ affabile, amabile.

ami·ably ['eɪmɪəblɪ] ADV affabilmente.

ami·cable ['æmɪkəbl] ADJ amichevole.

ami·cably ['æmɪkəblɪ] ADV amichevolmente; **to part amicably** lasciarsi senza rancori; (*divorcing couple*) separarsi consensualmente.

amid [ə'mɪd], **amidst** [ə'mɪdst] PREP (*frm, liter*) in mezzo a, fra, tra.

amid·ships [ə'mɪdʃɪps] ADV (*Naut*) a mezzanave.

ami·no acid [ə'miːnəʊ'æsɪd] N amminoacido.

amiss [ə'mɪs] ADJ, ADV: **there's something amiss** c'è qualcosa che non quadra; **don't take it amiss** non avertene a male.

am·meter ['æmˌmiːtəʳ] N amperometro.

ammo ['æməʊ] N ABBR (*fam*) = **ammunition**.

am·mo·nia [ə'məʊnɪə] N ammoniaca.

am·mo·nite ['æməˌnaɪt] N ammonite *f*.

am·mo·nium [ə'məʊnɪəm] N ammonio.

♦ **ammonium hydroxide** N idrossido di ammonio.

♦ **ammonium ion** N ione *m* ammonio *inv*.

am·mu·ni·tion [ˌæmjʊ'nɪʃən] N munizioni *fpl*; (*fig*) arma.

♦ **ammunition belt** N cartucciera.

♦ **ammunition dump** N deposito di munizioni.

am·ne·sia [æm'niːzɪə] N amnesia.

am·nes·ty ['æmnɪstɪ] N amnistia; **to grant an amnesty to** concedere l'amnistia a, amnistiare.

♦ **Amnesty International** N Amnesty International *f*.

am·ni·on ['æmnɪən] N (*pl* amnions *or* amnia ['æmnɪə]) amnio.

am·ni·ot·ic [ˌæmnɪ'ɒtɪk] ADJ amniotico(-a).

amoe·ba, (*Am*) **ame·ba** [ə'miːbə] N ameba.

am·oebia·sis [ˌæmɪ'baɪəsɪs] N (*pl* amoebiases [ˌæmɪ'baɪəˌsiːz]) amebiasi *f*.

amok [ə'mɒk] ADV = **amuck**.

among [ə'mʌŋ], **amongst** [ə'mʌŋst] PREP tra, fra, in mezzo a; **among friends** tra amici; **he is among those who** ... fa parte di quelli che..., è uno di quelli che...; **share it among yourselves** dividetevelo tra (di) voi; **among other things** tra l'altro, tra le altre cose.

amor·al [eɪ'mɒrəl] ADJ amorale.

amo·ral·ity [ˌeɪmə'rælɪtɪ] N amoralità.

amo·rous ['æmərəs] ADJ amoroso(-a); (*stronger*) appassionato(-a).

amor·phous [ə'mɔːfəs] ADJ amorfo(-a).

amortization [əˌmɔːtaɪ'zeɪʃən] N (*Comm*) ammortamento.

amount [ə'maʊnt] N (*sum of money*) somma, cifra; (*of invoice, bill etc*) importo; (*quantity*) quantità *f inv*; **in small amounts** poco per volta; **the total amount** (*of money*) l'importo totale; (*of things*) la quantità totale; **he has any amount of time/money** ha tutto il tempo/tutti i soldi che vuole

▶ **amount to** VI + PREP (*total*) ammontare a; (*fig: be equivalent to*) equivalere a, non essere altro che; **this amounts to a refusal** questo equivale a un rifiuto; **he'll never amount to much** non conterà mai granché.

amp [æmp], **am·père** ['æmpɛəʳ] N ampere *m inv*; **a 13**

amp(ère) plug una spina con fusibile da 13 ampere.

am·per·age ['æmpərɪdʒ] N amperaggio.

am·per·sand ['æmpəˌsænd] N "e" *f* commerciale.

am·pheta·mine [æm'fɛtəmiːn] N anfetamina.

am·phib·ian [æm'fɪbɪən] N (*Bio, vehicle*) anfibio.

am·phibi·ous [æm'fɪbɪəs] ADJ (*Bio, vehicle*) anfibio(-a).

am·phi·thea·tre, (*Am*) **am·phi·thea·ter** ['æmfɪˌθɪətəʳ] N anfiteatro.

am·pho·ter·ic [ˌæmfə'tɛrɪk] ADJ (*Chem*) anfotero(-a).

am·ple ['æmpl] ADJ (*comp* **-er**, *superl* **-est**) **a** (*large: boot of car*) ampio(-a), spazioso(-a); (*: garment*) ampio(-a) **b** (*more than enough: money*) in abbondanza; (*: space, means, resources*) abbondante, ampio(-a); **we have ample reason to believe that** ... abbiamo parecchie ragioni per credere che...; **we have ample time to finish it** abbiamo tutto il tempo (necessario) per finirlo; **that should be ample** (*time, money etc*) dovrebbe essere più che sufficiente.

am·pli·fi·ca·tion [ˌæmplɪfɪ'keɪʃən] N (*of sound*) sistema *m* di amplificazione; (*of idea, statement*) ampliamento.

am·pli·fi·er ['æmplɪfaɪəʳ] N amplificatore *m*.

am·pli·fy ['æmplɪfaɪ] VT (*sound*) amplificare; (*statement etc*) ampliare.

am·pli·tude ['æmplɪˌtjuːd] N (*Math, Phys*) ampiezza.

am·ply ['æmplɪ] ADV ampiamente.

am·poule, (*Am*) **am·pule** ['æmpuːl] N (*Med*) fiala.

am·pu·tate ['æmpjʊteɪt] VT amputare.

am·pu·ta·tion [ˌæmpjʊ'teɪʃən] N amputazione *f*.

am·pu·tee [æmpjʊ'tiː] N mutilato(-a) (*chi ha subito un'amputazione*).

Am·ster·dam [ˌæmstə'dæm] N Amsterdam *f*.

amt ABBR = **amount**.

amuck [ə'mʌk], **amok** [ə'mɒk] ADV: **to run amuck** (*madman*) essere preso(-a) da follia omicida; (*children, fans*) scatenarsi; (*animals*) correre all'impazzata.

amuse [ə'mjuːz] VT (*cause mirth*) divertire, far ridere; (*entertain*) (far) divertire; **to be amused at** essere divertito(-a) da; **he was not amused** non l'ha trovato divertente; **to amuse o.s. with sth/by doing sth** divertirsi con qc/a fare qc; **run along and amuse yourselves** andate a divertirvi.

amuse·ment [ə'mjuːzmənt] N **a** divertimento; **much to my amusement** con mio grande spasso; **a look of amusement** un'aria divertita **b** (*entertainment*) divertimento, svago; **they do it for amusement only** lo fanno solo per divertirsi *or* per svago.

♦ **amusement arcade** N sala *f* giochi *inv*.

♦ **amusement park** N luna park *m inv*.

amus·ing [ə'mjuːzɪŋ] ADJ divertente.

amus·ing·ly [ə'mjuːzɪŋlɪ] ADV in modo divertente.

am·yl·ase ['æmɪˌleɪz] N amilasi *f*.

an [æn, ən, n] INDEF ART see **a**.

ANA [ˌeɪɛn'eɪ] N ABBR **a** = *American Newspaper Association* **b** = *American Nurses Association*.

anabo·lism [ə'næbəˌlɪzəm] N anabolismo.

anach·ro·nism [ə'nækrənˌɪzəm] N anacronismo.

anach·ro·nis·tic [ə'nækrə'nɪstɪk] ADJ anacronistico(-a).

ana·con·da [ˌænə'kɒndə] N anaconda *m inv*.

anaemia, (*Am*) **anemia** [ə'niːmɪə] N anemia.

anaemic, (*Am*) **anemic** [ə'niːmɪk] ADJ anemico(-a).

an·aer·obe [æn'ɛərəʊb], **an·aero·bium** [æneə'rəʊbɪəm] N (*pl* anaerobia [æneə'rəʊbɪə]) anaerobio.

an·aes·the·sia, (*Am*) **an·es·the·sia** [ˌænɪs'θiːzɪə] N anestesia.

an·aes·thet·ic, (*Am*) **an·es·thet·ic** [ˌænɪs'θɛtɪk] 1 N

anestetico; **under (the) anaesthetic** sotto anestesia; **local/general anaesthetic** anestesia locale/totale.
[2] ADJ anestetico(-a).

anaes·the·tist, (Am) **anes·the·tist** [æ'ni:sθɪtɪst] N anestetista m/f.

anaes·the·tize, (Am) **anes·the·tize** [æ'ni:sθɪtaɪz] VT anestetizzare.

ana·gram ['ænəgræm] N anagramma m.

anal ['eɪnəl] ADJ anale.

an·alge·sic [ˌænæl'dʒi:zɪk] [1] ADJ analgesico(-a).
[2] N analgesico.

♦ **analog computer** N calcolatore m analogico.

ana·logi·cal·ly [ˌænə'lɒdʒɪklɪ] ADV analogicamente.

analo·gous [ə'næləgəs] ADJ: **analogous (to, with)** analogo (a), affine (a).

ana·logue, (Am) **ana·log** ['ænəlɒg] [1] ADJ (watch) analogico(-a).
[2] N cosa analoga.

anal·ogy [ə'nælədʒɪ] N analogia; **to draw an analogy between** fare un'analogia tra.

ana·lyse ['ænəlaɪz] VT (Brit) analizzare, fare l'analisi di.

analy·sis [ə'næləsɪs] N (pl **analyses** [ə'næləsi:z]) analisi f inv; (Psych) (psic)analisi f inv; **in the last analysis** in ultima analisi.

ana·lyst ['ænəlɪst] N (political, financial) analista m/f; (Am: also: **psychoanalyst**) (psic)analista m/f.

ana·lyti·cal [ˌænə'lɪtɪkəl], **ana·lyt·ic** [ˌænə'lɪtɪk] ADJ analitico(-a).

ana·lyti·cal·ly [ˌænə'lɪtɪklɪ] ADV analiticamente.

ana·lyze ['ænəlaɪz] VT (Am) = **analyse**.

an·ar·chic [æ'nɑ:kɪk] ADJ anarchico(-a).

an·ar·chi·cal [æ'nɑ:kɪkəl], **an·ar·chic** [æ'nɑ:kɪk] ADJ anarchico(-a).

an·ar·chism ['ænəˌkɪzm] N (Pol) anarchismo.

an·ar·chist ['ænəkɪst] N, ADJ anarchico(-a).

an·ar·chy ['ænəkɪ] N anarchia.

anath·ema [ə'næθɪmə] N (Rel, fig) anatema m; **it is anathema to him** non ne vuol neanche sentir parlare.

ana·tomi·cal [ˌænə'tɒmɪkəl] ADJ anatomico(-a).

ana·tomi·cal·ly [ˌænə'tɒmɪklɪ] ADV anatomicamente.

anato·mist [ə'nætəmɪst] N anatomista m/f.

anato·my [ə'nætəmɪ] N anatomia.

ANC [ˌeɪɛn'si:] N ABBR = African National Congress.

an·ces·tor ['ænsɪstə'] N antenato(-a), avo(-a).

an·ces·tral [æn'sɛstrəl] ADJ (of family) avito(-a); (of former times) ancestrale, atavico(-a); **ancestral home** casa avita.

an·ces·try ['ænsɪstrɪ] N (origin) lignaggio, ascendenza, stirpe f; (forebears) antenati mpl.

an·chor ['æŋkə'] [1] N ancora; (fig) ancora di salvezza; (of team, organization) perno, pilastro; **to be (lying) at anchor** essere alla fonda; **to drop anchor** gettare l'ancora; **to weigh anchor** salpare or levare l'ancora.
[2] VT (also fig) ancorare.
[3] VI ancorarsi.

an·chor·age ['æŋkərɪdʒ] N ancoraggio.

♦ **anchor·man** ['æŋkəmæn] N (pl **-men**) (Radio, TV) anchor man m inv.

an·cho·vy ['æntʃəvɪ] N acciuga, alice f.

♦ **anchovy paste** N pasta d'acciughe.

an·cient ['eɪnʃənt] ADJ (old: classical) antico(-a); (fam: person) decrepito(-a); (: object) vecchio(-a) come il cucco; **ancient monument** monumento storico; **ancient Rome** l'antica Roma.

an·cil·lary [æn'sɪlərɪ] ADJ ausiliario(-a).

and [ænd, ənd, nd, ən] CONJ e, ed (often used before vowel); **one and a half** uno e mezzo; **three hundred and ten** trecentodieci; **better and better** sempre meglio; **more and more** sempre di più; **without shoes and socks** senza scarpe né calze; **there are lawyers and lawyers!** ci sono avvocati e avvocati!; **he talked and talked** (e) parlava (e) parlava; **try and do it** prova a farlo; **wait and see** aspetta e vedrai; **come and sit here** vieni a sedere qui; **and so on** e così via.

An·des ['ændi:z] NPL: **the Andes** le Ande.

An·dor·ra [ˌæn'dɔ:rə] N Andorra.

an·dro·gyne ['ændrəˌdʒaɪn] N (Bio, frm) androgino.

an·drogy·nous [æn'drɒdʒɪnəs] ADJ (Bio, frm) androgino (-a).

Andromache [æn'drɒməkɪ] N Andromaca.

An·drom·eda [æn'drɒmɪdə] N Andromeda.

an·ec·do·tal [ænɪk'dəʊtl] ADJ aneddotico(-a).

an·ec·dote ['ænɪkdəʊt] N aneddoto.

anemia etc [ə'ni:mɪə] = **anaemia** etc.

an·emom·eter [ˌænɪ'mɒmɪtə'] N anemometro.

anemo·ne [ə'nɛmənɪ] N (Bot) anemone m; (also: **sea anemone**) anemone m di mare, attinia.

an·es·thet·ic etc [ˌænɪs'θɛtɪk] = **anaesthetic** etc.

anew [ə'nju:] ADV (liter) di nuovo; **to begin anew** ricominciare.

an·gel ['eɪndʒəl] N angelo; **be an angel and fetch my gloves** se mi vai a prendere i guanti sei proprio un angelo.

♦ **angel dust** N sedativo usato a scopo allucinogeno.

an·gel·ic [æn'dʒɛlɪk] ADJ angelico(-a).

an·gel·ica [æn'dʒɛlɪkə] N (Bot) angelica.

♦ **angel shark**, **angel fish** N squadro.

An·ge·lus ['ændʒɪləs] N Angelus m inv.

an·ger ['æŋgə'] [1] N rabbia, collera; **red with anger** rosso(-a) per or dalla rabbia; **in anger** nell'impeto della collera.
[2] VT far arrabbiare; **he is easily angered** si arrabbia facilmente.

an·gi·na [æn'dʒaɪnə] N angina.

♦ **an·gi·na pec·to·ris** [æn'dʒaɪnə'pɛktərɪs] N angina pectoris.

an·gle¹ ['æŋgl] N **a** (Geom) angolo; **right angle** angolo retto; **at right angles to** ad angolo retto con, perpendicolare a; **at an angle of 80** a un angolo di 80; **at an angle di sbieco**; **to cut sth at an angle** tagliare qc di traverso **b** (fig: point of view) punto di vista; **from their angle** dal loro punto di vista; **to look at sth from a different angle** (fig) considerare qc da un altro punto di vista or sotto un altro aspetto.

an·gle² ['æŋgl] VI (fish) pescare (con l'amo); **to angle for** (fig) cercare di avere.

an·gler ['æŋglə'] N pescatore m con la lenza.

An·gli·can ['æŋglɪkən] ADJ, N anglicano(-a).

An·gli·can·ism ['æŋglɪkənɪzəm] N anglicanesimo.

an·gli·cize ['æŋglɪsaɪz] VT anglicizzare.

an·gling ['æŋglɪŋ] N pesca con la lenza.

Anglo- ['æŋgləʊ] PREF anglo-.

♦ **Anglo-Italian** ['æŋgləʊɪ'tæljən] ADJ, N italo-britannico (-a).

an·glo·phile ['æŋgləʊfaɪl] N anglofilo(-a).

an·glo·phobe ['æŋgləʊfəʊb] N anglofobo(-a).

♦ **Anglo-Saxon** ['æŋgləʊ'sæksən] ADJ, N anglosassone m/f.

An·go·la [æŋ'gəʊlə] N Angola.

An·go·lan [æŋ'gəʊlən] ADJ, N angolano(-a).

an·go·ra [æŋ'gɔ:rə] [1] ADJ d'angora. [2] N angora.

an·gri·ly ['æŋgrɪlɪ] ADV con rabbia.

an·gry [ˈæŋgrɪ] ADJ (comp **-ier**, superl **-iest**) (gen) arrabbiato (-a), furioso(-a); (annoyed) irritato(-a); (wound) infiammato(-a); (sky) minaccioso(-a); **to be angry with sb/about** or **at sth** essere arrabbiato(-a) or in collera con qn/per qc; **to get angry** arrabbiarsi; **to make sb angry** far arrabbiare qn; **you won't be angry, will you?** non ti arrabbi, vero?; **he was angry at being treated so badly** era arrabbiato perché lo avevano trattato così male.

angst [æŋst] N (liter) ansietà f inv.

an·guish [ˈæŋgwɪʃ] N angoscia; **to be in anguish** essere angosciato(-a).

an·guished [ˈæŋgwɪʃt] ADJ (expression, look) angosciato (-a); (cry) angoscioso(-a).

an·gu·lar [ˈæŋgjʊlə'] ADJ angoloso(-a), spigoloso(-a); (measurement etc) angolare.

an·hy·dride [ænˈhaɪdraɪd] N anidride f.

an·hy·drous [ænˈhaɪdrəs] ADJ anidro(-a).

ani·line [ˈænɪlɪn] N anilina.

ani·mal [ˈænɪməl] [1] N animale m; (pej: person) bestia, bruto.
[2] ADJ animale.

♦ **animal husbandry** N allevamento di animali.

♦ **animal kingdom** N: **the animal kingdom** il regno animale.

♦ **animal rights** [1] NPL diritti mpl degli animali.
[2] ADJ (organization, activist) animalista.

♦ **animal spirits** NPL vivacità f inv.

ani·mate [adj ˈænɪmɪt; vb ˈænɪmeɪt] [1] ADJ (animal, plants) vivente; (capable of movement) animato(-a).
[2] VT animare.

ani·mat·ed [ˈænɪmeɪtɪd] ADJ animato(-a); **to become animated** animarsi.

♦ **animated cartoon** N cartone m animato.

ani·mat·ed·ly [ˈænɪmeɪtɪdlɪ] ADV animatamente.

ani·ma·tion [ˌænɪˈmeɪʃən] N animazione f.

ani·ma·tor [ˈænɪˌmeɪtə'] N (Cine) animatore(-trice).

ani·mos·ity [ˌænɪˈmɒsɪtɪ] N animosità.

ani·mus [ˈænɪməs] N animosità.

an·ion [ˈænˌaɪən] N anione m.

ani·seed [ˈænɪsiːd] N semi mpl di anice.

An·ka·ra [ˈæŋkərə] N Ankara.

an·kle [ˈæŋkl] N caviglia.

ankle·bone [ˈæŋklˌbəʊn] N astragalo.

♦ **ankle socks** NPL calzini mpl.

an·nals [ˈænəlz] NPL annali mpl.

an·neal [əˈniːl] VT (Tech: glass, metal) ricuocere.

an·neal·ing [əˈniːlɪŋ] N (: of glass, metal) ricottura.

an·nelid [ˈænəlɪd] N anellide m.

an·nex [vb əˈnɛks; n ˈænɛks] [1] VT (territory): **to annex (to)** annettere (a).
[2] N (Brit: also: **annexe**) (edificio) annesso.

an·nexa·tion [ˌænɛkˈseɪʃən] N annessione f.

an·ni·hi·late [əˈnaɪəleɪt] VT annientare, annichilire; (argument) demolire.

an·ni·hi·la·tion [əˌnaɪəˈleɪʃən] N annientamento.

an·ni·ver·sa·ry [ˌænɪˈvɜːsərɪ] [1] N anniversario.
[2] ADJ: **anniversary celebration** celebrazione f dell'anniversario; **anniversary dinner** pranzo per l'anniversario, cena commemorativa.

Anno Domi·ni [ˈænəʊˈdɒmɪnaɪ] ADV anno Domini.

an·no·tate [ˈænəʊteɪt] VT annotare.

an·no·ta·tion [ˌænəʊˈteɪʃən] N annotazione f.

an·nounce [əˈnaʊns] VT (gen) annunciare; **to announce the marriage/death of sb** annunciare le nozze/la morte di qn; **he announced that he wasn't going** ha dichiarato che non (ci) sarebbe andato.

an·nounce·ment [əˈnaʊnsmənt] N (declaration) comunicazione f, annuncio; (official: through media) comunicato; (private: in newspaper) annuncio; (letter, card) partecipazione f; **I'd like to make an announcement** ho una comunicazione da fare.

an·nounc·er [əˈnaʊnsə'] N (Radio, TV: linking programmes) annunciatore(-trice); (: introducing people) presentatore (-trice).

an·noy [əˈnɔɪ] VT dare fastidio a, infastidire, dare noia a; **to be annoyed about sth** essere seccato(-a) per qc, essere contrariato(-a) or irritato(-a) da qc; **to be annoyed (at sth/with sb)** essere seccato(-a) or irritato (-a) (per qc/con qn); **he's just trying to annoy you** sta solo cercando di stuzzicarti; **don't get annoyed!** non irritarti!

an·noy·ance [əˈnɔɪəns] N (state) fastidio, irritazione f; (cause of annoyance) seccatura, noia; **to her annoyance** con suo gran dispetto.

an·noy·ing [əˈnɔɪɪŋ] ADJ (person, habit, noise) irritante, seccante; **it's annoying to have to wait** è (una cosa) seccante dover aspettare.

an·noy·ing·ly [əˈnɔɪɪŋlɪ] ADV fastidiosamente.

an·nual [ˈænjʊəl] [1] ADJ (income) annuo(-a); (event, plant) annuale.
[2] N (book) pubblicazione f annuale, annuario; (children's comic book) almanacco; (Bot) pianta annuale.

♦ **annual general meeting** N (Brit) assemblea generale.

an·nual·ly [ˈænjʊəlɪ] ADV annualmente, ogni anno.

♦ **annual report** N relazione f annuale.

an·nu·ity [əˈnjuːɪtɪ] N annualità f inv, rendita annuale; (also: **life annuity**) vitalizio; **pension annuity** (policy) ≈ polizza di pensione integrativa.

an·nul [əˈnʌl] VT annullare; (law) rescindere.

an·nul·ment [əˈnʌlmənt] N annullamento; (of law) rescissione f.

an·nu·lus [ˈænjʊləs] N (pl **annules** or **annuli** [ˈænjʊˌlaɪ]) corona circolare.

an·num [ˈænəm] N see **per annum**.

An·nun·cia·tion [əˌnʌnsɪˈeɪʃən] N: **the Annunciation** l'Annunciazione f.

an·ode [ˈænəʊd] N anodo.

ano·dize [ˈænəˌdaɪz] VT anodizzare.

ano·dyne [ˈænəʊˌdaɪn] [1] N (Med) analgesico, calmante m; (fig liter) rimedio; **he used to speak of work as "the great anodyne"** soleva definire il lavoro la migliore delle medicine.
[2] ADJ (Med) analgesico(-a), calmante; (fig: bland, neutral) anodino.

anoint [əˈnɔɪnt] VT (Rel) ungere; **to anoint sb king** consacrare qn re.

anoma·lous [əˈnɒmələs] ADJ anomalo(-a).

anoma·ly [əˈnɒməlɪ] N anomalia.

anon [əˈnɒn] ADV (old, hum): **see you anon!** a presto!

anon. [əˈnɒn] ADJ ABBR = **anonymous**.

ano·nym·ity [ˌænəˈnɪmɪtɪ] N anonimato.

anony·mous [əˈnɒnɪməs] ADJ anonimo(-a); **to remain anonymous** mantenere l'anonimato.

anony·mous·ly [əˈnɒnɪməslɪ] ADV anonimamente; **to write anonymously to sb** scrivere una lettera anonima a qn.

ano·rak [ˈænəræk] N (esp Brit) giacca a vento.

ano·rexia [ænəˈrɛksɪə], **ano·rexia ner·vo·sa** [ænəˈrɛksɪə nɜːˈvəʊsə] N anoressia.

ano·rex·ic [ænəˈreksɪk] ADJ, N anoressico(-a).

an·oth·er [əˈnʌðə^r] ⓵ ADJ (*additional*) un altro/un'altra, ancora un(a); (*different*) un altro/un'altra; (*second*) un altro/un'altra, un(a) secondo(-a); **another book** (*one more*) un altro libro, ancora un libro; **another drink?** bevi ancora qualcosa?; **in another 5 years** fra altri 5 anni; **without another word** senza aggiungere una sola *or* nemmeno una parola; **that's quite another matter** è tutt'un'altra cosa; **he's another Shakespeare** è un nuovo *or* altro Shakespeare.

⓶ PRON un altro/un'altra, ancora uno(-a); **from one town to another** da una città all'altra; **they love one another** si vogliono bene; see also **one**.

ANSI [ˌeɪɛnɛsˈaɪ] N ABBR (= *American National Standards Institute*) *Istituto nazionale americano per la normalizzazione.*

an·swer [ˈɑːnsə^r] ⓵ N **a** (*reply*) risposta; **in answer to your question** in risposta *or* per rispondere alla tua domanda; **to know all the answers** (*fig*) saper tutto, saperla lunga

b (*solution*) soluzione *f*; (*Math etc*) soluzione, risposta; **there is no easy answer** non è un problema facile da risolvere.

⓶ VT **a** (*reply to*) rispondere a; **our prayers have been answered** le nostre preghiere sono state esaudite; **to answer the door** andare ad aprire (la porta); **to answer the phone** rispondere (al telefono)

b (*fulfil*: *needs*) rispondere a, soddisfare; (: *expectations, description*) corrispondere a, rispondere a; (: *purpose*) servire a, rispondere a; (*problem*) risolvere; (*prayer*) esaudire.

⓷ VI rispondere

▶ **answer back** VI + ADV (*fam*): **to answer (sb) back** rispondere (a qn) (con impertinenza)

▶ **answer for** VI + PREP (*action, crime*) rispondere di; (*sb's safety*) essere responsabile di; (*truth of sth*) garantire; **he's got a lot to answer for** ci sono molte cose di cui deve render conto

▶ **answer to** VI + PREP (*description*) corrispondere a; (*name*) rispondere a.

an·swer·able [ˈɑːnsərəbl] ADJ **a** (*responsible*) responsabile; **to be answerable (to sb for sth)** dover rispondere *or* render conto (a qn di qc); **I am answerable to no-one** non devo rispondere a nessuno **b** (*question*) (a) cui si può rispondere.

♦ **an·swer·ing ma·chine** [ˈɑːnsərɪŋməˈʃiːn] N segreteria telefonica.

ant [ænt] N formica.

ANTA [ˌeɪɛntiˈeɪ] N ABBR = *American National Theater and Academy.*

an·tago·nism [ænˈtæɡənɪzəm] N antagonismo.

an·tago·nist [ænˈtæɡənɪst] N antagonista *m/f.*

an·tago·nis·tic [ænˌtæɡəˈnɪstɪk] ADJ antagonistico(-a).

an·tago·nize [ænˈtæɡəˌnaɪz] VT provocare l'ostilità di, inimicarsi; **I don't want to antagonize her** non voglio inimicarmela.

Ant·arc·tic [ænˈtɑːktɪk] ⓵ ADJ antartico(-a). ⓶ N: **the Antarctic** l'Antartico.

Ant·arc·ti·ca [ænˈtɑːktɪkə] N Antartide *f.*

♦ **Antarctic Circle** N: **the Antarctic Circle** il Circolo polare antartico.

♦ **Antarctic Ocean** N: **the Antarctic Ocean** l'Oceano antartico.

ante [ˈæntɪ] N (*fam*): **to up the ante** (*in game, also fig*) alzare la posta.

ante... [ˈæntɪ] PREF anti..., ante..., pre.... .

ant·eater [ˈæntˌiːtə^r] N formichiere *m.*

ante·ced·ent [ˌæntɪˈsiːdənt] N antecedente *m*, precedente *m*; **antecedents** NPL (*past history*) antecedenti, precedenti; (*ancestors*) antenati *mpl.*

ante·cham·ber [ˈæntɪˌtʃeɪmbə^r] N anticamera.

ante·date [ˈæntɪˈdeɪt] VT **a** (*precede*) precedere **b** (*document etc*) retrodatare.

ante·di·lu·vian [ˈæntɪdɪˈluːvɪən] ADJ (*liter, hum*) antidiluviano(-a).

ante·lope [ˈæntɪləʊp] N antilope *f.*

ante·na·tal [ˈæntɪˈneɪtl] ADJ prenatale.

♦ **antenatal clinic** N assistenza medica preparto.

an·ten·na [ænˈtɛnə] N (*pl* **antennae** [ænˈtɛniː]) (*Radio, TV, Zool*) antenna.

ante·ri·or [ænˈtɪərɪə^r] ADJ (*frm: position*) anteriore; (: *time*) precedente.

ante·room [ˈæntɪˌruːm] N anticamera.

an·them [ˈænθəm] N inno; **national anthem** inno nazionale.

an·ther [ˈænθə^r] N antera.

♦ **ant hill** N formicaio.

an·tho·logi·cal [ˌænθəˈlɒdʒɪkəl] ADJ antologico(-a).

an·tholo·gist [ænˈθɒlədʒɪst] N antologista *m/f.*

an·thol·ogy [ænˈθɒlədʒɪ] N antologia.

an·thra·cite [ˈænθrəsaɪt] N antracite *f.*

an·thrax [ˈænθræks] N (*Med*) antrace *m.*

an·thro·poid [ˈænθrəʊpɔɪd] ADJ, N antropoide (*m*).

an·thro·po·logi·cal [ˌænθrəpəˈlɒdʒɪkəl] ADJ antropologico(-a).

an·thro·polo·gist [ˌænθrəˈpɒlədʒɪst] N antropologo(-a).

an·thro·pol·ogy [ˌænθrəˈpɒlədʒɪ] N antropologia.

an·thro·po·mor·phic [ˌænθrəpəˈmɔːfɪk] ADJ antropomorfo(-a).

anti... [ˈæntɪ] PREF anti...; **he's anti-everything** è un bastian contrario.

♦ **anti-aircraft** [ˈæntɪˈɛəkrɑːft] ADJ (*gun*) contraereo(-a), antiaereo(-a).

♦ **anti-aircraft defence** N difesa antiaerea.

♦ **anti-bal·lis·tic** [ˈæntɪbəˈlɪstɪk] ADJ antibalistico(-a).

anti·bi·ot·ic [ˈæntɪbaɪˈɒtɪk] ⓵ N antibiotico. ⓶ ADJ antibiotico(-a).

anti·body [ˈæntɪˌbɒdɪ] N anticorpo.

Anti·christ [ˈæntɪˌkraɪst] N: **the Antichrist** l'Anticristo.

an·tici·pate [ænˈtɪsɪpeɪt] VT **a** (*expect: trouble*) prevedere, aspettarsi; (: *pleasure*) pregustare, assaporare in anticipo; **this is worse than I anticipated** è peggio di quel che immaginavo *or* pensavo; **to anticipate that ...** prevedere che...; **I anticipate seeing him tomorrow** presumo *or* mi immagino che lo vedrò domani; **as anticipated** come previsto

b (*forestall: person*) prevenire, precedere; (*foresee: event*) prevedere; (: *question, objection, wishes*) prevenire.

an·tici·pa·tion [ænˌtɪsɪˈpeɪʃən] N: **in anticipation (of)** in previsione *or* attesa (di); **we waited in great anticipation** (*excitement*) abbiamo aspettato con grande impazienza; **in anticipation of an enjoyable week** pregustando una bella settimana; **thanking you in anticipation** vi ringrazio in anticipo.

anti·cleri·cal [ˌæntɪˈklɛrɪkl] ADJ, N anticlericale (*m/f*).

anti·cli·max [ˈæntɪˈklaɪmæks] N delusione *f*; **the game came as an anticlimax** la partita si rivelò una delusione.

anti·cline [ˈæntɪˌklaɪn] N anticlinale *f.*

anti·clock·wise [ˈæntɪˈklɒkwaɪz] ADV, ADJ in senso antiora-

rio.

anti·co·agu·lant [ˌæntɪkəʊ'ægjʊlənt] ADJ, N anticoagulante (m).

an·tics ['æntɪks] NPL (of clown etc) lazzi mpl, buffonerie fpl;
(of child, animal etc) buffe acrobazie fpl; (pej) scherzetti
mpl.

anti·cy·clone ['æntɪ'saɪkləʊn] N anticiclone m.

anti·cy·clon·ic [ˌæntɪsaɪ'klɒnɪk] ADJ anticiclonico(-a).

anti·dote ['æntɪdəʊt] N antidoto.

anti·fas·cist ['æntɪ'fæʃɪst] ADJ, N antifascista (m/f).

♦ **anti·flu** ['æntɪ'fluː] ADJ antinfluenzale.

anti·freeze ['æntɪ'friːz] N antigelo inv, anticongelante m.

anti·gen ['æntɪdʒən] N antigene m.

Antigone [æn'tɪgənɪ] N Antigone f.

anti·he·ro ['æntɪˌhɪərəʊ] N (pl antiheroes) antieroe m.

anti·his·ta·mine [ˌæntɪ'hɪstəmɪn] N antistaminico.

An·til·les [æn'tɪliːz] NPL: the Antilles le Antille.

anti·lock (device) ['æntɪ'lɒk] N dispositivo m antibloccaggio inv.

anti·loga·rithm [ˌæntɪ'lɒgəˌrɪðəm] N antilogaritmo.

anti·mat·ter ['æntɪˌmætə'] N antimateria.

anti·mili·ta·rism [ˌæntɪ'mɪlɪtərɪzəm] N antimilitarismo.

anti·mili·ta·ris·tic [ˌæntɪˌmɪlɪtə'rɪstɪk] ADJ antimilitaristico
(-a).

anti·mo·ny ['æntɪmənɪ] N antimonio.

anti·node ['æntɪˌnəʊd] N (Phys) ventre m, antinodo.

anti·nu·clear [ˌæntɪ'njuːklɪə'] ADJ antinucleare.

an·tipa·thy [æn'tɪpəθɪ] N antipatia.

anti·per·spi·rant [æntɪ'pɜːspɪrənt] N deodorante m (ad
azione) antitraspirante.

anti·phon ['æntɪfən] N (Rel) antifona.

an·tipo·dean [æn,tɪpə'diːən] ADJ degli antipodi.

An·tipo·des [æn'tɪpədiːz] NPL: the Antipodes gli antipodi.

anti·quar·ian [ˌæntɪ'kwɛərɪən] 1 ADJ: **antiquarian bookshop** libreria antiquaria.

2 N antiquario(-a).

anti·quary ['æntɪkwərɪ] N antiquario(-a).

anti·quat·ed ['æntɪkweɪtɪd] ADJ (pej) antiquato(-a),
sorpassato(-a).

an·tique [æn'tiːk] 1 ADJ (furniture etc) antico(-a),
d'epoca.

2 N oggetto antico, pezzo d'antiquariato; **antiques** NPL
antichità f inv; **he deals in antiques** commercia in
antiquariato.

♦ **antique dealer** N antiquario(-a).

♦ **antique shop** N bottega or negozio di antiquario,
negozio d'antichità.

an·tiq·uity [æn'tɪkwɪtɪ] N antichità; **of great antiquity**
molto antico(-a).

an·tir·rhi·num [ˌæntɪ'raɪnəm] N antirrino.

♦ **anti-Semitic** ['æntɪsɪ'mɪtɪk] ADJ antisemitico(-a), antisemita.

♦ **anti-Semitism** ['æntɪ'sɛmɪtɪzəm] N antisemitismo.

anti·sep·sis [ˌæntɪ'sɛpsɪs] N antisepsi f.

anti·sep·tic [ˌæntɪ'sɛptɪk] 1 ADJ antisettico(-a).

2 N antisettico.

anti·skid [ˌæntɪ'skɪd] ADJ antisdrucciolevole.

anti·so·cial ['æntɪ'səʊʃəl] ADJ (behaviour, tendency: against
society) antisociale; (unsociable) scorbutico(-a),
asociale.

anti·spas·mod·ic [ˌæntɪspæz'mɒdɪk] ADJ antispastico(-a).

anti·stat·ic [ˌæntɪs'tætɪk] ADJ antistatico(-a).

anti·tank [ˌæntɪ'tæŋk] ADJ anticarro inv.

anti·theft [ˌæntɪ'θɛft] ADJ antifurto inv.

an·tith·esis [æn'tɪθɪsɪs] N (pl antitheses [æn'tɪθɪsiːz]) anti-

tesi f inv; (contrast) carattere m antitetico.

anti·theti·cal [ˌæntɪθɛtɪkəl] ADJ antitetico(-a).

anti·tox·in [ˌæntɪ'tɒksɪn] N antitossina.

anti·trust ['æntɪ'trʌst] ADJ (Comm): **anti-trust law/legisla-
tion** legge f/legislazione f antitrust inv.

anti·vivi·sec·tion·ist ['æntɪˌvɪvɪ'sɛkʃənɪst] N antivivise-
zionista m/f.

ant·ler ['æntlə'] N palco; **antlers** NPL corna fpl.

an·to·no·ma·sia [ˌæntənə'meɪzɪə] N (frm) antonomasia.

an·to·nym ['æntənɪm] N (Gram) antonimo.

Ant·werp ['æntwɜːp] N Anversa.

anus ['eɪnəs] N ano.

an·vil ['ænvɪl] N incudine f.

anxi·ety [æŋ'zaɪətɪ] N **a** ansia, ansietà f inv; **I have no
anxieties about them** non sono in ansia per loro; **it is a
great anxiety to me** è una grossa preoccupazione per
me **b** (eagerness): **anxiety (to do sth)** smania (di fare
qc); **in his anxiety to be gone he forgot his case** nella
furia or fretta di andarsene si è dimenticato la borsa.

anx·ious ['æŋkʃəs] ADJ **a** (worried) preoccupato(-a),
ansioso(-a), in ansia, inquieto(-a); **I'm very anxious
about you** sono molto preoccupato or in pensiero per
te; **with an anxious glance** con uno sguardo pieno
d'ansia

b (causing worry: moment) angoscioso(-a)

c (eager): **anxious for sth/to do sth** impaziente di qc/di
fare qc; **I am anxious that she should do it** ci tengo
moltissimo che lo faccia; **he is anxious for success** ha un
grande desiderio di successo; **I'm not very anxious to go**
ho poca voglia di andarci.

anx·ious·ly ['æŋkʃəslɪ] ADV ansiosamente, con ansia.

any ['ɛnɪ]

1 ADJ

a (in questions etc: some) del (dell', dello) m, della
(dell') f, dei (degli) mpl, delle fpl, qualche;

▷ **is there any meat?** c'è (della) carne?

▷ **have you any money?** hai (dei) soldi?, hai qualche
soldo?

▷ **are there any others?** ce ne sono (degli) altri?

▷ **if there are any tickets left** se ci sono ancora (dei)
biglietti, se c'è ancora qualche biglietto

b (with negative) alcuno(-a), nessuno(-a);

▷ **I haven't any bread** non ho pane, sono senza pane

▷ **I don't see any cows** non vedo alcuna or nessuna
mucca, non vedo mucche

▷ **I haven't any money** non ho soldi, sono senza soldi

▷ **without any difficulty** senza (nessuna or alcuna)
difficoltà

▷ **I haven't any work** non ho lavoro, sono senza lavoro

c (no matter which) uno(-a)) qualsiasi, (uno(-a))
qualunque; (each and every) ogni inv, tutto(-a);

▷ **in any case** in ogni caso

▷ **any excuse will do** (una) qualunque or qualsiasi
scusa andrà bene, una scusa qualunque or qualsiasi andrà bene

▷ **any farmer will tell you** qualunque or qualsiasi or
ogni agricoltore te lo dirà

▷ **wear any hat (you like)** mettiti un cappello qualsiasi
or qualunque

▷ **at any moment** da un momento all'altro

▷ **at any rate** ad ogni modo

▷ **come (at) any time** vieni a qualsiasi ora.

2 PRON

a (*in negative and interrogative sentences*): **are there any?** ce ne sono?
▷*are* any of them *coming*? viene qualcuno di loro?
▷there *aren't* any left non ce ne sono più; (*emphatic*) non ne è rimasto nemmeno uno
▷*can* any of you *sing*? c'è qualcuno che sa cantare?
▷*have* you *got* any? ne hai?
▷I *haven't* got any (of them) non ne ho
b (*whichever one*) uno(-a) qualsiasi; (*anybody*) chiunque;
▷few, *if* any pochi, sempre che ce ne siano
▷take any *of* those books (you like) prendi qualsiasi libro.
3 ADV (*in negative sentences*) per niente; (*in interrogative sentences*) un po';
▷are you feeling any *better*? ti senti un po' meglio?
▷don't wait any *longer* non aspettare più
▷I can't hear him any *more* non lo sento più
▷do you want any *more* tea? vuoi ancora un po' di tè?, vuoi ancora del tè?
▷she's not any *more* intelligent than her sister sua sorella è altrettanto intelligente.

any·body ['ɛnɪbɒdɪ] PRON **a** (*in interrogative sentences*) qualcuno, nessuno; **did you see anybody** hai visto qualcuno *or* nessuno?
b (*in negative sentences*) nessuno; **I can't *or* don't see anybody** non vedo nessuno; **without anybody seeing him** senza che nessuno lo vedesse, senza esser visto da nessuno
c (*no matter who*) chiunque, qualsiasi persona; **anybody will tell you the same** chiunque ti dirà la stessa cosa; **anybody else would have laughed** chiunque altro avrebbe riso; **she's not going to marry just anybody** non sposerà il primo che le capita *or* uno qualunque.

any·how ['ɛnɪˌhaʊ] ADV **a** (*at any rate*) ad *or* in ogni modo, comunque; **I'm going anyhow** ci vado lo stesso **b** (*haphazard*) come capita, in qualsiasi modo; **do it anyhow you like** fallo come ti pare; **I finished it anyhow** in qualche modo l'ho finito; **he leaves things just anyhow** lascia tutto come (gli) capita.

any·one ['ɛnɪˌwʌn] PRON = **anybody**.

any·place ['ɛnɪˌpleɪs] PRON (*Am fam*) = **anywhere**.

any·thing ['ɛnɪˌθɪŋ] PRON **a** (*in interrogative sentences*) niente, qualcosa; **are you doing anything tonight?** fai qualcosa stasera?; **anything else?** (*in shop*) basta (così)?, nient'altro?, altro?; **is there anything else you want to tell me?** hai qualcos'altro *or* nient'altro da dirmi?; **can't anything be done?** (non) si può fare qualcosa *or* niente?
b (*in negative sentences*) non... niente, non... nulla; **it wasn't anything serious** non era niente di serio; **I saw hardly anything** non ho visto quasi niente; **the bridge is anything but safe** il ponte non è affatto sicuro; **it isn't anything like as cold as it was** non è più così freddo come prima
c (*no matter what*) qualsiasi cosa, qualunque cosa; **you can say anything you like** puoi dire quello che vuoi; **anything but that** tutto tranne questo; **they'll eat anything** mangiano qualsiasi cosa *or* di tutto; **it can cost anything between £15 and £20** può costare qualcosa come 15 o 20 sterline; **if anything, I have more to do now** se mai *or* piuttosto adesso ho più da fare.

any·time ['ɛnɪˌtaɪm] ADV (*happen*) in qualunque momento; (*come*) a qualsiasi ora.

any·way ['ɛnɪˌweɪ] ADV **a** (*besides*) in ogni caso; **I forgot to buy cough sweets - they don't do much good anyway** ho dimenticato di comprare le caramelle per la tosse - tanto non servono un granché
b (*just the same*) comunque; **thanks, anyway** grazie, comunque
c (*at least, at any rate*) almeno; **everything is ok, as far as I know anyway** va tutto bene, per quel che ne so io
d (*in narrative, conversation: well, then*) bene; **anyway, I've got to go** be', devo andare; **it's a long story ...anyway the upshot was that** ... è una lunga storia... a farla breve il risultato fu che... .

any·where ['ɛnɪˌwɛəʳ] ADV **a** (*in interrogative sentences*) da qualche parte, in qualche posto; **can you see him anywhere?** lo vedi da qualche parte?; **anywhere else?** da qualche *or* nessun'altra parte?, in qualche *or* nessun altro posto?
b (*in negative sentences*) da nessuna parte, in nessun posto; **I can't see him anywhere** non lo vedo da nessuna parte; **they never go anywhere else** non vanno mai da nessun'altra parte
c (*no matter where*) da qualsiasi *or* qualunque parte, in qualunque *or* qualsiasi posto, dovunque; **anywhere in the world** dovunque nel mondo; **put the books down anywhere** metti i libri dove ti capita.

An·zac ['ænzæk] N ABBR (= *Australia-New Zealand Army Corps*) A.N.Z.A.C. *m*; (*soldier*) soldato dell'A.N.Z.A.C.

♦ **Anzac Day** N *festa nazionale australiana e neozelandese in commemorazione dello sbarco a Gallipoli del 25 aprile 1915.*

AOB [ˌeɪəʊˈbiː] N ABBR (= *any other business*) *varie ed eventuali.*

aor·ta [eɪˈɔːtə] N aorta.

apace [əˈpeɪs] ADV (*liter*) rapidamente.

apart [əˈpɑːt] ADV **a** (*separated*) a distanza, separatamente; **we live 3 miles apart** abitiamo a 3 miglia di distanza (l'uno dall'altro); **their birthdays are two days apart** i loro compleanni sono a distanza di due giorni l'uno dall'altro; **she stood apart from the others** se ne stava *or* rimase in disparte; **to live apart** vivere separati; **he lives apart from his wife** vive separato da sua moglie; **I can't tell them apart** non li distinguo l'uno dall'altro; **joking apart** scherzi a parte, a parte gli scherzi; **these problems apart** a parte questi problemi; **apart from** a parte, eccetto; **apart from the fact that** a parte il fatto che; **with one's legs apart** con le gambe divaricate
b (*in pieces*) a pezzi; **to fall apart** cadere a pezzi, sfasciarsi; **to take sth apart** smontare qc.

apart·heid [əˈpɑːteɪt] N apartheid *m*.

apart·ment [əˈpɑːtmənt] N (*esp Am: flat*) appartamento; (*Brit: room in palace*) sala.

♦ **apartment building** N (*Am*) stabile *m*, caseggiato.

apa·thet·ic [ˌæpəˈθɛtɪk] ADJ apatico(-a), indifferente.

apa·theti·cal·ly [ˌæpəˈθɛtɪklɪ] ADV apaticamente.

apa·thy ['æpəθɪ] N apatia, indifferenza.

APB [ˌeɪpiːˈbiː] N ABBR (*Am: police expression: = all points bulletin*) *espressione della polizia che significa " priorità assoluta: trovate...".*

ape [eɪp] **1** N (*esp anthropoid*) scimmia; **to go ape** (*Am fam*) diventare stupido(-a).
2 VT scimmiottare.

Ap·en·nines ['æpəˌnaɪmz] NPL: **the Apennines** gli Apennini *mpl*.

aperi·ent [əˈpɪərɪənt] **1** ADJ lassativo(-a).
2 N lassativo.

ape·ri·tif [ə'pɛrɪtɪf] N aperitivo.

ap·er·ture ['æpət∫jʊə'] N fessura; (*Phot*) apertura.

APEX ['eɪpɛks] N ABBR **a** (*Brit*: = *Association of Professional, Executive, Clerical and Computer Staff*) *associazione dei professionisti, dirigenti, impiegati ed informatici* **b** (*Aer*: = *advance purchase excursion*) APEX *m inv*.

apex ['eɪpɛks] N (*Geom*) vertice *m*; (*fig*) vertice *m*, apice *m*.

aphid ['eɪfɪd] N afide *m*.

apho·rism ['æfərɪzəm] N aforisma *m*.

aph·ro·disi·ac [ˌæfrəʊ'dɪzɪæk] N, ADJ afrodisiaco(-a).

Aphrodite [ˌæfrə'daɪtɪ] N Afrodite *f*.

API [ˌeɪpi:'aɪ] N ABBR = *American Press Insitute*.

api·ary ['eɪpɪərɪ] N apiario.

apiece [ə'pi:s] ADV ciascuno(-a); **he gave them £10 apiece** ha dato loro dieci sterline (per) ciascuno; **these pens sell at 90p apiece** queste penne si vendono a 90 pence l'una.

aplomb [ə'plɒm] N disinvoltura; **with great aplomb** senza scomporsi, con gran disinvoltura.

APO [ˌeɪpi:'əʊ] N ABBR (*Am*: = *Army Post Office*) *ufficio postale dell'esercito*.

apoca·lypse [ə'pɒkəlɪps] N apocalisse *f*.

apoca·lyp·tic [əˌpɒkə'lɪptɪk] ADJ apocalittico(-a).

Apoc·ry·pha [ə'pɒkrɪfə] NPL (*Rel*): **the Apocrypha** i libri apocrifi.

apoc·ry·phal [ə'pɒkrɪfəl] ADJ apocrifo(-a).

apo·gee ['æpəʊdʒi:] N (*Astron, fig frm*) apogeo.

apo·liti·cal [ˌeɪpə'lɪtɪkəl] ADJ apolitico(-a).

Apollo [ə'pɒləʊ] N Apollo.

apolo·get·ic [əˌpɒlə'dʒɛtɪk] ADJ (*look, remark, letter*) di scusa; **he was very apologetic about it/for not coming** si è scusato moltissimo di ciò/per or di non essere venuto.

apolo·geti·cal·ly [əˌpɒlə'dʒɛtɪkəlɪ] ADV per scusarsi.

apolo·gist [ə'pɒlədʒɪst] N apologeta *m/f*.

apolo·gize [ə'pɒlədʒaɪz] VI: **to apologize (to sb for sth)** scusarsi (con qn per or di qc), chiedere scusa (a qn per or di qc); **they apologized for being late** si sono scusati per il ritardo; **there's no need to apologize** non è il caso di scusarsi.

apol·ogy [ə'pɒlədʒɪ] N scuse *fpl*; **I demand an apology** esigo delle scuse; **please accept my apologies** la prego di accettare le mie scuse; **an apology for a lunch** (*pej*) un tentativo mal riuscito di pranzo.

apo·plec·tic [ˌæpə'plɛktɪk] ADJ (*Med*) apoplettico(-a); **apoplectic with rage** (*fam*) livido(-a) per la rabbia.

apo·plexy ['æpəplɛksɪ] N apoplessia.

apos·tate [ə'pɒsteɪt] N (*frm*) apostata *m/f*.

apos·tle [ə'pɒsl] N apostolo.

♦ **Apostles' Creed** N: **the Apostles' Creed** il credo apostolico.

ap·os·tol·ic [ˌæpəs'tɒlɪk] ADJ apostolico(-a).

apos·tro·phe [ə'pɒstrəfɪ] N (*Gram: sign*) apostrofo.

apoth·ecary [ə'pɒθɪkərɪ] N farmacista *m/f*.

apoth·eo·sis [əˌpɒθɪ'əʊsɪs] N **a**: **apotheosis of** perfetto esempio di **b** (*Art*) apoteosi *f inv*.

ap·pal, (*Am*) **ap·pall** [ə'pɔ:l] VT sconvolgere, atterrire.

Ap·pa·la·chian Moun·tains [ˌæpə'leɪʃən 'maʊntɪnz] NPL: **the Appalachian Mountains** (*also*: **the Appalachians**) i (monti) Appalachi.

ap·pal·ling [ə'pɔ:lɪŋ] ADJ (*ignorance, conditions, destruction*) spaventoso(-a), impressionante; (*fam: film, taste*) pessimo(-a), spaventoso(-a); **she's an appalling cook** è un disastro come cuoca.

ap·pal·ling·ly [ə'pɔ:lɪŋlɪ] ADV spaventosamente; (*behave*)

molto male.

ap·pa·rat·us [ˌæpə'reɪtəs] N (*for heating etc*) impianto; (*for filming, camping, in gym*) attrezzatura; (*in lab*) strumenti *mpl*; (*Anat*) apparato; (*system*) sistema *m*.

ap·par·el [ə'pærəl] N (*frm*) abbigliamento, confezioni *fpl*.

ap·par·ent [ə'pærənt] ADJ (*seeming*) apparente; (*clear*) evidente, ovvio(-a); **to become apparent** manifestarsi, rivelarsi; **it is apparent that** è evidente che; **it was becoming increasingly apparent to me that ...** stava diventando sempre più evidente per me che... .

ap·par·ent·ly [ə'pærəntlɪ] ADV **a** (*it seems*) evidentemente; **did they give him the money? — apparently not** gli hanno dato i soldi? — no, a quanto pare **b** (*seemingly: unaffected, normal*) all'apparenza, apparentemente.

ap·pa·ri·tion [ˌæpə'rɪʃən] N fantasma *m*, apparizione *f*.

ap·peal [ə'pi:l] **1** VI **a** (*call, beg*): **to appeal (to sb)** implorare (qn), supplicare (qn); **to appeal for** chiedere (con insistenza); **he appealed for silence** ha invitato al silenzio; **he appealed to them for help** si è rivolto a loro per un aiuto; **she appealed to her attacker for mercy** ha supplicato il suo assalitore di avere pietà; **to appeal for funds** lanciare un appello per ottenere dei fondi

b (*Law*): **to appeal (against sth/to sb)** appellarsi (contro qc/presso qn), ricorrere in appello (contro qc/presso qn)

c (*attract*) attirare, attrarre; **it doesn't appeal to me** mi dice poco; **it appeals to the imagination** stimola la fantasia.

2 **a** (*call*) appello; (*request*) richiesta; **an appeal for funds** una richiesta di aiuti economici *or* di fondi; **he made an appeal for calm** ha fatto appello alla calma

b (*Law*) appello, ricorso (legale); **right of appeal** diritto d'appello

c (*attraction*) attrattiva, fascino; **a book of general appeal** un libro di interesse generale.

♦ **Appeal Court** N Corte *f* d'Appello.

ap·peal·ing [ə'pi:lɪŋ] ADJ (*attractive*) attraente; (*pleading*) supplichevole.

ap·peal·ing·ly [ə'pi:lɪŋlɪ] ADV (*attractively*) in modo attraente; (*pleadingly*) in modo supplichevole.

ap·pear [ə'pɪə'] VI **a** (*gen*) apparire, comparire; (*ghost*) apparire; **he appeared from nowhere** è saltato fuori all'improvviso

b (*in public*) esibirsi; (*Theatre*) recitare; (*book etc*) uscire, essere pubblicato(-a); **to appear on TV** apparire in televisione; **to appear in Hamlet** recitare nell'Amleto

c (*Law*) comparire, presentarsi; **who is appearing for the defendant?** chi è l'avvocato difensore?

d (*seem*) sembrare, parere; **she appears to want to leave** sembra che voglia andarsene; **the house appears to be empty** la casa sembra vuota; **he appears tired** sembra stanco, ha l'aria stanca; **it appears that ...** a quanto pare..., sembra che...; **it would appear that ...** sembrerebbe che; **so it would appear** pare proprio di sì.

ap·pear·ance [ə'pɪərəns] N **a** (*act*) apparizione *f*; (*Theatre*) comparsa, apparizione; (*of book etc*) uscita, pubblicazione *f*; **in order of appearance** in ordine di apparizione; **to make one's first appearance** fare il proprio debutto, debuttare; **to put in** or **make an appearance** fare atto di presenza

b (*look, aspect*) aspetto; **in appearance** a vedersi; **he was rather sickly in appearance** aveva un aspetto malaticcio or un'aria malaticcia; **appearances can be deceptive** non bisogna fidarsi delle apparenze, le

apparenze ingannano; **to all appearances** a giudicar dalle apparenze; **to keep up appearances** salvare le apparenze.

ap·pease [əˈpiːz] VT (*pacify*) placare; (*satisfy: curiosity*) appagare; (: *hunger*) calmare, soddisfare.

ap·pease·ment [əˈpiːzmənt] N (*Pol*) appeasement *m inv*.

ap·pel·late court [əˈpɛlɪt ˌkɔːt] N (*Law*) corte ʃdʼappello.

ap·pend [əˈpɛnd] VT (*frm: add: signature*) apporre; (: *attach*) allegare; (*Comput*) aggiungere (in coda).

ap·pend·age [əˈpɛndɪdʒ] N (*frm: adjunct*) appendice ʃ; (: *Bot, Zool*) peduncolo.

ap·pen·dec·to·my [ˌæpɛnˈdɛktəmɪ] N appendicectomia.

ap·pen·di·ci·tis [əˌpɛndɪˈsaɪtɪs] N appendicite ʃ.

ap·pen·dix [əˈpɛndɪks] N (*pl* **appendices** [əˈpɛndɪsiːz]) **a** (*Anat*) appendice ʃ; **to have one's appendix out** operarsi *or* farsi operare di appendicite **b** (*to book etc*) appendice ʃ.

ap·per·tain [ˌæpəˈteɪn] VI (*frm*): **to appertain to** essere pertinente a.

ap·pe·tite [ˈæpɪtaɪt] N: **appetite (for)** appetito (per); (*fig*) voglia (di), desiderio (di); **that walk has given me an appetite** la passeggiata mi ha messo *or* fatto venire appetito; **to have a good appetite** godere di *or* avere un ottimo appetito.

ap·pe·tiz·er [ˈæpɪtaɪzəʳ] N (*food*) stuzzichino; (*drink*) aperitivo.

ap·pe·tiz·ing [ˈæpɪtaɪzɪŋ] ADJ appetitoso(-a), invitante.

ap·plaud [əˈplɔːd] ①⃝ VT applaudire; (*fig*) lodare, approvare.

②⃝ VI applaudire.

ap·plause [əˈplɔːz] N applauso; (*fig*) lode ʃ, elogio.

ap·ple [ˈæpl] N (*fruit*) mela; **the apple of one's eye** (*fam*) la pupilla dei propri occhi; **apple tree** melo.

♦ **apple blossom** N fiore *m* di melo.

apple·cart [ˈæpəlˌkɑːt] N: **to upset the applecart** (*fig*) rompere le uova nel paniere.

♦ **apple core** N torsolo (della mela).

♦ **apple corer** N cavatorsoli *m inv*.

♦ **apple orchard** N meleto.

♦ **apple pie** N *crostata di mele ricoperta di pasta*; **in apple-pie order** in ordine perfetto.

♦ **apple sauce** N salsa di mele.

♦ **apple tart** N crostata di mele.

♦ **apple turnover** N sfogliatella alle mele.

ap·pli·ance [əˈplaɪəns] N apparecchio; **electrical appliances** elettrodomestici *mpl*.

ap·plic·abil·ity [ˌæplɪkəˈbɪlɪtɪ] N applicabilità.

ap·pli·cable [əˈplɪkəbl] ADJ applicabile; **the law is applicable from January** la legge entrerà in vigore in gennaio; **to be applicable to** essere valido(-a) per.

ap·pli·cant [ˈæplɪkənt] N (*for a post etc*) candidato(-a); (*Admin: for benefit, housing*) chi ha fatto domanda *or* richiesta.

ap·pli·ca·tion [ˌæplɪˈkeɪʃən] N **a** (*act of applying*) applicazione ʃ; **for external application only** (*Med*) (solo) per uso esterno

b (*request: for university place, grant etc*) domanda; **application for a job** domanda di assunzione; **on application** su richiesta; **further details may be had on application to X** per informazioni più dettagliate rivolgersi a X

c (*diligence*) applicazione ʃ, impegno.

♦ **application form** N modulo di domanda.

♦ **application program** N (*Comput*) programma applicativo.

♦ **applications package** N (*Comput*) software *m inv* applicativo.

ap·plied [əˈplaɪd] ADJ applicato(-a); **applied linguistics** linguistica applicata; **applied arts** arti ʃpl applicate.

ap·pli·qué [æˈpliːkeɪ] N (*Sewing*) applicazione ʃ.

ap·ply [əˈplaɪ] ①⃝ VT: **to apply (to)** (*ointment*) applicare (su); spalmare (su); (*plaster*) mettere (su), applicare (su); (*paint*) dare (a), stendere (su); (*rule, law, theory*) applicare (a); **to apply one's knowledge to sth** servirsi delle proprie nozioni per qc; **to apply one's mind to a problem** concentrarsi su un problema; **to apply o.s. (to one's studies)** applicarsi (nello studio); **to apply the brakes** azionare i freni, frenare.

②⃝ VI **a** (*be applicable*): **to apply (to)** applicarsi (a), essere valido(-a) (per); (*be suitable for, relevant to*) riguardare, riferirsi (a); **the law applies to everybody** la legge è valida *or* vale per tutti

b (*request*) fare *or* presentare domanda; **to apply for a job** fare domanda d'impiego; **to apply for a visa** chiedere un visto; **to apply to a university** fare domanda d'ammisione all'università; **to apply to sb for sth** rivolgersi a qn per qc.

ap·point [əˈpɔɪnt] VT **a** (*nominate*) nominare; **they appointed him chairman** lo hanno nominato presidente; **they appointed a new teacher** hanno assunto un nuovo insegnante **b** (*frm: time, place*) fissare, stabilire; **at the appointed time** all'ora stabilita **c** : **a well-appointed house** una casa ben attrezzata.

ap·poin·tee [əpɔɪnˈtiː] N incaricato(-a).

ap·point·ment [əˈpɔɪntmənt] N **a** (*arrangement to meet*) appuntamento; **by appointment** su *or* per appuntamento; **have you an appointment?** (*to caller*) ha un appuntamento?; **to keep an appointment** non mancare a un appuntamento; **she won't be able to keep the appointment** non potrà venire all'appuntamento; **to make an appointment with sb** prendere un appuntamento con qn

b (*to a job*) nomina; (*job*) posto, carica; (: *Press*): **"appointments (vacant)"** "offerte di impiego".

ap·por·tion [əˈpɔːʃən] VT (*praise, blame*) attribuire.

ap·po·site [ˈæpəzɪt] ADJ (*frm: question, remark*) appropriato(-a), pertinente.

ap·po·si·tion [ˌæpəˈzɪʃən] N (*Gram*) apposizione ʃ.

ap·prais·al [əˈpreɪzəl] N valutazione ʃ, stima; (*fig*) giudizio.

ap·praise [əˈpreɪz] VT (*value*) valutare, fare una stima di; (*fig*) dare *or* esprimere un giudizio su; (: *situation*) fare il bilancio di.

ap·pre·ci·able [əˈpriːʃəbl] ADJ (*increase, effect*) sensibile; (*change*) notevole.

ap·pre·ci·ably [əˈpriːʃəblɪ] ADV (*increase*) sensibilmente; (*change*) notevolmente.

ap·pre·ci·ate [əˈpriːʃɪeɪt] ①⃝ VT **a** (*be grateful for*) apprezzare, essere riconoscente di, essere grato(-a) per; **I appreciated your help** ti sono grato per l'aiuto

b (*value*) apprezzare; **I am not appreciated here** qui nessuno mi apprezza abbastanza

c (*understand: problem, difference*) rendersi conto di; **yes, I appreciate that** certo, me ne rendo conto.

②⃝ VI (*Comm: property*) aumentare (di valore).

ap·pre·cia·tion [əˌpriːʃɪˈeɪʃən] N **a** (*understanding*) comprensione ʃ; (*praise*) apprezzamento; (*gratitude*) riconoscimento; (*Art: critique*) critica; **he showed no appreciation of my difficulties** non ha dimostrato di rendersi conto delle mie difficoltà; **as a token of my**

appreciation in segno della mia gratitudine; **he has no appreciation of good music** non apprezza la buona musica

b (*Comm: rise in value*) aumento (del valore).

ap·pre·cia·tive [ə'pri:ʃɪətɪv] ADJ (*look*) di ammirazione; (*comment*) di elogio, elogiativo(-a); (*audience*) caloroso (-a); **he was very appreciative of what I had done** mi era molto grato di *or* ha dimostrato di apprezzare molto quello che avevo fatto.

ap·pre·cia·tive·ly [ə'pri:ʃɪətɪvlɪ] ADV (*look*) con ammirazione; (*applaud*) calorosamente.

ap·pre·hend [ˌæprɪ'hɛnd] VT (*frm: arrest*) arrestare; (: *understand*) comprendere.

ap·pre·hen·sion [ˌæprɪ'hɛnʃən] N **a** (*fear*) apprensione *f*, inquietudine *f*; **my chief apprehension is** ... la mia paura più grande è... **b** (*arrest*) arresto.

ap·pre·hen·sive [ˌæprɪ'hɛnsɪv] ADJ (*person*) in apprensione; (*expression*) apprensivo(-a).

ap·pre·hen·sive·ly [ˌæprɪ'hɛnsɪvlɪ] ADV apprensivamente.

ap·pren·tice [ə'prɛntɪs] ① N apprendista *m/f*; **a plumber's apprentice** OR **an apprentice plumber** un apprendista idraulico.

② VT: **to apprentice to** mettere come apprendista presso; **to be apprenticed to** lavorare come apprendista presso.

ap·pren·tice·ship [ə'prɛntɪsˌʃɪp] N apprendistato, tirocinio; **to serve one's apprenticeship** fare il proprio apprendistato *or* tirocinio.

ap·prise [ə'praɪz] VT (*frm*): **to apprise sb of sth** mettere qn a conoscenza di qc, informare qn di qc.

ap·pro [æ'prəʊ] N ABBR (*Brit Comm: fam*) = **approval**.

ap·proach [ə'prəʊtʃ] ① VT **a** (*come near: person*) avvicinarsi a, avvicinare; (: *animal*) avvicinarsi a; (: *place*) stare per arrivare a, avvicinarsi a; (*fig: subject, problem, job*) impostare, affrontare; **I approached it with an open mind** ho considerato la cosa senza pregiudizi; **he's approaching 50** si avvicina ai 50, va per i 50; **no other painter approaches him** (*fig*) nessun altro pittore lo uguaglia

b (*with request etc*): **to approach sb about sth** rivolgersi a qn per qc.

② VI avvicinarsi; **the approaching elections** le imminenti elezioni.

③ N **a** (*act*) l'avvicinarsi *m*, avvicinamento; **at the approach of night** all'avvicinarsi della notte

b (*to problem, subject*) modo di affrontare, approccio; **a new approach to maths** un nuovo approccio alla matematica

c (*access*) accesso; **the northern approaches to the city** le vie d'accesso a nord della città

d (*proposal, inquiry: about a job, project*) proposta; (: *to committee, department*) presa di contatto; **to make an approach to sb** contattare qn; **to make approaches to sb** (*amorous*) fare degli approcci *or* delle avances a qn.

④ ADJ di avvicinamento.

ap·proach·able [ə'prəʊtʃəbl] ADJ (*person*) avvicinabile, accessibile.

♦ **approach lights** NPL (*Aer*) sentiero luminoso di avvicinamento.

♦ **approach road** N strada d'accesso.

♦ **approach shot** N (*Tennis*) colpo d'approccio.

ap·pro·ba·tion [ˌæprə'beɪʃən] N (*frm*) approvazione *f*, benestare *m*.

ap·pro·pri·ate [*adj* ə'prəʊprɪɪt; *vb* ə'prəʊprɪeɪt] ① ADJ (*moment, name*) adatto(-a), opportuno(-a); (*remark*) opportuno(-a); (*word*) giusto(-a), adatto(-a); (*authority*) competente; **appropriate for** *or* **to** adatto(-a) a, appropriato(-a) a, adeguato(-a) a; **it would not be appropriate for me to comment** non sta a me fare dei commenti; **whichever seems more appropriate** ciò che sembra più adatto; **he is the appropriate person to ask** è lui il competente in materia.

② VT **a** (*take for one's own use*) appropriarsi di **b** (*frm: allocate*) destinare, stanziare.

ap·pro·pri·ate·ly [ə'prəʊprɪɪtlɪ] ADV in modo adatto *or* appropriato; **he was appropriately insured** era assicurato in modo adeguato *or* convenientemente.

ap·pro·pria·tion [əprəʊprɪ'eɪʃən] N (*taking for oneself*) appropriazione *f*; (*allocation*) stanziamento.

ap·prov·al [ə'pru:vəl] N (*consent*) approvazione *f*, consenso; **on approval** (*Comm*) in prova, in esame; **to meet with sb's approval** essere di gradimento di qn, soddisfare qn.

ap·prove [ə'pru:v] VT approvare

► **approve of** VI + PREP approvare; **I don't approve of kids going to pubs** non approvo *or* disapprovo che i ragazzi vadano al pub; **she doesn't approve of me** disapprova il mio modo di essere.

ap·proved [ə'pru:vd] ADJ **a** (*method, practice*) riconosciuto(-a), approvato(-a); **read and approved** letto e approvato **b** (*authorized*) autorizzato(-a).

♦ **approved school** [ə'pru:vd'sku:l] N (*Brit: old*) riformatorio.

ap·prov·ing [ə'pru:vɪŋ] ADJ d'approvazione.

ap·prov·ing·ly [ə'pru:vɪŋlɪ] ADV con approvazione.

approx. ABBR = **approximately**.

ap·proxi·mate [*adj* ə'prɒksɪmɪt; *vb* ə'prɒksɪmeɪt] ① ADJ approssimativo(-a), approssimato(-a).

② VI: **to approximate to** essere un'approssimazione di, avvicinarsi a.

ap·proxi·mate·ly [ə'prɒksɪmətlɪ] ADV approssimativamente, pressappoco, circa.

ap·proxi·ma·tion [ə'prɒksɪ'meɪʃən] N approssimazione *f*.

ap·pur·te·nances [ə'pɜ:tɪnənsɪz] NPL accessori *mpl*.

APR [ˌeɪpi:'ɑ:'] N ABBR (= *annual percentage rate*) tasso percentuale annuo.

après-ski [ˌæpreɪ'ski:] N attività ricreative in una località sciistica.

apri·cot ['eɪprɪˌkɒt] N (*fruit*) albicocca; **apricot tree** albicocco.

April ['eɪprəl] N aprile *m for usage see* **July**.

♦ **April fool** N (*victim*) pesce *m* d'aprile.

♦ **April Fools' Day** N il primo d'aprile.

a prio·ri [ɑ:prɪ'ɔ:rɪ] ADJ (*frm: argument*) a priori; (: *judgment, statement*) aprioristico(-a); **an a priori decision** una decisione presa a priori.

apron ['eɪprən] N **a** (*gen, workman's*) grembiule *m*; **tied to his mother's/wife's apron strings** attaccato alle sottane di sua madre/moglie **b** (*Aer*) area di stazionamento.

♦ **apron stage** N (*Theatre*) proscenio.

ap·ro·pos [ˌæprə'pəʊ] ① PREP (*with regard to*): **apropos (of)** a proposito di.

② ADV (*frm: incidentally*) a proposito.

③ ADJ (*frm*) appropriato(-a); **you look very apropos in that suit** sei proprio vestito nel modo giusto.

apse [æps] N (*Archit, Geom*) abside *f*.

APT [ˌeɪpi:'ti:] N ABBR (*Brit*: = *advanced passenger train*) treno ad alta velocità.

apt [æpt] ADJ (*comp* **-er**, *superl* **-est**) **a** (*suitable: remark*)

appropriato(-a), adatto(-a), pertinente; (: *description*) felice, indovinato(-a), giusto(-a)

b (*liable*): **to be apt to do sth** avere (la) tendenza a fare qc; **I am apt to be out on Mondays** generalmente di lunedì non ci sono; **we are apt to forget that ...** tendiamo a dimenticare che...

c (*pupil, student: able*) dotato(-a), capace.

Apt. ABBR = **apartment.**

ap·ti·tude ['æptɪtju:d] N (*ability*) abilità *f inv.*

♦ **aptitude test** N test *m inv* attitudinale.

apt·ly ['æptlɪ] ADV appropriatamente, in modo adatto; **she was aptly dressed for the occasion** aveva un vestito adatto all'occasione.

apt·ness ['æptnɪs] N opportunità *f inv.*

aq ABBR = **aqueous solution.**

aqua·lung ['ækwə,lʌŋ] N autorespiratore *m.*

aqua·marine [,ækwəmə'ri:n] 1 N acquamarina.
2 ADJ acquamarina *inv.*

aqua·plane ['ækwə,pleɪn] 1 N acquaplano.
2 VI **a** (*Sport*) praticare l'acquaplano **b** (*Aut*) andare in aquaplaning.

aquar·ium [ə'kwɛərɪəm] N acquario.

Aquar·ius [ə'kwɛərɪəs] N Acquario; **to be Aquarius** essere dell'Acquario.

aquat·ic [ə'kwætɪk] ADJ acquatico(-a).

aque·duct ['ækwɪ,dʌkt] N acquedotto.

aque·ous ['eɪkwɪəs] ADJ acquoso(-a); **aqueous solution** soluzione *f* acquosa.

aqui·fer ['ækwɪfəʳ] N (*Geol*) acquifero.

aqui·line ['ækwɪ,laɪn] ADJ aquilino(-a).

AR ABBR (*Am Post*) = **Arkansas.**

A & R [,eɪənd'ɑːʳ] N ABBR (*Mus*) = **Artists & Repertoire; A & R man** talent scout *m inv.*

ARA [,eɪɑ:r'eɪ] N ABBR (*Brit*) = **Associate of the Royal Academy.**

Arab ['ærəb] 1 N (*person*) arabo(-a); (*horse*) cavallo arabo.
2 ADJ arabo(-a).

ara·besque [,ærə'bɛsk] N arabesco.

Ara·bia [ə'reɪbɪə] N Arabia.

Ara·bian [ə'reɪbɪən] ADJ arabo(-a), arabico(-a).

♦ **Arabian Desert** N: **the Arabian Desert** il Deserto arabico.

♦ **Arabian Nights** N: **the Arabian Nights** le Mille e una Notte.

♦ **Arabian Sea** N: **the Arabian Sea** il mare *m* Arabico.

Ara·bic ['ærəbɪk] 1 N (*language*) arabo.
2 ADJ arabo(-a), arabico(-a).

♦ **Arabic numerals** NPL numeri *mpl* arabi, numerazione *fsg* araba.

ar·able ['ærəbl] ADJ arabile, arativo(-a); **arable farming** coltura del terreno.

Ara·gon ['ærəgən] N Aragona.

Ara·ma·ic [,ærə'meɪɪk] 1 N (*language*) aramaico.
2 ADJ aramaico(-a).

ar·bi·ter ['ɑːbɪtəʳ] N (*frm*) arbitro.

ar·bi·trari·ly ['ɑːbɪtrərəlɪ] ADV arbitrariamente.

ar·bi·trary ['ɑːbɪtrərɪ] ADJ arbitrario(-a).

ar·bi·trate ['ɑːbɪtreɪt] VI fare da arbitro, arbitrare.

ar·bi·tra·tion [,ɑːbɪ'treɪʃən] N (*Law*) arbitrato; (*Industry*) arbitraggio; **the dispute went to arbitration** la controversia è stata sottoposta ad arbitrato.

ar·bi·tra·tor ['ɑːbɪtreɪtəʳ] N arbitro.

ar·bour, (*Am*) **ar·bor** ['ɑːbəʳ] N pergolato.

ARC [,eɪɑ:'si:] N ABBR **a** (= *Aids Related Complex*) ARC *m* **b** (= *American Red Cross*) ≈ C.R.I. *f.*

arc [ɑːk] N arco.

ar·cade [ɑː'keɪd] N (*passage with shops*) galleria; (*series of arches*) portico; (*round public square*) porticato, portici *mpl.*

Ar·ca·dia [ɑː'keɪdɪə] N Arcadia.

Ar·ca·dian [ɑː'keɪdɪən] 1 ADJ arcadico(-a).
2 N arcade *m/f.*

ar·cane [ɑː'keɪn] ADJ (*frm*) arcano(-a).

arch¹ [ɑːtʃ] 1 N **a** (*Archit*) arco, arcata **b** (*of foot*) arco *or* arcata plantare.
2 VT (*back, body*) arcuare, inarcare; (*eyebrows*) inarcare.

arch² [ɑːtʃ] 1 ADJ grande (*before n*), per eccellenza; **an arch villain** un grande criminale; **the arch villain** il cattivo per eccellenza; **his arch rival** il suo rivale per eccellenza.

arch³ [ɑːtʃ] ADJ (*liter: playful: look, smile*) furbesco(-a); (: *tone*) malizioso(-a).

arch- [ɑːtʃ] PREF grande.

ar·chaeo·logi·cal [,ɑːkɪə'lɒdʒɪkəl] ADJ archeologico(-a).

ar·chae·olo·gist [,ɑːkɪ'ɒlədʒɪst] N archeologo(-a).

ar·chae·ol·ogy [,ɑːkɪ'ɒlədʒɪ] N archeologia.

ar·cha·ic [ɑː'keɪɪk] ADJ arcaico(-a).

ar·cha·ism ['ɑːkeɪɪzəm] N arcaismo.

arch·angel ['ɑːk,eɪndʒəl] N arcangelo.

arch·bishop ['ɑːtʃ'bɪʃəp] N arcivescovo.

arch·deacon ['ɑːtʃ'diːkən] N arcidiacono.

arch·duke ['ɑːtʃ'djuːk] N arciduca *m.*

arched [ɑːtʃt] ADJ arcuato(-a), ad arco.

♦ **arch·en·emy** [,ɑːtʃ'ɛnɪmɪ] N **a** (*chief enemy*) nemico per eccellenza **b** (*Rel*): **the Arch-enemy** (*the Devil*) il diavolo.

archeology etc [,ɑːkɪ'ɒlədʒɪ] (*esp Am*) = **archaeology** etc.

arch·er ['ɑːtʃəʳ] N arciere *m.*

ar·chery ['ɑːtʃərɪ] N tiro con l'arco.

ar·che·typ·al ['ɑːkɪtaɪpəl] ADJ tipico(-a).

ar·che·type ['ɑːkɪ,taɪp] N (*original*) archetipo; (*epitome*) prototipo.

Archimedes [,ɑːkɪ'miːdiːz] N Archimede *m.*

archi·pela·go [,ɑːkɪ'pɛlɪgəʊ] N (*pl* **archipelagos** *or* **archipelagoes**) arcipelago.

archi·tect ['ɑːkɪ,tɛkt] N architetto.

archi·tec·tur·al [,ɑːkɪ'tɛktʃərəl] ADJ architettonico(-a).

arch·itec·tur·al·ly ['ɑːkɪ,tɛktʃərəlɪ] ADV architettonicamente.

archi·tec·ture ['ɑːkɪ,tɛktʃəʳ] N architettura.

♦ **archive file** N (*Comput*) file *m inv* di archivio.

ar·chives ['ɑːkaɪvz] NPL archivio *msg*, archivi *mpl.*

archi·vist ['ɑːkɪvɪst] N archivista *m/f.*

arch·ly ['ɑːtʃli] ADV (*speak, smile*) maliziosamente.

arch·way ['ɑːtʃweɪ] N (*passage*) (passaggio a) volta; (*arch*) arco, arcata.

♦ **arc light** N lampada ad arco.

ARCM [,eɪɑ:si:'ɛm] N ABBR (*Brit*) = **Associate of the Royal College of Music.**

arc·tic ['ɑːktɪk] 1 ADJ artico(-a); (*fig: very cold*) polare.
2 N: **the Arctic** l'Artico.

♦ **Arctic Circle** N: **the Arctic Circle** il Circolo polare artico.

♦ **arctic fox** N volpe *f* polare *or* bianca.

♦ **Arctic Ocean** N: **the Arctic Ocean** l'Oceano artico.

♦ **arctic skua** ['ɑːktɪk'skjuːə] N labbo.

♦ **arc welding** N saldatura ad arco.

ar·dent ['ɑːdənt] ADJ (*supporter*) ardente, fervente; (*desire, lover*) ardente.

ar·dent·ly ['ɑːdəntlɪ] ADV ardentemente.

ar·dour, (*Am*) **ar·dor** ['ɑːdəʳ] N (*frm*) ardore *m.*

ar·du·ous [ˈɑːdjʊəs] ADJ arduo(-a).
ar·du·ous·ly [ˈɑːdjʊəslɪ] ADV a fatica, con difficoltà.
ar·du·ous·ness [ˈɑːdjʊəsnɪs] N difficoltà *f inv.*
are[1] [ɑːʳ, əʳ] 2ND PERS SG, 1ST, 2ND AND 3RD PERS PL PRESENT of **be**.
are[2] [ɑːʳ] N (*unit of measure*) ara.
area [ˈɛərɪə] N **a** (*surface extent*) area, superficie *f*; (*Geom*) area
  b (*region*) zona; (*district*) zona, settore *m*; **the London area** la zona di Londra
  c (*fig: of knowledge*) campo; (: *of responsibility etc*) sfera; **matters outside my area of responsibility** questioni che esulano dalla mia competenza; **in the area of £5000** sulle *or* intorno alle 5000 sterline.
♦ **area code** N (*Am Telec*) prefisso.
♦ **area manager** N direttore *m* di zona.
arena [əˈriːnə] N arena.
aren't [ɑːnt] = **are not**.
Ar·gen·ti·na [ˌɑːdʒənˈtiːnə] N l'Argentina.
Ar·gen·tin·ian [ˌɑːdʒənˈtɪnɪən] ADJ, N argentino(-a).
argie-bargie [ˈɑːdʒɪˈbɑːdʒɪ] N = **argy-bargy**.
ar·gon [ˈɑːɡɒn] N argo.
Ar·go·naut [ˈɑːɡənɔːt] N argonauta *m*.
ar·gu·able [ˈɑːɡjʊəbl] ADJ (*rather doubtful*) discutibile; (*capable of being argued for*); **it is arguable that ...** si può sostenere che...; **it is arguable whether ...** è una cosa discutibile se... *+sub.*
ar·gu·ably [ˈɑːɡjʊəblɪ] ADV: **it is arguably ...** si può sostenere che sia... .
ar·gue [ˈɑːɡjuː] 1 VI **a** (*dispute*) litigare; **to argue about sth (with sb)** litigare per *or* a proposito di qc (con qn); **don't argue!** senza tante discussioni!, non discutere!
  b (*reason*) ragionare; **to argue against/for** portare degli argomenti contro/in favore di.
  2 VT (*debate: case, matter*) dibattere, discutere; (*persuade*): **to argue sb into doing sth** persuadere *or* convincere qn a fare qc; **to argue that ...** (*maintain*) sostenere *or* affermare che... .
ar·gu·ment [ˈɑːɡjʊmənt] N **a** (*reasons*) argomento, ragione *f*, motivo; **argument for/against** argomento a *or* in favore di/contro; **I don't follow your argument** non ti seguo **b** (*discussion*) discussione *f*, dibattito; (*quarrel*) litigio, lite *f*; **to hear both sides of the argument** ascoltare entrambe le versioni.
ar·gu·men·ta·tive [ˌɑːɡjʊˈmɛntətɪv] ADJ polemico(-a).
argy-bargy [ˈɑːdʒɪˈbɑːdʒɪ] N (*fam*) discussione *f*, litigio.
aria [ˈɑːrɪə] N aria.
Ariadne [ˌærɪˈædnɪ] N Ariadne *f.*
ARIBA [əˈriːbə] N ABBR (*Brit*)= *Associate of the Royal Institute of British Architects*.
arid [ˈærɪd] ADJ arido(-a); (*fig*) piatto(-a).
arid·ity [əˈrɪdɪtɪ] N aridità.
ar·id·ly [ˈærɪdlɪ] ADV aridamente.
Aries [ˈɛəriːz] N Ariete *m*; **to be Aries** essere dell'Ariete.
aright [əˈraɪt] ADV **a** : **if I heard aright** se ho sentito bene **b** : **to set things aright** sistemare le cose.
arise [əˈraɪz] (*pt* arose, *pp* arisen [əˈrɪzn]) VI **a** (*occur: opportunity, problem*) presentarsi, offrirsi; (*result*): **to arise (from)** derivare (da); **difficulties have arisen** sono insorte *or* sorte delle difficoltà; **should the need arise** dovesse presentarsi la necessità, in caso di necessità; **a storm arose** si scatenò una tempesta; **the question does not arise** la questione non si pone **b** (*old: get up*) levarsi (*frm*), alzarsi.
aris·en [əˈrɪzn] PP of **arise**.
ar·is·toc·ra·cy [ˌærɪsˈtɒkrəsɪ] N aristocrazia.

aris·to·crat [ˈærɪstəˌkræt] N nobile *m/f*, aristocratico(-a).
aris·to·crat·ic [ˌærɪstəˈkrætɪk] ADJ aristocratico(-a).
aris·to·crati·cal·ly [ˌærɪstəˈkrætɪklɪ] ADV aristocraticamente.
Aristophanes [ˌærɪsˈtɒfəˌniːz] N Aristofane *m*.
Ar·is·to·telian [ˌærɪstəˈtiːlɪən] ADJ aristotelico(-a).
Aristotle [ˈærɪˌstɒtl] N Aristotele *m*.
arith·me·tic [*n* əˈrɪθmətɪk; *adj* ˌærɪθˈmɛtɪk] 1 N aritmetica; **mental arithmetic** calcolo mentale.
  2 ADJ aritmetico(-a); **arithmetic progression** progressione *f* aritmetica.
arith·meti·cal [ˌærɪθˈmɛtɪkəl] ADJ aritmetico(-a).
ark [ɑːk] N (*Bible*) arca; **Noah's Ark** l'arca di Noè; **it must have come out of the ark!** (*hum fam*) sembra un reperto archeologico.
arm [ɑːm] 1 N (*Anat*) braccio; (*of chair*) bracciolo; **arm in arm** a braccetto, sottobraccio; **with open arms** (*fig*) a braccia aperte; **within arm's reach** a portata di mano; **to keep sb at arm's length** (*fig*) tenere qn a distanza; **to put one's arm round sb** mettere un braccio intorno alle spalle di qn; see also **arms**.
  2 VT (*person, ship*) armare; **he armed himself with some good arguments** si è armato di validi argomenti.
ar·ma·da [ɑːˈmɑːdə] N armata (navale).
ar·ma·dil·lo [ˌɑːməˈdɪləʊ] N armadillo.
ar·ma·ments [ˈɑːməmənts] NPL (*weapons*) armamenti *mpl*.
ar·ma·ture [ˈɑːmətjʊəʳ] N (*Elec, Sculpture*) armatura.
arm·band [ˈɑːmˌbænd] N bracciale *m*.
arm·chair [ˈɑːmˌtʃɛəʳ] N poltrona.
armed [ɑːmd] ADJ armato(-a); **armed to the teeth** armato(-a) fino ai denti; **she was armed with all the facts** aveva in mano tutti i fatti.
♦ **armed forces** NPL forze *fpl* armate.
♦ **armed robbery** N rapina a mano armata.
Ar·me·nia [ɑːˈmiːnɪə] N Armenia.
Ar·me·nian [ɑːˈmiːnɪən] 1 ADJ armeno(-a).
  2 N (*person*) armeno(-a); (*language*) armeno.
arm·ful [ˈɑːmfʊl] N bracciata.
arm·hole [ˈɑːmˌhəʊl] N giro *m* manica *inv.*
ar·mi·stice [ˈɑːmɪstɪs] N armistizio.
ar·mour, (*Am*) **ar·mor** [ˈɑːməʳ] N armatura; (*also*: armour-plating) corazza, blindatura; (*Mil: tanks*) mezzi *mpl* blindati.
ar·moured, (*Am*) **ar·mored** [ˈɑːməd] ADJ **a** : **armoured divisions** divisioni *fpl* corazzate **b** (*Zool*) rivestito(-a) di aculei *or* corazza.
armoured car, (*Am*) **armored car** [ˈɑːməd ˈkɑːʳ] N autoblinda *f inv.*
♦ **armour-plated** [ˌɑːməˈpleɪtɪd] ADJ (*tank, warship*) corazzato(-a); (*fig: alibi*) di ferro.
ar·moury, (*Am*) **ar·mory** [ˈɑːmərɪ] N arsenale *m*, armeria.
arm·pit [ˈɑːmˌpɪt] N ascella.
arm·rest [ˈɑːmˌrɛst] N bracciolo.
arms [ɑːmz] NPL **a** (*weapons*) armi *fpl*; **to be up in arms** (*fig*) essere sul piede di guerra **b** (*Heraldry: also:* coat of arms) stemma *m*.
♦ **arms control** N controllo degli armamenti.
♦ **arms factory** N fabbrica d'armi.
♦ **arms race** N corsa agli armamenti.
army [ˈɑːmɪ] N (*Mil, fig*) esercito; **to join the army** arruolarsi.
♦ **army life** N vita militare.
aro·ma [əˈrəʊmə] N aroma *m*.
aroma·thera·py [əˌrəʊməˈθɛrəpɪ] N aromaterapia.
aro·mat·ic [ˌærəʊˈmætɪk] ADJ aromatico(-a).

arose [ə'rəʊz] PT of **arise**.
around [ə'raʊnd] [1] ADV **a** (place) attorno, intorno; **for miles around** nel raggio di molte miglia; **he must be somewhere around** dev'essere qui in giro *or* nei paraggi; **do you know your way around?** conosci il luogo?, sai come muoverti qui attorno?
  b (approximately) all'incirca, circa; **around 10 o'clock** verso le 10; **around 50** circa 50.
  [2] PREP intorno a; **it's just around the corner** è appena girato l'angolo; **I've travelled around the country** ho girato tutto il paese.
arous·al [ə'raʊzəl] N (sexual) eccitazione *f*; (awakening) risveglio.
arouse [ə'raʊz] VT (awaken: sleeper) svegliare; (fig: person) eccitare, stimolare; (: feelings) suscitare.
ar·range [ə'reɪndʒ] [1] VT **a** (put into order: books, thoughts, furniture) sistemare, ordinare; (hair) acconciare; (flowers) sistemare
  b (Mus) adattare, arrangiare
  c (decide on: meeting) combinare, organizzare; (: date) stabilire, fissare; (: programme) stabilire, preparare; **to arrange a time for** stabilire *or* fissare una data per; **everything is arranged** è tutto a posto; **it was arranged that ...** è stato deciso *or* stabilito che...; **what did you arrange with him?** per *or* su che cosa siete rimasti d'accordo?; **to arrange to do sth** mettersi d'accordo per fare qc.
  [2] VI mettersi d'accordo, combinare; **to arrange for sth/for sb to do sth** organizzare *or* predisporre qc/che qn faccia qc; **we have arranged for a taxi to pick you up** la faremo venire a prendere da un taxi; **I have arranged for you to go** ho dato disposizione in modo che lei vada.
ar·range·ment [ə'reɪndʒmənt] [1] N **a** (order, act of ordering) sistemazione *f*, disposizione *f*; (Mus) arrangiamento; **a flower arrangement** una composizione floreale
  b (agreement) accordo; **to come to an arrangement (with sb)** venire a un accordo (con qn), mettersi d'accordo *or* accordarsi (con qn); **by arrangement** su richiesta; **by arrangement with the tour operator** secondo gli accordi con l'operatore turistico; **by arrangement with La Scala** con l'autorizzazione del Teatro della Scala
  c (plan) piano, programma *m*; **arrangements** NPL (preparations) preparativi *mpl*; **I'll make arrangements for you to be met** darò disposizioni *or* istruzioni perché ci sia qualcuno ad incontrarla; **we must make arrangements to help** dobbiamo organizzarci per dare un aiuto; **all the arrangements for the party are made** sono stati ultimati i preparativi per la festa.
ar·rant ['ærənt] ADJ: **arrant nonsense** colossali sciocchezze *fpl*.
ar·ray [ə'reɪ] N **a** (of troops, police etc) schieramento; **in battle array** in ordine di battaglia; **a fine array of hats/cakes** tanti cappelli/tante torte in bella mostra **b** (Math) tabella; (Comput) array *m inv*, matrice *f*.
ar·rears [ə'rɪəz] NPL (of money) arretrati *mpl*; **arrears of filing** pratiche *fpl* arretrate da archiviare; **in arrears** in arretrato; **to be in arrears with one's rent** essere in arretrato con l'affitto.
ar·rest [ə'rɛst] [1] N arresto; **to be under arrest** essere in (stato di) arresto; **to place sb under arrest** mettere qn in stato di arresto, arrestare qn.
  [2] VT (criminal) arrestare; (attention, interest) fermare,

attirare; (halt: progress, decay etc) arrestare, bloccare.
ar·rest·ing [ə'rɛstɪŋ] ADJ (fig) che colpisce.
ar·rhyth·mia [ə'rɪðmɪə] N aritmia.
ar·ri·val [ə'raɪvəl] N (gen) arrivo; (person) arrivato(-a); **a new arrival** (newcomer) un(a) nuovo(-a) venuto(-a); (baby) un(a) neonato(-a); **on arrival** all'arrivo.
ar·rive [ə'raɪv] VI (gen) arrivare; (day, time) arrivare, giungere
  ▶ **arrive at** VI + PREP (place, price) arrivare a; (decision, solution) arrivare a, giungere a.
ar·ro·gance ['ærəgəns] N arroganza.
ar·ro·gant ['ærəgənt] ADJ arrogante.
ar·ro·gant·ly ['ærəgəntlɪ] ADV in modo arrogante.
ar·row ['ærəʊ] N freccia.
arrow·head ['ærəʊˌhɛd] N **a** punta di freccia **b** (Bot) sagittaria.
arse [ɑːs] N (Brit fam!) culo (fam!).
arse·hole ['ɑːsˌhəʊl] N (Brit fam!) **a** (anus) buco del culo (fam!) **b** coglionazzo(-a) (fam!).
ar·senal ['ɑːsɪnl] N arsenale *m*.
ar·senic ['ɑːsnɪk] N arsenico.
ar·son ['ɑːsn] N incendio doloso.
ar·son·ist ['ɑːsənɪst] N incendiario(-a).
art [ɑːt] [1] N **a** arte *f*; (craft) mestiere *m*; (Scol: subject) disegno e storia dell'arte; **to study art** fare degli studi artistici; **work of art** opera d'arte; see also **arts**.
  [2] ADJ d'arte.
♦ **art collection** N collezione *f* d'arte.
ar·te·fact, (Am) **ar·ti·fact** ['ɑːtɪfækt] N manufatto.
Artemis ['ɑːtɪmɪs] N Artemide *f*.
ar·te·rial [ɑːˈtɪərɪəl] ADJ (Anat) arterioso(-a); (road etc) di grande comunicazione; **arterial roads** le (grandi *or* principali) arterie.
ar·te·rio·sclero·sis [ɑːˈtɪərɪəʊsklɪˈrəʊsɪs] N arteriosclerosi *f*.
ar·tery ['ɑːtərɪ] N (Anat, fig) arteria.
ar·te·sian well [ɑːˈtiːzɪənˌwɛl] N pozzo artesiano.
art·ful ['ɑːtfʊl] ADJ (person) furbo(-a), abile; (trick) abile.
art·ful·ly ['ɑːtfəlɪ] ADV astutamente, abilmente.
art·ful·ness ['ɑːtfʊlnɪs] N astuzia, abilità *f inv*.
♦ **art gallery** N (museum) museo, galleria d'arte; (shop) galleria d'arte.
ar·thrit·ic [ɑːˈθrɪtɪk] ADJ, N artritico(-a).
ar·thri·tis [ɑːˈθraɪtɪs] N artrite *f*.
arthro·pod ['ɑːθrəˌpɒd] N artropode *m*.
Arthur ['ɑːθə] N: **King Arthur** re Artù.
Ar·thu·rian [ɑːˈθjʊərɪən] ADJ arturiano(-a), di re Artù.
ar·ti·choke ['ɑːtɪˌtʃəʊk] N (globe artichoke) carciofo; (Jerusalem artichoke) topinambur *m inv*.
ar·ti·cle ['ɑːtɪkl] N **a** (Admin, Law, Comm, Gram) articolo; (object) oggetto; **articles of clothing** articoli *mpl* di vestiario, indumenti *mpl* **b** : **articles** NPL (Brit Law, Admin) contratto di tirocinio; **to be in articles** fare il tirocinio.
♦ **article of faith** N credo.
♦ **articles of association** NPL (Comm) statuto sociale.
ar·ticu·late [adj ɑːˈtɪkjʊlɪt; vb ɑːˈtɪkjʊleɪt] [1] ADJ (account, diction) chiaro(-a); (person) che si esprime bene.
  [2] VT (words) articolare, pronunciare.
ar·ticu·lated lor·ry [ɑːˈtɪkjʊleɪtɪdˈlɒrɪ] N (Brit) autoarticolato.
ar·ticu·late·ly [ɑːˈtɪkjʊlɪtlɪ] ADV chiaramente.
ar·ticu·la·tion [ɑːˌtɪkjʊˈleɪʃən] N (of sounds) articolazione *f*; (of speech) dizione *f*.
ar·ti·fact ['ɑːtɪˌfækt] N (Am) = **artefact**.
ar·ti·fice ['ɑːtɪfɪs] N (frm: cunning) abilità, destrezza; (:

trick) artificio.

ar·ti·fi·cial [ˌɑːtɪˈfɪʃəl] ADJ (*synthetic*) artificiale; (*fig pej*: *smile, manner*) studiato(-a), affettato(-a); (: *tears, situation*) falso(-a).

♦ **artificial insemination** N inseminazione *f* or fecondazione *f* artificiale.

♦ **artificial intelligence** N intelligenza artificiale.

ar·ti·fi·ci·al·ity [ˌɑːtɪfɪʃɪˈælɪtɪ] N artificiosità.

ar·ti·fi·cial·ly [ˌɑːtɪˈfɪʃəlɪ] ADV (*gen*) artificialmente; (*behave, smile*) artificiosamente.

♦ **artificial respiration** N respirazione *f* artificiale.

ar·til·lery [ɑːˈtɪlərɪ] N artiglieria.

ar·ti·san [ˈɑːtɪˌzæn] N artigiano(-a).

art·ist [ˈɑːtɪst] N artista *m/f*.

ar·tiste [ɑːˈtiːst] N (*Cine, Theatre, TV*) artista *m/f*.

ar·tis·tic [ɑːˈtɪstɪk] ADJ artistico(-a); **to be artistic** avere una sensibilità artistica.

ar·tis·ti·cal·ly [ɑːˈtɪstɪkəlɪ] ADV artisticamente.

art·ist·ry [ˈɑːtɪstrɪ] N (*skill*) arte *f*, abilità artistica.

art·less [ˈɑːtlɪs] ADJ ingenuo(-a), semplice.

art·less·ly [ˈɑːtlɪslɪ] ADV ingenuamente.

arts [ɑːts] NPL (*Univ*) lettere *fpl*, studi *mpl* umanistici; **the arts** le belle arti; **arts and crafts** artigianato; **Faculty of Arts** facoltà di Lettere.

♦ **art school** N scuola d'arte.

♦ **Arts degree** N laurea in lettere.

♦ **Arts student** N studente(-essa) di discipline umanistiche.

♦ **art student** N studente(-essa) di belle arti.

art·work [ˈɑːtˌwɜːk] N materiale *m* illustrativo.

arty [ˈɑːtɪ] ADJ: **arty types** pseudo artisti *mpl*.

ARV [ˌeɪɑːˈviː] N ABBR (= *American Revised Version*) traduzione della Bibbia.

Aryan [ˈɛərɪən] ADJ, N ariano(-a).

AS [ˌeɪˈɛs] **1** N ABBR (*Am Univ*: = *Associate in/of Sciences*) titolo di studio.

2 ABBR (*Am Post*)= *American Samoa*.

---

as [æz, əz]

1 CONJ

a (*time*) mentre, quando;

▷ **as I get older, I** ... con l'età io...

▷ **as the years went by** col passare degli anni

▷ **he came in as I was leaving** è arrivato nel momento in cui *or* quando stavo per andarmene

▷ **as** *a* **child** ... da bambino...

▷ **as** *or* **so** *long* **as** finché

▷ **as** *soon* **as she arrived I left** me ne sono andato appena lei è arrivata

b (*because*) visto che, poiché, dal momento che, siccome;

▷ **as he had been up since 4 a.m. he was exhausted** era esausto perché si era alzato alle 4

c (*although*)

▷ *much* **as I like them,** ... per quanto mi siano simpatici, ...

▷ *try* **as he** *might*, **he couldn't do it** malgrado i suoi sforzi, non ha potuto farlo

▷ *young* **as he was he understood the situation perfectly** anche se giovane capì perfettamente la situazione

d (*way, manner: also preposition*) come;

▷ **you've got plenty as it** *is* ne hai già abbastanza

▷ **do as you** *wish* fa' come vuoi

▷ **leave things as they are** lascia tutto così com'è

▷ **as I've said before** ... come ho già detto...

e (*concerning*): **as** *for*, **as** *regards*, **as** *to* per quanto *or* quello che riguarda, quanto a

▷ **as** *for* **the children, they were exhausted** quanto ai bambini, erano sfiniti

▷ **as** *to* **that I can't say** su quello non ti so dire

f: **as** *if*, **as** *though* come se + *sub*

▷ **he fought as** *if* **his life depended on it** si è battuto come se ne andasse della sua vita

▷ **he got up as** *if* **to leave** si alzò come per andarsene

▷ **he looked as** *if* **he was ill** aveva l'aria di star male

g (*providing*): **as** *or* **so** *long* **as** purché.

2 ADV

(*in comparisons*)

▷ **as** *big* **as** tanto grande quanto

▷ **twice as** *big* **as** due volte più grande di

▷ **this car will go as** *fast* **as 120 m.p.h.** questa macchina raggiunge le 120 miglia all'ora;

▷ **I didn't know it could go as** *fast* **as that** non sapevo che fosse così veloce

▷ **as** *many* **(as)** tanti(-e) (... quanti(-e))

▷ **you've got as** *much* **as she has** ne hai (tanto) quanto ne ha lei

▷ **twice as** *old* due volte più vecchio(-a)

▷ **as** *pale* **as death** pallido (-a) come un morto

▷ **as** *quickly* **as possible** il più rapidamente possibile

▷ **as** *soon* **as possible** prima possibile

▷ **as** *tall* **as him** alto (-a) come lui.

3 PREP

a (*in the capacity of*) da;

▷ *disguised* **as a nun** travestito(-a) da suora

▷ **he** *gave* **it to me as a present** me lo ha regalato

▷ **he** *succeeded* **as a politician** come politico ha avuto successo

▷ **as** *such* come tale

b (*time*): **as** *of* **or** *from* **tomorrow** (a partire *or* a cominciare) da domani; see **be, same, such, so, well** etc.

ASA [ˌeɪɛsˈeɪ] N ABBR **a** (*Brit*)= *Advertising Standards Authority* **b** (*Brit*)= *Amateur Swimming Association* **c** (*Am*: = *American Standards Association*) associazione per la normalizzazione.

a.s.a.p. [ˌeɪɛseɪˈpiː] ADV ABBR (= *as soon as possible*) prima possibile.

as·bes·tos [æsˈbɛstɒs] N amianto, asbesto.

as·bes·to·sis [ˌæsbɛsˈtəʊsɪs] N asbestosi *f*.

as·cend [əˈsɛnd] **1** VT (*frm*: *stairs*) salire; (*mountain*) scalare; (*throne*) salire a, ascendere a.

2 VI salire.

as·cend·ancy [əˈsɛndənsɪ] N ascendente *m*.

as·cend·ant [əˈsɛndənt] N: **to be in the ascendant** essere in auge.

as·cend·ing [əˈsɛndɪŋ] ADJ ascendente.

as·cen·sion [əˈsɛnʃən] N (*Rel*): **the Ascension** l'Ascensione *f*.

♦ **Ascension Island** N isola dell'Ascensione.

as·cen·sion·ist [əˈsɛnʃənɪst] N (*Mountaineering*) ascensionista *m/f*.

as·cent [əˈsɛnt] N (*of mountain*) ascensione *f*, scalata; (*in plane*) salita; **we made a rapid ascent to our cruising altitude** siamo saliti rapidamente fino alla quota di crociera.

as·cer·tain [ˌæsəˈteɪn] VT (*frm*) accertare; **have you ascertained her real name yet?** ha accertato quale sia il suo vero nome?

as·cet·ic [əˈsetɪk] 1 ADJ ascetico(-a).
2 N asceta *m*.

as·ceti·cism [əˈsetɪsɪzəm] N ascetismo.

ASCII [ˈæskɪ] N ABBR (= *American Standard Code for Information Interchange*) ASCII *m*.

ascor·bic acid [əˌskɔːbɪkˈæsɪd] N acido ascorbico.

as·cribe [əˈskraɪb] VT: **to ascribe sth to sth/sb** attribuire qc a qc/qn.

ASCU [ˌeɪessiːˈjuː] N ABBR (*Am*)= *Association of State Colleges and Universities*.

ASE [ˌeɪesˈiː] N ABBR = *American Stock Exchange*.

asep·tic [eɪˈseptɪk] ADJ asettico(-a).

asexu·al [eɪˈseksjʊəl] ADJ asessuale.

ASH [æʃ] N ABBR (*Brit*: = *Action on Smoking and Health*) iniziativa contro il fumo.

ash¹ [æʃ] N (*of cigarette*) cenere *f*; **ashes** NPL (*of fire*) cenere *fsg*; (*of dead*) ceneri *fpl*; **burnt to ashes** carbonizzato(-a).

ash² [æʃ] N (*Bot*) frassino.

ashamed [əˈʃeɪmd] ADJ pieno(-a) di vergogna, vergognoso(-a); **to be** *or* **feel ashamed (of o.s.)** vergognarsi; **to be ashamed of sb/sth/to do sth** vergognarsi di qn/qc/di fare qc; **you ought to be ashamed of yourself!** dovresti vergognarti!, vergognati!; **it's nothing to be ashamed of** non è una cosa di cui ci si debba vergognare.

♦ **A shares** NPL (*Brit Stock Exchange*) azioni *fpl* con scarsi diritti di voto.

♦ **ash blond, ash blonde** ADJ biondo(-a) cenere *inv*.

♦ **ash can** N (*Am*) bidone *m* per le immondizie.

ash·en [ˈæʃn] ADJ cinereo(-a); (*pale*) livido(-a).

ashore [əˈʃɔː] ADV a terra; **to go ashore** scendere a terra, sbarcare.

ash·tray [ˈæʃˌtreɪ] N portacenere *m inv*, posacenere *m inv*.

♦ **Ash Wednesday** N mercoledì *m inv* delle Ceneri.

Asia [ˈeɪʃə] N Asia.

♦ **Asia Minor** N Asia minore.

Asian [ˈeɪʃn], **Asi·at·ic** [ˌeɪʃɪˈætɪk] ADJ, N asiatico(-a).

aside [əˈsaɪd] 1 ADV da parte; **to take sb aside** prendere qn da parte.
2 PREP: **aside from** (*as well as*) oltre a, a parte; (*except for*) a parte, salvo, eccetto.
3 N (*esp Theatre*) a parte *m inv*.

asi·nine [ˈæsɪnaɪn] ADJ (*liter*) asinesco(-a), asinino(-a).

ask [ɑːsk] 1 VT a (*inquire*): **to ask sb sth** domandare qc a qn, chiedere qc a qn; **she asked him about his father** gli domandò (notizie) di suo padre; **to ask sb a question** fare una domanda a qn; **to ask sb the time** chiedere l'ora a qn; **don't ask me!** (*fam*) non domandarlo a me!, a me lo chiedi?
b (*request*): **to ask sb for sth/sb to do sth** chiedere qc a qn/a qn di fare qc; **to ask sb a favour** chiedere un piacere *or* un favore a qn; **how much are they asking for it?** quanto chiedono per quello?; **that's asking a lot!** questo è pretendere un po' troppo!
c (*invite*): **to ask sb to sth/to do sth** invitare qn a qc/a fare qc; **to ask sb out** invitare qn fuori; **to ask sb to dinner** invitare qn a cena.
2 VI (*inquire*) chiedere; (*request*) richiedere; **to ask about sth** informarsi su *or* di qc; **you should ask at the information desk** dovresti rivolgerti all'ufficio informazioni; **it's yours for the asking** non hai che da chiederlo

▶ **ask after** VI + PREP chiedere di, domandare *or* chiedere (notizie) di, informarsi di

▶ **ask for** VI + PREP (*person*) chiedere di, cercare; (*help, information, money*) chiedere, domandare; **I asked him for help** gli ho chiesto aiuto *or* di aiutarmi; **it's just asking for trouble** è proprio (come) andarsele a cercare.

askance [əˈskɑːns] ADV: **to look askance at sb/sth** guardare qn/qc storto *or* di traverso.

askew [əˈskjuː] ADV di traverso, storto.

ask·ing price [ˈɑːskɪŋˈpraɪs] N prezzo.

asleep [əˈsliːp] ADJ addormentato(-a); **to be asleep** dormire; **to be fast asleep** dormire profondamente; **to fall asleep** addormentarsi; **my foot's asleep** mi si è addormentato *or* intorpidito il piede.

ASLEF [ˈæzlef] N ABBR (*Brit*: = *Associated Society of Locomotive Engineers and Firemen*) *sindacato dei conducenti dei treni e dei fuochisti.*

asp [æsp] N (*poisonous snake*) aspide *m*; (*Zool*) cobra *m inv* egiziano.

as·para·gus [əsˈpærəgəs] N (*plant*) asparago; (*food*) asparagi *mpl*.

♦ **asparagus tips** NPL punte *fpl* d'asparagi.

ASPCA [ˌeɪespiːsiːˈeɪ] N ABBR (= *American Society for the Prevention of Cruelty to Animals*) ≈ E.N.P.A. *m* (= *Ente Nazionale per la Protezione degli Animali*).

as·pect [ˈæspekt] N a (*of person, situation*) aspetto; **to study all aspects of a question** esaminare una questione sotto tutti gli aspetti b (*of building etc*) esposizione *f*; **a house with a northerly aspect** una casa esposta a nord.

as·pen [ˈæspən] N (*Bot*) tremolo.

as·per·ity [æˈsperɪtɪ] N (*frm: of manners, voice*) asprezza.

as·per·sion [əsˈpɜːʃən] N (*frm*) calunnia, maldicenza; **to cast aspersions on sth/sb** (*often hum*) diffamare qc/qn.

as·phalt [ˈæsfælt] N asfalto.

as·phyxia [æsˈfɪksɪə] N asfissia.

as·phyxi·ate [æsˈfɪksɪeɪt] VT, VI asfissiare.

as·phyxia·tion [æsˌfɪksɪˈeɪʃən] N asfissia.

as·pic [ˈæspɪk] N: **chicken in aspic** aspic *m inv* di pollo.

as·pi·dis·tra [ˌæspɪˈdɪstrə] N aspidistra.

as·pir·ant [ˈæspɪrənt] N aspirante *m/f*.

as·pi·rate [*adj, n* ˈæspɪrɪt; *vb* ˈæspəreɪt] 1 ADJ aspirato(-a).
2 N suono aspirato.
3 VT aspirare.

as·pi·ra·tion [ˌæspəˈreɪʃən] N aspirazione *f*.

as·pire [əsˈpaɪə] VI: **to aspire to** aspirare a, ambire a.

as·pi·rin [ˈæspɪrɪn] N aspirina.

as·pir·ing [əsˈpaɪərɪŋ] ADJ aspirante.

ass¹ [æs] N (*Zool*) asino, somaro; (*fig fam*) scemo(-a); **to make an ass of o.s.** rendersi ridicolo(-a).

ass² [æs] N (*Am fam!*) culo (*fam!*)

as·sail [əˈseɪl] VT: **to assail (with)** assalire (di).

as·sail·ant [əˈseɪlənt] N assalitore(-trice).

as·sas·sin [əˈsæsɪn] N assassino(-a).

as·sas·si·nate [əˈsæsɪneɪt] VT assassinare.

as·sas·si·na·tion [əˌsæsɪˈneɪʃən] N assassinio.

as·sault [əˈsɔːlt] 1 N: **assault (on)** (*Mil*) assalto (a); (*Law*) aggressione *f* (a); **assault and battery** (*Law*) minacce *fpl* e vie *fpl* di fatto.
2 VT (*Mil*) assaltare, assalire; (*Law*) aggredire; **to assault sexually** compiere atti di libidine violenta contro.

♦ **assault course** N percorso di guerra.

as·sem·ble [əˈsembl] 1 VT (*objects, ideas*) radunare, raccogliere; (*people*) radunare, riunire; (*Tech*) montare, assemblare.
2 VI radunarsi, riunirsi.

as·sem·bler [ə'sɛmblə'] N (Comput) programma m assemblatore.

as·sem·bly [ə'sɛmblɪ] N (meeting) assemblea; (of machine, furniture) assemblaggio, montaggio; (Comput) assemblaggio; **right of assembly** libertà di riunione.

♦ **assembly industry** N industria di assemblaggio.

♦ **assembly language** N (Comput) linguaggio assemblativo.

♦ **assembly line** N catena di montaggio.

♦ **assembly worker** N assemblatore m.

as·sent [ə'sɛnt] ☐ N benestare m, assenso, consenso; **by common assent** di comune accordo.

☐ VI assentire; **to assent (to sth)** approvare (qc).

as·sert [ə'sɜ:t] VT (declare) affermare, asserire; (insist on: rights) far valere; **to assert o.s.** farsi valere.

as·ser·tion [ə'sɜ:ʃən] N affermazione f, asserzione f.

as·ser·tive [ə'sɜ:tɪv] ADJ che sa imporsi.

as·ser·tive·ness [ə'sɜ:tɪvnɪs] N decisione f.

as·sess [ə'sɛs] VT (gen) valutare; (property, tax) accertare l'imponibile di; (damages) valutare; (fig: situation) giudicare.

as·sess·ment [ə'sɛsmənt] N (of value, damages) valutazione f; (of property, tax) accertamento; (judgment): **assessment (of)** giudizio (su).

as·ses·sor [ə'sɛsə'] N **a** (Scol) consulente esterno incaricato della valutazione di un curriculum o della preparazione degli studenti **b** (of taxes) ≈ perito dell'ufficio del catasto **c** (Law) perito.

as·set ['æsɛt] N (useful quality) bene m, qualità f inv, vantaggio; (person) elemento prezioso; **assets** NPL (Fin: of individual) beni mpl, disponibilità fpl; (: of company) attivo msg, attività fpl.

♦ **asset-stripping** ['æsɛt,strɪpɪŋ] N (Comm) acquisto di una società in fallimento allo scopo di rivenderne le attività.

as·si·du·ity [,æsɪ'djʊɪtɪ] N diligenza, assiduità.

as·sidu·ous [ə'sɪdjʊəs] ADJ assiduo(-a).

as·sidu·ous·ly [ə'sɪdjʊəslɪ] ADV diligentemente.

as·sign [ə'saɪn] VT: **to assign (to)** (allot: task, room, resources) assegnare (a); (reason, cause, meaning) dare (a), attribuire (a); (Law: property) cedere (a), trasferire (a); (appoint): **to assign sb to** dare a qn l'incarico di; **to assign a date to sth** fissare la data di qc.

as·sig·na·tion [,æsɪg'neɪʃən] N (frm: of lovers) convegno galante.

as·sign·ment [ə'saɪnmənt] N (task) incarico; (Scol) compito.

as·simi·late [ə'sɪmɪleɪt] VT assimilare.

as·simi·la·tion [ə,sɪmɪ'leɪʃən] N assimilazione f.

as·sist [ə'sɪst] ☐ VT: **to assist sb (to do or in doing sth)** aiutare qn (a fare qc), assistere qn (a or nel fare qc); **we assisted him to his car** lo abbiamo aiutato a raggiungere la sua macchina.

☐ VI (help): **to assist in sth** aiutare in qc, essere di aiuto in qc.

as·sis·tance [ə'sɪstəns] N aiuto, assistenza; **can I be of any assistance?** posso esserle utile (in qualcosa)?; (in shop) desidera?; **to come to sb's assistance** venire in aiuto a qn.

as·sis·tant [ə'sɪstənt] ☐ N aiutante m/f, assistente m/f, aiuto; (Brit: also: **shop assistant**) commesso(-a).

☐ ADJ aiuto inv.

♦ **assistant headmaster** N vicepreside m/f.

♦ **assistant librarian** N aiuto bibliotecario(-a).

♦ **assistant manager** N vicedirettore(-trice).

as·sizes [ə'saɪzɪz] NPL assise fpl.

as·so·ci·ate [vb ə'səʊʃɪeɪt; n, adj ə'səʊʃɪɪt] ☐ VT associare, collegare; **to associate o.s. with** associarsi a, unirsi a; **I don't wish to be associated with it** non voglio che si pensi che io abbia a che fare con la cosa.

☐ VI: **to associate with sb** frequentare qn.

☐ N (colleague) collega m/f, socio(-a); (accomplice) complice m/f; (member: of club) socio(-a) aggregato(-a); (: of learned society) membro aggregato.

☐ ADJ (company) consociato(-a); (member) aggregato(-a), aggiunto(-a).

as·so·ci·at·ed com·pa·ny [ə'səʊsɪeɪtɪd'kʌmpənɪ] N (Comm) consociata.

♦ **associate director** N amministratore m aggiunto.

as·so·cia·tion [ə,səʊsɪ'eɪʃən] N (most senses) associazione f; **his association with her family** i suoi legami con la famiglia di lei; **in association with** in collaborazione con; **full of historic associations** ricco(-a) di reminiscenze storiche; **the name has unpleasant associations** il nome è associato a qualcosa di spiacevole.

♦ **association football** N (Brit frm) (gioco del) calcio.

as·so·cia·tive [ə'səʊʃɪətɪv] ADJ (frm, Math) associativo(-a).

as·sort·ed [ə'sɔ:tɪd] ADJ assortito(-a); **in assorted sizes** in diverse taglie; **ill-/well-assorted** (matched) mal/ben assortito(-a).

as·sort·ment [ə'sɔ:tmənt] N (Comm: mixture) assortimento; **there was a strange assortment of guests** c'era uno strano miscuglio di invitati.

Asst. ABBR = **assistant**.

as·suage [ə'sweɪdʒ] VT (frm: feelings, pain) attenuare, alleviare; (: appetite) placare.

as·sume [ə'sju:m] VT **a** (suppose) supporre, presumere, presupporre; **assuming that ...** supponendo che... **b** (power, control, attitude) assumere, prendere; **to assume responsibility for** assumersi la responsabilità di.

as·sumed name [ə'sju:md'neɪm] N nome m falso; **under an assumed name** sotto falso nome.

as·sump·tion [ə'sʌmpʃən] N **a** (supposition) supposizione f, ipotesi f inv; **on the assumption that** partendo dal presupposto che; **to work on the assumption that** partire dal presupposto che

b: **the Assumption** (Rel) l'Assunzione f.

as·sur·ance [ə'ʃʊərəns] N **a** (guarantee) assicurazione f, garanzia; **I can give you no assurances** non posso assicurarle or garantirle niente

b (confidence) sicurezza, convinzione f; (self-confidence) fiducia in se stesso(-a), sicurezza di sé; **she spoke with assurance** ha parlato con convinzione

c (Brit): **life assurance** assicurazione f sulla vita.

as·sure [ə'ʃʊə'] VT (reassure): **to assure sb (of sth)** assicurare qn (di qc); **I assured him of my support** gli ho assicurato il mio appoggio.

as·sured [ə'ʃʊəd] ADJ (confident) sicuro(-a); (certain: promotion) assicurato(-a); **success was assured** il successo era garantito or assicurato.

as·sur·ed·ly [ə'ʃʊərɪdlɪ] ADV certamente, senza alcun dubbio.

AST [,eɪes'ti:] ABBR (Am: = Atlantic Standard Time) ora legale di New York.

as·ter ['æstə'] N astro della Cina.

as·ter·isk ['æstərɪsk] N asterisco.

astern [ə'stɜ:n] ADV a poppa.

as·ter·oid ['æstərɔɪd] N asteroide m.

asth·ma ['æsmə] N asma.
asth·mat·ic [æs'mætɪk] ADJ, N asmatico(-a).
astig·ma·tism [æs'tɪgmətɪzəm] N astigmatismo.
astir [ə'stɜːʳ] ADJ (*out of bed*) in piedi; (*on the move*) in movimento.
ASTMS [ˌeɪɛstiːɛmˈɛs] N ABBR (*Brit*: = *Association of Scientific, Technical and Managerial Staffs*) *sindacato del personale scientifico, tecnico e manageriale.*
aston·ish [ə'stɒnɪʃ] VT stupire, meravigliare; **you astonish me!** ma chi l'avrebbe mai detto!; **I was astonished to learn that** ... fui sorpreso nell'apprendere che... .
aston·ish·ing [ə'stɒnɪʃɪŋ] ADJ sorprendente, stupefacente; **I find it astonishing that** ... mi stupisce che... .
aston·ish·ing·ly [ə'stɒnɪʃɪŋlɪ] ADV straordinariamente, incredibilmente.
aston·ish·ment [ə'stɒnɪʃmənt] N stupore *m*, meraviglia; **in astonishment** in modo attonito; **she gave me a look of astonishment** mi ha lanciato uno sguardo stupito; **to my astonishment** con mia gran meraviglia, con mio grande stupore.
astound [ə'staʊnd] VT sbalordire; **he was astounded to hear** ... è rimasto stupefatto *or* allibito nel sentire... .
astound·ing [ə'staʊndɪŋ] ADJ (*resemblance*) sorprendente; (*price*) sbalorditivo(-a).
as·tra·khan [ˌæstrə'kæn] ☐1 ADJ di astrakan.
☐2 N astrakan *m*.
astray [ə'streɪ] ADV: **to go astray** perdere la strada, smarrirsi, perdersi; (*morally*) mettersi su una cattiva strada, traviarsi; **to go astray in one's calculations** sbagliare i calcoli; **to lead sb astray** portare qn su una cattiva strada.
astride [ə'straɪd] ☐1 PREP (*fence*) a cavalcioni di; (*animal*) a cavallo di; (*horse*) in sella a.
☐2 ADV a cavalcioni.
as·trin·gent [əs'trɪndʒənt] ADJ, N astringente *(m)*.
as·trol·o·ger [əs'trɒlədʒəʳ] N astrologo(-a).
as·tro·logi·cal [ˌæstrə'lɒdʒɪkəl] ADJ astrologico(-a).
as·trol·ogy [əs'trɒlədʒɪ] N astrologia.
as·tro·naut ['æstrə‚nɔːt] N astronauta *m/f*.
as·trono·mer [əs'trɒnəməʳ] N astronomo(-a).
as·tro·nomi·cal [ˌæstrə'nɒmɪkəl] ADJ (*also fig*) astronomico(-a).
as·tro·nomi·cal·ly [ˌæstrə'nɒmɪkəlɪ] ADV astronomicamente; **the wine is astronomically expensive** il vino ha un prezzo astronomico.
as·trono·my [əs'trɒnəmɪ] N astronomia.
as·tro·phys·ics ['æstrəʊ'fɪzɪks] NSG astrofisica.
as·tute [əs'tjuːt] ADJ (*shrewd*) accorto(-a).
as·tute·ly [əs'tjuːtlɪ] ADV accortamente.
as·tute·ness [əs'tjuːtnɪs] N accortezza.
asun·der [ə'sʌndəʳ] ADV (*liter*): **to tear asunder** strappare.
ASV [ˌeɪɛs'viː] N ABBR (= *American Standard Version*) *traduzione della Bibbia.*
asy·lum [ə'saɪləm] N **a** (*refuge*) asilo, rifugio; **to seek political asylum** chiedere asilo politico **b** (*also*: **lunatic asylum**) manicomio.
asym·met·rical [ˌeɪsɪ'mɛtrɪkəl], **asym·met·ric** [ˌeɪsɪ'mɛtrɪk] ADJ asimmetrico(-a).
asym·met·ri·cal·ly [ˌeɪsɪ'mɛtrɪklɪ] ADV asimmetricamente.
asym·me·try [æ'sɪmɪtrɪ] N asimmetria.

---

at [æt] PREP
☐a (*position*) a; (*direction*) verso;

▷to *aim* at the target mirare al bersaglio
▷at the *bottom* of the page a fondo pagina
▷at the *desk* al banco
▷to stand at the *door* stare sulla porta
▷at *home* a casa
▷at *John's* da John, a casa di John
▷to *look* at sth guardare qc
▷at *school* a scuola
▷at the *top* in cima
☐b (*time*)
▷at *Christmas* a *or* per Natale
▷at *night* di notte
▷at *4 o'clock* alle quattro
▷at a *time* like this in un momento come questo
▷at *times* talvolta
☐c (*rate*) a;
▷at *50p each* a 50 pence l'uno(-a)
▷two at a *time* due alla *or* per volta
☐d (*activity*)
▷to be *good* at sth riuscire bene in qc, essere bravo(-a) in qc *or* a fare qc
▷while you're at *it* (*fam*) già che ci sei
▷she's at *it* again (*fam*) eccola che ricomincia, ci risiamo
▷he's always *(on)* at me (*fam*) mi tormenta continuamente
▷to *play* at cowboys giocare ai cowboy
▷to be at *work* essere al lavoro, stare lavorando
☐e (*manner*)
▷at *50 km/h* a 50 km/h
▷at *peace* in pace
▷at a *run* di corsa, correndo
▷at full *speed* a tutta velocità
☐f (*cause*)
▷*annoyed* at seccato(-a) per
▷I was *shocked* at the news sono rimasto colpito dalla notizia
▷at his *suggestion* dietro suo consiglio
▷he was *surprised* at her reaction lo stupì la sua reazione.

---

ate [ɛt,eɪt] PT of **eat**.
athe·ism ['eɪθɪɪzəm] N ateismo.
athe·ist ['eɪθɪɪst] N ateo(-a).
athe·is·tical [ˌeɪθɪ'ɪstɪkəl], **athe·is·tic** [ˌeɪθɪ'ɪstɪk] ADJ (*person, philosophy*) ateo(-a); (*views, principles*) ateistico(-a).
Athena [ə'θiːnə], **Athene** [ə'θiːnɪ] N Atena.
Athe·nian [ə'θiːnɪən] ADJ, N ateniese *m/f*.
Ath·ens ['æθɪnz] N Atene *f*.
ath·lete ['æθliːt] N atleta *m/f*.
ath·let·ic [æθ'lɛtɪk] ADJ (*meeting etc*) di atletica, atletico (-a); (*person: muscular*) atletico(-a); (: *sporty*) sportivo (-a).
ath·leti·cal·ly [æθ'lɛtɪklɪ] ADV atleticamente.
ath·let·ics [æθ'lɛtɪks] NSG atletica.
At·lan·tic [ət'læntɪk] ☐1 ADJ dell'Atlantico, atlantico(-a).
☐2 N: **the Atlantic (Ocean)** l'(Oceano) Atlantico.
Atlas ['ætləs] N (*Myth*) Atlante *m*.
at·las ['ætləs] N atlante *m*.
♦ **Atlas Mountains** NPL: **the Atlas Mountains** i Monti dell'Atlante.
A.T.M. [ˌeɪtiː'ɛm] N ABBR (= *automated telling machine*) sportello automatico.
at·mos·phere ['ætməs‚fɪəʳ] N (*Geog, fig*) atmosfera; (*air*)

aria.

at·mos·pher·ic [ˌætməsˈfɛrɪk] ADJ atmosferico(-a); (*music*) che crea un'atmosfera; (*film*) pieno(-a) di atmosfera.

at·mos·pher·ics [ˌætməsˈfɛrɪks] NPL (*Radio*) scariche *fpl* elettriche.

at·oll [ˈætɒl] N atollo.

atom [ˈætəm] N atomo; (*fig*): **not an atom of truth** nemmeno un pizzico di verità.

atom·ic [əˈtɒmɪk] ADJ atomico(-a).

♦ **atomic bomb, atom bomb** N bomba atomica.

ato·mic·ity [ˌætəˈmɪsɪtɪ] N (*Chem*) atomicità.

♦ **atomic mass** N (*Chem*) massa atomica.

♦ **atomic number** N (*Chem*) numero atomico.

at·om·ize [ˈætəmaɪz] VT (*all senses*) atomizzare.

at·om·iz·er [ˈætəˌmaɪzəʳ] N atomizzatore *m*.

atone [əˈtəʊn] VI: **to atone for** (*frm: crime, sins*) espiare; (: *mistake, rudeness*) riparare a.

atone·ment [əˈtəʊnmənt] N (*frm*) espiazione *f*; (*Rel*) redenzione *f*; **to make atonement for a mistake** riparare ad un errore.

atop [əˈtɒp] PREP (*Am*) sopra; **atop the hill** in cima alla collina.

A.T.P. [ˌeɪtiːˈpiː] N ABBR (= *adenosine triphosphate*) A.T.P. *m*.

atrium [ˈeɪtrɪəm] N (*Archit, Anat*) atrio.

atro·cious [əˈtrəʊʃəs] ADJ atroce, pessimo(-a).

atro·cious·ly [əˈtrəʊʃəslɪ] ADV (*cruelly*) atrocemente; (*appallingly*) terribilmente.

atroc·ity [əˈtrɒsɪtɪ] N atrocità *f inv*.

at·ro·phy [ˈætrəfɪ] (*Med, fig*) [1] N atrofia.

[2] VT atrofizzare.

[3] VI atrofizzarsi.

at·tach [əˈtætʃ] VT: **to attach (to)** **a** (*fasten, stick*) attaccare (a); (*tie*) legare (a); (*join*) annettere (a), attaccare (a); (*document, letter*) allegare (a); **the attached letter** la lettera acclusa *or* allegata; **he attached himself to us** si è appiccicato a noi

b (*attribute: importance, value*) attribuire (a), dare (a)

c (*assign: troops, employee*) assegnare (a)

d (*Law: person*) trarre in arresto; (: *property*) sequestrare.

at·ta·ché [əˈtæʃeɪ] N addetto (di ambasciata), attaché *m inv*; **cultural attaché** addetto culturale.

♦ **attaché case** N valigetta *f* portadocumenti *inv*, valigetta (diplomatica).

at·tached [əˈtætʃt] ADJ (*fond*): **to be attached to sb** essere attaccato(-a) *or* affezionato(-a) a qn; (*fam: married, engaged*) impegnato(-a).

at·tach·ment [əˈtætʃmənt] N **a** (*device*) accessorio **b** (*affection*): **attachment (to)** attaccamento (per), affetto (per).

at·tack [əˈtæk] [1] N **a** (*Mil, fig*) attacco; (*on individual*) aggressione *f*; **surprise attack** attacco di sorpresa; **attack on sb's life** attentato alla vita di qn; **to be under attack (from)** essere attaccato(-a) (da); **to launch an attack (on)** (*Mil, Sport, fig*) sferrare un attacco (a) **b** (*Med*) attacco, accesso.

[2] VT (*Mil, Med, fig*) attaccare; (*person*) aggredire, assalire; (*tackle: job, problem*) affrontare.

at·tack·er [əˈtækəʳ] N aggressore *m*, assalitore(-trice).

at·tain [əˈteɪn] VT (*ambition*) realizzare; (*age, rank, happiness*) raggiungere, arrivare a.

at·tain·able [əˈteɪnəbl] ADJ (*see vb*) realizzabile; raggiungibile.

at·tain·ment [əˈteɪnmənt] (*frm*) N (*of ambition*) realizza-

zione *f*; (*of position, happiness*) raggiungimento; (*achievement*) risultato ottenuto; **attainments** (*accomplishments*) cognizioni *fpl* (acquisite); **linguistic attainments** abilità *fpl* linguistiche.

at·tempt [əˈtɛmpt] [1] N (*try*) tentativo; **he made no attempt to help** non ha (neanche) tentato *or* cercato di aiutare; **to make an attempt on sb's life** attentare alla vita di qn.

[2] VT: **to attempt sth/to do sth** tentare qc/di fare qc; **he attempted the exam** ha tentato l'esame; **attempted murder** (*Law*) tentato omicidio.

at·tend [əˈtɛnd] [1] VT **a** (*be present at: meeting etc*) andare a, assistere a, essere presente a; (*regularly: school, church*) frequentare; (: *course, classes*) seguire, frequentare; **the lecture was well attended** c'era molta gente alla conferenza

b (*subj: bridesmaid, lady-in-waiting*) accompagnare; (: *doctor*) avere in cura, curare, assistere.

[2] VI (*be present*) essere presente, esserci; (*pay attention to*) prestare attenzione, stare attento(-a)

▶ **attend to** VI + PREP (*needs, affairs*) prendersi cura di; (*customer, work*) occuparsi di; **are you being attended to?** (*in shop*) la stanno servendo?

at·tend·ance [əˈtɛndəns] N (*act*): **attendance (at)** presenza (a); (: *regular*) frequenza (a); (*those present*) persone *fpl* presenti; **what was the attendance at the meeting?** quanti erano i presenti alla riunione?; **there was a doctor in attendance on the queen** c'era un dottore al servizio della regina.

♦ **attendance officer** N *funzionario preposto a controllare la frequenza scolastica*.

at·tend·ant [əˈtɛndənt] N [1] (*in car park, museum*) custode *m/f*; (*servant*) attendente *m/f*, persona di servizio.

[2] ADJ (*frm*) concomitante.

at·ten·tion [əˈtɛnʃən] N **a** attenzione *f*; **to call sb's attention to sth** richiamare qc all'attenzione di qn; **it has come to my attention that …** sono venuto a conoscenza (del fatto) che…; **to pay attention (to)** stare attento(-a) (a), fare attenzione (a); **for the attention of** (*Admin*) all'attenzione di

b (*Mil*): **attention!** attenti!; **to come to/stand at attention** mettersi/stare sull'attenti

c: **attentions** NPL (*kindnesses*) attenzioni *fpl*, premure *fpl*.

♦ **attention-seeking** [əˈtɛnʃənˌsiːkɪŋ] ADJ *che fa di tutto per attirare l'attenzione altrui.*

♦ **attention span** N capacità *f inv* di concentrazione.

at·ten·tive [əˈtɛntɪv] ADJ (*audience*) attento(-a); (*escort*) premuroso(-a), sollecito(-a).

at·ten·tive·ly [əˈtɛntɪvlɪ] ADV attentamente.

at·ten·tive·ness [əˈtɛntɪvnɪs] N attenzione *f*; (*consideration*) sollecitudine *f*.

at·tenu·ate [əˈtɛnjʊeɪt] (*frm*) [1] VT ridurre, attenuare.

[2] VI attenuarsi.

at·test [əˈtɛst] (*frm*) [1] VT attestare; (*signature*) autenticare.

[2] VI: **to attest to** testimoniare, attestare.

at·tes·ta·tion [ˌætɛsˈteɪʃən] (*frm*) N dichiarazione *f*.

At·tic [ˈætɪk] ADJ attico(-a).

at·tic [ˈætɪk] N soffitta, solaio; (*room*) mansarda.

At·ti·ca [ˈætɪkə] N Attica.

Attila [əˈtɪlə] N Attila *m*.

at·tire [əˈtaɪəʳ] (*frm*) [1] N tenuta, abbigliamento.

[2] VT: **to attire (in)** abbigliare (con).

at·ti·tude [ˈætɪtjuːd] N (*view*) atteggiamento; (*posture*) posa; (*opinion*): **attitude (towards)** punto di vista (nei

confronti di); **attitude of mind** modo di pensare; **if that's your attitude** se la prendi così.

at·ti·tu·di·nize [,ætɪ'tjuːdɪnaɪz] vi posare, assumere un'aria affettata.

at·tor·ney [ə'tɜːnɪ] N (Am: lawyer) avvocato; (representative) procuratore m; (having proxy) mandatario; **power of attorney** procura.

♦ **Attorney General** N (Brit) Procuratore m Generale; (Am) ≈ Ministro della Giustizia.

at·tract [ə'trækt] vt (subj: magnet) attirare, attrarre; (fig: interest, attention etc) attirare, suscitare.

at·trac·tion [ə'trækʃən] N attrazione f, fascino; (pleasant feature) attrattiva; **city life has no attraction for me** la vita di città non mi attira affatto; **one of the attractions was a free car** uno dei vantaggi era quello di una macchina gratis.

at·trac·tive [ə'træktɪv] ADJ (person, dress, place) attraente, affascinante; (idea, offer, price) allettante, interessante.

at·trac·tive·ly [ə'træktɪvlɪ] ADV in modo attraente.

at·trac·tive·ness [ə'træktɪvnɪs] N (of proposition, offer) attrattiva; (of voice, person) fascino.

at·trib·ut·able [ə'trɪbjʊtəbl] ADJ attribuibile.

at·trib·ute [n 'ætrɪbjuːt; vb ə'trɪbjuːt] [1] N attributo.

  [2] vt: **to attribute sth to** attribuire qc a.

at·tribu·tion [,ætrɪ'bjuːʃən] N attribuzione f.

at·tribu·tive [ə'trɪbjʊtɪv] ADJ (Gram) attributivo(-a).

at·tri·tion [ə'trɪʃən] N usura (per attrito); **war of attrition** guerra di logoramento.

at·tuned [ə'tjuːnd] ADJ (person): **to be attuned to sth** poter apprezzare qc; (eye, ears): **attuned to** attento(-a) a.

Atty. Gen. ABBR = **Attorney General.**

ATV [,eɪtiː'viː] N ABBR a (Brit: = Associated Television) rete televisiva indipendente b (Mil: = all terrain vehicle) jeep f inv.

atypi·cal [eɪ'tɪpɪkəl] ADJ atipico(-a).

auber·gine ['əʊbəʒiːn] N (esp Brit) melanzana.

auburn ['ɔːbən] ADJ (hair) ramato(-a), color rame inv.

auc·tion ['ɔːkʃən] [1] N (also: **sale by auction**) asta.

  [2] vt (also: **to sell by auction**) vendere all'asta; (also: **to put up for auction**) mettere all'asta.

auc·tion·eer [,ɔːkʃə'nɪə'] N banditore(-trice).

♦ **auction room** N sala dell'asta.

♦ **auction sale** N vendita all'asta.

auda·cious [ɔː'deɪʃəs] ADJ (bold) audace; (impudent) sfrontato(-a).

audac·ity [ɔː'dæsɪtɪ] N (boldness) audacia; (impudence) sfacciataggine f, sfrontatezza.

audibil·ity [,ɔːdɪ'bɪlɪtɪ] N udibilità.

audible ['ɔːdɪbl] ADJ udibile, percettibile; **there was audible laughter** si è chiaramente sentita una risata; **he was hardly audible** si riusciva a malapena a sentirlo.

audibly ['ɔːdɪblɪ] ADV in modo che si senta, in modo chiaro.

audi·ence ['ɔːdɪəns] N a (gathering) pubblico; (Radio) ascoltatori mpl; (TV) telespettatori mpl; (of speaker) uditorio; **there was a big audience at the theatre** c'erano molti spettatori or c'era un gran pubblico al teatro b (formal interview) udienza.

♦ **audience participation** N partecipazione f del pubblico.

♦ **audience rating** N indice m di ascolto.

audio ['ɔːdɪəʊ] ADJ: **audio equipment** apparecchi mpl audiovisivi; **audio tape** audiocassetta.

♦ **audio-typist** ['ɔːdɪəʊ,taɪpɪst] N dattilografo(-a) che trascrive da nastro.

audio-visual [,ɔːdɪəʊ'vɪzjʊəl] ADJ audiovisivo(-a); **audio-visual aids** sussidi mpl audiovisivi.

audit ['ɔːdɪt] [1] N revisione f dei conti, verifica (ufficiale) dei conti.

  [2] vt (accounts) rivedere, verificare.

audi·tion [ɔː'dɪʃən] [1] N (Theatre) audizione f; (Cine) provino.

  [2] vt fare un'audizione (or un provino) a.

  [3] vi fare un'audizione (or un provino).

audi·tor ['ɔːdɪtə'] N revisore m dei conti.

audi·to·rium [,ɔːdɪ'tɔːrɪəm] N sala, auditorio.

audi·tory ['ɔːdɪtərɪ] ADJ uditivo(-a); **auditory canal** condotto uditivo.

AUEW [,eɪjuːiː'dʌblju:] N ABBR (Brit: = Amalgamated Union of Engineering Workers) sindacato dei metalmeccanici.

aug·ment [ɔːg'mɛnt] vt, vi (frm) aumentare.

aug·menta·tive [ɔːg'mɛntətɪv] ADJ (frm) accrescitivo(-a).

augur ['ɔːgə'] vi, vt (frm): **to augur well/ill** essere di buon/cattivo augurio or auspicio.

August ['ɔːgəst] N agosto; see also **July.**

august [ɔː'gʌst] ADJ (frm) augusto(-a).

aunt [ɑːnt] N zia; **my aunt and uncle** i miei zii, mia zia e mio zio.

auntie, aunty ['ɑːntɪ] N (fam) zietta; **auntie Jane** zia Jane.

au pair (girl) ['əʊ'pɛə'(,gɜːl)] N ragazza f alla pari inv.

aura ['ɔːrə] N aura.

auri·cle ['ɔːrɪkəl] N (of heart) orecchietta; (of ear) padiglione m auricolare.

auro·ra bo·real·is [ɔː'rɔːrəbɔːrɪ'eɪlɪs] N aurora boreale.

aus·pices ['ɔːspɪsɪz] NPL: **under the auspices of** sotto i buoni auspici di.

aus·pi·cious [ɔːs'pɪʃəs] (frm) ADJ (sign) di buon augurio or auspicio; (occasion) propizio(-a), favorevole; **to make an auspicious start** iniziare sotto buoni auspici.

aus·pi·cious·ly [ɔːs'pɪʃəslɪ] ADV (frm) favorevolmente, sotto buoni auspici; **to begin auspiciously** incominciare sotto buoni auspici.

Aus·sie ['ɒzɪ] (fam) = **Australian.**

aus·tere [ɒs'tɪə'] ADJ austero(-a).

aus·tere·ly [ɒs'tɪəlɪ] ADV in modo austero, austeramente.

aus·ter·ity [ɒs'tɛrɪtɪ] N austerità f inv.

Aus·tral·asia [,ɒstrə'leɪzɪə] N l'Australasia.

Aus·tralia [ɒs'treɪlɪə] N l'Australia.

Aus·tral·ian [ɒs'treɪlɪən] ADJ, N australiano(-a).

Aus·tria ['ɒstrɪə] N l'Austria.

Aus·trian ['ɒstrɪən] ADJ, N austriaco(-a).

AUT [,eɪjuː'tiː] N ABBR (Brit: = Association of University Teachers) associazione dei docenti universitari.

authen·tic [ɔː'θɛntɪk] ADJ autentico(-a).

authen·ti·cal·ly [ɔː'θɛntɪklɪ] ADV autenticamente.

authen·ti·cate [ɔː'θɛntɪkeɪt] vt (signature, document) autenticare; (statement, information) verificare, stabilire la veridicità di.

au·then·tic·ity [,ɔːθɛn'tɪsɪtɪ] N autenticità.

author ['ɔːθə'] N autore(-trice).

author·ess ['ɔːθərɪs] N autrice f.

authori·tar·ian [,ɔːθɒrɪ'tɛərɪən] ADJ autoritario(-a).

authori·tar·ianism [ɔː,θɒrɪ'tɛərɪənɪzm] N (Pol) autoritarismo.

authori·ta·tive [ɔː'θɒrɪtətɪv] ADJ (account, judgement) autorevole; (manner) autoritario(-a).

authori·ta·tive·ly [ɔː'θɒrɪtətɪvlɪ] ADV autorevolmente.

author·ity [ɔː'θɒrɪtɪ] [1] N a (power) autorità; (permission)

autorizzazione *f*; **those in authority** i dirigenti, i governanti; **to be in authority over** dare gli ordini a; **to have authority to do sth** avere l'autorizzazione a fare *or* il diritto di fare qc

b : **the authorities** NPL (*government, council*) le autorità; **the health authorities** l'autorità *sg* sanitaria

c (*expert*): **he's an authority (on)** è un'autorità (in materia di); **I have it on good authority that ...** so da fonte sicura *or* autorevole che... .

authori·za·tion [ˌɔːθəraɪ'zeɪʃən] N autorizzazione *f*.

author·ize ['ɔːθəraɪz] VT: **to authorize sth/sb (to do sth)** autorizzare qc/qn (a fare qc).

author·ized capi·tal ['ɔːθəˌraɪzd'kæpɪtl] N (*Fin*) capitale *m* nominale.

Author·ized Ver·sion ['ɔːθəraɪzd,vɜːʃən] N: **the Authorized Version** *traduzione inglese della Bibbia del 1611*.

author·ship ['ɔːθəˌʃɪp] N paternità (*letteraria etc*).

autism ['ɔːtɪzm] N autismo.

autis·tic [ɔː'tɪstɪk] ADJ autistico(-a).

auto ['ɔːtəʊ] N (*Am*) auto *f inv*.

auto... ['ɔːtəʊ] PREF auto... .

auto·bio·graph·ic ['ɔːtəʊˌbaɪəʊ'græfɪk], **auto·bio·graphi·cal** ['ɔːtəʊˌbaɪəʊ'græfɪkəl] ADJ autobiografico (-a).

auto·bi·og·ra·phy [ˌɔːtəʊbaɪ'ɒgrəfɪ] N autobiografia.

auto·clave ['ɔːtəˌkleɪv] N autoclave *f*.

auto·crat ['ɔːtəʊˌkræt] N autocrate *m*.

auto·crat·ic [ˌɔːtəʊ'krætɪk] ADJ autocratico(-a).

Auto·cue® ['ɔːtəʊˌkjuː] N (*Brit TV*) gobbo.

auto·graph ['ɔːtəˌgrɑːf] ① N autografo. ② VT firmare.

♦ **autograph album** N libro degli autografi.

♦ **autograph hunter** N cacciatore(-trice) di autografi.

auto·im·mune [ˌɔːtəʊɪ'mjuːn] ADJ autoimmune.

auto·mat ['ɔːtəˌmæt] N (*vending machine*) distributore *m* automatico; (*Am: room*) *tavola calda fornita esclusivamente di distributori automatici*.

automa·ta [ɔː'tɒmətə] NPL of **automaton**.

auto·mate ['ɔːtəˌmeɪt] VT automatizzare.

auto·mat·ed ['ɔːtəˌmeɪtɪd] ADJ automatizzato(-a).

auto·mat·ic [ˌɔːtə'mætɪk] ① ADJ automatico(-a). ② N (*pistol*) (pistola) automatica; (*car*) automobile *f* con cambio automatico; (*washing machine*) lavatrice *f* automatica.

auto·mati·cal·ly [ˌɔːtə'mætɪkəlɪ] ADV automaticamente.

♦ **automatic data processing** N elaborazione *f* automatica dei dati.

♦ **automatic pilot** N: **on automatic pilot** (*Aer, fig*) con pilota automatico.

♦ **automatic telling machine** [ˌɔːtə'mætɪk'telɪŋməˌʃiːn] N cassa prelievi automatica.

auto·ma·tion [ˌɔːtə'meɪʃən] N automazione *f*.

automa·ton [ɔː'tɒmətən] N (*pl* **automatons** *or* **automata** [ɔː'tɒmətə]) automa *m*.

auto·mo·bile ['ɔːtəməˌbiːl] N (*Am*) automobile *f*.

auto·mo·tive [ˌɔːtə'məʊtɪv] ADJ (*industry, design*) automobilistico(-a).

auto·nom·ic [ˌɔːtə'nɒmɪk] ADJ (*Med*) involontario(-a).

♦ **autonomic nervous system** N (*Med*) sistema *m* neurovegetativo.

autono·mous [ɔː'tɒnəməs] ADJ autonomo(-a).

autono·mous·ly [ɔː'tɒnəməslɪ] ADV autonomamente.

autono·my [ɔː'tɒnəmɪ] N autonomia.

auto·pi·lot [ˌɔːtəʊ'paɪlət] N (*Aer*) = **automatic pilot**.

autop·sy ['ɔːtɒpsɪ] N autopsia.

auto·radio·graph [ˌɔːtəʊ'reɪdɪəˌgrɑːf] N autoradiografia.

auto·sug·ges·tion ['ɔːtəʊsə'dʒestʃən] N autosuggestione *f*.

auto·troph·ic [ˌɔːtə'trɒfɪk] ADJ autotrofo(-a).

autumn ['ɔːtəm] ① N autunno. ② ADJ autunnale.

autum·nal [ɔː'tʌmnəl] ADJ autunnale, d'autunno.

aux·ilia·ry [ɔːg'zɪlɪərɪ] ① ADJ ausiliario(-a); (*Gram*) ausiliare.
② N (*assistant*) assistente *m/f*, aiuto; (*verb*) ausiliare *m*; **auxiliaries** NPL (*Mil*) truppe *fpl* ausiliarie.

aux·in ['ɔːksɪn] N auxina.

AV [ˌeɪ'viː] ① N ABBR (= *Authorized Version*) *traduzione inglese della Bibbia*.
② ABBR = **audiovisual**.

Av., Ave. ABBR = **avenue**.

avail [ə'veɪl] ① N: **of no avail** inutile; **to no avail** invano, inutilmente.
② VT: **to avail o.s. of** (*opportunity*) servirsi di, approfittare *or* approfittarsi di; (*rights*) (av)valersi di.

avail·abil·ity [əveɪlə'bɪlɪtɪ] N disponibilità.

avail·able [ə'veɪləbl] ADJ disponibile; **to make sth available to sb** mettere qc a disposizione di qn; **is the manager available?** è libero il direttore?; **every available means** tutti i mezzi disponibili.

ava·lanche ['ævəlɑːnʃ] N valanga.

♦ **avalanche warning** N avviso di valanghe.

avant-garde ['ævɒŋ'gɑːd] ① N avanguardia.
② ADJ d'avanguardia.

ava·rice ['ævərɪs] N avarizia.

ava·ri·cious [ˌævə'rɪʃəs] ADJ avaro(-a).

avdp. ABBR of **avoirdupois**.

Ave. ABBR = **avenue**.

avenge [ə'vendʒ] VT vendicare; **to avenge o.s. (on sb)** vendicarsi (di qn).

aveng·er [ə'vendʒəʳ] N vendicatore(-trice).

aveng·ing [ə'vendʒɪŋ] ADJ vendicatore(-trice).

av·enue ['ævənjuː] N viale *m*; (*fig*) strada, via.

aver [ə'vɜː] VT (*frm*) dichiarare, asserire.

av·er·age ['ævərɪdʒ] ① ADJ medio(-a); (*pej*) qualsiasi *inv*, ordinario(-a).
② N media; **on average** in media; **above/below (the) average** sopra/sotto la media.
③ VT fare una media di

▶ **average out** VT (*set of numbers*) fare *or* calcolare la media fra

▶ **average out at** VI (*reach an average of*) aggirarsi in media su, essere in media di.

averse [ə'vɜːs] ADJ: **averse to** (*opposed*) contrario(-a) a; (*disinclined*) restio(-a) a; **to be averse to sth/doing sth** essere contrario(-a) a qc/a fare qc; **I'm not averse to an occasional drink** non mi dispiace bere un bicchierino ogni tanto; **I wouldn't be averse to a drink** non avrei nulla in contrario a bere qualcosa.

aver·sion [ə'vɜːʃən] N (*dislike*): **aversion (for *or* to)** avversione *f* (per); **spiders are his aversion** ha la fobia dei ragni; **my pet aversion** ciò che detesto di più; **to have an aversion to sb/sth** avere *or* nutrire un'avversione nei confronti di qn/qc.

avert [ə'vɜːt] VT (*prevent: accident, danger*) evitare; (*turn away: eyes, thoughts*): **to avert (from)** distogliere (da), allontanare (da).

aviary ['eɪvɪərɪ] N voliera, uccelliera.

avia·tion [ˌeɪvɪ'eɪʃən] N aviazione *f*.

♦ **aviation industry** N industria aeronautica.

avia·tor ['eɪvɪeɪtə'] N aviatore *m*.

avid ['ævɪd] ADJ: **avid (for)** desideroso(-a) (di), avido(-a) (di); **an avid reader** un(a) accanito(-a) *or* appassionato (-a) lettore(-trice).

avid·ity [ə'vɪdɪtɪ] N avidità.

av·id·ly ['ævɪdlɪ] ADV avidamente.

avo·ca·do [ˌævə'kɑ:dəʊ] N (*Brit: also:* **avocado pear**) avocado *m inv.*

avoid [ə'vɔɪd] VT (*obstacle*) scansare, schivare, evitare; (*argument etc*) evitare; (*danger*) sfuggire a; **to avoid doing sth** evitare di fare qc; **try to avoid being seen** cerca di non farti vedere; **are you trying to avoid me?** stai cercando di evitarmi?

avoid·able [ə'vɔɪdəbl] ADJ evitabile.

avoid·ance [ə'vɔɪdəns] N: **her avoidance of me has been noticed by everyone** tutti hanno notato che mi evita; **his avoidance of his duty** la sua mancanza al dovere; see also **tax**.

av·oir·du·pois [ˌævədə'pɔɪz] N *sistema ponderale usato in Gran Bretagna basato su libbra, oncia e multipli.*

avow [ə'vaʊ] VT (*frm: declare*) dichiarare apertamente.

avow·al [ə'vaʊəl] N (*of intentions, innocence*) dichiarazione *f*; (*of guilt*) ammissione *f*.

avowed [ə'vaʊd] ADJ dichiarato(-a).

avow·ed·ly [ə'vaʊɪdlɪ] ADV apertamente, dichiaratamente; (*professedly*) dichiaratamente.

AVP [ˌeɪviː'piː] N ABBR (*Am*)= *assistant vice-president.*

avun·cu·lar [ə'vʌŋkjʊlə'] ADJ (*liter: man*) bonario(-a).

AWACS ['eɪwæks] N ABBR (= *airborne warning and control system*) *sistema di allarme e controllo in volo.*

await [ə'weɪt] VT aspettare, attendere; **long awaited** tanto atteso(-a); **awaiting attention** (*Comm: letter*) in attesa di risposta; (: *order*) in attesa di essere evaso(-a).

awake [ə'weɪk] **[1]** ADJ sveglio(-a); **to lie awake** rimanere sveglio(-a) a letto; **coffee keeps me awake** il caffè mi fa star sveglio; **to be awake to** (*fig*) essere cosciente *or* conscio(-a) *or* consapevole di.
[2] VT(*pt* **awoke** *or* **awaked**, *pp* **awoken** *or* **awaked**) svegliare; (*fig: emotions, memories*) risvegliare, ridestare; (: *suspicions*) destare.
[3] VI svegliarsi; **to awake to sth** (*fig*) rendersi conto di qc, aprire gli occhi su qc.

awak·en [ə'weɪkən] VT, VI = **awake 2, 3**.

awak·en·ing [ə'weɪknɪŋ] N risveglio.

award [ə'wɔ:d] **[1]** N (*prize*) premio; (*scholarship*) borsa di studio; (*Law: decision*) sentenza arbitrale, decreto; (: *sum*) ricompensa, risarcimento.
[2] VT **to award sb sth** [OR] **to award sth to sb** (*prize*) assegnare qc a qn; (*medal*) conferire qc a qn; **to award sb damages** concedere a qn il risarcimento dei danni.

aware [ə'wɛə'] ADJ: **to be aware of** (*conscious*) rendersi conto di; (*informed*) essere al corrente di, essere conscio (-a) di; **to become aware of** accorgersi di; **not that I am aware of** non che io sappia; **I am fully aware that** mi rendo perfettamente conto che; **to make sb aware of sth** rendere qn consapevole di qc; **to be politically/socially aware** aver coscienza politica/sociale.

aware·ness [ə'wɛənɪs] N (*consciousness*) coscienza; (*knowledge*) consapevolezza; **to develop people's awareness (of)** sensibilizzare la gente (su).

awash [ə'wɒʃ] ADJ: **awash (with)** inondato(-a) (da).

away [ə'weɪ] ADV **a** lontano; **away from** lontano da; **far away from home** molto lontano da casa; **the village is 3 miles away** il paese è a 3 miglia di distanza *or* è lontano 3 miglia; **two hours away by car** a due ore di distanza in

macchina; **away in the distance** in lontananza; **the holiday was two weeks away** mancavano due settimane alle vacanze

b (*absent*): **to be away** essere via; **he's away in Milan** è (andato) a Milano; **he's away for a week** è andato via per una settimana; **go away!** vai via (di qui)!, via di qui!; **to take away** portare via

c : **to turn away** girarsi, voltarsi; **to die away** (*sound*) spegnersi in lontananza; **the snow melted away** la neve si è completamente sciolta; **to play away** (*Sport*) giocare in trasferta *or* fuori casa; **to talk away** parlare in continuazione; **to work away** continuare a lavorare.

♦ **away game, away match** N (*Sport*) partita fuori casa *or* in trasferta.

awe [ɔ:] **[1]** N timore *m* reverenziale; **to stand in awe of** aver soggezione di.
[2] VT intimidire.

♦ **awe-inspiring** ['ɔ:ɪnˌspaɪərɪŋ], **awe·some** ['ɔ:səm] ADJ imponente.

♦ **awe-struck** ['ɔ:ˌstrʌk] ADJ sgomento(-a).

aw·ful ['ɔ:fəl] ADJ terribile, orribile; **an awful lot of** (*people, cars, dogs*) un numero incredibile di; (*jam, flowers*) una quantità incredibile di; **how awful!** che orrore!

aw·ful·ly ['ɔ:flɪ] ADV (*very*) terribilmente; **thanks awfully** mille grazie; **I'm awfully sorry** sono terribilmente spiacente.

awhile [ə'waɪl] ADV (per) un po'.

awk·ward ['ɔ:kwəd] ADJ **a** (*difficult: problem, question, situation, task*) delicato(-a), difficile; (*silence*) imbarazzante; (*Aut: corner*) brutto(-a); (*inconvenient*) scomodo(-a); (*time, moment*) poco opportuno(-a); (*tool*) poco maneggevole, scomodo(-a); (*shape*) difficile; **you've caught me at an awkward time** mi hai pescato in un momento poco opportuno; **Friday is awkward for me** venerdì mi riesce scomodo; **she's being awkward about it** sta rendendo la cosa un po' difficile; **he's an awkward customer** è un tipo difficile

b (*clumsy: person*) goffo(-a); (: *gesture, movement*) impacciato(-a); (*style, phrasing*) contorto(-a); **the awkward age** l'età difficile.

awk·ward·ly ['ɔ:kwədlɪ] ADV (*behave*) goffamente; (*move*) in modo impacciato; (*write*) in modo contorto.

awk·ward·ness ['ɔ:kwədnɪs] N (*of situation, problem*) difficoltà, delicatezza; (*of arrangement*) scomodità; (*of silence*) imbarazzo; (*of movement, behaviour*) goffaggine *f*; **the awkwardness of his prose style** lo stile contorto della sua prosa.

awl [ɔ:l] N punteruolo.

awn·ing ['ɔ:nɪŋ] N (*of shop, hotel etc*) tenda, tendone *m*; (*of tent*) veranda.

awoke [ə'wəʊk] PT of **awake**.

awok·en [ə'wəʊkən] PP of **awake**.

AWOL ['eɪwɒl] ADJ ABBR (*Mil*) = **absent without leave**; see **absent**.

awry [ə'raɪ] **[1]** ADV di traverso.
[2] ADJ storto(-a); **to go awry** andare a monte.

axe, (*Am*) **ax** [æks] **[1]** N ascia, scure *f*; **to have an axe to grind** (*fig*) fare i propri interessi *or* il proprio tornaconto.
[2] VT (*fig: expenditure*) ridurre drasticamente; (: *person*) liquidare (*per ragioni economiche*); (*write*) in annullare; (: *jobs*) sopprimere.

axi·om ['æksɪəm] N assioma *m*.

axio·mat·ic [ˌæksɪəʊ'mætɪk] ADJ assiomatico(-a).

Axis ['æksɪs] N: **the Axis** l'Asse.

axis ['æksɪs] N (*pl* **axes** ['æksi:z]) (*Geom, of the earth*) asse *m*.

axle ['æksl] N (*of wheel*) semiasse *m*; (*also:* **axletree**) asse *m*.

♦ **axle grease** N lubrificante *m* per gli assi.

axon ['æksɒn] N, **axone** ['æksəʊn] N assone *m*.

aye, ay [aɪ] ①①① EXCL (*esp Scot: yes*) sì.

　　②② N voto favorevole.

AYH [ˌeɪwaɪˈeɪtʃ] N ABBR (= *American Youth Hostels*) ≈ A.I.G. *f* (= *Associazione Italiana Alberghi per la Gioventù*).

AZ ABBR (*Am Post*)= *Arizona*.

azalea [əˈzeɪlɪə] N azalea.

Azer·bai·jan [ˌæzəbaɪˈdʒɑːn] N Azerbaigian *m*.

Azer·bai·ja·ni [ˌæzəbaɪˈdʒɑːnɪ], **Aze·ri** [əˈzɛərɪ] ①①① ADJ azerbaigiano(-a).

　　②② N azerbaigiano(-a), azero(-a); (*language*) azerbaigiano.

Azores [əˈzɔːz] NPL: **the Azores** le Azzorre.

AZT [ˌeɪzɛdˈtiː] N ABBR (= *azidothymidine*) AZT *m*.

Az·tec ['æztɛk] ①①① ADJ azteco(-a).

　　②② N (*person*) azteco(-a); (*language*) azteco.

az·ure ['eɪʒəʳ] ①①① ADJ azzurro(-a).

　　②② N azzurro.

B

B, b [bi:] N **a** (*letter*) B, b *f or m inv* **b** (*Mus*) si *m* **c** (*Scol: mark*) ≈ 8 (*buono*); **B for Benjamin**, (*Am*) **B for Baker** ≈ B come Bologna.

b. ABBR = **born.**

BA [ˌbiːˈeɪ] N ABBR **a** = **Bachelor of Arts b** = *British Academy.*

bab·ble [ˈbæbl] ⓵ N (*of voices*) mormorio; (*of baby*) balbettio; (*of stream*) gorgoglio; (*foolish*) ciance *fpl.*
⓶ VI (*indistinctly*) farfugliare; (*chatter*) cianciare; (*baby*) balbettare; (*stream*) gorgogliare.

bab·bling [ˈbæblɪŋ] ADJ (*stream*) che gorgoglia.

babe [beɪb] N (*old*) bimbo(-a), bebè *m inv*; (*esp Am fam: endearment*) piccolo(-a), tesoro; **babe in arms** bimbo (-a) in fasce; (*fig*) ingenuo(-a).

Ba·bel [ˈbeɪbəl] N Babele *f*; **the Tower of Babel** la torre di Babele.

ba·boon [bəˈbuːn] N babbuino.

baby [ˈbeɪbɪ] ⓵ N (*human*) bambino(-a), bimbo(-a); (*of animal*) piccolo; (*fam: as address: to woman*) piccola, bimba mia; (*: to man*) piccolo, bello; **the baby of the family** il/la piccolino(-a) di casa; **don't be such a baby!** non fare il bambino!; **to throw the baby out with the bathwater** (*fig*) buttar via il bambino con l'acqua sporca; **the new system was his baby** (*fam*) il nuovo sistema era la sua creatura; **I was left holding the baby** (*fam*) mi hanno piantato lì a sbrogliarmela da solo.
⓶ ADJ (*clothes, food*) per la prima infanzia.

♦ **baby-battering** [ˈbeɪbɪˌbætərɪŋ] N maltrattamento dei bambini.

♦ **baby bird** N uccellino.

♦ **baby boy** N maschietto.

♦ **baby carriage** N (*Am*) carrozzina.

♦ **baby-doll pyjamas** NPL baby-doll *m inv.*

♦ **baby face** N viso da bambino.

♦ **baby girl** N femminuccia.

♦ **baby grand** N (*also:* **baby grand piano**) pianoforte *m* a mezza coda.

ba·by·hood [ˈbeɪbɪhʊd] N prima infanzia.

ba·by·ish [ˈbeɪbɪʃ] ADJ puerile, infantile.

Baby·lon [ˈbæbɪlən] N Babilonia.

Baby·lo·nian [ˌbæbɪˈləʊnɪən] ⓵ ADJ babilonese.
⓶ N (*person*) babilonese *m/f*; (*language*) babilonese *m.*

♦ **baby-minder** [ˈbeɪbɪˌmaɪndəʳ] N bambinaia (*per madri che lavorano*).

♦ **baby rabbit** N coniglietto.

♦ **baby seat** N (*Aut*) sedile *m* per bambini.

♦ **baby-sit** [ˈbeɪbɪsɪt] VI: **to baby-sit (for sb)** guardare i bambini (a qn), fare il (*or* la) babysitter (per qn).

♦ **baby-sitter** [ˈbeɪbɪˌsɪtəʳ] N baby-sitter *m/f inv.*

♦ **baby-sitting** [ˈbeɪbɪˌsɪtɪŋ] N: **to go baby-sitting** fare il (*or* la) baby-sitter; **a baby-sitting service** un servizio di baby-sitting.

♦ **baby talk** N linguaggio infantile.

♦ **baby-walker** [ˈbeɪbɪˌwɔːkəʳ] N girello.

Bacchus [ˈbækəs] N Bacco.

bach·elor [ˈbætʃələʳ] N scapolo.

bach·elor·hood [ˈbætʃələhʊd] N celibato.

♦ **Bachelor of Arts** N (*Univ: degree*) ≈ laurea in lettere; (*: person*) ≈ laureato(-a) in lettere.

♦ **Bachelor of Science** N (*Univ: degree*) ≈ laurea in scienze; (*: person*) ≈ laureato(-a) in scienze.

♦ **bachelor party** N (*Am*) festa di addio al celibato.

♦ **Bachelor's Degree** N *in Gran Bretagna, diploma conferito a chi ha completato un corso di laurea di tre o quattro anni.*

ba·cil·lus [bəˈsɪləs] N (*pl* **bacilli** [bəˈsɪlaɪ]) bacillo.

back [bæk] ⓵ N **a** (*of person*) schiena; (*of animal*) dorso, schiena; **he fell on his back** è caduto di schiena; **with one's back to the light** con la luce alle spalle; **seen from the back** visto(-a) di spalle; **back to back** di spalle (uno(-a) contro l'altro(-a)), schiena contro schiena; **behind sb's back** alle spalle di qn; (*fig*) alle spalle *or* dietro le spalle di qn; **to break one's back** rompersi la schiena; **to break the back of a job** (*Brit*) fare il grosso *or* il peggio di un lavoro; **to put one's back into it** (*fam*) mettercela tutta; **to have one's back to the wall** (*fig*) essere *or* trovarsi con le spalle al muro; **to put sb's back up** (*fam*) far irritare qn; **to get off sb's back** (*fam*) lasciare qn in pace; **I was glad to see the back of him** (*fam*) ero contento che se ne fosse andato

b (*as opposed to front*) dietro; (*of cheque, envelope, medal, page*) retro, rovescio; (*of head*) nuca; (*of hand*) dorso; (*of hall, room*) fondo; (*of house, car*) parte *f* posteriore, dietro; (*of chair*) spalliera, schienale *m*; (*of train*) coda; **at the back of the class** in fondo alla classe; **back to front** all'incontrario; **at the back of my mind was the thought that ...** sotto sotto pensavo che...; **it's always there at the back of my mind** è sempre lì, non riesco a togliermelo dalla mente; **I know Naples like the back of my hand** conosco Napoli come il palmo della mia mano *or* come le mie tasche; **at the back of beyond** (*fam*) in capo al mondo; **he's at the back of all this** c'è lui dietro a questa storia

c (*Sport*) terzino; **right/left back** terzino destro/sinistro.

2 ADJ ATTR **a** (*rear*) di dietro; (: *wheel, seat*) posteriore; **back pass** (*Ftbl*) passaggio indietro; **back garden/room** giardino/stanza sul retro (della casa); **back cover** retro della copertina; **back kitchen** retrocucina *m*; **on the back page** in ultima pagina; **to take a back seat** (*fig*) restare in secondo piano; **he's a back seat driver** sta sempre a criticare chi guida; **back street** vicolo; **he grew up in the back streets of Glasgow** è cresciuto nei bassifondi di Glasgow

b (*overdue: rent*) arretrato(-a); **back payments** arretrati *mpl*.

3 ADV **a** (*again, returning*) (*often* ri- +*verb*): **to give back** ridare; **to be back** essere tornato(-a); **when will you be back?** quando torni?; **30 km there and back** 30 km fra andata e ritorno; **put it back on the shelf** rimettilo sullo scaffale; **she hit him back** gli restituì il colpo; **throw the ball back** rilancia la palla; **he called back** ha richiamato; **can I have it back?** posso riaverlo?; **he ran back** tornò indietro di corsa

b (*in distance*) indietro; **stand back!** indietro!; **back and forth** avanti e indietro; **a house set back from the road** una casa che non si affaccia sulla strada

c (*in time*): **some months back** mesi fa *or* addietro; **as far back as the 13th century** già nel duecento.

4 VT **a** (*car*): **to back (into)** far entrare a marcia indietro (in)

b (*support: plan, person, candidate*) appoggiare, sostenere, spalleggiare; (: *financially*) finanziare

c (*bet on: horse*) puntare su.

5 VI (*move: person*) indietreggiare; (: *car*) fare marcia indietro; **he backed into me** ha fatto un passo indietro e mi è venuto addosso; (*in car*) mi è venuto addosso a marcia indietro

▶ **back away** VI + ADV: **to back away (from)** indietreggiare (davanti a), tirarsi indietro (davanti a)

▶ **back down** VI + ADV (*fig*) abbandonare, arrendersi, fare marcia indietro

▶ **back off** VI + ADV tirarsi indietro

▶ **back on to** VI + ADV + PREP: **the house backs on to the golf course** il retro della casa dà sul campo da golf

▶ **back out** VI + ADV (*fig*) tirarsi indietro; **to back out of sth** (*undertaking*) sottrarsi a; (*deal*) ritirarsi da

▶ **back up** 1 VT + ADV **a** (*support: person*) appoggiare, sostenere; (: *claim, theory*) confermare, avvalorare

b (*car*): **to back the car up** far marcia indietro

c (*Comput*) copiare, fare una copia di riserva di.

2 VI + ADV **a** (*in car*) fare marcia indietro

b (*Am: traffic*) ingorgarsi.

back·ache ['bækˌeɪk] N mal *m* di schiena.

back·bencher ['bækˈbɛntʃəʳ] N *membro del Parlamento*

senza potere amministrativo.

back·benches ['bækˈbɛntʃəz] NPL *scanni del Parlamento inglese dove siedono i parlamentari che non hanno una carica al governo o all'opposizione.*

back·bit·ing ['bækˌbaɪtɪŋ] N maldicenze *fpl*.

back·bone ['bækˌbəʊn] N (*also fig*) spina dorsale; **the backbone of the organization** l'anima dell'organizzazione; **he's got no backbone** è uno smidollato.

back·break·ing ['bækˌbreɪkɪŋ] ADJ (*work, task*) massacrante.

back·chat ['bækˌtʃæt] N (*Brit fam*) impertinenza.

back·cloth ['bækˌklɒθ] N (*Brit: Theatre*) fondale *m*; (: *fig*) sfondo.

back·comb ['bækˌkəʊm] VT (*Brit*) cotonare.

back·comb·ing ['bækˌkəʊmɪŋ] N cotonatura.

back·date [ˌbækˈdeɪt] VT (*arrangement, document*) retrodatare; **backdated pay rise** aumento (di stipendio) retroattivo.

back·drop ['bækˌdrɒp] N = **backcloth**.

back·er ['bækəʳ] N (*supporter*) fautore(-trice), sostenitore(-trice); (*Comm*) finanziatore(-trice).

back·fire ['bækˈfaɪəʳ] VI (*Aut*) avere un ritorno di fiamma; (*fig: plan, policy*) avere effetto contrario; **to backfire on sb** ritorcersi contro qn.

back·gam·mon [bækˈgæmən] N backgammon *m*, tavola reale.

back·ground ['bækˌgraʊnd] 1 N **a** (*gen*) sfondo; (*fig*) sfondo, scenario; **in the background** sullo sfondo; (*fig*) nell'ombra; **on a red background** su sfondo rosso

b (*of person*) background *m inv*; (: *basic knowledge*) base *f*; (: *experience*) esperienza; (*of problem, event*) retroscena *m*, background *m inv*; **she comes from a wealthy background** è di famiglia ricca; **family background** ambiente familiare.

2 ADJ (*music, noise*) di fondo; (*Comput*) a bassa priorità.

♦ **background radiation** N radiazione *f* di fondo.

♦ **background reading** N letture *fpl* complementari.

back·hand ['bækˌhænd] N (*Tennis: also*: **backhand stroke**) rovescio.

back·hand·ed [ˌbækˈhændɪd] ADJ (*blow*) con il dorso della mano; (*Tennis: stroke*) di rovescio; **backhanded compliment** complimento ambiguo.

back·hand·er ['bækˌhændəʳ] N (*Brit: bribe*) bustarella.

back·ing ['bækɪŋ] N **a** (*support*) appoggio, sostegno; (*Comm*) finanziamento **b** (*Mus*) accompagnamento **c** (*protective layer of paper, cloth etc*) rivestimento, strato protettivo.

back·lash ['bækˌlæʃ] N (*fig*) reazione *f* (violenta).

back·log ['bækˌlɒg] N: **backlog of work** lavoro arretrato; **the strike has resulted in a backlog of orders** a causa dello sciopero si sono accumulate le ordinazioni.

♦ **back number** N (*of magazine*) numero arretrato.

back·pack ['bækˌpæk] N zaino.

back·packer ['bækˌpækəʳ] N *chi viaggia con zaino e sacco a pelo.*

backpack·ing ['bækˌpækɪŋ] N: **to go backpacking** viaggiare con zaino e sacco a pelo.

♦ **back passage** N (*Anat*) retto.

♦ **back pay** N arretrato di stipendio.

♦ **back·pedal** [ˌbækˈpɛdəl] VI (*on bicycle*) pedalare all'indietro; (*fig*) fare marcia indietro.

back·scratch·er ['bækˌskrætʃəʳ] N manina (grattaschiena *inv*).

♦ **back scrub·ber** ['bækˌskrʌbəʳ] N spazzola da bagno.

♦ **back-seat driver** [ˌbæksiːtˈdraɪvəʳ] N *passeggero che*

dà consigli non richiesti al guidatore.

back·side [ˌbæk'saɪd] N (*fam*) didietro *m inv*, sedere *m*.

back·slap·ping ['bækˌslæpɪŋ] N (*fam*) scambio di pacche sulle spalle.

back·slash ['bækˌslæʃ] N (*Typ*) barra obliqua inversa.

back·slid·ing ['bækˌslaɪdɪŋ] N ricaduta (*in vizio, errore*).

back·space ['bækˌspeɪs] VI (*in typing*) battere il tasto di ritorno.

back·stage [ˌbæk'steɪdʒ] ADV, ADJ dietro le quinte.

back·stairs ['bækˌstɛəz] NPL scala *sg* di servizio.

♦ **backstairs gossip** N pettegolezzi *mpl*, chiacchiere *fpl* di corridoio.

back·stay ['bækˌsteɪ] N (*Naut*) paterazzo.

back·street ['bækˌstriːt] 1 N vicolo.

2 ADJ (*shop, factory*) situato(-a) in un vicolo; (*fig: shady*) losco(-a); **a backstreet cafe** un bar d'infima categoria; **backstreet abortionist** praticante *m/f* di aborti clandestini.

back·stroke ['bækˌstrəʊk] N (*Swimming*) dorso.

back·swing ['bækˌswɪŋ] N (*Tennis*) movimento di apertura.

♦ **back-to-back** ['bæktə'bæk] ADJ (*Brit*): **back-to-back houses** *tipo di case a schiera con la parete posteriore in comune.*

back·track ['bækˌtræk] VI (*retrace one's steps*) tornare indietro; (*fig: backpedal*) fare marcia indietro.

back·up ['bækʌp] 1 ADJ (*gen, Comput*) di riserva.

2 N (*support*) sostegno, appoggio; (*substitute*) sostituto; (*Comput*) backup *m inv*.

back·ward ['bækwəd] ADJ **a** (*motion, glance*) all'indietro **b** (*pupil*) che è indietro, tardivo(-a); (*pej: country*) arretrato(-a) **c** (*reluctant*): **backward (in doing sth)** restio(-a) (a fare qc).

♦ **backward-looking** ['bækwədˌlʊkɪŋ] ADJ (*pej*) retrogrado(-a).

back·ward·ness ['bækwədnɪs] N (*pej: of country*) arretratezza.

back·wards ['bækwədz], (*Am*) **back·ward** ['bækwəd] ADV indietro; **to walk backwards** camminare all'indietro; **backwards and forwards** avanti e indietro; **to bend over backwards to do sth** (*fam*) farsi in quattro per fare qc; **to know sth backwards** (*fam*) sapere qc a menadito.

back·wash ['bækˌwɒʃ] N (*of waves*) risacca; (*of ship, aircraft*) risucchio; (*fig: repercussions*) strascico, ripercussione *f*.

back·water ['bækˌwɔːtəʳ] N acqua stagnante; (*fig pej*) buco, angolo sperduto; **this town is a cultural backwater** questa città è culturalmente arretrata.

back·woods ['bækwʊdz] 1 NPL (*Am*) zona *sg* rurale isolata.

2 ADJ rurale.

♦ **back yard** N (*Brit: paved area*) cortile *m* sul retro della casa; (*Am: garden*) giardino sul retro della casa.

ba·con ['beɪkən] N pancetta; **bacon and eggs** uova *fpl* con pancetta.

bac·te·ria [bæk'tɪərɪə] NPL batteri *mpl*.

bac·te·rial [bæk'tɪərɪəl] ADJ batterico(-a).

bac·te·rio·logi·cal [bækˌtɪərɪə'lɒdʒɪkəl] ADJ batteriologico (-a).

bac·te·ri·olo·gist [bækˌtɪərɪ'ɒlədʒɪst] N batteriologo(-a).

bac·te·ri·ol·ogy [bækˌtɪərɪ'ɒlədʒɪ] N batteriologia.

Bac·trian cam·el ['bæktrɪən'kæməl] N cammello (asiatico).

bad [bæd] ADJ (*comp* **worse**, *superl* **worst**) **a** (*gen*) cattivo (-a); (*child*) cattivello(-a); (*habit, news, weather*) brutto (-a), cattivo(-a); (*workmanship, film*) scadente, brutto (-a); (*mistake, illness, cut*) brutto(-a), grave; **bad language** parolacce *fpl*; **you bad boy!** (brutto) cattivo!; **he's bad at keeping appointments** non sa rispettare un impegno; **smoking is bad for you** il fumo fa male alla salute; **not bad** (*quite good*) non male; (*less enthusiastic*) così così; **how are you feeling? — not bad** come si sente? — non c'è male; **not bad, eh?** mica male, eh?; **that wouldn't be a bad thing** non sarebbe una cattiva idea; **that's too bad** (*sympathetic*) che peccato; **that's just too bad** (*unsympathetic*) tanto peggio per te (*or* lei *etc*); **it's too bad of you** è poco carino da parte tua; **business is bad** gli affari vanno male; **from bad to worse** di male in peggio; **to have a bad time of it** passarsela male; **to be in a bad way** (*in difficulties*) essere nei guai; (*ill*) stare molto male; **bad faith** malafede *f*

b (*rotten: food*) guasto(-a), andato(-a) a male; (: *smell*) cattivo(-a); (: *tooth*) cariato(-a), guasto(-a); **to go bad** andare a male

c : **to have a bad back/stomach** avere dei problemi alla schiena/allo stomaco; **his bad leg** la sua gamba malata; **to feel bad** (*sick*) sentirsi male; **I feel bad about it** (*guilty*) mi sento un po' in colpa; **there's no need for you to feel bad about it** non è il caso di prendersela.

♦ **bad cheque** N assegno a vuoto.

♦ **bad debt** N credito inesigibile.

bad·die ['bædɪ] N (*fam*) cattivo.

bade [bæd, beɪd] PT of **bid**.

badge [bædʒ] N (*of policeman, Scol*) distintivo; (*Mil*) mostrina; (*stick-on*) adesivo.

badg·er ['bædʒəʳ] 1 N (*Zool*) tasso.

2 VT tormentare.

bad·ly ['bædlɪ] ADV (*comp* **worse**, *superl* **worst**) **a** (*work, dress*) male; **a badly behaved child** un(a) bambino(-a) maleducato(-a); **things are going badly** le cose vanno male; **to treat sb badly** trattar male qn

b (*seriously: wounded*) gravemente; **badly hurt** gravemente ferito(-a)

c (*very much*): **I need it badly** ne ho assolutamente bisogno; **I want it badly** lo voglio ad ogni costo; **it badly needs painting** ha proprio bisogno di una mano di vernice; **he needs help badly** ha urgente bisogno di aiuto.

♦ **badly off** ADJ povero(-a).

♦ **bad-mannered** [ˌbæd'mænəd] ADJ maleducato(-a), sgarbato(-a).

bad·min·ton ['bædmɪntən] N badminton *m*.

bad·ness ['bædnɪs] N (*wickedness*) cattiveria.

♦ **bad-tempered** [ˌbæd'tɛmpəd] ADJ irascibile, irritabile; (*look*) antipatico(-a).

baf·fle ['bæfl] VT (*puzzle*) lasciare perplesso(-a), confondere; **it baffles me how she does it** non riesco a capire come faccia.

baf·fle·ment ['bæflmənt] N perplessità.

baf·fling ['bæflɪŋ] ADJ sconcertante.

bag [bæg] 1 N (*gen*) borsa; (*paper bag, carrier*) sacchetto; (*handbag*) borsa, borsetta; (*suitcase*) valigia; (*of hunter*) carniere *m*; (*animals taken by hunter*) carniere, bottino di caccia; **to pack one's bags** fare le valigie; **it's in the bag** (*fam*) ce l'ho (*or* ce l'hai *etc*) in tasca, è cosa fatta; **bags under the eyes** borse sotto gli occhi; **bags of** (*fam: lots*) un sacco di.

2 VT (*fam: seat, place*) accaparrarsi

▶ **bag up** VT + ADV (*flour*) insaccare.

bag·ful ['bægfʊl] N sacco (pieno).

bag·gage ['bægɪdʒ] N bagaglio, bagagli *mpl.*
♦ **baggage car** N (*Am*) bagagliaio.
♦ **baggage check** N controllo bagagli.
♦ **baggage handler** N addetto ai bagagli.
♦ **baggage identification tag** N tagliando (di) controllo (del) bagaglio.
♦ **baggage reclaim** N ritiro bagagli.
bag·gy ['bægɪ] ADJ largo(-a), sformato(-a).
Bagh·dad [bæg'dæd] N Bagdad *f.*
♦ **bag lady** N (*fam*) stracciona, barbona.
bag·pipes ['bæg,paɪps] NPL (*in Scotland*) cornamusa *sg*; (*in Italy*) zampogna *sg.*
♦ **bag-snatcher** ['bæg,snætʃəʳ] N (*Brit*) scippatore(-trice).
♦ **bag-snatching** ['bæg,snætʃɪŋ] N (*Brit*) scippo.
Ba·ha·mas [bə'hɑːməz] NPL: **the Bahamas** le Bahamas.
Bah·rain, Bah·rein [bɑː'reɪn] N il Bahrein *m.*
bail[1] [beɪl] N (*Law*) cauzione *f*; **he was granted bail** ha ottenuto la libertà provvisoria su cauzione; **to stand bail for sb** rendersi garante di *or* per qn; **to be released on bail** essere rilasciato(-a) su cauzione
▶ **bail out** VT + ADV (*Law*) mettere in libertà provvisoria su cauzione; (*fig*) tirare fuori dai guai.
bail[2] [beɪl] VT, VI see **bale out 1, 2a**.
bail·iff ['beɪlɪf] N (*Law*) ufficiale *m* giudiziario; (*on estate*) amministratore *m*, fattore *m.*
bairn [bɛən] N (*Scot*) bambino(-a).
bait [beɪt] [1] N (*also fig*) esca; **he didn't rise to the bait** (*fig*) non ha abboccato (all'amo).
[2] VT (*hook*) innescare; (*trap*) munire di esca; (*torment: person, animal*) stuzzicare, tormentare.
baize [beɪz] N panno.
bake [beɪk] [1] VT (*bread, cake*) cuocere (al forno); (*bricks*) cuocere; **she baked a cake today** ha fatto un dolce oggi; **baked potatoes** patate *fpl* (con la buccia) cotte al forno.
[2] VI cuocersi al forno.
♦ **baked beans** ['beɪk'bi:nz] NPL ≈ fagioli *mpl* all'uccelletto.
Ba·ke·lite® ['beɪkə,laɪt] N bachelite ® *f.*
bak·er ['beɪkəʳ] N fornaio(-a), panettiere(-a); **baker's (shop)** panetteria, forno; **at/to the baker's** dal panettiere, dal fornaio.
♦ **baker's dozen** N (*old*) *tredici cose.*
bak·ery ['beɪkərɪ] N panetteria, forno.
bak·ing ['beɪkɪŋ] [1] N cottura (al forno); **Monday was her day for doing the baking** il lunedì faceva il pane (e/o i dolci).
[2] ADJ (*fam: hot*): **it's baking in here** qui dentro è un forno.
♦ **baking dish** N pirofila.
♦ **baking powder** N lievito (minerale) in polvere.
♦ **baking sheet, baking tray** N placca da forno, teglia.
♦ **baking soda** N bicarbonato di soda.
♦ **baking tin** N stampo, tortiera.
bala·cla·va [,bælə'klɑːvə] N (*also:* **balaclava helmet**) passamontagna *m inv.*
bal·ance ['bæləns] [1] N **a** (*equilibrium*) equilibrio; **to lose one's balance** perdere l'equilibrio; **to throw sb off balance** far perdere l'equilibrio a qn; (*fig*) sconcertare qn, far mancare la terra sotto i piedi a qn; **balance of power** equilibrio di potere; **to strike the right balance** trovare il giusto mezzo; **on balance** (*fig*) a conti fatti, tutto sommato; **a nice balance of humour and pathos** una equilibrata combinazione di humour e pathos
b (*scales*) bilancia; **to hang in the balance** (*fig*) essere incerto(-a) *or* in bilico

c (*Comm*) bilancio; (: *difference*) saldo; (: *remainder*) resto; **balance brought** *or* **carried forward** saldo riportato, saldo da riportare.
[2] VT **a** tenere in equilibrio *or* in bilico; (*Aut: wheel*) fare l'equilibratura di; (*fig: compare*) soppesare, valutare; (*make up for*) compensare; **the two things balance each other out** le due cose si compensano; **this must be balanced against that** nel considerare questo fattore bisogna tener presente l'altro
b (*Comm: account*) saldare; (: *budget*) pareggiare, far quadrare; **to balance the books** fare il bilancio
c (*Chem, Math: equations*) bilanciare.
[3] VI **a** tenersi in equilibrio
b (*accounts*) quadrare, essere in pareggio.
bal·anced ['bælənst] ADJ (*views*) moderato(-a); (*personality, diet*) equilibrato(-a).
♦ **balance of payments** N bilancia dei pagamenti.
♦ **balance of trade** N bilancia commerciale.
♦ **balance sheet** N bilancio (di esercizio).
bal·anc·ing ['bælənsɪŋ] N **a** messa in equilibrio; (*Aut: of wheels*) equilibratura **b** (*Comm, Fin: of account*) saldo; (: *of budget*) pareggiamento; **balancing of the books** bilancio.
♦ **balancing act** N: **to do a balancing act** (*also fig*) fare dell'equilibrismo.
bal·co·ny ['bælkənɪ] N balcone *m*; (*Theatre*) prima galleria, balconata.
bald [bɔːld] ADJ (*person*) calvo(-a); (*tyre*) liscio(-a); (*statement*) asciutto(-a); (*style*) spoglio(-a); **to go bald** perdere i capelli.
bal·der·dash ['bɔːldə,dæʃ] N (*old*) sciocchezze *fpl*, stupidaggini *fpl.*
♦ **bald-headed** [,bɔːld'hɛdɪd] ADJ calvo(-a).
bald·ing ['bɔːldɪŋ] ADJ con una calvizie incipiente.
bald·ly ['bɔːldlɪ] ADV senza tanti complimenti.
bald·ness ['bɔːldnɪs] N calvizie *fsg.*
bale[1] [beɪl] N (*of cloth, hay*) balla.
bale[2] [beɪl] VT, VI see **bale out 1, 2a**.
▶ **bale out** [1] VT + ADV (*Naut: water*) vuotare; (: *boat*) sgottare, aggottare.
[2] VI + ADV **a** (*Naut*) saltare in acqua **b** (*Aer*) gettarsi col paracadute.
Bal·ear·ic [,bælɪ'ærɪk] ADJ: **the Balearic Islands** le (isole) Baleari.
bale·ful ['beɪlful] ADJ (*look*) malevolo(-a).
bale·ful·ly ['beɪlfəlɪ] ADV malevolmente.
balk, baulk [bɔːk] VI: **to balk (at the idea of)** (*person*) recalcitrare (all'idea di), tirarsi indietro (davanti a); (*horse*) recalcitrare *or* impennarsi (di fronte a).
Bal·kan ['bɔːlkən] ADJ balcanico(-a).
Bal·kans ['bɔːlkənz] NPL: **the Balkans** i Balcani.
ball[1] [bɔːl] N (*gen*) palla; (*inflated: Ftbl etc*) pallone *m*; (*for golf*) pallina; (*of wool, string*) gomitolo; **a glass ball** un globo di vetro; **he rolled the paper into a ball** ha appallottolato la carta; **the ball of the foot** la punta del piede; **the ball of the thumb** il polpastrello del pollice; **to be on the ball** (*fig: competent*) essere in gamba; (: *alert*) stare all'erta; **to play ball (with sb)** (*fig*) stare al gioco (di qn); **to start the ball rolling** (*fig*) fare la prima mossa; **to keep the ball rolling** (*fig*) mandare avanti le cose; **the ball is in your court** (*fig*) tocca a te.
ball[2] [bɔːl] N (*dance*) ballo; **to have a ball** (*fig fam*) divertirsi da matti.
bal·lad ['bæləd] N ballata.
bal·last ['bæləst] N zavorra.

♦ **ball bearing** N cuscinetto a sfere.
♦ **ball cock** ['bɔ:l,kɒk] N galleggiante m (in serbatoio).
bal·le·ri·na [,bælə'ri:nə] N ballerina (classica).
bal·let ['bæleɪ] N (dance) balletto; (art) danza classica.
♦ **ballet dancer** N ballerino(-a) (classico(-a)).
♦ **ball game** N (gen) gioco con la palla; (Am) partita di baseball; **it's a whole new ball game** (fam) è un altro paio di maniche.
bal·lis·tic [bə'lɪstɪk] ADJ balistico(-a); **intercontinental ballistic missile** missile m a gettata intercontinentale.
bal·lis·tics [bə'lɪstɪks] NSG balistica.
♦ **ball machine** N (Tennis) macchina f lanciapalle inv.
bal·loon [bə'lu:n] 1 N (toy) palloncino; (Aer) pallone m aerostatico, mongolfiera; (in comic strip) fumetto.
2 VI gonfiarsi.
bal·loon·ist [bə'lu:nɪst] N aeronauta m/f.
bal·lot ['bælət] 1 N votazione f (a scrutinio segreto); **on the first ballot** alla prima votazione.
2 VT (members) consultare tramite votazione.
♦ **ballot box** N urna (elettorale).
♦ **ballot paper** N scheda (elettorale).
ball·park ['bɔ:l,pɑ:k] N (Am) stadio di baseball.
♦ **ballpark figure** N (fam) cifra approssimativa.
♦ **ball-point** ['bɔ:l,pɔɪnt], **ball-point pen** ['bɔ:l,pɔɪnt'pɛn] N penna a sfera.
ball·room ['bɔ:l,rʊm] N sala da ballo.
♦ **ballroom dancing** N ballo liscio.
balls [bɔ:lz] (fam!) NPL coglioni mpl (fam!); (fig: bullshit) cazzate fpl (fam!)
♦ **balls up** (fam!) 1 VT + ADV incasinare.
2 N pasticcio; **you can rely on George to make a balls-up of everything** puoi star sicuro che George incasinerà tutto.
bal·ly·hoo [,bælɪ'hu:] N battage m inv.
balm [bɑ:m] N (also fig) balsamo.
balmy ['bɑ:mɪ] ADJ **a** (breeze, air) balsamico(-a) **b** (Brit fam) = **barmy**.
ba·lo·ney [bə'ləʊnɪ] N (Am fam) sciocchezze fpl, stupidaggini fpl.
BALPA ['bælpə] N ABBR = British Airline Pilots' Association.
bal·sa ['bɔ:lsə] N (also: **balsawood**) (legno di) balsa.
bal·sam ['bɔ:lsəm] N balsamo.
Bal·tic ['bɔ:ltɪk] ADJ, N baltico(-a); **the Baltic (Sea)** il (mar) Baltico.
bal·us·trade [,bæləs'treɪd] N balaustrata.
bam·boo [bæm'bu:] 1 N bambù m inv.
2 ADJ di bambù.
bam·boo·zle [bæm'bu:zl] VT (fam) abbindolare, infinocchiare.
ban [bæn] 1 N divieto, bando; **to put a ban on sth** proibire qc.
2 (pt, pp banned) VT (alcohol, book, film) proibire; **to ban sb from sth** proibire qc a qn; **to ban sb from doing sth** proibire a qn di fare qc; **to ban sb from a place** proibire a qn di andare in un posto; **they banned him from the competition** lo hanno escluso dalla gara; **he was banned from driving** (Brit) gli hanno tolto (or ritirato) la patente.
ba·nal [bə'nɑ:l] ADJ banale.
ba·nal·ity [bə'nælɪtɪ] N banalità f inv.
ba·nal·ly [bə'nɑ:lɪ] ADV banalmente.
ba·na·na [bə'nɑ:nə] N (fruit) banana; (tree) banano.
♦ **banana boat** N bananiera.
♦ **banana republic** N (fam pej) repubblica delle banane.
♦ **banana skin** N (also fig) buccia di banana.
♦ **banana split** N banana split f inv.

band[1] [bænd] N (gen) banda, striscia; (of hat, cigar) nastro.
band[2] [bænd] N **a** (Mus) banda (musicale); (jazz band, pop group) complesso; (Mil) fanfara **b** (group of people) banda
▶ **band together** VI + ADV mettersi in gruppo.
band·age ['bændɪdʒ] 1 N fascia, benda.
2 VT fasciare, bendare.
Band-Aid® ['bænd,eɪd] N (Am) cerotto.
ban·dana, **ban·dan·na** [bæn'dænə] N fazzolettone m.
ban·dit ['bændɪt] N bandito, brigante m.
ban·dit·ry ['bændɪtrɪ] N banditismo.
♦ **band saw** N segatrice f a nastro.
bands·man ['bændzmən] N (pl -men) suonatore di banda.
band·stand ['bænd,stænd] N palco coperto dell'orchestra (in parco pubblico).
band·wagon ['bænd,wægən] N: **to jump on the bandwagon** (fig) seguire la corrente.
ban·dy ['bændɪ] VT (jokes, insults) scambiarsi
▶ **bandy about** VT + ADV (word, phrase) ripetere con insistenza; **to bandy sb's name about** parlare con insistenza di qn.
♦ **bandy-legged** ['bændɪ'lɛgɪd] ADJ dalle or con le gambe storte.
bane [beɪn] N: **it (or he etc) is the bane of my life** è la mia rovina.
bane·ful ['beɪnfʊl] ADJ dannoso(-a), nocivo(-a).
bang[1] [bæŋ] 1 N (noise: of explosion, gun) scoppio, colpo; (: of sth falling) tonfo; (blow) botta, colpo; **he closed the door with a bang** ha sbattuto la porta; **it went with a bang** (fam) è stato una bomba.
2 ADV: **to go bang** esplodere, fare bang; **to be bang on time** (Brit fam) spaccare il secondo; **bang went £10** mi (or gli etc) sono volate 10 sterline.
3 VT (thump) battere, picchiare; (hit, knock, slam) sbattere, battere (violentemente); **he banged the receiver down** ha sbattuto giù il telefono; **to bang one's head against a wall** (fig) battere or picchiare la testa contro il muro.
4 VI (explode) scoppiare, esplodere; (slam: door) sbattere; **to bang at/on sth** picchiare a/su qc; **to bang at the door** picchiare alla porta; **to bang into sth** sbattere contro qc.
▶ **bang about** (fam)
1 VT + ADV sbatacchiare.
2 VI far rumore.
bang[2] [bæŋ] N (fringe) frangetta.
bang·er ['bæŋə] N (Brit fam) **a** (sausage) salsiccia **b** (firework) mortaretto **c** (old car) macinino.
Bang·kok [bæŋ'kɒk] N Bangkok f.
Bang·la·desh [bæŋglə'dɛʃ] N il Bangladesh m.
Bang·la·deshi [,bɑ:ŋglə'dɛʃɪ] 1 ADJ del Bangladesh.
2 N abitante m/f del Bangladesh.
ban·gle ['bæŋgl] N braccialetto.
ban·ish ['bænɪʃ] VT: **to banish (from)** (person) bandire (da), esiliare (da); (thought, fear) bandire (da).
ban·ish·ment ['bænɪʃmənt] N esilio, bando.
ban·is·ters ['bænɪstəz] NPL ringhiera sg.
ban·jo ['bændʒəʊ] N banjo m inv.
bank [bæŋk] 1 N **a** (Fin, Med) banca; (Gambling) banco **b** (of river) sponda, riva; (: embankment) argine m; (of road, racetrack) terrapieno **c** (heap: of earth, mud) mucchio; (: of snow) cumulo; (: of clouds, sand) banco **d** (Aer) virata.
2 VT (money) depositare in banca.

$\boxed{3}$ VI **a** servirsi di una banca; **they bank with Pitt's** (*Comm*) sono clienti di Pitt's; **where do you bank?** qual è la sua banca?

b (*Aviat*) inclinarsi in virata

▶ **bank on** VI + PREP far conto su, contare su

▶ **bank up** VT + ADV (*sand*) ammucchiare.

♦ **bank account** N (*gen*) conto in banca; (*frm*) conto bancario.

♦ **bank balance** N saldo; **a healthy bank balance** un solido conto in banca.

bank·book ['bæŋkˌbʊk] N libretto di banca, libretto di risparmio.

♦ **bank card** N = **cheque card**.

♦ **bank charges** NPL (*Brit*) spese *fpl* bancarie; (*on currency transaction*) commissioni *fpl* bancarie.

♦ **bank clerk** N impiegato(-a) di banca.

♦ **bank draft** N tratta bancaria.

bank·er ['bæŋkə'] N banchiere *m*.

♦ **banker's card** ['bæŋkəz'kɑːd] N (*Brit*) = **cheque card**.

♦ **banker's order** N = **standing order**.

♦ **bank giro** N bancogiro.

♦ **bank holiday** N (*Brit*) giorno di festa civile (*in cui le banche chiudono*).

bank·ing ['bæŋkɪŋ] N attività bancaria; **to study banking** fare studi bancari *or* di tecnica bancaria.

♦ **banking hours** NPL orario di sportello.

♦ **banking house** N istituto bancario *or* di credito.

♦ **bank loan** N prestito bancario.

♦ **bank manager** N direttore(-trice) di banca.

bank·note ['bæŋkˌnəʊt] N banconota.

♦ **bank rate** N tasso ufficiale di sconto.

bank·roll ['bæŋkˌrəʊl] (*Am*) $\boxed{1}$ VT finanziare.

$\boxed{2}$ N finanziamento.

bank·rupt ['bæŋkrʌpt] $\boxed{1}$ ADJ fallito(-a); (*fam: penniless*) senza una lira; **to go bankrupt** fallire, fare fallimento *or* bancarotta.

$\boxed{2}$ N fallito(-a).

$\boxed{3}$ VT portare al fallimento.

bank·rupt·cy ['bæŋkrəptsɪ] N fallimento, bancarotta; **bankruptcy proceedings** procedura fallimentare.

♦ **bank statement** N estratto *m* conto *inv*.

ban·ner ['bænə'] N stendardo, bandiera; (*with slogan*) striscione *m*.

♦ **banner headline** N titolo a tutta pagina.

ban·nis·ters ['bænɪstəz] NPL = **banisters**.

banns [bænz] NPL pubblicazioni *fpl* (di matrimonio); **to read** *or* **publish the banns** esporre le pubblicazioni.

ban·quet ['bæŋkwɪt] N banchetto.

ban·tam ['bæntəm] N gallo "bantam".

bantam·weight ['bæntəmˌweɪt] N (*Boxing*) peso gallo.

ban·ter ['bæntə'] N scherzi *mpl* bonari.

BAOR [ˌbiːeɪəʊˈɑː'] N ABBR = *British Army of the Rhine*.

bap·tism ['bæptɪzəm] N battesimo.

bap·tis·mal [bæpˈtɪzməl] ADJ (*font, ceremony*) battesimale; (*robes*) da battesimo.

Bap·tist ['bæptɪst] ADJ, N (*Rel*) battista (*m/f*); **St John the Baptist** San Giovanni Battista.

bap·tize [bæpˈtaɪz] VT battezzare.

bar[1] [bɑː'] $\boxed{1}$ N **a** (*pub*) bar *m inv*; (*counter: in pub*) banco

b (*piece: of wood, metal etc*) sbarra, barra; (*of chocolate*) tavoletta; (*of electric fire*) elemento; **bar of soap** saponetta

c (*of window, cage*) sbarra; (*on door*) spranga; **bar (to)** (*fig: obstacle*) barriera (a), ostacolo (a); **behind bars** (*prisoner*) dietro le sbarre

d (*Law: professional group*): **the Bar** l'ordine *m* degli avvocati; **the prisoner at the bar** (*area in court*) l'imputato(-a); **to be called to** *or* (*Am*) **admitted to the Bar** essere ammesso(-a) all'ordine degli avvocati

e (*Mus*) battuta.

$\boxed{2}$ VT (*obstruct: way*) sbarrare; (*fasten: door, window*) sbarrare, sprangare; (*ban: person*) escludere; (: *activity, thing*) proibire, interdire.

bar[2] [bɑː'] PREP ad esclusione di, tranne; **the fastest sprinter bar none** il velocista più veloce in assoluto.

barb [bɑːb] N (*of hook, arrow*) punta.

Bar·ba·dos [bɑːˈbeɪdɒs] N Barbados *fsg*.

bar·bar·ian [bɑːˈbɛərɪən] N barbaro(-a).

bar·bar·ic [bɑːˈbærɪk], **bar·ba·rous** ['bɑːbərəs] ADJ (*cruelty, behaviour*) barbaro(-a); (*splendour*) barbarico (-a).

bar·ba·rism ['bɑːbəˌrɪzəm] N (*of society*) barbarie *f inv*, barbarismo.

bar·bar·ity [bɑːˈbærɪtɪ] N barbarie *f inv*; **the barbarities of modern warfare** le atrocità della guerra moderna.

bar·becue ['bɑːbɪkjuː] $\boxed{1}$ N (*grill*) barbecue *m inv*; (*party*) grigliata all'aperto.

$\boxed{2}$ VT cuocere alla brace.

♦ **barbecue sauce** N salsa piccante per barbecue.

barbed ['bɑːbd] ADJ (*hook, arrow*) con barbigli; (*fig: wit, comment*) pungente, tagliente.

♦ **barbed wire** ['bɑːbdˌwaɪə'] N filo spinato.

bar·ber ['bɑːbə'] N barbiere *m*; **to go to the barber's (shop)** andare dal barbiere.

bar·bi·tu·rate [bɑːˈbɪtjʊrɪt] N barbiturico.

Bar·ce·lo·na [bɑːsɪˈləʊnə] N Barcellona.

♦ **bar chart** N diagramma *m* a colonna.

♦ **bar code** N codice *m* a barre.

bard [bɑːd] N bardo.

bare [bɛə'] $\boxed{1}$ ADJ **a** (*gen*) nudo(-a); (*arms, legs*) nudo(-a), scoperto(-a); (*head*) scoperto(-a); (*landscape*) spoglio (-a), brullo(-a); (*ground, tree, room*) nudo(-a), spoglio (-a); (*cupboard*) vuoto(-a); (*Elec: wire*) scoperto(-a); **there's a bare patch on the carpet** c'è un pezzo spelacchiato nella moquette; **with his bare hands** a mani nude; **the bare facts** i fatti nudi e crudi; **to lay bare** (*fig*) mettere a nudo, svelare

b (*meagre: majority*) risicato(-a); **to strip sth down to the bare essentials** (*structure, narrative*) ridurre qc all'essenziale; **the bare necessities** lo stretto necessario; **to earn a bare living** guadagnare appena da vivere.

$\boxed{2}$ VT scoprire, denudare; (*teeth*) mostrare; **to bare one's heart** (*fig*) mettere a nudo il proprio animo.

bare·back ['bɛəˌbæk] ADV senza sella.

bare·faced ['bɛəˌfeɪst] ADJ sfacciato(-a), spudorato(-a).

bare·foot ['bɛəˌfʊt], **bare·footed** [ˌbɛəˈfʊtɪd] ADJ, ADV scalzo(-a), a piedi nudi.

bare·headed [ˌbɛəˈhɛdɪd] ADJ, ADV a capo scoperto.

bare·legged [ˌbɛəˈlɛgd] ADJ a gambe scoperte.

bare·ly ['bɛəlɪ] ADV appena; **they had barely enough money** avevano appena denaro a sufficienza; **he was so drunk he could barely stand** era così ubriaco che riusciva a malapena a stare in piedi.

bare·ness ['bɛənɪs] N nudità.

Bar·ents Sea ['bærənts'siː] N: **the Barents Sea** il mar di Barents.

bar·gain ['bɑːgɪn] $\boxed{1}$ N **a** (*transaction*) affare *m*; **to make a bargain with sb** fare un patto con qn; (*business*) concludere un affare con qn; **it's a bargain!** affare fatto!; **you drive a hard bargain** lei mi pone delle condizioni

difficili; **into the bargain** (*fig*) per giunta, per di più

 b (*cheap thing*) affare *m*, occasione *f*; (*in sales*) occasione; **to get a bargain** fare un affare; **it's a (real) bargain** è un affarone, è un'occasione.

 [2] VI (*negotiate*) contrattare; (*haggle*) tirare sul prezzo

▶ **bargain for** VI + PREP (*fam*): **to bargain for sth** aspettarsi qc; **he got more than he bargained for** non si aspettava quello che è successo.

♦ **bargain basement** N reparto occasioni.

♦ **bargain hunter** N *chi va in giro per i negozi a caccia di occasioni.*

bar·gain·ing ['bɑːgɪnɪŋ] [1] ADJ: **bargaining position** posizione *f* di negoziato; **to be in a weak/strong bargaining position** non avere/avere potere contrattuale; (*fig*) non essere/essere nella posizione di poter trattare; **bargaining power** potere *m* contrattuale; **bargaining process** processo di negoziato.

 [2] N contrattazione *f*.

♦ **bargain offer** N affare *m*, occasione *f*.

♦ **bargain price** N prezzo d'occasione.

♦ **bargain sale** N svendita, liquidazione *f*.

barge [bɑːdʒ] N chiatta, barcone *m*; (*ceremonial*) lancia

▶ **barge in** VI + ADV (*fam pej: enter*) precipitarsi dentro, piombare dentro; (: *interrupt*) intromettersi

▶ **barge into** VI + PREP (*fam: knock*) andare a sbattere contro, urtare contro; (: *enter*) piombare in; (: *interrupt*) intromettersi in.

bar·gee [bɑːˈdʒiː] N, (*Am*) **barge·man** ['bɑːdʒmən] N barcaiolo.

♦ **barge pole** N: **I wouldn't touch it with a barge pole** (*fam: revolting*) non lo toccherei nemmeno con un dito; (: *risky*) girerei alla larga.

bari·tone ['bærɪtəʊn] N baritono.

bar·ium ['bɛərɪəm] N bario.

♦ **barium meal** N (pasto di) bario.

bark¹ [bɑːk] N (*of tree*) corteccia.

bark² [bɑːk] [1] N (*of dog*) latrato, abbaiare *m*; **his bark is worse than his bite** abbaia ma non morde.

 [2] VI: **to bark (at)** abbaiare a; **to be barking up the wrong tree** essere sulla strada sbagliata, sbagliarsi di grosso

▶ **bark out** VT + ADV (*order*) urlare, abbaiare.

bark·ing ['bɑːkɪŋ] N abbaiare *m*.

bar·ley ['bɑːlɪ] N orzo.

♦ **barley sugar** N zucchero d'orzo.

♦ **barley water** N orzata.

bar·maid ['bɑːˌmeɪd] N barista *f*.

bar·man ['bɑːmən] N (*pl* **barmen**) barista *m*.

bar·my ['bɑːmɪ] ADJ (*Brit fam*) tocco(-a), toccato(-a), suonato(-a).

barn [bɑːn] N fienile *m*, granaio; (*for animals*) stalla.

bar·na·cle ['bɑːnəkl] N cirripede *m*.

♦ **barnacle goose** N oca dalle guance bianche.

♦ **barn dance** N danza campestre.

♦ **barn owl** N barbagianni *m inv* nostrano.

barn·yard ['bɑːnˌjɑːd] N aia.

ba·rom·eter [bəˈrɒmɪtəʳ] N barometro.

baro·met·ric [ˌbærəˈmɛtrɪk] ADJ (*pressure, chart*) barometrico(-a); (*reading*) del barometro.

bar·on ['bærən] N barone *m*; (*fig*) magnate *m*; **the press barons** i baroni della stampa; **the oil barons** i magnati del petrolio.

bar·on·ess ['bærənɪs] N baronessa.

bar·on·et ['bærənɪt] N baronetto.

ba·roque [bəˈrɒk] ADJ barocco(-a).

bar·rack ['bærək] VT (*Brit*): **to barrack sb** subissare qn di

grida e fischi.

bar·rack·ing ['bærəkɪŋ] N (*Brit*): **to give sb a barracking** subissare qn di grida e fischi.

♦ **barrack-room** ['bærək'rʊm] ADJ: **to be a barrack-room lawyer** (*fig*) *dare pareri (non richiesti) legali senza avere alcuna competenza.*

bar·racks ['bærəks] NPL caserma *sg*; **confined to barracks** consegnato(-a) in caserma.

bar·ra·cu·da [ˌbærəˈkjuːdə] N barracuda *m inv*.

bar·rage ['bærɑːʒ] N (*dam*) (opera di) sbarramento; (*Mil*) sbarramento; **a barrage of questions** una raffica di *or* un fuoco di fila di domande.

♦ **barrage balloon** N pallone *m* di sbarramento.

bar·rel ['bærəl] N barile *m*; (*of gun*) canna.

♦ **barrel organ** N organetto.

bar·ren ['bærən] ADJ (*land*) arido(-a), povero(-a); (*tree*) infruttuoso(-a); (*animal*) sterile.

bar·ren·ness ['bærənnɪs] N (*of land*) sterilità.

bar·ri·cade [ˌbærɪˈkeɪd] [1] N barricata.

 [2] VT barricare.

bar·ri·er ['bærɪəʳ] N barriera; (*Brit also:* **crash barrier**) guardrail *m inv*; (*Rail: in station*) cancello; (*fig*) barriera, ostacolo.

♦ **barrier cream** N (*Brit*) crema protettiva.

bar·ring ['bɑːrɪŋ] PREP = **bar 2**.

bar·ris·ter ['bærɪstəʳ] N (*Brit*) avvocato(-essa) (*con diritto di parlare davanti a tutte le corti*).

bar·row¹ ['bærəʊ] N (*wheelbarrow*) carriola; (*market stall*) carretto, carrettino.

bar·row² ['bærəʊ] N (*Archeol*) tumulo.

Bart. ABBR (*Brit*) = **baronet**.

bar·tender ['bɑːˌtɛndəʳ] N (*Am*) barista *m*.

bar·ter ['bɑːtəʳ] [1] VT: **to barter sth (for sth)** barattare qc (con qc).

 [2] VI: **to barter with sb (for sth)** barattare (qc) con qn.

 [3] N baratto.

bas·alt ['bæsɔːlt] N basalto.

base¹ [beɪs] [1] N (*gen, Mil*) base *f*.

 [2] VT (*troops*): **to base at** mettere di stanza a; (*opinion, relationship*): **to base on** basare su, fondare su; **I'm based in London** sono di base *or* ho base a Londra; **the job is based in London** la sede di lavoro è a Londra; **a Paris-based firm** una ditta con sede centrale a Parigi; **coffee-based** a base di caffè.

base² [beɪs] ADJ (*liter: action, motive*) basso(-a); (: *behaviour*) ignobile.

base·ball ['beɪsˌbɔːl] N baseball *m*.

base·board ['beɪsbɔːd] N (*Am*) battiscopa *m inv*.

♦ **base camp** N campo *m* base *inv*.

Ba·sel ['bɑːzəl] N = **Basle**.

base·less ['beɪslɪs] ADJ (*gossip etc*) infondato(-a).

base·line ['beɪsˌlaɪn] N (*Tennis*) linea di fondo; (*Baseball*) linea di base.

base·ly ['beɪslɪ] ADV (*liter: act, behave*) ignobilmente.

base·ment ['beɪsmənt] N (*of house*) seminterrato; (*of shop*) scantinato.

♦ **base metal** N metallo vile.

base·ness ['beɪsnɪs] N (*liter: of action, behaviour*) bassezza (morale).

♦ **base rate** N (*Fin*) tasso base.

bases ['beɪsiːz, 'beɪsɪz] **a** NPL of **basis b** NPL of **base**.

bash [bæʃ] (*fam*) [1] N **a** (*blow*) botta; **the car has had a bash** la macchina ha preso una botta; **I'll have a bash (at it)** (*Brit fam*) ci proverò

 b (*fam: party*) festa.

2 VT (*fam*: *thing*) sbattere; (: *person*) picchiare, menare
► **bash in** VT + ADV (*fam*) sfondare; **to bash sb's head in** spaccare la testa a qn; **bashed in** sfondato(-a)
► **bash on** VI: **to bash on with** andare avanti con
► **bash up** VT + ADV (*fam*: *car*) sfasciare; (: *Brit*: *person*) riempire di botte.
bash·ful ['bæʃfʊl] ADJ timido(-a).
bash·ful·ly ['bæʃfʊlɪ] ADV timidamente.
bash·ful·ness ['bæʃfʊlnɪs] N timidezza.
bash·ing ['bæʃɪŋ] N: **to take a bashing** prendere una batosta; **union-bashing** denigrazione *f* sistematica dei sindacati.
BASIC ['beɪsɪk] N ABBR (*Comput*: = *Beginner's All-purpose Symbolic Introduction Code*) BASIC *m*.
ba·sic ['beɪsɪk] ADJ **a** (*fundamental*: *reason, problem*) fondamentale, base *inv (after n)*; (*rudimentary*: *knowledge*) rudimentale; (: *equipment*: *essential*) essenziale; (: *poor*) primitivo(-a); (*elementary*: *principles, precautions, rules*) elementare; (*salary*) base *inv (after n)*; "**Basic Italian**" "Italiano elementare" **b** (*Chem*: *oxide, salt*) basico(-a).
ba·si·cal·ly ['beɪsɪklɪ] ADV fondamentalmente, sostanzialmente.
♦ **basic rate** N (*of tax*) aliquota minima.
bas·il ['bæzl] N basilico.
ba·sili·ca [bə'zɪlɪkə] N basilica.
ba·sin ['beɪsn] N (*Brit*: *for food*) terrina; (*washbasin*) lavabo, lavandino; (*Geog*) bacino.
ba·sis ['beɪsɪs] N (*pl* **bases** ['beɪsiːz]) (*foundation*) base *f*, fondamento; **on the basis of what you've said** in base a quello che hai detto.
bask [bɑːsk] VI: **to bask in the sun** crogiolarsi al sole; **to bask in sb's favour** godere del favore di qn.
bas·ket ['bɑːskɪt] N (*gen, bread basket, wastepaper basket*) cestino; (*large*) cesto, cesta; (*shopping basket*) cestino della spesa; (*at supermarket*) cestello; (*wicker basket*) paniere *m*; (*Basketball*) canestro.
basket·ball ['bɑːskɪtˌbɔːl] N pallacanestro *f*, basket *m*.
♦ **basketball player** N cestista *m/f*.
bask·ing shark ['bɑːskɪŋ'ʃɑːk] N squalo elefante.
Basle [bɑːl] N Basilea.
bas·ma·ti rice [bæsˌmɑː'tɪ'raɪs] N riso basmati, *varietà di riso usato nella cucina indiana*.
Basque [bæsk] 1 ADJ basco(-a).
2 N (*person*) basco(-a); (*language*) basco.
bass[1] [beɪs] (*Mus*) 1 ADJ basso(-a).
2 N (*voice*) voce *f* di basso; (*singer*) basso; (*double bass*) contrabbasso; (*guitar*) basso (elettrico); (*on hi-fi*) basso.
bass[2] [bæs] N (*fish*: *freshwater*) pesce *m* persico; (: *seawater*) spigola.
♦ **bass clef** [ˌbeɪs'klɛf] N chiave *f* di basso.
bas·soon [bə'suːn] N fagotto.
bas·tard ['bɑːstəd] 1 N bastardo(-a); (*fam! pej*) figlio di puttana (*fam!*).
2 ADJ (*child*) illegittimo(-a).
baste [beɪst] VT (*Culin*) ungere, inumidire col suo sugo; (*Sewing*) imbastire.
bas·ti·on ['bæstɪən] N (*castle wall*) bastione *m*; (*stronghold*: *fig*) baluardo.
BASW [ˌbiːeɪɛs'dʌbljuː] N ABBR (= *British Association of Social Workers*) ≈ sindacato degli assistenti sociali.
bat[1] [bæt] N (*Zool*) pipistrello; **to have bats in the belfry** (*fig fam*) essere picchiato(-a) *or* suonato(-a); **like a bat out of hell** come un fulmine.
bat[2] [bæt] 1 N (*Cricket, Baseball*) mazza; (*Brit*: *Tabletennis*) racchetta; **off one's own bat** (*fam*) di testa

propria, di propria iniziativa.
2 VI (*Sport*) battere.
3 VT: **he didn't bat an eyelid** (*fam*) non ha battuto ciglio.
batch [bætʃ] N (*of applicants, letters*) gruppo; (*of work*) sezione *f*; (*of goods*) partita, lotto; (*of recruits*) contingente *m*; (*of bread*) infornata; (*of papers*) cumulo.
♦ **batch processing** N (*Comput*) elaborazione *f* a blocchi.
bat·ed ['beɪtɪd] ADJ: **with bated breath** col fiato sospeso.
bath [bɑːθ] 1 N (*pl* **baths** [bɑːðz]) **a** (*tub, wash*) bagno; **room with bath** camera con bagno; **to have a bath** fare *or* farsi un bagno **b** ESP PL: **swimming baths** piscina.
2 VI fare *or* farsi un bagno.
3 VT fare il bagno a.
bath·cap ['bɑːθˌkæp] N cuffia per la doccia.
Bath·chair ['bɑːθˌtʃɛəʳ] N (*Brit*) poltrona a rotelle.
bathe [beɪð] 1 N (*in sea, pool*) bagno.
2 VI **a** (*swim*) fare i bagni, bagnarsi; **to go bathing** andare a fare il bagno *or* a nuotare **b** (*Am*) = **bath** 2.
3 VT **a** (*wound*) lavare **b** (*Am*) = **bath** 3.
bath·er ['beɪðəʳ] N bagnante *m/f*.
bath·ing ['beɪðɪŋ] N bagni *mpl*; "**bathing is forbidden**" "è vietata la balneazione".
♦ **bathing cap** N cuffia da bagno.
♦ **bathing costume, bathing suit** N costume *m* da bagno.
♦ **bathing trunks** ['beɪðɪŋˌtrʌŋks] NPL pantaloncini *mpl* *or* costume *m* da bagno.
bath·mat ['bɑːθˌmæt] N tappetino da bagno.
♦ **bath oil** N olio da bagno.
bath·robe ['bɑːθˌrəʊb] N (*towelling*) accappatoio; (*Am*) = **dressing gown**.
bath·room ['bɑːθrʊm] N (*stanza da*) bagno.
♦ **bathroom cabinet** N armadietto (da bagno).
♦ **bathroom scales** NPL bilancia pesapersone.
baths [bɑːðz] NPL bagni *mpl* pubblici.
♦ **bath towel** N asciugamano da bagno.
bath·tub ['bɑːθˌtʌb] N (*old*) vasca da bagno.
bath·water ['bɑːθˌwɔːtəʳ] N acqua del bagno.
bathy·scaph ['bæθɪˌskæf] N batiscafo.
bat·man ['bætˌmæn] N (*pl* **batmen**) (*Brit Mil*) attendente *m*.
baton ['bætən] N (*Mus*) bacchetta; (*Mil*) bastone *m* di comando; (*of policeman*) sfollagente *m inv*, manganello; (*in race*) testimone *m*.
♦ **baton charge** N carica con lo sfollagente.
bats·man ['bætsmən] N (*pl* **-men**) **a** (*Cricket*) battitore *m* **b** (*Aer*) segnalatore *m*.
bat·tal·ion [bə'tælɪən] N battaglione *m*.
bat·ten ['bætən] N listello di legno; (*Carpentry*) assicella, correntino; (*for flooring*) tavola; (*Naut*) serretta; (: *on sail*) stecca
► **batten down** VT + ADV (*Naut*): **to batten down the hatches** chiudere i boccaporti; (*fig*) prepararsi per un'emergenza.
bat·ter[1] ['bætəʳ] N (*Culin*) pastella.
bat·ter[2] ['bætəʳ] VT (*person*) ridurre in cattivo stato; (*wife, baby*) maltrattare; (*subj*: *wind, waves*) colpire violentemente
► **batter down** VT + ADV abbattere, buttare giù.
bat·tered ['bætəd] ADJ (*car, building*) malridotto(-a); (*baby, wife*) maltrattato(-a), vittima *inv* di maltrattamenti; (*hat*) sformato(-a); (*pan*) ammaccato(-a).
bat·ter·ing ram ['bætərɪŋˌræm] N ariete *m*.
bat·tery ['bætərɪ] N (*Elec*) pila; (*Aut, Mil*) batteria; (*large number*: *of lights, tests*) batteria; (: *of questions*) pioggia,

raffica.
♦ **battery charger** N caricabatterie *m inv.*
♦ **battery farming** N allevamento in batteria.
♦ **battery lead connection** ['bætərɪ'liːdkə'nɛkʃən] N (*Aut*) morsetto della batteria.
bat·tle ['bætl] ⑴ N (*Mil*) battaglia, combattimento; (*fig*) lotta, battaglia; **killed in battle** ucciso in combattimento; **I had quite a battle to get permission** ho dovuto lottare per ottenere il permesso; **a battle of wits** una gara d'ingegno; **that's half the battle** (*fam*) è già una mezza vittoria; **to fight a losing battle** (*fig*) battersi per una causa persa.
⑵ VI (*fig*): **to battle (for)** lottare (per), combattere (per); **he battled to retain his self-control** dovette fare uno sforzo per controllarsi; **to battle against the wind** lottare con *or* contro il vento.
♦ **battle-axe** ['bætəlˌæks] N (*pej*): **she was a terrible old battle-axe** era proprio un carabiniere.
♦ **battle cruiser** N incrociatore *m* da battaglia.
♦ **battle cry** N grido di battaglia.
♦ **battle dress** N uniforme *f* da combattimento.
battle·field ['bætlˌfiːld], **battle·ground** ['bætlˌɡraʊnd] N campo di battaglia.
♦ **battle formation** N schieramento di battaglia.
bat·tle·ments ['bætlmənts] NPL bastioni *mpl.*
♦ **battle royal** N (*fig: quarrel*) violenta discussione *f.*
♦ **battle-scarred** ['bætəlˌskɑːd] ADJ (*person*) con cicatrici di guerra; (*town*) che mostra i segni della guerra.
battle·ship ['bætlˌʃɪp] N nave *f* da guerra.
♦ **battle zone** N zona del conflitto.
bat·ty ['bætɪ] ADJ (*comp* **-ier**, *superl* **-iest**) (*fam: person*) svitato(-a), strambo(-a); (: *behaviour, idea*) strampalato (-a); **I must be going batty!** sto proprio rimbambendo!
bau·ble ['bɔːbl] N ninnolo.
baud [bɔːd] N (*Comput*) baud *m inv.*
baulk [bɔːlk] VI = **balk**.
baux·ite ['bɔːksaɪt] N bauxite *f.*
Ba·varia [bə'vɛərɪə] N Baviera.
Ba·var·ian [bə'vɛərɪən] ADJ, N bavarese (*m/f*).
bawdy ['bɔːdɪ] ADJ piccante, spinto(-a), salace; **bawdy song** canzonaccia.
bawl [bɔːl] VI (*cry*) strillare; (*shout*) urlare, sbraitare
► **bawl out** VT + ADV **a** urlare (a squarciagola)
 b (*fam*): **to bawl sb out** fare una sfuriata *or* una lavata di testa a qn.
bay¹ [beɪ] N (*Geog*) baia; **the Bay of Biscay** il golfo di Biscaglia.
bay² [beɪ] N **a** (*Archit*) campata **b** (*Brit: for parking*) piazzola di sosta; (*for loading*) piazzale *m* di (sosta e) carico.
bay³ [beɪ] ⑴ VI (*hound*) abbaiare, latrare.
⑵ N (*bark*) latrato; **to keep sb/sth at bay** (*fig*) tenere a bada qn/qc.
bay⁴ [beɪ] ADJ (*horse*) baio(-a).
bay⁵ [beɪ] N (*also:* **bay tree**) alloro.
♦ **bay bar** N (*Geog*) barra.
♦ **bay leaf** ['beɪˌliːf] N foglia d'alloro.
bayo·net ['beɪənɪt] ⑴ N baionetta.
⑵ VT infilzare con la baionetta.
♦ **bayonet charge** N carica alla baionetta.
♦ **bay window** N bovindo.
ba·zaar [bə'zɑːʳ] N (*sale of work*) vendita di beneficenza; (*Oriental market*) bazar *m inv.*
ba·zoo·ka [bə'zuːkə] N bazooka *m inv.*

BB [ˌbiː'biː] N ABBR (*Brit*: = *Boys' Brigade*) *organizzazione giovanile a fine educativo.*
B & B, b. and b. [ˌbiːənd'biː] N ABBR = **bed and breakfast.**
BBB [ˌbiːbiː'biː] N ABBR (*Am*: = *Better Business Bureau*) *organismo per la difesa dei consumatori.*
BBC [ˌbiːbiː'siː] N ABBR (= *British Broadcasting Corporation*) *azienda statale che fornisce il servizio radiofonico e televisivo in Gran Bretagna.*
BC [ˌbiː'siː] ADV ABBR (= *before Christ*) a.C.
BCG [ˌbiːsiː'dʒiː] N ABBR (= *Bacillus Calmette-Guérin*) vaccino antitubercolare.
BD [ˌbiː'diː] N ABBR (= *Bachelor of Divinity*) ≈ laurea in teologia.
B/D ABBR = **bank draft.**
BDS [ˌbiːdiː'ɛs] N ABBR (= *Bachelor of Dental Surgery*) laurea in odontoiatria e protesi dentaria.

be [biː] (*present* **am, is, are**, *pt* **was, were**, *pp* **been**)
⑴ VI
ⓐ (*exist*) essere, esistere;
▷**leave it** *as* **it is** lascialo così
▷**the best singer that** *ever* **was** il miglior cantante mai esistito
▷*how much* **was it?** quanto è costato?, quant'era?
▷*let* **me be!** lasciami in pace!
▷*so* **be it** sia pure, e sia
▷**be** *that* **as it may** sia come sia, comunque sia
▷**his wife** *to* **be** la sua futura moglie
▷**to be or not to be** essere o non essere
ⓑ (*in place*) essere, trovarsi;
▷**she won't be** *here* **tomorrow** non ci sarà domani
▷**we've been** *here* **for ages** sono secoli che siamo qui
▷**Edinburgh is** *in* **Scotland** Edimburgo è *or* si trova in Scozia
▷**it's** *on* **the table** è *or* sta sul tavolo
ⓒ: **there is** c'è;
▷**there are** ci sono
▷**there were 3 of us** eravamo in 3
▷**there will be** *dancing* si ballerà
▷**there was once a** *house* **here** qua una volta c'era una casa
▷**let there be** *light* sia la luce
ⓓ (*presenting, pointing out*): **here is** ⓞᴿ **here are** ecco
▷**there is** ⓞᴿ **there are** (*over there*) ecco
▷*here* **you are (take it)** ecco qua (prendi)
▷**there's the church** ecco la chiesa
ⓔ (*come, go: esp in perfect tense*)
▷**I've been** *to* **China** sono stato in Cina
▷*where* **have you been?** dove sei stato?
⑵ COPULATIVE VB
ⓐ essere;
▷**2 and 2 are 4** 2 più 2 fa 4
▷**he's** *a* **pianist** è (un) pianista
▷**they're** *English* sono inglesi
▷**be** *good*! sii buono!
▷**I'm** *hot* ho caldo
▷**the book is** *in* **French** il libro è in francese
▷**I'm** *not* **Sue, I'm** *Mary* non sono Sue, sono Mary
▷**he's** *tall* è alto
ⓑ (*health*) stare;
▷**I'm** *better* **now** ora sto meglio
▷*how* **are you?** come stai (*or* sta)?
ⓒ (*age*): *how old* **is she? — she's** *9* quanti anni ha? — ne ha 9 *or* ha 9 anni.

3 IMPERS VB
a
▷ **it is *said* that** ... si dice che... + *sub*;
▷ **it is *possible* that** ... può darsi *or* essere che... + *sub*
b (*time*) essere;
▷ **it's the *3rd* of May** è il 3 (di) maggio
▷ **it's 8 *o'clock*** sono le 8
c (*measurement*)
▷ **it's 5 *km* to the village** da qui al paese sono 5 km
d (*weather*) fare;
▷ **it's too *hot*** fa troppo caldo
e (*emphatic*)
▷ **it's only *me*** sono solo io.
4 AUX VB
a (*with present participle*: *forming continuous tenses*);
▷ **they're *coming* tomorrow** vengono domani
▷ **what are you *doing*?** che fai?, che stai facendo?
▷ **he's always *grumbling*** brontola sempre, non fa che brontolare
▷ **I'll be *seeing* you** ci vediamo
▷ **I've been *waiting* for her for 2 hours** l'aspetto da 2 ore
b (*with past participle*: *forming passives*) essere;
▷ **what's to be *done*?** che fare?
▷ **he is nowhere to be *found*** non lo si trova da nessuna parte
▷ **to be *killed*** essere *or* venire ucciso (-a)
▷ **the box had been *opened*** la scatola era stata aperta
c (*in tag questions*)
▷ **he's back again, *is* he?** così è tornato, eh?
▷ **he's handsome, *isn't* he?** è un bell'uomo, vero?
▷ **it was fun, *wasn't* it?** è stato bello, no?
d (+ *to* + *infinitive*)
▷ **he's to be *congratulated* on his work** dobbiamo fargli i complimenti per il suo lavoro
▷ **you're to *do* as I tell you** devi fare come ti dico
▷ **he was to *have come* yesterday** sarebbe dovuto venire ieri
▷ **he's not to *open* it** non deve aprirlo
▷ **the car is to be *sold*** abbiamo (*or* hanno *etc*) intenzione di vendere la macchina
▷ **am I to *understand* that ...?** devo dedurre che...?
e (*modal: supposition*)
▷ **if it was or were to snow** ... (se) dovesse nevicare...
▷ **if I were you** ... se fossi in te...

▶ **be in for** VI + ADV + PREP: **you'll only be in for a disappointment** non puoi che restare deluso; **we may be in for some trouble here** mi sa che qui potremmo avere delle grane
▶ **be on to** VI + ADV + PREP: **to be on to something** essere sulla pista giusta; **I think they're on to us** penso che abbiano dei sospetti su di noi.
B/E ABBR = **bill of exchange**.
beach [biːtʃ] **1** N spiaggia.
    2 VT tirare in secco.
♦ **beach ball** N pallone *m* da mare *or* da spiaggia.
♦ **beach buggy** N dune buggy *f inv*.
beach·comber ['biːtʃˌkəumə'] N *persona che si aggira sulle spiagge alla ricerca di soldi, oggetti, ecc.*
beach·head ['biːtʃˌhɛd] N testa di sbarco.
beach·wear ['biːtʃˌwɛə'] N abbigliamento da spiaggia.

bea·con ['biːkən] N (*fire*) fuoco di segnalazione; (*lighthouse*) faro, fanale *m*; (*radio beacon*) radiofaro; (*marker*) segnale *m*.
bead [biːd] N perlina; (*of rosary*) grano; (*of dew, sweat*) goccia; **beads** NPL (*necklace*) collana; (*also*: **rosary beads**) corona (del rosario), rosario.
beady ['biːdɪ] ADJ: **beady eyes** occhi *mpl* piccoli e penetranti.
♦ **beady-eyed** ['biːdɪˈaɪd] ADJ dagli occhi piccoli e penetranti.
bea·gle ['biːgl] N bracchetto.
beak [biːk] N becco.
beak·er ['biːkə'] N coppa; (*Chem*) becher *m inv*.
♦ **be-all and end-all** [ˌbiːɔːlənd'ɛndɔːl]: **the be-all and end-all (of sth)** il fine ultimo (di qc).
beam [biːm] **1** N **a** (*Archit*) trave *f*
    b (*Naut*) baglio
    c (*of light, sunlight*) raggio; (*of torch*) fascio (di luce); (*Radio*) fascio (d'onde); **to drive with headlights on full** *or* (*Am*) **high beam** guidare con gli abbaglianti accesi
    d (*smile*) sorriso raggiante.
    2 VT (*Radio*) trasmettere con antenna direzionale.
    3 VI (*smile*) sorridere radiosamente; **to beam at sb** fare un largo sorriso a qn.
beam·ing ['biːmɪŋ] ADJ (*sun*) splendente; (*face, smile*) raggiante.
bean [biːn] N fagiolo; (*broad bean*) fava; (*runner bean*) fagiolino; (*of coffee*) grano, chicco; **full of beans** (*fam: child*) che ha l'argento vivo addosso; (: *adult*) in gran forma.
bean·pole ['biːnˌpəʊl] N (*fam*) spilungone(-a).
bean·sprouts ['biːnˌsprауts], **bean·shoots** ['biːnˌʃuːts] NPL germogli *mpl* di soia.
bear[1] [bɛə'] (*vb: pt* **bore**, *pp* **borne**) **1** VT **a** (*carry: burden, signature, date, name*) portare; (: *news, message*) recare; (: *traces, signs*) mostrare; **to bear some resemblance to** somigliare a; **he bore himself like a soldier** (*of posture*) aveva un portamento militare; (*of behaviour*) si comportò da soldato; **the love he bore her** l'amore che le portava; **to bear sb ill will** portare *or* serbare rancore a qn
    b (*support: weight*) reggere, sostenere; (: *cost*) sostenere; (: *responsibility*) assumere; (: *comparison*) reggere a; **the roof couldn't bear the weight of the snow** il tetto non ha retto il *or* al peso della neve
    c (*endure: pain*) sopportare; (*stand up to: inspection, examination*) reggere a; **it won't bear close examination** non bisogna guardarlo troppo da vicino; **I can't bear him** non lo posso soffrire *or* sopportare; **I can't bear to look** non ho il coraggio di guardare; **it doesn't bear thinking about** non ci si può neanche pensare
    d (*produce: fruit*) produrre, dare; (: *young*) partorire; (: *child*) generare, dare alla luce; (*Fin: interest*) fruttare.
    2 VI **a** (*move*): **to bear right/left** andare a destra/sinistra, piegare a destra/sinistra; **to bear away** (*Naut*) poggiare
    b : **to bring sth to bear (on)** (*influence, powers of persuasion*) esercitare qc (su); **to bring pressure to bear on sb** fare pressione su qn; **to bring one's mind to bear on sth** concentrarsi su qc
▶ **bear down** VI + ADV: **to bear down (on)** (*ship*) venire dritto (contro); (*person*) stare per piombare addosso (a)
▶ **bear on** VI + PREP (*frm*) essere in relazione con

▶ **bear out** VT + ADV (*theory, suspicion*) confermare, convalidare; (*person*) dare il proprio appoggio a

▶ **bear up** VI + ADV farsi coraggio; **he bore up well under the strain** ha sopportato bene lo stress

▶ **bear with** VI + PREP (*sb's moods, temper*) sopportare (con pazienza); **bear with me a minute** solo un attimo, prego; **if you'll bear with me** ... se ha la cortesia di aspettare (un attimo) ... .

bear² [bɛəʳ] N orso(-a); (*Stock Exchange*) ribassista *m/f*; **the Great Bear** (*Astron*) l'Orsa Maggiore; **to be like a bear with a sore head** (*hum*) avere la luna di traverso.

bear·able ['bɛərəbl] ADJ sopportabile.

♦ **bear cub** N cucciolo di orso.

beard [bɪəd] 1 N barba.
2 VT: **to beard the lion in his den** (*hum*) affrontare il nemico in casa sua.

beard·ed ['bɪədɪd] ADJ barbuto(-a).

bear·er ['bɛərəʳ] N (*of news, cheque*) portatore *m*; (*of passport*) titolare *m/f*.

♦ **bearer bond** N obbligazione *f* al portatore.

♦ **bear garden** N (*fig*) manicomio.

bear·ing ['bɛərɪŋ] N a (*of person*) portamento
b (*relevance*): **bearing (on)** attinenza (con)
c (*Tech*): **ball bearings** NPL cuscinetti *mpl* a sfere
d (*position*): **to take a compass bearing** effettuare un rilevamento con la bussola; **to take a ship's bearings** fare il punto nave; **to get** *or* **find one's bearings** (*fig*) orientarsi; **to lose one's bearings** (*fig*) perdere l'orientamento.

♦ **bear pit** N gabbia degli orsi.

bear·skin ['bɛəˌskɪn] N pelle *f* d'orso; (*hat*) colbacco.

beast [biːst] N (*animal, fam: disagreeable person*) bestia, animale *m*; (*cruel person*) bruto; **beast of burden** bestia da soma; **it's a beast of a job** (*fam*) è un lavoraccio.

beast·ly ['biːstlɪ] ADJ (*fam: person, behaviour*) insopportabile; (: *food*) orrendo(-a); (: *weather*) da cani.

beat [biːt] (*vb: pt* **beat**, *pp* **beaten**) 1 N a (*of drum: single beat*) colpo; (: *repeated beating*) rullo; (*of heart*) battito; (*Mus: rhythm*) ritmo; (: *quaver, crotchet*) battuta; **to give the beat** dare il tempo
b (*of policeman*) giro d'ispezione (a piedi), ronda; **on the beat** in giro d'ispezione, di ronda
c (*Phys*) battimento.
2 VT a (*hit*) battere, picchiare; (*person: as punishment*) picchiare; (: *with stick*) bastonare; (*carpet*) battere, sbattere; (*drum*) suonare; **the bird beat its wings** l'uccello batteva le ali; **to beat time** (*Mus*) battere il tempo; **beat it!** (*fam*) fila!, aria!
b (*defeat: team, army*) battere, sconfiggere; (*record*) battere; **I beat him to it** (*fam*) ci sono arrivato prima di lui; **nothing beats a good cup of coffee** (*fam*) non c'è niente di meglio di un bel caffè; **that beats everything!** (*fam*) questo è il colmo!; **it's got me beat(en)** (*fam*) devo arrendermi
c (*Culin*) sbattere, battere.
3 VI (*heart*) battere, palpitare; (*drums*) rullare; **to beat on a door** picchiare a una porta; **the rain was beating against the windows** la pioggia batteva contro le finestre; **don't beat about the bush** non menare il can per l'aia.
4 ADJ a (*pred: fam: tired*) sfinito(-a)
b (*usu attr: group, music*) beat *inv*

▶ **beat back** VT + ADV respingere

▶ **beat out** VT + ADV (*flames*) spegnere (battendo); (*dent*) ribattere, martellare; (*rhythm*) battere

▶ **beat down** 1 VT + ADV (*door*) abbattere, buttare giù; (*price*) far abbassare; (*seller*) far scendere.
2 VI + ADV (*rain*) scrosciare; (*sun*) picchiare

▶ **beat off** VT + ADV respingere

▶ **beat up** VT + ADV (*person*) picchiare, pestare; (*egg whites*) montare.

beat·en ['biːtn] 1 PP of **beat**.
2 ADJ (*metal*) battuto(-a); **off the beaten track** fuori mano.

♦ **beaten-up** [ˌbiːtən'ʌp] ADJ (*car etc*) malconcio(-a).

beat·er ['biːtəʳ] N (*Culin*) frullino; (*carpet beater*) battipanni *m inv*.

bea·tif·ic [ˌbiːə'tɪfɪk] ADJ (*liter: smile, expression*) beato(-a).

be·ati·fi·ca·tion [bɪˌætɪfɪ'keɪʃən] N (*Rel*) beatificazione *f*.

be·ati·fy [bɪ'ætɪfaɪ] VT (*Rel*) beatificare.

beat·ing ['biːtɪŋ] N a (*punishment*) botte *fpl*; **to give sb a beating** riempire qn di botte b (*defeat*) sconfitta, batosta; **to take a beating** prendere una (bella) batosta.

♦ **beating up** N (*pl* **beatings up**): **to give sb a beating up** pestare qn.

beat·nik ['biːtnɪk] N beatnik *m/f inv*.

♦ **beat-up** [ˌbiːt'ʌp] ADJ (*fam*) scassato(-a).

beau·ti·cian [bjuː'tɪʃən] N estetista *m/f*.

beau·ti·ful ['bjuːtɪfʊl] ADJ bello(-a), splendido(-a).

beau·ti·ful·ly ['bjuːtɪflɪ] ADV splendidamente, magnificamente.

beau·ti·fy ['bjuːtɪfaɪ] VT abbellire.

beau·ty ['bjuːtɪ] 1 N (*concept*) bello; (*of person, thing*) bellezza; **beauty is in the eye of the beholder** non è bello ciò che è bello, è bello ciò che piace; **the beauty of it is that** ... il bello è che...; **his car's a beauty!** (*fam*) ha una macchina che è una meraviglia *or* una bellezza!.
2 ADJ (*consultant, counter*) di bellezza.

♦ **beauty case** N beauty-case *m inv*.

♦ **beauty contest** N concorso di bellezza.

♦ **beauty queen** N miss *f inv*, reginetta di bellezza.

♦ **beauty salon** N istituto di bellezza.

♦ **beauty sleep** N: **to get one's beauty sleep** (*hum*) farsi un sonno ristoratore.

♦ **beauty spot** N (*in country*) luogo di particolare bellezza; (*on face*) neo.

♦ **beauty treatment** N trattamento di bellezza.

bea·ver ['biːvəʳ] N castoro.

▶ **beaver away** VI + ADV lavorare di buona lena.

be·calmed [bɪ'kɑːmd] ADJ: **to be becalmed** essere fermo (-a) per mancanza di vento.

be·came [bɪ'keɪm] PT of **become**.

be·cause [bɪ'kɒz] CONJ (*gen*) perché; **all the more surprising because** ancora più sorprendente dal momento che *or* poiché; **because of** a causa di.

beck [bɛk] N: **to be at sb's beck and call** dover essere a completa disposizione di qn.

beck·on ['bɛkən] VT, VI: **to beckon to sb** chiamare qn con un cenno; **he beckoned me in/over** mi ha fatto cenno di entrare/di avvicinarmi.

be·come [bɪ'kʌm] (*vb: pt* **became**, *pp* **become**) 1 VI diventare, divenire; **to become famous** diventare famoso(-a); **to become fat/thin** ingrassare/dimagrire; **to become angry** arrabbiarsi; **to become accustomed to sth** abituarsi a qc; **to become a doctor** diventare medico; **it became known that** si è venuto a sapere che.
2 IMPERS VB: **what has become of him?** che ne è stato di lui?; **whatever can have become of that book?** dove sarà mai finito quel libro?.
3 VT: **it does not become her** (*dress etc*) non le sta bene;

(*behaviour*) non le si addice.

be·com·ing [bɪ'kʌmɪŋ] ADJ (*frm*: *clothes*) grazioso(-a), che dona; (: *behaviour, language*) adatto(-a), che si addice alla situazione.

BECTU ['bɛktu:] N ABBR (*Brit*)= *Broadcasting Entertainment Cinematographic and Theatre Union*.

BEd [ˌbi:'ɛd] N ABBR (= *Bachelor of Education*) ≈ laurea con abilitazione all'insegnamento.

bed [bɛd] N **a** letto; **to go to bed** andare a letto; **to go to bed with sb** andare a letto con qn; **to get out of bed** alzarsi dal letto; **to get out of bed on the wrong side** alzarsi col piede sbagliato; **to make the bed** (ri)fare il letto; **to put sb to bed** mettere qn a letto; **I was in bed** ero a letto; **could you give me a bed for the night?** puoi tenermi a dormire per stanotte?; **his life's not a bed of roses** la sua vita non è tutta rose e fiori
 b (*of sea, lake*) fondo; (*of river*) letto
 c (*flower bed*) aiuola; **oyster bed** banco di ostriche; **vegetable bed** orticello
 d (*layer: of coal, ore, clay*) strato; (: *in roadbuilding*) massicciata
 ► **bed out** VT + ADV (*plants*) piantare a intervalli regolari
 ► **bed down** VI + ADV sistemarsi (per dormire).
 ◆ **bed and breakfast** N ≈ pensione *f* familiare; **to book in for bed and breakfast** prenotare una camera con prima colazione.

bed·bath ['bɛdˌbɑ:θ] N: **to give sb a bedbath** lavare qn a letto.

bed·bug ['bɛdˌbʌg] N cimice *f* (dei letti).

bed·clothes ['bɛdˌkləʊðz] NPL coperte e lenzuola *fpl*.

bed·cov·er ['bɛdˌkʌvəʳ] N copriletto.

bed·ding ['bɛdɪŋ] N coperte e lenzuola *fpl*; (*for animal*) lettiera.
 ◆ **bedding plane** N (*Geol*) piano di stratificazione.
 ◆ **bedding plant** N piantina da mettere a dimora.

be·deck [bɪ'dɛk] VT ornare, decorare.

be·dev·il [bɪ'dɛvl] VT (*person*) affliggere, tormentare; (*enterprise*) intralciare, ostacolare continuamente.

bed·fellow ['bɛdˌfɛləʊ] N: **they are strange bedfellows** (*fig*) fanno una coppia ben strana.

bed·head ['bɛdˌhɛd] N testata (del letto).
 ◆ **bed jacket** N liseuse *f inv*.

bed·lam ['bɛdləm] N baraonda.
 ◆ **bed linen** N biancheria da letto.

Bedou·in ['bɛdʊɪn] N, ADJ beduino(-a).

bed·pan ['bɛdˌpæn] N padella.

bed·post ['bɛdˌpəʊst] N colonnina del letto.

be·drag·gled [bɪ'drægld] ADJ (*person, clothes*) sbrindellato(-a); (*hair*) scompigliato(-a); (*wet*) bagnato(-a) fradicio(-a).

bed·rid·den ['bɛdˌrɪdən] ADJ costretto(-a) *or* inchiodato(-a) a letto.

bed·rock ['bɛdˌrɒk] N (*Geol*) basamento; (*fig*) fondamento, base *f*; **the moral bedrock of the nation** il fondamento morale della nazione.

bed·roll ['bɛdˌrəʊl] N sacco a pelo.

bed·room ['bɛdˌrʊm] N camera (da letto), stanza da letto.
 ◆ **bedroom farce** N (*Theatre*) pochade *f inv*.
 ◆ **bedroom slipper** N pantofola.
 ◆ **bedroom suite** N camera a letto (*mobili*).

Beds [bɛdz] N ABBR (*Brit*)= *Bedfordshire*.
 ◆ **bed settee** N divano *m* letto *inv*.

bed·side ['bɛdˌsaɪd] 1 N: **at his bedside** al suo capezzale.
 2 ADJ: **to have a good bedside manner** (*doctor*) saper trattare i pazienti.

◆ **bedside lamp** N lampada da comodino, abat-jour *m inv*.
 ◆ **bedside rug** N scendiletto.
 ◆ **bedside table** N comodino.
 ◆ **bed-sit** ['bɛdˌsɪt], **bed-sitter** ['bɛdˌsɪtəʳ], **bed-sitting room** [ˌbɛd'sɪtɪŋrʊm] N monolocale *m*.

bed·socks ['bɛdˌsɒks] NPL calze *fpl* da notte.

bed·sore ['bɛdˌsɔ:'] N piaga da decubito.

bed·spread ['bɛdˌsprɛd] N copriletto.

bed·stead ['bɛdˌstɛd] N fusto del letto.

bed·straw ['bɛdˌstrɔ:] N: **lady's bedstraw** (*Bot*) erba zolfina.

bed·time ['bɛdˌtaɪm] 1 N: **it's bedtime** è ora di andare a letto; **it's past your bedtime** a quest'ora dovresti già essere a letto; **John's bedtime is 8.00 pm** John va a letto alle 8.
 2 ADJ: **will you tell me a bedtime story?** mi racconti una storia prima di dormire?
 ◆ **bed-wetting** ['bɛdˌwɛtɪŋ] N incontinenza notturna.

bee[1] [bi:] N (*Zool*) ape *f*; **to have a bee in one's bonnet (about sth)** avere la fissazione (di qc).

bee[2] [bi:] N (*esp Am*): **spelling bee** gara di ortografia; **to have a sewing bee** riunirsi per cucire.

beech [bi:tʃ] N faggio.

beech·nut ['bi:tʃˌnʌt] N faggina.

beef [bi:f] N (*Culin*) manzo; **roast beef** roast beef *m inv*, arrosto di manzo
 ► **beef up** VT + ADV (*fam*) rinforzare.
 ◆ **beef breed** N razza da macello *or* da carne.

beef·bur·ger ['bi:fˌbɜ:gəʳ] N hamburger *m inv*.
 ◆ **beef cattle** NPL bovini *mpl* da macello.

beef·eater ['bi:fˌi:təʳ] N *guardia della Torre di Londra*.
 ◆ **beef olive** N (*Culin*) involtino di manzo.

beef·steak ['bi:fˌsteɪk] N bistecca di manzo.
 ◆ **beef tea** N brodo di manzo, consommé *m inv*.

beefy [ˌbi:fɪ] ADJ (*fam*) muscoloso(-a); **a big beefy fellow** un tipo grande e grosso.

bee·hive ['bi:ˌhaɪv] N alveare *m*.

bee·keeper ['bi:ˌki:pəʳ] N apicoltore *m*.

bee·keep·ing ['bi:ˌki:pɪŋ] N apicoltura.

bee·line ['bi:ˌlaɪn] N: **to make a beeline for sb/sth** (*fam*) andare diretto(-a) verso qn/qc.

been [bi:n] PP of **be**.

beep [bi:p] 1 N (*of horn*) colpo di clacson; (*of phone etc*) segnale *m* (acustico), bip *m inv*.
 2 VI (*horn*) suonare; (*computer, pager*) fare bip.

beep·er ['bi:pəʳ] N cicalino; (*of doctor etc*) cercapersone *m inv*.

beer [bɪəʳ] N birra.
 ◆ **beer belly** N (*fam*) stomaco da bevitore.
 ◆ **beer can** N lattina di birra.
 ◆ **beer glass** N boccale *m*, bicchiere *m* da birra.

bees·wax ['bi:zˌwæks] N cera d'api.

beet [bi:t] N barbabietola.

bee·tle ['bi:tl] 1 N (*Zool*) coleottero; (: *scarab*) scarabeo; (: *black beetle*) scarafaggio.
 2 VI (*fam*): **to beetle in/out** entrare/uscire di corsa; **to beetle off** correre via.
 ◆ **beetle-browed** ['bi:tlˌbraʊd] ADJ dalle folte sopracciglia.

beet·root ['bi:tˌru:t] N (*Brit*) barbabietola.

be·fall [bɪ'fɔ:l] (*pt* **befell** [bɪ'fɛl], *pp* **befallen** [bɪ'fɔ:lən]) VT accadere a.

be·fit [bɪ'fɪt] IMPERS VB (*frm*): **to befit sb** addirsi a qn, confarsi a qn; **it ill befits you to speak in this way** non ti

si addice *or* non ti si confa parlare così.

be·fit·ting [bɪ'fɪtɪŋ] ADJ adatto(-a); **in the manner befitting his status** come si conviene alla sua posizione.

be·fore [bɪ'fɔː'] ① PREP **a** (*in time*) prima di; **before 7 o'clock** prima delle 7; **the day before last** *or* **yesterday** due giorni fa, l'altro ieri, ieri l'altro; **before Christ** avanti Cristo; **before long** fra poco, fra non molto

b (*in place, rank, in the presence of*) davanti a; **a new life lay before him** una nuova vita si apriva davanti a lui; **to appear before a judge** comparire davanti *or* dinanzi a un giudice; **the question before us** la questione di cui ci dobbiamo occupare; **before my very eyes** proprio sotto i miei occhi; **ladies before gentlemen** prima le signore, la precedenza alle signore; **to put friendship before money** anteporre l'amicizia all'interesse.

② ADV prima; **the day before** il giorno prima *or* precedente; **I have read it before** l'ho già letto; **I've never seen it before** è la prima volta che lo vedo; **the week before** la settimana prima; **I knew long before that ...** sapevo da molto tempo che....

③ CONJ (*time*) prima di + *infin*, prima che + *sub*; (*rather than*) piuttosto che; **before doing it you ...** OR **before you do it, you ...** prima di farlo, tu..., prima che tu lo faccia, tu...; **he will die before he betrays his friends** morirebbe piuttosto che tradire gli amici.

before·hand [bɪ'fɔː,hænd] ADV prima, in anticipo; **let me know your plans beforehand** fammi sapere i tuoi piani in anticipo.

be·friend [bɪ'frɛnd] VT mostrare amicizia a.

be·fud·dled [bɪ'fʌdld] ADJ confuso(-a).

beg [bɛg] ① VT **a** (*entreat*) supplicare, pregare; (*favour*) chiedere; (*subj: beggar: food, money*) mendicare; **he begged me for mercy** mi supplicava di aver pietà; **he begged me to help him** mi ha supplicato *or* pregato di aiutarlo; **to beg forgiveness** implorare perdono; **I beg your pardon** (*apologising*) mi scusi; (*not hearing*) scusi?; **I beg to differ** mi permetto di non essere d'accordo

b : **this begs the question** questo dà per scontato ciò che dev'essere ancora dimostrato.

② VI (*entreat*): **to beg for** implorare; (*beggar*) chiedere l'elemosina *or* la carità; **it's going begging** (*fam*) non lo vuole proprio nessuno

► **beg off** VI + ADV disdire.

be·gan [bɪ'gæn] PT of **begin.**

be·get [bɪ'gɛt] VT (*pt* **begot**, *pp* **begotten**) originare; (*child*) generare.

beg·gar ['bɛgə'] ① N mendicante *m/f*; **lucky beggar!** (*fam*) che fortuna sfacciata!; **poor beggar!** (*fam*) povero diavolo!; **beggars can't be choosers** o mangiar questa minestra o saltar dalla finestra.

② VT (*ruin*) ridurre sul lastrico *or* in miseria; **it beggars description** è indescrivibile.

beg·gar·ly ['bɛgəlɪ] ADJ (*amount*) misero(-a), irrisorio(-a); (*existence*) miserabile; (*salary*) da fame.

be·gin [bɪ'gɪn] (*vb: pt* **began**, *pp* **begun**) ① VT (*gen*) cominciare, incominciare, iniziare; (*originate: fashion*) lanciare; (: *custom*) inaugurare; (: *war*) scatenare; **to begin doing sth** OR **to begin to do sth** incominciare *or* iniziare a fare qc; **it began to rain** ha cominciato *or* si è messo a piovere; **this skirt began life as an evening dress** questa gonna in origine era un abito da sera; **it doesn't begin to compare with ...** non c'è nemmeno da paragonarlo con...; **I can't begin to thank you** non so proprio come ringraziarti.

② VI incominciare, cominciare; (*fashion, custom*)

nascere; (*rumour*) spargersi; **to begin with sth/by doing sth** cominciare con qc/col fare qc; **to begin on sth** cominciare qc; **let me begin by saying ...** permettetemi di cominciare col dire...; **to begin with, I'd like to know ...** tanto per cominciare vorrei sapere...; **to begin with there were only two of us** all'inizio eravamo solo in due; **beginning on Monday** a partire da lunedì; **the service began at 9 a.m.** la funzione ha avuto inizio alle 9.

be·gin·ner [bɪ'gɪnə'] N principiante *m/f*; **it's just beginner's luck** è la solita fortuna del principiante.

be·gin·ning [bɪ'gɪnɪŋ] N inizio, principio; **at the beginning of the century** all'inizio *or* al principio del secolo; **right from the beginning** fin dal primo momento, fin dall'inizio; **start at the beginning and tell me all about it** raccontami tutto (cominciando *or* a partire) dall'inizio; **the beginning of the end** il principio della fine; **to make a beginning** cominciare; **the beginning of the world** le origini del mondo; **Buddhism had its beginnings ...** il buddismo nacque *or* ebbe origine... .

be·gonia [bɪ'gəʊnɪə] N begonia.

be·grudge [bɪ'grʌdʒ] VT = **grudge.**

be·guile [bɪ'gaɪl] VT (*enchant*) incantare.

be·guil·ing [bɪ'gaɪlɪŋ] ADJ seducente; (*charming*) allettante.

be·gun [bɪ'gʌn] PP of **begin.**

be·half [bɪ'hɑːf] N: **on behalf of** *or* (*Am*) **in behalf of** (*prep*) per conto di; (*thank, accept*) a nome di; **he spoke on my behalf** ha parlato a nome mio.

be·have [bɪ'heɪv] VI (*also:* **behave o.s.**: **conduct o.s.**) comportarsi; (: *conduct o.s. well*) comportarsi bene; **you behaved very wisely** hai agito saggiamente; **to behave well towards sb** comportarsi bene nei confronti di qn; **behave yourself!** comportati bene!

be·hav·iour, (*Am*) **be·hav·ior** [bɪ'heɪvjə'] N comportamento; **to be on one's best behaviour** sforzarsi di comportarsi bene.

be·hav·iour·al, (*Am*) **be·hav·ior·al** [bɪ'heɪvjərəl] ADJ comportamentale.

be·hav·iour·ism, (*Am*) **be·hav·ior·ism** [bɪ'heɪvjərɪzəm] N comportamentismo.

be·hav·iour·ist, (*Am*) **be·hav·ior·ist** [bɪ'heɪvjərɪst] N comportamentista *m/f*.

be·head [bɪ'hɛd] VT decapitare.

be·held [bɪ'hɛld] PT, PP of **behold.**

be·hest [bɪ'hɛst] N: **at his behest** su suo ordine.

be·hind [bɪ'haɪnd] ① PREP dietro; (*time*) in ritardo con; **look behind you!** guarda dietro di te!; **what's behind all this?** (*fig*) cosa c'è sotto?; **we're behind them in technology** (*fig*) siamo più indietro *or* più arretrati di loro nella tecnica; **his family is behind him** (*fig*) ha l'appoggio della famiglia; **behind the scenes** dietro le quinte.

② ADV dietro; **to stay behind (to do sth)** fermarsi (a fare qc); **to leave sth behind** dimenticare di prendere qc; **to be behind with sth** essere indietro con qc; (*payments*) essere in arretrato con qc.

③ N (*fam*) didietro *m inv*.

behind·hand [bɪ'haɪnd,hænd] ADV indietro.

be·hold [bɪ'həʊld] (*pt, pp* **beheld**) VT (*old, liter*) scorgere, vedere.

be·hold·en [bɪ'həʊldən] ADJ (*frm*): **to be beholden to sb for sth** sentirsi obbligato(-a) verso qn per qc.

be·hove [bɪ'həʊv], (*Am*) **be·hoove** [bɪ'huːv] IMPERS VT (*old, frm*): **to behove sb to do sth** stare a qn (il) fare qc.

beige [beɪʒ] ADJ, N beige *(m) inv*.

Bei·jing ['beɪ'dʒɪŋ] N Pechino *f*.

be·ing ['biːɪŋ] N **a** (*existence*) essere *m*, esistenza; **to come into being** nascere, essere creato(-a); **to bring sth into being** creare qc **b** (*creature*) essere *m*.

Bei·rut [beɪˈruːt] N Beirut *f*.

be·jew·elled [bɪˈdʒuːəld] ADJ ingioiellato(-a).

be·la·bour, (*Am*) **be·la·bor** [bɪˈleɪbəʳ] VT (*beat*) bastonare; **to belabour with** (*fig: questions*) tartassare di; (: *insults*) bombardare di.

be·lat·ed [bɪˈleɪtɪd] ADJ in ritardo; **his belated arrival** il suo ritardo.

be·lay [bɪˈleɪ] VT, VI (*Mountaineering*) assicurare.

belch [bɛltʃ] 1 N rutto.
2 VI ruttare.
3 VT (*also:* **belch out**: *smoke*) sputare (fuori); (*flames*) eruttare, vomitare.

be·lea·guered [bɪˈliːgəd] ADJ (*city*) assediato(-a); (*person*) assillato(-a); (*army*) accerchiato(-a); (*project, organization*) pieno(-a) di problemi.

Bel·fast [ˈbɛlfɑːst] N Belfast *f*.

bel·fry [ˈbɛlfrɪ] N campanile *m*.

Bel·gian [ˈbɛldʒən] ADJ, N belga (*m/f*).

Bel·gium [ˈbɛldʒəm] N Belgio.

Bel·grade [bɛlˈgreɪd] N Belgrado *f*.

be·lie [bɪˈlaɪ] VT (*prove false*) smentire; (*give false impression of*) nascondere.

be·lief [bɪˈliːf] N (*faith*) fede *f*; (*trust*) fiducia; (*tenet, doctrine, opinion*) convinzione *f*, opinione *f*; (*acceptance as true*) credenza; **belief in God** fede in Dio; **it's a belief held by all Christians** è credenza comune a tutti i cristiani; **it's beyond belief** è incredibile; **rich beyond belief** incredibilmente ricco(-a); **a man of strong beliefs** un uomo dalle ferme convinzioni; **it is my belief that** sono convinto che; **in the belief that** nella convinzione che.

be·liev·able [bɪˈliːvəbəl] ADJ credibile.

be·lieve [bɪˈliːv] 1 VT (*story, person*) credere a; **to believe (that)** (*be of the opinion that*) credere (che); **I don't believe he'll come** non credo che verrà *or* che venga; **don't you believe it!** non crederci!; **I don't believe a word of it!** non credo a una parola di tutto questo!; **he is believed to be abroad** si pensa (che) sia all'estero.
2 VI credere; **to believe in** (*God*) credere in; (*ghosts*) credere a; (*method*) avere fiducia in; **I don't believe in corporal punishment** sono contrario alle punizioni corporali.

be·liev·er [bɪˈliːvəʳ] N (*Rel*) credente *m/f*; **to be a believer in** (*in idea, activity*) essere a favore di.

Belisha bea·con [bəˈliːʃəˈbiːkən] N *segnale luminoso arancione che indica un attraversamento pedonale.*

be·lit·tle [bɪˈlɪtl] VT sminuire.

Be·lize [bɛˈliːz] N Belize *m*.

bell [bɛl] N (*small, on door, electric*) campanello; (*church bell*) campana; (*on cats, harness*) sonaglio; (*on cow*) campanaccio; (*of telephone*) soneria; **that rings a bell** (*fig*) mi ricorda qualcosa.

bel·la·don·na [ˌbɛləˈdɒnə] N (*Bot, Med*) belladonna.

♦ **bell-bottoms** [ˈbɛlˌbɒtəmz] NPL pantaloni *mpl* a zampa d'elefante.

bell·boy [ˈbɛlˌbɔɪ], (*Am*) **bell·hop** [ˈbɛlˌhɒp] N ragazzo d'albergo, fattorino d'albergo.

belle [bɛl] N: **the belle of the ball** la regina della festa.

♦ **bell heather** N erica campanulata di Scozia.

bel·li·cose [ˈbɛlɪkəʊs] ADJ bellicoso(-a).

bel·lig·er·ence [bɪˈlɪdʒərəns] N (*see adj*) belligeranza; bellicosità.

bel·lig·er·ent [bɪˈlɪdʒərənt] ADJ (*at war*) belligerante; (*fig*) bellicoso(-a).

bel·lig·er·ent·ly [bɪˈlɪdʒərəntlɪ] ADV bellicosamente.

♦ **bell jar** N campana di vetro.

bel·low [ˈbɛləʊ] 1 N (*of bull etc*) muggito; (*of person*) urlo.
2 VI (*see n*) muggire; urlare (a squarciagola).
3 VT (*also:* **bellow out**: *order, song*) urlare (a squarciagola).

bel·lows [ˈbɛləʊz] NPL (*of forge, organ*) mantice *m*; (*for fire*) soffietto.

♦ **bell push** N bottone *m or* pulsante *m* del campanello.

♦ **bell-ringer** [ˈbɛlˌrɪŋəʳ] N campanaro.

♦ **bell-shaped** [ˈbɛlˌʃeɪpt] ADJ a campana.

♦ **bell tent** N tenda conica.

♦ **bell tower** N torre *f* campanaria.

bel·ly [ˈbɛlɪ] N pancia.

belly·ache [ˈbɛlɪˌeɪk] (*fam*) 1 N mal *m* di pancia.
2 VI (*fam*) mugugnare.

belly·button [ˈbɛlˌbʌtn] N (*fam*) ombelico.

♦ **belly dance** N danza del ventre.

♦ **belly dancer** N *ballerina che esegue la danza del ventre.*

♦ **belly flop** N (*Swimming*) spanciata.

bel·ly·ful [ˈbɛlɪˌfʊl] N (*fam*): **to have had a bellyful of sb/sth** aver fatto un'indigestione di qn/qc.

♦ **belly landing** N (*Aer*) atterraggio sul ventre.

♦ **belly laugh** N grassa risata.

be·long [bɪˈlɒŋ] VI **a** : **to belong to sb/sth** (*be the property of*) appartenere a qn/qc; **who does this belong to?** questo di chi è?; **to belong to a club** essere socio(-a) di un club
b (*have rightful place*): **put it back where it belongs** rimettilo al suo posto; **it belongs on the shelf** va sullo scaffale; **I felt I didn't belong** mi sentivo un estraneo.

be·long·ings [bɪˈlɒŋɪŋz] NPL ciò che si possiede, cose *fpl* (*fam*); **he lost all his belongings** ha perso tutto ciò che possedeva; **personal belongings** effetti *mpl* personali.

Be·lo·rus·sia [ˌbɛləʊˈrʌʃə] N = Byelorussia.

Be·lo·rus·sian [ˌbɛləʊˈrʌʃən] ADJ, N = Byelorussian.

be·lov·ed [bɪˈlʌvɪd] ADJ, N adorato(-a).

be·low [bɪˈləʊ] 1 PREP sotto, al di sotto di; **temperatures below normal** temperature al di sotto del normale; **they live in the flat below us** abitano nell'appartamento sotto al nostro.
2 ADV sotto, di sotto; **the mountains below** le montagne sottostanti; **the flat below** l'appartamento al piano di sotto; **see below** (*on page*) vedi sotto *or* oltre.

belt [bɛlt] 1 N (*gen*) cintura; (*of trousers*) cintura, cinghia; (*Tech*) cinghia; (*Geog: zone*) zona, regione *f*; **industrial belt** zona industriale; **the cotton belt** la zona di coltivazione del cotone; **to tighten one's belt** (*fig*) tirare la cinghia; **that was below the belt** (*fig*) è stato un colpo basso.
2 VT (*fam: thrash*) usare la cinghia con, picchiare; **he belted me one** mi ha mollato un pugno.
3 VI (*fam: rush*): **to belt in/out** *etc* entrare/uscire *etc* di gran carriera; **he was belting up the motorway at 100 mph** filava sull'autostrada a 100 miglia all'ora

► **belt out** VT + ADV (*song*) cantare a squarciagola

► **belt up** VI + ADV (*fam: be quiet*) chiudere la boccaccia; **belt up!** chiudi quella boccaccia!

♦ **belt rack** N portacinture *m inv*.

belt·way [ˈbɛltˌweɪ] N (*Am Aut*) circonvallazione *f*; (*motorway*) raccordo anulare.

be·moan [bɪˈməʊn] VT lamentare.

be·mused [bɪˈmjuːzd] ADJ perplesso(-a), stupito(-a).

bench [bentʃ] N (*seat*: *with back*) panchina; (: *without back*) panca; (*in parliament, workbench*) banco; **to be on the Bench** (*Law*) essere giudice.

♦ **bench mark** N punto di riferimento.

bend [bend] (*vb*: *pt, pp* **bent**) ① N (*in road*) curva; (*in river*) ansa, gomito; (*in arm, knee*) piega; (*in pipe*) gomito; **he drives me round the bend!** (*fam*) mi fa diventare matto!.

② VT (*wire etc*) curvare, piegare; (*knee*) flettere, piegare; (*arm*) piegare; (*head*) piegare, chinare.

③ VI piegarsi, curvarsi; (*road*) fare una curva; (*river*) fare un gomito; (*person*) chinarsi

▶ **bend down** VI + ADV chinarsi

▶ **bend over** VI + ADV chinarsi, piegarsi; **to bend over backwards** (*fig*) farsi in quattro.

bend·er [ˈbendə'] N (*fam*) sbronza; **to go on a bender** prendersi una sbronza.

bends [bendz] NPL (*Med*): **the bends** un'embolia.

bendy [ˈbendɪ] ADJ (*comp* **-ier**, *superl* **-iest**) (*flexible*) flessibile; (*road*) tortuoso(-a).

be·neath [bɪˈniːθ] ① PREP sotto, al di sotto di; (*unworthy of*) indegno(-a) di; **it is beneath my notice** non è degno della mia attenzione; **it is beneath him to do such a thing** non si degnerebbe mai di fare una cosa del genere.

② ADV sotto, di sotto; **the flat beneath** l'appartamento al piano di sotto.

Ben·edic·tine [ˌbenɪˈdɪktɪn] ADJ, N benedettino(-a).

ben·edic·tion [ˌbenɪˈdɪkʃən] N benedizione *f*.

ben·efac·tor [ˈbenɪfæktə'] N benefattore *m*.

ben·efac·tress [ˈbenɪˌfæktrɪs] N benefattrice *f*.

ben·efice [ˈbenɪfɪs] N (*Rel*) beneficio ecclesiastico.

be·nefi·cence [bɪˈnefɪsəns] N (*frm*: *quality*) beneficenza; (: *act*) opera di carità.

be·nefi·cent [bɪˈnefɪsənt] ADJ (*frm*) benefico(-a).

ben·efi·cial [ˌbenɪˈfɪʃəl] ADJ benefico(-a); **beneficial to** che giova a, che fa bene a.

ben·efi·cial·ly [ˌbenɪˈfɪʃəlɪ] ADV beneficamente.

bene·fi·ciary [ˌbenɪˈfɪʃərɪ] N (*Law*) beneficiario(-a).

ben·efit [ˈbenɪfɪt] ① N **a** vantaggio, beneficio; **the benefits of a good education** i vantaggi di una buona educazione; **it might be of some benefit to you** potrebbe giovarti; **for the benefit of one's health** per la propria salute; **to give sb the benefit of the doubt** concedere a qn il beneficio del dubbio

b (*allowance*) indennità *f inv*, sussidio; **unemployment benefit** indennità di disoccupazione.

② VI trarre vantaggio *or* profitto da; **he'll benefit from it** ne trarrà beneficio *or* profitto.

③ VT giovare a, far bene a; **a service which will benefit rich and poor** un servizio che gioverà sia ai ricchi che ai poveri.

♦ **benefit association** N (*Am*) società di mutuo soccorso.

♦ **benefit performance** N spettacolo di beneficenza.

Bene·lux [ˈbenɪlʌks] ① ADJ: **the Benelux countries** i paesi del Benelux. ② N il Benelux *m*.

be·nevo·lence [bɪˈnevələns] N benevolenza.

be·nevo·lent [bɪˈnevələnt] ADJ benevolo(-a).

♦ **benevolent fund** N ≈ società di mutuo soccorso.

be·nevo·lent·ly [bɪˈnevələntlɪ] ADV con benevolenza.

BEng [ˌbiːˈendʒ] N ABBR (= *Bachelor of Engineering*) *laurea in ingegneria*.

Ben·ga·li [benˈɡɔːlɪ] ① ADJ bengalese.

② N **a** (*person*) bengalese *m/f inv* **b** (*language*) bengalese *m*.

be·nign [bɪˈnaɪn] ADJ benevolo(-a); (*Med*) benigno(-a).

be·nign·ly [bɪˈnaɪnlɪ] ADV con benevolenza.

bent¹ [bent] ① PT, PP of **bend**.

② ADJ **a** (*wire, pipe*) piegato(-a), storto(-a); (*fam*: *dishonest*) losco(-a); (*offensive*: *homosexual*) invertito(-a)

b (*fig*: *determined*): **to be bent on sth/on doing sth** essere deciso(-a) a qc/a fare qc; **to be bent on a quarrel** voler proprio litigare.

③ N (*aptitude*) inclinazione *f*, disposizione *f*; **to follow one's bent** seguire la propria inclinazione.

bent² [bent] N (*Bot*): **common bent** agrostide *f* bianca.

bent·wood [ˈbentˌwʊd] ADJ di legno ricurvo.

Ben·ze·drine® [ˈbenzɪˌdriːn] N benzedrina ®.

ben·zene [ˈbenziːn] N benzene *m*.

be·queath [bɪˈkwiːð] VT: **to bequeath sth to sb** lasciare qc in eredità a qn.

be·quest [bɪˈkwest] N lascito.

be·rate [bɪˈreɪt] VT rimproverare, redarguire.

be·reaved [bɪˈriːvd] ① ADJ in lutto.

② : **the bereaved** NPL i familiari in lutto.

be·reave·ment [bɪˈriːvmənt] N lutto.

be·reft [bɪˈreft] ADJ (*frm*): **to be bereft of sth** essere privo(-a) di qc.

be·ret [ˈbereɪ] N berretto.

berg·schrund [ˈbɜːkʃrʊnt] N crepaccio terminale.

Bering Sea [ˈbɛərɪŋˈsiː] N: **the Bering Sea** il mare di Bering.

Bering Strait [ˈbɛərɪŋˈstreɪt] N: **the Bering Strait** lo stretto di Bering.

berk [bɜːk] N (*Brit fam!*) povero(-a) scemo(-a).

Berks [bɑːks] N ABBR (*Brit*)= *Berkshire*.

Ber·lin [bɜːˈlɪn] N Berlino *f*; **East/West Berlin** Berlino est/ovest.

Ber·lin·er [bɜːˈlɪnə'] N berlinese *m/f*.

Ber·mu·da [bɜːˈmjuːdə] N: **the Bermudas** le Bermude.

♦ **Bermuda shorts** NPL bermuda *mpl*.

Bern [bɜːn] N Berna *f*.

ber·ry [ˈberɪ] N bacca; **brown as a berry** abbronzatissimo (-a).

ber·serk [bəˈsɜːk] ADJ: **to go berserk** dare in escandescenze; (*with anger*) andare *or* montare su tutte le furie.

berth [bɜːθ] ① N (*on ship, train*) cuccetta; (*Naut*: *place at wharf*) ormeggio; **to give sb a wide berth** (*fig*) tenersi alla larga da qn.

② VI ormeggiare; (*in harbour*) entrare in porto.

ber·yl [ˈberɪl] N berillo.

be·ryl·lium [beˈrɪlɪəm] N berillio.

be·seech [bɪˈsiːtʃ] (*pt, pp* **besought**) VT (*liter*) implorare.

be·seech·ing [bɪˈsiːtʃɪŋ] ADJ implorante.

be·seech·ing·ly [bɪˈsiːtʃɪŋlɪ] ADV in modo implorante.

be·set [bɪˈset] (*pt, pp* **beset**) VT (*afflict*) assillare; (*attack*) assalire; **a policy beset with dangers** una politica irta *or* piena di pericoli.

be·set·ting [bɪˈsetɪŋ] ADJ: **his besetting sin** il suo più grande difetto.

be·side [bɪˈsaɪd] PREP (*at the side of*) accanto a, vicino a; (*compared with*) rispetto a, in confronto a; **to be beside o.s. (with)** (*anger, joy etc*) essere fuori di sé (da); **that's beside the point** questo non c'entra niente.

be·sides [bɪˈsaɪdz] ① PREP (*in addition to*) oltre a; (*apart from*) all'infuori di, a parte; **besides which** ... per di più....

② ADV (*in addition*) inoltre; (*anyway*) poi, del resto, per di più; **and more besides** e altro ancora.

be·siege [bɪˈsiːdʒ] VT (*Mil, fig*) assediare, assalire; **we were**

besieged with inquiries siamo stati tempestati di domande.

be·sieg·er [bɪ'siːdʒəʳ] N assediante m/f.

be·smirch [bɪ'smɜːtʃ] VT (liter) screditare.

be·som ['biːzəm] N ramazza.

be·sot·ted [bɪ'sɒtɪd] ADJ: **besotted with sb** infatuato(-a) di qn.

be·sought [bɪ'sɔːt] PT, PP of **beseech**.

be·spat·tered [bɪ'spætəd] ADJ: **bespattered with** schizzato(-a) di.

be·spec·ta·cled [bɪ'spɛktɪkld] ADJ occhialuto(-a).

be·spoke [bɪ'spəʊk] ADJ (Brit: garment) su misura; **bespoke tailor** sarto (che lavora su ordinazione).

best [bɛst] [1] ADJ (superl of good) migliore; **to be best** essere il/la migliore; **the best pupil in the class** il/la primo(-a) della classe; **in her best dress** vestita del suo abito migliore; **my best friend** il/la mio(-a) migliore amico(-a); **the best thing about her is ...** la cosa più bella di lei è...; **the best thing to do is ...** la cosa migliore da fare or farsi è...; **for the best part of the year** per la maggior parte dell'anno; **may the best man win!** vinca il migliore!.

[2] ADV (superl of well) meglio; **the best liked** il/la più amato(-a); **the best dressed** il/la più elegante; **as best I could** meglio che ho potuto; **you know best** tu sai meglio di chiunque; **John came off best** John ha avuto la meglio; **you had best leave now** faresti meglio ad andartene ora.

[3] N il/la migliore; **she's the best at drawing** disegna meglio di tutti; **he deserves the best** si merita quanto c'è di meglio; **at best** nella migliore delle ipotesi, tutt'al più; **he wasn't at his best** non era in vena or in piena forma; **he's not exactly patient at the best of times** non è mai molto paziente; **I acted for the best** ho agito per il meglio; **let's hope for the best** speriamo che tutto vada per il meglio; **to the best of my knowledge** per quel che ne so io; **I did it to the best of my ability** l'ho fatto come meglio ho potuto; **to do one's best** fare del proprio meglio; **she looks her best in casual clothes** l'abbigliamento casual le dona molto; **to look its best** (house, flat) esser bello(-a) ed ordinato(-a); **to make the best of a bad job** far buon viso a cattivo gioco; **she can dance with the best of them** è una ballerina di prima classe.

bes·tial ['bɛstɪəl] ADJ bestiale.

bes·ti·al·ity [bɛstɪ'ælɪtɪ] N bestialità.

be·stir [bɪ'stɜːʳ] VT: **to bestir o.s.** muoversi.

♦ **best man** N testimone m dello sposo.

be·stow [bɪ'stəʊ] VT: **to bestow sth on sb** (title) conferire qc a qn; (honour, affections) accordare qc a qn.

best·sell·er [ˌbɛst'sɛləʳ] N bestseller m inv.

bet [bɛt] (vb: pt, pp **bet** or **betted**) [1] N scommessa; **to put a bet on** fare una scommessa su; **it's a safe bet** (fig) è molto probabile.

[2] VI: **to bet (on)** scommettere (su); **to bet on a horse** scommettere or puntare su un cavallo; **are you going? — you bet!** (fam) ci vai? — ci puoi giurare!; **I'm not a betting man** non sono uno scommettitore.

[3] VT scommettere; **he bet £5 on the favourite** ha giocato or puntato 5 sterline sul favorito; **I bet you a pound that ...** scommettiamo una sterlina che...; **I bet he doesn't come** (fam) scommetto che non viene; **you can bet your life that ...** (fam) puoi scommetterci la testa che... .

Beth·le·hem ['bɛθlɪˌhɛm] N Betlemme f.

be·to·ken [bɪ'təʊkən] VT (liter) denotare.

beto·ny ['bɛtənɪ] N erba betonica.

be·tray [bɪ'treɪ] VT (also fig) tradire; **to betray sb to the enemy** consegnare qn nelle mani del nemico; **his face betrayed his surprise** il suo viso tradiva la sorpresa.

be·tray·al [bɪ'treɪəl] N tradimento.

be·troth·al [bɪ'trəʊðəl] N fidanzamento.

be·troth·ed [bɪ'trəʊðd] (liter) [1] ADJ promesso(-a); **the betrothed couple** i promessi sposi.

[2] N sposo(-a) promesso(-a).

bet·ter[1] ['bɛtəʳ] [1] ADJ (comp of good) migliore; **I'm better at German than French** riesco meglio in tedesco che in francese; **he's better than his brother at mending cars** è più bravo di suo fratello ad aggiustare le macchine; **are you better now?** (in health) stai meglio adesso?; **to get better** migliorare; (Med) star meglio, rimettersi; **that's better!** così va meglio!; **it couldn't be better** non potrebbe andar meglio (di così); **it would be better to go now** sarebbe meglio andare adesso; **he's no better than a thief** non è né più né meno che un ladro; **it lasted the better part of a year** è durato quasi un anno.

[2] ADV (comp of well) meglio; **he speaks French better than Italian/his brother** parla il francese meglio dell'italiano/di suo fratello; **better known** meglio or più conosciuto(-a); **so much the better** OR **all the better** tanto meglio, meglio così; **he was all the better for it** ci ha guadagnato, gli ha fatto molto bene; **they are better off than we are** stanno meglio di noi; **you'd be better off staying where you are** faresti meglio a restare dove sei; **I had better go** dovrei andare; **hadn't you better ask him?** non sarebbe meglio se lo chiedessi a lui?; **to think better of it** cambiare idea.

[3] N: **a change for the better** un cambiamento in meglio; **for better or worse** nella buona o nella cattiva sorte; **to get the better of sb** avere la meglio su qn; **one's betters** i propri superiori.

[4] VT migliorare; **to better o.s.** migliorare la propria condizione.

bet·ter[2] ['bɛtəʳ] N scommettitore m.

♦ **better-off** [ˌbɛtə'ɒf] ADJ: **to be better-off** (gen) stare meglio; (financially) avere più soldi.

bet·ter·ment ['bɛtəmənt] N miglioramento.

bet·ting [bɛtɪŋ] N scommesse fpl; **what's the betting he'll be late?** (fig) quanto scommettiamo che arriverà in ritardo?

♦ **betting shop** N (Brit) ufficio dell'allibratore m.

♦ **betting slip** N talloncino per scommesse.

bet·tor ['bɛtəʳ] N (Am) = **better**[2].

be·tween [bɪ'twiːn] [1] PREP (gen) tra, fra; **the road between here and London** la strada da qui a Londra; **a village between Florence and Pisa** un paese tra Firenze e Pisa; **between now and next week we must ...** da qui alla settimana prossima dobbiamo...; **I sat (in) between John and Sue** ero seduto (in mezzo) tra John e Sue; **it's between 5 and 6 metres long** è lungo fra i 5 e i 6 metri; **we shared it between us** ce lo siamo diviso tra di noi; **just between you and me** or **ourselves ...** (sia detto) tra me e te..., sia detto tra noi (due)...; **we only had £5 between us** fra tutti e due avevamo solo 5 sterline.

[2] ADV (also: **in between**: of place) in mezzo; (of time) nel frattempo; **few and far between** rarissimi.

be·twixt [bɪ'twɪkst] ADV: **to be betwixt and between** essere una via di mezzo.

bev·el ['bɛvəl] [1] N (surface) superficie f obliqua; (bevel edge) spigolo smussato. [2] VT smussare.

♦ **bevel square** N squadra falsa or zoppa.

◆ **bevel wheel** N ruota conica dentata.
bev·er·age ['bevərɪdʒ] N bevanda.
bevy ['bevi] N banda; **a bevy of** una banda di.
be·wail [bɪ'weɪl] VT lamentare.
be·ware [bɪ'wɛə'] VI: **to beware of sb/sth** stare attento(-a) a qn/qc, guardarsi da qn/qc; **you must beware of falling** devi stare attento a non cadere; **beware of the dog!** attenti al cane!
be·wil·der [bɪ'wɪldə'] VT sconcertare, disorientare.
be·wil·dered [bɪ'wɪldəd] ADJ sconcertato(-a), disorientato(-a).
be·wil·der·ing [bɪ'wɪldərɪŋ] ADJ sconcertante, sbalorditivo(-a).
be·wil·der·ing·ly [bɪ'wɪldərɪŋlɪ] ADV in modo sconcertante, in modo sbalorditivo.
be·wil·der·ment [bɪ'wɪldəmənt] N perplessità, sbalordimento.
be·witch [bɪ'wɪtʃ] VT stregare; (fig) affascinare, ammaliare.
be·witch·ing [bɪ'wɪtʃɪŋ] ADJ (fig: person) affascinante, seducente; (: smile, look) ammaliatore(-trice).
be·witch·ing·ly [bɪ'wɪtʃɪŋlɪ] ADV (fig) in modo affascinante; **bewitchingly beautiful** bello(-a) da impazzire.
be·yond [bɪ'jɔnd] ①PREP (in place, time) al di là di; (: further than) più in là di; (exceeding) al di là di, al di sopra di; (apart from) oltre a; **beyond my reach** fuori della mia portata; **it would be unwise to delay it beyond 1998** sarebbe poco saggio rimandarlo oltre il 1998; **it's almost beyond belief** è incredibile; **that job is beyond him** quel lavoro è al di sopra delle sue capacità; **it's beyond me why ...** non arriverò mai a capire perché...; **that's beyond a joke** questo non è più uno scherzo; **beyond doubt** senza dubbio; **beyond repair** irreparabile.
② ADV più oltre, più in là, più avanti.
be·zique [bɪ'ziːk] N bazzica.
b/f ABBR = **brought forward.**
BFPO [,biːefpiː'əʊ] N ABBR (= British Forces Post Office) recapito delle truppe britanniche all'estero.
bhp [,biːeɪtʃ'piː] N ABBR (Aut: = brake horsepower) CV.
bi... [baɪ] PREF bi... .
bi·an·nual [baɪ'ænjʊəl] ADJ semestrale.
bias ['baɪəs] ①N a (inclination): **bias (towards** or **in favour of)** preferenza (per); **bias (against)** (prejudice) pregiudizio (contro); **a right-wing bias** una tendenza di destra b (of material) sbieco; **to cut sth on the bias** tagliare qc in sbieco.
② VT: **to bias sb towards** influenzare qn a favore di; **to bias sb against** prevenire qn contro.
◆ **bias binding** N (Sewing) fettuccia in sbieco.
bi·ased, bi·assed ['baɪəst] ADJ parziale; **to be biased against** essere prevenuto(-a) contro.
bi·ath·lon [baɪ'æθlən] N biathlon m inv.
bib [bɪb] N (for child) bavaglino; (on dungarees) pettorina; **in one's best bib and tucker** (fam) in ghingheri.
Bi·ble ['baɪbl] N: **the Bible** la Bibbia.
◆ **Bible–thumper** ['baɪbl'θʌmpə'], **Bible-basher** ['baɪbl'bæʃə'] N (fam) accanito sostenitore della Bibbia.
bib·li·cal ['bɪblɪkəl] ADJ biblico(-a).
bib·li·og·ra·pher [,bɪblɪ'ɒgrəfə'] N bibliografo(-a).
bib·lio·graph·ic [,bɪblɪəʊ'græfɪk], **bib·lio·graph·ical** [,bɪblɪəʊ'græfɪkəl] ADJ bibliografico(-a).
bib·li·og·ra·phy [,bɪblɪ'ɒgrəfɪ] N bibliografia.
bibu·lous ['bɪbjʊləs] ADJ (hum) avvinazzato(-a).
bi·car·bo·nate of soda [baɪ'kɑːbənɪtəv'səʊdə] N bicarbonato (di sodio).

bi·cen·tenary [,baɪsɛn'tiːnərɪ], (Am) **bi·cen·ten·nial** [baɪsɛn'tɛnɪəl] N, ADJ bicentenario.
bi·ceps ['baɪsɛps] NSG bicipite m.
bick·er ['bɪkə'] VI bisticciare.
bick·er·ing ['bɪkərɪŋ] N bisticci mpl.
bi·cy·cle ['baɪsɪkl] N bicicletta; **to ride a bicycle** andare in bicicletta; **bicycle parts** ricambi mpl per bicicletta.
◆ **bicycle pump** N pompa della bicicletta.
◆ **bicycle race** N gara ciclistica.
◆ **bicycle rack** N rastrelliera per biciclette; (on car) portabiciclette m inv.
◆ **bicycle shed** N rimessa per biciclette.
◆ **bicycle track** N sentiero ciclabile.
bid [bɪd] ①N offerta; (Comm: tender) offerta (di appalto); (attempt) tentativo; (Cards) dichiarazione f; **a suicide bid** un tentativo di suicidio; **to make a bid for freedom/power** fare un tentativo per ottenere la libertà/per impadronirsi del potere.
② VT a (pt, pp bid) offrire; **to bid £100 for** offrire 100 sterline per
b (pt bade, pp bidden) (frm: order): **to bid sb do sth** ingiungere a qn di fare qc
c (pt bade, pp bidden): **to bid sb good morning/farewell** dare il buon giorno/l'addio a qn, dire buon giorno/addio a qn.
③ VI a (pt, pp bid) (gen): **to bid (for)** fare un'offerta (per); (Cards) dichiarare; **to bid against sb** gareggiare contro qn
b (pt bade, pp bidden): **to bid fair to be/do sth** promettere di essere/fare qc.
bid·den ['bɪdn] PP of **bid.**
bid·der ['bɪdə'] N offerente m/f; (Cards) chi fa la dichiarazione; **the highest bidder** il/la miglior offerente.
bid·ding ['bɪdɪŋ] N a (at auction) offerte fpl; (Cards) dichiarazioni fpl; **the bidding opened at £50** le offerte sono partite da 50 sterline b : **I did his bidding** ho fatto ciò che voleva.
bide [baɪd] VT: **to bide one's time** aspettare il momento giusto.
bi·det ['biːdeɪ] N bidè m inv.
bi·di·rec·tion·al [,baɪdɪ'rɛkʃənəl] ADJ bidirezionale.
bi·en·nial [baɪ'ɛnɪəl] ①ADJ biennale.
② N (pianta) biennale f.
bier [bɪə'] N (for coffin) catafalco; (for corpse) feretro, bara.
biff [bɪf] N (Brit fam) botta.
bi·fo·cals [baɪ'fəʊkəlz] NPL occhiali mpl bifocali.
big [bɪg] ①ADJ (comp -ger, superl -gest) a (in height, age: building, tree, person) grande; (in bulk, amount: parcel, lie, increase) grosso(-a); (important) grande, importante; **my big brother** mio fratello maggiore
b : **to make the big time** sfondare; **to earn big money** guadagnare forte; **to have big ideas** avere delle grandi idee; **to do things in a big way** fare le cose in grande; **he's too big for his boots** (fam) ha delle belle pretese; **why don't you keep your big mouth shut!** (fam) ma perché non tieni chiusa quella boccaccia?; **that's big of you!** (iro) che generosità!; **big deal!** (iro) capirai!.
② ADV (fam): **to talk big** dirne tante; **to think big** avere delle grandi idee.
biga·mist ['bɪgəmɪst] N bigamo(-a).
biga·mous ['bɪgəməs] ADJ bigamo(-a).
biga·my ['bɪgəmɪ] N bigamia.
◆ **big-boned** [,bɪg'bəʊnd] ADJ che ha ossa grosse.
◆ **big brother** N Grande Fratello.

◆ **big business** N (*large organizations*) la grande industria; (*profitable activity*) un'attività redditizia; **pop music is big business** la musica pop è un grosso affare.

◆ **big dipper** N montagne *fpl* russe.

◆ **big end** N (*Aut*) testa di biella.

◆ **big game hunting** N caccia grossa.

big·gish ['bɪgɪʃ] ADJ (*see big*) piuttosto grande; piuttosto grosso(-a).

big·head ['bɪgˌhɛd] N (*fam*) montato(-a).

big·headed [bɪg'hɛdɪd] ADJ (*fam*) che si dà un sacco di arie.

◆ **big-hearted** [ˌbɪg'hɑːtɪd] ADJ generoso(-a), di buon cuore.

big·mouth ['bɪgˌmauθ] N (*fam*) chiacchierone(-a).

◆ **big noise, big shot** N (*fam*) pezzo grosso.

big·ot ['bɪgət] N (*pej*) fazioso(-a).

big·ot·ed ['bɪgətɪd] ADJ (*pej*) fazioso(-a).

big·ot·ry ['bɪgətrɪ] N (*pej*) faziosità.

◆ **big shot** N = **big noise.**

◆ **big time** N: "big time" politics politica con la 'p' maiuscola.

◆ **big toe** N alluce *m.*

◆ **big top** N (*circus*) circo; (*main tent*) tendone *m* del circo.

◆ **big wheel** N (*at fair*) ruota (panoramica); (*Am*) = **big noise.**

big·wig ['bɪgwɪg] N (*fam*) pezzo grosso.

bike [baɪk] N (*fam*) bici *f inv.*

bi·ki·ni [bɪ'kiːnɪ] N bikini *m inv.*

◆ **bikini briefs** NPL slip *m inv.*

bi·lat·er·al [baɪ'lætərəl] ADJ bilaterale.

bi·lat·er·al·ly [baɪ'lætərəlɪ] ADV bilateralmente.

bil·berry ['bɪlbərɪ] N mirtillo.

bile [baɪl] N (*Med, fig*) bile *f.*

bilge [bɪldʒ] N **a** (*Naut*) sentina; (*also:* **bilge water**) acqua di sentina **b** (*fam: nonsense*) idiozie *fpl*, cretinate *fpl.*

◆ **bilge pump** N pompa di sentina.

bi·lin·gual [baɪ'lɪŋgwəl] ADJ bilingue.

bili·ous ['bɪlɪəs] ADJ (*Med*) biliare; (*fig: irritable*) collerico(-a); **bilious attack** attacco di bile.

bill[1] [bɪl] [1] N **a** (*account*) fattura; (: *in hotel, restaurant*) conto; (: *for gas, electricity*) bolletta; **could I have the bill please?** il conto, per piacere
b (*Parliament*) progetto di legge
c (*Am: banknote*) banconota, biglietto
d (*notice*) avviso; **"post no bills"** "divieto di affissione"; **that fits the bill** (*fig*) quello fa proprio al caso mio (*or* tuo *etc*)
e (*Theatre*) cartellone *m*, manifesto; (: *smaller*) locandina; **to top the bill** essere in cima al cartellone; **on the bill** in cartellone
f (*Comm, Fin*) cambiale *f.*
[2] VT **a** (*customer*): **to bill sb for sth** mandare la fattura di qc a qn
b (*Theatre*) mettere in cartellone.

bill[2] [bɪl] [1] N (*of bird*) becco.
[2] VI: **to bill and coo** tubare.

bill·board ['bɪlˌbɔːd] N tabellone *m* pubblicitario.

bil·let ['bɪlɪt] [1] N acquartieramento.
[2] VT: **to billet sb (on sb)** acquartierare qn (presso qn).

bill·fold ['bɪlˌfəʊld] N (*Am*) portafoglio.

bill·hook ['bɪlˌhʊk] N falcetto.

◆ **billiard ball** N palla da biliardo.

◆ **billiard cue** N stecca da biliardo.

bil·liards ['bɪljədz] NSG biliardo.

◆ **billiard table** N tavolo da biliardo.

bill·ing ['bɪlɪŋ] N (*Theatre*): **to get top billing** figurare in testa al cartellone.

bil·lion ['bɪljən] N miliardo; (*Brit old*) mille miliardi.

◆ **bill of exchange** N cambiale *f*, tratta.

◆ **bill of fare** N lista delle vivande.

◆ **bill of health** N see **clean.**

◆ **bill of lad·ing** [ˌbɪləv'leɪdɪŋ] N polizza di carico.

◆ **bill of rights** N dichiarazione *f* dei diritti.

◆ **bill of sale** N atto di vendita.

bil·low ['bɪləʊ] [1] N (*of smoke*) nuvola; (*of sail*) rigonfiamento.
[2] VI (*smoke*) alzarsi in volute; (*sail*) gonfiarsi.

bill·poster ['bɪlˌpəʊstə'] N, (*Am*) **bill·sticker** ['bɪlˌstɪkə'] N attacchino.

◆ **bills payable** ['bɪlz'peɪəbl] NPL effetti *mpl* passivi.

◆ **bills receivable** ['bɪlzn'siːvəbl] NPL effetti *mpl* attivi.

bil·ly·can ['bɪlɪˌkæn] N pentolino.

bil·ly goat ['bɪlɪˌgəʊt] N caprone *m*, becco.

bill·yo, billy·oh ['bɪlɪˌəʊ] N (*Brit fam*): **they were fighting like billyo(h)** si riempivano di botte; **it was raining like billyo(h)** pioveva a dirotto.

bim·bo ['bɪmbəʊ] N (*pej*) pollastrella, svampitella.

bi·me·tal·lic [ˌbaɪmɪ'tælɪk] ADJ bimetallico(-a).

bi·month·ly [baɪ'mʌnθlɪ] [1] ADJ bimestrale.
[2] ADV bimestralmente.

bin [bɪn] N (*for coal, rubbish*) bidone *m*; (*for bread*) cassetta; (*Brit: dustbin*) pattumiera; (*litterbin*) cestino.

bi·na·ry ['baɪnərɪ] ADJ binario(-a); **binary system** (*Math*) sistema *m* binario.

◆ **binary fission** N (*Bio*) scissione *f* binaria.

bind [baɪnd] (*vb: pt, pp* **bound**) [1] VT **a** (*tie together, make fast*) legare; (: *fig*) legare, unire; (*Culin*) legare; (*Sewing: seam*) orlare; (*book*) rilegare; **bound hand and foot** legato(-a) mani e piedi
b (*encircle*) avvolgere; (: *wound, arm*) fasciare, bendare
c (*oblige*): **to bind sb to sth/to do sth** obbligare qn a qc/a fare qc.
[2] N (*fam: nuisance*) scocciatura

▶ **bind together** VT + ADV (*sticks etc*) legare (insieme); (*fig*) unire

▶ **bind over** VT + ADV (*Law*) dare la condizionale a

▶ **bind up** VT + ADV (*wound*) fasciare, bendare; **to be bound up in** (*work, research etc*) essere completamente assorbito(-a) da; **to be bound up with** (*person*) dedicarsi completamente a.

bind·er ['baɪndə'] N **a** (*file*) classificatore *m* **b** (*Agr*) mietilegatrice *f.*

bind·ing ['baɪndɪŋ] [1] N (*of book*) rilegatura, legatura; (*Sewing*) fettuccia, bordo; (*on skis*) attacco.
[2] ADJ (*agreement, contract*) vincolante; **to be binding on sb** essere vincolante per qn.

bind·weed ['baɪndˌwiːd] N convolvolo.

binge [bɪndʒ] (*fam*) [1] N: **to have a binge** far baldoria; **to go on a (shopping) binge** darsi alle spese folli; **to go on a (drinking) binge** prendersi una solenne sbronza.
[2] VI (*eat excessively*) mangiare in modo eccessivo.

bin·go ['bɪngəʊ] N ≈ tombola (*giocata in stabilimenti pubblici*).

◆ **bin-liner** ['bɪnˌlaɪnə'] N (*Brit*) sacchetto per l'immondizia.

bin·ocu·lar [bɪ'nɒkjʊlə'] ADJ binoculare.

bin·ocu·lars [bɪ'nɒkjʊləz] NPL binocolo *sg.*

bi·no·mial [baɪ'nəʊmɪəl] (*Math*) [1] ADJ binomio(-a).
[2] N binomiale *f.*

bio·chemi·cal [ˌbaɪəʊ'kɛmɪkəl] ADJ biochimico(-a).

bio·chem·ist ['baɪəʊ'kɛmɪst] N biochimico(-a).
bio·chem·is·try ['baɪəʊ'kɛmɪstrɪ] N biochimica.
bio·deg·ra·da·bil·ity [ˌbaɪəʊdɪgreɪdə'bɪlɪtɪ] N biodegradabilità.
bio·degrad·able ['baɪəʊdɪ'greɪdəbl] ADJ biodegradabile.
bio·di·ver·sity [ˌbaɪəʊdaɪ'vɜːsɪtɪ] N biodiversità.
bio·fuel ['baɪəʊfjʊəl] N carburante m biologico.
bi·og·raph·er [baɪ'ɒgrəfəʳ] N biografo(-a).
bio·graphi·cal [ˌbaɪəʊ'græfɪkəl] ADJ biografico(-a).
bi·og·ra·phy [baɪ'ɒgrəfɪ] N biografia.
bio·logi·cal [ˌbaɪə'lɒdʒɪkəl] ADJ biologico(-a).
♦ **biological clock** N orologio biologico.
bi·olo·gist [baɪ'ɒlədʒɪst] N biologo(-a).
bi·ol·ogy [baɪ'ɒlədʒɪ] N biologia.
bi·on·ics [baɪ'ɒnɪks] NSG bionica.
bio·physi·cal [ˌbaɪəʊ'fɪzɪkəl] ADJ biofisico(-a).
bio·physi·cist [ˌbaɪəʊ'fɪzɪsɪst] N biofisico(-a).
bio·phys·ics [ˌbaɪəʊ'fɪzɪks] NSG biofisica.
bio·pic ['baɪəʊpɪk] N film-biografia m inv.
bi·op·sy ['baɪɒpsɪ] N biopsia.
biorhythm ['baɪəʊˌrɪðəm] N bioritmo.
bio·sphere ['baɪəˌsfɪəʳ] N: **the biosphere** la biosfera.
bio·syn·the·sis [ˌbaɪəʊ'sɪnθɪsɪs] N biosintesi f.
bio·tech·nol·ogy [ˌbaɪəʊtɛk'nɒlədʒɪ] N biotecnologia.
bi·par·ti·san [ˌbaɪpɑːtɪ'zæn] ADJ bipartitico(-a).
bi·ped ['baɪpɛd] N bipede m.
bi·plane ['baɪˌpleɪn] N biplano.
birch [bɜːtʃ] N (tree, wood) betulla; (for whipping) frusta (di
betulla).
birch·ing ['bɜːtʃɪŋ] N fustigazione f.
bird [bɜːd] N uccello; (Brit fam: girl) tipa, bambola; **have
you put the bird in the oven?** hai messo il pollo (or il
tacchino etc) nel forno?; **a little bird told me** (hum) me
l'ha detto l'uccellino; **the early bird catches the worm**
(Proverb) chi dorme non piglia pesci; **a bird in the hand
is worth two in the bush** (Proverb) meglio un uovo oggi
che una gallina domani; **birds of a feather flock
together** (Proverb) chi si assomiglia si piglia; **to kill two
birds with one stone** prendere due piccioni con una
fava.
bird·bath ['bɜːdˌbɑːθ] N vasca per gli uccelli.
♦ **bird cage** N gabbia per uccelli.
♦ **bird of prey** N (uccello) rapace m.
♦ **bird sanctuary** N riserva per uccelli.
bird·seed ['bɜːdˌsiːd] N becchime m.
♦ **bird's-eye view** ['bɜːdzaɪ'vjuː] N vista a volo d'uccello.
♦ **bird-watcher** ['bɜːdˈwɒtʃəʳ] N bird watcher m/f inv.
♦ **bird-watching** ['bɜːdˌwɒtʃɪŋ] N bird-watching m.
Biro® ['baɪərəʊ] N biro ® f inv.
birth [bɜːθ] N (also fig) nascita; (childbirth) parto; **it was a
difficult birth** è stato un parto difficile; **at birth** alla
nascita; **Italian by birth** italiano di nascita; **place of birth**
luogo di nascita; **to give birth to** dare alla luce; (fig) dare
inizio a.
♦ **birth certificate** N certificato or atto di nascita.
♦ **birth control** N controllo delle nascite, contraccezione f.
birth·day ['bɜːθˌdeɪ] 1 N compleanno.
2 ADJ (present, party, cake) del or di compleanno; **in
my/his** etc **birthday suit** (fam) come mamma m'ha/l'ha
etc fatto.
birth·mark ['bɜːθˌmɑːk] N voglia (sulla pelle).
birth·place ['bɜːθˌpleɪs] N luogo di nascita; (town) città
natale.
♦ **birth rate** N (indice m or tasso di) natalità.

birth·right ['bɜːθˌraɪt] N (fig) diritto di nascita.
Biscay ['bɪskeɪ] N: **the Bay of Biscay** il golfo di Biscaglia.
bis·cuit ['bɪskɪt] N (Brit) biscotto; (Am) panino al latte; **to
take the biscuit** (fam) essere assolutamente incredibile.
bi·sect [baɪ'sɛkt] VT tagliare in due (parti); (Math) bisecare.
bi·sex·ual [baɪ'sɛksjʊəl] ADJ, N bisessuale (m/f), bisex (m/f)
inv.
bi·sexu·al·ity [baɪˌsɛksjʊ'ælɪtɪ] N bisessualità.
bish·op ['bɪʃəp] N vescovo; (Chess) alfiere m.
bish·op·ric ['bɪʃəprɪk] N vescovado.
bis·muth ['bɪzməθ] N bismuto.
bi·son ['baɪsn] N bisonte m.
bis·tro ['biːstrəʊ] N bistrot m inv.
bit[1] [bɪt] N a (piece) pezzo; (smaller) pezzetto; **a bit of**
(paper, wood, cake) un pezzo di; (wine, sunshine, peace)
un po' di; **a bit too much** un po' troppo; **a bit bigger/
smaller** un po' più grande/più piccolo(-a); **a little bit
dearer** un pochino più caro(-a); **a good bit cheaper**
molto più a buon mercato; **a bit of news** (fam) una
notizia; **a bit of advice** un (piccolo) consiglio; **a bit of
luck** una fortuna; **a bit mad/dangerous** un po' matto(-
a)/pericoloso(-a); **bit by bit** a poco a poco; **they have a
bit of money** hanno un po' di soldi; **it was a bit of a
shock** è stato un po' un colpo; **that's not a bit of help**
questo non aiuta affatto; **to come to bits** (break) andare
a pezzi; (be dismantled) essere smontabile; **in bits (and
pieces)** (broken) a pezzi; (dismantled) smontato(-a);
bring all your bits and pieces porta tutte le tue cose; **to
do one's bit** fare la propria parte
  b (short time): **a bit** un momento, un attimo
  c (considerable sum): **a good bit, quite a bit** un bel po'
  d (Am: coin) ottavo di dollaro.
bit[2] [bɪt] N (tool) punta; (of horse) morso.
bit[3] [bɪt] PT of **bite**.
bit[4] [bɪt] N (Comput) bit m inv.
bitch [bɪtʃ] 1 N a (of canines) femmina; (of dog) cagna; **a
terrier bitch** un terrier femmina b (offensive: woman)
stronza, puttana (offensivo).
  2 VI (fam: complain) mugugnare.
bitchy ['bɪtʃɪ] ADJ (comp -ier, superl -iest) maligno(-a); **a
bitchy remark** una cattiveria.
bite [baɪt] (vb: pt **bit**, pp **bitten**) 1 N a (act) morso;
(wound: of dog, snake) morsicatura; (: of insect) puntura;
to take a bite at dare un morso a, addentare
  b (of food) boccone m; **there's not a bite to eat** non c'è
niente da mettere sotto i denti; **do you fancy a bite (to
eat)?** ti va di mangiare qualcosa?
  c (Fishing): **he didn't get a single bite** non ha abboccato
neanche un pesce.
  2 VT (gen) mordere; (subj: dog) morsicare, mordere; (:
insect) pungere; **to bite one's nails** mangiarsi le unghie;
once bitten twice shy una volta scottati...; **to bite the
hand that feeds you** (fig) sputare nel piatto in cui si
mangia; **to bite the dust** (die) lasciarci la pelle.
  3 VI a (dog etc) mordere; (insect) pungere
  b (fish) abboccare
  c (fig: policy, action) farsi sentire
▶ **bite back** VT + ADV trattenersi dal dire
▶ **bite into** VI + PREP (subj: person) addentare, dare un
morso a; (: acid) intaccare
▶ **bite off** VT + ADV staccare con un morso; **to bite off more
than one can chew** (fig) fare il passo più lungo della
gamba; **to bite sb's head off** (fig) aggredire (verbalmente)
qn

▶ **bite through** VT + ADV tagliare con i denti.

bit·ing ['baitiŋ] ADJ (*cold, wind*) pungente; (*criticism, sarcasm*) pungente, mordace; (*remark*) caustico(-a).

bit·ing·ly ['baitiŋli] ADV (*speak*) in modo pungente, in modo caustico; **a bitingly cold wind** un vento freddo e pungente.

♦ **bit part** N (*in film, play*) particina, parte *f* secondaria.

bit·ten ['bitn] PP of **bite**.

bit·ter ['bitə'] ☐1 ADJ **a** (*taste*: *gen*) amaro(-a); (: *of fruit*) aspro(-a); **a bitter pill to swallow** (*fig*) un boccone amaro da ingoiare
b (*icy*: *weather*) gelido(-a); (*wind*) pungente
c (*enemy, hatred*) acerrimo(-a); (*quarrel*) aspro(-a); (*disappointment*) amaro(-a); (*person*) risentito(-a); **to the bitter end** fino all'ultimo, a oltranza.
☐2 N (*Brit*: *beer*) birra amara.

♦ **bitter lemon** N (*drink*) limonata amara.

bit·ter·ly ['bitəli] ADV (*disappoint, complain, weep*) amaramente; (*oppose, criticise*) aspramente; (*jealous*) profondamente; **it's bitterly cold** fa un freddo gelido.

bit·tern ['bitɜ:n] N tarabuso.

bit·ter·ness ['bitənis] N (*gen*) amarezza; (*of fruit, fig*: *of quarrel*) asprezza.

bitter·sweet ['bitə,swi:t] ADJ (*taste*) agrodolce; (*love affair*) dolceamaro(-a).

bit·ty ['biti] ADJ (*Brit fam*) frammentario(-a).

bi·tu·men ['bitjumin] N bitume *m*.

bi·tu·mi·nous [bi'tju:minəs] ADJ bituminoso(-a).

bivou·ac ['bivuæk] (*vb*: *pt, pp* **bivouacked**) ☐1 N bivacco.
☐2 VI bivaccare.

bi·zarre [bi'zɑ:'] ADJ bizzarro(-a).

bk ABBR **a** = **bank b** = **book**.

BL [,bi:'ɛl] N ABBR **a** (= *Bachelor of Law*) ≈ laurea in legge **b** (= *Bachelor of Letters, (Am) Bachelor of Literature*) ≈ laurea in lettere.

B/L, b/l, b.l. [,bi:'ɛl] N ABBR = **bill of lading**.

blab [blæb] (*fam*) ☐1 VT (*also*: **blab out**) spifferare.
☐2 VI (*chatter*) cianciare; (*to police*) vuotare il sacco.

blab·ber ['blæbə'] VI (*fam*) parlare a vanvera.

black [blæk] ☐1 ADJ **a** nero(-a); (*in darkness*) buio(-a); (*fig*: *gloomy*: *prospects*) poco allegro(-a); (: *despair*) nero(-a), cupo(-a); (: *future*) poco promettente; (: *wicked*: *thought, deed*) malvagio(-a); **things look pretty black** (*fig*) c'è poco da star allegri; **she looked as black as thunder** (*fig*) aveva un'aria furiosa; **black coffee** caffè *m inv* nero
b (*person*) nero(-a).
☐2 N **a** (*colour*) nero; **dressed in black** vestito(-a) di *or* in nero; **in the black** (*Fin*) in attivo; **to swear that black is white** (*obstinate person*) negare l'evidenza; (*liar*) mentire spudoratamente
b (*person*) nero(-a).
☐3 VT (*Brit Industry*: *goods, firm*) boicottare

▶ **black out** ☐1 VT + ADV **a** (*obliterate*) cancellare
b (*in wartime*) oscurare; (*subj*: *power cut*) far piombare nell'oscurità.
☐2 VI + ADV (*faint*) svenire.

♦ **black and blue** ADJ pieno(-a) di lividi, tutto(-a) pesto(-a); **to beat sb black and blue** riempire qn di lividi.

♦ **black and white** ADJ (*photograph, film, TV*) in bianco e nero; **there it is in black and white** (*fig*) eccolo nero su bianco; **he sees things in black and white terms** per lui non ci sono vie di mezzo.

black·ball ['blæk,bɔ:l] VT: **to blackball sb** votare a sfavore di qn.

♦ **black belt** N (*Sport*) cintura nera; (*Am*): **the black belt** zona abitata principalmente da afro-americani.

black·berry ['blækbəri] N mora (di rovo); **blackberry bush** cespuglio di more.

black·bird ['blæk,bɜ:d] N merlo.

black·board ['blæk,bɔ:d] N lavagna.

♦ **black box** N (*Aer*) scatola nera.

♦ **Black Country** N (*Brit*): **the Black Country** zona industriale dell'Inghilterra centrale.

black·cur·rant [,blæk'kʌrənt] N ribes *m inv* nero.

♦ **black economy** N (*Brit*) economia sommersa.

black·en ['blækən] ☐1 VI annerirsi; (*sky*) oscurarsi.
☐2 VT annerire; (*fig*: *reputation*) macchiare.

♦ **black eye** N occhio nero; **to give sb a black eye** fare un occhio nero a qn.

♦ **Black Forest** N: **the Black Forest** la Foresta Nera.

black·guard ['blægɑ:d] N (*old pej*) canaglia.

black·head ['blæk,hed] N punto nero, comedone *m*.

♦ **black hole** N (*Astron*) buco nero.

♦ **black humour** N umorismo nero.

♦ **black ice** N strato invisibile di ghiaccio (*su strada*).

black·ing ['blækiŋ] N (*for shoes, metal*) nero.

black·ish ['blækiʃ] ADJ nerastro(-a).

black·jack ['blæk,dʒæk] N (*Cards*) ventuno; (*at casino*) blackjack *m inv*; (*Am*: *truncheon*) manganello.

black·leg ['blæk,leg] N (*Brit*) crumiro(-a).

black·list ['blæk,list] ☐1 N lista nera.
☐2 VT mettere sulla lista nera.

♦ **black magic** N magia nera.

black·mail ['blækmeil] ☐1 N ricatto.
☐2 VT ricattare; **to blackmail sb into doing sth** ricattare qn affinché faccia qc.
☐3 ADJ (*letter, phone call*) ricattatorio(-a); (*attempt*) di ricatto.

black·mail·er ['blæk,meilə'] N ricattatore(-trice).

♦ **Black Maria** N (*furgone m*) cellulare.

♦ **black mark** N (*fig*) nota di demerito.

♦ **black market** N mercato nero; (*in wartime*) borsa nera; **on the black market** al mercato nero; alla borsa nera.

♦ **black marketeer** [blæk,mɑ:kə'tiə'] N borsanerista *m/f*.

black·ness ['blæknis] N colore *m* nero; (*darkness*) buio, oscurità.

black·out ['blæk,aut] N **a** (*of lights, TV*) black-out *m inv*; (*during war*) oscuramento **b** (*Med*) svenimento.

♦ **black pepper** N pepe *m* nero.

♦ **Black Power** N Black Power *m*, Potere *m* Nero.

♦ **black pudding** N sanguinaccio.

♦ **Black Sea** N: **the Black Sea** il mar Nero.

♦ **black sheep** N (*fig*) pecora nera.

Black·shirt ['blæk,ʃɜ:t] N (*Pol*) Camicia nera.

black·smith ['blæk,smiθ] N fabbro ferraio.

♦ **black spot** N = accident **blackspot**, N (*Aut*).

black·thorn ['blæk,θɔ:n] N prugnolo, pruno selvatico.

♦ **black tie** N: "**black tie**" (*on invitations*) "abito scuro".

blad·der ['blædə'] N (*Anat*) vescica (urinaria).

blade [bleid] N (*cutting edge*) lama; (: *of safety razor*) lametta; (*of propeller*) pala; **blade of grass** filo d'erba.

blah blah ['blɑ:'blɑ:] N (*fam*) blablà *m*.

blam·able ['bleiməbəl] ADJ biasimevole.

blame [bleim] ☐1 N (*responsibility*) colpa, responsabilità; (*censure*) biasimo; **to lay the blame for sth on sb** attribuire la responsabilità di qc a qn, dare la colpa di qc a qn.
☐2 VT **a** (*hold responsible*): **to blame sb for sth** dare la colpa a qn di qc, ritenere qn responsabile di qc; **to be to**

blame for essere responsabile di; **I'm not to blame** non è colpa mia; **you have only yourself to blame** puoi ringraziare solo te stesso
  b (*reproach*) criticare, biasimare; **and I don't blame him** e non gli dò torto.
blame·less ['bleɪmlɪs] ADJ irreprensibile.
blame·less·ly ['bleɪmlɪslɪ] ADV in modo irreprensibile.
blame·worthy ['bleɪm͵wɜ:ðɪ] ADJ biasimevole.
blanch [blɑ:ntʃ] 1 VI (*person*) sbiancare in viso.
  2 VT (*Culin*) scottare.
blanc·mange [blə'mɒnʒ] N biancomangiare *m*.
bland [blænd] ADJ (*smile*) blando(-a); (*character*) insulso (-a); (*food*) insipido(-a).
blan·dish·ments ['blændɪʃmənts] NPL (*frm*) lusinghe *fpl*.
blank [blæŋk] 1 ADJ (*paper, space*) bianco(-a); (*wall*) cieco(-a); (*empty: expression*) vacuo(-a); (*look*) distratto (-a); **a look of blank amazement** uno sguardo allibito; **my mind went blank** ho avuto un vuoto.
  2 N (*void*) vuoto; (*in form*) spazio in bianco; (*blank cartridge*) cartuccia a salve; **his mind was a blank** si sentiva la testa vuota; **to draw a blank** (*fig*) non aver nessun risultato.
♦ **blank cheque** N, (*Am*) **blank check** N assegno in bianco; **to give sb a blank cheque to do sth** (*fig*) dare carta bianca a qn per fare qc.
blan·ket ['blæŋkɪt] N coperta; (*fig: of snow, fog*) coltre *f*; (: *of smoke*) cappa.
♦ **blanket cover** N: **to give blanket cover** (*subj: insurance policy*) coprire tutti i rischi.
blank·ly ['blæŋklɪ] ADV (*say*) senza espressione; (*stare*) con aria assente.
♦ **blank verse** N versi *mpl* sciolti.
blare [blɛə'] 1 N (*of trumpet, car horn*) strombettio; (*of siren*) urlo; (*of radio*) frastuono.
  2 VT (*also:* **blare out**) far risuonare.
  3 VI (*see n*) strombettare; urlare; suonare a tutto volume.
blar·ney ['blɑ:nɪ] N (*fam*) moine *fpl*, lusinghe *fpl*.
blasé ['blɑ:zeɪ] ADJ blasé *inv*.
blas·pheme [blæs'fi:m] VI bestemmiare.
blas·phem·er [blæs'fi:mə'] N bestemmiatore(-trice).
blas·phe·mous ['blæsfɪməs] ADJ blasfemo(-a).
blas·phe·mous·ly ['blæsfɪməslɪ] ADV in modo blasfemo.
blas·phe·my ['blæsfɪmɪ] N bestemmia.
blast [blɑ:st] 1 N **a** (*of air, steam*) getto; (*of wind*) raffica; **(at) full blast** (*also fig*) a tutta forza
  b (*sound: of trumpet*) squillo; (: *of car horn, siren*) colpo; **(at) full blast** (*radio*) a tutto volume
  c (*of explosion*) spostamento d'aria; (*noise*) esplosione *f*.
  2 VT (*strike: with explosives*) far saltare; (: *by lightning*) bruciare; (*fig: hopes, future*) distruggere.
  3 EXCL (*Brit fam*) mannaggia!; **blast him!** mannaggia a lui!
▶ **blast away** VI + ADV **a** (*gun*) sparare a raffica
  b (*band*) suonare a tutto volume
▶ **blast off** VI + ADV (*Space*) essere lanciato(-a).
blast·ed ['blɑ:stɪd] ADJ (*fam*) maledetto(-a).
♦ **blast furnace** N altoforno.
blast·ing ['blɑ:stɪŋ] N (*Tech*) brillamento; "**blasting in progress**" "attenzione: esplosione mine".
blast·off ['blɑ:st͵ɒf] N (*of rockets*) lancio.
bla·tant ['bleɪtənt] ADJ sfacciato(-a).
bla·tant·ly ['bleɪtəntlɪ] ADV sfacciatamente; **it's blatantly obvious** è lampante.

blath·er ['blæðə'] VI blaterare.
blaze[1] [bleɪz] 1 N (*fire: of buildings*) incendio; (*glow: of fire, sun*) bagliore *m*; (*of gems, beauty*) splendore *m*; **a blaze of colour** un'esplosione di colori; **a blaze of anger** un impeto d'ira; **in a blaze of publicity** circondato(-a) da grande pubblicità; **go to blazes!** (*fam*) va' al diavolo!; **like the blazes** (*fam*) come un matto.
  2 VI (*fire*) ardere, fiammeggiare; (*conflagration*) divampare; (*building*) essere in fiamme; (*sun*) sfolgorare; (*light*) risplendere; **to blaze with anger** (*eyes*) fiammeggiare dalla rabbia; **to blaze with passion** ardere di passione
▶ **blaze away** VI + ADV: **to blaze away (at)** continuare a far fuoco (su)
▶ **blaze up** VI + ADV fare una fiammata; (*fig: feelings*) accendersi.
blaze[2] [bleɪz] 1 N (*mark: on horse*) stella; (: *on tree*) segno.
  2 VT (*tree*) segnare; **to blaze a trail** (*also fig*) aprire una nuova via.
blaz·er ['bleɪzə'] N blazer *m inv*.
blaz·ing ['bleɪzɪŋ] ADJ (*building*) in fiamme; (*fire*) ardente; (*sun*) infuocato(-a); (*light*) sfolgorante; (*jewel*) sfavillante; (*eyes*) fiammeggiante; (*colour, quarrel, anger*) acceso(-a).
bleach [bli:tʃ] 1 N decolorante *m*; **liquid bleach** acqua ossigenata; **household bleach** candeggina, varechina.
  2 VT (*material*) candeggiare; (*bones*) sbiancare; (*hair*) ossigenare.
bleached [bli:tʃt] ADJ (*hair*) decolorato(-a).
bleach·ers ['bli:tʃəz] NPL (*Am*) posti *mpl* di gradinata.
bleach·ing ['bli:tʃɪŋ] N decolorazione *f*; (*of hair*) ossigenazione *f*.
bleak [bli:k] ADJ (*landscape*) desolato(-a); (*weather*) gelido (-a); (*smile*) pallido(-a); (*prospect, future*) tetro(-a), deprimente; **the prospects of your getting a job here are bleak** le probabilità che tu trovi un lavoro qui sono molto scarse.
bleak·ly ['bli:klɪ] ADV in modo tetro, tetramente.
bleak·ness ['bli:knɪs] N (*of landscape, future*) desolazione *f*; (*of room, furnishings*) austerità; (*of weather*) rigidità; (*of smile*) tristezza.
blea·ri·ly ['blɪərɪlɪ] ADV: **he looked up blearily at Tom** fissò Tom con occhi annebbiati.
bleary ['blɪərɪ] ADJ (*eyes*) appannato(-a).
♦ **bleary-eyed** ['blɪərɪ'aɪd] ADJ: **to be bleary-eyed** avere gli occhi appannati.
bleat [bli:t] 1 N belato.
  2 VI belare; (*fig fam*) piagnucolare.
bled [blɛd] PT, PP of **bleed**.
bleed [bli:d] (*vb: pt, pp* **bled** [blɛd]) 1 VI sanguinare; **his nose is bleeding** gli sanguina il naso, gli esce il sangue dal naso; **to bleed to death** morire dissanguato(-a); **my heart bleeds for him** (*iro*) mi fa proprio compassione, poverino!.
  2 VT **a** salassare, dissanguare **b** (*brakes, radiator*) spurgare.
bleed·ing ['bli:dɪŋ] 1 ADJ **a** (*wound, person*) sanguinante; **bleeding gums** le gengive che sanguinano **b** (*Brit fam*) dannato(-a), maledetto(-a); **you bleeding idiot!** pezzo di cretino!.
  2 N perdita di sangue; (*serious*) emorragia.
bleep [bli:p] 1 N breve segnale *m* acustico, bip *m inv*.
  2 VI suonare.
  3 VT (*doctor*) chiamare con il cercapersone.
bleep·er ['bli:pə'] N (*of doctor etc*) cercapersone *m inv*.
blem·ish ['blɛmɪʃ] 1 N imperfezione *f*; (*on fruit*) ammac-

catura; (*on reputation*) macchia.
2 VT deturpare.
blench [blɛntʃ] VI (*flinch*) sussultare; (*turn pale*) impallidire.
blend [blɛnd] 1 N (*gen*) mescolanza, miscuglio; (*of tea, whisky*) miscela; (*of tobacco*) mistura.
2 VT (*teas*) mischiare; (*colours*) mescolare, mischiare; (*Culin*) amalgamare.
3 VI (*harmonize*): **to blend (with)** (*gen*) mescolarsi (a); (*sounds, perfumes*) confondersi (con); (*styles*) essere in armonia (con); (*opinions, races, colours*) fondersi (con).
blend·er [ˈblɛndə] N (*Culin*) frullatore *m*.
bless [blɛs] VT benedire; **God bless the queen!** Dio benedica la regina!; **bless you!** sei un angelo!; (*after sneezing*) salute!; **I'm blessed if I know!** (*fam*) non ne so un accidente!; **bless my soul!** santo cielo!; **to be blessed with** godere di.
bless·ed [ˈblɛsɪd] ADJ **a** (*Rel: holy*) benedetto(-a); (*: happy*) beato(-a); **Blessed Margaret Sinclair** Beata Margaret Sinclair **b** (*fam*) benedetto(-a); **every blessed day** tutti i santi giorni; **where's that blessed book?** dov'è quel benedetto libro?
♦ **Blessed Sacrament** N: **the Blessed Sacrament** il Santissimo Sacramento.
♦ **Blessed Virgin** N: **the Blessed Virgin** la Santa Vergine.
bless·ing [ˈblɛsɪŋ] N **a** (*Rel*) benedizione *f* **b** (*advantage*) vantaggio, fortuna; **to count one's blessings** ritenersi fortunato(-a); **what a blessing that ...** meno male che...; **it was a blessing in disguise** in fondo è stato un bene.
blest [blɛst] (*poetic*) PP of **bless**.
bleth·er [ˈblɛðə] VI = **blather**.
blew [bluː] PT of **blow**.
blight [blaɪt] 1 N (*Bot*) *malattia che fa avvizzire le piante*; (*fig*) piaga.
2 VT (*plants etc*) far avvizzire; (*fig: future, hopes*) rovinare, distruggere.
blight·er [ˈblaɪtə] N (*fam*) disgraziato(-a); **you lucky blighter!** beato te!
bli·mey [ˈblaɪmɪ] EXCL (*Brit fam*) accidenti!
blind [blaɪnd] 1 ADJ (*person, obedience, anger*) cieco(-a); **blind in one eye** cieco da un occhio, orbo; **blind as a bat** (*fam*) cieco come una talpa; **to go blind** diventare cieco; **he was blind to her faults** non vedeva i suoi difetti; **to turn a blind eye to** chiudere un occhio su; **it's not a blind bit of use** (*fam*) non serve a un bel niente; **he doesn't take a blind bit of notice of ...** (*fam*) non bada minimamente a....
2 N **a** : **the blind** NPL i ciechi; **it's a case of the blind leading the blind** è come mettere insieme uno storpio e uno sciancato
b (*shade*) tenda avvolgibile; **Venetian blind** veneziana.
3 ADV (*fly, land*) alla cieca; **blind drunk** (*fam*) ubriaco(-a) fradicio(-a).
4 VT accecare; **he was blinded in the war** ha perso la vista in guerra; **her love blinded her to his faults** il suo amore la rendeva cieca ai suoi difetti.
♦ **blind alley** N vicolo cieco.
♦ **blind corner** N (*Brit*) svolta cieca.
♦ **blind date** N *appuntamento galante con qualcuno che non si conosce*.
blind·ers [ˈblaɪndəz] NPL (*Am*) = **blinkers**.
blind·fold [ˈblaɪndˌfəʊld] 1 ADV con gli occhi bendati; **I could do it blindfold** potrei farlo a occhi chiusi.
2 N benda (per occhi).
3 VT bendare (gli occhi a).

blind·ing [ˈblaɪndɪŋ] ADJ (*flash, light*) accecante; (*pain*) atroce.
blind·ly [ˈblaɪndlɪ] ADV ciecamente.
♦ **blind man's buff** N moscacieca.
blind·ness [ˈblaɪndnɪs] N cecità; **blindness to the realities of life** rifiuto di guardare in faccia la realtà.
♦ **blind spot** N (*Anat*) punto cieco; (*Aut*) angolo in cui manca la visibilità; (*fig*) punto debole.
blink [blɪŋk] 1 N battito di ciglia; **to be on the blink** (*fam: car, machine*) essere scassato(-a).
2 VT: **to blink one's eyes** sbattere le palpebre.
3 VI sbattere le palpebre; (*light*) lampeggiare.
blink·ered [ˈblɪŋkəd] ADJ (*fig: person*) che ha i paraocchi; **to have a blinkered view of reality** vedere la realtà con i paraocchi.
blink·ers [ˈblɪŋkəz] NPL (*Brit*) paraocchi *mpl*.
blink·ing [ˈblɪŋkɪŋ] ADJ (*Brit fam*) dannato(-a), maledetto (-a); **this blinking ...** questo maledetto....
blip [blɪp] N (*on radar etc*) segnale *m* intermittente; (*on graph*) piccola variazione; (*fig*) momentanea battuta d'arresto.
bliss [blɪs] N (*Rel*) beatitudine *f*; (*happy state*) (immensa) felicità; **ignorance is bliss** (*Proverb*) beata ignoranza; **it's bliss!** (*fam*) è meraviglioso!
bliss·ful [ˈblɪsfʊl] ADJ (*event, day*) stupendo(-a), meraviglioso(-a); (*smile*) beato(-a); **in blissful ignorance** nella (più) beata ignoranza.
bliss·ful·ly [ˈblɪsfəlɪ] ADV (*sigh, smile*) beatamente; **blissfully happy** magnificamente felice.
blis·ter [ˈblɪstə] 1 N (*on skin*) vescica; (*of paint*) bolla.
2 VT (*skin*) far venire le vesciche a; (*paint*) produrre delle bolle in.
3 VI (*skin*) coprirsi di bollicine; (*paint*) formare delle bolle.
blis·ter·ing [ˈblɪstərɪŋ] ADJ (*sun*) che spacca le pietre; (*fig: attack*) sferzante.
♦ **blister pack** N (*Comm*) blister *m inv*.
blithe [blaɪð] ADJ (*thoughtless*) spensierato(-a); (*old: happy*) gioioso(-a), allegro(-a).
blithe·ly [ˈblaɪðlɪ] ADV (*unthinkingly*) spensieratamente; (*happily*) allegramente.
blith·er·ing [ˈblɪðərɪŋ] ADJ (*fam*): **this blithering idiot** questo pezzo d'idiota.
BLitt [ˌbiːˈlɪt] N ABBR (= *Bachelor of Literature*) ≈ laurea in lettere.
Blitz [blɪts] N: **the Blitz** *il bombardamento aereo della Gran Bretagna*.
blitz [blɪts] 1 N (*Mil*) blitz *m inv*; **to have a blitz on sth** (*fig*) prendere d'assalto qc.
2 VT bombardare.
blitz·krieg [ˈblɪtsˌkriːg] N guerra *f* lampo *inv*.
bliz·zard [ˈblɪzəd] N bufera di neve.
bloat·ed [ˈbləʊtɪd] ADJ (*also fig*): **bloated (with)** gonfio(-a) (di).
bloat·er [ˈbləʊtə] N (*herring*) aringa affumicata; (*mackerel*) sgombro affumicato.
blob [blɒb] N (*drop*) goccia; (*stain, spot*) macchia; (*lump: of mud*) pallina.
bloc [blɒk] N (*Pol*) blocco.
block [blɒk] 1 N **a** (*of stone, ice*) blocco; (*toy*) cubo (per fare le costruzioni); (*butcher's, executioner's*) ceppo; **to knock sb's block off** (*fam*) rompere la zucca a qn
b (*building*) palazzo; (*esp Am: group of buildings*) isolato; **block of flats** caseggiato; **to walk around the block** fare il giro dell'isolato; **3 blocks from here** a 3 isolati di

distanza da qui

c (*section*: *of tickets*) blocchetto; (: *of shares*) pacchetto; (*Comput*) blocco

d (*blockage*: *in pipe*) ingorgo; (*Med*) blocco; **mental block** blocco mentale.

[2] VT (*gen*, *Comput*) bloccare; (*pipe*) ingorgare, bloccare; (*Ftbl*) stoppare; **to block sb's way** sbarrare la strada a qn; **to block sb's view** coprire la vista a qn

▶ **block in** VT + ADV **a** : **to block sb in** (*with car*) chiudere qn (con l'auto)

b (*fill with paint*) colorare

▶ **block off** VT + ADV bloccare

▶ **block out** VT + ADV (*obscure*: *light*) escludere; (*obliterate*: *picture*) cancellare

▶ **block up** VT + ADV (*obstruct*: *passage*) bloccare; (: *pipe*) ingorgare, intasare; (*fill in*: *gap*) tappare; (: *window*, *entrance*) murare; **my nose is blocked up** ho il naso chiuso.

block·ade [blɒˈkeɪd] [1] N (*Mil*) blocco.
[2] VT bloccare.

block·age [ˈblɒkɪdʒ] N (*obstruction*) ingorgo; (*Med*) blocco.

◆ **block and tackle** N (*Tech*) paranco.

◆ **block booking** N prenotazione *f* in blocco.

block·bust·er [ˈblɒkˌbʌstəʳ] N (*fam*: *film*, *TV series*) successone *m*.

block·head [ˈblɒkˌhɛd] N (*fam*) testa di legno.

◆ **block letters**, **block capitals** NPL stampatello.

◆ **block release** N (*Brit*) *periodo pagato concesso al tirocinante per effettuare studi superiori*.

◆ **block vote** N (*Brit*) voto per delega.

bloke [bləʊk] N (*Brit fam*) tipo, tizio.

blond [blɒnd] [1] N (*man*) biondo.
[2] ADJ biondo(-a).

blonde [blɒnd] [1] N (*woman*) bionda.
[2] ADJ biondo(-a).

blood [blʌd] N sangue *m*; **to give blood** donare sangue; **of royal blood** di sangue reale; **there's bad blood between them** corre cattivo sangue fra di loro; **new blood** (*fig*) nuova linfa; **it's like trying to get blood out of a stone** è come voler cavare sangue dalle pietre; **in cold blood** a sangue freddo; **blood is thicker than water** (*Proverb*) il sangue non è acqua; **it's in the blood** ce l'ho (*or* l'hai *etc*) nel sangue; **he's after my blood** (*hum*) se mi prende m'ammazza; **my blood ran cold** mi son sentito gelare il sangue.

◆ **blood-and-thunder** [ˌblʌdənˈθʌndəʳ] ADJ (*novel*, *play*, *film*) a sensazione.

◆ **blood bank** N banca del sangue.

◆ **blood bath** N bagno di sangue.

◆ **blood brother** N fratello di sangue.

◆ **blood cell** N globulo.

◆ **blood count** N esame *m* emocromocitometrico.

blood·curdling [ˈblʌdˌkɜːdlɪŋ] ADJ raccapricciante, da far gelare il sangue.

◆ **blood donor** N donatore(-trice) di sangue.

◆ **blood group** N gruppo sanguigno.

◆ **blood heat** N temperatura corporea.

blood·hound [ˈblʌdˌhaʊnd] N segugio.

blood·less [ˈblʌdlɪs] ADJ (*pale*) smorto(-a), esangue; (*coup*) senza spargimento di sangue.

◆ **blood-letting** [ˈblʌdˌlɛtɪŋ] N (*fig*) spargimento di sangue; (*Med*) salasso.

◆ **blood lust** N sete *f* di sangue.

◆ **blood money** N denaro sporco (*somma pagata ad un*

killer o per una delazione).

◆ **blood orange** N arancia sanguigna.

◆ **blood poisoning** N setticemia.

◆ **blood pressure** N pressione *f* del sangue *or* sanguigna; **to have high/low blood pressure** avere la pressione alta/bassa.

◆ **blood red** ADJ rosso sangue *inv*.

◆ **blood relation** N consanguineo(-a).

blood·shed [ˈblʌdˌʃɛd] N spargimento di sangue.

blood·shot [ˈblʌdˌʃɒt] ADJ: **bloodshot eyes** occhi iniettati di sangue.

◆ **blood sports** NPL sport cruenti.

blood·stain [ˈblʌdˌsteɪn] N macchia di sangue.

blood·stained [ˈblʌdˌsteɪnd] ADJ insanguinato(-a), macchiato(-a) di sangue.

blood·stock [ˈblʌdˌstɒk] N purosangue *inv*.

blood·stone [ˈblʌdˌstəʊn] N eliotropio.

blood·stream [ˈblʌdˌstriːm] N (circolazione *f* del) sangue *m*.

blood·sucker [ˈblʌdˌsʌkəʳ] N (*also fig*) sanguisuga.

◆ **blood test** N analisi *fpl* del sangue.

blood·thirsty [ˈblʌdˌθɜːstɪ] ADJ sanguinario(-a), assetato (-a) di sangue.

◆ **blood transfusion** N trasfusione *f* di sangue.

◆ **blood type** N gruppo sanguigno.

◆ **blood vessel** N vaso sanguigno.

bloody [ˈblʌdɪ] [1] ADJ **a** (*bleeding*) sanguinante, che sanguina; (*bloodstained*) insanguinato(-a); (*cruel*: *battle*, *feud*) sanguinoso(-a)

b (*Brit fam*) maledetto(-a), dannato(-a); **this bloody ...** questo maledetto...; **bloody good** maledettamente buono(-a); **a bloody awful day** una giornata di merda; **bloody hell!** porca miseria!; **I'm a bloody genius!** madonna, che genio che sono!.

[2] ADV (*Brit fam*): **that's no bloody good!** questo non serve a un cavolo!; **she runs bloody fast!** cavolo, se corre veloce!

◆ **bloody-minded** [ˌblʌdɪˈmaɪndɪd] ADJ (*Brit fam*) indisponente.

◆ **bloody-mindedness** [ˌblʌdɪˈmaɪndɪdnɪs] N (*Brit fam*) ostinazione *f*.

bloom [bluːm] [1] N (*flower*) fiore *m*; (*on fruit*) lanugine *f*; (*on complexion*) colorito roseo; **in bloom** (*flower*) sbocciato(-a); (*tree*) in fiore; **in full bloom** in piena fioritura; **in the full bloom of youth** nel fiore della giovinezza.

[2] VI (*flower*) aprirsi; (*tree*) sfiorire.

bloom·ers [ˈbluːməz] NPL mutandoni *mpl* a sbuffo.

bloom·ing [ˈbluːmɪŋ] ADJ (*fam*) dannato(-a), maledetto (-a); **this blooming ...** questo dannato....

blos·som [ˈblɒsəm] [1] N (*with pl sense*) fiori *mpl*; (*single flower*) fiore *m*; **apple blossom** fiori di melo.

[2] VI fiorire; **to blossom into** (*fig*) diventare.

blot [blɒt] [1] N macchia; **to be a blot on the landscape** rovinare il paesaggio.

[2] VT **a** (*spot with ink*) macchiare d'inchiostro; **to blot one's copy book** (*fig*) farla grossa

b (*dry*: *ink*, *writing*) asciugare

▶ **blot out** VT + ADV (*memories*, *words*) cancellare; (*view*, *sun*) nascondere, offuscare; (*nation*, *city*) annientare.

blotch [blɒtʃ] N (*of ink*, *colour*) macchia, chiazza; (*on skin*) chiazza.

blotched [blɒtʃt] ADJ chiazzato(-a), macchiato(-a).

blotchy [ˈblɒtʃɪ] ADJ pieno(-a) *or* coperto(-a) di macchie.

blot·ter [ˈblɒtəʳ] N tampone *m* (di carta assorbente).

◆ **blot·ting pa·per** [ˈblɒtɪŋˌpeɪpəʳ] N carta assorbente,

carta asciugante.

blot·to ['blɒtəʊ] ADJ (*Brit fam*) sbronzo(-a); **to get blotto** sbronzarsi.

blouse [blaʊz] N camicetta.

blou·son ['bluːzɒn] N blouson *m inv*.

blow[1] [bləʊ] N (*gen*) colpo; (*with fist*) pugno; **a blow with a hammer** un colpo di martello; **at one blow** in un colpo (solo); **to come to blows** venire alle mani; **the news came as a great blow to her** la notizia fu un duro colpo per lei.

blow[2] [bləʊ] (*vb: pt* **blew**, *pp* **blown**) ☐ VT **a** (*subj: wind: ship*) spingere; (: *hair*) far svolazzare; **a gale blew the ship off course** una bufera ha fatto uscire di rotta la nave

b (*trumpet, horn*) suonare; **to blow a whistle** fischiare; **to blow one's own trumpet** cantare le proprie lodi

c (*bubbles*) fare; (*glass*) soffiare; (*kiss*) mandare; **to blow one's nose** soffiarsi il naso

d (*fuse, safe*) far saltare; **to blow money on sth** (*fam*) buttare via dei soldi per qc; **to blow a secret** spifferare un segreto; **to blow sb's cover** scoprire il gioco di qn; **to blow one's top** (*fam*) esplodere, andare su tutte le furie; **blow the expense!** crepi l'avarizia!; **well, blow me!** OR **well, I'll be blowed!** (*old: expressing surprise*) accidenti!; **I'll be blowed if ...** (*expressing indignation*) che mi venga un accidente se....

☐ VI **a** (*wind, person*) soffiare; (*leaves*) svolazzare; (*flag*) sventolare; **to blow on one's fingers** scaldarsi le mani soffiando; **to blow on one's soup** soffiare sulla minestra; **to see which way the wind blows** (*fig*) vedere che aria tira; **his hat blew out of the window** il suo cappello è volato fuori dalla finestra; **the door blew open/shut** un colpo di vento ha spalancato/chiuso la porta

b (*make sound: trumpet*) suonare; **the referee blew his whistle** l'arbitro fischiò

c (*fuse*) saltare; (*tyre*) scoppiare

▶ **blow away** ☐ VI + ADV volare via.
☐ VT + ADV (*papers, leaves*) far volare via; (*hat*) portare via

▶ **blow down** ☐ VI + ADV essere abbattuto(-a) dal vento.
☐ VT + ADV abbattere

▶ **blow in** VI + ADV (*window*) sfasciarsi; (*enter: leaves, dust*) volar dentro; **look who's just blown in!** (*fam*) ma guarda chi è arrivato!

▶ **blow off** ☐ VI + ADV (*hat*) volar via.
☐ VT + ADV (*hat*) portare via; **to blow off steam** (*fig fam*) sfogarsi

▶ **blow out** ☐ VT + ADV (*candle*) spegnere; (*swell out: cheeks*) gonfiare.
☐ VI + ADV scoppiare

▶ **blow over** ☐ VT + ADV (*tree*) abbattere.
☐ VI + ADV (*tree*) rovesciarsi; (*storm*) passare, calmarsi; (*fig: dispute*) calmarsi

▶ **blow up** ☐ VT + ADV (*bridge*) far saltare; (*tyre, balloon*) gonfiare; (*photo*) ingrandire; (*event*) esagerare.
☐ VI + ADV (*bomb, fig: person*) esplodere; (*row*) scoppiare; (*storm: gather*) arrivare.

♦ **blow-by-blow** ['bləʊbaɪˌbləʊ] ADJ (*account*) minuto per minuto.

♦ **blow-dry** ['bləʊˌdraɪ] ☐ N (*hairstyle*) messa in piega a phon.
☐ VT asciugare con il phon.

blow·er ['bləʊə'] N (*fam*) telefono.

blow·fly ['bləʊˌflaɪ] N moscone *m* della carne.

blow·hole ['bləʊˌhəʊl] N (*Geol*) sfiatatoio.

blow·lamp ['bləʊˌlæmp] N (*Brit*) cannello per saldare/

sverniciare.

blown [bləʊn] PP of **blow 2**.

blow·out ['bləʊˌaʊt] N (*fam: big meal*) abbuffata; (*of tyre*) scoppio; (*of fuse*) corto circuito.

blow·pipe ['bləʊˌpaɪp] N (*weapon*) cerbottana.

blowsy ['blaʊzɪ] ADJ = **blowzy**.

blow·torch ['bləʊˌtɔːtʃ] N (*Am*) = **blowlamp**.

♦ **blow-up** ['bləʊˌʌp] N (*Phot*) ingrandimento, esplosione *f*; (*fam: quarrel*) litigio, baruffa.

blowy ['bləʊɪ] ADJ ventoso(-a).

blowzy, blowsy ['blaʊzɪ] ADJ (*woman*) sciatto(-a), trasandato(-a).

blub·ber ['blʌbə'] ☐ N (*of whales*) grasso di balena.
☐ VI (*weep*) frignare.

bludg·eon ['blʌdʒən] VT prendere a randellate; **to bludgeon sb to death** ammazzare qn a randellate; **to bludgeon sb into doing sth** (*fig*) costringere qn a fare qc.

blue [bluː] ☐ ADJ **a** (*light blue*) azzurro(-a), celeste; (*darker*) blu *inv*; **bright blue** bluette *inv*; **blue with cold** livido(-a) dal freddo; **once in a blue moon** a ogni morte di papa; **you can talk till you're blue in the face** puoi parlare fino a domani; **to be in a blue funk** (*old*) avere una fifa nera

b (*obscene: film, book*) porno *inv*; (: *joke*) sporco(-a), sconcio(-a)

c (*fam: sad*): **to feel blue** sentirsi giù.
☐ N (*colour: see adj*) azzurro, celeste *m*; blu *m inv*; **the blue** (*sky*) l'azzurro; **out of the blue** (*fig*) all'improvviso.

♦ **blue baby** N neonato(-a) cianotico(-a).

blue·bell ['bluːˌbel] N giacinto dei boschi.

blue·berry ['bluːbərɪ] N (*Am*) mirtillo.

blue·bird ['bluːˌbɜːd] N uccello azzurro.

♦ **blue blood·ed** [bluːˈblʌdɪd] ADJ (*fig*) di sangue blu.

blue·bottle ['bluːˌbɒtl] N moscone *m*.

♦ **blue cheese** N ≈ gorgonzola.

♦ **blue-chip investment** ['bluːˈtʃɪpɪnˈvestmənt] N investimento sicuro.

♦ **blue-collar worker** ['bluːˌkɒlə'ˈwɜːkə'] N operaio(-a), tuta *f* blu *inv*.

♦ **blue-eyed** ['bluːˈaɪd] ADJ dagli occhi azzurri; **blue-eyed boy** (*fig*) favorito.

♦ **blue gum** N (*Bot*) blu gum *m inv* della Tasmania.

♦ **blue jeans** NPL (blue-)jeans *mpl*.

blue·print ['bluːˌprɪnt] N cianografia; **blueprint (for)** (*fig*) formula (di).

blues [bluːz] NPL (*Mus*): **the blues** il blues; **to have the blues** (*fam: depression*) essere giù.

blue·tit ['bluːˌtɪt] N cinciarella.

bluff[1] [blʌf] ADJ (*person*) senza peli sulla lingua, brusco (-a).

bluff[2] [blʌf] N (*cliff*) scogliera a picco.

bluff[3] [blʌf] ☐ N bluff *m inv*; **to call sb's bluff** far mettere le carte in tavola a qn.
☐ VT: **to bluff it out** cavarsela bluffando.
☐ VI bluffare.

bluff·er ['blʌfə'] N bluffatore(-trice).

blun·der ['blʌndə'] ☐ N (*serious mistake*) abbaglio; **to make a blunder** prendere un abbaglio.
☐ VI **a** (*see n*) prendere un abbaglio **b** (*move clumsily*): **to blunder about** andare *or* muoversi a tentoni; **to blunder into sb/sth** andare a sbattere contro qn/qc.

blun·der·er ['blʌndərə'] N imbranato(-a).

blun·der·ing ['blʌndərɪŋ] ADJ imbranato(-a); **you blundering idiot!** razza d'imbranato!

blunt [blʌnt] ☐ ADJ **a** (*not sharp: edge*) non tagliente,

smussato(-a); (: *knife*) che non taglia; (: *point*) spuntato (-a); **this pencil is blunt** questa matita non ha più la punta; **blunt instrument** (*Law*) corpo contundente **b** (*outspoken*) brutale; (*manners*) brusco(-a). 2 VT (*knife*) smussare; (*point*) spuntare; (*fig: nerves, feelings*) rendere insensibile.

blunt·ly ['blʌntlɪ] ADV (*speak*) senza mezzi termini.

blunt·ness ['blʌntnɪs] N (*fig: of person*) brutale franchezza.

blur [blɜːʳ] 1 N (*shape*) massa indistinta *or* confusa; **my mind was a blur** avevo la mente annebbiata. 2 VT (*writing*) rendere (quasi) illeggibile; (*outline, sight, memory, judgment*) offuscare. 3 VI (*see vt*) diventare (quasi) illeggibile; offuscarsi; **her eyes blurred with tears** gli occhi le si velarono di lacrime.

blurb [blɜːb] N (*publicity material*) trafiletto pubblicitario; (*on book jacket*) note *fpl* di copertina.

blurred [blɜːd] ADJ (*TV*) sfuocato(-a); (*photo*) mosso(-a).

blur·ry ['blɜːrɪ] ADJ (*comp* -**ier**, *superl* -**iest**) confuso(-a), indistinto(-a).

blurt [blɜːt] VT (*also:* **blurt out**) spifferare.

blush [blʌʃ] 1 N rossore *m*; **with a blush** arrossendo; **without a blush** senza neppure arrossire; **to spare sb's blushes** evitare di mettere in imbarazzo qn. 2 VI: **to blush (with)** arrossire (per *or* da).

blush·er ['blʌʃəʳ] N **a** (*Cosmetics*) fard *m inv* **b** (*mushroom*) tignosa vinata.

blush·ing ['blʌʃɪŋ] ADJ: **the blushing bride** (*hum*) la dolce sposina.

blus·ter ['blʌstəʳ] 1 N bravate *fpl*, spacconate *fpl*; (*threats*) vuote minacce *fpl*. 2 VI (*wind*) infuriare; (*person: boast*) fare lo/la spaccone (-a); (: *rage*) dare in escandescenze.

blus·ter·ing ['blʌstərɪŋ] ADJ (*tone, manner*) da spaccone.

blus·tery ['blʌstərɪ] ADJ (*wind*) a raffiche; (*day*) ventoso (-a); (*weather*) burrascoso(-a).

Blvd ABBR = **boulevard**.

BM [ˌbiːˈɛm] N ABBR **a** = *British Museum* **b** (*Univ*: = *Bachelor of Medicine*) ≈ laurea in medicina.

BMA [ˌbiːɛmˈeɪ] N ABBR = *British Medical Association*.

BMJ [ˌbiːɛmˈdʒeɪ] N ABBR = *British Medical Journal*.

♦ **B movie** N film *m inv* di serie B.

BMus ABBR of **Bachelor of Music**; *laurea in discipline musicali.*

BMX [ˌbiːɛmˈɛks] N ABBR (= *bicycle motorcross*) ciclocross *m inv*; **BMX bike** mountain bike *f inv* per cross, BMX *f inv*.

BO [ˌbiːˈəʊ] N ABBR (= *body odour*) odori *mpl* sgradevoli (del corpo).

boa ['bəʊə] N (*snake: also:* **boa constrictor**) (serpente *m*) boa *inv*; (*of feathers*) boa *m inv*.

boar [bɔːʳ] N (*male pig*) verro; (*wild boar*) cinghiale *m*.

board [bɔːd] 1 N **a** (*of wood*) asse *f*, tavola; (*for chess*) scacchiera; (*blackboard*) lavagna; (*on wall*) tabellone *m*; **across the board** (*fig: adv*) per tutte le categorie; (: *adj*) generale; **to go by the board** (*fig*) andare a monte, venir messo(-a) da parte; **above board** (*fig*) regolare **b** (*provision of meals*) vitto; **half board** (*Brit*) mezza pensione *f*, **full board** (*Brit*) pensione *f* completa **c** (*Naut, Aer*): **on board** a bordo; **to go on board** salire a bordo **d** (*group of officials*) commissione *f*; **board of directors** consiglio di amministrazione; **board of examiners** commissione esaminatrice *or* d'esame **e** (*institution*) ente *m*; **Board of Trade** (*Brit*) ministero

del Commercio. 2 VT (*ship, plane*) imbarcarsi su, salire a bordo di; (*enemy ship*) andare all'abbordaggio di; (*bus, train*) salire su *or* in. 3 VI: **to board with sb** essere a pensione da qn

▸ **board out** VT + ADV mettere a pensione presso
▸ **board up** VT + ADV (*door*) chiudere con assi.
♦ **board and lodging** N vitto e alloggio.

board·er ['bɔːdəʳ] N pensionante *m/f*; (*Scol*) collegiale *m/f*, convittore(-trice).

♦ **board game** N gioco da tavolo.

board·ing ['bɔːdɪŋ] N **a** (*floor*) impiantito (di legno); (*fence*) recinzione *f* di legno **b** (*of ship, plane*) imbarco.

♦ **boarding card**, **boarding pass** N (*Aviat, Naut*) carta d'imbarco.

♦ **boarding house** N pensione *f*.

♦ **boarding party** N (*to take control*) gruppo che assuma il controllo di una nave come forma di protesta; (*for inspection*) squadra di ispezione (*del carico di una nave*).

♦ **boarding school** N collegio, convitto.

♦ **board meeting** N riunione *f* di consiglio.

♦ **board room** N sala del consiglio.

board·walk ['bɔːdˌwɔːk] N (*Am*) passeggiata a mare.

boast [bəʊst] 1 N vanteria; **it is his boast that he's never lost a match** si fa vanto di non aver mai perso un incontro. 2 VT (*possession, achievement*): **the village boasted only one small store** nel paese c'era solo un negozietto. 3 VI: **to boast (about *or* of)** vantarsi (di).

boast·er ['bəʊstəʳ] N spaccone(-a).

boast·ful ['bəʊstfʊl] ADJ pieno(-a) di sé, che si vanta sempre.

boast·ful·ly ['bəʊstfəlɪ] ADV vantandosi.

boast·ful·ness ['bəʊstfəlnɪs] N vanagloria.

boast·ing ['bəʊstɪŋ] N vanterie *fpl*.

boat [bəʊt] N (*gen*) barca; (*ship*) nave *f*; **to go by boat** andare in barca *or* in nave; **we're all in the same boat** (*fig fam*) siamo tutti nella stessa barca.

boat·builder ['bəʊtˌbɪldəʳ] N costruttore *m* di barche.

boat·building ['bəʊtˌbɪldɪŋ] N costruzione *f* di barche.

boat·er ['bəʊtəʳ] N (*hat*) paglietta.

♦ **boat hook** N mezzo marinaio.

boat·house ['bəʊtˌhaʊs] N rimessa per barche.

boat·ing ['bəʊtɪŋ] N nautica da diporto.

♦ **boat neck** N (*of sweater, dress*) scollo a barchetta.

♦ **boat people** N boat people *mpl*.

♦ **boat race** N gara di canottaggio.

boat·swain ['bəʊsn] N nostromo.

♦ **boat train** N *treno in coincidenza con il traghetto.*

boat·yard ['bəʊtˌjɑːd] N cantiere *m* (*per costruzione e riparazione di barche*).

bob¹ [bɒb] 1 N (*curtsy*) riverenza, inchino. 2 VI (*also:* **bob up and down**) andare su e giù
▸ **bob up** VI + ADV spuntare, saltare fuori.

bob² [bɒb] N caschetto.

bob³ [bɒb] N, PL INV (*old: Brit fam*) scellino.

bob·bin ['bɒbɪn] N spoletta, bobina; (*of sewing machine*) rocchetto.

bob·ble ['bɒbl] N (*on hat*) pompon *m inv*.

bob·by ['bɒbɪ] N (*Brit fam*) poliziotto.

bob·cat ['bɒbˌkæt] N (*Am*) lince *f*.

bob·sleigh ['bɒbˌsleɪ] N bob *m inv*.

bod [bɒd] N (*Brit fam*) tipo; **he's an odd bod** è un tipo strano.

bode [bəʊd] VI: **to bode well** promettere bene; **to bode ill**

non promettere nulla di buono.

bodge [bɒdʒ] (*Brit*) [1] VT raffazzonare.
  [2] N lavoro raffazzonato.

bod·ice ['bɒdɪs] N (*of dress*) corpino, corpetto.

bodi·ly ['bɒdɪlɪ] [1] ADJ (*comfort, needs*) materiale; (*functions*) corporale.
  [2] ADV (*carry*) in braccio; (*lift*) di peso.

body ['bɒdɪ] N **a** (*of person, animal*) corpo; (*dead body*) corpo, cadavere *m*; **to keep body and soul together** tirare avanti; **over my dead body!** neanche se mi ammazzi!
  b (*main part: of structure*) corpo; (: *of car*) carrozzeria; (: *of plane*) fusoliera; (: *of ship*) scafo, corpo; (: *of speech, document*) parte *f* principale
  c (*mass, collection: of facts*) massa, quantità *f inv*; (: *of laws*) raccolta; (: *of people, water*) massa; (: *of troops*) grosso; **the student body** gli studenti; **in a body** in massa
  d (*organization*) associazione *f*, organizzazione *f*, ente *m*; **legislative body** organo legislativo; **ruling body** direttivo
  e (*of wine, hair*) corpo; **a wine with body** un vino corposo
  f (*also: body stocking*) body *m inv*.
♦ **body blow** N (*fig*) duro colpo.
♦ **body building** N culturismo.
body·guard ['bɒdɪˌgɑːd] N (*person, group*) guardia del corpo.
♦ **body language** N linguaggio del corpo.
♦ **body politic** N (*frm*): **the body politic** lo Stato.
♦ **body repairs** NPL (*Aut*) lavori *mpl* di carrozzeria.
♦ **body search** N perquisizione *f* personale; **to carry out a body search on sb** effettuare una perquisizione personale su qn; **to submit to** *or* **undergo a body search** essere sottoposto(-a) a perquisizione personale.
♦ **body stocking** N body *m inv*.
body·work ['bɒdɪˌwɜːk] N (*Aut*) carrozzeria.
Boer ['buəʳ] N, ADJ boero(-a).
bof·fin ['bɒfɪn] N (*Brit fam*) scienziato(-a).
bog [bɒg] N palude *f*; (*Brit fam: toilet*) cesso
► **bog down** VT + ADV: **to get bogged down (in)** impantanarsi (in).
bo·gey ['bəʊgɪ] N (*worry*) spauracchio.
bogey·man ['bəʊgɪˌmæn] N babau *m inv*.
bog·gle ['bɒgl] VI (*fam*): **the mind boggles!** è incredibile!; **his eyes boggled at the sight** ha fatto tanto d'occhi davanti a quella scena.
bog·gy ['bɒgɪ] ADJ paludoso(-a).
Bo·go·tá [ˌbəʊgə'tɑː] N Bogotà *f*.
bo·gus ['bəʊgəs] ADJ (*jewels, claim*) falso(-a), fasullo(-a); (*person, attitude*) finto(-a).
Bo·he·mia [bəʊ'hiːmɪə] N Boemia.
Bo·he·mian [bəʊ'hiːmɪən] [1] ADJ (*Geog*) boemo(-a); (*artist, life*) bohémien.
  [2] N (*Geog*) boemo(-a); (*artist, writer*) bohémien *m inv*.
boil[1] [bɔɪl] N (*Med*) foruncolo.
boil[2] [bɔɪl] [1] N: **to bring to the boil** (*Am*): **to bring to a boil** portare a ebollizione; **to come to the boil,** (*Am*) **to come to a boil** raggiungere l'ebollizione; **on the boil** che bolle; **it's off the boil** ha smesso di bollire.
  [2] VT (*far*) bollire; (*potatoes, meat*) (far) bollire, (far) lessare; **boiled egg** uovo alla coque; **boiled ham** prosciutto cotto; **boiled potatoes** patate *fpl* bollite *or* lesse.
  [3] VI (*water etc*) bollire; **the kettle is boiling** l'acqua bolle; **to let a saucepan boil dry** lasciar evaporare tutta

l'acqua da una pentola; **to boil with rage** (*fig*) bollire di rabbia
► **boil away** VI + ADV (*liquid*) evaporare; (*fig*) sfumare
► **boil down** VI + ADV (*fig*): **to boil down to** ridursi a
► **boil over** VI + ADV traboccare (bollendo); (*fig: anger*) esplodere
► **boil up** VT + ADV far bollire.
boil·er ['bɔɪləʳ] N (*gen*) caldaia; (*for domestic hot water*) scaldabagno, scaldaacqua *m inv*.
boiler·maker ['bɔɪləˌmeɪkəʳ] N operaio metallurgico.
♦ **boiler suit** N (*Brit*) tuta (da lavoro).
boil·ing ['bɔɪlɪŋ] ADJ (*also fig*) bollente; **a boiling hot day** un giorno torrido; **I'm boiling (hot)** (*fam*) sto morendo di caldo.
♦ **boiling point** N punto di ebollizione.
♦ **boil-in-the-bag** [ˌbɔɪlɪnðə'bæg] ADJ (*rice etc*) da bollire nel sacchetto.
bois·ter·ous ['bɔɪstərəs] ADJ (*meeting*) turbolento(-a); (*person*) chiassoso(-a); (*party*) animato(-a).
bold [bəʊld] ADJ **a** (*brave: person, attempt*) audace; (*fig: plan, move*) ardito(-a) **b** (*forward: child, remark*) sfacciato(-a), sfrontato(-a) **c** (*striking: line, pattern*) vistoso(-a), che salta all'occhio; (*colour*) deciso(-a).
bold·ly ['bəʊldlɪ] ADV (*see adj*) audacemente; arditamente; sfacciatamente; vistosamente.
bold·ness ['bəʊldnɪs] N (*of person, plan*) audacia; (*impudence*) sfacciataggine *f*, impudenza.
♦ **bold type** N (*Typ*) neretto, grassetto.
bo·lero [bə'lɛərəʊ] N bolero.
Bo·livia [bə'lɪvɪə] N Bolivia.
Bo·liv·ian [bə'lɪvɪən] ADJ, N boliviano(-a).
bol·lard ['bɒlɑd] N (*on quay*) bitta; (*Brit: to bar way*) pilastrino di chiusura al traffico; (*at junction*) colonnina luminosa.
bol·locks ['bɒləks] NPL (*fam!*): **to talk a load of bollocks** dire stronzate *or* cazzate (*fam!*)
Bol·she·vik ['bɒlʃəvɪk] ADJ, N bolscevico(-a).
Bol·she·vism ['bɒlʃəvɪzəm] N bolscevismo.
bol·shy ['bɒlʃɪ] ADJ (*comp* **-ier,** *superl* **-iest**) (*Brit fam*) piantagrane, ribelle; **to be in a bolshy mood** essere in vena di piantar grane.
bol·ster ['bəʊlstəʳ] [1] N capezzale *m*.
  [2] VT (*also:* **bolster up**) sostenere; **to bolster sb's courage** incoraggiare qn.
bolt [bəʊlt] [1] N **a** (*on door*) chiavistello, catenaccio; (*of lock*) catenaccio; (*Tech*) bullone *m*; (*of crossbow*) dardo; (*of cloth*) pezza; **he's shot his bolt** (*fig*) ha giocato la sua ultima carta
  b (*dash*): **to make a bolt for the door** fare un balzo *or* schizzare verso la porta; **to make a bolt for it** darsela a gambe
  c (*lightning*) fulmine *m*; **a bolt from the blue** (*fig*) un fulmine a ciel sereno.
  [2] ADV: **bolt upright** diritto(-a) come un fuso.
  [3] VT **a** (*door*) chiudere con il catenaccio *or* il chiavistello, serrare; (*Tech: also:* **bolt together**) imbullonare
  b (*food: also:* **bolt down**) ingollare.
  [4] VI (*run away: person*) darsela a gambe; (: *horse*) imbizzarrirsi; (*rush*) scappare via.
♦ **bolt hole** N (*Brit*) rifugio.
bomb [bɒm] [1] N bomba; **it went like a bomb** (*fam: party*) è andato a meraviglia; **it goes like a bomb** (*fam: car*) va come un razzo.
  [2] VT (*target*) bombardare
► **bomb out** VT + ADV (*building*) distruggere; **they**

were **bombed out** hanno dovuto abbandonare la casa bombardata.

bom·bard [bɒm'bɑ:d] VT (*Mil*): **to bombard (with)** bombardare (con); **I was bombarded with questions** sono stato bombardato di domande.

bom·bard·ment [bɒm'bɑ:dmənt] N bombardamento.

bom·bast ['bɒmbæst] N magniloquenza.

bom·bas·tic [bɒm'bæstɪk] ADJ magniloquente, ampolloso(-a).

♦ **bomb disposal expert** N artificiere *m*.

♦ **bomb disposal unit** N corpo degli artificieri.

bomb·er ['bɒmə^r] N (*aircraft*) bombardiere *m*; (*terrorist*) dinamitardo(-a), bombarolo(-a).

♦ **bomber jacket** N bomber *m inv*.

bomb·ing ['bɒmɪŋ] 1 N bombardamento.
2 ADJ (*expedition*) di bombardamento.

bomb·proof ['bɒm,pru:f] ADJ a prova di bomba.

♦ **bomb scare** N sospetta presenza di un ordigno esplosivo; **there was a bomb scare at Harrods** Harrods era in stato d'allarme per paura di una bomba.

bomb·shell ['bɒm,ʃɛl] N (*fig: news*) bomba; **a blonde bombshell** una bionda esplosiva.

♦ **bomb site** N luogo bombardato.

bona fide ['bəʊnə'faɪdɪ] ADJ (*antique, excuse*) autentico (-a); (*offer*) serio(-a), onesto(-a).

bo·nan·za [bə'nænzə] N periodo di boom.

bond [bɒnd] 1 N a (*link*) legame *m*, vincolo; **bonds** NPL (*chains etc*) catene *fpl*
b (*agreement*) impegno, accordo; **to enter into a bond (to do sth)** impegnarsi (a fare qc); **his word is his bond** ci si può fidare completamente della sua parola
c (*Fin*) obbligazione *f*
d (*Comm*): **in bond** in attesa di sdoganamento
e (*adhesion*) aderenza
f (*Chem*) legame *m*
g (*also:* **bond paper**) carta fine.
2 VT (*bricks*) cementare; (*subj: glue*) far aderire, incollare.
3 VI (*people*) stabilire un legame affettivo; (*objects*) incollarsi.

bond·age ['bɒndɪdʒ] N servitù, schiavitù.

bond·ed ware·house ['bɒndɪd'wɛəhaʊs] N magazzino doganale.

bonds·man ['bɒndzmən] N (*pl* **-men**) servo, schiavo.

bone [bəʊn] 1 N (*gen*) osso; (*of fish*) lisca, spina; **I feel it in my bones** me lo sento, qualcosa me lo dice; **I have a bone to pick with you** (*fam*) devo regolare un conto con te; **she made no bones about saying what she thought** ci ha detto quello che pensava senza fare tante cerimonie.
2 VT (*meat*) disossare; (*fish*) diliscare, spinare.
3 ADJ (*buttons*) d'osso.

♦ **bone china** N porcellana fine.

boned [bəʊnd] ADJ a (*meat*) disossato(-a); (*fish*) spinato (-a) b (*corset*) fornito(-a) di stecche.

♦ **bone-dry** ['bəʊn'draɪ] ADJ (*fam*) asciuttissimo(-a).

♦ **bone idle** ADJ: **to be bone idle** essere un(a) fannullone (-a).

♦ **bone marrow** N midollo osseo.

♦ **bone meal** N (*fertilizer*) farina d'ossa.

♦ **bone of contention** N pomo della discordia.

bon·er ['bəʊnə^r] N (*Am*) gaffe *f inv*.

bone·shaker ['bəʊn,ʃeɪkə^r] N (*hum: bicycle, car*) catorcio.

bon·fire ['bɒn,faɪə^r] N falò *m inv*.

♦ **bonfire night** N *notte del 5 novembre, anniversario*

dell'attentato al Parlamento del 1609 che viene celebrato con fuochi d'artificio e falò.

bon·go ['bɒŋgəʊ] N bongos *mpl*.

bon·ing ['bəʊnɪŋ] N (*see vb*) disossamento; diliscamento.

♦ **boning knife** N coltello per disossare.

bonk [bɒŋk] VT, VI (*Brit hum, fam*) scopare (*fam!*)

bonk·ers ['bɒŋkəz] ADJ (*Brit fam*): **to be bonkers** essere suonato(-a); **to go bonkers** diventare matto(-a).

Bonn [bɒn] N Bonn *f*.

bon·net ['bɒnɪt] N a (*Brit Aut*) cofano b (*woman's, baby's*) cuffia; (*esp Scot: man's*) berretto.

bon·ny ['bɒnɪ] ADJ (*esp Scot*) bello(-a), carino(-a).

bon·sai ['bɒnsaɪ] N bonsai *m inv*.

bo·nus ['bəʊnəs] N (*on wages*) gratifica; (*insurance etc*) dividendo; (*fig*) sovrappiù *m*; **Christmas bonus** ≈ tredicesima.

bony ['bəʊnɪ] ADJ (*comp* **-ier**, *superl* **-iest**) (*thin: person*) angoloso(-a), ossuto(-a); (*made of bone: frame*) osseo (-a); (: *fish*) pieno(-a) di lische; (: *meat*) con parecchio osso; (*like bone*) simile a osso.

boo [bu:] 1 EXCL bu!; **she wouldn't say boo to a goose** (*fam*) ha paura della sua ombra.
2 N: **boos** NPL fischi *mpl*.
3 VT fischiare; **he was booed off the stage** l'hanno cacciato di scena a suon di fischi.

boob [bu:b] N (*Brit fam: mistake*) gaffe *f inv*; (: *breast*) tetta.

boo·by prize ['bu:bɪ,praɪz] N premio per il peggior contendente.

boo·by trap ['bu:bɪ,træp] N trabocchetto; (*Mil*) congegno che esplode al contatto.

booby-trapped ['bu:bɪ,træpt] ADJ: **a booby-trapped car** una macchina carica di esplosivo.

boo·gie ['bu:gɪ] VI (*fam*) ballare.

book [bʊk] 1 N libro; (*notebook*) quaderno; (*of matches*) bustina; (*of tickets*) blocchetto; **the books** (*Comm*) i libri contabili; **to keep the books** tenere la contabilità; **to be in sb's bad books** essere nel libro nero di qn; **to bring sb to book (for sth)** costringere qn a render conto (di qc); **to throw the book at sb** (*in accusing*) imputare a qn tutte le accuse possibili; (*in punishing*) condannare qn al massimo della pena; **by the book** secondo le regole; **in my book** a mio avviso, a parer mio.
2 VT a (*reserve: seat, room, table*) prenotare, fissare, riservare; (*ticket*) prendere, comprare
b (*Police: driver*) fare una contravvenzione a, multare; (*Ftbl*) ammonire.
3 VI (*see vt a*) prenotare; (*prendere il biglietto*)

▶ **book in** 1 VI + ADV (*at hotel*) prendere una camera.
2 VT + ADV (*person*) prenotare (una camera) per

▶ **book up** VT + ADV riservare, prenotare; **the hotel is booked up** l'albergo è al completo; **tonight's performance is booked up** la rappresentazione di stasera è esaurita; **I'm booked up** (*fam*) sono occupatissimo.

book·able ['bʊkəbl] ADJ (*seat etc*) prenotabile, riservabile; **seats are bookable** si possono prenotare i posti.

book·binder ['bʊk,baɪndə^r] N rilegatore(-trice).

book·binding ['bʊk,baɪndɪŋ] N rilegatura.

book·case ['bʊk,keɪs] N libreria, scaffale *m*.

♦ **book club** N club *m inv* del libro.

♦ **book ends** NPL reggilibri *mpl*.

bookie ['bʊkɪ] N (*fam*) = **bookmaker**.

book·ing ['bʊkɪŋ] N (*Brit: in hotel*) prenotazione *f*; (: *Sport*) ammonizione *f*.

♦ **booking clerk** N impiegato(-a) della biglietteria.

♦ **booking office** N (*Rail*) biglietteria, ufficio *m* prenota-

zioni *inv*; (*Theatre*) botteghino.

book·ish ['bʊkɪʃ] ADJ (*person*) (troppo) studioso(-a); (*phrase*) libresco(-a).

♦ **book-keeper** ['bʊk͵kiːpəʳ] N contabile *m/f.*

♦ **book-keeping** ['bʊk͵kiːpɪŋ] N contabilità.

book·let ['bʊklɪt] N opuscolo, libretto.

book·maker ['bʊk͵meɪkəʳ] N bookmaker *m inv*, allibratore *m.*

book·mark ['bʊk͵maːk] N segnalibro.

book·mobile ['bʊkməͺbiːl] N (*Am*) biblioteca ambulante.

book·plate ['bʊk͵pleɪt] N ex libris *m inv.*

book·seller ['bʊk͵sɛləʳ] N libraio.

book·shelf ['bʊk͵ʃɛlf] N mensola per libri; **bookshelves** NPL (*bookcase*) libreria.

book·shop ['bʊk͵ʃɒp], (*Am*) **book·store** ['bʊk͵stɔːʳ] N libreria.

book·stall ['bʊk͵stɔːl] N (*in station*) edicola, chiosco (dei giornali); (*secondhand books*) bancarella (dei libri).

♦ **book token** N buono *m* libro *inv.*

♦ **book value** N valore *m* contabile.

book·worm ['bʊk͵wɜːm] N (*fig*) topo di biblioteca.

boom[1] [buːm] 1 N (*in prices, shares*) forte incremento; (*of product*) boom *m inv*, improvvisa popolarità; (*of sales*) esplosione *f*; (*period of growth*) boom (economico).
2 VI (*trade*) andare a gonfie vele; (*sales*) aumentare vertiginosamente; (*industry, town*) essere in forte espansione, svilupparsi enormemente.

boom[2] [buːm] 1 N (*of guns, thunder*) rombo, rimbombo; (*deeper*) boato.
2 VI (*voice, radio, sea*: also: **boom out**) rimbombare; (*gun*) tuonare.
3 VT (*also*: **boom out**) urlare con voce tonante.

boom[3] [buːm] N (*Naut*) boma; (*of crane*) braccio; (*across harbour*) sbarramento; (*of microphone*) giraffa.

boom·er·ang ['buːməræŋ] 1 N boomerang *m inv.*
2 VI (*fig*) avere effetto contrario; **to boomerang on sb** ritorcersi contro qn.

boom·ing[1] ['buːmɪŋ] ADJ (*sales*) in rapida ascesa; (*trade, business*) che va a gonfie vele.

boom·ing[2] ['buːmɪŋ] ADJ (*guns, voice*) tonante.

♦ **boom town** N ≈ città *f inv* in rapidissima espansione.

boon [buːn] N (*blessing*) benedizione *f.*

boor [bʊəʳ] N bifolco, zotico.

boor·ish ['bʊərɪʃ] ADJ (*manners*) da zoticone, da bifolco.

boor·ish·ly ['bʊərɪʃlɪ] ADV maleducatamente, da bifolco.

boor·ish·ness ['bʊərɪʃnɪs] N maleducazione *f.*

boost [buːst] 1 N a (*encouragement*) spinta, sprone *m*; **to give a boost to** (*morale*) tirar su; **it gave a boost to his confidence** è stata per lui un'iniezione di fiducia
b (*upward thrust*: *to person*) spinta (in su); (: *to rocket*) spinta propulsiva.
2 VT (*increase*: *sales, production*) incentivare; (*fig*: *hopes*) rinforzare; (*promote*: *product*) promuovere (sul mercato); (*Elec*: *voltage*) aumentare; (*radio signal*) amplificare; (*Space*) lanciare.

boost·er ['buːstəʳ] N (*TV*) amplificatore *m* di segnale; (*Elec*) amplificatore; (*booster rocket*) razzo vettore; (*Med*: *injection*) (iniezione *f* di) richiamo.

boot[1] [buːt] 1 N a (*gen*) stivale *m*; (*ankle boot*) stivaletto; (*of soldier, skier, workman*) scarpone *m*; (*for hiking*) scarpone *m* da montagna; (*football boot*) scarpa; **to give sb the boot** (*fam*) mettere qn alla porta
b (*Brit Aut*) portabagagli *m inv*, bagagliaio.
2 VT a (*fam*: *kick*) dare un calcio a; **to boot sb out** buttar fuori *or* cacciar via qn (a pedate)

b (*Comput*) inizializzare.

boot[2] [buːt] N (*old liter*): **to boot** (*in addition*) in (*or* per di) più, per giunta, come se non bastasse.

bootee [buːˈtiː] N (*baby's*) scarpetta; (*woman's*) stivaletto (da donna).

booth [buːð] N (*at fair*) bancarella, baraccone *m*; (*Telec, voting booth*) cabina.

boot·jack ['buːt͵dʒæk] N cavastivali *m inv.*

boot·lace ['buːt͵leɪs] N laccio, stringa.

boot·leg ['buːt͵lɛg] ADJ di contrabbando; **bootleg recording** registrazione *f* pirata *inv.*

boot·leg·ger ['buːt͵lɛgəʳ] N contrabbandiere *m* di alcolici.

♦ **boot-polish** ['buːt͵pɒlɪʃ] N lucido (da scarpe).

boot·strap ['buːt͵stræp] N (*Comput*) programma di innesco; **to pull o.s. up by one's bootstraps** (*fig*) tirarsi su con le proprie forze.

boo·ty ['buːtɪ] N bottino, refurtiva.

booze [buːz] (*fam*) 1 N alcolici *mpl*; **bring your own booze** portatevi da bere.
2 VI sbevazzare, alzare il gomito.

booz·er ['buːzəʳ] (*fam*) N (*person*) beone *m*; (*Brit*: *pub*) osteria.

♦ **booze-up** ['buːzʌp] N (*fam*) bevuta.

boozy ['buːzɪ] ADJ (*fam*: *person*) che alza spesso il gomito.

bo·ra·cic [bəˈræsɪk] ADJ boracico(-a).

bor·age ['bɒrɪdʒ] N borragine *f.*

bo·rax ['bɔːræks] N borace *m.*

bor·der ['bɔːdəʳ] 1 N a (*frontier*) confine *m*; **the Borders** NPL (*Brit*) zona al confine tra la Scozia e l'Inghilterra
b (*edge*: *as decoration*) bordo, orlatura, orlo; (: *as boundary*) margine *m*, limite *m*
c (*in garden*) aiuola (laterale).
2 VT (*line, adjoin*) fiancheggiare, costeggiare

► **border on**, **border upon** VI + PREP confinare con; (*fig*: *come close to being*) sfiorare, rasentare.

♦ **border incident** N incidente *m* di frontiera.

border·line ['bɔːdə͵laɪn] 1 ADJ (*case, candidate*) su cui è difficile decidere; **he was a borderline failure** è stato bocciato per poco.
2 N (*fig*) linea di demarcazione.

♦ **border raid** N incursione *f.*

♦ **border town** N città *f inv* di confine.

bore[1] [bɔːʳ] 1 N (*person*) noioso(-a), seccatore(-trice), noia; (*event*) noia, barba; **the party/office bore** l'attaccabottoni *m/f inv* (di una festa/un ufficio).
2 VT (*person*) annoiare.

bore[2] [bɔːʳ] 1 N (*also*: **bore hole**) foro di sonda; (*diameter*) diametro interno; (: *of gun*) calibro; **a 12-bore shotgun** un fucile calibro 12.
2 VT (*hole*) praticare; (*tunnel*) scavare.
3 VI: **to bore for** perforare *or* trivellare alla ricerca di.

bore[3] [bɔːʳ] PT of **bear** 2.

bored [bɔːd] ADJ annoiato(-a); **he's bored to tears** *or* **bored to death** *or* **bored stiff** è annoiato a morte, si annoia da morire.

bore·dom ['bɔːdəm] N noia.

bore·hole ['bɔː͵həʊl] N foro di trivellazione.

bor·ing ['bɔːrɪŋ] ADJ (*tedious*) noioso(-a).

born [bɔːn] ADJ nato(-a); **to be born** (*also fig*) nascere; **I was born in 1955** sono nato nel 1955; **born blind** cieco(-a) dalla nascita; **a Roman born and bred** un romano di Roma, un romano doc; **the revolution was born of the workers' discontent** la rivoluzione scaturì dallo scontento degli operai; **to be born again** rinascere; **I wasn't born yesterday!** (*fam*) non sono nato ieri!; **in all my born**

days (*fam*) in tutta la mia vita; **a born actor/musician** un attore/musicista nato; **a born liar** un(a) bugiardo(-a) matricolato(-a); **a born fool** un(a) perfetto(-a) cretino (-a).

♦ **born-again** [,bɔːnə'geɪn] ADJ: **born-again Christian** convertito(-a) alla chiesa evangelica.

borne [bɔːn] PP of **bear 2**.

Bor·neo ['bɔːnɪˌəʊ] N Borneo.

bo·ron ['bɔːrɒn] N boro.

bo·ro·sili·cate [,bɔːrəʊ'sɪlɪkɪt] N borosilicato.

♦ **borosilicate glass** N vetro al borosilicato.

bor·ough ['bʌrə] N comune *m*, circoscrizione *f* amministrativa; (*in London*) distretto.

bor·row ['bɒrəʊ] VT: **to borrow (from)** prendere in prestito (da), farsi prestare (da); (*idea, word*) prendere (da); **could I borrow your car?** puoi prestarmi la macchina?

bor·row·er ['bɒrəʊəʳ] N (*gen*) chi prende in prestito; (*Econ*) mutuatario(-a).

bor·row·ing ['bɒrəʊɪŋ] N prestito.

bor·stal ['bɔːstl] N (*Brit*) riformatorio.

Bos·nia ['bɒznɪə] N Bosnia.

Bosnia-Herzegovina [,bɒznɪəhɜːtsəgəʊ'viːnə], **Bosnia-Hercegovina** [,bɒznɪəhɜːtsə'gɒvɪnə] N Bosnia-Erzegovina.

Bos·nian ['bɒznɪən] ADJ, N bosniaco(-a).

bos·om ['bʊzəm] N (*of woman, fig*) seno; **in the bosom of the family** in seno alla famiglia.

♦ **bosom friend** N amico(-a) del cuore.

boss [bɒs] ①N (*employer, owner*) capo, padrone *m*, principale *m*; (*manager, of organization*) capo; (*of criminal organization*) boss *m inv*.

② VT (*also*: **boss about** or **around**: *pej*) comandare a bacchetta; **stop bossing everyone about!** smettila di dare ordini a tutti!

bossy ['bɒsɪ] ADJ (*person*) autoritario(-a); **don't you get bossy with me!** non cominciare a darmi ordini!

bo·sun ['bəʊsən] N = **boatswain**.

bo·tan·ical [bə'tænɪkəl)], **bo·tan·ic** [bə'tænɪk] ADJ botanico(-a).

♦ **botanic gardens** NPL orto botanico.

bota·nist ['bɒtənɪst] N botanico(-a).

bota·ny ['bɒtənɪ] N botanica.

botch [bɒtʃ] ①N (*of job*) pasticcio, macello.

② VT (*job*) raffazzonare; (*attempt*) fallire

▶ **botch up** VT (*job*) raffazzonare.

both [bəʊθ] ① ADJ tutti(-e) *pl* e due, entrambi(-e) *pl*, ambedue *inv*; **both books/boys** tutti e due or entrambi *or* ambedue i libri/ragazzi.

② PRON tutti(-e) *pl* e due, entrambi(-e) *pl*, ambedue *inv*; **they were both there** or **both of them were there** c'erano tutti e due; **both of us went** or **we both went** ci siamo andati tutt'e due; **both are to blame** la colpa è di tutti e due; **both of us agree** siamo d'accordo tutti e due; **come in both of you** entrate tutti e due; **she has 2 daughters: both are blonde** ha 2 figlie, bionde entrambe.

③ ADV: **John and I both went** ci siamo andati sia John che io; **both you and I saw it** l'abbiamo visto sia tu che io; **both this and that** sia questo che quello; **she was both laughing and crying** piangeva e rideva a un tempo *or* allo stesso tempo; **he both plays and sings** oltre a suonare canta; **they sell both meat and poultry** vendono sia carne che pollame.

both·er ['bɒðəʳ] ①N (*nuisance*) seccatura, noia; (*trouble*)

fastidio, disturbo; **it is a bother to have to go** è una seccatura dover andare; **that's no bother, I'll see to it** non c'è problema, ci penso io; **the children were no bother at all** i bambini non hanno dato nessun fastidio; **it wasn't any bother** (*don't mention it*) si figuri!, s'immagini!; **he had a spot of bother with the police** ha avuto delle noie con la polizia.

② VT (*worry*) preoccupare; (*annoy*) seccare, infastidire, dar fastidio a; **to bother doing** or **to do sth** darsi la pena di fare qc; **I'm sorry to bother you with my problems** mi spiace importunarti con i miei problemi; **does the noise bother you?** ti dà fastidio il rumore?; **don't bother me!** lasciami in pace!; **I can't be bothered going out** or **to go out** proprio non mi va di uscire; **his leg bothers him** gli fa un po' male la gamba; **he didn't even bother to write** non si è nemmeno sprecato a scrivere due righe.

③ VI: **to bother (about)** preoccuparsi (di *or* per); **please don't bother** non si scomodi.

④ EXCL uffa!, accidenti!

Bot·swa·na [,bɒts'wɑːnə] N Botswana *m*.

bot·tle ['bɒtl] ①N bottiglia; (*of perfume, shampoo*) flacone *m*; (*baby's*) biberon *m inv*, poppatoio; **bottle of wine/milk** bottiglia di vino/latte; **wine/milk bottle** bottiglia da vino/del latte.

② VT (*wine*) imbottigliare; (*fruit*) conservare (in vasetti)

▶ **bottle out** VI + ADV (*Brit*): **to bottle out (of sth)** tirarsi indietro (da qc)

▶ **bottle up** VT + ADV (*emotion*) soffocare, reprimere.

♦ **bottle bank** N contenitore *m* per la raccolta del vetro.

♦ **bottle-fed** ['bɒtl,fɛd] ADJ allattato(-a) artificialmente.

bottle·neck ['bɒtl,nɛk] N (*road*) strozzatura; (*traffic*) ingorgo.

♦ **bottle-nosed whale** ['bɒtlnəʊzd'weɪl] N iperdonte *m*.

♦ **bottle-opener** ['bɒtl,əʊpnəʳ] N apribottiglie *m inv*.

♦ **bottle party** N festa a cui gli invitati portano da bere.

bot·tom ['bɒtəm] ①N (*gen*) fondo; (*of mountain, tree*) piedi *mpl*; (*of shoe*) suola; (*of chair*) sedile *m*; (*of ship*) opera viva; (*of person*) sedere *m*; **at the bottom of** (*hill, ladder*) ai piedi di; (*road, list*) in fondo a; **at the bottom of the page** in fondo alla pagina, a piè di pagina; **to be bottom of the class** essere l'ultimo(-a) della classe; **on the bottom (of)** (*shoe etc*) sotto; (*sea, lake etc*) sul fondo (di); **the boat floated bottom up** la barca galleggiava capovolta; **I fell flat on my bottom** sono caduto battendo il sedere; **at bottom** in fondo; **from the bottom of my heart** con tutto il cuore, dal profondo del cuore; **to get to the bottom of sth** (*fig*) andare al fondo di *or* in fondo a qc; **he's at the bottom of it** (*fig*) qui ci dev'essere il suo zampino; **bottoms up!** (*fam*) cin-cin!.

② ADJ (*lowest: shelf, step*) più basso(-a), ultimo(-a); (*corner, part*) inferiore

▶ **bottom out** VI + ADV assestarsi al livello più basso.

♦ **bottom drawer** N (*fig*) dote *f*.

♦ **bottom gear** N (*Aut*) prima.

♦ **bottom half** N (*of box*) parte *f* inferiore; (*of list, class*) seconda metà.

bot·tom·less ['bɒtəmlɪs] ADJ (*pit*) senza fondo; (*funds, supply*) inesauribile.

♦ **bottom line** N: **the bottom line** (*Fin*) il risultato finanziario; (*essential point*) l'essenziale *m*; (*result*) il risultato.

bot·tom·most ['bɒtəm,məʊst] ADJ ultimo(-a) (in basso), più basso(-a).

botu·lism ['bɒtjuˌlɪzəm] N botulismo.

bou·clé ['buːkleɪ] ①N lana (*or* tessuto) bouclé.

② ADJ bouclé *inv*.

bou·gain·vil·lea, bou·gain·vil·laea [ˌbu:gən'vɪlɪə] N buganvillea.

bough [baʊ] N ramo.

bought [bɔ:t] PT, PP of buy.

boul·der ['bəʊldə'] N masso, macigno.

boule·vard ['bu:ləvɑ:'] N viale *m*.

bounce [baʊns] **1** N (*of ball*) rimbalzo; (*springiness: of hair, mattress*) elasticità; he's got plenty of bounce (*fig*) è molto esuberante.
2 VT (*ball*) far rimbalzare.
3 VI (*ball*) rimbalzare; (*child*) saltare, balzare; (*fam: cheque*) essere scoperto(-a) *or* a vuoto; the cheque he gave me bounced (*fam*) l'assegno che mi ha dato era scoperto (*or* a vuoto); to bounce in entrare di slancio *or* con foga
▶ bounce back VI + ADV (*person*) riprendersi.

bounc·er ['baʊnsə'] N (*fam*) buttafuori *m inv*.

bounc·ing ['baʊnsɪŋ] ADJ: bouncing baby bambino(-a) pieno(-a) di salute.

bouncy ['baʊnsɪ] ADJ (*comp* -ier, *superl* -iest) (*ball*) che rimbalza bene; (*hair*) vaporoso(-a); (*mattress*) (ben) molleggiato(-a); (*person*) dinamico(-a), esuberante.
♦ bouncy castle° N *grande castello gonfiabile per giocare*.

bound¹ [baʊnd] **1** PT, PP of bind.
2 ADJ **a** (*prisoner*) legato(-a); bound hand and foot legato(-a) mani e piedi
b (*book*) rilegato(-a)
c (*certain*): he's bound to say yes vedrai che dirà di sì; he's bound to fail sicuramente fallirà; it was bound to happen doveva succedere, era da prevedersi
d (*obliged*): to be bound to do sth essere obbligato(-a) a *or* tenuto(-a) a fare qc; I'm bound to say that ... devo dire che... .

bound² [baʊnd] ADJ (*destined*): bound for (*person, train, ship*) diretto(-a) a, in viaggio per; (*parcel*) indirizzato(-a) a, diretto(-a) a; where are you bound (for)? dove sei diretto?; California bound diretto(-a) in California; westbound traffic traffico diretto verso ovest.

bound³ [baʊnd] **1** N (*jump*) salto, balzo.
2 VI (*person, animal*) saltare, balzare; he bounded out of bed è saltato fuori *or* è balzato giù dal letto; his heart bounded with joy il cuore gli balzò in petto dalla gioia.

bound⁴ [baʊnd] VT: bounded by limitato(-a) da.

bounda·ry ['baʊndərɪ] N confine *m*.

bound·er ['baʊndə'] N maleducato(-a), cafone(-a).

bound·less ['baʊndlɪs] ADJ (*also fig*) illimitato(-a), sconfinato(-a).

bounds [baʊndz] NPL limiti *mpl*; out of bounds vietato *or* proibito l'accesso; within the bounds of modesty nei limiti della decenza; his ambition knows no bounds la sua ambizione è senza limiti *or* non conosce limiti.

boun·ti·ful ['baʊntɪfʊl] ADJ (*person*) munifico(-a); (*God*) misericordioso(-a); (*supply*) abbondante.

boun·ty ['baʊntɪ] N (*generosity*) liberalità, munificenza; (*reward*) taglia.
♦ bounty hunter N cacciatore *m* di taglie.

bou·quet ['bʊkeɪ] N (*of flowers, wine*) bouquet *m inv*.

Bourbon ['bʊəbən] ADJ, N borbonico(-a).

bour·bon ['bʊəbən] N (*Am also:* bourbon whiskey) bourbon *m inv*.

bour·geois ['bʊəʒwɑ:] ADJ, N borghese *(m/f)*.

bour·geoi·sie [ˌbʊəʒwɑ:'zi:] N borghesia.

bout [baʊt] N **a** (*of illness, malaria*) attacco, accesso; a severe bout of flu una brutta influenza; a drinking bout una sbronza; he's had several bouts of illness è stato ammalato diverse volte; a bout of hard work un periodo di intenso lavoro **b** (*boxing match*) incontro.

bou·tique [bu:'ti:k] N boutique *f inv*.

bo·vine ['bəʊvaɪn] ADJ (*also fig: pej*) bovino(-a).

bow¹ [bəʊ] N arco; (*Mus*) archetto; (*knot*) fiocco, nodo.

bow² [baʊ] **1** N inchino; to take a bow inchinarsi al pubblico *or* all'applauso del pubblico.
2 VT (*lower: head*) chinare; (*bend: back*) curvare, piegare; bowed down by cares schiacciato(-a) dalle preoccupazioni.
3 VI: to bow (to) inchinarsi (a), fare un inchino (a); (*fig: yield*) inchinarsi (di fronte a); to bow to the inevitable rassegnarsi all'inevitabile
▶ bow down VI + ADV: to bow down (to) prostrarsi (davanti a)
▶ bow out VI + ADV (*fig*) uscire di scena.

bow³ [baʊ] N (*Naut: also:* bows) prua; on the port/starboard bow di prua a sinistra/a destra.

bowd·ler·ize ['baʊdlə,raɪz] VT espurgare.

bow·el ['baʊəl] N (*gen pl*) intestini, intestini *mpl*; cancer of the bowel cancro all'intestino; bowels of the earth viscere *fpl* della terra.

bow·ing ['bəʊɪŋ] N (*Mus*) archeggio.

bowl¹ [bəʊl] N **a** (*for soup*) scodella; (*for cereal, fruit*) coppetta; (*mixing bowl*) terrina; (*for salad*) insalatiera; (*for washing up*) bacinella, catino; bowl of cornflakes ciotola di cornflakes; bowl of soup piatto di minestra
b (*hollow: of lavatory*) tazza; (: *of spoon*) incavo, cavo; (: *of pipe*) fornello
c (*Am: stadium*) stadio
▶ bowl over VT + ADV rovesciare (a terra); (*fig*) lasciare strabiliato(-a).

bowl² [bəʊl] **1** VT (*ball*) lanciare.
2 VI (*Cricket*) servire; (*Bowls*) tirare.
♦ bow-legged [ˌbəʊ'lɛgɪd] ADJ (*person*) con le gambe arcuate.

bowl·er ['bəʊlə'] N **a** (*Cricket*) lanciatore(-trice); (*Bowls*) giocatore(-trice) di bocce **b** (*Brit: also:* bowler hat) bombetta.

bow·line ['bəʊlɪn] N (*Naut: also:* bowline knot) gassa d'amante.

bowl·ing ['bəʊlɪŋ] N (*indoor*) bowling *m inv*; (*on grass*) gioco delle bocce.
♦ bowling alley N (pista da) bowling *m inv*.
♦ bowling green N campo da bocce (*su erba*).

bowls [bəʊlz] NSG gioco delle bocce.

bow·man ['bəʊmən] N (*pl* -men) (*Naut*) prodiere *m*.

bow·sprit ['bəʊ,sprɪt] N (*Naut*) bompresso.
♦ bow tie [ˌbəʊ'taɪ] N (cravatta a) farfalla.
♦ bow window ['bəʊ'wɪndəʊ] N bow-window *m inv*.
♦ bow-wow ['baʊ,waʊ] N (*dog, noise*) bau bau *m inv*.

box¹ [bɒks] N **a** scatola; (*crate, also for money*) cassetta; (*for jewels*) cofanetto; the box (*fam: tv*) la tele **b** (*Theatre*) palco; (*Law: for witness, press etc*) banco
▶ box in VT + ADV (*bath*) incassare; (*car*) incastrare; to feel boxed in sentirsi imprigionato(-a).

box² [bɒks] **1** N: a box on the ear uno scapaccione.
2 VT: to box sb's ears prendere qn a scapaccioni.
3 VI (*Sport*) fare il pugile; (: *fight*) combattere.

box³ [bɒks] N (*Bot*) bosso.

box·car ['bɒkskɑ:'] N (*Am*) carro merci *inv*.

box·er ['bɒksə'] N (*Sport*) pugile *m*, boxeur *m inv*; (*dog*) boxer *m inv*.
♦ box file N scatola di archivio.

box·ing ['bɒksɪŋ] N (Sport) pugilato, boxe f.
♦ **Boxing Day** N (Brit) il primo giorno infrasettimanale dopo Natale, ≈ Santo Stefano.
♦ **boxing gloves** NPL guantoni mpl (da pugile or da boxe).
♦ **boxing match** N incontro di pugilato.
♦ **boxing ring** N ring m inv.
♦ **box junction** N (Brit Aut) area d'incrocio.
♦ **box number** N (for advertisements) casella.
♦ **box office** N botteghino.
box·room ['bɒks,rʊm] N (Brit) ripostiglio, stanzino.
boy [bɔɪ] N ragazzo; (small) bambino; (son) figlio; (servant) servo; **she had a boy** ha avuto un maschio; **school for boys** scuola maschile; **when I was a boy** quand'ero piccolo; **boys will be boys** che vuoi, sono maschi; **he's out with the boys** è fuori con gli amici; **old boy** vecchio mio; **my dear boy** mio caro; **oh boy!** mamma mia!
boy·cott ['bɔɪkɒt] [1] N boicottaggio.
   [2] VT boicottare.
boy·friend ['bɔɪ,frɛnd] N ragazzo.
boy·hood ['bɔɪhʊd] N infanzia; (as teenager) adolescenza.
boy·ish ['bɔɪʃ] ADJ (appearance, manner) da ragazzo.
Bp ABBR = **bishop.**
BR [,bi:'ɑ:ʳ] N ABBR = **British Rail.**
bra [brɑ:] N reggiseno.
brace [breɪs] [1] N a (Constr) rinforzo, sostegno; (dental) apparecchio (ortodontico), macchinetta (per i denti); (Typ) graffa b (pl inv: pair: of game birds) coppia, paio.
   [2] VT (strengthen) rinforzare; **to brace o.s.** (also fig) tenersi forte.
♦ **brace and bit** N trapano a manubrio.
brace·let ['breɪslɪt] N braccialetto.
braces ['breɪsɪz] NPL (Brit) bretelle fpl.
brac·ing ['breɪsɪŋ] ADJ (air) tonificante, vivificante.
brack·en ['brækən] N (plant) felce f; (area of bracken) felci pl.
brack·et ['brækɪt] [1] N a (support) sostegno; (shelf) mensola
   b (Typ: usu pl) parentesi f inv; **round/square brackets** parentesi tonde/quadre; **in brackets** tra parentesi
   c (group) categoria, gruppo; **income bracket** fascia di reddito.
   [2] VT (Typ) mettere tra parentesi; (fig: also: **bracket together**) mettere insieme.
brack·ish ['brækɪʃ] ADJ (water) salmastro(-a).
brad·awl ['bræd,ɔ:l] N punteruolo.
brag [bræg] VT, VI: **to brag (about/that)** vantarsi (di).
brag·gart ['brægət] N (old) spaccone m.
brag·ging ['brægɪŋ] [1] N vanterie fpl.
   [2] ADJ (tone) da spaccone(-a).
Brah·min, Brah·man ['brɑ:mən] N brahmano, bramino.
braid [breɪd] [1] N (on dress) spighetta; (Mil, on dressing gown) cordoncino; (trimming) passamano; (of hair) treccia.
   [2] VT (hair) intrecciare.
Braille [breɪl] N braille m.
brain [breɪn] [1] N a (Anat) cervello; (Culin): **brains** NPL cervella sg; **to blow one's brains out** farsi saltare le cervella; **he's got cars on the brain** ha il chiodo fisso delle macchine
   b (fig fam: intelligence): **brains** NPL testa; **he's got brains** ha (del) cervello, è intelligente; **he's the brains of the family** è il cervellone di casa.
   [2] VT (fam) spaccare la testa a.
brain·child ['breɪn,tʃaɪld] N creatura, creazione f.
brain·dead ['breɪn,dɛd] ADJ (Med) che ha subìto morte

cerebrale; (fam) decelebrato(-a), deficiente.
♦ **brain death** N morte f clinica.
♦ **brain drain** N fuga di cervelli.
♦ **brain haemorrhage** N emorragia cerebrale.
brain·less ['breɪnlɪs] ADJ deficiente, stupido(-a).
brain·storm ['breɪn,stɔ:m] N (Brit fig) attacco di pazzia; (Am) = **brainwave.**
brain·storming ['breɪn,stɔ:mɪŋ] N brain-storming m inv.
♦ **brains trust** N trust m inv dei cervelli.
♦ **brain tumour** N tumore m al cervello.
brain·wash ['breɪn,wɒʃ] VT: **to brainwash sb (into doing sth)** fare il lavaggio del cervello a qn (per convincerlo a fare qc).
brain·wash·ing ['breɪn,wɒʃɪŋ] N lavaggio del cervello.
brain·wave ['breɪn,weɪv] N (fam) idea brillante, lampo di genio.
brainy ['breɪnɪ] ADJ (comp **-ier,** superl **-iest**) (fam) geniale.
braise [breɪz] VT (Culin) brasare.
brake [breɪk] [1] N (on vehicle) freno; **to put on** or **apply the brakes** (Aut) azionare i freni; **to put the brakes on sth** (fig) mettere un freno a qc.
   [2] VI frenare.
♦ **brake drum** N tamburo del freno.
♦ **brake fluid** N olio dei freni.
♦ **brake light** N (fanalino dello) stop m inv.
♦ **brake lining** N guarnizione f del freno, ferodo ®.
♦ **brake pedal** N pedale m del freno.
♦ **brake shoe** N ganascia.
brak·ing ['breɪkɪŋ] [1] N frenatura.
   [2] ADJ (distance, power) di frenatura.
bram·ble ['bræmbl] N rovo; (fruit) mora.
bran [bræn] N crusca.
branch [brɑ:ntʃ] [1] N (also fig) ramo; (in road, railway, pipe) diramazione f; (Comm: of company, bank) filiale f, succursale f.
   [2] VI (road) diramarsi, ramificarsi
► **branch off** VI + ADV (road, path) diramarsi; (speaker) divagare
► **branch out** VI + ADV: **to branch out into** (business) estendere la propria attività nel ramo di; (person) mettersi nel ramo di; **he's branched out on his own** si è messo in proprio.
♦ **branch line** N (Rail) linea secondaria.
♦ **branch manager** N direttore m di filiale.
♦ **branch office** N filiale f, succursale f.
brand [brænd] [1] N a (Comm) marca b (on cattle, prisoner) marchio.
   [2] VT (cattle, fig: person) marchiare; **his name is branded on my memory** il suo nome è impresso indelebilmente nella mia memoria; **he was branded (as) a traitor** (fig pej) fu tacciato di traditore.
brand·ed ['brændɪd] ADJ di marca.
branding-iron ['brændɪŋ,aɪən] N (ferro da) marchio.
bran·dish ['brændɪʃ] VT brandire.
♦ **brand name** N marca.
♦ **brand-new** ['brænd'nju:] ADJ nuovo(-a) di zecca, nuovo (-a) fiammante.
bran·dy ['brændɪ] N brandy m inv.
♦ **brandy snap** N cialda allo zenzero.
♦ **bran mash** N pastone m.
brash [bræʃ] ADJ (impudent) sfrontato(-a), sfacciato(-a).
Bra·sília [brə'zɪljə] N Brasilia.
brass [brɑ:s] [1] N a ottone m; **the brass** (Mus) gli ottoni
   b (fam): **to have the brass (neck) to do sth** avere la faccia tosta di fare qc; **the top brass** (Mil) i pezzi grossi

dell'esercito.

2 ADJ (*ornament etc*) d'ottone.

♦ **brass band** N fanfara.

♦ **brassed off** ADJ (*Brit*): **to be brassed off (with sth)** essere stufo(-a) (di qc).

bras·siere ['bræsɪə'] N reggiseno.

♦ **brass rub·bing** ['brɑ:s͵rʌbɪŋ] N *ricalco di figure e iscrizioni tombali*.

♦ **brass tacks** NPL: **to get down to brass tacks** (*fam*) venire al sodo.

brass·ware ['brɑ:s͵wɛə'] N ottoni *mpl*.

brassy ['brɑ:sɪ] ADJ (*comp* **-ier**, *superl* **-iest**) (*voice, sound*) squillante; (*colour*) chiassoso(-a); (*pej: tone*) insolente; (: *woman*) appariscente.

brat [bræt] N (*fam pej*) moccioso(-a).

bra·va·do [brə'vɑ:dəʊ] N spavalderia.

brave [breɪv] **1** ADJ coraggioso(-a); **be brave** coraggio!, sii forte!.

2 N (*Native American*) guerriero *m* pellerossa *inv*.

3 VT (*weather, danger*) sfidare; **to brave it out** affrontare la situazione.

brave·ly ['breɪvlɪ] ADV coraggiosamente.

brav·ery ['breɪvərɪ] N coraggio.

bra·vo ['brɑː'vəʊ] EXCL bravo!, bene!

brawl [brɔ:l] **1** N rissa.

2 VI azzuffarsi.

brawn [brɔ:n] N muscoli *mpl*; (*Culin*) ≈ soppressata.

brawny ['brɔ:nɪ] ADJ muscoloso(-a).

bray [breɪ] **1** N raglio.

2 VI ragliare.

bra·zen ['breɪzn] **1** ADJ (*shameless*) sfacciato(-a).

2 VT: **to brazen it out** continuare con la massima faccia tosta.

bra·zen·ly ['breɪzənlɪ] ADV sfacciatamente.

bra·zi·er ['breɪzɪə'] N braciere *m*.

Bra·zil [brə'zɪl] N Brasile *m*.

Bra·zil·ian [brə'zɪlɪən] ADJ, N brasiliano(-a).

♦ **Brazil nut** N noce *f* del Brasile.

breach [bri:tʃ] **1** N **a** (*violation: of law*) violazione *f*; (: *of rules*) infrazione *f*; (: *of duty*) abuso **b** (*gap: in wall*) apertura, varco; (*Mil*) breccia; (*estrangement*) rottura.

2 VT (*defences*) far breccia in.

♦ **breach of contract** N inadempienza di contratto.

♦ **breach of the peace** N violazione *f* dell'ordine pubblico.

♦ **breach of trust** N abuso di fiducia.

bread [brɛd] N pane *m*; (*fam: money*) grana; **sliced white bread** pancarrè *m*; **to earn one's daily bread** guadagnarsi il pane; **to know which side one's bread is buttered on** saper da che parte conviene stare.

♦ **bread and butter** N: **it's his bread and butter** (*livelihood*) è il suo pane.

bread·basket ['brɛd͵bɑ:skɪt] N cestino per il pane.

bread·bin ['brɛd͵bɪn] N (*Brit*) cassetta *f* portapane *inv*.

bread·board ['brɛd͵bɔ:d] N tagliere *m* (*per il pane*); (*Comput*) pannello per esperimenti.

bread·box ['brɛd͵bɒks] N (*Am*) cassetta *f* portapane *inv*.

bread·crumb ['brɛd͵krʌm] N mollica.

bread·crumbs ['brɛd͵krʌmz] NPL briciole *fpl*; (*Culin*) pangrattato; **fried in breadcrumbs** panato(-a) e fritto (-a).

bread·fruit ['brɛd͵fru:t] N frutto dell'albero del pane.

bread·knife ['brɛd͵naɪf] N (*pl* **-knives** ['brɛd͵naɪvz]) coltello per il pane *or* da pane.

bread·line ['brɛd͵laɪn] N: **to be on the breadline** sbarcare a malapena il lunario.

breadth [brɛtθ] N (*also fig*) larghezza; **to be 2 metres in breadth** misurare 2 metri di larghezza, essere largo(-a) 2 metri.

breadth·ways ['brɛtθ͵weɪz], **breadth·wise** ['brɛtθ͵waɪz] ADV nel senso della larghezza.

bread·winner ['brɛd͵wɪnə'] N chi mantiene la famiglia, chi porta i soldi a casa (*fam*).

break [breɪk] (*vb: pt* **broke**, *pp* **broken**) **1** N **a** (*gen*) rottura; (*fracture*) fenditura; (: *in bone*) frattura; (*in wall, fence*) apertura; (*gap*) breccia; (*in line, row, electric circuit*) interruzione *f*; **with a break in her voice** con voce rotta *or* incrinata dall'emozione; **a break in the clouds** una schiarita; **a break in the weather** un cambiamento di tempo; **at break of day** allo spuntare del giorno, sul far del giorno; **to make a break for it** darsela a gambe

b (*in conversation*) pausa, interruzione *f*; (*rest: in journey*) sosta; (*tea break*) intervallo; (*Scol*) ricreazione *f*, intervallo; (*holiday*) vacanza; **the Christmas break** le vacanze di Natale; **to have** *or* **take a break** (*few minutes*) fare una pausa; (*rest, holiday*) prendere un po' di riposo; **without a break** senza una pausa

c (*fam: chance*) possibilità *f inv*; **a lucky break** un colpo di fortuna; **give me a break!** dammi questa possibilità!; (*leave me alone*) lasciami respirare!.

2 VT **a** (*gen*) rompere; (*bone*) rompere, fratturare; (*skin*) lacerare; (*surpass: record*) battere; **to break one's back/ leg** rompersi la schiena/gamba; **to break the surface** (*submarine, diver*) affiorare (alla superficie); **to break sb's heart** (*fig*) spezzare il cuore a *or* di qn; **to break the ice** (*fig*) rompere il ghiaccio

b (*law, rule*) violare; (*promise*) mancare a; (*vow*) rompere; (*appointment*) disdire, mandare all'aria; **to break the law** infrangere la legge

c (*resistance, spirits*) fiaccare, annientare; (*health*) rovinare; (*strike*) domare, stroncare; **I can't break the habit** non riesco a perdere il vizio; **to break sb** (*financially*) mandare in rovina qn

d (*silence, spell*) rompere; (*journey*) spezzare, interrompere; (*electrical circuit*) interrompere

e (*soften: force*) smorzare; (: *fall, blow*) attutire

f (*bad news*): **to break the news to sb** comunicare per primo la notizia a qn; **try to break it to her gently** cerca di dirglielo con tatto.

3 VI **a** (*gen*) rompersi; (*wave*) frangersi, infrangersi; (*fig: heart*) spezzarsi; **to break into tiny pieces** andare in frantumi *or* in mille pezzi; **the stick broke in two** il bastone si è spezzato in due; **let's break for lunch** facciamo una sosta per pranzo; **to break with sb** (*fig*) rompere con qn; **to break free** *or* **loose** liberarsi

b (*dawn, day*) spuntare; (*storm*) scoppiare; (*news*) saltare fuori

c (*health, spirits*) cedere; (*weather*) cambiare; (*heatwave*) finire; (*voice: boy's*) cambiare; (: *in emotion*) rompersi

▶ **break away** VI + ADV: **to break away (from)** staccarsi (da); (*Ftbl etc*) scattare via (da)

▶ **break down** **1** VT + ADV **a** (*door*) buttare giù, abbattere; (*resistance*) stroncare

b (*analyse: figures*) analizzare; (: *substance*) scomporre.

2 VI + ADV (*machine*) rompersi, guastarsi; (*Aut*) restare in panne, avere un guasto, rompersi; (*person: under pressure*) crollare; (: *from emotion*) scoppiare in lacrime; (: *mentally*) avere un esaurimento (nervoso); (*health*) cedere; (*talks*) arenarsi

▶ **break even** VI (*in business*) coprire le spese; (*in gambling*) finire pari

▶ **break in** 1 VT + ADV **a** (*door*) sfondare
b (*train: horse*) domare; (: *new recruit*) addestrare.
2 VI **a** (*burglar*) fare irruzione
b (*interrupt*): **to break in (on sb/sth)** interrompere (qn/qc)

▶ **break into** VI + PREP **a** (*house*) fare irruzione in; (*safe*) scassinare, forzare; (*savings*) intaccare
b (*begin suddenly*): **to break into song/a trot** mettersi a cantare/trottare

▶ **break off** 1 VT + ADV (*piece*) staccare, spezzare; (*talks, engagement*) rompere.
2 VI + ADV **a** (*twig*) staccarsi
b (*speaker*) interrompersi; (*stop*): **to break off (from doing sth)** smettere (di fare qc); **to break off from work** interrompere il lavoro

▶ **break open** VT (*door*) sfondare

▶ **break out** VI + ADV **a** (*prisoners*): **to break out (of)** evadere (da)
b (*war, fire, argument*) scoppiare; (*violence*) esplodere; **to break out in spots** coprirsi di macchie

▶ **break through** 1 VI + ADV (*Mil*) aprirsi un varco, sfondare; **the sun broke through** il sole ha fatto capolino tra le nuvole.
2 VI + PREP (*defences, barrier*) penetrare in, sfondare; (*crowd*) aprirsi un varco in *or* tra, aprirsi un passaggio in *or* tra

▶ **break up** 1 VT + ADV (*rocks etc*) fare a pezzi, spaccare; (*marriage*) finire; (*crowd, clouds*) disperdere; (*fight etc*) interrompere, far cessare.
2 VI + ADV (*ship*) andare in *or* a pezzi, sfondarsi; (*ice*) spaccarsi, disintegrarsi; (*partnership, meeting*) sciogliersi; (*friends*) separarsi; (*marriage*) andare in pezzi; (*crowd, clouds*) disperdersi; **the schools break up tomorrow** le scuole chiudono domani.

break·able [ˈbreɪkəbl] ADJ fragile.

break·ables [ˈbreɪkəblz] NPL oggetti *mpl* fragili.

break·age [ˈbreɪkɪdʒ] N danni *mpl*; **to pay for breakages** pagare i danni.

break·away [ˈbreɪkəˌweɪ] ADJ (*group*) scissionista, dissidente.

♦ **break-dancing** [ˈbreɪkˌdɑːnsɪŋ] N breakdance *f*.

break·down [ˈbreɪkdaʊn] N **a** (*of machine*) guasto, rottura; (*in system, communications*) interruzione *f*, sospensione *f* di servizio; (*Aut*) guasto, panne *f inv*; (*of talks, in relations*) rottura; (*Med*) collasso; (: *mental*) esaurimento nervoso
b (*of figures*) resoconto analitico; (*Chem*) scomposizione *f*.

♦ **breakdown service** N servizio di soccorso stradale.

♦ **breakdown van** N carro *m* attrezzi *inv*.

break·er [ˈbreɪkəʳ] N (*wave*) frangente *m*.

break-even chart [ˈbreɪkiːvənˈtʃɑːt] N grafico del punto di pareggio.

break-even point [ˈbreɪkˌiːvənˈpɔɪnt] N punto di rottura *or* pareggio.

break·fast [ˈbrɛkfəst] 1 N (prima) colazione *f*.
2 VI: **to breakfast (on)** fare colazione (con).

♦ **breakfast cereal** N fiocchi *mpl* d'avena (*or* di mais etc).

♦ **breakfast television** N programmi *mpl* televisivi del mattino.

♦ **breakfast time** N ora di colazione.

♦ **break-in** [ˈbreɪkˌɪn] N irruzione *f*.

break·ing and en·ter·ing [ˈbreɪkɪŋəndˈɛntərɪŋ] N (*Law*) violazione *f* di domicilio con scasso.

break·ing point [ˈbreɪkɪŋˌpɔɪnt] N punto di rottura; (*fig: of person*) limite *m* di sopportazione.

break·neck [ˈbreɪkˌnɛk] ADJ: **at breakneck speed** a rotta di collo.

♦ **break-out** [ˈbreɪkˌaʊt] N evasione *f*.

break·through [ˈbreɪkˌθruː] N (*in research*) scoperta decisiva; (*Mil*) breccia.

♦ **break-up** [ˈbreɪkˌʌp] N (*of partnership, marriage*) rottura.

♦ **break-up value** N (*Comm*) valore *m* di realizzo.

break·water [ˈbreɪkˌwɔːtəʳ] N frangiflutti *m inv*.

bream [briːm] N abramide *m* comune.

breast [brɛst] 1 N (*Anat, Culin*) petto; (*of woman*) seno, mammella; **to make a clean breast of it** (*fig*) vuotare il sacco.
2 VT (*finishing tape*) toccare.

breast·bone [ˈbrɛstˌbəʊn] N sterno.

♦ **breast-fed** [ˈbrɛstˌfɛd] ADJ allattato(-a) al seno.

♦ **breast-feed** [ˈbrɛstˌfiːd] (*pt, pp* **breast-fed**) VT, VI allattare (al seno).

♦ **breast-feeding** [ˈbrɛstˌfiːdɪŋ] N allattamento al seno.

♦ **breast pocket** N taschino.

breast·stroke [ˈbrɛstˌstrəʊk] N (nuoto a) rana; **to swim** *or* **do the breaststroke** nuotare a rana.

breath [brɛθ] N fiato, alito; (*act of breathing*) respiro; **she drew a deep breath** fece un respiro profondo; **bad breath** alito cattivo; **in the same breath** nello stesso istante; **out of breath** senza fiato; **under one's breath** sotto voce; **to go out for a breath of air** uscire a prendere una boccata d'aria; **to hold one's breath** trattenere il fiato *or* il respiro; **to get one's breath back** riprendere fiato; **it took my breath away** mi ha lasciato senza fiato, mi ha mozzato il respiro.

breatha·lyse, (*Am*) **breatha·lyze** [ˈbrɛθəˌlaɪz] VT sottoporre ad alcoltest *or* alla prova del palloncino.

Breatha·lyz·er, **Breatha·lys·er®** [ˈbrɛθəˌlaɪzəʳ] N (*Brit*) alcoltest *m inv*.

breathe [briːð] 1 VT (*air*) respirare; (*sigh*) tirare; **he breathed garlic all over me** mi ha soffiato addosso il suo alito puzzolente d'aglio; **I won't breathe a word about it** non fiaterò; **to breathe new life into sb/sth** (*fig*) ridar vita a qn/qc.
2 VI respirare; **to breathe heavily** ansimare, avere il fiato grosso; **now we can breathe again** (*fig*) adesso possiamo riprendere fiato

▶ **breathe in** 1 VI + ADV inspirare.
2 VT + ADV respirare

▶ **breathe out** VT + ADV, VI + ADV espirare.

breath·er [ˈbriːðəʳ] N (*fam*) attimo di respiro.

breath·ing [ˈbriːðɪŋ] N respiro, respirazione *f*; **heavy breathing** (*on phone*) respiro ansimante (*di maniaco*).

♦ **breathing apparatus** N (*of diver*) autorespiratore *m*.

♦ **breathing rate** N frequenza respiratoria.

♦ **breathing space** N (*fig*) attimo di respiro.

breath·less [ˈbrɛθlɪs] ADJ (*exhausted*) senza fiato; (*with excitement*) con il fiato sospeso; (*silence*) religioso(-a); (*anticipation, anxiety*) vivissimo(-a); **his asthma makes him breathless** l'asma gli fa mancare il fiato.

breath·less·ly [ˈbrɛθlɪslɪ] ADV senza fiato.

breath·taking [ˈbrɛθˌteɪkɪŋ] ADJ (*sight*) mozzafiato *inv*.

♦ **breath test** N ≈ prova del palloncino.

bred [brɛd] PT, PP of **breed**.

-bred [brɛd] SUFF: **to be well/ill-bred** essere beneducato(-

a)/maleducato(-a).

breech [bri:tʃ] N (*of gun*) culatta.

♦ **breech birth** N parto podalico.

breeches ['brɪtʃɪz] NPL (*knee breeches*) calzoni *mpl* alla zuava; (*riding breeches*) pantaloni *mpl* da cavallo.

breed [bri:d] (*vb: pt, pp* bred) **1** N razza, varietà *finv*; (*fig*) tipo, specie *finv*.
2 VT allevare; (*fig: hate, suspicion*) generare, provocare.
3 VI (*animals*) riprodursi.

breed·er ['bri:də'] N **a** (*person*) allevatore(-trice) **b** (*Phys: also:* breeder reactor) reattore *m* autofertilizzante.

breed·ing ['bri:dɪŋ] N (*of stock*) allevamento; (*reproduction*) riproduzione *f*; (*of person: also:* good breeding) (buona) educazione *f*.

♦ **breeding ground** N (*of animal*) zona di riproduzione; (*fig*) terreno fertile (*fig*).

breeze [bri:z] **1** N brezza, venticello; **land/sea breeze** brezza di terra/di mare.
2 VI: **to breeze in/out** (*jauntily*) entrare/andarsene *etc* allegramente come se niente fosse; (*briskly*) entrare/andarsene *etc* in fretta.

♦ **breeze block** N (*Brit*) *mattone composto di scorie di coke.*

breezy ['bri:zɪ] ADJ (*day, weather*) ventoso(-a); (*spot*) ventilato(-a), ventoso(-a); (*optimism*) superficiale; (*person's manner*) brioso(-a), gioviale.

breth·ren ['brɛðrɪn] (*Rel*) NPL of **brother**.

Bret·on ['brɛtən] **1** ADJ bretone.
2 N (*person*) bretone *m/f*; (*language*) bretone *m*.

brev·ity ['brɛvɪtɪ] N brevità.

brew [bru:] **1** N (*of beer*) fermentazione *f*; (*of tea, herbs*) infuso; **a strong brew** (*of beer*) una qualità forte; (*of tea*) un tè forte.
2 VT (*beer*) produrre; (*tea, coffee*) fare; (*herbs*) fare un infuso di; (*fig: scheme, mischief*) macchinare, tramare.
3 VI (*beer*) fermentare; (*tea*) farsi; (*fig: storm, crisis*) prepararsi; (*: plot*) ordirsi; **there's trouble brewing** c'è aria di burrasca; **something's brewing** qualcosa bolle in pentola

▸ **brew up** VI + ADV (*Brit*) **a** (*make tea*) preparare il tè; **I'll be brewing up about ten** preparerò il tè verso le dieci
b (*storm, dispute*) prepararsi; **a big storm was brewing up** si preparava un grosso temporale.

brew·er ['bru:ə'] N birraio.

brew·ery ['bru:ərɪ] N fabbrica di birra.

brew·ing ['bru:ɪŋ] N fabbricazione *f* della birra.

♦ **brew-up** ['bru:ˌʌp] N (*fam*): **to have a brew-up** farsi un tè.

bri·ar ['braɪə'] N (*bramble*) rovo; (*wild rose*) rosa selvatica; (*pipe*) pipa in radica.

briar·root ['braɪəˌru:t], **briar·wood** ['braɪəˌwʊd] N radica.

bribe [braɪb] **1** N bustarella.
2 VT corrompere; **to bribe sb to do sth** pagare qn sottobanco perché faccia qc.

brib·ery ['braɪbərɪ] N corruzione *f*.

bric-a-brac ['brɪkəˌbræk] N, NO PL bric-à-brac *m inv*.

brick [brɪk] N (*single*) mattone *m*; (*material*) mattoni *mpl*; (*toy*) cubo; **building bricks** (*gioco delle*) costruzioni *fpl*; **he came down on me like a ton of bricks** (*fig*) ancora un po' e mi mangiava; **to drop a brick** (*fig fam*) fare una gaffe; **to meet** *or* **come up against a brick wall** (*fig*) trovarsi davanti a un ostacolo insormontabile; **I felt I was banging my head against a brick wall** mi sembrava di

parlare al muro; **you can't make bricks without straw** (*Proverb*) non si può far niente senza l'occorrente

▸ **brick in, brick up** VT + ADV murare.

brick·bat ['brɪkˌbæt] N pezzo di mattone; (*fig*) critica.

♦ **brick-built** ['brɪkˌbɪlt] ADJ di mattoni.

brick·layer ['brɪkˌleɪə'] N muratore *m*.

brick·work ['brɪkˌwɜ:k] N muratura in mattoni.

brick·works ['brɪkˌwɜ:ks] N fabbrica di mattoni.

brid·al ['braɪdl] ADJ (*veil, gown*) da sposa, nuziale; (*feast, procession*) nuziale; **bridal party** corteo nuziale.

bride [braɪd] N sposa; **the bride and groom** gli sposi, gli sposini.

bride·groom ['braɪdˌgru:m] N sposo.

brides·maid ['braɪdzˌmeɪd] N damigella d'onore.

bridge¹ [brɪdʒ] **1** N (*gen, Dentistry*) ponte *m*; (*Naut*) ponte di comando, plancia; **bridge of the nose** setto nasale.
2 VT gettare un ponte su; **to bridge a gap** (*fig: in knowledge*) colmare una lacuna; (*: in budget*) colmare un disavanzo.

bridge² [brɪdʒ] N (*Cards*) bridge *m inv*.

bridge·head ['brɪdʒˌhɛd] N (*Mil*) testa di ponte.

♦ **bridg·ing loan** ['brɪdʒɪŋˈləʊn] N (*Brit*) prefinanziamento.

bri·dle ['braɪdl] **1** N briglia.
2 VT mettere le briglie a, imbrigliare.
3 VI (*with indignation*) adombrarsi, adontarsi.

♦ **bridle path** N sentiero (per cavalli).

brief [bri:f] **1** ADJ (*visit, period, moment, speech*) breve; (*glimpse*) veloce, breve; **for a brief moment I thought ...** per un attimo ho creduto...; **I caught a brief glimpse of the queen** ho intravisto per un attimo la regina; **in brief** ... in breve..., a farla breve....
2 N **a** (*Law*) dossier *m inv*
b (*Mil, gen*) istruzioni *fpl*; **that's outside my brief** non è di mia competenza.
3 VT (*Mil*) dare istruzioni a; **to brief sb (about sth)** (*person*) mettere qn al corrente (di qc); (*Law*) affidare una causa a.

brief·case ['bri:fˌkeɪs] N cartella, ventiquattr'ore *f inv*.

brief·ing ['bri:fɪŋ] N briefing *m inv*, istruzioni *fpl*.

brief·ly ['bri:flɪ] ADV (*speak, visit*) brevemente; (*glimpse*) di sfuggita.

brief·ness ['bri:fnɪs] N brevità.

briefs [bri:fs] NPL (*man's*) slip *m inv*, mutande *fpl*; (*woman's*) slip *m inv*, mutandine *fpl*.

bri·er ['braɪə'] N = briar.

Brig. ABBR = brigadier.

bri·gade [brɪˈgeɪd] N (*Mil, also hum*) brigata.

briga·dier [ˌbrɪgəˈdɪə'] N generale *m* di brigata.

brig·and ['brɪgənd] N bandito, brigante *m*.

bright [braɪt] ADJ **a** (*day, weather*) sereno(-a); (*room*) luminoso(-a); (*eyes, star, gem, surface*) lucente, brillante; (*sunshine*) splendente; (*light, lamp*) forte; (*fire, flame*) vivo(-a); (*colour*) vivace; **bright intervals** (*Met*) schiarite *fpl*; **bright red** rosso acceso
b (*cheerful: person*) vispo(-a), allegro(-a); (*: expression*) radioso(-a), animato(-a); (*: future*) brillante, radioso (-a); **bright and early** di buon'ora, di buon mattino; **to look on the bright side** vedere il lato positivo delle cose
c (*clever: person*) intelligente, dotato(-a); (*: idea, move*) brillante, geniale.

bright·en ['braɪtn] **1** VT (*also:* brighten up: *colour*) ravvivare; (*television picture*) alzare la luminosità di; (*house, room*) rallegrare; (*situation*) migliorare; **a child will brighten up your life** un figlio allieterà la tua vita.

2 VI (*also:* **brighten up**: *person*) rianimarsi, rallegrarsi; (*eyes, expression*) illuminarsi; (*weather*) schiarirsi.
♦ **bright lights** NPL: **the bright lights of the big city** (*fig*) l'eccitante vita della metropoli.
bright·ly ['braɪtlɪ] ADV (*smile*) radiosamente; (*behave, talk*) con animazione; (*shine*) vivamente, intensamente.
bright·ness ['braɪtnɪs] N (*of room*) luminosità; (*of eyes, star*) lucentezza; (*of sunshine*) splendore *m*; (*of flame, colour*) vivacità.
♦ **bright spark** N genio.
brill [brɪl] EXCL (*Brit fam*) stupendo!, fantastico!
bril·liance ['brɪljəns] N (*of light*) intensità; (*of colour*) vivacità; (*fig: of person*) genialità.
bril·liant ['brɪljənt] ADJ (*sunshine*) sfolgorante; (*light, idea, person, success*) brillante.
brim [brɪm] 1 N (*of cup*) orlo; (*of hat*) tesa, falda.
2 VI: **to brim (over) with** traboccare di; **eyes brimming with tears** occhi colmi di lacrime.
brim·ful ['brɪm'fʊl] ADJ: **brimful (of)** pieno(-a) fino all'orlo (di), traboccante (di); (*fig: confidence, enthusiasm*) pieno (-a) (di); **brimful of happiness** traboccante di felicità.
brine [braɪn] N (*Culin*) salamoia; (*liter: sea water*) mare *m*; **tuna in brine** tonno al naturale.
bring [brɪŋ] (*pt, pp* **brought**) VT (*gen*) portare; (*dissatisfaction, storm*) provocare; (*consequences*) avere; **to bring relief** dare sollievo; **to bring luck** portare fortuna; **to bring tears to sb's eyes** fare venire a qn le lacrime agli occhi; **to bring sth to an end** mettere fine a qc; **to bring sth on o.s.** (*fig*) tirarsi qc addosso; **I can't bring myself to sack him** non so risolvermi a licenziarlo
▶ **bring along** VT + ADV portare con sé
▶ **bring about** VT + ADV **a** (*change, crisis*) causare, provocare
   b (*turn*): **to bring a boat about** far virare di bordo un'imbarcazione
▶ **bring back** VT + ADV (*person, object*) riportare; (*souvenir*) portarsi a casa; (*memories*) risvegliare; (*old method*) reintrodurre; **she brought a friend back for dinner** ha portato un'amica a casa per cena
▶ **bring down** VT (*lower: prices, temperature*) far scendere; (*opponent: also* Ftbl, Rugby) atterrare; (*enemy plane*) abbattere; (*government*) far cadere
▶ **bring forth** VT + ADV **a** (*protests, criticism*) suscitare
   b (*child*) mettere al mondo
▶ **bring forward** VT + ADV **a** (*person*) far venire avanti; (*chair*) spostare in avanti; (*witness, proof*) produrre
   b (*advance time of: meeting*) anticipare
   c (*Book-keeping*) riportare
▶ **bring in** VT + ADV **a** (*person*) fare entrare; (*object*) portare dentro; (*Parliament: bill*) presentare; (: *legislation*) introdurre; (*Law: verdict*) emettere
   b (*produce: income*) rendere
▶ **bring off** VT + ADV **a** (*plan, enterprise*) far riuscire, realizzare; (*deal*) concludere; **he didn't bring it off** (*fam*) (il colpo) non gli è riuscito
   b (*people from wreck*) portare in salvo
▶ **bring on** VT + ADV **a** (*illness*) provocare; (*crops, flowers*) far spuntare
   b (*Theatre: performer*) fare entrare; (: *object*) portare in scena; (*Sport: player*) mandare in sostituzione, far scendere in campo
▶ **bring out** VT + ADV (*meaning*) mettere in luce; (*colour, weaknesses*) far risaltare; (*qualities*) valorizzare, mettere

in luce; (*new product*) lanciare; (*book*) pubblicare, fare uscire
▶ **bring round** VT + ADV **a** (*persuade*): **to bring sb round (to the idea of sth)** persuadere qn (a fare qc)
   b (*steer: conversation*): **to bring round to** portare su, far cadere su
   c (*unconscious person*) far rinvenire, rianimare
▶ **bring to** VT (*unconscious person*) far rinvenire
▶ **bring together** VT + ADV (*people: introduce*) far incontrare; (: *reconcile*) riconciliare
▶ **bring up** VT + ADV (*person*) far salire; (*rear: child*) allevare; (*mention: question*) sollevare; (: *fact, problem*) far presente; (*vomit*) rimettere, rigurgitare.
♦ **bring-and-buy sale** [ˌbrɪŋənd'baɪseɪl] N ≈ vendita di beneficenza.
brink [brɪŋk] N orlo; **on the brink of doing sth** sul punto di fare qc; **she was on the brink of tears** era lì lì per piangere.
brink·man·ship ['brɪŋkmənˌʃɪp] N strategia del rischio calcolato.
brisk [brɪsk] ADJ (*person, tone*) spiccio(-a), sbrigativo(-a); (: *abrupt*) brusco(-a); (*walk*) svelto(-a); (*wind*) fresco(-a); (*trade*) vivace, attivo(-a); **business is brisk** gli affari vanno bene; **at a brisk pace** di buon passo; **to go for a brisk walk** fare una camminata di buon passo.
bris·ket ['brɪskɪt] N punta di petto.
brisk·ly ['brɪsklɪ] ADV (*move, speak*) bruscamente; (*walk*) di buon passo; (*act*) senza indugi; **the wind was blowing briskly** soffiava un vento fresco.
brisk·ness ['brɪsknɪs] N (*of person, tone*) sbrigatività; (*of walk*) rapidità; (*of trade*) vivacità; (*of wind*) freschezza.
bris·tle ['brɪsl] 1 N (*of beard, animal*) pelo; (*of boar, brush*) setola; **pure bristle brush** spazzola di pura setola; **brush with nylon bristles** spazzola di nylon.
2 VI (*also:* **bristle up**) rizzarsi; **to bristle with** (*fig: pins, difficulties*) essere irto(-a) di; (*policemen, guards*) brulicare di; **he bristled with anger** fremeva di rabbia.
bris·tly ['brɪslɪ] ADJ (*chin*) ispido(-a); (*beard, hair*) irsuto (-a), ispido(-a).
Brit [brɪt] N ABBR (*fam*: = *Briton*) inglese *m/f*.
Brit·ain ['brɪtən] N (*also:* **Great Britain**) la Gran Bretagna.
Bri·tan·nia [brɪ'tænɪə] N la Britannia.
Brit·ish ['brɪtɪʃ] 1 ADJ (*economy, team*) britannico(-a), inglese; (*ambassador*) della Gran Bretagna, inglese.
2 NPL: **the British** gli inglesi.
♦ **British Commonwealth** N: **the British Commonwealth** il Commonwealth britannico.
♦ **British Isles** NPL: **the British Isles** le Isole britanniche.
♦ **British Rail** N ≈ Ferrovie *fpl* dello Stato.
♦ **British Standards Institution** N: **the British Standards Institution** ≈ Ente *m* Nazionale Italiano di Unificazione.
♦ **British Summer Time** N ora legale (*in Gran Bretagna*).
Brit·on ['brɪtən] N inglese *m/f*, britannico(-a).
Brit·ta·ny ['brɪtənɪ] N Bretagna.
brit·tle ['brɪtl] ADJ fragile.
bro. ABBR = **brother**.
broach [brəʊtʃ] VT (*subject*) affrontare; (*bottle of wine*) stappare.
♦ **B-road** ['biːˌrəʊd] N (*Brit Aut*) ≈ strada secondaria.
broad [brɔːd] 1 ADJ (*street, smile*) largo(-a); (*mind, view*) aperto(-a); (*hint*) chiaro(-a), esplicito(-a); (*accent*) marcato(-a), spiccato(-a); (*distinction*) generale; **3 metres broad** largo 3 metri; **the broad outlines** le grandi

linee; **in broad daylight** in pieno giorno; **in the broadest sense** nel senso più ampio.

2 N (*Am fam offensive*) femmina.

♦ **broad bean** N fava.

broad·cast [ˈbrɔːdˌkɑːst] (*vb: pt, pp* **broadcast**) 1 N (*TV, Radio*) trasmissione *f*.

2 VT (*TV*) (tele)trasmettere, mandare in onda; (*Radio*) (radio)trasmettere, mandare in onda; (*fig: news, rumour*) diffondere; **don't broadcast it!** non spargerlo ai quattro venti!.

3 VI (*station*) trasmettere; (*person*) fare una trasmissione.

broad·cast·er [ˈbrɔːdˌkɑːstəʳ] N giornalista *m/f* radiotelevisivo(-a).

broad·cast·ing [ˈbrɔːdˌkɑːstɪŋ] N (*TV*) televisione *f*; (*Radio*) radiodiffusione *f*; (*broadcasts*) trasmissioni *fpl*.

♦ **broadcasting station** N stazione *f* trasmittente.

broad·en [ˈbrɔːdn] 1 VT (*scope, outlook*) allargare; **to broaden one's mind** allargare i propri orizzonti.

2 VI (*also*: **broaden out**) allargarsi.

broad·ly [ˈbrɔːdlɪ] ADV: **broadly speaking** parlando in senso lato, grosso modo.

♦ **broadly-based** [ˌbrɔːdlɪˈbeɪst] ADJ con ampia base; **he wants it to be a broadly-based movement** vuole che sia un movimento con un'ampia base.

♦ **broad-minded** [ˌbrɔːdˈmaɪndɪd] ADJ (*person*) di mente aperta, di larghe vedute; (*attitude*) aperto(-a).

♦ **broad-mindedness** [ˈbrɔːdˈmaɪndɪdnɪs] N larghezza di vedute.

broad·ness [ˈbrɔːdnɪs] N (*see adj*) larghezza; apertura; chiarezza; **the broadness of his accent** il suo accento marcato.

broad·sheet [ˈbrɔːdˌʃiːt] N (*Brit: newspaper*) quotidiano di grande formato.

♦ **broad-shouldered** [ˌbrɔːdˈʃəʊldəd] ADJ largo(-a) di spalle.

broad·side [ˈbrɔːdsaɪd] N (*Naut*) bordata; (*fig*) attacco.

bro·cade [brəʊˈkeɪd] N broccato.

broc·co·li [ˈbrɒkəlɪ] N (*Bot*) broccolo; (*Culin*) broccoli *mpl*.

bro·chure [ˈbrəʊʃjʊəʳ] N opuscolo, dépliant *m inv*.

brogue¹ [brəʊg] N (*shoe*) scarpone *m*.

brogue² [brəʊg] N (*accent*) accento irlandese.

broil [brɔɪl] VT (*Am Culin*) fare alla griglia.

broil·er [ˈbrɔɪləʳ] N **a** (*chicken*) galletto **b** (*pan*) griglia.

broke [brəʊk] 1 PT of **break**.

2 ADJ (*fam*) senza una lira, al verde, spiantato(-a); **to go broke** andare in fallimento.

bro·ken [ˈbrəʊkən] 1 PP of **break**.

2 ADJ **a** (*gen*) rotto(-a); (*stick*) spezzato(-a); (*fig: marriage*) fallito(-a); (: *promise, vow*) infranto(-a), non rispettato(-a); (: *appointment*) mancato(-a); (: *health*) rovinato(-a); (: *spirit*) a pezzi; (: *heart*) infranto(-a); **he comes from a broken home** i suoi sono divisi; **he's a broken old man** è un vecchio finito

b (*uneven: surface, coastline*) irregolare; (: *ground*) accidentato(-a); (*interrupted*: *line*) spezzato(-a); (: *sleep*) agitato(-a); **to have a broken night** non riuscire dormire una notte di filato; **he speaks broken English** parla un inglese stentato.

♦ **broken-down** [ˈbrəʊkənˈdaʊn] ADJ (*car*) in panne, rotto (-a); (*machine*) guasto(-a), fuori uso; (*house*) abbandonato(-a), in rovina.

♦ **broken-hearted** [ˌbrəʊkənˈhɑːtɪd] ADJ affranto(-a) dal dolore, col cuore spezzato; **to be broken-hearted** avere il cuore spezzato.

bro·ken·ly [ˈbrəʊkənlɪ] ADV (*say*) con voce rotta; (*sob*) convulsamente.

bro·ker [ˈbrəʊkəʳ] N (*Comm*) mediatore(-trice); (*stock broker*) agente *m/f* di cambio.

bro·ker·age [ˈbrəʊkərɪdʒ] N (*Comm*) commissione *f* di intermediazione.

brol·ly [ˈbrɒlɪ] N (*Brit fam*) ombrello.

bro·mide [ˈbrəʊmaɪd] N (*Chem*) bromuro.

bro·mine [ˈbrəʊmiːn] N bromo.

bron·chial [ˈbrɒŋkɪəl] ADJ bronchiale.

♦ **bronchial tubes** NPL bronchi *mpl*.

bron·chi·tis [brɒŋˈkaɪtɪs] N bronchite *f*.

bron·chus [ˈbrɒŋkəs] N (*pl* **bronchi** [ˈbrɒŋkaɪ]) bronco.

bron·to·sau·rus [ˌbrɒntəˈsɔːrəs] N brontosauro.

bronze [brɒnz] 1 N bronzo.

2 ADJ (*made of bronze*) di bronzo; (*colour*) bronzeo(-a), color del bronzo *inv*.

3 VI abbronzarsi.

4 VT (*skin*) abbronzare; (*metal*) bronzare.

♦ **Bronze Age** N: **the Bronze Age** l'età del bronzo.

bronzed [brɒnzd] ADJ (*person*) abbronzato(-a).

bronz·ing [ˈbrɒnzɪŋ] N (*of metal*) bronzatura.

brooch [brəʊtʃ] N spilla, fermaglio.

brood [bruːd] 1 N (*of chicks*) covata; (*of birds*) nidiata; (*hum: of children*) prole *f*.

2 VI (*bird*) covare; (*fig: person*) rimuginare, stare a pensare

▶ **brood on** VI + PREP rimuginare su, stare a pensare a.

♦ **brood mare** *f*.

broody [ˈbruːdɪ] ADJ (*fig*) cupo(-a) e taciturno(-a).

brook¹ [brʊk] N ruscello.

brook² [brʊk] VT (*frm: tolerate*) tollerare, ammettere.

broom [brʊm] N (*brush*) scopa; (*Bot*) ginestra.

broom·stick [ˈbrʊmˌstɪk] N manico di scopa.

Bros. ABBR (*Comm*: = *brothers*) F.lli.

broth [brɒθ] N minestra (in brodo), brodo.

broth·el [ˈbrɒθl] N bordello.

broth·er [ˈbrʌðəʳ] N (*gen, Rel*) fratello; (*Trade Union etc*) compagno.

brother·hood [ˈbrʌðəˌhʊd] N fratellanza, fraternità; (*group*) confraternita.

♦ **brother-in-law** [ˈbrʌðərɪnˌlɔː] N cognato.

broth·er·ly [ˈbrʌðəlɪ] ADJ fraterno(-a).

♦ **brother officers** NPL compagni *mpl* d'armi.

♦ **brother workers** NPL compagni lavoratori.

brought [brɔːt] PT, PP of **bring**.

♦ **brought forward** ADJ (*Comm*) riportato(-a).

brow [braʊ] N (*forehead*) fronte *f*; (*old: eyebrow*) sopracciglio; (*of hill*) cima; (: *on road*) dosso.

brow·beat [ˈbraʊˌbiːt] (*pt* **browbeat**, *pp* **browbeaten**) VT intimidire; **to browbeat sb into doing sth** costringere qn a fare qc con la prepotenza.

brown [braʊn] 1 ADJ (*gen*) marrone, bruno(-a); (*hair*) castano(-a); (*bronzed*: *skin*) scuro(-a), abbronzato(-a); **to go brown** (*person*) abbronzarsi; (*leaves*) ingiallire.

2 N marrone *m*.

3 VT (*Culin*: *meat*) rosolare; (: *onion*) dorare.

4 VI (*Culin*) rosolarsi.

♦ **brown ale** N birra scura.

♦ **brown bear** N orso bruno.

♦ **brown bread** N pane *m* integrale, pane nero.

♦ **browned off** [ˌbraʊndˈɒf] ADJ: **to be browned off (with sth)** (*fam*) essere stufo(-a) (di qc).

Brownie [ˈbraʊnɪ] N coccinella (*scout*), giovane esploratrice *f*.

brown·ish ['braʊnɪʃ] ADJ (*stain, mark*) marroncino(-a); (*colour, eyes*) sul marrone.

♦ **brown paper** N carta da pacchi *or* da imballaggio.

♦ **brown rice** N riso integrale.

♦ **brown sugar** N zucchero greggio.

browse [braʊz] ① VI (*in bookshop*) curiosare (*leggicchiando qua e là*); (*in other shop*) guardare in giro, curiosare; (*animal*) brucare; **to browse through a book** sfogliare un libro.

② N: **to have a browse (around)** dare un'occhiata (in giro).

bruise [bru:z] ① N (*on person*) livido; (*on fruit*) ammaccatura.

② VT (*leg etc*) farsi un livido a; (*fruit*) ammaccare; (*fig: feelings*) urtare.

③ VI (*fruit*) ammaccarsi; **I bruise easily** mi vengono facilmente i lividi sulla pelle.

bruis·er ['bru:zəʳ] N (*fam*) bullo.

bruis·ing ['bru:zɪŋ] ① N ecchimosi *f inv*.

② ADJ (*encounter, experience*) brutto(-a); (*criticism, defeat*) pesante.

Brum [brʌm], **Brum·ma·gem** ['brʌmədʒəm] N (*fam*)= Birmingham.

Brum·mie ['brʌmɪ] N (*fam: resident*) abitante *m/f* di Birmingham; (: *native*) originario(-a) di Birmingham.

brunch ['brʌntʃ] N (*fam*) *ricca colazione consumata a tarda mattina che sostituisce il pranzo*.

bru·nette [bru:'nɛt] N ragazza (*or* donna) bruna.

brunt [brʌnt] N: **to bear the brunt of sth** (*of attack, criticism*) sostenere l'urto di qc; (*of work, cost*) sostenere il peso di qc.

brush [brʌʃ] ① N **a** (*gen*) spazzola; (*broom*) scopa; (*hearth brush*) scopettino, scopino; (*scrubbing brush*) spazzola per pavimenti; (*paint brush*) pennello; **hair/shoe brush** spazzola per capelli/da scarpe

b (*act of brushing*) spazzolata, colpo di spazzola

c (*quarrel*) schermaglia; **to have a brush with sb** (*verbally*) avere uno scontro con qn; (*physically*) venire alle mani con qn; **to have a brush with the police** avere delle noie con la polizia

d (*light touch*) lieve tocco; **he felt the brush of her hair against his face** sentiva i capelli di lei che gli sfioravano il viso

e (*undergrowth*) boscaglia, sottobosco.

② VT **a** (*clean: floor*) scopare; (: *clothes, hair*) spazzolare; (: *shoes*) lucidare, spazzolare; (: *teeth*) lavarsi

b (*touch lightly*) sfiorare

▶ **brush against** VI + PREP sfiorare

▶ **brush aside** VT + ADV (*fig: protest, objection*) ignorare, rifiutarsi di ascoltare; (: *idea, feeling*) ignorare

▶ **brush away** VT + ADV (*dirt: on clothes*) togliere (con la spazzola); (: *on floor*) scopar via; (*tears*) asciugarsi; (*insects*) cacciare (via)

▶ **brush down** VT + ADV dare una spazzolata a

▶ **brush off** VT + ADV (*mud*) levare con la spazzola; (*fig: suggestion*) scartare; (: *criticism, attentions*) ignorare

▶ **brush past** VI + PREP sfiorare (passando)

▶ **brush up** VT + ADV

a (*crumbs*) raccogliere (con la spazzola)

b (*also*: **brush up on**: *revise*) dare una rinfrescata *or* una ripassata a.

brushed [brʌʃt] ADJ **a** (*Tech: steel, chrome*) sabbiato(-a) **b** (*nylon, denim*) pettinato(-a).

♦ **brush-off** ['brʌʃˌɒf] N (*fam*): **to give sb the brush-off** mandare qn a quel paese.

♦ **brush-up** ['brʌʃˌʌp] N ripulita.

brush·wood ['brʌʃˌwʊd] N (*undergrowth*) sottobosco; (*cuttings*) rami *mpl* tagliati.

brush·work ['brʌʃˌwɜːk] N (*Art*) tocco.

brusque [bru:sk] ADJ (*person, manner*) brusco(-a); (*tone*) secco(-a).

brusque·ly ['bru:sklɪ] ADV (*behave, speak*) bruscamente.

brusque·ness ['bru:sknɪs] N modi *mpl* bruschi, asprezza.

Brus·sels ['brʌslz] N Bruxelles *f*.

♦ **Brussels sprout** N cavoletto di Bruxelles.

bru·tal ['bru:tl] ADJ brutale.

bru·tal·ity [bru:'tælɪtɪ] N brutalità.

bru·tal·ize ['bru:təlaɪz] VT (*harden*) abbrutire; (*ill-treat*) brutalizzare.

bru·tal·ly ['bru:təlɪ] ADV brutalmente.

brute [bru:t] ① N (*animal*) bestia; (*person*) bruto; **you brute!** mostro!.

② ADJ (*force, strength*) bruto(-a); **by brute force** a viva forza, con la forza.

brut·ish ['bru:tɪʃ] ADJ da bruto.

Brutus ['bru:təs] N Bruto.

bs ABBR = **bill of sale**.

BSA [ˌbiːɛs'eɪ] N ABBR (*Am*)= **Boy Scouts of America**.

BSc [ˌbiːɛs'siː] N ABBR = **Bachelor of Science**.

BSE [ˌbiːɛs'iː] N ABBR (= *bovine spongiform encephalopathy*) encefalite *f* bovina spongiforme.

BSI [ˌbiːɛs'aɪ] N ABBR = **British Standards Institution**.

BST [ˌbiːɛs'tiː] N ABBR (= *British Summer Time*) ora legale.

Bt ABBR (*Brit*) = **baronet**.

btu [ˌbiːtiː'juː] N ABBR (= *British thermal unit*) Btu *f* (= *unità termica britannica*).

bub·ble ['bʌbl] ① N bolla; (*smaller*) bollicina; **soap bubble** bolla di sapone.

② VI ribollire, fare bollicine; (*champagne*) spumeggiare

▶ **bubble over** VI + ADV traboccare; **to bubble over (with)** (*fig*) scoppiare (di *or* da), traboccare (di).

♦ **bubble bath** N bagnoschiuma *m*.

♦ **bubble gum** N chewing-gum *m inv*.

bubblejet printer [ˌbʌbldʒɛt'prɪntəʳ] N stampante *f* a getto d'inchiostro.

bub·bly ['bʌblɪ] ① ADJ (*liquid*) effervescente; (*fig: personality*) spumeggiante.

② N (*fam*) champagne *m inv*.

bu·bon·ic plague [bjuː'bɒnɪk'pleɪg] ADJ peste *f* bubbonica.

buc·ca·neer [ˌbʌkə'nɪəʳ] N bucaniere *m*.

Bu·cha·rest [ˌbuːkə'rɛst] N Bucarest *f*.

buck [bʌk] ① N **a** (*Am fam: dollar*) dollaro

b (*Zool*) maschio

c (*of horse*) sgroppata; **to give a buck** dare una sgroppata

d : **to pass the buck** (*fam*) scaricare le proprie responsabilità (*or* colpe *etc*) sugli altri.

② VI (*horse*) sgroppare

▶ **buck up** (*fam*)

① VI + ADV (*cheer up*) tirarsi su; (*hurry up*) sbrigarsi, muoversi.

② VT + ADV **a** (*make cheerful*) tirar su (il morale di) **b** : **to buck one's ideas up** (*fam*) darsi una mossa.

buck·et ['bʌkɪt] ① N secchio; (*large*) secchia.

② VI (*Brit fam*): **the rain is bucketing (down)** piove a catinelle.

♦ **bucket seat** N sedile *m* anatomico.

♦ **bucket shop** N (*Brit*) *agenzia di viaggi che vende biglietti a prezzi scontati*.

Buck·ing·ham Pal·ace [ˌbʌkɪŋəmˈpælɪs] N *residenza ufficiale a Londra del sovrano britannico*.

buck·le [ˈbʌkl] ① N fibbia, fermaglio.

② VT **a** (*shoe, belt*) allacciare **b** (*wheel, girder*) distorcere, piegare; (*warp*) deformare. ③ VI (*see vt*) allacciarsi, chiudersi con una fibbia; distorcersi, piegarsi

▶ **buckle down** VI + ADV: **to buckle down to a job** mettersi a lavorare d'impegno *or* di buzzo buono, mettersi sotto.

buck·ram [ˈbʌkrəm] N tela rigida.

Bucks [bʌks] N ABBR (*Brit*)= *Buckinghamshire*.

buck·shee [ˌbʌkˈʃiː] ADJ, ADV (*fam: free*) gratis (*inv*).

buck·shot [ˈbʌkˌʃɒt] N pallettoni *mpl*.

buck·skin [ˈbʌkˌskɪn] N pelle *f* di daino.

♦ **buck teeth** NPL denti *mpl* da coniglio.

♦ **buck-toothed** [ˌbʌkˈtuːθt] ADJ che ha i denti sporgenti.

buck·wheat [ˈbʌkˌwiːt] N grano saraceno.

bu·col·ic [bjuːˈkɒlɪk] ADJ (*liter*) bucolico(-a), pastorale.

bu·coli·cal·ly [bjuːˈkɒlɪklɪ] ADV (*liter*) bucolicamente.

bud [bʌd] ① N (*of flower*) bocciolo, boccio; (*on tree, plant*) gemma, germoglio; **to be in bud** (*flower*) essere in boccio; (*tree*) germogliare.

② VI (*plant, tree*) germogliare, mettere le gemme; (*flower*) sbocciare.

Bu·da·pest [ˌbjuːdəˈpɛst] N Budapest *f*.

Buddha [ˈbʊdə] N Budda *m inv*.

Bud·dhism [ˈbʊdɪzəm] N buddismo.

Bud·dhist [ˈbʊdɪst] ADJ, N buddista (*m/f*).

bud·ding [ˈbʌdɪŋ] ① ADJ (*fig: talent*) in erba; (*flower*) in boccio.

② N (*Bot*) gemmazione *f*.

bud·dy [ˈbʌdɪ] N (*esp Am*) amico, compagno; **they've been buddies for years** sono amiconi da anni.

budge [bʌdʒ] ① VT (*move*) spostare, smuovere; **I couldn't budge him an inch** (*fig*) non sono riuscito a smuoverlo di un dito.

② VI muoversi, spostarsi; (*fig*) smuoversi

▶ **budge up** VI: **budge up, will you** fatti un po' più in là.

budg·eri·gar [ˈbʌdʒərɪgaː] N pappagallino.

Budget [ˈbʌdʒɪt] N (*Brit*): **the Budget** il bilancio (preventivo) dello Stato.

budg·et [ˈbʌdʒɪt] ① N bilancio (preventivo), budget *m inv*; **I'm on a tight budget** devo contare la lira; **she works out her budget every month** fa il preventivo delle spese ogni mese; **budget price** prezzo ridotto.

② VI fare un preventivo; (*household*) fare i propri conti

▶ **budget for** VI + PREP mettere in conto *or* in preventivo, preventivare.

budg·et·ary [ˈbʌdʒɪtərɪ] ADJ budgetario(-a); **the budgetary year** l'anno finanziario.

budgie [ˈbʌdʒɪ] N ABBR = **budgerigar**.

Bue·nos Aires [ˈbweɪnɒsˈaɪrɪz] N Buenos Aires *f*.

buff¹ [bʌf] ① ADJ (*colour*) color paglierino *inv or* camoscio *inv*.

② VT (*also:* **buff up**) lucidare, lustrare.

buff² [bʌf] N (*fam: enthusiast*) patito(-a), appassionato (-a).

buf·fa·lo [ˈbʌfələʊ] N (*pl* **buffaloes**) (*wild ox*) bufalo(-a); (*esp Am: bison*) bisonte *m*.

buff·er [ˈbʌfəʳ] N **a** (*for railway engine*) respingente *m*; (*fig*) cuscinetto **b** (*Comput*) buffer *m inv*.

buff·er·ing [ˈbʌfərɪŋ] N (*Comput*) bufferizzazione *f*, memorizzazione *f* transitoria.

♦ **buffer state** N stato *m* cuscinetto *inv*.

♦ **buffer zone** N zona *f* cuscinetto *inv*.

buf·fet¹ [ˈbʊfeɪ] N (*for refreshments*) buffet *m inv*, bar *m inv*; (*meal*) buffet, rinfresco.

buf·fet² [ˈbʌfɪt] ① N (*blow*) schiaffo; **the buffets of fate** (*fig*) le avversità della sorte.

② VT (*ship, car etc*) sballottare; (*house*) sferzare; (*fig: person*) travolgere.

♦ **buffet car** [ˈbʊfeɪˌkaː] N (*Brit Rail*) ≈ servizio ristoro.

buf·fet·ing [ˈbʌfɪtɪŋ] ① N (*of wind, waves*) violenza; **the ship took a buffeting in the storm** la nave fu sballottata violentemente durante la tempesta.

② ADJ (*wind*) violento(-a).

♦ **buffet lunch** [ˌbʊfeɪˈlʌntʃ] N pranzo in piedi.

♦ **buffet supper** [ˌbʊfeɪˈsʌpəʳ] N cena fredda.

buf·foon [bəˈfuːn] N buffone(-a); **to play the buffoon** fare il/la buffone(-a).

buf·foon·ery [bəˈfuːnərɪ] N buffoneria.

bug [bʌg] ① N **a** (*insect*) insetto; (*germ*) infezione *f*, virus *m inv*; (*fig: obsession*) mania, pallino; **I've got the travel bug** (*fig*) mi è presa la mania dei viaggi **b** (*bugging device*) microspia, cimice *f* **c** (*Comput: in program*) errore *m* (nel programma), bug *m inv*.

② VT **a** (*telephone*) mettere sotto controllo; (*room*) installare microspie in **b** (*fam: annoy*) scocciare; **it really bugs me** mi rompe da morire.

bug·bear [ˈbʌgˌbɛəʳ] N spauracchio.

bug·ger [ˈbʌgəʳ] ① N **a** (*Law*) sodomita *m* **b** (*fam!*) stronzo (*fam!*); **you stupid bugger!** stronzo!; **poor little bugger!** (*child*) povera bestia!.

② EXCL (*fam!*): **bugger (it)!** merda! (*fam!*).

③ ADV (*fam!*): **bugger all** un cazzo (*fam!*); **I know bugger all about it** non ne so un cazzo.

④ VT (*fam!: also:* **bugger up**) mandare a puttane *or* in vacca (*fam!*)

▶ **bugger about, bugger around** ① VI + ADV (*Brit fam!*) non fare un cazzo (*fam!*).

② VT: **to bugger sb about** *or* **around** rompere le palle a qn (*fam!*)

▶ **bugger off** VI + ADV (*Brit fam!*) togliersi dalle palle (*fam!*); **why don't you bugger off and leave me in peace?** perché non ti togli dalle palle e mi lasci in pace?

bug·gery [ˈbʌgərɪ] N sodomia.

bug·ging [ˈbʌgɪŋ] N utilizzazione *f* di microfoni nascosti.

♦ **bugging device** N microfono nascosto.

bug·gy [ˈbʌgɪ] N (*also:* **baby buggy**) passeggino; (*cart: two-wheeled*) calesse *m*; (*: four-wheeled*) baghero.

bu·gle [ˈbjuːgl] N (*Mus*) tromba.

bu·gler [ˈbjuːgləʳ] N trombettiere *m*.

build [bɪld] (*vb: pt, pp* **built**) ① N (*of person*) corporatura, fisico.

② VT (*house*) costruire, fabbricare; (*ship, town, machine*) costruire; (*nest*) fare; (*fig: relationship, career, empire*) costruire; **a new bridge is being built** è in costruzione un nuovo ponte

▶ **build on** ① VT + ADV aggiungere.

② VT + PREP (*fig*) fondare su, basare su

▶ **build up** ① VT + ADV (*develop: business*) consolidare; (*: reputation*) fare, consolidare; (*increase: production*) allargare, incrementare; (*stocks etc*) accumulare; (*collection*) mettere insieme; (*spirits, morale*) tirar su; (*hopes*) far crescere; **don't build your hopes up too soon** non sperarci troppo; **to build up one's strength** rimettersi in forze.

② VI + ADV (*pressure*) salire; (*Fin: interest*) accumularsi;

the music built up to a crescendo la musica aumentava in un crescendo continuo.

build·er ['bɪldə^r] N (contractor) costruttore m, imprenditore m (edile); (workman) muratore m; (fig) creatore(-trice).

build·ing ['bɪldɪŋ] N **a** (place) costruzione f, edificio; (block) palazzo **b** (no pl: activity) costruzione f.

♦ **building block** N componente m.

♦ **building contractor** N costruttore m, imprenditore m (edile).

♦ **building industry, building trade** N industria edilizia.

♦ **building site** N cantiere m di costruzione.

♦ **building society** N (Brit) ≈ istituto di credito immobiliare.

♦ **build-up** ['bɪldʌp] N **a** (of pressure, gas) aumento, accumulo; (Mil: of troops) ammassamento; (of traffic) aumento di volume, intensificarsi m; (fig: of tension) aumento **b** (publicity) campagna pubblicitaria; **to give sb/sth a good build-up** fare buona pubblicità a qn/qc.

built [bɪlt] PT, PP of build.

♦ **built-in** ['bɪlt,ɪn] ADJ (cupboard) a muro; (device, feature) incorporato(-a).

♦ **built-up** ['bɪlt,ʌp] ADJ: **built-up area** abitato.

bulb [bʌlb] N (Bot, of thermometer) bulbo; (Elec) lampadina.

bulb·ous ['bʌlbəs] ADJ a forma di bulbo, bulboso(-a).

Bul·garia [bʌl'gɛərɪə] N Bulgaria.

Bul·gar·ian [bʌl'gɛərɪən] **1** ADJ bulgaro(-a).
2 N **a** (person) bulgaro(-a) **b** (language) bulgaro.

bulge [bʌldʒ] **1** N **a** (in surface) rigonfiamento; (in plaster, metal) bolla; (curve: of thighs, hips) curva **b** (in birth rate, sales) punta, rapido aumento; **the postwar bulge** l'esplosione demografica del dopoguerra.
2 VI (stomach, muscles) sporgere; (pocket): **to bulge (with)** essere gonfio(-a) (di).

bulg·ing ['bʌldʒɪŋ] ADJ (see vi) sporgente, gonfio(-a); **to be bulging with** essere pieno(-a) or zeppo(-a) di.

bu·limia [bəˈlɪmɪə] N bulimia.

bulk [bʌlk] N (of thing) volume m, massa; (of person) corporatura massiccia; **the bulk of** la maggior parte di; **the bulk of the work** il grosso del lavoro; **to buy in bulk** comprare in grande quantità.

♦ **bulk buy·ing** ['bʌlk'baɪɪŋ] N acquisto di merce in grande quantità.

♦ **bulk carrier** N grossa nave f da carico.

bulk·head ['bʌlk,hɛd] N (Naut) paratia.

bulki·ness ['bʌlkɪnɪs] N (of person) corporatura massiccia; (of thing) voluminosità.

bulky ['bʌlkɪ] ADJ grosso(-a), voluminoso(-a).

bull¹ [bʊl] N **a** toro; (male of elephant, seal) maschio; **like a bull in a china shop** come un elefante; **to take the bull by the horns** (fig) prendere il toro per le corna **b** (Stock Exchange) rialzista m/f.

bull² [bʊl] N (Rel) bolla (papale).

bull·dog ['bʊl,dɒg] N bulldog m inv.

bull·doze ['bʊl,dəʊz] VT aprire or spianare col bulldozer; **I was bulldozed into doing it** (fig) mi ci hanno costretto con la prepotenza.

bull·doz·er ['bʊldəʊzə^r] N bulldozer m inv, apripista m inv.

bul·let ['bʊlɪt] N proiettile m, pallottola.

♦ **bullet hole** N foro di proiettile.

bul·letin ['bʊlɪtɪn] N (statement) comunicato (ufficiale); (journal) bollettino.

♦ **bulletin board** N (Comput) bulletin board m inv.

bullet·proof ['bʊlɪt,pruːf] ADJ a prova di proiettile; **bulletproof vest** giubbotto m antiproiettile inv.

bull·fight ['bʊl,faɪt] N corrida.

bull·fighter ['bʊl,faɪtə^r] N torero.

bull·fighting ['bʊl,faɪtɪŋ] N tauromachia.

bull·finch ['bʊl,fɪntʃ] N ciuffolotto.

bull·frog ['bʊl,frɒg] N rana toro.

bul·lion ['bʊljən] N oro (or argento) in lingotti.

♦ **bull-necked** ['bʊl,nɛkt] ADJ dal collo taurino.

bull·ock ['bʊlək] N manzo.

bull·ring ['bʊl,rɪŋ] N arena (per corride).

♦ **bull's-eye** ['bʊlz,aɪ] N (of target) centro (del bersaglio); **to hit the bull's-eye** (fig) far centro, colpire nel segno.

bull·shit ['bʊl,ʃɪt] (fam!) **1** N stronzate fpl (fam!).
2 VI, VT raccontare stronzate (a) (fam!)

♦ **bull terrier** N bull terrier m inv.

bul·ly¹ ['bʊlɪ] **1** N bullo, prepotente m/f.
2 VT (also: **bully around**) fare il/la prepotente con; (subj: children) fare le prepotenze a; **to bully sb into doing sth** far fare qc a qn con la prepotenza.

bul·ly² ['bʊlɪ] N (also: **bully beef**) carne f di manzo in scatola.

bul·ly·ing ['bʊlɪɪŋ] **1** N prepotenze fpl.
2 ADJ (person, tone, behaviour) prepotente.

bul·rush ['bʊl,rʌʃ] N stiancia.

bul·wark ['bʊlwək] N (Mil, fig) baluardo, bastione m; (Naut) parapetto.

bum¹ [bʌm] N (Brit fam: bottom) culo.

bum² [bʌm] (fam) **1** N (esp Am: idler) fannullone(-a); (tramp) barbone(-a), vagabondo(-a).
2 ADJ scadente; **bum advice** consiglio di merda (fam!).
3 VT (money, food) scroccare

▸ **bum around** VI + ADV (fam) vagabondare.

♦ **bum-bag** ['bʌm,bæg] N (fam) marsupio.

bum·ble ['bʌmbl] VI **a** (speak) borbottare; **what on earth are you bumbling about?** che diavolo stai borbottando? **b** (move) muoversi goffamente.

bumble·bee ['bʌmbl,biː] N (Zool) bombo.

bumf [bʌmf] N (fam: documents, forms) scartoffie fpl.

bum·mer ['bʌmə^r] N (fam) rottura.

bump [bʌmp] **1** N **a** (blow) botta, colpo; (noise) botto; (jolt of vehicle) botta, scossa **b** (lump) bernoccolo, bozzo, gonfiore m; (: on skin) gonfiore; (: on road) cunetta, bozzo.
2 VT (car) urtare, sbattere; **to bump one's head** sbattere la testa

▸ **bump along** VI procedere sobbalzando

▸ **bump into** VI + PREP **a** (vehicle) andare a sbattere contro **b** (fam: meet) imbattersi in, incontrare per caso; **fancy bumping into you!** ma guarda chi si vede!

▸ **bump off** VT + ADV (fam) far fuori

▸ **bump up** VT + ADV (fam, increase: prices) far salire, far aumentare; (: sales) incrementare.

bump·er¹ ['bʌmpə^r] N (Brit Aut) paraurti m inv.

bump·er² ['bʌmpə^r] ADJ: **bumper harvest** raccolto eccezionale.

♦ **bumper cars** NPL autoscontro.

bumph [bʌmf] N = bumf.

bump·tious ['bʌmpʃəs] ADJ arrogante, presuntuoso(-a).

bumpy ['bʌmpɪ] ADJ (surface, road) accidentato(-a), dissestato(-a), irregolare; (journey, flight) movimentato(-a); **we had a bumpy flight** abbiamo ballato or si ballava in volo.

bun [bʌn] N (Culin) panino dolce; (of hair) chignon m inv, crocchia; **to wear one's hair in a bun** portare lo chignon.

bunch [bʌntʃ] N (*of flowers, keys*) mazzo; (*posy*) mazzetto, mazzolino; (*of bananas*) casco; (*of grapes*) grappolo; (*set of people*) gruppo; **to wear one's hair in bunches** portare le codine; **the best of a bad bunch** il (*or* la *etc*) meno peggio

▶ **bunch together** 1 VT + ADV (*objects*) ammucchiare.
2 VI + ADV (*people*) ammucchiarsi.

bun·dle ['bʌndl] 1 N (*of clothes, rags*) fagotto, involto; (*of sticks*) fascina; (*of papers*) mucchio; (*of newspapers*) fascio; **to be a bundle of nerves** essere tesissimo(-a).
2 VT **a** (*also:* **bundle up:** *clothes*) fare un fagotto di, raccogliere in un mucchio; (: *papers*) fare un fascio di **b** (*put hastily*) riporre in fretta; (: *person*) spingere, caricare in gran fretta

▶ **bundle off** VT + ADV (*person*) mandare via in gran fretta; **he was bundled off to Australia** l'hanno spedito in fretta e furia in Australia

▶ **bundle out** VT + ADV far uscire (senza tante cerimonie).

♦ **bun fight** N (*Brit fam*) tè *m inv* (*ricevimento*).

bung [bʌŋ] 1 N tappo, turacciolo.
2 VT (*Brit fam: throw*) buttare

▶ **bung up** VT + ADV (*pipe, hole*) tappare, otturare; **my nose is bunged up** (*fam*) ho il naso otturato.

bun·ga·low ['bʌŋɡəˌləʊ] N bungalow *m inv*, villetta a un piano.

bun·gee jump·ing ['bʌndʒɪˌdʒʌmpɪŋ] N *salto nel vuoto da ponti, grattacieli ecc, con un cavo fissato alla caviglia.*

bun·gle ['bʌŋɡl] (*fam*) 1 VT fare un pasticcio di.
2 VI fare pasticci.

bun·gled ['bʌŋɡld] ADJ: **it is a bungled job** è un lavoro raffazzonato.

bun·gler ['bʌŋɡlə'] N pasticcione(-a).

bun·gling ['bʌŋɡlɪŋ] 1 ADJ imbranato(-a).
2 N incompetenza.

bunion ['bʌnjən] N callo (al piede).

bunk[1] [bʌŋk] N (*Naut, Rail*) cuccetta.

bunk[2] [bʌŋk] N (*Brit fam*): **to do a bunk** tagliare la corda

▶ **bunk off** VT, VI (*Brit fam*): **to bunk off (school)** marinare la scuola.

♦ **bunk beds** NPL letti *mpl* a castello.

bun·ker [bʌŋkə'] N (*coal bunker*) carbonaia; (*Mil, Golf*) bunker *m inv*.

bun·kum ['bʌŋkəm] N (*fam*) scempiaggini *fpl*.

bun·ny ['bʌnɪ] N (*also:* **bunny rabbit**) coniglietto.

♦ **bunny girl** N coniglietta.

♦ **bunny hill** N (*Am Skiing*) pista per principianti.

Bun·sen ['bʌnsn] N: **Bunsen burner** becco Bunsen.

bunt·ing ['bʌntɪŋ] N (*Naut*) gran pavese *m*; (*in street*) bandierine *fpl*.

buoy [bɔɪ] N boa, gavitello

▶ **buoy up** VT + ADV (*person, boat*) tenere a galla; (*fig: spirits*) tener su; (: *hopes*) alimentare.

buoy·an·cy ['bɔɪənsɪ] N (*Phys*) galleggiamento; (*of ship, object*) galleggiabilità; (*fig: of person*) ottimismo.

buoy·ant ['bɔɪənt] ADJ (*ship, log*) che galleggia (bene), galleggiante; (*fig: person*) di ottimo umore, su di corda; (: *nature*) ottimista; (*Fin: market*) sostenuto(-a); (*prices, currency*) stabile.

bur·ble ['bɜ:bl] VI **a** gorgogliare **b** (*pej*) borbottare; **what's he burbling (on) about?** che cosa sta borbottando?

bur·den ['bɜ:dn] 1 N (*load*) carico, peso; (*fig: of years, responsibility*) peso; (*of taxes, payment*) onere *m*; **the burden of proof lies with him** spetta a lui l'onere della prova; **to be a burden to sb** essere di peso a qn.

2 VT: **to burden (with)** (*cares etc*) opprimere (con); **burdened with debts** oberato(-a) di debiti.

bur·den·some ['bɜ:dnsəm] ADJ (*load, task*) pesante; (*taxes, payment*) gravoso(-a), oneroso(-a).

bu·reau ['bjʊərəʊ] N **a** (*office*) ufficio, agenzia; (*government department*) dipartimento, sezione *f* **b** (*Brit: desk*) secrétaire *m inv*, scrittoio; (*Am: chest of drawers*) cassettone *m*.

bu·reau·cra·cy [bjʊə'rɒkrəsɪ] N burocrazia.

bu·reau·crat ['bjʊərəʊˌkræt] N burocrate *m/f*.

bu·reau·crat·ic [ˌbjʊərəʊ'krætɪk] ADJ burocratico(-a).

bu·reau·crati·cal·ly [ˌbjʊərəʊ'krætɪkəlɪ] ADV burocraticamente.

bu·reaux ['bjʊərəʊz] NPL of **bureau**.

bu·rette [bjʊə'ret] N buretta.

bur·geon ['bɜ:dʒən] VI (*liter*) svilupparsi rapidamente.

burg·er ['bɜ:ɡə'] N hamburger *m inv*.

burgh·er ['bɜ:ɡə'] N cittadino(-a).

bur·glar ['bɜ:ɡlə'] N ladro(-a), scassinatore(-trice).

♦ **burglar alarm** N antifurto *m inv*.

bur·glar·ize ['bɜ:ɡləˌraɪz] VT (*Am*) svaligiare.

♦ **burglar-proof** ['bɜ:ɡləˌpru:f] ADJ antiscasso *inv*.

bur·gla·ry ['bɜ:ɡlərɪ] N furto (con scasso).

bur·gle ['bɜ:ɡl] VT (*house, shop*) svaligiare; **I've been burgled** mi hanno svaligiato la casa (*or* il negozio *etc*).

Bur·gun·dy ['bɜ:ɡəndɪ] N Borgogna.

bur·ial ['berɪəl] N sepoltura, seppellimento.

♦ **burial ground** N cimitero.

bur·lesque [bɜ:'lesk] N parodia.

bur·ly ['bɜ:lɪ] ADJ ben piantato(-a), robusto(-a).

Bur·ma ['bɜ:mə] N Birmania.

Bur·mese ['bɜ:'mi:z] 1 ADJ birmano(-a).
2 N (*person, cat*) birmano(-a); (*language*) birmano.

burn [bɜ:n] (*vb: pt, pp* **burned** *or* **burnt**) 1 N (*gen*) bruciatura; (*superficial*) scottatura; (*Med*) ustione *f*.
2 VT (*gen*) bruciare; (*set fire to*) incendiare; (*person, skin: also of sun*) bruciare, scottare; (*toast, meat etc*) (far) bruciare; **to burn wood/coal** (*use as fuel: boiler etc*) andare a legna/carbone; **the cigarette burnt a hole in her dress** si è fatta un buco nel vestito con la sigaretta; **to be burnt to death** morire tra le fiamme, morire bruciato(-a) *or* carbonizzato(-a); (*at stake*) essere bruciato(-a) vivo(-a); **I've burnt myself!** mi sono bruciato!; **to burn one's boats** *or* **bridges** (*fig*) bruciarsi i ponti alle spalle; **he's been burning the candle at both ends for too long** (*fig*) è da troppo tempo che abusa delle proprie energie.
3 VI (*gen*) bruciare; (*fire*) ardere; (*skin, person*) bruciarsi, scottarsi; (*meat, pastry etc*) bruciarsi; (*light, gas*) essere *or* rimanere acceso(-a); **to burn with anger** (*fig*) fremere di rabbia; **to burn with fever** scottare per la febbre; **to burn to do sth** morire dalla voglia di fare qc

▶ **burn down** 1 VT + ADV (*building*) bruciare, dare alle fiamme.
2 VI + ADV (*house*) essere distrutto(-a) dal fuoco, bruciarsi; (*candle, fire*) consumarsi, abbassarsi

▶ **burn off** VT + ADV (*paint*) togliere col fuoco

▶ **burn out** 1 VT + ADV (*subj: writer*): **to burn o.s. out** esaurirsi; (: *talent*): **to burn itself out** esaurirsi; (: *enthusiasm*) spegnersi.
2 VI (*fuse*) saltare; (*candle, lamp*) spegnersi; (*fire*) estinguersi.

▶ **burn up** 1 VI (*fire*) ravvivarsi, divampare.
2 VT + ADV (*rubbish*) bruciare

burn·er ['bɜ:nə'] N (*on cooker*) fornello; (*Tech*) bruciatore

m, becco (a gas).

burn·ing ['bɜ:nɪŋ] ⊞ N bruciato; **I can smell burning** sento odore di bruciato.

⊡ ADJ (*building, forest*) in fiamme; (*coals*) acceso(-a); (*flame*) vivo(-a), ardente; (*fig: thirst, fever, desire*) bruciante, divorante; (*tears*) cocente; (*question, topic, issue*) scottante.

bur·nish ['bɜ:nɪʃ] VT brunire.

bur·nish·ing ['bɜ:nɪʃɪŋ] N brunitura.

Burns' Night N *festa celebrata il 25 gennaio per commemorare il poeta scozzese Robert Burns (1759-1796).*

burnt [bɜ:nt] PT, PP of **burn**.

♦ **burnt sugar** N (*Brit*) caramello.

burp [bɜ:p] (*fam*) ⊞ N rutto; (*of baby*) ruttino.

⊡ VI ruttare, fare un rutto.

⊠ VT (*baby*) far fare il ruttino a.

burr, bur [bɜ:ʳ] ⊞ N **a** (*Bot*) lappa, bardana **b** (*Ling*): **to speak with a burr** arrotare la erre **c** (*sound*) ronzio.

⊡ VI (*plane*) ronzare; (*telephone*) suonare.

bur·row ['bʌrəʊ] ⊞ N (*of rabbit*) tana, cunicolo.

⊡ VT (*hole*) scavare; **to burrow one's way (under/through** *etc*) scavarsi un tunnel (sotto/attraverso *etc*).

⊠ VI (*rabbits*) scavare gallerie; **he burrowed under the bedclothes** si è rintanato sotto le coperte.

bur·sar ['bɜ:səʳ] N (*Univ*) economo(-a).

bur·sa·ry ['bɜ:sərɪ] N (*grant*) borsa di studio.

burst [bɜ:st] (*vb: pt, pp* **burst**) ⊞ N (*of shell etc*) scoppio, esplosione *f*; (*in pipe*) rottura; (*of shots*) raffica, scarica; **a burst of applause** uno scroscio d'applausi; **a burst of laughter/activity** uno scoppio di risa/attività; **a burst of speed** uno scatto (di velocità).

⊡ VT (*gen*) far scoppiare *or* esplodere; (*bag*) sfondare, spaccare; **the river has burst its banks** il fiume ha rotto gli argini *or* ha straripato.

⊠ VI **a** (*gen*) scoppiare; (*tyre: blow out*) scoppiare; (: *puncture*) bucarsi; (*shell, firework*) scoppiare, esplodere; (*bag*) sfondarsi, spaccarsi; (*dam*) cedere; (*blood vessel*) rompersi; **the door burst open** la porta si è spalancata di colpo; **filled to bursting point** pieno(-a) da scoppiare; **to be bursting with** (*health, energy*) scoppiare di; **to be bursting with pride** sprizzare soddisfazione da tutti i pori; **to be bursting at the seams (with)** essere pieno(-a) zeppo(-a) (di), traboccare (di); **the room was bursting at the seams** la stanza rigurgitava di persone; **I was bursting to tell you** (*fam*) morivo dalla voglia di dirtelo **b** (*go suddenly*): **to burst out of the room** scappare precipitosamente dalla stanza; **the sun burst through the clouds** è sbucato il sole

▶ **burst into** VI + PREP (*room*) irrompere in; **to burst into flames** prendere fuoco, andare in fiamme; **to burst into tears** scoppiare a piangere

▶ **burst out** VI + ADV

a (*exclaim*) esclamare

b (*start*): **to burst out laughing** scoppiare a ridere; **to burst out singing** mettersi (improvvisamente) a cantare.

bury [berɪ] VT (*body, treasure*) seppellire; (*plunge: claws, knife*): **to bury (in)** affondare (in); **he buried his face in his hands** si coprì il volto con le mani; **buried by an avalanche** travolto(-a) da una valanga; **to bury the hatchet** (*fig*) seppellire l'ascia di guerra; **to bury one's head in the sand** (*fig*) fare (la politica del)lo struzzo.

bus [bʌs] ⊞ N (*pl* **buses** *or* (*Am*) **busses**) autobus *m inv*; **to go by bus** andare in autobus.

⊡ ADJ (*driver, service, ticket*) d'autobus.

♦ **bus boy** N (*Am*) aiuto *m* cameriere $.

bush [bʊʃ] N **a** cespuglio **b** (*in Africa, Australia*): **the bush** la boscaglia.

bush·baby ['bʊʃ,beɪbɪ] N galagone *m*.

bushed [bʊʃt] ADJ (*fam: exhausted*) distrutto(-a).

bush·el ['bʊʃl] N staio.

bush·fire ['bʊʃ,faɪəʳ] N grande incendio in aperta campagna.

bushy ['bʊʃɪ] ADJ (*plant, tail, beard*) folto(-a); (*eyebrows*) irsuto(-a).

busi·ly ['bɪzɪlɪ] ADV con impegno, alacremente.

busi·ness ['bɪznɪs] ⊞ N **a** (*commerce, trading*) affari *mpl*; **selling books is her business** di mestiere vende libri; **he's in the insurance business** lavora nel campo delle assicurazioni; **he's in the wool business** è nel commercio della lana; **I'm here on business** sono qui per affari; **to be away on business** essere via per affari; **to do business with sb** fare affari con qn; **let's get down to business** (*fam*) bando alle chiacchiere; **business is business** gli affari sono affari; **now we're in business!** ci siamo!; **she means business** fa sul serio, non scherza **b** (*firm*) impresa, azienda; **to set up a business** metter su un'impresa; **it's a family business** è un'impresa familiare

c (*task, duty, concern, matter*) affare *m*; **to make it one's business to do sth** incaricarsi di fare qc; **that's none of your business** non sono affari tuoi, non ti riguarda; **that's my business** (è) affar mio, (sono) affari miei; **it's his business to see that ...** spetta a lui accertarsi che...; **you had no business to do that** non stava a te farlo; **mind your own business** bada ai fatti tuoi, non t'impicciare **d** (*fam: affair, matter*) storia, faccenda; **what an awful business it was!** che orrore che è stato!; **it's a nasty business** è una brutta faccenda, è un brutto affare.

⊡ ADJ (*deal, quarter, relationship*) d'affari; (*studies*) commerciale.

♦ **business address** N indirizzo sul lavoro.

♦ **business card** N biglietto da visita della ditta.

♦ **business college** N istituto commerciale.

♦ **business expenses** NPL spese *fpl*.

business·like ['bɪznɪs,laɪk] ADJ (*approach, transaction*) efficiente; (*firm, company*) serio(-a); (*person, manner*) pratico(-a), efficiente.

business·man ['bɪznɪsmən] N (*pl* **-men**) uomo d'affari, imprenditore.

♦ **business plan** N piano gestionale dell'impresa.

♦ **business sense** N senso degli affari.

♦ **business trip** N viaggio d'affari.

business·woman ['bɪznɪs,wʊmən] N (*pl* **-women**) imprenditrice.

busk [bʌsk] VI suonare (*or* cantare) per le strade.

busk·er ['bʌskəʳ] N (*Brit*) suonatore(-trice) ambulante.

♦ **bus lane** N (*Brit*) corsia preferenziale (per autobus).

♦ **bus route** N percorso dell'autobus.

♦ **bus shelter** N pensilina, fermata coperta.

♦ **bus station** N stazione *f* delle corriere, autostazione *f*.

♦ **bus stop** N fermata d'autobus.

bust[1] [bʌst] N (*bosom*) petto, seno; (*Art*) busto

▶ **bust up** VT + ADV (*fam*) sfasciare.

bust[2] [bʌst] (*fam*) ⊞ ADJ (*broken*) rotto(-a), scassato(-a); **to go bust** (*bankrupt*) fallire, fare fallimento.

⊡ VT **a** = **burst 2 b** (*Police: arrest*) pizzicare, beccare; (: *raid*) fare irruzione in **c** (*break*) scassare.

bust·er ['bʌstəʳ] N: **come here, buster!** ehi tu, vieni qui!

bus·tle ['bʌsl] ⊞ N trambusto.

2 VI (*person: also:* **bustle about**) darsi da fare, affaccendarsi; (*place*) essere animatissimo(-a).

bus·tling ['bʌslɪŋ] ADJ (*person*) affaccendato(-a), indaffarato(-a); (*place, town*) animatissimo(-a).

♦ **bust measurement** N giro *m* petto *inv.*

♦ **bust-up** ['bʌst,ʌp] N (*fam: argument*) lite *f*; **they had a bust-up** hanno rotto.

busty ['bʌstɪ] ADJ (*woman*) dal seno prosperoso.

busy ['bɪzɪ] 1 ADJ a (*occupied: person*) occupato(-a); **she's a busy woman** è una donna molto occupata; **she's busy** (*at the moment*) è occupata; **he's busy studying/ cooking** sta studiando/cucinando; **he's busy at his work** sta lavorando, è molto preso dal lavoro; **let's get busy** (*fam*) diamoci da fare

b (*active: day, time*) movimentato(-a), intenso(-a); (: *place, town*) animato(-a); **Christmas is a busy time of year** a Natale ci sono sempre mille cose da fare; **the roads are busy** c'è molto traffico sulle strade

c (*esp Am: telephone, line*) occupato(-a).

2 VT: **to busy o.s. (doing sth/with sth)** darsi da fare (a fare qc/con qc).

busy·body ['bɪzɪ,bɒdɪ] N ficcanaso *m/f*, impiccione(-a).

♦ **busy signal** N (*Am*) segnale *m* di occupato.

---

but [bʌt]

1 CONJ (*gen*) ma;

▷*never* **a week passes but she's ill** mai una settimana che non stia male

▷**it's small but comfortable** (*car*) è piccola ma comoda.

2 ADV solo, soltanto;

▷**she's but** *a* **child** è solo una bambina, non è che una bambina

▷**had I but** *known* se solo l'avessi saputo

▷**I cannot help but** *think* **that** ... non posso fare a meno di pensare che...

▷**you can but** *try* tentar non nuoce.

3 PREP eccetto, tranne, meno;

▷*all* **but finished** quasi finito(-a)

▷*anything* **but that** tutto ma non questo

▷*anything* **but finished** tutt'altro che finito(-a)

▷**but** *for* **you** (*Brit*) se non fosse per te

▷**the** *last* **but one** il/la penultimo(-a)

▷**I live in the** *next* **street but one** abito due strade più in su (*or* giù)

▷*no one* **but him** solo lui

▷*no one* **but him can do it** è l'unico che lo sappia fare

▷*nothing* **but** null'altro che

▷**he was** *nothing* **but trouble** non dava altro che guai.

4 N: **no buts about it!** non c'è ma che tenga!

---

bu·tane ['bjuːteɪn] N (*also:* **butane gas**) butano.

butch [bʊtʃ] ADJ (*woman: pej*) mascolina; (*man*) macho *inv.*

butch·er ['bʊtʃər] 1 N (*also fig*) macellaio; **butcher's knife** coltello da macellaio; (*Culin*) coltello per carne (cruda); **butcher's (shop)** macelleria; **at the butcher's** dal macellaio.

2 VT macellare.

♦ **butcher meat** N carne *f* macellata.

butch·ery ['bʊtʃərɪ] N a (*massacre*) massacro b (*work of a butcher*) macellazione *f*, macelleria.

but·ler ['bʌtlər] N maggiordomo.

butt[1] [bʌt] N (*end*) estremità più grossa; (*of gun*) cal-

cio; (*of cigar, cigarette*) mozzicone *m*

▶ **butt in** VI + ADV (*interrupt*) interrompere; (*meddle*) immischiarsi.

butt[2] [bʌt] N (*Shooting, Archery*): **the butts** il campo *or* poligono di tiro; (*Brit fig*) bersaglio, zimbello; **she's the butt of his jokes** è il bersaglio dei suoi scherzi, è il suo zimbello.

butt[3] [bʌt] 1 N (*push with head*) testata; (*of goat*) cornata.

2 VT dare una testata (*or* una cornata) a.

butt[4] [bʌt] N botte *f.*

but·ter ['bʌtər] 1 N burro; **he looks as if butter wouldn't melt in his mouth** ha una faccia d'angelo.

2 VT (*bread*) imburrare, spalmare di burro

▶ **butter up** VT + ADV: **to butter sb up** ruffianarsi con qn.

♦ **butter bean** N fagiolo bianco.

butter·cup ['bʌtə,kʌp] N ranuncolo.

♦ **butter curler** N arricciaburro *m inv.*

♦ **butter dish** N burriera.

butter·fingers ['bʌtə,fɪŋgəz] N (*fam*) mani *fpl* di ricotta.

butter·fly ['bʌtə,flaɪ] N a farfalla; **I've got butterflies (in my stomach)** ho il batticuore b (*Swimming: also:* **butterfly stroke**) (nuoto a) farfalla.

♦ **butter knife** N coltellino da burro.

butter·milk ['bʌtə,mɪlk] N latticello.

butter·scotch ['bʌtə,skɒtʃ] N *caramella dura a base di burro e zucchero di canna.*

but·tock ['bʌtək] N natica.

but·ton ['bʌtn] 1 N (*on garment*) bottone *m*; (*on doorbell, machine*) pulsante *m*, bottone.

2 VT (*also:* **button up**) abbottonare.

3 VI abbottonarsi.

button·hole ['bʌtn,həʊl] 1 N asola, occhiello; **to wear a buttonhole** portare un fiore all'occhiello.

2 VT (*person*) attaccar bottone a *or* con.

♦ **button lift** N skilift *m inv* (a piattello).

but·tress ['bʌtrɪs] 1 N contrafforte *m*, sperone *m.*

2 VT armare di contrafforti, rafforzare (con speroni); (*fig*) tener su, tenere in piedi; (: *argument*) avvalorare.

bux·om ['bʌksəm] ADJ formoso(-a).

buy [baɪ] (*vb: pt, pp* **bought**) 1 N: **a good/bad buy** un buon/cattivo acquisto *or* affare *m.*

2 VT comprare, acquistare; (*tickets, petrol*) fare, prendere; (*Comm: company*) acquistare; (*fig: time*) guadagnare; **to buy sb sth/sth from sb** comprare qc per qn/qc da qn; **the victory was dearly bought** la vittoria è stata pagata a caro prezzo; **to buy sb a drink** offrire da bere a qn; **he won't buy that explanation** (*fam*) quella scusa non se la beve

▶ **buy back** VT + ADV riprendersi, prendersi indietro

▶ **buy in** VT + ADV (*Brit: goods*) far provvista di

▶ **buy into** VI + PREP (*Brit Comm*) acquistare delle azioni di

▶ **buy off** VT + ADV (*fam: bribe*) comprare

▶ **buy out** VT + ADV (*business*) rilevare

▶ **buy up** VT + ADV (*property etc*) accaparrarsi.

buy·er ['baɪər] N acquirente *m/f.*

♦ **buyer's market** ['baɪəz'mɑːkɪt] N mercato favorevole ai compratori.

♦ **buy-out** ['baɪ,aʊt] N (*Comm*) *acquisto di una società da parte dei suoi dipendenti.*

buzz [bʌz] 1 N ronzio; (*of conversation*) brusio; **to give sb a buzz** (*fam: telephone call*) dare un colpo di telefono a qn.

2 VT (*call on intercom*) chiamare al citofono; (: *with buzzer*) chiamare col cicalino; (*Aer: plane, building*) passare rasente.

[3] VI (*insect, ears*) ronzare; **my head is buzzing** mi gira la testa

▶ **buzz off** VI + ADV (*Brit fam*) filare, levarsi di torno.

buz·zard ['bʌzəd] N poiana.

buzz·er ['bʌzə'] N cicalino; (*in factory*) sirena.

buzz·ing ['bʌzɪŋ] N ronzio.

♦ **buzz word** N (*fam*) termine *m* in voga.

by [baɪ]

[1] ADV (lì) vicino;

▷**by and by** (*in past*) poco dopo; (*in future*) fra breve

▷**by and large** nel complesso, nell'insieme

▷*close* **by** vicinissimo, molto vicino

▷**to** *go* **by** passare

▷*hard* **by** vicinissimo, molto vicino

▷**to** *lay* **sth by** mettere qc da parte

▷**to** *pass* **by** passare

▷**to** *put* **sth by** mettere qc da parte

▷**to** *rush* **by** passare correndo.

[2] PREP

[a] (*close to*) vicino a, accanto a, presso;

▷**I've got it by** *me* ce l'ho a portata di mano *or* sottomano

▷**the house by the** *river* la casa sul fiume

▷**a holiday by the** *sea* una vacanza al mare

[b] (*via, through*) per;

▷**we came by** *Dover* siamo venuti via Dover

[c] (*past*) davanti a;

▷**I** *go* **by the post office every day** passo davanti alla posta ogni giorno

▷**she** *walked* **by me** mi è passata accanto

[d] (*during*)

▷**by** *day* di giorno;

▷**by** *night* di notte

[e] (*not later than*) per;

▷**by** *then* **it was too late** ormai era troppo tardi

▷**by this** *time* **tomorrow I'll be in Spain** domani a quest'ora sarò in Spagna

▷**by the** *time* **I got there it was too late** quando sono arrivato era ormai troppo tardi

▷**by that** *time* **I knew** ormai lo sapevo

▷**it must be finished by** *4 o'clock* dev'essere terminato entro le 4

[f] (*amount*) a;

▷**by degrees** gradualmente

▷**by the** *hour* a ore

▷**to increase by the** *hour* aumentare di ora in ora

▷**by the** *kilo* a chili

▷*little* **by little** a poco a poco

▷**by the** *metre* a metri

▷*one* **by one** uno(-a) per uno(-a)

[g] (*agent, cause*) da;

▷*killed* **by lightning** ucciso(-a) da un fulmine

▷**a** *painting* **by Picasso** un quadro di Picasso

▷*surrounded* **by enemies** circondato(-a) da nemici

[h] (*method, manner, means*) per;

▷**by** *bus* in autobus, con l'autobus

▷**by** *car* in macchina, con la macchina

▷**to pay by** *cheque* pagare con (un) assegno

▷**by** *force* con la forza

▷**made by** *hand* fatto(-a) a mano

▷**to lead sb by the** *hand* portare qn per mano

▷**by** *land* **and by** *sea* per terra e per mare

▷**by** *moonlight* al chiaro di luna

▷**(all) by** *oneself* tutto(-a) solo(-a)

▷**by** *rail or train* con il treno, in treno

▷**by** *saving* **hard, he ... risparmiando** molto, lui...

[i] (*according to*) per;

▷**to** *play* **by the rules** attenersi alle regole

▷**it's all** *right* **by me** per me va bene

[j] (*measuring difference*) di;

▷**it missed me by** *inches* non mi ha preso *or* mi ha mancato per un millimetro

▷**it's wider by a** *metre* è un metro più largo

[k] (*Math, measure*) per;

▷**to** *divide/multiply* **by** dividere/moltiplicare per;

▷**a room 3** *metres* **by 4** una stanza di 3 metri per 4

[l] (*points of compass*): **north by north-east** nord-nordest

[m] (*in oaths*): **I** *swear* **by Almighty God** giuro dinanzi a Dio *or* nel nome di Dio

[n]: **by the** *way or* **by the** *by(e)* a proposito;

▷**this wasn't my idea by the** *way* tra l'altro l'idea non era mia.

bye [baɪ] EXCL (*fam: also:* **bye-bye**) ciao!, arrivederci.

♦ **by-election, bye-election** ['baɪɪˌlɛkʃən] N *in Gran Bretagna, elezioni indette per coprire un posto in Parlamento resosi vacante a governo ancora in carica.*

Bye·lo·rus·sia [ˌbjɛləʊˈrʌʃə] N Bielorussia.

Bye·lo·rus·sian [ˌbjɛləʊˈrʌʃən] [1] ADJ bielorusso(-a).

[2] N (*person*) bielorusso(-a); (*language*) bielorusso.

by·gone ['baɪˌgɒn] [1] ADJ passato(-a); **in bygone days** una volta.

[2] N: **let bygones be bygones** mettiamoci una pietra sopra.

by·lane ['baɪˌleɪn] N stradina.

♦ **by-law, bye-law** ['baɪˌlɔ] N ordinanza locale.

by·pass ['baɪˌpɑːs] [1] N (*road*) circonvallazione *f*; (*Med*) by-pass *m inv*.

[2] VT (*town*) (fare una deviazione per) evitare; (*fig: person*) scavalcare; (*difficulty*) aggirare.

♦ **by-product** ['baɪˌprɒdʌkt] N (*Chem etc*) sottoprodotto; (*fig*) conseguenza.

byre [baɪə'] N (*Brit*) vaccheria, stalla.

by·road ['baɪrəʊd], **by·way** ['baɪˌweɪ] N strada secondaria.

by·stander ['baɪˌstændə'] N astante *m/f*, spettatore(-trice).

byte [baɪt] N (*Comput*) byte *m inv*.

by·word ['baɪˌwɜːd] N: **his name is a byword for success** il suo nome è sinonimo di successo.

♦ **by-your-leave** ['baɪjʊəˈliːv] N: **without so much as a by-your-leave** senza nemmeno chiedere il permesso.

C

C, c [si:] N **a** (*letter*) C, c *f or m inv*; **C for Charlie** ≈ C come Como **b** (*Mus*) do *m inv* **c** (*Scol: mark*) ≈ 6 (*sufficiente*).

C ABBR = *Celsius*; *centigrade* C.

c. ABBR **a** (= *century*) sec. **b** (= *circa*) ca. **c** (*Am etc*) = cent(s).

CA [1] ABBR **a** = **Central America b** (*Am Post*)= *California*. [2] N ABBR (*Brit*) = **chartered accountant**.

ca. ABBR (= *circa*) ca.

c/a ABBR **a** = **capital account b** = **credit account c** = **current account**.

CAA [ˌsiːeɪˈeɪ] N ABBR (*Brit*)= *Civil Aviation Authority*; (*Am:* = *Civil Aeronautics Authority*) *organismo di controllo e di sviluppo dell'aviazione civile.*

CAB [ˌsiːeɪˈbi] N ABBR (*Brit:* = *Citizens' Advice Bureau*) *organizzazione di volontari che offre gratuitamente assistenza in materie legali e finanziarie.*

cab [kæb] N **a** (*taxi*) taxi *m inv*; **by cab** in taxi **b** (*of train, truck, lorry*) cabina **c** (*horsedrawn*) carrozza.

ca·bal [kəˈbæl] N (*intrigue*) intrigo; (*group*) cricca.

caba·ret [ˈkæbəreɪ] N cabaret *m inv*.

cab·bage [ˈkæbɪdʒ] N cavolo.

cab·by [ˈkæbɪ] N (*fam*) tassista *m/f*.

♦ **cab driver** N tassista *m/f*.

cab·in [ˈkæbɪn] N (*hut*) capanna; (*Naut, Aer*) cabina.

♦ **cabin baggage** N bagaglio a mano.

♦ **cabin boy** N mozzo.

♦ **cabin cruiser** N cabinato.

cabi·net [ˈkæbɪnɪt] N **a** (*cupboard*) armadietto; (*glass-fronted*) vetrina **b** (*Pol: also:* **Cabinet**) Consiglio dei Ministri.

♦ **cabinet-maker** [ˈkæbɪnɪtˌmeɪkəʳ] N ebanista *m*.

♦ **cabinet-making** [ˈkæbɪnɪtˌmeɪkɪŋ] N ebanisteria.

♦ **cabinet minister** N ministro (*membro del Consiglio*).

♦ **cabin trunk** N baule *m*.

ca·ble [ˈkeɪbl] [1] N (*rope*) cavo, fune *f*; (*Elec*) cavo; (*cablegram*) cablogramma *m*.

[2] VT (*information*) trasmettere per cablogramma, cablare; (*person*) mandare un cablogramma a, telegrafare a.

♦ **cable car** [ˈkeɪblˌkɑːʳ] N funivia; (*on rail*) funicolare *f*.

ca·ble·gram [ˈkeɪblˌgræm] N cablogramma *m*.

♦ **cable railway** N funicolare *f*.

♦ **cable stitch** N punto treccia.

♦ **cable television** N televisione *f* via cavo.

cable·way [ˈkeɪblˌweɪ] N teleferica.

cab·man [ˈkæbmən] N (*pl* **-men**) tassista *m/f*.

ca·boo·dle [kəˈbuːdl] N (*fam*): **the whole caboodle** baracca e burattini.

cache [kæʃ] N (*of arms, food*) deposito segreto.

ca·chet [ˈkæʃeɪ] N **a** (*seal*) sigillo; (*mark, stamp*) marchio; (*fig: prestige*) prestigio **b** (*capsule*) cachet *m inv*.

cack·le [ˈkækl] [1] N (*of hen*) coccodè *m*; (*laugh*) risolino (stridulo); (*chatter*) chiacchierio.

[2] VI (*hen*) fare coccodè; (*person: laugh*) ridacchiare.

ca·copho·nous [kəˈkɒfənəs] ADJ (*frm*) cacofonico(-a).

ca·copho·ny [kəˈkɒfənɪ] N (*frm*) cacofonia.

cac·tus [ˈkæktəs] N (*pl* **cactuses** *or* **cacti** [ˈkæktaɪ]) cactus *m inv*.

CAD [kæd] N ABBR (= *computer-aided design*) progettazione *f* assistita dall'elaboratore.

cad [kæd] N (*old pej*) mascalzone *m*.

ca·dav·er [kəˈdeɪvəʳ] N (*Med*) cadavere *m*.

ca·dav·er·ous [kəˈdævərəs] ADJ (*frm*) cadaverico(-a).

cad·die[1], **cad·dy** [ˈkædɪ] N (*in golf*) caddie *m inv*.

cad·dy[2] [ˈkædɪ] N (*tea caddy*) barattolo del tè.

ca·dence [ˈkeɪdəns] N cadenza.

ca·det [kəˈdɛt] N (*Mil etc*) cadetto; **police cadet** allievo poliziotto.

cadge [kædʒ] VT (*fam: money, cigarette etc*): **to cadge (from)** scroccare a; **to cadge a lift from sb** scroccare un passaggio a qn; **to cadge a meal (off sb)** scroccare un pranzo (a qn).

cadg·er [ˈkædʒəʳ] N (*fam*) scroccone(-a).

ca·dre [ˈkædrɪ] N (*Pol: group*) gruppo scelto.

cae·cum [ˈsiːkəm] N (*Anat*) intestino cieco.

Caesar [ˈsiːzəʳ] N Cesare *m*.

Cae·sar·ean, (*Am*) **Ce·sar·ean** [sɪˈzɛərɪən] N (*also:* **Caesarean section**) (*taglio*) cesareo.

CAF [ˌsiːeɪˈɛf] ABBR (*Brit:* = *cost and freight*) Caf *m*.

café [ˈkæfeɪ] N caffè *m inv*, bar *m inv* (*senza licenza per*

alcolici).

caf·eteria [ˌkæfɪˈtɪərɪə] N self-service *m inv*; (*in factory etc*) mensa.

caf·feine, caf·fein [ˈkæfiːn] N caffeina.

caf·tan, kaf·tan [ˈkæftæn] N caffettano.

cage [keɪdʒ] [1] N (*gen, in mine*) gabbia.
[2] VT mettere in gabbia
▶ **cage in** VT + ADV ingabbiare.

cag·ey [ˈkeɪdʒɪ] ADJ (*fam*) evasivo(-a); **to give a cagey answer** dare una risposta evasiva; **to be cagey about doing sth** esitare a fare qc.

cag·i·ly [ˈkeɪdʒɪlɪ] ADV prudentemente.

ca·goule [kəˈguːl] N K-way ® *m inv*.

ca·hoots [kəˈhuːts] NPL (*fam*): **to be in cahoots (with sb)** essere in combutta (con qn).

CAI [ˌsiːeɪˈaɪ] N ABBR (= *computer-aided instruction*) istruzione *f* assistita dall'elaboratore.

Cain [keɪn] N Caino.

cairn [kɛən] N tumulo (di pietre).

cairn·gorm [ˈkɛənˌɡɔːm] N quarzo affumicato.

Cai·ro [ˈkaɪərəʊ] N il Cairo *f*.

ca·jole [kəˈdʒəʊl] VT (*coax*) convincere con le buone; (: *deceitfully*) convincere con lusinghe; **to cajole sb into doing sth** convincere qn a fare qc.

ca·jol·ery [kəˈdʒəʊlərɪ] N (*see vb*) opera di convincimento; lusinghe *fpl*.

cake [keɪk] [1] N a (*large*) torta; (*small*) pasticcino; **piece of cake** fetta di torta; **it's a piece of cake** (*fam*) è una cosa facile *or* da nulla; **driving is a piece of cake** non ci vuole niente a guidare; **to sell like hot cakes** (*fam*) andare a ruba; **he wants to have his cake and eat it** (*fig*) vuole la botte piena e la moglie ubriaca
b (*of wax*) tavoletta; **cake of soap** saponetta.
[2] VT: **to cake (with)** incrostare (di).
[3] VI (*blood*) raggrumarsi; (*mud*) incrostarsi.

♦ **cake mix** N preparato per torta.
♦ **cake rack** N griglia per torte.
♦ **cake shop** N pasticceria.
♦ **cake slice** N paletta (da dolce).

cala·mine [ˈkæləˌmaɪn] N (*also*: **calamine lotion**) *lozione calmante a base di calamina*.

ca·lami·tous [kəˈlæmɪtəs] ADJ disastroso(-a).

ca·lam·ity [kəˈlæmɪtɪ] N calamità *f inv*.

cal·ci·fi·ca·tion [ˌkælsɪfɪˈkeɪʃən] N calcificazione *f*.

cal·ci·fy [ˈkælsɪfaɪ] [1] VT calcificare.
[2] VI calcificarsi.

cal·cium [ˈkælsɪəm] N (*Chem*) calcio.

cal·cu·late [ˈkælkjʊˌleɪt] [1] VT (*cost, distance etc*) calcolare; (*estimate: chances, effect*) valutare; **to be calculated to do sth** essere fatto(-a) *or* studiato(-a) per fare qc.
[2] VI (*Math*) fare (i) conti
▶ **calculate on** VI + PREP: **to calculate on sth/on doing sth** contare su qc/di fare qc, tenere conto di qc/di fare qc; **he hadn't calculated on the arrival of the night watchman** non aveva fatto i conti con l'arrivo del guardiano notturno.

cal·cu·lat·ed [ˈkælkjʊˌleɪtɪd] ADJ (*insult, action*) calcolato(-a), intenzionale; **a calculated risk** un rischio calcolato.

cal·cu·lat·ing [ˈkælkjʊˌleɪtɪŋ] ADJ (*scheming*) calcolatore(-trice).

♦ **calculating machine** N (macchina) calcolatrice *f*.

cal·cu·la·tion [ˌkælkjʊˈleɪʃən] N calcolo.

cal·cu·la·tor [ˈkælkjʊˌleɪtəʳ] N calcolatrice *f*.

cal·cu·lus [ˈkælkjʊləs] N calcolo; **differential/integral calculus** calcolo differenziale/integrale.

cal·de·ra [kælˈdɛərə] N (*Geol*) caldera.

cal·en·dar [ˈkælɪndəʳ] N calendario; **the Church calendar** il calendario ecclesiastico.
♦ **calendar month** N mese *m* civile.
♦ **calendar year** N anno civile.

calender [ˈkælɪndəʳ] N (*Tech*) calandra.

calf¹ [kaːf] N (*pl* **calves** [kaːvz]) a (*young cow*) vitello; **seal/elephant calf** piccolo di foca/elefante b = **calf-skin**.

calf² [kaːf] N (*pl* **calves** [kaːvz]) (*Anat*) polpaccio.

calf·skin [ˈkaːfˌskɪn] N (pelle *f* di) vitello.

cali·brate [ˈkælɪbreɪt] VT (*gun etc*) calibrare; (*scale of measuring instrument*) tarare.

cali·bra·tion [ˌkælɪˈbreɪʃən] N (*see vb*) calibratura; taratura.

cali·bre, (*Am***) cali·ber** [ˈkælɪbəʳ] N (*also fig*) calibro.

cali·co [ˈkælɪˌkəʊ] N (tela di) cotone *m* grezzo; (*Am*) cotonina stampata.

Caligula [kəˈlɪɡjʊlə] N Caligola *m*.

cali·pers [ˈkælɪpəz] NPL (*Am*) = **callipers**.

ca·liph [ˈkeɪlɪf] N califfo.

call [kɔːl] [1] N a (*shout*) richiamo, urlo, grido; (*of bird*) canto; **to give a call** lanciare un grido; **within call** a portata di voce; **please give me a call at 7** per piacere mi chiami alle 7; **whose call is it?** (*Cards*) a chi tocca (giocare)?
b (*Telec*) telefonata, chiamata; **long-distance call** chiamata interurbana; **to make a call** telefonare, fare una telefonata
c (*summons: for flight etc*) chiamata; (*fig: lure*) richiamo; **to be on call** essere a disposizione; (*doctor*) essere reperibile; **the call of the sea** il richiamo del mare; **to answer the call of duty** fare il proprio dovere
d (*short visit: also Med*) visita; **port of call** (porto di) scalo; **to pay a call on sb** fare (una) visita a qn
e (*need*): **there's not much call for these items** non c'è molta richiesta di questi articoli; **you had no call to say that** non c'era alcun bisogno che tu lo dicessi; **there is no call for alarm** non ci sono motivi di allarme
f (*claim*): **there are many calls on my time** sono molto preso, ho molti impegni.
[2] VT a chiamare; (*Telec*) chiamare, telefonare a; (*announce: flight*) annunciare; (*meeting, strike*) indire, proclamare; (*waken*) svegliare, chiamare
b (*name*) chiamare; (*describe as*) considerare; **can I call you by your first name?** posso chiamarti per nome?; **what are you called?** come ti chiami?; **she's called Jane** si chiama Jane; **would you call Italian a difficult language?** diresti che l'italiano è una lingua difficile?; **I call it an insult** questo lo chiamo un insulto, lo considero un insulto; **are you calling me a liar?** mi stai dando del bugiardo?; **let's call it £50** facciamo 50 sterline; **let's call it a day** (*fam*) smettiamo, basta per oggi.
[3] VI a (*shout: person*) chiamare; (*bird*) lanciare un richiamo; **to call to sb** gridare a qn
b (*Telec*): **who's calling?** chi parla?; **London calling** (*Radio*) qui Londra
c (*also*: **call in, call round**: *visit*) passare
▶ **call aside** VT + ADV chiamare da parte *or* in disparte
▶ **call at** VI + PREP (*subj: ship*) fare scalo a
▶ **call away** VT + ADV: **to be called away on business** dovere andare via per lavoro
▶ **call back** [1] VT + ADV (*Telec*) ritelefonare a, richiamare.
[2] VI + ADV (*Telec*) ritelefonare, richiamare; (*return*)

ritornare

▶ **call down** VT + PREP: **to call down sth (on sb)** (*curses*) invocare qc (su qn)

▶ **call for** VI + PREP (*summon*: *wine, the bill*) chiedere; (*demand*: *courage, action*) richiedere; (*collect*: *person*) passare a prendere; (: *goods*) ritirare; **this calls for a drink!** qui ci vuole un brindisi!

▶ **call forth** VT + ADV (*frm*: *protest, emotion*) suscitare

▶ **call in** ⓵ VT + ADV **a** (*doctor, expert, police*) chiamare, far venire

  b (*Comm etc*: *faulty goods*) riprendere; (: *currency*) mettere fuori corso.

  ⓶ VI + ADV = **call 3c**

▶ **call off** VT + ADV **a** (*meeting, race*) disdire, revocare; (*deal*) cancellare; **the strike was called off** lo sciopero è stato revocato

  b (*dog*) richiamare

▶ **call on** VI + PREP **a** (*visit*) far visita a, andare a trovare, passare da

  b (*invite*): **to call on sb to do sth** invitare qn a fare qc; (*request*) chiedere a qn di fare qc; **I now call on Mr Brown to speak** ora invito il signor Brown a parlare

▶ **call out** ⓵ VT + ADV (*doctor, police, troops*) chiamare; **to call workers out on strike** invitare gli operai a fare sciopero.

  ⓶ VI + ADV (*in pain*) urlare; (*to person*) chiamare; **to call out for help** invocare *or* chiamare aiuto

▶ **call round** VI + ADV passare; **to call round to see sb** passare da qn

▶ **call up** VT + ADV **a** (*Mil*) richiamare, mobilitare

  b (*Telec*) chiamare, telefonare a

  c (*fig*: *memories*) richiamare, evocare

▶ **call upon** VI + PREP = **call on b**.

Cal·lane·tics® [ˌkælə'netɪks] NSG *tipo di ginnastica basata sulla ripetizione di piccoli movimenti.*

call·box ['kɔːlˌbɒks] N (*Brit*) cabina telefonica.

cal·ler ['kɔːlə'] N (*visitor*) visitatore(-trice); (*Telec*) persona che chiama; **hold the line, caller!** rimanga in linea, signore (*or* signora)!

♦ **call girl** N ragazza *f* squillo *inv*.

cal·lig·ra·phy [kə'lɪɡrəfɪ] N calligrafia.

♦ **call-in** ['kɔːlˌɪn] N (*Am*) = **phone-in**.

call·ing ['kɔːlɪŋ] N vocazione *f*.

♦ **calling card** N (*Am*) biglietto da visita.

Cal·lio·pe [kə'laɪəpɪ] N Calliope *f*.

cal·li·pers, (*Am*) **cali·pers** ['kælɪpəz] NPL (*Med*) gambale *m*; (*Math*) calibro.

cal·lis·then·ics [ˌkælɪs'θenɪks] NSG ginnastica svedese.

cal·lous ['kæləs] ADJ (*person*) insensibile; (*remark*) crudele.

cal·loused ['kæləst] ADJ calloso(-a).

cal·lous·ly ['kæləslɪ] ADV (*behave*) in modo insensibile; (*speak*) con durezza; (*decide*) cinicamente.

cal·lous·ness ['kæləsnɪs] N (*of person*) insensibilità; (*of remark*) durezza.

cal·low ['kæləʊ] ADJ immaturo(-a).

♦ **call sign** N segnale *m* di chiamata.

♦ **call-up** ['kɔːlˌʌp] (*Mil*) N chiamata (alle armi).

♦ **call-up papers** NPL cartolina precetto.

calm [kɑːm] ⓵ ADJ (*gen*) calmo(-a); (*weather*) sereno(-a); **calm and collected** padrone(-a) di sé; **keep calm!** sta' calmo!.

  ⓶ N calma, pace *f*; **the calm before the storm** la quiete che precede la tempesta.

  ⓷ VT (*also*: **calm down**: *person*) calmare

▶ **calm down** ⓵ VT + ADV = **calm 3**.

  ⓶ VI + ADV calmarsi; **calm down!** calmati!

calm·ly ['kɑːmlɪ] ADV tranquillamente, con calma.

calm·ness ['kɑːmnɪs] N calma, tranquillità.

Cal·or Gas® ['kæləˌɡæs] N (*Brit*) liquigas ® *m*.

calo·rie ['kælərɪ] N caloria; **low-calorie product** prodotto a basso contenuto calorico.

calo·rif·ic [ˌkælə'rɪfɪk] ADJ: **calorific value** (*Phys*) valore *m* calorico.

cal·um·ny ['kæləmnɪ] N (*frm*) calunnia.

calve [kɑːv] VI figliare.

calves [kɑːvz] NPL of **calf**.

calv·ing ['kɑːvɪŋ] N parto (*di bovini*).

CAM [kæm] N ABBR (= *computer-aided manufacturing*) fabbricazione *f* assistita dall'elaboratore.

cam [kæm] N (*Tech*) camma, eccentrico.

ca·ma·ra·derie [ˌkæmə'rædərɪ] N cameratismo.

cam·ber ['kæmbə'] N (*of road*) curvatura, bombatura.

cam·bium ['kæmbɪəm] N (*pl* **cambiums** *or* **cambia** ['kæmbɪə]) (*Bot*) cambio.

Cam·bo·dia [kæm'bəʊdɪə] N Cambogia.

Cam·bo·dian [kæm'bəʊdɪən] ADJ, N cambogiano(-a).

Cambs ABBR (*Brit*)= *Cambridgeshire*.

cam·cord·er ['kæmkɔːdə'] N camcorder *f inv*.

came [keɪm] PT of **come**.

cam·el ['kæməl] ⓵ N cammello.

  ⓶ ADJ (*colour*) color cammello *inv*.

♦ **camel coat** N cappotto di cammello.

camel·hair ['kæməlˌheə'] N (pelo di) cammello.

ca·mel·lia [kə'miːlɪə] N camelia.

cameo ['kæmɪəʊ] ⓵ N cammeo.

  ⓶ ADJ (*ring, brooch*) con cammeo; (*Cine, Theatre*: *role, part*) breve apparizione *f* (*di un attore o un'attrice famoso/a*).

cam·era ['kæmərə] N **a** macchina fotografica; (*movie camera*) cinepresa; (*Cine, TV*) telecamera **b** (*Law*): **in camera** a porte chiuse.

camera·man ['kæmərəˌmæn] N (*pl* **-men**) cameraman *m inv*.

♦ **camera-ready copy** ['kæmərəˌredɪ 'kɒpɪ] N (*Typ*) testo pronto per la fotocomposizione.

♦ **camera-shy** ['kæmərəˌʃaɪ] ADJ che non ama essere fotografato(-a).

camera·work ['kæmərəˌwɜːk] N riprese *fpl*.

Cam·eroon [ˌkæmə'ruːn] N il Camerun *m*.

camo·mile ['kæməʊmaɪl] N camomilla.

camouflage ['kæməflɑːʒ] ⓵ N camuffamento; (*Mil*) mimetizzazione *f*.

  ⓶ VT camuffare; (*Mil*) mimetizzare.

camp¹ [kæmp] ⓵ N (*gen*) accampamento, campo; (*holiday camp*) campeggio; (*Pol etc*) campo, schieramento.

  ⓶ VI campeggiare, accamparsi; **to go camping** andare in campeggio

▶ **camp out** VI + ADV accamparsi, attendarsi, campeggiare.

camp² [kæmp] ADJ (*fam*: *theatrical*) melodrammatico(-a); (: *homosexual*) ostentatamente effeminato(-a).

cam·paign [kæm'peɪn] ⓵ N (*Mil, Pol etc*) campagna.

  ⓶ VI (*Mil, also fig*): **to campaign (for/against)** fare una campagna (per/contro).

cam·paign·er [kæm'peɪnə'] N (*Mil*): **old campaigner** veterano, vecchio combattente *m*; **campaigner for** fautore(-trice) di; **campaigner against** oppositore(-trice) di.

♦ **camp bed** N (*Brit*) brandina.

camp·er ['kæmpə'] N (person) campeggiatore(-trice); (vehicle) camper m inv.

♦ **camp follower** N (fig) simpatizzante m/f.

cam·phor ['kæmfə'] N canfora.

cam·pho·rat·ed ['kæmfə,reɪtɪd] ADJ canforato(-a).

camp·ing ['kæmpɪŋ] N campeggio.

cam·pi·on ['kæmpɪən] N: **white/red campion** licnide f bianca/rossa.

♦ **camp site**, **camping site** N (zona di) campeggio.

cam·pus ['kæmpəs] N campus m inv.

cam·shaft ['kæm,ʃæft] N albero a camme; **single camshaft** monoalbero.

---

can¹ [kæn] (neg **cannot**, **can't**, cond and pt **could**) MODAL AUX VB

a (be able to) potere;

▷**I'll tell you all I can** ti dirò tutto quello che posso

▷**she was as happy as could be** più felice di così non poteva essere

▷**she can be very annoying** lei a volte è molto seccante, lei riesce ad essere molto seccante

▷**he can do it if he tries hard** è capace di farlo se si sforza

▷**they couldn't help it** non potevano farci niente

▷**I can't or cannot go any further** non posso andare oltre

b (know how to) essere capace di, sapere;

▷**I can speak French** so parlare francese

▷**can you speak Italian?** parli italiano?

▷**I can swim** so nuotare

▷**he can't swim** non sa nuotare

c (may) potere;

▷**can't I come too?** non posso venire anch'io?

▷**could I have a word with you?** potrei parlarti un attimo?

▷**can I use your telephone?** posso usare il tuo telefono?

d (expressing disbelief, puzzlement)

▷**how could you lie to me!** come hai potuto dirmi una bugia!

▷**she can't possibly marry that creep!** (fam) non è possibile che sposi quell'essere!

▷**you can't be serious!** scherzi?

▷**this can't be true!** non può essere vero!

▷**what can he want?** cosa può mai volere?

▷**they can't have left already!** non è possibile che siano già partiti!

e (expressing possibility, suggestion etc)

▷**they could have forgotten** potrebbero essersene dimenticati

▷**he could be in the library** può darsi che sia in biblioteca, potrebbe essere in biblioteca

▷**I could have cried/screamed!** mi sarei messo a piangere/urlare!

f (not translated)

▷**can you hear me?** mi senti?

▷**I can't see you** non ti vedo.

---

can² [kæn] **1** N (container: for foodstuffs) scatola; (: for oil, water) latta; (esp Am: garbage can) bidone m; **a can of beer** una lattina di birra; **to carry the can** (Brit fam) prendere la colpa.

2 VT (food) inscatolare.

Cana·da ['kænədə] N Canada m.

Ca·na·dian [kə'neɪdɪən] ADJ, N canadese (m/f).

ca·nal [kə'næl] N canale m.

♦ **canal harbour** N porto canale m inv.

cana·li·za·tion [,kænəlaɪ'zeɪʃən] N canalizzazione f.

cana·lize ['kænə,laɪz] VT (frm) canalizzare, convogliare.

Ca·naries [kə'nɛərɪz] NPL: **the Canaries** le Canarie.

ca·nary [kə'nɛərɪ] N canarino.

Canary Islands NPL: **the Canary Islands** le isole fpl Canarie.

♦ **canary yellow** ADJ, N giallo canarino inv.

ca·nas·ta [kə'næstə] N canasta.

Can·ber·ra ['kænbərə] N Canberra.

can·cel ['kænsəl] VT **a** (call off: holiday, booking) cancellare, annullare, disdire; (meeting, event) cancellare, sospendere; (train) sopprimere; (annul: order, contract) annullare

b (obliterate: name) cancellare, radiare; (: stamp) timbrare, annullare; (: cheque) annullare

c (Math: figures) semplificare

▶ **cancel out** **1** VT + ADV (Math) semplificare; (fig) annullare; **they cancel each other out** (also fig) si annullano a vicenda.

2 VI + ADV (Math) semplificarsi.

can·cel·la·tion [,kænsə'leɪʃən] N (see vt a, c) cancellazione f, annullamento, disdetta; sospensione f; soppressione f; annullamento; semplificazione f.

Can·cer ['kænsə'] N (Astron, Geog) Cancro; **to be Cancer** (Astrol) essere del Cancro.

can·cer ['kænsə'] N (Med) cancro.

can·cer·ous ['kænsərəs] ADJ canceroso(-a).

♦ **cancer patient** N malato(-a) di cancro.

♦ **cancer research** N ricerca sul cancro.

♦ **cancer specialist** N cancerologo(-a).

can·de·la·bra [,kændɪ'lɑːbrə] N candelabro.

C and F [,siː.ənd'ɛf] ABBR (Brit: = cost and freight) Caf m.

can·did ['kændɪd] ADJ franco(-a), onesto(-a).

can·di·da·cy ['kændɪdəsɪ], (Brit) **can·di·da·ture** ['kændɪdətʃə'] N candidatura.

can·di·date ['kændɪ,deɪt] N candidato(-a).

can·did·ly ['kændɪdlɪ] ADV francamente, onestamente.

can·died ['kændɪd] ADJ candito(-a); **candied peel** scorzette fpl di frutta candita; **candied apple** (Am) mela caramellata.

can·dle ['kændl] N candela; (in church) cero.

♦ **candle grease** N sego.

candle·light ['kændl,laɪt] N lume m di candela; **by candlelight** a lume di candela.

Candle·mas ['kændəlməs] N Candelora.

candle·stick ['kændl,stɪk], **candle·holder** ['kændl,həʊldə'] N bugia, portacandele m inv; (large, ornate) candeliere m.

candle·wick ['kændl,wɪk] N ciniglia (di cotone).

can·dour, (Am) **can·dor** ['kændə'] N candore m, franchezza, sincerità.

can·dy ['kændɪ] **1** N (Am: sweet) caramella; (: sweets, confectionery) dolciumi mpl.

2 VT (fruit) candire.

candy·floss ['kændɪ,flɒs] N (Brit) zucchero filato.

♦ **candy store** N (Am) ≈ pasticceria.

♦ **candy-striped** ADJ (fabric) a righine bianche e rosa.

cane [keɪn] **1** N (Bot) canna; (for baskets, chairs) bambù m; (wicker) vimini m; (stick: for walking) bastone m (da passeggio); (: for punishment) bacchetta; **to get the cane** (Scol) prenderle con la bacchetta.

[2] VT (*Brit Scol: pupil*) picchiare con la bacchetta.

♦ **cane chair** N sedia di vimini *or* di bambù.

♦ **cane sugar** N zucchero di canna.

can·ine ['keɪnaɪn] [1] ADJ canino(-a).

[2] N (*canine tooth*) (dente *m*) canino.

ca·ning ['keɪnɪŋ] N: **to give sb a caning** dare bacchettate a qn (*per punizione*).

can·is·ter ['kænɪstəʳ] N (*for tea, coffee*) barattolo (*metallico*); (*for gas*) candelotto.

can·ker ['kæŋkəʳ] N **a** (*frm: evil*) cancro **b** (*Med*) afta, stomatite *f* **c** (*Bot*) cancro.

can·na·bis ['kænəbɪs] N canapa indiana.

canned [kænd] [1] PT, PP of **can²**.

[2] ADJ (*food*) in scatola; (*fam: recorded: music*) registrato (-a); (*Brit fam: drunk*) sbronzo(-a); (*Am fam: worker*) licenziato(-a).

can·nery ['kænərɪ] N conservificio.

can·ni·bal ['kænɪbəl] N cannibale *m/f.*

can·ni·bal·ism ['kænɪbəlɪzəm] N cannibalismo.

can·ni·bal·is·tic [ˌkænɪbə'lɪstɪk] ADJ cannibalesco(-a).

can·ni·bal·ize ['kænɪbəlaɪz] VT (*car etc*) smontare (*per riutilizzare alcuni singoli pezzi*).

can·ning ['kænɪŋ] N conservazione *f* dei cibi in scatola.

can·non ['kænən] [1] N (*pl* **cannon** *or* **cannons**) (*gun*) cannone *m*.

[2] VI: **to cannon into** *or* **against** sbattere violentemente contro.

cannon·ball ['kænən‚bɔːl] N palla di cannone.

♦ **cannon fodder** N carne *f* da cannone.

can·not ['kænɒt] = **can not.**

can·ny ['kænɪ] ADJ (*comp* **-ier**, *superl* **-iest**) furbo(-a).

ca·noe [kə'nuː] [1] N canoa.

[2] VI andare in canoa.

ca·noe·ing [kə'nuːɪŋ] N (*sport*) canottaggio.

ca·noe·ist [kə'nuːɪst] N canoista *m/f*, canottiere *m*.

can·on ['kænən] N **a** (*clergyman*) canonico **b** (*principle*) canone *m*.

can·oni·za·tion [ˌkænənaɪ'zeɪʃən] N canonizzazione *f*.

can·on·ize ['kænə‚naɪz] VT canonizzare.

♦ **canon law** N (*Rel*) diritto canonico.

ca·noo·dle [kə'nuːdl] VI (*fam*) sbaciucchiarsi.

♦ **can opener** N apriscatole *m inv.*

cano·py ['kænəpɪ] N (*above bed, throne*) baldacchino; (*Naut*) tandalino.

can't [kɑːnt] = **can not.**

cant¹ [kænt] N (*hypocritical talk*) discorsi *mpl* ipocriti; (*jargon*) gergo.

cant² [kænt] [1] VI (*tilt*) inclinarsi.

[2] VT inclinare; (*overturn*) rovesciare.

Cantab. ABBR (*Brit*: = *cantabrigiensis*) di Cambridge.

can·tan·ker·ous [kæn'tæŋkərəs] ADJ irascibile, stizzoso (-a).

can·teen [kæn'tiːn] N **a** (*restaurant*) mensa **b** (*Brit*): **a canteen of cutlery** un servizio di posate.

can·ter ['kæntəʳ] [1] N piccolo galoppo; **counter canter** galoppo rovescio.

[2] VI andare a piccolo galoppo.

can·ti·lever ['kæntɪ‚liːvəʳ] N trave *f* a sbalzo.

♦ **cantilever bridge** N ponte *m* a mensola.

can·ton ['kæntɒn] N cantone *m*.

can·vas ['kænvəs] N tela; **under canvas** (*in a tent*) in tenda; (*Naut*) a vele spiegate.

can·vass ['kænvəs] [1] VT (*Pol: district*) fare un giro elettorale di; (: *person*) fare propaganda elettorale a; (*Comm: district*) battere (*per raccogliere ordinazioni*); (:

citizens, opinions) fare un sondaggio di.

[2] VI (*Pol*) raccogliere voti; (*Comm*) battere la zona per raccogliere ordinazioni.

can·vass·er ['kænvəsəʳ] N (*Pol*) propagandista *m/f* (elettorale); (*Comm*) piazzista *m*.

can·vass·ing ['kænvəsɪŋ] N sollecitazione *f.*

can·yon ['kænjən] N canyon *m inv.*

CAP [ˌsiːeɪ'piː] N ABBR (= *Common Agricultural Policy*) PAC *f*, politica agricola comunitaria.

cap [kæp] [1] N **a** (*hat, also Sport*) berretto; (*for swimming*) cuffia; (*riding cap*) cap *m inv*; **cap in hand** (*fig*) umilmente; **if the cap fits wear it** chi ha orecchie per intendere intenda; **he's got his cap for England** (*Sport*) è stato scelto per la nazionale inglese

b (*of bottle, radiator etc*) tappo; (*of pen*) cappuccio; (*Brit: contraceptive: also:* **Dutch cap**) diaframma *m*.

[2] VT **a** (*bottle*) tappare; (*tooth*) ricoprire

b (*surpass: story, joke*) superare, essere meglio di; **and to cap it all, he ...** e per completare l'opera, lui...

c : **he's been capped 15 times for England** (*Brit Sport*) ha rappresentato l'Inghilterra 15 volte.

ca·pa·bil·ity [ˌkeɪpə'bɪlətɪ] N (*no pl: competence*) capacità, competenza, abilità; (*potential ability*) possibilità *f inv.*

ca·pable ['keɪpəbl] ADJ **a** (*competent*) capace, abile **b** (*able to*): **capable of (doing) sth** in grado di fare qc, capace di fare qc; **your son's capable of doing better at school** suo figlio potrebbe riuscire meglio a scuola; **she's quite capable of letting someone else take the blame** sarebbe capace di dar la colpa a un altro.

ca·pably ['keɪpəblɪ] ADV con abilità.

ca·pa·cious [kə'peɪʃəs] ADJ capace.

ca·paci·tor [kə'pæsɪtəʳ] N (*Phys*) condensatore *m*.

ca·pac·ity [kə'pæsɪtɪ] [1] N **a** (*Elec, Phys, of container etc*) capacità; (*of lift etc*) capienza; **seating capacity** capienza; **filled to capacity** pieno(-a) zeppo(-a); **to work at full capacity** (*factory etc*) lavorare a pieno ritmo

b (*position*) posizione *f*, funzione *f*; **in my capacity as chairman** nella mia veste di presidente, in qualità di presidente; **in an advisory capacity** a titolo consultativo; **in his official capacity** nell'esercizio delle sue funzioni

c (*ability*) capacità; **this work is beyond my capacity** questo lavoro è al di là delle mie possibilità.

♦ **capacity audience** N sala piena.

cape¹ [keɪp] N (*Geog*) capo.

cape² [keɪp] N (*garment*) cappa, mantello; (*of policeman, cyclist*) mantella.

♦ **Cape of Good Hope** N Capo di Buona Speranza.

ca·per¹ ['keɪpəʳ] N (*Culin*) cappero.

ca·per² ['keɪpəʳ] [1] N (*escapade*) scherzetto, birichinata; (*leap*) saltello.

[2] VI (*child*) saltellare.

cap·er·cail·lie [ˌkæpə'keɪljɪ] N gallo cedrone, urogallo.

♦ **Cape Town** N Città del Capo.

cap·ful ['kæpfʊl] N (*measure of liquid*): **3 capfuls to 4 litres of water** 3 tappi ogni 4 litri d'acqua.

ca·pil·lar·ity [ˌkæpɪ'lærɪtɪ] N (*Phys*) capillarità.

ca·pil·lary [kə'pɪlərɪ] ADJ, N capillare (*m*).

capi·ta ['kæpɪtə] see **per capita.**

capi·tal ['kæpɪtl] [1] N **a** (*also:* **capital letter**) (lettera) maiuscola **b** (*also:* **capital city**) capitale *f* **c** (*Fin*) capitale *m*; **to make capital out of sth** (*fig*) sfruttare qc.

[2] ADJ **a** (*letter*) maiuscolo(-a) **b** (*Law*): **capital offence** delitto passibile di pena capitale **c** (*old: idea*) meraviglioso(-a), splendido(-a).

♦ **capital account** N conto capitale.
♦ **capital allowance** N ammortamento fiscale.
♦ **capital assets** NPL capitale *msg* fisso.
♦ **capital expenditure** N spese *fpl* in capitale.
♦ **capital gains tax** N imposta sulla plusvalenza.
♦ **capital goods** N beni *mpl* d'investimento, beni capitali.
♦ **capital-intensive** ['kæpɪtlɪn'tɛnsɪv] ADJ ad alta intensità di capitale.
capi·tal·ism ['kæpɪtəlɪzəm] N capitalismo.
capi·tal·ist ['kæpɪtəlɪst] ADJ, N capitalista *(m/f).*
capi·tal·ist·ic [,kæpɪtə'lɪstɪk] ADJ *(pej)* capitalistico(-a).
capi·tali·za·tion [kæ,pɪtəlaɪ'zeɪʃən] N *(Fin)* capitalizzazione *f*; *(total sum of capital)* capitale *m* complessivo.
capi·tal·ize ['kæpɪtə,laɪz] VT **a** *(Fin: provide with capital)* capitalizzare **b** *(word)* scrivere (in) maiuscolo
▸ **capitalize on** VI + PREP *(fig)* trarre vantaggio da.
♦ **capital punishment** N pena capitale.
♦ **capital reserves** NPL riserve *fpl* (di capitale).
♦ **capital transfer tax** N *(Brit)* imposta sui trasferimenti di capitali.
Capi·tol ['kæpɪtəl] N: **the Capitol** il Campidoglio.
ca·pitu·late [kə'pɪtjʊleɪt] VI capitolare.
ca·pitu·la·tion [kə,pɪtjʊ'leɪʃən] N capitolazione *f*.
ca·pon ['keɪpən] N cappone *m*.
ca·price [kə'priːs] N capriccio.
ca·pri·cious [kə'prɪʃəs] ADJ capriccioso(-a).
ca·pri·cious·ly [kə'prɪʃəslɪ] ADV capricciosamente.
Cap·ri·corn ['kæprɪ,kɔːn] N Capricorno; **to be Capricorn** *(Astrol)* essere del Capricorno.
♦ **cap rock** N *(Geol)* roccia di copertura.
caps [kæps] NPL, ABBR of **capital letters**; see **capital**.
cap·si·cum ['kæpsɪkəm] N *(Bot)* capsico; *(Culin)* peperone *m*.
cap·size [kæp'saɪz] ① VT ribaltare, capovolgere.
② VI ribaltarsi, capovolgersi; *(boat)* ribaltarsi, scuffiare.
cap·stan ['kæpstən] N *(Naut)* argano.
cap·sule ['kæpsjuːl] N capsula.
Capt. ABBR *(= captain)* Cap.
cap·tain ['kæptɪn] ① N capitano, comandante *m*; **captain of industry** capitano d'industria.
② VT *(team)* essere capitano di, capitanare; *(ship)* comandare.
cap·tion ['kæpʃən] N *(heading)* intestazione *f*; *(to cartoon)* fumetto; *(for illustration, table)* didascalia.
cap·tious ['kæpʃəs] ADJ *(frm)* ipercritico(-a).
cap·ti·vate ['kæptɪ,veɪt] VT affascinare, incantare, avvincere.
cap·tive ['kæptɪv] ① ADJ *(person)* prigioniero(-a); *(animal)* in cattività; **he had a captive audience** i presenti hanno dovuto ascoltarlo per forza.
② N prigioniero(-a); **to hold sb captive** tenere prigioniero qn.
cap·tiv·ity [kæp'tɪvɪtɪ] N prigionia; *(of animal)* cattività; **in captivity** *(animal)* in cattività.
cap·tor ['kæptə] N *(lawful)* chi ha catturato; *(unlawful)* rapitore(-trice); **he managed to escape from his captors** riuscì a sfuggire a quelli che l'avevano catturato.
cap·ture ['kæptʃə] ① N *(of animal, soldier, escapee)* cattura; *(of city etc)* presa; *(thing caught)* preda; *(data capture)* registrazione *f* or rilevazione *f* di dati.
② VT *(animal)* catturare, prendere; *(escapee, soldier)* catturare, far prigioniero; *(city etc)* prendere; *(fig: attention)* attirare, cattivare; *(Art: atmosphere etc)* cogliere, rendere.

car [kɑː] N **a** *(Aut)* macchina, automobile *f*, auto *f inv*; **by car** in macchina **b** *(esp Am: in train)* carrozza; *(: in tram)* vettura.
ca·rafe [kə'ræf] N caraffa.
♦ **carafe wine** N *(in restaurant)* ≈ vino sfuso.
♦ **car allowance** N: **do you get a car allowance?** ti pagano le spese della macchina?
cara·mel ['kærəməl] ① N caramello; *(sweet)* caramella.
② ADJ *(custard, flavouring)* al caramello.
car·at ['kærət] N carato; **18 carat gold** oro a 18 carati.
cara·van ['kærə,væn] ① N **a** *(gipsies')* carrozzone *m*; *(Brit Aut)* roulotte *f inv* **b** *(in desert)* carovana.
② VI viaggiare con la roulotte.
cara·van·ette [,kærəvə'nɛt] N camper *m inv*.
cara·van·se·rai [,kærə'vænsə,raɪ] N caravanserraglio.
♦ **caravan site** N *(Brit)* campeggio per roulotte.
cara·way ['kærə,weɪ] N *(Bot)* cumino (dei prati); **caraway seed** seme *m* di cumino.
car·bine ['kɑːbaɪn] N carabina.
car·bo·hy·drate [,kɑːbəʊ'haɪdreɪt] N *(Chem, starchy food)* carboidrato.
car·bol·ic acid [kɑː'bɒlɪk'æsɪd] N acido fenico, fenolo.
♦ **car bomb** N autobomba *inv*.
car·bon ['kɑːbən] N *(Chem)* carbonio; *(also: carbon paper)* carta carbone.
car·bon·ate ['kɑːbənɪt] N carbonato.
car·bon·at·ed ['kɑːbə,neɪtɪd] ADJ *(drink)* gassato(-a).
♦ **carbon copy** N *(Typing)* copia (in carta carbone); *(fig)* copia *f* carbone *inv*; **he's a carbon copy of his father** è tutto suo padre, è la copia carbone di suo padre.
♦ **carbon cycle** N *(Chem)* ciclo del carbonio.
♦ **carbon dating** N *datazione effettuata per mezzo del carbonio 14.*
♦ **carbon dioxide** N anidride *f* carbonica, biossido di carbonio.
car·bon·ic [kɑː'bɒnɪk] ADJ carbonico(-a).
car·bon·if·er·ous [,kɑːbə'nɪfərəs] ADJ carbonifero(-a).
car·boni·za·tion [,kɑːbənaɪ'zeɪʃən] N carbonizzazione *f*.
car·bon·ize ['kɑːbənaɪz] VT carbonizzare.
♦ **carbon monoxide** N monossido di carbonio.
♦ **carbon paper** N carta carbone.
♦ **carbon ribbon** N nastro carbone.
♦ **carbon steel** N acciaio al carbonio.
♦ **car boot sale** N *(Brit) vendita di oggetti usati organizzata da privati.*
Car·bo·run·dum® [,kɑːbə'rʌndəm] N carborundum *m*.
car·bun·cle ['kɑː,bʌŋkl] N *(Med)* foruncolo.
car·bu·ret·tor, *(Am)* **carburetor** [,kɑːbjʊ'rɛtə'] N carburatore *m*.
car·cass, car·case ['kɑːkəs] N *(of animal)* carcassa.
car·cino·gen [kɑː'sɪnədʒən] N *(Med)* cancerogeno.
car·cino·gen·ic [,kɑːsɪnə'dʒɛnɪk] ADJ *(Med)* cancerogeno(-a).
car·ci·no·ma [,kɑːsɪ'nəʊmə] N *(Med)* carcinoma *m*.
card [kɑːd] N *(greetings card, visiting card)* biglietto; *(membership card)* tessera; *(index card)* scheda; *(playing card)* carta (da gioco); *(thin cardboard)* cartoncino; **to play cards** giocare a carte; **it's on the cards** *(fig)* è probabile; **to lay one's cards on the table** *(also fig)* mettere le carte in tavola; **to play one's cards right** *(fig)* giocare bene le proprie carte.
car·da·mom ['kɑːdəməm], **car·da·mon** ['kɑːdəmən] N cardamomo.
card·board ['kɑːd,bɔːd] N cartone *m*.
♦ **cardboard box** N *(scatola di)* cartone *m*.

♦ **cardboard city** N *luogo dove dormono (in scatole di cartone) emarginati senza tetto.*

♦ **card-carrying** ['kɑːd,kærɪŋ] ADJ (*member*) tesserato (-a).

♦ **card game** N gioco di carte.

car·di·ac ['kɑːdɪæk] ADJ (*Med*) cardiaco(-a).

♦ **cardiac arrest** N (*Med*) arresto cardiaco.

car·di·gan ['kɑːdɪgən] N cardigan *m inv*.

car·di·nal ['kɑːdɪnl] ADJ, N cardinale (*m*).

♦ **card index** N schedario.

car·di·oid ['kɑːdɪˌɔɪd] N (*Math*) cardioide *f*.

car·di·o·logi·cal [ˌkɑːdɪəˈlɒdʒɪkəl] ADJ (*Med*) cardiologico (-a).

car·di·olo·gist [ˌkɑːdɪˈɒlɪdʒɪst] N (*Med*) cardiologo(-a).

car·di·ol·ogy [ˌkɑːdɪˈɒlədʒɪ] N (*Med*) cardiologia.

card·phone ['kɑːdfəʊn] N telefono a scheda (magnetica).

♦ **card player** N giocatore(-trice) (di carte).

Cards ABBR (*Brit*)= Cardiganshire.

card·sharp ['kɑːd,ʃɑːp] N baro.

♦ **card table** N tavolo da gioco.

♦ **card vote** N (*Brit*) voto (palese) per delega.

CARE [kɛəʳ] N ABBR = *Cooperative for American Relief Everywhere.*

care [kɛəʳ] **1** N **a** (*worry*) preoccupazione *f*; **he hasn't a care in the world** non ha preoccupazioni di sorta; **the cares of State** i problemi di Stato

b (*carefulness*) attenzione *f*, cura; (*charge*) cura, custodia; "**with care**" "fragile"; **to take care to do sth** fare attenzione a *or* badare a fare qc; **take care!** (*as warning*) (stai) attento!; (*as good wishes*) stammi bene!; **to take care of** (*details, arrangements*) occuparsi di, curarsi di; **to take care of sb** (*child*) badare a qn; (*sick person*) curare qn; **I'll take care of him!** (*fam*) lo sistemo io!; **she can take care of herself** sa badare a se stessa; **take care not to drop it!** stai attento a non farlo cadere!; **care of** (*on letter*) presso; **I'll leave it/him in your care** te lo affido; **the child has been taken into care** il bambino è stato affidato ad un ente assistenziale.

2 VI (*be concerned*): **to care (about)** interessarsi (di), preoccuparsi (di); **I don't care** non m'importa, non me ne importa; **I couldn't care less** non me ne importa un bel niente; **to care deeply about** tenere molto a; **for all I care** per quello che mi interessa; **who cares?** chi se ne frega? (*fam!*).

3 VT **a** (*be concerned*): **I don't care what you think** non mi interessa quello che pensi; **I couldn't care less what people say** me ne infischio di quel che dice la gente

b (*frm*: *like*) volere, desiderare; **would you care to come this way?** le dispiacerebbe venire da questa parte?; **I wouldn't care to do it** non lo vorrei fare; **I shouldn't care to meet him** preferirei non incontrarlo

▶ **care for** VI + PREP

a (*look after*) curare, aver cura di

b (*be fond of*) voler bene a; **it's the most expensive model, but I don't care much for it** è il modello più costoso, ma non mi piace granché; **I don't care for coffee** non amo particolarmente il caffè; **would you care for a drink?** gradiresti qualcosa da bere?; **she no longer cares for him** non le importa più niente di lui.

ca·reen [kəˈriːn] **1** VI (*ship*) sbandare.

2 VT carenare.

ca·reer [kəˈrɪəʳ] **1** N (*occupation*) professione *f*; (*working life*) carriera.

2 VI (*also:* **career along**) sfrecciare, andare di gran carriera.

3 ADJ (*diplomat, soldier etc*) di carriera.

♦ **career girl** N donna in carriera.

♦ **career guidance** N orientamento professionale.

ca·reer·ist [kəˈrɪərɪst] N carrierista *m/f*.

♦ **careers officer** N consulente *m/f* d'orientamento professionale.

care·free ['kɛə,friː] ADJ spensierato(-a), libero(-a) da preoccupazioni.

care·ful ['kɛəfʊl] ADJ **a** (*taking care, cautious*) attento(-a), cauto(-a); (**be) careful!** (stai) attento!, attenzione!; **to be careful with sth** fare attenzione a qc; **he's very careful with his money** sta molto attento a quanto spende; **be careful what you say to him** stai attento a come gli parli; **he was careful not to offend her** badava a non offenderla

b (*painstaking: work*) accurato(-a); (: *writer, worker etc*) attento(-a), diligente, zelante.

care·ful·ly ['kɛəfəlɪ] ADV (*cautiously*) attentamente, con attenzione, cautamente; (*painstakingly*) con cura, accuratamente.

care·ful·ness ['kɛəfʊlnɪs] N (*see adj*) attenzione *f*; accuratezza.

care·less ['kɛəlɪs] ADJ (*worker, driver, driving*) distratto(-a), disattento(-a), negligente; (*work*) fatto(-a) con poco impegno; (*thoughtless: remark*) senza tatto, privo(-a) di tatto; **careless mistake** errore *m* di distrazione.

care·less·ly ['kɛəlɪslɪ] ADV (*act, drive*) con disattenzione, distrattamente; (*work*) con poco impegno, negligentemente; (*speak*) senza tatto.

care·less·ness ['kɛəlɪsnɪs] N (*see adj*) disattenzione *f*; mancanza d'impegno, negligenza; mancanza di tatto.

♦ **car·er** ['kɛərəʳ] N *familiare che bada a persone anziane o handicappate.*

ca·ress [kəˈrɛs] **1** N carezza.

2 VT carezzare, accarezzare.

care·taker ['kɛə,teɪkəʳ] N custode *m/f*; (*of school*) bidello (-a).

♦ **caretaker government** N (*Brit*) governo *m* ponte *inv or* provvisorio.

care·worn ['kɛə,wɔːn] ADJ sciupato(-a) (*dalle preoccupazioni*).

♦ **car-ferry** ['kɑː,fɛrɪ] N traghetto, nave *f* traghetto *inv*.

car·go ['kɑːgəʊ] N carico.

♦ **cargo boat** N cargo.

♦ **cargo plane** N aereo da carico.

♦ **car hire** N (*Brit*) autonoleggio.

Car·ib·bean [kærɪˈbiːən] **1** ADJ caraibico(-a).

2 N: **the Caribbean (Sea)** il Mar dei Caraibi.

cari·ca·ture ['kærɪkə,tjʊəʳ] **1** N caricatura.

2 VT fare una caricatura di.

cari·ca·tur·ist [ˌkærɪkəˈtjʊərɪst] N caricaturista *m/f*.

cari·es ['kɛərɪːz] N (*Dentistry*) carie *f*.

ca·ril·lon [kəˈrɪljən] N carillon *m inv*.

car·ing ['kɛərɪŋ] ADJ (*parent, person*) affettuoso(-a), premuroso(-a); (*society, organization*) umanitario(-a); **ours is not a caring society** viviamo in una società ben poco altruista.

♦ **car mat** N tappetino.

Car·mel·ite ['kɑːmə,laɪt] N carmelitano(-a).

car·mine ['kɑːmaɪn] ADJ, N carminio *inv*.

car·nage ['kɑːnɪdʒ] N carneficina.

car·nal ['kɑːnl] ADJ carnale.

car·na·tion [kɑːˈneɪʃən] N garofano.

car·nel·ian [kɑːˈniːljən] N cornalina.

car·ni·val ['kɑːnɪvəl] N (*public celebration*) carnevale *m*;

(*Am: funfair*) luna park *m inv*.

car·ni·vore ['kɑ:nɪvɔ:ʳ] N carnivoro.

car·nivo·rous [kɑ:'nɪvərəs] ADJ carnivoro(-a).

car·ob ['kærəb] N carrubo.

car·ol ['kærəl] N: (**Christmas**) **carol** canto di Natale.

ca·rot·id ar·tery [kəˌrɒtɪd'ɑ:tərɪ] N carotide *f*.

ca·rous·al [kə'rauzəl] N bevuta.

ca·rouse [kə'rauz] VI far baldoria.

carou·sel [ˌkærʊ:'sɛl] N (*Am: merry-go-round*) giostra; (: *at airport: conveyor belt*) nastro trasportatore.

carp[1] [kɑ:p] N (*fish*) carpa.

carp[2] [kɑ:p] VI (*complain*): **to carp at** avere *or* trovare da ridire su.

♦ **car park** N parcheggio.

car·pel ['kɑ:pəl] N (*Bot*) carpello.

car·pen·ter ['kɑ:pɪntəʳ] N carpentiere *m*.

car·pen·try ['kɑ:pɪntrɪ] N carpenteria.

car·pet ['kɑ:pɪt] [1] N tappeto; (*fitted carpet*) moquette *f inv*.
[2] VT (*floor, house*) coprire con tappeto; (: *with fitted carpet*) rivestire di moquette, mettere la moquette a.

carpet·bag·ger ['kɑ:pɪtˌbægəʳ] N (*Pol*) profittatore(-trice) (politico(-a)).

♦ **carpet bombing** N bombardamento a tappeto.

car·pet·ing ['kɑ:pɪtɪŋ] N moquette *f*.

♦ **carpet slippers** NPL pantofole *fpl*.

♦ **carpet sweeper** N battitappeto.

♦ **car phone** N telefonino per auto.

carp·ing ['kɑ:pɪŋ] [1] ADJ (*critic*) che trova sempre qualcosa da ridire.
[2] N lamentele *fpl*.

car·port ['kɑ:ˌpɔ:t] N tettoia (per automobile).

♦ **car rental** N (*Am*) autonoleggio.

car·riage ['kærɪdʒ] N **a** (*Brit Rail*) carrozza, vagone *m*, vettura; (*horse-drawn*) carrozza; (*of typewriter*) carrello **b** (*of person: bearing*) portamento **c** (*Comm: of goods*) trasporto; (*cost of carriage*) (spese *fpl* di) trasporto; **carriage free** franco di porto; **carriage paid** porto pagato; **carriage forward** porto assegnato.

♦ **carriage return** N (*on typewriter*) leva (*or* tasto) del ritorno a capo.

carriage·way ['kærɪdʒˌweɪ] N (*Brit: Aut*) carreggiata.

car·ri·er ['kærɪəʳ] N **a** (*of goods: person*) corriere *m*; (: *company*) impresa di trasporti, vettore *m*; **by carrier** per corriere **b** (*Med: of disease*) portatore(-trice) **c** (*aircraft carrier*) portaerei *f inv*.

♦ **carrier bag** N (*Brit*) sacchetto, borsa (di plastica).

♦ **carrier pigeon** N piccione *m* viaggiatore.

car·ri·on ['kærɪən] N carogna.

♦ **carrion crow** N cornacchia nera.

car·rot ['kærət] N carota.

car·roty ['kærətɪ] ADJ: **to have carroty hair** essere un pel di carota.

car·ry ['kærɪ] [1] VT **a** (*gen*) portare; (*have on one's person: money, documents*) portare *or* avere con sé; (*transport: goods*) trasportare; (: *passengers*) portare; (*message, news*) recare, portare; (*subj: pillar*) sostenere; (*involve: responsibilities etc*) comportare; **to carry sth about with one** portarsi dietro qc; **the wind carried the sound to him** il vento trasportò il suono verso di lui; **the offence carries a £50 fine** il reato prevede una multa di 50 sterline; **both papers carried the story** entrambi i giornali riportarono la storia; **he carries his drink well** regge bene l'alcool; **you're carrying things too far!** stai esagerando!

b (*Comm: stock*) tenere

c (*Math: figure*) riportare; (*Fin: interest*) avere; **this loan carries 10% interest** questo prestito ha un interesse del 10%

d (*approve: motion, bill*) approvare, far passare; (*win: election, point*) vincere; **to carry the day** avere successo

e : **he carries himself like a soldier** ha il portamento di un militare; **she carries herself well** ha un bel portamento.

[2] VI (*sound*) trasmettersi, farsi sentire, diffondersi

▶ **carry away** VT + ADV portare via; **to be carried away** (*fig*) farsi trascinare; **to get carried away by sth** (*fig*) farsi *or* lasciarsi prendere da qc

▶ **carry back** VT + ADV (*also fig: remind*) riportare

▶ **carry forward** VT + ADV (*Math, Fin*) riportare

▶ **carry off** VT + ADV (*seize, take away*) portare via; (*kidnap*) sequestrare, rapire; (*win: prize, medal*) vincere; **he carried it off very well** se l'è cavata molto bene

▶ **carry on** [1] VT + ADV (*continue: tradition etc*) portare avanti, continuare; (: *business, trade*) mandare avanti; **to carry on a conversation** conversare, parlare.
[2] VI + ADV **a** : **to carry on with sth/doing sth** continuare qc/a fare qc
b (*fam: make a fuss*) fare storie; **how you do carry on!** quante storie fai!
c (*fam: have an affair*): **to carry on (with)** intendersela (con), filare (con)

▶ **carry out** VT + ADV (*accomplish: plan*) realizzare; (*perform, implement: idea, threat*) mettere in pratica; (: *orders*) eseguire; (: *experiment, search, repairs*) effettuare; (: *investigation*) svolgere

▶ **carry over** VT + ADV riportare

▶ **carry through** VT + ADV (*accomplish: task*) portare a termine, realizzare; (*sustain: person*) sostenere.

carry·cot ['kærɪˌkɒt] N (*Brit*) porte-enfant *m inv*, culla portatile.

♦ **carry-on** [ˌkærɪ'ɒn] N (*fam: fuss*) casino, confusione *f*; (: *fuss*): **what a carry-on!** che casino!

car·sick ['kɑ:ˌsɪk] ADJ: **to be carsick** soffrire il mal d'auto.

car·sick·ness ['kɑ:ˌsɪknɪs] N mal *m* d'auto.

cart [kɑ:t] [1] N carretto; **to put the cart before the horse** (*fig*) mettere il carro davanti ai buoi.
[2] VT (*fam*) trascinare.

carte blanche ['kɑ:t'blɑ:nt∫] N: **to give sb carte blanche** dare carta bianca a qn.

car·tel [kɑ:'tɛl] N (*Comm*) cartello.

cart·er ['kɑ:təʳ] N carrettiere *m*.

Car·tesian [kɑ:'ti:zɪən] (*Philosophy*) [1] ADJ cartesiano(-a).
[2] N seguace *m/f* di Cartesio.

cart·ful ['kɑ:tˌfʊl] N carrettata.

Car·thage ['kɑ:θɪdʒ] N Cartagine *f*.

Car·tha·gin·ian [ˌkɑ:θə'dʒɪnɪən] ADJ, N cartaginese *(m/f)*.

cart·horse ['kɑ:tˌhɔ:s] N cavallo da tiro.

car·ti·lage ['kɑ:tɪlɪdʒ] N cartilagine *f*.

cart·load ['kɑ:tˌləud] N carrettata.

car·tog·ra·pher [kɑ:'tɒgrəfəʳ] N cartografo(-a).

car·tog·ra·phy [kɑ:'tɒgrəfɪ] N cartografia.

car·ton ['kɑ:tən] N (*of milk, yogurt*) cartone *m*; (*of ice cream*) vaschetta; (*of cigarettes*) stecca; (*box*) scatola di cartone.

car·toon [kɑ:'tu:n] N (*in newspaper etc*) vignetta; (*Cine, TV*) cartone *m* animato; (*Art*) cartone.

car·toon·ist [ˌkɑ:'tu:nɪst] N (*in newspaper*) vignettista *m/f*; (*Cine, TV*) cartonista *m/f*, disegnatore(-trice) di cartoni animati.

car·tridge ['kɑːtrɪdʒ] N (for gun, pen) cartuccia; (for camera) caricatore m; (music tape) cassetta; (of record player) testina.
♦ **cartridge paper** N carta da disegno (ruvida).
cart·wheel ['kɑːt̩wiːl] N: **to turn a cartwheel** (Sport etc) fare la ruota.
carve [kɑːv] ① VT (Culin: meat) tagliare; (stone, wood) scolpire, intagliare; (name on tree) incidere; **to carve out a career for o.s** farsi una carriera.
② VI (Culin) tagliare la carne
▶ **carve up** VT + ADV (meat) tagliare; (fig: country, money, profits) suddividere.
car·very ['kɑːvərɪ] N ristorante dove si servono arrosti, tagliati su richiesta del cliente.
carv·ing ['kɑːvɪŋ] N (Art: in wood, stone) scultura.
♦ **carving fork** N forchettone m.
♦ **carving knife, carv·er** ['kɑːvəʳ] N trinciante m.
♦ **car wash** N lavaggio auto; **automatic car wash** autolavaggio automatico.
♦ **car worker** N operaio(-a) dell'industria automobilistica.
cas·cade [kæsˈkeɪd] ① N cascata.
② VI scendere a cascata; **her hair cascaded over her shoulders** i capelli le ricadevano sulle spalle.
case¹ [keɪs] **a** (gen, Med, Gram) caso; **the doctor has a lot of cases to see today** il dottore oggi deve vedere molti pazienti; **in any case** in ogni caso, comunque; **in that case** in quel or questo caso; **(just) in case** non si sa mai, per precauzione, per sicurezza; **I think she knows you're coming, but just in case, you'd better phone her** penso che sappia del tuo arrivo, ma per sicurezza faresti meglio a telefonarle; **in case he changes his mind** caso mai lui cambiasse idea; **in case of emergency** in caso di emergenza; **a case in point** un esempio tipico; **it's a clear case of murder** è un chiaro caso di omicidio; **in most cases** nella maggior parte dei casi, in genere; **it's generally the case that people are selfish** di solito succede che la gente sia egoista; **as this was the case, we decided not to go** stando così le cose, decidemmo di non andare; **if that is the case** quand'è così, se così è; **as the case may be** a seconda del caso
b (Law) caso, processo, causa; (argument) motivo, ragione f; **the case for the defence/prosecution** le ragioni or argomentazioni della difesa/dell'accusa; **to state one's case** esporre le proprie ragioni; (fig) perorare la propria causa; **to have a good case** avere pretese legittime; **there's a strong case for reform** ci sono validi argomenti a favore della riforma.
case² [keɪs] N **a** (suitcase) valigia; (briefcase) valigetta, cartella; (packing case) cassa; (for camera) custodia; (for jewellery) scatolina, astuccio; (for spectacles) custodia, astuccio; (display case) vetrinetta; (of watch) cassa **b** (Typ): **lower/upper case** (carattere m) minuscolo/maiuscolo.
♦ **case file** N (Law, Med) dossier m inv.
♦ **case-hardened** ['keɪsˈhɑːdnd] ADJ (Tech) cementato (-a); (fig) indurito(-a) dall'esperienza.
♦ **case history** N (Med) cartella clinica.
ca·sein ['keɪsɪɪn] N (Chem) caseina.
♦ **case law** N (Law) giurisprudenza basata su sentenze precedenti.
case·ment ['keɪsmənt] N (window) finestra.
♦ **case study** [keɪs 'stʌdɪ] N casistica.
case·work ['keɪsˌwɜːk] N (Sociol) assistenza sociale.
cash [kæʃ] ① N **a** (coins, notes) soldi mpl, denaro; **to pay**

(in) cash pagare in contanti; **ready cash** (fam) (denaro) contante m; **cash in hand** fondo di cassa
b (immediate payment): **to pay cash down** pagare in contanti; **cash with order/on delivery** (Comm) pagamento all'ordinazione/alla consegna
c (fam: money) quattrini mpl; **he's got plenty of cash** ha un sacco di quattrini; **to be short of cash** essere a corto di soldi.
② VT (cheque) riscuotere, incassare
▶ **cash in** VT + ADV (insurance policy) riscuotere, riconvertire
▶ **cash in on** VI + ADV + PREP sfruttare.
♦ **cash account** N conto m cassa inv.
♦ **cash-and-carry** ['kæʃənd'kærɪ] N cash and carry m inv.
♦ **cash-book** ['kæʃˌbʊk] N libro or giornale m di cassa.
♦ **cash box** N cassetta f portavalori inv.
♦ **cash card** N carta per prelievi automatici, carta f bancomat inv.
♦ **cash crop** N prodotto agricolo coltivato su larga scala per la vendita.
♦ **cash desk** N (Brit) cassa.
♦ **cash discount** N sconto contanti.
♦ **cash dispenser** N sportello automatico, bancomat m.
cash·ew [kæˈʃuː] N (also: **cashew nut**) anacardio.
♦ **cash flow** N liquidità, cash-flow m inv.
cash·ier¹ [kæˈʃɪəʳ] N cassiere(-a).
cash·ier² [kæˈʃɪəʳ] VT (esp Mil: officer) destituire.
cash·mere [kæʃˈmɪəʳ] ① N cachemire m inv.
② ADJ di cachemire.
♦ **cash on delivery** N (Comm) pagamento alla consegna.
♦ **cash payment** N pagamento in contanti.
♦ **cash point** N sportello automatico, ≈ Bancomat ® m inv.
♦ **cash price** N prezzo per contanti.
♦ **cash prize** N premio in denaro.
♦ **cash register** N registratore m di cassa.
♦ **cash sale** N vendita per contanti.
cas·ing ['keɪsɪŋ] N (Tech) rivestimento; (of tyre) copertone m.
ca·si·no [kə'siːnəʊ] N casinò m inv.
cask [kɑːsk] N barile m, botte f.
cas·ket ['kɑːskɪt] N (for jewels) scrigno, cofanetto; (Am: coffin) bara.
Cas·pian ['kæspɪən] N: **the Caspian Sea** il mar Caspio.
Cassandra [kə'sændrə] N (Myth, fig) Cassandra.
cas·se·role ['kæsəˌrəʊl] N (utensil) casseruola (a due manici); (food): **chicken/veal casserole** pollo/vitello in casseruola.
cas·sette [kæ'sɛt] N cassetta.
♦ **cassette deck** N piastra di registrazione.
♦ **cassette player** N riproduttore m a cassetta.
♦ **cassette recorder** N registratore m a cassetta.
cas·sia ['kæsɪə] N (Bot) cassia.
Cassius ['kæsɪəs] N Cassio.
cas·sock ['kæsək] N tonaca.
cast [kɑːst] (vb: pt, pp **cast**) ① N **a** (Fishing) lancio
b (mould) stampo, forma; (Med: plaster cast) gesso, ingessatura; **cast of mind** mentalità f inv
c (Theatre) cast m inv
d (Med: squint) strabismo; **he has a cast in his right eye** ha l'occhio destro strabico.
② VT **a** (also fig: throw) gettare; (fishing line) lanciare; (shadow, light) gettare, proiettare; **to cast doubt on sth** far sorgere dubbi su qc; **to cast one's vote (for)** votare (per); **to cast one's eyes over sth** dare un'occhiata a qc

b (*shed*) spogliarsi di; (*horseshoe*) perdere; **the snake cast its skin** il serpente ha cambiato la pelle **c** (*metal*) colare, fondere; (*plaster*) gettare; (*bronze etc statue*) fondere, gettare **d** (*Theatre, Cine: part*) affidare; (: *actor*) scritturare, ingaggiare; **to cast sb as Hamlet** scegliere qn per la parte di Amleto
▶ **cast about for** VI + ADV + PREP cercare di trovare
▶ **cast aside** VT + ADV (*reject*) mettere da parte
▶ **cast away** VT + ADV (*Naut*): **to be cast away** naufragare
▶ **cast down** VT + ADV: **to be cast down** essere giù (di corda), essere depresso(-a)
▶ **cast off** [1] VT + ADV (*Knitting*) diminuire, calare.
[2] VI + ADV (*Naut*) levare gli ormeggi, salpare; (*Knitting*) diminuire, calare
▶ **cast on** (*Knitting*)
[1] VT + ADV avviare.
[2] VI + ADV avviare (le maglie)
▶ **cast out** VT + ADV (*liter*) abbandonare
▶ **cast up** VT + ADV: **to cast sth up (at sb)** rinfacciare qc (a qn).

cas·ta·nets [ˌkæstə'nɛts] NPL castagnette *fpl*, nacchere *fpl*.
cast·away ['kɑːstəweɪ] N naufrago(-a).
caste [kɑːst] [1] N casta.
[2] ADJ di casta.
cast·er, cas·tor ['kɑːstə'] N (*wheel*) rotella.
cas·ter sug·ar ['kɑːstə'ˌʃugə'] N zucchero semolato.
cas·ti·gate ['kæstɪgeɪt] VT (*frm*) castigare, punire.
Cas·tile [kæ'stiːl] N Castiglia.
Cas·til·ian [kæs'tɪlɪən] [1] ADJ castigliano(-a).
[2] N (*person*) castigliano(-a); (*language*) castigliano.
cast·ing ['kɑːstɪŋ] N (*object*) pezzo di fusione.
♦ **cast·ing vote** ['kɑːstɪŋ'vəʊt] N (*Brit*) voto decisivo.
♦ **cast-iron** ['kɑːst'aɪən] ADJ di ghisa; (*fig: will, alibi*) di ferro; **the police had a cast-iron case against the drug smuggler** la polizia aveva prove schiaccianti contro il trafficante di droga.
♦ **cast iron** N ghisa.
cas·tle ['kɑːsl] N castello; (*fortified*) rocca; (*Chess*) torre *f*; **castles in the air** (*fig*) castelli in aria.
cast·off ['kɑːstɒf] N (*garment*) indumento *or* vestito smesso.
♦ **cast-off** ['kɑːstˌɒf] ADJ (*clothing*) smesso(-a).
Castor ['kɑːstə'] N (*Myth, Astron*) Castore *m*.
cas·tor ['kɑːstə'] N = **caster**.
♦ **castor oil** N olio di ricino.
cas·trate [kæs'treɪt] VT castrare.
cas·tra·tion [kæs'treɪʃən] N castrazione *f*.
cas·ual ['kæʒʊəl] [1] ADJ **a** (*by chance: meeting*) fortuito (-a), casuale; (: *walk, stroll*) senza meta precisa; (: *glance*) di sfuggita; (: *remark*) fatto(-a) di sfuggita; **we're just casual acquaintances** ci conosciamo appena; **to have casual sex** avere avventure
b (*unconcerned: attitude, person*) noncurante, indifferente, disinvolto(-a); **he was very casual about it** si è mostrato indifferente
c (*informal: discussion, tone etc*) informale; (: *clothing*) sportivo(-a), casual *inv*; **casual wear** casual *m*
d (*irregular: work*) saltuario(-a); (: *worker*) saltuario(-a), avventizio(-a).
[2]: **casuals** NPL (*shoes*) calzature *fpl* sportive.
♦ **casual labour** N manodopera avventizia.
casu·al·ly ['kæʒʊlɪ] ADV (*see adj a, b, c*) casualmente; senza meta precisa; di sfuggita; con noncuranza, con disinvoltura; in modo informale; in modo sportivo *or*

informale.
casu·al·ty ['kæʒʊltɪ] N (*Mil: dead*) vittima, morto, caduto; (: *wounded*) ferito; (*in accident: dead*) vittima; (: *injured*) ferito; **heavy casualties** grosse perdite *fpl*.
♦ **casualty department** N (*Brit*) pronto soccorso.
CAT [kæt] N ABBR (= *computerized axial tomography*) TAC *f inv* (= *tomografia assiale computerizzata*); **CAT scanner** scanner *m inv* per TAC.
cat [kæt] N gatto(-a); (*species*) felino(-a); **that's put the cat among the pigeons!** ha suscitato un vespaio!; **that's let the cat out of the bag** questo non è più un segreto; **like a cat on hot bricks** sulle spine, sui carboni ardenti, come un'anima in pena; **to fight like cat and dog** essere come cane e gatto; **when the cat's away the mice will play** quando il gatto non c'è i topi ballano.
cata·clysm ['kætəˌklɪzəm] N cataclisma *m*.
cata·clys·mic [ˌkætə'klɪzmɪk] ADJ (*liter*) catastrofico(-a).
cata·combs ['kætəˌkuːmz] NPL catacombe *fpl*.
Cata·lan ['kætəˌlæn] [1] ADJ catalano(-a).
[2] N (*person*) catalano(-a); (*language*) catalano.
cata·logue, (*Am*) **cata·log** ['kætəˌlɒg] [1] N catalogo.
[2] VT catalogare.
Cata·lo·nia [ˌkætə'ləʊnɪə] N Catalogna.
ca·taly·sis [kə'tæləsɪs] N (*Chem*) catalisi *f*.
cata·lyst ['kætəlɪst] N (*all senses*) catalizzatore *m*.
cata·lyt·ic con·vert·er [ˌkætə'lɪtɪkˌkən'vɜːtə'] N (*Aut*) marmitta catalitica, catalizzatore *m*.
cata·ma·ran [ˌkætəmə'ræn] N catamarano.
♦ **cat-and-mouse** ['kætˌənd'maʊs] ADJ: **to play a cat-and-mouse game with sb** giocare al gatto e al topo con qn.
cata·pult ['kætəˌpʌlt] [1] N (*slingshot*) fionda; (*Mil, Aer*) catapulta.
[2] VT catapultare.
cata·ract ['kætəˌrækt] N (*Geog, Med*) cateratta.
ca·tarrh [kə'tɑː'] N catarro.
ca·tarrh·al [kə'tɑːrəl] ADJ catarrale.
ca·tas·tro·phe [kə'tæstrəfɪ] N catastrofe *f*.
cata·stroph·ic [ˌkætə'strɒfɪk] ADJ catastrofico(-a).
cata·stroph·ical·ly [ˌkætə'strɒfɪklɪ] ADV catastroficamente.
cat·call ['kætˌkɔːl] [1] N (*at meeting etc*) fischio.
[2] VI fischiare.
catch [kætʃ] (*vb: pt, pp* **caught**) [1] N **a** (*of ball*) presa; (*fish caught*) pescato; **he spent all day fishing without a single catch** passò tutta la giornata a pescare senza prendere niente; **he's a good catch** (*fig*) è un buon partito
b (*fastener: on suitcase, door*) gancio, fermo
c (*trick, snag*) tranello, inganno, trabocchetto; **where's the catch?** dove sta l'inganno?
d : **with a catch in one's voice** con la voce spezzata *or* rotta.
[2] VT **a** (*ball*) afferrare, prendere; (*fish*) prendere, pescare; (*thief*) prendere, acchiappare, acciuffare; (*bus, train*) prendere; (*entangle*) impigliare; **I caught my fingers in the door** mi son chiuso le dita nella porta; **I caught my coat on that nail** mi si è impigliato il cappotto in quel chiodo; **to catch sb's attention/eye** attirare l'attenzione/lo sguardo di qn; **to catch sight of** scorgere **b** (*take by surprise: person*) cogliere, sorprendere; **to catch sb doing sth** sorprendere qn a fare qc; **you won't catch me doing ...** non mi vedrai mai fare...; **caught in the act** colto(-a) sul fatto; **caught in the rain** sorpreso (-a) dalla pioggia
c (*hear, understand: remark*) afferrare, cogliere; (*portray: atmosphere, likeness*) cogliere

d (*disease*) prendere, contrarre; (*hit*) colpire; **to catch cold** prendere freddo; **to catch fire** prendere fuoco; **the punch caught him on the chin** è stato colpito al mento con un pugno; **to catch one's breath** (*from shock etc*) restare senza fiato; (*after effort*) riprendere fiato; **you'll catch it!** (*fam*) vedrai!.

3 VI **a** (*get entangled*) impigliarsi, restare impigliato(-a) **b** (*fire, wood*) prendere

▶ **catch at** VI + PREP (*object*) afferrare; (*opportunity*) cogliere

▶ **catch on** VI + ADV **a** (*understand*): **to catch on (to sth)** capire (qc)

b (*become popular*) affermarsi, far presa

▶ **catch out** VT + ADV (*Brit fig: with trick question*) cogliere in fallo, prendere in castagna; **to catch sb out in a lie** scoprire qn a dire una bugia

▶ **catch up** 1 VT + ADV (*snatch up*) afferrare; **to catch sb up** (*walking, working etc*) raggiungere qn.

2 VI + ADV: **to catch up with sb** raggiungere qn; **to catch up on one's work** mettersi in pari col lavoro; **to catch up with the news** aggiornarsi.

♦ **catch-22** ['kætʃ,twɛntɪ'tu:] N: **it's a catch-22 situation** non c'è via d'uscita.

♦ **catch-as-catch-can** ['kætʃəz,kætʃ'kæn] N (*Wrestling*) catch *m inv*.

catch·ing ['kætʃɪŋ] ADJ (*Med, fig*) contagioso(-a).

catch·ment ['kætʃmənt] N (*Geog*) bacino.

♦ **catchment area** N (*Brit: of school, hospital*) bacino di utenza; (*Geog*) bacino imbrifero.

♦ **catch phrase** N slogan *m inv*, tormentone *m*.

♦ **catch question** N domanda *f* trabocchetto *inv*.

catch·word ['kætʃ,wɜːd] N slogan *m inv*.

catchy ['kætʃɪ] ADJ (*tune*) orecchiabile.

cat·echism ['kætɪ,kɪzəm] N catechismo.

cat·echize ['kætɪ,kaɪz] VT catechizzare.

cat·egori·cal [,kætɪ'gɒrɪkəl], **cat·egor·ic** [,kætɪ'gɒrɪk] ADJ categorico(-a).

cat·egori·cal·ly [,kætɪ'gɒrɪkəlɪ] ADV categoricamente.

cat·ego·ri·za·tion [,kætɪgərər'zeɪʃən] N catalogazione *f*, classificazione *f*.

cat·ego·rize ['kætɪgə,raɪz] VT catalogare, classificare, dividere per categorie.

cat·ego·ry ['kætɪgərɪ] N categoria.

ca·tena·ry [kə'tiːnərɪ] N (*Phys*) catenaria.

ca·ter ['keɪtə'] 1 VI (*provide food*) provvedere alla ristorazione.

2 VT (*esp Am: wedding, party*) provvedere ai rinfreschi per

▶ **cater for** VI + PREP (*Brit: wedding, party*) provvedere ai rinfreschi per; (: *needs*) provvedere a; (: *readers, consumers*) incontrare i gusti di

▶ **cater to** VI + PREP (*Brit: whims, demands*) soddisfare.

ca·ter·er ['keɪtərə'] N chi si occupa di catering *or* ristorazione.

ca·ter·ing ['keɪtərɪŋ] N catering *m inv*, ristorazione *f* (collettiva).

♦ **catering trade** N settore *m* (della) ristorazione.

cat·er·pil·lar ['kætə,pɪlə'] N (*Zool*) bruco; (*vehicle*) cingolato.

♦ **caterpillar track** N cingolo.

cat·er·waul ['kætə,wɔːl] VI (*person, cat*) miagolare.

cat·er·waul·ing ['kætə,wɔːlɪŋ] N miagolio.

♦ **cat flap** N gattaiola.

ca·thedral [kə'θiːdrəl] N cattedrale *f*, duomo.

♦ **cathedral city** N sede *f* vescovile.

cath·erine wheel ['kæθərɪn,wiːl] N girandola.

cath·eter ['kæθɪtə'] N (*Med*) catetere *m*.

cath·ode ['kæθəud] N (*Elec*) catodo.

♦ **cathode-ray tube** ['kæθəud,reɪ'tjuːb] N (*Elec*) tubo a raggi catodici.

Catho·lic ['kæθəlɪk] (*Rel*) 1 ADJ (*Roman Catholic*) cattolico (-a); **the Catholic Church** la Chiesa Cattolica.

2 N cattolico(-a).

catho·lic ['kæθəlɪk] ADJ (*wide-ranging: taste, interests*) ampio(-a), vasto(-a), eclettico(-a).

Ca·tholi·cism [kə'θɒlɪsɪzəm] N Cattolicesimo.

Catiline ['kætɪ,lam] N Catilina *m*.

cati·on ['kætaɪən] N (*Chem*) catione *m*.

cat·kin ['kætkɪn] N (*Bot*) amento, gattino.

cat·like ['kæt,laɪk] ADJ felino(-a).

cat·mint ['kæt,mɪnt] N gattaia, nepeta.

cat·nap ['kæt,næp] N pisolino; **to take a catnap** fare un pisolino.

Cato ['keɪtəu] N Catone *m*.

♦ **cat-o'-nine-tails** ['kætənaɪn'teɪlz] N gatto a nove code.

♦ **CAT scanner** ['kæt,skænə'] N (*Med*) apparecchiatura per la TAC *f inv*.

♦ **cat's cradle** N (*game*) ripiglino.

♦ **cat's-eye** ['kæts,aɪ] N (*Brit Aut*) catarifrangente *m*.

cat·suit ['kætsuːt] N tutina-pantalone elasticizzata.

cat·sup ['kætsəp] N (*Am*) ketchup *m inv*.

cat·ti·ness ['kætnɪs] N malignità.

cat·tle ['kætl] NPL bestiame *m*.

♦ **cattle breeder** N allevatore *m* di bestiame.

♦ **cattle grid** N *griglia, attraverso strada o sentiero, che impedisce il passaggio del bestiame.*

cattle·man ['kætlmən] N (*pl* **-men**) bovaro.

♦ **cattle shed** N stalla.

♦ **cattle show** N mostra di bestiame.

♦ **cattle truck** N carro *m* bestiame *inv*.

cat·ty ['kætɪ] ADJ (*comp* **-ier**, *superl* **-iest**) (*fam*) maligno(-a), dispettoso(-a).

Catullus [kə'tʌləs] N Catullo.

cat·walk ['kæt,wɔːk] N passerella (*in sfilata di moda*).

Cau·ca·sian [kɔː'keɪzɪən] ADJ, N caucasico(-a).

Caucasus ['kɔːkəsəs] N Caucaso.

cau·cus ['kɔːkəs] N (*Am Pol*) (riunione *f* del) comitato elettorale; (*Brit Pol: group*) comitato di dirigenti.

caught [kɔːt] PT, PP of **catch**.

caul·dron ['kɔːldrən] N calderone *m*.

cau·li·flow·er ['kɒlɪ,flauə'] N cavolfiore *m*.

♦ **cauliflower cheese** N (*Culin*) cavolfiori *mpl* gratinati.

caus·al ['kɔːzəl] ADJ causale.

cau·sal·ity [kɔː'zælɪtɪ] N causalità.

causa·tive ['kɔːzətɪv] ADJ causativo(-a).

cause [kɔːz] 1 N **a** causa; (*reason*) motivo, ragione *f*; **cause and effect** causa ed effetto; **with good cause** a ragione; **to be the cause of** essere (la) causa di; **there's no cause for alarm** non c'è motivo di allarme; **there is no cause for concern** non c'è ragione di preoccuparsi

b (*purpose*) causa; **in the cause of justice** per la (causa della) giustizia; **to make common cause with** far causa comune con; **it's all in a good cause** (*fam*) è tutto a fin di bene.

2 VT causare; **to cause sth to be done** far fare qc; **to cause sb to do sth** far fare qc a qn.

cause·way ['kɔːz,weɪ] N strada rialzata.

caus·tic ['kɔːstɪk] ADJ (*Chem, fig*) caustico(-a).

caus·ti·cal·ly ['kɔːstɪklɪ] ADV causticamente.

♦ **caustic soda** N soda caustica.

cau·ter·ize ['kɔːtə,raɪz] VT cauterizzare.

cau·tion ['kɔːʃən] 1 N (care) attenzione f, prudenza; (warning) avvertimento, ammonizione f; (: from police) diffida.

2 VT: to caution sb (subj: official) ammonire qn; (: policeman) diffidare qn; to caution sb against doing sth diffidare qn dal fare qc.

cau·tion·ary ['kɔːʃənərɪ] ADJ: cautionary tale storiella ammonitrice.

cau·tious ['kɔːʃəs] ADJ cauto(-a), prudente.

cau·tious·ly ['kɔːʃəslɪ] ADV cautamente, prudentemente.

cau·tious·ness ['kɔːʃəsnɪs] N prudenza, cautela.

cav·al·cade [,kævəl'keɪd] N (of horses, cars) sfilata.

cava·lier [,kævə'lɪə'] 1 N (knight) cavaliere m.

2 ADJ (pej: offhand: person) brusco(-a); (: attitude) non curante.

cav·al·ry ['kævəlrɪ] N cavalleria.

cave [keɪv] 1 N grotta, caverna.

2 VI: to go caving fare speleologia

▶ cave in VI + ADV (ceiling, roof) sfondarsi, crollare; (ground) franare, cedere.

ca·veat ['kævɪ,æt] N ammonimento, avvertimento.

♦ cave-in ['keɪv,ɪn] N crollo.

cave·man ['keɪv,mæn] N (pl -men) cavernicolo, uomo delle caverne.

♦ cave painting N pittura rupestre.

cav·ern ['kævən] N caverna.

cav·ern·ous ['kævənəs] ADJ (eyes, cheeks) incavato(-a), infossato(-a); (pit) ampio(-a) e profondo(-a); (darkness) fitto(-a).

cavi·ar, cavi·are ['kævɪ,ɑː'] N caviale m.

cav·il ['kævɪl] VI (pt, pp cavilled, Am caviled): to cavil (at) cavillare (su).

cav·ity ['kævɪtɪ] N cavità.

♦ cavity-wall in·su·la·tion ['kævɪtɪ,wɔːlɪnsjʊ'leɪʃən] N isolamento per pareti a intercapedine.

ca·vort [kə'vɔːt] VI saltellare, far capriole.

caw [kɔː] 1 N gracchio.

2 VI gracchiare.

cay·enne ['keɪɛn] N: cayenne (pepper) pepe m di Caienna.

cay·man ['keɪmən] N caimano.

CB [,si:'bi:] N ABBR a (Brit: = Companion (of the Order) of the Bath) titolo onorifico b (= Citizens' Band (Radio)) C.B. m; CB radio (set) baracchino.

CBC [,si:bi:'si:] N ABBR = Canadian Broadcasting Corporation.

CBE [,si:bi:'i:] N ABBR (Brit: = Commander (of the Order) of the British Empire) titolo onorifico.

CBI [,si:bi:'aɪ] N ABBR (= Confederation of British Industry) ≈ Confindustria (= Confederazione Generale dell'Industria Italiana).

CBS [,si:bi:'ɛs] N ABBR (Am)= Columbia Broadcasting System.

CC [,si:'si:] ABBR (Brit)= county council.

cc [,si:'si:] ABBR a (= cubic centimetres) cc b (on letter) = carbon copy.

CCA [,si:si:'eɪ] N ABBR (Am: = Circuit Court of Appeals) corte f d'appello itinerante.

CCU [,si:si:'ju:] N ABBR (Am: = coronary care unit) unità coronarica.

CD [,si:'di:] 1 N ABBR a (= compact disc) CD m inv; CD player lettore m (di) CD b (Mil: Brit)= Civil Defence (Corps); (: Am) Civil Defense.

2 ABBR (Brit: = Corps Diplomatique) C.D.

CDC [,si:di:'si:] N ABBR (Am)= center for disease control.

CD-I® [,si:di:'aɪ] N ABBR = compact disc interactive.

Cdr. ABBR (= commander) Com.

CD-ROM [,si:di:'rɒm] N ABBR (= compact disc read-only memory) CD-rom m inv.

CDT [,si:di:'ti:] ABBR (Am: = Central Daylight Time) ora legale del centro.

cease [si:s] VT, VI cessare, smettere.

♦ cease-fire [,si:s'faɪə'] N cessate il fuoco m inv.

cease·less ['si:slɪs] ADJ incessante, continuo(-a), senza sosta.

cease·less·ly ['si:slɪslɪ] ADV continuamente, senza sosta.

CED [,si:i:'di:] N ABBR (Am)= Committee for Economic Development.

ce·dar ['si:də'] 1 N cedro.

2 ADJ di cedro.

♦ cedar of Lebanon N cedro del Libano.

cede [si:d] VT (territory) cedere; (argument) cedere su.

ce·dil·la [sɪ'dɪlə] N cediglia.

CEEB [,si:i:i:'bi:] N ABBR (Am: = College Entrance Examination Board) commissione per l'esame di ammissione al college.

cei·lidh ['keɪlɪ] N festa con musiche e danze popolari scozzesi o irlandesi.

ceil·ing ['si:lɪŋ] N (of room etc) soffitto; (of boat) pagliolato; (fig: upper limit) tetto, limite m massimo.

cel·an·dine ['sɛlən,daɪn] N (Bot) celidonia.

cel·ebrate ['sɛlɪ,breɪt] 1 VT (event, festival, birthday) celebrare, festeggiare; (mass) celebrare.

2 VI far festa.

cel·ebrat·ed ['sɛlɪ,breɪtɪd] ADJ celebre.

cel·ebra·tion [,sɛlɪ'breɪʃən] N (act) celebrazione f; (festivity) celebrazione, festa.

cel·ebra·tory [,sɛlɪ'breɪtrɪ] ADJ (frm) per celebrare.

ce·leb·rity [sɪ'lɛbrɪtɪ] N celebrità f inv.

ce·leri·ac [sə'lɛrɪ,æk] N sedano m rapa inv.

cel·ery ['sɛlərɪ] N sedano; head/stick of celery testa/gambo di sedano.

ce·les·tial [sɪ'lɛstɪəl] ADJ (also fig) celestiale, celeste.

celi·ba·cy ['sɛlɪbəsɪ] N celibato.

celi·bate ['sɛlɪbɪt] ADJ, N (man) celibe (m); (woman) nubile (f).

cell [sɛl] N (in prison, monastery) cella; (Bio) cellula; (Elec) elemento (di batteria); dry cell (Chem) cella a secco.

cel·lar ['sɛlə'] N cantina.

♦ cell differentiation N (Bio) differenziazione f cellulare.

♦ cell division N (Bio) divisione f cellulare.

cel·list ['tʃɛlɪst] N violoncellista m/f.

cel·lo ['tʃɛləʊ] N violoncello.

cel·lo·phane® ['sɛlə,feɪn] N cellophane ® m.

cell·phone ['sɛl,fəʊn] N cellulare m.

cel·lu·lar ['sɛljʊlə'] ADJ (Bio) cellulare; cellular blanket coperta a tessitura rada.

cel·lu·loid ['sɛljʊlɔɪd] N celluloide f.

cel·lu·lose ['sɛljʊləʊs] N cellulosa.

♦ cell wall N (Bio) parete f cellulare.

Celsius ['sɛlsɪəs] ADJ Celsius inv; Celsius scale of temperature scala Celsius.

Celt [kɛlt, sɛlt] N celta m/f.

Celt·ic ['kɛltɪk, 'sɛltɪk] 1 ADJ celtico(-a).

2 N (language) celtico.

ce·ment [sə'mɛnt] 1 N cemento; (glue) adesivo.

2 VT cementare.

♦ cement mixer N betoniera.

cem·etery ['sɛmɪtrɪ] N cimitero, camposanto.

ceno·taph ['sɛnə,tɑːf] N cenotafio.

cen·sor ['sɛnsə'] 1 N censore m.

2 VT censurare, sottoporre a censura.
cen·so·ri·ous [ˌsɛnˈsɔːrɪəs] ADJ critico(-a).
cen·sor·ship [ˈsɛnsəˌʃɪp] N censura.
cen·sure [ˈsɛnʃəʳ] 1 N biasimo, censura.
  2 VT biasimare, censurare.
cen·sus [ˈsɛnsəs] N censimento.
cent [sɛnt] N (Am: coin) centesimo (1:100 di un dollaro); **I haven't a cent** non ho una lira or un centesimo; see also **per cent**.
cen·taur [ˈsɛntɔːʳ] N centauro.
cen·te·nar·ian [ˌsɛntɪˈnɛərɪən] N centenario(-a).
cen·te·nary [sɛnˈtiːnərɪ] N centenario.
cen·ten·nial [sɛnˈtɛnɪəl] 1 ADJ centennale, centenario.
  2 N (Am) = **centenary**.
cen·ter [ˈsɛntəʳ] (Am) = **centre**.
cen·ti·grade [ˈsɛntɪˌgreɪd] ADJ centigrado(-a); **30 degrees centigrade** 30 gradi centigradi.
cen·ti·li·tre, (Am) **cen·ti·li·ter** [ˈsɛntɪˌliːtəʳ] N centilitro.
cen·ti·me·tre, (Am) **cen·ti·me·ter** [ˈsɛntɪˌmiːtəʳ] N centimetro.
cen·ti·pede [ˈsɛntɪˌpiːd] N millepiedi m inv, centopiedi m inv.
cen·tral [ˈsɛntrəl] ADJ centrale.
♦ **Central African Republic** N la Repubblica Centrafricana.
♦ **Central America** N l'America centrale.
♦ **Central Europe** N l'Europa centrale.
♦ **central government** N il governo.
♦ **central heating** N riscaldamento autonomo.
cen·tral·ism [ˈsɛntrəlɪzm] N (Pol) centralismo.
cen·tral·ity [ˌsɛnˈtrælɪtɪ] N (frm) centralità f inv.
cen·tral·ize [ˈsɛntrəˌlaɪz] VT centralizzare, accentrare.
cen·tral·ly [ˈsɛntrəlɪ] ADV: **centrally heated** che ha il riscaldamento autonomo.
♦ **central nervous system** N sistema m nervoso centrale.
♦ **central processing unit** N (Comput) unità f inv centrale di elaborazione.
♦ **central reservation** N (Brit Aut) banchina f spartitraffico inv.
cen·tre, (Am) **cen·ter** [ˈsɛntəʳ] 1 N centro; **she is the centre of attention** è al centro dell'attenzione.
  2 VT **a** centrare, mettere al centro
  b (concentrate): **to centre (on)** concentrare (su); **their demands centred round pay** gran parte delle loro richieste riguardavano il salario; **her plans centre on her child** i suoi progetti ruotano attorno al bambino.
  3 VI centrare.
centre·board [ˈsɛntəˌbɔːd] N (Naut) deriva.
centre·fold, (Am) **centerfold** [ˈsɛntəˌfəʊld] N (of magazine) paginone m centrale.
♦ **centre forward** N (Sport) centravanti m inv.
♦ **centre half** N (Sport) centromediano.
♦ **centre mark** N (Tennis) linea centrale di servizio.
♦ **centre of gravity** N baricentro, centro di gravità.
centre·piece, (Am) **centerpiece** [ˈsɛntəˌpiːs] N centrotavola m; (fig) pezzo forte, punta di diamante.
♦ **centre service line** N (Tennis) linea di divisione centrale.
♦ **centre spread** N (Brit) pubblicità f inv a doppia pagina.
♦ **centre-stage** [ˌsɛntəˈsteɪdʒ] N: **to take centre-stage** porsi al centro dell'attenzione.
cen·trif·u·gal [sɛnˈtrɪfjʊgəl] ADJ (Phys) centrifugo(-a).
cen·tri·fuge [ˈsɛntrɪˌfjuːʒ] N centrifuga.
cen·trip·etal [sɛnˈtrɪpɪtl] ADJ (Phys) centripeto(-a).

cen·trist [ˈsɛntrɪst] ADJ, N (Pol) centrista (m/f).
cen·tu·ri·on [sɛnˈtjʊərɪən] N centurione m.
cen·tu·ry [ˈsɛntjʊrɪ] N secolo; (in cricket) cento punti; **in the twentieth century** nel ventesimo secolo.
CEO [ˌsiːiːˈəʊ] N ABBR (Am) = **chief executive officer**.
cep [sɛp] N (mushroom) porcino.
ce·ram·ic [sɪˈræmɪk] 1 ADJ in or di ceramica; (arts) ceramico(-a).
  2: **ceramics** NPL ceramica.
Cerberus [ˈsɜːbərəs] N Cerbero.
ce·real [ˈsɪərɪəl] N (crop) cereale m; (breakfast cereal) cereali mpl.
cer·ebel·lum [ˌsɛrɪˈbɛləm] N (Anat) cervelletto.
cere·bral [ˈsɛrɪbrəl] ADJ (frm) cerebrale.
♦ **cerebral palsy** [ˌsɛrɪbrəlˈpɔːlzɪ] N paralisi f inv cerebrale.
cer·ebrum [ˈsɛrɪbrəm] N (Anat) cervello.
cer·emo·nial [ˌsɛrɪˈməʊnɪəl] 1 ADJ (rite) formale, solenne; (dress) da cerimonia.
  2 N cerimoniale m; (rite) rito.
cer·emo·ni·al·ly [ˌsɛrɪˈməʊnɪəlɪ] ADV secondo il rituale.
cer·emo·ni·ous [ˌsɛrɪˈməʊnɪəs] ADJ formale; (slightly pej) cerimonioso(-a).
cer·emo·ni·ous·ly [ˌsɛrɪˈməʊnɪəslɪ] ADV (see adj) in modo formale; in modo cerimonioso.
cer·emo·ny [ˈsɛrɪmənɪ] N (event) cerimonia; (no pl: formality) cerimonie fpl; **to stand on ceremony** attenersi all'etichetta, fare complimenti.
Ceres [ˈsɪəriːz] N Cerere f.
cert [sɜːt] N (Brit fam): **it's a dead cert** non c'è alcun dubbio.
cer·tain [ˈsɜːtən] ADJ **a** (sure) certo(-a), sicuro(-a); (inevitable: death, success) sicuro(-a); (cure) infallibile, garantito(-a); **he's certain to leave his job** è certo che lui lascerà il lavoro; **it is certain that ...** è certo che...; **I am certain of it** ne sono certo; **he is certain to be there** lui ci sarà certamente; **for certain** per certo, di sicuro; **I can't say for certain that ...** non posso dire con certezza che...; **be certain to tell her** ricordati or non dimenticarti di dirglielo; **to make certain of sth** accertarsi di qc
  b (before n: particular) certo(-a); **a certain gentleman called** ha telefonato un certo signore.
cer·tain·ly [ˈsɜːtənlɪ] ADV certamente, certo; **certainly!** (ma) certo!; **certainly not!** no di certo!; **I shall certainly be there** ci sarò sicuramente, ci sarò certamente.
cer·tain·ty [ˈsɜːtəntɪ] N certezza; **faced with the certainty of disaster** di fronte al sicuro disastro; **we know for a certainty that ...** sappiamo per certo che... .
cer·ti·fi·able [ˌsɜːtɪˈfaɪəbl] ADJ (fact, claim) dimostrabile; (fam: mad) pazzo(-a) da legare.
cer·tifi·cate [səˈtɪfɪkɪt] N (gen) certificato; (academic) diploma m.
cer·tifi·cat·ed [səˈtɪfɪˌkeɪtɪd] ADJ (gen) diplomato(-a); (doctor, teacher) abilitato(-a).
cer·ti·fi·ca·tion [ˌsɜːtɪfɪˈkeɪʃən] N (act) certificazione f; (document) certificato.
cer·ti·fied [ˈsɜːtɪfaɪd] ADJ (cheque) autenticato(-a); (translation) giurato(-a), autenticato(-a); (person: declared insane) malato(-a) di mente.
♦ **certified letter** N (Am) lettera raccomandata.
♦ **certified public accountant** N (Am) ≈ commercialista m/f.
cer·ti·fy [ˈsɜːtɪfaɪ] VT **a** certificare, attestare; **the will has been certified** il testamento è stato autenticato **b** (Med): **to certify sb** dichiarare malato(-a) di mente qn.

cer·ti·tude ['sɜːtɪˌtjuːd] N (*frm*) certezza, sicurezza.

cer·vi·cal ['sɜːvɪkəl] ADJ (*Anat*): **cervical cancer** cancro al collo dell'utero *or* alla cervice uterina.

♦ **cervical smear** N pap-test *m inv*, striscio (*fam*).

cer·vix ['sɜːvɪks] N (*pl* **cervices** [sə'vaɪsiːz]) (*Anat*) collo dell'utero, cervice *f* uterina.

Ce·sar·ean [siːˈzɛərɪən] N, ADJ (*Am*) = **Caesarean.**

ces·sa·tion [sɛˈseɪʃən] N (*frm*) cessazione *f*, arresto.

cess·pit ['sɛsˌpɪt], **cess·pool** ['sɛsˌpuːl] N pozzo nero.

CET [ˌsiːiːˈtiː] ABBR (= *Central European Time*) *fuso orario.*

Ceylon [sɪˈlɒn] N Ceylon *f.*

cf. ABBR (= *compare*) cf, cfr.

c/f ABBR (*Comm*)= *carried forward.*

CFC [ˌsiːɛfˈsiː] N ABBR = *chlorofluorocarbon* **CFCs** NPL CFC *mpl.*

CG [siːˈdʒiː] N ABBR (*Am*) = **coastguard.**

cg ABBR (= *centigram*) cg.

CH N ABBR (*Brit*: : = *Companion of Honour*) *titolo onorifico.*

ch. ABBR (= *chapter*) cap.

c.h. ABBR (*Brit*) = **central heating.**

Chad [tʃæd] N Ciad *m.*

chafe [tʃeɪf] ① VT (*irritate: skin*) sfregare contro, irritare; (*rub to warm*) frizionare.
② VI **a** (*become sore*) irritarsi **b** (*fig*): **to chafe (at)** irritarsi (per); **to chafe against** scontrarsi con.

chaff [tʃɑːf] N (*husks*) pula, loppa; (*animal food*) foraggio.

chaf·finch ['tʃæfɪntʃ] N fringuello.

cha·grin ['ʃægrɪn] N (*frm*) disappunto, dispiacere *m.*

chain [tʃeɪn] N (*gen*) catena; **gold chain** catenina d'oro.
② VT (*also:* **chain up**) incatenare
► **chain up** VT + ADV (*prisoner*) incatenare; (*dog*) mettere alla catena.

♦ **chain mail** N cotta di maglia.

♦ **chain reaction** N reazione *f* a catena.

♦ **chain saw** N motosega.

♦ **chain-smoke** ['tʃeɪnˌsməʊk] VI fumare una sigaretta dopo l'altra.

♦ **chain smoker** N fumatore(-trice) accanito(-a).

♦ **chain store** N *grande magazzino o supermercato che fa parte di una catena.*

chair [tʃɛəʳ] ① N sedia, seggiola; (*armchair*) poltrona; (*seat*) posto (a sedere); (*Univ*) cattedra; (*Am: electric chair*): **the chair** la sedia elettrica; **dentist's chair** poltrona del dentista; **to take the chair** (*at meeting*) assumere la presidenza.
② VT (*meeting*) presiedere.

♦ **chair lift** N seggiovia.

chair·man ['tʃɛəmən] N (*pl* -**men**) presidente *m.*

chair·man·ship ['tʃɛəmənˌʃɪp] N presidenza.

chair·person ['tʃɛəˌpɜːsn] N presidente(-essa).

chair·woman ['tʃɛəˌwʊmən] N (*pl* -**women**) presidentessa.

chal·cedo·ny [kælˈsɛdənɪ] N calcedonio.

cha·let ['ʃæleɪ] N (*in mountains*) chalet *m inv*; (*in holiday camp etc*) bungalow *m inv.*

chal·ice ['tʃælɪs] N calice *m.*

chalk [tʃɔːk] ① N gesso; **a (piece of) chalk** un gesso; (*child's*) un gessetto; **not by a long chalk** (*fam*) proprio per niente *or* nulla, niente affatto; **they are as different as chalk and cheese** sono diversi come il giorno e la notte.
② VT (*message*) scrivere col gesso; (*luggage*) segnare col gesso
► **chalk up** VT + ADV scrivere col gesso; (*fig: success*) ottenere; (: *victory*) riportare.

chalk·pit ['tʃɔːkˌpɪt] N cava di gesso.

chalky ['tʃɔːkɪ] ADJ (*water, soil*) calcareo(-a); (*complexion*)

biancastro(-a).

chal·lenge ['tʃælɪndʒ] ① N sfida; (*of sentry*) intimazione *f*; **to issue a challenge** lanciare una sfida; **to take up the challenge** accettare *or* raccogliere la sfida; **this task is a great challenge** questo compito è una grande sfida.
② VT (*to contest*) sfidare; (*subj: sentry*) intimare l'alt *etc* a; (*dispute: fact, point, statement, right*) mettere in dubbio, contestare; **to challenge sb to a fight/game** sfidare qn a battersi/ad una partita; **to challenge sb to do sth** sfidare qn a fare qc; **to challenge sb to a duel** sfidare qn a duello.

chal·leng·er ['tʃælɪndʒəʳ] N (*Sport*) sfidante *m/f.*

chal·leng·ing ['tʃælɪndʒɪŋ] ADJ (*situation, work*) impegnativo(-a); (*remark, look*) provocatorio(-a); (*book*) stimolante.

cham·ber ['tʃeɪmbəʳ] N (*of parliament*) camera; (*old: room*) stanza; **chambers** NPL (*of judge, lawyer*) studio.

cham·ber·lain ['tʃeɪmbəlɪn] N ciambellano.

chamber·maid ['tʃeɪmbəˌmeɪd] N cameriera al piano.

♦ **chamber music** N musica da camera.

♦ **chamber of commerce** N camera di commercio.

chamber·pot ['tʃeɪmbəˌpɒt] N vaso da notte.

cha·me·le·on [kəˈmiːlɪən] N camaleonte *m.*

cham·ois ['ʃæmwɑː] N (*Zool*) camoscio.

♦ **chamois leather** N (pelle *f* di) camoscio.

champ¹ [tʃæmp] ① VI masticare rumorosamente; **to champ at the bit** mordere il freno.
② VT (*gum*) masticare rumorosamente.

champ² [tʃæmp] N (*fam*: = *champion*) campione(-essa).

cham·pagne [ʃæmˈpeɪn] N champagne *m inv.*

cham·pers ['ʃæmpəz] NSG (*Brit fam*) sciampagnino.

cham·pi·on ['tʃæmpjən] ① N (*Sport*) campione(-essa); (*of cause*) difensore *m*; **boxing champion** campione di boxe.
② VT difendere, lottare per.

cham·pi·on·ship ['tʃæmpjənˌʃɪp] N (*contest*) campionato.

chance [tʃɑːns] ① N **a** (*possibility*) probabilità *f inv*; **the chances are that ...** probabilmente..., è probabile che... + *sub*; **he doesn't stand** *or* **he hasn't a chance of winning** non ha nessuna possibilità di vittoria; **there is little chance of his coming** è molto improbabile che venga **b** (*opportunity*) possibilità *f inv*, occasione *f*; **it's the chance of a lifetime** è un'occasione unica; **he never had a chance in life** non ha mai avuto nessuna possibilità nella vita; **to give sb a chance** dare a qn la possibilità (di fare qc); **to have an eye to the main chance** (*pej*) essere sempre pronto(-a) ad approfittare, non perdere occasioni **c** (*risk*) rischio; **an element of chance** una parte di fortuna; **to take a chance** rischiare; **I'm taking no chances** non voglio lasciar niente al caso **d** (*luck*) caso; **game of chance** gioco d'azzardo; **by chance** per caso; **do you by any chance know each other?** per caso vi conoscete?; **to leave nothing to chance** non lasciare nulla al caso.
② VT (*happen*): **to chance to do sth** (*frm*) fare per caso qc; **I'll chance it** (*risk*) ci provo, rischio.
③ ADJ (*meeting, remark, error*) casuale, fortuito(-a)
► **chance on, chance upon** VI + PREP (*person*) incontrare per caso, imbattersi in; (*thing*) trovare per caso.

chan·cel ['tʃɑːnsəl] N coro.

chan·cel·lor ['tʃɑːnsələʳ] N cancelliere *m*; (*of university*) rettore *m* (onorario).

♦ **Chancellor of the Exchequer** N (*Brit*) Cancelliere dello Scacchiere, ≈ Ministro del Tesoro.

chancy, chancey ['tʃɑːnsɪ] ADJ (comp -ier, superl -iest) rischioso(-a).

chan·de·lier [ˌʃændə'lɪəʳ] N lampadario.

change [tʃeɪndʒ] **1** N **a** cambiamento; **a change for the better/worse** un miglioramento/peggioramento, un mutamento per il meglio/peggio; **just for a change** tanto per cambiare; **he likes a change** gli piace cambiare; **change of address** cambiamento di indirizzo; **a change of clothes** un cambio (di vestiti); **to have a change of heart** cambiare idea; **to have a change of scene** cambiare aria; **there's been a change in the weather** il tempo è cambiato

b (small coins) moneta, spiccioli mpl; (money returned) resto; **small** or **loose change** spiccioli mpl; **can you give me change for £1?** mi può cambiare una sterlina?; **you don't get much change out of £5** non avanza molto da 5 sterline; **keep the change** tenga il resto.

2 VT **a** (by substitution) cambiare; **to change hands** cambiare padrone, passare di mano; **a sum of money changed hands** c'è stato un movimento di denaro; **to change gear** (Aut) cambiare (marcia); **to change places** (two people) scambiarsi di posto; **I changed places with him** ho scambiato il mio posto con il suo; **to change trains/buses (at)** cambiare treno/autobus (a); **to change the rein** (Horse-riding) cambiare di mano; **to change sides** (Pol etc) cambiare bandiera; **let's change the subject** cambiamo argomento

b (exchange: in shop) cambiare; **to change ends** (Tennis, Ftbl) effettuare il cambio di campo

c (alter: person, idea) cambiare; (transform: person) trasformare; (: thing) tramutare; **to change one's mind** cambiare idea

d (money) cambiare.

3 VI **a** (alter) cambiare, mutare; **you've changed!** come sei cambiato!

b (change clothes) cambiarsi

c (Rail) cambiare; **all change!** si cambia!

▶ **change down** VI + ADV (Aut) scalare (la marcia)

▶ **change into 1** VI + PREP **a** (become) trasformarsi in

b (different clothes): **she changed into an old skirt** si è cambiata e ha messo una vecchia gonna.

2 VT + PREP: **to change sb/sth into** trasformare qn/qc in

▶ **change over** VI + ADV (make complete change): **to change over from sth to sth** passare da qc a qc; (players etc) scambiarsi (di posto o di campo)

▶ **change up** VI + ADV (Aut) cambiare, mettere una marcia superiore.

change·abil·ity [ˌtʃeɪndʒə'bɪlɪtɪ] N (see adj) mutevolezza; variabilità.

change·able ['tʃeɪndʒəbl] ADJ (person) mutevole; (weather) mutevole, variabile.

change·less ['tʃeɪndʒlɪs] ADJ (frm) immutabile.

♦ **change machine** N distributore m automatico di monete.

♦ **change of life** N menopausa.

change·over ['tʃeɪndʒˌəʊvəʳ] N cambiamento, passaggio.

chang·ing ['tʃeɪndʒɪŋ] ADJ (face, expression) mutevole; (colours) cangiante.

♦ **Changing of the Guard** N: **the Changing of the Guard** il cambio della guardia.

♦ **changing-room** ['tʃeɪndʒɪŋˌrʊm] N (Brit: in shop) camerino; (: Sport) spogliatoio.

Chan·nel ['tʃænl] N: **the (English) Channel** il Canale della Manica, la Manica.

chan·nel ['tʃænl] **1** N (Geog, TV also fig) canale m; (of river,

sea) alveo; **to go through the usual channels** seguire la normale procedura; **green/red channel** (Customs) uscita "niente da dichiarare"/"merci da dichiarare".

2 VT (hollow out: course) scavare; (direct: river) far scorrere, convogliare; (fig: interest, energies): **to channel into** concentrare su, indirizzare verso, canalizzare.

♦ **Channel Islands** NPL: **the Channel Islands** le Isole Normanne or del Canale (della Manica).

♦ **Channel Tunnel** N: **the Channel Tunnel** il tunnel sotto la Manica.

chant [tʃɑːnt] **1** N (of crowd) slogan m inv; (Rel, Mus) canto, salmodia.

2 VT (Rel, Mus) cantare; (subj: crowd): **the demonstrators chanted their disapproval** i dimostranti lanciavano slogan di protesta.

3 VI (see vt) cantare, salmodiare; lanciare slogan.

cha·os ['keɪɒs] N caos m; **to be in chaos** essere nel caos.

♦ **chaos theory** N teoria del caos.

cha·ot·ic [keɪ'ɒtɪk] ADJ caotico(-a), confuso(-a).

cha·oti·cal·ly [keɪ'ɒtɪklɪ] ADV caoticamente.

chap¹ [tʃæp] N (Brit fam: man) tipo, tizio; **he's the sort of chap everyone likes** è il tipo di persona che piace a tutti; **old chap** vecchio mio; **poor little chap** povero piccolo.

chap² [tʃæp] **1** N (on lip) screpolatura.

2 VT (skin) screpolare.

chap·el ['tʃæpəl] N (of church, school) cappella; (small church) cappella, chiesetta.

chap·er·one, chap·er·on ['ʃæpəˌrəʊn] **1** N accompagnatore(-trice).

2 VT fare da accompagnatore(-trice), accompagnare.

chap·lain ['tʃæplɪn] N cappellano.

chapped [tʃæpt] ADJ (skin) screpolato(-a).

chap·ter ['tʃæptəʳ] N capitolo; **to quote chapter and verse** (fig) dare dei riferimenti precisi; **a chapter of accidents** una serie di imprevisti.

char¹ [tʃɑːʳ] VT (burn black) carbonizzare.

char² [tʃɑːʳ] (Brit) **1** N (charwoman) donna a ore.

2 VI lavorare come donna a ore.

chara·banc ['ʃærəˌbæŋ] N pullman per il trasporto di turisti.

char·ac·ter ['kærɪktəʳ] N (gen, Comput) carattere m; (in novel, play, film) personaggio; (eccentric) originale m; **a man of character** un uomo di polso; **a person of good character** una persona a modo; **it's quite in/out of character for him to be rude** è/non è nella sua natura essere maleducato; **he's quite a character** è un tipo originale; **Gothic characters** caratteri gotici.

♦ **character actor** N caratterista m.

♦ **character actress** N caratterista f.

♦ **character code** N (Comput) codice m di carattere.

char·ac·ter·is·tic [ˌkærɪktə'rɪstɪk] **1** ADJ caratteristico (-a), tipico(-a); **characteristic of** tipico(-a) di; **with (his) characteristic enthusiasm** con l'entusiasmo che lo caratterizza.

2 N caratteristica.

char·ac·ter·is·ti·cal·ly [ˌkærɪktə'rɪstɪkəlɪ] ADV tipicamente.

char·ac·teri·za·tion [ˌkærɪktəraɪ'zeɪʃən] N (in novel) caratterizzazione f.

char·ac·ter·ize ['kærɪktəˌraɪz] VT **a** (be characteristic of) caratterizzare **b** (describe): **to characterize (as)** descrivere (come).

char·ac·ter·less ['kærəktəlɪs] ADJ ordinario(-a).

cha·rade [ʃə'rɑːd] N **a** (pretence) farsa **b**: **charades** NPL (game) sciarada fsg.

char·coal ['tʃɑ:kəʊl] N carbone *m* di legna; (*for sketching*) carboncino.

charge [tʃɑ:dʒ] ① N **a** (*cost*) tariffa, prezzo; **is there a charge?** c'è da pagare?; **free of charge** gratis, gratuito (-a); (*adv*) gratuitamente; **extra charge** supplemento; **labour charges** costi *mpl* del lavoro
b (*Law*) accusa, imputazione *f*; **to bring a charge against sb** accusare qn, imputare qn; **he was arrested on a charge of murder** fu arrestato sotto accusa di omicidio
c (*control, responsibility*): **the person in charge** il/la responsabile; **who is in charge here?** chi è il responsabile qui?; **to be in charge of** essere responsabile di *or* per; **to take charge (of)** (*firm, situation*) assumere il controllo (di); (*project*) incaricarsi (di); **can you take charge here?** se ne occupa lei?; **to have charge of sb** aver cura di qn; **these children are my charges** questi bambini sono affidati a me
d (*Mil: attack*) carica
e (*Phys, Elec*) carica.
② VT **a** (*price*) chiedere, far pagare; (*customer*) far pagare a; **what did they charge you for it?** quanto te l'hanno fatto pagare?; **to charge an expense to sb** addebitare una spesa a qn; **charge it to my account** lo metta *or* addebiti sul mio conto
b (*Law*): **to charge sb (with)** accusare qn (di)
c (*gun, battery*) caricare
d (*Mil: attack*) caricare.
③ VI (*Mil etc*) caricare; (*fam: rush*) precipitarsi, lanciarsi; **to charge in/out** precipitarsi dentro/fuori; **to charge up/down the stairs** lanciarsi su/giù per le scale.
♦ **charge account** N (*Am*) conto.
♦ **charge card** N carta di credito commerciale.

charged [tʃɑ:ʒd] ADJ (*battery*) carico(-a); (*fig*): **charged with emotion** carico(-a) di; (*fig*): **there was a highly charged atmosphere** c'era molta elettricità nell'aria.

char·gé d'af·faires ['ʃɑ:ʒeɪdæ'fɛəʳ] N incaricato d'affari.
♦ **charge hand** N (*Brit*) caposquadra *m/f*.

charg·er ['tʃɑ:dʒəʳ] N (*Elec: also:* **battery charger**) carica-batterie *m inv*; (*old: warhorse*) destriero.

charg·ing ['tʃɑ:dʒɪŋ] N (*Phys*) elettrizzazione *f*.

chari·ot ['tʃærɪət] N cocchio, carro.

chari·ot·eer [ˌtʃærɪə'tɪəʳ] N auriga *m*.

cha·ris·ma [kə'rɪzmə] N carisma *m*.

char·is·mat·ic [ˌkærɪz'mætɪk] ADJ carismatico(-a).

chari·table ['tʃærɪtəbl] ADJ (*organization, society*) filantro-pico(-a), di beneficenza; (*person*) caritatevole; (*deed*) buono(-a), di carità, caritatevole; (*remark, view*) indul-gente, caritatevole.

chari·tably ['tʃærɪtəblɪ] ADV in modo caritatevole.

char·ity ['tʃærɪtɪ] N **a** (*virtue*) carità; **out of charity** per carità *or* misericordia; **to live on charity** vivere di elemosine; **charity begins at home** (*Proverb*) il primo prossimo è la tua famiglia **b** (*organization*) opera pia, associazione *f* benefica; **she gave all her money to charity** lasciò tutto il suo denaro in beneficenza.

char·lady ['tʃɑ:ˌleɪdɪ] N (*Brit*) = **charwoman**.

char·la·tan ['ʃɑ:lətən] N ciarlatano.

Charlemagne ['ʃɑ:ləˌmeɪn] N Carlo Magno.

char·lotte ['ʃɑ:lət] N (*Culin*) charlotte *f inv*.

charm [tʃɑ:m] ① N (*of person*) fascino; (*of object*) incanto; (*also fig: magic spell*) incanto, incantesimo; (*on bracelet*) ciondolo; **it worked like a charm** (*fig*) ha funzionato perfettamente.
② VT affascinare, incantare; **to lead a charmed life**

essere nato(-a) con la camicia.
♦ **charm bracelet** N braccialetto con ciondoli.

charm·er ['tʃɑ:məʳ] N persona affascinante.

charm·ing ['tʃɑ:mɪŋ] ADJ delizioso(-a), incantevole.

charm·ly ['tʃɑ:mɪŋlɪ] ADV deliziosamente.

Charon ['kɛərən] N Caronte *m*.

chart [tʃɑ:t] ① N (*table*) tabella, tavola; (*graph, Med*) grafico; (*Met: weather chart*) carta del tempo; (*Naut: map*) carta (nautica); **to be in the charts** (*record, pop group*) essere nella Hit Parade, essere in classifica.
② VT (*plot: course*) tracciare; (*: sales, progress*) tracciare il grafico di; (*Naut*) fare la carta nautica di.

char·ter ['tʃɑ:təʳ] ① N **a** (*document*) carta; (*of city, organization*) statuto **b** (*Naut, Aer etc: hire*) noleggio; **on charter** a nolo.
② VT (*plane etc*) noleggiare.
♦ **char·tered ac·count·ant** ['tʃɑ:tədə'kaʊntənt] N (*Brit*) ≈ commercialista *m/f*.
♦ **charter flight** N volo *m* charter *inv*.
♦ **charter party** N (*contract*) contratto di noleggio.
♦ **charter plane** N charter *m inv*.

char·woman ['tʃɑ:ˌwʊmən] N (*pl* **-women**) donna delle pulizie, donna a ore.

chary ['tʃɛərɪ] ADJ cauto(-a), attento(-a); **to be chary of doing sth** andare con i piedi di piombo prima di fare qc.

Cha·ryb·dis [kə'rɪbdɪs] N Cariddi *f*.

chase [tʃeɪs] ① N inseguimento, caccia; **the chase** (*Hunting*) la caccia; **to give chase** dare la caccia, mettersi all'inseguimento.
② VT inseguire.
③ VI: **to chase after sb** correre dietro a qn
▶ **chase away**, **chase off** VT + ADV cacciare via
▶ **chase up** VT + ADV, (*Am*) **chase down** VT + ADV (*information*) scoprire, raccogliere; (*person*) scovare.

chas·er ['tʃeɪsəʳ] N **a** (*drink*) *bibita alcolica bevuta dopo un'altra* **b** (*person*) inseguitore(-trice), cacciatore (-trice).

chasm ['kæzəm] N voragine *f*, abisso.

chas·sis ['ʃæsɪ] N (*Aut*) telaio.

chaste [tʃeɪst] ADJ casto(-a).

chaste·ly ['tʃeɪstlɪ] ADV castamente.

chas·tened ['tʃeɪsnd] ADJ abbattuto(-a), provato(-a).

chas·ten·ing ['tʃeɪsnɪŋ] ADJ che fa riflettere.

chas·tise [tʃæs'taɪz] VT (*frm: punish*) punire, castigare.

chas·tise·ment ['tʃæstɪzmənt] N (*frm*) punizione *f*, castigo.

chas·tity ['tʃæstɪtɪ] N castità.

chasu·ble ['tʃæzjʊbəl] N casula.

chat [tʃæt] ① N chiacchierata; **to have a chat** fare quattro chiacchiere.
② VI: **to chat (with** *or* **to)** chiacchierare (con)
▶ **chat up** VT + ADV (*Brit fam: girl*) agganciare, abbordare.

chat·line ['tʃætˌlaɪn] N chatline *f inv*.
♦ **chat show** N (*Brit*) talk show *m inv*.

chat·tel ['tʃætl] N see **goods**.

chat·ter ['tʃætəʳ] ① N (*talk*) parlottio, chiacchiere *fpl*, ciarle *fpl*.
② VI (*person*) chiacchierare, ciarlare; (*birds*) cinguet-tare; **her teeth were chattering** batteva i denti.

chatter·box ['tʃætəˌbɒks] N (*fam*) chiacchierone(-a).

chat·ter·ing classes ['tʃætərɪŋ'klɑ:sɪs] NPL: **the chat-tering classes** (*fam pej*) gli intellettualoidi.

chat·ty ['tʃætɪ] ADJ (*person*) ciarliero(-a); (*style*) familiare.

chauf·feur ['ʃəʊfəʳ] N autista *m/f*.

chau·vin·ism ['ʃəʊvɪˌnɪzəm] N (*male chauvinism*) maschili-

smo; (*nationalism*) sciovinismo.

chau·vin·ist ['ʃəʊvɪnɪst] N (*male chauvinist*) maschilista *m*; (*nationalist*) sciovinista *m/f*; **(male) chauvinist pig** (*fam pej*) sporco maschilista.

chau·vin·is·tic [ˌʃəʊvɪ'nɪstɪk] ADJ (*jingoistic*) sciovinistico (-a); (*sexist*) maschilista.

ChE ABBR = *chemical engineer*.

cheap [tʃiːp] ①ADJ (*comp* -**er**, *superl* -**est**) (*low cost: goods*) a buon mercato, a basso *or* buon prezzo, economico (-a); (*reduced: ticket*) a prezzo ridotto; (: *fare*) ridotto(-a); (*poor quality*) scadente, di cattiva qualità; (*vulgar, mean: joke, behaviour, trick*) volgare, grossolano(-a), dozzinale; **it was cheap at the price** sono stati soldi ben spesi; **this stuff is cheap and nasty** questa roba è veramente scadente; **cheaper** meno caro(-a), più economico(-a); **cheap money** (*Fin*) denaro a basso tasso di interesse; **to feel cheap (about)** provare vergogna *or* vergognarsi (di *or* per).

②ADV a buon prezzo *or* mercato.

③N: **on the cheap** (*fam*) a risparmio.

cheap·en ['tʃiːpən] VT: **to cheapen o.s.** svendersi, screditarsi; (*woman: sexually*) degradarsi.

cheap·ly ['tʃiːplɪ] ADV a buon prezzo, a buon mercato.

cheap·ness ['tʃiːpnɪs] N (*of goods etc*) basso prezzo; (*fig: of joke, behaviour*) bassezza.

cheap·skate ['tʃiːpˌskeɪt] N (*fam*) taccagno(-a).

cheat [tʃiːt] ①N (*deception*) imbroglio, truffa; (*person*) imbroglione(-a), truffatore(-trice).

②VT imbrogliare, truffare; (*rob*) soffiare, fregare; **to cheat sb out of sth** fregare qc a qn; **I was cheated out of the job** mi è stato soffiato il lavoro.

③VI (*at games*) barare, imbrogliare; (*in exam*) copiare; **he's been cheating on his wife** ha tradito sua moglie.

cheat·ing ['tʃiːtɪŋ] N truffe *fpl*, imbrogli *mpl*.

check [tʃɛk] ①N **a** (*inspection*) controllo, verifica; **to keep a check on sb/sth** controllare qn/qc, fare attenzione a qn/qc

b (*control, restraint*) limitazione *f*; **to hold** *or* **keep sb/sth in check** tenere qn/qc sotto controllo; **to act as a check on sth** fare da freno a qc

c (*Chess*): **in check** in scacco; **check!** scacco (al re)!

d (*Am: bill*) conto; (: *receipt*) scontrino

e (*Am*) = **cheque**

f : **checks** (*pattern*) quadretti *mpl*, quadri *mpl*, scacchi *mpl*.

②VT **a** (*examine: facts, figures*) verificare; (: *passport, ticket, tyres, oil*) controllare

b (*stop, halt*) bloccare, fermare, arrestare; (*restrain*) contenere, frenare, controllare; **to check o.s.** frenarsi, controllarsi, contenersi

c (*Am: tick*) spuntare.

③VI controllare; **to check with sb** chiedere a qn; (*official etc*) informarsi presso qn.

④ADJ (*also*: **checked**: *pattern, cloth*) a scacchi, a quadretti, a quadri

▶ **check in** ①VI + ADV (*at airport*) fare il check-in; (*at hotel: arrive*) arrivare; (: *register*) firmare il registro.

②VT + ADV (*luggage*) registrare, fare il check-in di

▶ **check off** VT + ADV controllare, spuntare

▶ **check on** VI + PREP (*facts, dates*) controllare, verificare; (*fam: person*) informarsi su

▶ **check out** ①VI + ADV (*from hotel*) lasciare la camera e saldare il conto.

②VT + ADV **a** (*luggage*) ritirare

b (*investigate: story*) controllare, verificare; (: *fam:*

person) prendere informazioni su

▶ **check up** VI + ADV controllare

▶ **check up on** VI + ADV + PREP (*story*) controllare, verificare; (*person*) controllare; **to check up (on sth)** investigare (qc).

check·book ['tʃɛkˌbʊk] N (*Am*) = **chequebook**.

checked [tʃɛkt] ADJ (*material*) a quadretti, a quadri, a scacchi.

check·er ['tʃɛkəʳ] N (*person*) controllore *m*, verificatore *m*.

checker·board ['tʃɛkəˌbɔːd] N (*Am*) scacchiera.

check·ered ['tʃɛkəd] ADJ (*Am*) = **chequered**.

check·ers ['tʃɛkəz] NPL (*Am*) dama.

♦ **check guarantee card** N (*Am*) carta *f* assegni *inv*.

♦ **check-in** ['tʃɛkˌɪn] N (*also*: **check-in desk**: *at airport*) check-in *m inv*, accettazione *f* bagagli *inv*.

check·ing ac·count ['tʃɛkɪŋə'kaʊnt] N (*Am*) conto corrente.

check·list ['tʃɛkˌlɪst] N lista di controllo.

check·mate ['tʃɛkˌmeɪt] ①N (*in chess, fig*) scacco matto, scaccomatto.

②VT dare scacco matto a; (*fig*) bloccare.

check·out ['tʃɛkˌaʊt] N (*in supermarket*) cassa.

check·point ['tʃɛkˌpɔɪnt] N posto di blocco.

check·room ['tʃɛkˌrʊm] N (*Am: for coats*) guardaroba *m inv*; (*for luggage*) deposito *m* bagagli *inv*.

check·up ['tʃɛkˌʌp] N (*Med*) check-up *m inv*, controllo medico globale; **to have a checkup** fare una visita di controllo.

ched·dar ['tʃɛdəʳ] N (*also*: **cheddar cheese**) tipo di formaggio.

cheek [tʃiːk] ①N **a** guancia; (*fam: buttock*) natica; **to dance cheek to cheek** ballare guancia a guancia; **cheek by jowl** gomito a gomito **b** (*fam: impudence*) faccia tosta, sfacciataggine *f*; **what a cheek!** che faccia tosta!.

②VT essere sfacciato(-a) con.

cheek·bone ['tʃiːkˌbəʊn] N zigomo.

cheeki·ly ['tʃiːkɪlɪ] ADV sfacciatamente, impudentemente.

cheeki·ness ['tʃiːkɪnɪs] N sfacciataggine *f*, impudenza.

cheeky ['tʃiːkɪ] ADJ sfacciato(-a), impudente.

cheep [tʃiːp] ①N (*of bird*) pigolio.

②VI pigolare.

cheer [tʃɪəʳ] ①N (*shout*) evviva *m inv*; (*applause*) applauso; **three cheers for the winner!** tre urrà per il vincitore!.

②VT **a** (*applaud: winner etc*) applaudire

b (*gladden*) rallegrare.

③VI applaudire

▶ **cheer on** VT + ADV (*person*) incitare

▶ **cheer up** ①VI + ADV rallegrarsi, farsi animo; **cheer up!** coraggio!, su con la vita!.

②VT + ADV rallegrare, tirar su di morale.

cheer·ful ['tʃɪəfʊl] ADJ allegro(-a).

cheer·ful·ly ['tʃɪəfəlɪ] ADV (*gen*) allegramente; (*willingly*) volentieri.

cheer·ful·ness ['tʃɪəfʊlnɪs] N allegria.

cheeri·ly ['tʃɪərɪlɪ] ADV allegramente.

cheeri·ness ['tʃɪərɪnɪs] N allegria.

cheer·ing ['tʃɪərɪŋ] ①ADJ (*news, sight*) confortante.

②N (*of crowd etc*) acclamazioni *fpl*.

cheerio [ˌtʃɪərɪ'əʊ] EXCL (*Brit fam*) ciao!

cheer·leader ['tʃɪəˌliːdəʳ] N cheerleader *f inv*.

cheer·less ['tʃɪəlɪs] ADJ (*atmosphere*) triste; (*room, place*) desolato(-a).

cheers [tʃɪəz] EXCL (*toast*) (alla) salute!, cin cin!; (*Brit fam: thank you*) grazie!; (: *goodbye*) ciao!

cheery ['tʃɪərɪ] ADJ allegro(-a).

cheese [tʃiːz] N formaggio; **say cheese!** (*Phot*) sorridi!

cheese·board ['tʃiːz‚bɔːd] N piatto portaformaggio (in legno).

cheese·burg·er ['tʃiːz‚bɜːɡəʳ] N cheesburger *m inv*, hamburger *m inv* al formaggio.

cheese·cake ['tʃiːz‚keɪk] N *torta al formaggio, a volte con frutta.*

cheese·cloth ['tʃiːz‚klɒθ] N tela indiana, garza.

cheesed off ['tʃiːzd'ɒf] ADJ (*Brit fam*) stufo(-a).

♦ **cheese knife** N coltello per formaggio.

cheese·paring ['tʃiːz‚pɛərɪŋ] 1 ADJ (*person*) taccagno (-a), spilorcio(-a); (*attitude, habits*) meschino(-a).
2 N (*see adj*) taccagneria, spilorceria; meschinità.

cheesy ['tʃiːzɪ] ADJ (*flavour, smell*) di formaggio; (*consistency*) del formaggio.

chee·tah ['tʃiːtə] N ghepardo.

chef [ʃɛf] N chef *m inv*, capocuoco.

chemi·cal ['kɛmɪkəl] 1 ADJ chimico(-a).
2 N prodotto chimico.

♦ **chemical engineering** N ingegneria chimica.

chemi·cal·ly ['kɛmɪkəlɪ] ADV chimicamente.

chem·ist ['kɛmɪst] N (*Brit: pharmacist*) farmacista *m/f*; (*scientist*) chimico(-a); **chemist's (shop)** (*Brit*) farmacia.

chem·is·try ['kɛmɪstrɪ] N chimica.

chemo·thera·py [‚kiːməʊ'θɛrəpɪ] N (*Med*) chemioterapia.

chemo·tro·pism [‚kɛməʊ'trəʊpɪzəm] N chemiotropismo.

cheque, (*Am*) **check** [tʃɛk] N assegno; **a cheque for £20** un assegno di 20 sterline; **to pay by cheque** pagare per assegno *or* con un assegno.

cheque·book, (*Am*) **check·book** ['tʃɛk‚bʊk] N libretto degli assegni.

♦ **cheque card** N (*Brit*) carta *f* assegni *inv*.

cheq·uered, (*Am*) **check·ered** ['tʃɛkəd] ADJ a scacchi, a quadretti, a quadri; (*fig*) movimentato(-a); **a chequered career** una carriera movimentata.

cher·ish ['tʃɛrɪʃ] VT (*person*) avere caro(-a); (*hope etc*) nutrire.

cher·ished ['tʃɛrɪʃt] ADJ (*memory*) caro(-a); (*hope, wish, ambition*) grande.

che·root [ʃə'ruːt] N sigaro spuntato.

cher·ry ['tʃɛrɪ] 1 N (*fruit*) ciliegia; (*cherry tree*) ciliegio.
2 ADJ (*pie, jam*) di ciliegie.

♦ **cherry brandy** N cherry brandy *m inv*.

♦ **cherry orchard** N ciliegeto.

♦ **cherry plum** N susino asiatico.

♦ **cherry red** ADJ rosso ciliegia *inv*.

cher·ub ['tʃɛrəb] N **a** (*pl* cherubs) (*child*) angioletto **b** (*pl* cherubim ['tʃɛrəbɪm]) (*Rel*) cherubino.

che·ru·bic [tʃɛ'ruːbɪk] ADJ da cherubino.

cher·vil ['tʃɜːvɪl] N cerfoglio.

Ches ABBR (*Brit*)= *Cheshire.*

chess [tʃɛs] N scacchi *mpl*.

chess·board ['tʃɛs‚bɔːd] N scacchiera.

chess·man ['tʃɛs‚mæn] N (*pl* -men) pezzo (degli scacchi).

chess·player ['tʃɛs‚pleɪəʳ] N scacchista *m/f*.

chest [tʃɛst] N **a** (*Anat*) petto, torace *m*; **to get sth off one's chest** (*fam*) togliersi un peso (dallo stomaco), alleggerirsi *or* scaricarsi la coscienza **b** (*box*) baule *m*, cassa, cassapanca.

♦ **chest cold** N: **to catch a chest cold** prendere una bronchite.

♦ **chest measurement** N giro *m* torace *inv*.

chest·nut ['tʃɛs‚nʌt] 1 N (*fruit*) castagna; (*chestnut tree*)

castagno; **sweet chestnut** (*tree*) castagno comune *or* dolce.
2 ADJ (*hair*) castano(-a); (*horse*) sauro(-a).

♦ **chest of drawers** N comò *m inv*, cassettone *m*.

♦ **chest specialist** N specialista *m/f* in malattie polmonari.

chesty ['tʃɛstɪ] ADJ (*comp* -**ier**, *superl* -**iest**) (*cough*) bronchitico(-a); (*Brit fam: person*) che soffre di bronchite.

chew [tʃuː] VT masticare; **to chew the cud** ruminare
▶ **chew over** VT + ADV rimuginare su
▶ **chew up** VT + ADV mangiucchiare.

chew·ing gum ['tʃuːɪŋ‚ɡʌm] N chewing-gum *m inv*, gomma (americana *or* da masticare).

chewy ['tʃuːɪ] ADJ (*fam*) gommoso(-a).

chic [ʃiːk] ADJ chic *inv*, elegante.

chi·can·ery [ʃɪ'keɪnərɪ] N (*frm*) cavillo.

chick [tʃɪk] N (*baby bird*) piccolo (*di volatile*), uccellino; (*baby hen*) pulcino; (*fam*) pollastrella.

chick·en ['tʃɪkɪn] 1 N pollo; (*fam: coward*) coniglio; **don't count your chickens before they're hatched** (*Proverb*) non dire quattro finché non l'hai nel sacco.
2 ADJ (*stock, breast, liver*) di pollo; (*farmer, farming*) di polli
▶ **chicken out** VI + ADV (*fam*) avere fifa; **to chicken out of sth** tirarsi indietro da qc per fifa *or* paura.

♦ **chicken feed** N (*fig*): **he earns chicken feed** guadagna una miseria.

chicken·pox ['tʃɪkɪn‚pɒks] N varicella.

♦ **chicken wire** N rete *f* metallica (a maglie esagonali).

chick·pea ['tʃɪk‚piː] N cece *m*.

chick·weed ['tʃɪk‚wiːd] N (*Bot*) centonchio.

chico·ry ['tʃɪkərɪ] N cicoria.

chide [tʃaɪd] VT riprendere, rimproverare.

chief [tʃiːf] 1 ADJ (*principal: reason etc*) principale; (*in rank*) capo *inv*; **chief steward** (*Aer*) commissario di bordo.
2 N capo.

♦ **Chief Constable** N (*Brit*) ≈ questore *m*.

♦ **chief executive**, (*Am*) **chief executive officer** N direttore *m* generale.

♦ **Chief Justice** N ≈ presidente *m* di Corte di Cassazione.

chief·ly ['tʃiːflɪ] ADV principalmente, per lo più.

♦ **Chief of Staff** N (*Mil*) Capo di Stato Maggiore.

chief·tain ['tʃiːftən] N capo tribù.

chif·fon ['ʃɪfɒn] 1 N chiffon *m inv*.
2 ADJ di chiffon.

chi·gnon ['ʃiːnjɒn] N chignon *m inv*.

chi·hua·hua [tʃɪ'wɑːwɑː] N chihuahua *m inv*.

chil·blain ['tʃɪl‚bleɪn] N gelone *m*.

child [tʃaɪld] N (*pl* children) (*gen*) bambino(-a); (*son/daughter*) figlio(-a), bambino(-a).

♦ **child abuser** ['tʃaɪldə'bjuːzəʳ] N molestatore(-trice) di bambini.

♦ **child-bearing** ['tʃaɪld‚bɛərɪŋ] 1 ADJ: **of child-bearing age** in età feconda.
2 N gravidanza, maternità; **constant child-bearing** gravidanze *fpl* ripetute.

♦ **child benefit** N (*Brit*) ≈ assegni *mpl* familiari.

child·birth ['tʃaɪld‚bɜːθ] N parto; **to die in childbirth** morire di parto.

♦ **child guidance** N consulenza psicopedagogica.

child·hood ['tʃaɪldhʊd] N infanzia; **from childhood** fin dall'infanzia, fin da piccolo(-a).

child·ish ['tʃaɪldɪʃ] ADJ (*pej*) infantile, puerile.

child·ish·ly ['tʃaɪldɪʃlɪ] ADV (*pej*) puerilmente, in modo

infantile.

child·ish·ness ['tʃaɪldɪʃnɪs] N (*pej*) puerilità.

♦ **child labour** N lavoro minorile.

child·less ['tʃaɪldlɪs] ADJ senza figli.

child·like ['tʃaɪld,laɪk] ADJ ingenuo(-a), innocente.

♦ **child minder** ['tʃaɪld,maɪndə'] N (*Brit*) bambinaia (*che sorveglia i bambini a casa propria*).

♦ **child prodigy** N bambino(-a) prodigio *inv*.

♦ **child-proof** ['tʃaɪld,pru:f] ADJ: **child-proof (door) lock** (*Aut*) sicura (della portiera) a prova di bambino.

chil·dren ['tʃɪldrən] NPL of **child**.

♦ **children's home** N istituto per l'infanzia (*abbandonata o maltrattata*).

♦ **child's play** ['tʃaɪldz,pleɪ] N: **it's child's play** è un gioco da ragazzi, è una cosa da nulla.

♦ **Child Support Agency** N *ente governativo incaricato di valutare e riscuotere da genitori separati i contributi per il mantenimento dei figli.*

Chile ['tʃɪlɪ] N Cile *m*.

Chil·ean ['tʃɪlɪən] ADJ, N cileno(-a).

♦ **Chile pine** N araucaria.

chili ['tʃɪlɪ] N (*Am*) = **chilli**.

chill [tʃɪl] **1** ADJ (*wind*) freddo(-a), gelido(-a).

2 N freddo; (*Med*) infreddatura, colpo di freddo; **there's a chill in the air** l'aria è fredda; **to take the chill off (a room)** riscaldare un po' (una stanza); **to catch a chill** (*Med*) prendere un colpo di freddo.

3 VT (*food, drink*) mettere in fresco; **"serve chilled"** "servire fresco"; **to chill sb's blood** (*fig*) far gelare il sangue a qn; **to be chilled to the bone** essere gelato(-a) fino alle ossa

► **chill out** VI (*esp Am fam*) darsi una calmata.

chilli, (*Am*) **chili** ['tʃɪlɪ] N peperoncino.

chill·ing ['tʃɪlɪŋ] ADJ (*story, thought*) agghiacciante; (*wind*) gelido(-a).

chill·ness, **chilli·ness** ['tʃɪl(ɪ)nɪs] N (*cold*) freddo; (*coolness*) fresco; (*fig*) freddezza.

chil·ly ['tʃɪlɪ] ADJ (*weather, room*) fresco(-a), freddo(-a); (*fig: person, look, reception*) freddo(-a), gelido(-a); (*sensitive to cold*) freddoloso(-a); **I feel chilly** ho *or* sento freddo, sono *or* mi sento infreddolito.

chime [tʃaɪm] **1** N rintocco.

2 VT, VI suonare.

► **chime in** VI + ADV (*fam: interrupt, join in*) intervenire; (: *echo*) fare eco, far coro.

chim·ney ['tʃɪmnɪ] N (*of house*) camino; (*of factory*) ciminiera.

♦ **chimney breast** N bocca del camino.

♦ **chimney pot** N comignolo.

♦ **chimney stack** N canna fumaria.

♦ **chimney sweep** N spazzacamino.

chimp [tʃɪmp] N (*fam*) scimpanzé *m inv*.

chim·pan·zee [,tʃɪmpæn'zi:] N scimpanzé *m inv*.

chin [tʃɪn] N mento; (**keep your) chin up!** (*fam*) coraggio!, testa alta!

Chi·na ['tʃaɪnə] N Cina; **People's Republic of China** Repubblica Popolare Cinese.

chi·na ['tʃaɪnə] **1** N (*porcelain*) porcellana; (*dishes*) porcellane *fpl*.

2 ADJ di porcellana.

♦ **China tea** N tè *m* cinese.

chin·chil·la [tʃɪn'tʃɪlə] N cincillà *m inv*.

Chi·nese ['tʃaɪ'ni:z] **1** ADJ cinese.

2 N (*person: pl inv*) cinese *m/f*; (*language*) cinese *m*.

chink¹ [tʃɪŋk] N (*opening*) fessura; **a chink in his armour**

(*fig*) il suo punto debole.

chink² [tʃɪŋk] **1** N (*noise*) tintinnio.

2 VT far tintinnare.

3 VI tintinnare.

chintz [tʃɪnts] N chintz *m inv*.

chin·wag ['tʃɪn,wæg] N (*Brit fam*): **to have a chinwag** fare una chiacchierata.

chip [tʃɪp] **1** N **a** (*piece*) frammento; (: *of glass, wood, stone*) scheggia; **he's a chip off the old block** (*fig*) è della stessa razza del padre; **he's got a chip on his shoulder because ...** gli è rimasto sullo stomaco il fatto che...

b (*gen pl: Culin: Brit: French fry*) patatina fritta; (: *Am: crisp*) patatina

c (*in crockery, furniture*) scheggiatura; **there's a chip in this cup** questa tazza è scheggiata

d (*in gambling*) fiche *f inv*; **when the chips are down** (*fig*) nei momenti critici, nel momento della verità, alla resa dei conti; **to have had one's chips** (*fig fam*) aver giocato l'ultima carta

e (*Comput: microchip*) chip *m inv*.

2 VT (*cup, plate*) scheggiare; **chipped potatoes** (*Culin*) patatine *fpl* fritte.

3 VI scheggiarsi

► **chip in** VI + ADV (*fam: contribute*) contribuire; (: *interrupt*) intromettersi

► **chip off 1** VI + ADV (*paint*) scrostarsi.

2 VT + ADV (*paint*) scrostare.

chip·board ['tʃɪp,bɔ:d] N truciolato, agglomerato.

chip·munk ['tʃɪp,mʌŋk] N tamia *m* striato.

chip·pings ['tʃɪpɪŋz] NPL: **loose chippings** brecciame *msg*.

♦ **chip shop** N (*also*: **fish-and-chip shop**) *friggitoria dove si vendono filetti di pesce impanati e patatine fritte.*

chi·ropo·dist [kɪ'rɒpədɪst] N (*Brit*) callista *m/f*, podiatra *m/f*.

chi·ropo·dy [kɪ'rɒpədɪ] N (*Brit*) chiropodia, podiatria, mestiere *m* di callista.

chi·ro·prac·tic [,kaɪrə'præktɪk] N chiroterapia.

chi·ro·prac·tor ['kaɪrə,præktə'] N chiropratico(-a).

chirp [tʃɜ:p], **chir·rup** ['tʃɪrəp] **1** N (*of birds*) cinguettio; (*of crickets*) cri cri *m*.

2 VI (*see n*) cinguettare; fare cri cri.

chirpy ['tʃɜ:pɪ] ADJ (*fam*) pimpante, frizzante.

chis·el ['tʃɪzl] **1** N scalpello; (*smaller*) cesello; (*for engraving*) bulino.

2 VT (*pt, pp* **chiselled**, *Am* **chiseled**) (*also*: **chisel out**) scolpire; cesellare; incidere con il bulino.

chit¹ [tʃɪt] N nota *f* spese *inv*.

chit² [tʃɪt] N (*old*): **a chit of a girl** una ragazzina.

chit·chat ['tʃɪt,tʃæt] N (*fam*) chiacchiere *fpl*.

chiv·al·rous ['ʃɪvəlrəs] ADJ cavalleresco(-a).

chiv·al·rous·ly ['ʃɪvəlrəslɪ] ADV cavallerescamente; (*gallantly*) con cavalleria.

chiv·al·ry ['ʃɪvəlrɪ] N cavalleria.

chives ['tʃaɪvz] NPL erba cipollina.

chiv·vy, (*Am*) **chivy** ['tʃɪvɪ] VT (*fam*) tormentare; **to chivvy sb into doing sth** tormentare qn perché faccia qc.

chlo·rate ['klɔ:reɪt] N (*Chem*) clorato.

chlo·ride ['klɔ:raɪd] N (*Chem*) cloruro.

chlo·rin·ate ['klɒrɪneɪt] VT clorare.

chlo·rine ['klɔ:ri:n] N cloro.

chlo·ro·form ['klɒrəfɔ:m] **1** N cloroformio.

2 VT cloroformizzare.

chlo·ro·phyll ['klɒrəfɪl] N (*Bot*) clorofilla.

chlo·ro·plast ['klɔ:rəʊ,plæst] N (*Bot*) cloroplasto.

chlo·ro·sis [klɔ:'rəʊsɪs] N (*Med, Bot*) clorosi *f*.

choc-ice ['tʃɒk,aɪs] N *barretta di gelato ricoperto di*

cioccolato.

chock [tʃɒk] N zeppa.

♦ **chock-a-block** ['tʃɒkə'blɒk] ADJ: **chock-a-block (with)** pieno(-a) zeppo(-a) (di).

♦ **chock-full** ['tʃɒk'fʊl] ADJ: **chock-full (of)** pieno(-a) zeppo(-a) (di).

choco·late ['tʃɒklɪt] [1] N (*substance*) cioccolato, cioccolata; (*individual sweet*) cioccolatino; (*drink*) cioccolata; **hot** or **drinking chocolate** cioccolata (calda).

[2] ADJ (*biscuit, cake*) al cioccolato; (*egg*) di cioccolato; (*colour*) (color) cioccolato *inv.*

choice [tʃɔɪs] [1] N scelta; **he's not really my choice** non è proprio quello che sceglierei io; **I did it by** or **from choice** l'ho fatto di mia volontà or per mia scelta; **a wide choice** un'ampia scelta; **she had no choice but to go** non aveva altra scelta che andare; **take your choice!** scegli pure!.

[2] ADJ (*fruit, wine*) di prima scelta; (*hum: example, remark*) bello(-a); **his language was really choice!** il suo tono non era esattamente garbato!

choir ['kwaɪə'] N coro.

choir·boy ['kwaɪə,bɔɪ] N corista *m* (*ragazzo*).

choir·mas·ter ['kwaɪə,mɑːstə'] N maestro(-a) del coro; (*in church*) maestro di cappella.

choir·stall ['kwaɪə,stɔːl] N stallo del coro.

choke [tʃəʊk] [1] N (*Aut*) (valvola dell')aria.

[2] VT (*person*) soffocare; (: *strangle*) strangolare; (*also: choke up: pipe*) intasare.

[3] VI soffocare

▶ **choke back** VT + ADV soffocare.

chok·er ['tʃəʊkə'] N collana girocollo.

chol·era ['kɒlərə] N colera *m.*

cho·les·ter·ol [kə'lɛstərɒl] N colesterolo.

chomp [tʃɒmp] VI, VT (*fam*) masticare rumorosamente.

choose [tʃuːz] (*vb: pt* chose, *pp* chosen) [1] VT scegliere; **to choose to do sth** scegliere or decidere di fare qc.

[2] VI scegliere; **to choose between** scegliere tra; **there is nothing to choose between them** uno vale l'altro; **to choose from** scegliere da or tra; **there were several to choose from** vi era parecchia scelta; **as/when I choose** come/quando voglio or decido io.

choosy ['tʃuːzɪ] ADJ (*comp* -**ier**, *superl* -**iest**) (*fam*): **to be choosy** fare lo/la schizzinoso(-a) or difficile.

chop[1] [tʃɒp] [1] N **a** (*blow*) colpo secco, colpo netto; **to get the chop** (*Brit fam: project*) essere bocciato(-a); (: *person: be sacked*) essere licenziato(-a)

b (*Culin*) costoletta; see also **chops**.

[2] VT (*wood*) tagliare, spaccare; (*meat, vegetables*) tagliare (a pezzetti)

▶ **chop down** VT + ADV (*tree*) abbattere

▶ **chop off** VT + ADV tagliare (via)

▶ **chop up** VT + ADV (*wood*) spaccare; (*vegetables, meat*) tagliare (a pezzetti).

chop[2] [tʃɒp] VI: **to chop and change** cambiare continuamente parere.

chop·per ['tʃɒpə'] N (*of butcher*) mannaia; (*Aer fam*) elicottero.

chop·ping ['tʃɒpɪŋ] ADJ: **chopping board** tagliere *m*; **chopping knife** coltello (per tritare).

chop·py ['tʃɒpɪ] ADJ (*comp* -**ier**, *superl* -**iest**) (*lake, sea*) increspato(-a), mosso(-a), agitato(-a); (*wind*) variabile; **choppy sea** maretta.

chops [tʃɒps] NPL (*jaws*) mascelle *fpl.*

chop·sticks ['tʃɒpstɪks] NPL bastoncini *mpl* (cinesi).

chop suey [tʃɒp'suːɪ] N (*Culin*) *spezzatino cinese.*

cho·ral ['kɔːrəl] ADJ corale; **choral society** coro.

chord [kɔːd] N (*Mus*) accordo; (*Geom*) corda; **to touch the right chord** (*fig*) toccare il tasto giusto.

chore [tʃɔː'] N faccenda; (*pej*) rottura; **household chores** faccende *fpl* (domestiche); **to do the chores** sbrigare or fare le faccende.

cho·reo·graph ['kɒrɪə,grɑːf] VI, VT (*ballet*) fare la coreografia (di).

cho·reog·ra·pher [,kɒrɪ'ɒgrəfə'] N coreografo(-a).

cho·reo·graph·ic [,kɒrɪəʊ'græfɪk] ADJ coreografico(-a).

cho·reo·graphi·cal·ly [,kɒrɪə'græfɪklɪ] ADV coreograficamente.

cho·reog·ra·phy [,kɒrɪ'ɒgrəfɪ] N coreografia.

chor·is·ter ['kɒrɪstə'] N (*Rel*) corista *m/f.*

cho·roid ['kɔːrɔɪd] N (*Anat*) coroide *f.*

chor·tle ['tʃɔːtl] VI ridacchiare, fare risolini.

cho·rus ['kɔːrəs] [1] N **a** (*musical work, people*) coro; **in chorus** in coro **b** (*refrain: also fig*) ritornello.

[2] VT (*answer*) rispondere in coro.

♦ **chorus girl** N girl *f inv*, ragazza che canta e balla.

chose [tʃəʊz] PT of **choose.**

cho·sen ['tʃəʊzn] [1] PP of **choose.**

[2] ADJ: **the chosen (people)** gli eletti.

choux pas·try ['ʃuː'peɪstrɪ] N pasta per bignè.

chow [tʃaʊ] N (*also: chow-chow, dog*) chow chow *m inv.*

chow·der ['tʃaʊdə'] N (*esp Am Culin*) zuppa di pesce.

Christ [kraɪst] N Cristo.

chris·ten ['krɪsn] VT battezzare.

Chris·ten·dom ['krɪsndəm] N cristianità.

chris·ten·ing ['krɪsnɪŋ] N battesimo.

Chris·tian ['krɪstɪən] [1] ADJ cristiano(-a); (*also: christian: fig*) caritatevole.

[2] N cristiano(-a).

Chris·ti·an·ity [,krɪstɪ'ænɪtɪ] N cristianesimo.

♦ **Christian name** N nome *m* (di battesimo).

Christ·mas ['krɪsməs] [1] N Natale *m*; **at Christmas** a Natale; **Happy** or **Merry Christmas!** Buon Natale!.

[2] ADJ (*tree, cake, present, party*) di Natale.

♦ **Christmas card** N biglietto di auguri natalizi.

♦ **Christmas Day** N il giorno di Natale.

♦ **Christmas Eve** N la vigilia di Natale.

♦ **Christmas Island** N Isola Christmas.

♦ **Christmas stocking** N ≈ calza della Befana.

Christ·mas·time ['krɪsməs,taɪm] N periodo natalizio or di Natale.

♦ **Christmas tree** N albero di Natale.

chro·mat·ic [krə'mætɪk] ADJ (*Mus*) cromatico(-a).

chro·mati·cism [krə'mætɪsɪzəm] N (*Mus*) cromatismo.

chro·ma·tog·ra·phy [,krəʊmə'tɒgrəfɪ] N (*Chem*) cromatografia.

chro·mium ['krəʊmɪəm], **chrome** [krəʊm] N cromo; (*also: chromium plating*) cromatura.

♦ **chromium-plated** ['krəʊmɪəm'pleɪtɪd] ADJ cromato (-a).

chro·mo·some ['krəʊməsəʊm] N cromosoma *m.*

chron·ic ['krɒnɪk] ADJ (*invalid, disease*) cronico(-a); (*fig: liar, drunkard*) incallito(-a); (*fam: weather, actor etc*) allucinante.

chroni·cal·ly ['krɒnɪklɪ] ADV in modo cronico, cronicamente; **he is chronically sick** è un malato cronico; **a hospital that is chronically short of finance** un ospedale affetto da una cronica mancanza di fondi.

chroni·cle ['krɒnɪkl] N cronaca.

chrono·logi·cal [,krɒnə'lɒdʒɪkəl] ADJ cronologico(-a); **in chronological order** in ordine cronologico.

chrono·logi·cal·ly [,krɒnə'lɒdʒɪkəlɪ] ADV cronologica-

mente.

chro·nol·ogy [krə'nɒlədʒɪ] N cronologia.

chro·nom·eter [krə'nɒmɪtə^r] N cronometro.

chrysa·lis ['krɪsəlɪs] N (pl -es) crisalide f.

chry·san·themum [krɪ'sænθəməm] N crisantemo.

chub [tʃʌb] N cavedano.

chub·by ['tʃʌbɪ] ADJ paffuto(-a), grassoccio(-a).

chuck[1] [tʃʌk] VT (fam) **a** (throw) gettare **b** (also: **chuck away**) buttare, gettare **c** (also: **chuck up, chuck in**: job) piantare **d** (boyfriend, girlfriend) piantare
► **chuck out** VT + ADV (fam: useless article) buttare via; (: person) sbattere or buttare fuori.

chuck[2] [tʃʌk] N (also: **chuck steak**) spalla.

chuck[3] [tʃʌk] N (Tech) mandrino.

chuck·le ['tʃʌkl] [1] N risolino.
[2] VI ridacchiare; **to chuckle at** or **over** ridere or ridacchiare per.

chuffed [tʃʌft] ADJ (Brit fam): **to be chuffed about sth** essere arcicontento(-a) di qc.

chug [tʃʌg] VI **a** (boat) sbuffare; (motor) scoppiettare **b** (also: **chug along**: boat) muoversi sbuffando.

chum [tʃʌm] N (fam) compagno(-a), amicone(-a)
► **chum up** VI + ADV (fam): **to chum up (with sb)** fare amicizia (con qn).

chum·my ['tʃʌmɪ] ADJ (fam): **to be chummy (with)** essere grande amico(-a) (di).

chump [tʃʌmp] N (fam) zuccone(-a).

chunk [tʃʌŋk] N (bel) pezzo; (of bread) tocco.

chunky ['tʃʌŋkɪ] ADJ (comp **-ier**, superl **-iest**) (furniture etc) basso(-a) e largo(-a); (person) ben piantato(-a); (knit-wear) di lana grossa.

Chun·nel ['tʃʌnəl] N (fam) = **Channel Tunnel**.

church [tʃɜːtʃ] N chiesa; **to go to church** andare in chiesa; **after church** dopo la funzione; (for Catholics) dopo la messa; **to enter the Church** prendere gli ordini.

church·goer ['tʃɜːtʃ,gəʊə^r] N fedele m/f; **his parents are regular churchgoers** i suoi genitori vanno regolarmente in chiesa.

♦ **Church of England** N: **the Church of England** la Chiesa anglicana.

church·warden [,tʃɜːtʃ'wɔːdən] N aiutante del vicario nell'amministrazione della parrocchia.

church·yard ['tʃɜːtʃjɑːd] N cimitero (annesso a una chiesa).

churl·ish ['tʃɜːlɪʃ] ADJ rozzo(-a), sgarbato(-a).

churl·ish·ly ['tʃɜːlɪʃlɪ] ADV rozzamente, sgarbatamente.

churl·ish·ness ['tʃɜːlɪʃnɪs] N rozzezza, sgarbataggine f.

churn [tʃɜːn] [1] N (for butter) zangola; (Brit: for milk) bidone m per il latte.
[2] VT (butter) fare (nella zangola); (fig: also: **churn up**: water) agitare.
[3] VI (water) agitarsi; (stomach) torcersi
► **churn out** VT + ADV (often pej) sfornare in gran quantità.

chute [ʃuːt] N (for parcels, coal, in swimming pool) scivolo; (also: **rubbish chute**) canale m di scarico; (fam) = **parachute**.

chut·ney ['tʃʌtnɪ] N salsa piccante (di frutta, zucchero e spezie).

CIA [,siː aɪ'eɪ] N ABBR (Am: = Central Intelligence Agency) CIA f.

ci·ca·da [sɪ'kɑːdə] N cicala.

Cicero ['sɪsə,rəʊ] N Cicerone m.

CID [,siː aɪ'diː] N ABBR (Brit) = **Criminal Investigation Department**.

ci·der ['saɪdə^r] N sidro.

c.i.f., CIF [,siː aɪ'ɛf] ABBR (= cost, insurance and freight) CIF, costo assicurazione e nolo.

ci·gar [sɪ'gɑː^r] N sigaro.

♦ **cigar case** N portasigari m inv.

ciga·rette [,sɪgə'rɛt] N sigaretta.

♦ **cigarette case** N portasigarette m inv.

♦ **cigarette end** N mozzicone m (di sigaretta), cicca.

♦ **cigarette holder** N bocchino.

♦ **cigarette lighter** N accendino.

♦ **cigarette paper** N cartina.

♦ **cigar lighter** N accendisigari m inv.

cil·ia ['sɪlɪə] NPL (Anat) ciglia fpl.

cili·ary ['sɪlɪərɪ] ADJ (Anat) ciliare.

C-in-C ABBR = **commander in chief**.

cinch [sɪntʃ] N (fam): **it's a cinch** (easy thing) è una cretinata or una sciocchezza, è presto fatto; (sure thing) è una cosa sicura.

Cincinnatus [,sɪnsɪ'nɑːtəs] N Cincinnato.

cin·der ['sɪndə^r] N cenere f, brace f; **burned to a cinder** (fig: food) carbonizzato(-a).

Cinderella [,sɪndə'rɛlə] N Cenerentola.

♦ **cinder track** N (Sport) pista di cenere.

cine camera ['sɪnɪ'kæmərə] N (Brit) cinepresa.

cine film ['sɪnɪfɪlm] N (Brit) film m inv.

cin·ema ['sɪnəmə] N cinema m inv.

Cin·ema·scope® ['sɪnɪmə,skəʊp] N cinemascope ® m.

cin·emat·ic [,sɪnɪ'mætɪk] ADJ cinematografico(-a).

cin·emato·graphi·cal·ly [,sɪnɪ,mætə'græfɪklɪ] ADV cinematograficamente.

cin·ema·tog·ra·phy [,sɪnɪmə'tɒgrəfɪ] N cinematografia.

cine projector ['sɪnɪprə'dʒɛktə^r] N (Brit) proiettore m.

cin·na·mon ['sɪnəmən] N cannella.

ci·pher ['saɪfə^r] N (code) codice m (cifrato); (Math) zero; (fig: faceless employee etc) persona di nessun conto, nullità f inv; **in cipher** in codice.

circa ['sɜːkə] PREP circa.

Circe ['sɜːsɪ] N Circe f.

cir·cle ['sɜːkl] [1] N (gen) cerchio; (of friends etc) circolo; (in theatre, cinema) galleria; **great/small circle** (Geom) cerchio massimo/minore; **to stand in a circle** mettersi in cerchio; **she moves in wealthy circles** frequenta l'alta società; **the family circle** la cerchia familiare; **to come full circle** (fig) ritornare al punto di partenza; **to go round in circles** (fam) girare sempre attorno allo stesso punto.
[2] VT (surround) accerchiare, circondare; (move round) girare attorno or intorno a; (draw round) segnare con un cerchio, cerchiare.
[3] VI girare in circolo.

cir·cuit ['sɜːkɪt] N (journey around) giro; (Sport, Elec) circuito; (of judge) distretto giudiziario; (Cine) rete f di distribuzione.

♦ **circuit board** N (Elec) piastra; (Comput) tavola dei circuiti.

♦ **circuit breaker** N salvavita m.

cir·cui·tous [sɜː'kjuːɪtəs] ADJ: **to go by a circuitous route** prendere la strada più lunga.

cir·cui·tous·ly [sɜː'kjuːɪtəslɪ] ADV facendo un lungo giro; (fig) indirettamente.

cir·cuit·ry ['sɜːkɪtrɪ] N circuiteria, circuiti mpl.

cir·cu·lar ['sɜːkjʊlə^r] [1] ADJ circolare.
[2] N (letter) circolare f; (as advertisement) volantino pubblicitario.

cir·cu·lar·ize ['sɜːkjʊlə,raɪz] VT inviare circolari a.

♦ **circular saw** N segatrice f a disco.

cir·cu·late ['sɜːkjʊˌleɪt] **1** VI (gen) circolare; (person: socially) girare e andare un po' da tutti. **2** VT far circolare.

cir·cu·lat·ing capi·tal ['sɜːkjʊˌleɪtɪŋ'kæpɪtl] N (Comm) capitale m d'esercizio.

cir·cu·la·tion [ˌsɜːkjʊ'leɪʃən] N (gen) circolazione f; (of news) diffusione f; (of newspaper etc) tiratura; **she has poor circulation** (Med) ha una cattiva circolazione; **to withdraw sth from circulation** togliere or ritirare qc dalla circolazione; **he's back in circulation** (fam) è tornato in circolazione.

cir·cu·la·tory [ˌsɜːkjʊ'leɪtərɪ] ADJ (Med) circolatorio(-a).

♦ **circulatory system** N (Med) apparato circolatorio.

cir·cum·cise ['sɜːkəmˌsaɪz] VT circoncidere.

cir·cum·ci·sion [ˌsɜːkəm'sɪʒən] N circoncisione f.

cir·cum·fer·ence [sə'kʌmfərəns] N circonferenza.

cir·cum·flex ['sɜːkəmˌfleks] N (also: circumflex accent) accento circonflesso.

cir·cum·lo·cu·tion [ˌsɜːkəmlə'kjuːʃən] N (frm) circonlocuzione f.

cir·cum·navi·gate [ˌsɜːkəm'nævɪgeɪt] VT circumnavigare.

cir·cum·navi·ga·tion ['sɜːkəmˌnævɪ'geɪʃən] N circumnavigazione f.

cir·cum·scribe ['sɜːkəmˌskraɪb] VT (limit) limitare; (Math) circoscrivere.

cir·cum·spect ['sɜːkəmˌspekt] ADJ circospetto(-a).

cir·cum·spec·tion [ˌsɜːkəm'spekʃən] N circospezione f.

cir·cum·spect·ly ['sɜːkəmspektlɪ] ADV con circospezione.

cir·cum·stances ['sɜːkəmstənsɪz] NPL **a** (conditions) circostanze fpl; **in the circumstances** date le circostanze; **under no circumstances** in nessun caso **b** (financial state) condizioni fpl finanziarie; **to be in easy/poor circumstances** trovarsi in buone/cattive condizioni finanziarie.

cir·cum·stan·tial [ˌsɜːkəm'stænʃəl] ADJ (report, statement) circostanziato(-a), dettagliato(-a).

♦ **circumstantial evidence** N prova indiziaria.

cir·cum·vent [ˌsɜːkəm'vɛnt] VT (frm: rule etc) aggirare.

cir·cus ['sɜːkəs] N (entertainment) circo (usu Circus: street name) piazza (di forma circolare).

cir·rho·sis [sɪ'rəʊsɪs] N (also: cirrhosis of the liver) cirrosi f inv (epatica).

cir·rus ['sɪrəs] N (pl cirri ['sɪraɪ]) (Met) cirro.

CIS [ˌsiːaɪ'ɛs] N ABBR (= Commonwealth of Independent States) CSI f.

cis·sy ['sɪsɪ] N (fam) femminuccia.

Cis·ter·cian [sɪ'stɜːʃən] ADJ, N cistercense (m).

cis·tern ['sɪstən] N serbatoio, cisterna; (in toilet) serbatoio d'acqua.

cita·del ['sɪtədl] N cittadella.

ci·ta·tion [saɪ'teɪʃən] N citazione f.

cite [saɪt] VT citare; **he was cited to appear in court** (Law) fu citato in tribunale; **to cite as an example** portare come esempio.

citi·zen ['sɪtɪzn] N (of state) cittadino(-a); (of city) abitante m/f; **the citizens of this town** gli abitanti di questa città.

♦ **Citizens' Advice Bureau** N (Brit) organizzazione di volontari che offre gratuitamente assistenza in materia legale e finanziaria.

♦ **Citizens' Band** N banda cittadina.

citi·zen·ship ['sɪtɪznˌʃɪp] N cittadinanza.

cit·ric acid [ˌsɪtrɪk'æsɪd] N acido citrico.

cit·rus fruit ['sɪtrəsˌfruːt] N agrume m.

City ['sɪtɪ] N: **the City** (Fin) la City di Londra.

city ['sɪtɪ] **1** N (grande) città f inv.

2 ADJ (centre) della città; (life) di città.

♦ **city dweller** N chi abita in città.

♦ **city fathers** NPL: **the city fathers** i notabili della città.

♦ **City Hall** N (Am) ≈ Comune m.

♦ **city page** N (in newspaper) pagina finanziaria.

♦ **city planner** N (Am) = **town planner**.

♦ **city slicker** ['sɪtɪ'slɪkəʳ] N (pej fam) cittadino(-a) sofisticato(-a).

♦ **City Technology College** N (Brit) istituto tecnico superiore (finanziato dall'industria).

civ·et ['sɪvɪt] N zibetto.

civ·ic ['sɪvɪk] ADJ civico(-a).

♦ **civic centre** N (Brit) centro civico.

civ·ics ['sɪvɪks] NSG educazione f civica.

civ·il ['sɪvɪl] ADJ **a** (war, law, marriage) civile **b** (polite) educato(-a), gentile.

♦ **Civil Aviation Authority** N organismo di controllo dell'aviazione civile.

♦ **civil defence** N protezione f civile.

♦ **civil disobedience** N resistenza passiva.

♦ **civil engineer** N ingegnere m civile.

♦ **civil engineering** N ingegneria civile.

ci·vil·ian [sɪ'vɪlɪən] **1** ADJ (clothes, government) civile, borghese; (life) da civile, da borghese. **2** N civile m/f, borghese m/f.

ci·vil·ity [sɪ'vɪlɪtɪ] N gentilezza.

civi·li·za·tion [ˌsɪvɪlaɪ'zeɪʃən] N civiltà f inv.

civi·lize ['sɪvɪˌlaɪz] VT civilizzare.

civi·lized ['sɪvɪˌlaɪzd] ADJ (country, society) civilizzato(-a), progredito(-a); (behaviour, manner) civile, cortese.

♦ **civil law** N codice m civile; (study) diritto civile.

♦ **civil liberties** NPL libertà fpl civili.

civ·il·ly ['sɪvɪlɪ] ADV civilmente, educatamente, gentilmente.

♦ **civil rights** NPL diritti mpl civili.

♦ **civil rights movement** N movimento per i diritti civili.

♦ **civil servant** N impiegato(-a) statale.

♦ **civil service** N: **the Civil Service** l'amministrazione f pubblica.

♦ **civil war** N guerra civile.

civ·vies ['sɪvɪz] NPL (fam): **in civvies** in borghese.

civ·vy street ['sɪvɪˌstriːt] N (Brit fam) vita da civile.

cl ABBR (= centilitre) cl.

clad [klæd] ADJ (old, liter) vestito(-a).

clad·ding ['klædɪŋ] N (of roof) rivestimento.

claim [kleɪm] **1** N **a** (demand: to title, right) pretesa, diritto; (: for expenses, damages, increased pay) richiesta; (insurance claim) domanda d'indennizzo; **the poor have a claim to our sympathy** i poveri hanno diritto alla nostra comprensione; **there are many claims on my time** sono molto preso; **to lay claim to sth** avanzare pretese su qc; **to put in a claim for sth** fare una richiesta di qc; **to put in a claim for petrol expenses** chiedere il rimborso delle spese per la benzina

b (assertion) affermazione f, pretesa; **I make no claim to be infallible** non pretendo di essere infallibile.

2 VT **a** (rights, territory) pretendere, rivendicare; (expenses, damages) (ri)chiedere; (lost property) reclamare; **something else claimed her attention** qualcosa distolse la sua attenzione

b (assert) dichiarare, sostenere; **the new system can claim many advantages over the old one** si può dire che il nuovo sistema offre molti vantaggi rispetto a quello vecchio; **to claim that/to be ...** affermare or sostenere

che/di essere...; **he claims to have seen her** sostiene di averla vista.

3 vi (*for insurance*) fare una domanda d'indennizzo.

claim·ant ['kleɪmənt] N (*to social benefit*) richiedente *m/f*; (*in court*) citante *m/f*; (*to throne etc*) pretendente *m/f*.

♦ **claim form** N (*gen*) modulo di richiesta; (*for expenses*) modulo di rimborso spese.

clair·voy·ance [klɛə'vɔɪəns] N chiaroveggenza.

clair·voy·ant [klɛə'vɔɪənt] ADJ, N chiaroveggente (*m/f*).

clam [klæm] N vongola

► **clam up** vi + ADV (*fam*) zittirsi.

clam·ber ['klæmbəʳ] vi arrampicarsi.

clam·my ['klæmɪ] ADJ (*comp* -ier, *superl* -iest) (*hands*) sudaticcio(-a), viscido(-a); (*weather*) appiccicoso(-a), caldo(-a) e umido(-a).

clam·or·ous ['klæmərəs] ADJ (*crowd, mob*) chiassoso(-a); (*demands*) insistente.

clam·our, (*Am*) **clam·or** ['klæməʳ] **1** N (*noise*) clamore *m*; (*protest*) protesta.

2 vi: **to clamour for sth** chiedere a gran voce qc.

clamp [klæmp] **1** N morsetto, morsa.

2 vT (*hold in a vice*) stringere con un morsetto; (*immobilize: car*) applicare i ceppi bloccaruote a

► **clamp down** vi + ADV (*fig*): **to clamp down (on)** dare un giro di vite a.

clamp·down [klæmp,daʊn] N stretta; **a clampdown on sth/sb** un giro di vite a qc/qn.

clan [klæn] N clan *m inv*.

clan·des·tine [klæn'dɛstɪn] ADJ clandestino(-a).

clan·des·tine·ly [klæn'dɛstɪnlɪ] ADV clandestinamente.

clang [klæŋ] **1** N suono metallico.

2 vi emettere un suono metallico; **the gate clanged shut** il cancello si chiuse con fragore.

clang·er ['klæŋəʳ] N (*Brit fam*) gaffe *f inv*; **to drop a clanger** fare una gaffe.

clank ['klæŋk] **1** N suono metallico.

2 vi emettere un suono metallico.

clan·nish ['klænɪʃ] (*pej*) ADJ (*group*) chiuso(-a); (*person*) selettivo(-a).

clans·man ['klænzmən] N membro di un clan.

clap [klæp] **1** N (*on shoulder*) pacca; (*of the hands*) battimano; (*applause*) applauso; **a clap of thunder** un tuono.

2 vT (*applaud*) applaudire; **to clap one's hands** battere le mani; **to clap a hand over sb's mouth** chiudere la bocca (con la mano) a qn; **they clapped him in prison** (*fam*) lo sbatterono dentro.

3 vi (*applaud*) applaudire.

clap·board ['klæp,bɔːd] N (*Am*): **a clapboard house** una casa rivestita di assicelle di legno.

♦ **clapped-out** ['klæpt,aʊt] ADJ (*fam*) malridotto(-a).

clapper·board ['klæpə,bɔːd] N ciac *m*, ciak *m*.

clap·ping ['klæpɪŋ] N applausi *mpl*.

clap·trap ['klæp,træp] N (*pej fam*) chiacchiere *fpl*, sciocchezze *fpl*.

clar·et ['klærət] N chiaretto (*originario della regione di Bordeaux*).

clari·fi·ca·tion [ˌklærɪfɪ'keɪʃən] N chiarificazione *f*, chiarimento.

clari·fy ['klærɪfaɪ] vT (*statement etc*) chiarire, chiarificare.

clari·net [ˌklærɪ'nɛt] N clarinetto.

clari·net·tist [ˌklærɪ'nɛtɪst] N clarinettista *m/f*.

♦ **clarion call** N (*liter*) appello.

clar·ity ['klærɪtɪ] N chiarezza.

clash [klæʃ] **1** N **a** (*noise*) fragore *m*, frastuono

b (*Mil, of personalities, interests*) scontro, conflitto; (*of dates, programmes*) conflitto; (*of colours*) contrasto, disarmonia; **a clash with the police** uno scontro con la polizia; **a clash of wills** uno scontro di idee.

2 vT (*cymbals*) far risuonare; (*swords*) far cozzare.

3 vi: **to clash (with)** (*fig: have an argument*) scontrarsi (con); (*personalities, interests*) scontrarsi (con), essere in conflitto (con); (*colours*) stridere (con); (*dates, events*) coincidere (con).

clasp [klɑːsp] **1** N fibbia, fermaglio.

2 vT afferrare; **to clasp one's hands (together)** stringere le mani; **to clasp sb in one's arms** stringere qn tra le braccia.

♦ **clasp knife** N coltello a serramanico.

class [klɑːs] **1** N (*social class, Bio, Scol, Univ*) classe *f*; (*group, category*) tipo, categoria; (*lesson*) lezione *f*; **to have class** (*fam*) avere classe; **to be in a class of one's own** essere impareggiabile.

2 vT: **to class sb as sth** definire qn qc.

♦ **class-conscious** ['klɑːsˌkɒnʃəs] ADJ che ha coscienza di classe.

♦ **class consciousness** N coscienza di classe.

♦ **class distinction** N (*Sociol*) distinzione *f* di classe.

clas·sic ['klæsɪk] **1** ADJ classico(-a).

2 N classico; see also **classics**.

clas·si·cal ['klæsɪkəl] ADJ classico(-a); **classical scholar** studioso(-a) di lettere antiche; **classical music** musica classica.

clas·si·cal·ly ['klæsɪklɪ] ADV classicamente.

clas·si·cism ['klæˌsɪsɪzəm] N classicismo.

clas·sics ['klæsɪks] NPL (*Scol, Univ*) studi *mpl* umanistici.

clas·si·fi·able ['klæsɪˌfaɪəbl] ADJ classificabile.

clas·si·fi·ca·tion [ˌklæsɪfɪ'keɪʃən] N classificazione *f*.

clas·si·fied ['klæsɪˌfaɪd] ADJ (*information*) segreto(-a), riservato(-a); **classified advertisements** or **ads** (*in newspaper*) piccola pubblicità.

clas·si·fy ['klæsɪˌfaɪ] vT classificare.

♦ **class interval** N (*Math*) intervallo di classe.

class·less ['klɑːslɪs] ADJ (*society*) aclassista, senza distinzioni di classe.

class·mate ['klɑːsˌmeɪt] N compagno(-a) di classe.

class·room ['klɑːsˌrʊm] N classe *f*, aula.

♦ **class war, class warfare** N (*Sociol*) lotta di classe.

classy ['klɑːsɪ] ADJ (*comp* -ier, *superl* -iest) (*fam*) di classe, chic *inv*.

clat·ter ['klætəʳ] **1** N (*of plates*) acciottolìo; (*of hooves*) scalpitìo.

2 vi (*metal object etc*) sferragliare; (*hooves*) scalpitare; **the gate clattered behind her** il cancello sbattè con fragore dietro di lei; **to clatter in/out** correre rumorosamente dentro/fuori.

3 vT (*plates*) acciottolare.

clause [klɔːz] N (*Gram*) proposizione *f*; (*in contract, law, will*) clausola.

claus·tro·pho·bia [ˌklɔːstrə'fəʊbɪə] N claustrofobia.

claus·tro·pho·bic [ˌklɔːstrə'fəʊbɪk] ADJ (*person*) claustrofobico(-a); (*atmosphere*) claustrofobico(-a), da claustrofobia.

clavi·cle ['klævɪkl] N (*Anat*) clavicola.

claw [klɔː] **1** N (*of cat, small bird*) unghia; (*of lion, eagle, bird of prey*) artiglio; (*of lobster*) chela, tenaglia.

2 vT graffiare; **to claw sth to shreds** dilaniare qc.

3 vi: **to claw at** graffiare; (*prey*) ghermire

► **claw back** vT + ADV (*tax, duty etc*) recuperare.

claw·back ['klɔːˌbæk] N (*of tax, duty etc*) recupero.

♦ **claw hammer** N martello a granchio.
clay [kleɪ] N (*gen*) argilla; (*for pottery*) creta, argilla.
♦ **clay court** N (*Tennis*) campo in terra battuta.
♦ **clay pigeon shooting** N tiro al piattello.
♦ **clay pipe** N pipa di terracotta.
clean [kli:n] [1] ADJ (*comp* **-er**, *superl* **-est**) (*gen*) pulito(-a); (*sheet of paper*) nuovo(-a); (*smooth, clear*: *outline, movement, break*) netto(-a); (*fair*: *fight, game*) leale, corretto(-a); **to wipe sth clean** pulire qc; **to make a clean sweep** fare piazza pulita; **the doctor gave me a clean bill of health** il medico ha garantito che godo di ottima salute; **to make a clean breast of sth** togliersi qc dalla coscienza; **a clean record** (*Police*) una fedina penale pulita; **to have a clean driving licence,** (*Am*) **to have a clean record** non aver mai preso contravvenzioni.
[2] ADV: **he clean forgot** si è completamente dimenticato; **he got clean away** se l'è svignata senza lasciare tracce; **the ball went clean through the window** la palla prese in pieno la finestra; **to come clean** (*fam*: *admit guilt*) confessare; (: *tell unpleasant truth*) dire veramente come stanno le cose; **I'm clean out of cigarettes** non ho neanche mezza sigaretta.
[3] N pulita, ripulitura.
[4] VT (*gen*) pulire; (*blackboard*) cancellare; (*shoes*) lucidare; **to clean one's teeth** (*Brit*) lavarsi i denti
► **clean off** VT + ADV (*mark*) togliere; (*chalk*) cancellare
► **clean out** VT + ADV (*also fig*) ripulire
► **clean up** [1] VT + ADV (*room, mess*) pulire, ripulire; (*fig*: *city, area*) fare un po' di pulizia in; **to clean o.s. up** darsi una ripulita.
[2] VI + ADV ripulire, far pulizia; (*fig*: *make profit*) fare una barca di soldi
► **clean up after** VT + ADV + PREP: **to clean up after sb** pulire lo sporco lasciato da qn.
♦ **clean-cut** ['kli:n'kʌt] ADJ (*line, shape*) netto(-a), nitido(-a); (*man*) curato(-a); (*situation etc*) ben definito(-a), chiaro(-a).
clean·er ['kli:nə'] N (*person*) addetto(-a) alle pulizie; (*product*) detersivo, detergente *m*; (*also*: **dry cleaner**) tintoria, lavanderia; **he took his coat to the cleaner's** ha portato il cappotto in lavanderia *or* tintoria.
clean·ing ['kli:nɪŋ] N pulizia; **to do the cleaning** fare le pulizie.
♦ **cleaning fluid** N (*stain remover*) smacchiatore *m*.
♦ **cleaning lady** N donna delle pulizie.
♦ **clean-limbed** ['kli:n'lɪmd] ADJ proporzionato(-a), ben fatto(-a).
clean·li·ness ['klɛnlɪnɪs] N pulizia.
♦ **clean-living** ['kli:n'lɪvɪŋ] ADJ onesto(-a).
clean·ly ['kli:nlɪ] ADV in modo netto.
clean·ness ['kli:nnɪs] N pulizia.
cleanse [klɛnz] VT pulire; (*fig*: *soul etc*) purificare.
cleans·er ['klɛnzə'] N (*detergent*) detersivo; (*cosmetic*) detergente *m* (*latte, gel, emulsione*).
♦ **clean-shaven** ['kli:n'ʃeɪvn] ADJ senza barba né baffi, sbarbato(-a).
cleans·ing ['klɛnzɪŋ] N (*see vb*) pulitura; purificazione *f.*
♦ **cleansing cream** N crema detergente.
♦ **cleansing department** N (*Brit*) nettezza urbana.
♦ **cleansing milk** N latte *m* detergente.
♦ **clean·up** ['kli:n.ʌp] N (*of house*) pulita, ripulita; **this room could do with a good cleanup** questa stanza avrebbe bisogno di una bella ripulita.
clear [klɪə'] [1] ADJ (*comp* **-er**, *superl* **-est**) a (*water*) chiaro(-a), limpido(-a); (*glass, plastic*) trasparente; (*air,*

sky, weather) sereno(-a); (*complexion*) senza brufoli o macchie; (*photograph, outline*) nitido(-a); (*conscience*) pulito(-a); **on a clear day** in una giornata limpida
b (*sound*) chiaro(-a), distinto(-a); (*impression, meaning, explanation*) chiaro(-a); (*motive, consequence*) ovvio(-a); (*understanding, proof*) certo(-a), sicuro(-a); (*profit, majority*) netto(-a); **a clear case of murder** un chiaro caso di omicidio; **to make o.s. clear** spiegarsi bene; **have I made myself clear?** mi sono spiegato?, sono stato chiaro?; **to make it clear to sb that** ... far capire a qn che...; **it is clear to me that** ... per me è evidente che...; **as clear as day** chiaro come il sole; **three clear days** tre giorni interi; **to win by a clear head** (*horse*) vincere di un'incollatura
c (*free*: *road, way, space*) libero(-a), sgombro(-a); **I have a clear day tomorrow** (*Brit*) non ho impegni domani; **we had a clear view** avevamo una buona visuale; **the ship was clear of the rocks** la nave aveva superato il pericolo delle rocce; **we're clear of the police now** ora siamo sufficientemente lontani dalla polizia; **all clear!** cessato pericolo!.
[2] ADV a see **loud**
b : **clear of** distante da; **to keep clear of sb/sth** tenersi lontano da qn/qc, stare alla larga da qn/qc; **to stand clear of sth** stare lontano da qc
c (*completely*) completamente; **to get clear away** svignarsela senza lasciar tracce.
[3] N: **to be in the clear** (*out of debt*) essere in attivo; (*out of suspicion*) essere a posto; (*out of danger*) essere fuori pericolo.
[4] VT a (*place, surface, road, railway track*) liberare, sgombrare; (*site, woodland*) spianare; (*pipe*) sbloccare; (*Med*: *blood*) purificare; **to clear a space for sth/sb** fare posto *or* spazio per qc/qn; **he cleared the path of leaves** ha sgombrato le foglie dal viale; **to clear the table** sparecchiare (la tavola); **to clear one's throat** schiarirsi la gola; **to clear the air** (*fig*) chiarire le cose; **to clear one's conscience** togliersi un peso dalla coscienza
b (*get over*: *fence etc*) scavalcare; (*get past*: *rocks*) evitare; **to clear 2 metres** (*athlete, horse*) superare i 2 metri
c (*declare innocent*) discolpare; **to clear sth (with sb)** (*get permission for*) ottenere il permesso (di qn) per qc; **he was cleared of murder** fu scagionato dall'accusa di omicidio; **to clear o.s.** provare la propria innocenza; **he'll have to be cleared by the security department** dovrà superare il controllo del dipartimento di sicurezza
d (*debt*) liquidare, saldare; (*stock*) svendere, liquidare; (*cheque*) fare la compensazione di; **to clear a profit** avere un profitto netto.
[5] VI (*weather, sky*) schiarirsi, rasserenarsi; (*smoke, fog*) dissolversi, andarsene
► **clear away** [1] VI + ADV (*mist, fog*) dissiparsi; (*clear the table*) sparecchiare.
[2] VT + ADV togliere
► **clear off** [1] VT + ADV (*debt*) saldare, liquidare.
[2] VI + ADV (*fam*: *go away*) tagliare la corda, squagliarsela
► **clear out** [1] VT + ADV (*cupboard*) liberare, sgombrare; (*rubbish*) gettare via.
[2] VI + ADV = **clear off** 2
► **clear up** [1] VT + ADV a (*matter, mystery*) chiarire, risolvere
b (*tidy*: *room etc*) mettere in ordine, rassettare.
[2] VI + ADV a (*weather*) schiarirsi, rasserenarsi
b (*tidy up*) fare ordine.

clear·ance ['klɪərəns] N **a** (*of road, room, surface*) sgombero; (*of woodland*) spianamento; (*of site, slum*) demolizione *f*; (*of rubbish, litter*) rimozione *f*
b (*for boat, car*) spazio libero
c (*authorization*) autorizzazione *f*, permesso; (*by customs*) sdoganamento; **clearance for take-off** (*Aer*) permesso di decollo
d (*Ftbl*) rinvio.
♦ **clearance sale** N svendita, (vendita di) liquidazione *f*.
♦ **clear-cut** ['klɪə‚kʌt] ADJ ben definito(-a) *or* delineato (-a), distinto(-a).
♦ **clear-headed** ['klɪə'hɛdɪd] ADJ lucido(-a).
clear·ing ['klɪərɪŋ] N (*in wood*) radura; (*Brit Banking*) clearing *m*.
♦ **clearing bank** N (*Brit Fin*) *banca che fa uso della camera di compensazione.*
♦ **clearing house** N (*Fin*) camera di compensazione.
clear·ly ['klɪəlɪ] ADV chiaramente.
clear·ness ['klɪənɪs] N (*of air, water, glass*) trasparenza; (*of sky*) serenità; (*of photograph, outline*) nitidezza; (*of sound, impression, thoughts*) chiarezza.
♦ **clear-sighted** ['klɪə'saɪtɪd] ADJ (*fig*) perspicace.
clear·way ['klɪə‚weɪ] N (*Brit Aut*) *strada in cui è vietata la sosta.*
cleat [kliːt] N (*Naut*) galloccia.
cleav·age ['kliːvɪdʒ] N décolleté *m inv*.
cleave [kliːv] (*pt* **cleave** *or* **cleft** *or* **clove**, *pp* **cleaved** *or* **cleft** *or* **cloven**) VT (*liter*) spaccare
► **cleave to** VI + PREP (*stick to*) aderire a; (*fig*) restare abbarbicato(-a).
cleav·er ['kliːvə'] N mannaia; **meat cleaver** (*Culin*) marrancio.
cleav·ers ['kliːvəz] NSG (*Bot*) attaccamani *m inv*, attaccavesti *m inv*.
clef [klɛf] N (*Mus*) chiave *f*.
cleft [klɛft] 1 PT, PP PP of **cleave**.
2 N (*in rock*) crepa, fenditura.
♦ **cleft palate** N (*Med*) palatoschisi *f*.
♦ **cleft stick** N: **in a cleft stick** (*fam*) in un vicolo cieco.
clema·tis ['klɛmətɪs] N clematide *f*.
clem·en·cy ['klɛmənsɪ] N (*frm*) clemenza.
clem·ent ['klɛmənt] (*frm*) ADJ (*person*) clemente; (*weather*) mite, clemente.
clem·en·tine ['klɛmən‚taɪn] N clementina, mandarancio.
clench [klɛntʃ] VT stringere; **to clench sth in one's hand** stringere in pugno qc.
Cleopatra [‚kliː:ə'pætrə] N Cleopatra.
cler·gy ['klɜ:dʒɪ] N clero.
clergy·man ['klɜ:dʒɪmən] N (*pl* -**men**) ecclesiastico.
cler·ic ['klɛrɪk] N ecclesiastico.
cleri·cal ['klɛrɪkəl] ADJ **a** (*Comm: job*) d'ufficio, da impiegato(-a); **clerical worker** impiegato(-a); **clerical error** svista **b** (*Rel*) clericale.
clerk [klɑ:k, *Am* [klɜ:k] N (*in office, bank*) impiegato(-a); (*Am: shop assistant*) commesso(-a); (: *in hotel*) impiegato (-a) della reception; **Clerk of the Court** (*Law*) cancelliere *m*.
♦ **clerk of the works** N sovrintendente *m/f* ai lavori.
clev·er ['klɛvə'] ADJ (*comp* -**er**, *superl* -**est**) (*gen*) intelligente; (*deft, skilful*) abile; (*ingenious: idea, person, device*) geniale; **to be clever at sth** essere abile in qc; **he is very clever with his hands** è molto abile *or* bravo nei lavori manuali; **he was too clever for us** era più furbo di noi.
♦ **clever Dick** ['klɛvə‚dɪk] N (*fam*) saputo(-a).
clev·er·ly ['klɛvəlɪ] ADV abilmente.

clev·er·ness ['klɛvənɪs] N (*intelligence*) intelligenza; (*deftness*) abilità; (*ingenuity*) genialità.
clew [kluː] N (*Am*) = **clue**.
cli·ché ['kliː:ʃeɪ] N cliché *m inv*.
click [klɪk] 1 N (*of camera etc*) scatto; (*of high heels*) tacchettio; (*of soldiers' boots*) battito; (*of tongue*) schiocco.
2 VT (*heels*) battere; (*tongue*) far schioccare.
3 VI (*camera etc*) scattare; (*heels*) ticchettare; **the door clicked shut** la porta si chiuse con uno scatto; **suddenly it all clicked (into place)** (*fig fam*) di colpo tutto è diventato chiaro.
click·ing ['klɪkɪŋ] N (*of typewriter*) ticchettio; (*of heels*) tacchettio.
cli·ent ['klaɪənt] N cliente *m/f*.
cli·en·tele [‚kliː:ã:n'tɛl] N clientela.
cliff [klɪf] N scogliera, rupe *f*.
cliff·hanger ['klɪf‚hæŋə'] N (*TV, fig*) *episodio o situazione ecc ricco di suspense.*
cli·mac·tic [klaɪ'mæktɪk] ADJ culminante.
cli·mate ['klaɪmɪt] N clima *m*; **the climate of popular opinion** l'opinione pubblica.
cli·mat·ic [klaɪ'mætɪk] ADJ climatico(-a).
cli·ma·tol·ogy [‚klaɪmə'tɒlədʒɪ] N climatologia.
cli·max ['klaɪmæks] N culmine *m*; (*of play etc*) momento più emozionante, climax *m inv*; (*sexual climax*) orgasmo.
climb [klaɪm] 1 N (*gen*) ascesa, salita; (*of mountain*) scalata, arrampicata; (*Aer*) ascesa.
2 VT (*also*: **climb up**: *tree, ladder etc*) salire su, arrampicarsi su; (: *staircase*) salire; (: *mountain, wall*) scalare; **to climb a rope** arrampicarsi su una corda.
3 VI (*road, person*) salire; (*plane*) prendere quota; (*plant*) arrampicarsi; **the pilot climbed into the cockpit** il pilota si è infilato nella cabina di pilotaggio; **to climb over a wall** scavalcare un muro
► **climb down** 1 VI + PREP scendere da.
2 VI + ADV scendere; (*fig: abandon one's position*) tornare sui suoi (*or* miei *etc*) passi.
♦ **climb-down** ['klaɪm‚daʊn] N ritirata.
climb·er ['klaɪmə'] N (*rock climber*) alpinista *m/f*, scalatore (-trice); (*Bot*) rampicante *m*.
climb·ing ['klaɪmɪŋ] N (*rock climbing*) alpinismo; **to go climbing** andare a far roccia.
♦ **climbing frame** N *struttura su cui i bambini possono arrampicarsi.*
clinch [klɪntʃ] 1 N: **in a clinch** (*fam: embrace*) abbracciati (-e) stretti(-e).
2 VT (*settle: deal*) concludere; (: *argument*) chiudere; **that clinches it** è fatta.
clinch·er ['klɪntʃə'] N (*fam*): **the clincher** il fattore decisivo.
cling [klɪŋ] VI (*pt, pp* **clung**) **a**: **to cling to** (*support, also fig*) aggrapparsi a; **to cling to one another** stringersi l'uno (-a) all'altro(-a) **b**: **to cling (to)** (*subj: clothes*) aderire strettamente (a); (: *smell*) impregnare; **the smell clung to her clothes** l'odore aveva impregnato i suoi abiti.
cling·film ['klɪŋ‚fɪlm], **clingwrap** ['klɪŋ‚ræp] N pellicola trasparente (*per alimenti*).
clin·ic ['klɪnɪk] N (*hospital, dental clinic etc*) clinica; (*for guidance etc*) centro; (*session*) seduta.
clini·cal ['klɪnɪkəl] ADJ clinico(-a); (*fig*) freddo(-a), distaccato(-a).
clini·cal·ly ['klɪnɪklɪ] ADV clinicamente; (*fig*) in modo impersonale.
clink [klɪŋk] 1 N tintinnio.
2 VT: **to clink glasses with sb** brindare *or* fare cin cin con

qn.

3 VI tintinnare.

clip[1] [klɪp] **1** N (*Cine*) sequenza.

2 VT (*cut: gen*) tagliare; (*sheep, dog*) tosare; (*hedge*) potare, tagliare; (*ticket*) forare; (*article from newspaper*) ritagliare; **to clip sb's wings** (*fig*) tarpare le ali a qn.

clip[2] [klɪp] **1** N (*paperclip*) graffetta; (*Brit: bulldog clip*) fermafogli *m inv*; (*hair clip*) molletta; (*brooch*) spilla, fermaglio; (*holding hose etc*) anello d'attacco.

2 VT (*also:* **clip together**: *papers*) attaccare (con una graffetta)

▶ **clip on** VT + ADV (*brooch*) agganciare; (*document: with paper clip etc*) attaccare

▶ **clip together** VT + ADV attaccare (con una graffetta).

clip·board ['klɪp,bɔːd] N fermabloc *m inv*.

clipped [klɪpt] ADJ: **in a clipped voice** scandendo bene le sillabe.

clip·per ['klɪpə'] N (*Naut*) clipper *m inv*.

clip·pers ['klɪpəz] NPL (*for nails*) tagliaunghie *m inv*; (*for hair*) macchinetta per capelli; (*for hedge*) tosasiepi *m inv*, cesoie *fpl*.

clip·ping ['klɪpɪŋ] N (*from newspaper*) ritaglio.

clique [kliːk] N cricca.

cli·quish ['kliːkɪʃ], **cli·quey** ['kliːkɪ] ADJ (*pej*) che tende ad unirsi in gruppi chiusi.

clito·ris ['klɪtərɪs] N clitoride *m or f*.

cloak [kləʊk] **1** N cappa, mantello; **under the cloak of darkness** (*fig*) sotto il manto delle tenebre.

2 VT avvolgere.

♦ **cloak-and-dagger** [,kləʊkən'dægə'] ADJ (*film etc*) del mistero; (*activities*) misterioso(-a).

cloak·room ['kləʊk,rʊm] N (*for coats*) guardaroba *m inv*; (*Brit euph*) toilette *f inv*.

♦ **cloakroom attendant** N guardarobiere(-a).

♦ **cloakroom ticket** N scontrino del guardaroba.

clob·ber ['klɒbə'] (*fam*) **1** N **a** (*belongings*) roba.

2 VT **a** (*hit*) pestare **b** (*defeat*) dare una batosta a, battere.

clock [klɒk] **1** N (*gen*) orologio; (*of taxi*) tassametro; **30,000 on the clock** (*Brit Aut*) 30.000 sul contachilometri; **around the clock** ventiquattr'ore su ventiquattro; **to sleep round the clock** *or* **the clock round** dormire un giorno intero; **to work against the clock** lavorare in gara col tempo.

2 VT (*time*) registrare; (: *of runner*) cronometrare

▶ **clock in, clock on** VI + ADV (*Brit*) timbrare il cartellino (all'entrata)

▶ **clock off, clock out** VI + ADV (*Brit*) timbrare il cartellino (all'uscita)

▶ **clock up** VT + ADV (*Aut*) registrare, fare; (*miles, hours etc*) fare.

clock·maker ['klɒk,meɪkə'] N orologiaio.

♦ **clock radio** N radiosveglia.

♦ **clock-watcher** ['klɒk,wɒtʃə'] N: **to be a clockwatcher** controllare con impazienza l'ora *or* l'orologio (*detto di lavoratore*).

clock·wise ['klɒk,waɪz] ADV in senso orario.

clock·work ['klɒk,wɜːk] **1** N: **to go like clockwork** (*fig*) funzionare alla perfezione.

2 ADJ (*toy, train*) a molla.

clod [klɒd] N zolla.

clog [klɒg] **1** N zoccolo.

2 VT (*also:* **clog up**: *pipe, drain*) ostruire, intasare; (: *machine, mechanism*) bloccare.

3 VI (*also:* **clog up**) intasarsi, bloccarsi.

clois·ter ['klɔɪstə'] N chiostro.

clois·tered ['klɔɪstəd] ADJ (*life*) da recluso(-a).

clone [kləʊn] **1** N clone *m*.

2 VT clonare.

clonk [klɒŋk] (*fam*) **1** N tonfo.

2 VT colpire.

close[1] [kləʊs] **1** ADV vicino, dappresso; **close by** [OR] **close at hand** qui *or* lì vicino; **to hold sb close** tenere stretto(-a) qn; **close together** vicino; **stay close to me** stammi vicino; **to follow close behind** seguire da vicino.

2 ADJ **a** (*near*) vicino(-a); (: *relative, connection, resemblance*) stretto(-a); (: *friend*) intimo(-a); (*almost equal: result*) quasi pari; (: *fight, contest, election, race*) combattuto(-a); **the house is close to the shops** la casa è vicina ai negozi; **they're very close** (*in age*) sono molto vicini come età; (*emotionally*) sono molto uniti; **at close quarters** da vicino; **close combat** combattimento corpo a corpo; **that was a close shave** (*fig fam*) l'ho (*or* l'hai *etc*) scampata per un pelo

b (*exact, detailed: examination, study*) accurato(-a), attento(-a); (: *investigation, questioning*) approfondito (-a); (: *surveillance, control, watch*) stretto(-a); **to pay close attention to sb/sth** stare ben attento(-a) a qn/qc; **to keep a close watch on sb** guardare qn a vista

c (*handwriting, texture, weave*) fitto(-a)

d (*stuffy: atmosphere, room*) soffocante; (*weather*) afoso (-a); **it's rather close in here** qui c'è aria viziata.

close[2] [kləʊz] **1** N (*end*) fine *f*, chiusura; **to bring sth to a close** terminare qc; **to draw to a close** avvicinarsi alla fine.

2 VI (*shut: shop etc*) chiudere; (: *lid, door etc*) chiudersi; (*end*) chiudersi, concludersi, finire.

3 VT **a** (*shut: door, road, shop etc*) chiudere; **to close the gap between two things** (*fig*) colmare il divario tra due cose; **to close one's eyes to sth** (*fig*) ignorare qc

b (*end: discussion, meeting*) chiudere, concludere; (: *bank account*) chiudere, estinguere; (: *bargain, deal*) concludere

▶ **close down** **1** VI + ADV (*business*) chiudersi, chiudere; (*TV, Radio*) terminare le trasmissioni.

2 VT + ADV chiudere (definitivamente).

▶ **close in** VI + ADV (*hunters*) stringersi attorno; (*evening, night, fog*) calare; **the days are closing in** le giornate si accorciano; **to close in on sb** accerchiare qn

▶ **close off** VT + ADV (*area*) chiudere

▶ **close round** VI + PREP stringersi attorno a

▶ **close up** **1** VI + ADV (*people in queue*) stringersi; (*wound*) rimarginarsi.

2 VT + ADV (*shop, house, opening*) chiudere; (*wound*) chiudere, suturare.

♦ **close-cropped** [,kləʊs'krɒpt] ADJ (*hair*) corti corti *pl*.

closed [kləʊzd] ADJ chiuso(-a); **sociology is a closed book to me** per me la sociologia è un mistero.

♦ **closed-circuit tele·vi·sion** ['kləʊzd,sɜːkɪt'telɪ,vɪʒən] N televisione *f* a circuito chiuso.

♦ **close-down** ['kləʊz,daʊn] N (*of shop, factory*) chiusura; (*TV, Radio*) fine *f* delle trasmissioni.

♦ **closed shop** N (*Industry*) *fabbrica, ditta* or *negozio che assume solo lavoratori iscritti al sindacato*.

♦ **close-fisted** [,kləʊs'fɪstɪd] ADJ avaro(-a), taccagno(-a).

♦ **close-fitting** [,kləʊs'fɪtɪŋ] ADJ aderente, attillato(-a).

♦ **close-hauled** [,kləʊs'hɔːld] ADJ (*Naut*) di bolina.

♦ **close-knit** [,kləʊs'nɪt] ADJ (*community, group, family*) molto unito(-a).

♦ **close-lipped**   [,kləʊs'lɪpt],   **close-mouthed**

[ˌkləʊs'maʊðd] ADJ riservato(-a); **the government is remaining very close-lipped about the matter** il governo non sta lasciando trapelare nulla sulla faccenda.

close·ly ['kləʊslɪ] ADV (*guard*) strettamente, attentamente; (*examine, study, watch, follow*) da vicino, attentamente; (*listen*) attentamente; (*resemble*) molto; (*connected*) strettamente; **a closely guarded secret** un segreto gelosamente custodito; **we are closely related** siamo parenti stretti.

close·ness ['kləʊsnɪs] N (*nearness*) vicinanza; (*of friendship*) profondità; (*of room*) mancanza d'aria; **the closeness of the weather** il tempo afoso; **the closeness of the resemblance** la stretta somiglianza.

♦ **close-run** [ˌkləʊs'rʌn] ADJ: **a close-run match** un incontro molto combattuto.

♦ **close season** ['kləʊsˌsiːsən] N (*Hunting*) stagione *f* di chiusura (*di caccia, pesca etc*).

♦ **close-set** [ˌkləʊs'sɛt] ADJ (*eyes*) ravvicinato(-a).

♦ **close-shaven** [ˌkləʊs'ʃeɪvn] ADJ ben rasato(-a).

clos·et ['klɒzɪt] **1** N (*Am: cupboard*) armadio; **to come out of the closet** (*fam*) uscire allo scoperto.

2 VT: **to be closeted with sb** essersi appartato(-a) con qn.

♦ **close-up** ['kləʊsˌʌp] N primo piano; **in close-up** in primo piano.

clos·ing ['kləʊzɪŋ] ADJ (*stages, remarks*) conclusivo(-a), finale; **closing speech** discorso di chiusura; **closing price** (*Stock Exchange*) prezzo di chiusura.

♦ **closing time** N (*of pub, shop*) orario di chiusura; **when is closing time?** a che ora chiude?

clo·sure ['kləʊʒəʳ] N chiusura.

clot [klɒt] **1** N (*Med: also:* **blood clot**) coagulo, grumo; (*fam: idiot*) scemo(-a), zuccone(-a); **to have a clot on the brain/in the leg** avere un grumo (di sangue) nel cervello/in una gamba.

2 VI coagularsi.

cloth [klɒθ] N (*material*) tessuto, stoffa; (*for cleaning*) panno, straccio; (*Brit: also:* **teacloth**) telo per i piatti; (*also:* **tablecloth**) tovaglia; **a man of the cloth** (*Rel*) un religioso, un ecclesiastico.

♦ **cloth cap** N berretto.

clothe [kləʊð] VT vestire.

♦ **cloth-eared** [ˌklɒθ'ɪəd] ADJ (*fam*) sordo(-a).

clothes [kləʊðz] NPL vestiti *mpl*, abiti *mpl*; **to put one's clothes on** vestirsi; **to take one's clothes off** togliersi i vestiti, svestirsi, spogliarsi.

♦ **clothes basket** N cesto *m* portabiancheria *inv*.

♦ **clothes brush** N spazzola per abiti.

♦ **clothes hanger** N gruccia, portabiti *m inv*.

♦ **clothes horse** N stendibiancheria *m inv*.

♦ **clothes line** N corda del bucato.

♦ **clothes peg**, (*Am*) **clothes pin** N molletta (da bucato).

♦ **clothes shop** N negozio di abbigliamento.

cloth·ing ['kləʊðɪŋ] N abbigliamento; **article of clothing** capo di vestiario *or* di abbigliamento.

♦ **clothing allowance** N indennità *f inv* per gli abiti da lavoro.

clot·ted cream [ˌklɒtɪd'kriːm] N (*Brit*) panna rappresa (*ottenuta per riscaldamento*).

cloud [klaʊd] **1** N (*Met*) nuvola, nube *f*; (*of dust, smoke, gas*) nube; (*of insects*) nugolo; **to be under a cloud** essere malvisto(-a); **he has his head in the clouds** ha la testa tra le nuvole; **to be on cloud nine** essere al settimo cielo; **every cloud has a silver lining** (*Proverb*) non tutto il male

vien per nuocere.

2 VT (*liquid*) intorbidire; (*mirror*) appannare; (*fig: judgement*) confondere; (: *mind*) turbare; **a clouded sky** un cielo nuvoloso; **to cloud the issue** imbrogliare la questione

▶ **cloud over** VI + ADV (*also fig*) rannuvolarsi, offuscarsi.

cloud·burst ['klaʊdˌbɜːst] N acquazzone *m*.

♦ **cloud chamber** N (*Phys*) camera a nube.

♦ **cloud-cuckoo-land** [ˌklaʊd'kʊkuːˌlænd] N mondo dei sogni.

cloudi·ness ['klaʊdnɪs] N (*see adj*) nuvolosità; torbidezza.

cloud·less ['klaʊdlɪs] ADJ sereno(-a), senza nubi.

cloudy ['klaʊdɪ] ADJ (*sky*) nuvoloso(-a), coperto(-a); (*liquid*) torbido(-a).

clout [klaʊt] **1** N (*blow*) ceffone *m*; (*fig: power, influence*) influenza.

2 VT colpire.

clove¹ [kləʊv] **1** PT of **cleave**.

2 N chiodo di garofano; **clove of garlic** spicchio d'aglio.

clove² [kləʊv] ADJ (*Naut*): **clove hitch** (nodo) parlato.

clo·ven ['kləʊvən] PP of **cleave**.

♦ **cloven hoof** N zoccolo fesso.

clo·ver ['kləʊvəʳ] N trifoglio; **a four-leaved clover** un quadrifoglio; **red clover** trifoglio pratense *or* rosso; **white clover** trifoglio bianco; **to be in clover** (*fam*) nuotare nell'abbondanza.

clover·leaf ['kləʊvəˌliːf] N (*Bot*) foglia di trifoglio; (*Aut*) raccordo (a quadrifoglio).

clown [klaʊn] **1** N (*in circus*) pagliaccio, clown *m inv*; (*fam*) buffone *m*.

2 VI (*also:* **clown about** *or* **around**) fare il buffone *or* il pagliaccio.

clown·ing ['klaʊnɪŋ] N pagliacciate *fpl*, buffonate *fpl*.

clown·ish ['klaʊnɪʃ] ADJ claunesco(-a).

cloy [klɔɪ] VI essere nauseante.

cloy·ing ['klɔɪɪŋ] ADJ (*taste, smell*) stucchevole.

club [klʌb] **1** N **a** (*society*) circolo, club *m inv*; **tennis club** circolo di tennis; **join the club!** (*fig*) non sei il solo!

b (*stick*) randello; (*of caveman*) clava; (*golf club*) mazza

c : **clubs** (*Cards*) fiori *mpl*; **he played a club** ha giocato (una carta di) fiori.

2 VT (*person*) bastonare; **clubbed to death with sticks** ucciso(-a) a colpi di bastone.

3 VI: **to club together (to buy)** mettersi insieme (per comprare).

♦ **club car** N (*Am Rail*) carrozza *or* vagone *m* ristorante.

♦ **club class** N (*Aer*) classe *f* club *inv*.

♦ **club foot** N (*Med*) piede *m* affetto da talismo.

club·house ['klʌbˌhaʊs] N circolo.

♦ **club member** N socio(-a) di un club.

♦ **club sandwich** N tramezzino *m*.

♦ **club soda** N (*Am*) soda.

cluck [klʌk] VI chiocciare.

clue [kluː] N indicazione *f*; (*in a crime etc*) indizio; (*in crosswords*) definizione *f*; **I'll give you a clue** ti metto sulla strada giusta; **I haven't a clue** (*fam*) non (ne) ho la minima idea.

♦ **clued-up** [kluːd'ʌp], **clued-in** [kluːd'ɪn] ADJ (*fam*) (ben) informato(-a).

clue·less ['kluːlɪs] ADJ (*fam*): **to be clueless** essere un(a) incapace.

clump¹ [klʌmp] N (*of trees*) gruppo; (*flowers*) macchia; (*of grass*) ciuffo.

clump² [klʌmp] **1** N rumore *m* sordo, tonfo.

2 VI: **to clump (about)** camminare con passo pesante.

clum·si·ly ['klʌmzɪlɪ] ADV goffamente, maldestramente; (*tactlessly*) senza (alcun) tatto; **a clumsily executed forgery** un falso mal eseguito; **a clumsily designed tool** un utensile poco pratico.

clum·si·ness ['klʌmzɪnɪs] N (*of person, action, apology*) goffaggine *f*; (*of remark*) mancanza di tatto; (*of painting, forgery*) cattiva esecuzione *f*; (*of tool*) scarsa praticità.

clum·sy ['klʌmzɪ] ADJ (*person, action, gesture*) goffo(-a), maldestro(-a); (*painting, forgery*) malfatto(-a); (*object*) mal costruito(-a); (*tool*) poco pratico(-a); (*remark*) maldestro(-a); (*apology*) goffo(-a).

clung [klʌŋ] PT, PP of **cling**.

clus·ter ['klʌstə'] 1 N (*of houses, people, trees*) gruppo; (*of grapes*) grappolo; (*of stars*) ammasso.

2 VI (*people, things*): **to cluster (round sb/sth)** raggrupparsi (intorno a qn/qc).

clutch[1] [klʌtʃ] 1 N **a** (*Aut*) frizione *f*; (*pedal*) (pedale *m* della) frizione **b** (*grip, grasp*) presa, stretta; **to fall into sb's clutches** cadere nelle grinfie di qn.

2 VT (*catch hold of*) afferrare; (*hold tightly*) tenere stretto (-a), stringere forte.

3 VI: **to clutch at** cercare di afferrare; **to clutch at straws** (*fig*) crearsi delle illusioni.

clutch[2] [klʌtʃ] N (*of eggs, chickens*) covata.

♦ **clutch bag** N pochette *f inv.*

♦ **clutch pedal** N (*Aut*) pedale *m* della frizione.

♦ **clutch plate** N (*Aut*) disco della frizione.

clut·ter ['klʌtə'] 1 N confusione *f*, disordine *m*; **in a clutter** in disordine.

2 VT (*also*: **clutter up**) ingombrare; **to be cluttered up with sth** essere pieno(-a) zeppo(-a) *or* ingombro(-a) di qc.

cm ABBR (= *centimetre*) cm.

CNAA [,si:ɛneɪ'eɪ] N ABBR (*Brit*: = *Council for National Academic Awards*) *organizzazione che conferisce titoli accademici.*

CND [,si:ɛn'di:] N ABBR = *Campaign for Nuclear Disarmament.*

CO 1 N ABBR **a** (= *commanding officer*) Com. **b** (*Brit*)= *Commonwealth Office.*

2 ABBR (*Am Post*)= *Colorado.*

co- [kəʊ] PREF co... .

Co. ABBR **a** (= *company*) C., C.ia **b** = *county.*

c/o ABBR (= *care of*) c/o.

coach [kəʊtʃ] 1 N **a** (*bus*) corriera, pullman *m inv*; (: *for excursions*) pullman *m inv*; (*Brit*: *of train*) carrozza, vettura; (*horse drawn*) carrozza; (: *stage coach*) diligenza **b** (*Sport*) allenatore(-trice); (*tutor*) chi dà ripetizioni.

2 VT (*team*) allenare; (*student*) dare ripetizioni a.

coach·load ['kəʊtʃ,ləʊd] N: **a coachload of football fans** un pullman di tifosi di calcio.

♦ **coach party** N gruppo di gitanti (*che viaggia in pullman*).

♦ **coach trip** N escursione *f or* viaggio in pullman.

co·agu·lant [kəʊ'ægjʊlənt] N coagulante *m.*

co·agu·late [kəʊ'ægjʊleɪt] 1 VT coagulare.

2 VI coagularsi.

co·agu·la·tion [kəʊ,ægjʊ'leɪʃən] N coagulazione *f.*

coal [kəʊl] 1 N carbone *m*; **to carry coals to Newcastle** (*fig*) portare acqua al mare.

2 ADJ (*fire*) di carbone; (*industry*) del carbone; (*stove*) a carbone.

♦ **coal-black** ['kəʊl'blæk] ADJ nero(-a) come il carbone.

♦ **coal cellar, coal shed** N carbonaia.

♦ **coal dust** N polvere *f* di carbone.

coa·lesce [,kəʊə'lɛs] VI (*frm*) fondersi, unirsi.

coal·face ['kəʊl,feɪs] N fronte *f* di abbattimento (*di filone carbonifero*).

coal·field ['kəʊl,fi:ld] N bacino carbonifero.

♦ **coal gas** N gas *m inv* illuminante.

coa·li·tion [,kəʊə'lɪʃən] N (*Pol*) coalizione *f.*

coal·man ['kəʊl,mæn] N (*pl* -men) carbonaio.

♦ **coal merchant** N negoziante *m* di carbone.

♦ **coal mine** N miniera di carbone.

♦ **coal miner** N minatore *m.*

♦ **coal mining** N estrazione *f* del carbone.

♦ **coal scuttle** N secchio del carbone.

♦ **coal shed** N = **coal cellar**.

♦ **coal tar** N catrame *m* minerale.

♦ **coal tit** N (*Zool*) cincia mora.

coarse [kɔ:s] ADJ (*comp* -er, *superl* -est) (*texture, skin, material*) ruvido(-a); (*salt, sand*) grosso(-a); (*sandpaper*) a grana grossa; (*vulgar*: *character, laugh, remark*) volgare.

♦ **coarse-grained** [,kɔ:s'greɪnd] ADJ (*sandpaper*) a grana grossa; (*person*) grossolano(-a).

coarse·ly ['kɔ:slɪ] ADV (*ground, woven*) grossolanamente; (*laugh, say*) volgarmente.

coars·en ['kɔ:sn] 1 VI (*skin*) irruvidirsi; (*person, manners*) diventare grossolano(-a).

2 VT (*see vi*) irruvidire; rendere grossolano(-a).

coarse·ness ['kɔ:snɪs] N (*of material*) ruvidezza; (*of salt, sand*) grossezza; (*of laugh, remark*) volgarità *f inv.*

coast [kəʊst] 1 N costa; (*also*: **coastline**) litorale *m*; **the coast is clear** (*fig*) la via è libera.

2 VI (*Aut*) andare in folle; (*Cycling*) andare a ruota libera.

coast·al ['kəʊstəl] ADJ costiero(-a).

coast·er ['kəʊstə'] N **a** (*Naut*) nave *f* da cabotaggio **b** (*for glass*) sottobicchiere *m.*

coast·guard ['kəʊst,gɑ:d] N (*person*) guardacoste *m inv*; (*organization*) guardia costiera.

♦ **coastguard vessel** N guardacoste *m inv* (*nave*).

coast·line ['kəʊst,laɪn] N litorale *m*, linea costiera.

coat [kəʊt] 1 N **a** (*garment*) cappotto, soprabito **b** (*of animal*) pelo, mantello **c** (*layer*) strato; (*of paint*) mano *f* **d** : **coat of arms** stemma *m*, blasone *m.*

2 VT: **to coat sth with** ricoprire qc con uno strato di; (*paint*) dare a qc una mano di.

♦ **coat hanger** ['kəʊt,hæŋə'] N gruccia, stampella.

coat·ing ['kəʊtɪŋ] N (*film, layer*) mano, strato; (*for protection*) rivestimento (esterno).

♦ **coat of mail** N cotta di maglia, giaco.

coat·stand ['kəʊt,stænd] N attaccapanni *m inv.*

♦ **coat-tails** ['kəʊt,teɪlz] NPL falde *fpl* del frac.

co·author ['kəʊ,ɔ:θə'] N coautore(-trice).

coax [kəʊks] VT: **to coax sth out of sb** ottenere qc da qn (con le buone); **to coax sb into/out of doing sth** convincere *or* indurre (con moine) qn a fare/non fare qc.

coax·ing ['kəʊksɪŋ] N moine *fpl.*

coax·ing·ly ['kəʊksɪŋlɪ] ADV con fare dolce, con fare accattivante.

cob [kɒb] N see **corn**.

co·balt ['kəʊbɒlt] N cobalto.

cob·ble ['kɒbl] N (*also*: **cobblestone**) ciottolo.

cob·bled ['kɒbld] ADJ: **cobbled street** strada pavimentata con ciottoli.

cob·bler ['kɒblə'] N calzolaio.

cobble·stones ['kɒbl,stəʊnz] NPL ciottoli *mpl.*

cob·nut ['kɒb,nʌt] N nocciola.

COBOL ['kəʊbɒl] N ABBR (*Comput*: = *common business*

orientated language) COBOL *m*.

co·bra ['kəʊbrə] N cobra *m inv*.

cob·web ['kɒb,wɛb] N ragnatela.

Coca-Cola® [,kəʊkə'kəʊlə] N coca-cola ® *f inv*.

co·caine [kə'keɪn] N cocaina.

coc·cyx ['kɒksɪks] N (*Anat*) coccige *m*.

coch·lea ['kɒklɪə] N (*pl* **cochleae** ['kɒklɪˌiː]) (*Anat*) coclea.

cock [kɒk] ⓵ N **a** (*rooster*) gallo; (*male bird*) maschio **b** (*fam!: penis*) cazzo (*fam!*).

⓶ VT (*gun*) armare; **to cock (up) one's ears** (*also fig*) drizzare le orecchie; **to cock a snook at** (*make rude gesture*) fare marameo a; (*fig*) burlarsi di

▶ **cock up** VT + ADV (*Brit fam*) incasinare; see also **cock-up**.

cock·ade [kɒ'keɪd] N coccarda.

♦ **cock-a-doodle-doo** [,kɒkə,duː'dəl'duː] N chicchirichì *m inv*.

♦ **cock-a-hoop** [,kɒkə'huːp] ADJ esultante, euforico(-a).

♦ **cock-and-bull** [,kɒkənd'bʊl] ADJ: **cock-and-bull story** frottola.

cocka·too [,kɒkə'tuː] N cacatoa *m inv*.

cock·chafer ['kɒk,tʃeɪfə'] N maggiolino.

cock·crow ['kɒk,krəʊ] N: **at cockcrow** al primo canto del gallo, all'alba.

cock·er ['kɒkə'] N (*also:* **cocker spaniel**) cocker (spaniel) *m inv*.

cock·er·el ['kɒkərəl] N galletto.

cock·eyed ['kɒk,aɪd] ADJ (*crooked*) storto(-a); (*absurd*) assurdo(-a), strampalato(-a).

cock·fight ['kɒk,faɪt] N combattimento di galli.

cocki·ness ['kɒkɪnɪs] N (*fam pej*) impertinenza.

cock·le ['kɒkl] N (*shellfish*) cardio; **it warmed the cockles of my heart** mi riempì il cuore di gioia.

cock·ney ['kɒknɪ] N (*person*) cockney *m/f inv*, abitante dei quartieri dell'East End di Londra; (*dialect*) cockney *m*.

cock·pit ['kɒk,pɪt] N (*Aer*) cabina di pilotaggio, abitacolo.

cock·roach ['kɒk,rəʊtʃ] N scarafaggio, blatta.

cock·sure [,kɒk'ʃʊə'] ADJ troppo sicuro(-a) di sé, baldanzoso(-a).

cock·tail ['kɒk,teɪl] N (*drink*) cocktail *m inv*; **fruit cocktail** macedonia di frutta; **prawn cocktail**, (*Am*) **shrimp cocktail** cocktail *m inv* di gamberetti.

♦ **cocktail bar** N bar *m inv* (*di un albergo*).

♦ **cocktail cabinet** N mobile *m* bar *inv*.

♦ **cocktail party** N cocktail *m inv*.

♦ **cock·tail shak·er** ['kɒt,teɪl'ʃeɪkə'] N shaker *m inv*.

♦ **cock-up** N (*Brit fam*) casino.

cocky ['kɒkɪ] ADJ (*comp* **-ier**, *superl* **-iest**) (*pej*) troppo sicuro(-a) di sé.

co·coa ['kəʊkəʊ] N cacao; (*drink*) cioccolata calda.

coco·nut ['kəʊkə,nʌt] N (*fruit*) noce *f* di cocco; (*tree: also:* **coconut palm**) palma di cocco; (*substance*) cocco.

♦ **coco·nut matting** ['kəʊkənʌt'mætɪŋ] N stuoia (di fibra) di cocco.

♦ **coconut shy** N gioco di tiro al bersaglio in cui si devono abbattere noci di cocco.

co·coon [kə'kuːn] N bozzolo.

co·cooned [kə'kuːnd] ADJ chiuso(-a) nel proprio bozzolo.

COD [,siːəʊ'diː] ABBR = **cash on delivery**, *Am* **collect on delivery**; see **collect**.

cod [kɒd] N merluzzo.

cod·dle ['kɒdl] VT (*Culin: esp eggs*) cuocere a fuoco lento; (*also:* **mollycoddle**) coccolare.

code [kəʊd] ⓵ N codice *m*; (*Telec*) prefisso; **in code** in

codice; **code of behaviour** regole *fpl* di condotta.

⓶ VT cifrare.

co·deine ['kəʊdiːn] N codeina.

♦ **code name** N nome *m* in codice.

♦ **code number** N (numero di) codice *m*.

♦ **code of practice** N codice *m* professionale.

codg·er ['kɒdʒə'] N: **an old codger** (*Brit fam*) un nonnetto.

codi·cil ['kɒdɪsɪl] N (*Law*) codicillo.

codi·fy ['kəʊdɪfaɪ] VT codificare (*leggi*).

cod·ing ['kəʊdɪŋ] N codificazione *f*.

♦ **cod-liver oil** ['kɒdlɪvər'ɔɪl] N olio di fegato di merluzzo.

♦ **co-driver** ['kəʊdraɪvə'] N (*in race*) copilota *m/f*; (*of lorry*) secondo autista *m*.

cods·wallop ['kɒdz,wɒləp] N (*Brit fam*) stupidaggini *fpl*, sciocchezze *fpl*.

♦ **co-ed** ['kəʊ'ɛd] (*fam*) ⓵ ADJ misto(-a).

⓶ N (*Am: female student*) studentessa di un'università mista; (*Brit: school*) scuola mista.

co·edu·ca·tion ['kəʊ,ɛdjʊ'keɪʃən] N (istruzione *f* in) scuole *fpl* miste.

co·edu·ca·tion·al [,kəʊɛdjʊ'keɪʃənl] ADJ misto(-a).

co·ef·fi·cient [,kəʊɪ'fɪʃənt] N coefficiente *m*.

co·erce [kəʊ'ɜːs] VT: **to coerce sb (into doing sth)** costringere qn (a fare qc).

co·er·cion [kəʊ'ɜːʃən] N forza; (*Law*) coercizione *f*.

co·er·cive [kəʊ'ɜːsɪv] ADJ coercitivo(-a).

co·ex·ist [,kəʊɪg'zɪst] VI coesistere.

co·ex·ist·ence [,kəʊɪg'zɪstəns] N coesistenza.

C. of C. [,siːəv'siː] N ABBR = **chamber of commerce**.

C. of E. [,siːə'viː] N ABBR = **Church of England**.

cof·fee ['kɒfɪ] N caffè *m inv*; **black coffee** caffè nero; **white coffee**, (*Am*) **coffee with cream** caffè con latte; **two white coffees, please** due caffè con latte, per favore.

♦ **coffee bar** N (*Brit*) caffè *m inv*.

♦ **coffee bean** N grano *or* chicco di caffè *m inv*.

♦ **coffee break** N pausa per il caffè.

coffee-cake ['kɒfɪ,keɪk] N (*Am*) panino dolce all'uva.

♦ **coffee cup** N tazzina da caffè.

♦ **coffee mill** N macinacaffè *m*, macinino da caffè.

♦ **coffee morning** N incontro a scopo benefico tenuto al mattino, con caffè e pasticcini.

♦ **coffee percolator** N caffettiera a pressione.

coffee-pot ['kɒfɪ,pɒt] N caffettiera.

♦ **coffee shop** N **a** (*bar*) caffè *m inv* **b** (*shop*) torrefazione *f*.

♦ **coffee spoon** N cucchiaino da caffè.

♦ **coffee table** N tavolino.

♦ **coffee-table book** N (*pej*) libro da mettere in mostra.

cof·fer ['kɒfə'] N (*chest*) forziere *m*.

cof·fin ['kɒfɪn] N bara.

cog [kɒg] N dente *m*; **a cog in the wheel** (*fig*) una rotella in un grande ingranaggio.

co·gen·cy ['kəʊdʒənsɪ] N (*frm*) forza (di persuasione).

co·gent ['kəʊdʒənt] ADJ (*frm*) convincente.

co·gent·ly ['kəʊdʒəntlɪ] ADV (*frm*) in modo convincente.

cogi·tate ['kɒdʒɪ,teɪt] VI (*frm*) meditare.

cogi·ta·tion [,kɒdʒɪ'teɪʃən] N (*frm*) meditazione *f*.

cog·nac ['kɒnjæk] N cognac *m inv*.

cog·ni·tion [,kɒg'nɪʃn] N (*frm*) apprendimento.

cog·ni·tive ['kɒgnɪtɪv] ADJ (*frm*) cognitivo(-a).

cog·ni·tiv·ism ['kɒgnɪtɪ,vɪzəm] N (*Philosophy*) cognitivismo.

cog·ni·zance, **cog·ni·sance** ['kɒgnɪzəns] N (*frm*) conoscenza; **to take cognisance of sth** tener conto di qc.

cog·ni·zant, **cog·ni·sant** [ˈkɒgnɪzənt] ADJ: **to be cognizant of** (frm) rendersi conto di.

co·gno·scen·ti [ˌkɒnjəʊˈʃɛntɪ] NPL: **the cognoscenti** (frm) gli esperti.

cog·wheel [ˈkɒgˌwiːl] N ruota dentata.

co·hab·it [kəʊˈhæbɪt] VI (frm): **to cohabit (with sb)** coabitare (con qn).

co·her·ence [kəʊˈhɪərəns] N coerenza.

co·her·ent [kəʊˈhɪərənt] ADJ coerente.

co·her·ent·ly [kəʊˈhɪərəntlɪ] ADV coerentemente.

co·he·sion [kəʊˈhiːʒən] N coesione f.

co·he·sive [kəʊˈhiːsɪv] ADJ (fig) unificante, coesivo(-a).

co·hort [ˈkəʊhɔːt] N (Mil) coorte f.

COHSE [ˈkəʊzɪ] N ABBR (Brit: = Confederation of Health Service Employees) confederazione dei dipendenti del Servizio Sanitario.

COI [ˌsiːəʊˈaɪ] N ABBR (Brit)= Central Office of Information.

coil [kɔɪl] **1** N **a** (roll) rotolo; (single loop) anello, giro; (of hair) ciocca; (of snake) spira; (of smoke) filo **b** (Aut, Elec) bobina **c** : **the coil** (contraceptive) la spirale.
2 VT avvolgere; **to coil sth up** avvolgere qc (in un rotolo).
3 VI attorcigliarsi.

coin [kɔɪn] **1** N moneta; **a 5p coin** una moneta da 5 pence.
2 VT (fam: money) fare soldi a palate; (fig: word etc) coniare; **to coin a phrase** (hum) come si suol dire.

coin·age [ˈkɔɪnɪdʒ] N **a** (money, system) moneta, sistema m monetario **b** (coining) coniazione f, invenzione f.

♦ **coin box** N (Brit) telefono pubblico a monete.

co·in·cide [ˌkəʊɪnˈsaɪd] VI: **to coincide (with)** coincidere (con).

co·in·ci·dence [kəʊˈɪnsɪdəns] N (chance) coincidenza, combinazione f.

co·in·ci·dent·al [kəʊˌɪnsɪˈdɛntl] ADJ: **it's entirely coincidental** è (una) pura combinazione.

co·in·ci·dent·al·ly [kəʊˌɪnsɪˈdɛntəlɪ] ADV per (pura) coincidenza.

coin·ing [ˈkɔɪnɪŋ] N (of money) coniazione f; (of word) invenzione f, coniazione f.

♦ **coin-op** [ˈkɔɪnˌɒp] N (fam) lavanderia a gettone or automatica.

♦ **coin-operated** [ˌkɔɪnˈɒpəreɪtɪd] ADJ (machine) (che funziona) a monete.

Coke® [kəʊk] N (Coca-Cola) coca ® f.

coke [kəʊk] N **a** (fuel) carbone m coke **b** (fam: cocaine) coca.

Col. ABBR = colonel.

col·an·der [ˈkʌləndə] N colapasta m inv.

cold [kəʊld] **1** ADJ (comp **-er**, superl **-est**) (also fig) freddo(-a); **it's cold** fa freddo; **it's a cold day** fa freddo oggi; **I'm cold** ho freddo; **my feet are cold** ho freddo ai piedi, ho i piedi freddi; **to catch cold** prendere freddo; **to get cold** (person) infreddolirsi; (food etc) freddarsi, diventare freddo(-a); **it's getting cold** (weather) comincia a far freddo; **the room's getting cold** comincia a far freddo in questa stanza; **to be out cold** (fam: unconscious) essere privo(-a) di sensi; **to knock sb (out) cold** mettere qn fuori combattimento; **in cold blood** a sangue freddo; **it leaves me cold** (fam) non mi fa né caldo, né freddo; **to get cold feet** (fig) avere fifa; **it's cold comfort** è una magra consolazione; **to put sth into cold storage** (food) mettere qc in cella frigorifera; (fig: project) accantonare qc.
2 N **a** (Met) freddo; **to feel the cold** sentire il freddo; **to**

be left out in the cold (fig) essere lasciato(-a) in disparte **b** (Med: also: **common cold**) raffreddore m; **to catch a cold** prendere un raffreddore.

♦ **cold-blooded** [ˌkəʊldˈblʌdɪd] ADJ a sangue freddo; (fig) spietato(-a).

♦ **cold-bloodedly** [ˌkəʊldˈblʌdɪdlɪ] ADV (fig) spietatamente.

♦ **cold cream** N crema emolliente.

♦ **cold frame** N cassetta di legno, coperta da un vetro per proteggere le piantine dal freddo.

♦ **cold-hearted** [ˌkəʊldˈhɑːtɪd] ADJ insensibile.

cold·ly [ˈkəʊldlɪ] ADV (fig) freddamente.

cold·ness [ˈkəʊldnɪs] N (of weather, room) freddo; (of person) freddezza.

♦ **cold-shoulder** [ˌkəʊldˈʃəʊldə] **1** VT trattare con freddezza.
2 N: **to give sb the cold shoulder** trattare qn con freddezza.

♦ **cold snap** N: **a sudden cold snap** un'improvvisa ondata di freddo.

♦ **cold sore** N (Med) febbre f (sulle labbra), herpes simplex m inv.

♦ **cold start** N, (Am) **cold starting** N (Comput) partenza a freddo.

♦ **cold sweat** N: **to be in a cold sweat (about sth)** sudare freddo (per qc).

♦ **cold turkey** N (fam): **to go cold turkey** avere la scimmia.

♦ **cold war** N: **the Cold War** la guerra fredda.

cole·slaw [ˈkəʊlˌslɔː] N, NO PL insalata di cavolo bianco.

col·ic [ˈkɒlɪk] N colica.

col·icky [ˈkɒlɪkɪ] ADJ che soffre di coliche.

co·li·tis [kɒˈlaɪtɪs] N (Med) colite f.

col·labo·rate [kəˈlæbəˌreɪt] VI: **to collaborate (with sb in or on sth)** collaborare (con qn a or in qc).

col·labo·ra·tion [kəˌlæbəˈreɪʃən] N collaborazione f.

col·labo·ra·tive [kəˈlæbərətɪv] ADJ (work) fatto(-a) in collaborazione, di gruppo.

col·labo·ra·tor [kəˈlæbəˌreɪtə] N (on project) collaboratore(-trice); (pej: with enemy) collaborazionista m/f.

col·lage [kɒˈlɑːʒ] N (Art) collage m inv.

col·la·gen [ˈkɒlədʒən] N collageno.

col·lapse [kəˈlæps] **1** N (gen) crollo; (of government) caduta; (of plans, scheme, business) fallimento; (of health) collasso.
2 VI (see n) crollare; cadere; fallire; avere un collasso; (fam: with laughter) piegarsi in due dalle risate.

col·laps·ible [kəˈlæpsəbl] ADJ pieghevole.

col·lar [ˈkɒlə] **1** N (of shirt, blouse, coat) colletto, collo; (for dog) collare m; (Tech) anello, fascetta; **to grab sb by the collar** afferrare qn per il bavero.
2 VT (fam: person, object) beccare.

collar·bone [ˈkɒləˌbəʊn] N clavicola.

♦ **collar stud** N bottone m del colletto.

col·late [kɒˈleɪt] VT collazionare.

col·lat·er·al [kɒˈlætərəl] N (Fin) garanzia.

col·la·tion [kəˈleɪʃən] N **a** (of information) collazione f **b** (frm: light meal) pasto leggero.

col·league [ˈkɒliːg] N collega m/f.

col·lect [kəˈlɛkt] **1** VT **a** (gen) raccogliere; (as hobby: stamps, valuables) fare collezione di, collezionare; **to collect o.s.** riprendersi; **to collect one's thoughts** raccogliere le idee
b (Brit: call for, pick up: person) andare or passare a prendere; (: post, ticket) ritirare; (: pension, rent, taxes)

riscuotere; (: *donations, subscriptions*) fare una colletta di; (: *rubbish*) portare via, raccogliere; (: *dust*) accumulare.

2 VI (*people*) riunirsi, adunarsi, radunarsi; (*water, dust*) accumularsi; (*rubbish etc*) ammucchiarsi, accumularsi; **to collect for charity** fare una raccolta di beneficenza; **collect on delivery** (*Am Comm*) pagamento alla consegna.

3 ADV (*Am*): **to call collect** (*Telec*) fare una chiamata a carico del destinatario

▶ **collect up** VT + ADV raccogliere.

col·lect·ed [kə'lɛktɪd] ADJ **a** (*works, poems*) raccolto(-a); **the collected works of Shakespeare** l'opera completa di Shakespeare **b** (*frm: person: composed*) padrone(-a) di sé.

col·lec·tion [kə'lɛkʃən] N (*of information etc*) raccolta; (*of taxes*) riscossione *f*; (*of refuse*) rimozione *f*; (*of stamps*) collezione *f*, raccolta; (*of miscellaneous objects, people*) miscuglio; (*Rel*) questua; (*for charity*) colletta, raccolta; (*Post*) levata.

col·lec·tive [kə'lɛktɪv] **1** N collettivo.

2 ADJ collettivo(-a).

♦ **collective bargaining** N trattative *fpl* (sindacali) collettive.

col·lec·tive·ly [kə'lɛktɪvlɪ] ADV collettivamente.

col·lec·tiv·ism [kə'lɛktɪvɪzəm] N collettivismo.

col·lec·tor [kə'lɛktə'] N (*of stamps etc*) collezionista *m/f*; (*of taxes*) esattore *m*; **collector's item** *or* **piece** pezzo da collezionista.

col·lege ['kɒlɪdʒ] N **a** (*of technology, agriculture etc*) istituto superiore; (*Brit, Am Univ*) college *m inv*; **college of art** scuola d'arte; **college of music** conservatorio; **to go to college** (*university*) andare all'università; (*other institution*) andare a un istituto di specializzazione **b** (*body*) collegio.

♦ **college of education** N ≈ facoltà *f inv* di Magistero.

col·lide [kə'laɪd] VI: **to collide (with)** scontrarsi (con).

col·lie ['kɒlɪ] N (*dog*) collie *m inv.*

col·li·er ['kɒlɪə'] N minatore *m* (di carbone).

col·liery ['kɒlɪərɪ] N (*Brit*) miniera di carbone.

col·li·ma·tion [ˌkɒlɪ'meɪʃən] N collimazione *f.*

col·li·ma·tor ['kɒlɪˌmeɪtə'] N collimatore *m.*

col·lin·ear [kɒ'lɪnɪə'] ADJ (*Math: points*) collineare.

col·li·sion [kə'lɪʒən] N scontro, collisione *f*; **to be on a collision course** (*also fig*) essere in rotta di collisione; **collision damage waiver** (*Insurance*) clausola che esclude la copertura per danni della vettura assicurata.

col·lo·cate [*n* 'kɒləkət; *vb* 'kɒləkeɪt] (*Ling*) **1** N collocazione *f.*

2 VI accordarsi.

col·loi·dal [kɒ'lɔɪdəl] ADJ colloidale.

col·lo·quial [kə'ləʊkwɪəl] ADJ (*word, phrase*) familiare; (*style*) colloquiale.

col·lo·qui·al·ism [kə'ləʊkwɪəlɪzəm] N colloquialismo.

col·lo·qui·al·ly [kə'ləʊkwɪəlɪ] ADV colloquialmente.

col·lude [kɒ'luːd] VI: **to collude with** (*frm*) mettersi d'accordo con.

col·lu·sion [kə'luːʒən] N collusione *f*; **in collusion with** in accordo segreto con.

col·ly·wob·bles ['kɒlɪˌwɒblz] NPL (*fam*): **to have the collywobbles** (*have stomach trouble*) avere mal di pancia; (*be scared*) avere la tremarella.

Co·logne [kə'ləʊn] N (*Geog*) Colonia.

co·logne [kə'ləʊn] N (*also:* **eau de cologne**) acqua di colonia.

Co·lom·bia [kə'lɒmbɪə] N Colombia.

Co·lom·bian [kə'lɒmbɪən] ADJ, N colombiano(-a).

co·lon ['kəʊlən] N **a** (*punctuation*) due punti *mpl* **b** (*Anat*) colon *m inv.*

colo·nel ['kɜːnl] N colonnello.

co·lo·nial [kə'ləʊnɪəl] ADJ coloniale; (*architecture*) di stile coloniale.

co·lo·ni·al·ism [kə'ləʊnɪəlɪzəm] N colonialismo.

co·lo·ni·al·ist [kə'ləʊnɪəlɪst] **1** ADJ colonialistico(-a).

2 N colonialista *m/f.*

colo·nist ['kɒlənɪst] N colonizzatore(-trice).

colo·ni·za·tion [ˌkɒlənaɪ'zeɪʃən] N colonizzazione *f.*

colo·nize ['kɒləˌnaɪz] VT colonizzare.

col·on·nade [ˌkɒlə'neɪd] N colonnato.

colo·ny ['kɒlənɪ] N colonia.

col·or *etc* ['kʌlə'] (*Am*) = **colour** *etc.*

Colo·ra·do [ˌkɒlə'rɑːdəʊ] N (*state, river*) il Colorado.

♦ **Colorado beetle** N dorifora.

col·ora·tion [ˌkʌlə'reɪʃən] N colorazione *f.*

co·los·sal [kə'lɒsl] ADJ colossale.

co·los·sus [kə'lɒsəs] N colosso.

co·los·to·my [kə'lɒstəmɪ] N (*Med*) colostomia.

col·our, (*Am*) **col·or** ['kʌlə'] **1** N **a** (*gen*) colore *m*; **what colour is it?** di che colore è?; **I want to see the colour of his money** voglio vederlo con i soldi in mano; **to change colour** cambiare colore

b (*complexion*) colore *m*, colorito; **to get one's colour back** riprendere colore; **the colour drained from his face** impallidì

c : **colours** NPL (*Mil, Naut*) colori *mpl*; (*of party, club*) emblemi *mpl*; **to salute the colours** salutare la bandiera; **to see sth in its true colours** (*fig: usu pej*) vedere qc come veramente è; **to show one's true colours** (*fig: usu pej*) rivelare la propria vera personalità; **to come through (sth) with flying colours** (*fig*) passare (qc) a pieni voti.

2 VT (*gen*) colorare; (*tint, dye*) tingere; (*fig: affect*) influenzare; **to colour sth green** tingere *or* colorare qc di verde.

3 VI (*blush: also:* **colour up**) arrossire.

4 ADJ (*film, slide, photograph, television*) a colori

▶ **colour in** VT + ADV colorare.

♦ **colour bar**, (*Am*) **color bar** N discriminazione *f* razziale (*in locali etc*).

♦ **colour-blind**, (*Am*) **color-blind** ['kʌlə,blaɪnd] ADJ daltonico(-a).

♦ **colour blindness**, (*Am*) **color-blindness** [ˌkʌlə'blaɪndnɪs] N daltonismo, discromatopsia.

coloured, (*Am*) **colored** ['kʌləd] **1** ADJ colorato(-a); (*person, race*) di colore; **a straw-coloured hat** un cappello color paglia; **highly-coloured** (*tale, account*) molto colorito(-a).

2 N: **coloureds** gente *f* di colore.

col·our·ful, (*Am*) **col·or·ful** ['kʌləful] ADJ (*dress*) dai colori vivaci; (*picture*) ricco(-a) di colore; (*personality*) originale, vivace; (*story*) avvincente.

col·our·ful·ly, (*Am*) **col·or·ful·ly** ['kʌləfəlɪ] ADV (*gen*) con colori vivaci; (*describe*) in modo pittoresco.

col·our·ing, (*Am*) **col·or·ing** ['kʌlərɪŋ] N colorazione *f*; (*substance*) colorante *m*; (*complexion*) colorito.

♦ **colouring book**, (*Am*) **coloring book** N album *m inv* da colorare.

col·our·less, (*Am*) **col·or·less** ['kʌləlɪs] ADJ incolore; (*fig: dull*) scialbo(-a).

♦ **colour scheme**, (*Am*) **color scheme** N combinazione *f* di colori.

♦ **colour supplement** N (*Brit Press*) supplemento a colori.

colt [kəʊlt] N puledro.

colts·foot ['kəʊltsˌfʊt] N (*Bot*) farfara.

col·um·bine ['kɒləmˌbaɪn] N aquilegia.

Co·lum·bus [kə'lʌmbəs] N: **Christopher Columbus** Cristoforo Colombo.

col·umn ['kɒləm] N (*gen*) colonna; (*in newspaper*) colonna; (: *fashion column, sports column etc*) rubrica; **the editorial column** l'articolo di fondo; **the advertising columns** gli annunci economici.

col·umn·ist ['kɒləmnɪst] N giornalista *m/f* (*che cura una rubrica*), articolista *m/f*.

coma ['kəʊmə] N (*Med*) coma *m inv*; **to go into a coma** entrare in coma.

co·ma·tose ['kəʊməˌtəʊs] ADJ comatoso(-a).

comb [kəʊm] 1 N pettine *m*; **to run a comb through one's hair** darsi una pettinata.

2 VT a (*hair*) pettinare; **to comb one's hair** pettinarsi b (*search*: *area, countryside etc*) rastrellare, setacciare, battere a tappeto.

com·bat ['kɒmbæt] 1 N lotta, combattimento; (*Mil*) combattimento.

2 VT (*fig*) combattere, lottare contro.

com·bat·ant ['kɒmbətənt] N combattente *m/f*.

com·bat·ive ['kɒmbətɪv] ADJ aggressivo(-a).

com·bi·na·tion [ˌkɒmbɪ'neɪʃən] N combinazione *f*.

♦ **combination lock** N serratura a combinazione.

com·bine [*vb* kəm'baɪn; *n* 'kɒmbaɪn] 1 VT: **to combine (with)** (*projects, proposals*) combinare (con); (*qualities*) unire a; **our combined incomes** i nostri stipendi messi insieme; **to combine business with pleasure** unire l'utile al dilettevole; **to combine forces with sb** unire le proprie forze con qn; **a combined effort** uno sforzo collettivo; **a combined operation** (*Mil*) operazione *f* combinata.

2 VI a unirsi, mettersi insieme; **to combine with** unirsi a; **to combine against sth/sb** unirsi contro qc/qn b (*Chem*): **to combine (with)** combinarsi (con); **combining power** valenza.

3 N lega; (*Comm, Fin*) trust *m inv*, associazione *f*; (*Agr*: *also*: **combine harvester**) mietitrebbia *f inv*.

com·bo ['kɒmbəʊ] N (*Jazz*) gruppo.

com·bus·tible [kəm'bʌstɪbl] ADJ combustibile.

com·bus·tion [kəm'bʌstʃən] N combustione *f*.

♦ **combustion chamber** N camera di combustione.

come [kʌm] VI (*pt* **came**, *pp* **come**) a (*gen*) venire; (*arrive*) venire, arrivare; (*have its place*) venire, trovarsi; **come with me** vieni con me; **come home** vieni a casa; **come and see us soon** vieni a trovarci presto; **we have come to help you** siamo venuti ad aiutarti; **she has come from London** è venuta da Londra; **we've just come from Paris** siamo appena arrivati da Parigi; **this necklace comes from Spain** questa collana viene dalla Spagna; **they have come a long way** vengono da lontano; (*fig*) hanno fatto molta strada; **people were coming and going all day** c'era gente che andava e veniva tutto il giorno; **to come running** venire di corsa; **to come for sb/sth** venire a prendere qn/qc; **we'll come after you** ti seguiamo; **coming!** vengo!, arrivo!; **we came to a village** siamo arrivati a un paese; **to come to a decision** arrivare *or* giungere a una decisione; **the water only came to her waist** l'acqua le arrivava solo alla vita; **it came to me that** (*idea*: *occur*) mi è venuto in mente che; **it may come as a surprise to you** ... può sorprenderti...; **it came as a shock to her** è stato un colpo per lei; **when it comes to**

choosing dovendo scegliere; **when it comes to mathematics** quanto alla matematica; **the time will come when** ... verrà il giorno in cui...; **the new ruling comes into force next year** il nuovo regolamento entrerà in vigore l'anno prossimo; **A comes before B** A viene prima di B; **he came 3rd in the race** è arrivato 3 nella gara

b (*happen*) accadere, succedere; **come what may** qualunque cosa succeda; **no good will come of it** andrà a finire male; **nothing came of it** non ne è saltato fuori niente, non ha portato a niente; **that's what comes of being careless** ecco cosa succede a non far attenzione; **how does this chair come to be broken?** come mai questa sedia è rotta?; **how come?** (*fam*) come mai?

c (*be, become*) diventare; **my dreams came true** i miei sogni si sono avverati; **to come undone/loose** slacciarsi/allentarsi; **my shoelaces have come undone** i lacci (delle scarpe) si sono sciolti; **your zip has come undone** ti si è aperta la chiusura lampo; **it comes naturally to him** gli viene spontaneo; **it'll all come right in the end** tutto si accomoderà alla fine; **those shoes come in two colours** quelle scarpe sono disponibili in due colori; **I have come to like her** ho finito col trovarla simpatica; **now I come to think of it** ora che ci penso

d (*phrases*): **in (the) years to come** negli anni futuri *or* a venire; **if it comes to it** in tal caso; **if it comes to that** ... se è per questo...; **come again?** (*fam*) come?; **he had it coming to him** ha avuto quello che si meritava; **I could see it coming** me lo aspettavo; **he's as daft as they come** è scemo come ce ne sono pochi; **to come between two people** mettersi fra due persone

▶ **come about** VI + ADV accadere, succedere

▶ **come across** 1 VI + ADV a (*gen*) attraversare b (*fig*): **to come across well/badly** fare una buona/cattiva impressione; **she came across as a very nice person** ha dato l'impressione di essere una persona molto simpatica.

2 VI + PREP (*find*) trovare (per caso)

▶ **come along** VI + ADV a : **come along!** sbrigati!, avanti!, andiamo!, forza! b (*accompany*) venire c (*progress*) far progressi, procedere, migliorare; (*pupil, work*) fare progressi; **how's your arm coming along?** come va il tuo braccio?

▶ **come apart** VI + ADV (*break*) andare in pezzi; (*become detached*: *sleeve, jacket*) staccarsi (scucendosi)

▶ **come at** VI + PREP a (*attack*) avventarsi su b (*reach*) arrivare; **to come at the truth** arrivare alla verità

▶ **come away** VI + ADV (*leave*) venir via; (*become detached*) staccarsi; **come away from there!** levati di lì!, vieni via da lì!

▶ **come back** VI + ADV a (*return*) tornare; **to come back to what we were discussing** ... per tornare all'argomento di prima... b (*reply*: *fam*): **can I come back to you on that one?** possiamo riparlarne più tardi? c (*return to mind*): **it's all coming back to me** mi sta tornando in mente

▶ **come by** VI + PREP: **to come by sth** procurarsi qc

▶ **come down** 1 VI + PREP scendere.

2 VI + ADV (*person*): **to come down (from/to)** scendere (da/a); (*building*) essere demolito(-a); (*prices, temperature*) diminuire, calare; **to come down in the world** ridursi male; **she came down on him like a ton of bricks**

gli ha fatto una sfuriata; **to come down with a cold** prendersi un raffreddore

▶ **come down to** VI + ADV + PREP: **it all comes down to ... è** tutta questione di..

▶ **come for** VI + PREP **a** (*attack*) avventarsi su
  b (*collect*) passare a prendere

▶ **come forward** VI + ADV farsi avanti, presentarsi

▶ **come from** VI + PREP venire *or* provenire da

▶ **come in** VI + ADV (*person*) entrare; (*train*) arrivare; (*tide*) salire; (*in race*) arrivare; (*in election*) salire al potere; **come in!** avanti!; **where do I come in?** dove entro in ballo io?; **they have no money coming in** non hanno entrate

▶ **come in for** VI + ADV + PREP (*criticism, blame*) essere oggetto di

▶ **come into** VI + PREP (*inherit*) ereditare; **where do I come into it?** (*be involved*) come vi entro io?; **money doesn't come into it** i soldi non c'entrano

▶ **come off** ⦁1⦁ VI + ADV **a** (*button etc*) staccarsi; (*stain*) andare via
  b (*event*) avere luogo; (*plans*) attuarsi; (*attempt, experiment*) riuscire
  c (*acquit o.s.*): **to come off best/worst** avere la meglio/la peggio.
  ⦁2⦁ VI + PREP: **a button came off my jacket** mi si è staccato un bottone dalla giacca; **she came off her bike** è caduta dalla bicicletta; **come off it!** (*fam*) piantala!, ma va'!

▶ **come on** VI + ADV **a** (*progress*) = **come along c**
  b (*exhortation*): **come on!** avanti!, andiamo!, forza!
  c (*protest*): **come on!** ma dai!
  d (*start*) cominciare; **I feel a cold coming on** mi sta venendo un raffreddore; **winter is coming on now** l'inverno si avvicina
  e (*lights, electricity*) accendersi
  f (*Theatre*) entrare in scena

▶ **come on to** VI + ADV + PREP (*turn to*) passare a

▶ **come out** VI + ADV (*person, object*) uscire; (*flower*) sbocciare; (*sun, stars*) apparire; (*news: esp scandal*) essere divulgato(-a); (*truth*) saltare fuori; (*book, film, magazine*) uscire, essere pubblicato(-a); (*qualities: show*) rivelarsi, mostrarsi; (*stain*) andare via; (*strike*) entrare in sciopero; **to come out of sth** uscire da qc; **it's bound to come out in the newspapers** apparirà senz'altro sui giornali; **he came out in a rash** gli è venuto uno sfogo; **the dye has come out of your jumper** il tuo maglione è scolorito; **to come out on strike** entrare in sciopero, fare sciopero; **to come out against sth** dichiararsi decisamente contrario(-a) a qc; **you never know what he is going to come out with next!** (*fam*) non si sa mai con cosa verrà fuori la prossima volta!

▶ **come over** ⦁1⦁ VI + ADV venire; **they came over to England for a holiday** sono venuti in Inghilterra per una vacanza; **you'll soon come over to my way of thinking** presto sarai anche tu della mia idea; **I came over all dizzy** mi è venuto un giramento di testa; **her speech came over very well** il suo discorso ha fatto una buona impressione, il suo discorso è riuscito bene.
  ⦁2⦁ VI + PREP: **I don't know what's come over him!** non so cosa gli sia preso!; **a feeling of weariness came over her** un forte senso di stanchezza la assalì

▶ **come round** VI + ADV **a** passare, venire; **he is coming round to see us** passa da noi, viene a trovarci
  b (*occur regularly*) ricorrere, venire; **Christmas seems to come round earlier every year** ogni anno sembra che il Natale venga prima
  c (*make detour*): **to come round (by)** passare (per); **we**

came round by the longer route abbiamo fatto la strada più lunga
  d (*change one's mind*) cambiare idea; **she'll soon come round to your way of thinking** presto la penserà come te
  e (*throw off bad mood*): **leave him alone, he'll soon come round** lascialo in pace *or* perdere, presto gli passerà
  f (*regain consciousness*) riprendere conoscenza, rinvenire

▶ **come through** ⦁1⦁ VI + ADV **a** (*survive*) sopravvivere, farcela
  b (*telephone call*): **the call came through** abbiamo ricevuto la telefonata.
  ⦁2⦁ VI + PREP (*survive: war, danger*) superare, uscire indenne da

▶ **come to** ⦁1⦁ VI + PREP (*add up to: amount*): **how much does it come to?** quanto costa?, quanto viene?.
  ⦁2⦁ VI + ADV (*regain consciousness*) riprendere conoscenza, rinvenire

▶ **come together** VI + ADV (*assemble*) riunirsi; (*meet*) incontrarsi

▶ **come under** VI + PREP (*heading*) trovarsi sotto; (*influence*) cadere sotto, subire

▶ **come up** ⦁1⦁ VI + ADV **a** salire; **he came up to us with a smile** ci si avvicinò sorridendo
  b (*matters for discussion*) essere sollevato(-a); **to come up (before)** (*accused*) comparire (davanti a); (*lawsuit*) essere ascoltato(-a) (da).
  ⦁2⦁ VI + PREP venire su, salire

▶ **come up against** VI + ADV + PREP (*resistance, difficulties*) urtare contro; **she came up against complete opposition to her proposals** le sue proposte hanno incontrato la più completa opposizione

▶ **come up to** VI + ADV + PREP arrivare (fino) a; **the film didn't come up to our expectations** il film ci ha deluso

▶ **come up with** VI + ADV + PREP (*suggest: idea, plan*) suggerire, proporre; (*offer: money, suggestion*) offrire; **he came up with an idea** venne fuori con un'idea

▶ **come upon** VI + PREP (*object, person*) trovare per caso.

come·back ['kʌmˌbæk] N **a** (*Theatre, Cine*) rentrée *f*, ritorno; **to make a comeback** tornare sulle scene **b** (*reaction*) reazione *f*; (*response*) risultato, risposta.

COMECON ['kɒmɪˌkɒn] N ABBR (= *Council for Mutual Economic Aid*) COMECON *m*.

co·median [kəˈmiːdɪən] N attore comico.

co·medi·enne [kəˌmiːdɪˈɛn] N attrice *f* comica.

come·down ['kʌmˌdaʊn] N, NO PL passo indietro.

com·edy ['kɒmɪdɪ] N (*gen*) commedia brillante; (*humour*) lato comico.

♦ **come-hither** [ˌkʌmˈhɪðəʳ] ADJ (*fam*): **a come-hither look** uno sguardo invitante.

come·ly ['kʌmlɪ] ADJ (*liter*) avvenente.

com·er ['kʌməʳ] N: **open to all comers** aperto(-a) a tutti; **the first comer** il/la primo(-a) venuto(-a).

com·et ['kɒmɪt] N cometa.

come·up·pance [ˌkʌmˈʌpəns] N: **she got her comeuppance** ha avuto quello che si meritava.

com·fort ['kʌmfət] ⦁1⦁ N **a** (*physical comfort*) comodità *f* inv, benessere *m*; **to live in comfort** vivere nell'agiatezza; **that car was a bit too close for comfort** quella macchina è passata troppo vicino per i miei gusti **b** (*solace*) consolazione *f*, conforto; **you're a great comfort to me** mi sei di gran conforto.
  ⦁2⦁ VT confortare, consolare.

com·fort·able ['kʌmfətəbl] ADJ (*house, chair, shoes, life*) comodo(-a); (*income, majority*) più che sufficiente;

(*temperature*) piacevole; **to make o.s. comfortable** mettersi a proprio agio; **are you comfortable, sitting there?** sta comodo, seduto lì?; **I don't feel very comfortable about it** non mi sento molto tranquillo.

com·fort·ably ['kʌmfətəblɪ] ADV (*sit etc*) comodamente; (*live*) bene; **to be comfortably off** vivere agiatamente; **to win comfortably** vincere agevolmente.

com·fort·er ['kʌmfətər] N (*person*) consolatore(-trice); (*scarf*) sciarpa di lana; (*baby's dummy*) ciuccio, succhiotto; (*Am: quilt*) trapunta.

com·fort·ing ['kʌmfətɪŋ] ADJ confortante.

com·fort·less ['kʌmfətlɪs] ADJ senza comodità, scomodo (-a).

♦ **comfort station** N (*Am euph*) toilette *f inv*.

com·fy ['kʌmfɪ] ADJ (*fam*) comodo(-a).

com·ic ['kɒmɪk] 1 ADJ comico(-a).
2 N (*person*) comico/attrice comica; (*magazine*) giornalino (a fumetti).

comi·cal ['kɒmɪkəl] ADJ divertente, buffo(-a), comico(-a).

comi·cal·ly ['kɒmɪkəlɪ] ADV comicamente, in modo buffo.

♦ **comic book** N (*Am*) fumetti *mpl*; **he reads a lot of comic books** legge un sacco di fumetti.

♦ **comic opera** N opera buffa.

♦ **comic relief** N parentesi *f* comica.

♦ **comic strip** N fumetto.

♦ **comic verse** N poesia umoristica.

com·ing ['kʌmɪŋ] 1 ADJ (*next*) prossimo(-a); (*future*) futuro(-a); **in the coming weeks/election** nelle prossime settimane/elezioni.
2 N avvento, arrivo.

♦ **coming and going** N, **comings and goings** NPL andirivieni *m inv*, viavai *m inv*; **there have been a lot of comings and goings** c'è stato un continuo andirivieni.

Com·in·tern ['kɒmɪn,tɜ:n] N KOMINTERN *m*.

com·ma ['kɒmə] N virgola.

com·mand [kə'mɑ:nd] 1 N (*esp Mil: order*) ordine *m*, comando; (: *control*) comando; (*mastery*) padronanza; (*Comput*) command *m inv*, comando; **by** or **at the command of** per ordine di; **under the command of** sotto il comando di; **to be in command (of)** essere al comando (di); **to have/take command of** avere/prendere il comando di; **to have at one's command** (*money, resources etc*) avere a propria disposizione; **to have a good command of English** avere una buona padronanza dell'inglese.
2 VT (*order*): **to command sb to do sth** ordinare or comandare a qn di fare qc; (*lead: men, ship*) essere al comando di; (*have at one's disposal: resources*) disporre di, avere a propria disposizione; (*respect*) incutere; **that picture will command a high price** quel quadro sarà venduto ad un prezzo elevato.

com·man·dant [,kɒmən'dænt] N comandante *m*.

♦ **command economy** N = **planned economy**.

com·man·deer [,kɒmən'dɪər] VT requisire.

com·mand·er [kə'mɑ:ndər] N capo; (*Mil*) comandante *m*.

♦ **commander in chief** N (*Mil*) comandante *m* in capo.

com·mand·ing [kə'mɑ:ndɪŋ] ADJ (*appearance*) imponente; (*voice, tone*) autorevole; (*lead, position*) dominante.

♦ **commanding officer** N comandante *m*.

com·mand·ment [kə'mɑ:ndmənt] N (*Bible*) comandamento.

♦ **command module** N (*Space*) modulo di comando.

com·man·do [kə'mɑ:ndəʊ] N (*group*) commando *m inv*; (*soldier*) soldato appartenente ad un commando.

♦ **command performance** N *serata di gala su richiesta del capo di Stato o sovrano.*

♦ **command post** N (*Mil*) posto di comando.

com·memo·rate [kə'mɛməreɪt] VT commemorare.

com·memo·ra·tion [kə,mɛmə'reɪʃən] N commemorazione *f*; **in commemoration of** in memoria di.

com·memo·ra·tive [kə'mɛmərətɪv] ADJ commemorativo (-a).

com·mence [kə'mɛns] 1 VT cominciare; **to commence doing sth** cominciare a fare qc.
2 VI cominciare.

com·mence·ment [kə'mɛnsmənt] N (*frm*) inizio.

com·mend [kə'mɛnd] VT a (*praise*) lodare b (*recommend*) raccomandare; **the proposal has little to commend it** la proposta dà poco affidamento c (*entrust*): **to commend (to)** affidare a.

com·mend·able [kə'mɛndəbl] ADJ lodevole.

com·mend·ably [kə'mɛndəblɪ] ADV lodevolmente.

com·men·da·tion [,kɒmɛn'deɪʃən] N (*for bravery etc*) encomio, lode *f*; (*recommendation*) raccomandazione *f*.

com·men·su·rate [kə'mɛnʃərɪt] ADJ: **commensurate with** proporzionato(-a) a, commisurato(-a) a.

com·ment ['kɒmɛnt] 1 N (*remark: written or spoken*) commento, osservazione *f*; (: *critical*) critica; **"no comment"** "(non ho) niente da dire"; **to cause comment** provocare critiche.
2 VI: **to comment (on)** fare commenti or dichiarazioni (su).
3 VT: **to comment that** osservare che.

com·men·tary ['kɒməntərɪ] N a (*Radio*) radiocronaca; (*TV*) telecronaca b (*on text*) commento.

com·men·tate ['kɒmɛnteɪt] VI commentare.

com·men·ta·tor ['kɒmɛnteɪtər] N (*Radio*) radiocronista *m/f*; (*TV*) telecronista *m/f*.

com·merce ['kɒmɜ:s] N commercio; **commerce between the two countries** scambi commerciali fra i due paesi.

com·mer·cial [kə'mɜ:ʃəl] 1 ADJ commerciale; **the commercial world** il mondo del commercio.
2 N (*TV: also:* **commercial break**) pubblicità *f inv*, spot *m inv* (pubblicitario).

♦ **commercial bank** N banca commerciale.

♦ **commercial college** N ≈ istituto commerciale.

com·mer·cial·ism [kə'mɜ:ʃə,lɪzəm] N (*pej*) affarismo.

com·mer·ciali·za·tion [kə,mɜ:ʃəlaɪ'zeɪʃən] N (*pej*) commercializzazione *f*.

com·mer·cial·ize [kə'mɜ:ʃə,laɪz] VT (*pej*) commercializzare.

com·mer·cial·ly [kə'mɜ:ʃəlɪ] ADV commercialmente.

♦ **commercial radio** N radio *f inv* privata.

♦ **commercial television** N televisione *f* privata.

♦ **commercial traveller**, (*Am*) **commercial traveler** N viaggiatore *m* or rappresentante di commercio, commesso viaggiatore.

♦ **commercial vehicle** N veicolo per il trasporto di merci, veicolo commerciale.

com·mis·er·ate [kə'mɪzəreɪt] VI: **to commiserate with** esprimere il proprio rincrescimento a.

com·mis·era·tion [kə,mɪzə'reɪʃən] N commiserazione *f*.

com·mis·sar ['kɒmɪsɑ:r] N commissario.

com·mis·sari·at [,kɒmɪ'sɛərɪət] N (*in former Soviet Union*) commissariato; (*Mil*) commissariato militare.

com·mis·sion [kə'mɪʃən] 1 N a (*order for work: esp of artist*) incarico
b (*for salesman*) commissione *f*, provvigione *f*; **to sell on commission** vendere a provvigione; **I get 10%**

commission ricevo il 10% sulle vendite **c** (*committee*) commissione *f*; **commission of inquiry** (*Brit*) commissione *f* d'inchiesta **d** (*Mil*): **to get one's commission** ricevere la nomina ad ufficiale **e** : **out of commission** (*machine*) fuori uso; (*Naut*) in disarmo. [2] VT **a** (*expert, consultant, artist*): **to commission sb to do sth** incaricare qn di fare qn; **to commission sth from sb** (*work of art*) commissionare qc a qn **b** (*Mil*) nominare ufficiale.

com·mis·sion·aire [kə,mɪʃə'nɛəʳ] N (*Brit*: *at shop, cinema etc*) portiere *m* in livrea.

com·mis·sioned of·fic·er [kə,mɪʃənd'ɒfɪsəʳ] N (*Mil*) ufficiale *m*.

com·mis·sion·er [kə'mɪʃənəʳ] N membro di una commissione; (*Police*) questore *m*; **commissioner of police** ≈ questore *m*.

com·mit [kə'mɪt] VT **a** (*crime, act*) commettere; **to commit suicide** suicidarsi **b** : **to commit o.s. (to sth/to doing sth)** impegnarsi (in qc/nel fare qc) **c** (*consign*): **to commit sth to sb's care** affidare qc a qn; **to commit to memory** imparare a memoria; **to commit to writing** mettere per iscritto; **to commit sb for trial** rinviare qn a giudizio.

com·mit·ment [kə'mɪtmənt] N (*responsibility*) impegno; (*devotion*) dedizione *f*; **he refused to make any commitment** ha rifiutato d'impegnarsi in alcun modo.

com·mit·tal [kə'mɪtl] N (*to prison*) imprigionamento, carcerazione *f*; (*to mental hospital*) ricovero.

com·mit·ted [kə'mɪtɪd] ADJ (*Christian*) convinto(-a); (*writer*) impegnato(-a).

com·mit·tee [kə'mɪtɪ] N (*takes* SG *or* PL VB) comitato, commissione *f*; (*Parliament*) commissione; **committee of inquiry** commissione d'inchiesta; **to be on a committee** far parte di un comitato *or* di una commissione.

♦ **committee meeting** N riunione *f* di comitato *or* di commissione.

com·mo·di·ous [kə'məʊdɪəs] ADJ spazioso(-a).

com·mod·ity [kə'mɒdɪtɪ] N prodotto, articolo; (*food*) derrata; **basic commodities** beni *mpl* di prima necessità.

♦ **commodity exchange** N borsa *f* merci *inv*.

com·mo·dore ['kɒmədɔ:ʳ] N commodoro.

com·mon ['kɒmən] [1] ADJ **a** comune; (*usual*) normale; **it's a common belief that ...** si tende a credere che...; **it's a common occurrence** succede di frequente; **it's common knowledge that ...** è risaputo *or* notorio che..., è di dominio pubblico che...; **it's common courtesy** è una questione di semplice cortesia; **in common use** di uso comune; **common or garden** ordinario(-a); **the common man** l'uomo della strada; **in common parlance** nel linguaggio corrente; **the common people** il popolo; **for the common good** nell'interesse generale, per il bene comune **b** (*pej*: *vulgar*) volgare, grossolano(-a). [2] N **a** (*land*) parco comunale **b** : **we have a lot in common** abbiamo molto in comune.

♦ **common cold** N: **the common cold** il raffreddore.

♦ **common denominator** N denominatore *m* comune.

com·mon·er ['kɒmənəʳ] N cittadino(-a) (non nobile).

♦ **common ground** N (*fig*) punto *mpl* d'incontro *or* d'intesa, terreno comune.

♦ **common land** N terreno di uso pubblico.

♦ **common-law** ['kɒmən,lɔ:] ADJ: **common-law wife** convivente *f* more uxorio.

♦ **common law** N diritto consuetudinario.

com·mon·ly ['kɒmənlɪ] ADV (*see adj*) comunemente, usualmente; in modo volgare.

♦ **Common Market** N: **the Common Market** il Mercato Comune.

com·mon·ness ['kɒmənnɪs] N (*of method, belief*) diffusione *f*; (*of occurrence*) frequenza; (*of person, accent*) grossolanità, volgarità.

common·place ['kɒmən,pleɪs] [1] ADJ comune; (*pej*) banale, ordinario(-a). [2] N (*statement*) luogo comune.

♦ **common room** N (*Scol*: *staff room*) sala dei professori; (: *for students*) sala di ritrovo.

Com·mons ['kɒmənz] NPL (*Brit Pol*): **the (House of) Commons** la Camera dei Comuni.

♦ **common sense** N buon senso.

♦ **common-sense** ['kɒmən,sɛns] ADJ sensato(-a).

Common·wealth ['kɒmən,wɛlθ] N: **the Commonwealth** il Commonwealth.

com·mo·tion [kə'məʊʃən] N confusione *f*, tumulto, trambusto; **to make** *or* **cause a commotion** causare confusione.

com·mu·nal ['kɒmjuːnl] ADJ (*facilities*) in comune; (*for common use*) pubblico(-a); (*life*) di comunità.

com·mu·nal·ly ['kɒmjuːnəlɪ] ADV (*see adj*) in comune; in una comunità.

com·mune [*n* 'kɒmjuːn; *vb* kə'mjuːn] [1] N (*group*) comune *f*. [2] VI: **to commune with nature** comunicare con la natura.

com·mu·ni·cabil·ity [kə,mjuːnɪkə'bɪlɪtɪ] N comunicabilità.

com·mu·ni·cant [kə'mjuːnɪkənt] N (*Rel*) comunicante *m/f*.

com·mu·ni·cate [kə'mjuːnɪ,keɪt] [1] VT: **to communicate sth (to sb)** (*thoughts, information*) comunicare qc (a qn); (*frm*: *disease*) trasmettere qc (a qn). [2] VI (*speak etc*): **to communicate (with)** comunicare (con), mettersi in contatto (con); **communicating rooms** stanze *fpl* comunicanti.

com·mu·ni·ca·tion [kə,mjuːnɪ'keɪʃən] N comunicazione *f*; **to be in communication with** (*frm*) essere in contatto con.

♦ **communication cord** N (*Brit Rail*) segnale *m* d'allarme.

♦ **communications network** N rete *f* delle comunicazioni.

♦ **communications satellite** N satellite *m* per telecomunicazioni.

com·mu·ni·ca·tive [kə'mjuːnɪkətɪv] ADJ (*gen*) loquace; **communicative skills** (*Scol*) capacità *f inv* espressive.

com·mu·ni·ca·tive·ness [kə'mjuːnɪkətɪvnɪs] N loquacità.

com·mun·ion [kə'mjuːnɪən] N (*also Rel*) comunione *f*; **to take communion** ricevere la comunione.

communiqué [kə'mjuːnɪ,keɪ] N comunicato, bollettino.

com·mun·ism ['kɒmjʊnɪzəm] N comunismo.

com·mun·ist ['kɒmjʊnɪst] ADJ, N comunista (*m/f*).

com·mu·nity [kə'mjuːnɪtɪ] N (*gen*) comunità *f inv*; (*of goods, interests*) comunanza; **the Italian community in Glasgow** la comunità italiana a Glasgow; **the student community** gli studenti.

♦ **community centre** N circolo ricreativo, centro sociale.

♦ **community chest** N (*Am*) fondo di beneficenza.

♦ **community health centre** N centro socio-sanitario (di quartiere).

♦ **community home** N (*Brit*) riformatorio.

♦ **community service** N (*Brit*) servizio civile (volontario o in sostituzione della pena per reati minori).

♦ **community singing** N canto corale.

♦ **community spirit** N (*responsibility*) spirito civico; (*solidarity*) spirito di solidarietà.

com·mu·ta·tion tick·et [ˌkɒmjuˈteɪʃənˈtɪkɪt] N (*Am*) biglietto di abbonamento.

com·mu·ta·tive [kəˈmjuːtətɪv] ADJ commutativo(-a).

com·mute [kəˈmjuːt] ⌐1⌐ VI fare il/la pendolare.

⌐2⌐ VT (*payment*): **to commute for** *or* **into** commutare in; (*Law: sentence*): **to commute (to)** commutare (a).

com·mut·er [kəˈmjuːtə²] N pendolare *m/f*; **the commuter belt** (*Brit*) la periferia abitata dai pendolari; **commuter aircraft** aereo interregionale.

com·pact¹ [kəmˈpækt] ADJ compatto(-a); **this house is very compact** questa casa è piccola ma funzionale.

com·pact² [ˈkɒmpækt] N **a** (*agreement*) patto, contratto **b** (*also:* **powder compact**) portacipria *m inv*.

♦ **compact disc** N compact disc *m inv*.

♦ **compact disc player** N lettore *m* di compact disc.

com·pact·ly [kəmˈpæktlɪ] ADV senza spreco di spazio.

com·pact·ness [kəmˈpæktnɪs] N compattezza.

com·pan·ion [kəmˈpænjən] N compagno(-a); (*lady's*) dama di compagnia; (*book*) manuale *m*, guida.

com·pan·ion·able [kəmˈpænjənəbl] ADJ (*person*) socievole, di compagnia; **we sat in companionable silence** sedevamo tranquillamente in silenzio.

com·pan·ion·ship [kəmˈpænjənˌʃɪp] N compagnia.

♦ **companion volume** N volume *m* complementare.

com·pan·ion·way [kəmˈpænjənˌweɪ] N (*Naut*) scala.

com·pa·ny [ˈkʌmpənɪ] N (*gen, also Mil, Theatre*) compagnia; (*Comm, Fin*) società *f inv*, compagnia; **ship's company** equipaggio; **he's good/poor company** è di buona/cattiva compagnia; **to keep sb company** tenere *or* fare compagnia a qn; **to get into bad company** farsi cattive amicizie; **to keep bad company** frequentare cattive compagnie; **to part company with sb** dividersi *or* separarsi da qn; **we have company this evening** abbiamo ospiti stasera; **Smith and Company** Smith e soci.

♦ **company car** N macchina (di proprietà) della ditta.

♦ **company director** N amministratore *m*, consigliere *m* di amministrazione.

♦ **company secretary** N (*Brit Comm*) segretario(-a) generale.

com·pa·rable [ˈkɒmpərəbl] ADJ simile; **comparable to** *or* **with** paragonabile a.

com·para·tive [kəmˈpærətɪv] ⌐1⌐ ADJ (*freedom, luxury, cost*) relativo(-a); (*adjective, adverb*) comparativo(-a); (*study, literature*) comparato(-a); **she's a comparative stranger** la conosco relativamente poco.

⌐2⌐ N (*Gram*) comparativo.

com·para·tive·ly [kəmˈpærətɪvlɪ] ADV (*see adj*) relativamente; comparativamente.

com·pare [kəmˈpɛə²] ⌐1⌐ VT: **to compare sth/sb with/to** paragonare qc/qn a, mettere a confronto *or* confrontare qc/qn con; **compared with** *or* **to** a paragone di, rispetto a; **to compare notes with sb** (*fig*) scambiare le proprie impressioni con qn.

⌐2⌐ VI: **to compare (with)** essere paragonabile (a), reggere il confronto (con); **how do they compare for speed?** che velocità fanno rispettivamente?; **how do the prices compare?** che differenza di prezzo c'è?; **it doesn't compare with yours** non è paragonabile al tuo.

⌐3⌐ N: **beyond compare** (*liter: adj*) senza confronto *or*

paragone; (: *adv*) incomparabilmente.

com·pari·son [kəmˈpærɪsn] N paragone *m*, confronto; **in comparison with** OR **by comparison with** rispetto a, in confronto a/di; **by comparison** a confronto.

com·part·ment [kəmˈpɑːtmənt] N comparto, scomparto; (*Brit Rail*) scompartimento.

com·part·men·tal·ize [ˌkɒmpɑːtˈmentəˌlaɪz] VT dividere in compartimenti.

com·pass [ˈkʌmpəs] N **a** (*Naut etc*) bussola **b** (*Math*): **(a pair of) compasses** un compasso **c** (*fig: range*) portata; **within the compass of** entro i limiti di.

com·pas·sion [kəmˈpæʃən] N compassione *f*.

com·pas·sion·ate [kəmˈpæʃənɪt] ADJ (*person*) compassionevole; **on compassionate grounds** per motivi personali.

♦ **compassionate leave** N congedo straordinario (*per gravi motivi di famiglia*).

com·pas·sion·ate·ly [kəmˈpæʃənɪtlɪ] ADV pietosamente, in modo compassionevole.

com·pat·ibil·ity [kəmˌpætəˈbɪlɪtɪ] N compatibilità.

com·pat·ible [kəmˈpætɪbl] ADJ: **compatible (with)** compatibile (con).

com·pat·ri·ot [kəmˈpætrɪət] N compatriota *m/f*.

com·pel [kəmˈpɛl] VT **a** (*force*): **to compel sb (to do sth)** forzare qn (a fare qc), costringere *or* obbligare qn (a fare qc)

b (*demand: obedience*) esigere; (: *respect*) incutere.

com·pel·ling [kəmˈpɛlɪŋ] ADJ (*argument, reason: powerful*) convincente; (*poem*) avvincente; (*painting*) affascinante.

com·pen·dium [kəmˈpɛndɪəm] N (*summary*) compendio, sommario; **compendium of games** (*Brit*) scatola di giochi vari.

com·pen·sate [ˈkɒmpənˌseɪt] ⌐1⌐ VT: **to compensate sb (for sth)** compensare qn (per qc); (*financially*) indennizzare *or* risarcire qn (per qc).

⌐2⌐ VI: **to compensate for** compensare.

com·pen·sa·tion [ˌkɒmpənˈseɪʃən] N (*see vb*) compensazione *f*; indennità, risarcimento; **in compensation (for)** come compenso (per), come indennizzo (per).

com·pen·sa·tory [kəmˈpɛnsətərɪ] ADJ compensativo (-a).

com·pere [ˈkɒmpɛə²] ⌐1⌐ N presentatore(-trice).

⌐2⌐ VT presentare.

com·pete [kəmˈpiːt] VI (*Comm*): **to compete (with)** essere in concorrenza (con), fare concorrenza (a); (*vie*) essere in competizione (con); **to compete for sth** contendersi qc; (*take part*) concorrere in qc; **to compete with one another** farsi concorrenza.

com·pe·tence [ˈkɒmpɪtəns], **com·pe·ten·cy** [ˈkɒmpɪtənsɪ] N competenza.

com·pe·tent [ˈkɒmpɪtənt] ADJ competente; **this court is not competent to deal with that** questa corte non è competente in materia.

com·pe·tent·ly [ˈkɒmpɪtəntlɪ] ADV con competenza.

com·pet·ing [ˌkɒmˈpiːtɪŋ] ADJ (*theories, ideas*) opposto (-a); (*companies*) in concorrenza; (*explanations*) in contrasto tra di loro.

com·pe·ti·tion [ˌkɒmprɪˈtɪʃən] N **a** (*Comm*) concorrenza; **in competition with** in concorrenza con

b (*gen, Sport*) gara, competizione *f*, concorso; **to go in for** *or* **enter a competition** partecipare ad una gara *or* un concorso; **she won £5000 in a newspaper competition** ha vinto 5000 sterline in un concorso organizzato da

un quotidiano.

com·peti·tive [kəm'pɛtɪtɪv] ADJ **a** (*sports*) agonistico(-a); (*person*) che ha spirito di competizione; (: *in sport*) che ha spirito agonistico, che ha spirito di competizione; **competitive examination** concorso **b** (*Comm: price*) concorrenziale, competitivo(-a); (: *goods*) a prezzo concorrenziale *or* competitivo; **to have a competitive advantage in sth** essere avvantaggiato(-a) sulla concorrenza in qc.

com·peti·tive·ly [kəm'pɛtɪtɪvlɪ] ADV (*see adj*) agonisticamente; competitivamente; in modo concorrenziale.

com·peti·tive·ness [kəm'pɛtɪtɪvnɪs] N competitività, spirito di competizione; (*in sport*) spirito agonistico.

com·peti·tor [kəm'pɛtɪtə'] N concorrente *m/f*.

com·pi·la·tion [ˌkɒmpɪ'leɪʃən] N compilazione *f*.

com·pile [kəm'paɪl] VT compilare.

com·pil·er [kəm'paɪlə'] N compilatore(-trice).

com·pla·cen·cy [kəm'pleɪsnsɪ] N autocompiacimento, eccessivo compiacimento.

com·pla·cent [kəm'pleɪsənt] ADJ compiaciuto(-a), soddisfatto(-a) di sé.

com·plain [kəm'pleɪn] VI: **to complain (to sb about sth)** lamentarsi (con qn di qc), lagnarsi (con qn di qc); (*make a formal complaint*) fare un reclamo (a qn per qc), reclamare (con qn per qc)

▶ **complain of** VI + PREP lamentarsi di; (*Med*) accusare.

com·plaint [kəm'pleɪnt] N lamentela; (*to manager of shop etc*) reclamo; (*Med: illness*) disturbo, malattia.

com·ple·ment [*n* 'kɒmplɪmənt; *vb* 'kɒmplɪˌmɛnt] **1** N **a** (*gen, Gram, Math*) complemento **b** (*staff, crew*) effettivo.
2 VT (*enhance*) accompagnarsi bene a, completare.

com·ple·men·ta·rity [ˌkɒmplɪmɛn'tærɪtɪ] N complementarità.

com·ple·men·tary [ˌkɒmplɪ'mɛntərɪ] ADJ complementare; **the food and wine were complementary** il cibo e il vino erano ben assortiti.

com·plete [kəm'pliːt] **1** ADJ (*whole*) completo(-a); (*finished*) completo(-a), finito(-a); **complete with** completo(-a) di; **it's a complete disaster** è un vero disastro.
2 VT (*set, collection*) completare; (*piece of work*) finire, completare; (*fill in: form*) riempire; **and to complete my misfortunes** e per colmo di sfortuna.

com·plete·ly [kəm'pliːtlɪ] ADV completamente.

com·plete·ness [kəm'pliːtnɪs] N completezza.

com·ple·tion [kəm'pliːʃən] N completamento; **to be nearing completion** essere in fase di completamento; **on completion of contract** alla firma del contratto.

com·plex ['kɒmplɛks] **1** ADJ (*all senses*) complesso(-a).
2 N **a** (*Psych*) complesso; **he's got a complex about his weight** ha il complesso del peso, è complessato per il peso **b** (*of buildings*) complesso; **sports/housing complex** complesso sportivo/edilizio.

com·plex·ion [kəm'plɛkʃən] N (*of face*) carnagione *f*; (*fig: aspect, appearance*) aspetto; **that puts a different complexion on it** (*fig*) ciò fa apparire la cosa sotto tutta un'altra luce *or* tutto un altro aspetto.

com·plex·ity [kəm'plɛksɪtɪ] N complessità *f inv*.

com·pli·ance [kəm'plaɪəns] N **a** (*with rules, orders, wishes*): **in compliance with** in conformità con **b** (*submissiveness*) arrendevolezza, acquiescenza.

com·pli·ant [kəm'plaɪənt] ADJ (*submissive*) arrendevole, acquiescente.

com·pli·ant·ly [kəm'plaɪəntlɪ] ADV arrendevolmente.

com·pli·cate ['kɒmplɪˌkeɪt] VT complicare.

com·pli·cat·ed ['kɒmplɪˌkeɪtɪd] ADJ complicato(-a), complesso(-a).

com·pli·ca·tion [ˌkɒmplɪ'keɪʃən] N complicazione *f*.

com·plic·ity [kəm'plɪsɪtɪ] N (*frm*) complicità *f inv*.

com·pli·ment [*n* 'kɒmplɪˌmənt; *vb* 'kɒmplɪmɛnt] **1** N **a** complimento; **to pay sb a compliment (on sth)** fare un complimento a qn (per qc)
b : **compliments** NPL (*frm: greetings*) rispetti *mpl*, ossequi *mpl*; **compliments of the season** auguri per le festività; **with the compliments of Mr X** con gli omaggi del Signor X.
2 VT: **to compliment sb (on sth/on doing sth)** congratularsi *or* complimentarsi con qn (per qc/per aver fatto qc).

com·pli·men·tary [ˌkɒmplɪ'mɛntərɪ] ADJ (*remark etc*) lusinghiero(-a), elogiativo(-a); (*free: ticket*) (in) omaggio *inv*.

♦ **compliments slip** N (*Comm*) cartoncino della società.

com·ply [kəm'plaɪ] VI: **to comply with** (*rules etc*) attenersi a, conformarsi a, osservare; (*wishes, request*) assecondare.

com·po·nent [kəm'pəʊnənt] ADJ, N componente (*m*).

com·pose [kəm'pəʊz] VT **a** (*music, poetry*) comporre; (*letter*) mettere insieme; **to be composed of** essere composto(-a) di **b** (*calm: thoughts*) riordinare; **to compose o.s.** ricomporsi.

com·posed [kəm'pəʊzd] ADJ (*person*) calmo(-a), composto(-a).

com·pos·ed·ly [kəm'pəʊzɪdlɪ] ADV con calma, tranquillamente.

com·pos·er [kəm'pəʊzə'] N (*Mus*) compositore(-trice).

com·po·site ['kɒmpəzɪt] ADJ (*gen, Math*) composto(-a); (*Archit*) composito(-a).

com·po·si·tion [ˌkɒmpə'zɪʃən] N composizione *f*.

com·posi·tor [kəm'pɒzɪtə'] N (*Typ*) compositore *m*.

com·pos men·tis ['kɒmpɒs'mɛntɪs] ADJ sano(-a) di mente.

com·post ['kɒmpɒst] N concime *m*.

com·po·sure [kəm'pəʊʒə'] N calma, padronanza di sé.

com·pote ['kɒmpəʊt] N (*Culin*) composta, conserva di frutta.

com·pound [*n* 'kɒmpaʊnd; *adj* kəm'paʊnd] **1** N **a** (*enclosed area*) recinto **b** (*Chem*) composto; (*Ling*) parola composta, composto.
2 ADJ composto(-a); **compound substance** composto.
3 VT (*fig: problem, difficulty*) peggiorare.

♦ **compound fracture** N frattura esposta.

♦ **compound interest** N interesse *m* composto.

com·pre·hend [ˌkɒmprɪ'hɛnd] VT capire, comprendere.

com·pre·hen·sible [ˌkɒmprɪ'hɛnsəbl] ADJ comprensibile.

com·pre·hen·sibly [ˌkɒmprɪ'hɛnsəblɪ] ADV in modo comprensibile.

com·pre·hen·sion [ˌkɒmprɪ'hɛnʃən] N (*understanding*) comprensione *f*; (*Scol*) esercizio di comprensione.

com·pre·hen·sive [ˌkɒmprɪ'hɛnsɪv] **1** ADJ (*study*) esauriente; (*knowledge*) esteso(-a); (*description*) dettagliato(-a); (*report, review*) completo(-a), esauriente; (*measures*) di vasta portata; **comprehensive insurance policy** (*Aut*) polizza *f* casco *inv*.
2 N (*Brit: also:* **comprehensive school**) *scuola secondaria dagli 11 ai 18 anni, aperta a tutti*.

com·pre·hen·sive·ly [ˌkɒmprɪ'hɛnsɪvlɪ] ADV (*study, review*) in modo esauriente; (*describe*) dettagliatamente.

com·press [*vb* kəm'prɛs; *n* 'kɒmprɛs] **1** VT (*substance*) comprimere; (*text etc*) condensare.

2 N (Med) compressa.
com·pres·sion [kəm'prɛʃən] N compressione f.
com·pres·sor [kəm'prɛsəʳ] N compressore m.
com·prise [kəm'praɪz] VT (also: **be comprised of:** be made up of) comprendere; (make up) costituire.
com·pro·mise ['kɒmprə,maɪz] 1 N compromesso.
2 VI: **to compromise (with sb over sth)** venire a un compromesso (con qn su qc).
3 VT compromettere.
4 ADJ (decision, solution) di compromesso.
com·pro·mis·ing ['kɒmprəmaɪzɪŋ] ADJ compromettente.
com·pul·sion [kəm'pʌlʃən] N **a** costrizione f, pressione f; **under compulsion** sotto costrizione, dietro or sotto pressione; **he is under no compulsion (to do it)** nessuno lo costringe (a farlo) **b** desiderio incontrollabile.
com·pul·sive [kəm'pʌlsɪv] ADJ **a** (Psych: desire, behaviour) incontrollabile; (: liar) patologico(-a); **he's a compulsive drinker/smoker/gambler** ha il vizio del fumo/del bere/del gioco **b** (novel, film) avvincente.
com·pul·sive·ly [kəm'pʌlsɪvlɪ] ADV **a** (Psych: eat) in modo incontrollato; (: lie) in modo patologico; **he gambles/drinks compulsively** ha il vizio del gioco/del bere **b** : **compulsively readable** che si legge d'un fiato.
com·pul·so·ri·ly [kəm'pʌlsərɪlɪ] ADV per forza; (Law) coattivamente.
com·pul·so·ry [kəm'pʌlsərɪ] ADJ obbligatorio(-a).
♦ **compulsory purchase** N espropriazione f.
♦ **compulsory retirement** N pensionamento obbligatorio.
com·punc·tion [kəm'pʌŋkʃən] N scrupolo; **to have no compunction about doing sth** non farsi scrupoli a fare qc.
com·pu·ta·tion [,kɒmpjʊ'teɪʃən] N calcolo.
com·pute [kəm'pju:t] VT calcolare, computare.
com·put·er [kəm'pju:təʳ] 1 N computer m inv, elaboratore m elettronico.
2 ADJ (printout) del computer; (software) per computer.
♦ **computer game** N computer game m inv, videogioco per computer.
com·put·eri·za·tion [kəm,pju:təraɪ'zeɪʃən] N computerizzazione f.
com·put·er·ize [kəm'pju:tə,raɪz] VT computerizzare.
com·put·er·ized [kəm'pju:tə,raɪzd] ADJ computerizzato (-a); **computerized axial tomography** tomografia assiale computerizzata.
♦ **computer language** N linguaggio m macchina inv.
♦ **computer-literate** [kəm'pju:tə'lɪtərɪt] ADJ: **to be computer-literate** avere dimestichezza coi computer.
♦ **computer operator** N terminalista m/f.
♦ **computer peripheral** N unità f inv periferica.
♦ **computer program** N programma m di computer.
♦ **computer programmer** N programmatore(-trice) di computer.
♦ **computer programming** N programmazione f di computer.
♦ **computer science** N informatica.
♦ **computer scientist** N informatico(-a).
com·put·ing [kəm'pju:tɪŋ] N informatica.
com·rade ['kɒmrɪd] N compagno(-a).
♦ **comrade-in-arms** ['kɒmrɪd,ɪn'ɑ:mz] N compagno d'armi.
com·rade·ly ['kɒmreɪdlɪ] ADJ (chat, spirit) amichevole.
com·rade·ship ['kɒmrɪdʃɪp] N cameratismo.
com·sat ['kɒmsæt] N ABBR = **communications satellite**.
con[1] [kɒn] (fam) 1 VT truffare; **to con sb into doing sth**

indurre qn a fare qc con raggiri; **I've been conned!** mi hanno fregato!.
2 N truffa.
con[2] [kɒn] N (disadvantage); see pro.
con·cat·ena·tion [kɒn,kætɪ'neɪʃən] N (frm: of events, ideas) concatenazione f.
con·cave ['kɒn'keɪv] ADJ concavo(-a).
con·ceal [kən'si:l] VT: **to conceal (sth from sb)** nascondere (qc a qn); (news) tenere nascosto(-a) (qc a qn); **concealed lighting** illuminazione f indiretta.
con·ceal·ment [kən'si:lmənt] N il nascondere; (of facts) occultazione f; (of feelings) dissimulazione f.
con·cede [kən'si:d] 1 VT (admit: point, defeat) ammettere; (: argument) riconoscere la validità di; (territory) cedere; **to concede victory** darla vinta.
2 VI cedere.
con·ceit [kən'si:t] N vanità f inv, presunzione f.
con·ceit·ed [kən'si:tɪd] ADJ pieno(-a) di sé, presuntuoso (-a), vanitoso(-a).
con·ceit·ed·ly [kən'si:tɪdlɪ] ADV vanitosamente.
con·ceiv·able [kən'si:vəbl] ADJ concepibile; **it is conceivable that ...** può anche darsi che... .
con·ceiv·ably [kən'si:vəblɪ] ADV: **he may conceivably be right** può anche darsi che abbia ragione.
con·ceive [kən'si:v] 1 VT (child, idea) concepire.
2 VI: **to conceive of sth/of doing sth** immaginare qc/di fare qc.
con·cel·ebrate [kən'sɛlɪ,breɪt] VT (Rel) concelebrare.
con·cel·ebra·tion [kən'sɛlɪ'breɪʃən] N (Rel) concelebrazione f.
con·cen·trate ['kɒnsən,treɪt] 1 VT concentrare; **concentrate one's thoughts on sth** concentrarsi su qc.
2 VI **a** (pay attention): **to concentrate (on)** concentrarsi (in or su); **concentrate on getting well** pensa soprattutto a guarire **b** (group closely) concentrarsi.
3 N (Chem) concentrato.
con·cen·trat·ed ['kɒnsən,treɪtɪd] ADJ (juice, attack) concentrato(-a).
con·cen·tra·tion [,kɒnsən'treɪʃən] N (of mind, also Tech) concentrazione f; (of people, troops) concentramento.
♦ **concentration camp** N campo di concentramento.
con·cen·tric [kən'sɛntrɪk] ADJ concentrico(-a).
con·cen·tric·ity [,kɒnsən'trɪsɪtɪ] N concentricità.
con·cept ['kɒnsɛpt] N concetto.
con·cep·tion [kən'sɛpʃən] N **a** (idea) concetto, concezione f **b** (of child) concepimento.
con·cep·tual [kən'sɛptjʊəl] ADJ concettuale.
con·cep·tu·al·ize [kən'sɛptjʊə,laɪz] VT (frm) concettualizzare.
con·cern [kən'sɜ:n] 1 N **a** : **what concern is it of yours?** non vedo come ti possa riguardare; **it's of no concern to me** or **it's no concern of mine** non mi riguarda **b** (anxiety) ansietà f inv, preoccupazione f; **it is a matter for concern that ...** è preoccupante che...
c (firm) impresa, azienda, ditta.
2 VT riguardare, interessare; **this shouldn't concern you** (affect) questo non dovrebbe cambiarti nulla; **"to whom it may concern"** "a tutti gli interessati"; **as far as I am concerned** per quanto mi riguarda; **the department concerned** (under discussion) l'ufficio in questione; (relevant) l'ufficio competente; **to be concerned with** occuparsi di; **to be concerned in** interessarsi a; **to concern o.s. with** occuparsi di.
con·cerned [kən'sɜ:nd] ADJ **a** (affected) interessato(-a) **b** (worried) preoccupato(-a), ansioso(-a); **to be concerned**

at or by or about sth/for or about sb preoccuparsi per or di qc/per qn, essere preoccupato(-a) per qc/per qn.

con·cern·ing [kən'sɜ:nɪŋ] PREP riguardo a, circa.

con·cert ['kɒnsət] ☐1 N (Mus) concerto; **in concert** in concerto; (fig) di concerto.
☐2 ADJ concertistico(-a).

con·cert·ed [kən'sɜ:tɪd] ADJ (effort, attack) concertato(-a), collettivo(-a).

concert·goer ['kɒnsət,gəʊəʳ] N frequentatore(-trice) di concerti.

♦ **concert hall** N sala da concerti.

con·cer·ti·na [,kɒnsə'ti:nə] ☐1 N piccola fisarmonica.
☐2 VI accartocciarsi, piegarsi come una fisarmonica.

con·cer·to [kən'tʃɛətəʊ] N concerto.

♦ **concert pianist** N concertista m/f (pianista).

♦ **concert tour** N serie f inv di concerti.

con·ces·sion [kən'sɛʃən] N concessione f.

con·ces·sion·aire [kən,sɛʃə'nɛəʳ] N (Comm) concessionario.

con·ces·sion·ary [kən'sɛʃənərɪ] ADJ (ticket, fare) a prezzo ridotto.

con·ces·sive [kən'sɛsɪv] ADJ: **concessive clause** (Gram) (proposizione f) concessiva.

conch [kɒntʃ] N (Zool) (conchiglia di) strombo.

con·cili·ate [kən'sɪlɪeɪt] VT (person) rabbonire, calmare; (opposing view) conciliare.

con·cili·ation [kən,sɪlɪ'eɪʃən] N conciliazione f.

con·cilia·tory [kən'sɪlɪətərɪ] ADJ conciliante, conciliatorio (-a), conciliativo(-a).

con·cise [kən'saɪs] ADJ conciso(-a).

con·cise·ly [kən'saɪslɪ] ADV concisamente, brevemente.

con·cise·ness [kən'saɪsnɪs], **con·ci·sion** [kən'sɪʒən] N concisione f.

con·clave ['kɒnkleɪv] N (meeting) riunione f segreta; (Rel) conclave m.

con·clude [kən'klu:d] ☐1 VT (all senses) concludere.
☐2 VI: **to conclude (with)** (events) concludersi (con); (speaker) concludere.

con·clud·ing [kən'klu:dɪŋ] ADJ (remarks etc) conclusivo (-a), finale.

con·clu·sion [kən'klu:ʒən] N (all senses) conclusione f; **in conclusion** in conclusione; **to come to the conclusion that** ... concludere che..., arrivare alla conclusione che... .

con·clu·sive [kən'klu:sɪv] ADJ conclusivo(-a).

con·coct [kən'kɒkt] VT (food, drink) mettere insieme; (lie, story, excuse) inventare; (scheme) architettare.

con·coc·tion [kən'kɒkʃən] N (food, drink) miscuglio.

con·comi·tant [kən'kɒmɪtənt] (frm) ☐1 ADJ concomitante.
☐2 N fatto concomitante.

con·cord ['kɒŋkɔ:d] N (harmony) armonia, concordia; (treaty) accordo.

con·cord·ant [kən'kɔ:dənt] ADJ (frm) concordante.

con·course ['kɒŋkɔ:s] N (of people) folla; (place) luogo di assembramento; (in station) atrio.

con·crete ['kɒnkri:t] ☐1 ADJ **a** (object, advantage) concreto(-a) **b** (Constr) di calcestruzzo.
☐2 N (Constr) calcestruzzo.
☐3 VT (path) rivestire di calcestruzzo.

con·crete·ly ['kɒnkri:tlɪ] ADV concretamente.

♦ **concrete mixer** N betoniera.

con·cur [kən'kɜ:ʳ] VI (frm) **a** (agree): **to concur (with)** (opinions etc) coincidere (con), concordare (con); (person) essere d'accordo (con) **b** (happen at the same time) coincidere.

con·cur·rent [kən'kʌrənt] ADJ simultaneo(-a); **to be concurrent with** coincidere con.

con·cur·rent·ly [kən'kʌrəntlɪ] ADV: **concurrently (with)** simultaneamente (a).

con·cussed [kən'kʌst] ADJ: **to be concussed** (Med) avere una commozione cerebrale.

con·cus·sion [kən'kʌʃən] N (Med) commozione f cerebrale.

con·demn [kən'dɛm] VT (person) condannare; (declare unfit: building) dichiarare inagibile; (: food) dichiarare immangiabile; **to condemn sb to death** condannare qn a morte.

con·dem·na·tion [,kɒndɛm'neɪʃən] N condanna.

♦ **condemned cell** N braccio della morte.

con·den·sa·tion [,kɒndɛn'seɪʃən] N condensazione f.

con·dense [kən'dɛns] ☐1 VT condensare.
☐2 VI condensarsi.

♦ **con·densed milk** [kən'dɛnst'mɪlk] N latte m condensato.

con·dens·er [kən'dɛnsəʳ] N condensatore m.

con·de·scend [,kɒndɪ'sɛnd] VI: **to condescend to sb** trattare qn con sussiego; **to condescend to do sth** degnarsi di fare qc, abbassarsi a fare qc.

con·de·scend·ing [,kɒndɪ'sɛndɪŋ] ADJ sussiegoso(-a).

con·de·scend·ing·ly [,kɒndɪ'sɛndɪŋlɪ] ADV con aria di sufficienza.

con·de·scen·sion [,kɒndɪ'sɛnʃən] N sussiego, aria di superiorità.

con·di·ment ['kɒndɪmənt] N condimento.

con·di·tion [kən'dɪʃən] ☐1 N **a** condizione f; **on condition that** a condizione di, a condizione che + sub; **under** or **in the present conditions** nelle attuali condizioni or circostanze; **in good/poor condition** in buone/cattive condizioni; **to be in no condition to do sth** non essere in condizione di fare qc; **to be out of condition** (person) essere fuori forma; **physical condition** (of person) condizioni fisiche; **physical conditions** condizioni ambientali; **weather conditions** condizioni meteorologiche; **conditions of sale** condizioni di vendita
b (disease) malattia; **to have a heart condition** soffrire di (mal di) cuore.
☐2 VT condizionare, regolare.

con·di·tion·al [kən'dɪʃənl] ADJ condizionale; **to be conditional upon** dipendere da.

con·di·tion·er [kən'dɪʃənəʳ] N (for hair) balsamo; (for clothes) ammorbidente m.

conditioning [kən'dɪʃənɪŋ] N condizionamento.

con·do ['kɒndəʊ] N ABBR (Am fam) = **condominium**.

con·dole [kən'dəʊl] VI (frm): **to condole with sb** porgere le proprie condoglianze a qn.

con·do·lences [kən'dəʊlənsɪz] NPL condoglianze fpl.

con·dom ['kɒndəm] N preservativo.

con·do·min·ium [,kɒndə'mɪnɪəm] N (Am) condominio.

con·done [kən'dəʊn] VT (forgive) perdonare, scusare; (overlook) passare sopra a.

con·du·cive [kən'dju:sɪv] ADJ: **to be conducive to** favorire, essere favorevole a.

con·duct [n 'kɒndʌkt; vb kən'dʌkt] ☐1 N condotta.
☐2 VT (gen, Phys) condurre; (guide) accompagnare; (Law) presentare; (Mus) dirigere; (manage) dirigere, amministrare; **to conduct o.s.** comportarsi.

♦ **con·duct·ed tour** [kən'dʌktɪd'tʊəʳ] N giro guidato, visita guidata.

con·duc·tion [kən'dʌkʃən] N (Elec, Phys) conduzione f.

con·duc·tiv·ity [,kɒndʌk'tɪvɪtɪ] N (Elec, Phys) conduttività.

con·duc·tor [kən'dʌktəʳ] N (of orchestra) direttore m d'orchestra; (on bus) bigliettaio; (Am Rail) controllore m; (Phys: of heat, electricity) conduttore m.

con·duc·tress [kən'dʌktrɪs] N (on bus) bigliettaia.

con·duit ['kɒndɪt] N (pipe) conduttura, condotto, tubo.

cone [kəʊn] N (gen, of ice cream) cono; (Aut) birillo; (Bot) pigna

▶ **cone off** VT + ADV chiudere al traffico (un'area o un tratto stradale, delimitandolo con birilli).

con·fab ['kɒnfæb] N (fam): **to have a confab** fare una chiacchieratina.

con·fec·tion·er [kən'fɛkʃənəʳ] N pasticciere m; **confectioner's (shop)** ≈ pasticceria.

con·fec·tion·ery [kən'fɛkʃənərɪ] N (sweets) dolciumi mpl.

con·fed·era·cy [kən'fɛdərəsɪ] N confederazione f; **the Confederacy** (Am) gli Stati della Confederazione.

con·fed·er·ate [kən'fɛdərɪt] **1** ADJ confederato(-a). **2** N (pej) complice m/f; (Am History) confederato.

con·fed·era·tion [kən,fɛdə'reɪʃən] N confederazione f.

con·fer [kən'fɜ:ʳ] **1** VT: **to confer sth on sb** conferire qc a qn. **2** VI: **to confer (with sb about sth)** consultarsi (con qn su qc).

con·fer·ence ['kɒnfərəns] N (convention, meeting) conferenza, convegno, congresso; (participants) partecipanti mpl alla conferenza or al convegno etc; **to be in conference** essere in riunione.

con·fess [kən'fɛs] **1** VT confessare, ammettere; **to confess o.s. guilty of** (sin, crime) confessare di essere colpevole di, dichiararsi colpevole di. **2** VI (make one's confession) confessarsi; (admit): **to confess (to sth/to doing sth)** confessare (qc/di aver fatto qc).

con·fes·sion [kən'fɛʃən] N confessione f; **to go to confession** andare a confessarsi; **to make one's confession** confessarsi; **to hear sb's confession** ascoltare la confessione di qn.

con·fes·sion·al [kən'fɛʃənl] N confessionale m.

con·fes·sor [kən'fɛsəʳ] N confessore m.

con·fet·ti [kən'fɛti:] N coriandoli mpl.

con·fi·dant [kɒnfɪ'dænt] N confidente m.

con·fi·dante [kɒnfɪ'dænt] N confidente f.

con·fide [kən'faɪd] **1** VT confidare. **2** VI: **to confide in sb (about sth)** confidarsi con qn (su qc).

con·fi·dence ['kɒnfɪdəns] N **a** (trust) fiducia; **to have (every) confidence in sb** avere (piena) fiducia in qn; **to have (every) confidence that** essere (assolutamente) certo(-a) che; **motion of no confidence** (Parliament) mozione f di sfiducia **b** (also: self-confidence) sicurezza di sé, fiducia in se stesso(-a); **to gain confidence** acquistare sicurezza **c** (secret) confidenza; **to take sb into one's confidence** confidarsi con qn; **to tell sb sth in strict confidence** dire qc a qn in via strettamente confidenziale; **to write in confidence to sb** scrivere a qn con la massima riservatezza.

♦ **confidence trick** N truffa.

♦ **confidence trickster** N truffatore(-trice).

confident ['kɒnfɪdənt] ADJ sicuro(-a), fiducioso(-a); (also: self-confident) sicuro(-a) (di sé); **to be confident of doing sth/that** essere sicuro di fare qc/che.

con·fi·den·tial [kɒnfɪ'dɛnʃəl] ADJ (letter, report, remark) confidenziale, riservato(-a); (secretary) particolare.

con·fi·den·ti·al·ity [kɒnfɪ,dɛnʃɪ'ælɪtɪ] N riservatezza,

carattere m confidenziale.

con·fi·den·tial·ly [kɒnfɪ'dɛnʃəlɪ] ADV in confidenza.

con·fi·dent·ly ['kɒnfɪdəntlɪ] ADV con sicurezza.

con·fid·ing [kən'faɪdɪŋ] ADJ fiducioso(-a).

con·figu·ra·tion [kən,fɪgjʊ'reɪʃən] N (Comput) configurazione f.

con·fine [kən'faɪn] VT **a** (imprison, shut up) rinchiudere; **confined to barracks** consegnato(-a) (in caserma); **confined to bed** costretto(-a) a letto **b** (limit) limitare; **to confine o.s. to doing sth** limitarsi a fare qc; see also **confines.**

con·fined [kən'faɪnd] ADJ (space) ristretto(-a); **a confined space** uno spazio ristretto.

con·fine·ment [kən'faɪnmənt] N **a** (imprisonment) reclusione f, detenzione f; (Mil) consegna **b** (Med) parto.

con·fines ['kɒnfaɪnz] NPL (bounds) confini mpl.

con·firm [kən'fɜ:m] VT **a** (gen) confermare; (strengthen: belief) rafforzare; (Rel) cresimare.

con·fir·ma·tion [kɒnfə'meɪʃən] N conferma; (Rel) cresima.

con·firmed [kən'fɜ:md] ADJ (smoker, habit etc) incallito (-a), inveterato(-a); (bachelor) impenitente; (admirer) fervente.

con·fis·cate ['kɒnfɪs,keɪt] VT: **to confiscate sth (from sb)** confiscare qc (a qn).

con·fis·ca·tion [,kɒnfɪs'keɪʃən] N confisca.

con·fla·gra·tion [,kɒnflə'greɪʃən] N (frm) conflagrazione f.

con·flict [n 'kɒnflɪkt; vb kən'flɪkt] **1** N conflitto. **2** VI: **to conflict (with)** essere in conflitto (con).

con·flict·ing [kən'flɪktɪŋ] ADJ (reports, evidence, opinions) contraddittorio(-a); (opinions) contrastante.

con·flu·ence ['kɒnfluəns] N (frm) **a** (of rivers) confluenza **b** (of interests, ideas) convergenza **c** (crowd) folla.

con·form [kən'fɔ:m] VI: **to conform (to)** conformarsi (a).

con·form·ist [kən'fɔ:mɪst] **1** ADJ conformistico(-a). **2** N conformista m/f.

con·form·ity [kən'fɔ:mɪtɪ] N: **in conformity with** in conformità a.

con·found [kən'faʊnd] VT (confuse) confondere; (amaze) sconcertare; (defeat) sconfiggere; **confound it!** al diavolo!

con·found·ed [kən'faʊndɪd] ADJ maledetto(-a).

con·front [kən'frʌnt] VT (enemy, danger) affrontare; (defiantly) fronteggiare; **to confront sb with sth** mettere qn a confronto con qc; **the problems which confront us** i problemi da affrontare.

con·fron·ta·tion [,kɒnfrən'teɪʃən] N scontro.

con·fron·ta·tion·al [,kɒnfrən'teɪʃənəl] ADJ polemico(-a), aggressivo(-a).

con·fuse [kən'fju:z] VT confondere.

con·fused [kən'fju:zd] ADJ confuso(-a); **in a confused state** (person) in stato confusionale; (room, papers) in disordine; **to get confused** confondersi.

con·fus·ed·ly [kən'fju:zɪdlɪ] ADV confusamente.

con·fus·ing [kən'fju:zɪŋ] ADJ (signals) ambiguo(-a); (plot, layout) confuso(-a).

con·fu·sion [kən'fju:ʒən] N confusione f.

con·geal [kən'dʒi:l] VI rapprendersi; (blood) coagularsi, rapprendersi.

con·gen·ial [kən'dʒi:nɪəl] ADJ (place, work, company) piacevole; (person) simpatico(-a).

con·geni·tal [kən'dʒɛnɪtl] ADJ (Med) congenito(-a).

con·ger ['kɒŋgəʳ] N (also: **conger eel**) grongo.

con·gest·ed [kən'dʒɛstɪd] ADJ (gen, Med) congestionato

(-a); (*telephone lines*) sovraccarico(-a).

con·ges·tion [kən'dʒɛstʃən] N (*with traffic, Med*) congestione *f*; (*with people*) sovraffollamento.

con·glom·er·ate [kən'glɒmərɪt] N (*Comm, Geol*) conglomerato.

con·glom·era·tion [kən,glɒmə'reɪʃən] N conglomerazione *f*.

Con·go ['kɒŋgəʊ] N: **the Congo** (*country, river*) il Congo.

con·gratu·late [kən'grætjʊ,leɪt] VT: **to congratulate sb (on sth/on doing sth)** congratularsi con qn (per qc/per aver fatto qc).

con·gratu·la·tions [kən,grætjʊ'leɪʃənz] NPL: **congratulations (on)** congratulazioni *fpl* (per); **to give sb one's congratulations** fare le (proprie) congratulazioni a qn; **congratulations!** congratulazioni!, rallegramenti!

con·gratu·la·tory [kən'grætjʊlətərɪ] ADJ (*telegram, speech*) di congratulazioni.

con·gre·gate ['kɒŋgrɪ,geɪt] VI radunarsi, congregarsi, riunirsi.

con·gre·ga·tion [,kɒŋgrɪ'geɪʃən] N (*worshippers*) assemblea (dei fedeli); (*parishioners*) parrocchiani *mpl*, congregazione *f*.

Con·gre·ga·tion·al·ism [,kɒŋgrɪ'geɪʃənə,lɪzəm] N congregazionalismo.

Con·gress ['kɒŋgrɛs] N (*Am*) il Congresso.

con·gress ['kɒŋgrɛs] N congresso.

Con·gres·sion·al [kɒŋ'grɛʃənl] ADJ (*Am*) del Congresso.

congress·man ['kɒŋgrɛsmən] N (*pl* **-men**) (*Am*) membro del Congresso.

congress·woman ['kɒŋgrɛs,wʊmən] N (*pl* **-women**) (*Am*) (donna) membro del Congresso.

con·gru·ent ['kɒŋgruənt] ADJ (*Geom: plane, solid*) congruente.

con·ic ['kɒnɪk] N (*also:* **conic section**, *Geog*) (sezione *f*) conica.

coni·cal ['kɒnɪkəl] ADJ conico(-a); **conical hat** cappello a cono.

co·ni·fer ['kɒnɪfə'] N conifera.

co·nif·er·ous [kə'nɪfərəs] ADJ (*forest*) di conifere; (*tree*) conifero(-a).

con·jec·tur·al [kən'dʒɛktʃərəl] ADJ congetturale.

con·jec·ture [kən'dʒɛktʃə'] ① N congettura.
② VT, VI (*frm*) congetturare.

con·ju·gal ['kɒndʒʊgəl] ADJ (*frm*) coniugale.

con·ju·gate ['kɒndʒʊ,geɪt] ① VT coniugare.
② VI coniugarsi.
③ ADJ (*Geom*) coniugato(-a).

con·ju·ga·tion [,kɒndʒʊ'geɪʃən] N (*Gram*) coniugazione *f*.

con·junc·tion [kən'dʒʌŋkʃən] N **a** (*Gram*) congiunzione *f*
b: **in conjunction with** in accordo con, insieme con *or* a.

con·junc·ti·vi·tis [kən,dʒʌŋktɪ'vaɪtɪs] N (*Med*) congiuntivite *f*.

con·junc·ture [kən'dʒʌŋktʃə'] N (*frm*) congiuntura.

con·jure ['kʌndʒə'] VI fare giochi di prestigio; **a name to conjure with** un nome prestigioso *or* molto importante
▶ **conjure up** VT + ADV (*memories*) evocare, rievocare; (*ghost, spirit*) evocare; (*meal*) inventare, improvvisare.

con·jur·er, **con·jur·or** ['kʌndʒərə'] N prestigiatore(-trice), illusionista *m/f*.

con·jur·ing ['kʌndʒərɪŋ] ① N giochi *mpl* di prestigio, prestidigitazione *f*.
② ADJ: **conjuring trick** gioco di prestigio.

conk·er ['kɒŋkə'] N (*Brit fam*) castagna (d'ippocastano).

conk out [,kɒŋk'aʊt] VI + ADV (*fam: break down*) rompersi.
♦ **con man** N truffatore *m*.

con·nect [kə'nɛkt] ① VT **a** (*gen*) collegare, connettere; (*install: cooker, telephone*) installare, allacciare; **to connect (with)** (*Telec: caller*) mettere in comunicazione (con); **to connect (to)** (*pipes, drains*) collegare (con); **I am trying to connect you** (*Telec*) sto cercando di darle la linea; **to connect sth (up) to the mains** (*Elec*) collegare qc alla rete
b (*associate*): **to connect sb/sth (with)** associare qn/qc (con), collegare qn/qc (con); **the evidence clearly connected him with the crime** le prove dimostravano chiaramente che era implicato nel delitto.
② VI collegarsi; (*train, planes*): **to connect with** essere in coincidenza con.

con·nect·ed [kə'nɛktɪd] ADJ (*languages, species*) connesso(-a); (*events*) collegato(-a); **to be connected (to/with)** (*language, family, species*) essere imparentato(-a) (con); (*event*) essere collegato(-a) (a/con); **these two things are in no way connected** non c'è alcun legame tra le due cose.

con·nec·tion, **con·nex·ion** [kə'nɛkʃən] N **a** (*Tech, Elec, Telec*) collegamento, connessione *f*; (*train, bus, plane*) coincidenza; (*connecting point*) giuntura; **to miss/make a connection** perdere/prendere la coincidenza
b (*relationship*) rapporto, relazione *f*, legame *m*; **connection between/with** rapporto tra/con; **what is the connection between them?** in che modo sono legati?; **in connection with** con riferimento a, a proposito di; **in this connection** riguardo a questo; **family connection** legame *m* di parentela; (*person*) parente *m/f*; **she has many business connections** ha molti rapporti d'affari; **she's got the right connections** conosce le persone giuste.

con·nec·tive [kə'nɛktɪv] ADJ connettivo(-a).

con·ning tow·er ['kɒnɪŋ,taʊə'] N (*of submarine*) torretta di comando.

con·niv·ance [kə'naɪvəns] N (*pej*) connivenza.

con·nive [kə'naɪv] VI: **to connive at** (*pej: pretend not to notice*) chiudere un occhio su; (: *aid and abet*) essere connivente in.

con·niv·ing ['kə'naɪvɪŋ] ADJ: **he's a conniving bastard** è un trafficone.

con·nois·seur [,kɒnə's3:'] N conoscitore(-trice), intenditore(-trice).

con·no·ta·tion [,kɒnəʊ'teɪʃən] N connotazione *f*.

con·no·ta·tive ['kɒnə,teɪtɪv] ADJ connotativo(-a).

con·note [kɒ'nəʊt] VT connotare.

con·nu·bial [kə'nju:bɪəl] ADJ (*frm*) coniugale.

con·quer ['kɒŋkə'] VT (*territory, nation, castle*) conquistare; (*enemy*) vincere, battere, sconfiggere; (*habit, feelings*) vincere, superare.

con·quer·ing ['kɒŋkərɪŋ] ADJ vincitore(-trice).

con·quer·or ['kɒŋkərə'] N conquistatore *m*.

con·quest ['kɒŋkwɛst] N conquista.

cons [kɒnz] NPL see **pro**, **convenience**.

con·science ['kɒnʃəns] N coscienza; **with a clear conscience** con la coscienza pulita *or* a posto; **to have sth on one's conscience** avere qc sulla coscienza; **in all conscience** onestamente, in coscienza.
♦ **conscience-stricken** ['kɒnʃəns,strɪkən] ADJ: **to be conscience-stricken** avere dei rimorsi (di coscienza).

con·sci·en·tious [,kɒnʃɪ'ɛnʃəs] ADJ coscienzioso(-a).

con·sci·en·tious·ly [,kɒnʃɪ'ɛnʃəslɪ] ADV coscienziosamente.

con·sci·en·tious·ness [,kɒnʃɪ'ɛnʃəsnɪs] N coscienziosità.
♦ **conscientious objector** N (*Mil*) obiettore *m* di

coscienza.

con·scious ['kɒnʃəs] ADJ **a** (*aware*): **conscious (of sth/of doing)** consapevole (di qc/di fare), conscio(-a) (di qc/di fare); **to become conscious of sth/that** rendersi conto di qc/che **b** (*deliberate*: *insult, error*) intenzionale, voluto(-a) **c** (*Med*) cosciente; **to become conscious** riprendere coscienza.

con·scious·ly ['kɒnʃəslɪ] ADV consciamente, consapevolmente.

con·scious·ness ['kɒnʃəsnɪs] N **a** (*awareness*): **consciousness (of)** consapevolezza *or* coscienza (di) **b** (*Med*) conoscenza; **to lose/regain consciousness** perdere/riprendere conoscenza *or* i sensi.

con·script [*n* 'kɒnskrɪpt; *vb* kən'skrɪpt] ☐1 N coscritto. ☐2 VT arruolare, chiamare alle armi.

con·scrip·tion [kən'skrɪpʃən] N arruolamento (obbligatorio), coscrizione *f*.

con·se·crate ['kɒnsɪˌkreɪt] VT consacrare.

con·se·cra·tion [ˌkɒnsɪ'kreɪʃən] N consacrazione *f*.

con·secu·tive [kən'sɛkjʊtɪv] ADJ consecutivo(-a); **consecutive clause** (*Gram*) proposizione *f* consecutiva; **on three consecutive occasions** tre volte di fila, tre volte consecutive.

con·sen·sus [kən'sɛnsəs] N consenso; **the consensus of opinion** l'opinione *f* unanime *or* comune.

con·sent [kən'sɛnt] ☐1 N consenso, benestare *m*; **by mutual consent** per mutuo consenso; **by common consent** di comune accordo. ☐2 VI: **to consent (to sth/to do sth)** acconsentire (a qc/a fare qc).

♦ **consenting adults** [kən'sɛntɪŋ'ædʌlts] NPL adulti *mpl* consenzienti.

con·se·quence ['kɒnsɪkwəns] N **a** (*result*) conseguenza, risultato; **in consequence** di conseguenza **b** (*importance*) importanza; **it is of no consequence** non ha nessuna importanza.

con·se·quent ['kɒnsɪkwənt] ADJ conseguente.

con·se·quen·tial [ˌkɒnsɪ'kwɛnʃəl] ADJ (*frm*) **a** (*important*) importante **b** (*consequent*) conseguente.

con·se·quent·ly ['kɒnsɪkwəntlɪ] ADV di conseguenza, dunque, quindi.

con·ser·va·tion [ˌkɒnsə'veɪʃən] N conservazione *f*, tutela; (*of nature*) tutela dell'ambiente; **energy conservation** risparmio energetico.

con·ser·va·tion·ist [ˌkɒnsə'veɪʃənɪst] N ambientalista *m/f*.

con·serva·tism [kən'sɜːvətɪzəm] N conservatorismo.

Con·serva·tive [kən'sɜːvətɪv] ADJ, N (*Brit Pol*) conservatore (-trice).

con·serva·tive [kən'sɜːvətɪv] ☐1 ADJ (*Pol, person, style*) conservatore(-trice); (*estimate, guess*) prudente. ☐2 N conservatore(-trice).

♦ **Conservative Party** N (*Brit*): **the Conservative Party** il partito conservatore.

con·serva·tory [kən'sɜːvətrɪ] N (*greenhouse*) serra; (*Mus*) conservatorio.

con·serve [kən'sɜːv] ☐1 VT conservare; **to conserve one's strength** risparmiare le forze. ☐2 N conserva di frutta.

con·sid·er [kən'sɪdə'] VT **a** (*think about*: *problem, possibility*) considerare, prendere in considerazione; (*question, matter, subject*) valutare, studiare; **to consider doing sth** considerare la possibilità di fare qc; **all things considered** tutto sommato *or* considerato; **it is my considered opinion that ...** sono fermamente convinto

che...

b (*take into account*) considerare, tener conto di **c** (*be of the opinion*) ritenere, considerare; **his teacher considers him too lazy to pass the exams** il suo insegnante lo considera *or* lo ritiene troppo pigro per superare gli esami; **consider yourself lucky** puoi dirti fortunato.

con·sid·er·able [kən'sɪdərəbl] ADJ considerevole, notevole; **to a considerable extent** in gran parte, in misura notevole.

con·sid·er·ably [kən'sɪdərəblɪ] ADV notevolmente, decisamente.

con·sid·er·ate [kən'sɪdərɪt] ADJ riguardoso(-a), premuroso(-a).

con·sid·er·ate·ly [kən'sɪdərɪtlɪ] ADV premurosamente.

con·sid·era·tion [kən,sɪdə'reɪʃən] N **a** NO PL (*thought, reflection*) considerazione *f*; **to be under consideration** essere in esame; **after due consideration** dopo un attento esame; **to take sth into consideration** considerare qc, prendere qc in considerazione; **taking everything into consideration** tutto considerato *or* sommato **b** NO PL (*thoughtfulness*) attenzione *f*, premura; **out of consideration for** per riguardo a; **to show consideration for sb's feelings** avere riguardo per qn **c** (*factor*) elemento; **my first consideration is my family** il mio primo pensiero è per la mia famiglia; **his age is an important consideration** la sua età è un fattore importante; **it's of no consideration** non ha nessuna importanza **d** (*payment*) rimunerazione *f*, ricompensa; **for a consideration** dietro compenso.

con·sid·ered [kən'sɪdəd] ADJ: **it is my considered opinion that ...** dopo lunga riflessione il mio parere è che ... .

con·sid·er·ing [kən'sɪdərɪŋ] ☐1 PREP considerando, considerato(-a). ☐2 CONJ: **considering (that)** se si considera *or* tiene conto (che). ☐3 ADV: **he did very well, considering** è stato molto bravo, tutto sommato.

con·sign [kən'saɪn] VT **a**: **to consign sb/sth (to)** (*frm*: *banish*) relegare qn/qc (in); (*commit, entrust*) affidare qn/qc (a) **b** (*Comm*: *send*) consegnare, spedire.

con·signee [ˌkɒnsaɪ'niː] N consegnatario(-a), destinatario(-a).

con·sign·ment [kən'saɪnmənt] N (*of goods*) partita, consegna, spedizione *f*.

♦ **consignment note** N (*Comm*) nota di spedizione.

con·sign·or [kən'saɪnə'] N mittente *m/f*.

con·sist [kən'sɪst] VI: **to consist of** essere composto(-a) di, constare di; **to consist in sth/in doing sth** consistere in qc/nel fare qc.

con·sist·en·cy [kən'sɪstənsɪ] N **a** (*of person, action*) coerenza **b** (*density*) consistenza.

con·sist·ent [kən'sɪstənt] ADJ **a** (*constant*: *results, action*) costante; (: *person*) costante **b** (*coherent*: *argument*) coerente, logico(-a); **to be consistent with** essere coerente con.

con·sist·ent·ly [kən'sɪstəntlɪ] ADV (*argue, behave, happen*) immancabilmente.

con·so·la·tion [ˌkɒnsə'leɪʃən] N consolazione *f*.

♦ **consolation prize** N premio di consolazione.

con·sole¹ [kən'səʊl] VT: **to console (sb for sth)** consolare (qn per qc).

con·sole² ['kɒnsəʊl] N (*control panel*) console *f inv*, quadro

di comando.

con·soli·date [kən'sɒlɪˌdeɪt] VT **a** (*position, influence*) consolidare **b** (*combine*) unire, fondere.

con·soli·da·tion [kənˌsɒlɪ'deɪʃən] N (*see vb*) consolidazione *f*; fusione *f*, unione *f*.

con·sol·ing [kən'səʊlɪŋ] ADJ confortante, consolante, consolatorio(-a).

con·sol·ing·ly [kən'səʊlɪŋlɪ] ADV (*smile, speak*) in modo confortante.

con·sols ['kɒnsɒlz] NPL (*Stock Exchange*) titoli *mpl* del debito consolidato.

con·som·mé [kɒn'sɒmeɪ] N (*Culin*) consommé *m inv*, brodo ristretto.

con·so·nant ['kɒnsənənt] N consonante *f*.

con·so·nan·tal [ˌkɒnsə'næntl] ADJ consonantico(-a).

con·sort [*n* 'kɒnsɔːt; *vb* kən'sɔːt] **1** N consorte *m/f*; **prince consort** principe *m* consorte.

 2 VI (*often pej*): **to consort with sb** frequentare qn.

con·sor·tium [kən'sɔːtɪəm] N (*pl* **consortia** [kən'sɔːtɪə]) consorzio.

con·spicu·ous [kən'spɪkjʊəs] ADJ (*person, behaviour*) che si fa notare; (*clothes*) vistoso(-a); (*sign, notice*) ben visibile; (*bravery, difference*) notevole, evidente; **a conspicuous lack of sth** una notevole mancanza di qc; **to make o.s. conspicuous** farsi notare; **to be conspicuous by one's absence** brillare per la propria assenza.

con·spicu·ous·ly [kən'spɪkjʊəslɪ] ADV (*behave*) in modo da farsi notare; (*successful*) notevolmente; (*dressed*) vistosamente.

con·spira·cy [kən'spɪrəsɪ] N cospirazione *f*, congiura.

con·spira·tor [kən'spɪrətəʳ] N cospiratore(-trice).

con·spira·to·rial [kənˌspɪrə'tɔːrɪəl] ADJ cospiratorio(-a).

con·spire [kən'spaɪəʳ] VI **a** (*people*): **to conspire (with sb against sb/sth)** congiurare *or* cospirare (con qn contro qn/qc) **b** (*events*): **to conspire to do sth** contribuire a fare qc; **everything had conspired to make him happy** tutto aveva contribuito a renderlo felice.

con·sta·ble ['kʌnstəbl] N (*Brit: also:* **police constable**) agente *m/f* (di polizia).

con·stabu·lary [kən'stæbjʊlərɪ] N polizia.

con·stan·cy ['kɒnstənsɪ] N (*of friend, affection*) costanza.

con·stant ['kɒnstənt] **1** ADJ (*interruptions*) continuo(-a), incessante; (*use*) continuo(-a), costante; (*speed, temperature, rhythm*) costante; (*affection*) costante, stabile; (*friend, love*) fedele.

 2 N (*Math, Phys*) costante *f*.

con·stant·ly ['kɒnstəntlɪ] ADV continuamente, costantemente.

con·stel·la·tion [ˌkɒnstə'leɪʃən] N costellazione *f*.

con·ster·na·tion [ˌkɒnstə'neɪʃən] N costernazione *f*, sgomento; **filled with consternation (at)** costernato(-a) (per).

con·sti·pate ['kɒnstɪˌpeɪt] VT (*Med*) causare stitichezza a.

con·sti·pat·ed ['kɒnstɪˌpeɪtɪd] ADJ (*Med*) stitico(-a).

con·sti·pa·tion [ˌkɒnstɪ'peɪʃən] N (*Med*) stitichezza.

con·stitu·en·cy [kən'stɪtjʊənsɪ] N (*district*) collegio elettorale; (*people*) elettori *mpl* (del collegio).

♦ **constituency party** N sezione *f* locale (del partito).

con·stitu·ent [kən'stɪtjʊənt] **1** N (*Pol: voter*) elettore(-trice); (*part*) ingrediente *m*, componente *m*.

 2 ADJ costitutivo(-a).

con·sti·tute ['kɒnstɪˌtjuːt] VT costituire.

con·sti·tu·tion [ˌkɒnstɪ'tjuːʃən] N costituzione *f*.

con·sti·tu·tion·al [ˌkɒnstɪ'tjuːʃənl] ADJ costituzionale.

con·sti·tu·tion·al·ity [ˌkɒnstɪˌtjuːʃə'nælɪtɪ] N costituzio-

nalità.

con·sti·tu·tion·al·ly [ˌkɒnstɪ'tjuːʃənəlɪ] ADV (*Pol*) costituzionalmente; (*by nature, inherently*) per natura.

♦ **constitutional monarchy** N monarchia costituzionale.

con·strain [kən'streɪn] VT costringere.

con·strained [kən'streɪnd] ADJ (*awkward*) forzato(-a); **to feel/be constrained to do sth** sentirsi/essere costretto (-a) a fare qc.

con·straint [kən'streɪnt] N, NO PL (*compulsion*) costrizione *f*; (*restraint*) limitazione *f*; (*embarrassment*) imbarazzo, soggezione *f*.

con·strict [kən'strɪkt] VT (*throat, waist, blood vessels*) stringere; (*movements*) impedire; (*freedom*) limitare.

con·strict·ed [kən'strɪktɪd] ADJ (*movements*) limitato(-a); (*point of view*) ristretto(-a).

con·stric·tion [kən'strɪkʃən] N costrizione *f*; (*feeling*) oppressione *f*.

con·struct [kən'strʌkt] VT costruire.

con·struc·tion [kən'strʌkʃən] N (*gen*) costruzione *f*; (*fig: interpretation*) interpretazione *f*; **under construction** in costruzione.

♦ **construction industry** N edilizia, industria edile.

con·struc·tive [kən'strʌktɪv] ADJ costruttivo(-a).

con·struc·tive·ly [kən'strʌktɪvlɪ] ADV costruttivamente.

con·strue [kən'struː] VT (*interpret*) interpretare.

con·sul ['kɒnsəl] N console *m*; **consul general** console generale.

con·su·lar ['kɒnsjʊləʳ] ADJ consolare.

con·su·late ['kɒnsjʊlɪt] N consolato.

con·sult [kən'sʌlt] **1** VT: **to consult sb (about sth)** consultare qn (su *or* riguardo a qc).

 2 VI: **to consult each other** consultarsi.

con·sul·tan·cy [kən'sʌltənsɪ] **1** N consulenza.

 2 ADJ (*fees, business*) di consulenza.

♦ **consultancy agreement** N contratto di consulenza.

♦ **consultancy fee** N onorario di consulenza.

con·sult·ant [kən'sʌltənt] N consulente *m/f*; (*Brit Med*) specialista *m/f*; **consultant engineer** ingegnere *m* consulente; **consultant paediatrician** specialista *m/f* in pediatria; **legal/management consultant** consulente legale/gestionale.

con·sul·ta·tion [ˌkɒnsəl'teɪʃən] N consultazione *f*; (*Med, Law*) consulto; **in consultation with** consultandosi con.

con·sul·ta·tive [kən'sʌltətɪv] ADJ (*document*) di consulenza; **in a consultative capacity** in veste di consulente.

con·sult·ing [kən'sʌltɪŋ] ADJ consulente.

♦ **consulting hours** NPL (*Med*) orario *msg* di visita.

♦ **consulting room** N (*Brit Med*) ambulatorio, studio medico.

con·sume [kən'sjuːm] VT (*gen*) consumare; **to be consumed with** (*envy*) essere roso(-a) da; (*grief*) consumarsi di.

con·sum·er [kən'sjuːməʳ] N consumatore(-trice); (*of electricity, gas etc*) utente *m/f*.

♦ **consumer credit** N credito al consumatore.

♦ **consumer durables** NPL prodotti *mpl* di consumo durevole.

♦ **consumer goods** NPL beni *mpl* di consumo.

con·sum·er·ism [kən'sjuːməˌrɪzəm] N (*consumer protection*) tutela del consumatore; (*Econ*) consumismo.

♦ **consumer organization** N organizzazione di consumatori.

♦ **consumer protection** N tutela dei consumatori.

♦ **consumer society** N società consumista *or* dei

consumi.
♦ **consumer watchdog** N comitato di difesa dei consumatori.

con·sum·ing [kən'sju:mɪŋ] ADJ (*passion, desire*) struggente.

con·sum·mate [*adj* kən'sʌmɪt; *vb* 'kɒnsəˌmeɪt] ① ADJ consumato(-a), abile; **with consummate ease** con estrema facilità.
② VT (*marriage*) consumare.

con·sum·ma·tion [ˌkɒnsə'meɪʃən] N (*of marriage*) consumazione *f*.

con·sump·tion [kən'sʌmpʃən] N **a** (*of food, fuel*) consumo; **not fit for human consumption** non commestibile **b** (*old: tuberculosis*) consunzione *f*.

con·sump·tive [kən'sʌmptɪv] ADJ, N (*old*) tisico(-a).

cont., cont'd ABBR (= *continued*) segue.

con·tact ['kɒntækt] ① N (*gen*) contatto; (*person*) conoscenza, contatto; **to be in contact with sb/sth** essere in contatto con qn/qc; **to make contact with sb** mettersi in contatto con qn; **to lose contact (with sb)** perdere i contatti (con qn), perdere di vista qn; **business contacts** contatti *mpl* d'affari.
② VT mettersi in contatto con, contattare.

♦ **contact adhesive** N adesivo istantaneo.
♦ **contact breaker** N (*Elec*) ruttore *m*.
♦ **contact lens** N (*pl* -es) lente *f* a contatto.

con·ta·gion [kən'teɪdʒən] N (*Med, frm*) contagio.

con·ta·gious [kən'teɪdʒəs] ADJ contagioso(-a), infettivo (-a).

con·ta·gious·ly [kən'teɪdʒəslɪ] ADV contagiosamente.

con·tain [kən'teɪn] VT contenere; (*fire, disease*) arginare; **to contain o.s.** contenersi.

con·tain·er [kən'teɪnə'] ① N (*box, jug*) contenitore *m*, recipiente *m*; (*Comm: for transport, shipping*) container *m inv*.
② ADJ (*train, lorry, ship*) da container; (*dock, depot, transport*) per container.

con·tain·eri·za·tion [kənˌteɪnəraɪ'zeɪʃən] N containerizzazione *f*.

con·tain·er·ize [kən'teɪnəˌraɪz] VT mettere in container.

con·tain·ment [kən'teɪnmənt] N contenimento.

con·tami·nate [kən'tæmɪˌneɪt] VT contaminare.

con·tami·na·tion [kənˌtæmɪ'neɪʃən] N contaminazione *f*.

cont'd ABBR = **cont.**

con·tem·plate ['kɒntɛmˌpleɪt] VT (*gaze at, reflect upon*) contemplare; **to contemplate sth/doing sth** (*consider*) pensare a qc/di fare qc.

con·tem·pla·tion [ˌkɒntɛm'pleɪʃən] N contemplazione *f*.

con·tem·pla·tive [kən'templətɪv] ADJ contemplativo(-a).

con·tem·po·ra·neous [kənˌtempə'reɪnɪəs] ADJ (*frm*): **contemporaneous (with)** contemporaneo(-a) (a).

con·tem·po·rary [kən'tempərərɪ] ① ADJ contemporaneo (-a); (*design*) moderno(-a).
② N contemporaneo(-a).

con·tempt [kən'tempt] N disprezzo, disdegno; **to hold sth/sb in contempt** disprezzare qc/qn; **contempt of court** (*Law*) oltraggio alla Corte; **it's beneath contempt** è oltremodo vergognoso.

con·tempt·ible [kən'temptəbl] ADJ vergognoso(-a), spregevole.

con·temp·tu·ous [kən'temptjʊəs] ADJ (*person*): **contemptuous (of)** sprezzante (di); (*manner, gesture*) sprezzante, altezzoso(-a), sdegnoso(-a).

con·temp·tu·ous·ly [kən'temptjʊəslɪ] ADV con disprezzo, sprezzantemente.

con·tend [kən'tend] ① VT: **to contend that** (*frm*) sostenere che, asserire che.
② VI (*fig*): **to contend (with sb) for sth** contendersi qc (con qn); **we have many problems to contend with** dobbiamo lottare contro molti problemi; **you'll have me to contend with** dovrai vedertela con me; **he has a lot to contend with** ha un sacco di guai.

con·tend·er [kən'tendə'] N contendente *m/f*, concorrente *m/f*.

con·tent¹ [kən'tent] ① ADJ: **content (with)** contento(-a) *or* soddisfatto(-a) (di); **to be content to do sth** essere contento(-a) di fare qc.
② N contentezza; **to one's heart's content** quanto si ha voglia; **to eat and drink to one's heart content** mangiare e bere a sazietà.
③ VT fare contento(-a), soddisfare, contentare; **to content o.s. with sth/with doing sth** accontentarsi di qc/di fare qc.

con·tent² ['kɒntent] N contenuto; **contents** NPL (*of box, case*) contenuto; **(table of) contents** (*of book*) indice *m*.

con·tent·ed [kən'tentɪd] ADJ: **contented (with)** contento (-a) (di), soddisfatto(-a) (di).

con·tent·ed·ly [kən'tentɪdlɪ] ADV con soddisfazione.

con·ten·tion [kən'tenʃən] N (*strife*) contesa, disputa; (*frm: assertion*) tesi *f inv*; **bone of contention** pomo della discordia.

con·ten·tious [kən'tenʃəs] ADJ polemico(-a).

con·tent·ment [kən'tentmənt] N contentezza, soddisfazione *f*.

con·test [*n* 'kɒntest; *vb* kən'test] ① N (*struggle*) gara, lotta; (*Boxing, Wrestling*) incontro; (*competition*) gara, concorso.
② VT (*dispute: argument*) contestare; (: *right*) contestare, disputare; (*Law*) impugnare; (*compete for*) contendersi, disputare; (: *election, seat*) essere in lizza per.

con·test·ant [kən'testənt] N (*in competition*) concorrente *m/f*; (*Sport*) contendente *m/f*, avversario(-a); **contestant for a title** aspirante *m/f* a un titolo.

con·text ['kɒntekst] N contesto; **in/out of context** nel/fuori dal contesto.

con·tex·tual [kən'tekstjʊəl] ADJ contestuale.

con·ti·nence ['kɒntɪnəns] N (*frm*) continenza.

con·ti·nent ['kɒntɪnənt] N **a** continente *m* **b** (*Brit*): **the Continent** l'Europa continentale; **on the Continent** in Europa.

con·ti·nen·tal [ˌkɒntɪ'nentl] ① ADJ continentale; (*Brit: European*) europeo(-a), dell'Europa continentale.
② N (*Brit*) abitante *m/f* dell'Europa continentale.

♦ **continental breakfast** N colazione *f* (*senza cibi caldi*).
♦ **continental drift** N deriva dei continenti.
♦ **continental quilt** N (*Brit*) piumino.

con·tin·gen·cy [kən'tɪndʒənsɪ] N contingenza, evenienza, eventualità *f inv*; **in certain contingencies** in certi frangenti.

♦ **contingency funds** NPL fondi *mpl* di previdenza.
♦ **contingency plan** N misura *or* piano d'emergenza.

con·tin·gent [kən'tɪndʒənt] (*frm*) ① ADJ: **to be contingent upon** dipendere da.
② N (*Mil*) contingente *m*; (*group*) gruppo.

con·tin·ual [kən'tɪnjʊəl] ADJ continuo(-a).

con·tin·u·al·ly [kən'tɪnjʊəlɪ] ADV continuamente, senza tregua, di continuo.

con·tinu·ance [kən'tɪnjʊəns] N (*continuation*) continuazione *f*; (*duration*) durata.

con·tinu·ation [kən‚tɪnjʊ'eɪʃən] N continuazione *f*; (*resumption*) ripresa; (*of serial story*) seguito.

con·tinue [kən'tɪnjuː] 1 VT (*gen*): **to continue (doing** *or* **to do sth)** continuare (a fare qc); (*start again*) riprendere, continuare; (*serial story*): **to be continued** continua; **continued on page 10** segue *or* continua a pagina 10.
2 VI (*gen*) continuare; (*resume*) riprendere, continuare; (*extend*) estendersi, proseguire; **to continue on one's way** continuare per la propria strada.

con·tinu·ing edu·ca·tion [kən'tɪnjuːɪŋɛdjʊ'keɪʃən] N corsi *mpl* per adulti.

con·ti·nu·ity [‚kɒntɪ'njuːɪtɪ] N continuità; (*Cine*) (ordine *m* della) sceneggiatura.

♦ **continuity girl** N (*Cine*) segretaria di produzione.

♦ **continuity man** N (*Cine*) segretario di produzione.

con·tinu·ous [kən'tɪnjʊəs] ADJ continuo(-a), ininterrotto (-a); **continuous performance** (*Cine*) spettacolo continuato; **continuous stationery** (*Comput*) (carta a) moduli *mpl* continui.

con·tinu·ous·ly [kən'tɪnjʊəslɪ] ADV (*unceasingly*) in continuazione; (*uninterruptedly*) ininterrottamente.

con·tin·uum [kən'tɪnjʊəm] N (*frm*) continuum *m inv*.

con·tort [kən'tɔːt] VT contorcere.

con·tor·tion [kən'tɔːʃən] N (*of acrobat*) contorsione *f*, contorcimento.

con·tor·tion·ist [kən'tɔːʃənɪst] N contorsionista *m/f*.

con·tour ['kɒntʊə] N contorno, profilo; (*also:* **contour line**) curva di livello, isoipsa.

♦ **contour map** N carta a curve di livello.

♦ **contour ploughing** N aratura a girapoggio.

contra·band ['kɒntrə‚bænd] 1 N contrabbando.
2 ADJ di contrabbando.

contra·cep·tion [‚kɒntrə'sɛpʃən] N contraccezione *f*.

contra·cep·tive [‚kɒntrə'sɛptɪv] 1 ADJ contraccettivo (-a), anticoncezionale.
2 N contraccettivo, anticoncezionale *m*.

♦ **contraceptive pill** N pillola anticoncezionale.

con·tract [*n, adj* 'kɒntrækt; *vb* kən'trækt] 1 N contratto; **contract of employment** contratto di lavoro; **to enter into a contract with sb to do sth/for sth** stipulare un contratto con qn per fare qc/per qc; **to be under contract to do sth** aver stipulato un contratto per fare qc; **to put work out to contract** dare del lavoro in appalto, appaltare un lavoro; **by contract** per contratto; **there's a contract out for him** (*fig fam*) c'è una taglia su di lui.
2 VT (*all senses*) contrarre; **to contract with sb to do sth** stipulare un contratto con qn per fare qc.
3 VI (*muscles, lips*) contrarsi; (*metal*) restringersi; (*economy*) essere in fase di contrazione.
4 ADJ (*date*) del contratto; (*price*) secondo contratto; (*work*) a contratto, in appalto

▶ **contract in** VI + ADV impegnarsi (con un contratto); (*Brit: into pension scheme*) *scegliere di pagare i contributi per una pensione*

▶ **contract out** VI + ADV: **to contract out (of)** ritirarsi (da); **to contract out of a pension scheme** (*Brit Admin*) cessare di pagare i contributi per una pensione.

♦ **contract bridge** N (*Cards*) bridge *m* contratto.

con·trac·tile [kən'træktaɪl] ADJ contrattile.

con·trac·tion [kən'trækʃən] N contrazione *f*; (*of metal*) restringimento.

♦ **contract labour** N manodopera a tempo determinato.

con·trac·tor [kən'træktə'] N (*Constr*) appaltatore *m*, imprenditore *m*; (*Law*) contraente *m*.

con·trac·tual [kən'træktʃʊəl] ADJ contrattuale.

con·trac·tu·al·ly [kən'træktʃʊəlɪ] ADV contrattualmente.

contra·dict [‚kɒntrə'dɪkt] VT contraddire.

contra·dic·tion [‚kɒntrə'dɪkʃən] N contraddizione *f*; **to be in contradiction with** discordare con; **contradiction in terms** contraddizione (in termini).

contra·dic·tory [‚kɒntrə'dɪktərɪ] ADJ contraddittorio(-a); **to be contradictory to** contraddire.

contra·in·di·ca·tion [‚kɒntrə‚ɪndɪ'keɪʃən] N (*Med*) controindicazione *f*.

con·tral·to [kən'træltəʊ] N contralto.

con·trap·tion [kən'træpʃən] N (*fam pej*) aggeggio.

con·tra·ri·ness [kən'trɛərɪnɪs] N testardaggine *f*, cocciutaggine *f*.

con·tra·ri·wise [kən'trɛərɪ‚waɪz] ADV (*on the other hand*) d'altro canto, d'altra parte; (*in the opposite direction*) nella direzione opposta, nel senso opposto.

con·tra·ry ['kɒntrərɪ; *adj b* kən'trɛərɪ] 1 ADJ **a** : contrary **(to)** contrario(-a) (a), opposto(-a) (a); **contrary to nature** contro natura; **contrary to what we thought** a differenza di *or* contrariamente a quanto pensavamo **b** (*self-willed*) difficile, cocciuto(-a), bisbetico(-a).
2 N contrario; **on the contrary** al contrario; **unless you hear to the contrary** salvo contrordine.

con·trast [*n* 'kɒntrɑːst; *vb* kən'trɑːst] 1 N contrasto; **in contrast to** *or* **with** a differenza di, contrariamente a.
2 VT: **to contrast (with)** mettere a confronto (con), opporre (a).
3 VI: **to contrast (with)** contrastare (con).

con·trast·ing [kən'trɑːstɪŋ] ADJ contrastante, di contrasto.

con·tras·tive [kən'trɑːstɪv] ADJ contrastivo(-a).

contra·vene [‚kɒntrə'viːn] VT (*frm*) contravvenire a.

contra·ven·tion [‚kɒntrə'vɛnʃən] N: **contravention (of)** (*frm*) contravvenzione *f*(a), infrazione *f*(di).

con·trib·ute [kən'trɪbjuːt] 1 VT (*sum of money*) offrire, donare, contribuire con; (*help*) offrire; **to contribute an article to a newspaper** contribuire ad un giornale con un articolo.
2 VI: **to contribute to** (*charity, collection, success*) contribuire a; (*discussion*) partecipare a; (*newspaper*) collaborare a *or* con, scrivere per; (*Admin*) pagare i contributi per.

con·tri·bu·tion [‚kɒntrɪ'bjuːʃən] N (*money, goods*) contributo, offerta, donazione *f*; (*help, assistance*) contributo, contribuzione *f*; (*Brit: payment*) contributi *mpl*; (*article, story*) contributo, collaborazione *f*; (*in discussion*) intervento.

con·tribu·tor [kən'trɪbjʊtə'] N (*of money*) donatore(-trice); (*to journal, newspaper*) collaboratore(-trice).

con·tribu·tory [kən'trɪbjʊtərɪ] ADJ (*cause*) che contribuisce; **it was a contributory factor in ...** quello ha contribuito a... .

♦ **contributory negligence** N (*Law*) concorso di colpa.

♦ **contributory pension scheme** N (*Brit*) *pensionamento finanziato da lavoratore e datore di lavoro*.

con·trite ['kɒntraɪt] ADJ mortificato(-a); (*Rel*) contrito(-a).

con·trite·ly [kən'traɪtlɪ] ADV compuntamente.

con·tri·tion [kən'trɪʃən] N (*see adj*) mortificazione *f*; contrizione *f*.

con·triv·ance [kən'traɪvəns] N (*machine, device*) congegno; (*scheme*) espediente *m*, stratagemma *m*.

con·trive [kən'traɪv] VT (*plan, scheme*) inventare, escogitare; **to contrive a means of doing sth** escogitare un

sistema per fare qc; **to contrive to do sth** trovare un modo per fare qc.

con·trived [kən'traɪvd] ADJ innaturale, forzato(-a).

con·trol [kən'trəʊl] ☐1☐ N **a** NO PL (*gen*) controllo; (*of traffic*) regolamentazione *f*; (*of pests*) eliminazione *f*; **the control of cancer** la lotta contro il cancro; **they have no control over their son** non hanno alcuna autorità sul figlio; **to keep sth/sb under control** tenere qc/qn sotto controllo; **to lose control of sth** perdere il controllo di qc; **to lose control of o.s.** perdere il controllo di sé; **to be in control of** tenere sotto controllo; **to take control of** assumere il controllo di; **to bring a fire under control** arginare *or* circoscrivere un incendio; **everything is under control** tutto è sotto controllo; **the car went out of control** la macchina non rispondeva più ai comandi; **the class was quite out of control** la classe era in subbuglio; **due to circumstances beyond our control** per circostanze *fpl* indipendenti dalla nostra volontà; **who is in control?** chi è il responsabile?

b (*Tech, TV, Radio*) comando; **to take over the controls** prendere i comandi

c : **wage/price controls** NPL (*restrictions*) limitazione *f* dei salari/prezzi

d (*in experiment*) gruppo di controllo.

☐2☐ VT (*check*) controllare; (*traffic*) dirigere, regolare; (*operation etc*) dirigere; (*company*) avere controllo di; (*crowd*) tenere sotto controllo; (*disease, fire*) arginare, limitare; (*emotions*) controllare, frenare, dominare; **to control o.s.** controllarsi.

♦ **control group** N (*Med, Psych etc*) gruppo di controllo.

♦ **control key** N (*Comput*) tasto di controllo.

con·trolled [kən'trəʊld] ADJ **a** (*emotion*) contenuto(-a); **she was very controlled** era padrona di sé **b** (*Econ*): **controlled economy** economia controllata.

con·trol·ler [kən'trəʊlə'] N controllore *m*.

con·trol·ling [kən'trəʊlɪŋ] ADJ (*factor*) dominante.

♦ **controlling interest** N (*Comm*) maggioranza delle azioni.

♦ **control panel** N (*on aircraft, ship, TV*) quadro dei comandi.

♦ **control point** N punto di controllo.

♦ **control room** N (*Naut, Mil*) sala di comando; (*Radio, TV*) sala di regia.

♦ **control tower** N (*Aer*) torre *f* di controllo.

♦ **control unit** N (*Comput*) unità *f inv* di controllo.

con·tro·ver·sial [ˌkɒntrə'vɜː'ʃəl] ADJ (*subject, speech, decision, book*) controverso(-a), discusso(-a), che suscita polemiche; (*person*) discusso(-a), polemico(-a).

con·tro·ver·sy [kən'trɒvəsɪ] N controversia, polemica; **it has caused a lot of controversy** ha causato molte polemiche.

con·tu·sion [kən'tjuːʒən] N (*Med*) contusione *f*.

co·nun·drum [kə'nʌndrəm] N indovinello.

con·ur·ba·tion [ˌkɒnɜː'beɪʃən] N conurbazione *f*.

con·va·lesce [ˌkɒnvə'lɛs] VI fare la convalescenza, rimettersi.

con·va·les·cence [ˌkɒnvə'lɛsəns] N convalescenza.

con·va·les·cent [ˌkɒnvə'lɛsənt] ADJ, N convalescente (*m/f*); **convalescent home** convalescenziario.

con·vec·tion [kən'vɛkʃən] N convezione *f*.

♦ **convection currents** NPL correnti *fpl* convettive.

con·vec·tor [kən'vɛktə'] N (*also*: **convector heater, convection heater**) convettore *m*.

con·vene [kən'viːn] ☐1☐ VT (*people*) convocare; (*meeting*) indire, convocare.

☐2☐ VI riunirsi, adunarsi, convenire.

con·ven·er [kən'viːnə'] N (*esp Brit*) presidente *m* (*di commissione etc*).

con·veni·ence [kən'viːnɪəns] N **a** (*of house, plan, person*) comodità; **at your earliest convenience** (*Comm*) appena possibile; **at your convenience** a suo comodo **b** : **conveniences** NPL (*amenities: of house*) comodità *fpl*; **all modern conveniences**, (*Brit*) **all mod cons** tutte le comodità moderne **c** (*frm: toilet*) gabinetto.

♦ **convenience foods** NPL cibi *mpl* precotti.

con·veni·ent [kən'viːnɪənt] ADJ (*tool, size, place etc*) comodo(-a); (*event, time, occasion*) adatto(-a), opportuno(-a); **the house is convenient for the shops** la casa è vicina ai *or* comoda per i negozi; **if it is convenient to you** se per lei va bene, se non la incomoda; **would tomorrow be convenient?** andrebbe bene domani?; **is it convenient to call tomorrow?** potrei passare domani?

con·veni·ent·ly [kən'viːnɪəntlɪ] ADV (*happen*) a proposito; (*situated*) in una posizione comoda; **very conveniently he arrived late** (*luckily*) è stata una fortuna che sia arrivato in ritardo.

con·vent ['kɒnvənt] N convento (di suore).

con·ven·tion [kən'vɛnʃən] N (*custom, agreement*) convenzione *f*; (*meeting*) congresso, convegno.

con·ven·tion·al [kən'vɛnʃənl] ADJ (*person, style, weapons*) convenzionale; (*methods*) tradizionale.

con·ven·tion·al·ly [kən'vɛnʃənlɪ] ADV (*dress, behave*) convenzionalmente.

♦ **convent school** N scuola retta da suore.

con·verge [kən'vɜːdʒ] VI: **to converge (on)** convergere (su).

con·ver·gence [kən'vɜːdʒəns] N convergenza.

con·ver·gent [kən'vɜːdʒənt], **con·ver·ging** [kən'vɜːdʒɪŋ] ADJ convergente.

con·ver·sant [kən'vɜːsənt] ADJ: **to be conversant with** (*car engines, machinery*) essere pratico(-a) di; (*facts*) essere al corrente di; (*language, subject*) avere una buona conoscenza di.

con·ver·sa·tion [ˌkɒnvə'seɪʃən] N conversazione *f*; **in conversation with** a colloquio con; **to have a conversation with sb** conversare con qn, parlare con qn; **what was your conversation about?** di che cosa parlavate?

con·ver·sa·tion·al [ˌkɒnvə'seɪʃənl] ADJ (*style, tone*) colloquiale; (*Comput*) conversazionale.

con·ver·sa·tion·al·ist [ˌkɒnvə'seɪʃnəlɪst] N conversatore (-trice).

con·ver·sa·tion·al·ly [ˌkɒnvə'seɪʃnəlɪ] ADV: **"lovely day"**, **he said conversationally** "bella giornata", ha detto per fare conversazione.

♦ **conversation mode** N (*Comput*) modo conversazionale.

♦ **conversation piece** N (*antique, curiosity*) oggetto di conversazione.

♦ **conversation stopper** N: **that was a conversation stopper** (*fam*) quello ha lasciato tutti a bocca aperta.

con·verse[1] [kən'vɜːs] VI: **to converse (with sb about sth)** (*frm*) conversare (con qn su *or* di qc).

con·verse[2] ['kɒnvɜːs] ☐1☐ N inverso, contrario, opposto; (*Math*) opposto.

☐2☐ ADJ opposto(-a), contrario(-a).

con·verse·ly [kɒn'vɜːslɪ] ADV al contrario, per contro.

con·ver·sion [kən'vɜːʃən] N (*gen, Rel*) conversione *f*; (*Brit: of house*) trasformazione *f*, rimodernamento; (*Rugby, Am Ftbl*) trasformazione *f*.

♦ **conversion table** N tavola *or* tabella di conversione.

con·vert [n 'kɒnvɜ:t; vb kən'vɜ:t] [1] N convertito(-a).
[2] VT **a** (Rel): **to convert (to)** convertire a **b** : **to convert (to, into)** (gen) convertire (in); (house) trasformare (in), convertire (in) **c** (Rugby, Am Ftbl) trasformare.

con·ver·ter [kən'vɜ:tə'] N (Elec) convertitore m.

con·vert·ibil·ity [kən,vɜ:tə'bılıtı] N convertibilità.

con·vert·ible [kən'vɜ:təbl] [1] ADJ (currency) convertibile; **convertible settee** divano letto.
[2] N (car) (auto f inv) decappottabile f.

con·vex ['kɒn'vɛks] ADJ convesso(-a).

con·vey [kən'veɪ] VT (goods, passengers) trasportare; (subj: pipeline) convogliare; (thanks, congratulations, sound, order) trasmettere; (meaning, ideas) comunicare, esprimere; **to convey to sb that** comunicare a qn che; **words cannot convey ...** le parole non possono esprimere...; **the name conveys nothing to me** il nome non mi dice niente.

con·vey·ance [kən'veɪəns] N (of goods) trasporto; (vehicle) mezzo di trasporto.

con·vey·anc·ing [kən'veɪənsɪŋ] N (Law) redazione f di transazioni di proprietà.

con·vey·or [kən'veɪə'] N (Law) concedente m/f.
♦ **conveyor belt** N (Industry) nastro trasportatore.

con·vict [n 'kɒnvɪkt; vb kən'vɪkt] [1] N carcerato(-a).
[2] VT: **to convict (of)** riconoscere colpevole (di), dichiarare colpevole (di); **convicted murderer** persona riconosciuta colpevole di omicidio.

con·vic·tion [kən'vɪkʃən] N **a** (belief) convinzione f; **it is my conviction that** sono convinto che; **to carry conviction** essere convincente **b** (Law) condanna.

con·vince [kən'vɪns] VT: **to convince sb (of sth/that)** convincere qn (di qc/che), persuadere qn (di qc/che).

con·vinc·ing [kən'vɪnsɪŋ] ADJ (gen) convincente; (win) netto(-a).

con·vinc·ing·ly [kən'vɪnsɪŋlı] ADV (see adj) in modo convincente; nettamente.

con·viv·ial [kən'vɪvɪəl] ADJ allegro(-a), gioviale.

con·vivi·al·ly [kən'vɪvɪəlɪ] ADV allegramente, giovialmente.

con·vo·ca·tion [,kɒnvə'keɪʃən] N (frm: summoning) convocazione f; (: assembly) assemblea.

con·vo·lut·ed ['kɒnvəlu:tɪd] (frm) ADJ (shape) attorcigliato(-a), avvolto(-a); (argument) involuto(-a).

con·vo·lu·tion [,kɒnvə'lu:ʃən] N (frm, curve) circonvoluzione f; (Art) voluta; (fig: of argument) involuzione f.

con·vol·vu·lus [kən'vɒlvjʊləs] N (Bot) convolvolo.

con·voy ['kɒnvɔɪ] N convoglio; (escort) scorta; **in convoy** in convoglio; **under convoy** sotto scorta.

con·vulse [kən'vʌls] VT sconvolgere; **to be convulsed with pain/laughter** contorcersi dal dolore/dalle risa.

con·vul·sion [kən'vʌlʃən] N (fit, seizure) convulsione f; **in convulsions** (fam: laughter) piegato(-a) in due (dalle risate).

con·vul·sive [kən'vʌlsɪv] ADJ (movement, laughter) convulso(-a); (Med) convulsivo(-a).

con·vul·sive·ly [kən'vʌlsɪvlɪ] ADV convulsamente.

coo [ku:] [1] VI (dove) tubare.
[2] VT sussurrare dolcemente; **to coo over a baby** fare versetti a un bimbo.

cook [kʊk] [1] N cuoco(-a); **head cook and bottlewasher** (fig hum) tuttofare m/f.
[2] VT **a** cuocere, cucinare; (meal) preparare; **shall I cook you an omelette?** ti cucino or ti faccio un'omelette?; **to cook sb's goose** (fig fam) rompere le uova nel paniere a qn; **to cook one's own goose** (fig fam) darsi la zappa sui piedi

b (fam: falsify: accounts) falsificare, alterare; **to cook the books** falsificare i libri contabili.
[3] VI (food) cuocere; (person) cucinare; **what's cooking?** (fig fam) cosa bolle in pentola?
▶ **cook up** VT + ADV (fam: excuse, story) inventare.

cook·book ['kʊk,bʊk] N (Am) = **cookery book**.

cook·er ['kʊkə'] N (stove) cucina (elettrodomestico); (cooking apple) mela da cuocere.
♦ **cooker hood** N cappa aspirante.

cook·ery ['kʊkərı] N cucina (attività).
♦ **cook·ery book** N (Brit) libro di ricette.

cook·house ['kʊk,haʊs] N (esp Am) cucina (da campo).

cookie ['kʊkı] N (Am: biscuit) biscotto.

cook·ing ['kʊkɪŋ] [1] N cucina (attività e cibo); **boys are just as keen on cooking as girls are** anche ai ragazzi piace cucinare; **she loves your cooking** adora quello che cucini tu.
[2] ADJ (apples, chocolate) da cuocere; (utensils, salt, foil) da cucina.

cook·out ['kʊk,aʊt] N (Am) pranzo cucinato all'aperto.

cool [ku:l] [1] ADJ (comp -er, superl -est) (gen) fresco(-a); (drink) freddo(-a); (dress) fresco(-a), leggero(-a); (calm) calmo(-a); (unenthusiastic, unfriendly) freddo(-a); (impertinent) sfacciato(-a); **it's cool** (weather) fa fresco; **to keep sth cool** or **in a cool place** tenere qc in fresco or al fresco; **to be cool towards sb** essere freddo(-a) con qn; **to keep cool** mantenersi fresco(-a); (fig) conservare la calma; **keep cool!** calma!; **play it cool!** fa' finta di niente!; **to be as cool as a cucumber** (fig) essere imperturbabile, conservare il sangue freddo; **he's a pretty cool customer** (fam) ha un gran sangue freddo; (pej) ha una bella faccia tosta; **that was very cool of you!** (fam) che sangue freddo!; **we paid a cool £90,000 for that house** (fam) abbiamo pagato la bellezza di 90.000 sterline per quella casa.
[2] N: **in the cool of the evening** nella frescura serale; **to keep sth in the cool** tenere qc al fresco; **to keep one's cool** (fam) conservare la calma; **to lose one's cool** (fam) perdere la calma or le staffe.
[3] VT (air) rinfrescare, raffreddare; (food) raffreddare; (engine) far raffreddare; **cool it!** (fam) calmati!; **to cool one's heels** (fam) aspettare (a lungo).
[4] VI (air, liquid) raffreddarsi
▶ **cool down** [1] VI + ADV raffreddarsi; (fig: person, situation) calmarsi.
[2] VT + ADV far raffreddare; (fig) calmare
▶ **cool off** VI + ADV (become less angry) calmarsi; (lose enthusiasm, become less affectionate) diventare più freddo(-a).

cool·ant ['ku:lənt] N (Tech) (liquido) refrigerante m.
♦ **cool box** N borsa termica.

cool·er ['ku:lə'] N (for food) ghiacciaia; **to send sb to the cooler** (fam: prison) mettere qn al fresco.

cool·ing ['ku:lɪŋ] ADJ rinfrescante; **cooling fan** (Aut) ventilatore m di raffreddamento.
♦ **cooling-off period** [,ku:lɪŋ'ɒf,pɪərɪəd] N (Industry) periodo di tregua sindacale.
♦ **cooling system** N (Aut) impianto di raffreddamento.
♦ **cooling tower** N torre f di raffreddamento or refrigerazione.

cool·ly ['ku:lı] ADV (calmly) con padronanza di sé; (audaciously) come se niente fosse; (unenthusiastically) freddamente.

cool·ness ['ku:lnıs] N (of air, weather) frescura, fresco; (of

drink) freschezza; (*calmness*) calma, controllo, sangue *m* freddo; (*of welcome*) freddezza; (*impudence*) sfacciataggine.

coop [ku:p] N stia

▶ **coop up** VT + ADV (*fig*) rinchiudere.

co-op [ˈkəʊˈɒp] N ABBR (= *cooperative (society)*) coop *f*.

co·oper·ate [kəʊˈɒpəˌreɪt] VI: **to cooperate (with sb in** *or* **on sth/to do sth)** cooperare (con qn in qc/per fare qc), collaborare (con qn in qc/per fare qc); **will he co-operate?** sarà disposto a collaborare?

co·opera·tion [kəʊˌɒpəˈreɪʃən] N cooperazione *f*, collaborazione *f*.

co·opera·tive [kəʊˈɒpərətɪv] **1** ADJ **a** (*person*) disposto (-a) a collaborare; **you're not very cooperative!** non sei di grande aiuto! **b** (*farm etc*) cooperativo(-a). **2** N cooperativa.

co·opera·tive·ly [kəʊˈɒpərətɪvlɪ] ADV (*jointly*) in cooperazione; (*obligingly*) con spirito di cooperazione.

♦ **co-operative society** N cooperativa.

co·opt [kəʊˈɒpt] VT: **to coopt sb onto/into sth** cooptare qn per qc.

co·or·di·nate [*n* kəʊˈɔ:dnɪt; *vb* kəʊˈɔ:dɪˌneɪt] **1** N (*Math*) coordinata; **coordinates** NPL (*clothes*) coordinati *mpl*. **2** VT coordinare.

co·or·di·na·tion [kəʊˌɔ:dɪˈneɪʃən] N coordinazione *f*.

co·or·di·na·tor [kəʊˈɔ:dɪˌneɪtəʳ] N coordinatore(-trice).

coot [ku:t] N (*Zool*) folaga.

♦ **co-ownership** [ˌkəʊˈəʊnəʃɪp] N comproprietà *f inv*.

cop [kɒp] (*fam*) **1** N **a** (*policeman*) poliziotto(-a); **to play at cops and robbers** giocare a guardie e ladri **b** : **it's not much cop** (*Brit*) non è un granché. **2** VT: **to cop it** buscarle

▶ **cop out** VI + ADV (*fam*) piantare tutto; **to cop out of sth** tirarsi indietro da qc.

cope [kəʊp] VI farcela; **to cope with** (*task, child*) farcela con; (*situation, difficulties, problems*: *tackle*) affrontare, far fronte a; (: *solve*) risolvere; **he's coping pretty well** se la cava abbastanza bene; **leave it to me, I'll cope** lascia stare, ci penso io.

Co·pen·ha·gen [ˌkəʊpnˈheɪgən] N Copenhagen *f*.

Co·per·ni·cus [kəˈpɜ:nɪkəs] N Copernico.

copi·er [ˈkɒpɪəʳ] N (*also*: **photocopier**) (foto)copiatrice *f*.

♦ **co-pilot** [ˈkəʊˈpaɪlət] N secondo pilota *m/f*, copilota *m/f*.

co·pi·ous [ˈkəʊpɪəs] ADJ (*tears*) copioso(-a); (*harvest*) abbondante, copioso(-a); (*notes, supply*) abbondante.

co·pi·ous·ly [ˈkəʊpɪəslɪ] ADV (*all senses*) abbondantemente, copiosamente.

co·pla·nar [kəʊˈpleɪnə] ADJ (*Geom*: *points, lines*) complanare.

cop·per [ˈkɒpəʳ] **1** N **a** rame *m*; (*coin*) monetina; **coppers** NPL spiccioli *mpl* **b** (*Brit fam*: *police*) poliziotto (-a). **2** ADJ (*wire, kettle*) di rame; (*colour*) (color) rame *inv*, ramato(-a).

♦ **copper beech** N faggio rosso.

♦ **copper chloride** N cloruro rameico.

♦ **copper-coloured** [ˈkɒpəˌkʌləd], **cop·pery** [ˈkɒpərɪ] ADJ (color) rame *inv*, ramato(-a).

copper·plate [ˈkɒpəˌpleɪt] N (*for engraving*) lastra di rame per incisione; (*also*: **copperplate handwriting**) calligrafia chiara e regolare.

cop·pice [ˈkɒpɪs], **copse** [kɒps] N bosco ceduo.

cop·ra [ˈkɒprə] N copra.

copu·late [ˈkɒpjʊleɪt] VI accoppiarsi.

copu·la·tion [ˌkɒpjʊˈleɪʃən] N copula, accoppiamento.

copu·la·tive [ˈkɒpjʊlətɪv] ADJ copulativo(-a).

copy [ˈkɒpɪ] **1** N **a** (*gen*) copia; (*book etc*) esemplare *m*; (*of painting*) copia, riproduzione *f*; **rough/fair copy** brutta/bella (copia). **b** (*material: for printing*) materiale *m*, testo; **to make good copy** (*story, scandal*) fare notizia. **2** VT (*imitate*) imitare; (*make copy of, cheat*) copiare; **he copied in the exam** all'esame ha copiato

▶ **copy out** VT + ADV ricopiare, trascrivere.

copy·book [ˈkɒpɪˌbʊk] N quaderno; **to blot one's copybook** (*fig*) rovinarsi la reputazione.

copy·cat [ˈkɒpɪˌkæt] N (*pej*) copione(-a).

copy·ing [ˈkɒpɪɪŋ] ADJ: **copying ink** inchiostro copiativo.

copy·right [ˈkɒpɪˌraɪt] N diritti *mpl* d'autore, copyright *m inv*; **copyright reserved** tutti i diritti riservati.

♦ **copy typist** N dattilografa.

copy·writer [ˈkɒpɪˌraɪtəʳ] N copywriter *m/f inv*, autore(-trice) di testi pubblicitari.

co·quet·ry [ˈkəʊkɪtrɪ] N (*frm*) civetteria.

co·quette [kəʊˈkɛt] N civetta (*fig*).

co·quet·tish [kəʊˈkɛtɪʃ] ADJ (*smile, girl*) civettuolo(-a).

cor [kɔ:ʳ] EXCL (*Brit: also*: **cor blimey!**) perbacco!

cor·al [ˈkɒrəl] **1** N corallo. **2** ADJ (*island*) corallino(-a); **coral necklace** collana di corallo.

♦ **coral reef** N barriera corallina.

♦ **Coral Sea** N: **the Coral Sea** il mar dei Coralli.

cor anglais [ˈkɔ:rˈɑ:ŋleɪ] N (*Brit*) corno inglese.

cord [kɔ:d] N **a** (*gen*) corda; (*for pyjamas*) cintura; (*round parcel etc*) corda, spago; (*Elec*) filo **b** (*fabric*) velluto a coste; **cords** NPL (*trousers*) calzoni *mpl* di velluto a coste.

cor·dial [ˈkɔ:dɪəl] **1** ADJ cordiale. **2** N cordiale *m*.

cor·di·al·ity [ˌkɔ:dɪˈælɪtɪ] N cordialità.

cor·di·al·ly [ˈkɔ:dɪəlɪ] ADV cordialmente.

cord·less [ˈkɔ:dlɪs] ADJ (*iron*) senza filo; (*telephone*) cordless *inv*.

cor·don [ˈkɔ:dn] N cordone *m*

▶ **cordon off** VT + ADV fare cordone intorno a.

cor·du·roy [ˈkɔ:dəˌrɔɪ] N velluto a coste.

CORE [kɔ:ʳ] N ABBR (*Am*)= *Congress of Racial Equality*.

core [kɔ:ʳ] **1** N (*of fruit*) torsolo; (*of cable*) centro; (*of earth, nuclear reactor*) nucleo; (*Mineralogy*: *sample*) carota; (*of problem*) cuore *m*, nocciolo; **a hard core of resistance** uno zoccolo duro di resistenza; **rotten to the core** marcio(-a) fino al midollo; **English to the core** inglese in tutto e per tutto. **2** VT (*fruit*) togliere il torsolo a.

cor·er [ˈkɔ:rəʳ] N cavatorsoli *m inv*.

♦ **co-respondent** [ˈkəʊrɪsˈpɒndənt] N (*Law*) correo(-a) (*di adulterio*).

Cor·fu [kɔ:ˈfu:] N Corfù *f*.

co·ri·an·der [ˌkɒrɪˈændəʳ] N coriandolo (*pianta*).

Co·rin·thian [kəˈrɪnθɪən] **1** ADJ corinzio(-a); **Corinthian order/capital** (*Archit*) ordine *m* /capitello corinzio. **2** N corinzio(-a).

cork [kɔ:k] **1** N (*substance*) sughero; (*of bottle*) tappo (di sughero), turacciolo; **to pull the cork out of a bottle** stappare una bottiglia. **2** VT (*bottle: also*: **cork up**) tappare. **3** ADJ di sughero.

cork·age [ˈkɔ:kɪdʒ] N *somma che il cliente di un ristorante paga per farsi stappare bottiglie (di vino) comprate altrove*.

corked [kɔ:kt], (*Am*) **corky** [ˈkɔ:kɪ] ADJ (*wine*) che sa di tappo.

♦ **cork oak** N quercia da sughero, sughera.

cork·screw ['kɔːkˌskruː] N cavatappi *m inv*.

corm [kɔːm] N (*Bot*) cormo.

cor·mo·rant ['kɔːmərənt] N cormorano.

Corn ABBR (*Brit*) = **Cornwall**.

corn[1] [kɔːn] N (*Brit: wheat*) grano, frumento; (*Am: maize*) granturco, mais *m*.

corn[2] [kɔːn] N (*on foot*) callo.

cor·nea ['kɔːnɪə] N (*Anat*) cornea.

corned beef ['kɔːnd'biːf] N carne *f* di manzo in scatola.

cor·ner ['kɔːnə[r]] 1 N a angolo; (*of table*) spigolo, angolo; **it's just around the corner** (*also fig*) è proprio dietro l'angolo; (: *in time*) è molto vicino; **to turn the corner** (*fig*) superare una crisi; **in odd corners** nei posti più strani *or* impensati; **the four corners of the world** i quattro angoli del mondo; **out of the corner of one's eye** con la coda dell'occhio; **to drive sb into a corner** (*fig*) mettere qn con le spalle al muro; **to be in a (tight) corner** (*fig*) essere nei pasticci *or* guai; **to cut a corner** (*Aut*) tagliare una curva; **to cut corners** (*fig*) prendere una scorciatoia

b (*Ftbl: also:* **corner kick**) calcio d'angolo, corner *m inv*.

2 VT a (*animal*) intrappolare; (*fugitive*) mettere in trappola; (*fig: person: catch to speak to*) bloccare

b (*Comm: market*) monopolizzare; (: *goods*) accaparrare.

3 VI (*Aut*) curvare, prendere una curva.

4 ADJ (*seat, table*) d'angolo.

♦ **corner cupboard** N angoliera.

♦ **corner flag** N (*Ftbl*) bandierina d'angolo.

♦ **corner kick** N (*Ftbl*) calcio d'angolo, corner *m inv*.

♦ **corner shop** N ≈ negozio sotto casa.

corner·stone ['kɔːnəˌstəʊn] N (*also fig*) pietra angolare.

cor·net ['kɔːnɪt] N a (*Mus*) cornetta b (*Brit: ice cream*) cornetto, cono.

♦ **cornet player** N cornettista *m/f*.

corn·field ['kɔːnˌfiːld] N (*Brit*) campo di grano; (*Am*) campo di granturco.

corn·flakes ['kɔːnˌfleɪks] NPL fiocchi *mpl* di granturco, cornflakes *mpl*.

corn·flour ['kɔːnˌflaʊə[r]] N (*Brit*) ≈ fecola di patate.

corn·flower ['kɔːnˌflaʊə[r]] N fiordaliso.

cor·nice ['kɔːnɪs] N (*Archit*) cornicione *m*; (: *interior*) cornice *f*.

Cor·nish ['kɔːnɪʃ] ADJ della Cornovaglia.

♦ **Cornish pasty** N *sfoglia salata ripiena di carne e verdura*.

♦ **corn oil** N olio di mais.

♦ **corn on the cob** N pannocchia cotta.

♦ **corn plaster** N callifugo (*cerotto*).

corn·starch ['kɔːnˌstɑːtʃ] N (*Am*) = **cornflour**.

cor·nu·co·pia [ˌkɔːnjʊˈkəʊpɪə] N (*frm*) grande abbondanza.

Corn·wall ['kɔːnwəl] N Cornovaglia.

corny ['kɔːnɪ] ADJ (*comp* **-ier**, *superl* **-iest**) (*fam: unoriginal*) banale; (: *sentimental*) sdolcinato(-a).

cor·ol·lary [kəˈrɒlərɪ] N corollario.

coro·nary ['kɒrənərɪ] 1 ADJ (*artery*) coronario(-a); (*disease*) coronarico(-a).

2 N (*heart attack*) infarto.

♦ **coronary thrombosis** N (*Med*) trombosi *f* coronarica.

coro·na·tion [ˌkɒrəˈneɪʃən] N incoronazione *f*.

coro·ner ['kɒrənə[r]] N coroner *m inv* (*pubblico ufficiale che indaga casi di morte sospetta*).

coro·net ['kɒrənɪt] N diadema *m*; (*of peer*) corona nobiliare.

Corp. ABBR = **corporation**.

cor·po·ral ['kɔːpərəl] N (*Mil*) caporalmaggiore *m*.

♦ **corporal punishment** N punizione *f* corporale.

cor·po·rate ['kɔːpərɪt] ADJ (*joint: action, effort*) congiunto (-a), unitario(-a); (*ownership, responsibility*) comune; (*Comm*) corporativo(-a), costituito(-a) (in corporazione); **corporate body** ente unico avente personalità giuridica.

♦ **corporate hospitality** N omaggi *mpl* aziendali (*consistenti in biglietti per spettacoli, cene ecc*).

♦ **corporate identity**, **corporate image** N (*of organization*) immagine *f* dell'azienda.

cor·po·ra·tion [ˌkɔːpəˈreɪʃən] N (*Comm*) società *f inv*; (: *Am*) società di capitali; (*of town*) consiglio comunale.

♦ **corporation tax** N ≈ imposta sul reddito di persone giuridiche.

cor·po·ra·tism ['kɔːpərətɪzəm] N corporativismo.

cor·po·real [kɔːˈpɔːrɪəl] ADJ (*frm*) corporeo(-a).

corps [kɔː[r]] N (*pl* **corps** [kɔːz]) corpo; **press corps** ufficio *m* stampa *inv*.

♦ **corps de bal·let** ['kɔːdəˈbæleɪ] N corpo di ballo.

corpse [kɔːps] N cadavere *m*.

cor·pu·lence ['kɔːpjʊləns] N corpulenza.

cor·pu·lent ['kɔːpjʊlənt] ADJ corpulento(-a).

cor·pus ['kɔːpəs] N (*pl* **corpora** ['kɔːpərə]) corpus *m*.

Cor·pus Chris·ti ['kɔːpəsˈkrɪstɪ] N (*feast*) Corpus Domini *m*.

cor·pus·cle ['kɔːpʌsl] N corpuscolo; (*of blood*) globulo (*sia rosso che bianco*).

cor·ral [kɒˈrɑːl] N recinto.

cor·rect [kəˈrɛkt] 1 ADJ (*answer*) corretto(-a), esatto(-a), giusto(-a); (*temperature, time, amount, forecast*) esatto (-a), giusto(-a); (*behaviour*) corretto(-a); (*dress*) adatto (-a); (*procedure*) giusto(-a), corretto(-a); **you are correct** ha ragione.

2 VT (*mistake, work, proofs*) correggere; **I stand corrected** (ametto che) ho torto.

♦ **correcting fluid**, **correction fluid** N bianchetto.

cor·rec·tion [kəˈrɛkʃən] N correzione *f*.

cor·rec·tive [kəˈrɛktɪv] 1 ADJ (*surgery*) correttivo(-a).

2 N correttivo.

cor·rect·ly [kəˈrɛktlɪ] ADV (*accurately*) correttamente; (*properly*) correttamente, in modo adatto.

cor·rect·ness [kəˈrɛktnɪs] N correttezza.

cor·re·late ['kɒrɪˌleɪt] 1 VT correlare, mettere in relazione *or* correlazione.

2 VI essere in correlazione; **to correlate with** essere in rapporto con.

cor·re·la·tion [ˌkɒrɪˈleɪʃən] N correlazione *f*.

cor·re·spond [ˌkɒrɪsˈpɒnd] VI a (*be in accordance*): **to correspond (with)** corrispondere a; **to correspond (to)** (*be equivalent*) corrispondere a, equivalere (a) b (*by letter*): **to correspond (with sb)** corrispondere (con qn), essere in corrispondenza (con qn); **they correspond** si scrivono.

cor·re·spond·ence [ˌkɒrɪsˈpɒndəns] N a (*agreement*): **correspondence (between)** accordo (tra) b (*letters*) corrispondenza; (*collection of letters*) carteggio c (*Math*) corrispondenza.

♦ **correspondence column** N (*Press*) rubrica delle lettere (al direttore).

♦ **correspondence course** N corso per corrispondenza.

cor·re·spond·ent [ˌkɒrɪsˈpɒndənt] N corrispondente *m/f*; **foreign correspondent** (*Press*) corrispondente dall'e-

stero.

cor·re·spond·ing [ˌkɒrɪs'pɒndɪŋ] ADJ corrispondente.

cor·ri·dor ['kɒrɪdɔː'] N corridoio.

cor·rie ['kɒrɪ] N (Geol) circo.

cor·robo·rate [kə'rɒbəˌreɪt] VT corroborare, confermare.

cor·robo·ra·tion [kəˌrɒbə'reɪʃən] N corroborazione f.

cor·robo·ra·tive [kə'rɒbərətɪv] ADJ comprovante.

cor·rode [kə'rəʊd] 1 VT corrodere.
2 VI corrodersi.

cor·ro·sion [kə'rəʊʒən] N corrosione f.

cor·ro·sive [kə'rəʊzɪv] ADJ corrosivo(-a).

cor·ro·sive·ly [kə'rəʊzɪvlɪ] ADV in modo distruttivo.

cor·ro·sive·ness [kə'rəʊsɪvnɪs] N corrosività.

cor·ru·gat·ed ['kɒrəˌgeɪtɪd] ADJ ondulato(-a), increspato (-a).

♦ **corrugated iron** N lamiera di ferro ondulata.

cor·rupt [kə'rʌpt] 1 ADJ corrotto(-a); **corrupt practices** (dishonesty, bribery) pratiche fpl illecite.
2 VT corrompere.

cor·rup·tion [kə'rʌpʃən] N corruzione f.

cor·rupt·ly [kə'rʌptlɪ] ADV correttamente.

cor·set ['kɔːsɪt] N (undergarment) corsetto, busto; (Med) busto (ortopedico).

Cor·si·ca ['kɔːsɪkə] N Corsica.

Cor·si·can ['kɔːsɪkən] ADJ, N corso(-a).

cor·tège [kɔː'teɪʒ] N corteo.

cor·tex ['kɔːtɛks] N (pl cortices ['kɔːtɪsiːz]) (Anat, Bot) corteccia.

cor·ti·sone ['kɔːtɪˌzəʊn] N cortisone m.

co·rus·cat·ing [ˌkɒrə'skeɪtɪŋ] ADJ (frm) scintillante.

c.o.s. ABBR (= cash on shipment) pagamento alla spedizione.

co·secant [kəʊ'siːkənt] N (Math) cosecante f.

cosh [kɒʃ] (Brit) 1 N manganello, randello.
2 VT (fam) pestare, manganellare.

co·sig·na·tory [kəʊ'sɪgnətərɪ] N cofirmatario(-a).

co·si·ly ['kəʊzɪlɪ] ADV (furnished) in modo accogliente; **she was cosily wrapped up in her shawl** era avvolta in uno scialle bello caldo.

co·sine ['kəʊsaɪn] N (Math) coseno.

co·si·ness ['kəʊzɪnɪs] N (of room) comodità; (of atmosphere) intimità, calore m.

cos lettuce ['kɒs'lɛtɪs] N lattuga romana.

cos·met·ic [kɒz'mɛtɪk] 1 ADJ (preparation) cosmetico(-a); (surgery) estetico(-a); (fig: reforms) solo apparente.
2 N cosmetico, prodotto di bellezza.

cos·mic ['kɒzmɪk] ADJ cosmico(-a).

cos·mog·ra·pher [kɒz'mɒgrəfə'] N cosmografo.

cos·mog·ra·phy [kɒz'mɒgrəfɪ] N cosmografia.

cos·mol·ogy [kɒz'mɒlədʒɪ] N cosmologia.

cos·mo·naut ['kɒzmə,nɔːt] N cosmonauta m/f.

cos·mo·poli·tan [ˌkɒzmə'pɒlɪtən] ADJ, N cosmopolita (m/f).

cos·mos ['kɒzmɒs] N cosmo.

cos·set ['kɒsɪt] VT coccolare, vezzeggiare.

cost [kɒst] 1 N costo; (Law): **costs** spese fpl; **to be ordered to pay costs** (Law) essere condannato(-a) a pagare le spese; **cost, insurance and freight** (Comm) costo, assicurazione e nolo; **to bear the cost of** sostenere la spesa di; **at great cost** a caro prezzo; **at cost (price)** a prezzo di costo; **at any cost** [OR] **at all costs** (fig) a tutti i costi, a ogni costo; **whatever the cost** (fig) costi quel che costi; **to my cost** (fig) a mie spese; **at the cost of his life/health** rimettendoci la vita/la salute.
2 VT a (pt, pp cost) costare; **how much does it cost?** quanto costa?, quanto viene?; **what will it cost to have it**

repaired? quanto costerà farlo riparare?; **it cost him a lot of money** gli è costato un sacco di soldi; **it costs the earth** (fam) costa un occhio della testa; **it cost him his life/job** gli è costato la vita/il lavoro; **it cost me a great deal of time/effort** mi è costato molto tempo/molta fatica; **it costs nothing to be polite** essere educati non costa nulla; **whatever it costs** (fig) costi quel che costi; **it costs £5/too much** costa 5 sterline/troppo
b (pt, pp costed) (Comm) stabilire il prezzo di.

♦ **cost accountant** N analizzatore m dei costi.

♦ **cost analysis** N analisi f inv dei costi.

♦ **co-star** ['kəʊstɑː'] N co-protagonista m/f.

Cos·ta Rica ['kɒstə'riːkə] N Costa Rica.

Cos·ta Ri·can ['kɒstə'riːkən] ADJ, N costaricano(-a).

♦ **cost centre** N (also: costing centre) centro di costo.

♦ **cost control** N controllo dei costi.

♦ **cost-effective** [ˌkɒstɪ'fɛktɪv] ADJ (Comm) redditizio(-a), efficiente; (gen) conveniente, economico(-a).

♦ **cost-effectiveness** [ˌkɒstɪ'fɛktɪvnɪs] N convenienza.

cos·ter·mon·ger ['kɒstə,mʌŋgə'] N (Brit old) venditore(-trice) ambulante di frutta e verdura.

cost·ing ['kɒstɪŋ] N (determinazione f dei) costi mpl.

cost·li·ness ['kɒstlɪnɪs] N alto costo.

cost·ly ['kɒstlɪ] ADJ costoso(-a), caro(-a).

♦ **cost of living** N costo della vita.

♦ **cost-of-living** [ˌkɒstəv'lɪvɪŋ] ADJ: **cost-of-living allowance** indennità f inv di contingenza; **cost-of-living index** indice m del costo della vita.

♦ **cost price** N (Brit) prezzo all'ingrosso.

cos·tume ['kɒstjuːm] N (gen) costume m; (Brit: also: swimming costume) costume da bagno.

♦ **costume ball** N ballo in maschera or in costume.

♦ **costume drama** N dramma m storico.

♦ **costume jewellery** N bigiotteria.

cosy, (Am) **cozy** ['kəʊzɪ] 1 ADJ (comp -ier, superl -iest) (room, atmosphere) accogliente, intimo(-a); (clothes) bello(-a) caldo(-a); **I'm very cosy here** sto proprio bene qui; **we had a cosy chat** abbiamo fatto due chiacchiere in confidenza.
2 N (tea cosy) copriteiera m inv; (egg cosy) copriuovo.

cot [kɒt] N (Brit: child's) lettino; (Am: folding bed) brandina.

co·tan·gent [kəʊ'tændʒənt] N (Math) cotangente f.

♦ **cot death** N (Brit) improvvisa e inspiegabile morte nel sonno di un neonato.

co·terie ['kəʊtərɪ] N (frm) gruppo ristretto.

Cots·wolds ['kɒts,wəʊldz] NPL: **the Cotswolds** zona collinare del Gloucestershire.

cot·tage ['kɒtɪdʒ] N villetta, cottage m inv.

♦ **cottage cheese** N fiocchi mpl di latte.

♦ **cottage hospital** N ospedale m di campagna.

♦ **cottage industry** N industria artigianale basata sul lavoro a cottimo.

♦ **cottage pie** N pasticcio di carne macinata e patate.

cot·ter ['kɒtə'] N (Tech): **cotter pin** copiglia.

cot·ton ['kɒtn] 1 N (cloth, plant) cotone m; (thread) (filo di) cotone.
2 ADJ (shirt, dress) di cotone

► **cotton on** VI + ADV (fam): **to cotton on (to sth)** afferrare (qc).

♦ **cotton buds** NPL cotton fioc ® m inv.

♦ **cotton candy** N (Am) zucchero filato.

♦ **cotton grass** N (Bot) erioforo.

♦ **cotton industry** N industria cotoniera.

♦ **cotton mill** N cotonificio.

♦ **cotton wool** N (Brit) cotone m idrofilo.

coty·le·don [ˌkɒtɪ'li:dən] N (Bot) cotiledone m.

couch [kaʊtʃ] **1** N (gen) divano, sofà m inv; (in doctor's surgery) lettino.
2 VT (statement, request) esprimere.

cou·chette [ku:'ʃɛt] N cuccetta.

♦ **couch potato** N (fam) pigrone(-a) teledipendente.

cou·gar ['ku:gə'] N coguaro.

cough [kɒf] **1** N (single instance) colpo di tosse; (illness) tosse f.
2 VI tossire

▶ **cough up** **1** VT + ADV (blood, phlegm) sputare; (fig fam: money) tirare fuori.
2 VI + ADV (fig fam) cacciare i soldi.

♦ **cough drop**, **cough sweet** N pasticca per la tosse.

♦ **cough mixture**, **cough syrup** N sciroppo per la tosse.

could [kʊd] PT, COND of **can**.

couldn't ['kʊdnt] PT, COND = **could not**.

cou·loir ['ku:lwa:] N canalone (di montagna) m inv.

coun·cil ['kaʊnsl] N consiglio; **council of war** consiglio di guerra; **city** or **town council** consiglio comunale; **the Security Council of the United Nations** il Consiglio di Sicurezza delle Nazioni Unite; **Council of Europe** Consiglio d'Europa.

♦ **council estate** N (Brit) complesso di case popolari.

♦ **council flat** N (Brit) casa popolare.

♦ **council house** N (Brit) casa popolare.

♦ **council housing** N (Brit) alloggi mpl popolari.

♦ **council housing estate** N (Brit) complesso di alloggi popolari.

coun·cil·lor ['kaʊnsɪlə'] N consigliere m.

♦ **council meeting** N seduta del consiglio.

♦ **council tax** N (Brit) imposta comunale sugli immobili.

coun·sel ['kaʊnsəl] **1** N **a** (advice) consiglio, consultazione f; **to keep one's own counsel** tenere le proprie opinioni per sé
b PL INV (Law) avvocato(-essa); **counsel for the defence/ the prosecution** avvocato difensore/di parte civile; **Queen's (or King's) Counsel** avvocato della Corona.
2 VT: **to counsel sth/sb to do sth** consigliare qc/a qn di fare qc; (caution) raccomandare qc/a qn di fare qc.

coun·sel·ling, (Am) **coun·sel·ing** ['kaʊnsəlɪŋ] N terapia; **marriage counselling** terapia di coppia.

coun·sel·lor, (Am) **coun·se·lor** ['kaʊnslə'] N (adviser) consulente m/f; (Psych) assistente m/f socio-psicologico (-a); (Am: lawyer) avvocato(-essa).

♦ **count**[1] [kaʊnt] **1** N **a** conteggio; (of votes at election) spoglio; **to be out for the count** (Boxing) essere fuori combattimento; (fam) essere K.O.; **to keep count of sth** tenere il conto di qc; **you made me lose count** mi hai fatto perdere il conto
b (Law): **he was found guilty on all counts** è stato giudicato colpevole di tutti i capi di accusa.
2 VT **a** (gen) contare; (one's change etc) controllare; **don't count your chickens before they're hatched** non vendere la pelle dell'orso prima di averlo ucciso, non dir quattro se non l'hai nel sacco; **to count sheep** (fig) contare le pecore; **to count the cost of** calcolare il costo di; (fig) valutare il prezzo di; **without counting the cost** (also fig) senza badare al prezzo; **count your blessings** considera la tua fortuna
b (include) contare; (consider): **to count sb among** annoverare qn tra; **not counting the children** senza contare i bambini; **ten counting him** dieci compreso lui; **count yourself lucky** considerati fortunato; **will you**

count it against me? te la prenderai con me?; **I count it an honour (to do/that)** mi ritengo onorato (a fare/che + sub).
3 VI **a** contare; **to count (up) to 10** contare fino a 10; **counting from today** a partire da oggi, oggi compreso
b (be considered, be valid) valere, contare; **two children count as one adult** due bambini valgono come un adulto; **that doesn't count** quello non conta; **it will count against him** deporrà a suo sfavore; **it counts for very little** non conta molto, non ha molta importanza

▶ **count in** VT + ADV comprendere nel conto; **count me in!** (fam) ci sto anch'io!

▶ **count on**, **count upon** VI + PREP contare su; **to count on doing sth** contare di fare qc

▶ **count out** VT + ADV
a (Boxing): **to be counted out** essere dichiarato(-a) K.O.
b (money, small objects) contare
c (fam): **count me out!** non ci sto!

▶ **count towards** VI + PREP (subj: payment) andare a incrementare

▶ **count up** VT + ADV contare; (column of figures) sommare, addizionare.

count[2] [kaʊnt] N (nobleman) conte m.

count·able ['kaʊntəbl] ADJ computabile; **a countable noun** (Gram) un sostantivo numerabile.

count·down ['kaʊnt,daʊn] N conto alla rovescia.

coun·te·nance ['kaʊntɪnəns] (frm) **1** N (face) (espressione f del) volto; **to keep one's countenance** restare impassibile.
2 VT (permit): **to countenance sth/sb doing sth** ammettere qc/che qn faccia qc.

counter... ['kaʊntə'] PREF contro....

count·er[1] ['kaʊntə'] N **a** (of shop, canteen) banco, bancone m; (position: in post office, bank) sportello; **to buy under the counter** (fig) comperare sottobanco **b** (in game) gettone m **c** (Tech) contatore m.

coun·ter[2] ['kaʊntə'] **1** ADV: **counter to** contrariamente a; **to run counter to** andare contro a.
2 VT: **to counter sth with sth/by doing sth** rispondere a qc con qc/facendo qc; **to counter an attack** rispondere ad un attacco.
3 VI: **to counter with** rispondere con; (words) ribattere con.

counter·act [ˌkaʊntər'ækt] VT (counterbalance) controbilanciare, agire in opposizione a; (neutralize) neutralizzare, annullare gli effetti di.

counter·at·tack ['kaʊntərə,tæk] **1** N contrattacco.
2 VT, VI contrattaccare.

counter·bal·ance ['kaʊntə,bæləns] **1** N contrappeso.
2 VT controbilanciare, fare da contrappeso a.

counter·clockwise [ˌkaʊntə'klɒk,waɪz] ADV (Am) in senso antiorario.

counter·es·pio·nage [ˌkaʊntər'espɪə,nɑ:ʒ] N controspionaggio.

counter·feit ['kaʊntəfɪt] **1** ADJ contraffatto(-a), falsificato(-a), falso(-a); (money) falso(-a).
2 N falso, contraffazione f; (coin) moneta falsa.
3 VT contraffare, falsificare.

counter·feit·er ['kaʊntə,fɪtə'] N contraffattore(-trice).

counter·foil ['kaʊntə,fɔɪl] N matrice f.

counter·in·tel·li·gence [ˌkaʊntərɪn'telɪdʒəns] N = counterespionage.

counter·mand ['kaʊntə,mɑ:nd] VT annullare.

countermeasure ['kaʊntə,mɛʒə'] N contromisura.

counteroffensive ['kaʊntərə,fɛnsɪv] N controffensiva.

counter·pane ['kaʊntə,peɪn] N copriletto *m inv.*

counter·part ['kaʊntə,pɑːt] N (*of person*) omologo(-a); (*of document etc*) copia, duplicato.

counter·pro·duc·tive [,kaʊntəprə'dʌktɪv] ADJ controproducente.

counter·pro·pos·al ['kaʊntəprə,pəʊzəl] N controproposta.

♦ **Counter-Reformation** [,kaʊntə,rɛfə'meɪʃən] N Controriforma.

♦ **counter-revolution** [,kaʊntə,rɛvə'luːʃən] N controrivoluzione *f.*

♦ **counter-revolutionary** [,kaʊntə,rɛvə'luːʃənrɪ] N, ADJ controrivoluzionario(-a).

counter·sign ['kaʊntə,saɪn] VT controfirmare.

counter·sink ['kaʊntə,sɪŋk] VT (*pt* **countersank**, *pp* **countersunk**) (*hole*) svasare; (*screw*) accecare.

counter·ten·or [,kaʊntə'tɛnə] N tenore *m* leggero.

♦ **counter-turn** ['kaʊntə,tɜːn] N (*Skiing*) controcurva.

coun·tess ['kaʊntɪs] N contessa.

count·less ['kaʊntlɪs] ADJ: **on countless occasions** in mille occasioni, in innumerevoli occasioni; **countless numbers of** un'infinità di.

coun·tri·fied ['kʌntrɪ,faɪd] ADJ rustico(-a), campagnolo (-a).

coun·try ['kʌntrɪ] ① N **a** (*gen*) paese *m*; (*native land*) patria; **to go to the country** (*Pol*) indire le elezioni; **to die for one's country** morire per la patria

  b (*as opposed to town*) campagna; (*terrain, land*) territorio; (*region*) regione *f*; **in the country** in campagna; **there is some lovely country further south** ci sono delle campagne bellissime più a sud; **mountainous country** territorio montagnoso; **unknown country** (*also fig*) terra sconosciuta.

  ② ADJ (*life, road*) di campagna.

♦ **country and western, country and western music** N musica country e western, country *m inv.*

♦ **coun·try bump·kin** ['kʌntrɪ'bʌmpkɪn] N (*pej*) burino (-a).

♦ **country club** N *circolo sportivo e ricreativo in campagna.*

♦ **country cottage** N villetta di campagna.

♦ **country cousin** N (*fig*) provinciale *m/f.*

♦ **country dancing** N (*Brit*) danza popolare.

♦ **country dweller** N campagnolo(-a).

♦ **country house** N villa di campagna.

country·man ['kʌntrɪmən] N (*pl* **-men**) (*compatriot*) compatriota *m*, connazionale *m*; (*country dweller*) campagnolo.

♦ **country seat** N residenza di campagna.

country·side ['kʌntrɪ,saɪd] N campagna.

♦ **country-wide** ['kʌntrɪ,waɪd] ① ADJ (su scala) nazionale, diffuso(-a) in tutto il paese.

  ② ADV in tutto il paese, su scala nazionale.

coun·ty ['kaʊntɪ] ① N contea.

  ② ADJ (*boundary, court*) di contea.

♦ **county council** N (*Brit*) consiglio di contea.

♦ **county town** N (*Brit*) capoluogo (di contea).

coup [kuː] N (*Pol: also:* **coup d'état**) colpo di stato, golpe *m inv*; (*triumph*) bel colpo.

coup de grace [,kuːdə'grɑːs] N (*frm*) colpo di grazia.

cou·pé ['kuːpeɪ] N (*Aut*) coupé *m inv.*

cou·ple ['kʌpl] ① N (*of animals, people*) coppia; **a couple of times/hours/books** (*two or three*) un paio di volte/ore/libri.

  ② VT **a** (*idea, name*): **to couple with** associare con

  b (*railway carriages*): **to couple (on** *or* **up)** agganciare.

cou·plet ['kʌplɪt] N distico.

cou·pling ['kʌplɪŋ] N (*Rail*) agganciamento.

cou·pon ['kuːpɒn] N (*voucher*) buono; (*Comm*) coupon *m inv*; (*football pools coupon*) schedina.

cour·age ['kʌrɪdʒ] N coraggio; **I haven't the courage to refuse** non ho il coraggio di rifiutare; **to have the courage of one's convictions** avere il coraggio delle proprie opinioni *or* convinzioni; **to take one's courage in both hands** prendere il coraggio a due mani.

cou·ra·geous [kə'reɪdʒəs] ADJ coraggioso(-a).

cou·ra·geous·ly [kə'reɪdʒəslɪ] ADV coraggiosamente.

cour·gette [,kʊə'ʒɛt] N (*Brit*) zucchina, zucchino.

cou·ri·er ['kʊrɪə] N (*messenger*) corriere *m*; (*for tourists*) accompagnatore(-trice) turistico(-a), tour leader *m/f inv.*

course [kɔːs] ① N **a**: **of course** naturalmente, ovviamente, senz'altro; **yes, of course!** sì, certo!; **(no) of course not!** certo che no!, no di certo!; **of course you can** certo che puoi; **of course I won't do it** certo che non lo farò

  b (*Scol, Univ*) corso; **to take a course in French** seguire un corso di francese; **a course of lectures on a subject** una serie di conferenze *or* lezioni su un argomento; **a course of treatment** (*Med*) una cura

  c (*part of meal*) piatto, portata; **a three-course meal** un pasto di tre portate; **first course** primo piatto

  d (*route: of ship*) rotta; (: *of river*) corso; (: *of planet*) orbita; **to set course for** (*Naut*) far rotta per; **to change course** (*Naut, fig*) cambiare rotta; **to go off course** deviare dalla rotta; **to hold one's course** seguire *or* mantenere la rotta; **to take/follow a course of action** (*fig*) imboccare/seguire una politica; **we have no other course but to ...** non possiamo far altro che...; **there are two courses open to us** abbiamo due possibilità; **the best course would be to ...** la cosa migliore sarebbe...; **to let things/events take** *or* **run their course** lasciare che le cose/gli eventi seguano il loro corso; **as a matter of course** come una cosa scontata

  e (*duration*): **in the course of** (*life, disease, events*) nel corso di; **in due course** a tempo debito; **in the course of time** col passare del tempo; **in the normal** *or* **ordinary course of events** normalmente; **in (the) course of construction** in (via di) costruzione; **in the course of the next few days** nel corso dei prossimi giorni

  f (*Sport*: **golf course**) campo (di golf); (: *race course*) pista.

  ② VI (*water, tears*) scorrere; **it sent the blood coursing through his veins** gli ha rimescolato il sangue nelle vene.

court [kɔːt] ① N **a** (*Law*) corte *f*; (: *room*) aula; **to take sb to court (over sth)** citare in tribunale qn (per qc); **to settle a case out of court** conciliare una causa in via amichevole; **to rule out of court** dichiarare inammissibile; **he was brought before the court on a charge of theft** fu processato sotto accusa di furto

  b (*Tennis*) campo

  c (*royal*) corte *f.*

  ② VT (*woo*) corteggiare, fare la corte a; (*fig: favour, popularity*) cercare di conquistare; (: *death, disaster*) sfiorare, rasentare.

  ③ VI (*old, Culin*) corteggiarsi.

♦ **court-bouillon** [,kɔːt'buːjɒn] N court-bouillon *m.*

♦ **court card** N (*Cards*) figura.

cour·teous ['kɜːtɪəs] ADJ cortese.

cour·teous·ly ['kɜːtɪəslɪ] ADV cortesemente.

cour·tesan [ˌkɔːtɪˈzæn] N cortigiana.

cour·tesy [ˈkɜːtɪsɪ] N (*politeness*) cortesia, gentilezza; (*polite act*) cortesia, piacere *m*; **by courtesy of** per gentile concessione di; **you might have had the courtesy to tell me** avresti potuto farmi la cortesia di dirmelo; **to exchange courtesies** scambiarsi convenevoli.

♦ **courtesy coach** N autobus *m inv* gratuito (*di hotel, aeroporto*).

♦ **courtesy light** N (*Aut*) luce *f* interna.

♦ **courtesy visit** N visita di cortesia.

court·house [ˈkɔːthaʊs] N (*Am*) tribunale *m*, palazzo di giustizia.

cour·ti·er [ˈkɔːtɪəʳ] N cortigiano(-a).

court·ing [ˈkɔːtɪŋ] ADJ: **courting couple** coppietta, coppia di innamorati.

court·ly [ˈkɔːtlɪ] ADJ (*comp* **-ier**, *superl* **-iest**) cortese, raffinato(-a).

♦ **court martial** [ˈkɔːtˈmɑːʃəl] N (*pl* **court martials** *or* **courts martial**) corte *f* marziale.

♦ **court-martial** [ˈkɔːtˈmɑːʃəl] VT processare in corte *f* marziale.

♦ **court of appeal** N corte d'appello.

♦ **court of inquiry** N commissione *f* d'inchiesta.

court·room [ˈkɔːtˌruːm] N aula (di tribunale).

court·ship [ˈkɔːtʃɪp] N corteggiamento.

♦ **court shoe** N scarpa *f* décolleté *inv*.

court·yard [ˈkɔːtˌjɑːd] N cortile *m*.

cous·cous [ˈkuːskuːs] N (*Culin*) cuscus *m inv*.

cous·in [ˈkʌzn] N cugino(-a).

cou·ture [kuːˈtʊəʳ] N couture *f inv*.

cou·tu·ri·er [kuːˈtʊərɪeɪ] N couturier *m inv*.

co·va·lent [kəʊˈveɪlənt] ADJ: **covalent bond** (*Chem*) legame *m* covalente.

cove [kəʊv] N piccola baia, cala.

cov·enant [ˈkʌvɪnənt] [1] N accordo (scritto).
[2] VT: **to covenant to do sth** impegnarsi (per iscritto) a fare qc; **to covenant £200 per year to a charity** impegnarsi a versare 200 sterline all'anno a un'organizzazione benefica.

Cov·en·try [ˈkɒvəntrɪ] N: **to send sb to Coventry** (*fig*) dare l'ostracismo a qn.

cov·er [ˈkʌvəʳ] [1] N **a** (*gen*) copertura; (*of dish, bowl, saucepan*) coperchio; (*of furniture, typewriter*) fodera; (*for merchandise, on vehicle*) telo, telone *m*; (*bedspread*) copriletto; (*often pl*: *blanket*) coperta; (*of book, magazine*) copertina; **under separate cover** (*Comm*) a parte, in plico separato; **to read a book from cover to cover** leggere un libro dalla prima all'ultima pagina
b (*shelter*) riparo; (*covering fire*) copertura; **to take cover** (*hide*) nascondersi; (*Mil, shelter*) ripararsi; **to break cover** uscire allo scoperto; **under cover** al coperto, al riparo; (*hiding*) nascosto(-a); **under cover of darkness** con il favore delle tenebre, protetto(-a) dall'oscurità
c (*Fin, Comm, Insurance, in espionage etc*) copertura; **without cover** (*Fin*) senza copertura; **fire cover** copertura contro i rischi d'incendio
d (*frm*: *at table*) coperto.
[2] VT **a** (*gen*): **to cover (with)** coprire (con *or* di); **covered with confusion** (*fig*) tutto(-a) confuso(-a); **covered with shame** pieno(-a) di vergogna; **to cover o.s. with glory/disgrace** coprirsi di gloria/infamia
b (*hide*: *facts, mistakes*) nascondere; (: *feeling*) nascondere, dissimulare; (: *noise*) coprire
c (*protect*: *Mil, Sport, Insurance*) coprire; **he only said**

that to cover himself lo disse solo per coprirsi le spalle; **I've got you covered!** ti copro io!
d (*be sufficient for, include*) coprire; **£100 will cover everything** 100 sterline saranno sufficienti; **we must cover all possibilities** dobbiamo prevedere tutte le possibilità
e (*distance*) coprire, percorrere; **to cover a lot of ground** (*also fig*) fare molta strada
f (*Press: report on*) fare un servizio su.
[3] VI: **to cover for sb** (*at work etc*) sostituire qn

▶ **cover over** VT + ADV (ri)coprire

▶ **cover up** [1] VT + ADV (*child, object*): **to cover up (with)** coprire (con *or* di); (*fig: hide: truth, facts*) nascondere; **to cover up one's tracks** (*also fig*) cancellare le tracce.
[2] VI + ADV (*warmly*) coprirsi; **to cover up for sb** (*fig*) coprire qn.

cov·er·age [ˈkʌvərɪdʒ] N (*Press, TV, Radio*): **to give full coverage to an event** fare un ampio servizio su un avvenimento, dare grande spazio *or* risonanza a un avvenimento; **the visit got nationwide coverage** (*Radio, TV*) la visita fu trasmessa su tutta la rete nazionale.

cover·alls [ˈkʌvərˌɔːlz] NPL (*Am*) tuta.

♦ **cover charge** N (*in restaurant*) coperto (*quota*).

♦ **cover girl** N cover girl *f inv*, ragazza-copertina.

cov·er·ing [ˈkʌvərɪŋ] N copertura; (*of snow, dust etc*) strato.

♦ **covering letter**, (*Am*) **cover letter** N nota esplicativa, lettera d'accompagnamento.

cov·er·let [ˈkʌvəlɪt] N copriletto.

♦ **cover note** N (*Insurance*) polizza (di assicurazione) provvisoria.

♦ **cover price** N prezzo di copertina.

cov·ert [ˈkʌvət] ADJ (*gen*) nascosto(-a); (*glance*) di sottecchi, furtivo(-a).

cov·ert·ly [ˈkʌvətlɪ] ADV (*glance, act*) di nascosto, furtivamente.

♦ **cover-up** [ˈkʌvərˌʌp] N occultamento (di informazioni).

cov·et [ˈkʌvɪt] VT concupire, bramare.

cov·et·ous [ˈkʌvɪtəs] ADJ avido(-a), bramoso(-a).

cov·et·ous·ly [ˈkʌvɪtəslɪ] ADV avidamente, bramosamente.

cov·et·ous·ness [ˈkʌvɪtəsnɪs] N avidità, brama.

cow [kaʊ] [1] N (*bovine*) mucca, vacca; (*female elephant*) elefantessa; (*female seal*) (foca) femmina; (*fam!: woman*) stronza (*fam!*); **you can cry till the cows come home, but you're not having it** puoi piangere quanto ti pare, tanto non te lo do.
[2] VT (*person*) intimidire; **a cowed look** un'aria da cane bastonato.
[3] ADJ femmina.

cow·ard [ˈkaʊəd] N vigliacco(-a).

cow·ard·ice [ˈkaʊədɪs], **cow·ard·li·ness** [ˈkaʊədlɪnɪs] N vigliaccheria.

cow·ard·ly [ˈkaʊədlɪ] ADJ vigliacco(-a).

cow·boy [ˈkaʊˌbɔɪ] N cowboy *m inv*; **to play cowboys and Indians** giocare agli indiani (e ai cowboys).

cow·er [ˈkaʊəʳ] VI acquattarsi (per paura).

cow·herd [ˈkaʊˌhɜːd] N vaccaro.

cow·hide [ˈkaʊˌhaɪd] N vacchetta.

cowl [kaʊl] N (*hood*) cappuccio.

cow·man [ˈkaʊmən] N (*pl* **-men**) vaccaro.

♦ **cow parsley** N (*Bot*) cerfoglio selvatico.

cow·pox [ˈkaʊˌpɒks] N vaiolo bovino.

cow·rie, **cow·ry** [ˈkaʊrɪ] N ciprea.

cow·shed [ˈkaʊˌʃed] N stalla.

cow·slip [ˈkaʊˌslɪp] N (*Bot*) primula odorosa.

cox [kɒks] **1** N (*Rowing*) timoniere *m*.
2 VT essere al timone di.
3 VI fare da timoniere.

cox·swain [ˈkɒksən] N nocchiere *m*.

coy [kɔɪ] ADJ (*comp* **-er**, *superl* **-est**) (*affectedly shy: person*) che fa il/la vergognoso(-a); (: *smile*) falsamente timido (-a); (*evasive*) evasivo(-a); (*coquettish*) civettuolo(-a).

coy·ly [ˈkɔɪlɪ] ADV (*smile*) con falsa timidezza; (*answer*) evasivamente; (*coquettishly*) con civetteria.

coy·ness [ˈkɔɪnɪs] N (*affected shyness*) falsa timidezza; (*evasiveness*) evasività; (*coquetry*) civetteria.

coy·ote [kɔɪˈəʊtɪ] N coyote *m inv*.

coy·pu [ˈkɔɪpuː] N (*pl* **coypu** *or* **coypus**) (*Zool*) nutria, castorino.

cozy [ˈkəʊzɪ] ADJ (*Am*) = **cosy**.

cp. ABBR (= *compare*) cfr.

c/p ABBR (*Brit*); see **carriage paid**.

CPI [ˌsiːpiːˈaɪ] N ABBR (*Am*: = *Consumer Price Index*) *indice dei prezzi al consumo*.

Cpl. ABBR = **corporal**.

CP/M [ˌsiːpiːˈɛm] N ABBR (= *Control Program for Microcomputers*) CP/M *m*.

c.p.s. [ˌsiːpiːˈɛs] ABBR (= *characters per second*) c.p.s.

CPSA [ˌsiːpiːɛsˈeɪ] N ABBR (*Brit*: = *Civil and Public Services Association*) *sindacato dei servizi pubblici*.

CPU [ˌsiːpiːˈjuː] N ABBR see **central processing unit**.

cr. ABBR **a** = **credit b** = **creditor**.

crab¹ [kræb] N granchio.

crab² [kræb] N (*Mountaineering*) moschettone *m*.

♦ **crab apple** N (*fruit*) mela selvatica; (*tree*) melo selvatico.

crab·by [ˈkræbɪ], **crab·bed** [ˈkræbɪd] ADJ (*fam*) acido(-a), scontroso(-a).

♦ **crab louse** N piattola.

♦ **crab meat** N polpa di granchio.

crack [kræk] **1** N **a** (*split, slit: in glass, pottery*) incrinatura, scheggiatura; (: *in wall, plaster, ground, paint*) crepa, spaccatura; (: *in skin*) screpolatura; **through the crack in the door** (*slight opening*) dalla fessura della porta; **at the crack of dawn** alle prime luci dell'alba
b (*noise: of twigs*) scricchiolio, crepitio; (: *of whip*) schiocco; (: *of rifle, of gun*) colpo; (: *of thunder*) boato
c (*blow*): **a crack on the head** una botta in testa
d (*fam: attempt*): **to have a crack at sth** tentare qc
e (*fam: joke, insult*) battuta
f (*Drugs*) crack *m inv*.
2 VT **a** (*break: glass, pottery*) incrinare; (: *wood*) schiantare; (: *nut*) schiacciare; (: *egg*) rompere; (*fig fam: safe*) scassinare; (: *bottle*) stappare, aprire; **to crack one's skull** spaccarsi la testa; **to crack sb over the head** dare un colpo in testa a qn
b (*cause to sound: whip, finger joints*) (far) schioccare; **to crack jokes** (*fam*) dire battute, scherzare
c (*case, mystery: solve*) risolvere; (*code*) decifrare.
3 VI **a** (*break: pottery, glass*) incrinarsi; (: *ground, wall*) creparsi; (*dry wood*) schiantarsi; (*skin*) screpolarsi; **to crack under the strain** (*person*) non reggere alla tensione
b (*whip*) schioccare; (*dry wood*) scricchiolare; **to get cracking** (*fam*) darsi una mossa.
4 ADJ (*team, regiment*) scelto(-a); (*athlete*) di prim'ordine; **a crack shot** un tiratore infallibile

▶ **crack down** VI + ADV: **to crack down (on)** prendere serie misure contro, porre freno a

▶ **crack up** (*fam*)
1 VI + ADV crollare; **I must be cracking up!** (*hum*) sto dando i numeri!.
2 VT + ADV: **he's not all he's cracked up to be** non è così meraviglioso come dicono.

crack·down [ˈkrækˌdaʊn] N repressione *f*.

cracked [krækt] ADJ (*fam: mad*) tocco(-a), matto(-a).

crack·er [ˈkrækəʳ] N **a** (*biscuit*) cracker *m inv* **b** (*firework*) petardo; (*Christmas cracker*) *specie di mortaretto natalizio con sorpresa* **c** (*Brit fam: girl, dress, car*) schianto; **a cracker of a ...** un(a) ...formidabile.

crack·ers [ˈkrækəz] ADJ (*Brit fam*) pazzo(-a), tocco(-a); **he's crackers** è un po' tocco.

crack·ing [ˈkrækɪŋ] **1** ADJ: **at a cracking pace** di buon passo.
2 N **a** (*Chem*) cracking *m* **b** (*of paint, varnish*) crepe *fpl*.

crack·le [ˈkrækl] **1** VI (*twigs burning*) crepitare, scoppiettare; (*sth frying*) sfrigolare.
2 N (*see vb*) crepitio, scoppiettio; sfrigolio; (*on telephone*) disturbo.

crack·ling [ˈkræklɪŋ] N **a** (*sound*) crepitio; (*on radio, telephone*) disturbo; (*of frying food*) sfrigolio **b** (*of pork*) cotenna (di maiale) arrostita.

crack·pot [ˈkrækˌpɒt] (*fam*) **1** N imbecille *m/f* con idee assurde.
2 ADJ (*idea*) assurdo(-a).

♦ **crack-up** [ˈkrækˌʌp] N (*fam*) crollo.

cra·dle [ˈkreɪdl] **1** N culla; (*of telephone*) forcella; (*Constr*) gabbia.
2 VT (*child*) tenere tra le braccia; (*object*) reggere tra le braccia.

♦ **cradle snatch·er** [ˈkreɪdlˈsnætʃəʳ] N (*pej*) chi se la fa con quelli(-e) più giovani.

cradle·song [ˈkreɪdlˌsɒŋ] N ninnananna.

craft [krɑːft] N **a** (*handicraft*) artigianato; (*art*) arte *f*, mestiere *m*; (*profession*) mestiere; (*fig: skill*) abilità, maestria **b** (*cunning: pej*) furbizia, astuzia **c** (*boat: pl inv*) barca, imbarcazione *f*.

crafti·ly [ˈkrɑːftɪlɪ] ADV (*see adj*) furbamente, astutamente; abilmente.

crafti·ness [ˈkrɑːftɪnɪs] N (*see adj*) furbizia, astuzia; abilità.

crafts·man [ˈkrɑːftsmən] N (*pl* **-men**) artigiano.

crafts·man·ship [ˈkrɑːftsmənˌʃɪp] N (*skill*) arte *f*, abilità, maestria; **a piece of craftmanship** un pezzo di artigianato.

crafty [ˈkrɑːftɪ] ADJ (*comp* **-ier**, *superl* **-iest**) (*person*) furbo (-a), astuto(-a); (*action*) abile.

crag [kræg] N rupe *f*.

crag·gy [ˈkrægɪ] ADJ (*comp* **-ier**, *superl* **-iest**) (*rock*) scosceso (-a), dirupato(-a); (*features*) marcato(-a); (*face*) dai tratti marcati.

cram [kræm] **1** VT (*stuff: books, papers*): **to cram into** infilare in, stipare in, pigiare in; (: *people, passengers*) ammassare in; (*fill*): **to cram sth with** riempire qc di; **to cram in** far stare, trovare posto per; **his head is crammed with strange ideas** ha la testa piena di idee strane; **the room was crammed with furniture/people** la stanza era stipata di mobili/affollata di gente; **she crammed her hat down over her eyes** si calcò il cappello sugli occhi; **to cram o.s. with food** abbuffarsi, rimpinzarsi.
2 VI **a** (*people*): **to cram (into)** affollarsi (in), accalcarsi (in), stiparsi (in)

b (*pupil: for exam*) fare una sgobbata finale.

cram·mer ['kræmə'] N (*school*) istituto che prepara agli esami; (*tutor*) insegnante *m/f* che cura la preparazione agli esami.

cramp [kræmp] **1** N (*Med*): **cramp (in)** crampo (a).
2 VT (*hinder: person*) impacciare, inibire; (: *progress*) ostacolare, frenare; **your presence is cramping my style** (*fam*) la tua presenza mi inibisce.

cramped [kræmpt] ADJ (*room etc*) angusto(-a); (*writing*) fitto(-a); (*position*) rannicchiato(-a).

cram·pon ['kræmpən] N (*Mountaineering*) rampone *m*.

cran·berry ['krænbərı] N mirtillo.

♦ **cranberry sauce** N salsa di mirtilli.

crane [kreın] **1** N (*Zool, Tech*) gru *f inv*.
2 VT, VI: **to crane forward, to crane one's neck** allungare il collo.

♦ **crane driver** N gruista *m*.

cra·nial ['kreınıəl] ADJ (*Anat*) cranico(-a).

cra·nium ['kreınıəm] N (*pl* **cranium**) (*Anat*) cranio.

crank [kræŋk] **1** N **a** (*Tech*) manovella **b** (*person*) eccentrico(-a), persona stramba.
2 VT (*also*: **crank up**) avviare a manovella.

crank·case ['kræŋk,keıs] N (*Aut*) basamento (del motore).

crank·pin ['kræŋk,pın] N (*Aut*) perno di biella.

crank·shaft ['kræŋkʃɑːft] N (*Aut*) albero motore, albero a gomiti.

cranky ['kræŋkı] ADJ (*comp* **-ier**, *superl* **-iest**) (*strange: ideas, people*) eccentrico(-a), strambo(-a); **to be cranky** (*bad-tempered*) avere i nervi.

cran·ny ['krænı] N see **nook**.

crap [kræp] (*fam!*) N merda (*fam!*); (*nonsense*) cazzate *fpl* (*fam!*); **to have a crap** cacare (*fam!*)

crape [kreıp] N = **crêpe**.

crap·py ['kræpı] ADJ (*comp* **-ier**, *superl* **-iest**) (*fam!*) di merda (*fam!*)

crash [kræʃ] **1** N **a** (*accident*) incidente *m*; **there has been a plane crash** un aereo è precipitato
b (*noise*) fragore *m*, fracasso; (*of thunder*) fragore
c (*of business*) fallimento; (*Stock Exchange*) crollo.
2 VT (*smash: car*) avere un incidente con, fracassare, sfasciare; **he crashed the car into a wall** andò a sbattere contro un muro con la macchina; **the pilot crashed the plane** il pilota ha fatto precipitare l'aereo.
3 VI **a** (*car*) avere un incidente; (*plane*) cadere, precipitare; (*collide: two vehicles*) scontrarsi; **to crash into sth** scontrarsi con qc, andare a sbattere contro qc, schiantarsi contro qc; **the plates came crashing down** i piatti sono andati in frantumi
b (*business*) fallire, andare in rovina; (*stock market*) crollare.
4 ADJ (*diet, course*) intensivo(-a), rapido(-a).

♦ **crash barrier** N (*Brit Aut*) guardrail *m inv*.

♦ **crash course** N corso intensivo.

♦ **crash helmet** N casco (di protezione).

crash·ing ['kræʃıŋ] ADJ (*fam old*): **it's/he's a crashing bore** è tremendamente noioso, è di una noia mortale.

♦ **crash landing** N atterraggio forzato, atterraggio di fortuna.

crass [kræs] ADJ crasso(-a).

crass·ly ['kræslı] ADV (*stupidly*) grossolanamente.

crass·ness ['kræsnıs] N (*of error*) grossolanità.

crate [kreıt] N cassa, cassetta.

cra·ter ['kreıtə'] N cratere *m*.

♦ **crater lake** N lago vulcanico.

cra·vat [krə'væt] N (*for men*) foulard *m inv* da collo.

crave [kreıv] **1** VT **a** (*desire*) desiderare disperatamente
b (*frm: pardon, permission*) implorare.
2 VI: **to crave for** = **1 a**.

cra·ven ['kreıvən] ADJ (*frm pej*) vigliacco(-a).

crav·ing ['kreıvıŋ] N: **craving (for)** (*for food, cigarettes etc*) (gran) voglia (di); (*in pregnancy*) voglia; (*for affection, attention*) desiderio estremo.

craw·fish ['krɔːfıʃ] N = **crayfish**.

crawl [krɔːl] **1** N **a** (*slow pace*) passo lento; **the traffic went at a crawl** il traffico procedeva a passo d'uomo
b (*Swimming*) stile *m* libero, crawl *m*; **to do the crawl** nuotare a stile libero, nuotare a crawl.
2 VI **a** (*drag o.s.*) trascinarsi, strisciare; (*child*) andare gattoni *or* carponi; (*traffic*) avanzare lentamente, procedere a passo d'uomo; (*time*) non passare mai; **to crawl in/out** etc trascinarsi carponi dentro/fuori etc; **to be crawling with ants** brulicare di formiche
b (*fam: suck up*): **to crawl to sb** arruffianarsi qn.

crawl·er ['krɔːlə'] N (*fam*) ruffiano(-a).

♦ **crawler lane** N (*Brit Aut*) corsia riservata al traffico lento.

cray·fish ['kreı,fıʃ] N gambero (d'acqua dolce).

cray·on ['kreıən] N (*wax*) pastello a cera; (*chalk*) gessetto; (*coloured pencil*) matita colorata.

craze [kreız] **1** N mania.
2 VT **a** far diventare pazzo(-a) **b** (*pottery, glaze*) incrinare.
3 VI (*pottery, glaze, windscreen*) incrinarsi.

crazed [kreızd] ADJ (*look, person*) folle, pazzo(-a); (*pottery, glaze*) incrinato(-a).

cra·zi·ly ['kreızılı] ADV pazzamente, follemente.

cra·zy ['kreızı] ADJ (*comp* **-ier**, *superl* **-iest**) **a** (*mad*) pazzo(-a), matto(-a), folle; **to go crazy** uscir di senno, impazzire; **crazy with jealousy** pazzo(-a) di gelosia; **it was a crazy idea** era un'idea folle; **you were crazy to do it** sei stato un pazzo a farlo
b (*fam: keen*): **to be crazy about sb** essere pazzo(-a) di qn; **to be crazy about sth** andare matto(-a) per qc
c (*angle, slope*) pericolante.

♦ **crazy paving** N (*Brit*) lastricato a mosaico irregolare.

creak [kriːk] **1** VI (*wood, shoe etc*) scricchiolare; (*hinge etc*) cigolare.
2 N (*see vb*) scricchiolio; cigolio.

creaky ['kriːkı] ADJ (*shoes, floorboards*) scricchiolante; (*hinge, joint*) cigolante, stridente.

cream [kriːm] **1** N **a** (*Culin*) panna; **single/double cream** panna da cucina liquida/densa; **whipped cream** panna montata; **a chocolate cream** (*a sweet*) un cremino al cioccolato; **cream of tomato soup** crema di pomodoro; **the cream of society** (*fig*) la crème della società
b (*lotion: for face, shoes etc*) crema.
2 ADJ (*colour*) (color) crema *inv*, (color) panna *inv*; (*Culin: made with cream*) alla panna.
3 VT (*mix: also*: **cream together**) amalgamare; **creamed potatoes** puré *m* di patate.

▶ **cream off** VT + ADV (*best talents, part of profits*) portarsi via.

♦ **cream cake** N torta alla panna.

♦ **cream cheese** N formaggio fresco spalmabile.

♦ **cream cracker** N *cracker da mangiare con i formaggi*.

cream·ery ['kriːmərı] N (*factory*) caseificio; (*shop*) latteria.

♦ **cream jug** N bricco per la panna.

♦ **cream tea** N *tè servito con "scones", "clotted cream" e marmellata*; see **scone, clotted cream**.

creamy ['kri:mɪ] ADJ (comp **-ier**, superl **-iest**) (taste, texture) cremoso(-a); (colour) crema inv, panna inv.

crease [kri:s] **1** N (fold: in trousers) piega; (wrinkle: in cloth) grinza; (: in face) ruga, grinza. **2** VT sgualcire, spiegazzare; **his face was creased with laughter** aveva il volto contratto dalle risate. **3** VI sgualcirsi.

♦ **crease-resistant** ['kri:srɪˌzɪstənt] ADJ ingualcibile.

cre·ate [kri:'eɪt] **1** VT (gen) creare; (impression, fuss, noise) fare; **to create a sensation** destare or fare scalpore; **he was created a peer by the Queen** fu nominato pari dalla Regina. **2** VI (fam) fare un sacco di storie.

crea·tion [kri:'eɪʃən] N creazione f.

crea·tive [kri:'eɪtɪv] ADJ creativo(-a).

crea·tive·ly [kri:'eɪtɪvlɪ] ADV creativamente.

crea·tiv·ity [ˌkri:eɪˈtɪvɪtɪ] N creatività.

crea·tor [krɪ'eɪtə'] N creatore(-trice).

crea·ture ['kri:tʃə'] N (gen) creatura; **the creatures of the deep** (liter) le creature degli abissi; **a creature from outer space** un extraterrestre; **the poor creature had no home** il poverino era senza casa; **a creature of habit** una persona abitudinaria.

♦ **creature comforts** NPL comodità fpl.

crèche [kreɪʃ] N asilo m nido inv.

cre·dence ['kri:dəns] N credenza, fede f.

cre·den·tials [krɪ'dɛnʃəlz] NPL (qualifications) titoli mpl; (identifying papers, of diplomat) credenziali fpl; (letters of reference) referenze fpl.

cred·ibil·ity [ˌkrɛdə'bɪlɪtɪ] N (see adj) credibilità; attendibilità.

cred·ible ['krɛdɪbl] ADJ (gen) credibile; (witness, source) attendibile.

cred·it ['krɛdɪt] **1** N **a** (Fin) credito; **to give sb credit** fare credito a qn; **you are £100 in credit** lei ha 100 sterline a suo credito; **on credit** a credito; **is his credit good?** gli si può dare credito?; **to be in credit** (person) essere creditore(-trice); (bank account) essere coperto(-a)
b (honour) onore m; **to one's credit** a proprio onore; **it is to his credit that ...** bisogna riconoscergli che...; **he's a credit to his family** fa onore alla sua famiglia; **to give sb credit for (doing) sth** riconoscere a qn il merito di (aver fatto) qc; **I gave you credit for more sense** ti reputavo più sensato; **it does you credit** ti fa onore; **to take credit for (doing) sth** attribuirsi il merito di (aver fatto) qc
c (Univ: esp Am) certificato di compimento di una parte di un corso universitario; see also **credits**. **2** VT **a** (believe: also: **give credit to**) credere, prestar fede a
b (attribute) attribuire il credito a; **to credit sb with sth** attribuire qc a qn; **I credited him with more sense** credevo che avesse più cervello; **he credited them with the victory** attribuì a loro il merito della vittoria
c (Comm): **to credit £50 to sb, to credit sb with £50** accreditare 50 sterline a qn. **3** ADJ (limit, agency etc) di credito; **on the credit side** (fig) a suo favore.

cred·it·able ['krɛdɪtəbl] ADJ che fa onore, lodevole, degno(-a) di lode.

cred·it·ably ['krɛdɪtəblɪ] ADV lodevolmente.

♦ **credit account** N (in shop etc) conto (di credito), conto (aperto).

♦ **credit agency**, (Am) **credit bureau** N agenzia di analisi di credito.

♦ **credit balance** N saldo attivo.

♦ **credit card** N carta di credito.

♦ **credit control** N controllo dei crediti.

♦ **credit entry** N (Comm) scrittura di accredito.

♦ **credit facilities** NPL agevolazioni fpl creditizie.

♦ **credit limit** N limite m di credito.

♦ **credit note** N (Brit) nota di credito.

credi·tor ['krɛdɪtə'] N creditore(-trice).

♦ **credit rating** N affidabilità f inv di credito.

cred·its ['krɛdɪts] NPL (Cine, TV: opening) titoli mpl di testa; (: closing) titoli mpl di coda.

♦ **credit squeeze** N limitazione f dei crediti, stretta creditizia.

♦ **credit terms** NPL condizioni fpl di credito.

♦ **credit transfer** N bancogiro, postagiro.

credit·worthy ['krɛdɪt,wɜ:ðɪ] ADJ autorizzabile al credito.

cre·du·lity [krɪ'dju:lɪtɪ] N credulità.

credu·lous ['krɛdjʊləs] ADJ credulo(-a).

credu·lous·ly ['krɛdjʊləslɪ] ADV con credulità.

creed [kri:d] N credo, dottrina.

creek [kri:k] N (inlet) insenatura; (Am) piccolo fiume m.

creel [kri:l] N cestino per il pesce; (also: **lobster creel**) nassa.

creep [kri:p] (vb: pt, pp **crept**) **1** VI (animal) strisciare; (plant) arrampicarsi; (person: stealthily) avanzare furtivamente; (: slowly) avanzare lentamente; **to creep in/out** entrare/uscire quatto(-a) quatto(-a); **to creep up on sb** avvicinarsi quatto(-a) quatto(-a) a qn; (fig: old age etc) cogliere qn alla sprovvista; **a feeling of peace crept over him** lo avvolse un senso di pace; **it made my flesh creep** mi fece accapponare la pelle; **an error has crept in** ci è scappato un errore. **2** N (fam): **it gives me the creeps** mi fa venire la pelle d'oca; **he's a creep** è un tipo viscido.

creep·er ['kri:pə'] N (Bot) rampicante m.

creep·ing ['kri:pɪŋ] ADJ (plant) rampicante; **creeping paralysis** paralisi f progressiva.

creepy ['kri:pɪ] ADJ (comp **-ier**, superl **-iest**) (frightening) che fa accapponare la pelle.

♦ **creepy-crawly** ['kri:pɪ,krɔ:lɪ] N (fam) bestiolina, insetto.

cre·mate [krɪ'meɪt] VT cremare.

cre·ma·tion [krɪ'meɪʃən] N cremazione f.

crema·to·rium [ˌkrɛmə'tɔ:rɪəm] N (pl **crematoria** [ˌkrɛmə'tɔ:rɪə]) (forno) crematorio.

cren·el·lat·ed ['krɛnɪˌleɪtɪd] ADJ merlato(-a).

cre·ole ['kri:əʊl] ADJ, N creolo(-a).

creo·sote ['krɪə,səʊt] **1** N creosoto. **2** VT dare il creosoto a.

crêpe [kreɪp] N **a** (fabric) crespo **b** (also: **crêpe rubber**) para **c** (pancake) crêpe f inv, crespella.

♦ **crêpe bandage** N (Brit) fascia elastica.

♦ **crêpe paper** N carta crespata.

♦ **crêpe sole** N (on shoes) suola di para.

crept [krɛpt] PT, PP OF **creep**.

cre·scen·do [krɪ'ʃɛndəʊ] N (Mus, fig) crescendo.

cres·cent ['krɛsnt] **1** ADJ (moon) crescente; (shape) a mezzaluna. **2** N (shape) mezzaluna; (street) via (a semicerchio).

cress [krɛs] N crescione m.

crest [krɛst] N (of bird, wave, mountain) cresta; (on helmet) pennacchio; (Heraldry) cimiero; **to be on the crest of the wave** (fig) essere sulla cresta dell'onda.

crest·fallen ['krɛst,fɔ:lən] ADJ abbattuto(-a), mortificato(-a); **to look crestfallen** avere un'aria mogia.

Cre·tan ['kri:tən] ADJ, N cretese *(m/f)*.
Crete [kri:t] N Creta.
cret·in ['krɛtɪn] N *(fam pej)* cretino(-a).
cret·in·ous ['krɛtɪnəs] ADJ *(fam pej)* da cretino(-a).
cre·vasse [krɪ'væs] N crepaccio.
crev·ice ['krɛvɪs] N crepa, fessura.
crew[1] [kru:] **1** N *(Naut, Aer)* equipaggio; *(Rowing etc: team)* squadra; *(Cine)* troupe *f inv*; *(gang)* banda, compagnia.
  2 VI *(Sailing)*: **to crew for sb** far parte dell'equipaggio di qn.
crew[2] [kru:] PT of **crow**.
♦ **crew cut** N: **to have a crew cut** avere i capelli a spazzola.
♦ **crew-neck** ['kru: nɛk] ADJ: **crew-neck sweater** maglione *m* a girocollo.
crib [krɪb] **1** N **a** *(small cot)* culla; *(Rel)* presepio; *(manger)* mangiatoia **b** *(plagiarism)* plagio; *(Scol: answer book)* traduttore *m*, bigino *(fam)*.
  2 VT *(Scol)* copiare.
crib·bage ['krɪbɪdʒ] N *tipo di gioco di carte*.
♦ **crib death** N *(Am)* = **cot death**.
crick [krɪk] **1** N: **crick in the neck** torcicollo; **crick in the back** dolore *m* alla schiena.
  2 VT: **to crick one's neck** prendere il torcicollo; **to crick one's back** farsi male alla schiena.
crick·et[1] ['krɪkɪt] N *(sport)* cricket *m*; **that's not cricket** *(fig)* questo non è leale.
crick·et[2] ['krɪkɪt] N *(insect)* grillo.
♦ **cricket ball** N palla da cricket.
crick·et·er ['krɪkɪtə'] N giocatore(-trice) di cricket.
♦ **cricket match** N partita di cricket.
cri·key ['kraɪkɪ] EXCL *(Brit fam)* cribbio.
crime [kraɪm] N *(in general)* criminalità; *(instance)* crimine *m*, delitto; **it's a crime** *(fig)* è una vergogna.
♦ **crime prevention** N prevenzione della criminalità.
♦ **crime wave** N ondata di criminalità.
crimi·nal ['krɪmɪnl] **1** N criminale *m/f*.
  2 ADJ criminale; *(fig)* vergognoso(-a); **criminal lawyer** (avvocato) penalista *m/f*; **to study criminal law** fare studi penalistici; **to take criminal proceedings against sb** istruire una causa penale contro qn.
♦ **Criminal Investigation Department** N ≈ polizia giudiziaria.
crimi·nal·ity [ˌkrɪmɪ'nælɪtɪ] N criminalità *f inv*.
crimi·nal·ly ['krɪmɪnəlɪ] ADV criminosamente.
crimi·nolo·gist [ˌkrɪmɪ'nɒlədʒɪst] N criminologo.
crimi·nol·ogy [ˌkrɪmɪ'nɒlədʒɪ] N criminologia.
crimp [krɪmp] VT *(hair)* arricciare; *(material)* pieghettare.
crim·son ['krɪmzn] ADJ, N cremisi *(m) inv*.
cringe [krɪndʒ] VI *(in terror)*: **to cringe (from)** ritrarsi impaurito(-a) (da); **to cringe (before)** *(in servility)* strisciare (davanti a); **the very thought of it makes me cringe** *(fam: in embarrassment)* solo a pensarci mi sento sprofondare.
crin·kle ['krɪŋkl] VT spiegazzare, sgualcire.
crin·kly ['krɪŋklɪ] ADJ *(comp* **-ier**, *superl* **-iest)** *(hair)* crespo (-a); *(paper etc)* crespato(-a).
crino·line ['krɪnəli:n] N crinolina.
crip·ple ['krɪpl] **1** N *(lame)* zoppo(-a); *(disabled)* invalido (-a); *(maimed)* mutilato(-a).
  2 VT **a** rendere invalido(-a); **crippled with arthritis** invalido(-a) per l'artrite **b** *(production, exports)* paralizzare.
crip·pled ['krɪpld] ADJ *(handicapped)* invalido(-a); *(production, exports)* paralizzato(-a); *(frm: seriously damaged)* seriamente danneggiato(-a).

crip·pling ['krɪplɪŋ] ADJ *(disease)* che provoca invalidità; *(taxes, debts)* esorbitante.
cri·sis ['kraɪsɪs] N *(pl* **crises** ['kraɪsi:z]) crisi *f inv*; **to come to a crisis** entrare in crisi; **we have a crisis on our hands** ci troviamo di fronte a una crisi.
crisp [krɪsp] ADJ *(comp* **-er**, *superl* **-est)** *(bacon, biscuit, lettuce)* croccante; *(snow)* fresco(-a); *(bank note)* nuovo (-a) di zecca; *(linen)* inamidato(-a); *(air)* fresco(-a), frizzante; *(manner, tone, reply)* secco(-a), brusco(-a); *(style)* conciso(-a) e vivace.
crisp·bread ['krɪsp brɛd] N cracottes ® *fpl*.
crisp·ly ['krɪsplɪ] ADV *(speak)* con tono secco; *(write)* in modo vivace.
crisp·ness ['krɪspnɪs] N *(of bacon, biscuit, snow)* friabilità; *(of linen)* freschezza; *(of apple)* sodezza; *(of style)* vivacità; **I like the crispness of new banknotes** mi piace toccare le banconote nuove di zecca.
crisps [krɪsps] NPL *(Brit)* patatine *fpl*.
crispy ['krɪspɪ] ADJ *(comp* **-ier**, *superl* **-iest)** croccante.
criss-cross ['krɪs krɒs] **1** ADJ *(lines)* incrociato(-a), intrecciato(-a); *(pattern)* a linee incrociate.
  2 VT incrociare.
cri·teri·on [kraɪ'tɪərɪən] N *(pl* **criteria** [kraɪ'tɪərɪə]) criterio.
crit·ic ['krɪtɪk] N critico(-a).
criti·cal ['krɪtɪkəl] ADJ *(all senses)* critico(-a); **to be critical of sb/sth** criticare qn/qc, essere critico(-a) verso qn/qc; **at a critical moment** in un momento critico; **a critical success** *(book, play)* un successo di critica.
criti·cal·ly ['krɪtɪkəlɪ] ADV criticamente; **to be critically ill** versare in gravi condizioni, essere gravemente malato (-a).
criti·cism ['krɪtɪsɪzəm] N critica.
criti·cize ['krɪtɪsaɪz] VT criticare.
cri·tique [krɪ'ti:k] N critica, saggio critico.
croak [krəʊk] **1** N *(of raven)* gracchio; *(of frog)* gracidio, gracidare *m*.
  2 VI *(raven)* gracchiare; *(frog)* gracidare; *(person)* dire con voce rauca.
Cro·at ['krəʊæt] N croato(-a).
Croa·tia [krəʊ'eɪʃə] N Croazia.
Croa·tian [krəʊ'eɪʃən] **1** ADJ croato(-a).
  2 N *(person)* croato(-a); *(language)* croato.
cro·chet ['krəʊʃeɪ] **1** N lavoro all' uncinetto.
  2 VT, VI lavorare all'uncinetto.
♦ **crochet hook** N uncinetto.
crock [krɒk] N coccio; *(fam: person: also:* **old crock)** rottame *m*; *(: car, bicycle)* rottame *m*, macinino.
crock·ery ['krɒkərɪ] N *(earthenware)* vasellame *m* (di terracotta); *(plates, cups)* stoviglie *fpl*.
croco·dile ['krɒkədaɪl] N coccodrillo; **to walk in a crocodile** *(Brit fam)* camminare in fila per due.
♦ **crocodile tears** NPL lacrime *fpl* di coccodrillo.
cro·cus ['krəʊkəs] N croco.
Croesus ['kri:səs] N Creso.
croft [krɒft] N *(Scot)* piccola fattoria.
croft·er ['krɒftə'] N *(Scot)* fattore *m* *(di piccola fattoria)*.
crois·sant ['krwæsɒŋ] N croissant *m inv*, cornetto.
crone [krəʊn] N vecchiarda.
cro·ny ['krəʊnɪ] N *(fam)* amicone(-a).
crook [krʊk] **1** N **a** *(fam: thief)* ladro(-a), truffatore(-trice) **b** : **the crook of one's arm** l'incavo del braccio **c** *(shepherd's)* bastone *m* (da pastore); *(bishop's)* pastorale *m*.
  2 VT *(arm, finger)* piegare.

crook·ed ['krʊkɪd] ADJ (*stick, person*) curvo(-a), storto(-a); (*picture*) storto(-a); (*path*) tortuoso(-a); (*smile*) forzato (-a); (*dishonest: deal, means, person*) disonesto(-a).

crook·ed·ly ['krʊkɪdlɪ] ADV (*hang etc*) di traverso; (*smile*) forzatamente.

crook·ed·ness ['krʊkɪdnɪs] N (*deformity*) deformità *f inv*; (*dishonesty*) disonestà.

croon [kruːn] VT, VI (*sing quietly*) canticchiare; (*professionally*) cantare.

croon·er ['kruːnəʳ] N cantante *m/f* melodico.

crop [krɒp] **1** N **a** (*produce*) coltivazione *f*; (*amount produced: of fruit, vegetables*) raccolto; (: *of cereals*) raccolto, messe *f*; (*fig: of problems, applicants*) serie *f inv*; **the crops** il raccolto
  b (*of bird*) gozzo, ingluvie *f*
  c (*of whip*) manico; (*riding crop*) frustino.
  2 VT (*cut: hair*) tagliare, rapare; (*subj: animals: grass*) brucare
► **crop up** VI + ADV (*fig: arise*) sorgere, presentarsi; **something must have cropped up** dev'essere capitato *or* successo qualcosa.

crop·per ['krɒpəʳ] N (*fam*): **to come a cropper** (*fall badly*) fare un capitombolo; (*fail completely*) fare fiasco.

♦ **crop rotation** N rotazione *f* delle colture.

♦ **crop spraying** N spruzzatura di antiparassitari.

cro·quet ['krəʊkeɪ] N croquet *m*.

cro·quette [krəʊˈkɛt] N (*Culin*) crocchetta.

cross [krɒs] **1** N **a** (*mark, symbol*) croce *f*; (*on questionnaire*) crocetta, croce; **Greek/Latin cross** croce greca/latina; **to mark with a cross** segnare con una crocetta; **we each have our cross to bear** (*fig*) ognuno ha la propria croce (da portare)
  b (*Zool, Bio*) incrocio, ibrido; **it's a cross between geography and sociology** è un misto di geografia e sociologia
  c (*bias*): **cut on the cross** tagliato(-a) in sbieco.
  2 ADJ (*comp* **-er**, *superl* **-est**) (*angry*) arrabbiato(-a), seccato(-a); **to be/get cross with sb (about sth)** essere arrabbiato(-a)/arrabbiarsi con qn (per qc); **it makes me cross when ...** mi fa arrabbiare quando....
  3 VT **a** (*gen*) attraversare; (*threshold*) varcare; **this road crosses the motorway** questa strada incrocia *or* interseca l'autostrada; **it crossed my mind that ...** mi è venuto in mente che...; **we'll cross that bridge when we come to it** (*fig*) ogni cosa a tempo debito
  b (*cheque, letter t*) sbarrare; **to cross o.s.** farsi il segno della croce, segnarsi; **cross my heart!** giuro (sulla mia vita)!
  c (*arms*) incrociare; (*legs*) accavallare, incrociare; **to keep one's fingers crossed** (*fig*) fare gli scongiuri; **to cross swords with sb** (*fig*) scontrarsi con qn; **we've got a crossed line** (*Brit: on telephone*) c'è un'interferenza; **they've got their lines crossed** (*fig*) si sono fraintesi
  d (*thwart: person, plan*) contrastare, ostacolare
  e (*animals, plants*) incrociare.
  4 VI **a** (*also:* **cross over**): **the boat crosses from Dieppe to Newhaven** il traghetto fa la traversata da Dieppe a Newhaven
  b (*roads*) intersecarsi; (*letters, people*) incrociarsi.
► **cross off, cross out** VT + ADV cancellare (tirandoci una riga sopra).
► **cross over** VI + ADV attraversare.

cross·bar ['krɒsˌbaːʳ] N (*of bicycle*) canna; (*of goal post*) traversa.

cross·bill ['krɒsˌbɪl] N (*Zool*) crociere *m*.

cross·bow ['krɒsˌbəʊ] N balestra.

cross·breed ['krɒsˌbriːd] N incrocio, ibrido.

♦ **cross-Channel fer·ry** [krɒsˌtʃænəlˈfɛrɪ] N traghetto che attraversa la Manica.

♦ **cross-check** [ˌkrɒsˈtʃɛk] **1** N controprova.
  2 VT fare una controprova di.
  3 VI fare una controprova.

♦ **cross-country** [ˌkrɒsˈkʌntrɪ] **1** ADJ (*race*) campestre, cross-country *inv*; **cross-country skiing** sci *m* di fondo.
  2 ADV (*walk, travel*) attraverso i campi.
  3 N (corsa) campestre, cross-country *m inv*.

cross·court ['krɒsˌkɔːt] ADJ (*Tennis*): **crosscourt shot** diagonale *m*.

♦ **cross-cultural** ['krɒsˌkʌltʃərəl] ADJ transculturale.

♦ **cross-dressing** [ˌkrɒsˈdrɛsɪŋ] N travestitismo.

crossed [krɒst] ADJ (*cheque*) sbarrato(-a).

♦ **cross-examination** ['krɒsɪgˌzæmɪˈneɪʃən] N (*Law*) interrogatorio in contraddittorio, controinterrogatorio.

♦ **cross-examine** [ˌkrɒsɪgˈzæmɪn] VT (*Law*) interrogare in contraddittorio, controinterrogare.

♦ **cross-eyed** ['krɒsaɪd] ADJ strabico(-a).

cross·fire ['krɒsˌfaɪəʳ] N fuoco incrociato.

cross·ing ['krɒsɪŋ] N (*sea-passage*) traversata; (*of equator*) attraversamento; (*road junction*) incrocio, crocicchio; (*also:* **pedestrian crossing**) strisce *fpl* pedonali, passaggio pedonale; (*level crossing*) passaggio a livello; **cross at the crossing** attraversare sulle strisce.

♦ **crossing point** N valico di frontiera.

♦ **cross-legged** [ˌkrɒsˈlɛgɪd] ADV a gambe incrociate.

cross·ly ['krɒslɪ] ADV in tono arrabbiato, con rabbia.

♦ **cross-multiply** [ˌkrɒsˈmʌltɪplaɪ] VT (*Math*) fare una moltiplicazione incrociata di.

cross·patch ['krɒsˌpætʃ] N (*fam*) permaloso(-a), musone (-a).

♦ **cross-purposes** [ˌkrɒsˈpɜːpəsɪz] NPL: **to be at cross-purposes with sb** (*disagree*) essere in contrasto con qn; (*misunderstand*) fraintendere qn; **to talk at cross-purposes** fraintendersi.

♦ **cross-question** ['krɒsˌkwɛstʃən] VT (*witness*) sottoporre a controinterrogatorio; (*fig*) interrogare.

♦ **cross-refer** ['krɒsrɪˈfɜː'] VT rimandare.

♦ **cross-reference** [ˌkrɒsˈrɛfərəns] N rinvio, rimando.

cross·roads ['krɒsˌrəʊdz] NSG incrocio, crocicchio.

♦ **cross section** N (*Bio etc*) sezione *f* trasversale; (*of population*) campione *m* (rappresentativo); (*Topography*) profilo trasversale.

cross·tree ['krɒsˌtriː] N (*Naut*) crocetta.

cross·walk ['krɒsˌwɔːk] N (*Am*) strisce *fpl* pedonali, passaggio pedonale.

cross·wind ['krɒsˌwɪnd] N vento di traverso.

cross·wise ['krɒsˌwaɪz] ADV (*in the form of a cross*) a forma di croce; (*across*) di traverso.

cross·word ['krɒsˌwɜːd] N: **crossword (puzzle)** parole *fpl* crociate, cruciverba *m inv*.

crotch [krɒtʃ] N (*also:* **crutch**: *Anat*) inforcatura; (*of garment*) cavallo.

crotch·et ['krɒtʃɪt] N (*Brit Mus*) semiminima.

crotch·ety ['krɒtʃɪtɪ] ADJ (*fam: person*) burbero(-a), irritabile, stizzoso(-a).

cro·ton ['krəʊtən] N (*Bot*) croton *m inv*.

crouch [kraʊtʃ] VI (*also:* **crouch down**: *person, animal*) accucciarsi, accovacciarsi, acquattarsi.

croup [kruːp] N (*Med*) crup *m*.

crou·pi·er ['kruːpɪeɪ] N croupier *m inv*.

crou·ton ['kruːtɒn] N (*Culin*) crostino.

crow [krəʊ] ① N **a** (*bird*) cornacchia; **hooded crow** cornacchia grigia; **as the crow flies** in linea d'aria
   b (*noise: of cock*) canto del gallo, chicchirichì *m inv*; (: *of baby, person*) gridolino.
   ② VI **a** (*pt* **crowed** *or* **crew**, *pp* **crowed**) (*cock*) cantare, fare chicchirichì
   b (*pt, pp* **crowed**) (*child*) lanciare gridolini; (*fig*): **to crow over** *or* **about sth** vantarsi di qc; **to crow with delight** lanciare gridolini di piacere.

crow·bar ['krəʊbɑːʳ] N piede *m* di porco.

crowd [kraʊd] ① N folla; **crowds of people** un sacco di gente; **the crowd** (*common humanity*) la massa; **to follow the crowd** (*fig*) seguire la massa; **I don't like that crowd at all** non mi piace affatto quella gente; **she is part of the university crowd** appartiene alla cricca dell'università.
   ② VT (*place*) affollare, gremire; **to crowd sth into** (*things*) ammassare qc in, stipare qc in.
   ③ VI affollarsi, ammassarsi; **to crowd in** entrare in massa; **to crowd round sb/sth** affollarsi attorno a qn/qc, accalcarsi intorno a qn/qc
► **crowd out** VT + ADV (*not let in*) escludere (dal proprio gruppo); **the bar was crowded out** il bar era così pieno(-a) che non si poteva entrare.

crowd·ed ['kraʊdɪd] ADJ (*meeting, event, place etc*) affollato(-a), gremito(-a); (*town*) molto popolato(-a); (*day*) pieno(-a); (*profession*) inflazionato(-a); **crowded with** pieno(-a) di, gremito(-a) di, stipato(-a) di.

♦ **crowd scene** N (*Cine, Theatre*) scena di massa.

crown [kraʊn] ① N **a** corona; **the Crown** (*Law*) ≈ il Pubblico Ministero
   b (*top: of hat, head*) cocuzzolo; (: *of hill*) cima, vetta, cocuzzolo; (: *of road: raised centre*) centro; (: *of tooth*) corona; (: *artificial*) capsula.
   ② VT **a** (*king etc, fig*) incoronare; (*tooth*) incapsulare; **and to crown it all ...** (*fig*) e per giunta..., e come se non bastasse...
   b (*fam: hit*) dare una botta in testa a; **I'll crown you if you do that again!** se lo fai ancora ti do una botta in testa!

♦ **crown court** N (*Brit Law*) ≈ corte *f* d'assise.

crown·ing ['kraʊnɪŋ] ADJ (*achievement, glory*) supremo(-a).

♦ **crown jewels** NPL gioielli *mpl* della Corona.

♦ **crown prince** N principe *m* ereditario.

♦ **crow's-feet** ['krəʊzˌfiːt] NPL zampe *fpl* di gallina.

♦ **crow's-nest** ['krəʊzˌnɛst] N (*Naut*) coffa.

cru·cial ['kruːʃəl] ADJ cruciale, decisivo(-a); **crucial to** essenziale per; **his approval is crucial to the success of the project** la sua approvazione è essenziale per il successo del progetto.

cru·cial·ly ['kruːʃəlɪ] ADV: **it is crucially important that ...** è di vitale importanza che... .

cru·ci·ble ['kruːsɪbl] N crogiolo.

cru·ci·fix ['kruːsɪfɪks] N crocifisso.

cru·ci·fix·ion [ˌkruːsɪˈfɪkʃən] N crocifissione *f*.

cru·ci·fy ['kruːsɪˌfaɪ] VT crocifiggere; (*fig: punish*) mettere in croce, fare a pezzi; (: *criticize: performance, actor*) stroncare; **if he catches us he'll crucify us** se ci pesca ci ammazza.

crude [kruːd] ① ADJ (*comp* **-r**, *superl* **-st**) **a** (*pej: clumsy, unsophisticated: method, idea*) rozzo(-a); (*light, colour*) violento(-a)
   b (*simple: device, tool*) rudimentale; (: *drawing*) (appena) abbozzato(-a); **to make a crude attempt at doing sth** fare un rozzo tentativo di fare qc
   c (*vulgar*) volgare, grossolano(-a)
   d (*unprocessed: materials*) grezzo(-a); (: *oil*) greggio(-a).
   ② N (*also:* **crude oil**) (petrolio) greggio.

crude·ly ['kruːdlɪ] ADV (*paint, make*) rozzamente; (*say, express*) brutalmente.

crude·ness ['kruːdnɪs], **crud·ity** ['kruːdɪtɪ] N (*of method, idea*) rozzezza; (*of device, drawing*) rudimentalità; (*of expression, language*) volgarità.

cru·el ['kruəl] ADJ (*comp* **-ler**, *superl* **-lest**): **cruel (to** *or* **towards)** crudele (con *or* nei confronti di).

cru·el·ly ['kruəlɪ] ADV crudelmente.

cru·el·ty ['kruəltɪ] N crudeltà *f inv*; **mental cruelty** crudeltà mentale.

cru·et ['kruːɪt] N saliera e pepiera.

cruise [kruːz] ① N crociera; **to go on a cruise** fare una crociera.
   ② VI (*ship, plane*) viaggiare a velocità di crociera; (*holidaymakers*) fare una crociera; (*taxi, patrol car*) circolare; **the car cruises at 100 kph** (*Aut*) la velocità di crociera dell'auto è di 100 kmh.

♦ **cruise missile** N missile *m* cruise *inv*.

cruis·er ['kruːzəʳ] N (*Naut*) incrociatore *m*.

♦ **cruis·ing speed** ['kruːzɪŋspiːd] N velocità *f inv* di crociera. .

crumb [krʌm] N (*of bread, cake etc*) briciola; (*inner part of bread*) mollica; **a crumb of comfort** (*fig*) un briciolo di conforto; **crumbs of information** ben poche informazioni; **crumbs!** (*fam*) accidenti!

crum·ble ['krʌmbl] ① VT sbriciolare.
   ② VI (*bread*) sbriciolarsi; (*earth, land*) sbriciolarsi, franare; (*building etc*) andare in rovina; (*plaster, bricks*) sgretolarsi; (*fig: hopes, power*) crollare.

crum·bly ['krʌmblɪ] ADJ friabile.

crum·my ['krʌmɪ] ADJ (*fam: flat*) scadente; (: *idea*) stupido(-a); **a crummy town** un postaccio.

crum·pet ['krʌmpɪt] N **a** (*Culin*) *specie di crespella piuttosto spessa da tostare e mangiare calda con burro, marmellata ecc*. **b** : **a piece of crumpet** (*fam!*) un bel tocco di ragazza.

crum·ple ['krʌmpl] ① VT (*also:* **crumple up**, *paper*) accartocciare; (: *clothes*) stropicciare, sgualcire, spiegazzare.
   ② VI (*see vt*) accartocciarsi; stropicciarsi, sgualcirsi, spiegazzarsi.

crunch [krʌntʃ] ① N (*of broken glass, gravel*) scricchiolio; **if it comes to the crunch** (*fig*) al momento cruciale.
   ② VT (*with teeth*) sgranocchiare.
   ③ VI (*gravel*) scricchiolare.

crunchy ['krʌntʃɪ] ADJ (*comp* **-ier**, *superl* **-iest**) croccante.

cru·sade [kruːˈseɪd] ① N crociata.
   ② VI (*fig*): **to crusade for/against** fare una crociata per/contro.

cru·sad·er [kruːˈseɪdəʳ] N (*History*) crociato; (*fig*): **crusader (for)** sostenitore(-trice) (di).

crush [krʌʃ] ① N **a** (*crowd*) ressa, calca, folla
   b (*fam: infatuation*) cotta; **to have a crush on sb** avere una cotta per qn
   c (*drink*): **orange/lemon crush** spremuta di arancia/limone.
   ② VT (*squash: also fig*) schiacciare; (*crumple: clothes, paper*) sgualcire; (: *garlic*) tritare, schiacciare; (: *ice*) tritare; (: *grapes*) pigiare; (: *scrap metal*) pressare; (: *stones*) frantumare; **to be crushed to a pulp** essere

ridotto(-a) in poltiglia.

3 VI (*clothes*) sgualcirsi, spiegazzarsi.

♦ **crush barrier** N (*Brit*) transenna.

crush·ing ['krʌʃɪŋ] ADJ (*defeat, blow*) schiacciante; (*reply*) mordace.

♦ **crush-resistant** ['krʌʃrɪˌzɪstənt] ADJ ingualcibile.

crust [krʌst] N crosta; (*layer*) strato; **the Earth's crust** la crosta terrestre.

crus·ta·cean [krʌs'teɪʃən] N (*Zool*) crostaceo.

crusty ['krʌstɪ] ADJ (*comp* -ier, *superl* -iest) (*bread*) croccante; (*fam: person*) brontolone(-a); (: *remark*) brusco(-a).

crutch [krʌtʃ] N **a** (*Med*) stampella, gruccia; (*support*) sostegno **b** = crotch b.

crux [krʌks] N **a** : **the crux of the matter** il nocciolo della questione **b** (*Mountaineering*) passaggio chiave.

cry [kraɪ] 1 N **a** (*call, shout*) grido, urlo; (*of animal*) verso; **to give a cry** emettere un grido; **a cry for help** un grido di aiuto; **it's a far cry from ...** (*fig*) è tutt'un'altra cosa da...; **"jobs, not bombs" was their cry** "lavoro non bombe" era il loro slogan

b (*weep*): **she had a good cry** si è fatta un bel pianto.

2 VI **a** (*also:* cry out: call out, shout) gridare, urlare; **he cried (out) with pain** urlò di dolore; **to cry for help** gridare aiuto; **to cry for mercy** invocare pietà

b (*weep*) piangere; **what are you crying about?** perché piangi?; **the child was crying for his mother** il bambino piangeva perché voleva la mamma; **I laughed till I cried** risi fino alle lacrime; **I'll give him something to cry about!** (*fam*) glielo darò io un motivo per piangere!; **it's no good crying over spilt milk** (*fig*) è inutile piangere sul latte versato.

3 VT **a** gridare, urlare

b : **to cry o.s. to sleep** piangere fino ad addormentarsi

► **cry off** VI + ADV (*fam*) ritirarsi

► **cry out** 1 VI + ADV (*shout*) urlare, gridare; **this car is crying out to be resprayed** (*fam*) questa macchina ha un gran bisogno di essere riverniciata.

2 VT + ADV **a** (*call*) gridare, urlare

b : **to cry one's eyes** *or* **heart out** piangere tutte le proprie lacrime

► **cry out against** VI + ADV + PREP protestare vigorosamente contro.

♦ **cry·baby** ['kraɪˌbeɪbɪ] N (*fam*) piagnone(-a).

cry·ing ['kraɪɪŋ] 1 ADJ (*child*) in lacrime, piangente; (*fam: need*) disperato(-a), urgente; (*injustice*) palese; **it's a crying shame** è una vera vergogna.

2 N (*weeping*) pianto.

cryo·lite ['kraɪəˌlaɪt] N criolite *f*.

cryo·sur·gery [ˌkraɪəʊ'sɜːdʒərɪ] N criochirurgia.

crypt [krɪpt] N cripta.

cryp·tic ['krɪptɪk] ADJ (*mysterious*) oscuro(-a); (*puzzling*) enigmatico(-a); **cryptic crossword** cruciverba *m* a crittogramma.

cryp·ti·cal·ly ['krɪptɪkəlɪ] ADV (*see adj*) in modo oscuro; in modo enigmatico.

cryp·to·gram ['krɪptəʊˌgræm] N crittogramma *m*.

cryp·to·graph ['krɪptəʊˌgrɑːf] N crittografia.

crys·tal ['krɪstl] 1 N (*gen*) cristallo; (*watch glass*) vetro.

2 ADJ (*glass, vase*) di cristallo; (*clear: water, lake*) cristallino(-a).

♦ **crystal ball** N sfera di cristallo.

♦ **crystal-clear** [ˌkrɪstl'klɪəʳ] ADJ (*water, wine*) cristallino (-a); (*fig*) chiaro(-a) (come il sole).

♦ **crystal-gazing** ['krɪstlˌgeɪzɪŋ] N predizione *f* del futuro.

crys·tal·line ['krɪstəˌlaɪn] ADJ cristallino(-a).

crys·tal·li·za·tion [ˌkrɪstəlaɪ'zeɪʃən] N cristallizzazione *f*.

crys·tal·lize ['krɪstəˌlaɪz] 1 VT (*Chem*) cristallizzare; (*fig*) concretizzare, concretare; **crystallized fruits** (*Brit*) frutta candita.

2 VI (*see vt*) cristallizzarsi; concretizzarsi, concretarsi.

CSA [ˌsiːɛs'eɪ] N ABBR (*Brit*) = Child Support Agency.

CSE [ˌsiːɛs'iː] N ABBR (*Brit*: = Certificate of Secondary Education) diploma di istruzione secondaria.

CSEU [ˌsiːɛsi:'juː] N ABBR (*Brit*: = Confederation of Shipbuilding and Engineering Unions) confederazione dei sindacati della costruzione navale e meccanica.

CS gas [ˌsiːɛs'gæs] N (*Brit*) tipo di gas lacrimogeno.

CST [ˌsiːɛs'tiː] N ABBR (*Am*: = central standard time) fuso orario.

CSU [ˌsiːɛs'juː] N ABBR (*Brit*: = Civil Service Union) sindacato dei dipendenti statali.

CT ABBR (*Am Post*) = Connecticut.

ct ABBR = carat.

CTC [ˌsiːtiː'siː] (*Brit*) N ABBR = City Technology College.

cu. ABBR = cubic.

cub [kʌb] N **a** cucciolo; **lion cub** leoncino; **wolf cub** lupetto **b** (*also:* cub scout) lupetto.

Cuba ['kjuːbə] N Cuba.

Cu·ban ['kjuːbən] ADJ, N cubano(-a).

cubby·hole ['kʌbɪˌhəʊl] N angolo, cantuccio.

cube [kjuːb] 1 N cubo; (*of sugar*) cubetto, zolletta; **to cut into cubes** tagliare a cubetti.

2 VT (*Math*) elevare al cubo *or* alla terza potenza.

♦ **cube root** N radice *f* cubica.

cu·bic ['kjuːbɪk] ADJ (*shape, volume*) cubico(-a); (*metre, foot*) cubo(-a); **cubic capacity** (*Aut*) cilindrata; **cubic function** (*Math*) funzione *f* cubica.

cu·bi·cle ['kjuːbɪkəl] N cabina.

cub·ism ['kjuːbɪzəm] N cubismo.

cub·ist ['kjuːbɪst] ADJ, N cubista (*m/f*).

cu·boid ['kjuːbɔɪd] 1 ADJ cuboide.

2 N parallelepipedo rettangolo.

cuck·old ['kʌkəld] (*old*) 1 N (*man*) becco, cornuto.

2 VT fare becco.

cuckoo ['kʊkuː] 1 N cuculo, cucù *m inv*.

2 ADJ (*fam*) tocco(-a), matto(-a).

♦ **cuckoo clock** N orologio a cucù.

cu·cum·ber ['kjuːkʌmbəʳ] N cetriolo.

cud [kʌd] N: **to chew the cud** (*cows*) ruminare; (*fig*) rimuginare.

cud·dle ['kʌdl] 1 N abbraccio, coccole *fpl*.

2 VT abbracciare, coccolare.

3 VI: **to cuddle down** accoccolarsi; **to cuddle up to sb** accoccolarsi contro qn.

cud·dly ['kʌdlɪ] ADJ (*comp* -ier, *superl* -iest) (*child, animal*) coccolone(-a); (*toy*) morbido(-a), da tenere stretto(-a).

cudg·el ['kʌdʒəl] 1 N (*weapon*) manganello, randello; **to take up the cudgels for sb/sth** (*fig*) mettersi a lottare per qn/qc.

2 VT: **to cudgel one's brains** scervellarsi, spremersi le meningi.

cue [kjuː] N **a** (*Theatre*: verbal, by signal) segnale *m*, imbeccata; (*Mus: by signal*) segnale; **to give sb his cue** suggerire a qn la battuta, dare l'imbeccata a qn; **to take one's cue from sb** (*fig*) prendere esempio da qn

b (*Billiards*) stecca

► **cue in** VT + ADV (*Theatre*) chiamare in scena; (*Radio, TV*) dare il segnale a.

cuff[1] [kʌf] 1 N (*blow*) schiaffo.

[2] VT dare uno schiaffo a.
cuff² [kʌf] N (*of shirt, coat*) polsino; (*Am: of trousers*) risvolto; **off the cuff** (*fig*) improvvisando.
♦ **cuff link** N gemello.
cu. ft. ABBR = cubic feet.
cu. in. ABBR = cubic inches.
cui·sine [kwɪˈziːn] N cucina.
cul-de-sac [ˈkʌldəˈsæk] N vicolo cieco.
culi·nary [ˈkʌlmərɪ] ADJ culinario(-a).
cull [kʌl] [1] VT (*select: fruit*) scegliere; (*kill selectively: animals*) selezionare e abbattere.
[2] N selezione *f*; **seal cull** abbattimento selettivo delle foche.
cull·ing [ˈkʌlɪŋ] N eliminazione *f* selettiva.
cul·mi·nate [ˈkʌlmɪˌneɪt] VI: **to culminate in** culminare con or in.
cul·mi·na·tion [ˌkʌlmɪˈneɪʃən] N culmine *m*; (*Astron*) culminazione *f*.
cu·lottes [kjuːˈlɒts] NPL gonna *f* pantalone *inv*.
cul·pable [ˈkʌlpəbl] ADJ colpevole.
cul·prit [ˈkʌlprɪt] N colpevole *m/f*.
cult [kʌlt] N (*Rel, fig*) culto; **to make a cult of sth** avere un culto per qc.
♦ **cult figure** N idolo.
cul·ti·vable [ˈkʌltɪvəbl] ADJ coltivabile.
cul·ti·vate [ˈkʌltɪˌveɪt] VT (*also fig*) coltivare.
cul·ti·vat·ed [ˈkʌltɪˌveɪtɪd] ADJ (*land*) coltivato(-a); (*refined: person, manner*) raffinato(-a); (*cultured*) colto(-a).
cul·ti·va·tion [ˌkʌltɪˈveɪʃən] N (*Agr*) coltivazione *f*, coltura.
cul·ti·va·tor [ˈkʌltɪˌveɪtəʳ] N **a** (*machine*) coltivatore *m* **b** (*person*) coltivatore(-trice).
cul·tur·al [ˈkʌltʃərəl] ADJ culturale.
cul·tur·al·ly [ˈkʌltʃərəlɪ] ADV culturalmente.
cul·ture [ˈkʌltʃəʳ] N **a** cultura; (*civilization*) civiltà **b** (*Bio, Agr*) coltura.
cul·tured [ˈkʌltʃəd] ADJ (*person, mind*) colto(-a); (*voice*) da persona colta; (*manners*) raffinato(-a); (*pearl*) coltivato (-a).
♦ **culture shock** N: **to experience culture shock** essere scioccato(-a) dall'impatto con una cultura diversa.
cum·ber·some [ˈkʌmbəsəm] ADJ ingombrante.
cum·in [ˈkʌmɪn] N (*spice*) cumino.
cum·mer·bund [ˈkʌməˌbʌnd] N fascia dello smoking.
cu·mu·la·tive [ˈkjuːmjʊlətɪv] ADJ cumulativo(-a); **cumulative frequency** (*Statistics*) frequenza cumulata.
cu·mu·lo·nim·bus [ˌkjuːmjʊləʊˈnɪmbəs] N (*Met*) cumulonembo.
cu·mu·lus [ˈkjuːmjələs] N cumulo.
cu·nei·form [ˈkjuːnɪˌfɔːm] ADJ, N cuneiforme (*m*).
cun·ning [ˈkʌnɪŋ] [1] ADJ (*pej: crafty*) furbo(-a), astuto(-a); (*clever: device, idea*) ingegnoso(-a).
[2] N furbizia, astuzia.
cun·ning·ly [ˈkʌnɪŋlɪ] ADV (*see adj*) ingegnosamente; astutamente.
cunt [kʌnt] N (*fam!*) figa (*fam!*); (*insult*) pezzo di merda (*fam!*)
cup [kʌp] [1] N (*for tea*) tazza; (*as prize, of brassière*) coppa; **a cup of tea** una tazza di tè; **tea cup** tazza da tè; **it's not everyone's cup of tea** (*fam*) non è una cosa che piace a tutti; **that's just not my cup of tea** (*fam*) non è proprio il mio genere.
[2] VT (*hands*) riunire (a coppa); **to cup one's hands round sth** prendere qc fra le mani.
cup·board [ˈkʌbəd] N armadio.
♦ **cupboard love** N (*Brit*) amore *m* interessato.

♦ **cup final** N (*Brit Ftbl*) finale *f* di coppa.
cup·ful [ˈkʌpfʊl] N tazza (*contenuto*).
Cupid [ˈkjuːpɪd] N (*Myth*) Cupido; **Cupid's bow** (*lip shape*) labbro arcuato.
cupid [ˈkjuːpɪd] N (*cherub*) cupido, amoretto.
cup·id·ity [kjuːˈpɪdɪtɪ] N cupidigia.
cu·po·la [ˈkjuːpələ] N cupola.
cup·pa [ˈkʌpə] N (*Brit fam*) tazza di tè.
♦ **cup tie** N (*Brit Ftbl*) partita eliminatoria.
cur [kɜːʳ] N **a** (*pej: dog*) cagnaccio **b** (*pej: man*) disgraziato.
cur·able [ˈkjʊərəbl] ADJ guaribile, curabile.
cu·rate [ˈkjʊərɪt] N curato, cappellano.
cu·ra·tive [ˈkjʊərətɪv] [1] ADJ curativo(-a).
[2] N cura, rimedio.
cu·ra·tor [kjʊəˈreɪtəʳ] N direttore(-trice) (di museo *etc*).
curb¹ [kɜːb] [1] N freno.
[2] VT (*fig: temper, impatience etc*) frenare, tenere a freno; (: *expenditure*) limitare.
curb² [kɜːb] N (*Am*) = **kerb**.
curd [kɜːd] N, USU PL: **curds** NPL latte *m* cagliato.
♦ **curd cheese** N cagliata.
cur·dle [ˈkɜːdl] [1] VT (*gen*) far cagliare; (*mayonnaise*) far impazzire.
[2] VI (*see vt*) cagliarsi, cagliare; impazzire; **it made my blood curdle** mi ha gelato il sangue nelle vene.
cure [kjʊəʳ] [1] N (*remedy*) cura; (*recovery*) guarigione *f*; **to take a cure** fare una cura.
[2] VT **a** (*Med: disease, patient*) guarire; (*fig: poverty, injustice, evil*) eliminare; **to be cured of sth** essere guarito(-a) da qc; **to cure sb of a habit** far perdere a qn un'abitudine
b (*preserve: in salt*) salare; (: *by smoking*) affumicare; (: *by drying*) seccare, essiccare; (: *animal hide*) conciare, trattare.
♦ **cure-all** [ˈkjʊərˌɔːl] N (*also fig*) panacea, toccasana *m inv*.
cur·few [ˈkɜːfjuː] N coprifuoco.
cu·rio [ˈkjʊərɪəʊ] N curiosità *f inv*, oggetto insolito.
cu·ri·os·ity [ˌkjʊərɪˈɒsɪtɪ] N curiosità *f inv*; **curiosity killed the cat** la curiosità si paga cara.
cu·ri·ous [ˈkjʊərɪəs] ADJ **a** (*inquisitive*) curioso(-a); **I'm curious about him** m'incuriosisce; **I'd be curious to know** sarei curioso di sapere **b** (*strange*) strano(-a), curioso(-a).
cu·ri·ous·ly [ˈkjʊərɪəslɪ] ADV (*see adj*) con curiosità; stranamente; **curiously enough, ...** per quanto possa sembrare strano,... .
curl [kɜːl] [1] N (*of hair*) ricciolo, riccio; (*of smoke*) anello.
[2] VT (*hair*) ondulare; (*tightly*) arricciare; **she curled her lip in scorn** arricciò sprezzantemente le labbra.
[3] VI (*hair*) arricciarsi; **it's enough to make your hair curl** (*fam*) è una cosa da far drizzare i capelli
▶ **curl up** VI + ADV (*leaves, paper*) accartocciarsi; (*cat*) acciambellarsi; (*person, dog*) accoccolarsi, rannicchiarsi; (*fam: with shame*) sprofondare (dalla vergogna); (*with laughter*) piegarsi in due (dalle risate).
curl·er [ˈkɜːləʳ] N **a** (*for hair*) bigodino **b** (*Sport*) giocatore (-trice) di curling.
cur·lew [ˈkɜːluː] N chiurlo.
curl·ing [ˈkɜːlɪŋ] N (*Sport*) curling *m*.
♦ **curling tongs**, (*Am*) **curling irons** NPL (*for hair*) arricciacapelli *m inv*.
curly [ˈkɜːlɪ] ADJ (*comp* **-ier**, *superl* **-iest**) (*gen*) riccio(-a), ricciuto(-a); (*eyelashes*) ricurvo(-a).
♦ **curly-haired** [ˌkɜːlɪˈhɛəd], **curly-headed** [ˌkɜːlɪˈhɛdɪd]

ADJ ricciuto(-a).

cur·rant ['kʌrənt] N (*dried grape*) uva passa; (*bush, fruit*) ribes *m inv.*

♦ **currant bun** N panino con l'uva passa.

cur·ren·cy ['kʌrənsɪ] N **a** moneta; **foreign currency** valuta estera; **hard currency** moneta forte; **paper currency** banconote *fpl* **b** (*fig: of ideas*): **to gain currency** acquistare larga diffusione, acquistare credito.

♦ **currency note** N banconota.

♦ **currency rate** N tasso di cambio.

cur·rent ['kʌrənt] 1 ADJ (*fashion, opinion, year*) corrente; (*tendency, price, event*) attuale; (*phrase*) di uso corrente; **in current use** in uso corrente, d'uso comune; **the current issue of a magazine** l'ultimo numero di una rivista; **her current boyfriend** il suo attuale ragazzo.
2 N (*of air, water, Elec, fig*) corrente *f*; **direct/alternating current** (*Elec*) corrente continua/alternata; **to go against the current** (*fig*) andare controcorrente.

♦ **current account** N (*Brit Bank*) conto corrente.

♦ **current affairs** ['kʌrəntə'fɛəz] NPL attualità *f inv.*

♦ **current assets** ['kʌrənt'æsɛts] NPL (*Fin*) attivo realizzabile e disponibile.

♦ **current liabilities** ['kʌrənt,laɪə'bɪlɪtɪz] NPL (*Fin*) passività *fpl* correnti.

cur·rent·ly ['kʌrəntlɪ] ADV attualmente, al momento.

♦ **current ratio** N (*Econ*) rapporto di liquidità.

cur·ric·u·lum [kə'rɪkjʊləm] N (*pl* **curricula** [kə'rɪkjʊlə] or **curriculums**) (*Scol, Univ*) programma *m.*

♦ **cur·ric·u·lum vi·tae** [kə,rɪkjʊləm'viːtaɪ] N curriculum vitae *m inv.*

cur·ried ['kʌrɪd] ADJ al curry.

cur·ry¹ ['kʌrɪ] 1 N (*dish*) pietanza al curry; (*spice*) curry *m inv*; **chicken curry** pollo al curry; **beef/vegetable curry** manzo/verdure al curry.
2 VT cucinare al curry.

cur·ry² ['kʌrɪ] VT: **to curry favour with sb** cercare di accattivarsi (il favore di) qn.

♦ **curry powder** N curry *m.*

curse [kɜːs] 1 N **a** maledizione *f*; **curses!** NPL (*fam*) maledizione!; **to put a curse on sb** maledire qn **b** (*bane*) rovina, flagello; **the curse of it is that ...** il guaio è che... **c** (*swearword*) imprecazione *f*; (*blasphemous*) bestemmia **d** (*fam: menstruation*): **she's got the curse** ha le sue cose.
2 VT maledire.
3 VI bestemmiare.

curs·ed ['kɜːsɪd] ADJ (*under a curse*) dannato(-a); **to be cursed with** (*fig*) essere tormentato(-a) da.

cur·sor ['kɜːsə'] N (*Comput*) cursore *m.*

cur·so·ri·ly ['kɜːsərɪlɪ] ADV (*glance*) di sfuggita, in fretta; (*read through*) rapidamente, in fretta.

cur·sory ['kɜːsərɪ] ADJ (*glance*) di sfuggita, superficiale; **a cursory reading** una rapida scorsa, una lettura veloce.

curt [kɜːt] ADJ brusco(-a), secco(-a); **with a curt nod** con un breve cenno del capo.

cur·tail [kɜː'teɪl] VT (*visit etc*) accorciare; (*wages, expenditure*) ridurre, decurtare, tagliare.

cur·tail·ment [kɜː'teɪlmənt] N (*of holiday*) interruzione *f*; (*of wages, financial support*) riduzione *f.*

cur·tain ['kɜːtn] N tenda; (*Theatre*) sipario; **to draw the curtains** (*together*) chiudere *or* tirare le tende; (*apart*) aprire le tende; **it'll be curtains for you!** (*fam*) per te sarà la fine!

▶ **curtain off** VT + ADV separare con una tenda.

♦ **curtain call** N (*Theatre*) chiamata alla ribalta.

♦ **curtain hook** N gancio della tenda.

♦ **curtain ring** N anello della tenda.

♦ **curtain rod** N asta *or* bastone *m* della tenda.

curt·ly ['kɜːtlɪ] ADV bruscamente, seccamente.

curt·ness ['kɜːtnɪs] N bruschezza.

curt·sy, curt·sey ['kɜːtsɪ] 1 N inchino, riverenza.
2 VI fare un inchino *or* una riverenza.

cur·va·ceous [kɜː'veɪʃəs] ADJ (*fam: woman*) formoso(-a).

cur·va·ture ['kɜːvətʃə'] N curvatura; **curvature of the spine** (*Med*) deviazione *f* della colonna vertebrale.

curve [kɜːv] 1 N (*gen*) curva; (*of river*) ansa; **simple closed curve** (*Math*) curva chiusa semplice.
2 VT curvare.
3 VI (*road, river*) fare una curva; (*line, surface, arch*) curvarsi.

curved [kɜːvd] ADJ curvo(-a).

cush·ion ['kʊʃən] 1 N cuscino; (*of billiard table*) sponda (elastica).
2 VT (*blow, fall, shock*) attutire, fare da cuscinetto a; **to cushion sb against sth** proteggere qn da qc.

cushy ['kʊʃɪ] ADJ (*comp* **-ier**, *superl* **-iest**) (*fam*): **a cushy job** un lavoro di tutto riposo.

cusp [kʌsp] N cuspide *f.*

cuss [kʌs] (*fam*) 1 N **a** (*oath*) bestemmia **b** (*person*) tipo(-a) palloso(-a).
2 VI bestemmiare.

cuss·ed ['kʌsɪd] ADJ (*fam*) ostinato(-a), testardo(-a).

cuss·ed·ness ['kʌsɪdnɪs] N (*fam*) ripicca, spirito di contraddizione.

cus·tard ['kʌstəd] N (*pouring*) crema (pasticcera); (*set*) ≈ budino.

♦ **custard cream** N (*biscuit*) biscotto farcito alla crema.

♦ **custard pie** N *tartina alla crema.*

♦ **custard powder** N (*Brit*) *preparato in polvere per crema.*

♦ **custard tart** N crostata alla crema.

cus·to·dial sen·tence [kʌs,təʊdɪəl'sɛntəns] N condanna ad una pena detentiva.

cus·to·dian [kʌs'təʊdɪən] N (*gen*) custode *m/f*; (*of museum etc*) soprintendente *m/f.*

cus·to·dy ['kʌstədɪ] N (*Law: of child*) custodia; (*for offenders*) arresto; (*police custody*) detenzione *f* (preventiva); **to take sb into custody** mettere qn in detenzione preventiva; **in safe custody** al sicuro; **in the custody of** alla custodia di.

cus·tom ['kʌstəm] N **a** costume *m*, usanza, consuetudine *f*; (*Law*) consuetudine; **social customs** convenzioni *fpl* sociali; **it is her custom to go for a walk each evening** è sua consuetudine fare una passeggiata ogni sera **b** (*Comm*): **to get sb's custom** ottenere qn per cliente; **the shop has lost a lot of custom** il negozio ha perso molti clienti; see also **customs.**

cus·tom·ary ['kʌstəmərɪ] ADJ consueto(-a); **it is customary to wear black** è consuetudine vestire di nero.

♦ **custom-built** ['kʌstəm,bɪlt] ADJ see **custom-made.**

cus·tom·er ['kʌstəmə'] N cliente *m/f*; **he's an awkward customer** (*fam*) è un tipo incontentabile; **ugly customer** (*fam*) brutto tipo.

♦ **customer profile** N profilo del cliente.

cus·tom·ized ['kʌstə,maɪzd] ADJ personalizzato(-a); (*car*) fuoriserie *inv.*

♦ **custom-made** ['kʌstəm'meɪd] ADJ (*clothes*) fatto(-a) su misura; (*other goods*: *also*: **custom-built**) fatto(-a) su ordinazione.

cus·toms ['kʌstəmz] NPL (*also*: **Customs**) dogana; **to go**

through (the) customs passare la dogana.

♦ **Customs and Excise** N (*Brit*) Ufficio Dazi e Dogana.

♦ **customs control** N controllo doganale.

♦ **customs duty** N dazio doganale.

♦ **customs house**, **customs post** N casotto *or* ufficio della dogana.

♦ **customs officer** N doganiere *m*.

cut [kʌt] (*vb*: *pt*, *pp* **cut**) ⊡ N **a** (*gen*) taglio; (*Med*) taglio, incisione *f*; (*Cards*) alzata; **the cut and thrust of politics** i vivaci contrasti della politica; **he's a cut above the others** è di gran lunga migliore degli altri

  b (*reduction*: *in salary, spending*) riduzione *f*, taglio; (*deletion*: *in film, text*) taglio; **power cut** interruzione di corrente elettrica; **to take a cut in salary** avere una riduzione dello stipendio

  c (*of clothes, hair*) taglio

  d (*of meat*: *piece*) taglio, pezzo, parte *f*; (*fam*: *share*) parte; **cold cuts** (*Am*) affettati *mpl*.

  ⊡ ADJ (*flowers*) reciso(-a); (*glass*) intagliato(-a).

  ⊡ VT **a** (*gen*) tagliare; (*Cards*) alzare; **to cut one's finger** tagliarsi un dito; **to cut a tooth** mettere un dente; **to cut sth in half/in two** tagliare qc a metà/in due; **he is cutting his own throat** (*fig*) si sta dando la zappa sui piedi; **to cut to pieces** (*army, fig*) fare a pezzi, distruggere; **to cut sth to size** tagliare qc su misura; **to cut open** aprire con un coltello (*or* con le forbici *etc*); **he cut his head open** si è spaccato la testa; **to cut sb free** liberare qn (*tagliando qc*); **it cut me to the quick** *or* **the heart** (*fig*) mi ha ferito profondamente

  b (*shape*: *gen, jewel*) tagliare; (*steps, channel*) scavare; (*key*) fare una copia di, riprodurre; (*glass*) lavorare; (*figure, statue*) scolpire; (*engrave*) incidere, intagliare; (*record*) incidere; **to cut one's way through** aprirsi la strada attraverso; **to cut one's coat according to one's cloth** (*fig*) non fare il passo più lungo della gamba

  c (*clip, trim*: *hair, nails, hedge etc*) tagliare; **to get one's hair cut** farsi tagliare i capelli

  d (*reduce*: *wages, prices, production etc*) ridurre; (*expenses*) ridurre, limitare, tagliare; (*speech*) abbreviare; (*text, film*) tagliare; (*interrupt*) interrompere; **to cut sb/sth short** interrompere qn/qc; **to cut 30 seconds off a record** (*Sport*) abbassare un record di 30 secondi

  e (*intersect*) intersecare, tagliare

  f (*fam*: *avoid*: *class, lecture, appointment*) saltare; **to cut sb dead** ignorare qn completamente.

  ⊡ VI **a** (*person, knife*) tagliare; **she cut into the melon** ha affondato il coltello nel melone; **it cuts both ways** (*fig*) è un'arma a doppio taglio; **to cut and run** (*fam*) tagliare la corda; **to cut loose (from sth)** (*fig*) staccarsi (da qc)

  b (*hurry*): **to cut across country/through the lane** tagliare per la campagna/per il sentiero; **I must cut along now** ora devo avviarmi

  c (*Cine*): **the film cut from the bedroom to the garden** la scena del film si è spostata dalla stanza da letto al giardino; **cut!** stop!

  d (*Cards*) tagliare il mazzo

▶ **cut away** VT + ADV tagliare via

▶ **cut across** VI + PREP (*fig*: *barriers, boundaries*) trascendere

▶ **cut back** ⊡ VI + ADV (*on costs etc*) limitare *or* tagliare le spese; (*on staff*) ridurre il personale.

  ⊡ VT + ADV (*plants*) potare; (*production, expenditure, staff*) ridurre

▶ **cut down** VT + ADV **a** (*tree*) abbattere; (*enemy*) falciare

  b (*reduce*: *consumption, expenses*) ridurre, tagliare; **to**

cut sb down to size (*fig*) sgonfiare *or* ridimensionare qn

▶ **cut down on** VI + ADV + PREP ridurre, diminuire

▶ **cut in** VI + ADV: **to cut in (on)** (*interrupt*: *conversation*) intromettersi (in); (*Aut*) tagliare la strada (a)

▶ **cut off** VT + ADV

  a (*gen*) tagliare; **to cut off one's nose to spite one's face** (*fam*) farsi dispetto

  b (*disconnect*: *telephone, gas*) tagliare; (*engine*) spegnere; **we've been cut off** (*Telec*) è caduta la linea

  c (*isolate*) isolare; **they feel very cut off** si sentono tagliati fuori dal mondo *or* isolati; **to cut o.s. off from sth/sb** allontanarsi *or* isolarsi da qc/qn; **to cut off the enemy's retreat** tagliare la ritirata al nemico; **to cut sb off without a penny** diseredare qn

▶ **cut out** ⊡ VI + ADV (*engine*) spegnersi.

  ⊡ VT + ADV **a** (*article, picture*) ritagliare; (*statue, figure*) scolpire; (*dress etc*) tagliare; **to be cut out for sth/to do sth** (*fig*) essere tagliato(-a) per qc/per fare qc; **you'll have your work cut out for you** avrai un bel daffare **b** (*delete*) eliminare, togliere **c** (*stop, give up*) eliminare; **cut it out!** (*fam*) dacci un taglio!

▶ **cut up** ⊡ VT + ADV **a** (*gen*) tagliare; (*chop*: *food*) sminuzzare

  b (*fam*): **to be cut up about sth** (*hurt*) rimanere sconvolto(-a) per qc; (*annoyed*) essere arrabbiato(-a) per qc.

  ⊡ VI + ADV: **to cut up rough** (*fam*) perdere le staffe.

♦ **cut-and-dried** [ˌkʌtənˈdraɪd] ADJ (*also*: **cut-and-dry**: *fig*) assodato(-a).

cut·a·way [ˈkʌtəˌweɪ] ADJ, N: **cutaway (drawing)** spaccato.

cut·back [ˈkʌtˌbæk] N **a** (*in expenditure, staff, production*) taglio, riduzione *f* **b** (*Cine*: *flashback*) flashback *m inv*.

cute [kjuːt] ADJ (*esp Am*: *sweet*) carino(-a), grazioso(-a); (*clever*) furbo(-a), astuto(-a).

♦ **cut glass** N cristallo.

cu·ti·cle [ˈkjuːtɪkl] N (*of fingernails*) cuticola, pellicina; (*Bot, Zool*) cuticola.

♦ **cuticle remover** N (*tool*) scalzapelli *m inv*; (*cream*) crema per le pellicine.

cut·lass [ˈkʌtləs] N (*History*) sciabola.

cut·ler [ˈkʌtlər] N coltellinaio.

cut·lery [ˈkʌtlərɪ] N posate *fpl*.

♦ **cutlery drainer** N scolaposate *m inv*.

♦ **cutlery tray** N portaposate *m inv*.

cut·let [ˈkʌtlɪt] N cotoletta, costoletta.

cut·off [ˈkʌtˌɒf] N (*also*: **cutoff point**) limite *m*.

♦ **cutoff switch** N interruttore *m*.

cut·out [ˈkʌtˌaʊt] N (*paper, cardboard figure*) ritaglio; (*switch*) interruttore *m*.

♦ **cut-price** [ˈkʌtˌpraɪs], (*Am*) **cut-rate** [ˈkʌtˌreɪt] ADJ (*goods*) scontato(-a), a prezzo ridotto; (*shop*) che fa prezzi bassi.

cut·ter [ˈkʌtər] N **a** (*person*) tagliatore(-trice); (*tool*) taglierina **b** (*sailing ship*) cutter *m inv*; (*ship's boat*) lancia.

cut·throat [ˈkʌtˌθrəʊt] ⊡ N assassino(-a).

  ⊡ ADJ (*razor*) da barbiere; (*business*) spietato(-a); **cutthroat competition** concorrenza spietata.

cut·ting [ˈkʌtɪŋ] ⊡ N **a** (*of plant*) talea **b** (*Brit*: *from newspaper*) ritaglio; (*Cine*) montaggio **c** (*Brit*: *for road, railway*) scavo.

  ⊡ ADJ **a** (*cold*: *wind etc*) pungente; (*fig*: *remark*) tagliente, mordace **b** (*Cine*): **cutting room** sala di montaggio.

♦ **cutting edge** N **a** (*of knife*) taglio, filo **b** (*fig*): **on** *or* **at the cutting edge of sth** all'avanguardia di qc.

cuttle·bone ['kʌtl̩ˌbəʊn] N osso di seppia.
cuttle·fish ['kʌtl̩ˌfɪʃ] N seppia.
♦ cut–up ['kʌtˌʌp] ADJ sconvolto(-a).
CV [ˌsiː'viː] N ABBR curriculum vitae.
C & W ['siːən'dʌbljʊ] N ABBR = country and western (music).
CWO ABBR = cash with order.
cwt. ABBR of hundredweight.
cya·nide ['saɪəˌnaɪd] N cianuro.
cya·not·ic [ˌsaɪə'nɒtɪk] ADJ cianotico(-a).
cy·ber·net·ics [ˌsaɪbə'nɛtɪks] NSG cibernetica.
cyc·la·men ['sɪkləmən] N ciclamino.
cy·cle ['saɪkl̩] ① N a (bicycle) bicicletta b (of seasons, poems) ciclo.
② VI andare in bicicletta.
♦ cycle path N pista ciclabile.
♦ cycle race N gara or corsa ciclistica.
♦ cycle rack N portabiciclette m inv.
♦ cycle shed N riparo per le biciclette.
cy·clic ['saɪklɪk] ADJ ciclico(-a).
cy·cli·cal ['saɪklɪkəl] ADJ ciclico(-a).
cy·cling ['saɪklɪŋ] N ciclismo.
♦ cycling holiday N vacanza in bicicletta; to go on a cycling holiday (Brit) fare una vacanza in bicicletta.
cy·clist ['saɪklɪst] N ciclista m/f.
cy·cloid ['saɪklɔɪd] N (Geom) cicloide f.
cy·clone ['saɪkləʊn] N ciclone m.
Cy·clops ['saɪklɒps] N (pl Cyclopes [saɪ'kləʊpiːz] or Cyclopses) ciclope m.
cy·clo·style ['saɪkləˌstaɪl] VT ciclostilare.
cy·clo·tron ['saɪkləˌtrɒn] N ciclotrone m.
cyg·net ['sɪgnɪt] N cigno giovane.
cyl·in·der ['sɪlɪndəʳ] N cilindro; a 6-cylinder engine un motore a 6 cilindri; to fire on all four cylinders avere tutti e quattro i cilindri in azione; (fig) andare a tutto gas.
♦ cylinder block N monoblocco.
♦ cylinder head N testata.
♦ cylinder head gasket N guarnizione f della testata del cilindro.
cy·lin·dri·cal [sɪ'lɪndrɪkəl] ADJ cilindrico(-a).
cym·bal ['sɪmbəl] N piatto (Mus).
cyn·ic ['sɪnɪk] N cinico(-a).
cyni·cal ['sɪnɪkəl] ADJ cinico(-a).
cyni·cal·ly ['sɪnɪklɪ] ADV cinicamente.
cyni·cism ['sɪnɪsɪzəm] N cinismo.
CYO [ˌsiː·waɪ'əʊ] N ABBR (Am)= Catholic Youth Organization.
cy·press ['saɪprɪs] N cipresso; Lawson's cypress cedro bianco.
Cyp·ri·ot ['sɪprɪət] ADJ, N cipriota (m/f).
Cy·prus ['saɪprəs] N Cipro; in Cyprus a Cipro.
Cy·re·ne [saɪ'riːnɪ] N: Simon of Cyrene il Cireneo.
cy·ril·lic [sɪ'rɪlɪk] ① ADJ cirillico(-a).
② N alfabeto cirillico.
cyst [sɪst] N cisti f inv.
cys·ti·tis [sɪs'taɪtɪs] N (Med) cistite f.
cy·to·plasm ['saɪtəʊˌplæzəm] N citoplasma m.
czar [zɑːʳ] N zar m inv.
cza·ri·na [zɑː'riːnə] N zarina.
czar·ist ['zɑːrɪst] ADJ, N zarista (m/f).
Czech [tʃɛk] ① ADJ ceco(-a).
② N (person) ceco(-a); (language) ceco.
Czecho·slo·vak [ˌtʃɛkəʊ'sləʊvæk], Czecho·slo·vakian ['tʃɛkəʊslə'vækɪən] ① ADJ cecoslovacco(-a).
② N (person) cecoslovacco(-a); (language) cecoslovacco.
Czecho·slo·va·kia ['tʃɛkəʊslə'vækɪə] N Cecoslovacchia.
♦ Czech Republic ADJ: the Czech Republic la repubblica Ceca.

D

D, d [di:] **1** N **a** (*letter*) D, d *f or m inv*; **D for David**, (*Am*) **D for Dog** ≈ D come Domodossola **b** (*Mus*) re *m inv*.

D ABBR (*Am Pol*) = **democrat(ic)**.

d [di:] ABBR (*Brit old*) = **penny**.

d. ABBR = *died*; see **die**.

DA [di:'eɪ] N ABBR (*Am*) = **district attorney**.

dab[1] [dæb] **1** N (*light stroke*) colpetto, tocco; (: *of paint*) pennellata; (*small amount*) pochino, punta; (: *of glue*) goccio; **a dab of paint** un colpetto di vernice. **2** ADJ: **to be a dab hand at sth/at doing sth** (*fam*) essere in gambissima in qc/a fare qc. **3** VT (*touch lightly: also:* **dab at**) picchiettare lievemente; (*eyes, wound*) tamponare; (*apply: paint, cream*): **to dab sth on sth** applicare qc con colpetti leggeri su qc.

dab[2] [dæb] N (*fish*) limanda.

dab·ble ['dæbl] **1** VT: **to dabble one's hands/feet in the water** sguazzare con le mani/i piedi nell'acqua. **2** VI (*fig*): **to dabble in sth** occuparsi di qc a tempo perso, dilettarsi di qc; **to dabble in politics** dilettarsi di politica.

dab·bler ['dæblə'] N (*pej*) dilettante *m/f*.

Dac·ca ['dækə] N Dacca.

da·cha ['dætʃə] N dacia.

dachs·hund ['dækshʊnd] N bassotto.

Da·cron® ['dækrɒn] N Dacron ® *m inv*.

dad [dæd], **dad·dy** ['dædɪ] N (*fam*) papà *m inv*, babbo.

♦ **daddy-long-legs** [ˌdædɪ'lɒŋlɛgz] N, PL INV zanzarone *m*, tipula (*Zool*).

dado ['deɪdəʊ] N (*of wall*) zoccolo decorato; (*Archit*) dado.

Daedalus ['di:dələs] N (*Myth*) Dedalo.

daf·fo·dil ['dæfədɪl] N trombone *m*, giunchiglia.

♦ **daffodil yellow 1** N giallo *m* brillante *inv*. **2** ADJ giallo brillante *inv*.

daft [dɑ:ft] ADJ (*comp* **-er**, *superl* **-est**) (*fam*) sciocco(-a); **to be daft about sb** aver perso la testa per qn; **to be daft about sth** andare pazzo(-a) per qc.

dag·ger ['dægə'] N pugnale *m*, stiletto; (*Typ*) croce *f*; **to be at daggers drawn (with sb)** essere ai ferri corti (con qn); **to look daggers at sb** fare gli occhiacci a qn.

dago ['deɪgəʊ] N (*offensive*) ≈ marocchino (*offensive*).

da·guerreo·type [də'gɛrəʊˌtaɪp] N dagherrotipo.

dahl·ia ['deɪlɪə] N dalia.

dai·ly ['deɪlɪ] **1** ADJ (*routine, task*) quotidiano(-a), giornaliero(-a); (*wage, output, consumption*) giornaliero(-a); **he takes a daily walk** fa una passeggiata ogni giorno; **our daily bread** il nostro pane quotidiano; **the daily grind** il tran-tran quotidiano. **2** ADV quotidianamente, ogni giorno, tutti i giorni; **twice daily** due volte al giorno. **3** N **a** (*also:* **daily paper**) quotidiano **b** (*Brit old: cleaner*) donna di servizio.

dain·ti·ly ['deɪntɪlɪ] ADV (*eat, hold*) delicatamente; (*move, walk*) con grazia.

dain·ti·ness ['deɪntɪnɪs] N (*of food, person*) delicatezza; (*of gestures, manners*) grazia.

dain·ty ['deɪntɪ] ADJ (*comp* **-ier**, *superl* **-iest**) (*person, figure*) minuto(-a); (*child, manners*) aggraziato(-a); (*flowers, gesture*) delicato(-a), grazioso(-a); (*dishes, food*) delicato (-a); (*dress, shoes*) grazioso(-a).

dairy ['dɛərɪ] **1** N (*shop*) latteria; (*organization, on farm*) caseificio. **2** ADJ casearo(-a); (*breed, cow*) da latte; **dairy farm** caseificio; **dairy farming** industria casearia; **dairy ice cream** gelato gusto crema; **dairy produce** latticini *mpl*.

dairy·ing ['dɛərɪɪŋ] N industria casearia.

dairy·maid ['dɛərɪˌmeɪd] N operaia di caseificio.

dairy·man ['dɛərɪmən] N (*pl* **-men**) operaio di caseificio.

dais ['deɪɪs] N pedana, palco.

dai·sy ['deɪzɪ] N (*wild*) pratolina, margheritina; (*cultivated*) margherita.

♦ **daisy chain** N ghirlanda di margherite.

♦ **daisy wheel** N (*on printer*) margherita.

♦ **daisy-wheel printer** ['deɪzɪˌwi:l'prɪntə'] N stampante *f* a margherita.

Da·kar ['dækə'] N Dakar *f*.

dale [deɪl] N (*in North of England, also liter*) valle *f*.

dal·ly ['dælɪ] VI (*delay*) dilungarsi; **to dally about** perdere tempo; **to dally over sth** perdere tempo con qc.

dal·ma·tian [dæl'meɪʃən] N (*dog*) dalmata *m*.

dam [dæm] **1** N (*wall*) diga, sbarramento; (*reservoir*) bacino artificiale.

② VT (*also*: **dam up**: *river*) sbarrare con una diga; (: *lake*) costruire una diga su; (: *fig*) arginare, frenare.

dam·age ['dæmɪdʒ] ① N **a** (*also fig*) danno, danni *mpl*; **damage to property** danni materiali; **to suffer damage** riportare *or* subire danni; **the fire did a lot of damage** l'incendio ha provocato danni ingenti; **to do damage to a relationship** pregiudicare un rapporto; **what's the damage?** (*fam*: *cost*) quanto ci tocca sborsare?

b : **damages** NPL (*Law*) danni *mpl*; **liable for damages** tenuto(-a) al risarcimento dei danni; **to pay £5000 in damages** pagare 5000 sterline di indennizzo.

② VT (*furniture, crops, machine*) danneggiare; (*health, eyesight*) rovinare; (*hopes, reputation*) compromettere; (*relationship*) guastare; (*cause*) compromettere, recar danno a.

dam·ag·ing ['dæmɪdʒɪŋ] ADJ: **damaging (to)** nocivo(-a) (a).

Da·mas·cus [də'mɑːskəs] N Damasco *f*.

dam·ask ['dæməsk] ① N damasco.

② ADJ damascato(-a).

dame [deɪm] N (*title, also Am fam*) donna, madama; (*in pantomime*) *personaggio comico di donna attempata recitato da un uomo*.

dam·mit ['dæmɪt] EXCL (*fam*) maledizione!

damn [dæm] ① VT (*Rel*) dannare; (*curse*) maledire; (*condemn*: *film, book*) stroncare; **damn it!** (*fam*) accidenti!; **damn him/you!** (*fam*) accidenti a lui/a te!; **well I'll be damned!** (*fam*) che mi venga un accidente!; **I'll be damned if I will!** (*fam*) (non lo faccio) manco morto!.

② N (*fam*): **I don't give a damn** me ne infischio, non me ne importa un fico; **it's not worth a damn** non vale un fico secco.

③ ADJ (*fam*: *also*: **damned**) maledetto(-a); **this damn machine won't work** questa maledetta macchina non funziona.

④ ADV (*fam*: *also*: **damned**): **it's damn hot** fa un caldo del diavolo; **he knew damn well** lo sapeva benissimo; **damn all** un bel niente, un accidente.

dam·nable ['dæmnəbl] ADJ (*old*: *behaviour*) vergognoso (-a); (: *weather*) orribile.

dam·na·tion [dæm'neɪʃən] ① N (*Rel*) dannazione *f*.

② EXCL (*old*) dannazione!, diavolo!

damned·est ['dæmdɪst] N (*fam*): **to do one's damnedest (to do sth)** fare l'impossibile (per fare qc).

♦ **damn-fool** ['dæmfuːl] ADJ cretino(-a); **another one of his damn-fool ideas!** un'altra delle sue cretinate!

damn·ing ['dæmɪŋ] ADJ (*implications*) fortemente negativo (-a); **damning evidence** prove *fpl* schiaccianti; **damning criticism** stroncatura.

damp [dæmp] ① ADJ (*comp* **-er**, *superl* **-est**) umido(-a); **damp with perspiration** madido(-a) di sudore; **that was a damp squib** (*fam*) è stato un vero fiasco.

② N (*dampness*) umidità, umido.

③ VT = **dampen**

▶ **damp down** VT (*fire*) coprire.

damp·course ['dæmp,kɔːs] N strato *m* isolante antiumido *inv*.

damp·en ['dæmpən] VT (*cloth, rag*) inumidire; (*fig*: *enthusiasm*) raffreddare; (: *hopes*) diminuire; **to dampen sb's courage** scoraggiare qn; **to dampen sb's spirits** buttar giù qn

▶ **dampen down** = **damp down**.

damp·er ['dæmpə'] N (*Mus*) sordina; (*of fire*) valvola di tiraggio; **to put a damper on sth** (*fig*: *atmosphere*) gelare; (: *enthusiasm*) raffreddare.

damp·ness ['dæmpnɪs] N umidità, umido.

♦ **damp-proof** ['dæmp,pruːf] ADJ impermeabile.

♦ **damp-proof course** N = **dampcourse**.

dam·sel ['dæmzəl] N (*old*) damigella.

dam·son ['dæmzən] N (*fruit*) susina *or* prugna selvatica; (*tree*) damaschino, susino selvatico.

dance [dɑːns] ① N (*activity*) ballo, danza; (*traditional, in ballet*) danza; (*event*) ballo, serata danzante; **to lead sb a dance** (*fig*) far girare qn come una trottola.

② VT (*waltz, tango*) ballare; **to dance attendance on sb** girare intorno a qn.

③ VI ballare, danzare; (*fig*: *flowers, boat on waves*) danzare; **will you dance with me?** vuoi ballare (con me)?; **to dance about** saltellare; **to dance for joy** ballare dalla gioia *or* dalla contentezza.

♦ **dance band** N orchestra da ballo.

♦ **dance floor** N pista da ballo.

♦ **dance hall** N dancing *m inv*, sala da ballo.

♦ **dance music** N musica da ballo.

danc·er ['dɑːnsə'] N ballerino(-a).

danc·ing ['dɑːnsɪŋ] N ballo.

D and C N ABBR (*Med*: = *dilation and curettage*) raschiamento.

dan·de·lion ['dændɪlaɪən] N dente *m* di leone.

dan·druff ['dændrəf] N forfora.

dan·dy ['dændɪ] ① N dandy *m inv*, elegantone *m*.

② ADJ (*comp* **-ier**, *superl* **-iest**) (*Am fam*) fantastico(-a).

Dane [deɪn] N danese *m/f*.

dan·ger ['deɪndʒə'] ① N pericolo; **in danger** in pericolo; **out of danger** fuori pericolo; **to put sb's life in danger** mettere in pericolo la vita di qn; **to be in danger of falling** rischiare di cadere; **there was no danger that he would be caught** non c'era pericolo che lo prendessero; **there is a danger of fire** c'è pericolo di incendio; **"danger! men at work"** "attenzione! lavori in corso"; **"danger! keep out"** "pericolo! vietato l'accesso".

② ADJ (*zone, sign*) di pericolo.

♦ **danger list** N (*Med*): **on the danger list** in prognosi riservata.

♦ **danger money** N indennità di rischio.

dan·ger·ous ['deɪndʒrəs] ADJ (*gen*) pericoloso(-a); (*illness*) grave, pericoloso(-a).

dan·ger·ous·ly ['deɪndʒrəslɪ] ADV (*gen*) pericolosamente; (*wounded*) gravemente; **dangerously ill** in pericolo di vita, gravemente malato(-a).

dan·gle ['dæŋgl] ① VT (*arm, leg*) (far) dondolare; (*object on string*) far oscillare; (*fig*: *tempting offer*): **to dangle sth in front of sb** allettare qn con qc.

② VI pendere, penzolare; **with one's legs dangling** con le gambe penzoloni.

Daniel ['dænjəl] N Daniele *m*.

Dan·ish ['deɪnɪʃ] ① ADJ danese.

② N (*language*) danese *m*.

♦ **Danish blue** N (*also*: **Danish blue cheese**) *formaggio tipo gorgonzola*.

♦ **Danish pastry** N *dolce di pasta sfoglia*.

dank [dæŋk] ADJ (*comp* **-er**, *superl* **-est**) freddo(-a) e umido(-a).

Dan·ube ['dænjuːb] N: **the Danube** il Danubio.

dap·per ['dæpə'] ADJ (*man*) azzimato(-a).

dap·pled ['dæpld] ADJ screziato(-a); (*horse*) pomellato (-a).

Dar·da·nelles [,dɑːdə'nɛlz] NPL: **the Dardanelles** i Dardanelli.

dare [deə'] ① VT **a** osare; **to dare (to) do sth** osare fare qc; **I don't dare tell him**, (*Brit*) **I daren't tell him** non oso

dirglielo; **how dare you!** come si permette!, come osa!

b : **I dare say** immagino; **I dare say he'll turn up** immagino che spunterà

c (*challenge*): **to dare (sb to do sth)** sfidare (qn a fare qc); **I dare you!** ti sfido a farlo!; **to dare death/sb's anger** sfidare la morte/l'ira di qn.

2 N sfida; **I did it for a dare** l'ho fatto per scommessa.

dare·devil ['dɛə‚dɛvl] N scavezzacollo *m/f.*

Dar es Sa·laam ['da:rɛssə'la:m] N Dar-es-Salaam *f.*

dar·ing ['dɛərɪŋ] 1 ADJ audace, ardito(-a).

2 N audacia.

dar·ing·ly ['dɛərɪŋlɪ] ADV audacemente.

dark [da:k] 1 ADJ (*comp* **-er**, *superl* **-est**) **a** (*lacking light*: *room, night*) scuro(-a), buio(-a); **it is/is getting dark** è/si sta facendo buio; **the dark side of the moon** l'altra faccia della luna

b (*in colour*) scuro(-a); (*complexion, hair, colour*) scuro (-a), bruno(-a); **dark blue/red** blu/rosso scuro *inv*; **dark brown hair** capelli castano scuro; **dark chocolate** cioccolata amara

c (*fig*: *sad, gloomy*) nero(-a), tetro(-a), cupo(-a); (: *sinister*: *secret, plan, threat*) oscuro(-a); **to keep sth dark** non far parola di qc.

2 N: **the dark** il buio, l'oscurità; **in the dark** al buio; **before dark** prima che faccia (*or* facesse) buio; **after dark** col buio, a notte fatta; **until dark** fino a sera; **to be in the dark about sth** (*fig*) essere all'oscuro di qc.

♦ **Dark Ages** NPL: **the Dark Ages** l'alto medioevo.

dark·en ['da:kən] 1 VT (*room*) oscurare; (*colour, photo*) scurire.

2 VI (*room, sky*) oscurarsi; (*colour*) scurirsi.

♦ **dark-eyed** ['da:k'aɪd] ADJ dagli occhi scuri.

♦ **dark glasses** NPL occhiali *mpl* scuri.

♦ **dark-haired** [‚da:k'hɛəd] ADJ bruno(-a), dai capelli scuri.

♦ **dark horse** N (*fig*): **to be a dark horse** essere un'incognita.

dar·kie, dar·ky ['da:kɪ] N (*fam*: *offensive*) negro(-a).

dark·ly ['da:klɪ] ADV (*sinisterly*) minacciosamente; (*gloomily*) cupamente, con aria cupa.

dark·ness ['da:knɪs] N oscurità, buio; (*of hair*) colore *m* scuro; **the house was in darkness** la casa era immersa nel buio *or* nell'oscurità.

dark·room ['da:krum] N camera oscura.

♦ **dark-skinned** [‚da:k'skɪnd] ADJ di pelle *or* carnagione scura.

dar·ling ['da:lɪŋ] 1 N **a** tesoro; **he's a little darling** è un amore; **be a darling ...** (*fam*) sii un angelo *or* un tesoro...; **come here darling** vieni qui tesoro **b** (*in shops*): **what can I do for you, darling?** desidera, cara?.

2 ADJ (*daughter, husband*) caro(-a); (*dress, house*) adorabile, delizioso(-a).

darn¹ [da:n] 1 VT (*socks, clothes*) rammendare.

2 N rammendo.

darn² [da:n] VT (*fam euph*) = **damn**.

darn·ing ['da:nɪŋ] 1 N (*action*) rammendo; (*items to be darned*) roba da rammendare.

2 ADJ (*needle, wool*) da rammendo.

dart [da:t] 1 N **a** dardo, freccia; (*Sport*) freccetta

b (*Sewing*) pince *f inv*, ripresa.

c : **to make a dart towards** precipitarsi verso.

2 VT (*look*) lanciare.

3 VI: **to dart in/out** *etc* entrare/uscire *etc* come una freccia; **to dart away** sfrecciar via; **to dart at sth** lanciarsi verso qc; **to dart towards** precipitarsi verso; **to dart along** passare come un razzo.

dart·board ['da:t‚bɔ:d] N bersaglio per freccette.

darts [da:ts] NSG tiro al bersaglio con freccette; **to play darts** giocare a freccette.

dash¹ [dæʃ] 1 N **a** (*rush*): **to make a dash (at, towards)** lanciarsi (verso), scattare (verso); **he had to make a dash for it** ha dovuto fare una corsa; **the 100-metre dash** (*Am*) i 100 metri piani

b (*small quantity*: *of liquid*) goccio, goccino; (: *of seasoning*) pizzico; (: *of colour*) tocco

c (*punctuation mark*) lineetta, trattino; (*Morse*) linea.

2 VT **a** (*throw*) scaraventare, gettare con violenza; **to dash sth to pieces** mandare qc in frantumi; **to dash one's head against sth** battere la testa contro qc

b (*fig*: *spirits*) abbattere; (: *hopes*) infrangere; **all his hopes were dashed** tutte le sue speranze naufragarono.

3 VI **a** (*smash*: *object, waves*): **to dash against** infrangersi su *or* contro

b (*rush*): **I must dash** (*fam*) devo scappare; **to dash away** scappare via; **to dash in/out** entrare/uscire di corsa; **to dash towards** precipitarsi verso

▶ **dash off** VT + ADV (*letter, drawing*) buttar giù.

dash² [dæʃ] VT (*fam euph*) = **damn**.

dash·board ['dæʃ‚bɔ:d] N (*Aut*) cruscotto.

dash·ing ['dæʃɪŋ] ADJ brillante, affascinante.

das·tard·ly ['dæstədlɪ] ADJ (*old*) vile.

DAT [‚di:eɪ'ti:] N ABBR (= *digital audio tape*) Dat *f inv*.

data ['deɪtə] NSG OR PL dati *mpl*.

♦ **data bank** N banca *f* dati *inv*.

♦ **data·base** ['deɪtə‚beɪs] N database *m inv*.

♦ **data capture** N registrazione *f* di dati.

♦ **data processing** N elaborazione *f* (elettronica) dei dati.

♦ **data transmission** N trasmissione *f* di dati.

date¹ [deɪt] 1 N **a** data; **what's the date today?** quanti ne abbiamo oggi?; **date of birth** data di nascita; **closing date** scadenza, termine *m*; **to date** fino a oggi; **to be up to date** (*person, document, information*) essere aggiornato (-a); (*person*: *fashionable*) essere alla moda; (: *with one's work*) essere nei termini; (*building*) essere moderno(-a); **to bring up to date** (*correspondence, information*) aggiornare; (*method*) modernizzare; (*person*) mettere al corrente, aggiornare; **to be out of date** (*information*) non essere aggiornato(-a); (*document*) essere scaduto(-a); (*person, style*) essere fuori moda

b (*fam*: *appointment*) appuntamento; (: *boyfriend*) ragazzo; (: *girlfriend*) ragazza; **to make a date with sb** fissare un appuntamento con qn; **he asked her for a date** le ha chiesto di uscire con lui.

2 VT **a** (*letter*) datare; (*ruin, manuscript*) attribuire una data a, datare; **dated the 13th** datato il 13; **thank you for your letter dated 5th July** *or* **July 5th** la ringrazio per la sua lettera in data 5 luglio; **his style of dress dates him** il suo abbigliamento tradisce la sua età

b (*fam*: *esp Am*: *girl, boy*) uscire con.

3 VI **a** : **to date (back) from** risalire a

b (*become old-fashioned*) passare di moda.

date² [deɪt] N (*fruit*) dattero; (*also*: **date palm**) palma da dattero.

dat·ed ['deɪtɪd] ADJ (*style*) antiquato(-a), fuori moda, passato(-a) di moda; (*film*) datato(-a).

date·less [‚deɪtlɪs] ADJ sempre attuale.

date·line ['deɪt‚laɪn] N linea del cambiamento di data.

♦ **date rape** N *stupro perpetrato da persona conosciuta.*

♦ **date stamp** N (*on library book*) timbro datario; (*on fresh*

food) scadenza; (*postmark*) timbro.

da·tive ['deɪtɪv] ① ADJ dativo(-a).
② N dativo; **in the dative** al dativo.

daub [dɔːb] VT: **to daub (with)** imbrattare (di).

daugh·ter ['dɔːtə'] N figlia.

♦ **daughter-in-law** ['dɔːtərɪnlɔː] N nuora.

daunt [dɔːnt] VT scoraggiare, intimidire; **nothing daunted** ... per nulla scoraggiato... .

daunt·ing ['dɔːntɪŋ] ADJ (*prospect*) non allettante.

daunt·less ['dɔːntlɪs] ADJ (*liter*) impavido(-a), intrepido (-a).

daunt·less·ly ['dɔːntlɪslɪ] ADV (*liter*) impavidamente.

David ['deɪvɪd] N Davide *m.*

daw·dle ['dɔːdl] VI (*in walking*) ciondolare, bighellonare; **to dawdle over one's work** gingillarsi con il lavoro.

daw·dler ['dɔːdlə'] N bighellone(-a), fannullone(-a).

daw·dling ['dɔːdlɪŋ] ① ADJ (*person, crowd*) ozioso(-a).
② N: **no dawdling in the corridors, please** non attardatevi nei corridoi, per favore.

dawn [dɔːn] ① N ⓐ alba; **at dawn** all'alba; **from dawn to dusk** dall'alba al tramonto
ⓑ (*fig: also:* **dawning:** *of civilization*) albori *mpl*; **the dawn of a new age** l'inizio di una nuova era.
② VI (*day*) spuntare

▶ **dawn on, dawn upon** VI + PREP: **the truth gradually dawned on us** poco a poco cominciammo a vederci chiaro; **the idea dawned upon me that** ... mi è balenata nella mente l'idea che...; **it suddenly dawned on him that** ... improvvisamente gli è venuto in mente che... .

♦ **dawn chorus** N (*Brit*) coro mattutino degli uccelli.

dawn·ing ['dɔːnɪŋ] ① ADJ (*day, hope*) appena nato(-a).
② N = **dawn 1b.**

day [deɪ] N ⓐ (*24 hours*) giorno; **what day is it today?** che giorno è oggi?; **2 days ago** 2 giorni fa; **one day** un giorno; **(on) the day that** ... il giorno che *or* in cui...; **(on) that day** quel giorno; **the day before** il giorno avanti *or* prima; **the day before yesterday** l'altroieri; **the day before his birthday** la vigilia del suo compleanno; **the day after** il giorno dopo; **the following day** il giorno seguente; **the day after tomorrow** dopodomani; **her mother died 3 years ago to the day** oggi sono 3 anni che è morta sua madre; **he works 8 hours a day** lavora 8 ore al giorno; **any day now** da un giorno all'altro; **every day** ogni giorno; **every other day** un giorno sì e uno no, ogni due giorni; **twice a day** due volte al giorno; **one of these days** uno di questi giorni, un giorno o l'altro; **the other day** l'altro giorno; **from one day to the next** da un giorno all'altro; **day after day** giorno dopo giorno; **day in day out** un giorno dopo l'altro, tutti i santi giorni; **for days on end** per giorni e giorni; **day by day** giorno per giorno; **to live from day to day** *or* **from one day to the next** vivere alla giornata; **it made my day to see him smile** (*fam*) mi ha fatto veramente felice vederlo sorridere; **he's fifty if he's a day!** (*fam*) cinquant'anni li ha di sicuro!; **that'll be the day, when he offers to pay!** (*fam*) figuriamoci se offre di pagare!
ⓑ (*daylight hours*) giorno, giornata; (*working hours*) giornata; **by day** di giorno; **to travel by day** *or* **during the day** viaggiare di giorno *or* durante il giorno; **to work all day** lavorare tutto il giorno; **to work day and night** lavorare giorno e notte; **it's a fine day** è una bella giornata; **to arrive on a fine/wet day** arrivare col bel tempo/con la pioggia; **one summer's day** un giorno d'estate; **a day off** un giorno libero; **to work an 8-hour day** avere una giornata lavorativa di 8 ore; **it's all in a**

day's work fa parte del mestiere; **paid by the day** pagato(-a) a giornata; **to work days** fare il turno di giorno
ⓒ (*period of time, age*) tempo, tempi *mpl*, epoca; **in this day and age** ai nostri tempi; **these days** di questi tempi, oggigiorno; **to this day** ... ancor oggi...; **in days to come** in futuro; **in those days** a quei tempi, a quell'epoca; **in the days when** ... all'epoca in cui...; **in Queen Victoria's day** ai tempi della regina Vittoria; **he was famous in his day** ai suoi tempi era famoso; **in his younger days** quand'era (più) giovane; **in the good old days** ai bei tempi; **the happiest days of one's life** il periodo più felice della propria vita; **during the early days of the strike** nelle prime fasi dello sciopero; **it's had its day** ha fatto il suo tempo.

♦ **day bed** N divano *m* letto *inv.*

day·book ['deɪbʊk] N (*Brit Book-keeping*) brogliaccio.

day·boy ['deɪbɔɪ] N (*esp Brit Scol*) alunno esterno.

day·break ['deɪbreɪk] N: **at daybreak** allo spuntar del giorno, all'alba.

♦ **day-care centre** ['deɪˌkɛə'sɛntə'] N (*Am*) scuola materna.

day·dream ['deɪˌdriːm] ① N sogno a occhi aperti.
② VI sognare a occhi aperti.

♦ **day girl** N (*esp Brit Scol*) alunna esterna.

day·light ['deɪˌlaɪt] N luce *f* (del giorno); **at daylight** (*dawn*) alle prime luci, all'alba; **in the daylight** OR **by daylight** alla luce del giorno; **it is still daylight** è ancora giorno; **I am beginning to see daylight** (*fig: understand*) ora comincio a vederci chiaro; (: *near the end of a job*) comincio a vedere uno spiraglio di luce; **daylight attack** attacco di giorno.

♦ **daylight hours** NPL ore *fpl* diurne *or* del giorno.

♦ **daylight robbery** N (*Brit fam*): **it's day light robbery!** è un vero furto!

♦ **daylight-saving time** ['deɪlaɪt'seɪvɪŋtaɪm] N (*Am*) ora legale.

♦ **day nursery** N scuola materna.

♦ **day of reckoning** N: **the day of reckoning** il giorno del giudizio.

♦ **day release** N: **to be on day release** avere un congedo *settimanale per formazione professionale.*

♦ **day release course** N *corso di formazione professionale esterno per dipendenti.*

♦ **day return** N (*Brit: also:* **day return ticket**) N biglietto giornaliero di andata e ritorno.

♦ **day school** N scuola privata (*che non prevede pernottamento*).

♦ **day shift** N turno di giorno; **to be on day shift** fare il turno di giorno.

day·time ['deɪˌtaɪm] ① N giorno; **in the daytime** di giorno.
② ADJ di giorno.

♦ **day-to-day** ['deɪtəˌdeɪ] ADJ (*routine*) quotidiano(-a); (*expenses*) giornaliero(-a); **on a day-to-day basis** a giornata.

♦ **day trip** N gita (di un giorno).

♦ **day tripper** N gitante *m/f.*

daze [deɪz] ① N: **in a daze** stordito(-a), inebetito(-a).
② VT (*subj: drug*) inebetire; (: *blow*) stordire.

daz·zle ['dæzl] VT abbagliare.

daz·zling ['dæzlɪŋ] ADJ (*light*) abbagliante; (*colour*) violento (-a); (*smile*) smagliante.

daz·zling·ly ['dæzlɪŋlɪ] ADV (*bright*) in modo abbagliante; (*beautiful*) in modo smagliante.

dB, db N ABBR = **decibel.**

DC [ˌdiː'siː] **1** N ABBR (*Elec*: = *direct current*) c.c..
2 ABBR (*Am Post*)= *District of Columbia*.

DCC® [ˌdiːsiː'siː] N ABBR (= *digital compact cassette*) D.C.C. ® *m inv.*

DD [ˌdiː'diː] ABBR **a** (= *Doctor of Divinity*) *titolare di un dottorato in teologia* **b** = **direct debit**.

dd. ABBR (*Comm*)= *delivered*.

♦ **D-day** ['diːˌdeɪ] N D-day *m, giorno dello sbarco alleato in Normandia.*

DDS [ˌdiːdiː'ɛs] N ABBR (*Am*: = *Doctor of Dental Surgery*) *titolare di un dottorato di odontoiatria.*

DDT [ˌdiːdiː'tiː] N ABBR (= *dichlorodiphenyl trichloroethane*) D.D.T. *m.*

DE [ˌdiː'iː] ABBR (*Am Post*)= *Delaware*.

DEA [ˌdiːiː'eɪ] N ABBR (*Am*: = *Drug Enforcement Administration*) ≈ squadra *f* narcotici *inv.*

dea·con ['diːkən] N diacono.

dea·con·ess ['diːkənɛs] N diaconessa.

de·ac·tiv·ate [diː'æktɪˌveɪt] VT disattivare.

dead [dɛd] **1** ADJ **a** (*person, animal, plant*) morto(-a); (*matter*) inanimato(-a); (*fingers, leg*): **to go dead** intorpidirsi; **to fall** *or* **drop (down) dead** morire; **he was shot dead** fu colpito a morte; **he's been dead for 2 years** è morto da due anni; **dead and buried** morto(-a) e sepolto(-a); **dead or alive** vivo(-a) o morto(-a); **over my dead body!** (*fam*) manco morto!; **I feel absolutely dead!** (*fig fam*) sono (stanco) morto!; **to be a dead duck** (*fam*) essere spacciato(-a)
b (*volcano, cigarette*) spento(-a); (*battery*) scarico(-a); (*telephone line*) caduto(-a); (*language, town, party*) morto (-a); (*custom*) scomparso(-a), estinto(-a); **the line has gone dead** (*Telec*) è caduta la linea; **he was dead to the world** (*fig*) era proprio partito (*fig*)
c (*complete: silence, calm*) assoluto(-a), totale; **to hit sth dead centre** centrare qc in pieno; **to come to a dead stop** fermarsi (del tutto); **to fall into a dead faint** cadere in svenimento.
2 ADV (*completely*): **dead certain** assolutamente certo (-a), sicurissimo(-a); **to stop dead** fermarsi di colpo; **dead ahead** sempre dritto; **it's dead ahead of us** è proprio davanti a noi; **dead on time** in perfetto orario; **to land dead on target** fare centro; **dead slow** (*Aut*) a passo d'uomo; (*Naut*) avanti piano; **to be dead set on doing sth** volere fare qc a tutti i costi; **to be dead set against sth** (*fam*) essere assolutamente contrario(-a) a qc; **dead broke** (*fam*) senza il becco di un quattrino; **dead drunk** (*fam*) ubriaco(-a) fradicio(-a); **dead tired** (*fam*) stanco (-a) morto(-a).
3 N **a** : **the dead** NPL i morti
b : **at dead of night** nel cuore della notte; **in the dead of winter** nel cuore dell'inverno.

♦ **dead ball line** N (*Rugby*) linea di pallone morto.

♦ **dead beat** ADJ (*fam*) stanco(-a) morto(-a).

dead·en ['dɛdn] VT (*noise, pain, blow, sound*) attutire; (*nerve*) rendere insensibile.

♦ **dead-end** [dɛd'ɛnd] ADJ: **a dead-end job** un lavoro senza sbocchi.

♦ **dead end** N (*also fig*) vicolo cieco.

dead·en·ing ['dɛdnɪŋ] ADJ (*boredom*) mortale; (*job, task*) alienante.

♦ **dead heat** N (*Sport*): **it was a dead heat** è stata una vittoria a pari merito; **to finish in a dead heat** finire alla pari.

♦ **dead-letter office** [dɛd'lɛtə'ɒfɪs] N ufficio della posta in giacenza.

dead·line ['dɛdˌlaɪn] N termine *m* (di consegna), scadenza; **to work to a deadline** avere una scadenza da rispettare.

dead·lock ['dɛdˌlɒk] N punto morto, impasse *f inv.*

dead·locked ['dɛdˌlɒkt] ADJ: **to be deadlocked** (*talks, negotiations*) essere in una fase di stallo.

♦ **dead loss** N (*fam*): **to be a dead loss** (*person, thing*) non valere niente.

dead·ly ['dɛdlɪ] **1** ADJ (*comp* **-ier,** *superl* **-iest**) (*gen*) mortale; (*weapon, poison, aim*) micidiale; (*disease*) letale; **they are deadly enemies** sono nemici mortali; **the seven deadly sins** i sette peccati capitali; **he is in deadly earnest** fa (*or* parla) sul serio, non scherza; **this book is deadly** (*fam: very boring*) questo libro è un mattone.
2 ADV: **deadly dull** di una noia mortale; **deadly pale** pallido(-a) come un cadavere.

♦ **dead-nettle** ['dɛdˌnɛtl] N ortica bianca, lamio.

dead-pan ['dɛdˌpæn] **1** ADJ (*face*) impassibile; (*humour*) all'inglese.
2 ADV (*with a straight face*) senza fare una piega.

♦ **Dead Sea** N: **the Dead Sea** il mar Morto.

♦ **dead season** N (*Tourism*): **the dead season** la stagione morta.

♦ **dead weight** N peso morto.

dead·wood ['dɛdˌwʊd] N (*also fig*) rami *mpl* secchi.

deaf [dɛf] **1** ADJ (*comp* **-er,** *superl* **-est**) sordo(-a); **deaf in one ear** sordo(-a) da un orecchio; **to be deaf to sth** (*fig*) restare sordo(-a) a qc; **to turn a deaf ear to sth** fare orecchi da mercante a qc; **as deaf as a (door)post** sordo(-a) come una campana.
2 NPL: **the deaf** i sordi.

♦ **deaf-aid** ['dɛfˌeɪd] N (*Brit fam*) apparecchio acustico.

♦ **deaf-and-dumb** ['dɛfən'dʌm] ADJ (*person*) sordomuto (-a); (*language*) dei sordomuti.

deaf·en ['dɛfn] VT assordare.

deaf·en·ing ['dɛfnɪŋ] ADJ assordante, fragoroso(-a).

deaf·en·ing·ly ['dɛfnɪŋlɪ] ADV in modo assordante.

♦ **deaf-mute** ['dɛfˌmjuːt] N sordomuto(-a).

deaf·ness ['dɛfnɪs] N sordità.

deal¹ [diːl] [*vb: pt, pp* **dealt**] **1** N **a** (*agreement*) accordo; (*also*: **business deal**) affare *m*; **to do** *or* **strike a deal with sb** fare un affare con qn; **perhaps we can do a deal?** forse ci si può aggiustare fra di noi?; **it's a deal!** (*fam*) affare fatto!; **a new deal** (*Pol, Econ, Sociol*) un piano di riforme; **to get a good/bad deal** (*Comm*) fare/non fare un buon affare; **he got a good deal from them** l'hanno trattato bene; **a fair deal for working mothers** un trattamento equo per le madri che lavorano
b (*Cards*) turno (*nel dare le carte*); **it's my deal** adesso tocca a me dare le carte
c (*in expressions of quantity*): **a good** *or* **great deal** molto, parecchio; **to have a great deal to do** avere molto da fare; **there's a good deal of truth in what he says** c'è molto di vero in quel che dice; **she spends a great deal of her time alone** passa buona parte del suo tempo da sola; **he thinks a great deal of his father** ha una grande stima di suo padre; **that's saying a good deal** non è dire poco; **it means a great deal to me** vuol dire molto per me; **a great deal cleverer** di gran lunga più intelligente.
2 VT **a** : **to deal sb a blow** assestare un colpo a qn
b (*Cards: also:* **deal out**) distribuire, dare

► **deal in** VI + PREP (*Comm*) occuparsi di; (*drugs*) spacciare

► **deal out** VT + ADV (*cards, money*) distribuire; **to deal out justice** far giustizia

► **deal with** VI + PREP

a (*handle: person, task, application*) occuparsi di; (: *problem*) affrontare; (: *Comm: order*) sbrigare; **I'll deal with you later!** con te facciamo i conti più tardi!; **to know how to deal with sb** sapere come prendere qn; **he's not easy to deal with** è un tipo difficile

b (*subj: book, film: be about*) trattare di

c (*Comm: company, organization, person*) trattare con.

deal² [diːl] **1** N legno di pino (*or* di abete).

2 ADJ di pino (*or* di abete).

deal·er ['diːlə'] N **a** (*Comm*): **dealer (in)** commerciante *m/f* (di); **an antique dealer** un(a) antiquario(-a) **b** (*also*: **drug dealer**) spacciatore(-trice) **c** (*Cards*) chi fa *or* dà le carte.

deal·er·ship ['diːlə‚ʃɪp] N (*Comm*) concessione *f*.

deal·ings ['diːlɪŋz] NPL **a** (*relationship*) rapporti *mpl*; **to have dealings with sb** avere a che fare con qn **b** (*Comm, Stock Exchange: in goods, shares*) transazioni *fpl*.

dealt [dɛlt] PT, PP of **deal**.

dean [diːn] N (*of college, university*) preside *m/f*; (*Rel*) decano.

dean·ery ['diːnərɪ] N (*Rel*) decanato.

dear [dɪə'] **1** ADJ (*comp* -**er**, *superl* -**est**) **a** (*loved, lovable*) caro(-a); **I hold it very dear** mi è molto caro; **my dearest wish** il mio più ardente desiderio; **what a dear little boy!** che amore di bambino!; **a dear little cottage** una casetta deliziosa

b (*in letter writing*): **Dear Daddy/Peter** Caro papà/Peter; **Dearest Paul** Carissimo Paul; **Dear Mr/Mrs Smith** Gentile Signor/Signora Smith; **Dear Mr and Mrs Smith** Gentili Signori Smith; **Dear Sir/Madam** Egregio Signore/Gentile Signora

c (*expensive*) caro(-a); **dear money** (*Comm*) denaro ad alto interesse.

2 EXCL: **oh dear!** oh Dio!, mamma mia!; **dear me!** Dio mio!.

3 N caro(-a); **my dear** caro(-a) mio(-a); **my dearest** amore mio; **(you) poor dear!** poverino!; **he's a dear!** (*fam*) è un tesoro!; **post this letter for me, there's a dear** (*fam*) sii gentile, imbucami questa lettera.

4 ADV caro: **to pay dear for sth** pagare caro qc; **he bought his freedom dear** la sua libertà gli è costata cara.

dear·est ['dɪərɪst] N, ADJ see **dear**.

dear·ly ['dɪəlɪ] ADV: **to love sb/sth dearly** amare qn/qc moltissimo; **I should dearly love to go there** mi piacerebbe moltissimo andarci; **to pay dearly for sth** (*esp fig*) pagar qc caro *or* a caro prezzo.

dearth [dɜːθ] N (*of food, resources, ideas, money*) penuria, mancanza.

death [dɛθ] N morte *f*; (*Med, Admin, Law*) decesso; (*of plans, hopes*) fine *f*; **to be burnt to death** morire carbonizzato(-a); **to drink o.s. to death** uccidersi a forza di bere; **to sentence sb to death** condannare a morte qn; **to put sb to death** mettere a morte qn, giustiziare qn; **a fight to the death** un duello all'ultimo sangue; **to be at death's door** essere in punto di morte; **it will be the death of him** sarà la sua rovina; **you'll be the death of me** (*fam fig*) mi farai morire; **you look like death warmed up** (*fam*) sembri un morto che cammina; **bored to death** (*fam*) annoiato(-a) a morte; **I'm sick** *or* **tired to death of it** (*fam*) ne ho fin sopra i capelli.

death·bed ['dɛθ‚bɛd] **1** N letto di morte; **on one's deathbed** in punto di morte.

2 ADJ (*confession*) in punto di morte.

death·blow ['dɛθ‚bləʊ] N colpo di grazia.

death certificate N (*Admin*) certificato di morte.

♦ **death duty** N, GEN PL (*Brit*) tassa di successione.

death·ly ['dɛθlɪ] **1** ADJ (*comp* -**ier**, *superl* -**iest**) (*pallor*) mortale; (*appearance*) cadaverico(-a); (*silence*) di tomba.

2 ADV: **deathly pale** pallido(-a) come un cadavere.

♦ **death march** N (*Mus*) marcia funebre.

♦ **death mask** N maschera mortuaria.

♦ **death penalty** N pena di morte.

♦ **death rate** N (tasso di) mortalità.

♦ **death rattle** N rantolo.

♦ **death row** N (*Am*): **to be on death row** essere nel braccio della morte.

♦ **death sentence** N condanna a morte, pena di morte.

♦ **death's-head** ['dɛθs‚hɛd] N teschio.

♦ **death squad** N squadra della morte.

♦ **death throes** NPL (*also fig*) ultimi spasimi *mpl*; **in one's death throes** agonizzante.

♦ **death toll** N numero delle vittime.

♦ **death·trap** ['dɛθ‚træp] N trappola mortale.

♦ **death warrant** N sentenza di morte.

♦ **death wish** N desiderio di morte.

deb [dɛb] N ABBR (*Brit fam*) = **debutante**.

de·ba·cle [deɪˈbɑːkl] N disastro; (*defeat*) disfatta; (*collapse*) sfacelo.

de·bar [dɪˈbɑː'] VT (*frm*): **to debar sb from sth** escludere qn da qc; **to debar sb from doing sth** vietare a qn di fare qc.

de·base [dɪˈbeɪs] VT (*person, relationship, word*) degradare, svilire; (*coinage*) svilire, adulterare.

de·base·ment [dɪˈbeɪsmənt] N (*of person, relationship, word*) degradazione *f*, svilimento.

de·bat·able [dɪˈbeɪtəbl] ADJ discutibile; **it is debatable whether ...** è in dubbio se... .

de·bate [dɪˈbeɪt] **1** VT (*discuss*) discutere, dibattere; (*consider*): **he debated the advisability of leaving** si chiedeva se fosse saggio partire; **we debated whether to go or not** discutemmo se andare o meno.

2 VI: **to debate (with sb about sth)** discutere (con qn di qc); **to debate with o.s. (about, (up)on sth)** essere in dubbio (su qc).

3 N dibattito, discussione *f*; **after much debate** dopo lunga discussione.

de·ba·ting so·ci·ety [dɪˈbeɪtɪŋ səˈsaɪətɪ] N (*Scol, Univ*) *circolo che organizza dibattiti con votazione finale*.

de·bauch [dɪˈbɔːtʃ] VT (*old frm*) corrompere.

de·bauched [dɪˈbɔːtʃt] ADJ (*old: person*) debosciato(-a); (: *taste, morals*) dissoluto(-a), vizioso(-a).

de·bauch·ery [dɪˈbɔːtʃərɪ] N dissolutezza.

de·ben·ture [dɪˈbɛntʃə'] N (*Fin*) obbligazione *f*.

de·bili·tate [dɪˈbɪlɪ‚teɪt] VT (*frm*) debilitare.

de·bil·ity [dɪˈbɪlɪtɪ] N (*frm*) debilitazione *f*.

deb·it ['dɛbɪt] (*Fin*) **1** N addebito.

2 VT addebitare; **to debit sb/sb's account with a sum** OR **to debit a sum to sb** *or* **to sb's account** addebitare una somma a qn/sul conto di qc.

♦ **debit balance** N saldo passivo *or* debitore.

♦ **debit note** N nota di addebito.

♦ **debit side** N colonna del dare; (*fig*): **on the debit side is the fact that ...** il lato negativo è che... .

debo·nair [‚dɛbəˈnɛə'] ADJ (*young man*) gioviale e disinvolto(-a).

de·brief [‚diːˈbriːf] VT (*Mil*) chiamare a rapporto (a operazione ultimata).

de·brief·ing [‚diːˈbriːfɪŋ] N rapporto *or* resoconto (a operazione ultimata).

de·bris ['dɛbriː] N detriti *mpl*.

debt [dɛt] N debito; **debts of £5000** debiti per 5000 sterline; **a debt of honour/gratitude** un debito d'onore/di gratitudine *or* di riconoscenza; **to be in debt (to sb)** essere indebitato(-a) (con qn), avere debiti (con qn); **I am £500 in debt** sono in debito di 500 sterline; **to be in sb's debt** (*fig*) essere in debito verso qn; **to get into debt** far debiti, indebitarsi; **to be out of debt** essere libero(-a) da debiti.

♦ **debt collector** N agente *m* di recupero crediti.

debt·or ['dɛtəʳ] N debitore(-trice).

♦ **debt-ridden** ['dɛt,rɪdn] ADJ oberato(-a) dai debiti.

de·bug [di:'bʌg] VT (*Comput: program*) localizzare e rimuovere errori da; (*room*) togliere i microfoni da.

de·bunk [,di:'bʌŋk] VT (*theory*) demistificare; (*claim*) smentire; (*person, institution*) screditare.

de·but ['deɪbjuː] N debutto; **to make one's debut** debuttare, fare il proprio debutto; **to make one's stage/film debut** debuttare sulle scene/sullo schermo.

debu·tante ['dɛbjuːtɑːnt] N debuttante *f.*

Dec. ABBR = **December**.

dec·ade ['dɛkeɪd] N decennio.

deca·dence ['dɛkədəns] N decadenza.

deca·dent ['dɛkədənt] ADJ decadente.

de·caf [di:'kæf] N ABBR [1] ADJ (*fam*) decaffeinato(-a). [2] N decaffeinato.

de·caf·fein·at·ed [di:'kæfɪ,neɪtɪd] ADJ decaffeinato(-a).

de·camp [dɪ'kæmp] VI filarsela.

de·cant [dɪ'kænt] VT (*wine*) decantare.

de·cant·er [dɪ'kæntəʳ] N bottiglia di cristallo (*per liquori o vini*).

de·capi·tate [dɪ'kæpɪteɪt] VT (*frm*) decapitare.

de·cath·lon [dɪ'kæθlən] N decathlon *m inv.*

de·cay [dɪ'keɪ] [1] VI (*teeth*) cariarsi; (*vegetation, flesh*) decomporsi; (*Phys: radioactive nucleus*) disintegrarsi; (*building, urban area*) andare in rovina; (*fig: civilization*) decadere; (: *one's faculties*) deteriorarsi.
[2] N (*of teeth*) carie *f*; (*of vegetation, body*) decomposizione *f*; (*of radioactivity*) disintegrazione *f*; (*of building, urban area*) stato di abbandono, decadimento; (*of civilization*) rovina; (*of faculties*) deterioramento; **urban decay** degrado urbano.

de·cay·ing [dɪ'keɪɪŋ] ADJ (*vegetation, flesh*) in decomposizione; (*teeth*) cariato(-a); (*building, urban area*) in rovina; (*civilization*) in declino.

de·cease [dɪ'siːs] (*Law*) [1] N decesso.
[2] VI decedere.

de·ceased [dɪ'siːst] (*Law, also frm*) [1] ADJ deceduto(-a).
[2] N: **the deceased** il/la defunto(-a).

de·ceit [dɪ'siːt] N (*quality*) disonestà; (*action*) inganno, truffa.

de·ceit·ful [dɪ'siːtfʊl] ADJ (*person*) falso(-a), disonesto(-a); (*words, behaviour*) menzognero(-a), ingannatore(-trice).

de·ceit·ful·ly [dɪ'siːtfəlɪ] ADV in modo falso, disonestamente.

de·ceit·ful·ness [dɪ'siːtfʊlnɪs] N falsità *f inv*, disonestà.

de·ceive [dɪ'siːv] VT ingannare; **she deceived me into thinking that ...** mi ha ingannato facendomi credere che...; **unless my eyes deceive me** se gli occhi non m'ingannano; **don't be deceived by appearances** non ti fare ingannare dalle apparenze; **to deceive o.s.** ingannarsi, illudersi.

de·ceiv·er [dɪ'siːvəʳ] N ingannatore(-trice).

de·cel·er·ate [di:'sɛləreɪt] VT, VI decelerare.

de·cel·era·tion ['di:,sɛlə'reɪʃən] N decelerazione *f.*

De·cem·ber [dɪ'sɛmbəʳ] N dicembre *m for usage see* **July**.

de·cen·cy ['di:sənsɪ] N (*moral sense*) rispetto per i valori umani; (*propriety*) decenza, decoro; **he has no sense of decency** non ha un minimo di rispetto; **to have the decency to do sth** avere la decenza di fare qc; **out of common decency** per gentilezza, se non altro.

de·cent ['di:sənt] ADJ **a** (*respectable: person, house*) perbene *inv*, ammodo *inv*; (*proper: clothes, behaviour, language*) decente
b (*kind*) gentile, bravo(-a); **he was very decent to me** si è comportato molto bene con me; **to do the decent thing** fare quello che è giusto; **they were very decent about it** sono stati molto corretti in merito
c (*satisfactory: meal, house*) decente, discreto(-a).

de·cent·ly ['di:səntlɪ] ADV (*respectably*) decentemente, convenientemente; (*kindly*) gentilmente.

de·cen·trali·za·tion [di:,sɛntrəlar'zeɪʃən] N (*Admin, Pol*) decentramento.

de·cen·tral·ize [di:'sɛntrə,laɪz] VT (*Admin, Pol*) decentrare.

de·cep·tion [dɪ'sɛpʃən] N inganno; **to practise deception on sb** raggirare qn.

de·cep·tive [dɪ'sɛptɪv] ADJ (*likely to deceive*) ingannevole; (*meant to deceive*) ingannatore(-trice).

de·cep·tive·ly [dɪ'sɛptɪvlɪ] ADV: **deceptively simple** (solo) apparentemente facile.

de·cep·tive·ness [dɪ'sɛptɪvnɪs] N carattere *m* ingannevole; (*deliberate*) carattere infido.

deci·bel ['dɛsɪbɛl] N decibel *m inv.*

de·cide [dɪ'saɪd] [1] VT (*question, argument*) decidere, risolvere; (*person*) far prendere una decisione a; **to decide to do sth** decidere di fare qc, decidersi a fare qc; **to decide that** decidere che.
[2] VI decidere, decidersi; **to decide for** *or* **in favour of sb** decidere a favore di qn; **to decide on/against sth** optare per/contro qc; **to decide on doing sth** scegliere *or* decidere di fare qc; **to decide against doing sth** decidere di non fare qc.

de·cid·ed [dɪ'saɪdɪd] ADJ (*tone, improvement*) deciso(-a); (*risk*) certo(-a); (*opinions, views*) chiaro(-a), preciso(-a).

de·cid·ed·ly [dɪ'saɪdɪdlɪ] ADV (*extremely*) decisamente; (*emphatically*) in modo deciso.

de·cid·er [dɪ'saɪdəʳ] N (*Sport*) spareggio.

de·cid·ing [dɪ'saɪdɪŋ] ADJ decisivo(-a).

de·cidu·ous [dɪ'sɪdjʊəs] ADJ deciduo(-a).

deci·mal ['dɛsɪməl] [1] ADJ decimale; **to 3 decimal places** al terzo decimale.
[2] N (numero) decimale *m.*

deci·mali·za·tion [,dɛsɪmələr'zeɪʃən] N (*Brit*) conversione *f* al sistema metrico decimale.

deci·mal·ize ['dɛsɪmə,laɪz] VT (*Brit*) convertire al sistema metrico decimale.

♦ **decimal point** N ≈ virgola (*in numero decimale*).

deci·mate ['dɛsɪ,meɪt] VT decimare.

de·ci·pher [dɪ'saɪfəʳ] VT decifrare.

de·ci·pher·able [dɪ'saɪfərəbl] ADJ decifrabile.

de·ci·sion [dɪ'sɪʒən] N decisione *f*; **to make a decision** prendere una decisione.

♦ **decision-making** [dɪ'sɪʒən,meɪkɪŋ] N: **to be good at decision-making** saper prendere decisioni.

de·ci·sive [dɪ'saɪsɪv] ADJ (*victory, factor*) decisivo(-a); (*influence*) determinante; (*manner, person*) risoluto(-a), deciso(-a); (*reply*) deciso(-a), categorico(-a).

de·ci·sive·ly [dɪ'saɪsɪvlɪ] ADV (*act*) con decisione.

de·ci·sive·ness [dɪ'saɪsɪvnɪs] N (*of manner, person*) risolutezza, decisione *f.*

deck [dɛk] [1] N **a** (*Naut*) (ponte *m* di) coperta; **to go up on**

deck salire in coperta; **below deck** sotto coperta; **to clear the decks** (*fig*) sgombrare il campo; **to hit the deck** (*fam*) cascare a terra (bocconi)
b (*of bus*): **top** or **upper deck** piano di sopra; **bottom** or **lower deck** piano di sotto
c (*of cards*) mazzo
d (*of record player*) piatto; **record deck** piatto (giradischi); **cassette deck** piastra (di registrazione).
2 VT (*also:* **deck out**): **to deck (with)** decorare (con).

deck·chair ['dɛk,tʃɛəʳ] N sedia *f* sdraio *inv*.
♦ **deck hand** N mozzo.
de·claim [dɪ'kleɪm] VI declamare.
dec·la·ma·tion [ˌdɛklə'meɪʃən] N declamazione *f*.
de·clama·tory [dɪ'klæmətərɪ] ADJ (*speech, tone*) declamatorio(-a).
dec·la·ra·tion [ˌdɛklə'reɪʃən] N dichiarazione *f*.
de·clara·tory [dɪ'klærətərɪ] ADJ (*Law*): **declaratory judgement** declamatorio(-a).
de·clare [dɪ'klɛəʳ] VT (*gen*) dichiarare; (*Fin, Pol: results*) annunciare; **have you anything to declare?** (*Customs*) ha qualcosa da dichiarare?, dichiara?; **to declare that** dichiarare che; **he declared that he was innocent** ha dichiarato di essere innocente, si è dichiarato innocente; **to declare war (on** or **against sb)** dichiarare guerra (a qn).
de·clas·si·fy [diː'klæsɪ,faɪ] VT (*documents, records*) declassificare.
de·clen·sion [dɪ'klɛnʃən] N (*Gram*) declinazione *f*.
de·cline [dɪ'klaɪn] 1 N: **decline (in)** (*decrease*) calo (di); (*deterioration*) declino (di); **decline in living standards** abbassamento del tenore di vita; **to be on the decline** (*gen*) essere in diminuzione; (*prices*) essere in ribasso.
2 VT **a** (*frm: refuse: invitation*) declinare, rifiutare; **to decline to do sth** rifiutare or rifiutarsi di fare qc.
b (*Gram*) declinare.
3 VI **a** (*power, influence*) diminuire, declinare; (*empire*) decadere; (*health*) deteriorare; **in his declining years** negli ultimi anni della sua vita; (*of public figure*) negli anni del suo declino; **to decline in importance** diminuire d'importanza
b (*Gram*) declinarsi.
de·clutch ['diː'klʌtʃ] VI (*Aut*) premere la frizione.
de·code ['diː'kəʊd] VT (*message*) decifrare; (*Comput, Ling*) decodificare.
de·cod·er [diː'kəʊdəʳ] N (*Comput, TV*) decodificatore *m*.
de·coke [*vb* diː'kəʊk; *n* 'diː'kəʊk] (*Aut*) 1 VT decarburare.
2 N decarburazione *f*.
de·colo·niza·tion [diːˌkɒlənaɪ'zeɪʃən] N decolonizzazione *f*.
de·colo·nize [diː'kɒlə,naɪz] VT decolonizzare.
de·com·pose [ˌdiː·kəm'pəʊz] 1 VI decomporsi.
2 VT decomporre.
de·com·po·si·tion [ˌdiː·kɒmpə'zɪʃən] N decomposizione *f*.
de·com·press [ˌdiː·kəm'prɛs] VT fare la decompressione di.
de·com·pres·sion [ˌdiː·kəm'prɛʃən] N decompressione *f*.
♦ **decompression chamber** N camera di decompressione.
de·con·gest·ant [ˌdiː·kən'dʒɛstənt] N decongestionante *m*.
de·con·secrat·ed [ˌdiː·'kɒnsɪ,kreɪtɪd] ADJ sconsacrato(-a).
de·con·tami·nate [ˌdiː·kən'tæmɪ,neɪt] VT decontaminare.
de·con·tam·in·ation [ˌdiː·kənˌtæmɪ'neɪʃən] N decontaminazione *f*.
de·con·trol [ˌdiː·kən'trəʊl] VT (*trade*) liberalizzare; (*prices*) togliere il controllo governativo a.

dé·cor ['deɪkɔːʳ] N arredamento, decorazione *f*.
deco·rate ['dɛkə,reɪt] VT **a** : **to decorate (with)** (*adorn*) decorare (con) **b** (*paint and wallpaper: room*) pitturare e tappezzare **c** (*honour: soldier*) decorare.
deco·rat·ing ['dɛkə,reɪtɪŋ] N: **to do some decorating** mettere la carta da parati (e pitturare).
deco·ra·tion [ˌdɛkə'reɪʃən] N decorazione *f*; **Christmas decorations** decorazioni natalizie.
deco·ra·tive ['dɛkərətɪv] ADJ decorativo(-a).
deco·ra·tor ['dɛkəreɪtəʳ] N decoratore(-trice).
deco·rous ['dɛkərəs] ADJ decoroso(-a).
deco·rous·ly ['dɛkərəslɪ] ADV decorosamente.
de·co·rum [dɪ'kɔːrəm] N decoro; **out of a sense of decorum** per rispetto delle convenienze; **a breach of decorum** una sconvenienza.
de·coy ['diːkɔɪ] N (*bird*) (uccello da) richiamo; (*fig: bait: thing*) tranello; (: *person*) esca; **police decoy** poliziotto in borghese (*usato come esca*).
de·crease [*n* 'diːkriːs; *vb* diː'kriːs] 1 N: **decrease (in)** (*amount, numbers, population, power*) diminuzione *f* (di); (*birth rate, value, production, enthusiasm*) calo (di); (*prices*) ribasso (di); (*strength, dose*) riduzione *f* (di); **to be on the decrease** essere in diminuzione.
2 VT (*see n*) diminuire; far calare; ribassare; ridurre.
3 VI (*amount, numbers etc*) diminuire; (*prices, birthrate etc*) calare; (*Knitting*) calare (le maglie); **to decrease by 10%** diminuire del 10%.
de·creas·ing [diː'kriːsɪŋ] ADJ in diminuzione.
de·cree [dɪ'kriː] 1 N (*Law, Pol*) decreto; (*municipal*) ordinanza; (*divorce*): **decree absolute** sentenza di divorzio definitiva; **decree nisi** sentenza provvisoria di divorzio.
2 VT: **to decree (that)** decretare (che) + *sub*.
de·crep·it [dɪ'krɛpɪt] ADJ (*building*) cadente; (*person*) decrepito(-a).
de·crepi·tude [dɪ'krɛpɪtjuːd] N (*frm*) decrepitezza.
de·cry [dɪ'kraɪ] VT (*frm*) condannare, deplorare.
dedi·cate ['dɛdɪ,keɪt] VT dedicare, consacrare; (*book etc*) dedicare; **to dedicate one's life** or **o.s. to sth/to doing sth** dedicare la propria esistenza a qc/a fare qc.
dedi·cat·ed ['dɛdɪ,keɪtɪd] ADJ coscienzioso(-a); (*Comput*) dedicato(-a).
dedi·ca·tion [ˌdɛdɪ'keɪʃən] N (*in book*) dedica; (*devotion*) dedizione *f*.
de·duce [dɪ'djuːs] VT: **to deduce sth from sth** dedurre qc da qc; **to deduce that** dedurre che.
de·duct [dɪ'dʌkt] VT: **to deduct (from)** (*gen*) dedurre (da); (*from wages*) trattenere (su); (*from price*) fare una riduzione (su); (*Scol: marks*) togliere (da).
de·duct·ible [dɪ'dʌktəbl] ADJ deducibile.
de·duc·tion [dɪ'dʌkʃən] N **a** (*inference*) deduzione *f* **b** (*subtraction*) detrazione *f*; (*from wages*) trattenuta.
de·duc·tive [dɪ'dʌktɪv] ADJ deduttivo(-a).
de·duc·tive·ly [dɪ'dʌktɪvlɪ] ADV deduttivamente.
deed [diːd] N **a** azione *f*, atto; **brave deed** impresa; **good deed** buona azione; **in deed** di fatto **b** (*Law*) atto (notarile); **deed of covenant** atto di donazione.
♦ **deed poll** N: **by deed poll** con atto unilaterale.
deem [diːm] VT (*frm*) giudicare, ritenere; **she deemed it wise to go** ha ritenuto prudente andarsene.
deep [diːp] 1 ADJ (*comp* **-er**, *superl* **-est**) **a** (*water, hole, wound*) profondo(-a); (*snow*) alto(-a); **the lake was 16 metres deep** il lago era profondo 16 metri; **knee-deep in water** in acqua fino alle ginocchia; **we were ankle-deep in mud** il fango ci arrivava alle caviglie; **to be in deep water** (*fig*) navigare in cattive acque; **the deep end** (*of*

swimming pool) la parte più profonda; **to be thrown in (at)
the deep end** (*fig fam*) avere il battesimo del fuoco; **to go
off (at) the deep end** (*fig fam: angry*) partire per la
tangente

b (*shelf, cupboard*) profondo(-a); (*border, hem*) lungo
(-a); **these kitchen units are 30 cm deep** questi mobili da
cucina hanno una profondità di 30 cm

c (*voice, sigh*) profondo(-a); **deep breathing exercises**
esercizi *mpl* respiratori; **he took a deep breath** fece un
respiro profondo

d (*feeling, sleep, writer, insight*) profondo(-a); (*colour*)
intenso(-a), cupo(-a); (*relief*) immenso(-a); (*interest,
concern*) vivo(-a); **to be deep in thought/in a book** essere
immerso(-a) nei propri pensieri/nella lettura.

2 ADV: **deep in her heart** in fondo al cuore; **the
spectators were standing 6 deep** c'erano 6 file di
spettatori in piedi; **don't go in too deep if you can't swim**
non andare nell'acqua alta se non sai nuotare; **to dig
deep** scavare in profondità; **deep in the forest** nel cuore
della foresta; **deep into the night** fino a tarda notte;
buried deep in snow coperto(-a) da uno spesso strato di
neve.

3 N: **the deep** (*liter*) il mare.

deep·en ['diːpən] 1 VT (*hole, knowledge, understanding*)
approfondire; (*sound, friendship, love*) rendere più
profondo(-a); (*colour*) scurire; (*interest*) ravvivare;
(*sorrow*) aggravare.

2 VI (*gen*) diventare più profondo(-a), approfondirsi;
(*colour*) diventare più intenso(-a); (*mystery*) infittirsi;
(*darkness*) farsi più intenso(-a).

deep·freeze [ˌdiːpˈfriːz] N congelatore *m*.

♦ **deep-freeze** [diːpˈfriːz] (*vb: pt* **deep-froze**, *pp* **deep-
frozen**) VT surgelare.

♦ **deep-fry** [ˌdiːpˈfraɪ] VT friggere in olio abbondante.

deep·ly ['diːplɪ] ADV (*breathe*) profondamente; (*dig*) in
profondità; (*drink*) a gran sorsi; (*interested, concerned*)
vivamente; (*moving*) estremamente; (*grateful, offended*)
profondamente; **to regret sth deeply** rammaricarsi
profondamente di qc; **to go deeply into sth** approfondire qc.

♦ **deep-rooted** [ˌdiːpˈruːtɪd] ADJ (*prejudice*) profondamente radicato(-a); (*affection*) profondo(-a); (*habit*)
inveterato(-a).

♦ **deep-sea** [ˌdiːpˈsiː] ADJ (*creatures, plants*) pelagico(-a),
abissale; (*fisherman, fishing*) d'alto mare; **deep-sea diver**
palombaro; **deep-sea diving** immersione *f* a grande
profondità.

♦ **deep-seated** [ˌdiːpˈsiːtɪd] ADJ (*beliefs*) radicato(-a).

♦ **deep-set** ['diːpˌsɛt] ADJ: **deep-set eyes** occhi *mpl* infossati.

deer [dɪəʳ] N, PL INV cervo(-a); **the deer family** la famiglia dei
cervidi.

deer·skin ['dɪəˌskɪn] N pelle *f* di daino.

deer·stalker ['dɪəˌstɔːkəʳ] N (*hat*) berretto da cacciatore.

deer·stalking ['dɪəˌstɔːkɪŋ] N caccia al cervo a piedi.

de-escalate [diːˈɛskəˌleɪt] VT (*crisis*) ridimensionare;
(*tension*) portare ad un rilassamento di.

de·face [dɪˈfeɪs] VT (*wall, monument*) deturpare; (*work of art*)
sfregiare; (*statue*) mutilare; (*poster*) imbrattare.

de facto [deɪˈfæktəʊ] ADJ, ADV (*frm*) de facto *inv*.

defa·ma·tion [ˌdɛfəˈmeɪʃən] N (*frm*) diffamazione *f*.

de·fama·tory [dɪˈfæmətərɪ] ADJ (*frm*) diffamatorio(-a).

de·fame [dɪˈfeɪm] VT (*frm*) diffamare.

de·fault [dɪˈfɔːlt] 1 N **a** : **by default** per esclusione;
judgement by default (*Law*) sentenza in contumacia; **to**

win by default vincere per abbandono dell'avversario;
in default of in mancanza di

b (*Comput: also:* **default value**) default *m inv*.

2 VI (*gen*) essere inadempiente; (*Law: not appear*) non
presentarsi in giudizio, essere contumace; (: *not pay*)
risultare inadempiente; **to default on a debt** non
onorare un debito.

de·fault·er [dɪˈfɔːltəʳ] N (*on debt*) inadempiente *m/f*, debi-
tore(-trice) moroso(-a); (*Law: at trial*) contumace *m/f*.

de·fault·ing [dɪˈfɔːltɪŋ] ADJ (*debtor, borrower*) inadempiente, moroso(-a); (*witness*) contumace.

♦ **default option** N (*Comput*) opzione *f* di default.

de·feat [dɪˈfiːt] 1 N (*of army, team*) sconfitta; (: *more
serious*) disfatta; (*of ambition, plan*) fallimento, insuccesso.

2 VT (*army, team, opponent*) sconfiggere, battere; (*plan,
ambition, efforts*) frustrare; (*Pol: party*) sconfiggere; (: *bill,
amendment*) respingere; **to defeat one's own ends** far
fallire i propri obiettivi.

de·feat·ism [dɪˈfiːtɪzəm] N disfattismo.

de·feat·ist [dɪˈfiːtɪst] N, ADJ disfattista (*m/f*).

def·ecate ['dɛfəkeɪt] VI (*frm*) defecare.

de·fect [*n* 'diːfɛkt; *vb* dɪˈfɛkt] 1 N (*gen*) difetto; **physical
defect** difetto fisico; **mental defect** anomalia mentale;
moral defect difetto.

2 VI (*from country*) scappare; (*from political party*) defezionare; **to defect to the enemy/the West** passare al
nemico/all'Ovest.

de·fec·tion [dɪˈfɛkʃən] N (*from country*) fuga; (*from political
party*) defezione *f*.

de·fec·tive [dɪˈfɛktɪv] ADJ (*machine, workmanship, eyesight*)
difettoso(-a); (*system, reasoning*) cattivo(-a); (*Gram*)
difettivo(-a); **to be defective in sth** mancare di qc.

de·fec·tor [dɪˈfɛktəʳ] N fuor(i)uscito(-a); (*political*) rifu-
giato(-a) politico(-a).

de·fence, (*Am*) **de·fense** [dɪˈfɛns] 1 N difesa; **in defence
of** in difesa di; **in his defence** in sua difesa; **the Ministry
of Defence**, (*Brit*) **the Department of Defense** (*Am*) il
Ministero della Difesa; **the case for the defence** la
difesa; **witness for the defence** teste *m/f* a difesa; **the
body's defences against disease** le difese naturali
dell'organismo contro la malattia; **as a defence against**
per ripararsi da, come difesa contro.

2 ADJ (*policy, strategy*) di difesa; **defence spending** *spese
per la difesa*.

de·fence·less, (*Am*) **de·fense·less** [dɪˈfɛnslɪs] ADJ
inerme, indifeso(-a), senza difesa.

♦ **defence mechanism** N (*Psych*) meccanismo di difesa.

de·fend [dɪˈfɛnd] VT (*gen*) difendere; (*decision, action*)
giustificare; (*opinion*) sostenere; **to defend o.s. (against)**
difendersi (da).

de·fend·ant [dɪˈfɛndənt] N (*Law*) imputato(-a).

de·fend·er [dɪˈfɛndəʳ] N (*Sport*) difensore/difenditrice; (:
of title) detentore(-trice); **Defender of the Faith** (*Brit: title
of monarch*) difensore *m* della fede.

de·fend·ing [dɪˈfɛndɪŋ] ADJ: **defending champion** (*Sport*)
campione(-essa) in carica; **defending counsel** (*Law*)
avvocato difensore.

de·fense [dɪˈfɛns] N (*Am*) = **defence**.

de·fen·sible [dɪˈfɛnsɪbl] ADJ giustificabile.

de·fen·sive [dɪˈfɛnsɪv] 1 ADJ difensivo(-a); (*person*) sulla
difensiva.

2 N: **on the defensive** sulla difensiva.

de·fer [dɪˈfɜːʳ] 1 VT (*postpone*) rimandare, rinviare; (*Law:
case*) aggiornare.

2 VI (*submit*): **to defer to sb/sth** rimettersi a qn/qc; **to defer to sb's (greater) knowledge** rimettersi alla scienza di qn.

def·er·ence ['dɛfərəns] N deferenza, riguardo; **out of** *or* **in deference to** per riguardo a.

def·er·en·tial [ˌdɛfə'rɛnʃəl] ADJ deferente.

de·fer·ment [dɪ'fɜ:mənt], **de·fer·ral** [dɪ'fɜ:rəl] N rinvio, differimento.

de·fi·ance [dɪ'faɪəns] N (atteggiamento di) sfida; **in defiance of** a dispetto di; **in defiance of orders/the law** sfidando gli ordini/la legge.

de·fi·ant [dɪ'faɪənt] ADJ (*person*) ribelle; (*tone, attitude*) di sfida; (*reply*) insolente.

de·fi·ant·ly [dɪ'faɪəntlɪ] ADV con aria (*or* tono) di sfida.

de·fi·cien·cy [dɪ'fɪʃənsɪ] N a (*of goods*) mancanza, insufficienza; (*of vitamins, minerals, protein*) carenza b (*in system, plan*) carenza.

♦ **deficiency disease** N malattia da carenza.

de·fi·cient [dɪ'fɪʃənt] ADJ deficiente, insufficiente; **to be deficient in sth** mancare di qc.

defi·cit ['dɛfɪsɪt] N (*Fin*) deficit *m inv*, disavanzo; **to be in deficit** essere in deficit.

de·file¹ [dɪ'faɪl] VT (*frm: pollute*) deturpare.

de·file² ['di:faɪl] 1 N (*liter: passage*) gola.
2 VI (*march*) sfilare.

de·file·ment [dɪ'faɪlmənt] N (*frm*) deturpazione *f*.

de·fin·able [dɪ'faɪnəbl] ADJ definibile, precisabile.

de·fine [dɪ'faɪn] VT (*all senses*) precisare, definire; **the skyscraper was clearly defined against the sky** il grattacielo si stagliava nettamente contro il cielo; **to define a block of text** (*Comput*) definire un blocco di testo.

defi·nite ['dɛfɪnɪt] ADJ a (*exact, clear: date, plan, intention*) preciso(-a); (: *answer, agreement*) definitivo(-a); (*positive, decided: sale, order*) sicuro(-a); (: *tone, manner*) deciso(-a); **is it definite that ...?** è sicuro che...?; **he was definite about it** (*certain*) ne era sicuro; (*unequivocal*) è stato chiaro al proposito
b (*clearly noticeable*) netto(-a)
c (*Gram*): **past definite tense** passato remoto.

♦ **definite article** N (*Gram*) articolo determinativo.

defi·nite·ly ['dɛfɪnɪtlɪ] ADV (*certainly*) di sicuro, certamente; (*emphatically*: *state*) categoricamente; (*appreciably*: *better, worse*) decisamente; **definitely!** assolutamente!

defi·ni·tion [ˌdɛfɪ'nɪʃən] N (*Ling, Phot, TV*) definizione *f*.

de·fini·tive [dɪ'fɪnɪtɪv] ADJ definitivo(-a).

de·flate [di:'fleɪt] VT a (*tyre*) sgonfiare; (*fig: person*) fare abbassare la cresta b (*Econ*) deflazionare.

de·fla·tion [di:'fleɪʃən] N (*Econ*) deflazione *f*.

de·fla·tion·ary [di:'fleɪʃənərɪ] ADJ (*Econ*) deflazionistico (-a).

de·flect [dɪ'flɛkt] VT (*ball, bullet, attention, criticism*) (far) deviare; (*person*): **to deflect sb (from)** distogliere (da).

de·flow·er [di:'flaʊəʳ] VT (*liter*) deflorare.

de·fog [di:'fɒg] VT (*Am Aut*) sbrinare.

de·fog·ger [di:'fɒgəʳ] N (*Am Aut*) sbrinatore *m*.

de·fo·li·ant [di:'fəʊlɪənt] N defogliante *m*.

de·fo·li·ate [di:'fəʊlɪeɪt] VT distruggere con il defogliante.

de·for·esta·tion [di:ˌfɒrɪs'teɪʃən] N deforestazione *f*.

de·form [dɪ'fɔ:m] VT deformare.

de·formed [dɪ'fɔ:md] ADJ (*person, limb, body*) deforme; (*structure*) deformato(-a).

de·form·ity [dɪ'fɔ:mɪtɪ] N (*of body*) deformità *f inv*.

de·fraud [dɪ'frɔ:d] VT: **to defraud (of)** defraudare (di).

de·fray [dɪ'freɪ] VT (*frm: expenses*) sostenere.

de·frost [di:'frɒst] VT (*refrigerator*) sbrinare; (*frozen food*) scongelare.

deft [dɛft] ADJ (*comp* **-er**, *superl* **-est**) abile, destro(-a).

deft·ly ['dɛftlɪ] ADV abilmente.

deft·ness ['dɛftnɪs] N abilità *f inv*, destrezza.

de·funct [dɪ'fʌŋkt] ADJ (*company*) scomparso(-a); (*scheme*) morto(-a) e sepolto(-a).

de·fuse [di:'fju:z] VT (*bomb*) disinnescare; **to defuse the situation** fare in modo che la situazione non degeneri.

defy [dɪ'faɪ] VT a (*person*) rifiutare di obbedire a; (*authority, death, danger*) sfidare; (*resist: efforts*) resistere a; **it defies description** supera ogni descrizione
b (*challenge*): **to defy sb (to do sth)** sfidare qn (a fare qc).

de·gen·era·cy [dɪ'dʒɛnərəsɪ] N degenerazione *f*.

de·gen·er·ate [*vb* dɪ'dʒɛnəˌreɪt; *adj, n* dɪ'dʒɛnərɪt] 1 VI: **to degenerate (into)** degenerare (in).
2 ADJ (*person*) degenere; (*morals, art*) degenerato(-a).
3 N degenerato(-a).

de·gen·era·tion [dɪˌdʒɛnə'reɪʃən] N degenerazione *f*.

de·gen·era·tive [dɪ'dʒɛnərɪtɪv] ADJ degenerativo(-a).

deg·ra·da·tion [ˌdɛgrə'deɪʃən] N degradazione *f*.

de·grade [dɪ'greɪd] VT degradare.

de·grad·ing [dɪ'greɪdɪŋ] ADJ degradante, umiliante.

de·gree [dɪ'gri:] N a (*gen, Math, Geog*) grado; **10 degrees below freezing** 10 gradi sotto zero
b (*amount*): **a high degree of uncertainty** un largo margine d'incertezza; **a considerable degree of risk** una grossa percentuale di rischio
c (*step in scale*): **by degrees** a poco a poco, gradualmente; **to some degree** OR **to a certain degree** in certa misura, fino a un certo punto
d (*Univ*) ≈ laurea; **first degree** ≈ laurea; **honorary degree** ≈ laurea ad honorem; **to get one's degree** ≈ prendere la laurea, laurearsi; **I'm doing a degree in languages** sono iscritto a lingue; **a (first) degree in maths** ≈ una laurea in matematica.

de·hu·man·ize [di:'hju:məˌnaɪz] VT disumanizzare.

de·hy·drate [ˌdi:'haɪdreɪt] VT disidratare; **dehydrating agent** disidratante *m*.

de·hy·dra·ted [di:haɪ'dreɪtɪd] ADJ (*person, vegetables*) disidratato(-a); (*milk, eggs*) in polvere.

de·hy·dra·tion [ˌdi:haɪ'dreɪʃən] N disidratazione *f*.

de-ice ['di:'aɪs] VT (*car windows*) sbrinare; (*roads*) liberare dal ghiaccio.

de-icer ['di:'aɪsəʳ] N (*thermal*) sbrinatore *m*; (*chemical*) scongelante *m*.

de-icing ['di:'aɪsɪŋ] N rimozione *f* del ghiaccio; **de-icing spray** (*Aut*) spray *m inv* sghiacciante.

dei·fy ['di:ɪfaɪ] VT (*frm*) divinizzare.

deign [deɪn] VT: **to deign to do sth** degnarsi di fare qc.

de·ity ['di:ɪtɪ] N divinità *f inv*, dio/dea; **the Deity** la Divinità, Dio.

déjà vu [ˌdeɪʒɑ:'vu:] N déjà vu *m inv*; **a feeling** *or* **sense of déjà vu** una sensazione di déjà vu.

de·ject·ed [dɪ'dʒɛktɪd] ADJ abbattuto(-a), avvilito(-a); **to become dejected** abbattersi.

de·ject·ed·ly [dɪ'dʒɛktɪdlɪ] ADV (*say, talk*) con tono abbattuto; (*move, act*) con aria abbattuta.

de·jec·tion [dɪ'dʒɛkʃən] N abbattimento, avvilimento.

dek·ko ['dɛkəʊ] N (*Brit: fam*): **to have a dekko at sth** dare un'occhiata a qc.

del. ABBR = **delete**.

de·lay [dɪ'leɪ] 1 N ritardo; **without delay** immediatamente; **without further delay** senza ulteriore indugio; **delays to traffic** rallentamenti *mpl* al traffico.

2 VT (*postpone*: *journey*) rimandare, rinviare; (: *payment*) differire; (*hold up*: *person*) trattenere; (: *traffic*) far rallentare; (: *action, event*) ritardare; **his train must have been delayed** il suo treno avrà fatto ritardo.

3 VI: **to delay (doing sth)** ritardare (a fare qc); **don't delay!** non perdere tempo!

de·layed-action [dɪleɪd'ækʃən] ADJ (*Phot*: *shutter*) ad azione ritardata; **delayed-action bomb** ordigno a scoppio ritardato.

de·lay·ing [dɪ'leɪɪŋ] ADJ: **delaying tactics** tattiche *fpl* per prendere tempo.

de·lec·table [dɪ'lɛktəbl] ADJ delizioso(-a).

de·lec·tably [dɪ'lɛktəblɪ] ADV deliziosamente.

de·lec·ta·tion [ˌdiːlɛk'teɪʃən] N (*frm*) diletto.

del·egate [*n* 'dɛlɪˌgɪt; *vb* 'dɛlɪgeɪt] 1 N: **delegate (to)** delegato(-a) (a).

2 VT (*duties, responsiblities, power*) delegare; **to delegate sth to sb** delegare qc a qn; **to delegate sb to do sth** delegare qn a fare qc.

del·ega·tion [ˌdɛlɪ'geɪʃən] N a (*of work, power*) delega b (*group*) delegazione *f*.

de·lete [dɪ'liːt] VT (*gen, Comput*) cancellare; **to delete (from)** (*item*: *from list, catalogue*) togliere (da); (*mistake, line*) cancellare (da).

del·eteri·ous [ˌdɛlɪ'tɪərɪəs] ADJ (*frm*): **deleterious (to)** deleterio(-a) (per).

de·letion [dɪ'liːʃən] N soppressione *f*, eliminazione *f*.

Del·hi ['dɛlɪ] N Delhi *f*.

deli ['dɛlɪ] N ABBR (*fam*) = **delicatessen**.

de·lib·er·ate [*adj* dɪ'lɪbərɪt; *vb* dɪ'lɪbəˌreɪt] 1 ADJ a (*intentional*: *insult, action*) intenzionale, voluto(-a); (: *mistake*) voluto(-a); (: *lie*) calcolato(-a)

b (*cautious, thoughtful*) ponderato(-a); (*unhurried*: *manner, voice*) posato(-a); (*pace*) misurato(-a).

2 VT (*think about*) considerare, riflettere su; (*discuss*) discutere.

3 VI: **to deliberate (on)** deliberare (su).

de·lib·er·ate·ly [dɪ'lɪbərɪtlɪ] ADV (*intentionally*) deliberatamente, volutamente; (*cautiously, slowly*) posatamente.

de·lib·era·tion [dɪˌlɪbə'reɪʃən] N a (*consideration*) riflessione *f*; (*discussion*) discussione *f*, deliberazione *f*; **after due deliberation** dopo matura riflessione b (*slowness*) ponderatezza, posatezza.

de·lib·era·tive [dɪ'lɪbərətɪv] ADJ (*assembly*) con potere deliberante.

deli·ca·cy ['dɛlɪkəsɪ] N a (*of person, thing*) delicatezza; (*of workmanship*) finezza b (*special food*) specialità *f inv*, ghiottoneria.

deli·cate ['dɛlɪkɪt] ADJ (*gen*) delicato(-a); (*workmanship, design*) fine.

deli·cate·ly ['dɛlɪkɪtlɪ] ADV (*gen*) delicatamente; (*act, express*) con delicatezza.

deli·ca·tes·sen [ˌdɛlɪkə'tɛsn] N ≈ salumeria.

de·li·cious [dɪ'lɪʃəs] ADJ delizioso(-a), squisito(-a).

de·light [dɪ'laɪt] 1 N (*feeling of joy*) piacere *m*, gioia; (*pleasurable thing*) delizia, (gran) piacere *m*; **the delights of good food** i piaceri della buona tavola; **to my delight** con mia grande gioia; **it is a delight to the eye** è un piacere guardarlo; **to take delight in sth/in doing sth** dilettarsi di qc/nel fare qc; **to be the delight of** essere la gioia di.

2 VT riempire di gioia

▶ **delight in** VI + PREP: **to delight in sth/in doing sth** dilettarsi di qc/nel fare qc.

de·light·ed [dɪ'laɪtɪd] ADJ: **delighted (with sb/sth)** conten-

tissimo(-a) (di qn/qc), felice (di qn/qc); **delighted at sth** contentissimo(-a) di qc, felice di qc; **to be delighted to do sth/that** essere felice di fare qc/che + *sub*; **I'd be delighted** con grande piacere.

de·light·ful [dɪ'laɪtfʊl] ADJ (*person, place, meal*) delizioso (-a); (*manner, smile*) incantevole.

de·light·ful·ly [dɪ'laɪtfəlɪ] ADV deliziosamente; **the hotel is delightfully situated** l'albergo è situato in una posizione incantevole.

de·lim·it [diː'lɪmɪt] VT (*frm*) delimitare.

de·lin·eate [dɪ'lɪnɪˌeɪt] VT (*frm*) delineare.

de·lin·ea·tion [dɪˌlɪnɪ'eɪʃən] N (*frm*) delineamento.

de·lin·quen·cy [dɪ'lɪŋkwənsɪ] N delinquenza.

de·lin·quent [dɪ'lɪŋkwənt] 1 ADJ (*behaviour*) delinquenziale, da delinquente; **a delinquent youth** un giovane delinquente.

2 N delinquente *m/f*.

de·liri·ous [dɪ'lɪrɪəs] ADJ (*Med, fig*) delirante, in delirio; **to be delirious** delirare; (*fig*) farneticare; **delirious with joy** pazzo(-a) di gioia.

de·liri·ous·ly [dɪ'lɪrɪəslɪ] ADV: **deliriously happy** fuori di sé dalla gioia.

de·lir·ium [dɪ'lɪrɪəm] N (*Med*) delirio; **delirium tremens** delirium *m inv* tremens *inv*.

de·liv·er [dɪ'lɪvə˞] VT a (*goods*) consegnare; (*letter, parcel*) recapitare, consegnare; **he delivered me home safely** mi ha portato a casa sano e salvo; **to deliver a message** dare un messaggio; **he delivered the goods** (*fig fam*) ha fatto quel che doveva fare

b (*speech, sermon, verdict*) pronunciare; (*lecture*) tenere, fare; (*ultimatum*) dare; (*blow, punch*) tirare

c (*subj*: *doctor, midwife*: *baby*) far nascere

d (*old*: *rescue*): **to deliver (from)** liberare (da).

de·liv·er·ance [dɪ'lɪvərəns] N (*old*) liberazione *f*.

de·liv·er·er [dɪ'lɪvərə˞] N (*old*) salvatore(-trice).

de·liv·ery [dɪ'lɪvərɪ] N a (*of goods, parcels*) consegna; (*of mail*) recapito; **there is no delivery on Sundays** (*Post*) non c'è posta la domenica; **to take delivery of** prendere in consegna b (*of speaker*) dizione *f* c (*Med*) parto.

♦ **delivery boy** N fattorino.

♦ **delivery note** N bolla di consegna.

♦ **delivery room** N (*Med*) sala *f* parto *inv*.

♦ **delivery van**, (*Am*) **delivery truck** N furgoncino (per le consegne).

dell [dɛl] N (*liter*) valletta.

de·louse [diː'laʊs] VT spidocchiare.

del·ta ['dɛltə] N delta *m inv*.

♦ **delta wing** N ala a delta.

de·lude [dɪ'luːd] VT illudere, ingannare; **to delude sb into thinking that** ... portare qn a credere che...; **to delude o.s** illudersi, farsi (delle) illusioni.

de·lud·ed [dɪ'luːdɪd] ADJ illuso(-a).

del·uge ['dɛljuːdʒ] 1 N diluvio; **a deluge of protests** un diluvio di proteste.

2 VT (*fig*): **to deluge (with)** subissare (di), inondare (di).

de·lu·sion [dɪ'luːʒən] N illusione *f*; (*Psych*) fissazione *f*.

de luxe [dɪ'lʌks] ADJ di lusso.

delve [dɛlv] VI: **to delve into** (*pocket, bag*) frugare in; (*subject*) far ricerche in.

Dem. (*Am Pol*) 1 N ABBR = **democrat**.

2 N, ADJ = **democratic**.

dema·gogue ['dɛməgɒg] N (*pej*) demagogo.

de·mand [dɪ'mɑːnd] 1 N a (*request*): **demand (for)** (*help, money*) richiesta (di); (*better pay*) richiesta (di), rivendicazione *f* (di); **by popular demand** a richiesta generale;

on demand a richiesta; **I have many demands on my time** sono impegnatissimo **b** (*Comm*): **demand (for)** domanda (di); **to be in demand** essere richiesto(-a).

2 VT (*ask for*): **to demand sth (from** *or* **of sb)** pretendere qc (da qn), esigere qc (da qn); (*need*) richiedere; **to demand that** richiedere che + *sub*; **I demand to see the manager** esigo di vedere il direttore.

♦ **demand draft** N (*Comm*) tratta a vista.

de·mand·ing [dɪˈmɑːndɪŋ] ADJ (*person*) esigente; (*work*: *physically*) stancante; (: *mentally*) impegnativo(-a).

de·mar·ca·tion [ˌdiːmɑːˈkeɪʃən] N (*frm*) demarcazione *f*; **demarcation dispute** controversia settoriale *or* di categoria; **demarcation line** linea di demarcazione.

de·ma·teri·al·ize [dɪməˈtɪərɪəˌlaɪz] VI smaterializzarsi.

de·mean [dɪˈmiːn] VT svilire; **to demean o.s** abbassarsi.

de·mean·ing [dɪˈmiːnɪŋ] ADJ degradante.

de·mean·our, (*Am*) **de·mean·or** [dɪˈmiːnəʳ] N (*frm*) contegno.

de·ment·ed [dɪˈmɛntɪd] ADJ folle, demente.

de·ment·ed·ly [dɪˈmɛntɪdlɪ] ADV come un(a) folle.

de·men·tia [dɪˈmɛnʃɪə] N (*Med*) demenza.

dem·erara [ˌdɛməˈrɛərə] N (*also*: **demerara sugar**) zucchero grezzo di canna.

de·mer·it [diːˈmɛrɪt] N (*frm*) difetto.

demi... [ˈdɛmɪ] PREF semi... .

demi·god [ˈdɛmɪˌɡɒd] N semidio.

demi·john [ˈdɛmɪˌdʒɒn] N damigiana.

de·mili·ta·ri·za·tion [ˈdiːˌmɪlɪtəraɪˈzeɪʃən] N smilitarizzazione *f*.

de·mili·ta·rize [ˈdiːˈmɪlɪtəˌraɪz] VT smilitarizzare.

de·mili·ta·rized zone [diːˈmɪlɪtəˌraɪzdˈzəʊn] N zona smilitarizzata.

de·mise [dɪˈmaɪz] N (*frm*) decesso.

de·mist [diːˈmɪst] VT (*Brit Aut*) sbrinare.

de·mist·er [diːˈmɪstəʳ] N (*Brit Aut*) sbrinatore *m*.

demo [ˈdɛməʊ] N ABBR (*Brit fam*: *demonstration*) manifestazione *f*.

de·mo·bi·li·za·tion [ˈdiːˌməʊbɪlaɪˈzeɪʃən] N smobilitazione *f*.

de·mo·bi·lize [diːˈməʊbɪlaɪz] VT smobilitare.

de·moc·ra·cy [dɪˈmɒkrəsɪ] N democrazia.

demo·crat [ˈdɛməˌkræt] N democratico(-a).

demo·crat·ic [ˌdɛməˈkrætɪk] ADJ democratico(-a).

demo·crati·cal·ly [ˌdɛməˈkrætɪkəlɪ] ADV democraticamente.

♦ **Democratic Party** N (*Am*): **the Democratic Party** il partito democratico.

de·moc·ra·tize [dɪˈmɒkrəˌtaɪz] VT democratizzare.

de·mog·ra·pher [dɪˈmɒɡrəfəʳ] N demografo(-a).

de·mo·graph·ic [ˌdɛməˈɡræfɪk] ADJ demografico(-a).

de·mog·ra·phy [dɪˈmɒɡrəfɪ] N demografia.

de·mol·ish [dɪˈmɒlɪʃ] VT (*gen*) demolire; (*hum*: *cake, food*) far fuori.

demo·li·tion [ˌdɛməˈlɪʃən] N demolizione *f*; **demolition squad** squadra di demolizione; **demolition zone** area *or* zona di demolizione.

de·mon [ˈdiːmən] **1** N (*also fig*) demonio; **he's a demon for work** (*fam*) è uno stacanovista.

2 ADJ: **a demon squash player** un mago dello squash; **a demon driver** un asso del volante.

de·mo·ni·ac [dɪˈməʊnɪæk], **de·mo·nia·cal** [ˌdiːməʊˈnaɪəkəl] ADJ demoniaco(-a), diabolico(-a).

de·mon·strable [ˈdɛmənstrəbl] ADJ dimostrabile.

de·mon·strably [ˈdɛmənstrəblɪ] ADV palesemente.

dem·on·strate [ˈdɛmənˌstreɪt] **1** VT **a** (*truth, ability*) dimostrare; (*emotion*) manifestare **b** (*appliance*) fare una dimostrazione di.

2 VI (*Pol*): **to demonstrate (for/against)** manifestare (per/contro).

dem·on·stra·tion [ˌdɛmənˈstreɪʃən] N dimostrazione *f*; (*Pol*) manifestazione *f*; **to hold a demonstration** (*Pol*) tenere una manifestazione.

de·mon·stra·tive [dɪˈmɒnstrətɪv] ADJ (*person*) espansivo (-a); (*Gram*) dimostrativo(-a).

de·mon·stra·tor [ˈdɛmənˌstreɪtəʳ] N (*Pol*) dimostrante *m/f*; (*Comm*: *sales person*) dimostratore(-trice); (: *Am*: *car, computer*) modello per dimostrazione.

de·mor·ali·za·tion [dɪˌmɒrəlaɪˈzeɪʃən] N demoralizzazione *f*.

de·mor·al·ize [dɪˈmɒrəˌlaɪz] VT demoralizzare.

de·mor·al·ized [dɪˈmɒrəˌlaɪzd] ADJ demoralizzato(-a).

de·mor·al·iz·ing [dɪˈmɒrəˌlaɪzɪŋ] ADJ demoralizzante.

de·mote [dɪˈməʊt] VT degradare.

de·mo·tion [dɪˈməʊʃən] N degradazione *f*.

de·mur [dɪˈmɜː] **1** VI (*frm*): **to demur (at)** sollevare obiezioni (a *or* su).

2 N: **without demur** senza obiezioni.

de·mure [dɪˈmjʊəʳ] ADJ (*girl*) pieno(-a) di contegno; (*smile*) contegnoso(-a).

de·mure·ly [dɪˈmjʊəlɪ] ADV contegnosamente.

de·mure·ness [dɪˈmjʊənɪs] N contegno.

de·mur·rage [dɪˈmʌrɪdʒ] N (*Comm*) controstallia.

de·mys·ti·fy [diːˈmɪstɪˌfaɪ] VT demistificare.

den [dɛn] N (*of wild animal*) tana, covo; (*room*) stanzetta; **he's up in his den reading** è su in camera sua a leggere; **a den of iniquity** un luogo di perdizione; **a den of thieves** un covo di ladri.

de·na·tion·ali·za·tion [diːˌnæʃnəlaɪˈzeɪʃən] N snazionalizzazione *f*, denazionalizzazione *f*.

de·na·tion·al·ize [diːˈnæʃnəˌlaɪz] VT snazionalizzare, denazionalizzare.

de·ni·able [dɪˈnaɪəbəl] ADJ negabile.

de·ni·al [dɪˈnaɪəl] N **a** (*of accusation, guilt*) diniego, rifiuto; **the government issued an official denial** il governo ha rilasciato una smentita ufficiale **b** (*refusal: of request*) rifiuto; (: *of rights*) mancato riconoscimento.

den·ier [ˈdɛnɪəʳ] N denaro (*di filati, calze*).

deni·grate [ˈdɛnɪˌɡreɪt] VT denigrare.

deni·gra·tory [ˈdɛnɪˌɡreɪtərɪ] ADJ denigratorio(-a).

den·im [ˈdɛnɪm] **1** N tessuto jeans; **denims** NPL (*clothes*) blue jeans *mpl*.

2 ADJ (*jacket, skirt*) di jeans.

deni·zen [ˈdɛnɪzn] N (*liter*: *inhabitant*) abitante *m/f*.

Den·mark [ˈdɛnmɑːk] N Danimarca.

de·nomi·na·tion [dɪˌnɒmɪˈneɪʃən] N (*Rel*) confessione *f*; (*of coin*) valore *m*.

de·nomi·na·tor [dɪˈnɒmɪˌneɪtəʳ] N (*Math*) denominatore *m*.

de·note [dɪˈnəʊt] VT (*indicate*) denotare, indicare; (*subj*: *word*) significare.

de·noue·ment, dénouement [deɪˈnuːmɒn] N epilogo.

de·nounce [dɪˈnaʊns] VT (*accuse publicly*) accusare; (*to police*) denunciare; **to denounce sb as a liar** accusare pubblicamente qn di essere un bugiardo.

dense [dɛns] ADJ (*comp* **-r**, *superl* **-st**) (*fog*) denso(-a), fitto(-a); (*forest, crowd*) fitto(-a); (*fur*) folto(-a); (*fam*: *person, stupid*) tonto(-a), ottuso(-a).

dense·ly [ˈdɛnslɪ] ADV: **densely populated** densamente popolato(-a); **densely wooded** coperto(-a) di fitti

boschi.

den·sity ['dɛnsɪtɪ] N densità *f inv*; **single-/double-density disk** (*Comput*) disco a singola/doppia densità.

dent [dɛnt] **1** N (*in metal*) ammaccatura, bozzo; (*in wood*) tacca, intaccatura; **to make a dent in** (*fig*) intaccare; **the holiday left a dent in our savings** la vacanza ha intaccato i nostri risparmi.

2 VT (*car, hat*) ammaccare; (*fig*) intaccare.

den·tal ['dɛntl] ADJ (*surgery, care*) dentistico(-a), odontoiatrico(-a); (*appointment*) dal dentista; **dental orthopaedics** ortodonzia; **dental technician** odontotecnico.

♦ **dental floss** N filo interdentale.

♦ **dental surgeon** N medico dentista *m/f*, odontoiatra *m/f*.

den·ti·frice ['dɛntɪfrɪs] N dentifricio.

den·tist ['dɛntɪst] N dentista *m/f*; **dentist's chair** poltrona del dentista; **dentist's surgery** (*Brit*) studio dentistico.

den·tis·try ['dɛntɪstrɪ] N odontoiatria.

den·ti·tion [dɛn'tɪʃən] N (*teeth*) dentatura; (*teething*) dentizione *f*.

den·tures ['dɛntʃəz] NPL (*false teeth*) dentiera.

de·nude [dɪ'njuːd] VT (*frm*): **to denude (of)** spogliare (di), denudare (di).

de·nun·cia·tion [dɪ,nʌnsɪ'eɪʃən] N denuncia; (*in public*) pubblica accusa.

deny [dɪ'naɪ] VT **a** (*possibility, truth of statement, charge*) negare; (*report*) smentire; **there's no denying it** è innegabile; **he denies having said it** nega di averlo detto **b** (*refuse*): **to deny sb sth** negare qc a qn, rifiutare qc a qn; **to deny o.s. sth** negarsi qc, privarsi di qc.

de·odor·ant [diː'əʊdərənt] N deodorante *m*.

de·odor·ize [diː'əʊdə,raɪz] VT deodorare.

de·part [dɪ'pɑːt] VI: **to depart (from)** (*train*) partire (da); (*person*) andar via (da), allontanarsi (da); **to depart from tradition/the truth** scostarsi dalla tradizione/dalla verità.

de·part·ed [dɪ'pɑːtɪd] **1** ADJ (*bygone: glory*) trascorso(-a), passato(-a); (*dead*) scomparso(-a).

2 N: **the dear departed** il/la caro(-a) estinto(-a).

de·part·ment [dɪ'pɑːtmənt] N (*Admin*) sezione *f*, reparto; (*in shop*) reparto; (*in government*) ministero; (*Univ*) istituto, dipartimento; **the English Department** (*Scol*) i professori d'inglese; **that's not my department** (*fig*) questo non è di mia competenza; **Department of Employment** (*Brit*) Ministero del Lavoro; **Department of State** (*Am*) Dipartimento di Stato; **Department of Trade and Industry** (*Brit*) Ministero del Commercio e dell'Industria.

de·part·men·tal [,diːpɑːt'mɛntl] ADJ (*meeting*) di sezione; **departmental manager** caporeparto *m/f*.

♦ **department store** N grande magazzino.

de·par·ture [dɪ'pɑːtʃəʳ] N (*gen*) partenza; (*fig: from custom, principle*) departure from deviazione *f* da, abbandono di; **a new departure** (*fig*) una svolta (decisiva); **departure board** (*Aer*) tabellone *m* (delle partenze); **departure lounge** (*Aer*) sala d'attesa.

de·pend [dɪ'pɛnd] VI **a** : **to depend (up)on** (*rely*) contare su, dipendere da; (*be dependent on*) dipendere (economicamente) da, essere a carico di; **you can depend on it** sta pur certo

b : **to depend (on)** (*be influenced by*) dipendere (da); **it (all) depends on the weather** (tutto) dipende dal tempo; **it (all) depends what you mean** dipende da che cosa vuoi dire; **that depends** OR **it depends** dipende; **depending on the result ...** a seconda del risultato... .

de·pend·abil·ity [dɪ,pɛndə'bɪlɪtɪ] N affidabilità.

de·pend·able [dɪ'pɛndəbl] ADJ (*person*) fidato(-a), serio (-a); (*machine, car*) affidabile.

de·pend·ant [dɪ'pɛndənt] N persona a carico.

de·pend·ence [dɪ'pɛndəns] N: **dependence (on)** dipendenza (da).

de·pend·en·cy [dɪ'pɛndənsɪ] N (*country*) possedimento.

de·pend·ent [dɪ'pɛndənt] **1** ADJ: **to be dependent (on)** (*gen*) dipendere (da); (*child, relative*) essere a carico (di).

2 N = **dependant**.

de·per·son·ali·za·tion [dɪ,pɜːsnəlaɪ'zeɪʃən] N (*frm*) spersonalizzazione *f*.

de·per·son·al·ize [diː'pɜːsənə,laɪz] VT (*frm*) spersonalizzare.

de·pict [dɪ'pɪkt] VT (*in picture*) rappresentare; (*in words*) descrivere, dipingere.

de·pic·tion [dɪ'pɪkʃən] N (*in picture*) rappresentazione *f*; (*in words*) descrizione *f*.

de·pila·tory [dɪ'pɪlətərɪ] N (*also:* **depilatory cream**) crema depilatoria.

de·plete [dɪ'pliːt] VT ridurre.

de·plet·ed [dɪ'pliːtɪd] ADJ diminuito(-a).

de·ple·tion [dɪ'pliːʃən] N riduzione *f*, impoverimento.

de·plor·able [dɪ'plɔːrəbl] ADJ (*frm*) deplorevole, lamentevole.

de·plor·ably [dɪ'plɔːrəblɪ] ADV (*frm*) deplorevolmente.

de·plore [dɪ'plɔːʳ] VT (*frm*) deplorare.

de·ploy [dɪ'plɔɪ] VT (*Mil: soldiers, forces*) schierare, spiegare; (*fig: resources*) impiegare, far uso di.

de·ploy·ment [dɪ'plɔɪmənt] N (*Mil*) schieramento, spiegamento; (*fig*) impiego.

de·popu·late [,diː'pɒpjʊleɪt] VT spopolare.

de·popu·la·tion [,diː:ˌpɒpjʊ'leɪʃən] N spopolamento.

de·port [dɪ'pɔːt] VT deportare.

de·por·ta·tion [,diːpɔː'teɪʃən] N deportazione *f*; **deportation order** ≈ foglio di via obbligatorio.

de·por·tee [diːpɔː'tiː] N deportato(-a).

de·port·ment [dɪ'pɔːtmənt] N (*old: bearing*) portamento; (: *behaviour*) comportamento.

de·pose [dɪ'pəʊz] VT (*monarch, leader*) deporre.

de·pos·it [dɪ'pɒzɪt] **1** N **a** (*in bank*) deposito; (*Comm: part payment*) acconto; (: *returnable security*) cauzione *f*; **to put down a deposit of £50** versare un acconto di 50 sterline

b (*Chem, Geol*) deposito, sedimento; (*of ore, oil*) giacimento.

2 VT **a** (*put down*) posare; (*leave: luggage*) mettere *or* lasciare in deposito, depositare

b (*money: in bank*) depositare.

♦ **deposit account** N ≈ libretto di risparmio.

de·posi·tary [dɪ'pɒzɪtərɪ] N = **depository b**.

depo·si·tion [,diːpə'zɪʃən] N (*Geol, Law, also of monarch*) deposizione *f*.

de·posi·tor [dɪ'pɒzɪtəʳ] N depositante *m/f*.

de·posi·tory [dɪ'pɒzɪtərɪ] N **a** (*place*) deposito **b** (*person*) depositario(-a).

de·pot ['dɛpəʊ, *Am* 'diːpəʊ] N **a** (*storehouse*) magazzino, deposito *m* merci *inv*; (*Brit: bus garage*) deposito; (*Am: railway station*) stazione *f* ferroviaria; (: *bus station*) stazione *f* degli autobus.

de·praved [dɪ'preɪvd] ADJ (*frm*) depravato(-a).

de·prav·ity [dɪ'prævɪtɪ] N (*frm*) depravazione *f*.

dep·re·cate ['dɛprɪˌkeɪt] VT (*frm*) deprecare.

dep·re·cat·ing ['dɛprɪˌkeɪtɪŋ], **dep·re·ca·tory** ['dɛprɪkətərɪ] ADJ (*disapproving*) di biasimo, di disapprova-

zione; (*apologetic*): **a deprecating smile** un sorriso di
scusa.

dep·re·cat·ing·ly ['dɛprɪkeɪtɪŋlɪ] ADV (*disapprovingly*) con
(aria di) disapprovazione; (*apologetically*) con aria di
scusa.

de·pre·ci·ate [dɪ'priːʃɪeɪt] ☐1 VI deprezzarsi, svalutarsi.
☐2 VT deprezzare, svalutare.

de·pre·cia·tion [dɪˌpriːʃɪ'eɪʃən] N deprezzamento, svalutazione *f*.

dep·re·da·tions [ˌdɛprɪ'deɪʃəns] NPL (*old*) saccheggi *mpl*.

de·press [dɪ'prɛs] VT **a** (*person*) deprimere; (*spirits*) buttar
giù **b** (*trade*) ridurre; (*prices*) far scendere, abbassare **c**
(*frm: press down: lever*) abbassare.

de·pres·sant [dɪ'prɛsnt] N (*Med*) sedativo.

de·pressed [dɪ'prɛst] ADJ **a** (*person*) depresso(-a); **to feel
depressed** sentirsi depresso(-a); **to get depressed**
deprimersi **b** (*area*) depresso(-a); (*industry*) in crisi;
(*Fin: market, trade*) stagnante, in ribasso.

de·press·ing [dɪ'prɛsɪŋ] ADJ deprimente, demoralizzante.

de·press·ing·ly [dɪ'prɛsɪŋlɪ] ADV in modo deprimente.

de·pres·sion [dɪ'prɛʃən] N (*gen, Med, Econ, Met*) depressione *f*; **the economy is in a state of depression** è in atto
una crisi economica; **the Depression** la Grande depressione.

de·pres·sive [dɪ'prɛsɪv] ☐1 ADJ depressivo(-a).
☐2 N (*Psych*) depresso(-a).

dep·ri·va·tion [ˌdɛprɪ'veɪʃən] N (*act*) privazione *f*; (*state*)
indigenza.

de·prive [dɪ'praɪv] VT: **to deprive sb of sth** privare qn di qc;
to deprive o.s. of sth privarsi di qc.

de·prived [dɪ'praɪvd] ADJ bisognoso(-a).

dept. ABBR = **department**.

depth [dɛpθ] N (*gen, of knowledge, thought*) profondità *f inv*;
(*of snow*) altezza, spessore *m*; (*of shelf*) profondità,
larghezza; (*of colour, feeling*) intensità *f inv*; **at a depth of
3 metres** a 3 metri di profondità, a una profondità di 3
metri; **the depths of the sea** gli abissi del mare; **to be out
of one's depth** (*swimmer*) non toccare; (*fig*) non sentirsi
all'altezza della situazione; **in the depths of the forest**
nel cuore della foresta; **in the depths of winter** in pieno
inverno, nel cuore dell'inverno; **in the depths of despair**
in preda alla disperazione; **to study sth in depth**
studiare qc in profondità.

♦ **depth charge** N (*Mil*) bomba di profondità.

♦ **depth gauge** N profondimetro.

depu·ta·tion [ˌdɛpjʊ'teɪʃən] N deputazione *f*, delegazione
f.

de·pute [dɪ'pjuːt] VT (*frm*): **to depute sth to sb** delegare qc a
qn; **to depute sb to do sth** deputare *or* delegare qn a fare
qc.

depu·tize ['dɛpjʊˌtaɪz] VI: **to deputize (for sb)** fare le veci
(di qn), sostituire (qn).

depu·ty ['dɛpjʊtɪ] ☐1 N (*second-in-command*) vice *m/f*;
(*replacement*) sostituto(-a), supplente *m/f*.
☐2 ADJ: **deputy chairman** vicepresidente *m*; **deputy head**
(*Scol*) vicepreside *m/f*; **deputy leader** (*Brit Pol*) sottosegretario; **deputy secretary** vicesegretario.

de·rail [dɪ'reɪl] VT far deragliare; **to be derailed** deragliare.

de·rail·leur [də'reɪljəʳ] N, **de·rail·leur gears** NPL (*Cycling*)
deragliatore *m*.

de·rail·ment [dɪ'reɪlmənt] N deragliamento.

de·ranged [dɪ'reɪndʒd] ADJ (*mind*) sconvolto(-a); (*person*)
squilibrato(-a); **to be (mentally) deranged** essere
uno(-a) squilibrato(-a).

der·by ['dɑːbɪ] N **a** (*sporting event*) derby *m inv* **b** (*Am: hat*)

bombetta.

Derbys ABBR (*Brit*)= *Derbyshire*.

de·regu·late [dɪ'rɛgjʊˌleɪt] VT deregolamentare.

de·regu·la·tion [dɪˌrɛgjʊ'leɪʃən] N deregolamentazione *f*.

der·elict ['dɛrɪlɪkt] ☐1 ADJ (*ruined*) cadente, fatiscente;
(*abandoned*) abbandonato(-a).
☐2 N (*frm: person*) derelitto(-a).

der·elic·tion [dɛrɪ'lɪkʃən] N: **dereliction of duty** (*frm*)
negligenza del dovere.

de·ride [dɪ'raɪd] VT deridere.

de rigueur [də rigœr] ADJ di rigore.

de·ri·sion [dɪ'rɪʒən] N derisione *f*.

de·ri·sive [dɪ'raɪsɪv] ADJ (*laughter*) di scherno, di derisione;
(*smile*) beffardo(-a).

de·ri·sive·ly [dɪ'raɪsɪvlɪ] ADV (*smile, laugh, gesture*) beffardamente.

de·ri·sory [dɪ'raɪsərɪ] ADJ **a** (*amount*) irrisorio(-a) **b** =
derisive.

deri·va·tion [ˌdɛrɪ'veɪʃən] N derivazione *f*.

de·riva·tive [dɪ'rɪvətɪv] ☐1 ADJ (*pej: literary work, style*) poco
originale.
☐2 N (*Chem, Ling*) derivato; (*Math*) derivata.

de·rive [dɪ'raɪv] ☐1 VT: **to derive (from)** (*profit, comfort,
pleasure*) ricavare (da), trarre (da); (*name*) derivare (da);
(*origins*) trarre (da).
☐2 VI: **to derive from** (*subj: word, language*) derivare da; (:
power, fortune) provenire da.

der·ma·ti·tis [ˌdɜːmə'taɪtɪs] N dermatite *f*.

der·ma·tolo·gist [ˌdɜːmə'tɒlədʒɪst] N dermatologo(-a).

der·ma·tol·ogy [ˌdɜːmə'tɒlədʒɪ] N dermatologia.

de·roga·tory [dɪ'rɒgətərɪ] ADJ (*remark*) denigratorio(-a);
(*term*) spregiativo(-a).

der·rick ['dɛrɪk] N (*in port*) albero di carico, gru *f inv*; (*over
oil well*) derrick *m inv*.

derv [dɜːv] N (*Brit*) gasolio.

der·vish ['dɜːvɪʃ] N (*Rel*) derviscio.

DES [ˌdiːiː'es] N ABBR (*Brit*: = *Department of Education and
Science*) ≈ ministero della Pubblica Istruzione.

de·sali·nate [diː'sælɪˌneɪt] VT dissalare.

de·sali·na·tion [diːˌsælɪ'neɪʃən] N desalinizzazione *f*,
dissalazione *f*.

des·cale [diː'skeɪl] VT disincrostare.

des·cant ['dɛskænt] N (*Mus*) discanto.

de·scend [dɪ'sɛnd] ☐1 VT **a** (*frm: stairs*) scendere
b : **to be descended from sb** (*Genealogy*) discendere da
qn.
☐2 VI **a** (*go down*): **to descend (from)** (di)scendere (da);
(*road*) scendere (da); **in descending order of importance**
in ordine decrescente d'importanza
b (*property, customs*): **to descend from ...to** passare da...
a; **to descend from generation to generation** traman-
darsi di generazione in generazione

▶ **descend on, descend upon** VI + PREP (*subj: enemy, large
group, angry person*) assalire, piombare su; (*liter: gloom,
silence*) scendere su; **visitors descended on us** ci sono
capitati ospiti inaspettati

▶ **descend to** VI + PREP (*lower o.s. to*): **to descend to sth**
abbassarsi a qc; **to descend to doing sth** abbassarsi a
fare qc.

de·scend·ant [dɪ'sɛndənt] N discendente *m/f*.

de·scent [dɪ'sɛnt] N (*going down*) discesa; (*ancestry*):
descent (from) discendenza (da), origine *f* (da).

de·scribe [dɪs'kraɪb] VT descrivere; **describe him for us**
descrivicelo; **she describes herself as a teacher** dice di
essere insegnante.

de·scrip·tion [dɪs'krɪpʃən] N **a** (*of person, scene, object*) descrizione *f*; (*of event*) racconto; (*of suspect*) connotati *mpl*, descrizione; **beyond description** oltre ogni dire **b** (*sort*) genere *m*, specie *f*; **he carried a gun of some description** aveva una pistola di qualche tipo; **of every description** di ogni genere e specie.

de·scrip·tive [dɪs'krɪptɪv] ADJ descrittivo(-a).

des·ecrate ['dɛsɪˌkreɪt] VT profanare.

des·ecra·tion [ˌdɛsɪ'kreɪʃən] N profanazione *f*.

de·seg·re·gate [di:'sɛgrɪˌgeɪt] VT abolire la segregazione in; **desegregated schools** scuole in cui non vige la segregazione razziale.

de·seg·re·ga·tion ['di:ˌsɛgrɪ'geɪʃən] N abolizione *f* della segregazione razziale.

de·sen·si·tize [di:'sɛnsɪˌtaɪz] VT desensibilizzare.

des·ert[1] ['dɛzət] [1] N deserto.

[2] ADJ (*climate, region*) desertico(-a).

de·sert[2] [dɪ'zɜ:t] [1] VT abbandonare, lasciare; **his courage deserted him** il coraggio l'ha abbandonato.

[2] VI (*Mil*): **to desert (from)** disertare (da); **to desert (to)** passare (a).

♦ **desert boot** [ˌdɛzət'bu:t] N scarponcino.

de·sert·ed [dɪ'zɜ:tɪd] ADJ (*streets*) deserto(-a); (*wife*) abbandonato(-a).

de·sert·er [dɪ'zɜ:tə^r] N (*Mil*) disertore *m*.

des·er·ti·fi·ca·tion [dɪˌzɜ:tɪfɪ'keɪʃən] N desertificazione *f*.

de·ser·tion [dɪ'zɜ:ʃən] N (*Mil*) diserzione *f*; (*of spouse*) abbandono del tetto coniugale.

♦ **desert island** [ˌdɛzət'aɪlənd] N isola deserta.

de·serts [dɪ'zɜ:ts] NPL: **to get one's just deserts** avere ciò che ci si merita.

de·serve [dɪ'zɜ:v] VT meritare; **he deserves to win** merita di vincere; **he got what he deserved** ha avuto quel che si meritava.

de·serv·ed·ly [dɪ'zɜ:vɪdlɪ] ADV meritatamente, giustamente.

de·serv·ing [dɪ'zɜ:vɪŋ] ADJ (*person, case, cause*) che merita aiuto; (*praiseworthy*) meritevole; **deserving of** degno(-a) di; **an idea deserving of consideration** un'idea degna di considerazione; **a crime deserving of severe punishment** un delitto che merita una severa punizione.

des·ic·ca·ted ['dɛsɪˌkeɪtɪd] ADJ essiccato(-a); **desiccated coconut** noce *f* di cocco essiccata.

de·sign [dɪ'zaɪn] [1] N **a** (*plan, drawing: of building*) progetto, disegno; (: *of dress, car*) modello; (: *of machine*) progettazione *f*; (*style*) linea, design *m inv*; (*pattern*) disegno, fantasia, motivo; (*art of design*) design *m*; **industrial design** disegno industriale; **dress with a floral design** vestito a fiori

b (*intention*) intenzione *f*; **by design** intenzionalmente, di proposito; **to have designs on sb/sth** avere delle mire su qn/qc.

[2] VT **a** (*building etc*) disegnare; (*Industry*) progettare; (*perfect crime, scheme*) concepire, elaborare

b (*intend*): **to be designed for sb/sth** essere fatto(-a) espressamente per qn/qc; **a well designed house** una casa progettata bene.

des·ig·nate [*vb* 'dɛzɪgˌneɪt, *adj* 'dɛzɪgnɪt] [1] VT: **to designate sb/sth (as)** designare qn/qc (come); **to designate sb to do sth** designare qn a fare qc.

[2] ADJ (*after n*) designato(-a).

des·ig·na·tion [ˌdɛzɪg'neɪʃən] N (*title*) titolo, designazione *f*.

de·sign·er [dɪ'zaɪnə^r] N (*fashion designer*) stilista *m/f*, disegnatore(-trice) di moda; (*of machines etc*)

disegnatore(-trice), progettista *m/f*; (*of furniture*) designer *m/f inv*; (*of theatre sets*) scenografo(-a).

de·sign·ing [dɪ'zaɪnɪŋ] ADJ (*scheming*) astuto(-a), intrigante.

de·sir·abil·ity [dɪˌzaɪərə'bɪlɪtɪ] N (*allure*) desiderabilità; (*value*) vantaggio.

de·sir·able [dɪ'zaɪərəbl] ADJ (*woman, man*) desiderabile; (*house, job*) attraente; (*offer*) vantaggioso(-a); **it is desirable that** è opportuno che + *sub*.

de·sire [dɪ'zaɪə^r] [1] N desiderio, voglia; (*sexual*) desiderio: **desire (for/to do sth)** desiderio (di/di fare qc); **I have no desire to see him** non ho nessuna voglia di vederlo.

[2] VT (*person*) desiderare; **to desire sth/to do sth/that** desiderare qc/di fare qc/che + *sub*; **it leaves much to be desired** lascia molto a desiderare.

de·sir·ous [dɪ'zaɪərəs] ADJ (*frm*): **desirous (of)** desideroso (-a) (di).

de·sist [dɪ'zɪst] VI (*frm*): **to desist (from)** desistere (da).

desk [dɛsk] N (*in office*) scrivania; (*Scol, in hotel, at airport*) banco; (*Brit: in shop, restaurant*) cassa; **desk diary** agenda da tavolo; **desk job** lavoro d'ufficio; **desk lamp** lampada da tavolo.

♦ **desk clerk** N (*Am*) receptionist *m/f inv*.

desk·top com·put·er ['dɛskˌtɒpkəm'pju:tə^r] N (*computer*) desk top *m inv*.

desk·top pub·lish·ing ['dɛskˌtɒp'pʌblɪʃɪŋ] N desktop publishing *m inv*.

deso·late ['dɛsəlɪt] ADJ (*place*) desolato(-a), deserto(-a); (*building*) abbandonato(-a); (*outlook, future*) nero(-a); (*person: grief-stricken*) affranto(-a) (dal dolore), desolato (-a); (: *friendless*) abbandonato(-a) da tutti.

deso·lat·ed ['dɛsəleɪtɪd] ADJ (*saddened*) desolato(-a); (*deserted: house*) abbandonato(-a).

deso·late·ly ['dɛsəlɪtlɪ] ADV (*weep, sigh*) con aria affranta.

deso·la·tion [ˌdɛsə'leɪʃən] N (*bleakness, grief*) desolazione *f*; (*liter: devastation*) devastazione *f*.

des·pair [dɪs'pɛə^r] [1] N disperazione *f*; **in despair** disperato(-a); **to drive sb to despair** far disperare qn.

[2] VI: **to despair (of)** disperare (di); **don't despair!** non disperare!

des·pair·ing [dɪs'pɛərɪŋ] ADJ disperato(-a).

des·pair·ing·ly [dɪs'pɛərɪŋlɪ] ADV disperatamente.

des·patch [dɪs'pætʃ] N, VT = **dispatch**.

des·pe·ra·do [ˌdɛspə'rɑ:dəʊ] N (*old*) bandito.

des·per·ate ['dɛspərɪt] ADJ (*gen*) disperato(-a); (*criminal*) capace di tutto; (*measures*) estremo(-a); **we are getting desperate** siamo sull'orlo della disperazione; **to be desperate to do sth** volere disperatamente fare qc; **I'm desperate for money** (*fam*) ho un disperato bisogno di soldi.

des·per·ate·ly ['dɛspərɪtlɪ] ADV (*say, look*) con disperazione; (*fight*) disperatamente; (*extremely*) terribilmente, estremamente; **desperately ill** gravemente malato(-a), tra la vita e la morte; **desperately in love** perdutamente innamorato(-a).

des·pera·tion [ˌdɛspə'reɪʃən] N disperazione *f*; **an act of desperation** un gesto disperato; **in (sheer) desperation** per (pura) disperazione.

des·pic·able [dɪs'pɪkəbl] ADJ spregevole; (*behaviour*) vergognoso(-a); (*person*) ignobile.

des·pi·cably [dɪs'pɪkəblɪ] ADV (*behave*) ignobilmente.

des·pise [dɪs'paɪz] VT (*person*) disprezzare, sdegnare; (*sb's attentions, offer*) disdegnare.

de·spite [dɪs'paɪt] PREP malgrado, a dispetto di, nonostante.

de·spond·en·cy [dɪs'pɒndənsɪ] N (frm) abbattimento, avvilimento.

de·spond·ent [dɪs'pɒndənt] ADJ (frm): **despondent (about)** avvilito(-a) (per), abbattuto(-a) (per); **he is despondent about his future** quanto al suo futuro è molto demoralizzato.

de·spond·ent·ly [dɪs'pɒndəntlɪ] ADV con aria avvilita or abbattuta.

des·pot ['dɛspɒt] N despota m.

des·pot·ic [dɛs'pɒtɪk] ADJ dispotico(-a).

des·poti·cal·ly [dɛs'pɒtɪkəlɪ] ADV dispoticamente.

des·pot·ism ['dɛspətɪzəm] N dispotismo.

des·sert [dɪ'zɜːt] N dessert m inv, dolce m; **dessert plate** piatto da dessert; **dessert wine** vino da dessert.

dessert·spoon [dɪ'zɜːt,spuːn] N cucchiaio da dessert.

de·sta·bi·lize [diː'steɪbɪ,laɪz] VT (regime) destabilizzare.

des·ti·na·tion [,dɛstɪ'neɪʃən] N destinazione f.

des·tine ['dɛstɪn] VT (frm) destinare.

des·tined ['dɛstɪnd] ADJ PRED **a** : **destined for sth/sb/to do sth** (by fate) destinato(-a) a qc/qn/a fare qc; **we were destined to meet** eravamo destinati a incontrarci **b** (bound for): **destined for London** con destinazione Londra, diretto(-a) a Londra.

des·ti·ny ['dɛstɪnɪ] N destino, sorte f.

des·ti·tute ['dɛstɪ,tjuːt] ADJ (frm) indigente; **utterly destitute** ridotto(-a) in miseria; **destitute of** privo(-a) di.

des·ti·tu·tion [,dɛstɪ'tjuːʃən] N (frm) indigenza.

de·stroy [dɪs'trɔɪ] VT (gen) distruggere; (kill: dangerous or diseased animal) abbattere; (: pet) sopprimere; (: vermin) eliminare; (mood, appetite) rovinare.

de·stroy·er [dɪs'trɔɪə'] N (Naut) cacciatorpediniere m.

de·struct [dɪs'trʌkt] (Mil) **1** VT (missile) distruggere.
2 VI (also: **selfdestruct**) autodistruggersi.

de·struct·ible [dɪs'trʌktəbl] ADJ distruttibile.

de·struc·tion [dɪs'trʌkʃən] N (gen) distruzione f; (caused by war, fire) danni mpl.

de·struc·tive [dɪs'trʌktɪv] ADJ (person) distruttore(-trice); (policy) rovinoso(-a); (action, power, criticism) distruttivo (-a).

de·struc·tive·ly [dɪs'trʌktɪvlɪ] ADV (act, criticise) in modo distruttivo.

de·struc·tive·ness [dɪs'trʌktɪvnɪs] N (gen) carattere m distruttivo; (of child) tendenza a distruggere.

de·struc·tor [dɪs'trʌktə'] N (for refuse) inceneritore m.

des·ul·tory ['dɛsəltərɪ] (frm) ADJ (conversation) sconnesso (-a); (reading) disordinato(-a); (contact) saltuario(-a), irregolare.

de·tach [dɪ'tætʃ] VT staccare, distaccare.

de·tach·able [dɪ'tætʃəbl] ADJ staccabile, smontabile.

de·tached [dɪ'tætʃt] ADJ **a** staccato(-a), separato(-a) **b** (impartial: opinion) imparziale, obiettivo(-a); (unemotional: manner, attitude) distaccato(-a), distante.

◆ **detached house** N villa.

de·tach·ment [dɪ'tætʃmənt] N **a** (aloofness) distacco **b** (Mil) distaccamento.

de·tail ['diːteɪl] **1** N **a** (gen) particolare m, dettaglio; (part of painting) particolare; **his attention to detail** la sua minuziosità; **in detail** nei particolari; **to go into detail(s)** entrare nei dettagli **b** (Mil) piccolo distaccamento.
2 VT **a** (list: items, facts) elencare dettagliatamente **b** (Mil) distaccare; **to detail sb (for)** assegnare qn (a).

de·tailed ['diːteɪld] ADJ dettagliato(-a), particolareggiato (-a).

de·tain [dɪ'teɪn] VT (delay) trattenere; (in custody) detenere.

de·tainee [,diːteɪ'niː] N detenuto(-a).

de·tect [dɪ'tɛkt] VT (signs, traces, drug, motive) scoprire; (feeling) avvertire; (Radar) individuare; (gas, smoke) avvertire la presenza di.

de·tect·able [dɪ'tɛktəbl] ADJ (see vb) scopribile; avvertibile; individuabile; (perceptible) percettibile.

de·tec·tion [dɪ'tɛkʃən] N scoperta, individuazione f; **crime detection** indagini fpl criminali; **to escape detection** (mistake) passare inosservato(-a); (criminal) eludere le ricerche.

de·tec·tive [dɪ'tɛktɪv] N investigatore(-trice); (private detective) investigatore(-trice) privato(-a).

◆ **detective story** N romanzo poliziesco, (romanzo) giallo.

de·tec·tor [dɪ'tɛktə'] N rivelatore m, detector m inv; **radiation detector** indicatore m di radiazioni.

de·tente, **dé·tente** [deɪ'tɑːnt] N (frm) distensione f.

de·ten·tion [dɪ'tɛnʃən] N (of criminal, spy) detenzione f; (of schoolchild) punizione f (trattenendo l'alunno alla fine delle lezioni).

de·ter [dɪ'tɜː'] VT: **to deter sb (from doing sth)** dissuadere qn (dal fare qc).

de·ter·gent [dɪ'tɜːdʒənt] N detersivo, detergente m.

de·terio·rate [dɪ'tɪərɪə,reɪt] VI deteriorarsi.

de·terio·ra·tion [dɪ,tɪərɪə'reɪʃən] N deterioramento.

de·ter·min·able [dɪ'tɜːmɪnəbl] ADJ determinabile.

de·ter·mi·nant [dɪ'tɜːmɪnənt] ADJ, N determinante (m).

de·ter·mi·na·tion [dɪ,tɜːmɪ'neɪʃən] N **a** (of person): **determination (to do)** determinazione f (di fare) **b** (of cause, position) determinazione f, individuazione f.

de·ter·mi·na·tive [dɪ'tɜːmɪnətɪv] **1** ADJ (determining) determinante; (Gram) determinativo(-a).
2 N (Gram) = **determiner**.

de·ter·mine [dɪ'tɜːmɪn] VT **a** (decide) determinare; (: outcome, situation) decidere
b (ascertain: cause, meaning) determinare, stabilire
c (resolve): **to determine to do sth** decidere di fare qc; **to determine sb to do sth** far decidere a qn di fare qc
▶ **determine on** VI + PREP decidersi per.

de·ter·mined [dɪ'tɜːmɪnd] ADJ (person) risoluto(-a), deciso (-a); **a determined effort** uno sforzo di volontà; **to be determined to do sth** essere determinato(-a) or deciso (-a) a fare qc.

de·ter·mined·ly [dɪ'tɜːmɪndlɪ] ADV grintosamente.

de·ter·min·er [dɪ'tɜːmɪnə'] N (Gram) determinante m.

de·ter·min·ing [dɪ'tɜːmɪnɪŋ] ADJ determinante.

de·ter·min·ism [dɪ'tɜːmɪ,nɪzəm] N determinismo.

de·ter·rence [dɪ'tɛrəns] N deterrenza.

de·ter·rent [dɪ'tɛrənt] N deterrente m; **to act as a deterrent** funzionare or fungere da deterrente.

de·test [dɪ'tɛst] VT detestare.

de·test·able [dɪ'tɛstəbl] ADJ detestabile.

de·test·ably [dɪ'tɛstəblɪ] ADV in modo detestabile.

de·tes·ta·tion [,diːtɛs'teɪʃən] N odio, avversione f.

de·throne [diː'θrəʊn] VT detronizzare.

deto·nate ['dɛtə,neɪt] **1** VT far detonare.
2 VI detonare.

deto·na·tion [,dɛtə'neɪʃən] N detonazione f.

deto·na·tor ['dɛtə,neɪtə'] N detonatore m.

de·tour ['diː,tʊə'] N giro più lungo, deviazione f; **to make a detour (through)** fare una deviazione (passando per).

de·tract [dɪ'trækt] VI: **to detract from** (value) sminuire; (reputation) intaccare; (pleasure) attenuare.

de·trac·tor [dɪ'træktə'] N detrattore(-trice).

det·ri·ment ['dɛtrɪmənt] N detrimento, danno; **to the**

detriment of a *or* con detrimento di, a danno di; **without detriment to** senza danno a.

det·ri·men·tal [ˌdɛtrɪ'mɛntl] ADJ: **detrimental (to)** dannoso (-a) (a), nocivo(-a) (a); **to be detrimental to sth** pregiudicare qc.

de·tri·tus [dɪ'traɪtəs] N **a** (*rubbish*) rifiuti *mpl*; (*fig*): **the detritus of society** i rifiuti della società **b** (*Geol*) rocce *fpl* detritiche.

de trop [də tro] ADJ (*frm*) di troppo.

deuce [dju:s] N (*Tennis*) deuce *m inv*, quaranta pari *m inv*.

Deu·ter·ono·my [ˌdjuːtə'rɒnəmɪ] N Deuteronomio.

de·valua·tion [ˌdɪvæljʊ'eɪʃən] N (*Fin*) svalutazione *f*.

de·value [ˈdiːˈvæljuː] VT (*Fin*) svalutare.

dev·as·tate [ˈdɛvəˌsteɪt] VT (*place*) devastare; (*opponent, opposition*) sbaragliare, annientare; (*upset greatly*) sconvolgere; **he was devastated by the news** la notizia l'aveva sconvolto.

dev·as·tat·ing [ˈdɛvəˌsteɪtɪŋ] ADJ (*flood, storm*) devastatore (-trice); (*news, effect*) micidiale; (*beauty*) travolgente.

dev·as·tat·ing·ly [ˈdɛvəˌsteɪtɪŋlɪ] ADV (*beautiful, funny*) da morire, irresistibilmente; (*critical, scornful*) terribilmente.

dev·as·ta·tion [ˌdɛvə'steɪʃən] N devastazione *f*.

de·vel·op [dɪ'vɛləp] **1** VT **a** (*skill, ability, also Phot*) sviluppare; (*mind*) allargare
  b (*acquire: habit*) prendere (a poco a poco *or* gradualmente); **to develop a taste for sth** imparare a gustare qc; **she has developed an interest in politics** è sorto in lei un interesse per la politica
  c (*resources*) sviluppare, valorizzare; (*region*) valorizzare, promuovere lo sviluppo di; **this land is to be developed** qui costruiranno.
  2 VI **a** (*gen*) svilupparsi; (*person: mentally, emotionally*) maturare; (*baby*) crescere; (*plot, illness*) progredire; **the area has developed industrially** la zona si è sviluppata sotto il profilo industriale; **to develop into** diventare
  b (*come into being: symptoms, feelings*) comparire, manifestarsi; (*come about: crisis, situation*) verificarsi, prodursi.

de·vel·op·er [dɪ'vɛləpə'] N **a** (*also*: **property developer**) costruttore *m* (edile) **b** (*Phot*) sviluppatore *m*.

de·vel·op·ing [dɪ'vɛləpɪŋ] **1** ADJ (*industry*) in via di sviluppo; (*crisis, storm*) che sta per scoppiare, imminente.
  2 N (*Phot*) sviluppo.

♦ **developing country** N paese *m* in via di sviluppo.

de·vel·op·ment [dɪ'vɛləpmənt] N **a** (*gen*) sviluppo; **to await developments** attendere ulteriori sviluppi; **the latest developments** gli ultimi sviluppi (della situazione); **development process** processo di sviluppo; **development grant** *finanziamento per un programma di sviluppo*.

♦ **development area** N (*Brit*) area di sviluppo industriale.

de·vi·ance [ˈdiːvɪəns] N devianza.

de·vi·ant [ˈdiːvɪənt] **1** ADJ (*behaviour*) deviante; (*development*) anormale; (*sexually*) pervertito(-a).
  2 N deviante *m/f*; (*also*: **sexual deviant**) pervertito(-a).

de·vi·ate [ˈdiːvɪˌeɪt] VI **to deviate (from)** deviare (da).

de·via·tion [ˌdiːvɪ'eɪʃən] N: **deviation (from)** deviazione *f* (da); **standard deviation** (*Math*) scarto quadratico medio.

de·vice [dɪ'vaɪs] N **a** (*gadget*) congegno, dispositivo **b** (*scheme*) stratagemma *m*; **leave him to his own devices** lascia che si arrangi da solo **c** (*also*: **explosive device**) ordigno esplosivo.

dev·il [ˈdɛvl] N **a** (*evil spirit*) diavolo; **the Devil** il Diavolo, il Demonio
  b (*fam: person*) diavolo; **poor devil** povero diavolo!; **be a devil!** fai uno strappo!; **you little devil!** monellaccio!; **she is a devil to work for** lavorare per lei è un inferno
  c (*fam: as intensifier*): **it's the devil of a job** è un lavoraccio; **he had the devil of a job to find it** ha sudato sette camicie per trovarlo; **I'm in the devil of a mess** sono in un pasticcio del diavolo; **to work/run like the devil** lavorare/correre come un dannato; **how/what/who the devil ...?** come/che/chi diavolo...?; **there will be the devil to pay** saranno guai
  d (*phrases*): **between the devil and the deep blue sea** tra Scilla e Cariddi; **go to the devil!** (*fam*) vai al diavolo!; **speak** *or* **talk of the devil!** (*fam*) lupus in fabula!, si parla del diavolo...; **(to) give the devil his due** ... bisogna riconoscerglielo..., siamo giusti... .

dev·il·ish [ˈdɛvlɪʃ] **1** ADJ (*wicked*) diabolico(-a); (*mischievous: child*) indiavolato(-a); (: *mood*) infernale.
  2 ADV (*old*) terribilmente.

dev·il·ish·ly [ˈdɛvlɪʃlɪ] ADV (*laugh etc*) in modo diabolico; (*old: extremely*) terribilmente.

♦ **devil-may-care** [ˈdɛvlmeɪ'kɛə'] ADJ (*attitude*) sprezzante.

dev·il·ment [ˈdɛvlmənt] (*old*) N (*mischief*) birichinate *fpl*; (*wickedness*) cattiveria.

dev·il·ry [ˈdɛvlrɪ] N (*old*) = **devilment**.

♦ **devil's advocate** [ˈdɛvəlz'ædvəˌkɪt] N: **to play (the) devil's advocate** fare l'avvocato del diavolo.

de·vi·ous [ˈdiːvɪəs] ADJ (*person, means, methods, mind*) subdolo(-a); (*path, argument*) tortuoso(-a).

de·vi·ous·ly [ˈdiːvɪəslɪ] ADV (*act*) subdolamente.

de·vi·ous·ness [ˈdiːvɪəsnɪs] N (*of scheme, behaviour*) disonestà, doppiezza; (*of person*) modi subdoli.

de·vise [dɪ'vaɪz] VT escogitare, concepire, ideare.

de·vi·tal·ize [diː'vaɪtəˌlaɪz] VT devitalizzare.

de·void [dɪ'vɔɪd] ADJ: **devoid of** privo(-a) di, senza.

de·vo·lu·tion [ˌdiːvə'luːʃən] N (*Pol*) decentramento.

de·volve [dɪ'vɒlv] **1** VT (*power, responsibility*) devolvere.
  2 VI: **to devolve (up)on** ricadere su; **it devolved on me to tell him** è stato compito mio dirglielo.

de·vote [dɪ'vəʊt] VT: **to devote (to)** dedicare (a); **to devote o.s. to** dedicarsi a; (*to a cause*) consacrarsi a, dedicarsi a.

de·vot·ed [dɪ'vəʊtɪd] ADJ (*friend, admirer*) devoto(-a); (*father, aunt*) amoroso(-a); **to be devoted to sb** essere molto attaccato(-a) a qn.

de·vot·ed·ly [dɪ'vəʊtɪdlɪ] ADV devotamente, con devozione.

devo·tee [ˌdɛvəʊ'tiː] N **a** : **devotee (of)** (*enthusiast*) appassionato(-a) di **b** (*Rel*) devoto(-a).

de·vo·tion [dɪ'vəʊʃən] N: **devotion (to)** (*studies etc*) devozione *f* (a), dedizione *f* (a); (*friend, family*) attaccamento (a), fedeltà (a); **devotions** NPL (*Rel*) devozioni *fpl*.

de·vo·tion·al [dɪ'vəʊʃənl] ADJ (*Rel*) devozionale.

de·vour [dɪ'vaʊə'] VT (*food*) divorare; **devoured by jealousy** divorato(-a) dalla gelosia.

de·vour·ing [dɪ'vaʊərɪŋ] ADJ (*flames, jealousy*) divoratore (-trice).

de·vout [dɪ'vaʊt] ADJ (*person*) devoto(-a), pio(-a); (*prayer, hope*) devoto(-a), fervido(-a).

de·vout·ly [dɪ'vaʊtlɪ] ADV (*frm: wish, hope*) fervidamente; (*live, pray*) devotamente.

dew [djuː] N rugiada.

dew·drop [ˈdjuːˌdrɒp] N goccia di rugiada; (*fig: on end of*

nose) goccia.

dewy ['dju:ɪ] ADJ bagnato(-a) di rugiada, rugiadoso(-a).

♦ **dewy-eyed** ['dju:ɪˈaɪd] ADJ (*innocent*) innocente.

dex·ter·ity [dɛksˈtɛrɪtɪ] N: **dexterity (in doing sth)** (*of hands*) destrezza (a fare qc); (*of mind*) abilità (nel fare qc).

dex·ter·ous, dex·trous ['dɛkstrəs] ADJ (*skilful*) destro(-a), abile; (*movement*) agile.

dex·ter·ous·ly, dex·trous·ly ['dɛkstrəslɪ] ADV (*with physical skill*) con destrezza; (*with mental skill*) sagacemente.

dg [ˌdi:ˈdʒi:] ABBR (= *decigram*) dg.

DH [ˌdi:ˈeɪtʃ] N ABBR = **Department of Health**; see **health**.

DHSS [ˌdi:eɪtʃˈɛsˈɛs] N ABBR (*Brit: old*)= *Department of Health and Social Security.*

dia·be·tes [ˌdaɪəˈbi:ti:z] N diabete *m*.

dia·bet·ic [ˌdaɪəˈbɛtɪk] [1] N diabetico(-a).

  [2] ADJ (*gen*) diabetico(-a); (*chocolate, jam*) per diabetici.

dia·boli·cal [ˌdaɪəˈbɒlɪkəl] ADJ (*fam: dreadful*) infernale, atroce; (: *incredible*) incredibile; (*satanic*) diabolico(-a).

dia·boli·cal·ly [ˌdaɪəˈbɒlɪkəlɪ] ADV (*see adj*) (*behave*) in modo diabolico; (*hot, dangerous*) terribilmente.

dia·crit·ic [ˌdaɪəˈkrɪtɪk] N segno diacritico.

dia·dem [ˈdaɪəˌdɛm] N diadema *m*.

di·aer·esis, di·er·esis [daɪˈɛrɪsɪs] N (*pl* **diaereses, diereses** [daɪˈɛrɪsi:z]) dieresi *f inv*.

di·ag·nose ['daɪəgnəʊz] VT diagnosticare; **it was diagnosed as bronchitis** hanno diagnosticato una bronchite.

di·ag·no·sis [ˌdaɪəgˈnəʊsɪs] N (*pl* **diagnoses** [ˌdaɪəgˈnəʊsi:z]) diagnosi *f inv*.

di·ag·nos·tic [ˌdaɪəgˈnɒstɪk] ADJ (*gen*) diagnostico(-a); (*probe, X-ray*) a scopo diagnostico.

di·ag·nos·ti·cian [ˌdaɪəgnɒsˈtɪʃən] N diagnostico(-a), diagnosta *m/f*.

di·ago·nal [daɪˈægənl] ADJ, N diagonale (*f*).

di·ago·nal·ly [daɪˈægənəlɪ] ADV (*cut, fold*) in diagonale, diagonalmente; **to go diagonally across** attraversare in senso *or* in direzione diagonale; **diagonally opposite** dall'altra parte in diagonale.

dia·gram ['daɪəˌgræm] N diagramma *m*, schema *m*; (*Math*) diagramma, grafico.

dia·gram·mat·ic [ˌdaɪəgrəˈmætɪk] ADJ schematico(-a).

dial ['daɪəl] [1] N (*of clock, instrument*) quadrante *m*; (*of radio*) scala; (*of telephone*) disco (combinatore).

  [2] VT (*Telec: number*) fare; (*more formal*) comporre; **to dial a wrong number** sbagliare numero; **can I dial London direct?** si può chiamare Londra in teleselezione?; **to dial 999** ≈ chiamare il 113.

dial. ABBR = **dialect**.

dia·lect ['daɪəˌlɛkt] N dialetto; **the local dialect** il dialetto del luogo; **dialect word** termine *m* dialettale.

dia·lec·tic [ˌdaɪəˈlɛktɪk] N (*Philosophy*) dialettica.

dia·lec·ti·cal [ˌdaɪəˈlɛktɪkəl] ADJ dialettico(-a).

dial·ling code ['daɪəlɪŋˌkəʊd], (*Am*) **dial code** N (*Telec*) prefisso.

dial·ling tone ['daɪəlɪŋˌtəʊn], (*Am*) **dial tone** N (*Telec*) segnale *m* di libero.

dia·logue ['daɪəlɒg] N dialogo.

di·aly·sis [daɪˈæləsɪs] N (*Med*) dialisi *f*.

di·am·eter [daɪˈæmɪtəʳ] N diametro; **it is one metre in diameter** misura un metro di diametro.

dia·met·ric [ˌdaɪəˈmɛtrɪk], **dia·met·ri·cal** [ˌdaɪəˈmɛtrɪkəl] ADJ diametrale.

dia·met·ri·cal·ly [ˌdaɪəˈmɛtrɪkəlɪ] ADV: **diametrically opposed (to)** diametralmente opposto(-a) (a).

dia·mond ['daɪəmənd] [1] N **a** (*stone*) diamante *m*, brillante *m*; (*shape*) rombo, losanga

  b (*Cards*): **diamonds** NPL quadri *mpl*; **the Queen of diamonds** la donna di quadri.

  [2] ADJ (*necklace*) di diamanti *or* brillanti; **diamond ring** anello di brillanti; (*with single diamond*) anello con brillante; **diamond-shaped** a forma di losanga.

♦ **diamond jubilee** N sessantesimo anniversario.

♦ **diamond wedding** N nozze *fpl* di diamante.

dia·per ['daɪəpəʳ] N (*Am*) pannolino.

di·apha·nous [daɪˈæfənəs] ADJ diafano(-a).

dia·phragm ['daɪəfræm] N diaframma *m*.

di·ar·rhoea, (*Am*) di·ar·rhea [ˌdaɪəˈrɪːə] N diarrea.

dia·ry ['daɪərɪ] N (*daily record*) diario; (*for engagements*) agenda; **to keep a diary** tenere un diario.

Di·as·po·ra [daɪˈæspərə] N Diaspora.

di·as·po·ra [daɪˈæspərə] N (*frm*) diaspora.

di·as·to·le [daɪˈæstəlɪ] N (*Med*) diastole *f*.

dia·tribe ['daɪəˌtraɪb] N (*frm*): **diatribe (against)** diatriba (contro).

di·ba·sic [ˌdaɪˈbeɪsɪk] ADJ (*Chem*) dibasico(-a).

dice [daɪs] [1] N, PL INV dado; **to play dice** giocare a dadi.

  [2] VT (*Culin*) tagliare a dadini.

  [3] VI: **to dice with death** scherzare con la morte.

dicey ['daɪsɪ] ADJ (*fam*): **it's a bit dicey** è un po' un rischio.

di·choto·my [dɪˈkɒtəmɪ] N (*frm*) dicotomia.

dick [dɪk] N (*fam!: penis*) cazzo (*fam!*)

dick·ens ['dɪkɪnz] N (*fam*) = **devil** c.

Dick·en·sian [dɪˈkɛnzɪən] ADJ dickensiano(-a).

dick·head ['dɪkˌhɛd] N (*fam!*) testa *m or f* di cazzo (*fam!*)

dicky ['dɪkɪ] [1] N (*of shirt*) pettino.

  [2] ADJ (*comp* **-ier**, *superl* **-iest**) (*Brit: fam: heart*) malandato (-a).

di·coty·ledon [daɪˌkɒtɪˈliːdən] N (*Bot*) dicotiledone *m*.

Dic·ta·phone® ['dɪktəˌfəʊn] N dittafono ®.

dic·tate [*vb* dɪkˈteɪt, *n* ˈdɪkteɪt] [1] VT, VI (*all senses*) dettare; **he decided to act as circumstances dictated** decise di agire come gli dettavano le circostanze.

  [2]: **dictates** NPL (*of heart, fashion*) dettami *mpl*

▶ **dictate to** VI + PREP (*person*) dare ordini a, dettar legge a; **I won't be dictated to** non ricevo ordini.

dic·ta·tion [dɪkˈteɪʃən] N (*to secretary*) dettatura; (*Scol*) dettato; **at dictation speed** a velocità di dettatura.

dic·ta·tor [dɪkˈteɪtəʳ] N dittatore(-trice).

dic·ta·to·ri·al [ˌdɪktətɔːrɪəl] ADJ dittatoriale, da dittatore.

dic·ta·to·ri·al·ly [ˌdɪktətɔːrɪəlɪ] ADV in modo dittatoriale, da dittatore.

dic·ta·tor·ship [dɪkˈteɪtəˌʃɪp] N dittatura.

dic·tion ['dɪkʃən] N dizione *f*.

dic·tion·ary ['dɪkʃənrɪ] N vocabolario, dizionario.

dic·tum ['dɪktəm] N (*pl* **dictums** *or* **dicta**) **a** (*pronouncement*) affermazione *f* **b** (*maxim*) massima.

did [dɪd] PT of **do**.

di·dac·tic [dɪˈdæktɪk] ADJ (*frm: educational*) didattico(-a); (*pej: person*) pedante.

di·dac·ti·cal·ly [dɪˈdæktɪklɪ] ADV didatticamente.

did·dle ['dɪdl] VT (*fam*) infinocchiare; **to diddle sb out of sth** fregare qc a qn.

didn't ['dɪdənt] = **did not**.

Dido ['daɪdəʊ] N (*Myth*) Didone *f*.

die¹ [daɪ] (*prp* **dying**) VI (*person, animal, plant*): **to die (of *or* from)** morire (di); (*engine*) spegnersi, fermarsi; (*fig: friendship*) finire; (: *interest, enthusiasm*) spegnersi; **to be dying** star morendo; **to be dying for sth/to do sth** morire dalla voglia di qc/di fare qc; **to die a natural/violent death** morire di morte naturale/violenta; **he died a hero** è morto da eroe; **the daylight was dying fast** si stava

facendo buio in fretta; **never say die** (*fig fam*) non bisogna disperare; **I nearly died** (*laughing*) per poco non morivo (dal ridere); (*with embarrassment*) avrei voluto sprofondare; **old habits die hard** il lupo perde il pelo ma non il vizio

▶ **die away** VI + ADV affievolirsi

▶ **die back** VI + ADV (*plant*) seccarsi

▶ **die down** VI + ADV (*fire*) spegnersi; (*flames*) abbassarsi, languire; (*storm, wind, emotion*) calmarsi

▶ **die off** VI + ADV (*plants, animals, people*) morire uno(-a) dopo l'altro(-a)

▶ **die out** VI + ADV estinguersi, scomparire.

die² [daɪ] N a (*pl* **dice**): **the die is cast** il dado è tratto b (*in minting*) conio; (*Tech*) matrice *f*; (*in press forging*) stampo.

die·hard ['daɪˌhɑːd] 1 N conservatore(-trice).

2 ADJ (*supporter, opponent*) convinto(-a).

di·er·esis [daɪˈɛrɪsɪs] N = **diaeresis**.

die·sel ['diːzəl] N (*car*) diesel *m inv*; (*fuel*) gasolio.

♦ **diesel engine** N motore *m* diesel *inv*.

♦ **diesel fuel, diesel oil** N gasolio (per motori diesel).

♦ **diesel train** N (treno con) locomotiva diesel.

diet ['daɪət] 1 N a (*customary food*) alimentazione *f*, regime *m* alimentare; **to live on a diet of** nutrirsi di b (*restricted food*) dieta; **to be/go on a diet** essere/mettersi a dieta.

2 VI seguire una dieta.

3 ADJ (*food, drink*) dietetico(-a); **diet yoghurt** yoghurt *m inv* magro.

di·etary ['daɪətərɪ] ADJ dietetico(-a).

di·etet·ic [ˌdaɪəˈtɛtɪk] ADJ dietetico(-a).

di·etet·ics [ˌdaɪəˈtɛtɪks] NSG dietetica.

di·eti·cian [ˌdaɪəˈtɪʃən] N dietista *m/f*.

dif·fer ['dɪfə'] VI a (*be unlike*): **to differ from sth** differire da qc, essere diverso(-a) da qc b (*disagree*): **to differ (with sb on** *or* **over** *or* **about sth)** dissentire (da qn su qc), discordare (da qn su qc); **we differed over the matter** ci siamo trovati in disaccordo sulla questione.

dif·fer·ence ['dɪfrəns] N a : **difference (in/between)** differenza (di/tra); **that makes all the difference** questo cambia tutto; **it makes no difference to me** per me è lo stesso; **a car with a difference** una macchina diversa dalle altre; **the difference in her is amazing** è incredibile com'è cambiata; **I'll make up the difference later** (*of money*) ti do il resto dopo; **common difference** (*Math*) ragione *f*

b (*quarrel*): **a difference of opinion** una divergenza di opinioni; **they could not settle their differences** non sono riusciti a mettersi d'accordo.

dif·fer·ent ['dɪfrənt] ADJ a (*not alike*): **different (from** *or* **to)** diverso(-a) (da), differente (da); (*changed*) altro(-a), diverso(-a); **that's quite a different matter** è tutt'altra cosa, è una faccenda completamente diversa; **I feel a different person** mi sento un altro

b (*various*) diverso(-a), vario(-a); **it comes in several different colours** è disponibile in diversi *or* vari colori.

dif·fer·en·tial [ˌdɪfəˈrenʃəl] 1 N (*Econ*) scarto salariale; (*Math, Aut*) differenziale *m*.

2 ADJ differenziale; **differential calculus** (*Math*) calcolo differenziale; **differential erosion** erosione *f* selettiva.

♦ **differential gear** N (*Aut*) differenziale *m*; **differential housing** scatola del differenziale.

dif·fer·en·ti·ate [ˌdɪfəˈrenʃɪˌeɪt] 1 VT: **to differentiate (from)** (*distinguish*) distinguere (fra); (*make different*) differenziare (da).

2 VI: **to differentiate (between)** (*perceive a difference*) distinguere (tra), differenziare (tra).

dif·fer·en·tia·tion [ˌdɪfəˌrenʃɪˈeɪʃən] N (*see vb*) distinzione *f*; differenziazione *f*.

dif·fer·ent·ly ['dɪfrəntlɪ] ADV in modo diverso *or* differente; **she thinks quite differently now** la pensa diversamente adesso.

dif·fi·cult ['dɪfɪkəlt] ADJ difficile; **difficult to understand** difficile da capire; **she is difficult to get on with** ha un carattere difficile; **I find it difficult to believe (that ...)** mi pare difficile da credere (che...); **getting started is the difficult thing** il difficile sta nel cominciare.

dif·fi·cul·ty ['dɪfɪkəltɪ] N difficoltà *f inv*; **he has difficulty in walking/breathing** ha difficoltà a camminare/di respirazione; **to have difficulties with** (*police, landlord*) avere noie con; **to get o.s. into difficulty** mettersi nei guai; **to be in difficulty** *or* **difficulties** essere *or* trovarsi in difficoltà; **to be in (financial) difficulties** avere delle difficoltà economiche.

dif·fi·dence ['dɪfɪdəns] N riservatezza.

dif·fi·dent ['dɪfɪdənt] ADJ (*person*) poco sicuro(-a) di sé; (*smile*) timido(-a), imbarazzato(-a); **to be diffident about doing sth** esitare a fare qc.

dif·fi·dent·ly ['dɪfɪdəntlɪ] ADV (*smile, answer, behave*) con esitazione.

dif·frac·tion [dɪˈfrækʃən] N (*Phys*) diffrazione *f*.

dif·fuse [*vb* dɪˈfjuːz; *adj* dɪˈfjuːs] 1 VT (*light, heat, gas, information*) diffondere; (*heat, perfume*) emanare.

2 VI diffondersi.

3 ADJ (*light*) diffuso(-a); (*style, writing*) prolisso(-a); (*organization*) ramificato(-a).

dif·fu·sion [dɪˈfjuːʒən] N (*of ideas, information*) diffusione *f*; (*of light, heat, substances*) spargimento.

dig [dɪg] (*vb: pt, pp* **dug**) 1 N a (*with elbow*) gomitata; **to give sb a dig in the ribs** dare una gomitata (nel fianco) a qn

b (*fam: taunt*) frecciata, insinuazione *f*; **to have a dig at sb/sth** lanciare una frecciata a qn/qc

c (*Archeol*) scavo, scavi *mpl*.

2 VT a (*ground, hole*) scavare; (*garden*) zappare, vangare b (*poke, thrust*): **to dig sth into sth** conficcare qc in qc; **to dig one's nails into** conficcare le unghie in

c (*old fam*): **dig that beat, man!** senti che forza quel ritmo!; **I don't dig that kind of scene** (*old fam*) quell'ambiente non mi va a genio; **he really digs jazz** (*old fam*) va pazzo per il jazz.

3 VI (*gen, Tech*) scavare; (*Archeol*) fare degli scavi; **to dig for minerals** scavare alla ricerca di minerali; **to dig into one's pockets for sth** frugarsi le tasche cercando qc

▶ **dig in** 1 VI + ADV a (*fam: eat*) attaccare a mangiare; **dig in!** dateci sotto!

b (*also*: **dig o.s. in**, *Mil*) trincerarsi; (: *fig*) insediarsi, installarsi.

2 VT + ADV (*compost*) interrare; (*knife, claw*) affondare; **to dig in one's heels** (*fig*) impuntarsi

▶ **dig out** VT + ADV (*survivors, car from snow*) tirar fuori (scavando), estrarre (scavando); (*fig*) scovare

▶ **dig up** VT + ADV (*potatoes, treasure, body*) dissotterrare; (*tree etc*) sradicare; (*weeds*) estirpare; (*fig fam: fact, information*) pescare.

di·gest [*vb* daɪˈdʒɛst; *n* ˈdaɪdʒɛst] 1 VT digerire; (*information*) assimilare; **it is easily digested** (*food*) è facilmente digeribile.

2 VI digerirsi.

3 N (*summary*) compendio.

di·gest·ible [dɪˈdʒɛstəbl] ADJ digeribile.

di·ges·tion [dɪ'dʒɛstʃən] N digestione *f*.
di·ges·tive [dɪ'dʒɛstɪv] ADJ digestivo(-a); **digestive system** apparato digerente; **digestive (biscuit)** *biscotto tipo frollino di farina integrale*.
dig·ger ['dɪgə'] N (*machine*) escavatore *m*.
dig·gings ['dɪgɪŋz] NPL (*Archeol*) scavi *mpl*.
dig·it ['dɪdʒɪt] N (*Math*) cifra; (*frm: finger, thumb, toe*) dito.
digi·tal ['dɪdʒɪtəl] ADJ (*clock, computer*) digitale.
♦ **digital compact cassette** N lettore-registratore *m* digitale.
dig·ni·fied ['dɪgnɪ,faɪd] ADJ dignitoso(-a), pieno(-a) di dignità.
dig·ni·fy ['dɪgnɪ,faɪ] VT **a** (*make impressive: building*) nobilitare **b** (*make respectable*) dare dignità a; **I wouldn't dignify that question with an answer** è una domanda che non merita risposta.
dig·ni·tary ['dɪgnɪtərɪ] N dignitario.
dig·nity ['dɪgnɪtɪ] N dignità; **it would be beneath his dignity to do it** non si abbasserebbe mai a farlo.
di·gress [daɪ'grɛs] VI: **to digress (from)** divagare (da), fare digressioni (da).
di·gres·sion [daɪ'grɛʃən] N digressione *f*.
digs [dɪgz] NPL (*Brit fam*): **to be in digs** affittare una camera (*presso privati*).
dike [daɪk] N = **dyke**.
di·lapi·da·ted [dɪ'læpɪ,deɪtɪd] ADJ (*building*) in pessime condizioni, cadente; (*vehicle*) sgangherato(-a), scassato (-a).
di·lapi·da·tion [dɪ,læpɪ'deɪʃən] N (*of building*) sfacelo, disfacimento.
di·late [daɪ'leɪt] **1** VI (*pupils, eyes, cervix*) dilatarsi.
2 VT dilatare.
di·la·tion [daɪ'leɪʃən] N dilatazione *f*.
dila·to·ri·ness ['dɪlətərmɪs] N (*frm: of person*) lentezza.
di·la·tory ['dɪlətərɪ] ADJ (*frm: person*) lento(-a); (*action, policy*) dilatorio(-a).
di·lem·ma [daɪ'lɛmə] N dilemma *m*; **to be in a dilemma** essere di fronte a un dilemma.
dil·et·tante [,dɪlɪ'tɑːntɪ] N dilettante *m/f*.
dili·gence ['dɪlɪdʒəns] N diligenza.
dili·gent ['dɪlɪdʒənt] ADJ (*person*) diligente, attento(-a); (*work, search*) accurato(-a), diligente.
dili·gent·ly ['dɪlɪdʒəntlɪ] ADV diligentemente.
dill [dɪl] N aneto.
dilly-dally ['dɪlɪ,dælɪ] VI (*fam*) gingillarsi.
di·lute [daɪ'luːt] **1** VT (*concentrated liquid*) diluire, allungare; (*wine*) annacquare; (*fig: statement, concept*) diluire; **"dilute to taste"** "aggiungere acqua a piacere".
2 ADJ diluito(-a).
di·lu·tion [daɪ'luːʃən] N diluizione *f*.
dim [dɪm] **1** ADJ (*comp* -**mer**, *superl* -**mest**) (*light*) debole, fioco(-a); (*sight*) debole; (*forest*) oscuro(-a); (*room*) in penombra; (*shape, outline, memory, sound*) indistinto (-a), vago(-a); (*fam: person*) tonto(-a), ottuso(-a); **to grow dim** (*light*) affievolirsi; (*eyesight*) indebolirsi; **to take a dim view of sth** (*fam*) non vedere qc di buon occhio.
2 VT (*light*) abbassare; (*Am: headlights*) abbassare; (*sound, memory, colour*) affievolire; (*shape, outline, beauty, glory*) offuscare; (*sight, senses*) annebbiare; (*metal*) annerire.
3 VI (*light, sight, memory*) affievolirsi; (*outline*) divenire indistinto(-a).
dime [daɪm] N (*USA and Canada*) *monetina da 10 cent*; **they're a dime a dozen** (*fam*) c'è ne un sacco.
di·men·sion [daɪ'mɛnʃən] N (*size*) dimensione *f*, propor-

zione *f*; (*Math, fig*) dimensione; **to add a new dimension to** (*fig*) dare una dimensione nuova a.
–dimensional [daɪ'mɛnʃənl] ADJ SUFF: **two-dimensional** bidimensionale; **three-dimensional** tridimensionale.
di·min·ish [dɪ'mɪnɪʃ] **1** VT (*effect, enthusiasm, authority, speed*) diminuire, ridurre; (*value, person*) sminuire.
2 VI diminuire, ridursi; (*value*) scendere.
di·min·ished [dɪ'mɪnɪʃt] ADJ (*value, importance*) ridotto(-a).
♦ **diminished responsibility** N (*Law*) incapacità d'intendere e di volere.
dimi·nu·tion [,dɪmɪ'njuːʃən] N (*of value, power*) diminuzione *f*; (*of strength, enthusiasm*) affievolimento.
di·minu·tive [dɪ'mɪnjʊtɪv] **1** ADJ (*frm*) minuto(-a), minuscolo(-a).
2 N (*Gram*) diminutivo.
dim·ly ['dɪmlɪ] ADV (*hear, remember*) vagamente; (*shine*) debolmente.
dim·mer ['dɪmə'] N (*also*: **dimmer switch**) dimmer *m inv*, interruttore *m* a reostato.
dim·mers ['dɪməz] NPL (*Am Aut: dipped headlights*) anabbaglianti *mpl*; (: *parking lights*) luci *fpl* di posizione.
dim·ness ['dɪmnɪs] N (*of light, sight*) debolezza; (*of place*) oscurità; (*of outline*) vaghezza; (*of sound*) carattere *m* indistinto; (*fam: of person*) stupidità.
dim·ple ['dɪmpl] N (*in cheek, chin etc*) fossetta.
dim·wit ['dɪm,wɪt] N (*fam*) cretino(-a).
♦ **dim-witted** [dɪm'wɪtɪd] ADJ (*fam*) sciocco(-a), stupido (-a).
din [dɪn] **1** N (*from people, in classroom*) chiasso, fracasso, baccano; (*from machine, factory, traffic*) rumore *m* infernale.
2 VT: **to din sth into sb** (*fam*) ficcare qc in testa a qn; **he tried to din it into her that** … ha cercato di ficcarle in testa che… .
dine [daɪn] VI (*frm*) cenare; **to dine (on)** pasteggiare (a *or* con); **to dine out** cenare fuori.
din·er ['daɪnə'] N (*person: in restaurant*) cliente *m/f*; (*Rail*) carrozza *or* vagone *m* ristorante *inv*; (*Am: eating place*) tavola calda.
ding-dong ['dɪŋdɒŋ] **1** N **a** (*of bells*) dindon *m inv* **b** (*Brit: fam*) rissa.
2 ADJ (*Brit: fam*): **a ding-dong argument** un battibecco.
din·ghy ['dɪŋgɪ] N (*rubber boat*) gommone *m*; (*sailing dinghy*) dinghy *m inv*.
din·gi·ness ['dɪndʒɪnɪs] N squallore *m*.
din·go ['dɪŋgəʊ] N (*Zool*) dingo.
din·gy ['dɪn(d)ʒɪ] ADJ (*shabby*) squallido(-a); (*dark*) scuro (-a), tetro(-a).
din·ing area ['daɪnɪŋ,ɛərɪə] N zona *f* pranzo *inv*.
din·ing car ['daɪnɪŋ,kɑː'] N carrozza *or* vagone *m* ristorante *inv*.
din·ing hall ['daɪnɪŋ,hɔːl] N refettorio.
din·ing room ['daɪnɪŋ,rʊm] N sala da pranzo.
din·ing ta·ble ['daɪnɪŋ,teɪbl] N tavola *or* tavolo da pranzo.
din·ner ['dɪnə'] N (*evening meal*) cena; (*lunch*) pranzo; (*banquet*) banchetto; **school dinners** refezione *f* scolastica; **we're having people to dinner this evening** abbiamo gente a cena stasera; **to go out to dinner in a restaurant/at friends** andare a cena fuori/da amici; **dinner's ready!** a tavola!
♦ **dinner jacket** N (*Brit*) smoking *m inv*.
♦ **dinner party** N cena (con amici).
♦ **dinner plate** N piatto piano.
♦ **dinner service** N servizio da tavola.

♦ **dinner time** N ora di pranzo (*or* cena).

di·no·saur ['daɪnəsɔ:'] N dinosauro.

dint [dɪnt] N: **by dint of (doing) sth** a forza di (fare) qc.

di·oc·esan [daɪ'ɒsɪsən] ADJ diocesano(-a).

dio·cese ['daɪəsɪs] N diocesi *f inv.*

diode ['daɪəʊd] N (*Elec*) diodo.

di·ox·ide [daɪ'ɒksaɪd] N (*Chem*) biossido; **carbon dioxide** anidride *f* carbonica.

dip [dɪp] ☐1 N **a** (*swim*) nuotatina; **to go for a dip** andare a fare una nuotatina

   b (*hollow*) cunetta; (*slope*) pendenza, discesa

   c (*Culin*) salsetta

   d (*for sheep*) bagno.

   ☐2 VT **a** (*into liquid*) immergere, bagnare; (*hand: into bag*) infilare; (*sheep*) immergere nel disinfestante; **to dip one's pen in ink** intingere la penna nell'inchiostro; **he dipped his bread in his soup** ha intinto il pane nella minestra

   b : **to dip one's headlights** (*Brit Aut*) abbassare i fari.

   ☐3 VI (*slope down: road*) essere in pendenza, andare in discesa; (*move down: bird, plane*) abbassarsi; (*temperature, sun*) calare; **to dip into one's pocket/savings** (*fig*) attingere al portafoglio/ai propri risparmi; **to dip into a book** scorrere un libro; **to dip into an author** leggere brani di un autore.

Dip. ABBR (*Brit*) = **diploma.**

diph·theria [dɪf'θɪərɪə] N difterite *f.*

diph·thong ['dɪfθɒŋ] N dittongo.

dip·loid ['dɪplɔɪd] N (*Bio*) diploide *f.*

di·plo·ma [dɪ'pləʊmə] N diploma *m*; **to have a diploma in** avere un diploma in, essere diplomato(-a) in.

di·plo·ma·cy [dɪ'pləʊməsɪ] N (*Pol, fig*) diplomazia.

dip·lo·mat ['dɪplə,mæt] N diplomatico.

dip·lo·mat·ic [,dɪplə'mætɪk] ADJ (*also fig*) diplomatico(-a); **diplomatic bag**, (*Am*) **diplomatic pouch** valigia diplomatica; **diplomatic service** diplomazia; **to break off diplomatic relations** rompere le relazioni diplomatiche.

dip·lo·mati·cal·ly [,dɪplə'mætɪkəlɪ] ADV diplomaticamente.

♦ **diplomatic corps** N corpo diplomatico.

♦ **diplomatic immunity** N immunità diplomatica.

di·pole ['daɪ,pəʊl] (*Elec*) N dipolo; **dipole aerial** antenna a dipolo.

dip·per ['dɪpə'] N (*ladle*) mestolo; (*Zool*) merlo acquaiolo.

dip·ping ['dɪpɪŋ] N (*of sheep*) bagno.

dip·so·ma·nia [,dɪpsəʊ'meɪnɪə] N dipsomania.

dip·so·ma·ni·ac [,dɪpsəʊ'meɪnɪæk] N dipsomane *m/f.*

dip·stick ['dɪp,stɪk] N (*Aut*) astina dell'olio.

dip·switch ['dɪp,swɪtʃ] N (*Aut*) levetta dei fari.

dire ['daɪə'] ADJ (*warning*) minaccioso(-a); (*consequences*) disastroso(-a); (*event*) terribile; (*poverty*) nero(-a); **dire necessity** dura necessità; **in dire straits** nei guai.

di·rect [daɪ'rɛkt] ☐1 ADJ (*gen*) diretto(-a); (*answer*) chiaro(-a); (*refusal*) esplicito(-a); (*manner, person*) franco(-a), diretto(-a); **direct object** (*Gram*) complemento oggetto; **to be a direct descendant of** discendere in linea diretta da; **the direct opposite of** esattamente il contrario di; **to make a direct hit** colpire in pieno.

   ☐2 ADV (*go*) direttamente; (*fly*) senza scalo; (*dial*) in teleselezione.

   ☐3 VT **a** (*aim: remark, gaze, attention*): **to direct at/to** dirigere a, rivolgere a; (*address: letter*): **to direct to** indirizzare a; **can you direct me to the station?** può indicarmi la strada per la stazione?

   b (*control: traffic, business, actors*) dirigere; (*play, film,*

programme) curare la regia di, dirigere

   c (*frm: instruct*): **to direct sb to do sth** dare direttive a qn di fare qc.

♦ **direct cost** N (*Comm*) costo diretto.

♦ **direct current** N (*Elec*) corrente *f* continua.

♦ **direct debit** N mandato di pagamento permanente.

♦ **direct dialling** [daɪ,rɛkt 'daɪəlɪŋ] N (*Telec*) ≈ teleselezione *f.*

di·rect·ed [dɪ'rɛktɪd] ADJ (*Math*): **directed numbers** numeri *mpl* ordinati.

♦ **direct hit** N (*Mil*) colpo diretto.

di·rec·tion [dɪ'rɛkʃən] ☐1 N **a** (*way*) direzione *f*; (*fig*) scopo, direzione; **in the direction of** in direzione di; **sense of direction** senso dell'orientamento

   b (*management: of business*) direzione *f*, amministrazione *f*; (*of play, film, programme*) regia

   c : **directions** NPL (*instructions: to a place*) indicazioni *fpl*; (*: for use*) istruzioni *fpl*; (*advice*) chiarimenti *mpl*; **to ask for directions** chiedere la strada; **stage directions** didascalie *fpl.*

di·rec·tion·al [dɪ'rɛkʃənl] ADJ direzionale.

♦ **di·rec·tion find·er** [dɪ,rɛkʃən'faɪndə'] N radiogoniometro.

di·rec·tive [dɪ'rɛktɪv] N direttiva, ordine *m*; **a government directive** una disposizione governativa.

♦ **direct labour** N manodopera diretta.

di·rect·ly [dɪ'rɛktlɪ] ☐1 ADV (*gen*) direttamente; (*at once*) subito; (*descended*) in linea diretta; (*frankly: speak*) con franchezza, senza peli sulla lingua; (*completely: opposite*) proprio.

   ☐2 CONJ (*non*) appena; **he'll come directly he's ready** verrà non appena sarà pronto.

♦ **direct mail** N mailing *m.*

♦ **direct mailshot** N (*Brit*) materiale *m* pubblicitario ad approccio diretto.

di·rect·ness [daɪ'rɛktnɪs] N (*of person, speech*) franchezza.

di·rec·tor [dɪ'rɛktə'] N (*Comm*) dirigente *m/f*, direttore (-trice) (d'azienda); (*of play, film, TV programme*) regista *m/f.*

♦ **Director of Public Prosecutions** N (*Brit*) ≈ Procuratore *m* della Repubblica.

di·rec·tor·ship [dɪ'rɛktə,ʃɪp] N direzione *f*; (*post*) carica di direttore.

di·rec·tory [dɪ'rɛktərɪ] N (*telephone directory*) elenco (telefonico); (*street directory*) stradario; (*trade directory*) repertorio del commercio; (*Comput*) directory *m inv.*

♦ **directory enquiries**, (*Am*) **directory assistance** N (*Telec*) servizio informazioni, informazioni *fpl* elenco abbonati.

♦ **direct tax** N imposta diretta.

dirge [dɜ:dʒ] N lamento funebre.

dirt [dɜ:t] N (*on face, clothes etc*) sporco, sporcizia; (*earth*) terra; (*mud*) fango; **dog dirt** bisogni *mpl* di un cane; **to treat sb like dirt** (*fam*) trattare qn come uno straccio; **to dig up dirt about sb** (*fam*) pescare nel torbido a proposito di qc; **to spread the dirt about sb** (*fam*) sparlare di qn; **have you heard the latest dirt on ...?** (*fam*) hai sentito l'ultimo scandalo riguardo a...?

♦ **dirt-cheap** [dɜ:t'tʃi:p] ADJ (*fam*) regalato(-a).

dirti·ly ['dɜ:tɪlɪ] ADV sudiciamente.

dirti·ness ['dɜ:tɪnɪs] N sporcizia, sudiciume *m.*

♦ **dirt road** N strada non asfaltata.

♦ **dirt track** N stradina sterrata.

dirty ['dɜ:tɪ] ☐1 ADJ (*comp* **-ier**, *superl* **-iest**) (*gen*) sporco(-a); (*cut, wound*) infetto(-a); (*indecent: novel, story, joke*)

sporco(-a), spinto(-a); **dirty trick** brutto scherzo; **to give sb a dirty look** (*fam*) lanciare un'occhiataccia a qn; **to play a dirty trick on sb** farla sporca a qn, giocare un brutto scherzo a qn; **to have a dirty mind** pensare solo a quello; **a dirty old man** un vecchio sporcaccione; **dirty word** parolaccia; **it's a dirty word these days** oggigiorno è un argomento tabù; **do your own dirty work!** non passare a me le tue gatte da pelare!.
[2] VT sporcare, insudiciare.

dis·abil·ity [ˌdɪsə'bɪlɪtɪ] N (*injury etc*) menomazione *f*, infermità *f inv*; (*state*) invalidità *f inv*, handicap *m inv*; (*Law, fig*) incapacità *f inv*; **disability allowance** ≈ pensione *f* d'invalidità.

dis·able [dɪs'eɪbl] VT (*subj: illness, accident*) rendere invalido(-a); (*tank, gun*) mettere fuori uso; (*Law: disqualify*) rendere inabile.

dis·abled [dɪs'eɪbld] [1] ADJ handicappato(-a), invalido (-a); (*maimed*) mutilato(-a); (*through illness, old age*) inabile; **disabled ex-serviceman** invalido di guerra.
[2]: **the disabled** NPL gli invalidi.

dis·able·ment [dɪs'eɪblmənt] N (*injury*) menomazione *f*; (*condition*) invalidità; **disablement pension** ≈ pensione di invalidità.

dis·abuse [ˌdɪsə'bjuːz] VT: **to disabuse sb (of sth)** (*frm*) disingannare qn (su qc).

dis·ad·vant·age [ˌdɪsəd'vɑːntɪdʒ] N svantaggio; **to be to sb's disadvantage** tornare a svantaggio *or* sfavore di qn; **to be at a disadvantage** essere svantaggiato(-a).

dis·ad·van·taged [ˌdɪsəd'vɑːntɪdʒd] ADJ (*person*) svantaggiato(-a).

dis·ad·van·ta·geous [ˌdɪsædvɑːn'teɪdʒəs] ADJ svantaggioso(-a), sfavorevole.

dis·af·fect·ed [ˌdɪsə'fɛktɪd] ADJ (*voters, supporters*) deluso (-a); (*young people*) ribelle.

dis·af·fec·tion [ˌdɪsə'fɛkʃən] N malcontento, insoddisfazione *f*.

dis·agree [ˌdɪsə'griː] VI **a** : **to disagree (with sb on** *or* **about sth)** essere in disaccordo (con qn su qc), dissentire (da qn su qc); (*quarrel*) litigare; (*stories, accounts, figures: conflict*) essere discordante; **I disagree with you** non sono d'accordo con te
  b : **to disagree with sth** (*oppose*) non essere d'accordo su qc
  c : **to disagree with** (*subj: climate, food*) non fare bene a; **a hot climate disagrees with me** il clima caldo non mi si confà; **onions disagree with me** non digerisco la cipolla.

dis·agree·able [ˌdɪsə'griːəbl] ADJ (*gen*) spiacevole; (*weather*) brutto(-a); (*person*) antipatico(-a); (*tone of voice*) sgradevole.

dis·agree·able·ness [ˌdɪsə'griːəblnɪs] N (*gen*) spiacevolezza; (*of person, tone of voice*) sgradevolezza.

dis·agree·ably [ˌdɪsə'griːəblɪ] ADV (*surprised*) sgradevolmente, in modo sgradevole; (*behave*) in modo spiacevole, in modo antipatico.

dis·agree·ment [ˌdɪsə'griːmənt] N (*with opinion*) disaccordo; (*quarrel*) dissapore *m*, litigio; (*between stories, accounts, figures*) discrepanza, discordanza; **to have a disagreement with sb** litigare con qn.

dis·al·low ['dɪsə'laʊ] VT respingere; (*Ftbl: goal*) annullare.

dis·ap·pear [ˌdɪsə'pɪə'] VI scomparire, sparire; **he disappeared from sight** è scomparso alla vista; **to make sth disappear** far sparire qc.

dis·ap·pear·ance [ˌdɪsə'pɪərəns] N scomparsa, sparizione *f*.

dis·ap·point [ˌdɪsə'pɔɪnt] VT deludere.

dis·ap·point·ed [ˌdɪsə'pɔɪntɪd] ADJ deluso(-a).

dis·ap·point·ing [ˌdɪsə'pɔɪntɪŋ] ADJ deludente.

dis·ap·point·ing·ly [ˌdɪsə'pɔɪntɪŋlɪ] ADV in modo deludente.

dis·ap·point·ment [ˌdɪsə'pɔɪntmənt] N (*cause of dejection*) delusione *f*; (*dejection*) disappunto.

dis·ap·prov·al [dɪsə'pruːvəl] N disapprovazione *f*.

dis·ap·prove [ˌdɪsə'pruːv] VI: **to disapprove (of sb/sth)** disapprovare (qn/qc).

dis·ap·prov·ing [ˌdɪsə'pruːvɪŋ] ADJ di disapprovazione.

dis·ap·prov·ing·ly [ˌdɪsə'pruːvɪŋlɪ] ADV con aria (*or* tono) di disapprovazione.

dis·arm [dɪs'ɑːm] [1] VT disarmare.
[2] VI (*Mil*) disarmarsi.

dis·arma·ment [dɪs'ɑːməmənt] N disarmo; **disarmament talks** conferenza sul disarmo.

dis·arm·ing [dɪs'ɑːmɪŋ] ADJ (*smile*) disarmante.

dis·arm·ing·ly [dɪs'ɑːmɪŋlɪ] ADV in modo disarmante.

dis·ar·range [ˌdɪsə'reɪndʒ] VT (*things*) buttare all'aria; (*hair*) scompigliare.

dis·ar·ray [ˌdɪsə'reɪ] N: **in disarray** (*troops*) in rotta; (*thoughts*) confuso(-a); (*clothes*) in disordine; **to throw into disarray** (*things, plans*) buttare all'aria; (*people*) portare lo scompiglio in.

dis·as·ter [dɪ'zɑːstə'] N (*also fig*) disastro; **disaster area** zona disastrata; **disaster fund** *raccolta di fondi a favore delle vittime di un disastro*.

dis·as·trous [dɪ'zɑːstrəs] ADJ disastroso(-a).

dis·as·trous·ly [dɪ'zɑːstrəslɪ] ADV disastrosamente.

dis·avow [ˌdɪsə'vaʊ] VT (*frm: one's opinions*) sconfessare; (: *one's words*) ritrattare; (: *one's faith*) rinnegare.

dis·band [dɪs'bænd] [1] VT (*army*) congedare, smobilitare; (*organization*) sciogliere.
[2] VI sciogliersi.

dis·be·lief ['dɪsbə'liːf] N incredulità; **in disbelief** incredulo (-a).

dis·be·lieve ['dɪsbə'liːv] VT (*person, story*) non credere a, mettere in dubbio; **I don't disbelieve you** non è che non ti creda.

dis·be·liev·ing [ˌdɪsbə'liːvɪŋ] ADJ (*smile, look*) incredulo (-a).

dis·be·liev·ing·ly [ˌdɪsbə'liːvɪŋlɪ] ADV in modo incredulo, con incredulità.

dis·burse [dɪs'bɜːs] VT (*frm*) sborsare.

dis·burse·ment [dɪs'bɜːsmənt] N (*frm*) esborso.

disc [dɪsk] N **a** (*gen, record, Anat*) disco; (*identity disc: of dog*) targhetta di riconoscimento; (: *of soldier*) piastrina di riconoscimento **b** (*Comput*) = **disk**.

dis·card [dɪs'kɑːd] VT (*clothes*) smettere; (*unwanted things*) sbarazzarsi di; (*idea, plan, playing card*) scartare; (*people*) abbandonare.

♦ **disc brakes** NPL (*Aut*) freni *mpl* a disco.

dis·cern [dɪ'sɜːn] VT (*frm*) distinguere, discernere.

dis·cern·ible [dɪ'sɜːnəbl] ADJ (*frm*) percepibile.

dis·cern·ing [dɪ'sɜːnɪŋ] ADJ (*buyer, reader, collector*) esperto(-a), perspicace; (*eye*) da intenditore(-trice); (*taste*) raffinato(-a), sicuro(-a).

dis·cern·ment [dɪ'sɜːnmənt] N discernimento.

dis·charge [*n* 'dɪstʃɑːdʒ; *vb* dɪs'tʃɑːdʒ] [1] N **a** (*of cargo*) operazione *f* di scarico; (*of gun*) scarica
  b (*of patient*) dimissione *f*; (*of worker*) licenziamento; (*of soldier*) congedo; (*of prisoner*) rilascio; (*of duty*) adempimento; (*of debt*) estinzione *f*
  c (*Elec*) scarica; (*of gas, chemicals*) emissione *f*; (*of water, waste*) scarico; (*Med: from wound*) secrezione *f*; (: *vaginal*

discharge) perdite *fpl* (bianche).

2 VT **a** (*ship, load*) scaricare; (*waste*) scaricare; (*shot*) far partire; (*liquid*) versare; (*Med: pus etc*) spurgare, emettere; **to discharge one's gun** fare fuoco

b (*dismiss: employee*) licenziare; (: *soldier*) congedare; (: *patient*) dimettere; (: *prisoner*) rilasciare; (: *defendant*) prosciogliere; **discharged bankrupt** *fallito cui il tribunale ha concesso la riabilitazione*

c (*settle: debt*) pagare, estinguere; (*complete: task*) assolvere, adempiere a; (*duties*) compiere.

3 VI (*wound, sore*) spurgare; (*Elec*) scaricarsi.

dis·ci·ple [dɪˈsaɪpl] N (*also fig*) discepolo(-a).

dis·ci·pli·nar·ian [ˌdɪsɪplɪˈnɛərɪən] N chi impone la disciplina; **to be a strict disciplinarian** far osservare rigorosamente la disciplina.

dis·ci·pli·nary [ˈdɪsɪplmərɪ] ADJ disciplinare; **to take disciplinary action against sb** prendere un provvedimento disciplinare contro qn.

dis·ci·pline [ˈdɪsɪplm] **1** N disciplina; (*punishment*) punizione *f*, castigo; **to keep/maintain discipline** tenere/mantenere la disciplina.

2 VT (*punish*) punire, castigare; **to discipline o.s. to do sth** imporsi di fare qc; **to discipline o.s** darsi una regola.

♦ **disc jockey** N disc jockey *m inv*.

dis·claim [dɪsˈkleɪm] VT (*frm*) negare, smentire; **to disclaim all knowledge of sth** negare di essere a conoscenza di qc.

dis·claim·er [dɪsˈkleɪməʳ] N (*frm*) smentita; **to issue a disclaimer** pubblicare una smentita.

dis·close [dɪsˈkləʊz] VT (*all senses*) rivelare, svelare.

dis·clo·sure [dɪsˈkləʊʒəʳ] N rivelazione *f*.

dis·co [ˈdɪskəʊ] N (*fam: place*) discoteca; (: *event*) festa (con disc jockey).

dis·col·our, (*Am*) **dis·col·or** [dɪsˈkʌləʳ] **1** VT scolorire, sbiadire; (*whites*) ingiallire.

2 VI scolorirsi, sbiadire; (*whites*) ingiallire.

dis·col·oura·tion, (*Am*) **dis·col·ora·tion** [dɪsˌkʌləˈreɪʃən] N (*see adj*) scolorimento; ingiallimento.

dis·col·oured, (*Am*) **dis·col·ored** [dɪsˈkʌləd] ADJ scolorito(-a), sbiadito(-a); (*whites*) ingiallito(-a).

dis·com·fit [dɪsˈkʌmfɪt] VT (*liter*) sconcertare.

dis·com·fi·ture [dɪsˈkʌmfɪtʃəʳ] N (*liter*) disagio, imbarazzo.

dis·com·fort [dɪsˈkʌmfət] N (*lack of comfort*) scomodità *f inv*; (*uneasiness*) disagio, imbarazzo; **his wound gave him some discomfort** la ferita gli procurava un certo disagio.

dis·con·cert [dɪskənˈsɜːt] VT sconcertare.

dis·con·cert·ed [ˌdɪskənˈsɜːtɪd] ADJ sconcertato(-a).

dis·con·cert·ing [ˌdɪskənˈsɜːtɪŋ] ADJ sconcertante.

dis·con·cert·ing·ly [ˌdɪskənˈsɜːtɪŋlɪ] ADV sorprendentemente, in modo sconcertante.

dis·con·nect [ˈdɪskəˈnɛkt] VT (*pipe, television*) staccare; (*electricity, gas, water*) sospendere (l'erogazione di); **I've been disconnected** (*Telec: for non-payment*) mi hanno staccato il telefono; (: *in mid-conversation*) è caduta la linea, si è interrotta la comunicazione.

dis·con·nec·ted [ˌdɪskəˈnɛktɪd] ADJ (*speech, thoughts, facts*) sconnesso(-a).

dis·con·so·late [dɪsˈkɒnsəlɪt] ADJ sconsolato(-a).

dis·con·so·late·ly [dɪsˈkɒnsəlɪtlɪ] ADV sconsolatamente.

dis·con·tent [ˈdɪskənˈtɛnt] N scontentezza, dispiacere *m*; (*Pol*) malcontento, scontento.

dis·con·tent·ed [ˈdɪskənˈtɛntɪd] ADJ: **discontented (with/about)** scontento(-a) (di), insoddisfatto(-a) (di).

dis·con·tent·ed·ly [ˌdɪskənˈtɛntɪdlɪ] ADV con insoddisfazione.

dis·con·tinue [ˈdɪskənˈtɪnjuː] VT interrompere, cessare; (*Comm*): **discontinued line** articolo fuori produzione.

dis·con·ti·nu·ity [dɪsˌkɒntɪˈnjuːɪtɪ] (*frm*) N (*quality*) discontinuità *f inv*; (*gap*) interruzione *f*.

dis·con·tinu·ous [ˌdɪskənˈtɪnjʊəs] ADJ (*process*) discontinuo(-a); (*speech*) incoerente.

dis·cord [ˈdɪskɔːd] N disaccordo, discordia; (*Mus*) dissonanza.

dis·cord·ant [dɪsˈkɔːdənt] ADJ (*gen*) discordante; (*sound*) dissonante, stonato(-a).

dis·co·theque [ˈdɪskəʊtɛk] N discoteca.

dis·count [*n* ˈdɪskaʊnt; *vb* dɪsˈkaʊnt] **1** N (*reduction*) sconto, riduzione *f*; **to be at a discount** (*Comm*) essere scontato(-a); (*fig: little valued*) essere svalutato(-a); **to buy at a discount** comprare a prezzo scontato; **to give sb a discount on sth** fare uno sconto a qn su qc; **discount for cash** sconto cassa *inv*; **discount rate** tasso di sconto.

2 VT (*Comm*) scontare; (*fig: report, idea, theory*) non badare a.

♦ **discount house** N **a** (*Brit Fin*) istituto di sconto, discount house *f inv* **b** (*Am*) = **discount store**.

♦ **discount store** N negozio di vendita diretta, discount *m inv*.

dis·cour·age [dɪsˈkʌrɪdʒ] VT **a** (*dishearten*) scoraggiare; **I don't want to discourage you, but ...** non vorrei scoraggiarti, ma... **b** (*dissuade, deter*) tentare di dissuadere; **to discourage sb from doing sth** tentare di dissuadere qn dal fare qc.

dis·cour·age·ment [dɪsˈkʌrɪdʒmənt] N (*dissuasion*) disapprovazione *f*; (*depression*) scoraggiamento; **to act as a discouragement to** scoraggiare.

dis·cour·ag·ing [dɪsˈkʌrɪdʒɪŋ] ADJ scoraggiante, avvilente.

dis·course [ˈdɪskɔːs] **1** N **a** (*disquisition*) dissertazione *f* **b** (*conversation*) conversazione *f*; (*written*) dissertazione *f*.

2 VI: **to discourse on/upon** dissertare su.

♦ **discourse analysis** N (*Ling*) analisi *f inv* del discorso.

dis·cour·teous [dɪsˈkɜːtɪəs] ADJ scortese.

dis·cour·teous·ly [dɪsˈkɜːtɪəslɪ] ADV scortesemente.

dis·cour·tesy [dɪsˈkɜːtɪsɪ] N scortesia.

dis·cov·er [dɪsˈkʌvəʳ] VT (*gen*) scoprire; (*after search*) scovare, trovare; (*notice: loss, mistake*) scoprire, accorgersi di.

dis·cov·er·er [dɪsˈkʌvərəʳ] N scopritore(-trice).

dis·cov·ery [dɪsˈkʌvərɪ] N scoperta.

dis·cred·it [dɪsˈkrɛdɪt] (*frm*) **1** N discredito; **to bring discredit on sb/sth** far cadere qn/qc in discredito.

2 VT screditare.

dis·cred·it·able [dɪsˈkrɛdɪtəbl] ADJ (*frm*) disonorevole.

dis·creet [dɪsˈkriːt] ADJ discreto(-a).

dis·creet·ly [dɪsˈkriːtlɪ] ADV discretamente, con discrezione.

dis·crep·an·cy [dɪsˈkrɛpənsɪ] N discrepanza.

dis·crete [dɪsˈkriːt] ADJ (*separate, distinct*) separato(-a), distinto(-a); (*Statistics*) discreto(-a).

dis·cre·tion [dɪsˈkrɛʃən] N discrezione *f*; **at your/his etc discretion** a tua/sua *etc* discrezione; **use your own discretion** giudica tu.

dis·cre·tion·ary [dɪsˈkrɛʃənərɪ] ADJ (*powers, payment*) discrezionale.

dis·crimi·nate [dɪsˈkrɪmɪˌneɪt] VI: **to discriminate (between)** (*gen*) distinguere (tra); **to discriminate against/in favour of** fare discriminazioni ai danni di/a favore di; **to discriminate against women** fare discriminazioni contro le donne.

dis·crimi·nat·ing [dɪsˈkrɪmɪˌneɪtɪŋ] ADJ (*person*) esigente; (*judgment*) acuto(-a); (*ear*) fine.

dis·crimi·na·tion [dɪsˌkrɪmɪˈneɪʃən] N **a** (*prejudice*): discrimination (against/in favour of) discriminazione *f* (ai danni di/a favore di); **racial/sexual discrimination** discriminazione razziale/sessuale **b** (*good judgment*) discernimento.

dis·crimi·na·tory [diˈskrɪmɪnətərɪ] ADJ discriminatorio (-a).

dis·cus [ˈdɪskəs] N disco; **discus thrower** lanciatore(-trice) di disco.

dis·cuss [dɪsˈkʌs] VT (*general topic*) discutere di; (*problem, plan*) discutere; (*debate*) dibattere; **to discuss sth at length** dibattere qc a lungo.

dis·cus·sion [dɪsˈkʌʃən] N discussione *f*; (*meeting*) colloquio, dibattito; **it's still under discussion** (*plan, policy*) non è ancora definitivo.

dis·dain [dɪsˈdeɪn] ① N disdegno.
② VT sdegnare; **to disdain to do sth** disdegnare di fare qc.

dis·dain·ful [dɪsˈdeɪnfʊl] ADJ (*person, tone*) sdegnoso(-a); (*look, laugh*) sprezzante.

dis·dain·ful·ly [dɪsˈdeɪnfəlɪ] ADV (*act, speak*) sdegnosamente; (*look, laugh*) in modo sprezzante.

dis·ease [dɪˈziːz] N malattia.

dis·eased [dɪˈziːzd] ADJ malato(-a).

dis·em·bark [ˌdɪsɪmˈbɑːk] VI, VT sbarcare.

dis·em·bar·ka·tion [ˌdɪsɛmbɑːˈkeɪʃən] N sbarco.

dis·em·bod·ied [ˈdɪsɪmˈbɒdɪd] ADJ incorporeo(-a); (*voice*) etereo(-a); (*soul, spirit*) disincarnato(-a).

dis·em·bow·el [dɪsɪmˈbaʊəl] VT sbudellare, sventrare.

dis·en·chant·ed [ˌdɪsɪnˈtʃɑːntɪd] ADJ disincantato(-a); **disenchanted (with)** deluso(-a) (da).

dis·en·chant·ment [ˌdɪsɪnˈtʃɑːntmənt] N disincanto.

dis·en·fran·chise [ˈdɪsɪnˈfræntʃaɪz] VT privare del diritto di voto; (*Comm*) togliere il privilegio commerciale a.

dis·en·gage [ˌdɪsɪnˈgeɪdʒ] ① VT (*object, hand*) liberare; (*Aut: clutch*) disinnestare; (*Mil: forces*) disimpegnare.
② VI (*see vt*): **to disengage (from)** disinnestarsi (da); disimpegnarsi (da).

dis·en·gage·ment [ˌdɪsɪnˈgeɪdʒmənt] N (*of clutch*) disinnesto; (*Pol*) disimpegno.

dis·en·tan·gle [ˈdɪsɪnˈtæŋgl] VT (*string, wool*) sbrogliare; **to disentangle o.s. from** (*fig*) districarsi da, sbrogliarsi da.

dis·fa·vour, (*Am*) **dis·fa·vor** [dɪsˈfeɪvəʳ] N (*frm*) disapprovazione *f*; **to fall into disfavour** cadere in disgrazia; **to be in disfavour with sb** avere la disapprovazione di qn; **to look with disfavour on** disapprovare.

dis·fig·ure [dɪsˈfɪgəʳ] VT (*person*) sfigurare; (*landscape*) deturpare.

dis·fig·ure·ment [dɪsˈfɪgəmənt] N: **to have a hideous disfigurement** essere orribilmente sfigurato(-a); **his disfigurement was caused by an accident** rimase sfigurato in un incidente.

dis·gorge [dɪsˈgɔːdʒ] VT (*contents*) scaricare; (*subj: vehicle, building*) scaricare.

dis·grace [dɪsˈgreɪs] ① N (*state of shame*) disonore *m*, vergogna; (*shameful thing*) vergogna; (*disfavour*) disgrazia; **he's a disgrace to the school/family** è il disonore della scuola/della famiglia; **he's brought disgrace upon himself** si è ricoperto di vergogna; **to be in disgrace** essere in disgrazia; (*child, dog*) essere in castigo; **it's a disgrace** è una vergogna.
② VT (*family, country*) disonorare, far cadere in disgrazia; **he disgraced himself** ha fatto una pessima figura; **he was**

publicly disgraced fu svergognato pubblicamente.

dis·grace·ful [dɪsˈgreɪsfʊl] ADJ vergognoso(-a), scandaloso(-a).

dis·grace·ful·ly [dɪsˈgreɪsfəlɪ] ADV vergognosamente, scandalosamente.

dis·grun·tled [dɪsˈgrʌntld] ADJ (*person*) di malumore, di cattivo umore; (*look*) seccato(-a).

dis·guise [dɪsˈgaɪz] ① N travestimento; **in disguise** travestito(-a).
② VT (*gen*) travestire; (*voice*) contraffare; (*feelings*) mascherare; **to disguise o.s. as** travestirsi da; **there's no disguising the fact that** ... non si può nascondere (il fatto) che... .

dis·gust [dɪsˈgʌst] ① N disgusto; **much to my disgust** con mio profondo disgusto; **she left in disgust** se n'è andata disgustata.
② VT disgustare, far schifo a.

dis·gust·ed [dɪsˈgʌstɪd] ADJ: **to be disgusted (at)** essere disgustato(-a) (di fronte a).

dis·gust·ed·ly [dɪsˈgʌstɪdlɪ] ADV con disgusto.

dis·gust·ing [dɪsˈgʌstɪŋ] ADJ schifoso(-a), disgustoso(-a).

dis·gust·ing·ly [dɪsˈgʌstɪŋlɪ] ADV disgustosamente.

dish [dɪʃ] N piatto, pietanza; **to wash** or **do the dishes** lavare or fare i piatti.
▶ **dish out** VT + ADV (*food*) servire; (*advice*) dispensare; (*money*) sganciare; (*exam papers*) distribuire
▶ **dish up** VT + ADV (*food*) servire; (*facts, statistics*) presentare.

dis·ha·bille [ˌdɪsæˈbiːl] N déshabillé *m inv*; **in dishabille** in déshabillé.

dis·har·mo·ny [dɪsˈhɑːmənɪ] N (*frm*) disaccordo.

dish·cloth [ˈdɪʃˌklɒθ] N strofinaccio dei piatti.

dis·heart·en [dɪsˈhɑːtn] VT scoraggiare.

dis·heart·en·ed [dɪsˈhɑːtənd] ADJ scoraggiato(-a), avvilito (-a).

dis·heart·en·ing [dɪsˈhɑːtnɪŋ] ADJ scoraggiante, deprimente.

di·shev·elled, (*Am*) **di·shev·eled** [dɪˈʃɛvəld] ADJ (*hair*) arruffato(-a); (*clothes*) tutto(-a) in disordine.

dish·mop [ˈdɪʃˌmɒp] N strofinaccio per i piatti.

dis·hon·est [dɪsˈɒnɪst] ADJ (*person, action*) disonesto(-a); (*means*) sleale.

dis·hon·est·ly [dɪsˈɒnɪstlɪ] ADV disonestamente, in modo disonesto.

dis·hon·es·ty [dɪsˈɒnɪstɪ] N (*see adj*) disonestà *f inv*; slealtà *f inv*.

dis·hon·our, (*Am*) **dis·hon·or** [dɪsˈɒnəʳ] ① N (*frm*) disonore *m*; **to bring dishonour on** gettare il disonore su, far disonore a.
② VT (*family, woman*) disonorare; (*cheque*) non onorare.

dis·hon·our·able, (*Am*) **dis·hon·or·able** [dɪsˈɒnərəbl] ADJ disonorevole.

dis·hon·our·ably, (*Am*) **dis·hon·or·ably** [dɪsˈɒnərəblɪ] ADV disonorevolmente.

dish·rack [ˈdɪʃˌræk] N scolapiatti *m inv*.

dish·towel [ˈdɪʃˌtaʊəl] N strofinaccio dei piatti.

dish·washer [ˈdɪʃˌwɒʃəʳ] N (*machine*) lavastoviglie *f inv*; (*person: in restaurant*) lavapiatti *m/f inv*.

dish·water [ˈdɪʃˌwɔːtəʳ] N sciacquatura dei piatti.

dishy [ˈdɪʃɪ] ADJ (*comp* **-ier**, *superl* **-iest**) (*Brit fam: esp man*) figo(-a).

dis·il·lu·sion [ˌdɪsɪˈluːʒən] ① VT disilludere, disingannare; **to become disillusioned (with)** perdere le illusioni (su).
② N = **disillusionment**.

dis·il·lu·sion·ment [ˌdɪsɪˈluːʒənmənt] N disillusione *f*,

dis·in·cen·tive [ˌdɪsɪnˈsɛntɪv] N (frm): **to act as a disincentive (to)** agire da freno (su); **to be a disincentive to** scoraggiare.

dis·in·cli·na·tion [ˌdɪsɪnklɪˈneɪʃən] N (frm): **disinclination (for/to do)** riluttanza (a/a fare).

dis·in·clined [ˈdɪsɪnˈklaɪnd] ADJ: **to be disinclined to do sth** essere poco propenso(-a) a fare qc.

dis·in·fect [ˌdɪsɪnˈfɛkt] VT disinfettare.

dis·in·fect·ant [ˌdɪsɪnˈfɛktənt] N disinfettante m.

dis·in·fec·tion [ˌdɪsɪnˈfɛkʃən] N disinfezione f.

dis·in·fla·tion [ˌdɪsɪnˈfleɪʃən] N (Econ) disinflazione f.

dis·in·for·ma·tion [ˌdɪsɪnfəˈmeɪʃən] N disinformazione f.

dis·in·genu·ous [ˌdɪsɪnˈdʒɛnjʊəs] ADJ insincero(-a).

dis·in·her·it [ˈdɪsɪnˈhɛrɪt] VT diseredare.

dis·in·te·grate [dɪsˈɪntɪgreɪt] VI disintegrarsi; (fig: society, theory) disgregarsi.

dis·in·te·gra·tion [dɪsˌɪntɪˈgreɪʃən] N (see vb) disintegrazione f; disgregamento.

dis·in·ter·est·ed [dɪsˈɪntrɪstɪd] ADJ (impartial) disinteressato(-a); (strictly incorrect: uninterested) non interessato(-a), indifferente.

dis·in·ter·est·ed·ness [dɪsˈɪntrɪstɪdnɪs] N (impartiality) disinteresse m, imparzialità f inv; (incorrect use: lack of interest) disinteresse m.

dis·joint·ed [dɪsˈdʒɔɪntɪd] ADJ sconnesso(-a), slegato(-a).

dis·joint·ed·ly [dɪsˈdʒɔɪntɪdlɪ] ADV in modo sconnesso, in modo slegato.

disk [dɪsk] N **a** = **disc b** (Comput) disco; **single-/double-sided disk** disco m monofaccia inv/a doppia faccia.

♦ **disk drive** N (Comput) disk drive m inv, unità f inv a dischi magnetici.

disk·ette [dɪsˈkɛt] N (Comput) dischetto, floppy disk m inv.

♦ **disk operating system** N (Comput) sistema m operativo a disco.

dis·like [dɪsˈlaɪk] [1] N: **dislike (of)** antipatia (per), avversione f (per); **to take a dislike to sb/sth** prendere in antipatia qn/qc.

[2] VT (thing, person): **I dislike it** non mi piace; **I dislike the idea** l'idea non mi va; **I dislike her intensely** mi è fortemente antipatica, mi è antipaticissima.

dis·lo·cate [ˈdɪsləʊkeɪt] VT (Med) slogare, lussare; (fig: plans) scombussolare; **he dislocated his shoulder** si è lussato una spalla.

dis·lo·ca·tion [ˌdɪsləʊˈkeɪʃən] N (Med) slogatura, lussazione f.

dis·lodge [dɪsˈlɒdʒ] VT (gen) rimuovere; (enemy) far sgomberare.

dis·loy·al [ˈdɪsˈlɔɪəl] ADJ: **disloyal (to)** sleale (verso).

dis·loy·al·ly [ˈdɪsˈlɔɪəlɪ] ADV slealmente.

dis·loy·al·ty [ˈdɪsˈlɔɪəltɪ] N slealtà.

dis·mal [ˈdɪzməl] ADJ (gloomy) tetro(-a), cupo(-a); (weather) grigio(-a); **it was a dismal failure** è stato un misero fallimento.

dis·mal·ly [ˈdɪzməlɪ] ADV tetramente, cupamente; **to fail dismally** fallire miseramente.

dis·man·tle [dɪsˈmæntl] VT (machine etc) smontare; (service, system) smantellare; (fort, warship) disarmare.

dis·may [dɪsˈmeɪ] [1] N sgomento, costernazione f; **in dismay** costernato(-a); **much to my dismay** con mio gran sgomento.

[2] VT costernare, sgomentare.

dis·mem·ber [dɪsˈmɛmbə'] VT (frm) smembrare.

dis·miss [dɪsˈmɪs] [1] VT **a** (worker) licenziare; (official) destituire; (assembly) sciogliere

b (gen) congedare; (charge, accusation) respingere; (problem, possibility, idea) scartare; **the judge dismissed the case** (Law) il giudice ha dichiarato il non luogo a procedere; **class dismissed!** (Scol) potete andare!.

[2] VI (Mil) rompere i ranghi.

dis·mis·sal [dɪsˈmɪsəl] N congedo; (of worker) licenziamento; (of official) destituzione f; (of assembly) scioglimento; **the dismissal of a case** (Law) il non luogo a procedere.

dis·miss·ive [dɪsˈmɪsɪv] ADJ: **dismissive (of)** sprezzante (nei confronti di).

dis·mount [dɪsˈmaʊnt] [1] VI: **to dismount (from)** smontare (da), scendere (da).

[2] VT **a** (gun) smontare **b** (rider) disarcionare.

dis·obedi·ence [ˌdɪsəˈbiːdɪəns] N disubbidienza.

dis·obedi·ent [ˌdɪsəˈbiːdɪənt] ADJ disubbidiente.

dis·obey [ˈdɪsəˈbeɪ] VT (person, order) disubbidire a; (rule) trasgredire.

dis·oblig·ing [ˈdɪsəˈblaɪdʒɪŋ] ADJ (frm) poco disponibile.

dis·or·der [dɪsˈɔːdə'] N **a** (confusion) confusione f, caos m; (untidiness) disordine m; **in disorder** in disordine **b** (Pol: rioting) disordini mpl, tumulto; **civil disorder** disordini mpl (interni) **c** (Med) disturbi mpl.

dis·or·dered [dɪsˈɔːdəd] ADJ (room) disordinato(-a), in disordine; (thoughts) disordinato(-a), confuso(-a); (Psych: mind) turbato(-a).

dis·or·der·ly [dɪsˈɔːdəlɪ] ADJ (room) disordinato(-a); (behaviour, crowd) turbolento(-a); (meeting) tumultuoso(-a), burrascoso(-a).

♦ **disorderly conduct** N (Law) comportamento atto a turbare l'ordine pubblico.

dis·or·gani·za·tion [dɪsˌɔːgənaɪˈzeɪʃən] N disorganizzazione f.

dis·or·gan·ize [dɪsˈɔːgənaɪz] VT disorganizzare.

dis·or·gan·ized [dɪsˈɔːgənaɪzd] ADJ (person, life) disorganizzato(-a); (system, meeting) male organizzato(-a).

dis·ori·ent [dɪsˈɔːrɪənt] VT disorientare.

dis·ori·en·tate [dɪsˈɔːrɪənˌteɪt] VT disorientare.

dis·own [dɪsˈəʊn] VT rinnegare, ripudiare.

dis·par·age [dɪsˈpærɪdʒ] VT (frm: person, achievements) denigrare.

dis·par·age·ment [dɪsˈpærɪdʒmənt] N (frm) denigrazione f, diffamazione f.

dis·par·ag·ing [dɪsˈpærɪdʒɪŋ] ADJ (comment, remark) denigratorio(-a); **to be disparaging about sb/sth** denigrare qn/qc.

dis·par·ag·ing·ly [dɪsˈpærɪdʒɪŋlɪ] ADV con tono denigratorio.

dis·par·ate [ˈdɪspərɪt] ADJ (frm) disparato(-a).

dis·par·ity [dɪsˈpærɪtɪ] N disparità f inv.

dis·pas·sion·ate [dɪsˈpæʃənɪt] ADJ (unbiased) spassionato(-a), imparziale; (unemotional) calmo(-a).

dis·pas·sion·ate·ly [dɪsˈpæʃənɪtlɪ] ADV (without bias) spassionatamente, in modo imparziale; (unemotionally) con calma.

dis·patch, des·patch [dɪsˈpætʃ] [1] N **a** (sending: of goods) spedizione f, invio; (: of person) invio; **dispatch department** reparto spedizioni

b (Mil, Press: report) dispaccio; **mentioned in dispatches** (Mil) citato(-a) all'ordine del giorno

c (promptness) prontezza, rapidità.

[2] VT **a** (send: letter, goods) spedire, inviare; (: messenger, troops) inviare

b (deal with: business) sbrigare

c (old: kill) uccidere, ammazzare; (hum) mandare all'al-

tro mondo.

♦ **dispatch rider** N (*Mil*) corriere *m*, portaordini *m inv*.

dis·pel [dɪs'pɛl] VT (*doubts, fears*) dissipare, scacciare.

dis·pen·sable [dɪs'pɛnsəbl] ADJ di cui si può fare a meno.

dis·pen·sa·ry [dɪs'pɛnsərɪ] N farmacia; (*clinic*) dispensario, ambulatorio.

dis·pen·sa·tion [ˌdɪspɛn'seɪʃən] N (*Law, Rel*) dispensa.

dis·pense [dɪs'pɛns] VT (*food, money*) dispensare, distribuire; (*justice*) amministrare; (*medicine*) preparare e dare; **to dispense prescriptions** preparare e dare medicine su ricetta.

▶ **dispense with** VT + PREP (*do without*) fare a meno di.

dis·pens·er [dɪs'pɛnsə'] N (*container*) distributore *m*.

dis·pens·ing chem·ist [dɪ'spɛnsɪŋ'kɛmɪst] N (*Brit: shop*) farmacia; (: *person*) farmacista *m/f*.

dis·per·sal [dɪs'pɜːsəl] N (*gen*) dispersione *f*; (*Bot*) disseminazione *f*.

dis·perse [dɪs'pɜːs] [1] VT (*crowd, demonstrators, oil slick*) disperdere.

[2] VI (*crowd*) disperdersi; (*mist*) dissiparsi.

dis·per·sion [dɪs'pɜːʃən] N = **dispersal**.

dis·pir·it·ed [dɪs'pɪrɪtɪd] ADJ abbattuto(-a), scoraggiato(-a); (*sigh*) di avvilimento.

dis·pir·it·ed·ly [dɪs'pɪrɪtɪdlɪ] ADV con aria abbattuta, con aria scoraggiata; (*speak*) con tono avvilito.

dis·pir·it·ing [dɪs'pɪrɪtɪŋ] ADJ deprimente.

dis·place [dɪs'pleɪs] VT (*move*) spostare; (*replace*) rimpiazzare, soppiantare; (*remove from office*) destituire; (*water: Naut*) dislocare; (: *Phys*) spostare.

dis·placed per·son [dɪs'pleɪsd'pɜːsn] N (*Pol*) profugo(-a).

dis·place·ment [dɪs'pleɪsmənt] N (*see vb*) spostamento; rimpiazzo; destituzione *f*; dislocamento.

dis·play [dɪs'pleɪ] [1] N a (*of goods for sale, paintings*) mostra, esposizione *f*; (*also*: **window display**) vetrina; (*of emotion*) manifestazione *f*; (*of strength, authority, force, interest*) dimostrazione *f*; (*pej: ostentation*) sfoggio, ostentazione *f*; **on display** (*gen*) in mostra; (*goods*) in vetrina; (*results, art*) esposto(-a); **display window** vetrina b (*military display*) parata (militare) c (*computer display*) display *m inv*.

[2] VT (*gen*) esporre; (*ostentatiously*) ostentare, far sfoggio di; (*emotion, ignorance*) mostrare, manifestare; (*notice, results*) affiggere; (*departure/arrival times*) indicare.

♦ **display advertisement** N (*Press*) locandina.

♦ **display advertising** N (*Press*) pubblicità tabellare.

dis·please [dɪs'pliːz] VT dispiacere a, scontentare; **displeased with** scontento(-a) di.

dis·pleas·ing [dɪs'pliːzɪŋ] ADJ: **displeasing (to)** sgradevole (a).

dis·pleas·ure [dɪs'plɛʒə'] N: **displeasure (at)** dispiacere *m* (per).

dis·pos·able [dɪs'pəʊzəbl] ADJ (*not reusable: razor, camera*) usa e getta *inv*; (*available: income*) disponibile; **disposable nappy** (*Brit*) pannolino.

dis·pos·al [dɪs'pəʊzəl] N (*of rubbish*) eliminazione *f*, smaltimento; (*of property etc: by selling*) vendita; (: *by giving away*) cessione *f*; **to put sth at sb's disposal** mettere qc a disposizione di qn; **to have at one's disposal** avere a propria disposizione.

dis·pose [dɪs'pəʊz] VT (*frm: arrange: furniture*) disporre; (: *troops*) disporre, schierare

▶ **dispose of** VI + PREP a (*get rid of: unwanted goods, evidence, rubbish*) sbarazzarsi di, disfarsi di; (*Comm: sell*) vendere b (*deal with: matter, problem*) sistemare.

dis·posed [dɪs'pəʊzd] ADJ: **to be disposed to do sth** essere

disposto(-a) a fare qc; **to be well disposed towards sb/sth** essere ben disposto(-a) verso qn/qc.

dis·po·si·tion [ˌdɪspə'zɪʃən] N (*frm*) a (*temperament*) indole *f*, temperamento; (*tendency*): **disposition to sth/to do sth** tendenza a qc/a fare qc, inclinazione *f*; **he was always of a nervous disposition** è sempre stato ansioso di carattere b (*arrangement*) disposizione *f*.

dis·pos·sess ['dɪspə'zɛs] VT: **to be dispossessed (of sth)** (*property*) essere spossessato(-a) (di qc).

dis·pro·por·tion [ˌdɪsprə'pɔːʃən] N sproporzione *f*.

dis·pro·por·tion·ate [ˌdɪsprə'pɔːʃnɪt] ADJ: **disproportionate (to)** sproporzionato(-a) (a or rispetto a).

dis·pro·por·tion·ate·ly [ˌdɪsprə'pɔːʃnɪtlɪ] ADV in modo sproporzionato; **disproportionately large** di una grandezza sproporzionata.

dis·prove [dɪs'pruːv] VT confutare.

dis·put·able [dɪs'pjuːtəbl] ADJ discutibile, contestabile.

dis·pute [dɪs'pjuːt] [1] N (*quarrel*) disputa; (*controversy*) discussione *f*, controversia; (*legal*) lite *f*; **industrial dispute** controversia sindacale; **beyond dispute** fuori discussione; **to be in dispute** (*matter*) essere in discussione; (*territory*) essere oggetto di contesa.

[2] VT a (*question: statement, claim*) contestare b (*debate: matter, question*) discutere c (*compete for: possession, victory*) disputarsi.

[3] VI (*argue*): **to dispute (about or over)** discutere (su).

dis·put·ed [dɪs'pjuːtɪd] ADJ (*territory*) contestato(-a).

dis·quali·fi·ca·tion [ˌdɪsˌkwɒlɪfɪ'keɪʃən] N (*from competition*) squalifica; (*of member*) espulsione *f*; (*Brit: from driving*) ritiro della patente.

dis·quali·fy [dɪs'kwɒlɪˌfaɪ] VT: **to disqualify sb (from)** (*from competition*) squalificare qn (da); **to disqualify sb from doing sth** vietare a qn di fare qc; **to disqualify sb from driving** (*Brit*) ritirare la patente a qn; **it disqualified him for the job** lo ha reso non adatto al lavoro.

dis·qui·et [dɪs'kwaɪət] N (*frm*) inquietudine *f*.

dis·qui·et·ing [dɪs'kwaɪətɪŋ] ADJ (*frm*) inquietante, allarmante.

dis·re·gard ['dɪsrɪ'gɑːd] [1] N (*indifference*): **disregard (for)** (*feelings*) insensibilità, indifferenza (verso); (*danger*) sprezzo (di); (*money*) disprezzo (di); (*non-observance*): **disregard (of)** (*law, rules*) inosservanza (di).

[2] VT (*remark, feelings, fact*) ignorare, non tenere conto di; (*duty*) trascurare; (*authority*) non curarsi di.

dis·re·pair ['dɪsrɪ'pɛə'] N cattivo stato; **to fall into disrepair** (*building*) andare in rovina; (*road*) deteriorarsi.

dis·repu·table [dɪs'rɛpjʊtəbl] ADJ (*person*) poco raccomandabile; (*clothing, behaviour*) indecente; (*area*) malfamato(-a), poco raccomandabile.

dis·repu·tably [dɪs'rɛpjʊtəblɪ] ADV (*behave, dress*) indecentemente.

dis·re·pute ['dɪsrɪ'pjuːt] N: **to bring into disrepute** rovinare la reputazione di; **to fall into disrepute** rovinarsi la reputazione.

dis·re·spect ['dɪsrɪs'pɛkt] N mancanza di rispetto.

dis·re·spect·ful [ˌdɪsrɪs'pɛktfʊl] ADJ (*person*) poco rispettoso(-a); (*comment*) irriverente; **to be disrespectful to or towards sb** mancare di rispetto a or verso.[*]

dis·re·spect·ful·ly [ˌdɪsrɪs'pɛktfəlɪ] ADV (*behave*) in modo irrispettoso; (*speak*) in modo irriverente.

dis·rupt [dɪs'rʌpt] VT (*meeting, lesson*) disturbare, interrompere; (*public transport*) creare il caos in; (*plans*) scombussolare.

dis·rup·tion [dɪs'rʌpʃən] N (*see vb*) interruzione *f*; caos *m*; scombussolamento.

dis·rup·tive [dɪsˈrʌptɪv] ADJ (*pupil*) indisciplinato(-a); (*influence*) negativo(-a), deleterio(-a); (*strike action*) paralizzante.

dis·sat·is·fac·tion [ˌdɪsˌsætɪsˈfækʃən] N scontentezza; **dissatisfaction (with)** insoddisfazione *f* (per), scontento (per *or* a causa di).

dis·sat·is·fied [ˈdɪsˈsætɪsfaɪd] ADJ: **dissatisfied (with)** insoddisfatto(-a) (di), scontento(-a) (di).

dis·sect [dɪˈsɛkt] VT (*animal, body, specimen*) sezionare; (*fig*) sviscerare.

dis·sec·tion [dɪˈsɛkʃən] N (*see vb*) dissezione *f*; sviscera-mento.

dis·sem·ble [dɪˈsɛmbl] VT, VI (*liter*) dissimulare.

dis·semi·nate [dɪˈsɛmɪˌneɪt] VT (*information*) diffondere.

dis·semi·na·tion [dɪˌsɛmɪˈneɪʃən] N diffusione *f*.

dis·sen·sion [dɪˈsɛnʃən] N (*frm*) dissenso.

dis·sent [dɪˈsɛnt] ①N dissenso.
　②VI (*gen*): **to dissent (from)** dissentire (da).

dis·sent·er [dɪˈsɛntəʳ] N (*Rel, Pol*) dissidente *m/f*.

dis·sent·ing [dɪˈsɛntɪŋ] ADJ dissenziente.

dis·ser·ta·tion [ˌdɪsəˈteɪʃən] N (*Univ*) tesi *f inv*, disserta-zione *f*.

dis·ser·vice [ˈdɪsˈsɜːvɪs] N: **to do sb a disservice** rendere un cattivo servizio a qn.

dis·si·dence [ˈdɪsɪdəns] N dissidenza.

dis·si·dent [ˈdɪsɪdənt] (*Pol*) ①N dissidente *m/f*.
　②ADJ (*speech, voice*) di dissenso; (*group*) dissidente.

dis·simi·lar [ˈdɪˈsɪmɪləʳ] ADJ: **dissimilar (to)** dissimile (da), diverso(-a) (da); **two very dissimilar cases** due casi molto diversi tra loro.

dis·simi·lar·ity [ˌdɪsɪmɪˈlærɪtɪ] N: **dissimilarity (between)** dissomiglianza (tra).

dis·simu·late [dɪˈsɪmjʊˌleɪt] VI (*frm*) dissimulare.

dis·simu·la·tion [dɪˌsɪmjʊˈleɪʃən] N (*frm*) dissimulazione *f*.

dis·si·pate [ˈdɪsɪˌpeɪt] VT (*frm*) dissipare.

dis·si·pat·ed [ˈdɪsɪˌpeɪtɪd] ADJ (*person, life*) dissipato(-a); (*behaviour*) dissoluto(-a).

dis·si·pa·tion [ˌdɪsɪˈpeɪʃən] N (*frm: of fears*) dissolvimento; (: *of money, fortune, effort*) dissipazione *f*; (*debauchery*) dissolutezza.

dis·so·ci·ate [dɪˈsəʊʃɪˌeɪt] VT: **to disassociate (from)** disso-ciare (da), separare (da); **to disassociate o.s. from** dichiarare di non avere niente a che fare con; (*from political line*) dissociarsi da.

dis·so·cia·tion [dɪˌsəʊsɪˈeɪʃən] N dissociazione *f*.

dis·so·lute [ˈdɪsəˌluːt] ADJ dissoluto(-a).

dis·so·lute·ly [ˈdɪsəˌluːtlɪ] ADV dissolutamente.

dis·so·lu·tion [ˌdɪsəˈluːʃən] N (*of partnership, Pol*) sciogli-mento; (*decay*) dissoluzione *f*.

dis·solve [dɪˈzɒlv] ①VT (*gen*) dissolvere, sciogliere; (*part-nership, business, marriage, Pol*) sciogliere.
　②VI dissolversi, sciogliersi; (*Pol*) sciogliersi; **it dissolves in water** si scioglie in acqua; **she dissolved into tears** si è sciolta in lacrime; **to dissolve into thin air** svanire nel nulla.

dis·so·nance [ˈdɪsənəns] N (*frm*) dissonanza.

dis·suade [dɪˈsweɪd] VT: **to dissuade sb (from doing)** dissuadere qc (dal fare), distogliere (dall'idea di fare).

dis·sua·sion [dɪˈsweɪʒən] N (*liter*) dissuasione *f*.

dis·sua·sive [dɪˈsweɪsɪv] (*liter*) ADJ (*person*) che cerca di dissuadere; (*powers*) di dissuasione.

distaff side [ˈdɪstɑːfˌsaɪd] N: **on the distaff side** per parte di madre.

dis·tance [ˈdɪstəns] ①N (*between two things*) distanza; **the distance between the houses** la distanza *or* lo spazio tra

le case; **it's a good distance** dista un bel po', è parecchio lontano; **it's within walking distance** ci si arriva a piedi; **at a distance of 2 metres** a 2 metri di distanza; **in the distance** in lontananza; **from a distance** da lontano; **distance race** gara di fondo; **distance runner** fondista *m/f*; **distance ratio** rapporto di distanza; **at this distance in time** a distanza di tanto tempo; **to keep sb at a distance** tenere qn a distanza; **to keep one's distance** tenersi a distanza.
　②VT (*fig*) allontanare; **to distance o.s from** allontanarsi da, staccarsi da.

dis·tant [ˈdɪstənt] ADJ (*gen*) lontano(-a); (*country*) distante, lontano(-a); (*likeness*) vago(-a), lontano(-a); (*fig: aloof: manner, person*) distaccato(-a); **in the distant past/future** nel lontano passato/futuro.

dis·tant·ly [ˈdɪstəntlɪ] ADV (*smile, say*) con distacco; (*resem-ble*) vagamente; **we are distantly related** siamo lontani parenti.

dis·taste [ˈdɪsˈteɪst] N: **distaste (for)** ripugnanza (per).

dis·taste·ful [dɪsˈteɪstful] ADJ sgradevole, ripugnante; **the very idea is distasteful to me** la sola idea mi ripugna.

Dist. Atty. ABBR (*Am*) = **district attorney**.

dis·tem·per[1] [dɪsˈtɛmpəʳ] N (*paint*) tempera.

dis·tem·per[2] [dɪsˈtɛmpəʳ] N (*disease*) cimurro.

dis·tend [dɪsˈtɛnd] ①VT dilatare.
　②VI dilatarsi.

dis·tend·ed [dɪsˈtɛndɪd] ADJ (*stomach*) dilatato(-a).

dis·til, (*Am*) **dis·till** [dɪsˈtɪl] VT distillare; **distilled water** acqua distillata.

dis·til·la·tion [ˌdɪstɪˈleɪʃən] N distillazione *f*.

dis·till·er [dɪsˈtɪləʳ] N (*person*) distillatore(-trice); (*company*) distilleria.

dis·till·ery [dɪsˈtɪlərɪ] N distilleria.

dis·tinct [dɪsˈtɪŋkt] ADJ **a** (*different: species, type*): **distinct (from)** diverso(-a) (da), distinto(-a) (da); **as distinct from** a differenza di
b (*clear: sound, shape*) chiaro(-a), distinto(-a); (*unmis-takable: increase, change*) palese, netto(-a); (*definite: preference, progress, feeling*) definito(-a).

dis·tinc·tion [dɪsˈtɪŋkʃən] N (*difference*) distinzione *f*, diffe-renza; (*mark of honour*) onorificenza; **a writer of distinction** un eminente scrittore; **to draw a distinction between** fare distinzione tra; **she got a distinction in English** (*Scol*) ha avuto il massimo dei voti in inglese; (*Univ*) ≈ ha ottenuto la lode.

dis·tinc·tive [dɪsˈtɪŋktɪv] ADJ tutto(-a) particolare.

dis·tinc·tive·ly [dɪsˈtɪŋktɪvlɪ] ADV in modo tutto partico-lare.

dis·tinct·ly [dɪsˈtɪŋktlɪ] ADV (*see, hear*) distintamente; (*promise, remember*) chiaramente; (*prefer*) nettamente; (*better, odd*) decisamente.

dis·tin·guish [dɪsˈtɪŋgwɪʃ] ①VT distinguere, discernere; **he could just distinguish the form of a man** riusciva a malapena a distinguere la sagoma di un uomo; **he can't distinguish red from green** non distingue il rosso dal verde; **to distinguish o.s. (as)** distinguersi (come).
　②VI: **to distinguish (between)** distinguere (tra).

dis·tin·guish·able [dɪsˈtɪŋgwɪʃəbl] ADJ (*discernible*) distin-guibile; **they were barely distinguishable from each other** si riusciva a distinguerli a malapena.

dis·tin·guished [dɪsˈtɪŋgwɪʃt] ADJ (*eminent: pianist, writer*) eminente, noto(-a); (: *scholar*) insigne; (: *career*) bril-lante; (*refined*) distinto(-a), signorile.

dis·tin·guish·ing [dɪsˈtɪŋgwɪʃɪŋ] ADJ (*marks, characteristics, features*) distintivo(-a), caratteristico(-a).

dis·tort [dɪs'tɔ:t] VT (*also fig*) distorcere; (*face, also Tech*) deformare; (*account, news*) falsare; **a distorted impression** una falsa impressione.

dis·tor·tion [dɪs'tɔ:ʃən] N (*gen*) distorsione *f*; (*of truth*) alterazione *f*; (*of facts*) travisamento; (*Tech*) deformazione *f*.

dis·tract [dɪs'trækt] VT (*person*): **to distract sb (from sth)** distrarre qn (da qc); **to distract sb's attention (from sth)** distrarre *or* sviare l'attenzione di qn (da qc).

dis·tract·ed [dɪs'træktɪd] ADJ (*confused*) confuso(-a); (*inattentive*) distratto(-a); **to drive sb distracted** far impazzire qn.

dis·tract·ed·ly [dɪs'træktɪdlɪ] ADV distrattamente.

dis·tract·ing [dɪs'træktɪŋ] ADJ: **to be distracting** deconcentrare, distrarre; **I find the noise very distracting** il rumore mi disturba molto.

dis·trac·tion [dɪs'trækʃən] N **a** (*interruption*) distrazione *f*; (*entertainment*) distrazione, diversivo **b** (*distress, madness*): **to drive sb to distraction** far impazzire qn.

dis·traint [dɪs'treɪnt] N (*Law*) pignoramento.

dis·traught [dɪs'trɔ:t] ADJ stravolto(-a), sconvolto(-a).

dis·tress [dɪs'trɛs] **1** N **a** (*mental anguish*) angoscia, pena; (*pain*) dolore *m*; **to be in great distress** essere sconvolto(-a) *or* affranto(-a) dal dolore **b** (*poverty*) bisogno **c** (*danger*) pericolo; **in distress** (*Brit: ship*) in difficoltà, in pericolo.
2 VT addolorare, affliggere.

dis·tressed [dɪs'trɛst] ADJ (*upset*) addolorato(-a); (*poor*) bisognoso(-a); **distressed area** zona sinistrata.

dis·tress·ing [dɪs'trɛsɪŋ] ADJ penoso(-a), doloroso(-a).

♦ **distress signal** N segnale *m* di richiesta di soccorso.

dis·trib·ute [dɪs'trɪˌbju:t] VT (*leaflets, prizes, load*) distribuire; (*tasks*) ripartire.

dis·tri·bu·tion [dɪstrɪ'bju:ʃən] N distribuzione *f*; **distribution costs** costi *mpl* di distribuzione.

dis·tribu·tive [dɪs'trɪbjʊtɪv] ADJ (*Comm, Gram*) distributivo (-a); **distributive law** (*Math*) legge *f* di distribuzione.

dis·tribu·tor [dɪs'trɪbjʊtəʳ] N **a** (*Comm*) concessionario; (*Cine*) distributore *m* **b** (*Aut, Tech*) distributore *m*; **distributor cap** calotta dello spinterogeno.

dis·trict ['dɪstrɪkt] N (*of country*) regione *f*; (*of town*) quartiere *m*; (*administrative area*) distretto; **district manager** responsabile *m* di zona.

♦ **district attorney** N (*Am*) ≈ Procuratore *m* della Repubblica.

♦ **district council** N (*Brit*) *organo amministrativo indipendente dei district.*

♦ **district nurse** N (*Brit*) infermiere(-a) (*che fa visite a domicilio*).

dis·trust [dɪs'trʌst] **1** N: **distrust (of)** diffidenza (verso), sfiducia (nei confronti di).
2 VT diffidare di, non fidarsi di.

dis·trust·ful [dɪs'trʌstfʊl] ADJ diffidente.

dis·trust·ful·ly [dɪs'trʌstfəlɪ] ADV con diffidenza.

dis·turb [dɪs'tɜ:b] VT **a** (*bother*) disturbare, importunare; (*inconvenience*) scomodare; **sorry to disturb you** scusi se la disturbo; **"please do not disturb"** "non disturbare" **b** (*worry: person*) turbare; (*disrupt: sleep, order, meeting*) turbare, disturbare; (*ruffle: water*) turbare **c** (*disarrange: papers*) scompigliare; (*move*) spostare.

dis·turb·ance [dɪs'tɜ:bəns] N **a** (*uneasiness, upset*) turbamento; (*interruption*) interruzione *f* **b** (*social, political*) disordini *mpl*, tumulto; (*affray*) tafferuglio.

dis·turbed [dɪs'tɜ:bd] ADJ turbato(-a); **to be emotionally disturbed** (*Psych*) avere problemi emotivi; **to be**
mentally disturbed (*Psych*) essere malato(-a) di mente.

dis·turb·ing [dɪs'tɜ:bɪŋ] ADJ inquietante.

dis·turb·ing·ly [dɪs'tɜ:bɪŋlɪ] ADV in modo inquietante.

dis·unite [ˌdɪsjʊ'naɪt] VT (*frm: government, political party*) creare divisioni all'interno di.

dis·unity [dɪs'ju:nɪtɪ] N (*frm*): **disunity (in** *or* **within/among)** disunione *f* (in *or* all'interno di/fra).

dis·use ['dɪs'ju:s] N: **to fall into disuse** cadere in disuso.

dis·used ['dɪs'ju:zd] ADJ abbandonato(-a), in disuso.

ditch [dɪtʃ] **1** N fosso; (*irrigation channel*) fosso *or* canale *m* d'irrigazione.
2 VT (*fam: get rid of: car*) abbandonare, mollare; (: *person*) piantare.

ditch·water ['dɪtʃˌwɔ:təʳ] N: **(as) dull as ditchwater** (*fam*) noioso(-a) da morire.

dith·er ['dɪðəʳ] (*fam*) **1** N: **to be in a dither** essere in agitazione.
2 VI titubare; **to dither over a decision** tentennare di fronte a una decisione.

dit·to ['dɪtəʊ] **1** N (*in lists*) idem come sopra; **ditto marks** virgolette *fpl*; **a coffee, please — ditto (for me)** (*fam*) per me caffè — per me idem.
2 ADV (*likewise*): **I'm really fed up — ditto!** sono proprio stufa — anch'io!

dit·ty ['dɪtɪ] N canzoncina.

di·uret·ic [ˌdaɪjʊ'rɛtɪk] **1** ADJ diuretico(-a).
2 N diuretico.

di·van [dɪ'væn] N divano; **divan bed** divano *m* letto *inv*.

dive [daɪv] **1** N **a** (*of swimmer, goalkeeper*) tuffo; (*of submarine*) immersione *f*; (*Aer*) picchiata
b (*pej fam: club etc*) bettola, buco.
2 VI **a** (*swimmer*): **to dive (into)** tuffarsi (in); (*submarine*) immergersi; (*Aer*) scendere in picchiata; (*Ftbl*) tuffarsi **b** (*fam: move quickly*): **to dive into** (*doorway, hole*) buttarsi dentro; (*car, taxi*) saltare su; **he dived into the crowd** si tuffò *or* si lanciò tra la folla; **he dived for cover** si è buttato al riparo; **he dived for the exit** si è lanciato *or* precipitato verso l'uscita.

♦ **dive-bomb** ['daɪvˌbɒm] VT (*town etc*) bombardare in picchiata; **dive-bombing** bombardamento in picchiata.

div·er ['daɪvəʳ] N **a** (*swimmer*) tuffatore(-trice); (*deep-sea diver*) palombaro; **diver's buoy** segnasub *m inv* **b** (*Zool*) strolaga.

di·verge [daɪ'vɜ:dʒ] VI divergere.

di·ver·gence [daɪ'vɜ:dʒəns] N divergenza.

di·ver·gent [daɪ'vɜ:dʒənt] ADJ divergente.

di·verse [daɪ'vɜ:s] ADJ svariato(-a), vario(-a).

di·ver·si·fi·ca·tion ['daɪˌvɜ:sɪfɪ'keɪʃən] N diversificazione *f*.

di·ver·si·fy [daɪ'vɜ:sɪfaɪ] **1** VT rendere vario(-a); (*Comm*) diversificare.
2 VI (*Comm*) diversificarsi.

di·ver·sion [daɪ'vɜ:ʃən] N (*Brit Aut*) deviazione *f*; (*of river*) diversione; (*distraction*) divertimento; (*old: pastime*) diversivo, distrazione *f*; **to create a diversion** creare un'azione diversiva.

di·ver·sion·ary tac·tics [daɪ'vɜ:ʃnərɪ'tæktɪks] NPL tattica *fsg* diversiva.

di·ver·sity [daɪ'vɜ:sɪtɪ] N varietà *f inv*, diversità *f inv*.

di·vert [daɪ'vɜ:t] VT **a** (*traffic, river*) deviare; (*conversation, attention, person*) sviare; (*train, plane*) dirottare **b** (*old: amuse*) distrarre, divertire.

di·vest [daɪ'vɛst] VT (*frm*): **to divest of** spogliare di.

di·vide [dɪ'vaɪd] **1** VT: **to divide (from/into)** dividere (da/in); **to divide (between** *or* **among)** dividere (tra), ripartire (tra); **to divide 6 into 36** *or* **36 by 6** dividere 36

per 6; **40 divided by 5** 40 diviso 5.

[2] VI (*road, river*) dividersi, biforcarsi; (*Math*) essere divisibile

▶ **divide off** [1] VI + ADV (*road*) separarsi.

[2] VT + ADV (*area*) separare

▶ **divide out** VT + ADV: **to divide out (between** *or* **among)** (*sweets, proceeds*) distribuire (tra); (*tasks*) distribuire *or* ripartire (tra)

▶ **divide up** VT + ADV dividere.

di·vid·ed [dɪ'vaɪdɪd] ADJ (*country, couple*) diviso(-a); **divided opinions** opinioni *fpl* discordi; **to be divided in one's mind about sth** essere indeciso(-a) su qc.

♦ **divided highway** N (*Am*) strada a doppia carreggiata.

♦ **divided skirt** N gonna *f* pantalone *inv*.

divi·dend ['dɪvɪˌdɛnd] N (*Fin*) dividendo.

di·vid·ers [dɪ'vaɪdəz] NPL (*Math*) compasso a punte fisse.

di·vid·ing [dɪ'vaɪdɪŋ] ADJ (*fence, wall, line*) divisorio(-a).

di·vine [dɪ'vaɪn] [1] ADJ (*Rel, fig old*) divino(-a); **what divine weather!** che tempo favoloso!.

[2] VT (*future*) divinare, predire; (*truth*) indovinare; (*water*) individuare (*tramite rabdomanzia*).

di·vine·ly [dɪ'vaɪnlɪ] ADV divinamente.

di·vin·er [dɪ'vaɪnə'] N (*water diviner*) rabdomante *m/f*.

div·ing ['daɪvɪŋ] N tuffi *mpl*.

♦ **diving bell** N campana da palombaro.

♦ **diving board** N trampolino.

♦ **diving suit** N scafandro.

di·vin·ing rod [dɪ'vaɪnɪŋˌrɒd] N bacchetta.

di·vin·ity [dɪ'vɪnɪtɪ] N divinità *f inv*; (*as study*) teologia.

di·vi·sible [dɪ'vɪzəbl] ADJ: **divisible (by)** divisibile (per).

di·vi·sion [dɪ'vɪʒən] N (*gen*) divisione *f*; (*Brit Ftbl*) serie *f inv*; **to call a division** (*Parliament*) procedere alla votazione, passare ai voti.

di·vi·sion·al [dɪ'vɪʒənl] ADJ di divisione.

♦ **division of labour** N divisione *f* del lavoro.

di·vi·sive [dɪ'vaɪsɪv] ADJ che causa discordia.

di·vi·sor [dɪ'vaɪzə'] N (*Math*) divisore *m*.

di·vorce [dɪ'vɔ:s] [1] N divorzio; **divorce proceedings** pratiche *fpl* per il divorzio.

[2] VI divorziare.

[3] VT divorziare da; (*fig*) separare; **she divorced him last year** ha divorziato da lui l'anno scorso.

divorcé [dɪ'vɔ:seɪ] N divorziato.

di·vorced [dɪ'vɔ:st] ADJ divorziato(-a).

di·vor·cee [dɪˌvɔ:'si:] N divorziata.

div·ot ['dɪvɪt] N (*Golf*) zolla di terra (*sollevata accidentalmente*).

di·vulge [daɪ'vʌldʒ] VT divulgare, rivelare; (*evidence, information*) rendere pubblico(-a).

D.I.Y. [ˌdi:aɪ'waɪ] N, ADJ ABBR (*Brit*) = **do-it-yourself**.

diz·zi·ly ['dɪzɪlɪ] ADV (*spin, rise, fall*) vertiginosamente; (*walk*) con un senso di vertigine.

diz·zi·ness ['dɪzɪnɪs] N capogiro, vertigini *fpl*; **an attack of dizziness** un capogiro.

diz·zy ['dɪzɪ] ADJ (*height*) vertiginoso(-a); **I am** *or* **feel dizzy** ho il capogiro, mi gira la testa; **to make sb dizzy** far girare la testa a qn; **the height made me dizzy** la grande altezza mi ha dato le vertigini.

DJ [di:'dʒeɪ] N ABBR (= *disc jockey*) disc jockey *m/f inv*.

dj [di:'dʒeɪ] N ABBR = **dinner jacket**.

Dja·kar·ta [dʒə'kɑ:tə] N Giacarta.

DJIA ['di:dʒeɪaɪ'eɪ] N ABBR (*Am Stock Exchange*: = *Dow-Jones Industrial Average*) indice *m* Dow-Jones.

dl ABBR (= *decilitre*) dl.

DLitt, DLit [di:'lɪt] N ABBR = *Doctor of Literature, Doctor of Letters*.

DLO [di:εl'əʊ] N ABBR = **dead-letter office**.

dm ABBR (= *decimetre*) dm.

DMus ABBR = *Doctor of Music*.

DMZ [di:ɛm'zɛd] N ABBR = **demilitarized zone**.

DNA [di:ɛn'eɪ] N ABBR (= *deoxyribonucleic acid*) DNA *m*.

do[1] [du:] (*3rd pers sg present* **does**, *pt* **did**, *pp* **done**)

[1] AUX VB

[a]

▷ **do you** *speak* **English?** parla inglese?

▷ **do you** *understand*? capisci?

▷ **I don't** *understand* non capisco

▷ **do you** *want* **some?** ne vuoi?

▷ **didn't you** *ask*? non (l')hai chiesto?

▷ **didn't you** *know*? non lo sapevi?

▷ **he didn't** *laugh* non ha riso

[b] (*for emphasis*)

▷ DO *come*! dai, vieni!

▷ **so you** DO *know* **him!** dunque è vero che lo conosci!

▷ **but I** DO *like* **it!** sì che mi piace!

▷ DO *shut up*! ma sta zitto!

▷ DO *sit down* (*polite*) si accomodi la prego, prego si sieda; (*annoyed*) insomma siediti

▷ DO *tell* me! su, dimmelo!

▷ **I** DO *wish* **I could …** magari potessi…

[c] (*used to avoid repeating verb*)

▷ *neither* **do we** nemmeno noi

▷ **he doesn't like it and** *neither* **do we** a lui non piace e a noi nemmeno

▷ *so* **does he** anche lui

▷ **you speak better** *than* **I do** parli meglio di me

[d] (*in question tags*)

▷ **he lives here, doesn't he?** abita qui, vero?, abita qui, no?

▷ **I don't know him, do I?** non lo conosco, vero?

[e] (*in answers, replacing verb*): **do you speak English?** — **yes, I do/no, I don't** parli inglese? — sì/no

▷ **do you agree?** — **I do** è d'accordo? — sì

▷ **may I come in?** — **please do!** posso entrare? — certo!

▷ **who made this mess?** — **I did** chi ha fatto questo disordine? — io!, sono stato io!

▷ **do you really?** davvero?, ah sì?

[2] VT

[a] (*gen*) fare;

▷ **I'll do** *all* **I can** farò tutto il possibile

▷ **I've got** *nothing* **to do** non ho niente da fare

▷ **I shall do** *nothing* **of the sort** non farò niente del genere

▷ *that's* **done it!** (*fam*) sono fregato! (*or* siamo fregati! etc)

▷ **have you done the** *washing*? hai fatto il bucato?

▷ **I'm going to do the** *washing up* adesso faccio i piatti

▷ *well* **done!** bravo!, benissimo!

▷ *what* **are you doing tonight?** che fai stasera?

▷ *what* **does he do for a living?** cosa fa per vivere?

▷ *what* **am I to do with you?** dimmi tu come devo fare con te!

▷ *what* **can I do for you?** (*in shop*) desidera?

▷ *what's* **to be done?** che fare?

▷ *what's* **done cannot be undone** quello che è fatto è fatto

▷it will have to be done again è tutto da rifare

b

▷I'll do the *flowers* i fiori li sistemo io

▷who does your *hair*? chi ti fa i capelli?

▷to do *Italian* fare italiano;

▷to do one's *nails* farsi le unghie

▷she does her guests *proud* i suoi ospiti li tratta da principi

▷this *room* needs doing questa stanza è ancora da fare

▷to do *Shakespeare* (*Scol*) fare Shakespeare

▷to do one's *teeth* pulirsi i denti

c (*only as past tense, past participle: finish*)

▷the *job's* done il lavoro è fatto;

▷I haven't done *telling* you (*fam*) non ho ancora finito la storia

d (*visit: city, museum*) fare, visitare

e (*Aut*) fare;

▷the car was doing *100* (mph) ≈ la macchina faceva i 160 (km/h)

▷we've done 200 *km* already abbiamo già fatto 200 km

f (*fam: be sufficient*) bastare; (: *be suitable*) andar bene;

▷that won't do him questo non gli basta

▷that'll do me nicely per me va benissimo

g (*play role of*) fare (la parte di); (*mimic*) imitare

h (*fam: cheat*) imbrogliare, fargliela a; (: *rob*) ripulire

▷to do sb *out of* sth fregare qc a qn

▷he did her *out of* a job le ha fregato *or* soffiato il posto

▷I've been done! mi hanno fregato!

i (*Culin*) fare;

▷to do the *cooking* cucinare

▷how do you like your steak done? come preferisci la bistecca?

▷the *meat's* done la carne è pronta

▷done to a *turn* (*meat*) cotto(-a) a puntino

▷*well* done ben cotto(-a).

3 VI

a (*act*) fare, agire;

▷do *as* I do fai come me, fai come faccio io

▷he did *well* to take your *advice* ha fatto bene a seguire il tuo consiglio

b (*get on, fare*) andare;

▷he's doing *badly* at school va male a scuola

▷how are you doing? (*fam*) come va?

▷how do you do? (*in introductions*) piacere

▷she did *well* at university era molto brava all'università

▷his business is doing *well* gli affari gli vanno bene

c (*finish: in past tenses only*)

▷I've done ho fatto, ho finito

▷have you done? hai fatto?, hai finito?

▷hasn't he done with that book yet? ancora non ha finito con quel libro?

d (*suit*) andare bene;

▷this coat will do *as* a cover questo cappotto potrà fare da coperta

▷to *make* do (*with*) arrangiarsi (con)

▷you'll have to *make* do with £10 dovrai arrangiarti con 10 sterline

▷this *room* will do questa stanza va bene

▷will it do? andrà bene?

▷that will never do! non se ne parla nemmeno!

▷will it do if I come back at 8? va bene se torno alle 8?

▷it doesn't do to upset her è meglio non agitarla

e (*be sufficient*) bastare;

▷will £5 do? bastano *or* vanno bene 5 sterline?

▷that'll do basta così

▷that'll do! (*in annoyance*) ora basta!

4 N (*fam*)

a (*party*) festa; (*formal gathering*) ricevimento;

▷it was rather a *grand* do è stato un ricevimento piuttosto imponente

▷we're having a *little* do on Saturday facciamo una festicciola sabato

b (*in phrases*)

▷the dos and *don'ts* le regole del gioco

▷*fair* dos! (*be fair*) quel che è giusto è giusto!

▷it's a *poor* do è brutto segno

▶ **do away with** VT + PREP (*abolish*) abolire; (*kill*) far fuori

▶ **do by** VI + PREP: **to do well/badly by sb** comportarsi bene/male con qn;

to be hard done by essere *or* venire trattato (-a) male

▶ **do down** VT + ADV (*fam*) screditare;

don't do yourself down! non sminuirti!

▶ **do for** VI + PREP **a** (*finish off: project*) mandare all'aria; (: *person*) spacciare;

he's done for! è spacciato!

b (*Brit old: clean for*) fare i servizi per

▶ **do in** VT + ADV (*fam: kill*) far fuori

▶ **do out** VT + ADV (*room*) fare

▶ **do over** VT + ADV (*fam*) **a** (*Am: do again: work, essay*) rifare; (: *redecorate: house*) rimettere a posto (*pitturare, tapezzare ecc*)

b (*Brit: rob: house*) ripulire

c (*Brit: hurt*) pestare

▶ **do up** VT + ADV **a** (*dress, shoes*) allacciare; (*zip*) tirar su; (*buttons*) abbottonare;

books done up in paper libri impacchettati

b (*renovate: house, room*) rimettere a nuovo, rifare; **to do o.s. up** farsi bello(-a)

▶ **do with** VT + PREP **a** (*with could: need*) avere bisogno di;

I could do with some help mi servirebbe una mano

I could do with a drink un bicchierino non guasterebbe

it could do with a wash una lavata non gli farebbe male

b: **what has that got to do with it?** che c'entra?;

it has to do with ... ha a che vedere *or* fare con...

money has a lot to do with it è una questione di soldi

that has nothing to do with you! non sono affari tuoi!, non ti riguarda!

I won't have anything to do with it non voglio aver niente a che farci

c: **what have you done with my slippers?** cosa hai fatto delle mie pantofole?;

what did he do with the cat? che ne ha fatto del gatto?

what's he done with his hair? che si è fatto ai capelli?

▶ **do without 1** VI + PREP fare a meno di.

2 VI + ADV fare senza.

do² [dəʊ] N (*Mus*) do *m inv.*

do. ABBR = ditto.

DOA [ˌdiːəʊˈeɪ] ABBR (= *dead on arrival*) morto(-a) durante il trasporto.

d.o.b. ABBR = date of birth.

Do·ber·man [ˈdeʊbəmən] N (*also:* **Doberman pinscher**) dobermann *m inv.*

doc [dɒk] N (*fam*) dottore(-essa).

doc·ile ['dəʊsaɪl] ADJ docile.

do·cil·ity [dəʊ'sɪlɪtɪ] N docilità.

dock¹ [dɒk] **1** N (*Naut*) bacino; (: *wharf*) molo; (: *for repairs*) darsena; **docks** dock *m inv*; **dock dues** diritti *mpl* di banchina.
2 VT mettere in bacino.
3 VI entrare in bacino.

dock² [dɒk] N (*in court*) banco degli imputati.

dock³ [dɒk] VT **a** (*tail*) mozzare **b** (*pay*) decurtare.

dock⁴ [dɒk] N (*Bot*) romice *m*.

dock·er ['dɒkəʳ] N scaricatore *m* (di porto), portuale *m*.

dock·et ['dɒkɪt] N (*on parcel etc*) etichetta, cartellino.

dock·ing ['dɒkɪŋ] N **a** (*of animals*) taglio della coda **b** (*of space vehicle*) aggancio.

dock·land ['dɒk,lænd] N, **dock·lands** ['dɒk,lændz] NPL zona portuale.

dock·yard ['dɒk,jɑːd] N cantiere *m* (navale).

doc·tor ['dɒktəʳ] **1** N **a** (*Med*) dottore(-essa), medico; **Doctor Brown** il Dottor Brown; **doctor's office** (*Am*) studio medico, ambulatorio
b (*Univ*: *Ph.D.*) dottore(-essa); **Doctor of Philosophy** (*degree*) ≈ dottorato di ricerca; (*person*) ≈ titolare *m/f* di un dottorato di ricerca.
2 VT **a** (*interfere with*: *food, drink*) adulterare; (: *text, document*) alterare, manipolare
b (*treat*: *cold*) curare
c (*fam*: *castrate*: *cat*) castrare.

doc·tor·ate ['dɒktərɪt] N ≈ dottorato di ricerca.

doc·tri·naire [,dɒktrɪ'nɛəʳ] ADJ (*pej*) dottrinario(-a).

doc·tri·nal ['dɒktraɪnl] ADJ dottrinale.

doc·trine ['dɒktrɪn] N dottrina.

docu·dra·ma [dɒkjʊ'drɑːmə] N (*TV*) ricostruzione *f* filmata.

docu·ment [*n* 'dɒkjʊmənt; *vb* 'dɒkjʊmənt] **1** N documento; **document case** cartella, borsa portadocumenti; **document wallet** cartelletta.
2 VT documentare.

docu·men·tary [,dɒkjʊ'mɛntərɪ] **1** ADJ documentario (-a); (*evidence*) documentato(-a); **documentary letter of credit** lettera di credito contro documenti.
2 N (*Cine, TV*) documentario.

docu·men·ta·tion [,dɒkjʊmɛn'teɪʃən] N documentazione *f*.

DOD [,diː əʊ'diː] N ABBR (*Am*) = **Department of Defense**.

dod·der ['dɒdəʳ] VI camminare con passo malfermo.

dod·der·er ['dɒdərəʳ] N (*fam*) vecchio(-a) decrepito(-a), rudere *m*.

dod·der·ing ['dɒdərɪŋ], **dod·dery** ['dɒdərɪ] ADJ malfermo (-a) sulle gambe.

dod·dle ['dɒdəl] N (*Brit fam*): **it's a doddle** è un gioco da ragazzi.

Do·deca·nese [,dəʊdɪkə'niːz] NPL: **the Dodecanese** il Dodecanneso; **the Dodecanese Islands** le isole del Dodecanneso.

dodge [dɒdʒ] **1** N (*fam*: *trick*) espediente *m*, trucco; **a tax dodge** un trucchetto per evadere le tasse.
2 VT (*blow, missile*) schivare; (*pursuer, question, difficulty*) eludere; (*tax*) evadere; (*work, duty*) sottrarsi a; **to dodge the issue** girare intorno all'argomento.
3 VI scansarsi; (*Sport*) fare una schivata; **to dodge out of the way** scansarsi; **to dodge through the traffic** destreggiarsi nel traffico; **to dodge behind a tree** nascondersi dietro un albero.

dodg·ems ['dɒdʒəmz] NPL (*also*: **dodgem cars**) autoscontro *msg*.

dodgy ['dɒdʒɪ] ADJ (*comp* **-ier**, *superl* **-iest**) (*fam*: *plan*) azzardato(-a), rischioso(-a); (: *deal*) sospetto(-a), poco chiaro(-a); (: *person*) losco(-a); **we're in a dodgy situation** navighiamo in cattive acque.

dodo ['dəʊdəʊ] N **a** (*Zool*) dodo; **as dead as a dodo** morto(-a) e sepolto(-a) **b** (*fam*: *fool*) scemo(-a).

DOE [,diː əʊ'iː] N ABBR (*Brit*) = **Department of the Environment**; (*Am*) = **Department of Energy**.

doe [dəʊ] N (*deer*) femmina di daino; (*rabbit*) coniglia.

doer ['duːəʳ] N tipo dinamico.

does [dʌz] 3RD PERS SG PRESENT of **do**.

doesn't ['dʌznt] = **does not**.

doff [dɒf] VT (*old*: *hat, coat*) togliere; **to doff one's hat to sb** levarsi il cappello davanti a qn.

dog [dɒg] **1** N (*male*) cane *m*; (*female*) cagna; (*male fox, wolf*) maschio; **he's a lucky dog** (*fam*) è nato con la camicia; **every dog has its day** ognuno ha il suo momento di gloria; **he's a dog in the manger** *non lascia che gli altri si godano ciò che lui non può godersi*; **to go to the dogs** (*person*) lasciarsi andare, ridursi male; (*nation*) andare in malora; **it's a dog's life!** che vita da cani!; **he hasn't a dog's chance** non ha la benché minima probabilità (di successo).
2 VT (*follow closely*) pedinare; (*fig*: *subj*: *problems, injuries*) perseguitare; **dogged by ill luck** perseguitato(-a) dalla scalogna; **he dogs my footsteps** mi sta alle costole, mi sta alle calcagna.
3 ADJ (*breed, show*) canino(-a); (*fox, wolf*) maschio; **dog biscuits** biscotti *mpl* per cani; **dog food** cibo per cani.

♦ **dog collar** N (*fam*: *clergyman's*) collarino; (*dog's*) collare *m*.

♦ **dog-eared** ['dɒg,ɪəd] ADJ (*book*) con orecchie.

♦ **dog·fight** ['dɒg,faɪt] N **a** (*planes*) combattimento ravvicinato fra aerei da caccia **b** (*dogs*) combattimento fra cani.

♦ **dog-fish** ['dɒg,fɪʃ] N (*also*: **lesser spotted dog-fish**) gattuccio.

dog·ged ['dɒgɪd] ADJ tenace, accanito(-a).

dog·ged·ly ['dɒgɪdlɪ] ADV tenacemente, accanitamente.

dog·ger·el ['dɒgərəl] N poesia di scarso valore.

dog·go ['dɒgəʊ] ADV (*fam*): **to lie doggo** fare il morto.

dog·gone ['dɒgɒn] ADJ (*Am*: *fam*) dannato(-a).

dog·gy, dog·gie ['dɒgɪ] N (*fam*) cane *m*, cagnolino.

♦ **doggy bag** N sacchetto per gli avanzi da portare a casa.

♦ **doggy paddle, doggie paddle** N: **to do the doggy paddle** (*fam*) nuotare a cagnolino.

dog·house ['dɒg,haʊs] N: **he's in the doghouse** (*fam*) è caduto in disgrazia.

dog·leg ['dɒg,lɛg] N (*in road*) curva a gomito.

dog·ma ['dɒgmə] N dogma *m*.

dog·mat·ic [dɒg'mætɪk] ADJ (*person, attitude*) dogmatico (-a); (*tone*) autoritario(-a).

dog·mati·cal·ly [dɒg'mætɪkəlɪ] ADV (*see adj*) dogmaticamente; con tono autoritario.

♦ **do-gooder** ['duː'gʊdəʳ] N (*fam pej*): **to be a do-gooder** fare il filantropo.

♦ **dog paddle** N = **doggy paddle**.

dogs·body ['dɒgz,bɒdɪ] N (*Brit fam*) tirapiedi *m/f inv*.

♦ **dog-tired** [,dɒg'taɪəd] ADJ (*fam*) stanco(-a) morto(-a).

doh [dəʊ] N (*Mus*) = **do²**.

doi·ly, doy·ley, doy·ly ['dɔɪlɪ] N centrino di carta sottopiatto.

do·ing ['duːɪŋ] N: **this is your doing** è opera tua!, sei stato tu!; **that takes some doing** non è una cosa facile.

do·ings ['duːɪŋz] NPL **a** (*exploits*) imprese *fpl* **b** (*Brit fam*: *thing*): **that doings over there** quel coso là.

◆ **do-it-yourself** ['du:ɪtjə'sɛlf] N fai da te *m inv*, bricolage *m inv*; do-it-yourself **magazine** rivista di bricolage; **do-it-yourself store** negozio di bricolage.

dol·drums ['dɒldrəmz] NPL (*fig*): **to be in the doldrums** (*person*) essere giù (di corda); (*business*) attraversare un momento difficile.

dole [dəʊl] N (*Brit fam*) sussidio di disoccupazione; **to be on the dole** ricevere un sussidio di disoccupazione

▶ **dole out** VT + ADV distribuire.

dole·ful ['dəʊlfʊl] ADJ (*expression*) afflitto(-a); (*song, prospect*) triste.

dole·ful·ly ['dəʊlfəlɪ] ADV (*see adj*) con aria afflitta; tristemente.

doll [dɒl] N bambola; **doll's house** casa delle bambole

▶ **doll up** VT + ADV: **to doll o.s. up** (*fam*) farsi bello(-a); **to get (all) dolled up** mettersi in ghingheri.

dol·lar ['dɒlə'] N dollaro; **dollar area** area del dollaro; **dollar bill** biglietto da un dollaro.

◆ **dollar diplomacy** N politica di penetrazione economica.

dol·ly ['dɒlɪ] N (*fam*) bambola.

dol·men ['dɒlmɛn] N dolmen *m inv*.

dol·phin ['dɒlfɪn] N (*Zool*) delfino.

dolt [dəʊlt] N imbecille *m/f*.

dolt·ish ['dəʊltɪʃ] ADJ (*person*) imbecille, stupido(-a); (*behaviour*) stupido(-a).

do·main [dəʊ'meɪn] N (*lands*) domini *mpl*; (*fig*) campo, sfera; (*Math*) dominio.

dome [dəʊm] N cupola.

domed [dəʊmd] ADJ (*roof*) a cupola; (*forehead*) bombato (-a).

Domes·day Book ['du:mzdeɪˌbʊk] N (*Brit*) *libro del Catasto fatto compilare da Guglielmo il Conquistatore.*

do·mes·tic [də'mɛstɪk] **1** ADJ **a** (*industry, flight*) nazionale; (*affairs, policy*) interno(-a); (*news*) dall'interno **b** (*chores, duties, animal*) domestico(-a); **domestic bliss** le gioie della famiglia; **domestic peace** pace in famiglia; **to be in domestic service** essere a servizio; **domestic servant** domestico(-a).   **2** N (*cleaner*) inserviente *m/f*.

do·mes·ti·cate [də'mɛstɪˌkeɪt] VT (*animal*) addomesticare.

do·mes·ti·cat·ed [də'mɛstɪˌkeɪtɪd] ADJ (*animal*) addomesticato(-a); (*person*) casalingo(-a).

do·mes·ti·city [ˌdəʊmɛsˈtɪsɪtɪ] N vita di famiglia.

◆ **domestic science** N economia domestica.

domi·cile ['dɒmɪˌsaɪl] N (*frm*) domicilio.

domi·ciled ['dɒmɪˌsaɪld] ADJ (*frm*) domiciliato(-a).

domi·nance ['dɒmɪnəns] N (*influence*) influenza; (*preeminence*) predominio.

domi·nant ['dɒmɪnənt] ADJ (*gen, Mus*) dominante; (*influence*) predominante.

domi·nate ['dɒmɪˌneɪt] VT, VI dominare.

domi·na·tion [ˌdɒmɪˈneɪʃən] N dominazione *f*.

domi·neer [ˌdɒmɪˈnɪə'] VI: **to domineer (over)** fare il tiranno (con).

domi·neer·ing [ˌdɒmɪˈnɪərɪŋ] ADJ dispotico(-a), autoritario(-a).

Do·mini·can[1] [də'mɪnɪkən] ADJ, N (*Rel*) domenicano(-a).

Do·mini·can[2] [də'mɪnɪkən] ADJ, N (*Geog*) dominicano(-a).

Dominican Republic N Repubblica Dominicana.

do·min·ion [də'mɪnɪən] N (*rule*) dominio, sovranità; (*territory*) dominio, possedimenti *mpl*; (*Brit Pol*) dominion *m inv*.

domi·no ['dɒmɪnəʊ] N tessera del domino; **dominoes** NPL

(*game*) domino *msg*.

don[1] [dɒn] N (*Brit Univ*) docente *m/f* universitario(-a).

don[2] [dɒn] VT (*old: garment*) indossare.

do·nate [dəʊ'neɪt] VT elargire.

do·na·tion [dəʊ'neɪʃən] N elargizione *f*.

done [dʌn] PP of **do**.

don·key ['dɒŋkɪ] N asino(-a); **I've known him for donkey's years** (*fam*) lo conosco da secoli.

◆ **donkey jacket** N giaccone *m* pesante.

◆ **donkey-work** ['dɒŋkɪwɜːk] N (*Brit fam*) *la parte meno interessante di un lavoro.*

do·nor ['dəʊnə'] N (*gen, Med*) donatore(-trice).

◆ **donor card** N tessera di donatore di organi, ≈ tessera dell'A.I.D.O.

don't [dəʊnt] = **do not**.

do·nut ['dəʊnʌt] N (*Am*) = **doughnut**.

doo·dah ['du:dɑ:], (*Am*) **doo·dads** ['du:dæd] N (*fam*) coso.

doo·dle ['du:dl] **1** N scarabocchio.   **2** VI scarabocchiare.

doom [du:m] **1** N (*ruin*) rovina; (*fate*) destino; **impending doom** disastro incombente.   **2** VT (*destine*): **to doom (to)** condannare (a); **doomed to failure** destinato(-a) al fallimento.

dooms·day ['du:mzˌdeɪ] N: **till doomsday** (*fig*) fino al giorno del giudizio.

door [dɔ:'] N (*gen*) porta; (*of vehicle*) sportello, portiera; (*of aircraft*) portello; **at the door** alla porta; "**pay at the door**" "pagare all'entrata"; **front/back door** porta principale/di servizio; **3 doors down the street** 3 case più giù; **from door to door** di porta in porta.

door·bell ['dɔːˌbɛl] N campanello.

◆ **do-or-die** ['du:ˌɔːˈdaɪ] ADJ disperato(-a).

◆ **door-handle** ['dɔːˌhændl] N maniglia della porta.

door·keeper ['dɔːˌkiːpə'] N portiere *m*.

door·knob ['dɔːˌnɒb] N pomello.

door·man ['dɔːˌmæn] N (*pl* -**men**) (*in hotel*) portiere *m* (in livrea); (*in block of flats*) portinaio.

door·mat ['dɔːˌmæt] N stoino, zerbino; (*fam: downtrodden person*) pezza da piedi.

door·nail ['dɔːˌneɪl] N: **as dead as a doornail** morto(-a) stecchito(-a).

door·step ['dɔːˌstɛp] N gradino della porta, soglia; **on our doorstep** (*close by*) a un passo.

◆ **door-to-door** ['dɔːtəˈdɔː'] ADJ (*selling*) porta a porta; (*salesman*) a domicilio.

door·way ['dɔːˌweɪ] N porta; **in the doorway** nel vano della porta.

dope [dəʊp] **1** N **a** (*fam: drugs*) roba (*fam*); (*Sport*) droga; **he takes dope** si droga; **dope test** (controllo) anti-doping *m inv* **b** (*fam: information*) informazioni *fpl*; **to give sb the dope (on sth)** fare una soffiata a qn (su qc) **c** (*fam: stupid person*) tonto(-a).   **2** VT (*horse, person, drink*) drogare.

dopey ['dəʊpɪ] (*fam*) ADJ (*comp* -**ier**, *superl* -**iest**) (*drugged*) inebetito(-a); (*stupid*) stupidotto(-a); (*sleepy*) addormentato(-a).

Doppler effect ['dɒplərɪˌfɛkt] N (*Phys*) effetto Doppler.

dor·mant ['dɔːmənt] ADJ (*Bot, volcano*) quiescente; (*energy*) latente; **to lie dormant** (*fig*) rimanere latente.

dor·mer ['dɔːmə'] N (*also:* **dormer window**) abbaino.

dor·mi·tory ['dɔːmɪtrɪ] N, ADJ dormitorio; (*Am: hall of residence*) casa dello studente; **dormitory town** città *f inv* dormitorio *inv*.

dor·mouse ['dɔːˌmaʊs] N (*pl* **dormice** ['dɔːˌmaɪs]) ghiro.

Dors ABBR (*Brit*)= **Dorset**.

dor·sal ['dɔ:sl] ADJ dorsale; **dorsal fin** pinna dorsale.

DOS [dɒs] N ABBR (*Comput*: = *disk operating system*) DOS *m*.

dos·age ['dəʊsɪdʒ] N (*on medicine bottle*) posologia.

dose [dəʊs] ① N (*of medicine*) dose *f*; (*Brit*: *of fever etc*) attacco; **to get a dose of flu** prendersi l'influenza; **in small doses** (*fig*) a piccole dosi.

② VT: **to dose sb with sth** somministrare qc a qn.

doss [dɒs] VI: **to doss (down)** (*fam*) sistemarsi (per la notte).

dos·ser ['dɒsə'] N (*Brit*: *fam*) barbone(-a).

doss·house ['dɒs,haʊs] N (*Brit*: *fam*) ≈ dormitorio pubblico.

dos·si·er ['dɒsɪeɪ] N: **dossier (on)** dossier *m inv* (su).

DOT [,di:əʊ'ti:] N ABBR (*Am*)= *Department of Transportation*.

dot [dɒt] ① N (*gen*) punto; (*on material*) pois *m inv*; (*stain*) macchiolina; (*in punctuation*): **dots** puntini *mpl* di sospensione; (*morse*): **dots and dashes** punti *mpl* e linee *fpl*; **on the dot** (*fig*) in punto.

② VT (*fig*): **to dot one's i's and cross one's t's** mettere i puntini sulle i; **a field dotted with flowers** un campo punteggiato di fiori; **they are dotted about the country** sono disseminati per il paese.

dot·age ['dəʊtɪdʒ] N: **to be in one's dotage** essere rimbambito(-a).

dote on ['dəʊt,ɒn] VI + PREP stravedere per.

dot·ing ['dəʊtɪŋ] ADJ: **doting mother** madre *f* che stravede per i figli; **doting husband** marito che stravede per la moglie.

♦ **dot-matrix printer** [,dɒt'meɪtrɪks'prɪntə'] N stampante *f* ad aghi.

dot·ted line ['dɒtɪd'laɪn] N linea punteggiata; **to sign on the dotted line** firmare (nell'apposito spazio); (*fig*) accettare; **to tear along the dotted line** strappare lungo la linea tratteggiata.

dot·ty ['dɒtɪ] ADJ (*Brit fam*: *mad*) tocco(-a), strambo(-a); **to be dotty about sth** andare pazzo(-a) per qc; **he's dotty about her** ha completamente perso la testa per lei.

dou·ble ['dʌbl] ① ADJ **a** (*gen*) doppio(-a); **a double whisky** un doppio whisky; **double spacing** (*Typ*) interlinea doppia

b (*dual*) duplice; **with a double meaning** a doppio senso; **to lead a double life** avere una doppia vita; **to play a double game** fare il doppio gioco

c (*Brit*: *repeated*): **double five two six (5526)** (*Telec*) cinque cinque due sei; **spelt with a double "l"** scritto con due elle *or* con doppia elle.

② ADV (*bend*) in due; (*see*) doppio; **double the amount (of sth)** il doppio (di qc).

③ N **a** (*amount*) doppio; (*person*) sosia *m inv*; (*Cine*) controfigura; **at the double** *or* **on the double** (*running*) a passo di corsa

b (*bet*) accoppiata.

④ VT **a** (*increase twofold*: *money, quantity etc*) raddoppiare

b (*fold*: *also*: **double over**) piegare in due.

⑤ VI **a** (*quantity etc*) raddoppiare

b (*have two uses*): **to double as** funzionare *or* servire anche da; (*Theatre, Cine*) fare anche la parte di

▶ **double back** VI + ADV (*person*) tornare sui propri passi

▶ **double up** VI + ADV **a** (*bend over*) piegarsi in due; **he doubled up with laughter** si sbellicava dal ridere

b (*share bedroom*) dividere la stanza.

♦ **double agent** N agente *m* segreto che fa il doppio gioco.

♦ **double-barrelled** [,dʌbl'bærəld] ADJ (*gun*) a doppia

canna; (*Brit*: *surname*) cognome *m* doppio.

♦ **double bass** [,dʌbl'beɪs] N contrabbasso.

♦ **double bed** N letto matrimoniale, letto a due piazze.

♦ **double bend** N (*Brit*) doppia curva.

♦ **double bluff** N: **it's a double bluff on his part** vuol farci credere che mente.

♦ **double-breasted** [,dʌbl'brɛstɪd] ADJ (*jacket*) doppiopetto *inv*.

♦ **double-check** [,dʌbl'tʃɛk] VT, VI ricontrollare.

♦ **double chin** N doppio mento.

♦ **double-clutch** ['dʌbl'klʌtʃ] VI (*Am Aut*) = **double-declutch**.

♦ **double cream** N (*Brit*) panna da cucina.

♦ **double-cross** [,dʌbl'krɒs] VT (*fam*) fare il doppio gioco con.

♦ **double-dealer** ['dʌbəl'di:lə'] N doppio-giochista *m/f*.

♦ **double-dealing** ['dʌbl'di:lɪŋ] N doppio gioco.

♦ **double-decker** [,dʌbl'dɛkə'] N (*also*: **double-decker bus**) autobus *m inv* a due piani; (*also*: **double-decker sandwich**) doppio tramezzino.

♦ **double-declutch** ['dʌbl,di:'klʌtʃ], (*Am*) **double-clutch** ['dʌbl'klʌtʃ] VI (*Aut*) fare la doppietta.

♦ **double-density** [,dʌbl'dɛnsɪtɪ] ADJ (*Comput*) a densità doppia.

♦ **double-Dutch** [,dʌbl'dʌtʃ] N (*Brit fam*): **it was double-Dutch to me** per me era come se parlasse turco *or* arabo.

♦ **double-edged** [,dʌbl'ɛdʒd] ADJ (*remark*) a doppio taglio.

♦ **dou·ble en·ten·dre** ['dʌblɑ:n'tɑ:ndrə] N doppio senso.

♦ **double exposure** N (*Phot*) sovrimpressione *f*.

♦ **double glazing** [,dʌbl'gleɪzɪŋ] N (*Brit*) doppiovetro; **to put in double glazing** mettere i doppivetri.

♦ **double-jointed** [,dʌbl'dʒɔɪntɪd] ADJ snodato(-a).

♦ **double negative** N (*Ling*) doppia negazione *f*.

♦ **double-page** ['dʌbl,peɪdʒ] ADJ: **double-page spread** pubblicità a doppia pagina.

♦ **double-park** [,dʌbl'pa:k] VI parcheggiare in doppia fila; **double-parking** parcheggio in doppia fila.

♦ **double-quick** [,dʌbl'kwɪk] ADV di corsa.

♦ **double room** N camera per due, (*camera*) doppia, (*camera*) matrimoniale *f*.

dou·bles ['dʌblz] NPL (*Tennis*) doppio; **a game of mixed/ladies' doubles** un doppio misto/femminile.

♦ **double standard** N: **to have double standards** avere due pesi e due misure.

dou·blet ['dʌblɪt] N (*History*: *jacket*) farsetto.

♦ **double take** N: **to do a double take** (*fig*) reagire a scoppio ritardato.

♦ **double talk** ['dʌbl,tɔ:k] N discorsi *mpl* ambigui.

♦ **double time** N *tariffa doppia per lavoro straordinario*.

♦ **dou·ble wham·my** [,dʌbl'wæmɪ] N (*fam*) doppia mazzata (*fig*).

dou·bly ['dʌblɪ] ADV doppiamente; **to be doubly careful** stare doppiamente attento(-a).

doubt [daʊt] ① N dubbio; **to be in doubt** essere in dubbio; **without (a) doubt** senza dubbio; **beyond doubt** fuor di dubbio; **if in doubt** nell'incertezza, in caso di dubbio; **no doubt he will come** è probabile che venga; **there is no doubt of that** su questo non c'è dubbio; **I have my doubts about whether he'll come** ho i miei dubbi che venga.

② VT **a** (*truth of statement*) dubitare di; **to doubt one's own eyes** non credere ai propri occhi; **I doubt it very much** ne dubito proprio; **you're a real doubting Thomas** sei proprio come San Tommaso

b (*be uncertain*): **to doubt whether** *or* **if** *or* **that** dubitare che + *sub*; **I don't doubt that he will come** non dubito *or* non ho dubbi che verrà.

doubt·er ['dautə] N scettico(-a).

doubt·ful ['dautful] ADJ (*uncertain: person*) poco convinto (-a); (: *look*) dubbioso(-a); (: *result, success, future*) dubbio(-a), incerto(-a); (*debatable: question*) discutibile; (*questionable: taste, reputation*) dubbio(-a); **to be doubtful about sth** non essere convinto(-a) di qc, avere dei dubbi su qc; **I'm a bit doubtful** non sono tanto sicuro; **it's doubtful whether ...** non è sicuro che... + *sub*.

doubt·ful·ly ['dautfəlɪ] ADV (*unconvincedly*) con aria dubbiosa, senza convinzione.

doubt·ful·ness ['dautfulnɪs] N (*hesitation*) esitazione *f*, indecisione *f*; (*uncertainty*) incertezza.

doubt·less ['dautlɪs] ADV senza dubbio, indubbiamente.

douche [du:ʃ] N (*shower*) doccia; (*Med: internal*) irrigazione *f*.

dough [dəu] N **a** impasto, pasta **b** (*fam: money*) grana.

dough·nut, (*Am*) **do·nut** ['dəunʌt] N krapfen *m inv*, bombolone *m*.

dough·ty ['dautɪ] ADJ (*comp* **-tier**, *superl* **-tiest**) (*old*) valoroso(-a).

doughy ['dəuɪ] ADJ (*bread*) molliccio(-a); (*fig: complexion*) pallidino(-a).

dour ['duə'] ADJ (*grim*) arcigno(-a).

douse [daus] VT (*with water*) infradiciare; (*flames*) spegnere.

dove [dʌv] N colombo(-a); (*fig Pol*) colomba; **collared dove** colombo(-a) dal collare.

dove·cote ['dʌv,kəut] N colombaia.

dove·tail ['dʌv,teɪl] ① N (*also: dovetail joint*) incastro a coda di rondine.
② VT (*fig*): **to dovetail with/into** connettere a/con.
③ VI (*fig*) combaciare, collimare.

dowa·ger ['dauədʒə'] N vedova titolata.

dow·di·ly ['daudɪlɪ] ADV (*dressed*) in modo scialbo.

dow·di·ness ['daudɪnɪs] N aspetto scialbo.

dowdy ['daudɪ] ADJ (*comp* **-ier**, *superl* **-iest**) scialbo(-a).

Dow-Jones average ['dau'dʒəunz'æverɪdʒ] N (*Am*): **the Dow-Jones average** l'indice *m* Dow-Jones.

down¹ [daun] ① ADV **a** (*movement*) giù; (*to the ground*) giù, a terra; (*to a dog*): **down!** a cuccia!; **get down!** scendi!; **to fall down** cadere; **to run down** correre giù; **he came down from Glasgow** è venuto giù da Glasgow; **from the year 1600 down to the present day** dal 1600 fino ai giorni nostri; **from the biggest down to the smallest** dal più grande al più piccolo; **down with traitors!** abbasso i traditori!

b (*position*) giù; **down there** là in fondo, laggiù; **down here** quaggiù; **the blinds are down** le tapparelle sono tirate giù *or* abbassate; **to kick a man when he's down** (*fig*) uccidere un uomo morto; **I'll be down in a minute** scendo tra un minuto; **I've been down with flu** sono stato a letto con l'influenza; **he lives down south** abita nel sud; **the tyres are down** le gomme sono sgonfie *or* a terra; **his temperature is down** la febbre gli è scesa; **England is two goals down** l'Inghilterra sta perdendo per due goal; **the price of meat is down** il prezzo della carne è sceso; **write this down** scrivi; **I've got it down in my diary** ce l'ho sulla mia agenda; **you're down for the next race** sei iscritto alla prossima gara

c (*as deposit*): **to pay £20 down** dare 20 sterline in acconto *or* di anticipo.

② PREP (*indicating movement*) giù per; (*at a lower point on*) più giù; **he ran his finger down the list** percorse la lista col dito; **he went down the hill** discese la collina; **he's down the hill** è in fondo alla collina; **he lives down the street** abita un po' più giù; **looking down this road, you can see** ... guardando in fondo alla strada, vedrai...; **down the ages** nel corso della storia; **he's gone down the pub/down town** (*fam*) è andato al pub/in città.

③ ADJ (*train, line*) che parte da una grande città; **I'm feeling a bit down** (*fam*) mi sento un po' giù.

④ VT (*opponent*) atterrare; (*fam: drink*) scolarsi; **he downed a pint of beer** si è scolato una pinta di birra; **to down tools** (*fig*) incrociare le braccia (*fig*).

⑤ N: **to have a down on sb** (*fam*) avercela con qn.

down² [daun] N (*on bird, in quilts*) piumino *m inv*; (*on person, fruit*) peluria, lanugine *f*.

down³ [daun] N (*hill*) collina, colle *m*.

♦ **down-and-out** ['daunənd'aut] ① ADJ (*destitute*) sul lastrico.
② N (*tramp*) barbone *m*.

♦ **down-at-heel** [,daunət'hi:l] ADJ scalcagnato(-a); (*fig*) trasandato(-a).

down·beat ['daun,bi:t] ① N (*Mus*) tempo in battere ② ADJ (*fam: gloomy*) pessimistico(-a); (: *relaxed*) distaccato(-a).

down·cast ['daun,ka:st] ADJ (*sad*) abbattuto(-a), avvilito (-a); (*eyes*) basso(-a).

down·er ['daunə'] N (*fam: drug*) sedativo; **to be on a downer** (*depressed*) essere giù.

down·fall ['daun,fɔ:l] N rovina, caduta.

down·grade ['daun,greɪd] VT (*job, hotel*) declassare; (*person*) degradare.

down·hearted [,daun'ha:tɪd] ADJ scoraggiato(-a), demoralizzato(-a); **don't be downhearted!** non scoraggiarti!

down·hill [,daun'hɪl] ADV: **to go downhill** (*road*) andare in discesa; (*car*) andare giù per la discesa; (*fig: person*) lasciarsi andare; (: *business*) andare sempre peggio; **downhill race** (*Ski*) gara di discesa (libera); **downhill racer** discesista *m/f*; **downhill ski** sci *m inv* a valle.

Downing Street ['daunɪŋ,stri:t] N (*Brit*): **10 Downing Street** *residenza del primo ministro inglese.*

♦ **down-in-the-mouth** ['daunɪnðə'mauθ] ADJ: **to look down-in-the-mouth** avere un'aria abbattuta.

down·load ['daun,ləud] VT (*Comput*) trasferire.

♦ **down-market** ['daun,ma:kɪt] ① ADJ rivolto(-a) ad una fascia di mercato inferiore; (*product*) dozzinale.
② ADV: **to go down-market** rivolgersi ad una fascia inferiore di pubblico.

♦ **down payment** N acconto.

down·play ['daun,pleɪ] VT (*Am*) minimizzare.

down·pour ['daun,pɔ:'] N acquazzone *m*.

down·right ['daun,raɪt] ① ADJ (*person, manner*) franco(-a); (*lie, liar*) bell'e buono(-a); (*refusal*) categorico(-a), assoluto(-a).
② ADV (*rude, disgusting*) davvero.

Downs [daunz] NPL (*Brit*): **the Downs** *colline di gesso nel sud-est dell'Inghilterra.*

down·size ['daun,saɪz] VT (*workforce*) ridurre.

Down's syndrome ['daunz,sɪndrəum] N sindrome *f* di Down; **a Down's syndrome baby** un(a) bambino(-a) Down.

down·stairs ['daun'stɛəz] ① ADJ (*on the ground floor*) al pianterreno, al pianterra; (*on the floor underneath*) al piano di sotto.
② ADV di sotto, giù; **to come** *or* **go downstairs** scendere (al piano di sotto); **she lives downstairs** abita al piano di sotto.

down·stream ['daʊn'striːm] ADV: **downstream (from)** a valle (di).

down·swing ['daʊnˌswɪŋ], **down·turn** ['daʊnˌtɜːn] N (*Statistics*) calo.

down·time ['daʊntaɪm] N (*Comm*) tempi *mpl* morti.

♦ **down-to-earth** ['daʊntʊˈɜːθ] ADJ (*person*) coi piedi per terra, pratico(-a); (*advice, approach*) pratico(-a).

down·town ['daʊn'taʊn] 1 ADV (*Am*) in città, in centro.
2 ADJ: **downtown San Francisco** il centro di San Francisco.

down·trod·den ['daʊnˌtrɒdn] ADJ oppresso(-a).

down·turn ['daʊnˌtɜːn] N = **downswing**.

♦ **down under** (*fam*) 1 N gli antipodi.
2 ADV agli antipodi.

down·ward ['daʊnwəd] ADJ (*curve, movement etc*) in giù, verso il basso; (*slope*) in discesa; **a downward trend** una diminuzione progressiva; **a downward trend in prices** una tendenza al ribasso dei prezzi.

down·ward(s) ['daʊnwəd(z)] ADV (*go*) in giù, in discesa; (*look*) verso il basso; **face downwards** (*person*) bocconi; (*object*) a faccia in giù; **from the President downwards** dal Presidente in giù.

down·wind ['daʊn'wɪnd] ADV: **downwind (of** or **from)** sottovento (rispetto a).

downy ['daʊnɪ] ADJ (*skin, peach*) ricoperto(-a) di peluria, lanuginoso(-a).

dow·ry ['daʊrɪ] N dote *f*.

dowse [daʊz] VI praticare la rabdomanzia.

doy·en ['dɔɪən] N: **the doyen of** (*frm*) il decano di.

doy·enne [dɔɪ'ɛn] N: **the doyenne of** (*frm*) la decana di.

doz. ABBR = **dozen**.

doze [dəʊz] 1 N sonnellino, pisolino.
2 VI sonnecchiare
▸ **doze off** VI + ADV appisolarsi.

doz·en ['dʌzn] N dozzina; **80p a dozen** 80 pence la dozzina; **a dozen eggs** una dozzina d'uova; **dozens of times** centinaia *or* migliaia di volte; **dozens of people** decine *fpl* di persone.

dozy ['dəʊzɪ] ADJ (*comp* **-ier**, *superl* **-iest**) (*sleepy*) assonnato (-a); (*fam: stupid*) addormentato(-a).

DPhil [ˌdiːˈfɪl], **DPh** N ABBR (= *Doctor of Philosophy*) ≈ dottorato di ricerca.

DPP [ˌdiːpiːˈpiː] N ABBR (*Brit*)= *Director of Public Prosecution*.

DPW [diːpiːˈdʌbljuː] N ABBR (*Am*)= *Department of Public Works*.

dr ABBR (*Comm*) = **debtor**.

Dr. ABBR (= *doctor*) Dott./Dott.ssa; (*in street names*) = **drive**.

drab [dræb] ADJ (*comp* **-ber**, *superl* **-best**) (*colour*) cupo(-a); (*clothes*) triste; (*life*) grigio(-a), tetro(-a).

drab·ness ['dræbnɪs] N (*of colour*) cupezza; (*of clothes*) aspetto triste; (*of life*) grigiore *m*.

drach·ma ['drækmə] N (*pl* **drachmas** or **drachmae** ['drækmiː]) (*coin*) dracma.

dra·co·nian [drə'kəʊnɪən] ADJ draconiano(-a).

draft [drɑːft] 1 N a (*outline*) abbozzo, brutta (copia); (*of contract, document*) minuta; **draft letter** prima stesura (di una lettera)
b (*Mil: detachment*) distaccamento; **the draft** (*Am Mil*: *conscription*) la leva
c (*Comm: also:* **banker's draft**) tratta
d (*Am*) = **draught**.
2 VT a (*also:* **draft out**) abbozzare; (: *plan*) tracciare; (: *document, report*) stendere (in versione preliminare)
b (*Mil: for specific duty*) distaccare; (*Am Mil: conscript*)

arruolare.

♦ **draft dodg·er** ['drɑːftˌdɒdʒəʳ] N (*Am Mil*) renitente *m* alla leva.

drafts·man ['drɑːftsmən] N (*Am*) = **draughtsman**.

drafts·man·ship ['drɑːftsmənˌʃɪp] N (*Am*) = **draughtsmanship**.

drafty ['drɑːftɪ] N (*Am*) = **draughty**.

drag [dræg] 1 N a (*Aer, Naut: resistance*) resistenza (aerodinamica)
b (*fam: boring thing, task, person*) noia, strazio; **what a drag!** che scocciatura!
c (*on cigarette*) tirata
d (*women's clothing worn by men*): **in drag** travestito (da donna).
2 VT a (*object*) trascinare, tirare; (*person*) trascinare; **to drag one's feet over sth** (*fig*) farla lunga con qc, trascinare qc
b (*sea bed, river*) dragare.
3 VI a (*anchor*) arare
b (*go very slowly: evening, conversation etc*) trascinarsi, non finire mai
▸ **drag along** VT + ADV (*person*) trascinare (controvoglia); (*object*) tirare
▸ **drag away** VT + ADV: **to drag away (from)** tirare via (da)
▸ **drag down** VT + ADV trascinare giù, trascinare in basso; **to drag sb down to one's own level** (*fig*) far abbassare qn al proprio livello
▸ **drag in** VT + ADV (*subject, topic*) tirare in ballo
▸ **drag into** VT + PREP: **to drag sb/sth into** (*introduce unnecessarily*) trascinare qn/qc in
▸ **drag on** VI + ADV (*meeting, conversation*) trascinarsi, passare lentamente
▸ **drag up** VT + ADV (*mention unnecessarily*) ritirare in ballo, tirar fuori di nuovo.

♦ **drag coefficient, drag factor** N (*Aut*) coefficiente *m* di resistenza.

drag·net ['drægˌnɛt] N rete *f* a strascico; (*fig*) rastrellamento.

drag·on ['drægən] N drago.

dragon·fly ['drægənˌflaɪ] N libellula.

dra·goon [drə'guːn] 1 N (*Mil: cavalryman*) dragone *m*.
2 VT: **to dragoon sb into doing sth** (*Brit*) costringere qn a fare qc.

drain [dreɪn] 1 N a (*outlet*) scarico, canale *m* di scolo; (: *pipe*) tubatura di scarico; (*drain cover*) tombino; **to throw one's money down the drain** (*fig*) buttare i soldi dalla finestra
b : **the drains** NPL (*sewage system*) le fognature
c (*fig: source of loss*): **a drain on** (*energies, resources*) un salasso per; **it has been a great drain on her** l'ha veramente spossata.
2 VT (*land, lake*) prosciugare; (*marshes*) bonificare, drenare; (*vegetables, pasta*) scolare; (*glass, bottle of wine*) svuotare; (*radiator*) (far) svuotare; (*Med: wound*) drenare; **to feel drained (of energy)** (*fig*) sentirsi svuotato(-a) (di energie), sentirsi sfinito(-a).
3 VI (*washed dishes, vegetables*) scolare; (*liquid, stream*): **to drain (into)** defluire (in)
▸ **drain away** 1 VT + ADV (*liquid*) far scolare.
2 VI + ADV (*liquid*) scolare; (*strength*) esaurirsi
▸ **drain off** VT + ADV (*liquid*) far scolare.

drain·age ['dreɪnɪdʒ] N (*of land: natural*) scolo; (: *artificial*) drenaggio; (*of lake*) prosciugamento; (*system of drains*) fognature *fpl*.

drain·er ['dreɪnəʳ] N scolapiatti *m inv*.

drain·ing board ['dreɪnɪŋ,bɔːd], (*Am*) **drain·board** ['dreɪmbɔːd] N piano del lavello.

drain·pipe ['dreɪn,paɪp] N **a** tubo di scarico **b** : **drain-pipes** (*trousers*) pantaloni *mpl* a tubo.

drake [dreɪk] N maschio dell'anatra.

dram [dræm] N bicchierino (di whisky *etc*).

dra·ma ['drɑːmə] N (*gen*) dramma *m*, teatro; (*play*) commedia; (*event*) dramma; **drama critic** critico teatrale; **drama student** studente(-essa) di arte drammatica.

dra·mat·ic [drə'mætɪk] ADJ (*change*) spettacolare; (*event, improvement, effect*) straordinario(-a); (*entrance*) teatrale; (*art*) drammatico(-a).

dra·mati·cal·ly [drə'mætɪkəlɪ] ADV (*improve, change*) in modo straordinario, moltissimo; (*enter, pause*) in modo teatrale.

dra·mat·ics [drə'mætɪks] NPL **a** : **amateur dramatics** filodrammatica **b** (*histrionics*) modi *mpl* teatrali.

dra·ma·tis per·so·nae ['dræmətɪspɜː'səʊnaɪ] N personaggi *mpl*.

drama·tist ['dræmətɪst] N drammaturgo(-a).

drama·ti·za·tion [,dræmətaɪ'zeɪʃən] N (*adaptation of novel*: *for cinema*) riduzione *f* cinematografica; (: *for TV*) riduzione televisiva.

drama·tize ['dræmətaɪz] VT (*events, situation*) drammatizzare; (*adaptation of novel*: *for TV*) ridurre *or* adattare per la televisione; (: *for cinema*) ridurre *or* adattare per lo schermo.

drank [dræŋk] PT of **drink**.

drape [dreɪp] **1** N see **drapes**.

2 VT: **to drape (with)** (*altar*) drappeggiare (con); (*shoulders*) avvolgere (in); **to drape (over)** (*cloth, clothing*) avvolgere (intorno a).

drap·er ['dreɪpə'] N (*Brit old*) negoziante *m/f* di stoffe.

dra·pery ['dreɪpərɪ] N (*hanging folds*) drappeggio; (*shop*) negozio di tessuti; **draperies** NPL (*rich and heavy*) drappi *mpl*.

drapes [dreɪps] NPL (*Am*) tende *fpl*.

dras·tic ['dræstɪk] ADJ drastico(-a).

dras·ti·cal·ly ['dræstɪkəlɪ] ADV drasticamente.

drat [dræt] EXCL (*old fam*) **drat it!** accidenti!

draught, (*Am*) **draft** [drɑːft] N **a** (*of air*) corrente *f* (d'aria), spiffero; (*for fire*) tiraggio; (*Naut*) pescaggio **b** (*drink*): **he took a long draught of beer** ha bevuto una lunga sorsata di birra; **on draught** alla spina.

◆ **draught beer** N birra alla spina.

draught·board ['drɑːft,bɔːd] N scacchiera.

draughts ['drɑːfts] N (*Brit*) (gioco della) dama.

draughts·man, (*Am*) **draftsman** ['drɑːftsmən] N (*pl* -men) (*in drawing office*) disegnatore(-trice).

draughts·man·ship, (*Am*) **drafts·man·ship** ['drɑːftsmənʃɪp] N (*skill*) arte *f* del disegno.

draughty, (*Am*) **drafty** ['drɑːftɪ] ADJ (*comp* -ier, *superl* -iest) (*room*) pieno(-a) di spifferi; (*street corner*) ventoso (-a).

draw [drɔː] (*vb*: *pt* **drew**, *pp* **drawn**) **1** N **a** (*lottery*) lotteria, riffa; (*picking of tickets*) estrazione *f*, sorteggio; (*for sporting events*) sorteggio

b (*Sport*: *equal score*) pareggio; **the match ended in a draw** la partita è finita con un pareggio

c (*attraction*) attrazione *f*

d : **to be quick on the draw** essere veloce con la pistola; (*fig*) avere i riflessi pronti.

2 VT **a** (*pull*: *bolt, curtains*) tirare; (: *caravan, trailer*) trainare, rimorchiare; (: *bow*) tendere la corda di; **he drew his finger along the table** ha passato il dito sul tavolo; **he drew his hat over his eyes** si è calato il cappello sugli occhi; **she drew him to one side** lo tirò da una parte

b (*extract*: *from pocket, bag*) tirar fuori; (: *from well, tap*) attingere; (: *sword*) sguainare; (: *teeth*) estrarre; (: *cork*) cavare; (*salary, money from bank*) ritirare; (*cheque*) cambiare, riscuotere; (*Culin*: *fowl*) pulire; **to draw a bath** preparare un bagno; **to draw blood** fare uscir il sangue; (*fig*) colpire nel vivo; **to draw a card** estrarre una carta (dal mazzo); **to draw a breath** tirare un respiro; **to draw breath** (ri)prendere fiato; **to draw comfort from sth** trovare conforto in qc; **to draw a smile from sb** strappare un sorriso a qn

c (*attract*: *attention, crowd, customer*) attrarre, attirare; **to feel drawn to sb** sentirsi attratto(-a) verso qn, provare attrazione per qn

d (*sketch*: *picture, portrait*) fare; (: *object, person*) disegnare; (: *plan, line, circle*) tracciare; (: *map*) disegnare, fare; (*fig*: *situation*) fare un quadro di; (: *character*) disegnare; **I draw the line at (doing) that** mi rifiuto (di farlo)

e (*formulate*: *conclusion*): **to draw (from)** trarre (da), ricavare (da); (: *comparison, distinction*): **to draw (between)** fare (tra)

f (*Ftbl etc*): **to draw a match** pareggiare.

3 VI **a** (*move*): **to draw (towards)** avvicinarsi (a), avanzare (verso); **he drew to one side** si è tirato da parte *or* in disparte; **the train drew into the station** il treno è entrato in stazione; **the car drew over to the kerb** la macchina si è accostata al marciapiede; **he drew ahead of the other runners** ha staccato gli altri corridori; **to draw level** affiancarsi; **to draw near** avvicinarsi; **to draw to an end** *or* **to a close** volgere alla fine, avvicinarsi alla conclusione

b (*in cards*): **to draw for trumps** scegliere il seme *or* la briscola

c (*chimney*) tirare

d (*Sport*: *be equal*: *two teams*) pareggiare; **the teams drew for second place** le due squadre sono arrivate seconde a pari merito

e (*sketch*) disegnare

▶ **draw aside 1** VI + ADV (*person*) scostarsi.

2 VT + ADV (*person*) tirare in disparte; (*object*) spostare (da un lato)

▶ **draw away 1** VI + ADV: **to draw away (from)** (*go away*) allontanarsi (da); (*move ahead*: *athlete*) portarsi in vantaggio (su).

2 VT + ADV (*person*) allontanare, portare via; (*object*) togliere

▶ **draw back 1** VT + ADV (*object, hand*) tirare indietro, ritirare; (*curtains*) tirare.

2 VI + ADV (*move back*): **to draw back (from)** indietreggiare (di fronte a), tirarsi indietro (di fronte a)

▶ **draw down 1** VT + ADV (*gen*) abbassare; (*blame*): **to draw down (on)** tirare addosso a

▶ **draw in 1** VI + ADV **a** (*Brit*: *car*) accostarsi; (: *train*) entrare in stazione

b : **the days are drawing in** le giornate si accorciano.

2 VT + ADV (*breath*) tirare; (*air*) aspirare; (*pull back in*: *claws*) ritirare; (*attract*: *crowds*) richiamare

▶ **draw off** VT + ADV (*siphon off*) spillare

▶ **draw on 1** VI + ADV (*time*) avanzare.

2 VT + ADV (*gloves, stockings*) infilare lentamente.

3 VI + PREP (*resources*) attingere a; (*imagination, person*)

far ricorso a
- ▶ **draw out** 1 VI + ADV (*lengthen*) allungarsi.
  - 2 VT + ADV **a** (*take out: handkerchief*) tirar fuori; (*money from bank*) ritirare; **to draw sb out (of his shell)** (*fig*) tirare qn fuori dal suo guscio
  - **b** (*prolong: meeting*) tirare per le lunghe
- ▶ **draw up** 1 VT + ADV **a** (*formulate: will*) redigere; (: *contract*) stendere; (: *plans*) formulare; (: *document*) compilare
  - **b** (*chair*) avvicinare; (*troops*) schierare; **to draw o.s. up (to one's full height)** raddrizzarsi (con tutta la persona).
  - 2 VI + ADV (*stop*) arrestarsi, fermarsi; **to draw up (beside sth/sb)** accostarsi (a qc/qn).

draw·back ['drɔːˌbæk] N inconveniente *m*, svantaggio.
draw·bridge ['drɔːˌbrɪdʒ] N ponte *m* levatoio.
drawee [drɔːˈiː] N (*Fin*) trassato, trattario.
draw·er [drɔːʳ] N **a** (*furniture*) cassetto **b** (*of cheque*) traente *m/f*.
draw·ing ['drɔːɪŋ] N (*picture*) disegno; **I'm no good at drawing** non so disegnare; **drawing pen** (*Art*) tiralinee *m inv*.
- ♦ **drawing board** N tavolo da disegno; **back to the drawing board!** (*fig*) ricominciamo da capo!
- ♦ **drawing pin** N (*Brit*) puntina da disegno.
- ♦ **drawing room** N salotto.

drawl [drɔːl] 1 N cadenza strascicata.
  - 2 VT strascicare.
  - 3 VI strascicare le parole.
drawn [drɔːn] 1 PP of **draw**.
  - 2 ADJ (*haggard: with tiredness*) tirato(-a); (: *with pain*) contratto(-a) (dal dolore).
- ♦ **drawn-out** [drɔːnˈaʊt] ADJ prolungato(-a).
draw·string ['drɔːˌstrɪŋ] N cordone *m*, cordoncino.
dread [drɛd] 1 N terrore *m*.
  - 2 VT avere il terrore di, tremare all'idea di.
dread·ful ['drɛdfʊl] ADJ (*crime, sight, suffering*) terribile, spaventoso(-a); (*weather*) tremendo(-a); **I feel dreadful!** (*ill*) mi sento uno straccio!; (*ashamed*) vorrei scomparire (dalla vergogna)!
dread·fully ['drɛdfəlɪ] ADV terribilmente; **I'm dreadfully sorry** sono terribilmente spiacente.
dream [driːm] (*vb: pt, pp* **dreamed** *or* **dreamt**) 1 N sogno; **to have a dream about sb/sth** sognare di qn/qc; **I had a bad dream** ho fatto un brutto sogno; **sweet dreams!** sogni d'oro!; **that museum is an archaeologist's dream** quel museo è un paradiso per gli archeologi; **it worked like a dream** ha funzionato a meraviglia; **she goes about in a dream** ha sempre la testa tra le nuvole; **rich beyond his wildest dreams** ricco come non si era mai sognato in vita sua; **isn't he a dream?** non è un sogno *or* un amore?; **it's my dream house** è la casa dei miei sogni; **dream world** mondo immaginario.
  - 2 VT sognare; (*imagine*) sognarsi, credersi; **I didn't dream that ...** non mi sarei mai sognato che... + *sub*.
  - 3 VI sognare; (*imagine*) sognarsi; **to dream (of** *or* **about sb/sth)** sognare ((di) qn/qc); **I wouldn't dream of it!** non me lo sognerei neanche!; **I'm sorry, I was dreaming** mi scusi, stavo fantasticando; **there were more than I'd ever dreamed of** ce n'erano di più di quanto avessi mai immaginato
- ▶ **dream up** VT + ADV (*reason, excuse*) inventare; (*plan, idea*) escogitare.
dream·er ['driːməʳ] N sognatore(-trice).
dream·ily ['driːmɪlɪ] ADV con aria sognante.
dream·land ['driːmˌlænd] N paese *m* dei sogni.

dream·less ['driːmlɪs] ADJ senza sogni.
dream·like ['driːmlaɪk] ADJ irreale.
dreamt [drɛmt] PT, PP of **dream**.
dreamy ['driːmɪ] ADJ (*comp* **-ier**, *superl* **-iest**) (*person*) distratto(-a), sognatore(-trice); (*look, voice*) sognante; (*music, quality*) di sogno.
dreari·ly ['drɪərɪlɪ] ADV (*dressed*) in modo deprimente; (*speak*) in modo noioso.
dreari·ness ['drɪərɪnɪs] N (*of landscape, weather*) tetraggine *f*; (*of life*) squallore *m*; (*of book, speech*) monotonia.
dreary ['drɪərɪ] ADJ (*comp* **-ier**, *superl* **-iest**) (*landscape*) tetro(-a); (*weather*) deprimente; (*life*) squallido(-a); (*work, book, speech*) noioso(-a), monotono(-a).
dredge[1] [drɛdʒ] VT (*river*) dragare
- ▶ **dredge up** VT + ADV tirare alla superficie; (*fig: unpleasant facts*) rivangare.
dredge[2] [drɛdʒ] VT (*Culin*): **to dredge with** (*sugar, flour*) spolverizzare di.
dredg·er[1] ['drɛdʒəʳ], **dredge** [drɛdʒ] N (*ship*) draga.
dredg·er[2] ['drɛdʒəʳ] N (*also*: **sugar dredger**) spargizucchero *m inv*.
dredg·ing ['drɛdʒɪŋ] N dragaggio.
dregs [drɛgz] NPL (*also fig*) feccia *fsg*.
drench [drɛntʃ] VT inzuppare, infradiciare; **drenched to the skin** bagnato(-a) fradicio(-a), bagnato(-a) fino all'osso.
drench·ing ['drɛntʃɪŋ] 1 ADJ (*rain*) torrenziale.
  - 2 N: **to get a drenching** inzupparsi fino all'osso.
Dres·den ['drɛzdən] N Dresda.
- ♦ **Dresden china** N porcellana di Meissen.
dress [drɛs] 1 N (*frock*) vestito, abito; (*no pl: clothing*) abbigliamento; **in summer dress** in abiti estivi.
  - 2 VT **a** vestire; **to dress o.s.** OR **to get dressed** vestirsi; **dressed in green** vestito(-a) di verde
  - **b** (*Culin: salad*) condire; (: *chicken, crab*) preparare
  - **c** (*Med: wound*) medicare, fasciare
  - **d** (*decorate: shop window*) allestire.
  - 3 VI vestirsi; **she dresses very well** veste molto bene
- ▶ **dress down** VI + ADV **a** (*Brit: casually*) mettersi qualcosa di meno elegante (del solito)
  - **b** (*scold*): **to dress sb down** fare una lavata di capo a qn; see also **dressing-down**
- ▶ **dress up** 1 VI + ADV (*in smart clothes*) mettersi elegante; (*in fancy dress*) vestirsi in costume, mascherarsi.
  - 2 VT + ADV (*improve appearance of: facts*) presentare sotto una veste migliore.
dres·sage ['drɛsɑːʒ] N (*Horse-riding*) dressage *m*.
- ♦ **dress circle** N prima galleria.
- ♦ **dress designer** N stilista *m/f*.
dress·er ['drɛsəʳ] N **a** (*in kitchen*) credenza; (*Am: dressing table*) toilette *f inv* **b** (*Theatre*) assistente *m/f* di camerino.
dress·ing ['drɛsɪŋ] 1 N **a** (*act*) il vestirsi; (*style*) (modo di) vestire **b** (*Med: bandage*) fasciatura, benda **c** (*Culin: salad dressing*) condimento.
- ♦ **dressing-down** [ˌdrɛsɪŋ'daʊn] N lavata di capo.
- ♦ **dressing gown** N (*Brit*) vestaglia, veste *f* da camera.
- ♦ **dressing room** N (*in theatre*) camerino; (*Sport*) spogliatoio.
- ♦ **dressing table** N toilette *f inv*.
dress·maker ['drɛsˌmeɪkəʳ] N sarto(-a).
dress·making ['drɛsˌmeɪkɪŋ] N sartoria; (*school subject*) taglio e cucito.
- ♦ **dress rehearsal** N prova generale.
- ♦ **dress shirt** N camicia da sera.
dressy ['drɛsɪ] ADJ (*comp* **-ier**, *superl* **-iest**) (*fam*) elegante.

drew [dru:] PT of **draw**.
drib·ble ['drɪbl] ⓵ N (*of saliva*) bava, filo di saliva; (*Ftbl*) dribbling *m*.
　⓶ VT (*liquid*) sbrodolare.
　⓷ VI (*baby*) sbavare; (*liquid*) sgocciolare; (*Ftbl*) dribblare, fare un dribbling; (*people*): **to dribble in/out** entrare/uscire alla spicciolata.
dribs and drabs ['drɪbzən'dræbz] NPL: **in dribs and drabs** (*pay, send etc*) un po' alla volta; (*arrive*) alla spicciolata.
dried [draɪd] ADJ (*fruit, beans, flowers, herbs*) secco(-a); (*milk, eggs*) in polvere; (*soup*) liofilizzato(-a).
dri·er ['draɪəʳ] N = **dryer**.
drift [drɪft] ⓵ N **a** (*direction: of current*) direzione *f*; (: *of events*) corso; (: *of conversation, opinion*) tendenza
　b (*meaning: of questions*) senso; **to catch sb's drift** capire dove qn vuole arrivare
　c (*loss of direction*) deriva
　d (*mass of snow, sand*) cumulo, mucchio.
　⓶ VI (*in wind, current*) andare alla deriva; (*clouds*) essere sospinto(-a) dal vento; (*boat*) essere trasportato(-a) dalla corrente; (*sand, snow*) accumularsi, ammucchiarsi; (*person*) vagare; (*events*): **to drift (towards)** scivolare (verso); **to drift downstream** venir portato(-a) a valle dalla corrente; **he drifted into marriage** ha finito con lo sposarsi; **to let things drift** lasciare che le cose vadano come vogliono; **to drift apart** (*friends*) perdersi di vista; (*lovers*) allontanarsi l'uno dall'altro
　▶ **drift off** VI + ADV (*fall asleep*) scivolare nel sonno.
drift·er ['drɪftəʳ] N *persona che ha una vita instabile*.
drift·wood ['drɪftwud] N legno portato dalla corrente.
drill¹ [drɪl] ⓵ N (*for wood, metal, dentist's drill*) trapano; (*in mine, quarry*) perforatrice *f*; (*in oilfield*) trivella; (*pneumatic drill*) martello pneumatico.
　⓶ VT (*wood etc*) forare, trapanare; (*tooth*) trapanare; (*oil well*) trivellare, scavare.
　⓷ VI: **to drill (for)** fare trivellazioni (alla ricerca di).
drill² [drɪl] ⓵ N (*Scol: exercises*) esercizi *mpl*; (*Mil*) esercitazione *f*.
　⓶ VT (*soldiers*) esercitare, addestrare; (*pupils: in grammar*) fare esercitare, far fare esercizi a; **to drill good manners into a child** fare entrare la buona educazione in testa a un bambino.
　⓷ VI (*Mil*) fare esercitazioni.
drill³ [drɪl] N (*fabric*) *spesso tessuto di cotone*.
drill·ing ['drɪlɪŋ] N (*of metal, wood*) perforazione *f*; (*for oil*) trivellazione *f*; (*by dentist*) trapanazione *f*; **drilling ship** nave *f* per la trivellazione.
◆ **drilling rig** N (*on land*) torre *f* di perforazione; (*at sea*) piattaforma (per trivellazioni subacquee).
dri·ly ['draɪlɪ] ADV = **dryly**.
drink [drɪŋk] (*vb: pt* **drank**, *pp* **drunk**) ⓵ N **a** (*liquid to drink*) bevanda, bibita; **there's food and drink in the kitchen** c'è da mangiare e da bere in cucina; **could I have a drink?** posso avere qualcosa da bere?; **can I have a drink of water, please?** mi dai un po' d'acqua?; **to give sb a drink** dare qualcosa da bere a qn
　b (*glass of alcohol*): **a drink** un bicchierino; **we had drinks before lunch** abbiamo preso l'aperitivo; **let's have a drink** beviamo qualcosa; **I need a drink** ho bisogno di bere qualcosa di forte; **to invite sb for drinks** invitare qn a bere qualcosa
　c (*alcoholic liquor*) alcolici *mpl*; **he has a drink problem** è uno che beve, ha il vizio del bere; **to take to drink** darsi al bere; **to smell of drink** puzzare d'alcool; **his worries drove him to drink** le preoccupazioni lo hanno spinto al

bere.
　⓶ VT (*gen*) bere; (*soup*) mangiare; **would you like something to drink?** vuole qualcosa da bere?; **to drink sb under the table** far finire qn sotto il tavolo (completamente ubriaco(-a)).
　⓷ VI (*gen*) bere; **he doesn't drink** non beve (alcolici); **"don't drink and drive"** "non bevete se dovete guidare"; **he drinks like a fish** beve come una spugna; **to drink to sth/sb** bere a qc/alla salute di qn
　▶ **drink in** VT + ADV (*subj: person: fresh air*) aspirare; (: *story*) ascoltare avidamente; (: *sight*) ammirare, bersi con gli occhi
　▶ **drink up** ⓵ VT + ADV bere tutto.
　⓶ VI + ADV finire di bere; **drink up!** (*to child*) su, finiscilo!; (*in pub*) finisci il bicchiere!
drink·able ['drɪŋkəbl] ADJ (*not polluted: water*) potabile; (*palatable*) bevibile.
◆ **drink-driving** ['drɪŋk'draɪvɪŋ] N guida in stato di ebbrezza.
◆ **drink-driving campaign** N campagna sociale contro la guida in stato di ebbrezza.
◆ **drink-driving offence** N reato di guida in stato di ebbrezza.
drink·er ['drɪŋkəʳ] N bevitore(-trice); **a heavy drinker** un forte bevitore.
drink·ing ['drɪŋkɪŋ] N (*of alcohol*) il bere; **drinking song** ≈ canzone *f* goliardica; **an all-night drinking bout** una notte passata a ubriacarsi.
◆ **drinking fountain** N fontanella.
◆ **drinking water** N acqua potabile.
drip [drɪp] ⓵ N **a** (*droplet*) goccia; (: *of blood, dew*) stilla; (*sound: of water*) sgocciolio
　b (*fam: spineless person*) lavativo(-a)
　c (*Med*) fleboclisi *f inv*; **he's on a drip** gli stanno facendo la flebo.
　⓶ VT (*liquid*) sbrodolare; **you're dripping paint everywhere!** stai schizzando vernice dappertutto!.
　⓷ VI (*tap*) perdere, gocciolare; (*washing*) sgocciolare; (*wall*) trasudare; **to be dripping with sweat/blood** grondare sudore/sangue.
◆ **drip-dry** ['drɪp'draɪ] ADJ (*shirt*) che non si stira.
◆ **drip-feed** ['drɪp,fi:d] VT alimentare mediante fleboclisi.
drip·ping ['drɪpɪŋ] ⓵ N (*Culin*) grasso (dell'arrosto).
　⓶ ADJ (*tap*) che gocciola; (*washing, coat*) tutto(-a) bagnato(-a).
　⓷ ADV: **dripping wet** (*fam*) bagnato(-a) fradicio(-a).
drive [draɪv] (*vb: pt* **drove**, *pp* **driven**) ⓵ N **a** (*outing*) giro; (*journey*) tragitto; **to go for a drive** andare a fare un giro in macchina; **it's a long drive** è un lungo viaggio; **it's 3 hours' drive from London** è a 3 ore di macchina da Londra
　b (*leading to house*) vialetto (d'accesso)
　c (*Tennis*) diritto; (*Golf*) drive *m inv*
　d (*energy*) grinta, energia; (*motivation*) spinta, stimolo; (*Psych*) impulso; (*effort*) sforzo eccezionale; **sex drive** libido *f inv*
　e (*Comm, Pol*) campagna; **sales drive** campagna di vendita
　f (*Tech*) trasmissione *f*; (*Aut*): **front-/rear-wheel drive** trazione *f* anteriore/posteriore; **left-/right-hand drive** guida a sinistra/destra
　g (*Comput: also:* **disk drive**) disk drive *m inv*, unità *f inv* a dischi magnetici.
　⓶ VT **a** (*cause to move: people, animals*) condurre; (: *clouds, leaves*) sospingere; **the gale drove the ship off**

course la tempesta ha spinto la nave fuori rotta; **to drive sb hard** (*fig*) far sgobbare qn; **to drive sb to (do) sth** spingere qn a (fare) qc; **I was driven to it** sono stato costretto a farlo; **he is driven by greed/ambition** è spinto dall'avidità/dall'ambizione; **to drive sb mad** far impazzire qn; **to drive sb to despair** ridurre qn alla disperazione

b (*vehicle*) guidare; (*passenger*) portare (in macchina *etc*); **he drives a taxi** fa il tassista; **he drives a Mercedes** ha una Mercedes; **I'll drive you home** ti porto a casa (in macchina)

c (*operate: machine*) azionare; **steam-driven train** treno a vapore; **machine driven by electricity** macchina che funziona a elettricità

d (*nail, stake*): **to drive (into)** conficcare (in), piantare (in); **to drive this point home, she pointed out that ...** per farsi capire bene, ha sottolineato che....

3 VI (*drive a car*) guidare; (*travel by car*) andare in macchina; **to drive away/back** partire/ritornare in macchina; **can you drive?** sai guidare?; **to drive at 50 km an hour** guidare *or* andare a 50 km all'ora; **to drive on the left** guidare a sinistra

▶ **drive at** VI + PREP (*fig: intend, mean*) mirare a, voler dire

▶ **drive back** VT + ADV (*person, army*) respingere, ributtare indietro

▶ **drive off** VT + ADV (*enemy*) cacciare

▶ **drive on** **1** VI + ADV proseguire, andare (più) avanti.
  2 VT + ADV (*incite, encourage*) sospingere, spingere

▶ **drive out** VT + ADV cacciare; (*fig*) fare allontanare

▶ **drive up** VI + ADV (*car*) sopraggiungere, arrivare; (*person*) arrivare (in macchina).

◆ **drive-by** ['draɪvˌbaɪ] N (*also:* **drive-by shooting**) sparatoria dalla macchina; **he was killed in a drive-by shooting** lo hanno ammazzato sparandogli da una macchina in corsa.

◆ **drive-in** ['draɪvˌɪn] **1** N (*esp Am*) drive-in *m inv*.
  2 ADJ: **drive-in cinema/restaurant/bank** cinema/fast-food/banca drive-in; **drive-in window** sportello di drive-in.

driv·el ['drɪvl] N (*fam: nonsense*) stupidaggini *fpl*, sciocchezze *fpl*

▶ **drivel on** VI + ADV (*fam*): **to drivel on (about)** non smettere di cianciare (di).

driv·en ['drɪvn] PT of **drive**.

driv·er ['draɪvəʳ] N (*of car*) guidatore(-trice); (*professional: of car, lorry*) autista *m/f*; (*: of bus*) conducente *m/f*, autista *m/f*; (*of taxi*) tassista *m/f*; **to be in the driver's seat** essere seduto(-a) nel posto del conducente; (*fig*) essere al timone; **he's a good driver** guida bene.

◆ **driver's license** N (*Am*) = **driving licence**.

drive·way ['draɪvˌweɪ] N vialetto d'accesso.

driv·ing ['draɪvɪŋ] **1** N (*Aut*) guida; **his driving is awful** guida veramente male.
  2 ADJ **a** (*Aut*) di guida; **driving instructor** istruttore(-trice) di (scuola) guida; **driving lesson** lezione *f* di guida; **driving mirror** specchietto retrovisore; **driving school** scuola guida *inv*; **driving test** esame *m* di guida; **to pass/fail one's driving test** superare/non superare l'esame di guida

  b (*necessity*) impellente; (*force*) trainante; (*rain, sleet*) battente, sferzante.

◆ **driving licence,** (*Am*) **driver's license** N patente *f* (di guida).

driz·zle ['drɪzl] **1** N pioggerella, acquerugiola.
  2 VI piovigginare.

driz·zly ['drɪzlɪ] ADJ piovigginoso(-a).

droll [drəʊl] ADJ (*old: humour*) ameno(-a); (*: expression*) buffo(-a), strambo(-a).

drom·edary ['drɒmɪdərɪ] N dromedario.

drone [drəʊn] **1** N **a** (*male bee*) fuco, pecchione *m* **b** (*noise: of bees, aircraft*) ronzio; (*: of voices*) brusio.
  2 VI (*bee, engine, aircraft*) ronzare; (*person: also:* **drone on**) continuare a parlare (in modo monotono); (*voice*) continuare a ronzare.

drool [druːl] VI (*baby*) sbavare; **to drool over sb/sth** (*fig*) andare in estasi per qn/qc.

droop [druːp] VI (*head*) chinarsi; (*: with sleep*) cadere; (*shoulders*) piegarsi; (*flower, plant*) afflosciarsi; (*person*) abbattersi; **she was drooping with tiredness** cascava di stanchezza; **his spirits drooped** si è molto abbattuto, si è avvilito.

droopy ['druːpɪ] ADJ (*comp* **-ier,** *superl* **-iest**) (*moustache*) cascante.

drop [drɒp] **1** N **a** (*gen*) goccia; (*of wine, tea*) goccio, goccino; **drop by drop** goccia a goccia; **a drop in the ocean** (*fig*) una goccia nel mare; **he's had a drop too much** (*fam*) ha bevuto un bicchiere di troppo; **drops** NPL (*Med*) gocce *fpl*; **lemon drops** (*sweets*) caramelle *fpl* al limone

  b (*fall: in price*) calo, ribasso; (*: in temperature*) abbassamento; (*: in salary*) riduzione *f*, taglio; **a drop of 10%** un calo del 10%; **at the drop of a hat** in quattro e quattr'otto

  c (*downward slope*) salto, dislivello; (*fall*) salto; **a drop of 10 metres** un salto di 10 metri

  d (*unloading by parachute: of supplies, arms*) lancio.

  2 VT **a** (*let fall*) far *or* lasciar cadere; (*: bomb*) lanciare, sganciare; (*: liquid*) gocciolare; (*: stitch*) lasciar cadere; (*lower: hemline*) allungare; (*: price, eyes, voice*) abbassare; (*set down from car: object, person*) lasciare; (*from boat: cargo, passengers*) sbarcare; **to drop anchor** gettare l'ancora

  b (*utter casually: remark, name, clue*) lasciar cadere; **to drop a word in sb's ear** dire una parolina nell'orecchio a qn; **to drop (sb) a hint about sth** far capire qc (a qn)

  c (*postcard, note*) mandare, scrivere; **to drop sb a line** mandare due righe a qn

  d (*omit: word, letter*) dimenticare; (*: aitches*) omettere, non pronunciare; (*: intentionally: person*) escludere; (*: thing*) omettere

  e (*abandon: work*) lasciare; (*: topic*) lasciar cadere; (*: idea*) abbandonare; (*: candidate*) escludere; (*: boyfriend, girlfriend*) piantare; **let's drop the subject** lasciamo perdere; **drop it!** (*fam: subject*) piantala!; (*: gun*) buttalo!
  f (*lose: money, game*) perdere.

  3 VI **a** (*fall: object*) cadere, cascare; **I'm ready to drop** (*fam*) sto morendo; **drop dead!** (*fam*) va' al diavolo!

  b (*decrease: wind, temperature, price*) calare; (*: numbers, attendance*) diminuire; (*: voice*) abbassare

▶ **drop back** VI + ADV (rallentare per) restare indietro; **he dropped back on purpose** ha rallentato apposta per restare indietro

▶ **drop behind** VI + ADV restare indietro

▶ **drop down** VI + ADV cadere, cascare

▶ **drop in** VI + ADV (*fam: visit*): **to drop in (on)** fare un salto (da), passare (da)

▶ **drop off** **1** VI + ADV **a** (*fall asleep*) addormentarsi
  b (*decline: sales, interest*) calare, diminuire; (*: craze*) passare.
  2 VT + ADV: **to drop sb off** (*from car*) far scendere qn; **to drop sth off** lasciare qc

▶ **drop out** VI + ADV (*contents*) cascar fuori; (*fig: from contest*) ritirarsi; (: *student*) smettere di studiare; **to drop out of society/university** abbandonare la società/gli studi universitari.

♦ **drop-leaf table** ['drɒpˌliːfˈteɪbl] N tavolo con piano ribaltabile.

drop·let ['drɒplɪt] N gocciolina.

♦ **drop-off** ['drɒpˌɒf] N: **drop-off (in)** (*sales, demand*) calo (di).

drop·out ['drɒpaʊt] N **a** (*from school, university*) chi ha abbandonato gli studi; (*from society*) chi si mette ai margini della società; **the school/college dropout rate** la percentuale di abbandono della scuola/università **b** (*Rugby*) calcio di rinvio.

drop·per ['drɒpəʳ] N (*Med*) contagocce *m inv*.

drop·pings ['drɒpɪŋz] NPL (*of bird, animal*) escrementi *mpl*, sterco *msg*.

♦ **drop shot** N (*Tennis*) smorzata; **drop volley** volée *f inv* smorzata.

dross [drɒs] N (*Metallurgy*) scoria; (*fig: rubbish*) spazzatura.

drought [draʊt] N siccità.

drove [drəʊv] **1** PT of **drive**.
2 N (*of cattle*) mandria; **droves of people** centinaia *fpl* di persone; **they came in droves** sono arrivati a frotte.

drown [draʊn] **1** VT (*people, animals*) affogare, annegare; (*land*) allagare; (*also*: **drown out**: *sound*) coprire; **you look like a drowned rat** (*fam*) sei tutto fradicio!.
2 VI (*also*: **to be drowned**) annegare, affogare.

drown·ing ['draʊnɪŋ] **1** ADJ che sta annegando *or* affogando.
2 N annegamento.

drowse [draʊz] VI sonnecchiare, essere mezzo assopito (-a).

drowsi·ly ['draʊzɪlɪ] ADV con aria assonnata; **she answered drowsily** rispose con voce assonnata.

drowsi·ness ['draʊzɪnɪs] N sonnolenza.

drowsy ['draʊzɪ] ADJ (*comp* **-ier**, *superl* **-iest**) (*sleepy: person, smile, look*) assonnato(-a); (*soporific: afternoon, atmosphere*) sonnolento(-a); **to feel drowsy** sentirsi insonnolito(-a).

drudge [drʌdʒ] N (*person*) uomo/donna di fatica.

drudg·ery ['drʌdʒərɪ] N fatica; **housework is sheer drudgery** sbrigare le faccende domestiche è un lavoro pesante e ingrato.

drug [drʌg] **1** N (*Med*) medicina, medicinale *m*, farmaco; (*addictive substance*) droga, stupefacente *m*; **he's on drugs** si droga; (*Med*) è in cura.
2 ADJ di droga; **drug dealer** spacciatore(-trice) di droga; **drug runner** trafficante *m/f* di droga; **drug running** = **drug traffic**; **drug traffic** traffico di droga.
3 VT (*person, wine, food*) drogare; **to be in a drugged sleep** dormire sotto l'effetto di narcotici.

♦ **drug abuser** N chi fa abuso di droghe.

♦ **drug addict** N tossicodipendente *m/f*, tossicomane *m/f*.

♦ **drug addiction** N tossicodipendenza.

drug·gist ['drʌgɪst] N (*Am*) farmacista *m/f*.

drug·store ['drʌgˌstɔːʳ] N (*Am*) *negozio di generi vari con un bar*.

♦ **drug-taker** ['drʌgˌteɪkəʳ] N chi fa uso di droga *or* di stupefacenti.

♦ **drug-taking** ['drʌgˌteɪkɪŋ] N uso di droga.

drum [drʌm] **1** N **a** (*Mus*) tamburo; **the drums** la batteria; **big drum** grancassa; **drum roll** rullio di tamburi **b** (*container: for oil, petrol*) bidone *m*, fusto; (*Tech: cylinder, machine part*) tamburo.

2 VT: **to drum one's fingers on the table** tamburellare con le dita sul tavolo; **to drum sth into sb** (*fig*) ficcare qc in testa a qn.
3 VI (*Mus*) battere *or* suonare il tamburo; (*tap: with fingers*) tamburellare; **the noise was drumming in my ears** il rumore mi martellava nel cervello

▶ **drum up** VT + ADV (*enthusiasm, support*) conquistarsi.

drum·beat ['drʌmˌbiːt] N colpo di tamburo.

♦ **drum brake** N (*Aut*) freno a tamburo.

drum·lin ['drʌmlɪn] N collina morenica.

♦ **drum major** N tamburo maggiore.

♦ **drum majorette** N majorette *f inv*.

drum·mer ['drʌməʳ] N (*in military band*) tamburo; (*in jazz band, pop group*) batterista *m/f*.

drum·stick ['drʌmˌstɪk] N **a** (*Mus*) bacchetta **b** (*chicken leg*) coscia di pollo.

drunk [drʌŋk] **1** PP of **drink**.
2 ADJ ubriaco(-a); (*fig*) ebbro(-a), ubriaco(-a); **to get drunk** ubriacarsi; **to arrest sb for being drunk and disorderly** arrestare qn per ubriachezza molesta.
3 N ubriaco(-a).

drunk·ard ['drʌŋkəd] N beone(-a), ubriacone(-a).

drunk·en ['drʌŋkən] ADJ (*intoxicated*) ubriaco(-a); (: *habitually*) alcolizzato(-a); (*brawl, orgy*) di ubriachi; (*rage*) provocato(-a) dall'alcol; (*voice*) da ubriaco; **drunken driving** guida in stato di ebbrezza.

drunk·en·ness ['drʌŋkənnɪs] N (*state*) ubriachezza, ebbrezza; (*habit, problem*) abuso di alcolici.

drunk·om·eter [drʌŋ'kɒmɪtəʳ] N (*Am*) alcoltest *m inv*.

dry [draɪ] **1** ADJ (*comp* **-ier**, *superl* **-iest**) **a** (*gen*) secco(-a); (*clothes*) asciutto(-a); (*day*) senza pioggia; (*battery*) a secco; **on dry land** sulla terraferma; **as dry as a bone** completamente asciutto(-a); **to be dry** (*thirsty*) avere la gola secca; **the reservoir ran dry** il lago artificiale si è prosciugato
b (*humour*): **a dry sense of humour** un senso dell'umorismo all'inglese; (*uninteresting: lecture, subject*) poco avvincente.
2 VT (*subj: person: hair, hands, clothes, child*) asciugare; (: *herbs, figs, flowers*) far seccare; (*subj: sun, wind*) seccare; **to dry one's hands/hair/eyes** asciugarsi le mani/i capelli/gli occhi; **to dry the dishes** asciugare i piatti; **to dry o.s** asciugarsi.
3 VI asciugarsi

▶ **dry off 1** VI + ADV (*clothes etc*) asciugarsi.
2 VT + ADV asciugare

▶ **dry out 1** VI + ADV seccarsi; (*alcoholic*) disintossicarsi.
2 VT + ADV asciugare

▶ **dry up** VI + ADV **a** (*river, well*) seccarsi; (*moisture*) asciugarsi; (*source of supply*) esaurirsi; (*fig: imagination*) inaridirsi
b (*dry the dishes*) asciugare (i piatti)
c (*fall silent: speaker*) azzittirsi; **dry up!** (*fam*) chiudi il becco!

♦ **dry-clean** [ˌdraɪ'kliːn] VT pulire *or* lavare a secco; **"dry-clean only"** (*on label*) "pulire a secco".

♦ **dry-cleaner's** [ˌdraɪ'kliːnəz] N lavasecco *m inv*, tintoria.

♦ **dry-cleaning** [ˌdraɪ'kliːnɪŋ] N lavaggio a secco; **shall I pick up your dry-cleaning for you?** vado a prenderti la roba in tintoria?

♦ **dry dock** N (*Naut*) bacino di carenaggio.

dry·er, dri·er ['draɪəʳ] N (*for hair*) föhn *m inv*, asciugacapelli *m inv*; (*at hairdresser's*) casco *m* asciugacapelli *inv*; (*for clothes*) asciugabiancheria *m inv*.

♦ **dry-eyed** [ˌdraɪ'aɪd] ADJ: **she remained dry-eyed**

throughhout the funeral non ha pianto per tutto il funerale.

♦ **dry goods** NPL (*Am Comm*) tessuti *mpl* e mercerie *fpl*; **dry goods store** negozio di stoffe.

♦ **dry ice** N ghiaccio secco.

dry·ing ['draɪɪŋ] N (*of clothes*) asciugatura; (*of herbs, flowers*) essiccazione *f*; **drying cupboard** ambiente *m* riscaldato per asciugare i panni.

♦ **drying-up** [ˌdraɪɪŋ'ʌp] N: **to do the drying-up** asciugare i piatti.

♦ **dry iron** N ferro da stiro (a secco).

dry·ly, dri·ly ['draɪlɪ] ADV (*coldly*) con fare distaccato; (*with dry humour*) con una punta d'ironia.

dry·ness ['draɪnɪs] N (*gen*) secchezza; (*of ground*) aridità; **she remarked with some dryness that ...** osservò con una punta d'ironia che... .

♦ **dry rot** N fungo del legno.

♦ **dry run** N (*fig*) prova.

♦ **dry ski slope** N pista artificiale.

♦ **dry-stone wall** ['draɪsteʊn'wɔ:l] N muro a secco.

DSc N ABBR = *Doctor of Science*.

DSS [ˌdi:ɛs'ɛs] N ABBR (*Brit*: = *Department of Social Security*) ≈ ministero della previdenza sociale.

DST [ˌdi:ɛs'ti:] ABBR (*Am*) = **Daylight Saving Time**.

DTI [ˌdi:ti:'aɪ] N ABBR (*Brit*) = **Department of Trade and Industry**.

DTP [ˌdi:ti:'pi:] N ABBR = **desktop publishing**.

DT's [ˌdi:'ti:z] NPL (*fam*): **the DT's** delirium *m inv* tremens *inv*.

dual ['djʊəl] 1 ADJ doppio(-a), duplice; **dual controls** doppi comandi *mpl*; **dual nationality** doppia nazionalità. 2 N (*Gram*) duale *m*; (*Geom*) duale *f*.

♦ **dual carriageway** N (*Brit*) strada a doppia carreggiata.

dual·ism ['dju:əlɪzəm] N dualismo.

dual·ist ['dju:əlɪst] N dualista *m/f*.

♦ **dual-purpose** ['dju:əl'pɜ:pəs] ADJ a doppio uso.

dub [dʌb] VT **a** (*Cine*) doppiare **b** (*nickname*) ribattezzare, soprannominare; **they dubbed him "Shorty"** l'hanno ribattezzato *or* soprannominato "Shorty".

dubbed [dʌbd] ADJ (*film*) doppiato(-a).

dub·bing ['dʌbɪŋ] N (*Cine*) doppiaggio.

du·bi·ety [dju:'baɪətɪ] N (*frm*) incertezza.

du·bi·ous ['dju:bɪəs] ADJ (*gen*) dubbio(-a); (*look, smile*) dubbioso(-a); (*character, manner*) ambiguo(-a), equi-voco(-a); **to feel dubious about** *or* **as to what to do next** essere incerto(-a) sul da farsi; **I'm very dubious about it** ho i miei dubbi in proposito.

du·bi·ous·ly ['dju:bɪəslɪ] ADV con esitazione.

du·bi·ous·ness ['dju:bɪəsnɪs] N (*uncertainty*) incertezza.

Dub·lin ['dʌblɪn] N Dublino *f*.

♦ **Dublin Bay prawn** N gamberone *m*.

Dub·lin·er ['dʌblɪnə'] N dublinese *m/f*.

duch·ess ['dʌtʃɪs] N duchessa.

duchy ['dʌtʃɪ] N ducato.

duck [dʌk] 1 N anatra; **wild duck** anatra selvatica; **she's taken to her new school like a duck to water** si è trovata subito benissimo nella nuova scuola; **to play (at) ducks and drakes** tirare i sassi a fior d'acqua. 2 VT (*plunge in water*: *person, head*) spingere sotto (acqua); **to duck one's head** abbassare la testa. 3 VI (*also*: **duck down**) accucciarsi; (*in fight*) fare una schivata; (*under water*) tuffarsi sott'acqua

▸ **duck out of** VI + PREP (*fam*): **to duck out of doing sth** svignarsela per evitare di fare qc.

duck·board ['dʌkˌbɔ:d] N passerella.

♦ **duck-egg blue** ['dʌkɛg,blu:] 1 ADJ, N verdazzurro(-a)

chiaro(-a).

duck·ing ['dʌkɪŋ] N: **to give sb a ducking** spingere qn sott'acqua (*per gioco*).

duck·ling ['dʌklɪŋ] N anatroccolo.

duct [dʌkt] N (*Tech, Anat*) condotto, canale *m*.

duc·tile ['dʌktaɪl] ADJ (*metal*) duttile.

dud [dʌd] (*fam*) 1 ADJ (*shell, bomb*) inesploso(-a); (*not working*: *machine*) inservibile; (*false*: *coin, note*) fasullo (-a); (: *cheque*) a vuoto. 2 N: **to be a dud** (*object, tool*) non servire a un bel niente, non funzionare; (*person*) essere una nullità; (*shell*) fare cilecca.

dudg·eon ['dʌdʒən] N: **in high dudgeon** profondamente indignato(-a).

due [dju:] 1 ADJ **a** (*owing*: *sum, money*) dovuto(-a); **due date** (*Comm*) data di scadenza; **the rent's due on the 30th** l'affitto scade il 30; **our thanks are due to him** gli è dovuto un grazie; **I am due 6 days' leave** mi spettano 6 giorni di ferie

b (*proper*: *care, respect, attention*) dovuto(-a), giusto(-a); **with all due respect** con rispetto parlando; **after due consideration** dopo un attento esame; **in due course** a tempo debito

c (*expected*) atteso(-a); **the train is due at 8** il treno è atteso per le 8; **she is due back tomorrow** dovrebbe essere di ritorno domani; **it is due to be demolished** è destinato alla demolizione

d : **due to** (*caused by*) dovuto(-a) a; (*because of*) a causa di; (*thanks to*) grazie a.

2 ADV: **due west of** direttamente a ovest di; **to go due north** andare dritto verso nord; **to face due south** guardare dritto verso sud.

3 N: **to give him his due, he did try hard** per essere onesti (nei suoi confronti), bisogna riconoscere che ce l'ha messa tutta; see also **dues**.

duel ['djʊəl] 1 N duello. 2 VI battersi in duello.

dues [dju:z] NPL (*club, union fees*) quota; **harbour dues** diritti *mpl* di porto.

duet [dju:'ɛt] N duetto; **to sing/play a duet** cantare/ suonare un duetto; **a violin/piano duet** (*performance*) un duetto al violino/al piano; (*composition*) un duetto per violino/per piano.

duff [dʌf] ADJ (*Brit fam*: *effort, attempt*) balordo(-a)

▸ **duff up** VT + ADV (*Brit*: *fam*) tempestare di pugni.

duf·fel, duf·fle ['dʌfəl] N montgomery *m inv*.

♦ **duffel bag** N sacca da viaggio di tela.

♦ **duffel coat** N = **duffel**.

duf·fer ['dʌfə'] N (*fam*) schiappa.

dug [dʌg] PT, PP of **dig**.

dug·out ['dʌgˌaʊt] N **a** (*Mil*) trincea coperta; (*Sport*) panchina **b** (*canoe*) canoa ricavata da un tronco d'albero.

duke [dju:k] N duca *m*.

dul·cet ['dʌlsɪt] ADJ (*liter, hum*) soave; **I thought I heard your dulcet tones** (*hum*) mi pareva di aver sentito la tua dolce voce.

dull [dʌl] 1 ADJ (*comp* **-er**, *superl* **-est**) **a** (*boring*: *book, evening*) noioso(-a); (: *person, style*) insulso(-a); **as dull as ditchwater** una vera pizza

b (*dim*: *colour, eyes*) spento(-a); (*metal*) opaco(-a); (*overcast*: *weather, day, sky*) cupo(-a), scuro(-a), fosco (-a); (*muffled*: *sound, pain, thud*) sordo(-a); (*Comm*: *trade, business*) stagnante; (*lacking spirit*: *person, mood*) svogliato(-a); (*blade*) smussato(-a)

c (*sight, hearing*) debole; (*slow-witted: person, mind*) ottuso(-a); (: *pupil*) lento(-a). [2] VT (*mind, senses*) ottundere, annebbiare; (*blade*) smussare; (*impression, memory*) offuscare; (*pleasure, pain, grief*) attenuare, attutire; (*sound, colour*) smozzare; (*metal*) rendere opaco(-a).

dull·ard ['dʌləd] N (*old*) tonto(-a).

dull·ness ['dʌlnɪs] N **a** (*of life, evening*) tedio; (*of person: uninteresting character*) l'essere noioso(-a); (: *slow-witted-ness*) ottusità; (: *lack of vitality*) inerzia; (*of books, ideas, approach*) mancanza di originalità **b** (*of colour, metal*) opacità; (*of sound*) tono sordo.

dul·ly ['dʌllɪ] ADV (*listen*) con aria imbambolata; (*act*) senza mostrare interesse; (*talk, write*) in modo monotono, in modo insipido.

duly ['dju:lɪ] ADV (*properly*) come si deve, debitamente; (*as expected*) come previsto, secondo le previsioni; (*on time*) a tempo debito; **he duly arrived at 3** è arrivato alle 3 come previsto; **everybody was duly shocked** tutti sono rimasti debitamente scioccati.

dumb [dʌm] ADJ (*comp* **-er**, *superl* **-est**) **a** (*Med*) muto(-a); (*with surprise*) senza parole, ammutolito(-a); **a dumb person** un(a) muto(-a); **dumb animals** gli animali; **to be struck dumb** (*fig*) restare senza parole, ammutolire **b** (*fam: stupid*) stupido(-a); **to act dumb** fare lo gnorri; **a dumb blonde** una bionda svampita.

dumb·bell ['dʌm‚bɛl] N (*Sport*) manubrio, peso.

dumb·found [dʌm'faʊnd] VT sbigottire.

dumb·found·ed [‚dʌm'faʊndɪd] ADJ: **to be dumbfounded** rimanere sbigottito(-a).

dumb·ness ['dʌmnɪs] N **a** (*Med*) mutismo **b** (*fam: stupidity*) idiozia, stupidità.

dumbo ['dʌmbəʊ] N (*fam*) scemo(-a).

dumb·struck ['dʌm‚strʌk] ADJ: **to be dumbstruck** restare senza parole.

dumb·waiter ['dʌm‚weɪtəʳ] N montavivande *m*.

dum·my ['dʌmɪ] [1] N **a** (*Comm: imitation*) cosa finta, riproduzione *f*; (*tailor's model*) manichino; (*ventriloquist's dummy*) pupazzo; (*Sport*) finta; (*Bridge*) morto **b** (*Brit: for baby*) tettarella, succhiotto **c** (*fam: idiot*) tonto(-a). [2] ADJ (*not real*) finto(-a), falso(-a).

♦ **dummy run** N giro di prova.

dump [dʌmp] [1] N **a** (*pile of rubbish*) mucchio di immondizie *or* di rifiuti; (*place for refuse*) discarica pubblica; **to be (down) in the dumps** (*fam*) essere giù di corda **b** (*Mil*) deposito **c** (*pej fam: town, hotel etc*) buco; (: *house*) catapecchia; **d** (*Comput*) stampa della memoria, dump *m inv*. [2] VT **a** (*get rid of: rubbish etc*) buttare; (: *Comm: goods*) svendere; (*fam: person*) piantare, scaricare **b** (*put down: load*) scaricare; (: *fam: parcel, passenger, coat*) mollare **c** (*Comput*) riversare.

dump·ing ['dʌmpɪŋ] N **a** (*of rubbish*) scarico; "**no dumping**" (*of waste, rubbish*) "vietato lo scarico" **b** (*Econ*) dumping *m inv*.

dump·ling ['dʌmplɪŋ] N (*Culin*) gnocco di pasta.

♦ **dump truck** N (*also:* **dumper truck**) autocarro con cassone ribaltabile.

dumpy ['dʌmpɪ] ADJ tracagnotto(-a).

dun [dʌn] ADJ bigio(-a), grigiastro(-a).

dunce [dʌns] N (*Scol*) asino(-a), somaro(-a).

dune [dju:n] N duna.

dung [dʌŋ] N (*of horse, cow*) sterco; (*as manure*) letame *m*,

concime *m*.

dun·ga·rees [‚dʌŋgə'ri:z] NPL (*child's*) tutina; (*adult's*) salopette *f inv*; (*of workmen*) tuta.

dun·geon ['dʌndʒən] N segreta, prigione *f* sotterranea.

dung·hill ['dʌŋ‚hɪl] N letamaio.

dunk [dʌŋk] VT intingere, inzuppare; **to dunk one's bread in one's soup** inzuppare il pane nella minestra.

duo ['dju:əʊ] N (*gen, Mus*) duo *m inv*.

duo·deci·mal [‚dju:əʊ'dɛsɪməl] ADJ duodecimale.

duo·de·nal [‚dju:əʊ'di:nl] ADJ (*ulcer*) duodenale.

duo·denum [‚dju:əʊ'di:nəm] N duodeno.

dupe [dju:p] [1] N zimbello(-a); **to be sb's dupe** lasciarsi ingannare da qn. [2] VT ingannare, gabbare; **to dupe sb into doing sth** ingannare qn per fargli fare qc.

du·plex ['dju:plɛks] N (*Am: also:* **duplex apartment**) appartamento su due piani.

du·pli·cate [*vb* 'dju:plɪ‚keɪt; *n, adj* 'dju:plɪkɪt] [1] VT (*document*) fare una doppia copia di; (*on machine*) riprodurre, duplicare; (*repeat: action*) ripetere, riprodurre. [2] N (*document*) duplicato; **in duplicate** in duplice copia, in doppia copia; **duplicate key** doppione *m* della chiave. [3] ADJ (*copy*) conforme, esattamente uguale; **duplicate receipt pad** bollettario.

du·pli·cat·ing ma·chine ['dju:plɪ‚keɪtɪŋmə‚ʃi:n], **du·pli·ca·tor** ['dju:plɪkeɪtəʳ] N duplicatore *m*.

du·pli·ca·tion [‚dju:plɪ'keɪʃən] N (*gen*) ripetizione *f*; **we want to avoid duplication of work/effort** vogliamo evitare un doppio lavoro/sforzo.

du·plic·ity [dju:'plɪsɪtɪ] N (*frm*) doppiezza, duplicità.

du·rabil·ity [‚djʊərə'bɪlɪtɪ] N (*of materials*) resistenza; (*of relationship*) durevolezza.

du·rable ['djʊərəbl] ADJ (*material, clothes*) resistente; (*Comm*) durevole; (*friendship*) duraturo(-a).

du·ra·tion [djʊə'reɪʃən] N durata; **of 6 years' duration** della durata di 6 anni.

du·ress [djʊə'rɛs] N: **under duress** sotto costrizione, con la coercizione.

Durex® ['djʊərɛks] N, PL INV (*Brit*) preservativo.

dur·ing ['djʊərɪŋ] PREP durante.

dur·mast ['dɜ:mɑ:st] N (*Bot: also:* **durmast oak**) eschia.

dusk [dʌsk] N (*twilight*) crepuscolo; (*gloom*) (semi)oscurità; **at dusk** sul far della sera, al crepuscolo; **in the dusk** (*liter*) nella semioscurità.

dusky ['dʌskɪ] ADJ (*complexion, room, light*) scuro(-a); **dusky pink** rosa antico *inv*.

dust [dʌst] [1] N (*on furniture etc*) polvere *f*. [2] VT, VI (*furniture*) spolverare; **she dusted the cake with sugar** ha spolverato il dolce di zucchero

▶ **dust off** VT + ADV rispolverare.

dust·bin ['dʌst‚bɪn] N bidone *m* della spazzatura.

♦ **dust bowl** N (*Geog*) regione *semi-arida soggetta a tempeste di polvere*.

dust·cart ['dʌst‚kɑ:t] N camion *m inv* della nettezza urbana *or* delle immondizie.

dust·er ['dʌstəʳ] N (*cloth*) straccio per la polvere; (*for blackboard*) cancellino, cimosa.

dust·ing ['dʌstɪŋ] [1] N: **to do the dusting** spolverare; **to give sth a dusting** dare una spolverata a qc. [2] ADJ: **dusting powder** borotalco.

♦ **dust jacket**, **dust cover** N (*of book*) sopraccoperta, copertina.

dust·man ['dʌstmən] N (*pl* **-men**) (*Brit*) netturbino.

dust·pan ['dʌst‚pæn] N paletta.

♦ **dust sheet** N (*Brit*) telo di protezione.

♦ **dust storm** N tempesta di sabbia.

♦ **dust-up** ['dʌst,ʌp] N (fam) zuffa.

dusty ['dʌstɪ] ADJ (comp **-ier**, superl **-iest**) polveroso(-a); **to get dusty** impolverarsi.

Dutch [dʌtʃ] ☐1 ADJ olandese; **Dutch elm disease** fungo parassita dell'olmo.

☐2 N **a** : **the Dutch** NPL (people) gli olandesi **b** (language) olandese m.

☐3 ADV: **to go Dutch** or **dutch** (fam) fare alla romana.

♦ **Dutch auction** N asta all'olandese.

♦ **Dutch cap** N diaframma m.

♦ **Dutch courage** N: **to give o.s. Dutch courage** farsi coraggio con un bicchierino.

Dutch·man ['dʌtʃmən] N (pl **-men**) olandese m.

Dutch·woman ['dʌtʃ,wʊmən] N (pl **-women**) olandese f.

du·ti·able ['dju:tɪəbl] ADJ soggetto(-a) a dazio.

du·ti·ful ['dju:tɪfʊl] ADJ (child) rispettoso(-a); (husband) premuroso(-a); (employee) coscienzioso(-a).

du·ti·ful·ly ['dju:tɪfəlɪ] ADV (obey, act) con il dovuto rispetto; (work) coscienziosamente.

duty ['dju:tɪ] N **a** (moral, legal) dovere m; **to do one's duty (by sb)** fare il proprio dovere (verso qn); **to make it one's duty to do sth** assumersi l'obbligo di fare qc

b (often pl: task, responsibility) mansione f, funzione f; **on duty** (Med: in hospital) di guardia; (Mil) di servizio; (Admin, Scol) di turno; **off duty** (gen) fuori servizio; (Mil) in libera uscita; **duty rota** piano dei turni di lavoro

c (tax) tassa; (: at customs) dazio; **to pay duty on sth** pagare il dazio su qc.

♦ **duty-bound** ['dju:tɪ,baʊnd] ADJ (frm): **to be duty-bound to do sth** avere il dovere morale di fare qc.

♦ **duty-free** [,dju:tɪ'fri:] ADJ (goods) esente da dogana or dazio; (at airport) duty-free inv.

♦ **duty-free shop** N duty free m inv.

♦ **duty officer** N (Mil) ufficiale m di servizio.

du·vet ['du:veɪ] N (Brit) piumone ® m.

DV [,di:'vi:] ADV ABBR = Deo volente.

DVLA [,di:vi:ɛl'eɪ] N ABBR (= Driver and Vehicle Licensing Authority) ≈ I.M.C.T.C. m (= Ispettorato generale della Motorizzazione Civile e dei Trasporti in Concessione).

DVLC [,di:vi:ɛl'si:] N ABBR (Brit)= Driver and Vehicle Licensing Centre.

DVM [,di:vi:'ɛm] N ABBR (Am)= Doctor of Veterinary Medicine.

dwarf [dwɔ:f] ☐1 ADJ, N nano(-a).

☐2 VT (subj: building, person) fare sembrare piccolissimo (-a), far scomparire; (achievement) eclissare.

dwarf·ism ['dwɔ:fɪzəm] N (Med) nanismo.

dwell [dwɛl] (pt, pp **dwelt**) VI (poetic) dimorare

▶ **dwell (up)on** VI + PREP (think about) rimuginare; (talk about) soffermarsi su, indugiare su; (subj: conversation) aggirarsi su; **don't let's dwell upon it** non insistiamo su questo punto.

dwell·er ['dwɛlə'] N abitante m/f; **city dweller** cittadino(-a).

dwell·ing ['dwɛlɪŋ] N (frm, liter) dimora; **dwelling house** (Law) abitazione f.

dwelt [dwɛlt] PT, PP of dwell.

dwin·dle ['dwɪndl] VI (numbers, supplies) assottigliarsi, diminuire, decrescere; (interest) affievolirsi; **to dwindle to** ridursi a.

dwin·dling ['dwɪndlɪŋ] ADJ (strength, interest) che si affievolisce; (resources, supplies) in diminuzione.

dye [daɪ] ☐1 N colore m; (chemical) colorante m, tintura; **hair dye** tinta per capelli; **the dye has run** si è stinto.

☐2 VT (fabric) tingere; **to dye sth red** tingere qc di or in rosso; **to dye one's hair blond** farsi biondo(-a); **dyed hair** capelli mpl tinti.

dyed-in-the-wool ['daɪdnðə'wʊl] ADJ (fig) inveterato(-a).

dye·ing ['daɪɪŋ] N tintura.

dyer ['daɪə'] N tintore(-a).

dye·stuffs ['daɪ,stʌfs] NPL sostanze fpl coloranti (per tintura).

dye·works ['daɪ,wɜ:ks] NSG tintoria.

dy·ing ['daɪɪŋ] ☐1 N (death) morte f; **the dying** NPL i morenti.

☐2 ADJ (person, plant) morente; (custom, race) in via di estinzione; **his dying words were** ... le sue ultime parole furono...; **to my dying day** finché vivrò.

dyke [daɪk] N **a** (barrier) diga, argine m; (channel) canale m di scolo; (causeway) sentiero rialzato **b** (offensive: lesbian) lesbica.

dy·nam·ic [daɪ'næmɪk] ADJ dinamico(-a).

dy·nam·ics [daɪ'næmɪks] NSG dinamica.

dy·na·mism ['daɪnəmɪzəm] N dinamismo.

dy·na·mite ['daɪnə,maɪt] ☐1 N **a** dinamite f **b** (fig fam): **he's dynamite!** è una bomba!; **the story is dynamite** è una storia esplosiva.

☐2 VT far saltare con la dinamite.

dy·na·mo ['daɪnəməʊ] N dinamo f inv.

dy·nas·tic [daɪ'næstɪk] ADJ dinastico(-a).

dyn·as·ty ['dɪnəstɪ, Am 'daɪnəstɪ] N dinastia.

d'you [dju:] = do you.

dys·en·tery ['dɪsɪntrɪ] N dissenteria.

dys·lexia [dɪs'lɛksɪə] N dislessia.

dys·lex·ic [dɪs'lɛksɪk] ADJ, N dislessico(-a).

dys·pep·sia [dɪs'pɛpsɪə] N dispepsia.

dys·pep·tic [dɪs'pɛptɪk] ADJ (Med) dispeptico(-a).

dys·tro·phy ['dɪstrəfɪ] N distrofia; **muscular dystrophy** distrofia muscolare.

E

E, e [iː] N **a** (*letter*) E, e *f or m inv*; **E for Edward**, (*Am*) **E for Easy** ≈ E come Empoli **b** (*Mus*) mi *m inv*.

E ① ABBR (= *east*) E.

② N ABBR (*fam*) = **ecstasy**.

E111 [ˌiːwʌnɪˈlɛvn] N ABBR (*also:* **form E111**) E111 (*modulo CEE per rimborso spese mediche all'estero*).

ea. ABBR = **each**.

each [iːtʃ] ① ADJ ogni *inv*, ciascuno(-a); **in each hand** in ciascuna mano; **each day** ogni giorno; **each one** ognuno (-a); **each one of them** ciascuno(-a) *or* ognuno(-a) di loro.

② PRON **a** ognuno(-a), ciascuno(-a); **each of us** ciascuno(-a) *or* ognuno(-a) di noi; **a little of each please** un po' di tutto, per favore

b : **each other** l'un(a) l'altro(-a), si (*or* ci *etc*); **they love each other** si amano; **we hate each other** ci odiamo; **you know each other** vi conoscete; **people must help each other** ci si deve aiutare a vicenda *or* l'un l'altro; **separated from each other** separati l'uno dall'altro; **next to each other** uno accanto all'altro; **you are jealous of each other** siete gelosi l'uno dell'altro.

③ ADV l'uno(-a), per uno(-a), ciascuno(-a); **we gave them an apple each** abbiamo dato una mela a ciascuno; **they cost £5 each** costano 5 sterline l'uno; **they have 2 books each** hanno 2 libri ciascuno.

eager [ˈiːɡəʳ] ADJ (*keen: pupil*) appassionato(-a), attento (-a); (*: search, desire*) appassionato(-a); **to be eager to do sth** (*impatient*) essere impaziente *or* ansioso(-a) di fare qc, non veder l'ora di fare qc; **to be eager for** (*knowledge, power*) essere avido(-a) di; (*affection*) essere desideroso(-a) di; (*happiness*) desiderare ardentemente; **he gave me an eager look** mi ha guardato speranzoso.

♦ **eager beaver** N (*fam: worker*) stacanovista *m/f*; (*: student*) secchione(-a).

eager·ly [ˈiːɡəlɪ] ADV (*listen, watch*) attentamente; (*speak, work*) con entusiasmo; (*wait*) ansiosamente.

eager·ness [ˈiːɡənɪs] N (*see adj*) passione *f*; impazienza, ansia; (*for happiness, affection*) desiderio; (*for knowledge, power*) sete *f*.

eagle [ˈiːɡl] N aquila.

♦ **eagle-eyed** [ˈiːɡlˈaɪd] ADJ (*person*) dagli occhi di lince.

E and OE [ˌiːəndˈəʊiː] ABBR (= *errors and omissions excepted*) S.E. e O. (= *salvo errori e omissioni*).

ear[1] [ɪəʳ] N orecchio, orecchia; **to keep one's ears open** tenere le orecchie aperte; **to be all ears** essere tutt'orecchi; **he could not believe his ears** non credeva alle proprie orecchie; **your ears must have been burning** non ti fischiavano le orecchie?; **it goes in one ear and out the other** mi (*or* ti *etc*) entra da un orecchio ed esce dall'altro; **to be up to one's ears in debt** essere nei debiti fino al collo; **to be up to one's ears in work** avere una mole enorme di lavoro; **to have a good ear for music** avere molto orecchio; **to have a good ear for languages** avere molto orecchio per le lingue; **to play sth by ear** (*tune*) suonare qc a orecchio; **I'll play it by ear** (*fig*) vedrò come si mettono le cose.

ear[2] [ɪəʳ] N (*of wheat, barley*) spiga; (*of corn*) pannocchia.

ear·ache [ˈɪərˌeɪk] N mal *m* d'orecchi.

ear·drum [ˈɪəˌdrʌm] N timpano.

ear·ful [ˈɪəfʊl] N: **to give sb an earful** fare una ramanzina a qn.

earl [ɜːl] N conte *m*.

ear·ly [ˈɜːlɪ] (*comp* **-ier**, *superl* **-iest**) ① ADV presto; (*ahead of time*) in anticipo; **I came home early** sono tornato a casa presto; **as early as possible** il più presto possibile; **early in the morning/afternoon** nelle prime ore del mattino/del pomeriggio; **early in the spring/19th century** all'inizio della primavera/dell'Ottocento; **he was 10 minutes early** è arrivato con 10 minuti di anticipo; **to book early** prenotare in anticipo; **I can't come any earlier** non posso venire prima; **earlier on** poco tempo prima.

② ADJ (*man*) primitivo(-a); (*Christians, settlers*) primo (-a); (*fruit, plant*) precoce; (*death*) prematuro(-a); (*reply*) pronto(-a); **it's still early** è ancora presto; **an early general election** elezioni *fpl* generali anticipate; **at an early date** prossimamente; **an early edition of the book** una precedente edizione del libro; **you're early!** sei in anticipo!; **to be an early riser** *or* **an early bird** essere

mattiniero(-a); **at an early hour** presto; **in the early morning** al mattino presto; **in the early 19th century** ai primi dell'Ottocento; **she's in her early forties** ha appena passato la quarantina; **from an early age** fin dall'infanzia; **his early youth** la sua prima giovinezza; **Shakespeare's early work** le prime opere di Shakespeare; **an early Victorian table** un tavolo del primo periodo vittoriano; **to have an early night/start** andare a letto/iniziare presto; **at your earliest convenience** (*Comm*) non appena possibile.

♦ **early closing** N (*Brit Comm*) chiusura pomeridiana settimanale; **early closing day** giorno di chiusura pomeridiana settimanale.

♦ **early retirement** N pensionamento anticipato, prepensionamento.

♦ **early warning system** N sistema *m* di preallarme.

ear·mark ['ɪəˌmɑːk] VT: **to earmark (for)** (*money*) mettere da parte (per); (*person, job*) destinare (a).

earn [ɜːn] VT (*money, salary*) guadagnare; (*Fin: interest*) maturare; (*praise, reward, rest*) meritare, meritarsi; **to earn one's living** guadagnarsi da vivere; **this earned him much praise** OR **he earned much praise for this** si è attirato grandi lodi per questo.

earned income ['ɜːnd'ɪnkʌm] N (*Brit Fin*) reddito derivante da lavoro.

earn·er ['ɜːnə'] N: **to be the sole earner** essere l'unico in famiglia ad avere un reddito; **families with a sole earner** famiglie *fpl* monoreddito *inv*; **it is a nice little earner** è una buona fonte di guadagno.

ear·nest ['ɜːnɪst] [1] ADJ (*person, character, request*) serio (-a); (*wish*) sincero(-a).
[2] N **a**: **in earnest** (*with determination*) con serietà, con coscienza; (*seriously*) sul serio **b** (*Law: also:* **earnest money**) caparra.

ear·nest·ly ['ɜːnɪstlɪ] ADV (*speak*) con serietà; (*work*) con coscienza; (*pray*) con fervore.

ear·nest·ness ['ɜːnɪstnɪs] N serietà.

earn·ings ['ɜːnɪŋz] NPL (*of individual*) guadagni *mpl*; (*salary*) stipendio *sg*; (*of company*) proventi *mpl*.

♦ **ear nose and throat specialist** N otorinolaringoiatra *m/f*.

ear·phones ['ɪəˌfəʊnz] NPL (*Telec*) cuffia *sg*.

ear·piece ['ɪəˌpiːs] N **a** auricolare *m* **b** (*of glasses*) stanghetta.

ear·plug ['ɪəˌplʌg] N tappo per le orecchie.

ear·ring ['ɪərɪŋ] N orecchino.

ear·shot ['ɪəˌʃɒt] N: **out of/within earshot** fuori portata/a portata d'orecchio; **wait till he's out of earshot before you say anything** aspetta che si allontani prima di parlare.

♦ **ear-splitting** ['ɪəˌsplɪtɪŋ] ADJ (*yell*) lacerante; (*din*) assordante.

earth [ɜːθ] [1] N **a** (*the world*) terra; **(the) Earth** la Terra; **on earth** sulla terra; **the silliest man on earth** l'uomo più stupido del mondo; **it tasted like nothing on earth** (*fam*) aveva un sapore tremendo; **it must have cost the earth!** (*fam*) deve essere costato un occhio della testa!; **where/who/what on earth ...?** (*fam*) dove/chi/che diavolo...?
b (*ground*) terra; (*soil*) terra, terreno; **to fall to earth** cadere a terra, cadere al suolo
c (*of fox, badger*) tana; **to run to earth** (*animal*) inseguire fino alla tana; (*person*) scovare, stanare
d (*Brit Elec*) terra, massa.
[2] VT (*Brit Elec: apparatus*) mettere *or* collegare a terra.

earth·en ['ɜːθən] ADJ (*of earth*) di terra; (*of baked clay*) di terracotta.

earthen·ware ['ɜːθənweə'] [1] N terraglie *fpl*, terracotta.
[2] ADJ di terracotta.

earth·ly ['ɜːθlɪ] ADJ terreno(-a); **earthly paradise** paradiso terrestre; **there is no earthly reason to think ...** non vi è nessunissima ragione di pensare...; **it's of no earthly use** non serve assolutamente a nulla.

earth·quake ['ɜːθˌkweɪk] N terremoto.

earth·shaking ['ɜːθˌʃeɪkɪŋ] ADJ (*fig*) sconvolgente.

♦ **earth-shattering** ['ɜːθˌʃætərɪŋ] ADJ stupefacente; (*momentous*) molto importante.

♦ **earth tremor** N scossa sismica.

earth·ward(s) ['ɜːθwəd(z)] ADV verso terra.

earth·work ['ɜːθˌwɜːk] N (*Mil*) terrapieno.

earthworks ['ɜːθˌwɜːks] NPL lavori *mpl* di sterro.

earth·worm ['ɜːθˌwɜːm] N lombrico.

earthy ['ɜːθɪ] ADJ **a** (*taste, smell*) di terra **b** (*person*) terra terra *inv*; (*humour*) grossolano(-a).

ear·wax ['ɪəˌwæks] N cerume *m*.

ear·wig ['ɪəˌwɪg] N (*insect*) forbicina.

ease [iːz] [1] N **a** disinvoltura, scioltezza; **with ease** senza difficoltà
b (*freedom from worry*) tranquillità, agio; **a life of ease** una vita comoda; **to feel at ease/ill at ease** sentirsi a proprio agio/a disagio; **to put sb at his** *or* **her ease** mettere qn a suo agio; **(stand) at ease!** (*Mil*) riposo!.
[2] VT (*task*) facilitare; (*pain*) alleviare, calmare; (*rope, strap, pressure*) allentare; (*collar*) slacciare; **to ease sb's mind** tranquillizzare *or* rassicurare qn; **to ease sth out/in** facilitare l'uscita/l'entrata di qc; **to ease in the clutch** (*Aut*) rilasciare la frizione dolcemente.
[3] VI (*situation*) distendersi

▶ **ease off** VI + ADV (*slow down*) rallentare; (*work, business*) diminuire; (*pressure, tension*) allentarsi; (*pain*) calmarsi; (*relax*) rilassarsi

▶ **ease up** VI + ADV (*person*) calmarsi; (*situation*) distendersi; **ease up a bit!** prenditela calma!

easel ['iːzl] N cavalletto.

easi·ly ['iːzɪlɪ] ADV (*without effort: win, climb*) facilmente, agevolmente; **he may easily change his mind** potrebbe benissimo cambiare idea; **it's easily the best** è senza dubbio il migliore; **there were easily 500 at the meeting** c'erano almeno 500 persone alla riunione.

easi·ness ['iːzɪnɪs] N **a** facilità, semplicità **b** (*of manners*) disinvoltura.

east [iːst] [1] N est *m*, oriente *m*; **the mysterious East** l'Oriente misterioso; **the East** (*Geog*) l'Oriente; (*Pol: formerly*) i Paesi dell'Est; **the wind is in the east** *or* **from the east** il vento viene da est; **to the east of** a est di; **in the east of** nella parte orientale di.
[2] ADJ (*side, coast*) orientale; (*wind*) dell'est, di levante; **the East End** il quartiere dell'est di Londra; **East Africa** l'Africa orientale.
[3] ADV (*travel*) a est, verso est, a oriente; **east of the border** a est della frontiera.

east·bound ['iːstˌbaʊnd] ADJ (*traffic*) diretto(-a) a est; (*carriageway*) che porta a est.

East·er ['iːstə'] [1] N Pasqua; **at Easter** a Pasqua.
[2] ADJ (*holidays*) pasquale, di Pasqua; (*week*) di Pasqua.

♦ **Easter egg** N uovo di Pasqua.

♦ **Easter Island** N Isola di Pasqua.

east·er·ly ['iːstəlɪ] ADJ (*point, aspect*) orientale; (*wind*) da est, di levante, dell'est; **in an easterly direction** in direzione est.

♦ **Easter Monday** N Pasquetta.

east·ern ['i:stən] ADJ orientale, d'oriente; **Eastern Europe** l'Europa orientale; **the Eastern bloc** (*Pol: formerly*) i Paesi *mpl* dell'Est; **Eastern Standard Time** (*Am*) *fuso orario della costa orientale degli Stati Uniti*.

east·ern·er ['i:stənə^r] N originario(-a) della parte orientale del paese.

east·ern·most ['i:stən,məʊst] ADJ più a est.

♦ **Easter Sunday** N domenica di Pasqua.

♦ **East Germany** N la Germania dell'Est.

east·ward ['i:stwəd] ADJ (*direction*) est *inv.*

east·ward(s) ['i:stwəd(z)] ADV a est, verso est, verso levante.

easy ['i:zɪ] ① (*comp* **-ier**, *superl* **-iest**) ADJ **a** (*not difficult*) facile; **it is easy to see that ...** è facile comprendere che...; **he's easy to get on with** ha un buon carattere; **he came in an easy first** ha vinto di larga misura; **easier said than done** si fa presto a dirlo; **easy money** facili guadagni *mpl*

b (*carefree: life*) agiato(-a), tranquillo(-a); (: *relationship*) cordiale; (*relaxed: manners, style*) disinvolto(-a); **to feel easy in one's mind** sentirsi tranquillo(-a); **payment on easy terms** (*Comm*) facilitazioni *fpl* di pagamento; **I'm easy** (*fam*) non ho problemi.

② ADV: **easy does it!** piano!; **to take it** *or* **things easy** prendersela con calma; **take it easy!** (*don't worry*) non prendertela!; (*don't rush*) calma!; **go easy with the sugar** vacci piano con lo zucchero; **go easy on him** non essere troppo duro con lui; **stand easy!** (*Mil*) riposo!

♦ **easy chair** N poltrona.

♦ **easy-going** [,i:zɪ'gəʊɪŋ] ADJ (*person*) accomodante; (*attitude*) tollerante.

♦ **easy touch** N (*fam*): **to be an easy touch** lasciarsi spillare denaro facilmente.

eat [i:t] (*vb: pt* ate, *pp* eaten) ① VT (*food*) mangiare; **to eat one's fill** mangiare a sazietà; **he's eating us out of house and home** (*fam*) è un mangiapane a tradimento; **he won't eat you** (*fam*) non ti mangia mica; **what's eating you?** (*fam*) che cosa ti rode?; **to eat one's words** (*fig*) rimangiarsi quello che si è detto.

② VI mangiare; **he eats like a horse** mangia come un lupo; **I've got him eating out of my hand** pende dalle mie labbra, fa tutto quello che voglio io

► **eat away** VT + ADV (*subj: sea*) erodere; (: *acid*) corrodere; (: *mice*) rosicchiare

► **eat away at** VI + PREP rodere

► **eat in** VI + ADV mangiare a casa

► **eat into** VI + PREP rodere; (*subj: acid*) corrodere; (*savings*) intaccare

► **eat out** ① VI + ADV mangiare fuori.

② VT + ADV: **to eat one's heart out** mangiarsi *or* rodersi il fegato

► **eat up** ① VT + ADV (*meal*) finire di mangiare; **it eats up electricity** consuma un sacco di corrente; **this car eats up the miles** questa macchina macina i chilometri.

② VI + ADV: **eat up!** finisci di mangiare!

eat·able ['i:təbl] ADJ (*fit to eat*) mangiabile; (*safe to eat*) commestibile.

eat·en ['i:tn] PP of eat.

eat·er ['i:tə^r] N: **a big eater** un(a) gran mangiatore(-trice), una buona forchetta.

eat·ery ['i:tərɪ] N (*fam*) posto per mangiare.

eat·ing ['i:tɪŋ] ADJ (*apple*) da mangiare.

♦ **eating hall** N (*Am*) mensa.

eau de Co·logne ['əʊdəkə'ləʊn] N acqua di colonia.

eaves ['i:vz] NPL gronda *sg.*

eaves·drop ['i:vzdrɒp] VI: **to eavesdrop (on a conversation)** origliare (una conversazione).

eaves·drop·per ['i:vz,drɒpə^r] N chi origlia.

ebb [ɛb] ① N (*of tide*) riflusso; **ebb and flow** flusso e riflusso; **to be at a low ebb** (*fig: person, spirits*) avere il morale a terra; (: *business*) andar male, diminuire.

② VI rifluire; (*fig: also:* **ebb away**); **to ebb and flow** (*tide*) fluire e rifluire; **his strength was ebbing fast** le forze gli venivano meno rapidamente.

♦ **ebb tide** N marea discendente.

eb·ony ['ɛbənɪ] N ebano.

ebul·lience [ɪ'bʌlɪəns] N esuberanza.

ebul·lient [ɪ'bʌlɪənt] ADJ esuberante.

ebul·lient·ly [ɪ'bʌlɪəntlɪ] ADV con esuberanza.

EC [,i:'si:] N ABBR (= *European Community*) CE *f* (= *Comunità Europea*).

ec·cen·tric [ɪk'sɛntrɪk] ADJ, N eccentrico(-a).

ec·cen·tri·cal·ly [ɪk'sɛntrɪkəlɪ] ADV eccentricamente.

ec·cen·tri·city [,ɛksən'trɪsɪtɪ] N eccentricità *f inv.*

Ec·cle·si·as·tes [ɪ,kli:zɪ'æstiːz] N Ecclesiaste *m.*

ec·cle·si·as·tic [ɪ,kli:zɪ'æstɪk] N, ADJ ecclesiastico(-a).

ec·cle·si·as·ti·cal [ɪ,kli:zɪ'æstɪkəl] ADJ ecclesiastico(-a).

ECG [,i:si:'dʒi:] N ABBR = **electrocardiogram.**

ECGD [,i:si:dʒi:'di:] N ABBR (= *Export Credits Guarantee Department*) *servizio di garanzia finanziaria per l'esportazione*.

eche·lon ['ɛʃə,lɒn] N **a** grado **b** (*Mil*) scaglione *m.*

echi·no·derm [ɪ'ki:nə,dɜ:m] N echinoderma *m.*

echo ['ɛkəʊ] ① N (*pl* **echoes**) eco *m or f.*

② VI (*sound*) echeggiare, riecheggiare; **the room echoed with their laughter** la stanza riecheggiava delle loro risate.

③ VT fare eco a, ripetere.

♦ **echo chamber** N camera sonora.

echo·graph [,ɛkəʊ'grɑ:f] N ecografo.

echo·graph·ic [,ɛkəʊ'græfɪk] ADJ ecografico(-a).

♦ **echo sounder** N ecoscandaglio.

éclair ['eɪkleə^r] N ≈ bignè *m inv.*

ec·lec·tic [ɪ'klɛktɪk] ADJ eclettico(-a).

ec·lec·ti·cism [ɪ'klɛktɪsɪzəm] N eclettismo.

eclipse [ɪ'klɪps] ① N eclissi *f inv.*

② VT eclissare.

ECM [,i:si:'ɛm] N ABBR (*Am:* = *European Common Market*) MEC *m.*

eco... ['i:kəʊ] PREF eco... .

eco-friendly ['i:kəʊ'frɛndlɪ] ADJ ecologico(-a), che rispetta l'ambiente.

eco·logi·cal [,i:kəʊ'lɒdʒɪkəl] ADJ ecologico(-a).

eco·logi·cal·ly [,i:kəʊ'lɒdʒɪkəlɪ] ADV ecologicamente.

ecolo·gist [ɪ'kɒlədʒɪst] N (*scientist*) ecologo(-a); (*conservationist*) ecologista *m/f.*

ecol·ogy [ɪ'kɒlədʒɪ] N ecologia.

eco·nom·ic [,i:kə'nɒmɪk] ADJ **a** (*problems, development, geography*) economico(-a) **b** (*profitable: price*) vantaggioso(-a); (: *business*) redditizio(-a).

eco·nomi·cal [,i:kə'nɒmɪkəl] ADJ (*method, appliance, car*) economico(-a); (*person*) parsimonioso(-a), economo (-a).

eco·nomi·cal·ly [,i:kə'nɒmɪkəlɪ] ADV **a** con economia **b** (*regarding economics*) dal punto di vista economico.

eco·nom·ics [,i:kə'nɒmɪks] ① NSG (*science*) economia.

② NPL (*financial aspects*) aspetto *or* lato economico.

♦ **economies of scale** [ɪ'kɒnəmɪzəv'skeɪl] NPL (*Econ*) economie *fpl* di scala.

econo·mist [ɪ'kɒnəmɪst] N economista *m/f*.

econo·mize [ɪ'kɒnə̩maɪz] VI: **to economize (on)** fare economia (di), risparmiare (su).

econo·my [ɪ'kɒnəmɪ] N (*all senses*) economia; **we must make economies** dobbiamo fare economia.

♦ **economy class** N (*Aer*) classe *f* turistica.

♦ **economy drive** N: **to have an economy drive** adottare una politica del risparmio.

♦ **economy size** N confezione *f* economica.

eco·sys·tem ['i:kəʊ̩sɪstəm] N ecosistema *m*.

eco-tourism [̩i:kəʊ'tʊərɪzəm] N ecoturismo.

ECSC [̩i:si:ɛs'si:] N ABBR (= *European Coal & Steel Community*) C.E.C.A. *f* (= *Comunità Europea del Carbone e dell'Acciaio*).

ec·sta·sy ['ɛkstəsɪ] N **a** (*Rel*, *fig*) estasi *f inv*; **to go into ecstasies over** andare in estasi per **b** (*drug*) ecstasy *f*.

ec·stat·ic [ɛks'tætɪk] ADJ estatico(-a), in estasi.

ec·stati·cal·ly [ɛk'stætɪkəlɪ] ADV estaticamente.

ECT [̩i:si:'ti:] N ABBR = **electroconvulsive therapy**.

ECU ['eɪkju:] N ABBR (= *European Currency Unit*) ECU *m or f inv*, ecu *m or f inv*.

Ecua·dor ['ɛkwə̩dɔ:'] N Ecuador *m*.

ecu·meni·cal [̩i:kjʊ'mɛnɪkəl] ADJ ecumenico(-a).

ecu·meni·cism [̩i:kjʊ'mɛnɪsɪzəm], **ecu·meni·cal·ism** [̩i:kjʊ'mɛnɪkəlɪzəm] N ecumenismo.

ec·ze·ma ['ɛksɪmə] N eczema *m*.

eddy ['ɛdɪ] ①VI (*water*) far mulinelli; (*wind*, *air*) turbinare. ②N (*of water*) mulinello, gorgo; (*of wind*, *air*) turbine *m*.

♦ **eddy current** N (*Phys*) corrente *f* di Foucault.

edge [ɛdʒ] ①N (*of table*, *plate*, *cup*) orlo, bordo; (*of cube*, *brick*) spigolo; (*of page*) margine *m*; (*of lake*) sponda; (*of road*) ciglio; (*of forest*) limitare *m*; (*of knife*, *razor*) taglio, filo; (*of ski*) lamina; **the water's edge** il bagnasciuga; **on the edge of the town** ai margini della città; **the trees at the edge of the road** gli alberi lungo il ciglio della strada; **a book with gilt edges** un libro con i bordi dorati; **to be on edge** (*fig*) essere nervoso(-a), avere i nervi a fior di pelle; **it sets my teeth on edge** (*voice*, *accent*) mi dà sui nervi; **to be on the edge of disaster** essere sull'orlo del disastro; **that took the edge off my appetite** mi ha calmato i morsi della fame; **to have the edge on sb/sth** essere in vantaggio su qn/qc. ②VT **a** : **to edge (with)** (*garment*, *garden*) bordare (di) **b** (*move carefully*) spostare piano piano. ③VI **a** : **to edge past** passar rasente; **to edge forward** avanzare a poco a poco; **to edge away from sb/sth** allontanarsi piano piano da qn/qc **b** (*Skiing*) spigolare.

edge·ways ['ɛdʒ̩weɪz] ADV di fianco; **I couldn't get a word in edgeways** (*fam*) non sono riuscito a infilare neppure una parola.

edgi·ness ['ɛdʒɪnɪs] N irritabilità.

edg·ing ['ɛdʒɪŋ] N bordo.

♦ **edging shears** NPL cesoie *fpl*.

edgy ['ɛdʒɪ] ADJ nervoso(-a), teso(-a).

ed·ibil·ity [̩ɛdɪ'bɪlɪtɪ] N commestibilità.

ed·ible ['ɛdɪbl] ADJ (*fit to eat*) mangiabile; (*produce*, *mushrooms*) commestibile.

edict ['i:dɪkt] N editto.

edi·fi·ca·tion [̩ɛdɪfɪ'keɪʃən] N (*often iro*) cultura, educazione *f*.

edi·fice ['ɛdɪfɪs] N costruzione *f*, edificio.

edi·fy ['ɛdɪ̩faɪ] VT edificare.

edi·fy·ing ['ɛdɪ̩faɪɪŋ] ADJ edificante.

Ed·in·burgh ['ɛdɪnbərə] N Edimburgo *f*.

edit ['ɛdɪt] VT (*newspaper*, *magazine*) dirigere; (*book*, *series*) curare; (*article*, *speech*, *text*) fare la revisione di; (*tape*, *film*, *TV*: *programme*) montare; (*Comput*) editare, correggere e modificare

► **edit out** VT + ADV tagliare.

edi·tion [ɪ'dɪʃən] N edizione *f*.

edi·tor ['ɛdɪtə'] N (*of newspaper*, *magazine*: *managing director*) direttore(-trice); (: *editorial director*) redattore(-trice) capo; (*of section of newspaper*, *magazine*) redattore(-trice); (*publisher's editor*: *of series*) editore(-trice); (: *of text*) redattore(-trice); (: *of author's work*) curatore(-trice); (*film editor*) responsabile *m/f* del montaggio.

edi·to·rial [̩ɛdɪ'tɔ:rɪəl] ① ADJ redazionale, editoriale; **editorial assistant** assistente *m/f* di redazione; **editorial staff** redazione *f*. ②N (*in newspaper*) editoriale *m*, articolo di fondo.

edi·to·ri·al·ize [̩ɛdɪ'tɔ:rɪəlaɪz] VI (*Press*: *in article*) esprimere delle opinioni (*invece di limitarsi ad esporre i fatti*).

edi·tor·ship ['ɛdɪtəʃɪp] N direzione *f* (*di pubblicazione*).

EDP [̩i:di:'pi:] N ABBR = **electronic data processing**.

EDT [̩i:di:'ti:] N ABBR (*Am*: = *Eastern Daylight Time*) ora legale di New York.

edu·cable ['ɛdjʊkəbl] ADJ educabile.

edu·cate ['ɛdjʊkeɪt] VT (*pupil*) istruire; (*the public*, *the mind*) educare; (*tastes*) affinare; **I was educated abroad** ho fatto i miei studi all'estero.

edu·cat·ed ['ɛdjʊ̩keɪtɪd] ADJ (*person*) istruito(-a), colto (-a).

♦ **educated guess** N supposizione *f inv* ben fondata.

edu·ca·tion [̩ɛdjʊ'keɪʃən] N (*schooling*) istruzione *f*; (*teaching*) insegnamento; (*knowledge*, *culture*) cultura; (*studies*) studi *mpl*; (*training*) formazione *f*; (*Univ*: *subject etc*) pedagogia; **Ministry of Education** Ministero della Pubblica Istruzione; **primary education**, (*Am*) **elementary education** scuola elementare or primaria; **secondary education** scuola secondaria; **physical education** educazione *f* fisica.

edu·ca·tion·al [̩ɛdjʊ'keɪʃənl] ADJ (*establishment*, *institution*) scolastico(-a); (*methods*) didattico(-a), d'insegnamento; (*system*) pedagogico(-a); (*film*, *visit*, *role*) educativo(-a); (*experience*, *event*) istruttivo(-a); **educational technology** tecnologie *fpl* applicate alla didattica.

edu·ca·tion·al·ist [̩ɛdjʊ'keɪʃnəlɪst], **edu·ca·tion·ist** [̩ɛdjʊ'keɪʃnɪst] N (*theorist*) pedagogista *m/f*; (*teacher*) pedagogo(-a).

edu·ca·tion·al·ly [̩ɛdjʊ'keɪʃnəlɪ] ADV dal punto di vista dell'istruzione; **the educationally deprived** le persone culturalmente svantaggiate.

edu·ca·tive ['ɛdjʊkətɪv] ADJ (*experience*, *event*) istruttivo (-a); (*film*, *visit*, *role*) educativo(-a); (*method*) didattico (-a).

edu·ca·tor ['ɛdjʊkeɪtə'] N educatore(-trice), docente *m/f*.

Ed·ward·ian [ɛd'wɔ:dɪən] ADJ edoardiano(-a).

EEC [̩i:i:'si:] N ABBR (= *European Economic Community*) C.E.E. *f* (= *Comunità Economica Europea*).

EEG [̩i:i:'dʒi:] N ABBR = **electroencephalogram**.

eel [i:l] N anguilla.

EENT [̩i:i:ɛn'ti:] N ABBR (*Am Med*)= *eye*, *ear*, *nose and throat*.

EEOC [̩i:i:əʊ'si:] N ABBR (*Am*) = **Equal Employment Opportunity Commission**.

eerie ['ɪərɪ] ADJ sinistro(-a), che fa accapponare la pelle.

EET [̩i:i:'ti:] N ABBR (= *Eastern European Time*) fuso orario dell'Europa orientale.

ef·face [ɪ'feɪs] VT (*frm*) cancellare.
ef·fect [ɪ'fɛkt] ① N **a** (*result*) effetto; **to have an effect on sb/sth** avere *or* produrre un effetto su qn/qc; **to have no effect** non avere *or* produrre alcun effetto; **to no effect** invano; **to such good effect that** con risultati così buoni che; **to recover from the effects of an illness** rimettersi dai postumi di una malattia; **to put into effect** (*rule*) rendere operativo; (*plan*) attuare; **to take effect** (*drug*) fare effetto; **to come into** *or* **take effect** (*Law*) entrare in vigore; **in effect** in realtà, effettivamente, in effetti; **his letter is to the effect that ...** (*frm*) il tenore della sua lettera è che...; **or words to that effect** o qualcosa di simile

b (*impression*) effetto, impressione *f*; **to create an effect** fare effetto; **he said it for effect** l'ha detto per far colpo; see also **effects**.
② VT (*bring about*) effettuare; (: *saving, transformation, reunion*) operare.
ef·fec·tive [ɪ'fɛktɪv] ADJ **a** (*efficient*) efficace; **to become effective** (*Law*) entrare in vigore **b** (*striking: display, outfit*) che fa colpo **c** (*actual*) effettivo(-a); **effective date** data d'entrata in vigore.
ef·fec·tive·ly [ɪ'fɛktɪvlɪ] ADV (*efficiently*) efficacemente; (*in effect*) in effetti; (*strikingly*) ad effetto; (*in reality*) di fatto.
ef·fec·tive·ness [ɪ'fɛktɪvnɪs] N efficacia.
ef·fects [ɪ'fɛkts] NPL **a** (*Cine, Theatre: visual*) effetti *mpl* scenici; (: *sound*) effetti *mpl* sonori **b** (*property*) effetti *mpl*.
ef·fec·tual [ɪ'fɛktjʊəl] ADJ (*frm*) efficace.
ef·fec·tu·al·ly [ɪ'fɛktjʊəlɪ] ADV (*frm*) efficacemente.
ef·femi·na·cy [ɪ'fɛmɪnəsɪ] N effeminatezza.
ef·femi·nate [ɪ'fɛmɪnɪt] ADJ effeminato(-a).
ef·fer·vesce [ˌɛfə'vɛs] VI (*also fig*) essere in effervescenza; **she effervesced with excitement** sprizzava felicità da tutti i pori.
ef·fer·ves·cence [ˌɛfə'vɛsns] N effervescenza.
ef·fer·ves·cent [ˌɛfə'vɛsnt] ADJ effervescente.
ef·fete [ɪ'fiːt] ADJ (*pej*) decadente.
ef·fi·ca·cious [ˌɛfɪ'keɪʃəs] ADJ (*frm*) efficace.
ef·fi·ca·cy ['ɛfɪkəsɪ] N (*frm*) efficacia.
ef·fi·cien·cy [ɪ'fɪʃənsɪ] N (*see adj*) efficienza; efficacia; rendimento.
♦ **efficiency apartment** N (*Am*) miniappartamento.
ef·fi·cient [ɪ'fɪʃənt] ADJ (*person*) efficiente; (*remedy, product, system*) efficace; (*machine, car*) che ha un buon rendimento.
ef·fi·cient·ly [ɪ'fɪʃəntlɪ] ADV (*see adj*) efficientemente; efficacemente; **the new machine works efficiently** il nuovo macchinario ha un buon rendimento.
ef·fi·gy ['ɛfɪdʒɪ] N effigie *f*.
ef·flo·res·cence [ˌɛflɔː'rɛsns] N (*Chem, Med*) efflorescenza.
ef·flu·ent ['ɛflʊənt] N effluente *m*.
ef·fort ['ɛfət] N sforzo; **to make an effort to do sth** sforzarsi di fare qc; **to make every effort to do sth** fare il possibile per fare qc; **he made no effort to be polite** non si è sforzato minimamente di essere gentile; **he won a prize for effort** gli è stato dato un premio per l'impegno dimostrato; **it's not worth the effort** non vale la pena; **that's a good effort** (*fam*) non è niente male; **his latest effort** (*fam pej*) la sua ultima fatica.
ef·fort·less ['ɛfətlɪs] ADJ (*success*) facile; (*movement*) disinvolto(-a).
ef·fort·less·ly ['ɛfətlɪslɪ] ADV senza sforzo.
ef·fron·tery [ɪ'frʌntərɪ] N sfrontatezza, sfacciataggine *f*.

ef·fu·sion [ɪ'fjuːʒən] N effusione *f*.
ef·fu·sive [ɪ'fjuːsɪv] ADJ (*person*) espansivo(-a); (*welcome, letter*) caloroso(-a); (*thanks, apologies*) interminabile.
ef·fu·sive·ly [ɪ'fjuːsɪvlɪ] ADV calorosamente; **he apologised effusively** si è profuso in scuse interminabili.
EFL [ˌiːɛf'ɛl] N ABBR (*Scol*)= *English as a Foreign Language*.
EFTA ['ɛftə] N ABBR (= *European Free Trade Association*) E.F.T.A *f*.
e.g. [ˌiː'dʒiː] ADV ABBR (= *exempli gratia: for example*) ad es.
egali·tar·ian [ɪˌgælɪ'tɛərɪən] ADJ egualitario(-a).
egali·tari·an·ism [ɪˌgælɪ'tɛərɪənɪzəm] N egualitarismo.
egg [ɛg] N uovo; (*Bio: seed*) ovulo; **egg custard** ≈ crema pasticciera; **don't put all your eggs in one basket** (*fig*) non puntare tutto su una sola carta; **to get egg on one's face** (*fig*) fare una brutta figura
▶ **egg on** VT + ADV: **to egg sb on (to do sth)** incitare *or* spingere qn (a fare qc).
egg·beater ['ɛgˌbiːtəʳ] N = **egg whisk**.
♦ **egg cup** N portauovo *m inv*.
egg·head ['ɛgˌhɛd] N (*pej fam*) intellettualoide *m/f*.
egg·nog [ˌɛg'nɒg], **egg flip** ['ɛgˌflɪp] N ≈ zabaione *m*.
egg·plant ['ɛgplɑːnt] N (*esp Am*) melanzana.
♦ **egg-shaped** ['ɛgˌʃeɪpt] ADJ ovoidale.
egg·shell ['ɛgˌʃɛl] ① N guscio d'uovo.
② ADJ (*paint finish*) a guscio d'uovo; (*colour*) color guscio d'uovo *inv*.
♦ **egg-timer** ['ɛgˌtaɪməʳ] N clessidra (*per misurare il tempo di cottura delle uova*).
♦ **egg whisk** N frusta (*da cucina*).
♦ **egg white** N albume *m*, bianco d'uovo.
♦ **egg yolk** N tuorlo, rosso (d'uovo).
ego ['iːgəʊ] N (*Psych*) ego, io; (*pride*) amor *m* proprio.
ego·cen·trical [ˌɛgəʊ'sɛntrɪkəl], **ego·cen·tric** [ˌɛgəʊ'sɛntrɪk] ADJ egocentrico(-a).
ego·ism ['ɛgəʊɪzəm] N egoismo.
ego·ist ['ɛgəʊɪst] N egoista *m/f*.
ego·is·tic [ˌɛgəʊ'ɪstɪk], **ego·is·tical** [ˌɛgəʊ'ɪstɪkəl] ADJ egoista, egoistico(-a).
ego·ma·nia [ˌɛgəʊ'meɪnɪə] N egocentrismo.
ego·ma·ni·ac [ˌiːgəʊ'meɪnɪæk] N egocentrico(-a).
ego·tism ['ɛgəʊˌtɪzəm] N egotismo.
ego·tist ['ɛgəʊtɪst] N egotista *m/f*.
ego·tis·tical [ˌɛgəʊ'tɪstɪkəl], **ego·tis·tic** [ˌɛgəʊ'tɪstɪk] ADJ egotistico(-a).
♦ **ego trip** N (*fam*): **to be on an ego trip** gasarsi.
Egypt ['iːdʒɪpt] N Egitto.
Egyp·tian [ɪ'dʒɪpʃən] ① ADJ egiziano(-a), egizio(-a).
② N (*person*) egiziano(-a); (: *ancient*) egizio(-a); (*language*) egiziano.
eider ['aɪdəʳ] N (*also*: **eider duck**) edredone *m*.
eider·down ['aɪdəˌdaʊn] N (*quilt*) trapunta di piuma.
eight [eɪt] ① ADJ otto *inv*.
② N otto *m inv*; **he's had one over the eight** (*fam*) ha alzato troppo il gomito *for usage see* **five**.
eight·een ['eɪ'tiːn] ① ADJ diciotto *inv*.
② N diciotto *m inv for usage see* **five**.
eight·eenth ['eɪ'tiːnθ] ① ADJ diciottesimo(-a).
② N (*in series*) diciottesimo(-a); (*fraction*) diciottesimo *for usage see* **fifth**.
eighth [eɪtθ] ① ADJ ottavo(-a).
② N (*in series*) ottavo(-a); (*fraction*) ottavo *for usage see* **fifth**.
eighti·eth ['eɪtɪəθ] ① ADJ ottantesimo(-a).
② N (*in series*) ottantesimo(-a); (*fraction*) ottantesimo *for usage see* **fifth**.

eighty ['eɪtɪ] ① ADJ ottanta *inv.*
② N ottanta *m inv for usage see* **five**.
Eire ['ɛərə] N Repubblica d'Irlanda.
either ['aɪðəʳ] ① ADJ **a** (*one or other*) l'uno(-a) o l'altro (-a); **either day would suit me** mi va bene sia un giorno che l'altro
b (*each*) entrambi(-e), ciascuno(-a); **on either side** su entrambi i lati; **in either hand** in ciascuna mano.
② PRON: **either (of them)** (o) l'uno(-a) o l'altro(-a); **I don't want either of them** non voglio né l'uno né l'altro; **give it to either of them** dallo a uno dei due; **which bus will you take? — either** che autobus prendi? — uno qualsiasi dei due; **I don't like either** non mi piace né l'uno né l'altro.
③ CONJ: **either …or** o… o; (*after neg*) né… né; **either today or tomorrow** oggi o domani; **either come in or stay out** o entri o stai fuori; **I have never been to either Paris or Rome** non sono mai stato né a Parigi né a Roma; **I haven't seen either one or the other** non ho visto né l'uno né l'altro.
④ ADV neanche, nemmeno, neppure; **he can't sing either** non sa neppure cantare; **no, I don't/haven't either** no, neanch'io, no, nemmeno io.
ejacu·late [ɪ'dʒækjʊˌleɪt] VI, VT **a** (*semen*) eiaculare **b** (*liter: cry out*) esclamare.
ejacu·la·tion [ɪˌdʒækjʊ'leɪʃən] N (*see vb*) eiaculazione *f*; esclamazione *f*.
eject [ɪ'dʒɛkt] ① VT (*Tech*) sganciare, eiettare; (*flames*) emettere; (*cartridge*) espellere; (*troublemaker*) espellere, allontanare.
② VI (*pilot*) catapultarsi.
ejec·tion [ɪ'dʒɛkʃən] N (*gen*) espulsione *f*; (*of bomb*) sganciamento, lancio.
ejec·tor seat [ɪ'dʒɛktəʳˌsi:t] N (*in plane*) seggiolino eiettabile.
eke [i:k] VT: **to eke out** (*food, supplies, money*) far bastare, far durare; (*income*) arrotondare; **to eke out a living** sbarcare il lunario.
EKG [ˌi:keɪ'dʒi:] N ABBR (*Am*) = **electrocardiogram**.
el [ɛl] N ABBR (*Am fam*) = **elevated railroad**.
elabo·rate [*adj* ɪ'læbərɪt; *vb* ɪ'læbəˌreɪt] ① ADJ (*gen*) elaborato(-a); (*design, pattern*) complicato(-a); (*plan*) minuzioso(-a), particolareggiato(-a); (*hairstyle*) elaborato(-a); (*style of writing*) elaborato(-a), ricercato(-a); (*meal*) raffinato(-a).
② VT (*work out*) elaborare; (*describe*) illustrare.
③ VI entrare in dettagli; **to elaborate on sth** approfondire qc.
elabo·rate·ly [ɪ'læbərɪtlɪ] ADV (*done, prepared, planned*) minuziosamente; (*written, dressed, styled etc*) con ricercatezza.
elapse [ɪ'læps] VI (*time*) trascorrere, passare.
elas·tic [ɪ'læstɪk] ① ADJ elastico(-a).
② N elastico.
♦ **elastic band** N (*Brit*) elastico.
♦ **elas·tici·ty** [ˌi:læs'tɪsɪtɪ] N elasticità.
♦ **elastic stockings** NPL calze *fpl* elastiche.
elate [ɪ'leɪt] VT esaltare, rendere euforico(-a).
elat·ed [ɪ'leɪtɪd] ADJ esultante, euforico(-a).
ela·tion [ɪ'leɪʃən] N esultanza, euforia.
el·bow ['ɛlbəʊ] ① N (*Anat*) gomito; **at his elbow** al suo fianco, accanto.
② VT: **to elbow sb aside** scostare qn a gomitate; **to elbow one's way through the crowd** farsi largo tra la folla a gomitate.

♦ **elbow grease** N (*fam*) olio di gomito.
elbow·room ['ɛlbəʊˌrʊm] N spazio; **give me some elbowroom** fammi spazio.
el·der¹ ['ɛldəʳ] ① ADJ (*brother, sister*) maggiore, più vecchio(-a).
② N **a** : **he is your elder** è più anziano di te; **one's elders** i più anziani; **you should respect your elders** devi rispettare chi è più anziano di te **b** : **elders** NPL (*of tribe*) anziani *mpl*.
el·der² ['ɛldəʳ] N (*Bot*) sambuco.
elder·berry ['ɛldəˌbɛrɪ] N (*fruit*) bacca di sambuco; (*tree*) = **elder**.
♦ **elderberry wine** N vino di sambuco.
el·der·ly ['ɛldəlɪ] ① ADJ anziano(-a).
② NPL: **the elderly** gli anziani.
♦ **elder statesman** N (*Pol*) uomo politico di grande esperienza e prestigio.
eld·est ['ɛldɪst] ADJ maggiore; **my eldest brother** il maggiore dei miei fratelli; **the eldest (child)** il/la maggiore (dei bambini).
elect [ɪ'lɛkt] ① VT **a** (*Pol etc*): **to elect (to)** eleggere (a); **he was elected chairman** è stato eletto presidente **b** : **to elect to do** (*decide*) decidere *or* scegliere di fare; **he elected to remain** ha deciso di restare.
② ADJ futuro(-a); **the president elect** il presidente designato.
elec·tion [ɪ'lɛkʃən] N elezione *f*; (*of Government*) elezioni *fpl*; **to hold an election** indire un'elezione; **the election will be held next week** l'elezione avrà luogo la settimana prossima.
♦ **election campaign** N campagna elettorale.
♦ **election day** N giorno delle elezioni.
elec·tion·eer [ɪˌlɛkʃə'nɪəʳ] VI fare propaganda elettorale.
elec·tion·eer·ing [ɪˌlɛkʃə'nɪərɪŋ] N propaganda elettorale.
elec·tive [ɪ'lɛktɪv] ADJ elettivo(-a).
elec·tor [ɪ'lɛktəʳ] N elettore(-trice).
elec·tor·al [ɪ'lɛktərəl] ADJ elettorale.
♦ **electoral college** N collegio elettorale.
♦ **electoral roll, electoral register** N (*Brit*) liste *fpl* elettorali.
elec·tor·ate [ɪ'lɛktərɪt] N elettorato.
Electra [ɪ'lɛktrə] N Elettra.
elec·tric [ɪ'lɛktrɪk] ADJ elettrico(-a); **the atmosphere was electric** (*fig*) l'atmosfera era elettrica.
elec·tri·cal [ɪ'lɛktrɪkəl] ADJ elettrico(-a).
♦ **electrical engineer** N elettrotecnico.
♦ **electrical engineering** N elettrotecnica.
♦ **electrical failure** N guasto all'impianto elettrico.
elec·tri·cal·ly [ɪ'lɛktrɪkəlɪ] ADV elettricamente.
♦ **electric blanket** N coperta elettrica, termocoperta.
♦ **electric-blue** [ɪ'lɛktrɪkblu:] ① ADJ blu *inv* elettrico.
② N blu *m inv* elettrico.
♦ **electric chair** N sedia elettrica.
♦ **electric cooker** N cucina elettrica.
♦ **electric current** N corrente *f* elettrica.
♦ **electric fire** N (*Brit*) stufa elettrica.
elec·tri·cian [ɪlɛk'trɪʃən] N elettricista *m*.
elec·tri·city [ɪlɛk'trɪsɪtɪ] N elettricità; **to switch on/off the electricity** attaccare/staccare la corrente.
♦ **electricity board** N (*Brit*) ente *m* regionale per l'energia elettrica.
♦ **electric light** N luce *f* elettrica.
♦ **electric shock** N scossa (elettrica).
♦ **electric storm** N tempesta elettromagnetica.

elec·tri·fi·ca·tion [ɪˈlɛktrɪfɪˈkeɪʃən] N (*of railway*) elettrificazione *f*; (*of audience*) elettrizzazione *f*.

elec·tri·fy [ɪˈlɛktrɪˌfaɪ] VT (*railway system, fence*) elettrificare; (*audience*) elettrizzare.

elec·tri·fy·ing [ɪˈlɛktrɪfaɪɪŋ] ADJ elettrizzante.

electro... [ɪˈlɛktrəʊ] PREF elettro... .

elec·tro·car·dio·gram [ɪˌlɛktrəʊˈkɑːdɪəˌgræm] N elettrocardiogramma *m*.

elec·tro·car·dio·graph [ɪˌlɛktrəʊˈkɑːdɪəˌgræf] N elettrocardiografo.

elec·tro·chemi·cal [ɪˌlɛktrəʊˈkɛmɪkəl] ADJ elettrochimico (-a).

elec·tro·chem·istry [ɪˌlɛktrəʊˈkɛmɪstrɪ] N elettrochimica.

elec·tro·con·vul·sive thera·py [ɪˌlɛktrəʊkənˈvʌlsɪvˈθɛrəpɪ], **elec·tro·shock thera·py** [ɪˈlɛktrəʊˌʃɒkˈθɛrəpɪ] N elettroshockterapia.

elec·tro·cute [ɪˈlɛktrəˌkjuːt] VT (*see n*) folgorare (*con la corrente elettrica*); giustiziare sulla sedia elettrica.

elec·tro·cu·tion [ɪˌlɛktrəˈkjuːʃən] N (*electric shock*) folgorazione *f*; (*Am: execution*) elettroesecuzione *f*, elettrocuzione *f*.

elec·trode [ɪˈlɛktrəʊd] N elettrodo.

elec·tro·dy·nam·ics [ɪˌlɛktrəʊdaɪˈnæmɪks] NSG elettrodinamica.

elec·tro·en·cepha·lo·gram [ɪˌlɛktrəʊɛnˈsɛfələˌgræm] N elettroencefalogramma *m*.

elec·tro·en·cepha·lo·graph [ɪˈlɛktrəʊɛnˈsɛfələˌgræf] N elettroencefalografo.

elec·troly·sis [ɪlɛkˈtrɒlɪsɪs] N elettrolisi *f*.

elec·tro·lyte [ɪˈlɛktrəʊˌlaɪt] N elettrolita *m*.

elec·tro·mag·net [ɪˈlɛktrəʊˈmægnɪt] N elettromagnete *m*.

elec·tro·mag·net·ic [ɪˈlɛktrəʊmægˈnɛtɪk] ADJ elettromagnetico(-a).

elec·tro·mo·tive [ɪˌlɛktrəʊˈməʊtɪv] ADJ elettromotore (-trice).

♦ **electromotive force** N (*Phys*) forza elettromotrice.

elec·tron [ɪˈlɛktrɒn] N elettrone *m*.

elec·tro·nega·tiv·ity [ɪˌlɛktrəʊˌnɛgəˈtɪvɪtɪ] N elettronegatività.

♦ **electron gun** N proiettore *m* elettronico.

elec·tron·ic [ɪlɛkˈtrɒnɪk] ADJ elettronico(-a); **electronic configuration** (*Chem*) configurazione *f* degli elettroni.

elec·troni·cal·ly [ɪlɛkˈtrɒnɪkəlɪ] ADV elettronicamente.

♦ **electronic data processing** N elaborazione *f* elettronica di dati.

♦ **electronic mail** N posta elettronica.

elec·tron·ics [ɪlɛkˈtrɒnɪks] NSG elettronica.

♦ **electron microscope** N microscopio elettronico.

elec·tro·plat·ed [ɪˈlɛktrəʊˌpleɪtɪd] ADJ galvanizzato(-a), placcato(-a) (mediante galvanostegia).

elec·tro·scope [ɪˈlɛktrəʊˌskəʊp] N elettroscopio.

elec·tro·shock treat·ment [ɪˈlɛktrəʊˌʃɒkˌtriːtmənt] N = electroconvulsive therapy.

elec·tro·thera·py [ɪˌlɛktrəʊˈθɛrəpɪ] N elettroterapia.

elec·tro·va·lent [ɪˌlɛktrəʊˈveɪlənt] ADJ elettrovalente.

el·egance [ˈɛlɪgəns] N eleganza.

el·egant [ˈɛlɪgənt] ADJ elegante.

el·egant·ly [ˈɛlɪgəntlɪ] ADV in modo elegante, con eleganza.

el·egi·ac [ˌɛlɪˈdʒaɪək] ADJ (*liter*) elegiaco(-a).

el·egy [ˈɛlɪdʒɪ] N elegia.

el·ement [ˈɛlɪmənt] N (*gen*) elemento; (*of surprise, luck*) fattore *m*, componente *f*; (*of heater, kettle*) resistenza; **the elements** (*weather*) gli elementi; **the elements of mathematics** i fondamenti della matematica; **to be in**

one's element essere nel proprio elemento *or* ambiente naturale.

el·ement·al [ˌɛlɪˈmɛntl] ADJ (*basic*) fondamentale; (*Chem, Phys*) elementare; (*forces*) della natura.

el·emen·ta·ry [ˌɛlɪˈmɛntərɪ] ADJ elementare; **elementary physics** i primi rudimenti di fisica.

♦ **elementary school** N *negli Stati Uniti e in Canada, un istituto scolastico dove i bambini ricevono un'istruzione per un periodo che va dai 6 agli 8 anni.*

el·ephant [ˈɛlɪfənt] N elefante(-essa).

el·ephan·tine [ˌɛlɪˈfæntaɪn] ADJ (*fig*) mastodontico(-a), elefantesco(-a).

el·evate [ˈɛlɪˌveɪt] VT **a** (*raise in rank, importance*): **to elevate (to)** elevare (a) **b** (*fig: mind*) elevare.

el·evat·ed [ˈɛlɪˌveɪtɪd] ADJ (*gen*) elevato(-a); (*railway*) soprelevato(-a); (*thoughts*) nobile.

♦ **elevated railroad** N (*Am*) (ferrovia) soprelevata.

el·evat·ing [ˈɛlɪˌveɪtɪŋ] ADJ (*fig*) esaltante.

el·eva·tion [ˌɛlɪˈveɪʃən] N (*gen*) elevazione *f*; (*Archit*) prospetto; (*of style, thought*) alto livello; (*altitude*) altitudine *f*, altezza.

el·eva·tor [ˈɛlɪˌveɪtəʳ] N (*Am: lift*) ascensore *m*; (*hoist*) montacarichi *m inv*.

elev·en [ɪˈlɛvn] ① ADJ undici *inv*.
② N undici *m inv*; **the first eleven** (*Sport*) la prima squadra *for usage see* **five**.

elev·en·ses [ɪˈlɛvnzɪz] NPL (*Brit fam*) ≈ pausa per il caffè a metà mattina.

elev·enth [ɪˈlɛvnθ] ① ADJ undicesimo(-a); **at the eleventh hour** (*fig*) all'ultimo minuto.
② N (*in series*) undicesimo(-a); (*fraction*) undicesimo *for usage see* **fifth**.

elf [ɛlf] N (*pl* **elves**) elfo.

elf·in [ˈɛlfɪn] ADJ da elfo; (*belonging to elves*) degli elfi.

elic·it [ɪˈlɪsɪt] VT: **to elicit sth (from sb)** (*truth, secret*) strappare qc (a qn); (*admission, reply*) ottenere qc (da qn).

elide [ɪˈlaɪd] VT (*Ling*) elidere.

eli·gibil·ity [ˌɛlɪdʒəˈbɪlɪtɪ] N (*see adj*) idoneità; eleggibilità.

eli·gible [ˈɛlɪdʒəbl] ADJ (*suitable*): **eligible (for)** idoneo(-a) (a); (*for membership*) che ha i requisiti richiesti (per); (*public office*) eleggibile a; **to be eligible for a pension** essere pensionabile; **he's a very eligible young man** è un buon partito.

elimi·nate [ɪˈlɪmɪˌneɪt] VT (*gen*) eliminare; (*suspect, possibility*) scartare.

elimi·na·tion [ɪˌlɪmɪˈneɪʃən] N eliminazione *f*; **by process of elimination** per eliminazione.

eli·sion [ɪˈlɪʒən] N elisione *f*.

élite [eɪˈliːt] N élite *f inv*.

élit·ism [eɪˈliːtɪzəm] N elitarismo.

élit·ist [eɪˈliːtɪst] ADJ elitario(-a).

elix·ir [ɪˈlɪksəʳ] N elisir *m inv*.

Eliza·bethan [ɪˌlɪzəˈbiːθən] ADJ, N elisabettiano(-a).

elk [ɛlk] N alce *m*.

el·lipse [ɪˈlɪps] N ellisse *f*.

el·lip·sis [ɪˈlɪpsɪs] (*pl* **ellipses** [ɪˈlɪpsiːz]) N (*Gram*) ellissi *f inv*.

el·lip·tical [ɪˈlɪptɪkəl], **el·lip·tic** [ɪˈlɪptɪk] ADJ ellittico(-a).

elm [ɛlm] N olmo; **English elm** olmo inglese.

elo·cu·tion [ˌɛləˈkjuːʃən] N dizione *f*, elocuzione *f*.

elon·gate [ˈiːlɒŋˌgeɪt] VT allungare.

elon·gat·ed [ˈiːlɒŋˌgeɪtɪd] ADJ allungato(-a).

elon·ga·tion [ˌiːlɒŋˈgeɪʃən] N allungamento.

elope [ɪˈləʊp] VI (*lovers*) fuggire insieme (*per sposarsi*).

elope·ment [ɪˈləʊpmənt] N fuga romantica.

elo·quence ['ɛləkwəns] N eloquenza.

elo·quent ['ɛləkwənt] ADJ eloquente.

elo·quent·ly ['ɛləkwəntlɪ] ADV eloquentemente.

El Sal·va·dor [ɛl'sælvə,dɔː] N El Salvador *m*.

else [ɛls] ADV **a** (*other*) altro; **anybody else would have done it** chiunque altro l'avrebbe fatto; **is it anybody else's?** è di qualcun altro?; **I'd prefer anything else rather than ...** preferirei qualsiasi altra cosa piuttosto che...; **is there anything else I can do?** posso fare qualcos'altro?; **anything else, sir?** (*shop assistant*) desidera altro, signore?; **I'd go anywhere else but there** andrei ovunque fuorché lì; **have you tried anywhere else?** hai provato da qualche altra parte?; **everyone else** tutti gli altri; **everything else** tutto il resto; **everywhere else** in qualsiasi altro luogo; **nobody else** nessun altro/nessun'altra; **nothing else** nient'altro; **nothing else, thank you** (*in shop*) è tutto, grazie; **nowhere else** nessun altro posto; **I went nowhere else** non sono andato in nessun altro posto; **somebody else** qualcun altro/qualcun'altra; **something else** qualcos'altro; **it's something else!** (*fam*) è qualcosa di speciale!; **somewhere else** da qualche altra parte, altrove; **who/what/where/how else?** chi/che/dove/come altro?; **where else?** in quale altro luogo?; **little else** poco altro; **there is little else to be done** rimane ben poco da fare; **he said that, and much else** ha detto questo e altro ancora

b (*otherwise*): **or else** altrimenti; **keep quiet or else go away** stai zitto, altrimenti vai via; **do as I say, or else!** (*fam*) fai come ti dico, se no vedi!

else·where ['ɛls'wɛə'] ADV altrove; **these flowers cannot be found elsewhere** questi fiori non si trovano da nessun'altra parte.

ELT [ɛlt] N ABBR (*Scol*)= *English Language Teaching*.

elu·ci·date [ɪ'luːsɪ,deɪt] VT delucidare.

elu·ci·da·tion [ɪ,luːsɪ'deɪʃən] N delucidazione *f*.

elude [ɪ'luːd] VT (*arrest, pursuit, enemy, observation*) sfuggire a; (*question*) eludere; **success has eluded him** il successo non gli ha arriso.

elu·sive [ɪ'luːsɪv] ADJ (*prey, enemy*) inafferrabile; (*thoughts, word, success etc*) che sfugge; (*glance*) sfuggevole; **he is very elusive** è proprio inafferrabile.

elves [ɛlvz] NPL of **elf.**

ema·ci·at·ed [ɪ'meɪsɪ,eɪtɪd] ADJ emaciato(-a).

ema·cia·tion [ɪ,meɪsɪ'eɪʃən] N deperimento, dimagrimento.

♦ E-mail, e-mail ['iː,meɪl] **①** N ABBR (= *electronic mail*) posta elettronica. **②** VT: **to E-mail sb** comunicare con qn mediante posta elettronica.

ema·nate ['ɛmə,neɪt] VI: **to emanate from** (*frm*) provenire da, emanare da.

ema·na·tion [,ɛmə'neɪʃən] N (*frm*) emanazione *f*.

eman·ci·pate [ɪ'mænsɪ,peɪt] VT (*women, slaves*) emancipare; (*fig*) liberare.

eman·ci·pa·tion [ɪ,mænsɪ'peɪʃən] N emancipazione *f*.

emas·cu·late [ɪ'mæskjʊ,leɪt] VT (*fig*) rendere impotente.

emas·cu·la·tion [ɪ'mæskjʊ,leɪʃən] N indebolimento.

em·balm [ɪm'baːm] VT imbalsamare.

em·balm·er [ɪm'baːmə'] N imbalsamatore(-trice).

em·bank·ment [ɪm'bæŋkmənt] N (*of path*) terrapieno; (*of road, railway*) massicciata; (*of canal, river*) argine *m*; (*dyke*) diga.

ern·bar·go [ɪm'baːgəʊ] N (*pl* **-es**) **①** (*Comm, Naut*) embargo; **to put an embargo on sth** mettere l'embargo su qc.

② VT mettere l'embargo su.

em·bark [ɪm'baːk] (*Naut, Aer*) **①** VI imbarcarsi.

② VT imbarcare

▶ embark on VI + PREP (*journey*) intraprendere; (*business venture, explanation, discussion*) imbarcarsi in.

em·bar·ka·tion [,ɛmbaː'keɪʃən] N imbarco.

♦ embarkation card N carta d'imbarco.

em·bar·rass [ɪm'bærəs] VT mettere in imbarazzo, imbarazzare; **to be embarrassed** essere imbarazzato(-a); **I was embarrassed by the question** la domanda mi ha messo in imbarazzo; **to be financially embarrassed** avere difficoltà economiche.

em·bar·rass·ing [ɪm'bærəsɪŋ] ADJ imbarazzante.

em·bar·rass·ment [ɪm'bærəsmənt] N imbarazzo; **to be an embarrassment to sb** essere fonte d'imbarazzo per qn; **financial embarrassments** difficoltà *fpl* economiche.

em·bas·sy ['ɛmbəsɪ] N ambasciata; **the Italian Embassy** l'ambasciata italiana.

em·bat·tled [ɪm'bætld] ADJ **a** (*castle*) assediato(-a) **b** (*person, government*) in difficoltà.

em·bed [ɪm'bɛd] VT (*in wood, cement, rock*) incastrare; (*weapon, teeth*) conficcare; (*jewel*) incastonare; **it is embedded in my memory** è impresso nella mia memoria.

em·bel·lish [ɪm'bɛlɪʃ] VT: **to embellish (with)** (*decorate*) abbellire (con); (*fig: story, truth*) infiorettare (con).

em·bel·lish·ment [ɪm'bɛlɪʃmənt] N (*see vb*) abbellimento; infiorettatura.

em·bers ['ɛmbəz] NPL braci *fpl*.

em·bez·zle [ɪm'bɛzl] VT appropriarsi indebitamente di.

em·bez·zle·ment [ɪm'bɛzlmənt] N appropriazione *f* indebita, malversazione *f*.

em·bez·zler [ɪm'bɛzlə'] N malversatore(-trice).

em·bit·ter [ɪm'bɪtə'] VT amareggiare, inasprire; **embittered by constant failure** amareggiato(-a) dai continui fallimenti.

em·bla·zon [ɪm'bleɪzən] VT: **to emblazon with** decorare con.

em·blem ['ɛmbləm] N emblema *m*.

em·blem·at·ic [,ɛmblə'mætɪk] ADJ emblematico(-a).

em·bodi·ment [ɪm'bɒdɪmənt] N incarnazione *f*, personificazione *f*.

em·body [ɪm'bɒdɪ] VT **a** (*spirit, quality*) incarnare; (*thought, theory, ideas*): **to embody (in)** esprimere (in) **b** (*include: features*) comprendere, racchiudere.

em·bold·en [ɪm'bəʊldən] VT incitare, incoraggiare.

em·bo·lism ['ɛmbəlɪzəm] N (*Med*) embolia.

em·boss [ɪm'bɒs] VT (*metal*) lavorare a sbalzo; (*leather, paper*) imprimere in rilievo, goffrare.

em·bossed [ɪm'bɒst] ADJ (*see vb*) a sbalzo; impresso(-a) in rilievo, goffrato(-a); **embossed with ...** con in rilievo... .

em·brace [ɪm'breɪs] **①** VT **a** (*person, religion, cause*) abbracciare **b** (*include*) comprendere.

② VI abbracciarsi.

③ N abbraccio.

em·bro·ca·tion [,ɛmbrəʊ'keɪʃən] N (*lotion*) linimento.

em·broi·der [ɪm'brɔɪdə'] VT ricamare; (*fig: truth, facts, story*) ricamare su, abbellire.

em·broi·dery [ɪm'brɔɪdərɪ] N ricamo; **embroidery thread** filo da ricamo.

em·broil [ɪm'brɔɪl] VT: **to embroil sb in sth** coinvolgere qn in qc; **to become embroiled (in sth)** restare invischiato (-a) (in qc).

em·bryo ['ɛmbrɪ,əʊ] N (*also fig*) embrione *m*; **in embryo** in

embrione.

em·bry·on·ic [ˌɛmbrɪ'ɒnɪk] ADJ (*also fig*) embrionale.

♦ **embryo sac** ['ɛmbrɪəʊ'sæk] N sacco embrionale.

em·cee [ˌɛm'siː] N ABBR = **master of ceremonies**.

emend [ɪ'mɛnd] VT (*text*) correggere, emendare.

emen·da·tion [ˌiːmɛn'deɪʃən] N correzione *f*, emendamento.

em·er·ald ['ɛmərəld] 1 N (*stone*) smeraldo; (*colour*) verde *m* smeraldo.

2 ADJ (*necklace, bracelet etc*) di smeraldi; (*colour: also:* **emerald green**) verde smeraldo *inv*.

♦ **Emerald Isle** N: **The Emerald Isle** (*liter*) l'Isola di Smeraldo (*Irlanda*).

emerge [ɪ'mɜːdʒ] VI: **to emerge (from)** spuntare (da); (*from water, fig: truth, facts, theory*) emergere (da); (: *problems, new nation*) sorgere (da); **it emerged that** (*Brit*) è risultato che.

emer·gence [ɪ'mɜːdʒəns] N (*of new ideas, theory*) apparizione *f*; (*of submarine*) emersione *f*; (*of nation*) nascita.

emer·gen·cy [ɪ'mɜːdʒənsɪ] 1 N emergenza; **in an emergency** in caso di emergenza; **prepared for any emergency** pronto(-a) ad ogni emergenza; **to declare a state of emergency** dichiarare lo stato di emergenza.

2 ADJ (*measures, powers*) di sicurezza; (*repairs*) di fortuna; (*Med: operation*) d'urgenza; (*rations, fund*) di riserva.

♦ **emergency case** N caso urgente.

♦ **emergency exit** N uscita di sicurezza.

♦ **emergency landing** N atterraggio di fortuna.

♦ **emergency lane** N (*Am Aut*) corsia d'emergenza.

♦ **emergency road service** N (*Am*) servizio di soccorso stradale.

♦ **emergency service** N servizio di pronto intervento.

♦ **emergency stop** N (*Aut Brit*) frenata d'emergenza.

♦ **emergency ward** N reparto di pronto soccorso.

emer·gent [ɪ'mɜːdʒənt] ADJ emergente; **emergent nation** paese *m* in via di sviluppo.

em·ery ['ɛmərɪ] N smeriglio.

♦ **emery board** N limetta (di carta smerigliata) per unghie.

♦ **emery paper** N carta vetrata, carta smerigliata.

emet·ic [ɪ'mɛtɪk] N emetico.

emi·grant ['ɛmɪɡrənt] N emigrante *m/f*.

emi·grate ['ɛmɪɡreɪt] VI emigrare.

emi·gra·tion [ˌɛmɪ'ɡreɪʃən] N emigrazione *f*.

émi·gré ['ɛmɪˌɡreɪ] N (*frm*) esule *m*.

emi·nence ['ɛmɪnəns] N a (*fame*) eminenza, reputazione *f*; **to gain** *or* **win eminence** farsi un nome *or* una reputazione b (*Rel*): **His Eminence** Sua Eminenza c (*frm: hill*) altura.

emi·nent ['ɛmɪnənt] ADJ (*person*) eminente, insigne; (*quality*) eccellente.

emi·nent·ly ['ɛmɪnəntlɪ] ADV assolutamente, perfettamente.

emir [ɛ'mɪər] N emiro.

emir·ate [ɛ'mɪərɪt] N emirato.

em·is·sary ['ɛmɪsərɪ] N emissario.

emis·sion [ɪ'mɪʃən] N (*of fumes, gas*) esalazione *f*.

emit [ɪ'mɪt] VT (*radiation*) emettere; (*fumes*) esalare.

emolu·ment [ɪ'mɒljʊmənt] N (*often pl: frm*) emolumento.

emo·tion [ɪ'məʊʃən] N emozione *f*; (*love, jealousy etc*) sentimento.

emo·tion·al [ɪ'məʊʃənl] ADJ (*person, nature*) emotivo(-a); (*moment, experience, story, scene*) commovente; (*tone, speech*) carico(-a) d'emozione; **emotional state** condi-

zione *f* mentale; **to be in a very emotional state** essere in uno stato di estrema confusione mentale; **some films have a strong emotional appeal** certi film fanno presa sui sentimenti dello spettatore *or* coinvolgono emotivamente lo spettatore.

emo·tion·al·ism [ɪ'məʊʃnəlɪzəm] N (*pej*) sentimentalismo.

emo·tion·al·ly [ɪ'məʊʃnəlɪ] ADV (*behave, be involved*) sentimentalmente; (*speak*) con emozione; **to be emotionally deprived** soffrire di carenze affettive; **to be emotionally disturbed** avere turbe emotive.

emo·tive [ɪ'məʊtɪv] ADJ che fa presa sui sentimenti; **emotive power** capacità di commuovere.

em·pa·thize ['ɛmpəˌθaɪz] VI simpatizzare.

em·pa·thy ['ɛmpəθɪ] N immedesimazione *f*; **to feel empathy with sb** immedesimarsi nei sentimenti di qn.

Empedocles [ɛm'pɛdəˌkliːz] N Empedocle *m*.

em·per·or ['ɛmpərər] N imperatore *m*.

em·pha·sis ['ɛmfəsɪs] N (*pl* **emphases** ['ɛmfəsiːz]) enfasi *f inv*; (*in word, phrase*) accento; **to speak with emphasis** parlare con enfasi; **to lay** *or* **place emphasis on sth** (*fig*) mettere in risalto *or* in evidenza qc; **the emphasis is on sport** si dà molta importanza allo sport.

em·pha·size ['ɛmfəˌsaɪz] VT (*word, fact, point, feature*) sottolineare; (*subj: garment etc*) mettere in evidenza; **I must emphasize that** ... devo sottolineare il fatto che... .

em·phat·ic [ɪm'fætɪk] ADJ (*tone, manner, person*) energico (-a), vigoroso(-a); (*speech*) enfatico(-a); (*condemnation, denial*) categorico(-a), netto(-a).

em·phati·cal·ly [ɪm'fætɪkəlɪ] ADV (*speak*) con enfasi; (*deny, refuse*) categoricamente.

em·phy·sema [ˌɛmfɪ'siːmə] N (*Med*) enfisema *m*.

em·pire ['ɛmpaɪər] N impero.

♦ **empire builder** N (*fam pej*) accentratore(-trice) di potere (economico).

♦ **empire building** N (*fam pej*) accentramento di potere (economico).

em·piri·cal [ɛm'pɪrɪkəl] ADJ empirico(-a).

em·piri·cal·ly [ɛm'pɪrɪkəlɪ] ADV empiricamente.

em·piri·cism [ɛm'pɪrɪˌsɪzəm] N empirismo.

em·piri·cist [ɛm'pɪrɪsɪst] N, ADJ empirista (*m/f*).

em·ploy [ɪm'plɔɪ] 1 VT (*give job to*) dare lavoro a, impiegare; (*appoint*) assumere; (*make use of: thing, method, person*) servirsi di, impiegare; (: *time*) impiegare; **he's employed in a bank** lavora in banca; **we employed a painter to decorate the house** ci siamo serviti di un imbianchino per pitturare la casa.

2 N (*frm*): **in the employ of sb** alle dipendenze di qn.

em·ployee [ˌɛmplɔɪ'iː] N dipendente *m/f*.

em·ploy·er [ɪm'plɔɪər] N datore(-trice) di lavoro; **employer's contribution** (*to National Insurance*) contributi *mpl* (*versati dal datore di lavoro*).

em·ploy·ment [ɪm'plɔɪmənt] N occupazione *f*, impiego; (*a job*) lavoro; **to take up employment** prendere servizio; **to find employment** trovare impiego *or* lavoro; **without employment** disoccupato(-a); **full employment** piena occupazione; **place of employment** (*frm*) sede dell'attività lavorativa.

♦ **employment agency** N agenzia di collocamento.

♦ **employment exchange** N (*old*) ufficio *m* di collocamento.

♦ **employment office** N (*Brit*) ufficio *m* di collocamento.

♦ **Employment Training** N *corso di formazione professionale per disoccupati*.

em·po·rium [ɛm'pɔːrɪəm] N (*old*) emporio.

em·pow·er [ɪm'paʊəʳ] VT: **to empower sb to do sth** concedere l'autorità a qn di fare qc.

em·press ['ɛmprɪs] N imperatrice f.

emp·ties ['ɛmptɪz] NPL (bottles) vuoti mpl.

emp·ti·ness ['ɛmptɪnɪs] N vuoto.

emp·ty ['ɛmptɪ] 1 (comp **-ier**, superl **-iest**) ADJ (gen) vuoto(-a); (street, area) deserto(-a); (post) vacante; (fig: threat, promise) vano(-a); (words) vacuo(-a), privo(-a) di significato; **on an empty stomach** a stomaco vuoto.

2 VT (contents, container) vuotare; (liquid) versare; **to empty (out) one's pockets** vuotarsi le tasche; **to empty a liquid from or out of sth into sth** travasare un liquido da qc in qc; **she emptied everything out of her bag onto the bed** ha rovesciato sul letto il contenuto della borsa.

3 VI (room, container) vuotarsi; (liquid) scaricarsi; (river): **to empty into** gettarsi in.

♦ empty-handed [,ɛmptɪ'hændɪd] ADJ a mani vuote; **to arrive/leave empty-handed** arrivare/andarsene a mani vuote.

♦ empty-headed [,ɛmptɪ'hɛdɪd] ADJ sciocco(-a).

EMS [,i:ɛm'ɛs] N ABBR (= European Monetary System) S.M.E. m (= Sistema Monetario Europeo).

EMU [,i:ɛm'ju:] N ABBR = Economic Monetary Union.

emu ['i:mju:] N emù m inv.

emu·late ['ɛmjʊ,leɪt] VT emulare.

emul·si·fy [ɪ'mʌlsɪ,faɪ] 1 VT emulsionare.

2 VI emulsionarsi.

emul·sion [ɪ'mʌlʃən] N (liquid) emulsione f; (also: **emul·sion paint**) pittura (murale).

en·able [ɪ'neɪbl] VT: **to enable sb to do sth** consentire or permettere a qn di fare qc.

en·act [ɪn'ækt] VT a (law) emanare b (play, scene) rappresentare.

en·act·ment [ɪ'næktmənt] N a emanazione f b (in play) rappresentazione f.

enam·el [ɪ'næməl] 1 N smalto.

2 VT smaltare.

3 ADJ smaltato(-a).

♦ enamel paint N vernice f a smalto.

enam·el·ware [ɪ'næməl,wɛəʳ] N stoviglie fpl smaltate.

en·am·oured, (Am) en·am·ored [ɪ'næməd] ADJ: **enam·oured** of innamorato(-a) di.

enc. ABBR = encl.

en·camp [ɪn'kæmp] VI (frm) accamparsi.

en·camp·ment [ɪn'kæmpmənt] N accampamento.

en·cap·su·late [ɪn'kæpsjʊ,leɪt] VT (fig) racchiudere.

en·case [ɪn'keɪs] VT: **to encase in** (contain) racchiudere in; (cover) rivestire di.

encash [ɪn'kæʃ] VT (Brit frm) incassare.

en·cepha·li·tis [,ɛnsɛfə'laɪtɪs] N encefalite f.

en·chant [ɪn'tʃɑːnt] VT incantare; (subj: magic spell) stregare.

en·chant·er [ɪn'tʃɑːntəʳ] N incantatore m.

en·chant·ing [ɪn'tʃɑːntɪŋ] ADJ incantevole, affascinante.

en·chant·ing·ly [ɪn'tʃɑːntɪŋlɪ] ADV incantevolmente.

en·chant·ment [ɪn'tʃɑːntmənt] N (charm, spell) incantesimo; (delight): **to fill with enchantment** incantare.

en·chant·ress [ɪn'tʃɑːntrɪs] N incantatrice f.

en·cir·cle [ɪn'sɜːkl] VT circondare; (Mil) accerchiare; (waist, shoulders) stringere.

encl., enc. ABBR (on letters: = enclosed, enclosure) all., alleg.

en·clave ['ɛnkleɪv] N enclave f inv.

en·clit·ic [ɪn'klɪtɪk] ADJ enclitico(-a).

en·close [ɪn'kləʊz] VT a (land, garden) recintare, recin-
gere, circondare b (with letter): **to enclose (with)** allegare (a); **please find enclosed a copy of** ... qui allegata è una copia di... .

en·closed [ɪn'kləʊzd] ADJ (garden, field) recintato(-a); (space) chiuso(-a); (in letter) allegato(-a).

en·clo·sure [ɪn'kləʊʒəʳ] N (act) recinzione f; (place) recinto; (at racecourse) tondino; (in letter) allegato.

en·code [ɪn'kəʊd] VT codificare.

en·cod·er [ɪn'kəʊdəʳ] N (Comput) codificatore m.

en·com·pass [ɪn'kʌmpəs] VT comprendere.

en·core [ɒŋ'kɔːʳ] 1 EXCL bis.

2 N bis m inv; **to give an encore** concedere un bis.

en·coun·ter [ɪn'kaʊntəʳ] 1 VT (person) incontrare; (difficulty, danger, enemy) imbattersi in.

2 N incontro.

en·cour·age [ɪn'kʌrɪdʒ] VT (person) incoraggiare; (industry, growth etc) favorire; **to encourage sb (to do sth)** incoraggiare qn (a fare qc).

en·cour·age·ment [ɪn'kʌrɪdʒmənt] N incoraggiamento.

en·cour·ag·ing [ɪn'kʌrɪdʒɪŋ] ADJ incoraggiante.

en·cour·ag·ing·ly [ɪn'kʌrɪdʒɪŋlɪ] ADV in modo incoraggiante.

en·croach [ɪn'krəʊtʃ] VI: **to encroach (up)on** (rights) usurpare; (land: of neighbour) sconfinare in; (subj: sea: land) avanzare sopra; (time) abusare di.

en·croach·ment [ɪn'krəʊtʃmənt] N violazione f.

en·crust·ed [ɪn'krʌstɪd] ADJ: **encrusted with** (diamonds) tempestato(-a) di; (rust) incrostato(-a) di.

en·cum·ber [ɪn'kʌmbəʳ] VT: **to encumber (with)** (person: with luggage) caricare (di); (: with debts) gravare (di); (room) ingombrare (di).

en·cum·bered [ɪn'kʌmbəd] ADJ: **to be encumbered (with)** essere carico(-a) di.

en·cum·brance [ɪn'kʌmbrəns] N peso; **to be an encumbrance to sb** essere di peso or di impaccio a qn.

en·cyc·li·cal [ɪn'sɪklɪkəl] N enciclica.

en·cy·clo·pedia, en·cy·clo·paedia [ɪn,saɪkləʊ'piːdɪə] N enciclopedia.

en·cy·clo·pedic, en·cy·clo·paedic [ɪn,saɪkləʊ'piːdɪk] ADJ enciclopedico(-a).

end [ɛnd] 1 N a (of line, table, rope) estremità f inv; (of pointed object) punta; (of town) parte f; **3rd from the end** il 3 a partire dalla fine; **at the end of the street** in fondo alla strada; **to place end to end** mettere un'estremità contro l'altra; **from end to end** da un'estremità all'altra; **to stand sth on end** mettere qc in piedi or ritto(-a); **his hair stood on end** gli si sono rizzati i capelli; **to change ends** (Sport) cambiare campo; **it's the end of the road or line for us** (fig) non abbiamo futuro; **to make ends meet** (fig) far quadrare il bilancio, sbarcare il lunario; **to keep one's end up** (fam) difendersi abbastanza bene; **to get hold of the wrong end of the stick** (fig) prendere fischi per fiaschi

b (conclusion) fine f; **at the end of the day** (Brit fig) in fin dei conti; **it's not the end of the world** (fam) non è poi la fine del mondo; **we'll never hear the end of it** (fam) non avremo più pace; **there's no end to it** (fam) non finisce mai; **that was the end of that!** e quella fu la fine!; **to the bitter end** fino all'ultimo sangue; **to come to a bad end** finire male; **in the end** alla fine, da ultimo; **to be at an end** essere finito(-a), arrivare alla fine; **to get to the end of** (book, supplies, work etc) finire; **to be at the end of** (strength, patience) essere al limite di; **to bring to an end** (work, speech) concludere; **to draw to an end** stare per finire; **to come to an end** finire; **to put an end to**

(*argument, relationship, sb's tricks*) porre fine a; **for hours on end** per ore e ore; **for 5 hours on end** per 5 ore di fila; **no end of trouble** (*fam*) problemi a non finire; **it upset me no end** (*adv: fam*) mi ha turbato enormemente; **without end** a non finire; **that's the end!** (*fam*) è il colmo!; **he's the end!** (*fam*) è impossibile!

c (*remnant: of loaf, meat*) avanzo; (: *of candle*) moccolo; **cigarette end** mozzicone *m* di sigaretta

d (*aim*) fine *m*, scopo; **to achieve one's end** raggiungere i propri scopi; **it's an end in itself** è fine a se stesso; **to no end** invano; **to this end, with this end in view** a questo fine; **the end justifies the means** il fine giustifica i mezzi.

2 VI finire, terminare; (*road, period of time*) terminare; **to end by saying** concludere dicendo; **to end in** (*dispute, conflict*) sfociare in; (*subj: word*) finire per *or* in.

3 VT (*gen*) porre fine a; (*speech, writing, broadcast*): **to end (with)** concludere (con); **to end one's life** mettere fine ai propri giorni; **to end it all** (*fam*) farla finita; **that was the meal to end all meals!** (*fam*) quel pranzo era imbattibile!

▶ **end up** VI + ADV (*finish*) finire, terminare; **to end up in prison** finire in prigione.

en·dan·ger [ɪnˈdeɪndʒəʳ] VT mettere in pericolo; **to endanger one's life** mettere a repentaglio la propria vita; **an endangered species** (*of animal*) una specie in via di estinzione.

en·dear [ɪnˈdɪəʳ] VT: **to endear sb to** rendere qn caro(-a) (a); **to endear o.s. to sb** accattivarsi le simpatie di qn.

en·dear·ing [ɪnˈdɪərɪŋ] ADJ (*smile*) accattivante; (*characteristic, personality*) simpatico(-a).

en·dear·ing·ly [ɪnˈdɪərɪŋlɪ] ADV (*see adj*) in modo accattivante; simpaticamente.

en·dear·ment [ɪnˈdɪəmənt] N: **to whisper endearments** sussurrare tenerezze; **term of endearment** vezzeggiativo, appellativo affettuoso.

en·deav·our, (*Am*) **en·deav·or** [ɪnˈdɛvəʳ] (*frm*) 1 VT: **to endeavour to do** cercare *or* sforzarsi di fare.

2 N (*attempt*) sforzo, tentativo; **to make every endeavour to do sth** fare ogni sforzo per fare qc.

en·dem·ic [ɛnˈdɛmɪk] ADJ endemico(-a).

end·ing [ˈɛndɪŋ] N fine *f*, conclusione *f*; (*Gram*) desinenza; **film with a happy ending** film a lieto fine.

en·dive [ˈɛndaɪv] N (*curly*) indivia (riccia); (*smooth, flat*) indivia belga.

end·less [ˈɛndlɪs] ADJ (*gen*) senza fine; (*road, speech*) interminabile, senza fine; (*attempts*) innumerevole; (*arguments*) continuo(-a); (*patience*) infinito(-a); (*possibilities*) illimitato(-a); (*resources*) inesauribile.

end·less·ly [ˈɛndlɪslɪ] ADV senza fine.

endo·crine [ˈɛndəʊˌkraɪn] ADJ endocrino(-a); **endocrine (ductless) gland** ghiandola endocrina a secrezione interna.

en·dorse [ɪnˈdɔːs] VT (*approve: opinion, claim, plan*) approvare, appoggiare; (*Brit: driving licence*) annotare un'infrazione su; (*sign: cheque*) girare.

en·dor·see [ˌɪndɔːˈsiː] N giratario(-a).

en·dorse·ment [ɪnˈdɔːsmənt] N (*approval*) approvazione *f*; (*Brit: on driving licence*) infrazione *f* annotata; (*signature*) girata, firma.

en·dor·ser [ɪnˈdɔːsəʳ] N girante *m/f*.

endo·skel·eton [ˌɛndəʊˈskɛlɪtən] N endoscheletro.

endo·ther·mic [ˌɛndəʊˈθɜːmɪk] ADJ endotermico(-a).

en·dow [ɪnˈdaʊ] VT **a** (*equip*): **to endow with** fornire di, dotare di; **to be endowed with** (*fig*) essere dotato(-a) di **b** (*prize*) istituire; (*hospital*) fondare; (*provide with money: institution*) devolvere denaro a; **to endow sth with sth** devolvere qc a favore di qc.

en·dow·ment [ɪnˈdaʊmənt] N **a** (*gift of money*) donazione *f* **b** (*see vt b*) istituzione *f*; fondazione *f*; donazione **c** (*frm: talent*) talento.

♦ **endowment assurance, endowment insurance** N assicurazione *f* mista.

♦ **endowment mortgage** N *mutuo garantito da un'assicurazione sulla vita*.

♦ **endowment policy** N assicurazione *f* sulla vita a polizza mista.

end·papers [ˈɛndˌpeɪpəz] NPL (*of book*) risguardi *mpl*.

♦ **end product** N (*Industry*) prodotto finale *or* finito; (*fig*) risultato.

♦ **end result** N risultato finale.

en·dur·able [ɪnˈdjʊərəbl] ADJ sopportabile.

en·dur·ance [ɪnˈdjʊərəns] N resistenza; **to come to the end of one's endurance** arrivare al limite della propria sopportazione; **past or beyond endurance** al di là di ogni sopportazione; **tried beyond endurance** messo(-a) a dura prova.

♦ **endurance test** N prova di resistenza.

en·dure [ɪnˈdjʊəʳ] 1 VT sopportare; **I can't endure being teased** non sopporto di essere preso in giro.

2 VI (*friendship, memory, peace*) durare; (*book, building*) resistere.

en·dur·ing [ɪnˈdjʊərɪŋ] ADJ duraturo(-a).

♦ **end user** N (*Econ*) consumatore(-trice) finale; (*Comput*) utente *m/f* finale.

end·ways [ˈɛndˌweɪz], (*Am*) **end·wise** [ˈɛndˌwaɪz] ADV (*endways on*) longitudinalmente; (*end to end*) l'uno(-a) contro l'altro(-a) (longitudinalmente).

en·ema [ˈɛnɪmə] N (*Med*) clistere *m*.

en·emy [ˈɛnəmɪ] 1 N (*person*) nemico(-a); (*Mil*) nemico; **to make an enemy of sb** inimicarsi qn; **he is his own worst enemy** è il peggior nemico di se stesso.

2 ADJ (*territory, forces, aircraft*) nemico(-a); (*morale, strategy*) del nemico.

♦ **enemy-occupied** [ˈɛnəmɪˌɒkjʊpaɪd] ADJ occupato(-a) dal nemico.

en·er·get·ic [ˌɛnəˈdʒɛtɪk] ADJ (*person, protest etc*) energico (-a); (*day*) attivo(-a); **do you feel energetic enough to go for a walk?** sei abbastanza in forze per fare una passeggiata?

en·er·geti·cal·ly [ˌɛnəˈdʒɛtɪkəlɪ] ADV energicamente.

en·er·gize [ˈɛnədʒaɪz] VT (*invigorate*) stimolare; (*Elec*) alimentare (a corrente).

en·er·gy [ˈɛnədʒɪ] N energia; **I haven't the energy** non ho la forza; **to put all one's energy into sth** dedicare tutte le proprie energie *or* forze a qc; **Department of Energy** ≈ ministero dell'Industria (del Commercio e dell'Artigianato).

♦ **energy crisis** N crisi *f* energetica.

♦ **energy-giving** [ˈɛnədʒɪˌgɪvɪŋ] ADJ energetico(-a).

♦ **energy-saving** [ˈɛnədʒɪˌseɪvɪŋ] 1 ADJ (*policy*) di risparmio energetico; (*device*) che risparmia energia.

2 N risparmio energetico.

en·er·vate [ˈɛnəˌveɪt] VT snervare.

en·er·va·ting [ˈɛnəˌveɪtɪŋ] ADJ snervante.

en·fee·bled [ɪnˈfiːbld] ADJ indebolito(-a).

en·fold [ɪnˈfəʊld] VT (*frm: hug*) abbracciare; (: *wrap*) avvolgere.

en·force [ɪnˈfɔːs] VT (*decision, policy*) attuare; (*law, regulation*) far osservare, far rispettare; (*obedience*) imporre; (*argument*) rafforzare.

en·forc·ed [ɪnˈfɔːst] ADJ imposto(-a), forzato(-a).

en·force·ment [ɪnˈfɔːsmənt] N (of discipline) imposizione f.

en·fran·chise [ɪnˈfræntʃaɪz] VT (frm: give vote to) concedere il diritto di voto a; (: set free) affrancare.

en·fran·chise·ment [ɪnˈfræntʃɪzmənt] N (frm: see vb): enfranchisement (of) concessione f del diritto di voto a; affrancamento (di).

en·gage [ɪnˈgeɪdʒ] 1 VT (occupy: attention, interest) assorbire; (attract: attention) attrarre; (hire: servant, worker) assumere; (: actor) ingaggiare; (: lawyer) incaricare; (reserve: room) prenotare; (Mil: enemy) attaccare; to engage to do sth impegnarsi a fare qc; to engage sb in conversation attaccare conversazione con qn; to engage gear/the clutch (Tech) innestare la marcia/la frizione.
2 VI (Tech) innestarsi, ingranare; to engage in (discussion, politics) impegnarsi in.

en·gaged [ɪnˈgeɪdʒd] ADJ a (to be married) fidanzato(-a); to get engaged fidanzarsi b (occupied): to be engaged in doing sth essere impegnato(-a) a fare qc; she is engaged in research/a survey si occupa di ricerca/di un'inchiesta; to be engaged on sth occuparsi di qc c (Brit: phone number, lavatory) occupato(-a).
♦ engaged tone N (Brit Telec) segnale m di occupato.

en·gage·ment [ɪnˈgeɪdʒmənt] N a (appointment, undertaking) impegno; I have a previous engagement ho già un impegno
b (of worker, servant) assunzione f; (of actor, speaker) ingaggio; (of lawyer) nomina
c (to marry) fidanzamento; to break off one's engagement rompere il fidanzamento
d (Mil: battle) scontro, combattimento.
♦ engagement ring N anello di fidanzamento.

en·gag·ing [ɪnˈgeɪdʒɪŋ] ADJ attraente.

en·gag·ing·ly [ɪnˈgeɪdʒɪŋlɪ] ADV in modo attraente.

en·gen·der [ɪnˈdʒɛndər] VT produrre, causare.

en·gine [ˈɛndʒɪn] N (motor: in car, ship, plane) motore m; (Rail) locomotiva; facing/with your back to the engine nel senso della/in senso contrario alla marcia; front-to-back engine (Aut) motore longitudinale.
♦ engine block N (Aut) blocco motore.
♦ engine driver N (Brit: of train) macchinista m.

en·gi·neer [ˌɛndʒɪˈnɪər] 1 N (gen) ingegnere m; (mechanic) meccanico; (Brit: for electrical appliances) tecnico; (Naut, Am Rail) macchinista m; civil/mechanical engineer ingegnere civile/meccanico; the Engineers (Mil) il Genio.
2 VT (contrive) architettare, organizzare.

en·gi·neer·ing [ˌɛndʒɪˈnɪərɪŋ] 1 N ingegneria.
2 ADJ (works, factory, worker) metalmeccanico(-a).
♦ engine failure N guasto al motore.
♦ engine pod N (Aer) gondola del motore.
♦ engine room N (Naut) sala f macchine inv.
♦ engine trouble N panne f inv.

Eng·land [ˈɪŋglənd] N Inghilterra.

Eng·lish [ˈɪŋglɪʃ] 1 ADJ inglese.
2 N a : the English (people) gli inglesi b (language) inglese m; in plain English in parole povere; the King's or Queen's English l'inglese corretto.
♦ English breakfast N colazione f all'inglese.
♦ English Channel N: the English Channel il Canale della Manica.

Eng·lish·man [ˈɪŋglɪʃmən] (pl -men) N inglese m.
♦ English-speaker [ˈɪŋglɪʃˌspiːkər] N anglofono(-a).
♦ English-speaking [ˈɪŋglɪʃˌspiːkɪŋ] ADJ di lingua inglese.

English·woman [ˈɪŋglɪʃˌwʊmən] (pl -women) N inglese f.

en·grave [ɪnˈgreɪv] VT (Art, Typ etc) incidere; (: wood) intagliare; (fig) imprimere.

en·grav·er [ɪnˈgreɪvər] N incisore m.

en·grav·ing [ɪnˈgreɪvɪŋ] N (picture) incisione f.

en·grossed [ɪnˈgrəʊst] ADJ: engrossed in assorto(-a) in, immerso(-a) in, preso(-a) da.

en·gross·ing [ɪnˈgrəʊsɪŋ] ADJ (study, game) appassionante; (book) avvincente.

en·gulf, in·gulf [ɪnˈgʌlf] VT (also fig) inghiottire.

en·hance [ɪnˈhɑːns] VT (beauty, attraction) valorizzare; (position, reputation) migliorare; (chances, value) aumentare, accrescere.

enig·ma [ɪˈnɪgmə] N enigma m.

en·ig·mat·ic [ˌɛnɪgˈmætɪk] ADJ enigmatico(-a).

en·ig·mati·cal·ly [ˌɛnɪgˈmætɪkəlɪ] ADV enigmaticamente.

en·join [ɪnˈdʒɔɪn] VT (frm: obedience, silence, discretion): to enjoin (on) imporre (a); to enjoin sb to do sth ingiungere a qn di fare qc.

en·joy [ɪnˈdʒɔɪ] VT a (take delight in): did you enjoy the film/wine/book? ti è piaciuto il film/vino/libro?; I enjoy reading mi piace leggere; he enjoys (going for) long walks gli piace fare lunghe passeggiate; to enjoy life godersi la vita; to enjoy o.s divertirsi; enjoy yourself! divertiti!
b (have: success, fortune) avere; (have benefit of: health, respect) godere (di); (: income, advantage) fruire di.

en·joy·able [ɪnˈdʒɔɪəbl] ADJ piacevole.

en·joy·ment [ɪnˈdʒɔɪmənt] N piacere m; to find enjoyment in sth/in doing sth provare piacere in qc/nel fare qc.

en·large [ɪnˈlɑːdʒ] VT (Phot) ingrandire; (house, circle of friends) ampliare
▶ enlarge on, enlarge upon VI + ADV (subject) dilungarsi su.

en·larged [ɪnˈlɑːdʒd] ADJ (edition) ampliato(-a); (Med: organ, gland) ingrossato(-a); (: pores) dilatato(-a).

en·large·ment [ɪnˈlɑːdʒmənt] N (gen) ampliamento; (Med) ingrossamento; (Phot) ingrandimento.

en·larg·er [ɪnˈlɑːdʒər] N (Phot) ingranditore m.

en·light·en [ɪnˈlaɪtn] VT (inform): to enlighten sb (about or on sth) illuminare qn (su qc).

en·light·ened [ɪnˈlaɪtnd] ADJ illuminato(-a).

en·light·en·ing [ɪnˈlaɪtnɪŋ] ADJ istruttivo(-a).

en·light·en·ment [ɪnˈlaɪtnmənt] N (explanations) chiarimenti mpl; the (Age of) Enlightenment (History) l'Illuminismo.

en·list [ɪnˈlɪst] 1 VT a (Mil: men) arruolare b (support) assicurarsi, procurarsi.
2 VI (Mil): to enlist (in) arruolarsi (in); enlisted man (Am Mil) soldato semplice.

en·list·ment [ɪnˈlɪstmənt] N arruolamento.

en·liv·en [ɪnˈlaɪvn] VT (people) rallegrare; (events) ravvivare.

en·mesh [ɪnˈmɛʃ] VT impigliare; to become or be enmeshed in rimanere impigliato(-a) in; (fig) rimanere coinvolto(-a) in.

en·mity [ˈɛnmɪtɪ] N inimicizia.

en·no·ble [ɪˈnəʊbl] VT nobilitare; (with title) conferire un titolo nobiliare a.

enor·mity [ɪˈnɔːmɪtɪ] N (of crime, action) atrocità f inv; (of problem) gravità.

enor·mous [ɪˈnɔːməs] ADJ (gen) enorme; (patience) infinito(-a); (strength) prodigioso(-a); (risk) immenso(-a); an enormous number of (people, things) una moltitu-

dine di.

enor·mous·ly [ɪ'nɔ:məslɪ] ADV enormemente.

enough [ɪ'nʌf] **1** ADJ, N (*sufficient*) abbastanza; **enough people/money/time** abbastanza gente/soldi/tempo; **more than enough money** denaro più che sufficiente; **have you had enough to eat?** hai mangiato abbastanza?; **have you got enough?** ne hai abbastanza *or* a sufficienza?; **we earn enough to live on** guadagniamo quel tanto che basta per vivere; **will £5 be enough?** bastano 5 sterline?; **that's enough, thank you** basta, grazie; **there's more than enough for everyone** ce n'è più che a sufficienza per tutti; **enough!** basta!; **enough! enough!** (*fam*) adesso basta!; **I've had enough!** (*protest*) non ne posso più!; **I've had enough of (doing) this** ne ho avuto abbastanza di (fare) questo; **it's enough to drive you mad** (*fam*) è sufficiente a farti diventare matto; **you can never have enough of this scenery** non ci si stancherebbe mai di questo paesaggio; **it was enough to prove his innocence** è stato sufficiente a dimostrare la sua innocenza.

2 ADV abbastanza; **big enough** abbastanza grande; **it's hot enough (as it is!)** fa già abbastanza caldo (così)!; **he's old enough to go alone** è abbastanza grande da poterci andare da solo; **she was fool enough** *or* **enough of a fool to listen to him** è stata così stupida da dargli retta; **he was kind enough to lend me the money** è stato così gentile da prestarmi i soldi; **you know well enough that ...** sai molto bene che...; **he has not worked enough** non ha lavorato abbastanza; **oddly enough, ...** stranamente...; **sure enough** come volevasi dimostrare; **fair enough!** (*fam*) d'accordo!

en·quire [ɪn'kwaɪə'] VT, VI = **inquire** *etc.*

en·rage [ɪn'reɪdʒ] VT fare arrabbiare.

en·rap·ture [ɪn'ræptʃə'] VT estasiare, rapire.

en·rich [ɪn'rɪtʃ] VT arricchire.

en·rich·ment [ɪn'rɪtʃmənt] N arricchimento.

en·rol, (*Am*) **en·roll** [ɪn'rəʊl] **1** VT (*gen*) iscrivere; (*Univ*) immatricolare.

2 VI: **to enrol (in)** iscriversi a.

en·rol·ment, (*Am*) **en·roll·ment** [ɪn'rəʊlmənt] N (*see vb*) iscrizione *f*; immatricolazione *f*.

♦ **enrol(l)ment fee** N tasse *fpl* d'iscrizione; (*Univ*) tasse d'immatricolazione.

en route [ɒn'ru:t] ADV: **en route for/from/to** in viaggio per/da/a; **it was stolen en route** è stato rubato durante il viaggio.

en·sconce [ɪn'skɒns] VT: **to ensconce o.s** sistemarsi bene.

en·sem·ble [ã:n'sã:mbl] N **a** (*gen*) insieme *m* **b** (*Mus*) ensemble *m inv* **c** (*outfit*) completo.

en·shrine, in·shrine [ɪn'ʃraɪn] VT custodire.

en·sign [*a, b* 'ɛnsən, *c* 'ɛnsaɪn] N **a** (*flag*) insegna, bandiera **b** (*Mil*) portabandiera *m inv* **c** (*Am Naut*) guardiamarina *m inv.*

en·slave [ɪn'sleɪv] VT rendere schiavo(-a), schiavizzare.

en·slave·ment [ɪn'sleɪvmənt] N asservimento.

en·snare [ɪn'snɛə'] VT prendere in trappola; (*fig*) intrappolare.

en·sue [ɪn'sju:] VI (*follow*) seguire; **to ensue (from)** (*result*) risultare (da).

en·su·ing [ɪn'sju:ɪŋ] ADJ (*chaos, event*) che segue.

en suite [ã sɥit] ADV (*in hotel*): **with bathroom en suite** con stanza da bagno annessa.

en·sure [ɪn'ʃʊə'] VT garantire, assicurare; **to ensure that ...** assicurarsi che... .

ENT [ˌiɛn'ti:] N ABBR (= *Ear, Nose & Throat*) O.R.L. (=

Otorinolaringoiatria).

en·tail [ɪn'teɪl] VT comportare; **it entailed buying a new car** comportava l'acquisto di una nuova macchina.

en·tan·gle [ɪn'tæŋgl] VT (*thread*) impigliare; **to become entangled in sth** (*fig*) rimanere impegolato(-a) in qc.

en·tan·gle·ment [ɪn'tæŋglmənt] N (*fig: gen*) coinvolgimento; (: *romantic*) relazione *f* sentimentale.

en·ter ['ɛntə'] **1** VT **a** (*go into: house, vehicle*) entrare in; (*road*) prendere; (*navy, army*) arruolarsi in; (*profession*) intraprendere; (*college, school*) iscriversi a; (*club*) associarsi a; (*debate, discussion, contest, competition*) partecipare a; **the thought never entered my head** non mi è mai passato per la testa *or* l'anticamera del cervello; **he entered the Church** si è fatto prete

b (*write down: name, amount, order*) registrare; (*Comput: data*) immettere, inserire, introdurre; **to enter sb/sth for sth** (*enrol: pupil, candidate, racehorse*) iscrivere qn/qc a qc.

2 VI entrare; **enter Othello** (*Theatre*) entra Otello; **to enter for** (*competition, race*) iscriversi a

▶ **enter into** VI + PREP **a** (*participate in*) entrare in; (*negotiations, argument, debate*) prendere parte a, partecipare a; (*explanation*) lanciarsi in; (*agreement*) concludere; **to enter into conversation with sb** intavolare una conversazione con qn

b (*sb's plans, calculations*) rientrare in; **that doesn't enter into it** questo non c'entra

c : **to enter into the spirit of things** entrare nello spirito delle cose

▶ **enter upon** VI + PREP cominciare.

en·teri·tis [ˌɛntə'raɪtɪs] N enterite *f.*

en·ter·prise ['ɛntə,praɪz] N **a** (*firm, undertaking, company*) impresa **b** (*initiative*) iniziativa.

en·ter·pris·ing ['ɛntə,praɪzɪŋ] ADJ (*person*) intraprendente; (*venture*) audace.

en·ter·pris·ing·ly ['ɛntəpraɪzɪŋlɪ] ADV con intraprendenza.

en·ter·tain [ˌɛntə'teɪn] **1** VT **a** (*audience*) divertire; (*guest*) intrattenere, ricevere; **to entertain sb to dinner** invitare qn a cena **b** (*consider: idea, proposal, plan*) prendere in considerazione; (*hopes, doubts*) nutrire.

2 VI (*have visitors*) avere ospiti.

en·ter·tain·er [ˌɛntə'teɪnə'] N artista *m/f* (di cabaret, radio, TV).

en·ter·tain·ing [ˌɛntə'teɪnɪŋ] **1** ADJ divertente.

2 N: **to do a lot of entertaining** ricevere molti ospiti.

en·ter·tain·ment [ˌɛntə'teɪnmənt] N **a** (*amusement*) divertimento; (*of guests*) trattenimento **b** (*show*) spettacolo.

♦ **entertainment allowance** N spese *fpl* di rappresentanza.

♦ **entertainment world** N: **the entertainment world** il mondo dello spettacolo.

en·thral, (*Am*) **en·thrall** [ɪn'θrɔ:l] VT affascinare, avvincere.

en·thral·ling [ɪn'θrɔ:lɪŋ] ADJ affascinante, avvincente.

en·throne [ɛn'θrəʊn] VT (*frm, king, queen*) intronizzare, collocare sul trono.

en·thuse [ɪn'θu:z] VI: **to enthuse (over** *or* **about)** entusiasmarsi (per).

en·thu·si·asm [ɪn'θu:zɪˌæzəm] N entusiasmo; **it failed to arouse my enthusiasm** non mi ha entusiasmato.

en·thu·si·ast [ɪn'θu:zɪˌæst] N appassionato(-a); **a jazz** *etc* **enthusiast** un(a) appassionato(-a) di jazz *etc.*

en·thu·si·as·tic [ɪnˌθu:zɪ'æstɪk] ADJ (*response*) entusia-

stico(-a); (*person*) entusiasta; **to be enthusiastic about sth/sb** essere entusiasta di qc/qn; **to become enthusiastic about sth** entusiasmarsi per qc.

en·thu·si·as·ti·cal·ly [ɪnˌθju:zɪˈæstɪkəlɪ] ADV entusiasticamente, con entusiasmo.

en·tice [ɪnˈtaɪs] VT allettare, attirare; **to entice sb away from sb/sth** persuadere qn a lasciare qn/qc; **to entice sb into doing sth** indurre qn a fare qc; **to entice sb with food/an offer** *etc* allettare qn col cibo/con un'offerta *etc*.

en·tice·ment [ɪnˈtaɪsmənt] N (*act*) allettamento; (*attraction*) attrattiva.

en·tic·ing [ɪnˈtaɪsɪŋ] ADJ allettante, attraente.

en·tic·ing·ly [ɪnˈtaɪsɪŋlɪ] ADV in modo allettante.

en·tire [ɪnˈtaɪə'] ADJ (*whole*) intero(-a), tutto(-a); (*complete*) completo(-a), intero(-a); (*unreserved*) assoluto(-a), pieno(-a).

en·tire·ly [ɪnˈtaɪəlɪ] ADV completamente, interamente; (*agree*) assolutamente, pienamente.

en·tirety [ɪnˈtaɪərətɪ] N: **in its entirety** nel suo complesso.

en·ti·tle [ɪnˈtaɪtl] VT **a** (*book, poem*) intitolare **b** (*give right*) dare diritto a; **this entitles him to a free ticket/to do it** questo gli dà diritto ad un biglietto gratis/a farlo; **to be entitled to sth/to do sth** avere diritto a qc/a fare qc; **you are quite entitled to do as you wish** sei libero di fare come credi.

en·ti·tled [ɪnˈtaɪtld] ADJ (*book*) che si intitola, dal titolo.

en·ti·tle·ment [ɪnˈtaɪtəlmənt] N: **entitlement (to sth)** diritto (a qc).

en·tity [ˈɛntɪtɪ] N entità *f inv*.

ento·mo·logi·cal [ˈɛntəməˈlɒdʒɪkəl] ADJ entomologico (-a).

ento·mo·lo·gist [ˌɛntəˈmɒlədʒɪst] N entomologo(-a).

ento·mol·ogy [ˌɛntəˈmɒlədʒɪ] N entomologia.

en·tou·rage [ˌɒntuˈrɑːʒ] N entourage *m inv*.

entrails [ˈɛntreɪlz] NPL interiora *fpl*.

en·trance¹ [ˈɛntrəns] N **a** (*way in, of person*) entrata, ingresso; (*right to enter*) ammissione *f*, ingresso; **to gain entrance to** (*university etc*) essere ammesso(-a) a; **to make one's entrance** (*Theatre*) fare il proprio ingresso.

en·trance² [ɪnˈtrɑːns] VT estasiare, incantare.

♦ **entrance examination** N (*to school*) esame *m* di ammissione.

♦ **entrance fee** N (*for club etc*) quota di ammissione, tassa d'iscrizione; (*to museum etc*) biglietto d'ingresso.

en·tranc·ing [ɪnˈtrɑːnsɪŋ] ADJ incantevole.

en·tranc·ing·ly [ɪnˈtrɑːnsɪŋlɪ] ADV incantevolmente.

en·trant [ˈɛntrənt] N (*in race, competition*) concorrente *m/f*, partecipante *m/f*; (*Brit: in exam*) candidato(-a); **he's a new entrant to teaching** è nuovo all'insegnamento.

en·trap [ɪnˈtræp] VT (*frm*) intrappolare.

en·treat [ɪnˈtriːt] VT: **to entreat sb (to do sth)** implorare *or* supplicare qn (di fare qc).

en·treaty [ɪnˈtriːtɪ] N supplica; **a look of entreaty** uno sguardo supplichevole; **at his earnest entreaty** dietro sua viva supplica.

en·trée [ˈɒntreɪ] N (*Culin*) entrée *f inv*.

en·trenched [ɪnˈtrɛntʃt] ADJ (*Mil*) trincerato(-a); (*fig*) radicato(-a).

en·trench·ment [ɪnˈtrɛntʃmənt] N trincea.

en·tre·pre·neur [ˌɒntrəprəˈnɜː'] N imprenditore(-trice).

en·tre·pre·neur·ial [ˌɒntrəprəˈnɜːrɪəl] ADJ imprenditoriale.

en·tro·py [ˈɛntrəpɪ] N entropia.

en·trust [ɪnˈtrʌst] VT: **to entrust sth to sb** OR **to entrust sb**

with sth affidare qc a qn.

en·try [ˈɛntrɪ] N **a** (*way in*) ingresso, entrata **b** (*act*) ingresso; **"no entry"** "vietato l'ingresso", "ingresso vietato"; (*Aut*) "divieto d'accesso" **c** (*Sport etc: total*) numero degli iscritti; (: *thing, person entered in competition*) iscrizione *f* **d** (*in reference book*) voce *f*; (*in diary, ship's log*) annotazione *f*; (*in account book, ledger, list*) registrazione *f*; **single/double entry book-keeping** partita semplice/doppia.

♦ **entry form** N modulo d'iscrizione.

en·try·ism [ˈɛntrɪɪzm] N entrismo.

♦ **entry permit** N visto d'ingresso.

♦ **entry phone** N (*Brit*) citofono.

en·twine [ɪnˈtwaɪn] VT intrecciare.

♦ **E-number** [ˈiːˌnʌmbə'] N additivo (alimentare).

enu·mer·ate [ɪˈnjuːməreɪt] VT enumerare.

enu·mera·tion [ɪˌnjuːməˈreɪʃən] N enumerazione *f*.

enun·ci·ate [ɪˈnʌnsɪeɪt] VT (*words*) articolare, pronunciare; (*sound*) articolare; (*theory, idea*) enunciare, esporre.

enun·cia·tion [ɪˌnʌnsɪˈeɪʃən] N (*see vt*) articolazione *f*; enunciazione.

enu·resis [ˌɛnjʊˈriːsɪs] N enuresi *f*.

enu·ret·ic [ˌɛnjəˈrɛtɪk] ADJ enuretico(-a).

en·vel·op [ɪnˈvɛləp] VT: **to envelop (in)** avvolgere (in), avviluppare (in).

en·velope [ˈɛnvələʊp] N busta; **in a sealed envelope** in busta sigillata *or* chiusa.

en·vi·able [ˈɛnvɪəbl] ADJ invidiabile.

en·vi·ably [ˈɛnvɪəblɪ] ADV invidiabilmente.

en·vi·ous [ˈɛnvɪəs] ADJ: **envious (of sb/sth)** invidioso(-a) (di qn/qc).

en·vi·ous·ly [ˈɛnvɪəslɪ] ADV con invidia.

en·vi·ron·ment [ɪnˈvaɪərənmənt] N ambiente *m*; **Department of the Environment** (*Brit*) ≈ Ministero dell'Ambiente.

en·vi·ron·men·tal [ɪnˌvaɪərənˈmɛntl] ADJ ambientale; **environmental studies** *or* **science** (*in school*) ecologia.

en·vi·ron·men·tal·ist [ɪnˌvaɪərənˈmɛntəlɪst] N ambientalista *m/f*.

en·vi·ron·men·tal·ly [ɪnˌvaɪərənˈmɛntəlɪ] ADV: **environmentally friendly** che rispetta l'ambiente.

♦ **Environmental Protection Agency** N (*Am*) ≈ Agenzia nazionale di protezione ambientale.

en·vi·rons [ɪnˈvaɪrənz] NPL dintorni *mpl*.

en·vis·age [ɪnˈvɪzɪdʒ], (*Am*) en·vi·sion [ɪnˈvɪʒən] VT (*expect*) prevedere; (*imagine*) prefigurare.

en·voy [ˈɛnvɔɪ] N (*gen*) inviato(-a); (*diplomat*) ministro plenipotenziario.

envy [ˈɛnvɪ] ① N invidia; **her new car was the envy of all the neighbours** la sua macchina nuova era l'invidia di tutto il vicinato. ② VT: **to envy (sb sth)** invidiare (qn per qc).

en·zyme [ˈɛnzaɪm] N enzima *m*.

eon [ˈiːɒn] N = aeon.

ephem·er·al [ɪˈfɛmərəl] ADJ effimero(-a).

epic [ˈɛpɪk] ① ADJ epico(-a). ② N poema *m* epico, epopea; (*film*) epopea.

epi·cen·tre, (*Am*) epi·cen·ter [ˈɛpɪˌsɛntə'] N epicentro.

epi·cure [ˈɛpɪkjʊə'] N buongustaio(-a).

epi·cu·rean [ˌɛpɪkjʊəˈriːən] ADJ, N epicureo(-a).

Epicurus [ˌɛpɪˈkjʊərəs] N Epicuro.

epi·dem·ic [ˌɛpɪˈdɛmɪk] ① ADJ epidemico(-a). ② N epidemia.

epi·der·mis [ˌɛpɪ'dɜːmɪs] N (*Anat, Bot, Zool*) epidermide *f*.
epi·dur·al [ˌɛpɪ'djʊərəl] [1] ADJ epidurale.
[2] N anestesia epidurale.
epi·glot·tis [ˌɛpɪ'glɒtɪs] N epiglottide *f*.
epi·gram ['ɛpɪˌgræm] N epigramma *m*.
epi·gram·mat·ical [ˌɛpɪgrə'mætɪkəl], **epi·gram·mat·ic** [ˌɛpɪgrə'mætɪk] ADJ epigrammatico(-a).
epi·graph ['ɛpɪˌgrɑːf] N epigrafe *f*.
epi·lep·sy ['ɛpɪˌlɛpsɪ] N epilessia.
epi·lep·tic [ˌɛpɪ'lɛptɪk] ADJ, N epilettico(-a).
epi·logue ['ɛpɪˌlɒg] N epilogo.
Epipha·ny [ɪ'pɪfənɪ] N Epifania.
epis·co·pal [ɪ'pɪskəpəl] ADJ episcopale.
Epis·co·pa·lian [ɪˌpɪskə'peɪlɪən] ADJ, N episcopaliano(-a).
epi·sode ['ɛpɪsəʊd] N episodio.
epi·sod·ic [ˌɛpɪ'sɒdɪk] ADJ episodico(-a).
epi·sodi·cal·ly [ˌɛpɪ'sɒdɪkəlɪ] ADV episodicamente.
epis·temol·ogy [ɪˌpɪstə'mɒlədʒɪ] N epistemologia.
epis·tle [ɪ'pɪsl] N epistola.
epi·taph ['ɛpɪtɑːf] N epitaffio.
epi·thelium [ˌɛpɪ'θiːlɪəm] N epitelio.
epi·thet ['ɛpɪθɛt] N epiteto.
epito·me [ɪ'pɪtəmɪ] N (*frm*): **the epitome of kindness** la personificazione della gentilezza.
epito·mize [ɪ'pɪtəmaɪz] VT (*frm*) incarnare.
epoch ['iːpɒk] N (*period*) epoca, era.
♦ **epoch–making** ['iːpɒkˌmeɪkɪŋ] ADJ che fa epoca.
epony·mous [ɪ'pɒnɪməs] ADJ (*liter*) eponimo.
eq·uable ['ɛkwəbl] ADJ (*character*) tranquillo(-a); (*climate*) costante.
eq·uably ['ɛkwəblɪ] ADV tranquillamente.
equal ['iːkwəl] [1] ADJ: **equal (to)** uguale (a); **an equal amount of time** lo stesso tempo; **to be equal in strength** avere la stessa forza; **all things being equal** se tutto va bene; **with equal ease/indifference** con la stessa facilità/indifferenza; **on equal terms** su un piano di parità; **to be/feel equal to** (*task*) essere/sentirsi all'altezza di.
[2] N (*person, thing*) pari *m/f inv*, simile *m/f*, uguale *m/f*; **without equal** senza pari.
[3] VT (*Math*) fare; (*record, rival*) uguagliare; **there is nothing to equal it** non ha rivali.
♦ **Equal Employment Opportunity Commission** N (*Am*) Commissione *f* per le pari opportunità.
equali·ty [ɪ'kwɒlɪtɪ] N uguaglianza; (*parity*) parità.
equal·ize ['iːkwəˌlaɪz] [1] VT (*society*) livellare; (*wealth, possessions*) distribuire uniformemente; (*salaries*) equiparare; (*pressure, temperature*) rendere uniforme.
[2] VI (*Sport*) pareggiare.
equal·iz·er ['iːkwəˌlaɪzəʳ] N a (*Sport*) pareggio b (*Tech*) equalizzatore *m*.
equal·ly ['iːkwəlɪ] ADV ugualmente; (*share*) in parti uguali; **they are equally clever** sono intelligenti allo stesso modo; **she is equally clever** è altrettanto intelligente; **equally, you must remember** ... allo stesso modo, ti devi ricordare... .
♦ **Equal Opportunities Commission** N Commissione *f* per le pari opportunità.
♦ **equal(s) sign** N (*Math*) segno d'uguale *or* d'uguaglianza.
equa·nim·ity [ˌɛkwə'nɪmɪtɪ] N equanimità, serenità d'animo.
equate [ɪ'kweɪt] VT a : **to equate (with)** identificare (con), considerare uguale a; (*compare*) paragonare (a) b (*Math: make equal*) uguagliare; **to equate A to B** mettere in equazione A e B.

equa·tion [ɪ'kweɪʒən] N (*Math*) equazione *f*; **equations of motion** (*Phys*) equazioni del moto.
equa·tor [ɪ'kweɪtəʳ] N: **the equator** l'equatore *m*.
equa·to·rial [ˌɛkwə'tɔːrɪəl] ADJ equatoriale.
♦ **Equatorial Guinea** N Guinea Equatoriale.
eques·trian [ɪ'kwɛstrɪən] [1] ADJ equestre.
[2] N (*man*) cavaliere *m*; (*woman*) amazzone *f*.
equi·dis·tant ['iːkwɪ'dɪstənt] ADJ equidistante.
equi·lat·eral [ˌiːkwɪ'lætərəl] ADJ equilatero: **equilateral triangle** triangolo equilatero.
equi·lib·rium [ˌiːkwɪ'lɪbrɪəm] N equilibrio.
equine ['ɛkwaɪn] ADJ equino(-a).
equi·nox ['iːkwɪnɒks] N equinozio.
equip [ɪ'kwɪp] VT: **to equip (with)** (*room etc*) equipaggiare (con), attrezzare (con); (*person*) preparare a; **equipped with** (*machinery etc*) dotato(-a) di; (*supplies etc*) fornito (-a) di; **he is well equipped for the job** ha i requisiti necessari per quel lavoro; **ill/poorly equipped** (*hospital, expedition*) male equipaggiato(-a)/attrezzato(-a).
equip·ment [ɪ'kwɪpmənt] N, NO PL attrezzatura; (*Tech, Elec*) apparecchiatura.
equi·table ['ɛkwɪtəbl] ADJ equo(-a).
equi·tably ['ɛkwɪtəblɪ] ADV equamente.
equi·ties ['ɛkwɪtɪz] NPL (*Brit: shares*) azioni *fpl* ordinarie.
equi·ty ['ɛkwɪtɪ] N equità.
♦ **equity capital** N capitale *m* azionario.
equiva·lence [ɪ'kwɪvələns] N equivalenza.
equiva·lent [ɪ'kwɪvələnt] [1] ADJ equivalente; **to be equivalent to** equivalere a.
[2] N equivalente *m*.
equivo·cal [ɪ'kwɪvəkəl] ADJ equivoco(-a); (*open to suspicion*) dubbio(-a).
equivo·cal·ly [ɪ'kwɪvəkəlɪ] ADV in modo equivoco.
equivo·cate [ɪ'kwɪvəˌkeɪt] VI esprimersi in modo equivoco.
equivo·ca·tion [ɪˌkwɪvə'keɪʃən] N parole *fpl* equivoche.
ER ABBR (*Brit*)= *Elizabeth Regina*.
ERA [ˌiːɑːr'eɪ] N ABBR (*Am Pol*)= *Equal Rights Amendment*.
era ['ɪərə] N era.
eradi·cate [ɪ'rædɪˌkeɪt] VT sradicare.
eradi·ca·tion [ɪˌrædɪ'keɪʃən] N sradicamento.
eras·able [ɪ'reɪzəbl] ADJ cancellabile.
erase [ɪ'reɪz] VT cancellare.
eras·er [ɪ'reɪzəʳ] N (*frm, Am: rubber*) gomma (da cancellare).
eras·ure [ɪ'reɪʒəʳ] N (*frm*) cancellatura.
erect [ɪ'rɛkt] [1] (*frm*) VT (*statue, monument, temple*) erigere; (*flats, factory*) costruire; (*barricade, mast*) innalzare; (*machinery, tent*) montare; (*theory, system*) edificare; (*obstacles*) creare.
[2] ADJ eretto(-a), dritto(-a); **with head erect** a testa alta.
erec·tion [ɪ'rɛkʃən] N a (*act: gen*) erezione *f*; (*of building*) costruzione *f*; (*of machinery*) montaggio b (*Anat*) erezione *f*.
ergo ['ɜːgəʊ] ADV ergo.
er·go·nom·ics [ˌɜːgə'nɒmɪks] NSG ergonomia.
Eri·trea [ˌɛrɪ'treɪə] N Eritrea.
ERM [ˌiːɑːr'ɛm] N ABBR = **Exchange Rate Mechanism**.
er·mine ['ɜːmɪn] N ermellino.
ERNIE ['ɜːnɪ] N ABBR (*Brit*: = *Electronic Random Number Indicator Equipment*) *sistema che seleziona i numeri vincenti di buoni del Tesoro*.
erode [ɪ'rəʊd] VT (*Geol*) erodere; (*metal, fig*) corrodere.
erog·enous [ɪ'rɒdʒɪnəs] ADJ: **erogenous zone** zona erogena.

Eros [ˈiːrɒs] N Eros *m*.

ero·sion [ɪˈrəʊʒən] N (*see vb*) erosione *f*; corrosione *f*.

ero·sive [ɪˈrəʊzɪv] ADJ (*see vb*) erosivo(-a); corrosivo(-a).

erot·ic [ɪˈrɒtɪk] ADJ erotico(-a).

eroti·ca [ɪˈrɒtɪkə] N (*art*) arte *f* erotica; (*literature*) letteratura erotica.

eroti·cal·ly [ɪˈrɒtɪkəlɪ] ADV eroticamente.

eroti·cism [ɪˈrɒtɪˌsɪzəm] N erotismo.

err [ɜːʳ] VI (*be mistaken*) sbagliare, errare; (*sin*) peccare; **it is better to err on the side of caution** la prudenza non è mai troppa.

er·rand [ˈɛrənd] N commissione *f*; **to run errands** fare commissioni; **errand of mercy** atto di carità.

♦ **errand boy** N fattorino.

er·rant [ˈɛrənt] ADJ (*frm: wrong*) in errore; (: *unfaithful*) infedele.

er·ra·ta [ɪˈrɑːtə] N (*Typ*) errore *m* di stampa.

er·rat·ic [ɪˈrætɪk] **1** ADJ (*person, conduct, opinions, mood*) incostante, imprevedibile; (*results etc*) irregolare, discontinuo(-a); (*driving*) irregolare; (*Geol*) erratico(-a). **2** N (*Geol*) masso erratico.

er·rati·cal·ly [ɪˈrætɪkəlɪ] ADV in modo erratico.

er·ro·neous [ɪˈrəʊnɪəs] ADJ erroneo(-a).

er·ror [ˈɛrəʳ] N errore *m*; **typing/spelling error** errore di battitura/di ortografia; **in error** per errore; **to see the error of one's ways** riconoscere i propri errori.

♦ **error message** N (*Comput*) messaggio di errore.

er·satz [ˈɛəzæts] ADJ surrogato(-a); **ersatz coffee** caffè surrogato.

erst·while [ˈɜːstˌwaɪl] (*old*) **1** ADJ di un tempo. **2** ADV un tempo, tempo addietro.

eru·dite [ˈɛrʊˌdaɪt] ADJ erudito(-a).

eru·dite·ly [ˈɛrʊˌdaɪtlɪ] ADV eruditamente.

eru·di·tion [ˌɛrʊˈdɪʃən] N erudizione *f*.

erupt [ɪˈrʌpt] VI (*volcano*) entrare in eruzione *or* in attività; (*spots*) spuntare; (*anger*) esplodere; (*fighting, quarrel*) scoppiare; **he erupted into the room** ha fatto irruzione nella stanza.

erup·tion [ɪˈrʌpʃən] N (*of volcano, spots*) eruzione *f*; (*of anger, violence*) esplosione *f*.

eryth·ro·cyte [ɪˈrɪθrəʊˌsaɪt] N eritrocita *m*.

ESA [ˌiːɛsˈeɪ] N ABBR (= *European Space Agency*) A.S.E. *f* (= *Agenzia spaziale europea*).

es·ca·late [ˈɛskəˌleɪt] **1** VI **a** (*violence, fighting, bombing*) intensificarsi **b** (*costs*) salire. **2** VT intensificare.

es·ca·la·tion [ˌɛskəˈleɪʃən] N escalation *f inv*; (*of prices*) aumento.

es·ca·la·tor [ˈɛskəˌleɪtəʳ] N scala mobile.

♦ **escalator clause** N clausola di indicizzazione *or* di revisione.

es·ca·lope [ˈɛskəˌlɒp] N scaloppina.

es·ca·pade [ˌɛskəˈpeɪd] N (*adventure*) avventura; (*misdeed*) scappatella.

es·cape [ɪsˈkeɪp] **1** N (*gen*) fuga; (*of prisoner*) fuga, evasione *f*; (*of gas*) fuga, fuoriuscita; **to have a lucky escape** scamparla bella; **to make one's escape** evadere. **2** VT (*capture, pursuers, punishment*) sfuggire a; (*death*) scampare; (*danger*) scampare a; (*consequences*) sottrarsi a; **he narrowly escaped being killed** per poco non è rimasto ucciso; **his name escapes me** il suo nome mi sfugge; **to escape notice** passare inosservato(-a); **it had escaped his notice** era sfuggito alla sua attenzione; **nothing escapes her (attention)** non le sfugge nulla. **3** VI (*gen*) scappare; (*prisoner*) evadere; (*liquid, gas*) fuoriuscire; (*Comput*) uscire; **to escape from** (*person*) sfuggire a; (*prison*) fuggire di; **to escape to** (*another place*) fuggire in; (*freedom, safety*) fuggire verso; **he escaped with a few bruises** (*fig*) se l'è cavata con qualche livido; **an escaped prisoner** un(a) evaso(-a).

♦ **escape artist** N = escapologist.

♦ **escape clause** N (*in agreement*) clausola liberatoria.

es·capee [ɪskeɪˈpiː] N evaso(-a).

♦ **escape hatch** N (*in submarine, space rocket*) portello di sicurezza.

♦ **escape key** N (*Comput*) tasto di escape *or* di scambio codice.

♦ **escape plan** N piano di fuga.

♦ **escape route** N percorso di fuga.

♦ **escape velocity** N (*Astron*) velocità di fuga.

es·cap·ism [ɪsˈkeɪpɪzəm] N escapismo, evasione *f* (dalla realtà).

es·cap·ist [ɪsˈkeɪpɪst] **1** ADJ d'evasione. **2** N persona che cerca di evadere dalla realtà.

es·ca·polo·gist [ˌɛskəˈpɒlədʒɪst] N (*Brit*) *illusionista specializzato nel liberarsi da funi, catene ecc*.

es·carp·ment [ɪsˈkɑːpmənt] N scarpata.

eschew [ɪsˈtʃuː] VT (*frm*) evitare.

es·cort [*n* ˈɛskɔːt; *vb* ɪsˈkɔːt] **1** N (*Mil, Naut*) scorta; (*male companion*) cavaliere *m*, accompagnatore *m*; (*female companion*) accompagnatrice *f*. **2** VT accompagnare; (*Mil, Naut*) scortare.

♦ **escort agency** N agenzia di accompagnatrici.

♦ **escort duty** N servizio di scorta.

♦ **escort vessel** N battello di scorta.

Es·ki·mo [ˈɛskɪˌməʊ] (*pl* **Eskimos** *or* **Eskimo**) **1** ADJ eschimese. **2** N (*person*) eschimese *m/f*; (*language*) eschimese *m*.

ESL [ˌiːɛsˈɛl] N ABBR (*Scol*) = *English as a Second Language*.

esopha·gus [ɪˈsɒfəgəs] N (*Am*) = **oesophagus**.

eso·ter·ic [ˌɛsəʊˈtɛrɪk] ADJ esoterico(-a).

ESP [iːɛsˈpiː] N ABBR **a** = **extrasensory perception b** (*Scol*) = *English for Special Purposes*.

esp. ABBR (= *especially*) spec.

es·pa·drilles [ˌɛspəˈdrɪlz] NPL espadrilles *fpl*.

es·pe·cial [ɪsˈpɛʃəl] ADJ particolare.

es·pe·cial·ly [ɪsˈpɛʃəlɪ] ADV (*particularly*) particolarmente; (*above all*) soprattutto, specialmente; (*expressly*) appositamente, espressamente; **it is especially difficult** è particolarmente difficile; **especially when it rains** soprattutto quando piove; **why me, especially?** perché proprio io?

Es·pe·ran·tist [ˌɛspəˈræntɪst] N esperantista *m/f*.

Es·pe·ran·to [ˌɛspəˈræntəʊ] **1** N esperanto. **2** ADJ in esperanto.

es·pio·nage [ˌɛspɪəˈnɑːʒ] N spionaggio.

es·pla·nade [ˌɛspləˈneɪd] N lungomare *m*.

es·pous·al [ɪsˈpaʊzl] N: **espousal of** (*frm*) appoggio a.

es·pouse [ɪsˈpaʊz] VT (*fig frm*) abbracciare.

espy [ɪsˈpaɪ] VT (*old*) notare.

Esq. ABBR (*Brit frm: on an envelope*) = **Esquire**.

es·quire [ɪsˈkwaɪəʳ] N: **Colin Smith Esquire** Egregio Signor Colin Smith.

es·say [ˈɛseɪ] N (*Literature*) saggio; (*Scol*) tema *m*, composizione *f*.

es·say·ist [ˈɛseɪɪst] N saggista *m/f*.

es·sence [ˈɛsəns] N (*gen, Culin*) essenza; **in essence** in sostanza; **speed is of the essence** la velocità è di estrema importanza.

es·sen·tial [ɪˈsɛnʃəl] **1** ADJ (*gen*) essenziale; (*basic*)

fondamentale; (*important*) indispensabile; **it is essential that** è essenziale che + *sub*.

2 N, OFTEN PL elemento essenziale.

es·sen·tial·ly [ɪˈsɛnʃəlɪ] ADV essenzialmente, fondamentalmente.

EST [ˌiːɛsˈtiː] N ABBR (*Am*)= *Eastern Standard Time*; see **eastern**.

est. ABBR **a** = *established* **b** = *estimate(d)*.

es·tab·lish [ɪsˈtæblɪʃ] VT **a** (*set up*: *company*) costituire; (: *business*) avviare; (: *state*) creare; (: *committee*) istituire; (: *custom*, *precedent*, *relations*) stabilire; (: *power*, *authority*, *reputation*) affermare; (: *peace*, *order*) ristabilire; **he established his reputation as an architect** si è affermato come architetto

b (*prove*: *fact*, *identity*, *sb's innocence*) dimostrare.

es·tab·lished [ɪsˈtæblɪʃt] ADJ (*person*) affermato(-a); (*business*) avviato(-a); (*custom*) radicato(-a); (*fact*) stabilito(-a); **the Established Church** la religione di Stato; **a well-established business** un'attività ben avviata.

es·tab·lish·ment [ɪsˈtæblɪʃmənt] N **a** (*of company*) costituzione *f*; (*of state*) creazione *f*; (*of committee*) istituzione *f*; (*of law*) instaurazione *f*; (*of reputation*) affermazione *f*

b (*business*) azienda; (*Admin*, *Mil*, *Naut*: *personnel*) effettivo; **a teaching establishment** un istituto d'istruzione; **the Establishment** la classe dirigente, l'establishment *m inv*; **the values of the Establishment** i valori tradizionali; **the cultural Establishment** l'establishment culturale.

es·tate [ɪsˈteɪt] N **a** (*land*) proprietà *f inv*, tenuta; (*Brit*: *also*: **housing estate**) complesso edilizio; **country estate** tenuta in campagna **b** (*Law*: *on death*) patrimonio, beni *mpl*.

♦ **estate agency** N (*Brit*) agenzia immobiliare.

♦ **estate agent** N (*Brit*) agente *m/f* immobiliare.

♦ **estate car** N (*Brit*) auto modello familiare, station wagon *f inv*.

♦ **estate duty** N tassa di successione.

es·teem [ɪsˈtiːm] (*frm*) 1 N stima; **I hold him in high esteem** gode della mia più alta stima.

2 VT (*think highly of*) stimare; (*consider*) considerare; **I would esteem it an honour** sarebbe un onore per me.

es·ter [ˈɛstə] N estere *m*.

es·thet·ic [iːsˈθɛtɪk] ADJ (*Am*) = **aesthetic** *etc*.

Es·thon·ia [ɛˈstəʊnɪə] N = **Estonia**.

Es·tho·nian [ɛˈstəʊnɪən] ADJ, N = **Estonian**.

es·ti·mable [ˈɛstɪməbl] ADJ stimabile.

es·ti·mate [*n* ˈɛstɪmɪt; *vb* ˈɛstɪmeɪt] 1 N (*judgment*) valutazione *f*, stima; (*Comm*: *for work to be done*) preventivo; **to give sb an estimate of** fare a qn un preventivo (*or* una stima) di; **at a rough estimate** ad un calcolo approssimativo.

2 VT valutare, stimare; (*Comm*) preventivare; **we estimate the cost to be £150** preventiviamo un costo di circa 150 sterline.

3 VI (*Comm*): **to estimate for** fare il preventivo per.

es·ti·ma·tion [ˌɛstɪˈmeɪʃən] N **a** (*judgment*) giudizio; **in my estimation** a mio giudizio, a mio avviso **b** (*esteem*) stima, opinione *f*; **she has gone up in my estimation** ho maggiore stima di lei.

es·ti·ma·tor [ˈɛstɪmeɪtə] N estimatore(-trice).

Es·ton·ia, **Es·thon·ia** [ɛˈstəʊnɪə] N Estonia.

Es·to·nian, **Es·thon·ian** [ɛˈstəʊnɪən] 1 ADJ estone.

2 N (*person*) estone *m/f*; (*language*) estone *m*.

es·tranged [ɪˈstreɪndʒd] ADJ separato(-a); **to become**

estranged allontanarsi, disaffezionarsi.

es·trange·ment [ɪsˈtreɪndʒmənt] N allontanamento.

es·tro·gen [ˈiːstrədʒən] N (*Am*) = **oestrogen**.

es·tu·ary [ˈɛstjʊərɪ] N estuario.

ET [ˌiːˈtiː] 1 N ABBR (*Brit*)= *Employment Training*.

2 ABBR (*Am*: = *Eastern Time*) fuso orario della costa orientale.

ETA [ˌiːtiːˈeɪ] N ABBR **a** (= *estimated time of arrival*) ora di arrivo prevista **b** (*Basque separatist organization*: = *Euzkadi ta Askatsuna*) ETA *f*.

et al. [ɛtˈæl] ABBR (= *et alii*: *and others*) ed altri.

etc ABBR (= *et cetera*) ecc., etc.

etch [ɛtʃ] VT incidere all'acquaforte.

etch·ing [ˈɛtʃɪŋ] N (*process*) incisione *f* all'acquaforte; (*print made from plate*) acquaforte *f*.

ETD [ˌiːtiːˈdiː] N ABBR (= *estimated time of departure*) ora di partenza prevista.

eter·nal [ɪˈtɜːnl] ADJ eterno(-a); (*pej*: *complaints etc*) continuo(-a); **the eternal triangle** il classico triangolo.

eter·nal·ly [ɪˈtɜːnəlɪ] ADV eternamente.

eter·nity [ɪˈtɜːnɪtɪ] N eternità.

ethane [ˈiːθeɪn] N etano.

etha·nol [ˈɛθəˌnɒl] N alcol *m* etilico.

eth·ene [ˈɛθiːn] N = **ethylene**.

ether [ˈiːθə] N etere *m*.

ethe·real [ɪˈθɪərɪəl] ADJ etereo(-a).

eth·ic [ˈɛθɪk] N etica; **the work ethic** l'etica del lavoro, la deontologia professionale.

ethi·cal [ˈɛθɪkəl] ADJ etico(-a), morale.

ethi·cal·ly [ˈɛθɪkəlɪ] ADV eticamente.

eth·ics [ˈɛθɪks] N (*sg*: *study*) etica; (*pl*: *principles*, *system*) morale *f*.

Ethio·pia [ˌiːθɪˈəʊpɪə] N Etiopia.

Ethio·pian [ˌiːθɪˈəʊpɪən] 1 ADJ etiopico(-a), etiope.

2 N (*person*) etiope *m/f*; (*language*) etiope *m*.

eth·nic [ˈɛθnɪk] ADJ etnico(-a).

eth·ni·cal·ly [ˈɛθnɪkəlɪ] ADV etnicamente.

♦ **ethnic cleansing** N pulizia etnica.

eth·nog·ra·phy [ɛθˈnɒgrəfɪ] N etnografia.

eth·no·logi·cal [ˌɛθnəʊˈlɒdʒɪkəl] ADJ etnologico(-a).

eth·nolo·gist [ɛθˈnɒlədʒɪst] N etnologo(-a).

eth·nol·ogy [ɛθˈnɒlədʒɪ] N etnologia.

ethos [ˈiːθɒs] N (*of culture*, *group*) ethos *m*, norma di vita.

ethyl [ˈiːθaɪl] N etile *m*.

♦ **ethyl acetate** N acetato di etile.

eth·yl·ene [ˈɛθɪliːn] N etilene *m*.

ethyne [ˈiːθaɪn] N acetilene *m*.

eti·quette [ˈɛtɪˌkɛt] N etichetta; **court etiquette** (*royal*) cerimoniale di corte; **medical etiquette** prassi *f* medica.

Etrus·can [ɪˈtrʌskən] ADJ etrusco(-a).

ETU [ˌiːtiːˈjuː] N ABBR (*Brit*: = *Electrical Trades Union*) sindacato dei lavoratori dell'industria elettrica.

ETV [ˌiːtiːˈviː] N ABBR (*Am*)= *Educational Television*.

ety·mo·logi·cal [ˌɛtɪməˈlɒdʒɪkəl] ADJ etimologico(-a).

ety·mo·logi·cal·ly [ˌɛtɪməˈlɒdʒɪkəlɪ] ADV etimologicamente.

ety·mol·ogy [ˌɛtɪˈmɒlədʒɪ] N etimologia.

EU [ˌiːˈjuː] N ABBR (= *European Union*) U.E. *f*.

euca·lyp·tus [ˌjuːkəˈlɪptəs] N eucalipto.

Eucha·rist [ˈjuːkərɪst] N Eucaristia.

Euclid [ˈjuːklɪd] N Euclide *m*.

Euclid·ean [juːˈklɪdɪən] ADJ euclideo(-a).

eugen·ics [juːˈdʒɛnɪks] NSG eugenica.

eulo·gize [ˈjuːləˌdʒaɪz] VT elogiare, encomiare.

eulogy [ˈjuːlədʒɪ] N elogio, encomio.

eunuch ['ju:nək] N eunuco.

eu·phe·mism ['ju:fə,mɪzəm] N eufemismo.

euphemis·tic [,ju:fə'mɪstɪk] ADJ eufemistico(-a).

euphemis·ti·cal·ly [,ju:fɪ'mɪstɪkəlɪ] ADV eufemisticamente.

euphon·ic [ju:'fɒnɪk] ADJ eufonico(-a).

eupho·ria [ju:'fɔ:rɪə] N euforia.

euphor·ic [ju:'fɒrɪk] ADJ euforico(-a).

euphor·ical·ly [ju:'fɒrɪkəlɪ] ADV euforicamente.

Eura·sia [jʊə'reɪʃə] N Eurasia.

Eura·sian [jʊə'reɪʃn] ①ADJ eurasiatico(-a).
②N eurasiano(-a).

Euratom [jʊə'rætəm] N ABBR (= *European Atomic Energy Community*) EURATOM *f.*

Euripides [jʊ'rɪpɪ,di:z] N Euripide *m.*

Euro- [jʊərəʊ] PREF euro-.

Euro·cheque ['jʊərəʊ,tʃɛk] N eurochèque *m inv.*

Euro·crat ['jʊərəʊ,kræt] N eurocrate *m/f.*

Euro·dol·lar ['jʊərəʊ,dɒlə'] N eurodollaro.

Europa [jʊ'rəʊpə] N (*Myth*) Europa.

Europe ['jʊərəp] N Europa; **to go into** or **join Europe** (*Pol*) entrare nella Comunità Europea.

Euro·pean [jʊərə'pi:ən] ①ADJ europeo(-a); **European plan** (*Am*: *in hotel*) solo pernottamento (pasti esclusi).
②N europeo(-a).

♦ **European Court of Justice** N Tribunale *m* della Comunità Europea.

♦ **European Economic Community** N Comunità Economica Europea.

♦ **Euro-sceptic** ['jʊərəʊ,skɛptɪk] N euroscettico(-a).

Euro·vis·ion ['jʊərəʊ,vɪʒən] N (*TV*) eurovisione *f.*

Eurydice [jʊ'rɪdɪsɪ] N Euridice *f.*

Eusta·chian tube [ju:'steɪʃən'tju:b] N tromba di Eustachio.

eutha·na·sia [,ju:θə'neɪzɪə] N eutanasia.

evacu·ate [ɪ'vækjʊ,eɪt] VT (*people*) sfollare; (*building, area, Med*) evacuare.

evacu·ation [ɪ,vækjʊ'eɪʃən] N (*see vb*) sfollamento; evacuazione *f.*

evac·uee [ɪ,vækjʊ'i:] N sfollato(-a).

evade [ɪ'veɪd] VT (*capture, pursuers*) sfuggire a; (*punishment, blow*) schivare; (*question*) eludere; (*issue, truth, sb's gaze*) evitare; (*responsibility, duties, obligation, military service*) sottrarsi a; (*tax, customs duty*) evadere.

evalu·ate [ɪ'væljʊ,eɪt] VT valutare.

evalu·ation [ɪ,væljʊ'eɪʃən] N valutazione *f.*

eva·nesce [,ɛvə'nɛs] VI (*liter*) svanire.

evan·geli·cal [,i:væn'dʒɛlɪkəl] ADJ evangelico(-a).

evan·gelism [ɪ'vændʒə,lɪzm] N evangelizzazione *f.*

evan·gelist [ɪ'vændʒəlɪst] N (*writer*: *also*: **Evangelist**) evangelista *m*; (*preacher*) predicatore *m* evangelista.

evan·gelize [ɪ'vændʒɪ,laɪz] ①VT evangelizzare.
②VI predicare il vangelo.

evapo·rate [ɪ'væpəreɪt] ①VT (*liquid*) far evaporare.
②VI (*liquid*) evaporare; (*fig: hopes, fears, anger*) svanire.

evapo·rat·ed milk [ɪ'væpə,reɪtɪd'mɪlk] N latte *m* condensato.

evapo·ra·tion [ɪ,væpə'reɪʃən] N evaporazione *f.*

eva·sion [ɪ'veɪʒən] N evasione *f.*

eva·sive [ɪ'veɪsɪv] ADJ (*answer*) evasivo(-a); (*person*) sfuggente; **to take evasive action** defilarsi.

eva·sive·ly [ɪ'veɪsɪvlɪ] ADV evasivamente.

Eve [i:v] N Eva.

eve [i:v] N vigilia; **on the eve of** alla vigilia di.

even ['i:vən] ① ADV **a** perfino, anche; **not even** ...

nemmeno..., neppure...; **even on Sundays** perfino di domenica; **and she even sings** e sa anche *or* addirittura cantare; **even though** OR **even if** anche se; **even as** proprio nel momento in cui; **even now he can't do it** non lo sa fare nemmeno ora; **without even reading it** senza neppure leggerlo; **he can't even read** non sa nemmeno leggere; **even so** ciò nonostante; **not even if/when** nemmeno *or* neppure se/quando

b (+ *comp adj or adv*) ancora; **even faster** ancora più veloce; **even more** ancora di più.

② ADJ **a** (*smooth*) liscio(-a); (*level*): **even (with)** allo stesso livello (di); **to make even** livellare

b (*uniform: speed, breathing*) regolare; (*temperature*) costante; (*temper*) calmo(-a); (*tone, voice, colour*) uniforme

c (*equal: quantities*) uguale; (: *score*) di parità, pari *inv*; **to have an even chance (of doing sth)** avere una buona probabilità (di fare qc); **to get even with sb** vendicarsi di qn; **to break even** (*Fin*) chiudere in pareggio; **that makes us even** (*in game, fig*) siamo pari; **they are an even match** sono allo stesso livello

d (*numbers*) pari *inv*

▶ **even out** ①VT + ADV (*smooth*: *also fig*) appianare; (*number, score*) pareggiare.
②VI + ADV pareggiarsi

▶ **even up** VT + ADV livellare; (*fig*) appianare.

♦ **even-handed** [,i:vən'hændɪd] ADJ imparziale, equo(-a).

eve·ning ['i:vnɪŋ] ①N sera; (*as duration, event*) serata; **in the evening** di sera, la sera; **this evening** stasera, questa sera; **tomorrow/yesterday evening** domani/ieri sera; **on Sunday evening** domenica sera; **on the evening of the 30th** la sera del 30; **she spends her evenings knitting** trascorre le sue serate a fare la maglia; **good evening!** buona sera!.
②ADJ (*paper, prayers, service*) della sera; (*performance*) serale.

♦ **evening class** N corso serale.

♦ **evening dress** N (*woman's*) abito da sera; **in evening dress** (*man*) in abito scuro; (*woman*) in abito lungo.

♦ **evening star** N stella della sera.

even·ly ['i:vənlɪ] ADV (*distribute, space, spread*) uniformemente; (*divide*) in parti uguali; (*breathe*) in modo regolare.

even·song ['i:vən,sɒŋ] N ≈ vespro.

event [ɪ'vɛnt] N avvenimento; (*Sport*: *in a programme*) gara; **"Events"** "Spettacoli e manifestazioni"; **at all events** OR **in any event** in ogni caso; **in either event** in entrambi i casi; **in the event of/that** ... in caso di/che + *sub*...; **in the event** in realtà, di fatto; **in that event** in quel caso; **in the normal course of events** secondo le regole, nel corso naturale delle cose; **in the course of events** nel corso degli eventi.

♦ **even-tempered** [,i:vən'tɛmpəd] ADJ equilibrato(-a).

event·ful [ɪ'vɛntfʊl] ADJ (*life*) ricco(-a) di avvenimenti; (*match, day*) movimentato(-a), denso(-a) di eventi.

event·ing [ɪ'vɛntɪŋ] N (*Sport*) concorso ippico.

even·tual [ɪ'vɛntʃʊəl] ADJ finale; **it resulted in the eventual loss of many lives** ha avuto come risultato finale la perdita di molte vite umane.

even·tu·al·ity [ɪ,vɛntʃʊ'ælɪtɪ] N eventualità *f inv*, possibilità *f inv*; **to be ready for any eventuality** essere pronto(-a) a ogni evenienza.

even·tu·al·ly [ɪ'vɛntʃʊəlɪ] ADV (*at last*) alla fine, finalmente; **eventually the species will become extinct** (*given time*) la specie finirà per estinguersi.

ever [ˈɛvəʳ] ADV **a** (*always*) sempre; **ever ready** sempre pronto(-a); **ever since (then) they have been very careful** da allora in poi sono stati molto prudenti; **ever since I've known him** sin da quando lo conosco; **with ever increasing frequency** con sempre maggior frequenza; **they lived happily ever after** e vissero per sempre felici e contenti; **as ever** come sempre; **for ever** per sempre; **they are for ever fighting** litigano di continuo; **yours ever** (*Brit: in letters*) sempre tuo(-a)

b (*at any time*) mai; **hardly ever** quasi mai; **nothing ever happens** non succede mai nulla; **if you ever go there se** ti capita di andarci; **did you ever meet him?** l'hai mai incontrato?; **have you ever been there?** ci sei mai stato?; **we haven't ever tried it** non l'abbiamo mai provato; **more handsome than ever** più bello che mai; **now if ever is the time** *or* **moment to ...** ora o mai più è il momento di...; **the best ever** il/la migliore che ci sia mai stato(-a); **the best film ever** il miglior film che si sia mai visto; **he's a liar if ever there was one** se c'è un bugiardo al mondo quello è lui

c (*emphasizing*): **as soon as ever you can** al più presto possibile; **why ever did you do it?** perché mai l'hai fatto?; **why ever not?** ma perché no?; **never ever** mai e poi mai; **ever so pretty** così bello(-a); **he's ever so strong** è fortissimo; **ever so slightly drunk** leggermente sbronzo; **we're ever so grateful** siamo estremamente grati; **thank you ever so much** grazie mille; **as if I ever would!** non sia mai detto!

Ev·er·est [ˈɛvərɪst] N (*also:* **Mount Everest**) l'Everest *m*, il monte *m* Everest.

ever·green [ˈɛvəˌgriːn] ADJ, N sempreverde *(m or f)*.

ever·lasting [ˌɛvəˈlɑːstɪŋ] ADJ eterno(-a); (*pej*) continuo (-a).

ever·lasting·ly [ˌɛvəˈlɑːstɪŋlɪ] ADV (*see adj*) eternamente, in eterno; continuamente, incessantemente.

ever·more [ˌɛvəˈmɔːʳ] ADV sempre; **for evermore** per sempre.

every [ˈɛvrɪ] ADJ (*each*) ogni *inv*; (*all*) tutti(-e) *pl*; **every one of them** ognuno(-a) di loro; **I gave you every assistance** ti ho dato tutta l'assistenza; **I have every confidence in him** ho piena fiducia in lui; **we wish you every success** ti auguriamo ogni successo; **every day** ogni giorno, tutti i giorni; **every other day** un giorno sì e uno no; **every other car** una macchina su due; **every second month** ogni due mesi; **every three days** OR **every third day** ogni tre giorni; **every few days** ogni due o tre giorni; **every so often** OR **every now and then** OR **every now and again** di tanto in tanto, di quando in quando, ogni tanto; **every time that** ogni volta che; **every single time** proprio tutte le volte; **her every wish** ogni suo desiderio; **I enjoyed every minute of the party** mi sono divertito moltissimo alla festa; **every bit of the carpet** proprio tutto il tappeto; **every bit as clever as** tanto intelligente quanto; **in every way** sotto tutti i profili; **every man for himself** ognuno per sé.

every·body [ˈɛvrɪˌbɒdɪ] PRON ognuno, ciascuno; (*all*) tutti(-e) *pl*; **everybody knows about it** lo sanno tutti; **everybody has their** *or* (*frm*) **his own view** ognuno *or* ciascuno la pensa come crede; **everybody else** tutti gli altri.

every·day [ˈɛvrɪˌdeɪ] ADJ quotidiano(-a), di ogni giorno; (*expression*) di uso corrente; (*use, occurrence, experience*) comune; (*shoes, clothes*) di tutti i giorni; **it is not an everyday event** non capita tutti i giorni.

every·one [ˈɛvrɪˌwʌn] PRON = **everybody**.

every·place [ˈɛvrɪˌpleɪs] ADV (*Am*) = **everywhere**.

every·thing [ˈɛvrɪˌθɪŋ] PRON tutto, ogni cosa; **everything is ready** è tutto pronto; **everything you say is true** tutto ciò che dici è vero; **this shop sells everything** questo negozio vende di tutto; **he did everything possible** ha fatto tutto il possibile.

every·where [ˈɛvrɪˌwɛəʳ] ADV dappertutto, in ogni luogo; (*wherever*) ovunque; **everywhere you go you meet ...** ovunque tu vada trovi... .

evict [ɪˈvɪkt] VT sfrattare.

evic·tion [ɪˈvɪkʃən] N sfratto.

♦ **eviction notice** N avviso di sfratto.

evi·dence [ˈɛvɪdəns] N INV (*proof*) prova; (*testimony*) testimonianza; (*sign*) indizio, traccia; **to show evidence of** mostrare segni di; **evidence of a break-in** tracce di scasso; **to give evidence** testimoniare, deporre; **to turn King's** *or* **Queen's** *or* (*Am*) **State's evidence** testimoniare contro i propri complici; **to be in evidence** essere visibile *or* in vista; **she was nowhere in evidence** non la si vedeva da nessuna parte.

evi·dent [ˈɛvɪdənt] ADJ evidente, chiaro(-a); **it is evident from his speech that ...** risulta chiaro *or* evidente dal suo discorso che... .

evi·dent·ly [ˈɛvɪdəntlɪ] ADV (*clearly*) chiaramente; (*apparently*) evidentemente; **evidently he cannot come** evidentemente non può venire.

evil [ˈiːvl] **1** N male *m*; **the lesser of two evils** il minore tra due mali.

2 ADJ (*person, deed*) malvagio(-a), cattivo(-a); (*reputation, influence*) pessimo(-a); (*spirit, spell, influence*) malvagio(-a); (*unhappy: hour, times*) infausto(-a).

evil·doer [ˈiːvlˌduːəʳ] N persona malvagia.

♦ **evil eye** N: **to put the evil eye on sb** gettare il malocchio su qn.

evil·ly [ˈiːvɪlɪ] ADV malvagiamente.

♦ **evil-minded** [ˌiːvlˈmaɪndɪd] ADJ malvagio(-a).

evince [ɪˈvɪns] VT (*frm*) manifestare.

evo·ca·tion [ˌɛvəˈkeɪʃən] N evocazione *f*.

evoca·tive [ɪˈvɒkətɪv] ADJ: **evocative (of)** evocativo(-a) (di).

evoca·tive·ly [ɪˈvɒkətɪvlɪ] ADV in modo evocativo.

evoke [ɪˈvəʊk] VT (*memories*) evocare; (*admiration*) suscitare.

evo·lu·tion [ˌiːvəˈluːʃən] N (*development*) sviluppo; (*Bio*) evoluzione *f*.

evo·lu·tion·ary [ˌiːvəˈluːʃənrɪ] ADJ evolutivo(-a).

evo·lu·tion·ist [ˌiːvəˈluːʃənɪst] **1** ADJ evoluzionistico(-a). **2** N evoluzionista *m/f*.

evolve [ɪˈvɒlv] **1** VT (*system, theory, plan*) elaborare, sviluppare.

2 VI (*species*) evolversi; (*system, plan, science*) svilupparsi.

ewe [juː] N pecora.

ewer [ˈjuːəʳ] N (*old*) brocca.

ex [ɛks] **1** N (*ex-husband, ex-wife*) ex *m/f inv*.

2 PREP (*out of*): **the price ex works** il prezzo franco fabbrica.

ex- [ɛks] PREF (*former: husband, president*) ex-.

ex·ac·er·bate [ɪgˈzæsəˌbeɪt] (*frm*) VT (*pain*) aggravare; (*relations, situation*) esacerbare, inasprire.

ex·ac·er·ba·tion [ɪgˌzæsəˈbeɪʃən] N (*see vb*) aggravamento; esacerbazione *f*, inasprimento.

ex·act [ɪgˈzækt] **1** ADJ (*number, value, meaning, time*) esatto(-a); (*instructions, description*) preciso(-a); **it's an exact copy of the original** è una copia perfetta

dell'originale; **her exact words were ...** le sue precise parole sono state...; **to be exact, there were three of us** per essere precisi eravamo in tre; **the exact opposite (of)** l'esatto contrario (di).

2 VT: **to exact sth (from)** (*frm*) esigere qc (da).

ex·act·ing [ɪgˈzæktɪŋ] ADJ (*task, profession, work*) impegnativo(-a); (*person*) esigente.

ex·acti·tude [ɪgˈzæktɪtjuːd] N precisione *f*, esattezza.

ex·act·ly [ɪgˈzæktlɪ] ADV (*describe, know, resemble*) esattamente; (*of time*) in punto; **exactly!** esatto!; **that's exactly what I thought** è proprio quello che pensavo; **it's exactly 5 o'clock** sono le 5 in punto.

ex·act·ness [ɪgˈzæktnɪs] N esattezza, precisione *f*.

ex·ag·ger·ate [ɪgˈzædʒəˌreɪt] 1 VT (*overstate*) esagerare; (*emphasize*) accentuare.

2 VI esagerare.

ex·ag·ger·at·ed [ɪgˈzædʒəˌreɪtɪd] ADJ esagerato(-a); **to have an exaggerated opinion of o.s.** stimarsi troppo.

ex·ag·gera·tion [ɪgˌzædʒəˈreɪʃən] N esagerazione *f*.

ex·alt [ɪgˈzɔːlt] VT (*frm*) **a** (*in rank*) promuovere **b** (*praise*) esaltare, magnificare.

ex·al·ta·tion [ˌɛgzɔːlˈteɪʃən] (*frm*) N esaltazione *f*.

ex·alt·ed [ɪgˈzɔːltɪd] ADJ (*frm: high: rank, position, person*) elevato(-a); (: *elated*) esaltato(-a).

exam [ɪgˈzæm] N ABBR (*Scol*) = **examination.**

ex·ami·na·tion [ɪgˌzæmɪˈneɪʃən] N (*Scol*) esame *m*; (*inspection: of machine, premises*) ispezione *f*; (: *of accounts, passport, at Customs*) controllo; (*of witness, suspect*) interrogatorio; (*Med*) visita; **to take** *or* **sit an examination** sostenere *o* dare un esame; **on examination** in seguito all'esame; **the matter is under examination** la questione è all'esame.

ex·am·ine [ɪgˈzæmɪn] VT (*inspect: machine, wreckage*) ispezionare; (: *luggage, passport*) controllare; (*Med*) visitare, esaminare; (*witness, suspect*) interrogare; (*test: pupil, candidate*): **to examine sb in** esaminare qn in; (*orally*) interrogare qn in.

ex·am·in·er [ɪgˈzæmɪnə'] N esaminatore(-trice).

ex·am·ple [ɪgˈzɑːmpl] N (*gen*) esempio; (*person*) esempio, modello; (*copy*) esemplare *m*; **for example** ad *or* per esempio; **to quote sth/sb as an example** portare qc/qn come esempio; **to set a good/bad example** dare il buon/cattivo esempio; **to make an example of sb** dare l'esempio (punendo qn); **to punish sb as an example** punire qn per dare l'esempio.

ex·as·per·ate [ɪgˈzɑːspəˌreɪt] VT esasperare; **exasperated by** *or* **at** *or* **with** esasperato(-a) da; **to become exasperated** esasperarsi.

ex·as·per·at·ing [ɪgˈzɑːspəˌreɪtɪŋ] ADJ esasperante.

ex·as·per·at·ing·ly [ɪgˈzɑːspəˌreɪtɪŋlɪ] ADV in modo esasperante.

ex·as·pera·tion [ɪgˌzɑːspəˈreɪʃən] N esasperazione *f*.

ex·ca·vate [ˈɛkskəˌveɪt] VT (*ground*) scavare; (*Archeol*) effettuare gli scavi di.

ex·ca·va·tion [ˌɛkskəˈveɪʃən] N scavo; (*Archeol*) scavi *mpl*.

ex·ca·va·tor [ˈɛkskəˌveɪtə'] N (*machine*) escavatrice *f*, escavatore *m*.

ex·ceed [ɪkˈsiːd] VT (*gen, speed limit*): **to exceed (by)** superare (di); (*limit, bounds*) oltrepassare; (*powers, instructions, duty*) eccedere; (*time limit*) superare.

ex·ceed·ing·ly [ɪkˈsiːdɪŋlɪ] ADV estremamente.

ex·cel [ɪkˈsɛl] 1 VT superare; **to excel o.s.** superare se stesso.

2 VI: **to excel at** *or* **in** eccellere in; **to excel as** primeggiare come.

ex·cel·lence [ˈɛksələns] N superiorità.

Ex·cel·len·cy [ˈɛksələnsɪ] N: **His Excellency** Sua Eccellenza.

ex·cel·lent [ˈɛksələnt] ADJ eccellente, ottimo(-a).

ex·cel·lent·ly [ˈɛksələntlɪ] ADV eccellentemente, ottimamente.

ex·cept [ɪkˈsɛpt] 1 PREP (*also:* **except for, excepting**) eccetto, salvo, tranne; **except that/if/when** salvo che/se/quando; **there is nothing we can do except wait** non c'è nulla che possiamo fare se non aspettare; **except for** ad eccezione di; **except for one old lady** ad eccezione di *or* tranne una vecchia signora.

2 VT: **to except (from)** escludere (da); **present company excepted** esclusi i presenti; **always excepting the possibility ...** sempre se si esclude la possibilità...; **not excepting ...** senza esclusione di... .

ex·cep·tion [ɪkˈsɛpʃən] N eccezione *f*; **with the exception of** ad eccezione di, fatta eccezione per; **without exception** senza eccezioni; **to make an exception** fare un'eccezione; **the exception proves the rule** l'eccezione conferma la regola; **to take exception to** fare obiezione a, trovare da ridire su.

ex·cep·tion·al [ɪkˈsɛpʃənl] ADJ eccezionale; (*unusual*) insolito(-a).

ex·cep·tion·al·ly [ɪkˈsɛpʃənəlɪ] ADV eccezionalmente.

ex·cerpt [ˈɛksɜːpt] N (*from film*) spezzone *m*; (*from TV play*) estratto; (*from book, Mus*) brano.

ex·cess [ɪkˈsɛs] 1 N eccesso; **the excess of losses over profits** l'eccedenza delle perdite sui guadagni; **in excess of** al di sopra di; **to excess** all'eccesso; **to carry sth to excess** spingere qc all'eccesso.

2 ADJ (*profit, weight*) in eccesso.

♦ **excess baggage, excess luggage** N bagaglio in eccedenza.

♦ **excess fare** N supplemento di prezzo *or* di tariffa.

ex·ces·sive [ɪkˈsɛsɪv] ADJ (*drinking, spending, interest*) smodato(-a); (*charges, rates*) eccessivo(-a); (*fear*) esagerato(-a).

ex·ces·sive·ly [ɪkˈsɛsɪvlɪ] ADV (*see adj*) smodatamente; eccessivamente; esageratamente.

♦ **excess luggage** N = **excess baggage.**

♦ **excess supply** N eccesso di offerta.

ex·change [ɪksˈtʃeɪndʒ] 1 N **a** scambio; **in exchange for** in cambio di; **an exchange of gunfire** uno scontro a fuoco

b (*Comm*): **foreign exchange** cambio

c (*also:* **telephone exchange**) centralino.

2 VT: **to exchange sth for sth/with sb** scambiare qc con qc/con qn; (*prisoners, stamps, greetings*) scambiarsi; **to exchange blows** venire alle mani.

ex·change·able [ɪksˈtʃeɪndʒəbl] ADJ cambiabile.

♦ **exchange control** N (*Fin*) controllo dei cambi.

♦ **exchange market** N mercato dei cambi.

♦ **exchange rate** N tasso di cambio.

♦ **Exchange Rate Mechanism** N meccanismo dei tassi di cambi.

Ex·cheq·uer [ɪksˈtʃɛkə'] N: **the Exchequer** (*Brit*) ≈ il ministero delle Finanze.

ex·cis·able [ɪkˈsaɪzəbl] ADJ soggetto(-a) a dazio.

ex·cise [*n* ˈɛksaɪz; *vb* ɪkˈsaɪz] 1 N (*also:* **excise tax**) dazio.

2 VT (*frm*) asportare.

♦ **excise duties** [ˈɛksaɪzˈdjuːtɪz] NPL dazi *mpl*.

ex·cit·abil·ity [ɪkˌsaɪtəˈbɪlɪtɪ] N eccitabilità.

ex·cit·able [ɪkˈsaɪtəbl] ADJ eccitabile.

ex·cite [ɪkˈsaɪt] VT **a** (*person*) far agitare; (: *pleasantly*)

riempire di gioia (*or* interesse *etc*); (: *sexually*) eccitare; **to excite sb to anger** far arrabbiare qn **b** (*anger*) provocare; (*interest, enthusiasm*) suscitare.

ex·cit·ed [ɪk'saɪtɪd] ADJ: **excited (about)** eccitato(-a) (per); **to get excited (about sth)** agitarsi (per qc); **it's nothing to get excited about** (*fig*) non è niente di particolare.

ex·cit·ed·ly [ɪk'saɪtɪdlɪ] ADV con eccitazione.

ex·cite·ment [ɪk'saɪtmənt] N eccitazione *f*, agitazione *f*; **in the excitement of the departure/preparations** nell'eccitazione *or* agitazione della partenza/dei preparativi; **the book caused great excitement** il libro ha fatto sensazione; **she enjoys excitement** le piacciono le emozioni.

ex·cit·ing [ɪk'saɪtɪŋ] ADJ (*gen*) emozionante; (*idea, fashion, person*) entusiasmante; (*film, book*) appassionante.

excl. ABBR **a** = *excluding* **b** = *exclusive (of)*.

ex·claim [ɪks'kleɪm] **1** VT esclamare.

2 VI: **to exclaim at sth** (*indignantly*) indignarsi per qc; (*admiringly*) esprimere meraviglia davanti a qc.

ex·cla·ma·tion [ˌɛksklə'meɪʃən] N esclamazione *f*.

♦ **exclamation mark**, (*Am*) **exclamation point** N (*Gram*) punto esclamativo.

ex·clude [ɪks'klu:d] VT (*gen*) escludere; (*possibility*) scartare; **I'm excluded from taking part** non ho il diritto di partecipare.

ex·clud·ing [ɪks'klu:dɪŋ] PREP: **excluding VAT** IVA esclusa; **excluding the cleaners** escluse le donne delle pulizie.

ex·clu·sion [ɪks'klu:ʒən] N esclusione *f*; **to the exclusion of** escludendo.

♦ **exclusion clause** N clausola di esclusione di rischi.

♦ **exclusion zone** N area interdetta.

ex·clu·sive [ɪks'klu:sɪv] ADJ **a** (*gen, club*) esclusivo(-a); (*district*) snob *inv*; (*interest, attention*) totale; **exclusive agency agreement** (*Comm*) accordo di esclusiva; **exclusive rights** *mpl* esclusivi; **an interview exclusive to ...** un'intervista in esclusiva a...

b (*not including*): **exclusive of postage** spese postali escluse; **exclusive of service** servizio escluso; **exclusive of VAT** IVA esclusa.

ex·clu·sive·ly [ɪks'klu:sɪvlɪ] ADV esclusivamente.

ex·com·muni·cate [ˌɛkskə'mju:nɪˌkeɪt] VT scomunicare.

ex·com·mu·ni·ca·tion ['ɛkskəˌmju:nɪ'keɪʃən] N scomunica.

ex·cre·ment ['ɛkskrɪmənt] N (*frm*) escremento.

ex·cres·cence [ɪks'krɛsns] N (*frm*) escrescenza.

ex·cre·ta [ɪks'kri:tə] NPL (*frm*) escrementi *mpl*, escrezioni *fpl*.

ex·crete [ɪks'kri:t] VT (*frm*) espellere.

ex·cre·tion [ɪks'kri:ʃən] N (*frm*) escrezione *f*.

ex·cru·ci·at·ing [ɪks'kru:ʃɪˌeɪtɪŋ] ADJ (*pain, suffering, fam: film*) atroce; (*noise*) insopportabile.

ex·cru·ci·at·ing·ly [ɪks'kru:ʃɪˌeɪtɪŋlɪ] ADV (*see adj*) atrocemente; insopportabilmente; **my leg is excruciatingly painful** ho un dolore atroce alla gamba.

ex·cul·pate ['ɛkskʌlˌpeɪt] VT (*frm*): **to exculpate (from)** scagionare (da), discolpare (da).

ex·cur·sion [ɪks'kɜ:ʃən] N (*journey*) escursione *f*, gita; (*fig*) digressione *f*.

♦ **excursion ticket** N biglietto a tariffa turistica.

♦ **excursion train** N treno speciale (per escursioni).

ex·cus·able [ɪks'kju:zəbl] ADJ scusabile, perdonabile.

ex·cuse [*n* ɪks'kju:s; *vb* ɪks'kju:z] **1** N scusa; **there's no excuse for this** non ci sono scuse *or* scusanti per questo; **on the excuse that ...** con la scusa *or* il pretesto che...; **to make excuses for sb** trovare giustificazioni per

qn.

2 VT **a** (*forgive*) scusare; **excuse me!** mi scusi!; **now, if you will excuse me ...** ora mi scusi ma...; **excuse me?** (*Am*) come (dice), scusi?

b (*justify*) giustificare; **to excuse o.s. (for (doing) sth)** giustificarsi (per (aver fatto) qc)

c (*exempt*): **to excuse sb (from sth/from doing sth)** esonerare *or* dispensare qn (da qc/dal fare qc); **to excuse o.s. (from sth/from doing sth)** farsi esonerare *or* dispensare (da qc/dal fare qc); **to ask to be excused** chiedere di essere scusato(-a).

♦ **ex·directory** [ˌɛksdɪ'rɛktərɪ] ADJ (*Brit*) fuori elenco; **to go ex-directory** non avere il numero di telefono sull'elenco; **ex-directory (phone) number** numero (telefonico) fuori elenco.

ex·ecrable ['ɛksɪkrəbl] ADJ (*frm*: *gen*) pessimo(-a); (: *manners*) esecrabile.

ex·ecrably ['ɛksɪkrəblɪ] (*frm*) ADV (*see adj*) pessimamente; in modo esecrabile.

ex·ecrate ['ɛksɪˌkreɪt] VT (*frm*) esecrare, aborrire.

ex·ecra·tion [ˌɛksɪ'kreɪʃən] N (*frm*) esecrazione *f*.

ex·ecute ['ɛksɪkju:t] VT **a** (*put to death*: *prisoner*) giustiziare **b** (*carry out*: *plan, movement*) eseguire; (: *scheme*) attuare; (*work of art*) realizzare; (*Law*: *will*) rendere esecutivo(-a).

ex·ecu·tion [ˌɛksɪ'kju:ʃən] N (*see vb*) esecuzione *f*; attuazione *f*; realizzazione *f*; **in the execution of one's duty** nell'adempimento del proprio dovere.

ex·ecu·tion·er [ˌɛksɪ'kju:ʃnəʳ] N boia *m inv*.

ex·ecu·tive [ɪg'zɛkjutɪv] **1** ADJ (*powers, committee*) esecutivo(-a); (*position, job, duties*) direttivo(-a); (*secretary*) di direzione; (*offices, suite*) della direzione; (*car, plane*) dirigenziale.

2 N (*Admin, Industry*) dirigente *m/f*, manager *m/f*; **the executive** (*Pol*) l'esecutivo.

♦ **executive director** N amministratore(-trice).

ex·ecu·tor [ɪg'zɛkjutəʳ] N (*of will*) esecutore(-trice) testamentario(-a).

ex·egesis [ˌɛksɪ'dʒi:sɪs] N (*frm*) esegesi *f*.

ex·em·plar [ɪg'zɛmpləʳ] (*frm*) N (*example*) esempio; (*model*) modello.

ex·em·pla·ry [ɪg'zɛmplərɪ] ADJ esemplare.

ex·em·pli·fi·ca·tion [ɪgˌzɛmplɪfɪ'keɪʃən] N esemplificazione *f*.

ex·em·pli·fy [ɪg'zɛmplɪˌfaɪ] VT (*illustrate*) spiegare con esempi, esemplificare; (*be an example of*) essere un esempio di.

ex·empt [ɪg'zɛmpt] **1** ADJ: **exempt (from)** (*person: from tax*) esentato(-a) (da); (: *from military service etc*) esonerato(-a) (da); (*goods*) esente (da).

2 VT: **to exempt (from)** (*see adj*) esentare (da); esonerare (da).

ex·emp·tion [ɪg'zɛmpʃən] N (*see adj*) esenzione *f*; esonero.

ex·er·cise ['ɛksəˌsaɪz] **1** N (*gen*) esercizio; (*physical activity*) esercizio fisico; (*Mil*) esercitazione *f*; **in the exercise of one's duties** nell'esercizio delle proprie funzioni; **to take** *or* **do exercise** fare del movimento *or* moto.

2 VT **a** (*use: authority, right, influence*) esercitare; (: *patience, restraint, tact*) usare

b (*mind, muscle, limb*) tenere in esercizio; (*dog*) fare passeggiare, portar fuori.

3 VI fare del movimento *or* moto.

♦ **exercise bike**, **exercise cycle** N cyclette ® *f inv*.

♦ **exercise book** N quaderno.
ex·ert [ɪgˈzɜːt] VT (force) impiegare; (influence, authority) esercitare; **to exert o.s** (physically) fare uno sforzo; **don't exert yourself!** (hum) non sforzarti troppo!
ex·er·tion [ɪgˈzɜːʃən] N sforzo.
ex·eunt [ˈɛksɪˌʌnt] VI (Theatre) escono.
ex·fo·lia·tion [ɛksˌfəʊlɪˈeɪʃən] N esfoliazione f.
♦ **ex gra·tia** [ˌɛksˈgreɪʃə] ADJ: **ex gratia payment** gratifica.
ex·hale [ɛksˈheɪl] VT, VI espirare.
ex·haust [ɪgˈzɔːst] 1 N (also: **exhaust pipe**) tubo di scappamento.
  2 VT (gen) esaurire; (tire out: person) stremare; **an exhausting journey/day** un viaggio/una giornata estenuante; **to exhaust o.s** sfiancarsi.
ex·haust·ed [ɪgˈzɔːstɪd] ADJ (tired) esausto(-a), sfinito(-a); (used up: supplies) esaurito(-a).
♦ **exhaust fumes** NPL gas m inv di scarico.
ex·haust·ing [ɪgˈzɔːstɪŋ] ADJ estenuante, sfibrante.
ex·haus·tion [ɪgˈzɔːstʃən] N esaurimento; **nervous exhaustion** sovraffaticamento mentale, surmenage m.
ex·haus·tive [ɪgˈzɔːstɪv] ADJ (research, inquiry, inspection) approfondito(-a), minuzioso(-a); (account, description) esauriente; (list) completo(-a).
ex·haus·tive·ly [ɪgˈzɔːstɪvlɪ] ADV (see adj) minuziosamente, in modo approfondito; in modo esauriente.
♦ **exhaust system** N scappamento.
ex·hib·it [ɪgˈzɪbɪt] 1 VT (painting) esporre; (signs of emotion) mostrare; (courage) dar prova di; (skill, ingenuity) dimostrare.
  2 VI (painter) esporre.
  3 N (object on show) oggetto esposto; (Law) reperto.
ex·hi·bi·tion [ˌɛksɪˈbɪʃən] N (act) esposizione f, dimostrazione f; (of rudeness) dimostrazione; (a public show) mostra; **to be on exhibition** essere esposto(-a); **to make an exhibition of o.s** dare spettacolo di sé.
ex·hi·bi·tion·ism [ˌɛksɪˈbɪʃəˌnɪzəm] N (also Psych) esibizionismo.
ex·hi·bi·tion·ist [ˌɛksɪˈbɪʃənɪst] N esibizionista m/f.
ex·hibi·tor [ɪgˈzɪbɪtəʳ] N espositore(-trice).
ex·hila·rate [ɪgˈzɪləˌreɪt] VT (subj: sea, air) tonificare; (: good company, wine) rallegrare.
exhilarating [ɪgˈzɪləreɪtɪŋ] ADJ (see vb) tonificante; che rallegra.
ex·hila·ra·tion [ɪgˌzɪləˈreɪʃən] N allegria.
ex·hort [ɪgˈzɔːt] VT (frm): **to exhort sb (to sth/to do sth)** esortare qn (a qc/a fare qc).
ex·hor·ta·tion [ˌɛgzɔːˈteɪʃən] N (frm): **exhortation (to)** esortazione f (a).
ex·hu·ma·tion [ˌɛkshjʊˈmeɪʃən] N (frm) esumazione f.
ex·hume [ɛksˈhjuːm] VT (frm) esumare.
exi·gen·cy [ˈɛksɪdʒənsɪ] N (frm) esigenza.
ex·ile [ˈɛksaɪl] 1 N (state) esilio; (person) esule m/f; **in(to) exile** in esilio.
  2 VT esiliare.
ex·ist [ɪgˈzɪst] VI **a** (live) vivere; **to exist on sth** vivere di qc
  b (be in existence) esistere; (: doubt) sussistere; (occur) trovarsi.
ex·ist·ence [ɪgˈzɪstəns] N esistenza; **to be in existence** esistere; **to come into existence** essere creato(-a); **the only one in existence** l'unico esistente.
ex·ist·ent [ɪgˈzɪstənt] ADJ (frm) esistente.
ex·is·ten·tial [ˌɛgzɪsˈtɛnʃəl] ADJ (frm) esistenziale.
ex·is·ten·tial·ism [ˌɛgzɪsˈtɛnʃəˌlɪzəm] N esistenzialismo.
ex·is·ten·tial·ist [ˌɛgzɪsˈtɛnʃəlɪst] ADJ, N esistenzialista (m/f).

ex·ist·ing [ɪgˈzɪstɪŋ] ADJ (law, state of affairs) attuale.
exit [ˈɛksɪt] 1 N uscita; **to make one's exit** uscire.
  2 VI (Theatre, Comput) uscire.
♦ **exit poll** N exit poll m inv.
♦ **exit ramp** N (Am Aut) rampa di uscita.
♦ **exit runway** N (Aer) bretella.
♦ **exit visa** N visto d'uscita.
exo·dus [ˈɛksədəs] N (gen, Rel) esodo.
♦ **ex of·fi·cio** [ˌɛksəˈfɪʃɪəʊ] 1 ADV (act) d'ufficio.
  2 ADJ (member) di diritto.
ex·on·er·ate [ɪgˈzɒnəˌreɪt] VT (frm): **to exonerate sb (from sth)** discolpare qn (da qc).
ex·or·bi·tance [ɪgˈzɔːbɪtəns] N eccessività.
ex·or·bi·tant [ɪgˈzɔːbɪtənt] ADJ (price) esorbitante; (demands) spropositato(-a).
ex·or·bi·tant·ly [ɪgˈzɔːbɪtəntlɪ] ADV eccessivamente.
ex·or·cise, ex·or·cize [ˈɛksɔːsaɪz] VT esorcizzare.
ex·or·cism [ˈɛksɔːsɪzəm] N esorcismo.
ex·or·cist [ˈɛksɔːsɪst] N esorcista m.
exo·skel·eton [ˌɛksəʊˈskɛlɪtən] N esoscheletro.
exo·ther·mic [ˌɛksəʊˈθɜːmɪk] ADJ esotermico(-a).
ex·ot·ic [ɪgˈzɒtɪk] ADJ esotico(-a).
ex·oti·cal·ly [ɪgˈzɒtɪkəlɪ] ADV esoticamente.
ex·oti·cism [ɪgˈzɒtɪˌsɪzəm] N esotismo.
ex·pand [ɪksˈpænd] 1 VT (chest, muscles, economy) sviluppare; (market, operations) espandere; (business) ingrandire; (statement, notes) ampliare; (knowledge) approfondire; (horizons) allargare; (influence) estendere.
  2 VI (see vt) svilupparsi; espandersi; ingrandirsi; (gas) espandersi; (metal, lungs) dilatarsi; **to expand on** (notes, story etc) ampliare.
ex·pand·ing [ɪksˈpændɪŋ] ADJ (universe, industry) in espansione; **after six months her expanding waistline became impossible to hide** dopo sei mesi le riuscì impossibile nascondere il pancione.
ex·panse [ɪksˈpæns] N distesa, estensione f.
ex·pan·sion [ɪksˈpænʃən] N (gen) espansione f; (of town, economy, idea) sviluppo; (of production) aumento; (of knowledge) approfondimento; (of influence) estendersi m; (of gas) espansione, dilatazione f; (of metal) dilatazione.
♦ **expansion bolt** N vite f a espansione.
ex·pan·sion·ism [ɪksˈpænʃənɪzəm] N espansionismo.
ex·pan·sion·ist [ɪksˈpænʃənɪst] ADJ espansionistico(-a).
ex·pan·sive [ɪksˈpænsɪv] ADJ (fig: sociable) espansivo(-a); (frm: extensive) considerevole.
ex·pan·sive·ly [ɪksˈpænsɪvlɪ] ADV (fig) in modo espansivo.
ex·pa·ti·ate [ɪksˈpeɪʃɪˌeɪt] VI (frm): **to expatiate on or upon** dilungarsi (su).
ex·pat·ri·ate [ɛksˈpætrɪˌeɪt] 1 N espatriato.
  2 ADJ espatriato(-a).
  3 VT espatriare.
ex·pect [ɪksˈpɛkt] 1 VT **a** (anticipate) aspettarsi, prevedere; (count on) contare su; (hope for) sperare in; (wait for: letter, guests, baby) aspettare; **it's easier than I expected** è più facile del previsto; **to expect to do sth** pensare or contare di fare qc; **I expected as much** me l'aspettavo; **we'll expect you for supper** ti aspettiamo per cena; **that was (only) to be expected** non potevamo che aspettarcelo; **I did not know what to expect** non sapevo che cosa aspettarmi; **as expected** come previsto; **I'll expect you when I see you** (fam) ci vediamo quando ci vediamo
  b (suppose) pensare, supporre; **I expect so** credo di sì; **yes, I expect it is** sì, non ne dubito

c (*require*): **to expect sth (from sb)** esigere qc (da qn); **to expect sb to do sth** pretendere *or* esigere che qn faccia qc; **I expect you to be punctual** esigo che tu sia puntuale; **you can't expect too much from him** non puoi pretendere troppo da lui; **what do you expect me to do about it?** cosa vuoi che ci faccia?.

2 VI: **to be expecting** (*a baby*) essere incinta *or* in stato interessante.

ex·pec·tan·cy [ɪks'pɛktənsɪ] N attesa; **life expectancy** speranza (media) di vita.

ex·pec·tant [ɪks'pɛktənt] ADJ (*person, crowd*) in attesa; (*look*) di attesa.

ex·pect·ant·ly [ɪks'pɛktəntlɪ] ADV (*look, listen*) con un'aria d'attesa; **the crowds waited expectantly** c'era un'aria di attesa tra la folla.

♦ **expectant mother** N gestante *f*.

ex·pec·ta·tion [ˌɛkspɛk'teɪʃən] N attesa, aspettativa; **there is little expectation of sunshine today** ci sono poche speranze che venga fuori il sole oggi; **in expectation of** in previsione di; **against** *or* **contrary to all expectation(s)** contro ogni aspettativa; **to come** *or* **live up to sb's expectations** rispondere alle aspettative di qn; **beyond (all) expectation** al di là di ogni aspettativa.

ex·pec·to·rant [ɪk'spɛktərənt] N (*Med*) espettorante *m*.

ex·pe·di·ence [ɪks'pi:dɪəns], **ex·pe·di·en·cy** [ɪk'pi:dɪənsɪ] N (*advisability*) convenienza, opportunità *f inv*; (*pej*) interesse personale; **for the sake of expedience** per una questione di convenienza.

ex·pe·di·ent [ɪks'pi:dɪənt] 1 N espediente *m*.

2 ADJ (*convenient, politic*) conveniente, opportuno(-a).

ex·pe·dite ['ɛkspɪdaɪt] VT (*frm: speed up*) accelerare; (: *official matter, legal matter*) sollecitare; (: *task*) affrettare.

ex·pe·di·tion [ˌɛkspɪ'dɪʃən] N spedizione *f*.

ex·pe·di·tion·ary force [ˌɛkspɪ'dɪʃənərɪ'fɔ:s] N (*Mil*) corpo di spedizione.

ex·pe·di·tious [ˌɛkspɪ'dɪʃəs] ADJ (*frm*) spedito(-a), sollecito (-a).

ex·pe·di·tious·ly [ˌɛkspɪ'dɪʃəslɪ] ADV (*frm*) speditamente, sollecitamente.

ex·pel [ɪks'pɛl] VT espellere.

ex·pend [ɪks'pɛnd] VT (*frm: money*) spendere; (: *time, effort, energy*) consacrare; (: *use up*) consumare.

ex·pend·able [ɪks'pɛndəbl] ADJ sacrificabile.

ex·pen·di·ture [ɪks'pɛndɪtʃə'] N (*of money etc*) spesa; (*of time, effort*) dispendio; **an item of expenditure** una spesa.

ex·pense [ɪks'pɛns] N (*cost*) spesa; **at the expense of** (*fig*) a spese di; **at the expense of his life** a prezzo della vita; **at great expense** con grande impiego di mezzi; **at my expense** a mie spese; (*fig*) alle mie spalle; **to go to the expense (of)** sobbarcarsi la spesa (di); **regardless of expense** senza badare a spese; **to put sb to the expense of** fare affrontare a qn la spesa di; **to meet the expense of** affrontare la spesa di.

♦ **expense account** N conto *m* spese *inv*.

ex·penses [ɪks'pɛnsɪz] NPL (*Comm*) spese *fpl*; **all expenses paid** spesato(-a) di tutto; **it's on expenses** paga la ditta.

ex·pen·sive [ɪks'pɛnsɪv] ADJ (*dear*) caro(-a); (*costly*) costoso(-a); (*fig: victory*) a caro prezzo; **she has expensive tastes** le piacciono le cose costose.

ex·pen·sive·ly [ɪks'pɛnsɪvlɪ] ADV (*dress*) in modo costoso.

ex·pen·sive·ness [ɪks'pɛnsɪvnɪs] N dispendiosità.

ex·peri·ence [ɪks'pɪərɪəns] 1 N (*all senses*) esperienza; **to learn by experience** imparare per esperienza; **I know from bitter experience** ho imparato a mie spese; **he has no experience of grief/being out of work** non sa che cosa voglia dire il dolore/restare senza lavoro; **she has plenty of experience** ha moltissima esperienza; **have you any previous experience?** ha esperienza in questo campo?; **practical/teaching experience** esperienza pratica/d'insegnamento; **to have a pleasant/frightening experience** avere un'esperienza piacevole/terrificante; **it was quite an experience** (*also iro*) è stata una bella esperienza.

2 VT (*feel: emotions, sensations, pleasure*) provare; (*suffer: defeat, losses, hardship etc*) subire; **she experiences some difficulty in walking** ha qualche difficoltà a camminare.

ex·peri·enced [ɪks'pɪərɪənst] ADJ (*teacher, lawyer*) che ha esperienza; (*driver, politician*) consumato(-a); **experienced (in)** esperto(-a) (di).

ex·peri·ment [*n* ɪks'pɛrɪˌmənt; *vb* ɪks'pɛrɪmɛnt] 1 N esperimento; **to perform** *or* **carry out an experiment** fare un esperimento; **as an experiment** a titolo di esperimento.

2 VI fare un esperimento, sperimentare; **to experiment with a new vaccine** sperimentare un nuovo vaccino.

ex·peri·men·tal [ɪks,pɛrɪ'mɛntl] ADJ sperimentale; **the process is still at the experimental stage** il procedimento è ancora allo stadio sperimentale.

ex·peri·men·tal·ly [ɪks,pɛrɪ'mɛntəlɪ] ADV sperimentalmente.

ex·peri·men·ta·tion [ɪks,pɛrɪmɛn'teɪʃən] N sperimentazione *f*.

ex·peri·ment·er [ɪk'spɛrɪməntə'] N sperimentatore(-trice).

ex·pert ['ɛkspɜ:t] 1 ADJ (*gen*) esperto(-a); (*advice, help*) da esperto; **expert in** *or* **at doing sth** esperto(-a) nel fare qc.

2 N esperto(-a); **an expert on sth/in** *or* **at doing sth** un(a) esperto(-a) di qc/nel fare qc.

♦ **expert evidence** N (*Law*) testimonianza di perito.

ex·per·tise [ˌɛkspə'ti:z] N (*frm*) competenza.

ex·pert·ly ['ɛkspɜ:tlɪ] ADV abilmente, con perizia.

♦ **expert opinion** N (*Law*) perizia.

♦ **expert witness** N (*Law*) perito.

ex·pi·ate ['ɛkspɪˌeɪt] VT (*fam*) espiare.

ex·pi·ra·tion [ˌɛkspɪ'reɪʃən] N **a** (*frm: end*) scadenza; **after the expiration of a year** allo scadere di un anno **b** (*Med*) espirazione *f*.

ex·pire [ɪks'paɪə'] VI (*document, time limit*) scadere; (*die*) spirare.

ex·pi·ry [ɪks'paɪərɪ] N scadenza.

ex·plain [ɪks'pleɪn] VT (*gen*) spiegare; (*mystery*) chiarire; **to explain o.s.** spiegarsi

► **explain away** VT cercare di dare una motivazione a.

ex·plain·able [ɪks'pleɪnəbl] ADJ spiegabile.

ex·pla·na·tion [ˌɛksplə'neɪʃən] N spiegazione *f*; **to find an explanation for sth** trovare una spiegazione per qc; **what have you to say in explanation?** qual è la sua giustificazione?

ex·plana·tory [ɪks'plænətərɪ] ADJ (*words*) di spiegazione; (*notes*) esplicativo(-a).

ex·ple·tive [ɪks'pli:tɪv] N (*frm: swear word*) imprecazione *f*.

ex·pli·cable [ɛks'plɪkəbəl] ADJ (*frm*) spiegabile; **for no explicable reason** senza un motivo plausibile.

ex·plic·it [ɪks'plɪsɪt] ADJ (*definite*) netto(-a); (*instructions, intention, denial*) esplicito(-a); (*details*) chiaro(-a).

ex·plic·it·ly [ɪk'splɪsɪtlɪ] ADV (*see adj*) nettamente; esplicitamente; chiaramente.

ex·plode [ɪks'pləʊd] 1 VI esplodere; **to explode with laughter** scoppiare dalle risa.

2 VT far esplodere; (*fig: theory*) demolire; **to explode a myth** distruggere un mito; **exploded drawing** disegno

esploso.

ex·ploit [vb ıks'plɔıt; n 'ɛksplɔıt] 1 VT sfruttare.
2 N impresa.

ex·ploit·able [ɛks'plɔıtəbəl] ADJ sfruttabile.

ex·ploi·ta·tion [ˌɛksplɔı'teıʃən] N sfruttamento.

ex·ploita·tive [ɛks'plɔıtətıv] ADJ (frm) profittatore(-trice).

ex·ploit·er [ɛks'plɔıtəʳ] N sfruttatore(-trice); **they were the first exploiters of Lebanon timber** furono i primi a sfruttare il legname del Libano.

ex·plo·ra·tion [ˌɛksplɔː'reıʃən] N esplorazione f.

ex·plora·tory [ıks'plɒrətərı] ADJ (talks) esplorativo(-a); (expedition) d'esplorazione; (step, discussion) preliminare; **exploratory operation** (Med) intervento esplorativo.

ex·plore [ıks'plɔː'] VT (gen, Med) esplorare; (fig: problems, subject, possibilities) esaminare; **to explore every avenue** sondare tutte le possibilità.

ex·plor·er [ıks'plɔːrəʳ] N esploratore(-trice).

ex·plo·sion [ıks'pləʊʒən] N (also fig) esplosione f.

ex·plo·sive [ıks'pləʊzıv] 1 ADJ (also fig) esplosivo(-a).
2 N esplosivo.

ex·po·nent [ıks'pəʊnənt] N **a** (person) esponente m/f **b** (Math) esponente m.

ex·po·nen·tial [ˌɛkspəʊ'nɛnʃəl] ADJ (Math, also fig) esponenziale.

ex·port [n 'ɛkspɔːt; vb ıks'pɔːt] 1 N esportazione f; (item) merce f d'esportazione.
2 VT esportare.
3 ADJ (goods, permit, duty) d'esportazione.

ex·por·ta·tion [ˌɛkspɔː'teıʃən] N esportazione f.

♦ **export drive** N campagna a favore dell'esportazione.

ex·port·er [ıks'pɔːtəʳ] N esportatore(-trice).

♦ **export licence** N licenza d'esportazione.

♦ **export manager** N dirigente m/f responsabile dei rapporti con i mercati esteri.

♦ **export trade** N esportazioni fpl.

ex·pose [ıks'pəʊz] VT (gen, also Phot) esporre; (uncover) scoprire; (sexual parts) esibire; (fig: reveal: plot) rivelare; (: criminal) smascherare; (one's ignorance) mettere a nudo; **to be exposed to view** offrirsi alla vista; **to expose sb/o.s. to ridicule** esporre qn/esporsi al ridicolo; **to expose o.s.** (indecently) fare l'esibizionista.

ex·posed [ıks'pəʊzd] ADJ (land, house, town) esposto(-a); (Elec: wire, Mil: terrain, country) scoperto(-a); (pipe, beam) a vista; **as a politician, he is in a very exposed position** come politico, è in una posizione molto vulnerabile.

ex·po·si·tion [ˌɛkspə'zıʃən] N (frm) esposizione f.

ex·pos·tu·late [ıks'pɒstjʊˌleıt] VI (frm): **to expostulate with sb about sth** fare le proprie rimostranze a qn per qc.

ex·pos·tu·la·tion [ıksˌpɒstjʊ'leıʃən] N (frm) rimostranza.

ex·po·sure [ıks'pəʊʒəʳ] N (gen) esposizione f; (of plot) smascheramento; (Phot) esposizione f; (: photo) posa; (Med) assideramento; **to die of exposure** morire assiderato(-a); **to threaten sb with exposure** minacciare di denunciare qn.

♦ **exposure meter** N (Phot) esposimetro.

ex·pound [ıks'paʊnd] VT (theory, text) spiegare; (one's views) esporre.

ex·press [ıks'prɛs] 1 ADJ (all senses) espresso(-a); **express letter** espresso.
2 ADV: **to send sth express** spedire qc per espresso.
3 N (also: **express train**) espresso.
4 VT esprimere; **to express o.s** esprimersi.

ex·pres·sion [ıks'prɛʃən] N (all senses) espressione f; **set expression** modo di dire.

ex·pres·sion·ism [ıks'prɛʃənızəm] N espressionismo.

ex·pres·sion·ist [ık'sprɛʃənıst] ADJ, N espressionista (m/f).

ex·pres·sion·less [ık'sprɛʃənlıs] ADJ (pej: face) impassibile; (: of artistic performance) senza sentimento; **an expressionless voice** una voce che non tradisce (or tradiva) emozioni.

ex·pres·sive [ıks'prɛsıv] ADJ (look, face, language) espressivo(-a); (gesture) eloquente.

ex·pres·sive·ly [ıks'prɛsıvlı] ADV (see adj) in modo espressivo; in modo eloquente.

ex·press·ly [ıks'prɛslı] ADV espressamente.

ex·press·way [ıks'prɛsˌweı] N (esp Am) autostrada urbana.

ex·pro·pri·ate [ɛks'prəʊprıˌeıt] VT espropriare.

ex·pul·sion [ıks'pʌlʃən] N espulsione f.

♦ **expulsion order** N ordine m di espulsione.

ex·punge [ık'spʌndʒ] VT (frm) espungere.

ex·pur·gate ['ɛkspəˌgeıt] VT (frm) espurgare.

ex·quis·ite [ıks'kwızıt] ADJ (gen) squisito(-a); (manners, sensibility, charm) raffinato(-a); (sense of humour) sottile; (pain) acuto(-a); (joy, pleasure) vivo(-a).

ex·quis·ite·ly [ıks'kwızıtlı] ADV **a** (paint, embroider) squisitamente; (dress) in modo raffinato **b** (extremely) estremamente.

♦ **ex-serviceman** [ˌɛks'sɜ:vısmən] N (Brit) ex combattente m.

ext. ABBR (Telec: = extension) int. (= interno).

ex·tant [ɛks'tænt] ADJ (frm) esistente.

ex·tem·po·re [ıks'tɛmpərı] (frm) 1 ADV senza preparazione.
2 ADJ estemporaneo(-a).

ex·tem·po·rize, ex·tem·po·rise [ıks'tɛmpəˌraız] VI (frm) improvvisare.

ex·tend [ıks'tɛnd] 1 VT **a** (frm: stretch out: hand, arm) tendere; (: offer: friendship, help, hospitality) offrire; (: thanks, condolences, welcome) porgere; (: invitation) estendere; (Fin: credit) accordare
b (prolong: road, line, deadline) prolungare; (: visit) protrarre; (enlarge: building, business, vocabulary) ampliare; (knowledge, research) approfondire; (powers) estendere; (frontiers) allargare; **extended walk/trot** (Horse-riding) passo/trotto allungato.
2 VI (land, wall): **to extend to** or **as far as** estendersi fino a; **to extend to/for** (term, meeting) protrarsi fino a/per; **the contract extends to/for ...** il contratto è valido fino a/per... .

ex·tend·able [ık'stɛndəbəl] ADJ (ladder, tentacles) allungabile; (tenancy) prorogabile.

ex·ten·sion [ıks'tɛnʃən] N (for table, electric flex) prolunga; (of road, term) prolungamento; (of contract, deadline) proroga; (building) annesso; (telephone: in private house) derivazione f; (: in office) interno; **extension 3718** interno 3718; **to have an extension built onto one's house** far ingrandire la casa.

♦ **extension cable,** (Brit) **extension lead,** (Am) **extension cord** N (Elec) prolunga.

♦ **extension ladder** N scala allungabile.

ex·ten·sive [ıks'tɛnsıv] ADJ (grounds, forest, damage) vasto (-a), esteso(-a); (knowledge, research) approfondito(-a); (inquiries, reforms, investments) su vasta scala; (use) largo(-a); (alterations) radicale; **extensive farming** agricoltura estensiva.

ex·ten·sive·ly [ıks'tɛnsıvlı] ADV (altered, damaged etc) radi-

calmente; (*study, investigate*) a fondo; (*use, travel*)
molto; **he's travelled extensively** ha viaggiato molto.
ex·tent [ɪksˈtɛnt] N (*of land*) estensione *f*; (*of road*)
lunghezza; (*of knowledge, activities, power*) portata;
(*degree: of damage, loss*) proporzioni *fpl*; **to what extent**
in che misura, fino a che punto; **to a certain/large
extent** in certa/larga misura; **to such an extent that** a tal
punto che; **to the extent of** fino al punto di; **to some
extent** fino a un certo punto.
ex·ten·u·at·ing [ɪksˈtɛnjʊˌeɪtɪŋ] ADJ (*frm*): **extenuating
circumstances** (circostanze) attenuanti *fpl*.
ex·ten·u·ation [ɪkˌstɛnjʊˈeɪʃən] N attenuante *f*.
ex·te·ri·or [ɪksˈtɪərɪə'] 1 ADJ esterno(-a), esteriore.
   2 N (*of house, box*) esterno; (*of person*) aspetto esteriore;
on the exterior all'esterno; (*fig*) in apparenza.
ex·ter·mi·nate [ɪksˈtɜːmɪˌneɪt] VT sterminare.
ex·ter·mi·na·tion [ɪksˌtɜːmɪˈneɪʃən] N sterminio.
ex·ter·mi·na·tor [ɪkˈstɜːmɪˌneɪtə'] N addetto(-a) alla
disinfestazione.
ex·ter·nal [ɛksˈtɜːnl] 1 ADJ (*walls etc*) esterno(-a); (*appearance*) esteriore; **external affairs** (*Pol*) affari *mpl*
esteri; **for external use only** (*Med*) solo per uso esterno;
external examiner esaminatore(-trice) esterno(-a);
external processes (*Geol*) fenomeni *mpl* esogeni.
   2 N: **the externals** le apparenze.
ex·ter·nal·ize [ɪkˈstɜːnəˌlaɪz] VT (*frm*) esternare.
ex·ter·nal·ly [ɛksˈtɜːnəlɪ] ADV dall'esterno, esternamente.
ex·tinct [ɪksˈtɪŋkt] ADJ (*volcano*) spento(-a), inattivo(-a);
(*animal, race*) estinto(-a).
ex·tinc·tion [ɪksˈtɪŋkʃən] N (*of fire*) estinzione *f*, spegnimento; (*of race*) estinzione *f*.
ex·tin·guish [ɪksˈtɪŋgwɪʃ] VT (*frm: fire*) estinguere,
spegnere; (: *cigarette*) spegnere; (*fig*) annientare.
ex·tin·guish·er [ɪksˈtɪŋgwɪʃə'] N estintore *m*.
ex·tol, (*Am*) **ex·toll** [ɪksˈtəʊl] VT (*frm: merits, virtues*)
magnificare; (*person*) celebrare.
ex·tort [ɪksˈtɔːt] VT: **to extort (from)** (*money, confession*)
estorcere a; (*promise*) strappare a.
ex·tor·tion [ɪksˈtɔːʃən] N estorsione *f*.
ex·tor·tion·ate [ɪksˈtɔːʃənɪt] ADJ esorbitante.
ex·tra [ˈɛkstrə] 1 ADJ in più; **she needs extra help** ha
bisogno di maggior aiuto; **an extra charge** un supplemento; **wine is extra** il vino è escluso; **take extra care!**
stai molto attento!; **for extra safety** per maggior sicurezza; **extra transport** corse *fpl* supplementari *or*
straordinarie.
   2 ADV (*specially*) eccezionalmente; (*in addition: pay,
charge*) di più; **extra fine** extra sottile; **wine will cost
extra** il vino è extra; **extra large sizes** taglie *fpl* forti.
   3 N extra *m inv*; (*Cine, Theatre: actor*) comparsa.
extra... PREF extra... .
ex·tract [*n* ˈɛkstrækt; *vb* ɪksˈtrækt] 1 N (*from book*) brano;
(*from film*) spezzone *m*; (*Culin, Chem*) estratto.
   2 VT: **to extract (from)** (*take out*) estrarre (da); (*obtain:
promise, confession, money*) estorcere a, strappare a;
(*select: from book etc*) stralciare (da).
ex·trac·tion [ɪksˈtrækʃən] N estrazione *f*; (*descent*) origine
f; **of German extraction** di origine tedesca.
ex·trac·tor fan [ɪkˈstræktəˌfæn] N aspiratore *m*.
extra·cur·ricu·lar [ˈɛkstrəkəˈrɪkjʊlə'] ADJ (*Scol*) parascolastico.
extra·dite [ˈɛkstrəˌdaɪt] VT: **to extradite sb (from/to)**
estradare qn (da/in).
extra·di·tion [ˌɛkstrəˈdɪʃən] N estradizione *f*.
extra·mari·tal [ˈɛkstrəˈmærɪtl] ADJ extraconiugale.

extra·mu·ral [ˈɛkstrəˈmjʊərəl] ADJ (*Univ*): **extramural
course** *corso libero tenuto da docenti accreditati presso
l'università.*
extra·neous [ɪksˈtreɪnɪəs] ADJ (*frm*): **extraneous (to)** estra-
neo(-a) (a).
extraor·di·nari·ly [ɪksˈtrɔːdnrɪlɪ] ADV straordinariamente.
extraor·di·nary [ɪksˈtrɔːdnrɪ] ADJ (*gen*) straordinario(-a);
(*very strange*) strano(-a); **the extraordinary thing is that**
... la cosa strana è che... .
♦ **extraordinary general meeting** N assemblea generale straordinaria.
ex·trapo·late [ɛksˈtræpəˌleɪt] VT estrapolare.
ex·trapo·la·tion [ˌɪkstræpəʊˈleɪʃən] N estrapolazione *f*.
extra·sen·so·ry per·cep·tion [ˈɛkstrəˈsɛnsərɪpəsɛpʃən] N
percezione *f* extrasensoriale.
extra·ter·res·trial [ˌɛkstrətɪˈrɛstrɪəl] ADJ extraterrestre.
♦ **extra time** N (*Ftbl*) tempo supplementare.
ex·trava·gance [ɪksˈtrævəgəns] N (*excessive spending*)
sperpero; (*wastefulness*) spreco; (*thing bought*) stravaganza.
ex·trava·gant [ɪksˈtrævəgənt] ADJ stravagante; (*spending,
claim, opinion*) eccessivo(-a); (*lavish: person*) prodigo
(-a); (: *tastes*) dispendioso(-a); (*exaggerated: praise*)
esagerato(-a); (: *prices*) esorbitante; **don't be extravagant with the butter** non esagerare con il burro.
ex·trava·gant·ly [ɪksˈtrævəgəntlɪ] ADV (*lavishly*) in modo
dispendioso; (*exaggeratedly*) esageratamente.
ex·trava·gan·za [ɪkˌstrævəˈgænzə] N rappresentazione *f*
spettacolare.
ex·treme [ɪksˈtriːm] 1 ADJ estremo(-a); (*sorrow, anger*)
profondo(-a); **the extreme left/right** (*Pol*) l'estrema
sinistra/destra; **the extreme end of sth** l'estremità di qc;
there's no need to be so extreme non c'è bisogno di
essere così drastico.
   2 N estremo; **extremes of temperature** gli estremi *mpl*
della scala termica; **dangerous in the extreme** estremamente pericoloso(-a); **to go/be driven to extremes**
arrivare/essere spinto(-a) agli estremi.
ex·treme·ly [ɪksˈtriːmlɪ] ADV estremamente.
ex·trem·ism [ɪksˈtriːmɪzəm] N estremismo.
ex·trem·ist [ɪksˈtriːmɪst] ADJ, N estremista (*m/f*).
ex·trem·ity [ɪksˈtrɛmɪtɪ] N (*gen*) estremità *f inv*; (*fig: of
despair etc*) culmine.
ex·tri·cate [ˈɛkstrɪˌkeɪt] VT (*object*) liberare; **to extricate
sth (from)** districare qc (da); **to extricate sb/o.s. from a
difficult situation** togliere qn/togliersi d'impaccio.
extro·vert [ˈɛkstrəʊvɜːt] ADJ, N estroverso(-a).
exu·ber·ance [ɪgˈzuːbərəns] N esuberanza.
exu·ber·ant [ɪgˈzuːbərənt] ADJ esuberante.
exu·ber·ant·ly [ɪgˈzuːbərəntlɪ] ADV in modo esuberante.
ex·ude [ɪgˈzjuːd] VT, VI trasudare, stillare; (*fig*) emanare.
ex·ult [ɪgˈzʌlt] VI (*frm*): **to exult in** *or* **over** *or* **at** esultare per.
ex·ult·ant [ɪgˈzʌltənt] ADJ (*frm: person, smile*) esultante; (:
shout, expression) di giubilo.
ex·ul·ta·tion [ˌɛgzʌlˈteɪʃən] N giubilo; **in exultation** per la
gioia.
eye [aɪ] 1 N occhio; (*of needle*) cruna; (*for hook*) occhiello;
he gave him a black eye gli ha fatto un occhio nero; **eyes
right/left!** (*Mil*) attenti a destra/sinistra!; **as far as the
eye can see** a perdita d'occhio; **it happened before my
very eyes** mi è successo proprio sotto gli occhi; **I saw it
with my own eyes** l'ho visto con i miei occhi; **keep your
eyes on the road ahead!** guarda la strada!; **I could hardly
keep my eyes open** non riuscivo a tenere gli occhi

aperti; **he didn't take his eyes off her** non le toglieva gli occhi di dosso; **to catch sb's eye** attirare l'attenzione di qn; **to look sb (straight) in the eye** guardare qn (dritto) negli occhi; **to be in the public eye** essere in vista; **in the eyes of** agli occhi di; **under the (watchful) eye of** sotto lo sguardo (vigile) di; **to keep an eye on sb/sth** tenere d'occhio qn/qc; **to keep an eye on things** (*fam*) tenere d'occhio la situazione; **to keep an eye out for sth/sb** OR **one's eyes open for sth/sb** tenere gli occhi aperti per trovare qc/qn; **to look at sth with the eye of an expert** guardare qc con l'occhio dell'esperto; **with an eye to sth** in vista di qc; **with an eye to doing sth** (*Brit*) con l'idea di fare qc; **with one's eyes (wide) open** (*fig*) perfettamente conscio(-a) di ciò che si fa; **to shut one's eyes to sth** (*fig*: *to the truth, dangers, evidence*) chiudere gli occhi di fronte a qc; (: *to sb's shortcomings*) chiudere un occhio su qc; **to be up to one's eyes in work** essere pieno(-a) di lavoro fin sopra i capelli; **to have an eye for sth** avere occhio per qc; **there's more to this than meets the eye** non è così semplice come sembra; **I don't see eye to eye with him** non condivido il suo punto di vista; **it's five years since I last set** *or* **laid eyes on him** sono cinque anni che non lo vedo; **use your eyes!** (*fam*) guarda un po' meglio!; **that's one in the eye for him** (*fig fam*) gli sta bene; **to make eyes at sb** (*fam*) fare gli occhi dolci a qn; **she was all eyes** era tutt'occhi; **an eye for an eye and a tooth for a tooth** occhio per occhio dente per dente.

2 VT (*look at carefully*) scrutare; (*ogle*) adocchiare

▶ **eye up** VT + ADV (*fam*) occhieggiare; **he's been eyeing me up all evening** non mi ha staccato gli occhi di dosso per tutta la sera.

eye·ball ['aɪˌbɔːl] N bulbo oculare; **eyeball to eyeball** (*fig*) faccia a faccia.

eye·bath ['aɪˌbɑːθ], (*Am*) **eye cup** N occhino.

eye·brow ['aɪˌbraʊ] N sopracciglio; **to raise one's eyebrows** inarcare le sopracciglia.

♦ **eyebrow pencil** N matita per le sopracciglia.

♦ **eyebrow tweezers** NPL pinzette *fpl* per le sopracciglia.

♦ **eye-catching** ['aɪˌkætʃɪŋ] ADJ che attira l'attenzione.

♦ **eye clinic** N studio oculistico.

♦ **eye cup** N = eyebath.

eye·drops ['aɪˌdrɒps] N collirio.

eye·ful ['aɪful] N (*fam*): **to get an eyeful (of)** avere l'occasione di dare una bella sbirciata.

eye·glass ['aɪˌglɑs] N monocolo.

eye·lash ['aɪˌlæʃ] N ciglio.

eye·let ['aɪlɪt] N occhiello.

eye·lev·el ['aɪˌlɛvl] ADJ all'altezza degli occhi.

eye·lid ['aɪˌlɪd] N palpebra.

eye·liner ['aɪˌlaɪnə] N eye-liner *m inv*.

♦ **eye-opener** ['aɪˌəʊpnə] N rivelazione *f*.

eye·shade ['aɪˌʃeɪd] N visiera.

eye·shadow ['aɪˌʃædəʊ] N ombretto.

eye·sight ['aɪˌsaɪt] N vista.

eye·sore ['aɪˌsɔː] N pugno in un occhio.

eye·strain ['aɪˌstreɪn] N: **to get eyestrain** stancarsi gli occhi.

eye·tooth [ˌaɪ'tuːθ] N (*pl* -teeth) canino superiore; **to give one's eye-teeth for sth/to do sth** (*fam fig*) dare non so che cosa per qc/per fare qc.

eye·wash ['aɪˌwɒʃ] N (*liquid*) collirio; (*fam*: *nonsense*) balle *fpl*.

eye·witness ['aɪˌwɪtnɪs] N testimone *m/f* oculare.

ey·rie ['ɪərɪ] N nido d'aquila.

F

F, f [ɛf] N **a** (*letter*) F, f *form inv*; **F for Frederick**, (*Am*) **F for fox** ≈ F come Firenze **b** (*Mus*): **F fa** *m*.

F. ABBR (= *Fahrenheit*) F.

FA [ɛf'eɪ] N ABBR (*Brit*)= *Football Association*.

fa [fɑː] N (*Mus*) fa *m inv*.

FAA [ˌɛfeɪ'eɪ] N ABBR (*Am*)= *Federal Aviation Administration*.

fa·ble ['feɪbl] N favola.

fa·bled ['feɪbld] ADJ favoloso(-a), leggendario(-a).

fab·ric ['fæbrɪk] N **a** (*cloth*) stoffa, tessuto **b** (*Archit*) struttura; **the fabric of society** (*fig*) la struttura della società.

fab·ri·cate ['fæbrɪkeɪt] VT fabbricare.

fab·ri·ca·tion [ˌfæbrɪ'keɪʃən] N fabbricazione *f*.

♦ **fabric ribbon** N (*Typ*) nastro dattilografico.

fabu·lous ['fæbjʊləs] ADJ (*mythical*) favoloso(-a); (*fam: wonderful*) meraviglioso(-a), fantastico(-a).

fabu·lous·ly ['fæbjʊləslɪ] ADV favolosamente.

fa·çade, fa·cade [fə'sɑːd] N (*Archit*) facciata; (*fig*) facciata, apparenza.

face [feɪs] **1** N (*gen*) faccia; (*Anat*) faccia, volto, viso; (*expression*) faccia, espressione *f*; (*grimace*) smorfia; (*of dial, watch, clock*) quadrante *m*; (*surface: of the earth*) superficie *f*, faccia; (*of building*) facciata; (*of mountain, cliff*) parete *f*; **face down(wards)** (*person*) a faccia in giù, bocconi; (*object*) a faccia in giù; (*card*) coperto(-a); **face up(wards)** (*person, object*) a faccia in su; (*card*) scoperto (-a); **in the face of** (*difficulties etc*) di fronte a; **to laugh in sb's face** ridere in faccia a qn; **to look sb in the face** guardare qn in faccia; **to say sth to sb's face** dire qc in faccia a qn; **I told him to his face** gliel'ho detto in faccia; **you can shout till you're black** *or* **blue in the face** ... puoi urlare fino a sgolarti...; **don't show your face here again!** non farti più vedere qui!; **it's vanished off the face of the earth** è sparito(-a) dalla faccia della terra; **to have a good memory for faces** essere un(a) buon(a) fisionomista; **to pull a long face** fare la faccia lunga, fare il muso; **to keep a straight face** rimanere serio(-a); **to pull a face** fare una smorfia; **to make** *or* **pull faces (at sb)** fare le boccacce (a qn); **his face fell** (*fig*) ha fatto una facciata!; **on the face of it** a prima vista; **they put a brave face on it** hanno fatto buon viso a cattivo gioco; **to lose/save face** perdere/salvare la faccia.

2 VT **a** (*be facing, be opposite*) essere di fronte a; (*overlook: road*) dare su; (: *sea*) guardare verso; **face the wall!** girati verso il muro!; **to sit facing the engine** (*on train*) sedersi nella direzione della marcia; **the picture facing page 20** la figura a fianco di pagina 20; **the difficulties facing us** i problemi che ci aspettano

b (*confront: attacker, danger*) affrontare, fronteggiare; **I can't face him** (*ashamed*) non ho il coraggio di guardarlo in faccia; (*reluctant*) non ho nessuna voglia di vederlo; **I can't face doing it** non ho nessuna voglia di farlo; **to face the music** (*fig*) far fronte alla tempesta; **to face facts** affrontare la realtà; **to face the fact that** ... riconoscere *or* ammettere che...; **we are faced with serious problems** ci troviamo di fronte a gravi problemi; **let's face it!** (*fam*) diciamocelo chiaramente!

c (*Tech*) rivestire, ricoprire; **a wall faced with concrete** un muro rivestito di cemento

3 VI (*person*): **to face this way** girarsi da questa parte; **it faces east/towards the east** è esposto(-a) a/guarda verso est

▶ **face down** VT + ADV (*Am, fig*): **to face sb down** sfidare qn

▶ **face out** VT + ADV (*Brit*) affrontare

▶ **face up to** VI + ADV + PREP (*difficulty etc*) affrontare, far fronte a; **to face up to the fact that** ... accettare che... .

♦ **face card** N (*Am*) figura.

♦ **face cloth** N (*Brit*) ≈ guanto di spugna.

♦ **face cream** N crema per il viso.

♦ **face flannel** N (*Brit*) ≈ guanto di spugna.

face·less ['feɪslɪs] ADJ anonimo(-a).

♦ **face lift** N lifting *m inv*; (*of façade, building*) ripulita, restauro.

♦ **face pack** N maschera di bellezza.

♦ **face powder** N cipria.

♦ **face-saver** [feɪseɪvəʳ] N: **it was clearly a face-saver on their part** l'hanno ovviamente fatto per salvarsi la faccia.

♦ **face-saving** ['feɪsˌseɪvɪŋ] ADJ che salva la faccia.

fac·et ['fæsɪt] N (*of gem*) sfaccettatura, faccetta; (*fig*)

sfaccettatura, aspetto, lato.

fa·cetious [fə'siːʃəs] ADJ faceto(-a); **don't be facetious** non fare lo spiritoso.

fa·cetious·ly [fə'siːʃəslɪ] ADV spiritosamente.

♦ **face-to-face** [ˌfeɪstə'feɪs] ADV, ADJ faccia a faccia, a quattr'occhi.

♦ **face value** N (of coin) valore m facciale or nominale; **to take sth at face value** (fig) giudicare qc dalle apparenze.

fa·cia ['feɪʃə] N = fascia.

fa·cial ['feɪʃəl] [1] ADJ del viso, facciale.
[2] N trattamento di bellezza per il viso.

fa·cial·ly ['feɪʃəlɪ] ADV di faccia.

fac·ile ['fæsaɪl] ADJ (gen pej: remark, answer) superficiale; (: victory) facile.

fa·cili·tate [fə'sɪlɪˌteɪt] VT facilitare, agevolare.

fa·cil·ity [fə'sɪlɪtɪ] N **a** (easiness) facilità; (skill) abilità; (with languages) predisposizione f **b** : **facilities** NPL (gen) servizi mpl; (educational, leisure) attrezzature fpl; (transport) mezzi mpl; **credit facilities** facilitazioni fpl di credito.

fac·ing ['feɪsɪŋ] N (Constr: of wall etc) rivestimento; (Sewing) passafino.

fac·simi·le [fæk'sɪmɪlɪ] N facsimile m inv.

♦ **facsimile machine** N facsimile m inv, telecopiatrice f.

♦ **facsimile publication** N pubblicazione f in facsimile.

fact [fækt] N fatto; **it's a fact that** ... è un dato di fatto che...; **to know for a fact that** ... sapere per certo che...; **the facts of life** (sex) i fatti riguardanti la vita sessuale; (realities) le realtà della vita; **facts and figures** dati mpl e cifre fpl; **fact and fiction** realtà e fantasia; **story founded on fact** storia basata sui fatti; **it has no basis in fact** non si basa su fatti realmente accaduti; **as a matter of fact** OR **in point of fact** per la verità; **the fact (of the matter) is that** ... la verità è che...; **in fact** in realtà.

♦ **fact-finding** ['fækt ˌfaɪndɪŋ] ADJ: **a fact-finding tour/ mission** un viaggio/una missione d'inchiesta.

fac·tion ['fækʃən] N fazione f.

fac·tion·al ['fækʃənəl] ADJ (fighting) tra fazioni.

fac·ti·tious [fæk'tɪʃəs] ADJ (frm) artificiale.

fac·tor ['fæktə'] [1] N **a** (fact) fattore m, elemento; **human factor** elemento umano; **safety factor** coefficiente m di sicurezza **b** (Math) fattore m **c** (Comm: company) società f inv di factoring; (: agent) factor m inv.
[2] VI (Comm) esercitare il factoring.

fac·torial [fæk'tɔːrɪəl] ADJ (Math) fattoriale.

fac·to·ry ['fæktərɪ] [1] N fabbrica, stabilimento.
[2] ADJ (inspector, work) di fabbrica.

♦ **factory farming** N (Brit) allevamento su scala industriale.

♦ **factory floor** N: **the factory floor** (workers) gli operai; (area) il reparto produzione; **on the factory floor** nel reparto produzione.

♦ **factory ship** N nave f fattoria inv.

fac·to·tum [fæk'təutəm] N factotum m/f inv.

fac·tual ['fæktjʊəl] ADJ (report, description) che si limita ai fatti; (error) che riguarda i fatti.

fac·tu·al·ly ['fæktjʊəlɪ] ADV riguardo ai fatti.

fac·ul·ty ['fækəltɪ] N facoltà f inv; (Am: teaching staff) corpo insegnante.

fad [fæd] N (fashion) moda, mania; (personal) capriccio, mania, fisima.

fad·dy ['fædɪ] ADJ capriccioso(-a); **to be a faddy eater** essere schizzinoso(-a).

fade [feɪd] VI **a** (flower) appassire; (colour, fabric) scolorire or scolorirsi, sbiadire or sbiadirsi

b (also: **fade away**: light) affievolirsi, attenuarsi; (: eyesight, hearing, memory) indebolirsi; (: hopes, smile) svanire; (: sounds) affievolirsi, attutirsi; (: person) deperire; (object): **to fade from sight** scomparire alla vista

▶ **fade in** [1] VT + ADV (TV, Cine) aprire in dissolvenza; (Radio: sound) aumentare gradualmente d'intensità.
[2] VI + ADV (TV, Cine) aprirsi in dissolvenza; (Radio) aumentare gradualmente d'intensità

▶ **fade out** [1] VT + ADV (TV, Cine) chiudere in dissolvenza; (Radio) diminuire gradualmente l'intensità di.
[2] VI + ADV (TV, Cine) chiudere in dissolvenza; (Radio) diminuire gradualmente d'intensità.

fad·ed ['feɪdɪd] ADJ (material) scolorito(-a); (flower, beauty) sfiorito(-a).

♦ **fade-in** ['feɪd ɪn] N (Cine) dissolvenza in apertura; (Radio) aumento graduale del suono.

♦ **fade-out** ['feɪd ˌaʊt] N (Cine) dissolvenza in chiusura; (Radio) diminuzione f graduale del suono.

fae·ces, (Am) **fe·ces** ['fiːsiːz] NPL feci fpl.

fag¹ [fæg] [1] N **a** (Brit fam: effort, job, chore) faticata, sfacchinata **b** (Brit: Scol) studente che fa piccoli servizi ad uno più anziano.
[2] VT (fam: also: **fag out**) stancare, affaticare.

fag² [fæg] N (Brit fam: cigarette) sigaretta, cicca.

fag³ [fæg] N (Am offensive) = **faggot¹**.

♦ **fag end** N fine f, sgoccioli mpl; (Brit fam: of cigarette) mozzicone m, cicca.

fagged [fægd] ADJ (Brit fam: also: **fagged out**) stanco(-a) morto(-a).

fag·got¹ ['fægət] N (Am offensive) frocio (offensivo).

fag·got² ['fægət] N **a** (wood) fascina **b** (Brit Culin): **faggots** NPL polpette a base di fegato di maiale.

fah [fɑː] N (Mus) fa m inv.

Fahr·en·heit ['færənhaɪt] ADJ Fahrenheit inv; **Fahrenheit scale** scala Fahrenheit.

fail [feɪl] [1] VI **a** (gen) fallire; (in exam: candidate) essere respinto(-a) or bocciato(-a); (show, play) essere un fiasco; **to fail in one's duty** mancare al proprio dovere
b (power, light, supplies) mancare; (crops) andare perduto(-a); (sight, light) indebolirsi; (strength, health) venire a mancare; (engine) fermarsi; (brakes) non funzionare.
[2] VT **a** (exam, subject) non superare, essere bocciato (-a) in; (candidate) respingere, bocciare, rimandare
b (subj: person, memory, nerve) abbandonare, mancare a; **don't fail me!** non deludermi!; **his courage failed him** gli è mancato il coraggio; **words fail me!** mi mancano le parole!
c : **to fail to do sth** (neglect) non fare qc, mancare di fare qc; (be unable) non riuscire a fare qc; **I fail to see why/what** etc non vedo perché/che cosa etc.
[3] N: **without fail** senza fallo, senz'altro.

failed [feɪld] ADJ fallito(-a).

fail·ing ['feɪlɪŋ] [1] PREP in mancanza di; **failing that** se questo non è possibile.
[2] N difetto.

fail·safe ['feɪlˌseɪf] ADJ (device etc) di sicurezza.

fail·ure ['feɪljə'] N (gen) fallimento; (in exam) bocciatura; (of crops) perdita; (breakdown) guasto, avaria; (person) fallito(-a); (omission): **his failure to come/answer** il fatto che non sia venuto/abbia risposto; **to end in failure** fallire; **it was a complete failure** è stato un vero fiasco; **failure rate** (gen) numero di insuccessi; (Scol) numero di respinti.

faint [feɪnt] [1] ADJ (comp **-er**, superl **-est**) (smell, breeze,

trace) leggero(-a); (*outline, mark*) indistinto(-a); (*sound, voice*) fievole, debole; (*hope*) debole; (*idea, recollection, resemblance*) vago(-a); **to feel faint** sentirsi svenire; **I haven't the faintest (idea)** (*fam*) non ne ho la più pallida idea; **faint with hunger** debole per la fame.

2 N svenimento.

3 VI: **to faint (from)** svenire (da).

♦ **faint-hearted** [ˌfeɪntˈhɑːtɪd] 1 ADJ pusillanime.

2 NPL: **the faint-hearted** tipi impressionabili.

faint·ly [ˈfeɪntlɪ] ADV (*call, say, shine, smile*) debolmente; (*write, mark*) leggermente; **faintly reminiscent of** che ricorda vagamente.

faint·ness [ˈfeɪntnɪs] N (*of voice, sound etc*) debolezza.

fair¹ [fɛəʳ] 1 ADJ (*comp* **-er,** *superl* **-est**) a (*person, decision etc*) giusto(-a), equo(-a); (*hearing*) imparziale; (*sample*) rappresentativo(-a); (*fight, competition, match*) leale; **it's not fair!** non è giusto!; **to be fair (to her)** ... per essere giusti (nei suoi confronti)...; **it's only fair that ...** è più che giusto che...; **it's fair to say that ...** bisogna riconoscere che...; **fair enough!** d'accordo!, va bene!; **by fair means** *or* **foul** con ogni mezzo; **his fair share of** la sua buona parte di

b (*reasonable, average*: *work, result*) discreto(-a); **he has a fair chance** *or* **hope of success** ha buone probabilità di riuscire

c (*quite large*: *sum*) discreto(-a), bello(-a), considerevole; (: *speed, pace*) buono(-a); **a fair amount of** un bel po' di

d (*light-coloured*: *hair, person*) biondo(-a); (: *complexion, skin*) chiaro(-a)

e (*fine*: *weather*) bello(-a).

2 ADV: **to play fair** giocare correttamente; **to act/win fair and square** agire/vincere onestamente; **the ball hit me fair and square in the face** la palla mi ha colpito in piena faccia.

fair² [fɛəʳ] N (*market*) fiera, mercato; (*trade fair*) fiera campionaria; (*Brit: funfair*) luna park *m inv*.

♦ **fair copy** N bella copia.

♦ **fair game** N: **to be fair game** (*person*) essere bersaglio legittimo.

fair·ground [ˈfɛəˌgraʊnd] N luna park *m inv*.

♦ **fair-haired** [ˌfɛəˈhɛəd] ADJ (*person*) biondo(-a).

fair·ly [ˈfɛəlɪ] ADV a (*justly*) in modo imparziale *or* equo, equamente; (*according to the rules*) lealmente, correttamente b (*quite*) abbastanza, piuttosto; **I'm fairly sure** sono abbastanza sicuro; **fairly good** discreto(-a) c (*fam*: *utterly*) completamente; **she was fairly raging** era completamente fuori di sé.

♦ **fair-minded** [ˈfɛəˈmaɪndɪd] ADJ equo(-a), imparziale.

fair·ness [ˈfɛənɪs] N a onestà, equità, giustizia; (*of decision*) imparzialità; **in all fairness** per essere giusti, a dire il vero; **in (all) fairness to him** per essere giusti nei suoi confronti b (*of hair, skin*) chiarezza.

♦ **fair play** N correttezza.

♦ **fair sex** N (*old, hum*): **the fair sex** il gentil sesso.

♦ **fair-sized** [ˈfɛəˈsaɪzd] ADJ (*crowd, audience*) numeroso (-a); (*piece*) bello(-a).

♦ **fair-skinned** [ˌfɛəˈskɪnd] ADJ di carnagione chiara.

fair·way [ˈfɛəˌweɪ] N: **the fairway** (*Golf*) il fairway *m inv*.

fairy [ˈfɛərɪ] N a fata; **fairy queen** regina delle fate b (*offensive*: *homosexual*) finocchio.

♦ **fairy godmother** N fata buona.

fairy·land [ˈfɛərɪˌlænd] N paese *m* delle fate.

♦ **fairy lights** NPL (*Brit*) lanternine *fpl* colorate.

♦ **fairy tale** N fiaba; (*lie*) frottola.

fait ac·com·pli [ˌfɛtəkɒmˈpliː] N fatto compiuto.

faith [feɪθ] N a (*trust*) fiducia; **to have faith in sb/sth** avere fiducia in qn/qc; **to put one's faith in sb/sth** fidarsi di qn/qc; **to keep/break faith with sb** mantenere la parola/mancare di parola con qn; **in (all) good faith** in buona fede; **in bad faith** in malafede

b (*Rel*: *belief*) fede *f*, religione *f*; **Faith, Hope and Charity** Fede, Speranza e Carità.

faith·ful [ˈfeɪθfʊl] 1 ADJ: **faithful (to)** fedele (a).

2 NPL: **the faithful** (*Rel*) i fedeli.

faith·ful·ly [ˈfeɪθfəlɪ] ADV fedelmente; **he promised faithfully to come** ci ha dato la sua parola che sarebbe venuto; **yours faithfully** (*Brit: in letters*) distinti saluti.

faith·ful·ness [ˈfeɪθfʊlnɪs] N: **faithfulness (to)** fedeltà (a).

♦ **faith healer** N guaritore(-trice).

♦ **faith healing** N guarigione *f* mistica.

faith·less [ˈfeɪθlɪs] ADJ infedele.

faith·less·ness [ˈfeɪθlɪsnɪs] N: **faithlessness (to)** infedeltà *f inv* (a).

fake [feɪk] 1 N (*picture*) falso; (*thing*) imitazione *f*; (*person*) impostore(-a); **his illness is a fake** fa finta di essere malato.

2 ADJ falso(-a), fasullo(-a).

3 VT (*accounts*) falsificare; (*illness*) fingere; (*painting*) contraffare.

4 VI fingere.

fal·con [ˈfɔːlkən] N falco, falcone *m*.

fal·con·ry [ˈfɔːlkənrɪ] N (*skill*) falconeria.

Falk·land Islands [ˈfɔːlkləndˌaɪləndz], **Falk·lands** [ˈfɔːlkləndz] NPL: **the Falkland Islands** OR **Falklands** le isole *fpl* Falkland, le isole Malvine.

fall [fɔːl] (*vb*: *pt* **fell**, *pp* **fallen**) 1 N a (*gen*) caduta; (*decrease*) diminuzione *f*, calo; (: *in prices*) ribasso; (: *in temperature*) abbassamento; **he had a bad fall** ha fatto una brutta caduta; **a fall of earth** uno smottamento; **a fall of snow** (*Brit*) una nevicata; **a heavy/light fall of rain** una pioggia forte/leggera

b (*Am*: *autumn*) autunno; **in the fall** in autunno; see also **falls.**

2 VI a (*gen*) cadere; (*building*) crollare; (*decrease*: *temperature, price*) abbassarsi, diminuire; **night is falling** scende la notte; **darkness is falling** si fa buio; **to fall to** *or* **on one's knees** cadere in ginocchio; **to fall on one's feet** cadere in piedi; **to let sth fall** lasciar cadere qc; **to let fall that ...** lasciar capire che...; **to fall into bad habits** *or* **bad ways** prendere delle cattive abitudini; **to fall into conversation with sb** mettersi a parlare con qn; **his poems fall into three categories** le sue poesie si dividono in tre categorie; **to fall from grace** (*Rel*) perdere la grazia di Dio; (*fig*) cadere in disgrazia; **he fell in my estimation** ha perso ai miei occhi; **it all began to fall into place** (*fig*) ha cominciato a prendere forma; **the responsibility falls on you** la responsabilità ricade su di te; **my birthday falls on a Saturday** il mio compleanno cade di sabato; **he fell to wondering if ...** si mise a pensare se...; **it falls to me to say ...** (*frm*) tocca a me *or* è mio compito dire...; **to fall short of** (*sb's expectations*) non corrispondere a; (*perfection*) non raggiungere; **the dart fell short of the board** la freccetta è caduta poco prima del bersaglio; **to fall flat** (*on one's face*) cadere bocconi; (*subj*: *joke, party*) essere un fiasco; (: *plan*) fallire, fare cilecca; **to fall foul of** scontrarsi con

b (*become*): **to fall asleep** addormentarsi; **to fall into arrears** accumulare degli arretrati; **to fall due** scadere; **to fall ill** ammalarsi; **to fall in love (with sb/sth)** innamo-

rarsi (di qn/qc); **to fall silent** farsi silenzioso(-a)
▶ **fall about** VI + ADV (*fig fam*) torcersi dalle risa
▶ **fall apart** VI + ADV cadere a pezzi; (*fig*) crollare
▶ **fall away** VI + ADV (*slope steeply: ground*) scendere; (*crumble: plaster*) scrostarsi, sgretolarsi; (*fig: diminish*) diminuire
▶ **fall back** VI + ADV (*retreat*) indietreggiare; (*Mil*) ritirarsi
▶ **fall back on** VI + ADV + PREP (*also fig*): **to have sth to fall back on** avere qc di riserva
▶ **fall behind** VI + ADV (*in race etc*) rimanere indietro; (*fig: with payments*) essere in arretrato; (: *with work*) essere indietro
▶ **fall down** VI + ADV (*person*) cadere; (*building, hopes*) crollare; **but it falls down in one aspect** (*fig*) ma ha un punto debole; **to fall down on the job** (*fig*) non essere all'altezza del lavoro
▶ **fall for** VI + PREP **a** (*fam: person*) prendere una cotta per, innamorarsi di
b (*fam: be deceived by*): **to fall for a trick** (*or a story etc*) cascarci
▶ **fall in** ① VI + ADV **a** (*person*) cadere dentro; (*roof, walls*) crollare
b (*Mil*) mettersi in riga, allinearsi.
② VI + PREP: **to fall in(to)** cadere in
▶ **fall in with** VI + ADV + PREP; **to fall in with sb** (*meet*) trovare qn; **to fall in with sb's plans** (*person*) trovarsi d'accordo con i progetti di qn; (*event*) coincidere con i progetti di qn
▶ **fall off** ① VI + ADV (*person, leaf*) cadere; (*part*) staccarsi; (*diminish: demand, numbers, interest*) diminuire, abbassarsi; (: *quality*) scadere.
② VI + PREP cadere da
▶ **fall on, fall upon** VI + PREP (*attack*) scagliarsi su; (*responsibility*) ricadere su
▶ **fall out** VI + ADV **a** (*person, object*): **to fall out (of)** cadere (da)
b (*Mil*) rompere le righe
c (*fig: quarrel*): **to fall out (with sb over sth)** litigare (con qn per qc)
d (*happen*): **it fell out that ...** è andata a finire che...; **events fell out (just) as we had hoped** andò a finire proprio come avevamo sperato
▶ **fall over** ① VI + ADV cadere.
② VI + PREP: **he fell over the table** è inciampato nel tavolino ed è caduto; **he was falling over himself** *or* **over backwards to be polite** (*fam*) si faceva in quattro per essere gentile; **they were falling over each other to get it** (*fam*) si accapigliavano per averlo
▶ **fall through** VI + ADV (*plan, project*) fallire
▶ **fall upon** VI + PREP = **fall on**.
fal·la·cious [fə'leɪʃəs] ADJ (*frm*) fallace.
fal·la·cy ['fæləsɪ] N errore *m*.
fall·back ['fɔːl,bæk] ADJ: **fallback position** posizione *f* di ripiego.
fall·en ['fɔːlən] ① PP of **fall**.
② ADJ caduto(-a); (*morally: woman, angel*) perduto(-a).
③ NPL: **the fallen** (*Mil*) i caduti.
♦ **fallen arches** N piedi *mpl* piatti; **to have fallen arches** (*Med*) avere i piedi piatti.
fal·libil·ity [,fælɪ'bɪlɪtɪ] N fallibilità *f inv*.
fal·lible ['fæləbl] ADJ (*frm*) fallibile.
fall·ing ['fɔːlɪŋ] ADJ: **falling market** (*Fin*) mercato in ribasso.
♦ **falling-off** ['fɔːlɪŋ'ɒf] N calo.
♦ **falling star** N stella cadente.

♦ **fall line** N (*Skiing*) linea di massima pendenza.
fal·lo·pian tube [fə'ləʊpɪən'tjuːb] N (*Anat*) tuba di Fallopio.
fall·out ['fɔːl,aʊt] N pioggia radioattiva; (*fig: repercussions*) ripercussione *f*; **fallout shelter** rifugio antiatomico.
fal·low ['fæləʊ] ADJ incolto(-a), a maggese; **to lie fallow** rimanere a maggese.
fallow deer N, PL INV daino(-a).
falls [fɔːlz] NPL (*waterfall*) cascate *fpl*; **the Niagara Falls** le cascate del Niagara.
false [fɔːls] ADJ (*gen*) falso(-a); **false ceiling** controsoffitto; **a false step** un passo falso; **under false pretences** con l'inganno; **with a false bottom** con doppio fondo.
♦ **false alarm** N falso allarme *m*.
false·hood ['fɔːls,hʊd] N (*frm: lie*) menzogna; **truth and falsehood** il vero e il falso.
false·ly ['fɔːlslɪ] ADV (*accuse*) a torto; (*state*) falsamente.
♦ **false move** N passo falso.
false·ness ['fɔːlsnɪs] N falsità.
♦ **false start** N falsa partenza.
♦ **false teeth** NPL (*Brit*) denti *mpl* finti, dentiera.
fal·set·to [fɔːl'setəʊ] ① N falsetto.
② ADJ di falsetto.
fal·si·fi·ca·tion [,fɔːlsɪfɪ'keɪʃən] N falsificazione *f*.
fal·si·fy ['fɔːlsɪ,faɪ] VT falsificare; (*figures*) alterare.
fal·sity ['fɔːlsɪtɪ] N = **falseness**.
fal·ter ['fɔːltəʳ] VI (*voice, speaker*) esitare; (*interest*) scemare; (*engine*) perder colpi; **his voice faltered with emotion** la sua voce era rotta dall'emozione; **his steps faltered** ha vacillato.
fal·ter·ing ['fɔːltərɪŋ] ADJ incerto(-a).
fame [feɪm] N fama, celebrità; **his fame as a musician** la sua fama di musicista.
famed [feɪmd] ADJ famoso(-a), celebre.
fa·mil·ial [fə'mɪlɪəl] ADJ (*frm*) familiare.
fa·mili·ar [fə'mɪljəʳ] ADJ **a** (*well-known: face, person, place*) conosciuto(-a), familiare; (*common: experience, complaint, event*) comune; **her face looks familiar** la sua faccia non mi è nuova; **to be on familiar ground** (*fig*) trovarsi sul proprio terreno
b (*well-acquainted*): **to be familiar (with sb/sth)** conoscere bene (qn/qc); **to make o.s. familiar with** familiarizzarsi con, acquistare dimestichezza con
c (*language*) familiare; (*intimate: tone of voice*) di eccessiva confidenza; **to be on familiar terms with** essere in confidenza con; **to get too familiar with sb** (*pej*) prendersi troppa confidenza con qn.
fa·mili·ar·ity [fə,mɪlɪ'ærɪtɪ] N (*knowledge*): **familiarity (with)** conoscenza (di), dimestichezza (con); (*of tone etc*) confidenza, familiarità, intimità; **familiarity breeds contempt** dar troppa confidenza fa perdere il rispetto.
fa·mil·iar·ize [fə'mɪlɪə,raɪz] VT: **to familiarize o.s. with** familiarizzarsi con; **to familiarize sb with sth** far conoscere qc a qn.
fa·mili·ar·ly [fə'mɪljəlɪ] ADV con molta confidenza.
fami·ly ['fæmɪlɪ] ① N (*gen*) famiglia; **it runs in the family** è di famiglia; **she's quite one of the family** è come se facesse parte della famiglia.
② ADJ (*jewels, life, business*) di famiglia, familiare.
♦ **family allowance** N (*Brit: old*) assegni *mpl* familiari.
♦ **family butcher** N macellaio di quartiere.
♦ **family credit** N (*Brit*) ≈ assegni *mpl* familiari.
♦ **family doctor** N (*Brit*) medico di famiglia.
♦ **family man** N uomo amante della famiglia, padre *m* di

famiglia.
♦ **family name** N = surname.
♦ **family planning** N pianificazione *f* familiare.
♦ **family planning clinic** N consultorio familiare.
♦ **family tree** N albero genealogico.
fam·ine ['fæmɪn] N carestia.
fam·ished ['fæmɪʃt] ADJ affamato(-a); **I'm famished!** (*fam*) ho una fame da lupi!
fa·mous ['feɪməs] ADJ famoso(-a), celebre; **famous last words!** (*fam hum*) le ultime parole famose!
fa·mous·ly ['feɪməslɪ] ADV (*get on*) a meraviglia.
fan[1] [fæn] [1] N ventaglio; (*machine*) ventilatore *m*.
  [2] VT (*face, person*) fare aria a, fare vento a; (*fire*) alimentare; **to fan the flames** (*fig*) soffiare sul fuoco
► **fan out** VI + ADV spargersi (a ventaglio).
fan[2] [fæn] N (*gen*) fan *m/f inv*, ammiratore(-trice); (*Sport*) tifoso(-a), fan *m/f inv*; **he's a jazz fan** è un patito del jazz.
fa·nat·ic [fə'nætɪk] N fanatico(-a).
fa·nati·c(al) [fə'nætɪk(əl)] ADJ fanatico(-a).
fa·nati·cal·ly [fə'nætɪkəlɪ] ADV fanaticamente.
fa·nati·cism [fə'nætɪˌsɪzəm] N fanatismo.
♦ **fan belt** N (*Aut*) cinghia della ventola.
fan·cied ['fænsɪd] ADJ **a** (*imaginary*) immaginario(-a) **b** (*horse, candidate*) favorito(-a).
fan·ci·ful ['fænsɪfʊl] ADJ (*explanation*) fantastico(-a); (*person, idea, drawing*) fantasioso(-a); (*object*) di fantasia.
fan·ci·ful·ly ['fænsɪfəlɪ] ADV (*see adj*) fantasticamente; in modo fantasioso.
♦ **fan club** N fan club *m inv*.
fan·cy ['fænsɪ] [1] N **a** (*whim*) voglia, capriccio; **a passing fancy (for sth)** una voglia passeggera (di qc); **when the fancy takes him** quando ne ha voglia; **to take a fancy to** (*person, thing*) affezionarsi a, incapricciarsi di; **to catch or take sb's fancy** entusiasmare qn; **it took or caught my fancy** mi è piaciuto
  b (*imagination*) fantasia, immaginazione *f*; **in the realm of fancy** nel regno della fantasia; **I have a fancy that he'll be late** (*vague idea*) ho la vaga impressione che arriverà tardi; **is it just my fancy, or did I hear a knock at the door?** mi sbaglio o hanno bussato alla porta?
  [2] ADJ (*comp* **-ier**, *superl* **-iest**) **a** (*ornamental*) elaborato (-a); **a fancy design** un disegno fantasia; **nothing fancy** niente di speciale; **fancy cakes** pasticcini *mpl*
  b (*pej: price*) esorbitante; (: *idea*) stravagante.
  [3] VT **a** (*imagine*) immaginare, credere; **to fancy that** immaginare che; **I rather fancy he's gone out** credo proprio che sia uscito; **fancy that!** (*fam*) pensa un po'!, ma guarda!; **fancy meeting you here!** (*fam*) che combinazione incontrarti qui!
  b (*feel like, want*) avere voglia di; **do you fancy (going for) a stroll?** hai voglia *or* ti va di fare una passeggiatina?; **I don't fancy the idea** l'idea non mi attira; **he fancies himself** (*fam*) ha un'alta opinione di sé; **he fancies himself as a footballer** (*fam*) crede di essere un gran calciatore; **she fancies him** (*fam*) lui le piace (*sessualmente*)
  c (*predict success for: team, horse*) dare per vincente; **I don't fancy his chances of winning** non credo che vincerà.
♦ **fancy dress** N costume *m*, maschera; **fancy-dress ball** ballo in maschera; **fancy-dress party** festa mascherata.
♦ **fancy goods** NPL articoli *mpl* da regalo.
♦ **fancy man** N (*old pej*) amico.
♦ **fancy woman** N (*old pej*) amica.

fan·dan·go [fæn'dæŋgəʊ] N fandango.
fan·fare ['fænfɛə] N fanfara.
fang [fæŋ] N zanna; (*of snake*) dente *m*.
♦ **fan heater** N (*Brit*) termoventilatore *m*.
fan·light ['fænˌlaɪt] N lunetta (a ventaglio).
♦ **fan mail** N lettere *fpl* degli ammiratori.
fan·ny ['fænɪ] N (*Brit fam!*) figa (*fam!*); (*Am fam*) culo.
fan·ta·size ['fæntəˌsaɪz] VI fantasticare, sognare.
fan·tas·tic [fæn'tæstɪk] ADJ (*gen*) fantastico(-a); (*idea*) assurdo(-a).
fan·tas·ti·cal·ly [fæn'tæstɪkəlɪ] ADV in modo fantastico, fantasticamente; **he is fantastically rich** è incredibilmente *or* favolosamente ricco.
fan·ta·sy ['fæntəsɪ] N (*imagination*) fantasia, immaginazione *f*; (*fanciful idea, wish*) sogno, idea fantastica, chimera; **in a world of fantasy** in un mondo fantastico.
fan·zine ['fænˌziːn] N fanzine *f inv*.
FAO [ˌɛfeɪ'əʊ] N ABBR (= *Food and Agriculture Organization*) FAO *f*.
f.a.q, FAQ [ˌɛfeɪ'kjuː] ABBR (= *free alongside quay*) FAQ, franco lungo banchina.
far [fɑː] (*comp* **farther** *or* **further**, *superl* **farthest** *or* **furthest**) [1] ADV **a** lontano; **is it far (away)?** è lontano?; **is it far to London?** è lontana Londra?; **how far is it to the river?** quanto è lontano il fiume?; **it's not far (from here)** non è lontano (da qui); **as far as** fino a; **as far as the eye can see** a perdita d'occhio; **to go as far as Milan** andare fino a Milano; **to come from as far away as Milan** venire addirittura da Milano; **she swam as far as the others** ha nuotato tanto lontano quanto gli altri; **as far back as I can remember** per quanto *or* per quello che posso ricordare; **as far back as 1945** già nel 1945; **as** *or* **so far as I know** per quel che ne so, per quanto ne sappia; **as** *or* **so far as I am concerned** per quanto mi riguarda; **as far as possible** nei limiti del possibile; **I would go** *or* **go so far as to say that** ... arriverei al punto di dire...; **from far and near** da ogni parte; **to come from far and wide** venire da ogni parte; **to travel far and wide** viaggiare in lungo e in largo; **far away** *or* **off** lontano, distante; **far away** *or* **off in the distance** in lontananza; **not far away** *or* **off** non lontano; **far away from one's family** lontano dalla famiglia; **Christmas is not far off** Natale non è lontano, non manca molto a Natale; **far beyond** molto al di là di; **far from** (*place*) lontano da; **far from (doing sth)** invece di (fare qc); **we are far from having finished** siamo ben lungi dall'aver finito; **far from it!** al contrario!; **he is far from well** non sta affatto *or* per niente bene; **far be it from me to interfere, but** ... non ho la minima intenzione di immischiarmi, ma...; **far from easy** tutt'altro che facile; **far into the night** fino a notte inoltrata; **far out at sea** in alto mare; **our calculations weren't far out** i nostri calcoli non erano poi così sbagliati; **to go far** (*person*) andare lontano; **he'll go far** farà molta strada; **it won't go far** (*money, food*) non basterà; **how are you going?** fin dove vai?; **how far have you got with your work?** dove sei arrivato con il tuo lavoro?; **he's gone too far this time** questa volta ha esagerato *or* oltrepassato i limiti; **he's gone too far to back out now** si è spinto troppo oltre per tirarsi indietro adesso; **the plans are too far advanced** i piani sono a uno stadio troppo avanzato; **he was far gone** (*fam: ill*) era molto malato; (: *drunk*) era ubriaco fradicio; **this far** (*in distance*) fin qui; **so far** (*in time*) finora; **so far so good** fin qui tutto a posto; **so** *or* **thus far and no further** fin qui e non oltre
  b (*with comp: very much*) di gran lunga; **far better** assai

migliore; **it's far and away the best** *or* **it's by far the best** è di gran lunga il migliore; **this car is far faster (than)** questa macchina è molto più veloce (di); **she's the prettiest by far** è di gran lunga la più carina; **it is far better not to go** è molto meglio non andare.

[2] ADJ: **the Far North** l'estremo Nord; **the far east** *etc* of the country la zona orientale *etc* del paese; **on the far side of** dall'altra parte di; **at the far end of** in fondo a, all'altro capo di; **the far left/right** (*Pol*) l'estrema sinistra/destra.

far·away [ˈfɑːrəˌweɪ] ADJ (*distant*) lontano(-a); (*voice, look*) assente.

farce [fɑːs] N (*Theatre, fig*) farsa.

far·ci·cal [ˈfɑːsɪkl] ADJ farsesco(-a), ridicolo(-a); **the trial was farcical** il processo fu una farsa.

♦ **far-distant** [ˌfɑːˈdɪstənt] ADJ lontano(-a).

fare [feəʳ] [1] N **a** (*cost: on trains, buses*) tariffa; (: *in taxi*) prezzo della corsa; **"fares please!"** (*conductor on bus*) "biglietti?"

b (*passenger in taxi*) passeggero(-a), cliente *m/f*

c (*frm: food*) cibo, vitto; **bill of fare** (*menu*) lista delle vivande.

[2] VI: **how did you fare?** com'è andata?; **I think they will fare badly if** ... penso che le cose si metteranno male per loro se... .

♦ **Far East** N: **the Far East** l'Estremo Oriente *m*.

♦ **fare stage** N (*for bus*) tronco.

fare·well [ˌfeəˈwel] [1] N, EXCL addio; **to bid farewell (to sb)** salutare (qn), dire addio (a qn).

[2] ADJ (*party*) d'addio; (: *dinner, speech*) d'addio, di commiato.

♦ **far-fetched** [ˌfɑːˈfetʃt] ADJ (*explanation*) stiracchiato (-a), forzato(-a); (*idea, scheme, story*) inverosimile.

♦ **far-flung** [ˌfɑːˈflʌŋ] ADJ (*remote*) remoto(-a); (*widely distributed: empire, operations*) esteso(-a).

farm [fɑːm] [1] N fattoria, podere *m*; **farm produce** prodotti *mpl* agricoli.

[2] VT coltivare.

[3] VI (*as profession*) fare l'agricoltore

▶ **farm out** VT + ADV (*work*): **farm out (to sb)** dare in consegna (a qn); (*children*): **to farm out (on)** affidare (a).

farm·er [ˈfɑːməʳ] N agricoltore *m*, contadino(-a), coltivatore(-trice); (*owner of farm*) proprietario(-a) terriero(-a).

farm·hand [ˈfɑːmˌhænd], **farm labourer**, (*Am*) **farm laborer** N bracciante *m/f*.

farm·house [ˈfɑːmˌhaʊs] N casa colonica, fattoria.

farm·ing [ˈfɑːmɪŋ] N agricoltura; **sheep farming** allevamento di pecore; **farming community** comunità *f inv* agricola; **farming methods** metodi *mpl* di coltivazione.

farm·land [ˈfɑːmˌlænd] N terreno coltivo.

farm·stead [ˈfɑːmˌsted] N fattoria.

♦ **farm worker** N = **farmhand**.

farm·yard [ˈfɑːmˌjɑːd] N aia.

Faroe Is·lands [ˈfeərəʊˈaɪləndz], **Faroes** [ˈfeərəʊz] NPL: **the Faroe Islands** le isole *fpl* Faeroer.

♦ **far-off** [ˈfɑːˌrɒf] ADJ lontano(-a), distante.

♦ **far-reaching** [ˌfɑːˈriːtʃɪŋ] ADJ (*effect*) di larga *or* vasta portata.

far·ri·er [ˈfærɪəʳ] N maniscalco.

far·row [ˈfærəʊ] VI (*Zool*) figliare (*di scrofa*).

♦ **far-sighted** [ˌfɑːˈsaɪtɪd] ADJ **a** (*person*) previdente, lungimirante; (*plan, decision, measure*) lungimirante **b** (*Am: long-sighted*) presbite.

fart [fɑːt] (*fam!*) [1] N scoreggia, peto (*fam!*).

[2] VI scoreggiare, fare un peto (*fam!*)

far·ther [ˈfɑːðəʳ] COMP of far [1] ADV see **further 1 a**.

[2] ADJ più lontano(-a); **on the farther side of the street** dall'altra parte della strada.

far·thest [ˈfɑːðɪst] ADJ, ADV, SUPERL of **far**; see **furthest**.

far·thing [ˈfɑːðɪŋ] N (*coin*) moneta da un quarto di penny, *non più in circolazione*; **it does not matter a brass farthing if** ... (*old fam*) non me ne importa un fico secco se... .

FAS, f.a.s. ABBR (*Brit*: = *free alongside ship*) F.A.S., franco banchina nave.

fas·cia, fa·cia [ˈfeɪʃə] N (*Aut*) cruscotto.

fas·ci·nate [ˈfæsɪˌneɪt] VT affascinare; **it fascinates me how/why** ... sono affascinato da come/perché... .

fas·ci·nat·ing [ˈfæsɪˌneɪtɪŋ] ADJ affascinante.

fas·ci·nat·ingly [ˈfæsɪˌneɪtɪŋlɪ] ADV in modo affascinante.

fas·ci·na·tion [ˌfæsɪˈneɪʃən] N fascino.

fas·cism [ˈfæʃɪzəm] N fascismo.

fas·cist [ˈfæʃɪst] ADJ, N fascista (*m/f*).

fash·ion [ˈfæʃən] [1] N **a** (*manner*) modo, maniera; **after a fashion** (*finish, manage etc*) così così; **in his usual fashion** nel solito modo; **in the Greek fashion** alla greca

b (*vogue: in clothing, speech etc*) moda; **to set a fashion for sth** lanciare la moda di qc; **to be in fashion** essere di/alla moda; **to be out of fashion** essere fuori moda, essere passato(-a) di moda; **to come into/go out of fashion** diventare/passare di moda; **the latest fashion** l'ultima moda; **the new Spring fashions** i nuovi modelli per la primavera; **it's no longer the fashion** non va più di moda; **women's/men's fashions** moda femminile/maschile.

[2] VT (*gen*) fabbricare; (*in clay*) modellare.

[3] ADJ (*editor, house, show*) di moda.

fash·ion·able [ˈfæʃnəbl] ADJ alla moda, di moda; (*writer*) di grido; **it is fashionable to do** ... è/va di moda fare... .

fash·ion·ably [ˈfæʃnəblɪ] ADV: **to be fashionably dressed** essere vestito(-a) alla moda.

♦ **fashion designer** N stilista *m/f*, disegnatore(-trice) di moda.

♦ **fashion model** N indossatore(-trice), modello(-a).

fast[1] [fɑːst] (*comp* -**er**, *superl* -**est**) [1] ADJ **a** (*speedy*) veloce, svelto(-a), rapido(-a); (*film*) ad alta sensibilità; **fast train** rapido; **he's a fast worker** (*fig*) non perde certo tempo; **to pull a fast one on sb** (*fam*) giocare un brutto tiro a qn

b (*clock*): **to be fast** andare avanti; **my watch is 5 minutes fast** il mio orologio va avanti di 5 minuti

c (*dissipated: woman*) dissoluto(-a); (: *life*) dissipato(-a), dissoluto(-a)

d (*firm: friend*) devoto(-a), fedele; (: *colour, dye*) resistente, che non stinge; **to make a boat fast** (*Brit*) ormeggiare una barca.

[2] ADV **a** (*quickly*) in fretta, velocemente, rapidamente; **as fast as I can** più in fretta possibile; **he ran off as fast as his legs would carry him** è corso via come il vento *or* più veloce che poteva; **how fast can you type?** a che velocità scrivi a macchina?; **not so fast!** piano!; **the rain was falling fast** pioveva forte *or* a dirotto

b (*firmly: stuck, held*) saldamente, bene; **tie it fast** legalo bene; **it's stuck fast** (*door*) è saldamente bloccato; (*nail, screw*) è completamente incastrato; **fast asleep** profondamente addormentato(-a).

fast[2] [fɑːst] [1] N digiuno.

[2] VI digiunare.

fas·ten [ˈfɑːsn] [1] VT (*with rope, string etc*) legare; (*with nail*) inchiodare; (*secure: belt, dress, seat belt*) allacciare; (:

door, box, window) chiudere; (*attach*) attaccare, fissare; **to fasten the blame/responsibility (for sth) on sb** (*fig*) dare la colpa/addossare la responsabilità (di qc) a qn. ②ᵥₗ (*door etc*) chiudersi; (*dress*) allacciarsi, abbottonarsi

▶ **fasten down** ᵥₜ + ᴀᴅᵥ fissare bene
▶ **fasten on** ᵥₜ + ᴀᴅᵥ fissare
▶ **fasten up** ᵥₜ + ᴀᴅᵥ (*clothing, coat*) allacciare, abbottonare
▶ **fasten (up)on** ᵥₗ + ᴘʀᴇᴘ (*idea*) cogliere al volo; (*excuse*) ricorrere a.

fas·ten·er ['faːsnə'], **fas·ten·ing** ['faːsnɪŋ] ɴ chiusura, fermaglio; (*zip*) chiusura *f* lampo *inv*.

♦ **fast food** ɴ fast food *m inv*.

fas·tidi·ous [fæ'stɪdɪəs] ᴀᴅᴊ (*person: about cleanliness*) pignolo(-a); (: *in taste*) difficile, esigente.

fas·tidi·ous·ly [fæs'tɪdɪəslɪ] ᴀᴅᵥ (*examine, check, clean*) meticolosamente, scrupolosamente.

fas·tidi·ous·ness [fæ'stɪdɪəsnɪs] ɴ pignoleria; (*excessive cleanliness*) mania della pulizia.

fast·ing [faːstɪŋ] ɴ digiuno.

♦ **fast lane** ɴ (*Aut*) ≈ corsia di sorpasso; **in the fast lane** nella corsia di sorpasso.

fast·ness ['faːstnɪs] ɴ (*liter*) roccaforte *f*.

fat [fæt] (*comp* **-ter**, *superl* **-test**) ① ᴀᴅᴊ (*person, meat*) grasso(-a); (*face, cheeks*) paffuto(-a); (*arm, leg*) grassoccio(-a); (*book*) grosso(-a); (*wallet*) gonfio(-a); (*wage packet*) cospicuo(-a); **to get fat** ingrassare, diventare grasso(-a); **he grew fat on the proceeds/profits** (*fig*) si è arricchito con i guadagni/gli incassi; **a fat lot he knows about it!** (*fam iro*) che vuoi che ne sappia lui!; **a fat lot of good that is!** (*fam iro*) bella roba!.
② ɴ grasso; (*Anat*) adipe *m*; **to fry in deep fat** friggere in molto olio; **to live off the fat of the land** vivere nel lusso, avere ogni ben di Dio; **the fat's in the fire** (*fig*) adesso son guai.

fa·tal ['feɪtl] ᴀᴅᴊ (*injury, disease, accident*) fatale, mortale; (*mistake*) fatale; (*consequences, result*) disastroso(-a); (*influence*) nefasto(-a); (*fateful: words, decision*) fatidico (-a); **it was fatal to mention that** è stato un grave errore parlarne.

fa·tal·ism ['feɪtə,lɪzəm] ɴ fatalismo.

fa·tal·ist ['feɪtəlɪst] ɴ fatalista *m/f*.

fa·tal·is·tic [,feɪtə'lɪstɪk] ᴀᴅᴊ fatalistico(-a).

fa·tal·ity [fə'tælɪtɪ] ɴ (*death*) incidente *m* mortale; (*person killed*) morto(-a), vittima.

fa·tal·ly ['feɪtəlɪ] ᴀᴅᵥ (*wounded, injured*) mortalmente, a morte; (*damaged, flawed*) irrimediabilmente; (*exposed, incriminated*) in modo disastroso; **fatally ill** condannato (-a).

fate [feɪt] ɴ **a** (*force*) destino, sorte *f*, fato; **the Fates** (*Myth*) le Parche; **what has fate in store for us?** cosa ci riserva il destino? **b** (*person's lot*) sorte *f*, destino; **to leave sb to his fate** abbandonare qn alla propria sorte *or* al proprio destino; **to meet one's fate** (*death*) trovare la morte.

fat·ed ['feɪtɪd] ᴀᴅᴊ (*governed by fate*) destinato(-a); (*person, project, friendship etc*) destinato(-a) a finire male; **it was fated that ...** era destino che... .

fate·ful ['feɪtful] ᴀᴅᴊ (*momentous: day, event*) fatale; (*prophetic: words*) fatidico(-a).

♦ **fat-free** ['fæt'friː] ᴀᴅᴊ senza grassi.

fat·head ['fæt,hed] ɴ (*fam*) scemo(-a), babbeo(-a).

fa·ther ['faːðə'] ɴ (*gen*) padre *m*; **Our Father** (*Rel*) Padre Nostro; **from father to son** di padre in figlio; **like father**

like son tale padre tale figlio; **Old Father Time** il Tempo.

♦ **Father Christmas** ɴ Babbo Natale.

♦ **father confessor** ɴ (*Rel*) padre confessore; (*fig*) refugium peccatorum *m inv*.

♦ **father-figure** ['faːðə,fɪgə'] ɴ figura paterna.

father·hood ['faːðə,hud] ɴ paternità.

♦ **father-in-law** ['faːðəm,lɔː] ɴ suocero.

father·land ['faːðə,lænd] ɴ patria.

fa·ther·less ['faːðəlɪs] ᴀᴅᴊ orfano(-a) di padre.

fa·ther·ly ['faːðəlɪ] ᴀᴅᴊ paterno(-a).

fath·om ['fæðəm] ① ɴ (*Naut*) braccio (= *1,83m*).
② ᵥₜ (*fig: also:* **fathom out**) capire; (*mystery*) penetrare, sondare; **I can't fathom why** non riesco a capire perché; **I can't fathom it out** non ci capisco assolutamente niente.

fath·om·less ['fæðəmlɪs] ᴀᴅᴊ insondabile, inesplorabile; (*fig*) incomprensibile.

fa·tigue [fə'tiːg] ① ɴ stanchezza, fatica; **to be on fatigue** (*Mil*) essere di corvé.
② ᵥₜ (*frm*) affaticare, stancare.

fa·tigued [fə'tiːgd] ᴀᴅᴊ (*person*) affaticato(-a).

fat·less ['fætlɪs] ᴀᴅᴊ senza grassi.

fat·ness ['fætnɪs] ɴ grassezza.

fat·ted ['fætɪd]: **to kill the fatted calf** (*old*) uccidere il vitello grasso.

fat·ten ['fætn] ᵥₜ, ᵥₗ (*also:* **fatten up**) ingrassare.

fat·ten·ing ['fætnɪŋ] ᴀᴅᴊ ingrassante; **chocolate is fattening** la cioccolata fa ingrassare.

fat·ty ['fætɪ] ① ᴀᴅᴊ (*foods*) grasso(-a); (*Anat: tissue*) grasso (-a), adiposo(-a).
② ɴ (*fam*) ciccione(-a).

fa·tu·ity [fə'tjuːɪtɪ], **fatu·ous·ness** ['fætjʊəsnɪs] ɴ fatuità.

fatu·ous ['fætjʊəs] ᴀᴅᴊ fatuo(-a).

fatu·ous·ly ['fætjʊəslɪ] ᴀᴅᵥ stupidamente.

fau·cet ['fɔːsɪt] ɴ (*Am*) rubinetto.

fault [fɔːlt] ① ɴ **a** (*defect*) difetto; (*mistake*) errore *m*; (*Tennis*) fault *m inv*, fallo; (*Geol*) faglia; **generous to a fault** eccessivamente generoso(-a); **to find fault with sb/sth** trovare da ridire su qn/qc; **to be at fault** avere torto; **your memory is at fault** non ricordi bene
b (*responsibility*) colpa; **it's all your fault** è tutta colpa tua; **whose fault is it (if ...)?** di chi è la colpa (se...)?.
② ᵥₜ trovare da ridire su, criticare.

♦ **fault-finding** ['fɔːlt,faɪndɪŋ] ① ᴀᴅᴊ ipercritico(-a).
② ɴ critica pedante.

fault·less ['fɔːltlɪs] ᴀᴅᴊ (*person, behaviour*) irreprensibile; (*work, English*) impeccabile, perfetto(-a).

fault·less·ly ['fɔːltlɪslɪ] ᴀᴅᵥ (*gen*) perfettamente; (*dress*) in modo impeccabile.

faulty ['fɔːltɪ] ᴀᴅᴊ (*comp* **-ier**, *superl* **-iest**) difettoso(-a).

fau·na ['fɔːnə] ɴ fauna.

faux pas [fəʊ'paː] ɴ gaffe *f inv*.

fa·vor *etc* ['feɪvə'] (*Am*) = **favour** *etc*.

fa·vour, (*Am*) **fa·vor** ['feɪvə'] ① ɴ **a** (*kindness*) favore *m*; **to do sb a favour** fare un favore *or* una cortesia a qn; **to ask a favour of sb** chiedere un favore a qn; **as a favour to me** per farmi un favore; **do me a favour and close the window** fammi un favore, chiudi la finestra
b (*approval*) favore *m*; **to be in favour (with sb)** (*person*) essere nelle grazie di qn; (*idea*) essere ben visto(-a) (da qn); **to be out of favour** (*person*) essere in disgrazia; (*idea, practice*) essere mal visto(-a); **to find favour with sb** (*subj: person*) entrare nelle buone grazie di qn; (: *suggestion*) avere l'approvazione di qn; **to gain sb's favour** *or* **gain favour with sb** guadagnarsi la stima di qn

c (*support, advantage*) favore *m*; **to be in favour of sth/of doing sth** essere favorevole a qc/a fare qc; **that's a point in his favour** è un punto a suo favore; **to decide in favour of sb/sth** decidere in favore di qn/qc; **to decide in favour of doing sth** decidere di fare qc; **to show favour to sb** mostrarsi parziale verso qn, favorire qn.

2 VT (*approve: idea, scheme, approach*) essere a favore di; (*prefer: person, party, proposition*) preferire, essere favorevole a; (: *pupil*) favorire; (: *team*) essere per; **he eventually favoured us with a visit** finalmente ci ha fatto l'onore di una visita.

fa·vour·able, (*Am*) **fa·vor·able** ['feɪvərəbl] ADJ: **favourable (to sb/sth, for doing sth)** favorevole (a qn/qc, a fare qc).

fa·vour·ably, (*Am*) **fa·vor·ably** ['feɪvərəblɪ] ADV favorevolmente.

fa·voured, (*Am*) **fa·vored** ['feɪvəd] ADJ favorito(-a); **the favoured few** i pochi privilegiati.

fa·vour·ite, (*Am*) **fa·vor·ite** ['feɪvərɪt] **1** ADJ favorito(-a), preferito(-a).

2 N favorito(-a), preferito(-a); (*Horse-racing*) favorito (-a); **it's a favourite of mine** è uno dei miei preferiti, è tra i miei favoriti; **he sang some old favourites** ha cantato dei vecchi successi.

fa·vour·it·ism, (*Am*) **fa·vor·it·ism** ['feɪvərɪˌtɪzəm] N favoritismo.

fawn[1] [fɔːn] **1** N **a** (*Zool*) cerbiatto **b** (*colour*) marroncino.

2 ADJ (*also:* **fawn-coloured**) marroncino(-a).

fawn[2] [fɔːn] VI: **to fawn (up)on sb** (*subj: dog*) fare le feste a qn; (: *person: fig*) adulare servilmente qn.

fawn·ing ['fɔːnɪŋ] ADJ (*person*) servile, untuoso(-a); (*dog*) espansivo(-a), affettuoso(-a).

fax [fæks] **1** N (*document, machine*) facsimile *m inv*, fax *m inv*.

2 VT spedire via fax, teletrasmettere.

FBI [ˌɛfbiːˈaɪ] N ABBR (*Am*: = *Federal Bureau of Investigation*) FBI *f*.

FCC [ˌɛfsiːsiː] N ABBR (*Am*)= *Federal Communications Commission*.

FCO [ˌɛfsiːˈəʊ] N ABBR (*Brit*: = *Foreign and Commonwealth Office*) ≈ Ufficio Affari Esteri.

FD [ˌɛfˈdiː] N ABBR (*Am*) = **fire department**.

FDA [ˌɛfdiːˈeɪ] N ABBR (*Am*)= *Food and Drug Administration*.

FE [ˌɛfˈiː] N ABBR = **further education**.

fe·al·ty ['fiːəltɪ] N fedeltà.

fear [fɪə] **1** N paura, timore *m*; **there are fears that ...** si teme che...; **grave fears have arisen for ...** si nutrono seri timori per...; **for fear of sb/of doing sth** per paura di qn/di fare qc; **for fear that** per paura di (*or* che + *sub*); **to live in fear of sb/sth/doing sth** vivere con la paura di qn/qc/fare qc; **to go in fear of one's life/of being discovered** temere per la propria vita/di essere scoperto(-a); **fear of heights** vertigini *fpl*; **fear of enclosed spaces** claustrofobia; **have no fear!** non temere!; **in fear and trembling** tremante di paura; **to put the fear of God into sb** (*fam*) far venire una paura del diavolo a qn; **without fear nor favour** imparzialmente; **no fear!** (*fam*) neanche per sogno!; **there's no fear of that!** neanche per sogno!; **there's not much fear of his coming** non c'è pericolo che venga.

2 VT (*person, God*) temere, avere paura di; **to fear the worst** temere il peggio; **to fear that** temere di (*or* che +*sub*), avere paura di (*or* che +*sub*); **I fear I/he may be late** temo di essere in ritardo/che sia in ritardo; **I fear so/not**

temo di sì/di no, ho paura di sì/di no.

3 VI: **to fear for** temere per, essere in ansia per.

fear·ful ['fɪəfʊl] ADJ **a** (*frightened*): **to be fearful of** temere, avere paura di; **to be fearful that ...** temere *or* avere paura che... **b** (*frightening: accident*) pauroso(-a), spaventoso(-a); (: *sight, noise*) terrificante, spaventoso (-a), terribile.

fear·ful·ly ['fɪəfəlɪ] ADV **a** (*timidly*) timorosamente **b** (*fam: very*) terribilmente, spaventosamente.

fear·ful·ness ['fɪəfʊlnɪs] N paura, timore *m*.

fear·less ['fɪəlɪs] ADJ intrepido(-a), senza paura; **to be fearless of** non aver paura di.

fear·less·ly ['fɪəlɪslɪ] ADV intrepidamente, senza paura.

fear·less·ness ['fɪəlɪsnɪs] N coraggio.

fear·some ['fɪəsəm] ADJ (*opponent*) formidabile, terribile; (*sight*) terrificante.

fea·sibil·ity [ˌfiːzəˈbɪlɪtɪ] N fattibilità, attuabilità.

♦ **feasibility study** N studio di fattibilità, studio delle possibilità di realizzazione.

fea·sible ['fiːzəbl] ADJ **a** (*practicable: plan, suggestion*) realizzabile, fattibile, attuabile **b** (*likely: theory, explanation*) verosimile, credibile.

feast [fiːst] **1** N (*meal*) pranzo, banchetto; (*Rel, fig*) festa; **feast day** festa, festività *f inv*.

2 VT: **to feast one's eyes on sth/sb** deliziarsi alla vista di qc/qn.

3 VI banchettare; **to feast on sth** banchettare a qc.

feast·ing ['fiːstɪŋ] N banchetto.

feat [fiːt] N impresa, prodezza; **a feat of engineering** un trionfo dell'ingegneria; **that was quite a feat** è stata un'impresa non da poco.

feath·er ['fɛðə] **1** N penna, piuma; **as light as a feather** leggero(-a) come una piuma; **that is a feather in his cap** è un fiore all'occhiello per lui; **you could have knocked me down with a feather** (*fam*) avresti potuto farmi cadere con un soffio.

2 VT: **to feather one's nest** (*fig*) arricchirsi.

3 ADJ (*mattress, bed, pillow*) di piuma.

♦ **feather boa** N boa *m inv* (di piume).

feather-brained ['fɛðəˌbreɪnd] ADJ sciocco(-a), sventato (-a).

♦ **feather duster** N piumino.

feath·ered ['fɛðəd] ADJ piumato(-a); **our feathered friends** i nostri amici pennuti.

feather·weight ['fɛðəˌweɪt] (*Boxing*) **1** ADJ dei pesi piuma.

2 N peso *m* piuma *inv*.

fea·ture ['fiːtʃə] **1** N **a** (*gen, Comm, Tech*) caratteristica **b** (*of face*): **features** NPL lineamenti *mpl*, fisionomia *fsg*, fattezze *fpl*

c (*also:* **feature film**) film *m inv* (principale), lungometraggio

d (*Press*) articolo, servizio speciale; **a regular feature in** (*newspapers*) un articolo che appare regolarmente in; **a (special) feature on sth/sb** un servizio speciale su qc/qn.

2 VT (*person*) avere come protagonista; (*event, news*) presentare, dare risalto a.

3 VI (*Cine*) apparire, essere protagonista, figurare; **it featured prominently in ...** (*gen*) ha avuto un posto di primo piano in... .

fea·ture·less ['fiːtʃəlɪs] ADJ privo(-a) di carattere, anonimo(-a).

Feb. ABBR (= *February*) feb.

Feb·ru·ary ['fɛbrʊərɪ] N febbraio *for usage see* **July.**

feces ['fi:si:z] NPL (*Am*) = **faeces.**
feck·less ['fɛklɪs] ADJ irresponsabile, incosciente.
fe·cund ['fi:kənd] ADJ (*liter*) fecondo(-a).
fe·cun·dity [fɪ'kʌndɪtɪ] N fecondità.
Fed [fɛd] ABBR (*Am*) **a** = **federal b** = **federation.**
fed [fɛd] PT, PP of **feed.**
Fed. N ABBR (*Am fam*) = **Federal Reserve Board.**
fed·er·al ['fɛdərəl] ADJ federale.
♦ **Federal Republic of Germany** N Repubblica Federale Tedesca.
♦ **Federal Reserve Board** N (*Am*) *organo di controllo del sistema bancario statunitense.*
♦ **Federal Trade Commission** N (*Am*) *organismo di tutela contro pratiche commerciali abusive.*
federate [*vb* 'fɛdə,reɪt; *adj* 'fɛdərɪt] [1] VI federarsi.
[2] ADJ federato(-a).
fed·era·tion [,fɛdə'reɪʃən] N federazione *f.*
♦ **fed up** ADJ (*fam*): **to be fed up (with** *or* **of)** essere stufo(-a) (di); **to be fed up doing sth** essere stufo(-a) di fare qc.
fee [fi:] N pagamento; (*of doctor, lawyer*) onorario, parcella; (*entrance fee, membership fee*) quota d'iscrizione; **course** *or* **tuition fees** (*Univ*) tasse *fpl* universitarie; **school fees** tasse *fpl* scolastiche; (*for examination*) tassa d'esame; **for a small fee** per una somma modesta.
fee·ble ['fi:bl] ADJ (*comp* **-er,** *superl* **-est**) (*gen*) debole; (*joke*) pietoso(-a); (*fam: person*) rammollito(-a).
♦ **feeble-minded** [,fi:bl'maɪndɪd] ADJ deficiente, sciocco (-a).
♦ **feeble-mindedness** [,fi:bl'maɪndɪdnɪs] N debolezza mentale.
fee·ble·ness ['fi:blnɪs] N debolezza.
fee·bly ['fi:blɪ] ADV (*move, smile*) a fatica; (*say, explain*) in modo poco convincente.
feed [fi:d] (*vb: pt, pp* fed) [1] N (*baby's*) pappa; (*fodder*) mangime *m*, foraggio; (*amount, portion*) razione *f*; (*fam: meal*): **to have a good feed** fare una bella mangiata.
[2] VT **a** (*gen*) nutrire; (*horse etc*) dare da mangiare a; **to feed sth to sb** *or* **sb sth** dare qc da mangiare a qn
b (*fire, machine*) alimentare; (*information*) fornire; **to feed sth into a machine** introdurre qc in una macchina; **to feed material into sth** introdurre materiale in qc; **to feed information into a computer** introdurre dati in un computer.
[3] VI (*baby, animal*) mangiare; (*at breast/on bottle*) poppare; **to feed on sth** nutrirsi di qc
▶ **feed back** VT + ADV (*results*) riferire
▶ **feed in** VT + ADV (*wire, tape*) introdurre
▶ **feed on** VI + PREP nutrirsi di
▶ **feed up** VT + ADV (*person, animal*) ingrassare.
feed·back ['fi:d,bæk] N (*from person*) reazioni *fpl*; (*from computer*) feed-back *m.*
feed·er ['fi:də'] N **a** (*baby, animal*) mangiatore(-trice); **a heavy feeder** un(-a) mangione(-a) **b** (*road, rail*) secondario(-a).
feed·ing ['fi:dɪŋ] N alimentazione *f.*
♦ **feeding bottle** N (*Brit*) biberon *m inv*, poppatoio.
♦ **feeding ground** N pascolo; (*for birds*) zona dove si trova da mangiare.
feel [fi:l] (*vb: pt, pp* felt) [1] N (*sense of touch*) tatto; (*sensation*) sensazione *f*; (*of substance*) consistenza; **to be rough to the feel** essere ruvido(-a) al tatto; **to know sth by the feel of it** riconoscere qc al tatto; **let me have a feel!** fammi toccare!; **to get the feel of sth** (*fig*) abituarsi a qc.

[2] VT **a** (*touch*) tastare, sentire, toccare; **to feel sb's pulse** sentire *or* tastare il polso a qn; **to feel one's way (towards)** avanzare a tastoni (verso); **I'm still feeling my way** (*fig*) sto ancora tastando il terreno
b (*be aware of*) sentire; (*experience: pain, pity, anger*) provare, sentire; **he doesn't feel the cold** non sente il freddo; **she felt a hand on her shoulder** sentì una mano sulla spalla; **I felt something move** ho sentito qualcosa che si muoveva; **we are beginning to feel the effects** cominciamo a sentire gli effetti; **I felt a great sense of relief** ho sentito un grande sollievo; **he feels the loss of his father very deeply** sta risentendo molto della morte del padre
c (*think, believe*): **to feel (that)** credere (che), pensare (che); **I feel that you ought to do it** penso che dovresti farlo; **he felt it necessary to point out that ...** ritenne necessario far notare che...; **since you feel so strongly about it ...** visto che ci tieni tanto...; **I feel it in my bones that ...** me lo sento nelle ossa che...; **what do you feel about it?** cosa ne pensi?.
[3] VI **a** (*physically, mentally*) sentirsi; **to feel cold/hungry/ sleepy** avere freddo/fame/sonno; **to feel ill** sentirsi male; **I don't feel well** non mi sento bene; **I feel much better** mi sento molto meglio; **to feel lonely** sentirsi solo(-a); **she's not feeling quite herself** non si sente molto bene; **I felt (as if I was going to) faint** mi sono sentito svenire; **to feel ashamed** avere vergogna; **I feel sure that ...** sono sicuro che...; **I feel sorry for sb** dispiacersi per qn; **I feel very cross/sorry** *etc* sono molto arrabbiato/triste *etc*; **he feels bad about leaving his wife alone** gli dispiace lasciare sola la moglie; **I feel as if there is nothing we can do** ho la sensazione che non ci possiamo fare niente; **how do you feel about him/about the idea?** che ne pensi di lui/dell'idea?; **to feel like sth/doing sth** avere voglia di qc/di fare qc; **what does it feel like to do that?** che effetto ti fa fare ciò?; **I don't feel up to (doing) it** non me la sento (di farlo); **I felt (like) a fool** mi sono sentito uno stupido; **I feel for you!** (*sympathize*) come ti capisco!
b (*objects*): **to feel hard/cold/damp (to the touch)** essere duro(-a)/freddo(-a)/umido(-a) al tatto; **it feels soft** è morbido al tatto; **the house feels damp** la casa sembra umida; **it feels like silk** sembra seta al tatto; **it feels colder out here** sembra più freddo qui fuori; **it feels like (it might) rain** sembra che voglia piovere; **it felt like being drunk** *or* **as if I was drunk** mi sentivo come se fossi ubriaco
c (*grope*) cercare a tastoni; **to feel about** *or* **around for** cercare a tastoni; **to feel about** *or* **around for sth in the dark** cercare a tastoni qc al buio; **to feel (about** *or* **around) in one's pocket for** frugarsi in tasca per cercare.
feel·er ['fi:lə'] N (*of insect, snail*) antenna; (*of octopus*) tentacolo; **to put out feelers** (*fig*) tastare il terreno.
♦ **feeler gauge** N spessimetro.
feel·ing ['fi:lɪŋ] N **a** (*physical*) senso, sensazione *f*; **a cold feeling** una sensazione di freddo; **to have no** *or* **to have lost all feeling in one's arm** aver perso completamente la sensibilità in un braccio
b (*emotion*) sentimento, emozione *f*; (*sensitivity*) sensibilità; **bad** *or* **ill feeling** ostilità, rancore *m*; **to speak/sing with feeling** parlare/cantare con sentimento; **he shows no feeling for her** non mostra nessuna simpatia per lei; **a woman of great feeling** una donna molto sensibile; **what are your feelings about the matter?** che cosa ne pensi?; **you can imagine my feelings** puoi immaginare

quello che sento/ho sentito; **to hurt sb's feelings** offendere i sentimenti di qn, ferire qn; **feelings ran high about it** la cosa aveva provocato grande eccitazione; **no hard feelings!** senza rancore!

c (*impression*) senso, impressione *f*; **a feeling of security/isolation** un senso di sicurezza/di isolamento; **my feeling is that** ... ho l'impressione che...; **I have a (funny) feeling that** ... ho la (strana) sensazione che...; **I got the feeling that** ... ho avuto l'impressione che...; **there was a general feeling that** ... il sentimento generale era che... .

feel·ing·ly ['fiːlɪŋlɪ] ADV (*speak*) infervoratamente.

♦ **fee-paying** ['fiːˌpeɪɪŋ] ADJ (*pupil*) che paga; **fee-paying school** scuola privata.

feet [fiːt] NPL of **foot**.

feign [feɪn] VT (*liter*) fingere, simulare.

feint [feɪnt] ① N finta.
② VI fare una finta.

fe·lici·tous [fɪˈlɪsɪtəs] ADJ (*frm*) felice.

fe·lic·ity [fɪˈlɪsɪtɪ] N (*frm*) felicità.

fe·line ['fiːlaɪn] ADJ felino(-a).

fell[1] [fɛl] PT of **fall**.

fell[2] [fɛl] VT (*with a blow: person*) atterrare; (: *tree*) abbattere.

fell[3] [fɛl] ADJ: **with one fell blow** con un colpo terribile; **at one fell swoop** in un colpo solo.

fell[4] [fɛl] N (*Brit: mountain*) monte *m*; (: *uplands*): **the fells** NPL *versante montuoso con scarsa vegetazione*; **fell-walking** passeggiate *fpl* in montagna.

fel·low ['fɛləʊ] ① N **a** (*fam: man, boy*) uomo, individuo, tipo; (: *boyfriend*) ragazzo; **poor fellow!** povero diavolo!; **my dear fellow** mio caro, caro mio
  b (*comrade*) compagno; (*equal*) pari *m inv*
  c (*of association, society etc*) membro; (*Univ*) ≈ docente *m/f*.
② ADJ: **fellow citizen** concittadino(-a); **fellow countryman/woman** compatriota *m/f*; **one's fellow creatures** i/le propri(e) simili; **fellow doctor** collega *m/f* (medico); **their fellow prisoners/students/workers** i loro compagni di prigione/studio/lavoro; **fellow men** simili *mpl*.

♦ **fellow feeling** N simpatia.

fel·low·ship ['fɛləʊˌʃɪp] N (*companionship*) compagnia; (*club, society*) associazione *f*; (*Univ: research post*) incarico come ricercatore(-trice).

♦ **fellow traveller** N compagno(-a) di viaggio; (*Pol: with communists*) compagno(-a) di strada.

fel·on ['fɛlən] N (*Law*) criminale *m/f*.

fe·lo·ni·ous [fɪˈləʊnɪəs] ADJ (*Law*) criminale.

felo·ny ['fɛlənɪ] N (*Law*) reato, crimine *m*.

felt[1] [fɛlt] PT, PP of **feel**.

felt[2] [fɛlt] ① N feltro.
② ADJ di feltro; **felt hat** cappello di feltro.

♦ **felt-tip pen** ['fɛltˌtɪp'pɛn] N (*also:* **felt-tip**) N pennarello.

fe·male ['fiːmeɪl] ① ADJ (*animal, plant, Elec*) femmina *inv*; (*subject, member, worker*) di sesso femminile; (*company, vote*) di donne; (*sex, quality, character*) femminile; **female labour** manodopera femminile; **female student/worker** studentessa/operaia; **male and female students** studenti e studentesse.
② N (*animal, woman: pej*) femmina.

♦ **female impersonator** N (*Theatre*) *attore comico che fa parti da donna*.

femi·nine ['fɛmɪnɪn] ① ADJ femminile; **the feminine form** (*Gram*) il femminile.
② N (*Gram*) femminile *m*; **in the feminine** al femminile.

femi·nin·ity [ˌfɛmɪˈnɪnɪtɪ] N femminilità.

femi·nism ['fɛmɪˌnɪzəm] N femminismo.

femi·nist ['fɛmɪnɪst] ADJ, N femminista *(m/f)*.

femme fatale ['fɛmfə'tæl] N donna fatale.

fen [fɛn] N (*often pl: Brit*) zona paludosa; see also **Fens**.

fence [fɛns] ① N **a** recinto, steccato; (*Racing*) ostacolo; **to sit on the fence** (*fig*) rimanere neutrale
  b (*fam: receiver of stolen goods*) ricettatore(-trice).
② VT recintare.
③ VI (*Sport*) tirare di scherma
▶ **fence in** VT + ADV **a** (*field*) recintare, recingere
  b (*fig*): **to feel fenced in** sentirsi imprigionato(-a)
▶ **fence off** VT + ADV separare con un recinto.

fenced [fɛnst] ADJ recintato(-a).

fenc·er ['fɛnsəʳ] N schermidore(-trice).

fenc·ing ['fɛnsɪŋ] N **a** (*Sport*) scherma; **fencing match** incontro di scherma **b** (*material*) materiale *m* per recintare.

fend [fɛnd] VI: **to fend for o.s.** arrangiarsi, badare a se stesso(-a)
▶ **fend off** VT + ADV (*attack, attacker*) respingere, difendersi da; (*blow*) parare; (*awkward question*) eludere.

fend·er ['fɛndəʳ] N (*round fire*) paracenere *m*, parafuoco; (*Am Aut: wing*) parafango; (*Am Rail*) paraurti *m inv*; (*Naut*) parabordo.

fen·nel ['fɛnl] N finocchio.

Fens [fɛnz] NPL (*Brit*): **the Fens** la regione delle Fens (*regione paludosa dell'Inghilterra centrale*).

fer·ment [*n* 'fɜːmɛnt; *vb* fə'mɛnt] ① N (*excitement*) eccitazione *f*, agitazione *f*, fermento; **to be in a state of ferment** essere in fermento *or* in uno stato di agitazione.
② VT far fermentare; (*fig*) fomentare.
③ VI fermentare.

fer·men·ta·tion [ˌfɜːmɛnˈteɪʃən] N fermentazione *f*.

fer·ment·ed [ˌfəˈmɛntɪd] ADJ fermentato(-a).

fern [fɜːn] N felce *f*.

fe·ro·cious [fəˈrəʊʃəs] ADJ feroce.

fe·ro·cious·ly [fəˈrəʊʃəslɪ] ADV ferocemente, con ferocia.

fe·roc·ity [fəˈrɒsɪtɪ] N ferocia.

fer·ret ['fɛrɪt] ① N furetto.
② VI cacciare con il furetto
▶ **ferret about, ferret around** VI + ADV (*fam*) frugare
▶ **ferret out** VT + ADV (*fam: secret, truth*) scoprire; (: *person*) scovare, scoprire.

fer·ro·con·crete ['fɛrəʊˈkɒŋkriːt] N cemento armato.

fer·rous ['fɛrəs] ADJ ferroso(-a).

fer·rule ['fɛruːl] N puntale *m*.

fer·ry ['fɛrɪ] ① N (*also: ferryboat: small*) traghetto; (: *large: for cars etc*) nave *f inv* traghetto.
② VT: **to ferry sth/sb across** *or* **over** traghettare qc/qn da una parte all'altra; **to ferry sb to and fro** portare qn avanti e indietro.

ferry·man ['fɛrɪmən] N (*pl* **ferrymen**) traghettatore *m*.

fer·tile ['fɜːtaɪl] ADJ (*gen*) fertile; (*creature, plant*) fecondo (-a); **fertile period** periodo di fecondità.

fer·til·ity [fəˈtɪlɪtɪ] N (*see adj*) fertilità; fecondità.

♦ **fertility drug** N farmaco contro la sterilità.

fer·ti·li·za·tion [ˌfɜːtɪlaɪˈzeɪʃən] N (*see vb*) fecondazione *f*; fertilizzazione *f*.

fer·ti·lize ['fɜːtɪˌlaɪz] VT (*egg*) fecondare; (*Agr: land, soil*) fertilizzare.

fer·ti·lized ['fɜːtɪˌlaɪzd] ADJ fecondato(-a).

fer·ti·liz·er ['fɜːtɪˌlaɪzəʳ] N fertilizzante *m*.

fer·vent ['fɜːvənt], **fer·vid** ['fɜːvɪd] ADJ (*believer, supporter*)

fervente; (*desire*) ardente, fervido(-a).

fer·vent·ly ['fɜ:vəntlɪ], **fer·vid·ly** ['fɜ:vɪdlɪ] ADV (*believe, support*) con passione, appassionatamente; (*desire*) intensamente, ardentemente.

fer·vour, (*Am*) **fer·vor** ['fɜ:və'] N (*frm*) fervore *m*, ardore *m*.

fes·ter ['fɛstə'] VI (*Med*) suppurare; (*anger, resentment*) covare.

fes·ti·val ['fɛstɪval] N (*Rel etc*) festa; (*Art, Mus*) festival *m inv*.

fes·tive ['fɛstɪv] ADJ di festa; **the festive season** (*Brit: Christmas*) il periodo delle feste natalizie; **in a festive mood** di umore allegro.

fes·tiv·ity [fɛs'tɪvɪtɪ] N **a** (*festival*) festa **b** (*celebrations*): **festivities** NPL festeggiamenti *mpl*.

fes·toon [fɛs'tu:n] VT: **to festoon with** ornare di, decorare con.

fe·tal ['fi:tl] (*Am*) ADJ = **foetal**.

fetch [fɛtʃ] VT **a** (*bring*) portare; (*go and get*) andare a prendere; (*: doctor*) andare a chiamare; **fetch it!** (*to dog*) prendi!
b (*sell for*) essere venduto(-a) per; **how much did it fetch?** a *or* per quanto lo hai venduto?
▶ **fetch in** VT + ADV (*object*) portare dentro; (*person*) far venire
▶ **fetch out** VT + ADV (*person*) far uscire; (*object*) tirare fuori
▶ **fetch up** VI + ADV (*Brit*) andare a finire.

fetch·ing ['fɛtʃɪŋ] ADJ attraente.

fetch·ing·ly ['fɛtʃɪŋlɪ] ADV (*dressed*) graziosamente.

fête [feɪt] **1** N festa all'aperto (*spesso a scopo di beneficenza*).
2 VT festeggiare.

fet·id, **foet·id** ['fi:tɪd] ADJ (*frm*) fetido(-a).

fet·ish ['fɛtɪʃ] N (*obsession*) fissazione *f*, mania; (*object of cult*) feticcio.

fet·ish·ism ['fɛtɪˌʃɪzəm] N feticismo.

fet·ish·ist ['fɛtɪʃɪst] N feticista *m/f*.

fet·lock ['fɛtˌlɒk] N (*joint*) nocca; (*hair*) barbetta.

fet·ter ['fɛtə'] VT (*person*) incatenare; (*fig*) ostacolare.

fet·ters ['fɛtəz] NPL catene *fpl*; (*fig*) restrizioni *fpl*.

fet·tle ['fɛtl] N (*Brit*): **in fine fettle** in gran forma.

fe·tus ['fi:təs] (*Am*) N = **foetus**.

feud [fju:d] **1** N faida, contesa, lotta; **a family feud** una faida familiare.
2 VI: **to feud (with sb)** essere in lotta (con qn).

feu·dal ['fju:dl] ADJ feudale.

feu·dal·ism ['fju:dəˌlɪzəm] N feudalesimo.

fe·ver ['fi:və'] N **a** (*high temperature*) febbre *f*; **he has a fever** ha la febbre; **a bout of fever** un accesso di febbre; **a high/slight fever** una febbre alta/leggera
b (*excitement*) eccitazione *f*; **the gambling fever** (*fig*) la febbre del gioco; **in a fever of excitement** in uno stato di eccitazione febbrile; **it reached fever pitch** ha raggiunto il colmo dell'emozione.

fe·vered ['fi:vəd] ADJ febbrile; (*person*) febbricitante.

fe·ver·ish ['fi:vərɪʃ] ADJ (*also fig*) febbrile; (*person*) febbricitante.

fe·ver·ish·ly ['fi:vərɪʃlɪ] ADV (*fig*) febbrilmente.

few [fju:] ADJ (*comp* **-er**, *superl* **-est**) PRON **a** (*not many*) pochi(-e); **few books** pochi libri; **few of them** pochi di loro; **few (people) managed to do it** pochi riuscirono a farlo; **few succeed** pochi ci riescono; **she is one of the few (people) who ...** è una delle poche persone che...; **the few who ...** i pochi che...; **in** *or* **over the past few days** in questi ultimi giorni, negli ultimi giorni; **in** *or* **over the**

next **few days** nei prossimi giorni; **every few days/ months** ogni due o tre giorni/mesi; **with few exceptions** con *or* salvo poche eccezioni; **every few weeks** a intervalli di qualche settimana; **they are few and far between** sono rari; **there are very few of us** *or* **we are very few** siamo pochi; **the last** *or* **remaining few minutes** i pochi minuti che rimangono; **as few as three of them** solo tre di loro; **too few** troppo pochi; **there were three too few** ne mancavano tre
b (*some, several*): **a few** alcuni(-e), qualche; **a few books** alcuni libri, qualche libro; **I know a few** ne conosco alcuni; **a few of them** alcuni di loro; **a few more days** qualche altro giorno; **in a few more days** fra qualche giorno; **a good few** *or* **quite a few** parecchi; **a good few** *or* **quite a few books** parecchi libri, un bel po' di libri; **a good few** *or* **quite a few (people) came** parecchie persone sono venute.

few·er ['fju:ə'] ADJ, PRON, COMP of **few**; meno *inv*, meno numerosi(-e); **fewer than 10** meno di 10; **fewer than you** meno di te; **no fewer than...** non meno di...; **there are fewer of them now** adesso ce ne sono di meno.

few·est ['fju:ɪst] ADJ, PRON, SUPERL of **few**; il minor numero di; **we were fewest in number** eravamo i meno numerosi.

fez [fɛz] N (*pl* **fezzes**) fez *m inv*.

FFA [ˌɛfɛf'eɪ] N ABBR = *Future Farmers of America*.

FH ABBR (*Brit*) = **fire hydrant**.

FHA [ˌɛfeɪtʃ'eɪ] N ABBR (*Am*)= *Federal Housing Administration*.

fi·an·cé [fi:'ãnseɪ] N fidanzato.

fi·an·cée [fi:'ãnseɪ] N fidanzata.

fi·as·co [fɪ'æskəʊ] N fiasco.

fiat ['faɪət] N (*frm*) ordine *m*.

fib [fɪb] (*fam*) **1** N bugia, frottola; **to tell a fib** dire una bugia.
2 VI dire bugie, raccontare storie.

fib·ber ['fɪbə'] N (*fam*) bugiardo(-a).

fi·bre, (*Am*) **fi·ber** ['faɪbə'] N fibra.

fibre·board, (*Am*) **fiber·board** ['faɪbəˌbɔ:d] N pannello di fibre.

fibre·glass, (*Am*) **fiber·glass** ['faɪbəˌglɑ:s] **1** N fibra di vetro.
2 ADJ di fibra di vetro.

♦ **fibre optics** NSG ottica a fibre.

fi·bril·la·tion [ˌfaɪbrɪ'leɪʃən] N fibrillazione *f*.

fi·broid ['faɪbrɔɪd] N fibroma *m*.

fi·bro·ma [faɪ'brəʊmə] N fibroma *m*.

fi·bro·sis [faɪ'brəʊsɪs] N fibrosi *f*.

fi·bro·si·tis [ˌfaɪbrə'saɪtɪs] N fibrosite *f*, cellulite *f*.

fi·brous ['faɪbrəs] ADJ fibroso(-a).

fi·brous·ness ['faɪbrəsnɪs] N fibrosità.

fibu·la ['fɪbjʊlə] N (*Anat*) fibula, perone *m*.

fick·le ['fɪkl] ADJ incostante, volubile.

fick·le·ness ['fɪklnɪs] N incostanza, volubilità.

fic·tion ['fɪkʃən] N **a** (*Literature*) narrativa; **a work of fiction** un'opera di narrativa; **light fiction** narrativa leggera **b** (*sth made up*) finzione *f*.

fic·tion·al ['fɪkʃənl] ADJ immaginario(-a).

fictionalize ['fɪkʃənəˌlaɪz] VT romanzare.

fic·tion·al·ized ['fɪkʃənəˌlaɪzd] ADJ romanzato(-a).

fic·ti·tious [fɪk'tɪʃəs] ADJ **a** = **fictional b** (*false*) falso(-a), fittizio(-a).

fic·ti·tious·ly [fɪk'tɪʃəslɪ] ADV in modo fittizio.

fid·dle ['fɪdl] **1** N **a** (*violin*) violino; **to play second fiddle to sb** (*fig*) avere un ruolo di secondo piano rispetto a qn **b** (*fam: cheating*) imbroglio, truffa; **it's a fiddle** è un

imbroglio; **tax fiddle** frode *f* fiscale; **to work a fiddle** fare un imbroglio; **to be on the fiddle** imbrogliare.

[2] VI (*fidget*) giocherellare, gingillarsi; **do stop fiddling!** stai fermo!; **to fiddle (about) with sth** giocherellare/gingillarsi con qc.

[3] VT (*Brit fam: accounts, results etc*) falsificare, alterare

▶ **fiddle about**, **fiddle around** VT + ADV gingillarsi, giocherellare.

fid·dler [ˈfɪdləʳ] N **a** (*Mus*) violinista *m/f* **b** (*fam: cheat*) imbroglione(-a).

fiddle·sticks [ˈfɪdlˌstɪks] EXCL (*old*): **fiddlesticks!** sciocchezze!

fid·dling [ˈfɪdlɪŋ] [1] ADJ insignificante; **fiddling little job** lavoretto.

[2] N (*fam: cheating*) imbrogli *mpl.*

fid·dly [ˈfɪdlɪ] ADJ (*comp* **-ier**, *superl* **-iest**) (*task*) da certosino; (*object*) complesso(-a).

fi·del·ity [fɪˈdɛlɪtɪ] N (*in relationships*) fedeltà; (*accuracy*) esattezza, accuratezza.

fidg·et [ˈfɪdʒɪt] [1] N (*person*) persona irrequieta; **to have the fidgets** essere irrequieto(-a) *or* agitato(-a).

[2] VI (*also:* **fidget about** *or* **around**) agitarsi; **to fidget with sth** giocherellare con qc.

fidg·ety [ˈfɪdʒɪtɪ] ADJ agitato(-a), irrequieto(-a).

fi·du·ci·ary [fɪˈduːʃɪərɪ] ADJ, N (*Law*) fiduciario(-a).

fief [fiːf] N feudo.

field [fiːld] [1] N (*gen*, *Comput*) campo; (*Geol*) giacimento; (*sphere of activity*) campo, settore *m*; **to give sth a year's trial in the field** (*fig*) sperimentare qc sul campo per un anno; **to study sth in the field** osservare *or* studiare qc sul campo; **to die in the field** (*Mil*) cadere sul campo di battaglia; **to take the field** (*Sport*) scendere in campo; **to lead the field** (*Sport*, *Comm*) essere in testa, essere al primo posto; **my particular field** la mia specialità, il mio campo *or* settore; **field of vision** campo visivo.

[2] VT (*team*) far giocare, far scendere in campo; (*Cricket: catch: ball*) prendere.

♦ **field day** N (*Mil*) giorno di grandi manovre; **to have a field day** (*fig*) divertirsi, spassarsela.

field·er [ˈfiːldəʳ] N (*Cricket*) giocatore che deve afferrare e rilanciare la palla.

♦ **field events** NPL (*Athletics*) atletica leggera.

field·fare [ˈfiːldˌfɛəʳ] N (*Zool*) viscarda.

♦ **field glasses** NPL (*binoculars*) binocolo *msg.*

♦ **field hockey** N (*Am*) hockey *m inv* (su prato).

♦ **field hospital** N ospedale *m* da campo.

♦ **field marshal** N feldmaresciallo.

♦ **field mushroom** N prataiolo.

♦ **field sports** NPL caccia e pesca.

♦ **field-test** [ˈfiːldˌtɛst] [1] N prova pratica.

[2] VT testare sul campo.

♦ **field·work** [ˈfiːldˌwɜːk] N (*Sociol etc*) ricerche *fpl* esterne; (*Archeology*, *Geo*) lavoro sul campo.

fiend [fiːnd] N demonio; **you little fiend!** (*fam*) piccolo delinquente!; **a tennis fiend** un fanatico *or* patito del tennis.

fiend·ish [ˈfiːndɪʃ] ADJ (*cruelty*, *smile*, *plot*) diabolico(-a); (*fam: difficult and unpleasant*) tremendo(-a); **I had a fiendish time trying to ...** è stato un lavoraccio tentare di... .

fiend·ish·ly [ˈfiːndɪʃlɪ] ADV (*see adj*) diabolicamente; tremendamente.

fierce [fɪəs] ADJ (*comp* **-er**, *superl* **-est**) (*gen*) feroce; (*opponent*) accanito(-a); (*enemy*) acerrimo(-a); (*look*, *fighting*) fiero(-a); (*wind*, *storm*) furioso(-a); (*heat*) intenso(-a).

fierce·ly [ˈfɪəslɪ] ADV (*extremely*) intensamente; (*fight*) con accanimento; (*rage*) furiosamente.

fierce·ness [ˈfɪəsnɪs] N (*also fig*) ferocia; (*of heat*) intensità.

fiery [ˈfaɪərɪ] ADJ (*comp* **-ier**, *superl* **-iest**) (*gen*) infocato(-a), ardente; (*red*) di fuoco; (*temperament*, *person*) focoso (-a); (*liquor*) che brucia la gola.

fi·es·ta [fɪˈɛstə] N fiesta *f inv.*

FIFA [ˈfiːfə] N ABBR (= *Fédération Internationale de Football Association*) F.I.F.A. *f.*

fif·teen [fɪfˈtiːn] [1] ADJ quindici *inv*; **about fifteen people** una quindicina di persone.

[2] N quindici *m inv*; (*Rugby*) squadra *for usage see* **five**.

fif·teenth [fɪfˈtiːnθ] [1] ADJ quindicesimo(-a).

[2] N (*in series*) quindicesimo(-a); (*fraction*) quindicesimo *for usage see* **fifth**.

fifth [fɪfθ] [1] ADJ quinto(-a); **I was (the) fifth to arrive** sono stato il quinto ad arrivare; **he came fifth in the competition** è arrivato quinto al concorso, si è piazzato al quinto posto; **Henry the Fifth** Enrico Quinto; **the fifth of July, July the fifth** il cinque luglio; **I wrote to him on the fifth** gli ho scritto il cinque; **fifth form** (*Brit Scol*) ≈ terzo anno di scuola superiore.

[2] N (*in series*) quinto(-a); (*fraction*) quinto; (*Mus*) quinta.

♦ **fifth column** N (*Pol*) quinta colonna.

♦ **fifth columnist** N appartenente *m/f* alla quinta colonna.

fif·ti·eth [ˈfɪftɪɪθ] [1] ADJ cinquantesimo(-a).

[2] N (*in series*) cinquantesimo(-a); (*fraction*) cinquantesimo *for usage see* **fifth**.

fif·ty [ˈfɪftɪ] [1] ADJ cinquanta *inv*; **about fifty people/cars** una cinquantina di persone/di macchine; **he'll be fifty (years old) next birthday** al prossimo compleanno avrà/compirà cinquant'anni; **he's about fifty** è sulla cinquantina.

[2] N cinquanta *m inv*; **the fifties** (*1950s*) gli anni cinquanta; **to be in one's fifties** avere passato la cinquantina; **the temperature was in the fifties** la temperatura era al di sopra dei cinquanta gradi (Fahrenheit); **to do fifty** (*Aut*) andare a 50 (all'ora).

♦ **fifty-fifty** [ˈfɪftɪˈfɪftɪ] ADJ, ADV: **to go fifty-fifty with sb** fare a metà con qn; **we have a fifty-fifty chance of success** abbiamo una probabilità su due di successo.

fig [fɪg] N fico.

fight [faɪt] (*vb: pt, pp* **fought**) [1] N (*Mil*) combattimento, lotta; (*Boxing*) incontro; (*between 2 persons*) lite *f*; (*brawl*) zuffa, rissa; (*fighting spirit*) combattività; (*struggle*, *campaign*): **fight (for/against)** lotta (a favore di/contro); (*argument*): **fight (over)** disputa (su); **to have a fight with sb** (*quarrel*, *struggle*) avere una lite con qn, litigare con qn; **to put up a good fight** battersi *or* difendersi bene; **there was no fight left in him** aveva perduto la sua combattività.

[2] VT (*Mil: enemy*, *battle*) combattere; (*fire*, *disease*, *proposals*) lottare contro, combattere; (*Law: case*) difendere; **to fight a duel** battersi in duello; **to fight one's way through a crowd/across a room** farsi strada a fatica tra la folla/attraverso una stanza.

[3] VI (*person*) azzuffarsi; (*animal*) battersi; (*troops*, *countries*): **to fight (against)** combattere (contro); (*quarrel*): **to fight (with sb)** litigare (con qn); (*fig*): **to fight (for/against)** lottare (per/contro); **to fight for one's life** lottare per la (propria) vita

▶ **fight back** [1] VI + ADV difendersi; (*Sport, after illness*) riprendersi.

[2] VT + ADV (*tears*) trattenere; (*anger*) reprimere; (*despair, doubts*) scacciare

▶ **fight down** VT + ADV (*anger, anxiety*) vincere; (*urge*) reprimere

▶ **fight off** VT + ADV (*attack, attacker*) respingere; (*disease, sleep, urge*) lottare contro

▶ **fight on** VI + ADV continuare a combattere

▶ **fight out** VT + ADV: **to fight it out** risolvere la questione a pugni.

fight·er ['faɪtə'] N combattente *m/f*; (*plane*) caccia *m inv*; **he's a fighter for the cause of** ... lotta per la causa di... .

♦ **fighter-bomber** ['faɪtə'bɒmə'] N cacciabombardiere *m*.

♦ **fighter pilot** N pilota *m* di caccia.

fight·ing ['faɪtɪŋ] [1] N (*Mil*) combattimento; (*in streets*) scontri *mpl*; (*in pub etc*) risse *fpl*, zuffe *fpl*.

[2] ADJ (*forces, strength, troops*) da combattimento; **fighting spirit** spirito combattivo; **a fighting chance** una buona probabilità.

♦ **fig leaf** N foglia di fico.

fig·ment ['fɪgmənt] N: **it's a figment of the imagination** è frutto dell'immaginazione, è un parto della fantasia.

fig·ura·tive ['fɪgərətɪv] ADJ (*meaning*) figurato(-a); (*Art*) figurativo(-a).

fig·ura·tive·ly ['fɪgərətɪvlɪ] ADV in modo figurato.

fig·ure ['fɪgə'] [1] N **a** (*number*) cifra; **to be good at figures** essere bravo(-a) a fare i conti; **a mistake in the figures** un errore nei calcoli, un errore di calcolo; **to reach double/three figures** raggiungere le due/tre cifre

  b (*body, outline*) figura, forma; **he's a fine figure of a man** è un bell'uomo; **he cuts a fine figure** ha molta classe; **to lose one's figure** perdere la linea

  c (*person*) figura, personaggio; **public figure** personaggio pubblico

  d (*drawing, Geom*) figura; (*diagram*) illustrazione *f*.

[2] VI **a** (*appear*) figurare

  b (*esp Am: make sense*) essere logico(-a), spiegarsi; **that figures!** (*fam*) è logico!.

[3] VT (*esp Am: think, calculate*) pensare, immaginare

▶ **figure on** VI + PREP (*Am*) contare su; **I figured on him arriving by 6 o'clock** contavo sul fatto che sarebbe arrivato entro le 6

▶ **figure out** VT + ADV (*understand*) riuscire a capire; (*calculate: sum*) calcolare; **I just can't figure it out!** non ci arrivo!

figure·head ['fɪgə,hɛd] N (*Naut*) polena; (*fig*) figura rappresentativa; (*pej*) prestanome *m/f inv*.

♦ **figure of eight** N un otto.

♦ **figure of speech** N figura retorica; **it's just a figure of speech** (*fig*) è solo un modo di dire.

♦ **figure skating** N pattinaggio artistico.

figu·rine [,fɪgə'riːn] N figurina, statuetta.

Fiji ['fiːdʒiː] N: **the Fiji Islands** le isole *fpl* Figi.

fila·ment ['fɪləmənt] N filamento.

filch [fɪltʃ] VT (*fam: steal*) grattare.

file¹ [faɪl] [1] N (*folder*) cartella, cartellina; (*ring binder*) raccoglitore *m*; (*dossier*) pratica, incartamento; (*in cabinet*) scheda; (*Comput*) archivio, file *m inv*.

[2] VT **a** (*also:* **file away***: notes, information, papers*) raccogliere; (: *under heading*) archiviare

  b (*Law: claim, application, complaint*) presentare; **to file a suit against sb** (*Law*) intentare causa contro qn.

file² [faɪl] [1] N (*tool*) lima; (*for nails*) limetta.

[2] VT (*metal, wood*) limare; **to file one's nails** limarsi le unghie.

file³ [faɪl] [1] N (*row*) fila; **in single file** in fila indiana.

[2] VI: **to file in/out** entrare/uscire in fila; **to file past (sth/sb)** sfilare (davanti a qc/qn), marciare in fila (davanti a qc/qn).

♦ **file clerk** N = **filing clerk**.

filename ['faɪl,neɪm] N (*Comput*) nome *m* del file.

fil·ial ['fɪljəl] ADJ filiale.

fili·bus·ter ['fɪlɪ,bʌstə'] (*esp Am Pol*) [1] N ostruzionismo.

[2] VI fare ostruzionismo.

fili·bus·ter·er ['fɪlɪ,bʌstərə'] N (*esp Am Pol*) ostruzionista *m/f*.

fili·gree ['fɪlɪ,griː] [1] N filigrana.

[2] ADJ a filigrana.

fil·ing ['faɪlɪŋ] N archiviazione *f*; see also **filings**.

♦ **filing cabinet** N schedario, casellario.

♦ **filing clerk**, (*Am*) **file clerk** N archivista *m/f*.

fil·ings ['faɪlɪŋz] NPL limatura.

Fili·pi·no [,fɪlɪ'piːnəʊ] [1] ADJ filippino(-a).

[2] N **a** (*person*) filippino(-a) **b** (*language*) tagal *m*.

fill [fɪl] [1] VT (*gen*) riempire; (*tooth*) otturare; (*position*) coprire; (*subj: wind: sails*) gonfiare; (*supply: order, requirements, need*) soddisfare; **to fill with** riempire di *or* con; **we've already filled that vacancy** abbiamo già assunto qualcuno per quel posto; **they asked her to fill the vacancy** le hanno offerto il posto; **the position is already filled** il posto è già preso; **filled with admiration (for)** pieno(-a) di ammirazione (per); **filled with remorse/despair** in preda al rimorso/alla disperazione; **that fills the bill** è quello che ci vuole.

[2] VI: **to fill (with)** riempirsi (di *or* con).

[3] N: **to eat/drink one's fill** mangiare/bere a sazietà; **to have one's fill of sth** (*fig*) averne le tasche piene di qc

▶ **fill in** [1] VT + ADV **a** (*hole, gap, outline*) riempire

  b (*one's name*) mettere; (*form*) riempire, compilare; (*details, report*) completare; **to fill sb in on sth** (*fam*) mettere qn al corrente di qc.

[2] VI + ADV: **to fill in for sb** sostituire qn

▶ **fill out** [1] VT + ADV (*form, receipt*) riempire, compilare.

[2] VI + ADV (*person, face*) ingrassare, ingrassarsi; (*sail*) gonfiarsi

▶ **fill up** [1] VI + ADV **a** (*Aut*) fare il pieno

  b (*room etc*) riempirsi, gremirsi.

[2] VT + ADV (*container*) riempire; **fill it** *or* **her up, please** (*fam: Aut*) mi faccia il pieno, per piacere.

filled [fɪld] ADJ: **filled with** (*room*) completamente occupato(-a) da; **to be filled with resentment** essere colmo(-a) di rancore; **eyes filled with tears** occhi pieni di lacrime.

fill·er ['fɪlə'] N (*for cracks: in wood, plaster*) stucco.

fil·let ['fɪlɪt] [1] N filetto.

[2] VT (*meat*) disossare; (*fish*) tagliare a filetti, sfilettare; **filleted cod** filetti *mpl* di merluzzo.

♦ **fillet steak** N (bistecca di) filetto.

fill·ing ['fɪlɪŋ] [1] N (*for tooth*) otturazione *f*; (*Culin*) ripieno.

[2] ADJ (*food*) sostanzioso(-a).

♦ **filling station** N stazione *f* di rifornimento.

fil·lip ['fɪlɪp] N stimolo.

fil·ly ['fɪlɪ] N puledra.

film [fɪlm] [1] N **a** (*at cinema*) film *m inv*; (*Phot*) pellicola; **a 36 exposure film** un rullino da 36 pose; **film buff** appassionato(-a) di cinema; **film camera** macchina da presa **b** (*thin layer*) strato sottile, velo; (*wrap*) pellicola.

[2] VT (*scene*) filmare.

♦ **film crew** N troupe *f inv* cinematografica.

film·ing ['fɪlmɪŋ] N: **filming started last week** hanno cominciato a girare (il film) la settimana scorsa.

♦ **film library** N cineteca.

♦ **film rights** NPL diritti *mpl* di produzione.

♦ **film script** N copione *m*.

film·set ['fɪlm,sɛt] VT (*Typ*) fotocomporre.

film·setting ['fɪlm,sɛtɪŋ] N (*Typ*) fotocomposizione *f*.

♦ **film star** N divo(-a) del cinema.

film·strip ['fɪlm,strɪp] N filmina.

♦ **film studio** N studio cinematografico.

♦ **film theatre** N cineteca.

filmy ['fɪlmɪ] ADJ trasparente.

Filo·fax® ['faɪləʊ,fæks] N filofax *f inv*, *agenda ad anelli*.

fil·ter ['fɪltə'] [1] N filtro.

[2] VT filtrare.

[3] VI: **to filter to the left** (*Aut*) immettersi nella corsia di svincolo

▶ **filter in, filter through** VI + ADV (*news*) trapelare.

♦ **filter coffee** N caffè *m* da passare al filtro.

♦ **filter feeding** N (*Bio*) filtrazione *f*.

♦ **filter lane** N (*Brit Aut*) corsia di svincolo.

♦ **filter light** N (*Brit Aut*) freccia di svolta continua (*nei semafori*).

♦ **filter paper** N carta da filtro *or* filtrante.

♦ **filter tip** N filtro.

♦ **filter-tipped** ['fɪltə,tɪpt] ADJ con filtro.

filth [fɪlθ] N sudiciume *m*, sporcizia; (*fig*) oscenità; **it's just sheer filth** non è altro che una porcheria.

filthi·ness ['fɪlθɪnɪs] N (*of room, person*) sporcizia; (*of language*) sudiceria.

filthy ['fɪlθɪ] ADJ (*comp* **-ier**, *superl* **-iest**) sudicio(-a), sozzo(-a); (*language*) volgare, osceno(-a); **what filthy weather!** che tempaccio!; **he's got a filthy mind** è uno sporcaccione.

fin [fɪn] N (*of fish*) pinna; (*of plane, bomb*) impennaggio verticale.

fi·nal ['faɪnl] [1] ADJ (*last*) ultimo(-a); (*conclusive*) finale, definitivo(-a); (*victory*) conclusivo(-a); (*exam*) finale; **final demand** (*Comm*) ingiunzione *f* (di pagamento); **the judge's decision is final** la decisione del giudice è inappellabile; ... **and that's final!** ...e basta!.

[2] N (*Sport*) finale *f*; see also **finals**.

fi·na·le [fɪ'nɑːlɪ] N finale *m*; **the grand finale** (*also fig*) il gran finale.

fi·nal·ist ['faɪnəlɪst] N (*Sport*) finalista *m/f*.

fi·nal·ity [faɪ'nælɪtɪ] N irrevocabilità; **with an air of finality** con risolutezza.

fi·na·li·za·tion [,faɪnəlaɪ'zeɪʃən] N (*see vb*) messa a punto; definizione *f*; stesura definitiva.

fi·nal·ize ['faɪnə,laɪz] VT (*preparations, arrangements, plans*) mettere a punto; (*agreement, decision, contract*) definire; (*report, text*) dare una stesura definitiva a; (*date*) fissare.

fi·nal·ly ['faɪnəlɪ] ADV (*lastly*) alla fine; (*in conclusion*) in fine; (*eventually*) finalmente; (*once and for all*) definitivamente.

fi·nals ['faɪnlz] NPL (*Univ*) esami *mpl* dell'ultimo anno.

fi·nance [faɪ'næns] [1] N **a** (*money management*) finanza; (*funds*) fondi *mpl*, capitale *m*; **Minister of Finance** Ministro delle Finanze **b** (*resources*): **finances** NPL finanze *fpl*.

[2] VT finanziare.

[3] ADJ (*page, section, company*) finanziario(-a).

fi·nan·cial [faɪ'nænʃəl] ADJ finanziario(-a); **financial management** gestione *f* finanziaria; **financial statement** estratto conto finanziario.

fi·nan·cial·ly [faɪ'nænʃəlɪ] ADV finanziariamente.

♦ **financial year** N anno finanziario, esercizio finanziario.

fi·nan·ci·er [fɪ'nænsɪə'] N finanziatore(-trice).

finch [fɪntʃ] N fringillide *m*.

find [faɪnd] (*vb: pt, pp* **found**) [1] VT **a** (*gen*) trovare; (*sth lost*) trovare, ritrovare; (*learn*) scoprire; **the book is nowhere to be found** il libro non si trova da nessuna parte; **this plant is found all over Europe** questa pianta si trova in tutta Europa; **it has been found that ...** è stato *or* si è scoperto che...; **if you can find the time** se riesci a trovare il tempo; **no cure has been found** non è stata trovata nessuna cura; **I found it impossible to tell the difference** non riuscivo a distinguerli; **he finds it easy/difficult to do ...** non trova/trova difficoltà a *or* nel fare...; **to find (some) difficulty in doing sth** trovare delle difficoltà nel fare qc; **I find him very pleasant** lo trovo molto simpatico; **we found him in bed/reading** l'abbiamo trovato a letto/che stava leggendo; **I found myself at a loss** non sapevo cosa dire, non riuscivo a trovare le parole; **can you find your (own) way to the station?** sai come andare alla stazione?; **this found its way into my drawer** questo è andato a finire nel mio cassetto; **leave everything as you find it** lascia tutto come trovi; **to find fault with sb/sth** trovare da ridire sul conto di qn/su qc; **to find sb guilty** (*Law*) giudicare qn colpevole; **he was found innocent** (*Law*) fu dichiarato innocente; **to find one's feet** (*fig*) ambientarsi

b (*obtain*) trovare; **go and find me a pencil** vai a cercarmi una matita; **there are no more to be found** non ce ne sono più; **wages all found** stipendio più vitto e alloggio.

[2] VI (*Law*): **to find for/against sb** emettere un verdetto a favore di/contro qn.

[3] N scoperta, trovata

▶ **find out** [1] VT + ADV informarsi di; (*truth, secret, answer*) scoprire; **to find out that ...** scoprire che...; **to find sb out** smascherare qn.

[2] VI + ADV: **to find out about** scoprire; (*by investigation*) informarsi su; **we found out about his death** abbiamo scoperto che era morto; **we found out all about ...** abbiamo scoperto tutto su... .

find·ings ['faɪndɪŋz] NPL (*of report, of inquiry*) conclusioni *fpl*; (*Law*) verdetto *msg*.

fine¹ [faɪn] [1] ADJ (*comp* **-r**, *superl* **-st**) **a** (*small, delicate, narrow*) fine; (*rain*) leggero(-a); (*fig: distinction*) sottile; **not to put too fine a point on it** per dirlo con schiettezza; **he's got it down to a fine art** lo fa alla perfezione

b (*not coarse: metal*) fino(-a); (: *sense*) sottile; (: *taste*) raffinato(-a); (: *feelings*) elevato(-a); **fine workmanship** lavorazione *f* raffinata

c (*good*) ottimo(-a); (*beautiful, imposing*) bello(-a); (*clothes*) elegante; **the weather is fine** se il tempo è bello; **it's a fine day today** è una bella giornata oggi; **he's a fine man** è un'ottima persona; **that's fine** va benissimo; **he's fine** sta bene; **a fine friend you are!** bell'amico sei!; **you're a fine one to talk!** senti chi parla!; **a fine thing!** bella roba!; **one fine day** un bel giorno.

[2] ADV **a** (*well*) molto bene; **you're doing fine** te la cavi benissimo

b (*finely*) finemente; **to cut it fine** (*of time, money*) farcela per un pelo

▶ **fine down** VT + ADV affinare.

fine² [faɪn] [1] N multa; **to get a fine for sth/doing sth** ricevere una multa per qc/per aver fatto qc.

2 VT: **to fine sb (for sth/for doing sth)** multare qn *or* fare una multa a qn (per qc/per aver fatto qc).

♦ **fine arts** NPL: **the fine arts** (le) belle arti *fpl*.

fine·ly ['faɪnlɪ] ADV **a** (*written, sewn*) con raffinatezza **b** (*chop*) finemente; (*adjust*) con precisione.

fine·ness ['faɪnnɪs] N (*of silk*) finezza, sottigliezza.

♦ **fine print** N: **the fine print** i caratteri minuti.

fin·ery ['faɪnərɪ] N abiti *mpl* eleganti; **to be dressed in all one's finery** essere tutto(-a) in ghingheri.

fi·nesse [fɪ'nɛs] N finezza; (*Cards*) impasse *f*.

♦ **fine-tooth comb** ['faɪnˌtuːθ'kəʊm] N: **to go through sth with a fine-tooth comb** (*fig*) passare qc al setaccio.

fin·ger ['fɪŋgəʳ] 1 N dito; **his fingers are all thumbs** OR he **is all fingers and thumbs** è molto maldestro; **keep your fingers crossed** fai gli scongiuri; **they never laid a finger on her** non l'hanno mai nemmeno toccata; **he didn't lift a finger to help** non ha mosso un dito per aiutare; **I can't quite put my finger on what's wrong** non riesco a vedere cosa c'è di sbagliato; **to twist sb round one's little finger** fare quello che si vuole di qn; **to have a finger in every pie** avere le mani in pasta dappertutto; **to pull one's finger out** (*fig fam*) darsi una mossa.

2 VT toccare, tastare; (*keyboard*) far scorrere le dita su.

♦ **finger board** N manico.

♦ **finger bowl** N sciacquadita *m inv*.

finger·mark ['fɪŋgəˌmaːk] N ditata.

finger·nail ['fɪŋgəˌneɪl] N unghia.

♦ **finger painting** N dipingere con le mani: **to do finger painting** dipingere con le mani.

finger·print ['fɪŋgəˌprɪnt] 1 N impronta digitale.

2 VT (*person*) prendere le impronte digitali di *or* a.

finger·stall ['fɪŋgəˌstɔːl] N ditale *m*.

finger·tip ['fɪŋgəˌtɪp] N punta del dito; **to have sth at one's fingertips** (*fig*) avere qc sulla punta delle dita; **fingertip hold** (*Mountaineering*) gratton *m inv*.

fin·icky ['fɪnɪkɪ] ADJ **a** (*person*): **finicky (about)** pignolo(-a) (su), difficile (per) **b** (*job*) minuzioso(-a).

fin·is ['fɪnɪs] N fine *f*.

fin·ish ['fɪnɪʃ] 1 N **a** (*end: esp Sport*) fine *f*; (*Sport: line*) traguardo; (*Mountaineering*) uscita; **to be in at the finish** essere presente alla fine; **a fight to the finish** un combattimento all'ultimo sangue **b** (*appearance*) finitura.

2 VT (*gen*) finire, terminare; (*use up*) esaurire; **to finish doing sth** finire di fare qc; **that last mile nearly finished me** (*fam*) quell'ultimo miglio mi ha quasi distrutto.

3 VI (*session*) finire, terminare; (*book, game*) finire, concludersi; (*contract*) scadere; (*Mountaineering*) uscire; **the party was finishing** la festa stava per finire; **she finished by saying that ...** ha concluso dicendo che...; **to finish first/second** (*Sport*) arrivare primo(-a)/secondo (-a); **I've finished with the paper** ho finito col giornale; **he's finished with politics** ha chiuso con la politica; **she's finished with him** (*broken relationship*) ha chiuso con lui

▶ **finish off** VT + ADV finire; (*kill*) uccidere

▶ **finish up** 1 VI + ADV finire; **he finished up in Paris** è finito a Parigi; **it finished up as ...** ha finito col diventare....

2 VT + ADV (*food etc*) finire.

fin·ished ['fɪnɪʃt] ADJ **a** (*product*) finito(-a); (*performance*) perfetto(-a) **b** (*fam: tired*) sfinito(-a); (: *done for*) finito (-a).

fin·ish·ing line ['fɪnɪʃɪŋˌlaɪn] N (*Sport*) traguardo, linea d'arrivo.

fin·ish·ing ma·chine ['fɪnɪʃɪŋməˈʃiːn] N (*Tech*) finitrice *f*.

fin·ish·ing school ['fɪnɪʃɪŋˌskuːl] N scuola privata di perfezionamento (*per signorine*).

fin·ish·ing touches [ˌfɪnɪʃɪŋˈtʌtʃɪz] NPL ultimi ritocchi *mpl*; **to put the finishing touches to sth** dare gli ultimi ritocchi a qc.

fi·nite ['faɪnaɪt] ADJ **a** (*limited*) limitato(-a) **b** (*Gram: verb*) finito(-a).

fink [fɪŋk] N (*Am*) informatore(-trice).

Fin·land ['fɪnlənd] N la Finlandia.

Finn [fɪn] N finlandese *m/f*.

Finn·ish ['fɪnɪʃ] 1 ADJ finlandese.

2 N (*language*) finlandese *m*.

fiord [fjɔːd] N = **fjord**.

fir [fɜːʳ] N (*also:* **fir tree**) abete *m*.

♦ **fir cone** N pigna.

fire ['faɪəʳ] 1 N **a** (*gen*) fuoco; (*house fire etc*) incendio; **electric/gas fire** stufa elettrica/a gas; **forest fire** incendio boschivo; **to set fire to sth** *or* **set sth on fire** dar fuoco a qc, incendiare qc; **to catch fire** prendere fuoco; **to be on fire** essere in fiamme; **insured against fire** assicurato(-a) contro gli incendi; **to play with fire** (*fig*) scherzare col fuoco

b (*Mil*) fuoco; **to open fire (on sb)** aprire il fuoco (contro *or* su qn); **to hold one's fire** cessare il fuoco; **to be/come under fire (from)** essere/finire sotto il fuoco *or* il tiro (di); **the government has come under fire from the opposition** il governo è finito sotto il tiro dell'opposizione.

2 VT **a** (*gun, shot, salute*) sparare; (*rocket etc*) lanciare; **to fire a gun at sb** fare fuoco contro qn; **to fire questions at sb** bombardare qn di domande

b (*pottery: in kiln*) cuocere; (*fig: imagination*) accendere, infiammare

c (*fam: dismiss*) licenziare; **you're fired!** sei licenziato!.

3 VI **a** (*Mil etc*): **to fire (at)** sparare (a), far fuoco (contro); **fire away** *or* **ahead!** (*fig fam*) spara!

b (*Aut: subj: engine*) accendersi.

♦ **fire alarm** N allarme *m* antincendio *inv*.

fire·arm ['faɪərˌɑːm] N arma da fuoco.

fire·ball ['faɪəˌbɔːl] N (*Astron*) bolide *m*; (*nuclear*) palla di fuoco; (*lightning*) fulmine *m* globulare.

fire·brand ['faɪəˌbrænd] N (*person*) agitatore(-trice), sobillatore(-trice).

fire·break ['faɪəˌbreɪk] N tagliafuoco.

fire·brick ['faɪəˌbrɪk] N mattone *m* refrattario.

♦ **fire brigade**, (*Am*) **fire department** N (corpo dei) pompieri *mpl* *or* vigili *mpl* del fuoco.

fire·bug ['faɪəˌbʌg] N (*fam*) incendiario(-a).

♦ **fire chief** N (*Am*) comandante *m* dei vigili del fuoco.

fire·cracker ['faɪəˌkrækəʳ] N petardo.

♦ **fire department** N (*Am*) = **fire brigade**.

fire·dogs ['faɪəˌdɒgz] NPL alari *mpl*.

♦ **fire door** N porta *f* tagliafuoco *inv*.

♦ **fire drill**, **fire practice** N esercitazione *f* antincendio *inv*.

♦ **fire-eater** ['faɪərˌiːtəʳ] N (*performer*) mangiatore *m* di fuoco; (*fig*) attaccabrighe *m/f*.

♦ **fire engine** N autopompa.

♦ **fire escape** N scala di sicurezza.

♦ **fire exit** N uscita di sicurezza.

♦ **fire extinguisher** N estintore *m*.

♦ **fire-fighting** ['faɪəʳˌfaɪtɪŋ] N: **attempts at fire-fighting** tentativi di spegnere l'incendio; **fire-fighting equipment** attrezzatura antincendio *f inv*.

fire·fly ['faɪə‚flaɪ] N (pl **-flies**) lucciola.
fire·guard ['faɪə‚gɑːd] N (Brit) parafuoco.
♦ **fire hazard** N: **that's a fire hazard** può provocare un incendio.
♦ **fire hydrant** N idrante m.
♦ **fire insurance** N assicurazione f contro gli incendi.
♦ **fire-irons** ['faɪər‚aɪəns] N molle fpl.
fire·light ['faɪə‚laɪt] N bagliore m del fuoco; **by firelight** alla luce del fuoco.
♦ **fire lighter** N esca (per accendere il fuoco).
fire·man ['faɪəmən] N (pl **-men**) vigile m del fuoco, pompiere m.
fire·place ['faɪə‚pleɪs] N caminetto, focolare m.
fire·plug ['faɪə‚plʌg] N (Am) = **fire hydrant**.
♦ **fire practice** N = **fire drill**.
♦ **fire prevention** N prevenzione f antincendio.
fire·proof ['faɪə‚pruːf] ADJ (material) resistente al fuoco; (dish) resistente al calore.
♦ **fire rais·er** ['faɪə‚reɪzəʳ] N incendiario(-a).
♦ **fire-raising** ['faɪəʳ‚reɪzɪŋ] N piromania.
♦ **fire regulations** NPL norme fpl antincendio.
♦ **fire risk** N rischio d'incendio.
♦ **fire sale** N svendita di prodotti danneggiati da un incendio; **we got them at fire-sale prices** li abbiamo comprati a prezzi stracciati.
♦ **fire screen** N = **fireguard**.
fire·side ['faɪə‚saɪd] N angolo del focolare; **by the fireside** intorno al focolare.
♦ **fire station** N caserma dei pompieri.
♦ **fire trap** N: **it's a fire trap** in caso di incendio si trasformerà in una trappola.
fire·wood ['faɪə‚wʊd] N legna da ardere.
fire·work ['faɪə‚wɜːk] N fuoco d'artificio.
fire·works ['faɪə‚wɜːks] NPL (show) fuochi mpl d'artificio; (fig: temper) parole fpl grosse; (: virtuosity) virtuosismi mpl.
fir·ing ['faɪərɪŋ] N (Mil) spari mpl, tiro.
♦ **firing line** N linea del fuoco; **to be in the firing line** (fig: liable to be criticized) essere sulla linea del fuoco.
♦ **firing squad** N plotone m d'esecuzione.
firm¹ ['fɜːm] ADJ (comp **-er**, superl **-est**) (gen) solido(-a); (steady) saldo(-a); (belief) fermo(-a); (measures) severo (-a); (look, voice) risoluto(-a); (prices) stabile; (offer, decision) definitivo(-a); **as firm as a rock** solido(-a) come una roccia; **to be a firm believer in sth** credere fermamente in qc; **to be firm with sb** essere deciso(-a) con qn; **they are firm friends** sono molto amici; **to keep a firm hold on** tenere saldamente; **to be on firm ground** (fig) andare sul sicuro; **to stand firm** or **take a firm stand over sth** (fig) tener duro per quanto riguarda qc.
firm² [fɜːm] N azienda, ditta, impresa.
firm·ly ['fɜːmlɪ] ADV (fixed) saldamente, solidamente; (speak) con fermezza; (believe) fermamente.
firm·ness ['fɜːmnɪs] N (of voice, decision etc) fermezza; (of object) solidità.
first [fɜːst] **1** ADJ primo(-a); **the first of January** il primo (di) gennaio; **the first time** la prima volta; **Charles the First** Carlo Primo; **to win first place** arrivare primo; **in the first place** per prima cosa, innanzitutto; **in the first instance** in primo luogo, prima di tutto; **first thing in the morning** la mattina presto; **I'll do it first thing tomorrow** lo farò per prima cosa domani; **first things first!** prima le cose più importanti!; **I don't know the first thing about it** (fam) non ne so un bel niente.
2 ADV **a** (firstly) prima; (before other things) per primo

(-a); (when listing reasons etc) per prima cosa; **first one, then another** prima uno, poi un altro; **first of all** prima di tutto; **first and foremost** prima di tutto, innanzitutto; **first and last** (above all) prima di tutto; **ladies first!** prima le signore!; **we arrived first** siamo arrivati per primi; **she came first in the race** è arrivata prima nella gara; **at first** sulle prime, all'inizio, dapprima; **finish this work first** finisci questo lavoro prima; **head first** a capofitto
b (for the first time) per la prima volta; **I first met him in Paris** l'ho incontrato per la prima volta a Parigi
c (rather) piuttosto; **I'd die first!** piuttosto morirei!.
3 N (person: in race) primo(-a); **the first to arrive** il/la primo(-a) ad arrivare; **first come, first served** chi tardi arriva, male alloggia; **from the (very) first** fin dall'inizio, fin dal primo momento; **from first to last** dall'inizio alla fine; **in first (gear)** (Aut) in prima (marcia); **he gained a first in French** (Brit Univ: class of degree) si è laureato in francese col massimo dei voti.
♦ **first-aid** ['fɜːst'eɪd] ADJ: **first-aid classes** corso di pronto soccorso; **first-aid kit** or **box** cassetta di pronto soccorso; **first-aid post** posto di pronto soccorso.
♦ **first aid** N pronto soccorso.
♦ **first-class** ['fɜːst'klɑːs] **1** ADJ **a** di prima classe; **first-class ticket** (Rail etc) biglietto di prima classe; **first-class compartment** (Rail) scompartimento di prima classe; **first-class honours degree** (Univ) ≈ laurea con centodieci e lode
b (very good) di prima qualità.
2 ADV: **to travel first-class** viaggiare in prima classe; **to send a letter first-class** ≈ spedire una lettera per espresso.
♦ **first-class mail** N ≈ espresso.
♦ **first cousin** N cugino di primo grado.
♦ **first-day cover** [fɜːst'deɪ'kʌvəʳ] N busta con francobolli del primo giorno di emissione.
♦ **first-degree** ['fɜːst'dɪ'griː] ADJ (burn) di primo grado.
♦ **first edition** N prima edizione f.
♦ **first-ever** [fɜːst'ɛvəʳ] ADJ primo(-a) in assoluto.
♦ **first floor** N: **the first floor** (Brit) il primo piano; (Am) il pianoterreno; **on the first floor** (Brit) al primo piano.
♦ **first form, first year** N (Scol) ≈ prima media.
♦ **first fruits** N: **the first fruits** i primi risultati.
♦ **first-generation** ['fɜːst‚dʒɛnə'reɪʃən] ADJ (immigrant) di prima generazione; (computer) della prima generazione.
♦ **first-hand** ['fɜːst'hænd] **1** ADJ diretto(-a), di prima mano.
2 ADV direttamente.
♦ **First Lady** N (Am) moglie f del presidente.
♦ **first language** N prima lingua.
first·ly ['fɜːstlɪ] ADV prima, innanzitutto, in primo luogo.
♦ **first name** N nome m (di battesimo).
♦ **first night** N (Theatre) prima.
♦ **first offender** N (Law) incensurato(-a).
♦ **first person** N: **a novel in the first person** un romanzo in prima persona.
♦ **first-rate** ['fɜːst'reɪt] ADJ di prim'ordine, ottimo(-a).
♦ **first school** N ≈ scuola elementare.
♦ **first-time buyer** ['fɜːst'taɪm'baɪəʳ] N acquirente m/f di prima casa.
♦ **First World War** N: **the First World War** la prima guerra mondiale.
♦ **first year** N = **first form**.
FIS [‚ɛfaɪ'ɛs] N ABBR (Brit: old: = Family Income Supplement) ≈

A.F. (= *assegni familiari*).

fis·cal ['fɪskəl] ADJ fiscale.

♦ **fiscal year** N (*Am*) anno fiscale.

fish [fɪʃ] ①① N (*pl* fish *or* fishes) pesce *m*; **fish and chips** pesce con patatine fritte; **to be like a fish out of water** sentirsi come un pesce fuor d'acqua; **I've got other fish to fry** (*fam*) ho altro da fare.

② VI pescare; **to go fishing** andare a pesca; **to go salmon fishing** andare a pesca di salmoni; **to fish for trout** pescare (le) trote; **to fish for compliments/for information** (*fig*) andare a caccia di complimenti/di informazioni; **to fish (around) in one's pockets for sth** frugarsi le tasche in cerca di qc.

③ VT (*river, pond*) pescare in; (*trout, salmon*) pescare

▶ **fish out** VT + ADV (*from water*) ripescare; (*from box etc*) tirare fuori.

♦ **fish-and-chip shop** ['fɪʃənd'tʃɪp'ʃɒp] N (*Brit*); see **chip shop**.

fish·bone ['fɪʃˌbəʊn] N lisca, spina.

fish·bowl ['fɪʃˌbəʊl] N vaschetta per pesci.

fish·cake ['fɪʃˌkeɪk] N crocchetta di pesce.

fisher·man ['fɪʃəmən] N (*pl* -men) pescatore *m*.

fish·ery ['fɪʃərɪ] N zona di pesca.

♦ **fish farm** N vivaio.

♦ **fish farming** N piscicoltura.

♦ **fish fingers** NPL (*Brit*) bastoncini *mpl* di pesce (surgelati).

♦ **fish-hook** ['fɪʃˌhʊk] N amo.

fish·ing ['fɪʃɪŋ] N pesca.

♦ **fishing boat** N peschereccio.

♦ **fishing fleet** N flotta di pescherecci.

♦ **fishing grounds** NPL zona di pesca.

♦ **fishing industry** N industria della pesca.

♦ **fishing line** N lenza.

♦ **fishing net** N rete *f* da pesca.

♦ **fishing port** N porto di pesca.

♦ **fishing rod** N canna da pesca.

♦ **fishing tackle** N attrezzatura da pesca.

♦ **fish kettle** N pesciera.

♦ **fish knife** N coltello da pesce.

♦ **fish market** N mercato del pesce.

fish·monger ['fɪʃˌmʌŋgəʳ] N (*Brit*) pescivendolo; **fishmonger's (shop)** pescheria.

fish·pond ['fɪʃˌpɒnd] N (*in garden*) vasca per i pesci.

♦ **fish shop** N pescheria.

♦ **fish slice** N (*Brit*) paletta forata *or* per fritti.

♦ **fish sticks** ['fɪʃˌstɪks] NPL (*Am*) = **fish fingers**.

♦ **fish tank** N acquario.

fish·wife ['fɪʃˌwaɪf] N (*pej*) pescivendola.

fishy ['fɪʃɪ] ADJ (*comp* -ier, *superl* -iest) **a** (*smell, taste: usu pej*) di pesce **b** (*fam: suspicious*) losco(-a), sospetto(-a).

fis·sion ['fɪʃən] N fissione *f*; **atomic/nuclear fission** fissione atomica/nucleare.

fis·sure ['fɪʃəʳ] N fessura, fenditura.

fist [fɪst] N pugno; **to shake one's fist (at sb)** minacciare (qn) con il pugno.

fist·fight ['fɪstˌfaɪt] N scazzottata.

fist·ful ['fɪstfʊl] N pugno, manciata.

fisti·cuffs ['fɪstɪˌkʌfs] NPL scazzottata.

fis·tu·la ['fɪstjʊlə] N fistola.

fit¹ [fɪt] ① ADJ (*comp* -ter, *superl* -test) **a** (*suitable*) adatto(-a); (*proper*) appropriato(-a), conveniente; **fit for** adatto a; **to be fit for sth** andare bene per qc; **to be fit for nothing** non essere buono(-a) a niente; **a meal fit for a king** un pranzo da re; **he's not fit for the job** non è la persona adatta per questo lavoro; **fit for habitation** abitabile; **he is not fit company for my daughter** non è la compagnia adatta per mia figlia; **he's not fit to teach** non è adatto all'insegnamento; **he's not fit to drive** non è in condizione di guidare; **you're not fit to be seen** non sei presentabile; **it's not fit to eat** *or* **to be eaten** non è mangiabile *or* commestibile; **I'm fit to drop** (*fam*) sto per crollare; **do as you think** *or* **see fit** fai come meglio credi

b (*in health*) in forma; (*Sport*) in buone condizioni fisiche, in forma; **to keep fit** tenersi in forma; **to be fit for work** (*after illness*) essere in grado di riprendere il lavoro; **to be (as) fit as a fiddle** essere sano(-a) come un pesce.

② N: **to be a good fit** (*shoes*) calzare bene; (*clothes*) andare *or* stare bene; **it's a rather tight fit** mi sta un po' stretto.

③ VT **a** (*subj: clothes*) andare/stare bene a; (: *key etc*) adattarsi a; **it fits you well** ti sta bene; **it fits me like a glove** mi sta a pennello

b (*match: facts etc*) concordare con; (: *description*) corrispondere a; **the punishment should fit the crime** la punizione dovrebbe essere adeguata al reato

c (*put in place*) mettere, fissare; **to fit a key in the lock** mettere una chiave nella serratura; **to have a carpet fitted** far mettere la moquette; **to fit sth into place** sistemare qc; **to fit sth on sth** mettere qc a *or* su qc

d (*equip*) fornire, dotare, equipaggiare; **a car fitted with a radio** una macchina fornita di radio; **she has been fitted with a new hearing aid** le hanno messo un nuovo apparecchio acustico

e (*make fit*) rendere adatto(-a); (*adjust*) aggiustare; **to fit a dress (on sb)** provare un vestito (a qn); **her experience fits her for the job** la sua esperienza la rende adatta a questo lavoro.

④ VI **a** (*clothes*) andare *or* stare bene; (*part*) adattarsi; (*key, object*) andare, entrare

b (*match: facts*) quadrare; (: *story*) reggere; (: *description*) calzare; **it all fits now!** tutto è chiaro adesso!

▶ **fit in** ① VI + ADV (*person*) adattarsi; **to fit in (with)** (*fact, statement*) corrispondere (con), concordare (con); **to fit in with sb's plans** adattarsi ai progetti di qn; **he left because he didn't fit in** se ne è andato perché non riusciva ad integrarsi.

② VT + ADV (*object*) far entrare; (*fig: appointment, visitor*) trovare il tempo per; (*plan, activity*): **to fit in (with)** conciliare (con)

▶ **fit out** VT + ADV (*Brit: ship*) allestire, equipaggiare; (: *person*) fornire, equipaggiare

▶ **fit up** VT + ADV **a** (*provide*): **to fit sb up with sth** fornire qc a qn

b (*arrange: room etc*) attrezzare

c (*fam: incriminate*) incastrare.

fit² [fɪt] N **a** (*Med*) attacco; **to have** *or* **suffer a fit** avere un attacco di convulsioni; **fit of coughing** attacco di tosse

b (*outburst*) accesso; **fit of anger/enthusiasm** accesso d'ira/d'entusiasmo; **to have a fit of crying** scoppiare in un pianto dirotto; **to get a fit of the giggles** avere un attacco di ridarella; **to have** *or* **throw a fit** (*fam*) andare su tutte le furie; **to be in fits (of laughter)** scoppiare dalle risa; **by** *or* **in fits and starts** a sbalzi.

fit·ful ['fɪtfʊl] ADJ saltuario(-a); (*breeze, showers*) intermittente; (*wind*) a raffiche; (*sleep*) agitato(-a).

fit·ful·ly ['fɪtfəlɪ] ADV (*work*) in modo discontinuo; **to sleep**

fitfully avere il sonno agitato.
fit·ment ['fɪtmənt] N **a** (*accessory: of machine*) accessorio **b** = **fitting 2b.**
fit·ness ['fɪtnɪs] N **a** (*suitability: for post etc*): **fitness (for)** idoneità (a); (: *of remark*) appropriatezza **b** (*health*) forma fisica.
fit·ted ['fɪtɪd] ADJ (*garment*) modellato(-a); **fitted carpet** moquette *f inv*; **fitted cupboards** armadi *mpl* a muro; **fitted kitchen** (*Brit*) cucina componibile; **fitted sheet** lenzuolo con gli angoli.
fit·ter ['fɪtəʳ] N (*Tech*) installatore(-trice); (*of garment*) sarto(-a).
fit·ting ['fɪtɪŋ] [1] ADJ (*suitable*) adatto(-a), appropriato (-a); **it is fitting that** (*frm*) è opportuno che.
[2] N (*of dress*) prova; (*of piece of equipment*) installazione *f*; see also **fittings.**
fit·ting·ly ['fɪtɪŋlɪ] ADV opportunamente.
♦ **fitting room** N (*in shop*) camerino.
fittings ['fɪtɪŋz] NPL (*of house*) accessori *mpl*, attrezzature *fpl*; **bathroom fittings** accessori per il bagno.
five [faɪv] [1] ADJ cinque *inv*; **she is five (years old)** ha cinque anni; **they live at number five/at five Green Street** vivono al numero cinque/al numero cinque di Green Street; **there are five of us** siamo in cinque; **all five of them came** sono venuti tutti e cinque; **it costs five pounds** costa cinque sterline; **five and a quarter/half** cinque e un quarto/e mezzo; **it's five (o'clock)** sono le cinque.
[2] N cinque *m inv*; **to divide sth into five** dividere qc in cinque parti; **they are sold in fives** sono venduti in gruppi di cinque.
♦ **five-day week** ['faɪv'deɪ'wi:k] N settimana di cinque giorni (lavorativi).
five·fold ['faɪv͵fəʊld] [1] ADJ quintuplo(-a).
[2] ADV cinque volte tanto.
♦ **five o'clock shadow** N (*hum*): **you've got a five o'clock shadow** dovresti farti la barba.
fiv·er ['faɪvəʳ] N (*fam: Brit*) biglietto da cinque sterline; (: *Am*) biglietto da cinque dollari.
♦ **five-star** ['faɪv͵stɑ:ʳ] ADJ (*hotel*) a cinque stelle; (*restaurant*) ≈ di lusso.
♦ **five-year** ['faɪv'jɪəʳ] ADJ quinquennale; **five-year plan** piano quinquennale.
fix [fɪks] [1] N **a** (*fam: predicament*) pasticcio, guaio; **to be in a fix** essere in un pasticcio, essere nei guai; **to get o.s. into a fix** cacciarsi nei guai
  b (*fam: of drug*) pera
  c : **the fight was a fix** (*fam*) l'incontro è stato truccato
  d (*Aer, Naut*) posizione *f*; **to take a fix on** fare il punto su.
[2] VT **a** (*gen, Phot, fig*) fissare; (*with string etc*) legare, fissare; **to fix one's gaze on** fermare lo sguardo su; **to fix the blame on sb/sth** dare *or* attribuire la colpa a qn/qc; **to fix sth in one's mind** imprimersi qc nella mente
  b (*date, price*) fissare, stabilire; (*fight, race*) truccare; **I'll fix everything** ci penso io, sistemo tutto io; **I'll fix him!** (*fam*) lo sistemo io!, lo metto a posto io!
  c (*repair*) accomodare, riparare
  d (*Am: make ready: meal, drink*) preparare; **can I fix you a drink?** cosa posso offrirti da bere?; **to fix one's hair** darsi una pettinata
▶ **fix on** [1] VT + ADV (*badge, lid*) fissare, attaccare.
[2] VI + PREP (*decide on*) fissare
▶ **fix up** VT + ADV (*arrange: date, meeting*) fissare, stabilire; **to fix sb up with sth** procurare qc a qn.

fixa·tion [fɪk'seɪʃən] N (*Psych, fig*) fissazione *f*, ossessione *f*; **to have a fixation on sth** avere la mania di qc.
fixa·tive ['fɪksətɪv] N fissativo.
fixed [fɪkst] ADJ **a** (*gen*) fisso(-a); **at a fixed time** ad un'ora stabilita; **fixed price** prezzo fisso; **there's a fixed charge** c'è una quota fissa **b** : **how are you fixed for money?** (*fam*) a soldi come stai?; **how are you fixed for this evening?** cosa fai stasera?
♦ **fixed assets** NPL beni *mpl* patrimoniali.
fix·ed·ly ['fɪksɪdlɪ] ADV fissamente.
fix·ings ['fɪksɪŋz] NPL (*Am Culin*) guarnizioni *fpl*.
fix·ture ['fɪkstʃəʳ] N **a** (*of house etc*): **fixtures** NPL impianti *mpl* **b** (*Sport*) incontro.
fizz [fɪz] [1] N effervescenza.
[2] VI frizzare
▶ **fizz up** VI + ADV spumeggiare.
fiz·zle ['fɪzl] VI (*sputter*) sibilare
▶ **fizzle out** VI + ADV (*fire, firework*) finire per spegnersi; (*enthusiasm, interest*) smorzarsi, svanire; (*plan*) fallire.
fizzy ['fɪzɪ] ADJ (*comp* **-ier**, *superl* **-iest**) (*drink*) gassato(-a), frizzante, effervescente.
fjord, fiord [fjɔ:d] N fiordo.
FL ABBR (*Am Post*) = *Florida.*
flab·ber·gast·ed ['flæbə͵gɑ:stɪd] ADJ sbalordito(-a).
flab·bi·ness ['flæbɪnɪs] N (*of flesh*) flaccidezza.
flab·by ['flæbɪ] ADJ (*comp* **-ier**, *superl* **-iest**) flaccido(-a), floscio(-a).
flag[1] [flæg] N (*gen*) bandiera; (*for charity etc*) bandierina; **flag of convenience** bandiera di convenienza
▶ **flag down** VT + ADV (*taxi, motorist*) fare cenno (di fermarsi) a.
flag[2] [flæg] VI (*strength*) indebolirsi; (*person*) stancarsi; (*enthusiasm etc*) affievolirsi; (*conversation*) languire.
flag[3] [flæg] N (*also:* **flag stone**) pietra per lastricare.
♦ **flag day** N ≈ giornata in cui si vendono bandierine per beneficenza.
flag·el·late ['flædʒɪ͵leɪt] VT (*frm*) fustigare; **to flagellate o.s** flagellarsi, fustigarsi.
flag·el·la·tion [͵flædʒə'leɪʃən] N flagellazione *f*.
flagged [flægd] ADJ lastricato(-a).
flag·ging ['flægɪŋ] ADJ (*interest, enthusiasm*) affievolito(-a).
flag·on ['flægən] N bottiglione *m*.
flag·pole ['flæg͵pəʊl] N pennone *m*.
fla·grant ['fleɪgrənt] ADJ flagrante.
fla·grant·ly ['fleɪgrəntlɪ] ADV palesemente; **it is flagrantly unjust** è una flagrante ingiustizia.
flag·ship ['flæg͵ʃɪp] N nave *f* ammiraglia; (*fig*) fiore all'occhiello.
♦ **flag stop** N (*Am: for bus*) fermata a richiesta, fermata facoltativa.
flail [fleɪl] VI (*arms, legs*) agitare.
flair [flɛəʳ] N (*for business etc*) fiuto; (*for languages etc*) predisposizione *f*; **to have a flair (for)** essere portato(-a) per.
flak [flæk] N **a** (*Mil*) fuoco d'artiglieria **b** (*fam: criticism*) critiche *fpl*.
flake [fleɪk] [1] N (*of paint, rust*) scaglia; (*of skin*) squama; (*of snow, cereal*) fiocco.
[2] VI (*also:* **flake off**: *paint*) scrostarsi; (: *skin*) squamarsi; (*stone*) sfaldarsi
▶ **flake out** VI + ADV (*fam: collapse*) svenire; (: *fall asleep*) crollare.
flaked [fleɪkt] ADJ: **flaked almonds** scaglie *fpl* di mandorle.
flaky ['fleɪkɪ] ADJ (*comp* **-ier**, *superl* **-iest**) (*paintwork*) scrostato(-a); (*skin*) squamoso(-a).

♦ **flaky pastry** N (*Culin*) pasta sfoglia.
flam·bé ['flɒmbeɪ] VT cucinare alla fiamma.
flam·boy·ance [flæm'bɔɪəns] N (*of person, style*) stravaganza.
flam·boy·ant [flæm'bɔɪənt] ADJ (*character, speech*) stravagante; (*dress etc*) sgargiante, vistoso(-a); (*style*) fiorito(-a), ornato(-a).
flam·boy·ant·ly [flæm'bɔɪəntlɪ] ADV (*dress*) vistosamente, in modo sgargiante; (*behave*) teatralmente.
flame [fleɪm] ① N fiamma; **to burst into flames** divampare.
② VI (*also:* **flame up**) divampare; **her cheeks flamed with embarrassment** arrossì per l'imbarazzo.
fla·men·co [flə'mɛŋkəʊ] N flamenco.
flame·proof ['fleɪm,pruːf] ADJ resistente al calore.
♦ **flame test** N (*Chem*) test *m inv* alla fiamma.
♦ **flame-thrower** ['fleɪm,θrəʊə'] N lanciafiamme *m inv.*
flam·ing ['fleɪmɪŋ] ADJ **a** (*red, orange*) acceso(-a) **b** (*Brit fam: furious*) furibondo(-a), furioso(-a) **c** (*Brit fam: damn*) maledetto(-a).
fla·min·go [flə'mɪŋgəʊ] N fenicottero.
flam·mabil·ity [,flæmə'bɪlɪtɪ] N infiammabilità.
flam·mable ['flæməbl] ADJ infiammabile.
flan [flæn] N (*Brit Culin*) flan *m inv.*
Flan·ders ['flɑːndəz] NSG le Fiandre *fpl.*
flange [flændʒ] N (*Tech: on wheel*) flangia.
flank [flæŋk] ① N (*gen, Mil*) fianco.
② VT fiancheggiare.
flan·nel ['flænl] ① N (*fabric*) flanella; (*Brit: also:* **face flannel**) guanto di spugna; see also **flannels**.
② ADJ di flanella.
flan·nel·ette [,flænə'lɛt] N flanella di cotone.
flan·nels ['flænlz] NPL pantaloni *mpl* di flanella.
flap [flæp] ① N **a** (*of pocket*) patta, battente *m*; (*of envelope*) linguetta; (*of table*) ribalta; (*Aer*) flap *m inv* **b** (*movement*): **to give sth a flap** sbattere qc; **they could hear the flap of the sails** (*sound*) sentivano sbattere le vele; **to be in a flap** (*fam*) essere in agitazione; **to get into a flap** (*fam*) farsi prendere dal panico.
② VT (*subj: bird: wings*) sbattere, battere; (*shake: sheets, newspaper*) agitare, sbattere.
③ VI **a** (*wings, sails, flag*) sbattere **b** (*fam: panic*) farsi prendere dal panico.
flap·jack ['flæp,dʒæk] N (*Brit: biscuit*) biscotto di avena; (*Am: pancake*) frittella.
flare [flɛə'] ① N **a** (*blaze*) chiarore *m*; (*signal*) segnale *m* luminoso; (*Mil: for target*) razzo illuminante **b** (*in skirt*) svasatura **c** (*trousers*): **flares** NPL pantaloni *mpl* a zampa d'elefante.
② VI (*match, torch*) accendersi con una fiammata
▶ **flare up** VI + ADV (*fire*) divampare; (*fig: person*) infiammarsi di rabbia, saltar su; (: *revolt, situation etc*) scoppiare.
flared ['flɛəd] ADJ (*skirt, trousers*) svasato(-a).
♦ **flare-up** ['flɛər,ʌp] N (*of fire*) fiammata; (*of quarrel, fighting*) recrudescenza; (*outburst of rage*) scoppio d'ira; (*sudden dispute*) battibecco.
flash [flæʃ] ① N **a** (*of light*) sprazzo, lampo; (*Am: torch*) torcia elettrica, lampadina tascabile; **flash of lightning** lampo; **flash of inspiration** lampo di genio; **a flash in the pan** (*fig*) un fuoco di paglia; **in a flash** in un baleno, in un lampo
b (*also:* **news flash**) flash *m inv*, notizia *f* lampo *inv*
c (*Phot*) flash *m inv.*

② VT (*light, torch*) far lampeggiare; (*look*) lanciare; (*send: message*) trasmettere; **to flash one's headlights** (*Aut*) lampeggiare; **to flash sth about** (*fig fam: flaunt*) ostentare qc; **stop flashing your money about!** smettila di ostentare i tuoi soldi!.
③ VI **a** (*light, eyes*) lampeggiare; (*lightning*) guizzare, balenare; (*jewels*) brillare, scintillare
b (*move quickly: person, vehicle*): **to flash by** or **past** passare come un lampo; **he flashed by** or **past us** sfrecciò davanti a noi.
flash·back ['flæʃ,bæk] N (*Cine*) flashback *m inv.*
flash·bulb ['flæʃ,bʌlb] N flash *m inv.*
♦ **flash burn** N ustione *f* causata da un'esplosione.
♦ **flash card** N (*Scol*) scheda didattica.
flash·cube ['flæʃ,kjuːb] N (*Phot*) cubo-flash *m inv.*
flash·er ['flæʃə'] N **a** (*Aut*) lampeggiatore *m* **b** (*Brit fam: man*) esibizionista *m.*
♦ **flash flood** N inondazione *f.*
flash·gun ['flæʃ,gʌn] N (*Phot*) lampeggiatore *m.*
flashi·ly ['flæʃɪlɪ] ADV in modo vistoso.
flash·ing ['flæʃɪŋ] N scossalina.
flash·light ['flæʃ,laɪt] N (*Am: torch*) torcia elettrica, lampadina tascabile.
flash·point ['flæʃ,pɔɪnt] N punto di infiammabilità; (*fig*) livello critico.
flashy ['flæʃɪ] ADJ (*comp* **-ier**, *superl* **-est**) (*pej: car, clothes*) vistoso(-a); (*person*) appariscente.
flask [flɑːsk] N (*for brandy etc*) fiaschetta; (*also:* **vacuum flask**) thermos ® *m inv*; (*Chem*) pallone *m*, beuta.
flat[1] [flæt] ① ADJ (*comp* **-ter**, *superl* **-test**) **a** (*gen*) piatto (-a); (*smooth*) liscio(-a), piano(-a); (*tyre*) sgonfio(-a) or a terra; **as flat as a pancake** (*fam*) completamente piatto (-a); (: *Aut: tyre*) completamente sgonfio(-a) or a terra; **to fall flat on one's face** cadere a terra lungo(-a) disteso(-a), finire faccia a terra; **flat race** corsa piana **b** (*final: refusal, denial*) categorico(-a), netto(-a); **I'm not going, and that's flat!** (*fam*) non ci vado e basta!
c (*Mus: key*) bemolle *inv*; (: *voice*) stonato(-a); (: *instrument*) scordato(-a); **C flat** do *m inv* bemolle
d (*dull, lifeless: taste, style*) piatto(-a); (: *joke*) che non fa ridere; (*drink*) che ha perso l'effervescenza, sgassato (-a); (*battery*) scarico(-a); (*colour*) scialbo(-a); **to be feeling rather flat** sentirsi giù di corda or di morale
e (*fixed*): **flat rate of pay** tariffa unica di pagamento; **at a flat rate** a una tariffa unica.
② ADV **a** (*absolutely: refuse, tell etc*) seccamente, recisamente; **flat broke** (*fam*) al verde, in bolletta; **in ten minutes flat** in dieci minuti spaccati; **(to work) flat out** (*lavorare*) a più non posso
b : **to spread a map out flat on the floor** stendere una cartina sul pavimento; **to be flat out** (*lying*) essere disteso(-a) or sdraiato(-a); (*asleep*) dormire della grossa
c (*Mus: sing, play*) in modo stonato.
③ N (*of hand*) palmo; (*of sword*) parte *f* piatta; (*Mus*) bemolle *m inv*; (*Aut*) gomma a terra.
flat[2] [flæt] N (*Brit*) appartamento; **to go flat-hunting** cercare un appartamento.
♦ **flat-bottomed** ['flæt'bɒtəmd] ADJ (*boat etc*) a fondo piatto.
♦ **flat cap** N berretto.
♦ **flat-chested** ['flæt'tʃɛstɪd] ADJ piatta, che ha poco seno.
flat·fish ['flætfɪʃ] N pesce *m* piatto.
♦ **flat-footed** ['flæt'fʊtɪd] ADJ: **to be flat-footed** avere i piedi piatti.
flat·iron ['flæt,aɪən] (*old*) N ferro da stiro.

flat·let ['flætlɪt] N (Brit) appartamentino.

flat·ly ['flætlɪ] ADV (refuse etc) categoricamente, nettamente.

flat·mate ['flæt‚meɪt] N: **he's my flatmate** (Brit) divide l'appartamento con me.

flat·ness ['flætnɪs] N (gen) piattezza; (dullness) piattezza, monotonia; (of land) assenza di rilievi.

♦ **flat racing** N (Horse-racing) corse fpl piane or in piano.

♦ **flat-screen** ['flæt'skriːn] ADJ a schermo piatto.

flat·ten ['flætn] VT (road, field) spianare, appiattire; (house, city) abbattere, radere al suolo; (map) spiegare, aprire; **to flatten o.s. against sth** appiattirsi contro qc

▶ **flatten out** 1 VI + ADV (road, countryside) appiattirsi. 2 VT + ADV (path, paper) spianare.

flat·tened ['flætənd] ADJ appiattito(-a).

flat·ter ['flætə'] VT (praise) adulare, lusingare; (show to advantage) donare a; **this photo flatters you** in questa foto sei venuto molto bene; **to flatter o.s. that one is ...** illudersi di essere... .

flat·tered ['flætəd] ADJ lusingato(-a).

flat·ter·er ['flætərə'] N adulatore(-trice).

flat·ter·ing ['flætərɪŋ] ADJ (person, remark) lusinghiero (-a); (clothes etc) che dona, che abbellisce; **this photo of you is not very flattering** questa foto non ti fa onore.

flat·ter·ing·ly ['flætərɪŋlɪ] ADV in modo lusinghiero.

flat·tery ['flætərɪ] N adulazione f, lusinghe fpl.

flat·ties ['flætɪz] NPL (fam) scarpe fpl basse.

flatu·lence ['flætjʊləns] N flatulenza.

flat·worm ['flæt‚wɜːm] N verme m piatto, platelminta m.

flaunt [flɔːnt] VT (pej) sfoggiare, ostentare.

flau·tist ['flɔːtɪst] N flautista m/f.

fla·vour, (Am) **fla·vor** ['fleɪvə'] 1 N sapore m, gusto; (of ice-cream etc) gusto; (flavouring) aroma m; (fig) atmosfera.
2 VT: **to flavour (with)** (Culin: cake etc) aromatizzare (con); (: savoury dish) condire (con), insaporire (con); **vanilla-flavoured** al gusto di vaniglia.

fla·vour·ing, (Am) **fla·vor·ing** ['fleɪvərɪŋ] N (for cake etc) aroma m, essenza (artificiale); (for savoury dish) condimento; **vanilla flavouring** aroma di vaniglia.

flaw [flɔː] N (gen) difetto; (crack: in china) incrinatura.

flawed [flɔːd] ADJ (complexion) imperfetto(-a); (china etc) difettoso(-a); (argument) debole; (character) pieno(-a) di difetti.

flaw·less ['flɔːlɪs] ADJ perfetto(-a), senza difetti.

flaw·less·ly ['flɔːlɪslɪ] ADV perfettamente.

flax [flæks] N lino.

flax·en ['flæksən] ADJ biondo(-a).

♦ **flaxen-haired** ['flæksən'hɛəd] ADJ dai capelli biondi.

flay [fleɪ] VT (skin) scorticare; (criticize) criticare aspramente, stroncare.

flea [fliː] N pulce f; **to send sb off with a flea in his ear** (fam) mandare qn a quel paese.

flea·bite ['fliː‚baɪt] N morso di pulce; (fig) piccola seccatura.

♦ **flea-bitten** ['fliː‚bɪtn] ADJ pulcioso(-a); (fig) pidocchioso(-a).

♦ **flea market** N mercato delle pulci.

flea·pit ['fliː‚pɪt] N (fam) teatrucolo.

fleck [flɛk] 1 N (of mud, paint, colour) macchiolina; (of dust) granello.
2 VT (with blood, mud etc) macchiettare; **brown flecked with white** marrone screziato di bianco.

fled [flɛd] PT, PP of **flee**.

fledg·ling, fledge·ling ['flɛdʒlɪŋ] N uccellino.

flee [fliː] (pt, pp **fled**) 1 VT (town, country) fuggire da, scappare da; (danger, enemy) sfuggire a.
2 VI: **to flee (from)** fuggire (da or davanti a); **to flee to sb/sth** correre da qn/verso qc; **to flee to safety** mettersi in salvo.

fleece [fliːs] 1 N vello.
2 VT (fig fam: rob) pelare.

fleecy ['fliːsi] ADJ (comp -ier, superl -iest) (blanket) soffice; (cloud) come ovatta.

fleet[1] [fliːt] N flotta; (of cars) parco; (of lorries etc) convoglio; **they were followed by a fleet of cars** erano seguiti da un corteo di macchine.

fleet[2] [fliːt] ADJ (poetic: also: **fleet-footed**) svelto(-a).

fleet·ing ['fliːtɪŋ] ADJ (glimpse) fuggevole; (moment, beauty) fugace, passeggero(-a), effimero(-a); (visit) volante, veloce.

fleet·ing·ly ['fliːtɪŋlɪ] ADV fugacemente.

Flem·ing ['flɛmɪŋ] N fiammingo(-a).

Flem·ish ['flɛmɪʃ] 1 ADJ fiammingo(-a).
2 N a (language) fiammingo b (people): **the Flemish** NPL i Fiamminghi.

flesh [flɛʃ] N (gen) carne f; (of fruit) polpa; **in the flesh** in carne ed ossa; **my own flesh and blood** la mia famiglia; **it's more than flesh and blood can stand** è più di quanto un essere umano possa sopportare; **to demand one's pound of flesh** (fig) esigere tutto il dovuto.

flesh·ly ['flɛʃlɪ] ADJ sensuale.

flesh·pot ['flɛʃ‚pɒt] N locale m porno.

♦ **flesh wound** N ferita superficiale.

fleshy ['flɛʃɪ] ADJ (comp -ier, superl -iest) carnoso(-a); (Bot: fruit) polposo(-a).

flew [fluː] PT of **fly**.

flex [flɛks] 1 N (of lamp, telephone) filo (flessibile).
2 VT (body, knees) piegare, flettere; (muscles) contrarre.

flexi·bil·ity [‚flɛksɪ'bɪlɪtɪ] N flessibilità, elasticità.

flex·ible ['flɛksɪbl] ADJ flessibile; **flexible working hours** orario di lavoro flessibile.

flex·ibly ['flɛksɪblɪ] ADV in modo flessibile.

flexi·time ['flɛksɪ‚taɪm] N orario flessibile.

flick [flɪk] 1 N a (gen) colpetto; see also **flicks**.
2 VT (with finger) dare un colpetto a; **she flicked her hair out of her eyes** buttò i capelli da una parte.
3 VI: **the snake's tongue flicked in and out** la lingua del serpente guizzava

▶ **flick off** VT + ADV (dust, ash) mandar via con un colpetto

▶ **flick through** VI + PREP (book, pages) sfogliare, scartabellare.

flick·er ['flɪkə'] 1 N (of light, flame) tremolio; (of eyelid) battito; (of hope) barlume m; **a flicker of light** un breve bagliore.
2 VI (light) tremolare; (flame) guizzare.

flick·er·ing ['flɪkərɪŋ] ADJ (flame, eyelids) tremolante.

♦ **flick knife** N (Brit) coltello a serramanico.

flicks [flɪks] NPL: **the flicks** (Brit fam) il cine.

fli·er ['flaɪə'] N aviatore(-trice).

flies [flaɪz] NPL of **fly**.

flight[1] [flaɪt] N a (Aer, gen) volo; (of bullet) traiettoria; **in flight** in volo; **how long does the flight take?** quanto dura il volo?; **"flight closing"** (Aer) "volo in chiusura"; **flights of fancy** (fig) voli di fantasia; **in the top flight** (fig) fra i migliori b : **flight (of stairs)** rampa (di scale); **he lives two flights up** abita due piani sopra.

flight[2] [flaɪt] N (act of fleeing) fuga; **to put to flight** mettere in fuga; **to take flight** darsi alla fuga.

♦ **flight attendant** N (Am) steward m, hostess f inv.

◆ **flight coupon** N tagliando di volo.

◆ **flight crew** N equipaggio.

◆ **flight deck** N (*on aircraft carrier*) ponte *m* di volo; (*of aeroplane*) cabina di pilotaggio.

◆ **flight path** N (*of aircraft*) aerovia; (*of rocket, projectile*) traiettoria.

◆ **flight plan** N piano di volo.

◆ **flight recorder** N registratore *m* di volo.

◆ **flight simulator** N simulatore *m* di volo.

flighty ['flaɪtɪ] ADJ (*comp* **-ier**, *superl* **-iest**) capriccioso(-a), frivolo(-a).

flim·si·ly ['flɪmzɪlɪ] ADV (*dressed*) leggero; **flimsily built** costruito(-a) poco solidamente.

flim·si·ness ['flɪmzɪnɪs] N (*of dress*) leggerezza; (*of structure, argument*) scarsa solidità.

flim·sy ['flɪmzɪ] ADJ (*comp* **-ier**, *superl* **-iest**) (*thin: dress*) leggero(-a); (*weak: construction*) poco solido(-a); (: *excuse, argument*) che non sta in piedi, inconsistente.

flinch [flɪntʃ] VI trasalire; **without flinching** senza batter ciglio; **to flinch from sth** tirarsi indietro di fronte a qc.

fling [flɪŋ] (*vb: pt, pp* flung) 1 N (*love affair*) avventura; **to have a last fling** fare un'ultima follia; **to have one's fling** godersela; **to have a fling at doing sth** cercare *or* tentare di fare qc.

2 VT (*stone etc*) lanciare, gettare, scagliare; **to fling one's arms round sb** gettare le braccia al collo di qn; **the door was flung open** la porta fu spalancata; **to fling o.s. into a chair** buttarsi su una poltrona; **to fling o.s. into a job** gettarsi a capofitto in un lavoro; **to fling on one's clothes** vestirsi in fretta e furia

▶ **fling away** VT + ADV (*waste*) gettare via, sperperare

▶ **fling off** VT + ADV togliersi in fretta e furia

▶ **fling on** VT + ADV (*clothes*) mettersi in fretta e furia

▶ **fling out** VT + ADV (*unwanted object*) buttare via; (*person*) buttar fuori

▶ **fling up** VT + ADV lanciare in aria; **to fling up one's arms** alzare le braccia al cielo; **she flung up her head** ha buttato la testa all'indietro.

flint [flɪnt] N (*Geol*) selce *f*; (*for lighter*) pietrina.

flint·lock ['flɪnt‚lɒk] N fucile *m* ad acciarino.

flip [flɪp] 1 N colpetto.

2 VT (*switch*) dare un colpetto a; (*Am: pancake*) rivoltare (*dando un colpo alla padella*); **to flip a coin** lanciare una moneta in aria, fare a testa e croce; **he flipped the book open** ha aperto il libro con un rapido gesto della mano.

3 VI **a** (*fam: lose temper*) uscire dai gangheri

b : **to flip for sth** (*Am*) fare a testa e croce per qc.

4 ADJ (*fam: remark*) poco serio(-a)

▶ **flip through** VI + PREP (*book, records*) dare una scorsa a.

◆ **flip chart** N blocco di fogli per lavagna.

◆ **flip-flops** ['flɪp‚flɒps] NPL (*sandals*) infradito *mpl*.

flip·pan·cy ['flɪpənsɪ] N frivolezza.

flip·pant ['flɪpənt] ADJ (*remark, tone*) poco serio(-a); (*attitude*) frivolo(-a).

flip·pant·ly ['flɪpəntlɪ] ADV (*speak*) in modo poco serio.

flip·per ['flɪpə'] N pinna.

flip·ping ['flɪpɪŋ] ADJ (*fam*) maledetto(-a).

◆ **flip side** N (*of record*) retro.

flirt [flɜːt] 1 N (*woman*) civetta; (*man*): **he's a terrible flirt** è un gran donnaiolo.

2 VI: **to flirt (with)** flirtare (con); (*woman only*) civettare (con); **to flirt with an idea** trastullarsi con un'idea.

flir·ta·tion [flɜː'teɪʃən] N flirt *m inv*.

flir·ta·tious [flɜː'teɪʃəs] ADJ civettuolo(-a).

flit [flɪt] 1 VI (*bats, butterflies*) svolazzare; **to flit in/out** (*person*) entrare/uscire svolazzando.

2 N (*Brit*): **to do a (moonlight) flit** squagliarsela (*per non pagare l'affitto, il conto in albergo etc*).

float [fləʊt] 1 N galleggiante *m*; (*cork*) sughero; (*vehicle in parade*) carro; (*cash*) soldi *mpl* in cassa (*per dare il resto*).

2 VT (*boat, logs*) far galleggiare; (*refloat*) riportare a galla; (*launch: project, plan*) lanciare; (*Fin: company*) lanciare (*emettendo azioni*); (: *currency*) far fluttuare; **to float an idea** ventilare un'idea.

3 VI (*gen*) galleggiare; (*ship*) stare a galla; (*bather*) fare il morto; (*Fin: currency*) fluttuare; **to float downstream** essere trascinato(-a) dalla corrente

▶ **float away**, **float off** VI + ADV (*in water*) andare alla deriva; (*in air*) volare via.

float·ing ['fləʊtɪŋ] ADJ a galla.

◆ **floating voter** N elettore *m* indeciso.

flock [flɒk] 1 N (*of sheep, also Rel*) gregge *m*; (*of birds*) stormo; (*of people*) stuolo, folla.

2 VI (*crowd*) affollarsi, ammassarsi; **to flock around sb** affollarsi intorno a qn.

floe [fləʊ] N (*also:* **ice floe**) banchisa.

flog [flɒg] VT frustare, flagellare; **to flog a dead horse** (*fig fam*) perdere il proprio tempo; **to flog o.s. to death** (*fig fam*) ammazzarsi di fatica.

flog·ging ['flɒgɪŋ] N fustigazione *f*.

flood [flʌd] 1 N inondazione *f*, alluvione *f*; (*of words, tears*) diluvio; **the river is in flood** il fiume è in piena; **the Flood** (*Rel*) il diluvio universale; **a flood of letters** una marea di lettere; **she was in floods of tears** era in un mare di lacrime.

2 VT (*town, fields, fig*) inondare, allagare; (*Aut: carburettor*) ingolfare; **to flood the market** (*Comm*) inondare il mercato.

3 VI (*river*) straripare; **the crowd flooded into the streets** la folla si riversò nelle strade

▶ **flood in** VI + ADV entrare in grande quantità; **the light flooded in through the window** una gran luce entrava dalla finestra

▶ **flood out** VT + ADV (*house*) inondare; **they were flooded out** l'inondazione li ha costretti ad abbandonare le loro case.

flood·gates ['flʌd‚geɪts] NPL: **to open the floodgates to** aprire le porte a.

flood·ing ['flʌdɪŋ] N inondazione *f*.

flood·light ['flʌd‚laɪt] (*vb: pt, pp* **floodlighted** *or* **floodlit**) 1 N riflettore *m*; **to play a match under floodlights** giocare una partita in notturna.

2 VT illuminare a giorno.

flood·lit ['flʌd‚lɪt] 1 PT, PP *of* **floodlight**.

2 ADJ illuminato(-a) a giorno.

◆ **flood tide** N alta marea, marea crescente.

flood·water ['flʌd‚wɔːtə'] N acque *fpl* (*di inondazione*).

floor [flɔː] 1 N **a** (*gen*) suolo; (*of room*) pavimento; (*of sea, valley*) fondo; (*dance floor*) pista; (*fig: at meeting*): **the floor** il pubblico; **on the floor** per terra, sul pavimento; **to take the floor** (*dancer*) mettersi a ballare; **to have the floor** (*speaker*) prendere la parola

b (*storey*) piano; **ground floor** (*Brit*) pianterreno; **on the first floor** (*Brit*) al primo piano; (*Am*) al pianterreno; **top floor** ultimo piano.

2 VT **a** (*room*): **to floor (with)** pavimentare (con)

b (*fam: knock down: opponent*) atterrare; (: *baffle*)

confondere.

floor·board ['flɔ:ˌbɔ:d] N asse f di pavimento.

♦ **floor cleaner** N detersivo per pavimenti.

floor·cloth ['flɔ:ˌklɒθ] N straccio per il pavimento.

♦ **floor covering** N rivestimento (di pavimento).

floored [flɔ:d] ADJ: **room floored with oak** stanza con il pavimento di quercia.

floor·ing ['flɔ:rɪŋ] N (floor) pavimento; (material) materiale m per pavimentazioni.

♦ **floor lamp** N (Am) lampada a stelo.

♦ **floor polish** N cera per pavimenti.

♦ **floor pol·ish·er** ['flɔ:ˌpɒlɪʃə'] N lucidatrice f.

♦ **floor show** N spettacolo di varietà.

floor·walker ['flɔ:ˌwɔ:kə'] N (esp Am) caporeparto m/f (in grande magazzino).

floo·zy ['flu:zɪ] N (fam) putanella.

flop [flɒp] 1 N (fam: failure) fiasco.
2 VI a (person): **to flop (into/on)** lasciarsi cadere (in/su) b (fam: play) far fiasco; (: scheme) fallire.

flop·py ['flɒpɪ] ADJ (comp **-ier**, superl **-iest**) floscio(-a), molle; **floppy hat** cappello floscio.

♦ **floppy disk** N floppy disk m inv.

flo·ra ['flɔ:rə] N flora.

flo·ral ['flɔ:rəl] ADJ (arrangement) floreale; (fabric, dress) a fiori; **floral tribute** omaggio floreale.

Flor·ence ['flɒrəns] N Firenze f.

Flor·en·tine ['flɒrənˌtaɪn] ADJ, N fiorentino(-a).

flo·ret ['flɔ:rɪt] N (Bot) flosculo.

flor·id ['flɒrɪd] ADJ (complexion) florido(-a); (style) fiorito (-a).

flo·rist ['flɒrɪst] N fioraio(-a); **at the florist's (shop)** dal fioraio.

floss [flɒs] 1 N filamenti mpl; (thread) seta da ricamo; **dental floss** filo interdentale.
2 VT (teeth) pulire col filo interdentale.

flo·ta·tion [fləʊˈteɪʃən] N (Fin) lancio.

flot·sam ['flɒtsəm] N: **flotsam and jetsam** rifiuti mpl portati dal mare; (people) relitti mpl.

flounce[1] [flaʊns] 1 VI: **to flounce in/out** entrare/uscire stizzito(-a).
2 N balzo.

flounce[2] [flaʊns] N (frill) balza.

floun·der[1] ['flaʊndə'] VI (also: **flounder about**: in water, mud) dibattersi, annaspare; (: in speech etc) impappinarsi, esitare.

floun·der[2] ['flaʊndə'] N (fish) passera di mare.

flour ['flaʊə'] N farina.

floured ['flaʊəd] ADJ infarinato(-a).

flour·ish ['flʌrɪʃ] 1 N abbellimento; (movement) gran gesto; (under signature) svolazzo; (Mus: fanfare) fanfara; **to do sth with a flourish** fare qc con ostentazione.
2 VI (gen) fiorire; (person) essere in piena forma; (writer, artist) avere successo; (business etc) prosperare.
3 VT (weapon, stick) brandire.

flour·ish·ing ['flʌrɪʃɪŋ] ADJ (plant) rigoglioso(-a); (person) florido(-a), in gran forma; (business) fiorente, prospero (-a).

floury ['flaʊərɪ] ADJ (hands) infarinato(-a); (potato) farinoso(-a).

flout [flaʊt] VT (order) contravvenire a; (advice) ignorare deliberatamente; (conventions, society) sfidare.

flow [fləʊ] 1 N (of river, also Elec) corrente f; (of tide) flusso; (of blood: from wound) uscita; (: in veins) circolazione f; (of words) fiume m; (of insults, orders) caterva, sfilza; **the flow of traffic** la circolazione.

2 VI (gen) fluire; (tide) salire; (blood in veins, traffic) circolare; (hair) ricadere (morbidamente), scendere; **money flowed in** (fig) i soldi sono arrivati in grande quantità; **the river flows into the sea** il fiume sfocia nel mare; **to keep the conversation flowing** mantenere viva la conversazione.

♦ **flow chart** N schema m di flusso.

♦ **flow diagram** N diagramma m di flusso, organigramma m.

flow·er ['flaʊə'] 1 N fiore m; **in flower** in fiore.
2 VI fiorire.

♦ **flower arrangement** N composizione f floreale.

flow·er·bed ['flaʊəˌbɛd] N aiuola.

flow·ered ['flaʊəd] ADJ a fiori.

♦ **flower girl** N (in street) fioraia; (at wedding) damigella.

flow·er·ing ['flaʊərɪŋ] 1 N fioritura.
2 ADJ (in flower) in fiore; (which flowers) fiorifero(-a), da fiore.

flow·er·pot ['flaʊəˌpɒt] N vaso da fiori.

♦ **flower shop** N negozio di fiori, fioraio.

♦ **flower show** N mostra di fiori.

flow·ery ['flaʊərɪ] ADJ (meadow) fiorito(-a), in fiore; (dress, material) a fiori; (style, speech) fiorito(-a).

flow·ing ['fləʊɪŋ] ADJ (style) scorrevole, fluido(-a); (movement) sciolto(-a); (dress) di linea morbida; (hair) fluente; **flowing robes** abiti mpl dalle linee fluide.

flown [fləʊn] PP of **fly**.

fl. oz N = **fluid ounce**.

flu [flu:] N (fam) influenza.

fluc·tu·ate ['flʌktjʊˌeɪt] VI (cost, rate, speed) fluttuare, oscillare; (person): **he fluctuated between fear and excitement** passava da uno stato di paura a uno stato di eccitazione.

fluc·tu·at·ing ['flʌktjʊˌeɪtɪŋ] ADJ oscillante.

fluc·tua·tion [ˌflʌktjʊˈeɪʃən] N fluttuazione f, oscillazione f.

flue [flu:] N canna fumaria.

flu·en·cy ['flu:ənsɪ] N facilità, scioltezza; **his fluency in English** la sua scioltezza nel parlare l'inglese.

flu·ent ['flu:ənt] ADJ (style) fluido(-a), scorrevole; (speaker) dalla parola facile; (speech) facile, sciolto(-a); (French) corrente; **he's a fluent speaker/reader** si esprime/legge senza difficoltà; **he speaks fluent Italian** OR **he's fluent in Italian** parla l'italiano correntemente.

flu·ent·ly ['flu:əntlɪ] ADV (speak a language) correntemente; (speak, write) con scioltezza, con facilità.

fluff [flʌf] 1 N (from blankets etc) pelucchi mpl; (of chicks, kittens) lanugine f.
2 VT a (also: **fluff out**) rendere soffice or vaporoso(-a); (feathers) arruffare; **to fluff up the pillows** sprimacciare i cuscini b (fam: make mistake in) impaperarsi nel recitare.

fluffi·ness ['flʌfɪnɪs] N morbidezza.

fluffy ['flʌfɪ] ADJ (toy) di peluche; (kitten, chick) coperto(-a) di lanugine; (pullover) morbido(-a) e peloso(-a).

flu·id ['flu:ɪd] 1 ADJ (substance, movement) fluido(-a); (plan, arrangements) flessibile, elastico(-a).
2 N fluido, liquido; (in diet) liquido.

flu·id·ity [flu:ˈɪdɪtɪ] N (of substance) fluidità; (of movement) scioltezza; (of arrangements) elasticità.

♦ **fluid ounce** N unità di misura di capacità pari a 0.028 l (Brit) o 0.030 l (Am).

fluke [flu:k] N (fam) colpo di fortuna; **by a fluke** per puro caso.

flum·mox ['flʌməks] VT (*fam*) sconcertare, rendere perplesso(-a).

flung [flʌŋ] PT, PP of **fling**.

flunk [flʌŋk] VT (*esp Am fam: course, exam*) essere bocciato (-a) *or* respinto(-a) in *or* a.

flunky ['flʌŋkɪ] N tirapiedi *m/f inv*.

fluo·res·cence [ˌfluə'rɛsəns] N fluorescenza.

fluo·res·cent [ˌfluə'rɛsənt] ADJ (*lighting, tube*) fluorescente.

fluori·da·tion [ˌfluərɪ'deɪʃən] N fluorizzazione *f*.

fluo·ride ['fluəˌraɪd] N fluoruro.

♦ **fluoride toothpaste** N dentifricio al fluoro.

fluo·rine ['fluəri:n] N fluoro.

flur·ried ['flʌrɪd] ADJ agitato(-a).

flur·ry ['flʌrɪ] N (*of snow*) turbine *m*; (*of wind*) folata; **a flurry of activity/excitement** una grande attività/un'improvvisa agitazione; **in a flurry** in uno stato di agitazione *or* eccitazione.

flush [flʌʃ] **1** N **a** (*lavatory flush*) sciacquone *m*
b (*blush*) rossore *m*
c (*of beauty, health, youth*) rigoglio, pieno vigore *m*; (*fig: exhilaration*) ebbrezza; **in the first flush of victory** nell'ebbrezza della vittoria; **in a flush of excitement** in uno stato di eccitazione
d (*in poker*) colore *m*; see also **hot flush**.
2 ADJ **a** (*level*): **flush (with)** a livello (di *or* con); **a door flush with the wall** una porta a livello con la parete
b (*fam*): **to be flush (with money)** essere pieno(-a) di soldi.
3 VI (*person, face*): **to flush (with)** arrossire (di); **flushed with success** eccitato(-a) dal successo.
4 VT **a** pulire con un getto d'acqua; **to flush the lavatory** *or* **the toilet** tirare l'acqua
b (*also*: **flush out**: *game, birds*) far alzare in volo; (: *fig: criminal*) stanare

▶ **flush away** VT + ADV (*down lavatory*) buttare nel gabinetto (e tirare l'acqua).

flushed [flʌʃt] ADJ tutto(-a) rosso(-a).

flus·ter ['flʌstə'] **1** N agitazione *f*.
2 VT (*confuse, upset*) mettere in agitazione, innervosire; **to get flustered** agitarsi.

flus·tered ['flʌstəd] ADJ sconvolto(-a).

flute [flu:t] N flauto.

flut·ist ['flu:tɪst] N (*Am*) = **flautist**.

flut·ter ['flʌtə'] **1** N agitazione *f*; (*of eyelashes*) battito; (*of wings*) battito, frullio; **to be in a flutter** (*fig*) essere in uno stato di agitazione; **to have a flutter** (*fam: gamble*) fare una scommessa.
2 VT (*wings*) battere; **to flutter one's eyelashes at sb** fare gli occhi dolci a qn.
3 VI svolazzare; (*bird etc*) battere le ali; (*flag*) sventolare; (*heart*) palpitare.

flux [flʌks] N **a**: **to be in a state of flux** essere in continuo mutamento **b** (*Med, Phys*) flusso; (*Metallurgy*) fondente *m*.

fly[1] [flaɪ] N (*insect*) mosca; **he wouldn't hurt a fly** non farebbe male a una mosca; **they were dropping like flies** morivano come mosche; **the fly in the ointment** (*fig*) la piccola pecca che sciupa tutto; **there are no flies on him** (*fig*) non è nato ieri, non si fa prendere per il naso.

fly[2] [flaɪ] (*vb: pp* **flew**, *pt* **flown**) **1** VI **a** (*gen*) volare; (*passengers*) andare in aereo; (*flag*) sventolare; **the plane flew over London** l'aereo ha sorvolato Londra
b (*move quickly: time*) volare, passare in fretta; **to fly past sb** (*subj: car, person*) sfrecciare davanti a qn; **the door flew open** la porta si è spalancata all'improvviso; **to knock** *or* **send sth/sb flying** far volare qc/qn; **I must fly!** devo scappare!; **to let fly at sb** scagliarsi contro qn; **to fly into a rage** infuriarsi; **to fly off the handle** perdere le staffe
c (*flee*) fuggire, scappare; **to fly for one's life** salvare la pelle scappando.
2 VT (*aircraft*) pilotare; (*passenger, cargo*) trasportare (in aereo); (*distances*) percorrere; (*flag*) battere; **to fly the Atlantic** sorvolare l'Atlantico; **to fly a kite** far volare un aquilone.
3 N (*on trousers: also*: **flies**) patta

▶ **fly away** VI + ADV volar via

▶ **fly in** **1** VI + ADV (*plane*) arrivare; (*person*) arrivare in aereo; **he flew in from Rome** è venuto da Roma in aereo.
2 VT + ADV (*supplies, troops*) trasportare in aereo

▶ **fly off** VI + ADV volare via

▶ **fly out** VI + ADV (*plane*) partire; (*person*) partire in aereo.

fly·blown ['flaɪˌbləun] ADJ (*meat*) infestato(-a) di uova di mosca.

fly·by ['flaɪˌbaɪ] N (*Am*) parata aerea.

♦ **fly-fishing** ['flaɪˌfɪʃɪŋ] N pesca con la mosca.

fly·ing ['flaɪɪŋ] **1** ADJ (*gen*) volante; **to pass an exam with flying colours** superare un esame con risultati brillanti; **to take a flying leap** *or* **jump** fare un gran balzo.
2 N (*action*) volo; (*activity*) aviazione *f*; **he doesn't like flying** non gli piace viaggiare in aereo.

♦ **flying ambulance** N aereo ambulanza.

♦ **flying boat** N idrovolante *m*.

♦ **flying buttress** N (*Archit*) arco rampante.

♦ **flying doctor** N medico volante.

♦ **flying fish** N pesce *m* volante.

♦ **flying fox** N pteropo.

♦ **flying picket** N picchetto (*proveniente da fabbriche ecc non direttamente coinvolte nello sciopero*).

♦ **flying saucer** N disco volante.

♦ **flying squad** N (*Police*) (squadra) volante *f*.

♦ **flying start** N partenza lanciata; **to get off to a flying start** (*fig*) partire come un razzo, avere un inizio brillante.

♦ **flying time** N (*of flight*) durata del volo.

♦ **flying visit** N (*of official*) visita-lampo; (*of friends*) breve visita.

fly·leaf ['flaɪˌli:f] N (*pl* **-leaves**) risguardo.

fly·over ['flaɪˌəuvə'] N (*Brit: bridge*) cavalcavia *m inv*.

fly·paper ['flaɪˌpeɪpə'] N carta moschicida.

fly·past ['flaɪpɑːst] N parata aerea.

fly·sheet [flaɪˌʃi:t] N (*for tent*) soprattetto.

♦ **fly spray** N (spray *m inv*) moschicida *m*.

♦ **fly swat, fly swatter** N acchiappamosche *m inv*.

fly·weight ['flaɪˌweɪt] (*Boxing*) **1** N peso *m* mosca *inv*.
2 ADJ (*contest*) di pesi mosca.

fly·wheel ['flaɪˌwi:l] N (*Tech*) volano.

FM [ˌɛf'ɛm] **1** ABBR (*Radio:* = *frequency modulation*) FM.
2 (*Brit Mil*) = **field marshal**.

FMB [ˌɛfɛm'bi:] N ABBR (*Am*) = *Federal Maritime Board*.

FMCS [ˌɛfɛmsi:'ɛs] N ABBR (*Am*: = *Federal Mediation and Conciliation Services*) organismo di conciliazione in caso di conflitti sul lavoro.

FO [ˌɛf'əu] N ABBR (*Brit*) = **Foreign Office**.

foal [fəul] N puledro.

foam [fəum] **1** N (*gen*) schiuma.
2 VI (*sea*) spumeggiare; **to foam at the mouth** avere la schiuma alla bocca.

♦ **foam-backed** ['fəʊmˌbækt] ADJ (*carpet*) con il rovescio in gomma.
♦ **foam bath** N bagnoschiuma *m inv*.
♦ **foam rubber** N gommapiuma ®.
foamy ['fəʊmɪ] ADJ (*comp* **-ier**, *superl* **-iest**) spumeggiante.
FOB, f.o.b. ABBR (= *free on board*) f.o.b., franco a bordo.
fob [fɒb] [1] VT: **to fob sb off (with sth)** appioppare *or* rifilare (qc) a qn; **to fob sb off with promises** tenere qn buono(-a) con delle promesse.
[2] N (*also*: **watch fob**: *chain*) catena per orologio; (: *band of cloth*) nastro per orologio.
► **fob off on** VT + ADV + PREP rifilare a.
FOC ABBR (*Brit*) = **free of charge**.
fo·cal ['fəʊkl] ADJ (*Tech*) focale.
♦ **focal point** N (*fig*) centro; (*of lens, mirror*) punto focale.
fo'c'sle ['fəʊksl] N = **forecastle**.
fo·cus ['fəʊkəs] [1] N (*pl* **focuses** *or* **foci** ['fəʊkaɪ]) (*gen*) fuoco; (*of attention, interest*) centro; **to be out of focus** (*Phot*) essere sfocato(-a); **in focus** a fuoco.
[2] VT: **to focus (on)** (*camera, instrument, field glasses*) mettere a fuoco (su); (*attention, eyes*) focalizzare (su); (*light rays*) far convergere (su).
[3] VI: **to focus (on)** (*light, heat, rays*) convergere (su); (*person*) fissare lo sguardo (su); **to focus on sth** (*eyes, person*) mettere a fuoco qc.
fod·der ['fɒdə'] N foraggio.
♦ **fodder crop** N coltura foraggera.
FOE [ˌɛfəʊ'iː] N ABBR **a** (= *Friends of the Earth*) ≈ Lega Ambiente **b** (*Am*: = *Fraternal Order of Eagles*) *organizzazione filantropica.*
foe [fəʊ] N (*liter*) nemico(-a).
foe·tal, (*Am*) **fe·tal** ['fiːtl] ADJ fetale.
foet·id ['fiːtɪd] ADJ = **fetid**.
foe·tus, (*Am*) **fe·tus** ['fiːtəs] N feto.
fog [fɒg] [1] N nebbia.
[2] VT (*lens*) far appannare; **to fog the issue** (*fig*) confondere le cose.
♦ **fog bank** N banco di nebbia.
♦ **fog·bound** ['fɒgˌbaʊnd] ADJ fermo(-a) a causa della nebbia.
fo·gey, fogy ['fəʊgɪ] N (*fam*): **old fogey** matusa *m inv*.
fog·gi·ness ['fɒgɪnɪs] N nebbiosità.
fog·gy ['fɒgɪ] ADJ (*comp* **-ier**, *superl* **-iest**) nebbioso(-a); **it's foggy** c'è nebbia; **I haven't the foggiest (idea)** (*fam*) non ne ho la più pallida idea.
fog·horn ['fɒgˌhɔːn] N corno da nebbia; **a voice like a foghorn** una voce tonante.
♦ **fog light**, (*Brit*) **fog lamp** N (*Aut*) faro *m* antinebbia *inv*.
♦ **fog signal** N (*Rail*) segnale *m* da nebbia.
fogy ['fəʊgɪ] N = **fogey**.
foi·ble ['fɔɪbl] N debolezza, mania.
foil[1] [fɔɪl] N **a** lamina di metallo; (*also*: **tinfoil, kitchen foil**) carta stagnola *or* d'alluminio; **to act as a foil to sb/sth** (*fig*) far risaltare qn/qc **b** (*Fencing*) fioretto.
foil[2] [fɔɪl] VT (*thief*) fermare; (*attempt*) far fallire, sventare.
foist [fɔɪst] VT: **to foist sth on sb** rifilare qc a qn.
fold[1] [fəʊld] N (*Agr*) ovile *m*; **to come back to the fold** (*fig*) tornare all'ovile.
fold[2] [fəʊld] [1] N (*bend, crease, also Geol*) piega.
[2] VT (*gen*) piegare; (*wings*) ripiegare; **she folded the paper in two** piegò in due la carta; **to fold one's arms** incrociare le braccia.
[3] VI (*chair, table*) piegarsi; (*fam*: *fail*: *business venture*) crollare; (: *play*) chiudere
► **fold away** [1] VI + ADV (*table, bed*) piegarsi, essere pieghevole.
[2] VT + ADV (*clothes, linen*) piegare, mettere a posto
► **fold back** VT + ADV ripiegare
► **fold over** VT + ADV ripiegare
► **fold up** [1] VI + ADV (*fam*: *fail*: *business*) fallire, crollare.
[2] VT + ADV (*map, paper*) piegare, ripiegare.
♦ **fold·away** ['fəʊldəˌweɪ] ADJ (*bed, table*) pieghevole.
♦ **fold·ed** ['fəʊldɪd] ADJ (*paper*) piegato(-a); (*closed*) chiuso(-a).
fold·er ['fəʊldə'] N (*file*: *for papers*) cartella, cartellina; (*binder*) raccoglitore *m*.
fold·ing ['fəʊldɪŋ] ADJ (*chair, doors, bed*) pieghevole.
♦ **folding money** N (*Am*) banconote *fpl*.
♦ **fold mountains** NPL montagne *fpl* a pieghe.
fo·li·age ['fəʊlɪɪdʒ] N fogliame *m*.
fo·lia·tion [ˌfəʊlɪ'eɪʃən] N fogliazione *f*.
fo·lio ['fəʊlɪəʊ] N (*book*) volume *m* in folio; (*sheet*) foglio.
folk [fəʊk] N **a** (*people*) gente *f*; **country/city folk** gente di campagna/di città; **my folks** (*fam*) i miei **b** (*also*: **folk music**) folk *m inv*.
folk·lore ['fəʊkˌlɔː'] N folclore *m*.
♦ **folk music** N musica *f* folk *inv*.
♦ **folk singer** N cantante *m/f* folk *inv*.
♦ **folk song** ['fəʊkˌsɒŋ] N canto popolare, canzone *f* folk *inv*.
folk·sy ['fəʊksɪ] ADJ (*comp* **-ier**, *superl* **-iest**) (*often pej*: *person*) senza pretese; (: *art, humour*) popolare.
fol·li·cle ['fɒlɪkl] N follicolo.
♦ **follicle-stimulating hormone** ['fɒlɪkl'stɪmjʊˌleɪtɪŋ'hɔːməʊn] N ormone *m* follicolo-stimolante.
fol·low ['fɒləʊ] [1] VT (*gen*) seguire; (*football team*) fare il tifo per; **the road follows the coast** la strada segue la costa; **we're being followed** qualcuno ci sta seguendo; **to follow sb's advice** seguire il consiglio di qn; **he followed suit** ha fatto altrettanto; **I don't quite follow you** non sono sicuro di capirti *or* seguirti.
[2] VI **a** (*gen*) seguire; **as follows** come segue; **to follow in sb's footsteps** seguire le orme di qn; **what is there to follow?** che c'è dopo?; **I don't follow** non capisco **b** (*result, deduction etc*) risultare, conseguire; **it follows that** ... ne consegue che...; **it doesn't follow that** ... non vuol dire che...; **that doesn't follow** non necessariamente
► **follow about, follow around** VT + ADV seguire dappertutto
► **follow on** VI + ADV (*continue*): **to follow on from** seguire
► **follow out** VT + ADV (*implement*: *idea, plan*) eseguire, portare a termine
► **follow through** [1] VT + ADV = **follow out**.
[2] VI + ADV (*Golf*) portare a termine l'azione; (*Tennis*) accompagnare la palla
► **follow up** [1] VT + ADV **a** (*investigate*: *case, clue*) esaminare, seguire
b (*take further action on*: *offer, suggestion*) seguire
c (*reinforce*: *success, victory*) rafforzare, sfruttare; (*letter, offer*) fare seguito a.
[2] VI + ADV (*Ftbl etc*): **to follow up with another goal** segnare di nuovo.
fol·low·er ['fɒləʊə'] N (*disciple*) seguace *m/f*, discepolo(-a); (*of team*) tifoso(-a).
fol·low·ing ['fɒləʊɪŋ] [1] ADJ seguente, successivo(-a); **following wind** vento in poppa; **the following day** il giorno seguente, l'indomani.
[2] N **a** (*Pol etc*) seguito, proseliti *mpl*; (*Sport*) tifosi *mpl*; **they have a large following** hanno un grande seguito

b : he said the following ha detto quanto segue; **see the following** (*in document etc*) vedi quanto segue.
♦ **follow-my-leader** ['fɒləʊmaːˈliːdəʳ] N *gioco in cui tutti i bambini ripetono i gesti del capofila.*
♦ **follow-up** ['fɒləʊˌʌp] N seguito.
♦ **follow-up letter** N lettera (*informativa o di risposta*).
♦ **follow-up visit** N (*Med*) visita di controllo.
fol·ly ['fɒlɪ] N follia, pazzia.
fo·ment [fəˈmɛnt] VT (*frm: trouble, discord, revolution*) fomentare; (*Med*) applicare impacchi caldi.
fond [fɒnd] ADJ (*comp* **-er**, *superl* **-est**) (*loving: memory, look*) affettuoso(-a), tenero(-a); (*doting*) che stravede; (*foolish: hope, desire*) vano(-a); **to be fond of sb** voler bene a qn; **she's fond of swimming** le piace nuotare; **she's fond of dogs** le piacciono i cani.
fon·dant ['fɒndənt] N fondente *m.*
fon·dle ['fɒndl] VT accarezzare.
fond·ly ['fɒndlɪ] ADV (*lovingly*) affettuosamente; (*naïvely*) ingenuamente; **he fondly believed that …** ha avuto l'ingenuità di credere che… .
fond·ness ['fɒndnɪs] N: **fondness (for sth)** predilezione *f* (per qc); **fondness (for sb)** affetto (per qn).
fon·due ['fɒnduː] N fonduta, fondue *f inv.*
font [fɒnt] N **a** (*in church*) fonte *m* battesimale **b** (*Typ*) carattere *m* (di scrittura).
food [fuːd] N cibo; (*for plants*) fertilizzante *m*; **I've no food left in the house** non c'è più niente da mangiare in casa; **the food at the hotel is terrible** si mangia malissimo in albergo; **to be off one's food** (*fam*) aver perso l'appetito; **food for thought** (*fig*) qualcosa su cui riflettere.
♦ **food chain** N catena alimentare.
♦ **food mixer** N frullatore *m.*
♦ **food parcel** N pacco *m* viveri *inv.*
♦ **food poisoning** N intossicazione *f* alimentare.
♦ **food processor** N tritatutto *m inv* elettrico.
♦ **food rationing** N razionamento alimentare.
♦ **food stamp** N (*Am*) *buono alimentare dato agli indigenti.*
food·stuffs ['fuːdˌstʌfs] NPL generi *mpl* alimentari.
♦ **food supplies** NPL derrate *fpl* alimentari.
fool [fuːl] ① N **a** sciocco(-a), stupido(-a), fesso(-a); (*jester*) buffone *m*, giullare *m*; **you fool!** stupido!; **don't be a fool!** non fare lo stupido!; **I was a fool not to go** sono stato stupido a non andarci; **some fool of a civil servant** uno stupido di impiegato statale; **to play the fool** fare lo/la stupido(-a); **to live in a fool's paradise** (*fig*) vivere di illusioni; **he is nobody's fool** non è mica scemo; **to make a fool of sb** far fare a qn la figura dello scemo, prendere in giro qn; **to make a fool of o.s.** rendersi *or* coprirsi di ridicolo(-a); **to go on a fool's errand** fare la strada per niente
  b (*Culin*) frullato.
  ② ADJ (*Am*) sciocco(-a).
  ③ VT (*deceive*) ingannare, far fesso(-a); **you can't fool me** non mi inganni.
  ④ VI scherzare; **I was only fooling** stavo solo scherzando
▶ **fool about, fool around** VI + ADV **a** (*waste time*) perdere tempo
  b (*act the fool*) fare lo/la stupido(-a).
fool·ery ['fuːlərɪ] N stupidaggini *fpl.*
fool·har·di·ness ['fuːlˌhaːdɪnɪs] N imprudenza, avventatezza.
fool·hardy ['fuːlˌhaːdɪ] ADJ (*rash*) avventato(-a), imprudente.

fool·ish ['fuːlɪʃ] ADJ (*senseless*) sciocco(-a), stupido(-a), insensato(-a); (*ridiculous*) ridicolo(-a), assurdo(-a); (*unwise*) imprudente; **that was very foolish of you** è stato molto sciocco da parte tua.
fool·ish·ly ['fuːlɪʃlɪ] ADV stupidamente.
fool·ish·ness ['fuːlɪʃnɪs] N stupidità.
fool·proof ['fuːlˌpruːf] ADJ (*method, plan etc*) infallibile, sicurissimo(-a); (*machine*) facile da usare.
fools·cap ['fuːlzˌkæp] N carta protocollo.
foot [fʊt] ① N (*pl* **feet**) **a** (*gen*) piede *m*; (*of animal*) zampa; (*of page, stairs etc*) fondo; **on foot** a piedi; **to be on one's feet** essere in piedi; (*after illness*) essersi rimesso(-a); **to jump/rise to one's feet** balzare/alzarsi in piedi; **it's wet under foot** è bagnato per terra
  b (*fig phrases*): **to fall on one's feet** cadere in piedi; **to find one's feet** ambientarsi; **to get cold feet** avere fifa; **to get under sb's feet** stare tra i piedi a qn; **to have one foot in the grave** avere un piede nella fossa; **to put one's foot down** (*say no*) imporsi; (*Aut*) schiacciare l'acceleratore; **to get a foot in the door** fare il primo passo; **to put one's foot in it** fare una gaffe; **to put one's feet up** (*fam*) riposarsi; **I've never set foot there** non ci ho mai messo piede; **to put one's best foot forward** (*hurry*) sbrigarsi; **to get off on the right/wrong foot** partire col piede giusto/sbagliato; **she didn't put a foot wrong** non ha fatto neanche un errore
  c (*measure*) piede *m* (= 304 mm *or* 12 inches); **he's 6 foot** *or* **feet tall** ≈ è alto 1 metro e 80.
  ② VT: **to foot the bill** (*fam*) pagare il conto.
foot·age ['fʊtɪdʒ] N (*Cine*) sequenza; (*material*) ≈ metraggio.
♦ **foot-and-mouth (disease)** ['fʊtənd'maʊθ(dɪziːz)] N afta epizootica.
foot·ball ['fʊtˌbɔːl] ① N (*ball*) pallone *m*; (*Sport: Brit*) calcio; (: *Am*) football *m* americano.
  ② ADJ (*team, supporters*) di calcio.
♦ **football coupon** N schedina del totocalcio.
foot·ball·er ['fʊtˌbɔːləʳ] N (*Brit*) calciatore(-trice).
♦ **football ground** N campo di calcio.
♦ **football league** N campionato di calcio.
♦ **football match** N (*Brit*) partita di calcio.
♦ **football player** N (*Brit*) calciatore(-trice); (*Am*) giocatore *m* di football americano.
♦ **football pools** NPL totocalcio *msg*; **to do the football pools** giocare la schedina.
♦ **football special** N treno straordinario per tifosi (di calcio).
♦ **foot brake** N freno a pedale.
foot·bridge ['fʊtˌbrɪdʒ] N passerella.
foot·fall ['fʊtˌfɔːl] N passo.
♦ **foot fault** N (*Tennis*) fallo di piede.
foot·gear ['fʊtˌɡɪəʳ] N calzatura.
foot·hills ['fʊtˌhɪlz] NPL contrafforti *fpl*, colline *fpl* pedemontane.
foot·hold ['fʊtˌhəʊld] N punto d'appoggio; **to gain a foothold** (*fig: idea, movement*) prendere piede; (: *newcomer*) farsi accettare; **to gain a foothold in a market** (*Comm*) imporsi sul mercato.
foot·ing ['fʊtɪŋ] N (*foothold*) punto d'appoggio; (*fig: basis*) posizione *f*; **to lose one's footing** perdere l'equilibrio, mettere un piede in fallo; **on an equal footing** (*fig*) su un piano di parità, in condizioni di parità; **to be on a friendly footing with sb** essere in rapporti d'amicizia con qn.
foot·le ['fuːtl] VI: **to footle about** bighellonare.

foot·lights ['fʊt,laɪts] NPL (*in theatre*) luci *fpl* della ribalta.

foot·ling ['fʊtlɪŋ] ADJ stupido(-a), insignificante.

foot·loose ['fʊt,luːs] ADJ: **footloose and fancy-free** libero (-a) e spensierato(-a).

foot·man ['fʊtmən] N (*pl* -**men**) lacchè *m inv*.

foot·mark ['fʊt,mɑːk] N orma.

foot·note ['fʊt,nəʊt] N nota a piè di pagina.

foot·path ['fʊt,pɑːθ] N (*track*) sentiero.

foot·plate ['fʊt,pleɪt] N (*Rail*) piattaforma del macchinista.

foot·print ['fʊt,prɪnt] N orma, impronta.

foot·pump ['fʊt,pʌmp] N pompa a pedale.

foot·rest ['fʊt,rɛst] N poggiapiedi *m inv*.

foot·sie ['fʊtsɪ] N (*fam*): **to play footsie with sb** fare piedino a qn.

♦ **foot soldier** N soldato di fanteria, fante *m*.

foot·sore ['fʊt,sɔː'] ADJ: **to be footsore** avere i piedi doloranti, avere mal di piedi.

foot·step ['fʊt,stɛp] N passo.

foot·stool ['fʊt,stuːl] N poggiapiedi *m inv*.

foot·way ['fʊt,weɪ] N passaggio pedonale.

foot·wear ['fʊtwɛəʳ] N calzatura.

foot·work ['fʊt,wɜːk] N (*Sport*) gioco di gambe.

fop [fɒp] N gagà *m inv*.

FOR [,ɛfəʊ'ɑː'] ABBR (= *free on rail*) franco vagone.

---

for [fɔː]
1 PREP
a (*indicating destination, intention*) per;
▷he *left* for Rome è partito per Roma
▷here's a *letter* for you ecco una lettera per te
▷is this for *me*? è per me questo?
▷for *sale* in vendita, vendesi
▷he *swam* for the shore nuotò verso la riva
▷it's *time* for lunch è ora di pranzo
▷the *train* for London il treno per Londra
b (*indicating purpose*) per;
▷*clothes* for children vestiti per bambini
▷a *cupboard* for toys un armadio per i giocattoli
▷*fit* for nothing buono(-a) a niente
▷to *pray* for peace pregare per la pace
▷he *went down* for the paper è sceso a prendere il giornale
▷*what* for? perché?, per cosa?
▷*what's* this button for? a cosa serve questo bottone?
c (*representing*) per;
▷I'll *ask* him for you glielo chiederò a nome tuo
▷*G* for George G come George
▷*member* for Hove deputato che rappresenta Hove
▷I *took* him for his brother l'ho scambiato *or* preso per suo fratello
d (*in exchange for*) per;
▷to *pay* 50 pence for a ticket pagare 50 penny per un biglietto
▷I *sold* it for £50 l'ho venduto per 50 sterline
e (*with regard to*) per;
▷*anxious* for success avido(-a) di successo
▷*as* for him/that quanto a lui/ciò
▷it's *cold* for July è freddo per essere luglio
▷for *each* one who voted yes, 50 voted no per ogni voto a favore ce n'erano 50 contro
▷a *gift* for languages un dono per le lingue
▷he's *mature* for his age è maturo per la sua età

▷there's *nothing* for it but to jump (*Brit*) non c'è altro da fare che saltare
f (*in favour of*) per, a favore di;
▷are you for or *against* us? sei con noi o contro di noi?
▷I'm *all* for it sono completamente a favore
▷the *campaign* for la campagna a favore di *or* per
▷*vote* for me! votate per me!
g (*because of*) per, a causa di;
▷*famous* for its cathedral famoso(-a) per la sua cattedrale
▷for *fear* of being criticised per paura di essere criticato(-a)
▷to shout for *joy* gridare di gioia
▷for this *reason* per questa ragione
▷do it for my *sake* fallo per me
▷if it were not for *you* se non fosse per te
h (*in spite of*)
▷for all *that* malgrado ciò;
▷for all his *money* malgrado tutto il suo denaro
i (*distance*) per;
▷there were *roadworks* for 5 km c'erano lavori in corso per 5 km
▷we *walked* for miles abbiamo camminato per chilometri
j (*time*)
▷can you do it for *tomorrow*? lo puoi fare per domani?
▷I haven't seen him for a *week* non lo vedo da una settimana, è una settimana che non lo vedo
▷I'll be away for 3 *weeks* starò via (per) 3 settimane
▷it has not rained for 3 *weeks* non piove da 3 settimane
▷he won't be back for a *while* non tornerà per un po'
▷he was away for 2 *years* è stato via per 2 anni
▷I have known her for *years* la conosco da anni
k (*with infinitive clauses*): **for this** *to be* **possible** ... perché ciò sia possibile...
▷it would be *best* for you to go sarebbe meglio che te ne andassi
▷he *brought* it for us to see l'ha portato per farcelo vedere
▷*it's not* for me to decide non sta a me decidere
▷there is still *time* for you to do it hai ancora tempo per farlo
l (*phrases*)
▷you're for *it*! (*fam*) vedrai adesso!
▷*oh* for a cup of tea! cosa non darei per una tazza di tè!
2 CONJ dal momento che, poiché.

---

for·age ['fɒrɪdʒ] **1** N piante *fpl* foraggere.
2 VI: **to forage (for)** andare in cerca (di).
♦ **forage cap** N bustina.

for·ay ['fɒreɪ] N (*esp Mil*) incursione *f*.

for·bade, for·bad [fə'bæd] PT of **forbid**.

for·bear [fɔː'bɛəʳ] (*pt* **forbore**, *pp* **forborne**) VI: **to forbear from doing, to forbear to do** astenersi dal fare.

for·bear·ance [fɔː'bɛərəns] N pazienza, tolleranza.

for·bear·ing [fɔː'bɛərɪŋ] ADJ paziente, tollerante.

for·bid [fə'bɪd] (*pt* **forbad** *or* **forbade**, *pp* **forbidden**) VT proibire, vietare; **to forbid sb sth** proibire qc a qn; **to forbid sb to do sth** proibire a qn di fare qc; "**smoking forbidden**" "vietato fumare"; **God forbid!** Dio non

voglia!
forbidden [fə'bɪdn] ADJ vietato(-a).
♦ **forbidden fruit** N frutto proibito.
for·bid·ding [fə'bɪdɪŋ] ADJ arcigno(-a), d'aspetto minaccioso.
for·bid·ding·ly [fə'bɪdɪŋlɪ] ADV minacciosamente.
for·bore [fɔː'bɔːʳ], **for·borne** [fɔː'bɔːn] PT, PP of **forbear**.
force [fɔːs] [1] N **a** (gen) forza; **to resort to force** ricorrere alla violenza; **force of gravity** forza di gravità; **a force 5 wind** un vento forza 5; **the forces of evil** (fig) le forze del male; **by force** con la forza; **by force of habit** per abitudine; **by sheer force of character, he …** grazie alla sua forza di carattere, lui…; **to be in force** (Law) essere in vigore; **to come into force** (Law) entrare in vigore; **to turn out in force** manifestare in gran numero or in massa
 b (body of men) gruppo; (Mil) forza; **the force** (police force) la polizia, il corpo di polizia; **the sales force** (Comm) l'effettivo dei rappresentanti
 c : **the Forces** (Brit: Mil) le forze armate.
 [2] VT **a** (compel: person) forzare, costringere; **to force sb to do sth** costringere qn a fare qc
 b (impose): **to force sth on sb** imporre qc a qn; **to force o.s. on sb** imporsi a qn, imporre la propria presenza a qn
 c (push, squeeze) schiacciare; **he forced the clothes into the suitcase** ha fatto entrare a forza i vestiti nella valigia; **to force one's way into** entrare con la forza in; **to force one's way through** (crowd) farsi strada tra; (opening) penetrare a forza in, passare a forza attraverso
 d (break open: lock) forzare; **to force an entry** entrare con la forza; **to force sb's hand** (fig) forzare la mano a qn
 e (produce with effort): **to force a smile/a reply** sforzarsi di sorridere/rispondere; **don't force the situation** non forzare le cose
 f (obtain by force: smile, confession) strappare
▶ **force back** VT + ADV (crowd, enemy) respingere; (urge) reprimere; (tears) ingoiare
▶ **force down** VT + ADV (food) sforzarsi di mangiare; (aircraft) forzare ad atterrare
▶ **force out** VT + ADV (person) costringere ad uscire; (cork) far uscire con la forza.
forced [fɔːst] ADJ (labour, marriage) forzato(-a).
♦ **force-feed** ['fɔːsˌfiːd] (pt, pp **force-fed**) VT sottoporre ad alimentazione forzata.
♦ **force field** N (Phys) campo di forze.
force·ful ['fɔːsfʊl] ADJ (personality) forte; (argument) valido(-a).
force·ful·ly ['fɔːsfəlɪ] ADV (argue) efficacemente.
force·ful·ness ['fɔːsfʊlnɪs] N forza.
force·meat ['fɔːsˌmiːt] N (Brit Culin) ripieno.
for·ceps ['fɔːsɛps] NPL forcipe msg.
for·cible ['fɔːsəbl] ADJ (done by force) fatto(-a) con la forza; (effective: argument, style) convincente, efficace.
for·cibly ['fɔːsəblɪ] ADV (by force: take) con la forza; (vigorously: argue) energicamente, vigorosamente.
ford [fɔːd] [1] N guado.
 [2] VT guadare, passare a guado.
ford·able ['fɔːdəbl] ADJ guadabile.
fore [fɔːʳ] [1] ADJ (section, part: of animal, ship, aircraft) anteriore.
 [2] ADV (Naut): **fore and aft** da prua a poppa.
 [3] N: **to the fore** in primo piano; **to come to the fore** mettersi in evidenza or in luce.

fore·arm ['fɔːrˌɑːm] N avambraccio.
fore·bear ['fɔːˌbɛəʳ] N antenato(-a).
fore·bod·ing [fɔː'bəʊdɪŋ] N (cattivo) presagio, presentimento.
fore·cast ['fɔːˌkɑːst] (vb: pt, pp **forecast** or **forecasted**) [1] N pronostico, previsione f; (also: **weather forecast**) previsioni fpl del tempo; (Horse-racing) accoppiata.
 [2] VT (also Met) prevedere.
fore·cas·tle, fo'c's'le ['fəʊksl] N (Naut) castello di prua.
fore·close [fɔː'kləʊz] VT (Law: also: **foreclose on**) pignorare.
fore·clo·sure [fɔː'kləʊʒəʳ] N pignoramento.
fore·court ['fɔːˌkɔːt] N (of garage) spiazzo; (of station) piazzale m.
fore·doomed [fɔː'duːmd] ADJ: **to be foredoomed to failure** essere destinato(-a) a fallire.
fore·fathers ['fɔːˌfɑːðəz] NPL progenitori mpl, antenati mpl, avi mpl.
fore·finger ['fɔːˌfɪŋgəʳ] N (dito) indice m.
fore·foot ['fɔːˌfʊt] N (pl -feet) zampa anteriore.
fore·front ['fɔːˌfrʌnt] N: **to be in the forefront of** essere all'avanguardia in.
fore·go [fɔː'gəʊ] VT = **forgo**.
fore·going [fɔː'gəʊɪŋ] ADJ precedente.
fore·gone ['fɔːˌgɒn] [1] PP of **forego**.
 [2] ADJ: **it was a foregone conclusion** era un risultato scontato.
fore·ground ['fɔːˌgraʊnd] [1] N (Art) primo piano; **in the foreground** (fig) in una posizione di primo piano.
 [2] ADJ (Comput) foreground inv, di primo piano.
fore·hand ['fɔːˌhænd] N (Tennis) diritto.
fore·head ['fɔːˌhɛd] N fronte f.
for·eign ['fɒrɪn] ADJ **a** (language, tourist) straniero(-a); (policy, trade) estero(-a); **foreign investment** investimento all'estero **b** (not natural) estraneo(-a); **deceit is foreign to his nature** ingannare non è nel suo carattere.
♦ **foreign bill** N (Fin) cambiale f pagabile all'estero.
♦ **foreign body** N (frm) corpo estraneo.
♦ **foreign currency** N valuta estera.
for·eign·er ['fɒrɪnəʳ] N straniero(-a).
♦ **foreign exchange** N cambio di valuta; (currency) valuta estera; **foreign exchange market** mercato dei cambi.
♦ **foreign minister** N ministro degli Esteri.
♦ **Foreign Office** N (Brit) ministero degli Esteri.
♦ **foreign secretary** N (Brit) ministro degli Esteri.
fore·leg ['fɔːˌlɛg] N zampa anteriore.
fore·man ['fɔːmən] N (pl -men) (of workers) caposquadra m; (Law: of jury) portavoce m della giuria.
fore·mast ['fɔːmɑːst] N (Naut) (albero di) trinchetto.
fore·most ['fɔːˌməʊst] [1] ADJ (outstanding: writer, politician) più importante, principale, più in vista.
 [2] ADV: **first and foremost** innanzitutto.
fore·name ['fɔːˌneɪm] N nome m di battesimo.
fore·noon ['fɔːˌnuːn] N (frm) mattina.
fo·ren·sic [fə'rɛnsɪk] ADJ (evidence, laboratory) medico-legale; **forensic scientist** or **expert** esperto(-a) della (polizia) scientifica.
♦ **forensic medicine** N medicina legale.
fore·part ['fɔːˌpɑːt] N (frm) parte f anteriore.
fore·play ['fɔːˌpleɪ] N preliminari mpl (nel rapporto sessuale).
fore·run·ner ['fɔːˌrʌnəʳ] N precursore m; (Skiing) apripista m/f inv.
fore·sail ['fɔːˌseɪl] N (Naut) (vela di) trinchetto.

fore·see [fɔː'siː] (*pt* **foresaw**, *pp* **foreseen**) VT prevedere.

fore·see·able [fɔː'siːəbl] ADJ (*opportunity*) prevedibile; **in the foreseeable future** nell'immediato futuro.

fore·seen [fɔː'siːn] PP of **foresee**.

fore·shad·ow [fɔː'ʃædəʊ] VT (*liter*) presagire, far prevedere.

fore·shore ['fɔː.ʃɔːʳ] N battigia.

fore·short·en [fɔː'ʃɔːtn] VT (*figure*) rappresentare in scorcio.

fore·short·ened [fɔː'ʃɔːtənd] ADJ di scorcio.

fore·sight ['fɔː.saɪt] N previdenza.

fore·skin ['fɔː.skɪn] N (*Anat*) prepuzio.

for·est ['fɒrɪst] N foresta.

fore·stall [fɔː'stɔːl] VT (*anticipate: event, accident*) prevenire; (: *rival, competitor*) anticipare.

fore·stay ['fɔː.steɪ] N (*Naut*) strallo di trinchetto.

for·est·er ['fɒrɪstəʳ] N guardia forestale.

for·est·ry ['fɒrɪstrɪ] N selvicoltura.

♦ **Forestry Commission** N ≈ Corpo forestale dello Stato.

fore·summit ['fɔː.sʌmɪt] N (*Mountaineering*) antecima.

fore·taste ['fɔː.teɪst] N assaggio.

fore·tell [fɔː'tɛl] (*pt, pp* **foretold**) VT predire.

fore·thought ['fɔː.θɔːt] N previdenza; **to act with forethought** essere previdente.

fore·told [fɔː'təʊld] PT, PP of **foretell**.

for·ever [fər'ɛvəʳ] ADV (*eternally*) per sempre, eternamente; (*for good*) per sempre; (*fam: incessantly, repeatedly*) sempre, di continuo; (: *for ages*): **it lasted forever** è durato un'eternità; **it'll take forever** ci vorrà una vita.

fore·warn [fɔː'wɔːn] VT avvisare in precedenza; **forewarned is forearmed** uomo avvisato è mezzo salvato.

forewent [fɔː'wɛnt] PT of **forego**.

fore·woman ['fɔː.wʊmən] N (*pl* **-women**) caporeparto *f inv*; (*of jury*) portavoce *f inv* della giuria.

fore·word ['fɔː.wɜːd] N prefazione *f*.

for·feit ['fɔːfɪt] **1** N (*penalty*) ammenda; (*in game*) penitenza.
2 VT (*esp Law: one's right, status*) perdere; (*one's happiness, health*) giocarsi.

for·gave [fə'geɪv] PT of **forgive**.

forge [fɔːdʒ] **1** N (*of blacksmith*) fucina.
2 VT **a** (*metal, iron*) fucinare, forgiare; (*fig: friendship, plan, unity*) forgiare, formare
b (*falsify: signature, document*) contraffare, falsificare
▶ **forge ahead** VI + ADV andare avanti (con determinazione).

forged [fɔːdʒd] ADJ (*document*) falsificato(-a), contraffatto (-a); (*banknote, signature*) falso(-a).

forg·er ['fɔːdʒəʳ] N falsario(-a), contraffattore(-trice).

for·gery ['fɔːdʒərɪ] N (*activity*) falsificazione *f*, contraffazione *f*; (*thing*) falso.

for·get [fə'gɛt] (*pt* **forgot**, *pp* **forgotten**) **1** VT dimenticare; **to forget to do sth** dimenticare di fare qc; **to forget how to do sth** dimenticare come si fa qc; **she never forgets a face** è molto fisionomista; **never to be forgotten** indimenticabile; **forget it!** (*fam*) lascia perdere!; **to forget o.s.** (*lose self-control*) perdere la testa.
2 VI dimenticarsi, scordarsi; **I've forgotten all about it** me ne sono completamente dimenticato; **let's forget about it!** non ne parliamo più!

for·get·ful [fə'gɛtfʊl] ADJ (*absent-minded*) distratto(-a), di poca memoria; **forgetful of** dimentico(-a) di; **it was very forgetful of me not to ...** è stata una grande dimenti-

canza quella di non... .

for·get·ful·ness [fə'gɛtfʊlnɪs] N smemoratezza; (*oblivion*) oblio.

♦ **forget-me-not** [fə'gɛtmɪ.nɒt] N nontiscordardimé *m inv*.

for·get·table [fə'gɛtəbl] ADJ non degno(-a) di nota.

for·giv·able [fə'gɪvəbl] ADJ perdonabile.

for·giv·ably [fə'gɪvəblɪ] ADV comprensibilmente.

for·give [fə'gɪv] (*pt* **forgave**, *pp* **forgiven**) VT (*person, fault*) perdonare; **to forgive sb for sth/for doing sth** perdonare qc a qn/a qn di aver fatto qc.

for·give·ness [fə'gɪvnɪs] N (*pardon*) perdono; (*willingness to forgive*) clemenza, indulgenza.

for·giv·ing [fə'gɪvɪŋ] ADJ indulgente.

for·go [fɔː'gəʊ] (*pt* **forwent**, *pp* **forgone**) VT (*do without*) rinunciare a, fare a meno di.

for·got [fə'gɒt] PT of **forget**.

for·got·ten [fə'gɒtn] PP of **forget**.

fork [fɔːk] **1** N (*for eating*) forchetta; (*for gardening*) forca, forcone *m*; (*in road*) bivio, biforcazione *f*.
2 VI (*road*) biforcarsi
▶ **fork out** **1** VT + ADV (*fam: money, cash*) sborsare, tirare fuori.
2 VI + ADV tirare fuori i soldi, pagare.

forked [fɔːkt] ADJ (*tail, tongue, branch*) biforcuto(-a).

♦ **forked lightning** N (fulmine *m* a) saetta.

♦ **fork-lift truck** ['fɔːk.lɪft'trʌk] N carrello elevatore.

for·lorn [fə'lɔːn] ADJ (*person*) sconsolato(-a); (*deserted: place, house*) abbandonato(-a); (*desperate: attempt*) disperato(-a); **a forlorn hope** una speranza vana.

for·lorn·ly [fə'lɔːnlɪ] ADV sconsolatamente; (*hope*) vanamente.

form [fɔːm] **1** N **a** (*gen*) forma; **in the form of** a forma di, sotto forma di; **the same thing in a new form** la stessa cosa presentata in modo diverso; **a form of apology** una specie di scusa; **form and content** forma e contenuto; **to take form** prendere forma; **the correct form of address for a bishop** il corretto modo di rivolgersi a un vescovo
b (*Sport, fig*): **to be in good form** essere in forma; **in top form** in gran forma; **true to form** come sempre; **he was in great form last night** era in piena forma ieri sera
c (*document*) modulo
d (*old: etiquette*) forma; **it's a matter of form** è una questione di forma; **it's bad form** è maleducato
e (*bench*) banco
f (*Brit Scol*) classe *f*; **in the first form** ≈ in prima media.
2 VT (*gen*) formare; (*plan*) concepire; (*idea, opinion*) formarsi, farsi; (*habit*) prendere; **to form a circle/a queue** fare *or* formare un cerchio/una coda; **he formed it out of a lump of clay** l'ha plasmato *or* modellato su un blocco di creta; **to form a government/group** formare un governo/gruppo; **those who formed the group** quelli che facevano parte del gruppo; **to form part of sth** far parte di qc.
3 VI formarsi.

for·mal ['fɔːməl] ADJ (*gen*) formale; (*person*) cerimonioso (-a); (*official: visit, offer, acceptance*) ufficiale; **there was no formal agreement** non c'era un contratto formale; **formal garden** giardino all'italiana; **formal training** preparazione *f* specifica.

for·mal·de·hyde [fɔː'mældɪ.haɪd] N formaldeide *f*.

♦ **formal dress** N abito da cerimonia; (*evening dress*) abito da sera.

for·ma·lin ['fɔːməlɪn] N formalina.

for·mal·ism ['fɔːmə.lɪzəm] N formalismo.

for·mal·ist ['fɔ:mə'lɪst] ADJ, N formalista *(m/f)*.
for·mal·is·tic [ˌfɔ:mə'lɪstɪk] ADJ formalistico(-a).
for·mal·ity [fɔ:'mælɪtɪ] N formalità *f inv*; **it's a mere formality** è una semplice formalità.
for·mal·ize ['fɔ:mə,laɪz] VT rendere ufficiale.
for·mal·ly ['fɔ:məlɪ] ADV *(see adj)* in modo formale; ufficialmente; **formally dressed** in abito da cerimonia; **to be formally invited** ricevere un invito ufficiale.
for·mat ['fɔ:ˌmæt] [1] N formato.
[2] VT *(Comput)* formattare.
for·ma·tion [fɔ:'meɪʃən] N formazione *f*.
forma·tive ['fɔ:mətɪv] ADJ formativo(-a); **formative years** anni *mpl* formativi.
for·mer ['fɔ:mə'] [1] ADJ **a** *(earlier, previous)* vecchio(-a) *(before n)*, precedente; (: *chairman, wife etc)* ex *inv (before n)*; **in former days** nei tempi passati, in altri tempi; **the former president** l'ex presidente; **the former Yugoslavia/Soviet Union** l'ex Jugoslavia/Unione Sovietica
b *(of two)* primo(-a).
[2] PRON: **the former (** ...**the latter)** il/la primo(-a) (... l'ultimo(-a)), quello(-a)... (questo(-a)).
for·mer·ly ['fɔ:məlɪ] ADV in passato, precedentemente.
♦ **form feed** N *(on printer)* alimentazione *f* della carta.
For·mi·ca® [fɔ:'maɪkə] N Fòrmica ®.
for·mi·dable ['fɔ:mɪdəbl] ADJ *(task, difficulties)* formidabile, terribile; *(person, appearance)* che incute rispetto.
for·mi·dably ['fɔ:mɪdəblɪ] ADV tremendamente; **a formidably difficult task** un compito tremendamente difficile.
form·less ['fɔ:mlɪs] ADJ *(shape)* informe; *(feelings)* nebuloso(-a).
♦ **form master** N ≈ coordinatore *m* del Consiglio di classe.
♦ **form mistress** N ≈ coordinatrice *f* del Consiglio di classe.
for·mu·la ['fɔ:mjʊlə] N *(pl* **formulae** *or* **formulas** ['fɔ:mjʊ,li:]) *(Math, Chem, fig: plan)* formula; *(Am: baby's feed)* latte *m* in polvere.
♦ **Formula One** N *(Aut)* formula uno.
for·mu·late ['fɔ:mjʊ,leɪt] VT formulare.
for·mu·la·tion [ˌfɔ:mjʊ'leɪʃən] N formulazione *f*.
for·ni·cate ['fɔ:nɪ,keɪt] VI fornicare.
for·ni·ca·tion [ˌfɔ:nɪ'keɪʃən] N fornicazione *f*.
for·sake [fə'seɪk] *(pt* **forsook**, *pp* **forsaken)** VT *(person)* abbandonare; *(place)* lasciare.
for·sythia [fɔ:'saɪθɪə] N forsizia.
fort [fɔ:t] N *(Mil)* forte *m*.
for·te ['fɔ:tɪ] N forte *m*.
forth [fɔ:θ] ADV *(old)* **a** in avanti; **to go back and forth** andare avanti e indietro; **to set forth** mettersi in cammino; **from this day forth** d'ora in poi **b** : **and so forth** e così via, e via dicendo.
forth·com·ing [ˌfɔ:θ'kʌmɪŋ] ADJ *(event, election)* prossimo(-a); *(film)* che sta per uscire, imminente; *(book)* di prossima pubblicazione; *(character)* aperto(-a), comunicativo(-a); **if help is forthcoming** se c'è chi è disposto ad aiutare; **he wasn't very forthcoming about it** non sembrava molto disposto a parlarne.
forth·right ['fɔ:θ,raɪt] ADJ *(person, answer etc)* franco(-a), schietto(-a).
forth·with [ˌfɔ:θ'wɪθ] ADV *(frm)* immediatamente, subito.
for·ti·eth ['fɔ:tɪɪθ] [1] ADJ quarantesimo(-a).
[2] N *(in series)* quarantesimo(-a); *(fraction)* quarantesimo *for usage see* **fifth**.
for·ti·fi·ca·tion [ˌfɔ:tɪfɪ'keɪʃən] N fortificazione *f*.

for·ti·fied wine ['fɔ:tɪ,faɪd'waɪn] N vino ad alta gradazione alcolica.
for·ti·fy ['fɔ:tɪ,faɪ] VT *(Mil)* fortificare; *(fig: person)* rinvigorire, rafforzare; *(enrich: food)* arricchire.
for·tis·si·mo [fɔ:'tɪsɪ,məʊ] *(Mus)* [1] ADV fortissimo.
[2] ADJ fortissimo *inv*.
for·ti·tude ['fɔ:tɪ,tju:d] N forza d'animo.
fort·night ['fɔ:t,naɪt] N *(Brit)* quindici giorni *mpl*, quindicina di giorni, due settimane *fpl*; **to go on a fortnight's holiday** fare due settimane di vacanza; **a fortnight (from) today** oggi a quindici; **it's a fortnight since ...** sono due settimane da quando... .
fort·night·ly ['fɔ:t,naɪtlɪ] *(Brit)* [1] ADJ quindicinale, bimensile.
[2] ADV ogni quindici giorni.
FORTRAN, For·tran ['fɔ:træn] N FORTRAN *m*.
for·tress ['fɔ:trɪs] N fortezza, rocca.
for·tui·tous [fɔ:'tju:ɪtəs] ADJ fortuito(-a).
for·tui·tous·ly [fɔ:'tju:ɪtəslɪ] ADV fortuitamente, per caso.
for·tu·ity [fɔ:'tju:ɪtɪ] N accidentalità.
for·tu·nate ['fɔ:tʃənɪt] ADJ *(coincidence, event, person)* fortunato(-a); **he is fortunate to have ...** ha la fortuna di avere...; **it is fortunate that** è una fortuna che *+ sub*.
for·tu·nate·ly ['fɔ:tʃənɪtlɪ] ADV fortunatamente.
for·tune ['fɔ:tʃən] N **a** *(chance)* fortuna; **the fortunes of war** le vicende della guerra; **by good fortune** per fortuna; **to tell sb's fortune** predire l'avvenire a qn **b** *(money)* fortuna; **to come into a fortune** ereditare una fortuna; **to make a fortune** farsi una fortuna *or* un patrimonio; **a small fortune** *(fam)* un patrimonio.
♦ **fortune-hunter** ['fɔ:tʃən,hʌntə'] N cacciatore *m* di dote.
♦ **fortune-teller** ['fɔ:tʃən,tɛlə'] N indovino(-a), chiromante *m/f*.
♦ **fortune-telling** ['fɔ:tʃən,tɛlɪŋ] N chiromanzia.
for·ty ['fɔ:tɪ] [1] N quaranta *m inv*.
[2] ADJ quaranta *inv*; **to have forty winks** *(fam)* fare *or* schiacciare un pisolino *for usage see* **fifty**.
fo·rum ['fɔ:rəm] N *(History)* foro; *(fig)* tribuna.
for·ward ['fɔ:wəd] [1] ADJ **a** *(in movement, position)* in avanti; *(in time)* in anticipo; *(Naut)* prodiero(-a); **forward line** *(Sport)* linea d'attacco; *(Mil)* prima linea; **forward planning** sollecita programmazione *f*, **forward thinking** *(person)* dalle idee innovatrici
b *(precocious: child)* precoce; *(presumptuous: person, remark)* insolente, sfacciato(-a)
c *(Comm: delivery, sales, exchange)* a termine.
[2] N *(Sport)* attaccante *m*, avanti *m inv*.
[3] VT *(dispatch: parcel, goods)* spedire; *(send on: letter)* inoltrare; *(fig: sb's plans)* promuovere, appoggiare; **"please forward"** "si prega di inoltrare".
for·ward·ing ad·dress ['fɔ:wədɪŋə'drɛs] N: **he didn't leave a forwarding address** non ha lasciato un nuovo recapito.
♦ **forward-looking** ['fɔ:wəd,lʊkɪŋ] ADJ che guarda al futuro, progressista.
for·ward·ness ['fɔ:wədnɪs] N *(of child)* precocità; *(boldness)* insolenza.
♦ **forward pass** N *(Rugby)* passaggio in avanti.
for·ward(s) ['fɔ:wəd(s)] ADV *(in place)* in avanti; *(in time)* avanti, innanzi; **to push o.s. forward** farsi avanti, mettersi in evidenza; **to come forward** farsi avanti; **to move sth forward** spostare qc in avanti; **from this time forward** d'ora in poi, d'ora innanzi.
for·went [fɔ:'wɛnt] PT OF **forgo**.
fos·sil ['fɒsl] N, ADJ fossile *(m)*.

♦ **fossil fuel** N combustibile *m* fossile.
fos·sil·za·tion [ˌfɒsɪlaɪˈzeɪʃən] N fossilizzazione *f*.
fos·sil·ize [ˈfɒsɪˌlaɪz] vi fossilizzarsi.
fos·sil·ized [ˈfɒsɪˌlaɪzd] ADJ fossilizzato(-a).
fos·ter [ˈfɒstə^r] 1 VT (*child*) avere in affidamento; (*hope, ambition*) nutrire, accarezzare; (*encourage*) incoraggiare.
2 ADJ (*parent, mother, father*) affidatario(-a); (*child*) preso(-a) in affido; **foster brother** fratellastro, fratello adottivo; **foster sister** sorellastra, sorella adottiva.
fos·ter·ing [ˈfɒstərɪŋ] N affidamento.
fought [fɔːt] PT, PP of **fight**.
foul [faʊl] 1 ADJ (*putrid, disgusting: smell, breath, taste*) disgustoso(-a), rivoltante; (: *water, air*) puzzolente, fetido(-a); (*nasty: weather*) brutto(-a), orribile; (: *mood*) nero(-a); (*obscene: language*) volgare, osceno(-a); (*deed*) infame; **to use foul language** parlare sboccatamente; **to fall foul of sb/the law** entrare in contrasto con qn/con la giustizia.
2 N (*Football*) fallo; (*Boxing*) colpo basso.
3 VT **a** (*pollute: air*) appestare; **the dog fouled the pavement** il cane ha sporcato il marciapiede
b (*Sport: opponenet*) commettere un fallo su
c (*entangle: anchor, propeller*) impigliare
▶ **foul up** VT + ADV (*fam: plan, project*) rovinare.
♦ **foul-mouthed** [ˈfaʊlˈmaʊðd] ADJ sboccato(-a).
♦ **foul play** N **a** (*murder*) delitto, atto criminale; (*dishonesty*) imbroglio, raggiro; **the police suspect foul play** la polizia sospetta si tratti di un delitto; **a body has been found, but foul play is not suspected** è stato rinvenuto un cadavere, ma si è scartata l'ipotesi di un omicidio **b** (*Sport*) gioco scorretto.
♦ **foul-smelling** [ˈfaʊlˈsmɛlɪŋ] ADJ puzzolente, fetido (-a).
found[1] [faʊnd] PT, PP of **find**.
found[2] [faʊnd] VT (*establish*) fondare; (*opinion, belief*) fondare, basare; **a statement founded on fact** una dichiarazione basata sulla realtà.
foun·da·tion [faʊnˈdeɪʃən] N **a** (*founding, organization*) fondazione *f*
b : **foundations** NPL (*Archit*) fondamenta *fpl*; **to lay the foundations** gettare le fondamenta; (*fig*) gettare le basi
c (*basis*) fondamento, base *f*
d (*justification*): **the story is without foundation** la storia è infondata.
♦ **foundation course** N corso propedeutico.
♦ **foundation cream** N (*also:* **foundation**) fondotinta *m inv*.
♦ **foundation stone** N: **to lay the foundation stone** posare la prima pietra.
found·er[1] [ˈfaʊndə^r] N fondatore(-trice).
found·er[2] [ˈfaʊndə^r] VI (*Naut, also fig*) affondare, colare a picco.
♦ **founder member, founding member** N (*Brit*) socio (-a) fondatore(-trice).
found·ing [ˈfaʊndɪŋ] 1 ADJ (*principle, assumption*) di base.
2 N fondazione *f*.
♦ **founding fathers** NPL (*esp Am*) padri *mpl* fondatori.
found·ling [ˈfaʊndlɪŋ] N trovatello(-a).
found·ry [ˈfaʊndrɪ] N fonderia.
fount [faʊnt] N **a** (*liter: source*) fonte *f*, sorgente *f* **b** (*Typ*) carattere *m* (di stampa).
foun·tain [ˈfaʊntɪn] N (*also fig*) fontana.
♦ **fountain pen** N penna stilografica.
four [fɔː] 1 ADJ quattro *inv*.

2 N quattro *m inv*; **on all fours** (a) carponi *for usage see* **five**.
♦ **four-door** [ˈfɔːˈdɔː^r] ADJ (*Aut*) a quattro porte.
four·fold [ˈfɔːˈfəʊld] 1 ADJ quadruplo(-a).
2 ADV quattro volte tanto.
♦ **four-footed** [ˈfɔːˈfʊtɪd] ADJ quadrupede.
♦ **four-leaf clover** [ˈfɔːˌliːfˈkləʊvə^r], **four-leaved clover** [ˈfɔːˌliːvdˈkləʊvə^r] N quadrifoglio.
♦ **four-letter word** [ˈfɔːˌlɛtəˈwɜːd] N parolaccia.
♦ **four-ply** [fɔːplaɪ] ADJ (*wood*) a quattro strati; (*wool*) a quattro capi.
♦ **four-poster** [ˈfɔːˌpəʊstə^r] N (*also:* **four-poster bed**) letto a baldacchino.
four·score [ˈfɔːˈskɔː^r] ADJ (*old*) ottanta *inv*.
four·some [ˈfɔːsəm] N (*game*) partita a quattro; **we went in a foursome** siamo andati in quattro.
four·square [ˌfɔːˈskwɛə^r] 1 ADJ (*firm*) solido(-a); (*square*) quadrato(-a); (*forthright*) schietto(-a), franco(-a).
2 ADV (*firmly*) solidamente.
four·teen [ˈfɔːˈtiːn] ADJ, N quattordici (*m*) *inv for usage see* **five**.
four·teenth [ˈfɔːˈtiːnθ] 1 ADJ quattordicesimo(-a).
2 N (*in series*) quattordicesimo(-a); (*fraction*) quattordicesimo *for usage see* **fifth**.
fourth [fɔːθ] 1 ADJ quarto(-a); **fourth finger** anulare *m*.
2 N (*in series*) quarto(-a); (*fraction*) quarto; (*Aut: also:* **fourth gear**) quarta *for usage see* **fifth**.
♦ **fourth dimension** N: **the fourth dimension** la quarta dimensione.
fourth·ly [ˈfɔːθlɪ] ADV in quarto luogo.
♦ **Fourth of July** N: **the Fourth of July** il quattro luglio (*anniversario dell'indipendenza americana*).
♦ **four-wheel drive** [ˈfɔːˌwiːlˈdraɪv] N (*Aut*): **with four-wheel drive** con quattro ruote motrici.
fowl [faʊl] N pollame *m*, volatile *m*.
fox [fɒks] 1 N volpe *f*; **a sly fox** (*fig*) una volpe, un furbacchione.
2 VT (*puzzle*) lasciare perplesso(-a), confondere; (*deceive*) ingannare.
♦ **fox cub** N volpacchiotto.
♦ **fox fur** N (pelliccia di) volpe *f*.
fox·glove [ˈfɒksˌglʌv] N (*Bot*) digitale *f*.
♦ **fox hound** N foxhound *m inv*.
♦ **fox-hunting** [ˈfɒksˌhʌntɪŋ] N caccia alla volpe.
♦ **fox terrier** N fox-terrier *m inv*.
fox·trot [ˈfɒksˌtrɒt] N fox-trot *m inv*.
foxy [ˈfɒksɪ] ADJ astuto(-a), scaltro(-a).
foy·er [ˈfɔɪeɪ] N (*Theatre*) ridotto, foyer *m inv*.
FP [ˌɛfˈpiː] N ABBR **a** (*Brit*)= *former pupil* **b** (*Am*) = **fireplug**.
FPA [ˌɛfpiːˈeɪ] N ABBR (*Brit*: = *Family Planning Association*) ≈ A.I.E.D. (= *Associazione Italiana Educazione Demografica*).
Fr. ABBR (*Rel*) = **father**.
fr. ABBR (= *franc*) fr.
fra·cas [ˈfrækɑː] N rissa, lite *f*.
frac·tion [ˈfrækʃən] N (*Math*) frazione *f*; **move it just a fraction** (*fig*) spostalo un pochino.
frac·tion·al [ˈfrækʃənl] ADJ (*Math*) frazionario(-a); (*fig*) insignificante.
frac·tion·al·ly [ˈfrækʃnəlɪ] ADV un tantino, minimamente.
frac·tious [ˈfrækʃəs] ADJ (*person, mood*) irritabile; **to be in a fractious mood** essere irritato *or* di cattivo umore.
frac·ture [ˈfræktʃə^r] 1 N frattura.
2 VT fratturare; **to fracture one's arm** fratturarsi un braccio.

3 VI fratturarsi.

frag·ile ['frædʒaɪl] ADJ fragile; **I'm feeling rather fragile this morning** (*hum: esp after drinking*) mi sento piuttosto debole stamattina.

fra·gil·ity [frə'dʒɪlɪtɪ] N fragilità.

frag·ment [*n* 'frægmənt: *vb* fræg'mɛnt] 1 N frammento; **fragments of conversation** brani *mpl* di conversazione.
2 VI frammentarsi.

frag·men·tary ['frægməntərɪ] ADJ frammentario(-a).

frag·men·ta·tion [ˌfrægmɛn'teɪʃən] N frammentazione *f*.

frag·ment·ed ['frægməntɪd] ADJ frammentario(-a).

fra·grance ['freɪgrəns] N (*of flowers*) fragranza, profumo; (*perfume, of toiletries*) profumo.

fra·grant ['freɪgrənt] ADJ fragrante, profumato(-a).

frail [freɪl] ADJ (*comp* -**er**, *superl* -**est**) (*person, health, structure*) fragile, delicato(-a); (*fig: hope, relationship*) tenue, debole.

frail·ty ['freɪltɪ] N (*see adj*) fragilità; (*imperfection*) debolezza.

frame [freɪm] 1 N **a** (*of person*) corpo, ossatura; (*of ship, building, tent*) struttura, armatura; (*of bicycle*) telaio; (*of picture*) cornice *f*; (*of window, door*) telaio, intelaiatura
  b (*Cine*) immagine *f*
  c (*of spectacles*): **frames** NPL montatura.
2 VT **a** (*picture*) incorniciare
  b (*formulate: plan*) ideare; (: *question*) formulare; (: *sentence*) costruire
  c : **to frame sb** (*fam: incriminate*) incastrare qn.

framed [freɪmd] ADJ incorniciato(-a).

♦ **frame of mind** N stato d'animo, umore *m*; **in a happy frame of mind** di buon umore.

♦ **frame of reference** N (*Sociol*) sistema *m* di riferimento.

♦ **frame-up** ['freɪmˌʌp] N (*fam*) montatura.

frame·work ['freɪmˌwɜːk] N (*also fig*) struttura.

franc [fræŋk] N franco.

France [frɑːns] N la Francia.

fran·chise ['fræntʃaɪz] N (*Pol*) diritto di voto; (*Comm*) concessione *f*; (*Marine Insurance*) franchigia.

fran·chisee ['fræntʃaɪ'zɪ:] N concessionario(-a).

fran·chis·er ['fræntʃaɪzə] N concedente *m*.

Franco-... ['fræŋkəʊ] PREF franco-...; **Franco-British** franco-britannico(-a).

Fran·co·phile ['fræŋkəʊˌfaɪl] N francofilo(-a).

frank¹ [fræŋk] ADJ (*comp* -**er**, *superl* -**est**) franco(-a), sincero(-a), aperto(-a).

frank² [fræŋk] VT (*letter*) affrancare.

Frank·furt ['fræŋkfɜːt] N Francoforte *f*.

frank·fur·ter ['fræŋkfɜːtə'] N würstel *m inv*.

frank·in·cense ['fræŋkɪnˌsɛns] N incenso.

frank·ing ma·chine ['fræŋkɪŋməˌʃiːn] N affrancatrice *f*.

frank·ly ['fræŋklɪ] ADV francamente, sinceramente.

frank·ness ['fræŋknɪs] N franchezza.

fran·tic ['fræntɪk] ADJ (*activity, pace*) frenetico(-a); (*desperate: desire*) pazzo(-a), sfrenato(-a); (: *need*) disperato(-a); (: *search*) affannoso(-a); (*person*) fuori di sé; **frantic with worry** fuori di sé dalla preoccupazione; **frantic with joy** pazzo(-a) di gioia.

fran·ti·cal·ly ['fræntɪkəlɪ] ADV (*gen*) freneticamente, affannosamente.

fra·ter·nal [frə'tɜːnl] ADJ fraterno(-a).

fra·ter·nal·ly [frə'tɜːnəlɪ] ADV fraternamente.

fra·ter·nity [frə'tɜːnɪtɪ] N fraternità; (*club*) associazione *f*; (*spirit*) fratellanza; (*Am Univ*) *associazione studentesca maschile.*

frat·er·ni·za·tion [ˌfrætənaɪ'zeɪʃən] N il fraternizzare.

frat·er·nize ['frætəˌnaɪz] VI: **to fraternize (with)** fraternizzare (con).

fraud [frɔːd] N (*Law*) frode *f*; (*trickery, trick*) truffa; (*person*) imbroglione(-a), impostore(-a).

fraudu·lence ['frɔːdjʊləns] N fraudolenza.

fraudu·lent ['frɔːdjʊlənt] ADJ (*behaviour*) disonesto(-a); (*claims*) fraudolento(-a).

fraudu·lent·ly ['frɔːdjʊləntlɪ] ADV con la frode.

fraught [frɔːt] ADJ (*tense*) teso(-a); **the situation is rather fraught** la situazione è un po' tesa; **fraught with** pieno(-a) *or* carico(-a) di; **fraught with danger** pieno(-a) di pericoli.

fray¹ [freɪ] N (*old: fight*) zuffa, baruffa; **ready for the fray** (*also fig*) pronto(-a) a battersi; **to return to the fray** ributtarsi nella mischia.

fray² [freɪ] 1 VT (*cloth, cuff, rope*) consumare, logorare; **tempers were getting frayed** (tutti) cominciavano a innervosirsi; **her nerves were frayed** aveva i nervi a pezzi.
2 VI consumarsi, logorarsi.

frayed [freɪd] ADJ sdrucito(-a), logoro(-a).

fraz·zle ['fræzl] N (*fam*): **burnt to a frazzle** (*dinner*) completamente carbonizzato(-a); **worn to a frazzle** (*person*) ridotto(-a) a uno straccio.

fraz·zled ['fræzəld] ADJ (*fam, person*) logorato(-a); (*bacon*) bruciato(-a).

FRB [ˌɛfɑː'biː] N ABBR (*Am*) = **Federal Reserve Board.**

FRCM [ˌɛfɑːsiː'ɛm] N ABBR (*Brit*)= *Fellow of the Royal College of Music.*

FRCO [ˌɛfɑːsiː'əʊ] N ABBR (*Brit*)= *Fellow of the Royal College of Organists.*

FRCP [ˌɛfɑːsiː'piː] N ABBR (*Brit*)= *Fellow of the Royal College of Physicians.*

FRCS [ˌɛfɑːsiː'ɛs] N ABBR (*Brit*)= *Fellow of the Royal College of Surgeons.*

freak [friːk] 1 N (*abnormal: person*) fenomeno da baraccone; (: *animal, plant*) mostro; (: *event*) avvenimento eccezionale; (*fam: enthusiast*) fanatico(-a); **a freak of nature** un capriccio della natura; **the result was a freak** il risultato è stato un caso eccezionale; **health freak** (*fam*) salutista *m/f*.
2 ADJ (*storm, conditions*) anormale; (*victory*) inatteso(-a)

▶ **freak out** VI + ADV (*fam: get angry*) uscire dai gangheri; (: *get excited*) andare su di giri; (: *on drugs*) andare fuori di testa.

freak·ish ['friːkɪʃ] ADJ (*result, appearance*) strano(-a), bizzarro(-a); (*moods*) capriccioso(-a); (*weather*) anormale.

freak·ish·ly ['friːkɪʃlɪ] ADV stranamente.

freck·le ['frɛkl] N lentiggine *f*.

freck·led ['frɛkld] ADJ lentigginoso(-a).

free [friː] 1 ADJ (*comp* -**r**, *superl* -**st**) **a** (*at liberty*): **free (from** *or* **of)** libero(-a) (da); **free from ties/cares** senza legami/preoccupazioni; **to be free of pain** non soffrire; **feel free** fai pure; **to break free (of)** liberarsi (da); **to set free** liberare; **free and easy** rilassato(-a); **he is not free to choose** non è libero di scegliere; **to give free rein to one's anger** *etc* dare libero sfogo alla propria rabbia *etc*; **to give sb a free hand** dare carta bianca a qn
  b (*not occupied*) libero(-a); **is this seat free?** è libero questo posto?; **are you free tomorrow?** sei libero domani?; **to have one's hands free** avere le mani libere
  c : **free (with)** (*generous*) prodigo(-a) (di); **to be free with one's money** spendere con facilità; **he's too free with his**

remarks è sempre pronto alla critica

d (*costing nothing*: *ticket, delivery*) gratuito(-a), gratis *inv*; **free of charge** gratuito(-a); **admission free** entrata libera; **free baggage allowance** (*Aer*) franchigia bagaglio

e (*improper*: *behaviour*) sfrontato(-a); (*language*) spinto (-a).

2 ADV (*without charge*) gratuitamente, gratis; **I got in free** *or* **for free** (*fam*) sono entrato gratis.

3 VT (*gen*) liberare; (*jammed object*) districare; (*untie*: *person, animal*) sciogliere; **to free o.s. from** *or* **of sth** sbarazzarsi di qc.

♦ **free agent** N persona indipendente.

free·bie ['fri:bɪ] N (*fam*): **it's a freebie** è in omaggio.

free·board ['fri:bɔːd] N (*Naut*) bordo libero.

♦ **free climbing** N (*Mountaineering*) arrampicata libera.

free·dom ['fri:dəm] N: **freedom (from)** libertà (da); **to give sb the freedom of one's house** mettere la propria casa a disposizione di qn; **the freedom of the press** la libertà di stampa; **to give sb the freedom of the city** dare a qn la cittadinanza onoraria; **freedom of speech** libertà di parola; **freedom of movement** libertà di movimento.

♦ **freedom fighter** N combattente *m/f* per la libertà.

♦ **free enterprise** N liberalismo economico.

♦ **free fall** N (*Parachuting*): **in free fall** in caduta libera.

♦ **free-floating** [fri:'fləʊtɪŋ] ADJ (*currency, exchange rate*) fluttuante.

Free·fone® ['fri:ˌfəʊn] N (*Brit*) ≈ numero verde.

♦ **free-for-all** ['fri:fɔ'rɔ:l] N parapiglia *m* generale.

♦ **free form** ADJ (*poetry*) libero(-a).

♦ **free gift** N regalo, omaggio.

free·hand ['fri:ˌhænd] ADJ, ADV a mano libera.

♦ **free-handed** [fri:'hændɪd] ADJ generoso(-a).

free·hold ['fri:ˌhəʊld] N (*Law*) proprietà assoluta.

♦ **free kick** N (*Ftbl*) calcio di punizione.

free·lance ['fri:la:ns] 1 ADJ: **freelance contributor** collaboratore(-trice) esterno(-a); **freelance work** collaborazione *f* esterna.

2 N collaboratore(-trice) esterno(-a).

3 VI (*journalist*) essere un(a) giornalista *m/f* indipendente.

free·loader ['fri:ˌləʊdə'] N (*pej*) scroccone(-a).

♦ **free love** N libero amore *m*.

free·ly ['fri:lɪ] ADV (*confess, speak*) liberamente, francamente; (*generously*) generosamente; **you may come and go freely** puoi andare e venire come vuoi.

free·man ['fri:mən] N (*pl* **-men**): **freeman of a city** cittadino(-a) onorario(-a) di una città.

♦ **free-market economy** ['fri:ˌmɑ:kɪt'kɒnəmɪ] N economia di libero mercato.

Free·mason ['fri:ˌmeɪsən] N massone *m*.

free·masonry ['fri:ˌmeɪsənrɪ] N massoneria.

♦ **free pardon** N condono.

♦ **free pass** N biglietto gratis.

♦ **free port** N porto franco.

Free·post® ['fri:ˌpəʊst] N (*Brit Post*) affrancatura a carico del destinatario.

♦ **free-range** ['fri:ˌreɪndʒ] ADJ (*hen*) ruspante; (*eggs*) di gallina ruspante.

♦ **free sample** N campione *m* gratuito.

free·sia ['fri:zɪə] N fresia.

♦ **free speech** N libertà di parola.

♦ **free spirit** N spirito indipendente.

free·style ['fri:staɪl] N (*in swimming*) stile *m* libero.

free·thinker [ˌfri:'θɪŋkə'] N libero(-a) pensatore(-trice).

♦ **free trade** N libero scambio.

♦ **free verse** N verso libero.

free·way ['fri:ˌweɪ] N (*Am*) superstrada.

free·wheel [ˌfri:'wi:l] VI (*coast*: *on bicycle*) andare a ruota libera; (: *in car*) andare in folle.

free·wheel·ing [ˌfri:'wi:lɪŋ] ADJ (*fam*: *person*) indipendente.

♦ **free will** N libero arbitrio; **of one's own free will** di spontanea volontà.

freeze [fri:z] (*vb*: *pt* **froze**, *pp* **frozen**) 1 VT (*water*) gelare; (*food*) congelare; (*industrially*) surgelare; (*prices, assets, salaries*) bloccare, congelare.

2 VI (*Met*) gelare; (*water, lake*) ghiacciare; (*food*) congelarsi; (*keep still*) bloccarsi; **freezing fog** nebbia gelata; **to freeze to death** morire assiderato(-a); **he froze in his tracks** si bloccò; **freeze!** non muoverti!.

3 N (*Met*) gelata; (*of prices, wages etc*) blocco

▸ **freeze over** VI + ADV (*lake, river*) ghiacciarsi; (*windows, windscreen*) coprirsi di ghiaccio

▸ **freeze up** VI + ADV gelarsi.

♦ **freeze-dried** ['fri:zˌdraɪd] ADJ liofilizzato(-a).

♦ **freeze-dry** [ˌfri:zˌdraɪ] VT liofilizzare.

♦ **freeze-frame** ['fri:zˌfreɪm] N fotogramma *m*; (*on video*) fermo immagine.

freez·er ['fri:zə'] N (*cabinet*) congelatore *m*; (*also*: **freezer compartment**) freezer *m inv*.

♦ **freeze-up** ['fri:zˌʌp] N (*Met*) gelo, gelata.

freez·ing ['fri:zɪŋ] 1 N (*also*: **freezing point**) punto di congelamento; **5 degrees below freezing** 5 gradi sotto zero.

2 ADJ (*room, weather*) gelido(-a); **I'm freezing** sono congelato.

freight [freɪt] 1 N (*goods transported*) merce *f*, merci *fpl*; (*charge*) spese *fpl* di trasporto; **freight forward** (*Comm*) spese a carico del destinatario; **freight inward** spese di trasporto sulla merce in entrata.

2 VT (*transport*: *goods*) trasportare.

3 ADJ (*yard*) merci *inv*.

4 ADV: **to send sth freight** spedire qc per via ordinaria.

♦ **freight car** N (*Am*) carro *m* merci *inv*.

freight·er ['freɪtə'] N (*Naut*) nave *f* mercantile *or* da carico, mercantile *m*; (*Aer*) aereo da trasporto merci.

♦ **freight for·ward·er** ['freɪt'fɔ:wədə'] N spedizioniere *m*.

♦ **freight han·dling** ['freɪt'hændlɪŋ] N facchinaggio merci.

♦ **freight train** N (*Am*) treno *m* merci *inv*.

French [frɛntʃ] 1 ADJ francese; (*lesson, teacher etc*) di francese.

2 N **a** (*language*) francese *m* **b** (*people*): **the French** NPL i francesi.

♦ **French bean** N fagiolino.

♦ **French bread** N baguette *f inv*.

♦ **French Canadian** ADJ, N franco-canadese (*m/f*).

♦ **French chalk** N steatite *f*, pietra da sarto.

♦ **French doors** NPL = **French windows**.

♦ **French dressing** N (*Culin*) condimento per insalata.

♦ **French fried potatoes**, (*esp Am*) **French fries** NPL patate *fpl* fritte.

♦ **French Gui·ana** ['frɛntʃgɑr'ænə] N la Guiana francese.

♦ **French horn** N (*Mus*) corno da caccia.

♦ **French knickers** NPL culottes *fpl*.

♦ **French leave** N: **to take French leave** filarsela all'inglese.

♦ **French loaf** N filoncino.

French·man ['frɛntʃmən] N (pl -men) francese m.
♦ **French polish** N vernice ƒ all'alcol or allo spirito.
♦ **French Riviera** N: the French Riviera la Costa Azzurra.
♦ **French stick, French loaf** N filoncino.
♦ **French windows,** (esp Am) **French doors** NPL porta-finestra.
French·woman ['frɛntʃˌwʊmən] N (pl -women) francese ƒ.
fre·net·ic [frɪ'nɛtɪk] ADJ frenetico(-a).
fre·neti·cal·ly [frɪ'nɛtɪkəlɪ] ADV freneticamente.
fren·zied ['frɛnzɪd] ADJ (person) frenetico(-a); (efforts, shouts) convulso(-a).
fren·zied·ly ['frɛnzɪdlɪ] ADV (work) freneticamente; **his heart was beating frenziedly** il cuore gli batteva all'impazzata.
fren·zy ['frɛnzɪ] N frenesia; **he was in a frenzy of anxiety** era quasi impazzito dall'ansia.
fre·quen·cy ['fri:kwənsɪ] N frequenza; **high/low frequency** alta/bassa frequenza.
♦ **frequency modulation** N modulazione ƒ di frequenza.
fre·quent [adj 'fri:kwənt; vb 'fri:kwɛnt] [1] ADJ (gen) frequente; (visitor) abituale.
[2] VT frequentare.
fre·quent·ly ['fri:kwəntlɪ] ADV frequentemente, spesso.
fres·co ['frɛskəʊ] N affresco.
fresh [frɛʃ] [1] ADJ (comp -er, superl -est) **a** (gen: not stale) fresco(-a); (new: sheet of paper, supplies, approach) nuovo(-a); (: news) recente; **to put fresh courage into sb** ridare coraggio a qn; **to make a fresh start** ricominciare da capo; **as fresh as a daisy** fresco(-a) come una rosa
b (invigorating: breeze) fresco(-a); **it's a bit fresh** (Met) fa un po' freschino
c (not salt: water) dolce
d (fam: cheeky) sfacciato(-a); **to get fresh with sb** prendersi delle libertà con qn.
[2] ADV (baked, picked) appena, da poco; **bread fresh from the oven** pane appena uscito dal forno; **to come fresh from New York** essere arrivato(-a) fresco(-a) fresco(-a) da New York.
♦ **fresh air** N aria fresca; **I need some fresh air** ho bisogno di un po' d'aria; **in the fresh air** all'aria aperta.
fresh·en ['frɛʃn] VI (wind, air) rinfrescare.
▶ **freshen up** [1] VI + ADV rinfrescarsi.
[2] VT + ADV rinfrescare; **to freshen o.s. up** darsi una rinfrescata.
fresh·en·er ['frɛʃnə'] N (also: skin freshener) tonico rinfrescante.
fresh·er ['frɛʃə'] N (Brit Univ fam) = **freshman.**
fresh·ly ['frɛʃlɪ] ADV di recente, di fresco, appena.
fresh·man ['frɛʃmən] N (pl -men) (Univ) matricola ƒ.
fresh·ness ['frɛʃnɪs] N (of food, air) freschezza; (of approach) novità; (impertinence) impertinenza.
fresh·water ['frɛʃˌwɔ:tə'] ADJ: **freshwater fish** pesce m d'acqua dolce.
fret [frɛt] VI (worry) preoccuparsi, agitarsi, affliggersi; **don't fret** non preoccuparti; **the baby is fretting for its mother** il/la bambino(-a) piange perché vuole la madre.
fret·ful ['frɛtfʊl] ADJ (child) irritabile.
fret·ful·ly ['frɛtfəlɪ] ADV in modo irritato.
fret·ful·ness ['frɛtfʊlnɪs] N irritabilità.
fret·saw ['frɛtˌsɔ:] N sega da traforo.
fret·ted ['frɛtɪd] ADJ intagliato(-a), traforato(-a).
fret·work ['frɛtˌwɜ:k] N lavoro di traforo.
Freud·ian ['frɔɪdɪən] ADJ freudiano(-a).

♦ **Freudian slip** N lapsus m inv freudiano.
FRG [ˌɛfɑ:'dʒi:] N ABBR (= Federal Republic of Germany) RFT ƒ (= Repubblica Federale Tedesca).
Fri. [a] ABBR (= Friday) ven.
fri·abil·ity [ˌfraɪə'bɪlɪtɪ] N (frm) friabilità.
fri·able ['fraɪəbəl] ADJ (frm) friabile.
fri·ar ['fraɪə'] N frate m.
fric·as·see [ˌfrɪkə'si:] N (Culin) fricassea.
frica·tive ['frɪkətɪv] N (Ling) fricativa.
fric·tion ['frɪkʃən] N frizione ƒ, attrito.
♦ **friction feed** N (on printer) trascinamento ad attrito.
♦ **friction tape** N (Am) nastro isolante.
Fri·day ['fraɪdɪ] N venerdì m inv for usage see **Tuesday.**
fridge [frɪdʒ] N (Brit) frigorifero, frigo.
♦ **fridge-freezer** ['frɪdʒ'fri:zə'] N frigocongelatore m.
fried [fraɪd] [1] PT, PP of **fry.**
[2] ADJ (Culin) fritto(-a); **fried egg** uovo fritto or al tegamino.
friend [frɛnd] N amico(-a); (at school) compagno(-a); (at work) collega m/f; **a friend of mine** un(a) mio(-a) amico(-a); **to make friends with sb** fare amicizia con qn; **let's be friends** facciamo pace; **we're just good friends** siamo solo buoni amici.
friend·li·ness ['frɛndlɪnɪs] N cordialità.
friend·ly ['frɛndlɪ] [1] ADJ (comp -ier, superl -iest) cordiale, amichevole; **to be friendly to sb** essere cordiale con qn; **to be friendly with sb** essere amico di qn.
[2] N (also: friendly match) (partita) amichevole ƒ.
♦ **friendly fire** N (Mil) fuoco amico.
♦ **friendly society** N società ƒ inv di mutuo soccorso.
friend·ship ['frɛndʃɪp] N amicizia.
frieze [fri:z] N (Archit) fregio.
frig·ate ['frɪgɪt] N (Naut) fregata.
frig·ging ['frɪgɪŋ] ADJ (fam) dannato(-a).
fright [fraɪt] N paura, spavento; **to get** or **have a fright** spaventarsi; **what a fright you gave me!** mi hai fatto paura!; **to take fright (at)** spaventarsi (all'idea di); **she looked a fright** (fam) era conciata da far paura.
fright·en ['fraɪtn] VT spaventare, far paura a; **to frighten sb out of their wits** far morire qn dallo spavento; **to be frightened of sth** avere paura di qc; **he was frightened into doing it** l'ha fatto per paura; **I was frightened to death** ero morto di paura
▶ **frighten away, frighten off** VT + ADV (birds, children) scacciare (facendogli paura).
fright·ened ['fraɪtnd] ADJ: **to be frightened (of)** avere paura (di).
fright·en·ing ['fraɪtnɪŋ] ADJ pauroso(-a), spaventoso(-a).
fright·en·ing·ly ['fraɪtnɪŋlɪ] ADV spaventosamente.
fright·ful ['fraɪtfʊl] ADJ terribile, spaventoso(-a), orribile.
fright·ful·ly ['fraɪtfəlɪ] ADV (fam: late, cold) terribilmente, spaventosamente; **it was frightfully good of her** è stato estremamente gentile da parte sua; **I'm frightfully sorry** mi dispiace moltissimo.
fright·ful·ness ['fraɪtfʊlnɪs] N (of crime) atrocità ƒ inv.
frig·id ['frɪdʒɪd] ADJ (atmosphere, look) glaciale; (Psych) frigido(-a).
fri·gid·ity [frɪ'dʒɪdɪtɪ] N (of manners, look) freddezza; (sexual) frigidità.
frig·id·ly ['frɪdʒɪdlɪ] ADV (see n) freddamente; frigidamente.
frill [frɪl] N (on dress) fronzolo, balza; **without frills** (fig) senza fronzoli.
frilled [frɪld] ADJ (blouse) con la gala, volant; (curtain, skirt) a balze.

frilly ['frɪlɪ] ADJ (*dress*) con pizzi e merletti.

fringe [frɪndʒ] **1** N **a** (*on shawl, rug*) frangia; (*Brit: of hair*) frangia, frangetta **b** : **fringes** NPL (*of forest*) margine *m*; (*of city*) periferia; **on the fringe(s) of society** ai margini della società.

2 VT (*shawl*) frangiare; **a road fringed with trees** una strada fiancheggiata da alberi.

♦ **fringe benefits** NPL benefici *mpl* aggiuntivi, fringe benefits *mpl*.

fringed [frɪndʒd] ADJ (*lampshade, curtains*) con le frange; **fringed with** (*surrounded by*) contornato(-a) da.

♦ **fringe theatre** N teatro d'avanguardia.

frip·pery ['frɪpərɪ] N (*pej*): **fripperies** cianfrusaglie *fpl*.

Fris·bee® ['frɪzbi:] N frisbee ® *m inv*.

frisk [frɪsk] **1** VT (*fam: suspect*) perquisire.

2 VI (*frolic*) saltellare allegramente.

frisky ['frɪskɪ] ADJ (*comp* **-ier**, *superl* **-iest**) (*person, horse*) vispo(-a), vivace.

frit·ter ['frɪtə'] N (*Culin*) frittella

► **fritter away** VT + ADV sprecare.

fri·vol·ity [frɪ'vɒlɪtɪ] N frivolezza.

frivo·lous ['frɪvələs] ADJ frivolo(-a).

frivo·lous·ly ['frɪvələslɪ] ADV frivolamente.

frizz [frɪz] **1** VT increspare.

2 N riccio.

frizzed [frɪzd] ADJ crespo(-a).

friz·zle ['frɪzl] VI sfrigolare; **frizzled (up)** troppo croccante.

friz·zy ['frɪzɪ] ADJ (*comp* **-ier**, *superl* **-iest**) (*hair*) crespo(-a); **to go frizzy** incresparsi.

fro [frəʊ] ADV: **to and fro** avanti e indietro; **to go to and fro between** fare la spola tra.

frock [frɒk] N (*woman's*) abito, vestito; (*of monk*) tonaca.

frog [frɒg] N rana; **to have a frog in one's throat** avere la voce rauca.

frog·ging ['frɒgɪŋ] N alamaro.

frog·man ['frɒgmən] N (*pl* **-men**) sommozzatore *m*, uomo *m* rana *inv*.

frog·march ['frɒg,mɑːtʃ] VT (*Brit*): **to frogmarch sb in/out** portar qn dentro/fuori con la forza.

frol·ic ['frɒlɪk] (*pt, pp* **frolicked**) VI saltellare allegramente.

from [frɒm] PREP

a (*indicating starting place*) da;

▷**where has he** *come* **from?** da dove arriva?

▷**to** *escape* **from sb/sth** fuggire da qn/qc

▷**from London** *to* **Glasgow** da Londra a Glasgow

▷**from house** *to* **house** di casa in casa

▷*where* **is he from?** da dove viene?, di dov'è?

b (*indicating time*) da;

▷**(as) from** *Friday* (*a partire*) da venerdì

▷**from** *January* da gennaio in poi

▷**from** *now* **on** d'ora in poi, d'ora innanzi

▷**from** *time* **to time** ogni tanto, di tanto in tanto

▷**from one o'clock** *to* **or** *until* **or** *till* **two** dall'una alle due

c (*indicating distance*) da;

▷**the hotel is 1** *km* **from the beach** l'albergo è a 1 km dalla spiaggia

▷**a long** *way* **from home** lontano(-a) da casa

d (*indicating source, origin*) da;

▷**a telephone** *call* **from Mr Smith** una telefonata dal Signor Smith

▷**to** *drink* **from a stream/the bottle** bere a un ruscello/dalla bottiglia

▷**where did you** *get* **that from?** dove l'hai trovato?

▷**a** *letter* **from my sister** una lettera da mia sorella

▷*painted* **from life** dipinto(-a) dal vero

▷**a** *quotation* **from Shakespeare** una citazione da Shakespeare

▷**to** *steal* **sth from sb** rubare qc a qn

▷*take* **the gun from him!** levagli la pistola!

▷*tell* **him from me** diglielo da parte mia

e (*indicating price, number*) da;

▷**prices** *range* **from £10 to £50** i prezzi vanno dalle 10 alle 50 sterline

▷**there were from 10** *to* **15 people there** c'erano tra le 10 e le 15 persone

▷**we have shirts from £18** *(upwards)* abbiamo camicie da 18 sterline in su

f (*indicating change*)

▷**things went from** *bad* **to worse** le cose andarono di male in peggio

▷ **the interest rate** *increased* **from 6% to 10%** il tasso d'interesse è aumentato dal 6% al 10%

g (*indicating difference*)

▷**to be** *different* **from sb** essere diverso(-a) da qn

▷**he can't** *tell* **red from green** non sa distinguere il rosso dal verde

h (*because of, on the basis of*)

▷**to act from** *conviction* agire per convinzione

▷**from** *experience* per esperienza

▷**to die from** *exposure* morire assiderato(-a)

▷**weak from** *hunger* debole per la fame

▷**from** *what* **I can see** a quanto vedo

▷**from** *what* **I understood** da quanto ho capito

▷**from** *what* **he says** a quanto dice

i (*with preposition*)

▷**from** *above* **sth** da sopra qc, dall'alto di qc

▷**from** *among* **the crowd** dalla folla

▷**from** *beneath* **sth** da sotto qc

▷**from** *inside* **the house** dall'interno della casa

▷**from** *outside* **the house** dall'esterno della casa

▷**from** *over* **sth** da sopra qc, dall'alto di qc

▷**from** *underneath* **sth** da sotto qc

frond [frɒnd] N fronda.

front [frʌnt] **1** ADJ (*tooth*) davanti *inv*; (*garden*) sul davanti; (*wheel*) anteriore; (*row, page*) primo(-a); (*carriage*) di testa; (*view*) frontale.

2 N **a** (*gen*) davanti *m inv*; (*of house*) facciata, davanti; (*of book*) copertina; (*of train*) testa; (*fig: appearance*) facciata; **in front** davanti; **in front of** davanti a; (*opposite*) di fronte a; **at the front of the line** *or* **queue** in cima *or* all'inizio della fila; **to be in front** (*Sport*) essere in testa; **he sat at the front of the class** era seduto nei primi banchi (della classe); **to put on a bold front** (*fig*) mostrare coraggio; **to be a front for sth** (*fam*) servire da copertura per qc

b (*Mil, Pol, Met*) fronte *m*; **on all fronts** su tutti i fronti; **a united front** un fronte unito

c (*also: sea front: promenade*) lungomare *m*.

3 VI: **to front onto sth** dare su qc, guardare verso qc.

front·age ['frʌntɪdʒ] N facciata.

front·al [frʌntl] ADJ frontale.

♦ **front bench** N (*Brit Pol*): **the front bench** (*government ministers*) i ministri; (*opposition leaders*) *i principali esponenti dell'opposizione*.

front·bench·er [,frʌnt'bentʃə'] N *parlamentare che*

detiene una carica presso il governo o l'opposizione.

front·benches [ˌfrʌntˈbɛntʃəz] NPL *nel Parlamento britannico, scanni della House of Commons alla sinistra e alla destra dello speaker, occupati dai frontbencher.*

♦ **front desk** N (*Am: in hotel*) reception *f inv*; (: *at doctor's*) accettazione *f*.

♦ **front door** N porta d'ingresso.

♦ **front end** N (*Aut*) avantreno.

fron·tier [ˈfrʌntɪəʳ] N frontiera, confine *m*.

fron·tiers·man [ˈfrʌntɪəzmən] N pioniere *m*.

♦ **frontier town** N città *f inv* di frontiera.

fron·tis·piece [ˈfrʌntɪsˌpiːs] N frontespizio.

♦ **front line** N (*Mil*) prima linea.

♦ **front man** N (*fam: representative*) prestanome *m inv*; (: *presenter*) presentatore *m*.

♦ **front-page** [ˈfrʌntˌpeɪdʒ] ADJ (*news, article*) di prima pagina.

♦ **front room** N (*Brit*) salotto.

♦ **front runner** N (*fig*) favorito(-a).

♦ **front seat** N (*Aut*) sedile *m* anteriore.

♦ **front-wheel drive** [ˈfrʌntˌwiːlˈdraɪv] N (*Aut*) trazione *f* anteriore.

frost [frɒst] ① N gelo; (*also: hoar frost*) brina; (*on window*) ghiaccio; **an overnight frost** gelata notturna; **4 degrees of frost** 4 gradi sotto zero.

② VT (*esp Am: ice: cakes*) glassare.

frost·bite [ˈfrɒstˌbaɪt] N congelamento.

frost·bitten [ˈfrɒstˌbɪtn] ADJ congelato(-a).

frost·ed [ˈfrɒstɪd] ADJ (*glass*) smerigliato(-a); (*esp Am: cake*) glassato(-a).

frosti·ly [ˈfrɒstɪlɪ] ADV gelidamente.

frostiness [ˈfrɒstɪ£nɪs] N freddezza.

frost·ing [ˈfrɒstɪŋ] N (*esp Am: icing*) glassa.

frosty [ˈfrɒstɪ] ADJ (*comp* -ier, *superl* -iest) (*weather, also fig*) gelido(-a); (*surface, window*) coperto(-a) di ghiaccio *or* di brina; **it was frosty last night** ha gelato durante la notte.

froth [frɒθ] ① N schiuma, spuma.

② VI schiumare, spumare; **the dog was frothing at the mouth** il cane aveva la schiuma alla bocca.

frothy [ˈfrɒθɪ] ADJ (*beer, mixture*) spumoso(-a), schiumoso(-a); (*lace, nightdress*) vaporoso(-a); (*play, entertainment*) leggero(-a).

frown [fraʊn] ① N: **he gave me a worried frown** mi ha guardato con aria preoccupata; **he gave me a frown of disapproval** mi ha lanciato un'occhiata di disapprovazione.

② VI aggrottare le sopracciglia; **to frown at sth/sb** guardare qc/qn con cipiglio

▶ **frown upon, frown on** VI + PREP (*fig*) disapprovare.

frown·ing [ˈfraʊnɪŋ] ADJ corrucciato(-a).

frowsy, frowzy [ˈfraʊzɪ] ADJ (*person, clothes*) trasandato(-a), sciatto(-a); (*room*) che puzza di chiuso.

froze [frəʊz] PT of **freeze**.

fro·zen [ˈfrəʊzn] ① PP of **freeze**.

② ADJ (*food*) congelato(-a); (*industrially deep frozen*) surgelato(-a); (*Econ: assets*) bloccato(-a); **I'm frozen stiff** sono gelato fino alle ossa.

FRS [ˌɛfɑːrˈɛs] N ABBR **a** (*Brit*)= *Fellow of the Royal Society* **b** (*Am: = Federal Reserve System*) *sistema bancario degli Stati Uniti.*

fruc·tose [ˈfrʌktəʊs] N fruttosio.

fru·gal [ˈfruːɡəl] ADJ (*person*) economo(-a); (*meal*) frugale.

fru·gal·ity [fruːˈɡælɪtɪ] N frugalità.

fru·gal·ly [ˈfruːɡəlɪ] ADV (*live*) frugalmente; (*give out*) con parsimonia.

fruit [fruːt] N (*collectively*) frutta; (*Bot*) frutto; **would you like some fruit?** vuoi della frutta?; **to bear fruit** dare frutti; (*fig*) dare frutto; **the fruits of one's labour** (*fig*) i frutti del proprio lavoro.

fruit·cake [ˈfruːtˌkeɪk] N plumcake *m inv*; (*fam: person*) picchiatello(-a).

♦ **fruit cocktail** N macedonia di frutta.

♦ **fruit dish** N fruttiera.

fruit·er·er [ˈfruːtərəʳ] N (*esp Brit*) fruttivendolo(-a); **at the fruiterer's (shop)** dal fruttivendolo.

♦ **fruit farm** N azienda ortofrutticola.

♦ **fruit fly** N mosca della frutta.

fruit·ful [ˈfruːtfʊl] ADJ (*profitable*) fruttuoso(-a); (*soil*) fertile.

fruit·ful·ly [ˈfruːtfəlɪ] ADV (*fig*) fruttuosamente.

fruit·ful·ness [ˈfruːtfʊlnɪs] N (*of discussion etc*) buon esito; (*of soil*) fertilità.

frui·tion [fruːˈɪʃən] N: **to come to fruition** (*frm*) realizzarsi.

♦ **fruit juice** N succo di frutta.

fruit·less [ˈfruːtlɪs] ADJ (*fig*) vano(-a), inutile.

♦ **fruit machine** N (*Brit*) slot-machine *f inv*, macchina *f* mangiasoldi *inv*.

♦ **fruit salad** N macedonia.

♦ **fruit tree** N albero da frutto.

fruity [ˈfruːtɪ] ADJ (*comp* -ier, *superl* -iest) (*taste*) che sa di frutta; (*wine*) fruttato(-a); (*voice*) pastoso(-a).

frump [frʌmp] N (*woman*) donnetta scialba; **I felt a frump** mi son sentita goffa e scialba.

frump·ish [ˈfrʌmpɪʃ], **frumpy** [ˈfrʌmpɪ] ADJ scialbo(-a) e fuori moda.

frus·trate [frʌˈstreɪt] VT (*plan, effort, hope*) rendere vano (-a); (*person*) frustrare.

frus·trat·ed [frʌˈstreɪtɪd] ADJ (*person*) frustrato(-a); (*effort*) reso(-a) vano(-a); **he's a frustrated artist** è un artista mancato; **I got more and more frustrated with it** ci sono impazzito.

frus·trat·ing [frʌˈstreɪtɪŋ] ADJ (*job*) frustrante; (*day*) disastroso(-a); **how frustrating!** che seccatura!

frus·tra·tion [frʌˈstreɪʃən] N (*feeling: of hopes*) frustrazione *f*; (*of plans*) inutilità; (*setback*) scocciatura.

fry[1] [fraɪ] VT, VI friggere.

fry[2] [fraɪ] NPL (*Zool*) avannotti *mpl*; see also **small fry**.

fry·ing pan [ˈfraɪŋˈpæn] N padella; **to jump out of the frying pan into the fire** cadere dalla padella nella brace.

♦ **fry-up** [fraɪʌp] N (*Brit*) ≈ fritto misto.

FT [ˌɛfˈtiː] N ABBR (*Brit*: = *Financial Times*) *giornale finanziario*; **the FT index** l'indice del Financial Times.

ft. ABBR = **foot, feet**.

FTC [ˌɛftiːˈsiː] N ABBR (*Am*) = **Federal Trade Commission**.

FT-SE 100 Index [ˈfʊtsɪwʌnˌhʌndrədˈɪndɛks] N ABBR *indice borsistico del financial times*.

fuch·sia [ˈfjuːʃə] ① N (*Bot*) fucsia; (*colour*) fucsia *m*.

② ADJ fucsia *inv*.

fuck [fʌk] (*fam!*) ① VT **a** fottere

b: **fuck you!** va' a farti fottere! (*fam!*).

② EXCL: **fuck!** cazzo!

▶ **fuck about** (*fam!*) ① VI + ADV: **to fuck about** *or* **around** cazzeggiare; **he's fucking about all day** non fa un cazzo tutto il giorno; **what is he fucking about with my stereo for?** che cazzo fa con il mio stereo?.

② VT + ADV: **to fuck sb about** *or* **around** prendere qn per il culo.

▶ **fuck off** VI + ADV (*fam!*): **fuck off!** vaffanculo! (*fam!*)

fud·dled ['fʌdld] ADJ (*muddled*) confuso(-a); (*tipsy*) brillo (-a).

fuddy-duddy ['fʌdɪˌdʌdɪ] N (*pej*) parruccone *m*.

fudge [fʌdʒ] 1 N (*Culin*) *specie di caramella a base di latte, burro e zucchero.*

2 VT (*figures, results*) falsificare; (*question, issue*) eludere.

fuel [fjʊəl] 1 N (*gen*) combustibile *m*; (*for engine*) carburante *m*; **to add fuel to the flames** (*fig*) soffiare sul fuoco, gettar olio sul fuoco.

2 VT (*furnace etc*) alimentare; (*aircraft, ship*) rifornire di carburante.

3 VI (*aircraft, ship*) rifornirsi di carburante.

♦ **fuel cell** N cella a combustione.

♦ **fuel oil** N olio combustibile, nafta.

♦ **fuel pump** N (*Aut*) pompa del carburante.

♦ **fuel-saving** ['fjʊəlˌseɪvɪŋ] ADJ: **fuel-saving device** economizzatore *m*.

♦ **fuel tank** N (*industrial, domestic*) serbatoio del carburante, deposito *m* nafta *inv*; (*on vehicle*) serbatoio (della benzina).

fug [fʌg] N (*Brit*) aria viziata.

fu·gi·tive ['fjuːdʒɪtɪv] 1 N fuggitivo(-a), profugo(-a); (*from prison*) evaso(-a).

2 ADJ fuggitivo(-a); (*liter: fleeting*) fugace, fuggevole.

fugue [fjuːg] N (*Mus*) fuga.

ful·crum ['fʊlkrəm] N fulcro.

ful·fil, (*Am*) **ful·fill** [fʊl'fɪl] VT (*duty, function*) compiere; (*promise*) mantenere; (*ambition*) realizzare; (*wish, desire*) soddisfare, appagare; (*order*) eseguire; **to fulfil o.s.** realizzarsi.

ful·filled [fʊl'fɪld] ADJ (*person*) realizzato(-a), soddisfatto (-a).

ful·fil·ling [fʊl'fɪlɪŋ] ADJ (*work*) soddisfacente.

ful·fil·ment, (*Am*) **ful·fill·ment** [fʊl'fɪlmənt] N (*see vb*) compimento; mantenimento; realizzazione *f*; soddisfazione *f*, appagamento; esecuzione *f*; **sense of fulfilment** soddisfazione.

full [fʊl] 1 ADJ (*comp* -**er**, *superl* -**est**) **a** (*gen*) pieno(-a); (*vehicle, hotel*) completo(-a); (*timetable*) denso(-a); **to be full of …** essere pieno(-a) di…; **full of people** gremito(-a) di gente; **to be full of o.s.** essere pieno(-a) di sé; **we are full up for July** siamo al completo per luglio; **he's had a full life** ha avuto una vita piena *or* intensa; **I'm full (up)** (*fam*) sono pieno

b (*complete*) completo(-a); (: *member*) effettivo(-a); (: *price*) intero(-a); (*details*) ampio(-a); **to pay full fare** pagare la tariffa intera *or* completa; **to fall full length** cadere lungo(-a) disteso(-a); **in full bloom** in piena fioritura; **in full colour** (*illustration*) a colori; **in full dress** in abito da cerimonia; **army at full strength** esercito al gran completo; **to be in full swing** essere in pieno fervore; **in the fullest sense of the word** nel pieno senso della parola; **at full speed** a tutta velocità; **full speed ahead** (*Naut*) avanti tutta; **the full particulars** tutti i particolari; **I waited a full hour** ho aspettato un'ora intera

c (*rounded: face*) pieno(-a); (: *figure*) pienotto(-a); (: *lips*) carnoso(-a); (: *skirt, sleeves*) largo(-a), ampio(-a).

2 ADV: **to know full well that** sapere benissimo che; **it hit him full in the face** l'ha colpito in pieno viso.

3 N: **to write sth in full** scrivere qc per intero; **to pay in full** pagare tutto; **to the full** fino in fondo, al massimo.

full·back ['fʊlˌbæk] N (*Ftbl, Rugby*) terzino.

♦ **full-blooded** [ˌfʊl'blʌdɪd] ADJ (*vigorous: attack, support*) vigoroso(-a); (*virile*) virile.

♦ **full-blown** [ˌfʊl'bləʊn] ADJ (*disease, heart attack*) vero (-a) e proprio(-a); (*doctor, architect*) a tutti gli effetti.

♦ **full board** N pensione *f* completa.

♦ **full-bodied** [ˌfʊl'bɒdɪd] ADJ (*wine*) corposo(-a).

♦ **full-cream** [ˌfʊl'kriːm] ADJ (*Brit*): **full-cream milk** latte *m* intero.

♦ **full dress** N (*Mil*) abito da cerimonia.

♦ **full employment** N (*Econ*) piena occupazione.

♦ **full-face** [ˌfʊl'feɪs] ADJ, ADV di faccia.

♦ **full-grown** [ˌfʊl'grəʊn] ADJ maturo(-a).

♦ **full house** N (*Theatre*) il tutto esaurito.

♦ **full-length** [ˌfʊl'lɛŋθ] ADJ (*portrait*) in piedi; (*dress*) lungo(-a); (*film*) a lungometraggio.

♦ **full moon** N luna piena.

♦ **full name** N nome *m* e cognome *m*.

full·ness ['fʊlnɪs] N (*of detail*) abbondanza; (*of figure, hips*) rotondità; (*of dress*) ampiezza; **in the fullness of time** (*eventually*) col tempo; (*at predestined time*) a tempo debito.

♦ **full-page** [ˌfʊl'peɪdʒ] ADJ a tutta pagina.

♦ **full-scale** ['fʊl'skeɪl] ADJ (*search, retreat*) su vasta scala; (*drawing, model*) a grandezza naturale.

♦ **full-sized** [ˌfʊl'saɪzd], **full-size** [ˌfʊl'saɪz] ADJ (*full-grown*) adulto(-a); (*portrait, model*) a grandezza naturale.

♦ **full stop** N punto.

♦ **full-throated** [ˌfʊl'θrəʊtɪd] ADJ (*shout*) a piena gola.

♦ **full-time** [ˌfʊl'taɪm] ADJ, ADV (*work*) a tempo pieno.

♦ **full time** 1 N (*Sport*) fine *f* partita.

ful·ly ['fʊlɪ] ADV **a** (*completely*) completamente, pienamente, interamente; **fully dressed** completamente vestito(-a) **b** (*at least*) almeno; **fully as big** almeno così grosso(-a).

♦ **fully fashioned** ['fʊlɪ'fæʃənd] ADJ (*sweater*) sciancrato (-a); (*stockings*) modellato(-a).

♦ **fully-fledged** ['fʊlɪ'flɛdʒd] ADJ (*bird*) adulto(-a); (*fig: teacher, member*) a tutti gli effetti.

ful·mar ['fʊlmə'] N procellaria dei ghiacci.

ful·mi·nate ['fʌlmɪˌneɪt] VI: **to fulminate (against)** scagliare fulmini (contro).

ful·mi·na·tion [ˌfʌlmɪ'neɪʃən] N invettiva.

ful·some ['fʊlsəm] ADJ (*pej: praise*) esagerato(-a), eccessivo(-a); (: *manner*) insincero(-a).

fum·ble ['fʌmbl] 1 VI (*also:* **fumble about**): **to fumble (about) in one's pockets** frugare *or* rovistare nelle tasche; **to fumble in the dark** andare a tastoni *or* a tentoni, brancolare; **to fumble with sth** armeggiare con qc.

2 VT: **to fumble a catch** mancare una presa; **to fumble a ball** lasciarsi sfuggire di mano una palla.

fume [fjuːm] VI (*angry person*) essere furioso(-a); (*car exhaust*) fumare; **to be fuming with rage at** *or* **about sth** fumare di rabbia per qc.

fumes [fjuːmz] NPL esalazioni *fpl*, vapori *mpl*.

fu·mi·gate ['fjuːmɪˌgeɪt] VT (*room*) suffumicare, fumigare.

fu·mi·ga·tion [ˌfjuːmɪ'geɪʃən] N fumigazione *f*.

fun [fʌn] N (*enjoyment*) divertimento, spasso; **for** *or* **in fun** per scherzo, per ridere; **it's great fun** è molto divertente; **it's not much fun** non è molto divertente; **don't spoil our fun** non fare il guastafeste; **there'll be fun and games with that** (*fig iro*) ci sarà da divertirsi; **to do sth for the fun of it** fare qc tanto per ridere; **to have fun** divertirsi; **to make fun of** *or* **poke fun at sb** canzonare *or* prendere in giro qn.

func·tion [ˈfʌŋkʃən] [1] N [a] (purpose, Math) funzione f [b] (reception) ricevimento; (official ceremony) cerimonia, funzione f.
[2] VI (operate) funzionare; **to function as** fungere da.
func·tion·al [ˈfʌŋkʃnəl] ADJ funzionale.
func·tion·al·ly [ˈfʌŋkʃənəlɪ] ADV dal punto di vista funzionale.
func·tion·ary [ˈfʌŋkʃənərɪ] N funzionario(-a).
♦ **function key** N (Comput) tasto di funzioni.
fund [fʌnd] [1] N [a] (reserve of money) fondo, cassa; (supply) provvista, riserva; **to be a fund of information** essere una miniera d'informazioni [b] (cash): **funds** NPL fondi mpl; **to raise funds for** raccogliere fondi per.
[2] VT (project) finanziare.
fun·da·men·tal [ˌfʌndəˈmɛntl] ADJ fondamentale; **his fundamental honesty** la sua innata onestà.
fun·da·men·tal·ism [ˌfʌndəˈmɛntəˌlɪzəm] N fondamentalismo.
fun·da·men·tal·ist [ˌfʌndəˈmɛntəlɪst] ADJ, N fondamentalista (m/f).
fun·da·men·tal·ly [ˌfʌndəˈmɛntəlɪ] ADV fondamentalmente, essenzialmente.
fun·da·men·tals [ˌfʌndəˈmɛntlz] NPL basi fpl, fondamenti mpl, principi mpl fondamentali.
fund·ing [ˈfʌndɪŋ] N finanziamento, fondi mpl.
♦ **fund-raising** [ˈfʌndˌreɪzɪŋ] [1] N raccolta di fondi.
[2] ADJ (event) per la raccolta di fondi.
fu·ner·al [ˈfjuːnərəl] N funerale m; (procession) corteo funebre; (state funeral) funerali mpl; **that's your funeral!** (fam) è affar tuo!
♦ **funeral director** N impresario di pompe funebri.
♦ **funeral parlour**, (Am) **funeral parlor** N impresa di pompe funebri.
♦ **funeral service** N ufficio funebre.
fu·ner·ary [ˈfjuːnərərɪ] ADJ (frm) funebre.
fu·nereal [fjuːˈnɪərɪəl] ADJ funereo(-a), lugubre.
fun·fair [ˈfʌnˌfɛəˈ] N (Brit) luna park m inv.
fun·gi [ˈfʌŋgaɪ] NPL of **fungus**.
fun·gi·cide [ˈfʌndʒɪˌsaɪd] N fungicida m; (for plants) anticrittogamico.
fun·gus [ˈfʌŋgəs] N (pl **fungi** [ˈfʌŋgaɪ]) fungo; (mould) muffa.
fu·nicu·lar [fjuːˈnɪkjʊləˈ] [1] N (also: **funicular railway**) funicolare f.
[2] ADJ funicolare.
funk [fʌŋk] [1] N (old): **to be in a (blue) funk** (fam) avere una gran fifa.
[2] VT (old) evitare (per paura).
funky [ˈfʌŋkɪ] ADJ (comp **-ier**, superl **-iest**) (music) funky inv; (fam: excellent) figo(-a).
♦ **fun-loving** [ˈfʌnˌlʌvɪŋ] ADJ a cui piace divertirsi.
fun·nel [ˈfʌnl] N (for pouring) imbuto; (of steam engine, ship) fumaiolo, ciminiera.
fun·ni·ly [ˈfʌnɪlɪ] ADV [a] in modo divertente [b] (oddly) stranamente; **funnily enough** strano a dirsi, per una strana coincidenza.
fun·ny [ˈfʌnɪ] [1] ADJ (comp **-ier**, superl **-iest**) [a] divertente, buffo(-a); **that's not funny** c'è poco da ridere; **to try to be funny** fare lo spiritoso(-a)
[b] (strange) strano(-a), bizzarro(-a); **this tastes funny** ha uno strano sapore; **a funny feeling came over me** mi sono sentito strano; **the funny thing about it is that** ... la cosa strana è che...; **there's some funny business going on here** (fam) qui c'è qualcosa di losco.
[2] N: **the funnies** (Am fam) i fumetti.

♦ **funny bone** N (fam) osso cubitale.
♦ **fun run** N marcia non competitiva.
fur [fɜː'] N (of animal) pelo, pelame m; (single skin) pelle f; (as clothing) pelliccia; (Brit: in kettle) incrostazione f, calcare m.
fur·bish [ˈfɜːbɪʃ] VT (polish) lucidare; (renovate, smarten) ravvivare.
♦ **fur coat** N pelliccia.
Furies [ˈfjʊərɪz] NPL (Myth): **the Furies** le Furie.
fu·ri·ous [ˈfjʊərɪəs] ADJ (person) furioso(-a), infuriato(-a); (argument) violento(-a); (effort) grande; **at a furious speed** a velocità folle; **to be furious with sb** essere furioso(-a) con qn; **to be furious at sth/at having done sth** essere furioso(-a) per qc/per aver fatto qc.
fu·ri·ous·ly [ˈfjʊərɪəslɪ] ADV furiosamente, accanitamente.
furl [fɜːl] VT (sail) piegare.
furled [fɜːld] ADJ (flag, umbrella) ripiegato(-a).
fur·long [ˈfɜːˌlɒŋ] N = 201,17 m.
fur·lough [ˈfɜːləʊ] N (esp Am) licenza, permesso, congedo.
fur·nace [ˈfɜːnɪs] N fornace f.
fur·nish [ˈfɜːnɪʃ] VT [a] (room, house): **to furnish (with)** arredare (con), ammobiliare (con); **furnishing fabric** tessuto da arredamento; **furnished flat** or (Am) **furnished apartment** appartamento ammobiliato [b] (frm: supply: excuse, information) fornire, dare; **to furnish sb with sth** dare qc a qn.
fur·nish·ings [ˈfɜːnɪʃɪŋz] NPL mobili mpl, mobilia.
fur·ni·ture [ˈfɜːnɪtʃəˈ] N mobili mpl, mobilia; **a piece of furniture** un mobile; **to be part of the furniture** (fig fam) confondersi con la tappezzeria.
♦ **furniture polish** N cera per mobili.
♦ **furniture removers** N (firm) impresa di traslochi.
♦ **furniture shop** N negozio di mobili.
♦ **furniture van** N camion m inv per or dei traslochi.
fu·ro·re [fjʊəˈrɔːrɪ], (Am) **fu·ror** [fjʊəˈrɔː'] N (protests) scalpore m; (enthusiasm) entusiasmo.
furred [fɜːd] ADJ (kettle, pipe) incrostato(-a); **to have a furred tongue** avere la bocca impastata.
fur·ri·er [ˈfʌrɪəˈ] N pellicciaio(-a).
fur·row [ˈfʌrəʊ] [1] N (Agr) solco; (on forehead) solco, ruga.
[2] VT (forehead, brow) segnare di rughe, solcare.
fur·rowed [ˈfʌrəʊd] ADJ corrucciato(-a).
fur·ry [ˈfɜːrɪ] ADJ (animal) peloso(-a); (toy) di peluche.
fur·ther [ˈfɜːðəˈ] COMP of **far** [1] ADV [a] (in time) oltre, più avanti; (in place) più lontano, oltre, più avanti; **further back** più indietro; **further on** (also fig) più avanti; **how much further is it?** quanto manca or dista?; **I got no further with him** (fig) non sono riuscito a cavare un ragno dal buco; **nothing is further from my thoughts** non ci penso neanche
[b] (more) inoltre, di più; **and I further believe that** ... e inoltre or per di più credo che...; **further to your letter of** ... (Comm) con riferimento alla vostra lettera del...; **he heard nothing further** non c'è stato alcun seguito.
[2] ADJ [a] = **farther**
[b] (additional) ulteriore, altro(-a), supplementare; **until further notice** fino a nuovo avviso; **after further consideration** dopo un più attento esame.
[3] VT (a cause) appoggiare, promuovere, favorire; **to further one's interests** fare i propri interessi.
fur·ther·ance [ˈfɜːðərəns] N: **in furtherance of sth** a favore di qc.
♦ **further education** N (Brit) ≈ corsi mpl di formazione.

further·more ['fɜːðə,mɔː'] ADV inoltre, per di più.

further·most ['fɜːðə,məʊst] ADJ più lontano(-a).

fur·thest ['fɜːðɪst] SUPERL of **far** [1] ADV: **this is the furthest you can go** non puoi andare più lontano.

[2] ADJ più lontano(-a), più distante.

fur·tive ['fɜːtɪv] ADJ (*glance, action*) furtivo(-a); (*person*) circospetto(-a).

fur·tive·ly ['fɜːtɪvlɪ] ADV furtivamente.

fury ['fjʊərɪ] N (*of storm, person*) furia, furore *m*; **she flew into a fury** andò su tutte le furie; **like fury** (*fam*) come una furia; **she's a little fury** è una piccola furia; see also **Furies.**

furze [fɜːz] N ginestrone *m*.

fuse, (*Am*), **fuze** [fjuːz] [1] N (*Elec*) fusibile *m*, valvola; (*of bomb*) spoletta, miccia; **to blow a fuse** far saltare una valvola; **a fuse has blown** è saltata una valvola, è saltato un fusibile.

[2] VT **a** (*Elec*): **to fuse the lights** far saltare le valvole **b** (*metals*) fondere.

[3] VI **a** (*Elec*): **the lights have fused** sono saltate le valvole **b** (*metals*) fondersi.

♦ **fuse box** N scatola *or* cassetta dei fusibili.

fused [fjuːzd] ADJ con fusibile incorporato.

fu·selage ['fjuːzəlaːʒ] N fusoliera.

♦ **fuse wire** N (filo) fusibile *m*.

fu·si·lier [,fjuːzɪ'lɪə'] N fuciliere *m*.

fu·sil·lade [,fjuːzɪ'leɪd] N scarica, raffica; (*fig*) raffica.

fu·sion ['fjuːʒən] N fusione *f*.

fuss [fʌs] [1] N (*complaints, arguments*) storie *fpl*; (*anxious preparations*) agitazione *f*; **to make a fuss about sth** fare storie per qc; **he made a lot of fuss about nothing** ha fatto un sacco di storie per nulla; **don't make such a fuss!** non fare tante storie!; **to make a fuss of sb** (*Brit*) coprire qn di attenzioni.

[2] VI agitarsi.

[3] VT (*person*) infastidire, scocciare

▶ **fuss about, fuss around** VI + ADV affannarsi

▶ **fuss over** VI + PREP (*person*) circondare di premure.

fussi·ly ['fʌsɪlɪ] ADV meticolosamente; **she was fussily dressed** era carica di fronzoli.

fussi·ness ['fʌsɪnɪs] N schifiltosità.

fuss·pot ['fʌs,pɒt] N (*Brit fam*) pignolo(-a).

fussy ['fʌsɪ] ADJ (*comp* **-ier**, *superl* **-iest**) (*person: difficult to please*) difficile, esigente; (: *excessively punctilious*) puntiglioso(-a), pignolo(-a); (*clothes*) pieno(-a) di fronzoli; (*style*) elaborato(-a); **I'm not fussy** (*fam*) per me è lo stesso.

fus·ty ['fʌstɪ] ADJ (*comp* **-ier**, *superl* **-iest**) (*pej: musty: smell*) che sa di stantio; (: *old-fashioned: ideas, outlook*) stantio (-a).

fu·tile ['fjuːtaɪl] ADJ futile, vano(-a).

fu·tile·ly ['fjuːtaɪlɪ] ADV futilmente.

fu·til·ity [fjuː'tɪlɪtɪ] N futilità.

fu·ton [,fuː'tɒn] N futon *m inv*, materasso giapponese.

fu·ture ['fjuːtʃə'] [1] ADJ futuro(-a); **the future tense** il futuro; **at some future date** in futuro.

[2] N futuro, avvenire *m*; (*Gram*) futuro; **in future** in futuro; **in the near future** in un prossimo futuro; **in the immediate future** nell'immediato futuro; **there's no future in it** non c'è futuro in questo campo.

fu·tures ['fjuːtʃəz] NPL (*Fin*) futures *mpl*.

fu·tur·ism ['fjuːtʃə,rɪzəm] N futurismo.

fu·tur·ist ['fjuːtʃərɪst] N futurista *m/f*.

fu·tur·is·tic [,fjuːtʃə'rɪstɪk] ADJ futurista, futuristico(-a).

fu·tur·olo·gist [,fjuːtʃər'ɒlədʒɪst] N futurologo(-a).

fu·tur·ol·ogy [,fjuːtʃər'ɒlədʒɪ] N futurologia.

fuze [fjuːz] N, VT, VI (*Am*) = **fuse.**

fuzz [fʌz] N (*frizzy hair*) capelli *mpl* crespi; (*on chin*) peluria; **the fuzz** (*fam*) la polizia.

fuzzi·ly ['fʌzɪlɪ] ADV confusamente.

fuzzy ['fʌzɪ] ADJ (*comp* **-ier**, *superl* **-iest**) (*hair*) crespo(-a); (*blurred: photo*) sfocato(-a), indistinto(-a); (: *memory*) confuso(-a).

G

G, g [dʒiː] N **a** (*letter*) G, g *for m inv*; **G for George** ≈ G come Genova **b** (*Mus*) sol *m*.

G [dʒiː] N ABBR **a** (*Brit Scol: mark:* = *good*) ≈ buono **b** (*Austrl Cine:* = *general audience*) per tutti.

g [dʒiː] ABBR **a** (= *gram*) **g b** = *gravity*.

G7 ['dʒiː'sɛvn] N ABBR (*Pol:* = *Group of Seven*) G7 *mpl*.

GA ABBR (*Am Post*)= *Georgia*.

gab [gæb] N (*fam*): **to have the gift of the gab** avere parlantina.

gab·ar·dine ['gæbəˌdiːn] N = **gaberdine**.

gab·ble ['gæbl] **1** VT borbottare.
  2 VI farfugliare; **they were gabbling away in French** chiacchieravano come macchinette in francese.

gab·er·dine [ˌgæbə'diːn] N (*material*) gabardine *m*; (*coat*) (soprabito di) gabardine.

ga·ble ['geɪbl] N frontone *m*.

Ga·bon [gə'bɒn] N Gabon *m*.

gad·about ['gædəˌbaut] N (*fam*) girellone(-a).

gad about ['gædə'baut] VI + ADV (*fam old*) bighellonare, vagabondare.

gad·fly ['gædˌflaɪ] N tafano *m*.

gadg·et ['gædʒɪt] N aggeggio, arnese *m*.

gadg·et·ry ['gædʒɪtrɪ] N aggeggi *mpl*, arnesi *mpl*.

Gaea ['dʒiːə] N Gaia.

Gael·ic ['geɪlɪk] **1** ADJ gaelico(-a).
  2 N (*language*) gaelico.

gaff [gæf] N **a** (*fam*): **to blow the gaff** spifferare un segreto **b** (*Fishing*) arpione *m*.

gaffe [gæf] N gaffe *f inv*.

gaf·fer ['gæfər] N (*Brit fam*) capo.

gag [gæg] **1** N **a** (*over mouth*) bavaglio **b** (*fam: joke*) battuta, gag *f inv*.
  2 VT (*silence: prisoner etc*) imbavagliare.
  3 VI (*choke*) soffocare; (*retch*) avere conati di vomito.

gaga ['gɑːgɑː] ADJ (*fam*): **to go gaga** rimbambire.

gage [geɪdʒ] N, VT (*Am*) = **gauge**.

gag·gle ['gægl] N (*of geese*) branco.

gai·ety ['geɪtɪ] N allegria, gaiezza.

gai·ly ['geɪlɪ] ADV (*sing, chatter*) allegramente, gaiamente; (*painted, decorated*) vivacemente; **gaily coloured** dai colori allegri.

gain [geɪn] **1** N (*increase*) aumento; (*improvement*) miglioramento; (*advantage*) vantaggio, utile *m*; (*profit*) guadagno, profitto; **gain in weight** aumento di peso; **to do sth for gain** fare qc per lucro; **his loss is our gain** lui ci perde, noi ci guadagniamo; **the Conservatives made several gains** i Conservatori hanno guadagnato parecchi seggi.
  2 VT (*obtain, acquire: respect, approval*) ottenere; (: *reputation*) farsi; (: *experience, wealth, knowledge, territory*) acquistare; (*reach: summit, shore*) raggiungere, guadagnare; (: *objective*) raggiungere; (*increase: weight*) aumentare di; **to gain 3lbs/kilos (in weight)** aumentare di 3 libbre/chili; **what do I have to gain by staying here?** che ci guadagno restando qui?; **to gain strength** (*person*) riprendere le forze; (*theory*) avvalorarsi; **to gain possession of** impadronirsi di, impossessarsi di; **to gain ground** guadagnare terreno; **to gain speed** prendere velocità; **my watch has gained 5 minutes** il mio orologio va avanti di 5 minuti; **to gain an advantage over sb** avvantaggiarsi rispetto a qn.
  3 VI (*person*) guadagnare; (*watch*) andare avanti; **to gain in/by** aumentare di/con; **to gain in weight** aumentare di peso; **to gain in popularity** acquistare popolarità
  ▶ **gain upon, gain on** VI + PREP accorciare le distanze da, riprendere.

gain·ful ['geɪnful] ADJ (*employment*) remunerativo(-a).

gain·ful·ly ['geɪnfəlɪ] ADV: **to be gainfully employed** avere un lavoro retribuito.

gain·say [ˌgeɪn'seɪ] (*pt, pp* **gainsaid** [ˌgeɪn'sɛd]) VT (*frm: fact, argument*) contestare, negare; (: *person*) contraddire.

gait [geɪt] N (*frm*) passo, andatura.

gait·er ['geɪtər] N ghetta.

gal. ABBR = **gallon**.

gala ['gɑːlə] N (*festive occasion*) festa; (: *important*) gran galà *m inv*; **swimming gala** manifestazione *f* di nuoto.

ga·lac·tic [gə'læktɪk] ADJ galattico(-a).

Ga·la·pa·gos Is·lands [gə'læpəgəs'aɪləndz] NPL: **the Galapagos Islands** le (isole) Galapagos *fpl*.

♦ **gala performance** N serata di gala.

gal·axy ['gæləksɪ] N galassia.

gale [geɪl] N (*strong wind*) bufera, vento forte; (*at sea*) burrasca; **gale force 10** vento forza 10.

♦ **gale force wind** N vento di bufera.

♦ **gale warning** N avviso di bufera.

gall [gɔ:l] 1 N (*Anat*) bile *f*; (*fig: impudence*) fegato, faccia (tosta).

2 VT seccare; **it galled him to have to ask permission** gli seccava dover chiedere il permesso.

gal·lant ['gælənt] ADJ (*brave*) valoroso(-a), prode; (*towards ladies*) galante.

gal·lant·ly ['gæləntlɪ] ADV (*see adj*) valorosamente, prodemente; galantemente.

gal·lant·ry ['gæləntrɪ] N (*see adj*) valore *m* militare, prodezza; galanteria.

♦ **gall bladder** N cistifellea.

gal·leon ['gælɪən] N galeone *m*.

gal·lery ['gælərɪ] N (*also*: **art gallery**: *state owned*) museo; (: *private*) galleria, loggia; (*for spectators*) tribuna; (*in theatre*) loggione *m*, balconata; **to play to the gallery** parlare (*per accattivarsi il pubblico*).

gal·ley ['gælɪ] N (*ship*) galea; (*ship's kitchen*) cambusa.

♦ **galley proof** N (*Typ*) bozza in colonna.

♦ **galley slave** N galeotto; (*fam: drudge*) schiavo(-a).

Gal·lic ['gælɪk] ADJ (*of Gaul*) gallico(-a); (*French*) francese.

gall·ing ['gɔ:lɪŋ] ADJ (*irritating*) seccante, irritante; (*humiliating*) umiliante.

gal·li·vant ['gælɪˌvænt] VI andare in giro a divertirsi.

gal·lon ['gælən] N gallone *m* (*Brit* = 4,55 *litri*; *Am* = 3,79 *litri*).

gal·lop ['gæləp] 1 N (*pace*) galoppo; (*ride*) galoppata; **at a gallop** al galoppo.

2 VI (*horse, rider*) galoppare, andare al galoppo; **to gallop away** galoppare via; (*fig*) andarsene di gran carriera; **he galloped through his homework** (*fig*) ha fatto i compiti di volata.

gal·lop·ing ['gæləpɪŋ] ADJ (*horse*) al galoppo; (*fig: inflation, pneumonia*) galoppante.

gal·lows ['gæləʊz] NPL forca, patibolo.

♦ **gallows bird** N (*fam*) pendaglio da forca, avanzo di galera.

gall·stone ['gɔ:lˌstəʊn] N calcolo biliare.

Gal·lup poll® ['gæləpˌpəʊl] N sondaggio d'opinione, ≈ sondaggio Doxa.

ga·lore [gə'lɔ:'] ADV a iosa, a profusione.

ga·loshes [gə'lɒʃɪz] N calosce *fpl*.

gal·van·ic [gæl'vænɪk] ADJ (*Elec*) galvanico(-a); (*fig: effect*) galvanizzante.

gal·va·ni·za·tion [ˌgælvənarˈzeɪʃən] N galvanizzazione *f*.

gal·va·nize ['gælvəˌnaɪz] VT galvanizzare; (*fig*) galvanizzare, elettrizzare; **to galvanize sb into action** spronare qn all'azione.

gal·va·nized iron ['gælvəˌnaɪzd'aɪən] N ferro zincato.

Gam·bia ['gæmbɪə] N: **the Gambia** il Gambia.

gam·bit ['gæmbɪt] N (*Chess*) gambetto; (*fig*) mossa; **opening gambit** prima mossa.

gam·ble ['gæmbl] 1 N azzardo, rischio; **to take a gamble** rischiare; **the gamble came off** è valsa la pena rischiare; **it's a gamble** è un salto nel buio.

2 VT (*money*) giocare.

3 VI giocare (d'azzardo); **to gamble on the Stock Exchange** giocare in Borsa; **to gamble on sth** puntare su qc, giocare su qc

▶ **gamble away** VT + ADV (*money*) perdere al gioco, giocarsi.

gam·bler ['gæmblə'] N giocatore(-trice) d'azzardo.

gam·bling ['gæmblɪŋ] N gioco (d'azzardo).

♦ **gambling debts** NPL debiti *mpl* di gioco.

♦ **gambling den** N bisca.

♦ **gambling house** N casinò *m inv*, casa da gioco.

gam·bol ['gæmbəl] VI saltellare.

game [geɪm] 1 N a (*gen*) gioco; (*match*) partita; **games** NPL (*Scol*) attività *fpl* sportive; **that's three games to you and two to me** siamo tre a due; **to have a game of cards/chess/tennis** fare una partita a carte/scacchi/tennis; **he plays a good game of golf** gioca bene al golf; **game of chance** gioco d'azzardo; **game, set and match** (*Tennis*) game, set e partita; **he was off his game** non era nella sua forma migliore; **to play the game** (*also fig*) rispettare le regole del gioco; **to play sb's game** fare il gioco di qn; **come on lads, play the game** su ragazzi, siate sportivi; **to beat sb at his own game** battere qn con le sue stesse armi; **the game is up** è finita, è la fine; **I wonder what his game is?** mi chiedo a che gioco stia giocando; **two can play at that game** ti (*or* lo *etc*) ripagherò con la stessa moneta; **how long have you been in this game?** (*fam*) da quant'è che fai questo mestiere?; **to be on the game** (*prostitute*) essere nel giro (della prostituzione).

b (*Culin, Hunting*) selvaggina; **big game** caccia grossa.

2 ADJ (*willing*): **to be game** starci; **to be game (for sth/to do sth)** (*ready*) essere pronto(-a) (a qc/a fare qc); **game for anything** pronto(-a) a tutto.

♦ **game bird** N uccello da cacciagione.

game·keeper ['geɪmˌki:pə'] N guardacaccia *m inv*.

game·ly ['geɪmlɪ] ADV coraggiosamente.

♦ **game reserve** N riserva di caccia.

♦ **games console** N console *f inv* del videogame.

game·show ['geɪmˌʃəʊ] N gioco a premi (*televisivo o radiofonico*).

games·man·ship ['geɪmzmən,ʃɪp] N: **to be a master of gamesmanship** essere una vecchia volpe.

♦ **games master** N insegnante *m* di educazione fisica.

♦ **games mistress** N insegnante *f* di educazione fisica.

gam·ete ['gæmi:t] N gamete *m*.

♦ **game warden** N (*on reserve*) guardacaccia *m inv*.

gam·ing ['geɪmɪŋ] N (*frm: old*) gioco d'azzardo.

gam·ma ['gæmə] N gamma *m or f*.

♦ **gamma rays** NPL raggi *mpl* gamma.

gam·mon ['gæmən] N (*ham*) ≈ prosciutto; (: *smoked*) ≈ prosciutto affumicato; (*bacon*) ≈ pancetta.

gam·my ['gæmɪ] ADJ (*fam: leg*) zoppo(-a).

gam·ut ['gæmət] N gamma; **to run the (whole) gamut of emotions** provare uno dopo l'altro tutti i sentimenti possibili.

gan·der ['gændə'] N (*Zool*) oca maschio.

gang [gæŋ] N (*of thieves, youths*) banda; (*of friends*) comitiva; (*of workmen*) squadra

▶ **gang up** VI + ADV: **to gang up (with)** mettersi insieme (a *or* con); **to gang up on *or* against sb** far comunella contro qn.

Gan·ges ['gændʒi:z] N: **the Ganges** il Gange.

gang·land ['gæŋˌlænd] ADJ della malavita; **gangland killer** sicario.

gang·ling ['gæŋglɪŋ] ADJ allampanato(-a).

gan·gli·on ['gæŋglɪən] N ganglio.

gan·gly ['gæŋglɪ] ADJ = gangling.

gang·plank ['gæŋˌplæŋk] N passerella.

gang·grene ['gæŋgri:n] N cancrena.

gan·gre·nous ['gæŋgrɪnəs] ADJ in cancrena.

gang·ster ['gæŋstə'] N gangster *m inv*.

gang·way ['gæŋ,weɪ] N (*Naut*) passerella; (*Brit*: *aisle*: *in theatre, cinema*) corsia; (: *in train*) corridoio; (: *in bus*) passaggio; **gangway!** largo!

gan·net ['gænɪt] N (*Zool*) sula bassana.

gan·try ['gæntrɪ] N (*for crane, railway signal*) cavalletto; (*for rocket*) torre *f* di lancio.

Ganymede ['gænɪˌmiːd] N Ganimede *m*.

GAO [ˌdʒiːeɪ'əʊ] N ABBR (*Am*: = *General Accounting Office*) ≈ Corte *f* dei Conti.

gaol *etc* [dʒeɪl], VT (*Brit*) = **jail**.

gaol·er ['dʒeɪlə'] N (*Brit*) carceriere *m*.

gap [gæp] VI N a (*gen*) spazio vuoto; (*in line, traffic*) interruzione *f*; (*in trees, crowd, defences*) vuoto; (*in wall, fence*) apertura, buco; (*mountain pass*) passo, valico; (*between teeth*) spazio; (*between floorboards*) interstizio; (*fig*: *in knowledge*) lacuna; (: *in conversation*) pausa; (*in time*) intervallo; **he left a gap which will be hard to fill** ha lasciato un vuoto difficile da colmare

b (*difference*): **gap (between)** divario (tra); **the generation gap** il gap *m inv* generazionale; **the gap between them widened** la distanza tra di loro si fece più grande.

gape [geɪp] VI a (*mouth, hole*) essere spalancato(-a) b (*person*) restare a bocca aperta; **to gape (at sb/sth)** guardare (qn/qc) a bocca aperta.

gap·ing ['geɪpɪŋ] ADJ (*wound*) aperto(-a); (*hole*) grosso(-a); **gaping seam** larga scucitura.

gar·age ['gærɑːʒ] N (*of private house*) garage *m inv*; (*for car repairs*) officina, autofficina; (*filling station*) stazione *f* di servizio.

♦ **garage mechanic** N meccanico.

♦ **garage proprietor** N proprietario dell'officina *or* della stazione di servizio.

garb [gɑːb] N abiti *mpl*, vesti *fpl*.

gar·bage ['gɑːbɪdʒ] N (*esp Am*) immondizie *fpl*, spazzatura, rifiuti *mpl*; (*fig*: *film, book*) porcheria, robaccia; (: *nonsense*) fesserie *fpl*.

♦ **garbage can** N (*Am*) bidone *m* della spazzatura.

♦ **garbage collector** N (*Am*) netturbino(-a).

♦ **garbage disposal unit** N (*Am*) tritarifiuti *m inv*.

♦ **garbage truck** N (*Am*) camion *m inv* della nettezza urbana.

gar·ble ['gɑːbl] VT (*story, facts*) ingarbugliare.

gar·bled ['gɑːbld] ADJ (*speech, account*) ingarbugliato(-a), distorto(-a); (*words*) incomprensibile.

gar·den ['gɑːdn] a ① N giardino; **gardens** NPL (*public*) giardino *sg* (pubblico); (*of stately home*) parco *sg*, giardino; **the Garden of Eden** il Paradiso Terrestre, l'Eden *m*.

② VI fare (lavori di) giardinaggio.

♦ **garden centre** N vivaio.

♦ **garden city** N (*Brit*) città giardino *f inv*.

gar·den·er ['gɑːdnə'] N giardiniere(-a).

gar·denia [gɑːˈdiːnɪə] N gardenia.

gar·den·ing ['gɑːdnɪŋ] N giardinaggio.

♦ **garden party** N festa all'aperto, garden-party *m inv*.

♦ **garden path** N (*fig*): **to lead sb up the garden path** darla a bere a qn.

♦ **garden shears** NPL tosasiepi *f inv*, cesoie *fpl*.

♦ **garden shed** N capanno.

♦ **garden tools** NPL attrezzi *mpl* da giardinaggio.

gar·gan·tuan [gɑːˈgæntjʊən] ADJ (*frm*) gargantuesco(-a).

gar·gle ['gɑːgl] a ① N (*act*) gargarismo; (*liquid*) collutorio.

② VI fare gargarismi.

gar·goyle ['gɑːgɔɪl] N gargolla, gargouille *f inv*.

gar·ish ['gɛərɪʃ] ADJ sgargiante, vistoso(-a); (*light*) abbagliante.

gar·ish·ly ['gɛərɪʃlɪ] ADV (*see adj*) in modo sgargiante, in modo vistoso; in modo abbagliante.

gar·ish·ness ['gɛərɪʃnɪs] N vistosità.

gar·land ['gɑːlənd] N ghirlanda.

gar·lic ['gɑːlɪk] N aglio.

♦ **garlic bread** N ≈ bruschetta.

gar·licky ['gɑːlɪkɪ] ADJ (*sauce, food*) con molto aglio; (*flavour*) di aglio; (*breath*) che puzza di aglio.

♦ **garlic press** N spremiaglio.

♦ **garlic sausage** N salamino all'aglio.

gar·ment ['gɑːmənt] N (*frm*) articolo di vestiario, indumento.

gar·ner [gɑːnə'] VT (*frm*) raccogliere.

gar·net ['gɑːnɪt] N granato.

gar·nish ['gɑːnɪʃ] ① N (*Culin*) decorazione *f*.

② VT: **to garnish (with)** guarnire (con).

gar·ret ['gærət] N soffitta, mansarda.

gar·ri·son ['gærɪsən] ① N guarnigione *f*.

② VT (*town*) piazzare truppe in; (: *subj*: *troops*) presidiare.

♦ **garrison town** N città *f inv* di guarnigione.

gar·rotte [gəˈrɒt] ① N garrotta.

② VT garrottare.

gar·ru·lous ['gærʊləs] ADJ loquace, ciarliero(-a).

gar·ru·lous·ness ['gærʊləsnɪs] N loquacità.

gar·ter ['gɑːtə'] N giarrettiera; (*Am*: *suspender*) gancio (di reggicalze).

♦ **garter belt** N (*Am*) reggicalze *m inv*.

♦ **garter stitch** N (*punto*) legaccio.

gas [gæs] ① a (*gen*) gas *m inv*; (*as anaesthetic*) etere *m*; **Calor gas®** gas liquido *or* in bombole b (*Am*: *also*: **gasoline**) benzina.

② VT (*person*) asfissiare (col gas); (*Mil*) uccidere col gas asfissiante, gassare; **to gas o.s.** asfissiarsi, suicidarsi col gas.

③ VI (*fam*: *chatter*) chiacchierare, cianciare.

④ ADJ (*industry, pipe*) del gas.

gas·bag ['gæsˌbæg] N (*fam*) chiaccherone(-a).

♦ **gas burner** N becco a gas.

♦ **gas chamber** N camera a gas.

Gas·co·ny ['gæskənɪ] N Guascogna.

♦ **gas cooker** N (*Brit*) cucina a gas.

♦ **gas cylinder** N bombola del gas.

gas·eous ['gæsɪəs] ADJ gassoso(-a).

♦ **gas fire** N (*Brit*) stufa a gas.

♦ **gas-fired** ['gæsˌfaɪəd] ADJ (*central heating*) alimentato(-a) a gas.

♦ **gas fitter** N gas(s)ista *m*, operaio addetto al gas.

gash [gæʃ] ① N (*in flesh*) taglio profondo, squarcio; (*on face*) sfregio; (*in material*) spacco.

② VT (*arm, head*) fare un brutto taglio in; (*face*) sfregiare; (*seat*) squarciare.

♦ **gas jet** N becco a gas.

gas·ket ['gæskɪt] N (*Tech*) guarnizione *f*.

♦ **gas laws** NPL (*Chem*) leggi *fpl* dei gas.

gas·light ['gæsˌlaɪt] N illuminazione *f* a gas.

♦ **gas lighter** N accendisigari *m inv* a gas.

♦ **gas main** N conduttura del gas.

gas·man ['gæsˌmæn] N (*pl* **-men**) (*fam*): **the gasman** l'uomo del gas.

♦ **gas mask** N maschera *f* antigas *inv*.

♦ **gas meter** N contatore *m* del gas.

gaso·line ['gæsəʊliːn] N (*Am*) benzina.

gas·om·eter [gæ'sɒmɪtə⁽ʳ⁾] N gas(s)ometro.

gasp [gɑːsp] 1 N ansito; **she gave a gasp of surprise** la sorpresa le mozzò il fiato; **to be at one's last gasp** star tirando l'ultimo respiro.

2 VI ansare, ansimare; (in surprise) restare senza fiato; **to gasp for breath** respirare a fatica

▶ **gasp out** VT + ADV dire affannosamente.

♦ **gas pipeline** N gasdotto.

♦ **gas ring** N fornello a gas.

♦ **gas station** N (Am) distributore m di benzina.

♦ **gas stove** N cucina a gas.

gas·sy ['gæsɪ] ADJ (usu pej) troppo gassato(-a).

♦ **gas tank** N (Am Aut) serbatoio (della benzina).

♦ **gas tap** N (on pipe) rubinetto del gas; (on cooker) manopola del gas.

gas·tric ['gæstrɪk] ADJ gastrico(-a); **gastric flu** influenza m inv gastro-intestinale.

♦ **gastric ulcer** N ulcera gastrica.

gas·tri·tis [gæs'traɪtɪs] N gastrite f.

gas·tro·en·teri·tis [ˌgæstrəʊˌentə'raɪtɪs] N gastroenterite f.

gas·tro·nome ['gæstrənəʊm] N gastronomo(-a).

gas·tro·nom·ic [ˌgæstrə'nɒmɪk] ADJ gastronomico(-a).

gas·tro·nomi·cal·ly [ˌgæstrə'nɒmɪkəlɪ] ADV gastronomicamente.

gas·trono·my [gæs'trɒnəmɪ] N gastronomia.

♦ **gas turbine** N turbina a gas.

♦ **gas worker** N lavoratore(-trice) dell'industria del gas.

gas·works ['gæsˌwɜːks] NSG OR NPL impianto di produzione del gas.

gate [geɪt] N a (in garden, field) cancello; (of castle, town, Skiing) porta; (at airport) uscita; (at level crossing) barriera b (Sport: attendance) (numero di) spettatori mpl, presenze fpl; (: entrance money) incassi mpl.

ga·teau ['gætəʊ] N (pl gateaux ['gætəʊz]) torta.

♦ **gate–crash** ['geɪtˌkræʃ] VT (fam: party) intrufolarsi in, imbucarsi in; (: enter without paying) fare il portoghese.

♦ **gate–crasher** ['geɪtˌkræʃə⁽ʳ⁾] N (fam: at party) intruso(-a), imbucato(-a); (: at concert etc) portoghese m/f.

gate·house ['geɪtˌhaʊs] N casetta del custode (all'entrata di un parco).

gate·post ['geɪtˌpəʊst] N pilastrino del cancello; **between you, me and the gatepost** (fig fam) che resti tra noi.

gate·way ['geɪtˌweɪ] N porta; **the gateway to success** la strada del successo.

gath·er ['gæðə⁽ʳ⁾] 1 VT a (also: **gather together**: people) radunare, riunire; (: objects) raccogliere, radunare; (also: **gather up**: papers, possessions) raccogliere; (also: **gather in**: material) riprendere, increspare; (: taxes) riscuotere; **to gather the harvest** fare il raccolto; **to gather dust** raccogliere polvere; **to gather one's thoughts/strength** raccogliere i propri pensieri/le proprie forze; **she gathered her mink around her** si avvolse nel visone

b (gain): **to gather speed** prendere or acquistare velocità; **to gather strength** (wind, waves) aumentare d'intensità

c (understand): **to gather (from/that)** comprendere (da/che), dedurre (da/che); **I gather (that) you are leaving** ho saputo che parti; **as you will have gathered** come avrai indovinato; **as far as I can gather** da quel che ho potuto capire; **from what he says I gather that ...** da quel che dice mi pare di capire che....

2 VI (people: also: **gather together**) raccogliersi, radunarsi; (: crowd) assembrarsi; (dust) accumularsi;

(clouds) addensarsi

▶ **gather round** VI + ADV radunarsi.

gath·er·ing ['gæðərɪŋ] N (meeting) raduno, riunione f; (crowd) gruppo.

GATT [gæt] N ABBR (= General Agreement on Tariffs and Trade) GATT m (= accordo generale sulle tariffe e sul commercio).

gauche [gəʊʃ] ADJ goffo(-a).

gauche·ly ['gəʊʃlɪ] ADV goffamente.

gauche·ness ['gəʊʃnɪs] N goffaggine f.

gaudi·ly ['gɔːdɪlɪ] ADV in modo vistoso, in modo chiassoso.

gaudy ['gɔːdɪ] ADJ (comp -ier, superl -iest) vistoso(-a), chiassoso(-a).

gauge [geɪdʒ] 1 N (standard measure: of bullet) calibro; (: of pipe, wire) diametro; (: of railway track) scartamento; (instrument) indicatore m di livello; (fig) metro, criterio; **petrol gauge**, (Am) **gas gauge** indicatore m or spia della benzina; **oil gauge** spia dell'olio; **pressure gauge** manometro.

2 VT (temperature, pressure) misurare; (fig: sb's capabilities, character) valutare, stimare; **to gauge the right moment** calcolare il momento giusto.

Gaul [gɔːl] N a (country) Gallia b (person) gallo.

gaunt [gɔːnt] ADJ emaciato(-a); (face) smunto(-a), scarno (-a); (grim, desolate) desolato(-a).

gaunt·let ['gɔːntlɪt] N (of knight) guanto d'armatura, manopola; (of motorcyclist) guanto; **to run the gauntlet of an angry crowd** (fig) sottoporsi al fuoco di fila di una folla ostile; **to throw down the gauntlet** gettare il guanto.

gaunt·ness ['gɔːntnɪs] N (of person, face) estrema magrezza.

gauze [gɔːz] N garza.

gave [geɪv] PT of **give**.

gav·el ['gævl] N martelletto.

Gawd [gɔːd] N (fam) = **God**.

gawk [gɔːk] VI (fam): **to gawk at** restare a bocca aperta davanti a.

gawki·ness ['gɔːkɪnɪs] N goffaggine f.

gawky ['gɔːkɪ] ADJ (comp -ier, superl -iest) goffo(-a), sgraziato(-a).

gawp [gɔːp] VI = **gape b**.

gay [geɪ] 1 ADJ (comp -er, superl -est) a (homosexual) omosessuale, gay inv b (liter: person) allegro(-a), gaio (-a); (colour) vivace, vivo(-a).

2 N (homosexual) gay m.

♦ **gay lib, gay liberation** N movimento per la liberazione dei gay.

gaze [geɪz] 1 N sguardo (insistente or fisso).

2 VI: **to gaze at** guardare (con insistenza or fisso), fissare; **to gaze in wonderment at sb/sth** guardare rapito(-a) qn/qc; **to gaze into space** guardare nel vuoto.

ga·zelle [gə'zɛl] N gazzella.

ga·zette [gə'zɛt] N (newspaper) gazzetta; (official publication) pubblicazione f ufficiale.

gaz·et·teer [ˌgæzɪ'tɪə⁽ʳ⁾] N (book) dizionario di nomi geografici; (section of book) indice m dei nomi geografici.

ga·zump [gə'zʌmp] VT (Brit fam) venir meno ad una promessa di vendita di un immobile per accettare un'offerta migliore; **he was gazumped** non è riuscito a comprare la casa perché qualcun altro ha fatto un'offerta migliore.

ga·zump·ing [gə'zʌmpɪŋ] N (Brit fam) il fare un'offerta

d'acquisto molto alto per un immobile facendo così annullare un impegno di vendita precedente.

GB [ˌdʒiː'biː] ABBR (= *Great Britain*) GB.

GBH [ˌdʒiːbiː'eɪtʃ] N ABBR (*Brit Law*) = **grievous bodily harm**.

GC [ˌdʒiː'siː] N ABBR (*Brit*: = *George Gross*) *decorazione al valore.*

GCE [ˌdʒiːsiː'iː] N ABBR (*Brit*: = *General Certificate of Education*) ≈ diploma *m*; **GCE A level** ≈ di maturità.

GCHQ [ˌdʒiːsiːeɪtʃ'kjuː] N ABBR (*Brit*: = *Government Communications Headquarters*) *centro per l'intercettazione delle telecomunicazioni straniere.*

GCSE [ˌdʒiːsiːɛs'iː] N ABBR (*Brit*: = *General Certificate of Secondary Education*) *serie di esami sostenuti alla fine del quinto anno della scuola secondaria in Inghilterra e Galles.*

Gdns. ABBR = *gardens*.

GDP [ˌdʒiːdiː'piː] N ABBR = **gross domestic product**.

GDR [ˌdʒiːdiː'ɑː] N ABBR (*old*) = **German Democratic Republic**.

gear [gɪə] ① N **a** (*Aut*: *mechanism*) cambio; (: *speed*) marcia; **in gear** in marcia; **the car is in gear** la marcia è innestata; **out of gear** in folle; **first** *or* **bottom gear** prima; **low gear** marcia bassa; **top gear**, (*Am*) **high gear** marcia alta; **to put the car into gear** innestare *or* ingranare la marcia; **to change gear** cambiare marcia; **she changed into second gear** ha messo *or* ingranato la seconda; **to move into top gear** ingranare la quinta; **production has moved into high** *or* **top gear** la produzione ha subito una forte accelerazione
b (*equipment*) attrezzatura, equipaggiamento; (*belongings*) roba, cose *fpl*; (*clothing*) vestiti *mpl*; **dressed in the latest gear** (*fam*) bardato(-a) all'ultima moda
c (*Tech*) ruota dentata.
② VT (*fig*: *adapt*) adattare; **the book is geared to adult students** il libro si rivolge a studenti di età adulta; **our service is geared to meet the needs of the disabled** la nostra organizzazione risponde espressamente alle esigenze degli handicappati
▶ **gear up** VI + ADV: **to gear up (to do)** prepararsi (a fare); **we are geared up (and ready) to do it** siamo tutti pronti a farlo.

gear·box ['gɪəˌbɒks] N (*Aut*) scatola del cambio.

♦ **gear lever**, (*Am*) **gear·shift** ['gɪəˌʃɪft] N leva del cambio.

♦ **gear ratio** N (*Cycling*) moltiplica.

♦ **gear stick** N leva del cambio.

gear·wheel ['gɪəˌwiːl] N ruota dentata.

GED [ˌdʒiːiː'diː] N ABBR (*Am Scol*)= *general educational development*.

gee [dʒiː] EXCL (*Am*) cribbio.

geese [giːs] NPL of **goose**.

gee·zer ['giːzə] N (*Brit fam*) tizio.

Geiger count·er ['gaɪgəˌkaʊntə] N (contatore *m*) geiger *m inv*.

gel [dʒɛl] N gel *m inv*.

gela·tine ['dʒɛləˌtiːn], **gela·tin** ['dʒɛlətɪn] N gelatina; **in gelatin(e)** in gelatina.

geld·ing ['gɛldɪŋ] N castrone *m*.

gel·ig·nite ['dʒɛlɪgˌnaɪt] N gelatina esplosiva, gelignite *f*.

gem [dʒɛm] N gemma, pietra preziosa; (*fig*: *person*) gioiello, perla; **I must read you this gem** (*fam*) senti questa perla.

Gemi·ni ['dʒɛmɪˌnaɪ] N Gemelli *mpl*; **to be Gemini** essere dei Gemelli.

gem·ol·ogy [dʒɛ'mɒlədʒɪ] N gemmologia.

gem·stone ['dʒɛmˌstəʊn] N gemma, pietra preziosa.

gen [dʒɛn] N (*Brit fam*): **to give sb the gen on sth** mettere qn al corrente di qc.

Gen. ABBR (*Mil*: = *General*) Gen.

gen. ABBR (= *general; generally*) gen.

gen·darme ['ʒɒndɑːm] N (*French policeman*) gendarme *m inv*.

gen·der ['dʒɛndə] N (*Gram*) genere *m*; (*frm*: *sex*) sesso.

gene [dʒiːn] N (*Bio*) gene *m*.

ge·nea·logi·cal [ˌdʒiːnɪə'lɒdʒɪkəl] ADJ genealogico(-a).

ge·nealo·gist [ˌdʒiːnɪ'ælədʒɪst] N genealogista *m/f*.

ge·neal·ogy [ˌdʒiːnɪ'ælədʒɪ] N genealogia.

gen·er·al ['dʒɛnərəl] ① ADJ (*gen*) generale; (*not detailed*: *plan, view*) generale, complessivo(-a); (: *enquiry*) generico(-a); (*not specialized*: *trader, store*) di generi vari; **in general use** d'uso comune *or* corrente; **in general terms** in termini generici, in generale; **as a general rule** di norma, di regola; **the general idea is to ...** l'idea base sarebbe di....
② ADV: **in general** (*usually*) generalmente; (*as a whole*) nel complesso.
③ N (*Mil*) generale *m*.

♦ **general anaesthetic** N anestesia totale.

♦ **general delivery** N (*Am*) fermo posta *m*.

♦ **general election** N elezioni *fpl* politiche.

♦ **general headquarters** NPL (*Mil*) quartier *msg* generale.

♦ **general hospital** N ospedale *m* generico, policlinico.

gen·er·al·ity [ˌdʒɛnə'rælɪtɪ] N (*frm*) principio generale; **to talk in generalities** parlare in termini generici.

gen·er·ali·za·tion [ˌdʒɛnərəlaɪ'zeɪʃən] N (*often pej*) generalizzazione *f*.

gen·er·al·ize ['dʒɛnərəˌlaɪz] VI: **to generalize (about)** generalizzare (per quel che riguarda); **to generalize from** generalizzare sulla base di.

♦ **general knowledge** N cultura generale.

gen·er·al·ly ['dʒɛnərəlɪ] ADV (*usually*) in genere, di solito, generalmente; (*for the most part*) nel complesso; **he's generally disliked** è antipatico a tutti; **generally speaking** in genere.

♦ **general manager** N direttore *m* generale.

♦ **General Post Office** N (*building*) Posta Centrale; (*Brit*: *organization*) ≈ Poste *fpl* e Telegrafi.

♦ **general practice** N: **to go into general practice** fare il medico generico.

♦ **general practitioner** N medico generico; (*personal doctor*) medico di famiglia.

♦ **general public** N: **the general public** il grande pubblico.

♦ **general-purpose** ['dʒɛnərəl'pɜːpəs] ADJ per tutti gli usi.

♦ **general secretary** N segretario(-a) generale.

♦ **general staff** N (*Mil*) stato maggiore.

♦ **general strike** N sciopero generale.

gen·er·ate ['dʒɛnəˌreɪt] VT generare.

gen·era·tion [ˌdʒɛnə'reɪʃən] N **a** (*age group*) generazione *f*; **the younger/older generation** la nuova/vecchia generazione; **the generation gap** il gap *m inv* generazionale **b** (*of electricity*) produzione *f*.

gen·era·tive ['dʒɛnərətɪv] ADJ (*Ling*) generativo(-a).

gen·era·tor ['dʒɛnəˌreɪtə] N generatore *m*.

ge·ner·ic [dʒɪ'nɛrɪk] ADJ generico(-a).

ge·neri·cal·ly [dʒɪ'nɛrɪkəlɪ] ADV genericamente.

gen·er·os·ity [ˌdʒɛnə'rɒsɪtɪ] N generosità.

gen·er·ous ['dʒɛnərəs] ADJ (gen) generoso(-a); (plentiful: supply, quantity) abbondante, generoso(-a); **to be generous with sth** essere prodigo(-a) di qc.

gen·er·ous·ly ['dʒɛnərəslɪ] ADV generosamente.

gen·esis ['dʒɛnɪsɪs] N genesi f; **Genesis** (Bible) la Genesi.

ge·net·ic [dʒɪ'nɛtɪk] ADJ genetico(-a).

ge·neti·cal·ly [dʒɪ'nɛtɪkəlɪ] ADV geneticamente.

♦ **genetic code** N codice m genetico.

♦ **genetic engineering** N ingegneria genetica.

♦ **ge·net·ic finger·print·ing** [dʒɪ'nɛtɪk'fɪŋgə,prɪntɪŋ] N rilevamento delle impronte genetiche.

ge·neti·cist [dʒɪ'nɛtɪsɪst] N genetista m/f.

ge·net·ics [dʒɪ'nɛtɪks] NSG genetica.

Ge·neva [dʒɪ'ni:və] N Ginevra; **Lake Geneva** il lago di Ginevra.

Ge·nevan [dʒɪ'ni:vən] ADJ, N ginevrino(-a).

gen·ial ['dʒi:nɪəl] ADJ (manner, person) cordiale, affabile.

ge·ni·al·ity [,dʒi:nɪ'ælɪtɪ] N cordialità, affabilità.

gen·ial·ly ['dʒi:nɪəlɪ] ADV cordialmente, affabilmente.

ge·nie ['dʒi:nɪ] N genio.

geni·ta·lia [,dʒɛnɪ'teɪlɪə] N (frm) genitali mpl.

geni·tals ['dʒɛnɪtlz] NPL genitali mpl.

geni·tive ['dʒɛnɪtɪv] ① ADJ genitivo(-a).
② N genitivo; **in the genitive** al genitivo.

ge·ni·us ['dʒi:nɪəs] N genio; **to have a genius for sth/for doing sth** essere molto bravo(-a) in qc/a fare qc.

genned up ['dʒɛnd'ʌp] ADJ (Brit) al corrente.

Genoa ['dʒɛnəʊə] N Genova.

genoa ['dʒɛnəʊə] N (Naut) genoa m inv.

geno·cide ['dʃɛnəʊ,saɪd] N genocidio.

Geno·ese ['dʒɛnəʊ'i:z] ADJ, N, PL INV genovese (m/f).

geno·type ['dʒɛnəʊ'taɪp] N genotipo.

gen·re ['ʒã:nrə] N (frm) genere m.

gent [dʒɛnt] N ABBR (Brit fam: = gentleman) signore m.

gen·teel [dʒɛn'ti:l] ADJ (affectedly polite) affettato(-a); (old: refined) distinto(-a), raffinato(-a).

Gen·tile ['dʒɛntaɪl] N, ADJ gentile (m/f); (non-Jewish) non ebreo(-a).

gen·til·ity [dʒɛn'tɪlɪtɪ] N (see adj) affettazione f; distinzione f.

gen·tle ['dʒɛntl] ADJ (comp **-r**, superl **-st**) (person, slope, voice) dolce; (touch) delicato(-a); (hint, reminder) velato (-a); (rebuke) discreto(-a); (heat, exercise) moderato(-a); (breeze, sound) leggero(-a); **to be gentle with sb** trattare qn con delicatezza.

gentle·man ['dʒɛntlmən] N (pl **-men**) signore m; (well-mannered, well-bred man) gentiluomo, signore m; **gentlemen!** signori!; **(to be) a perfect gentleman** (dimostrarsi) un vero gentiluomo; **gentleman's agreement** impegno sulla parola, gentleman's agreement m inv.

♦ **gentleman farmer** N signorotto di campagna.

gentle·man·ly ['dʒɛntlmənlɪ] ADJ da gentiluomo.

gen·tle·ness ['dʒɛntlnɪs] N (see adj) dolcezza; delicatezza; discrezione f; leggerezza.

gen·tly ['dʒɛntlɪ] ADV (say, smile) dolcemente; (touch) lievemente, delicatamente; **gently does it!** piano!

gen·try ['dʒɛntrɪ] NPL piccola nobiltà.

gents [dʒɛnts] N (fam: public toilet) toilette f inv or bagno degli uomini.

genu·flect ['dʒɛnjʊ,flɛkt] VI genuflettersi.

genu·ine ['dʒɛnjʊɪn] ADJ **a** (person, belief) sincero(-a) **b** (authentic: leather, silver) vero(-a); (: painting, antique) autentico(-a).

genu·ine·ly ['dʒɛnjʊɪnlɪ] ADV (believe, welcome) sinceramente, veramente.

ge·nus ['dʒɛnəs] N (pl **genera** ['dʒɛnərə]) genere m.

ge·og·ra·pher [dʒɪ'ɒgrəfə'] N geografo(-a).

geo·graph·ic [dʒɪə'græfɪk], **geo·graph·ical** [dʒɪə'græfɪkəl] ADJ geografico(-a).

geo·graphi·cal·ly [,dʒɪə'græfɪkəlɪ] ADV geograficamente.

ge·og·ra·phy [dʒɪ'ɒgrəfɪ] N geografia.

geo·logi·cal [dʒɪəʊ'lɒdʒɪkəl] ADJ geologico(-a).

geo·logi·cal·ly [,dʒɪəʊ'lɒdʒɪkəlɪ] ADV geologicamente.

ge·olo·gist [dʒɪ'ɒlədʒɪst] N geologo(-a).

ge·ol·ogy [dʒɪ'ɒlədʒɪ] N geologia.

geo·met·rical [dʒɪəʊ'mɛtrɪkəl], **geo·met·ric** [dʒɪəʊ'mɛtrɪk] ADJ geometrico(-a).

geo·met·ri·cal·ly [,dʒɪə'mɛtrɪkəlɪ] ADV geometricamente.

♦ **geometric mean** N media geometrica.

♦ **geometric progression** N progressione f geometrica.

ge·om·etry [dʒɪ'ɒmɪtrɪ] N geometria.

geo·phys·ics [,dʒi:əʊ'fɪzɪks] NSG geofisica.

geo·poli·tics [,dʒi:əʊ'pɒlɪtɪks] N geopolitica.

Geor·die ['dʒɔ:dɪ] (fam) ① ADJ di Tyneside.
② N abitante m/f or originario(-a) del Tyneside.

Geor·gia ['dʒɔ:dʒɪə] N Georgia.

Geor·gian ['dʒɔ:dʒən] ① ADJ (History, Geog) georgiano (-a).
② N (Geog) georgiano(-a); (language) georgiano.

geo·syn·cline [,dʒi:əʊ'sɪnklaɪn] N geosinclinale f.

ge·ot·ro·pism [dʒɪ'ɒtrə,pɪzəm] N geotropismo.

ge·ra·nium [dʒɪ'reɪnɪəm] N geranio.

ger·bil ['dʒɜ:bɪl] N gerbillo.

geri·at·ric [,dʒɛrɪ'ætrɪk] ADJ geriatrico(-a).

geri·at·rics [,dʒɛrɪ'ætrɪks] NSG geriatria.

germ [dʒɜ:m] N (Med) microbo; (Bio, also fig) germe m.

Ger·man ['dʒɜ:mən] ① ADJ tedesco(-a).
② N **a** (person) tedesco(-a) **b** (language) tedesco.

♦ **German Democratic Republic** N (formerly) Repubblica Democratica Tedesca.

ger·mane [dʒɜ:'meɪn] ADJ (frm): **to be germane to sth** essere attinente a qc.

Ger·man·ic [dʒɜ:'mænɪk] ADJ germanico(-a).

♦ **German measles** N rosolia.

Ger·ma·ny ['dʒɜ:mənɪ] N Germania; **East/West Germany** Germania dell'Est/dell'Ovest.

♦ **germ-free** ['dʒɜ:m,fri:] ADJ asettico(-a).

ger·mi·cid·al [,dʒɜ:mɪ,saɪdl] ADJ germicida.

ger·mi·cide ['dʒɜ:mɪ,saɪd] N germicida m.

ger·mi·nate ['dʒɜ:mɪ,neɪt] VI germinare, germogliare.

ger·mi·na·tion [dʒɜ:mɪ'neɪʃən] N germinazione f.

♦ **germ warfare** N guerra batteriologica.

ger·on·tolo·gist [,dʒɛrɒn'tɒlədʒɪst] N gerontologo(-a).

ger·on·tol·ogy [,dʒɛrɒn'tɒlədʒɪ] N gerontologia.

ger·ry·man·der·ing [,dʒɛrɪ'mændərɪŋ] N alterazione del confine dei distretti elettorali che avvantaggia un solo partito.

ger·und ['dʒɛrənd] N gerundio.

ge·run·dive [dʒɪ'rʌndɪv] ① ADJ gerundivo(-a).
② N gerundivo.

ge·stalt [gə'ʃtɑ:lt] N gestalt f inv.

♦ **gestalt psychology** N gestaltismo.

ges·tate [dʒɛs'teɪt] VI essere in gravidanza.

ges·ta·tion [dʒɛs'teɪʃən] N (Bio) gestazione f.

ges·ticu·late [dʒɛs'tɪkjʊ,leɪt] VI gesticolare.

ges·ture ['dʒɛstʃə'] ① N gesto; **as a gesture of friendship** in segno d'amicizia.
② VI: **he gestured towards the door** fece un gesto verso la porta; **to gesture to sb to do sth** far segno a qn di

fare qc.

get [gɛt] (*vb: pt, pp* **got**, *pp (Am)* **gotten**)
1 VT
a (*obtain by effort: money, visa*) ottenere, procurarsi; (: *results, permission*) avere, ottenere; (*find: job, flat*) trovare; (*buy*) comprare, prendere; (*fetch: person, doctor*) chiamare; (: *object*) prendere; (*Telec: number*) avere; (*TV, Radio: channel, station*) prendere;
▷**to get** *breakfast* preparare la colazione
▷**can I get you a** *drink*? bevi qualcosa?
▷**to get sth** *for* **sb** prendere *or* procurare qc a qn
▷**I'll get it** *for* **you** vado a prendertelo io
▷**I've still got** *one* **to get** me ne manca ancora uno
▷**I've been trying to get** *you* **(on the phone) all morning** ti ho cercato tutta la mattina al telefono
b (*receive: present, letter*) ricevere; (: *prize*) ricevere, vincere; (*acquire: reputation*) farsi
▷**how much did you get** *for* **it?** quanto ti hanno dato?
▷**he got 5 years** *for* **robbery** si è beccato 5 anni per rapina
▷**he gets it** *from* **his father** in questo prende da suo padre
▷**where did you get that idea** *from*? come ti sei fatta quest'idea?
▷**I didn't get much** *from* **the film** quel film non mi è parso un granché
▷**get it** *into* **your head that ...** mettiti bene in testa che...
▷**I'll get** *it*! (*phone*) rispondo io!; (*door*) vado io!
▷**this room gets very little** *sun* questa stanza è poco soleggiata
▷**he's in it for** *what* **he can get** lo fa per interesse
c (*catch*) prendere, acchiappare; (*hit: target*) colpire;
▷**the** *bullet* **got him in the leg** il proiettile l'ha colpito alla gamba
▷**to get sb** *by* **the arm/throat** afferrare qn per un braccio/alla gola
▷**I'll get you** *for* **that!** (*fam*) ti faccio vedere io!
▷**you've got** *me* **there!** (*fam*) m'hai preso in castagna!
▷**got** *you*! (*fam*) beccato!
d (*take, move*) portare;
▷**crying won't get you** *anywhere* piangere non serve a niente
▷**the discussion got us** *nowhere* la discussione non è servita a nulla
▷**to get sth** *past* **customs** riuscire a far passare qc alla dogana
▷**we'll get you** *there* **somehow** in un modo o nell'altro ti ci portiamo
▷**to get sth** *to* **sb** far avere qc a qn
▷**I'll never get this** *upstairs* non riuscirò mai a portarlo di sopra
▷*where* **will that get us?** (*fam*) ma a che pro?
e (*understand*) afferrare, capire, comprendere; (*hear*) sentire;
▷**I've got** *it*! ci sono arrivato!, ci sono!
▷**get** *it*? (*fam*) capito?
▷**I don't get** *it* (*fam*) non capisco, non ci arrivo
▷**sorry, I didn't get your** *name* scusi, non ho capito il suo nome
f (*fam: annoy*) dare ai nervi a
g (*fam: thrill*) toccare
h (*have, possess*): **to** *have* **got** avere

▷**how many** *have* **you** *got*? quanti ne hai?
i: **to get sth** *done* (*do o.s.*) fare qc; (*have done by sb else*) far fare qc
▷**I wonder how he got his leg** *broken* mi chiedo come abbia fatto a rompersi la gamba
▷**to get one's hair** *cut* farsi tagliare i capelli
▷**to get one's hands** *dirty* sporcarsi le mani
▷**to get the washing/dishes** *done* fare il bucato/i piatti
▷**to get sb** *drunk* (far) ubriacare qn
▷**to get the car** *going or to go* mettere in moto *or* far partire la macchina
▷**to get sb/sth** *ready* preparare qn/qc
▷**to get sb** *to do* **sth** far fare qc a qn
▷**I can't get the lock** *to turn* non riesco a far scattare la serratura.
2 VI
a (*go*) andare; (*reach*) arrivare;
▷**I've got** *as far as* **page 10** sono arrivato (fino) a pagina 10
▷**he won't get** *far* non andrà lontano
▷**to get** *from* andare da
▷**how did you get** *here*? come sei venuto?
▷**to get** *home* arrivare *or* tornare a casa
▷**to get** *nowhere* (*fig*) non approdare a nulla
▷**to get** *somewhere* avere dei risultati
▷**to get** *to* andare a; (*reach*) arrivare a
b (*become, be*) diventare, farsi;
▷**to get** (o.s.) *dirty* sporcarsi
▷**to get** *killed* venire *or* rimanere ucciso(-a)
▷**it's getting** *late* si sta facendo tardi
▷**how did it get** *like that*? (*fam*) come ha fatto a ridursi così?
▷**to get** *married* sposarsi
▷**to get** *old* invecchiare
▷**when do I get** *paid*? quando mi pagate?
▷**to get** *tired* stancarsi
▷**to get** *used* **to sth** abituarsi a qc
▷**I'm not getting any** *younger*! il tempo passa anche per me!
c (*begin*) mettersi a, cominciare a;
▷**let's get** *going or started* muoviamoci!
▷**to get** *talking* **to sb** mettersi a parlare con *or* a qn
▷**to get** *to know* **sb** cominciare a conoscere meglio qn
▷**I'm getting** *to like* **him** incomincia a piacermi
d MODAL AUX VB
▷**why have I got** *to do* **it?** perché devo farlo?
▷**you've got** *to tell* **the police** devi dirlo alla polizia
e (*be allowed to*)
▷**I never get** *to go* **on holiday on my own** non riesco mai ad andare in vacanza da sola

▶ **get about** VI + ADV (*go out: socially, after illness*) uscire, muoversi; (*fig: news, rumour*) spargersi, diffondersi
▶ **get across 1** VT + ADV far capire;
to get sth across to sb (*message, meaning*) comunicare qc a qn.
2 VI + ADV **a** (*cross road*) attraversare
b : **to get across to** comunicare con
▶ **get after** VT + PREP inseguire
▶ **get ahead** VI + ADV andare avanti, farsi strada;
to get ahead of sb sorpassare *or* superare qn
▶ **get along** VI + ADV **a** (*leave*) andarsene, scappare;

get along with you! vattene!
b (*progress*) procedere; (*manage*) farcela, cavarsela;
how is your son getting along at school? come va tuo
figlio a scuola?
c (*to be on good terms*) essere in buoni rapporti;
to get along well with sb andare d'accordo con qn
▶ **get around** [1] VI + ADV **a** = **get about**
b = **get round 2.**
[2] VI + PREP = **get round 1**
▶ **get at** VI + PREP **a** (*gain access to*: *object*) arrivare a
(prendere); (: *place*) raggiungere, arrivare a; (*ascertain*:
facts, truth) accertare, scoprire;
just let me get at him! (*fam*) lascia che mi capiti fra le
mani!
b : **to get at sb** (*fam*: *criticize, attack*) prendersela con qn
c (*fam*: *imply*) avere in mente; .
what are you getting at? dove vuoi arrivare?
▶ **get away** VI + ADV (*depart*) partire; (*go on holiday*) andar
via;
to get away (from) (*work, party*) andarsene (da) (*escape*)
liberarsi (da), scappare (da)
to get away from it all andarsene lontano da tutto e da
tutti
there's no getting away from it (*fam*) non c'è niente da
fare
▶ **get away with** VI + ADV + PREP **a** (*steal*) dileguarsi con
b (*fam*: *go unpunished*): **to get away with sth/with doing
sth** fare qc e passarla liscia
he'll never get away with it! non riuscirà a passarla
liscia!
to get away with murder essere libero(-a) di fare tutto
quello che si vuole
▶ **get back** [1] VT + ADV **a** (*recover*: *possessions*) recuperare; (: *sth borrowed*) farsi restituire; (: *strength*)
riprendere
b (*return*: *object, person*) riportare.
[2] VI + ADV (ri)tornare;
get back! indietro!
to get back (home) ritornare a casa, rincasare
to get back to (*start again*) ritornare a; (*contact again*)
rimettersi in contatto con
to get back to sleep riaddormentarsi
▶ **get back at** VI + ADV + PREP (*fam*): **to get back at sb (for
sth)** rendere pan per focaccia a qn (per qc)
▶ **get behind** VI + ADV rimanere indietro
▶ **get by** VI + ADV **a** (*pass*) passare
b (*manage*) cavarsela; (*be acceptable*) essere passabile;
I can get by in Dutch mi arrangio in olandese
don't worry, he'll get by non preoccuparti, se la caverà
▶ **get down** [1] VT + ADV **a** (*take down*) tirar giù
b (*swallow*) mandar giù
c (*note down*) prender nota di
d (*fam*: *depress*) buttar giù;
don't let it get you down non devi abbatterti per questo.
[2] VI + ADV (*descend*): **to get down (from** *or* **off)** scendere
(da);
quick, get down! giù presto!
▶ **get down to** VI + PREP: **to get down to (doing) sth**
mettersi a (fare) qc;
to get down to business venire al dunque
▶ **get in** [1] VT + ADV **a** (*bring in*: *harvest*) raccogliere; (*buy,
obtain*: *coal, shopping, supplies*) fare provvista di
b (*plant*: *bulbs, seeds*) piantare
c (*summon*: *expert*) chiamare, far venire
d (*insert*: *object*) far entrare, infilare; (: *comment, word*)

infilare.
[2] VI + ADV **a** (*enter*) entrare
b (*arrive*: *train*) arrivare; (*reach home*: *person*) rientrare
c (*be admitted*: *to club*) entrare; (*be elected*: *party*) salire
al potere; (: *MP*) essere eletto(-a);
he got in with a bad crowd si è messo con una banda di
cattivi soggetti
▶ **get in on** VI + ADV + PREP (*fam*) intrufolarsi in
▶ **get into** VI + PREP (*house, clothes*) entrare in; (*vehicle*)
salire in, montare in; (*club*) entrare in, essere ammesso
(-a) a;
to get into difficulties trovarsi in difficoltà
to get into trouble ficcarsi nei guai
to get into the habit of doing sth prendere l'abitudine di
fare qc
to get into bed mettersi a letto
to get into a rage andare su tutte le furie
▶ **get off** [1] VT + ADV **a** (*remove*: *clothes, stain*) levare,
togliere
b (*send off*) spedire;
she got the baby off to sleep ha fatto addormentare il
bambino
c (*save from punishment*) far assolvere, tirar fuori
d (*have as holiday*: *day, time*) prendersi;
we got 2 days off abbiamo avuto 2 giorni liberi.
[2] VI + PREP (*bus, train, plane, bike*) scendere da; (*fam*:
escape: *chore, lessons*) evitare, sfuggire a.
[3] VI + ADV **a** (*from bus, train, plane, bike*) scendere;
to tell sb where to get off (*fam*) dire a qn di andare a farsi
benedire
to get off to a good start (*fig*) cominciare bene
b (*depart*: *person*) andare via
c (*escape injury, punishment*) cavarsela;
he got off with a fine se l'è cavata con una multa
d (*from work*) staccare
▶ **get off with** VI + ADV + PREP (*fam*: *start relationship with*)
mettersi con
▶ **get on** [1] VI + PREP (*vehicle*): **to get on the bus/train** salire
or montare in autobus/in treno, salire *or* montare
sull'autobus/sul treno;
to get on a horse montare a cavallo
[2] VI + ADV **a** (*mount*) montare, salire
b : **to get on (with sth)** (*proceed*) continuare a fare (qc);
get on with it! su, muoviti!
c (*progress*) far progressi; (*fare*: *in exam, interview*): **how
did you get on?** com'è andata?
how are you getting on? come va (la vita)?
to be getting on (*person*) essere avanti negli anni
he's getting on for 70 va per i 70
time is getting on si sta facendo tardi
d (*succeed*) farsi strada
e (*be on good terms*): **to get on (with sb)** andare
d'accordo (con qn)
▶ **get on to** VI + ADV + PREP (*fam*: *contact*: *on phone*)
contattare, rintracciare; (*deal with*) occuparsi di
▶ **get out** [1] VT + ADV: **to get out (of)** (*take out*) tirare fuori
(da); (*money*: *from bank*) ritirare (da); (*stain*) levare (da),
togliere (da); (*book*: *from library*) prendere in prestito
(da);
get those children out of here! leva quei bambini di
torno!
[2] VI + ADV (*news*) venirsi a sapere, spargersi: **to get out
(of)** (*go out*) uscire (da); (*leave*) andar via (da), uscire
(da); (*from vehicle*) scendere (da); (*escape*) scappare (da)
▶ **get out of** [1] VT + ADV + PREP (*extract*: *confession, words*)

tirare fuori di bocca a; (*gain from: pleasure, benefit*) trarre da;
to get sb out of bed far alzare qn.
2 VI + ADV + PREP **a** see also **get out 2**; (*difficulty*) togliersi da; (*escape: duty, punishment*) sottrarsi a
b : **to get out of the habit of doing sth** perdere l'abitudine di fare qc
▶ **get over** 1 VI + ADV (*cross*) attraversare.
2 VI + PREP **a** (*cross*) attraversare
b (*recover from: illness*) riprendersi da, rimettersi da; (: *disappointment*) superare; (: *surprise, shock*) riaversi da; **I can't get over it!** non riesco a crederci!
you'll get over it! ti passerà!
c (*overcome: difficulty*) superare; (: *shyness*) vincere.
3 VT + ADV **a** (*transport across*) far passare
b (*have done with*) finire una buona volta;
let's get it over (with) facciamolo, così ci togliamo il pensiero
c (*communicate: idea*) comunicare, passare
▶ **get round** 1 VI + PREP (*difficulty, problem*) aggirare, superare; (*law, regulation*) eludere; (*fig: person*) rigirare; **she knows how to get round him** sa come prenderlo.
2 VI + ADV: **to get round to doing sth** trovare il tempo di fare qc;
I'll get round to it prima o poi lo farò
▶ **get through** 1 VI + PREP **a** (*pass through: window*) passare per *or* da; (: *crowd*) passare attraverso, farsi strada attraverso
b (*finish: work*) sbrigare; (: *book*) finire; (*use up: food, money*) far fuori, dar fondo a;
we got through a lot of work today abbiamo sbrigato molto lavoro oggi
c (*pass: exam*) passare.
2 VT + PREP (*cause to succeed: student*) far passare; (: *proposal, bill*) far passare a, far approvare a.
3 VT + ADV (*succeed in sending: message, supplies*) far arrivare *or* pervenire; (*Pol: bill*) far passare *or* approvare.
4 VI + ADV **a** (*pass through*) passare; (*news, supplies: arrive*) raggiungere
b (*pass, be accepted*) passare;
they got through to the semifinal sono entrati in semifinale
c (*finish*) finire, terminare
d (*Telec*) ottenere la comunicazione *or* la linea;
to get through to sb mettersi in contatto con qn (*fig: communicate with*) comunicare con qn
▶ **get together** 1 VT + ADV (*people*) radunare; (*objects, thoughts, ideas*) raccogliere.
2 VI + ADV (*group, club*) riunirsi;
to get together about sth vedersi per discutere qc
▶ **get up** 1 VI + ADV **a** (*rise: from chair, bed*) alzarsi; (*wind*) alzarsi, levarsi
b (*climb up*) salire.
2 VT + ADV **a** (*person: from chair, floor*) sollevare, tirar su; (: *wake*) far alzare, svegliare
b (*gather: strength, speed*) prendere;
to get up enthusiasm for sth entusiasmarsi per qc
c (*fam: organize: celebrations*) organizzare
d (*fam: dress up: person*): **to get o.s. up in** farsi bello(-a) con
to get o.s. up as travestirsi da.
3 VI + PREP (*tree*) arrampicarsi su; (*ladder*) salire su per
▶ **get up to** VI + ADV + PREP **a** (*reach*) raggiungere, arrivare a;
I've got up to chapter 4 sono arrivato *or* sono al

capitolo 4
b : **to get up to mischief** combinarne di tutti i colori;
what have you been getting up to? cosa hai combinato?
♦ **get-at-able** [ˌgɛtˈætəbl] ADJ (*fam*) accessibile.
♦ **get·away** [ˈgɛtəˌweɪ] N: **to make one's getaway** darsi alla fuga.
♦ **getaway car** N macchina per la fuga.
Geth·sema·ne [gɛθˈsɛmənɪ] N Getsemani *m*.
♦ **get-together** [ˈgɛttəˌgɛðəʳ] N (piccola) riunione *f*; (*party*) festicciola.
♦ **get-up** [ˈgɛtˌʌp] N (*fam: outfit*) tenuta.
♦ **get-well card** [gɛtˈwɛlˌkɑːd] N cartolina di auguri di pronta guarigione.
gey·ser [ˈgiːzəʳ] N (*Geog*) geyser *m inv*; (*water heater*) scaldabagno.
Gha·na [ˈgɑːnə] N Gana *m*.
Gha·na·ian [gɑːˈneɪən] 1 ADJ del Ghana, ganaense.
2 N ganaense *m/f*.
ghast·ly [ˈgɑːstlɪ] ADJ (*horrible*) atroce, spaventoso(-a); (*pale*) spettrale; (*fam: very bad: mistake, experience*) pauroso(-a); **we had a ghastly time last night** è stata una serata orribile ieri sera.
gher·kin [ˈgɜːkɪn] N cetriolino.
ghet·to [ˈgɛtəʊ] N ghetto.
♦ **ghetto blaster** N maxistereo portatile.
ghost [gəʊst] 1 N fantasma *m*, spettro; **the ghost of a smile** (*fig*) una parvenza di sorriso; **he hasn't the ghost of a chance** (*fig*) non ha la minima possibilità.
2 VT (*book*) scrivere per conto di altri.
ghost·ly [ˈgəʊstlɪ] ADJ spettrale; **a ghostly apparition** uno spettro.
♦ **ghost story** N storia di fantasmi.
♦ **ghost town** N città *f inv* fantasma *inv*.
ghost·writ·er [ˈgəʊstˌraɪtəʳ] N ghost writer *m/f inv*, scrittore (-trice) fantasma *inv*.
ghoul [guːl] N *vampiro che si nutre di cadaveri*; **she's a ghoul** (*fig*) ha proprio il gusto del macabro.
ghoul·ish [ˈguːlɪʃ] ADJ (*tastes*) macabro(-a).
ghoul·ish·ly [ˌguːlɪʃlɪ] ADV in modo macabro, morbosamente.
GHQ [ˌdʒiːeɪtʃˈkjuː] N ABBR (*Mil*: = *general headquarters*) Q.G. (= *quartier generale*).
GI [ˌdʒiːˈaɪ] N ABBR (*Am fam*: = *government issue*) *soldato americano*.
gi·ant [ˈdʒaɪənt] 1 N gigante(-essa); (*fig*) gigante *m*, colosso.
2 ADJ (*fern, panda*) gigante; (*strides*) da gigante; **giant (size) packet** confezione *f* gigante.
♦ **giant killer** N (*Sport*) *atleta o squadra minore che riesce a battere un avversario più forte*.
♦ **giant slalom** N (*Skiing*) slalom *m inv* gigante.
gib·ber [ˈdʒɪbəʳ] VI (*monkey*) squittire confusamente; (*idiot*) farfugliare; **to gibber with rage** non connettere più dalla rabbia.
gib·ber·ish [ˈdʒɪbərɪʃ] N parole *f pl* senza senso.
gib·bet [ˈdʒɪbɪt] N patibolo.
gib·bon [ˈgɪbən] N gibbone *m*.
gibe [dʒaɪb] 1 N frecciata, malignità *f inv*.
2 VI: **to gibe (at)** lanciare frecciate (a).
gib·lets [ˈdʒɪblɪts] NPL rigaglie *f pl*.
Gi·bral·tar [dʒɪˈbrɔːltəʳ] N Gibilterra.
gid·di·ness [ˈgɪdɪnɪs] N vertigini *f pl*; **I had a bout of giddiness** ho avuto un attacco di vertigini.
gid·dy [ˈgɪdɪ] ADJ (*comp* **-ier**, *superl* **-iest**) (*dizzy*): **to be giddy** aver le vertigini; (*causing dizziness: height*) vertiginoso

(-a); (: *speed*) folle; **I feel giddy** mi gira la testa.

gift [gɪft] N **a** (*present*) dono, regalo; (*Comm*: *also*: **free gift**) omaggio; **as a free gift** in omaggio, in dono; **it's a gift!** (*fam*: *easy*) è uno scherzo! **b** (*talent*): **to have a gift for sth** avere il dono di qc.

gift·ed ['gɪftɪd] ADJ: **gifted (at)** dotato(-a) (per).

♦ **gift voucher, gift token** N buono (acquisto *inv*).

gift-wrap ['gɪft,ræp] VT incartare in confezione regalo.

gift-wrap·ping ['gɪft,ræpɪŋ] N confezione *f* regalo *inv*.

gig [gɪg] N (*fam*: *of musician*) serata.

giga·byte ['gaɪgə,baɪt] N gigabyte *m inv*.

gi·gan·tic [dʒaɪ'gæntɪk] ADJ gigantesco(-a).

gig·gle ['gɪgl] 1 N risolino (sciocco); **to get the giggles** farsi prendere dalla risarella.

2 VI ridacchiare (scioccamente), avere la risarella.

gig·gly ['gɪglɪ] ADJ ridanciano(-a).

GIGO ['gaɪgəʊ] ABBR (*Comput*: *fam*: = *garbage in, garbage out*) (= *qualità di input* = *qualità di output*).

gild [gɪld] VT (*metal, frame*) dorare; (*fig*) indorare; **to gild the lily** (*fig*) aggiungere inutili fronzoli.

gild·ed ['gɪldɪd] ADJ dorato(-a).

gill¹ [gɪl] N (*of fish*) branchia; **to be green around the gills** (*fig fam*) essere verde per la paura.

gill² [dʒɪl] N (*measure*) ≈ 0,142 l.

gilt [gɪlt] 1 N doratura.

2 ADJ dorato(-a).

♦ **gilt-edged** ['gɪlt,ɛdʒd] ADJ **a** (*Fin*: *stocks, securities*) della massima sicurezza **b** (*book*) dal taglio dorato.

gim·crack ['dʒɪm,kræk] ADJ (*pej*) dozzinale.

gim·let ['gɪmlɪt] N (*for wood*) succhiello.

gim·mick ['gɪmɪk] N trovata; **sales gimmick** trovata commerciale.

gim·micky ['gɪmɪkɪ] ADJ (*fam*): **a gimmicky film** un film pieno di trovate ad effetto.

gin [dʒɪn] N (*liquor*) gin *m inv*; **gin and tonic** gin tonic *m inv*.

gin·ger ['dʒɪndʒəʳ] 1 N zenzero.

2 ADJ (*hair*) rossiccio(-a); **ginger snap** biscotto allo zenzero

▶ **ginger up** VT + ADV animare.

♦ **ginger ale** N *bibita gassata allo zenzero*.

♦ **ginger beer** N (*Brit*) *bibita leggermente alcolica allo zenzero*.

ginger·bread ['dʒɪndʒə,brɛd] N pan *m* pepato *or* di zenzero.

♦ **gingerbread man** N omino di pan pepato.

♦ **ginger group** N (*Brit*: *within organization*) gruppo di pressione.

♦ **ginger-haired** [,dʒɪndʒə'hɛəd] ADJ rossiccio(-a).

gin·ger·ly ['dʒɪndʒəlɪ] ADV con circospezione, cautamente.

gin·gery ['dʒɪndʒərɪ] ADJ rossiccio(-a).

ging·ham ['gɪŋəm] N (*material*) percalle *m* a righe (*or* quadretti).

gin·seng ['dʒɪnsɛŋ] N ginseng *m inv*.

gip·sy ['dʒɪpsɪ] = **gypsy**.

gi·raffe [dʒɪ'rɑːf] N giraffa.

gird·er ['gɜːdəʳ] N trave *f*.

gir·dle ['gɜːdl] N (*corset*) busto, corsetto; (*belt*) cintura.

girl [gɜːl] N (*child*) bambina, ragazzina; (*young unmarried woman*) signorina, ragazza; (*daughter*) figlia, figliola; (*fam*: *girlfriend*) ragazza; **a little girl** una bambina; **factory girl** operaia; **shop girl** commessa; **the old girl next door** (*fam*) la vecchia qui accanto.

♦ **girl Friday** N impiegata *f* tuttofare *inv*.

girl·friend ['gɜːl,frɛnd] N (*of boy*) ragazza; (*of girl*) amica.

♦ **Girl Guide** N (*Brit*: *old*) = **guide 1b**.

girl·hood ['gɜːl,hʊd] N giovinezza.

girlie ['gɜːlɪ] ADJ (*fam*: *magazine, calendar*) con donnine nude.

girl·ish ['gɜːlɪʃ] ADJ da ragazza.

♦ **Girl Scout** N (*Am*) = **guide 1b**.

Giro ['dʒaɪrəʊ] N: **the National Giro** (*Brit*) ≈ la *or* il Bancoposta.

giro ['dʒaɪrəʊ] N (*Brit fam*: *also*: **giro check**) assegno postale (*per indennità di disoccupazione o malattia*); (*also*: **bank giro**) bancogiro; (*also*: **post office giro**) postagiro.

girth [gɜːθ] N (*for saddle*) sottopancia *m inv*; (*measure*: *of tree*) circonferenza; (: *of person's waist*) (giro) vita.

gist [dʒɪst] N (*of speech, conversation*) succo, nocciolo.

give [gɪv] (*vb*: *pt* **gave**, *pp* **given**) 1 VT **a** (*gen*) dare; (*as gift*) regalare, dare (in dono); (*description, promise, surprise*) fare; (*particulars*) dare, fornire; (*decision*) annunciare; (*title, honour*) conferire, dare; (*assign*: *job*) assegnare, dare; (*dedicate*: *life, time*) consacrare, dedicare; **to give sb sth** *or* **sth to sb** dare qc a qn; **one must give and take** bisogna fare delle concessioni; **how much did you give for it?** quanto (l')hai pagato?; **to give sb a kick/push** dare un calcio/una spinta a qn; **to give sb a cold** passare *or* attaccare il raffreddore a qn; **to give sb news of sth** dar notizie di qc a qn; **to give sb something to eat** dare (qualcosa) da mangiare a qn; **12 o'clock, give or take a few minutes** mezzogiorno, minuto più minuto meno; **give or take ten miles** dieci miglia in più o meno; **to give as good as one gets** rendere pan per focaccia; **he gave it everything he'd got** (*fig*) ce l'ha messa tutta; **I'd give a lot/the world/anything to know** ... (*fam*) darei moltissimo/tutto l'oro del mondo/non so che cosa per sapere...; **I can give you 10 minutes** posso darti 10 minuti; **give them my regards** salutali da parte mia; **give yourself an hour to get there** calcola un'ora per arrivare; **that gave me an idea** mi ha fatto venire un'idea; **he's honest, I'll give you that** è onesto, te lo concedo **b** (*produce*) dare, produrre; (*result, help, advice*) dare; **3 times 4 gives 12** 3 per 4 fa 12; **to give the right/wrong answer** dare la risposta giusta/sbagliata **c** (*perform etc*: *jump, smile*) fare; (*deliver*: *speech, lecture*) fare, tenere; (*utter*: *cry*) lanciare; (: *sigh*) tirare, fare; **give us a song** cantaci qualcosa; **he gave a good performance** (*musician*) è stata una buona esecuzione; (*actor*) ha recitato bene.

2 VI **a** (*give presents*) dare, donare; **to give to charity** fare della beneficenza **b** (*also*: **give way**: *collapse*: *roof, ground, door*) cedere; (: *knees*) piegarsi; **something's got to give!** (*fam*) non si può andare avanti così.

3 N (*of material*) elasticità; (*of bed*) morbidezza

▶ **give away** VT + ADV **a** (*money, goods*) dar via, donare; (*bride*) condurre all'altare; (*distribute*: *prizes*) distribuire **b** (*reveal*: *secret*) rivelare; (*betray*: *person*) tradire; **to give the game away** (*fig*) farsi scoprire

▶ **give back** VT + ADV (*return*: *sb's property*): **to give back (to)** restituire (a), rendere (a), ridare (a)

▶ **give in** 1 VT + ADV (*hand in*: *form, essay*) consegnare; **to give in one's name** dare il proprio nome.

2 VI + ADV (*yield*): **to give in (to sb)** cedere (a qn); (*in guessing game*): **I give in!** mi arrendo!

▶ **give off** VT + ADV (*smell, smoke, heat*) emettere, sprigionare

▶ **give onto** VI + PREP (*subj*: *door, window*) dare su

▶ **give out** 1 VT + ADV **a** (*distribute*) distribuire

b (*make known: news*) annunciare.

② VI + ADV (*be exhausted: supplies*) esaurirsi, venir meno; (*fail: engine*) fermarsi; (: *strength*) mancare; (: *legs*) non reggere più

▶ **give over** ① VT + ADV **a** (*devote*): **to give over to** dedicare a

b (*transfer*): **to give over to** consegnare a.

② VI + ADV (*fam: stop*) piantarla, smetterla; **give over!** piantala!, smettila!

▶ **give up** ① VT + ADV **a** (*surrender: place*) cedere; (*hand over: ticket*) consegnare; **to give o.s. up** arrendersi; **to give o.s. up to the police** costituirsi alla polizia

b (*renounce: friend, boyfriend, job*) lasciare; (*abandon: idea*) rinunciare a, abbandonare; (*abandon hope for: patient*) dare per spacciato(-a); (: *expected visitor*) non aspettare più; **I gave it up as a bad job** (*fam*) ci ho rinunciato, ho abbandonato l'idea; **to give up drinking/smoking** smettere di bere/fumare

c (*devote: one's life, time*): **to give up (to)** dedicare (a); **to give up (for)** (*sacrifice: one's life, career*) donare (per), dare (per).

② VI + ADV (*stop trying*) rinunciare, arrendersi; **I give up!** (*trying to guess*) mi arrendo!

▶ **give way** VI + ADV **a** see **give 2b**

b (*yield*): **to give way (to)** cedere (a); **to give way to despair** lasciarsi andare alla disperazione

c (*make room for*): **to give way (to)** lasciare il posto (a)

d (*Brit Aut*) dare la precedenza.

♦ **give-and-take** [ˌgɪvən'teɪk] N (*fam*) elasticità; **there has to be a bit of give-and-take** bisogna venirsi un po' incontro.

give·away ['gɪvə,weɪ] ① N (*fam*): **her expression was a dead giveaway** le si leggeva tutto in volto; **the exam was a giveaway!** l'esame è stato uno scherzo!.

② ADJ: **giveaway prices** prezzi *mpl* stracciati.

giv·en ['gɪvn] ① PP of **give**.

② ADJ **a** (*fixed: time, amount*) dato(-a), determinato(-a) **b** : **to be given to doing sth** essere incline *or* propenso (-a) a fare qc.

③ CONJ: **given (that)** ... ammesso che..., supposto che...; **given the circumstances** ... date le circosanze...; **given time, it would be possible** se ci fosse tempo, sarebbe possibile.

♦ **given name** N (*esp Am*) nome *m* di battesimo.

giv·er ['gɪvəʳ] N donatore(-trice).

gla·cé ['glæseɪ] ADJ (*fruit*) candito(-a).

gla·cial ['gleɪsɪəl] ADJ glaciale; **glacial advance** espansione *f* glaciale; **glacial retreat** ritiro dei ghiacciai.

gla·cia·tion [ˌgleɪsɪ'eɪʃən] N glaciazione *f*.

glaci·er ['glæsɪəʳ] N ghiacciaio.

glad [glæd] ADJ (*comp* **-der**, *superl* **-dest**) (*pleased*) contento(-a), compiaciuto(-a); (*news, occasion*) lieto (-a); **to be glad about sth** essere contento(-a) *or* lieto(-a) di qc/che + *sub*; **I am glad to hear it** mi fa molto piacere, ne sono felice; **I was glad of his help** gli sono stato grato del suo aiuto; **he was only too glad to do it** non chiedeva di meglio che farlo.

glad·den ['glædn] VT rallegrare, allietare.

glade [gleɪd] N radura.

gladia·tor ['glædɪˌeɪtəʳ] N gladiatore *m*.

gladio·lus [ˌglædɪ'əʊləs] N gladiolo.

glad·ly ['glædlɪ] ADV (*joyfully*) lietamente; (*willingly*) con piacere, volentieri.

glad·ness ['glædnɪs] N contentezza, felicità.

glad·rags ['glæd,rægz] NPL (*fam*) vestito della festa; **she's**

in her gladrags tonight è tutta in ghingheri stasera.

glam·or·ize ['glæmə,raɪz] VT (*job, event, place*) far apparire (più) prestigioso(-a).

glam·or·ous, glam·our·ous ['glæmərəs] ADJ (*gen*) favoloso(-a); (*person*) affascinante; (*occasion*) brillante, elegante.

glam·our, (*Am*) **glam·or** ['glæməʳ] N fascino.

♦ **glamour girl,** (*Am*) **glamor girl** N cover girl *f inv*.

glance [glɑːns] ① N sguardo, occhiata; **to take** *or* **have a glance at** dare un'occhiata a; **at a glance** a colpo d'occhio; **at first glance** a prima vista; **without a backward glance** senza voltarsi indietro; (*fig*) senza rimpianti.

② VI (*look*): **to glance at** (*person*) lanciare uno sguardo *or* un'occhiata a; (*headlines*) dare uno sguardo *or* un'occhiata a; **to glance away** distogliere lo sguardo; **to glance through a report** dare una scorsa a un rapporto

▶ **glance off** VI + PREP (*bullet*): **to glance off sth** rimbalzare di striscio su qc.

glanc·ing ['glɑːnsɪŋ] ADJ (*blow*) di striscio.

gland [glænd] N (*Anat*) ghiandola.

glan·du·lar ['glændjʊləʳ] ADJ ghiandolare.

♦ **glandular fever** N mononucleosi *f inv*.

glare [gleəʳ] ① N **a** (*of light, sun*) luce *f or* bagliore *m* accecante; **the glare of publicity** (*fig*) il chiasso della pubblicità **b** (*look*) occhiata fulminante, sguardo furioso.

② VI **a** (*light*) sfolgorare **b** (*look*): **to glare at** fulminare con lo sguardo.

glar·ing ['gleərɪŋ] ADJ (*dazzling: sun, light*) sfolgorante, accecante; (: *colour*) sgargiante; (*obvious: evidence*) lampante; (: *mistake*) palese.

glar·ing·ly ['gleərɪŋlɪ] ADV: **it is glaringly obvious that** ... è più che evidente che...'.

glas·nost ['glæs,nɒst] N glasnost *f inv*.

glass [glɑːs] ① N **a** (*material, pane of glass*) vetro; (*glassware*) cristalleria; (*drinking vessel, glassful*) bicchiere *m*; (*barometer*) barometro; (*mirror*) specchio; **a wine glass** un bicchiere da vino, calice *m*; **grown under glass** di serra, coltivato(-a) in serra; see also **glasses**.

② ADJ (*bottle, eye*) di vetro; (*industry*) del vetro.

♦ **glass-blowing** ['glɑːs,bləʊɪŋ] N soffiatura del vetro.

♦ **glass case** N teca di vetro.

♦ **glass ceiling** N (*fig*) barriera invisibile.

♦ **glass cloth** N asciugapiatti *m inv* (*per bicchieri*).

♦ **glass cutter** N (*tool*) rotella tagliavetro.

glasses ['glɑːsɪz] NPL (*spectacles*) occhiali *mpl*.

♦ **glass fibre** N fibra di vetro.

glass·ful ['glɑːsfʊl] N bicchiere *m* (pieno).

glass·house ['glɑːs,haʊs] N (*for plants*) serra.

♦ **glass paper** N carta vetrata (fine).

glass·ware ['glɑːs,weəʳ] N cristalleria, articoli *mpl* di vetro.

♦ **glass wool** N lana di vetro.

glass·works ['glɑːs,wɜːks] NSG vetreria, fabbrica di vetri.

glassy ['glɑːsɪ] ADJ (*comp* **-ier**, *superl* **-iest**) (*sea, lake*) come uno specchio; (*eye, look*) vitreo(-a).

Glas·we·gian [glæz'wiːdʒən] ① ADJ di Glasgow.

② N abitante *m/f or* originario(-a) di Glasgow.

glau·co·ma [glɔː'kəʊmə] N glaucoma *m*.

glaze [gleɪz] ① N (*on pottery*) smalto; (*Culin*) glassa.

② VT **a** (*window, door*) mettere i vetri a, fornire di vetri **b** (*pottery*) invetriare; (*Culin*) glassare.

③ VI: **his eyes glazed over** i suoi occhi si fecero vitrei.

glazed [gleɪzd] ADJ (*tiles, pottery*) invetriato(-a); (*fig: eye*)

vitreo(-a).

gla·zi·er ['gleɪzɪə'] N vetraio.

GLC [ˌdʒi:el'si:] N ABBR (*Brit: old:* = *Greater London Council*) *consiglio municipale di Londra e sobborghi.*

gleam [gli:m] **1** N (*of light*) bagliore *m*; (*of moonlight*) chiarore *m*; (*of metal, water*) lucichio; **with a gleam in one's eye** con gli occhi scintillanti; (*mischievous*) con uno sguardo furbesco; **a gleam of hope** un barlume di speranza.

2 VI (*light, furniture*) brillare; (*metal, water*) luccicare; (*eyes*): **to gleam (with)** brillare (di).

gleam·ing ['gli:mɪŋ] ADJ brillante, lucente; **the house was gleaming** la casa era uno specchio.

glean [gli:n] VT (*gather: information*) racimolare.

glee [gli:] N: **with glee** (*gen*) con gioia; (*laugh*) di gusto.

glee·ful ['gli:fʊl] ADJ (*smile, laugh*) gioioso(-a), allegro(-a); (: *malicious*) malizioso(-a).

glee·ful·ly ['gli:fəlɪ] ADV (*see adj*) gioiosamente; maliziosamente.

glen [glɛn] N vallone *m*.

glib [glɪb] ADJ (*person*) dalla lingua sciolta; (*explanation, excuse*) facile, disinvolto(-a).

glib·ly ['glɪblɪ] ADV con disinvoltura.

glide [glaɪd] **1** N (*of dancer etc*) volteggio; (*Aer*) planata; (*Skiing*) scivolata.

2 VI (*move smoothly*) scivolare silenziosamente; (: *dancer*) volteggiare; (*Aer, birds*) planare; **to glide in** (*person*) entrare silenziosamente.

♦ **glide path** N (*Aer*) sentiero di avvicinamento.

glid·er ['glaɪdə'] N (*Aer*) aliante *m*.

glid·ing ['glaɪdɪŋ] N (*Aer*) volo a vela.

glim·mer ['glɪmə'] **1** N (*of light, also fig*) barlume *m*; (*of water*) lucichio.

2 VI (*light*) baluginare; (*water*) luccicare.

glim·mer·ing ['glɪmərɪŋ] **1** ADJ baluginante.

2 N barlume *m*.

glimpse [glɪmps] **1** N: **to catch a glimpse of** vedere di sfuggita.

2 VT intravedere.

glint [glɪnt] **1** N (*of metal etc*) scintillio, lucichio; **he had a glint in his eye** nei suoi occhi brillava una luce strana; **he had an angry glint in his eye** aveva uno sguardo arrabbiato.

2 VI brillare, luccicare.

glis·ten ['glɪsn] VI (*wet surface, water*) luccicare; (*eyes*): **to glisten (with)** brillare (di).

glit·ter ['glɪtə'] **1** N (*of gold etc*) scintillio; (*on Christmas cards etc*) polvere *f* d'oro.

2 VI (*gold etc*) luccicare, scintillare; **all that glitters is not gold** non è tutt'oro quel che luccica.

glit·ter·ing ['glɪtərɪŋ] ADJ (*jewels*) scintillante; (*eyes*) lucido(-a); (*career*) brillante; (*prize*) prestigioso(-a).

glitz [glɪts] N (*fam*) vistosità, chiassosità.

gloat [gləʊt] VI gongolare; **to gloat over** (*money etc*) covare con gli occhi; (*victory, enemy's misfortune*) gongolare (di gioia) per, esultare per.

glob·al ['gləʊbl] ADJ (*world-wide*) mondiale; (*comprehensive*) globale.

♦ **global warming** N riscaldamento dell'atmosfera terrestre.

globe [gləʊb] N globo, sfera; (*spherical map*) mappamondo, globo.

globe·flower ['gləʊb,flaʊə'] N luparia.

globe·trotter ['gləʊb,trɒtə'] N giramondo *m/f inv*.

globe·trotting ['gləʊb'trɒtɪŋ] N viaggi *mpl* per il mondo.

globu·lar ['glɒbjʊlə'] ADJ (*frm*) globulare.

glob·ule ['glɒbju:l] N (*of water etc*) gocciolina; (*Anat*) globulo.

globu·lin ['glɒbjʊlm] N globulina.

glo·meru·lus [glɒ'mɛrʊləs] N glomerulo.

gloom [glu:m] N **a** (*darkness*) oscurità, buio; **in the gloom** nell'oscurità, al buio **b** (*sadness*) tristezza, malinconia.

gloomi·ly ['glu:mɪlɪ] ADV cupamente.

gloomy ['glu:mɪ] ADJ (*comp* **-ier**, *superl* **-iest**) (*place, character*) cupo(-a), tetro(-a); (*person*) triste; (*atmosphere, weather, day*) deprimente; (*sky*) fosco(-a); (*outlook*) nero(-a); **to feel gloomy** sentirsi giù *or* depresso(-a); **to take a gloomy view of things** vedere tutto nero; **to feel gloomy about sth** essere pessimista su qc.

glo·ri·fi·ca·tion [ˌglɔ:rɪfɪ'keɪʃən] N glorificazione *f*.

glo·ri·fy ['glɔ:rɪ,faɪ] VT (*exalt: God*) glorificare; (: *person*) onorare; (*pej: war, deeds*) magnificare, esaltare; **it was just a glorified** ... non era altro che... .

glo·ri·ous ['glɔ:rɪəs] ADJ (*deeds, victory*) glorioso(-a); (*weather, view*) stupendo(-a), magnifico(-a); (*colours*) festoso(-a).

glo·ry ['glɔ:rɪ] **1** N gloria; (*splendour*) splendore *m*, magnificenza; **Rome at the height of its glory** Roma all'apogeo della gloria; **she's in her glory there** (*fam*) ci sguazza in quella situazione; **there she was in all her glory** (*fam*) stava lì in tutto il suo splendore; **glory be!** (*fam*) buon Dio!.

2 VI: **to glory in sth** (*one's success etc*) gloriarsi di qc; (*another's misfortune*) gustare *or* assaporare qc.

♦ **glory hole** N (*fam*) ripostiglio.

Glos ABBR (*Brit*)= *Gloucestershire.*

gloss [glɒs] N **a** (*explanation*) glossa, nota esplicativa **b** (*shine*) lucentezza, lustro; (*also:* **gloss paint**) vernice *f* lucida

▶ **gloss over** VT + ADV (*play down*) sorvolare su; (*hide*) coprire, mascherare.

glos·sa·ry ['glɒsərɪ] N glossario.

♦ **gloss finish** N: **with a gloss finish** (*paint*) lucido(-a); (*photo*) su carta lucida.

glossy ['glɒsɪ] ADJ (*comp* **-ier**, *superl* **-iest**) (*gen*) lucido(-a).

♦ **glossy magazine** N rivista (su carta patinata).

glot·tis ['glɒtɪs] N glottide *f*.

glove [glʌv] N guanto.

♦ **glove compartment** N (*Aut*) vano portaoggetti.

gloved [glʌvd] ADJ inguantato(-a).

♦ **glove puppet** N burattino (di stoffa).

glow [gləʊ] **1** N (*of lamp, sunset etc*) luce *f* (diffusa); (*of cigarette, fire, city*) bagliore *m*; (*of bright colour*) luminosità; (*of cheeks*) colorito acceso; (*warm feeling: of pride etc*) vampata.

2 VI (*lamp, sunset etc*) ardere; (*fire*) sfavillare; (*colour, face*) essere luminoso(-a); **to glow with health** sprizzare salute (da tutti i pori).

glow·er ['glaʊə'] VI: **to glower (at sb)** guardare (qn) in cagnesco.

glow·er·ing ['glaʊərɪŋ] ADJ astioso(-a), torvo(-a).

glow·ing ['gləʊɪŋ] ADJ (*light etc*) caldo(-a); (*fire*) ardente; (*complexion*) luminoso(-a); (*cheeks, colour*) acceso(-a); (*person: with health*) florido(-a); (: *with pleasure*) raggiante; (*fig: report, description etc*) entusiasta; **to paint sth in glowing colours** (*fig*) dire meraviglie di qc.

♦ **glow-worm** ['gləʊ,wɜ:m] N lucciola.

glu·cose ['glu:kəʊs] N glucosio.

glue [glu:] **1** N colla.

2 VT: **to glue (to)** incollare (a); **to glue two things**

together incollare due cose insieme; **she was glued to the television** (*fig*) stava incollata alla televisione; **he was glued to the spot** (*fig*) rimase di sasso.

♦ **glue-sniffing** ['gluː,snɪfɪŋ] N lo sniffare *m* (colla).

gluey ['gluːɪ] ADJ appiccicoso(-a).

glum [glʌm] ADJ (*comp* **-mer**, *superl* **-mest**) (*person*) abbattuto(-a); (*mood*) nero(-a); (*expression*) cupo(-a); **to feel glum** sentirsi giù.

glut [glʌt] 1 N sovrabbondanza, surplus *m inv*, eccesso. 2 VT (*market*) inondare, saturare; (*with food*) saziare.

glu·ti·nous ['gluːtɪnəs] ADJ colloso(-a), appiccicoso(-a).

glut·ton ['glʌtn] N goloso(-a), ghiottone(-a); **a glutton for work** uno(-a) stacanovista, un(a) patito(-a) del lavoro; **a glutton for punishment** un(a) masochista.

glut·ton·ous ['glʌtənəs] ADJ ghiotto(-a), goloso(-a).

glut·tony ['glʌtənɪ] N ghiottoneria, golosità; (*sin*) gola.

glyc·er·in ['glɪsərɪn], **glyc·er·ine** [,glɪsə'riːn] N glicerina.

gly·co·gen ['glaɪkəʊdʒən] N glicogeno.

gly·col ['glaɪkɒl] N glicol *m*.

gm (*pl* **gms**) ABBR = **gramme(s)**.

GMAT [,dʒiːeɪ'tiː] N ABBR (*Am*: = *Graduate Management Admissions Test*) esame di ammissione all'ultimo biennio di scuola superiore.

GMB [,dʒiːɛm'biː] N ABBR (*Brit*)= *General Municipal and Boilermakers (Union)*.

GMT [,dʒiːɛm'tiː] ABBR (= *Greenwich Mean Time*) T.M.G. (= *Tempo Medio di Greenwich*).

GMWU [,dʒiːɛmdʌblju'juː] N ABBR (*Brit*: = *General and Municipal Workers' Union*) *sindacato degli operai non specializzati e comunali*.

gnarled [nɑːld] ADJ nodoso(-a).

gnash [næʃ] VT: **to gnash one's teeth** digrignare i denti.

gnat [næt] N moscerino.

gnaw [nɔː] 1 VT (*chew*) rosicchiare, rodere; (*fig*: *subj*: *remorse*) rodere; (: *hunger*, *pain*) tormentare. 2 VI: **to gnaw through** rosicchiare da una parte all'altra; **to gnaw at** rosicchiare; (*fig*) rodere.

gnaw·ing ['nɔːɪŋ] ADJ (*hunger*, *pain*) che attanaglia; (*remorse*, *anxiety*) attanagliante; (*doubt*) assillante.

gnome [nəʊm] N gnomo.

gno·mic ['nəʊmɪk] ADJ (*liter*) gnomico(-a).

GNP [,dʒiːɛn'piː] N ABBR = **gross national product**.

gnu [nuː] N gnu *m inv*.

go [gəʊ] (*vb*: *3rd pers sg present* **does**, *pt* **went**, *pp* **gone**) 1 VI **a** (*gen*) andare; **to go to London** andare a Londra; **to go by car/on foot** andare in macchina/a piedi; **to go at 50 km/h** andare a 50 km l'ora *or* a 50 all'ora; **to go looking for sb/sth** andare in cerca di qn/qc; **to go swimming/shopping** *etc* andare a nuotare/a fare spese *etc*; **to go for a walk/swim** andare a fare due passi/una nuotata; **to go to a party/to the dentist's** andare a una festa/dal dentista; **to go and see sb** andare a trovare qn; halt, **who goes there?** alt, chi va là?; **you go first** (vai) prima tu; **there he goes!** eccolo (là)!; **he went that way** è andato di là; **there you go again!** (*fam*) ci risiamo!

b (*depart*) andar via, andarsene; (*train etc*) partire; (*disappear*: *person*, *object*) sparire; (: *time*) passare; (: *money*): **to go (on)** andarsene (in); (*be sold*): **to go (for)** essere venduto(-a) (per); **my voice has gone** mi è andata via la voce; **the cake is all gone** il dolce è finito; **that cupboard will have to go** dobbiamo sbarazzarci di quell'armadio; **go!** (*Sport*) via!; **here goes!** (*fam*) Dio me la mandi buona!; **gone are the days when ...** sono finiti i tempi in cui...; **the day went slowly** la giornata non passava mai; **it's just gone 7** sono appena passate le 7;

only 2 days to go mancano solo 2 giorni; **going, going, gone!** uno, due, tre, aggiudicato!; **it went for £100** è stato venduto per 100 sterline; **it's going cheap** (*fam*) costa poco

c (*extend*) arrivare; **the garden goes down to the lake** il giardino arriva fino al lago; **money doesn't go far nowadays** non si fa molto coi soldi oggigiorno; **it's good as far as it goes, but ...** quello che c'è va bene, ma...; **as cooks go, she's quite good** come cuoca non è male; **as hotels in Milan go, it's quite cheap** questo albergo non è molto caro, per essere a Milano

d (*function*: *machine etc*) andare; **I couldn't get the car to go at all** non sono riuscito a far partire la macchina; **to keep going** (*person*, *also fig*) andare avanti; (*machine*) andare; **to make sth go** OR **to get sth going** far funzionare qc; (*engine*, *machine*) mettere in moto qc; **let's get going** muoviamoci

e (*progress*, *turn out*) andare; **the meeting went well** la riunione è andata bene; **how did the exam go?** com'è andato l'esame?; **how's it going?** (*fam*) come va (la vita)?; **we'll see how things go** (*fam*) vediamo come vanno *or* come si mettono le cose; **he has a lot going for him** molte cose giocano a suo favore; **how does that song go?** come fa quella canzone?

f : **to go (with)** (*match*) andare (con); (*coincide*, *co-occur*) accompagnarsi a; **the curtains don't go with the carpet** le tende non si intonano col tappeto; **the house goes with the job** la casa è parte integrante del suo contratto di lavoro; **to go with sb** (*also fam*) andare con qn

g (*become*) diventare, farsi; **to go blind** perdere la vista; **to go hungry** fare la fame; **to go without sth** non avere qc; **to go bad** (*food*) andare a male, guastarsi; **to go mad** impazzire; **to go to sleep** addormentarsi

h (*fit, be contained*) andare, starci; **it won't go in the case** non sta nella valigia; **4 into 3 won't go** il 4 nel 3 non ci sta

i (*be acceptable*) andare, essere ammesso(-a) *or* ammissibile; **anything goes** (*fam*) tutto è permesso; **that goes for me too** questo vale anche per me; **what he says goes** la sua parola è legge

j (*break etc*: *material*) consumarsi, logorarsi; (: *rope*) rompersi, cedere; (: *fuse*, *button*) saltare; (: *health*, *eyesight etc*) deteriorarsi; **this jumper has gone at the elbows** questo golf ha i gomiti bucati

k (*be available*): **there are several jobs going** ci sono diversi posti disponibili; **is there any tea going?** c'è un po' di tè?; **I'll take whatever is going** (*Brit*) prendo quello che mi offrono

l (*prize*, *inheritance*): **to go (to)** andare (a), toccare (a); **the money goes to charity** il denaro va in beneficenza; **the money will go towards our holiday** questi soldi li mettiamo da parte per la vacanza; **all his money goes on drink** tutti i suoi soldi se ne vanno in alcolici; **the qualities which go to make him a great writer** le qualità che fanno di lui un grande scrittore

m (*make*: *sound*, *movement*) fare; (*doorbell*, *phone*) suonare; **go like that (with your right hand)** fai così (con la destra)

n (*Am*): **...to go** (*food*) ... da portar via, da asporto.

2 AUX VB: **I'm going to do it** lo farò; (*intention*) ho intenzione di farlo; **I was going to do it** stavo per farlo; (*intention*) volevo farlo; **it's going to rain** sta per piovere; **there's going to be trouble** saranno guai.

3 VT (*fam*): **to go it alone** farlo da solo(-a); **to go one better** (*action*) fare di meglio; (*story*) avere di meglio.

4 N (*pl* goes) **a** (*fam*: *energy*) dinamismo; **he's always on the go** non si ferma un minuto; **I've got two projects on the go** ho due progetti per le mani; **it's all go** non c'è un attimo di respiro

b (*success*): **to make a go of sth** riuscire in qc; (*scheme*) mandare in porto qc; **it's no go** (*fam*) (non c'è) niente da fare

c (*attempt*) tentativo; **to have a go (at doing sth)** provare (a fare qc); **at** *or* **in one go** in un sol colpo; **it's your go** tocca a te

d : **from the word go** (*fam*) (*fin*) dal primo momento; **all systems (are) go** tutto a posto

▶ **go about** 1 VI + PREP **a** (*set to work on*: *task*) affrontare; **how does one go about getting the tickets?** come si fa a procurarsi i biglietti?; **how do I go about this?** qual è la prassi per questo?

b (*busy o.s. with*) continuare a fare; **to go about one's business** occuparsi delle proprie faccende.

2 VI + ADV (*also*: **go around**: *wander about*) aggirarsi; (*circulate*: *flu etc*) esserci in giro; (: *rumour*) correre, circolare

▶ **go after** VI + PREP (*pursue*) correr dietro a, rincorrere; (*criminal etc*) inseguire; (*job, record etc*) mirare a; (*girl*) star dietro (a), fare il filo (a)

▶ **go against** VI + PREP (*be unfavourable to*: *result, events*) essere contro; (*be contrary to*: *principles, conscience, sb's wishes*) andare contro

▶ **go ahead** VI + ADV (*carry on*) andare *or* tirare avanti; **he went ahead with his plan** mise in atto il suo piano; **go (right) ahead!** fai pure!

▶ **go along** VI + ADV (*proceed*) andare avanti, avanzare; **check as you go along** verifica man mano che procedi; **as we went along ...** andando avanti...; **to go along with** (*accompany*) andare con, accompagnare; (*agree with*: *idea*) sottoscrivere, appoggiare; (: *person*) essere d'accordo con

▶ **go around** VI + ADV see **go about** 2; see **go round** a

▶ **go at** VI + PREP (*fam*: *attack*) scagliarsi contro; (*tackle, job etc*) buttarsi in; **he really went at it** si è veramente buttato

▶ **go away** VI + ADV (*depart*) andarsene

▶ **go back** VI + ADV **a** : **to go back (to)** (*return, revert*) (ri)tornare (a); **there's no going back now** non si può più tornare indietro

b (*date back*) risalire; **the controversy goes back to 1929** la controversia risale al 1929 **c** (*extend*: *garden, cave*) estendersi; (*go again*) andare di nuovo

▶ **go back on** VI + ADV + PREP (*word, promise*) rimangiarsi, ritirare; (*decision*) tornare su

▶ **go before** VI + ADV (*happen before*) accadere prima, succedere prima

▶ **go by** 1 VI + PREP **a** (*be guided by*: *watch, compass*) seguire, basarsi su, attenersi a; **to go by appearances** giudicare dalle apparenze; **going by what he says ...** stando a ciò che dice...

b : **to go by the name of X** farsi chiamare X.

2 VI + ADV (*pass by*: *person, car etc*) passare; (*opportunity*) scappare; (*years, time*) scorrere; **as time goes by** col passare del tempo

▶ **go down** VI + ADV **a** (*sun*) tramontare, calare; (*person*: *downstairs*) scendere, andar giù; (*sink*: *ship*) affondare; (: *person*) andar sotto; (*be defeated*) crollare; **that should go down well with him** dovrebbe incontrare la sua approvazione

b (*be written down*) venire registrato(-a); **to go down in**

history/to posterity passare alla storia/ai posteri

c (*decrease*: *price, temperature etc*) scendere, calare; **he has gone down in my estimation** è sceso nella mia stima

▶ **go down with** VI + ADV + PREP (*fam*): **to go down with flu** beccarsi l'influenza

▶ **go for** VI + PREP **a** (*attack*) lanciarsi contro *or* su, avventarsi su *or* contro; (*fig*) dare addosso a, attaccare

b (*fam*: *apply to*): **that goes for me too** questo vale anche per me

c (*fam*: *like, fancy*) andar matto(-a) per; **I don't go for his films** i suoi film non mi dicono un granché

▶ **go forward** VI + ADV **a** (*proceed*: *with plan etc*): **to go forward (with)** procedere con **b** (*be put forward*: *suggestion*) essere avanzato(-a), venire avanzato(-a)

▶ **go in** VI + ADV **a** (*enter*) entrare **b** : **the sun went in** il sole si è oscurato *or* nascosto **c** (*fit*) entrarci, andarci

▶ **go in for** VI + ADV + PREP **a** (*enter for*: *race, competition*) prendere parte a; (*exam*) presentarsi a

b (*be interested in*: *hobby, sport*) interessarsi di, essere appassionato(-a) di; (*take as a career*) scegliere; **she goes in for the latest styles** le piace vestirsi all'ultima moda

▶ **go into** VI + PREP **a** (*investigate, examine*) indagare, esaminare a fondo; (*embark on*) lanciarsi in, imbarcarsi in; **to go into details** entrare nei particolari; **let's not go into all that now** non parliamone per ora

b (*embark on*: *career*) darsi a

c (*trance, coma*) entrare in; **to go into fits of laughter** essere preso(-a) da un convulso di risa

▶ **go off** 1 VI + ADV **a** (*leave*) partire, andarsene; **to go off (to sleep)** addormentarsi

b (*cease to operate*: *lights etc*) spegnersi

c (*explode*) esplodere, scoppiare; (*alarm clock*) suonare; **the gun went off by accident** è partito un colpo accidentalmente

d (*food*) andare a male, guastarsi

e (*event*) andare; **the party went off well** la festa è riuscita bene.

2 VI + PREP (*cease to like*: *thing*) perdere il gusto di; (: *person*) non poter più vedere; **I've gone off chocolate** la cioccolata non mi piace più

▶ **go off with** VI + ADV + PREP (*boyfriend*) scappare con; (*book*) andarsene con

▶ **go on** 1 VI + PREP (*be guided by*: *evidence etc*) basarsi su, fondarsi su; **there's nothing to go on** non abbiamo niente su cui basarci.

2 VI + ADV **a** (*continue*: *war, talks*) protrarsi, continuare; (: *on journey*) proseguire; **to go on doing** continuare a fare; **he went on to say that ...** ha aggiunto che...; **to go on about sth** (*fam*) non finirla più con qc; **what a way to go on!** (*pej*) bel modo di comportarsi!

b (*lights*) accendersi; (*machine*) partire, mettersi in moto

c (*happen*) succedere, svolgersi; **what's going on here?** che succede *or* che sta succedendo qui?

d (*pass*: *time, years*) passare; **as time went on** con l'andar del tempo

▶ **go on at** VI + ADV + PREP (*nag*) assillare

▶ **go on for** VI + ADV + PREP: **it's going on for 3 years now** sono quasi tre anni ormai; **he's going on for 60** va per la sessantina; **it' going on for 2 o' clock** sono quasi le 2

▶ **go on with** VI + ADV + PREP continuare, proseguire

▶ **go out** VI + ADV **a** (*be estinguished*: *fire, light*) spegnersi

b (*leave*) uscire, andar fuori; (*socially*) uscire; (*in cards*) chiudere; (*ebb*: *tide*) calare; **to go out shopping/for a**

meal andare a far spese/a mangiare fuori; **to go out (of fashion)** passare (di moda); **to go out with sb** uscire con qn; **they've been going out together for 2 years** sono due anni che stanno insieme, fanno coppia fissa da due anni

▶ **go over** ⒈ VI + PREP **a** (*examine: report etc*) riguardare, controllare **b** (*rehearse, review: speech, lesson etc*) ripassare; **to go over sth in one's mind** pensare bene a qc. ⒉ VI + ADV **a** : **to go over (to)** (*cross over*) andare (a *or* in); (*fig: change habit, size etc*) passare (a) **b** (*be received*) essere accolto(-a); **his speech went over well** il suo discorso è stato accolto bene

▶ **go round** VI + ADV **a** (*revolve*) girare; (*circulate: news, rumour*) circolare; **there is a rumour going round that ...** corre voce che... **b** (*suffice*) bastare (per tutti); **is there enough food to go round?** c'è abbastanza da mangiare per tutti? **c** (*visit*): **to go round (to sb's)** passare (da qn); **let's go round to John's place** facciamo un salto da John **d** (*make a detour*): **to go round (by)** passare (per)

▶ **go through** ⒈ VI + PREP **a** (*suffer*) passare **b** (*examine: list, book*) leggere da capo a fondo; (*search through*) frugare in **c** (*use up: money*) spendere, mangiarsi; (*consume, wear out*) consumare **d** (*perform*) fare; (: *formalities*) sbrigare; **let's go through that scene again** rifacciamo quella scena (da capo) **e** (*town etc*) attraversare. ⒉ VI + ADV (*bill, law*) essere approvato(-a); (*deal*) essere concluso(-a)

▶ **go through with** VI + ADV + PREP (*plan, crime*) mettere in atto, eseguire; **I couldn't go through with it** non sono riuscito ad andare fino in fondo

▶ **go under** VI + ADV (*sink: ship*) affondare, colare a picco; (: *person*) andare sotto; (*fig: business, firm*) fallire

▶ **go up** ⒈ VI + ADV **a** (*rise: temperature, prices etc*) salire, aumentare; **to go up in price** aumentare (di prezzo) **b** (*ascend*) andare su **c** (*be built: tower block etc*) venire costruito(-a); (: *new district etc*) sorgere; (: *scaffolding etc*) venire montato(-a) **d** (*explode*) saltare in aria; **to go up in flames** andare in fiamme. ⒉ VI + PREP (*ascend*) salire su per

▶ **go without** VI + PREP fare a meno di.

goad [gəʊd] VT: **to goad sb into doing sth** (*fig*) pungolare qn perché faccia qc; **to goad sb on** (*fig*) spronare qn, incitare qn.

◆ **go-ahead** ['gəʊə,hɛd] ⒈ ADJ (*firm, director*) intraprendente, pieno(-a) d'iniziativa; (*policy, ideas*) avanzato(-a). ⒉ N: **to give sb/sth the go-ahead** dare l'okay a qn/qc.

goal [gəʊl] N **a** (*Sport: score*) goal *m inv*, gol *m inv*; (: *net etc*) rete *f*, porta; **to win by 4 goals to 2** vincere per 4 reti a 2; **to play in goal** giocare in porta **b** (*aim: in life*) scopo, fine *m*, obiettivo; (: *in journey*) meta.

◆ **goal area** N (*Sport*) area della porta.

◆ **goal difference** N differenza *f* reti *inv*.

goalie ['gəʊlɪ] N (*Brit fam*) portiere *m*.

goal·keeper ['gəʊl,ki:pəʳ] N portiere *m*.

◆ **goal kick** N (*Ftbl*) rimessa (in gioco) dalla linea di fondo.

◆ **goal line** N linea di porta.

goal·mouth ['gəʊl'maʊθ] N: **in the goalmouth** proprio davanti ai pali.

goal·post ['gəʊlpəʊst] N palo (della porta).

goat [gəʊt] N capra; **to act the goat** (*fam*) fare lo(-a) stupido(-a); **to get sb's goat** (*fam*) far uscire qn dai gangheri.

goatee ['gəʊti:] N pizzo.

gob·ble ['gɒbl] VT (*also*: **gobble down, gobble up**) tranguiare, ingurgitare.

gob·ble·dy·gook, gob·ble·de·gook ['gɒbəldɪ,gu:k] N (*fam*) burocratese *m*.

◆ **go-between** ['gəʊbɪ,twi:n] N intermediario(-a).

Gobi De·sert ['gəʊbɪ'dɛzət] N: **the Gobi Desert** il Deserto del Gobi.

gob·let ['gɒblɪt] N calice *m*.

◆ **goblet cell** N (*Bio*) cellula calciforme.

gob·lin ['gɒblɪn] N folletto.

◆ **go-cart** ['gəʊ,ka:t] N go-kart *m inv*.

god [gɒd] N **a** : **God** Dio; **God save the Queen** Dio salvi la Regina; **(my) God!** (*fam*) Dio (mio)!; **for God's sake!** per amor di Dio!; **God forbid!** per carità!; (*stronger*) Dio ce ne scampi e liberi!; **God willing** a Dio piacendo; **God (only) knows** Dio (solo) lo sa **b** (*Myth*) dio **c** (*Brit Theatre*): **the gods** la piccionaia *sg*, il loggione *sg*.

◆ **god-awful** ['gɒd,ɔ:fəl] ADJ (*fam*) orrendo(-a).

god·child ['gɒd,tʃaɪld] N (*pl* **-children**) figlioccio(-a).

god·damn(ed) ['gɒd'dæm(d)] (*esp Am fam*) ⒈ EXCL: **goddamn!** dannazione!, maledizione!. ⒉ ADJ dannato(-a). ⒊ ADV dannatamente.

god·daughter ['gɒd,dɔ:təʳ] N figlioccia.

god·dess ['gɒdɪs] N dea.

god·father ['gɒd,fɑ:ðəʳ] N padrino.

◆ **god-fearing** ['gɒd,fɪərɪŋ] ADJ timorato(-a) di Dio, (molto) pio(-a).

god·forsaken ['gɒdfə,seɪkən] ADJ (*fam: place*) dimenticato(-a) da Dio e dagli uomini, sperduto(-a).

god·head ['gɒd,hɛd] N divinità.

god·less ['gɒdlɪs] ADJ empio(-a).

god·like ['gɒd,laɪk] ADJ divino(-a).

god·ly ['gɒdlɪ] ADJ (*comp* **-ier**, *superl* **-iest**) pio(-a).

god·mother ['gɒd,mʌðəʳ] N madrina.

god·parents ['gɒd,pɛərənts] NPL: **the godparents** il padrino e la madrina.

god·send ['gɒd,sɛnd] N dono del cielo; **it was a godsend to us** è stata una vera manna per noi.

god·son ['gɒd,sʌn] N figlioccio.

goes [gəʊz] 3RD PERS SG PRESENT of **go**.

go·fer ['gəʊfəʳ] N (*fam*) galoppino(-a).

◆ **go-getter** ['gəʊ,gɛtəʳ] N arrivista *m/f*.

gog·gle ['gɒgl] VI (*look astonished*) sbarrare gli occhi, sgranare tanto d'occhi; **to goggle (at)** (*stare*) stare con gli occhi incollati *or* appiccicati (a *or* addosso a).

gog·gles ['gɒglz] NPL (*of skin-diver*) maschera; (*of skier*) occhiali *mpl* da sci; (*for workman*) occhiali (di protezione).

go·ing ['gəʊɪŋ] ⒈ N **a** (*pace*) andatura, ritmo; **it was slow going** si andava a rilento; **that was good going** è stata una cosa veloce **b** (*state of road surface etc*) percorribilità; (*in horse-racing etc*) terreno; **let's get out while the going is good** è meglio uscirne finché sia possibile; **it's heavy going talking to her** parlare con lei è una faticaccia. ⒉ ADJ **a** : **a going concern** un'azienda avviata **b** (*current: price*) corrente, attuale; **the going rate** la tariffa in vigore.

◆ **going-over** [,gəʊɪŋ'əʊvəʳ] N (*fam*) **a** (*check*) controllata; **they gave the car a thorough going-over** hanno

dato una bella controllata alla macchina **b** (*search*): **to give a house a going-over** perquisire una casa **c** (*violent attack*) pestaggio; **to give sb a going-over** pestare qn.

♦ **goings-on** ['gəʊɪŋz'ɒn] NPL (*fam*) fatti *mpl* strani, cose *fpl* strane.

goi·tre, (*Am*) **goi·ter** ['gɔɪtəʳ] N gozzo.

♦ **go-kart** ['gəʊˌkɑ:t] N = go-cart.

gold [gəʊld] **1** N oro; **it's made of gold** è d'oro; **rolled gold** oro laminato.

2 ADJ (*bracelet, tooth, mine*) d'oro; (*reserves*) aureo(-a); **gold braid** gallone *m* d'oro.

gold·crest ['gəʊldˌkrɛst] N (*Zool*) regolo.

gold·digger ['gəʊldˌdɪgəʳ] N (*fam pej*): **she's a gold digger** è un'avventuriera.

♦ **gold dust** N polvere *f* d'oro; **good jobs are like gold dust these days** un buon lavoro è una rarità al giorno d'oggi.

gold·en ['gəʊldən] ADJ (*made of gold*) d'oro, in oro; (*hair etc*) biondo oro *inv*; (*era*) d'oro; (*afternoon*) meraviglioso (-a); (*gold in colour*) dorato(-a); **a golden opportunity** un'occasione d'oro; **the golden mean** il giusto mezzo; **golden wedding (anniversary)** nozze *fpl* d'oro.

♦ **golden age** N età *f inv* d'oro.

♦ **golden eagle** N aquila reale.

♦ **golden handshake** N (*Brit*) gratifica di fine servizio.

♦ **golden jubilee** N cinquantenario, giubileo.

golden·rod ['gəʊldənˌrɒd] N (*Bot*) verga d'oro.

♦ **golden rule** N regola d'oro.

♦ **golden syrup** N melassa (raffinata).

gold·finch ['gəʊldˌfɪntʃ] N cardellino.

gold·fish ['gəʊldfɪʃ] N pesce *m* rosso.

♦ **goldfish bowl** N boccia dei pesci rossi.

♦ **gold leaf** N lamina d'oro.

♦ **gold medal** N (*Sport*) medaglia d'oro.

gold·mine ['gəʊldˌmaɪn] N miniera d'oro.

♦ **gold plate** N vasellame *m* d'oro.

♦ **gold-plated** [ˌgəʊld'pleɪtɪd] ADJ laminato(-a) *or* placcato(-a) d'oro.

♦ **gold-rimmed** [ˌgəʊld'rɪmd] ADJ bordato(-a) d'oro; **a pair of gold-rimmed glasses** un paio di occhiali con la montatura d'oro; **a gold-rimmed cup** una tazza con bordo d'oro.

♦ **gold rush** N corsa all'oro.

gold·smith ['gəʊldˌsmɪθ] N (*dealer*) orefice *m*; (*artisan*) orafo.

♦ **gold standard** N tallone *m* aureo.

golf [gɒlf] **1** N golf *m*; **to play golf** giocare a golf.

2 VI: **to go golfing** giocare a golf.

♦ **golf ball** N palla da golf; (*on typewriter*) pallina.

♦ **golf club** N (*organization*) circolo di golf; (*stick*) bastone *m or* mazza da golf.

♦ **golf course** N campo di golf.

golf·er ['gɒlfəʳ] N giocatore(-trice) di golf.

golf·ing ['gɒlfɪŋ] N il giocare a golf.

Gol·go·tha ['gɒlgəθə] N Golgota *m*.

Goliath [gəʊ'laɪəθ] N Golia *m*.

gol·li·wog, gol·ly·wog ['gɒlɪˌwɒg] N *bambolotto di pezza con la faccia da negretto*.

gol·ly ['gɒlɪ] **1** EXCL **a** : **golly! Have you seen the time!** santo cielo! Hai visto che ora è?; **golly, I didn't know he was an expert!** perbacco, non sapevo fosse un esperto! **b** per Giove; **he said he'd do it, and by golly he's succeeded** ha detto che l'avrebbe fatto e, per Giove, ci è riuscito!

2 N = golliwog.

gon·ad ['gəʊnæd] N gonade *f*.

gon·do·la ['gɒndələ] N gondola.

gon·do·lier [ˌgɒndə'lɪəʳ] N gondoliere *m*.

gone [gɒn] PP of go.

gon·er ['gɒnəʳ] N (*fam*): **I thought you were a goner** pensavo che ormai fossi spacciato.

gong [gɒŋ] N gong *m inv*.

gon·na ['gɒnə] VI (*esp Am* = going to): **what are we gonna do?** che facciamo?, cosa faremo?

gon·or·rhoea [ˌgɒnə'rɪə] N gonorrea.

goo [gu:] N (*fam*) sostanza appiccicosa.

good [gʊd] **1** ADJ (*comp* **better**, *superl* **best**) **a** (*gen*) buono(-a); **to lead a good life** condurre una vita virtuosa; **he's a good man** è una brava persona; (*saintly*) è un sant'uomo; **good manners** buona educazione *f*, buone maniere; **he has good judgment** sa giudicare; **be good!** fai il bravo!; **good for you!** bravo!; **she's too good for him** lui non se la merita; **it's just not good enough!** è inaccettabile!; **the job is as good as done** il lavoro è praticamente finito; **as good as new** come nuovo(-a); **she has been as good as gold** è stata un angelo; **(that's) good!** bene!, ottimo!; **that's a good one!** (*iro*) questa sì che è bella!

b (*pleasant: holiday, day, weather*) bello(-a); (: *news*) buono(-a, good); **to feel good** sentirsi bene; **have a good journey!** buon viaggio!; **it's good to see you** mi fa piacere vederti

c (*handsome: looks, features*) bello(-a); **you look good in that dress** quel vestito ti dona *or* ti sta bene; **she has a good figure** ha un bel personale

d (*beneficial, advantageous, wholesome*) buono(-a); **good to eat** buono(-a) da mangiare; **he's on to a good thing** ha trovato una miniera d'oro; **it's good for you** ti fa bene; **it's a good thing you were there** meno male che c'eri

e (*child*) bravo(-a); (*competent: teacher, doctor*) bravo (-a), buono(-a); **to be good at** essere bravo(-a) in; **he's good at English/telling jokes** è bravo in inglese/a raccontare barzellette; **she's good with children** ci sa fare coi bambini; **to be good for** andar bene per; **a ticket good for 3 months** un biglietto valido (per) 3 mesi; **he's good for £10** 10 sterline le sgancia; **are you good for another kilometre?** ce la fai a fare un altro chilometro?

f (*kind*) gentile, buono(-a); **to be good to sb** essere gentile con *or* verso qn; **he's a good sort** (*fam*) è una brava persona; **would you be so good as to sign here?** avrebbe la gentilezza di firmare qui?; **that's very good of you** è molto gentile da parte sua; **good deeds** *or* **works** buone azioni *fpl*, opere *fpl* buone

g (*considerable, not less than*) buono(-a); **a good many/ few people** parecchia/un bel po' di gente; **a good deal of money** un bel po' di soldi; **a good deal of work** parecchio lavoro; **a good 3 hours** 3 ore buone; **it's a good distance from here** dista parecchio *or* un bel po' da qui

h (*thorough*) bello(-a); **to give sb a good scolding** fare una bella ramanzina a qn; **to have a good cry** farsi un bel pianto; **to take a good look (at sth)** guardare bene (qc)

i (*in greetings*): **good morning** buongiorno; **good afternoon** buongiorno; **good evening** buonasera; **good night** buonanotte.

2 ADV **a** : **a good strong stick** un bel bastone robusto; **good and strong** (*fam*) bello forte; **to hold good (for)** valere (per), reggere (in)

b (*esp Am fam: well*) bene.

3 N **a** (*what is morally right*) bene *m*; **to do good** fare del bene; **good and evil** il bene e il male; **he's up to no good**

ne sta combinando qualcuna

b (*advantage, benefit*) bene *m*, interesse *m*; **for your own good** per il tuo bene; **for the common good** nell'interesse generale, per il bene comune; **to come to no good** andare a finire male; **what's the good of that?** a che pro?, a che serve?; **is this any good?** (*will it do?*) va bene questo?; (*what's it like?*) com'è ?; **that's no good to me** non mi va bene, non fa al caso mio; **that's all to the good!** tanto meglio!, tanto di guadagnato!; **it's no good complaining** brontolare non serve a niente; **a (fat) lot of good that will do you** (*iro fam*) sai quanto ne ricavi

c (*people of virtue*): **the good** NPL i buoni

d (*for ever*): **for good (and all)** per sempre, definitivamente; see also **goods**.

good·bye [ˌɡʊdˈbaɪ] **1** EXCL arrivederci.

2 N saluto, addio; **to say goodbye to** (*person*) salutare; (*fig: holiday, promotion etc*) dire addio a.

♦ **good faith** N buona fede.

♦ **good-for-nothing** [ˈɡʊdfəˌnʌθɪŋ] ADJ, N buono(-a) a nulla.

♦ **Good Friday** N Venerdì *m* Santo.

♦ **good-hearted** [ˌɡʊdˈhɑːtɪd] ADJ buono(-a) (d'animo).

♦ **good-humoured** [ˌɡʊdˈhjuːməd] ADJ (*person*) di buon umore; (*remark, joke*) bonario(-a); (*discussion*) cordiale; **to be good-humoured about doing sth** fare qc di buon grado.

♦ **good-humouredly** [ˌɡʊdˈhjuːmədlɪ] ADV (*see adj*) con buon umore; bonariamente; cordialmente.

♦ **good-looker** [ˌɡʊdˈlʊkəʳ] N (*fam: person*) bellezza.

♦ **good-looking** [ˌɡʊdˈlʊkɪŋ] ADJ bello(-a), piacente.

good·ly [ˈɡʊdlɪ] ADJ (*frm*) consistente.

♦ **good-natured** [ˌɡʊdˈneɪtʃəd] ADJ (*person*) affabile; (*discussion*) amichevole, cordiale.

good·ness [ˈɡʊdnɪs] **1** N (*virtue, kindness*) bontà (d'animo); (*good quality*) (buona) qualità *f*.

2 EXCL (*fam*): **(my) goodness!** OR **goodness gracious!** santo cielo!, mamma mia!; **for goodness' sake!** per amor del cielo!

goods [ɡʊdz] NPL (*Comm etc*) merci *fpl*, articoli *mpl*; **leather goods** articoli di *or* in pelle; **canned goods** scatolame *m*; **all my worldly goods** (*frm*) tutti i miei beni *or* i miei averi; **all his goods and chattels** tutti i suoi beni ed effetti.

♦ **goods train** N (*Brit*) treno *m* merci *inv*.

♦ **goods yard** N (*Brit*) scalo *m* merci *inv*.

♦ **good-tempered** [ˌɡʊdˈtɛmpəd] ADJ buono(-a).

♦ **good-time** [ˈɡʊdˌtaɪm] ADJ: **a good-time girl** una ragazza che non pensa ad altro che a divertirsi.

good·will [ˌɡʊdˈwɪl] N buona volontà, buona fede *f*; (*Comm*) (valore *m* d')avviamento; **as a gesture of goodwill** in segno di buona volontà; **to gain sb's goodwill** ingraziarsi qn.

♦ **goodwill mission** N missione *f* di mediazione.

goody [ˈɡʊdɪ] **1** EXCL bene!.

2 N **a** (*Culin*): **goodies** NPL cose *fpl* buone **b** (*Cine: character*) buono(-a).

♦ **goody-goody** [ˈɡʊdɪˌɡʊdɪ] N (*pej*) santarellino(-a).

goo·ey [ˈɡuːɪ] (*Brit fam*) ADJ (*comp* **-ier**, *superl* **-iest**) (*mess*) appiccicoso(-a); (*cake, dessert*) molto ricco(-a); (*fig: sentimental*) sdolcinato(-a).

goof [ɡuːf] (*Am*) **1** VI **a** (*fail*): **they had their chance, and they goofed** avevano avuto un'opportunità e se la sono lasciata sfuggire **b** (*skive*): **to goof off** perdere tempo.

2 N **a** (*fool*) gonzo(-a) **b** (*blunder*): **what a goof!** che gaffe!

goofy [ˈɡuːfɪ] ADJ (*comp* **-ier**, *superl* **-iest**) (*Am*) ridicolo(-a).

goos·an·der [ɡuːˈsændəʳ] N smergo maggiore.

goose [ɡuːs] N (*pl* **geese**) oca; **the goose that lays the golden eggs** la gallina dalle uova d'oro; **don't be such a goose!** (*fam*) non essere così stupido!

goose·berry [ˈɡʊzbərɪ] N uva spina; **to play gooseberry** (*Brit*) tenere *or* reggere la candela.

goose·flesh [ˈɡuːsˌflɛʃ] N, **goose·pimples** [ˈɡuːsˌpɪmplz] NPL pelle *f inv* d'oca.

goose·grass [ˈɡuːsˌɡrɑːs] N attaccamani *m inv*, attaccavesti *m inv*.

♦ **goose step** N (*Mil*) passo dell'oca.

GOP [ˌdʒiːəʊˈpiː] N ABBR (*Am Pol fam*: = *Grand Old Party*) partito repubblicano.

go·pher [ˈɡəʊfəʳ] N geomio borsario.

gore[1] [ɡɔːʳ] N sangue *m*.

gore[2] [ɡɔːʳ] VT (*subj: bull etc*) incornare.

gore[3] [ɡɔːʳ] N (*of skirt*) godet *m inv*; (*of umbrella*) spicchio.

gorge [ɡɔːdʒ] **1** N (*Geog, Anat*) gola.

2 VT: **to gorge o.s. (with** *or* **on)** rimpinzarsi (di), ingozzarsi (di).

gor·geous [ˈɡɔːdʒəs] ADJ (*woman, dress, holiday*) stupendo (-a), magnifico(-a); (*meal etc*) fantastico(-a).

Gor·gon [ˈɡɔːɡən] N Gorgone *f*.

go·ril·la [ɡəˈrɪlə] N gorilla *m inv*.

gorm·less [ˈɡɔːmlɪs] ADJ (*Brit fam*) tonto(-a); (: *stronger*) deficiente.

gorse [ɡɔːs] N ginestrone *m*.

gory [ˈɡɔːrɪ] ADJ (*comp* **-ier**, *superl* **-iest**) (*battle, death*) sanguinoso(-a); **the gory details** (*hum*) i dettagli più scabrosi, i particolari più piccanti.

gosh [ɡɒʃ] EXCL (*fam*) cribbio!, perdinci!

gos·hawk [ˈɡɒsˌhɔːk] N astore *m* nostrano.

♦ **go-slow** [ˌɡəʊˈsləʊ] N (*Brit*) ≈ sciopero bianco.

gos·pel [ˈɡɒspəl] N (*Rel*) vangelo; **the Gospel according to St John** il Vangelo secondo (San) Giovanni; **you can take it as gospel** (*fam*) puoi giurarci su.

♦ **gospel truth** N: **it's the gospel truth** è la sacrosanta verità.

gos·sa·mer [ˈɡɒsəməʳ] N (*fabric*) garza, mussolina; (*cobweb*) filo di ragnatela.

gos·sip [ˈɡɒsɪp] **1** N (*talk*) chiacchiere *fpl*; (*scandal*) pettegolezzi *mpl*; (*person*) pettegolo(-a), chiacchierone (-a); **a piece of gossip** un pettegolezzo.

2 VI (*talk*) chiacchierare; **to gossip (about)** (*talk scandal*) fare pettegolezzi (su), chiacchierare (sul conto di).

♦ **gossip column** N cronaca mondana.

gos·sip·ing [ˈɡɒsɪpɪŋ] **1** ADJ pettegolo(-a).

2 N pettegolezzi *mpl*.

♦ **gossip writer**, **gossip columnist** N giornalista *m/f* scandalistico(-a).

gos·sipy [ˈɡɒsɪpɪ] ADJ **a** (*pej*) pettegolo(-a); **a gossipy letter** una lettera piena di pettegolezzi **b** (*tone*) frivolo (-a).

got [ɡɒt] PT, PP of **get**.

Goth [ɡɒθ] N Goto.

Goth·ic [ˈɡɒθɪk] ADJ gotico(-a).

got·ta [ˈɡɒtə] VI (*esp Am* = *have got to*): **I gotta get dressed** devo vestirmi; **I've gotta get back** devo tornare.

got·ten [ˈɡɒtn] (*Am*) PP of **get**.

gouge [ɡaʊdʒ] VT (*also*: **gouge out**: *hole etc*) scavare; (: *initials*) scolpire; (: *sb's eyes*) cavare.

gou·lash [ˈɡuːlæʃ] N gulasch *m inv*.

gourd [ɡʊəd] N zucca.

gour·mand [ˈɡʊəmənd] N buona forchetta, ghiottone(-a).

gour·met ['guɜmeɪ] N gourmet *m inv*, buongustaio(-a).

gout [gaut] N (*Med*) gotta.

gov·ern ['gʌvən] VT (*rule: country*) governare; (*subj: king*) regnare (in); (*control: business*) dirigere; (: *city*) amministrare; (: *choice, decision*) regolare; (: *person*) guidare; (: *emotions*) dominare; (*Gram*) reggere.

gov·er·ness ['gʌvənɪs] N governante *f*, istitutrice *f*.

gov·ern·ing ['gʌvənɪŋ] ADJ (*Pol*) al potere, al governo; **governing class** classe *f* dirigente.

♦ **governing body** N consiglio di amministrazione.

gov·ern·ment ['gʌvənmənt] N governo; **local government** amministrazione *f* locale.

gov·ern·men·tal [ˌgʌvən'mɛntl] ADJ governativo(-a).

♦ **government department** N dipartimento ministeriale.

♦ **government housing** N (*Am*) alloggi *mpl* popolari.

♦ **government loan** N prestito statale.

♦ **government policy** N (*gen*) politica governativa; (*of current government*) politica del governo.

♦ **government stock** N titoli *mpl* di stato.

gov·er·nor ['gʌvənəʳ] N **a** (*of colony, state, bank etc*) governatore *m*; (*director: of school, hospital*) membro del consiglio di amministrazione; (*Brit: of prison*) direttore (-trice) **b** (*of engine*) controllo automatico della velocità.

Govt ABBR = **government**.

gown [gaun] N (*dress*) abito; (*Law, Univ*) toga.

GP [ˌdʒiː'piː] N ABBR (= *general practitioner*) medico generico; **who's your GP?** qual è il suo medico di famiglia?

GPMU [ˌdʒiːpiːɛm'juː] N ABBR (*Brit*) = *Graphical, Paper and Media Union*.

GPO [ˌdʒiːpiːˈəʊ] N ABBR **a** (*Brit old*) = **General Post Office** **b** (*Am*: = *Government Printing Office*) ≈ Poligrafici *mpl* dello Stato.

gr. ABBR (*Comm*) = **gross**.

grab [græb] [1] N **a** (*snatch*): **to make a grab at** *or* **for sth** cercare di afferrare qc **b** (*Tech*) benna. [2] VT (*seize*) afferrare, acchiappare; (: *property, power*) impossessarsi di, impadronirsi di; (*greedily*) agguantare; (*fig: chance etc*) cogliere al volo; **to grab sth from sb** strappare qc di mano a qn. [3] VI: **to grab at** tentare disperatamente di afferrare; (*in falling*) cercare di aggrapparsi a.

grace [greɪs] [1] N (*Rel, elegance: of form, movement etc*) grazia; (*graciousness*) garbo, cortesia; **the Graces** (*Myth*) le (tre) Grazie; **he had the grace to apologise** ha avuto la buonagrazia di scusarsi; **to do sth with good/bad grace** fare qc volentieri/malvolentieri; **his sense of humour is his saving grace** il suo senso dell'umorismo è quello che lo salva; **three days' grace** tre giorni di proroga, una dilazione *f* di tre giorni; **by the grace of God** per grazia di Dio; **to say grace** dire il benedicite; **to be in sb's good graces** essere nelle grazie di qn; **His Grace** (*duke, archbishop*) Sua Eccellenza. [2] VT (*adorn*) adornare; (*honour: occasion, event*) onorare con la propria presenza; **he graced the meeting with his presence** ci ha fatto l'onore di presenziare alla riunione.

grace·ful ['greɪsful] ADJ (*gen*) aggraziato(-a), pieno(-a) di grazia; (*apology*) garbato(-a).

grace·ful·ly ['greɪsfəlɪ] ADV (*see adj*) con grazia; con garbo.

grace·ful·ness ['greɪsfulnɪs] N grazia.

grace·less ['greɪslɪs] ADJ (*dress*) poco elegante; (*rude*) sgarbato(-a).

gra·cious ['greɪʃəs] [1] ADJ (*hostess, permission*) cortese; (*smile*) benevolo(-a); (*mansion*) di raffinata eleganza; (*God*) misericordioso(-a); **gracious living** vita da gran signore. [2] EXCL: **(good) gracious!** madonna (mia)!

gra·cious·ly ['greɪʃəslɪ] ADV (*see adj*) cortesemente; benevolmente; in modo raffinato ed elegante; misericordiosamente.

gra·cious·ness ['greɪʃəsnɪs] N gentilezza, cortesia.

gra·date [grə'deɪt] [1] VT graduare. [2] VI: **the colours/tones gradate** ci sono delle sfumature di colore/di tono.

gra·da·tion [grə'deɪʃən] N gradazione *f*.

grade [greɪd] [1] N **a** (*on scale*) categoria, livello; (*in hierarchy, also Mil*) grado; (*Comm*) qualità *f inv*; (*size*) misura, grandezza; **grade A fruit** frutta di prima scelta; **to make the grade** (*fig*) essere all'altezza **b** (*Scol: mark*) voto; (: *Am: class*) classe *f*, anno **c** (*Am: gradient*) pendenza, gradiente *m*. [2] VT **a** (*goods, eggs*) classificare; (*level of difficulty*) graduare; **graded profile** (*Geol*) profilo di equilibrio **b** (*Scol: mark*) giudicare, dare un voto a.

♦ **grade crossing** N (*Am Rail*) passaggio a livello.

♦ **grade school** N (*Am*) scuola elementare *or* primaria.

gra·di·ent ['greɪdɪənt] N **a** (*of road*) pendenza, gradiente *m*; **a gradient of 1 in 7** una pendenza del 7 per cento **b** (*Math, Phys*) gradiente *m*.

grad·ual ['grædjʊəl] ADJ (*change*) graduale; (*slope*) dolce, lieve.

gradu·al·ly ['grædjʊəlɪ] ADV gradualmente, poco alla volta.

gradu·ate [*n* 'grædjʊɪt; *vb* 'grædjʊˌeɪt] [1] N (*Univ*) laureato (-a); (*Am Scol*) diplomato(-a), licenziato(-a); **he's a French graduate** *or* **a graduate in French** è laureato *or* ha la laurea in francese. [2] VT (*thermometer etc*) graduare. [3] VI (*Univ*) ≈ laurearsi; (*Am Scol*) ≈ dare gli esami di maturità; **to graduate from the University of Aberdeen** laurearsi all'università di Aberdeen.

gradu·at·ed pen·sion ['grædjʊˌeɪtɪd'pɛnʃən] N *pensione calcolata sugli ultimi stipendi*.

♦ **graduate school** N (*Am*) scuola di specializzazione.

gradua·tion [ˌgrædjʊ'eɪʃən] N (*Univ: ceremony*) consegna delle lauree; (*Am Scol*) consegna dei diplomi.

graf·fi·ti [grə'fiːtɪ] NPL graffiti *mpl*.

graft [grɑːft] [1] N **a** (*Bot, Med*) innesto; **skin graft** innesto di pelle; **kidney graft** trapianto del rene **b** (*fam: corruption*) corruzione *f*; (: *hard work*) duro lavoro. [2] VT innestare.

grain [greɪn] N **a** (*no pl: cereals*) cereali *mpl*; (*Am: corn*) grano **b** (*single seed: of wheat, rice etc*) chicco, granello; (*particle: of sand, salt, sense*) grano, granello; **there's not a grain of truth in what you say** non c'è un briciolo di verità in quello che dici **c** (*of wood, marble*) venatura; (*of leather, also Phot*) grana; **it goes against the grain** (*fig*) va contro la mia (*or* la sua *etc*) natura.

♦ **grain elevator** N (*Am*) silo per cereali.

♦ **grain prices** NPL prezzo del grano.

grainy ['greɪnɪ] ADJ (*comp* **-ier**, *superl* **-iest**) granuloso(-a); (*skin*) butterato(-a).

gram, gramme [græm] N grammo.

gram·mar ['græməʳ] N grammatica; **that's bad grammar** è sgrammaticato.

gram·mar·ian [grəˈmɛərɪən] N grammatico(-a).

♦ **grammar school** N (*Brit*) ≈ liceo.

gram·mati·cal [grəˈmætɪkəl] ADJ (*exercise*) di grammatica; (*structure*) grammaticale; **to be grammatical** (*sentence, language*) essere corretto(-a) grammaticalmente.

gram·mati·cal·ly [grəˈmætɪkəlɪ] ADV grammaticalmente.

gramme [græm] N = **gram**.

gramo·phone [ˈgræməˌfəʊn] N (*Brit*) grammofono.

♦ **gramophone needle** N puntina (del grammofono).

♦ **gramophone record** N disco.

gran [græn] N (*Brit*) nonna.

grana·ry [ˈgrænərɪ] N granaio.

grand [grænd] ①ADJ (*comp* **-er**, *superl* **-est**) (*splendid*: *occasion, person*) splendido(-a), magnifico(-a); (*person*: *important*) altolocato(-a); (*style, house*) sontuoso(-a), grandioso(-a); (*fam*: *very pleasant*) eccezionale, stupendo(-a); **we had a grand time** ce la siamo proprio spassata; **the grand old man of** ... il grande vecchio di.... ②N (*fam*) mille dollari *mpl* (*or* sterline *fpl*).

grand·ad, grand·dad [ˈgrænˌdæd] N (*Brit fam*) = **grandpa**.

grand·child [ˈgrænˌtʃaɪld] N (*pl* **-children**) nipote *m/f*, nipotino(-a) (*di nonno*).

grand·daughter [ˈgrænˌdɔːtə'] N nipote *f*, nipotina (*di nonno*).

♦ **grand duke** N granduca *m*.

gran·deur [ˈgrændjə'] N (*of occasion, scenery etc*) grandiosità, maestà; (*of style, house*) splendore *m*.

grand·father [ˈgrændˌfɑːðə'] N nonno.

♦ **grandfather clock** N orologio a pendolo.

♦ **grand finale** N gran finale *m*.

gran·di·ose [ˈgrændɪəʊz] ADJ grandioso(-a); (*pej*) pomposo(-a).

♦ **grand jury** N (*Am*) giuria (*formata da 12 a 23 membri*).

grand·ma [ˈgrænˌmɑː], **grand·mama** [ˈgrænməˌmɑː] N (*fam*) nonna, nonnina.

grand·mother [ˈgrænˌmʌðə'] N nonna.

♦ **grand opera** N opera lirica.

grand·pa [ˈgrænˌpɑː], **grand·papa** [ˈgrænpəˌpɑː] N (*fam*) nonno, nonnino.

grand·parent [ˈgrænˌpɛərənt] N nonno(-a).

♦ **grand piano** N pianoforte *m* a coda.

Grand Prix [grɒnˈpriː] N (*Aut*) Gran Premio, Grand Prix *m inv*.

♦ **grand slam** N grande slam *m inv*.

grand·son [ˈgrænˌsʌn] N nipote *m*, nipotino (*di nonno*).

grand·stand [ˈgrænˌstænd] N (*Sport*) tribuna coperta.

♦ **grand total** N somma complessiva.

♦ **Grand Tour** N (*old*) il giro dell'Europa; **we did a** *or* **the Grand Tour of Venice** abbiamo fatto il giro completo di Venezia.

gran·ite [ˈgrænɪt] N granito.

gran·ny, gran·nie [ˈgrænɪ] N (*pl* **grannies**) (*fam*) nonna, nonnina.

grant [grɑːnt] ①N (*Admin*: *of money*) sovvenzione *f*, sussidio; (*Brit Univ*) ≈ borsa di studio. ②VT (*allow*: *extension, favour*) accordare; (: *pension*) assegnare; (: *a request*) accogliere; (*admit*): **to grant (that)** ammettere (che), concedere (che); **granted** *or* **granting that** ... ammesso che...; **I grant him that** glielo concedo; **to take sth for granted** dare qc per scontato; **to take sb for granted** dare per scontata la presenza di qn.

♦ **grant-aided** [ˌgrɑːntˈeɪdɪd] ADJ sovvenzionato(-a).

granu·lar [ˈgrænjʊlə'] ADJ granulare.

granu·lat·ed [ˈgrænjʊleɪtɪd] ADJ: **granulated sugar** zucchero semolato.

gran·ule [ˈgrænjuːl] N granello.

granu·lo·ma [ˌgrænjʊˈləʊmə] N granuloma *m*.

grape [greɪp] N acino, chicco d'uva; **grapes** NPL uva; **a bunch of grapes** un grappolo d'uva.

grape·fruit [ˈgreɪpˌfruːt] N pompelmo.

♦ **grapefruit knife** N coltellino ricurvo.

♦ **grape harvest** N vendemmia.

♦ **grape juice** N succo d'uva.

grape·vine [ˈgreɪpˌvaɪn] N vite *f*; **I heard it on the grapevine** (*fig*) l'ho sentito dire.

graph [grɑːf] N grafico, diagramma *m*.

graph·ic [ˈgræfɪk] ADJ (*gen*) grafico(-a); (*vivid*: *description etc*) di grande efficacia, vivido(-a); **the graphic arts** le arti grafiche.

graphi·cal·ly [ˈgræfɪkəlɪ] ADV graficamente.

♦ **graphic designer** N grafico(-a).

♦ **graphic equalizer** N equalizzatore *m* grafico.

graph·ics [ˈgræfɪks] N (*sg*: *art, process*) grafica; (*pl*: *drawings*) illustrazioni *fpl*.

graph·ite [ˈgræfaɪt] N grafite *f*.

graph·olo·gist [græˈfɒlədʒɪst] N grafologo(-a).

graph·ol·ogy [græˈfɒlədʒɪ] N grafologia.

♦ **graph paper** N carta millimetrata.

grap·ple [ˈgræpl] VI (*wrestlers etc*): **to grapple (with)** essere alle prese (con), lottare (con); **to grapple with a problem** (*fig*) essere alle prese con un problema.

grap·pling iron [ˈgræplɪŋˌaɪən] N (*Naut*) grappino.

grasp [grɑːsp] ①N (*grip*) presa; **to lose one's grasp on reality** (*fig*) perdere contatto con la realtà; **to have sth within one's grasp** avere qc a portata di mano; **it is within everybody's grasp** (*fig*) è alla portata di tutti; **it is beyond my grasp** non ci arrivo; **to have a good grasp of** (*subject*) avere una buona padronanza di; **he has a good grasp of the difficulties** si rende perfettamente conto dei problemi. ②VT **a** (*take hold of*) afferrare; (*hold firmly*) stringere; (*fig*: *chance, opportunity*) cogliere (al volo) **b** (*understand*: *meaning, hint*) afferrare

▶ **grasp at** VI + PREP (*rope etc*) afferrarsi a, aggrapparsi a; (*fig*: *opportunity*) non farsi sfuggire, approfittare di.

grasp·ing [ˈgrɑːspɪŋ] ADJ (*fig*) avido(-a).

grass [grɑːs] ①N **a** (*plant*) erba; (*lawn*) prato; (*pasture*) pascolo, prato; **"keep off the grass"** "vietato calpestare l'erba"; **not to let the grass grow under one's feet** (*fig*) non tirarla per le lunghe; **to put out to grass** (*also fig*) mettere a riposo **b** (*slang*: *marijuana*) erba **c** (*Brit fam*: *informer*) informatore(-trice); (: *ex-terrorist*) pentito(-a). ②VI (*prison slang*): **to grass (on sb)** fare una soffiata (sul conto di qn)

▶ **grass over** VT + ADV mettere a prato.

grass·hopper [ˈgrɑːsˌhɒpə'] N cavalletta.

grass·land [ˈgrɑːsˌlænd] N prateria.

♦ **grass roots** NPL (*fig*) base *f*.

♦ **grass snake** N biscia d'erba.

♦ **grass widow** N vedova bianca.

grassy [ˈgrɑːsɪ] ADJ (*comp* **-ier**, *superl* **-iest**) erboso(-a).

grate[1] [greɪt] N (*in fireplace*) grata, griglia.

grate[2] [greɪt] ①VT **a** (*cheese etc*) grattugiare, grattare **b** (*scrape*: *metallic object, chalk etc*) far stridere; **to grate one's teeth** digrignare i denti.

2 VI (*hinge*) cigolare, stridere; **to grate (on** *or* **against)** (*chalk*) stridere (su); **it really grates (on me)** (*fig*) mi dà veramente ai *or* sui nervi.

grate·ful ['greɪtfʊl] ADJ: **grateful (for)** grato(-a) (per), riconoscente (per); **I am most grateful to you** le sono enormemente grato.

grate·ful·ly ['greɪtfəlɪ] ADV con gratitudine.

grat·er ['greɪtəʳ] N grattugia.

grati·fi·ca·tion [ˌgrætɪfɪ'keɪʃən] N soddisfazione *f*.

grati·fied ['grætɪˌfaɪd] ADJ soddisfatto(-a).

grati·fy ['grætɪˌfaɪ] VT (*person*) far piacere a, dare soddisfazione a; (*desire, whim etc*) soddisfare, appagare.

grati·fy·ing ['grætɪˌfaɪɪŋ] ADJ gradito(-a), soddisfacente.

grat·in [gra'tɛ̃] N **= au gratin**.

grat·ing[1] ['greɪtɪŋ] N (*in wall, pavement*) grata.

grat·ing[2] ['greɪtɪŋ] ADJ (*sound*) stridulo(-a), stridente.

gra·tis ['grætɪs] ADV gratis.

grati·tude ['grætɪtjuːd] N gratitudine *f*, riconoscenza.

gra·tui·tous [grə'tjuːɪtəs] ADJ gratuito(-a).

gra·tui·tous·ly [grə'tjuːɪtəslɪ] ADV **a** (*for no reason*) gratuitamente **b** (*without payment*) gratis.

gra·tu·ity [grə'tjuːɪtɪ] N (*Mil*) indennità *f inv* di congedo; (*frm: tip*) mancia.

grave[1] [greɪv] ADJ (*comp* **-r**, *superl* **-st**) (*gen*) grave, serio (-a); **it had grave consequences for the nation** si ripercosse pesantemente su tutta la nazione.

grave[2] [greɪv] N tomba.

grave·dig·ger ['greɪvˌdɪgəʳ] N becchino, affossatore *m*.

grav·el ['grævəl] 1 N ghiaia.
2 ADJ (*path, pit*) di ghiaia.

grav·el·ly ['grævəlɪ] ADJ (*soil, shore*) ghiaioso(-a); (*voice*) rauco(-a), roco(-a).

grave·ly ['greɪvlɪ] ADV gravemente, solennemente; **gravely ill** in pericolo di vita.

grave·ness ['greɪvnɪs] N gravità, serietà.

♦ **grave robber** N ladro(-a) di tombe, tombarolo(-a).

grave·stone ['greɪvˌstəʊn] N pietra tombale, lapide *f*.

grave·yard ['greɪvˌjɑːd] N cimitero.

gravi·tate ['grævɪˌteɪt] VI (*fig*): **to gravitate (towards)** gravitare (verso).

gravi·ta·tion [ˌgrævɪ'teɪʃən] N gravitazione *f*.

gravi·ta·tion·al [ˌgrævɪ'teɪʃənl] ADJ gravitazionale.

grav·ity ['grævɪtɪ] N (*all senses*) gravità; **the law of gravity** la legge di gravità.

♦ **gravity feed** N alimentazione *f* a gravità.

gra·vy ['greɪvɪ] N (*Culin*) sugo dell'arrosto, intingolo della carne.

♦ **gravy boat** N salsiera.

♦ **gravy train** N: **to ride the gravy train** (*esp Am fam*) aver trovato la cuccagna.

gray [greɪ] ADJ **= grey**.

graze[1] [greɪz] 1 VI pascolare, pascere.
2 VT (*grass, field*) mettere *or* lasciare a pascolo; (*cattle*) far pascolare.

graze[2] [greɪz] 1 N (*injury*) scorticatura, escoriazione *f*.
2 VT (*touch lightly*) sfiorare, rasentare; (*scrape: skin*) scorticare, escoriare; **to graze one's knees** sbucciarsi le ginocchia.

graz·ing ['greɪzɪŋ] N pascolo.

grease [griːs] 1 N (*fat*) grasso, unto; (*lubricant*) grasso, lubrificante *m*.
2 VT (*baking tin*) ungere; (*Aut etc*) ingrassare, lubrificare; **like greased lightning** (*fam*) come una saetta; **to grease the skids** (*Am fig*) spianare la strada.

♦ **grease gun** N ingrassatore *m*.

grease·paint ['griːsˌpeɪnt] N cerone *m*.

grease·proof pa·per ['griːsˌpruːf'peɪpəʳ] N (*Brit*) carta oleata.

♦ **grease-stained** ['griːsˌsteɪnd] ADJ macchiato(-a) di unto.

greasi·ness ['griːsɪnɪs] N (*gen*) untuosità; (*of road, surface*) scivolosità.

greasy ['griːsɪ] ADJ (*comp* **-ier**, *superl* **-iest**) (*substance etc*) grasso(-a); (*hair*) untuoso(-a), grasso(-a); (*Brit: road, surface*) scivoloso(-a); (*hands, clothes*) unto(-a); (*stains*) d'unto.

great [greɪt] ADJ (*comp* **-er**, *superl* **-est**) **a** (*gen*) grande; (*pain, heat*) forte, intenso(-a); (*care etc*) molto(-a); (*age*) venerando(-a); **they're great friends** sono grandi amici; **he was in great pain** soffriva molto; **it's of no great importance** non ha molta importanza; **he's a great reader** è un lettore accanito; **great big** (*fam*) enorme; **Alexander the Great** Alessandro Magno *or* il Grande; **you're a great one for arriving at the wrong moment!** (*fam*) sei speciale per arrivare al momento sbagliato!; **the great thing is that ...** il bello è che...; **great Scott!** (*fam*) perbacco!

b (*fam: excellent*) meraviglioso(-a), magnifico(-a), favoloso(-a); **it was great!** è stato fantastico!; **he's great at football** nel calcio è una cannonata; **he's great on jazz** sa tutto sul jazz; **we had a great time** ci siamo divertiti un mondo; **you look great** hai un aspetto splendido; **you look great in that outfit** quel completo ti sta benissimo.

♦ **great-aunt** [ˌgreɪt'ɑːnt] N prozia.

♦ **Great Barrier Reef** N: **the Great Barrier Reef** la grande barriera corallina.

♦ **Great Britain** N la Gran Bretagna.

great·coat ['greɪtˌkəʊt] N cappotto pesante.

great·er ['greɪtəʳ] ADJ (*comp of* **great**) più grande; **Greater London** Londra e sobborghi.

great·est ['greɪtɪst] ADJ (*superl of* **great**) il/la più grande; **he's the greatest!** (*fam*) è grande!

♦ **great-grandchild** [ˌgreɪt'grænˌtʃaɪld] N (*pl* **-children**) pronipote *m/f* (*di bisnonno*).

♦ **great-granddaughter** [ˌgreɪt'grænˌdɔːtəʳ] N pronipote *f* (*di bisnonno*).

♦ **great-grandfather** [ˌgreɪt'grænˌfɑːðəʳ] N bisnonno.

♦ **great-grandmother** [ˌgreɪt'grænˌmʌðəʳ] N bisnonna.

♦ **great-grandparent** [ˌgreɪt'grænˌpɛərənt] N bisnonno (-a).

♦ **great-grandson** [ˌgreɪt'grænsʌn] N pronipote *m* (*di bisnonno*).

♦ **great-hearted** [ˌgreɪt'hɑːtɪd] ADJ magnanimo(-a).

♦ **Great Lakes** NPL: **the Great Lakes** i Grandi Laghi.

great·ly ['greɪtlɪ] ADV (*gen*) molto; **greatly superior** di gran lunga superiore; **it is greatly to be regretted that ...** (*frm*) ci rincresce infinitamente che...; **you are greatly mistaken** ti sbagli di grosso.

♦ **great-nephew** [ˌgreɪt'nɛvjuː] N pronipote *m* (*di prozio*).

great·ness ['greɪtnɪs] N grandezza.

♦ **great-niece** [ˌgreɪt'niːs] N pronipote *f* (*di prozio*).

♦ **great northern diver** N (*Zool*) tuffatore *m* dei ghiacci.

♦ **great tit** N (*Zool*) cinciallegra.

♦ **great-uncle** [ˌgreɪt'ʌŋkl] N prozio.

♦ **Great War** N: **the Great War** la Grande Guerra.

grebe [griːb] N (*Zool*) svasso; **great crested grebe** svasso *m* maggiore.

Gre·cian ['griːʃən] ADJ greco(-a).

Greece [griːs] N Grecia.

greed [griːd] N: **greed (for)** (for money, power) avidità (di), desiderio smodato (di); (for food: also: **greediness**) golosità (per), ingordigia (di).

greedi·ly ['griːdɪlɪ] ADV (see adj) avidamente; golosamente, ghiottamente, ingordamente.

greedy ['griːdɪ] ADJ (comp -ier, superl -iest): **greedy (for)** (gen) avido(-a) (di); (for food) goloso(-a) (di), ghiotto(-a) (di), ingordo(-a) (di).

Greek [griːk] **1** ADJ greco(-a).
2 N **a** (person) greco(-a) **b** (language) greco; **ancient/modern Greek** greco antico/moderno; **it's (all) Greek to me** (fam) per me è arabo.

♦ **Greek Orthodox Church** N Chiesa Greco-Ortodossa.

green [griːn] **1** ADJ (comp -er, superl -est) (colour, Pol) verde; (unripe) acerbo(-a), verde; (inexperienced) alle prime armi, inesperto(-a); (gullible) ingenuo(-a); **to have green fingers**, (Am) **to have a green thumb** (fig) avere il pollice verde; **to turn green** (fig: with nausea) sbiancare; (: with envy) diventare verde; **I'm not as green as I look!** (fig fam) non sono mica nato ieri!; **green salad** insalata verde.
2 N **a** (colour) verde m; (grassy area) prato, spiazzo erboso; (bowling green) campo da bocce; (of golf course) green m inv; (also: **village green**) ≈ piazza del paese; **greens** NPL (Culin) verdura sg
b (Pol): **the Greens** i verdi.

green·back ['griːnˌbæk] N (Am fam) biglietto da un dollaro.

♦ **green beans** NPL fagiolini mpl.

♦ **green belt** N (round town) cintura di verde.

♦ **Green Beret** N: **Green Berets** (Mil) Berretti mpl Verdi.

♦ **green card** N (Brit Aut) carta verde; (Am: residence permit) permesso di soggiorno.

green·ery ['griːnərɪ] N verde m.

green·finch ['griːnˌfɪntʃ] N verdone m.

green·fly ['griːnˌflaɪ] N afide m.

green·gage ['griːnˌgeɪdʒ] N susina Regina Claudia.

green·grocer ['griːnˌgrəʊsəʳ] N (Brit) fruttivendolo(-a); "greengrocer's" "frutta e verdura"; **to go to the greengrocer's** andare dal fruttivendolo.

green·house ['griːnˌhaʊs] N serra.

♦ **greenhouse effect** N: **the greenhouse effect** l'effetto serra.

♦ **greenhouse gas** N gas m inv responsabile dell'effetto serra.

green·ish ['griːnɪʃ] ADJ verdognolo(-a), verdastro(-a).

Green·land ['griːnlənd] N Groenlandia.

Green·land·er ['griːnləndəʳ] N groenlandese m/f.

♦ **green light** N: **to give sb/sth the green light** dare il via libera a qn/qc.

green·ness ['griːnnɪs] N verde m.

♦ **Green Paper** N (Brit Pol) ≈ libro bianco.

♦ **Green Party** N: **the Green Party** i Verdi.

♦ **green pepper** N peperone m verde.

green·room ['griːnˌruːm] N (Theatre) camerino.

green·stuff ['griːnˌstʌf] N verdura.

Green·wich Mean Time ['grɪnɪdʒˌmiːnˌtaɪm], **Green·wich Time** ['grɪnɪdʒˌtaɪm] N tempo medio di Greenwich.

greet [griːt] VT accogliere, salutare; **a strange sight greeted his eyes** una strana scena si presentò ai suoi occhi; **the statement was greeted with loud laughter** l'affermazione fu salutata da or con grasse risate.

greet·ing ['griːtɪŋ] N saluto; (welcome) accoglienza; **greetings** NPL saluti mpl; **Season's greetings** Buone Feste; **Christmas/birthday greetings** auguri mpl di Natale/di compleanno.

♦ **greeting card**, **greetings card** N biglietto d'auguri.

gre·gari·ous [grɪˈgɛərɪəs] ADJ (animal) gregario(-a); (person) socievole.

grem·lin ['grɛmlɪn] N spiritello.

Gre·na·da [grɛˈneɪdə] N Grenada.

gre·nade [grɪˈneɪd] N (also: **hand grenade**) granata, bomba a mano.

grew [gruː] PT of **grow**.

grey [greɪ] **1** ADJ (comp -er, superl -est) grigio(-a); (complexion) smorto(-a); (outlook, prospect) poco roseo(-a); **to go grey** diventar grigio(-a); **to go grey with fear** (person) sbiancarsi in viso dalla paura; **grey skies** cielo grigio.
2 N (colour) grigio.
3 VI (hair) diventare grigio(-a).

♦ **grey area** N (fig) punto oscuro.

grey·beard ['greɪˌbɪəd] N vecchio.

♦ **grey·haired** [ˌgreɪˈhɛəd] ADJ dai capelli grigi.

grey·hound ['greɪˌhaʊnd] N levriero.

grey·lag ['greɪˌlæg] N (also: **greylag goose**) oca cenerina.

♦ **grey matter** N (fig fam) materia grigia.

grid [grɪd] N (grating) grata, griglia; (Elec, Gas: network) rete f; (on map) reticolato; (Am Aut) area d'incrocio; **the national grid** la rete elettrica nazionale.

grid·dle ['grɪdl] N (esp Am) piastra.

grid·iron ['grɪdˌaɪən] N graticola.

grid·lock ['grɪdˌlɒk] N (traffic jam) paralisi f inv del traffico.

♦ **grid reference** N coordinate fpl chilometriche.

grief [griːf] N (sorrow) dolore m; (cause of sorrow) dolore, pena; **to come to grief** (plan) naufragare; (person) finire male; **good grief!** (fam) mio Dio!

♦ **grief-stricken** ['griːfˌstrɪkən] ADJ affranto(-a).

griev·ance ['griːvəns] N (complaint) lagnanza, rimostranza; (cause for complaint) motivo di risentimento.

grieve [griːv] **1** VT addolorare; **it grieves me to see ...** mi rattrista vedere.... **2** VI addolorarsi, soffrire; **to grieve for sb** compiangere qn; (dead person) piangere qn.

griev·ous ['griːvəs] ADJ (pain) atroce, intenso(-a); (injuries, fault, loss) grave; (blow) pesante; (news) triste, doloroso (-a); (crime) atroce, orrendo(-a).

♦ **grievous bodily harm** N (Law) lesione f personale grave.

griev·ous·ly ['griːvəslɪ] ADV (see adj) atrocemente; gravemente; pesantemente; tristemente; orribilmente.

grif·fin ['grɪfɪn] N (Myth) grifone m.

grif·fon ['grɪfən] N (Myth, Zool) grifone m.

grill [grɪl] **1** N **a** (Brit: on cooker) griglia; (gridiron) graticola; (in restaurant: also: **grillroom**) grill-room m inv; **a mixed grill** una grigliata mista **b** (also: **grille**: grating) griglia; (: at window) grata.
2 VT **a** (Culin) cuocere ai ferri or alla griglia; **grilled meat** carne ai ferri or alla griglia **b** (fam: interrogate) fare il terzo grado a.

grille [grɪl] N grata; (Aut) griglia.

grill·room ['grɪlˌrʊm] N grill-room m inv.

grim [grɪm] ADJ (comp -mer, superl -mest) (hard, unpleasant: gen) duro(-a); (: struggle) accanito(-a); (: silence) sinistro (-a); (: landscape) desolato(-a); (: humour, tale) macabro (-a); (determined: face) risoluto(-a), determinato(-a); (determination) feroce; **to hold on (to sth) like grim death** attaccarsi (a qc) con le unghie e coi denti; **to feel grim** (fam: ill) sentirsi poco bene, sentirsi giù.

gri·mace [grɪˈmeɪs] **1** N smorfia.

2 VI fare smorfie.

grime [graɪm] N sporcizia, sudiciume m.

grim·ly ['grɪmlɪ] ADV (frown, look) cupamente; (continue, hold on) risolutamente; (fight) accanitamente.

grimy ['graɪmɪ] ADJ sudicio(-a), sporco(-a).

grin [grɪn] 1 N (smile) sorriso smagliante; (cheeky) sorrisetto.

2 VI: **to grin (at)** fare un gran sorriso (a); **to grin and bear it** stringere i denti e andare avanti.

grind [graɪnd] (vb: pt, pp **ground**) 1 VT (coffee, corn) macinare; (Am: meat) tritare, macinare; (car gears) grattare; (sharpen: knife) arrotare; (polish: gem, lens) molare; **to grind one's teeth** digrignare i denti; **to grind sth into the earth** schiacciare qc col piede.

2 VI stridere, cigolare; **to grind to a halt** (vehicle) rallentare fino a fermarsi; (fig: talks, scheme) insabbiarsi; (: work, production) cessare del tutto.

3 N (fam: work) sgobbata; **the daily grind** (fam) il trantran m inv quotidiano

▶ **grind away** VI + ADV (fam) sgobbare

▶ **grind down** VT + ADV (substance) levigare; (fig: oppress) schiacciare, opprimere

▶ **grind on** VI + ADV continuare; **the years grind on** gli anni avanzano inesorabilmente

▶ **grind up** VT + ADV polverizzare.

grind·er ['graɪndə'] N (machine: for coffee, pepper) macinino; (: for sharpening) affilacoltelli m inv.

grind·ing ['graɪndɪŋ] ADJ (sound) stridente; (fig: poverty) opprimente.

grind·stone ['graɪnd,stəun] N: **to keep one's nose to the grindstone** darci sotto or dentro.

grip [grɪp] 1 N a presa; **to have a firm grip on sb/sth** tenere saldamente qn/qc; **he held her arm in a vice-like grip** le stringeva il braccio come in una morsa; **to take a grip on** afferrare; **to lose one's grip** perdere or allentare la presa; (fig) perdere la grinta; **in the grip of the recession** (fig) nel pieno della recessione; **to get to grips with sb/sth** (also fig) venire alle prese con qn/qc; **to come to grips with** affrontare, cercare di risolvere; **to have a good grip of a subject** avere una buona padronanza di una materia; **get a grip on yourself!** (fam) controllati!

b (of racket, oar) impugnatura

c (holdall) sacca, borsa da viaggio.

2 VT a (hold) afferrare, stringere; **to grip the road** (tyres) far presa sulla strada; (càr) tenere bene la strada b (fig: enthral) far presa su; (: subj: fear) prendere.

gripe [graɪp] 1 N (fam: complaint) lagna; **the gripes** (stomach ache) colica.

2 VI (fam: complain): **to gripe (about)** lagnarsi (di).

grip·ing ['graɪpɪŋ] 1 ADJ (pain) lancinante.

2 N (fam: complaining) lagne fpl, lamentele fpl.

grip·ping ['grɪpɪŋ] ADJ (story, novel) avvincente, appassionante.

gris·ly ['grɪzlɪ] ADJ (comp -ier, superl -iest) (murder) raccapricciante.

grist [grɪst] N (fig): **it's (all) grist to the mill** tutto aiuta.

gris·tle ['grɪsl] N cartilagine f.

gris·tly ['grɪslɪ] ADJ (meat) tutto(-a) nervi.

grit [grɪt] 1 N (gravel) ghiaia; (fig: courage) fegato; **I've got a piece of grit in my eye** ho un bruscolino nell'occhio; see also **grits**.

2 VT a (road) ricoprire di ghiaia b: **to grit one's teeth** stringere i denti.

grits [grɪts] NPL (Am) macinato grosso (di granturco).

grit·ty ['grɪtɪ] ADJ (texture) granuloso(-a); (person) coraggioso(-a).

griz·zle ['grɪzl] VI (Brit: cry) piagnucolare.

griz·zled ['grɪzld] ADJ (hair) brizzolato(-a).

griz·zly ['grɪzlɪ] N (also: **grizzly bear**) orso grigio, grizzly m inv.

groan [grəun] 1 N (of pain) gemito.

2 VI gemere; (tree, floorboard) scricchiolare.

gro·cer ['grəusə'] N negoziante m/f di (generi) alimentari; **grocer's (shop)** negozio di (generi) alimentari.

gro·ceries ['grəusərɪz] NPL (generi) alimentari mpl; **to go out for some groceries** fare la spesa.

gro·cery ['grəusərɪ] N (shop) negozio di (generi) alimentari.

grog [grɒg] N grog m inv.

grog·gy ['grɒgɪ] ADJ (comp -ier, superl -iest) (dazed) stordito(-a), intontito(-a); (shaky) malfermo(-a), barcollante.

groin [grɔɪn] N inguine m.

groom [gru:m] 1 N (in stable) palafreniere m; (also: **bridegroom**) sposo.

2 VT a (horse) pulire, strigliare b (prepare: person): **to groom sb for** avviare qn alla carriera di.

groom·ing ['gru:mɪŋ] N (of horse) strigliatura; **she's known for her immaculate grooming** è famosa per essere sempre curata e perfetta.

groove [gru:v] N (in wood, metal) solco, scanalatura; (of record) solco.

groovy ['gru:vɪ] ADJ (comp -ier, superl -iest) favoloso(-a).

grope [grəup] 1 VI (also: **grope around**, **grope about**) brancolare, andare a tentoni; **to grope for sth** cercare qc a tentoni or a tastoni; (fig: for words) cercare (disperatamente).

2 VT: **to grope one's way through** farsi strada a tentoni in or tra; **to grope one's way towards** andare a tentoni verso; **to grope sb** (fam: sexually) mettere le mani addosso a qn.

gros·grain ['grəu,greɪn] N gros-grain m.

gross [grəus] 1 ADJ (comp -er, superl -est) a (fat: body) obeso(-a); (vegetation) lussureggiante; (behaviour, language, error) grossolano(-a); (impertinence) sfacciato (-a)

b (total: profit, income) complessivo(-a), totale; (Comm: weight, income) lordo(-a); **£10,000 gross** 10.000 sterline lorde.

2 N, PL INV (twelve dozen) grossa.

3 VT (Comm) incassare, avere un incasso lordo di.

♦ **gross domestic product** N prodotto interno lordo.

gross·ly ['grəuslɪ] ADV (exaggerate) enormemente; (overestimate) di molto; **it's grossly unfair!** è proprio ingiusto!

♦ **gross national product** N prodotto nazionale lordo.

gro·tesque [grəu'tesk] ADJ grottesco(-a).

gro·tesque·ly [grəu'tesklɪ] ADV grottescamente.

grot·to ['grɒtəu] N grotta.

grot·ty ['grɒtɪ] ADJ (Brit fam) squallido(-a); **I feel grotty** mi sento a terra.

grouch [grautʃ] 1 VI (fam) brontolare.

2 N (person) brontolone(-a); **she's always got a grouch** (complaint) ha sempre da brontolare.

grouchy ['grautʃɪ] ADJ (fam) brontolone(-a).

ground¹ [graund] 1 N a (soil) terra, suolo, terreno

b (terrain) terreno; **high ground** altura; **hilly ground** zona collinosa; **to gain/lose ground** guadagnare/perdere terreno; **to be on dangerous ground** muoversi

su un terreno minato; **it suits me down to the ground** mi sta *or* va benissimo; **to cut the ground from under sb's feet** tagliare le gambe a qn

c (*surface*) terra; (*background*) terreno, sfondo; **on the ground** per terra, a terra; **above ground** in superficie; **below ground** sottoterra; **to fall to the ground** cadere a *or* per terra *or* al suolo; (*fig*) andare in fumo; **to get off the ground** (*aircraft*) decollare; (*plans*) prendere il via; **to stand one's ground** mantenere le proprie posizioni; **he covered a lot of ground in his lecture** ha toccato molti argomenti nel corso della conferenza

d (*Sport*) campo; (*also:* **football ground**) campo di calcio; **grounds** NPL (*gardens*) giardini *mpl*

e : **grounds** NPL (*of coffee*) fondi *mpl* (di caffè)

f (*Am Elec: also:* **ground wire**) (presa a) terra

g (*reason: usu pl*) ragione *f*, motivo; **on medical grounds** per motivi di salute; **grounds for complaint** motivo *or* ragione di lamentarsi; **on the ground(s) that** per il motivo che.

2 VT **a** (*plane, pilot*) bloccare a terra; (*ship*) far incagliare

b (*argument, hope*) basare

c (*Am Elec*) mettere a terra.

3 VI (*Naut*) incagliarsi, arenarsi.

ground² [graʊnd] **1** PT, PP of **grind**.

2 ADJ (*coffee, pepper*) macinato(-a); **ground glass** vetro smerigliato; **ground rice** farina di riso.

♦ **ground cloth** N (*Am*) = **groundsheet**.

♦ **ground control** N (*Aer, Space*) base *f* di controllo.

♦ **ground floor** N pianterreno, pianoterra *m*.

♦ **ground forces** NPL (*Mil*) forze *fpl* di terra.

♦ **ground frost** N brina.

♦ **ground handling** N (*Aer*) assistenza a terra.

ground·ing [ˈgraʊndɪŋ] N (*educational*) fondamento, basi *fpl*; **he has a good grounding in French** ha delle buone basi in francese.

ground·less [ˈgraʊndlɪs] ADJ infondato(-a).

♦ **ground level** N (*of house*) pianterreno, pianoterra *m*; **at ground level** al livello del suolo.

ground·nut [ˈgraʊndˌnʌt] N arachide *f*.

♦ **ground plan** N pianta.

♦ **ground rent** N (*Brit*) canone *m* di affitto di un terreno.

♦ **ground rule** N: **the ground rules** le regole del gioco.

♦ **ground rules** NPL: **the ground rules** i principi fondamentali.

ground·sel [ˈgraʊnsl] N erba calderina.

ground·sheet [ˈgraʊndˌʃiːt] N (*Brit: in tent*) telone *m* impermeabile.

grounds·man [ˈgraʊndzmən] N (*pl* **-men**), (*Am*) **grounds·keep·er** [ˈgraʊndzˌkiːpəʳ] N (*Sport*) custode *m* (di campo sportivo).

♦ **ground staff** N (*Aer*) personale *m* di terra.

♦ **ground stroke** N (*Tennis*) colpo di rimbalzo.

grounds·well [ˈgraʊndˌswɛl] N mareggiata; (*fig*) ondata.

♦ **ground-to-air** [ˈgraʊndtuːˈɛəʳ] ADJ terra-aria *inv*.

♦ **ground-to-ground** [ˈgraʊndtəˈgraʊnd] ADJ terra-terra *inv*; **ground-to-ground missile** missile *m* terra-terra.

♦ **ground water** N acqua freatica.

♦ **ground wire** N (*Am Elec*) filo di massa *or* di terra.

ground·work [ˈgraʊndˌwɜːk] N lavoro preparatorio, preparazione *f*.

group [gruːp] **1** N (*gen*) gruppo; (*set, clique: of people*) circolo, gruppo; (*Mus: pop group*) complesso, gruppo.

2 VT (*also:* **group together**) raggruppare.

3 VI (*also:* **group together**) raggrupparsi.

4 ADJ (*discussion, photo*) di gruppo, collettivo(-a).

♦ **group captain** N (*Aer*) comandante *m* di gruppo.

groupie [ˈgruːpɪ] N (*fam*) groupie *m/f*, *fanatico seguace di un gruppo (o un cantante) rock*.

♦ **group practice** N (*Med*) *ambulatorio medico con più dottori*.

♦ **group therapy** N (*Psych*) terapia di gruppo.

grouse¹ [graʊs] N, PL INV gallo cedrone, urogallo.

grouse² [graʊs] (*fam*) **1** N (*complaint*) mugugno.

2 VI: **to grouse (about)** brontolare (su).

grove [graʊv] N boschetto.

grov·el [ˈgrɒvl] VI (*also fig*): **to grovel to** *or* **before sb** strisciare di fronte a qn.

grow [graʊ] (*vb: pt* **grew**, *pp* **grown**) **1** VT (*Agr*) coltivare, far crescere; (*beard*) farsi crescere.

2 VI **a** (*plant, person, hair*) crescere; (*increase: in numbers*) aumentare, salire; (: *in membership*) ingrandirsi; (*develop: friendship, love*) rafforzarsi; (: *custom, idea*) affermarsi, diffondersi; **to grow in stature/popularity** veder aumentare il proprio prestigio/la propria popolarità

b (*become*) farsi, diventare; **to grow dark** farsi buio; **to grow rich/weak** arricchirsi/indebolirsi; **to grow tired of waiting** stancarsi di aspettare; **to grow to like sb** imparare ad apprezzare qn

▶ **grow apart** VI + ADV (*fig*) estraniarsi

▶ **grow away from** VI + ADV + PREP (*fig*) allontanarsi da, staccarsi da; **we have grown away from each other** i nostri rapporti si sono gradatamente raffreddati

▶ **grow in** VI + ADV (*nail*) incarnarsi

▶ **grow into** VI + PREP **a** (*clothes*): **he'll grow into them** quando crescerà gli andranno bene

b (*become*) farsi, diventare; **she has grown into a beautiful woman** si è fatta una gran bella donna

▶ **grow on** VI + PREP: **that painting is growing on me** quel quadro più lo guardo più mi piace

▶ **grow out of** VI + ADV + PREP **a** (*clothes*) non entrare più in; (*habit*) perdere (col tempo); **he'll grow out of it** gli passerà

b (*arise from*) nascere da, essere la conseguenza di

▶ **grow up** VI + ADV **a** (*become adult*) diventar grande, crescere; **I grew up in the country** sono cresciuto in campagna; **grow up!** (*fam*) non fare il bambino!

b (*develop: idea, friendship*) nascere.

grow·er [ˈgraʊəʳ] N (*Agr*) coltivatore(-trice); (*of wine*) viticoltore(-trice).

grow·ing [ˈgraʊɪŋ] ADJ (*fear, amount*) crescente; **to have a growing desire to do sth** avere un desiderio sempre più forte di fare qc.

♦ **growing pains** NPL problemi *mpl* della crescita; (*fig: of organization*) problemi di avviamento.

growl [graʊl] **1** N (*of animal*) ringhio; (*of thunder*) brontolio; **the dog gave a growl** il cane ringhiò.

2 VI ringhiare; (*person, thunder*) brontolare.

grown [graʊn] **1** PP of **grow**.

2 ADJ (*also:* **fully grown**) adulto(-a), grande; **he's a grown man** è un adulto.

♦ **grown-up** [ˌgraʊnˈʌp] **1** ADJ da grande; **he's very grown-up** è molto maturo.

2 N grande *m/f*, adulto(-a).

growth [graʊθ] N **a** (*increase*) crescita, aumento; (*development*) sviluppo; **he has 5 days' growth (of beard)** ha una barba di 5 giorni; **to reach full growth** raggiungere il pieno sviluppo **b** (*Med*) tumore *m*.

♦ **growth rate** N (*Econ*) tasso di crescita.

groyne [grɔɪn] N frangiflutti *m inv*.

grub [grʌb] N a (*larva*) bruco b (*fam: food*) roba da mangiare; **grub('s) up!** si mangia!, a tavola!

grub·bi·ness ['grʌbɪnɪs] N sporcizia.

grub·by ['grʌbɪ] ADJ (*comp* -ier, *superl* -iest) sudicio(-a), sporco(-a).

grudge [grʌdʒ] 1 N: **grudge (against)** risentimento (verso), rancore *m* (verso); **to bear a grudge against sb** portare *or* serbare rancore a qn.

2 VT: **to grudge sb sth** (*money*) dare qc a qn malvolentieri *or* a malincuore; **it's not the money I grudge, but the time** non me la prendo per i soldi ma per il tempo; **I don't grudge you your success** non t'invidio il tuo successo; **to grudge doing sth** fare qc malvolentieri *or* a malincuore.

grudg·ing ['grʌdʒɪŋ] ADJ (*praise, respect*) dato(-a) a malincuore; **she gave him her grudging support** gli ha dato a malincuore il suo appoggio.

grudg·ing·ly ['grʌdʒɪŋlɪ] ADV (*accept, support*) malvolentieri, a malincuore.

gru·el ['gruːəl] N pappa d'avena.

gru·el·ling, (*Am*) **gru·el·ing** ['gruəlɪŋ] ADJ estenuante.

grue·some ['gruːsəm] ADJ orrendo(-a), orribile, agghiacciante.

gruff [grʌf] ADJ (*comp* -er, *superl* -est) burbero(-a).

gruff·ly ['grʌflɪ] ADV in modo burbero, burberamente.

gruff·ness ['grʌfnɪs] N rudezza, scontrosità.

grum·ble ['grʌmbl] 1 N (*complaint*) lamentela; (*noise*) brontolio; (: *of guns*) rombo; **without a grumble** (*agree, accept*) senza lagnarsi.

2 VI (*person: complain*): **to grumble (about)** brontolare (su), lagnarsi (di); (*thunder*) rombare.

grum·bling ap·pen·dix ['grʌmblɪŋə'pɛndɪks] N appendice *f* infiammata.

grumpi·ly ['grʌmpɪlɪ] ADV in modo scorbutico, scorbuticamente.

grumpi·ness ['grʌmpɪnɪs] N scontrosità, irritabilità.

grumpy ['grʌmpɪ] ADJ (*comp* -ier, *superl* -iest) scorbutico (-a).

grunge [grʌndʒ] N (*Mus*) grunge *m*; (*style*) moda grunge.

grunt [grʌnt] 1 N grugnito; **to give a grunt** emettere un grugnito.

2 VI grugnire.

♦ **G-string** ['dʒiːˌstrɪŋ] N (*garment*) tanga *m inv*.

GT [ˌdʒiːˈtiː] N ABBR (*Aut: = gran turismo*) GT *f*.

GU ABBR (*Am Post*) = Guam.

gua·no ['gwɑːnəʊ] N guano.

guar·an·tee [ˌgærənˈtiː] 1 N garanzia; (*guarantor*) garante *m/f*, mallevadore *m*; **a year's guarantee** (*on appliances, watch etc*) un anno di garanzia; **there's no guarantee that it won't happen again** nessuno ti garantisce che non accadrà di nuovo.

2 VT (*gen*) garantire; **I can't guarantee that he did it** non posso garantire che lo abbia fatto; **he can't guarantee (that) he'll come** non può garantire che verrà.

guar·an·tor [ˌgærənˈtɔː] N garante *m/f*, mallevadore *m*.

guard [gɑːd] 1 N a (*gen, also Mil, Sport*) guardia; (*security guard*) guardia giurata; (*esp Am: prison guard*) secondino; (*Brit Rail*) ≈ capotreno; (*also:* **guard duty:** *watch*) (turno di) guardia; (*fig: watchfulness*) vigilanza; **to change guard** (*Mil*) cambiare la guardia; **to be on guard** (*Mil*) essere di guardia; **to be on one's guard** (*fig*) stare in guardia; **to keep sb under guard** tenere qn sotto vigilanza; **to catch sb off his/her guard** cogliere *or*

prendere qn alla sprovvista; **to keep guard over sb/sth** (*Mil, fig*) fare la guardia a qn/qc.

b (*safety device: on machine*) schermo protettivo; (*protection*) riparo, protezione *f*; (*also:* **fire guard**) parafuoco; (*mud guard*) parafango.

2 VT (*prisoner, treasure*) fare la guardia a, stare a guardia di; (*secret*) custodire; (*protect*): **to guard (against** *or* **from)** proteggere (da), salvaguardare (da).

3 ADJ: **guard duty** turno di guardia; **on guard duty** di guardia

▸ **guard against** VI + PREP (*take care to avoid: illness*) guardarsi da; (: *suspicion, accidents*) premunirsi contro; **to guard against doing sth** guardarsi dal fare qc.

♦ **guard dog** N cane *m* da guardia.

guard·ed ['gɑːdɪd] ADJ (*reply, tone*) guardingo(-a), cauto (-a), circospetto(-a).

guard·ed·ly ['gɑːdɪdlɪ] ADV in modo guardingo, con circospezione.

guard·house ['gɑːdˌhaʊs] N (*for guards*) corpo di guardia; (*for prisoners*) sala di disciplina.

guard·ian ['gɑːdɪən] N custode *m/f*; (*of minor*) tutore(-trice).

♦ **guardian angel** N angelo custode.

♦ **Guardian Angels** NPL (*vigilantes*) *organizzazione di vigilantes volontari.*

guard·rail ['gɑːdˌreɪl] N guardrail *m inv*.

guard·room ['gɑːdˌrʊm] N (*Mil*) corpo di guardia.

guards·man ['gɑːdzmən] N (*pl* -men) (*Brit*) soldato della Guardia Reale; (*Am*) soldato della Guardia Nazionale.

♦ **guard's van** N (*Brit Rail*) vagone *m* di servizio.

Gua·te·ma·la [ˌgwɑːtɪˈmɑːlə] N Guatemala *m*.

Gua·te·ma·lan [ˌgwɑːtɪˈmɑːlən] ADJ, N guatemalteco(-a).

gudg·eon ['gʌdʒən] N (*fish*) gobione *m*.

Guern·sey ['gɜːnzɪ] N (*island*) (isola di) Guernsey *f*; (*cow*) mucca di Guernsey.

guer·ril·la [gəˈrɪlə] N guerrigliero(-a); **guerrilla group** gruppo di guerriglieri; **guerrilla tactics** tattica di guerriglia.

♦ **guerrilla warfare** N guerriglia.

guess [gɛs] 1 N supposizione *f*, congettura; **to take** *or* **make** *or* **have a guess** cercare di indovinare, provare a indovinare; **at a (rough) guess** a occhio e croce; **my guess is that ...** suppongo che...; **it's anybody's guess** Dio solo (lo) sa; **your guess is as good as mine** ne so quanto te.

2 VT a (*gen*) indovinare; **guess what!** (*fam*) sai l'ultima?; **I guessed as much** me lo immaginavo

b (*esp Am: suppose*) supporre, credere; **I guess so** direi di sì; **I guess you're right** forse hai ragione.

3 VI a indovinare; **to guess at sth** provare a indovinare qc; **to guess correctly** azzeccarci; **she's just guessing** sta tirando a indovinare; **to keep sb guessing** tenere qn in sospeso *or* sulla corda.

b (*esp Am: suppose*) supporre, credere; **he's happy, I guess** è felice, immagino.

guess·ti·mate ['gɛstɪmɪt] N (*fam*) stima approssimativa.

guess·work ['gɛsˌwɜːk] N: **I got the answer by guesswork** ho azzeccato la risposta.

guest [gɛst] N (*in house, on TV programme*) ospite *m/f*; (*at party*) invitato(-a); (*at hotel*) cliente *m/f*; (*in boarding house*) pensionante *m/f*; **guest of honour** ospite d'onore; **be my guest** (*fam*) fai come ti pare.

guest·house ['gɛstˌhaʊs] N pensione *f*.

♦ **guest room** N stanza *or* camera degli ospiti.

guff [gʌf] N (*fam*) stupidaggini *fpl*, assurdità *fpl*.

guf·faw [gʌˈfɔː] 1 N risata fragorosa or sonora. 2 VI ridere fragorosamente.

guid·ance [ˈgaɪdəns] N (counselling) consigli mpl, guida; (leadership) guida, direzione f; **for your guidance** a titolo informativo.

guide [gaɪd] 1 N a (gen) guida; (manual) guida, manuale m; (fig: indication, model) indicazione f; **let conscience be your guide** lasciati guidare dalla coscienza; **as a rough guide** approssimativamente b : Guide (Brit) giovane esploratrice f. 2 VT guidare; **to be guided by sb/sth** farsi or lasciarsi guidare da qn/qc.

guide·book [ˈgaɪdˌbʊk] N guida.

guid·ed [ˈgaɪdɪd] ADJ (tour) guidato(-a).

♦ **guided missile** N missile m teleguidato.

♦ **guide dog** N cane m per ciechi.

guide·lines [ˈgaɪdˌlaɪnz] NPL (fig) direttive fpl.

guid·ing [ˈgaɪdɪŋ] ADJ (principle) informatore(-trice); **he needs a guiding hand** ha bisogno di qualcuno che lo guidi; **guiding light** or **star** (fig) guida.

guild [gɪld] N (History) corporazione f, arte f, gilda; (club) associazione f.

guild·hall [ˈgɪldˌhɔːl] N (Brit: town hall) (palazzo del) municipio.

guile [gaɪl] N astuzia.

guile·less [ˈgaɪllɪs] ADJ franco(-a), candido(-a).

guil·le·mot [ˈgɪlɪˌmɒt] N uria.

guil·lo·tine [gɪləˈtiːn] N ghigliottina; (for paper) taglierina.

guilt [gɪlt] N (being guilty) colpevolezza; (feeling guilty) colpa, senso di colpa; **tormented by guilt** tormentato (-a) dal senso di colpa.

♦ **guilt complex** N (Psych) complesso di colpa.

guilti·ly [ˈgɪltɪlɪ] ADV colpevolmente.

guilt·less [ˈgɪltlɪs] ADJ senza colpa, innocente.

guilty [ˈgɪltɪ] ADJ (comp **-ier**, superl **-iest**) (gen, Law) colpevole; (conscience) sporco(-a); **guilty of sth** colpevole di qc; **the guilty person** or **party** il/la responsabile; **to feel guilty (about)** sentirsi in colpa (per); **to find sb guilty** riconoscere qn colpevole; **to plead guilty/not guilty** dichiararsi colpevole/innocente.

Guinea [ˈgɪnɪ] N: **Republic of Guinea** la Repubblica di Guinea.

guinea [ˈgɪnɪ] N (Brit old) ghinea, ≈ 21 shillings.

♦ **guinea fowl** N faraona.

♦ **guinea pig** N porcellino d'India, cavia; (fig) cavia.

guise [gaɪz] N maschera, parvenza.

gui·tar [gɪˈtɑːʳ] N chitarra.

gui·tar·ist [gɪˈtɑːrɪst] N chitarrista m/f.

gulch [gʌltʃ] N (Am) burrone m.

gulf [gʌlf] N (bay) golfo; (chasm, also fig) abisso; **the (Persian) Gulf** il Golfo Persico.

♦ **Gulf States** NPL: **the Gulf States** gli stati del Golfo Persico.

♦ **Gulf Stream** N: **the Gulf Stream** la corrente del Golfo.

gull [gʌl] N gabbiano.

gul·let [ˈgʌlɪt] N gargarozzo.

gul·li·bil·ity [ˌgʌlɪˈbɪlɪtɪ] N credulità, semplicioneria.

gul·lible [ˈgʌlɪbl] ADJ credulone(-a), sempliciotto(-a).

gul·ly [ˈgʌlɪ] N (ravine) burrone m, gola; (channel) canale m di scolo.

gulp [gʌlp] 1 N (of liquid) sorso; (of food) boccone m; **in** or **at one gulp** in un sorso, d'un fiato. 2 VT (also: **gulp down**) tranguiare, tracannare, inghiottire. 3 VI (while drinking) deglutire; (through fear) sentirsi

serrare la gola; (from emotion) avere un nodo alla gola.

gum[1] [gʌm] N (Anat) gengiva

gum[2] [gʌm] 1 N (glue) colla; (also: **gum tree**) albero della gomma; (chewing gum) gomma americana, chewing-gum m inv; (sweet) caramella gommosa. 2 VT (stick together) incollare, ingommare; (also: **gum down**: label) attaccare, incollare; **gummed label** etichetta adesiva.

▶ **gum up** VT + ADV: **to gum up the works** (fam) mettere il bastone tra le ruote.

♦ **gum arabic** N gomma arabica.

gum·boil [ˈgʌmˌbɔɪl] N ascesso gengivale.

gum·boots [ˈgʌmˌbuːts] NPL (Brit) stivali mpl di gomma.

gump·tion [ˈgʌmpʃən] N (fam: initiative) spirito d'iniziativa; (: common sense) buon senso, senso pratico.

gum·shield [ˈgʌmˌʃiːld] N (Sport) paradenti m inv.

gun [gʌn] 1 N (handgun) pistola, rivoltella; (rifle) fucile m, carabina; (shotgun) fucile da caccia; (cannon) cannone m; **gun barrel** canna di fucile; **to draw a gun on sb** spianare la pistola contro qn; **to carry a gun** portare la pistola; **the big guns** (Mil) l'artiglieria pesante; (fig fam: people) i pezzi grossi; **to stick to one's guns** (fig) tener duro; **to be going great guns** (fam) andare a tutto gas. 2 VT (also: **gun down**) abbattere a colpi di pistola or fucile

▶ **gun for** VI + PREP (fig) avercela a morte con.

gun·boat [ˈgʌnˌbəʊt] N cannoniera.

♦ **gun dog** N cane m da caccia.

gun·fight [ˈgʌnˌfaɪt] N scontro a fuoco.

gun·fire [ˈgʌnˌfaɪəʳ] N colpi mpl d'arma da fuoco, spari mpl.

gunge [gʌndʒ] N (fam) pappa schifosa.

gung-ho [ˈgʌŋˈhəʊ] ADJ (fam) stupidamente entusiasta.

gunk [gʌŋk] N porcherie fpl.

♦ **gun licence** N porto d'armi.

gun·man [ˈgʌnmən] N (pl **-men**) bandito; (hired) sicario.

gun·ner [ˈgʌnəʳ] N artigliere m.

gun·point [ˈgʌnˌpɔɪnt] N: **at gunpoint** sotto la minaccia delle armi.

gun·powder [ˈgʌnˌpaʊdəʳ] N polvere f da sparo.

gun·runner [ˈgʌnˌrʌnəʳ] N trafficante m/f or contrabbandiere(-a) di armi.

gun·running [ˈgʌnˌrʌnɪŋ] N traffico or contrabbando d'armi.

gun·shot [ˈgʌnˌʃɒt] N (noise) sparo; **within gunshot** a portata di tiro.

♦ **gunshot wound** N ferita da arma da fuoco.

gun·smith [ˈgʌnˌsmɪθ] N armaiolo.

gun·wale [ˈgʌnl] N (Naut) falchetta.

gur·gle [ˈgɜːgl] 1 N (all senses) gorgoglio. 2 VI gorgogliare, ciangottare.

gur·nard [ˈgɜːnəd] N (Zool) cappone m; **grey gurnard** triglia grigia.

guru [ˈguːruː] N (Rel, fig) guru m inv.

gush [gʌʃ] 1 N (of liquid) getto, fiotto; (of blood) fiotto; (of feeling) ondata. 2 VI a (also: **gush out**: water, blood): **to gush (from)** sgorgare (da) b (pej: enthuse): **to gush (about** or **over)** abbandonarsi ad effusioni.

gush·ing [ˈgʌʃɪŋ] ADJ (water) zampillante; (pej: person) svenevole; (: compliments) affettato.

gus·set [ˈgʌsɪt] N (in tights, pants) rinforzo; (in skirt) gherone m; (in glove) quadrello.

gust [gʌst] N (of wind) folata; (: stronger) raffica; (of rain) scroscio; (of smoke) sbuffo; (of laughter) scoppio.

gus·to [ˈgʌstəʊ] N: **with gusto** di or con gusto.

gusty ['gʌstɪ] ADJ (comp **-ier**, superl **-iest**) (wind) a raffiche; (day) tempestoso(-a).

gut [gʌt] **1** N **a** (Anat) intestino; (for violin, racket) minugia, budello
b : **guts** NPL (fam: innards) budella fpl; (: of animals) interiora fpl; (fig: courage) fegato; **to hate sb's guts** odiare qn a morte.
2 VT **a** (poultry, fish) levare le interiora a, sventrare
b (building): **the blaze gutted the entire building** le fiamme hanno sventrato completamente l'edificio.
♦ **gut feeling** N sensazione f istintiva.
gut·less ['gʌtlɪs] ADJ (fam) vigliacco(-a), che non ha fegato.
♦ **gut reaction** N reazione f istintiva.
gutsy ['gʌtsɪ] ADJ (comp **-ier**, superl **-iest**) (fam: style) che ha mordente; (: plucky) coraggioso(-a).
gutted ['gʌtɪd] ADJ (fam: upset) distrutto(-a).
gut·ter ['gʌtə^r] N (in street) cunetta, scolo; (on roof) grondaia; **to rise from the gutter** (fig) venire dai bassi-fondi or dalla strada.
♦ **gutter press** N: **the gutter press** la stampa scandali-stica.
gutter·snipe ['gʌtə‚snaɪp] N scugnizzo.
gut·tur·al ['gʌtərəl] ADJ gutturale.
guv [gʌv] N (fam) capo.
guy[1] [gaɪ] N (fam: man) tizio, tipo; (effigy) fantoccio che si brucia la notte di Guy Fawkes; **a tough guy** un duro; **he's a nice guy** è simpatico; see also **wise guy**.
guy[2] [gaɪ] N (also: **guy-rope**, for tent) tirante m, cavo.
Guy·ana [gaɪ'ænə] N Guayana.
♦ **Guy Fawkes' Night** N serata di festeggiamenti il 5 novembre in commemorazione del fallimento della Congiura delle Polveri contro Giacomo I nel 1605.
guz·zle ['gʌzl] **1** VT (food) ingozzare; (drink) tracannare; (hum: petrol) bere.

2 VI gozzovigliare.
gybe, jibe [dʒaɪb] VI (Naut) strambare.
gym [dʒɪm] N (gymnasium) palestra; (gymnastics) ginna-stica.
gym·kha·na [dʒɪm'kɑ:nə] N gimcana.
gym·na·sium [dʒɪm'neɪzɪəm] N palestra.
gym·nast ['dʒɪmnæst] N ginnasta m/f.
gym·nas·tic [dʒɪm'næstɪk] ADJ (display) di ginnastica; (skills) da ginnasta.
gym·nas·tics [dʒɪm'næstɪks] **1** NSG (art) ginnastica.
2 NPL (exercises) ginnastica.
♦ **gym shoes** NPL scarpe fpl da ginnastica.
gymslip ['dʒɪm‚slɪp] N (Brit) ≈ grembiule m di scuola (per ragazze).
gy·nae·co·logi·cal, (Am) **gy·ne·co·logi·cal** ['gaɪnɪkə'lɒdʒɪkəl] ADJ (disorder, examination) ginecolo-gico(-a); (specialist) in ginecologia.
gy·nae·co·logi·cal·ly, (Am) **gy·ne·co·logi·cal·ly** [‚gaɪnɪkə'lɒdʒɪkəlɪ] ADV dal punto di vista ginecologico.
gy·nae·colo·gist, (Am) **gy·ne·colo·gist** [‚gaɪnɪ'kɒlədʒɪst] N ginecologo(-a).
gy·nae·col·ogy, (Am) **gy·ne·col·ogy** [‚gaɪnɪ'kɒlədʒɪ] N ginecologia.
gy·noe·cium, (Am) **gy·ne·cium** [dʒaɪ'ni:sɪəm] N (Bot) gineceo.
gyp·sy, gip·sy ['dʒɪpsɪ] **1** N zingaro(-a).
2 ADJ (life) da zingaro, zingaresco(-a); (caravan) degli zingari; (music) zigano(-a).
gy·rate [‚dʒaɪə'reɪt] VI (spin) roteare, girare (su se stesso); (dance) volteggiare.
gy·ra·tion [‚dʒaɪə'reɪʃən] N (spinning) rotazione f; (when dancing: usu pl) giravolta.
gyro... ['dʒaɪərəʊ] PREF giro... .
gy·ro·scope ['dʒaɪərəskəʊp] N giroscopio.

H

H, h [eɪtʃ] N (*letter*) H, h *for m inv*; **H for Harry**, (*Am*) **H for How** ≈ H come hotel.

ha·beas cor·pus ['heɪbɪəs 'kɔːpəs] N (*Law*) habeas corpus *m inv.*

hab·er·dash·er ['hæbə,dæʃə'] N (*Brit*) merciaio(-a); (*Am*) camiciaio(-a).

hab·er·dash·ery [,hæbə'dæʃərɪ] N merceria; (*Am*) camiceria.

hab·it ['hæbɪt] N **a** (*customary behaviour, individual habit*) abitudine *f*; **a bad habit** una brutta *or* cattiva abitudine; **to be in the habit of doing sth** avere l'abitudine di fare qc; **to fall into bad habits** prendere delle cattive abitudini; **to get out of/into the habit of doing sth** perdere/prendere l'abitudine di fare qc; **to get sb into the habit of doing sth** abituare qn a fare qc; **out of sheer habit** solo per abitudine; **don't make a habit of it!** che non diventi un'abitudine!

b (*dress: of monk, nun*) tonaca; (: *riding habit*) costume *m* da amazzone

c (*fam: addiction*) assuefazione.

hab·it·able ['hæbɪtəbl] ADJ abitabile.

habi·tat ['hæbɪ,tæt] N habitat *m inv.*

habi·ta·tion [,hæbɪ'teɪʃən] N abitazione *f*; **fit for human habitation** abitabile.

♦ **habit-forming** ['hæbɪt,fɔːmɪŋ] ADJ: **to be habit-forming** causare assuefazione.

ha·bitu·al [hə'bɪtjʊəl] ADJ abituale, consueto(-a); (*drunkard, smoker*) incallito(-a); (*liar*) inveterato(-a).

ha·bitu·al·ly [hə'bɪtjʊəlɪ] ADV abitualmente, d'abitudine.

hack¹ [hæk] ①① N (*of sword, axe*) colpo; (*of sabre*) fendente *m.*

②② VT **a** (*cut*) tagliare; **to hack one's way through** aprirsi un varco (a colpi d'ascia *etc*) tra; **to hack sth to pieces** tagliare a pezzi qc

b : **to hack into** (*Comput: program, system*) inserirsi illegalmente in

► **hack about** VT + ADV tagliare; **my book's been hacked about terribly by the editor** il mio libro è stato tagliato senza pietà dal redattore

► **hack down** VT + ADV (*tree etc*) abbattere (a colpi d'ascia *etc*).

hack² [hæk] ①① N **a** (*old horse*) ronzino; (*ride*) passeggiata a cavallo **b** (*pej: writer*) scribacchino(-a); **to do hack writing** fare lo scribacchino(-a).

②② VI: **to go hacking** (andare a) fare una passeggiata a cavallo.

hack·er ['hækə'] N (*Comput*) hacker *m/f inv.*

hack·ing ['hækɪŋ] ADJ: **a hacking cough** una brutta tosse.

♦ **hacking jacket** N giacca da equitazione.

hack·les ['hæklz] NPL: **to make sb's hackles rise** (*fig*) far arrabbiare qn.

hack·ney cab ['hæknɪ,kæb] N carrozza a nolo.

hack·ney car·riage ['hæknɪ,kærɪdʒ] N (*frm*) autopubblica.

hack·neyed ['hæknɪd] ADJ (*saying*) trito(-a); **hackneyed expression** luogo comune.

hack·saw ['hæk,sɔː] N seghetto per metalli.

hack·work ['hæk,wɜːk] N *prodotto letterario scadente, scritto su ordinazione.*

had [hæd] PT, PP **of have.**

had·dock ['hædək] N eglefino (*tipo di merluzzo*).

Ha·des ['heɪdiːz] N Ade *m.*

hadn't ['hædnt] = **had not.**

haema·tol·ogy, (*Am*) **hema·tol·ogy** [,hiːmə'tɒlədʒɪ] N ematologia.

haemo·glo·bin, (*Am*) **hemo·glo·bin** [,hiːməʊ'gləʊbɪn] N emoglobina.

hae·moly·sis, (*Am*) **he·moly·sis** [hɪ'mɒlɪsɪs] N emolisi *f.*

haemo·philia, (*Am*) **hemo·philia** [,hiːməʊ'fɪlɪə] N emofilia.

haemo·phili·ac, (*Am*) **hemo·phili·ac** [,hiːməʊ'fɪlɪæk] N emofiliaco(-a).

haem·or·rhage, (*Am*) **hem·or·rhage** ['hemərɪdʒ] ①① N emorragia.

②② VI avere un'emorragia.

haem·or·rhoids, (*Am*) **hem·or·rhoids** ['hemə,rɔɪdz] NPL emorroidi *fpl.*

haemo·stat·ic [,hiːməʊ'stætɪk] ADJ (*action, remedy*) antiemorragico(-a).

hag [hæg] N (*ugly*) befana; (*nasty*) megera; (*witch*) strega.

hag·gard ['hægəd] ADJ (*careworn*) tirato(-a); (*gaunt*)

smunto(-a).

hag·gis ['hægɪs] N (*Scot Culin*) *insaccato a base di avena e frattaglie di pecora.*

hag·gle ['hægl] VI: **to haggle (over)** (*bargain*) contrattare (su); (*argue*) discutere (su).

hag·gling ['hæglɪŋ] N contrattazione *f*.

♦ **hag-ridden** ['hæg,rɪdn] ADJ tormentato(-a).

Hague [heɪg] N: **the Hague** l'Aia.

hail¹ [heɪl] 1 N (*Met*) grandine *f*; (*fig: of bullets*) pioggia; (: *of abuse*) valanga.
2 VI grandinare.

hail² [heɪl] 1 N (*greeting, call*) grido di saluto; **within hail** a portata d'orecchio.
2 EXCL (*old, liter*): **hail, Caesar!** ave, Cesare!.
3 VT (*acclaim*): **to hail (as)** acclamare (come); (*greet*) salutare; (*signal: taxi*) fermare; (*call*) chiamare.
4 VI: **where does that ship hail from?** qual è il porto di provenienza di quella nave?; **he hails from Scotland** viene dalla Scozia.

♦ **hail-fellow-well-met** ['heɪl,fɛləʊwɛl'mɛt] ADJ (*pej*) che si prende troppa confidenza.

♦ **Hail Mary** N Ave Maria *f inv.*

hail·stone ['heɪl,stəʊn] N chicco di grandine.

hail·storm ['heɪl'stɔ:m] N grandinata.

hair [hɛə'] N **a** (*collective: of person*) capelli *mpl*; (: *on body*) peli *mpl*; (: *of animal*) pelo; **to comb one's hair** pettinarsi; **to do one's hair** acconciarsi; **to put one's hair up** raccogliersi i capelli; **to have one's hair done** andare dal parrucchiere; **to get one's hair cut** farsi tagliare i capelli; **to remove unwanted hair** (*from legs, armpits*) depilarsi; **to make sb's hair stand on end** far rizzare i capelli (in testa) a qn; **to let one's hair down** (*fig*) lasciarsi andare; **keep your hair on!** (*fam*) datti una calmata!
b (*single hair: of head*) capello; (: *of body, animal*) pelo; **to split hairs** (*fig*) spaccare il capello in quattro, cercare il pelo nell'uovo; **he didn't turn a hair** non ha battuto ciglio; **try a hair of the dog (that bit you)** (*fam*) prendi un bicchierino per farti passare la sbornia.

♦ **hair appointment** N appuntamento dal parrucchiere.

hair·ball ['hɛə,bɔ:l] N palla di pelo.

hair·band ['hɛə,bænd] N (*elastic*) fascia per i capelli; (*rigid*) cerchietto.

hair·brained ['hɛə,breɪnd] ADJ = harebrained.

hair·brush ['hɛə,brʌʃ] N spazzola per capelli.

hair·cut ['hɛə,kʌt] N taglio (di capelli); **to have** *or* **get a haircut** farsi tagliare i capelli; **I need a haircut** devo tagliarmi i capelli.

hair·do ['hɛə,du:] N (*fam*) pettinatura.

hair·dresser ['hɛə,drɛsə'] N parrucchiere(-a); **at the hair-dresser's** dal parrucchiere.

hair·dressing ['hɛə,drɛsɪŋ] N mestiere *m* di parrucchiere; **to study hair dressing** seguire un corso per parrucchieri.

♦ **hair-dryer** ['hɛə,draɪə'] N asciugacapelli *m inv*, föhn *m inv.*

-haired [hɛəd] ADJ SUFF: **fair/long-haired** dai capelli biondi/lunghi.

hair·grip ['hɛə,grɪp] N molletta (per i capelli).

hair·line ['hɛə,laɪn] N attaccatura dei capelli; **to have a receding hairline** essere stempiato(-a).

♦ **hairline crack** N incrinatura, sottilissima crepa.

♦ **hairline fracture** N (*Med*) frattura capillare.

hair·net ['hɛə,nɛt] N retina (per capelli).

♦ **hair oil** N brillantina.

hair·piece ['hɛə,pi:s] N toupet *m inv.*

hair·pin ['hɛə,pɪn] N forcina.

hairpin bend, (*Am*) **hairpin curve** N tornante *m.*

♦ **hair-raising** ['hɛə,reɪzɪŋ] ADJ (*story, adventure*) da far rizzare i capelli, terrificante.

♦ **hair remover** N crema depilatoria.

♦ **hair's-breadth** ['hɛəz,brɛtθ] N: **by a hair's breadth** per un pelo.

♦ **hair slide** N fermacapelli *m inv.*

hair·splitting ['hɛə,splɪtɪŋ] 1 ADJ pedante, cavilloso(-a).
2 N pedanteria.

♦ **hair spray** N lacca per capelli.

hair·style ['hɛə,staɪl] N pettinatura, acconciatura.

hairy ['hɛərɪ] ADJ (*comp* **-ier**, *superl* **-iest**) **a** peloso(-a), irsuto(-a) **b** (*fam: frightening*) da far rizzare i capelli.

Hai·ti ['heɪtɪ] N Haiti *f.*

hake [heɪk] N nasello.

hal·cy·on ['hælsɪən] ADJ sereno(-a).

hale [heɪl] ADJ: **hale and hearty** che scoppia di salute.

half [hɑ:f] 1 N (*pl* **halves**) **a** (*part*) metà *f inv*, mezzo(-a); **half (of it)** la metà; **half (of)** *or* **half the amount of** la metà di; **one half of the apple** la *or* una metà della mela; **half an orange** mezza arancia; **half a dozen** mezza dozzina; **half a pound** mezza libbra; **two and a half** due e mezzo; **half an hour** mezz'ora; **3 and a half hours** tre ore e mezza; **half of my friends** (la) metà dei miei amici; **to cut in half/into halves** tagliare a metà/in due; **his** (*or* **her**) **better half** (*fam hum*) la sua (dolce) metà; **she doesn't do things by halves** non fa mai le cose a metà; **to go halves (with sb)** fare a metà (con qn); **bigger by half** una volta e mezzo più grande; **he's too clever by half** (*fam*) è troppo furbo per i miei gusti
b (*Sport: of match*) tempo; (: *of ground*) metà campo; (*player*) mediano; **left/right half** mediano sinistro/destro
c (*of beer*) mezza pinta
d (*child's ticket*) (ridotto per) bambino.
2 ADJ (*bottle, quantity, fare, pay*) mezzo(-a), metà *inv*; **half a glass** *or* **a half glass** (un) mezzo bicchiere; **half measures** mezze misure *fpl*.
3 ADV **a** (a) metà, (a) mezzo; **half empty/closed** mezzo(-a) vuoto(-a)/chiuso(-a), semivuoto(-a)/semichiuso(-a); **half asleep** mezzo(-a) addormentato(-a); **she's half French, half Italian** è mezza francese, mezza italiana; **half as big (as)** la metà (di); **half as big again** una volta e mezzo più grande; **I was half afraid that ...** avevo un po' paura che... + *sub*; **not half!** (*fam*) altroché!, eccome!; **it isn't half hot!** (*fam*) scotta!
b (*time*): **half past 3** le 3 e mezza; **half past 12** le 12 e mezza.

♦ **half-and-half** ['hɑ:fən'hɑ:f] ADV metà e metà.

half·back ['hɑ:f,bæk] N (*Sport*) mediano.

♦ **half-baked** [,hɑ:f'beɪkt] ADJ (*fig fam: idea, scheme*) mal combinato(-a), che non sta in piedi.

♦ **half-breed** ['hɑ:f,bri:d] N mezzosangue *m.*

♦ **half-brother** ['hɑ:f,brʌðə'] N fratellastro.

♦ **half-caste** ['hɑ:f,kɑ:st] N meticcio(-a).

♦ **half-circle** [,hɑ:f'sɜ:kl] N semicerchio.

♦ **half-crown** [,hɑ:f'kraʊn] N (*Brit: old coin*) mezza corona.

♦ **half-dead** [,hɑ:f'dɛd] ADJ: **half-dead (with)** mezzo(-a) morto(-a) (da *or* per).

♦ **half-fill** [,hɑ:f'fɪl] VT riempire a metà.

♦ **half-hearted** [,hɑ:f'hɑ:tɪd] ADJ (*effort*) poco convinto(-a), svogliato(-a); **he made a half-hearted attempt** ha fatto un mezzo tentativo.

♦ **half-heartedly** [,hɑ:f'hɑ:tɪdlɪ] ADV svogliatamente.

♦ **half holiday** N mezza giornata di festa.

♦ **half-hour** [,hɑ:f'aʊə'] N mezz'ora.

♦ **half-hourly** [ˌhɑːfˈaʊəlɪ] ADJ, ADV ogni mezz'ora.

♦ **half-life** [ˌhɑːfˈlaɪf] N (*Phys*) tempo di dimezzamento.

♦ **half-light** [ˌhɑːfˈlaɪt] N semioscurità.

♦ **half-mast** [ˌhɑːfˈmɑːst] N: **at half-mast** (*flag*) a mezz'asta.

♦ **half-moon** [ˌhɑːfˈmuːn] N mezzaluna; **half-moon spectacles** mezze lunette *fpl*.

♦ **half-nelson** [ˌhɑːfˈnɛlsən] N (*Wrestling*) mezza elson *f inv*.

half·penny [ˈheɪpnɪ] N (*pl* **-pennies** *or* **-pence** [ˈheɪpəns]) (*Brit*) mezzo penny *m inv*.

♦ **half-price** [ˌhɑːfˈpraɪs] ADV, ADJ a metà prezzo.

♦ **half-sister** [ˌhɑːfˈsɪstəʳ] N sorellastra.

♦ **half term** N (*Brit Scol*) vacanza a *or* di metà trimestre.

♦ **half-time** [ˌhɑːfˈtaɪm] 1 N (*Sport*) intervallo.

 2 ADJ, ADV all'intervallo; **to work half-time** lavorare mezza giornata.

♦ **half-truth** [ˈhɑːfˈtruːθ] N mezza verità *f inv*.

♦ **half volley** N (*Tennis*) demi-volée *f inv*.

half·way [ˈhɑːfˈweɪ] 1 ADV a metà strada; **halfway up (** *or* **down) the stairs** a metà delle scale; **to meet sb halfway** (*fig*) arrivare a un compromesso con qn; **halfway through sth** a metà di qc; **we are halfway through the work** abbiamo fatto metà del lavoro.

 2 ADJ (*mark*) di mezzo; **halfway line** (*Ftbl*) linea mediana.

♦ **halfway house** N (*hostel*) centro di riadattamento alla vita sociale per ex detenuti; (*fig*) via di mezzo.

♦ **half-wit** [ˈhɑːfˌwɪt] N grullo(-a), idiota *m/f*.

♦ **half-witted** [ˌhɑːfˈwɪtɪd] ADJ (*reply, action*) da idiota; **a half-witted person** un(a) idiota.

♦ **half-yearly** [ˌhɑːfˈjɪəlɪ] 1 ADV semestralmente, ogni sei mesi.

 2 ADJ semestrale.

hali·but [ˈhælɪbət] N ippoglosso, halibut *m inv*.

hali·to·sis [ˌhælɪˈtəʊsɪs] N alitosi *f*.

hall [hɔːl] N **a** (*entrance hall*) ingresso, entrata; (*Am: passage*) corridoio **b** (*large room*) salone *m*, sala; **church hall** sala dell'oratorio **c** (*mansion*) palazzo, maniero, grande villa; (*Brit Univ: also:* **hall of residence**) ≈ casa dello studente.

hal·le·lu·jah [ˌhælɪˈluːjə] N, EXCL alleluia *m inv*.

hall·mark [ˈhɔːlˌmɑːk] N (*also fig*) marchio.

hal·lo [həˈləʊ] EXCL = **hello**.

Hal·low·e'en [ˈhæləʊˈiːn] N vigilia d'Ognissanti.

♦ **hall porter** N portiere(-a).

♦ **hall stand** N attaccapanni *m inv* a stelo.

hal·lu·ci·nate [həˈluːsɪˌneɪt] VI avere le allucinazioni.

hal·lu·ci·na·tion [həˌluːsɪˈneɪʃən] N allucinazione *f*.

hal·lu·ci·no·gen·ic [həˌluːsɪnəʊˈdʒɛnɪk] ADJ allucinogeno(-a).

hall·way [ˈhɔːlˌweɪ] N (*corridor*) corridoio; (*entrance*) ingresso.

halo [ˈheɪləʊ] N (*of saint*) aureola; (*Astron*) alone *m*.

halo·gen [ˈhæləˌdʒɛn] N alogeno.

♦ **halogen light** N luce *f* alogena.

halt [hɔːlt] 1 N sosta, fermata; (*train stop*) fermata; **to come to a halt** fermarsi, arrestarsi; **to call a halt (to sth)** (*fig*) mettere *or* porre fine (a qc).

 2 VT (*vehicle, production*) fermare, arrestare.

 3 VI fermarsi, arrestarsi; **halt!** alt!

hal·ter [ˈhɔːltəʳ] N (*for horse*) cavezza.

halter·neck [ˈhɔːltəˌnɛk] ADJ allacciato(-a) dietro il collo.

halt·ing [ˈhɔːltɪŋ] ADJ titubante.

halt·ing·ly [ˈhɔːltɪŋlɪ] ADV con titubanza.

♦ **halt sign** N segnale *m* d'arresto.

halve [hɑːv] VT (*divide*): **to halve (between)** dividere a metà

or in due (tra); (*reduce by half*) dimezzare, ridurre della metà.

halves [hɑːvz] NPL of **half**.

hal·yard [ˈhæljəd] N (*Naut*) drizza.

ham [hæm] N **a** (*Culin*) prosciutto; **ham and eggs** uova *fpl* al prosciutto **b** (*fam: radio ham*) radioamatore(-trice); (: *ham actor*) gigione(-a)

▶ **ham up** VT + ADV: **to ham it up** (*fam*) fare l'esagerato(-a).

Ham·burg [ˈhæmbɜːg] N Amburgo *f*.

ham·burg·er [ˈhæmˌbɜːɡəʳ] N hamburger *m inv*.

♦ **ham-fisted** [ˌhæmˈfɪstɪd], (*Am*) **ham-handed** [ˌhæmˈhændɪd] ADJ maldestro(-a).

ham·let [ˈhæmlɪt] N paesetto, paesino.

ham·mer [ˈhæməʳ] 1 N (*tool*) martello; (*of gun*) percussore *m*; **to go at it hammer and tongs** (*fam: work*) darci dentro; (: *argue*) azzuffarsi.

 2 VT martellare; (*fig fam: defeat*) stracciare; (: *thrash*) picchiare; **to hammer nails into wood** piantare chiodi nel legno; **to hammer sth into shape** (*metal*) dare una forma a qc col martello; (*fig: team, plan*) mettere a punto qc; **to hammer a point home to sb** cacciare un'idea in testa a qn.

 3 VI dare colpi di martello; **to hammer on** *or* **at the door** picchiare alla porta

▶ **hammer down** VT + ADV (*lid*) fissare con colpi di martello; (*nail*) piantare (a martellate)

▶ **hammer out** VT + ADV (*metal*) spianare (a martellate); (*fig: solution, agreement*) mettere a punto.

♦ **hammer and sickle** N: **the hammer and sickle** la falce e il martello.

♦ **hammer drill** N martello pneumatico.

hammer·head [ˈhæməˌhɛd] N (*shark*) pesce *m* martello *inv*.

ham·mock [ˈhæmək] N amaca.

ham·per¹ [ˈhæmpəʳ] N (*basket*) cesto, cestino.

ham·per² [ˈhæmpəʳ] VT (*hinder*) impedire, ostacolare.

ham·ster [ˈhæmstəʳ] N criceto.

ham·string [ˈhæmˌstrɪŋ] (*vb: pt, pp* **hamstrung**) 1 N (*Anat*) tendine *m* del ginocchio; (*of horse*) corda del garretto.

 2 VT tagliare i tendini delle gambe a; (*fig*) tagliare le gambe a.

hand [hænd] 1 N **a** (*of person*) mano *f*; (*of clock*) lancetta; **to have in one's hand** (*knife, victory*) avere in mano *or* in pugno; (*book, money*) avere in mano; **to take sb by the hand** prendere per mano qn; **on (one's) hands and knees** carponi, a quattro zampe; **hands up!** (*during hold-up*) mani in alto!; (*to pupils*) alzate la mano!; **hands off!** (*fam*) giù le mani!; **to be clever** *or* **good with one's hands** avere le mani d'oro; **made/delivered by hand** fatto(-a) / consegnato(-a) a mano; **to live from hand to mouth** vivere alla giornata; **they gave him a big hand** (*fig*) gli hanno fatto un bell'applauso

 b (*worker: in factory*) operaio(-a), manovale *m*; (: *farm hand*) bracciante *m/f*; (: *deck hand*) marinaio; **all hands on deck!** (*Naut*) tutti in coperta!; **to be an old hand** essere vecchio(-a) del mestiere

 c (*liter: handwriting*) scrittura, mano *f*; **in one's own hand** di proprio pugno, di propria mano

 d (*Cards*) mano *f*; **a hand of bridge/poker** una mano a bridge/poker

 e (*measurement: of horse*) ≈ dieci centimetri

 f (*phrases with verb*): **to be hand in glove with sb** essere in combutta con qn; **to change hands** (*property*) cambiare (di) mano; **to force sb's hand** forzare la mano a qn; **to give** *or* **lend sb a hand** dare una mano a qn; **to keep one's hand in** tenersi in esercizio, non perdere la mano; **she**

can turn her hand to anything sa fare un po' di tutto; he asked for her hand (in marriage) ha chiesto la sua mano; to wait on sb hand and foot essere a totale disposizione di qn; to have one's hands full (with sb/sth) essere troppo preso(-a) (con qn/qc); to win hands down vincere senza difficoltà; to be making/losing money hand over fist fare/perdere un sacco di soldi; to have a free hand avere carta bianca; to have the upper hand avere la meglio or il sopravvento; to have a hand in sth essere immischiato(-a) in qc

g (phrases with prep before n): at hand a portata di mano; to be near or close at hand essere a due passi; at first hand di prima mano; hand in hand mano nella mano; to go hand in hand (with) (fig) andare insieme (a); to be in sb's hands essere nelle mani di qn; in hand (work) in corso; to have £50 in hand avere ancora 50 sterline a disposizione; we have the situation in hand abbiamo la situazione sotto controllo; we have the matter in hand ci stiamo occupando della cosa; to take sb in hand controllare qn; to play into sb's hands fare il gioco di qn; to fall into the hands of the enemy cadere in mano al nemico; on hand (person) disponibile; (object) sottomano, a portata di mano; (emergency services) pronto(-a) a intervenire; on the right/left hand sulla destra/sinistra; (on the one hand) ...on the other hand (da una parte)... d'altra parte; to have sth left on one's hands ritrovarsi con qc, rimanere con qc; to take sth off sb's hands togliere qc di torno a qn; to condemn sb out of hand condannare qn a priori; to get out of hand sfuggire di mano; to hand (information) a portata di mano.

[2] VT (pass): to hand sb sth, hand sth to sb passare qc a qn; you've got to hand it to him (fam) questo glielo devi riconoscere; it was handed to him on a plate (fam) glielo hanno dato su un piatto d'argento

▶ **hand back** VT + ADV restituire

▶ **hand down** VT + ADV (suitcase) passare, dare (con movimento dall'alto al basso); (tradition) tramandare; (heirloom) lasciare in eredità; (Am: sentence, verdict) emettere

▶ **hand in** VT + ADV (form) consegnare; (resignation) rassegnare, dare

▶ **hand on** VT + ADV trasmettere, dare, passare

▶ **hand out** VT + ADV (leaflets) distribuire; (advice) elargire

▶ **hand over** VT + ADV consegnare; (powers, property, business) cedere

▶ **hand round** VT + ADV (information, papers) far circolare; (distribute: chocolates, cakes) far girare; (subj: hostess) offrire.

hand·bag ['hænd͵bæg] N borsa, borsetta.

♦ **hand baggage** N bagaglio a mano.

hand·ball ['hænd͵bɔːl] N pallamano f.

hand·basin ['hænd͵beɪsn] N lavandino.

hand·bell ['hænd͵bɛl] N campanello (strumento musicale).

hand·bill ['hænd͵bɪl] N volantino.

hand·book ['hænd͵bʊk] N (manual) manuale m, libretto di istruzioni; (for tourists) guida (turistica).

hand·brake ['hænd͵breɪk] N freno a mano.

♦ **handbrake lever** N leva del freno a mano.

♦ **hand controls** NPL (Aut) comandi mpl manuali.

♦ **hand cream** N crema per le mani.

hand·cuff ['hænd͵kʌf] [1] VT ammanettare.

[2] N: handcuffs NPL manette fpl.

hand·ful ['hændfʊl] N (quantity) manciata, pugno; a handful of people uno sparuto gruppo di persone; that

child's a real handful (fam) quel bambino è proprio un terremoto.

♦ **hand grenade** N bomba a mano.

♦ **hand-held** ['hænd'hɛld] ADJ a mano.

handi·cap ['hændɪ͵kæp] [1] N (fig, Sport) handicap m inv.

[2] VT (disable) handicappare, menomare; (hamper) ostacolare.

handi·capped ['hændɪ͵kæpt] ADJ handicappato(-a), portatore(-trice) di handicap.

handi·craft ['hændɪ͵krɑːft] N (art) lavoro artigianale; **handicrafts** NPL (products) prodotti di artigianato.

handi·work ['hændɪ͵wɜːk] N (work) lavoro, opera; (craft work) lavorazione f a mano; this looks like his handiwork (pej) qui c'è il suo zampino.

hand·ker·chief ['hæŋkətʃɪf] N fazzoletto.

♦ **hand-knitted** [͵hænd'nɪtɪd] ADJ (jumper) fatto(-a) a mano.

han·dle ['hændl] [1] N (gen) manico; (of knife) manico, impugnatura; (of door, drawer) maniglia; (of wheelbarrow) stanga; (of pump) braccio; (for winding) manovella; (of cup) ansa; to fly off the handle (fig) perdere le staffe, uscire dai gangheri.

[2] VT **a** (touch) toccare; "handle with care" "fragile"; the police handled him roughly è stato malmenato dalla polizia; to handle the ball (Ftbl) fare un fallo di mano

b (deal with: theme) trattare; (: situation) far fronte a; (: resources) amministrare; (cope with: people) saper come prendere; (: animals) occuparsi di; (Comm: goods) trattare, occuparsi di; (ship, car) manovrare; (use: gun, machine, money) maneggiare; I'll handle this me ne occupo io, ci penso io; she knows how to handle her son sa come prendere suo figlio; we handle 2000 travellers a day abbiamo un traffico di 2000 passeggeri al giorno.

[3] VI (ship, plane, car) rispondere ai comandi.

handle·bars ['hændl͵bɑːz] NPL, **handle·bar** ['hændl͵bɑː'] N (on bicycle) manubrio.

han·dler ['hændlə'] N (dog handler) addestratore(-trice) (di cane).

han·dling ['hændlɪŋ] N **a** (touching, fingering) maneggio; these goods have been damaged through too much handling questa merce è danneggiata perché è stata maneggiata troppo

b (of theme, animals) trattamento; (of resources) amministrazione f; (of car, ship) controllo; (of gun) maneggiamento; he was criticized for his handling of the situation/the crowd fu criticato per il suo modo di affrontare or trattare la situazione/la folla.

♦ **handling charges** NPL (for goods) commissione f per la prestazione; (Banking) spese fpl bancarie.

♦ **hand-luggage** ['hænd͵lʌgɪdʒ] N bagaglio a mano.

hand·made [͵hænd'meɪd] ADJ (clothes, paper) fatto(-a) a mano; (biscuits) fatto(-a) in casa.

♦ **hand-me-down** ['hændmɪ͵daʊn] N vestito smesso.

hand·out ['hænd͵aʊt] N (leaflet) volantino; (press handout) comunicato stampa; (at lecture) fotocopia; (fam: money) elemosina.

♦ **hand-picked** [͵hænd'pɪkt] ADJ (staff, team) scelto(-a); (produce) scelto(-a), selezionato(-a).

hand·rail ['hænd͵reɪl] N (on staircase) corrimano.

hand·saw ['hænd͵sɔː] N sega a mano.

hand·set ['hændsɛt] N (Telec) ricevitore m.

hand·shake ['hænd͵ʃeɪk] N stretta di mano.

hand·shaking ['hænd͵ʃeɪkɪŋ] N (Comput) procedura di sincronizzazione delle comunicazioni.

hand·some ['hænsəm] ADJ (comp -r, superl -st) (gen)

bello(-a); (*salary*) buono(-a); (*considerable*: *profit, fortune*) considerevole, grosso(-a); (*reward*) genero-so(-a).

hand·some·ly ['hænsəmlɪ] ADV (*generously*) generosa-mente; (*attractively*) graziosamente.

♦ **hands-on** [ˌhændz'ɒn] ADJ (*approach*) pragmatico(-a); (*training*) pratico(-a); **hands-on experience** esperienza diretta *or* pratica.

hand·spring ['hænd,sprɪŋ] N salto sulle mani.

hand·stand ['hænd,stænd] N: **to do a handstand** fare la verticale.

♦ **hand-to-hand** ['hændtə'hænd] ADJ, ADV corpo a corpo.

♦ **hand-to-mouth** [ˌhændtə'maʊθ] ADJ (*existence*) preca-rio(-a).

♦ **hand towel** N asciugamani *m inv*.

hand·writing ['hænd,raɪtɪŋ] N scrittura, calligrafia.

hand·written ['hænd,rɪtn] ADJ (*gen*) scritto(-a) a mano, manoscritto(-a); (*text, musical score*) manoscritto(-a).

handy ['hændɪ] ADJ (*comp* **-ier**, *superl* **-iest**) **a** (*close at hand*) a portata di mano, sottomano
  b (*convenient*) comodo(-a); (*useful*: *machine, gadget*) pratico(-a), utile; **to come in handy** tornare utile; **that would come in very handy** farebbe proprio molto comodo
  c (*fam*: *skilful*) bravo(-a); **he's handy with a paintbrush** è proprio bravo come imbianchino.

handy·man ['hændɪ,mæn] N (*pl* **-men**) (*paid*) tuttofare *m inv*; (*amateur*) *uno bravo a fare piccole riparazioni e lavoretti*; **tools for the handyman** arnesi per il fai da te.

hang [hæŋ] (*pt, pp* **hung**) ① VT **a** (*gen*) appendere; (*washing*) stendere; (*door*) montare (sui cardini); (*wall-paper*) mettere, incollare; (*coat, hat*): **to hang (on)** appendere (a); **the walls were hung with tapestries** i muri erano coperti di arazzi; **the Christmas tree was hung with lights** l'albero di Natale era decorato di *or* con luci colorate
  b (*pt, pp* **hanged**) (*criminal*) impiccare; **hang (it)!** (*fam*) accidenti!, porca miseria!
  c: **to hang one's head** abbassare la testa (per la vergogna).
  ② VI **a** (*rope, dangling object*): **to hang (from)** penzolare (da), pendere (da); (*garment*) cadere; (*hair*) scendere; (*criminal*) essere impiccato(-a); **that dress hangs well** quel vestito cade bene
  b: **to hang over** (*smoke, fog*) sovrastare; (*threat*) incom-bere su; (*hawk*) essere sospeso(-a) su.
  ③ N: **he couldn't get the hang of the game** (*fam*) non riusciva ad afferrare il senso del gioco; **you'll soon get the hang of this** (*fam*) ti farai presto la mano a questo

▸ **hang about** ① VI + ADV (*also*: **hang around**) (*loiter*) gironzolare, ciondolare; (: *wait*) rimanere ad aspettare; **to keep sb hanging about** far aspettare qn; **don't hang about, there's work to do** non perder tempo, c'è un sacco di lavoro da fare.
  ② VI + PREP (*the streets*) aggirarsi per

▸ **hang back** VI + ADV (*hesitate*): **to hang back (from doing)** essere riluttante (a fare)

▸ **hang down** ① VI + ADV ricadere.
  ② VT + ADV far ricadere

▸ **hang on** ① VI + PREP **a** (*depend on*: *decision*) dipendere da
  b (*listen eagerly*) bersi le parole di; **she hung on his every word** pendeva dalle sue labbra.
  ② VI + ADV **a** (*keep hold*): **to hang on (to)** aggrapparsi (a), attaccarsi (a); **to hang on to** (*keep*) tenere

  b (*fam*: *wait*) aspettare; **hang on a minute!** aspetta un momento!; (*polite*: *on phone*) attenda un attimo!

▸ **hang out** ① VT + ADV (*washing*) stendere (fuori); (*flags*) metter fuori.
  ② VI + ADV **a**: **to hang out of sth** penzolare *or* pendere fuori da qc; **his shirt was hanging out** gli usciva la camicia dai pantaloni
  b (*fam*: *frequent*) frequentare; **he hangs out in the local bars** bazzica nei bar locali

▸ **hang together** VI + ADV (*fam*: *people*) stare insieme; (*cohere*: *argument*) stare in piedi

▸ **hang up** ① VT + ADV (*coat*) appendere; (*picture*) attac-care, appendere.
  ② VI + ADV (*Telec*) riattaccare, riagganciare; **to hang up on sb** metter giù il ricevitore a qn.

hang·ar ['hæŋəʳ] N hangar *m inv*, aviorimessa.

hang·dog ['hæŋ,dɒg] ADJ (*guilty*: *look, expression*) da cane bastonato.

hang·er ['hæŋəʳ] N (*for clothes*) ometto, gruccia.

♦ **hanger-on** [ˌhæŋə'rɒn] N (*pl* **hangers-on**) (*pej*) parassita *m/f*.

♦ **hang-glider** ['hæŋ,glaɪdəʳ] N deltaplano (*velivolo*).

♦ **hang-gliding** ['hæŋ,glaɪdɪŋ] N (*volo col*) deltaplano.

hang·ing ['hæŋɪŋ] ① N **a** (*execution*) impiccagione *f* **b** (*curtains*): **hangings** NPL tende *fpl*, tendaggi *mpl*.
  ② ADJ (*bridge*) sospeso(-a); (*offence, matter*) da punire con l'impiccagione; **hanging lamp** lampadario.

hang·man ['hæŋmən] N (*pl* **-men**) boia *m inv*.

♦ **hang-out** ['hæŋ,aʊt] N (*fam*) ritrovo.

hang·over ['hæŋ,əʊvəʳ] N **a** (*after drinking*) postumi *mpl* della sbornia; **I've got an awful hangover** ho un terribile cerchio alla testa **b** (*sth left over*) residuato.

♦ **hang-up** ['hæŋ,ʌp] N (*fam*) complesso, ossessione *f*.

hank [hæŋk] N (*of wool*) matassa; (*of hair*) ciocca; (*Naut*) garroccio.

hank·er ['hæŋkəʳ] VI: **to hanker after** *or* **for** (*fame, power*) essere assetato(-a) di, bramare; (*sympathy, possessions*) desiderare intensamente.

hank·er·ing [ˈhæŋkərɪŋ] N: **to have a hankering for sth/to do sth** avere una voglia matta di qc/di fare qc.

hanky ['hæŋkɪ] N (*fam*: *handkerchief*) fazzoletto.

♦ **hanky-panky** ['hæŋkɪ'pæŋkɪ] N (*fam*): **there's some hanky-panky going on here** qui c'è del losco; **you can drive me home, but no hanky-panky!** puoi portarmi a casa se tieni le mani a posto!

Hannibal ['hænɪbəl] N Annibale *m*.

Hants ABBR (*Brit*)= *Hampshire*.

ha'penny ['heɪpnɪ] N = **halfpenny**.

hap·haz·ard [ˌhæp'hæzəd] ADJ (*fatto(-a)*) a caso *or* a casaccio; (*arrangement*) casuale, fortuito(-a).

hap·haz·ard·ly [ˌhæp'hæzədlɪ] ADV a caso, a casaccio.

hap·less ['hæplɪs] (*liter*) ADJ (*wretched*) disgraziato(-a); (*unfortunate*) sventurato(-a).

hap·loid ['hæplɔɪd] ADJ, N (*Bio*) aploide (*m*).

hap·pen ['hæpən] VI **a** succedere, accadere, capitare; **what's happening?** cosa succede?, cosa sta succe-dendo?; **these things will happen** sono cose che capitano *or* succedono; **don't let it happen again** che non si ripeta *or* succeda mai più; **as if nothing had happened** come se niente fosse; **what has happened to him?** (*befallen*) cosa gli è successo?; (*become of*) che fine ha fatto?; **if anything should happen to him …** se gli dovesse accadere qualcosa…
  b (*chance*): **it happened that …** si dava il caso che…; **do you happen to know if …** sai per caso se…; **if anyone**

should happen to see John se a qualcuno capita di vedere John; **I happen to know that** ... si dà il caso che io sappia che...; **she happened to be free** per caso era libera; **as it happens** (per) combinazione; **it so happened that** ... guarda caso...

▶ **happen (up)on** VI + PREP imbattersi in.

hap·pen·ing ['hæpnɪŋ] N (*event*) avvenimento, evento; (*in theatre*) happening *m inv*.

hap·pen·stance ['hæpən,stæns] N (*Am fam*) combinazione *f*.

hap·pi·ly ['hæpɪlɪ] ADV (*contentedly*: *play, work*) tranquillamente; (*cheerfully*: *say*) con gioia; (: *laugh*) con allegria; (*fortunately*) per fortuna, fortunatamente; **and they lived happily ever after** e vissero per sempre felici e contenti.

hap·pi·ness ['hæpɪnɪs] N felicità, contentezza, gioia.

hap·py ['hæpɪ] ADJ (*comp* **-ier**, *superl* **-iest**) **a** (*pleased, content*) contento(-a), felice; (*cheerful*) allegro(-a); (*at ease, unworried*) tranquillo(-a); **happy with** (*arrangements*) soddisfatto(-a) di; **we are not entirely happy about the plan** non siamo del tutto contenti del progetto; **we're very happy for you** ci rallegriamo per te, siamo molto felici per te; **yes, I'd be happy to** (certo,) con piacere, (ben) volentieri; **I am happy to tell you that** ... sono felice *or* ho il piacere di informarti che...; **a happy ending** un lieto fine; **to be as happy as a lark** essere felice *or* contento(-a) come una pasqua; **happy birthday!** buon compleanno!; **happy Christmas/New Year!** buon Natale/anno!

b (*well-chosen*: *phrase, idea*) felice, indovinato(-a); (*lucky*: *position*) fortunato(-a), favorevole; **by a happy chance** per fortuna.

◆ **happy event** N (*euph*) lieto evento.

◆ **happy-go-lucky** ['hæpɪgəʊ,lʌkɪ] ADJ spensierato(-a).

◆ **happy hour** N *orario in cui le consumazioni alcoliche in un bar hanno prezzi ridotti*.

◆ **happy medium** N giusta via di mezzo.

Hapsburg ['hæps,bɜːg] N Asburgo.

ha·rangue [hə'ræŋ] 1 N tirata, arringa.

2 VT arringare.

har·ass ['hærəs] VT (*attack persistently*) tormentare; (*trouble*) assillare.

har·assed ['hærəst] ADJ (*under attack*) tormentato(-a); (*troubled*) assillato(-a); (*under pressure*) stressato(-a); **you look harassed** hai una faccia sconvolta.

har·ass·ment ['hærəsmənt] N (*action*) persecuzione *f*; (*less severe*) molestia; (*feeling*) insofferenza.

har·bour, (*Am*) **har·bor** ['hɑːbəʳ] 1 N porto.

2 VT (*hold*: *grudge, resentment*) covare, nutrire; (*shelter*: *criminal, spy*) dar rifugio a, tener nascosto(-a).

◆ **harbour dues**, (*Am*) **harbor dues** NPL diritti *mpl* portuali.

◆ **harbour master**, (*Am*) **harbor master** N capitano di porto.

hard [hɑːd] (*comp* **-er**, *superl* **-est**) 1 ADJ **a** (*substance*) duro(-a); (*mud*) indurito(-a); **to grow hard** indurirsi; **hard cover** (*of book*) copertina cartonata; **a hard nut to crack** (*problem, person*) un osso duro

b (*severe, tough*: *gen*) duro(-a); (: *climate, weather, winter*) rigido(-a); (: *frost*) forte; **to take a long hard look at sth** esaminare qc attentamente; **the hard fact is that** ... la verità nuda e cruda è che...; **hard lines!** OR **hard luck!** (*Brit fam*) peccato!, scalogna!; **a hard luck story** una storia pietosa; **he's as hard as nails** (*physically*) è forte come un toro *or* una quercia; (*in temperament*) è duro di cuore; **to take a hard line over sth** adottare una linea

dura in merito a qc; **to be hard on sb** essere severo(-a) con qn; **to be a hard worker** essere un(a) gran/grande lavoratore(-trice)

c (*difficult*: *gen*) arduo(-a), difficile; **I find it hard to believe that** ... stento *or* faccio fatica a credere che... + *sub*; **to be hard to please** essere esigente, essere difficile da accontentare.

2 ADV (*push*) forte; (*work*) sodo; (*think, try*) bene; (*hit*) forte, duramente; **to freeze hard** gelare; **it's snowing/raining hard** sta nevicando/piovendo forte; **he was breathing hard** respirava affannosamente; **to be hard hit** (*fig*) essere duramente colpito(-a); **to be hard done by** (*fam*) essere trattato(-a) ingiustamente *or* molto male; **to be hard at it** (*fam*) darci dentro; **to be hard put (to it) to do sth** essere in difficoltà a fare qc; **to try one's hardest to do sth** fare di tutto per fare qc; **to take sth hard** prendere (molto) male qc; **to be hard up for sth** essere a corto di qc; **to look hard at** guardare fissamente, esaminare attentamente; **to drink hard** essere un(a) forte bevitore(-trice).

◆ **hard-and-fast** [,hɑːdən'fɑːst] ADJ ferreo(-a).

hard·back ['hɑːd,bæk] 1 N (*book*) libro con copertina rigida *or* in edizione rilegata.

2 ADJ (*edition*) rilegato(-a).

◆ **hard-bitten** [,hɑːd'bɪtn] ADJ duro(-a).

hard·board ['hɑːd,bɔːd] N faesite *f*.

◆ **hard-boiled** [,hɑːd'bɔɪld] ADJ (*egg*) sodo(-a); (*fig*: *tough, cynical*) duro(-a).

◆ **hard cash** N (*denaro*) contante.

◆ **hard copy** N (*Comput*) hard copy *f inv*.

◆ **hard-core** [,hɑːd'kɔː] 1 ADJ **a** (*pornography*) hard-core *inv* **b** (*supporters*) irriducibile.

2 N **a** (*supporters*) zoccolo duro **b** (*for roads, foundations*) massicciata.

◆ **hard court** N (*Tennis*) campo in terra battuta.

◆ **hard disk** N (*Comput*) hard disk *m inv*, disco rigido.

◆ **hard drink** N l'alcol *m*.

◆ **hard drug** N droga pesante.

◆ **hard-earned** ['hɑːd,ɜːnd] ADJ (*money*) sudato(-a), guadagnato(-a) a fatica; (*rest, praise*) meritato(-a).

hard·en ['hɑːdn] 1 VT (*gen*) indurire; (*steel*) temprare; (*fig*: *determination*) rafforzare; **to harden one's heart** non lasciarsi commuovere.

2 VI (*substance*) indurirsi.

hard·ened ['hɑːdnd] ADJ (*criminal*) incallito(-a); **to be hardened to sth** essere (diventato(-a)) insensibile a qc.

hard·en·ing ['hɑːdnɪŋ] N indurimento.

◆ **hard feeling** N rancore *m*; **no hard feelings?** amici come prima!

◆ **hard-fought** [,hɑːd'fɔːt] ADJ (*battle, campaign*) accanito(-a).

◆ **hard graft** N: **by sheer hard graft** lavorando da matti.

◆ **hard hat** N (*for worker*) casco; (*for horse rider*) cap *m inv*.

◆ **hard-headed** [,hɑːd'hedɪd] ADJ pratico(-a).

◆ **hard-hearted** [,hɑːd'hɑːtɪd] ADJ che non si lascia commuovere, dal cuore duro.

◆ **hard-hitting** [,hɑːd'hɪtɪŋ] ADJ molto duro(-a); **a hard-hitting documentary** un documentario verità *inv*.

har·di·ness ['hɑːdɪnɪs] N robustezza.

◆ **hard labour** N lavori *mpl* forzati.

◆ **hard-liner** [,hɑːd'laɪnəʳ] N sostenitore(-trice) *or* fautore(-trice) della linea dura.

◆ **hard-luck story** [,hɑːd'lʌk,stɔːrɪ] N storia lacrimosa (*per commuovere qn*).

hard·ly ['hɑːdlɪ] ADV (*scarcely*) appena, a mala pena; **she**

can hardly read riesce a malapena a leggere; **that can hardly be true** non può essere vero; **I hardly know him** lo conosco appena; **it's hardly the case** non è proprio il caso; **I can hardly believe it** stento a crederci; **I need hardly point out that** ... non c'è bisogno che io faccia notare che...; **this is hardly the time** non è di sicuro il momento; **hardly anyone/anything** quasi nessuno/niente; **hardly ever** quasi mai; **hardly anywhere** quasi da nessuna parte; **hardly!** figuriamoci!, neanche per idea!

hard·ness ['hɑ:dnɪs] N (gen) durezza.

♦ **hard-nosed** [,hɑ:d'nəʊzd] ADJ (fam: person) duro(-a); (: attitude) da duro.

♦ **hard of hearing** ADJ duro(-a) d'orecchio.

♦ **hard-pressed** [,hɑ:d'prɛst] ADJ in difficoltà.

♦ **hard sell** N (Comm) tecnica aggressiva di vendita; **I don't like his hard sell approach** non mi piace quel suo approccio così aggressivo.

hard·ship ['hɑ:dʃɪp] N privazioni fpl, avversità f inv; (suffering) sofferenze fpl; **a life of hardship** una vita di sacrifici e privazioni.

♦ **hard shoulder** N (Brit Aut) corsia d'emergenza.

♦ **hard-up** [,hɑ:d'ʌp] ADJ (fam) al verde.

hard·ware ['hɑ:d,wɛə'] N (for domestic use) ferramenta fpl; (Mil) armamenti mpl; (Comput) hardware m.

♦ **hardware shop**, **hardware store** N (negozio di) ferramenta.

♦ **hard-wearing** [,hɑ:d'wɛərɪŋ] ADJ (gen) resistente, robusto(-a); (shoes) robusto(-a).

♦ **hard-won** [,hɑ:d'wʌn] ADJ sudato(-a).

hard·wood ['hɑ:d,wʊd] N legno duro.

♦ **hard-working** [,hɑ:d'wɜ:kɪŋ] ADJ che lavora duro.

har·dy ['hɑ:dɪ] ADJ (comp -ier, superl -iest) forte, robusto (-a); (Bot) resistente al gelo.

hare [hɛə'] N lepre f.

hare·bell ['hɛə,bɛl] N campanella scozzese.

hare·brained, **hair·brained** ['hɛə,breɪnd] ADJ scervellato(-a).

hare·lip [,hɛə'lɪp] N labbro leporino.

har·em [hɑ:'ri:m] N harem m inv.

hari·cot ['hærɪkəʊ] N (also: **haricot bean**) fagiolo bianco.

hark [hɑ:k] VI: **hark!** (liter) udite!; **hark at him!** (fam) ma sentilo!

▶ **hark back** VI + PREP: **to hark back to** (former days) rievocare; (earlier occasion) ritornare a or su.

harm [hɑ:m] ① N (gen) male m; (damage) danno; **to do sb harm** far del male a qn; **to do harm to** (reputation, interests) danneggiare; **out of harm's way** al sicuro; **to keep out of harm's way** tenersi alla larga; **there's no harm in trying** tentar non nuoce; **it does more harm than good** fa più male che bene; **you will come to no harm** non ti succederà nulla; **he means no harm** non ha nessuna cattiva intenzione; **he meant no harm by what he said** non l'ha detto con cattiveria.

② VT (person) far male a; (reputation, interests, health) danneggiare, nuocere a; (object, crops) danneggiare.

harm·ful ['hɑ:mfʊl] ADJ: **harmful (to)** dannoso(-a) (a), nocivo(-a) (a).

harm·less ['hɑ:mlɪs] ADJ (gen) innocuo(-a), inoffensivo (-a); (innocent: conversation, joke) innocente.

har·mon·ic [hɑ:'mɒnɪk] ADJ armonico(-a).

har·mon·i·ca [hɑ:'mɒnɪkə] N armonica a bocca.

har·mon·ics [hɑ:'mɒnɪks] ① NPL (Mus) armonia.

② NSG (Phys) armonica.

har·mo·ni·ous [hɑ:'məʊnɪəs] ADJ armonioso(-a).

har·mo·nium [hɑ:'məʊnɪəm] N armonium m inv.

har·mo·nize ['hɑ:mə,naɪz] ① VT (Mus) armonizzare; (colours) intonare, armonizzare.

② VI (Mus) armonizzare; **to harmonize (with)** (colours) armonizzarsi con, intonarsi (a).

har·mo·ny ['hɑ:mənɪ] N armonia.

har·ness ['hɑ:nɪs] ① N (for horse) bardatura, finimenti mpl; (for baby) briglie fpl; (safety harness) imbracatura; **to get back into harness** (fig) tornare al lavoro consueto; **to die in harness** (fig) morire sul lavoro or sulla breccia.

② VT (horse) bardare, mettere i finimenti a; (: to carriage) attaccare a; (resources) sfruttare.

harp [hɑ:p] N arpa

▶ **harp on** VI + ADV (fam): **to harp on (about)** continuare a menarla (con).

harp·ist ['hɑ:pɪst] N arpista m/f.

har·poon [hɑ:'pu:n] ① N arpione m.

② VT arpionare.

harp·si·chord ['hɑ:psɪ,kɔ:d] N clavicembalo, cembalo.

Har·py ['hɑ:pɪ] N (Myth, fig) arpia.

har·row ['hærəʊ] (Agr) ① N erpice m.

② VT erpicare.

har·row·ing ['hærəʊɪŋ] ADJ (experience, story) straziante, sconvolgente.

har·ry ['hærɪ] VT (pester) assillare; (attack persistently) attaccare.

harsh [hɑ:ʃ] ADJ (comp -er, superl -est) **a** (punishment, person) severo(-a), duro(-a); (words) duro(-a); (weather) rigido(-a); (taste) pungente **b** (discordant: voice) sgradevole; (: colour) chiassoso(-a), squillante; (light) troppo forte; (contrast) brusco(-a).

harsh·ly ['hɑ:ʃlɪ] ADV (treat, punish) duramente; (speak) duramente, aspramente.

harsh·ness ['hɑ:ʃnɪs] N **a** (of punishment, person) durezza; (of weather) inclemenza; (of taste) asprezza; (of cloth) ruvidezza **b** (of voice) sgradevolezza; (of colour) chiassosità; (of light) intensità; (of contrast) violenza.

har·te·beest ['hɑ:tɪ,bi:st] N alcelafo.

harum-scarum ['hɛərəm'skɛərəm] ① ADJ sfrenato(-a), scatenato(-a).

② ADV sfrenatamente, in modo scatenato.

har·vest ['hɑ:vɪst] ① N (of crop) raccolto; (of grapes) vendemmia.

② VT (gen) fare il raccolto di, raccogliere; (grain) mietere; (grapes) vendemmiare.

③ VI (on farm) fare il raccolto, mietere; (in vineyard) vendemmiare.

har·vest·er ['hɑ:vɪstə'] N (person) mietitore(-trice); (machine) mietitrice f; (combine harvester) mietitrebbia.

♦ **harvest festival** N festa del raccolto.

har·vest·ing ['hɑ:vɪstɪŋ] N mietitura.

♦ **harvest moon** N plenilunio (più vicino all'equinozio d'autunno).

♦ **harvest mouse** N topolino nano.

has [hæz] 3RD PERS SG PRESENT of have.

♦ **has-been** ['hæz,bi:n] N (fam: person): **he's/she's a has-been** ha fatto il suo tempo; (: thing) anticaglia.

hash [hæʃ] N **a** (Culin) spezzatino fatto con avanzi di carne cotta **b** (fam): **to make a hash of sth** fare un bel pasticcio di qc **c** (fam: hashish) erba.

hash·ish ['hæʃɪʃ] N hascisc m.

hasn't ['hæznt] = has not.

has·sle ['hæsl] (fam) ① N seccatura, scocciatura.

② VT seccare, scocciare.

has·sock ['hæsək] N (kneeler) cuscino (di inginocchiatoio).

haste [heɪst] N fretta, premura; **to make haste** sbrigarsi,

affrettarsi; **more haste less speed** (*Proverb*) presto e bene raro avviene.

has·ten ['heɪsn] ① VT (*growth*) accelerare; (*steps*) affrettare, accelerare; **to hasten sb's departure** affrettare la partenza di qn.

② VI: **to hasten (to do sth)** affrettarsi (a fare qc); **I hasten to add that ...** mi preme aggiungere che... .

hasti·ly ['heɪstɪlɪ] ADV (*hurriedly*) in (gran) fretta, in fretta e furia; (*without thinking*) senza riflettere, precipitosamente; **he hastily suggested that ...** s'è affrettato a proporre che... .

has·ty ['heɪstɪ] ADJ (*comp* **-ier**, *superl* **-iest**) (*hurried*) frettoloso(-a); (*rash*) affrettato(-a), precipitoso(-a).

hat [hæt] N cappello; **to pass the hat round** (*fig*) fare la colletta; **I take my hat off to him** (*fig*) gli faccio tanto di cappello; **to keep sth under one's hat** (*fig*) tenere qc per sé; **keep it under your hat!** acqua in bocca!; **to talk through one's hat** (*fam*) dire delle stupidaggini; **that's old hat!** (*fam*) sono storie vecchie.

hat·band ['hæt,bænd] N nastro del cappello.

hat·box ['hæt,bɒks] N cappelliera.

hatch[1] [hætʃ] N (*Naut: hatchway*) boccaporto; (*Brit: service hatch*) sportello passavivande; **down the hatch!** (*fam: when drinking*) salute!

hatch[2] [hætʃ] ① VT (*chick*) fare nascere; (*eggs*) fare schiudere; (*fig: scheme, plot*) elaborare, mettere a punto.

② VI (*chick*) uscire dal *or* rompere il guscio; (*egg*) schiudersi.

hatch·back ['hætʃ,bæk] N (*car*) auto a tre (*or* cinque) porte.

♦ **hatch cover** N (*Naut*) tambucio.

hatch·et ['hætʃɪt] N accetta, ascia.

♦ **hatchet-faced** ['hætʃɪt,feɪst] ADJ dal volto affilato.

♦ **hatchet job** N (*fam*) stroncatura.

♦ **hatchet man** N (*fam*) scagnozzo.

hate [heɪt] ① N odio.

② VT (*person, thing*) odiare; (*weaker*) detestare; **I hate having to do it** detesto doverlo fare; **I hate to trouble you, but ...** mi dispiace disturbarla, ma...; **she hates to be** *or* **she hates being corrected** non sopporta le critiche *or* le osservazioni.

hate·ful ['heɪtfʊl] ADJ odioso(-a), detestabile.

hate·ful·ly ['heɪtfəlɪ] ADV odiosamente.

hat·pin ['hæt,pɪn] N spillone *m*.

ha·tred ['heɪtrɪd] N: **hatred (of)** odio (per).

♦ **hat stand** N attaccapanni *m*.

hat·ter ['hætə'] N cappellaio; **as mad as a hatter** matto(-a) da legare.

♦ **hat trick** N (*Brit Sport, also fig*) tripletta.

haugh·ti·ly ['hɔːtɪlɪ] ADV altezzosamente, in modo altero.

haugh·ti·ness ['hɔːtɪnɪs] N altezzosità, alterigia.

haugh·ty ['hɔːtɪ] ADJ (*comp* **-ier**, *superl* **-iest**) altezzoso(-a), altero(-a).

haul [hɔːl] ① N **a** (*distance*) tragitto, viaggio; **it's a long haul** è una lunga tirata

b (*amount taken: from robbery*) bottino; (*: of fish*) retata, pescata.

② VT (*drag: person, heavy object*) tirare, trascinare; **to haul sb over the coals** (*fig*) dare una strigliata a qn

► **haul down** VT + ADV (*gen*) tirare giù; (*flag, sail*) ammainare

► **haul in** VT + ADV (*subj: police, authorities: suspect*) fare una retata di; (*net, catch, drowning person*) tirare a riva

► **haul up** VT + ADV (*flag, sail, load*) issare; (*suspect*) portare.

haul·age ['hɔːlɪdʒ] N (*road transport*) trasporto, autotra-

sporto; (*cost*) costo del trasporto.

♦ **haulage contractor** N (*Brit: firm*) impresa di trasporti; (*: person*) autotrasportatore *m*.

haul·ier ['hɔːljə], (*Am*) **haul·er** ['hɔːlə] N autotrasportatore *m*.

haunch [hɔːntʃ] N (*of person, animal*) anca; (*Culin*) coscia; **to sit on one's haunches** (*person*) accoccolarsi; (*animal*) sedersi (sulle zampe posteriori); **a haunch of venison** una coscia di cervo.

haunt [hɔːnt] ① N (*of criminals*) covo; **it's one of his favourite haunts** è un dei suoi posticini favoriti.

② VT (*subj: ghost*) abitare; (*fig: memory*) perseguitare; (*: fear*) pervadere; **he haunts the local bars** frequenta assiduamente i bar della zona; **a ghost haunts this house** questa casa è abitata da un fantasma.

haunt·ed ['hɔːntɪd] ADJ (*castle, house*) abitato(-a) dai fantasmi *or* dagli spiriti; (*look*) ossessionato(-a), tormentato(-a).

haunt·ing ['hɔːntɪŋ] ADJ (*sight, music*) che non si riesce a togliere dalla mente, ossessionante.

Ha·vana [hə'vænə] N L'Avana.

have [hæv] (*3rd pers sg present* **has**, *pt, pp* **had**)

① AUX VB

a (*gen*) avere; (*with many intransitive verbs*) essere;

▷**to have arrived** essere arrivato(-a)

▷**he has been kind/promoted** è stato gentile/promosso

▷**to have eaten** aver mangiato

▷**having finished** *or* **when he had finished, he left** dopo aver finito se n'è andato

▷**has/hasn't she told you?** te l'ha/non te l'ha detto?

b (*in tag questions*): **you've done it, haven't you?** l'hai fatto, (non è) vero?;

▷**he hasn't done it, has he?** non l'ha fatto, vero?

c (*in short answers and questions*): **you've made a mistake — no I haven't/so I have** hai fatto uno sbaglio — ma no, niente affatto/eh sì, è vero

▷**we haven't paid — yes we have!** non abbiamo pagato — sì che abbiamo pagato!

▷**I've been there before, have you?** ci sono già stato, e tu?

② MODAL AUX VB (*be obliged*): **to have (got) to do** sth dover fare qc

▷**I had better leave** è meglio che io vada

▷**this has got to be a mistake** dev'essere un errore, deve trattarsi di un errore

▷**she has to do it** lo deve fare

▷**I have (got) to finish this work** devo finire questo lavoro

▷**it will have to wait till tomorrow** bisogna rimandarlo a domani

▷**I don't have to wear glasses** non ho bisogno di portare gli occhiali.

③ VT

a (*possess*) avere;

▷**he has (got) blue eyes** ha gli occhi azzurri

▷**I haven't got blue eyes** OR **I don't have blue eyes** non ho gli occhi azzurri

▷**I have (got) an idea** ho un'idea, mi è venuta un'idea

▷**have you (got)** *or* **do you have a pen?** hai una penna?

▷**I've got somebody staying next week** ho un ospite la settimana prossima

▷**I have (got) no Spanish** non so una parola di spagnolo

b (*meal, shower*) fare; (*drink*) prendere;
▷to have *breakfast* far colazione
▷she had a *cigarette* fumò una sigaretta
▷I'll have a *coffee* prendo un caffè
▷to have *dinner* cenare
▷I must have a *drink* devo bere qualcosa
▷to have *lunch* pranzare
▷will you have some *more*? ne vuoi ancora?
▷*what* will you have? cosa bevi *or* prendi?
c (*receive, obtain*) avere, ricevere;
▷let me have your *address* dammi il tuo indirizzo
▷there was no *bread* to be had non avevano più *or* non c'era più pane
▷I must have it *by* tomorrow mi occorre per domani
▷to have a *child* avere un figlio
▷you can have it *for* £5 te lo lascio per 5 sterline
▷I have it *on* good authority that ... so da fonte sicura che...
d (*hold*) avere, tenere;
▷he had him *by* the throat lo teneva per la gola
▷I have (got) him *where* I want him ce l'ho in mano *or* in pugno
e (*maintain, allow*)
▷she will have *it* that she is right sostiene *or* asserisce di aver ragione
▷rumour has *it* (that) ... si dice *or* corre voce che...
▷I won't have *it* questo non mi va affatto
▷she won't have *it* said that ... non permette che si dica che...
▷I won't have this *nonsense* non tollero queste assurdità
f (*causative*): to have sth *done* far fare qc;
▷to have one's luggage *brought up* farsi portar su le valigie
▷to have one's hair *cut* farsi tagliare i capelli
▷he had them all *dancing* è riuscito a farli ballare tutti
▷to have sb *do* sth far fare qc a qn
▷what would you have me *do*? cosa vuoi che faccia?
▷I'd have you *know* that ... voglio che tu sappia che...
▷he had a suit *made* si fece fare un abito
g (*experience, suffer*)
▷to have an *operation* avere *or* subire un'operazione
▷she had her bag *stolen* le hanno rubato la borsa
h (+ *noun* = *verb identical with noun*)
▷let's have a *look* diamo un'occhiata
▷to have a *swim* fare una nuotata
▷let me have a *try* fammi *or* lasciami provare
▷to have a *walk* fare una passeggiata
i (*phrases*)
▷to have a pleasant *evening* passare una piacevole serata
▷you've been *had*! (*fam*) ci sei cascato!
▷let him have it! (*fam*) dagliele!, picchialo!
▷you've had it! (*fam*) sei fritto!, sei fregato!
▷thank you for having *me* grazie dell'ospitalità
▷you have *me* there! questo proprio non lo so!
▷to have a *party* dare una festa
▷to have a good *time* divertirsi

▶ **have in** VT + ADV a (*visitor*) avere (in casa); (*candidate*) far passare *or* entrare; (*doctor*) chiamare
b: to have it in *for* sb (*fam*) avercela con qn
▶ **have on** 1 VT + ADV a (*garment*) avere addosso

b (*Brit*: *be busy with*) avere da fare, avere in programma; **have you anything on tomorrow?** hai qualcosa in programma per domani?
c (*Brit fam*): **to have sb on** prendere in giro qn.
2 VT + PREP (*money*): **I don't have any money on me** non ho soldi con me
▶ **have out** VT + ADV a (*tooth, tonsils*) farsi togliere *or* levare
b: to have sth out *with* sb chiarire *or* mettere in chiaro qc con qn.
▶ **have up** VT + ADV: **to be had up** (*fam*: *in court*) essere chiamato(-a) in tribunale
ha·ven ['heɪvn] N rifugio, riparo; **a haven of peace** un'oasi di pace.
♦ **have-nots** ['hæv,nɒts] NPL see **haves**.
haven't ['hævnt] = **have not**.
hav·er·sack ['hævə,sæk] N zaino.
haves [hævz] NPL: **the haves and the have-nots** gli abbienti e i non abbienti.
hav·oc ['hævək] N distruzione *f*, devastazione *f*; **to wreak havoc on** devastare; **to play havoc with** (*fig*) scombussolare.
haw [hɔ:] N (*Bot*) bacca di biancospino.
Ha·waii [hə'waɪɪ] N le Hawaii.
Ha·wai·ian [hə'waɪjən] 1 ADJ hawaiano(-a).
2 N a (*person*) hawaiano(-a) b (*language*) hawaiano.
hawk[1] [hɔ:k] N (*also fig*) falco.
hawk[2] [hɔ:k] VT (*goods for sale*) vendere per strada.
hawk·er ['hɔ:kə] N venditore(-trice) ambulante.
♦ **hawk-eyed** ['hɔ:k,aɪd] ADJ dagli occhi di falco.
hawk·ish ['hɔ:kɪʃ] ADJ (*politician*) che sostiene la linea dura.
haw·thorn ['hɔ:,θɔ:n] N biancospino.
hay [heɪ] N fieno; **to make hay while the sun shines** (*Proverb*) battere il ferro finché è caldo.
hay·cock ['heɪ,kɒk] N mucchio di fieno.
♦ **hay fever** N raffreddore *m* da fieno.
hay·making ['heɪ,meɪkɪŋ] N fienagione *f*.
hay·stack ['heɪ,stæk] N pagliaio.
hay·wire ['heɪ,waɪə] ADJ (*fam*): **to go haywire** (*person*) dare i numeri, perdere la testa; (*machine*) impazzire; (*scheme, system*) andare a catafascio.
haz·ard ['hæzəd] 1 N (*risk*) rischio; (*more serious*) pericolo; (*chance*) azzardo; **occupational hazard** rischio del mestiere; **natural hazard** calamità naturale; **to be a health hazard** essere dannoso(-a) alla salute.
2 VT (*one's life*) rischiare, mettere a repentaglio; (*remark*) azzardare; **to hazard a guess** tirare a indovinare.
haz·ard·ous ['hæzədəs] ADJ rischioso(-a), pericoloso(-a).
♦ **hazard warning lights** NPL (*Aut*) luci *fpl* di emergenza.
haze [heɪz] N (*mist*) foschia; (*of smoke*) velo.
ha·zel ['heɪzl] 1 N (*tree*) nocciolo.
2 ADJ (*eyes*) (*color*) nocciola *inv*.
ha·zel·nut ['heɪzl,nʌt] N nocciola.
hazy ['heɪzɪ] ADJ (*comp* -**ier**, *superl* -**iest**) (*day*) di foschia; (*weather*) caliginoso(-a); (*view*) indistinto(-a); (*photograph*) leggermente sfocato(-a); (*uncertain: person*) confuso(-a); (*unclear: memory, details, idea*) vago(-a).
♦ **H-bomb** ['eɪtʃ,bɒm] N bomba H.
h & c ABBR (*Brit*)= hot and cold (water).
HE [,eɪtʃ'i:] ABBR a = high explosive b (*Diplomacy*: = *His (or Her) Excellency*) S.E. (= *sua eccellenza*); (*Rel*: = *His Eminence*) S.E. (= *Sua Eminenza*).
he [hi:] 1 PERS PRON lui, egli; **he has gone out** è uscito;

there/here he is eccolo; **it is he who ... è lui che...;** HE **didn't do it** non è stato lui a farlo; **he who hesitates is lost** chi si ferma è perduto.

2 N: **it's a he** (*animal, fam: baby*) è un maschio.

head [hɛd] 1 N **a** (*Anat*) testa, capo; **head of hair** capigliatura; **head down** a testa bassa; **head first** a capofitto, di testa; **my head is aching** mi fa male la testa, ho mal di testa; **to fall head over heels in love with sb** innamorarsi perdutamente *or* follemente di qn; **from head to foot** dalla testa ai piedi; **his head's in the clouds** ha la testa fra le nuvole; **to keep one's head above water** (*fig*) mantenersi a galla; **the horse won by a head** il cavallo ha vinto per una testa; **on your head be it** a tuo rischio e pericolo; **I could do it standing on my head** (*fam*) potrei farlo a occhi chiusi; **they went over my head to the manager** mi hanno scavalcato e sono andati direttamente dal direttore; **wine goes to my head** il vino mi dà *or* va alla testa; **success has gone to his head** il successo gli ha dato alla testa; **to shout one's head off** (*fam*) sgolarsi

b (*intellect, mind*) cervello, testa; **two heads are better than one** (*Proverb*) due occhi vedono meglio di uno; **it never entered my head** non mi è mai passato per la testa; **to have a head for business** essere tagliato(-a) per gli affari; **to have no head for heights** soffrire di vertigini; **to lose/to keep one's head** perdere/non perdere la testa; **let's put our heads together** pensiamoci insieme; **it was above** *or* **over their heads** non erano all'altezza di capirlo; **to do a sum in one's head** fare un calcolo a mente; **I couldn't tell you off the top of my head** (*fam*) non te lo saprei dire così su due piedi; **to get sth into one's head** ficcarsi in testa qc; **to be off one's head** (*fam*) essere fuori di testa

c (*leader: of family, business*) capo; (: *of school*) direttore (-trice), preside *m/f*; **head of state** (*Pol*) capo di Stato

d (*on coin*) testa; **heads or tails?** testa o croce?; **I couldn't make head nor tail of it** per me non aveva né capo né coda

e (*no pl: unit*): **20 head of cattle** 20 capi *mpl* di bestiame; **£10 a** *or* **per head** 10 sterline a testa

f (*of hammer, bed, flower*) testa; (*of nail*) capocchia; (*of arrow*) punta; (*of lettuce*) cespo; (*of river*) sorgente *f*; (*of stairs, page*) cima; (*of beer*) schiuma; (*on tape recorder, computer*) testina; **at the head of** (*organization*) a capo di; (*train, procession*) in testa a, alla testa di; (*queue*) all'inizio di; **to sit at the head of the table** sedersi a capotavola; **to come to a head** (*abscess*) maturare; (*fig: situation*) precipitare

g (*Naut: of ship*) prua; (*of sail*) penna.

2 VT **a** (*parade, list, poll*) essere in testa a; (*company, group*) essere a capo di

b (*Ftbl*): **to head a ball** colpire di testa una palla

c (*chapter*) intitolare.

3 VI dirigersi; **to head for** dirigersi *or* andare verso; **to head home** andare a casa; **she was heading up the stairs** stava salendo le scale; **he is heading for trouble** sta andando incontro a dei guai.

4 ADJ **a** (*clerk, typist*) capo *inv*

▶ **head for** VI + PREP dirigersi verso

▶ **head off** VT + ADV (*threat, danger*) sventare; (*person, animal*) far cambiare direzione a

▶ **head up** VT + ADV (*Am: team, group*) essere a capo di.

head·ache ['hɛdˌeɪk] N (*pain*) mal *m* di testa; (*fig*) grattacapo; **to have a headache** avere mal di testa.

head·band ['hɛdˌbænd] N fascia per i capelli.

head·board ['hɛdˌbɔːd] N testiera (del letto).

♦ **head cold** N raffreddore *m* di testa.

♦ **head collar**, (*Am*) **head·stall** ['hɛdˌstɔːl] N capezza.

head·dress ['hɛdˌdrɛs] N (*made of feathers*) copricapo; (*of bride*) acconciatura.

head·ed note·paper [ˌhɛdɪd'nəʊtˌpeɪpəʳ] N carta intestata.

head·er ['hɛdəʳ] N (*Brit fam: Ftbl*) colpo di testa; (: *fall*) caduta di testa; **he took a header into the water** fece un tuffo di testa nell'acqua.

♦ **head·first** [ˌhɛd'fɜːst] ADV a testa in giù, a capofitto; (*fig*) senza pensare.

♦ **head gardener** N capo giardiniere *m*.

head·gear ['hɛdˌgɪəʳ] N (*hat*) copricapo.

head·hunt ['hɛdˌhʌnt] VT: **to be headhunted** avere un'offerta di lavoro da un cacciatore di teste.

head·hunt·er ['hɛdˌhʌntəʳ] N cacciatore *m* di teste.

head·ing ['hɛdɪŋ] N (*title*) titolo; (*section*) sezione *f*; (*on letter*) intestazione *f*.

head·land ['hɛdlənd] N punta, promontorio.

head·light ['hɛdˌlaɪt], **head·lamp** ['hɛdˌlæmp] N (*Aut*) faro, fanale *m*.

head·line ['hɛdˌlaɪn] N (*in newspaper*) titolo; (*TV, Radio*): **headlines** NPL (*main points*) sommario; **to hit the headlines** far titolo.

head·long ['hɛdˌlɒŋ] 1 ADJ (*fall, dive*) a capofitto, a testa in giù; (*rush*) a tutta velocità.

2 ADV (*fall*) a capofitto, a tutta velocità; (*rush*) precipitosamente.

head·man ['hɛdmən] N (*pl* **-men**) capotribù *m inv*.

head·master [ˌhɛd'mɑːstəʳ] N (*of primary school*) direttore *m*; (*of secondary school*) preside *m*.

head·mistress [ˌhɛd'mɪstrɪs] N (*of primary school*) direttrice *f*; (*of secondary school*) preside *f*.

♦ **head office** N sede *f* centrale.

♦ **head·on** [ˌhɛd'ɒn] 1 ADJ (*collision*) frontale; (*confrontation*) diretto(-a), faccia a faccia.

2 ADV (*collide*) frontalmente.

head·phones ['hɛdˌfəʊnz] NPL cuffia *fsg*.

head·quarters [ˌhɛd'kwɔːtəz] NPL (*Mil*) quartier *msg* generale; (*of party, organization*) sede *f* centrale; (*Police*) centrale *f*.

head·rest ['hɛdˌrɛst] N poggiatesta *m inv*.

head·room ['hɛdˌrʊm] N (*under ceiling*) spazio (per la testa); (*under bridge*) altezza libera di passaggio; (*in car*) altezza dell'abitacolo.

head·scarf ['hɛdˌskɑːf], **head·square** ['hɛdˌskwɛəʳ] N foulard *m inv*.

head·set ['hɛdˌsɛt] N cuffia.

head·stall ['hɛdˌstɔːl] N = **head collar**.

head·stand ['hɛdˌstænd] N: **to do a headstand** fare una verticale.

♦ **head start** N (*Sport, fig*): **to have a head start** partire avvantaggiato(-a).

head·stone ['hɛdˌstəʊn] N (*on grave*) lapide *f*, pietra tombale.

head·strong ['hɛdˌstrɒŋ] ADJ testardo(-a), cocciuto(-a).

♦ **head waiter** N capocameriere *m*.

head·way ['hɛdˌweɪ] N (*Naut*) abbrivio; **to make headway** (*fig*) fare progressi *or* passi avanti; (*Naut*) avanzare.

head·wind ['hɛdˌwɪnd] N vento di prua; **to cycle against a headwind** pedalare controvento.

heady ['hɛdɪ] ADJ (*comp* **-ier**, *superl* **-iest**) (*wine, scent, success*) inebriante; (*atmosphere*) euforico(-a).

heal [hiːl] 1 VT (*wound*) guarire, cicatrizzare; (*person*)

guarire; (*fig: differences*) appianare.
2 VI (*also: heal up*) cicatrizzarsi.
heal·er ['hiːlə'] N guaritore(-trice).
heal·ing ['hiːlɪŋ] 1 ADJ (*waters, power*) curativo(-a); (*ointment*) curativo(-a), medicamentoso(-a); **to have healing hands** essere un(a) pranoterapeuta *m/f*.
2 N guarigione *f.*
health [hɛlθ] N (*gen*) salute *f*; **Ministry of Health** ministero della Sanità; **Health Minister** ministro della Sanità; **Department of Health** ≈ ministero della Sanità; **to be in good/bad health** essere in buona/cattiva salute; **to drink sb's health** bere alla salute di qn; **your health!** (alla tua) salute!
♦ **health care** N assistenza sanitaria.
♦ **health centre** N (*Brit*) poliambulatorio.
♦ **health fanatic** N salutista *m/f.*
♦ **health food** N cibo macrobiotico.
♦ **health–giving** ['hɛlθˌgɪvɪŋ] ADJ (*food, air, exercise*) sano (-a), salutare.
♦ **health hazard** N pericolo per la salute.
healthi·ly ['hɛlθɪlɪ] ADV (*live, eat*) in modo sano.
♦ **Health Service** N: **the Health Service** (*Brit*) ≈ il Servizio Sanitario Nazionale.
healthy ['hɛlθɪ] ADJ (*comp* **-ier**, *superl* **-iest**) (*person*) sano (-a), in buona salute; (*skin, diet, attitude*) sano(-a); (*air, place, climate*) salubre; (*appetite*) robusto(-a); (*exercise, food, fig: respect*) salutare; (: *interest*) vivace; (: *economy*) florido(-a); (: *bank balance*) in attivo.
heap [hiːp] 1 N (*pile*) mucchio, cumulo; (*fam: old car*) macinino; (: *lots*): **heaps (of)** un sacco (di), un mucchio (di); **we have heaps of time** abbiamo un mucchio *or* sacco di tempo; **I was struck** *or* **knocked all of a heap** (*fam*) sono rimasto di stucco.
2 VT: **to heap sth onto sth** ammucchiare qc su qc; **the waitress heaped potatoes onto my plate** la cameriera mi ha dato una montagna *or* un mucchio di patate; **to heap sth with sth** colmare qc di qc; **to heap favours/praise/gifts on sb** ricolmare qn di favori/lodi/regali; **heaped spoonful** (*Culin*) cucchiaio colmo
▶ **heap up** VT + ADV accumulare, ammucchiare.
hear [hɪə'] (*pt, pp* **heard** [hɜːd]) 1 VT (*gen*) sentire; (*be informed of: piece of news*) apprendere, sentire; (*news on radio, TV*) ascoltare; (*lecture*) assistere a; (*Law: case*) esaminare; **I can't hear you** non ti sento; **I could hardly make myself heard** facevo fatica a farmi sentire; **I hear you've lost your watch** ho saputo che hai perso l'orologio; **to hear him speak you'd think ...** a sentirlo parlare si direbbe che...; **have you heard the one about the Irishman who ...** la sai quella dell'irlandese che....
2 VI (*gen*) sentire; (*get news*) aver notizie; **to hear about** sentire parlare di; (*have news of*) avere notizie di; **I heard about her from her mother** ho avuto sue notizie tramite sua madre; **did you hear about the move?** hai saputo del trasloco?; **to hear from sb** ricevere notizie da qn; **she was never heard of again** non se ne seppe più nulla; **I've never heard of that book** non ho mai sentito parlare di quel libro; **I've never heard of such a thing** non ho mai sentito una cosa simile; **I won't hear of it** (*allow*) non ne voglio proprio sapere; **I won't hear of you paying for this** non è proprio il caso che tu paghi; **hear! hear!** (*bravo*) bravo!, bene!
▶ **hear out** VT + ADV ascoltare senza interrompere; **hear me out!** fammi finire!
heard [hɜːd] PT, PP of **hear**.
hear·er ['hɪərə'] N uditore(-trice).

hear·ing ['hɪərɪŋ] N **a** (*sense of hearing*) udito; **to be within/out of hearing (distance)** essere/non essere a portata di voce; **in my hearing** in mia presenza **b** (*Law*) udienza; **to give sb a hearing** dare udienza a qn; (*of witnesses*) audizione *f*, escussione *f.*
♦ **hearing aid** N apparecchio acustico.
hear·say ['hɪəˌseɪ] N diceria, chiacchiere *fpl*; **by hearsay** per sentito dire.
hearse [hɜːs] N carro funebre.
heart [hɑːt] 1 N **a** (*also fig*) cuore *m*; **to have a weak heart** avere il cuore debole; **he's a man after my own heart** è proprio il tipo che mi piace; **he's a good boy at heart** in fondo è un bravo ragazzo; **to have sb's interests at heart** avere a cuore gli interessi di qn; **from the (bottom of one's) heart** dal profondo del cuore, con tutto il cuore; **in her heart of hearts** nel suo intimo; **heart and soul** anima e corpo; **his heart was in his boots** (*dejected*) aveva la morte nel cuore; **to wear one's heart on one's sleeve** non fare mistero dei propri sentimenti; **my heart sank** mi sono scoraggiato; **to learn/know/recite by heart** imparare/sapere/ripetere a memoria; **to one's heart's content** quanto si ha voglia; **her heart is in the right place** è di buon cuore; **to cry one's heart out** piangere disperatamente *or* a calde lacrime; **have a heart!** (*fam*) sii buono!; **she has a heart of gold** ha un cuore d'oro; **to take sth to heart** prendersi a cuore qc; **his heart was not in it** gli mancava l'entusiasmo; **to set one's heart on sth/on doing sth** tenere molto a qc/a fare qc; **with all one's heart** con tutto il cuore; **to break sb's heart** spezzare il cuore a qn; **to be in good heart** essere su di morale; **I did not have the heart to tell her** non ho avuto cuore *or* il coraggio di dirglielo; **to have one's heart in one's mouth** avere il cuore in gola; **to lose heart** perdersi di coraggio *or* d'animo, scoraggiarsi; **to take heart** farsi coraggio *or* animo; **in the heart of the country** in mezzo alla campagna; **the heart of the matter** il nocciolo della questione
b (*Cards*): **hearts** NPL cuori *mpl.*
2 ADJ cardiaco(-a); **to have a heart complaint** OR **to have heart trouble** avere un disturbo cardiaco *or* una cardiopatia; **to have a heart condition** essere cardiopatico(-a).
heart·ache ['hɑːtˌeɪk] N pene *fpl*, dolori *mpl.*
♦ **heart attack** N (*Med*) infarto.
heart·beat ['hɑːtˌbiːt] N (*single*) pulsazione *f*; (*rate*) battiti *mpl* del cuore.
heart·break ['hɑːtˌbreɪk] N immenso dolore *m.*
heart·breaking ['hɑːtˌbreɪkɪŋ] ADJ penoso(-a), straziante.
heart·broken ['hɑːtˌbrəʊkən] ADJ affranto(-a); **to be heartbroken** essere heartbroken *or* cuore spezzato.
heart·burn ['hɑːtbɜːn] N (*Med*) bruciore *m* di stomaco.
-hearted ['hɑːtɪd] SUFF: **a kind-hearted person** una persona di buon cuore.
heart·en ['hɑːtn] VT rincuorare, incoraggiare.
heart·en·ing ['hɑːtnɪŋ] ADJ incoraggiante.
♦ **heart failure** N (*Med*) (*malfunction*) collasso cardiaco; (*arrest*) arresto cardiaco.
heart·felt ['hɑːtˌfɛlt] ADJ profondo(-a), sincero(-a).
hearth [hɑːθ] N focolare *m.*
♦ **hearth rug** N tappeto (*che si mette davanti al camino*).
hearti·ly ['hɑːtɪlɪ] ADV (*agree*) in pieno, completamente; (*laugh*) di cuore, di gusto; (*eat*) di buon appetito, di gusto; (*thank, welcome*) calorosamente; **to be heartily sick of** (*Brit*) essere veramente stufo(-a) di, essere arcistufo(-a) di.
heart·land ['hɑːtˌlænd] N zona centrale; **Italy's industrial**

heartland il cuore dell'industria italiana.
heart·less ['hɑːtlɪs] ADJ spietato(-a), crudele, senza cuore, insensibile.
heart·less·ly ['hɑːtlɪslɪ] ADV spietatamente, crudelmente.
heart·less·ness ['hɑːtlɪsnɪs] N crudeltà.
heart·rend·ing ['hɑːt,rɛndɪŋ] ADJ straziante.
♦ **heart-searching** ['hɑːt,sɜːtʃɪŋ] N: **after much heart-searching** dopo lunghe meditazioni; **he came to his decision after much heart-searching** la sua fu una decisione lunga e sofferta.
hearts·ease ['hɑːts,iːz] N (Bot) viola del pensiero selvatica.
heart·strings ['hɑːt,strɪŋs] NPL: **to tug (at) sb's heartstrings** toccare il cuore a qn, toccare qn nel profondo.
♦ **heart surgeon** N cardiochirurgo.
♦ **heart-throb** ['hɑːt,θrɒb] N: **a teenage heart-throb** un idolo delle ragazzine.
♦ **heart-to-heart** [,hɑːttə'hɑːt] ☐1 ADJ, ADV a cuore aperto. ☐2 N (conversation): **to have a heart to heart** parlare a cuore aperto.
♦ **heart transplant** N trapianto di cuore.
♦ **heart-warming** ['hɑːt,wɔːmɪŋ] ADJ toccante.
hearty ['hɑːtɪ] ADJ (comp -ier, superl -iest) (person) gioviale; (support) caloroso(-a); (dislike) vivo(-a); (laugh) di cuore, di gusto; (appetite) robusto(-a); (meal) abbondante, sostanzioso(-a); (welcome, thanks) cordiale, caloroso (-a); **a hearty eater** una buona forchetta.
heat [hiːt] ☐1 N a (gen) calore m; (fig) ardore m; **I can't stand the heat** non sopporto il caldo; **at low heat** (Culin: on stove) a fuoco basso; (: in oven) a calore moderato; **in the heat of the moment** (fig) nella foga del momento; **in the heat of the battle** nella furia della battaglia; **to put the heat on sb** fare pressione a or su qn; **he replied with some heat** rispose piuttosto irritato
  b (Sport: also: **qualifying heat**) batteria, prova eliminatoria
  c (Zool): **in** or **on heat** in calore.
☐2 VT (far) scaldare.
☐3 VI scaldarsi
► **heat up** ☐1 VI + ADV (liquids) scaldarsi; (room) riscaldarsi. ☐2 VT + ADV riscaldare.
heat·ed ['hiːtɪd] ADJ riscaldato(-a); (fig: discussion, argument) acceso(-a), animato(-a); **heated words** parole fpl di fuoco; **to grow heated** (discussion) accendersi.
heat·ed·ly ['hiːtɪdlɪ] ADV (discuss, argue) animatamente.
heat·er ['hiːtər] N calorifero, termosifone m, radiatore m; (stove) stufa.
heath [hiːθ] N (Brit: moor) landa, brughiera; (plant) erica, brugo.
♦ **heat haze** N foschia dovuta all'afa.
hea·then ['hiːðən] ADJ, N pagano(-a).
hea·then·ish ['hiːðənɪʃ] ADJ (pej: pagan) pagano(-a); (: uncivilized) barbaro(-a).
heath·er ['hɛðər] N erica.
heat·ing ['hiːtɪŋ] N riscaldamento.
♦ **heat loss** N perdita di calore.
♦ **heat rash** N (Med) eritema m (da calore).
♦ **heat-resistant** ['hiːtrɪˌzɪstənt] ADJ termoresistente.
♦ **heat-seeking** ['hiːt,siːkɪŋ] ADJ (missile) termoguidato(-a).
heat·stroke ['hiːt,strəʊk] N (Med) colpo di calore.
♦ **heat-treatment** ['hiːt,triːtmənt] N (Med) termoterapia; **to have heat-treatment** fare i forni.
heat·wave ['hiːt,weɪv] N ondata di caldo.
heave [hiːv] ☐1 N sforzo; (of waves) movimento; (Geol)

rigetto.
☐2 VT (pull) tirare con forza; (drag) trascinare a fatica; (lift) sollevare a fatica; (throw) scagliare; **to heave a sigh** emettere or mandare un sospiro; **to heave a sigh of relief** tirare un sospiro di sollievo; **to heave anchor** (Naut) salpare l'ancora.
☐3 VI a (sea, chest, stomach) alzarsi ed abbassarsi; **to heave at** or **to heave on** (pull) tirare con forza; **he heaved with all his might** ha tirato con tutta la sua forza
  b (feel sick) avere i conati di vomito; **her stomach heaved** le si rivoltò lo stomaco
  c (liter: pt, pp hove): **to heave in sight** or **into view** comparire all'orizzonte
► **heave to** (pt, pp hove) VI + ADV (Naut) navigare in cappa.
heav·en ['hɛvn] N a (Rel) cielo, paradiso; (fig) paradiso; **to go to heaven** andare in paradiso; **(good) heavens!** santo cielo!; **thank heaven!** grazie al cielo!; **heaven forbid!** Dio ce ne guardi!; **for heaven's sake!** (protesting) santo cielo!, in nome del cielo!; **this is heaven!** (fam) che meraviglia!; **to move heaven and earth to do sth** muovere mari e monti or farsi in quattro per fare qc; **in seventh heaven** al settimo cielo; **heaven on earth** il paradiso terrestre
  b: **the heavens** NPL (liter: sky) il cielo, la volta celeste; **the heavens opened** si è messo a diluviare.
heav·en·ly ['hɛvnlɪ] ADJ (Rel) celeste, divino(-a); (fam: delightful) divino(-a); **heavenly kingdom** regno dei cieli.
♦ **heavenly body** N (Astron) corpo celeste.
♦ **heaven-sent** ['hɛvn,sɛnt] ADJ provvidenziale, mandato (-a) dal cielo.
heavi·ly ['hɛvɪlɪ] ADV (move) con pesantezza; (tax) fortemente; (rain, snow, gamble) forte; (breathe) con difficoltà; (sigh, sleep) profondamente; (rely, drink, smoke, load) molto; **it weighs heavily on him** questo gli pesa molto.
♦ **heavily-built** [,hɛvɪlɪ'bɪlt] ADJ di corporatura robusta, massiccio(-a).
♦ **heavily-laden** [,hɛvɪlɪ'leɪdn] ADJ (molto) carico(-a).
heavi·ness ['hɛvɪnɪs] N (weight) pesantezza; (of expense, taxation) gravosità, onerosità; (of traffic) intensità.
heavy ['hɛvɪ] ADJ (comp -ier, superl -iest) (gen, fig) pesante; (sigh) profondo(-a); (sleep) profondo(-a), pesante; (blow, rain, taxation) forte; (sea) grosso(-a) (after n); (expense, casualties) ingente; (traffic) intenso(-a); (atmosphere) opprimente; (crop) abbondante; (Mil: fighting) accanito(-a); (: fire) nutrito(-a), fitto(-a); (loss) grave; (smoker) accanito(-a); **how heavy are you?** quanto pesi?; **to have a heavy cold** avere un forte raffreddore; **it's a heavy burden for her to bear** è un peso troppo grande per lei; **with a heavy heart** col cuore gonfio; **air heavy with scent** aria carica di profumo; **to be a heavy drinker** essere un(a) forte bevitore(-trice); **my car is heavy on petrol** la mia macchina consuma troppo; **to be a heavy sleeper** avere il sonno duro or pesante; **it's heavy going** è una gran fatica.
♦ **heavy cream** N (Am) panna da montare.
♦ **heavy-duty** [,hɛvɪ'djuːtɪ] ADJ molto resistente.
♦ **heavy goods vehicle** N (Brit) autoveicolo pesante da trasporto.
♦ **heavy-handed** [,hɛvɪ'hændɪd] ADJ (clumsy, tactless) pesante; (harsh: person) che ha la mano pesante, severo(-a).
♦ **heavy-hearted** [,hɛvɪ'hɑːtɪd] ADJ: **to be heavy-hearted** avere il cuore gonfio.
♦ **heavy industry** N industria pesante.
♦ **heavy metal** N (Mus) heavy metal m inv.
♦ **heavy-set** [,hɛvɪ'sɛt] ADJ (esp Am) tarchiato(-a).

heavy·weight ['hɛvɪ,weɪt] **1** N (Boxing) (peso) massimo; (fig: important or influential person) autorità f inv, pezzo m grosso.

2 ADJ (issue, subject) importante.

Hebe ['hi:bɪ] N Ebe f.

He·brew ['hi:bru:] **1** ADJ (language) ebraico(-a); (person, nation) ebreo(-a).

2 N (person) ebreo(-a); (language) ebraico.

Heb·ri·des ['hɛbrɪ,di:z] NPL: **the Hebrides** le Ebridi.

Heca·te ['hɛkətɪ] N Ecate f.

heck [hɛk] (fam) **1** EXCL: **oh heck!** oh cavolo!.

2 N: **a heck of a lot of** un casino di.

heck·le ['hɛkl] VT, VI: **to heckle (sb)** interrompere continuamente (qn) (un oratore).

heck·ler ['hɛklə'] N disturbatore(-trice).

heck·ling ['hɛklɪŋ] N interruzioni fpl.

hec·tare ['hɛktɑ:'] N ettaro.

hec·tic ['hɛktɪk] ADJ (busy) frenetico(-a); (eventful) movimentato(-a).

Hector ['hɛktə'] N Ettore m.

hec·tor ['hɛktə'] VT fare il prepotente con.

hec·tor·ing ['hɛktərɪŋ] ADJ prepotente.

he'd [hi:d] = **he would, he had.**

hedge [hɛdʒ] **1** N siepe f; (fig) difesa; **as a hedge against inflation** per cautelarsi contro l'inflazione.

2 VT (Agr) recintare con una siepe; **to be hedged about** or **around** or **in with** (restricted) essere limitato(-a) da, essere vincolato(-a) da; **to hedge one's bets** (fig) cercare di non compromettersi.

3 VI tergiversare, essere elusivo(-a).

hedge·hog ['hɛdʒ,hɒg] N riccio.

hedge·hop ['hɛdʒ,hɒp] VI volare raso terra.

hedge·row ['hɛdʒrəu] N siepe f.

he·don·ism ['hi:dənɪzəm] N (frm) edonismo.

he·don·ist ['hi:dənɪst] N (frm) edonista m/f.

heebie-jeebies ['hi:bɪ'dʒi:bɪz] NPL (fam): **I had the heebie-jeebies** le gambe mi facevano giacomo giacomo; **it gives me the heebie-jeebies** mi fa venire la tremarella.

heed [hi:d] (frm) **1** N: **to pay (no) heed to, to take (no) heed of** (non) ascoltare, (non) tener conto di.

2 VT fare attenzione a.

heed·less ['hi:dlɪs] ADJ (not thinking) avventato(-a); (not caring) noncurante; **to be heedless of** essere insensibile or sordo(-a) a.

heed·less·ly ['hi:dlɪslɪ] ADV (see adj) avventatamente; con noncuranza.

heel[1] [hi:l] **1** N a (of foot, sock) tallone m, calcagno; (of shoe) tacco; **heel, boy!** (to dog) qui!; **to bring sb to heel** (fig) riportare qn all'ordine; **to be at sb's heels** stare alle calcagna di qn; **to take to one's heels** (liter) darsela a gambe; **to turn on one's heel** girare i tacchi

b (fam: person) carogna.

2 VT (shoe) fare or rifare i tacchi a; (ball) colpire di tacco.

heel[2] [hi:l] VI (also: **heel over**: ship, truck) inclinarsi (pericolosamente).

heel·ing ['hi:lɪŋ] N (Rugby) tallonaggio.

heel·piece ['hi:l,pi:s] N talloniera.

hefty ['hɛftɪ] (fam) ADJ (comp **-ier**, superl **-iest**) (load) pesante; (person) robusto(-a), solido(-a); (piece, profit) grosso(-a) (before n); (price) alto(-a), bello(-a) (before n).

heif·er ['hɛfə'] N giovenca.

height [haɪt] N a (measurement) altezza; (of person) altezza, statura; (altitude) altezza, altitudine f; (high ground) altura; **what height are you?** quanto sei alto?; **of average height** di statura media; **to be 20 metres in**

height essere alto(-a) 20 metri; **height above sea level** altitudine sopra il livello del mare; **to be afraid of heights** soffrire di vertigini

b (fig: of career, success, glory) apice m; (: of rudeness, stupidity) colmo; **at the height of** (storm, battle) nel momento culminante di; **it's the height of fashion** è l'ultimo grido della moda; **in the height of summer** nel pieno dell'estate.

height·en ['haɪtn] VT (raise) alzare; (increase) far aumentare; (enhance: effect) mettere in risalto, accrescere; (: experience) rendere più intenso(-a).

hei·nous ['heɪnəs] ADJ (frm) nefando(-a), atroce.

heir [ɛə'] N erede m/f.

♦ **heir apparent** N erede m/f legittimo(-a).

heir·ess ['ɛərɛs] N erede f; (rich) ereditiera.

heir·loom ['ɛəlu:m] N: **this picture is a family heirloom** è un quadro di famiglia.

heist [haɪst] N (Am fam: hold-up) rapina.

held [hɛld] PT, PP of **hold.**

Helen ['hɛlɪn] N Elena.

heli·cal ['hɛlɪkəl] ADJ elicoidale.

heli·cop·ter ['hɛlɪ,kɒptə'] N elicottero.

heli·port ['hɛlɪ,pɔ:t] N eliporto.

he·lium ['hi:lɪəm] N elio.

he·lix ['hi:lɪks] (pl **helices** ['hɛlɪ,si:z] or **helixes**) N elica.

hell [hɛl] N inferno; **in hell** all'inferno; **to go hell for leather** andare or correre come un demonio; **all hell broke loose** è successo il or un finimondo; **a hell of a noise** (fam) un casino infernale, un fracasso del diavolo; **a hell of a lot of** (fam) un sacco or mucchio or casino di; **we had a hell of a time** (fam: good) ci siamo divertiti da pazzi; (: bad) è stato terribile; **to have a hell of a time doing sth** (fam) diventar matto(-a) a fare qc; **to make sb's life hell** (fam) rendere la vita un inferno a qn; **to give sb hell** (fam: address harshly) dirne di tutti i colori a qn; **to run like hell** (fam) correre come un matto(-a); **what the hell do you want?** (fam) che diavolo vuoi?; **just for the hell of it** (fam) per il gusto di farlo; **go to hell!** (fam) va' all'inferno!, va' al diavolo!; **to hell with it!** (fam) al diavolo!; **oh hell!** (fam) porca miseria!, accidenti!

he'll [hi:l] = **he will, he shall.**

Hel·las ['hɛləs] N Ellade f.

hell·bent [,hɛl'bɛnt] ADJ: **hellbent on doing sth** deciso(-a) a fare qc a tutti i costi.

Hel·len·ic [hɛ'lɛnɪk] ADJ ellenico(-a).

hell·ish ['hɛlɪʃ] ADJ (fam) infernale, bestiale.

hell·ish·ly ['hɛlɪʃlɪ] ADV (fam) mostruosamente, atrocemente.

hel·lo [hə'ləu] EXCL (on meeting sb) ciao!; (: more formal) buon giorno!; (in surprise) ma guarda!; (Telec) pronto!; (to attract attention) ehi!

helm [hɛlm] N (Naut) timone m; **to be at the helm** (fig) essere al comando.

hel·met ['hɛlmɪt] N (of motorcyclist, construction worker) casco; (of miner, soldier, policeman) elmetto; (of knight) elmo.

helms·man ['hɛlmzmən] N (pl **-men**) timoniere m.

help [hɛlp] **1** N a (assistance) aiuto; **with the help of** con l'aiuto di; **without the help of sb/sth** senza l'aiuto di qn/qc; **to be of help to sb** essere di aiuto or essere utile a qn; **to call for help** chiedere or gridare aiuto; **he gave me no help** non mi ha dato nessun aiuto; **he is beyond help** è un caso senza speranza; **there's no help for it** non c'è altro or nient'altro da fare; **help!** aiuto!

b (employee) aiutante m/f; (domestic) domestico(-a);

(*daily*) donna di servizio.

2 VT **a** (*aid, assist*) aiutare; (*scheme, project*) contribuire a; (*progress*) favorire; (*pain*) far passare, alleviare; **to help sb (to) do sth** aiutare qn a far qc; **to help sb with sth** aiutare qn con qc; **I helped him with his luggage** l'ho aiutato a portare i bagagli; **I got my sister to help me** mi sono fatta aiutare da mia sorella; **that won't help much** non servirà a gran che; **can I help you?** (*in shop*) desidera?; **to help sb on/off with his/her coat** aiutare qn a mettersi/togliersi il cappotto; **to help sb across/up/down** aiutare qn ad attraversare/a salire/a scendere **b** (*at table*): **to help sb to soup** servire la minestra a qn; **to help o.s.** (*to food*) servirsi, prendere; (*to other things: steal*) prendersi, arraffare

c: **he can't help coughing** non può fare a meno di tossire; **she can't help being stupid** cosa può farci se è stupida?; **I couldn't help thinking** ... non potevo fare a meno di pensare...; **it can't be helped** non ci si può fare (più) niente, non c'è niente da fare; **he won't do it if I can help it** farò il possibile per impedirglielo; **he can't help himself** non può farne a meno

▶ **help out** **1** VI + ADV aiutare, dare una mano.

2 VT + ADV aiutare, dare una mano a.

help·er ['hɛlpəʳ] N aiutante *m/f*, assistente *m/f*.

help·ful ['hɛlpfʊl] ADJ (*person: willing*) che si rende utile; (: *useful*) di grande aiuto; (*object, advice*) utile.

help·ful·ly ['hɛlpfəlɪ] ADV gentilmente.

help·ful·ness ['hɛlpfʊlnɪs] N disponibilità.

help·ing ['hɛlpɪŋ] N porzione *f*; **you've had two helpings of dessert already** ti sei già servito due volte di dolce.

♦ **helping hand** N aiuto; **to give sb a helping hand** dare una mano a qn.

help·less ['hɛlplɪs] ADJ (*rage, person: powerless*) impotente; (*person: vulnerable*) indifeso(-a); (: *physically weak*) debole; **a helpless invalid** un infermo; **a helpless old lady** una povera vecchietta; **helpless with laughter** morto(-a) dalle risate.

help·less·ly ['hɛlplɪslɪ] ADV (*struggle, try*) in vano; (*lie, remain*) senza potersi muovere; (*say*) con fare impotente; **he watched helplessly as his parents were shot** guardava impotente mentre i genitori venivano fucilati; **to laugh helplessly** ridere senza potersi fermare.

help·less·ness ['hɛlplɪsnɪs] N impotenza.

help·line ['hɛlp‚laɪn] N ≈ telefono amico; (*Comm*) servizio *m* informazioni *inv* (*a pagamento*).

Hel·sin·ki ['hɛlsɪŋkɪ] N Helsinki *f*.

helter-skelter ['hɛltə'skɛltəʳ] **1** ADV in fretta e furia, in quattro e quattr'otto.

2 N (*Brit: in funfair*) scivolo (a spirale).

hem [hɛm] **1** N (*hemline*) orlo; **to let the hem down on a skirt** allungare una gonna.

2 VT fare l'orlo a

▶ **hem in** VT + ADV cingere, circondare; **to feel hemmed in** (*fig*) sentirsi soffocare.

♦ **he-man** ['hiː‚mæn] N (*pl -men*) (*fam*) vero maschio.

hema·tol·ogy *etc* [‚hiːmə'tɒlədʒɪ] (*Am*) = **haematology**.

hemi·sphere ['hɛmɪsfɪəʳ] N emisfero.

hem·lock ['hɛm‚lɒk] N cicuta.

hemo·glo·bin [‚hiːməʊ'gləʊbɪn] N (*Am*) = **haemoglobin**.

hemo·philia [‚hiːməʊ'fɪlɪə] N (*Am*) = **haemophilia**.

hem·or·rhage ['hɛmərɪdʒ] N (*Am*) = **haemorrhage**.

hem·or·rhoids ['hɛmɔrɔɪdz] NPL (*Am*) = **haemorrhoids**.

hemp [hɛmp] N (*for rope*) canapa; (*drug*) canapa indiana, hascisc *m inv*.

hen [hɛn] N (*fowl*) gallina; (*with chicks*) chioccia; (*female bird*) femmina; **hen pheasant** fagiano femmina.

hence [hɛns] ADV **a** (*frm: therefore*) per cui, dunque **b** (*old: place*) da qui, di qui **c** (*frm: time*): **5 years hence** da qui a 5 anni.

hence·forth [‚hɛns'fɔːθ] ADV (*frm*) d'ora innanzi *or* in poi.

hench·man ['hɛntʃmən] N (*pl -men*) (*follower*) accolito; (*pej*) scagnozzo.

hen·house ['hɛn‚haʊs] N pollaio.

hen·na ['hɛnə] N henna.

♦ **hen party** N (*fam*) festa di sole donne.

hen·pecked ['hɛn‚pɛkt] ADJ (*fam*): **he is henpecked** è succube della moglie.

hepa·ti·tis [‚hɛpə'taɪtɪs] N epatite *f*.

her [hɜːʳ] **1** PERS PRON **a** (*direct: unstressed*) la, l'+ *vowel*; (: *stressed*) lei; **I hear her** la sento; **I heard her** l'ho sentita; **I've never seen HER** lei, non l'ho mai vista **b** (*indirect*) le; **I gave her the book** le ho dato il libro; **I spoke to her** le ho parlato

c (*after prep, in comparisons*) lei; **without her** senza di lei; **I was thinking of her** pensavo a lei; **she had a case with her** aveva con sé una valigia; **if I were her** se fossi in lei; **it's her** è lei; **I'm older than her** sono più vecchio di lei.

2 POSS ADJ il/la suo(-a); PL i/le suoi/sue; **this is her house** questa è la sua casa; **her brother** suo fratello.

Hera ['hɪərə] N Era.

her·ald ['hɛrəld] **1** N araldo; (*fig*) messaggero.

2 VT annunciare.

he·ral·dic [hɛ'rældɪk] ADJ araldico(-a).

her·ald·ry ['hɛrəldrɪ] N araldica.

herb [hɜːb] N (*Med*) erba medicinale; **herbs** NPL (*Culin*) erbe *fpl* aromatiche, odori *mpl*.

her·ba·ceous [hɜː'beɪʃəs] ADJ erbaceo(-a).

herb·al ['hɜːbəl] ADJ di erbe; **herbal tea** tisana.

herb·al·ist ['hɜːbəlɪst] N erborista *m/f*.

♦ **herb garden** N orticello di odori.

herbi·cide ['hɜːbɪ‚saɪd] N erbicida *m*.

her·bi·vore ['hɜːbɪ‚vɔː] N erbivoro.

her·bivo·rous [hɜː'bɪvərəs] ADJ erbivoro(-a).

Hercules ['hɜːkjʊliːz] N Ercole *m*.

herd [hɜːd] **1** N (*of cattle, horses*) mandria; (*of wild animals, swine*) branco; (*of people: pej*): **the (common) herd** il gregge.

2 VT (*drive, gather: animals*) guidare; (: *people*) radunare

▶ **herd together** **1** VT + ADV radunare.

2 VI + ADV stringersi uno vicino all'altro.

♦ **herd instinct** N istinto gregale.

here [hɪəʳ] **1** ADV (*place*) qui, qua; (*at this point*) qui, a questo punto; **come here!** vieni qui!; **here!** (*at roll call*) presente!; **over here** da questa parte, di qua; **here I am** eccomi qua; **here are the books** ecco (qua) i libri; **here you are!** (*giving sb sth*) ecco qui!; **here she comes** eccola (che viene); **here and there** qua e là; **here, there and everywhere** dappertutto; **winter is here** l'inverno è arrivato; **my friend here will do it** il mio amico qui lo farà; **that's neither here nor there** non ha molta importanza; **here's to John!** alla salute di John!.

2 EXCL ehi!

here·abouts ['hɪərə‚baʊts] ADV da queste parti.

here·after [‚hɪər'ɑːftəʳ] **1** ADV (*frm*) d'ora in poi, da qui in avanti, in futuro.

2 N: **the hereafter** l'aldilà *m*.

here·by [‚hɪə'baɪ] (*frm*) ADV con questo (*documento or atto etc*); (*in letter*) con la presente.

he·redi·tary [hɪ'rɛdɪtərɪ] ADJ ereditario(-a).

he·red·ity [hɪ'rɛdɪtɪ] N eredità.

her·esy ['hɛrəsɪ] N eresia.

her·etic ['hɛrətɪk] N eretico(-a).

he·reti·cal [hɪ'rɛtɪkəl] ADJ eretico(-a).

he·reti·cal·ly [hɪ'rɛtɪkəlɪ] ADV ereticamente.

here·upon [,hɪərə'pɒn] ADV (*frm*) su ciò, su questo.

here·with [,hɪə'wɪθ] ADV (*Comm*) con la presente.

her·it·age ['hɛrɪtɪdʒ] N (*inheritance*) eredità; (*of country, nation*) retaggio; **our national heritage** il nostro patrimonio nazionale.

her·met·ic [hɜ:'mɛtɪk] ADJ ermetico(-a).

her·meti·cal·ly [hɜ:'mɛtɪkəlɪ] ADV ermeticamente; **hermetically sealed** ermeticamente chiuso(-a).

her·mit ['hɜ:mɪt] N eremita *m*.

♦ **hermit crab** N paguro, bernardo l'eremita.

her·nia ['hɜ:nɪə] N ernia.

hero ['hɪərəʊ] N (*pl* **heroes**) eroe *m*.

Herod ['hɛrəd] N Erode *m*.

Herodotus [hɪ'rɒdətəs] N Erodoto.

he·ro·ic [hɪ'rəʊɪk] ADJ eroico(-a).

he·roi·cal·ly [hɪ'rəʊɪkəlɪ] ADV eroicamente.

he·ro·ics [hɪ'rəʊɪks] NPL (*pej: words*) parolone *fpl*; (: *actions*) eroismi *mpl* inutili.

hero·in ['hɛrəʊɪn] N eroina.

♦ **heroin addict** N eroinomane *m/f*.

♦ **heroin addiction** N eroinomania.

hero·ine ['hɛrəʊɪn] N eroina.

hero·ism ['hɛrəʊɪzəm] N eroismo.

her·on ['hɛrən] N airone *m*.

♦ **hero worship** N culto degli eroi.

her·pes ['hɜ:pi:z] N herpes *m*.

her·ring ['hɛrɪŋ] N aringa.

herring·bone ['hɛrɪŋ,bəʊn] ① N (*pattern*) disegno a spina di pesce.

② ADJ spigato(-a), spinato(-a).

♦ **herring gull** N gabbiano reale.

hers [hɜ:z] POSS PRON il/la suo(-a); PL i/le suoi/sue; **a friend of hers** un suo amico; **hers is red, mine is green** il suo è rosso, il mio è verde; **this is hers** questo è (il) suo.

her·self [hɜ:'sɛlf] PERS PRON (*reflexive*) si; (*emphatic*) lei stessa; (*after preposition*) sé, se stessa; **she's not herself today** ha qualcosa che non va oggi; **she did it (all) by herself** l'ha fatto (tutto) da sola; *see also* **oneself**.

Herts ABBR (*Brit*)= **Hertfordshire**.

he's [hi:z] = **he is, he has.**

hesi·tan·cy ['hɛzɪtənsɪ] N titubanza.

hesi·tant ['hɛzɪtənt] ADJ esitante, indeciso(-a), titubante; **to be hesitant about doing sth** esitare a fare qc.

hesi·tant·ly ['hɛzɪtəntlɪ] ADV con esitazione.

hesi·tate ['hɛzɪ,teɪt] VI esitare; **to hesitate to do sth** esitare a fare qc; **to hesitate about** *or* **over sth** esitare in qc; **don't hesitate to ask (me)** non aver timore *or* paura di chiedere.

hesi·ta·tion [,hɛzɪ'teɪʃən] N esitazione *f*; **I have no hesitation in saying (that)** ... non esito a dire che... .

Hesperides [hɛ'spɛrɪ,di:z] NPL Esperidi *fpl*.

hes·sian ['hɛsɪən] N tela di canapa.

hetero·geneous ['hɛtərəʊ'dʒi:nɪəs] ADJ eterogeneo(-a).

hetero·sex·ual ['hɛtərəʊ'sɛksjʊəl] ADJ, N eterosessuale (*m/f*).

het up [,hɛt'ʌp] ADJ (*fam*) agitato(-a); **to get het up** scaldarsi.

HEW [,eɪtʃi:'dʌblju:] N ABBR (*Am*: = *Department of Health, Education and Welfare*) *ministero della sanità, della pubblica istruzione e della previdenza sociale*.

hew [hju:] (*pt* **hewed**, *pp* **hewed** *or* **hewn**) VT (*wood*) tagliare;

(*stone, coal*) scavare; (*statue*) scolpire.

hex [hɛks] (*Am*) ① N stregoneria.

② VT stregare.

hexa·deci·mal [,hɛksə'dɛsɪməl] N (*also*: **hexadecimal notation**: *Comput*) notazione *f* esadecimale.

hexa·gon ['hɛksəgən] N esagono.

hex·ago·nal [hɛk'sægənəl] ADJ esagonale.

hey [heɪ] EXCL ehi!

hey·day ['heɪ,deɪ] N età *or* tempi *mpl* d'oro; **in his heyday** quand'era in auge, ai bei tempi.

HF [,eɪtʃ'ɛf] N ABBR (= *high frequency*) A.F. (= *alta frequenza*).

HGV [,eɪtʃdʒi:'vi:] N ABBR = **heavy goods vehicle.**

HI ABBR (*Am Post*) = **Hawaii.**

hi [haɪ] EXCL ciao!, salve!

hia·tus [haɪ'eɪtəs] N (*frm: gap*) vuoto; (*Gram*) iato.

hi·ber·nate ['haɪbə,neɪt] VI andare in letargo, ibernare.

hi·ber·na·tion [,haɪbə'neɪʃən] N letargo, ibernazione *f*.

hi·bis·cus [hɪ'bɪskəs] N ibisco.

hic·cough, hic·cup ['hɪkʌp] ① N singhiozzo; **to have hiccoughs** avere il singhiozzo.

② VI avere il singhiozzo, singhiozzare.

hick [hɪk] (*Am fam*) ① N burino(-a).

② ADJ (*ideas*) da burino(-a); (*town*) provinciale.

hid [hɪd] PT of **hide.**

hid·den ['hɪdn] ① PP of **hide.**

② ADJ (*gen*) nascosto(-a); (*meaning*) recondito(-a); **there are no hidden extras** è veramente tutto compreso nel prezzo.

♦ **hidden agenda** N programma *m* non dichiarato.

hide[1] [haɪd] (*pt* **hid**, *pp* **hidden**) ① VT (*gen*) nascondere; (*feelings, truth*) dissimulare; **the clouds hid the sun** le nuvole hanno nascosto *or* coperto il sole; **to hide sth from sb** nascondere qc a qn.

② VI nascondersi; **he's hiding behind his illness** si trincera dietro la sua malattia; **to hide one's light under a bushel** (*fig*) tenere nascoste le proprie virtù

▶ **hide away** ① VI + ADV nascondersi, rifugiarsi.

② VT + ADV nascondere

▶ **hide out** VI + ADV nascondersi.

hide[2] [haɪd] N (*skin*) pelle *f*; (*leather*) cuoio.

♦ **hide-and-seek** [,haɪdən'si:k] N nascondino, rimpiattino.

hide·away ['haɪdə,weɪ] N (*hiding place*) nascondiglio; (*secluded spot*) rifugio.

hide·bound ['haɪd,baʊnd] ADJ limitato(-a), gretto(-a).

hid·eous ['hɪdɪəs] ADJ (*sight, person*) orribile, orrendo(-a); (*crime*) atroce.

hid·eous·ly ['hɪdɪəslɪ] ADV (*deformed, tortured*) orrendamente; (*fig: expensive, disappointed*) estremamente, terribilmente.

♦ **hide-out** ['haɪd,aʊt] N nascondiglio.

hid·ing[1] ['haɪdɪŋ] N: **to be in hiding** tenersi nascosto(-a); **to go into hiding** darsi alla macchia.

hid·ing[2] ['haɪdɪŋ] N botte *fpl*; **to give sb a good hiding** (*fam*) suonarle a qn.

♦ **hiding place** N nascondiglio.

hi·er·ar·chy ['haɪə,rɑ:kɪ] N (*frm*) gerarchia.

hi·ero·glyph·ic [,haɪərə'glɪfɪk] ADJ geroglifico(-a).

hieroglyphics [,haɪərə'glɪfɪks] NPL geroglifici *mpl*.

hi-fi ['haɪ'faɪ] ADJ, N ABBR (= *high fidelity*) hi-fi (*m*) *inv*; **hi-fi system** impianto hi-fi.

higgledy-piggledy ['hɪgldɪ'pɪgldɪ] ① ADJ buttato(-a) alla rinfusa.

② ADV alla rinfusa.

high [haɪ] ① ADJ (*comp* **-er**, *superl* **-est**) **a** (*gen*) alto(-a); **a**

building **60 metres high** un palazzo alto 60 metri; **how high is Ben Nevis?** quanto è alto il Ben Nevis?; **since she was so high** (*fam*) fin da quando era grande *or* alta così; **to leave sb high and dry** (*fig*) piantare in asso qn; **to be on one's high horse** (*fig*) montare *or* salire in cattedra; **to be** *or* **act high and mighty** darsi delle arie

b (*frequency, pressure, temperature, salary, price*) alto (-a); (*speed, wind*) forte; (*character, ideals*) nobile; (*value, respect, number*) grande; **to pay a high price for sth** pagare (molto) caro(-a) qc; **his colour is very high** è molto rosso in viso; **to have a high old time** (*fam*) spassarsela; **it's high time you were in bed** (*fam*) dovresti essere già a letto da un pezzo

c (*Mus: note*) alto(-a); (*sound, voice*) acuto(-a)

d (*fam: on drugs*) fatto(-a); (: *on drink*) su di giri

e (*Brit Culin: meat, game*) frollato(-a); (: *spoilt*) andato(-a) a male.

2 ADV (*fly, aim, climb*) in alto; **the doves flew high in the sky** le colombe volavano alte nel cielo; **high up** molto in alto; **high above the clouds** in alto sopra le nuvole; **higher and higher** sempre più (in) alto; **the bidding went as high as £500** le offerte sono arrivate fino a 500 sterline; **to hunt high and low** cercare per mare e per terra; **feelings were running high** c'era molta tensione.

3 N **a** : **on high** (*in heaven*) nell'alto dei cieli; **orders from on high** (*also hum*) ordini dall'alto

b : **exports have reached a new high** le esportazioni hanno toccato un nuovo record

c (*Met*) anticiclone *m*, area di alta pressione.

♦ **high altar** N altare *m* maggiore.

high·ball ['haɪˌbɔːl] N (*Am: drink*) *whisky (or brandy) e soda con ghiaccio*.

high·boy ['haɪˌbɔɪ] N (*Am*) cassettone *m*.

high·brow ['haɪˌbraʊ] N, ADJ intellettualoide (*m/f*).

high·chair ['haɪˌtʃɛə'] N seggiolone *m*.

♦ **high-class** ['haɪˌklɑːs] ADJ (*neighbourhood*) elegante; (*hotel*) di prim'ordine; (*person*) di gran classe; (*food*) raffinato(-a).

♦ **high command** N (*Mil*) stato maggiore.

♦ **high commissioner** N alto commissario.

♦ **high court** N (*Law*) Corte *f* Suprema.

high·er ['haɪə'] **1** ADJ (*form of life, study*) superiore.

2 ADV più in alto, più in su.

♦ **higher education** N istruzione *f* superiore *or* universitaria.

♦ **highest common factor** N: **the highest common factor** il massimo comun divisore.

♦ **high explosive** N esplosivo ad alto potenziale.

high·fa·lu·tin [ˌhaɪfə'luːtɪn] ADJ (*fam*) pomposo(-a).

♦ **high fidelity** N alta fedeltà.

♦ **high finance** N alta finanza.

♦ **high-flier**, **high-flyer** [ˌhaɪ'flaɪə'] N (*ambitious*) rampante *m/f*, ambizioso(-a); (*gifted*) giovane *m/f* di talento.

♦ **high-flown** [ˌhaɪ'fləʊn] ADJ (*speech*) altisonante(-a); (*language*) ampolloso(-a).

♦ **high-flying** ['haɪˌflaɪɪŋ] ADJ (*aircraft*) da alta quota; (*fig: person, aim*) ambizioso(-a).

♦ **high frequency** N alta frequenza.

♦ **high-handed** [ˌhaɪ'hændɪd] ADJ dispotico(-a), autoritario(-a).

♦ **high-handedly** [ˌhaɪ'hændɪdlɪ] ADV dispoticamente, in modo autoritario.

♦ **high-handedness** [ˌhaɪ'hændɪdnɪs] N dispotismo, autoritarismo.

♦ **high-heeled** [ˌhaɪ'hiːld] ADJ con il tacco alto.

high·jack ['haɪˌdʒæk] VT, N = **hijack**.

♦ **high jinks** ['haɪˌdʒɪŋks] NPL: **to have high jinks** (*fam*) far baldoria.

♦ **high jump** N (*Sport*) salto in alto; **you'll be for the high jump when Dad finds out** (*fam*) papà ti ammazza quando lo viene a sapere.

high·lands ['haɪləndz] NPL zona montuosa; **the Highlands** le Highlands scozzesi.

♦ **high-level** ['haɪˌlɛvl] ADJ (*talks, conference*) ad alto livello; (*Comput: language*) di alto livello.

♦ **high life** N: **the high life** la vita dell'alta società *or* del bel mondo.

high·light ['haɪˌlaɪt] **1** VT (*fig*) mettere in evidenza; (*in painting, drawing*) lumeggiare.

2 N (*fig: of evening, trip*) clou *m inv*; (*Art*) luce *f*; **highlights** NPL (*in hair*) colpi *mpl* di sole, riflessi *mpl*.

high·light·er ['haɪˌlaɪtə'] N (*pen*) evidenziatore *m*.

high·ly ['haɪlɪ] ADV estremamente, molto; **highly paid** pagato(-a) molto bene; **highly spiced dishes** piatti molto piccanti; **highly specialized** altamente specializzato(-a); **to think highly of sb** avere molta stima di qn; **to speak highly of** parlare molto bene di.

♦ **highly-strung** [ˌhaɪlɪ'strʌŋ] ADJ nervoso(-a), teso(-a).

♦ **High Mass** N messa cantata *or* solenne.

♦ **high-minded** [ˌhaɪ'maɪndɪd] ADJ (*person*) retto(-a), di alti principi; (*ideals, ambitions*) nobile.

♦ **high-necked** [ˌhaɪ'nɛkt] ADJ (*pullover, blouse*) a collo alto.

high·ness ['haɪnɪs] N: **Your Highness** Vostra Altezza.

♦ **high noon** N mezzogiorno.

♦ **high-pitched** [ˌhaɪ'pɪtʃt] ADJ acuto(-a).

♦ **high point** N: **the high point** (*of show, evening, holiday*) il clou *m inv*.

♦ **high-powered** [ˌhaɪ'paʊəd] ADJ (*engine*) molto potente, ad alta potenza; (*fig: person*) di prestigio.

♦ **high-pressure** [ˌhaɪ'prɛʃə'] ADJ ad alta pressione; (*fig*) aggressivo(-a).

♦ **high priest** N gran sacerdote *m*.

♦ **high-ranking** [ˌhaɪ'ræŋkɪŋ] ADJ di alto rango.

♦ **high-rise** ['haɪˌraɪz] ADJ: **high-rise building** palazzone *m*.

high·road ['haɪˌrəʊd] N strada principale *or* maestra.

♦ **high school** N (*Brit*) ≈ scuola media inferiore e superiore (*dagli 11 ai 18 anni*); (*Am*) ≈ scuola media superiore.

♦ **high seas** N: **on the high seas** in altomare.

♦ **high season** N (*Brit*) alta stagione *f*.

♦ **high society** N alta società.

♦ **high-sounding** [ˌhaɪ'saʊndɪŋ] ADJ (*speech, ideas*) altisonante; (*language*) ampolloso(-a).

♦ **high-speed** ['haɪˌspiːd] ADJ (*film*) ultrarapido(-a); **high-speed train** treno rapido.

♦ **high spirits** NPL buonumore *msg*; **to be in high spirits** essere euforico(-a).

♦ **high spot** N clou *m inv*.

♦ **high street** N (*Brit*) strada principale, corso.

♦ **high summer** N piena estate *f*.

♦ **high table** N (*Univ*) tavola dei professori (*nella sala della mensa*).

♦ **high tea** N (*Brit*) *pasto consumato verso le sei di sera al posto della cena*.

♦ **high tide** N alta marea; **at high tide** *or* **water** quando c'è l'alta marea.

♦ **high treason** N alto tradimento.

♦ **high-up** [ˌhaɪ'ʌp] N (*person*) pezzo grosso.

high·way ['haɪˌweɪ] **1** N strada principale *or* maestra;

public highway strada pubblica; **he knows all the highways and byways of Tuscany** conosce tutte le strade e stradine della Toscana.

♦ **Highway Code** N (*Brit*): **the Highway Code** il codice *m* della strada.

highway·man ['haɪ,weɪmən] N (*pl* **-men**) ≈ bandito.

hi·jack ['haɪ,dʒæk] ①ᴠᴛ (*aircraft*) dirottare; (*lorry, car*) impadronirsi di.
②ɴ dirottamento.

hi·jack·er ['haɪ,dʒækə'] N (*of aircraft*) dirottatore(-trice).

hi·jack·ing ['haɪ,dʒækɪŋ] N pirateria aerea; (*incident*) dirottamento.

hike [haɪk] ①ɴ a escursione *f* a piedi; **to go on** or **for a hike** fare un'escursione or una gita a piedi b (*fam: in prices*) aumento.
②ᴠɪ fare un'escursione or una gita a piedi; **to go hiking** fare escursioni a piedi.
③ᴠᴛ (*fam*) aumentare.

hik·er ['haɪkə'] N escursionista *m/f*.

hi·lari·ous [hɪ'lɛərɪəs] ADJ spassosissimo(-a).

hi·lar·ity [hɪ'lærɪtɪ] N ilarità.

hill [hɪl] N collina; (*lower*) colle *m*; (*slope*) pendio, costa; **up hill and down dale** per monti e per valli; **to be over the hill** (*fig fam*) essere sul viale del tramonto; **as old as the hills** vecchio(-a) come Matusalemme.

hill·bil·ly ['hɪl,bɪlɪ] N (*Am*) montanaro del sud degli Stati Uniti; (*pej*) zotico(-a).

♦ **hill farming** N ≈ alpeggio.

hill·ock ['hɪlək] N collinetta, poggio.

hill·side ['hɪl,saɪd] N pendio.

♦ **hill start** N (*Aut*) partenza in salita.

hill·top ['hɪl,tɒp] N sommità *f inv* della collina; **on the hilltop** in cima alla collina.

hilly ['hɪlɪ] ADJ (*comp* **-ier,** *superl* **-iest**) collinoso(-a), montagnoso(-a); **this road is very hilly** questa strada è un continuo saliscendi.

hilt [hɪlt] N (*of sword*) elsa, impugnatura; **to back sb to the hilt** dare il proprio appoggio incondizionato a qn; **to mortgage sth up to the hilt** ipotecare completamente qc.

him [hɪm] PERS PRON a (*direct: unstressed*) lo, l'+ *vowel*; (: *stressed*) lui; **I hear him** lo sento; **I heard him** l'ho sentito; **I've never seen HIM** lui, non l'ho mai visto b (*indirect*) gli; **I gave him the book** gli ho dato il libro; **I spoke to him** gli ho parlato c (*after prep, in comparatives*) lui; **without him** senza di lui; **I was thinking of him** pensavo a lui; **he had a case with him** aveva con sé una valigia; **if I were him** se fossi in lui; **it's him** è lui; **I'm older than him** sono più vecchio di lui.

Hima·la·yas [,hɪmə'leɪəz] NPL: **the Himalayas** l'Himalaia *msg*.

him·self [hɪm'sɛlf] PERS PRON (*reflexive*) si; (*emphatic*) lui stesso; (*after preposition*) sé, se stesso; **(all) by himself** (tutto) da solo or da sé; **he's not himself today** ha qualcosa che non va oggi; see also **oneself**.

hind[1] [haɪnd] ADJ (*leg*) posteriore; **he would talk the hind leg off a donkey** (*fam*) parla come una macchinetta.

hind[2] [haɪnd] N (*Zool*) cerva.

hin·der ['hɪndə'] ᴠᴛ (*prevent*): **to hinder sb (from doing sth)** impedire a qn (di fare qc); (*delay*) ritardare; (*obstruct*) ostacolare, intralciare.

Hin·di ['hɪndɪ] N (*language*) hindi *m*.

hind·quarters ['haɪnd,kwɔːtəz] NPL (*Zool*) posteriore *msg*.

hin·drance ['hɪndrəns] N intralcio, impedimento, ostacolo; **to be a hindrance to** intralciare, ostacolare.

hind·sight ['haɪnd,saɪt] N senno di poi; **with the benefit of hindsight** con il senno di poi.

Hin·du ['hɪn'duː] ADJ, N indù *(m/f) inv*.

Hin·du·ism ['hɪndu:,ɪzəm] N (*Rel*) induismo.

hinge [hɪndʒ] ① N (*of door, gate*) cardine *m*; (*of box*) cerniera.
②ᴠɪ: **to hinge on** (*fig*) dipendere da.

hinged [hɪndʒd] ADJ (*door*) provvisto(-a) di cardini; (*box, lid*) incernierato(-a).

hint [hɪnt] ① N (*suggestion*) allusione *f*, accenno; (*advice*) consiglio; **hints on do-it-yourself** consigli pratici per il fai-da-te; **a gentle hint** una velata allusione; **to give sb a broad hint** far capire chiaramente a qn; **to drop a hint** lasciar capire; **to take the hint** capire l'antifona; **with a hint of irony/sadness** con una punta d'ironia/tristezza; **give me a hint** (*clue*) dammi almeno un'idea, dammi un'indicazione.
②ᴠᴛ: **to hint (to sb) that** ... lasciar capire (a qn) che...
▶ **hint at** ᴠɪ + PREP accennare a, alludere a, fare allusione a; **just what are you hinting at?** cosa vuoi insinuare?

hinter·land ['hɪntə,lænd] N hinterland *m inv*.

hip[1] [hɪp] N (*Anat*) anca; (*side*) fianco; **to put one's hands on one's hips** mettersi le mani sui fianchi.

hip[2] [hɪp] N (*Bot*) frutto della rosa canina.

hip[3] [hɪp] ADJ (*fam: trendy*) all'ultima moda, in *inv*.

♦ **hip bath** N semicupio.

♦ **hip·bone** ['hɪp,bəʊn] N ileo, osso iliaco.

♦ **hip flask** N fiaschetta.

♦ **hip hop** N hip-hop *m inv*.

♦ **hip joint** N articolazione *f* dell'anca.

hip·pie, hip·py ['hɪpɪ] N hippy *m/f inv*.

♦ **hip pocket** N tasca posteriore dei calzoni.

Hippocrates [hɪ'pɒkrə,tiːz] N Ippocrate *m*.

Hippolytus [hɪ'pɒlɪtəs] N Ippolito.

hippo·pota·mus [,hɪpə'pɒtəməs] N (*pl* **hippopotamuses** or **hippopotami** [,hɪpə'pɒtəmaɪ]) ippopotamo.

hippy ['hɪpɪ] N = **hippie**.

hip·sters ['hɪpstəz] NPL (*trousers*) NPL pantaloni *mpl* a vita bassa.

hire ['haɪə'] ① N noleggio; (*cost*) nolo; **"for hire"** "a nolo", "noleggiasi"; (*taxi*) "libero"; **on hire** a nolo.
②ᴠᴛ (*Brit: car, equipment*) noleggiare; (*employee*) ingaggiare; **hired hand** bracciante *m/f*, **hired assassin** sicario prezzolato
▶ **hire out** ᴠᴛ + ADV noleggiare, dare a nolo or noleggio, affittare.

hired car [,haɪəd'kɑː], **hire car** N (*Brit*) macchina a nolo.

♦ **hire-purchase** [,haɪə'pɜːtʃɪs] N (*Brit*) acquisto (*or* vendita) a rate; **to buy sth on hire-purchase** comprare qc a rate.

his [hɪz] POSS ADJ, PRON il/la suo(-a); PL i/le suoi/sue; **his house** la sua casa; **his brother** suo fratello; **a friend of his** un suo amico; **his is red, mine is green** il suo è rosso, il mio è verde; **this is his** questo è (il) suo.

hiss [hɪs] ①ɴ (*of snake*) sibilo; (*of kettle, protest*) fischio; (*of cat*) soffio.
②ᴠɪ (*see n*) sibilare; fischiare; soffiare.
③ᴠᴛ (*speaker*) fischiare; **"get out"** she hissed "sparisci" sibilò.

his·to·gram ['hɪstə,græm] N istogramma *m*.

his·to·rian [hɪs'tɔːrɪən] N storico(-a).

his·tor·ic [hɪs'tɒrɪk] ADJ storico(-a).

his·tori·cal [hɪs'tɒrɪkəl] ADJ storico(-a).

his·to·ri·og·ra·pher [hɪ,stɔːrɪ'ɒgrəfə'] N storiografo(-a).

his·to·ry ['hɪstərɪ] N storia; **a history book** un libro di

storia; **to make history** fare storia; **to go down in history** passare alla storia; **there's a long history of that illness in his family** ci sono molti precedenti (della malattia) nella sua famiglia.

his·tri·on·ic [ˌhɪstrɪ'ɒnɪk] ADJ (pej) istrionesco(-a).

his·tri·on·ics [ˌhɪstrɪ'ɒnɪks] NPL (pej) scene fpl.

hit [hɪt] (vb: pt, pp hit) **1** N **a** (blow) colpo; (Sport) tiro, colpo; **she made three hits and two misses** ha messo a segno tre colpi e ne ha mancati due; **to score a direct hit** colpire in pieno

b (Mus, Theatre, Cine) successo; **to be a hit** essere un (gran) successo; **the song is a big hit** è una canzone di successo; **she's a hit with everyone** (fam) ha successo con tutti, fa colpo su tutti.

2 VT **a** (strike, affect: gen) colpire; (thrash: person) picchiare; (knock against) battere; (collide with: car) urtare, sbattere contro; **to hit sb a blow** dare un colpo a qn; **to hit a man when he's down** (fig) infierire su chi non può difendersi; **to hit the mark** colpire nel segno, raggiungere lo scopo; **then it hit me** (realization: fam) solo allora me ne sono reso conto; **the news hit him hard** la notizia è stata un brutto colpo per lui

b (reach: target, musical note) raggiungere; (: road) trovare, raggiungere; (: speed) toccare; (: difficulty, snag) incontrare, imbattersi in; (fam: arrive at: town) arrivare in; **to hit the papers** finire sui giornali; **to hit the headlines** far titolo; **to hit the front page** apparire in prima pagina; **to hit the bottle** (fam) darsi al bere; **to hit the ceiling** (fam) andare su tutte le furie; **to hit the road** or **the trail** (fam) levare le tende; **to hit the hay** or **the sack** (fam) andare a letto.

3 VI: **to hit against** sbattere contro.

4 ADJ (song, film) di successo

▶ **hit back** **1** VI + ADV restituire il colpo; **to hit back at sb** (fig) reagire contro qn.

2 VT + ADV: **to hit sb back** restituire il colpo a qn

▶ **hit off** VT + ADV: **to hit it off with sb** andare d'accordo con qn

▶ **hit out at** VI + ADV + PREP sferrare (dei) colpi contro; (fig) attaccare.

▶ **hit (up)on** VI + PREP (answer) imbroccare, azzeccare; (solution) trovare (per caso)

◆ **hit-and-run** ['hɪtən'rʌn] ADJ: **hit-and-run driver** pirata m della strada; **hit-and-run raid** (Mil) attacco m lampo inv; **hit-and-run tactics** (Mil) tattica dell'attacco lampo.

hitch [hɪtʃ] **1** N (impediment, obstacle) intoppo, contrattempo; (difficulty) difficoltà f inv; **technical hitch** difficoltà tecnica; **without a hitch** senza intoppi, a gonfie vele.

2 VT **a** (fasten) attaccare; (: to post) legare; **to get hitched** (fam) sposarsi

b (fam): **to hitch a lift** fare l'autostop.

3 VI (fam) = **hitchhike**

▶ **hitch up** VT + ADV (trousers) tirarsi su; (horse, cart) attaccare.

hitch·hike ['hɪtʃ,haɪk] VI fare l'autostop; **we hitchhiked through Europe** abbiamo girato tutta l'Europa in autostop.

hitch·hiker ['hɪtʃ,haɪkə'] N autostoppista m/f.

hitch·hiking ['hɪtʃ,haɪkɪŋ] N autostop m.

hi-tech ['haɪ'tɛk] **1** ADJ (Industry) tecnologicamente avanzato(-a), hi-tech inv.

2 N (Industry) tecnologia avanzata; (Archit, Design) hi-tech m or f inv.

hith·er ['hɪðə'] ADV (old) qui, qua; **hither and thither** (liter) qua e là.

hither·to ['hɪðə'tu:] ADV (frm) finora.

◆ **hit list** N: **to be on a hit list** essere un bersaglio.

◆ **hit man** N (fam) sicario, killer m inv.

◆ **hit-or-miss** ['hɪtɔ:'mɪs] ADJ (approach) disinvolto(-a); (work) così cosà; **the service in this hotel is very hit-or-miss** il servizio in questo albergo lascia a desiderare.

◆ **hit parade** N hit-parade f inv.

HIV [ˌeɪtʃaɪ'vi:] N ABBR (= human immunodeficiency virus) HIV m inv.

hive [haɪv] N alveare m; (bees collectively) sciame m; **the shop was a hive of activity** (fig) c'era una grande attività nel negozio

▶ **hive off** **1** VI + ADV: **to hive off (from)** staccarsi (da).

2 VT + ADV staccare; (privatize) privatizzare.

◆ **HIV-negative** [ˌeɪtʃaɪˌvi:'nɛgətɪv] ADJ sieronegativo(-a).

◆ **HIV-positive** [ˌeɪtʃaɪˌvi:'pɒzɪtɪv] ADJ sieropositivo(-a).

hl ABBR (= hectolitre) hl.

HM [ˌeɪtʃ'ɛm] N ABBR (= His (or Her) Majesty) S.M. (= Sua Maestà).

HMG [ˌeɪtʃɛm'dʒi:] N ABBR (Brit)= His (or Her) Majesty's Government.

HMI [ˌeɪtʃɛm'aɪ] N ABBR (Brit Scol: = His (or Her) Majesty's Inspector) ≈ ispettore(-trice) scolastico(-a).

HMO [ˌeɪtʃɛm'əʊ] N ABBR (Am: = health maintenance organization) organo per la salvaguardia della salute pubblica.

HMS [ˌeɪtʃɛm'ɛs] N ABBR (Brit)= His (or Her) Majesty's Ship.

HMSO [ˌeɪtʃɛmɛs'əʊ] N ABBR (Brit: = His (or Her) Majesty's Stationery Office) ≈ istituto poligrafico dello Stato.

HNC [ˌeɪtʃɛn'si:] N ABBR (Brit: = Higher National Certificate) diploma di istituto tecnico o professionale.

HND [ˌeɪtʃɛn'di:] N ABBR (Brit: = Higher National Diploma) diploma in materie tecniche equivalente ad una laurea.

hoard [hɔːd] **1** N (of food) provviste fpl, scorta; (of money) gruzzolo.

2 VT (also: hoard up: provisions) fare incetta or provvista di; (: money) ammonticchiare; (: old newspapers) accumulare.

hoard·ing ['hɔːdɪŋ] N (Brit: for advertisements) tabellone m or riquadro per affissioni; (wooden fence) staccionata, palizzata.

hoar·frost ['hɔː'frɒst] N brina.

hoarse [hɔːs] ADJ (comp -r, superl -st) rauco(-a); **they shouted themselves hoarse** si sono sgolati a forza di urlare.

hoarse·ly ['hɔːslɪ] ADV con voce roca, raucamente.

hoarse·ness ['hɔːsnɪs] N raucedine f.

hoary ['hɔːrɪ] ADJ (comp -ier, superl -iest) (liter: hair) bianco(-a); (: person) canuto(-a), dai capelli bianchi; (ancient) vetusto(-a); **it's a hoary old joke** è una barzelletta vecchia.

hoax [həʊks] **1** N scherzo; (bomb scare) falso allarme m.

2 VT prendere in giro; **he hoaxed me into believing that ...** mi ha fatto credere che... .

hob [hɒb] N piastra (con fornelli).

Ho·bart ['həʊbɑːt] N Hobart f.

hob·ble ['hɒbl] VI zoppicare; **to hobble in/out** entrare/uscire zoppicando.

hob·by ['hɒbɪ] N hobby m inv, passatempo (preferito).

◆ **hobby-horse** ['hɒbɪ,hɔːs] N **a** (fig) chiodo fisso **b** (toy) giocattolo di legno raffigurante la testa di un cavallo montata su un bastone.

hob·nail(ed) boots [ˌhɒbneɪl(d)'buːts] NPL scarponi mpl chiodati.

hob·nob ['hɒb,nɒb] VI (fam): **to hobnob (with)** essere in confidenza (con).

hobo ['həʊbəʊ] N (*Am*) vagabondo.

Hobson's choice ['hɒbsənz'tʃɔɪs] N: **it's Hobson's choice** è una questione di prendere o lasciare.

hock¹ [hɒk] N (*of animal, Culin*) garretto.

hock² [hɒk] N (*Brit: wine*) vino bianco del Reno.

hock³ [hɒk] (*fam*) 1 N: **to be in hock** (*debt*) essere indebitato(-a).

2 VT (*pawn*) impegnare.

hock·ey ['hɒkɪ] N hockey *m* (su prato).

♦ **hockey stick** N bastone *m* da hockey.

hocus-pocus ['həʊkəs'pəʊkəs] N (*trickery*) trucco; (*words: of magician*) abracadabra *m inv*; (*talk*) ciance *fpl*.

hod [hɒd] N (*Tech*) cassetta per portare i mattoni.

hodge·podge ['hɒdʒ,pɒdʒ] N = **hotchpotch**.

hoe [həʊ] 1 N zappa.

2 VT (*ground*) zappare; (*weeds*) sarchiare.

hog [hɒg] 1 N porco, maiale *m*; **to go the whole hog** (*fig*) fare le cose fino in fondo.

2 VT (*fam*) accaparrarsi; **to hog the road** guidare nel mezzo della strada.

Hog·man·ay ['hɒgmə,neɪ] N (*in Scotland*) ≈ San Silvestro.

hog·wash ['hɒg,wɒʃ] N (*fam*) stupidaggini *fpl*, cretinate *fpl*.

hog·weed ['hɒg,wiːd] N panace *m*, sedano dei prati.

hoi pol·loi ['hɔɪpə'lɔɪ] N (*pej*): **the hoi polloi** la plebe.

hoist [hɔɪst] 1 VT issare.

2 N paranco; (*goods lift*) montacarichi *m inv*; see also **petard**.

hoity-toity [,hɔɪtɪ'tɔɪtɪ] ADJ (*fam*) altezzoso(-a).

hold [həʊld] (*vb: pt, pp* **held**) 1 N a **presa; to seize** *or* **grab hold of sth/sb** afferrare qc/qn; **to catch** *or* **get (a) hold of** afferrare, attaccarsi a; **to get hold of sb** (*fig: contact*) mettersi in contatto con qn; **where can I get hold of some red paint?** dove posso trovare della vernice rossa?; **to get (a) hold of o.s.** (*fig*) trattenersi, controllarsi; **no holds barred** (*fig*) senza esclusione di colpi; **to have a hold over sb** (*fig*) avere un forte ascendente *or* molta influenza su qn

b (*Naut, Aer*) stiva

c (*Mountaineering*) appiglio.

2 VT a (*gen*) tenere; (*contain*) contenere; (*fig: audience*) mantenere viva l'attenzione di; (: *attention, interest*) mantenere; (: *belief, opinion*) avere; **to hold hands** tenersi per mano; **to hold a baby** tenere in braccio un bambino; **the hall holds 500 people** nella sala c'è posto per 500 persone; **the chair won't hold you** la sedia non sopporterà il tuo peso; **to hold o.s. upright/ready** tenersi dritto(-a)/pronto(-a); **to hold one's head high** andare a testa alta; **to hold sb to a promise** far mantenere una promessa a qn; **to hold one's own** sapersi difendere, difendersi bene; **she holds the view that ...** è del parere che...; **to hold the line** (*Telec*) rimanere *or* restare in linea; **this car holds the road well** questa macchina tiene bene la strada; **what does the future hold?** cosa ci riserva il futuro?

b (*restrain: person*) trattenere; **to hold sb prisoner** tenere prigioniero qn; **there's no holding him** non lo ferma più nessuno; **to hold one's breath** trattenere il respiro *or* il fiato; **I held my breath in amazement** sono rimasto a bocca aperta per lo stupore; **to hold one's tongue** (*fig*) tacere, star zitto(-a); **hold it!** (*fam*) alt!, fermati!

c (*position, title, passport*) avere; (*shares: Fin*) possedere, avere; (*record: Sport*) detenere; (*position: Mil*) tenere, mantenere; **to hold office** (*Pol*) essere in carica

d (*meeting, election*) tenere, indire; (*conversation*) tenere, sostenere; (*Rel: service*) celebrare

e (*consider*): **to hold (that)** ritenere (che), sostenere (che); **to hold sb in high esteem** avere molta stima di qn; **to hold sth/sb dear** tenere molto a qc/qn; **to hold sb responsible for sth** considerare *or* ritenere qn responsabile di qc.

3 VI (*rope, nail*) tenere; (*continue*) mantenersi, durare; (*be valid*) essere valido(-a); **to hold firm** *or* **fast** resistere bene, tenere

▶ **hold against** VT + PREP: **to hold sth against sb** (*fig*) volerne a qn per qc

▶ **hold back** 1 VI + ADV: **to hold back from sth** tirarsi indietro da qc; **to hold back from doing sth** trattenersi dal fare qc; **he always holds back when he meets new people** quando incontra gente nuova è sempre poco espansivo.

2 VT + ADV a (*restrain: crowd, river*) trattenere, contenere; (: *emotions, tears*) trattenere, frenare; **to hold sb back from doing sth** impedire a qn di fare qc

b (*information, name*) nascondere, non dare, celare; **he's holding something back** non sta dicendo tutta la verità

▶ **hold down** VT + ADV a (*keep low, on ground*) tener giù; (*keep in place*) tener fermo(-a)

b (*job*) conservare, mantenere

▶ **hold forth** VI + ADV fare *or* tenere una concione

▶ **hold in** VT + ADV (*stomach*) tirare *or* tenere in dentro; **to hold o.s. in** (*fig*) frenarsi, trattenersi

▶ **hold off** 1 VT + ADV (*enemy*) tenere a distanza; (*attack*) sventare; (*visitor*) far aspettare.

2 VI + ADV (*rain*): **if the rain holds off** se non si mette a piovere

▶ **hold on** 1 VI + ADV (*endure*) resistere; (*wait*) aspettare; **hold on!** (*Telec*) resti in linea!.

2 VT + ADV tenere a posto

▶ **hold on to** VI + ADV + PREP (*grasp*) tenersi (attaccato(-a)) a, tenersi (stretto(-a)) a; (*keep*) tenere, conservare; (*fig: retain: hope*) rimanere aggrappato(-a) a

▶ **hold out** 1 VI + ADV a (*supplies*) durare.

b (*stand firm*) tener duro; **to hold out for more money** (*fam*) continuare a chiedere più soldi; **to hold out (against)** resistere (a).

2 VT + ADV: **to hold out (sth to sb)** allungare (qc a qn); (*one's arms, hand*) tendere; (*fig: offer*) presentare, offrire; (: *hope*) nutrire

▶ **hold out on** VI + ADV + PREP: **you've been holding out on me!** (*fam*) mi hai tenuto nascosto qualcosa!

▶ **hold over** VT + ADV (*meeting*) rimandare, rinviare

▶ **hold together** 1 VI + ADV (*group*) restare unito(-a).

2 VT + ADV (*factions*) tenere uniti(-e)

▶ **hold up** 1 VT + ADV a (*raise*) sollevare, alzare; **hold up your hand** alza la mano; **to hold sth up to the light** alzare qc verso la luce

b (*support: roof*) sostenere

c (*delay: person*) trattenere; (: *traffic*) rallentare; (*stop*) bloccare

d (*rob: bank*) assaltare; (: *person*) assalire.

2 VI + ADV (*survive, last*) resistere; **how are your shoes holding up?** in che stato sono le tue scarpe?

▶ **hold with** VI + PREP (*fam*): **she doesn't hold with gambling** è contraria al gioco d'azzardo.

hold·all ['həʊld,ɔːl] N (*Brit*) sacca *or* borsa da viaggio, borsone *m*.

hold·er ['həʊldə'] N a (*of ticket*) possessore *m*; (*owner: of property*) proprietario(-a); (*tenant*) affittuario(-a); (*of

bonds, shares) titolare m/f, intestatario(-a); (of title) chi ha or possiede; (of passport, office, post) titolare; (of record) detentore(-trice) **b** (container) contenitore m; **pencil holder** portamatite m inv.

hold·ing ['həʊldɪŋ] N (land) podere m, tenuta; **holdings** terre fpl, proprietà fpl terriere; **holdings** NPL (Comm) azioni fpl, titoli mpl.

♦ **holding company** N (Comm) holding f inv.

♦ **holding pattern** N (Aer) circuito di attesa.

♦ **holding position** N (Aer) area di attesa.

♦ **hold-up** ['həʊld,ʌp] N (robbery) rapina a mano armata; (stoppage, delay) intoppo; (Brit: of traffic) ingorgo.

hole [həʊl] ① N **a** (in ground, road, also Golf) buca; (in wall, fence, clothes) buco; (in dam, ship) falla; (in defences) breccia; (of rabbit, fox) tana; **to wear a hole in sth** usare qc tanto da farci un buco; **to pick holes in** (fig: argument) dimostrare che fa acqua; **it made a hole in my savings** ha mangiato gran parte dei miei risparmi **b** (fig fam: difficulty): **to be in a hole** essere nei guai; **she got me out of a hole** mi ha tirato fuori dai pasticci or dai guai **c** (fam pej: place) buco.

② VT bucare; (Golf: ball) mandare in buca; **the boat was holed when it hit the rocks** quando la barca ha urtato gli scogli si è aperta una falla nello scafo

▶ **hole out** VI + ADV andare in buca

▶ **hole up** VI + ADV nascondersi, rifugiarsi.

♦ **hole-and-corner** [,həʊlənd'kɔ:nə'] ADJ (fam) furtivo(-a).

♦ **hole in the heart** N morbo blu.

holey ['həʊlɪ] ADJ pieno(-a) di buchi.

holi·day ['hɒlədɪ] ① N (vacation) vacanza; (from work) ferie fpl; (day off) giorno di vacanza; **the school holidays** le vacanze scolastiche; **holiday with pay** ferie pagate or retribuite; **public holiday** festa (nazionale); **to be on holiday** essere in vacanza.

② ADJ (town) di villeggiatura; **holiday atmosphere** aria di vacanza; **holiday spirit** spirito vacanziero.

♦ **holiday camp** N (Brit) ≈ villaggio turistico.

♦ **holiday-maker** ['hɒlədɪ,meɪkə'] N (Brit) villeggiante m/f, vacanziere(-a).

♦ **holiday pay** N: **do you get holiday pay?** hai le ferie pagate?

♦ **holiday resort** N luogo di villeggiatura.

♦ **holiday season** N stagione f delle vacanze.

♦ **holiday traffic** N traffico dell'esodo (or del rientro).

Ho·li·ness ['həʊlɪnɪs] N: **his Holiness** Sua Santità.

ho·li·ness ['həʊlɪnɪs] N santità.

hol·is·tic [həʊ'lɪstɪk] ADJ olistico(-a).

Hol·land ['hɒlənd] N Olanda.

hol·ler ['hɒlə'] VT, VI (fam) urlare, gridare.

hol·low ['hɒləʊ] ① ADJ (comp -er, superl -est) cavo(-a), vuoto(-a); (eyes, cheeks) infossato(-a); (sound, voice) cupo(-a); (sympathy) falso(-a); (promises) vano(-a); **a hollow victory** una vittoria di Pirro; **to give a hollow laugh** ridere a denti stretti.

② ADV: **to beat sb hollow** (fam) stracciare qn.

③ N (of back) incavo; (of hand) cavo; (in ground) cavità f inv, affossamento; (small valley) conca; (in landscape) valletta, depressione f

▶ **hollow out** VI + ADV scavare, incavare.

♦ **hollow-cheeked** [,hɒləʊ'tʃi:kt] ADJ dalle guance incavate.

♦ **hollow-eyed** [,hɒləʊ'aɪd] ADJ dagli occhi infossati.

hol·ly ['hɒlɪ] N (also: holly tree) agrifoglio.

hol·ly·hock ['hɒlɪ,hɒk] N malvone m.

holm oak ['həʊm'əʊk] N leccio.

holo·caust ['hɒlə,kɔ:st] N olocausto.

holo·gram ['hɒlə,græm] N ologramma m.

ho·lo·gra·phy [hɒ'lɒgrəfɪ] N olografia.

holo·phyt·ic [,hɒlə'fɪtɪk] ADJ olofitico(-a).

hols [hɒlz] NPL (Brit fam): **the hols** le vacanze fpl.

hol·ster ['həʊlstə'] N fondina.

holy ['həʊlɪ] ① ADJ (comp -ier, superl -iest) (gen) santo(-a); (ground, bread) consacrato(-a), benedetto(-a); (person) pio(-a); (vow) religioso(-a); **the Holy Trinity** la Santissima Trinità; **a holy terror** (fam) un demonio.

♦ **Holy Bible** N: **the Holy Bible** la Sacra Bibbia.

♦ **Holy City** N: **the Holy City** (Jerusalem) la città santa.

♦ **Holy Communion** N la comunione, l'eucaristia.

♦ **Holy Father** N: **the Holy Father** il Santo Padre.

♦ **Holy Land** N: **the Holy Land** la Terra Santa.

♦ **holy of holies** N sancta sanctorum m inv.

♦ **holy orders** NPL ordini mpl (sacri).

♦ **Holy Spirit, Holy Ghost** N: **the Holy Spirit, the Holy Ghost** lo Spirito Santo.

♦ **Holy Week** N la settimana santa.

hom·age ['hɒmɪdʒ] N omaggio; **to pay homage to** rendere omaggio a.

home [həʊm] ① N **a** (residence, house) casa; (country, area) patria, paese m natale or natio; (Bot, Zool) habitat m inv; **to have a home of one's own** avere una casa propria; **it's near my home** è vicino a casa mia; **it's a home from home** è come essere a casa propria; **there's no place like home** non si sta mai bene come a casa propria; **she comes from a good home** viene da una buona famiglia; **he comes from a broken home** i suoi sono divisi; **to give sb/sth a home** prendersi in casa qn/qc; **he made his home in Italy** si è stabilito in Italia; **Scotland is the home of the haggis** la Scozia è la patria dell'haggis; **at home** a casa; **Celtic is playing at home on Saturday** il Celtic gioca in casa sabato; **make yourself at home** fai come se fossi a casa tua; **to make sb feel at home** mettere qn a proprio agio; **she is at home with the topic** conosce la materia benissimo; **I'm not at home to anyone** (fig) non ci sono per nessuno

b (institution) istituto; (for old people) casa di riposo.

② ADV **a** a casa; **to go home** andare a casa; **to come home** tornare (a casa) or restare in casa; **I got home at 10 o'clock** sono rientrato alle 10; **on the way home** sulla via di casa; **can I see you home?** posso accompagnarti a casa?; **it's nothing to write home about** (fam) non è gran che, non è niente di speciale; **we're home and dry** (fig) siamo salvi

b (right in) a fondo, fino in fondo; **to drive a nail home** conficcare un chiodo; **to bring sth home to sb** (fig) aprire gli occhi a qn su qc; **that remark hit home** ciò che ha detto ha colpito nel segno.

③ VI (pigeons) tornare alla base.

④ ADJ (life) familiare; (cooking) casalingo(-a); (improvements) alla casa; (comforts) di casa; (native: village) natale, natio(-a); (Econ: trade, market) nazionale, interno(-a); (: product, industries) nazionale; (news) dall'interno; (Sport: team) di casa; (: match, win) in casa

▶ **home in on** VI + ADV + PREP (missiles) dirigersi (automaticamente) verso.

♦ **home address** N indirizzo di casa or privato.

♦ **home-baked** [,həʊm'beɪkt] ADJ fatto(-a) in casa.

♦ **home-brew** [həʊm'bru:] N birra or vino fatto(-a) in casa.

home·coming ['həʊm,kʌmɪŋ] N ritorno.

♦ **home computer** N home computer *m inv.*
♦ **Home Counties** NPL: **the Home Counties** le contee intorno a Londra.
♦ **home economics** N economia domestica.
♦ **home front** N fronte *m* interno.
♦ **home ground** N (*fig*): **to be on home ground** essere sul proprio terreno.
♦ **home-grown** [ˌhəʊmˈɡrəʊn] ADJ (*in locality*) nostrano (-a), di produzione locale.
♦ **home help** N (*Brit*) assistente a domicilio per anziani o disabili stipendiata dai servizi sociali.
home·land [ˈhəʊmˌlænd] N patria.
♦ **home leave** N (*Mil*) licenza ordinaria.
home·less [ˈhəʊmlɪs] ①ADJ senza tetto.
②: **the homeless** NPL i senzatetto.
♦ **home loan** N mutuo per la casa.
♦ **home-lover** [ˈhəʊmˌlʌvə'] N persona cui piace stare a casa.
♦ **home-loving** [ˈhəʊmˌlʌvɪŋ] ADJ affezionato(-a) alla casa.
home·ly [ˈhəʊmlɪ] ADJ (*comp* **-ier,** *superl* **-iest**) (*food, person*) semplice, alla buona; (*atmosphere*) familiare, accogliente; (*advice*) pratico(-a); (*Am: plain: person, features*) insignificante.
♦ **home-made** [ˌhəʊmˈmeɪd] ADJ fatto(-a) in casa, casalingo(-a).
♦ **Home Office** N (*Brit*): **the Home Office** il Ministero degli Interni.
homeo·path, homoeo·path [ˈhəʊmɪəʊpæθ] N omeopatico(-a).
homeo·path·ic, homoeo·path·ic [ˌhəʊmɪəʊˈpæθɪk] ADJ omeopatico(-a).
homeopa·thy, homoeopa·thy [ˌhəʊmɪˈɒpəθɪ] N omeopatia.
homeo·sta·sis [ˌhəʊmɪəʊˈsteɪsɪs] N omeostasi *f.*
♦ **home port** N (*Naut*) porto d'origine.
Homer [ˈhəʊmə'] N Omero; **even Homer nods** errare humanum est.
♦ **home rule** N autogoverno, autonomia.
♦ **Home Secretary** N (*Brit*) ministro degli Interni.
home·sick [ˈhəʊmˌsɪk] ADJ: **to be homesick** avere la nostalgia, sentire la mancanza di casa.
home·sick·ness [ˈhəʊmˌsɪknɪs] N nostalgia (di casa).
home·spun [ˈhəʊmˌspʌn] ①ADJ (*fig*) alla buona; **homespun philosophy** filosofia spicciola.
②N tessuto filato a mano.
home·stead [ˈhəʊmˌstɛd] N casa colonica.
♦ **home straight, home stretch** N (*Sport*) dirittura d'arrivo; **in the home straight** (*fig*) quasi arrivato(-a).
♦ **home town** N città *f inv* natale.
♦ **home truths** NPL: **to tell sb a few home truths** dire a qn quello che si merita.
home·ward [ˈhəʊmwəd] ADJ (*journey*) di ritorno.
home·ward(s) [ˈhəʊmwədz] ADV verso casa.
home·work [ˈhəʊmˌwɜːk] N (*Scol*) compiti *mpl* (per casa).
homi·ci·dal [ˌhɒmɪˈsaɪdl] ADJ omicida.
homi·cide [ˈhɒmɪˌsaɪd] N omicidio.
homi·ly [ˈhɒmɪlɪ] N (*frm*) omelia.
hom·ing [ˈhəʊmɪŋ] ADJ (*device, missile*) autoguidato(-a).
♦ **homing pigeon** N piccione *m* viaggiatore.
homi·nid [ˈhɒmɪnɪd] N ominide *m.*
homoeopa·thy *etc* [ˌhəʊmɪˈɒpəθɪ] = **homeopathy** *etc.*
homo·genei·ty [ˌhɒməʊdʒəˈniːɪtɪ] N omogeneità.
homo·geneous [ˌhɒməˈdʒiːnɪəs], **homo·genous** [həˈmɒdʒɪnəs] ADJ omogeneo(-a).

ho·mog·enize [həˈmɒdʒəˌnaɪz] VT omogeneizzare.
homo·graph·ic [ˌhɒməˈɡræfɪk] ADJ omografo(-a).
ho·molo·gous [həʊˈmɒləɡəs] ADJ omologo(-a).
homo·nym [ˈhɒmənɪm] N omonimo.
ho·mony·my [həˈmɒnɪmɪ] N omonimia.
homo·sex·ual [ˌhɒməʊˈsɛksjʊəl] ADJ, N omosessuale *(m/f).*
homo·sex·ual·ity [ˈhɒməʊsɛksjʊˈælɪtɪ] N omosessualità.
homo·zy·gote [ˌhəʊməʊˈzaɪɡəʊt] N omozigote *m.*
Hon. ABBR **a** = **honourable b** = **honorary**.
Hon·du·ras [hɒnˈdjʊərəs] N Honduras *m.*
hone [həʊn] VT (*sharpen*) affilare; (*fig*) affinare.
hon·est [ˈɒnɪst] ADJ (*person, face, actions*) onesto(-a); (*answer*) franco(-a), schietto(-a); (*means, method*) onesto (-a), lecito(-a); (*wages, profit*) decente, ragionevole; (*opinion*) sincero(-a); **to be quite honest with you ...** se devo dirti la verità...; **please be honest with me** ti prego di essere sincero con me.
hon·est·ly [ˈɒnɪstlɪ] ADV onestamente; (*truly*) sinceramente, francamente; **I didn't do it, honestly!** non l'ho fatto, sul serio!; **honestly?** davvero?; **honestly!** (*exasperated*) (ma) veramente!
hon·es·ty [ˈɒnɪstɪ] N **a** onestà; **in all honesty** a voler essere *or* per essere proprio sincero(-a) **b** (*Bot*) monete *fpl* del Papa.
hon·ey [ˈhʌnɪ] N miele *m*; (*Am fam*) tesoro, amore *m.*
honey·bee [ˈhʌnɪˌbiː] N ape *f.*
honey·comb [ˈhʌnɪˌkəʊm] ①N favo; (*fig*) disegno *or* struttura a nido d'ape.
②VT (*fig*) sforacchiare, perforare; **honeycombed with tunnels** pieno(-a) di gallerie.
honey·dew [ˈhʌnɪˌdjuː] N melata.
♦ **honeydew melon** N *tipo di melone con buccia gialla.*
hon·eyed [ˈhʌnɪd] ADJ (*words*) dolce (come il miele).
honey·moon [ˈhʌnɪˌmuːn] ①N luna di miele, viaggio di nozze.
②VI fare la luna di miele, andare in viaggio di nozze.
♦ **honeymoon couple** N coppia in luna di miele.
honey·suckle [ˈhʌnɪˌsʌkl] N caprifoglio.
Hong Kong [ˈhɒŋˈkɒŋ] N Hong Kong *f.*
honk [hɒŋk] ①VI (*car*) suonare il clacson; (*goose*) schiamazzare.
②N (*of horn*) colpo di clacson.
Hono·lu·lu [ˌhɒnəˈluːluː] N Honolulu *f.*
hon·or·ary [ˈɒnərərɪ] ADJ (*person*) onorario(-a); (*duty, title*) onorifico(-a); **an honorary degree** una laurea honoris causa *or* ad honorem.
hon·our, (*Am*) **hon·or** [ˈɒnə'] ①N **a** (*gen*) onore *m*; (*esteem, respect*) stima, rispetto; **in honour of** in onore di; **on my honour!** sul mio onore!; **to be on one's honour to do sth** aver dato la propria parola (d'onore) di fare qc; **to do honour to sb** *or* **to do sb honour** (*enhance reputation of*) fare onore a qn; **she did me the honour of attending my exhibition** mi ha fatto l'onore di presenziare alla mostra; **to be an honour to one's profession** fare onore alla propria professione; **it's a great honour to be invited** (*frm*) è un grande onore essere invitati; **I had the honour of meeting him** (*frm*) ho avuto l'onore d'incontrarlo; **(in) honour bound** moralmente obbligato(-a)
b : **honours** NPL (*distinction, award*) onorificenze *fpl*; (*Univ*): **she got first-class honours in French** ≈ si è laureata in francese con la lode; **to be buried with full honours** essere sepolto(-a) con grandi onori; **to do the honours** (*fam*) fare gli onori di casa
c (*title*): **Your Honour** (*judge*) Vostro Onore; (*Am: mayor*) signor sindaco.

2 VT (*dignify*): **to honour sb (with)** onorare qn (con); **to honour sb with a title** conferire a qn un titolo.

hon·our·able, (*Am*) **hon·or·able** ['ɒnərəbl] ADJ (*gen*) onorevole; (*person*) d'onore.

♦ **honourable mention**, (*Am*) **honorable mention** N menzione *f* onorevole, attestato di merito.

hon·our·ably, (*Am*) **hon·or·ably** ['ɒnərəblɪ] ADV onorevolmente, con onore.

♦ **honour-bound**, (*Am*) **honor-bound** ['ɒnəˌbaʊnd] ADJ: **to be honour-bound to do** dover fare per una questione di onore.

♦ **honours degree**, (*Am*) **honors degree** N (*Univ*) *laurea (con corso di studi di 4 o 5 anni).*

♦ **honours list** N (*Brit*) *elenco di titoli e onoreficenze conferiti dal sovrano ai cittadini britannici o del Commonwealth che si sono distinti in un dato di campo.*

Hons. ABBR (*Univ*) = **honours degree**.

hooch [hu:tʃ] N (*Am fam*) liquore *m* (distillato illegalmente).

hood [hʊd] N **a** (*of cloak, raincoat*) cappuccio; (*on pram, Aut*) capote *f inv*; (*Am Aut*) cofano; (*on cooker*) cappa **b** (*Am fam*) malvivente *m/f*.

hood·ed ['hʊdɪd] ADJ incappucciato(-a); (*robber*) mascherato(-a).

hood·lum ['hu:dləm] N teppista *m/f*.

hood·wink ['hʊdˌwɪŋk] VT gabbare, imbrogliare, infinocchiare.

hoo·ey ['hu:ɪ] N (*fam*) fesserie *f pl*.

hoof [hu:f] N (*pl* **hoofs** *or* **hooves**) zoccolo.

hoo-ha ['hu:ˌhɑ:] N (*fam*) casino; **there was a great hoo-ha about it** la cosa ha fatto scalpore.

hook [hʊk] **1** N (*gen, also Boxing*) gancio; (*Fishing*) amo; (*on dress*) gancetto; **hooks and eyes** gancetti; **to leave the phone off the hook** lasciare staccato il ricevitore; **by hook or (by) crook** in un modo o nell'altro, di riffa o di raffa; **to get sb off the hook** salvare qn; **he fell for it hook, line and sinker** (*fig*) l'ha bevuta tutta.

2 VT (*fasten*) agganciare, attaccare; (*Fishing*) prendere all'amo; **to hook one's arms/legs around sth** aggrapparsi a qc con le braccia/le gambe; **she finally hooked him** (*fam*) è finalmente riuscita a incastrarlo; **to be hooked on** (*fam*) essere fanatico(-a) di; **he's hooked on heroin** *or* **cocaine** (*fam*) è un eroinomane *or* cocainomane.

3 VI (*fasten*) agganciarsi

▶ **hook on** **1** VI + PREP: **to hook on(to)** agganciarsi (a), attaccarsi (a).

2 VT + PREP: **to hook on(to)** agganciare (a)

▶ **hook up** VT + ADV (*dress*) agganciare; (*Radio, TV*) allacciare, collegare.

hook·ah ['hʊkə] N narghilè *m inv*.

hook·nosed ['hʊkˌnəʊzd] ADJ dal naso adunco.

♦ **hook-up** N (*TV, Comput: fam*) collegamento.

hooky ['hʊkɪ] N (*fam*): **to play hooky** marinare la scuola.

hoo·li·gan ['hu:lɪgən] N teppista *m/f*, hooligan *m/f inv*.

hoo·li·gan·ism ['hu:lɪgənɪzəm] N teppismo.

hoop [hu:p] N (*gen*) cerchio; (*for skirt*) guardinfante *m*; (*croquet hoop*) archetto; **to put sb through the hoops** (*fig*) mettere qn sotto il torchio.

hoop·la ['hu:plɑ:] N tiro dei cerchi (*nei luna-park, per vincere premi*).

hoo·poe ['hu:pu:] N upupa.

hoot [hu:t] **1** N (*of owl*) verso; (*of horn*) colpo di clacson; (*of siren*) ululato; **a hoot of derision** una risata di scherno; **I don't give a hoot** (*fam*) non me ne importa un accidente,

me ne infischio; **it was a hoot** (*fam*) è stato divertentissimo *or* uno spasso.

2 VI (*owl*) gufare; (*person: in scorn*) farsi una risata (di scherno); (*Aut: person*) strombazzare, suonare il clacson; (*ship, train, factory hooter*) fischiare; **to hoot with laughter** farsi una gran risata.

hoot·er ['hu:tə'] N (*Brit: of ship, factory*) sirena; (*Aut*) clacson *m inv*, tromba (d'automobile); (*Brit fam: nose*) nasone *m*.

hoo·ver® ['hu:və'] (*Brit*) **1** N aspirapolvere *m inv*.

2 VT pulire con l'aspirapolvere.

hooves [hu:vz] NPL of **hoof**.

hop[1] [hɒp] **1** N (*jump*) saltello; (*dance: fam*) ballo; (*Aer*): **it's a short hop from Paris to London** è un salto da Parigi a Londra in aereo; **to catch sb on the hop** (*fam*) prendere qn alla sprovvista.

2 VI (*person, bird, animal*) saltellare; **he hopped over the wall** è balzato al di là del muro; **to hop out of bed** saltar giù *or* fuori dal letto; **hop in!** (*car*) salta dentro!, salta su!, monta su!; **hop it!** (*fam*) sparisci!, smamma!

hop[2] [hɒp] N (*Bot*) luppolo; see also **hops**.

hope [həʊp] **1** N speranza; **he is past** *or* **beyond all hope** per lui non c'è più nessuna speranza; **to live in hope** vivere sperando *or* nella speranza; **in the hope of doing sth** nella speranza di fare qc; **in the hope of sth** nella speranza di avere *or* ottenere qc; **there is no hope of that** non c'è da farci nessun conto; **with high hopes** con grandi speranze; **to raise sb's hopes** far nascere delle speranze in qn; **to lose hope** perdere ogni speranza *or* tutte le speranze; **what a hope!** or **some hopes!** (*fam*) figurati!.

2 VT: **to hope that/to do** sperare che/di fare.

3 VI sperare, augurarsi; **to hope for the best** sperare in bene *or* per il meglio; **I hope so/not** spero di sì/no; **let's hope for success** speriamo di riuscire; **to hope against hope** sperare malgrado tutto.

♦ **hope chest** N (*Am*) cassa del corredo.

hope·ful ['həʊpfʊl] **1** ADJ (*person*) ottimista *m/f*, pieno(-a) di speranza, fiducioso(-a); (*future, situation*) promettente; (*sign, response*) incoraggiante, buono(-a) (*before n*); **I'm hopeful that she'll manage to come** ho buone speranze che venga.

2 N: **a young hopeful** un(a) giovane *m/f* di belle speranze.

hope·ful·ly ['həʊpfəlɪ] ADV **a** (*optimistically: speak*) con ottimismo, con speranza; **to look hopefully at sb** guardare speranzoso(-a) qn **b** (*one hopes: incorrect use*) si spera; **hopefully he will recover** speriamo che si riprenda.

hope·less ['həʊplɪs] ADJ (*impossible, useless: situation*) impossibile; (: *outlook, case*) disperato(-a), senza speranza; (*drunkard*) incorreggibile, inguaribile; (*bad: work: fam*) disastroso(-a); **I'm hopeless at it** (*fam*) sono completamente negato per questo; **it's hopeless trying to convince her** è perfettamente inutile *or* è fiato sprecato cercare di convincerla.

hope·less·ly ['həʊplɪslɪ] ADV (*live*) senza speranza; (*involved, complicated*) spaventosamente; (*late*) disperatamente, irrimediabilmente; **I'm hopelessly confused/lost** sono completamente confuso/perso; **hopelessly in love** perdutamente innamorato(-a).

hop·per ['hɒpə'] N (*chute*) tramoggia.

♦ **hop-picker** ['hɒpˌpɪkə'] N raccoglitore(-trice) di luppolo.

hops [hɒps] NPL coni *m pl* di luppolo.

hop·scotch ['hɒp,skɒtʃ] N campana (*gioco infantile*).

Horace ['hɒrɪs] N Orazio.

horde [hɔːd] N orda; **hordes of screaming children** un'orda di bambini urlanti.

ho·ri·zon [hə'raɪzn] N (*also fig*) orizzonte *m*; **on the horizon** all'orizzonte; **to widen one's horizons** allargare i propri orizzonti.

hori·zon·tal [,hɒrɪ'zɒntl] [1] ADJ orizzontale; **the shelf is horizontal to the floor** la mensola è parallela al pavimento.

[2] N linea *or* piano orizzontale.

hori·zon·tal·ly [,hɒrɪ'zɒntəlɪ] ADV orizzontalmente.

hor·mo·nal [hɔː'məunəl] ADJ ormonale.

hor·mone ['hɔːməun] N ormone *m*.

♦ **hormone replacement therapy** N terapia ormonale (*usata in menopausa*).

horn [hɔːn] N (*gen*, *Mus*) corno; (*of snail*) antenna; (*Aut*) clacson *m inv*; **to draw in one's horns** (*fig: back down*) cedere; (: *spend less*) ridurre le spese.

horn·beam ['hɔːn,biːm] N (*Bot*) carpino bianco.

horned [hɔːnd] ADJ (*animal*) cornuto(-a).

hor·net ['hɔːnɪt] N calabrone *m*.

♦ **horn-rimmed** ['hɔːn'rɪmd] ADJ (*spectacles*) con la montatura di tartaruga.

horny ['hɔːnɪ] ADJ (*comp* **-ier**, *superl* **-iest**) (*like horn*) corneo(-a); (*hands*) incallito(-a), calloso(-a); (*fam: randy*) arrapato(-a), eccitato(-a).

horo·scope ['hɒrə,skəup] N oroscopo.

hor·ren·dous [hɒ'rɛndəs] N orrendo(-a).

hor·ri·ble ['hɒrɪbl] ADJ (*gen*) orribile, tremendo(-a), orrendo(-a); (*accident*) spaventoso(-a).

hor·ri·bly ['hɒrɪblɪ] ADV (*see adj*) in modo orribile *or* orrendo, tremendamente; spaventosamente.

hor·rid ['hɒrɪd] ADJ (*unpleasant: person*) odioso(-a), antipatico(-a); (: *thing*, *weather*) orribile, orrendo(-a); (: *meal*) schifoso(-a); (*unkind*) cattivo(-a).

hor·rif·ic [hɒ'rɪfɪk] ADJ (*accident*) spaventoso(-a); (*murder*) terrificante.

hor·rifi·cal·ly [hɒ'rɪfɪkəlɪ] ADV orrendamente.

hor·ri·fy ['hɒrɪ,faɪ] VT lasciare inorridito(-a).

hor·ri·fy·ing ['hɒrɪ,faɪɪŋ] ADJ terrificante.

hor·ror ['hɒrə] N (*terror*, *dread*) spavento, terrore *m*; (*loathing*, *hatred*) orrore *m*; (*fam*) peste *f*; **he ran away in horror** è scappato terrorizzato; **to have a horror of** avere il terrore di; **that gives me the horrors** (*fam*) quello mi fa venire i brividi.

♦ **horror film** N film *m inv* dell'orrore.

♦ **horror-struck** ['hɒrə,strʌk], **horror-stricken** ['hɒrə,strɪkən] ADJ inorridito(-a).

hors d'oeuvres [ɔː'dɜːvr] NPL (*course*) antipasto; (*individual items*) antipasti *mpl*.

horse [hɔːs] [1] N cavallo; **it's straight from the horse's mouth** (*fam*) è di fonte sicura; **never look a gift horse in the mouth** (*Proverb*) a caval donato non si guarda in bocca

► **horse about**, **horse around** VI + ADV (*fam*) fare lo/la sciocco(-a).

horse·back ['hɔːs,bæk]: **on horseback** ADV a cavallo.

horse·box ['hɔːs,bɒks] N carro *or* furgone *m* per il trasporto dei cavalli.

♦ **horse brass** N ornamento d'ottone per finimenti.

♦ **horse chestnut** N (*tree*) ippocastano; (*nut*) castagna d'India.

♦ **horse dealer** N commerciante *m* di cavalli.

♦ **horse-drawn** ['hɔːs,drɔːn] ADJ a cavalli, tirato(-a) da

cavalli.

horse·flesh ['hɔːs,flɛʃ] N (*horses*) cavalli *mpl*; (*meat*) carne *f* equina *or* di cavallo.

horse·fly ['hɔːs,flaɪ] N tafano, mosca cavallina.

horse·hair ['hɔːs,hɛə] N crine *m* (di cavallo).

♦ **horse laugh** N risata cavallina.

horse·man ['hɔːsmən] N (*pl* **-men**) cavaliere *m*.

horse·man·ship ['hɔːsmən,ʃɪp] N (*riding*) equitazione *f*; (*skill*) abilità di cavaliere.

♦ **horse mushroom** N prataiolo maggiore.

♦ **horse opera** N (*hum*) western *m inv*.

horse·play ['hɔːs,pleɪ] N giochi *mpl* scatenati.

horse·power ['hɔːs,pauə] N cavallo (vapore).

♦ **horse-racing** ['hɔːs,reɪsɪŋ] N (*sport*) ippica; (*events*) corse *fpl* dei cavalli.

horse·radish ['hɔːs,rædɪʃ] N rafano.

♦ **horse sense** N (*fam*) buonsenso.

horse·shoe ['hɔːʃ,ʃuː] [1] N ferro di cavallo.

[2] ADJ a ferro di cavallo.

♦ **horse show** N, **horse trials** NPL concorso ippico, gare *fpl* ippiche.

♦ **horse-trader** ['hɔːs,treɪdə] N commerciante *m/f* di cavalli; (*fig*) vecchia volpe *f*.

♦ **horse-trading** ['hɔːs,treɪdɪŋ] N mercanteggiamento.

horse·whip ['hɔːswɪp] VT frustare.

horse·woman ['hɔːs,wumən] N amazzone *f*.

horsey, **horsy** ['hɔːsɪ] ADJ (*comp* **-ier**, *superl* **-iest**) (*fam: person*) che adora i cavalli; (*appearance*) cavallino(-a), da cavallo.

hor·ti·cul·tur·al [,hɔːtɪ'kʌltʃərəl] ADJ di orticoltura.

hor·ti·cul·ture ['hɔːtɪ,kʌltʃə] N orticoltura.

hor·ti·cul·tur·ist [,hɔːtɪ'kʌltʃərɪst] N orticoltore(-trice).

hose [həuz] N **a** (*hosepipe*) tubo di gomma; (*also*: **garden hose**) tubo per annaffiare; (*Aut*) manicotto **b** (*pl*: *stockings*, *socks*) calze *fpl*, calzini *mpl*; (: *old*) calzamaglia

► **hose down** VT + ADV lavare con un getto d'acqua.

hose·pipe ['həuz,paɪp] N = **hose a**.

ho·siery ['həuʒərɪ] N maglieria; (*in shop*) (reparto di) calze *fpl* e calzini *mpl*.

hos·pice ['hɒspɪs] N *ospedale specializzato nell'assistenza ai malati terminali*.

hos·pi·table [hɒs'pɪtəbl] ADJ ospitale.

hos·pi·tably [hɒs'pɪtəblɪ] ADV in modo ospitale.

hos·pi·tal ['hɒspɪtl] [1] N ospedale *m*; **in hospital**, (*Am*) **in the hospital** in ospedale.

[2] ADJ (*staff*, *treatment*) ospedaliero(-a); (*bed*) di *or* dell'ospedale.

♦ **hospital case** N caso da ricovero (in ospedale).

♦ **hospital facilities** NPL attrezzatura ospedaliera.

hos·pi·tal·ity [,hɒspɪ'tælɪtɪ] N ospitalità.

hos·pi·tal·ize ['hɒspɪtə,laɪz] VT ricoverare (in *or* all'ospedale).

Host [həust] N (*Rel*) ostia.

host¹ [həust] [1] N ospite *m/f*; (*TV*, *Radio*) presentatore(-trice); (*Bot*, *Zool*) ospite *m*.

[2] VT (*TV programme*, *games*) presentare.

host² [həust] N (*crowd*) moltitudine *f*; **for a whole host of reasons** per tutta una serie di ragioni.

hos·tage ['hɒstɪdʒ] N ostaggio; **to take sb hostage** prendere qn in ostaggio.

♦ **host country** N paese *m* ospite, paese che ospita.

hos·tel ['hɒstəl] N (*for students*, *nurses*) pensionato; (*for homeless people*) ospizio, ricovero; (*also*: **youth hostel**) ostello della gioventù.

hos·tel·ler ['hɒstələ] N frequentatore(-trice) di ostelli

(della gioventù).

hos·tel·ling ['hɒstəlɪŋ] N: **to go (youth) hostelling** passare le vacanze negli ostelli della gioventù.

host·ess ['həʊstɛs] N ospite *f*; (*Aer*) hostess *f inv*; (*in nightclub*) entraîneuse *f inv*.

hos·tile ['hɒstaɪl] ADJ: **hostile (to)** ostile (a).

hos·tile·ly ['hɒstaɪllɪ] ADV ostilmente.

hos·til·ity [hɒs'tɪlɪtɪ] N ostilità *f inv*.

hot [hɒt] **1** ADJ (*comp* **-ter**, *superl* **-test**) **a** caldo(-a); **to be hot** (*person*) avere caldo; (*thing*) essere caldo(-a); (*weather*) fare caldo; **to get hot** (*person*) incominciare ad avere caldo; (*thing*) scaldarsi; (*weather*) incominciare a fare caldo; **this room is hot** fa caldo in questa stanza; **I don't like hot weather** non sopporto il caldo; **to get hot under the collar** (*fam*) scaldarsi; **to be all hot and bothered** essere tutto accaldato(-a); (*flustered*) essere tutto agitato(-a); **to be/get into hot water** essere/cacciarsi nei guai; **you're getting hot!** (*fig: when guessing*) fuochino!

b (*curry, spice*) piccante; (*news*) fresco(-a); (*temperament*) focoso(-a), ardente; (*conflict, contest*) accanito(-a); **she's got a hot temper** è un tipo collerico; **hot favourite** grande favorito(-a); **I've got a hot tip for the Derby** ho un cavallo sicuro per il Derby; **I'll make things hot for you** (*fam*) ti renderò la vita difficile; **to be in hot pursuit of sb** stare alle calcagna di qn; **she's pretty hot at maths** (*fam*) se la cava bene in matematica; **those goods are hot** (*fam: stolen*) è roba che scotta.

2 ADV: **to be hot on sb's trail** essere sulle tracce di qn; **to be hot on the heels of sb** essere alle calcagna di qn

▶ **hot up** (*fam*) **1** VI + ADV (*situation*) farsi più teso(-a); (*party*) scaldarsi.

2 VT + ADV (*pace*) affrettare; (*car engine*) truccare.

♦ **hot air** N (*fam pej*) ciance *fpl*.

♦ **hot-air balloon** [,hɒt,ɛəbə'lu:n] N (*Aer*) mongolfiera.

hot·bed ['hɒt,bɛd] N (*fig*) focolaio.

♦ **hot-blooded** [,hɒt'blʌdɪd] ADJ dal sangue caldo, appassionato(-a).

hotch·potch ['hɒtʃ,pɒtʃ] N (*Brit*) pot-pourri *m*.

♦ **hot dog** N (*Culin*) hot dog *m inv*.

♦ **hot-dogging** [,hɒt'dɒgɪŋ] N (*Am Skiing*) sci *m* acrobatico.

ho·tel [həʊ'tɛl] N albergo, hotel *m inv*; **hotel room** camera d'albergo; **hotel workers** personale *m* alberghiero.

ho·tel·ier [həʊ'tɛlɪə'] N albergatore(-trice).

♦ **hot flush**, (*Am*) **hot flash** N scalmana, caldana.

hot·foot ['hɒt,fʊt] ADV di gran carriera.

hot·head ['hɒt,hɛd] N (*fig*) testa calda.

♦ **hot-headed** [,hɒt'hɛdɪd] ADJ impetuoso(-a), focoso(-a).

♦ **hot-headedness** [,hɒt'hɛdɪdnɪs] N impetuosità.

hot·house ['hɒt,haʊs] N serra.

♦ **hot line** N (*Pol*) telefono rosso.

hot·ly ['hɒtlɪ] ADV accanitamente, con accanimento, violentemente; **he was hotly pursued by the policeman** il poliziotto lo rincorreva senza dargli tregua.

hot·plate ['hɒt,pleɪt] N (*on cooker*) piastra (riscaldante); (*for keeping food warm*) scaldavivande *m inv*.

hot·pot ['hɒt,pɒt] N (*Brit Culin*) stufato.

♦ **hot potato** N (*fam*) patata bollente; **to drop sb/sth like a hot potato** piantare in asso qn/qc.

♦ **hot rod** N (*Aut: fam*) macchina truccata.

♦ **hot seat** N (*fig*): **to be in the hot seat** avere un posto che scotta.

♦ **hot spot** N (*fig*) zona calda.

♦ **hot spring** N sorgente *f* termale.

♦ **hot stuff** N: **to be hot stuff** (*fam*) essere eccezionale.

♦ **hot-tempered** [,hɒt'tɛmpəd] ADJ irascibile.

♦ **hot-water bottle** [,hɒt'wɔːtə,bɒtl] N borsa dell'acqua calda, boule *f inv*.

♦ **hot-wire** ['hɒt,waɪə'] VT (*fam: car*) avviare mettendo in contatto i fili dell'accensione.

hound [haʊnd] **1** N segugio; **the hounds** la muta; **to follow the hounds** [OR] **to ride to hounds** fare la caccia alla volpe.

2 VT (*fig*) perseguitare

▶ **hound down** VT + ADV riuscire a stanare

▶ **hound out** VT + ADV: **to hound out of** cacciare da.

hour ['aʊə'] N ora; **at 30 miles an hour** a 30 miglia all'ora; **hour by hour** ora per ora; **on the hour** ad ogni ora precisa; **in the early** *or* **small hours** alle ore piccole; **at all hours (of the day and night)** a tutte le ore (del giorno e della notte); **at this late hour** in questa fase avanzata; **he thought his (last) hour had come** pensò che fosse giunta la sua ora; **in the hour of danger** nel momento del pericolo; **to pay sb by the hour** pagare qn a ore; **to wait (for) hours** aspettare per (delle) ore; **hours and hours** ore e ore; **to keep regular hours** fare una vita regolare; **out of hours** fuori orario; **after hours** (*at office*) dopo le ore d'ufficio; (*at shop, pub*) dopo l'ora di chiusura.

hour·glass ['aʊə,glɑːs] N clessidra.

♦ **hour hand** N lancetta delle ore.

hour·ly ['aʊəlɪ] **1** ADJ (*intervals*) di un'ora; (*bus service*) (ad) ogni ora; (*rate*) orario(-a).

2 ADV ogni ora; **hourly paid workers** operai(-e) pagati a ore; **we expected him hourly** lo aspettavamo da un momento all'altro.

house [*n* haʊs; *vb* haʊz] **1** N (*pl* **houses**) **a** casa; **at** (*or* **to) my house** a casa mia; **to keep house** mandare avanti la casa; **to set up house** metter su casa; **house of cards** castello di carte; **to put** *or* **set one's house in order** (*fig*) sistemare i propri affari; **to get on like a house on fire** (*two people: fam*) andare d'amore e d'accordo

b (*Pol*) camera

c (*Theatre*) sala; **"house full"** "biglietti esauriti"; **in the front of the house** tra gli spettatori, in sala; **to bring the house down** (*fig*) scatenare un uragano di applausi; **the second house** il secondo spettacolo

d (*Comm*) ditta, casa; **it's on the house** (*paid by company*) paga la ditta; (*free*) è offerto dalla casa

e (*family, line*) casa, casato.

2 VT ospitare; **this building houses 6 families** in quest'edificio abitano 6 famiglie.

♦ **house arrest** N arresti *mpl* domiciliari; **to put sb under house arrest** mettere qn agli arresti domiciliari.

house·boat ['haʊs,bəʊt] N house boat *f inv*.

house·bound ['haʊs,baʊnd] ADJ confinato(-a) in casa.

♦ **house-break** ['haʊs,breɪk] VT (*Am*) = **house-train**.

house·break·er ['haʊs,breɪkə'] N svaligiatore(-trice), scassinatore(-trice).

house·break·ing ['haʊs,breɪkɪŋ] N furto con scasso.

♦ **house-broken** ['haʊs,brəʊkən] ADJ (*Am: animal*) che non sporca in casa.

house·coat ['haʊs,kəʊt] N vestaglia.

♦ **house doctor** N ≈ (*medico*) interno.

house·father ['haʊs,fɑːðə'] N responsabile *m* di gruppo (*in un collegio*).

house·fly ['haʊs,flaɪ] N (*pl* **-flies**) mosca (comune).

house·ful ['haʊsfʊl] N: **we had a houseful of children** abbiamo avuto la casa piena di bambini.

♦ **house guest** N ospite *m/f* (della casa).

house·hold ['haʊs,həʊld] **1** N casa, famiglia.

2 ADJ (*accounts, expenses, equipment*) della casa, dome-

stico(-a).

♦ **Household Cavalry** N (*Mil*) cavalleria della guardia reale.

house·holder ['haʊsˌhəʊldə'] N padrone(-a) di casa; (*head of house*) capofamiglia *m/f*.

♦ **household name, household word** N nome *m* che tutti conoscono *or* conosciuto da tutti.

house·hunting ['haʊsˌhʌntɪŋ] N: **to go househunting** mettersi a cercar casa.

house·keeper ['haʊsˌkiːpə'] N governante *f*.

house·keeping ['haʊsˌkiːpɪŋ] N (*work*) andamento *or* governo della casa; (*also:* **housekeeping money**) soldi *mpl* per le spese di casa; (*Comput*) ausilio.

house·maid ['haʊsˌmeɪd] N cameriera, domestica.

♦ **housemaid's knee** N (*Med*) ginocchio della lavandaia.

house·man ['haʊsmən] N (*pl* **-men**) (*Brit: in hospital*) ≈ (medico) interno.

house·mother ['haʊsˌmʌðə'] N responsabile *f* di gruppo (*in un collegio*).

♦ **House of Commons** N (*Brit*): **the House of Commons** la Camera dei Comuni.

♦ **House of Lords** N (*Brit*): **the House of Lords** la Camera dei Lords.

♦ **House of Representatives** N (*Am*): **the House of Representatives** la Camera dei Rappresentanti.

♦ **house–owner** ['haʊsˌəʊnə'] N proprietario(-a) di una casa.

♦ **house party** N riunione *f* di ospiti (*in una casa di campagna*).

♦ **house physician** N = **house doctor**.

♦ **house plant** N pianta da appartamento.

♦ **house–proud** ['haʊsˌpraʊd] ADJ che ha la mania della pulizia.

house·room ['haʊsˌrʊm] N: **I wouldn't give it houseroom** (*fam*) non lo vorrei avere in casa mia neanche se me lo regalassero.

♦ **Houses of Parliament** (*Brit*) NPL: **the Houses of Parliament** (*building*) il palazzo del Parlamento; (*members*) il Parlamento.

♦ **house-to-house** [ˌhaʊstə'haʊs] ADJ (*search*) casa per casa; (*collection*) porta a porta.

house·top ['haʊsˌtɒp] N: **to proclaim** *or* **shout sth from the housetops** (*fig*) proclamare qc ai quattro venti.

♦ **house–train** ['haʊsˌtreɪn] VT (*Brit: pet animal*) addestrare a non sporcare in casa.

♦ **house–trained** ['haʊsˌtreɪnd] ADJ (*Brit: animal*) che non sporca in casa.

♦ **house–warming** ['haʊsˌwɔːmɪŋ] N (*also:* **house-warming party**) festa per inaugurare la casa nuova.

house·wife ['haʊsˌwaɪf] N (*pl* **-wives**) massaia, casalinga.

house·wife·ly ['haʊsˌwaɪflɪ] ADJ della massaia *or* casalinga.

house·work ['haʊsˌwɜːk] N faccende *fpl*, lavori *mpl* di casa, lavori domestici; **to do the housework** fare i lavori di casa, sbrigare le faccende.

hous·ing ['haʊzɪŋ] **1** N **a** alloggiamento **b** (*houses*) alloggi *mpl*, case *fpl*.
2 ADJ (*problem, shortage*) degli alloggi.

♦ **housing association** N cooperativa edilizia.

♦ **housing benefit** N (*Brit*) *sussidio assegnato ad affittuari in difficoltà economiche.*

♦ **housing conditions** NPL condizioni *fpl* di abitazione.

♦ **housing development** N *zona residenziale con case popolari e/o private.*

♦ **housing estate** N (*Brit*) quartiere *m* residenziale.

hove [həʊv] PT, PP of **heave 3c**.

hov·el ['hɒvəl] N tugurio.

hov·er ['hɒvə'] VI (*bird*) librarsi; (*helicopter*) volare a punto fisso; **a smile hovered on her lips** un sorriso indugiava sulle sue labbra; **to hover on the brink of disaster** essere sull'orlo del disastro

▶ **hover about, hover around** VI + ADV stare *or* girare intorno; **to hover round sb** aggirarsi intorno a qn.

hover·craft ['hɒvəˌkrɑːft] N hovercraft *m inv*.

hover·port ['hɒvəˌpɔːt] N porto per hovercraft.

how [haʊ] ADV **a** (*gen*) come; **how did you do it?** come hai fatto?, come l'hai fatto?; **I know how you did it** so come hai fatto; **to know how to do sth** sapere come fare qc; **how are you?** come stai?, come va?; **how's life?** (*fam*) come va (la vita)?; **how is school?** come va la scuola?; **how was the film?** com'era il film?; **how is it that ...?** com'è che...?; **how do you do?** molto lieto!, piacere!; **how come?** (*fam*) come mai?; **how come he's leaving?** (*fam*) come mai se ne va?; **how about (going for) a drink?** che ne diresti di (andare a) bere qualcosa?; **and how!** (*fam*) eccome!
b (*to what degree*) quanto(-a); **how much is it?** quanto costa?; **how long have you been here?** da quanto tempo stai qui?; **how old are you?** quanti anni hai?; **how far is it to ...?** quanto è lontano...?; **how many people?** quante persone?; **how much milk?** quanto latte?; **how often do you go?** quanto spesso ci vai?; **how lovely!** che bello!; **how kind of you!** è molto gentile da parte sua!
c (*that*) che, di come; **she told me how she'd found the money in an old suitcase** mi ha raccontato di come aveva trovato il denaro in una vecchia valigia.

how·dy ['haʊdɪ] EXCL (*Am*) salve!

how·ever [haʊ'ɛvə'] **1** CONJ (*still, nevertheless*) però, comunque, tuttavia.
2 ADV: **however I do it** in qualunque modo lo faccia; **however cold it is** per quanto freddo faccia; **however much I try** per quanto ci possa provare; **however did you do it?** (*fam*) come diavolo hai fatto?; **however that may be** comunque sia.

how·itz·er ['haʊɪtsə'] N (*Mil*) obice *m*.

howl [haʊl] **1** N (*of animal*) ululato; **a howl of pain** un urlo di dolore; **a howl of protest** un grido di protesta; **howls of laughter** scrosci *mpl* di risate.
2 VI (*person*) gridare, urlare; (*animal, wind*) ululare; (*weep*) piangere; **to howl with laughter** rotolarsi dalle risate.
3 VT urlare

▶ **howl down** VT + ADV zittire a forza di urla.

howl·er ['haʊlə'] N (*fam*) abbaglio; (: *in homework*) strafalcione *m*.

howl·ing ['haʊlɪŋ] ADJ (*wind, gale*) che ulula; **howling success** (*fig*) successo travolgente.

HP [ˌeɪtʃ'piː] N ABBR (*Brit*) = **hire-purchase**.

hp [ˌeɪtʃ'piː] N ABBR (*Aut*: = *horsepower*) C.V. (= *cavallo vapore*).

HQ [ˌeɪtʃ'kjuː] N ABBR (= *headquarters*) Q.G. (= *quartier generale*).

HR [ˌeɪtʃ'ɑː'] N ABBR (*Am*) = **House of Representatives**.

hr (*pl* **hrs**) ABBR (= *hour*) h (= *ora*).

HRH [ˌeɪtʃɑː'r'eɪtʃ] ABBR (= *His or Her Royal Highness*) S.A.R. (= *Sua Altezza Reale*).

HRT [ˌeɪtʃɑː'tiː] N ABBR = **hormone replacement therapy**.

HS ABBR (*Am*) = **high school**.

HT ABBR (= *high tension*) A.T. (= *alta tensione*).

hub [hʌb] N (*of wheel*) mozzo; (*fig*) centro, fulcro.

hub·bub ['hʌbʌb] N baccano.
hub·cap ['hʌbˌkæp] N (*Aut*) coprimozzo.
HUD [hʌd] N ABBR (*Am*)= *Department of Housing and Urban Development*.
hud·dle ['hʌdl] 1 N gruppetto, capannello; **to go into a huddle** (*fam*) fare capannello.
2 VI raggomitolarsi, rannicchiarsi
▸ **huddle down** VI + ADV accucciarsi, rannicchiarsi
▸ **huddle together** VI + ADV stringersi l'uno(-a) vicino all'altro(-a)
▸ **huddle up** VI + ADV rannicchiarsi, raggomitolarsi.
hue [hju:] N (*colour*) colore *m*, tinta.
♦ **hue and cry** N clamorosa protesta.
huff [hʌf] N: **in a huff** (*fam*) imbronciato(-a), stizzito(-a).
huffi·ly ['hʌfılı] ADV (*fam*) con aria imbronciata.
huffi·ness ['hʌfınıs] N (*fam*) cattivo umore *m*.
huffy ['hʌfı]) ADJ (*comp* **-ier**, *superl* **-iest**) (*fam*) imbronciato (-a); **to get huffy** fare il broncio.
hug [hʌg] 1 N abbraccio, stretta; **to give sb a hug** abbracciare qn.
2 VT abbracciare, tener stretto(-a) a sé; (*subj: bear*) stringere; (*keep close to: kerb*) tenersi vicino a; **to hug the coast** tenersi sotto costa.
huge [hju:dʒ] ADJ (*comp* **-r**, *superl* **-st**) (*gen*) enorme; (*appetite, helping*) smisurato(-a); (*success*) strepitoso (-a), immenso(-a).
huge·ly ['hju:dʒlı] ADV enormemente.
hulk [hʌlk] N (*abandoned ship*) nave *f* in disarmo; (*building*) costruzione *f* mastodontica; **a great hulk of a man** (*fam*) un colosso.
hulk·ing ['hʌlkıŋ] ADJ (*fam*) mastodontico(-a); **hulking (great)** grosso(-a) e goffo(-a).
hull [hʌl] N (*of ship*) scafo.
hul·la·ba·loo [ˌhʌləbə'lu:] N (*fam: noise*) fracasso.
hul·lo [hʌ'ləʊ] EXCL = hello.
hum [hʌm] 1 N (*also Elec*) ronzio; (*of traffic, machines*) rumore *m*; (*of voices*) mormorio, brusio.
2 VT (*tune*) canticchiare.
3 VI (*insect*) ronzare; (*person*) canticchiare a labbra chiuse; (*engine, machine*) rombare; (*wireless*) mandare un brusio; (*fig fam: be busy*) animarsi; **to make things hum** (*fam*) fare procedere le cose speditamente; **to hum with activity** pullulare di attività; **to hum and haw** essere incerto(-a) sul da farsi.
hu·man ['hju:mən] 1 ADJ umano(-a); **she's only human** nessuno è perfetto.
2 N essere *m* umano.
♦ **human being** N essere *m* umano.
hu·mane [hju:'meın] ADJ umanitario(-a).
hu·mane·ly [hju:'meınlı] ADV con umanità.
hu·man·ism ['hju:məˌnızəm] N umanesimo.
hu·man·ist ['hju:mənıst] N umanista *m/f*.
hu·mani·tar·ian [hju:ˌmænı'tɛərıən] ADJ umanitario(-a).
hu·man·ity [hju:'mænıtı] N umanità; **the humanities** gli studi letterari *or* umanistici, le lettere.
hu·man·ly ['hju:mənlı] ADV umanamente.
♦ **human nature** N la natura umana; **it's human nature** è nella natura umana; è umano.
hu·man·oid ['hju:mənɔɪd] 1 ADJ che sembra umano(-a).
2 N umanoide *m/f*.
♦ **human rights** NPL diritti *mpl* dell'uomo.
hum·ble ['hʌmbl] 1 ADJ (*comp* **-r**, *superl* **-st**) umile; (*opinion, occupation*) modesto(-a); **of humble origins** di umili origini; **to eat humble pie** rimangiarsi tutto.
2 VT umiliare; **to humble o.s.** abbassarsi, umiliarsi.

hum·bly ['hʌmblı] ADV umilmente, modestamente.
hum·bug ['hʌmˌbʌg] N (*person*) impostore *m*; (*nonsense*) frottole *fpl*, falsità; (*Brit: sweet*) caramella alla menta.
hum·ding·er ['hʌmˌdıŋəʳ] N (*fam*): **it's a humdinger!** è una cannonata!; **he's** (*or* **she's**) **a humdinger!** è uno schianto!
hum·drum ['hʌmˌdrʌm] ADJ monotono(-a), banale.
hu·mer·us ['hju:mərəs] N omero.
hu·mid ['hju:mıd] ADJ umido(-a).
hu·midi·fi·er [hju:'mıdıˌfaıəʳ] N umidificatore *m*.
hu·mid·ity [hju:'mıdıtı] N umidità.
hu·mili·ate [hju:'mılıˌeıt] VT umiliare.
hu·mili·at·ing [hju:'mılıˌeıtıŋ] ADJ umiliante.
hu·milia·tion [hju:ˌmılı'eıʃən] N umiliazione *f*.
hu·mil·ity [hju:'mılıtı] N umiltà.
humming·bird ['hʌmıŋˌbɜ:d] N colibrì *m inv*.
hu·mor·ist ['hju:mərıst] N umorista *m/f*.
hu·mor·ous ['hju:mərəs] ADJ (*person*) spiritoso(-a); (*book, story*) divertente, umoristico(-a); (*tone*) scherzoso(-a).
hu·mor·ous·ly ['hju:mərəslı] ADV (*see adj*) (*describe*) in modo spiritoso; in modo divertente; (*say*) scherzosamente, con fare scherzoso.
hu·mour, (*Am*) **hu·mor** ['hju:məʳ] 1 N **a** (*comic sense*) umorismo; (*of situation*) lato divertente *or* umoristico; **sense of humour** senso dell'umorismo **b** (*mood*) umore *m*; **to be in a good/bad humour** essere di buon/cattivo umore.
2 VT (*person*) accontentare, compiacere; (*sb's whims*) assecondare.
hu·mour·less, (*Am*) **hu·mor·less** ['hju:məlıs] ADJ privo (-a) di umorismo.
hu·mour·less·ly ['hju:məlıslı] ADV senza umorismo.
hump [hʌmp] 1 N (*Anat*) gobba; **it gives me the hump** (*Brit fam*) mi mette di malumore; **we're over the hump** (*fig*) il peggio è passato, il più è fatto.
2 VT **a** (*arch: back*) inarcare **b** (*fam: carry*) portare.
hump·back ['hʌmpˌbæk] N (*also:* **humpback bridge**) ponte *m* a schiena d'asino.
hump·backed ['hʌmpˌbækt] ADJ (*offensive: person*) gobbo(-a); (*animal*) con la gobba, gibboso(-a).
hu·mus ['hju:məs] N humus *m*.
Hun [hʌn] N (*History*) Unno; (*offensive: German*) crucco(-a).
hunch [hʌntʃ] 1 N **a** (*fam: idea*) impressione *f*; (*premonition*) intuizione *f*; **I have a hunch that** ... ho la vaga impressione che...; **she's acting on a hunch** sta andando a naso; **to follow one's hunch** seguire il proprio fiuto **b** (*hump*) gobba.
2 VT (*also:* **hunch up**) incurvare.
3 VI star curvo(-a); **to sit hunched up** star seduto(-a) curvo(-a).
hunch·back ['hʌntʃˌbæk] N (*offensive*) gobbo(-a).
hunch·back·ed ['hʌntʃˌbækt] ADJ (*offensive: person*) gobbo (-a).
hunched ['hʌntʃt] ADJ incurvato(-a).
hun·dred ['hʌndrıd] 1 ADJ cento *inv*; **about a hundred people** un centinaio di persone; **a hundred and one** centouno; **hundred and first** centounesimo(-a); **I'm a hundred per cent sure** sono sicuro(-a) al cento per cento.
2 N cento *m inv*; **to live to be a hundred** vivere fino all'età di cent'anni; (*less exactly*) diventare centenario(-a); **hundreds of people** centinaia *fpl* di persone; **they came in their hundreds** sono arrivati a centinaia.
hun·dredth ['hʌndrıdθ] 1 ADJ centesimo(-a).
2 N (*in series*) centesimo(-a); (*fraction*) centesimo.
hundred·weight ['hʌndrıdˌweıt] N (*Brit: 112 lb*) ≈ 50.8 kg;

(*Am: 100 lb*) ≈ 45.3 kg.

hung [hʌŋ] **1** PT, PP of **hang**.

2 ADJ: **a hung jury** una giuria divisa (sul verdetto).

Hun·gar·ian [hʌŋˈgɛərɪən] **1** ADJ ungherese.

2 N **a** (*person*) ungherese *m/f* **b** (*language*) ungherese *m*.

Hun·ga·ry [ˈhʌŋgərɪ] N Ungheria.

hun·ger [ˈhʌŋgəʳ] N fame *f*; (*also fig*): **hunger (for)** sete *f* (di)

► **hunger after, hunger for** VI + PREP desiderare ardentemente, morire dalla voglia di.

♦ **hunger strike** N sciopero della fame.

hung·over [ˌhʌŋˈəʊvəʳ] ADJ (*fam*): **to be hungover** avere i postumi della sbornia.

hun·gri·ly [ˈhʌŋgrɪlɪ] ADV (*fig*) avidamente; (*eat*) voracemente.

hun·gry [ˈhʌŋgrɪ] ADJ (*comp* **-ier**, *superl* **-iest**): **to be hungry** aver fame, essere affamato(-a); **to make sb hungry** far venire fame a qn; **to go hungry** (*starve*) patire la fame; (*skip a meal*) saltare il pasto; **hungry for** (*fig*) assetato(-a) di; (*lit*) affamato(-a) di.

♦ **hung up** ADJ (*fam*) complessato(-a).

hunk [hʌŋk] N (*of bread, cheese*) bel pezzo; **a gorgeous hunk of a man** (*fam*) un bel fusto.

hunky-dory [ˈhʌŋkɪˈdɔːrɪ] (*fam*) ADJ (*okay*) soddisfacente; (*fine*) magnifico(-a), meraviglioso(-a); **everything's hunky-dory** va tutto bene.

hunt [hʌnt] **1** N (*gen*) caccia; (*huntsmen*) cacciatori *mpl*; (*search*): **hunt (for)** ricerca (di); **tiger hunt** caccia alla tigre; **I've had a hunt for the book** ho cercato il libro dappertutto.

2 VT (*animal*) andare a caccia di; (*search*) cercare; **I've hunted the house for it** ho messo la casa sottosopra per trovarlo.

3 VI (*Sport*) cacciare; **to go hunting** andare a caccia; **to hunt for** (*animal*) cacciare; (*object, information*) cercare dappertutto; **she hunted in her bag for the keys** ha rovistato nella borsa per trovare le chiavi

► **hunt down** VT + ADV (*criminal, enemy*) dar la caccia a

► **hunt out** VT + ADV scovare

► **hunt up** VT + ADV scovare.

hunt·er [ˈhʌntəʳ] N cacciatore(-trice); (*Brit: horse*) cavallo da caccia.

hunt·ing [ˈhʌntɪŋ] N (*Sport*) caccia.

♦ **hunting lodge** N casino di caccia.

hunts·man [ˈhʌntsmən] N (*pl* **-men**) cacciatore *m*.

hur·dle [ˈhɜːdl] N (*for fence*) graticcio; (*fig, Sport*) ostacolo; **the 100 metre hurdles** (*race*) i cento metri a ostacoli.

♦ **hurdle race** N (*Horse-racing*) corsa a ostacoli.

hurl [hɜːl] VT (*throw*) scagliare, scaraventare; **to hurl o.s. at sb/sth** scagliarsi su qn/qc; **they were hurled to the ground by the blast** vennero scagliati a terra dall'esplosione; **to hurl abuse** *or* **insults at sb** scagliare *or* lanciare (degli) insulti a qn.

hurl·ing [ˈhɜːlɪŋ] N (*Sport*) hurling *m*.

hurly-burly [ˌhɜːlɪˈbɜːlɪ] N chiasso, baccano.

hur·rah [huˈrɑː], **hur·ray** [huˈreɪ] EXCL urrà!, evviva!; **hurrah for Mr Jones!** viva Mr Jones!

hur·ri·cane [ˈhʌrɪkən] N uragano.

♦ **hurricane lamp** N lampada controvento.

hur·ried [ˈhʌrɪd] ADJ (*gen*) affrettato(-a); (*steps*) frettoloso (-a); (*work*) fatto(-a) in fretta; **to eat a hurried meal** buttare giù due bocconi.

hur·ried·ly [ˈhʌrɪdlɪ] ADV in fretta (e furia).

hur·ry [ˈhʌrɪ] **1** N fretta, premura; **to be in a hurry (to do)** avere una gran fretta (di fare); **done in a hurry** fatto(-a)

in fretta; **are you in a hurry for this?** ti serve subito?; **what's the hurry?** che fretta c'è?; **there's no hurry** non c'è fretta *or* premura; **he won't do that again in a hurry** (*fam*) non lo rifarà tanto facilmente.

2 VT (*person*) far fretta a; (*work*) fare in fretta; **to hurry to do sth** affrettarsi a fare qc; **he won't be hurried** non gli si può far fretta; **she hurried him into the car** l'ha spinto in macchina; **he was hurried to the hospital** è stato portato d'urgenza all'ospedale; **he hurried his lunch** ha mangiato il pranzo alla svelta; **troops were hurried to the spot** le truppe furono spedite in fretta sul posto.

3 VI fare in fretta; **to hurry back/home** affrettarsi a tornare indietro/a casa; **to hurry after sb** precipitarsi dietro a qn; **to hurry in/out** entrare/uscire in fretta

► **hurry along 1** VI + ADV camminare in fretta.

2 VT + ADV = **hurry up 2**

► **hurry away, hurry off 1** VI + ADV andarsene in fretta.

2 VT + ADV spedire fuori in fretta; **to be hurried off to** essere spedito(-a) in fretta a

► **hurry on 1** VI + ADV: **to hurry on to** passare in fretta a.

2 VT + ADV far fretta a

► **hurry up 1** VI + ADV sbrigarsi, affrettarsi.

2 VT + ADV (*person*) far fretta a; (*work*) fare in fretta; **hurry him up will you!** digli di fare in fretta!

hurt [hɜːt] (*vb: pt, pp* **hurt**) **1** VT **a** (*injure, also fig*) ferire; (*cause pain to, harm*) far male a; **I hurt my arm** mi sono fatto male al braccio; **to hurt o.s.** farsi male; **where does it hurt you?** dove ti fa male?; **to get hurt** farsi male; (*emotionally*) essere ferito(-a); **to hurt sb's feelings** colpire la suscettibilità di qn

b (*business, interests*) colpire, danneggiare.

2 VI far male; **my arm hurts** mi fa male il braccio; **where does it hurt?** dove ti fa male?; **that hurts!** che male!.

3 N dolore *m*.

4 ADJ (*foot*) ferito(-a); (*feelings, look, tone*) offeso(-a).

hurt·ful [ˈhɜːtfʊl] ADJ (*upsetting: remark*) che fa male, che ferisce.

hurt·le [ˈhɜːtl] **1** VI sfrecciare; **to hurtle past/down** passare/scendere a razzo; **she hurtled down the stairs** si è precipitata giù per le scale.

2 VT scagliare.

hus·band [ˈhʌzbənd] **1** N marito.

2 VT dosare; **to husband one's resources** misurare le proprie risorse.

hush [hʌʃ] **1** N silenzio, calma, pace *f*; **hush!** silenzio!, zitto(-a)!.

2 VT quietare, calmare

► **hush up** VT + ADV (*fact*) cercare di far passare sotto silenzio; (*scandal*) mettere a tacere; (*person*) far star zitto(-a), zittire.

hushed [hʌʃt] ADJ (*tone, voice*) sommesso(-a); (*silence*) profondo(-a).

♦ **hush-hush** [ˈhʌʃˈhʌʃ] ADJ (*fam*) segretissimo(-a).

♦ **hush money** N: **to pay sb hush money** (*fam*) comprare il silenzio di qn.

husk [hʌsk] N (*of wheat, rice, seed*) pula; (*of maize*) cartoccio.

huski·ly [ˈhʌskɪlɪ] ADV con voce roca.

huski·ness [ˈhʌskɪnɪs] N raucedine *f*.

husky¹ [ˈhʌskɪ] ADJ (*comp* **-ier**, *superl* **-iest**) (*voice*) roco(-a); (*tough: person*) ben piantato(-a).

husky² [ˈhʌskɪ] N (*pl* **-ies**) husky *m inv*, cane *m* eschimese.

hus·tings [ˈhʌstɪŋz] NPL (*Brit Pol*) campagna elettorale.

hus·tle [ˈhʌsl] **1** N: **hustle and bustle** trambusto, via vai *m*

inv.

[2] VT (*push: person*) spingere, incalzare; **to hustle in/out** spintonare dentro/fuori; **we'll have to hustle things along** dobbiamo fare più in fretta.

[3] VI: **to hustle in/out** entrare/uscire in fretta.

hut [hʌt] N (*primitive dwelling*) capanna; (*in mountains*) baita, rifugio; (*Mil*) baracca; (*shed*) capanno.

hutch [hʌtʃ] N gabbia (per conigli).

hya·cinth ['haɪəsɪnθ] N giacinto.

hy·brid ['haɪbrɪd] [1] N ibrido.

[2] ADJ ibrido(-a).

hy·dran·gea [haɪ'dreɪndʒə] N ortensia.

hy·drant ['haɪdrənt] N (*also:* **fire hydrant**) idrante *m*.

hy·drate ['haɪdreɪt] N idrato.

hy·drau·lic [haɪ'drɒlɪk] ADJ idraulico(-a); **hydraulic ramp** (*Aut*) ponte *m* (sollevatore).

hy·drau·lics [haɪ'drɒlɪks] NSG idraulica.

hy·dride ['haɪdraɪd] N idruro.

hydro... ['haɪdrəʊ] PREF idro... .

hydro·car·bon ['haɪdrəʊ'kɑːbən] N idrocarburo.

hydro·chlo·ric acid [,haɪdrəʊ'klɒrɪk'æsɪd] N acido cloridrico *or* muriatico.

hydro·dy·nam·ics ['haɪdrəʊdaɪ'næmɪks] NSG idrodinamica.

hydro·elec·tric ['haɪdrəʊɪ'lɛktrɪk] ADJ idroelettrico(-a).

hydro·elec·tric·ity ['haɪdrəʊɪlɛk'trɪsɪtɪ] N idroelettricità.

hydro·foil ['haɪdrə,fɔɪl] N aliscafo.

hydro·gen ['haɪdrɪdʒən] N idrogeno.

♦ **hydrogen bomb** N bomba all'idrogeno, bomba H.

♦ **hydrogen carbonate** N carbonato acido, bicarbonato.

♦ **hydrogen chloride** N acido cloridrico.

♦ **hydrogen ion** N ione *m* idrogeno.

♦ **hydrogen peroxide** N acqua ossigenata.

♦ **hydrogen sulphide** N acido solfidrico.

hydro·logi·cal [,haɪdrə'lɒdʒɪkəl] ADJ idrologico(-a).

hy·droly·sis [haɪ'drɒlɪsɪs] N idrolisi *f*.

hy·drom·eter [haɪ'drɒmɪtə̍ʳ] N idrometro.

hydro·phil·lic [,haɪdrəʊ'fɪlɪk] ADJ idrofilo(-a).

hydro·pho·bia [,haɪdrə'fəʊbɪə] N idrofobia.

hydro·pho·bic [,haɪdrəʊ'fəʊbɪk] ADJ idrofobo(-a); (*Chem*) idrofugo(-a).

hydro·plane ['haɪdrəʊ,pleɪn] N idrovolante *m*.

hydro·pon·ics [,haɪdrə'pɒnɪks] NSG idroponica.

hy·drot·ro·pism [haɪ'drɒtrə,pɪzəm] N idrotropismo.

hy·drox·ide [haɪ'drɒksaɪd] N ossidrile *m*.

hy·ena [haɪ'iːnə] N iena.

hy·giene ['haɪdʒiːn] N igiene *f*.

hy·gien·ic [haɪ'dʒiːnɪk] ADJ igienico(-a).

hy·gieni·cal·ly [haɪ'dʒiːnɪkəlɪ] ADV igienicamente.

hy·grom·eter [haɪ'grɒmɪtə̍ʳ] N igrometro.

hygro·scop·ic [,haɪgrə'skɒpɪk] ADJ igroscopico(-a).

hymn [hɪm] N inno (sacro).

hym·nal ['hɪmnəl] N libro dei canti.

♦ **hymn book** N libro dei canti.

hype [haɪp] N (*fam*) battage *m inv.*

hyper... ['haɪpə] PREF iper... .

hyper·ac·tive [,haɪpər'æktɪv] ADJ iperattivo(-a).

hyper·bo·le [haɪ'pɜːbəlɪ] N iperbole *f*.

hyper·criti·cal [,haɪpə'krɪtɪkəl] ADJ ipercritico(-a).

hyper·mar·ket ['haɪpə,mɑːkɪt] N (*Brit*) ipermercato.

hyper·sen·si·tive [,haɪpə'sɛnsɪtɪv] ADJ (*physically*) ipersensibile; (*easily offended: pej*) permaloso(-a).

hyper·ten·sion [,haɪpə'tɛnʃən] N (*Med*) ipertensione *f*.

hyper·ven·ti·la·tion [,haɪpə,vɛntɪ'leɪʃən] N (*Med*) iperventilazione *f*.

hy·phen ['haɪfən] N trattino, lineetta.

hy·phen·ate ['haɪfə,neɪt] VT unire con un trattino.

hyp·no·sis [hɪp'nəʊsɪs] N ipnosi *f*.

hyp·not·ic [hɪp'nɒtɪk] ADJ ipnotico(-a).

hyp·no·tism ['hɪpnətɪzəm] N ipnotismo.

hyp·no·tist ['hɪpnətɪst] N ipnotizzatore(-trice).

hyp·no·tize ['hɪpnə,taɪz] VT ipnotizzare; **to hypnotize sb into doing sth** far fare qc a qn sotto ipnosi.

hypo·al·ler·gen·ic ['haɪpəʊ,ælə'dʒɛnɪk] ADJ anallergico(-a).

hypo·chon·dria [,haɪpəʊ'kɒndrɪə] N ipocondria.

hypo·chon·dri·ac [,haɪpəʊ'kɒndrɪæk] N ipocondriaco (-a).

hy·poc·ri·sy [hɪ'pɒkrɪsɪ] N ipocrisia.

hypo·crite ['hɪpəkrɪt] N ipocrita *m/f.*

hypo·criti·cal [,hɪpə'krɪtɪkəl] ADJ ipocrita.

hypo·criti·cal·ly [,hɪpə'krɪtɪkəlɪ] ADV ipocritamente, in modo ipocrita.

hypo·der·mic [,haɪpə'dɜːmɪk] [1] ADJ ipodermico(-a).

[2] N (*syringe*) siringa ipodermica.

hy·pot·enuse [haɪ'pɒtɪnjuːz] N (*Geom*) ipotenusa.

hypo·ther·mia [,haɪpəʊ'θɜːmɪə] N (*Med*) ipotermia.

hy·poth·esis [haɪ'pɒθɪsɪs] N (*pl* **hypotheses** [haɪ'pɒθɪsiːz]) ipotesi *f inv.*

hy·poth·esize [haɪ'pɒθɪ,saɪz] VI (*frm*) ipotizzare.

hypo·theti·cal [,haɪpəʊ'θɛtɪkəl] ADJ ipotetico(-a).

hypo·theti·cal·ly [,haɪpəʊ'θɛtɪkəlɪ] ADV ipoteticamente, per ipotesi.

hys·ter·ec·to·my [,hɪstə'rɛktəmɪ] N (*Med*) isterectomia.

hys·te·ria [hɪs'tɪərɪə] N (*gen*) isterismo; (*Psych*) isteria.

hys·teri·cal [hɪs'tɛrɪkəl] ADJ isterico(-a); **to become hysterical** avere una crisi isterica.

hys·teri·cal·ly [hɪs'tɛrɪkəlɪ] ADV istericamente; **it was hysterically funny** era buffo da morire.

hys·ter·ics [hɪs'tɛrɪks] NPL (*tears*) crisi *f inv* isterica; (*laughter*) attacco di riso; **to be in** *or* **have hysterics** avere una crisi isterica; (*fam: laugh*) crepar dal ridere.

Hz ABBR (= *herz*) Hz.

I

I, i [aɪ] N (letter) I, i f or m inv; **I for Isaac**, (Am) **I for Item** ≈ I come Imola.

I [aɪ] PERS PRON io; **I'll do it** lo faccio io; **he and I were at school together** io e lui eravamo a scuola insieme.

I. ABBR (= island, isle) I., Is.

IA ABBR (Am Post)= Iowa.

IAEA [ˌaɪeɪiː'eɪ] N ABBR (= International Atomic Energy Agency) A.I.E.A. f (= Agenzia Internazionale per l'Energia Atomica).

IATA [aɪ'ɑːtə] N ABBR (= International Air Transport Association) Associazione Internazionale per il Trasporto Aereo.

ib. ABBR = **ibid.**

IBA [ˌaɪbiː'eɪ] N ABBR (Brit: = Independent Broadcasting Authority) organo di controllo sulle reti televisive.

Iberian [aɪ'bɪərɪən] ADJ iberico(-a).

♦ **Iberian Peninsula** N: **the Iberian Peninsula** la penisola iberica.

IBEW [ˌaɪbiː'iː'dʌbljuː] N ABBR (Am: = International Brotherhood of Electrical Workers) associazione internazionale degli elettrotecnici.

ibex ['aɪbɛks] N (Zool) stambecco.

ibid. ['ɪbɪd] ABBR (= ibidem: from the same source) ibid.

i/c ABBR (Brit) = **in charge.**

Icarus ['ɪkərəs] N Icaro.

ICBM [ˌaɪsiːbiː'ɛm] N ABBR (= intercontinental ballistic missile) ICBM m inv.

ICC [ˌaɪsiː'siː] N ABBR **a** (= International Chamber of Commerce) C.C.I. f(= camera di commercio internazionale) **b** (Am: = Interstate Commerce Commission) commissione per il commercio tra gli stati degli USA.

ice [aɪs] **1** N **a** ghiaccio; (on road) ghiaccio, strato di ghiaccio; **to be as cold as ice** essere freddo(-a) come il ghiaccio, essere un pezzo di ghiaccio; **to break the ice** (fig) rompere il ghiaccio; **it cuts no ice with me** con me non attacca; **to keep sth on ice** (fig: plan, project) accantonare qc; **to skate on thin ice** (fig) essere sul filo del rasoio
b (ice cream) gelato; **strawberry ice** gelato alla fragola.
2 VT (cake) glassare

▶ **ice over, ice up** VI + ADV (river) gelarsi, ghiacciarsi; (windscreen, wings of plane) incrostarsi di ghiaccio.

♦ **Ice Age** N: **the Ice Age** l'era glaciale.

♦ **ice axe** N piccozza da ghiaccio.

ice·berg ['aɪsbɜːg] N iceberg m inv; **this is only the tip of the iceberg** (fig) questa è solo la punta dell'iceberg.

ice·bound ['aɪsˌbaʊnd] ADJ bloccato(-a) dal ghiaccio.

ice·box ['aɪsˌbɒks] N (Am: refrigerator) frigorifero; (Brit: freezer compartment) freezer m inv.

ice·breaker ['aɪsˌbreɪkə'] N rompighiaccio m inv; (fig: for group of students) gioco o esercizio fatto per rompere il ghiaccio all'inizio di una lezione.

♦ **ice bucket** N secchiello del ghiaccio.

ice·cap ['aɪsˌkæp] N calotta glaciale; **polar icecap** calotta polare.

♦ **ice-cold** [ˌaɪs'kəʊld] ADJ ghiacciato(-a), gelato(-a).

♦ **ice cream** N gelato.

♦ **ice-cream soda** ['aɪskriːm'səʊdə] N (Am) (gelato) affogato al seltz.

♦ **ice cube** N cubetto di ghiaccio.

iced [aɪst] ADJ **a** (drink) ghiacciato(-a); (coffee, tea) freddo (-a) **b** (cake) glassato(-a).

ice·fall ['aɪsˌfɔːl] N seraccata.

♦ **ice floe** N banco di ghiaccio, banchisa.

♦ **ice hammer** N martello-piccozza m inv.

♦ **ice hockey** N hockey m su ghiaccio.

Ice·land ['aɪslənd] N l'Islanda.

Ice·land·er ['aɪsləndə'] N islandese m/f.

Ice·land·ic [aɪs'lændɪk] **1** ADJ islandese.
2 N (language) islandese m.

♦ **ice lolly** N (Brit) ghiacciolo.

♦ **ice pack** N impacco di ghiaccio.

♦ **ice pick** N piccone m per ghiaccio.

♦ **ice rink** N pista di pattinaggio su ghiaccio.

♦ **ice sheet** N ghiacciaio continentale.

♦ **ice-skate** ['aɪsˌskeɪt] VI pattinare sul ghiaccio.

♦ **ice skate** N pattino da ghiaccio.

♦ **ice-skating** ['aɪsˌskeɪtɪŋ] N pattinaggio sul ghiaccio.

♦ **ice tray** N vaschetta per il ghiaccio.

ici·cle ['aɪsɪkl] N ghiacciolo.

ici·ly ['aɪsɪlɪ] ADV gelidamente.

ic·ing ['aɪsɪŋ] N a (on cake) glassa; vanilla icing glassa alla vaniglia b (Aer) patina di ghiaccio.

♦ icing sugar N zucchero a velo.

ICJ [ˌaɪsiːˈdʒeɪ] N ABBR = International Court of Justice.

icon ['aɪkɒn] N (also Comput) icona.

icono·clast [aɪˈkɒnəklæst] N (frm) iconoclasta m/f.

icono·clas·tic [aɪˌkɒnəˈklæstɪk] (frm) ADJ (opinions) iconoclastico(-a), iconoclasta; (person) iconoclasta.

ico·nog·ra·phy [ˌaɪkɒˈnɒɡrəfɪ] N iconografia.

ICR [ˌaɪsiːˈɑː] N ABBR (Am)= Institute for Cancer Research.

ICRC [ˌaɪsiːɑːˈsiː] N ABBR (= International Committee of the Red Cross) CICR m.

ic·tus ['ɪktəs] N ictus m inv.

ICU [ˌaɪsiːˈjuː] N ABBR = intensive care unit.

icy ['aɪsɪ] ADJ (comp -ier, superl -iest) (road, hand) ghiacciato(-a); (weather, temperature, stare) gelido(-a); it's icy cold si gela.

ID [ˌaɪˈdiː] ① N ABBR = identification.
② ABBR (Am Post)= Idaho.

id [ɪd] N (Psych) Id m, Es m.

I'd [aɪd] = I would, I had.

♦ ID card N = identity card.

IDD [ˌaɪdiːˈdiː] N ABBR (Brit Telec: = international direct dialling) teleselezione f internazionale.

idea [aɪˈdɪə] N idea; good idea! buon'idea!; that was a brilliant idea è stata un'idea splendida; she had no idea of the answer non aveva idea della risposta; to have an idea that ... aver l'impressione che...; I haven't the least or slightest or foggiest idea non ne ho la minima or la più pallida idea; it wouldn't be a bad idea to paint it non sarebbe una cattiva idea verniciarlo; to put ideas into sb's head mettere delle idee in testa a qn; it wasn't my idea non è stata un'idea mia, non sono io che ho avuto l'idea; if that's your idea of a joke ... se credi di essere spiritoso...; I've got the general idea mi sono fatto un'idea; that's the idea ecco, proprio così; what's the big idea? (fam) cosa credi di fare?; the idea is to sell it si tratta di venderlo.

ideal [aɪˈdɪəl] ADJ, N ideale (m).

ideal·ism [aɪˈdɪəˌlɪzəm] N idealismo.

ideal·ist [aɪˈdɪəlɪst] N idealista m/f.

ideal·is·tic [aɪˌdɪəˈlɪstɪk] ADJ (person) idealista; (views) idealistico(-a).

ideal·ize [aɪˈdɪəˌlaɪz] VT idealizzare.

ideal·ly [aɪˈdɪəlɪ] ADV perfettamente; it is ideally situated si trova in un posto ideale; they are an ideally matched couple sono una coppia ideale; ideally the book should have ... l'ideale sarebbe che il libro avesse... .

iden·ti·cal [aɪˈdentɪˌkəl] ADJ identico(-a).

iden·ti·cal·ly [aɪˈdentɪkəlɪ] ADV in modo identico.

♦ identical twins NPL gemelli(-e) monoovulari.

iden·ti·fi·able [aɪˈdentɪˌfaɪəbl] ADJ identificabile.

iden·ti·fi·ca·tion [aɪˌdentɪfɪˈkeɪʃən] N (recognition) identificazione f; (document) documento (di riconoscimento or di identità).

iden·ti·fy [aɪˈdentɪfaɪ] ① VT (recognize, specify) identificare, riconoscere; (point out) individuare; to identify o.s. with identificarsi con.
② VI: to identify with identificarsi con.

Iden·ti·kit® [aɪˈdentɪˌkɪt] N: Identikit (picture) identikit m inv.

iden·tity [aɪˈdentɪtɪ] N identità f inv; a case of mistaken identity uno scambio di persona.

♦ identity card N carta d'identità.

♦ identity disc N piastrina di riconoscimento.

♦ identity parade N (Brit) confronto all'americana.

ideo·gram ['ɪdɪəʊˌɡræm], ideo·graph [ˌɪdɪˈɒɡrəf] N ideogramma m.

ideo·logi·cal [ˌaɪdɪəˈlɒdʒɪkəl] ADJ ideologico(-a).

ideol·ogy [ˌaɪdɪˈɒlədʒɪ] N ideologia.

idio·cy ['ɪdɪəsɪ] N idiozia.

idi·om ['ɪdɪəm] N (phrase) locuzione f idiomatica; (style of expression) stile m.

idio·mat·ic [ˌɪdɪəˈmætɪk] ADJ idiomatico(-a).

idio·mati·cal·ly [ˌɪdɪəˈmætɪkəlɪ] ADV in modo idiomatico.

idio·syn·cra·sy [ˌɪdɪəˈsɪŋkrəsɪ] N (peculiarity, foible) (piccola) mania; (characteristic) particolarità f inv.

idio·syn·crat·ic [ˌɪdɪəsɪŋˈkrætɪk] ADJ particolare.

idi·ot ['ɪdɪət] N deficiente m/f, stupido(-a).

idi·ot·ic [ˌɪdɪˈɒtɪk] ADJ (person) idiota; (price, question) assurdo(-a).

idi·oti·cal·ly [ˌɪdɪˈɒtɪkəlɪ] ADV (stare) con aria da ebete; (behave) stupidamente, da idiota.

idle ['aɪdl] ① ADJ (comp -r, superl -st) a (lazy: student) pigro(-a), poltrone(-a); (inactive: machine, factory, workers) inattivo(-a); (unemployed: worker) disoccupato (-a); the idle rich i ricchi sfaccendati; in my idle moments nei miei momenti liberi; an idle life una vita d'ozio; to stand or lie idle (factory, machine) rimaner fermo(-a) or inattivo(-a)
b (fear, speculation) infondato(-a); (gossip, pleasures) futile; (question) ozioso(-a); (threat) campato(-a) in aria; out of idle curiosity per pura curiosità.
② VI (person) oziare; (engine) girare al minimo
▶ idle away VT + ADV (time) sprecare, buttar via.

idle·ness ['aɪdlnɪs] N pigrizia, ozio.

idler ['aɪdlə'] N fannullone(-a), sfaccendato(-a).

♦ idle time N (esp Comm) tempi mpl morti.

idly ['aɪdlɪ] ADV pigramente; he stood idly by, watching the others working è rimasto lì senza far niente a guardare gli altri che lavoravano.

idol ['aɪdl] N idolo.

idola·trous [aɪˈdɒlətrəs] ADJ (pej) idolatra.

idola·try [aɪˈdɒlətrɪ] N (old) idolatria.

idol·ize ['aɪdəˌlaɪz] VT idolatrare.

id·yll ['ɪdɪl] N idillio.

idyl·lic [ɪˈdɪlɪk] ADJ idilliaco(-a).

i.e. [ˌaɪˈiː] ABBR (= id est: that is) cioè.

if [ɪf] ① CONJ a se; if anyone comes in se viene or venisse qualcuno; I'll go if you come with me ci vado se vieni anche tu; I'd be pleased if you could do it sarei molto contento se potessi farlo; if necessary se (è) necessario; if I were you se fossi in te, io al tuo posto; if you ask me ... secondo me...
b (whenever) tutte le volte or ogni volta che, quando; if we are in Scotland, we always go to see her quando siamo in Scozia, andiamo sempre a trovarla
c (although): (even) if anche se + sub; I am determined to do it, (even) if it takes all week sono deciso a farlo, dovessi impiegarci tutta la settimana
d (whether) se; I don't know if he is here non so se c'è
e (in phrases): if so se è così; if not se no; if only se solo or soltanto; if only she were here se solo fosse qui; if only I could se soltanto potessi, magari (potessi); I would like to see her if only for a few minutes vorrei vederla magari or anche solo per pochi minuti; if only to show him my gratitude se non altro per esprimergli la mia gratitudine; as if come se; as if by chance come per caso; see also as, even etc.
② N: there are a lot of ifs and buts ci sono molti se e ma;

that's *or* it's a big if è un grosso punto interrogativo.

if·fy ['ɪfɪ] ADJ (*comp* -ier, *superl* -iest) (*fam*) incerto(-a).

ig·loo ['ɪgluː] N igloo *m inv*.

ig·ne·ous ['ɪgnɪəs] ADJ (*rock*) eruttivo(-a).

ig·nite [ɪg'naɪt] ☐ VT (*fire, match*) accendere; (*wood*) incendiare.

☐ VI accendersi.

ig·ni·tion [ɪg'nɪʃən] N (*Aut*) accensione *f*; (*Chem*) ignizione *f*; **to switch on/off the ignition** accendere/spegnere il motore.

♦ **ignition key** N (*Aut*) chiave *f* dell'accensione.

♦ **ignition switch** N (*Aut*) interruttore *m* dell'accensione.

ig·no·ble [ɪg'nəʊbl] ADJ ignobile.

ig·no·mini·ous [ˌɪgnə'mɪnɪəs] ADJ vergognoso(-a), ignominioso(-a).

ig·no·mini·ous·ly [ˌɪgnə'mɪnɪəslɪ] ADV vergognosamente, in modo ignominioso.

ig·no·miny ['ɪgnəˌmɪnɪ] N (*frm*) ignominia.

ig·no·ra·mus [ˌɪgnə'reɪməs] N ignorante *m/f*.

ig·no·rance ['ɪgnərəns] N: **ignorance (of)** ignoranza (di); **to keep sb in ignorance of sth** tenere qn all'oscuro di qc; **to show one's ignorance** dimostrare la propria ignoranza; **it's no use pleading ignorance of the law** la legge non ammette ignoranza.

ig·no·rant ['ɪgnərənt] ADJ (*lacking education*) ignorante; **to be ignorant of** (*fact, situation, subject*) ignorare; (*events*) essere all'oscuro di.

ig·no·rant·ly ['ɪgnərəntlɪ] ADV per ignoranza.

ig·nore [ɪg'nɔː'] VT (*person*) ignorare; (*problem, fact*) trascurare; (*remark*) non far caso a; (*advice, letter*) non tener in nessun conto; (*danger*) non curarsi di; (*sb's behaviour*) chiudere un occhio su.

igua·na [ɪ'gwɑːnə] N iguana.

ikon ['aɪkɒn] N = **icon**.

IL ABBR (*Am Post*)= *Illinois*.

ILEA ['ɪlɪə] N ABBR (*Brit*: = *Inner London Education Authority*) *nel passato, provveditorato agli studi della zona centrale di Londra*.

il·eum ['ɪlɪəm] N ileo (*intestino*).

ilk [ɪlk] N: **of that ilk** di quel genere.

ill [ɪl] ☐ ADJ (*comp* **worse**, *superl* **worst**) **a** (*sick*) ammalato (-a), malato(-a); **to fall** *or* **be taken ill** ammalarsi; **to feel ill (with)** star male (per *or* a causa di); **to be in ill health** essere malaticcio(-a); **she is seriously ill in hospital** è ricoverata in gravi condizioni all'ospedale

b (*bad*) cattivo(-a); **ill fortune** *or* **ill luck** sfortuna, scalogna; **ill effects** brutte conseguenze *fpl*; **to be in an ill humour** *or* **temper** essere di cattivo umore; **it's an ill wind that blows nobody any good** (*Proverb*) non tutto il male viene per nuocere.

☐ ADV male; **we can ill afford to lose him/to buy it** non possiamo certo permetterci di perderlo/di comprarlo; **to speak/think ill of sb** parlar/pensar male di qn.

☐: **ills** NPL (*old frm*) mali *mpl*, malanni *mpl*.

I'll [aɪl] = **I will, I shall**.

♦ **ill-advised** [ˌɪləd'vaɪzd] ADJ (*plan, remark, decision, person*) sconsiderato(-a), avventato(-a); see also **advise**.

♦ **ill-assorted** [ˌɪlə'sɔːtɪd] ADJ mal assortito(-a).

♦ **ill at ease** ADJ a disagio.

♦ **ill-bred** [ˌɪl'bred] ADJ maleducato(-a).

♦ **ill-considered** [ˌɪlkən'sɪdəd] ADJ (*plan*) avventato(-a).

♦ **ill-disposed** [ˌɪldɪs'pəʊzd] ADJ: **to be ill-disposed towards sb/sth** essere maldisposto(-a) verso qn/qc *or* nei riguardi di qn/qc.

il·legal [ɪ'liːgəl] ADJ illegale.

il·legal·ity [ˌɪliː'gælɪtɪ] N illegalità.

il·legal·ly [ɪ'liːgəlɪ] ADV illegalmente.

il·leg·ible [ɪ'ledʒəbl] ADJ illeggibile.

il·leg·ibly [ɪ'ledʒəblɪ] ADV in modo illeggibile.

il·legiti·ma·cy [ˌɪlɪ'dʒɪtɪməsɪ] N illegittimità.

il·legiti·mate [ˌɪlɪ'dʒɪtɪmɪt] ADJ illegittimo(-a).

il·legiti·mate·ly [ˌɪlɪ'dʒɪtɪmɪtlɪ] ADV illegittimamente.

♦ **ill-equipped** [ɪlɪ'kwɪpt] ADJ (*lacking necessary qualities*) impreparato(-a); (*lacking equipment*) mal equipaggiato (-a); **they were ill-equipped for the part** non avevano i requisiti necessari per la parte.

♦ **ill-fated** [ˌɪl'feɪtɪd] ADJ (*person*) sventurato(-a); (*enterprise*) sfortunato(-a).

♦ **ill-favoured**, (*Am*) **ill-favored** [ˌɪl'feɪvəd] ADJ (*ugly*) sgraziato(-a), brutto(-a); (*objectionable*) sgradevole.

♦ **ill feeling** N rancore *m*.

♦ **ill-founded** [ɪl'faʊndɪd] ADJ (*gossip*) infondato(-a); (*argument*) senza fondamento.

♦ **ill-gotten** ['ɪl,gɒtn] ADJ (*frm*): **ill-gotten gains** guadagni *mpl* illeciti.

♦ **ill health** N problemi *mpl* di salute.

il·lib·er·al [ɪ'lɪbərəl] ADJ illiberale.

il·lic·it [ɪ'lɪsɪt] ADJ illecito(-a).

il·lic·it·ly [ɪ'lɪsɪtlɪ] ADV illecitamente.

♦ **ill-informed** [ˌɪlɪn'fɔːmd] ADJ (*person*) male informato (-a); (*comment, criticism*) che rivela ignoranza.

il·lit·era·cy [ɪ'lɪtərəsɪ] N analfabetismo.

il·lit·er·ate [ɪ'lɪtərɪt] ☐ ADJ (*person*) analfabeta, illetterato (-a); (*letter*) sgrammaticato(-a).

☐ N analfabeta *m/f*, illetterato(-a).

♦ **ill-judged** [ˌɪl'dʒʌdʒd] ADJ (*remark*) inopportuno(-a).

♦ **ill-mannered** [ˌɪl'mænəd] ADJ maleducato(-a), sgarbato(-a).

♦ **ill-natured** [ˌɪl'neɪtʃəd] ADJ d'indole cattiva.

ill·ness ['ɪlnɪs] N malattia.

il·logi·cal [ɪ'lɒdʒɪkəl] ADJ illogico(-a).

il·logi·cal·ity [ɪ'lɒdʒɪ'kælɪtɪ] N illogicità *f inv*.

il·logi·cal·ly [ɪ'lɒdʒɪkəlɪ] ADV illogicamente.

♦ **ill-omened** [ɪl'əʊmənd] ADJ nefasto(-a).

♦ **ill-starred** [ɪl'stɑːd] ADJ (*liter, person*) nato(-a) sotto una cattiva stella; (*day*) sfortunato(-a). ·

♦ **ill-suited** [ˌɪl'suːtɪd] ADJ (*couple*) mal assortito(-a); **he is ill-suited to the job** è inadatto a quel lavoro.

♦ **ill-timed** [ˌɪl'taɪmd] ADJ intempestivo(-a), inopportuno (-a).

♦ **ill-treat** [ˌɪl'triːt] VT maltrattare.

♦ **ill-treatment** [ˌɪl'triːtmənt] N maltrattamenti *mpl*.

il·lu·mi·nate [ɪ'luːmɪˌneɪt] VT (*light up*) illuminare; (*fig: problem, question*) chiarire.

il·lu·mi·nat·ed [ɪ'luːmɪˌneɪtɪd] ADJ **a** (*sign, advertising*) luminoso(-a) **b** (*manuscript*) miniato(-a).

il·lu·mi·nat·ing [ɪ'luːmɪˌneɪtɪŋ] ADJ (*comments, remark*) chiarificatore(-trice); (*experience, book*) istruttivo(-a).

il·lu·mi·na·tion [ɪ,luːmɪ'neɪʃən] N **a** (*lighting*) illuminazione *f* **b** (*of manuscript*) miniatura **c**: **illuminations** NPL (*coloured lights*) luminarie *fpl*.

il·lu·sion [ɪ'luːʒən] N illusione *f*; **to be under an illusion** illudersi; **to be under the illusion that** illudersi che; **to have no illusions** non farsi illusioni.

il·lu·sive [ɪ'luːsɪv], **il·lu·sory** [ɪ'luːsərɪ] ADJ illusorio(-a).

il·lus·trate ['ɪləˌstreɪt] VT illustrare.

il·lus·tra·tion [ˌɪləs'treɪʃən] N illustrazione *f*; (*example*) esemplificazione *f*; **by way of illustration** a titolo d'esempio.

il·lus·tra·tive ['ɪləstrətɪv] ADJ illustrativo(-a).

il·lus·tra·tor ['ɪləs‚treɪtəʳ] N illustratore(-trice).

il·lus·tri·ous [ɪ'lʌstrɪəs] ADJ illustre.

♦ **ill will** N rancore *m*; **I bear you no ill will** non ti serbo rancore.

ILO [‚aɪɛl'əʊ] N ABBR (= *International Labour Organization*) O.I.L. *f* (= *Organizzazione Internazionale del Lavoro*).

I'm [aɪm] = **I am.**

im·age ['ɪmɪdʒ] N (*of person, group, organization*) immagine *f*; **to be the very** *or* **the spitting image of sb** essere il ritratto sputato di qn; **she's the image of her mother** è il ritratto di sua madre; **mirror image** immagine speculare; **she has to think of her image** deve pensare alla sua immagine.

im·age·ry ['ɪmɪdʒərɪ] N (*Art, Literature*) immagini *fpl*; (*Psych*) immaginario.

im·agi·nable [ɪ'mædʒɪnəbl] ADJ immaginabile, che si possa immaginare.

im·agi·nary [ɪ'mædʒɪnərɪ] ADJ immaginario(-a).

im·agi·na·tion [ɪ‚mædʒɪ'neɪʃən] N immaginazione *f*; (*inventiveness*) immaginazione, fantasia; **it's all imagination!** sono tutte fantasie!; **it's all in your imagination** è tutto frutto della tua immaginazione; **to have a vivid imagination** avere una fervida fantasia *or* una viva immaginazione; **she lets her imagination run away with her** si lascia trasportare dalla fantasia; **use your imagination!** su, un po' di fantasia!

im·agi·na·tive [ɪ'mædʒɪnətɪv] ADJ fantasioso(-a), immaginoso(-a).

im·agi·na·tive·ly [ɪ'mædʒɪnətɪvlɪ] ADV con fantasia *or* immaginazione.

im·ag·ine [ɪ'mædʒɪn] VT **a** (*visualize*) immaginare, immaginarsi; **just imagine!** pensa un po'!; **you can imagine how I felt** puoi immaginare *or* immaginarti come mi sono sentito; **you are just imagining things** che idee!, è tutto frutto della tua immaginazione **b** (*suppose, think*) immaginare, credere; **I never imagined that he would be there** non avrei mai immaginato che lui sarebbe stato lì.

im·ag·in·ings [ɪ'mædʒɪnɪŋs] N (*liter*) fantasie *fpl*.

im·bal·ance [ɪm'bæləns] N squilibrio.

im·becile ['ɪmbəsi:l] N ebete *m/f*, imbecille *m/f*.

im·becil·ity [‚ɪmbɪ'sɪlɪtɪ] N imbecillità.

im·bibe [ɪm'baɪb] VT (*frm also hum: drink*) bere; (*fig: absorb*) assorbire, assimilare.

im·bue [ɪm'bju:] VT (*frm*): **to imbue sth with** impregnare qc di.

IMF [‚aɪɛm'ɛf] N ABBR = **International Monetary Fund.**

imi·tate ['ɪmɪ‚teɪt] VT imitare.

imi·ta·tion [‚ɪmɪ'teɪʃən] **1** N imitazione *f*; **in imitation of** a imitazione di; **a painting in imitation of the famous work by Picasso** un dipinto che riproduce la famosa opera di Picasso. **2** ADJ finto(-a).

♦ **imitation jewels** NPL gioielli *mpl* falsi.

imi·ta·tive ['ɪmɪtətɪv] ADJ imitativo(-a).

imi·ta·tor ['ɪmɪ‚teɪtəʳ] N imitatore(-trice).

im·macu·late [ɪ'mækjʊlɪt] ADJ (*spotless*) immacolato(-a); (*flawless*) impeccabile.

♦ **Immaculate Conception** N: **the Immaculate Conception** (*Rel*) l'Immacolata Concezione *f*.

im·macu·late·ly [ɪ'mækjʊlɪtlɪ] ADV impeccabilmente.

im·ma·terial [‚ɪmə'tɪərɪəl] ADJ irrilevante, insignificante; **it is immaterial whether** poco importa se *or* che + *sub*; **that's quite immaterial to me** questo non ha alcuna importanza per me.

im·ma·ture [‚ɪmə'tjʊəʳ] ADJ immaturo(-a).

im·ma·tu·rity [‚ɪmə'tjʊərɪtɪ] N immaturità.

im·meas·ur·able [ɪ'mɛʒərəbl] ADJ incommensurabile.

im·meas·ur·ably [ɪ'mɛʒərəblɪ] ADV incommensurabilmente.

im·media·cy [ɪ'mi:dɪəsɪ] N immediatezza.

im·medi·ate [ɪ'mi:dɪət] ADJ (*decision, answer, reaction*) immediato(-a); (*need, problem*) impellente, immediato (-a); (*neighbour*) della casa accanto; **in the immediate area** nelle immediate vicinanze; **in the immediate future** nell'immediato futuro; **to take immediate action** prendere immediati provvedimenti.

im·medi·ate·ly [ɪ'mi:dɪətlɪ] **1** ADV **a** (*at once: reply, come, agree*) immediatamente **b** (*directly: affect, concern*) direttamente; **immediately in front of sb/sth** proprio davanti a qn/qc. **2** CONJ (non) appena.

im·memo·ri·al [‚ɪmɪ'mɔːrɪəl] ADJ remotissimo(-a); **from time immemorial** da tempo immemorabile.

im·mense [ɪ'mɛns] ADJ (*distance*) smisurato(-a); (*size, difference*) enorme; (*enjoyment*) immenso(-a).

im·mense·ly [ɪ'mɛnslɪ] ADV (*differ*) enormemente; (*difficult, rich*) estremamente; (*like, enjoy*) immensamente.

im·men·si·ty [ɪ'mɛnsɪtɪ] N (*of size, difference, problem*) vastità; (*of space*) immensità.

im·merse [ɪ'mɜːs] VT: **to immerse sth in water** immergere qc nell'acqua; **immersed in sth** (*fig*) immerso(-a) *or* assorto(-a) in qc; **to immerse o.s. in sth** (*fig*) buttarsi anima e corpo in qc.

im·mer·sion [ɪ'mɜːʃən] N immersione *f*.

♦ **immersion heater** N (*Brit*) scaldabagno elettrico.

im·mi·grant ['ɪmɪgrənt] ADJ, N (*newly arrived*) immigrante (*m/f*); (*already established*) immigrato(-a).

im·mi·grate ['ɪmɪ‚greɪt] VI immigrare.

im·mi·gra·tion [‚ɪmɪ'greɪʃən] N immigrazione *f*.

♦ **immigration authorities** NPL ufficio *m* stranieri *inv*.

♦ **immigration laws** NPL leggi *fpl* relative all'immigrazione.

im·mi·nence ['ɪmɪnəns] N imminenza.

im·mi·nent ['ɪmɪnənt] ADJ imminente.

im·mis·cible [ɪ'mɪsɪbəl] ADJ (*frm*) immiscibile.

im·mo·bile [ɪ'məʊbaɪl] ADJ immobile.

im·mo·bil·ity [‚ɪməʊ'bɪlɪtɪ] N immobilità.

im·mo·bi·lize [ɪ'məʊbɪ‚laɪz] VT immobilizzare.

im·mo·der·ate [ɪ'mɒdərɪt] ADJ (*person*) smodato(-a), sregolato(-a); (*opinion, reaction, demand*) eccessivo(-a).

im·mod·est [ɪ'mɒdɪst] ADJ (*indecent*) indecente; (*boastful*) immodesto(-a).

im·mod·est·ly [ɪ'mɒdɪstlɪ] ADV (*see adj*) indecentemente; immodestamente.

im·mod·es·ty [ɪ'mɒdɪstɪ] N (*see adj*) indecenza; immodestia.

im·mor·al [ɪ'mɒrəl] ADJ immorale.

im·mo·ral·ity [ɪ'mɒrælɪtɪ] N immoralità.

im·mor·al·ly [ɪ'mɒrəlɪ] ADV immoralmente.

im·mor·tal [ɪ'mɔːtl] ADJ, N immortale (*m/f*).

im·mor·tal·ity [‚ɪmɔː'tælɪtɪ] N immortalità.

im·mor·tal·ize [ɪ'mɔːtə‚laɪz] VT immortalare.

im·mov·able [ɪ'muːvəbl] ADJ (*object*) non movibile; (*person*) irremovibile.

im·mune [ɪ'mjuːn] ADJ: **immune (to, against)** (*naturally*) immune (da); (*after injection*) immunizzato(-a) (contro); **immune (from)** (*fig*) immune (a).

♦ **immune system** N sistema *m* immunitario.

im·mu·nity [ɪ'mjuːnɪtɪ] N (*also fig*) immunità; **diplomatic**

immunity immunità diplomatica.

im·mu·ni·za·tion [ˌɪmjʊnaɪˈzeɪʃən] N immunizzazione f.

im·mu·nize [ˈɪmjʊˌnaɪz] VT immunizzare.

im·mu·no·thera·py [ˌɪmjʊnəʊˈθɛrəpɪ] N immunoterapia.

im·mu·table [ɪˈmjuːtəbl] ADJ (frm) immutabile.

im·mu·tably [ɪˈmjuːtəblɪ] ADV (frm) immutabilmente.

imp [ɪmp] N (small devil) folletto; (child) diavoletto.

im·pact [n ˈɪmpækt; vb ɪmˈpækt] **1** N (force of collision) impatto, (forza d') urto; (fig: effect) effetto; **on impact** nell'urto, nell'impatto; **the book made a great impact on me/the public** il libro ha prodotto una forte impressione su di me/sul pubblico.
2 VT (drive) conficcare.
3 VI (fig: influence): **to impact on** influire su.

im·pact·ed [ɪmˈpæktɪd] ADJ: **an impacted tooth** un dente incluso.

im·pair [ɪmˈpɛəʳ] VT (health) danneggiare, pregiudicare; (sight, hearing) deteriorare, menomare; (visibility) ridurre; (relations) deteriorare.

im·paired [ɪmˈpɛəd] ADJ (faculties, hearing) deteriorato (-a), indebolito(-a); **visually impaired** videoleso(-a).

im·pa·la [ɪmˈpɑːlə] N impala m inv.

im·pale [ɪmˈpeɪl] VT impalare.

im·part [ɪmˈpɑːt] VT (frm) **a** (make known) comunicare **b** (bestow) impartire.

im·par·tial [ɪmˈpɑːʃəl] ADJ imparziale.

im·par·ti·al·ity [ɪmˌpɑːʃɪˈælɪtɪ] N imparzialità.

im·par·tial·ly [ɪmˈpɑːʃəlɪ] ADV con imparzialità.

im·pass·able [ɪmˈpɑːsəbl] ADJ (road, mountain pass) intransitabile, impraticabile; (barrier) insuperabile; (river) non attraversabile.

im·passe [æmˈpɑːs] N impasse f inv.

im·pas·sioned [ɪmˈpæʃnd] ADJ appassionato(-a).

im·pas·sive [ɪmˈpæsɪv] ADJ impassibile.

im·pa·tience [ɪmˈpeɪʃəns] N impazienza; **impatience (with sb/to do sth)** impazienza (nei confronti di qn/di fare qc).

im·pa·tient [ɪmˈpeɪʃənt] ADJ (eager) impaziente; (irascible) insofferente; **to get** or **grow impatient (with sb/over sth)** perdere la pazienza (con qn/per qc); **impatient to do sth** impaziente di fare qc.

im·pa·tient·ly [ɪmˈpeɪʃəntlɪ] ADV con impazienza.

im·peach [ɪmˈpiːtʃ] VT **a** (esp Am: prosecute: public official) mettere in stato d'accusa **b** (challenge: character, motive) mettere in dubbio.

im·peach·ment [ɪmˈpiːtʃmənt] N (Law) impeachment m inv.

im·pec·cable [ɪmˈpɛkəbl] ADJ impeccabile.

im·pec·cably [ɪmˈpɛkəblɪ] ADV impeccabilmente.

im·pecu·ni·ous [ˌɪmpɪˈkjuːnɪəs] ADJ (frm) indigente.

im·pede [ɪmˈpiːd] VT ostacolare.

im·pedi·ment [ɪmˈpɛdɪmənt] N **a** (obstacle) ostacolo **b** (Law) impedimento **c** (Med) difetto; **speech impediment** difetto di pronuncia.

im·pedi·men·ta [ɪmˌpɛdɪˈmɛntə] N (frm) impedimenti mpl.

im·pel [ɪmˈpɛl] VT (force): **to impel sb (to do sth)** costringere or obbligare qn (a fare qc); (drive) spingere qn (a fare qc).

im·pend·ing [ɪmˈpɛndɪŋ] ADJ (birth, storm, retirement) imminente; (doom, disaster) incombente.

im·pen·etrable [ɪmˈpɛnɪtrəbl] ADJ (jungle) impenetrabile; (fortress) inespugnabile; (fig) incomprensibile.

im·pen·etrably [ɪmˈpɛnɪtrəblɪ] ADV impenetrabilmente.

im·peni·tent [ɪmˈpɛnɪtənt] ADJ non pentito(-a); **she was quite impenitent about it** non ne era affatto pentita.

im·peni·tent·ly [ɪmˈpɛnɪtəntlɪ] ADV senza pentirsi.

im·pera·tive [ɪmˈpɛrətɪv] **1** ADJ **a** (essential) essenziale; **it is imperative that he comes** è indispensabile che lui venga **b** (authoritative: manner, voice) imperioso(-a); (Gram) imperativo(-a).
2 N (Gram) imperativo; **in the imperative** all'imperativo.

im·per·cep·tible [ˌɪmpəˈsɛptəbl] ADJ impercettibile.

im·per·cep·tibly [ˌɪmpəˈsɛptəblɪ] ADV impercettibilmente.

im·per·fect [ɪmˈpɜːfɪkt] **1** ADJ **a** (gen) difettoso(-a) **b** (Gram) imperfetto(-a).
2 N (Gram: also: imperfect tense) imperfetto; **in the imperfect** all'imperfetto.

im·per·fec·tion [ˌɪmpəˈfɛkʃən] N (poor quality) imperfezione f; (flaw) difetto, imperfezione.

im·per·fect·ly [ɪmˈpɜːfɪktlɪ] ADV in modo imperfetto; **an imperfectly produced copy** una copia imperfetta.

im·perial [ɪmˈpɪərɪəl] ADJ (gen) imperiale; (imperious) imperioso(-a); (Brit: weights, measures) misurato secondo un sistema non metrico.

im·peri·al·ism [ɪmˈpɪərɪəˌlɪzəm] N imperialismo.

im·peri·al·ist [ɪmˈpɪərɪəlɪst] ADJ, N imperialista (m/f).

im·per·il [ɪmˈpɛrɪl] VT (frm) mettere in pericolo.

im·peri·ous [ɪmˈpɪərɪəs] ADJ imperioso(-a).

im·peri·ous·ly [ɪmˈpɪərɪəslɪ] ADV imperiosamente.

im·per·ma·nent [ɪmˈpɜːmənənt] ADJ transitorio(-a).

im·per·meable [ɪmˈpɜːmɪəbl] ADJ (frm) impermeabile.

im·per·son·al [ɪmˈpɜːsnl] ADJ **a** (manner, treatment) impersonale, distaccato(-a) **b** (Gram) impersonale.

im·per·son·al·ly [ɪmˈpɜːsnlɪ] ADV impersonalmente.

im·per·son·ate [ɪmˈpɜːsəˌneɪt] VT (person) fingersi; (Theatre) imitare.

im·per·sona·tion [ɪmˌpɜːsəˈneɪʃən] N (gen, Theatre) imitazione f; (fraudulent) usurpazione f d'identità.

im·per·sona·tor [ɪmˈpɜːsəˌneɪtəʳ] N (gen, Theatre) imitatore(-trice).

im·per·ti·nence [ɪmˈpɜːtɪnəns] N impertinenza.

im·per·ti·nent [ɪmˈpɜːtɪnənt] ADJ: **impertinent (to)** impertinente (con or nei confronti di).

im·per·ti·nent·ly [ɪmˈpɜːtɪnəntlɪ] ADV con impertinenza.

im·per·turb·able [ˌɪmpəˈtɜːbəbl] ADJ imperturbabile.

im·per·turb·ably [ˌɪmpəˈtɜːbəblɪ] ADV imperturbabilmente.

im·per·vi·ous [ɪmˈpɜːvɪəs] ADJ: **impervious (to)** impermeabile (a); (fig) indifferente (a), imperturbato(-a) (di fronte a).

im·peti·go [ˌɪmpɪˈtaɪgəʊ] N (Med) impetigine f.

im·petu·os·ity [ɪmˌpɛtʊˈɒsɪtɪ] N impetuosità.

im·petu·ous [ɪmˈpɛtjʊəs] ADJ impetuoso(-a).

im·petu·ous·ly [ɪmˈpɛtjʊəslɪ] ADV impetuosamente.

im·petus [ˈɪmpɪtəs] N (force) spinta, impeto; (fig) impulso.

im·pi·ety [ɪmˈpaɪətɪ] N (frm) empietà.

im·pinge [ɪmˈpɪndʒ] VI: **to impinge on** (person, situation) influire su; (freedom, independence) violare; (rights) ledere.

im·pi·ous [ˈɪmpɪəs] ADJ (frm) empio(-a).

imp·ish [ˈɪmpɪʃ] ADJ malizioso(-a), birichino(-a).

im·plac·able [ɪmˈplækəbl] ADJ implacabile.

im·plac·ably [ɪmˈplækəblɪ] ADV implacabilmente.

im·plant [vb ɪmˈplɑːnt; n ˈɪmplɑːnt] **1** VT (Med) innestare; (fig: idea, principle) inculcare.
2 N (Med) innesto.

im·plan·ta·tion [ˌɪmplɑːnˈteɪʃən] N (Med) innesto.

im·plau·sible [ɪmˈplɔːzəbl] ADJ poco plausibile.

im·ple·ment [vb 'ɪmplɪˌmɛnt; n 'ɪmplɪmənt] ⬚1⬚ VT (decision, plan, idea) attuare; (law) applicare.
⬚2⬚ N (for cooking) utensile m; (for garden, farm) attrezzo.

im·pli·cate ['ɪmplɪˌkeɪt] VT: **to implicate sb in sth** implicare qn in qc.

im·pli·ca·tion [ˌɪmplɪ'keɪʃən] N **a** (hint, suggestion) insinuazione f; **the implication of your remark is that ...** la tua osservazione implica che...; **by implication** implicitamente
b (in crime, scandal) implicazione f
c : **implications** NPL (repercussions) conseguenze fpl, ripercussioni fpl; **this event had serious implications for industry** quest'avvenimento ebbe (delle) importanti conseguenze per l'industria; **we must study all the implications** dobbiamo considerare tutte le (possibili) conseguenze.

im·plic·it [ɪm'plɪsɪt] ADJ **a** (implied: threat) implicito(-a); (: agreement) tacito(-a) **b** (unquestioning: faith, belief) assoluto(-a).

im·plic·it·ly [ɪm'plɪsɪtlɪ] ADV **a** (agree) tacitamente; (condone) implicitamente **b** (believe) senza riserve.

im·plore [ɪm'plɔː] VT: **to implore sb (to do sth)** implorare qn (di fare qc); **to implore sb's forgiveness** implorare il perdono di qn.

im·plor·ing [ɪm'plɔːrɪŋ] ADJ implorante.

im·plor·ing·ly [ɪm'plɔːrɪŋlɪ] ADV in modo implorante.

im·ply [ɪm'plaɪ] VT (hint, suggest) insinuare; (indicate) implicare; **it implies a lot of work** implica un sacco di lavoro.

im·po·lite [ˌɪmpə'laɪt] ADJ (person, remark) maleducato (-a).

im·po·lite·ly [ˌɪmpə'laɪtlɪ] ADV maleducatamente.

im·po·lite·ness [ˌɪmpə'laɪtnɪs] N (of person, remark) maleducazione f.

im·poli·tic [ɪm'pɒlɪtɪk] ADJ (frm) impolitico(-a).

im·pon·der·able [ɪm'pɒndərəbl] ADJ imponderabile.

im·port [n 'ɪmpɔːt; vb ɪm'pɔːt] ⬚1⬚ N **a** (Comm: article) articolo importato; (: importation) importazione f; **import-export** import-export m inv
b (frm: significance) significato.
⬚2⬚ VT importare.
⬚3⬚ ADJ (duty, licence) d'importazione.

im·por·tance [ɪm'pɔːtəns] N importanza; **to attach great importance to sth** dare or attribuire molta importanza a qc; **to be of great/little importance** essere molto/poco importante.

im·por·tant [ɪm'pɔːtənt] ADJ importante; **it's not important** non ha importanza; **it is important that** è importante che + sub; **to try to look important** (pej) darsi arie d'importanza.

im·por·tant·ly [ɪm'pɔːtəntlɪ] ADV significativamente; (pej) con (aria d')importanza; **but, more importantly, ...** ma, quel che più conta or importa,... .

im·por·ta·tion [ˌɪmpɔː'teɪʃən] N importazione f.

im·port·ed [ɪm'pɔːtɪd] ADJ importato(-a).

im·port·er [ɪm'pɔːtə'] N importatore(-trice).

im·por·tu·nate [ɪm'pɔːtjʊnɪt] ADJ (frm) importuno(-a).

im·por·tune [ˌɪmpɔː'tjuːn] VT (frm) importunare.

im·por·tun·ity [ˌɪmpɔː'tjuːnɪtɪ] N (frm) insistenza fpl.

im·pose [ɪm'pəʊz] VT (conditions, fine, tax): **to impose (sth on sb)** imporre (qc a qn)
► **impose (up)on** VI + PREP (person) approfittare di.

im·pos·ing [ɪm'pəʊzɪŋ] ADJ imponente.

im·po·si·tion [ˌɪmpə'zɪʃən] N (of tax, fine, punishment) imposizione f; **it's a bit of an imposition** è pretendere un po' troppo; **to be an imposition on** (person) abusare della gentilezza di.

im·pos·sibil·ity [ɪmˌpɒsə'bɪlɪtɪ] N: **impossibility (of sth/of doing sth)** impossibilità (di qc/di fare qc).

im·pos·sible [ɪm'pɒsəbl] ADJ **a** (task, enterprise, situation) impossibile; **it is impossible for me to leave now** mi è impossibile andar via adesso; **it is impossible/not impossible for her to do that** le è impossibile/non le è impossibile farlo; **to make it impossible for sb to do sth** mettere qn nell'impossibilità di fare qc; **to do the impossible** fare l'impossibile
b (fam: child, person: difficult, intolerable) impossibile, insopportabile.

im·pos·sibly [ɪm'pɒsəblɪ] ADV (extremely: late, early, difficult) incredibilmente; (intolerably: behave, act) insopportabilmente.

im·pos·tor [ɪm'pɒstə'] N impostore(-trice).

im·pos·ture [ɪm'pɒstʃə'] N (frm) impostura.

im·po·tence ['ɪmpətəns] N (frm, Med) impotenza.

im·po·tent ['ɪmpətənt] ADJ (frm, Med) impotente.

im·pound [ɪm'paʊnd] VT (gen) sequestrare, confiscare; (stray animal) rinchiudere.

im·pov·er·ished [ɪm'pɒvərɪʃt] ADJ impoverito(-a).

im·pov·er·ish·ment [ɪm'pɒvərɪʃmənt] N impoverimento.

im·prac·ti·cabil·ity [ɪmˌpræktɪkə'bɪlɪtɪ] N inattuabilità.

im·prac·ti·cable [ɪm'præktɪkəbl] ADJ inattuabile.

im·prac·ti·cal [ɪm'præktɪkəl] ADJ (person) privo(-a) di senso pratico; (plan) poco realistico(-a), poco pratico (-a).

im·prac·ti·cal·ity [ɪmˌpræktɪ'kælɪtɪ] N (of person) mancanza di praticità; (of plan) poca praticità.

im·pre·ca·tion [ˌɪmprɪ'keɪʃən] N (frm) imprecazione f.

im·pre·cise [ˌɪmprɪ'saɪs] ADJ impreciso(-a).

im·pre·ci·sion [ˌɪmprɪ'sɪʒən] N imprecisione f.

im·preg·nable [ɪm'prɛgnəbl] ADJ (fortress, defences) inespugnabile; (fig: person, group) inattaccabile.

im·preg·nate ['ɪmprɛgˌneɪt] VT (fertilize) fecondare; (saturate): **to impregnate (with)** impregnare (di).

im·pre·sa·rio [ˌɪmprɛ'sɑːrɪəʊ] N impresario(-a).

im·press [ɪm'prɛs] VT **a** (make good impression on) fare una buona impressione a or su, colpire favorevolmente; **how did she impress you?** che impressione ti ha fatto?; **he impressed me quite favourably** mi ha fatto un'impressione abbastanza buona; **I'm not impressed** non ne sono rimasto colpito
b (mark, stamp) imprimere; **to impress sth on sb** (fig) far comprendere qc a qn.

im·pres·sion [ɪm'prɛʃən] N **a** (most senses) impressione f; **to be under** or **have the impression that** avere l'impressione che; **he gives the impression of knowing a lot about it** dà l'impressione di saperne molto; **to make a good/bad impression on sb** fare una buona/cattiva impressione a or su qn; **my words made no impression on him** le mie parole non hanno avuto nessun effetto su di lui
b (imitation) imitazione f; **to do impressions** fare delle imitazioni.

im·pres·sion·able [ɪm'prɛʃnəbl] ADJ (person) impressionabile; **to be at an impressionable age** essere nell'età in cui si è facilmente influenzabili.

im·pres·sion·ism [ɪm'prɛʃəˌnɪzəm] N (Art) impressionismo.

im·pres·sion·ist [ɪm'prɛʃənɪst] ADJ, N (Art) impressionista (m/f); (mimic) imitatore(-trice).

im·pres·sion·is·tic [ɪmˌprɛʃə'nɪstɪk] ADJ (account, story)

approssimativo(-a); (*Art*) impressionista, impressioni-
stico(-a).

im·pres·sive [ɪm'presɪv] ADJ (*person, achievement*) notevole; (*occasion, event*) di notevole imponenza; (*building*)
imponente.

im·pres·sive·ly [ɪm'presɪvlɪ] ADV (*tall, rich, bright*) straordinariamente; (*displayed, organized*) in modo imponente.

im·print [*n* 'ɪmprɪnt; *vb* ɪm'prɪnt] ① N (*Publishing*) sigla
editoriale. ② VT imprimere.

im·print·ed [ɪm'prɪntɪd] ADJ: **imprinted on** impresso(-a)
in.

im·pris·on [ɪm'prɪzn] VT incarcerare; **after being imprisoned for three weeks** dopo tre settimane di *or* in carcere.

im·pris·on·ment [ɪm'prɪznmənt] N reclusione *f*; **during his
imprisonment** mentre era in carcere; **life imprisonment**
l'ergastolo.

im·prob·abil·ity [ɪm,prɒbə'bɪlɪtɪ] N (*see adj*) improbabilità; inverosimiglianza.

im·prob·able [ɪm'prɒbəbl] ADJ (*event*) improbabile, poco
probabile; (*excuse, story*) inverosimile.

im·promp·tu [ɪm'prɒmptju:] ① ADJ improvvisato(-a),
estemporaneo(-a).
② ADV (*speak*) improvvisando, a braccio.

im·prop·er [ɪm'prɒpə'] ADJ (*unseemly, indecent*) sconveniente; (*wrong*) scorretto(-a); (*unsuitable*) impro-
prio(-a), inadatto(-a).
♦ **improper fraction** N (*Math*) frazione *f* impropria.

im·prop·er·ly [ɪm'prɒpəlɪ] ADV (*see adj*) sconvenientemente; scorrettamente; impropriamente, in modo
inadatto.

im·pro·pri·ety [,ɪmprə'praɪətɪ] N (*frm: of behaviour*) scorrettezza; (: *unseemliness, indecency*) sconvenienza; (*of
expression*) improprietà *f inv*.

im·prove [ɪm'pru:v] ① VT (*gen*) migliorare; (*property, land*)
apportare migliorie a; (*production, yield, salary*) aumentare; **to improve one's Italian** perfezionare il proprio
italiano; **to improve one's chances of success** aumentare le proprie probabilità di successo; **to improve one's
mind** migliorare la propria cultura.
② VI (*gen*) migliorare; (*person: in skill*) fare (dei)
progressi; **to improve in sth** migliorare *or* fare (dei)
progressi in qc; **to improve with age/use** migliorare con
gli anni/con l'uso; **this wine improves with age** questo
vino migliora con l'invecchiamento
▶ **improve (up)on** VI + PREP (*offer*) aumentare; (*work*)
ottenere dei risultati migliori rispetto a; (*method*) perfezionare; (*quality*) migliorare; **I can't improve on my offer
to you** non posso farti un'offerta migliore.

im·prove·ment [ɪm'pru:vmənt] N: **improvement (in)** (*gen*)
miglioramento (in); (*in production, salary*) aumento (di
or in); **it's an improvement on the old one** è meglio di
quello vecchio; **there is room for improvement** si può
migliorare *or* far meglio; **to make improvements to**
migliorare; (*property*) apportare migliorie a; (*method*)
perfezionare.
♦ **improvement grant** N *sussidio per la modernizzazione di edifici.*

im·provi·dence [ɪm'prɒvɪdəns] N (*frm*) imprevidenza.

im·provi·dent [ɪm'prɒvɪdənt] (*frm*) ADJ (*not providing for
future*) imprevidente; (*thriftless*) prodigo(-a); (*heedless*)
imprudente.

im·prov·ing [ɪm'pru:vɪŋ] ADJ (*book*) edificante.

im·provi·sa·tion [,ɪmprəvaɪ'zeɪʃən] N improvvisazione *f*.

im·pro·vise ['ɪmprəvaɪz] VT, VI improvvisare.

im·pru·dence [ɪm'pru:dəns] N imprudenza.

im·pru·dent [ɪm'pru:dənt] ADJ imprudente.

im·pru·dent·ly [ɪm'pru:dəntlɪ] ADV imprudentemente.

im·pu·dence ['ɪmpjʊdəns] N impudenza.

im·pu·dent ['ɪmpjʊdənt] ADJ impertinente, impudente.

im·pu·dent·ly ['ɪmpjʊdəntlɪ] ADV impertinentemente,
impudentemente.

im·pugn [ɪm'pju:n] VT (*frm*) attaccare, contestare.

im·pulse ['ɪmpʌls] N impulso; **to act on impulse** agire
d'impulso *or* impulsivamente.
♦ **impulse buy** N acquisto fatto d'impulso.

im·pul·sion [ɪm'pʌlʃən] N impulso.

im·pul·sive [ɪm'pʌlsɪv] ADJ impulsivo(-a).

im·pul·sive·ly [ɪm'pʌlsɪvlɪ] ADV impulsivamente.

im·pul·sive·ness [ɪm'pʌlsɪvnɪs] N impulsività.

im·pu·nity [ɪm'pju:nɪtɪ] N: **with impunity** impunemente.

im·pure [ɪm'pjʊə'] ADJ (*Chem, morally*) impuro(-a); (*air*)
inquinato(-a).

im·pu·rity [ɪm'pjʊərɪtɪ] N impurità *f inv*.

im·pu·ta·tion [,ɪmpjʊ'teɪʃən] N (*frm*) capo d'imputazione
or d'accusa.

im·pute [ɪm'pju:t] VT (*frm*): **to impute (to)** (*change, development*) attribuire (a); (*crime, blame*) imputare (a).

IN ABBR (*Am Post*)= *Indiana*.

in [ɪn]
① PREP
Ⓐ (*place, position*) in;
▷ **in** the *country* in campagna
▷ **in** the *garden* in giardino
▷ **in** my *hand* in mano
▷ **in** *here* qui dentro
▷ **in** the *house* in casa
▷ **in** *school* a scuola
▷ **in** the *school* nella scuola
▷ **in** *there* lì dentro
▷ **in** the *town* in città
Ⓑ (*with place names: of town*) a; (: *of region, country*) in;
▷ **in** *England* in Inghilterra
▷ it's **in** *France* è in Francia
▷ **in** *London* a Londra
▷ **in** *Sicily* in Sicilia
▷ it's **in** the *United States* è negli Stati Uniti
▷ **in** *Yorkshire* nello Yorkshire
Ⓒ (*time: during*) in;
▷ **in** *1994* nel 1994
▷ at 4 o'clock **in** the *afternoon* alle 4 del pomeriggio
▷ **in** *autumn* in autunno
▷ **in** the 20th *century* nel ventesimo secolo
▷ **in** those *days* a quei tempi, allora
▷ **in** the *daytime* di *or* durante il giorno, durante la
giornata
▷ **in** the *eighties* negli anni ottanta
▷ **in** *May* in maggio, a maggio, nel mese di maggio
▷ **in** the *morning* di *or* alla mattina, la mattina, nella
mattinata
▷ **in** the *mornings* di *or* alla mattina, la mattina
▷ **in** the *past* nel *or* in passato
▷ **in** *spring* in primavera
▷ **in** (the) *summer* in estate, d'estate
▷ **in** (the) *winter* in inverno, d'inverno
▷ she has not been here **in** *years* sono anni che non
viene qui
Ⓓ (*time: in the space of*) in; (*after*) tra, fra;

▷**it will be ready in 2 *days*** sarà pronto fra due giorni
▷**I did it in 3 *hours*** l'ho fatto in 3 ore
▷**she will return the money in a *month*** restituirà i soldi tra un mese
e (*manner, means*)
▷**a statue *carved* in wood** una statua intagliata nel legno
▷**to pay in *dollars*** pagare in dollari
▷***dressed* in green/a skirt/trousers** vestito(-a) di verde/con una gonna/con i calzoni
▷**in *English*** in inglese
▷**in *ink*** a penna
▷**in *Italian*** in italiano
▷**the *man* in the hat** l'uomo con il cappello
▷**in alphabetical *order*** in ordine alfabetico
▷***painted* in red** dipinto(-a) di rosso
▷**in *part*** in parte
▷**in *pencil*** a matita
▷**in *person*** di persona
▷**in large/small *quantities*** in grandi/piccole quantità
▷**in a loud/soft *voice*** a voce alta/bassa
▷**in *watercolour*** ad acquerello
▷**in a *whisper*** sussurrando
▷**in *writing*** per iscritto
f (*circumstance*)
▷**in the *dark(ness)*** al buio, nell'oscurità
▷**in (the) *daylight*** alla *or* con la luce del giorno
▷**to be 10 metres in *height*** essere alto(-a) 10 metri
▷**to be 10 metres in *length*** essere lungo(-a) 10 metri
▷**in the *moonlight*** al chiaro di luna
▷**a change in *policy*** un cambiamento di prassi
▷**a rise in *prices*** un aumento dei prezzi
▷**in the *rain*** sotto la pioggia
▷**in the *shade*** all'ombra
▷**in the *sun*** al sole
▷**in all *weathers*** con qualsiasi tempo, qualsiasi tempo faccia
▷**to be 10 metres in *width*** essere largo(-a) 10 metri
g (*mood, state*)
▷**to act in *anger*** agire per rabbia
▷**in good *condition* or *repair*** in buono stato, in buone condizioni
▷**in *despair*** disperato(-a)
▷**lame in the left *leg*** zoppo(-a) dalla gamba sinistra
▷**to live in *luxury*** vivere nel lusso
▷**in *private*** in privato
▷**to be in a *rage*** essere su tutte le furie
▷**in *secret*** in segreto
▷**in *tears*** in lacrime
h (*ratio, number*)
▷**in *hundreds*** a centinaia
▷***once* in a hundred years** una volta ogni cento anni
▷***one* person/car in ten** una persona/macchina su dieci
▷**20 pence in the *pound*** 20 pence per sterlina
▷**in *twos*** a due a due
i (*people, works*) in;
▷**this is *common* in children/cats** questo è comune nei *or* per i bambini/gatti
▷**she *has* it in her to succeed** ha in sé la capacità di riuscire
▷**they *have* a good leader in him** hanno in lui un ottimo capo
▷**in (the works of) *Shakespeare*** in Shakespeare

j (*in profession*)
▷**to be in the *army*** essere nell'esercito
▷**to be in *publishing*** lavorare nell'editoria
▷**to be in *teaching*** fare l'insegnante, insegnare
▷**to be in the motor *trade*** lavorare nel settore automobilistico
k (*after superlative*) di;
▷**the *best* pupil in the class** il migliore alunno della classe
▷**the *biggest* in Europe** il più grande d'Europa
▷**the *smallest* in Europe** il più piccolo d'Europa
l (*with present participle*): **in *saying* this** dicendo questo, nel dir questo
m: **in *that*** dal momento che, visto che;
▷**in *all*** in tutto.
2 ADV: **to *be* in** (*person*) esserci; (*train, ship, plane*) essere arrivato(-a); (*crops, harvest*) essere raccolto (-a); (*in fashion*) essere di moda; (*fam*: *in power*) essere al potere;
▷**to *ask* sb in** invitare qn a entrare
▷***day* in, *day* out** (*pej*) dalla mattina alla sera
▷**we're in *for* a snow storm** si prepara una tormenta
▷**he is in *for* trouble** lo aspettano dei guai
▷**he's in *for* it** (*fam*) è nei guai, lo aspettano guai seri
▷**to *have* it in for sb** (*fam*) avercela con qn
▷***is* he in?** lui c'è?
▷**to *limp* in** entrare zoppicando
▷**my *luck* is in** la fortuna è dalla mia (parte)
▷**to be in *on* a plan/secret** essere al corrente di un progetto/segreto
▷**to be in and *out* of work** non durare mai molto in un impiego
▷**to be in and *out* of hospital/prison** essere sempre dentro e fuori dall'ospedale/di prigione
▷**their *party* is in** il loro partito è al potere
▷**to *run* in** entrare correndo.
3 N: **the *ins* and *outs* of the problem** tutti i particolari del problema.
4 ADJ (*fam*) in *inv*;
▷**it's an in *club*** è un club molto 'in'
▷**it's an in *joke*** è una cosa nostra
▷**it's the in *thing* to do** (*fam*) è la cosa 'in' del momento
▷**hang-gliding is the in *thing* to do** fare del deltaplano è 'in'.

in. ABBR (*pl* **ins.**) = **inch**.
in·abil·ity [ˌɪnəˈbɪlɪtɪ] N (*physical, mental*) incapacità; **inability to do sth** incapacità di fare qc; **inability to pay** impossibilità di pagare.
in·ac·ces·sibil·ity [ˈɪnækˌsɛsəˈbɪlɪtɪ] N inaccessibilità.
in·ac·ces·sible [ˌɪnækˈsɛsəbl] ADJ: **inaccessible (to)** inaccessibile (a).
in·ac·cu·ra·cy [ɪnˈækjʊrəsɪ] N (*see adj*) inaccuratezza; inesattezza; imprecisione *f*; (*usu pl*: *mistake*) errore *m*.
in·ac·cu·rate [ɪnˈækjʊrɪt] ADJ (*statement, report, story*) inaccurato(-a); (*figures*) inesatto(-a); (*translation*) impreciso(-a).
in·ac·cu·rate·ly [ɪnˈækjʊrɪtlɪ] ADV (*state, report, describe*) in modo inaccurato; (*add up, multiply*) in modo inesatto; (*translate*) in modo impreciso.
in·ac·tion [ɪnˈækʃən] N inerzia, inazione *f*.
in·ac·tive [ɪnˈæktɪv] ADJ inattivo(-a).
in·ac·tiv·ity [ˌɪnækˈtɪvɪtɪ] N inattività.

in·ad·equa·cy [ɪn'ædɪkwəsɪ] N inadeguatezza, insufficienza; (of person) incapacità f inv.

in·ad·equate [ɪn'ædɪkwɪt] ADJ (insufficient) inadeguato (-a), insufficiente; (person) non all'altezza; **he felt quite inadequate** non si sentiva assolutamente all'altezza.

in·ad·equate·ly [ɪn'ædɪkwɪtlɪ] ADV inadeguatamente, insufficientemente.

in·ad·mis·si·ble [ˌɪnəd'mɪsəbl] ADJ (evidence) inammissibile.

in·ad·vert·ent [ˌɪnəd'vɜ:tənt] ADJ (unintentional) involontario(-a); (unthinking) inconsapevole.

in·ad·vert·ent·ly [ˌɪnəd'vɜ:təntlɪ] ADV (unintentionally) inavvertitamente, involontariamente; (unawares) inconsapevolmente.

in·ad·vis·abil·ity ['ɪnədˌvaɪzə'bɪlɪtɪ] N: **the inadvisability (of)** l'inopportunità (di).

in·ad·vis·able [ˌɪnəd'vaɪzəbl] ADJ sconsigliabile.

in·al·ien·able [ɪn'eɪlɪənəbl] ADJ (frm: right) inalienabile.

in·ane [ɪ'neɪn] ADJ (remark) sciocco(-a), stupido(-a).

in·ani·mate [ɪn'ænɪmɪt] ADJ inanimato(-a).

in·an·ity [ɪ'nænɪtɪ] N sciocchezza, stupidità f inv.

in·ap·pli·cable [ɪn'æplɪkəbl] ADJ inapplicabile.

in·ap·pro·pri·ate [ˌɪnə'prəuprɪɪt] ADJ (action, punishment, treatment) inadeguato(-a), non appropriato(-a); (word, phrase, expression) non appropriato(-a); (behaviour) sconveniente.

in·ap·pro·pri·ate·ly [ˌɪnə'prəuprɪɪtlɪ] ADV (punish, treat) inadeguatamente; (use: word) poco appropriatamente; (behave, act) sconvenientemente.

in·apt [ɪn'æpt] ADJ (remark, behaviour) poco appropriato (-a).

in·ap·ti·tude [ɪn'æptɪˌtju:d], **in·apt·ness** [ɪn'æptnɪs] N (of remark) improprietà.

in·ar·ticu·late [ˌɪnɑ:'tɪkjulɪt] ADJ (person) che non sa esprimersi, che si esprime male; (speech) inarticolato (-a), confuso(-a).

in·ar·tis·tic [ˌɪnɑ:'tɪstɪk] ADJ (work) di scarso valore artistico; (person) che manca di senso artistico.

in·as·much as [ˌɪnəz'mʌtʃəz] CONJ (insofar as) in quanto, nella misura in cui; (seeing that) poiché.

in·at·ten·tion [ˌɪnə'tɛnʃən] N: **inattention (to)** mancanza di attenzione (per or nei confronti di), disattenzione f (per or nei confronti di).

in·at·ten·tive [ˌɪnə'tɛntɪv] ADJ disattento(-a), distratto (-a).

in·at·ten·tive·ly [ˌɪnə'tɛntɪvlɪ] ADV distrattamente.

in·audible [ɪn'ɔ:dəbl] ADJ appena percettibile.

in·audibly [ɪn'ɔ:dəblɪ] ADV (speak) in modo appena percettibile.

in·augu·ral [ɪ'nɔ:gjurəl] ADJ inaugurale.

in·augu·rate [ɪ'nɔ:gjureɪt] VT (president, official) insediare; (start officially: organization, festival) inaugurare; (frm: system, idea) inaugurare, instaurare.

in·augu·ra·tion [ɪˌnɔ:gju'reɪʃən] N (of president) insediamento (in carica); (opening) inaugurazione f; **the inauguration of a new era** l'inizio di una nuova era.

in·aus·pi·cious [ˌɪnɔ:s'pɪʃəs] ADJ poco propizio(-a).

in·aus·pi·cious·ly [ˌɪnɔ:s'pɪʃəslɪ] ADV in modo poco propizio.

♦ **in-between** [ɪnbɪ'twi:n] ADJ intermedio(-a).

in·board ['ɪnˌbɔ:d] N (also: **inboard motor**) entrobordo m inv.

in·born ['ɪn'bɔ:n] ADJ (feeling) innato(-a); (defect) congenito(-a).

in·bred ['ɪn'brɛd] ADJ (tendency) innato(-a); **an inbred family** (pej) una famiglia con un alto indice di unioni fra consanguinei.

in·breed·ing ['ɪn'bri:dɪŋ] N (Zool) inbreeding m inv; (of people) unioni fpl fra consanguinei.

♦ **in-built** ['ɪn'bɪlt] ADJ innato(-a); **inbuilt limitations** limiti mpl intrinseci.

Inc. ABBR = **incorporated**.

Inca [ɪŋkə] **1** ADJ (also: **Incan**) incaico(-a), inca inv. **2** N inca m/f inv.

in·cal·cu·lable [ɪn'kælkjuləbl] ADJ incalcolabile.

in·can·des·cence [ˌɪnkæn'dɛsns] N (frm) incandescenza.

in·can·des·cent [ˌɪnkæn'dɛsnt] ADJ (frm) incandescente.

in·can·ta·tion [ˌɪnkæn'teɪʃən] N incantesimo.

in·ca·pabil·ity [ɪnˌkeɪpə'bɪlɪtɪ] N incapacità.

in·ca·pable [ɪn'keɪpəbl] ADJ: **incapable (of doing sth)** incapace (di fare qc); **a question incapable of solution** (frm) un problema irrisolvibile or insolubile.

in·ca·paci·tate [ˌɪnkə'pæsɪˌteɪt] VT (person) rendere inabile; (Law) inabilitare; **to incapacitate sb from doing sth** rendere qn inabile a fare qc.

in·ca·paci·tat·ed [ˌɪnkə'pæsɪˌteɪtɪd] ADJ (disabled) inabile; (Law) inabilitato(-a); **physically incapacitated** inabile fisicamente.

in·ca·pac·ity [ˌɪnkə'pæsɪtɪ] N incapacità; (Law) inabilitazione.

in·car·cer·ate [ɪn'kɑ:səˌreɪt] VT (frm) incarcerare.

in·car·nate [adj ɪn'kɑ:nɪt; vb ɪn'kɑ:neɪt] **1** ADJ (Rel) incarnato(-a); **the devil incarnate** il diavolo personificato or in persona. **2** VT incarnare.

in·car·na·tion [ˌɪnkɑ:'neɪʃən] N (Rel) incarnazione f.

in·cau·tious [ɪn'kɔ:ʃəs] ADJ incauto(-a).

in·cen·di·ary [ɪn'sɛndɪərɪ] **1** ADJ incendiario(-a). **2** N (bomb) ordigno incendiario.

in·cense [n 'ɪnsɛns; vb ɪn'sɛns] **1** N incenso. **2** VT (anger) fare infuriare.

♦ **incense burner** N incensiere m.

in·censed [ɪn'sɛnst] ADJ furente, furibondo(-a).

in·cen·tive [ɪn'sɛntɪv] N incentivo; **there is no incentive to work** non c'è alcun incentivo al lavoro; **it gave me an incentive** mi è servito da incentivo.

♦ **incentive bonus** N premio d'incentivazione.

♦ **incentive scheme** N piano di incentivazione.

in·cep·tion [ɪn'sɛpʃən] N (frm) inizio, principio.

in·cer·ti·tude [ɪn'sɜ:tɪtju:d] N (frm) incertezza.

in·ces·sant [ɪn'sɛsnt] ADJ incessante.

in·ces·sant·ly [ɪn'sɛsntlɪ] ADV incessantemente.

in·cest ['ɪnsɛst] N incesto.

in·ces·tu·ous [ɪn'sɛstjuəs] ADJ incestuoso(-a).

inch [ɪntʃ] N pollice m (cm 2.54; 12 per foot); **a few inches** ≈ qualche centimetro; **the car missed me by inches** c'è mancato un pelo che la macchina mi investisse; **to lose a few inches** (fam) perdere un po' di ciccia; **inch by inch** a poco a poco; **every inch of it was used** è stato utilizzato tutto fino all'ultimo millimetro or centimetro; **he's every inch a soldier** è un soldato dalla testa ai piedi; **within an inch of** a un pelo da; **to be within an inch of death/disaster** essere a un passo dalla morte/dalla rovina; **he didn't give** or **budge an inch** (fig) non ha ceduto di un millimetro.

► **inch forward** VI + ADV avanzare pian piano

► **inch up** VI + ADV salire a poco a poco.

♦ **inch tape** N metro a nastro (da sarto).

in·ci·dence ['ɪnsɪdəns] N (extent, rate: of disease, crime) incidenza; **the angle of incidence** (Phys) l'angolo d'inci-

denza.

in·ci·dent ['ɪnsɪdənt] N (gen) caso, avvenimento; (diplomatic, on border) incidente m; (in book) episodio; (in play) scena; **without incident** (uneventful) senza incidenti (di rilievo); (without trouble) senza problemi.

in·ci·den·tal [ˌɪnsɪ'dɛntl] ⊡ ADJ (secondary) secondario (-a); (unplanned) fortuito(-a); **incidental to** connesso(-a) con; **incidental expenses** spese fpl accessorie.

⊡ N (minor point) punto di secondaria importanza; **incidentals** NPL (expenses) spese fpl accessorie.

in·ci·den·tal·ly [ˌɪnsɪ'dɛntəlɪ] ADV (by the way) fra parentesi, tra l'altro, per inciso; **the system prevents heat loss and incidentally saves you money** il sistema impedisce perdite di calore e tra l'altro fa risparmiare; **incidentally, I saw your sister yesterday** fra parentesi, ho visto tua sorella ieri.

♦ **incidental music** N sottofondo musicale, musica di sottofondo.

♦ **incident room** N (Police) centrale f operativa.

in·cin·er·ate [ɪn'sɪnəˌreɪt] VT incenerire.

in·cin·era·tion [ɪnsɪnə'reɪʃən] N incenerimento.

in·cin·era·tor [ɪn'sɪnəˌreɪtə'] N inceneritore m.

in·cipi·ent [ɪn'sɪpɪənt] ADJ (disease, baldness) incipiente; (revolt) nascente.

in·cise [ɪn'saɪz] VT (frm) incidere.

in·ci·sion [ɪn'sɪʒən] N incisione f.

in·ci·sive [ɪn'saɪsɪv] ADJ (mind, remark) acuto(-a); (criticism) tagliente; (speech, style) incisivo(-a).

in·ci·sive·ly [ɪn'saɪsɪvlɪ] ADV (remark, question, describe) incisivamente.

in·ci·sor [ɪn'saɪzə'] N (Anat) incisivo.

in·cite [ɪn'saɪt] VT: **to incite sb (to sth/to do sth)** incitare qn (a qc/a fare qc), istigare qn (a qc/a fare qc).

in·cite·ment [ɪn'saɪtmənt] N incitamento, istigazione f.

in·ci·vil·ity [ˌɪnsɪ'vɪlɪtɪ] N inciviltà f inv.

incl. ABBR = **including, inclusive (of)**.

in·clem·ent [ɪn'klɛmənt] ADJ inclemente.

in·cli·na·tion [ˌɪnklɪ'neɪʃən] N **a** (wish) tendenza, inclinazione f; **he felt no inclination to join in the fun** non aveva nessuna voglia di unirsi alla gazzarra; **her inclination was to ignore him** avrebbe voluto ignorarlo; **against my inclination** controvoglia; **to follow one's inclination** seguire le proprie inclinazioni

b (slope) pendio, china

c (bow) cenno.

in·cline [n 'ɪnklaɪn; vb ɪn'klaɪn] ⊡ N pendenza, pendio.

⊡ VT (bend: head, body) chinare, inclinare.

⊡ VI **a** (slope) declinare **b** (tend to): **to incline to(wards)** tendere a; **I incline to the belief/opinion that ...** sono propenso a credere che... .

in·clined [ɪn'klaɪnd] ADJ **a** (liable, apt): **to be inclined to do sth** essere incline a fare qc; (: out of habit) tendere a fare qc; (: from preference) essere propenso(-a) a fare qc; **it is inclined to break** ha la tendenza a rompersi

b (gifted): **artistically/musically inclined** portato(-a) per l'arte/la musica

c (disposed): **if you feel so inclined** se lo desideri, se ne hai voglia; **to be well inclined towards sb** essere ben disposto(-a) verso qn.

in·clude [ɪn'kluːd] VT comprendere, includere; **your name is not included in the list** il tuo nome non è incluso nella lista; **he sold everything, books included** ha venduto tutto, compresi i libri; **service is/is not included** il servizio è compreso/escluso.

in·clud·ing [ɪn'kluːdɪŋ] PREP compreso(-a), incluso(-a);

including VAT IVA compresa; **seven books including this one** sette libri compreso or incluso questo; **up to and including Chapter 12** fino al capitolo 12 compreso or incluso.

in·clu·sion [ɪn'kluːʒən] N inclusione f.

in·clu·sive [ɪn'kluːsɪv] ⊡ ADJ (sum, price) tutto compreso inv; **inclusive of** incluso(-a); **£500, inclusive of VAT** 500 sterline, IVA compresa.

⊡ ADV: **from the 10th to the 15th inclusive** dal 10 al 15 incluso or compreso.

in·clu·sive·ly [ɪn'kluːsɪvlɪ] ADV inclusivamente.

♦ **inclusive terms** NPL (Brit) (prezzo m) tutto compreso inv.

in·cog·ni·to [ˌɪnkɒg'niːtəʊ] ADV (travel) in incognito; **to remain incognito** mantenere l'incognito.

in·co·her·ence [ˌɪnkəʊ'hɪərəns] N incoerenza.

in·co·her·ent [ˌɪnkəʊ'hɪərənt] ADJ (person) incoerente; **he was incoherent with rage** non connetteva per la rabbia.

in·co·her·ent·ly [ˌɪnkəʊ'hɪərəntlɪ] ADV incoerentemente.

in·com·bus·tible [ˌɪnkəm'bʌstəbl] ADJ incombustibile.

in·come ['ɪnkʌm] N (gen) reddito; (from receipts) introito; **gross/net income** reddito lordo/netto; **private income** rendita; **to live within/beyond one's income** vivere secondo i propri mezzi/al di sopra dei propri mezzi.

♦ **income and expenditure account** N conto entrate e uscite.

in·comer ['ɪnˌkʌmə'] N nuovo(-a) venuto(-a).

♦ **incomes policy** N politica dei redditi.

♦ **income support** N (Brit) sussidio di indigenza or povertà.

♦ **income tax** N imposta sul reddito.

♦ **income tax inspector** N ispettore m delle imposte sul reddito.

♦ **income tax return** N dichiarazione f dei redditi.

in·com·ing ['ɪnˌkʌmɪŋ] ADJ (passengers) in arrivo; (tide) montante; (government) entrante; (tenant) subentrante.

in·com·mu·ni·ca·do [ˌɪnkəˌmjuːnɪ'kɑːdəʊ] ADJ: **to hold sb incommunicado** tenere segregato(-a) qn.

in·com·pa·rable [ɪn'kɒmpərəbl] ADJ incomparabile.

in·com·pa·rably [ɪn'kɒmpərəblɪ] ADV incomparabilmente.

in·com·pat·ibil·ity ['ɪnkəmˌpætə'bɪlɪtɪ] N incompatibilità.

in·com·pat·ible [ˌɪnkəm'pætəbl] ADJ incompatibile.

in·com·pe·tence [ɪn'kɒmpɪtəns] N incompetenza.

in·com·pe·tent [ɪn'kɒmpɪtənt] ADJ (work) da incompetenti; (person): **incompetent (at)** incompetente (in fatto di).

in·com·plete [ˌɪnkəm'pliːt] ADJ (partial) incompleto(-a); (unfinished: work) non finito(-a); (: book, painting) incompiuto(-a).

in·com·pre·hen·sible [ɪnˌkɒmprɪ'hɛnsəbl] ADJ incomprensibile.

in·com·pre·hen·sibly [ɪnˌkɒmprɪ'hɛnsəblɪ] ADV incomprensibilmente.

in·com·pre·hen·sion [ˌɪnkɒmprɪ'hɛnʃən] N: **he gave me a look of incomprehension** mi fissava senza capire.

in·con·ceiv·able [ˌɪnkən'siːvəbl] ADJ inconcepibile.

in·con·ceiv·ably [ˌɪnkən'siːvəblɪ] ADV (stupid, long) incredibilmente.

in·con·clu·sive [ˌɪnkən'kluːsɪv] ADJ (debate, discussion) inconcludente, non risolutivo(-a); (evidence, experiment) che lascia dubbi, inconcludente; (argument) poco convincente.

in·con·gru·ity [ˌɪnkɒn'gruːɪtɪ] N assurdità f inv.

in·con·gru·ous [ɪn'kɒŋgrʊəs] ADJ (appearance, behaviour)

stonato(-a), assurdo(-a); (*remark, act*) fuori luogo.

in·con·gru·ous·ly [ɪn'kɒŋgrʊəslɪ] ADV assurdamente.

in·con·sequen·tial [ɪn,kɒnsɪ'kwɛnʃəl], **in·con·sequent** [ɪn'kɒnsɪkwənt] ADJ (*conversation*) senza importanza; (*remark*) irrilevante.

in·con·sid·er·able [,ɪnkən'sɪdərəbl] ADJ: **not inconsiderable** non trascurabile.

in·con·sid·er·ate [,ɪnkən'sɪdərɪt] ADJ (*person*) privo(-a) di riguardo; (*behaviour*) poco gentile.

in·con·sist·en·cy [,ɪnkən'sɪstənsɪ] N **a** (*of actions*) contraddizione *f*, incoerenza; (*of work*) irregolarità **b** (*of statement*) incongruenza.

in·con·sist·ent [,ɪnkən'sɪstənt] ADJ (*contradictory: action*) contraddittorio(-a), incoerente; (*uneven: work*) irregolare, non costante; **his actions were inconsistent with his principles** le sue azioni non erano coerenti con i suoi principi; **that is inconsistent with what you told me earlier** questo è in contraddizione con quanto mi avevi riferito prima.

in·con·sol·able [,ɪnkən'səʊləbl] ADJ inconsolabile.

in·con·spicu·ous [,ɪnkən'spɪkjʊəs] ADJ (*place*) che non dà nell'occhio, poco in vista; (*colour*) poco appariscente; (*person, dress*) dimesso(-a); **to make o.s. inconspicuous** cercare di passare inosservato(-a).

in·con·spicu·ous·ly [,ɪnkən'spɪkjʊəslɪ] ADV (*behave, move*) senza dare nell'occhio; (*dress*) in modo poco appariscente, modestamente; (*marked, placed*) in modo da non attirare l'attenzione.

in·con·stan·cy [ɪn'kɒnstənsɪ] N incostanza.

in·con·stant [ɪn'kɒnstənt] ADJ incostante, volubile.

in·con·test·able [,ɪnkən'tɛstəbl] ADJ incontestabile.

in·con·ti·nence [ɪn'kɒntɪnəns] N (*Med*) incontinenza.

in·con·ti·nent [ɪn'kɒntɪnənt] ADJ (*Med*) incontinente.

in·con·tro·vert·ible [ɪn,kɒntrə'vɜːtəbl] ADJ incontrovertibile.

in·con·ven·ience [,ɪnkən'viːnɪəns] **1** N (*see adj*) scomodità *f inv*; scarsa funzionalità; inopportunità; **not having a car was a great inconvenience** non aver la macchina era una gran scomodità; **to put sb to great inconvenience** creare degli inconvenienti a qn, recare disturbo a qn.
2 VT disturbare, incomodare; **don't inconvenience yourself** non si disturbi *or* incomodi.

in·con·ven·ient [,ɪnkən'viːnɪənt] ADJ (*time, appointment, location*) scomodo(-a); (*house, design*) poco funzionale; (*arrival*) inopportuno(-a); **that time is very inconvenient for me** non è un'ora adatta per me; **if it is not inconvenient (to you)** se non è un problema; **could you let me have the key tomorrow, if it is not inconvenient** mi puoi dare la chiave domani, se non è un problema?

in·con·vert·ible [,ɪnkən'vɜːtəbl] ADJ inconvertibile.

in·cor·po·rate [ɪn'kɔːpəˌreɪt] VT (*include*) includere, comprendere; (*integrate*) incorporare.

in·cor·po·rat·ed [ɪn'kɔːpəˌreɪtɪd] ADJ (*Am Comm*): **incorporated company** ≈ società *f inv* per azioni.

in·cor·rect [,ɪnkə'rɛkt] ADJ (*statement, fact*) inesatto(-a); (*conclusion*) errato(-a); (*behaviour*) scorretto(-a); (*dress*) sconveniente; **that is incorrect** questo è inesatto; **you are incorrect in stating that ...** ti sbagli quando dici che... .

in·cor·rect·ly [,ɪnkə'rɛktlɪ] ADV (*state*) in modo inesatto; (*conclude*) in modo errato; (*behave, dress*) in modo sconveniente.

in·cor·ri·gible [ɪn'kɒrɪdʒəbl] ADJ incorreggibile.

in·cor·rupt·ible [,ɪnkə'rʌptəbl] ADJ incorruttibile.

in·crease [*vb* ɪn'kriːs; *n* 'ɪnkriːs] **1** VI (*prices, salaries*) aumentare; (*population, demand, supply, sales*) aumentare, crescere; (*excitement, tension*) farsi più intenso(-a); (*rain, wind*) aumentare, intensificarsi; **to increase in number/size** crescere di numero/di dimensioni; **to increase in volume/weight** aumentare di volume/di peso; **to increase in value** aumentare di valore; **to increase by 100** aumentare di 100; **the hole is increasing in size** il buco si sta allargando.
2 VT (*see vi*) aumentare; accrescere; intensificare; **to increase speed** aumentare la velocità; **to increase one's efforts** moltiplicare *or* intensificare i propri sforzi.
3 N (*see vi*) aumento; crescita; intensificazione *f*; **an increase in size/volume** un aumento di dimensioni/di volume; **an increase of £5/10%** un aumento di 5 sterline/del 10%; **to be on the increase** essere in aumento; (*prices*) essere in aumento *or* in rialzo; (*sales, trade*) essere in aumento *or* in fase di espansione.

in·creas·ing [ɪn'kriːsɪŋ] ADJ (*number*) crescente, in aumento.

in·creas·ing·ly [ɪn'kriːsɪŋlɪ] ADV sempre più.

in·cred·ible [ɪn'krɛdəbl] ADJ incredibile.

in·cred·ibly [ɪn'krɛdəblɪ] ADV incredibilmente.

in·cre·du·lity [,ɪnkrɪ'djuːlɪtɪ] N incredulità.

in·credu·lous [ɪn'krɛdjʊləs] ADJ incredulo(-a).

in·credu·lous·ly [ɪn'krɛdjʊləslɪ] ADV incredulamente.

in·cre·ment ['ɪnkrɪmənt] N (*in salary*) aumento; (*Math*) incremento.

in·cre·men·tal [,ɪnkrɪ'mɛntl] ADJ (*increase*) progressivo (-a).

in·crimi·nate [ɪn'krɪmɪˌneɪt] VT incriminare.

in·crimi·na·ting [ɪn'krɪmɪˌneɪtɪŋ] ADJ incriminante.

in·cu·bate ['ɪnkjʊˌbeɪt] **1** VT (*eggs*) covare.
2 VI (*egg*) essere in incubazione; (*disease*) avere un'incubazione.

in·cu·ba·tion [,ɪnkjʊ'beɪʃən] N incubazione *f*.

♦ **incubation period** N (periodo di) incubazione *f*.

in·cu·ba·tor ['ɪnkjʊˌbeɪtə'] N (*for eggs, baby*) incubatrice *f*.

in·cul·cate ['ɪnkʌlˌkeɪt] VT (*frm*): **to inculcate sth in(to) sb** inculcare qc a qn.

in·cum·ben·cy [ɪn'kʌmbənsɪ] N (*tenure*) incarico.

in·cum·bent [ɪn'kʌmbənt] (*frm*) **1** ADJ: **it is incumbent on him to do it ...** spetta a lui farlo... .
2 N (*gen*) titolare *m/f*; (*Rel*) beneficiato.

in·cur [ɪn'kɜː'] VT (*debt, obligation*) contrarre; (*expenses*) andare incontro a; (*loss*) subire; (*anger*) attirarsi; (*risk*) esporsi a.

in·cur·able [ɪn'kjʊərəbl] ADJ (*disease*) incurabile; (*habit*) incorreggibile; (*fig: optimist*) inguaribile.

in·cur·ably [ɪn'kjʊərəblɪ] ADV: **the incurably ill** i malati incurabili; **to be incurably optimistic** essere un(a) inguaribile ottimista.

in·cu·ri·ous [ɪn'kjʊərɪəs] ADJ indifferente.

in·cur·sion [ɪn'kɜːʃən] N incursione *f*.

in·debt·ed [ɪn'dɛtɪd] ADJ (*fig*): **to be indebted to sb (for sth)** essere molto obbligato(-a) a qn (per *or* di qc).

in·debt·ed·ness [ɪn'dɛtɪdnɪs] N l'essere in debito; (*Fin*) indebitamento.

in·de·cen·cy [ɪn'diːsnsɪ] N indecenza.

in·de·cent [ɪn'diːsnt] ADJ (*dress, behaviour*) indecente.

♦ **indecent assault** N (*Brit Law*) atti *mpl* di libidine violenta.

♦ **indecent exposure** N esibizionismo (di organi genitali).

in·de·cent·ly [ɪn'diːsntlɪ] ADV (*dress, behave*) indecente-

mente.

in·de·ci·pher·able [ˌɪndɪ'saɪfərəbl] ADJ indecifrabile.

in·de·ci·sion [ˌɪndɪ'sɪʒən] N indecisione *f*.

in·de·ci·sive [ˌɪndɪ'saɪsɪv] ADJ (*person*) indeciso(-a), esitante; (*result, discussion*) non decisivo(-a).

in·de·ci·sive·ly [ˌɪndɪ'saɪsɪvlɪ] ADV (*act*) con indecisione *or* esitazione; (*finish: game, argument*) in modo inconcludente; **the discussion ended indecisively** la discussione è finita senza un risultato preciso.

in·deco·rous [ɪn'dɛkərəs] ADJ indecoroso(-a).

in·deco·rous·ly [ɪn'dɛkərəslɪ] ADV indecorosamente.

in·deed [ɪn'diːd] ADV **a** veramente, infatti, in effetti; **I feel, indeed I know he is wrong** ho l'impressione, anzi sono certo che si sbaglia; **there are indeed mistakes, but ...** ci sono certamente degli errori, però...; **thank you very much indeed** grazie infinite; **that is praise indeed** questa è decisamente una lode; **it is indeed difficult** è proprio difficile

b (*in answer to question*): **yes indeed!** certamente!; **isn't that right? — indeed it is** non è vero? — altroché; **are you coming? — indeed I am** vieni? — certo; **was I mistaken? — indeed you weren't** mi sbagliavo? — no, per niente.

in·de·fati·gable [ˌɪndɪ'fætɪgəbl] ADJ infaticabile, instancabile.

in·de·fati·gably [ˌɪndɪ'fætɪgəblɪ] ADV infaticabilmente, instancabilmente.

in·de·fen·sible [ˌɪndɪ'fɛnsəbl] ADJ (*town*) indifendibile; (*conduct*) ingiustificabile.

in·de·fin·able [ˌɪndɪ'faɪnəbl] ADJ indefinibile.

in·defi·nite [ɪn'dɛfɪnɪt] ADJ (*answer, plans*) vago(-a); (*time, period, number*) indeterminato(-a), indefinito(-a); (*Gram*) indefinito(-a).

♦ **indefinite article** N (*Gram*): **the indefinite article** l'articolo indeterminativo.

in·defi·nite·ly [ɪn'dɛfɪnɪtlɪ] ADV (*postpone*) a tempo indeterminato; (*wait*) indefinitamente, all'infinito.

in·del·ible [ɪn'dɛləbl] ADJ (*also fig*) indelebile.

in·del·ibly [ɪn'dɛləblɪ] ADV (*also fig*) indelebilmente.

in·deli·ca·cy [ɪn'dɛlɪkəsɪ] N (*lack of tact*) indelicatezza, mancanza di tatto; (*impoliteness*) indelicatezza.

in·deli·cate [ɪn'dɛlɪkɪt] ADJ (*tactless*) indelicato(-a), privo (-a) di tatto; (*not polite*) indelicato(-a).

in·dem·ni·fi·able [ɪnˌdɛmnɪ'faɪəbl] ADJ indennizzabile, risarcibile.

in·dem·ni·fy [ɪn'dɛmnɪˌfaɪ] VT (*compensate*): **to indemnify sb for sth** indennizzare qn per qc, risarcire qn di qc; **to indemnify sb against sth** (*safeguard*) assicurare qn contro qc.

in·dem·nity [ɪn'dɛmnɪtɪ] N (*see vb*) indennizzo, risarcimento; assicurazione *f*.

in·dent [ɪn'dɛnt] ①VT (*Typ: text*) far rientrare dal margine. ②VI (*Comm*): **to indent for sth** ordinare *or* commissionare qc.

in·den·ta·tion [ˌɪndɛn'teɪʃən] N (*dent, hollow mark*) tacca; (: *in metal, car*) ammaccatura; (*Typ*) rientranza, rientro; (*notched edge*) dentellatura; (*in coastline*) frastagliatura.

in·dent·ed [ɪn'dɛntɪd] ADJ (*Typ*) rientrante; (*surface*) intaccato(-a), ammaccato(-a); (*coastline*) frastagliato(-a).

in·den·ture [ɪn'dɛntʃə] N contratto *m* formazione *inv*.

in·de·pend·ence [ˌɪndɪ'pɛndəns] N indipendenza; **the country gained independence in 1964** il paese ha conquistato l'indipendenza nel 1964.

♦ **Independence Day** N (*Am*) *anniversario dell'indipendenza americana al 4 luglio*.

in·de·pend·ent [ˌɪndɪ'pɛndənt] ADJ indipendente, autonomo(-a); **of independent means** finanziariamente indipendente; **to ask for an independent opinion** chiedere un parere imparziale; **independent suspension** (*Aut*) sospensioni *fpl* indipendenti.

in·de·pen·dent·ly [ˌɪndɪ'pɛndəntlɪ] ADV (*move, decide*) indipendentemente, autonomamente; (*arrive*) separatamente; **independently of** indipendentemente da.

♦ **in-depth** [ɪn'dɛpθ] ADJ (*investigation, study*) approfondito(-a).

in·de·scrib·able [ˌɪndɪs'kraɪbəbl] ADJ indescrivibile.

in·de·scrib·ably [ˌɪndɪs'kraɪbəblɪ] ADV indescrivibilmente; **indescribably horrible/beautiful** di una bruttezza/bellezza indescrivibile.

in·de·struct·ible [ˌɪndɪs'trʌktəbl] ADJ indistruttibile.

in·de·ter·mi·nable [ˌɪndɪ'tɜːmɪnəbl] ADJ indeterminabile.

in·de·ter·mi·nate [ˌɪndɪ'tɜːmɪnɪt] ADJ (*gen*) indeterminato (-a), indefinito(-a); (*plans, ideas*) indefinito(-a), vago (-a).

In·dex ['ɪndɛks] N (*Rel*): **the Index** l'indice dei libri proibiti.

in·dex ['ɪndɛks] N **a** (*pl indexes*) (*in book*) indice *m*; (: *in library*) catalogo **b** (*pl indices*) (*pointer, sign*) indicazione *f*, indizio; (: *Math*) indice *m*, esponente *m*; **standard index form** forma esponenziale.

♦ **index card** N scheda.

♦ **index finger** N (dito) indice *m*.

♦ **index-link** [ˌɪndɛks'lɪŋk] VT indicizzare.

♦ **index-linked** [ˌɪndɛks'lɪŋkt], (*Am*) **in·dexed** ['ɪndɛkst] ADJ indicizzato(-a).

In·dia ['ɪndɪə] N India.

In·dian ['ɪndɪən] ① ADJ **a** (*from India*) indiano(-a) **b** (*American Indian*) indiano(-a) (d'America). ② N **a** (*from India*) indiano(-a) **b** (*American Indian*) indiano(-a) (d'America).

♦ **Indian elephant** N elefante *m* indiano.

♦ **Indian ink** N (inchiostro di) china.

♦ **Indian Ocean** N: **the Indian Ocean** l'Oceano Indiano.

♦ **Indian summer** N (*fig*) estate *f* di San Martino.

♦ **India paper** N carta d'India, carta bibbia.

♦ **India rubber** N (*material*) caucciù *m*; (*eraser*) gomma da cancellare.

in·di·cate ['ɪndɪˌkeɪt] ① VT **a** (*point out: place*) indicare; (: *with finger*) additare; (*register: temperature, speed*) segnare, indicare

b (*show: feelings*) denotare; (*suggest*) indicare, lasciar intendere.

② VI (*Aut Brit*) segnalare (il cambiamento di direzione), mettere la freccia; **to indicate left/right** mettere la freccia a sinistra/a destra.

in·di·ca·tion [ˌɪndɪ'keɪʃən] N indicazione *f*; **there is no indication that** non c'è niente che faccia pensare che; **this is some indication that** questo fa pensare *or* sembra indicare che.

in·dica·tive [ɪn'dɪkətɪv] ① ADJ **a**: **to be indicative of sth** essere indicativo(-a) *or* un indice di qc **b** (*Gram*) indicativo(-a).

② N (*Gram*) indicativo; **in the indicative** all'indicativo.

in·di·ca·tor ['ɪndɪˌkeɪtə] N (*sign*) segno; (: *fig*) indice *m*; (*in station, airport*) tabellone *m*; (*Brit Aut*) indicatore *m* di direzione, freccia; (*Chem*) indicatore.

in·di·ces ['ɪndɪsiːz] NPL of **index b**.

in·dict [ɪn'daɪt] VT (*Law*): **to indict sb for** incriminare qn per.

in·dict·able [ɪn'daɪtəbl] ADJ (*Law*): **indictable offence** reato perseguibile a norma di legge.

in·dict·ment [ɪnˈdaɪtmənt] N (*Law*) atto d'accusa, imputazione *f*; **to bring an indictment against sb** formulare un'accusa *or* imputazione contro qn.

in·dif·fer·ence [ɪnˈdɪfrəns] N (*see adj*) indifferenza; mediocrità.

in·dif·fer·ent [ɪnˈdɪfrənt] ADJ **a** (*apathetic*): **indifferent (to)** indifferente (a) **b** (*mediocre*) mediocre.

in·dif·fer·ent·ly [ɪnˈdɪfrəntlɪ] ADV (*apathetically*) con indifferenza; (*not well*) mediocremente.

in·dig·enous [ɪnˈdɪdʒɪnəs] ADJ indigeno(-a).

in·di·gent [ˈɪndɪdʒənt] ADJ (*frm*) indigente.

in·di·gest·ible [ˌɪndɪˈdʒɛstəbl] ADJ (*food*) indigesto(-a), poco digeribile; (*fig: style*) indigesto(-a).

in·di·ges·tion [ˌɪndɪˈdʒɛstʃən] N cattiva digestione *f*; (*chronic*) dispepsia; **to have indigestion** non riuscire a digerire.

in·dig·nant [ɪnˈdɪgnənt] ADJ indignato(-a); **to be indignant at** *or* **about sth/with sb** essere indignato(-a) per qc/contro qn; **to make sb indignant** far indignare qn.

in·dig·nant·ly [ɪnˈdɪgnəntlɪ] ADV con indignazione.

in·dig·na·tion [ˌɪndɪgˈneɪʃən] N indignazione *f*.

in·dig·nity [ɪnˈdɪgnɪtɪ] N umiliazione *f*.

in·di·go [ˈɪndɪgəʊ] 1 N indaco. 2 ADJ (*color*) indaco *inv*.

in·di·rect [ˌɪndɪˈrɛkt] ADJ (*gen, Gram*) indiretto(-a); (*road, route, answer*) non diretto(-a).

♦ **indirect costs** NPL (*Comm*) costi *mpl* indiretti.

in·di·rect·ly [ˌɪndɪˈrɛktlɪ] ADV indirettamente.

in·dis·cern·ible [ˌɪndɪˈsɜːnəbl] ADJ indiscernibile.

in·dis·ci·pline [ɪnˈdɪsɪplɪn] N indisciplina.

in·dis·creet [ˌɪndɪsˈkriːt] ADJ (*tactless*) indiscreto(-a); (*incautious*) imprudente.

in·dis·creet·ly [ˌɪndɪsˈkriːtlɪ] ADV (*tactlessly*) indiscretamente; (*incautiously*) imprudentemente.

in·dis·cre·tion [ˌɪndɪsˈkrɛʃən] N **a** (*see adj*) indiscrezione *f*; imprudenza **b** (*action, remark*) indiscrezione.

in·dis·crimi·nate [ˌɪndɪsˈkrɪmɪnɪt] ADJ (*killings*) indiscriminato(-a); (*person*) che non fa distinzioni; (*admiration*) cieco(-a).

in·dis·crimi·nate·ly [ˌɪndɪsˈkrɪmɪnɪtlɪ] ADV indiscriminatamente.

in·dis·pen·sable [ˌɪndɪsˈpɛnsəbl] ADJ indispensabile; **no-one is indispensable** nessuno è indispensabile.

in·dis·posed [ˌɪndɪsˈpəʊzd] ADJ (*frm*) **a** (*unwell*) indisposto(-a) **b** (*unwilling*) poco incline.

in·dis·po·si·tion [ˌɪndɪspəˈzɪʃən] N (*frm*) **a** (*illness*) indisposizione *f* **b** (*unwillingness*) poca inclinazione *f*.

in·dis·put·able [ˌɪndɪsˈpjuːtəbl] ADJ (*evidence*) inconfutabile, incontestabile; (*fact*) indiscutibile, incontestabile; (*winner*) incontestabile.

in·dis·put·ably [ˌɪndɪsˈpjuːtəblɪ] ADV (*demonstrate*) indiscutibilmente, inconfutabilmente, incontestabilmente; **indisputably the winner** senza dubbio il vincitore.

in·dis·sol·uble [ˌɪndɪˈsɒljʊbl] ADJ indissolubile.

in·dis·sol·ubly [ˌɪndɪˈsɒljʊblɪ] ADV indissolubilmente.

in·dis·tinct [ˌɪndɪsˈtɪŋkt] ADJ (*voice, words*) indistinto(-a); (*memory, noise*) vago(-a).

in·dis·tinct·ly [ˌɪndɪsˈtɪŋktlɪ] ADV (*mumble, appear*) indistintamente.

in·dis·tin·guish·able [ˌɪndɪsˈtɪŋgwɪʃəbl] ADJ indistinguibile.

in·di·vid·ual [ˌɪndɪˈvɪdjʊəl] 1 ADJ **a** (*separate: member, case*) (ogni) singolo(-a) **b** (*own, personal: taste, style*) personale, individuale; (*for one person: portion*) individuale.

2 N individuo.

in·di·vidu·al·ism [ˌɪndɪˈvɪdjʊəˌlɪzəm] N individualismo.

in·di·vidu·al·ist [ˌɪndɪˈvɪdjʊəlɪst] N individualista *m/f*.

in·di·vidu·al·is·tic [ˌɪndɪˌvɪdjʊəˈlɪstɪk] ADJ individualistico (-a).

in·di·vidu·al·ity [ˌɪndɪˌvɪdjʊˈælɪtɪ] N individualità *f inv*.

in·di·vidu·al·ize [ˌɪndɪˈvɪdjʊəlaɪz] VT (*frm*) caratterizzare.

in·di·vid·ual·ly [ˌɪndɪˈvɪdjʊəlɪ] ADV singolarmente, uno(-a) per uno(-a).

in·di·vis·ible [ˌɪndɪˈvɪzəbl] ADJ indivisibile.

Indo- [ˈɪndəʊ] PREF indo... .

Indo·china [ˌɪndəʊˈtʃaɪnə] N l'Indocina.

in·doc·tri·nate [ɪnˈdɒktrɪˌneɪt] VT indottrinare.

in·doc·tri·na·tion [ɪnˌdɒktrɪˈneɪʃən] N indottrinamento.

in·do·lence [ˈɪndələns] N indolenza.

in·do·lent [ˈɪndələnt] ADJ indolente.

in·do·lent·ly [ˈɪndələntlɪ] ADV indolentemente.

in·domi·table [ɪnˈdɒmɪtəbl] ADJ (*spirit, character*) indomabile.

In·do·nesia [ˌɪndəʊˈniːzɪə] N l'Indonesia.

In·do·nesian [ˌɪndəʊˈniːzɪən] 1 ADJ indonesiano(-a). 2 N (*person*) indonesiano(-a); (*language*) indonesiano.

in·door [ˈɪnˌdɔːʳ] ADJ (*shoes*) da casa; (*plant*) da appartamento; (*sport: table tennis, squash*) praticato(-a) al coperto; (: *athletics*) indoor *inv*; (*tennis court*) al coperto; (*swimming pool*) coperto(-a); (*photography*) di interni; (*hobby*) da praticare a casa; **indoor aerial** antenna interna; **indoor sports stadium** palasport *m inv*.

in·doors [ˌɪnˈdɔːz] ADV (*in building*) all'interno; (*at home*) in casa; (*under cover*) al coperto; **to go indoors** rientrare, andar dentro.

in·du·bi·table [ɪnˈdjuːbɪtəbl] ADJ indubitabile.

in·du·bi·tably [ɪnˈdjuːbɪtəblɪ] ADV indubbiamente.

in·duce [ɪnˈdjuːs] VT (*persuade*) persuadere, convincere; (*bring about: sleep*) provocare; (: *birth*) indurre; **to induce sb to do sth** persuadere *or* convincere qn a fare qc.

in·duce·ment [ɪnˈdjuːsmənt] N (*incentive*) incentivo.

in·duct [ɪnˈdʌkt] VT (*frm: install*) insediare; (*Am Mil*) reclutare.

in·duc·tion [ɪnˈdʌkʃən] N (*Elec, Philosophy*) induzione *f*; (*Med: of birth*) parto indotto.

♦ **induction course** N (*Brit*) corso introduttivo.

in·duc·tive [ɪnˈdʌktɪv] ADJ induttivo(-a).

in·duc·tor [ɪnˈdʌktəʳ] N (*Phys*) induttore *m*.

in·dulge [ɪnˈdʌldʒ] VT (*give into: desire, appetite*) soddisfare, appagare; (: *person*) assecondare (i desideri di), accontentare; (*spoil: child*) viziare; **why not indulge yourself and have an ice-cream?** dai, concediti un gelato

▶ **indulge in** VI + PREP (*activity*) darsi a; (*emotion*) lasciarsi andare a; (*chocolate, sweets*) concedersi.

in·dul·gence [ɪnˈdʌldʒəns] N (*extravagance*) piccolo lusso (che ci si concede); (*habit*) vizio; (*leniency, Rel*) indulgenza.

in·dul·gent [ɪnˈdʌldʒənt] ADJ: **indulgent (to** *or* **towards sb)** indulgente (con *or* verso qn).

in·dul·gent·ly [ɪnˈdʌldʒəntlɪ] ADV con indulgenza.

in·dus·trial [ɪnˈdʌstrɪəl] ADJ (*area, town, processes*) industriale; (*worker*) dell'industria; (*accident, injury*) sul lavoro; (*disease*) del lavoro.

♦ **industrial action** N (*strikes, working to rule*) agitazione *f* sindacale.

♦ **industrial estate**, (*Am*) **industrial park** N zona industriale.

in·dus·tri·al·ism [ɪn'dʌstrɪə,lɪzəm] N industrialismo.

in·dus·tri·al·ist [ɪn'dʌstrɪəlɪst] N industriale *m/f.*

in·dus·tri·ali·za·tion [ɪn,dʌstrɪəlaɪ'zeɪʃən] N industrializzazione *f.*

in·dus·tri·al·ize [ɪn'dʌstrɪə,laɪz] VT industrializzare.

in·dus·tri·al·ized [ɪn'dʌstrɪə,laɪzd] ADJ industrializzato (-a).

in·dus·tri·al·ly [ɪn'dʌstrɪəlɪ] ADV industrialmente.

♦ **industrial park** (*Am*) N = **industrial estate.**

♦ **industrial relations** [1] NPL relazioni *fpl* sindacali. [2] N (*field of study*) relazioni *fpl* industriali.

♦ **industrial tribunal** N (*Brit*) *organo competente a decidere le controversie di lavoro.*

♦ **industrial unrest** N (*Brit*) agitazione *f* sindacale.

in·dus·tri·ous [ɪn'dʌstrɪəs] ADJ diligente.

in·dus·tri·ous·ly [ɪn'dʌstrɪəslɪ] ADV diligentemente.

in·dus·tri·ous·ness [ɪn'dʌstrɪəsnɪs] N diligenza, zelo.

in·dus·try ['ɪndəstrɪ] N a l'industria; **light/heavy industry** industria leggera/pesante; **the tourist industry** il turismo b (*frm: industriousness*) operosità.

in·ebri·at·ed [ɪ'niːbrɪ,eɪtɪd] ADJ (*frm*) ubriaco(-a).

in·ed·ible [ɪn'ɛdɪbl] ADJ (*not to be eaten*) non commestibile; (*not fit to be eaten*) immangiabile.

in·ef·fable [ɪn'ɛfəbl] ADJ (*frm*) ineffabile.

in·ef·fec·tive [,ɪnɪ'fɛktɪv] ADJ (*remedy*) inefficace; (*minister, leader*) poco capace.

in·ef·fec·tive·ly [,ɪnɪ'fɛktɪvlɪ], **in·ef·fec·tu·al·ly** [,ɪnɪ'fɛktjʊəlɪ] ADV inefficacemente.

in·ef·fec·tual [,ɪnɪ'fɛktʊəl] ADJ (*policy*) inefficace; (*person*) inetto(-a); **to be ineffectual** essere un(-a) incapace.

in·ef·fi·cien·cy [,ɪnɪ'fɪʃənsɪ] N inefficienza.

in·ef·fi·cient [,ɪnɪ'fɪʃənt] ADJ inefficiente.

in·ef·fi·cient·ly [,ɪnɪ'fɪʃəntlɪ] ADV inefficientemente.

in·el·egant [ɪn'ɛlɪgənt] ADJ poco elegante.

in·el·egant·ly [ɪn'ɛlɪgəntlɪ] ADV poco elegantemente.

in·eli·gible [ɪn'ɛlɪdʒəbl] ADJ: **to be ineligible for sth/to do sth** non avere diritto a qc/a fare qc; **they are ineligible for unemployment benefit** non hanno diritto all'indennità di disoccupazione.

in·eluc·table [,ɪnɪ'lʌktəbl] ADJ (*frm*) ineluttabile.

in·ept [ɪ'nɛpt] ADJ (*person*) inetto(-a); (*remark, behaviour*) inopportuno(-a); (*management, handling*) poco abile.

in·epti·tude [ɪ'nɛptɪtjuːd] N (*see adj*) inettitudine *f*; inopportunità; scarsa abilità.

in·equal·ity [,ɪnɪ'kwɒlɪtɪ] N (*gen*) ineguaglianza, disuguaglianza; (*Math*) disuguaglianza.

in·equi·table [ɪn'ɛkwɪtəbl] ADJ iniquo(-a).

in·equi·ty [ɪn'ɛkwɪtɪ] N (*frm*) ingiustizie *fpl.*

in·eradi·cable [,ɪnɪ'rædɪkəbl] ADJ (*frm: feeling*) tenace; (: *sign, memory*) incancellabile.

in·ert [ɪ'nɜːt] ADJ inerte.

♦ **inert gas** N gas *m* inerte *or* nobile.

in·er·tia [ɪ'nɜːʃə] N inerzia.

♦ **inertia-reel seat belt** [ɪ,nɜːʃə,riːl'siːt,bɛlt] N cintura di sicurezza con pretensionatore.

in·es·cap·able [,ɪnɪs'keɪpəbl] ADJ ineluttabile, inevitabile.

in·es·sen·tial [,ɪnɪ'sɛnʃl] ADJ superfluo(-a).

in·es·ti·mable [ɪn'ɛstɪməbl] ADJ inestimabile, incalcolabile.

in·evi·tabil·ity [ɪn,ɛvɪtə'bɪlɪtɪ] N inevitabilità.

in·evi·table [ɪn'ɛvɪtəbl] ADJ inevitabile; **I was offered the inevitable cup of tea** mi venne offerta l'immancabile tazza di tè.

in·evi·tably [ɪn'ɛvɪtəblɪ] ADV inevitabilmente; **as inevitably happens** ... come immancabile succede ... .

in·ex·act [,ɪnɪg'zækt] ADJ inesatto(-a), impreciso(-a).

in·ex·act·ly [,ɪnɪg'zæktlɪ] ADV in modo inesatto, in modo impreciso.

in·ex·cus·able [,ɪnɪks'kjuːzəbl] ADJ imperdonabile.

in·ex·cus·ably [,ɪnɪks'kjuːzəblɪ] ADV imperdonabilmente; **inexcusably lazy** di una pigrizia imperdonabile.

in·ex·haust·ible [,ɪnɪg'zɔːstəbl] ADJ (*patience, supply*) inesauribile; (*person*) instancabile, infaticabile.

in·exo·rable [ɪn'ɛksərəbl] ADJ inesorabile.

in·exo·rably [ɪn'ɛksərəblɪ] ADV inesorabilmente.

in·ex·pen·sive [,ɪnɪks'pɛnsɪv] ADJ a buon mercato, poco costoso(-a).

in·ex·pen·sive·ly [,ɪnɪks'pɛnsɪvlɪ] ADV (*buy*) a buon mercato; (*dress*) con poca spesa; (*live*) frugalmente.

in·ex·pe·ri·ence [,ɪnɪks'pɪərɪəns] N inesperienza.

in·ex·pe·ri·enced [,ɪnɪks'pɪərɪənst] ADJ inesperto(-a); **to be inexperienced in sth** essere poco pratico(-a) di qc.

in·ex·pert [ɪn'ɛkspɜːt] ADJ (*attempt*) maldestro(-a).

in·ex·pert·ly [ɪn'ɛkspɜːtlɪ] ADV in modo poco esperto.

in·ex·pli·cable [,ɪnɪks'plɪkəbl] ADJ inesplicabile.

in·ex·pli·cable·ness [,ɪnɪks'plɪkəblnɪs] N inesplicabilità.

in·ex·pli·cably [,ɪnɪks'plɪkəblɪ] ADV inesplicabilmente.

in·ex·press·ible [,ɪnɪks'prɛsəbl] ADJ inesprimibile.

in·ex·pres·sive [,ɪnɪks'prɛsɪv] ADJ (*style*) piatto(-a), inespressivo(-a); (*look, face*) senza espressione.

in·ex·tri·cable [,ɪnɪks'trɪkəbl] ADJ inestricabile.

in·ex·tri·cably [,ɪnɪks'trɪkəblɪ] ADV inestricabilmente.

in·fal·libil·ity [ɪn,fælə'bɪlɪtɪ] N infallibilità.

in·fal·lible [ɪn'fæləbl] ADJ infallibile.

in·fal·libly [ɪn'fæləblɪ] ADV infallibilmente; **she's infallibly correct** ha sempre ragione; **he infallibly arrives just as we are sitting down to eat** arriva puntualmente quando stiamo per sederci a tavola.

in·fa·mous ['ɪnfəməs] ADJ (*person*) famigerato(-a); (*crime*) infame.

in·fa·my ['ɪnfəmɪ] N infamia.

in·fan·cy ['ɪnfənsɪ] N (*childhood*) infanzia; (*Law*) minore età *finv*; **in its infancy** (*fig: early stage*) ai primi passi.

in·fant ['ɪnfənt] N bambino(-a); (*Law*) minorenne *m/f*, minore *m/f.*

in·fan·ti·cide [ɪn'fæntɪsaɪd] N infanticidio.

in·fan·tile ['ɪnfən,taɪl] ADJ infantile.

♦ **infant mortality** N mortalità infantile.

in·fan·try ['ɪnfəntrɪ] N fanteria.

in·fantry·man ['ɪnfəntrɪmən] N (*pl* **-men**) fante *m.*

♦ **infant school** N (*Brit*) scuola elementare (*per bambini dai 5 ai 7 anni*).

in·fatu·at·ed [ɪn'fætjʊ,eɪtɪd] ADJ: **infatuated (with sb)** infatuato(-a) (di qn); **to become infatuated (with sb)** infatuarsi (di qn).

in·fatu·a·tion [ɪn,fætjʊ'eɪʃən] N infatuazione *f.*

in·fect [ɪn'fɛkt] VT (*wound*) infettare; (*person*) contagiare; (*food, air*) contaminare; (*fig: poison*) corrompere; (: *influence*) influenzare; **to infect sb with a disease** trasmettere una malattia a qn; **he's infected everybody with his enthusiasm** ha contagiato tutti con il suo entusiasmo.

in·fect·ed [ɪn'fɛktɪd] ADJ (*wound*) infetto(-a); (*person*) contagiato(-a); **to become infected** (*wound*) infettarsi; **infected with measles** affetto(-a) da morbillo.

in·fec·tion [ɪn'fɛkʃən] N infezione *f.*

in·fec·tious [ɪn'fɛkʃəs] ADJ (*disease*) infettivo(-a), contagioso(-a); (*person, laughter*) contagioso(-a).

in·fer [ɪn'fɜː'] VT: **to infer (from)** dedurre (da).

in·fer·ence ['ɪnfərəns] N deduzione *f*, illazione *f.*

in·fe·ri·or [ɪn'fɪərɪəʳ] [1] ADJ (*in quality, rank*): **inferior (to)** inferiore (a); (*work, goods*) scadente; **to feel inferior** sentirsi inferiore.

  [2] N inferiore *m/f*; (*in rank*) subalterno(-a).

in·fe·ri·or·ity [ɪn,fɪərɪ'ɒrɪtɪ] N inferiorità.

♦ **inferiority complex** N complesso di inferiorità.

in·fer·nal [ɪn'fɜːnl] ADJ (*fires*) dell'inferno; (*spirit, powers*) infernale; (*fig: cruelty*) diabolico(-a); (*fam: noise*) infernale, terribile.

in·fer·nal·ly [ɪn'fɜːnəlɪ] ADV (*difficult*) terribilmente; **it is infernally hot** fa un caldo infernale.

in·fer·no [ɪn'fɜːnəʊ] N inferno.

in·fer·tile [ɪn'fɜːtaɪl] ADJ sterile.

in·fer·til·ity [,ɪnfɜː'tɪlɪtɪ] N sterilità.

in·fest [ɪn'fɛst] VT infestare.

in·fes·ta·tion [,ɪnfɛs'teɪʃən] N infestazione *f*.

in·fest·ed [,ɪn'fɛstɪd] ADJ: **infested (with)** infestato(-a) (di *or* da).

in·fi·del ['ɪnfɪdəl] (*liter*) [1] N infedele *m/f*.

  [2] ADJ miscredente.

in·fi·del·ity [,ɪnfɪ'dɛlɪtɪ] N infedeltà *f inv*.

♦ **in-fighting** ['ɪnfaɪtɪŋ] N lotte *fpl* interne *or* intestine.

in·fil·trate ['ɪnfɪl,treɪt] [1] VT (*troops*) far penetrare; (*enemy line, political organization*) infiltrarsi in.

  [2] VI: **to infiltrate (into)** infiltrarsi (in).

in·fil·tra·tion [,ɪnfɪl'treɪʃən] N infiltrazione *f*.

in·fi·nite ['ɪnfɪnɪt] ADJ infinito(-a); **we haven't got an infinite amount of time/money** non abbiamo un'illimitata quantità di tempo/denaro.

in·fi·nite·ly ['ɪnfɪnɪtlɪ] ADV infinitamente.

in·fini·tesi·mal [,ɪnfɪnɪ'tɛsɪməl] ADJ infinitesimale.

in·fini·tive [ɪn'fɪnɪtɪv] [1] ADJ (*Gram*) infinito(-a).

  [2] N infinito; **in the infinitive** all'infinito.

in·fini·tude [ɪn'fɪnɪtjuːd] N (*frm*) infinità *f inv*.

in·fin·ity [ɪn'fɪnɪtɪ] N (*infiniteness*) infinità; (*in time, space, Math*) infinito.

in·firm [ɪn'fɜːm] ADJ infermo(-a).

in·fir·ma·ry [ɪn'fɜːmərɪ] N (*hospital*) ospedale *m* ; (*in school, prison, barracks*) infermeria.

in·fir·mity [ɪn'fɜːmɪtɪ] N infermità *f inv*.

in·flame [ɪn'fleɪm] VT **a** (*Med: wound*) infiammare; **to become inflamed** infiammarsi **b** (*fig: feelings, passions*) accendere; (*: person*) far incollerire.

in·flamed [ɪn'fleɪmd] ADJ (*Med*) infiammato(-a).

in·flam·mable [ɪn'flæməbl] ADJ (*substance, fabric*) infiammabile; (*fig: situation*) esplosivo(-a).

in·flam·ma·tion [,ɪnflə'meɪʃən] N infiammazione *f*.

in·flam·ma·tory [ɪn'flæmətərɪ] ADJ (*speech*) incendiario (-a).

in·flat·able [ɪn'fleɪtəbl] ADJ gonfiabile.

in·flate [ɪn'fleɪt] [1] VT (*tyre, balloon*) gonfiare; (*fig: prices, profits*) gonfiare, far salire; (*: idea, opinion*) esagerare, gonfiare.

  [2] VI (*tyre, balloon*) gonfiarsi; (*fig: prices, profits*) salire.

in·flat·ed [ɪn'fleɪtɪd] ADJ (*price, fee*) gonfiato(-a); (*idea, opinion, value*) esagerato(-a), gonfiato(-a); (*style, language*) ampolloso(-a); (*tyre*) gonfio(-a).

in·fla·tion [ɪn'fleɪʃən] N (*Econ*) inflazione *f*.

in·fla·tion·ary [ɪn'fleɪʃnərɪ] ADJ inflazionistico(-a).

in·flect [ɪn'flɛkt] [1] VT (*voice*) modulare; (*Gram*) flettere.

  [2] VI (*Gram*) flettersi.

in·flec·tion [ɪn'flɛkʃən] N (*of voice*) intonazione *f*, modulazione *f*; (*Gram*) flessione *f*; **the inflection of nouns/verbs** la flessione nominale/verbale; **point of inflection** (*Math*) punto di flesso.

in·flex·ibil·ity [ɪn,flɛksɪ'bɪlɪtɪ] N (*see adj*) rigidità; inflessibilità.

in·flex·ible [ɪn'flɛksəbl] ADJ (*object*) rigido(-a); (*fig: person, ideas*) inflessibile, rigido(-a).

in·flict [ɪn'flɪkt] VT: **to inflict (on)** (*penalty*) infliggere (a); (*tax*) imporre (a); (*suffering, damage*) procurare (a); **to inflict a blow/wound on sb** assestare un colpo a/ferire qn; **to inflict o.s. on sb** imporre la propria presenza a qn.

in·flic·tion [ɪn'flɪkʃən] N l'infliggere *m*.

♦ **in-flight** ['ɪn,flaɪt] ADJ a bordo; **in-flight service** servizio a bordo.

in·flow ['ɪn,fləʊ] N afflusso.

in·flu·ence ['ɪnflʊəns] [1] N influenza; **to have an influence on sb/sth** (*subj: person*) avere un'influenza su qn/qc; (*: event*) influenzare qn/qc; (*: weather*) influire su qn/qc; **to have influence with sb** avere un ascendente su qn; **to be a good/bad influence on sb** avere *or* esercitare una buona/cattiva influenza su qn; **under the influence of drugs** sotto l'effetto della droga; **under the influence of drink** sotto l'effetto dell'alcol; (*Law*) in stato di ebbrezza; **he was under the influence** (*fam*) aveva alzato il gomito.

  [2] VT (*person*) influenzare; (*action, decision*) influire su, influenzare; **to be easily influenced** essere facilmente influenzabile.

in·flu·en·tial [,ɪnflʊ'ɛnʃəl] ADJ influente.

in·flu·en·za [,ɪnflʊ'ɛnzə] N (*Med*) influenza.

in·flux ['ɪnflʌks] N (*of people, objects*) afflusso; (*of ideas*) flusso.

in·fo ['ɪnfəʊ] N (*fam*) informazione *f*.

in·form [ɪn'fɔːm] [1] VT informare, avvertire; **to inform sb about/of sth** informare *or* avvertire qn di qc; **I am happy to inform you that** sono lieto di comunicarle che; **keep me informed** tienimi informato; **a well-informed person** una persona di cultura.

  [2] VI: **to inform on sb** denunciare qn.

in·for·mal [ɪn'fɔːməl] ADJ (*person, manner*) semplice, alla mano; (*tone: of letter*) non formale; (*language, style*) colloquiale; (*dinner, party*) fra amici; (*visit, announcement, invitation*) non ufficiale; (*meeting, arrangement, discussion*) informale; **"dress informal"** "non è richiesto l'abito da sera".

in·for·mal·ity [,ɪnfɔː'mælɪtɪ] N (*of person, manner*) semplicità; (*of tone*) mancanza di formalità; (*of language, style*) tono colloquiale; (*of occasion*) tono familiare; (*of meeting, negotiations, announcement*) carattere *m* non ufficiale.

in·for·mal·ly [ɪn'fɔːməlɪ] ADV (*discuss, chat*) alla buona; (*invite, meet*) in modo non ufficiale; **the Queen visited the hospital informally** la regina ha visitato l'ospedale in forma privata; **I have been informally told that ...** mi è stato comunicato ufficiosamente che... .

in·form·ant [ɪn'fɔːmənt] N informatore(-trice).

in·for·mat·ics [,ɪnfə'mætɪks] NSG informatica.

in·for·ma·tion [,ɪnfə'meɪʃən] N: **information (about** *or* **on)** informazioni *fpl* (riguardo a *or* su); **a piece of information** un'informazione; **to give sb information about** *or* **on sb/sth** dare a qn informazioni su qn/qc; **to get information on** informarsi su; **for your information** (*on document*) a titolo d'informazione; (*fam iro*) per tua norma e regola.

♦ **information bureau** N ufficio *m* informazioni *inv*.

♦ **information processing** N (*Comput*) elaborazione *f* delle informazioni.

♦ **information retrieval** N (*Comput*) ricupero delle informazioni.

♦ **information science** N scienza dell'informazione.

♦ **information superhighway** N: **the information superhighway** (*Comput*) l'autostrada telematica.

♦ **information technology** N informatica.

in·forma·tive [ɪnˈfɔːmətɪv] ADJ (*speech, book*) istruttivo (-a); **she wasn't very informative about it** non si è sbottonata sulla faccenda.

in·formed [ɪnˈfɔːmd] ADJ (*observer*) (ben) informato(-a); **an informed guess** un'ipotesi ƒ fondata.

in·form·er [ɪnˈfɔːməʳ] N informatore(-trice); **to turn informer** (*Police*) diventare un informatore(-trice).

in·fra dig [ˈɪnfrəˈdɪg] ADJ poco dignitoso(-a); **it would be infra dig for him to ...** non si abbasserebbe mai a... .

infra·red [ˌɪnfrəˈrɛd] 1 ADJ infrarosso(-a). 2 N (*raggio*) infrarosso.

infra·sound [ˈɪnfrəˌsaʊnd] N (*Phys*) infrasuono.

infra·struc·ture [ˈɪnfrəˌstrʌktʃəʳ] N infrastruttura.

in·fre·quen·cy [ɪnˈfriːkwənsɪ] N rarità.

in·fre·quent [ɪnˈfriːkwənt] ADJ poco frequente, raro(-a).

in·fre·quent·ly [ɪnˈfriːkwəntlɪ] ADV raramente.

in·fringe [ɪnˈfrɪndʒ] 1 VT (*law*) infrangere, violare; (*rights, copyright*) violare. 2 VI (*encroach*): **to infringe on** or **upon** (*rights*) violare; (*privacy*) invadere.

in·fringe·ment [ɪnˈfrɪndʒmənt] N (*of law, rule*) infrazione ƒ, violazione ƒ; (*of rights, copyright*) violazione ƒ.

in·furi·ate [ɪnˈfjʊərɪˌeɪt] VT far infuriare, rendere furioso (-a); **to become infuriated** infuriarsi, andare in bestia.

in·furi·at·ing [ɪnˈfjʊərɪˌeɪtɪŋ] ADJ esasperante, estremamente irritante.

in·furi·at·ing·ly [ɪnˈfjʊərɪeɪtɪŋlɪ] ADV in modo esasperante, in modo estremamente irritante.

in·fuse [ɪnˈfjuːz] VT **a** (*with courage, enthusiasm*): **to infuse sb with sth** infondere qc a qn; **to infuse courage into sb** infondere coraggio a qn **b** (*Culin: herbs, tea*) lasciare in infusione.

in·fu·sion [ɪnˈfjuːʒən] N (*tea*) infuso.

in·gen·ious [ɪnˈdʒiːnɪəs] ADJ ingegnoso(-a).

in·gen·ious·ly [ɪnˈdʒiːnɪəslɪ] ADV ingegnosamente.

in·genu·ity [ˌɪndʒɪˈnjuːɪtɪ] N ingegnosità.

in·genu·ous [ɪnˈdʒɛnjʊəs] ADJ ingenuo(-a).

in·genu·ous·ly [ɪnˈdʒɛnjʊəslɪ] ADV ingenuamente.

in·genu·ous·ness [ɪnˈdʒɛnjʊəsnɪs] N ingenuità.

in·glo·ri·ous [ɪnˈɡlɔːrɪəs] ADJ inglorioso(-a).

♦ **in-goal** [ˈɪnˈɡəʊl] ADJ (*Rugby*): **in-goal area** area di meta.

in·got [ˈɪŋɡət] N lingotto.

in·grained [ˈɪnˈɡreɪnd] ADJ (*dirt*) incrostato(-a); (*fig: ideas, tradition*) radicato(-a); (*habit, prejudice*) inveterato(-a).

in·gra·ti·ate [ɪnˈɡreɪʃɪˌeɪt] VT: **to ingratiate o.s. with sb** ingraziarsi qn.

in·gra·ti·at·ing [ɪnˈɡreɪʃɪˌeɪtɪŋ] ADJ (*smile, speech*) suadente, accattivante; (*person*) compiacente.

in·grati·tude [ɪnˈɡrætɪtjuːd] N ingratitudine ƒ.

in·gre·di·ent [ɪnˈɡriːdɪənt] N (*Culin*) ingrediente *m*; (*fig*) fattore *m*, elemento.

in·grow·ing [ˈɪnˌɡrəʊɪŋ], **in·grown** [ˈɪnˌɡrəʊn] ADJ: **ingrowing (toe)nail** unghia incarnita.

in·gulf [ɪnˈɡʌlf] VT = **engulf**.

in·hab·it [ɪnˈhæbɪt] VT (*house*) abitare (in); (*town, country*) vivere in.

in·hab·it·able [ɪnˈhæbɪtəbl] ADJ abitabile.

in·hab·it·ant [ɪnˈhæbɪtənt] N abitante *m/f*.

in·hab·it·ed [ɪnˈhæbɪtɪd] ADJ abitato(-a).

in·hal·ant [ɪnˈheɪlənt] N inalante *m*.

in·ha·la·tion [ˌɪnhəˈleɪʃən] N inalazione ƒ.

in·hale [ɪnˈheɪl] 1 VT (*gas, smoke, air*) respirare; (*Med*) inalare. 2 VI (*smoker*) aspirare; (*Med*) inspirare.

in·hal·er [ɪnˈheɪləʳ], **in·ha·la·tor** [ˈɪnhəˌleɪtəʳ] N inalatore *m*.

in·her·ent [ɪnˈhɪərənt] ADJ: **inherent (in)** intrinseco(-a) (a); (*kindness, cruelty*) innato(-a) (a).

in·her·ent·ly [ɪnˈhɪərəntlɪ] ADV (*easy, difficult*) di per se stesso(-a), di per sé; **inherently inefficient** sostanzialmente inefficiente.

in·her·it [ɪnˈhɛrɪt] VT ereditare.

in·her·it·ance [ɪnˈhɛrɪtəns] N eredità ƒ inv; (*fig*) retaggio.

in·heri·tor [ɪnˈhɛrɪtəʳ] N erede *m/f*.

in·hib·it [ɪnˈhɪbɪt] VT inibire; **to inhibit sb from doing sth** impedire a qn di fare qc.

in·hib·it·ed [ɪnˈhɪbɪtɪd] ADJ (*person*) inibito(-a).

in·hi·bit·ing [ɪnˈhɪbɪtɪŋ] ADJ inibitorio(-a).

in·hi·bi·tion [ˌɪnhɪˈbɪʃən] N inibizione ƒ.

in·hos·pi·table [ˌɪnhɒsˈpɪtəbl] ADJ inospitale.

♦ **in-house** [ˈɪnˈhaʊs] 1 ADJ (*magazine, video*) per il personale, aziendale; (*training*) all'interno dell'azienda. 2 ADV (*train, produce*) all'interno dell'azienda.

in·hu·man [ɪnˈhjuːmən] ADJ (*cruelty, conditions, treatment*) disumano(-a); (*appearance*) non umano(-a).

in·hu·mane [ˌɪnhjuːˈmeɪn] ADJ inumano(-a).

in·hu·mane·ly [ˌɪnhjuːˈmeɪnlɪ] ADV inumanamente, disumanamente.

in·hu·man·ity [ˌɪnhjuːˈmænɪtɪ] N inumanità ƒ inv, disumanità ƒ inv.

in·imi·cal [ɪˈnɪmɪkəl] ADJ ostile.

in·imi·table [ɪˈnɪmɪtəbl] ADJ inimitabile.

in·imi·tably [ɪˈnɪmɪtəblɪ] ADV in modo inimitabile.

in·iqui·tous [ɪˈnɪkwɪtəs] ADJ iniquo(-a); **it's an iniquitous system** è un sistema di un'ingiustizia mostruosa.

in·iqui·tous·ly [ɪˈnɪkwɪtəslɪ] ADV iniquamente.

in·iquity [ɪˈnɪkwɪtɪ] N iniquità ƒ inv.

ini·tial [ɪˈnɪʃəl] 1 ADJ iniziale; **in the initial stages** nella fase iniziale; **in the initial stages of their relationship** agli inizi della loro storia. 2 N iniziale ƒ; **to sign sth with one's initials** siglare qc con le proprie iniziali. 3 VT siglare.

ini·tial·ize [ɪˈnɪʃəˌlaɪz] VT (*Comput*) inizializzare.

ini·tial·ly [ɪˈnɪʃəlɪ] ADV all'inizio, inizialmente.

ini·ti·ate [ɪˈnɪʃɪˌeɪt] VT **a** (*begin*) iniziare; (: *talks*) iniziare, avviare; (: *reform*) promuovere; **to initiate proceedings against sb** (*Law*) intentare causa a or contro qn **b** (*admit*): **to initiate sb (into sth)** iniziare qn (a qc).

ini·tia·tion [ɪˌnɪʃɪˈeɪʃən] N iniziazione ƒ.

♦ **initiation ceremony** N rito iniziatico.

ini·tia·tive [ɪˈnɪʃətɪv] N iniziativa; **on one's own initiative** di propria iniziativa, da sé; **to take the initiative** prendere l'iniziativa; **she's got initiative** è una che ha spirito d'iniziativa; **an important initiative** un'importante iniziativa.

ini·tia·tor [ɪˈnɪʃɪˌeɪtəʳ] N promotore(-trice).

in·ject [ɪnˈdʒɛkt] VT (*drug*) iniettare; (*person*) fare un'iniezione a; (*fig: money*): **to inject into** immettere in; **to inject sb with sth** iniettare qc a qn; **to inject enthusiasm into sth/sb** dare una carica di entusiasmo a qc/qn.

in·jec·tion [ɪnˈdʒɛkʃən] N (*Med*) iniezione ƒ, puntura; (*Tech, fig*) iniezione; **to give sb an injection** fare un'iniezione

or una puntura a qn; **to have an injection** farsi fare un'iniezione *or* una puntura.

in·jec·tor [ɪnˈdʒɛktəʳ] N (*Tech*) iniettore *m*.

in·ju·di·cious [ˌɪndʒʊˈdɪʃəs] ADJ (*frm*) poco saggio(-a).

in·ju·di·cious·ly [ˌɪndʒʊˈdɪʃəslɪ] ADV (*frm*) poco saggiamente.

in·junc·tion [ɪnˈdʒʌŋkʃən] N (*Law*) ingiunzione *f*, intimazione *f*, ordinanza.

in·jure [ˈɪndʒəʳ] VT **a** (*physically*) ferire; **he injured his arm** si è fatto male a *or* si è ferito a un braccio; **to injure o.s.** farsi male, ferirsi **b** (*fig: reputation, trade etc*) nuocere a; (: *feelings*) offendere; (: *wrong: person*) fare (un) torto a.

in·jured [ˈɪndʒəd] 1 ADJ (*person, leg*) ferito(-a); (*tone, feelings*) offeso(-a).

2 NPL: **the injured** i feriti.

♦ **injured party** N (*Law*) parte *f* lesa.

in·ju·ri·ous [ɪnˈdʒʊərɪəs] ADJ: **injurious (to)** nocivo(-a) (a), pregiudizievole (per).

in·ju·ry [ˈɪndʒərɪ] N (*physical*) ferita, lesione *f*; (*fig: to reputation*) danno; (: *to feelings*) offesa; (: *wrong*) torto; **to escape without injury** rimanere illeso(-a).

♦ **injury time** N (*Sport*) (minuti *mpl* di) recupero.

in·jus·tice [ɪnˈdʒʌstɪs] N ingiustizia; **you do me an injustice** sei ingiusto verso di me.

ink [ɪŋk] N inchiostro; **in ink** a penna.

♦ **ink-cap** [ˈɪŋkˌkæp] N (*Bot*) fungo dell'inchiostro.

♦ **ink-jet printer** [ˈɪŋkˌdʒɛtˈprɪntəʳ] N stampante *f* a getto d'inchiostro.

ink·ling [ˈɪŋklɪŋ] N (*hint*) indizio; (*suspicion, vague idea*) mezza idea; **to give sb an inkling that** lasciar capire *or* intuire a qn che; **I had no inkling that** non avevo la minima idea che.

♦ **ink pad** N tampone *m or* cuscinetto per timbri.

ink·stand [ˈɪŋkˌstænd] N calamaio.

ink·well [ˈɪŋkˌwɛl] N calamaio.

inky [ˈɪŋkɪ] ADJ (*comp* **-ier**, *superl* **-iest**) macchiato(-a) *or* sporco(-a) d'inchiostro; (*fig: darkness*) nero(-a) come l'inchiostro.

INLA [ˌaɪɛnɛlˈeɪ] N (= *Irish National Liberation Army*) organizzazione paramilitare repubblicana irlandese.

in·laid [ˈɪnˈleɪd] ADJ (*table, box*): **inlaid (with)** intarsiato(-a) (di).

in·land [ˈɪnlænd] 1 ADJ (*town*) dell'interno; (*mail*) nazionale, interno(-a); (*sea, waterway*) interno(-a).

2 ADV (*location*) nell'entroterra; (*travel*) verso l'interno.

♦ **Inland Revenue** N (*Brit*): **the Inland Revenue** il fisco.

♦ **in-laws** [ˈɪnˌlɔːz] N (*fam*) NPL (*parents-in-law*) suoceri *mpl*; (*other family members*) famiglia del marito (*or* della moglie).

in·let [ˈɪnˌlɛt] N **a** (*Geog*) insenatura, baia; (*of sea*) braccio di mare **b** (*Tech*) apertura di ammissione.

♦ **inlet pipe** N (*Tech*) tubo d'immissione.

♦ **inlet valve** N valvola d'aspirazione.

in loco pa·ren·tis [ɪnˈləʊkəʊpəˈrɛntɪs] ADV (*frm*): **to be in loco parentis** fare le veci dei genitori.

in·mate [ˈɪnˌmeɪt] N (*of prison*) detenuto(-a), carcerato(-a); (*of asylum*) internato(-a), ricoverato(-a).

in·most [ˈɪnˌməʊst] ADJ più profondo(-a), più intimo(-a); **one's inmost being** il proprio intimo; **in one's inmost heart** nel profondo del proprio cuore, nel proprio intimo.

inn [ɪn] N locanda.

in·nards [ˈɪnədz] NPL (*fam*) budella *fpl*.

in·nate [ɪˈneɪt] ADJ innato(-a).

in·ner [ˈɪnəʳ] ADJ (*place*) interno(-a), interiore; (*thoughts,*

emotions) intimo(-a), profondo(-a).

♦ **inner city** N centro di una zona urbana (*in degrado socio-economico*).

inner·most [ˈɪnəˌməʊst] ADJ = **inmost**.

♦ **inner sole** N (*in shoe*) soletta.

♦ **inner tube** N camera d'aria.

in·nings [ˈɪnɪŋz] NSG (*in cricket*) turno di battuta; **he has had a good innings** (*Brit fig*) ha vissuto bene e a lungo; **that car has had a good innings** quella macchina ha fatto i suoi anni.

inn·keeper [ˈɪnˌkiːpəʳ] N locandiere(-a).

in·no·cence [ˈɪnəsns] N innocenza.

in·no·cent [ˈɪnəsnt] ADJ innocente; **to put on an innocent air** fare l'innocente *or* l'ingenuo(-a).

in·no·cent·ly [ˈɪnəsntlɪ] ADV innocentemente.

in·nocu·ous [ɪˈnɒkjʊəs] ADJ innocuo(-a).

in·no·vate [ˈɪnəʊˌveɪt] VI introdurre delle innovazioni.

in·no·va·tion [ˌɪnəʊˈveɪʃən] N innovazione *f*.

in·no·va·tive [ˈɪnəʊˌveɪtɪv] ADJ innovativo(-a).

in·no·va·tor [ˈɪnəʊˌveɪtəʳ] N innovatore(-trice).

in·nu·en·do [ˌɪnjʊˈɛndəʊ] N (*insinuation*) insinuazione *f*; (*sexual*) allusione *f*.

in·nu·mer·able [ɪˈnjuːmərəbl] ADJ innumerevole.

in·ocu·late [ɪˈnɒkjʊˌleɪt] VT: **to inoculate sb with sth** inoculare qn con qc; **to inoculate sb against sth** vaccinare qn contro qc.

in·ocu·la·tion [ɪˌnɒkjʊˈleɪʃən] N inoculazione *f*.

in·of·fen·sive [ˌɪnəˈfɛnsɪv] ADJ inoffensivo(-a), innocuo (-a).

in·op·er·able [ɪnˈɒpərəbl] ADJ **a** (*Med*) inoperabile **b** (*regulation, plan*) inattuabile; **this machine is inoperable without the help of a technician** questa macchina non può essere messa in funzione senza l'aiuto di un tecnico.

in·op·era·tive [ɪnˈɒpərətɪv] ADJ (*plan, rule*) inoperante.

in·op·por·tune [ɪnˈɒpətjuːn] ADJ inopportuno(-a).

in·op·por·tune·ly [ɪnˈɒpətjuːnlɪ] ADV inopportunamente.

in·op·por·tune·ness [ɪnˈɒpəˌtjuːnnɪs] N inopportunità.

in·or·di·nate [ɪˈnɔːdɪnɪt] ADJ esagerato(-a).

in·or·di·nate·ly [ɪˈnɔːdɪnɪtlɪ] ADV: **an inordinately large sum of money** una cifra esorbitante *or* astronomica; **an inordinately large amount of food** una quantità esagerata di cibo; **an inordinately long time** un'infinità di tempo.

in·or·gan·ic [ˌɪnɔːˈgænɪk] ADJ inorganico(-a).

in·pa·tient [ˈɪnˌpeɪʃənt] N degente *m/f*, ricoverato(-a).

in·put [ˈɪnpʊt] 1 N **a** (*outlay: of funds, labour, energy*) impiego; (*contribution: of ideas, work*) contributo **b** (*Comput*) dati *mpl*, input *m inv* **c** (*Elec*) alimentazione *f*; (*in amplifiers*) ingresso.

2 VT (*Comput*) introdurre.

in·quest [ˈɪnkwɛst] N (*Law*) inchiesta giudiziaria.

in·quire [ɪnˈkwaɪəʳ] 1 VT: **to inquire when/where/whether** domandare quando/dove/se; **to inquire sth of sb** domandare qc a qn.

2 VI: **to inquire (about sth)** informarsi (di *or* su qc), chiedere informazioni (su qc)

▶ **inquire after** VI + PREP (*person*) chiedere di; (*sb's health*) informarsi di

▶ **inquire into** VI + PREP indagare su, svolgere delle indagini su.

in·quir·er [ɪnˈkwaɪərəʳ] N (*frm*): **we told all inquirers to phone again later** abbiamo detto a tutti quelli che chiedevano informazioni di ritelefonare più tardi.

in·quir·ing [ɪnˈkwaɪərɪŋ] ADJ (*mind*) pieno(-a) di curiosità;

(*look*) interrogativo(-a), indagatore(-trice).

in·quir·ing·ly [ɪnˈkwaɪərɪŋlɪ] ADV (*look*) interrogativamente, con aria interrogativa.

in·quiry [ɪnˈkwaɪərɪ] N **a** (*question*) domanda, richiesta di informazioni; **"Inquiries"** (*on sign*) "Informazioni"; **on inquiry he found that ...** essendosi informato scoprì che...; **to make inquiries (about sth)** chiedere informazioni (su qc), informarsi (di *or* su qc) **b** (*Admin, Law*) inchiesta; **committee of inquiry** commissione *f* d'inchiesta; **to hold an inquiry into sth** svolgere un'inchiesta su qc; **the police are making inquiries** la polizia sta indagando, la polizia sta svolgendo delle indagini.

♦ **inquiry desk** N (*Brit*) (banco delle) informazioni *fpl*.
♦ **inquiry office** N (*Brit*) ufficio *m* informazioni *inv*.

In·qui·si·tion [ˌɪnkwɪˈzɪʃən] N (*Rel*): **the Inquisition** l'Inquisizione *f*.

in·qui·si·tion [ˌɪnkwɪˈzɪʃən] N inquisizione *f*.

in·quisi·tive [ɪnˈkwɪzɪtɪv] ADJ (*troppo*) curioso(-a).

in·quisi·tive·ly [ɪnˈkwɪzɪtɪvlɪ] ADV con troppa curiosità.

in·quisi·tive·ness [ɪnˈkwɪzɪtɪvnɪs] N indiscrezione *f*.

in·quisi·tor [ɪnˈkwɪzɪtəʳ] N (*Rel*) inquisitore *m*.

in·quisi·to·rial [ɪnˌkwɪzɪˈtɔːriəl] ADJ inquisitorio(-a).

in·roads [ˈɪnˌrəʊdz] NPL: **to make inroads into** (*savings, supplies*) intaccare (seriamente).

ins ABBR of **inches**.

in·sa·lu·bri·ous [ˌɪnsəˈluːbrɪəs] ADJ (*frm*) insalubre.

in·sane [ɪnˈseɪn] **1** ADJ (*person*) pazzo(-a), matto(-a); (*Med*) malato(-a) di mente; (*act*) folle, demenziale; **to drive sb insane** (*fig*) far impazzire *or* far diventar matto(-a) qn. **2** NPL: **the insane** i malati di mente; **an asylum for the insane** un manicomio.

in·sane·ly [ɪnˈseɪnlɪ] ADV (*behave*) da pazzo(-a); **insanely jealous** follemente geloso(-a).

in·sani·tary [ɪnˈsænɪtərɪ] ADJ malsano(-a), antigienico (-a).

in·san·ity [ɪnˈsænɪtɪ] N (*Med*) infermità mentale; (*gen*) pazzia, follia.

in·sa·tiable [ɪnˈseɪʃəbl] ADJ insaziabile.

in·sa·tiably [ɪnˈseɪʃəblɪ] ADV insaziabilmente.

in·scribe [ɪnˈskraɪb] VT **a** (*engrave*) incidere; (*write*) scrivere **b** (*dedicate: book*) scrivere una dedica su; **to inscribe sth to sb** dedicare qc a qn.

in·scrip·tion [ɪnˈskrɪpʃən] N (*on stone*) iscrizione *f*; (*in book*) dedica.

in·scru·table [ɪnˈskruːtəbl] ADJ (*person*) imperscrutabile; (*face, eyes, gaze*) impenetrabile.

in·sect [ˈɪnsɛkt] N insetto.
♦ **insect bite** N puntura *or* morsicatura di insetto.

in·sec·ti·cide [ɪnˈsɛktɪsaɪd] N insetticida *m*.

in·sec·ti·vore [ɪnˈsɛktɪ.vɔː] N insettivoro.

in·sec·tivo·rous [ˌɪnsɛkˈtɪvərəs] ADJ insettivoro(-a).
♦ **insect powder** N polvere *f* insetticida.
♦ **insect repellent** N insettifugo.

in·secure [ˌɪnsɪˈkjʊəʳ] ADJ (*structure, lock, door*) malsicuro (-a); (*Psych: person*) insicuro(-a).

in·secu·rity [ˌɪnsɪˈkjʊərɪtɪ] N (*of person*) insicurezza; (*of lock, employment, finances*) scarsa sicurezza.

in·semi·nate [ɪnˈsɛmɪˌneɪt] VT inseminare.

in·semi·na·tion [ɪnˌsɛmɪˈneɪʃən] N inseminazione *f*.

in·sen·sibil·ity [ɪnˌsɛnsəˈbɪlɪtɪ] N **a** (*Med: unconsciousness*) incoscienza **b** (*fig: unfeelingness*): **insensiblity (towards)** indifferenza (di fronte a).

in·sen·sible [ɪnˈsɛnsəbl] ADJ **a** (*unconscious*) privo(-a) di

sensi *or* di conoscenza **b** (*unaware*): **insensible of** ignaro(-a) di.

in·sen·sibly [ɪnˈsɛnsəblɪ] ADV (*imperceptibly*) impercettibilmente.

in·sen·si·tive [ɪnˈsɛnsɪtɪv] ADJ (*person*): **insensitive (to)** insensibile (a); (*action, behaviour*) privo(-a) di sensibilità.

in·sen·si·tive·ly [ɪnˈsɛnsɪtɪvlɪ] ADV insensibilmente, senza sensibilità.

in·sen·si·tiv·ity [ɪnˌsɛnsɪˈtɪvɪtɪ] N mancanza di sensibilità.

in·sepa·rable [ɪnˈsɛpərəbl] ADJ inseparabile.

in·sepa·rably [ɪnˈsɛpərəblɪ] ADV indissolubilmente.

in·sert [*n* ˈɪnsɜːt; *vb* ɪnˈsɜːt] **1** N inserto. **2** VT inserire; (*needle*) introdurre.

in·ser·tion [ɪnˈsɜːʃən] N inserimento.
♦ **in–service** [ˌɪnˈsɜːvɪs] ADJ: **in-service training** corso di aggiornamento.

in·shore [ˈɪnˈʃɔː] **1** ADV (*fish*) sotto costa; (*sail*) verso riva; (*blow*) dal mare. **2** ADJ (*fishing*) costiero(-a); (*wind*) dal mare.

in·shrine [ɪnˈʃraɪm] VT = **enshrine**.

in·side [ˈɪnˈsaɪd] **1** N **a** interno, parte *f* interiore; (*of road: Brit*) sinistra; (: *Am, in Europe etc*) destra; **to overtake on the inside** (*Brit*) sorpassare a sinistra; (*Am, Europe etc*) sorpassare a destra; **to know sth from the inside** conoscere qc per esperienza diretta **b** : **to be inside out** essere alla rovescia; **to turn sth inside out** rivoltare qc; **to know sth inside out** conoscere qc a fondo; (*place*) conoscere qc come le proprie tasche **c** (*fam: stomach*): **insides** NPL budella *fpl*, pancia. **2** ADV dentro, all'interno; **to be inside** (*fam: in prison*) essere dentro *or* al fresco. **3** PREP **a** (*of place*) dentro, all'interno di; **come inside the house** vieni dentro (casa) **b** (*of time*) nel giro di; **inside 10 minutes** nel giro di 10 minuti; **he is inside the record** sta battendo il record; **just inside the speed limit** sotto il limite di velocità. **4** ADJ interno(-a).
♦ **inside forward** N (*Sport*) mezzala.
♦ **inside information** N informazioni *fpl* riservate.
♦ **inside job** N (*fam: robbery*) *rapina organizzata con l'aiuto di un complice interno*.
♦ **inside lane** N (*Brit*) corsia di sinistra; (*Am, Europe*) corsia di destra.
♦ **inside left** N mezzala sinistra.
♦ **inside leg measurement** N (*Brit*) *lunghezza della gamba dei pantaloni partendo dal cavallo*.

in·sid·er [ɪnˈsaɪdəʳ] N uno(-a) degli adetti ai lavori.
♦ **insider dealing, insider trading** N (*Stock Exchange*) insider trading *m inv*.
♦ **inside right** N mezzala destra.
♦ **inside story** N storia segreta.

in·sidi·ous [ɪnˈsɪdɪəs] ADJ insidioso(-a).

in·sidi·ous·ly [ɪnˈsɪdɪəslɪ] ADV insidiosamente.

in·sight [ˈɪnˌsaɪt] N (*perception*) perspicacia, intuito; (*glimpse, idea*) intuizione *f*; **to gain** *or* **get an insight into sth** potersi render conto di qc; **to give sb an insight into sth** permettere a qn di capire qc.

in·sig·nia [ɪnˈsɪgnɪə] NPL insegne *fpl*.

in·sig·nifi·cance [ˌɪnsɪgˈnɪfɪkəns] N scarsa importanza.

in·sig·nifi·cant [ˌɪnsɪgˈnɪfɪkənt] ADJ insignificante.

in·sin·cere [ˌɪnsɪnˈsɪəʳ] ADJ (*person,*) falso(-a), insincero (-a), ipocrita; (*smile, behaviour*) falso(-a), ipocrita.

in·sin·cer·ity [ˌɪnsɪnˈsɛrɪtɪ] N falsità, ipocrisia.

in·sinu·ate [ɪnˈsɪnjʊˌeɪt] VT insinuare; **to insinuate o.s.**

into sb's favour insinuarsi nelle grazie di qn.

in·sin·ua·tion [ɪnˌsɪnjʊˈeɪʃən] N insinuazione *f*.

in·sip·id [ɪnˈsɪpɪd] ADJ (*food, drink*) insipido(-a); (*fig*) insulso(-a), insipido(-a).

in·sist [ɪnˈsɪst] ① VI: **to insist (on sth/on doing sth)** insistere (su qc/nel fare qc); **she insists on leaving tomorrow** vuole assolutamente partire domani, insiste nel voler partire domani.
② VT: **to insist that** (*order*) insistere che + *sub*; (*maintain*) sostenere *or* affermare di; **I insist that you let me pay** insisto che tu mi lasci pagare; **he insists that he is innocent** sostiene di essere innocente.

in·sist·ence [ɪnˈsɪstəns] N insistenza; **at her insistence** dietro sua insistenza, perché lei ha insistito (molto).

in·sist·ent [ɪnˈsɪstənt] ADJ insistente.

in·sist·ent·ly [ɪnˈsɪstəntlɪ] ADV insistentemente, con insistenza.

in·so·far as [ˌɪnsəʊˈfɑːrəz] CONJ in quanto, nella misura in cui.

in·sole [ˈɪnˌsəʊl] N soletta; **orthopaedic insole** plantare *m*.

in·so·lence [ˈɪnsələns] N insolenza.

in·so·lent [ˈɪnsələnt] ADJ insolente.

in·sol·uble [ɪnˈsɒljʊbl] ADJ insolubile.

in·sol·ven·cy [ɪnˈsɒlvənsɪ] N insolvenza.

in·sol·vent [ɪnˈsɒlvənt] ADJ insolvente.

in·som·nia [ɪnˈsɒmnɪə] N insonnia.

in·som·ni·ac [ɪnˈsɒmnɪæk] N chi soffre di insonnia.

in·sou·ci·ant [ɪnˈsuːsɪənt] ADJ (*liter*) noncurante.

in·spect [ɪnˈspɛkt] VT (*examine*) ispezionare; (*Brit*: *ticket*) controllare; (*Mil*: *troops*) passare in rassegna; **to inspect sth for faults** sottoporre qc a controllo *or* verifica.

in·spec·tion [ɪnˈspɛkʃən] N (*of goods*) controllo, ispezione *f*; (*of ticket, document*) controllo; (*Mil, of school*) ispezione; **on inspection it was found that** ad un controllo si scoprì che.

in·spec·tor [ɪnˈspɛktəʳ] N (*police inspector*) ispettore(-trice) (di polizia); (*schools inspector*) ispettore(-trice) scolastico(-a); (*on bus, train*) controllore *m*; **inspector of taxes** ispettore *m* del fisco.

in·spec·tor·ate [ɪnˈspɛktərɪt] N ispettorato.

in·spi·ra·tion [ˌɪnspɪˈreɪʃən] N ispirazione *f*; **to have a sudden inspiration** avere un lampo di genio; **to be an inspiration to sb** ispirare qn, essere una fonte d'ispirazione per qn; **you've been an inspiration to us all** sei stato di esempio per tutti noi.

in·spi·ra·tion·al [ˌɪnspɪˈreɪʃənəl] ADJ ispiratore(-trice).

in·spire [ɪnˈspaɪəʳ] VT: **to inspire sth in sb, to inspire sb with sth** ispirare qc a qn; **to inspire sb (to do sth)** ispirare qn (a fare qc).

in·spired [ɪnˈspaɪəd] ADJ (*writer, book etc*) ispirato(-a); **in an inspired moment** in un momento d'ispirazione.

in·spir·ing [ɪnˈspaɪərɪŋ] ADJ ispiratore(-trice), stimolante.

inst. ABBR (*Brit Comm*: = *instant: of the present month*) c.m. (= *corrente mese*).

in·stabil·ity [ˌɪnstəˈbɪlɪtɪ] N instabilità.

in·stall [ɪnˈstɔːl] VT (*machine, equipment, telephone*) installare; (*mayor, official etc*) insediare.

in·stal·la·tion [ˌɪnstəˈleɪʃən] N (*see vb*) installazione *f*; insediamento.

in·stal·ment, (*Am*) **in·stall·ment** [ɪnˈstɔːlmənt] N **a** (*Comm*: *part payment*) rata, pagamento rateale; **to pay in instalments** pagare a rate **b** (*of serial, story*) puntata, episodio; (*of publication*) dispensa.

♦ **instalment plan** N (*Am Comm*) sistema *m* di vendita rateale.

in·stance [ˈɪnstəns] N (*example*) esempio, caso; **for instance** per *or* ad esempio; **in that instance** in quel caso; **in the first instance** in primo luogo.

in·stant [ˈɪnstənt] ① ADJ **a** (*reply, reaction, success*) immediato(-a); (*coffee*) solubile; (*food*) liofilizzato(-a); **instant potatoes** fiocchi *mpl* di patate
b (*Comm: of the present month*) corrente mese *inv*; **the 10th instant** il 10 corrente mese.
② N istante *m*, attimo; **come here this instant** vieni immediatamente *or* subito qui; **in an instant** in un attimo; **I came the instant I got the news** sono venuto non appena ho ricevuto la notizia.

in·stan·ta·neous [ˌɪnstənˈteɪnɪəs] ADJ istantaneo(-a).

in·stan·ta·neous·ly [ˌɪnstənˈteɪnɪəslɪ] ADV istantaneamente.

in·stant·ly [ˈɪnstəntlɪ] ADV immediatamente, subito.

♦ **instant replay** N (*Am TV*) replay *m inv*.

in·stead [ɪnˈstɛd] ① ADV invece; **don't take Tom, take Fred instead** non prendere Tom, prendi piuttosto Fred; **I haven't got any coffee, will cocoa do instead?** non ho caffè, va bene lo stesso il cacao?; **if you're not going, I'll go instead** se non vai tu, andrò io al posto tuo.
② PREP: **instead of** invece di; **instead of sb** al posto di qn; **instead of doing sth** invece di fare qc.

in·step [ˈɪnˌstɛp] N (*of foot*) collo del piede; (*of shoe*) collo della scarpa.

in·sti·gate [ˈɪnstɪˌgeɪt] VT (*rebellion, strike, crime*) istigare a; (*new ideas*) promuovere.

in·sti·ga·tion [ˌɪnstɪˈgeɪʃən] N istigazione *f*; **at sb's instigation** per *or* in seguito al suggerimento di qn.

in·sti·ga·tor [ˈɪnstɪgeɪtəʳ] N istigatore(-trice).

in·stil, (*Am*) **in·still** [ɪnˈstɪl] VT: **to instil sth into sb** instillare qc a qn.

in·stinct [ˈɪnstɪŋkt] N istinto; **by instinct** per istinto, istintivamente.

in·stinc·tive [ɪnˈstɪŋktɪv] ADJ istintivo(-a).

in·stinc·tive·ly [ɪnˈstɪŋktɪvlɪ] ADV istintivamente, per istinto.

in·sti·tute [ˈɪnstɪtjuːt] ① N istituto, ente *m*.
② VT (*start: reform*) introdurre; (: *inquiry, investigation*) avviare, aprire; (: *legal proceedings*) intentare.

in·sti·tu·tion [ˌɪnstɪˈtjuːʃən] N **a** (*organization*) istituzione *f*; (*charitable institution*) istituto di beneficenza; (*mental institution*) istituto psichiatrico **b** (*custom, tradition*) istituzione *f*.

in·sti·tu·tion·al [ˌɪnstɪˈtjuːʃənl] ADJ **a** (*reforms*) istituzionale
b (*food, furniture*) tipico(-a) degli istituti assistenziali; **institutional care** (*for children*) ricovero presso un istituto; (*for handicapped people*) assistenza medica presso un istituto; **institutional life** la vita all'interno di un istituto.

in·sti·tu·tion·al·ized [ˌɪnstɪˈtjuːʃnəˌlaɪzd] ADJ **a** (*procedure, religion*) istituzionalizzato(-a) **b** (*pej*): **the prisoner had become institutionalized** il detenuto era incapace di provvedere a se stesso a causa della lunga permanenza in carcere.

in·struct [ɪnˈstrʌkt] VT **a** (*teach*) istruire; **to instruct sb in sth/in how to do sth** insegnare qc a qn/a qn come fare qc **b** (*order*): **to instruct sb to do sth** dare istruzioni *or* ordini a qn di fare qc.

in·struc·tion [ɪnˈstrʌkʃən] N **a** (*teaching*) istruzione *f* **b** : **instructions** NPL (*orders, directions*) istruzioni *fpl*; **to give sb instructions (to do sth)** dare istruzioni a qn (di fare qc); **instructions for use** istruzioni per l'uso.

♦ **instruction book** N libretto di istruzioni.

in·struc·tive [ɪn'strʌktɪv] ADJ istruttivo(-a).

in·struc·tor [ɪn'strʌktəʳ] N (gen) istruttore(-trice); (Skiing) maestro(-a).

in·stru·ment ['ɪnstrəmənt] N (also Mus) strumento; **to fly on instruments** (Aer) fare il volo strumentale.

in·stru·men·tal [ˌɪnstrə'mɛntl] ADJ **a** : **to be instrumental in sth/in doing sth** avere un ruolo importante in qc/nel fare qc **b** (music etc) strumentale.

in·stru·men·tal·ist [ˌɪnstrə'mɛntəlɪst] N strumentista m/f.

♦ **instrument panel** N (Aer) quadro degli strumenti di bordo.

in·sub·or·di·nate [ˌɪnsə'bɔːdənɪt] ADJ insubordinato(-a).

in·sub·or·di·na·tion ['ɪnsəˌbɔːdɪ'neɪʃən] N insubordinazione f.

in·sub·stan·tial [ˌɪnsəb'stænʃəl] ADJ (structure) poco solido(-a); (evidence) inconsistente; (vision) irreale.

in·suf·fer·able [ɪn'sʌfərəbl] ADJ intollerabile.

in·suf·fer·ably [ɪn'sʌfərəblɪ] ADV intollerabilmente; **she's insufferably rude** è di una maleducazione intollerabile.

in·suf·fi·ciency [ˌɪnsə'fɪʃənsɪ] N insufficienza.

in·suf·fi·cient [ˌɪnsə'fɪʃənt] ADJ insufficiente.

in·suf·fi·cient·ly [ˌɪnsə'fɪʃəntlɪ] ADV insufficientemente, in modo insufficiente.

in·su·lar ['ɪnsjʊləʳ] ADJ (climate) insulare; (fig: person) di mentalità ristretta; **insular attitude** chiusura mentale, ristrettezza di idee.

in·su·late ['ɪnsjʊˌleɪt] VT (against cold) isolare termicamente; (against noise) isolare acusticamente; (Elec: wire) isolare; (fig: person): **to insulate sb (from)** tener qn lontano (da).

in·su·lat·ing tape ['ɪnsjʊˌleɪtɪŋˌteɪp] N nastro isolante.

in·su·la·tion [ˌɪnsjʊ'leɪʃən] N (see vb) isolamento termico; isolamento acustico; isolamento (elettrico); (material) (materiale m) isolante.

in·su·la·tor ['ɪnsjʊˌleɪtəʳ] N isolante m.

in·su·lin ['ɪnsjʊlɪn] N insulina; **insulin injection** iniezione f d'insulina.

in·sult [n 'ɪnsʌlt; vb ɪn'sʌlt] **1** N insulto.
2 VT insultare, offendere.

in·sult·ing [ɪn'sʌltɪŋ] ADJ offensivo(-a).

in·sult·ing·ly [ɪn'sʌltɪŋlɪ] ADV in modo offensivo.

in·su·per·able [ɪn'suːpərəbl] ADJ insormontabile.

in·sup·port·able [ˌɪnsə'pɔːtəbl] ADJ insopportabile.

in·sur·ance [ɪn'ʃʊərəns] **1** N assicurazione f; **life insurance** assicurazione sulla vita; **fire insurance** assicurazione contro gli incendi; **to take out insurance (against)** fare un'assicurazione (contro), assicurarsi (contro).
2 ADJ (certificate, company) di assicurazione.

♦ **insurance agent** N agente m/f d'assicurazioni.

♦ **insurance broker** N broker m inv d'assicurazioni.

♦ **insurance policy** N polizza d'assicurazione.

♦ **insurance premium** N premio assicurativo.

in·sure [ɪn'ʃʊəʳ] VT (house, car, parcel): **to insure (against)** assicurare (contro); **to insure o.s.** or **one's life** assicurarsi (sulla vita); **to insure sb** or **sb's life** assicurare qn sulla vita; **to be insured for £50,000** essere assicurato (-a) per 50.000 sterline.

in·sured [ɪn'ʃʊəd] N: **the insured** l'assicurato(-a).

in·sur·er [ɪn'ʃʊərəʳ] N assicuratore(-trice).

in·sur·gent [ɪn'sɜːdʒənt] **1** ADJ ribelle.
2 N insorto(-a), rivoltoso(-a).

in·sur·mount·able [ˌɪnsə'maʊntəbl] ADJ insormontabile.

in·sur·rec·tion [ˌɪnsə'rɛkʃən] N insurrezione f.

in·tact [ɪn'tækt] ADJ intatto(-a).

in·take ['ɪnˌteɪk] N **a** (Tech: of air, water, gas) immissione f **b** (quantity: of pupils) (numero di) iscrizioni fpl; (: of workers) (numero di) assunzioni fpl; (: of food) consumo.

in·tan·gible [ɪn'tændʒəbl] ADJ **a** (fears, hopes) indefinibile **b** (Comm: asset) immateriale.

in·te·ger ['ɪntɪdʒəʳ] N (Math) intero.

in·te·gral ['ɪntɪgrəl] **1** ADJ (essential: part) integrante; **to be an integral part of** essere parte integrante di.
2 N (Math) integrale m.

♦ **integral calculus** N (Math) calcolo integrale.

in·te·grate ['ɪntɪˌgreɪt] VT (gen, Math) integrare; (Am: school, community) operare l'integrazione razziale in.

in·te·grat·ed ['ɪntɪˌgreɪtɪd] ADJ (population, school) in cui si è operata l'integrazione razziale; (personality) equilibrato(-a); **integrated steelworks** impianto metallurgico a ciclo integrale.

♦ **integrated circuit** N (Comput) circuito integrato.

in·te·gra·tion [ˌɪntɪ'greɪʃən] N integrazione f; **racial integration** integrazione razziale.

in·teg·rity [ɪn'tɛgrɪtɪ] N integrità.

in·tegu·ment [ɪn'tɛgjʊmənt] N tegumento.

in·tel·lect ['ɪntɪlɛkt] N intelletto.

in·tel·lec·tual [ˌɪntɪ'lɛktjʊəl] **1** ADJ (person) intellettuale; (interests) culturale.
2 N intellettuale m/f.

in·tel·lec·tu·al·ly [ˌɪntɪ'lɛktjʊəlɪ] ADV intellettualmente.

in·tel·li·gence [ɪn'tɛlɪdʒəns] N (cleverness) intelligenza; (information) informazioni fpl.

♦ **intelligence quotient** N quoziente m d'intelligenza.

♦ **Intelligence Service** N servizio segreto.

♦ **intelligence test** N test m inv d'intelligenza.

in·tel·li·gent [ɪn'tɛlɪdʒənt] ADJ intelligente.

in·tel·li·gent·ly [ɪn'tɛlɪdʒəntlɪ] ADV intelligentemente.

in·tel·li·gent·sia [ɪnˌtɛlɪ'dʒɛntsɪə] N intellighenzia.

in·tel·li·gibil·ity [ɪnˌtɛlɪdʒə'bɪlɪtɪ] N intelligibilità.

in·tel·li·gi·ble [ɪn'tɛlɪdʒəbl] ADJ intelligibile.

in·tel·li·gibly [ɪn'tɛlɪdʒəblɪ] ADV intelligibilmente.

in·tem·per·ate [ɪn'tɛmpərɪt] ADJ (remarks, response, opinion) privo(-a) di autocontrollo; (climate) rigido(-a); (habits) smoderato(-a); (person: lacking moderation) intemperante; (: drinking too much) intemperante nel bere.

in·tend [ɪn'tɛnd] VT (mean): **to intend to do sth** avere (l')intenzione di fare qc, intendere fare qc; (remark, gift): **to intend sth for sb/sth** destinare qc a qn/qc; **I intend him to come too** voglio che venga anche lui; **it was intended as a compliment** voleva essere un complimento; **I intended no harm** non intendevo fare del male; **did you intend that?** (do on purpose) l'hai fatto intenzionalmente?

in·tend·ed [ɪn'tɛndɪd] **1** ADJ **a** (deliberate: insult) intenzionale **b** (planned: effect) voluto(-a); (: journey, route) programmato(-a).
2 N (old often hum) fidanzato(-a); **he was not the intended victim** non era lui la vittima designata.

in·tense [ɪn'tɛns] ADJ (heat, cold, expression) intenso(-a); (interest, enthusiasm) vivo(-a), profondo(-a); (person) di forti sentimenti.

in·tense·ly [ɪn'tɛnslɪ] ADV (difficult, hot, cold) estremamente; (moved) profondamente.

in·ten·si·fi·er [ɪn'tɛnsɪfaɪəʳ] N (Gram) rafforzativo.

in·ten·si·fy [ɪn'tɛnsɪˌfaɪ] **1** VT intensificare.
2 VI intensificarsi.

in·ten·sity [ɪnˈtɛnsɪtɪ] N intensità *f inv.*

in·ten·sive [ɪnˈtɛnsɪv] ADJ (*study*) intenso(-a); (*course*) intensivo(-a); (*bombing*) a tappeto; **intensive farming** agricoltura intensiva.

◆ **intensive care** N rianimazione *f*; **to be in intensive care** essere in rianimazione; **intensive care unit** reparto *or* centro di rianimazione.

in·ten·sive·ly [ɪnˈtɛnsɪvlɪ] ADV (*study*) intensamente; (*farm*) intensivamente.

in·tent [ɪnˈtɛnt] ⬛1 ADJ **a** (*determined*): **to be intent on doing sth** essere deciso(-a) a fare qc **b** (*absorbed*) assorto(-a); **to be intent on sth** essere intento(-a) a qc; **intent stare** sguardo attento.
⬛2 N (*frm*) intenzione *f*, intento; **with intent to kill** con l'intento di uccidere; **to all intents and purposes** praticamente, a tutti gli effetti.

in·ten·tion [ɪnˈtɛnʃən] N intenzione *f*; **I have no intention of going** non ho nessuna intenzione di andare; **I have every intention of going** ho proprio intenzione di andare; **with the best of intentions** con le migliori intenzioni del mondo.

in·ten·tion·al [ɪnˈtɛnʃənl] ADJ intenzionale, deliberato (-a); **it wasn't intentional** non l'ho (*or* l'ha *etc*) fatto apposta.

in·ten·tion·al·ly [ɪnˈtɛnʃənlɪ] ADV intenzionalmente, deliberatamente.

in·tent·ly [ɪnˈtɛntlɪ] ADV attentamente.

in·ter [ɪnˈtɜː] VT (*frm*) seppellire.

inter... [ˈɪntəʳ] PREF inter... .

inter·act [ˌɪntərˈækt] VI interagire.

inter·ac·tion [ˌɪntərˈækʃən] N interazione *f*.

inter·ac·tive [ˌɪntərˈæktɪv] ADJ (*gen, Comput*) interattivo (-a).

◆ **interactive computing** N elaborazione *f* conversazionale.

◆ **interactive video** N (*Comput*) video interattivo.

inter·cede [ˌɪntəˈsiːd] VI: **to intercede with sb/on behalf of sb** intercedere presso qn/a favore di qn.

inter·cept [*vb* ˌɪntəˈsɛpt; *n* ˈɪntəˌsɛpt] ⬛1 VT intercettare.
⬛2 N (*Math*) intersezione *f*.

inter·cep·tion [ˌɪntəˈsɛpʃən] N intercettazione *f*.

inter·ces·sion [ˌɪntəˈsɛʃən] N intercessione *f*.

inter·change [*n* ˈɪntəˌtʃeɪndʒ; *vb* ˌɪntəˈtʃeɪndʒ] ⬛1 N **a** (*of views, ideas*) scambio **b** (*on motorway*) interscambio, svincolo. ⬛2 VT (*views*) scambiarsi.

inter·change·abil·ity [ˌɪntəˌtʃeɪndʒəˈbɪlɪtɪ] N intercambiabilità.

inter·change·able [ˌɪntəˈtʃeɪndʒəbl] ADJ intercambiabile.

inter·city [ˌɪntəˈsɪtɪ] ADJ: **intercity (train)** (treno) intercity *m inv.*

inter·com [ˈɪntəˌkɒm] N (*fam*) interfono.

inter·con·nect [ˌɪntəkəˈnɛkt] VI (*rooms*) essere in comunicazione.

inter·con·nect·ed [ˌɪntəkəˈnɛktɪd] ADJ interconnesso(-a); **interconnected parts** parti *fpl* legate tra loro.

inter·con·ti·nen·tal [ˈɪntəˌkɒntɪˈnɛntl] ADJ intercontinentale.

inter·con·ver·sion [ˌɪntəkənˈvɜːʃən] N (*Comput*) transcodificazione *f*.

inter·cos·tal [ˌɪntəˈkɒstəl] ADJ (*Anat*) intercostale.

inter·course [ˈɪntəˌkɔːs] N **a** (*also*: **sexual intercourse**) rapporti *mpl* sessuali; **to have (sexual) intercourse with sb** avere rapporti sessuali con qn **b** (*frm: communication*) rapporti *mpl*, relazioni *fpl*.

inter·de·nomi·na·tion·al [ˈɪntədɪˌnɒmɪˈneɪʃənl] ADJ inter-

confessionale.

inter·de·part·ment·al [ˈɪntəˌdiːpɑːtˈmɛntl] ADJ interdipartimentale.

inter·de·pend·ent [ˌɪntədɪˈpɛndənt] ADJ interdipendente.

inter·dict [ˈɪntədɪkt] N interdizione *f*.

inter·dis·ci·pli·nary [ˌɪntəˈdɪsɪˌplɪnərɪ] ADJ interdisciplinare.

in·ter·est [ˈɪntrɪst] ⬛1 N **a** (*involvement, curiosity*) interesse *m*; **to have** *or* **take an interest in sth** interessarsi di *or* a qc; **to have** *or* **take no interest in sth** non interessarsi di qc; **to be of interest to sb** interessare qn; **to lose interest in sth** perdere l'interesse per qc; **I have lost interest in motor racing** le corse automobilistiche non mi interessano più
b (*profit, advantage*) interesse *m*; **in one's own interest (s)** nel proprio interesse; **to act in sb's interest(s)** agire nell'interesse di qn; **to have a vested interest in sth** essere direttamente interessato(-a) in *or* a qc; **in the public interest** nell'interesse pubblico
c (*Comm: stake, share*) interessi *mpl*; **business interests** attività *fpl* commerciali; **British interests in the Middle East** gli interessi britannici nel Medio Oriente
d (*Comm: on loan, shares etc*) interesse *m*; **compound/ simple interest** interesse composto/semplice; **at an interest of 5%** all'interesse del 5%; **to bear interest at 5%** fruttare il 5% (di interesse); **to lend at interest** prestare denaro a interesse.
⬛2 VT interessare; **to interest o.s. in sth** interessarsi a qc; **to interest sb in sth** (fare) interessare qn a qc.

in·ter·est·ed [ˈɪntrɪstɪd] ADJ (*expression*) interessato(-a), pieno(-a) di interesse; (*person*) che s'interessa; **to be interested in sth** interessarsi di qc; **he's interested in buying a car** è interessato all'acquisto di una macchina; **interested party** parte *f* interessata.

◆ **interest-free** [ˈɪntrɪstˈfriː] ADJ (*loan*) senza interesse.

in·ter·est·ing [ˈɪntrɪstɪŋ] ADJ interessante.

in·ter·est·ing·ly [ˈɪntrɪstɪŋlɪ] ADV in modo interessante; **interestingly enough** ... la cosa interessante è che... .

◆ **interest rate** N tasso di interesse.

inter·face [ˈɪntəˌfeɪs] N (*Comput*) interfaccia.

inter·fere [ˌɪntəˈfɪəʳ] VI **a** : **to interfere (in sth)** (*quarrel, other people's business*) interferire (in qc), intromettersi (in qc); **to interfere with sth** (*object*) manomettere qc; (*plans*) intralciare qc; (*process, activity*) interferire con qc; (*Radio, TV*) causare delle interferenze in qc; **he is always interfering** si intromette sempre in tutto; **stop interfering!** smettila di interferire!
b (*euph: sexually*): **to interfere with sb** molestare sessualmente qn.

inter·fer·ence [ˌɪntəˈfɪərəns] N interferenza, intromissione *f*; (*Radio, TV, Phys*) interferenza.

inter·fer·ing [ˌɪntəˈfɪərɪŋ] ADJ invadente.

in·ter·im [ˈɪntərɪm] ⬛1 N: **in the interim** nel frattempo.
⬛2 ADJ (*report*) provvisorio(-a); (*government*) ad interim; **interim dividend** (*Comm*) acconto di dividendo.

in·te·ri·or [ɪnˈtɪərɪəʳ] ⬛1 ADJ interno(-a); (*life, world, monologue*) interiore.
⬛2 N interno; (*of country*) entroterra *m*; **Department of the Interior** Ministero degli Interni.

◆ **interior decorator** N (*designer*) arredatore(-trice); (*painter*) imbianchino; (*wallpaper hanger*) tappezziere.

inter·ject [ˌɪntəˈdʒɛkt] VT intervenire (con).

inter·jec·tion [ˌɪntəˈdʒɛkʃən] N interiezione *f*.

inter·link [ˌɪntəˈlɪŋk] VT: **to be interlinked (with)** essere connesso(-a) (con).

inter·lock [ˌɪntə'lɒk] **1** vi ingranarsi.
2 vt ingranare.
inter·locu·tor [ˌɪntə'lɒkjʊtə'] N (frm) interlocutore(-trice).
inter·lop·er ['ɪntələʊpə'] N intruso(-a).
inter·lude ['ɪntəluːd] N parentesi f inv, intervallo; (Theatre) intermezzo; **musical interlude** interludio.
inter·mar·ry ['ɪntə'mærɪ] vi (races, groups) fare matrimonii misti; (blood relations) sposarsi tra consanguinei.
inter·medi·ary [ˌɪntə'miːdɪərɪ] N mediatore(-trice), intermediario(-a).
inter·medi·ate [ˌɪntə'miːdɪət] ADJ (stage, position, course, level) intermedio(-a); (student) che frequenta un corso intermedio.
in·ter·ment [ɪn'tɜːmənt] N (frm) inumazione f.
in·ter·mi·nable [ɪn'tɜːmɪnəbl] ADJ interminabile.
in·ter·mi·nably [ɪn'tɜːmɪnəblɪ] ADV interminabilmente.
inter·min·gle [ˌɪntə'mɪŋgl] vi: **to intermingle (with)** mescolarsi (a).
inter·mis·sion [ˌɪntə'mɪʃən] N (pause) interruzione f, pausa; (Theatre, Cine) intervallo.
inter·mit·tent [ˌɪntə'mɪtənt] ADJ intermittente.
inter·mit·tent·ly [ˌɪntə'mɪtəntlɪ] ADV a intermittenza.
in·tern [vb ɪn'tɜːn; n 'ɪntɜːn] **1** vt internare.
2 N (Am: doctor) (medico) interno.
in·ter·nal [ɪn'tɜːnl] ADJ interno(-a); **internal injuries** lesioni fpl interne; **internal processes** (Geol) fenomeni mpl endogeni.
♦ **internal-combustion engine** [ɪnˌtɜːnlkəm'bʌstʃən-ˌɛndʒɪn] N motore m a combustione interna or a scoppio.
in·ter·nal·ize [ɪn'tɜːnəˌlaɪz] vt (frm) interiorizzare.
in·ter·nal·ly [ɪn'tɜːnəlɪ] ADV internamente; **to bleed internally** avere un'emorragia interna; **"not to be taken internally"** "per uso esterno".
♦ **Internal Revenue Service** N (Am) fisco.
inter·na·tion·al [ˌɪntə'næʃnəl] **1** ADJ internazionale.
2 N (Sport: game) incontro internazionale; (: player) giocatore(-trice) della squadra nazionale.
♦ **International Court of Justice** N Corte f Internazionale di Giustizia.
♦ **International Date Line** N linea del cambiamento di data.
inter·na·tion·al·ly [ˌɪntə'næʃnəlɪ] ADV: **internationally famous** di fama internazionale; **internationally, the situation is even worse** a livello internazionale la situazione è anche peggiore.
♦ **International Monetary Fund** N Fondo monetario internazionale.
♦ **international relations** NPL rapporti mpl internazionali.
inter·necine [ˌɪntə'niːsaɪn] ADJ distruttivo(-a) per entrambe le parti.
in·ternee [ˌɪntɜː'niː] N internato(-a).
in·tern·ist [ɪn'tɜːnɪst] N (Am Med) internista m/f.
in·tern·ment [ɪn'tɜːnmənt] N internamento.
inter·per·son·al [ˌɪntə'pɜːsnl] ADJ interpersonale.
inter·play ['ɪntəˌpleɪ] N interazione f.
Inter·pol ['ɪntəˌpɒl] N Interpol f.
in·ter·po·late [ɪn'tɜːpəˌleɪt] vt (frm: remark) interpolare; **to interpolate (into)** (phrase, passage) inserire (in).
in·ter·po·la·tion [ɪnˌtɜːpə'leɪʃən] N (frm) interpolazione f.
inter·pose [ˌɪntə'pəʊz] vt intervenire; **to interpose oneself between** frapporsi fra.
in·ter·pret [ɪn'tɜːprɪt] **1** vt **a** (translate orally): **to inter-**

pret sth (into) tradurre qc (in) **b** (explain, understand) interpretare.
2 vi fare da interprete.
in·ter·pre·ta·tion [ɪnˌtɜːprɪ'teɪʃən] N interpretazione f.
in·ter·pret·er [ɪn'tɜːprɪtə'] N interprete m/f.
in·ter·pret·ing [ɪn'tɜːprɪtɪŋ] N (profession) interpretariato.
inter·reg·num [ˌɪntə'rɛgnəm] N interregno.
inter·re·late [ˌɪntərɪ'leɪt] **1** vt mettere in connessione, connettere; **interrelated facts** fatti mpl connessi fra loro.
2 vi essere connesso(-a).
inter·re·lat·ed [ˌɪntərɪ'leɪtɪd] ADJ correlato(-a), in relazione (l'uno(-a) con l'altro(-a)).
in·ter·ro·gate [ɪn'tɛrəˌgeɪt] vt interrogare.
in·ter·ro·ga·tion [ɪnˌtɛrə'geɪʃən] N (of suspect, witness) interrogatorio.
in·ter·rogative [ˌɪntə'rɒgətɪv] **1** ADJ interrogativo(-a).
2 N (Gram) interrogativo.
in·ter·roga·tive·ly [ˌɪntə'rɒgətɪvlɪ] ADV interrogativamente, con aria interrogativa; (Gram) in forma interrogativa.
in·ter·ro·ga·tor [ɪn'tɛrəˌgeɪtə'] N interrogatore(-trice).
in·ter·rupt [ˌɪntə'rʌpt] vt, vi interrompere.
in·ter·rup·tion [ˌɪntə'rʌpʃən] N interruzione f.
inter·sect [ˌɪntə'sɛkt] **1** vt (Math) intersecare.
2 vi (Math) intersecarsi; (roads) incrociarsi, intersecarsi.
inter·sec·tion [ˌɪntə'sɛkʃən] N (crossroads) incrocio; (Math) intersezione f.
inter·sperse [ˌɪntə'spɜːs] vt: **to intersperse sth with sth** inframmezzare qc con qc.
inter·state [ˌɪntə'steɪt] ADJ fra stati.
inter·stel·lar [ˌɪntə'stɛlə'] ADJ (frm) interstellare.
inter·twine [ˌɪntə'twaɪn] **1** vt intrecciare.
2 vi intrecciarsi.
in·ter·val ['ɪntəvəl] N intervallo; **at intervals** di tanto in tanto, a tratti; **at regular intervals** a intervalli regolari; **sunny intervals** (Met) schiarite fpl.
inter·vene [ˌɪntə'viːn] vi (event, circumstances) sopraggiungere; (time) intercorrere; (person): **to intervene (in)** intervenire (in); **in the intervening years** negli anni che sono intercorsi.
inter·ven·tion [ˌɪntə'vɛnʃən] N intervento.
inter·ven·tion·ism [ˌɪntə'vɛnʃənɪzəm] N interventismo.
inter·ven·tion·ist [ˌɪntə'vɛnʃənɪst] ADJ, N interventista (m/f).
inter·view ['ɪntəˌvjuː] **1** N (for job, position) colloquio; (in paper, on radio, TV) intervista; **to have an interview with the director** avere un colloquio con il direttore.
2 vt (see n) sottoporre a colloquio; intervistare.
inter·viewee [ˌɪntəvjuː'iː] N (Media) intervistato(-a); (for job) chi viene sottoposto ad un colloquio di lavoro.
inter·view·er ['ɪntəvjuːə'] N (on radio, TV) intervistatore(-trice).
inter·weave [ˌɪntə'wiːv] **1** vt intrecciare.
2 vi intrecciarsi.
in·tes·tate [ɪn'tɛstɪt] ADJ (Law): **to die intestate** morire intestato(-a).
in·tes·ti·nal [ɪn'tɛstɪnl] ADJ intestinale.
in·tes·tine [ɪn'tɛstɪn] N intestino; **large intestine** (intestino) crasso; **small intestine** (intestino) tenue m.
in·ti·ma·cy ['ɪntɪməsɪ] N (friendship) intimità; (sexual intimacy) rapporti mpl intimi.
in·ti·mate [adj 'ɪntɪˌmɪt; vb 'ɪntɪmeɪt] **1** ADJ intimo(-a); (knowledge) profondo(-a); **to be/become intimate with**

sb (*friendly*) essere/diventare amico(-a) intimo(-a) di qn; (*sexually*) avere rapporti intimi con qn.
2 VT: **to intimate (that)** far *or* lasciar capire (che).

in·ti·mate·ly ['ɪntɪmɪtlɪ] ADV intimamente; **to talk intimately with sb** scambiare confidenze con qn; **to be intimately involved in sth** essere direttamente coinvolto (-a) in qc.

in·ti·ma·tion [ˌɪntɪ'meɪʃən] N (*hint*) accenno.

in·timi·date [ɪn'tɪmɪˌdeɪt] VT intimidire; (*witness*) minacciare, sottoporre ad intimidazione.

in·timi·da·tion [ɪnˌtɪmɪ'deɪʃən] N intimidazione *f*.

into ['ɪntu:] PREP **a** (*of place*) in, dentro; **put it into the box** mettilo nella *or* dentro la scatola; **come into the house** vieni dentro casa; **to go into the wood** entrare nel bosco; **to walk into a wall** sbattere contro un muro; **he drove into a tree** andò a sbattere contro un albero; **to go into town/the country** andare in città/in campagna; **to get into the car** salire in macchina
b (*change in condition*) in; **to translate sth into Italian** tradurre qc in italiano; **to burst into tears** scoppiare in lacrime; **to change pounds into dollars** cambiare delle sterline in dollari; **to cut into pieces** tagliare a pezzi; **to change into clean clothes** mettersi dei vestiti puliti; **he is really into jazz** (*fam*) è un appassionato di jazz, ha la passione del jazz
c (*Math*): **2 into 6 goes 3 times** il 2 nel 6 sta 3 volte; **to divide 3 into 12** dividere 12 per 3.

in·tol·er·able [ɪn'tɒlərəbl] ADJ intollerabile.

in·tol·er·ably [ɪn'tɒlərəblɪ] ADV intollerabilmente.

in·tol·er·ance [ɪn'tɒlərəns] N intolleranza.

in·tol·er·ant [ɪn'tɒlərənt] ADJ: **intolerant (of)** intollerante (verso).

in·tol·er·ant·ly [ɪn'tɒlərəntlɪ] ADV in modo intollerante.

in·to·na·tion [ˌɪntəʊ'neɪʃən] N (*Linguistics*) intonazione *f*.

in·toxi·cant [ɪn'tɒksɪkənt] N (*frm*) bevanda alcolica.

in·toxi·cate [ɪn'tɒksɪˌkeɪt] VT (*subj: alcohol*) ubriacare; (*subj: success*) inebriare.

in·toxi·cat·ed [ɪn'tɒksɪˌkeɪtɪd] ADJ ubriaco(-a); **intoxicated (with)** (*fig*) inebriato(-a) (di); **to become intoxicated** ubriacarsi.

in·toxi·ca·tion [ɪnˌtɒksɪ'keɪʃən] N (*see adj*) ubriachezza; ebbrezza.

intra... ['ɪntrə] PREF intra... .

in·trac·table [ɪn'træktəbl] (*frm*) ADJ (*person, mood*) intrattabile; (*illness*) difficile da curare; (*problem*) insolubile.

intra·mus·cu·lar [ˌɪntrə'mʌskjʊləʳ] ADJ intramuscolare.

in·tran·si·gence [ɪn'trænsɪdʒəns] N intransigenza.

in·tran·si·gent [ɪn'trænsɪdʒənt] ADJ intransigente.

in·tran·si·tive [ɪn'trænsɪtɪv] ADJ (*Gram*) intransitivo(-a).

♦ **intra-uterine device** [ˌɪntrə'ju:tərəmdɪ'vaɪs] N dispositivo anticoncezionale intrauterino, spirale *f*.

intra·venous [ˌɪntrə'vi:nəs] ADJ endovenoso(-a).

intra·venous·ly [ˌɪntrə'vi:nəslɪ] ADV endovena.

♦ **in-tray** ['ɪnˌtreɪ] N vassoio della corrispondenza in arrivo.

in·trep·id [ɪn'trepɪd] ADJ intrepido(-a).

in·tre·pid·ity [ˌɪntrɪ'pɪdɪtɪ] N intrepidezza.

in·tri·ca·cy [ɪntrɪkəsɪ] N complessità *f inv*.

in·tri·cate ['ɪntrɪkɪt] ADJ (*plot, problem*) intricato(-a), complicato(-a); (*pattern, machinery, mechanism*) complicato(-a), complesso(-a).

in·tri·cate·ly ['ɪntrɪkɪtlɪ] ADV (*see adj*) in modo intricato; in modo complesso.

in·trigue [ɪn'tri:g] **1** N (*plot*) intrigo; (*amorous*) tresca.

2 VT (*fascinate*) intrigare, affascinare; (*make curious*) incuriosire.
3 VI complottare, tramare.

in·tri·guer [ɪn'tri:gəʳ] N cospiratore(-trice).

in·tri·guing [ɪn'tri:gɪŋ] **1** ADJ (*fascinating*) affascinante, intrigante; (*arousing curiosity*) che suscita curiosità.
2 N intrighi *mpl*.

in·trin·sic [ɪn'trɪnsɪk] ADJ intrinseco(-a).

in·trin·si·cal·ly [ɪn'trɪnsɪklɪ] ADV intrinsecamente.

intro·duce [ˌɪntrə'dju:s] VT **a** (*bring in: reform, new fashion, idea*) introdurre; (: *Pol*: bill, TV, *Radio*: programme) presentare; **to introduce sb into a firm** far entrare qn in una ditta
b (*make acquainted*): **to introduce sb to sb** presentare qn a qn; **to introduce sb to sth** (*pastime, technique*) far conoscere qc a qn, iniziare qn a qc; **she introduced us to the delights of Indian cookery** ci ha iniziato ai piaceri della cucina indiana; **may I introduce ...?** permette che le presenti...?

intro·duc·tion [ˌɪntrə'dʌkʃən] N (*see vb*) introduzione *f*; presentazione *f*; **my introduction to maths** il mio primo contatto con la matematica; **a letter of introduction** una lettera di presentazione.

intro·duc·tory [ˌɪntrə'dʌktərɪ] ADJ introduttivo(-a); **introductory remarks** osservazioni *fpl* preliminari; **an introductory offer** un'offerta di lancio.

intro·spec·tion [ˌɪntrəʊ'spekʃən] N introspezione *f*.

intro·spec·tive [ˌɪntrəʊ'spektɪv] ADJ introspettivo(-a).

intro·ver·sion [ˌɪntrəʊ'vɜ:ʃən] N introversione *f*.

intro·vert ['ɪntrəʊˌvɜ:t] N, ADJ introverso(-a).

intro·ver·ted ['ɪntrəʊˌvɜ:tɪd] ADJ = **introvert**.

in·trude [ɪn'tru:d] VI intromettersi; **to intrude on** *or* **upon** (*person*) importunare; (*conversation*) intromettersi in; **I hope I'm not intruding** spero di non disturbare.

in·trud·er [ɪn'tru:dəʳ] N (*trespasser*) intruso(-a); (*burglar*) ladro(-a).

in·tru·sion [ɪn'tru:ʒən] N intrusione *f*.

in·tru·sive [ɪn'tru:sɪv] ADJ importuno(-a).

in·tui·tion [ˌɪntju:'ɪʃən] N (*no pl: power*) intuito, intuizione *f*; (*feeling*) intuito.

in·tui·tive [ɪn'tju:ɪtɪv] ADJ intuitivo(-a).

in·tui·tive·ly [ɪn'tju:ɪtɪvlɪ] ADV intuitivamente.

in·un·date ['ɪnʌnˌdeɪt] VT: **to inundate (with)** inondare (di); (*fig*) sommergere (di).

in·ure [ɪn'jʊəʳ] VT: **to inure (to)** assuefare (a).

in·vade [ɪn'veɪd] VT (*Mil, gen, fig*) invadere; (*privacy, sb's rights*) violare.

in·vad·er [ɪn'veɪdəʳ] N invasore *m*.

in·vad·ing [ɪn'veɪdɪŋ] ADJ (*army, troops*) d'invasione.

in·va·lid[1] ['ɪnvəlɪd] **1** N (*sick person*) infermo(-a); (*disabled person*) invalido(-a).
2 ADJ (*see n*) infermo(-a); invalido(-a).
▶ **invalid out** VT + ADV (*Mil*) congedare per invalidità.

in·val·id[2] [ɪn'vælɪd] ADJ (*document, cheque*) invalido(-a), non valido(-a); (*excuse, argument*) non valido(-a); (*marriage*) nullo(-a).

in·vali·date [ɪn'vælɪˌdeɪt] VT (*law, contract*) invalidare; (*argument, conclusion*) smentire; **the will was invalidated** il testamento è stato invalidato.

♦ **invalid chair** N (*Brit*) sedia a rotelle.

in·valu·able [ɪn'væljʊəbl] ADJ estremamente prezioso (-a).

in·vari·able [ɪn'vɛərɪəbl] ADJ costante, invariabile.

in·vari·ably [ɪn'vɛərɪəblɪ] ADV invariabilmente; **she is invariably late** è immancabilmente in ritardo.

in·vari·ant [ɪn'vɛərɪənt] ADJ (*Math*) invariante *f*.

in·va·sion [ɪn'veɪʒən] N invasione *f*; **an invasion of sb's privacy** una violazione della privacy di qn.

in·vec·tive [ɪn'vɛktɪv] N invettiva; **a stream of invective** una sfilza d'ingiurie, una sequela di improperi.

in·veigh [ɪn'veɪ] VI: **to inveigh against** (*frm*) inveire contro.

in·vei·gle [ɪn'viːgl] VT: **to inveigle sb into (doing) sth** circuire qn per fargli/farle fare qc.

in·vent [ɪn'vɛnt] VT inventare.

in·ven·tion [ɪn'vɛnʃən] N invenzione *f*.

in·ven·tive [ɪn'vɛntɪv] ADJ (*genius*) inventivo(-a), creativo(-a); (*mind*) ricco(-a) d'inventiva.

in·ven·tive·ness [ɪn'vɛntɪvnɪs] N inventiva.

in·ven·tor [ɪn'vɛntə'] N inventore(-trice).

in·ven·tory ['ɪnvəntrɪ] N inventario; **to draw up/take an inventory** fare l'inventario.

♦ **inventory control** N (*Comm*) controllo delle giacenze.

in·verse ['ɪn'vɜːs] [1] ADJ inverso(-a); **in inverse proportion (to)** inversamente proporzionale (a); **to be in inverse proportion** essere inversamente proporzionale.

[2] N inverso, contrario.

in·verse·ly [ɪn'vɜːslɪ] ADV all'inverso; **Inversely proportionate** inversamente proporzionale.

in·ver·sion [ɪn'vɜːʃən] N (*of elements, words, roles*) inversione *f*; (*of object*) capovolgimento, ribaltamento; (*of values*) rovesciamento, capovolgimento.

in·vert [ɪn'vɜːt] VT (*object*) capovolgere, rovesciare; (*elements, words*) invertire.

in·ver·tebrate [ɪn'vɜːtɪbrɪt] N, ADJ invertebrato(-a).

in·vert·ed com·mas [ɪn,vɜːtɪd'kɒməz] NPL (*Brit*) virgolette *fpl*; **in inverted commas** tra virgolette.

in·vest [ɪn'vɛst] [1] VT **a** (*money, capital*) investire; (*fig: time, effort*) impiegare **b** (*endow*): **to invest sb with sth** investire qn di qc.

[2] VI: **to invest in** (*company, property*) investire in, fare (degli) investimenti in; (*acquire*) comprarsi.

in·ves·ti·gate [ɪn'vɛstɪ,geɪt] VT (*crime, motive*) indagare su, investigare su; (*possibilities*) studiare, esaminare.

in·ves·ti·ga·tion [ɪn,vɛstɪ'geɪʃən] N (*of crime*) indagine *f*, investigazione *f* giudiziaria; **police investigations** le indagini della polizia.

in·ves·ti·gative [ɪn'vɛstɪgətɪv] ADJ: **investigative journalism** giornalismo investigativo.

in·ves·ti·ga·tor [ɪn'vɛstɪ,geɪtə'] N investigatore(-trice); **a private investigator** un investigatore privato, un detective.

in·ves·ti·ture [ɪn'vɛstɪtʃə'] N investitura.

in·vest·ment [ɪn'vɛstmənt] N (*Comm*) investimento.

♦ **investment grant** N incentivo agli investimenti.

♦ **investment income** N reddito da investimenti.

♦ **investment trust** N fondo comune di investimento.

in·ves·tor [ɪn'vɛstə'] N (*gen*) investitore(-trice); (*shareholder*) azionista *m/f*.

in·vet·er·ate [ɪn'vɛtərɪt] ADJ (*habit, gambler*) inveterato (-a); (*liar, smoker*) incallito(-a).

in·vidi·ous [ɪn'vɪdɪəs] ADJ (*comparison*) ingiusto(-a); (*task*) poco invidiabile, antipatico(-a); (*choice*) imbarazzante, difficile.

in·vigi·late [ɪn'vɪdʒɪ,leɪt] VT, VI (*Brit Scol*) sorvegliare.

in·vigi·la·tor [ɪn'vɪdʒɪ,leɪtə'] N (*Brit*) chi sorveglia agli esami.

in·vig·or·ate [ɪn'vɪgə,reɪt] VT (*subj: exercise, air*) tonificare, invigorire.

in·vig·or·at·ing [ɪn'vɪgə,reɪtɪŋ] ADJ (*exercise, walk, air,*

breeze) tonificante.

in·vin·cible [ɪn'vɪnsəbl] ADJ invincibile.

in·vio·lable [ɪn'vaɪələbl] ADJ (*frm*) inviolabile.

in·vio·late [ɪn'vaɪəlɪt] ADJ inviolato(-a).

in·vis·ibil·ity [ɪn,vɪzə'bɪlɪtɪ] N invisibilità.

in·vis·ible [ɪn'vɪzəbl] ADJ invisibile.

♦ **invisible assets** NPL (*Brit: Econ*) beni *mpl* immateriali.

♦ **invisible earnings** NPL (*Econ*) partite *fpl* invisibili.

♦ **invisible ink** N inchiostro simpatico.

♦ **invisible mending** N rammendo invisibile.

in·vis·ibly [ɪn'vɪzəblɪ] ADV in modo invisibile.

in·vi·ta·tion [,ɪnvɪ'teɪʃən] N invito; **by invitation only** esclusivamente su invito; **at sb's invitation** dietro *or* su invito di qn.

in·vite [ɪn'vaɪt] VT (*person*): **to invite sb (to do)** invitare qn (a fare); (*subscriptions, applications*) sollecitare, richiedere (cortesemente); (*opinions*) chiedere; (*discussion*) invitare a; (*ridicule*) provocare, suscitare; (*disbelief*) incoraggiare; **to invite sb to dinner** invitare qn a cena; **to invite sb in/up** invitare qn a entrare/salire; **to invite trouble** cercare guai

► **invite out** VT + ADV invitare fuori; **he invited us out to dinner** ci ha invitato a cena fuori

► **invite over** VT + ADV invitare (a casa).

in·vit·ing [ɪn'vaɪtɪŋ] ADJ (*prospect, goods*) invitante, allettante; (*smile*) invitante; (*food, smell*) invitante, appetitoso(-a).

in·vit·ing·ly [ɪn'vaɪtɪŋlɪ] ADV (*smile, describe*) in modo invitante.

in vitro [ɪn'viːtrəʊ] ADJ, ADV in vitro.

♦ **in vitro fertilization** N (*Med*) fecondazione *f* in vitro.

in·vo·ca·tion [,ɪnvəʊ'keɪʃən] N invocazione *f*.

in·voice ['ɪnvɔɪs] [1] N fattura.

[2] VT (*goods*) fatturare; **to invoice sb for goods** intestare a qn la fattura per le *or* delle merci.

♦ **invoice clerk** N fatturista *m/f*.

in·voke [ɪn'vəʊk] VT invocare.

in·vol·un·tari·ly [ɪn'vɒləntərɪlɪ] ADV involontariamente.

in·vol·un·tary [ɪn'vɒləntərɪ] ADJ involontario(-a).

in·volve [ɪn'vɒlv] VT **a** (*associate*) coinvolgere; (*implicate*) implicare, coinvolgere; **to be/become involved in sth** essere/rimanere coinvolto(-a) in qc; **to involve o.s./sb in sth** (*politics etc*) impegnarsi/coinvolgere qn in qc; **don't involve me in your quarrels!** non tiratemi in mezzo alle vostre beghe!; **don't involve yourself in unnecessary expense** non metterti a fare spese inutili; **how did he come to be involved?** come ha fatto a trovarcisi in mezzo?; **the factors involved** i fattori in causa *or* in gioco; **the persons involved** le persone in questione *or* coinvolte; **to feel involved** sentirsi coinvolto(-a); **to become** *or* **get involved with sb** (*socially*) legarsi a qn; (*emotionally*) legarsi sentimentalmente a qn

b (*entail*) implicare, comportare; **it involves a lot of expense/trouble** comporta un mucchio di spese/difficoltà.

in·volved [ɪn'vɒlvd] ADJ (*situation, discussion*) complicato (-a), complesso(-a); see also **involve**.

in·volve·ment [ɪn'vɒlvmənt] N **a** (*being involved*) impegno, partecipazione *f*, coinvolgimento; (*emotional*) legame *m*, relazione *f*; **we don't know the extent of his involvement** non sappiamo fino a che punto sia coinvolto; **financial involvements** impegni *mpl* finanziari **b** (*complexity*) complessità.

in·vul·ner·abil·ity [ɪn,vʌlnərə'bɪlɪtɪ] N invulnerabilità.

in·vul·ner·able [ɪn'vʌlnərəbl] ADJ invulnerabile.

in·ward ['ɪnwəd] ① ADJ (*peace, happiness*) interiore; (*thought, feeling*) intimo(-a); (*movement*) verso l'interno.
② ADV = **inwards**.
♦ **inward-looking** ['ɪnwəd'lʊkɪŋ] ADJ (*society*) chiuso(-a); **an inward-looking individual** un introverso.

in·ward·ly ['ɪnwədlɪ] ADV (*feel, think*) nel proprio intimo, dentro di sé.

in·wards ['ɪnwədz] ADV verso l'interno.

I/O ABBR (*Comput*: = *input/output*) I/O.

IOC [ˌaɪəʊ'siː] N ABBR (= *International Olympic Committee*) C.I.O. *m* (= *Comitato Internazionale Olimpico*).

iodide ['aɪəˌdaɪd] N ioduro.

iodine ['aɪəˌdiːn] N iodio.

IOM ABBR (*Brit*)= *Isle of Man*.

ion ['aɪən] N ione *m*.

♦ **ion exchange** N scambio ionico.

Ionian Sea [aɪ'əʊnɪən'siː] N: **the Ionian Sea** il mar Ionio.

Ion·ic [aɪ'ɒnɪk] ADJ (*Archit*) ionico(-a).

ion·ic [aɪ'ɒnɪk] ADJ (*Phys, Chem*) ionico(-a).

ioni·za·tion [ˌaɪənaɪ'zeɪʃən] N ionizzazione *f*.

ion·iz·er [ˈaɪənˌaɪzəʳ] N ionizzatore *m*.

iono·sphere [aɪ'ɒnəˌsfɪəʳ] N ionosfera.

iota [aɪ'əʊtə] N (*letter*) iota; (*of truth, commonsense*) briciolo.

IOU [ˌaɪəʊ'juː] N ABBR (= *I owe you*) pagherò *m inv.*

IOW ABBR (*Brit*)= *Isle of Wight*.

IPA [ˌaɪpiː'eɪ] N ABBR (= *International Phonetic Alphabet*) A.F.I. *m* (= *Alfabeto Fonetico Internazionale*).

Iphigenia [ˌɪfɪdʒɪ'naɪə] N Ifigenia.

IQ [ˌaɪ'kjuː] N ABBR (= *intelligence quotient*) Q.I. *m.*

IRA [ˌaɪɑː'reɪ] N ABBR (= *Irish Republican Army*) I.R.A. *f.*

Iran [ɪ'rɑːn] N l'Iran *m.*

Ira·nian [ɪ'reɪnɪən] ① ADJ iraniano(-a).
② N (*person*) iraniano(-a); (*language*) iranico.

Iraq [ɪ'rɑːk] N l'Iraq *m.*

Ira·qi [ɪ'rɑːkɪ] ① ADJ iracheno(-a).
② N (*person*) iracheno(-a).

iras·cibil·ity [ɪˌræsɪ'bɪlɪtɪ] N irascibilità.

iras·cible [ɪ'ræsɪbl] ADJ irascibile.

irate [aɪ'reɪt] ADJ irato(-a), infuriato(-a).

Ire·land ['aɪələnd] N l'Irlanda; **Northern Ireland** l'Irlanda del Nord; **Republic of Ireland** la Repubblica d'Irlanda, l'Eire *f.*

iri·des·cent [ˌɪrɪ'dɛsnt] ADJ (*frm*) iridescente.

iris ['aɪərɪs] N **a** (*Anat*) iride *f* **b** (*Bot*) iris *f inv*, giaggiolo.

Irish ['aɪərɪʃ] ① ADJ irlandese.
② N **a** : **the Irish** NPL gli irlandesi **b** (*language*) irlandese *m.*

Irish·man ['aɪərɪʃmən] N (*pl* **-men**) irlandese *m.*

♦ **Irish Sea** N: **the Irish Sea** il mar d'Irlanda.

Irish·woman ['aɪərɪʃˌwʊmən] N (*pl* **-women**) irlandese *f.*

irk [ɜːk] VT seccare.

irk·some ['ɜːksəm] ADJ noioso(-a), seccante.

IRO [ˌaɪːɑːr'əʊ] N ABBR (*Am*)= *International Refugee Organization.*

iron ['aɪən] ① N (*also fig*) ferro; (*Golf*) mazza da golf di ferro; (*for ironing clothes*) ferro (da stiro); **a will of iron** una volontà ferrea *or* di ferro; **he rules his children with a rod of iron** comanda a bacchetta i figli; **to strike while the iron is hot** (*fig*) battere finché il ferro è caldo; **to have a lot of/too many irons in the fire** (*fig*) avere molta/troppa carne al fuoco; see also **irons**.
② VT (*clothes*) stirare.
③ VI: **this dress irons well** questo vestito è facile da

stirare.
④ ADJ (*bridge, bar, tool etc*) di ferro; (*fig*: *will, determination*) ferreo(-a), di ferro; **an iron fist in a velvet glove** un pugno di ferro in un guanto di velluto
▶ **iron out** VT + ADV (*creases*) far sparire col ferro; (*fig*: *problems, disagreements*) appianare.

♦ **Iron Age** N: **the Iron Age** l'età del ferro.

♦ **iron and steel industry** N l'industria siderurgica, la siderurgia.

♦ **iron chloride** N cloruro di ferro.

♦ **iron constitution** N (*fig*) costituzione *f* robusta.

♦ **Iron Curtain** N (*Pol*): **the Iron Curtain** la cortina di ferro; **Iron Curtain countries** *or* **countries behind the Iron Curtain** gli stati d'oltrecortina.

♦ **iron foundry** N fonderia.

iron·ic [aɪ'rɒnɪk], **ironi·cal** [aɪ'rɒnɪkəl] ADJ ironico(-a); **it's ironic that ...** è un'ironia (della sorte) che... .

ironi·cal·ly [aɪ'rɒnɪkəlɪ] ADV ironicamente; **ironically ...** per ironia... .

iron·ing ['aɪənɪŋ] N (*act*) stirare *m*; (*clothes*) roba da stirare; **mother is doing the ironing** la mamma sta stirando.

♦ **ironing board** N asse *f* da stiro.

♦ **iron lung** N (*Med*) polmone *m* d'acciaio.

iron·monger ['aɪənˌmʌŋgəʳ] N (*Brit*): **ironmonger's (shop)** (negozio di) ferramenta.

iron·mongery ['aɪənˌmʌŋgərɪ] N (*goods*) ferramenta.

♦ **iron ore** N minerale *m* di ferro.

♦ **iron oxide** N ossido di ferro.

♦ **iron rations** NPL viveri *mpl* di riserva.

irons ['aɪənz] NPL (*chains*) catene *fpl.*

iron·stone ['aɪənstəʊn] N minerale *m* di ferro.

♦ **iron sulphate** N solfato ferroso.

iron·works ['aɪənˌwɜːks] NSG stabilimento siderurgico.

iro·ny ['aɪərənɪ] N ironia; **the irony of it is that ...** l'ironia maggiore è che...; **it's one of life's ironies** è un'ironia della sorte *or* del destino.

ir·ra·di·ate [ɪ'reɪdɪˌeɪt] VT (*Phys*) irradiare.

ir·ra·dia·tion [ɪˌreɪdɪ'eɪʃən] N (*Phys*) irradiazione *f.*

ir·ra·tion·al [ɪ'ræʃənl] ADJ irrazionale; **an irrational fear** una paura irrazionale; **he had become quite irrational about it** era diventato piuttosto irragionevole al riguardo.

ir·ra·tion·al·ly [ɪ'ræʃnəlɪ] ADV irrazionalmente.

ir·rec·on·cil·able [ɪˌrɛkən'saɪləbl] (*frm*) ADJ (*persons*) irreconciliabile; (*foes, enemies*) irriducibile; **irreconcilable with** (*opinion, proposal, view*) inconciliabile con.

ir·re·deem·able [ˌɪrɪ'diːməbl] ADJ **a** (*failing*) incorreggibile; (*selfishness*) assoluto(-a) **b** (*Comm*) irredimibile.

ir·re·den·tist [ˌɪrɪ'dɛntɪst] N irredentista *m/f.*

ir·refu·table [ˌɪrɪ'fjuːtəbl] ADJ irrefutabile.

ir·regu·lar [ɪ'rɛgjʊləʳ] ADJ irregolare.

ir·regu·lar·ity [ɪˌrɛgjʊ'lærɪtɪ] N irregolarità *f inv.*

ir·rel·evance [ɪ'rɛləvəns] N non pertinenza.

ir·rel·evant [ɪ'rɛləvənt] ADJ non pertinente; **if he has the qualifications, his age is irrelevant** se ha i titoli la sua età non ha importanza.

ir·re·li·gious [ˌɪrɪ'lɪdʒəs] ADJ irreligioso(-a).

ir·re·medi·able [ˌɪrɪ'miːdɪəbl] ADJ (*frm*) irreparabile.

ir·repa·rable [ɪ'rɛpərəbl] ADJ irrimediabile, irreparabile.

ir·repa·rably [ɪ'rɛpərəblɪ] ADV (*damage, harm*) irrimediabilmente, irreparabilmente.

ir·re·place·able [ˌɪrɪ'pleɪsəbl] ADJ insostituibile.

ir·re·press·ible [ˌɪrɪ'prɛsəbl] ADJ irrefrenabile.

ir·re·proach·able [ˌɪrɪ'prəʊtʃəbl] ADJ (*conduct*) irreprensi-

bile.

ir·re·sist·ible [ˌɪrɪ'zɪstəbl] ADJ irresistibile.

ir·re·sist·ibly [ˌɪrɪ'zɪstəblɪ] ADV irresistibilmente.

ir·reso·lute [ɪ'rezəluːt] ADJ (*person, character*) irresoluto (-a), indeciso(-a).

ir·re·spec·tive [ˌɪrɪ'spɛktɪv]: **irrespective of** PREP a prescindere da; **irrespective of the weather** qualunque tempo faccia.

ir·re·spon·sible [ˌɪrɪs'pɒnsəbl] ADJ (*person, behaviour*) irresponsabile.

ir·re·spon·sibly [ˌɪrɪs'pɒnsəblɪ] ADV irresponsabilmente.

ir·re·triev·able [ˌɪrɪ'triːvəbl] ADJ (*object*) irrecuperabile; (*loss, damage*) irreparabile.

ir·rev·er·ence [ɪ'rɛvərəns] N irriverenza.

ir·rev·er·ent [ɪ'rɛvərənt] ADJ irriverente.

ir·rev·er·ent·ly [ɪ'rɛvərəntlɪ] ADV in modo irriverente.

ir·re·vers·ible [ˌɪrɪ'vɜːsəbl] ADJ irreversibile.

ir·revo·cable [ɪ'rɛvəkəbl] ADJ irrevocabile.

ir·revo·cably [ɪ'rɛvəkəblɪ] ADV irrevocabilmente.

ir·ri·gate ['ɪrɪˌgeɪt] VT irrigare.

ir·ri·ga·tion [ˌɪrɪ'geɪʃən] N irrigazione *f*.

ir·ri·tabil·ity [ˌɪrɪtə'bɪlɪtɪ] N irritabilità.

ir·ri·table ['ɪrɪtəbl] ADJ irritabile.

ir·ri·tably ['ɪrɪtəblɪ] ADV (*speak*) con tono i.rritato; (*shrug*) in modo scontroso.

ir·ri·tant ['ɪrɪtənt] N (*annoyance*) fastidio; (*substance*) sostanza irritante.

ir·ri·tate ['ɪrɪˌteɪt] VT (*annoy*) irritare, seccare; (*skin*) irritare.

ir·ri·tat·ing ['ɪrɪˌteɪtɪŋ] ADJ (*annoying*) irritante, seccante; (*itchy*) irritante.

ir·ri·ta·tion [ˌɪrɪ'teɪʃən] N (*gen, Med*) irritazione *f*; (*fig: irritating thing*) seccatura.

IRS [ˌaɪɑːr'ɛs] N ABBR (*Am*) = **Internal Revenue Service**.

is [ɪz] 3RD PERS SG PRESENT of **be**.

Isaac ['aɪzək] N Isacco.

Isaiah [aɪ'zaɪə] N Isaia *m*.

ISBN [ˌaɪɛsbiː'ɛn] N ABBR (= *International Standard Book Number*) I.S.B.N. *m*.

Is·lam ['ɪzlɑːm] N Islam *m inv*.

Is·lam·ic [ɪz'læmɪk] ADJ islamico(-a).

is·land ['aɪlənd] N isola; (*also:* **traffic island**) isola *f* spartitraffico *inv*, salvagente *m*.

is·land·er ['aɪləndəʳ] N isolano(-a).

♦ **island people** NPL isolani *mpl*.

isle [aɪl] N (*liter*) isola.

isn't ['ɪznt] = **is not**.

iso·bar ['aɪsəʊˌbɑːʳ] N (*Phys*) elemento isobaro; (*Met*) isobara.

iso·hy·et [ˌaɪsəʊ'haɪɪt] N isoieta.

iso·late ['aɪsəˌleɪt] VT (*gen, Med*): **to isolate (from)** isolare (da); (*pinpoint: cause*) individuare, isolare.

iso·lat·ed ['aɪsəˌleɪtɪd] ADJ isolato(-a).

iso·la·tion [ˌaɪsə'leɪʃən] N isolamento.

iso·la·tion·ism [ˌaɪsə'leɪʃəˌnɪzəm] N isolazionismo.

iso·la·tion·ist [ˌaɪsə'leɪʃənɪst] ADJ, N isolazionista (*m/f*).

♦ **isolation ward** N reparto d'isolamento.

iso·mer ['aɪsəməʳ] N isomero.

iso·met·ric [ˌaɪsəʊ'mɛtrɪk] ADJ (*Math, Geog, Poetry*) isometrico(-a).

isom·etry [aɪ'sɒmɪtrɪ] N (*Math*) isometria.

iso·mor·phic [ˌaɪsəʊ'mɔːfɪk], **iso·mor·phous** [ˌaɪsəʊ'mɔːfəs] ADJ isomorfo(-a).

iso·mor·phism [ˌaɪsəʊ'mɔːfɪzəm] N isomorfismo.

isos·celes [aɪ'sɒsɪˌliːz] ADJ isoscele.

iso·therm ['aɪsəʊˌθɜːm] N isoterma.

iso·tope ['aɪsəˌtəʊp] N isotopo.

Is·ra·el ['ɪzreɪəl] N Israele *m*.

Is·rae·li [ɪz'reɪlɪ] 1 ADJ israeliano(-a), d'Israele. 2 N israeliano(-a).

Is·rael·ite ['ɪzrɪəˌlaɪt] N israelita *m/f*.

is·sue ['ɪʃjuː] 1 N a (*matter, question*) questione *f*, problema *m*; **a political issue** una questione politica; **the (real/main) issue is whether ...** la questione (reale/fondamentale) è quella di sapere se...; **to confuse** *or* **obscure the issue** confondere le acque; **to avoid the issue** eludere il (vero) problema; **to face the issue** affrontare la questione; **to make an issue of sth** fare un problema di qc; **the point/matter at issue** il punto in discussione; **to take issue with sb (over sth)** prendere posizione contro qn (riguardo a qc); **I must take issue with you over your last remark** mi dispiace, ma non sono affatto d'accordo sulla tua ultima osservazione

b (*of stamps, banknotes, shares*) emissione *f*; (*of passports, driving licences*) rilascio; (*of rations*) distribuzione *f*; **these coins are a new issue** queste monete sono di recente emissione

c (*copy: of newspaper, magazine etc*) numero; **back issue** (numero) arretrato

d (*frm: outcome*) risultato, esito

e (*Law: offspring*) prole *f*, discendenti *mpl*; **to die without issue** morire senza lasciare discendenti.

2 VT (*book*) pubblicare; (*stamps, cheques, banknotes, shares*) emettere; (*passports, documents*) rilasciare; (*rations, goods, equipment*) distribuire; (*tickets for performance*) mettere in vendita; (*orders*) dare, impartire; (*statement*) rilasciare, diramare; (*warrant, writ, summons*) spiccare, emettere; **to issue sth to sb** *or* **to issue sb with sth** consegnare qc a qn; **the police issued a warning to people to remain indoors** la polizia ha raccomandato alla popolazione di rimanere in casa.

3 VI: **to issue (from)** uscire (da), venir fuori (da).

Is·tan·bul [ˌɪstæn'buːl] N Istanbul *f*.

isth·mus ['ɪsməs] N istmo.

IT [ˌaɪ'tiː] N ABBR = **information technology**.

it [ɪt] PRON

a (*specific: subject*) esso(-a) (*often not translated*); (*: direct object*) lo/la, l' (*before vowel*); (*: indirect object*) gli/le;

▷**I spoke to him** *about* **it** gliene ho parlato

▷**she asked him** *about* **it yesterday** glielo ha chiesto ieri

▷**I didn't expect to meet her** *at* **it** non mi aspettavo di incontrarci lei

▷**what's** *behind* **it?** cosa ci sta dietro?, cosa c'è lì dietro?

▷**I** *doubt* **it** ne dubito

▷**I've come** *from* **it** vengo da lì

▷**there's a mistake** *in* **it** c'è un errore

▷**you're just** *in front of* **it** ci stai di fronte

▷**I'm afraid** *of* **it** ne ho paura, mi spaventa

▷**I'm proud** *of* **it** ne sono fiero

▷**it's** *on* **it** è lì sopra

▷**where's my book?** — **it's** *on* **the table** dov'è il mio libro? — è sul tavolo

▷**you won't get anything** *out of* **it** non ne ricaverai niente

▷**put a cover** *over* **it** mettici sopra una coperta

▷**he agreed** *to* **it** ha acconsentito

▷**did you go** *to* **it?** ci sei andato?

▷**there's nothing** *under* **it** non ci sta niente sotto, sotto non c'è niente

▷**have you seen my pen/book? — I can't find it anywhere** hai visto la mia penna/il mio libro? — non la/lo trovo da nessuna parte

▷**here's the book — give it to me** ecco il libro — dammelo

b (*impersonal*)

▷**it's the** *10th* **of October** è il 10 ottobre

▷**I'm** *against* **it** sono contrario

▷**it's** *cold* **today** oggi fa freddo

▷**it's** *easy* **to talk** parlare è facile

▷**I'm (all)** *for* **it** sono pro

▷**it's** *Friday* **tomorrow** domani è venerdì

▷**it's 2** *hours* **on the train** sono *or* ci vogliono 2 ore di treno

▷**it was** *kind* **of you** è stato gentile da parte tua

▷**it's** *me* sono io

▷**how far is it? — it's 10** *miles* quanto dista? — 10 miglia

▷**it's 6** *o'clock* sono le 6

▷**it was** *Peter* **who phoned** è Peter che ha telefonato

▷**I like it here, it's** *quiet* qui mi piace, è tranquillo

▷**it's** *raining* sta piovendo, piove

▷*that's* **it!** (*approval, agreement*) ecco!, è proprio così!; (*disapproval*) basta!; (*finishing*) (questo) è tutto

▷**it's no** *use* **worrying** preoccuparsi è inutile

▷*what* **is it?** (*what do you want?*) cosa c'è?

▷*where* **is it?** dov'è?

▷*who* **is it?** chi è?

c (*in games*): *you're* **it!** tocca a te!

ITA [ˌaɪtiːˈeɪ] N ABBR (*Brit*: = *initial teaching alphabet*) *alfabeto fonetico semplificato per insegnare a leggere.*

Ital·ian [ɪˈtæljən] 1 ADJ italiano(-a); (*lesson, teacher, dictionary*) d'italiano; (*king*) d'Italia.

2 N (*person*) italiano(-a); (*language*) italiano; **the Italians** gli italiani.

ital·ic [ɪˈtælɪk] ADJ (*handwriting*) corsivo(-a).

ital·ics [ɪˈtælɪks] NPL (*Typ*) (carattere *m*) corsivo; **in italics** in corsivo.

Ita·ly [ˈɪtəlɪ] N l'Italia; **in Italy** in Italia.

itch [ɪtʃ] 1 N prurito; **to have an itch to do sth** (*fig*) avere la smania di fare qc.

2 VI (*person*) avere prurito; (*part of body*) prudere; **my leg itches** mi prude la gamba; **to be itching for sth/to do sth** (*fig fam*) aver una gran voglia di qc/di fare qc.

itch·ing [ˈɪtʃɪŋ] ADJ: **itching powder** polverina che dà prurito.

itchy [ˈɪtʃɪ] ADJ (*comp* -**ier**, *superl* -**iest**) (*feeling*) di prurito; **my leg is itchy** ho prurito alla gamba; **I've got itchy feet** (*fig*) mi scotta la terra sotto i piedi.

it'd [ˈɪtd] PRON = **it would, it had.**

item [ˈaɪtəm] N (*in list, catalogue, newspaper*) articolo; (*in bill, account*) voce *f*; (*on agenda*) argomento *or* punto all'ordine del giorno; (*in programme*) numero; **items of clothing** capi *mpl* di abbigliamento; **the main item of news** la notizia più importante.

item·ize [ˈaɪtəˌmaɪz] VT specificare (uno(-a) per uno(-a)), dettagliare.

item·ized bill [ˈaɪtəˌmaɪzdˈbɪl] N (*of restaurant etc*) conto dettagliato; (*Telec*) bolletta con documentazione del traffico telefonico.

it·er·ate [ˈɪtəˌreɪt] VT (*frm*) iterare.

it·era·tive [ˈɪtərətɪv] ADJ iterativo(-a).

itin·er·ant [ɪˈtɪnərənt] ADJ (*actors*) girovago(-a); (*seller*) ambulante; (*preacher*) itinerante.

itin·er·ary [aɪˈtɪnərərɪ] N itinerario.

it'll [ˈɪtl] PRON = **it will, it shall.**

ITN [ˌaɪtiːˈɛn] N ABBR (*Brit*: = *Independent Television News*) *agenzia d'informazioni per la televisione.*

its [ɪts] POSS ADJ il suo/la sua; PL i suoi/le sue; **the dog hurt its paw** il cane si è fatto male alla zampa; **this doll has lost its leg** questa bambola ha perso una gamba.

it's [ɪts] PRON = **it is, it has.**

it·self [ɪtˈsɛlf] PRON a (*reflexive*) si; **the dog injured itself** il cane si è fatto male; **the cat is washing itself** il gatto si pulisce; **the door closed by itself** la porta si è chiusa da sé

b (*emphatic*): **the theatre itself** il teatro stesso; **Barra, itself a beautiful island ...** Barra, di per sé un'isola bellissima...; **she is kindness itself** è la bontà fatta persona.

ITV [ˌaɪtiːˈviː] N ABBR (*Brit*: = *Independent Television*) *emittente televisiva indipendente.*

IUD [ˌaɪjuːˈdiː] N ABBR (= *intra-uterine device*) iud *m inv.*

I've [aɪv] = **I have.**

ivo·ry [ˈaɪvərɪ] 1 N avorio.

2 ADJ (*colour*) avorio *inv*; (*object*) d'avorio.

♦ **Ivory Coast** N: **the Ivory Coast** la Costa d'Avorio.

♦ **ivory tower** N torre *f* d'avorio.

ivy [ˈaɪvɪ] N (*Bot*) edera.

♦ **Ivy League** N *le otto università più prestigiose del Nord-Est degli Stati Uniti (Brown, Columbia, Cornell, Dartmouth College, Harvard, Princeton, University of Pennsylvania e Yale).*

J

J, j [dʒeɪ] N (*letter*) J, j *f or m inv*; **J for Jack**, (*Am*) **J for Jig** ≈ J come jolly.

J/A ABBR = **joint account**.

jab [dʒæb] **1** N (*poke*) colpo (di punta); (*Boxing*) diretto; (*fam: injection*) puntura.

2 VT: **to jab sth into** conficcare qc in; **to jab a finger at sb** puntare un dito contro qn.

3 VI: **to jab at** dare colpi a.

jab·ber ['dʒæbəʳ] **1** VI (*person*) ciarlare, chiacchierare; (*monkey*) schiamazzare; **they were jabbering away in Russian** parlavano fitto fitto in russo.

2 VT farfugliare, borbottare.

3 N (*of person*) chiacchierio, cicaleccio; (*of monkey*) schiamazzo.

jack [dʒæk] N (*Tech, Aut*) cric *m inv*; (*Cards*) fante *m*; (*Bowls*) boccino, pallino; **before you could say Jack Robinson** (*fam*) in men che non si dica; **every man jack of them** (*fam*) ognuno di loro

▶ **jack in** VT + ADV (*fam*) piantare; **I've had enough: let's jack it in** smettiamo, non ne posso più

▶ **jack up** VT + ADV **a** (*Tech, Aut*) sollevare con il cric **b** (*fam: raise: prices, wages*) alzare.

jack·al ['dʒækɔ:l] N sciacallo.

jack·ass ['dʒæk‚æs] N (*also fig: old*) asino, somaro.

jack·boots ['dʒæk‚bu:ts] NPL (*Mil*) stivali *mpl* alti.

jack·daw ['dʒæk‚dɔ:] N taccola.

jack·et ['dʒækɪt] N (*garment*) giacca; (*of book*) sopraccopertina; (*of boiler*) incamiciatura; (*of potato*) buccia.

♦ **jacket potato** N *patata cotta al forno con la buccia.*

♦ **jack-in-the-box** ['dʒækɪnðə‚bɒks] N (*toy*) *scatola con pupazzo a molla*; **she popped up like a jack-in-the-box** è saltata fuori dal nulla.

♦ **jack-knife** ['dʒæk‚naɪf] **1** N coltello a serramanico.

2 VI: **the lorry jack-knifed** il rimorchio del camion si è messo di traverso.

♦ **jack-of-all-trades** [‚dʒækəv'ɔ:l‚treɪdz] N uno(-a) che sa fare un po' di tutto.

♦ **jack plug** N (*Brit*) jack *m inv*.

jack·pot ['dʒæk‚pɒt] N primo premio (in denaro); **to hit the jackpot** (*fam*) vincere il primo premio; (: *fig*) fare centro.

Jaco·bean [‚dʒækə'bi:ən] ADJ (*Brit*) dell'epoca di Giacomo I.

ja·cuz·zi® [dʒə'ku:zi] N vasca per idromassaggio.

jade [dʒeɪd] **1** N (*stone*) giada; (*colour: also:* **jade green**) verde *m* giada *inv*.

2 ADJ (*statue, carving, necklace*) di giada; (*also:* **jade-green**) verde giada *inv*.

jad·ed ['dʒeɪdɪd] ADJ (*person*) annoiato(-a), sfibrato(-a); **to have a jaded appetite** essere un po' svogliato(-a) nel mangiare.

jag·ged ['dʒægɪd] ADJ (*edge*) dentellato(-a); (*rock, cliffs*) frastagliato(-a).

jagu·ar ['dʒægjʊəʳ] N giaguaro.

jail, (*Brit*) **gaol** [dʒeɪl] **1** N carcere *m*, prigione *f*; **in jail** in prigione; **to send sb to jail** mandare qn in prigione.

2 VT mandare in prigione; **he was jailed for 10 years** è stato condannato a 10 anni di carcere.

jail·bird, (*Brit*) **gaol·bird** ['dʒeɪl‚bɜ:d] N (*fam old*) avanzo di galera.

jail·break ['dʒeɪl‚breɪk] N evasione *f*.

jail·breaker ['dʒeɪl‚breɪkəʳ] N evaso(-a).

jail·er, (*Brit*) **gaol·er** ['dʒeɪləʳ] N carceriere *m*.

ja·lopy [dʒə'lɒpɪ] N (*fam: old car*) macinino, carretta.

jam¹ [dʒæm] **1** N (*food*) marmellata, confettura; **strawberry jam** marmellata di fragole; **you want jam on it!** (*fig fam*) vuoi troppo!, sei incontentabile!; **that's money for jam!** (*fig fam*) ti (*or* lo *etc*) pagano per far niente!.

2 ADJ (*tart*) alla marmellata; (*sandwich*) con la marmellata.

jam² [dʒæm] **1** VT **a** (*block: mechanism, drawer*) bloccare; (: *machine*) far inceppare; (*subj: people, cars: passage, exit*) bloccare, ingombrare, ostruire; (*Radio: station, broadcast*) disturbare con interferenze; **to jam a door open** (*or* **shut**) bloccare una porta; **streets jammed with people** strade molto affollate; **streets jammed with cars** strade congestionate; **the telephone lines are jammed** le linee sono sovraccariche; **to jam one's brakes on** frenare bruscamente

b (*cram*): **to jam sth into sth** (*drawer, suitcase*) ficcare *or*

infilare qc a forza dentro qc; (*room, vehicle*) far entrare qc dentro qc; **he jammed his hat on his head** si è ficcato il cappello in testa; **I jammed my finger in the door** mi sono schiacciato il dito nella porta.

2 VI **a** (*get stuck: mechanism, sliding part*) bloccarsi, incepparsi; (: *gun*) incepparsi

b (*press tightly: people*): **to jam into** affollare

c (*Mus fam*) improvvisare.

3 N **a** (*of people*) folla, calca; (*of shoppers*) ressa; (*of cars: also:* **traffic jam**) ingorgo

b (*fig fam*): **to be in/get into a jam** essere/ficcarsi nei pasticci; **to get sb out of a jam** tirare qn fuori dai pasticci.

Ja·mai·ca [dʒəˈmeɪkə] N la Giamaica.

Ja·mai·can [dʒəˈmeɪkən] ADJ, N giamaicano(-a).

jamb [dʒæm] N stipite *m*.

jam·bo·ree [ˌdʒæmbəˈriː] N (*party, merrymaking*) baldoria; (*of scouts*) raduno.

♦ **jam jar** N barattolo *or* vasetto da marmellata.

jam·ming [ˈdʒæmɪŋ] N (*Radio*) jamming *m inv*, *disturbo intenzionale di una trasmissione*.

♦ **jam-packed** [ˌdʒæmˈpækt] ADJ: **jam-packed (with)** pieno (-a) zeppo(-a) (di), strapieno(-a) (di).

♦ **jam session** N (*Mus fam*) jam-session *f inv*.

Jan. ABBR (= *January*) gen., genn.

jan·gle [ˈdʒæŋgl] **1** VI (*bells*) scampanellare; (*bracelets, keys, chains*) tintinnare.

2 VT far risuonare.

3 N (*see vi*) scampanio; tintinnio.

jan·gled [ˈdʒæŋgld] ADJ (*nerves*) scosso(-a).

jan·gling [ˈdʒæŋglɪŋ] ADJ (*bells*) scampanellante; (*bracelets, keys*) tintinnante; (*nerves*) scosso(-a).

jani·tor [ˈdʒænɪtəʳ] (*esp Am, Scot*) N (*caretaker*) custode *m*; (*Scol*) bidello.

Janu·ary [ˈdʒænjʊərɪ] N gennaio *for usage see* **July**.

Janus [ˈdʒeɪnəs] N Giano.

Ja·pan [dʒəˈpæn] N il Giappone *m*.

Japa·nese [ˌdʒæpəˈniːz] **1** ADJ giapponese.

2 N (*person: pl inv*) giapponese *m/f*; (*language*) giapponese *m*.

ja·poni·ca [dʒəˈpɒnɪkə] N cotogno del Giappone.

jar¹ [dʒɑːʳ] N (*container*) vasetto; (: *of glass*) barattolo; (: *of earthenware*) vaso.

jar² [dʒɑːʳ] **1** VI (*clash: sounds*) stridere; **to jar (with)** (*colours*) stonare (con); (*opinions*) discordare (da); **to jar on sb's nerves** dare ai nervi a qc; **to jar on sb's ears** dar fastidio alle orecchie di qc.

2 VT (*also fig*) scuotere; (*elbow*) urtare.

3 N (*jolt*) scossa, scossone *m*; (*fig*) colpo, scossone.

jar·gon [ˈdʒɑːgən] N gergo.

jar·ring [ˈdʒɑːrɪŋ] ADJ (*sound, colour*) stonato(-a); **to strike a jarring note (in, at)** (*fig*) portare una nota stonata (in, a).

Jas. ABBR = *James*.

jas·mine [ˈdʒæzmɪn] N gelsomino.

Jason [ˈdʒeɪsən] N Giasone *m*.

jaun·dice [ˈdʒɔːndɪs] N itterizia.

jaun·diced [ˈdʒɔːndɪst] ADJ (*fig: cynical*) cinico(-a); (*Med*) itterico(-a); **with a jaundiced eye** con occhio cinico; **to have a jaundiced view of things** vedere le cose cinicamente.

jaunt [dʒɔːnt] N gita; **to go for a jaunt** fare una gita.

jaun·ti·ly [ˈdʒɔːntɪlɪ] ADV con fare baldanzoso; **his hat was perched jauntily on his head** portava il cappello sulle ventitré.

jaun·ty [ˈdʒɔːntɪ] ADJ baldanzoso(-a); **at a jaunty angle** (*hat*) sulle ventitré.

Java [ˈdʒɑːvə] N Giava.

jave·lin [ˈdʒævlɪn] N giavellotto; **to throw the javelin** (*Sport*) lanciare il giavellotto; **javelin throwing** lancio del giavellotto.

jaw [dʒɔː] N **a** (*Anat*) mascella **b** : **jaws** NPL (*Tech: of vice, machine*) ganascia.

jaw·bone [ˈdʒɔːˌbəʊn] N mandibola.

jay [dʒeɪ] N ghiandaia.

jay·walk·er [ˈdʒeɪˌwɔːkəʳ] N pedone *m* indisciplinato (*nell'attraversare la strada*).

jazz [dʒæz] N (*Mus*) jazz *m*; **...and all that jazz** (*fig fam usu pej*) ... eccetera eccetera

▶ **jazz up** VT + ADV **a** (*party, room, outfit*) vivacizzare **b** (*Mus: play*) suonare a ritmo di jazz; (: *arrange*) adattare a ritmo di jazz.

♦ **jazz band** N banda *f* jazz *inv*.

jazzy [ˈdʒæzɪ] ADJ (*comp* **-ier**, *superl* **-iest**) (*pattern, design*) vistoso(-a), chiassoso(-a); (*rhythm*) jazzistico(-a).

JCB® [ˌdʒeɪsiːˈbiː] N scavatrice *f*.

JCS [ˌdʒeɪsiːˈɛs] N ABBR (*Am*) = *Joint Chiefs of Staff*.

JD [ˌdʒeɪˈdiː] N ABBR (*Am*) **a** (= *Doctor of Laws*) ≈ dottore *m* in legge **b** (= *Justice Department*) ≈ Ministero di Grazia e Giustizia.

jeal·ous [ˈdʒeləs] ADJ: **jealous (of)** geloso(-a) (di); **to make sb jealous** far ingelosire qn.

jeal·ous·ly [ˈdʒeləslɪ] ADV (*enviously*) con gelosia; (*possessively*) gelosamente.

jeal·ousy [ˈdʒeləsɪ] N gelosia.

jeans [dʒiːnz] NPL jeans *mpl*.

jeep [dʒiːp] N jeep *f inv*.

jeer [dʒɪəʳ] **1** N grido di scherno.

2 VI: **to jeer (at sb)** schernire (qn).

jeer·ing [ˈdʒɪərɪŋ] **1** ADJ (*crowd*) che lancia grida di scherno; (*remark, laughter*) di scherno.

2 N grida *fpl* di scherno.

Je·ho·vah [dʒɪˈhəʊvə] N Geova *m*.

♦ **Jehovah's Witness** N testimone *m/f* di Geova.

jell [dʒel] VI, N = **gel**.

jel·lo [ˈdʒeləʊ] N (*Am*) gelatina di frutta.

jel·ly [ˈdʒelɪ] N gelatina.

jelly·fish [ˈdʒelɪˌfɪʃ] N medusa.

jem·my, (*Am*) **jim·my** [ˈdʒemɪ] N piede *m* di porco.

jeop·ard·ize [ˈdʒepəˌdaɪz] VT mettere in pericolo, mettere a repentaglio.

jeop·ardy [ˈdʒepədɪ] N: **in jeopardy** a rischio, in pericolo; **to place** *or* **put in jeopardy** mettere a repentaglio *or* in pericolo.

Jeremiah [ˌdʒerɪˈmaɪə] N Geremia *m*.

Jeri·cho [ˈdʒerɪˌkəʊ] N Gerico *f*.

jerk [dʒɜːk] **1** VT (*pull*) tirare con uno strattone; **he jerked it away from me** me l'ha strappato di mano.

2 VI muoversi a scatti; **to jerk along** procedere a sbalzi; **the bus jerked to a halt** l'autobus si fermò con un sobbalzo.

3 N **a** (*movement*) sobbalzo, scossa; (*reflex*) spasmo muscolare, contrazione *f* nervosa; **he sat up with a jerk** balzò a sedere di scatto.

b (*esp Am fam*) stronzo.

jerki·ly [ˈdʒɜːkɪlɪ] ADV (*move*) a scatti; (*speak, laugh*) in modo convulso.

jer·kin [ˈdʒɜːkɪn] N gilè *m inv*.

jerky [ˈdʒɜːkɪ] ADJ (*comp* **-ier**, *superl* **-iest**) (*motion, speech*) convulso(-a), a scatti; (*ride*) pieno(-a) di scossoni.

jerry-build ['dʒɛrɪˌbɪld] (*pt, pp* **jerry-built**) VT *costruire utilizzando materiali e tecnologie scadenti.*

jerry-built ['dʒɛrɪˌbɪlt] ADJ *costruito con materiali scadenti.*

jer·ry can ['dʒɛrɪˌkæn] N tanica.

Jer·sey ['dʒɜːzɪ] N (*island*) Jersey *f*; **a Jersey (cow)** una mucca di razza Jersey.

jer·sey ['dʒɜːzɪ] N (*garment*) maglia; (*fabric*) jersey *m*.

Je·ru·sa·lem [dʒə'ruːsələm] N Gerusalemme *f*.

jest [dʒɛst] [1] N scherzo, facezia; **in jest** per scherzo.
[2] VI scherzare.

jest·er ['dʒɛstə'] N (*also:* **court jester**) buffone *m* (di corte).

Jesu·it ['dʒɛzjʊɪt] ADJ, N gesuita (*m*).

Jesus ['dʒiːzəs] N Gesù *m*; **Jesus Christ** Gesù Cristo.

jet¹ [dʒɛt] [1] N **a** (*plane*) jet *m inv*, aereo a reazione **b** (*of liquid, steam, gas*) getto; (*of fountain*) zampillo **c** (*nozzle: of gas burner*) becco, ugello; (*Aut*) spruzzatore *m*.
[2] ADJ (*aircraft, propulsion*) a reazione; (*fuel*) per aviogetto.
[3] VI (*fam: fly*) volare.

jet² [dʒɛt] N (*mineral*) giaietto.

♦ **jet-black** [ˌdʒɛt'blæk] ADJ nero(-a) come l'ebano; **jet-black hair** capelli *mpl* corvini.

♦ **jet engine** N motore *m* a reazione.

♦ **jet lag** N jet lag *m inv*.

♦ **jet-propelled** [ˌdʒɛtprə'pɛld] ADJ (*aeroplane*) a reazione.

jet·sam ['dʒɛtsəm] N *oggetti gettati in mare e portati a riva dalla corrente*; see also **flotsam**.

♦ **jet set** N: **the jet set** il jet-set *m inv*.

♦ **jet-setter** ['dʒɛtˌsɛtə'] N membro del jet set.

jet·ti·son ['dʒɛtɪsn] VT (*burden*) alleggerirsi di; (*hopes, chances*) abbandonare; (*Naut*) gettare in mare.

jet·ty ['dʒɛtɪ] N (*landing pier*) imbarcadero; (*breakwater*) molo.

Jew [dʒuː] N ebreo(-a).

jew·el ['dʒuːəl] N (*stone*) pietra preziosa; (*ornament*) gioiello; (*of watch*) rubino; (*fig*) gioiello, perla.

♦ **jewel box, jewel case** N (cofanetto) portagioie *m inv*.

jew·elled, (*Am*) **jew·eled** ['dʒuːəld] ADJ ornato(-a) di pietre preziose.

jew·el·ler, (*Am*) **jew·el·er** ['dʒuːələ'] N gioielliere(-a), orefice *m*; **jeweller's (shop)** gioielleria, oreficeria.

jew·el·lery, (*Am*) **jew·el·ry** ['dʒuːəlrɪ] N gioielli *mpl*, gioie *fpl*; **a piece of jewellery** un gioiello; **jewellery box** (cofanetto) portagioie *m inv*.

Jew·ess ['dʒuːɪs] N (*offensive*) ebrea.

Jew·ish ['dʒuːɪʃ] ADJ (*mother, people*) ebreo(-a); (*festival, religion, tradition*) ebraico(-a); **Jewish joke** *battuta improntata al tipico umorismo degli ebrei.*

Jew·ry ['dʒʊərɪ] N (*frm*) il popolo ebraico, gli ebrei, la comunità ebraica.

♦ **jew's-harp** [ˌdʒuːz'hɑːp] N scacciapensieri *m inv*.

JFK [ˌdʒeɪɛf'keɪ] N ABBR (*Am*) **a** = John Fitzgerald Kennedy **b** = John Fitzgerald Kennedy International Airport.

jib¹ [dʒɪb] VI (*horse*) impennarsi; (*person*) impuntarsi, recalcitrare; **to jib at doing sth** essere restio(-a) a fare qc.

jib² [dʒɪb] N (*Naut*) fiocco; (*of crane*) braccio.

jibe [dʒaɪb] N = **gibe**.

jif·fy ['dʒɪfɪ] N (*fam*): **in a jiffy** in un baleno, in un batter d'occhio; **wait a jiffy** aspetta un attimo.

Jiffy bag® N busta imbottita.

jig [dʒɪg] N (*dance, tune*) giga.

jig·saw ['dʒɪgˌsɔː] N **a** (*also:* **jigsaw puzzle**) puzzle *m inv* **b** (*tool*) sega da traforo.

jilt [dʒɪlt] VT piantare (*fidanzato(a)*).

jim·my ['dʒɪmɪ] N (*Am*) = **jemmy**.

jin·gle ['dʒɪŋgl] [1] N (*of keys, coins*) tintinnio; (*of bells*) scampanellio; (*advert*) jingle *m inv*, ritornello pubblicitario.
[2] VT (*see n*) far tintinnare; far scampanellare.
[3] VI (*see n*) tintinnare; scampanellare.

jin·go·ism ['dʒɪŋgəʊˌɪzəm] N sciovinismo.

jin·go·is·tic [ˌdʒɪŋgəʊ'ɪstɪk] ADJ sciovinista.

jinx [dʒɪŋks] N (*curse*) malocchio; (*person*) iettatore (-trice); (*thing*) cosa che porta sfortuna; **there's a jinx on him** è iellato; **to put a jinx on sb** gettare il malocchio su qn.

jit·ters ['dʒɪtəz] NPL (*fam*) fifa *fsg*; **to have the jitters** avere fifa; **to get the jitters** prendersi uno spavento.

jit·tery ['dʒɪtərɪ] ADJ (*fam*) nervoso(-a), agitato(-a).

jiu·jit·su [dʒuː'dʒɪtsuː] N = **jujitsu**.

Jnr. ABBR = **junior**.

Job [dʒəʊb] N Giobbe *m*; **to have the patience of Job** avere la pazienza di Giobbe.

job [dʒɒb] N **a** (*work*) lavoro; (*post*) posto, impiego; **to look for a job** cercare lavoro; **to be out of a job** essere disoccupato(-a) *or* senza lavoro; **a part-time/full-time job** un lavoro a mezza giornata/a tempo pieno; **this is a case of jobs for the boys** (*fam pej*) questo è il modo di sistemare amici e parenti; **the government is creating new jobs** il governo sta creando nuovi posti di lavoro **b** (*piece of work*) lavoro; (*task*) compito; **on the job** sul lavoro; **to make a good/bad job of sth** fare bene/male qc; **he's done a good job of work** ha fatto un buon lavoro; **that's not my job** non è compito mio; **to know one's job** conoscere il proprio mestiere; **he's only doing his job** sta solo facendo il suo dovere; **I had the job of telling him** è stato compito mio dirglielo; **that car is a nice little job** (*fam*) quella macchina è un gioiellino **c** : **that's just the job!** è proprio quello che ci vuole!; **to give sth up as a bad job** lasciar perdere qc perché è un'impresa impossibile; **it's a good job that …** meno male che…; **a good job too!** meno male!; **we had quite a job getting here** *or* **to get here** è stata un'impresa arrivare qui; **he was caught doing a bank job** (*fam*) l'hanno preso mentre faceva un colpo alla banca.

job·ber ['dʒɒbə'] N (*Brit Stock Exchange*) jobber *m/f inv*, *intermediario tra agenti di cambio.*

job·bing ['dʒɒbɪŋ] ADJ (*Brit: worker, gardener*) a cottimo.

Job·centre ['dʒɒbˌsɛntə'] N (*Brit*) ufficio di collocamento.

♦ **job creation scheme** N (*Brit*) programma *m* per la creazione di posti di lavoro.

♦ **job description** N mansionario, descrizione *f* delle mansioni (*relative ad un lavoro*).

♦ **job evaluation** N valutazione *f* delle mansioni (*relative ad un lavoro*).

♦ **job hunting** N: **to go job hunting** cercare lavoro.

job·less ['dʒɒblɪs] [1] ADJ disoccupato(-a).
[2] : **the jobless** NPL i disoccupati, i senza lavoro *m inv*.

♦ **job lot** N partita di articoli disparati.

♦ **job satisfaction** N soddisfazione *f* nel lavoro.

♦ **job security** N sicurezza del posto di lavoro.

♦ **job sharing** ['dʒɒbˌʃɛərɪŋ] N job sharing *m inv*, *suddivisione di un posto di lavoro tra due persone che lavorano part-time.*

♦ **job specification** N specifica (*relativa ad un lavoro*).

Jock [dʒɒk] N (*Brit fam pej*) *termine spregiativo usato dagli inglesi per chiamare uno scozzese.*

jock·ey ['dʒɒkɪ] [1] N fantino.
[2] VI: **to jockey for position** (fig) manovrare per mettersi in una posizione vantaggiosa.
[3] VT: **to jockey sb into doing sth** indurre qn a fare qc (con manovre).
♦ **jockey cap** N berretto da fantino.
Jockey shorts® NPL boxer mpl.
jock·strap ['dʒɒk‚stræp] N sospensorio, conchiglia.
jocu·lar ['dʒɒkjʊlə'] ADJ (person) gioviale; (remark) scherzoso(-a).
jodh·purs ['dʒɒdpəz] NPL calzoni mpl alla cavallerizza.
jog [dʒɒg] [1] VI (Sport) fare jogging.
[2] VT (push) urtare, spingere; (fig: sb's memory) rinfrescare; **to jog sb into doing sth** (fig) spingere qn a fare qc.
[3] N [a] (pace: also: **jog trot**) passo lento di corsa; (: of horse) piccolo trotto; (run): **to go for a jog** andare a fare jogging
[b] (push) spinta, colpetto
► **jog along** VI + ADV (vehicle) procedere con leggeri scossoni; (fig): **we're jogging along** si tira avanti; **the work is jogging along nicely** il lavoro procede senza alti né bassi.
jog·ger ['dʒɒgə'] N persona che fa jogging.
jog·ging ['dʒɒgɪŋ] N (Sport) jogging m.
jog·gle ['dʒɒgl] VT (fam) scuotere leggermente.
John [dʒɒn] N (Bible) Giovanni.
john [dʒɒn] N (esp Am fam): **the john** il gabinetto.
join [dʒɔɪn] [1] VT [a] (fasten): **to join (together)** unire, congiungere; (link) collegare; (: fig) unire; **to join hands** prendersi per mano; **to join battle (with)** (frm) attaccare battaglia (con); **to join A and B** or **A to B** unire A e B or A a B; **to join forces (with)** allearsi (con or a); (fig) mettersi insieme (a)
[b] (procession) unirsi a; (club) divenire socio(-a) di; (university) entrare a; (army, navy, religious order, firm) entrare in; (political party) iscriversi a; **to join a queue** mettersi in fila; **to join one's ship** imbarcarsi; **to join one's regiment** raggiungere il proprio reggimento
[c] (person) unirsi a; **may I join you?** posso?, permette?; **will you join us?** (come with us) viene con noi?; (in restaurant, bar) vuole sedersi con noi?; **will you join us for dinner?** viene a cena con noi?; **will you join me in a drink?** posso offrirle qualcosa da bere?; **I'll join you later** vi raggiungo più tardi; **they joined us in protesting** si sono uniti a noi nel protestare
[d] (river) confluire in, gettarsi in; (road) immettersi in.
[2] VI [a]: **to join (together)** (parts, people) unirsi; (lines) incontrarsi; (roads) congiungersi; (rivers) confluire.
[b] (club member) divenire socio(-a).
[3] N (in wood, wallpaper) giuntura; (Sewing) cucitura
► **join in** [1] VI + PREP (game, discussion, protest) prendere parte a, partecipare a; **they all joined in the chorus** tutti si unirono al ritornello.
[2] VI + ADV partecipare; (in singing): **join in!** cantate con noi!
► **join on** [1] VT + ADV fissare, attaccare.
[2] VI + ADV (in queue) mettersi in coda; (part) unirsi
► **join up** [1] VI + ADV (Mil) arruolarsi.
[2] VT + ADV (wires) unire, collegare.
join·er ['dʒɔɪnə'] N falegname m.
join·ery ['dʒɔɪnərɪ] N falegnameria.
joint [dʒɔɪnt] [1] ADJ (action, effort, work) comune; (responsibility) collettivo(-a); (committee) misto(-a); **joint authors** coautori(-trici); **to make a joint declaration on sth** rilasciare una dichiarazione congiunta su qc.

[2] N [a] (Anat) articolazione f, giuntura; **out of joint** slogato(-a); **to put sb's nose out of joint** (fig fam) far indispettire qn
[b] (join) giuntura, giunto
[c] (Brit: of meat) pezzo di carne; (: cooked) arrosto (al forno)
[d] (fam: place: esp Am) locale m
[e] (fam: cannabis cigarette) spinello.
[3] VT (chicken) tagliare a pezzi.
♦ **joint account** N (at bank) conto comune.
♦ **Joint Chiefs of Staff** N (Am) ≈ gabinetto dei ministri.
joint·ed ['dʒɔɪntɪd] ADJ [a] (doll) snodabile; (fishing rod, tent poles) smontabile [b] (chicken) (tagliato(-a)) a pezzi.
joint·ly ['dʒɔɪntlɪ] ADV (held, funded) in comune; (agree, organize, act) di comune accordo.
♦ **joint ownership** N comproprietà.
♦ **joint-stock company** [‚dʒɔɪnt'stɒk‚kʌmpənɪ] N società f inv per azioni.
♦ **joint venture** N joint venture f inv, società f inv a capitale misto.
joist [dʒɔɪst] N trave f.
joke [dʒəʊk] [1] N (verbal) battuta; (practical joke) scherzo; (funny story) barzelletta; **to tell a joke** raccontare una barzelletta; **to make a joke about sth** fare una battuta su qc; **for a joke** per scherzo; **what a joke!** (iro) bello scherzo!; **it's no joke** non è uno scherzo; **the joke is that** ... la cosa buffa è che...; **the joke is on you** chi ci perde, comunque, sei tu; **it's (gone) beyond a joke** lo scherzo sta diventando pesante; **to play a joke on sb** fare uno scherzo a qn; **I don't see the joke** non capisco cosa ci sia da ridere; **he can't take a joke** non sa stare allo scherzo.
[2] VI scherzare; **I was only joking** stavo solo scherzando; **you're** or **you must be joking!** stai scherzando!, scherzi!
jok·er ['dʒəʊkə'] N [a] (amusing) burlone(-a); (fam pej) buffone(-a) [b] (Cards) jolly m inv, matta.
jok·ing ['dʒəʊkɪŋ] [1] ADJ scherzoso(-a).
[2] N scherzi mpl.
jok·ing·ly ['dʒəʊkɪŋlɪ] ADV scherzosamente.
jol·li·fi·ca·tion [‚dʒɒlɪfɪ'keɪʃən] N (hum) festeggiamento.
jol·lity ['dʒɒlɪtɪ] N allegria.
jol·ly ['dʒɒlɪ] [1] ADJ (comp -ier, superl -iest) (person) allegro(-a), gioviale; (laugh) allegro(-a), gioioso(-a); (old: party) piacevole.
[2] ADV (Brit fam) veramente, proprio; **he's jolly lucky!** è fortunatissimo!; **you've jolly well got to** devi assolutamente or proprio farlo; **it jolly well serves you right** te lo meriti proprio; **jolly good!** (old) benissimo!.
[3] VT: **to jolly sb along** (Brit: cheer up) cercare di tenere qn su di morale; (: encourage) incoraggiare dolcemente qn.
jolt [dʒəʊlt] [1] VT (gen) urtare; (fig) scuotere; **to jolt sb into doing sth** spingere qn a fare qc.
[2] VI (vehicle) sobbalzare; **to jolt along** avanzare a sbalzi.
[3] N (jerk) scossa, sobbalzo; (fig) colpo; **it gave me a jolt** (fig) mi ha fatto venire un colpo.
Jonah ['dʒəʊnə] N Giona m; (fig) iettatore(-trice).
jon·quil ['dʒɒŋkwɪl] N giunchiglia.
Jor·dan ['dʒɔ:dn] N (country) la Giordania; (river) Giordano.
Jor·da·nian [dʒɔ:'deɪnɪən] ADJ, N giordano(-a).
Joshua ['dʒɒʃʊə] N Giosuè m.
joss stick ['dʒɒs‚stɪk] N bastoncino d'incenso.
jos·tle ['dʒɒsl] [1] VT urtare, spintonare.
[2] VI darsi gomitate; **to jostle against sb** urtare qn; **to jostle for a place** farsi largo a gomitate.

jos·tling ['dʒɒslɪŋ] **1** ADJ (*crowd*) che spinge. **2** N pigia pigia *m*.

jot [dʒɒt] N briciolo; **there's not a jot of evidence** non c'è la ben che minima prova; **not one jot** nemmeno un po' ▶ **jot down** VT + ADV (*ideas, notes*) buttar giù; (*address, number*) prendere.

jot·ter ['dʒɒtə'] N (*Brit*) blocchetto.

jot·tings ['dʒɒtɪŋz] NPL appunti *mpl* disordinati.

jour·nal ['dʒɜ:nl] N (*periodical*) rivista (specializzata); (*newspaper*) giornale *m*; (*diary*) diario; (*Book-keeping*) brogliaccio.

jour·nal·ese ['dʒɜ:nə'li:z] N (*pej*) giornalese.

jour·nal·ism ['dʒɜ:nə‚lɪzəm] N giornalismo.

jour·nal·ist ['dʒɜ:nəlɪst] N giornalista *m/f*.

jour·nal·is·tic [‚dʒɜ:nə'lɪstɪk] ADJ giornalistico(-a).

jour·ney ['dʒɜ:nɪ] **1** N (*trip*) viaggio; (*distance, time*) tragitto; **a 5-hour journey** un viaggio *or* un tragitto di 5 ore; **to reach one's journey's end** (*liter*) giungere a destinazione; **the outward/return journey** il viaggio di andata/di ritorno; **the journey there and back** il viaggio di andata e ritorno. **2** VI viaggiare.

journey·man ['dʒɜ:nɪmən] N (*pl* -**men**) (*old*) operaio qualificato.

joust [dʒaʊst] **1** N giostra. **2** VI giostrare.

Jove [dʒəʊv] N Giove *m*; **by Jove!** (*old*) per Giove!

jo·vial ['dʒəʊvɪəl] ADJ gioviale.

jo·vi·al·ity ['dʒəʊvɪ'ælɪtɪ] N giovialità.

jo·vi·al·ly ['dʒəʊvɪəlɪ] ADV giovialmente, con giovialità.

jowl [dʒaʊl] N (*cheek*) guancia; (*jaw*) mandibola; **a man with heavy jowls** un uomo con le guance cascanti.

joy [dʒɔɪ] N gioia; **to jump for joy** fare salti di gioia; **I wish you joy of it!** (*iro*) buon pro ti faccia!; **the joys of camping** (*also iro*) i piaceri del campeggio; **it's a joy to hear him** è un piacere ascoltarlo; **did you have any joy?** ci sei riuscito?; **no joy!** (*fam*) niente da fare!

joy·ful ['dʒɔɪfʊl] ADJ (*happy*) lieto(-a); (*cheerful*) gioioso (-a).

joy·ful·ly ['dʒɔɪfəlɪ] ADV (*see adj*) lietamente; gioiosamente.

joy·ous ['dʒɔɪəs] ADJ (*liter*) = **joyful**.

♦ **joy-ride** ['dʒɔɪ‚raɪd] **1** VI: **to go joy-riding** rubare una macchina per farsi un giro. **2** N: **to go for a joy-ride** rubare una macchina per farsi un giro.

joy·rider ['dʒɔɪ‚raɪdə'] N chi ruba una macchina per farsi un giro.

joy·stick ['dʒɔɪ‚stɪk] N (*Aer*) barra di comando; (*Comput*) joystick *m inv*.

JP [‚dʒeɪ'pi:] N ABBR = **Justice of the Peace**.

Jr ABBR = **junior**.

ju·bi·lant ['dʒu:bɪlənt] ADJ giubilante; **to be jubilant** essere esultante.

ju·bi·la·tion [‚dʒu:bɪ'leɪʃən] N (*emotion*) giubilo; **she was full of jubilation at the news of her win** esultò quando seppe di aver vinto.

ju·bi·lee ['dʒu:bɪ‚li:] N giubileo; **silver jubilee** venticinquesimo anniversario.

Ju·da·ism ['dʒu:deɪ‚ɪzəm] N giudaismo.

Judas ['dʒu:dəs] N Giuda *m*; (*fig: traitor*) giuda *m*.

Ju·dea [dʒu:'di:ə] N Giudea.

judge [dʒʌdʒ] **1** N giudice *m*; **to be a good/bad judge of sth** sapere/non sapere giudicare qc; **I'm no judge of wines** non sono un intenditore di vini; **he's no judge of character** non sa giudicare le persone.

2 VT (*Law, assess*) giudicare; (*estimate: weight, size*) calcolare, valutare; (*consider*) ritenere; **he judged the moment well** ha saputo scegliere il momento giusto; **I judged it necessary to inform him** ho ritenuto necessario informarlo; **I judged it to be right** l'ho ritenuto giusto.

3 VI (*act as judge*) fare da giudice; **judging** *or* **to judge by his expression** a giudicare dalla sua espressione; **to judge for o.s.** giudicare da sé; **as far as I can judge** a mio giudizio.

♦ **judge advocate** N (*Brit Mil*) magistrato militare.

♦ **Judge Advocate General** N (*Brit Mil*) *consigliere principale in materia di diritto militare*.

judg·ment, judge·ment ['dʒʌdʒmənt] N giudizio; **error of judgement** errore *m* di valutazione; **to pass judgement (on)** (*Law*) pronunciare una sentenza (nei confronti di); (*fig*) giudicare; **in my judgement** a mio giudizio; **it's against my better judgement, but ...** non ne sono affatto convinto, ma... .

♦ **Judgment Day** N il giorno del giudizio.

ju·di·cial [dʒu:'dɪʃəl] ADJ **a** (*enquiry, decision*) giudiziario (-a); **to bring judicial proceedings against sb** procedere per vie legali contro qn **b** (*mind, faculty*) critico(-a).

ju·di·ci·ary [dʒu:'dɪʃɪərɪ] N: **the judiciary** la magistratura.

ju·di·cious [dʒu:'dɪʃəs] ADJ (*frm*) giudizioso(-a).

ju·di·cious·ly [dʒu:'dɪʃəslɪ] ADV (*frm*) giudiziosamente.

judo ['dʒu:dəʊ] N judo.

jug [dʒʌg] N **a** (*container*) brocca, caraffa; (*for milk*) lattiera, bricco **b** (*fam: prison*) gattabuia.

jugged hare [‚dʒʌgd'hɛə'] N (*Brit*) lepre *f* in salmì.

jug·ger·naut ['dʒʌgə‚nɔ:t] N (*Brit: lorry*) bisonte *m* della strada.

jug·gle ['dʒʌgl] **1** VI fare giochi di destrezza. **2** VT fare giochi di destrezza con; (*fig*) manipolare.

jug·gler ['dʒʌglə'] N giocoliere *m*.

jug·gling ['dʒʌglɪŋ] N giochi *mpl* di destrezza; (*fig*) manipolazione *f*.

Ju·go·slav ['ju:gəʊ‚slɑ:v] ADJ, N = **Yugoslav**.

Ju·go·sla·via ['ju:gəʊ'slɑ:vɪə] N = **Yugoslavia**.

jugu·lar ['dʒʌgjʊlə'] N (*also*: **jugular vein**) (vena) giugulare *f*.

juice [dʒu:s] N **a** (*of fruit*) succo; (*of meat*) sugo **b** (*in stomach*): **juices** NPL succhi *mpl* gastrici **c** (*fam: petrol*) benzina; (: *electricity*) corrente *f*; **turn on the juice** accendi la luce.

♦ **juice extractor**, (*Am*) **jui·cer** ['dʒu:sə'] N centrifuga elettrica.

juici·ness ['dʒu:sɪnɪs] N (*of fruit*) succosità, succulenza; (*of meat*) succulenza; (*of story*) succosità.

juicy ['dʒu:sɪ] ADJ (*comp* -**ier**, *superl* -**iest**) (*fruit*) succoso (-a); (*meat*) sugoso(-a); (*story*) piccante.

ju·jit·su [‚dʒu:'dʒɪtsu:] N jujitsu *m*.

juke·box ['dʒu:k‚bɒks] N juke-box *m inv*.

Jul. ABBR (= *July*) lug., lu.

July [dʒu:'laɪ] N luglio; **the first of July** il primo luglio; **(on) the eleventh of July** l'undici luglio; **in the month of July** nel mese di luglio; **at the beginning/end of July** all'inizio/alla fine di luglio; **in the middle of July** a metà luglio; **during July** durante (il mese di) luglio; **in July of next year** a luglio dell'anno prossimo; **each** *or* **every July** ogni anno a luglio; **July was wet this year** è piovuto molto a luglio, quest'anno.

jum·ble ['dʒʌmbl] **1** N **a** (*of objects, ideas*) miscuglio, accozzaglia **b** (*old clothes etc*) roba usata. **2** VT (*also*: **jumble together**, **jumble up**) mettere alla

rinfusa.

♦ **jumble sale** N (*Brit*) *vendita (di beneficenza) di roba usata.*

jum·bo ['dʒʌmbəʊ] **1** ADJ (*fam*) maxi *inv*; **jumbo size** formato gigante.
  2 N (*also:* **jumbo jet**) jumbo *m inv* (jet *m inv*).

jump [dʒʌmp] **1** VI (*gen Sport*) saltare; (*in fright*) fare un salto, trasalire; (*prices*) aumentare di colpo; **to jump about** fare salti, saltellare; **to jump over sth** saltare oltre qc; **to jump in/out** saltare dentro/fuori; **to jump off/on (to) sth** saltare giù da/su qc; **to jump out (of) the window** saltare giù dalla finestra; **to jump out of bed** saltare fuori dal letto; **he jumped into a taxi** è saltato su un tassì; **she jumped to her feet** si alzò di scatto, balzò in piedi; **to jump up** saltare in piedi; **to jump down** saltare giù; **to jump up and down** saltellare; **there's no need to jump down my throat!** (*fam*) non è il caso di aggredirmi così!; **I almost jumped out of my skin!** (*fam*) ho fatto un salto!; **jump to it!** (*fam*) presto, sbrigati!; **to jump to conclusions** arrivare a conclusioni affrettate.
  2 VT (*ditch, fence*) saltare; (*horse*) far saltare; **to jump the rails** (*train*) deragliare; **to jump bail** (*Law*) *scappare quando si è in libertà provvisoria sotto cauzione*; **don't jump the gun!** (*fig fam*) non correre troppo!; **to jump the lights** (*Aut*) passare con il (semaforo) rosso; **to jump the queue** (*Brit*) passare davanti agli altri (*in una coda*); **to jump ship** lasciare la nave senza permesso; **to jump sb** (*fam*) assalire qn.
  3 N **a** (*gen, Sport*) salto; **to give a jump** (*also: fig:* *nervously*) fare un salto; **my heart gave a jump** ho provato un tuffo al cuore; **in** or **at one jump** in un salto; **a jump in prices** un'impennata dei prezzi; **to be one jump ahead of sb** (*fig*) essere un passo avanti a qn
  b (*Showjumping*) salto; (*: fence*) ostacolo
  ▶ **jump at** VI + PREP (*fig*) cogliere or afferrare al volo; **he jumped at the offer** si affrettò ad accettare l'offerta.

jumped-up ['dʒʌmpt'ʌp] ADJ (*Brit pej*) presuntuoso(-a).

jump·er ['dʒʌmpə'] N (*Brit: sweater*) maglione *m*; (*Am: pinafore dress*) scamiciato; (*Sport*) saltatore(-trice).

♦ **jump leads,** (*Am*) **jumper cables** NPL (*Aut*) cavi *mpl* per batteria.

♦ **jump-off** ['dʒʌmp,ɒf] N (*Horse-riding*) barrage *m inv*.

♦ **jump seat** N (*Aut*) strapuntino, seggiolino (pieghevole).

♦ **jump-start** ['dʒʌmp,stɑːt] **1** N: **to give the car a jump-start** dare una spinta alla macchina per farla partire; (*with jump leads*) mettere in moto una macchina usando i cavi per la batteria.
  2 VT: **to jump-start the car** far partire la macchina spingendola; **to jump-start the economy** dare una spinta all'economia.

♦ **jump suit** N tuta intera.

jumpy ['dʒʌmpɪ] ADJ (*comp* **-ier,** *superl* **-iest**) nervoso(-a), agitato(-a).

Jun. ABBR **a** (= *June*) giu. **b** = *junior.*

junc·tion ['dʒʌŋkʃən] N (*Brit: of roads*) bivio, incrocio; (*: Rail*) nodo ferroviario.

junc·ture ['dʒʌŋktʃə'] N (*fig: critical point*) momento critico; **at this juncture** in questo frangente.

June [dʒuːn] N giugno *for usage see* July.

jun·gle ['dʒʌŋgl] **1** N giungla.
  2 ADJ della giungla.

jun·ior ['dʒuːnɪə'] **1** ADJ (*on staff, in rank*) subalterno(-a); (*section: in competition*) per ragazzi; (*with name*): **Roy Smith, Junior** Roy Smith junior; **he's junior to me** ho più

anzianità di lui; **junior sizes** (*Comm*) taglie *fpl* per ragazzi.
  2 N (*in organization*) persona più giovane; (*Brit: school-child*) ≈ allievo delle scuole elementari (*da 7 a 11 anni*); **3 years my junior** or **my junior by 3 years** più giovane di me di 3 anni.

♦ **junior executive** N dirigente *m/f* di livello inferiore.

♦ **junior high school** N (*Am*) ≈ scuola media (*da 11 a 14 anni*).

♦ **junior minister** N (*Brit Pol*) ≈ sottosegretario di Stato.

♦ **junior miss** N (*Comm: also:* **junior miss size**) misura per giovanette (*11-14 anni*).

♦ **junior partner** N socio meno anziano.

♦ **junior school** N (*Brit*) ≈ scuola elementare (*da 7 a 11 anni*).

ju·ni·per ['dʒuːnɪpə'] N ginepro; **juniper berry** bacca di ginepro.

junk¹ [dʒʌŋk] **1** N (*stuff*) roba; (*fam: goods of poor quality*) porcherie *fpl.*
  2 VT disfarsi di.

junk² [dʒʌŋk] N (*boat*) giunca.

♦ **junk bond** N (*Fin*) junk bond *m inv*, titolo *m* spazzatura *inv.*

♦ **junk dealer** N rigattiere *m*, robivecchi *m inv.*

jun·ket ['dʒʌŋkɪt] **a** (*fam pej*): **to go on a junket** fare bisboccia; (*trip*) farsi un viaggetto pagato (*dallo stato*) **b** (*Culin*) giuncata.

jun·ket·ing ['dʒʌŋkɪtɪŋ] N (*fam pej*): **to go junketing** fare bisboccia; (*trip*) farsi un viaggetto pagato (*dallo stato*).

♦ **junk food** N cibo a scarso valore nutritivo.

junkie, junky ['dʒʌŋkɪ] N (*fam*) tossico(-a).

♦ **junk mail** N posta spazzatura *f inv.*

♦ **junk room** N ripostiglio.

♦ **junk shop** N (*fam*) (bottega di) rigattiere.

junky ['dʒʌŋkɪ] N (*fam*) = **junkie.**

junk·yard ['dʒʌŋk,jɑːd] N deposito di robivecchi e anticaglie.

Juno ['dʒuːnəʊ] N (*Myth, Astron*) Giunone *f.*

Junr, junr ABBR = *junior.*

jun·ta ['dʒʌntə] N giunta.

Ju·pi·ter ['dʒuːpɪtə'] N (*Myth, Astron*) Giove *m.*

ju·ris·dic·tion [,dʒʊərɪs'dɪkʃən] N (*frm*) giurisdizione *f*; **it falls** or **comes within/outside our jurisdiction** è/non è di nostra competenza.

jur·is·pru·dence [,dʒʊərɪs'pruːdəns] N giurisprudenza.

ju·ror ['dʒʊərə'] N (*Law*) giurato(-a); (*for contest*) membro della giuria.

jury ['dʒʊərɪ] N (*Law, for contest*) giuria; **to serve on a jury** far parte di una giuria.

♦ **jury box** N banco dei giurati.

jury·man ['dʒʊərɪmən] N (*pl* **-men**) giurato.

jury·woman ['dʒʊərɪ,wʊmən] N (*pl* **-women**) giurata.

just¹ [dʒʌst] ADJ (*fair*) giusto(-a).

just² [dʒʌst] ADV **a** (*exactly*) proprio, esattamente; **just here/there** proprio qui/là; **just behind/in front of/near** proprio dietro a/davanti a/vicino a; **just when it was going well ...** proprio quando tutto andava a gonfie vele...; **just then** or **just at that moment** proprio in quel momento; **it's just on 10 o'clock** sono le 10 in punto or precise; **it costs just (on) £20** costa 20 sterline tonde tonde; **it's just what I wanted** è proprio quello che volevo; **just right** proprio giusto; **just what did he say?** cosa ha detto esattamente?; **come just as you are** vieni così come sei; **leave it just as it is** lascialo com'è; **they are just like brothers** sono proprio come

fratelli; **that's just it!** OR **that's just the point!** precisamente!, proprio così!, per l'appunto!; **that's just (like) him, always late** è proprio da lui arrivare sempre in ritardo; **just as I thought/expected** proprio come pensavo/mi aspettavo; **just as he was leaving** proprio mentre se ne stava andando; **just as you like** come vuoi; **he likes everything just so** (*fam*) gli piace che tutto sia fatto a puntino

b (*recently, soon*) appena, or ora; **he's just done it/left** lo ha appena fatto/è appena partito; **just this minute** proprio adesso; **the book is just out** il libro è appena stato pubblicato; **we were just going** stavamo giusto andando; **I was just about to phone** stavo proprio per telefonare

c (*only*) soltanto, solo; **it's just me** sono solo io; **just the two of us** soltanto noi due; **it's just 3 o'clock** sono le 3; **just yesterday/this morning** soltanto ieri/stamattina; **just for a laugh** tanto per ridere; **it's just around the corner** è appena dietro l'angolo; **just a minute!** OR **just one moment!** un attimo!

d (*simply*) semplicemente, soltanto; **it's just a mistake** non è che uno sbaglio; **I just told him to go away** gli ho semplicemente detto di andarsene; **just ask someone the way** basta che tu chieda la strada a qualcuno; **I just wanted to say that ...** volevo solo dire che...; **I just can't imagine** non riesco proprio a immaginare; **it's just that I don't like it** il fatto è che non mi piace; **it's just one of those things** (*fam*) così è la vita

e (*slightly*) poco; **just over/under 2 kilos** un po' più/meno di 2 chili; **just before 5 o'clock** poco prima delle 5; **just after 5 o'clock** poco dopo le 5; **it's just after 10 (o'clock)** sono le 10 passate; **just after I arrived** subito dopo il mio arrivo; **it's just to the left/right** è subito a sinistra/destra

f (*barely*) appena; (*almost not*) per un pelo; **just in time** giusto *or* appena in tempo; **I had just enough money** avevo giusto i soldi che mi servivano; **just enough money for sth/to do sth** soldi appena sufficienti per qc/per fare qc; **he (only) just caught/missed it** OR **he caught/missed it, but only just** l'ha preso/perso proprio per un pelo

g (*in comparison*): **it's just as good** è altrettanto buono; **it's just as good as ...** è buono quanto...; **he speaks Italian just as well as I do** il suo italiano è buono almeno quanto il mio

h (*with imperatives*) un po'; **just imagine!** pensa un po'!; **just look at this mess!** guarda un po' che disordine!; **just wait a minute!** aspetta un momento!; **just let me get my hands on him!** (*fam*) se lo prendo!

i (*emphatic*) veramente, proprio; **that's just fine!** va bene così!; **so you regret buying it? — don't I just!** ti sei pentito di averlo comprato? — eccome!

j (*phrases*): **I've had just about enough of this noise!** (*fam*) ne ho proprio avuto abbastanza di questo rumore!; **it's just as well you didn't go** per fortuna non ci sei andato; **it would be just as well if you didn't mention it** faresti bene a non parlarne; **not just yet** non ancora; **just now** proprio ora; **not just now** non proprio ora; **take an umbrella just in case** prendi un'ombrello, che non si sa mai; **just in case I don't see you** caso mai non ti vedessi; **just the same, I'd rather...** ciononostante, preferirei...; **I'd just as soon not go** preferirei non andarci; **just my luck!** la mia solita sfortuna!

jus·tice ['dʒʌstɪs] N **a** (*Law*) giustizia; **to bring sb to justice** consegnare qn alla giustizia

b (*fairness*): **in justice to her, she ...** per essere giusti, lei...; **she never does herself justice** non dimostra mai quello che vale; **this biography doesn't do him justice** questa biografia non gli rende giustizia; **this photo doesn't do you justice** questa foto non ti fa giustizia; **to do justice to a meal** fare onore a un pranzo

c (*judge*) giudice *m*; **Lord Chief Justice** (*Brit*) ≈ presidente *m* della Corte d'Appello.

♦ **Justice of the Peace** N (*Brit*) giudice *m* di pace.

jus·ti·fi·able [ˌdʒʌstɪ'faɪəbl] ADJ giustificabile.

jus·ti·fi·ably [ˌdʒʌstɪ'faɪəblɪ] ADV legittimamente, a ragione.

jus·ti·fi·ca·tion [ˌdʒʌstɪfɪ'keɪʃən] N giustificazione *f*; **in justification of or for** a giustificazione di.

jus·ti·fy ['dʒʌstɪˌfaɪ] VT (*behaviour, action, also Typ*) giustificare; **to be justified in doing sth** avere ragione di fare qc; **am I justified in thinking that ...?** mi sbaglio o...?

just·ly ['dʒʌstlɪ] ADV giustamente.

just·ness ['dʒʌstnɪs] N (*of decision*) giustezza.

jut [dʒʌt] VI (*also:* **jut out**) sporgere; **a cliff jutting out over the sea** una scogliera a strapiombo sul mare.

jute [dʒuːt] N iuta.

ju·venile ['dʒuːvəˌnaɪl] **1** ADJ (*offender*) minorenne; (*crime*) minorile; (*books, sports*) per ragazzi; (*pej*) puerile, infantile.

2 N (*Law*) minorenne *m/f*.

♦ **juvenile court** N tribunale *m* dei minori.

♦ **juvenile delinquency** N delinquenza minorile.

♦ **juvenile delinquent** N delinquente *m/f* minorenne.

jux·ta·pose [ˌdʒʌkstə'pəʊz] VT giustapporre.

jux·ta·po·si·tion [ˌdʒʌkstəpə'zɪʃən] N giustapposizione *f*; **to be in juxtaposition** essere in giustapposizione.

K

K, k [keɪ] N (*letter*) K, k *f or m inv*; **K for King** ≈ K come kursaal.

K [keɪ] ① ABBR (= *chilo*) kg.
② N ABBR **a** (*fam: one thousand*): **he's on 25k** prende 25.000 (sterline) **b** (*Comput*)= *kilobyte*.

kaf·tan ['kæftæn] N caffettano.

Ka·la·ha·ri [ˌkælə'hɑːrɪ] N: **the Kalahari (Desert)** il deserto del Kalahari.

kale [keɪl] N cavolo verde.

ka·lei·do·scope [kə'laɪdəˌskəʊp] N caleidoscopio.

ka·lei·do·scopic [kə'laɪdəˌskɒpɪk] ADJ caleidoscopico(-a).

ka·mi·ka·ze [ˌkæmɪ'kɑːzɪ] ① N (*also:* **kamikaze pilot**) kamikaze *m inv*.
② ADJ da kamikaze.

Kam·pa·la [kæm'pɑːlə] N Kampala.

Kam·pu·chea [ˌkæmpʊ'tʃɪə] N la Cambogia.

kan·ga·roo [ˌkæŋgə'ruː] N canguro.

♦ **kangaroo court** N *commissione giudicante (in carcere o all'interno di un sindacato) che si arroga il diritto di far giustizia sommaria, normalmente su questioni disciplinari.*

kao·lin ['keɪəlɪn] N caolino.

ka·pok ['keɪpɒk] N kapok *m*.

ka·put [kə'pʊt] ADJ (*fam*) kaputt *inv*.

kara·oke [ˌkɑːrɪ'əʊkɪ] N karaoke *m inv*.

ka·ra·te [kə'rɑːtɪ] N karatè *m*.

kart [kɑːt] ① N go-kart *m inv*.
② VI: **to go karting** andare in go-kart.

kas·bah ['kæzbɑː] N casba.

Kash·mir [kæʃ'mɪə] N Kashmir *m*.

kay·ak ['kaɪæk] N kayak *m inv*.

Ka·zakh·stan [ˌkæzæk'stɑːn] N Kazakistan *m*.

KC [ˌkeɪ'siː] N ABBR (*Brit Law*: = *King's Counsel*) avvocato della Corona.

KD [ˌkeɪ'diː] ABBR (*Am Comm*: = *knocked down*) da montare.

ke·bab [kə'bæb] N kebab *m inv* (*spiedino di carne e verdura*).

ked·geree [ˌkedʒə'riː] N *riso pilaf con pesce e uova sode.*

keel [kiːl] N (*Naut*) chiglia; **on an even keel** (*Naut*) di pescaggio uniforme; **to keep things on an even keel** (*fig*) mantenere un certo equilibrio

▶ **keel over** VI + ADV (*person*) crollare; (*Naut*) capovolgersi.

keen [kiːn] ADJ (*comp* **-er**, *superl* **-est**) **a** (*Brit*: *person*) entusiasta; **he's a keen gardener** è un appassionato di giardinaggio; **to be keen on sth** (*opera, theatre*) essere appassionato(-a) di qc; (*plan, idea*) essere entusiasta di qc; **she's keen on the music master** il maestro di musica le piace molto; **she's very keen on pop music** le piace molto la musica pop; **to be keen to do** *or* **on doing sth** avere una gran voglia di fare qc; **I'm not keen on going** non mi va di andare; **I'm not keen to do it** non ci tengo a farlo
b (*edge, blade*) affilato(-a), tagliente; (*wind, air*) tagliente; (*hearing*) fine; (*appetite*) robusto(-a); (*intelligence, eyesight, observation*) acuto(-a); (*desire, delight, sense*) intenso(-a), forte; (*interest*) vivo(-a); (*price, rate*) competitivo(-a); (*competition, match, struggle*) duro(-a).

keen·ly ['kiːnlɪ] ADV **a** (*acutely*) intensamente; (*deeply*) profondamente; (*fiercely*) duramente; **to feel sth keenly** sentire qc profondamente; **he looked at her keenly** le rivolse uno sguardo penetrante **b** (*enthusiastically*) con entusiasmo.

keen·ness ['kiːnnɪs] N (*eagerness*) entusiasmo.

keep [kiːp] (*vb*: *pt*, *pp* **kept**) ① VT **a** (*retain, maintain*) tenere; **keep the change** tenga il resto; **he keeps himself to himself** se ne sta per conto suo; **to keep sb busy** tenere qn occupato(-a); **to keep time** (*clock*) andar bene; **to keep sth clean** tenere qc pulito(-a); **to keep a place tidy** tenere un posto in ordine; **she keeps herself fit** si tiene *or* si mantiene in forma; **the garden is well kept** il giardino è tenuto bene; **he has kept his looks** è ancora un bell'uomo; **to keep sb waiting** far aspettare qn; **keep him at it!** spingilo a continuare!; **to keep the engine running** tenere il motore acceso; **I'll keep you to your promise** ti farò mantenere la promessa; **to keep sth from sb** (*fig*) tenere qc nascosto(-a) a qn; **to keep sth to o.s.** tenere qc per sé; **keep it to yourself** *or* **under your hat** (*fam*) tienilo per te
b (*put aside*) mettere da parte; (*store*) tenere, conservare; **keep it in a safe place** *or* **somewhere safe** tienilo in un posto sicuro; **"keep in a cool place"** "conservare in

un luogo fresco"

c (*detain, restrain*) trattenere; **to keep sb in prison** tenere qn in prigione; **I mustn't** *or* **don't let me keep you** non voglio trattenerti; **what kept you?** come mai sei in ritardo?; **to keep sb from doing sth** impedire a qn di fare qc; **to keep sth from happening** impedire che qc succeda; **to keep o.s. from doing sth** trattenersi dal fare qc; **you're keeping me from my work** mi stai impedendo di lavorare, così non riesco a lavorare; **keep him from school** non mandarlo a scuola

d (*fulfil, observe: promise, vow*) mantenere; (: *law, rule, Lent*) osservare; (: *treaty, agreement*) rispettare; (: *Christmas, Easter*) celebrare; **to keep an appointment** rispettare un appuntamento

e (*own, have, also Comm: stock*) avere; (*Agr: animals*) allevare

f (*support: family*) mantenere; **he earns enough to keep himself** guadagna abbastanza per mantenersi da solo; **to keep sb in food and clothing** nutrire e vestire qn

g (*accounts, diary*) tenere; **to keep a record** *or* **note of sth** prendere nota di qc; **keep a note of how much you spend** segnati quanto spendi.

2 VI **a** (*continue*) continuare; (*remain*) stare, restare; **to keep (to the) left/right** tenere la sinistra/la destra; **to keep straight on** continuare dritto(-a); **to keep to** (*promise*) mantenere; (*subject, text*) attenersi a; **to keep doing sth** continuare a fare qc; **to keep fit** tenersi *or* mantenersi in forma; **to keep in good health** mantenersi in buona salute; **keep going!** forza!; **to keep at sb** (*fam: pester*) non dare pace a qn; **to keep at sth** (*fam: continue*) continuare a fare qc; **keep at it!** (*fam*) continua, dai!; **to keep still** stare *or* rimanere fermo(-a); **to keep quiet** stare zitto(-a); **to keep together** rimanere insieme; **to keep from doing sth** trattenersi *or* frenarsi dal fare qc; **to keep to one's room/bed** rimanere in camera/a letto; **they keep to themselves** si tengono in disparte, stanno per conto loro

b (*in health*): **how are you keeping?** come stai?; **I hope you're keeping well** spero che stia bene; **she's keeping better** sta meglio

c (*food*) mantenersi, conservarsi; (*fig: wait*): **this business can keep** quest'affare può aspettare.

3 N **a** (*livelihood*) vitto e alloggio; **to earn one's keep** guadagnarsi di che vivere

b (*of castle*) torrione *m*, maschio; see also **keeps**

▶ **keep away** **1** VT + ADV: **to keep sth/sb away from sb** tenere qc/qn lontano(-a) da qn; **they kept him away from school** non l'hanno mandato a scuola.

2 VI + ADV: **to keep away (from)** stare lontano(-a) (da)

▶ **keep back** **1** VT + ADV **a** (*crowds, tears, money*) trattenere

b (*conceal: information*): **to keep sth back from sb** nascondere qc a qn.

2 VI + ADV tenersi indietro; **please keep back!** indietro per favore!

▶ **keep down** **1** VT + ADV **a** (*control: prices, spending*) contenere; (: *anger*) controllare, contenere; (: *dog*) tenere a bada; (*rebellion*) soffocare, reprimere; (*population*) opprimere; **you can't keep a good man down** una persona valida prima o poi emerge

b (*food*) trattenere, ritenere

c (*Scol*): **he was kept down a year** gli hanno fatto ripetere l'anno.

2 VI + ADV tenersi giù, stare giù

▶ **keep in** **1** VT + ADV (*invalid, child*) tenere a casa; (*Scol*)

trattenere un alunno oltre l'orario scolastico, per punizione; (*stomach*) tenere dentro; (*elbows*) tenere giù.

2 VI + ADV (*fam*): **to keep in with sb** tenersi buono(-a) qn

▶ **keep off** **1** VT + ADV: **keep your hands off!** giù le mani!, non toccare!.

2 VT + PREP (*dog, person*) tenere lontano(-a) da; **keep your hands off that cake** non toccare quella torta.

3 VI + PREP: **"keep off the grass"** "non calpestare l'erba".

4 VI + ADV: **if the rain keeps off** se non piove

▶ **keep on** **1** VI + ADV (*continue*) continuare; **keep on along this road until ...** continui per questa strada finché...; **to keep on doing sth** continuare a fare qc; **to keep on at sb about sth** (*nag*) non dare pace a qc per qc; **don't keep on so!** *or* **don't keep on about it!** basta! smettila!.

2 VT + ADV (*hat, employee*) tenere; (*light*) tenere acceso (-a)

▶ **keep out** **1** VI + ADV (*not enter*) restare fuori; **"keep out"** "vietato l'ingresso"; **to keep out of trouble** tenersi fuori dai guai; **to keep out of a quarrel** non immischiarsi in una lite; **you keep out of this!** non immischiarti!.

2 VT + ADV (*exclude: person, dog*) tenere fuori; **this coat keeps out the cold** questo cappotto protegge dal freddo; **to keep sb out of trouble** tenere qn lontano dai guai

▶ **keep up** **1** VT + ADV **a** (*continue: tradition, subscription*) mantenere; **I did French at school, but I haven't kept it up** non ho più studiato francese dai tempi della scuola; **keep up the good work!** bravo, continua così!; **he'll never keep it up!** non ce la farà mai!

b (*maintain: property*) mantenere

c (*hold up*) tenere su, sorreggere; **to keep up one's spirits** (*fig*) tenersi su di morale, non perdersi d'animo; **the noise kept me up all night** il rumore mi ha tenuto sveglio tutta la notte.

2 VI + ADV **a**: **to keep up with sb** (*in race*) mantenersi al passo con qn; (*fig: in comprehension*) seguire qn; (: *by correspondence*) mantenere i rapporti con qn; **to keep up with sth** (*work, payments, price rises*) tener dietro a qc; **to keep up with the times** mantenersi al passo con i tempi; **to keep up with the Joneses** (*fig*) non essere da meno dei vicini

b (*weather*) continuare; (*prices*) mantenersi allo stesso livello.

keep·er ['ki:pə'] N **a** (*in park, zoo*) guardiano; (*in museum*) custode *m* **b** (*also: gamekeeper*) guardacaccia *m inv* **c** (*also: goalkeeper*) portiere *m*.

◆ **keep-fit** [ˌki:p'fɪt] **1** N ginnastica.

2 ADJ (*class, exercises*) di ginnastica.

keep·ing ['ki:pɪŋ] N **a**: **in keeping/out of keeping (with)** in armonia/disaccordo (con); **that modern building is out of keeping with the houses round about** quella costruzione moderna stona con le case intorno **b** (*care*) custodia; **in the keeping of** in custodia a; **in safe keeping** al sicuro.

keeps [ki:ps] N: **for keeps** (*fam*) per sempre.

keep·sake ['ki:p.seɪk] N ricordo.

keg [kɛg] N barile *m*, fusto.

◆ **keg beer** N birra alla spina.

kelp [kɛlp] N (*seaweed*) laminaria.

ken [kɛn] N (*old*): **beyond one's ken** al di là della propria comprensione.

ken·nel ['kɛnl] N **a** (*dog house*) canile *m* **b**: **kennels** NPL OR NSG (*establishment: for boarding*) canile; (: *for breeding*) allevamento di cani; **to put a dog in kennels** portare un cane al canile.

Ken·ya ['kɛnjə] N il Kenia *m*.

Ken·yan ['kɛnjən] ADJ, N keniano(-a), keniota *(m/f)*.

kept [kɛpt] ① PT, PP of **keep**.

② ADJ: **a kept woman/man** un(a) mantenuto(-a).

kera·tin ['kɛrətɪn] N cheratina.

kerb [kɜːb] N (*Brit*) bordo *or* orlo del marciapiede.

♦ **kerb crawler** ['kɜːb,krɔːləʳ] N (*Brit*) *chi va in macchina in cerca di una prostituta*.

♦ **kerb crawling** ['kɜːb,krɔːlɪŋ] N: **to go kerb crawling** *andare in macchina in cerca di una prostituta*.

ker·chief ['kɜːtʃɪf] N (*old*) foulard *m inv*.

ker·fuf·fle [kə'fʌfl] N (*Brit*) bagarre *f inv*.

ker·nel ['kɜːnl] N (*of nut*) gheriglio; (*of fruit stone*) nocciolo, seme *m*.

kero·sene, kero·sine ['kɛrəsiːn] N (*esp Am*) cherosene *m*.

kes·trel ['kɛstrəl] N gheppio.

ketch·up ['kɛtʃəp] N (*also:* **tomato ketchup**) ketchup *m inv*.

ket·tle ['kɛtl] N bollitore *m*; **that's a different** *or* **another kettle of fish** (*fig*) questo è un altro paio di maniche.

kettle·drum ['kɛtl,drʌm] N timpano.

key [kiː] ① N **a** (*also fig*) chiave *f*; (*for winding clock, toy*) chiave, chiavetta; (*can opener*) chiavetta; (*on map*) leg(g)enda; **the key to success** la chiave del successo **b** (*of piano, computer, typewriter*) tasto; (*of wind instrument*) chiave *f* **c** (*Mus*) chiave *f*; **in the key of C/F** in chiave di do/fa; **major/minor key** tonalità maggiore/minore; **to change key** cambiare tonalità; **to be in/off key** essere in/fuori tono.

② ADJ (*vital: position, industry, man*) chiave *inv*

► **key in** VT + ADV (*on computer: text*) digitare, battere.

key·board ['kiː,bɔːd] ① N tastiera.

② VT (*text*) digitare, battere.

key·board·er ['kiː,bɔːdəʳ] N (*on typewriter*) dattilografo (-a); (*on computer*) tastierista *m/f*.

♦ **keyed up** ['kiːd'ʌp] ADJ: **to be (all) keyed up** essere (tutto(-a)) agitato(-a).

key·hole ['kiː,həʊl] N buco della serratura.

♦ **keyhole surgery** N chirurgia mininvasiva.

key·note ['kiː,nəʊt] ① N (*Mus*) tonica; (*fig*) nota dominante.

② ADJ (*speech*) programmatico(-a).

key·pad ['kiː,pæd] N tastiera numerica.

♦ **key ring** N portachiavi *m inv*.

♦ **key signature** N (*Mus*) armatura.

key·stone ['kiː,stəʊn] N chiave *f* di volta.

key·stroke ['kiː,strəʊk] N (*on keyboard*) battuta.

kg ABBR (= *kilogram*) kg.

KGB [,keɪdʒiː'biː] N ABBR: **the KGB** il KGB.

kha·ki ['kɑːkɪ] ① N (*cloth*) tela cachi; (*colour*) cachi *m*.

② ADJ cachi *inv*.

Khmer [kmɛəʳ] ① ADJ khmer *inv*.

② N (*person*) khmer *m/f inv*; (*language*) khmer *m*.

♦ **Khmer Rouge** N, PL INV: **the Khmer Rouge** i khmer *mpl* rossi.

kib·butz [kɪ'bʊts] N (*pl* **kibbutzim**) kibbutz *m inv*.

ki·bosh ['kaɪ,bɒʃ] N (*fam*): **to put the kibosh on sth** mettere fine a qc.

kick [kɪk] ① VT (*person*) dare *or* tirare calci a; (*ball*) calciare; (*subj: horse*) tirare un calcio a; **to kick sb downstairs** scaraventare qn giù per le scale; **to kick sth out of the way** spostare qc con un calcio; **I could have kicked myself** (*fig fam*) mi sarei preso a schiaffi; **to kick the bucket** (*fig fam*) tirare le cuoia; **to kick a habit** (*fig fam*) liberarsi da un vizio.

② VI (*person*) dare calci, tirare calci; (*baby, horse*) scalciare; **to kick at sth** dare *or* tirare un calcio a qc.

③ N **a** (*action*) calcio; (*of firearm*) contraccolpo, rinculo; **to take a kick at sth/sb** tirare un calcio a qc/qn; **to give sth/sb a kick** dare un calcio a qc/qn; **this cocktail's got a kick to it** (*fam*) è forte questo cocktail; **it was a kick in the teeth for him** (*fig fam*) per lui è stato uno schiaffo morale; **he needs a kick in the pants** (*fig fam*) ha bisogno di un bel calcio nel sedere

b (*fam: thrill*): **he gets a kick out of it** ci prova un gusto matto; **to do something for kicks** fare qc per divertimento

► **kick about, kick around** ① VT + ADV: **to kick a ball about** *or* **around** giocare a pallone.

② VI + ADV (*fam: object*) essere in giro

► **kick against** VI + PREP lottare contro

► **kick back** ① VI + ADV (*gun*) rinculare.

② VT + ADV (*ball*) rinviare, rimandare

► **kick down** VT + ADV abbattere a calci

► **kick in** VT + ADV abbattere, sfasciare; **to kick sb's teeth in** (*fam*) spaccare la faccia a qn

► **kick off** VI + ADV (*Ftbl*) dare il calcio d'inizio; (*fig fam: meeting etc*) cominciare

► **kick out** ① VI + ADV: **to kick out (at)** tirare calci (a).

② VT + ADV (*fig fam*): **to kick sb out (of)** cacciare qn via (da), buttare qn fuori (da)

► **kick up** VT + ADV (*fig fam*): **to kick up a row** *or* **a din** scatenare un putiferio; **to kick up a fuss about** *or* **over sth** piantare un casino per qc.

kick·back ['kɪk,bæk] N tangente *f*.

kick·er ['kɪkəʳ] N (*Rugby*) *giocatore che effettua un calcio piazzato*.

kick·off ['kɪk,ɒf] N (*Ftbl*) calcio d'inizio; (*fig*) inizio.

kick·stand ['kɪk,stænd] N cavalletto.

♦ **kick-start** ['kɪk,stɑːt] (*Brit*) ① N (*also:* **kick-starter**) pedale *m* d'avviamento.

② VT mettere in moto (col pedale); (*fig*): **to kick-start the economy** dare una spinta all'economia.

♦ **kick turn** N (*Skiing*) dietro-front *m inv* da fermo.

kid [kɪd] ① N **a** (*fam: child*) bambino(-a); (: *teenager*) ragazzo(-a); (: *son, daughter*) figlio(-a) **b** (*goat, leather*) capretto.

② VT (*fam*): **to kid sb (on) that ...** dar da bere a qn che...; **to kid sb about sth** prendere in giro qn per qc; **don't kid yourself!** non illuderti!.

③ VI (*fam: also:* **kid on**) scherzare; **I'm only kidding** sto solo scherzando; **no kidding!** sul serio!.

④ ADJ **a** (*fam: brother, sister*) più giovane **b** (*gloves, leather*) di capretto.

kid·die ['kɪdɪ] N (*fam*) bambino(-a).

♦ **kid gloves** NPL: **to treat sb with kid gloves** trattare qn coi guanti.

kid·nap ['kɪdnæp] VT rapire, sequestrare.

kid·nap·per ['kɪdnæpəʳ] N rapitore(-trice), sequestratore (-trice).

kid·nap·ping ['kɪdnæpɪŋ] N sequestro di persona.

kid·ney ['kɪdnɪ] ① N (*Anat*) rene *m*; (*Culin*) rognone *m*.

② ADJ (*disease, failure, transplant*) renale, del rene.

♦ **kidney bean** N fagiolo comune.

♦ **kidney machine** N rene *m* artificiale.

♦ **kidney-shaped** ['kɪdnɪ,ʃeɪpt] ADJ a forma di fagiolo.

♦ **kidney stone** N calcolo renale.

Kili·man·ja·ro [,kɪlɪmən'dʒɑːrəʊ] N (*also:* **Mount Kilimanjaro**) il Kilimangiaro.

kill [kɪl] ① VT a uccidere, ammazzare; **to be killed in action** essere ucciso(-a) in combattimento; **to kill two birds with one stone** (fig) prendere due piccioni con una fava; **this heat is killing me** (fig fam) sto morendo di caldo; **my feet are killing me** (fam) i piedi mi fanno male da morire; **he was killing himself laughing** (fam) moriva dal ridere or dalle risate; **he certainly wasn't killing himself!** (fig hum) di sicuro non si ammazzava di fatica! b (fig: pain) togliere; (: rumour) mettere fine a; (: story) rovinare, guastare; (: paragraph, line) sopprimere; (newspaper article) impedire la pubblicazione di, far saltare; (: feeling, hope) distruggere; (: flavour, smell) soffocare; (: sound) attutire, smorzare; (: engine, motor) fermare, spegnere; **to kill time** ammazzare il tempo.
② N (Hunting, Bullfighting) uccisione f; **to be in at the kill** (fig) essere presente al colpo di grazia
▶ **kill off** VT + ADV sterminare; (fig) eliminare; (: rumour) soffocare.

kill·er ['kɪlə'] ① N (murderer) assassino(-a); (: hired) killer m/f inv; **flu can be a killer** si può morire per un'influenza.
② ADJ (disease) mortale.

♦ **killer instinct** N (fig): **he has the killer instinct** sa essere spietato.

♦ **killer whale** N orca.

kill·ing ['kɪlɪŋ] ① N (murder) uccisione f; (massacre) strage f; (fam: profit): **to make a killing** fare un colpaccio.
② ADJ (blow) mortale; (fig: work) estenuante; (fam: funny) divertentissimo(-a).

kill·joy ['kɪl,dʒɔɪ] N guastafeste m/f.

kiln [kɪln] N fornace f.

kilo ['kiːləʊ] N chilo.

kilo·byte ['kɪləʊbaɪt] N kilobyte m inv.

kilo·gram, kilo·gramme ['kɪləʊɡræm] N chilogrammo.

kilo·hertz ['kɪləʊˌhɜːts] N chilohertz m inv.

kilo·metre ['kɪləʊˌmiːtə'], (Am) **kilo·meter** [kɪ'lɒmɪtə'] N chilometro.

kilo·watt ['kɪləʊwɒt] N chilowatt m inv.

kilt [kɪlt] N kilt m inv.

kilt·ed ['kɪltɪd] ADJ (man) in kilt; **a kilted skirt** un kilt m inv.

kil·ter ['kɪltə'] N (fam): **out of kilter** fuori fase.

ki·mo·no [kɪ'məʊnəʊ] N chimono.

kin [kɪn] N parenti mpl, familiari mpl; see also **kith, next of kin.**

kind [kaɪnd] ① N (species) sorta, specie f, genere m; **all kinds of things** ogni genere di cose; **some kind of fish** qualche tipo di pesce; **he's not the kind of person to ...** non è il tipo da...; **what kind of an answer is that?** OR **what kind of an answer do you call that?** che razza di risposta è questa?; **what kind of person do you take me for?** per chi mi prendi?; **I had a kind of feeling that would happen** avevo come il presentimento che sarebbe successo; **you know the kind of thing I mean** sai cosa intendo or voglio dire; **something of the kind** qualcosa del genere; **nothing of the kind!** niente affatto!; **it's not his kind of film** non è il tipo or genere di film che piace a lui, non è il suo genere di film; **they're two of a kind** (pej) sono della stessa pasta; **it's the only one of its kind** è l'unico nel suo genere; **it was tea of a kind** (pej) era una sottospecie di tè; **I kind of thought this would happen** (fam) quasi me l'aspettavo; **she looked kind of worried** (fam) sembrava come preoccupata; **payment in kind** pagamento in natura; **to repay sb in kind** (after good deed) ricambiare la cortesia a qn; (after bad deed) ripagare qn con la stessa moneta.
② ADJ (comp -er, superl -est) gentile, buono(-a); **to be**

kind to sb essere gentile con qn; **would you be kind enough to ...?** sarebbe così gentile da...?; **would you be so kind as to ...?** le spiacerebbe...?; **it's very kind of you (to do ...)** è molto gentile da parte sua (fare...); **thank you for your kind assistance** (frm) la ringrazio per il gentile aiuto.

kin·der·gar·ten ['kɪndə,ɡɑːtn] N asilo.

♦ **kind-hearted** [,kaɪnd'hɑːtɪd] ADJ buono(-a), di buon cuore.

♦ **kind-heartedness** [,kaɪnd'hɑːtɪdnɪs] N bontà, buon cuore m.

kin·dle ['kɪndl] VT (wood) appiccare il fuoco a; (fire) accendere; (emotion, interest) suscitare.

kind·li·ness ['kaɪndlɪnɪs] N gentilezza.

kin·dling ['kɪndlɪŋ] N frasche fpl, ramoscelli mpl.

kind·ly ['kaɪndlɪ] ① ADJ (comp -ier, superl -iest) (person, smile, tone) benevolo(-a), affabile; (gesture) gentile.
② ADV (speak, act) con gentilezza, gentilmente; **kindly wait a moment** abbia la cortesia or gentilezza di aspettare un momento; **will you kindly ...** vuole... per cortesia; **he doesn't take kindly to being kept waiting** non gli piace affatto dover aspettare; **he didn't take it kindly** non l'ha presa molto bene.

kind·ness ['kaɪndnɪs] N (towards sb) gentilezza, bontà; (act) gentilezza; **out of the kindness of her heart** per bontà d'animo; **to do sb a kindness** fare una cortesia or una gentilezza a qn.

kin·dred ['kɪndrɪd] ① ADJ (tribes, peoples) imparentato (-a); (language) affine; **to have a kindred feeling for sb** sentirsi molto vicino(-a) a qn.
② N (relations) familiari mpl, parenti mpl.

♦ **kindred spirit** N spirito affine.

ki·net·ic [kɪ'netɪk] ADJ cinetico(-a).

ki·net·ics [kɪ'netɪks] NSG cinetica.

king [kɪŋ] N (also fig, Chess, Cards) re m inv; (Draughts) dama.

king·cup ['kɪŋ,kʌp] N (flower) botton m d'oro.

king·dom ['kɪŋdəm] N regno, reame m; **the Kingdom of Heaven** il Regno dei Cieli; **till kingdom come** (fam) fino al giorno del giudizio.

king·fisher ['kɪŋ,fɪʃə'] N martin m inv pescatore.

king·ly ['kɪŋlɪ] ADJ (virtues, bearing) regale; (palace) reale.

king·pin ['kɪŋ,pɪn] N (Tech, fig) perno.

♦ **king-size** ['kɪŋ,saɪz], **king-sized** ['kɪŋ,saɪzd] ADJ (gen: object, bed) king size inv, più grande del normale; (packet) formato gigante inv; (cigarette) king size, lungo (-a).

kink [kɪŋk] ① N (in rope) attorcigliamento; (in hair) riccio; (fig: emotional, psychological, sexual) aberrazione f.
② VI attorcigliarsi.

kinky ['kɪŋkɪ] ADJ (comp -ier, superl -iest) (hair) crespo(-a); (fam: sexually) dai gusti particolari; (: person, idea, fashion) stravagante, eccentrico(-a).

kin·ship ['kɪnʃɪp] N parentela.

kins·man ['kɪnzmən] N (pl -men) (old) congiunto.

kins·woman ['kɪnz,wʊmən] N (pl -women) (old) congiunta.

ki·osk ['kiːɒsk] N (gen) chiosco; (Brit: also: **telephone kiosk**) cabina telefonica; (also: **newspaper kiosk**) edicola.

kip [kɪp] (fam) ① VI dormire.
② N dormita; **to get some kip** fare una dormita.

kip·per ['kɪpə'] N aringa affumicata.

Kir·ghi·zia [,kɜː'ɡɪzɪə] N Kirghizistan m.

kirk [kɜːk] N (Scot) chiesa; **the Kirk** la Chiesa presbiteriana

scozzese.

kiss [kɪs] **1** VT baciare; **to kiss sb goodbye** congedarsi da qn con un bacio; **to kiss sb goodnight** dare a qn il bacio della buonanotte; **to kiss sb's hand** baciare la mano a qn.
2 VI: **to kiss (each other)** baciarsi.
3 N bacio.

kissa·gram ['kɪsə,græm] N *servizio-burla in cui un(a) modello(a) viene incaricato(a) di porgere gli auguri baciando il(la) festeggiato(a).*

♦ **kiss of death** N (*fam*): **the kiss of death** il colpo di grazia.

♦ **kiss of life** N (*esp Brit*): **to give the kiss of life** fare la respirazione bocca a bocca.

kit [kɪt] N **a** (*equipment: gen*) kit *m inv*, attrezzatura; (*Mil*) equipaggiamento; (*Sport: outfit*) tenuta; (: *gear*) attrezzi *mpl*; (*tools*) arnesi *mpl*
b (*parts for assembly*) kit *m inv* di montaggio; **kitchen units in kit form** mobili *mpl* per cucina in kit di montaggio; **toy aircraft kit** kit per aeromodellismo
▶ **kit out** VT + ADV (*Brit*) attrezzare, equipaggiare.

kit·bag ['kɪt,bæg] N (*Mil*) sacco militare; (*Sport*) sacca sportiva.

kitch·en ['kɪtʃɪn] **1** N cucina.
2 ADJ (*cupboard, equipment etc*) da cucina.

kitch·en·ette [,kɪtʃɪ'nɛt] N cucinino.

♦ **kitchen foil** N carta di alluminio.

♦ **kitchen garden** N orto.

♦ **kitchen knife** N coltello da cucina.

♦ **kitchen roll**, (*Brit*) **kitchen paper, kitchen towel** N Scottex ® *f inv*, carta assorbente (da cucina).

♦ **kitchen sink** N lavello, acquaio; **to take everything but the kitchen sink** (*fam hum*) portarsi dietro tutta la casa.

♦ **kitchen sink drama** N (*fam*) *teatro degli anni '50 rappresentante gli aspetti quotidiani della vita della classe operaia.*

♦ **kitchen unit** N (*Brit*) (mobile *m*) componibile *m* da cucina.

kitchen·ware ['kɪtʃɪn,wɛə] N (*dishes*) stoviglie *fpl*; (*equipment*) utensili *mpl* da cucina.

kite [kaɪt] N (*toy*) aquilone *m*; (*bird*) nibbio.

kith [kɪθ] N: **kith and kin** (*old*) amici *mpl* e parenti *mpl*.

kitsch [kɪtʃ] **1** N kitsch *m inv*.
2 ADJ kitsch *inv*.

kit·ten ['kɪtn] N gattino(-a); **I had kittens when ...** (*fig fam*) mi è venuto un colpo quando... .

kit·ten·ish ['kɪtənɪʃ] ADJ da gattina.

kit·ti·wake ['kɪtɪ,weɪk] N gabbiano tridattilo.

kit·ty ['kɪtɪ] N **a** (*funds*) cassa comune; (: *Cards*) posta **b** (*fam: cat*) micio(-a), micino(-a).

kiwi ['ki:wi:] N kiwi *m inv*; (*fam: New Zealander*) neozelandese *m/f*.

♦ **kiwi fruit** N kiwi *m inv*.

KKK [,keɪkeɪ'keɪ] N ABBR = *Ku Klux Klan*.

Kleen·ex® ['kli:nɛks] N kleenex ® *m inv*, fazzoletto di carta.

klep·to·ma·nia [,klɛptəʊ'meɪnɪə] N (*Psych*) cleptomania.

klep·to·ma·ni·ac [,klɛptəʊ'meɪnɪæk] N cleptomane *m/f*.

km ABBR (= *kilometre*) km.

km/h ABBR (= *kilometre per hour*) km/h.

knack [næk] N abilità, capacità; **to get the knack of sth** farsi la mano in qc; **to have the knack of doing sth** avere l'abilità di fare qc; **to learn the knack of doing sth** imparare la tecnica per fare qc; **there's a knack to doing this** c'è un trucco per fare questo.

knack·ered ['nækəd] ADJ (*Brit fam*) fuso(-a).

knap·sack ['næp,sæk] N (*rucksack*) zainetto; (*shoulder bag*) tascapane *m*.

knave [neɪv] N (*old*) furfante *m*; (*Cards*) fante *m*.

knead [ni:d] VT (*dough, clay*) impastare, lavorare; (*muscle*) massaggiare.

knee [ni:] N (*Anat, of garment*) ginocchio; **on one's knees** in ginocchio; **on one's hands and knees** carponi; **to go down on one's knees (to sb)** inginocchiarsi (davanti a qn).

♦ **knee-bend** ['ni:,bɛnd] N flessione *for* piegamento delle ginocchia.

knee·cap ['ni:,kæp] **1** N (*Anat*) rotula.
2 VT gambizzare.

knee·cap·ping ['ni:,kæpɪŋ] N gambizzazione *f*.

♦ **knee-deep** ['ni:'di:p] ADJ fino al ginocchio; **the water was knee-deep** l'acqua ci arrivava alle ginocchia.

♦ **knee-high** ['ni:'haɪ] ADJ che arriva al ginocchio.

kneel [ni:l] VI (*pt, pp* **knelt**) (*also:* **kneel down**) inginocchiarsi.

knee·pad ['ni:,pæd] N ginocchiera.

♦ **knees-up** ['ni:zʌp] N (*Brit*): **to have a knees-up** (*old: to dance*) fare quattro salti; (*drink*) farsi una bevuta.

knell [nɛl] N (*liter: also:* **death knell**) campana a morto.

knelt [nɛlt] PT, PP of **kneel**.

knew [nju:] PT of **know**.

knick·er·bock·ers ['nɪkə,bɒkəz] N knickerbockers *mpl*.

knick·ers ['nɪkəz] NPL (*Brit*) slip *m inv* (*da donna*), mutandine *fpl*.

knick-knack ['nɪk,næk] N ninnolo.

knife [naɪf] **1** N (*pl* **knives**) (*gen*) coltello; (*also:* **penknife**) temperino; **knife, fork and spoon** coperto; **I can't wait to get my knife into him** (*fig*) non vedo l'ora di cavargli gli occhi.
2 VT (*stab*) accoltellare; **to knife sb to death** uccidere qn a coltellate.

♦ **knife edge** N: **to be on a knife edge** (*fig: person*) stare *or* camminare sul filo del rasoio; (: *hope, result*) essere appeso(-a) a un filo; **the success of the scheme was balanced on a knife edge** la riuscita del progetto era appesa ad un filo.

♦ **knife grinder** N arrotino.

♦ **knife pleat** N: **a skirt with knife pleats** una gonna a pieghe sovrapposte.

♦ **knife-sharpener** ['naɪf,ʃɑ:pnə'] N (*tool*) affilacoltelli *m inv*.

knight [naɪt] **1** N cavaliere *m*; (*Chess*) cavallo.
2 VT nominare cavaliere.

knight·hood ['naɪthʊd] N (*Brit: title*) cavalierato; **to get a knighthood** essere nominato cavaliere.

knit [nɪt] **1** VT (*garment*) lavorare a maglia *or* a ferri; **to knit together** (*fig*) unire; **to knit one's brows** aggrottare le sopracciglia.
2 VI **a** (*make garment*) lavorare a maglia **b** (*also:* **knit together**: *broken bones*) saldarsi; (: *people*) andare d'accordo.

knit·ted ['nɪtɪd] ADJ lavorato(-a) a maglia.

knit·ting ['nɪtɪŋ] N (*activity*) il lavorare *m* a maglia; (*product*) lavoro a maglia.

♦ **knitting machine** N macchina per maglieria.

♦ **knitting needle** N ferro da calza.

♦ **knitting pattern** N modello per maglia.

knit·wear ['nɪt,wɛə'] N maglieria.

knives [naɪvz] NPL of **knife**.

knob [nɒb] N pomo, pomello; (*on radio, TV*) manopola; **a knob of butter** (*Brit*) una noce *f* di burro.

knob·bly ['nɒblɪ], (Am) **knob·by** ['nɒbi] ADJ (comp **-ier**, superl **-iest**) (wood, surface) nodoso(-a); (knee) ossuto (-a).

knock [nɒk] **1** VT **a** (strike) colpire; **to knock a nail into sth** conficcare un chiodo in qc; **to knock sb on the head** colpire qn in or alla testa; **to knock one's head on/against sth** battere or sbattere la testa su/contro qc; **to knock sb unconscious** or **out** or **cold** tramortire qn; **to knock the bottom out of sth** (box) sfondare qc; (fig: argument) demolire qc; **he knocked the knife out of her hand** con un colpo le ha fatto cadere il coltello di mano; **to knock spots off sb/sth** (fig fam) dare dei punti a qn/qc; **to knock sb sideways** or **for six** (fig fam) lasciare qn di stucco; **to knock some sense into sb** (fam) far entrare un po' di buonsenso in testa a qn
b (fam: criticize) criticare.
2 VI **a** (strike) bussare; **he knocked at** or **on the door** ha bussato alla porta; **his knees were knocking** gli tremavano le ginocchia
b (bump): **to knock into** or **against sb/sth** sbattere or urtare contro qn/qc
c (engine) battere in testa.
3 N **a** (blow) colpo; (in collision) botta; **there was a knock at the door** hanno bussato alla porta; **I heard a knock** ho sentito bussare; **his pride took a knock** il suo orgoglio ha subito un duro colpo
b (in engine) battito in testa
▶ **knock about, knock around** **1** VT + ADV (person, object) maltrattare.
2 VI + ADV (fam: person) vagabondare; (: thing): **it's knocking around here somewhere** è qui in giro, da qualche parte
▶ **knock back** VT + ADV (fam) **a** (drink) scolare, tracannare
b (cost): **it knocked me back £100** mi è costato la bellezza di 100 sterline
▶ **knock down** VT + ADV **a** (building) demolire; (person) gettare a terra, stendere; (pedestrian) investire; (tree) abbattere; (door) buttare giù; **you could have knocked me down with a feather!** mi sono cadute le braccia!
b (price) abbassare; (object at auction) aggiudicare
▶ **knock in** VT + ADV (nail) conficcare
▶ **knock off** **1** VT + ADV **a** (strike off: vase on shelf) far cadere; (fig: from price, record): **to knock off £10** or **knock £10 off the price** fare uno sconto di 10 sterline
b (fam: steal) sgraffignare, fregare
c (fam: do quickly) buttare giù
d (fam: stop): **knock it off!** piantala!.
2 VI + ADV (fam: stop work) smontare, staccare
▶ **knock out** VT + ADV **a** (stun) stordire, stendere; (Boxing) mettere k.o. or fuori combattimento
b (nails) far uscire, levare; (in fight: teeth) spaccare; **to knock out one's pipe** svuotare la pipa
c (eliminate: in competition) eliminare
▶ **knock over** VT + ADV (object) far cadere; (pedestrian) investire
▶ **knock together** VT + ADV **a** (two objects) battere uno contro l'altro
b (make hastily) mettere insieme alla svelta, arrangiare alla meglio
▶ **knock up** VT + ADV **a** (handle, lever) tirare in alto
b (Brit: waken) svegliare bussando alla porta
c (make hastily) = **knock together b**.
knock·down ['nɒk‚daʊn] ADJ (price) stracciato(-a).
knock·er ['nɒkə'] N (on door) battente m.

♦ **knock-for-knock agree·ment** ['nɒkfə'nɒkə'griːmənt] N (Brit) accordo fra assicurazioni auto per risarcire i propri clienti indipendentemente dalla responsabilità.
knock·ing ['nɒkɪŋ] N colpi mpl.
♦ **knocking-off time** ['nɒkɪŋ'ɒf‚taɪm] N: **knocking-off time is six o'clock** si stacca or si smonta alle sei.
♦ **knock-kneed** [‚nɒk'niːd] ADJ che ha le gambe a X.
♦ **knock-on** ['nɒk'ɒn] ADJ: **knock-on effect** reazione f a catena.
knock·out ['nɒk‚aʊt] N **a** (Boxing) knock out m inv **b** (fam: person) schianto, cannonata.
♦ **knockout competition** N gara ad eliminazione.
♦ **knockout drops** NPL (fam) sonnifero.
♦ **knock-up** ['nɒk‚ʌp] N (Tennis) palleggio; **to have a knock-up** palleggiare.
knoll [nəʊl] N poggio.
knot [nɒt] **1** N (in rope, wood, also Naut: speed) nodo; (group: of people) capannello; **to tie a knot** fare un nodo; **to tie o.s. up in knots** (fig) ingarbugliarsi.
2 VT fare un nodo a, annodare; **to knot together** annodare insieme.
knot·grass ['nɒt‚grɑːs] N centinodia.
knot·ty ['nɒtɪ] ADJ (comp **-ier**, superl **-iest**) (wood) nodoso (-a); (fig: problem) spinoso(-a).
know [nəʊ] (vb: pt **knew**, pp **known**) **1** VT **a** (facts, dates) sapere; **to know that …** sapere che…; **to get to know sth** venire a sapere qc; **to know how to do sth** saper fare qc; **he knows all the answers** sa rispondere a tutte le domande; (pej) sa sempre tutto; **he knows what he's talking about** parla con cognizione di causa; **to know one's (own) mind** sapere ciò che si vuole; **I know nothing about it** non ne so niente; **there's no knowing what may happen** chissà cosa succederà; **it soon became known that …** si è presto venuto a sapere che…; **to make sth known to sb** far sapere qc a qn; **he is known to have been there** si sa che c'è stato; **it's worth knowing what/how** etc … vale la pena sapere che cosa/come etc…; **to know sth backwards** conoscere qc a menadito; **let me know how you get on** fammi sapere come va; **you know how it is** sai com'è; **I knew it!** lo sapevo!
b (be acquainted with: person, place, author, subject) conoscere; **I don't know him** non lo conosco; **to know sb by sight/by name** conoscere qn di vista/di nome; **to get to know sb** conoscere meglio qn; **I don't know him to speak to** lo conosco solo di vista; **to make o.s. known to sb** presentarsi a qn; **he is known as X** è conosciuto con or sotto il nome di X
c (recognize) riconoscere; **I knew him by his voice** l'ho riconosciuto dalla voce; **she knows a good painting when she sees one** sa riconoscere un buon dipinto; **to know the difference between …** saper distinguere fra…; **to know right from wrong** distinguere il bene dal male.
2 VI sapere; **as far as I know …** che io sappia…, per quanto ne so io…; **we'll let you know** le faremo sapere; **how should I know?** come vuoi che lo sappia?; **no, not that I know of** no, che io sappia; **there's no (way of) knowing** non c'è modo di saperlo; **it's not easy, you know** non è facile, sai; **yes, I know** sì, lo so; **I don't know** non lo so; **you ought to know better (than to …)** dovresti saperlo da solo (che non è il caso di…); **she says she didn't do it, but I know better** ha detto che non è stata lei, ma a me non la fa; **he doesn't know any better** non ha criterio or giudizio; **you know best** nessuno può saperlo meglio di te; **(well,) what do you know!** (fam) chi

l'avrebbe mai detto!; **to know about** *or* **of sth** essere a conoscenza di qc; **to know about** *or* **of sb** aver sentito parlare di qn; **to get to know about sth** venire a sapere qc; **how many "don't knows" are there?** quanti sono gli incerti?.

3 N: **to be in the know** (*fam*) essere al corrente, essere beninformato(-a).

know·able ['nəʊəbl] ADJ conoscibile.

♦ **know-all** ['nəʊɔːl] N (*Brit pej*) sapientone(-a).

♦ **know-how** ['nəʊˌhaʊ] N know-how *m inv*.

know·ing ['nəʊɪŋ] ADJ (*look, smile*) d'intesa; (*shrewd*) scaltro(-a).

know·ing·ly ['nəʊɪŋlɪ] ADV (*intentionally*) deliberatamente; (*smile, look*) con aria d'intesa.

♦ **know-it-all** ['nəʊɪtˌɔːl] N (*Am*) = know-all.

knowl·edge ['nɒlɪdʒ] N **a** (*information, awareness, understanding*) conoscenza; **to have no knowledge of** ignorare, non sapere; **not to my knowledge** non che io sappia; **without my knowledge** a mia insaputa; **to (the best of) my knowledge** per quanto io ne sappia; **it is common knowledge that …** è risaputo che…; **it has come to my knowledge that …** sono venuto a sapere che…

b (*learning*) conoscenza, sapere *m*; **to have a working knowledge of Italian** avere una conoscenza pratica dell'italiano; **to have a thorough knowledge of sth** conoscere qc a fondo.

knowl·edge·able ['nɒlɪdʒəbl] ADJ (*person*) ben informato (-a); (*remark*) pertinente.

known [nəʊn] **1** PP of **know**.

2 ADJ (*thief, facts*) noto(-a); (*expert*) riconosciuto(-a), famoso(-a).

knuck·le ['nʌkl] N (*Anat*) nocca

▶ **knuckle down** VI + ADV (*fam*): **to knuckle down to some hard work** mettersi sotto a lavorare

▶ **knuckle under** VI + ADV (*fam*) cedere.

knuckle·duster ['nʌklˌdʌstəʳ] N tirapugni *m inv*.

KO, k.o. ['keɪ'əʊ] **1** N ABBR (*pl* **KO's**) (= *knockout*) K.O.

2 VT (*pt, pp* **KO'd**) (= *knock out*) mettere k.o.

koa·la [kəʊˈɑːlə] N (*also:* **koala bear**) koala *m inv*.

kohl [kəʊl] N kajal *m inv*.

kook [kuːk] N (*Am fam*) svitato(-a).

Ko·ran [kɒˈrɑːn] N: **the Koran** il Corano.

Ko·ran·ic [kɒˈrænɪk] ADJ coranico(-a).

Ko·rea [kəˈrɪə] N Corea; **North/South Korea** Corea del Nord/del Sud.

Ko·rean [kəˈriːən] ADJ, N coreano(-a).

ko·sher ['kəʊʃəʳ] ADJ kasher *inv*.

kow·tow [ˌkaʊˈtaʊ] VI (*fam*): **to kowtow to sb** prostrarsi davanti a qn (*fig*).

kph [ˌkeɪpiːˈaɪtʃ] N km/h.

Krem·lin ['kremlɪn] N: **the Kremlin** il Cremlino.

kremlin·olo·gist ['kremlɪˈnɒlədʒɪst] N cremlinologo(-a).

kremlin·ol·ogy [kremlɪˈnɒlədʒɪ] N cremlinologia.

kryp·ton ['krɪptɒn] N cripto.

KS ABBR (*Am Post*)= *Kansas*.

Kt ABBR (*Brit*)= *knight*.

Kua·la Lum·pur ['kwɑːləˈlʊmpʊəʳ] N Kuala Lumpur *f*.

ku·dos ['kjuːdɒs] NSG gloria, fama.

Ku Klux Klan ['kuːˈklʌksˈklæn] N: **the Ku Klux Klan** il Ku Klux Klan.

kung fu ['kʌŋˈfuː] N kung fu *m*.

Kurd [kɜːd] N curdo(-a).

Kurd·ish ['kɜːdɪʃ] **1** ADJ curdo(-a).

2 N (*language*) curdo.

Ku·wait [kʊˈweɪt] N il Kuwait *m*.

Ku·wai·ti [kʊˈweɪtɪ] ADJ, N kuwaitiano(-a).

kw ABBR (= *kilowatt*) kW.

KY ABBR = *Kentucky*.

L

L, l [ɛl] N (letter) L, l for m inv; **L for Lucy**, (Am) **L for Love** ≈ L come Livorno.

L [ɛl] ABBR 1 **a** (= large) L f **b** (Brit Aut: = learner) P (= principiante); see also **L-plates**.

2 N ABBR (Am fam): **the L** (= the elevated (railroad)) la soprelevata.

l ABBR (= litre) l.

L., l. ABBR **a** (lake) l **b** (left) sin.

LA [ˌɛlˈeɪ] (Am) N ABBR 1 = Los Angeles.

2 (Post) = Louisiana.

la [lɑː] N (Mus) = **lah**.

lab [læb] N (fam) laboratorio.

la·bel [ˈleɪbl] 1 N etichetta, cartellino; (brand: of record) casa discografica, etichetta; **he records on the E.M.I. label** incide per la E.M.I.

2 VT **a** (goods) mettere l'etichetta su, marcare; (fig) classificare, etichettare; **a bottle labelled "poison"** una bottiglia con l'etichetta "veleno".

la·bor etc [ˈleɪbəʳ] (Am) = **labour** etc.

la·bora·tory [ləˈbɒrətərɪ] 1 N laboratorio.

2 ADJ di laboratorio.

♦ **Labor Day** N il primo lunedì di settembre, festa del lavoro negli Stati Uniti e in Canada.

la·bo·ri·ous [ləˈbɔːrɪəs] ADJ faticoso(-a), laborioso(-a).

la·bo·ri·ous·ly [ləˈbɔːrɪəslɪ] ADV faticosamente, laboriosamente.

♦ **labor union** (Am) N sindacato.

La·bour [ˈleɪbəʳ] 1 N (Brit Pol: also: **the Labour Party**) il partito laburista, i laburisti; **she votes Labour** vota (per il partito) laburista.

2 ADJ laburista; **official Labour policy** politica ufficiale dei laburisti.

la·bour, (Am) **la·bor** [ˈleɪbəʳ] 1 N **a** (toil, task) lavoro; **hard labour** (Law) lavori forzati; **labour of love** lavoro fatto per il puro piacere di farlo

b (workforce) manodopera

c (Med) doglie fpl, travaglio (del parto); **to be in labour** avere le doglie.

2 VT (point) insistere su.

3 VI: **to labour at** (with effort) lavorare sodo or duro a; (with difficulty) faticare a fare; (engine, motor) essere sotto sforzo; **to labour under a delusion/misapprehension** essere vittima di un'illusione/di un malinteso; **to labour up a hill** arrancare su per una collina.

4 ADJ di lavoro.

♦ **labour camp**, (Am) **labor camp** N campo di lavoro.

♦ **labour cost**, (Am) **labor cost** N costo del lavoro.

♦ **labour dispute**, (Am) **labor dispute** N conflitto tra lavoratori e datori di lavoro.

la·boured, (Am) **la·bored** [ˈleɪbəd] ADJ (breathing) affannoso(-a); (style) pesante.

la·bour·er, (Am) **la·bor·er** [ˈleɪbərəʳ] N (on building site) manovale m; (on farm) bracciante m.

♦ **Labour Exchange** N (Brit old) ufficio di collocamento.

♦ **labour force**, (Am) **labor force** N manodopera.

♦ **labour-intensive**, (Am) **labor-intensive** [ˈleɪbər-ɪnˌtɛnsɪv] ADJ che assorbe molta manodopera.

La·bour·ite [ˈleɪbəˌraɪt] N laburista m/f.

♦ **labour market**, (Am) **labor market** N mercato del lavoro.

♦ **labour pains**, (Am) **labor pains** NPL doglie fpl.

♦ **labour relations**, (Am) **labor relations** NPL relazioni fpl industriali.

♦ **labour-saving**, (Am) **labor-saving** [ˈleɪbəˌseɪvɪŋ] ADJ che fa risparmiare fatica or lavoro.

♦ **labour unrest**, (Am) **labor unrest** N agitazioni fpl operaie.

la·bur·num [ləˈbɜːnəm] N maggiociondolo.

laby·rinth [ˈlæbɪrɪnθ] N labirinto.

laby·rin·thine [ˌlæbəˈrɪnθaɪn] (frm) ADJ labirintico(-a).

lace [leɪs] 1 N **a** (fabric) pizzo, merletto **b** (of shoe) laccio, stringa; (of corset) laccio.

2 ADJ di pizzo.

3 VT **a** (also: **lace up**: shoes etc) allacciare **b** (drink: with spirits) correggere; (: with poison) avvelenare.

lace·ma·ker [ˈleɪsˌmeɪkəʳ] N merlettaia.

lace·making [ˈleɪsˌmeɪkɪŋ] N fabbricazione f dei pizzi or dei merletti.

lac·er·ate [ˈlæsəˌreɪt] VT lacerare.

lac·era·tion [ˌlæsəˈreɪʃən] N lacerazione f.

♦ **lace-up** ['leɪsˌʌp] ADJ (*shoes*) con i lacci *or* le stringhe.

♦ **lace-ups** ['leɪsˌʌps] NPL scarpe *fpl* con i lacci *or* le stringhe.

lack [læk] ☐ N mancanza, scarsità; **for *or* through lack of** per mancanza *or* scarsità di; **there is no lack of money** i soldi non mancano.

   ☐ VT: **we lack (the) time to do it** ci manca il tempo di *or* per farlo; **he lacks confidence** non è sicuro di sé.

   ☐ VI: **to be lacking in** mancare di; **he is lacking in confidence** non è sicuro di sé; **he lacks for nothing** non gli manca niente.

lacka·dai·si·cal [ˌlækə'deɪzɪkəl] ADJ (*careless*) noncurante; (*lacking enthusiasm*) svogliato(-a).

lacka·dai·si·cal·ly [ˌlækə'deɪzɪkəlɪ] ADV (*see adj*) con noncuranza; svogliatamente.

lack·ey ['lækɪ] N (*also pej*) lacchè *m inv*.

lack·lustre, (*Am*) **lack·luster** ['lækˌlʌstəʳ] ADJ (*performance*) scialbo(-a); (*eyes*) spento(-a).

la·con·ic [lə'kɒnɪk] ADJ laconico(-a).

la·coni·cal·ly [lə'kɒnɪkəlɪ] ADV laconicamente.

lac·quer ['lækəʳ] ☐ N (*for wood, hair*) lacca.

   ☐ VT (*wood*) laccare; (*hair*) mettere la lacca su.

la·crosse [lə'krɒs] N (*sport*) lacrosse *m inv*.

lac·tic ['læktɪk] ADJ lattico(-a).

lac·tose ['læktəʊs] N lattosio.

lacy ['leɪsɪ] ADJ (*comp* -**ier**, *superl* -**iest**) (*made of lace*) di pizzo; (*like lace*) che sembra un pizzo.

lad [læd] N ragazzo, giovanotto; (*Brit: in stable*) mozzo *or* garzone *m* di stalla; **when I was a lad** quand'ero ragazzo *or* giovane; **come on, lads!** forza, *or* dai, ragazzi!; **a drink with the lads** una bevuta con gli amici; **he's a bit of a lad** (*fam*) è uno a cui piace far bisboccia.

lad·der ['lædəʳ] ☐ N scala a pioli; (*stepladder*) scala a libretto; (*Brit: in tights*) smagliatura; **social ladder** scala sociale; **it's the first step up the ladder** è il primo passo sulla via del successo.

   ☐ VT (*Brit: tights*) smagliare.

   ☐ VI (*Brit: tights*) smagliarsi.

lad·der·proof ['lædəˌpruːf] ADJ (*Brit*) indemagliabile.

lad·en ['leɪdn] ADJ: **laden (with)** carico(-a) *or* caricato(-a) (di); **fully laden** (*truck, ship*) a pieno carico.

la-di-da [ˌlɑːdɪ'dɑː] ADJ (*fam: person*) affettato(-a) e pretenzioso(-a); (: *voice*) affettato(-a).

la·dies ['leɪdɪz] NSG, **ladies' room** N (*lavatory*): **the ladies** i gabinetti per signore, la toilette *f inv*; **"Ladies"** "signore"; **where is the Ladies?** dov'è la toilette? (*per signore*).

♦ **ladies' man** N *uomo premuroso con le donne e che si trova bene in loro compagnia*.

la·dle ['leɪdl] ☐ N (*Culin*) mestolo.

   ☐ VT (*soup*) servire con il mestolo

▶ **ladle out** VT + ADV (*soup*) servire con il mestolo; (*fig: advice*) elargire, distribuire; **to ladle out money to sb** dare un sacco di soldi a qn.

lady ['leɪdɪ] N **a** signora; **the lady of the house** la padrona di casa; **young lady** (*married*) signora; (*unmarried*) signorina; **ladies' hairdresser** parrucchiere *m* per signora; **Ladies and Gentlemen!** signore e signori! **b** : **Our Lady** (*Rel*) la Madonna **c** : **Lady Jane Grey** lady Jane Grey.

lady·bird ['leɪdɪˌbɜːd], (*Am*) **lady·bug** ['leɪdɪˌbʌg] N coccinella.

♦ **Lady Day** N Annunciazione *f*.

♦ **lady doctor** N dottoressa.

♦ **lady friend** N (*old, hum*) amica.

♦ **lady-in-waiting** ['leɪdɪɪn'weɪtɪŋ] N dama di corte.

lady·killer ['leɪdɪˌkɪləʳ] N dongiovanni *m inv*, rubacuori *m inv*.

lady·like ['leɪdɪˌlaɪk] ADJ (*person*) ben educato(-a), distinto(-a); (*manners*) da signora, distinto(-a).

♦ **lady mayoress** N (*Brit*) moglie *f* (*or* figlia) del Lord Mayor.

lady·ship ['leɪdɪʃɪp] N: **Her Ladyship the Countess** la signora contessa; **Your Ladyship** signora contessa.

lag[1] [læg] ☐ VI (*also:* **lag behind**) restare indietro; **we lag behind in space exploration** siamo ancora indietro nel campo dell'esplorazione spaziale.

   ☐ N (*also:* **time-lag**) lasso *or* intervallo di tempo; see also **jet lag**.

lag[2] [læg] VT (*boiler, pipes*) rivestire con *or* di materiale isolante.

lag[3] [læg] N (*fam*): **old lag** vecchia conoscenza della polizia.

la·ger ['lɑːgəʳ] N birra chiara, birra bionda.

la·ger lout ['lɑːgəˌlaʊt] N (*Brit fam*) giovinastro ubriaco.

lag·gard ['lægəd] N (*old*) lento (-a) tiratardi *m/f inv*.

lag·ging ['lægɪŋ] N (*Tech*) rivestimento termo-isolante.

la·goon [lə'guːn] N laguna.

La·gos ['leɪgɒs] N Lagos *f*.

lah [lɑː] N (*Mus*) la *m inv*.

lah-di-dah [ˌlɑːdɪ'dɑː] = **la-di-da**.

laid [leɪd] PT, PP of **lay 3**.

♦ **laid-back** [ˌleɪd'bæk] ADJ (*fam*) rilassato(-a).

lain [leɪn] PP of **lie 2**.

lair [lɛəʳ] N (*of animal*) tana, covo; (*of thieves*) covo.

laissez-faire [ˌlɛseɪ'fɛəʳ] ☐ N liberismo.

   ☐ ADJ liberistico(-a).

la·ity ['leɪɪtɪ] COLLECTIVE N: **the laity** (*as opposed to the clergy*) i laici, il laicato; (*as opposed to professionals*) i non appartenenti ad una categoria professionale.

lake [leɪk] N lago.

♦ **Lake District** N: **the Lake District** (*Brit*) la regione dei laghi (nel nord dell'Inghilterra).

lama ['lɑːmə] N (*Rel*) lama *m inv*.

lamb [læm] ☐ N (*animal, meat*) agnello; **my poor lamb!** oh, povero tesoro!; **he took it like a lamb** ha accettato docilmente; **Lamb of God** Agnello di Dio.

   ☐ VI figliare, partorire (*di pecora*).

♦ **lamb chop** N cotoletta d'agnello.

lamb·ing ['læmɪŋ] N agnellatura.

lamb·skin ['læmˌskɪn] N (pelle *fd'*) agnello.

lambs·wool ['læmzˌwʊl] N lambswool *m inv*.

lame [leɪm] ☐ ADJ (*comp* -**r**, *superl* -**st**) zoppo(-a); (*also fig: argument, excuse*) zoppicante; **to be lame** zoppicare, essere zoppo(-a); **to be lame in one foot** esser zoppo da un piede.

   ☐ VT (*person*) rendere zoppo(-a); (*horse*) azzoppare.

lamé ['lɑːmeɪ] N lamé *m inv*.

♦ **lame duck** N (*person*) persona inetta; (*firm*) azienda traballante; **a lame duck president** (*Am*) *presidente uscente*.

lame·ly ['leɪmlɪ] ADV (*fig*) in modo poco convincente.

lame·ness ['leɪmnɪs] N zoppia.

la·ment [lə'mɛnt] ☐ VT lamentare, piangere; **to lament sb** piangere qn.

   ☐ VI: **to lament over sth** lamentarsi di qc; **to lament for sb** affliggersi per qn.

   ☐ N (*poetic*) lamento, elegia.

lam·en·table ['læməntəbl] ADJ (*performance*) penoso(-a); (*disregard, waste*) deplorevole.

lam·en·tably ['læməntəblɪ] ADV deplorevolmente; **we are lamentably short of good staff** purtroppo siamo vera-

mente a corto di personale in gamba.

la·men·ta·tion [ˌlæmənˈteɪʃən] N (frm) lamento; **there was much lamentation over the news that the president had died** la notizia della morte del presidente ha causato profonda afflizione.

lami·na·ted [ˈlæmɪˌneɪtɪd] ADJ (gen) laminato(-a); (card) plastificato(-a).

lamp [læmp] N (for table) lampada; (in street) lampione m; (Aut) faro, luce f; (Rail) lanterna; (bulb) lampadina.

lamp·light [ˈlæmp,laɪt] N: **by lamplight** a lume della lampada.

lam·poon [læmˈpuːn] ①N satira.
②VT fare oggetto di satira, satirreggiare.

lamp·post [ˈlæmp,pəʊst] N lampione m.

lamp·shade [ˈlæmp,ʃeɪd] N paralume m.

lamp·stand [ˈlæmp,stænd] N base f (di lampada).

♦ **lamp standard** N palo della luce.

lance [lɑːns] ①N lancia.
②VT (Med) incidere.

♦ **lance corporal** N (Brit) caporale m.

lanc·er [ˈlɑːnsəʳ] N (Mil) lanciere m.

lan·cet [ˈlɑːnsɪt] N (Med) bisturi m inv.

Lancs [læŋks] N ABBR (Brit)= Lancashire.

land [lænd] ①N **a** terra; (soil, ground) terreno; (estate) terreni mpl, terre fpl; **to go/travel by land** andare/viaggiare per via di terra; **(dry) land** terraferma; **to work on the land** lavorare la terra; **to live off the land** vivere dei prodotti della terra; **to own land** possedere dei terreni, avere delle proprietà (terriere); **to see how the land lies** (fig) tastare il terreno
b (nation, country) paese m; **throughout the land** in tutto il paese; **to be in the land of the living** essere nel mondo dei vivi.
②VT **a** (cargo, goods) scaricare, (far) sbarcare; (passengers) (far) sbarcare; (aircraft) far atterrare; (catch: fish) tirare in secco; (fig: job, contract) accaparrarsi
b (fam: place): **to land a blow on sb** assestare un colpo a qn; **it landed him in jail** gli è costato la galera; **to land sb in trouble** cacciare qn nei guai; **to land sb in debt** far indebitare qn; **I got landed with the job** è toccato a me fare il lavoro; **I got landed with him** mi è toccato restare con lui, me lo sono dovuto sorbire io.
③VI **a** (plane, passenger) atterrare; (from boat, ship) sbarcare
b (after fall, jump) atterrare; (fig: fall) cadere; **to land on** (bird) posarsi su; **to land on one's feet** (to be lucky) cadere in piedi; **the hat landed in my lap** il cappello è finito sulle mie ginocchia; **the bomb landed on the building** la bomba è caduta sul palazzo; **the first man to land on the moon** il primo uomo a mettere piede sulla luna

▶ **land up** VI + ADV (fig fam) andare a finire.

lan·dau [ˈlændɔ:] N landò m inv.

♦ **land defences** NPL difese fpl terrestri.

land·ed [ˈlændɪd] ADJ (estate) terriero(-a).

♦ **landed gentry** N proprietari mpl terrieri.

land·fall [ˈlænd,fɔ:l] N: **to make landfall** approdare, toccare terra.

land·fill site [ˈlændfɪl,saɪt] N discarica pubblica (in cui i rifiuti vengono interrati).

♦ **land forces** NPL (Mil) forze fpl terrestri.

land·ing [ˈlændɪŋ] N **a** (of aircraft) atterraggio; (of troops) sbarco **b** (in house) pianerottolo.

♦ **landing card** N carta di sbarco.

♦ **landing craft** N mezzo da sbarco.

♦ **landing fees** NPL (Aer) diritti mpl d'atterraggio.

♦ **landing gear** N (Aer) carrello d'atterraggio.

♦ **landing net** N (Fishing) retino (da pesca).

♦ **landing party** N (Naut) reparto da sbarco.

♦ **landing stage** N pontile m da sbarco.

♦ **landing strip** N pista d'atterraggio.

land·lady [ˈlænd,leɪdɪ] N (of flat, house) padrona di casa; (of pub) proprietaria.

land·locked [ˈlænd,lɒkt] ADJ senza sbocco sul mare.

land·lord [ˈlænd,lɔ:d] N (landowner) proprietario (di beni immobili); (of flat) padrone m di casa; (of pub) proprietario.

land·lub·ber [ˈlænd,lʌbəʳ] N (fam) marinaio d'acqua dolce.

land·mark [ˈlænd,mɑːk] N punto di riferimento; (event) pietra miliare; **a landmark in history** una pietra miliare nella storia.

♦ **land mass** N continente m.

land·mine [ˈlænd,maɪn] N mina terrestre.

land·owner [ˈlænd,əʊnəʳ] N proprietario(-a) terriero(-a).

♦ **land reform** N riforma fondiaria.

Land·rover® [ˈlænd,rəʊvəʳ] N Land Rover ® f inv.

land·scape [ˈlænd,skeɪp] ①N paesaggio.
②VT abbellire con criteri architettonici.

♦ **landscape architect** N architetto del paesaggio.

♦ **landscape architecture** N architettura del paesaggio.

♦ **landscape gardener** N architetto dei giardini, paesaggista m/f.

♦ **landscape gardening** N architettura dei giardini.

♦ **landscape painter** N (Art) paesaggista m/f, paesista m/f.

♦ **landscape painting** N (Art) paesaggistica.

land·scap·ing [ˈlænd,skeɪpɪŋ] N architettura del paesaggio.

land·slide [ˈlænd,slaɪd] N (Geol) frana; (fig: Pol) valanga di voti, maggioranza schiacciante.

♦ **landslide victory** N (Pol) vittoria schiacciante.

land·slip [ˈlænd,slɪp] N smottamento.

♦ **land tax** N tassa or imposta fondiaria.

lane [leɪn] N (in country) stradina, viottolo; (in town) stradina, viuzza; (Sport, Aut) corsia; **"keep in lane"** (Aut) "divieto di sorpasso"; **"get into lane"** (Aut) "immettersi in corsia"; **I'm in the wrong lane** (Aut) sono sulla corsia sbagliata; **a 3-lane motorway** un'autostrada a 3 corsie.

lang·lauf [ˈlɑː,laʊf] N (Skiing) sci m di fondo.

lan·guage [ˈlæŋgwɪdʒ] N (faculty, style of speech) linguaggio; (national tongue, also fig) lingua; **the Italian language** la lingua italiana; **legal/scientific language** linguaggio legale/scientifico; **we don't speak the same language** (fig) non parliamo la stessa lingua; **to use bad language** dire parolacce, usare un linguaggio volgare; **watch your language!** attento a come parli!

♦ **language degree** N laurea in lingue.

♦ **language laboratory** N laboratorio linguistico.

♦ **language studies** NPL studi mpl linguistici.

lan·guid [ˈlæŋgwɪd] ADJ (liter: graceful, affected) languido (-a); (: indolent) fiacco(-a).

lan·guid·ly [ˈlæŋgwɪdlɪ] ADV (liter) languidamente.

lan·guish [ˈlæŋgwɪʃ] VI: **to languish for love/over sb/in prison** languire d'amore/per qn/in prigione.

lan·guish·ing [ˈlæŋgwɪʃɪŋ] ADJ languido(-a).

lan·guor [ˈlæŋgəʳ] N (liter) languore m.

lan·guor·ous [ˈlæŋgərəs] ADJ (liter) languido(-a).

lank [læŋk] ADJ (hair) diritto(-a) e opaco(-a).

lanky ['læŋkɪ] ADJ (*comp* **-ier**, *superl* **-iest**) (*person*) allampanato(-a).

lano·lin, **lano·line** ['lænəlɪn] N lanolina.

lan·tern ['læntən] N lanterna.

♦ **lantern-jawed** ['læntən,dʒɔːd] ADJ con il volto affilato e incavato.

Laocoon [leɪ'ɒkəʊ,ɒn] N Laocoonte.

Laos [laʊs] N Laos *m*.

Lao·tian ['laʊʃɪən] ADJ, N laotiano(-a).

lap[1] [læp] N (*Anat*) grembo, ginocchia *fpl*; **to sit in** *or* **on sb's lap** sedersi in grembo a *or* sulle ginocchia di qn; **to live in the lap of luxury** vivere nel lusso; **in the lap of the gods** (*fig*) nelle mani di Dio

▶ **lap up** VT + ADV (*milk*: *cat*) leccare; (: *dog*) lappare; (*fig*: *compliments*, *attention*) bearsi di.

lap[2] [læp] N (*Sport*) giro; **to run a lap** fare un giro della pista; **we're on the last lap now** (*fig*) siamo quasi arrivati al traguardo.

lap[3] [læp] ① VT = **lap up**.

    ② VI (*waves*) sciabordare; **to lap against** lambire.

La Paz [læ'pæz] N La Paz *f*.

lap·dog ['læp,dɒg] N cagnolino da salotto; (*fig*: *person*) cagnolino.

la·pel [lə'pɛl] N risvolto.

lap·is lazu·li ['læpɪs 'læzjʊlaɪ] N lapislazzuli *m inv*.

Lap·land ['læp,lænd] N Lapponia.

Lap·land·er ['læp,lændə'] N lappone *m/f*.

♦ **lap of honour** N giro d'onore.

Lapp [læp] ① ADJ lappone.

    ② N (*person*) lappone *m/f*; (*language*) lappone *m*.

Lapp·ish ['læpɪʃ] ① ADJ Lappone.

    ② N (*language*) lappone *m*.

lapse [læps] ① N **a** (*fault*) mancanza; (*in behaviour*) scorrettezza; **a lapse (of memory)** un vuoto (di memoria); **a lapse into bad habits** un ritorno alle cattive abitudini

    b (*of time*) intervallo.

    ② VI **a** (*err*) sgarrare; **to lapse in one's duty** mancare al proprio dovere

    b (*fall slowly*): **to lapse into bad habits** prendere cattive abitudini; **to lapse into one's old ways** ritornare a poco a poco alle vecchie abitudini; **to let one's attention lapse** distrarsi; **to lapse into silence** tacere; **she lapsed into unconsciousness** scivolò in uno stato di incoscienza

    c (*law*, *act*) cadere, andare in prescrizione; (*membership*, *passport*, *ticket*) scadere.

lapsed [læpst] ADJ (*contract*, *law*, *passport*) scaduto(-a); **lapsed Catholic** cattolico(-a) non praticante.

lap·top ['læp,tɒp] N (*also*: **laptop computer**) laptop *m inv*.

lap·wing ['læp,wɪŋ] N pavoncella.

lar·ceny ['lɑːsənɪ] N (*Law*) furto.

larch [lɑːtʃ] N larice *m*.

lard [lɑːd] ① N strutto.

    ② VT (*speech*, *writing*): **to lard with** infarcire di.

lar·der ['lɑːdə'] N dispensa.

large [lɑːdʒ] ① ADJ (*comp* **-r**, *superl* **-st**) (*gen*) grande; (*item of clothing*) di taglia grande; (*garden*, *room*) grande, ampio(-a); (*person*) grande e grosso(-a); (*animal*) grosso(-a); (*sum*, *loss*) grosso(-a), ingente; (*family*, *population*) numeroso(-a); (*meal*) lauto(-a); **a large number of people** molta gente; **we had a large meal** abbiamo mangiato tanto; **on a large scale** su vasta scala; **as large as life** in carne e ossa; **larger than life** portato(-a) all'estremo; **to grow large(r)** ingrandirsi; **to make large (r)** ingrandire.

    ② N: **at large** (*criminal*, *dangerous animal*) in libertà; (*generally*) in generale, nell'insieme; **the world at large** il mondo nel complesso.

    ③ ADV: **by and large** generalmente.

large·ly ['lɑːdʒlɪ] ADV in gran parte, per la maggior parte.

large·ness ['lɑːdʒnɪs] N grandezza.

♦ **large-scale** ['lɑːdʒ'skeɪl] ADJ (*map*, *drawing*) a grande scala; (*reforms*, *business activities*) su vasta *or* larga scala.

♦ **large-size** ['lɑːdʒ'saɪz], **large-sized** [,lɑːdʒ'saɪzd] ADJ grande.

lar·gesse, **lar·gess** [lɑː'dʒɛs] N (*frm*) generosità.

lark[1] [lɑːk] N (*bird*) allodola.

lark[2] [lɑːk] N (*Brit fam*: *joke*) scherzo, gioco; **for a lark** per scherzo; **what a lark!** che spasso!

▶ **lark about**, **lark around** VI + ADV: **to lark about (with)** (*Brit fam*) divertirsi (con).

lark·spur ['lɑːk,spɜː'] N delfinio.

lar·va ['lɑːvə] N (*pl* **larvae** ['lɑːviː]) larva.

lar·val ['lɑːvəl] ADJ larvale.

lar·yn·gi·tis [,lærɪn'dʒaɪtɪs] N laringite *f*.

lar·ynx ['lærɪŋks] N (*Anat*) laringe *f*.

la·sa·gne [lə'zænjə] N lasagne *fpl*.

las·civi·ous [lə'sɪvɪəs] ADJ lascivo(-a).

las·civi·ous·ly [lə'sɪvɪəslɪ] ADV lascivamente.

la·ser ['leɪzə'] N laser *m inv*.

♦ **laser beam** N raggio *m* laser *inv*.

♦ **laser printer** N stampante *f* laser *inv*.

lash [læʃ] ① N **a** (*also*: **eye lash**) ciglio

    b (*thong*) laccio (di cuoio); (*stroke*) frustata, colpo di frusta; (*of tail*) colpo.

    ② VT **a** (*beat etc*) frustare; (*subj*: *rain*, *waves*: *also*: **lash against**) picchiare (contro), sbattere (contro); **the wind lashed the sea into a fury** il vento ha trasformato il mare in una furia

    b (*esp Naut*: *tie*) legare.

▶ **lash down** ① VT + ADV assicurare (con corde).

    ② VI + ADV (*rain*) scrosciare

▶ **lash out** VI + ADV **a** : **to lash out (at** *or* **against sb/sth)** menare colpi (contro qn/a qc); (*fig*) attaccare violentemente (qn/qc), inveire (contro qn/qc)

    b (*fam*): **to lash out (on sth)** (*spend*) spendere un sacco di soldi (per qc).

lash·ing ['læʃɪŋ] N **a** (*beating*) frustata, sferzata **b** : **lashings of** (*Brit fam*) un mucchio di, una montagna di.

lass [læs] N (*esp in Northern Britain*) ragazza.

las·si·tude ['læsɪtjuːd] N (*frm*) apatia.

las·so [læ'suː] ① N lazo *m inv*, laccio.

    ② VT prendere al lazo *or* al laccio.

last[1] [lɑːst] ① ADJ **a** (*most recent*) ultimo(-a); (*week*, *month*, *year*) scorso(-a), passato(-a); **last Monday** lunedì scorso; **last night** ieri sera *or* notte, la notte scorsa; **during (the) last week** nel corso della settimana scorsa; **during the last 2 years** negli ultimi 2 anni; **the night before last** l'altro ieri sera *or* notte; **(the) last time** l'ultima volta

    b (*final*: *in series*) ultimo(-a); **the last page** l'ultima pagina; **the last slice of cake** l'ultima fetta di torta; **last thing at night** prima di andare a letto; **that was the last thing I expected** era l'ultima cosa che mi sarei aspettato; **you're the last person I'd trust with it** sei l'ultima persona al mondo di cui mi fiderei per questo; **last but one** OR **second last** penultimo(-a).

    ② N: **the last of the wine/bread** quello che resta del vino/del pane; **they were the last to arrive** erano gli ultimi arrivati, sono arrivati per ultimi; **the last in the**

series l'ultimo della serie; **each one better than the last** uno meglio dell'altro; **I shall be glad to see the last of this** sarò contento di vederne la fine; **we'll never hear the last of it** chissà per quanto ne sentiremo parlare; **at (long) last** finalmente; **to the last** fino all'ultimo.

3 ADV (per) ultimo; **to do/come/arrive last (of all)** fare come/venire per/arrivare ultimo(-a); **last but not least** ... come ultimo, ma non per questo meno importante...; **when I last saw them** *or* **saw them last** l'ultima volta che li ho visti.

last² [lɑːst] **1** VI (*rain, film, pain*) durare; (*also:* **last out:** *person*) resistere; (: *money, resources*) durare, bastare; **it lasts (for) 2 hours** dura 2 ore; **this material will last (for) years** questa stoffa durerà degli anni; **he didn't last long in the job** non ha resistito a lungo in quell'impiego; **it's too good to last** OR **it can't last** è troppo bello per durare.

2 VT durare; **he won't last the winter** non sopravviverà all'inverno; **it will last you a lifetime** ti durerà una vita.

♦ **last-ditch** [ˈlɑːstˌdɪtʃ] ADJ (*attempt*) ultimo(-a) e disperato(-a).

last·ing [ˈlɑːstɪŋ] ADJ duraturo(-a), durevole; **to his lasting shame** con sua profonda vergogna.

♦ **Last Judgement, Last Judgment** N: **the Last Judgement** il Giudizio Universale.

last·ly [ˈlɑːstlɪ] ADV infine, per finire, per ultimo.

♦ **last-minute** [ˈlɑːstˌmɪnɪt] ADJ (*decision*) dell'ultimo momento; (*preparation*) fatto(-a) all'ultimo momento.

♦ **last post** N (*Mil*): **the last post** il silenzio.

latch [lætʃ] N (*metal bar*) chiavistello; (*lock*) serratura a scatto; **the door is on the latch** la porta non è chiusa a chiave

▶ **latch on to** VI + ADV + PREP **a** (*cling to: person*) attaccarsi a, appiccicarsi a **b** (*idea*) afferrare, capire.

latch·key [ˈlætʃˌkiː] N chiave ƒ di casa.

♦ **latchkey child** N *bambino i cui genitori lavorano e che perciò ha le chiavi per rientrare a casa.*

late [leɪt] (*comp* **-r**, *superl* **-st**) **1** ADJ **a** (*not on time*) in ritardo; **to be (10 minutes) late** essere in ritardo (di 10 minuti); **to be late arriving** arrivare tardi *or* in ritardo; **to make sb late** far far tardi a qn; **to be late with one's work** essere in ritardo con il proprio lavoro; **the late arrival of the flight** il ritardo del volo; **late delivery** consegna ritardata

b (*towards end of period*) tardivo(-a); (*far on in day etc*) tardo(-a); (*composition, concerto*) ultimo(-a); **to be/be getting late** essere/farsi tardi; **to keep late hours** stare alzato(-a) fino a tardi, fare le ore piccole; **at this late hour** a un'ora così tarda, a quest'ora; **at this late stage** al punto in cui stanno ormai le cose; **in (the) late spring** nella tarda primavera, a fine primavera; **she's in her late sixties** è vicina ai settanta

c (*recent*) recente; **his late remarks on industry** le sue recenti osservazioni sull'industria

d (*euph: dead*) defunto(-a); **the late Mrs Smith** la defunta signora Smith; **my late-lamented husband** il mio povero marito

e (*former*) ex *inv*; **our late prime minister** il nostro ex primo ministro.

2 ADV **a** (*not on time*) in ritardo, tardi; **to arrive/leave 10 minutes late** arrivare/partire con 10 minuti di ritardo; **to arrive/leave too late** arrivare/partire troppo tardi; **better late than never** meglio tardi che mai

b (*towards end of period*) tardi; **to work late** lavorare fino a tardi; **late at night** a tarda notte; **late into the night** fino

a tarda notte, fino a notte fonda; **in the late afternoon** nel tardo pomeriggio; **in late May** verso la fine di maggio; **late in life** in età avanzata; **late in 1978** verso la fine del 1978

c (*recently*): **as late as 1991** ancora nel 1991; **of late** negli ultimi tempi, di recente, recentemente.

late·comer [ˈleɪtˌkʌməʳ] N ritardatario(-a).

late·ly [ˈleɪtlɪ] ADV ultimamente, di recente, recentemente; **till lately** fino a poco *or* non molto tempo fa.

late·ness [ˈleɪtnɪs] N (*of person, vehicle*) ritardo; (*of event*) ora tarda.

♦ **late-night** [ˈleɪtˈnaɪt] ADJ: **a late-night movie** l'ultimo spettacolo; **late-night shopping is on Thursdays** i negozi chiudono più tardi del solito il giovedì.

la·tent [ˈleɪtənt] ADJ latente.

lat·er [ˈleɪtəʳ] **1** ADV (*comp* of **late**) **a** (*not on time*) più tardi **b** (*after*) dopo, più tardi; **a few years later** pochi anni dopo *or* più tardi

c : **later on** (*in series of events*) più avanti; (*in time*) più tardi; **later on today** più tardi.

2 ADJ (*comp* of **late**) (*meeting, train*) successivo(-a); (*edition, version*) più recente, successivo(-a); (*date etc*) posteriore; **he was later than usual** è arrivato più tardi del solito; **Easter is later this year** Pasqua cade più tardi quest'anno; **at a later stage** *or* **date** in un secondo momento; **his later symphonies** le sue ultime sinfonie; **this version is later than that one** questa versione è posteriore a *or* più recente di quella.

lat·er·al [ˈlætərəl] ADJ laterale.

♦ **lateral thinking** N pensiero laterale.

lat·est [ˈleɪtɪst] **1** ADJ (*superl* of **late**) (*gen*) ultimo(-a), più recente; **her latest exhibition** la sua ultima mostra; **the latest news** le ultime notizie.

2 N **a** (*fam: most recent*) ultima novità; **the latest in skin care** l'ultima novità nel campo della cosmesi; **have you heard the latest?** (*news*) hai sentito l'ultima?

b : **at the latest** al più tardi; **it'll arrive tomorrow at the latest** arriverà al più tardi domani.

la·tex [ˈleɪtɛks] N latice *m*.

lath [lɑːθ] N (*pl* **laths**) listello, assicella.

lathe [leɪð] N tornio.

lath·er [ˈlɑːðəʳ] **1** N (*soap*) schiuma (di sapone); **in a lather of sweat** tutto(-a) sudato(-a); **the horse was in a lather** il cavallo era coperto di sudore; **in a lather** (*fig*) tutto affannato(-a) *or* scalmanato(-a).

2 VT (*one's face*) insaponarsi, insaponare.

3 VI (*soap*) far schiuma.

Lat·in [ˈlætɪn] **1** ADJ (*language, temperament*) latino(-a); (*textbook, scholar, lessons*) di latino.

2 N (*language*) latino.

♦ **Latin America** [ˈlætɪnəˈmɛrɪkə] N America Latina.

♦ **Latin American** [ˈlætɪnəˈmɛrɪkən] **1** ADJ dell'America Latina, latino-americano(-a).

2 N latino-americano(-a).

lati·tude [ˈlætɪtjuːd] N **a** (*Geog*) latitudine ƒ **b** (*fig: freedom*) libertà d'azione.

la·trine [ləˈtriːn] N latrina.

lat·ter [ˈlætəʳ] **1** N: **the latter** quest'ultimo(-a); **of the two, the latter is better** fra i due è meglio il secondo.

2 ADJ **a** (*later*) ultimo(-a); **the latter years of his life** gli ultimi anni della sua vita **b** (*of two*): **the latter part of the story** la seconda *or* l'ultima parte della storia.

♦ **latter-day** [ˈlætəˌdeɪ] ADJ moderno(-a), del giorno d'oggi.

lat·ter·ly [ˈlætəlɪ] ADV negli ultimi tempi.

lat·tice ['lætɪs] N (gen) reticolato; (for plants) graticcio, traliccio; (Chem) reticolo cristallino.
♦ **lattice window** N finestra con vetrata a losanghe.
♦ **lattice work** N graticcio.
Lat·via ['lætvɪə] N Lettonia.
Lat·vian ['lætvɪən] ① ADJ lettone.
　② N (person) lettone m/f; (language) lettone m.
laud·able ['lɔːdəbl] ADJ (frm) lodevole, degno(-a) di lode.
lau·da·num ['lɔːdənəm] N laudano.
lauda·tory ['lɔːdətərɪ] ADJ (frm) elogiativo(-a).
laugh [lɑːf] ① VI ridere; **to laugh** or **about sth** ridere di or per qc; **we all laughed about it later** più tardi ci abbiamo riso sopra; **it's nothing to laugh about** non c'è niente da ridere; **to laugh to o.s.** ridere dentro di sé or fra sé e sé; **I laughed till I cried** ho riso fino alle lacrime; **to laugh in sb's face** ridere in faccia a qn; **then we'll be laughing** (fig) poi saremo tranquilli; **to laugh up one's sleeve** ridere sotto i baffi.
　② VT: **to laugh sb/sth out of court** ridicolizzare qn/qc; **they tried to laugh me out of my fears** hanno cercato di farmi passare la paura ridendo; **to laugh sb to scorn** deridere qn.
　③ N risata; **to get** or **raise a laugh (from sb)** far ridere (qn); **to have a good laugh at sth** farsi una bella risata su or sopra qc; **do you want a laugh?** vuoi farti due risate?; **to do sth for a laugh** (fam) fare qc per scherzo or per ridere; **what a laugh!** che ridere!; (iro) che ridicolo!; **good for a laugh** divertente; **he's always good for a laugh** ci fa sempre fare due risate; **we'll see who has the last laugh** (fig) staremo a vedere chi l'avrà vinta
　▶ **laugh at** VI + PREP (person, sb's behaviour, also fig) ridere di; **I laughed at his joke** la sua barzelletta mi fece ridere
　▶ **laugh off** VT + ADV (pain, accusation) ridere sopra, prendere alla leggera; **to laugh one's head off** (fam) sbellicarsi dalle risate.
laugh·able ['lɑːfəbl] ADJ ridicolo(-a).
laugh·ing ['lɑːfɪŋ] ADJ (face) ridente; **this is no laughing matter** non è una cosa da ridere.
♦ **laughing gas** N gas m esilarante.
laugh·ing·ly ['lɑːfɪŋlɪ] ADV ridendo allegramente; **it is laughingly called ...** viene scherzosamente chiamato.... .
♦ **laughing stock** N zimbello; **to make a laughing stock of o.s.** rendersi ridicolo(-a).
laugh·ter ['lɑːftəʳ] N risata; (laughing) riso; **he roared with laughter** si è fatto una fragorosa risata.
launch [lɔːntʃ] ① VT (gen, also fig) lanciare; (ship, plan) varare; (shore lifeboat) far uscire; (ship's boat) calare (in mare).
　② N **a** (of rocket, product) lancio; (of boat) varo **b** (also: motor launch) motolancia; (pleasure boat) battello
　▶ **launch into** VI + ADV (speech, task) lanciarsi (in)
　▶ **launch out** VI + ADV: **to launch out (into)** lanciarsi (in).
launch·er ['lɔːntʃəʳ] N (Aer) lanciamissili m inv.
launch·ing ['lɔːntʃɪŋ] N lancio; (of ship) varo; (of shore lifeboat) uscita; (of ship's boat) calo, calata (in mare).
♦ **launching pad, launch pad** N rampa di lancio.
laun·der ['lɔːndəʳ] VT lavare e stirare; (fig: money) riciclare.
laun·der·ette, laun·drette [ˌlɔːndəˈrɛt], (Am) **laun·dro·mat** ['lɔːndrəˌmæt] N lavanderia (automatica).
laun·dry ['lɔːndrɪ] N (establishment) lavanderia; (clothes) bucato, biancheria; **to do the laundry** fare il bucato, lavare la biancheria.
♦ **laundry bag** N sacca portabiancheria.
lau·reate ['lɔːrɪɪt] N: **Nobel laureate in Physics** insignito (-a) del Nobel per la fisica; see also **poet laureate.**

lau·rel ['lɒrəl] N alloro, lauro; **to rest on one's laurels** riposare or dormire sugli allori.
Lau·sanne [ləʊ'zæn] N Losanna.
lava ['lɑːvə] N lava.
♦ **lava flow** N effusione ƒ lavica.
♦ **lava plateau** N altopiano basaltico.
lava·tory ['lævətrɪ] N (Brit: room) gabinetto, toilette ƒ inv; (: appliance) water m inv, gabinetto.
♦ **lavatory brush** N (Brit) scopino del gabinetto.
♦ **lavatory paper** N (Brit) carta igienica.
♦ **lavatory seat** N (Brit) sedile m del gabinetto.
lav·en·der ['lævɪndəʳ] N lavanda.
♦ **lavender bag** N sacchettino di lavanda.
♦ **lavender water** N (acqua di) lavanda.
lav·ish ['lævɪʃ] ① ADJ (person) prodigo(-a); (meal) lauto (-a); (surroundings, apartment) sontuoso(-a), lussuoso (-a); (expenditure) considerevole; (: excessive) eccessivo (-a); **to be lavish with one's gifts** non badare a spese in fatto di regali; **to bestow lavish praise on sb** coprire qn di elogi or lodi.
　② VT: **to lavish sth on sb/on sth** colmare qn/qc di qc.
lav·ish·ly ['lævɪʃlɪ] ADV (give, spend) generosamente; (furnished) sontuosamente, lussuosamente.
lav·ish·ness ['lævɪʃnɪs] N (of person) prodigalità; (of meal) abbondanza; (of surroundings, apartment) sontuosità, lusso.
law [lɔː] N legge ƒ; **law of gravity** legge di gravità; **law of constant energy** legge della conservazione dell'energia; **against the law** contro la legge; **by law** a norma di or per legge; **by British law** secondo la legge britannica; **civil/criminal law** diritto civile/penale; **to study law** studiare giurisprudenza or legge; **Faculty of Law** facoltà di giurisprudenza; **court of law** corte ƒ di giustizia, tribunale m; **to go to law** ricorrere alle vie legali; **to have the law on one's side** avere la legge dalla propria (parte); **to be above the law** essere al di sopra della legge; **to be a law unto o.s.** non conoscere altra legge che la propria; **there's no law against it** nessuna legge lo vieta or impedisce; **to take the law into one's own hands** farsi giustizia da sé; **his word is law** la sua parola è legge.
♦ **law-abiding** ['lɔːəˌbaɪdɪŋ] ADJ rispettoso(-a) delle leggi.
♦ **law and order** N l'ordine m pubblico.
law·breaker ['lɔːˌbreɪkəʳ] N persona che viola la legge.
♦ **law court** N (aula del) tribunale m, corte ƒ di giustizia.
♦ **law-enforcement** [lɔːɪn'fɔːsmənt] N (Am): **law-enforcement agency/official** organismo/funzionario preposto al controllo della corretta appplicazione delle leggi.
law·ful ['lɔːfʊl] ADJ legale.
law·ful·ly ['lɔːfəlɪ] ADV legalmente.
law·giver ['lɔːˌgɪvəʳ], **law·maker** ['lɔːˌmeɪkəʳ] N legislatore m.
law·less ['lɔːlɪs] ADJ (time, place) privo(-a) di legge; (action) illegale.
♦ **Law Lords** NPL (Brit Pol) ≈ Corte ƒ Suprema.
lawn[1] [lɔːn] N prato all'inglese.
lawn[2] [lɔːn] N (fabric) batista.
lawn·mower, lawn mower ['lɔːnˌməʊəʳ] N tagliaerba m inv, tosaerba m inv.
♦ **lawn tennis** N tennis m sull'erba.
♦ **law school** N (Am) facoltà ƒ inv di giurisprudenza or legge.
♦ **law student** N studente(-essa) di giurisprudenza or legge.
law·suit ['lɔːˌsuːt] N causa, processo; **to bring a lawsuit against** intentare causa a.

law·yer ['lɔːjəʳ] N (*in court*) avvocato(-essa); (*consultant*) legale *m/f*; (*for sales, wills*) notaio; **I have put the matter in the hands of my lawyer** ho affidato la questione al mio avvocato.

lax [læks] ADJ (*comp* -**er**, *superl* -**est**) (*conduct*) lassista; (*person: careless*) negligente; (: *on discipline*) permissivo (-a); **to be lax about punctuality** non tenere *or* badare alla puntualità.

laxa·tive ['læksətɪv] N lassativo.

lax·ity ['læksɪtɪ], **lax·ness** ['læksnɪs] N (*see adj*) lassismo; negligenza; permissività.

lay[1] [leɪ] ADJ (*Rel*) laico(-a), secolare; (: *brother, sister*) laico(-a); (*fig: non-specialist*) profano(-a).

lay[2] [leɪ] PT of **lie**[2].

lay[3] [leɪ] (*pt, pp* **laid**) [1] VT **a** (*put, set*) mettere, posare; (*carpet*) stendere; (*bricks*) posare; (*cable, pipe*) installare, fare la posa di; (*trail*) lasciare; (*subj: bird: egg*) deporre, fare; **to lay sth over sth** stendere qc su qc; **to lay sth on sth** coprire qc con qc; **to lay the facts/one's proposals before sb** presentare i fatti/delle proposte a qn; **to be laid low with flu** essere costretto(-a) a letto con l'influenza; **to be laid to rest** (*euph: buried*) essere sepolto(-a); **to get laid** (*fam!*) scopare (*fam!*); **I don't know where to lay my hands on it** non saprei dove trovarlo; **to lay o.s. open to attack/criticism** esporsi agli attacchi/alle critiche; **to lay the blame (for sth) on sb** dar la colpa (di qc) a qn; **to lay claim to sth** reclamare qc, accampare diritti *mpl* su qc; **to lay odds** *or* **a bet on sth** scommettere su qc

b (*prepare: fire*) preparare; (: *trap, snare*) tendere; (: *mine*) posare, piantare; (: *table*) apparecchiare

c (*settle: ghost*) placare, esorcizzare; (: *doubts, fears*) eliminare, dissipare.

[2] VI (*bird*) fare le uova, deporre le uova

► **lay alongside** VI + ADV (*Naut*) affiancarsi
► **lay aside** VT + ADV mettere da parte
► **lay by** VT + ADV mettere da parte
► **lay down** VT + ADV **a** (*put down: luggage*) posare, metter giù; (: *arms*) deporre, posare; (: *wine*) mettere in cantina; **to lay down one's life for sb/sth** sacrificare la propria vita per qn/qc

b (*dictate: conditions*) stabilire, fissare; (: *principle, rule, policy*) formulare, fissare; **to lay down the law** (*fig*) dettar legge

► **lay in** VT + ADV fare una scorta di
► **lay into** VI + PREP (*fam: attack, scold*) aggredire
► **lay off** [1] VT + ADV (*permanently*) licenziare; (*temporarily*) ≈ mettere in cassa integrazione.

[2] VI + ADV (*fam*) smettere.

[3] VI + PREP (*fam*): **lay off it!** piantala!; **lay off him!** non rompergli le scatole!, lascialo in pace!

► **lay on** VT + ADV (*provide: water, electricity, gas*) installare, mettere; (: *meal etc*) fornire; (*paint*) applicare; **to lay on (for)** (*meal, entertainment*) offrire (a); (*facilities, transport*) mettere a disposizione (di); **to lay it on thick** (*fam: flatter*) andarci pesante con i complimenti; (: *exaggerate*) metterla giù dura

► **lay out** VT + ADV **a** (*plan: garden, house, town*) pianificare, progettare; (: *page, letter*) impostare; **the way the house is laid out** la disposizione della casa

b (*put ready: clothes*) preparare; (*display: goods for sale*) sistemare, disporre, presentare; (*make ready: body for burial*) preparare, comporre

c (*spend*) sborsare

d (*knock out*) stendere

► **lay over** VI + ADV (*Am*) fermarsi, far tappa
► **lay up** VT + ADV

a (*store: provisions*) far scorta *or* provvista di, accumulare; **to lay up trouble for o.s** crearsi dei guai

b (*put out of service: boat*) mettere in disarmo, ritirare in cantiere; (*subj: illness*) costringere a letto; **to be laid up with flu** essere costretto(-a) a letto con l'influenza.

lay·about ['leɪəˌbaʊt] N (*fam*) sfaccendato(-a), fannullone(-a).

♦ **lay-by** ['leɪˌbaɪ] N (*Brit Aut*) piazzola (di sosta).

lay·er ['leɪəʳ] N strato.

lay·ered ['leɪəd] ADJ (*rocks*) stratificato(-a); (*potatoes, mushrooms*) a strati.

lay·ette [leɪ'ɛt] N corredino (per neonato).

lay·man ['leɪmən] N (*pl* -**men**) (*Rel*) laico; (*fig: non-professional*) profano.

♦ **lay-off** ['leɪˌɒf] N (*permanent*) licenziamento; (*temporary*) ≈ messa in cassa integrazione.

lay·out ['leɪˌaʊt] N (*of town*) piano urbanistico; (*of house, garden*) disposizione *f*; (*Typing*) impostazione *f*; (*Press*) impaginazione *f*.

lay·over ['leɪˌəʊvəʳ] N (*Am*) sosta.

Lazarus ['læzərəs] N Lazzaro.

laze [leɪz] VI (*also:* **laze around** *or* **about**) oziare.

la·zi·ly ['leɪzɪlɪ] ADV pigramente.

la·zi·ness ['leɪzɪnɪs] N pigrizia.

lazy ['leɪzɪ] ADJ (*comp* -**ier**, *superl* -**iest**) pigro(-a).

lazy·bones ['leɪzɪˌbəʊnz] N (*fam*) poltrone(-a).

lb. ABBR (= *libra: pound*) lb.

lbw [ˌɛlbiːˈdʌbəljuː] N ABBR (*Cricket*: = *leg before wicket*) *fallo dovuto al fatto che il giocatore ha la gamba davanti alla porta.*

LC [ˌɛlˈsiː] N ABBR (*Am*)= *Library of Congress*.

lc ABBR (*Typ*) = **lower-case.**

L/C, l/c ABBR = **letter of credit.**

LCD [ˌɛlsiːˈdiː] N ABBR = **liquid crystal display.**

Ld ABBR (*Brit*: = *lord*) *titolo.*

LDS [ˌɛldiːˈɛs] N ABBR (= *Licentiate in Dental Surgery*) specializzato(-a) in odontoiatria.

LEA [ˌɛliːˈeɪ] N ABBR (*Brit*: = *Local Education Authority*) ≈ Provveditorato agli Studi.

lead[1] [liːd] (*vb: pt, pp* **led**) [1] VT **a** (*conduct*) condurre; **to lead the way** fare strada; **to lead astray** sviare; **he is easily led** si lascia facilmente convincere *or* influenzare

b (*be the leader of: government*) essere a capo di; (: *party*) essere alla guida *or* a capo di; (: *expedition, movement*) guidare; (: *revolution*) capeggiare; (: *team*) capitanare; (: *league, procession*) essere in testa a; (: *orchestra: Brit*) essere il primo violino di; (: *Am*) dirigere; **to lead the field** essere in testa; (*fig*) essere all'avanguardia nel campo

c (*life, existence*) condurre

d (*induce*) indurre, portare; **to lead sb to do sth** portare qn a fare qc; **to lead sb to believe that …** far credere a qn che…; **it led me to the conclusion that …** mi ha portato alla conclusione che….

[2] VI **a** (*go in front*) andare avanti; (*Cards*) essere di mano

b (*in match, race*) essere in testa; **to lead by 3 goals** avere 3 gol di vantaggio

c (*street, corridor*) portare; **where does this door lead?** cosa c'è oltre questa porta?

d (*result in*): **to lead to** portare a; **one thing led to another …** una cosa tira l'altra….

[3] N **a** (*front position*) posizione *f* di testa; (*distance, time*

ahead) vantaggio; **to be in the lead** (*Sport*) essere in testa; (*fig*) essere all'avanguardia; **to be in the lead by 5 points to 4** condurre *or* essere in testa per 5 a 4; **to take the lead** (*Sport*) passare in testa; (*fig*) prendere l'iniziativa; **to have a 3-second lead** avere un vantaggio di 3 secondi; **to follow sb's lead** seguire l'esempio di qn; **it's your lead** (*Cards*) sei tu di mano

  b (*Elec*) filo (elettrico)

  c (*for dog*) guinzaglio

  d (*clue*) indizio, pista

  e (*Theatre*) parte *f or* ruolo principale; **male/female lead** protagonista *m/f* maschile/femminile

► **lead away** VT + ADV condurre via, portar via

► **lead back** VT + ADV riportare, ricondurre

► **lead off** [1] VT + ADV **a** portare; **he led us off on a visit of the museum** ci ha portato a visitare il museo **b** (*fig: begin*) dare inizio a, cominciare [2] VI + PREP partire da; **a street leading off the main road** una traversa della strada principale

► **lead on** VT + ADV **a** (*deceive*) prendere in giro, ingannare

  b (*incite*): **to lead sb on (to do sth)** incoraggiare *or* spingere *or* trascinare qn (a fare qc)

► **lead up to** VI + ADV + PREP portare (a); (*fig*) preparare la strada per; **what's all this leading up to?** dove vuoi andare a parare?

lead² [lɛd] [1] N (*metal*) piombo; (*in pencil*) mina; (*for sounding*) scandaglio.

  [2] ADJ (*pipes*) di piombo; (*paint*) a base di piombo.

lead·ed ['lɛdɪd] ADJ: **leaded windows** vetrate *fpl* (artistiche).

lead·en ['lɛdn] ADJ (*colour, sky*) plumbeo(-a); (*fig: atmosphere*) teso(-a); (: *silence*) opprimente; **with a leaden heart** con la morte nel cuore.

lead·er ['li:dəʳ] N **a** (*of group, expedition*) capo; (*of party, union*) capo, leader *m/f inv*; (*Mus: of orchestra: Brit*) primo violino; (: *Am*) direttore *m* d'orchestra; (*guide*) guida; (*Mountaineering*) capocordata *m inv*; **the Leader of the House** (*Pol*) capo della maggioranza ministeriale alla Camera; **he's a born leader** è nato per comandare **b** (*Sport: in race*) chi è in testa, leader *m/f inv*; **the leaders of the First Division** (*Ftbl*) la squadra in testa alla classifica di serie A; **they are leaders in their field** (*fig*) sono all'avanguardia nel loro campo

  c (*Brit: in newspaper*) articolo di fondo, editoriale *m*.

lead·er·ship ['li:dəʃɪp] N **a** direzione *f*, leadership *f inv*; **under the leadership of ...** sotto la direzione *or* guida di...; **qualities of leadership** qualità *fpl* di un capo **b** (*leaders*) dirigenti *mpl*, dirigenza.

♦ **lead-free** ['lɛd'fri:] ADJ (*petrol*) senza piombo.

♦ **lead-in** ['li:d‚ɪn] N introduzione *f*, presentazione *f*.

lead·ing ['li:dɪŋ] ADJ (*horse, car: in race*) (che è) in testa, di testa; (: *in procession*) che apre la sfilata; (*chief: member etc*) principale, preminente; (: *Theatre etc: role, character*) principale, di primo piano; **one of the leading figures of this century** una delle più importanti figure di questo secolo.

♦ **leading article** N = **leader c**.

♦ **leading lady** N (*Theatre*) prima attrice.

♦ **leading light** N (*person*) personaggio di primo piano.

♦ **leading man** N (*Theatre*) primo attore.

♦ **leading question** N *domanda formulata in modo da influenzare la risposta.*

♦ **lead pencil** [‚lɛd'pɛnsəl] N matita con la mina di grafite.

♦ **lead poisoning** ['lɛd‚pɔɪzənɪŋ] N saturnismo.

♦ **lead time** ['li:d‚taɪm] N (*Comm*) tempo di consegna.

♦ **lead weight** [‚lɛd'weɪt] N piombino, piombo.

leaf [li:f] N (*pl* **leaves**) **a** (*of plant*) foglia **b** (*of book*) foglio, pagina; **to turn over a new leaf** (*fig*) voltare pagina, cambiar vita; **to take a leaf out of sb's book** (*fig*) prendere esempio da qn **c** (*of table*: *fold-down*) ribalta; (: *extending*) asse *f* estraibile

► **leaf through** VT + PREP (*book*) sfogliare.

leaf·let ['li:flɪt] N (*gen*) dépliant *m inv*; (*single sheet*) volantino.

♦ **leaf spring** N (*Tech*) molla a balestra.

leafy ['li:fɪ] ADJ (*comp* **-ier**, *superl* **-iest**) (*suburb*) ricco(-a) di verde; (*branch*) ricco(-a) di foglie.

league [li:g] N **a** (*alliance*) associazione *f*, lega; **to be in league with** essere in associazione con; (*pej*) essere in combutta con, essere in lega con; **to form a league against** far lega contro **b** (*Ftbl, Rugby*) campionato; **they're not in the same league** (*fig fam*) non c'è paragone.

♦ **league table** N (*Ftbl etc*) classifica del campionato.

leak [li:k] [1] N (*in pipe*) perdita, fuoriuscita; (*in boat*) falla; (*in roof, wall*) infiltrazione *f*; (*of gas*) fuga, perdita, fuoriuscita; (*fig: of information*) fuga di notizie; **to have** *or* **take a leak** (*fam*) andare al bagno, andare a far pipì.

  [2] VI (*roof, bucket*) perdere; (*ship*) far acqua; (*shoes*) lasciar passare l'acqua; **water was leaking into the cellar** l'acqua si stava infiltrando nella cantina.

  [3] VT (*liquid*) gocciolare, perdere; (*fig: information*) divulgare

► **leak out** VI + ADV (*liquid*) uscire (fuori); (*gas*) esalare, uscire; (*fig: news*) trapelare.

leak·age ['li:kɪdʒ] N (*of water, gas etc*) perdita.

leaky ['li:kɪ] ADJ (*comp* **-ier**, *superl* **-iest**) (*pipe, bucket, roof*) che perde; (*shoe*) che lascia passare l'acqua; (*boat*) che fa acqua.

lean¹ [li:n] [1] ADJ (*comp* **-er**, *superl* **-est**) magro(-a); **the lean years** i tempi di magra.

  [2] N (*of meat*) magro, parte *f* magra (della carne).

lean² [li:n] (*pt, pp* **leaned** *or* **leant**) [1] VI **a** (*gatepost, wall, slope*) essere inclinato(-a), pendere; **to lean to(wards) the left/right** (*Pol*) avere tendenze di sinistra/di destra **b** (*for support: person*): **to lean on, lean against** appoggiarsi a; **to be leaning against** (*ladder*) essere appoggiato(-a) a *or* contro; **to lean on sb** (*also fig: for support*) appoggiarsi a qn; (*fig: put pressure on*) far pressione su qn.

  [2] VT (*ladder, bicycle*): **to lean sth against/on sth** appoggiare qc a *or* contro/su qc; **to lean one's head on sth** appoggiare la testa su qc

► **lean back** VI + ADV sporgersi indietro; (*against sth*) appoggiarsi all'indietro; **she leaned back against the pillows** si è adagiata sui cuscini

► **lean forward** VI + ADV piegarsi in avanti

► **lean out** VI + ADV: **to lean out (of)** sporgersi (da)

► **lean over** [1] VI + ADV (*person*) chinarsi; (*thing*) piegarsi, inclinarsi; **to lean over backwards to help sb** (*fig fam*) farsi in quattro per aiutare qn.

  [2] VI + PREP (*balcony, gate*) sporgersi da, affacciarsi a; (*desk*) piegarsi su, chinarsi su.

lean·ing ['li:nɪŋ] [1] N: **leaning (towards)** tendenza (a), propensione *f* (per).

  [2] ADJ inclinato(-a), pendente; **the leaning Tower of Pisa** la torre (pendente) di Pisa.

leant [lɛnt] PT, PP of **lean²**.

♦ **lean-to** ['li:n‚tu:] N (*roof*) tettoia; (*building*) *edificio con*

tetto appoggiato ad altro edificio.

leap [li:p] (*vb: pp, pt* **leaped** *or* **leapt**) **1** VI saltare, balzare; he leapt into/out of the train saltò sul/giù dal treno; **to leap to one's feet** scattare in piedi; **to leap about** saltellare qua e là; **to leap out** saltare fuori; **to leap out at sb** saltare addosso a qn; **to leap over sth** saltare qc con un balzo; **my heart leapt** ho avuto un tuffo al cuore; **to leap at an offer** afferrare al volo una proposta.

2 VT (*fence, ditch*) saltare.

3 N salto, balzo; **a leap in the dark** (*fig*) un salto nel buio; **by leaps and bounds** a passi da gigante

▶ **leap up** VI + ADV (*person*) balzare in piedi; (*flames*) divampare.

leap·frog ['li:p,frɒg] **1** N gioco della cavallina.

2 VI: **to leapfrog over sb/sth** saltare (alla cavallina) qn/qc.

leapt [lɛpt] PT, PP of **leap**.

♦ **leap year** N anno bisestile.

learn [lɜ:n] (*pt, pp* **learned** *or* **learnt**) **1** VT (*study*) imparare; (*hear*) (venire a) sapere; **to learn (how) to do sth** imparare a fare qc; **to learn that ...** apprendere che..., venire a sapere che...; **we were sorry to learn that it was closing down** la notizia della chiusura ci ha fatto dispiacere; **I think he's learnt his lesson** (*fig*) penso che gli sia servito di lezione.

2 VI: **to learn about sth** (*study*) studiare qc, imparare qc; (*hear*) sentire qc, apprendere qc; **I've learnt from experience not to trust him** l'esperienza mi ha insegnato a non fidarmi di lui; **you learn from your mistakes** sbagliando s'impara; **you'll learn!** un giorno capirai!

▶ **learn off** VT + ADV imparare a memoria.

learn·ed ['lɜ:nɪd] ADJ (*person*) erudito(-a), dotto(-a); (*book*) dotto(-a); **a member of the learned profession** un principe del foro.

learn·er ['lɜ:nə'] N principiante *m/f*; **she's a fast learner** è una che impara subito *or* con facilità; **slow learner** (*Scol*) alunno(-a) che ha difficoltà di apprendimento; **he's a learner (driver)** (*Brit*) sta imparando a guidare, è un principiante.

learn·ing ['lɜ:nɪŋ] N cultura, erudizione *f*, sapere *m*.

learnt [lɜ:nt] PT, PP of **learn**.

lease [li:s] **1** N contratto di affitto (*a lungo termine con responsabilità simili a quelle di un proprietario*); **on lease** in affitto; **to give sb a new lease of life** (*fig*) ridare nuova vita a qn.

2 VT (*take*) affittare, prendere in affitto; (*give: also:* **lease out**) affittare, dare in affitto

▶ **lease back** VT + ADV effettuare un lease-back *inv*.

lease·back ['li:s,bæk] N lease-back *m inv*.

lease·hold ['li:s,həʊld] **1** ADJ in affitto.

2 N (*property*) proprietà *f inv* in affitto; (*tenure*) diritto di godimento (della proprietà).

lease·holder ['li:s'həʊldə'] N locatario(-a), affittuario(-a) (*in possesso di un contratto a lungo termine e con diritti simili a quelli del proprietario*).

leash [li:ʃ] N guinzaglio; **on a leash** al guinzaglio.

least [li:st] (*superl of* **little**) **1** ADJ minimo(-a), più piccolo(-a); **I haven't the least idea** non ne ho la minima idea; **she wasn't in the least bit interested** non era minimamente interessata; **she always orders whatever costs the least money** ordina sempre quello che costa di meno; **that's the least of my worries** è la cosa che mi preoccupa di meno *or* che meno mi preoccupa, quella è l'ultima delle mie preoccupazioni.

2 N minimo; **it's the least one can do** è il minimo che si

possa fare; **to say the least** a dir poco; **the least said about the meeting, the better** meno parliamo della riunione e meglio è; **at least** almeno; **I can at least try** posso sempre *or* almeno provarci; **at the very least** come minimo; **not in the least** per nulla *or* niente, affatto.

3 ADV meno; **the least expensive car** l'auto meno cara; **the least qualified girl** la ragazza meno qualificata; **she is least able to afford it** è quella che se lo può permettere meno di tutti; **least of all me** e men che meno io, tanto meno io; **for a number of reasons, not least ...** per una serie di motivi, non ultimo il fatto che... .

leath·er ['lɛðə'] **1** N (*hide: soft*) pelle *f*; (: *hard*) cuoio; (*wash leather*) pelle di daino.

2 ADJ (*see n*) di *or* in pelle; di *or* in cuoio; **leather goods** (articoli di) pelletteria.

Leath·er·ette® [,lɛðə'rɛt] N similpelle *f*, vinilpelle ® *f*.

leath·er·ing ['lɛðərɪŋ] N: **to give sb a leathering** (*fam*) prendere qn a cinghiate.

leath·ery ['lɛðərɪ] ADJ (*meat, substance, skin*) coriaceo(-a).

leave [li:v] (*vb: pt, pp* **left**) **1** VT **a** (*go away from: town*) lasciare, andarsene da; (: *room*) lasciare, uscire da; (: *station*) partire da; (: *hospital*) uscire da; (: *person*) lasciare; **to leave school** (*complete studies*) finire la scuola; (*prematurely*) lasciare la scuola; **to leave home** uscire di casa; (*permanently*) andarsene di casa; **they have left this address** se ne sono andati da qui; **may I leave the room?** (*Scol euph: to go to the lavatory*) posso uscire?; **to leave the table** alzarsi da tavola; **the car left the road** la macchina è uscita di strada; **the train is leaving in 10 minutes** il treno parte fra 10 minuti

b (*forget*) lasciare, dimenticare; (*give: in will, as tip*) lasciare

c (*allow to remain*) lasciare; **to leave the window open** lasciare la finestra aperta; **let's leave it at that** per ora basta (così); **leave it to me!** ci penso io!, lascia fare a me!; **leave it with me** lascia che me ne occupi io; **I'll leave it to you to decide** decidi tu, lo lascio decidere a te; **she left him to it** lo ha lasciato alle sue occupazioni; **he leaves a wife and a child** lascia la moglie e un figlio; **to leave sb alone** lasciare qn (da) solo(-a); **leave me alone** *or* **in peace!** lasciami in pace!; **don't leave anything to chance** non lasciar niente al caso; **it leaves much to be desired** lascia molto a desiderare; **take it** *or* **leave it!** prendere o lasciare!; **3 from 10 leaves 7** 10 meno 3 fa 7

d (*remaining*): **to be left (over)** rimanere, restare, avanzare; **all the money I have left (over)** tutti i soldi che mi restano *or* che mi sono avanzati; **there's some milk left over** c'è rimasto del latte; **how many are (there) left?** quanti ne restano?, quanti ce ne sono ancora?; **nothing was left for me (to do) but to sell it** non mi rimaneva *or* restava altro (da fare) che venderlo.

2 VI (*plane, train*) partire; (*person*) uscire, andarsene; **he's already left for the airport** è già uscito per andare all'aeroporto.

3 N **a** (*permission*) permesso, autorizzazione *f*; **without so much as a "by your leave"** senza nemmeno chiedere il permesso

b (*permission to be absent*) permesso; (: *of public employee*) congedo; (: *Mil*) licenza; **unpaid leave** ≈ aspettativa; **on leave** in congedo; **on leave of absence** in permesso; (*public employee*) in congedo; (*Mil*) in licenza

c: **to take (one's) leave of sb** accomiatarsi da qn, congedarsi da qn; **have you taken leave of your senses?**

ma sei uscito di senno?, ma sei impazzito?

► **leave about, leave around** VT + ADV lasciare in giro

► **leave behind** VT + ADV (*also fig*) lasciare indietro; (*forget*) dimenticare; **she leaves everybody else behind** è superiore a tutti gli altri; **you'll be left behind by the rest** rimarrai indietro rispetto agli altri

► **leave in** VT + ADV lasciare, non togliere

► **leave off** 1 VT + ADV **a** (*cover, lid, clothes*) non mettere; (*heating, light*) non accendere; (*name: from list*) non inserire

    b (*fam: stop*): **to leave off doing sth** smetterla *or* piantarla di fare qc.

    2 VI + ADV (*Brit fam: stop*) smetterla

► **leave on** VT + ADV (*lid*) lasciare su; (*light, fire, cooker*) lasciare acceso(-a); (*coat*) non togliersi

► **leave out** VT + ADV **a** (*omit*) tralasciare; (: *in reading etc*) saltare; **he feels left out** si sente escluso *or* lasciato in disparte

    b (*not put back*) lasciare fuori

► **leave over** VT + ADV (*postpone*) rimandare.

leav·en ['lɛvn] 1 N lievito.

    2 VT far lievitare.

leaves [li:vz] NPL of **leaf**.

leave·taking ['li:vˌteɪkɪŋ] N commiato, addio.

leav·ings ['li:vɪŋz] NPL avanzi *mpl*, rimasugli *mpl*.

Leba·nese [ˌlɛbə'ni:z] 1 ADJ libanese.

    2 N, PL INV libanese *m/f*.

Leba·non ['lɛbənən] N: **(the) Lebanon** (il) Libano.

lech·er ['lɛtʃə'] N satiro (*fig*).

lech·er·ous ['lɛtʃərəs] ADJ lascivo(-a).

lech·er·ous·ly ['lɛtʃərəslɪ] ADV in modo lascivo.

lech·ery ['lɛtʃərɪ] N lascivia.

lec·tern ['lɛktən] N leggio.

lec·ture ['lɛktʃə'] 1 N **a** (*Univ*) lezione *f*; (*by visitor*) conferenza; **to deliver** *or* **give a lecture on** tenere una conferenza *or* una lezione su

    b (*reproof*) paternale *f*, sermone *m*.

    2 VI: **to lecture (in sth)** essere professore incaricato (di qc); **to lecture (to sb on sth)** (*Univ*) fare lezione (a qn di qc); (: *visiting lecturer*) tenere una conferenza (a qn su qc).

    3 VT (*reprove*) rimproverare, fare una ramanzina a.

♦ **lecture hall, lecture theatre** N aula magna.

♦ **lecture notes** NPL appunti *mpl* (del corso *or* delle lezioni).

lec·tur·er ['lɛktʃərə'] N (*Brit: Univ*) professore(-essa), docente *m/f* (universitario(-a)); (*speaker*) conferenziere (-a); **assistant lecturer** (*Brit*) ≈ professore(-essa) associato(-a); **senior lecturer** (*Brit*) ≈ professore(-essa) ordinario(-a).

lec·ture·ship ['lɛktʃəˌʃɪp] N docenza.

LED [ˌɛli:'di:] N ABBR (*Elec*: = *light-emitting diode*) LED *m inv*.

led [lɛd] PT, PP of **lead**.

ledge [lɛdʒ] N (*on wall etc*) sporgenza; (*of window*) davanzale *m*; (*of mountain*) cengia, cornice *f*.

ledg·er ['lɛdʒə'] N libro mastro, registro.

lee [li:] 1 N lato *m* sottovento *inv*; **in the lee of** a ridosso di, al riparo di.

    2 ADJ sottovento *inv*; **to have a lee helm** (*ship*) essere poggiero(-a).

leech [li:tʃ] N sanguisuga.

leek [li:k] N porro.

leer [lɪə'] 1 N (*lustful*) espressione *f* libidinosa; (*evil*) espressione *f* malvagia.

    2 VI: **to leer at sb** (*lustfully*) guardare qn con occhi

vogliosi; (*cruelly*) guardare qn con malvagità.

leery ['lɪərɪ] ADJ: **to be leery of** (*fam*) essere sospettoso(-a) di.

lee·ward ['li:wəd] (*Naut*) 1 ADJ sottovento *inv*.

    2 ADV sottovento; **to drift leeward** scarrocciare.

    3 N lato sottovento; **to leeward** sottovento.

lee·way ['li:ˌweɪ] N (*Naut*) deriva; (*fig*) margine *m*; **they gave him a great deal of leeway** gli hanno lasciato ampia libertà di azione.

left[1] [lɛft] PT, PP of **leave**.

left[2] [lɛft] 1 ADJ sinistro(-a).

    2 ADV a sinistra.

    3 N sinistra; **on my left, to my left** sulla *or* alla mia sinistra; **on the left, to the left** sulla *or* a sinistra; **the Left** (*Pol*) la sinistra; **he has always been on the Left** ha sempre avuto idee di sinistra.

♦ **left-hand** ['lɛftˌhænd] ADJ a sinistra; **left-hand page** pagina a *or* di sinistra; **left-hand side** (*parte f*) sinistra; **on the left-hand side** sulla *or* a sinistra, sul lato sinistro.

♦ **left-hand drive** ADJ (*Brit*) guida a sinistra.

♦ **left-handed** [ˌlɛft'hændɪd] ADJ mancino(-a); (*fig: compliment*) ambiguo(-a); **left-handed scissors** forbici *fpl* per mancini.

♦ **left-hander** [ˌlɛft'hændə'] N mancino(-a).

leftie ['lɛftɪ] N (*fam*) uno(-a) di sinistra.

left·ist ['lɛftɪst] (*Pol*) 1 ADJ di sinistra.

    2 N uno(-a) di sinistra.

♦ **left-luggage** [ˌlɛft'lʌgɪdʒ] N: **left-luggage office** deposito *m* bagagli *inv*; **left-luggage locker** armadietto per depositare i bagagli.

♦ **left-of-centre** [lɛftəv'sɛntə'] ADJ di centro sinistra.

♦ **left-overs** ['lɛftˌəʊvəz] NPL avanzi *mpl*.

♦ **left-wing** [ˌlɛft'wɪŋ] ADJ (*Pol*) di sinistra.

♦ **left wing** N (*Mil, Sport*) ala sinistra; (*Pol*) sinistra.

♦ **left-winger** [ˌlɛft'wɪŋə'] N (*Sport*) ala sinistra; (*Pol*) uno(-a) di sinistra.

lefty ['lɛftɪ] N = **leftie**.

leg [lɛg] 1 N **a** (*gen*) gamba; (*of animal, bird*) zampa; (*Culin: of chicken, turkey*) coscia; (: *of lamb, pork*) cosciotto; (*of furniture*) piede *m*; **to be on one's last legs** (*person, animal*) stare in piedi per miracolo; (*machine, car*) funzionare per miracolo; **he hasn't got a leg to stand on** (*fig*) non ha una scusa *or* una ragione che stia in piedi; **to pull sb's leg** (*fig*) prendere in giro qn; **to stretch one's legs** sgranchirsi le gambe; **to give sb a leg up** aiutare qn a salire; **shake a leg!** (*Brit fam*) muoviti!, sbrigati!; **show a leg!** (*fam*) alzati!

    b (*stage: of journey*) tappa; (*of relay race*) frazione *f*; (*of competition*) girone *m*.

    2 VT: **to leg it** (*fam*) darsela a gambe.

lega·cy ['lɛgəsɪ] N eredità *f inv*; (*fig*) retaggio.

le·gal ['li:gəl] ADJ **a** (*lawful*) legale; (: *requirement*) di legge; **these coins are no longer legal currency** queste monete sono fuori corso

    b (*relating to the law: gen*) legale; (: *error*) giudiziario(-a); **as a member of the legal profession** come legale; **to take legal action** *or* **proceedings against sb** intentare un'azione legale contro qn, far causa a qn; **legal department** (*of a firm*) ufficio legale, contenzioso; **legal aid** assistenza legale gratuita, patrocinio legale gratuito.

♦ **legal adviser** N consulente *m/f* legale.

le·gal·is·tic [ˌli:gə'lɪstɪk] ADJ legalista.

le·gal·ity [lɪ'gælɪtɪ] N legalità.

le·gali·za·tion [ˌliːgəlaɪˈzeɪʃən] N legalizzazione f.

le·gal·ize ['liːgəˌlaɪz] VT legalizzare.

leg·al·ly ['liːgəlɪ] ADV legalmente; **to be legally binding** essere (legalmente) vincolante.

♦ **legal tender** N moneta in corso legale.

le·ga·tion [lɪˈgeɪʃən] N legazione f.

leg·end ['lɛdʒənd] N leggenda.

leg·end·ary ['lɛdʒəndərɪ] ADJ leggendario(-a).

-legged ['lɛgɪd] SUFF: **two-legged** a due gambe (or zampe), bipede.

leg·gings ['lɛgɪŋz] NPL (women's) pantacollant mpl, fuseaux mpl; (men's) gambali mpl.

leg·gy ['lɛgɪ] ADJ (comp **-ier**, superl **-iest**) dalle gambe lunghe.

leg·ibil·ity [ˌlɛdʒɪˈbɪlɪtɪ] N leggibilità.

leg·ible ['lɛdʒəbl] ADJ leggibile.

leg·ibly ['lɛdʒəblɪ] ADV in modo leggibile.

le·gion ['liːdʒən] 1 N legione f; (fig) schiera, stuolo.
2 ADJ (frm: very many) innumerevole.

le·gion·ary ['liːdʒənərɪ] N (Roman history) legionario.

le·gion·naire [ˌliːdʒəˈnɛəʳ] N (French Foreign Legion) legionario.

♦ **legionnaire's disease, legionnaires' disease** N morbo or malattia del legionario, legionellosi f inv.

leg·is·late ['lɛdʒɪsˌleɪt] VI legiferare, promulgare delle leggi.

leg·is·la·tion [ˌlɛdʒɪsˈleɪʃən] N legislazione f; **a piece of legislation** una legge.

leg·is·la·tive ['lɛdʒɪslətɪv] ADJ legislativo(-a).

leg·is·la·tor ['lɛdʒɪsˌleɪtəʳ] N legislatore m.

leg·is·la·ture ['lɛdʒɪslətʃəʳ] N organi mpl legislativi, potere m legislativo.

le·giti·ma·cy [lɪˈdʒɪtɪməsɪ] N (gen) legittimità; (of argument, excuse) validità.

le·giti·mate [lɪˈdʒɪtɪmɪt] ADJ (lawful) legittimo(-a); (argument, cause, excuse) buono(-a), valido(-a); (complaint) legittimo(-a); (conclusion) logico(-a).

le·giti·mize [lɪˈdʒɪtɪˌmaɪz] VT (gen) convalidare, rendere legittimo(-a).

leg·less ['lɛglɪs] ADJ (Brit fam) sbronzo(-a), fatto(-a).

♦ **leg-pull** ['lɛgˌpʊl] N (fam) scherzo.

♦ **leg-pulling** ['lɛgˌpʊlɪŋ] N (fam) scherzi mpl.

♦ **leg-room** ['lɛgˌrʊm] N spazio per le gambe.

♦ **leg-warmers** ['lɛgˌwɔːməz] NPL scaldamuscoli mpl.

Leics ABBR (Brit)= Leicestershire.

lei·sure ['lɛʒəʳ] 1 N svago, tempo libero; **a life of leisure** una vita comoda; **to be a lady of leisure** (hum) fare la bella vita; **do it at your leisure** fallo con comodo.
2 ADJ (activities) del tempo libero; **in one's leisure time** durante il proprio tempo libero.

♦ **leisure centre** N (Brit) centro sportivo e ricreativo.

lei·sure·ly ['lɛʒəlɪ] ADJ (day, stroll, trip) tranquillo(-a); **in a leisurely way** (fatto(-a)) con comodo or senza fretta.

♦ **leisure suit** N (Am) tuta da ginnastica.

leit·mo·tiv, leit·mo·tif ['laɪtməʊˌtiːf] N (Mus, fig) leitmotiv m inv.

lem·ming ['lɛmɪŋ] N lemming m inv.

lem·on ['lɛmən] 1 N (fruit) limone m.
2 ADJ (colour) giallo limone inv.

lem·on·ade [ˌlɛməˈneɪd] N (fizzy drink) gassosa; (: with lemon flavour) limonata.

♦ **lemon cheese, lemon curd** N crema di limone (da spalmare sul pane).

♦ **lemon juice** N succo di limone.

♦ **lemon sole** N sogliola limanda.

♦ **lemon squeez·er** ['lɛmənˌskwiːzəʳ] N spremilimoni m inv, spremiagrumi m inv.

♦ **lemon tea** N tè m inv al limone.

♦ **lemon tree** N (albero di) limone m.

♦ **lemon zest·er** ['lɛmənˌzɛstəʳ] N rigalimoni m inv.

le·mur ['liːməʳ] N lemuride m.

lend [lɛnd] (pt, pp lent) VT (gen) prestare; (fig: impart: importance, mystery, authority) conferire; **to lend out** prestare, dare in prestito; **to lend a hand** dare una mano; **to lend an ear to sb/sth** prestare ascolto a qn/qc; **it does not lend itself to being filmed** non si presta ad essere filmato.

lend·er ['lɛndəʳ] N chi presta, prestatore(-trice).

lend·ing ['lɛndɪŋ] N prestito.

♦ **lending library** N biblioteca (con servizio di prestito di libri).

♦ **lending rate** N tasso di interesse.

length [lɛŋθ] N a (size, extent) lunghezza; (duration) durata; **it is 2 metres in length** è lungo 2 metri; **what is its length?** OR **what length is it?** quant'è lungo?; **throughout the length and breadth of Italy** in tutta Italia; **to fall full length** cadere lungo(-a) disteso(-a); **length of time** periodo (di tempo); **for what length of time?** per quanto tempo?; **1000 words in length** di 1000 parole; **their team won the boat race by 2 lengths** (Sport) la loro squadra ha vinto la gara di canottaggio per 2 lunghezze; **at length** (at last) finalmente; (lengthily) a lungo; **to speak at length** dilungarsi, parlare a lungo; **I even went to the length of sending her flowers** sono perfino arrivato al punto di mandarle i fiori; **to go to any lengths to do sth** fare qualsiasi cosa pur di or per fare qc; **she went to great lengths to make sure that ...** fece di tutto per assicurarsi che...

b (piece: of road, pipe etc) pezzo, tratto; (: material) taglio, altezza; **a dress/skirt length** un taglio per vestito/gonna.

length·en ['lɛŋθən] 1 VT (distance) allungare; (time) prolungare.
2 VI allungarsi.

lengthi·ly ['lɛŋθɪlɪ] ADV a lungo.

length·ways ['lɛŋθˌweɪz], **length·wise** ['lɛŋθˌwaɪz] ADV per la lunghezza, per lungo.

lengthy ['lɛŋθɪ] ADJ (comp **-ier**, superl **-iest**) lungo(-a); (tedious) interminabile.

le·ni·ence ['liːnɪəns], **le·ni·en·cy** ['liːnɪənsɪ] N (of person) clemenza, indulgenza; (of sentence, punishment) mitezza.

le·ni·ent ['liːnɪənt] ADJ (person) indulgente, clemente; (sentence, punishment) leggero(-a).

le·ni·ent·ly ['liːnɪəntlɪ] ADV con indulgenza.

Len·in·ism ['lɛnɪˌnɪzəm] N leninismo.

Len·in·ist ['lɛnɪˌnɪst] ADJ, N leninista (m/f).

lens [lɛnz] N (Anat: of the eye) cristallino; (of spectacles) lente f; (of camera etc) obiettivo.

♦ **lens holder** N (Phot) portaobiettivi m inv.

♦ **lens hood** N (Phot) paraluce m inv.

Lent [lɛnt] N Quaresima; **I'm giving it up for Lent** vi rinuncio come fioretto (quaresimale).

lent [lɛnt] PT, PP of lend.

len·ten ['lɛntən] ADJ (Rel) quaresimale.

len·til ['lɛntl] N lenticchia.

Leo ['liːəʊ] N (Astron, Astrol) Leone m; **to be Leo** essere del Leone.

leop·ard ['lɛpəd] N leopardo; **the leopard cannot or doesn't change its spots** il lupo perde il pelo ma non il

vizio.

leop·ard·ess [ˌlɛpə'dɛs] N femmina del leopardo.

leo·tard ['liːətɑːd] N body *m inv* (*per ginnastica, danza*).

lep·er ['lɛpə'] N lebbroso(-a).

♦ **leper colony** N lebbrosario.

lep·ro·sy ['lɛprəsɪ] N lebbra.

lep·rous ['lɛprəs] ADJ lebbroso(-a).

les·bian ['lɛzbɪən] ① ADJ lesbico(-a).

② N lesbica.

les·bi·an·ism ['lɛzbɪəˌnɪzəm] N lesbismo.

le·sion ['liːʒən] N (*Med*) lesione *f*.

Le·so·tho [ləˈsəutəu] N Lesotho *m*.

less [lɛs] (*comp of little*) ① ADJ meno; **now we eat less bread** ora mangiamo meno pane; **she has less time to spare** ha meno tempo a disposizione; **of less importance** di minor importanza.

② PRON meno; **we see less of them now** li vediamo di meno adesso; **the less you read the less you learn** meno leggi meno impari; **can't you let me have it for less?** mi potrebbe fare un piccolo sconto?; **the less said about it the better** meno se ne parla e meglio è; **less than half** meno della metà; **less than £1/a kilo/3 metres** meno di una sterlina/un chilo/3 metri; **less than you think** meno di quanto tu creda; **less than you/ever** meno di te/che mai; **the holiday was less than perfect** la vacanza non è stata proprio stupenda; **it's nothing less than a disaster** è un disastro bell'e buono; **a tip of £10, no less!** (*fam*) nientemeno che 10 sterline di mancia!.

③ ADV meno, di meno; **to go out less (often)** uscire di meno; **less and less** sempre meno; **still less** ancora meno; **none the less ...** ugualmente..., lo stesso....

④ PREP meno; **less 5%** meno il 5%.

-less SUFF senza; **breathless** senza fiato; **meaningless** privo(-a) di significato, senza senso.

les·see [lɛ'siː] N affittuario(-a), locatario(-a).

less·en ['lɛsn] ① VT (*gen*) diminuire, ridurre; (*pain*) alleviare; (*cost, tension*) ridurre; (*shock*) attutire, attenuare.

② VI (*gen*) diminuire, ridursi; (*shock*) attenuarsi.

less·en·ing ['lɛsnɪŋ] N diminuzione *f*.

less·er ['lɛsə'] ADJ (*importance, degree*) minore; (*size*) più piccolo(-a); **to a lesser extent** *or* **degree** in grado *or* misura minore; **the lesser of two evils** il minore dei due mali.

les·son ['lɛsn] N lezione *f*; **to give lessons in** dare *or* impartire lezioni di; **a French lesson** una lezione di francese; **to teach sb a lesson** (*fig*) dare una lezione a qn; **it taught him a lesson** (*fig*) gli è servito di lezione.

les·sor [lɛ'sɔː'] N locatore(-trice).

lest [lɛst] CONJ (*old, frm*) nel timore che + *sub*, per paura che + *sub*; **lest we forget** per non dimenticare.

let¹ [lɛt] (*pt, pp let*) VT **a** (*permit*) lasciare, permettere; **to let sb past** lasciar *or* far passare qn; **to let sb do sth** lasciar fare qc a qn, lasciare che qn faccia qc; **let him come** lascialo venire; **let me have a look** fammi vedere; **to let sb have sth** dare qc a qn; **to let sb know sth** far sapere qc a qn; **don't let him get away with it** (*fam*) non lasciare che la passi liscia; **I'll let you have it back tomorrow** te lo ridò *or* restituisco domani; **don't let me catch** *or* **see you copying again!** che non ti peschi *or* sorprenda mai più a copiare!; **let him alone** *or* **be** lascialo stare *or* in pace; **to let go of sb/sth** mollare *or* lasciar andare qn/qc; **he let me go** mi ha lasciato andare; **let the water boil then ...** fate bollire l'acqua e quindi...

b (*in verb forms*): **let's** *or* **let us go!** andiamo!; **let's see, what was I saying?** dunque, cosa stavo dicendo?; **let them wait** che aspettino (pure); **let that be a warning to you!** che questo ti serva di lezione!; **let x = 1 and y = 2** sia x=1 e y=2

c (*Brit: rent out*) affittare, dare in affitto; **"To Let"** "Affittasi"

▶ **let away** VT + ADV lasciare andare (via)

▶ **let down** VT + ADV **a** (*lower*) abbassare; (*dress*) allungare; (*hem*) allungare, lasciar giù; (*Brit: tyre*) sgonfiare; (*one's hair*) sciogliersi; (*on rope*) calare (giù)

b (*disappoint*) deludere; **that car always lets me down** quella macchina mi molla sempre in asso

▶ **let go** ① VI + ADV mollare.

② VT + ADV mollare; (*allow to go*) lasciare andare

▶ **let in** VT + ADV far *or* lasciar entrare, far *or* lasciar passare; **to let sb in** far *or* lasciar entrare qn; **shoes which let the water in** scarpe che lasciano passare l'acqua; **to let sb in for a lot of trouble** procurare *or* dare un mucchio di fastidi a qn; **what have you let yourself in for?** in che guai *or* pasticci sei andato a cacciarti?; **to let sb in on a secret** rivelare *or* confidare un segreto a qn

▶ **let into** VT + PREP **a** (*allow in*) lasciar entrare in

b (*allow to share*): **to let sb into** far partecipe qn di

c (*inset*) inglobare

▶ **let off** VT + ADV **a** (*explode*) far esplodere; (*fireworks*) accendere, lasciar partire; (*smell etc*) emettere; **to let off steam** (*fig fam*) sfogarsi, scaricarsi

b (*allow to go*) lasciar andare *or* uscire; (*not punish*) non punire; **to let sb off lightly** non calcare la mano nel punire qn; **to let sb off with a warning** limitarsi ad ammonire qn

c (*subj: taxi driver, bus driver*) far scendere

▶ **let on** VI + ADV (*fam*) dire, lasciar capire; **to let on to sb about sth** far capire qc a qn; **to let on (that ...)** dare a intendere (che...)

▶ **let out** VT + ADV **a** (*gen*) far *or* lasciare uscire; (*secret*) spifferare; (*news*) divulgare; **don't get up, I'll let myself out** non occorre che mi accompagni alla porta; **to let out a cry/sigh/scream** emettere un grido/un sospiro/un urlo; **to let the air out of a tyre** sgonfiare una gomma; **that lets her out** questo la esonera

b (*dress, seam*) allargare

c (*rent out*) affittare, dare in affitto

▶ **let up** ① VI + ADV (*bad weather*) diminuire; (*talker, worker*) smettere, fermarsi.

② VT + ADV far alzare.

let² [lɛt] N (*Tennis*) colpo nullo.

♦ **let-down** ['lɛtˌdaʊn] N (*disappointment*) delusione *f*.

le·thal ['liːθəl] ADJ: **lethal (to)** (*gen*) letale (per); (*wound, blow*) mortale (per).

le·thar·gic [lɪ'θɑːdʒɪk] ADJ (*physically*) fiacco(-a); (*mentally*) apatico(-a).

leth·ar·gy ['lɛθədʒɪ] N (*see adj*) fiacchezza; apatia.

let·ter ['lɛtə'] N **a** (*missive*) lettera; **by letter** per lettera; **letter of introduction/application/protest** lettera di presentazione/di domanda/di protesta

b (*of alphabet*) lettera; **the letter G** la (lettera) G; **small/capital letter** lettera minuscola/maiuscola; **she's got a lot of letters after her name** ha un mucchio di titoli; **the letter of the law** (*fig*) la lettera della legge; **to follow instructions to the letter** seguire alla lettera le istruzioni.

♦ **letter bomb** ['lɛtəˌbɒm] N lettera esplosiva.

letter·box ['lɛtəˌbɒks] N cassetta *or* buca delle lettere.

♦ **letter card** N biglietto postale.
letter·head ['lɛtə,hɛd] N intestazione f.
let·ter·ing ['lɛtərɪŋ] N (engraving) iscrizione f; (letters) caratteri mpl.
♦ **letter of credit** N lettera di credito; **documentary letter of credit** lettera di credito documentata.
♦ **letter-opener** ['lɛtər,əupnəˈ] N tagliacarte m inv.
♦ **letter-perfect** [,lɛtə'pɜ:fɪkt] ADJ (Am): **to be letter-perfect in sth** conoscere qc a menadito.
letter·press ['lɛtə,prɛs] (Typ) N (method) rilievografia; (printed page) testo.
♦ **letter quality printer** N stampante f ad alta definizione.
let·ters ['lɛtəz] NPL (Literature): **man of letters** uomo di lettere.
♦ **letter scales** NPL pesalettere m inv.
♦ **letters patent** NPL brevetto di invenzione.
♦ **letter tray** N cestello per la corrispondenza.
♦ **letter-writer** ['lɛtə,raɪtəˈ] N corrispondente m/f.
let·ting ['lɛtɪŋ] N affitto.
let·tuce ['lɛtɪs] N lattuga.
♦ **let-up** ['lɛt,ʌp] N (fam) rallentamento; **without (a) let-up** ininterrottamente, senza smettere.
leu·co·cyte ['lu:kə,saɪt] N leucocita m.
leu·kae·mia, (Am) **leu·ke·mia** [lu:'ki:mɪə] N leucemia.
levee ['lɛvɪ] N (esp Am) argine m.
lev·el ['lɛvl] [1] ADJ **a** (flat: ground, surface) piano(-a), piatto(-a); (: shelf) diritto(-a), orizzontale; **I'll do my level best** (fam) farò del mio meglio, farò tutto il possibile; **a level spoonful** (Culin) un cucchiaio raso
b (steady: voice, tone) pacato(-a); (: gaze) diretto(-a), sicuro(-a); **to keep a level head** mantenere il sangue freddo or la calma
c (equal) alla pari; **to be level with sb** (in race, league, studies) essere allo stesso livello di; (in rank) avere lo stesso grado di qn; **to draw level with** (team) mettersi alla pari di; (runner, car) affiancarsi a.
[2] N **a** livello; **above/at/below sea level** sotto il/sul/al livello del mare; **talks at ministerial level** colloqui a livello ministeriale; **to be on a level with** essere al livello di; (fig) essere allo stesso livello di; **to come down to sb's level** (fig) scendere or abbassarsi al livello di qn; **to find one's own level** trovare la giusta dimensione; **on the level** piatto(-a); (fig) onesto(-a); **he's on the level** (fig fam) è a posto
b (also: spirit level) livella (a bolla d'aria)
c (Brit Scol): **A-levels** diploma di studi superiori; **O-levels** (formerly) esame che si sosteneva in Inghilterra a 16 anni, ora sostituito dal GSCE.
[3] VT **a** (make level: ground, site) livellare, spianare; (raze: building) radere al suolo; (fig) livellare
b (aim): **to level (at)** (blow) tirare (a), allungare (a); (gun) puntare (verso); **to level an accusation against** lanciare un'accusa contro
► **level off, level out** VI + ADV (prices, curve on graph etc) stabilizzarsi; (ground) diventare pianeggiante; (aircraft) volare in quota
► **level with** VI + PREP (fam): **to level with sb** esser franco (-a) con qn.
♦ **level crossing** N (Brit) passaggio a livello.
♦ **level-headed** [,lɛvl'hɛdɪd] ADJ equilibrato(-a), con la testa a posto or sulle spalle.
lev·el·ling, (Am) **lev·el·ing** ['lɛvəlɪŋ] ADJ (process, effect) di livellamento.

♦ **level playing field** N: **to compete on a level playing field** competere ad armi pari.
lev·er ['li:vəˈ, Am 'lɛvəˈ] [1] N (also fig) leva.
[2] VT: **to lever sth up/off/out** sollevare/togliere/estrarre qc (con una leva).
lev·er·age ['li:vərɪdʒ, Am 'lɛvərɪdʒ] N: **leverage (on)** forza (su); (fig) ascendente m (su); **to exert leverage on sth/sb** far leva su qc/qn.
♦ **lever arch file** N cartella con macchinetta a leva.
levi·tate ['lɛvɪ,teɪt] VI levitare.
Le·viti·cus [lɪ'vɪtɪkəs] N Levitico.
lev·ity ['lɛvɪtɪ] (frm) N (frivolity) frivolezza; (flippancy) leggerezza.
levy ['lɛvɪ] [1] N (amount) imposta, tassa; (collection) riscossione f.
[2] VT (tax, contributions) imporre; (fine) elevare; (army) arruolare.
lewd [lu:d] ADJ (comp **-er**, superl **-est**) osceno(-a).
lewd·ness ['lu:dnɪs] N oscenità.
lexi·cal ['lɛksɪkəl] ADJ lessicale.
lexi·cog·ra·pher [,lɛksɪ'kɒgrəfəˈ] N lessicografo(-a).
lexi·cog·ra·phy [,lɛksɪ'kɒgrəfɪ] N lessicografia.
lexi·colo·gist [,lɛksɪ'kɒlədʒɪst] N lessicologo(-a).
lexi·col·ogy [,lɛksɪ'kɒlədʒɪ] N lessicologia.
lexi·con ['lɛksɪkən] N lessico.
LI ABBR (Am)= Long Island.
liabil·ities [,laɪə'bɪlɪtɪz] NPL (Comm) debiti mpl; (on balance sheet) passivo msg, passività f inv.
lia·bil·ity [,laɪə'bɪlɪtɪ] N (Law: responsibility) responsabilità f inv; (burden) peso; (person) peso morto; see also **liabilities**.
lia·ble ['laɪəbl] ADJ **a** (likely): **liable to do** propenso(-a) a fare; **she's liable to get cross** è probabile che si arrabbi; **it's liable to break** è probabile che si rompa; **we are liable to get shot at here** qui c'è il rischio che ci sparino; **he's liable to colds** è soggetto a frequenti raffreddori, prende facilmente il raffreddore
b (subject): **to be liable for military service** essere tenuto(-a) a svolgere il servizio militare; **to be liable to a fine** essere passibile di multa
c (responsible): **to be liable for** essere responsabile di.
li·aise [li:'eɪz] VI: **to liaise (with)** mantenere i contatti (con).
liai·son [li:'eɪzɒn] N (also euph) relazione f; (coordination) coordinamento; (Mil) collegamento.
♦ **liaison committee** N comitato di coordinamento.
♦ **liaison officer** N ufficiale m di collegamento.
lia·na [lɪ'ɑ:nə] N liana.
liar ['laɪəˈ] N bugiardo(-a).
li·bel ['laɪbəl] [1] N (Law: crime) diffamazione f; (: written statement) libello.
[2] VT diffamare.
li·bel·lous, (Am) **li·bel·ous** ['laɪbələs] ADJ diffamatorio (-a).
Lib·er·al ['lɪbərəl] N (Pol) liberale m/f.
lib·er·al ['lɪbərəl] ADJ (generous) liberale, generoso(-a); (views) liberale; **to be liberal with** essere prodigo(-a) di.
♦ **Liberal Democrat** ADJ, N liberaldemocratico(-a).
lib·er·al·ism ['lɪbərə,lɪzəm] N liberalismo.
lib·er·al·ity [,lɪbə'rælɪtɪ] N (generosity) liberalità, generosità.
lib·er·al·ize ['lɪbərə,laɪz] VT liberalizzare.
lib·er·al·ly ['lɪbərəlɪ] ADV generosamente.

♦ **liberal-minded** [ˌlɪbərəl'maɪndɪd] ADJ tollerante.

lib·er·ate ['lɪbəˌreɪt] VT liberare; **a liberated woman** una donna emancipata.

lib·er·at·ed ['lɪbəˌreɪtɪd] ADJ (*woman, lifestyle*) emancipato (-a).

lib·era·tion [ˌlɪbə'reɪʃən] N liberazione *f*.

♦ **liberation theology** N teologia della liberazione.

lib·era·tor ['lɪbəˌreɪtə'] N liberatore(-trice).

Li·beria [laɪ'bɪərɪə] N Liberia.

Li·berian [laɪ'bɪərɪən] ADJ, N liberiano(-a).

lib·er·tar·ian [ˌlɪbə'tɛərɪən] 1 ADJ (*frm*) libertario(-a). 2 N liberale *m/f*.

lib·er·ty ['lɪbətɪ] N libertà *f inv*; **liberty of conscience** libertà di coscienza; **at liberty** (*not detained*) in libertà; **to be at liberty to do sth** essere libero(-a) di fare qc; **to take the liberty of doing sth** prendersi la libertà di fare qc, permettersi di fare qc; **to take liberties** prendersi delle libertà; **what a liberty!** (*fam*) come ti permetti? (*or* si permette? *etc*).

li·bidi·nous [lɪ'bɪdɪnəs] ADJ (*frm*) libidinoso(-a).

li·bi·do [lɪ'bi:dəʊ] N (*Psych*) libido *f inv*.

Li·bra ['li:brə] N (*Astron, Astrology*) Bilancia; **to be Libra** essere della Bilancia.

li·brar·ian [laɪ'brɛərɪən] N bibliotecario(-a).

li·brar·ian·ship [laɪ'brɛərɪənʃɪp] N biblioteconomia.

li·brary ['laɪbrərɪ] N biblioteca.

♦ **library book** N libro della biblioteca.

♦ **library ticket** N tesserino della biblioteca.

li·bret·tist [lɪ'brɛtɪst] N librettista *m/f*.

li·bret·to [lɪ'brɛtəʊ] N libretto.

Libya ['lɪbɪə] N Libia.

Liby·an ['lɪbɪən] ADJ, N libico(-a).

lice [laɪs] NPL of **louse**.

li·cence, (*Am*) **li·cense**[1] ['laɪsəns] N **a** (*permit*) autorizzazione *f*, permesso; (*for car*) bollo, tassa di circolazione; (*also*: **driving licence**: Am: *also*: **driver's licence**) patente *f* di guida; (*Comm*) licenza; (*for dog*) tassa; (*TV, Radio*) abbonamento; (: *amount paid*) canone *m*, abbonamento; **they were married by special licence** si sono sposati con dispensa; **provisional driving licence** ≈ foglio rosa; **pilot's licence** brevetto (di pilota); **import licence** licenza di importazione; **produced under licence** prodotto(-a) su licenza **b** (*freedom*) libertà; (*excessive freedom*) licenza, eccessiva libertà.

♦ **licence number** N (*Brit Aut*) numero di targa.

li·cense[2] ['laɪsəns] VT **a** (*person*): **to license sb to do** autorizzare qn a fare **b** (*car*: *subj*: *owner*) pagare la tassa di circolazione; (: *subj*: *licensing authority*) rilasciare il bollo (di circolazione).

li·censed ['laɪsənst] ADJ (*restaurant, premises*) autorizzato (-a) alla vendita di bevande alcoliche.

♦ **licensed trade** N commercio di bevande alcoliche con licenza speciale.

li·cen·see [ˌlaɪsən'si:] N (*in pub*) titolare *m/f* di licenza per la vendita di bevande alcoliche.

♦ **license plate** N (*esp Am Aut*) targa (automobilistica).

li·cens·ing laws ['laɪsənsɪŋ ˌlɔːz] N (*Brit*) leggi *fpl* che regolamentano la vendita di alcolici.

li·cen·tious [laɪ'sɛnʃəs] ADJ (*frm*) licenzioso(-a).

li·chee [ˌlaɪ'tʃi:] N = **lychee**.

li·chen ['laɪkən] N lichene *m*.

lick [lɪk] 1 VT **a** (*with tongue*) leccare; (*subj*: *flames*) lambire; **to lick one's plate clean** pulire il piatto con la lingua; **to lick one's lips** leccarsi le labbra; (*hungrily*) leccarsi i baffi; **to lick one's wounds** (*also fig*) leccarsi le ferite; **to lick sb's boots** (*fig fam*) leccare i piedi a qn; **to lick sth into shape** (*fig fam*) mettere a punto qc **b** (*fam*: *defeat*) suonarle a, stracciare. 2 N **a** leccata; **a lick of paint** una passata di vernice; **a lick and a promise** (*fig fam*) una pulitina sommaria **b** (*fam*: *speed*): **at full lick** a tutta birra.

lick·ing ['lɪkɪŋ] N (*fam*: *beating*) pestata, botte *fpl*; (: *defeat*) batosta.

lico·rice ['lɪkərɪs] N = **liquorice**.

lid [lɪd] N coperchio; **to take the lid off sth** (*fig*) smascherare qc; **that puts the lid on it** (*fam*) ci mancava solo questo.

lido ['li:dəʊ] N (*esp Brit*: *swimming pool*) piscina (all'aperto); (*part of the beach*) lido, stabilimento balneare.

lie[1] [laɪ] 1 N bugia, menzogna; **to tell lies** raccontare *or* dir bugie; **to give the lie to** smentire. 2 VI (*prp* **lying**) mentire.

lie[2] [laɪ] (*pt* **lay**, *pp* **lain**, *prp* **lying**) VI **a** (*also*: **lie down**) sdraiarsi, distendersi; (*be lying*) essere sdraiato(-a) *or* disteso(-a), giacere; (*dead body*) giacere; **he lay where he had fallen** giaceva a terra nel punto in cui era caduto; **to lie still** giacere immobile; **she lay in bed until 10 o'clock** è rimasta a letto fino alle 10; **to lie low** (*fig*) tenersi nell'ombra; (: *hide*) nascondersi **b** (*be situated*) trovarsi, essere; (*remain*) rimanere; **the book lay on the table** il libro giaceva sul tavolo; **the snow lay half a metre deep** la neve formava una coltre di mezzo metro; **the town lies in a valley** la città è situata *or* si trova in una valle; **the plain lay before us** la pianura si stendeva dinanzi a noi; **in spite of the obstacles lying in his way** nonostante gli ostacoli che aveva di fronte; **where does the difficulty/difference lie?** dov'è *or* qual è la difficoltà/differenza?; **the fault lies with you** l'errore è tuo; **the best remedy lies in ...** il miglior rimedio consiste nel...

► **lie about, lie around** VI + ADV (*things*) essere in giro; (*person*) bighellonare; **it must be lying about somewhere** dev'essere in giro da qualche parte

► **lie back** VI + ADV stendersi; **lie back and enjoy yourself!** rilassati e divertiti!

► **lie behind** VI + PREP essere dietro; **what lies behind his refusal?** cosa c'è dietro il suo rifiuto?; **the real cause that lay behind the rise in divorce** la vera causa all'origine dell'incremento dei divorzi

► **lie down** VI + ADV stendersi, sdraiarsi; **lie down!** (*to dog*) cuccia!; **to take sth lying down** (*fig*) accettare supinamente qc

► **lie in** VI + ADV (*stay in bed*) rimanere a letto (*al mattino*)

► **lie up** VI + ADV (*hide*) nascondersi.

Liech·ten·stein ['lɪktənˌstaɪn] N Liechtenstein *m*.

♦ **lie detector** N macchina della verità.

♦ **lie-down** ['laɪˌdaʊn] N (*Brit fam*) riposino.

♦ **lie-in** ['laɪˌɪn] N: **to have a lie-in** (*Brit fam*) rimanere a letto (*al mattino*).

lieu [luː] N: **in lieu of** invece di, al posto di.

Lieut. ABBR (= **lieutenant**) Ten.

lieu·ten·ant [lɛf'tɛnənt, Am luː'tɛnənt] N (*Mil*) tenente *m*; (*Naut*) tenente *m* di vascello.

♦ **lieutenant-colonel** [lɛf'tɛnənt'kɜːnl, Am luː'tɛnənt'kɜːnl] N tenente *m* colonnello.

♦ **lieutenant-general** [lɛf'tɛnənt'dʒɛnərəl, Am luː'tɛnənt'dʒɛnərəl] N tenente *m* generale, generale *m* di divisione.

life [laɪf] ① N (*pl* **lives**) **a** (*gen*) vita; **life on earth** vita terrestre *or* sulla terra; **bird life** gli uccelli; **a matter of life and death** una questione di vita o di morte; **to bring sb back to life** riportare in vita qn; **to come to life** rianimarsi, riprendere vita

b (*existence*) vita; (*of battery etc*) durata; **to spend one's life doing sth** passare la vita a fare qc; **during the life of this government** durante questo governo, nel corso di questa amministrazione; **to begin life as** cominciare come; **to be sent to prison for life** essere condannato (-a) all'ergastolo; **in early life** in gioventù; **in later life** nella maturità; **a quiet/hard life** una vita tranquilla/dura; **country/city life** vita di campagna/di città; **how's life?** (*fam*) come va (la vita)?; **that's life** così è la vita; **to lose one's life** perdere la vita; **three lives were lost** tre persone sono morte *or* hanno perso la vita; **to take one's own life** (*euph: commit suicide*) togliersi la vita; **a danger to life and limb** un pericolo mortale; **to risk life and limb** rischiare l'osso del collo; **you'll be taking your life in your hands if you climb up there** (*fam*) rischi la pelle se ti arrampichi lassù; **his life won't be worth living** rimpiangerà di esser nato; **not on your life!** (*fam*) neanche morto!, fossi matto!; **to see life** vedere il mondo; **to run for one's life** correre per mettersi in salvo; **I can't for the life of me imagine ...** (*fam*) non riesco assolutamente a immaginare...; **true to life** fedele alla realtà; **to paint from life** dipingere dal vero

c (*liveliness: of place*) vita, animazione *f*; (: *of person*) vita, vivacità; **the life and soul of the party** l'anima della festa; **to put** *or* **breathe new life into** (*person*) ridare entusiasmo a; (*project, area etc*) ridare nuova vita a.

② ADJ (*for life: membership*) a vita; (*in life: chances*) di vita.

♦ **life-and-death** [ˈlaɪfənˌdɛθ] ADJ: **life-and-death struggle** lotta all'ultimo sangue.

♦ **life annuity** N rendita vitalizia.

♦ **life assurance** N (*Brit*) = **life insurance**.

♦ **life belt**, **life buoy** N salvagente *m*.

life·blood [ˈlaɪfˌblʌd] N (*fig*) linfa vitale.

life·boat [ˈlaɪfˌbəʊt] N (*from shore*) lancia di salvataggio; (*from ship*) scialuppa di salvataggio.

♦ **life cycle** N ciclo vitale.

♦ **life expectancy** N durata media della vita.

life·guard [ˈlaɪfˌgɑːd] N (*on beach*) bagnino(-a).

♦ **life history** N (*Bio*) ciclo biologico; **a significant event in his life history** un avvenimento importante nella sua vita.

♦ **life imprisonment** N ergastolo.

♦ **life insurance** N, (*Brit*) **life assurance** N assicurazione *f* sulla vita.

♦ **life jacket** N giubbotto di salvataggio.

life·less [ˈlaɪflɪs] ADJ (*body*) privo(-a) di vita, inanimato (-a); (*fig: person*) privo(-a) di energia; (: *style*) piatto(-a); (: *hair*) senza corpo.

life·less·ness [ˈlaɪflɪsnɪs] N (*fig*) mancanza di vigore.

life·like [ˈlaɪfˌlaɪk] ADJ che sembra vero(-a), realistico(-a).

life·line [ˈlaɪfˌlaɪn] N (*on ship*) sagola di salvataggio; (*for diver*) cavo di recupero *or* di salvataggio; **it was his lifeline** (*fig*) era vitale per lui.

life·long [ˈlaɪfˌlɒŋ] ADJ (*ambition etc*) di tutta la mia *or* sua *etc* vita; (*friend*) di sempre.

♦ **life peer** N pari *m inv* a vita.

♦ **life peerage** N titolo di pari a vita.

♦ **life pre·serv·er** [ˈlaɪfprɪˌzɜːvəʳ] N **a** (*Am: life belt*) salvagente *m*; (: *life jacket*) giubbotto di salvataggio **b** (*Brit: bludgeon*) sfollagente *m inv*.

lif·er [ˈlaɪfəʳ] N (*fam*) ergastolano(-a).

♦ **life raft** N zattera di salvataggio.

♦ **life-saver** [ˈlaɪfˌseɪvəʳ] N (*person*) bagnino(-a); **it/he etc was a life-saver** (*fig*) mi ha salvato la vita.

♦ **life-saving** [ˈlaɪfˌseɪvɪŋ] ① N (*rescuing*) salvataggio. ② ADJ (*treatment, drug*) che salva (*or* salvano *etc*) la vita.

♦ **life science** N scienze *fpl* naturali.

♦ **life sentence** N condanna all'ergastolo.

♦ **life-size(d)** [ˈlaɪfˌsaɪz(d)] ADJ in *or* a grandezza naturale.

♦ **life span** N (durata della) vita.

♦ **life story** N biografia; **her life story** la sua biografia, la storia della sua vita.

♦ **life style** N stile *m* di vita.

♦ **life support system** N (*Med*) respiratore *m* automatico.

life·time [ˈlaɪfˌtaɪm] N vita; **a lifetime's work** OR **the work of a lifetime** il lavoro di tutta una vita; **in my lifetime** nel corso della mia vita, durante la mia vita; **in a lifetime** nell'arco della vita, in tutta la vita; **the chance of a lifetime** un'occasione unica *or* che capita una sola volta nella vita; **it seemed a lifetime** sembrò (che fosse passata) un'eternità *or* una vita.

LIFO [ˈlaɪfəʊ] N ABBR (= *last in first out*) lifo *m inv*.

lift [lɪft] ① VT **a** (*thing, person*) sollevare, alzare; **to lift sb over sth** far passare qn sopra qc; **to lift one's head** alzare *or* sollevare la testa; **she never lifts a finger to help** non alza *or* muove mai neanche un dito per aiutare

b (*fig: restrictions, ban*) revocare

c (*fam: steal: idea, quotation*) riprendere *or* copiare pari pari.

② VI sollevarsi, alzarsi; (*fog*) alzarsi.

③ N **a** (*Brit: elevator*) ascensore *m*; (*for goods*) montacarichi *m inv*

b (*esp Brit: in car*) passaggio; **to give sb a lift** dare un passaggio a qn

c (*Aer*) spinta; **it gave him a tremendous lift** (*fig*) lo ha tirato su moltissimo

▶ **lift down** VT + ADV tirar giù

▶ **lift off** ① VT + ADV togliere. ② VI + ADV (*aircraft, rocket*) decollare

▶ **lift out** VT + ADV tirar fuori; (*troops, evacuees etc*) far evacuare per mezzo di elicotteri (*or* aerei)

▶ **lift up** VT + ADV sollevare, alzare.

♦ **lift attendant** N ascensorista *m/f*.

lift·boy [ˈlɪftˌbɔɪ], **lift·man** [ˈlɪftˌmæn] N (*pl* -boys *or* -men) lift *m inv*, ascensorista *m/f*.

♦ **lift-off** [ˈlɪftˌɒf] N decollo.

♦ **lift-off tape** N (*for typewriter*) nastrino *m* correttore *inv* per macchina da scrivere.

♦ **lift shaft** N tromba dell'ascensore.

liga·ment [ˈlɪɡəmənt] N legamento.

light[1] [laɪt] (*vb: pt, pp* **lit** *or* **lighted**) ① N **a** (*gen*) luce *f*; **electric light** illuminazione *f or* luce elettrica; **at first light** alle prime luci dell'alba; **by the light of the moon** alla luce della luna, al chiaro di luna; **in the cold light of day** (*also fig*) alla luce del giorno; **you're (standing) in my light** mi fai ombra; **to hold sth up to** *or* **against the light** tenere qc controluce

b (*fig*): **in the light of** alla luce di; **to bring to light** portare alla luce; **to come to light** venire in luce, emergere; **to cast** *or* **shed** *or* **throw light on** gettare *or* far luce su; **I was hoping that you could shed some light on it (for me)** speravo che tu potessi darmi dei chiarimenti su questo; **to see the light** (*Rel*) convertirsi; (*fig*) ravve-

dersi; **to reveal sb/sth in a new light** mostrare qn/qc sotto una nuova luce; **according to my lights** (*frm*) secondo quanto mi è dato da capire

c (*single light*) luce *f*; (*lamp*) luce, lampada; (*Aut, Aer*) fanale *m*, faro, luce; **to turn the light on/off** accendere/ spegnere la luce; **rear lights** luci di posizione posteriori; **the (traffic) lights were red** il semaforo era rosso

d (*flame*) fiamma; **pilot light** (*on stove, water heater*) fiammella di sicurezza; **have you got a light?** (*for cigarette*) hai da accendere?; **to put a light to sth** dar fuoco a qc.

2 ADJ (*comp* -er, *superl* -est) a (*bright*) chiaro(-a); **to get lighter** rischiararsi, schiarirsi

b (*colour, skin, hair, room*) chiaro(-a); **light yellow** giallo (-a) chiaro *inv*.

3 VT a (*illuminate*) illuminare, rischiarare; **to light sb's way** far luce a qn; **lit by electricity** illuminato(-a) elettricamente

b (*cigarette, fire, candle*) accendere; **to light a bonfire** accendere un falò; **to light the fire** accendere il fuoco.

4 VI (*ignite*) accendersi

▶ **light up** 1 VI + ADV a (*lamp*) accendersi; (*face, eyes*) illuminarsi

b (*fam: smoke*) accendersi una sigaretta (*or* la pipa *etc*)

2 VT + ADV illuminare, rischiarare

▶ **light upon** VI + PREP: **her eyes lit upon the jewels** il suo sguardo cadde sui gioielli.

light² [laɪt] 1 ADJ (*comp* -er, *superl* -est) (*gen*) leggero(-a); **light ale** birra chiara; **some light reading** una lettura leggera; **she is a light sleeper** ha il sonno leggero; **as light as a feather** leggero(-a) come una piuma; **to be light on one's feet** avere il passo leggero; **with a light heart** a cuor leggero; **to make light work of sth** fare qc con molta facilità; **to make light of sth** (*fig*) prendere alla leggera qc, non dar peso a qc.

2 ADV (*travel*) leggero, con poco bagaglio.

♦ **light bulb** N lampadina.

♦ **light-coloured** [ˈlaɪtˈkʌləd] ADJ di colore chiaro.

light·en¹ [ˈlaɪtn] 1 VT (*darkness*) rischiarare, illuminare; (*hair, colour*) schiarire.

2 VI schiarirsi; (*room*) rischiararsi.

light·en² [ˈlaɪtn] VT (*load*) alleggerire; (*fig: make cheerful: heart, atmosphere*) sollevare.

light·er [ˈlaɪtəʳ] N a (*also:* **cigarette lighter**) accendino, accendisigari *m inv* b (*boat*) chiatta.

♦ **lighter fuel** N gas *m inv* per accendini.

♦ **light-fingered** [ˈlaɪtˈfɪŋɡəd] ADJ lesto(-a) di mano.

♦ **light-haired** [ˌlaɪtˈhɛəd] ADJ dai capelli chiari.

♦ **light-headed** [ˌlaɪtˈhɛdɪd] ADJ (*by temperament*) svampito(-a); (*dizzy*) intontito(-a), stordito(-a); (*with fever*) vaneggiante; (*with excitement*) eccitato(-a); **the drink made him feel light-headed** il liquore gli ha fatto girare la testa.

♦ **light-hearted** [ˈlaɪtˈhɑːtɪd] ADJ (*person, laugh*) spensierato(-a), gaio(-a); (*discussion*) non impegnato(-a).

light·house [ˈlaɪthaʊs] N faro.

light·ing [ˈlaɪtɪŋ] N (*system*) illuminazione *f*; (*in theatre*) luci *fpl*.

♦ **lighting-up time** [ˌlaɪtɪŋˈʌpˌtaɪm] N (*Brit Aut*) ora in cui bisogna accendere i fari.

light·ly [ˈlaɪtlɪ] ADV leggermente; **to fry sth lightly** (*Culin*) far soffriggere qc; **to sleep lightly** avere il sonno leggero; **to get off lightly** cavarsela a buon mercato.

♦ **light meter** N (*Phot*) esposimetro.

light·ness [ˈlaɪtnɪs] N a (*brightness*) chiarezza b (*in*

weight etc) leggerezza.

light·ning [ˈlaɪtnɪŋ] N fulmine *m*, lampo; **a lot of lightning** molti lampi; **as quick as lightning** OR **like (greased) lightning** (*fam*) (veloce) come un fulmine, in un lampo.

♦ **lightning attack** N incursione *f* lampo.

♦ **lightning conductor**, (*Am*) **lightning rod** N parafulmine *m*.

♦ **lightning strike** N sciopero a sorpresa *or* a gatto selvaggio.

♦ **light opera** N operetta.

♦ **light pen** N penna luminosa *or* ottica, light pen *f inv*.

lights [laɪts] NPL (*old: of animal*) polmone *m*.

light·ship [ˈlaɪtˌʃɪp] N battello *m* faro *inv*.

light·weight [ˈlaɪtˌweɪt] 1 ADJ (*also fig*) leggero(-a); (*Boxing*) dei pesi leggeri.

2 N (*Boxing*) peso leggero.

♦ **light year** [ˈlaɪtˌjɪəʳ] N anno *m* luce *inv*.

lig·nite [ˈlɪɡnaɪt] N lignite *f*.

Li·gu·rian [lɪˈɡjʊərɪən] ADJ, N ligure (*m/f*).

like¹ [laɪk] 1 PREP a (*similar to*) come, uguale a; (*in comparisons*) come; **to be like sb/sth** essere come qn/qc; **they are very like each other** si somigliano molto; **a house like mine** una casa come la mia; **what's he like?** che tipo è?, com'è?; **what's the weather like?** che tempo fa?; **this portrait is not like him** questo ritratto non gli somiglia affatto; **he thinks like us** la pensa come noi; **she behaved like an idiot** si è comportata come una *or* da cretina; **that's just like him** è proprio da lui; **it's not like him to do that** non è da lui fare così, non è tipo da fare cose del genere; **I never saw anything like it** non ho mai visto una cosa simile, non ho mai visto niente di simile; **that's more like it** (*fam*) così va meglio; **that's nothing like it** non ha niente a che vedere con quello; **something like that** qualcosa del genere; **don't talk like that** non parlare così; **there's nothing like a holiday** non c'è niente di meglio di una vacanza; **it happened like this** ... è andata così...; **like father like son** tale padre tale figlio; **we ran like mad** (*fam*) abbiamo fatto una corsa pazzesca; **it rained like mad** (*fam*) ha piovuto a dirotto; **I feel like a drink** avrei voglia di bere qualcosa, berrei volentieri qualcosa; **it looks like a diamond** sembra un diamante

b (*such as*) come.

2 ADJ simile, uguale; **in like cases** in casi simili *or* analoghi; **rabbits, mice and like creatures** conigli, topi e animali simili; **to be as like as two peas (in a pod)** essere come due gocce d'acqua.

3 ADV: **it's nothing like as hot as it was** non fa più così caldo come faceva prima; **as like as not** (molto) probabilmente.

4 CONJ (*as*) come; **like we used to (do)** come facevamo una volta.

5 N: **we shall not see his like again** non ci sarà mai più uno come lui; **did you ever see the like (of it)?** hai mai visto niente del genere?; **the like of which I never saw** come non ne avevo mai visti; **sparrows, blackbirds and the like** passeri, merli e altri uccelli simili; **the likes of him** (*fam pej*) quelli come lui.

like² [laɪk] 1 VT a : **I like swimming/that book/chocolate** mi piace nuotare/quel libro/il cioccolato; **I like hats** mi piacciono i cappelli; **I like her** mi piace; **which do you like best?** quale preferisci?; **well, I like that!** (*fam hum*) questa sì che è bella!

b (*want*) desiderare, volere; **I would like** OR **I'd like** mi piacerebbe, vorrei; **would you like a coffee?** vuole un

caffè?, gradirebbe un caffè?; **I would like more time** vorrei *or* mi piacerebbe avere più tempo; **I should like to know why** vorrei *or* mi piacerebbe sapere perché; **would you like me to wait outside?** vuoi *or* desideri che aspetti fuori?; **I didn't like to (do it)** non volevo (farlo); **as you like** come vuoi; **if you like** se vuoi; **whenever you like** quando vuoi.

2: **likes** NPL gusti *mpl*, preferenze *fpl*; **his likes and dislikes** i suoi gusti.

like·able ['laɪkəbl] ADJ simpatico(-a).

like·li·hood ['laɪklɪˌhʊd] N probabilità; **in all likelihood** con ogni probabilità, molto probabilmente; **there is no likelihood of that** è da escludersi; **there is little likelihood that he'll come** è difficile che venga.

like·ly ['laɪklɪ] 1 ADJ (*comp* **-ier**, *superl* **-iest**) (*outcome, winner*) probabile; (*place*) adatto(-a), buono(-a); (*story, explanation*) plausibile; **a likely explanation** una spiegazione attendibile *or* plausibile; **a likely story!** (*iro*) ma a chi la racconti?, e io dovrei crederci?; **when is the likeliest time to find you at home?** quando è più probabile trovarti a casa?; **it's likely that I'll be late** molto probabilmente sarò in ritardo; **an incident likely to cause trouble** un incidente che probabilmente causerà dei problemi; **it's not likely that he'll come** OR **he is not likely to come** è difficile che venga; **he's likely to leave** è probabile che parta, probabilmente partirà.

2 ADV probabilmente; **most** *or* **very likely they've lost it** con molta probabilità *or* molto probabilmente l'hanno perso; **not likely!** (*fam*) neanche per sogno!

♦ **like-minded** [ˌlaɪk'maɪndɪd] ADJ che la pensa allo stesso modo.

lik·en ['laɪkən] VT: **to liken sth to** paragonare qc a.

like·ness ['laɪknɪs] N a (*similarity*) somiglianza; **there is a family likeness** ci sono tratti caratteristici della famiglia; **that's a good likeness of you** ti rassomiglia molto b (*form*): **in the likeness of** sotto le apparenze *or* l'aspetto di.

like·wise ['laɪkˌwaɪz] ADV (*similarly*) nello *or* allo stesso modo; (*also*) anche; (*moreover*) inoltre, per di più; **to do likewise** fare altrettanto.

lik·ing ['laɪkɪŋ] N (*for person*) simpatia; (*for thing*) predilezione *f*; **to have a liking for sb/sth** avere un debole per qn/qc; **to be to sb's liking** essere di gusto *or* gradimento di qn; **to take a liking to sb** prendere qn in simpatia; **to take a liking to sth/to doing sth** scoprire il piacere di qc/di fare qc; **is the meal to your liking?** è di tuo gradimento il pranzo?

li·lac ['laɪlək] 1 N (*flower*) lillà *m inv*; (*colour*) lilla *m inv*. 2 ADJ lilla *inv*.

Lil·li·pu·tian [ˌlɪlɪ'pjuːʃɪən] ADJ, N (*liter*) lillipuziano(-a).

Lilo® ['laɪləʊ] N (*Brit*) *materassino gonfiabile*.

lilt [lɪlt] N cadenza.

lilt·ing ['lɪltɪŋ] ADJ melodioso(-a).

lily ['lɪlɪ] N giglio.

♦ **lily-livered** ['lɪlɪˌlɪvəd] ADJ (*old*) codardo(-a).

♦ **lily of the valley** N mughetto.

Lima ['liːmə] N Lima.

limb [lɪm] N (*Anat*) arto; (*of tree*) (grosso) ramo; **a man with strong limbs** un uomo dalle membra robuste; **to be out on a limb** (*fig*) trovarsi in difficoltà; **to go out on a limb** (*fig*) esporsi; **to tear limb from limb** sbranare, fare a pezzettini.

lim·ber up [ˌlɪmbər'ʌp] VI + ADV scaldarsi (i muscoli).

limbo ['lɪmbəʊ] N (*Rel, also fig*) limbo.

lime¹ [laɪm] N (*Chem, Geol*) calce *f*; **slaked lime** calce

spenta.

lime² [laɪm] N (*Bot: linden*) tiglio.

lime³ [laɪm] N (*Bot: citrus fruit*) limetta.

♦ **lime juice** N succo di limetta.

lime·light ['laɪmˌlaɪt] N: **to be in the limelight** essere alla ribalta, essere in vista.

lim·er·ick ['lɪmərɪk] N *poesiola umoristica di 5 versi*.

lime·stone ['laɪmˌstəʊn] N (*Geol*) calcare *m*, pietra calcarea.

♦ **limestone pavement** N (*Geol*) campi *mpl* solcati.

lime·water ['laɪmˌwɔːtəʳ] N acqua di calce.

lim·it ['lɪmɪt] 1 N limite *m*; **weight/speed limit** limite di peso/di velocità; **there's a limit to my patience** la mia pazienza ha un limite; **within limits** entro certi limiti; **there is a limit to what one can do** c'è un limite a quello che si può fare; **he's the limit!** (*fam*) lui passa tutti i limiti!; **well, that's the limit!** (*fam*) questo è il massimo *or* il colmo!.

2 VT limitare; **to limit o.s. to a few remarks** limitarsi ad alcune osservazioni; **I limit myself to 10 cigarettes a day** mi limito a (fumare) 10 sigarette al giorno.

limi·ta·tion [ˌlɪmɪ'teɪʃən] N limitazione *f*, restrizione *f*; **he has/knows his limitations** ha/conosce i suoi limiti.

lim·it·ed ['lɪmɪtɪd] ADJ limitato(-a), ristretto(-a); (*means, income*) scarso(-a); **to a limited extent** entro certi limiti, fino a un certo punto; **they are limited in what they can do** hanno una possibilità di agire limitata; **limited edition** edizione *f* numerata.

♦ **limited company**, **limited liability company** N (*Brit*) ≈ società *f inv* a responsabilità limitata.

lim·it·less ['lɪmɪtlɪs] ADJ illimitato(-a).

lim·ou·sine ['lɪməziːn] N limousine *f inv*.

limp¹ [lɪmp] 1 VI zoppicare; **to limp in/out** entrare/uscire zoppicando; **the ship limped home** la nave è tornata faticosamente in porto.

2 N: **to walk with** *or* **have a limp** zoppicare.

limp² [lɪmp] ADJ (*gen*) molle; (*dress*) floscio(-a); (*person*) fiacco(-a); **she went limp** si afflosciò; **let your arm go limp** rilassa completamente il braccio; **limp cover(s)** (*on book*) rilegatura in brossura.

lim·pet ['lɪmpɪt] N (*Zool*) patella; (*fig*) persona appiccicosa.

♦ **limpet mine** N (*Mil*) mignatta.

lim·pid ['lɪmpɪd] ADJ (*liter*) limpido(-a).

limp·ly ['lɪmplɪ] ADV (*see adj*) mollemente; flosciamente; fiaccamente.

limp·ness ['lɪmpnɪs] N (*see adj*) mollezza; flaccidità; fiacchezza.

linch·pin ['lɪntʃˌpɪn] N (*in axle*) acciarino, bietta; (*fig*) perno.

Lincs [lɪŋks] ABBR (*Brit*) = Lincolnshire.

linc·tus ['lɪŋktəs] N (*Med*) sciroppo per la tosse.

lin·den ['lɪndən] N = **lime²**.

line¹ [laɪn] N a (*gen*) linea; (*pen stroke*) tratto; (*wrinkle*) ruga; **to draw a line under sth** sottolineare qc; **to draw a line through sth** tirare una riga sopra qc; **to draw the line at (doing) sth** rifiutarsi di fare qc; **to know where to draw the line** (*fig*) saper rispettare i limiti; **in line to the throne** nella linea di successione al trono; **she comes from a long line of teachers** i suoi sono insegnanti da generazioni

b (*rope*) corda, fune *f*; (*fishing line*) lenza; (*wire*) filo; (*Elec*) linea; **clothes line** filo *or* corda del bucato

c (*Telec*) linea; **the line went dead** è caduta la linea; **hold the line please** resti in linea per cortesia; **Mr Smith is on**

the line c'è in linea il signor Smith

d (*row, series*) fila; (*queue*) fila, coda; **to stand in line** mettersi in fila; **to be in line for sth** (*fig*) essere in lista per qc; **to bring sth into line with sth** mettere qc al passo con qc; **to fall into line with sb/sth** adeguarsi a qn/qc; **to step out of line** (*fig*) sgarrare; **to cut in line** (*Am*) passare avanti

e (*direction, course*) linea, direzione *f*; **line of inquiry** pista; **in the line of fire** (*Mil*) sulla linea di tiro; **line of attack** (*Mil*) piano d'attacco; (*fig*) piano d'azione; **to follow** *or* **take the line of least resistance** seguire la via più facile; **in the line of duty** nell'esercizio delle proprie funzioni; **line of argument** filo del ragionamento; **line of research/business** settore *m* di ricerca/d'attività; **in his line of business** nel suo ramo (di affari); **line of interest** sfera di interesse; **it's not my line** (*fam: speciality*) non sono un esperto in materia; **to take a strong** *or* **firm line on sth** essere deciso(-a) per quanto riguarda qc; **to take the line that ...** essere del parere che...; **to toe** *or* **follow the party line** attenersi alla *or* seguire la linea politica del partito; **in line with** in linea con, d'accordo con; **along the same lines** dello stesso tipo *or* genere; **we are thinking along the same lines** la pensiamo più o meno allo stesso modo; **to be on the right lines** andare tutto sommato bene

f (*of print*) riga; (*of verse*) verso; **to learn one's lines** (*Theatre*) imparare le battute; **to read between the lines** (*fig*) leggere fra le righe; **drop me a line** scrivimi due righe

g (*Rail: route*) linea; (*shipping company*) compagnia di navigazione; **all along the line** (*fig*) fin da principio; **to reach** *or* **come to the end of the line** (*fig: relationship*) arrivare a un punto di rottura

h (*Comm*) linea; **a new line in cosmetics** una nuova linea di cosmetici

▶ **line up** ①**VT + ADV** (*people, objects*) allineare, mettere in fila; **have you got anyone lined up for the job?** hai già in mente qualcuno per quel posto?; **to have sth lined up** avere qc in programma. ②**VI + ADV** (*in queue*) mettersi in fila; (*in row*) allinearsi.

line² [laɪn] **VT: to line (with)** (*clothes*) foderare (di); (*box*) rivestire (di), foderare (di); (*subj: trees, crowd*) fiancheggiare; **the streets were lined with people/trees** c'erano file di persone/di alberi ai bordi delle strade.

lin·eage ['lɪnɪɪdʒ] N (*frm*) stirpe *f*, lignaggio, schiatta.

lin·ear ['lɪnɪə'] ADJ lineare.

lined¹ [laɪnd] ADJ (*paper*) a righe, rigato(-a); (*face*) rugoso (-a).

lined² [laɪnd] ADJ (*clothes*) foderato(-a).

♦ **line drawing** N disegno a tratteggio.

♦ **line feed** N (*Comput*) avanzamento di una interlinea.

line·man ['laɪnmən] N (*pl* **-men**) (*Am Elec*) guardafili *m inv*; (*Rail*) guardalinee *m inv*; (*American Football*) attaccante *m*.

lin·en ['lɪnɪn] ①N (*cloth*) (tela di) lino; (*sheets, tablecloth etc*) biancheria; **to wash one's dirty linen in public** (*fig*) lavare i panni sporchi in pubblico. ②ADJ (*garment*) di lino; (*basket, cupboard*) della biancheria.

♦ **line of sight**, **line of vision** N visuale *f*.

♦ **line-out** ['laɪn,aʊt] N (*Rugby*) touche *f inv*.

♦ **line printer** N stampante *f* parallela.

lin·er ['laɪnə'] N **a** (*ship*) nave *f* di linea, transatlantico **b** : dustbin liner sacchetto per la pattumiera.

lines·man ['laɪnzmən] N (*pl* **-men**) (*Sport*) guardalinee *m*

inv, segnalinee *m inv*; (*Telec*) guardafili *m inv*.

♦ **line-up** ['laɪn,ʌp] N (*row*) fila, allineamento; (*Sport*) formazione *f*; (*Am: identity parade*) confronto all'americana.

ling¹ [lɪŋ] N (*Bot*) brugo.

ling² [lɪŋ] N (*fish*) molva.

lin·ger ['lɪŋgə'] VI (*person: dawdle*) indugiare; (: *wait*) attardarsi; (: *be on the point of death*) trascinarsi; (*smell, memory, tradition*) persistere; **to linger over a meal** attardarsi a tavola; **to linger on a subject** dilungarsi su un argomento.

lin·gerie ['lænʒəri:] N lingerie *f inv*, biancheria intima (femminile).

lin·ger·ing ['lɪŋgərɪŋ] ADJ (*smell, doubt*) persistente; (*look*) insistente, lungo(-a); (*death*) lento(-a).

lin·go ['lɪŋgəʊ] N (*fam pej*) *qualunque lingua straniera che risulti incomprensibile*; (: *jargon*) gergo.

lin·gua fran·ca ['lɪŋgwə'fræŋkə] N lingua franca.

lin·guist ['lɪŋgwɪst] N (*academic*) linguista *m/f*; **I'm no linguist** sono negato per le lingue; **he's an excellent linguist** è molto portato per le lingue.

lin·guis·tic [lɪŋ'gwɪstɪk] ADJ linguistico(-a).

lin·guis·tics [lɪŋ'gwɪstɪks] NSG linguistica.

lini·ment ['lɪnɪmənt] N linimento.

lin·ing ['laɪnɪŋ] N (*of clothes etc*) fodera; (*Tech*) rivestimento (interno); (*of brake*) guarnizione *f*.

link [lɪŋk] ①N (*of chain*) anello; (*fig: connection*) legame *m*, collegamento, rapporto; **cultural links** rapporti culturali; **rail link** collegamento ferroviario; see also **links**. ②VT (*also fig*) collegare, congiungere, unire; **to link arms with sb** prendere sottobraccio qn

▶ **link up** ①VI + ADV (*people: meet*) ritrovarsi, riunirsi; (: *join*) unirsi, associarsi; (*spaceships etc*) agganciarsi; (*railway lines, roads*) congiungersi. ②VT collegare, unire.

link·age ['lɪŋkɪdʒ] N connessione *f*; **the linkage between cause and effect** il nesso fra causa ed effetto.

link·man ['lɪŋkmən] N (*pl* **-men**) annunciatore.

links [lɪŋks] NPL (*golf links*) terreno *or* campo da golf.

♦ **link-up** ['lɪŋk,ʌp] N legame *m*; (*of roads*) nodo; (*of spaceships*) aggancio; (*Radio, TV*) collegamento.

lin·net ['lɪnɪt] N fanello.

lino ['laɪnəʊ], **li·no·leum** [lɪ'nəʊlɪəm] N linoleum *m inv*.

Li·no·type® ['laɪnəʊ,taɪp] N linotype ® *f inv*.

lin·seed oil ['lɪnsiːd'ɔɪl] N olio di semi di lino.

lint [lɪnt] N (*Med*) garza.

lin·tel ['lɪntl] N architrave *m*.

lion ['laɪən] N leone *m*; (*fig: person*) celebrità *f inv*; **to get** *or* **take the lion's share** fare la parte del leone; **to put one's head in the lion's mouth** (*fig*) cacciarsi nei guai.

♦ **lion cub** N leoncino.

li·on·ess ['laɪənɪs] N leonessa.

♦ **lion-hearted** ['laɪən,hɑːtɪd] ADJ molto coraggioso(-a).

♦ **lion-tamer** ['laɪən,teɪmə'] N domatore(-trice) di leoni.

lip [lɪp] N (*Anat*) labbro; (*of jug*) beccuccio; (*of glass, of cup etc*) orlo; (*fam: insolence*) sfacciataggine *f*.

♦ **lip gloss** N lucidalabbra *m inv*.

li·pid ['laɪpɪd] N (*Biochemistry*) lipide *m*.

lipo·suc·tion ['lɪpəʊ,sʌkʃən] N liposuzione *f*.

♦ **lip-read** ['lɪp,riːd] VI, VT leggere (sul)le labbra.

♦ **lip-reading** ['lɪp,riːdɪŋ] N lettura delle labbra, labiolettura.

♦ **lip salve** N burro di cacao.

♦ **lip service** N: **to pay lip service to sth** essere favorevole a qc solo a parole; **he pays lip service to environ-**

mentalism but … si professa ambientalista ma… .

lip·stick ['lɪpˌstɪk] N rossetto.

liq·ue·fac·tion [ˌlɪkwɪ'fækʃən] N (*Tech*) liquefazione *f*.

liq·ue·fy ['lɪkwɪˌfaɪ] ① VT liquefare; **liquefied gas** gas *m* liquido.
② VI liquefarsi.

li·queur [lɪ'kjʊəʳ] N liquore *m*.

liq·uid ['lɪkwɪd] ① ADJ (*gen*) liquido(-a).
② N liquido.

♦ **liquid assets** NPL (*Fin*) attività *fpl* liquide.

liq·ui·date ['lɪkwɪdeɪt] VT liquidare.

liq·ui·da·tion [ˌlɪkwɪ'deɪʃən] N liquidazione *f*; **to go into liquidation** (*Fin*) andare in liquidazione.

♦ **liquidation sale** N (*Am*) liquidazione *f*.

liq·ui·da·tor ['lɪkwɪˌdeɪtəʳ] N (*Fin*) liquidatore *m*.

♦ **liquid crystal display** N visualizzatore *m* a cristalli liquidi.

li·quid·ity [lɪ'kwɪdɪtɪ] N (*Fin*) liquidità.

♦ **liquidity ratio** N (*Fin*) rapporto di liquidità.

liq·uid·ize ['lɪkwɪˌdaɪz] VT (*Brit Culin*) passare al frullatore.

liq·uid·iz·er ['lɪkwɪˌdaɪzəʳ] N (*Brit Culin*) frullatore *m* (a brocca).

♦ **liquid paraffin** N olio di paraffina.

liq·uor ['lɪkəʳ] N (*esp Am*) bevanda alcolica, alcolico.

liquo·rice ['lɪkərɪs] N liquirizia.

♦ **liquor store** N (*Am*) negozio di alcolici.

lira ['lɪərə] N lira.

Lis·bon ['lɪzbən] N Lisbona.

lisle [laɪl] ① N filo di Scozia.
② ADJ (*socks*) di filo di Scozia.

lisp [lɪsp] ① N lisca (*fam*); **with a lisp** con la lisca (*fam*).
② VI parlare con la lisca (*fam*).

lis·som ['lɪsəm] ADJ (*liter*) leggiadro(-a).

list[1] [lɪst] ① N lista, elenco; (*Comm*) listino; **shopping list** lista *or* nota della spesa.
② VT (*include in list*) mettere in lista; (*write down*) fare una lista di; (: *expenses etc*) fare la nota di; (*enumerate*) elencare; (*Comput*) listare; **it is not listed** non è *or* non figura nell'elenco.

list[2] [lɪst] ① VI (*ship*) inclinarsi, sbandare.
② N (*of ship*) sbandamento.

list·ed build·ing ['lɪstɪd'bɪldɪŋ] N (*Brit Archit*) edificio sotto la protezione delle Belle Arti.

list·ed com·pa·ny ['lɪstɪd'kʌmpənɪ] N società *f inv* le cui azioni sono quotate in Borsa.

lis·ten ['lɪsn] VI ascoltare; **to listen to sb/sth** ascoltare qn/qc; **listen!** ascolta!, senti!; **he wouldn't listen to me** non mi ha voluto dar retta *or* ascolto; **he wouldn't listen to reason** non ha voluto sentire ragione; **listen (out) for the car** senti se arriva la macchina; **listen (out) for your name** aspetta che ti chiamino; **to listen in on a conversation** ascoltare di nascosto una conversazione.

lis·ten·er ['lɪsnəʳ] N (*to speaker*) ascoltatore(-trice); (*to radio*) radioascoltatore(-trice); **to be a good listener** saper ascoltare.

lis·teria [ˌlɪs'tɪərɪə] N listeria.

list·ing ['lɪstɪŋ] N (*entry*) voce *f*; (*Comput*) lista stampata.

list·less ['lɪstlɪs] ADJ (*gen*) fiacco(-a), svogliato(-a); (*uninterested*) apatico(-a).

list·less·ly ['lɪstlɪslɪ] ADV (*see adj*) fiaccamente, svogliatamente; apaticamente.

list·less·ness ['lɪstlɪsnɪs] N (*see adj*) fiacchezza, svogliatezza; apatia.

♦ **list price** N prezzo di listino.

lists [lɪsts] NPL (*History*) lizza; **to enter the lists (against**

sb/sth) (*fig*) entrare in lizza (contro qn/qc).

lit [lɪt] PT, PP of **light**[1].

lita·ny ['lɪtənɪ] N litania.

li·ter ['liːtəʳ] N (*Am*) = **litre**.

lit·era·cy ['lɪtərəsɪ] N il saper leggere e scrivere.

♦ **literacy campaign** N lotta contro l'analfabetismo.

lit·er·al ['lɪtərəl] ① ADJ (*meaning, translation*) letterale; (*account*) testuale; (*person*) prosaico(-a).
② N (*Brit: Typ*) refuso.

lit·er·al·ly ['lɪtərəlɪ] ADV (*gen*) letteralmente; (*interpret*) alla lettera; **it was literally impossible to work there** era letteralmente impossibile lavorare lì.

lit·er·ary ['lɪtərərɪ] ADJ letterario(-a); **a literary man** un letterato.

lit·er·ate ['lɪtərɪt] ADJ che sa leggere e scrivere; **highly literate** molto colto(-a), molto istruito(-a).

lit·era·ture ['lɪtərɪtʃəʳ] N (*publications, Literature*) letteratura; (*brochures etc*) opuscoli *mpl*, materiale *m*, informativo.

lithe [laɪð] ADJ (*frm*) agile, flessuoso(-a).

lith·ium ['lɪθɪəm] N litio.

litho·graph ['lɪθəʊgrɑːf] N litografia.

li·thog·ra·pher [lɪ'θɒɡrəfəʳ] N litografo(-a).

li·thog·ra·phy [lɪ'θɒɡrəfɪ] N litografia.

Lithua·nia [ˌlɪθju'eɪnɪə] N Lituania.

Lithua·nian [ˌlɪθju'eɪnɪən] ① ADJ lituano(-a).
② N lituano(-a); (*language*) lituano.

liti·gant ['lɪtɪɡənt] N litigante *m/f*.

liti·gate ['lɪtɪˌɡeɪt] VI essere in causa.

liti·ga·tion [ˌlɪtɪ'ɡeɪʃən] N causa (giudiziaria).

li·ti·gious [lɪ'tɪdʒəs] ADJ (*frm: person*) *che fa eccessivo ricorso all'autorità giudiziaria*.

lit·mus pa·per ['lɪtməsˌpeɪpəʳ] N (*also fig*) cartina al tornasole.

lit·mus test ['lɪtməsˌtɛst] N (*also fig*) cartina al tornasole.

li·tre ['liːtəʳ] N litro.

lit·ter ['lɪtəʳ] ① N a (*rubbish*) rifiuti *mpl*; (*papers*) cartacce *fpl*
b (*young animals*) nidiata, figliata; (: *of dogs*) cucciolata
c (*Agr: bedding*) lettiera.
② VT (*subj: person*) lasciare rifiuti in; (: *books, rubbish*) coprire; **littered with** coperto(-a) di; **the room was littered with books** nella stanza c'erano libri dappertutto; **a pavement littered with papers** un marciapiede pieno di cartacce.

♦ **litter bin, litter basket** N cestino dei rifiuti.

♦ **litter lout**, (*Am*) **litter·bug** ['lɪtəˌbʌɡ] N *persona che butta per terra le cartacce o i rifiuti*.

lit·tle[1] ['lɪtl] ADJ a (*small: gen*) piccolo(-a); **a little chair** una seggiolina; **a little cup** una tazzina; **my little brother** il mio fratellino; **a little girl** una bambina; **little finger** mignolo; **poor little thing!** poverino!
b (*short*) breve; **we went for a little ride/walk** siamo andati a fare un giretto/una passeggiatina; **for a little while** per un po'; **it's only a little way to the station** la stazione non è lontana; **a little holiday** una breve vacanza.

lit·tle[2] ['lɪtl] (*comp* less, *superl* least) ① ADJ, PRON (*not much*) poco(-a); (*some*) un poco *or* un po' di; **a little milk** un po' di latte; **little money** pochi soldi; **with little difficulty** senza fatica *or* difficoltà; **to see/do little** non vedere/fare molto, vedere/fare molto poco; **we did what little we could** abbiamo fatto quel poco che abbiamo potuto; **little or nothing** poco o nulla; **that has little to do with it!** questo c'entra ben poco!; **as little as £5** soltanto 5

sterline; **to make little of sth** (*fail to understand*) capire poco di qc; (*belittle*) tenere qc in poco conto, dare poca importanza a qc; **little by little** poco a poco.

2 ADV a : **a little** un po'; **a little too big** un po' troppo grande; **a little longer** un po' più a lungo; **we were a little surprised** eravamo un po' sorpresi; **a little more milk** un po' più di latte; **a little more** ancora un po' b (*not much*): **a little-known fact** un fatto poco noto; **it's little better** non va molto meglio; **as little as possible** il meno possibile; **little more than a month ago** appena più di un mese fa; **I like it as little as you do** non mi piace più di quanto piaccia a te; **little does he know that ...** quello di cui non si rende conto è che... .

li·tur·gi·cal [lɪ'tɜːdʒɪkəl] ADJ liturgico(-a).

lit·ur·gy ['lɪtədʒɪ] N liturgia.

liv·able ['lɪvəbl] ADJ (*gen*) vivibile; (*house*) abitabile; **he's not livable with** (*fam*) è insopportabile.

live¹ [lɪv] 1 VI a (*exist, survive*) vivere; **to live to be 100** vivere fino all'età di *or* a 100 anni; **he hasn't long to live** non gli resta molto da vivere; **as long as I live** finché vivo *or* campo; **to live through an experience** sopravvivere a un'esperienza; **he lived through two wars** ha visto due guerre; **to live like a lord** vivere da signore *or* come un re; **she lives for her family** vive solo per la famiglia; **I'm living for the day when ...** vivo solo nell'attesa del giorno in cui...; **the doctors have given her three months to live** i medici le hanno dato tre mesi di vita; **you'll live!** (*iro*) vedrai che non morirai!; **to live with a memory** essere perseguitato(-a) da un ricordo; **he's not easy to live with** non è facile vivere con lui; **you live and learn** c'è sempre qualcosa da imparare; **live and let live** vivi e lascia vivere; **to live by.../by doing ...** guadagnarsi da vivere con.../facendo...; **long live the King!** viva il re!

b (*reside*) abitare, vivere; **to live in London** abitare *or* vivere a Londra; **I live in Grange Road** abito in Grange Road.

2 VT: **to live a happy life/a life of hardship** avere una vita felice/dura; **to live life to the full** godersi la vita; **to live a life of luxury** vivere nel lusso; **to live the part** (*Theatre, fig*) immedesimarsi nella parte

► **live down** VT + ADV (*disgrace*) far dimenticare (alla gente)

► **live in** VI + ADV (*students, nurses*) essere interno(-a); (*servants*) avere vitto e alloggio

► **live off** VI + PREP (*land, food*) vivere di; (*pej: parents*) vivere alle spalle *or* a spese di

► **live on** 1 VI + PREP (*food, fruit, salary*) vivere di; **to live on £50 a week** vivere con 50 sterline la settimana; **enough to live on** abbastanza per vivere.

2 VI + ADV continuare a vivere, sopravvivere

► **live out** 1 VI + ADV (*Brit: students*) essere esterno(-a); (*housekeeper*) essere a mezzo servizio.

2 VT + ADV: **to live out one's days** *or* **life** trascorrere gli ultimi anni

► **live together** VI + ADV (*cohabit*) vivere insieme, convivere

► **live up** VT + ADV: **to live it up** (*fam*) fare la bella vita

► **live up to** VI + ADV + PREP (*principles*) tenere fede a, non venir meno a; (*reputation*) essere all'altezza di; **the film didn't live up to our expectations** il film ci ha deluso

► **live with** VI + PREP (*cohabit with*) vivere con; (*put up with*): **I'll learn to live with it** mi ci abituerò; **I can't live with that pink door any more** non sopporto più quella porta rosa.

live² [laɪv] 1 ADJ a (*animal*) vivo(-a); (*issue*) scottante, d'attualità; (*Radio, TV: broadcast*) in diretta; (*music,*

concert) dal vivo; **a real live crocodile** un coccodrillo in carne e ossa; **live yoghurt** yogurt ricco di fermenti lattici vivi

b (*shell, ammunition: not blank*) carico(-a); (: *unexploded*) inesploso(-a); (*Elec: rail*) sotto tensione; (: *wire*) ad alta tensione; (*still burning: coal*) ardente.

2 ADV: **to be broadcast live** essere trasmesso(-a) in diretta.

♦ **live-in** ['lɪvɪn] ADJ (*fam: partner*) convivente; (: *servant*) che vive in casa; **he has a live-in girlfriend** la sua ragazza vive con lui.

live·li·hood ['laɪvlɪˌhʊd] N mezzi *mpl* di sostentamento; **to earn one's livelihood** guadagnarsi da vivere.

live·li·ness ['laɪvlɪnɪs] N vivacità, brio.

live·long ['lɪvˌlɒŋ] ADJ (*liter*): **all the livelong day** tutto il santo giorno.

live·ly ['laɪvlɪ] ADJ (*comp* **-ier**, *superl* **-iest**) (*gen*) vivace, vivo(-a); (*imagination*) fervido(-a); (*conversation, argument*) animato(-a); (*interest*) vivo(-a); (*party, scene etc*) movimentato(-a); (*pace*) sostenuto(-a); **things are getting lively** l'ambiente *or* l'atmosfera comincia a scaldarsi.

liv·en up [ˌlaɪvən'ʌp] 1 VT + ADV (*room etc*) ravvivare; (*discussion, evening*) animare.

2 VI + ADV animarsi.

liv·er ['lɪvəʳ] 1 N (*Anat, Culin*) fegato.

2 ADJ di fegato.

♦ **liver fluke** N distoma *m* epatico.

liv·er·ish ['lɪvərɪʃ] ADJ: **to be liverish** *or* **feel liverish** sentirsi il fegato ingrossato, avere mal di fegato; (*fig*) scontroso (-a).

Liv·er·pud·lian [ˌlɪvə'pʌdlɪən] 1 ADJ di Liverpool.

2 N abitante *m/f or* originario(-a) di Liverpool.

liv·ery ['lɪvərɪ] N livrea.

♦ **livery stable** N scuderia (di cavalli da nolo).

lives [laɪvz] NPL of **life**.

live·stock ['laɪvˌstɒk] N bestiame *m*.

♦ **live wire** ['laɪvwaɪəʳ] N (*fam*): **to be a live wire** essere pieno(-a) di vitalità.

liv·id ['lɪvɪd] ADJ a (*furious*) furioso(-a), livido(-a) di rabbia, furibondo(-a) b (*in colour: complexion*) livido (-a); (: *sky*) plumbeo(-a); (: *bruise*) bluastro(-a).

liv·ing ['lɪvɪŋ] 1 ADJ (*alive: gen*) vivo(-a); (: *person*) vivente, in vita; **within living memory** a memoria d'uomo; **the greatest living pianist** il più grande pianista vivente; **there wasn't a living soul** non c'era anima viva.

2 N vita; **what do you do for a living?** come ti guadagni da vivere?; **to earn** *or* **make a living** guadagnarsi da vivere; **the living** (*people*) i vivi.

♦ **living conditions** NPL condizioni *fpl* di vita.

♦ **living expenses** NPL spese *fpl* di mantenimento.

♦ **living quarters** NPL alloggi *mpl*.

♦ **living room** N soggiorno, salotto.

♦ **living space** N spazio per vivere.

♦ **living standards** NPL tenore *m or* livello di vita.

♦ **living wage** N salario sufficiente per vivere.

Livy ['lɪvɪ] N Tito Livio.

liz·ard ['lɪzəd] N lucertola.

lla·ma ['lɑːmə] N lama *m inv*.

LLB [ˌelel'biː] N ABBR (= *Bachelor of Laws*) ≈ laurea in Giurisprudenza.

LLD [ˌelel'diː] N ABBR (= *Doctor of Laws*) ≈ dottorato in Giurisprudenza.

LMT [ˌelem'tiː] ABBR (*Am*: = *Local Mean Time*) tempo medio locale.

lo [ləʊ] EXCL (old): **lo and behold** ... quand'ecco che... .

load [ləʊd] **1** N **a** (Elec, Tech, burden) carico; (weight) peso **b** (fig): **that's (taken) a load off my mind** mi sono tolto un peso; **loads of, a load of** (fam) un sacco or un mucchio di; **it's a load of old rubbish** (fam) sono un mucchio di sciocchezze. **2** VT (also: **load up**): **to load (with)** (lorry, ship) caricare (di); (gun, camera): **to load (with)** caricare (con); **he's loaded (down) with debts/worries** è carico di debiti/preoccupazioni; **to load a program** (Comput) caricare un programma.

load·ed ['ləʊdɪd] ADJ **a** : **a loaded question** una domanda tendenziosa **b** (dice) truccato(-a); **the dice are loaded against him** (fig) ha tutto contro di lui **c** : **to be loaded** (fam: rich) essere pieno(-a) di soldi.

load·er ['ləʊdə'] N caricatore m.

load·ing bay ['ləʊdɪŋˌbeɪ] N piazzola di carico.

loaf¹ [ləʊf] N (pl **loaves**) pagnotta, pane m; **half a loaf is better than no bread** (Proverb) meglio poco che niente.

loaf² [ləʊf] VI (also: **loaf about, loaf around**) oziare, bighellonare.

loaf·er ['ləʊfə'] N (fam) scansafatiche m/f inv; (shoes): **loafers** mocassini mpl.

♦ **loaf tin** N stampo (per il pane).

loam [ləʊm] N terriccio (fertile).

loan [ləʊn] **1** N prestito; **to give sb the loan of sth** prestare or dare in prestito qc a qn; **to ask for the loan of** chiedere in prestito; **on loan** (book, painting) in prestito; (employee) distaccato(-a); **to raise a loan** (money) ottenere un prestito or un mutuo. **2** VT prestare, dare in prestito.

♦ **loan capital** N capitale m di prestito.

♦ **loan-shark** ['ləʊnˌʃɑːk] N (fam pej) strozzino(-a).

♦ **loan word** N prestito linguistico.

loath [ləʊθ] ADJ: **to be loath to do sth** essere riluttante or restio(-a) a fare qc.

loathe [ləʊð] VT (thing, person) detestare, odiare; **I loathe doing it** detesto farlo; **to loathe sb's doing sth** detestare che qn faccia qc.

loath·ing ['ləʊðɪŋ] N (hatred) odio; (disgust) ribrezzo, disgusto; **it fills me with loathing** mi riempie di disgusto, mi fa ribrezzo.

loath·some ['ləʊðsəm] ADJ (gen) ripugnante, disgustoso (-a); (person) detestabile, odioso(-a).

loaves [ləʊvz] NPL of **loaf**.

lob [lɒb] VT (ball) lanciare; **to lob sth over to sb** lanciare qc a qn.

lob·by ['lɒbɪ] **1** N **a** atrio, hall f inv **b** (Pol: pressure group) gruppo di pressione, lobby f inv. **2** VT (Pol) far pressione su. **3** VI fare pressioni; **to lobby for a reform** fare pressioni per ottenere una riforma.

lob·by·ist ['lɒbɪɪst] N appartenente m/f ad un gruppo di pressione, lobbista m/f.

lobe [ləʊb] N (Anat) lobo.

lo·belia [ləʊ'biːlɪə] N lobelia.

lo·boto·my [ləʊ'bɒtəmɪ] N (Med) lobotomia.

lob·ster ['lɒbstə'] N aragosta.

♦ **lobster pot** N nassa per aragoste.

lo·cal ['ləʊkəl] **1** ADJ (gen) locale; (resident, shop) del posto; **local doctor** medico della zona. **2** N (fam) **a** : **he's a local** è uno del posto; **the locals** la gente del posto **b** (Brit: pub) ≈ bar m inv sotto casa.

♦ **local anaesthetic**, (Am) **local anesthetic** N aneste-

sia locale.

♦ **local authority** N autorità f inv locale; **local education authority** ≈ provveditorato agli studi; **local health authority** ≈ unità f inv sanitaria locale.

♦ **local call** N (Telec) telefonata urbana.

♦ **local colour** N colore m locale.

lo·cale [ləʊ'kɑːl] N (frm: gen) ambiente m; (: of film, book) ambientazione f.

♦ **local government** N amministrazione f locale; **local government officer** or **official** funzionario dell'amministrazione locale; **local government elections** elezioni fpl amministrative.

lo·cal·ity [ləʊ'kælɪtɪ] N (place) località f inv; (neighbourhood) vicinanze fpl.

lo·cal·ize ['ləʊkəlaɪz] VT localizzare.

lo·cal·ly ['ləʊkəlɪ] ADV (nearby) nei paraggi, nelle vicinanze; (in the locality) sul posto, in loco; **there will be showers locally** il tempo sarà localmente piovoso, ci saranno locali rovesci.

♦ **local time** N ora locale.

lo·cate [ləʊ'keɪt] VT (situate) situare, collocare; (find) trovare; (: cause) individuare, trovare; **where can he be located?** dove si può rintracciare?

lo·ca·tion [ləʊ'keɪʃən] N **a** (place) posto; (placing) posizione f, ubicazione f; (Geog) localizzazione f **b** (Cine): **to be on location in Mexico** girare gli esterni in Messico; **film shot on location** film girato in esterni.

loch [lɒx] N (Scot) lago.

lock¹ [lɒk] N (of hair) ciocca; **locks** (liter) chioma.

lock² [lɒk] **1** N **a** (on door, box) serratura; **under lock and key** sotto chiave; **lock stock and barrel** (fig) in blocco; **he moved out, lock stock and barrel** se n'è andato con armi e bagagli **b** (of canal) chiusa **c** (Brit: Aut: turning) sterzo; **on full lock** a tutto sterzo. **2** VT (door) chiudere a chiave; (Tech: immobilize) bloccare; **she locked the steering mechanism** ha messo il bloccasterzo; **to lock sb/sth in a place** chiudere qn/qc in un posto; **behind locked doors** a porte chiuse; **they were locked in each other's arms** erano abbracciati stretti; **to be locked in combat** lottare corpo a corpo. **3** VI (door etc) chiudersi; (wheels) bloccarsi, incepparsi

▶ **lock away** VT + ADV (valuables) tenere (rinchiuso(-a)) al sicuro; (criminal) mettere dentro; (mental patient) rinchiudere

▶ **lock in** VT + ADV chiudere dentro (a chiave)

▶ **lock out** VT + ADV chiudere fuori; **to lock workers out** (Industry) fare una serrata

▶ **lock up 1** VT + ADV (object) mettere al sicuro, chiudere (a chiave); (criminal) mettere dentro; (mental patient) rinchiudere; (funds) vincolare, immobilizzare; **she checked that the house was properly locked up** ha controllato che tutto fosse ben chiuso. **2** VI + ADV chiudere tutto (a chiave).

lock·er ['lɒkə'] N armadietto; (Naut) gavone m.

♦ **locker room** N spogliatoio.

lock·et ['lɒkɪt] N medaglione m (portaritratti).

lock·jaw ['lɒkˌdʒɔː] N tetano.

lock·out ['lɒkˌaʊt] N (Industry) serrata.

lock·smith ['lɒkˌsmɪθ] N fabbro.

♦ **lock-up** ['lɒkˌʌp] N (prison) prigione f; (cell) guardina; (Brit: also: **lock-up garage**) box m inv.

lo·co·mo·tion [ˌləʊkə'məʊʃən] N locomozione f.

lo·co·mo·tive [ˌləʊkə'məʊtɪv] N (Rail) locomotiva.

lo·cum ['ləʊkəm] N (doctor) medico sostituto; (priest)

vicario.

lo·cus ['ləʊkəs] N (pl **loci** ['ləʊsaɪ]) (Math) luogo geometrico.

lo·cust ['ləʊkəst] N locusta, cavalletta.

♦ **locust tree** N robinia.

lo·cu·tion [ləʊ'kjuː.ʃən] N (frm) locuzione f.

lodge [lɒdʒ] [1] N (house) casetta del guardiano; (porter's lodge) portineria, guardiola; (Freemasonry) loggia.

[2] VT (person: give lodging) dare alloggio a; (: find lodging) trovare alloggio per; (money) depositare; (complaint, appeal etc) fare, presentare; (statement) rilasciare; **to lodge an appeal** (Law) ricorrere in corte d'appello.

[3] VI **a** (person): **to lodge (with)** (landlady) essere a pensione (presso or da); (friends) alloggiare (con)

b (bullet) conficcarsi; **to lodge (itself) in/between** piantarsi dentro/fra.

lodg·er ['lɒdʒə'] N (with room and meals) pensionante m/f; (room only) persona che ha una camera in affitto; **she takes in lodgers** fa l'affittacamere.

lodg·ing ['lɒdʒɪŋ] N (accommodation) alloggio; see also **board**.

♦ **lodging house** N (Brit) casa con camere in affitto.

lodg·ings ['lɒdʒɪŋz] NPL (room) camera in affitto, camera ammobiliata; (small flat) appartamentino; **to look for lodgings** cercarsi un alloggio.

loft [lɒft] N soffitta, solaio; (also: **hayloft**) granaio, fienile m; (Am) loft m inv.

lofti·ly ['lɒftɪlɪ] ADV (frm) altezzosamente.

lofty ['lɒftɪ] ADJ (comp **-ier**, superl **-iest**) (frm: sentiments, aims) nobile; (: haughty: manner) di superiorità, altezzoso(-a); (liter: mountain) alto(-a).

log [lɒg] [1] N **a** (for fire) ceppo; (tree trunk) tronco

b = **logbook**.

[2] N ABBR (= logarithm) log.

[3] VT **a** (Naut, Aer) annotare or registrare sul giornale di bordo

b (Aut: also: **log up**: speed) fare; (distance) coprire; **to log 50 mph** ≈ fare 80 km/h

▶ **log in**, **log on** VI + ADV (Comput) aprire una sessione (con codice di riconoscimento)

▶ **log off**, **log out** VI + ADV (Comput) terminare una sessione.

logan·berry ['ləʊgənberɪ] N mora.

loga·rithm ['lɒgə.rɪðəm] N logaritmo; **common logarithm** logaritmo decimale or volgare.

log·book ['lɒg.bʊk] N (Naut, Aer) giornale m or diario di bordo; (Aut: registration document) libretto di circolazione; (of events, movement of goods) registro.

♦ **log cabin** N capanna di tronchi.

♦ **log fire** N fuoco di legna.

log·ger ['lɒgə'] N boscaiolo, taglialegna m inv.

log·ger·heads ['lɒgə.hɛdz] NPL: **at loggerheads (with sb)** in violento contrasto (con qn), ai ferri corti (con).

log·ging ['lɒgɪŋ] N disboscamento.

log·ic ['lɒdʒɪk] N logica.

logi·cal ['lɒdʒɪkəl] ADJ logico(-a).

logi·cal·ly ['lɒdʒɪkəlɪ] ADV logicamente; **logically, we should ...** a rigor di logica, dovremmo... .

lo·gi·cian [lɒ'dʒɪʃən] N logico.

lo·gis·tic [lɒ'dʒɪstɪk] [1] N logistica.

[2] ADJ logistico(-a).

lo·gis·tics [lɒ'dʒɪstɪks] NSG logistica.

log·jam ['lɒg.dʒæm] N: **to break the logjam** superare l'impasse f inv.

logo ['ləʊgəʊ] N logo m inv.

loin [lɔɪn] N (of meat) lombata.

♦ **loin chop** N (Culin) lombatina, bistecca di lombo.

♦ **loin cloth** N perizoma m.

loins [lɔɪnz] NPL (frm) reni fpl, fianchi mpl.

loi·ter ['lɔɪtə'] VI (idle) bighellonare; (lag behind) attardarsi, fermarsi (ad ogni passo); **to loiter (about)** indugiare, bighellonare; **to loiter (with intent)** (Law) aggirarsi (con intenzioni sospette).

loll [lɒl] VI (head, tongue) ciondolare; **to loll about** or **around** starsene pigramente sdraiato(-a), essere stravaccato(-a); **to loll against sth**, **loll back on sth** appoggiarsi pigramente a qc.

lol·li·pop ['lɒlɪ.pɒp] N lecca lecca m inv.

♦ **lollipop man**, **lollipop lady** N (Brit fam) persona incaricata di regolare il traffico in prossimità delle scuole e di aiutare i bambini ad attraversare la strada.

lol·lop ['lɒləp] VI (Brit) camminare (or correre) goffamente.

lol·ly ['lɒlɪ] N (Brit fam) **a** (lollipop) lecca lecca m inv; (also: **ice lolly**) ghiacciolo **b** (money) grana, quattrini mpl.

Lom·bardy ['lɒmbədɪ] N Lombardia.

Lon·don ['lʌndən] N Londra.

Lon·don·er ['lʌndənə'] N londinese m/f.

lone [ləʊn] ADJ (frm: person) solitario(-a), solo(-a); (: house) solitario(-a); **to play a lone hand** (fig) agire da solo.

lone·li·ness ['ləʊnlɪnɪs] N solitudine f.

lone·ly ['ləʊnlɪ] ADJ (comp **-ier**, superl **-iest**) (person) solitario(-a); (place: isolated) isolato(-a); (: deserted) deserto(-a); **to be** or **feel lonely** sentirsi solo(-a).

♦ **lonely hearts** ADJ: **lonely hearts ad** annuncio per cuori solitari; **lonely hearts column** messaggi mpl personali; **lonely hearts club** club m inv dei cuori solitari.

♦ **lone parent** N (mother) madre single (o divorziata o vedova); (father) padre single (o divorziato o vedovo).

lon·er ['ləʊnə'] N tipo solitario, persona solitaria, solitario (-a).

lone·some ['ləʊnsəm] ADJ (esp Am) solo(-a).

♦ **lone wolf** N (fig) tipo solitario.

long¹ [lɒŋ] [1] ADJ (comp **-er**, superl **-est**) **a** (in size) lungo(-a); **how long is it?** quant'è lungo?; **how long is this river?** quanto è lungo questo fiume?; **it is 6 metres long** è lungo 6 metri; **to get longer** allungarsi

b (in time) lungo(-a); **(for) a long time** (per) molto tempo; **how long is the film?** quanto dura il film?; **2 hours long** che dura 2 ore, di 2 ore; **a long walk/holiday** una lunga camminata/vacanza; **a long job** un lavoro lungo; **to have a long memory** avere buona memoria; **it's been a long day** (fig) è stata una giornata lunga; **to take a long look at sth** esaminare ben bene qc; **at long last** finalmente.

[2] ADV a lungo, per molto tempo; **I shan't be long** non ne avrò per molto; **he won't be long finishing** non ci metterà molto a finire; **we didn't stay (for) long** non ci siamo fermati a lungo; **I have long believed that ...** è da molto tempo che credo che...; **he had long understood that ...** aveva capito da molto tempo che...; **long before** molto tempo prima; **long before now** molto prima; **long before you came** molto prima che tu arrivassi; **before long** (+ future) presto, fra poco; (+ past) poco tempo dopo; **he's long since departed** se n'è andato molto tempo fa; **how long is it since you saw them?** da quant'è che non li vedi?; **long ago** molto tempo fa; **how long ago?** quanto tempo fa?; **as long ago as 1960** niente meno che nel 1960; **he no longer comes** non viene più; **all day long** tutto il giorno; **so long as** [OR] **as long as**

(*while*) finché; (*provided that*) sempre che + *sub*; **so long!** (*fam esp Am*) ciao!; **don't be long!** fai presto!; **it won't take long** è questione di poco.

3 N: **the long and the short of it is that ...** (*fig*) a farla breve... .

long² [lɒŋ] VI: **to long for sth/sb** desiderare molto qc/qn; **to long to do sth** morire dalla voglia di fare qc; **to long for sb to do sth** desiderare tanto che qn faccia qc.

♦ **long-awaited** ['lɒŋə,weɪtɪd] ADJ tanto atteso(-a), sospirato(-a).

long·bow ['lɒŋ,bəʊ] N arco.

♦ **long-distance** [,lɒŋ'dɪstəns] ADJ (*Telec*: *call*) interurbano(-a); (*race*) di fondo; **long-distance runner** fondista *m/f*.

♦ **long division** N divisione *f* scritta per esteso.

♦ **long-drawn-out** [,lɒŋdrɔːn'aʊt] ADJ che va per le lunghe, interminabile.

♦ **long drink** N long drink *m inv*.

longed-for ['lɒŋd,fɔː'] ADJ tanto sospirato(-a).

lon·gev·ity [lɒn'dʒevɪtɪ] N longevità.

♦ **long face** N: **to pull a long face** fare il muso (lungo).

♦ **long-forgotten** ['lɒŋfə'gɒtn] ADJ dimenticato(-a) da tempo.

♦ **long-haired** ['lɒŋ'hɛəd] ADJ (*person*) dai capelli lunghi; (*animal*) dal pelo lungo.

long·hand ['lɒŋ,hænd] N scrittura (normale).

long·ing ['lɒŋɪŋ] **1** N desiderio; (*for food*) voglia; (*nostalgia*) nostalgia.

2 ADJ (*look*) pieno(-a) di desiderio *or* di nostalgia.

long·ing·ly ['lɒŋɪŋlɪ] ADV con desiderio (*or* nostalgia).

lon·gi·tude ['lɒŋgɪtjuːd] N longitudine *f*.

♦ **long johns** NPL (*fam*) mutandoni *mpl*.

♦ **long jump** N salto in lungo.

♦ **long-legged** ['lɒŋ,lɛgd] ADJ (*person*) dalle gambe lunghe; (*animal*) con le zampe lunghe.

♦ **long-life** ['lɒŋ'laɪf] ADJ a lunga conservazione; **long-life milk** latte *m* a lunga conservazione.

♦ **long-lived** ['lɒŋ'lɪvd] ADJ longevo(-a); **women are longer-lived** *or* **more long-lived than men** le donne vivono più a lungo degli uomini.

♦ **long-lost** ['lɒŋ'lɒst] ADJ perduto(-a) da tempo; (*friend*) che non si vede da molto tempo.

♦ **long-playing** ['lɒŋ'pleɪɪŋ] ADJ: **long-playing record** (disco a) 33 giri *m inv*, long-playing *m inv*.

♦ **long-range** ['lɒŋ'reɪndʒ] ADJ (*gun, missile*) a lunga portata *or* gittata; (*aircraft*) a lungo raggio d'azione; (*weather forecast*) a lungo termine.

long·shore ['lɒŋ,ʃɔː'] ADJ litoraneo(-a); **longshore drift** trasporto litoraneo.

long·shore·man ['lɒŋ,ʃɔːmən] N (*pl* -men) (*Am*) portuale *m*, scaricatore *m* di porto.

♦ **long shot** N: **it's a long shot** (*fam*) le probabilità sono minime.

♦ **long-sighted** [,lɒŋ'saɪtɪd] ADJ presbite; (*Med*) ipermetrope; (*fig*) lungimirante.

♦ **long-sightedness** [,lɒŋ'saɪtɪdnɪs] N presbiopia; (*Med*) ipermetropia; (*fig*) lungimiranza.

♦ **long-sleeved** ['lɒŋ'sliːvd] ADJ a maniche lunghe.

♦ **long-standing** ['lɒŋ'stændɪŋ] ADJ di vecchia data.

♦ **long-suffering** ['lɒŋ'sʌfərɪŋ] ADJ estremamente paziente, infinitamente tollerante.

♦ **long-term** ['lɒŋ'tɜːm] ADJ (*plans, effects*) a lungo termine; **to take a long-term view of sth** proiettare qc nel futuro.

♦ **long-time** ['lɒŋ,taɪm] ADJ (*friend*) di vecchia data.

♦ **long vacation** N (*Univ*) vacanze *fpl* estive.

♦ **long wave** N (*Radio*) onde *fpl* lunghe.

long·ways ['lɒŋ,weɪz] ADV longitudinalmente.

♦ **long-winded** [,lɒŋ'wɪndɪd] ADJ (*speaker*) prolisso(-a); (*account, explanation*) interminabile.

loo [luː] N (*Brit fam: toilet*) gabinetto, cesso.

loo·fah, loo·fa ['luːfə] N luffa.

look [lʊk] **1** VI **a** (*see, glance*) guardare; **I'm just looking** (*in shop*) sto solo dando un'occhiata; **I'll look and see** vado a vedere; **look who's here!** (ma) guarda chi si vede!; **to look the other way** guardare dall'altra parte; (*fig*) far finta di non vedere; **to look ahead** guardare avanti; (*fig*) cominciare a pensare al futuro; **to look south** (*building etc*) essere esposto(-a) a sud, dare a sud; **look before you leap** (*fig*) non buttarti alla cieca

b (*seem, appear*) sembrare, aver l'aria; **he looks (as if he's) happy** sembra *or* ha l'aria felice; **she looked prettier than ever** era più graziosa che mai; **he looks about 60 (years old)** dimostra una sessantina d'anni; **it looks about 4 metres long** sarà lungo un 4 metri; **you don't look yourself** non mi sembri in forma; **you look** *or* **you're looking well** ti trovo bene; **it looks good on you** ti sta bene, ti dona; **it makes you look younger** ti ringiovanisce, ti fa sembrare più giovane; **it looks all right to me** a me pare che vada bene

c : **to look like** assomigliare a; **he looks like his brother** assomiglia a suo fratello; **this photo doesn't look like him** in questa foto non sembra lui; **it looks like cheese to me** mi sembra formaggio; **it certainly looks like it** ne ha tutta l'aria; **the party looks like being fun** la festa promette bene; **it looks like rain** mi sa che sta per piovere; **it looks as if** *or* **as though the train will be late** mi sa tanto che il treno sarà in ritardo.

2 VT guardare; **to look sb (straight) in the eye** *or* **in the face** guardare qn (dritto) negli occhi *or* in faccia; **to look sb up and down** squadrare qn da capo a piedi; **look where you're going!** guarda dove vai!; **to look one's best** essere in gran forma; **you must look your best for this interview** dovresti cercare di presentarti a questo colloquio ben vestito e ben curato; **to look one's age** dimostrare la propria età.

3 N **a** (*glance*) occhiata; (*expression*) sguardo, aria; **with a look of despair** con un'aria *or* un'espressione disperata; **to have a look at sth** dare un'occhiata a qc; **let me have a look** fammi vedere; **to take a good look at sb/sth** guardare (per) bene qn/qc; **to have a look for sth** cercare qc; **shall we have a look round the town?** andiamo a visitare la città?; **she gave me a dirty look** mi ha lanciato un'occhiataccia

b (*air, appearance*) aspetto, aria; **he has a look of his mother about him** ha qualcosa di sua madre; **there's a mischievous look about that child** quel bambino ha un'aria birichina; **by the look of things** it's going to rain ha tutta l'aria di (voler) piovere; **by the look of him** a vederlo; **I don't like the look of him** ha un'aria che non mi piace; **the new look for summer** (*Fashion*) il nuovo look *m inv* per l'estate; see also **looks**

▶ **look after** VI + PREP (*gen*) occuparsi di; (*possessions*) prendersi cura di; (*keep an eye on*) guardare, badare a; **to look after sth for sb** dare un'occhiata a qc per qn; **he doesn't look after himself** si trascura; **she's old enough to look after herself** è abbastanza grande per badare a se stessa

▶ **look around** VI + ADV guardarsi intorno; **to look around for sb/sth** cercare qn/qc

▶ **look at** VI + PREP (*person, object*) guardare; (*problem, situation*) considerare; **it isn't much to look at but ...** (*fam*) non è bellissimo(-a) ma...; **could you look at the engine for me?** puoi dare un'occhiata al motore?; **I wouldn't even look at such a low offer** non prenderei nemmeno in considerazione un'offerta così bassa

▶ **look away** VI + ADV distogliere lo sguardo

▶ **look back** VI + ADV girarsi *or* voltarsi indietro; (*remember*) ripensare al passato; **to look back at sth/sb** voltarsi a guardare qc/qn; **he's never looked back** (*fig*) non ha fatto che migliorare; **to look back on** (*event, period*) ripensare a

▶ **look down** VI + ADV abbassare gli occhi *or* lo sguardo; (*from height*) guardare giù; **to look down at sb/sth** guardare giù verso qn/qc

▶ **look down on** VI + ADV + PREP guardare giù verso; (*fig*) guardare dall'alto in basso, disprezzare

▶ **look for** VI + PREP cercare; **to look for sb/sth** cercare qn/qc

▶ **look forward to** VI + ADV + PREP: **to look forward to doing sth** non veder l'ora di fare qc; **I'm looking forward to his visit/the film** non vedo l'ora che venga/di vedere il film; **I'm not looking forward to it** non ne ho nessuna voglia; **looking forward to hearing from you** (*in letter*) aspettando tue notizie

▶ **look in** VI + ADV guardar dentro

▶ **look in on** VI + ADV + PREP (*visit*) fare un salto da

▶ **look into** VI + PREP (*matter, possibility*) esaminare

▶ **look on** ⟦1⟧ VI + ADV rimanere a guardare, fare da spettatore.
⟦2⟧ VI + PREP considerare

▶ **look onto** VI + PREP dare su, affacciarsi su; **to look onto the sea** dare sul mare; **my room looks onto the garden** la mia camera si affaccia *or* dà sul giardino

▶ **look out** ⟦1⟧ VI + ADV **a** (*watch*) guardar fuori
b : **to look out (for)** stare attento(-a) (a); **look out!** attento!.
⟦2⟧ VT + ADV (*find*) tirar fuori

▶ **look out for** VI + PREP (*seek*) cercare; **to look out for sb/sth** (*watch out for*) guardare se arriva qn/qc

▶ **look over** VT + ADV (*essay*) dare un'occhiata a, riguardare; (*building*) ispezionare; (*person*) esaminare

▶ **look round** ⟦1⟧ VI + ADV (*turn*) girarsi, voltarsi; (*in shops*) dare un'occhiata; **to look round for sb/sth** guardarsi intorno per cercare qn/qc.
⟦2⟧ VI + PREP (*museum, factory*) visitare; (*shops*) dare un'occhiata a

▶ **look through** VI + PREP **a** (*papers, book*) esaminare; (: *briefly*) scorrere; (: *revise*) rivedere
b (*telescope*) guardare attraverso

▶ **look to** VI + PREP (*turn to*) rivolgersi a; (*look after*) badare a, stare attento(-a) a; (*rely on*) contare su

▶ **look up** ⟦1⟧ VI + ADV **a** (*glance*) alzare gli occhi
b (*improve: prospects*) migliorare; (: *business*) riprendersi; (: *sales*) aumentare; (: *shares*) essere in rialzo; (: *weather*) mettersi al bello; **things are looking up** le cose stanno migliorando.
⟦2⟧ VT + ADV **a** (*information, word*) cercare
b (*visit: friend*) andare a trovare

▶ **look upon** VT + PREP considerare, ritenere

▶ **look up to** VI + ADV + PREP avere rispetto per.

look·alike ['lʊkə,laɪk] N sosia *m/f*.

looker-on [,lʊkər'ɒn] N (*pl* **lookers-on**) astante *m/f*.

♦ **look-in** ['lʊk,ɪn] N (*fam*): **not to get a look-in** non avere la minima possibilità di (partecipare, vincere *etc*).

looking-glass ['lʊkɪŋ,glɑːs] N (*old*) specchio.

♦ **look-out** ['lʊk,aʊt] ⟦1⟧ N **a** : **to keep a look-out** fare la guardia; **keep a look-out for a post box** guarda se vedi una buca per le lettere; **to be on the look-out for sth** cercare qc
b (*viewpoint*) posto di vedetta, posto d'osservazione; (*person: thief*) palo; (: *Mil*) sentinella; (: *Naut*) vedetta
c (*prospect*) prospettiva; **it's a grim** *or* **poor look-out** è una prospettiva poco allegra; **that's his look-out!** questo è affar suo!

♦ **look-out post** N posto di vedetta, posto di osservazione.

♦ **look-out tower** N torre *f* di osservazione.

looks [lʊks] NPL (*appearance*) aspetto; (*attractiveness*) bellezza; **she has kept her (good) looks** è rimasta bella; **you can't go by looks** non si può giudicare dalle apparenze.

loom¹ [luːm] N (*weaving loom*) telaio.

loom² [luːm] VI (*also:* **loom up**: *building, mountain*) apparire in lontananza; **the ship loomed (up) out of the mist** nella nebbia apparve la nave; **to loom large** (*fig*) essere imminente, incombere.

loony ['luːnɪ] ADJ, N (*fam*) pazzo(-a), matto(-a).

♦ **loony bin** N (*fam*) manicomio.

loop [luːp] ⟦1⟧ N (*in string etc*) cappio; (*fastening*) asola; (*for belt*) passante *m*; (*bend: in river*) ansa; (*Comput*) iterazione *f*, anello.
⟦2⟧ VT: **to loop a rope round a post** passare una corda intorno a un palo; **to loop the loop** (*Aer*) fare il giro della morte.

loop·hole ['luːp,həʊl] N (*fig*) scappatoia, via d'uscita.

loose [luːs] ⟦1⟧ ADJ (*comp* **-r,** *superl* **-st**) **a** (*not firm, attached*: *plaster, button*) che si stacca; (: *knot, shoelace, screw*) allentato(-a); (: *hair*) sciolto(-a); (: *skin*) floscio(-a); (: *tooth*) che tentenna; (: *page*) staccato(-a); (: *sheet of paper*) volante; (: *stone*) sconnesso(-a); (*animal*) in libertà, scappato(-a); **to come** *or* **work loose** allentarsi; **to turn** *or* **let loose** (*animal*) lasciare in libertà; **to get loose** (*animal*) scappare; **loose chippings** (*Aut*) ghiaino; **loose connection** (*Elec*) filo che fa contatto
b (*not tight: clothes*) ampio(-a), largo(-a); **loose weave** a trama *or* maglia larga
c (*not packed: fruit, cheese*) non confezionato(-a), sfuso(-a)
d (*fig: translation*) libero(-a); (: *style*) prolisso(-a); (: *discipline*) rilassato(-a); (: *associations, links, thinking*) vago(-a), poco rigoroso(-a); (: *life, morals*) dissoluto(-a); **loose living** vita dissipata.
⟦2⟧ N (*fam*): **to be on the loose** (*criminal, animal*) essere in libertà.
⟦3⟧ VT (*frm: free*) liberare; (: *untie*) sciogliere; (: *slacken*) allentare; (*also:* **loose off**: *arrow*) scoccare; **to loose one's gun (off)** *or* sparare a *or* contro; **to loose the dogs on** *or* **at sb** sguinzagliare i cani dietro a *or* contro qn.

♦ **loose change** N spiccioli *mpl*, moneta.

♦ **loose cover** N (*on settee, chair*) foderina.

♦ **loose end** N dettaglio in sospeso; **to tie up loose ends** (*fig*) sistemare gli ultimi dettagli; **to be at a loose end**, (*Am*) **to be at loose ends** (*fig*) non saper cosa fare.

♦ **loose-fitting** ['luːs,fɪtɪŋ] ADJ ampio(-a), largo(-a).

♦ **loose-leaf** ['luːs'liːf] ADJ: **loose-leaf binder** *or* **folder** raccoglitore *m* a fogli mobili.

♦ **loose-limbed** ['luːs'lɪmd] ADJ snodato(-a), agile.

loose·ly ['luːslɪ] ADV (*hold, tie*) senza stringere; (*associate*) vagamente; (*translate*) liberamente; (*use word*) in modo

improprio.

♦ **loosely-knit** ['lu:slɪ'nɪt] ADJ non rigidamente struttu-rato(-a).

loos·en ['lu:sn] ① VT (*slacken: screw, belt, knot*) allentare; (: *rope, grip*) mollare; (: *clothing*) slacciare; (*untie*) disfare; (*fig: tongue*) sciogliere.
　② VI (*all senses*) allentarsi

▶ **loosen up** VI + ADV (*before game*) sciogliere i muscoli, scaldarsi; (*fam: relax*) rilassarsi.

loose·ness ['lu:snɪs] N (*of knot, screw*) lentezza; (*of rope*) scarsa tensione *f*; (*of clothes*) ampiezza; (*of translation*) approssimazione *f*; (*of behaviour*) dissipazione *f*, disso-lutezza.

loot [lu:t] ① N bottino.
　② VT saccheggiare, depredare.
　③ VI: **to go looting** darsi al saccheggio.

loot·er ['lu:tə'] N saccheggiatore(-trice).

loot·ing ['lu:tɪŋ] N saccheggio.

lop [lɒp] VT (*also:* **lop off**) tagliar (via), recidere.

lope [ləʊp] VI: **to lope along/off** *etc* procedere/partire *etc* a grandi balzi.

♦ **lop-eared** ['lɒp͵ɪəd] ADJ dalle orecchie pendenti.

♦ **lop-sided** ['lɒp'saɪdɪd] ADJ (*smile*) di traverso; (*structure*) sbilenco(-a).

lo·qua·cious [lə'kweɪʃəs] ADJ (*frm*) loquace.

lo·qua·cious·ly [lə'kweɪʃəslɪ] ADV (*frm*) loquacemente.

lo·quac·ity [lə'kwæsɪtɪ] N (*frm*) loquacità.

lord [lɔ:d] ① N **a** signore *m*; **lord of the manor** signore del castello; **lord and master** signore e padrone; **to live like a lord** vivere da signore *or* come un re
　b (*Brit*): **Lord Smith** Lord Smith; **my Lord** (*to bishop, noble*) Eccellenza; (*to judge*) signor giudice
　c: **Our Lord** (*Rel*) Nostro Signore; **the Lord** il Signore; **the Lord's prayer** il Padrenostro; **good Lord!** Dio mio!.
　② VT: **to lord it over sb** (*fam*) darsi arie da gran signore con qn.

lord·li·ness ['lɔ:dlɪnɪs] N altezzosità.

lord·ly ['lɔ:dlɪ] ADJ (*pej: person, manner*) altero(-a), altez-zoso(-a); (*bearing, castle*) nobile, maestoso(-a).

Lords [lɔ:dz] NPL: **the Lords = House of Lords.**

lord·ship ['lɔ:dʃɪp] N: **his lordship the Count** *etc* Sua Signoria il conte *etc*; **your Lordship** (*Brit*) Vostra Signo-ria.

lore [lɔ:'] N tradizioni *fpl*; **plant/weather lore** cognizioni *fpl* sulle piante/sul tempo.

Lor·raine [lɒ'reɪn] N Lorena.

lor·ry ['lɒrɪ] N (*Brit*) camion *m inv*.

♦ **lorry driver** N (*Brit*) camionista *m/f*.

♦ **lorry load** N (*Brit*) carico (*di camion*).

lose [lu:z] (*pt, pp* lost) ① VT **a** (*gen*) perdere; **to get lost** (*object*) andare perso(-a) *or* perduto(-a) *or* smarrito(-a); (*person*) perdersi, smarrirsi; **get lost!** (*fam*) vattene!, sparisci!; **to lose one's life** perdere la vita; **many lives were lost** ci sono state molte vittime; **there were no lives lost** non ci sono stati morti, non ci sono state vittime; **he's lost his licence** (*Aut*) gli è stata ritirata la patente; **you've got nothing to lose** non hai niente da perdere; **to lose one's way** perdersi; **to lose interest/one's appetite** perdere interesse/l'appetito; **to lose weight** dimagrire; **to lose patience** perdere la pazienza, spazientirsi; **to lose no time (in doing sth)** non perdere tempo (a fare qc); **there's no time to lose** non c'è tempo da perdere; **he managed to lose his pursuers** è riuscito a seminare i suoi inseguitori; **you've lost me there** (*fig*) ho perso il filo

b: **that mistake lost us the game** quell'errore ci ha fatto perdere il gioco
　c: **this watch loses 5 minutes every day** quest'orologio resta indietro di 5 minuti al giorno.
　② VI perdere; **they lost (by) 3 goals to 2** hanno perso (per) 3 a 2; **to lose to sb** perdere contro qn; **to lose (out) on sth** (*deal*) rimetterci in qc; (*trip*) perdersi; **you can't lose** in tutti i casi ci guadagni; **the clock is losing** l'orologio resta indietro.

los·er ['lu:zə'] N perdente *m/f*; **he's a born loser** è un perdente nato; **to be a good/bad loser** saper/non saper perdere.

los·ing ['lu:zɪŋ] ADJ perdente; **to fight a losing battle** (*fig*) combattere una battaglia perduta; **on a losing streak** in un periodo nero.

loss [lɒs] N **a** perdita; **heavy losses** (*Mil*) gravi perdite; **without loss of life** senza perdita di vite umane; **to cut one's losses** rimetterci il meno possibile; **it's your loss!** quello che ci rimette sei tu!; **he's a dead loss** (*fam*) è un disastro; **he's no great loss** (*fam*) nessuno lo rimpiange di certo; **to make a loss** perderci; (*Comm*) subire una perdita; **to sell sth at a loss** vendere qc perdendoci
　b: **to be at a loss** essere perplesso(-a); **to be at a loss to explain sth** non saper come fare a spiegare qc; **to be at a loss for words** essere senza parole.

♦ **loss adjuster** N (*Insurance*) liquidatore *m/f*.

♦ **loss leader** N (*Comm*) articolo *m* civetta *inv*.

lost [lɒst] ① PT, PP of **lose.**
　② ADJ (*gen, fig*) perso(-a); (*bewildered*) smarrito(-a); **a lost sheep** una pecorella smarrita; **some lost children** dei bambini che si erano smarriti; **lost in thought** immerso(-a) *or* perso(-a) nei propri pensieri; **to feel a bit lost** sentirsi smarrito(-a); **the remark/joke was lost on him** non ha capito l'osservazione/la barzelletta; **my advice was lost on her** non ha ascoltato il mio consiglio; **I feel lost without my car/him** mi sento perso senza la mia macchina/di lui; **to make up for lost time** recupe-rare il tempo perduto; **to give sth up for lost** dare qc per perso(-a); **lost baggage claim** ritiro bagagli smarriti; **lost at sea** perito(-a) in mare.

♦ **lost cause** N causa persa.

♦ **lost property,** (*Am*) **lost and found property** N oggetti *mpl* smarriti; **lost property office** *or* **department** ufficio oggetti smarriti.

lot [lɒt] N **a** (*large amount*) molto; **a lot of money** [OR] (*fam*) **lots of money** un sacco di soldi; **a lot of people** [OR] (*fam*) **lots of people** molta gente, molti; **quite a lot of noise** parecchio rumore; **such a lot of people** talmente tanta gente; **there was not a lot we could say/do** c'era ben poco da dire/da fare; **I'd give a lot to know …** darei non so cosa per sapere…; **I read a lot** leggo molto; **he feels a lot** *or* (*fam*) **lots better** si sente molto meglio; **thanks a lot!** (*also: iro*) grazie tante!
　b (*fam*): **the lot** (*all, everything*) tutto(-a) (quanto(-a)); **he took the lot** ha preso tutto (quanto); **that's the lot** (questo) è tutto; **the (whole) lot of them** tutti quanti
　c (*destiny*) sorte *f*, destino; **the common lot** il destino comune; **it fell to my lot to do it** è toccato a me farlo; **to throw in one's lot with sb** unirsi a qn
　d (*random selection*) sorte *f*; **to draw lots (for sth)** tirare a sorte (per qc)
　e (*at auction*) lotto, partita; **he's a bad lot** (*fig*) è un pessimo soggetto
　f (*plot of land*) lotto di terreno; **building lot** lotto edificabile.

lo·tion ['ləʊʃən] N lozione *f.*
lot·tery ['lɒtərɪ] N lotteria.
lo·tus ['ləʊtəs] N loto.
♦ **lotus position** N posizione *f* del loto.
loud [laʊd] [1] ADJ (*comp* **-er**, *superl* **-est**) (*gen*) forte; (*laugh, applause, thunder*) fragoroso(-a), forte; (*noisy: behaviour, party, protests*) rumoroso(-a); (*pej: gaudy: colour, clothes*) chiassoso(-a), vistoso(-a), sgargiante; **the radio's too loud** il volume della radio è troppo alto.
  [2] ADV (*speak etc*) forte; **out loud** ad alta voce; **loud and clear** chiaro e forte, molto chiaramente.
loud·hailer [ˌlaʊd'heɪlə] N megafono.
loud·ly ['laʊdlɪ] ADV (*gen*) forte; (*laugh, applaud*) fragorosamente; (*protest*) rumorosamente; (*proclaim: out loud*) ad alta voce; (*: on banner etc*) a lettere cubitali.
♦ **loud-mouthed** [ˌlaʊd'maʊθd] ADJ (*person*) sguaiato (-a); (*protests*) rumoroso(-a).
loud·ness ['laʊdnɪs] N (*see adj*) forza; fragorosità; rumorosità, chiassosità.
loud·speaker [ˌlaʊd'spiːkə] N altoparlante *m.*
lounge [laʊndʒ] [1] N soggiorno, salotto; (*of hotel*) salone *m*; (*of airport*) sala d'attesa.
  [2] VI (*also:* **lounge about**) oziare, poltrire, starsene colle mani in mano.
♦ **lounge bar** N (*Brit*) bar *m inv* con servizio a tavolino.
loung·er ['laʊndʒə] N lettino da spiaggia.
♦ **lounge suit** N (*Brit*) completo da uomo.
louse [laʊs] N (*pl* **lice**) pidocchio; (*pej fam: person*) verme *m*
  ▶ **louse up** VT + ADV (*Am fam*) rovinare.
lousy ['laʊzɪ] ADJ (*Med*) pidocchioso(-a); (*fam: very bad*) schifoso(-a); (*: headache, cough*) orrendo(-a); **to feel lousy** stare da cani; **she's a lousy cook** fa schifo come cuoca; **a lousy trick** uno sporco trucco.
lout [laʊt] N giovinastro.
lout·ish ['laʊtɪʃ] ADJ rozzo(-a), da zotico(-a).
lou·vre, (*Am*) **lou·ver** ['luːvə] ADJ (*door, window*) con apertura a gelosia.
lov·able ['lʌvəbl] ADJ adorabile, carino(-a).
love [lʌv] [1] N **a** : **love (of, for)** amore *m* (di, per); (*of hobby, object*) passione *f* (per); **it was love at first sight** è stato amore a prima vista *or* un colpo di fulmine; **he studies history for the love of it** studia storia per il puro piacere di farlo; **to be in love (with sb)** essere innamorato(-a) (di qn); **to fall in love (with sb)** innamorarsi (di qn); **to make love** fare l'amore; **to make love to sb** (*old: woo*) fare la corte a qn; **there is no love lost between them** non si possono soffrire; **love from Anne** [OR] **love, Anne** (*in letter*) con affetto, Anne; **to send one's love to sb** mandare i propri saluti a qn
  b : **(my) love** amore *m* (mio), tesoro (mio)
  c (*Tennis etc*): **love all** zero a zero; **"15 love"** "15 a zero".
  [2] VT (*person: spouse, child*) amare; (*: relative, friend*) voler bene a; (*food, activity, place*) amare, adorare; **he loves tennis/Florence** gli piace (molto) il tennis/Firenze; **he loves swimming** *or* **to swim** gli piace (molto) nuotare; **I'd love to come** mi piacerebbe molto venire.
♦ **love affair** N relazione *f.*
love·bird ['lʌvˌbɜːd] N (*fig*) picciončino(-a).
♦ **love child** N (*euph*) figlio(-a) dell'amore.
loved ones ['lʌvd'wʌnz] NPL: **my loved ones** i miei cari.
♦ **love-hate relationship** ['lʌvˌheɪtrɪ'leɪʃənʃɪp] N rapporto *m* amore-odio *inv.*
love·less ['lʌvlɪs] ADJ senza amore.
♦ **love letter** N lettera d'amore.
♦ **love life** N vita sentimentale.

love·li·ness ['lʌvlɪnɪs] N (*of person*) grazia.
love·lorn ['lʌvˌlɔːn] ADJ infelice in amore.
love·ly ['lʌvlɪ] ADJ (*comp* **-ier**, *superl* **-iest**) (*beautiful, gen*) bello(-a); (*delightful: meal, voice*) delizioso(-a); (*: evening, party*) bellissimo(-a); (*: holiday, weather*) bello(-a); (*: delicious: smell, meal, food*) buono(-a); **it's lovely and warm** fa un bel calduccio; **it's been lovely seeing you** è stato un vero piacere vederti; **we had a lovely time** ci siamo divertiti molto.
♦ **love-making** ['lʌvˌmeɪkɪŋ] N il fare l'amore.
♦ **love match** N matrimonio d'amore.
♦ **love nest** N nido d'amore.
lov·er ['lʌvə] N **a** (*sexually*) amante *m/f*; (*romantically*) innamorato(-a) **b** : **lover (of)** (*enthusiast*) appassionato (-a) (di); **he's a lover of good food** è un buongustaio, è un amante della buona tavola.
love·sick ['lʌvˌsɪk] ADJ malato(-a) d'amore.
love·song ['lʌvˌsɒŋ] N canzone *f* d'amore.
♦ **love story** N storia d'amore, love story *f inv.*
lovey-dovey ['lʌvɪ'dʌvɪ] ADJ (*fam*) melenso(-a).
lov·ing ['lʌvɪŋ] ADJ affettuoso(-a); (*care*) tenero(-a), amoroso(-a); **his loving parents** i suoi genitori che gli vogliono molto bene.
lov·ing·ly ['lʌvɪŋlɪ] ADV affettuosamente; (*stronger*) amorosamente.
low¹ [ləʊ] [1] ADJ (*comp* **-er**, *superl* **-est**) (*gen*) basso(-a); (*bow*) profondo(-a); (*murmur*) sommesso(-a); (*intelligence*) scarso(-a); (*quality*) scadente; (*Bio, Zool: form of life*) primitivo(-a); (*pej: opinion, taste*) cattivo(-a); (*: character*) pessimo(-a); (*: behaviour*) ignobile; (*: café, place*) malfamato(-a); **a low trick** un tiro mancino, uno scherzo ignobile; **to feel low** (*depressed*) sentirsi (un po') giù; **he's very low** (*ill*) è molto debole; **supplies are low** le scorte si stanno esaurendo; **we are low on flour** non c'è rimasta molta farina; **in a low voice** a bassa voce; **in low gear** (*Aut*) in una marcia bassa; **on low ground** in pianura; **lower down** più in basso; **lower deck/floor** ponte/piano inferiore.
  [2] ADV (*aim*) in basso; (*sing*) a bassa voce; (*fly*) a bassa quota, basso; (*bow*) profondamente; **to sink lower** sprofondare sempre di più; **to fall** *or* **sink low** (*fig*) cadere in basso; **to turn sth down low** (*gas, radio etc*) abbassare qc; **supplies are running** *or* **getting low** le scorte stanno per finire.
  [3] N **a** (*Met*) depressione *f*, zona di bassa pressione
  b (*fig: low point*): **to reach a new** *or* **an all-time low** toccare il livello più basso *or* il minimo.
low² [ləʊ] VI (*cow*) muggire.
♦ **low-alcohol** ['ləʊ'ælkəˌhɒl] ADJ a basso contenuto alcolico.
low·brow ['ləʊˌbraʊ] [1] ADJ (*pej: person*) poco colto(-a); (*: interests, entertainment*) senza pretese intellettuali.
  [2] N persona poco colta *or* senza pretese intellettuali.
♦ **low-budget** ['ləʊ'bʌdʒɪt] ADJ a basso costo.
♦ **low-calorie** ['ləʊ'kælərɪ] ADJ a basso contenuto calorico.
♦ **low-cost** ['ləʊ'kɒst] ADJ a basso prezzo.
♦ **Low Countries** N: **the Low Countries** i Paesi Bassi.
♦ **low-cut** ['ləʊ'kʌt] ADJ (*dress*) scollato(-a).
♦ **low-down** ['ləʊˌdaʊn] [1] N (*fam*): **he gave me the low-down on it** mi ha messo al corrente dei fatti.
  [2] ADJ (*mean*) ignobile.
low·er¹ ['ləʊə] [1] ADJ (*comp of* **low**).
  [2] ADV (*comp of* **low**).
  [3] VT (*gen*) calare; (*flag, sail*) ammainare; (*reduce: price*)

abbassare, ridurre; (*resistance*) indebolire; **to lower sb's morale** demoralizzare qn; **to lower one's guard** (*Boxing, also fig*) abbassare la guardia; **to lower one's voice** abbassare la voce; **to lower o.s. to do sth** (*fig*) abbassarsi a fare qc.

low·er² ['ləʊəʳ] VI (*person*): **to lower (at sb)** dare un'occhiataccia (a qn); (*sky*) oscurarsi, essere minaccioso(-a).

♦ **lower-case** ['ləʊə'keɪs] ADJ (*Typ*) minuscolo(-a).

♦ **Lower Chamber** N (*Pol*): **the Lower Chamber** la Camera Bassa.

♦ **lower-class** [,ləʊə'klɑːs] ADJ proletario(-a).

♦ **lower classes** NPL: **the lower classes** le classi inferiori.

low·er·ing¹ ['ləʊərɪŋ] 1 N (*of price*) riduzione *f*, diminuzione *f*; (*of temperature, pressure*) abbassamento; (*of resistance*) indebolimento; (*of boat*) messa in acqua; **the lowering of morale** il calo del morale; **the lowering of the flag** l'ammainabandiera.
2 ADJ umiliante, degradante.

low·er·ing² ['ləʊərɪŋ] ADJ (*look, sky*) minaccioso(-a).

low·est common denominator ['ləʊɪst,kɒmənndɪ'nɒmɪ,neɪtəʳ] N minimo comune denominatore *m*.

low·est common multiple ['ləʊɪst,kɒmən'mʌltɪpl] N minimo comune multiplo.

♦ **low-fat** ['ləʊ'fæt] ADJ magro(-a).

♦ **low-flying** ['ləʊ,flaɪɪŋ] ADJ che vola a bassa quota.

♦ **low-grade** ['ləʊ,greɪd] ADJ di qualità inferiore.

♦ **low-heeled** ['ləʊ'hiːld] ADJ basso(-a), coi tacchi bassi.

low·ing ['ləʊɪŋ] N muggito.

♦ **low-key** [,ləʊ'kiː] ADJ moderato(-a); (*operation*) condotto(-a) con discrezione; **to keep sth low-key** fare qc con discrezione.

low·land ['ləʊlənd] N bassopiano, pianura; **the Lowlands of Scotland** le Lowlands scozzesi.

♦ **Low Latin** N basso latino.

♦ **low-level** ['ləʊ,lɛvl] ADJ a basso livello; (*flying*) a bassa quota.

♦ **low-loader** [,ləʊ'ləʊdəʳ] N camion *m inv* a pianale basso.

low·ly ['ləʊlɪ] ADJ modesto(-a), umile.

♦ **low-lying** ['ləʊ,laɪɪŋ] ADJ (*land*) a basso livello.

♦ **low-necked** ['ləʊ'nɛkt] ADJ (*dress*) scollato(-a).

low·ness ['ləʊnɪs] N (*gen*) bassezza.

♦ **low-paid** [,ləʊ'peɪd] ADJ mal pagato(-a).

♦ **low-priced** [,ləʊ'praɪst] ADJ a buon prezzo, a basso prezzo.

♦ **low-rise** ['ləʊ'raɪz] ADJ (*Archit*) di altezza contenuta, basso(-a).

♦ **low season** N: **the low season** la bassa stagione.

♦ **low-spirited** [,ləʊ'spɪrɪtɪd] ADJ abbacchiato(-a), giù (di morale).

♦ **Low Sunday** N Domenica in Albis.

♦ **low-tech** ['ləʊ'tɛk] ADJ a basso contenuto tecnologico.

♦ **low tide, low water** N: **at low tide** quando c'è la bassa marea.

loy·al ['lɔɪəl] ADJ (*comp* -**er**, *superl* -**est**) leale, fedele.

loy·al·ist ['lɔɪəlɪst] N, ADJ lealista (*m/f*).

loy·al·ly ['lɔɪəlɪ] ADV con lealtà, lealmente.

loy·al·ty ['lɔɪəltɪ] N lealtà *f inv*, fedeltà *f inv*.

loz·enge ['lɒzɪndʒ] N (*Med*) pastiglia; (*Geom*) losanga.

LP [,ɛl'piː] N ABBR (= *long-playing record*) LP *m inv*, ellepi *m inv*.

♦ **L-plates** ['ɛl,pleɪts] NPL (*Brit*) *cartelli bianchi con L rossa per learner* (= *principiante obbligatori su veicoli di chi sta imparando a guidare*).

LPN [,ɛlpiː'ɛn] N ABBR (*Am*: = *Licensed Practical Nurse*) ≈ infermiere(-a) diplomato(-a).

LRAM [,ɛlɑːreɪ'ɛm] N ABBR (*Brit*: = *Licentiate of the Royal Academy of Music*) diploma di conservatorio.

LSD [,ɛlɛs'diː] N ABBR **a** (= *lysergic acid diethylamide*) LSD *m* **b** (*Brit*: = *pounds, shillings and pence*) sistema monetario in vigore in Gran Bretagna fino al 1971.

LSE [,ɛlɛs'iː] N ABBR = *London School of Economics*.

LT [,ɛl'tiː] N ABBR (*Elec*: = *low tension*) B.T. (= *bassa tensione*).

Lt. ABBR (= *lieutenant*) Ten.

Ltd ABBR (*Comm*: = *limited*) ≈ s.r.l.

lub·ri·cant ['luːbrɪkənt] N lubrificante *m*.

lu·bri·cate ['luːbrɪ,keɪt] VT lubrificare; **lubricating oil** lubrificante *m*.

lu·bri·ca·tion [,luːbrɪ'keɪʃən] N lubrificazione *f*.

lu·bri·ca·tor ['luːbrɪ,keɪtəʳ] N (*liquid*) lubrificante *m*; (*device*) ingrassatore *m*.

lu·cerne [luː'sɜːn] N erba medica.

lu·cid ['luːsɪd] ADJ (*person*) lucido(-a); (*instructions*) chiaro (-a); (*moments*) di lucidità.

lu·cid·ity [luː'sɪdɪtɪ] N (*of person*) lucidità; (*of instructions*) chiarezza.

lu·cid·ly ['luːsɪdlɪ] ADV (*think*) con lucidità; (*explain*) con chiarezza.

luck [lʌk] N fortuna, sorte *f*; **good luck** (buona) fortuna; **bad luck** mala sorte, sfortuna; **good luck!** buona fortuna!; **bad luck!** che sfortuna!; **it's good/bad luck to do** ... porta fortuna/sfortuna fare...; **no such luck!** magari!, purtroppo no!; **with any luck** con un po' di fortuna; **to be in luck** essere fortunato(-a); **to be out of luck** essere sfortunato(-a); **to be down on one's luck** essere scalognato(-a); **I had the luck to** ho avuto la fortuna di; **better luck next time!** andrà meglio la prossima volta!; **he's got the luck of the devil!** (*fam*) ha una fortuna sfacciata!; **to trust to luck** affidarsi al caso; **as luck would have it** come volle il caso; **it's the luck of the draw** (*fig*) è una questione di fortuna.

lucki·ly ['lʌkɪlɪ] ADV per fortuna, fortunatamente.

luck·less ['lʌklɪs] ADJ (*liter*) sfortunato(-a).

lucky ['lʌkɪ] ADJ (*comp* -**ier**, *superl* -**iest**) (*gen*) fortunato (-a); (*horseshoe, number*) portafortuna *inv*, che porta fortuna; **lucky break** colpo di fortuna; **lucky charm** portafortuna *m inv*; **it was a lucky guess** è stata tutta fortuna; **he's lucky to be alive** è vivo per miracolo; **lucky you!** OR **you lucky thing!** beato te!; **it was very lucky for you (that ...)** per fortuna (che...).

♦ **lucky dip** N (*at fair*) pesca miracolosa.

luc·ra·tive ['luːkrətɪv] ADJ lucrativo(-a), redditizio(-a).

lu·cre ['luːkəʳ] N (*old*) lucro.

Lud·dite ['lʌdaɪt] N, ADJ (*frm*) luddista (*m/f*).

lu·di·crous ['luːdɪkrəs] ADJ ridicolo(-a), assurdo(-a).

lu·di·crous·ly ['luːdɪkrəslɪ] ADV in modo ridicolo.

ludo ['luːdəʊ] N (*Brit*) ≈ gioco dell'oca.

luff [lʌf] VI (*Naut*) fileggiare.

lug [lʌg] VT (*fam*) trascinare.

lug·gage ['lʌgɪdʒ] N bagagli *mpl*, bagaglio.

♦ **luggage rack** N (*on train etc*) reticella (per i bagagli); (*Aut*) portapacchi *m inv*, portabagagli *m inv*.

♦ **luggage van** N (*Brit Rail*) bagagliaio.

lug·hole ['lʌg,həʊl] N (*Brit*) orecchio.

lu·gu·bri·ous [lʊ'guːbrɪəs] ADJ (*liter*) lugubre.

lu·gu·bri·ous·ly [lʊ'guːbrɪəslɪ] ADV (*liter*) lugubremente.

lug·worm ['lʌg,wɜːm] N arenicola.

luke·warm [,luːk'wɔːm] ADJ **a** (*tepid*: *water*) tiepido(-a) **b** (*unenthusiastic*: *support, response*) tiepido(-a); (: *person*)

poco entusiasta.

lull [lʌl] **1** N (gen) momento di calma; (in business) periodo di stasi; (in conversation) pausa; (in fighting) tregua.

2 VT (fear) calmare; (person) calmare, acquietare; (child) cullare; **to lull a baby to sleep** cullare un bambino finché si addormenta; **to be lulled into a false sense of security** illudersi che tutto vada bene.

lulla·by ['lʌləˌbaɪ] N ninnananna.

lum·ba·go [lʌm'beɪgəʊ] N lombaggine f.

lum·bar ['lʌmbə'] ADJ (Med) lombare.

lum·ber¹ ['lʌmbə'] **1** N (wood: esp Am) legname m; (junk: esp Brit) roba vecchia.

2 VT (Brit: fam): **to lumber sb with sth/sb** affibbiare or rifilare qc/qn a qn; **he got lumbered with the job** è toccato a lui fare quel lavoro; **I got lumbered with him for the evening** me lo sono dovuto sorbire per tutta la serata.

lum·ber² ['lʌmbə'] VI (also: **lumber about, lumber along**) muoversi pesantemente; **to lumber past** (vehicle) passare facendo fracasso.

lum·ber·ing ['lʌmbərɪŋ] ADJ goffo(-a).

lumber·jack ['lʌmbəˌdʒæk] N taglialegna m inv, boscaiolo.

♦ **lumber room** N ripostiglio, sgabuzzino.

♦ **lumber yard** N (Am) segheria.

lu·mi·nary ['lu:mɪnərɪ] N (liter) luminare m/f.

lu·mi·nous ['lu:mɪnəs] ADJ luminoso(-a).

lump [lʌmp] **1** N (gen) pezzo; (of earth) zolla; (of sugar) zolletta; (in sauce) grumo; (swelling) gonfiore m; (hard swelling) nodulo; (bump) bernoccolo; (person: fam pej) bestione m; **with a lump in one's throat** (fig) con un nodo alla gola.

2 VT (fam: endure): **if he doesn't like it he can lump it** dovrà mandarla giù, che gli piaccia o no

▶ **lump together** VT + ADV mettere insieme, riunire.

♦ **lump sugar** N zucchero in zollette.

♦ **lump sum** N somma globale; (payment) pagamento unico.

lumpy ['lʌmpɪ] ADJ (comp **-ier**, superl **-iest**) (sauce) grumoso(-a); (mattress) bitorzoluto(-a).

lu·na·cy ['lu:nəsɪ] N demenza; (fig) pazzia, follia; **it's sheer lunacy!** ma è una vera pazzia!

lu·nar ['lu:nə'] ADJ lunare; **lunar landing** allunaggio; **lunar module** modulo lunare.

lu·na·tic ['lu:nətɪk] **1** N (idiot) pazzo(-a); (old: mentally-ill person) matto(-a).

2 ADJ (person) pazzo(-a); (idea: crazy) pazzo(-a), pazzesco(-a); (: stupid) idiota; (driving) da pazzi.

♦ **lunatic asylum** N (old offensive) manicomio.

♦ **lunatic fringe** N: **the lunatic fringe** la frangia estremista.

lunch [lʌntʃ] N pranzo, (seconda) colazione f; **to invite sb to** or **for lunch** invitare qn a pranzo; **to have lunch** pranzare.

♦ **lunch break** N intervallo del pranzo.

lunch·eon ['lʌntʃən] N (frm) pranzo.

♦ **luncheon meat** N ≈ mortadella.

♦ **luncheon voucher** N buono m pasto inv.

♦ **lunch hour** N = **lunch break**.

lunch·time ['lʌntʃˌtaɪm] N ora di pranzo.

lung [lʌŋ] N polmone m; **to shout at the top of one's lungs** gridare a squarciagola.

♦ **lung cancer** N cancro del polmone.

♦ **lung disease** N malattia polmonare or dei polmoni.

lunge [lʌndʒ] **1** N balzo (in avanti); (Fencing) affondo.

2 VI (also: **lunge forward**) fare un balzo in avanti; **to lunge at sb** balzare su qn; **to lunge out with one's fists/feet** tirare dei pugni/calci.

lu·pin, (Am) **lu·pine** ['lu:pɪn] N lupino.

lurch¹ [lɜ:tʃ] **1** N sobbalzo; (of ship, plane) rollata.

2 VI (person) barcollare, vacillare; (car) sobbalzare; (ship, plane) rollare; **to lurch along** (person) procedere barcollando; (car) procedere a scatti.

lurch² [lɜ:tʃ] N scatto improvviso; **to leave sb in the lurch** (fam) piantare in asso qn.

lure [ljʊə'] **1** N (decoy, bait) richiamo, esca; (fig: charm) attrazione f, lusinga.

2 VT attirare (con l'inganno); **to lure sb into a trap** attirare qn in una trappola; **to lure out** far uscire con l'inganno.

lur·gy ['lɜ:gɪ] N (Brit): **I've got the dreaded lurgy again** mi sento di nuovo poco bene.

lu·rid ['ljʊərɪd] ADJ **a** (details, description etc: gruesome) impressionante, sconvolgente; (: sensational) sensazionale, scandalistico(-a), **b** (colour) violento(-a), sgargiante; (sunset) fiammeggiante.

lurk [lɜ:k] VI (person: hide) stare in agguato, appostarsi; (: creep about) girare furtivamente; (danger) stare in agguato; (doubt) persistere.

lurk·ing ['lɜ:kɪŋ] ADJ (fear, suspicion etc) vago(-a).

lus·cious ['lʌʃəs] ADJ (food) appetitoso(-a), succulento(-a); (taste, smell) delizioso(-a); **a luscious blonde** una bionda appetitosa.

lush [lʌʃ] ADJ rigoglioso(-a), lussureggiante.

lust [lʌst] N (sexual) libidine f, desiderio; **lust for** (greed) sete f di

▶ **lust after, lust for** VI + PREP (person) desiderare; (power, wealth etc) aver sete di.

lust·ful ['lʌstfʊl] ADJ pieno(-a) di desiderio.

lus·tre, (Am) **lus·ter** ['lʌstə'] N lustro, splendore m.

lus·trous ['lʌstrəs] ADJ lucente, splendente.

lusty ['lʌstɪ] ADJ (comp **-ier**, superl **-iest**) (person) vigoroso(-a), robusto(-a); (cry etc) forte.

lute [lu:t] N liuto.

Luther ['lu:θə'] N Lutero.

Lu·ther·an ['lu:θərən] ADJ, N luterano(-a).

Lu·ther·an·ism ['lu:θərənɪzəm] N luteranesimo.

luv [lʌv] N gioia.

Lux·em·bourg ['lʌksəmˌbɜ:g] N (city) Lussemburgo f; (state) Lussemburgo m.

luxu·ri·ance [lʌg'zjʊərɪəns] N (of growth) rigoglio; (of beard) foltezza.

luxu·ri·ant [lʌg'zjʊərɪənt] ADJ (growth, jungle) lussureggiante, rigoglioso(-a); (beard) folto(-a); (fig: imagination) ricco(-a), fervido(-a).

luxu·ri·ant·ly [lʌg'zjʊərɪəntlɪ] ADV (grow) rigogliosamente.

luxu·ri·ate [lʌg'zjʊərɪˌeɪt] VI: **to luxuriate in** indulgere in, abbandonarsi al piacere di.

luxu·ri·ous [lʌg'zjʊərɪəs] ADJ (gen) lussuoso(-a), di lusso; (surroundings) di lusso; (meal, tastes) raffinato(-a), di lusso.

luxu·ri·ous·ly [lʌg'zjʊərɪəslɪ] ADV lussuosamente.

luxu·ry ['lʌkʃərɪ] **1** N (gen) lusso; (article) (oggetto di) lusso.

2 ADJ (goods, apartment) di lusso.

LV ABBR (Brit) = **luncheon voucher**.

LW ABBR (Radio: = long wave) O.L. (= onde lunghe).

ly·chee, li·chee [ˌlaɪ'tʃi:] N litchi m inv.

Ly·cra® ['laɪkrə] **1** N lycra ®.

2 ADJ di lycra.

ly·ing ['laɪŋ] [1] ADJ (*statement, story*) falso(-a); (*person*) bugiardo(-a).
  [2] N bugie *fpl*, menzogne *fpl*.
♦ **lying-in** [ˌlaɪŋ'ɪn] N (*old*): **the lying-in period** la degenza post-natale.
lymph [lɪmf] N linfa.
lym·phat·ic [lɪmˈfætɪk] ADJ linfatico(-a).
♦ **lymph nodes** NPL linfonodi *mpl*.
lynch [lɪntʃ] VT linciare.
lynch·ing ['lɪntʃɪŋ] N linciaggio.
lynch·pin ['lɪntʃpɪn] N = **linchpin**.

lynx [lɪŋks] N lince *f*.
Ly·ons ['laɪənz] N Lione *f*.
lyre ['laɪəʳ] N lira.
lyre·bird ['laɪəˌbɜːd] N uccello *m* lira *inv*.
lyr·ic ['lɪrɪk] [1] ADJ lirico(-a).
  [2] N (*poem*) lirica; **lyrics** NPL (*words of song*) parole *fpl*.
lyri·cal ['lɪrɪkəl] ADJ lirico(-a); (*fig*) entusiasta; **to wax** *or* **become lyrical about sth** infervorarsi a parlare di qc.
lyri·cal·ly ['lɪrɪkəlɪ] ADV liricamente.
lyri·cism ['lɪrɪˌsɪzəm] N lirismo.
lyri·cist ['lɪrɪsɪst] N paroliere(-a).

M

M, m [ɛm] N (*letter*) M, m *for m inv*; **M for Mary**, (*Am*) **M for Mike** ≈ M come Milano.

M [ɛm] ①️ N ABBR (*Brit*: = *motorway*) ≈ A *f* (= *autostrada*).
②️ ABBR (= *medium*) M *f* (*taglia media*).

m [ɛm] ABBR **a** (= *metre*) m **b** = **mile** **c** = **million.**

MA [ɛm'eɪ] ①️ N ABBR **a** (*Univ*) = **Master of Arts** **b** (*Am*)= *Military Academy*; see **academy.**
②️ ABBR (*Am Post*)= *Massachusetts.*

ma [mɑː] N (*fam*) mamma.

mac [mæk] N ABBR (*Brit fam*: = *mackintosh*) impermeabile *m.*

ma·ca·bre [mə'kɑːbrə] ADJ macabro(-a).

mac·ad·am [mə'kædəm] N macadam *m.*

mac·ad·am·ize [mə'kædə,maɪz] VT macadamizzare.

ma·caque [mə'kɑːk] N (*animal*) macaco.

maca·ro·ni [,mækə'rəʊnɪ] N maccheroni *mpl.*

♦ **macaroni cheese** N *pasta con formaggio gratinata al forno.*

maca·roon [,mækə'ruːn] N ≈ amaretto (*biscotto*).

ma·caw [mə'kɔː] N (*bird*) ara.

mace[1] [meɪs] N (*weapon, ceremonial*) mazza.

mace[2] [meɪs] N (*spice*) macis *m or f.*

mace·bearer ['meɪs,bɛərəʳ] N mazziere *m.*

Mac·edo·nia [,mæsɪ'dəʊnɪə] N la Macedonia.

Mac·edo·nian [,mæsɪ'dəʊnɪən] ①️ ADJ macedone.
②️ N (*person*) macedone *m/f*; (*language*) macedone *m.*

mac·er·ate ['mæsə,reɪt] ①️ VT macerare.
②️ VI macerarsi.

Mach [mæk] N (*Aer*: also: **Mach number**) (numero di) mach *m inv.*

ma·chete [mə'ʃetɪ] N machete *m inv.*

Machia·vel·lian [,mækɪə'velɪən] ADJ machiavellico(-a).

machi·na·tions [,mækɪ'neɪʃənz] NPL macchinazioni *fpl*, intrighi *mpl.*

ma·chine [mə'ʃiːn] ①️ N (*gen*) macchina; (*Pol*) apparato, macchina.
②️ VT (*Tech*) lavorare (a macchina); (*Sewing*) cucire a macchina.

♦ **machine code** N (*Comput*) codice *m* (di) macchina.

♦ **machine-gun** [mə'ʃiːn,gʌn] VT mitragliare.

♦ **machine gun** N mitragliatrice *f.*

♦ **machine-gunner** [mə'ʃiːn,gʌnəʳ] N mitragliere *m.*

♦ **machine language** N (*Comput*) linguaggio *m* macchina *inv.*

♦ **machine operator** N = **machinist.**

♦ **machine-readable** [mə'ʃiːn,riːdəbl] ADJ (*Comput*) leggibile dalla macchina.

ma·chin·ery [mə'ʃiːnərɪ] N (*machines*) macchine *fpl*, macchinari *mpl*; (*mechanism*) meccanismo; (*fig*) macchina, apparato; **a piece of machinery** un macchinario.

♦ **machine shop** N officina meccanica.

♦ **machine-stitch** [mə'ʃiːn,stɪtʃ] VT cucire a macchina.

♦ **machine tool** N macchina utensile.

♦ **machine washable** ADJ lavabile in lavatrice.

ma·chin·ist [mə'ʃiːnɪst] N (*Tech*) macchinista *m/f*; (*Sewing*) operaio(-a) addetto(-a) alla macchina da cucire.

ma·chis·mo [mæ'kɪzməʊ] N atteggiamenti *mpl* da macho, machismo.

macho ['mætʃəʊ] ADJ (da) macho *inv.*

macke·rel ['mækrəl] N, PL INV sgombro.

mack·in·tosh ['mækɪn,tɒʃ] N impermeabile *m.*

mac·ra·me [mə'krɑːmɪ] N macramè *m.*

macro... ['mækrəʊ] PREF macro... .

macro·bi·ot·ic [,mækrəʊbaɪ'ɒtɪk] ADJ macrobiotico(-a).

macro·bi·ot·ics [,mækrəʊbaɪ'ɒtɪks] NSG macrobiotica.

macro·cosm ['mækrə,kɒzəm] N macrocosmo.

macro·eco·nom·ics [,mækrəʊ,iːkə'nɒmɪks] NSG macroeconomia.

macro·mol·ecule [,mækrəʊ'mɒlɪ,kjuːl] N macromolecola.

mad [mæd] ADJ (*comp* **-der**, *superl* **-dest**) **a** (*deranged*: *person*) pazzo(-a), matto(-a); (: *bull*) furioso(-a); (: *dog*) rabbioso(-a); (*foolish*) sciocco(-a); (*rash*: *person, idea, plan*) folle; **to go mad** impazzire, diventare matto(-a); **to drive sb mad** far diventare matto(-a) qn, far impazzire qn; **as mad as a hatter** *or* **a March hare** matto(-a) da legare; **are you mad?** sei matto?, sei impazzito?; **mad with grief** pazzo(-a) di dolore; **I'm in a mad rush** ho una fretta terribile; **like mad** (*adv phrase*: *fam*) come un(a) pazzo(-a); **to be mad (keen) about** *or* **on sth** (*fam*) andar

pazzo(-a) *or* matto(-a) per qc

b (*fam: angry*): **mad (at** *or* **with sb)** furioso(-a) *or* furibondo(-a) (con qn); **he's hopping mad** (*fam*) è furibondo.

mad·am ['mædəm] N **a** signora; **can I help you madam?** (la signora) desidera?; **Madam Chairman** Signora Presidentessa; **a little madam** una bambinetta prepotente **b** (*of brothel*) tenutaria.

mad·cap ['mæd,kæp] ADJ (*fam*) senza senso, assurdo(-a).

♦ **mad cow disease** N encefalite *f* bovina spongiforme.

mad·den ['mædn] VT (*infuriate*) far impazzire, esasperare.

mad·den·ing ['mædnɪŋ] ADJ esasperante.

mad·den·ing·ly ['mædnɪŋlɪ] ADV in modo esasperante; **he's maddeningly slow** è di una lentezza esasperante; **she's maddeningly well-organized** è così organizzata che dà sui nervi.

made [meɪd] PT, PP of **make**.

Ma·dei·ra [mə'dɪərə] N (*Geog*) Madera; (*wine*) madera *m*.

♦ **made-to-measure** [,meɪdtə'mɛʒəʳ] ADJ (*Brit*) (fatto(-a)) su misura.

♦ **made-to-order** [,meɪdtə'ɔːdəʳ] ADJ fatto(-a) su ordinazione.

♦ **made-up** [,meɪd'ʌp] ADJ (*story*) inventato(-a); (*face, person, eyes*) truccato(-a).

mad·house ['mædhaʊs] N (*also fig*) manicomio.

mad·ly ['mædlɪ] ADV (*behave*) come un(a) pazzo(-a); (*love*) alla follia; **to be madly in love with sb** essere follemente innamorato(-a) di qn; **I'm not madly keen on the idea** l'idea non mi entusiasma.

mad·man ['mædmən] N (*pl* **-men**) pazzo, folle *m*.

mad·ness ['mædnɪs] N pazzia, follia.

Ma·drid [mə'drɪd] N Madrid *f*.

mad·ri·gal ['mædrɪgəl] N madrigale *m*.

mad·woman ['mæd,wʊmən] N (*pl* **-women**) pazza, folle *f*.

mael·strom ['meɪlstrəʊm] N (*frm*) turbine *m*, vortice *m*.

maes·tro ['maɪstrəʊ] N maestro.

Ma·fia ['mæfɪə] N: **the Mafia** la mafia.

mag. ABBR (*Brit fam*) = **magazine a.**

maga·zine [,mægə'ziːn] N **a** (*Press*) rivista **b** (*of firearm*) caricatore *m*; (*Mil: store*) deposito, magazzino.

ma·gen·ta [mə'dʒentə] N, ADJ (*color m*) magenta *inv*.

mag·got ['mægət] N verme *m*, baco.

mag·goty ['mægətɪ] ADJ bacato(-a), con i vermi.

mag·ic ['mædʒɪk] 1 ADJ (*spell*) magico(-a); (*beauty*) straordinario(-a); **to say the magic word** pronunciare la parola magica.
2 N magia; (*conjuring tricks*) giochi *mpl* di prestigio; **like magic** come per magia *or* per incanto.

magi·cal ['mædʒɪkəl] ADJ magico(-a).

magi·cal·ly ['mædʒɪkəlɪ] ADV magicamente.

♦ **magic carpet** N tappeto volante.

ma·gi·cian [mə'dʒɪʃən] N mago(-a); (*conjuror*) illusionista *m/f*.

♦ **magic lantern** N lanterna magica.

♦ **magic wand** N bacchetta magica.

mag·is·te·rial [,mædʒɪ'stɪərɪəl] ADJ (*frm*) di magistrato; (: *authoritative*) autorevole.

mag·is·trate ['mædʒɪ,streɪt] N magistrato.

mag·ma ['mægmə] N magma *m*.

mag·na·nim·ity [,mægnə'nɪmətɪ] N magnanimità *f inv*.

mag·nani·mous [mæg'nænɪməs] ADJ magnanimo(-a).

mag·nani·mous·ly [mæg'nænɪməslɪ] ADV con magnanimità, magnanimamente.

mag·nate ['mægneɪt] N magnate *m*.

mag·ne·sia [mæg'niːʃə] N magnesia.

mag·ne·sium [mæg'niːzɪəm] N magnesio.

mag·net ['mægnɪt] N calamita, magnete *m*.

mag·net·ic [mæg'netɪk] ADJ magnetico(-a).

mag·neti·cal·ly [mæg'netɪkəlɪ] ADV magneticamente.

♦ **magnetic disk** N (*Comput*) disco magnetico.

♦ **magnetic field** N campo magnetico.

♦ **magnetic tape** N nastro magnetico.

mag·net·ism ['mægnɪ,tɪzəm] N magnetismo.

mag·net·ize ['mægnɪ,taɪz] VT magnetizzare.

mag·ne·to [mæg'niːtəʊ] N (*Elettr*) magnete *m*.

mag·ni·fi·ca·tion [,mægnɪfɪ'keɪʃən] N ingrandimento.

mag·nifi·cence [mæg'nɪfɪsəns] N magnificenza.

mag·nifi·cent [mæg'nɪfɪsənt] ADJ magnifico(-a).

mag·nifi·cent·ly [mæg'nɪfɪsəntlɪ] ADV magnificamente.

mag·ni·fy ['mægnɪ,faɪ] VT **a** (*gen*) ingrandire; (*sound*) amplificare **b** (*exaggerate*) esagerare.

♦ **mag·ni·fy·ing glass** ['mægnɪfaɪŋ,glɑːs] N lente *f* d'ingrandimento.

mag·ni·tude ['mægnɪtjuːd] N (*gen*) vastità *f inv*, grandezza, ampiezza; (*importance*) importanza; (*Astron*) magnitudine *f*.

mag·no·lia [mæg'nəʊlɪə] N magnolia.

mag·num ['mægnəm] N (*bottle*) magnum *m inv*.

mag·pie ['mæg,paɪ] N gazza.

ma·ha·ra·jah, ma·ha·ra·ja [,mɑːhə'rɑːdʒə] N maragià *m inv*.

ma·hoga·ny [mə'hɒgənɪ] 1 N mogano.
2 ADJ di *or* in mogano.

Mahomet [mə'hɒmɪt] N = **Mohammed.**

maid [meɪd] N **a** (*servant*) domestica; (*in hotel*) cameriera **b** (*old, liter: young girl*) ragazza, fanciulla.

maid·en ['meɪdn] 1 N (*old, liter*) fanciulla, ragazza.
2 ADJ (*flight, voyage*) inaugurale.

♦ **maiden aunt** N zia nubile; (*pej*) zia zitella.

maiden·hair ['meɪdn,hɛəʳ] N (*also:* **maidenhair fern**) capelvenere *m*.

♦ **maiden name** N nome *m* da ragazza *or* da nubile.

♦ **maiden speech** N primo discorso (*in Parlamento*).

♦ **maid of honour** N damigella d'onore.

mail [meɪl] 1 N posta; **by mail** per posta.
2 VT spedire (per posta), inviare (per posta).

mail·bag ['meɪl,bæg] N sacco postale, sacco delle poste.

mail·box ['meɪl,bɒks] N (*Am*) cassetta delle lettere; (*Comput*) mailbox *m or f inv*.

♦ **mail car** N (*Am Rail*) carrozza *or* vagone *m* postale.

♦ **mail carrier** N (*Am*) postino(-a), portalettere *m/f inv*.

♦ **mail clerk** N (*Am*) impiegato(-a) delle poste.

mail·ing list ['meɪlɪŋ,lɪst] N elenco di indirizzi, indirizzario (*per l'invio di materiale pubblicitario*).

mail·man ['meɪl,mæn] N (*pl* **-men**) (*Am*) portalettere *m inv*, postino.

♦ **mail-order** ['meɪl,ɔːdəʳ] ADJ: **mail-order firm** *or* **house** ditta di vendita per corrispondenza.

♦ **mail order** ['meɪl,ɔːdəʳ] N (*selling*) vendita per corrispondenza; (*buying*) acquisto per corrispondenza.

mail·shot ['meɪl,ʃɒt] N campagna promozionale a mezzo posta, mailing *m inv*.

♦ **mail train** N treno postale.

♦ **mail truck** N (*Am: Aut*) furgone *m* postale.

♦ **mail van** N (*Brit: Aut*) furgone *m* postale; (: *Rail*) vagone *m* postale.

maim [meɪm] VT storpiare, mutilare.

main [meɪn] 1 ADJ (*gen*) principale; **the main body of an army** il grosso di un esercito; **the main thing is to ...** l'essenziale è...; **the main thing to remember is ...**

soprattutto non bisogna dimenticare che.... **2** N **a** (*pipe: for water, gas*) conduttura *or* tubatura principale; (*Elec*) linea principale; **main (sewer)** collettore *m*; see also **mains b**: **in the main** nel complesso, nell'insieme.

♦ **main course** N (*Culin*) piatto principale, piatto forte, secondo.

♦ **main deck** N (*of ship*) ponte *m* principale; (: *Mil*) ponte di batteria.

main·frame ['meɪn,freɪm] N (*also:* **mainframe computer**) mainframe *m inv.*

main·land ['meɪnlənd] N continente *m*, terraferma; **the Greek mainland** la Grecia continentale.

main·line ['meɪn,laɪn] (*slang*) **1** VT (*heroin*) bucarsi di. **2** VI bucarsi.

♦ **main-line** ['meɪn,laɪn] ADJ (*Rail*) della linea principale.

♦ **main line** N (*Rail*) linea principale.

main·ly ['meɪnlɪ] ADV principalmente, soprattutto.

main·mast ['meɪn,mɑːst] N albero maestro.

♦ **main road** N strada principale.

mains [meɪnz] NPL: **the mains** (*supply: gas, water, electricity*) le condutture; **water from the mains** acqua delle condutture; **mains operated** che funziona a elettricità; **it works by battery or from the mains** funziona a pile o a corrente; **to turn sth off at the mains** (*water*) chiudere le condutture; (*electricity, gas*) chiudere il contatore.

main·sail ['meɪn,seɪl] N randa.

main·spring ['meɪn,sprɪŋ] N (*of clock, watch*) molla principale; (*fig*) molla.

main·stay ['meɪn,steɪ] N (*support*) sostegno, pilastro.

main·stream ['meɪn,striːm] N (*fig*) corrente *f* principale.

main·tain [meɪn'teɪn] VT **a** (*keep up: gen*) mantenere; (: *attack*) continuare; (: *lead in race*) mantenere, conservare; **if the improvement is maintained** se il miglioramento continua
  b (*support: family, army*) mantenere
  c (*keep in good condition*) mantenere in buono stato
  d (*claim*): **to maintain that ...** sostenere che... .

main·te·nance ['meɪntɪnəns] N (*gen*) mantenimento; (*of car, building*) manutenzione *f*; (*alimony*) alimenti *mpl.*

♦ **maintenance contract** N contratto di manutenzione.

♦ **maintenance costs** NPL spese *fpl* di manutenzione.

♦ **maintenance grant** N (*for student*) presalario; (*for worker*) indennità *f inv* di trasferta.

♦ **maintenance order** N (*Law*) obbligo degli alimenti.

mai·son·ette [,meɪzə'nɛt] N (*Brit*) appartamentino su due piani.

maize [meɪz] N granturco, mais *m.*

♦ **maize flour** N farina di granoturco *or* di mais.

Maj. ABBR (*Mil*) = **major.**

ma·jes·tic [mə'dʒɛstɪk] ADJ maestoso(-a).

ma·jes·ti·cal·ly [mə'dʒɛstɪkəlɪ] ADV maestosamente.

maj·es·ty ['mædʒɪstɪ] N maestà *f inv*; **His Majesty** Sua Maestà.

ma·jor ['meɪdʒəʳ] **1** ADJ (*greater, also Math, Mus*) maggiore; (*in importance*) principale, importante; (*repairs*) grosso(-a), sostanziale; (*disaster, loss*) grave; (*interest, artist, success*) grande; **a major operation** (*Med*) un complesso intervento chirurgico; (*undertaking*) un'operazione considerevole; **major road** strada con diritto di precedenza.
  2 N **a** (*Mil*) maggiore *m*
  b (*Law*) maggiorenne *m/f*
  c (*Am Univ*) materia di specializzazione.

  3 VI (*Am Univ*): **to major (in)** specializzarsi (in).

Ma·jor·ca [mə'jɔːkə] N Maiorca.

♦ **major general** N (*Mil*) generale *m* di divisione.

ma·jor·ity [mə'dʒɒrɪtɪ] **1** N **a** maggioranza; **the majority of people** la maggior parte della gente; **elected by a majority of two** eletto con una maggioranza di due voti; **to be in the majority** essere in maggioranza **b** (*Law*): **the age of majority** la maggiore età.
  2 ADJ (*verdict*) maggioritario(-a); (*government*) di maggioranza.

♦ **majority holding** N (*Fin*): **to have a majority holding** essere il/la maggiore azionista.

make [meɪk] (*pt, pp* **made**) **1** VT **a** (*gen*) fare; (*Comm*) produrre, fabbricare; (*building*) costruire; (*points, score*) fare, segnare; **God made the world** Dio creò il mondo; **she made the material into a dress** con la stoffa ha fatto un vestito; **made of silver** (fatto(-a)) d'argento; **made in Italy** fabbricato(-a) in Italia; (*on label*) made in Italy; **to show what one is made of** far vedere di che tempra *or* che stoffa si è fatti; **they were made for each other** erano fatti l'uno per l'altra
  b (*cause to be or become*) fare; (+ *adj*) rendere; **to make sb happy/sad** rendere *or* far felice/triste qn; **to make sb angry** far arrabbiare qn; **to make sth difficult** render difficile qc; **to make sth into sth else** fare di qc qualcos'altro; **to make sb a judge** nominare qn giudice; **let's make it 6 o'clock** facciamo alle 6; **to make o.s. heard** farsi sentire; **make yourself comfortable** si accomodi; **you'll make yourself ill!** starai male!
  c (*cause to do*) fare; (: *stronger*) costringere; **to make sb do sth** far fare qc a qn; costringere qn a fare qc; **to make sb wait** far aspettare qn; **to make o.s. do sth** sforzarsi a fare qc; **if you don't want to I can't make you** se non vuoi non posso costringerti; **this made him leave** questo lo ha fatto partire, questo ha fatto sì che partisse; **what made you say that?** perché hai detto questo?; **what makes you think that?** cosa te lo fa pensare?; **to make sth do** OR **to make do with sth** arrangiarsi con qc
  d (*earn*) guadagnare; **to make money** far soldi; **to make a profit of £500** ricavare un profitto di 500 sterline; **to make a loss of £500** subire una perdita di 500 sterline; **he made a profit/loss** ci ha rimesso/guadagnato; **he made £500 on the deal** l'affare gli ha fruttato 500 sterline
  e (*reach: destination*) arrivare a; (*catch: bus, train*) prendere; **they made (it to) the finals** sono entrati in finale; **to make it** (*in time*) arrivare; (*achieve sth*) farcela; **can you make it for 4 o'clock?** ce la fai per le 4?; **to make it in life** riuscire nella vita; **to make good** (*succeed*) aver successo; **to make port** raggiungere il porto
  f (*cause to succeed*): **he's made for life** il suo avvenire è assicurato, è a posto per sempre; **this film made her** questo film l'ha resa celebre; **that's made my day!** questo ha trasformato la mia giornata!; **to make or break sb** essere il successo o la rovina di qn
  g (*equal, constitute*) fare; **2 and 2 make 4** 2 più 2 fa 4; **that makes 20** questo fa 20; **does that book make good reading?** è un libro interessante?; **these records make a set** questi dischi formano un set; **he made a good husband** è stato un buon marito
  h (*estimate*): **how far do you make it to the village?** quanto pensi che ci sia da qui al paese?; **what time do you make it?** — **I make it 6 o'clock** che ora fai? — io faccio le 6; **what do you make of this?** cosa pensi che voglia dire questo?; **what do you make of him?** che te ne

pare di lui?.

2 VI **a** (*go*): **to make towards the door** dirigersi verso la porta; **to make after sb** inseguire qn

b : **to make as if to do sth** fare (come) per fare qc.

3 N **a** (*action*) fabbricazione *f*; (*brand*) marca; **it's our own make** è di nostra produzione

b : **to be on the make** (*fam*) essere a caccia di successo

▶ **make away** VI + ADV = **make off**

▶ **make away with** VI + ADV + PREP (*kill*) far fuori, togliere di mezzo

▶ **make for** VI + PREP **a** (*place*) essere diretto(-a) a, avviarsi verso; (*subj: ship*) far rotta verso

b (*fig: result in*) produrre; (: *contribute to*) contribuire a

▶ **make off** VI + ADV svignarsela; **to make off with sth** svignarsela con qc

▶ **make out** **1** VT + ADV **a** (*write out: cheque, receipt, list*) fare; (: *document*) redigere; (: *form*) riempire, compilare; **to make out a case for sth** presentare delle valide ragioni in favore di qc

b (*see, discern*) riuscire a vedere, distinguere; (*decipher*) decifrare; (*understand*) (riuscire a) capire; **how do you make that out?** che cosa te lo fa pensare?

c (*claim, imply*): **to make out (that ...)** voler far credere (che...), darla ad intendere (che...); **to make sb out to be stupid** far passare qn per stupido.

2 VI + ADV (*fam: get on*) cavarsela

▶ **make out with** VI + ADV + PREP (*fam*): **to make out with sb** farsi qn; **did you make out with her, then?** sei poi riuscito a fartela?

▶ **make over** VT + ADV (*assign*): **to make over (to)** passare (a), trasferire (a)

▶ **make up** **1** VT + ADV **a** (*invent: story*) inventare

b (*put together, prepare: list, parcel, bed*) fare; (*food, medicine*) preparare; **she made the books up into a parcel** ha impacchettato i libri

c (*settle: dispute*) mettere fine a; **to make it up with sb** far la pace con qn

d (*complete: total, quantity*) completare; **I need £5 to make up the sum we require** mi occorrono 5 sterline per raggiungere la somma stabilita

e (*compensate for: loss, deficit, lost time*) recuperare, compensare, colmare; **to make it up to sb (for sth)** compensare qn (per qc)

f (*constitute*) comporre; **to be made up of** essere composto(-a) di *or* formato(-a) da

g (*apply cosmetics to*) truccare.

2 VI + ADV **a** (*after quarrelling*) fare la pace, riconciliarsi

b (*apply cosmetics*) truccarsi

c (*catch up*): **to make up on sb** riprendere qn

▶ **make up for** VI + ADV + PREP (*lost time*) recuperare; (*trouble caused*) farsi perdonare; (*mistake*) rimediare a; (*loss, injury*) compensare

▶ **make up to** VI + ADV + PREP (*fam: curry favour with*) cercare di entrare nelle simpatie di *or* di accattivarsi il favore di, lisciare.

♦ **make-believe** ['meɪkbɪˌliːv] N: **the land of make-believe** il mondo delle favole; **it's just make-believe** (*activity*) è solo per finta; (*story*) sono frottole, è tutta un'invenzione.

mak·er ['meɪkə'] N (*manufacturer*) fabbricante *m*; (*creator*) creatore(-trice); (*originator*) autore(-trice); (*Rel*): **our Maker** il Creatore.

make·shift ['meɪkˌʃɪft] ADJ di fortuna, improvvisato(-a).

♦ **make-up** ['meɪkˌʌp] N **a** (*cosmetics*) trucco, cosmetici *mpl* **b** (*nature: of object, group*) composizione *f*; (: *of*

football team) formazione *f*; (: *of person*) carattere *m*.

♦ **make-up artist** N truccatore(-trice).

♦ **make-up bag** N borsa del trucco.

♦ **make-up remover** N struccante *m*.

make·weight ['meɪkˌweɪt] N (*thing*) *cosa aggiunta per completare un insieme*; (*person*): **I'm only in the team as a sort of make-weight** sono nella squadra solo per far numero.

mak·ing ['meɪkɪŋ] N **a** (*Comm, gen*) fabbricazione *f*; (*of dress, food*) confezione *f*; **it's still in the making** non è ancora finito; **it's history in the making** è un momento storico; **it was the making of him** ha fatto di lui un uomo

b : **he has the makings of an actor** (*qualities, potential*) ha la stoffa dell'attore; **the makings of a good film** quello che ci vuole per fare un buon film.

mala·chite ['mæləˌkaɪt] N malachite *f*.

mal·ad·just·ed [ˌmæləˈdʒʌstɪd] ADJ (*Psych*) disadattato (-a).

mala·droit [ˌmæləˈdrɔɪt] ADJ maldestro(-a).

mala·dy ['mælədɪ] N (*old*) male *m*, malattia.

ma·laise [mæˈleɪz] N malessere *m*.

ma·laria [məˈlɛərɪə] N malaria.

ma·lar·ial [məˈlɛərɪəl] ADJ malarico(-a).

Ma·la·wi [məˈlɑːwɪ] N il Malawi.

Ma·lay [məˈleɪ] **1** ADJ malese.

2 N (*person*) malese *m/f*; (*language*) malese *m*.

Ma·la·ya [məˈleɪə] N la Malesia.

Ma·lay·an [məˈleɪən] ADJ, N = **Malay**.

Ma·lay·sia [məˈleɪzɪə] N la Malaysia.

Ma·lay·sian [məˈleɪzɪən] ADJ, N malaysiano(-a).

mal·con·tent ['mælkənˌtɛnt] N (*frm*) malcontento(-a), insoddisfatto(-a).

Mal·dive Islands ['mɔːldaɪvˌaɪləndz], **Mal·dives** ['mɔːldaɪvz] NPL: **the Maldive Islands, the Maldives** le (isole *fpl*) Maldive.

male [meɪl] **1** ADJ (*gen, sex*) maschile; (*animal, child*) maschio *inv*; **male and female students** studenti e studentesse.

2 N (*Bio, Elec*) maschio.

♦ **male chauvinism** N maschilismo.

♦ **male chauvinist** N maschilista *m*.

♦ **male chauvinist pig** N (*fam*) sporco maschilista *m*.

mal·efac·tor ['mælɪˌfæktə'] N (*frm*) malfattore *m*.

♦ **male nurse** N infermiere *m*.

ma·levo·lence [məˈlɛvələns] N malevolenza, malanimo.

ma·levo·lent [məˈlɛvələnt] ADJ malevolo(-a).

ma·levo·lent·ly [məˈlɛvələntlɪ] ADV con malevolenza.

mal·for·ma·tion [ˌmælfɔːˈmeɪʃən] N malformazione *f*.

mal·func·tion [ˌmælˈfʌŋkʃən] N cattivo funzionamento.

mal·ice ['mælɪs] N cattiveria, malevolenza; **I bear him no malice** non gli serbo nessun rancore.

♦ **mal·ice afore·thought** [ˌmælɪsəˈfɔːˌθɔːt] N (*Law*) premeditazione *f*.

ma·li·cious [məˈlɪʃəs] ADJ cattivo(-a), malevolo(-a); (*Law*) doloso(-a); **malicious gossip** malignità *fpl*.

ma·li·cious·ly [məˈlɪʃəslɪ] ADV con cattiveria, malignamente; (*Law*) dolosamente.

ma·li·cious·ness [məˈlɪʃəsnɪs] N cattiveria, malignità *f inv*.

ma·lign [məˈlaɪn] **1** ADJ malefico(-a), nocivo(-a).

2 VT diffamare, calunniare, malignare su.

ma·lig·nan·cy [məˈlɪgnənsɪ] N (*of person, remark*) malignità *f inv*; (*of tumour*) carattere *m* maligno.

ma·lig·nant [məˈlɪgnənt] ADJ maligno(-a), malevolo(-a); (*Med: tumour*) maligno(-a).

ma·lin·ger [məˈlɪŋgə'] VI fingersi malato(-a) (*per non*

lavorare).

ma·lin·ger·er [mə'lɪŋgərəʳ] N uno(-a) che si finge malato (-a) (*per non lavorare*), scansafatiche *m/f inv*.

mall [mɔːl] N (*Am: also:* **shopping mall**) centro commerciale.

mal·lard ['mæləd] N (*duck*) germano reale.

mal·le·able ['mælɪəbl] ADJ malleabile.

mal·let ['mælɪt] N (*tool*) mazzuolo; (*in croquet*) maglio; (*in polo*) mazza.

mal·low ['mæləʊ] N (*plant*) malva.

mal·nour·ished [mæl'nʌrɪʃt] ADJ (*frm*) denutrito(-a).

mal·nu·tri·tion [,mælnjʊ'trɪʃən] N denutrizione *f*, malnutrizione *f*.

mal·odor·ous [mæl'əʊdərəs] ADJ (*liter*) maleodorante.

mal·prac·tice [,mæl'præktɪs] N (*by doctor*) negligenza (colposa); (*by minister, lawyer*) prevaricazione *f*.

malt [mɔːlt] ① N malto; (*also:* **malt whisky**) whisky di malto.
② ADJ (*vinegar, whisky*) di malto.

Mal·ta ['mɔːltə] N Malta.

♦ **malt bread** N pane *m* al malto.

malt·ed milk ['mɔːltɪd,mɪlk] ADJ latte *m* al malto.

Mal·tese [,mɔː'tiːz] ① ADJ maltese.
② N INV (*person*) maltese *m/f*; (*language*) maltese *m*.

♦ **Maltese cross** N croce di Malta.

mal·treat [,mæl'triːt] VT maltrattare.

mal·treat·ment [,mæl'triːtmənt] N maltrattamento.

mama, mam·ma [mə'mɑː] N (*fam*) mamma.

mam·mal ['mæməl] N mammifero.

mam·ma·lian [mæ'meɪlɪən] ADJ (*Bio, species, behaviour*) dei mammiferi.

mam·mon ['mæmən] N (*pej: money*) mammona *m or f*.

mam·moth ['mæməθ] ① N mammut *m inv*.
② ADJ colossale, mostruoso(-a), enorme, gigantesco (-a).

man [mæn] ① N (*pl* men) **a** (*gen, Mil, Sport*) uomo; (*in office, shop*) impiegato; (*Chess*) pezzo; (*Draughts*) pedina; **an old man** un vecchio; **a blind man** un cieco; **man and wife** marito e moglie; **her man is in the army** il suo uomo è nell'esercito; **the man in the street** l'uomo della strada; **he was man enough to apologize** ha avuto il coraggio di scusarsi; **he's a man about town** è un uomo di mondo; **a man of the world** un uomo di mondo *or* di grande esperienza; **men say that ...** si dice che...; **no man** nessuno; **any man** chiunque; **that man Jones** quel Jones; **as one man** come un sol uomo; **they're communists to a man** sono tutti comunisti, dal primo all'ultimo; **he's not the man for the job** non è l'uomo adatto per questo lavoro; **I'm not a drinking man** non sono un bevitore; **he's a family man** è un uomo tutto casa e famiglia; **he's a Glasgow man** è di Glasgow; **the ice-cream man** il gelataio; **come on, man!** dai, forza!; **good man!** bravo!
b (*humanity*): **Man** l'uomo, l'umanità *f inv*.
② VT (*ship, fortress*) fornire di uomini; (*fleet*) armare; **the ship is manned by Americans** l'equipaggio della nave è americano; **the telephone is manned all day** c'è sempre una persona che risponde al telefono; **man the guns!** uomini ai cannoni!

mana·cle ['mænəkl] VT ammanettare, mettere le manette a.

mana·cles ['mænəklz] NPL manette *fpl*.

man·age ['mænɪdʒ] ① VT **a** (*direct: company, organization, hotel*) dirigere; (: *shop, restaurant*) gestire; (: *household, property, affairs*) amministrare; (: *football team, pop star*)

essere il manager di; **the election was managed** (*pej*) le elezioni erano truccate
b (*handle, control: tool*) maneggiare; (: *ship, vehicle*) manovrare; (: *person, child*) saper prendere *or* trattare; **I can manage him** so come trattarlo *or* prenderlo
c : **to manage to do sth** riuscire a fare qc; **he managed not to get his feet wet** è riuscito a non bagnarsi i piedi; **£5 is the most I can manage** posso metterci 5 sterline ma non di più; **I shall manage it** ce la farò; **can you manage the cases?** ce la fai a portare le valigie?; **can you manage 8 o'clock?** alle 8 ti va bene?.
② VI farcela; **can you manage?** ce la fai?; **how do you manage?** come riesci a farcela?; **I have to manage on £20** mi devo arrangiare con 20 sterline; **to manage without sb/sth** fare a meno di qn/qc.

man·age·able ['mænɪdʒəbl] ADJ (*car, boat, size, proportions*) maneggevole; (*person*) trattabile, arrendevole; (*task*) fattibile; **manageable hair** capelli *mpl* docili al pettine.

man·age·ment ['mænɪdʒmənt] N **a** (*act: see vb 1a*) direzione *f*; gestione *f*; amministrazione *f* **b** (*persons: of business, firm*) dirigenti *mpl*, direzione *f*; (: *of hotel, shop, theatre*) direzione *f*; **"under new management"** "nuova gestione"; **management and workers** i dirigenti e i lavoratori.

♦ **management accounting** N contabilità *f inv* di gestione.

♦ **management consultant** N consulente *m/f* aziendale.

♦ **management potential** N potenzialità *fpl* manageriali.

man·ag·er ['mænɪdʒəʳ] N (*gen*) direttore *m*; (*of shop, restaurant*) gestore *m*, gerente *m*; (*of football team, pop star, artiste*) manager *m inv*; (*of estate*) amministratore *m*; **sales manager** direttore *m* delle vendite.

man·ag·er·ess [,mænɪdʒə'rɛs] N (*gen*) direttrice *f*; (*of shop, restaurant*) gerente *f*.

mana·gerial [,mænə'dʒɪərɪəl] ADJ (*class*) dirigente, manageriale, dirigenziale; (*ability, post*) direttivo(-a), manageriale, dirigenziale.

man·ag·ing di·rec·tor ['mænɪdʒɪŋ,dɪ'rɛktəʳ] N amministratore *m* delegato.

mana·tee [,mænə'tiː] N (*mammal*) lamantino.

Man·cu·nian [mæŋ'kjuːnɪən] ① ADJ di Manchester.
② N (*resident*) abitante *m/f* di Manchester; (*native*) originario(-a) di Manchester.

man·da·rin ['mændərɪn] N **a** (*person*) mandarino **b** (*also:* **mandarin orange**) mandarino.

man·date ['mændeɪt] N delega, mandato.

man·da·tory ['mændətərɪ] ADJ obbligatorio(-a).

man·do·lin, man·do·line ['mændəlɪn] N mandolino.

man·drill ['mændrɪl] N (*monkey*) mandrillo.

mane [meɪn] N criniera.

♦ **man-eater** ['mæn,iːtəʳ] N (*animal*) mangiatore *m* di uomini; (*person*) cannibale *m/f*, antropofago(-a).

♦ **man-eating** ['mæn,iːtɪŋ] ADJ (*animal*) che si nutre di carne umana; (*tribe*) antropofago(-a).

ma·neu·ver *etc* [mə'nuːvəʳ] (*Am*) = **manoeuvre** *etc*.

man·ful ['mænfʊl] ADJ coraggioso(-a), valoroso(-a).

man·ful·ly ['mænfəlɪ] ADV coraggiosamente, valorosamente.

man·ga·nese [,mæŋgə'niːz] N manganese *m*.

man·gel·wur·zel ['mæŋgəl,wɜːzəl], **man·gel** ['mæŋgəl] N bietola da foraggio.

man·ger ['meɪndʒəʳ] N mangiatoia.

mange·tout ['mɑ̃ʒ'tuː] N pisello dolce, taccola.

man·gle[1] ['mæŋgl] VT (*mutilate*: *body*) straziare, maciullare; (: *object*) stritolare.

man·gle[2] ['mæŋgl] N strizzatoio.

man·go ['mæŋgəʊ] N mango.

♦ **mango chutney** N *salsa piccante a base di mango*.

man·grove ['mæŋ,grəʊv] N mangrovia.

man·gy ['meɪndʒɪ] ADJ rognoso(-a).

man·handle ['mæn,hændl] VT (*treat roughly*) malmenare; (*move by hand*: *goods*) spostare a mano.

man·hole ['mæn,həʊl] N botola stradale.

♦ **manhole cover** N tombino, chiusino.

man·hood ['mænhʊd] N **a** (*state*) età *f inv* virile **b** (*manliness*) virilità *f inv* **c** (*men*) uomini *mpl*.

♦ **man·hour** ['mæn,aʊəʳ] N (*Industry*) ora di lavoro.

man·hunt ['mæn,hʌnt] N caccia all'uomo.

ma·nia ['meɪnɪə] N mania; **to have a mania for (doing) sth** avere la mania di (fare) qc.

ma·ni·ac ['meɪnɪæk] N maniaco(-a); **sports maniac** (*fig fam*) maniaco(-a) dello sport; **he drives like a maniac!** guida come un pazzo!

ma·nia·cal [mə'naɪəkəl] ADJ (*behaviour*) da folle.

man·ic ['mænɪk] ADJ (*Psych*) maniaco(-a), maniacale.

♦ **manic depression** N (*Psych*) psicosi *f inv* maniacodepressiva.

♦ **manic-depressive** [,mænɪkdɪ'prɛsɪv] (*Psych*) [1] ADJ maniaco-depressivo(-a). .

[2] N persona affetta da psicosi maniaco-depressiva.

mani·cure ['mænɪ,kjʊəʳ] [1] N manicure *f inv*.

[2] VT: **to manicure one's hands** (*or* one's nails) fare manicure; **well-manicured hands** mani ben curate.

♦ **manicure set** N trousse *f inv* della manicure.

mani·cur·ist ['mænɪ,kjʊərɪst] N manicure *f inv*.

mani·fest ['mænɪ,fɛst] [1] ADJ evidente, manifesto(-a), palese.

[2] VT manifestare.

[3] N (*Aer*, *Naut*) manifesto.

mani·fes·ta·tion [,mænɪfɛs'teɪʃən] N manifestazione *f*.

mani·fest·ly ['mænɪ,fɛstlɪ] ADV manifestamente, palesemente.

mani·fes·to [,mænɪ'fɛstəʊ] N (*pl* **manifestoes**) manifesto.

mani·fold ['mænɪ,fəʊld] [1] ADJ molteplice.

[2] N (*Aut*): **exhaust manifold** collettore *m* di scarico; **intake manifold** collettore *m* di aspirazione.

Ma·nila [mə'nɪlə] N Manila.

ma·nila, ma·nil·la [mə'nɪlə] ADJ (*paper*, *envelope*) manilla *inv*.

ma·nipu·late [mə'nɪpjʊleɪt] VT (*tool*) maneggiare; (*controls*) azionare; (*Med*, *fig*: *person*) manipolare; (*situation*, *system*) manovrare.

ma·nipu·la·tion [mə,nɪpjʊ'leɪʃən] N (*see vb*) maneggiare *m*; capacità *f inv* di azionare; manipolazione *f*; capacità *f inv* di manovrare.

ma·nipu·la·tive [mə'nɪpjʊ,lətɪv] ADJ: **to be manipulative** (*person*) cercare di manipolare gli altri; **manipulative behaviour** comportamento teso alla manipolazione altrui.

man·kind [mæn'kaɪnd] N l'umanità *f inv*, il genere *m* umano.

man·like ['mæn,laɪk] ADJ (*appearance*, *qualities*) umano (-a); (*pej*: *woman*) mascolino(-a).

man·li·ness ['mænlɪnɪs] N virilità *f inv*.

man·ly ['mænlɪ] ADJ (*comp* **-ier**, *superl* **-iest**) virile, coraggioso(-a).

♦ **man-made** ['mæn,meɪd] ADJ artificiale, sintetico(-a).

man·na ['mænə] N manna.

manned ['mænd] ADJ pilotato(-a) da un equipaggio (a bordo).

man·ne·quin ['mænɪkɪn] N (*dummy*) manichino; (*fashion model*) indossatrice *f*.

man·ner ['mænəʳ] N **a** (*mode*) modo, maniera; **in this manner** in questo modo, così; **in such a manner that ...** in modo tale che + *indic* (*actual result*) *or* + *sub* (*intended result*); **he spoke in such a manner as to offend them** ha parlato in modo tale da offenderli *or* che li ha offesi; **after** *or* **in the manner of X** alla maniera di X, nello stile di X; **in a manner of speaking** per così dire; **(as) to the manner born** come se ce l'avesse nel sangue

b (*behaviour*) comportamento; (*attitude*) atteggiamento; **I don't like his manner** ha un modo di fare che non mi piace

c : (good) **manners** buona educazione *f*, buone maniere *fpl*; **bad manners** maleducazione *f*; **it's bad manners to talk with your mouth full** è da maleducati parlare con la bocca piena; **she has no manners** non conosce le buone maniere; **to teach sb manners** insegnare l'educazione a qn; **a novel of manners** un romanzo di costume

d (*class*, *type*): **all manner of** ogni sorta di.

man·nered ['mænəd] ADJ affettato(-a).

man·ner·ism ['mænə,rɪzəm] N **a** (*habit*) vezzo, tic *m inv* **b** (*Art*) manierismo.

man·ner·ly ['mænəlɪ] ADJ educato(-a), civile.

man·nish ['mænɪʃ] ADJ (*pej*) mascolino(-a).

ma·noeu·vrabil·ity [mə,nuː'vrəˈbɪlɪtɪ] N manovrabilità *f inv*, maneggevolezza.

ma·noeu·vrable, (Am**) ma·neu·ver·able** [mə'nuː'vrəbl] ADJ (*gen*) facile da manovrare; (*car*) maneggevole; (*ship*, *plane*) manovriero(-a).

ma·noeu·vre, (Am**) ma·neu·ver** [mə'nuː'vəʳ] [1] N manovra; **the soldiers were out on manoeuvres** i soldati stavano facendo le manovre *or* le esercitazioni.

[2] VT (*also Mil*) manovrare; **I couldn't manoeuvre the settee through the door** non sono riuscito a far passare il divano attraverso la porta; **he manoeuvred himself into a job** è riuscito a ottenere un posto con abili manovre; **to manoeuvre sb into doing sth** costringere abilmente qn a fare qc.

[3] VI (*Mil*, *fig*) manovrare; (*Aut*) far manovra.

man·oeu·vring, (Am**) man·euve·ring** [mə'nuː'vərɪŋ] N manovre *fpl*.

ma·nom·eter [mə'nɒmɪtəʳ] N manometro.

man·or ['mænəʳ] N (*also*: **manor house**) maniero.

man·power ['mæn,paʊəʳ] N (*gen*, *Industry*) manodopera; (*Mil*) effettivi *mpl*.

♦ **Manpower Services Commission** N (*Brit*) *ente nazionale per l'occupazione, non più esistente*.

man·sard ['mænsɑːd] N **a** (*also*: **mansard roof**) tetto mansardato **b** (*attic*) mansarda.

manse [mæns] N canonica.

man·servant ['mæn,sɜːvənt] N (*pl* **menservants**) servitore *m*, domestico.

man·sion ['mænʃən] N (*in town*) palazzo (signorile); (*in country*) villa, maniero.

♦ **man-sized** ['mæn,saɪzd] ADJ (*fig*) grande.

man·slaughter ['mæn,slɔːtəʳ] N omicidio colposo.

man·ta ['mæntə] N (*also*: **manta ray**) manta.

mantel·piece ['mæntl,piːs] N mensola del caminetto.

man·til·la [mæn'tɪlə] N mantiglia.

man·tle ['mæntl] N (*old*: *garment*) mantello, manto; (*also*:

gas mantle) reticella; (*Geol*) mantello; **a mantle of snow** un manto di neve.

♦ **man-to-man** [ˌmæntə'mæn] ADJ, ADV da uomo a uomo.

man-trap ['mæn ˌtræp] N trappola per l'uomo.

Man-tua ['mæntjʊə] N Mantova.

manu-al ['mænjʊəl] [1] ADJ manuale.

[2] N (*book*) manuale *m*.

manu-al-ly ['mænjʊəlɪ] ADV manualmente.

♦ **manual worker** N manovale *m*; **manual workers** la manovalanza.

manu-fac-tur-able [ˌmænjʊ'fæktʃərəbl] ADJ fabbricabile.

manu-fac-ture [ˌmænjʊ'fæktʃəʳ] [1] N (*act*) fabbricazione *f*, manifattura; (*of clothes*) confezione *f*; (*product*) manufatto.

[2] VT (*gen*) fabbricare; (*clothes*) confezionare; (*fig: excuse, lie*) architettare, inventare.

♦ **manu-fac-tured goods** [ˌmænjʊ'fæktʃəd'gʊdz] NPL manufatti *mpl*.

manu-fac-tur-er [ˌmænjʊ'fæktʃərəʳ] N fabbricante *m*.

♦ **manu-fac-tur-ing in-dus-tries** [ˌmænjʊ'fæktʃə-rɪŋ'ɪndəstrɪz] NPL industrie *fpl* manifatturiere.

ma-nure [mə'njʊəʳ] [1] N concime *m*; (*organic*) letame *m*.

[2] VT concimare.

manu-script ['mænjʊ skrɪpt] N manoscritto.

Manx [mæŋks] ADJ dell'isola di Man.

many ['mɛnɪ] ADJ, PRON molti(-e), tanti(-e); **too many difficulties** troppe difficoltà; **many a ...** più di un(a)..., molti(-e)...; **a great many** un gran numero (di), moltissimi(-e); **so many books** (così) tanti libri; **many people** molta *or* tanta gente, molte persone; **there were as many as 100 at the meeting** alla riunione c'erano ben 100 persone; **many a man** più d'uno, molti; **many a time** più volte; **he has as many as I have** ne ha tanti quanti ne ho io; **there's one too many** ce n'è uno in più; **he's had one too many** ha bevuto un bicchiere di troppo; **as many again** altrettanti; **twice as many** due volte tanto; **a good** *or* **great many houses** moltissime case, un gran numero di case; **how many?** quanti(-e)?; **how many people?** quanta gente?, quante persone?; **there are too many of you** siete (in) troppi; **however many there may be** per quanti ce ne siano; **many of them came** molti di loro sono venuti.

♦ **many-coloured** [ˌmɛnɪ'kʌləd] ADJ multicolore.

♦ **many-sided** [ˌmɛnɪ'saɪdɪd] ADJ (*object*) che ha molti lati; (*fig: problem, question*) complesso(-a), che ha molte sfaccettature.

Mao-ri ['maʊrɪ] ADJ, N maori (*m/f*) *inv*.

map [mæp] [1] N (*gen*) carta (geografica); (*of town*) pianta; **treasure map** mappa del tesoro; **this will put Eastdean on the map** (*fig*) questo renderà famoso *or* farà conoscere Eastdean; **off the map** (*fig*) in capo al mondo.

[2] VT tracciare una carta (*or* una pianta *or* una mappa) di

► **map out** VT + ADV tracciare una carta (*or* una pianta *or* una mappa) di; (*fig: career, holiday, essay*) pianificare.

ma-ple ['meɪpl] N acero; **field maple** acero campestre.

map-ping ['mæpɪŋ] N (*Math*) funzione *f*.

mar [mɑː] VT sciupare, guastare.

Mar. ABBR (= *March*) mar.

mara-bou ['mærə bu:] N (*bird*) marabù *m inv*.

ma-ras-ca [mə'ræskə] N (*tree*) marasco.

mara-schi-no [ˌmærə'ski:nəʊ] N (*liqueur*) maraschino.

♦ **maraschino cherry** N marasca.

mara-thon ['mærəθən] [1] N maratona.

[2] ADJ (*debate*) lunghissimo; **a marathon session** una

seduta fiume.

♦ **marathon runner** N maratoneta *m/f*.

ma-raud [mə'rɔːd] VI darsi al saccheggio.

ma-raud-er [mə'rɔːdəʳ] N predone *m*, saccheggiatore(-trice), predatore(-trice).

ma-raud-ing [mə'rɔːdɪŋ] ADJ che si dà al saccheggio.

mar-ble ['mɑːbl] [1] N a (*material, sculpture*) marmo b (*toy*) bilia, biglia; **to play marbles** giocare a bilie.

[2] ADJ di marmo.

March [mɑːtʃ] N marzo *for usage see* **July**.

march [mɑːtʃ] [1] N (*gen*) marcia; (*demonstration*) marcia, dimostrazione *f*; **on the march** in marcia; **a day's march** una giornata di marcia.

[2] VI (*Mil*) marciare; **quick march!** avanti, marsc!; **to march into a room** entrare a passo deciso in una stanza; **to march past** sfilare; **to march past sb** sfilare davanti a qn; **to march up to sb** andare risolutamente da qn.

[3] VT (*Mil*) far marciare; **to march sb off to prison/to bed** spedire qn in prigione/a letto.

march-er ['mɑːtʃəʳ] N dimostrante *m/f*.

march-ing or-ders ['mɑːtʃɪŋ'ɔːdəz] NPL (*Mil*) ordini *mpl* di partenza; **to give sb his marching orders** (*fig*) dare il benservito a qn.

mar-chion-ess ['mɑːʃənɪs] N marchesa.

♦ **march past** N (*Mil*) sfilata.

mare [mɛəʳ] N giumenta, cavalla.

marg, marge [mɑːdʒ] N ABBR (*Brit fam*) = **margarine**.

mar-ga-rine [ˌmɑːdʒə'ri:n] N margarina.

mar-gin ['mɑːdʒɪn] N (*gen, fig*) margine *m*; **to win by a wide/narrow margin** vincere con largo margine/di stretta misura.

mar-gin-al ['mɑːdʒɪnl] [1] ADJ marginale.

[2] N (*Brit Pol: also:* **marginal seat**) *collegio elettorale con una stretta maggioranza a favore del partito al governo.*

mar-gin-al-ly ['mɑːdʒɪnəlɪ] ADV (*bigger, better*) lievemente, di poco; (*different*) un po'.

mar-gue-rite [ˌmɑːgə'riːt] N margherita.

mari-gold ['mærɪ gəʊld] N calendola.

ma-ri-jua-na, ma-ri-hua-na [ˌmærɪ'hwɑːnə] N marijuana.

ma-ri-na [mə'riːnə] N porticciolo, marina.

mari-nade [ˌmærɪ'neɪd] [1] N marinata.

[2] VT = **marinate**.

mari-nate, mari-nade ['mærɪ neɪt] VT marinare.

ma-rine [mə'riːn] [1] ADJ (*animal, plant*) marino(-a); (*products*) del mare; (*vegetation, forces*) marittimo(-a); (*engineering*) navale.

[2] N a : **merchant** *or* **mercantile marine** marina mercantile b (*Mil*) fante *m* di marina; (*Am*) marine *m inv*; **tell that to the marines!** (*fam*) va' a raccontarla a un altro!

♦ **marine insurance** N assicurazione *f* marittima.

mari-ner ['mærɪnəʳ] N marinaio.

mari-on-ette [ˌmærɪə'nɛt] N marionetta.

mari-tal ['mærɪtl] ADJ coniugale, maritale.

♦ **marital status** N stato civile.

mari-time ['mærɪ taɪm] ADJ (*climate, nation, museum*) marittimo(-a); (*plant, creature*) marino(-a).

♦ **maritime law** N diritto marittimo.

mar-jo-ram ['mɑːdʒərəm] N maggiorana.

mark¹ [mɑːk] [1] N a (*gen*) segno; (*stain*) macchia; (*of shoes, fingers: in mud*) impronta; (*of skid*) traccia; **to leave a mark on sth** lasciare un segno su qc; **to leave one's mark on sth** (*fig*) lasciare un segno in qc; **there wasn't a**

mark on him *or* on his body non aveva nemmeno un graffio; **it's the mark of a gentleman** è da gentiluomo; **it bears the mark of genius** ha l'impronta del genio; **to make one's mark (as)** *(fig)* farsi un nome (come); **as a mark of my gratitude** come segno della mia gratitudine; **punctuation marks** segni di punteggiatura

b *(instead of signature)* croce *f*; **to make one's mark** fare una croce

c *(Brit Scol)* voto; **good/bad mark** buon *or* bel/brutto voto; **he failed by 2 marks** l'hanno bocciato per 2 punti; **full marks for trying!** un bravo per aver tentato!; **there are no marks for guessing where I've been!** non ci vuole un genio per sapere dove sono stato!

d *(Brit Tech)*: **Mark 1/2** prima/seconda serie *f*

e *(Sport: target)* bersaglio; **to hit the mark** far centro; *(fig)* azzeccare in pieno; **to be wide of the mark** essere lontano(-a) dal bersaglio; *(fig)* essere lontano(-a) dal vero

f *(Sport: starting line)* linea di partenza; **on your marks! get set! go!** ai vostri posti! pronti! (attenti!) via!; **to be quick off the mark (in doing sth)** *(fig)* non perdere tempo (per fare qc); **up to the mark** *(in health)* in forma; *(in efficiency)* all'altezza.

2 VT **a** *(make a mark on)* segnare; *(stain)* macchiare, lasciare dei segni su

b *(indicate: score)* segnare; *(: price)* mettere; *(: place)* indicare, segnare; *(: change, improvement)* indicare; **this marks the frontier** questo segna la frontiera; **the qualities which mark a good swimmer** le qualità che contraddistinguono un buon nuotatore

c *(heed)*: **mark my words** fa' attenzione a quello che ti dico

d *(Brit Scol: correct)* correggere; *(: exam)* dare un voto a; **to mark sth wrong** segnare qc come errore

e *(Sport: player)* marcare

f : **to mark time** *(Mil, fig)* segnare il passo.

3 VI macchiarsi

▶ **mark down** VT + ADV **a** *(reduce: prices, goods)* ribassare, ridurre

b *(note down)* prendere nota di

▶ **mark off** VT + ADV **a** *(separate)* dividere, separare

b *(tick off)* spuntare, cancellare

▶ **mark out** VT + ADV **a** *(zone, road)* delimitare

b *(single out: for promotion)* designare; *(characterize)* distinguere

▶ **mark up** VT + ADV **a** *(write up)* segnare

b *(increase: goods)* aumentare il prezzo di; *(: price)* aumentare.

mark² [mɑːk] N *(currency)* marco.

marked [mɑːkt] ADJ *(accent, contrast, bias)* marcato(-a); *(improvement, increase)* sensibile, spiccato(-a), chiaro (-a); **he's a marked man** è sotto tiro.

mark·ed·ly ['mɑːkɪdlɪ] ADV visibilmente, notevolmente, marcatamente.

mark·er ['mɑːkə'] N *(stake)* paletto; *(pen)* pennarello; *(sign)* segno; *(in book)* segnalibro; *(Brit Scol)* persona addetta a correggere le prove d'esame; *(scorekeeper in games)* segnapunti *m inv*.

mar·ket ['mɑːkɪt] **1** N *(gen)* mercato; *(also: stock market)* mercato azionario *or* dei titoli; **to go to market** andare al mercato; **open market** mercato libero; **there is a good market for videos** c'è una grossa richiesta di video; **is there a market for that?** c'è uno sbocco sul mercato per quello?; **it appeals to the Italian market** è richiesto sul mercato italiano; **to be in the market for sth** avere

intenzione di comprare qc; **to be on the market** essere (messo(-a)) in vendita *or* in commercio; **to come on(to) the market** essere introdotto(-a) sul mercato; **to play the market** giocare *or* speculare in borsa.

2 VT *(Comm: sell)* vendere, mettere in vendita; *(: promote)* lanciare sul mercato.

mar·ket·abil·ity [ˌmɑːkɪtə'bɪlɪtɪ] N commerciabilità *f inv*.

mar·ket·able ['mɑːkɪtəbl] ADJ commercializzabile.

♦ **market analysis** N analisi *f inv* di mercato.

♦ **market day** N giorno di mercato.

♦ **market demand** N domanda del mercato.

♦ **market economy** N economia di mercato.

♦ **market forces** NPL forze *fpl* di mercato.

♦ **market garden** N *(Brit)* orto (industriale).

♦ **market gardener** N *(Brit)* ortofrutticoltore *m*.

♦ **market gardening** N *(Brit)* ortofrutticoltura.

mar·ket·ing ['mɑːkɪtɪŋ] N marketing *m inv*.

♦ **marketing manager** N direttore *m* del marketing.

♦ **market leader** N leader *m inv* del mercato.

market·place ['mɑːkɪtˌpleɪs] N *(square)* (piazza del) mercato; *(world of trade)* piazza, mercato.

♦ **market potential** N possibilità *f inv* di mercato.

♦ **market price** N prezzo di mercato.

♦ **market research** N indagine *f or* ricerca di mercato.

♦ **market share** N quota di mercato.

♦ **market trend** N tendenza del mercato.

♦ **market value** N valore *m* di mercato.

mark·ing ['mɑːkɪŋ] N **a** *(on animal)* marcatura di colore; *(on road)* segnaletica orizzontale **b** *(Brit Scol)* correzione *f* (dei compiti) **c** *(Ftbl)* marcamento, marcatura.

♦ **marking ink** N inchiostro indelebile.

marks·man ['mɑːksmən] N *(pl* **-men**) tiratore *m* scelto.

marks·man·ship ['mɑːksmənˌʃɪp] N abilità *f inv* nel tiro.

♦ **mark-up** ['mɑːkˌʌp] N *(Comm: margin)* margine *m* di vendita; *(: increase)* aumento.

marl [mɑːl] N *(Geol)* marna.

mar·ma·lade ['mɑːməˌleɪd] N marmellata d'arance.

♦ **marmalade orange** N arancia amara.

mar·mo·set ['mɑːməʊˌzɛt] N callitricide *m*.

mar·mot ['mɑːmət] N marmotta.

ma·roon¹ [mə'ruːn] ADJ, N *(colour)* bordeaux *(m) inv*.

ma·roon² [mə'ruːn] VT *(on island)* abbandonare; *(subj: sea, traffic, snow)* bloccare; **to be marooned (in *or* at)** *(fig)* essere abbandonato(-a) (in).

mar·quee [mɑː'kiː] N grande tenda, padiglione *m*.

mar·quis, mar·quess ['mɑːkwɪs] N marchese *m*.

Mar·ra·kech, Mar·ra·kesh [ˌmærə'kɛʃ] N Marrakesh *f*.

mar·riage ['mærɪdʒ] **1** N matrimonio; **he's my uncle by marriage** è uno zio acquisito.

2 ADJ *(vows)* di matrimonio; *(bed)* coniugale.

mar·riage·able ['mærɪdʒəbl] ADJ: **of marriageable age** *(woman)* da marito, in età da marito; *(man)* che deve prendere moglie.

♦ **marriage bureau** N agenzia matrimoniale.

♦ **marriage certificate** N certificato di matrimonio.

♦ **marriage guidance**, *(Am)* **marriage counseling** N consulenza matrimoniale.

♦ **marriage licence** N licenza matrimoniale.

♦ **marriage lines** NPL *(Brit old)* certificato di matrimonio.

♦ **marriage of convenience** N matrimonio di convenienza.

mar·ried ['mærɪd] ADJ *(person)* sposato(-a); *(life, love)* coniugale, matrimoniale; *(name)* da sposata.

mar·row ['mærəʊ] N **a** (*Anat*) midollo; **to be frozen to the marrow** sentirsi il gelo *or* il freddo nelle ossa **b** (*vegetable*) zucca; **baby marrow** zucchino.

marrow·bone ['mærəʊ͵bəʊn] N ossobuco, osso con il midollo.

mar·ry ['mærɪ] **1** VT (*take in marriage*) sposare, sposarsi con; (*subj: father, priest*) dare in matrimonio.
2 VI (*also:* **to get married**) sposarsi; **to marry again** risposarsi; **to marry into a rich family** imparentarsi con una famiglia ricca
▶ **marry up** VT + ADV (*pattern*) far combaciare.

Mars [mɑːz] N (*Astron, Myth*) Marte *m*.

Mar·seilles [mɑːˈseɪlz] N Marsiglia.

marsh [mɑːʃ] N palude *f*.

mar·shal ['mɑːʃəl] **1** N (*Mil*) maresciallo; (*for demonstration, meeting*) membro del servizio d'ordine; (*Am: also:* **fire marshal**) capo; (: *also:* **police marshal**) capitano.
2 VT (*soldiers, procession*) schierare, adunare; (*fig: facts*) ordinare.

mar·shal·ling yard ['mɑːʃəlɪŋ ͵jɑːd] N (*Brit*) scalo smistamento.

♦ **marsh gas** N gas *m inv* delle paludi.
♦ **marsh harrier** N (*bird*) falco di palude.

marsh·mal·low ['mɑːʃ͵mæləʊ] N (*sweet*) *caramella soffice e gommosa.*

♦ **marsh mallow** N (*plant*) altea.
♦ **marsh marigold** N (*plant*) calta, farferugine *f* di palude.

marshy ['mɑːʃɪ] ADJ (*comp* **-ier**, *superl* **-iest**) paludoso(-a).

mar·su·pial [mɑːˈsuːpɪəl] ADJ, N marsupiale *(m)*.

mar·ten ['mɑːtɪn] N (*animal*) martora; **pine marten** martora degli alberi; **stone marten** faina.

mar·tial ['mɑːʃəl] ADJ marziale.

♦ **martial art** N arte *f* marziale.
♦ **martial law** N legge *f* marziale.

Mar·tian ['mɑːʃən] N marziano(-a).

mar·tin ['mɑːtɪn] N (*bird, also:* **house martin**) balestruccio; **sand martin** topino.

mar·ti·net [͵mɑːtɪˈnɛt] N: **to be a martinet** essere molto rigido(-a), essere molto intransigente.

mar·tyr ['mɑːtəʳ] **1** N martire *m/f*; **to be a martyr to arthritis** essere torturato(-a) dall'artrite.
2 VT martirizzare.

mar·tyr·dom ['mɑːtədəm] N martirio.

mar·tyred ['mɑːtəd] ADJ (*look, expression, sigh*) da martire.

mar·vel ['mɑːvəl] **1** N (*of nature*) meraviglia; (*of science, skill*) prodigio; **if she gets there it will be a marvel** (*fam*) se ci arriva è un miracolo; **it's a marvel to me how she does it** (*fam*) non so proprio come riesca a farlo; **you're a marvel!** (*fam*) sei un fenomeno!.
2 VI: **to marvel (at)** (*awestruck*) rimanere incantato(-a) (davanti a); (*surprised*) stupirsi (di fronte a), meravigliarsi (di).

mar·vel·lous, (*Am*) **mar·ve·lous** ['mɑːvələs] ADJ meraviglioso(-a).

mar·vel·lous·ly ['mɑːvələslɪ] ADV meravigliosamente.

Marx·ism ['mɑːksɪzəm] N marxismo.

Marx·ist ['mɑːksɪst] ADJ, N marxista *(m/f)*.

Mary ['mɛərɪ] N Maria.

♦ **Mary Mag·da·lene** ['mɛərɪˈmægdə͵liːn] N Maria Maddalena, Maria di Magdala.

mar·zi·pan [͵mɑːzɪˈpæn] N marzapane *m*.

mas·cara [mæsˈkɑːrə] N mascara *m inv*.

mas·cot ['mæskət] N mascotte *f inv*, portafortuna *m inv*.

mas·cu·line ['mæskjʊlɪn] **1** ADJ (*also Gram*) maschile;

(*pej: woman*) mascolino(-a).
2 N (*Gram*) (genere *m*) maschile *m*.

mas·cu·lin·ity [͵mæskjʊˈlɪnɪtɪ] N virilità *f inv*, mascolinità *f inv*; (*pej: of woman*) mascolinità *f inv*.

MASH [mæʃ] N ABBR (*Am Mil*: = *mobile army surgical hospital*) *ospedale da campo di unità mobile dell'esercito.*

mash [mæʃ] **1** N **a** (*Brit fam: also:* **mashed potatoes**) purè *m* (di patate) **b** (*for animals*) pastone *m*.
2 VT (*Culin*) passare, schiacciare.

mask [mɑːsk] **1** N (*gen, Elec*) maschera.
2 VT mascherare.

masked ball ['mɑːskt͵bɔːl] N ballo in maschera, ballo mascherato.

mask·ing tape ['mɑːskɪŋ͵teɪp] N (*during painting, spraying*) nastro adesivo di carta.

maso·chism ['mæsəʊ͵kɪzəm] N masochismo.

maso·chist ['mæsəʊkɪst] N masochista *m/f*.

maso·chis·tic [͵mæsəʊˈkɪstɪk] ADJ masochistico(-a).

ma·son ['meɪsn] N **a** (*builder*) muratore *m*; (*also:* **stonemason**) scalpellino **b** (*also:* **freemason**) massone *m*.

ma·son·ic [məˈsɒnɪk] ADJ massonico(-a).

ma·son·ry ['meɪsnrɪ] N **a** (*stonework*) muratura; (*skill*) arte *f* muratoria **b** (*also:* **freemasonry**) massoneria.

mas·quer·ade [͵mæskəˈreɪd] **1** N (*fig: pretence*) mascherata, finzione *f*, montatura; (*masked ball*) ballo in maschera. **2** VI: **to masquerade as** farsi passare per.

mass¹ [mæs] N (*Rel*) messa; **to say mass** dire (la) messa; **to go to mass** andare a *or* alla messa.

mass² [mæs] **1** N (*gen*) massa, moltitudine *f*; (*Phys*) massa; **he's a mass of bruises** è coperto di lividi; **in the mass** nella gran maggioranza; **the masses** le masse; **masses (of)** (*fam*) un sacco (di), un mucchio (di).
2 VI (*Mil*) adunarsi, concentrarsi; (*crowd*) radunarsi, ammassarsi; (*clouds*) addensarsi.
3 VT adunare.
4 ADJ (*culture, demonstration*) di massa; (*education*) delle masse; (*hysteria*) collettivo(-a); (*murders*) in massa.

mas·sa·cre ['mæsəkəʳ] **1** N massacro.
2 VT massacrare.

mas·sage ['mæsɑːʒ] **1** N massaggio.
2 VT massaggiare.

♦ **massage parlour** N centro *m* massaggi *inv*.

massed [mæst] ADJ (*bands, troops*) radunato(-a) in massa; (*artillery*) ammassato(-a).

mas·seur [mæˈsɜːʳ] N massaggiatore *m*.

mas·seuse [mæˈsɜːz] N massaggiatrice *f*.

mas·sive ['mæsɪv] ADJ massiccio(-a), enorme.

♦ **mass market** N mercato di massa.
♦ **mass media** NPL mass media *mpl*, mezzi *mpl* di comunicazione *f* di massa.
♦ **mass meeting** N (*of everyone concerned*) riunione *f* generale; (*huge*) adunata popolare.
♦ **mass number** N (*Phys*) numero di massa.
♦ **mass-produce** ['mæsprə͵djuːs] VT produrre in serie.
♦ **mass production** N produzione *f* in serie.

mast [mɑːst] N (*Naut*) albero; (*flagpole*) asta; (*Radio, TV*) pilone *m* (a traliccio).

mastectomy [͵mæsˈtɛktəmɪ] N mastectomia.

mas·ter ['mɑːstəʳ] **1** N **a** (*of servant, dog*) padrone *m*; **the master of the house** il padrone di casa; **to be one's own master** non aver padroni; **I am (the) master now** ora comando io; **to be master of the situation** essere padrone della situazione
b (*Naut: of ship*) capitano

c (*musician, painter*) maestro

d (*Brit*: *teacher*: *in primary school*) maestro; (: *in secondary school*) professore *m*; **fencing master** maestro di scherma

e (*title for boys*): **Master Paul Moran** il signorino Paul Moran; (*on letters*) (il) signor Paul Moran.

2 VT **a** (*animal*) domare; (*person*) dominare; (*one's emotions*) controllare

b (*theory*: *understand*) conoscere a fondo; (*learn*: *subject, skill*) imparare a fondo.

♦ **master baker** N mastro pasticciere.

♦ **master bedroom** N camera da letto principale.

♦ **master builder** N capomastro.

♦ **master cylinder** N (*Tech*) pompa idraulica.

♦ **master disk** N (*Comput*) disco *m* master *inv*, disco principale.

mas·ter·ful ['mɑːstəfʊl] ADJ (*imperious*) imperioso(-a); (*authoritative*) magistrale.

mas·ter·ful·ly ['mɑːstəfəlɪ] ADV (*see adj*) imperiosamente; magistralmente.

♦ **master key** N passe-partout *m inv*.

mas·ter·ly ['mɑːstəlɪ] ADJ magistrale, da maestro.

master·mind ['mɑːstəˌmaɪnd] **1** N (*genius*) mente *f* superiore; (*in crime*) cervello.

2 VT ideare e dirigere, essere il cervello di.

♦ **Master of Arts/Science** N (*degree*) master *m inv* in lettere/scienze; (*person*) *titolare di un master in lettere/ scienze*.

♦ **master of ceremonies** N maestro di cerimonie.

master·piece ['mɑːstəˌpiːs] N capolavoro.

♦ **master plan** N piano generale, progetto di massima.

♦ **master race** N razza superiore.

♦ **mas·ter's** ['mɑːstəz] N (*also*: **master's degree**) master *m inv*.

master·stroke ['mɑːstəˌstrəʊk] N colpo magistrale *or* da maestro.

♦ **master switch** N interruttore *m* centrale.

mas·tery ['mɑːstərɪ] N: **mastery (of)** (*subject, musical instrument*) padronanza (di); (*of the seas*) dominio (su), supremazia (su); **mastery (at)** (*skill*) virtuosità *f inv* (a *or* in), maestria (a *or* in); **mastery (over)** (*competitors*) superiorità *f inv* (su).

mas·ti·cate ['mæstɪˌkeɪt] VT, VI masticare.

mas·tiff ['mæstɪf] N mastino.

mas·toid ['mæstɔɪd] N **a** (*also*: **mastoide bone**) mastoide *f*

b (*Med fam*: *inflammation*) = **mastoiditis**.

mas·toid·itis [ˌmæstɔɪ'daɪtɪs] N mastoidite *f*.

mas·tur·bate ['mæstəˌbeɪt] **1** VI masturbarsi

1 VT masturbare.

mas·tur·ba·tion [ˌmæstə'beɪʃən] N masturbazione *f*.

mat¹ [mæt] N (*on floor*) tappetino; (: *of straw*) stuoia; (*also*: **doormat**) zerbino, stoino; (*on table*) tovaglietta all'americana.

mat² [mæt] ADJ = **matt**.

match¹ [mætʃ] **1** N **a** (*of colours*): **to be a good match (for)** intonarsi a, andar bene con; **Paul and Jane make a good match** Paul e Jane sono una bella coppia

b (*equal*) uguale *m/f*, pari *m/f inv*; **to be a match/no match for sb** riuscire/non riuscire a tenere testa a qn; **to meet one's match** trovare pane per i propri denti

c (*marriage*) partito

d (*game*) incontro; (: *Ftbl, Rugby*) partita, incontro.

2 VT **a** (*find similar to*: *also*: **match up**): **can you match this wool for me?** ha della lana che vada bene con questa?; **to match sb against sb** opporre qn a qn; **they**

are well matched (*opponents*) son ben assortiti; (*two friends*) sono una coppia bene assortita; (*husband and wife*) sono una bella coppia

b (*equal*) uguagliare; **the results did not match our hopes** i risultati non hanno corrisposto alle nostre speranze; **I can't match that** per me è troppo

c (*go well with*: *colours*) intonarsi a; (: *clothes*) andare benissimo con; **his tie matches his socks** la sua cravatta s'intona ai calzini.

3 VI (*colours, materials*) intonarsi; **with a skirt to match** OR **with a matching skirt** con una gonna adatta *or* intonata

▶ **match up to** VI + ADV + PREP essere all'altezza di.

match² [mætʃ] N fiammifero; **to put a match to sth** dar fuoco a qc.

match·box ['mætʃˌbɒks] N scatola fiammiferi.

match·ing ['mætʃɪŋ] ADJ (*colours*) intonato(-a), ben assortito(-a); **with matching shoes and bag** con scarpe e borsa intonate.

match·less ['mætʃlɪs] ADJ senza pari.

match·make ['mætʃˌmeɪk] VI: **she's always matchmaking** cerca sempre di combinare matrimoni.

match·maker ['mætʃˌmeɪkə'] N (*arranger of marriages*) sensale *m/f* di matrimoni; (*Sport*) organizzatore(-trice) di incontri sportivi; **she is a great matchmaker** ha combinato molte unione felici.

♦ **match point** N (*Tennis*) match point *m inv*.

match·stick ['mætʃˌstɪk] N fiammifero.

match·wood ['mætʃˌwʊd] N legno per fiammiferi; **the boat was smashed to matchwood** (*fig*) la barca fu completamente sfasciata.

mate¹ [meɪt] **1** N **a** (*at work*) compagno(-a) di lavoro; (*fam*: *friend*) amico(-a); **look here, mate** ehi tu, senti **b** (*assistant*) aiutante *m/f* **c** (*Zool*) compagno(-a), maschio (*or* femmina) **d** (*in merchant navy*) secondo.

2 VT (*Zool*) accoppiare.

3 VI (*Zool*) accoppiarsi.

mate² [meɪt] N (*Chess*) scaccomatto.

ma·terial [mə'tɪərɪəl] **1** ADJ **a** (*things, needs, success*) materiale

b (*important*) sostanziale, essenziale; (*relevant*): **material to** pertinente a; (*Law*: *evidence*) determinante; **a material witness** un testimone chiave.

2 N **a** (*substance*) materiale *m*, materia; (*cloth*) stoffa, tessuto; **she is university material** è una che dovrebbe continuare gli studi; **he is officer material** ha la stoffa dell'ufficiale

b (*equipment*): **materials** NPL occorrente *m*; **building materials** materiali *mpl* da costruzione; **have you any writing materials?** hai l'occorrente per scrivere?

c (*for novel, report*) materiale *m*, documentazione *f*.

ma·teri·al·ism [mə'tɪərɪəˌlɪzəm] N materialismo.

ma·teri·al·ist [mə'tɪərɪəlɪst] N materialista *m/f*.

ma·teri·al·is·tic [məˌtɪərɪə'lɪstɪk] ADJ materialista.

ma·teri·al·ize [mə'tɪərɪəˌlaɪz] VI materializzarsi; (*idea, hope*) avverarsi, realizzarsi; **so far he hasn't materialized** (*fam*) per ora non si è visto.

ma·teri·al·ly [mə'tɪərɪəlɪ] ADV (*see adj*) dal punto di vista materiale; sostanzialmente.

ma·ter·nal [mə'tɜːnl] ADJ materno(-a).

ma·ter·nal·ly [mə'tɜːnəlɪ] ADV maternamente.

ma·ter·nity [mə'tɜːnɪtɪ] **1** N maternità *f inv*.

2 ADJ di maternità.

♦ **maternity benefit** N sussidio di maternità.

♦ **maternity dress** N vestito *m* pre-maman *inv*.

♦ **maternity home**, **maternity hospital** N ≈ clinica ostetrica.

♦ **maternity leave** N congedo per maternità.

♦ **maternity ward** N reparto *m* maternità *inv*.

matey ['meɪtɪ] ADJ (*Brit fam*) amicone(-a).

math [mæθ] N ABBR (*Am*) = **mathematics**.

math·emati·cal [ˌmæθə'mætɪkəl] ADJ matematico(-a).

math·emati·cal·ly [ˌmæθə'mætɪkəlɪ] ADV matematicamente.

math·ema·ti·cian [ˌmæθəmə'tɪʃən] N matematico(-a).

math·emat·ics [ˌmæθə'mætɪks] NSG matematica.

maths [mæθs] N ABBR (*Brit fam*) = **mathematics**.

mati·née ['mætɪˌneɪ] N matinée *f inv*.

mat·ing ['meɪtɪŋ] 1 N accoppiamento.

2 ADJ dell'accoppiamento.

♦ **mating call** N chiamata all'accoppiamento.

♦ **mating season** N stagione *f* degli amori.

mat·ins ['mætɪnz] NSG OR NPL mattutino.

ma·tri·arch ['meɪtrɪɑːk] N matriarca.

ma·tri·ar·chal [ˌmeɪtrɪ'ɑːkl] ADJ matriarcale.

ma·tri·ar·chy ['meɪtrɪɑːkɪ] N matriarcato.

ma·tri·ces ['meɪtrɪsiːz] NPL of **matrix**.

mat·ri·cide ['mætrɪˌsaɪd] N (*crime*) matricidio; (*person*) matricida *m/f*.

ma·tricu·late [mə'trɪkjʊˌleɪt] VI immatricolarsi.

ma·tricu·la·tion [məˌtrɪkjʊ'leɪʃən] N immatricolazione *f*.

mat·ri·mo·nial [ˌmætrɪ'məʊnɪəl] ADJ (*vows*) di matrimonio; (*state, troubles*) coniugale, matrimoniale.

mat·ri·mo·ny ['mætrɪmənɪ] N matrimonio.

ma·trix ['meɪtrɪks] N (*pl* **matrices** *or* **matrixes**) matrice *f*.

ma·tron ['meɪtrən] N (*Brit: in hospital*) capoinfermiera; (: *in school*) infermiera; (*older woman*) matrona.

ma·tron·ly ['meɪtrənlɪ] ADJ (*figure, behaviour*) da matrona.

♦ **matron-of-honour** [ˌmeɪtrənəv'ɒnə˞] N dama d'onore.

matt [mæt] ADJ opaco(-a).

mat·ted ['mætɪd] ADJ (*hair*) arruffato(-a); (*sweater*) infeltrito(-a).

mat·ter ['mætə˞] 1 N **a** (*substance: gen, Phys*) materia, sostanza; **colouring matter** colorante *m*; **foreign matter** sostanza estranea; **advertising matter** pubblicità *f inv*; **reading matter** (*Brit*) qualcosa da leggere

b (*content*) contenuto

c (*question, affair*) questione *f*, faccenda; **money matters** questioni finanziarie; **the matter in hand** l'argomento *or* la faccenda in questione; **there's the matter of my wages** ci sarebbe la questione del mio stipendio; **and to make matters worse** ... e come se non bastasse...; **that will only make matters worse** questo servirà solo a peggiorare la situazione; **it's a matter of great concern to us** è una cosa che ci preoccupa molto; **it's no laughing matter** è una cosa *or* faccenda seria; **it will be a matter of a few weeks** ci vorrà qualche settimana; **it's a matter of a few pounds** si tratta di poche sterline; **in the matter of** in fatto di, per quanto riguarda; **for that matter** peraltro; **as a matter of course** di conseguenza, come cosa naturale; **as a matter of fact** per (dire) la verità, in verità; **it's a matter of opinion** è una questione di punti di vista; **that's another matter** quella è un'altra faccenda; **it's a matter of habit** è una questione di abitudine

d (*importance*): **no matter!** non importa!; **do it, no matter how** non importa come, basta che tu lo faccia; **no matter how you do it** comunque tu lo faccia; **no matter what** qualsiasi cosa accada; **no matter what he says** qualsiasi *or* qualunque cosa dica; **no matter how**

big it is per quanto grande sia; **no matter when** in qualunque momento; **no matter who** chiunque

e (*difficulty, problem*): **what's the matter?** cosa c'è (che non va)?; **what's the matter with you?** cos'hai?; **what's the matter with my hair?** cos'hanno i miei capelli che non va?; **there's something the matter with my arm** c'è qualcosa che non va al braccio; **as if nothing was the matter** come se niente fosse; **something's the matter with the lights** le luci hanno qualcosa che non va; **nothing's the matter** non è successo niente; **nothing's the matter with me** non ho niente

f (*Med: pus*) pus *m*.

2 VI importare; **it doesn't matter** (*I don't mind*) non importa, non fa niente; **what does it matter?** cosa importa?, che importanza ha?; **what does it matter to you?** ma a te che te ne importa?; **why should it matter to me?** e perché dovrebbe importarmi?

Mat·ter·horn ['mætəˌhɔːn] N: **the Matterhorn** il Cervino.

♦ **matter-of-fact** [ˌmætərəv'fækt] ADJ (*person, attitude*) pratico(-a), prosaico(-a); (*tone, voice*) neutro(-a), piatto (-a); (*account*) che si limita ai fatti.

mat·ting ['mætɪŋ] N stuoia.

mat·tins ['mætɪnz] NSG OR PL = **matins**.

mat·tress ['mætrɪs] N materasso.

ma·ture [mə'tjʊə˞] 1 ADJ (*comp* **-r**, *superl* **-st**) (*gen*) maturo(-a); (*cheese*) stagionato(-a); **he's much more mature** è molto più maturo.

2 VI (*gen*) maturarsi, maturare; (*Fin*) maturare, scadere; (*cheese*) stagionarsi, stagionare.

♦ **mature student** N studente(-essa) universitario(-a) di età superiore ai 25 anni.

ma·tur·ity [mə'tjʊərɪtɪ] N maturità *f inv*.

maud·lin ['mɔːdlɪn] ADJ piagnucoloso(-a).

maul [mɔːl] VT (*subj: tiger*) dilaniare, sbranare; **mauled to death** sbranato(-a) a morte.

Maun·dy Thurs·day ['mɔːndɪ'θɜːzdɪ] N giovedì *m inv* santo.

Mau·ri·ta·nia [ˌmɔːrɪ'teɪnɪə] N la Mauritania.

Mau·ri·tius [mə'rɪʃəs] N (l'isola di) Maurizio *f*.

mau·so·leum [ˌmɔːsə'lɪəm] N mausoleo.

mauve [məʊv] ADJ (*color*) malva *inv*.

mav·er·ick ['mævərɪk] 1 N chi sta fuori del branco.

2 ADJ anticonformista.

mawk·ish ['mɔːkɪʃ] ADJ svenevole, sdolcinato(-a), insipido(-a).

max. ABBR (= *maximum*) max.

max·im ['mæksɪm] N massima.

maxi·ma ['mæksɪmə] NPL of **maximum**.

maxi·mal·ism ['mæksɪməˌlɪzəm] N massimalismo.

max·im·ize ['mæksɪˌmaɪz] VT (*profits*) massimizzare; (*chances*) aumentare al massimo.

maxi·mum ['mæksɪməm] 1 N (*pl* **maxima** *or* **maximums**) massimo.

2 ADJ massimo(-a).

May [meɪ] N maggio *for usage see* **July**.

may [meɪ] (*pt* **might**) MODAL AUX VB **a** (*possibility*): **she may come** può darsi che venga, può venire; **he might come** potrebbe venire, può anche darsi che venga; **I might well go** potrei anche andare; **he might be there** può darsi che ci sia; **he may not be hungry** potrebbe non aver fame, può darsi che non abbia fame; **they may well be connected** può darsi benissimo che ci sia un legame; **that's as may be** può anche darsi; **be that as it may** comunque sia, sia come sia; **you may well ask!** è quello che mi chiedo anch'io!

b (*of permission*): **may I smoke?** posso fumare?; **may I have a cigarette? — yes, of course** potrei avere una sigaretta? — sì, prego; **may I sit here?** le dispiace se mi siedo qua?; **if I may say so** se mi è concesso dirlo; **may I? permette?; might I suggest that …?** con il suo permesso suggerirei che…; **he said I might leave** mi ha detto che potevo andare

c : **I hope he may succeed** (*frm*) spero che ci riesca; **I hoped he might succeed this time** speravo che stavolta ci sarebbe riuscito; **we may** *or* **might as well go** tanto vale che ci andiamo; **he might have offered to help** avrebbe potuto offrirsi di aiutare; **as you might expect** come c'era da aspettarsi; **you might like to try** forse le piacerebbe provare

d (*in wishes*): **may you have a happy life together** possiate vivere insieme felici; **may God bless you!** (che) Dio la benedica!

may·be ['meɪbi:] ADV forse, può darsi; **maybe not** forse no, può darsi di no; **maybe tomorrow** forse *or* magari domani; **maybe he'll come** può darsi che venga, magari *or* forse verrà.

♦ **May Day** N il primo maggio (*in cui si festeggia l'arrivo della primavera*).

may·day ['meɪ,deɪ] N (*Aer, Naut*) mayday *m inv*, S.O.S. *m inv*.

may·fly ['meɪ,flaɪ] N efemera.

may·hem ['meɪhɛm] N cagnara.

may·on·naise [,meɪə'neɪz] N maionese *f*.

mayor [mɛə] N sindaco.

mayor·ess ['mɛərɛs] N (*wife*) moglie *f* del sindaco; (*holding office*) sindaco (*donna*).

may·pole ['meɪ,pəʊl] N *palo ornato di fiori attorno a cui si danza durante la festa del primo maggio.*

maze [meɪz] N dedalo, labirinto.

ma·zur·ka [mə'zɜ:kə] N mazurca.

MB [ɛm'bi:] 1 N ABBR **a** (*Med*)= Bachelor of Medicine **b** (*Comput*)= megabyte.
2 ABBR = *Manitoba*.

MBA [,ɛmbi:'eɪ] N ABBR (= *Master of Business Administration*) ≈ Master in discipline aziendali.

MBBS [,ɛmbi:bi:'ɛs], **MBChB** N ABBR (*Brit*: = *Bachelor of Medicine and Surgery*) ≈ Laurea in Medicina e Chirurgia.

MBE [,ɛmbi:'i:] N ABBR (*Brit*: = *Member of the Order of the British Empire*) *titolo onorifico.*

MC [,ɛm'si:] N ABBR **a** = *master of ceremonies* **b** (*Am*: = *Member of Congress*) membro del Congresso.

MCAT [,ɛmsi:er'ti:] N ABBR (*Am*: = *Medical College Admissions Test*) *esame di ammissione alla Facoltà di Medicina.*

McCoy [mə'kɔɪ] (*fam*): **this is the real McCoy!** questo è quello originale!

MCP [,ɛmsi:'pi:] N ABBR (*Brit fam*: = *male chauvinist pig*) sporco maschilista *m*.

MD [,ɛm'di:] 1 N ABBR **a** (= *Doctor of Medicine*) Dottore *m* in Medicina **b** (*Comm*: = *managing director*) A.D. *m* (= *Amministratore Delegato*).
2 ABBR (*Am Post*)= Maryland.

MDT [,ɛmdi:'ti:] ABBR (*Am*: = *Mountain Daylight Time*) *ora legale delle Montagne Rocciose.*

ME [,ɛm'i:] 1 N ABBR (*Med*) **a** = *myalgic encephalomyelitis* **b** = *medical examiner*.
2 ABBR (*Am Post*)= Maine.

me [mi:] PERS PRON **a** (*direct: unstressed*) mi, m' + *vowel or silent 'h'*; (: *stressed*) me; **he can hear me** mi sente; **he heard me** mi ha *or* m'ha sentito; **he heard ME!** ha sentito ME!

b (*indirect*) mi, m'+ *vowel or silent 'h'*; **he gave me the money, he gave the money to me** mi ha *or* m'ha dato i soldi; **he gave them to me** me li ha dati; **give them to me** dammeli

c (*stressed, after prep*) me; **it's for me** è per me; **without me** senza (di) me; **it's me** sono io.

mead¹ [mi:d] N idromele *m*.

mead² [mi:d] N (*liter: meadow*) prato.

mead·ow ['mɛdəʊ] N prato, pascolo.

meadow·sweet ['mɛdəʊ,swi:t] N (*plant*) olmaria, barba di capra.

mea·gre, (*Am*) **mea·ger** ['mi:gə] ADJ magro(-a).

meal¹ [mi:l] N (*flour*) farina.

meal² [mi:l] N pasto; **to have a meal** mangiare; **to have a good meal** mangiar bene; **to go out for a meal** mangiare fuori; **what a lovely meal** che pranzo delizioso (*or* cena deliziosa); **to make a meal of sth** (*fam*) fare di qc un affare di stato.

♦ **meals on wheels** N SG (*Brit*) *distribuzione di pasti caldi a domicilio a persone malate o anziane.*

♦ **meal ticket** N (*Am*) buono *m* pasto *inv*; (*fig fam: job*) che dà di che vivere; **a meal ticket for life** (*fig*) la pagnotta assicurata a vita.

meal·time ['mi:l,taɪm] N ora di mangiare.

mealy ['mi:lɪ] ADJ farinoso(-a).

♦ **mealy-mouthed** ['mi:lɪ,maʊðd] ADJ evasivo(-a).

mean¹ [mi:n] (*pt, pp* **meant**) VT **a** (*signify*) significare, voler dire; **what does that word mean?** che significa quella parola?; **what do you mean by that?** cosa vuoi dire con questo?; **you don't mean that, do you?** non parli sul serio, vero?; **do you really mean it?** dici sul serio?; **he said it as if he meant it** l'ha detto senza scherzare *or* sul serio; **I mean what I say** parlo sul serio; **it means a lot of expense for us** per noi questo vuol dire una grossa spesa; **the play didn't mean a thing to me** la commedia non mi ha detto niente; **her name means nothing to me** il suo nome non mi dice niente; **your friendship means a lot to me** la tua amicizia è molto importante per me; **he means nothing to me** non conta niente per me

b (*intend*) intendere; **to mean to do sth** aver l'intenzione di fare qc, intendere fare qc; **to be meant for** essere destinato(-a) a; **I meant it for her** era destinato a lei; **I meant it as a joke** volevo solo scherzare; **what do you mean to do?** cosa intendi fare?, cosa pensi di fare?; **he didn't mean to do it** non intendeva *or* non era sua intenzione farlo; **do you mean me?** (*are you speaking to me?*) dici a me?; (*about me*) ti riferisci a me?; **was that remark meant for me?** quell'osservazione era diretta a me?; **Roberta is meant to do it** è Roberta che lo deve fare; **I mean to be obeyed** intendo essere ubbidito; **he means well** le sue intenzioni sono buone.

mean² [mi:n] ADJ (*comp* **-er**, *superl* **-est**) **a** (*with money*) avaro(-a), spilorcio(-a), gretto(-a); **mean with** avaro(-a) con

b (*unkind, spiteful*) meschino(-a), maligno(-a); **a mean trick** uno scherzo ignobile; **you mean thing!** (*fam*) che meschino!; **it made me feel mean** mi ha fatto sentire un verme

c (*Am: vicious: animal*) cattivo(-a); (: *person*) perfido (-a)

d (*poor: appearance, district*) misero(-a); **she's no mean cook** è una cuoca tutt'altro che disprezzabile.

mean³ [mi:n] N 1 (*middle term*) mezzo; (*Math*) media; **the**

golden or **happy mean** il giusto mezzo; see also **means**.
[2] ADJ (*average*) medio(-a).
me·ander [mɪˈændəʳ] [1] N meandro.
[2] VI (*river*) fare dei meandri; (*person*) girovagare; (*fig*)
divagare.
♦ **mean deviation** N (*Statistics*) scarto medio.
mean·ing [ˈmiːnɪŋ] N significato, senso; **a look full of
meaning** uno sguardo eloquente; **do you get my
meaning?** capisci cosa voglio dire?; **what's the meaning
of this?** (*as reprimand*) e questo cosa significa?
mean·ing·ful [ˈmiːnɪŋfʊl] ADJ (*word, look*) significativo
(-a), eloquente; (*relationship*) profondo(-a).
mean·ing·ful·ly [ˈmiːnɪŋfəlɪ] ADV (*look, speak*) eloquentemente.
mean·ing·less [ˈmiːnɪŋlɪs] ADJ senza senso; **your remarks
are quite meaningless** i tuoi commenti non vogliono
dire niente.
mean·ly [ˈmiːnlɪ] ADV **a** (*stingily*) avaramente **b** (*unkindly*)
meschinamente, grettamente **c** (*Am: viciously*) perfidamente.
mean·ness [ˈmiːnnɪs] N (*see adj*) avarizia, spilorceria;
meschinità *f inv*; cattiveria; perfidia.
means [miːnz] [1] N INV (*method or way of doing*) mezzo,
modo; **to find a means to do** or **of doing sth** trovare il
modo per fare qc; **there is no means of doing it** non c'è
mezzo or modo di farlo; **a means to an end** un modo or
mezzo per raggiungere i propri fini; **by means of** per
mezzo di; **by this means** in questo modo, così; **by some
means or other** in un modo o nell'altro; **by all means!**
ma certamente!; **by no means** [OR] **not by any means** per
niente, niente affatto; **by all manner of means** in tutti i
modi.
[2] NPL (*Fin*) mezzi *mpl*; **private means** rendite *fpl*; **to live
within/beyond one's means** vivere secondo i/al di sopra
dei propri mezzi.
♦ **means test** N (*Admin*) accertamento dei redditi (*per
concedere di prestito*).
♦ **means-tested** [ˈmiːnzˌtɛstɪd] ADJ basato(-a) sul
reddito; **the grant is not means-tested** la borsa di studio
non dipende dal reddito.
meant [mɛnt] PT, PP of **mean**.
mean·time [ˈmiːnˌtaɪm], **mean·while** [ˈmiːnˌwaɪl] ADV
(*also:* **in the meantime**) nel frattempo, (e) intanto.
mea·sles [ˈmiːzlz] N morbillo.
mea·sly [ˈmiːzlɪ] ADJ (*comp* **-ier**, *superl* **-iest**) (*fam*) misero
(-a), miserabile.
meas·ur·able [ˈmɛʒərəbl] ADJ misurabile.
meas·ure [ˈmɛʒəʳ] [1] N **a** (*gen*) misura; (*also:* **tape
measure**) metro; **a litre measure** una misura da un litro;
to give full measure dare il peso giusto (*or* la quantità
giusta); **for good measure** (*fig*) in più, in aggiunta; **her
happiness was beyond measure** era immensamente
felice; **in some/large measure** in parte/gran parte; **some
measure of success** un certo successo; **I've got her
measure** (*fig*) so quanto vale
b (*step, action*) misura, provvedimento; **to take measures to do sth** prendere provvedimenti per fare qc.
[2] VT misurare; (*take sb's measurements*) prendere le
misure di or a; **to measure one's length** (*fig: fall*) cadere
lungo(-a) disteso(-a)
▶ **measure against** VT + PREP: **to measure sb/sth against
sb/sth** valutare qn/qc confrontandolo a qn/qc
▶ **measure off** VT + ADV misurare
▶ **measure out** VT + ADV dosare
▶ **measure up** VI + ADV: **to measure up (to)** dimostrarsi

or essere all'altezza (di).
meas·ured [ˈmɛʒəd] ADJ misurato(-a).
meas·ure·ment [ˈmɛʒəmənt] N (*act*) misurazione *f*;
(*measure*) misura; **to take sb's measurements** prendere
le misure di or a qn; **chest/hip measurement** giro
petto/fianchi.
meas·ur·ing [ˈmɛʒərɪŋ] N misurazione *f*.
♦ **measuring jug** N bicchiere *m* graduato.
♦ **measuring tape** N metro a nastro.
meat [miːt] N carne *f*; **cold meats** (*Brit*) affettati *mpl*; **meat
and drink** da mangiare e da bere; **this is meat and drink
to them** (*fig*) questo per loro è una delizia; **one man's
meat is another man's poison** (*proverb*) ciò che giova a
uno nuoce a un altro.
meat·ball [ˈmiːtˌbɔːl] N polpetta di carne.
♦ **meat-eater** [ˈmiːtˌiːtəʳ] N carnivoro(-a).
♦ **meat-eating** [ˈmiːtˌiːtɪŋ] ADJ carnivoro(-a).
♦ **meat extract** N estratto di carne.
♦ **meat pie** N *torta salata in pasta frolla con ripieno di
carne.*
meaty [ˈmiːtɪ] ADJ (*comp* **-ier**, *superl* **-iest**) (*flavour*) di
carne; (*fig: book, talk*) sostanzioso(-a).
Mec·ca [ˈmɛkə] N La Mecca; **it has become a Mecca for
tourists** (*fig*) è diventato la mecca dei turisti.
me·chan·ic [mɪˈkænɪk] N meccanico; **motor mechanic**
motorista *m*.
me·chani·cal [mɪˈkænɪkəl] ADJ (*also fig*) meccanico(-a).
♦ **mechanical engineer** N ingegnere *m* meccanico.
♦ **mechanical engineering** N (*science*) ingegneria
meccanica; (*industry*) costruzioni *fpl* meccaniche.
me·chani·cal·ly [mɪˈkænɪkəlɪ] ADV meccanicamente.
me·chan·ics [mɪˈkænɪks] N **a** (*sg: science*) meccanica **b**
(*pl: of car*) meccanismo, meccanica; (: *fig: of legal
system*) meccanismo; (: *of writing, novel, plot*) meccanismo.
mecha·nism [ˈmɛkəˌnɪzəm] N meccanismo.
mecha·nis·tic [ˌmɛkəˈnɪstɪk] ADJ (*Philosophy*) meccanici-
stico(-a).
mecha·ni·za·tion [ˌmɛkənaɪˈzeɪʃən] N (*see vb*) meccanizzazione *f*; motorizzazione *f*.
mecha·nize [ˈmɛkəˌnaɪz] VT (*process, industry*) meccanizzare; (*troops*) motorizzare.
MEd [ˌɛmˈɛd] N ABBR (= *Master of Education*) *titolo di studio
post-universitario.*
med·al [ˈmɛdl] N medaglia.
me·dal·lion [mɪˈdæljən] N medaglione *m*.
med·al·list [ˈmɛdəlɪst] (*Am*) **med·al·ist** [ˈmɛdəlɪst] N (*Sport*): **to be a
gold/silver medallist** essere medaglia d'oro/d'argento.
med·dle [ˈmɛdl] VI (*interfere*): **to meddle (in)** immischiarsi
(in); **to meddle with sth** (*tamper*) toccare qc; **stop
meddling!** smettila di impicciarti!
med·dler [ˈmɛdləʳ] N (*busybody*) impiccione(-a).
med·dle·some [ˈmɛdlsəm], **med·dling** [ˈmɛdlɪŋ] ADJ
(*interfering*) impiccione(-a), ficcanaso *m/f*.
Medea [mɪˈdɪə] N Medea.
me·dia [ˈmiːdɪə] NPL **a** (*Press, Radio, TV*): **the media** i mass
media; **all the media were there** stampa, radio e
televisione erano tutte sul posto **b** (*frm*) *pl* of **medium b**.
♦ **media circus** N carrozzone *m* dell'informazione.
me·di·aeval [ˌmɛdɪˈiːvəl] ADJ = **medieval**.
me·dian [ˈmiːdɪən] N (*Math, Statistics*) mediana; (*Am: also:
median strip*) banchina *f* spartitraffico *inv*.
♦ **media research** N sondaggio tra gli utenti dei mass
media.
me·di·ate [ˈmiːdɪˌeɪt] [1] VI fare da mediatore(-trice).

2 VT (*settlement*) mediare.

me·dia·tion [ˌmiːdɪˈeɪʃən] N mediazione *f*.

me·dia·tor [ˈmiːdɪeɪtəʳ] N mediatore(-trice).

med·ic [ˈmɛdɪk] N (*fam: doctor*) dottore(-essa); (: *student*) studente(-essa) di medicina; **a final year medic** uno studente all'ultimo anno di medicina.

Medi·caid [ˈmɛdɪˌkeɪd] N (*Am*) *programma di assistenza medica ai poveri*.

medi·cal [ˈmɛdɪkəl] 1 ADJ (*school, ward*) di medicina; (*test, treatment*) medico(-a); **the medical profession** il corpo dei medici.

2 N = **medical examination**.

♦ **medical board** N commissione *f* sanitaria.

♦ **medical certificate** N certificato medico.

♦ **medical examination** N visita medica.

♦ **medical examiner** N (*Am*) medico legale.

♦ **medical jurisprudence** N medicina legale.

medi·cal·ly [ˈmɛdɪkəlɪ] ADV dal punto di vista medico; **medically treated** curato(-a) da un medico.

♦ **medical officer** N (*Mil*) medico militare; (*Admin*) ufficiale *m* sanitario.

♦ **medical school** N facoltà *f inv* di medicina.

♦ **medical student** N studente(-essa) di medicina.

Medi·care [ˈmɛdɪˌkɛəʳ] N (*Am*) *programma di assistenza medica agli anziani*.

medi·ca·ted [ˈmɛdɪˈkeɪtɪd] ADJ medicato(-a).

medi·ca·tion [ˌmɛdɪˈkeɪʃən] N (*medicine*) medicinali *mpl*, farmaci *mpl*.

me·dici·nal [mɛˈdɪsɪnl] ADJ medicinale, medicamentoso (-a).

medi·cine [ˈmɛdsɪn, ˈmɛdɪsɪn] 1 N **a** (*drug*) medicina; **to give sb a taste of his own medicine** (*fig*) rendere pan per focaccia a qn **b** (*science*) medicina.

♦ **medicine cabinet, medicine chest** N armadietto farmaceutico *or* dei medicinali.

♦ **medicine man** N stregone *m*.

me·dieval [ˌmɛdɪˈiːvəl] ADJ medievale, del medio evo; **medieval studies** medievalistica *sg*.

me·dio·cre [ˌmiːdɪˈəʊkəʳ] ADJ mediocre.

me·di·oc·rity [ˌmiːdɪˈɒkrɪtɪ] N mediocrità *f inv*.

medi·tate [ˈmɛdɪˌteɪt] 1 VI: **to meditate (on** *or* **about)** meditare (su).

2 VT meditare.

medi·ta·tion [ˌmɛdɪˈteɪʃən] N meditazione *f*.

medi·ta·tive [ˈmɛdɪtətɪv] ADJ meditativo(-a).

Medi·ter·ra·nean [ˌmɛdɪtəˈreɪnɪən] ADJ mediterraneo (-a); **the Mediterranean (Sea)** il (mar) Mediterraneo.

me·dium [ˈmiːdɪəm] 1 ADJ medio(-a); **medium walk/trot** (*Horse-riding*) passo/trotto ordinario.

2 N **a** (*spiritualist*) medium *m/f inv*

b (*pl* **media** *or* **mediums**) (*gen, Phys*) mezzo; **through the medium of the press** per mezzo della stampa; **an advertising medium** un organo di pubblicità; **the artist's medium** i mezzi espressivi dell'artista; see also **media**

c (*midpoint*): **a happy medium** una giusta misura *or* una via di mezzo

d (*environment*) ambiente *m*, habitat *m inv*.

♦ **medium-dry** [ˈmiːdɪəmˈdraɪ] ADJ (*wine*) semisecco(-a), demi-sec *inv*.

♦ **medium-sized** [ˈmiːdjəmˌsaɪzd] ADJ (*tin, packet*) di grandezza media; (*clothes*) di taglia media.

♦ **medium-term** [ˈmiːdɪəmˈtɜːm] N: **to look at the medium term** fare una valutazione a medio termine.

♦ **medium term** ADJ a medio termine.

♦ **medium wave** N (*Radio*) onde *fpl* medie.

med·lar [ˈmɛdləʳ] N (*also:* **medlar tree**) nespolo; (*fruit*) nespola.

med·ley [ˈmɛdlɪ] N (*mixture*) miscuglio, accozzaglia; (*Mus*) pot-pourri *m inv*, selezione *f*.

me·dul·la [mɪˈdʌlə] N (*Anat: also:* **medulla oblungata**) midollo allungato.

Medusa [mɪˈdjuːzə] N Medusa.

meek [miːk] ADJ (*comp* -er, *superl* -est) mite, umile; **meek and mild** mite come un agnello.

meek·ly [ˈmiːklɪ] ADV docilmente, umilmente.

meek·ness [ˈmiːknɪs] N mitezza, umiltà *f inv*.

meet [miːt] (*pt, pp* met) 1 VT **a** (*gen*) incontrare; (*coming in opposite direction*) incrociare; (*by arrangement*) rivedere, ritrovare; **to arrange to meet sb** dare appuntamento a qn; **she ran out to meet us** ci è corsa incontro; **to meet sb off the train** (andare a) aspettare *or* andare a prendere qn al treno; **the car will meet the train** ci sarà una macchina all'arrivo del treno; **I'll meet you at the station** verrò a prenderla alla stazione; **to meet sb's eye** *or* **gaze** incrociare lo sguardo di qn; **a terrible sight met him** *or* **his eyes** gli si presentò un orrendo spettacolo; **there's more to this than meets the eye** è molto più complicato di quanto possa sembrare a prima vista

b (*for the first time*) fare la conoscenza di, essere presentato(-a) a; **meet my brother** le presento mio fratello; **pleased to meet you!** lieto di conoscerla!, piacere!

c (*encounter: team, difficulty*) incontrare; (*face: enemy, danger, death*) affrontare; **to meet one's death** trovare la morte

d (*satisfy: requirement, demand, need*) soddisfare, andare incontro a; (: *criticism, objection*) ribattere a; (*pay: bill, expenses*) far fronte a; **we agree to meet your expenses** siamo d'accordo a rimborsarle le spese.

2 VI **a** (*gen*) incontrarsi; (*by arrangement*) darsi appuntamento, trovarsi; (*committee, society*) riunirsi; **until we meet again!** arrivederci (alla prossima volta)!; **haven't we met before?** non ci conosciamo già?

b (*join: rivers, teams, armies*) incontrarsi.

3 N (*Brit Hunting*) raduno (*dei partecipanti alla caccia alla volpe*); (*Am Sport*) raduno (sportivo).

▶ **meet up** VI + ADV incontrarsi, vedersi; **to meet up with sb** incontrare qn

▶ **meet with** VI + PREP **a** (*success, difficulties, praise*) incontrare; (*welcome*) ricevere; **they met with an accident** hanno avuto un incidente

b (*have meeting with*) incontrarsi con.

meet·ing [ˈmiːtɪŋ] 1 N **a** (*between individuals*) incontro; (*arranged*) appuntamento; (*interview*) intervista, colloquio; **the minister had a meeting with the ambassador** il ministro ha avuto un colloquio con *or* si è incontrato con l'ambasciatore

b (*session: of club, committee, council*) riunione *f*; (: *of members, citizens, employees*) assemblea; **to call a meeting** convocare una riunione; **Mrs Stark is in a meeting** la signora Stark è in riunione

c (*Sport: rally*) raduno; (*Horse-racing*) riunione *f* ippica.

♦ **meeting place** N luogo d'incontro.

♦ **meeting point area** N (*at airport, station*) area *f* convocazione gruppi *inv*, meeting point *m inv*.

mega... [ˈmɛgə] PREF mega... .

mega·byte [ˈmɛgəˌbaɪt] N megabyte *m inv*.

mega·hertz [ˈmɛgəˌhɜːts] N megahertz *m inv*.

mega·lith ['mɛgəlɪθ] N megalite *m*.

mega·lo·ma·nia [ˌmɛgələʊ'meɪnjə] N megalomania.

mega·lo·ma·ni·ac [ˌmɛgələʊ'memɪæk] N megalomane *m/f*.

mega·phone ['mɛgəˌfəʊn] N megafono.

mega·ton ['mɛgəˌtʌn] N megaton *m inv*.

mega·watt ['mɛgəˌwɒt] N megawatt *m inv*.

meio·sis [maɪ'əʊsɪs] N meiosi *f*.

mela·mine ['mɛləˌmiːn] N melammina.

mel·an·cho·lia [ˌmɛlən'kəʊljə] N (*old Psych*) malinconia.

mel·an·chol·ic [ˌmɛlən'kɒlɪk] ADJ malinconico(-a).

mel·an·choly ['mɛlənkəlɪ] 1 ADJ (*person*) malinconico (-a); (*duty, subject*) triste.
2 N malinconia.

mê·lée ['mɛleɪ] N confusione *f*, mischia.

mel·low ['mɛləʊ] 1 (*comp* **-er**, *superl* **-est**) ADJ (*fruit*) ben maturo(-a); (*wine*) maturo(-a) e pastoso(-a); (*colour, light*) caldo(-a) e morbido(-a); (*person, character*) addolcito(-a) dall'età; (*sound*) melodioso(-a).
2 VI (*fruit, wine*) maturare, maturarsi; (*colour, sound*) attenuarsi, smorzarsi; (*person, character*) addolcirsi.
3 VT: **old age has mellowed him** con l'età si è addolcito.

mel·low·ness ['mɛləʊnɪs] N (*of wine*) pastosità *f inv*; (*of colour, character*) dolcezza.

me·lo·dious [mɪ'ləʊdɪəs] ADJ melodioso(-a).

me·lo·di·ous·ly [mɪ'ləʊdɪəslɪ] ADV melodiosamente.

melo·dra·ma ['mɛləʊˌdrɑːmə] N melodramma *m*.

melo·dra·mat·ic [ˌmɛləʊdrə'mætɪk] ADJ melodrammatico(-a).

melo·dra·mati·cal·ly [ˌmɛləʊdrə'mætɪkəlɪ] ADV in modo melodrammatico.

melo·dy ['mɛlədɪ] N melodia.

mel·on ['mɛlən] N melone *m*.

melt [mɛlt] 1 VT **a** (*gen*) sciogliere, struggere; (*metal*) fondere; **melted butter** burro fuso
b (*fig: heart*) intenerire; (: *anger*) far svanire; (: *person*) commuovere.
2 VI **a** (*gen*) sciogliersi, struggersi; (*metals*) fondersi; **it melts in the mouth** si scioglie in bocca
b (*fig: anger, determination*) svanire; (: *heart*) intenerirsi; **he melted into the crowd** si confuse tra la folla

▶ **melt away** VI + ADV (*snow, ice*) sciogliersi completamente; (*fog*) dileguarsi; (*fig: anger, anxiety, opposition*) svanire; (: *savings*) andare in fumo; (: *crowd*) dispersi; **he melted away into the crowd** svanì tra la folla

▶ **melt down** VT + ADV fondere.

melt·down ['mɛltˌdaʊn] N melt-down *m inv*.

melt·ing ['mɛltɪŋ] 1 ADJ (*snow*) che si scioglie (*or* scioglieva *etc*); (: *voice, look*) tenero(-a).
2 N (*Chem*) fusione *f*.

♦ **melting point** N punto di fusione.

♦ **melting pot** N (*fig*) crogiolo; **to be in the melting pot** essere ancora in discussione.

melt·water ['mɛltˌwɔːtə'] N acque *fpl* di fusione.

mem·ber ['mɛmbə'] N (*gen*) membro; (*of club*) socio(-a), iscritto(-a); (*of political party*) iscritto(-a); **she's like a member of the family** è come una di famiglia; **"members only"** "riservato ai soci"; **member of staff** (*Scol, Univ*) insegnante *m/f*; **a member of the staff** (*gen*) un(a) dipendente *m/f*; **member of the public** privato(-a) cittadino(-a).

♦ **member countries** NPL paesi *mpl* membri.

♦ **Member of Parliament** N (*Brit*) deputato(-a).

♦ **Member of the European Parliament** N eurodeputato(-a).

♦ **Member of the House of Representatives** N (*Am*) membro della Camera dei Rappresentanti.

mem·ber·ship ['mɛmbəˌʃɪp] N **a** (*state*): **membership (of)** iscrizione *f* a, adesione *f* a **b** (*number of members*): **the club has a membership of 950** il club ha 950 iscritti.

♦ **membership card** N tessera (di iscrizione).

♦ **membership fee** N tassa d'iscrizione.

♦ **member state** N stato membro.

mem·brane ['mɛmbreɪn] N membrana.

me·men·to [mə'mɛntəʊ] N ricordo, souvenir *m inv*.

memo ['mɛməʊ] N ABBR (= *memorandum*) promemoria *m inv*; (*to staff*) comunicazione *f* interna *or* di servizio.

mem·oir ['mɛmwɑː'] N (*essay*) saggio monografico; (*biography*) nota biografica.

mem·oirs ['mɛmwɑːz] NPL memorie *fpl*.

♦ **memo pad** N blocchetto per appunti.

memo·ra·bilia [ˌmɛmərə'bɪlɪə] NPL cimeli *mpl*.

memo·rable ['mɛmərəbl] ADJ (*day*) memorabile; (*beauty*) notevole.

memo·ran·dum [ˌmɛmə'rændəm] N (*pl* **memoranda**) (*gen*) promemoria *m inv*; (*Diplomacy, Comm*) memorandum *m inv*; (*within company*) comunicazione *f* interna *or* di servizio.

me·mo·rial [mɪ'mɔːrɪəl] 1 ADJ commemorativo(-a).
2 N monumento commemorativo; **as a memorial to** in commemorazione di.

♦ **Memorial Day** N (*Am*) *festa nazionale per la commemorazione dei caduti in guerra*.

memo·rize ['mɛməˌraɪz] VT imparare a memoria, memorizzare.

memo·ry ['mɛmərɪ] N **a** (*faculty, of computer*) memoria; **to have a good/bad memory** aver buona/cattiva memoria; **loss of memory** amnesia, perdita di memoria; **I have a bad memory for faces** non sono molto fisionomista; **he recited the poem from memory** ha recitato la poesia a memoria; **volatile/nonvolatile memory** (*Comput*) memoria volatile/permanente
b (*recollection*) ricordo; **I have no memory of it** non me lo ricordo affatto
c : **in memory of** in memoria *or* ricordo di; **to the memory of** alla memoria di.

men [mɛn] NPL of **man**.

men·ace ['mɛnɪs] 1 N (*threat*) minaccia; (*fam: nuisance*) peste *f*, piaga; **a public menace** un pericolo pubblico.
2 VT minacciare.

men·ac·ing ['mɛnɪsɪŋ] ADJ minaccioso(-a).

men·ac·ing·ly ['mɛnɪsɪŋlɪ] ADV minacciosamente.

me·nage [meɪ'nɑːʒ] N (*frm*) ménage *m inv*.

me·nag·erie [mɪ'nædʒərɪ] N serraglio.

mend [mɛnd] 1 VT (*repair: fence, car, clothes*) aggiustare, riparare; (*darn*) rammendare; **to mend one's ways** (*improve*) correggersi; **to mend matters** risolvere le cose.
2 VI (*broken bone*) rimettersi a posto.
3 N: **to be on the mend** star migliorando, essere in via di guarigione.

mend·ing ['mɛndɪŋ] N (*act*) rammendo; (*items to be mended*) cose *fpl* da rammendare.

Menelaus [ˌmɛnɪ'leɪəs] N Menelao.

men·folk ['mɛnˌfəʊk] NPL uomini *mpl*.

me·nial ['miːnɪəl] ADJ (*position*) subalterno(-a); (*work, task*) umile, servile.

men·in·gi·tis [ˌmɛnɪn'dʒaɪtɪs] N meningite *f*.

me·nis·cus [mɪ'nɪskəs] N (*pl* **meniscuses** *or* **menisci** [mɪ'nɪsaɪ]) menisco.

meno·pau·sal [ˌmɛnəʊ'pɔːzəl] ADJ (*woman*) in menopausa; (*symptoms, problems*) della menopausa.

meno·pause ['mɛnəʊpɔːz] N menopausa.

men·or·rha·gia [ˌmɛnɔː'reɪdʒɪə] N menorragia.

men·servants ['mɛnˌsɜːvənts] NPL of **manservant**.

♦ **men's room** N (*esp Am*): **the men's room** la toilette degli uomini.

men·strual ['mɛnstrʊəl] ADJ mestruale.

men·stru·ate ['mɛnstrʊˌeɪt] VI avere le mestruazioni, mestruare.

men·strua·tion [ˌmɛnstrʊ'eɪʃən] N mestruazione *f.*

men·su·ra·tion [ˌmɛnsjʊə'reɪʃən] N (*also Math*) misurazione *f.*

mens·wear ['mɛnzˌwɛəʳ] N (*Comm*: *clothing*) abbigliamento maschile; (*also:* **menswear department**) (*reparto*) abbigliamento uomo.

men·tal ['mɛntl] ADJ **a** (*gen*) mentale, della mente; (*ability, powers*) intellettuale; (*treatment*) psichiatrico (-a); **to make a mental note of sth** prendere mentalmente nota di qc; **mental patient** malato(-a) di mente; **mental strain** tensione *f* **b** (*fam: mad*) pazzo(-a).

♦ **mental age** N età *f inv* mentale.

♦ **mental arithmetic** N calcolo mentale.

♦ **mental defective** N (*offensive*) ritardato(-a) mentale.

♦ **mental handicap** N handicap *m inv* mentale.

♦ **mental hospital, mental home, mental institution** N ospedale *m* psichiatrico.

♦ **mental illness** N malattia mentale.

men·tal·ity [mɛn'tælɪtɪ] N mentalità *f inv.*

men·tal·ly ['mɛntəlɪ] ADV (*calculate*) mentalmente, a mente; **to be mentally handicapped** avere un handicap mentale; **she is mentally ill** è malata di mente; **the mentally handicapped** i portatori di handicap mentale.

men·thol ['mɛnθɒl] ①N mentolo. ②ADJ al mentolo.

men·tion ['mɛnʃən] ①N menzione *f*, accenno; **it's hardly worth a mention** non è neanche il caso di parlarne. ②VT (*gen*) accennare a; (*name, person*) fare il nome di, menzionare; **I mentioned it to him** glielo ho accennato; **just mention my name** basta che tu faccia il mio nome; **all those people, too numerous to mention, who** ... tutti coloro che qui sarebbe troppo lungo elencare, i quali...; **I need hardly mention that** ... inutile dire che...; **not to mention** OR **without mentioning** per non parlare di, senza contare; **don't mention it!** non c'è di che!, prego!

men·tor ['mɛntɔː] N mentore *m.*

menu ['mɛnjuː] N (*also Comput*) menù *m inv.*

♦ **menu-driven** ['mɛnjuːˌdrɪvn] ADJ (*Comput*) guidato(-a) da menù.

mer·can·tile ['mɜːkənˌtaɪl] ADJ mercantile; (*law*) commerciale.

mer·ce·nary ['mɜːsɪnərɪ] ①ADJ (*person*) mercenario(-a); (*motive*) venale. ②N mercenario.

mer·cer·ize ['mɜːsəˌraɪz] VT mercerizzare.

♦ **mer·cer·ized cot·ton** ['mɜːsəˌraɪzd'kɒtn] N cotone *m* mercerizzato.

mer·chan·dise ['mɜːtʃənˌdaɪz] ①N merce *f*, merci *fpl.* ②VT commercializzare.

mer·chan·dis·er ['mɜːtʃənˌdaɪzəʳ] N merchandiser *m inv.*

mer·chant ['mɜːtʃənt] N (*trader*) commerciante *m/f*; (*shopkeeper*) negoziante *m/f*, commerciante *m/f*; **timber/wine merchant** commerciante di legname/vino.

♦ **merchant bank** N (*Brit*) banca d'affari.

mer·chant·man ['mɜːtʃəntmən] N (*pl* **-men**) (*ship*)

mercantile *m.*

♦ **merchant navy**, (*Am*) **merchant marine** N marina mercantile.

♦ **merchant seaman** N marinaio (di nave mercantile).

mer·ci·ful ['mɜːsɪfʊl] ADJ (*Rel*) misericordioso(-a); (*person*) compassionevole, pietoso(-a), clemente; **it was a merciful release** è stata una vera liberazione.

mer·ci·ful·ly ['mɜːsɪfəlɪ] ADV (*act*) con clemenza, con misericordia; (*fortunately*) per fortuna.

mer·ci·less ['mɜːsɪlɪs] ADJ spietato(-a).

mer·ci·less·ly ['mɜːsɪlɪslɪ] ADV spietatamente.

mer·cu·rial [mɜː'kjʊərɪəl] ADJ (*unpredictable*) volubile.

Mer·cu·ry ['mɜːkjʊrɪ] N (*Astron, Myth*) Mercurio.

mer·cu·ry ['mɜːkjʊrɪ] N (*Chem*) mercurio.

mer·cy ['mɜːsɪ] N pietà *f inv*, clemenza; (*Rel*) misericordia; **to be at the mercy of sb/sth** essere alla mercé *or* in balia di qn/qc; **to have mercy on sb** avere pietà di qn; **to be left to the tender mercies of sb** essere lasciato(-a) alle buone cure di qn; **it's a mercy that** ... è una fortuna che + *sub.*

♦ **mercy killing** N eutanasia.

mere [mɪəʳ] ADJ (*formality*) semplice, puro(-a) (*before n*); (*thought*) solo(-a) (*before n*); (*chance, coincidence*) puro(-a) (*before n*); **she's a mere child** non è che una bambina, è solo una bambina; **the mere sight of him irritates her** solo a vederlo s'arrabbia; **she's a mere secretary** è una semplice segretaria; **by the merest chance** per mero caso.

mere·ly ['mɪəlɪ] ADV soltanto, semplicemente, non... che.

merge [mɜːdʒ] ①VT (*Comm*) fondere, unire; (*Comput: files, text*) unire. ②VI **a** (*colours, sounds, shapes*): **to merge (into, with)** fondersi (con), confondersi (con); **to merge (with)** (*roads*) unirsi (a); (*river*) confluire (in) **b** (*Comm*) fondersi, unirsi.

mer·ger ['mɜːdʒəʳ] N (*Comm*) fusione *f.*

me·rid·ian [mə'rɪdɪən] N meridiano.

me·ringue [mə'ræŋ] N meringa.

me·ri·no [mə'riːnəʊ] N merino.

mer·it ['mɛrɪt] ①N merito, valore *m*; **to look** *or* **inquire into the merits of sth** valutare *or* pesare i pro e i contro di qc; **to treat a case on its merits** trattare un caso con obiettività. ②VT meritare.

meri·toc·ra·cy [ˌmɛrɪ'tɒkrəsɪ] N meritocrazia.

meri·to·ri·ous [ˌmɛrɪ'tɔːrɪəs] ADJ (*frm: deed, service*) meritorio(-a).

mer·maid ['mɜːmeɪd] N sirena.

mer·ri·ly ['mɛrɪlɪ] ADV allegramente.

mer·ri·ment ['mɛrɪmənt] N allegria, gaiezza; (*laughter*) ilarità *f inv.*

mer·ry ['mɛrɪ] ADJ (*comp* **-ier**, *superl* **-iest**) (*cheerful*) allegro (-a), gaio(-a), festoso(-a); (*Brit fam: tipsy*) brillo(-a); **Merry Christmas!** Buon Natale!

♦ **merry-go-round** ['mɛrɪɡəʊˌraʊnd] N giostra, carosello.

merry·making ['mɛrɪˌmeɪkɪŋ] N festeggiamenti *mpl.*

me·sa ['meɪsə] N (*tableland*) mesa.

mes·ca·line ['mɛskəˌliːn] N mescalina.

mesh [mɛʃ] ①N **a** (*in net*) maglia; **a 6-cm mesh net** una rete con maglie di 6 cm **b** (*network, net*) rete *f*; **wire mesh** rete *f* metallica **c** (*gears*): **in mesh** ingranato(-a). ②VI (*gears*) ingranare.

mes·mer·ize ['mɛzməˌraɪz] VT ipnotizzare; **she was mesmerized** (*fig*) non riusciva a distogliere lo sguardo.

mess [mɛs] N **a** (*confusion of objects*) disordine *m*, confu-

sione *f*; (*dirt*) sporcizia; (*awkward predicament*) pasticcio; **you look a mess!** guarda in che stato sei!; **to be (in) a mess** (*house, room*) essere in disordine, essere molto sporco(-a); (*fig: marriage, life*) essere un caos *or* un disastro; **to make a mess** fare un gran disordine dappertutto, sporcare dappertutto; **the dog has made a mess** il cane ha sporcato; **to make a mess of** (*dirty*) sporcare; (*tear*) strappare; (*wreck*) sfasciare; **to make a mess of one's life/career** rovinarsi la vita/la carriera; **I made a mess of the exam** ho fatto un pasticcio all'esame; **to be/get (o.s.) in a mess** (*fig*) essere/cacciarsi in un pasticcio

 b (*Mil*) mensa

▶ **mess about, mess around** (*fam*) ⬚1 VI + ADV (*waste time*) perdere tempo, trastullarsi; (*play the fool*) far confusione; (*in water, mud*) pasticciare; **what are you doing? — just messing about** cosa fai? — niente di speciale.

 ⬚2 VT + ADV (*person*) menare per il naso; (*plans*) scombinare; **stop messing me about!** smettila di farmi perdere tempo!

▶ **mess about with, mess around with** (*fam*) VI + ADV + PREP (*plans*) fare un pasticcio di; **to mess about with sth** armeggiare *or* trafficare con qc; **to mess about with sb** divertirsi con qn

▶ **mess up** VT + ADV (*room*) mettere sottosopra; (*dress*) sporcare; (*hair*) scompigliare; (*fig: plan, marriage, situation*) mandare a monte, rovinare.

mes·sage ['mɛsɪdʒ] N messaggio; **to get the message** (*fig fam*) capire l'antifona.

♦ **message switching** N (*Comput*) smistamento messaggi.

mes·sen·ger ['mɛsɪndʒəʳ] N (*gen*) messaggero(-a); (*in office*) messo.

♦ **messenger boy** N fattorino.

Mes·si·ah [mɪ'saɪə] N Messia *m*.

Messrs ['mɛsəz] MPL ABBR (*on letters*: = *messieurs*) Spett.

messy ['mɛsɪ] ADJ (*comp* **-ier,** *superl* **-iest**) (*dirty: clothes*) sporco(-a); (: *job*) che insudicia; (*untidy*) disordinato(-a); (*confused: situation*) ingarbugliato(-a).

Met [mɛt] N ABBR: **the Met a** (*Am*)= *the Metropolitan Opera* **b** (*Brit*)= *the Metropolitan Police*.

met [mɛt] PT, PP of **meet**.

meta·bol·ic [ˌmɛtə'bɒlɪk] ADJ metabolico(-a).

me·tabo·lism [mə'tæbəˌlɪzəm] N metabolismo.

met·al ['mɛtl] ⬚1 N metallo; **road metal** pietrisco.

 ⬚2 ADJ in metallo.

 ⬚3 VT massicciare.

♦ **metal detector** N metaldetector *m inv*.

♦ **metal fatigue** N fatica del metallo.

me·tal·lic [mɪ'tælɪk] ADJ metallico(-a).

met·al·loid ['mɛtəˌlɔɪd] N metalloide *m*.

met·al·lur·gist [mɛ'tælədʒɪst] N metallurgista *m*.

met·al·lur·gy [mɛ'tælədʒɪ] N metallurgia.

♦ **metal polish** N lucido per metalli.

metal·work ['mɛtlˌwɜːk] N (*craft*) lavorazione *f* del metallo.

meta·mor·phic [ˌmɛtə'mɔːfɪk] ADJ metamorfico(-a).

meta·mor·phose [ˌmɛtə'mɔːfəʊz] VI: **to metamorphose into** (*frm*) trasformarsi in.

meta·mor·pho·sis [ˌmɛtə'mɔːfəsɪs] N (*pl* **metamorphoses** [ˌmɛtə'mɔːfəsiːz]) metamorfosi *f inv*.

meta·phor ['mɛtəfəʳ] N metafora.

meta·phor·ic [ˌmɛtə'fɒrɪk], **meta·phor·ical** [ˌmɛtə'fɒrɪkəl] ADJ metaforico(-a).

meta·phori·cal·ly [ˌmɛtə'fɒrɪkəlɪ] ADV metaforicamente.

meta·physi·cal [ˌmɛtə'fɪzɪkəl] ADJ metafisico(-a).

meta·physi·cal·ly [ˌmɛtə'fɪzɪkəlɪ] ADV metafisicamente.

meta·phys·ics [ˌmɛtə'fɪzɪks] NSG metafisica.

me·tas·ta·sis [mɪ'tæstəsɪs] N metastasi *f inv*.

meta·tar·sus [ˌmɛtə'tɑːsəs] N metatarso.

mete [miːt] VI: **to mete out** (*punishment*) infliggere.

me·teor ['miːtɪəʳ] N meteora.

me·teor·ic [ˌmiːtɪ'ɒrɪk] ADJ meteorico(-a); (*fig*) fulmineo(-a).

me·teor·ite ['miːtɪəˌraɪt] N meteorite *m*.

me·teoro·logi·cal [ˌmiːtɪərə'lɒdʒɪkəl] ADJ meteorologico(-a).

me·teor·olo·gist [ˌmiːtjə'rɒlədʒɪst] N meteorologo(-a).

me·teor·ol·ogy [ˌmiːtɪə'rɒlədʒɪ] N meteorologia.

me·ter¹ ['miːtəʳ] N (*gen*) contatore *m*; (*parking meter*) parchimetro; **electricity meter** contatore dell'elettricità.

me·ter² ['miːtəʳ] N (*Am*) = **metre**.

♦ **meter maid** N (*Brit, old fam*) vigilessa.

me·thane ['miːθeɪn] N metano.

metha·nol ['mɛθəˌnɒl] N metanolo.

meth·od ['mɛθəd] N **a** (*manner, way*) metodo, sistema *m*; **my method of working** il mio metodo di lavoro; **method of payment** modo *or* modalità *fpl* di pagamento **b** (*orderliness*) metodo; **there's method in his madness** la sua follia non è priva di logica.

me·thodi·cal [mɪ'θɒdɪkəl] ADJ metodico(-a).

me·thodi·cal·ly [mɪ'θɒdɪkəlɪ] ADV metodicamente, con metodo, con ordine.

Meth·od·ism ['mɛθədɪzəm] N metodismo.

Meth·od·ist ['mɛθədɪst] ADJ, N metodista (*m/f*).

meth·od·ol·ogy [ˌmɛθə'dɒlədʒɪ] N metodologia.

meths [mɛθs] N (*Brit fam*)= *methylated spirit(s)*.

me·thyl ['mɛθɪl] N metile *m*.

meth·yl·at·ed spir·it ['mɛθɪˌleɪtɪd'spɪrɪt] N, **meth·yl·at·ed spir·its** ['mɛθɪˌleɪtɪd'spɪrɪts] NPL (*Brit*) alcol *m inv* denaturato.

me·ticu·lous [mɪ'tɪkjʊləs] ADJ meticoloso(-a).

me·ticu·lous·ly [mɪ'tɪkjʊləslɪ] ADV meticolosamente.

Met Office N (*Brit*): **the Met Office** l'Ufficio meteorologico.

me·tre, (*Am*) **me·ter** ['miːtəʳ] N metro.

met·ric ['mɛtrɪk] ADJ metrico(-a); **to go metric** adottare il sistema metrico decimale.

met·ri·cal ['mɛtrɪkəl] ADJ (*also Poetry*) metrico(-a).

met·ri·ca·tion [ˌmɛtrɪ'keɪʃən] N conversione *f* al sistema metrico decimale.

♦ **metric system** N sistema *m* metrico decimale.

♦ **metric ton** N tonnellata.

met·ro·nome ['mɛtrəˌnəʊm] N metronomo.

me·tropo·lis [mɪ'trɒpəlɪs] N metropoli *f inv*.

met·ro·poli·tan [ˌmɛtrə'pɒlɪtən] ADJ metropolitano(-a).

♦ **Metropolitan Police** N (*Brit*): **the Metropolitan Police** la polizia di Londra.

met·tle ['mɛtl] N: **to be on one's mettle** essere pronto(-a) a dare il meglio di se stesso(-a).

mew [mjuː] ⬚1 N miagolio.

 ⬚2 VI miagolare.

mews flat [mjuːz flæt] N (*Brit*) *appartamentino ricavato da una vecchia scuderia*.

Mexi·can ['mɛksɪkən] ADJ, N messicano(-a).

Mexi·co ['mɛksɪkəʊ] N il Messico.

♦ **Mexico City** N Città *f inv* del Messico.

mez·za·nine ['mɛzəniːn] N (*also:* **mezzanine floor**) mezzanino.

mezzo-soprano [ˌmɛtsəʊsəˈprɑːnəʊ] N (voice, singer) mezzosoprano sm.

MFA [ˌɛmɛfˈeɪ] N ABBR (Am: = Master of Fine Arts) diploma post-universitario di Belle Arti.

mfr ABBR a = manufacture b = manufacturer.

mg ABBR (= milligram) mg.

Mgr ABBR a (= Monseigneur, Monsignor) mons. b (Comm) = manager.

MHR [ˌɛmeɪtʃˈɑːʳ] N ABBR (Am) = Member of the House of Representatives.

MHz ABBR (= megahertz) MHz.

MI ABBR (Am Post)= Michigan.

mi [miː] N (Mus) mi m inv.

MI5 [ˌɛmaɪˈfaɪv] N ABBR (Brit: = Military Intelligence 5) agenzia di controspionaggio.

MI6 [ˌɛmaɪˈsɪks] N ABBR (Brit: = Military Intelligence 6) agenzia di spionaggio.

MIA [ˌɛmaɪˈeɪ] ABBR see missing in action.

mi·aow [miːˈaʊ] ① N miao. ② VI miagolare.

mica [ˈmaɪkə] N mica.

mice [maɪs] NPL of mouse.

Mich·ael·mas [ˈmɪklməs] N festa di San Michele.

♦ **Michaelmas daisy** N margherita settembrina.

mick·ey [ˈmɪkɪ] N (Brit fam): to take the mickey out of sb prendere qn per i fondelli or in giro.

mi·cro [ˈmaɪkrəʊ] N microcomputer m inv.

micro... [ˈmaɪkrəʊ] PREF micro... .

mi·crobe [ˈmaɪkrəʊb] N microbio, microbo.

micro·bi·ol·ogy [ˌmaɪkrəʊbaɪˈɒlədʒɪ] N microbiologia.

micro·chip [ˈmaɪkrəʊˌtʃɪp] N (Elec) microcircuito integrato, microchip m inv.

micro·cir·cuit [ˈmaɪkrəʊˌsɜːkɪt] N microcircuito.

micro·com·put·er [ˌmaɪkrəʊkəmˈpjuːtəʳ] N microcomputer m inv.

micro·cosm [ˈmaɪkrəʊˌkɒzəm] N microcosmo.

micro·eco·nom·ics [ˌmaɪkrəʊˌiːkəˈnɒmɪks] NSG microeconomia.

micro·elec·tron·ics [ˌmaɪkrəʊɪlɛkˈtrɒnɪks] NSG microelettronica.

micro·fiche [ˈmaɪkrəʊˌfiːʃ] N microfiche f inv.

micro·film [ˈmaɪkrəʊˌfɪlm] ① N microfilm m inv. ② VT microfilmare.

micro·graph [ˈmaɪkrəʊˌɡræf] N microfotografia.

mi·crog·ra·phy [maɪˈkrɒɡrəfɪ] N microfotografia.

micro·light [ˈmaɪkrəʊˌlaɪt] N aereo m biposto inv.

micro·mesh [ˈmaɪkrəʊˌmɛʃ] ADJ (stockings) a rete finissima, velato(-a).

mi·crom·eter [maɪˈkrɒmɪtəʳ] N micrometro, palmer m inv.

micro·or·gan·ism [ˌmaɪkrəʊˈɔːɡəˌnɪzəm] N microorganismo.

micro·phone [ˈmaɪkrəˌfəʊn] N microfono.

micro·pro·ces·sor [ˌmaɪkrəʊˈprəʊsɛsəʳ] N microprocessore m.

micro·scope [ˈmaɪkrəskəʊp] N microscopio; **light microscope** microscopio ottico; **electron microscope** microscopio elettronico; **under the microscope** al microscopio.

micro·scop·ic [ˌmaɪkrəˈskɒpɪk], **micro·scop·ical** [ˌmaɪkrəˈskɒpɪkəl] ADJ microscopico(-a).

micro·sec·ond [ˈmaɪkrəʊˌsɛkənd] N microsecondo.

micro·wave [ˈmaɪkrəʊˌweɪv] N microonda; (also: microwave oven) (forno a) microonde m.

mid [mɪd] ADJ: **mid morning** a metà (della) mattina; **mid afternoon** metà pomeriggio; **in mid journey** a metà del viaggio; **in mid June** a metà giugno; **in mid air** a

mezz'aria; **to leave sth in mid air** (fig) lasciare qc in sospeso; **in mid Atlantic** in mezzo all'Atlantico; **he's in his mid thirties** avrà circa trentacinque anni.

Midas [ˈmaɪdəs] N Mida m; **he has the Midas touch** (fig) tutto ciò che tocca si trasforma in oro.

mid·day [ˈmɪdˈdeɪ] ① N mezzogiorno; **at midday** a mezzogiorno.
② ADJ di mezzogiorno.

mid·dle [ˈmɪdl] ① ADJ (of place) di mezzo, centrale; (in quality, size) medio(-a); **the middle chair in the row** la sedia nel centro della fila.
② N (centre) mezzo, centro; (fam: waist) vita, cintura; **in the middle of the field** in mezzo al campo; **a village in the middle of nowhere** un paese sperduto; **in the middle of summer** in piena estate; **in the middle of the night** nel cuore della notte, a notte fonda; **I'm in the middle of reading it** sto proprio leggendolo ora.

♦ **middle age** N mezza età f inv.

♦ **middle-aged** [ˌmɪdlˈeɪdʒd] ADJ di mezza età.

♦ **Middle Ages** NPL: **the Middle Ages** il Medioevo.

middle·brow [ˈmɪdəlˌbraʊ] (pej) ① ADJ (fiction, play, film) per il lettore o spettatore ecc medio.
② N chi ha una cultura media.

♦ **middle C** N (Mus) do sotto il rigo.

♦ **middle-class** [ˌmɪdlˈklɑːs] ADJ borghese, della borghesia.

♦ **middle class** N: **the middle class(es)** ≈ la borghesia.

♦ **middle-distance** [ˌmɪdlˈdɪstəns] ADJ (runner) di mezzofondo.

♦ **middle distance** N (Art): **in the middle distance** in secondo piano.

♦ **Middle East** N: **the Middle East** il Medio Oriente.

♦ **middle finger** N medio.

middle·man [ˈmɪdlˌmæn] N (pl -men) (gen) intermediario; (Comm) (agente m) rivenditore m.

♦ **middle management** N quadri mpl intermedi.

♦ **middle name** N secondo nome m.

♦ **middle-of-the-road** [ˌmɪdləvðəˈrəʊd] ADJ moderato (-a).

♦ **middle school** N ≈ scuola media (per ragazzi dagli 8 o 9 anni ai 12 o 13 anni in Gran Bretagna e dagli 11 anni ai 14 anni negli Stati Uniti).

middle·weight [ˈmɪdlˌweɪt] (Boxing) ① ADJ dei pesi medi.
② N peso medio.

♦ **Middle West** N (Am): **the Middle West** = Midwest.

mid·dling [ˈmɪdlɪŋ] ADJ così così, medio(-a).

Middx. ABBR (Brit)= Middlesex.

midge [mɪdʒ] N moscerino; (biting) pappataci m inv.

midg·et [ˈmɪdʒɪt] N nano(-a).

midi system [ˈmɪdɪˌsɪstəm] N compatto.

Mid·lands [ˈmɪdləndz] NPL: **the Midlands** le contee del centro dell'Inghilterra.

mid·night [ˈmɪdˌnaɪt] ① N mezzanotte f; **at midnight** a mezzanotte.
② ADJ (gen) di mezzanotte; (attack) a mezzanotte.

♦ **midnight oil** N: **to burn the midnight oil** lavorare or studiare fino a tarda notte.

mid·point [ˈmɪdpɔɪnt] N: **at the midpoint of** (road, event) nel mezzo di.

mid·riff [ˈmɪdrɪf] N (diaphragm) diaframma m; (stomach) stomaco.

mid·ship·man [ˈmɪdˌʃɪpmən] N (pl -men) aspirante guardiamarina m inv.

midst [mɪdst] N: **in the midst of** in mezzo a; (during) durante; **in our midst** tra di noi, in mezzo a noi.

mid·stream ['mɪd,striːm] N: **in midstream** (*of river*) al centro della corrente; **she paused** *or* **stopped midstream** (*fig*) si interruppe nel bel mezzo del discorso.

mid·sum·mer ['mɪd,sʌmə^r] N piena estate *f*.

♦ **Midsummer('s) Day** ['mɪd,sʌmə(z)deɪ] N festa di San Giovanni (*24 giugno*).

mid·term ['mɪd'tɜːm] N (*Scol, Univ: holiday*) *vacanza a metà trimestre.*

mid·way [,mɪd'weɪ] ADV, ADJ: **midway (between)** a mezza strada (fra).

mid·week [,mɪd'wiːk] ADV, ADJ a metà settimana.

Mid·west [,mɪd'wɛst] N (*Am*): **the Midwest** il Midwest *m* (*regione medio-occidentale degli Stati Uniti*).

mid·wife ['mɪd,waɪf] N (*pl* **-wives**) ostetrica.

mid·wife·ry ['mɪd,wɪfərɪ] N ostetricia.

mid·win·ter [,mɪd'wɪntə^r] N pieno inverno.

mien [miːn] N (*liter*) contegno.

miffed [mɪft] ADJ (*fam*) seccato(-a), stizzito(-a).

might¹ [maɪt] PT of **may**.

might² [maɪt] N forza, potere *m*, forze *fpl*; **with all one's might** con tutte le proprie forze.

mighty ['maɪtɪ] ① ADJ (*comp* **-ier**, *superl* **-iest**) (*ruler, nation*) forte, potente; (*warrior*) possente; (*ocean*) vasto(-a). ② ADV (*fam*) molto.

mi·graine ['miːgreɪn] N emicrania.

mi·grant ['maɪgrənt] ① ADJ (*bird, animal*) migratore(-trice); (*worker*) emigrante, emigrato(-a); (*herdsman*) nomade. ② N (*see adj*) migratore(-trice); emigrante *m/f*; nomade *m/f*.

mi·grate [maɪ'greɪt] VI (*bird*) migrare; (*worker*) emigrare.

mi·gra·tion [maɪ'greɪʃən] N (*see vb*) migrazione *f*; emigrazione *f*.

mike [maɪk] N ABBR (*fam*: = *microphone*) microfono.

Mi·lan [mɪ'læn] N Milano *f*.

Mil·an·ese [,mɪlə'niːz] ① ADJ milanese, alla milanese. ② N INV milanese *m/f*.

mild [maɪld] ① ADJ (*comp* **-er**, *superl* **-est**) (*climate, punishment, weather*) mite; (*character, person, cheese, voice*) dolce; (*flavour, taste*) delicato(-a), non piccante; (*curry*) non piccante; (*illness, sedative, beer, cigar*) leggero(-a); (*effect*) blando(-a); **it's mild today** non fa freddo oggi. ② N (*Brit*) birra leggera.

mil·dew ['mɪldjuː] N muffa.

mil·dewed ['mɪl,djuːd] ADJ ammuffito(-a).

mild·ly ['maɪldlɪ] ADV (*gently*) gentilmente, dolcemente, delicatamente; (*slightly*) vagamente; **to put it mildly** (*fam*) per usare un eufemismo, a dir poco.

♦ **mild-mannered** [,maɪld'mænəd] ADJ: **to be mild-mannered** essere dal carattere docile.

mild·ness ['maɪldnɪs] N (*of climate, punishment, weather, effect*) mitezza; (*of character, person*) mitezza, dolcezza; (*of cheese, dish*) sapore *m* delicato, delicatezza; (*of sedative, beer, cigar*) leggerezza; (*of illness*) non gravità *f* inv.

mile [maɪl] N miglio (*1609,33 m*); **nautical mile** miglio nautico; **to do 20 miles per gallon** ≈ fare cento chilometri con 14 litri; **miles and miles** ≈ chilometri e chilometri; **they live miles away** abitano lontanissimo; **it stands** *or* **sticks out a mile** si capisce *or* si vede lontano un miglio.

mile·age ['maɪlɪdʒ] N ≈ chilometraggio; **what mileage does your car do?** ≈ quanti chilometri al litro fa la tua macchina?

♦ **mileage allowance** N ≈ rimborso per chilometro.

mile·om·eter [maɪ'lɒmɪtə^r] N (*Brit*) = **milometer**.

mile·stone ['maɪl,stəʊn] N (*also fig*) pietra miliare.

mi·lieu ['miːljɜ:] N ambiente *m* sociale.

mili·tan·cy ['mɪlɪtənsɪ] N militanza.

mili·tant ['mɪlɪtənt] ADJ, N militante (*m/f*).

mili·ta·rism ['mɪlɪtə,rɪzəm] N militarismo.

mili·ta·ris·tic [,mɪlɪtə'rɪstɪk] ADJ militaristico(-a).

mili·tary ['mɪlɪtərɪ] ① ADJ militare. ② NPL: **the military** i militari, l'esercito.

♦ **military service** N servizio militare.

mili·tate ['mɪlɪ,teɪt] VI: **to militate against** pregiudicare, essere di ostacolo a.

mi·li·tia [mɪ'lɪʃə] N milizia, milizie *fpl*.

milk [mɪlk] ① N latte *m*; **it's no good crying over spilt milk** (*Proverb*) è inutile piangere sul latte versato. ② VT (*cow*) mungere; (*fig: person*) spillare quattrini a; (: *situation*) sfruttare fino in fondo.

♦ **milk chocolate** N cioccolato al latte.

♦ **milk churn** N bidone *m* per il latte.

♦ **milk float** N (*Brit*) furgone *m* del lattaio.

milk·ing ['mɪlkɪŋ] N mungitura.

♦ **milking machine** N mungitrice *f*.

♦ **milking parlour** N sala di mungitura.

♦ **milk jug** N bricco del latte.

milk·man ['mɪlkmən] N (*pl* **-men**) lattaio.

♦ **milk of magnesia** N latte di magnesia.

♦ **milk pan** N bollilatte *m* inv.

♦ **milk pudding** N budino al latte.

♦ **milk shake** N frappé *m* inv, frullato.

♦ **milk tooth** N dente *m* di latte.

♦ **milk truck** N (*Am*) = **milk float**.

milky ['mɪlkɪ] ADJ (*comp* **-ier**, *superl* **-iest**) (*substance*) lattiginoso(-a); (*colour*) latteo(-a); (*coffee*) con tanto latte.

♦ **Milky Way** N: **the Milky Way** la Via Lattea.

mill [mɪl] ① N **a** (*gen*) mulino; (*Industry: for grain*) macina; (*also: windmill*) mulino a vento; (*small: for coffee, pepper*) macinino; **to go through the mill** (*fig*) passare un periodo duro; **to put sb through the mill** (*fig*) mettere qn sotto torchio. **b** (*factory*) fabbrica, stabilimento. ② VT (*coffee, pepper, flour*) macinare; (*metal*) laminare; (*coin*) zigrinare

▶ **mill about, mill around** VI + ADV (*crowd*) brulicare, formicolare.

mil·len·nium [mɪ'lɛnɪəm] N (*pl* **millennia**) (*period*) millennio; (*anniversary*) millenario; **the millennium** periodo (*futuro*) di pace e felicità.

mil·ler ['mɪlə^r] N mugnaio.

mil·let ['mɪlɪt] N miglio.

milli... ['mɪlɪ] PREF milli... .

mil·li·bar ['mɪlɪ,bɑ:^r] N millibar *m* inv.

mil·li·gram, **mil·li·gramme** ['mɪlɪ,græm] N milligrammo.

mil·li·li·tre, (*Am*) **mil·li·li·ter** ['mɪlɪ,li:tə^r] N millilitro.

mil·li·metre, (*Am*) **mil·li·meter** ['mɪlɪ,mi:tə^r] N millimetro.

mil·li·ner ['mɪlɪnə^r] N modista.

mil·li·nery ['mɪlɪnərɪ] N (*articoli mpl di*) modisteria.

mill·ing ['mɪlɪŋ] ADJ: **the milling crowd** la folla in movimento.

mil·lion ['mɪljən] N milione *m*; **a million women** un milione di donne; **thanks a million!** (*fam*) grazie mille!; **she's one in a million** (*fam*) come lei ce ne sono poche; **millions of** (*fam*) migliaia di, miliardi di; **you look like a**

million dollars (*fam*) sei in forma smagliante.

mil·lion·aire [ˌmɪljə'nɛəʳ] N ≈ miliardario(-a).

mil·lionth ['mɪljənθ] **1** ADJ milionesimo(-a).

2 N (*in series*) milionesimo(-a); (*fraction*) milionesimo.

mil·li·pede ['mɪlɪˌpiːd] N millepiedi *m inv*.

mill·pond ['mɪlˌpɒnd] N: **the sea is like a millpond** il mare è liscio come l'olio.

mill·race ['mɪlˌreɪs] N *corrente d'acqua che fa girare la ruota di un mulino*.

mill·stone ['mɪlˌstəʊn] N macina, mola; **it's a millstone round his neck** è un grosso peso per lui, è una palla al piede per lui.

mill·wheel ['mɪlˌwiːl] N ruota di mulino.

♦ **mill worker** N operaio(-a) di cotonificio.

mi·lom·eter, mile·om·eter [maɪ'lɒmətəʳ] N (*Brit*) ≈ contachilometri *m inv*.

mime [maɪm] **1** N (*play*) mimo; (*skill, gestures*) mimica; (*actor*) mimo(-a).

2 VT, VI mimare.

mim·ic ['mɪmɪk] **1** N imitatore(-trice).

2 VT (*subj: comedian*) imitare; (*: animal, person*) scimmiottare.

mim·ic·ry ['mɪmɪkrɪ] N imitazioni *fpl*; (*Zool*) mimetismo.

mi·mo·sa [mɪ'məʊzə] N mimosa.

Min. ABBR (*Brit Pol*: = *ministry*) Min.

min. ABBR **a** (= *minute or minutes*) min. **b** (= *minimum*) min.

mina·ret [ˌmɪnə'rɛt] N minareto.

mince [mɪns] **1** N (*Brit Culin*) macinato, carne *f* macinata.

2 VT tritare, macinare; **he does not mince (his) words** non ha peli sulla lingua.

3 VI (*in walking*) camminare a passettini; (*in talking*) parlare con affettazione.

mince·meat ['mɪnsˌmiːt] N *composto di frutta secca tritata e spezie usato in pasticceria*; **to make mincemeat of** (*fig: person*) ridurre in polpette; (*: argument*) demolire.

♦ **mince pie** N *tortino ripieno di frutta secca*.

minc·er ['mɪnsəʳ] N (*for meat*) tritacarne *m inv*; (*all-purpose*) tritatutto *m inv*.

minc·ing ['mɪnsɪŋ] ADJ affettato(-a), lezioso(-a).

mind [maɪnd] **1** N **a** (*gen*) mente *f*; (*intellect*) intelletto; **a case of mind over matter** una vittoria dello spirito sulla materia; **one of Britain's finest minds** uno dei più grandi cervelli della Gran Bretagna; **I am not clear in my mind about the idea** non ho le idee chiare in proposito; **to be uneasy in one's mind** avere dei dubbi, essere un po' preoccupato(-a); **what's on your mind?** cosa c'è che ti preoccupa?; **I can't get it out of my mind** non riesco a togliermelo dalla mente; **to put** *or* **set** *or* **give one's mind to sth** concentrarsi su qc, applicarsi a qc; **that will take your mind off it** questo ti aiuterà a non pensarci (più); **to bear** *or* **keep sth in mind** (*take account of*) tener presente qc; (*remember*) tenere a mente qc, non dimenticare qc; **it went right out of my mind** mi è completamente passato di mente, me ne sono completamente dimenticato; **to bring** *or* **call sth to mind** riportare *or* richiamare qc alla mente

b (*inclination, intention*) intenzione *f*, idea; **to have sb/sth in mind** avere in mente qn/qc; **to have in mind to do sth** avere intenzione *or* in mente di fare qc; **I have a good mind to do it** avrei molta voglia di farlo; **I have half a mind to do it** ho una mezza idea di farlo; **nothing was further from my mind** non mi era nemmeno passato per l'anticamera del cervello; **to change one's mind** cambiare idea

c (*opinion*): **to make up one's mind** decidersi; **to be in two minds about sth** essere incerto(-a) *or* indeciso(-a) su qc; **to be in two minds about doing sth** non sapersi decidere se fare qc o no; **of one mind** della stessa idea; **I am still of the same mind** sono ancora dello stesso parere; **to have a mind of one's own** (*person: think for o.s.*) saper pensare con la propria testa; (*: not conform*) avere delle idee proprie; **my car has a mind of its own** la mia macchina fa un po' quello che vuole lei; **to my mind** a mio parere, secondo me

d (*sanity*) cervello, mente *f*, testa; **to go out of** *or* **lose one's mind** impazzire, perdere la testa; **to be out of one's mind** essere pazzo(-a), essere uscito(-a) di senno, essere fuori di sé.

2 VT **a** (*pay attention to, be careful of*) fare attenzione a, stare attento(-a) a; **never mind** (*don't worry*) non preoccuparti; (*it makes no difference*) non importa, non fa niente; **"please mind the step"** "attenti *or* attenzione al gradino"; **mind you don't fall** attento a non cadere; **mind your language!** bada a come parli!, controlla le tue parole!; **mind you, ...** (*fam*) sì, però va detto che...; **mind your own business!** (*fam*) fatti gli affari tuoi!; **never mind him** non badargli, non fargli caso; **never mind the expense** se costa caro, pazienza!; **don't mind me!** (*iro*) per carità, non fare caso a me!

b (*attend to, look after: shop, machine, children*) occuparsi di, badare a

c (*be put out by, object to*): **I don't mind what he does** non m'importa cosa fa; **which? — I don't mind** quale? — è indifferente; **I don't mind the cold/noise** il freddo/rumore non mi dà noia *or* fastidio; **would you mind opening the door?** le dispiace aprire la porta?; **do you mind if I open the window? — I don't mind** le dispiace se apro la finestra? — faccia pure!; **I wouldn't mind a cup of tea** prenderei volentieri una tazza di tè.

♦ **mind-blowing** ['maɪndˌbləʊɪŋ] ADJ (*fam*) allucinante, che fa sballare.

♦ **mind-boggling** ['maɪndˌbɒglɪŋ] ADJ (*fam*) inconcepibile, incredibile.

mind·ed ['maɪndɪd] ADJ (*frm*): **to be minded to do sth** essere intenzionato(-a) a fare qc.

-minded ['maɪndɪd] ADJ SUFF: **fair-minded** imparziale; **an industrially-minded nation** una nazione orientata verso l'industria.

mind·er ['maɪndəʳ] N (*Brit*: *child minder*) bambinaia; (*: bodyguard*) guardia del corpo.

mind·ful ['maɪndfʊl] ADJ: **mindful of** conscio(-a) *or* consapevole di, attento(-a) a, memore di.

mind·less ['maɪndlɪs] ADJ (*violence, crime*) insensato(-a); (*task*) che non richiede nessuna intelligenza, idiota.

♦ **mind-reader** ['maɪndˌriːdəʳ] N chi legge nel pensiero; **you must be a mind-reader!** mi devi aver letto nel pensiero!

mine[1] [maɪn] POSS PRON il/la mio(-a), PL i/le miei/mie; **a friend of mine** un mio amico; **his is red, mine is green** il suo è rosso, il mio è verde; **this is mine** questo è (il) mio; **this book is mine** questo libro è mio.

mine[2] [maɪn] **1** N **a** (*pit*) miniera; **to work down the mines** lavorare in miniera; **a mine of information** (*fig*) una miniera di informazioni **b** (*explosive*) mina; **to lay mines** posare delle mine.

2 VT **a** (*coal, metal*) estrarre **b** (*Mil, Naut*) minare.

3 VI fare degli scavi minerari; **to mine for sth** estrarre qc.

♦ **mine detector** N rivelatore *m* di mine.

♦ **mine disposal** N disinnesco di mine.

mine·field ['maɪn̩fiːld] N (*also fig*) campo minato.

mine·layer ['maɪnˌleɪə'] N posamine *m or f inv*.

min·er ['maɪnə'] N minatore *m*.

min·er·al ['mɪnərəl] [1] ADJ (*substance, kingdom*) minerale; (*wealth, deposits, ore*) minerario(-a); **mineral salts** sali *mpl* minerali.

[2] N minerale *m*; (*Brit: soft drink*): **minerals** NPL bevande *fpl* gasate.

min·er·al·ogic [ˌmɪnərə'lɒdʒɪk], **min·er·al·ogical** [ˌmɪnərə'lɒdʒɪkl] ADJ mineralogico(-a).

min·er·alo·gist [ˌmɪnə'rælədʒɪst] N mineralogista *m/f*.

min·er·al·ogy [ˌmɪnə'rælədʒɪ] N mineralogia.

♦ **mineral water** N acqua minerale.

Minerva [mɪ'nɜːvə] N Minerva.

mine·sweeper ['maɪnˌswiːpə'] N dragamine *m inv*.

♦ **mine sweep·ing** ['maɪnˌswiːpɪŋ] N dragaggio di mine.

min·gle ['mɪŋgl] [1] VT: **to mingle (with)** mescolare *or* mischiare (a *or* con).

[2] VI: **to mingle (with)** (*sounds*) mescolarsi *or* mischiarsi (a *or* con); **to mingle with one's guests** mescolarsi agli ospiti.

min·gy ['mɪndʒɪ] ADJ (*Brit fam: person*) tirchio(-a), spilorcio (-a); (: *share, portion, amount*) misero(-a), scarso(-a).

mini ['mɪnɪ] N (*also:* **miniskirt**) mini *f inv*.

mini... ['mɪnɪ] PREF mini... .

minia·ture ['mɪnɪtʃə'] [1] N miniatura; **in miniature** in miniatura.

[2] ADJ (*gen*) in miniatura; (*poodle*) nano(-a).

minia·tur·ist ['mɪnɪtʃərɪst] N miniaturista *m/f*.

minia·turi·za·tion [ˌmɪnɪtʃəraɪ'zeɪʃən] N miniaturizzazione *f*.

minia·tur·ize ['mɪnɪtʃəˌraɪz] VT miniaturizzare.

minia·tur·iz·ed ['mɪnɪtʃəˌraɪzd] ADJ miniaturizzato(-a).

mini·bus ['mɪnɪˌbʌs] N minibus *m inv*, pulmino.

mini·cab ['mɪnɪˌkæb] N (*Brit*) ≈ taxi *m inv*.

mini·com·put·er [ˌmɪnɪkəm'pjuːtə'] N minielaboratore *m*, minicomputer *m inv*.

min·im ['mɪnɪm] N (*Brit: Mus*) minima.

mini·ma ['mɪnɪmə] NPL of **minimum**.

mini·mal ['mɪnɪməl] ADJ minimo(-a).

mini·mal·ist ['mɪnɪməlɪst] ADJ, N minimalista *(m/f)*.

mini·market ['mɪnɪˌmɑːkɪt] N minimarket *m inv*.

mini·mize ['mɪnɪˌmaɪz] VT minimizzare.

mini·mum ['mɪnɪməm] [1] N (*pl* **minimums** *or* **minima**) minimo; **he does the minimum of work** lavora il meno possibile *or* il minimo indispensabile; **to reduce to a minimum** ridurre al minimo.

[2] ADJ minimo(-a); **the minimum temperature** la (temperatura) minima; **minimum wage** salario minimo garantito.

♦ **minimum lending rate** N (*Brit*) ≈ tasso ufficiale di sconto.

min·ing ['maɪnɪŋ] [1] N **a** estrazione *f* mineraria, industria mineraria **b** (*Mil, Naut*) posa di mine.

[2] ADJ (*industry, engineer, area*) minerario(-a); (*community, family*) di minatori.

minion ['mɪnjən] N (*pej*) galoppino.

♦ **mini–series** ['mɪnɪˌsɪəriːz] NSG miniserie *f sg*.

♦ **mini–ski** ['mɪnɪˌskiː] N minisci *m inv*.

mini·skirt ['mɪnɪˌskɜːt] N minigonna.

min·is·ter ['mɪnɪstə'] [1] N (*Brit Pol*) ministro; (*Rel*) pastore *m*; **Minister for Defence** Ministro della Difesa.

[2] VI: **to minister to** (*sick person*) assistere; **to minister to sb's needs** provvedere ai bisogni di qn; **ministering**

angel (*fig*) angelo del paradiso.

min·is·terial [ˌmɪnɪs'tɪərɪəl] ADJ (*Brit Pol*) ministeriale.

mini·stra·tions [ˌmɪnɪ'streɪʃənz] NPL assistenza, cure *fpl*.

min·is·try ['mɪnɪstrɪ] N **a** (*Brit Pol*) ministero; **Ministry of Defence** Ministero della Difesa **b** (*Rel*): **the ministry** il ministero sacerdotale; **to go into** *or* **enter the ministry** diventare sacerdote (*or* pastore).

mink [mɪŋk] N visone *m*; **European mink** lutreola.

♦ **mink coat** N pelliccia di visone.

min·now ['mɪnəʊ] N *pesciolino d'acqua dolce*.

mi·nor ['maɪnə'] [1] ADJ (*also Math, Mus*) minore; (*detail, role*) secondario(-a), di poca importanza; (*importance*) secondario(-a); (*repairs, operation, expense*) piccolo(-a).

[2] N **a** (*Law*) minore *m/f*, minorenne *m/f* **b** (*Am Univ*) materia complementare.

Mi·nor·ca [mɪ'nɔːkə] N Minorca.

mi·nor·ity [maɪ'nɒrɪtɪ] [1] N minoranza; **to be in a minority** essere in minoranza.

[2] ADJ (*verdict*) minoritario(-a); (*government*) di minoranza.

Minos ['maɪnɒs] N Minosse *m*.

Minotaur ['maɪnətɔː'] N Minotauro.

min·ster ['mɪnstə'] N (*Brit*) cattedrale *f* (*annessa a monastero*).

min·strel ['mɪnstrəl] N giullare *m*, menestrello.

mint¹ [mɪnt] [1] N (*Fin*) zecca; **to be worth a mint (of money)** valere un patrimonio; **the (Royal) Mint** (*Brit*), **the (US) Mint** (*Am*) la Zecca.

[2] ADJ: **in mint condition** in perfette condizioni, che sembra nuovo(-a) di zecca.

[3] VT (*coins*) battere, coniare; **he's minting money** (*fig*) sta facendo soldi a palate.

mint² [mɪnt] [1] N (*plant*) menta; (*sweet*) mentina, caramella di menta.

[2] ADJ alla menta.

mint·ing ['mɪntɪŋ] N coniazione *f*.

♦ **mint sauce** N salsa di menta.

minu·et [ˌmɪnjʊ'ɛt] N minuetto.

mi·nus ['maɪnəs] [1] PREP (*Math*) meno; (*fam: without*) senza.

[2] ADJ: **minus quantity** (*Math*) quantità *f inv* negativa; **minus sign** (segno) meno *inv*.

[3] N (segno) meno *inv*.

mi·nus·cule ['mɪnəskjuːl] ADJ piccolissimo(-a), minuscolo (-a).

min·ute¹ ['mɪnɪt] [1] N **a** (*of time*) minuto; (*of degree*) minuto, primo; **it is 5 minutes past 3** sono le 3 e 5 (minuti); **I'll come in a minute** vengo subito *or* tra un attimo; **wait a minute!** (aspetta) un momento!; **come here this minute!** vieni subito!; **I won't be a minute** vengo (*or* torno) subito; (*I've nearly finished*) faccio subito; **at the last minute** all'ultimo momento; **at that minute the phone rang** in quel (preciso) istante suonò il telefono; **tell me the minute he arrives** (non) appena arriva dimmelo; **up to the minute** (*fashions, news*) ultimissimo; (*equipment*) modernissimo

b: **minutes** NPL (*of meeting*) verbale *m*, verbali *mpl*; **to take the minutes of a meeting** redigere i verbali di una riunione.

min·ute² [maɪ'njuːt] ADJ (*small*) minuscolo(-a); (: *change, improvement*) piccolissimo(-a); (*detailed, exact*) minuzioso(-a); **in minute detail** minuziosamente.

♦ **minute book** ['mɪnɪtˌbʊk] N libro dei verbali.

♦ **minute hand** ['mɪnɪtˌhænd] N lancetta dei minuti.

mi·nute·ly [maɪ'njuːtlɪ] ADV (*by a small amount*) di poco; (*in*

detail) minuziosamente.

♦ **minute steak** [ˈmɪnɪtˌsteɪk] N fettina (di carne), paillard *f inv.*

mi·nu·tiae [mɪˈnjuːʃɪˌiː] NPL minuzie *fpl.*

mira·cle [ˈmɪrəkl] N (*also fig*) miracolo; **it's a miracle that ...** è un miracolo che... + *sub*; **by some miracle** per qualche miracolo; **to work miracles** (*also fig*) far miracoli.

♦ **miracle cure** N cura miracolosa.

♦ **miracle drug** N medicina miracolosa.

♦ **miracle play** N (*Theatre*) miracolo.

mi·racu·lous [mɪˈrækjʊləs] ADJ miracoloso(-a).

mi·racu·lous·ly [mɪˈrækjʊləslɪ] ADV miracolosamente.

mi·rage [ˈmɪrɑːʒ] N miraggio.

mire [maɪə] N pantano, melma.

mir·ror [ˈmɪrə*r*] **1** N specchio; (*Aut*) specchietto (retrovisore); **hand mirror** specchio a mano; **pocket mirror** specchietto da borsetta; **to look at o.s. in the mirror** guardarsi allo specchio. **2** VT riflettere, rispecchiare.

♦ **mirror image** N immagine *f* speculare.

mirth [mɜːθ] N ilarità *f inv*, gaiezza.

mirth·less [ˈmɜːθlɪs] ADJ (*smile, laugh*) mesto(-a).

mis·ad·ven·ture [ˌmɪsədˈventʃə*r*] N sfortuna, disavventura; **death by misadventure** (*Brit Law*) morte *f* accidentale.

mis·an·throp·ic [ˌmɪzənˈθrɒpɪk] ADJ misantropico(-a).

mis·an·thro·pist [mɪˈzænθrəpɪst] N misantropo(-a).

mis·an·thro·py [mɪˈzænθrəpɪ] N misantropia.

mis·ap·pli·ca·tion [ˌmɪsæplɪˈkeɪʃən] N (*of technique*) uso improprio; (*of resources*) cattivo uso.

mis·ap·ply [ˌmɪsəˈplaɪ] VT impiegare male, usare erroneamente.

mis·ap·pre·hen·sion [ˈmɪsˌæprɪˈhenʃən] N equivoco, malinteso; **to be (labouring) under a misapprehension** sbagliarsi.

mis·ap·pro·pri·ate [ˌmɪsəˈprəʊprɪˌeɪt] VT appropriarsi indebitamente di.

mis·ap·pro·pria·tion [ˈmɪsəˌprəʊprɪˈeɪʃən] N appropriazione *f* indebita.

mis·be·have [ˌmɪsbɪˈheɪv] VI comportarsi male.

mis·be·hav·iour, (*Am*) **mis·be·hav·ior** [ˌmɪsbɪˈheɪvjə*r*] N comportamento scorretto.

misc. ABBR = **miscellaneous**.

mis·cal·cu·late [ˌmɪsˈkælkjʊˌleɪt] VT, VI calcolare male.

mis·cal·cu·la·tion [ˈmɪsˌkælkjʊˈleɪʃən] N errore *m* di calcolo.

mis·car·riage [ˌmɪsˈkærɪdʒ] N **a** (*Med*) aborto spontaneo. **b** : **miscarriage of justice** (*fig*) errore *m* giudiziario.

mis·car·ry [ˌmɪsˈkærɪ] VI **a** (*Med*) abortire **b** (*fail: plans*) andare a monte, fallire.

mis·cast [ˌmɪsˈkɑːst] ADJ: **to be miscast** non essere adatto (-a) al ruolo.

mis·cel·la·neous [ˌmɪsəˈleɪnɪəs] ADJ (*items*) vario(-a), diverso(-a); (*collection*) misto(-a), eterogeneo(-a); **miscellaneous expenses** spese *fpl* varie.

mis·cel·la·ny [mɪˈselənɪ] N misto; (*Literature*) miscellanea, raccolta; (*Radio, TV*) selezione *f*.

mis·chance [ˌmɪsˈtʃɑːns] N: **by (some) mischance** per sfortuna.

mis·chief [ˈmɪstʃɪf] N (*roguishness*) furberia; (*naughtiness*) birichinate *fpl*; (*maliciousness*) cattiveria, malizia; (*harm*) male *m*, danno; **he's always getting into mischief** ne combina sempre una; **to keep sb out of mischief** tenere qn occupato(-a) così che non possa combinare guai; **full of mischief** birichino(-a); **to make mischief (for**

sb) rendere la vita difficile (a qn); **to make mischief between** seminare zizzania tra; **to do o.s. a mischief** (*Brit: hum*) farsi male.

♦ **mischief-maker** [ˈmɪstʃɪfˌmeɪkə*r*] N (*troublemaker*) chi semina discordia; (*gossip*) maldicente *m/f*.

mis·chie·vous [ˈmɪstʃɪvəs] ADJ (*roguish*) malizioso(-a); (: *child*) birichino(-a); (*harmful*) pieno(-a) di cattiveria; **mischievous rumours** (*troublemaking*) malignità *fpl*.

mis·chie·vous·ly [ˈmɪstʃɪvəslɪ] ADV (*roguishly*) maliziosamente; (*naughtily*) con aria birichina.

mis·chie·vous·ness [ˈmɪstʃɪvəsnɪs] N (*roguishness*) maliziosità *f inv*; (*naughtiness*) birbanteria.

mis·cible [ˈmɪsɪbəl] ADJ miscibile.

mis·con·ceived [ˌmɪskənˈsiːvd] ADJ (*plan*) sbagliato(-a).

mis·con·cep·tion [ˌmɪskənˈsepʃən] N (*false idea/opinion*) idea/convinzione *f* sbagliata; (*misunderstanding*) malinteso.

mis·con·duct [ˌmɪsˈkɒndʌkt] N cattiva condotta, comportamento scorretto; (*sexual*) adulterio; **professional misconduct** reato professionale.

mis·con·struc·tion [ˌmɪskənˈstrʌkʃən] N interpretazione errata *f*.

mis·con·strue [ˌmɪskənˈstruː] VT interpretare male.

mis·count [ˌmɪsˈkaʊnt] **1** N (*gen*) calcolo errato; (*in election*) conteggio erroneo. **2** VT contare male. **3** VI sbagliare il conto.

mis·deed [ˌmɪsˈdiːd] N (*old*) misfatto.

mis·de·mean·our, (*Am*) **mis·de·mean·or** [ˌmɪsdɪˈmiːnə*r*] N infrazione *f*, trasgressione *f*, misfatto.

mis·di·rect [ˌmɪsdɪˈrekt] VT (*letter*) mettere l'indirizzo sbagliato su; (*person*) dare indicazioni sbagliate a, mal indirizzare; (*operation*) organizzare male; (*Law: jury*) dare istruzioni sbagliate a.

mis·di·rect·ed [ˌmɪsdɪˈrektd] ADJ (*energies*) mal indirizzato(-a).

mi·ser [ˈmaɪzə*r*] N avaro(-a).

mis·er·able [ˈmɪzərəbl] ADJ **a** (*unhappy*) infelice; (*deplorable: sight, failure*) penoso(-a); **to feel miserable** sentirsi avvilito(-a) *or* giù di morale; (*physically*) sentirsi a terra; **don't look so miserable!** non fare quella faccia da funerale!
b (*filthy, wretched*) miserabile; (*unpleasant: weather*) deprimente
c (*contemptible*) miserabile; **a miserable £2** 2 miserabili sterline.

mis·er·ably [ˈmɪzərəblɪ] ADV (*smile, answer*) tristemente; (*fail, live, pay*) miseramente.

mi·ser·li·ness [ˈmaɪzəlɪnɪs] N taccagneria.

mi·ser·ly [ˈmaɪzəlɪ] ADJ taccagno(-a), avaro(-a).

mis·ery [ˈmɪzərɪ] N (*unhappiness*) tristezza; (*pain*) sofferenza, tormento, dolore *m*; (*wretchedness*) miseria; (*fam: person*) lagna; **to put an animal out of its misery** uccidere un animale (per non farlo soffrire più); **to put sb out of his misery** (*fig*) mettere fine alle sofferenze di qn; **to make sb's life a misery** rovinare la vita a qn.

mis·fire [ˌmɪsˈfaɪə*r*] VI (*gun, plan, joke*) far cilecca; (*engine*) perdere colpi.

mis·fit [ˈmɪsˌfɪt] N (*person*) disadattato(-a), spostato(-a).

mis·for·tune [mɪsˈfɔːtʃən] N disgrazia, sventura, sfortuna; **she has the misfortune to be blind** ha la sventura di essere cieca; **that's YOUR misfortune!** peggio per te!

mis·giv·ing [mɪsˈgɪvɪŋ] N (*often pl*) diffidenza, apprensione *f*, dubbi *mpl*, sospetti *mpl*; **to have misgivings about sth** essere diffidente verso qc, avere dei dubbi su qc.

mis·guid·ed [ˌmɪsˈgaɪdɪd] ADJ (*person*) malaccorto(-a); (*conduct, belief*) poco assennato(-a).

mis·guid·ed·ly [ˌmɪsˈgaɪdɪdlɪ] ADV (*attempt, try*) malaccortamente; (*believe, think*) in modo poco assennato.

mis·han·dle [ˌmɪsˈhændl] VT (*object*) maneggiare senza precauzioni; (*person*) non prendere per il verso giusto; (*mismanage*) condurre male; **he mishandled the whole situation** ha sbagliato tutto.

mis·hap [ˈmɪsˌhæp] N incidente *m*; **without mishap** senza incidenti.

mis·hear [ˈmɪsˈhɪəʳ] (*pt, pp* misheard) VT, VI capire male.

mish·mash [ˈmɪʃˌmæʃ] N (*fam*) minestrone *m*, guazzabuglio.

mis·in·form [ˌmɪsɪnˈfɔːm] VT informare male, dare informazioni erronee.

mis·in·for·ma·tion [ˌmɪsɪnfəˈmeɪʃən] N disinformazione *f*.

mis·in·ter·pret [ˌmɪsɪnˈtɜːprɪt] VT interpretare male.

mis·in·ter·pre·ta·tion [ˈmɪsɪnˌtɜːprɪˈteɪʃən] N interpretazione errata *f*; **open to misinterpretation** che dà adito ad un'interpretazione errata.

mis·judge [ˌmɪsˈdʒʌdʒ] VT (*distance, amount*) calcolare male; (*person*) giudicare male.

mis·judge·ment, **mis·judg·ment** [ˌmɪsˈdʒʌdʒmənt] N errore *m* di valutazione.

mis·lay [ˌmɪsˈleɪ] (*pt, pp* mislaid) VT smarrire.

mis·lead [ˌmɪsˈliːd] (*pt, pp* misled) VT trarre in inganno, sviare; **to mislead sb into thinking that ...** far credere a qn che..., indurre qn a credere che... .

mis·lead·ing [ˌmɪsˈliːdɪŋ] ADJ ingannevole, fuorviante.

mis·led [mɪsˈlɛd] PT, PP of **mislead**.

mis·man·age [ˌmɪsˈmænɪdʒ] VT amministrare *or* gestire *or* condurre male.

mis·man·age·ment [ˌmɪsˈmænɪdʒmənt] N cattiva amministrazione *for* gestione *f*.

mis·no·mer [ˌmɪsˈnəʊməʳ] N: **to call her a cook is a misnomer** non si può certo definirla una cuoca.

mi·sogy·nist [mɪˈsɒdʒɪnɪst] N misogino.

mis·place [ˌmɪsˈpleɪs] VT **a** (*mislay*) smarrire **b**: **to be misplaced** (*trust*) essere malriposto(-a).

mis·print [ˈmɪsˌprɪnt] N errore *m* di stampa, refuso.

mis·pro·nounce [ˌmɪsprəˈnaʊns] VT pronunciare male.

mis·pro·nun·ci·a·tion [ˈmɪsprəˌnʌnsɪˈeɪʃən] N pronuncia errata; **a mispronounciation** un errore di pronuncia.

mis·quo·ta·tion [ˌmɪskwəʊˈteɪʃən] N citazione *f* errata.

mis·quote [ˌmɪsˈkwəʊt] VT citare erroneamente.

mis·read [ˌmɪsˈriːd] (*pt, pp* misread) VT leggere male; (*misinterpret*) interpretare male.

mis·rep·re·sent [ˈmɪsˌrɛprɪˈzɛnt] VT (*facts*) travisare; (*person*) dare un'impressione sbagliata di.

miss¹ [mɪs] **1** N (*shot*) colpo mancato *or* a vuoto; **it was a near miss** (*fig*) c'è mancato poco *or* un pelo; **to give sth a miss** (*fam*) lasciar perdere qc.
2 VT **a** (*gen: train, opportunity, film*) perdere; (*appointment, class*) mancare a, saltare; (*target*) mancare; (*remark: not hear*) non sentire; (: *not understand*) non capire; (*omit: meal, page*) saltare; **you haven't missed much!** non hai perso molto!; **I missed you at the station** non ti ho visto alla stazione; **to miss the boat** *or* **bus** (*fig*) perdere il treno, lasciarsi sfuggire (di mano) l'occasione; **we must have missed the sign for London** ci dev'essere sfuggito il cartello per Londra; **you can't miss our house, it's ...** non puoi sbagliarti: la nostra casa è...; **don't miss this film** non perderti questo film; **I missed what you said** mi è sfuggito quello che hai detto;

you're missing the point non capisci
b (*escape or avoid: accident, bad weather*) evitare, scampare; **the bus just missed the wall** l'autobus per un pelo non è andato a finire contro il muro; **he narrowly missed being run over** per poco non è stato investito
c (*notice loss of: money*) accorgersi di non avere più; **then I missed my wallet** allora mi sono accorto che mi mancava *or* che non avevo più il portafoglio
d (*regret the absence of: person*): **I miss you so** mi manchi tanto; **I miss him/it** sento la sua mancanza, mi manca; **do you miss Trieste?** senti la mancanza di *or* ti manca Trieste?.
3 VI (*person, shot*) mancare il bersaglio; **you can't miss!** non puoi fallire!

▶ **miss out** VT + ADV (*Brit*) saltare, omettere

▶ **miss out on** VI + ADV + PREP (*fun, party*) perdersi; (*chance, bargain*) lasciarsi sfuggire; **I feel I've been missing out on life** sento di non aver goduto la vita come avrei potuto.

miss² [mɪs] N **a** signorina; **the modern miss** la ragazza moderna **b** : **Miss Smith** la signorina Smith; (*on envelope*) Sig.na Smith; (*in letter*): **Dear Miss Smith** Cara Signorina Smith; (*more frm*) Gentile Signorina Smith; **Miss World 1994** Miss Mondo 1994.

mis·sal [ˈmɪsəl] N messale *m*.

mis·shap·en [ˌmɪsˈʃeɪpən] ADJ deforme.

mis·sile [ˈmɪsaɪl] N (*Mil*) missile *m*; (*frm: projectile*) proiettile *m*.

♦ **missile base** N base *f* missilistica.

♦ **mis·sile launch·er** [ˈmɪsaɪlˌlɔːntʃəʳ] N lanciamissili *m inv*.

mis·sing [ˈmɪsɪŋ] ADJ (*not able to be found*) smarrito(-a), perso(-a); (*not there*) mancante; (*person: also Mil*) disperso(-a); **to be missing** mancare; **to go missing** sparire; **there are several books missing** mancano diversi libri; **the missing link** l'anello mancante; **missing in action** (*Mil*) disperso(-a); **missing person** disperso (-a), scomparso(-a); **reported missing** (*Mil*) dato(-a) per disperso.

mis·sion [ˈmɪʃən] N (*all senses*) missione *f*; **on a mission to sb** in missione da qn; **it's her mission in life** è la sua missione nella vita.

mis·sion·ary [ˈmɪʃənrɪ] N (*Rel*) missionario(-a).

Mis·sis·sip·pi [ˌmɪsɪˈsɪpɪ] N (*state*) Mississippi *m*; (*river*): **the Mississippi** il Mississippi.

mis·sive [ˈmɪsɪv] N (*old*) missiva.

mis·spell [ˌmɪsˈspɛl] (*pt, pp* misspelled *or* misspelt) VT sbagliare l'ortografia di.

mis·spell·ing [ˌmɪsˈspɛlɪŋ] N errore *m* di ortografia.

mis·spent [ˈmɪsˌspɛnt] ADJ: **his misspent youth** la sua gioventù dissoluta.

mis·sus [ˈmɪsɪz] N (*fam*) **a** : **the missus** (*wife*) mia moglie; **how's your missus?** come sta tua moglie? **b** (*Brit: term of addresss*) signora.

mist [mɪst] **1** N (*Met*) foschia, nebbia, nebbiolina; (*on glass*) appannamento; (*of perfume*) nuvola; **through a mist of tears** attraverso un velo di lacrime; **lost in the mists of time** (*fig*) perduto nella notte dei tempi.
2 VI (*also: mist over: eyes*) velarsi; (*also: mist over or up: scene, landscape*) annebbiarsi, offuscarsi; (: *mirror, window, windscreen*) appannarsi.

mis·take [mɪsˈteɪk] (*vb: pt mistook, pp mistaken*) **1** N errore *m*, sbaglio; **to make a mistake** (*in writing, calculating*) fare uno sbaglio *or* un errore; **to make a mistake (about sb/sth)** sbagliarsi (sul conto di qn/su qc); **my mistake!** è colpa mia!; **you're making a big mistake** commetti un grosso *or* grave errore; **I made the mistake**

of trusting him ho fatto l'errore di fidarmi di lui; **by mistake** per sbaglio; **he took my hat in mistake for his** ha preso il mio cappello credendo fosse il suo; **there must be some mistake** ci dev'essere un errore; **make no mistake (about it)** non aver paura, sta' tranquillo; **she's pretty and no mistake** (*fam*) è proprio una bella ragazza.

2 VT (*meaning, remark*) capir male, fraintendere; (*road*) sbagliare; (*time*) sbagliarsi su; **to mistake A for B** prendere *or* scambiare A per B.

mis·tak·en [mɪs'teɪkən] 1 PP of **mistake**.

2 ADJ (*wrong: idea, conclusion*) sbagliato(-a), errato(-a); (*misplaced: loyalty, generosity*) malriposto(-a); **in the mistaken belief that …** credendo erroneamente che…; **to be mistaken** sbagliarsi; **if I'm not mistaken** se non sbaglio.

♦ **mistaken identity** N errore *m* di persona.

mis·tak·en·ly [mɪs'teɪkənlɪ] ADV (*believe*) erroneamente; (*by mistake*) per errore.

mis·ter ['mɪstə'] N (*fam*) signore *m*; see also **Mr.**

mis·time [ˌmɪs'taɪm] VT (*action, blow*) calcolare male; **to mistime one's arrival** (*arrive inopportunely*) arrivare al momento sbagliato; (*miscalculate time*) sbagliarsi su *or* calcolare male il proprio orario d'arrivo; **the government mistimed its announcement** il governo ha emesso il comunicato al momento sbagliato; **a mistimed remark** un'osservazione poco opportuna.

mis·tle thrush ['mɪsl̩ˌθrʌʃ] N tordela.

mis·tle·toe ['mɪsl̩ˌtəʊ] N vischio.

mis·took [mɪs'tʊk] PT of **mistake**.

mis·tral ['mɪstrəl] N: **the mistral** il mistral.

mis·trans·late [ˌmɪstræns'leɪt] VT tradurre in modo sbagliato.

mis·trans·la·tion [ˌmɪstrænz'leɪʃən] N errore *m* di traduzione, traduzione *f* errata.

mis·treat [ˌmɪs'triːt] VT maltrattare, trattare male.

mis·tress ['mɪstrɪs] N a (*of servant*) padrona; **the mistress of the house** la padrona di casa b (*lover*) amante *f* c (*Brit Scol: teacher*) insegnante *f.*

mis·trust [ˌmɪs'trʌst] 1 N: **mistrust (of)** diffidenza (nei confronti di).

2 VT (*person, motives*) diffidare di; (*one's own abilities*) dubitare di.

mis·trust·ful [mɪs'trʌstfʊl] ADJ: **mistrustful (of)** diffidente (nei confronti di).

mis·trust·ful·ly [mɪs'trʌstfəlɪ] ADV con diffidenza.

misty ['mɪstɪ] ADJ (*comp* **-ier**, *superl* **-iest**) (*day, morning*) brumoso(-a), nebbioso(-a); (*mirror, window*) appannato(-a); **it's misty today** c'è foschia oggi.

♦ **misty-eyed** [ˌmɪstɪ'aɪd] ADJ trasognato(-a).

mis·under·stand [ˌmɪsʌndə'stænd] (*pt, pp* **misunderstood**) VT fraintendere, capire male.

mis·under·stand·ing [ˌmɪsʌndə'stændɪŋ] N malinteso, equivoco.

mis·under·stood [ˌmɪsʌndə'stʊd] 1 PT, PP of **misunderstand**.

2 ADJ incompreso(-a).

mis·use [*n* ˌmɪs'juːs; *vb* ˌmɪs'juːz] 1 N (*of power, authority*) abuso; (*of word, tool*) uso improprio; (*of resources, time, energies*) cattivo uso.

2 VT (*see n*) abusare di; usare impropriamente; fare cattivo uso di.

MIT [ˌɛmaɪ'tiː] N ABBR (*Am*)= *Massachusetts Institute of Technology.*

mite [maɪt] N a (*small quantity*) briciolo; **the widow's mite**

(*Bible*) l'obolo della vedova b (*Brit: small child*): **poor mite!** povera creaturina! c (*Zool*) acaro.

mi·ter ['maɪtə'] N (*Am*) = **mitre.**

miti·gate ['mɪtɪˌgeɪt] VT (*punishment*) mitigare; (*suffering*) alleviare.

miti·gat·ing cir·cum·stances ['mɪtɪˌgeɪtɪŋˈsɜːkəmstənsɪz] NPL circostanze *fpl* attenuanti.

miti·ga·tion [ˌmɪtɪ'geɪʃən] N (*see vb*) mitigazione *f;* alleviamento.

mi·to·sis [maɪ'təʊsɪs] N (*Bio*) mitosi *f.*

mi·tral ['maɪtrəl] ADJ (*Anat*) mitralico(-a); **mitral valve** valvola mitrale.

mi·tre, (*Am*) **mi·ter** ['maɪtə'] N a (*Rel*) mitra b (*Tech: also:* **mitre joint**) giunto ad angolo retto.

mitt [mɪt] N a (*also: mitten: with cut-off fingers*) mezzo guanto; (*: no separate fingers*) muffola, manopola b (*baseball glove*) guantone *m.*

mix [mɪks] 1 N mescolanza; **the school has a good social mix** gli studenti di questa scuola provengono da diverse classi sociali.

2 VT mescolare; (*cocktail, sauce*) preparare (mescolando); **mix to a smooth paste** mescolare fino ad ottenere una pasta omogenea; **to mix sth with sth** mischiare qc a qc; **to mix business with pleasure** unire l'utile al dilettevole.

3 VI mescolarsi; **he doesn't mix well** non riesce a legare; **he mixes with all sorts of people** ha a che fare con persone di ogni tipo; **they just don't mix** (*people*) non legano fra di loro; (*patterns*) non stanno bene insieme

▶ **mix in** VT + ADV (*eggs*) incorporare

▶ **mix together** VT + ADV mescolare

▶ **mix up** VT + ADV a (*prepare: drink, medicine*) preparare b (*get in a muddle: documents*) confondere, mescolare; (*confuse*): **to mix sb/sth up (with)** scambiare qn/qc (per) c : **to mix sb up in sth** (*involve*) coinvolgere *or* immischiare qn in qc; **to be mixed up in sth** essere coinvolto(-a) in qc; **she got herself mixed up with some shady characters** ha avuto a che fare con dei tipi loschi.

mixed [mɪkst] ADJ (*biscuits, nuts*) assortito(-a); (*school*) misto(-a); **in mixed company** in presenza di persone di entrambi i sessi; **we had mixed weather** il tempo è stato un po' bello e un po' brutto; **I have mixed feelings** sono combattuto; **the announcement got a mixed reception** non tutti hanno accolto favorevolmente l'annuncio; **mixed metaphor** metafora che non sta in piedi.

♦ **mixed-ability** [ˌmɪkstə'bɪlɪtɪ] ADJ (*class, teaching*) alunni di capacità diverse.

♦ **mixed bag** N miscuglio, accozzaglia; **it's a mixed bag** (*fig fam*) c'è un po' di tutto.

♦ **mixed blessing** N: **it's a mixed blessing** è una cosa buona che ha il suo risvolto negativo.

♦ **mixed doubles** NPL (*Sport*) doppio misto.

♦ **mixed economy** N economia mista.

♦ **mixed farming** N agricoltura e allevamento di bestiame insieme.

♦ **mixed grill** N (*Brit*) grigliata mista.

♦ **mixed marriage** N matrimonio misto.

♦ **mixed-up** [ˌmɪkst'ʌp] ADJ (*person, ideas*) confuso(-a); (*papers*) mescolato(-a), in disordine; **I'm all mixed-up** sono disorientato.

mix·er ['mɪksə'] N a (*for food: electric*) frullatore *m*, mixer *m inv*; (*: hand*) frullino b (*person*): **he's a good mixer** è molto socievole.

♦ **mixer tap** N (*Brit*) miscelatore *m.*

♦ **mix·ing bowl** ['mɪksɪŋˌbəʊl] N terrina.

mix·ture ['mɪkstʃəʳ] N mistura, miscuglio, mescolanza; (*Med*) sciroppo; (*blend*: *of tobacco*) miscela.

♦ **mix-up** ['mɪks'ʌp] N (*fam*) confusione *f*.

MK [ˌɛm'keɪ] ABBR (*Brit Tech*) = **mark¹ 1** d.

mk ABBR = **mark²**.

mkt ABBR = **market**.

MLitt ['ɛm'lɪt] N ABBR (= *Master of Literature, Master of Letters*) Master *m* in Lettere.

MLR [ˌɛmɛl'ɑː'] N ABBR (*Brit Fin*: = *minimum lending rate*) TUS *m* (= *tasso ufficiale di sconto*).

mm ABBR (= *millimetre*) mm.

MN [ˌɛm'ɛn] N ABBR a (*Brit*) = **Merchant Navy** b (*Am Post*)= Minnesota.

MO [ˌɛm'əʊ] 1 N ABBR a (*Brit*)= *medical officer* b (*fam*: = *modus operandi*) modo d'agire.

 2 ABBR (*Am Post*)= Missouri.

m.o. [ˌɛm'əʊ] N ABBR = **money order**.

moan [məʊn] 1 N (*gen*) gemito, lamento; (*complaint*) lamentela, lagna.

 2 VI (*gen*) gemere; **to moan (about)** (*fam*: *complain*) lamentarsi (di).

moan·er ['məʊnəʳ] N (*fam*) brontolone(-a).

moan·ing ['məʊnɪŋ] N gemiti *mpl*, lamenti *mpl*.

moat [məʊt] N fossato.

mob [mɒb] 1 N (*of people*) folla, massa; (*disorderly*) calca; (*rioting, violent*) folla inferocita; (*fam*: *criminal gang*) cricca, banda; **the mob** (*pej*: *Mafia*) la Mafia; (: *rabble*) la plebaglia.

 2 VT (*person*) assalire, accalcarsi intorno a; (*place*) prendere d'assalto, accalcarsi intorno a.

mob·cap ['mɒbˌkæp] N cuffia (*da donna*) con pizzi.

mo·bile ['məʊbaɪl] 1 ADJ (*gen*) mobile; **the old man is no longer mobile** il vecchio non può più muoversi; **are you mobile today?** hai un mezzo oggi?; **applicants must be mobile** (*Brit*) i candidati devono essere disposti a viaggiare; **mobile studio** (*Radio, TV*) studio mobile.

 2 N (*Art*) mobile *m inv*.

♦ **mobile home** N grande roulotte *f inv* (*utilizzata come domicilio*).

♦ **mobile library** N (*Brit*) biblioteca ambulante.

♦ **mobile phone** N telefonino.

♦ **mobile shop** N (*Brit*) negozio ambulante.

♦ **mobile unit** N unità *f inv* mobile.

mo·bil·ity [məʊ'bɪlɪtɪ] N mobilità *f inv*; (*of applicant*) disponibilità *f inv* a viaggiare.

♦ **mobility allowance** N *indennità che i portatori di handicap in Gran Bretagna ricevono dallo stato come rimborso alle spese sostenute per spostarsi o viaggiare.*

mo·bi·li·za·tion [ˌməʊbɪlaɪ'zeɪʃən] N mobilitazione *f*.

mo·bi·lize ['məʊbɪˌlaɪz] 1 VT mobilitare.

 2 VI mobilitarsi.

mob·ster ['mɒbstəʳ] N (*Am*) gangster *m inv*.

moc·ca·sin ['mɒkəsɪn] N mocassino.

mock [mɒk] 1 ADJ (*gen*) finto(-a), falso(-a); (*battle, exams*) simulato(-a); **mock Tudor** in stile Tudor.

 2 VT (*ridicule*: *person*) canzonare, deridere, farsi beffe di; (: *plan, efforts*) ridicolizzare, farsi beffe di; (*mimic*) scimmiottare.

 3 VI: **to mock at** farsi beffe di

▶ **mock up** VT + ADV costruire un modello di.

mock·er ['mɒkəʳ] N chi prende in giro.

mock·ery ['mɒkərɪ] N (*derision*) scherno, derisione *f*; **it was a mockery of a trial** il processo è stato tutto una farsa; **to make a mockery of** rendere ridicolo(-a).

mock·ing ['mɒkɪŋ] ADJ (*gen*) beffardo(-a), derisorio(-a), di scherno.

mocking·bird ['mɒkɪŋˌbɜːd] N mimo (*uccello*).

mock·ing·ly ['mɒkɪŋlɪ] ADV (*smile*) beffardamente; (*speak*) con tono di scherno.

♦ **mock turtle soup** N *zuppa di testina di vitello, a imitazione della zuppa di tartaruga.*

♦ **mock-up** ['mɒkˌʌp] N modello dimostrativo, abbozzo.

MOD [ˌɛməʊ'diː] N ABBR: **the MOD** (*Brit*) = **Ministry of Defence**; see **defence**.

mod [mɒd] N (*fam*: *person*) mod *inv*.

mod·al ['məʊdl] ADJ modale.

mod cons [ˌmɒd'kɒnz] NPL ABBR = *modern conveniences*; **all mod cons** (*fam*) tutti i comfort.

mode [məʊd] N a (*gen*) modo, maniera; (*of transport*) mezzo; (*Mus*) modo; (*Comput*) modalità *f inv* b (*fashion, Math*) moda.

mod·el ['mɒdl] 1 N (*gen, fig, Archit*) modello; (*small-scale*) modellino; (*also*: **fashion model**) indossatore(-trice), modello(-a); (*also*: **artist's model**) modello(-a); **male model** indossatore, modello; **4-door model** (*of car*) versione *f* 4 porte.

 2 VT a: **to model sth on** modellare qc su; **to model sb on** prendere a modello per qn; **to model o.s. on sb** prendere a modello qn

 b (*make a model*: *in clay*) modellare, plasmare; (: *in wood*) scolpire

 c (*clothes*) indossare.

 3 VI (*Art, Phot*) fare da modello(-a), posare; (*fashion*) sfilare, fare l'indossatore(-trice) *or* il/la modello(-a).

 4 ADJ a (*small-scale*: *village, aircraft*) in miniatura b (*prison, school, husband*) modello *inv*.

♦ **model car** N modellino di auto.

mod·el·ling, (*Am*) **mod·el·ing** ['mɒdlɪŋ] N a (*Fashion*) professione *f* d'indossatore(-trice) *or* modello(-a) b (*Sculpture*) modellamento.

♦ **modelling clay** N creta per modellare.

♦ **model railway** N modellino di ferrovia.

mo·dem ['məʊdɛm] N modem *m inv*.

mod·er·ate [*adj* 'mɒdərɪt; *vb* 'mɒdəˌreɪt] 1 ADJ (*gen*) moderato(-a); (*climate*) temperato(-a); (*size, income*) medio(-a); (*demands, price*) modico(-a), ragionevole; (*language, terms*) misurato(-a); (*quality, ability*) mediocre, modesto(-a).

 2 N (*Pol*) moderato(-a).

 3 VT moderare.

 4 VI (*pain, wind, anger*) calmarsi, attenuarsi, placarsi.

mod·er·ate·ly ['mɒdərɪtlɪ] ADV (*act*) con moderazione; (*expensive, difficult*) non troppo, moderatamente; (*pleased, happy*) abbastanza, discretamente; **moderately priced** a prezzo modico; **it was moderately successful** ha avuto un discreto successo.

mod·era·tion [ˌmɒdə'reɪʃən] N moderazione *f*, misura; **in moderation** (*eat, drink*) in quantità moderata, con moderazione.

moderator ['mɒdəˌreɪtəʳ] N (*gen*) moderatore(-trice); (*Rel*) *moderatore in importanti riunioni della chiesa presbiteriana.*

mod·ern ['mɒdən] ADJ moderno(-a); **all modern conveniences** tutti i comfort.

mod·ern·ism ['mɒdənɪzəm] N (*Art*) modernismo.

mo·der·nity [mɒ'dɜːnɪtɪ] N modernità *f inv*.

mod·erni·za·tion [ˌmɒdənaɪ'zeɪʃən] N rimodernamento, modernizzazione *f*.

mod·ern·ize ['mɒdəˌnaɪz] VT modernizzare.

♦ **modern languages** NPL lingue *fpl* moderne.

mod·est ['mɒdɪst] ADJ (*all senses*) modesto(-a); **to be modest about sth** non vantarsi di qc.

mod·est·ly ['mɒdɪstlɪ] ADV modestamente.

mod·es·ty ['mɒdɪstɪ] N modestia; **in all modesty** in tutta modestia.

modi·cum ['mɒdɪkəm] N: **a modicum of** un minimo di.

modi·fi·ca·tion [ˌmɒdɪfɪ'keɪʃən] N: **modification (to, in)** modifica (a); **to make modifications** fare *or* apportare delle modifiche.

modi·fi·er ['mɒdɪˌfaɪəʳ] N (*Gram*) modificatore *m*.

modi·fy ['mɒdɪˌfaɪ] VT (*change: also Gram*) modificare; (*moderate: demands*) moderare.

mod·ish ['məʊdɪʃ] ADJ (*liter*) à la page *inv*.

Mods [mɒdz] N ABBR (*Brit:* = (*Honour*) *Moderations*) *primo esame all'università di Oxford*.

modu·lar ['mɒdjʊləʳ] ADJ (*furniture, unit*) modulare.

modu·late ['mɒdjʊˌleɪt] VT modulare.

modu·la·tion [ˌmɒdjʊ'leɪʃən] N modulazione *f*.

mod·ule ['mɒdjuːl] N modulo.

modu·lus ['mɒdjʊləs] N (*Math, Phys*) modulo.

Moga·dishu [ˌmɒgə'dɪʃuː] N Mogadiscio *f*.

mog·gy, mog·gie ['mɒgɪ] N (*Brit*) micio.

mo·gul ['məʊgəl] N a (*fig*) magnate *m*, pezzo grosso b (*Skiing*) cunetta.

MOH [ˌɛməʊ'eɪtʃ] N ABBR (*Brit:* = *Medical Officer of Health*) ≈ ufficiale *m* sanitario.

mo·hair ['məʊˌhɛəʳ] N mohair *m*.

Mohammed [məʊ'hæmɪd] N Maometto.

Mo·ham·med·an [məʊ'hæmɪdən] ADJ, N maomettano (-a).

Mo·ham·med·an·ism [məʊ'hæmɪdəˌnɪzəm] N maomettismo.

moi·ré ['mwɑːreɪ] ADJ moiré *inv*, marezzato(-a).

moist [mɔɪst] ADJ (*comp* **-er**, *superl* **-est**) (*gen*) umido(-a); (*cake*) soffice; **eyes moist with tears** occhi umidi di lacrime.

mois·ten ['mɔɪsn] VT inumidire; **to moisten one's lips** umettarsi le labbra.

moist·ness ['mɔɪstnɪs] N (*see adj*) umidità *f inv*; sofficità *f inv*.

mois·ture ['mɔɪstʃəʳ] N (*gen*) umidità *f inv*; (*on glass*) vapore *m* condensato.

mois·tur·ize ['mɔɪstʃəˌraɪz] VT (*skin*) idratare.

mois·tur·iz·er ['mɔɪstʃəˌraɪzəʳ] N (prodotto) idratante *m*.

mo·lar ['məʊləʳ] ADJ, N molare (*m*).

mo·las·ses [məʊ'læsɪz] NSG melassa.

mold *etc* [məʊld] (*Am*) = **mould** *etc*.

Mol·da·via [ˌmɒl'deɪvɪə], **Mol·dova** [mɒl'dəʊvə] N la Moldavia.

Mol·da·vian [ˌmɒl'deɪvɪən], **Mol·dovan** [mɒl'dəʊvən] ADJ, N moldavo(-a).

mole[1] [məʊl] N (*Zool, fig*) talpa.

mole[2] [məʊl] N (*on skin*) neo.

mole[3] [məʊl] N (*Chem*) mole *f*.

mole[4] [məʊl] N (*breakwater*) frangiflutti *m inv*.

mo·lecu·lar [məʊ'lɛkjʊləʳ] ADJ molecolare.

mol·ecule ['mɒlɪkjuːl] N molecola.

mole·hill ['məʊlˌhɪl] N *cumulo di terra vicino alla tana scavata da una talpa*.

mole·skin ['məʊlˌskɪn] N (*fur*) (pelliccia di) talpa; (*Textiles*) fustagno.

mo·lest [məʊ'lɛst] VT (*trouble*) importunare; (*harm, Law: sexually*) molestare.

mol·li·fy ['mɒlɪˌfaɪ] VT rabbonire, ammansire.

mol·lusc, (Am) mol·lusk ['mɒləsk] N mollusco.

molly·coddle ['mɒlɪˌkɒdl] VT (*pej*) coccolare, vezzeggiare.

Molotov cock·tail ['mɒləˌtɒf'kɒkˌteɪl] N (bottiglia) Molotov *f inv*.

molt [məʊlt] VI (*Am*) = **moult**.

mol·ten ['məʊltən] ADJ (*metal*) fuso(-a); (*lava*) allo stato liquido.

mom [mɒm] N (*Am fam*) = **mum**.

mo·ment ['məʊmənt] N a momento, istante *m*; **(at) any moment** *or* **any moment now** da un momento all'altro; **at the (present) moment** OR **at this moment in time** al momento, in questo momento; **at the last moment** all'ultimo momento; **for a** *or* **one moment** per un momento; **for the moment** per il momento, per ora; **not for a** *or* **one moment** neanche per un istante; **in a moment** (*very soon*) tra un momento; (*quickly*) in un attimo; **one moment!** OR **wait a moment!** (aspetta) un momento *or* un attimo!; **I won't be a moment** vengo (*or* torno) subito; (*I've nearly finished*) faccio subito; **it won't take a moment** è (solo) questione di un attimo; **I've just this moment heard about it** l'ho saputo in questo (preciso) istante; **the moment he arrives** (non) appena arriva; **from the moment I saw him** dal primo momento in cui l'ho visto; **the man of the moment** l'uomo del momento; **"one moment please"** (*Telec*) "attenda, prego"
b (*Phys*) momento
c (*frm: importance*) importanza, rilievo.

mo·men·tari·ly ['məʊməntərɪlɪ] ADV (*for a second*) per un momento; (*Am: very soon*) da un momento all'altro.

mo·men·tary ['məʊməntərɪ] ADJ momentaneo(-a), passeggero(-a).

♦ **moment of truth** N: **the moment of truth** il momento della verità.

mo·men·tous [məʊ'mɛntəs] ADJ (*molto*) importante, di grande importanza.

mo·men·tum [məʊ'mɛntəm] N (*Phys*) momento, quantità *f inv* di moto; (*fig*) slancio, impeto, velocità *f inv* acquisita; **to gather** *or* **gain momentum** (*vehicle, person*) acquistare *or* prendere velocità, aumentare di velocità; (*fig*) prendere *or* guadagnare terreno; **to lose momentum** (*vehicle, person*) perdere velocità; (*fig*) perdere vigore.

mom·ma ['mɒmə] N (*Am fam*) mamma.

mom·my ['mɒmɪ] N (*Am*) = **mummy**.

Mon. ABBR (= *Monday*) lun.

Mona·co ['mɒnəˌkəʊ] N Monaco *f* (Principato).

mon·ad ['mɒnæd] N (*Chem, Philosophy*) monade *f*.

mon·arch ['mɒnək] N monarca *m*.

mon·ar·chism ['mɒnəkɪzəm] N monarchia.

mon·ar·chist ['mɒnəkɪst] ADJ, N monarchico(-a).

mon·ar·chy ['mɒnəkɪ] N monarchia.

mon·as·tery ['mɒnəstərɪ] N monastero.

mo·nas·tic [mə'næstɪk] ADJ monastico(-a).

mo·nas·ti·cism [mə'næstɪˌsɪzəm] N monachesimo.

Mon·day ['mʌndɪ] N lunedì *m inv for usage see* **Tuesday**.

Mon·egasque [ˌmɒnə'gæsk] ADJ, N monegasco(-a).

mon·etar·ism ['mʌnɪtəˌrɪzəm] N monetarismo.

mon·etar·ist ['mʌnɪtərɪst] [1] ADJ monetaristico(-a).
[2] N monetarista *m/f*.

mon·etary ['mʌnɪtərɪ] ADJ monetario(-a).

mon·ey ['mʌnɪ] N denaro, soldi *mpl*; **paper money** banconote *fpl*; **Italian money** moneta italiana; **there's money in it** c'è da farci i soldi; **I've got no money left** non ho più neanche una lira; **to make money** (*person*) fare (i) soldi; (*business*) rendere; **we didn't make any money on that**

deal in quell'affare non ci abbiamo guadagnato niente; **that's the one for my money!** *(fam)* è quello su cui sono pronto a scommettere!; **it's money for jam** *or* **old rope** *(fam)* son soldi guadagnati senza fatica; **to be in the money** nuotare nell'oro, essere pieno(-a) di soldi; **to get one's money's worth** spender bene i propri soldi; **to earn good money** guadagnare bene; **money doesn't grow on trees!** non me li tirano mica dietro i soldi!; **I'm not made of money** non nuoto nell'oro; **your money or your life!** o la borsa o la vita!; **danger money** *(Brit)* indennità *f inv* di rischio.

money·bags ['mʌnɪˌbægz] N *(fam pej)* riccone(-a).

♦ **money-box** ['mʌnɪbɒks] N salvadanaio.

mon·eyed ['mʌnɪd] ADJ danaroso(-a), ricco(-a); **the moneyed classes** le classi più abbienti.

♦ **money-grubbing** ['mʌnɪˌɡrʌbɪŋ] ADJ *(pej)* avido(-a) di denaro.

money·lender ['mʌnɪˌlɛndəʳ] N chi presta soldi; *(pej)* usuraio(-a).

money·maker ['mʌnɪˌmeɪkəʳ] N *(Brit fam: business)* affare *m* d'oro.

money·making ['mʌnɪˌmeɪkɪŋ] ADJ che rende (bene *or* molto), lucrativo(-a).

♦ **money market** N mercato monetario.

♦ **money order** N vaglia *m inv* (postale).

♦ **money-spinner** ['mʌnɪˌspɪnəʳ] N *(fam)* miniera d'oro *(fig)*.

♦ **money supply** N liquidità *f inv* monetaria.

Mon·gol ['mɒŋɡəl] [1] N *(person)* mongolo(-a); *(language)* mongolo.
[2] ADJ mongolo(-a).

mon·gol ['mɒŋɡəl] N, ADJ *(offensive)* mongoloide *(m/f)*.

Mon·go·lia [mɒŋˈɡəʊlɪə] N la Mongolia.

Mon·go·lian [mɒŋˈɡəʊlɪən] [1] ADJ *(people, tribe)* mongolo(-a); *(language)* mongolico(-a).
[2] N *(person)* mongolo(-a).

mon·go·lism ['mɒŋɡəˌlɪzəm] N *(offensive)* mongolismo.

mon·goose ['mɒŋɡuːs] N mangusta.

mon·grel ['mʌŋɡrəl] N *(dog)* (cane *m*) bastardo.

moni·tor ['mɒnɪtəʳ] [1] N **a** *(Brit Scol)* ≈ capoclasse *m/f*; *(Am Scol)* chi sorveglia agli esami **b** *(TV, Tech: screen)* monitor *m inv*; *(Radio: person)* addetto(-a) all'ascolto delle trasmissioni dall'estero.
[2] VT *(foreign station, broadcast)* ascoltare le trasmissioni di; *(machine, progress)* controllare; *(discussion)* dirigere, fare da moderatore(-trice) in *or* di.

monk [mʌŋk] N frate *m*, monaco.

mon·key ['mʌŋkɪ] N scimmia; *(fig: child)* birbante *m*
▶ **monkey about, monkey around** VI + ADV *(fam)* far lo/la scemo(-a); **to monkey about with sth** armeggiare con qc.

♦ **monkey business** N, **monkey tricks** NPL *(fam)* scherzi *mpl*.

♦ **monkey nut** N *(Brit)* nocciolina americana, arachide *f*.

♦ **monkey puzzle** N *(tree)* araucaria.

♦ **monkey wrench** N chiave *f* inglese a rullino.

monk·ish ['mʌŋkɪʃ] ADJ da monaco.

mono ['mɒnəʊ] [1] ADJ mono *inv*; *(broadcast)* in mono.
[2] N: **in mono** in mono.

mono... ['mɒnəʊ] PREF mono... .

mono·atom·ic [ˌmɒnəʊəˈtɒmɪk] ADJ monoatomico(-a).

mono·ba·sic [ˌmɒnəʊˈbeɪsɪk] ADJ monobasico(-a).

mono·chro·ma·tism [ˌmɒnəʊˈkrəʊməˌtɪzəm] N monocromatismo.

mono·chrome ['mɒnəˌkrəʊm] ADJ *(painting, print)* mono-

cromatico(-a), monocromo(-a); *(television)* in bianco e nero.

mono·cle ['mɒnəkl] N monocolo.

mono·coque ['mɒnəˌkɒk] ADJ, N monoscocca *(f) inv*.

mono·coty·ledon [ˌmɒnəʊˌkɒtɪˈliːdən] N *(Bot)* monocotiledone *m*.

mono·cul·ture ['mɒnəʊˌkʌltʃəʳ] N monocoltura.

mo·noga·mous [mɒˈnɒɡəməs] ADJ monogamo(-a).

mo·noga·my [mɒˈnɒɡəmɪ] N monogamia.

mono·gram ['mɒnəˌɡræm] N monogramma *m*.

mono·grammed ['mɒnəɡræmd] ADJ *(shirt, handkerchief)* con il monogramma.

mono·graph ['mɒnəˌɡrɑːf] N monografia.

mono·lith ['mɒnəʊlɪθ] N monolito.

mono·lithic ['mɒnəʊˌlɪθɪk] ADJ *(also fig)* monolitico(-a).

mono·logue ['mɒnəlɒɡ] N monologo.

mono·ma·nia [ˌmɒnəʊˈmeɪnjə] N monomania.

mono·ma·ni·ac [ˌmɒnəʊˈmeɪnɪæk] N monomaniaco(-a).

mono·mer ['mɒnəməʳ] N *(Chem)* monomero.

mo·no·mial [mɒˈnəʊmɪəl] [1] ADJ monomiale.
[2] N monomio.

mono·plane ['mɒnəʊpleɪn] N monoplano.

♦ **Monopolies and Mergers Commission** N *(Brit)* commissione *f* antimonopoli.

mo·nopo·lize [məˈnɒpəˌlaɪz] VT monopolizzare.

Mo·nopo·ly® [məˈnɒpəlɪ] N *(game)* monopoli ® *m*.

mo·nopo·ly [məˈnɒpəlɪ] N monopolio.

mono·rail ['mɒnəʊˌreɪl] N monorotaia.

mono·sac·cha·ride [ˌmɒnəʊˈsækəˌraɪd] N monosaccaride *m*.

mono·so·dium glu·ta·mate [ˌmɒnəʊˈsəʊdɪəmˈɡluːtə,meɪt] N glutammato di sodio.

mono·syl·lab·ic [ˌmɒnəʊsɪˈlæbɪk] ADJ *(word, reply)* monosillabico(-a); *(person)* che parla a monosillabi.

mono·syl·la·ble ['mɒnəˌsɪləbl] N monosillabo; **to speak/ answer in monosyllables** parlare/rispondere a monosillabi.

mono·theism ['mɒnəʊθɪˌɪzəm] N monoteismo.

mono·theis·tic [ˌmɒnəʊθɪˈɪstɪk] ADJ monoteistico(-a).

mono·tone ['mɒnəˌtəʊn] N: **in a monotone** con voce monotona, con tono monotono.

mo·noto·nous [məˈnɒtənəs] ADJ monotono(-a).

mo·noto·nous·ly [məˈnɒtənəslɪ] ADV in modo monotono, monotonamente.

mo·noto·ny [məˈnɒtənɪ] N monotonia.

Mono·type® ['mɒnəˌtaɪp] N monotype ® *f inv*.

mon·ox·ide [mɒˈnɒksaɪd] N monossido.

mon·soon [mɒnˈsuːn] N monsone *m*.

mon·ster ['mɒnstəʳ] [1] N mostro.
[2] ADJ *(enormous)* gigantesco(-a).

mon·strance ['mɒnstrəns] N ostensorio.

mon·stros·ity [mɒnsˈtrɒsɪtɪ] N mostruosità *f inv*.

mon·strous ['mɒnstrəs] ADJ *(huge)* colossale, enorme; *(dreadful)* mostruoso(-a); **it is monstrous that ...** è scandaloso *or* pazzesco che... + *sub*.

mon·strous·ly ['mɒnstrəslɪ] ADV mostruosamente.

mon·tage [mɒnˈtɑːʒ] N montaggio.

Mont Blanc [mɔ̃ˈblɑ̃] N il Monte Bianco.

month [mʌnθ] N mese *m*; **in the month of May** nel mese di maggio, in maggio; **300 dollars a month** 300 dollari al mese; **paid by the month** pagato(-a) mensilmente; **which day of the month is it?** quanti ne abbiamo (oggi)?; **every month** *(happen)* tutti i mesi; *(pay)* mensilmente, ogni mese.

month·ly ['mʌnθlɪ] [1] ADJ *(gen)* mensile; *(ticket)* valevole

per un mese.

2 ADV mensilmente, ogni mese, al mese; **twice monthly** due volte al mese.

3 N (*magazine*) (rivista) mensile *m*.

monu·ment ['mɒnjʊmənt] N monumento.

monu·men·tal [ˌmɒnjʊ'mentl] ADJ (*also: fig*) monumentale, colossale.

♦ **monumental mason, monumental sculptor** N marmista *m*, lapidario.

moo [mu:] **1** N muggito.

2 VI muggire, mugghiare.

mooch [mu:tʃ] VI (*fam*): **to mooch about** *or* **around** bighellonare.

mood[1] [mu:d] N umore *m*; **what kind of mood are you in?** di che umore sei?; **to be in a good/bad mood** essere di buonumore/di cattivo umore; **to be in a generous mood** sentirsi generoso(-a); **she's in one of her moods** ha la luna; **to be in the mood for sth/to do sth** sentirsi in vena *or* aver voglia di qc/di fare qc; **I'm not in the mood** non mi sento in vena; **I'm in no mood to argue** non ho voglia di discutere.

mood[2] [mu:d] N (*Gram*) modo.

moodi·ly ['mu:dɪlɪ] ADV (*reply*) sgarbatamente; (*stare*) con aria imbronciata.

moodi·ness ['mu:dɪnɪs] N (*changeability*) volubilità *f inv*; (*sulkiness*) malumore *m*.

moody ['mu:dɪ] ADJ (*comp* **-ier**, *superl* **-iest**) (*variable*) lunatico(-a), capriccioso(-a); (*morose*) imbronciato (-a), intrattabile.

moon [mu:n] N luna; **full/new moon** luna piena/nuova; **by the light of the moon** al chiaro di luna; **once in a blue moon** a ogni morte di papa; **to be over the moon** (*fam*) essere al settimo cielo

▶ **moon about, moon around** VI + ADV aggirarsi con aria trasognata

▶ **moon over** VI + PREP: **to moon over sb** sospirare per qn.

moon·beam ['mu:nˌbi:m] N raggio di luna.

♦ **moon landing** N allunaggio.

moon·light ['mu:nˌlaɪt] **1** N chiaro di luna; **in the moonlight** al chiaro di luna.

2 VI (*fam*) fare del lavoro nero.

3 ADJ (*walk*) al chiaro di luna; **to do a moonlight flit** (*Brit fam*) *traslocare di notte per non pagare l'affitto*.

moon·light·ing ['mu:nˌlaɪtɪŋ] N lavoro nero.

moon·lit ['mu:nˌlɪt] ADJ illuminato(-a) dalla luna; **on a moonlit night** in una notte rischiarata dalla luna.

moon·rise ['mu:nˌraɪz] N il sorgere della luna.

moon·shine ['mu:nˌʃaɪn] N (*fam: nonsense*) fandonie *fpl*; (*Am: liquor: illegally made*) *liquore distillato clandestinamente*; (: *smuggled*) *liquore di contrabbando*.

moon·shot ['mu:nˌʃɒt] N lancio sulla luna.

moon·stone ['mu:nˌstəʊn] N lunaria, pietra della luna.

moon·struck ['mu:nˌstrʌk] ADJ pazzo(-a).

moony ['mu:nɪ] ADJ (*comp* **-ier**, *superl* **-iest**) (*eyes*) sognante.

Moor [mʊəʳ] N moro(-a).

moor[1] [mʊəʳ] N (*land*) brughiera.

moor[2] [mʊəʳ] **1** VT (*ship*) ormeggiare.

2 VI ormeggiarsi, attraccare.

moor·hen ['mʊəˌhen] N gallinella d'acqua.

moor·ing ['mʊərɪŋ] N (*place*) ormeggio.

♦ **moor·ing buoy** N gavitello.

moor·ings ['mʊərɪŋz] NPL (*chains, ropes*) ormeggi *mpl*; (*place*) ormeggio.

Moor·ish ['mʊərɪʃ] ADJ moresco(-a).

moor·land ['mʊələnd] N brughiera.

moose [mu:s] N, PL INV alce *m*.

moot [mu:t] **1** ADJ: **it's a moot point** è un punto discutibile *or* controverso.

2 VT: **it has been mooted whether ...** è stata sollevata la questione se... .

mop [mɒp] **1** N (*for floor*) mocio *m* Vileda ® *inv*; (*for dishes*) spazzolino per i piatti; (*fam: hair*) cespuglio *or* testa di capelli.

2 VT (*floor*) lavare; **to mop one's brow** asciugarsi la fronte

▶ **mop up** VT + ADV **a** asciugare con uno straccio **b** (*Mil*) eliminare.

mope [məʊp] VI essere depresso(-a) *or* avvilito(-a)

▶ **mope about, mope around** VI + ADV trascinarsi *or* aggirarsi con aria avvilita.

mo·ped ['məʊped] N (*Brit*) ciclomotore *m*.

mopping-up op·era·tions [mɒpɪŋˈʌpˌɒpəˈreɪʃəns] NPL (*Mil*) operazioni *fpl* di rastrellamento.

MOR [ˌɛməʊˈɑːʳ] (*Mus*) ADJ ABBR = *middle-of-the-road*; **MOR music** musica melodica.

mo·raine [mɒˈreɪn] N morena.

mor·al ['mɒrəl] **1** ADJ (*gen*) morale; (*person*) di saldi principi morali; **to lower moral standards** rilassare i costumi.

2 N **a** (*lesson*) morale *f* **b**: **morals** NPL principi *mpl* morali, moralità *f inv*.

mo·rale [mɒˈrɑːl] N morale *m*; **to raise sb's morale** risollevare il morale di qn.

mor·al·ist ['mɒrəlɪst] N moralista *m/f*.

mor·al·is·tic [mɒrəˈlɪstɪk] ADJ (*pej: attitude*) moralistico (-a).

mo·ral·ity [məˈrælɪtɪ] N moralità *f inv*.

♦ **morality play** N (*Theatre*) moralità *f inv*.

mor·al·ize ['mɒrəˌlaɪz] VI: **to moralize (about)** fare il/la moralista (riguardo a), moraleggiare (riguardo a).

mor·al·ly ['mɒrəlɪ] ADV (*act*) moralmente; **morally wrong** moralmente sbagliato(-a).

♦ **moral philosophy** N filosofia morale.

♦ **moral support** N appoggio morale.

♦ **moral victory** N vittoria morale.

mo·rass [məˈræs] N pantano, palude *f*; (*fig*) pantano.

mora·to·rium [ˌmɒrəˈtɔːrɪəm] N moratoria.

mor·bid ['mɔːbɪd] ADJ morboso(-a).

mor·bid·ly ['mɔːbɪdlɪ] ADV morbosamente.

mor·dant ['mɔːdənt] ADJ (*frm: wit, humour*) mordace.

more [mɔːʳ] (*comp of many, much*)

1 ADJ (*greater in number*) più *inv*; (*in addition*) altro(-a), ancora *inv*;

▷ **is there any more wine?** c'è ancora del vino?, c'è dell'altro vino?

▷ **a few more weeks** ancora qualche settimana, qualche altra settimana

▷ **many more people** molta più gente

▷ **I have no more pennies** non ho più un penny

▷ **do you want some more tea?** vuoi ancora un po' di tè?, vuoi dell'altro tè?

▷ **I have more wine/money than you** ho più vino/soldi di te

▷ **I have more wine than beer** ho più vino che birra

▷ **there was more snow this winter than last** c'è stata più neve quest'inverno che l'inverno scorso

▷ **more letters than we expected** più lettere di

quante ne aspettavamo
▷*the* more fool you for giving her the money sei ancora più stupido tu che le hai dato i soldi.
2 PRON
a (*greater amount*) più *inv*; (*further or additional amount*) ancora;
▷*4* more ancora 4
▷*a few* more ancora qualcuno
▷*a little* more ancora un po', un altro po'
▷is there *any* more? ce n'è ancora?, ce n'è dell'altro?
▷you couldn't *ask for* more non potresti chiedere di più
▷it *cost* more than we had expected è costato (di) più di quanto pensavamo
▷*many* more molti altri
▷*much* more molto di più
▷there's *no* more non ce n'è più
▷let's say *no* more about it non parliamone più
▷more *than* 10 più di 10
▷more *than* ever più che mai
▷I *want* more ne voglio ancora *or* di più
▷and *what's* more ... e per di più...
b : *(all) the* more (molto) di più;
▷*the* more you give him the more he wants più gliene dai e più ne vuole
▷*the* more the merrier più gente c'è, meglio è.
3 ADV (di) più;
▷more *and* more sempre di più
▷it's more *and* more difficult to ... è sempre più difficile...
▷I don't want to go *any* more non ci voglio più andare
▷more *dangerous* than più pericoloso(-a) di *or* che
▷more *difficult* più difficile
▷more *easily* più facilmente
▷*no* more non... più
▷*not any* more non... più
▷*once* more ancora (una volta), un'altra volta
▷(all) the more *so as* ... tanto più che...
▷he was more *surprised* than angry era più sorpreso che arrabbiato
▷it will more *than* meet the demand supererà ampiamente la richiesta
▷more *or* less più o meno.

mo·rel [mɒˈrɛl] N (*mushroom*) morchella.
more·over [mɔːˈrəʊvəʳ] ADV per di più, inoltre.
mor·es [ˈmɔːreɪz] NPL (*frm*) costumi *mpl.*
mor·ga·nat·ic [ˌmɔːgəˈnætɪk] ADJ morganatico(-a).
morgue [mɔːg] N obitorio.
MORI [ˈmɔːrɪ] N ABBR (*Brit*: = *Market & Opinion Research Institute*) *istituto di sondaggio.*
mori·bund [ˈmɒrɪˌbʌnd] ADJ moribondo(-a).
Mor·mon [ˈmɔːmən] N, ADJ mormone *(m/f).*
morn·ing [ˈmɔːnɪŋ] **1** N (*part of day*) mattina, mattino; (*expressing duration*) mattinata; this morning stamattina, questa mattina; yesterday morning ieri mattina; tomorrow morning domani mattina, domattina; on Monday morning lunedì mattina; a morning's work il lavoro di una mattinata; in the morning di mattina, la mattina; (*tomorrow*) domattina; I work in the mornings lavoro la mattina; at 7 o'clock in the morning alle 7 del mattino; on the morning of September 19th la mattina del 19 settembre.

2 ADJ (*walk*) mattutino(-a); (*papers*) del mattino.
♦ **morning-after pill** [ˌmɔːnɪŋˈɑːtəˌpɪl] N pillola del giorno dopo.
♦ **morning dress** N frac *m inv.*
♦ **morning prayer**, **morning service** N mattutino.
♦ **morning sickness** N (*Med*) nausee *fpl* mattutine.
♦ **morning star** N stella del mattino.
Mo·roc·can [məˈrɒkən] ADJ, N marocchino(-a).
Mo·roc·co [məˈrɒkəʊ] N **a** il Marocco **b** (*also*: **Morocco leather**) marocchino.
mor·on [ˈmɔːrɒn] N (*fam*) idiota *m/f*, deficiente *m/f.*
mo·ron·ic [mɒˈrɒnɪk] ADJ cretino(-a), idiota, deficiente.
mo·rose [məˈrəʊs] ADJ cupo(-a), tetro(-a), imbronciato (-a).
mo·rose·ly [məˈrəʊslɪ] ADV cupamente.
mor·pheme [ˈmɔːfiːm] N morfema *m.*
mor·phine [ˈmɔːfiːn], **mor·phia** [ˈmɔːfɪə] N morfina.
♦ **morphine addict**, **morphia addict** N morfinomane *m/f.*
mor·pho·logi·cal·ly [ˌmɔːfəˈlɒdʒɪkəlɪ] ADV morfologicamente.
mor·phol·ogy [mɔːˈfɒlədʒɪ] N morfologia.
mor·ris danc·ing [ˈmɒrɪsˌdɑːnsɪŋ] N (*Brit*) *antica danza tradizionale inglese.*
mor·row [ˈmɒrəʊ] N: the morrow (*old*) domani *m inv*; on the morrow domani.
Morse [mɔːs] N (*also*: **Morse code**) alfabeto Morse.
mor·sel [ˈmɔːsl] N (*of food*) boccone *m*; (*fig*) briciolo.
mor·tal [ˈmɔːtl] ADJ, N mortale *(m/f).*
mor·tal·ity [mɔːˈtælɪtɪ] N mortalità *f inv.*
♦ **mortality rate** N tasso di mortalità.
mor·tal·ly [ˈmɔːtəlɪ] ADV mortalmente.
mor·tar [ˈmɔːtəʳ] N **a** (*cannon, bowl*) mortaio **b** (*cement*) malta.
mortar·board [ˈmɔːtəˌbɔːd] N *tradizionale copricapo nero, con cupola piatta e quadrata indossato da studenti, docenti universitari a cerimonie ufficiali.*
mort·gage [ˈmɔːgɪdʒ] **1** N (*in house buying*) mutuo ipotecario; (*second loan*) ipoteca; to take out a mortgage contrarre un mutuo (*or* un'ipoteca); to pay off a mortgage pagare un mutuo (*or* un'ipoteca).
2 VT ipotecare.
♦ **mortgage company** N (*Am*) società *f inv* immobiliare.
mort·ga·gee [ˌmɔːgɪˈdʒiː] N creditore *m* ipotecario.
mort·gag·or [ˈmɔːgɪdʒəʳ] N debitore *m* ipotecario.
mor·tice [ˈmɔːtɪs] N = mortise.
mor·ti·cian [mɔːˈtɪʃən] N (*Am*) impresario di pompe funebri.
mor·ti·fi·ca·tion [ˌmɔːtɪfɪˈkeɪʃən] N mortificazione *f.*
mor·ti·fied [ˈmɔːtɪˌfaɪd] ADJ mortificato(-a).
mor·ti·fy [ˈmɔːtɪˌfaɪ] VT mortificare.
mor·ti·fy·ing [ˈmɔːtɪˌfaɪɪŋ] ADJ mortificante.
mor·tise, **mor·tice** [ˈmɔːtɪs] N mortasa.
♦ **mortise lock** N serratura incastrata.
mor·tu·ary [ˈmɔːtjʊərɪ] N camera mortuaria.
mo·sa·ic [məʊˈzeɪɪk] N mosaico.
Mos·cow [ˈmɒskəʊ] N Mosca.
Moses [ˈməʊzɪs] N (*Brit*) Mosè *m.*
♦ **Moses basket** N (*Brit*) culla di vimini.
Mos·lem [ˈmɒzləm] ADJ, N = **Muslim**.
mosque [mɒsk] N moschea.
mos·qui·to [mɒsˈkiːtəʊ] N (*pl* mosquitoes) zanzara.
♦ **mosquito net** N zanzariera.
moss [mɒs] N (*Bot*) muschio.
mossy [ˈmɒsɪ] ADJ (*comp* -ier, *superl* -iest) muscoso(-a).

most [məʊst] (*superl of* **many, much**) [1] ADJ **a** più (di tutti); **the most pleasure** il piacere più grande; **who has (the) most money?** chi ha più soldi (di tutti)?; **for the most part** in gran parte, per la maggior parte
b (*the majority of*): **most men** la maggior parte *or* la grande maggioranza degli uomini; **most fish** la maggior parte dei pesci.
[2] PRON: **most of it/them** quasi tutto/tutti; **most of the money/her friends/the time** la maggior parte dei soldi/dei suoi amici/del tempo; **do the most you can** fai più che puoi; **at most** *or* **at the (very) most** al massimo; **to make the most of sth** sfruttare al massimo qc, trarre il massimo vantaggio da qc; **make the most of it!** approfittane!.
[3] ADV **a** (*spend, eat, work, sleep*) di più; **I saw most** ho visto più io; **the most attractive/difficult/comfortable** il/la più attraente/difficile/confortevole; **which one did it most easily?** chi ha avuto più facilità a farlo?
b (*very*): **most likely** molto probabilmente; **a most interesting book** un libro estremamente interessante.
most·ly [ˈməʊstlɪ] ADV (*chiefly*) per lo più; (*usually*) in genere.
MOT [ˌɛməʊˈtiː] N ABBR (*Brit*: = *Ministry of Transport*) ministero dei Trasporti; MOT (*test*) *revisione obbligatoria degli autoveicoli*; **the car passed/failed its** MOT ≈ la macchina ha passato/non ha passato la revisione.
mo·tel [məʊˈtɛl] N motel *m inv.*
moth [mɒθ] N falena, farfalla notturna; (*also:* **clothes moth**) tarma.
moth·ball [ˈmɒθˌbɔːl] N pallina di naftalina.
♦ **moth-eaten** [ˈmɒθˌiːtn] ADJ tarmato(-a).
moth·er [ˈmʌðəʳ] [1] N madre *f.*
[2] VT (*care for*) fare da madre a; (*spoil*) essere troppo chioccia con.
moth·er·board [ˈmʌðəˌbɔːd] N (*Comput*) scheda *f* madre *inv.*
moth·er·hood [ˈmʌðəˌhʊd] N maternità *f inv.*
Moth·er·ing Sun·day [ˈmʌðərɪŋˌsʌndɪ] N (*Brit*) ≈ la festa della mamma.
♦ **mother-in-law** [ˈmʌðərɪnlɔː] N (*pl* **mothers-in-law**) suocera.
mother·land [ˈmʌðəˌlænd], **mother country** N madrepatria, patria.
♦ **mother love** N amore *m* materno.
moth·er·ly [ˈmʌðəlɪ] ADJ materno(-a).
♦ **Mother Nature** N madre *f* natura.
♦ **mother-of-pearl** [ˌmʌðərəvˈpɜːl] N madreperla.
♦ **Mother's Day** N la festa della mamma.
♦ **mother's help** N bambinaia.
♦ **Mother Superior** N madre superiora.
♦ **mother-to-be** [ˌmʌðətəˈbiː] N (*pl* **mothers-to-be**) futura mamma.
♦ **mother tongue** N lingua materna, madrelingua.
moth·proof [ˈmɒθˌpruːf] ADJ antitarmico(-a).
mo·tif [məʊˈtiːf] N motivo.
mo·tion [ˈməʊʃən] [1] N **a** (*movement*) moto, movimento; **perpetual motion** moto perpetuo; **to be in motion** (*vehicle*) essere in moto; (*machine*) essere in funzione; **to set in motion** avviare; **to go through the motions of doing sth** (*fig*) fare qc pro forma
b (*gesture*) cenno, gesto; (*proposal: at meeting*) mozione *f*
c (*Brit: also:* **bowel motion**) evacuazione *f* (intestinale).
[2] VT, VI: **to motion (to) sb to do sth** far cenno *or* segno a qn di fare qc.

mo·tion·less [ˈməʊʃənlɪs] ADJ immobile.
♦ **motion picture** N (*Am*) film *m inv.*
♦ **motion-picture in·dus·try** [ˌməʊʃənˈpɪktʃərˌɪndəstrɪ] N (*Am*) l'industria cinematografica.
♦ **motion sickness** N mal *m* d'auto (*or* d'aria *or* di mare).
mo·ti·vate [ˈməʊtɪˌveɪt] VT (*act, decision*) dare origine a, motivare; (*person*) spingere, motivare.
mo·ti·vat·ed [ˈməʊtɪˌveɪtɪd] ADJ motivato(-a).
mo·ti·va·tion [ˌməʊtɪˈveɪʃən] N motivazione *f.*
mo·tive [ˈməʊtɪv] [1] N (*gen*) motivo, ragione *f*; (*for crime*) movente *m*; **from the best motives** con le migliori intenzioni. [2] ADJ motore(-trice).
mot·ley [ˈmɒtlɪ] ADJ (*many-coloured*) variopinto(-a); (*mixed*) eterogeneo(-a), molto vario(-a); **a motley crew** una banda eterogenea.
mo·to·cross [ˈməʊtəˌkrɒs] N motocross *m.*
mo·tor [ˈməʊtəʳ] [1] N **a** (*engine*) motore *m* **b** (*Brit fam: car*) macchina.
[2] VI andare in automobile.
[3] ADJ motore(-trice).
♦ **motor accident** N incidente *m* automobilistico.
motor·bike [ˈməʊtəˌbaɪk] N moto *f inv.*
motor·boat [ˈməʊtəˌbəʊt] N motoscafo.
motor·cade [ˈməʊtəˌkeɪd] N corteo di auto.
motor·car [ˈməʊtəkɑː] N (*Brit frm*) automobile *f.*
♦ **motor caravan** N (*Brit*) camper *m inv.*
motor·coach [ˈməʊtəˌkəʊtʃ] N (*Brit*) pullman *m inv.*
motor·cycle [ˈməʊtəˌsaɪkl] N motocicletta.
motor·cycling [ˈməʊtəˌsaɪklɪŋ] N motociclismo.
motor·cyclist [ˈməʊtəˌsaɪklɪst] N motociclista *m/f.*
♦ **motor industry** N industria automobilistica.
mo·tor·ing [ˈməʊtərɪŋ] [1] ADJ (*accident*) d'auto, automobilistico(-a); (*offence*) di guida; **motoring holiday** vacanza in macchina; **the motoring public** gli automobilisti.
[2] N (*Brit*) turismo automobilistico; **the hazards of motoring** i rischi dell'andare in macchina.
mo·tor·ist [ˈməʊtərɪst] N automobilista *m/f.*
mo·tori·za·tion [ˌməʊtəraɪˈzeɪʃən] N motorizzazione *f.*
mo·tor·ize [ˈməʊtəˌraɪz] VT motorizzare.
motor·man [ˈməʊtəˌmæn] N (*pl* **-men**) (*Am: of electric train*) macchinista *m.*
♦ **motor mechanic** N meccanico.
♦ **motor muscle** N muscolo motore.
♦ **motor oil** N olio lubrificante.
♦ **motor racing** N (*Brit*) corse *fpl* automobilistiche.
♦ **motor scooter** N motorscooter *m inv.*
♦ **motor show** N salone *m* dell'automobile.
♦ **motor vehicle** N (*frm*) automezzo, autoveicolo.
motor·way [ˈməʊtəˌweɪ] N (*Brit*) autostrada.
mott·led [ˈmɒtld] ADJ (*leaves, bird*) variopinto(-a), variegato(-a), screziato(-a); (*marble*) variegato(-a); (*animal*) pezzato(-a), marezzato(-a); (*complexion*) a chiazze, chiazzato(-a).
mot·to [ˈmɒtəʊ] N (*pl* **mottoes**) motto.
mouf·lon [ˈmuːflɒn] N (*sheep*) muflone *m.*
mould[1], (*Am*) **mold** [məʊld] N (*fungus*) muffa.
mould[2], (*Am*) **mold** [məʊld] [1] N (*Art, Culin, Tech*) stampo, forma.
[2] VT (*clay, figure*) plasmare, modellare; (*fig: character*) plasmare, formare, foggiare.
mould·er, (*Am*) **mold·er** [ˈməʊldəʳ] VI (*decay*) ammuffire; (*building*) sgretolarsi, andare in rovina.
mould·ing, (*Am*) **mold·ing** [ˈməʊldɪŋ] N (*Archit*) modanatura.

mouldy, (*Am*) **moldy** ['məʊldɪ] ADJ (*comp* **-ier**, *superl* **-iest**) ammuffito(-a); **to smell mouldy** avere odore di muffa; **to go mouldy** ammuffire.

moult, (*Am*) **molt** [məʊlt] VI far la muta.

mound [maʊnd] N rialzo, collinetta.

mount[1] [maʊnt] N (*liter*) monte *m*, montagna; **Mount Everest** il monte Everest; **Mount of Olives** (*Rel*) il Monte degli Ulivi.

mount[2] [maʊnt] ⓵ N a (*horse*) cavalcatura

  b (*support, base*) piedistallo; (*of machine*) incastellatura di sostegno; (*of jewel, photo*) montatura; (*of slide*) telaietto

  ⓶ VT a (*horse*) montare; (*platform*) salire su; (*stairs*) salire

  b (*exhibition*) organizzare; (*play*) metter su; (*attack*) sferrare, condurre

  c (*picture, stamp*) sistemare; (*jewel*) montare

  d : **to mount guard (on** *or* **over)** fare la guardia a; (*Mil*) montare la guardia a.

  ⓷ VI a (*get on a horse*) montare a cavallo

  b (*quantity, price: also:* **mount up**) aumentare, salire.

moun·tain ['maʊntɪn] ⓵ N (*also fig*) montagna; **in the mountains** sulle montagne, in montagna; **to have a holiday in the mountains** fare una vacanza in montagna; **to make a mountain out of a molehill** fare di una mosca un elefante; **butter mountain** (*Econ*) montagna di burro. ⓶ ADJ (*people*) montanaro(-a), di montagna; (*shoes*) da montagna; (*animal, plant, path*) di montagna.

♦ **mountain bike** N mountain bike *f inv*.

♦ **mountain breed** N razza montana.

♦ **mountain cat, mountain lion** N puma *m inv*.

moun·tain·eer [ˌmaʊntɪ'nɪə'] N alpinista *m/f*.

moun·tain·eer·ing [ˌmaʊntɪ'nɪərɪŋ] N alpinismo; **to go mountaineering** fare dell'alpinismo.

moun·tain·ous ['maʊntɪnəs] ADJ (*country*) montagnoso (-a), montuoso(-a); (*fig*) gigantesco(-a).

♦ **mountain range** N catena montuosa *or* di montagne.

♦ **mountain rescue team** N ≈ squadra di soccorso alpino.

moun·tain·side ['maʊntɪn,saɪd] N fianco della montagna.

mount·ed ['maʊntɪd] ADJ a cavallo.

mourn [mɔːn] ⓵ VT piangere, lamentare.

  ⓶ VI: **to mourn (for sb)** piangere (la morte di qn).

mourn·er ['mɔːnə'] N chi piange un defunto.

mourn·ful ['mɔːnfʊl] ADJ (*person*) triste, malinconico(-a); (*tone, sound*) lugubre, funereo.

mourn·ful·ly ['mɔːnfəlɪ] ADV (*gaze, speak*) tristemente, malinconicamente.

mourn·ful·ness ['mɔːnfʊlnɪs] N tristezza, malinconia.

mourn·ing ['mɔːnɪŋ] ⓵ N lutto; **to be in mourning** essere in lutto; **to wear mourning** portare il lutto.

  ⓶ ADJ (*dress*) da lutto.

mouse [maʊs] N (*pl* **mice**) (*gen*) topo; (*Comput*) mouse *m inv*; **house mouse** topo domestico.

mous·er ['maʊzə'] N (*cat*) cacciatore *m* di topi.

mouse·trap ['maʊs,træp] N trappola per i topi.

mous·sa·ka [ˌmʊ'sɑːkə] N moussaka, *sorta di parmigiana di melanzane con ragù di carne, specialità greca*.

mousse [muːs] N mousse *f inv*.

mous·tache [mə'stɑːʃ] N baffi *mpl*.

mousy, mousey ['maʊsɪ] ADJ (*comp* **-ier**, *superl* **-iest**) (*person*) timido(-a), schivo(-a); **mousy hair** capelli color castano spento.

mouth [*n* maʊθ; *vb* maʊð] ⓵ N (*pl* **mouths** [maʊðz]) (*gen*) bocca; (*of cave*) imboccatura, imbocco; (*of river*) foce *f*,

bocca; (*opening*) orifizio; **to keep one's mouth shut** (*fig*) tener la bocca chiusa; **shut your mouth!** ma sta' un po' zitto!.

  ⓶ VT (*insincerely*) blaterare; (*soundlessly*) esprimere col semplice movimento delle labbra.

mouth·ful ['maʊθfʊl] N (*of food*) boccone *m*; (*of drink*) sorsata.

♦ **mouth organ** N armonica (a bocca).

mouth·piece ['maʊθ,piːs] N (*Mus*) imboccatura, bocchino; (*of breathing apparatus*) boccaglio; (*of telephone*) microfono; (*fig: person*) portavoce *m/f*.

♦ **mouth-to-mouth** ['maʊθə'maʊθ], **mouth-to-mouth resuscitation** N respirazione *f* bocca a bocca.

mouth·wash ['maʊθ,wɒʃ] N collutorio.

mouth·water·ing ['maʊθ,wɔːtərɪŋ] ADJ che fa venire l'acquolina in bocca.

mov·able ['muːvəbl] ADJ mobile, movibile.

move [muːv] ⓵ N a (*movement*) movimento, mossa; **to be on the move** (*travelling*) spostarsi; (*active, busy*) essere indaffarato(-a); (*fig: developments*) essere in continuo progresso; **to get a move on** (*fam*) affrettarsi, sbrigarsi; **get a move on (with that)!** (*fam*) sbrigati (con quello)!, datti una mossa (con quello)!; **to make a move** (*start to leave, go*) andarsene; (*begin to take action*) muoversi; **he made a move towards her** fece un passo verso di lei

  b (*in game*) mossa; (: *turn to play*) turno; (*fig: step, action*) passo; **it's my move** tocca a me; **a good/bad move** una mossa buona/sbagliata; **what's the next move?** e adesso cosa facciamo?; **to make the first move** (*fig*) fare il primo passo; **his first move after his victory** la prima cosa che ha fatto dopo la sua vittoria; **there was a move to oust him from the party** ci fu un tentativo di estrometterlo dal partito

  c (*change of house*) trasloco; (*to different job*) trasferimento.

  ⓶ VT a (*change place of*) spostare; (: *limbs, chesspiece*) muovere; (*transport*) trasportare; (*transfer: employee, troops*) trasferire; **move those children off the grass!** fate andare via i bambini dal prato!; **to move house** traslocare, cambiar casa; **we asked a (removal) firm to move us** abbiamo chiesto a una ditta (di traslochi) di farci il trasloco

  b (*fig: sway*): **to move somebody from an opinion** smuovere qn da un'idea; **to move sb to do sth** indurre *or* spingere qn a fare qc; **he will not be easily moved** non cambierà facilmente idea

  c (*cause emotion in*) commuovere; **to be moved** essere commosso(-a); **to move sb to tears** commuovere qn fino alle lacrime; **to move sb to anger/pity** far arrabbiare/impietosire qn

  d (*frm: propose*): **to move a resolution** avanzare una proposta; **to move that ...** proporre che... + *sub*.

  ⓷ VI a (*gen*) muoversi; (*traffic*) circolare; (*from a place*) spostarsi; **move!** muoviti!, spostati!; **let's move!** andiamo!; **to move towards** andare verso; **she moves beautifully** si muove con molta grazia; **I'll not move from here** di qui non mi muovo; **to move freely** (*piece of machinery*) aver gioco; (*person*) circolare liberamente; (*traffic*) scorrere; **the policeman kept the traffic moving** il vigile ha fatto scorrere il traffico; **things are moving at last** finalmente qualcosa si è mosso; **to move in high society** frequentare l'alta società

  b (*move house*) cambiar casa, traslocare; **the family moved to a new house** la famiglia è andata ad abitare in

una nuova casa
c (*in games*) muovere; **it's you to move** tocca a te
d (*take steps*) intervenire
▶ **move about**, **move around** ① VT + ADV (*furniture*) spostare; (*person*) far spostare.
② VI + ADV (*fidget*) agitarsi; (*walk about*) muoversi; (*travel*) spostarsi, viaggiare
▶ **move along** ① VT + ADV (*crowd*) far circolare; (*car*) far spostare.
② VI + ADV spostarsi in avanti, scorrere
▶ **move away** ① VT + ADV (*demonstrators*) allontanare; (*employee*) trasferire; (*object*) spostare.
② VI + ADV, VI (*move aside*) spostarsi; (*leave*) allontanarsi, andarsene; (*move house*) traslocare
▶ **move back** ① VT + ADV **a** (*to former place: person*) far tornare; (*: object*) rimettere dov'era
b (*cause to give ground: crowd*) sospingere indietro; (*: troops*) far indietreggiare.
② VI + ADV **a** (*return*) ritornare
b (*give ground*) indietreggiare
▶ **move down** ① VT + ADV (*person*) far scendere; (*object*) spostare in basso; (*demote*) far retrocedere.
② VI + ADV scendere; (*be demoted*) retrocedere
▶ **move forward** ① VT + ADV (*object*) spostare in avanti; (*people, troops, chesspiece*) far avanzare; (*fig: date*) anticipare.
② VI + ADV avanzare
▶ **move in** ① VT + ADV (*police*) far intervenire; (*take inside*) portar dentro; **we haven't moved the furniture in yet** non ci abbiamo ancora messo i mobili.
② VI + ADV **a** (*to a house*) traslocare, andare ad abitare
b (*police*) intervenire; (*pej: try to take control*) cercare di imporsi
▶ **move off** ① VT + ADV (*object*) togliere.
② VI + ADV **a** (*go away*) allontanarsi
b (*start moving*) partire
▶ **move on** ① VT + ADV (*crowd*) far circolare; (*hands of clock*) spostare in avanti.
② VI + ADV ripartire, riprendere la strada; **the policeman asked them to move on** il vigile ha chiesto loro di circolare; **to move on to** (*fig: point*) passare a
▶ **move out** ① VT + ADV (*gen*) portar fuori; (*person*) mandare fuori; (*troops*) far ritirare; **move the chair out of the corner** togli la sedia dall'angolo.
② VI + ADV (*of house*) sgombrare, trasferirsi; (*withdraw: troops*) ritirarsi
▶ **move over** ① VT + ADV spostare.
② VI + ADV spostarsi
▶ **move up** ① VT + ADV (*person*) portare su; (*object*) spostare in alto; (*promote: employee*) promuovere.
② VI + ADV **a** (*move along*) andare avanti, avanzare
b (*fig: shares*) salire; (*: rates*) aumentare; (*be promoted*) passare di grado.
move·ment ['muːvmənt] N (*gen*) movimento; (*gesture*) gesto; (*of stars, water, physical*) moto; **movement (of the bowels)** (*Med*) evacuazione *f* (*intestinale*); **the police questioned him about his movements** la polizia lo ha interrogato circa i suoi spostamenti.
mov·er ['muːvəʳ] N proponente *m/f*.
movie ['muːvɪ] (*esp Am*) ① N film *m inv*; **to go to the movies** andare al cinema.
② ADJ (*star*) del cinema; (*industry*) cinematografico(-a).
♦ **movie camera** N (*Am*) cinepresa.
movie·goer ['muːvɪˌgəʊəʳ] N (*Am*) frequentatore(-trice) di cinema.

mov·ing ['muːvɪŋ] ADJ **a** (*parts, staircase*) mobile; (*vehicle*) in moto, in corsa **b** (*fig: instigating*) animatore(-trice) **c** (*causing emotion*) commovente, toccante.
mov·ing·ly ['muːvɪŋlɪ] ADV in modo commovente.
mow [məʊ] (*pt* **mowed**, *pp* **mown** *or* **mowed**) VT (*corn*) falciare; (*grass*) tagliare
▶ **mow down** VT + ADV falciare.
mow·er ['məʊəʳ] N (*machine, Agr*) falciatrice *f*; (*also:* **lawn mower**) tagliaerba *m inv*, tosaerba *m inv*.
Mo·zam·bique [ˌməʊzəmˈbiːk] N il Mozambico.
MP [ˌɛmˈpiː] N ABBR **a** = *Military Police* **b** (*Canada*)= *Mounted Police* **c** (*Brit*: = *Member of Parliament*) deputato (-a); (*on envelope*): **Paul Smith, MP** ≈ On. Paul Smith.
mpg [ˌɛmpiːˈdʒiː] N ABBR (= *miles per gallon*) ≈ km/l.
mph [ˌɛmpiːˈeɪtʃ] N ABBR (= *miles per hour*) ≈ km/h.
MPhil [ˌɛmˈfɪl] N ABBR (= *Master of Philosophy*) *diploma post-laurea.*
Mr ['mɪstəʳ] N signore *m*; **Mr Smith** il signor Smith; (*on letter*) Sig. Smith; (*direct address*) signor Smith.
MRC [ˌɛmɑːˈsiː] N ABBR (*Brit*: = *Medical Research Council*) *ufficio governativo per la ricerca medica in Gran Bretagna e nel Commonwealth.*
MRCP [ˌɛmɑːsiːˈpiː] N ABBR (*Brit*)= *Member of the Royal College of Physicians.*
MRCS [ˌɛmɑːsiːˈɛs] N ABBR (*Brit*)= *Member of the Royal College of Surgeons.*
MRCVS [ˌɛmɑːsiːviːˈɛs] N ABBR (*Brit*)= *Member of the Royal College of Veterinary Surgeons.*
Mrs ['mɪsɪz] N signora; **Mrs Black** la signora Black; (*on letter*) Sig.ra Black; (*direct address*) signora Black.
MS [ˌɛmˈɛs] ① N ABBR **a** (*Am*: = *Master of Science*) Master *m inv* in Scienze naturali **b** (*Med*) = **multiple sclerosis**.
② ABBR (*Am: Post*)= *Mississippi*.
Ms [mɪz] N ABBR *termine usato per evitare di distinguere tra signora e signorina.*
MS., ms. (*pl* **MSS., mss.**) ABBR (= *manuscript*) ms.
MSA [ˌɛmɛsˈeɪ] N ABBR (*Am*: = *Master of Science in Agriculture*) Master *m inv* in Scienze Agrarie.
MSc [ˌɛmɛsˈsiː] N ABBR = **Master of Science**.
MSG [ˌɛmɛsˈdʒiː] ABBR = **monosodium glutamate**.
MST [ˌɛmɛsˈtiː] ABBR (*Am*: = *Mountain Standard Time*) *ora invernale delle Montagne Rocciose.*
MT [ˌɛmˈtiː] ① N ABBR = *machine translation*.
② ABBR (*Am Post*)= *Montana*.
Mt ABBR (*Geog*: = *mount*) M.
mth ABBR (= *month*) m.
MTV [ˌɛmtiːˈviː] N ABBR (= *music television*) MTV *f*.

much [mʌtʃ] (*comp* **more**, *superl* **most**)
① ADJ, PRON
a molto(-a);
▷ **how much money?** quanti soldi?
▷ **how much is it?** quanto costa?
▷ **it's *not* much** non è tanto
▷ **there's *not* much to do** non c'è molto da fare
▷ **much *of* this is true** molto di questo è vero
▷ **I'm not much *of* a cook/singer** non sono un granché come cuoco/cantante
▷ **that wasn't much *of* a party** la festa non è stata un granché
▷ **we don't see much *of* each other** non ci vediamo molto spesso
▷ **he/it isn't *up to* much** (*fam*) non vale granché
b: *as* **much**: **as much *again*** altrettanto(-a)

▷*as* much *as* you want (tanto) quanto vuoi

▷he drinks as much *beer* as I do beve tanta birra quanto me

▷it's as much as he *can* do to stand up stare in piedi è il massimo che riesce a fare

▷he spends as much as he *earns* spende tanto quanto guadagna

▷he has (just) as much *money* as you ha tanti soldi quanto te

▷I *thought* as much c'era da aspettarselo

▷three *times* as much tea tre volte tanto tè

C: *so* much talmente tanto(-a), così (tanto(-a))

▷*at* so much a pound un tot *or* un tanto alla libbra

▷so much *for* that! pazienza!

▷the problem is *not* so much one of money as time non è tanto una questione di soldi quanto di tempo

d: *too* much troppo(-a);

▷ *that's* too much! *or* a *bit* (too) much! (*fam*) questo è (un po') troppo!

▷the job is too much *for* her quel lavoro è al di sopra delle sue capacità

e

▷to *make* much of sb (*treat as important*) coprire qn di attenzioni

▷to *make* much of (*success, failure*) fare un sacco di storie per; (*item of news, scandal*) dare rilievo a

▷I couldn't *make* much of that (*fam*) non ci ho capito molto.

2 ADV

a molto;

▷much *as* I would like to go I can't per quanto abbia *or* anche se ho una gran voglia di andarci, non posso

▷he was much *embarrassed* era molto imbarazzato

▷*how* much? quanto?

▷*however* much he tries per quanto ci provi

▷I hardly know her, much *less* her mother conosco appena lei e ancora meno sua madre

▷it doesn't much *matter* non ha molta importanza

▷I like it *so* much mi piace così tanto

▷*so* much (tanto)

▷much *to* my surprise con mia grande sorpresa, con mio grande stupore

▷*too* much troppo

▷I like it *very* much mi piace moltissimo

▷thank you *very* much molte grazie

b (*by far*) di gran lunga;

▷much the *biggest* di gran lunga il/la più grande

▷I would much *rather* stay preferirei di gran lunga restare

c (*almost*) pressappoco, quasi;

▷they're much the *same* sono praticamente uguali.

much·ness ['mʌtʃnɪs] N (*fam*): **they're much of a muchness** sono più o meno uguali.

mu·ci·lage ['mju:sɪlɪdʒ] N mucillagine *f*.

muck [mʌk] N a (*dirt*) sporcizia, sudiciume *m*; (*mud*) fango; (*manure*) letame *m*

b (*fig*) porcherie *fpl*

▶ **muck about, muck around** (*fam*) 1 VT + ADV: **to muck sb about** complicare la vita a qn.

2 VI + ADV a (*lark about*) fare lo/la stupido(-a); (*do nothing in particular*) non fare niente di speciale, gingillarsi

b (*tinker*) armeggiare

▶ **muck in** VI + ADV (*Brit fam*) mettersi insieme

▶ **muck out** VT + ADV (*stable*) pulire

▶ **muck up** VT + ADV (*fam*)

a (*dirty*) sporcare

b (*spoil*) rovinare.

mucki·ness ['mʌkɪnɪs] N (*see adj*) fangosità; sporcizia.

muck·rak·ing ['mʌkˌreɪkɪŋ] (*fig fam*) 1 N scandalismo.

2 ADJ scandalistico(-a).

♦ **muck-up** ['mʌkˌʌp] N (*fam*) casino, pasticcio.

mucky ['mʌkɪ] ADJ (*comp* -**ier**, *superl* -**iest**) (*muddy*) fangoso (-a); (*filthy*) sudicio(-a), sporco(-a), lordo(-a).

mu·cous ['mju:kəs] ADJ (*of mucus*) mucoso(-a); (*producing mucus*) muciparo(-a).

mu·cus ['mju:kəs] N muco.

mud [mʌd] N a fango b (*fig*): **his name is mud** non è molto ben visto; **to sling mud at sb** gettar fango addosso a qn.

♦ **mud bath** N: **to have a mud bath** fare i fanghi.

mud·di·ness ['mʌdɪnɪs] N (*of road, ground*) fangosità *f inv*; (*of liquid*) torbidità *f inv*; (*of complexion*) colore *m* terreo.

mud·dle ['mʌdl] 1 N (*perplexity*) confusione *f*; (*disorder*) disordine *m*; **to be in a muddle** (*room, books*) essere in disordine; (*person*) essere molto confuso(-a), non riuscire a raccapezzarsi; (*plan, arrangements*) essere per aria; **to get into a muddle** (*person: while explaining*) imbrogliarsi, fare confusione; (*things*) finire sottosopra; **there's been a muddle over the seats** è successo un pasticcio con i posti.

2 VT (*also:* **muddle up**) a (*papers*) mettere sottosopra; **you've muddled up A and B** hai confuso A con B

b (*person, story, details*) confondere

▶ **muddle along, muddle on** VI + ADV andare avanti a casaccio

▶ **muddle through** VI + ADV cavarsela alla meno peggio.

♦ **muddle-headed** ['mʌdlˌhedɪd] ADJ (*person*) confusionario(-a); (*ideas*) confuso(-a).

mud·dler ['mʌdlə'] N confusionario(-a), pasticcione(-a).

mud·dy ['mʌdɪ] ADJ (*comp* -**ier**, *superl* -**iest**) (*road, ground, field*) fangoso(-a); (*hands*) coperto(-a) di fango; (*clothes, shoes*) infangato(-a); (*liquid*) torbido(-a); (*complexion*) smorto(-a), terreo(-a).

♦ **mud flap** N (*Aut, Brit*) paraspruzzi *m inv*.

♦ **mud flat** N distesa fangosa.

mud·guard ['mʌdˌgɑ:d] N (*Brit*) parafango.

♦ **mud hut** N capanna di fango.

mud·pack ['mʌdˌpæk] N maschera di fango.

♦ **mud pie** N formina di fango.

♦ **mud-slinging** ['mʌdˌslɪŋɪŋ] N (*fig*) infangamento.

mues·li ['mju:zlɪ] N müsli *msg*.

mu·ez·zin [mu:'ɛzɪn] N muezzin *m inv*.

muff[1] [mʌf] N manicotto.

muff[2] [mʌf] VT (*shot, catch*) mancare, sbagliare; **to muff it** sbagliare tutto; **to muff one's lines** (*actor*) impappinarsi.

muf·fin ['mʌfɪn] N (*Brit*) specie di pasticcino soffice da tè.

muf·fle ['mʌfl] VT a (*wrap warmly: also:* **muffle up**) imbacuccare b (*deaden: sound*) smorzare, attutire; (*: screams*) soffocare.

muf·fled ['mʌfld] ADJ (*sound*) attutito(-a), smorzato(-a).

muf·fler ['mʌflə'] N (*scarf*) sciarpa (pesante); (*Am: Aut*) marmitta; (*: on motorbike*) silenziatore *m*.

muf·ti ['mʌftɪ] N: **in mufti** in borghese.

mug [mʌg] 1 N a (*cup*) tazzone *m*; (*for beer*) boccale *m* b (*Brit fam: fool*) salame *m*, scemo(-a); **it's a mug's game** è proprio (una cosa) da fessi c (*fam: face*) muso.

2 VT (*attack and rob*) aggredire, assalire

▶ **mug up** VT + ADV (*Brit fam*: *also*: **mug up on**) studiare bene.

mug·ger ['mʌgə'] N aggressore *m*, rapinatore(-trice).

mug·ging ['mʌgɪŋ] N aggressione *f* (*a scopo di rapina*).

mug·gins ['mʌgɪnz] NSG (*Brit fam*) fesso(-a), salame *m*; (: *oneself*): **muggins had to do it** come sempre è toccato a me.

mug·gy ['mʌgɪ] ADJ (*comp* **-ier**, *superl* **-iest**) (*weather*) afoso(-a).

♦ **mug shot** N (*fam*) foto *f inv* segnaletica.

mu·lat·to [mjuː'lætəʊ] N (*pl* **mulattoes**) (*offensive*) mulatto (-a).

mul·berry ['mʌlbərɪ] N (*fruit*) mora (di gelso); (*tree*) gelso, moro; **black mulberry** gelso nero.

mulch [mʌltʃ] N pacciame *m*.

mule [mjuːl] N mulo(-a); (**as**) **stubborn as a mule** testardo (-a) come un mulo.

mul·ish ['mjuːlɪʃ] ADJ testardo(-a).

mull [mʌl] VT (*wine*) scaldare con aromi e zucchero

▶ **mull over** VT + ADV rimuginare.

mul·lah ['mʌlə] N mullah *m inv*.

mulled wine ['mʌld,waɪn] N vin brûlé *m inv*, vino caldo.

mul·let ['mʌlɪt] N: **red mullet** triglia; **grey mullet** muggine *m*, cefalo.

mul·li·ga·taw·ny [,mʌlɪgə'tɔːnɪ] N minestra al curry.

multi... ['mʌltɪ] PREF multi... .

multi·ac·cess [,mʌltɪ'æksɛs] ADJ (*Comput*) ad accesso multiplo.

multi·cel·lu·lar [mʌltɪ'sɛljʊlə'] ADJ pluricellulare.

multi·col·oured, (*Am*) **multi·col·ored** ['mʌltɪ'kʌləd] ADJ multicolore, variopinto(-a).

multi·fari·ous [,mʌltɪ'fɛərɪəs] ADJ molteplice, svariato (-a).

multi·hull ['mʌltɪ,hʌl] N multiscafo.

multi·lat·er·al [,mʌltɪ'lætərəl] ADJ (*Pol*) multilaterale; **multilateral trade** interscambio.

♦ **multi-level** ['mʌltɪ,lɛvl] ADJ (*Am*) = **multistorey**.

multi·lin·gual [,mʌltɪ 'lɪŋgwəl] ADJ multilingue.

multi·mil·lion·aire [,mʌltɪ,mɪljə'nɛə'] N multimiliardario (-a).

multi·na·tion·al [,mʌltɪ'næʃənl] 1 N multinazionale *f*. 2 ADJ multinazionale.

multi·ple ['mʌltɪpl] 1 ADJ **a** WITH SG N multiplo(-a) **b** (*with pl n*: *many*) molteplici. 2 N **a** (*Math*) multiplo **b** (*Brit*: *also*: **multiple store**) *grande magazzino che fa parte di una catena*.

♦ **multiple choice** N esercizi *mpl* a scelta multipla.

♦ **multiple crash** N serie *f inv* di incidenti a catena.

♦ **multiple purpose resource management** N gestione *f* multiuso delle risorse.

♦ **multiple sclerosis** N sclerosi *f* a placche.

♦ **multiple socket** N (*Elec*) presa multipla.

multi·plex ['mʌltɪ,plɛks] N (*also*: **multiplex cinema**) cinema multisale *m inv*.

multi·pli·ca·tion [,mʌltɪplɪ'keɪʃən] N moltiplicazione *f*.

♦ **multiplication table** N tavola pitagorica; **to learn one's multiplication tables** imparare le tabelline.

multi·plic·ity [,mʌltɪ'plɪsɪtɪ] N molteplicità *f inv*; **for a multiplicity of reasons** per una serie di ragioni.

multi·ply ['mʌltɪ,plaɪ] 1 VT (*Math*) moltiplicare. 2 VI **a** (*Math*) moltiplicare; **she can't multiply** non sa fare le moltiplicazioni **b** (*increase*) moltiplicarsi.

multi·pur·pose [,mʌltɪ'pɜːpəs] ADJ multiuso *inv*.

multi·racial [,mʌltɪ'reɪʃəl] ADJ multirazziale.

multi·sto·rey [,mʌltɪ'stɔːrɪ], (*Am*) **multi-level** ADJ (*building, car park*) a più piani.

multi·tude ['mʌltɪ,tjuːd] N moltitudine *f*.

mum[1] [mʌm] N (*Brit fam*: *mother*) mamma.

mum[2] [mʌm] ADJ: **to keep mum (about sth)** non fare parola (di qc), non aprire bocca (su qc); **mum's the word!** acqua in bocca!

mum·ble ['mʌmbl] VT, VI borbottare.

mum·bo jum·bo [,mʌmbəʊ'dʒʌmbəʊ] N (*pej*) sfilza di paroloni.

mum·mi·fy ['mʌmɪ,faɪ] VT mummificare.

mum·my[1] ['mʌmɪ] N (*Brit fam*: *mother*) mamma; **he's a mummy's boy** è un mammone.

mum·my[2] ['mʌmɪ] N (*embalmed corpse*) mummia.

mumps [mʌmps] NSG orecchioni *mpl*.

munch [mʌntʃ] VT, VI sgranocchiare.

mun·dane [,mʌn'deɪn] ADJ (*worldly*) di questo mondo; (*pej*: *humdrum*) banale, terra terra *inv*.

Mu·nich ['mjuːnɪk] N Monaco *f* (di Baviera).

mu·nici·pal [mjuː'nɪsɪpəl] ADJ municipale, comunale.

mu·nici·pal·ity [mjuː,nɪsɪ'pælɪtɪ] N (*place*) comune *m*, municipio.

mu·nifi·cence [mjuː'nɪfɪsns] N (*frm*) munificenza.

mu·nifi·cent [mjuː'nɪfɪsnt] ADJ munifico(-a).

mu·ni·tions [mjuː'nɪʃənz] NPL munizioni *fpl*.

♦ **munitions dump** N deposito di munizioni.

mu·ral ['mjʊərəl] 1 ADJ murale. 2 N dipinto murale.

mur·der ['mɜːdə'] 1 N **a** omicidio, assassinio; **to commit murder** commettere un omicidio **b** (*fam*): **it was murder!** è stato pazzesco!; **to scream blue murder** strepitare; **she gets away with murder** se la cava sempre. 2 VT (*person*) assassinare; (*fig, song*) massacrare.

♦ **murder case** N caso di omicidio.

mur·der·er ['mɜːdərə'] N assassino, omicida *m*.

mur·der·ess ['mɜːdərɪs] N assassina, omicida *f*.

mur·der·ous ['mɜːdərəs] ADJ (*intentions*) omicida; (*look*) assassino(-a); (*climate, road*) micidiale.

♦ **murder weapon** N arma del delitto.

mu·rex ['mjʊərɛks] N murice *m*.

murk [mɜːk] N oscurità *f inv*, buio.

murky ['mɜːkɪ] ADJ (*comp* **-ier**, *superl* **-iest**) (*gen*) oscuro (-a), cupo(-a), tenebroso(-a), buio(-a); (*thick*: *darkness*) fitto(-a); (: *smoke*) denso(-a); (*fig*) torbido(-a).

mur·mur ['mɜːmə'] 1 N (*soft speech*) mormorio; (*of traffic, voices*) brusio; (*of bees*) ronzio; (*of leaves*) fruscio; **there were murmurs of disagreement** c'era un mormorio di disapprovazione; **without a murmur** senza fiatare; **heart murmur** (*Med*) soffio al cuore. 2 VT, VI borbottare, mormorare.

MusB, **MusBac** N ABBR (= *Bachelor of Music*) *diploma universitario in Musica*.

mus·cle ['mʌsl] N muscolo; (*fig*) energia, forza; **he never moved a muscle** rimase fermo immobile

▶ **muscle in** VI + ADV: **to muscle in (on sth)** (*fam*) intromettersi *or* immischiarsi (in qc).

mus·cle·man ['mʌsl,mæn] N (*pl* **-men**) mister muscolo *m inv*.

mus·cu·lar ['mʌskjʊlə'] ADJ muscolare; (*person, arm*) muscoloso(-a).

♦ **muscular dystrophy** N distrofia muscolare.

MusD, **MusDoc** N ABBR (= *Doctor of Music*) ≈ diploma in Musica.

Muse [mjuːz] N (*Myth*) Musa.

muse¹ [mju:z] N (*fig*) musa.
muse² [mju:z] VI: **to muse on** *or* **about sth** rimuginare *or* meditare su qc.
mu·seum [mju:'zɪəm] N museo.
♦ **museum piece** N pezzo da museo.
mush [mʌʃ] N pappa.
mush·room ['mʌʃrum] ⓵ N (*Bot*) fungo.
　⓶ ADJ (*soup, omelette*) ai *or* coi funghi; (*flavour*) di funghi; (*colour*) color beige rosato *inv*.
　⓷ VI **a** (*town*) svilupparsi rapidamente; (*houses*) spuntare come funghi; **the cloud of smoke went mushrooming up** la nuvola di fumo si alzò prendendo la forma di un fungo
　b: **to go mushrooming** andare per funghi, andare a cercare funghi.
♦ **mushroom cloud** N fungo di un'esplosione nucleare.
mushy ['mʌʃɪ] ADJ (*comp* **-ier**, *superl* **-iest**) come pappa; (*fig*) sdolcinato(-a).
♦ **mushy peas** NPL *piatto a base di piselli grandi stracotti e mescaloti fino a ridurli in poltiglia.*
mu·sic ['mju:zɪk] ⓵ N musica; **to set to music** mettere in musica *or* musicare; **it was music to her ears** (*fig*) era musica per le sue orecchie.
　⓶ ADJ (*teacher, lesson*) di musica.
mu·si·cal ['mju:zɪkəl] ⓵ ADJ (*gen*) musicale; **he's very musical** (*fond of*) è amante della musica; (*skilled*) è portato per la musica; **she comes from a musical family** viene da una famiglia di musicisti.
　⓶ N (*Cine, Theatre*) musical *m inv*, commedia musicale.
♦ **musical chairs** NSG gioco delle sedie (*in cui bisogna sedersi non appena cessa la musica*); (*fig*) scambio delle poltrone.
♦ **musical instrument** N strumento musicale.
mu·si·cal·ly ['mju:zɪkəlɪ] ADV musicalmente.
♦ **music box, musical box** N carillon *m inv*.
♦ **music centre** N stereo *m inv* compatto.
♦ **music critic** N critico musicale.
♦ **music festival** N festival *m inv* musicale.
♦ **music hall** N teatro di varietà.
mu·si·cian [mju:'zɪʃən] N musicista *m/f*.
mu·si·cian·ship [mju:'zɪʃənʃɪp] N tecnica (musicale).
♦ **music lover** N appassionato(-a) di *or* amante *m/f* della musica.
mu·si·colo·gist [,mju:zɪ'kɒlədʒɪst] N musicologo(-a).
mu·si·col·ogy [,mju:zɪ'kɒlədʒɪ] N musicologia.
♦ **music stand** N leggio.
musk [mʌsk] N muschio.
mus·ket ['mʌskɪt] N moschetto.
♦ **musk ox** N bue *m* muschiato.
musk·rat ['mʌsk,ræt] N (*animal*) topo muschiato, ondatra; (*fur*) rat musqué *m inv*.
♦ **musk rose** N (*Bot*) rosa muschiata.
musky ['mʌskɪ] ADJ (*comp* **-ier**, *superl* **-iest**) muschiato(-a).
Mus·lim, Mos·lem ['muslɪm] ADJ, N musulmano(-a).
mus·lin ['mʌzlɪn] ⓵ N mussola (di cotone).
　⓶ ADJ di mussola.
mus·quash ['mʌskwɒʃ] N (*fur*) rat musqué *m inv*.
muss [mʌs] VT (*also*: **muss up**: *Am fam*: *hair*) scompigliare; (: *dress*) spiegazzare.
mus·sel ['mʌsl] N cozza.
must¹ [mʌst] MODAL AUX VB ⓵ **a** (*obligation*) dovere; **I must do it** devo farlo; **if you must** se proprio devi; **one must not be too hopeful** non bisogna sperare troppo; **there must be a reason** ci deve (pur) essere un motivo; **I must say** francamente

　b (*probability*): **he must be there by now** dovrebbe essere arrivato ormai; **it must be cold up there** dev'essere freddo lassù; **I must have made a mistake** devo essermi sbagliato.
　⓶ N (*fam*): **this programme/trip is a must** è un programma/viaggio da non perdere.
must² [mʌst] N = **mustiness**.
must³ [mʌst] N (*in wine-making*) mosto.
mus·tache [mə'stɑ:ʃ] N (*Am*) = **moustache**.
mus·tard ['mʌstəd] N senape *f*; (*also*: **grain mustard**) mostarda; **as keen as mustard** molto entusiasta.
♦ **mustard gas** N (*Chem*) iprite *f*.
♦ **mustard plaster** N senapismo.
mus·ter ['mʌstə'] ⓵ N (*gathering*) adunata; (*roll-call*) appello; **to pass muster** (*fig*) essere (considerato(-a)) accettabile *or* passabile.
　⓶ VT (*men, helpers*) radunare, mettere insieme; (*money, sum*) mettere insieme; (*also*: **muster up**: *strength, courage*) fare appello a; **I can't muster up any enthusiasm** non riesco ad entusiasmarmi.
　⓷ VI radunarsi.
musti·ness ['mʌstɪnɪs] N odor di muffa *or* di stantio.
mustn't ['mʌsnt] = **must not**.
mus·ty ['mʌstɪ] ADJ (*comp* **-ier**, *superl* **-iest**) (*smell*) (che sa) di stantio *or* di muffa; (*ideas*) ammuffito(-a), stantio(-a); **to smell musty** aver odore di stantio.
mu·tant ['mju:tənt] ADJ, N mutante (*m/f*).
mu·tate [mju:'teɪt] VI subire una mutazione.
mu·ta·tion [mju:'teɪʃən] N mutazione *f*.
mute [mju:t] ⓵ ADJ (*comp* **-r**, *superl* **-st**) muto(-a).
　⓶ N (*person*) muto(-a); (*Mus*) sordina.
mut·ed ['mju:tɪd] ADJ (*noise*) attutito(-a), smorzato(-a); (*criticism*) attenuato(-a); (*Mus*) in sordina; (: *trumpet*) con sordina.
mu·ti·late ['mju:tɪ,leɪt] VT mutilare.
mu·ti·la·tion [,mju:tɪ'leɪʃən] N mutilazione *f*.
mu·ti·neer [,mju:tɪ'nɪə'] N ammutinato(-a).
mu·ti·nous ['mju:tɪnəs] ADJ (*sailor, troops*) ammutinato(-a); (*attitude*) ribelle.
mu·ti·ny ['mju:tɪnɪ] ⓵ N ammutinamento.
　⓶ VI ammutinarsi.
mut·ter ['mʌtə'] ⓵ N borbottio.
　⓶ VT borbottare, bofonchiare.
　⓷ VI borbottare; (*thunder*) brontolare.
mut·ton ['mʌtn] N carne *f* di montone, montone *m*; **a leg of mutton** un cosciotto di montone; **mutton dressed as lamb** (*fig*) *una vecchia che vuol sembrare una giovincella.*
mu·tu·al ['mju:tjʊəl] ADJ (*affection, suspicion*) reciproco(-a); (*interests*) mutuo(-a), reciproco(-a), comune; (*friend, cousin*) comune; **to our mutual satisfaction** in modo da soddisfare entrambi, con reciproca soddisfazione.
mu·tu·al·ism ['mju:tjʊə,lɪzəm] N simbiosi *f* mutualistica.
mu·tu·al·ly ['mju:tjʊəlɪ] ADV reciprocamente.
Mu·zak® ['mju:zæk] N *musica di sottofondo trasmessa in ristoranti, posti di lavoro ecc.*
muz·zle ['mʌzl] ⓵ N (*snout*) muso; (*of gun*) bocca (da fuoco); (*for dog*) museruola.
　⓶ VT (*dog*) mettere la museruola a; (*fig*: *person*) costringere a tacere.
muz·zy ['mʌzɪ] ADJ (*comp* **-ier**, *superl* **-iest**) (*outline, ideas*) confuso(-a); (*person*) intontito(-a).
MV [,ɛm'vi:] ABBR (= *motor vessel*) motonave *f*.
MW ABBR (*Radio*: = *medium wave*) O.M.

my [maɪ] POSS ADJ il/la mio(-a), *pl* i/le miei(-mie); **this is my house** questa è la mia casa; **my brother** mio fratello.

Myanmar ['maɪænmɑːʳ] N la Myanma.

my·co·sis [maɪ'kəʊsɪs] N micosi *f*.

myo·pia [maɪ'əʊpɪə] N (*frm*) miopia.

my·op·ic [maɪ'ɒpɪk] ADJ miope.

myri·ad ['mɪrɪəd] N miriade *f*.

myr·tle ['mɜːtl] N mirto.

my·self [maɪ'sɛlf] PERS PRON (*reflexive*) mi; (*emphatic*) io stesso(-a); (*after preposition*) me, me stesso(-a); **I did it (all) by myself** l'ho fatto (tutto) da solo; **I'm not myself today** non mi sento in forma oggi; see also **oneself**.

mys·teri·ous [mɪs'tɪərɪəs] ADJ misterioso(-a).

mys·teri·ous·ly [mɪs'tɪərɪəslɪ] ADV misteriosamente.

mys·tery ['mɪstərɪ] ① N mistero; **it's a mystery to me where it can have gone** dove sia finito (per me) è un mistero.
② ADJ (*man, woman*) misterioso(-a).

♦ **mystery play** N mistero.

♦ **mystery ship** N nave *f* fantasma *inv*.

♦ **mystery story** N racconto del mistero.

♦ **mystery tour** N *viaggio con destinazione a sorpresa*.

mys·tic ['mɪstɪk] ADJ, N mistico(-a).

mys·ti·cal ['mɪstɪkəl] ADJ mistico(-a).

mys·ti·cism ['mɪˌstɪsɪzəm] N misticismo.

mys·ti·fi·ca·tion [ˌmɪstɪfɪ'keɪʃən] N (*bewilderment*) perplessità *f inv*.

mys·ti·fy ['mɪstɪˌfaɪ] VT (*bewilder*) lasciare perplesso(-a), disorientare.

mys·tique [mɪs'tiːk] N fascino.

myth [mɪθ] N mito.

myth·ic ['mɪθɪk] ADJ mitico(-a).

mythi·cal ['mɪθɪkəl] ADJ mitico(-a).

mytho·logi·cal [ˌmɪθə'lɒdʒɪkəl] ADJ mitologico(-a).

my·thol·ogy [mɪ'θɒlədʒɪ] N mitologia.

mytho·ma·nia [ˌmɪθəʊ'meɪnɪə] N mitomania.

myxo·ma·to·sis [ˌmɪksəʊmə'təʊsɪs] N mixomatosi *f*.

N

N, n [ɛn] N (*letter*) N, n *form inv*; **N for Nellie,** (*Am*) **N for Nan**
≈ N come Napoli.

N ABBR (= *north*) N (= *nord*).

NA [ˌɛn'eɪ] N ABBR **a** (*Am*: = *Narcotics Anonymous*) *associazione in aiuto dei tossicodipendenti* **b** (*Am*)= *National Academy*.

n/a ABBR **a** (= *not applicable*) non pertinente **b** (*Comm etc*)= *no account*.

NAACP [ˌɛneɪeɪsi:'pi:] N ABBR (*Am*)= *National Association for the Advancement of Colored People*.

NAAFI ['næfɪ] N ABBR (*Brit*: = *Navy, Army & Air Force Institute*) *organizzazione che fornisce negozi, mense ecc. per il personale militare*.

nab [næb] VT (*fam: thief etc*) acciuffare, beccare; (: *person to speak to*) beccare, bloccare.

NACU [ˌɛneɪsi:'ju:] N ABBR (*Am*)= *National Association of Colleges and Universities*.

na·dir ['neɪdɪər] N (*Astron*) nadir *m*; (*fig*) punto più basso.

nag¹ [næg] N (*pej: horse*) ronzino.

nag² [næg] **1** VT (*also: nag at*) assillare, tormentare; **the children nagged (at) their parents to take them to the fair** i bambini hanno tormentato i genitori per farsi portare alle giostre; **the family nagged me into buying a new car** a forza di insistere in famiglia mi hanno fatto comprare una macchina nuova.

2 VI lagnarsi, brontolare in continuazione.

3 N (*person*) brontolone(-a).

nag·ging ['nægɪŋ] **1** ADJ (*person*) brontolone(-a); (*pain*) insistente, persistente; (*doubt, fear etc*) tormentoso(-a), angoscioso(-a).

2 N brontolii *mpl*, osservazioni *fpl* continue.

nai·ad ['naɪæd] N (*Myth*) naiade *f*.

nail [neɪl] **1** N **a** (*Anat*) unghia; **to bite one's nails** mangiarsi le unghie

b (*metal*) chiodo; **to hit the nail on the head** (*fig*) cogliere *or* colpire nel segno; **to pay cash on the nail** (*Brit*) pagare subito e in contanti, pagare sull'unghia (*fam*).

2 VT (*also fig fam: criminal*) inchiodare; **to nail the lid on a box** inchiodare il coperchio di una cassa

▶ **nail down** VT + ADV fissare con chiodi, inchiodare; (*fig*): **to nail sb down to a date** costringere qn a una data; **to nail sb down to a promise** costringere qn a fare una promessa; **to nail sb down to a price** costringere qn ad accettare un prezzo

▶ **nail up** VT + ADV (*picture, sign*) fissare con un chiodo; (*door*) chiudere con chiodi.

nail·brush ['neɪl,brʌʃ] N spazzolino per unghie.

nail·file ['neɪl,faɪl] N lima *or* limetta per unghie.

♦ **nail polish** N smalto per unghie.

♦ **nail polish remover,** (*Brit*) **nail varnish remover** N acetone *m*, solvente *m*.

♦ **nail scissors** NPL forbicine *fpl* per unghie.

♦ **nail varnish** N (*Brit*) = **nail polish**.

Nai·ro·bi [naɪ'rəʊbɪ] N Nairobi *f*.

na·ïve [naɪ'i:v] ADJ ingenuo(-a).

na·ïve·ly [naɪ'i:vlɪ] ADV ingenuamente.

na·ïve·té [ˌnɑ:i:v'teɪ], **na·ïve·ty** [naɪ'i:vtɪ] N ingenuità *f inv*.

na·ked ['neɪkɪd] ADJ (*person*) nudo(-a); (*hillside, trees*) spoglio(-a), nudo(-a); **the naked truth** la verità nuda e cruda; **visible to the naked eye** che si può vedere a occhio nudo; **with the naked eye** a occhio nudo.

na·ked·ness ['neɪkɪdnɪs] N nudità.

NAM [ˌɛneɪ'ɛm] N ABBR (*Am*)= *National Association of Manufacturers*.

namby-pamby [ˌnæmbɪ'pæmbɪ] ADJ, N (*fam*) rammollito(-a).

name [neɪm] **1** N nome *m*; (*of book etc*) titolo; (*reputation*) (buon) nome, fama, reputazione *f*; **what's your name?** come ti chiami?; **my name is Peter** mi chiamo Peter; **by the name of Jones** di nome Jones; **to go by** *or* **under the name of** farsi chiamare; **she knows them all by name** li conosce tutti per nome; **I know him only by name** lo conosco solo di nome; **in the name of the law/of God** in nome della legge/di Dio; **in the name of all those present** a nome di tutti i presenti; **in name only** solo di nome; **to take sb's name and address** prendere nome e indirizzo di qn; (*Police*) prendere le generalità di qn; **to put one's name down for** (*ticket*) mettersi in lista per avere; (*school, course*) mettersi in lista per; **to call sb**

names insultare qn; **he's a big name in show business** è una personalità *or* un grosso nome nel mondo dello spettacolo; **he has a name for being honest** è noto *or* famoso per la sua onestà; **to protect one's (good) name** salvaguardare il proprio buon nome; **to make a name for o.s.** farsi un nome; **the firm has a good name** l'azienda ha una buona reputazione; **to get (o.s.) a bad name** farsi una cattiva fama *or* una brutta reputazione.

[2] VT **a** (*baby etc*) chiamare; (*ship*) battezzare; **a man named Jones** un uomo di nome Jones; **he was named after his father** gli è stato dato il nome del padre; **they haven't named him yet** non gli hanno ancora dato un nome

b (*mention*) nominare, fare il nome di; (*identify*) identificare; (: *accomplice*) fare il nome di, rivelare il nome di; **to name sb for a post** proporre la candidatura di qn a una carica, proporre qn per una carica; **you name it, we've got it** abbiamo tutto quello che vuoi

c (*date, price etc*) stabilire, fissare; **have you named the day yet?** (*for wedding*) avete già fissato la data?

♦ **name-drop** ['neɪmˌdrɒp] VI: **he's always name-dropping** si dà tante arie vantando amicizie importanti.

♦ **name-dropping** ['neɪmˌdrɒpɪŋ] N: **there was a lot of name-dropping in his speech** il suo discorso era infarcito di nomi di gente famosa.

name·less ['neɪmlɪs] ADJ (*unknown*) senza nome; (*anonymous*) ignoto(-a), anonimo(-a); (*indefinable: fears, crimes*) indescrivibile, indefinibile; **a certain person who shall be nameless** una persona di cui non verrà fatto il nome.

name·ly ['neɪmlɪ] ADV vale a dire.

name·plate ['neɪmˌpleɪt] N (*on door etc*) targa, targhetta.

name·sake ['neɪmˌseɪk] N omonimo(-a).

nan bread ['nɑːnˌbrɛd] N *tipo di pane indiano poco lievitato di forma schiacciata.*

nan·ny ['nænɪ] N (*children's*) bambinaia, tata (*fam*).

♦ **nanny goat** N capra.

nap[1] [næp] N [1] (*sleep*) sonnellino, pisolino; **to have** *or* **take a nap** fare *or* farsi un sonnellino, schiacciare un pisolino.

[2] VI: **to be caught napping** essere preso(-a) alla sprovvista.

nap[2] [næp] N (*on cloth*) peluria; **against the nap** contropelo.

NAPA [ˌeneɪpiːˈeɪ] N ABBR (*Am:* = National Association of Performing Arts*) associazione nazionale degli artisti di palcoscenico.*

na·palm ['neɪpɑːm] N napalm *m*.

♦ **napalm bomb** N bomba al napalm.

nape [neɪp] N: **nape of the neck** nuca.

naph·tha ['næfθə] N nafta.

nap·kin ['næpkɪn] N (*also:* **table napkin**) tovagliolo, salvietta.

♦ **napkin ring** N portatovagliolo (*ad anello*).

Na·ples ['neɪplz] N Napoli *f*.

Napoleon [nəˈpəʊlɪən] N Napoleone *m*.

Na·po·leon·ic [nəˌpəʊlɪˈɒnɪk] ADJ napoleonico(-a).

nap·py ['næpɪ] N (*Brit*) pannolino.

♦ **nappy liner** N (*Brit*) fogliettino igienico (*per pannolini*).

nar·cis·sist ['nɑːsɪsɪst] N (*frm*) narcisista *m/f*.

nar·cis·sis·tic [ˌnɑːsɪˈsɪstɪk] ADJ (*frm*) narcisistico(-a).

Narcissus [nɑːˈsɪsəs] N (*Myth*) Narciso.

nar·cis·sus [nɑːˈsɪsəs] N (*pl* narcissi [nɑːˈsɪsaɪ]) (*flower*) narciso.

♦ **Narcissus complex** N: **to have a Narcissus complex** essere narcisista.

nar·cot·ic [nɑːˈkɒtɪk] [1] ADJ narcotico(-a).

[2] N (*Med*) narcotico; **narcotics** NPL (*drugs*) narcotici *mpl*, stupefacenti *mpl*.

nark [nɑːk] VT (*Brit fam*) scocciare.

narked [nɑːkt] ADJ (*Brit fam*) scocciato(-a).

nar·rate [nəˈreɪt] VT narrare, raccontare.

nar·ra·tion [nəˈreɪʃən] N narrazione *f*.

nar·ra·tive ['nærətɪv] [1] ADJ narrativo(-a).

[2] N narrazione *f*; (*technique*) narrativa.

nar·ra·tor [nəˈreɪtəʳ] N narratore(-trice).

nar·row ['nærəʊ] [1] ADJ (*comp* -er, *superl* -est) (*gen*) stretto(-a); (*advantage, majority*) scarso(-a); (*outlook, mind*) ristretto(-a), limitato(-a); (*interpretation*) limitato (-a); (*means*) limitato(-a), modesto(-a); **to have a narrow escape** farcela per un pelo, scamparla bella; **to take a narrow view of** avere una visione limitata di.

[2] VT **a** (*also:* **narrow down**: *road, investigations*) restringere; (: *choice*) restringere, ridurre; **to narrow sth down to** ridurre qc a; **we have narrowed the field (down) to three candidates** abbiamo ristretto la scelta a tre candidati

b (*eyes*) stringere.

[3] VI (*road*) restringersi; (*majority*) ridursi; (*eyes*) stringersi; **so the question narrows down to this** la questione, quindi, si riduce a questo.

♦ **narrow-gauge** ['nærəʊˌgeɪdʒ] ADJ (*Rail*) a scartamento ridotto.

nar·row·ly ['nærəʊlɪ] ADV **a** (*miss, escape etc*): **Maria narrowly escaped drowning** per un pelo Maria non è affogata; **he narrowly missed hitting the cyclist** per poco non ha investito il ciclista **b** (*interpret: rules etc*) rigorosamente.

♦ **narrow-minded** [ˌnærəʊˈmaɪndɪd] ADJ (*pej: person*) di idee ristrette; (: *views, outlook etc*) ristretto(-a).

♦ **narrow-mindedness** [ˌnærəʊˈmaɪndɪdnɪs] N chiusura mentale.

nar·row·ness ['nærəʊnɪs] N strettezza.

nar·whal ['nɑːwəl] N narvalo.

NAS [ˌeneɪˈɛs] N ABBR (*Brit*)= National Academy of Sciences.

NASA ['næsə] N ABBR (*Am:* = National Aeronautics and Space Administration*) N.A.S.A. *f*.

na·sal ['neɪzəl] ADJ nasale.

na·sal·ize ['neɪzəˌlaɪz] VT nasalizzare.

nas·cent ['næsnt] ADJ (*frm*) nascente.

Nas·sau ['næsaʊ] N Nassau *f*.

nas·ti·ly ['nɑːstɪlɪ] ADV (*unpleasantly*) sgradevolmente; (*spitefully*) malignamente, con cattiveria.

nas·ti·ness ['nɑːstɪnɪs] N (*of person, remark*) malignità, cattiveria.

na·stur·tium [nəˈstɜːʃəm] N cappuccina, nasturzio (indiano).

nas·ty ['nɑːstɪ] ADJ (*comp* -ier, *superl* -iest) (*smell, taste*) cattivo(-a), sgradevole; (*moment, experience, situation*) brutto(-a), spiacevole; (*accident, wound, corner, trick*) brutto(-a); (*person*) antipatico(-a), villano(-a); (: *spiteful: also: remark, mind*) maligno(-a), cattivo(-a); (*temper, nature*) brutto(-a); (*weather*) brutto(-a), cattivo(-a); (*book, film etc*) di cattivo gusto; (: *violent*) violento(-a); **to smell nasty** non avere un buon odore; **to turn nasty** (*situation*) mettersi male; (*weather*) guastarsi; (*person*) incattivirsi; **he's a nasty piece of work** (*fam*) è un farabutto; **what a nasty mind you have!** quanto sei maligno!; **he had a nasty time of it** se l'è passata brutta; **she gave me a nasty look** mi ha dato un'occhiataccia;

it's a nasty business è una brutta faccenda, è un brutto affare.

NAS/UWT [ɛneɪˈɛsˌjuːdʌbljuːˈtiː] N ABBR (*Brit*: = *National Association of Schoolmasters/Union of Women Teachers*) *sindacato di insegnanti in Inghilterra e Galles*.

na·tion [ˈneɪʃən] N nazione *f*.

na·tion·al [ˈnæʃənl] [1] ADJ nazionale; **national news** notizie *fpl* dall'interno; **national press** stampa (a diffusione) nazionale.

[2] N cittadino(-a).

♦ **national anthem** N inno nazionale.

♦ **National Coal Board** N (*Brit old*) *ente nazionale per l'industria carbonifera*.

♦ **National Curriculum** N (*Brit*) ≈ programma *m* (scolastico) ministeriale (*in Inghilterra e Galles*).

♦ **national debt** N debito pubblico.

♦ **national dress, national costume** N costume *m* nazionale.

♦ **national grid** N: **the national grid** la rete elettrica nazionale.

♦ **National Guard** N (*Am*): **the National Guard** la milizia nazionale (*volontaria, in ogni stato*).

♦ **National Health** N (*Brit*: *also*: **National Health Service**) *servizio nazionale di assistenza sanitaria*; **I got it on the National Health** l'ho avuto con la mutua.

♦ **national income** N (*Econ*) reddito nazionale.

♦ **National Insurance** N (*Brit*) ≈ Previdenza Sociale.

na·tion·al·ism [ˈnæʃnəˌlɪzəm] N nazionalismo.

na·tion·al·ist [ˈnæʃnəlɪst] [1] ADJ nazionalista; (*sympathies*) nazionalistico(-a).

[2] N nazionalista *m/f*.

na·tion·al·is·tic [ˌnæʃnəˈlɪstɪk] ADJ (*pej*) nazionalistico (-a).

na·tion·al·ity [ˌnæʃəˈnælɪtɪ] N nazionalità *f inv*; (*citizenship*) cittadinanza, nazionalità.

na·tion·ali·za·tion [ˌnæʃnəlaɪˈzeɪʃən] N nazionalizzazione *f*.

na·tion·al·ize [ˈnæʃnəˌlaɪz] VT nazionalizzare.

na·tion·al·ized [ˈnæʃnəˌlaɪzd] ADJ nazionalizzato(-a).

na·tion·al·ly [ˈnæʃnəlɪ] ADV (*consider*) da un punto di vista nazionale; (*broadcast*) in tutto il paese; (*apply etc*) a livello nazionale.

♦ **national park** N parco nazionale.

♦ **National Security Council** N (*Am*) consiglio nazionale di sicurezza.

♦ **national service** N (*Mil*) servizio militare.

♦ **National Trust** N (*Brit*): **the National Trust** ≈ soprintendenza ai beni culturali e ambientali.

♦ **nation-state** [ˈneɪʃənsteɪt] N stato-nazione *m*.

♦ **nation-wide** [ˈneɪʃənˌwaɪd] ADJ, ADV su scala nazionale.

na·tive [ˈneɪtɪv] [1] ADJ **a** (*country, town*) natale, natio(-a), nativo(-a); (*dialect*) nativo(-a); **he's a native Italian speaker** è di madrelingua italiana; **native language** lingua materna, madrelingua; **native land** paese *m* natio, patria

b (*innate*: *ability*) innato(-a), naturale

c (*indigenous*: *animal, plant*) indigeno(-a), originario (-a); (: *product, resources*) del luogo, del paese; **native to** originario(-a) di; **Britain's native red squirrel** lo scoiattolo rosso originario della Gran Bretagna

d (*of the natives*: *customs, costume, rites*) del luogo, del paese

e (*offensive*: *non-Western*) indigeno(-a).

[2] N **a** (*of birth, nationality*) abitante *m/f* del luogo; **he's a native of Japan** è giapponese di nascita; **he's a native of**

Salzburg è originario di Salisburgo; **he speaks Italian like a native** parla l'italiano come un madrelingua

b (*offensive*: *esp in colonies*) indigeno(-a).

♦ **Native American** N *discendente di tribù nordamericana dell'America settentrionale*.

Na·tiv·ity [nəˈtɪvɪtɪ] N (*Rel*): **the Nativity** la Natività.

♦ **nativity play** N rappresentazione *f* della Natività.

NATO [ˈneɪtəʊ] N ABBR (= *North Atlantic Treaty Organisation*) N.A.T.O. *f*.

nat·ter [ˈnætəʳ] (*fam*) [1] N chiacchierata; **to have a natter** fare quattro chiacchiere.

[2] VI chiacchierare.

nat·ty [ˈnætɪ] ADJ (*comp* **-ier**, *superl* **-iest**) (*fam*) elegante, chic *inv*.

natu·ral [ˈnætʃrəl] [1] ADJ (*gen*) naturale; (*ability*) innato (-a); (*manner*) semplice; **death from natural causes** (*Law*) morte *f* per cause naturali; **he died a natural death** è morto di morte naturale; **in its natural state** allo stato naturale; **he never knew his natural parents** non ha mai conosciuto i suoi veri genitori; **it's natural to be tired after a long journey** è naturale essere stanchi dopo un lungo viaggio; **it seemed the natural thing to do** è sembrata la cosa più ovvia *or* più naturale da farsi; **it is natural that ...** è naturale che... + *sub*; **he's a natural painter** è un pittore nato; **C natural** (*Mus*) do naturale.

[2] N **a** (*Mus*: *sign*) bequadro

b: **she's a natural!** ci è nata!

♦ **natural childbirth** N parto naturale.

♦ **natural gas** N gas *m* metano.

♦ **natural history** N storia naturale.

natu·ral·ism [ˈnætʃrəˌlɪzəm] N (*Art, Literature*) naturalismo.

natu·ral·ist [ˈnætʃrəlɪst] N naturalista *m/f*.

natu·ral·is·tic [ˌnætʃrəˈlɪstɪk] ADJ (*Art*) naturalistico(-a).

natu·rali·za·tion [ˌnætʃrəlaɪˈzeɪʃən] N (*see vb*) naturalizzazione *f*; acclimatazione *f*.

natu·ral·ize [ˈnætʃrəˌlaɪz] VT: **to be naturalized** (*person*) naturalizzarsi; **to become naturalized** (*animal, plant*) acclimatarsi.

natu·ral·ly [ˈnætʃrəlɪ] ADV **a** (*gen*) naturalmente

b (*by nature*: *gifted*) di natura, per natura; **he is naturally lazy** è pigro per natura; **my hair is naturally curly** i miei capelli sono ricci per natura; **a naturally optimistic person** un ottimista per natura; **it comes naturally to him to do ...** gli viene spontaneo fare...

c (*unaffectedly*: *behave, speak*) con naturalezza, in modo naturale

d (*of course*) naturalmente, certo.

natu·ral·ness [ˈnætʃrəlnɪs] N naturalezza.

♦ **natural resources** NPL risorse *fpl* naturali.

♦ **natural selection** N selezione *f* naturale.

♦ **natural wastage** N (*Industry*) naturale diminuzione *f* di personale (*per pensionamento, decesso, ecc.*)

na·ture [ˈneɪtʃəʳ] [1] N **a** natura; **a law of nature** una legge di natura; **the laws of nature** le leggi naturali *or* della natura; **to draw/paint from nature** disegnare/dipingere dal vero

b (*character*: *of person*) natura, indole *f*; (: *of thing*) natura; **by nature** per natura, di natura; **it is not in his nature to say that** non è nella sua natura *or* nel suo carattere parlare così; **it's second nature to him to do that** gli viene quasi istintivo farlo

c (*kind, type*) natura; **things of this nature** cose *fpl* di questo genere; **documents of a confidential nature** documenti *mpl* di natura riservata; **something in the**

nature of an apology una specie di scusa.

-natured ['neɪtʃəd] SUFF: **ill-natured** maldisposto(-a); **jealous-natured** geloso(-a) di natura, di temperamento geloso.

♦ **nature lover** N amante *m/f* della natura.

♦ **nature reserve** N (*Brit*) parco naturale.

♦ **nature study** N scienze *fpl* naturali.

♦ **nature trail** N *percorso tracciato in parchi nazionali ecc. con scopi educativi*.

na·tur·ism ['neɪtʃə‚rɪzm] N naturismo, nudismo.

na·tur·ist ['neɪtʃə‚rɪst] N naturista *m/f*, nudista *m/f*.

naught [nɔːt] N a (*Math*) = **nought** b (*old liter: nothing*) niente *m*, nulla *m*; **to come to naught** finire in nulla.

naugh·ti·ly ['nɔːtɪlɪ] ADV (*behave*) male, con cattiveria; (*say*) maliziosamente.

naugh·ti·ness ['nɔːtɪnɪs] N cattiveria.

naugh·ty ['nɔːtɪ] ADJ (*comp* **-ier**, *superl* **-iest**) a (*child*) cattivo(-a), cattivello(-a), birichino(-a); **that was a naughty thing to do** non si fanno queste cose b (*joke, song, story, film*) spinto(-a).

nau·sea ['nɔːzɪə] N (*Med*) nausea; (*fig: disgust*) schifo, disgusto.

nau·seate ['nɔːzɪ‚eɪt] VT (*Med*) nauseare; (*fig*) far schifo a, disgustare.

nau·seat·ing ['nɔːzɪ‚eɪtɪŋ] ADJ nauseante; (*fig*) disgustoso (-a).

nau·seous ['nɔːzɪəs] ADJ (*Med, fig*) nauseabondo(-a); **to be nauseous** avere la nausea.

nau·ti·cal ['nɔːtɪkəl] ADJ nautico(-a).

♦ **nautical mile** N miglio nautico *or* marino.

na·val ['neɪvəl] ADJ (*battle, strength, base, academy*) navale; (*affairs, barracks*) della marina; **naval forces** forze *fpl* navali, marina militare; **naval officer** ufficiale *m* di marina.

nave [neɪv] N (*of church*) navata centrale.

na·vel ['neɪvəl] N ombelico.

navi·gable ['nævɪgəbl] ADJ (*river etc*) navigabile.

navi·gate ['nævɪ‚geɪt] 1 VT (*ship, plane*) pilotare, governare; (*seas, river*) navigare, percorrere navigando. 2 VI navigare; (*Aut*) fare da navigatore.

navi·ga·tion [‚nævɪ'geɪʃən] N navigazione *f*.

navi·ga·tor ['nævɪ‚geɪtə'] N (*Naut, Aer*) navigatore *m*, ufficiale *m* di rotta; (*explorer*) navigatore *m*; (*Aut*) secondo pilota *m*, copilota *m/f*.

nav·vy ['nævɪ] N (*Brit*) sterratore *m*, manovale *m*.

navy ['neɪvɪ] N marina (militare *or* da guerra); **to join the navy** arruolarsi in marina; **Department of the Navy** (*Am*) Ministero della Marina.

♦ **navy-blue** [‚neɪvɪ'bluː] ADJ (*also:* **navy**) blu scuro *inv*.

nay [neɪ] ADV (*old: no*) no.

Naza·rene [‚næzə'riːn] N: **Jesus the Nazarene** Gesù Nazareno, il Nazareno.

Naza·reth ['næzərɪθ] N Nazareth *f*.

Nazi ['nɑːtsɪ] ADJ, N nazista (*m/f*).

Na·zism ['nɑːtsɪzəm] N nazismo.

NB [‚ɛn'biː] 1 N ABBR (= *nota bene*) N.B. 2 ABBR (*Canada*)= *New Brunswick*.

NBA [‚ɛnbiː'eɪ] N ABBR a (*Am*: = *National Basket Association*) ≈ F.I.P. *f* (= *Federazione Italiana Pallacanestro*) b = *National Boxing Association*.

NBC [‚ɛnbiː'siː] N ABBR (*Am*: = *National Broadcasting Company*) *compagnia nazionale di radiodiffusione*.

NBS [‚ɛnbiː'ɛs] N ABBR (*Am*: = *National Bureau of Standards*) *istituto per la normalizzazione*.

NC ABBR a (*Comm*: = *no charge*) gratis b (*Am Post*)= *North*

Carolina.

NCB [‚ɛnsiː'biː] N ABBR (*Brit*: *old*) = **National Coal Board**.

NCC [‚ɛnsiː'siː] N ABBR a (= *Nature Conservancy Council*) *organismo per la protezione dei beni naturali* b (*Am*)= *National Council of Churches*.

NCCL [‚ɛnsiːsiː'ɛl] N ABBR (*Brit*: = *National Council for Civil Liberties*) *associazione per la difesa della libertà civili*.

NCO [‚ɛnsiː'əu] N ABBR = **noncommissioned officer**.

ND ABBR (*Am Post*)= *North Dakota*.

NE ABBR (*Am Post*)= *Nebraska*, = *New England*.

NEA ['ɛniː'eɪ] N ABBR (*Am*)= *National Education Association*.

Ne·an·der·thal [nɪ'ændə‚tɑːl] 1 ADJ a (*Archeol*) neandertaliano(-a) b (*pej: brutish: person, behaviour*) da bruto; (: *reactionary: politician, attitude*) reazionario(-a). 2 N (*pej: brute*) bruto(-a); (: *reactionary*) reazionario(-a).

♦ **Neanderthal man** N l'Uomo di Neandertal.

neap [niːp] N (*also:* **neap tide**) marea di quadratura.

Nea·poli·tan [nɪə'pɒlɪtən] ADJ, N napoletano(-a).

near [nɪə'] 1 ADV vicino; **I like to know that you are near** mi piace sapere che tu sei (qui) vicino *or* accanto; **near at hand** a portata di mano; (*event*) imminente, alle porte; **to come** *or* **draw near** (*person, event*) avvicinarsi; **come nearer** vieni più vicino, avvicinati; **to bring sth nearer (to)** portare qc più vicino (a); **he came near to being drowned** per poco non è annegato; **near to tears** sul punto di piangere; **that's near enough** va bene così; **there were 100 people there, near enough** c'erano pressappoco 100 persone; **nowhere near full** ben lontano(-a) dall'essere pieno(-a). 2 PREP (*also:* **near to**: *of place*) vicino a, presso; (*in time*) circa, quasi; **near here/there** qui/lì vicino; **he was standing near the door** era in piedi vicino alla porta; **it was somewhere near midnight** era circa mezzanotte; **it's somewhere near here** dev'essere da queste parti; **the passage is near the end of the book** il brano è verso la fine del libro; **his views are very near my own** è di vedute molto simili alle mie; **nobody comes anywhere near her at cooking** nessuno può competere con lei in cucina. 3 ADJ (*comp* **-er**, *superl* **-est**) a (*in space, time*) vicino(-a); **in the near distance** a breve distanza; **the nearest way** la via *or* strada più breve; **£25,000** *or* **nearest offer** (*Brit*) 25.000 sterline trattabili; **in the near future** in un prossimo futuro b (*relation*) stretto(-a), prossimo(-a) c : **their win was a near thing** hanno vinto di misura; **that was a near thing!** per un pelo!. 4 VT (*place, event*) avvicinarsi a; **the building is nearing completion** il palazzo è quasi terminato *or* ultimato.

near·by [nɪə'baɪ] 1 ADV (qui *or* lì) vicino. 2 ADJ vicino(-a).

♦ **Near East** N: **the Near East** il Medio Oriente.

near·ly ['nɪəlɪ] ADV a (*gen*) quasi; **not nearly** non... affatto; **it's not nearly ready** non è affatto pronto; **that's not nearly enough** non basta per niente b (*with vb*): **I nearly lost it** per poco non lo perdevo; **she was nearly crying** era lì lì per piangere; **he very nearly died** ha rischiato di morire; **did you win? — very nearly!** hai vinto? — c'è mancato poco!

♦ **near miss** N (*Aer*) incidente mancato; **that was a near miss** (*fig*) c'è mancato poco; **he had a near miss with that car** per un pelo non ha investito quella macchina.

near·ness ['nɪənɪs] N prossimità, vicinanza.

near·side ['nɪə‚saɪd] 1 N (*Aut: right-hand drive*) lato sinistro; (: *left-hand drive*) lato destro.

2 ADJ (*see n*) sinistro(-a); destro(-a).

♦ **near-sighted** [ˌnɪəˈsaɪtɪd] ADJ miope.

neat [niːt] ADJ (*comp* **-er**, *superl* **-est**) **a** (*tidy: person, handwriting*) ordinato(-a); (: *room, house, desk*) ordinato (-a), in ordine; (: *work*) accurato(-a), pulito(-a); (*well-dressed*) curato(-a) nel vestire; (*skilful: plan, solution*) indovinato(-a), azzeccato(-a); (*Am fam: excellent*) figo (-a); **she is a neat worker** è molto accurata nel lavoro; **he has made a neat job of the bathroom** ha fatto un buon lavoro *or* un lavoro accurato nel bagno; **she has a neat figure** è ben proporzionata; **a neat little car** una bella macchinetta
b (*undiluted: spirits*) liscio(-a).

neat·ly [ˈniːtlɪ] ADV **a** (*tidily: fold, wrap, dress*) accuratamente, con cura; (: *write*) bene, in bella calligrafia **b** (*skilfully*) abilmente; **neatly put** ben espresso(-a).

neat·ness [ˈniːtnɪs] N **a** (*tidiness*) ordine *m* **b** (*skilfulness*) abilità.

nebu·la [ˈnɛbjʊlə] N nebulosa.

nebu·lous [ˈnɛbjʊləs] ADJ nebuloso(-a); (*fig*) nebuloso (-a), vago(-a).

nec·es·sari·ly [ˈnɛsɪsərɪlɪ] ADV necessariamente, per forza; (*lead to, give rise to*) inevitabilmente; **not necessarily** non necessariamente, non è detto.

nec·es·sary [ˈnɛsɪsərɪ] **1** ADJ (*gen*) necessario(-a); (*result, effect*) inevitabile; **a necessary evil** un male necessario; **is it necessary to make so much noise?** è proprio necessario *or* indispensabile far tanto rumore?; **it is necessary for you to go** *or* **that you go** è necessario che *or* bisogna che tu vada; **don't do more than is necessary** non fare più del necessario; **if necessary** se necessario; **the necessary qualifications (for)** i requisiti necessari (per); **necessary to health** necessario(-a) alla salute.
2 N (*fam: what is needed*): **to do the necessary** fare il necessario; **the necessary** (*money*) i quattrini.

ne·ces·si·tate [nɪˈsɛsɪˌteɪt] VT rendere necessario(-a).

ne·ces·sity [nɪˈsɛsɪtɪ] N **a** necessità; **there is no necessity for you to do that** non è necessario che *or* non c'è bisogno che tu lo faccia; **the necessity of doing sth** la necessità di fare qc; **is there any necessity?** è proprio necessario?, c'è proprio bisogno?; **of necessity** di necessità, necessariamente; **from** *or* **out of necessity** per necessità *or* bisogno; **in case of necessity** in caso di necessità
b (*necessary thing*) cosa indispensabile, necessità *f inv*; **the bare necessities** lo stretto necessario, il minimo indispensabile.

neck [nɛk] **1** N (*Anat, of bottle*) collo; (*of garment*) collo, colletto; (: *Dressmaking*) scollo; **to break one's neck** rompersi il collo; (*fig*) affannarsi; **to have a stiff neck** avere il torcicollo; **the favourite won by a neck** (*Horse-racing*) il favorito ha vinto per un'incollatura; **neck and neck** testa a testa; **to be up to one's neck in work** (*fam*) essere immerso(-a) nel lavoro fino al collo; **he is in it up to his neck** (*fam*) c'è dentro fino al collo; **to risk one's neck** rischiare l'osso del collo, rischiare la pelle; **to save one's neck** salvare la pelle; **to stick one's neck out** (*fam*) rischiare (forte); **in this neck of the woods** (*fam*) in questi paraggi, da queste parti; **dress with a low neck** [OR] **to low-necked dress** vestito scollato.
2 VI (*fam*) pomiciare, sbaciucchiarsi.

neck·ing [ˈnɛkɪŋ] N (*fam*) pomiciate *fpl*.

neck·lace [ˈnɛklɪs] N collana; **pearl necklace** collana di perle.

neck·line [ˈnɛkˌlaɪn] N scollatura.

neck·tie [ˈnɛkˌtaɪ] N (*esp Am*) cravatta.

nec·ro·man·cy [ˈnɛkrəʊˌmænsɪ] N (*frm*) negromanzia.

nec·ro·philia [ˌnɛkrəʊˈfɪlɪə] N necrofilia.

nec·ro·phili·ac [ˌnɛkrəʊˈfɪlɪæk] N necrofilo(-a).

ne·cro·sis [nɛˈkrəʊsɪs] N necrosi *f inv*.

nec·tar [ˈnɛktə] N nettare *m*.

nec·tar·ine [ˈnɛktərɪn] N nocepesca.

NEDC [ˌɛniːdiːˈsiː] N ABBR (*Brit*: = *National Economic Development Council*) ≈ C.N.E.L. *m* (= *Consiglio Nazionale dell'Economia e del Lavoro*).

ned·dy [ˈnɛdɪ] N ABBR (*Brit fam*) = **NEDC**.

née [neɪ] ADJ nata; **Mary Green neé Smith** Mary Green nata Smith.

need [niːd] **1** N **a** (*necessity, obligation*) bisogno, necessità *f inv*; **if need(s) be** se necessario; **in case of need** in caso di bisogno *or* necessità; **there's no need to worry** non c'è bisogno di preoccuparsi; **there's no need for you to come too** non c'è bisogno *or* non occorre che venga anche tu; **what need is there to buy it?** che bisogno c'è di comprarlo?
b (*want, lack*) bisogno; (*poverty*) povertà, bisogno; **to be in need of** [OR] **to have need of** aver bisogno di; **she felt in need of a friend** sentiva il bisogno di un amico; **there's a great need for a book on this subject** c'è molto bisogno di un libro su questo argomento; **in times of need** nei momenti difficili; **to be in need** essere bisognoso(-a)
c (*thing needed*) bisogno, necessità *f inv*; **£100 will meet my immediate needs** 100 sterline mi basteranno per le necessità più urgenti; **his needs are few** non ha grosse esigenze; **the needs of industry** le esigenze dell'industria.
2 VT aver bisogno di; **he needs money** ha bisogno di soldi, gli occorrono soldi; **I need it** ne ho bisogno, mi serve; **it's just what I need** è proprio quel che mi ci vuole; **a signature is needed** occorre *or* ci vuole una firma; **a much needed holiday** una vacanza di cui si ha proprio bisogno; **all that you need** tutto ciò che occorre; **he doesn't need me to tell him what to do** non c'è bisogno che sia io a dirgli cosa deve fare; **he needs watching** *or* **to be watched** va tenuto d'occhio; **this book needs careful reading** questo libro richiede un'attenta lettura; **the report needs no comment** il rapporto non ha bisogno di commenti; **he needs to have everything explained to him** bisogna spiegargli proprio tutto; **he doesn't need to be told all the details** non c'è bisogno di *or* non occorre dirgli tutti i particolari; **you only needed to ask** bastava che lo chiedessi; **it needed a war to alter things** c'è voluta una guerra per cambiare le cose.
3 MODAL AUX VB: **need I go?** devo (proprio) andarci?; **I need hardly tell you that ...** non c'è bisogno che io le dica *or* di dirle che...; **I need to do it** bisogna che io lo faccia, lo devo fare; **you don't need to go** non c'è bisogno *or* non è necessario che tu vada, non devi andare per forza; **you needn't wait** non c'è bisogno *or* non è necessario che aspetti; **you needn't have bothered to come** non occorreva che venissi; **it need not be done now** non c'è bisogno di farlo ora; **it need not follow that ...** non ne consegue necessariamente che...
+ sub.

need·ful [ˈniːdfʊl] ADJ (*old*) necessario(-a).

nee·dle [ˈniːdl] **1** N ago; (*on record player*) puntina; **knitting needle** ferro (da calza); **it's like looking for a needle in a haystack** è come cercare un ago in un

pagliaio; **to give sb the needle** (*fam*: *annoy*) dare ai nervi a qn.

[2] VT (*fam*: *annoy*) irritare, dare ai nervi a; (: *tease, provoke*) punzecchiare; **she was needled into replying** punzecchiata, ha risposto.

needle·cord ['niːdl‚kɔːd] N (*Brit*) velluto a coste sottili.

needle·point ['niːdl‚pɔɪnt] N ricamo ad ago.

need·less ['niːdlɪs] ADJ inutile; **needless to say he didn't keep his promise** inutile dire che non ha mantenuto la promessa.

need·less·ly ['niːdlɪslɪ] ADV inutilmente.

needle·woman ['niːdəl‚wʊmən] N (*pl* **-women**) (*old*) cucitrice *f*.

needle·work ['niːdl‚wɜːk] N cucito; (*embroidery*) ricamo.

needn't ['niːdnt] = **need not**.

needy ['niːdɪ] ADJ (*comp* **-ier**, *superl* **-iest**) bisognoso(-a).

ne'er [nɛəʳ] ADV (*poetic*) = **never**.

ne'er-do-well ['nɛəduː‚wel] N buono(-a) a nulla.

ne·fari·ous [nɪ'fɛərɪəs] ADJ (*liter*) scellerato(-a).

ne·gate [nɪ'geɪt] VT (*frm*: *nullify*) annullare; (: *deny*) negare.

ne·ga·tion [nɪ'geɪʃən] N negazione *f*.

nega·tive ['nɛgətɪv] [1] ADJ negativo(-a).

[2] N [a] (*answer*): **his answer was a firm negative** ha risposto con un fermo no *or* con un fermo diniego; **an answer in the negative** una risposta negativa; **to answer in the negative** rispondere negativamente *or* di no [b] (*Gram*) negazione *f*; **to put a sentence into the negative** mettere una frase in forma negativa [c] (*Phot*) negativa, negativo [d] (*Elec*) polo negativo.

♦ **negative equity** N *situazione in cui l'ammontare del mutuo su un immobile supera il suo valore sul mercato.*

nega·tive·ly ['nɛgətɪvlɪ] ADV negativamente.

ne·glect [nɪ'glɛkt] [1] VT (*friends, children, garden*) trascurare; (*opportunity*) lasciarsi sfuggire; (*obligations*) mancare a; **to neglect to do sth** trascurare *or* tralasciare di fare qc.

[2] N (*lack of care*) trascuratezza; (*of child*) il trascurare; (*of duty*) negligenza; (*of rule etc*) mancata osservanza; **neglect of one's appearance** trascuratezza nel vestire; **his neglect of his friends** l'aver trascurato gli amici; **in a state of neglect** (*house, garden*) in stato di abbandono.

ne·glect·ed [nɪ'glɛktɪd] ADJ trascurato(-a).

ne·glect·ful [nɪ'glɛktfʊl] ADJ (*gen*) negligente; (*parent*) che trascura; **to be neglectful of sb/sth** trascurare qn/qc.

neg·li·gee ['nɛglɪ‚ʒeɪ] N négligé *m inv*.

neg·li·gence ['nɛglɪdʒəns] N negligenza; **through negligence** per negligenza; **criminal negligence** (*Law*) reato d'omissione.

neg·li·gent ['nɛglɪdʒənt] ADJ [a] (*careless*) negligente; **she has become negligent in her work** è diventata trascurata nel lavoro [b] (*offhand*: *gesture, manner*) noncurante, disinvolto(-a).

neg·li·gent·ly ['nɛglɪdʒəntlɪ] ADV con negligenza.

neg·li·gible ['nɛglɪdʒəbl] ADJ trascurabile, insignificante.

ne·go·tiable [nɪ'gəʊʃɪəbl] ADJ [a] (*Comm etc*) negoziabile; (: *cheque*) trasferibile; **not negotiable** non trasferibile [b] (*road*) transitabile; (*river*) navigabile; (*hill*) valicabile.

ne·go·ti·ate [nɪ'gəʊʃɪ‚eɪt] [1] VT [a] (*Comm*: *treaty, loan, sale*) negoziare, trattare [b] (*obstacle, difficulty, hill*) superare; (*river*) passare; (*bend in road*) prendere.

[2] VI trattare, condurre (le) trattative; **to negotiate with sb for sth** trattare con qn per ottenere qc.

ne·go·tiat·ing ta·ble [nɪ'gəʊʃɪ‚eɪtɪŋ'teɪbl] N tavolo delle trattative.

ne·go·tia·tion [nɪ‚gəʊʃɪ'eɪʃən] N (*gen*) trattativa; (*Pol*) negoziato, trattativa; **to enter into negotiations with sb** entrare in trattative *or* intavolare i negoziati con qn.

ne·go·tia·tor [nɪ'gəʊʃɪ‚eɪtəʳ] N negoziatore(-trice).

Ne·gress ['niːgrɪs] N (*old offensive*) negra.

Ne·gro ['niːgrəʊ] (*offensive*) [1] ADJ negro(-a).

[2] N (*pl* **-es**) negro(-a).

ne·groid ['niːgrɔɪd] ADJ negroide.

neigh [neɪ] [1] VI nitrire.

[2] N nitrito.

neigh·bour, (*Am*) **neigh·bor** ['neɪbəʳ] N vicino(-a); (*Bible etc*) prossimo(-a).

neigh·bour·hood, (*Am*) **neigh·bor·hood** ['neɪbə‚hʊd] N (*district*) quartiere *m*, vicinato; (*surrounding area*) vicinanze *fpl*; **the whole neighbourhood knows her** tutto il vicinato *or* il quartiere la conosce; **in the neighbourhood of the station** nelle vicinanze *or* nei paraggi della stazione; (*something*) **in the neighbourhood of £1,000** qualcosa come 1.000 sterline.

♦ **neighbourhood watch** N (*Brit*: *also*: **neighbourhood watch scheme**) *sistema di vigilanza reciproca in un quartiere.*

neigh·bour·ing, (*Am*) **neigh·bor·ing** ['neɪbərɪŋ] ADJ vicino(-a), confinante, limitrofo(-a).

neigh·bour·ly, (*Am*) **neigh·bor·ly** ['neɪbəlɪ] ADJ (*action*) da buon vicino; (*feelings*) amichevole; **people here aren't very neighbourly** la gente qua non ha il senso del vicinato.

nei·ther ['naɪðəʳ] [1] ADV né; **neither he nor I can go** né io né lui possiamo andare; **neither good nor bad** né buono(-a) né cattivo(-a); **he neither smokes nor drinks** non fuma né beve; **he likes neither the house nor the people** non gli piace né la casa né la gente; **that's neither here nor there** (*fig*) questo non c'entra.

[2] CONJ neanche, nemmeno, neppure; **if you aren't going, neither am I** se tu non ci vai, non ci vado neanch'io *or* nemmeno io; **I don't like it — neither do I** non mi piace — nemmeno a me; **I didn't move and neither did he** io non mi mossi e nemmeno lui; **...neither did I refuse** ... ma non ho nemmeno rifiutato.

[3] ADJ: **on neither side** né da una parte né dall'altra; **neither story is true** nessuna delle due storie è vera.

[4] PRON né l'uno(-a) né l'altro(-a), nessuno(-a) dei/delle due; **neither of them has any money** né l'uno né l'altro *or* nessuno dei due ha soldi, non hanno soldi né l'uno né l'altro.

Nemesis ['nɛmɪsɪs] N (*Myth*) Nemesi *f*; (*fig*): **nemesis** nemesi *f*.

neo... ['niːəʊ] PREF neo... .

neo·clas·si·cal [‚niːəʊ'klæsɪkl] ADJ neoclassico(-a).

neo·co·lo·ni·al·ism [‚niːəʊkə'ləʊnɪə‚lɪzəm] N neocolonialismo.

neo·fasc·ism [‚niːəʊ'fæʃɪzəm] N neofascismo.

neo·fasc·ist [‚niːəʊ'fæʃɪst] ADJ, N neofascista (*m/f*).

neo·lith·ic [‚niːəʊ'lɪθɪk] ADJ neolitico(-a).

ne·olo·gism [nɪ'ɒlə‚dʒɪzəm] N neologismo.

neon ['niːɒn] [1] N neon *m inv*.

[2] ADJ al neon.

neo·nazi [‚niːəʊ'nɑːtsɪ] ADJ, N neonazista (*m/f*).

neo·nazism [‚niːəʊ'nɑːtsɪzəm] N neonazismo.

♦ **neon light** N luce *f* al neon.

♦ **neon sign** N insegna al neon.

neo·prene ['niːəʊ‚priːn] N neoprene *m*.

Ne·pal [nɪ'pɔːl] N il Nepal *m*.

neph·ew ['nɛvjuː] N nipote *m* (*di zii*).

ne·phrit·ic [nɪ'frɪtɪk] ADJ (*Med*) nefritico(-a).
ne·phri·tis [nɪ'fraɪtɪs] N (*Med*) nefrite *f*.
nepo·tism ['nɛpətɪzəm] N nepotismo.
Nep·tune ['nɛptjuːn] N (*Myth, Astron*) Nettuno.
nerd [nɜːd] N (*fam pej*) sfigato(-a).
Ne·reid ['nɪərɪɪd] N (*Myth*) nereide *f*.
Nero ['nɪərəʊ] N Nerone *m*.
nerve [nɜːv] ❶ N **a** (*Anat*) nervo; (*Bot*) nervatura; **she suffers from nerves** soffre di nervi; **my nerves are on edge** ho i nervi tesi; **a fit of nerves** una crisi di nervi; **it/he gets on my nerves** mi dà ai nervi, mi fa venire i nervi
b (*fig: courage*) coraggio; (: *calm*) sangue *m* freddo; (: *self-confidence*) fiducia in se stesso(-a); (*fam: impudence*) sfacciataggine *f*, faccia tosta; **a man of nerve** un uomo che ha fegato; **to lose one's nerve** (*self-confidence*) perdere la fiducia in se stesso(-a); **I lost my nerve** (*courage*) mi è mancato il coraggio; **I hadn't the nerve to do it** non ho avuto il coraggio di farlo; (*cheek*) non ho avuto la faccia tosta di farlo; **he's got a nerve!** ha una bella faccia tosta!.
❷ VT: **to nerve o.s. to do sth** farsi coraggio *or* animo per fare qc, armarsi di coraggio per fare qc.
♦ **nerve cell** N cellula nervosa, neurone *m*.
♦ **nerve centre** N (*Anat*) centro nervoso; (*fig*) cervello, centro vitale.
♦ **nerve gas** N gas *m* nervino.
nerve·less ['nɜːvlɪs] ADJ (*without strength*) privo(-a) di forza; (*calm*) che ha sangue freddo.
♦ **nerve-racking** ['nɜːv,rækɪŋ] ADJ logorante.
nerv·ous ['nɜːvəs] ADJ (*Anat, Med*) nervoso(-a); (*edgy*) nervoso(-a), agitato(-a), teso(-a); (*apprehensive*) ansioso(-a), apprensivo(-a); **he's full of nervous energy** è tutto nervi; **he is making me nervous** mi innervosisce; **I was nervous about speaking to her** (*apprehensive*) l'idea di parlarle mi agitava; (*excited*) ero emozionato all'idea di parlarle; **I'm nervous about flying** ho un po' paura di volare.
♦ **nervous breakdown** N esaurimento nervoso.
nerv·ous·ly ['nɜːvəslɪ] ADV nervosamente; (*apprehensively*) con ansia.
nerv·ous·ness ['nɜːvəsnɪs] N nervosismo; (*anxiousness*) ansia.
♦ **nervous system** N sistema *m* nervoso.
♦ **nervous wreck** N (*fam*): **to be a nervous wreck** avere i nervi a pezzi.
nervy ['nɜːvɪ] ADJ (*comp* **-ier**, *superl* **-iest**) (*fam: Brit: tense*) teso(-a), nervoso(-a); (: *Am: cheeky*) sfacciato(-a).
nest [nɛst] ❶ N **a** nido **b** : **nest of tables** tris *m* di tavolini.
❷ VI fare il nido, nidificare.
♦ **nest egg** N (*fig*) gruzzolo.
nes·tle ['nɛsl] VI accoccolarsi; **to nestle up to** *or* **against sb** accoccolarsi vicino a qn, rannicchiarsi accanto a qn; **to nestle down in bed** sistemarsi ben bene nel letto; **a village nestling among hills** un paesetto annidato tra le colline.
nest·ling ['nɛslɪŋ] N uccellino di nido, nidiaceo.
net¹ [nɛt] ❶ N **a** (*gen, fig*) rete *f*; (*for hair*) retina (per capelli); (*fabric*) tulle *m* **b** (*Geom*) sviluppo.
❷ VT (*fish, game*) prendere con la rete.
net² [nɛt] ❶ ADJ (*weight, price, salary*) netto(-a); **net assets** patrimonio netto, attività *fpl* nette; **he earns £30,000 net per year** guadagna 30.000 sterline nette all'anno; **net of tax** al netto delle tasse.

❷ VT (*get, obtain*) ottenere; (*make: profit*) fare; (*subj: deal, sale*) dare un utile netto di.
net·ball ['nɛt,bɔːl] N *sport simile alla pallacanestro*.
♦ **net call judge** N (*Tennis*) giudice *m* di rete.
♦ **net curtains** NPL tende *fpl* di tulle.
neth·er ['nɛðəʳ] ADJ (*old*): **the nether regions** *or* **world** gli inferi.
Neth·er·lands ['nɛðələndz] NPL: **the Netherlands** i Paesi Bassi.
♦ **net profit** N utile *m* netto.
nett [nɛt] ADJ = **net²**.
net·ting ['nɛtɪŋ] N (*nets*) reti *fpl*; (*mesh*) rete; (*also:* **wire netting**: *for fence etc*) rete metallica, reticolato; (*fabric*) tulle *m*.
net·tle ['nɛtl] ❶ N ortica.
❷ VT esasperare; **he is easily nettled** è una persona facilmente irritabile.
♦ **nettle rash** N orticaria.
net·work ['nɛt,wɜːk] ❶ N (*Elec, TV, fig*) rete *f*; **network of roads** rete stradale; **spy network** rete spionistica *or* di spie.
❷ VT (*TV*) trasmettere su rete nazionale.
neu·ral ['njʊərəl] ADJ (*Anat*) neurale.
neu·ral·gia [njʊə'rældʒə] N nevralgia.
neuro... ['njʊərəʊ] PREF neuro... .
neu·ro·logi·cal [njʊərəʊ'lɒdʒɪkəl] ADJ neurologico(-a).
neu·rolo·gist [njʊ'rɒlədʒɪst] N neurologo(-a).
neu·rol·ogy [njʊ'rɒlədʒɪ] N neurologia.
neu·ron ['njʊərɒn] N (*Bio*) neurone *m*.
neu·ro·path ['njʊərəʊ,pæθ] N neuropatico(-a).
neu·ro·path·ic [,njʊərəʊ'pæθɪk] ADJ neuropatico(-a).
neu·ropa·thy [njʊ'rɒpəθɪ] N neuropatia.
neu·ro·psy·chia·trist [,njʊərəʊsaɪ'kaɪətrɪst] N neuropsichiatra *m/f*.
neu·ro·psy·chia·try [,njʊərəʊsaɪ'kaɪətrɪ] N neuropsichiatria.
neu·ro·sis [njʊ'rəʊsɪs] N (*pl* **neuroses** [njʊ'rəʊsiːz]) nevrosi *f inv*.
neu·ro·sur·geon [,njʊərəʊ'sɜːdʒən] N neurochirurgo.
neu·ro·sur·gery [,njʊərəʊ'sɜːdʒərɪ] N neurochirurgia.
neu·rot·ic [njʊ'rɒtɪk] ❶ ADJ (*person, disease*) nevrotico (-a); **she's getting quite neurotic about it** (*fig*) se ne sta facendo un'ossessione.
❷ N nevrotico(-a).
neu·ter ['njuːtəʳ] ❶ ADJ neutro(-a).
❷ N (*Gram*) neutro.
❸ VT (*cat etc*) castrare.
neu·tral ['njuːtrəl] ❶ ADJ **a** (*person, country, opinion*) neutrale **b** (*Chem, colour*) neutro(-a).
❷ N (*Aut*) folle *f*; **in neutral** in folle.
neu·tral·ity [njuː'trælɪtɪ] N neutralità.
neu·trali·za·tion [,njuːtrəlaɪ'zeɪʃən] N neutralizzazione *f*.
neu·tral·ize ['njuːtrə,laɪz] VT neutralizzare.
neu·tri·no [njuː'triːnəʊ] N neutrino.
neu·tron ['njuːtrɒn] N neutrone *m*.
♦ **neutron bomb** N bomba al neutrone.
nev·er ['nɛvəʳ] ADV **a** non... mai; **they never go out** non escono mai; **I have never read it** non l'ho mai letto; **have you been to Rome? — never** è mai stato a Roma? — no, mai; **never before had he been so bored** non si era mai annoiato tanto; **she's never been here before** non è mai venuta qui prima; **never again!** mai più!; **I'll never go there again** non ci andrò mai più; **never in my life** mai in vita mia
b (*emphatic negative*): **I never slept a wink all night** non

ho chiuso occhio per tutta la notte; **he never so much as smiled** non ha nemmeno accennato un sorriso; **I told the boss what I thought of him — never!** *or* **you never did!** ho detto al capo quel che pensavo di lui — no, non mi dire! *or* non ci credo!; **well I never!** chi l'avrebbe (mai) detto!, ma guarda un po'!; **never mind** non fa niente.

♦ **never-ending** [ˌnɛvərˈɛndɪŋ] ADJ interminabile.

♦ **never-never** [ˌnɛvəˈnɛvəʳ] N: **to buy sth on the never-never** (*Brit fam*) comprare qc a rate.

♦ **never-never land** N mondo dei sogni.

never·the·less [ˌnɛvəðəˈlɛs] ADV tuttavia, ciononondimeno, ciononostante.

♦ **never-to-be-forgotten** [ˌnɛvətəbiːfəˈgɒtən] ADJ indimenticabile.

new [njuː] ADJ (*comp* **-er,** *superl* **-est**) nuovo(-a); (*brand new*) nuovo(-a) di zecca; (*different*) nuovo(-a), altro(-a); (*bread*) fresco(-a); **he buys a new car every year** (*brand-new*) si compra una macchina nuova ogni anno; (*different*) si compra una nuova macchina *or* una macchina diversa ogni anno; **bring me a new glass** portami un altro bicchiere; **new potatoes** patate *fpl* novelle; **as good as new** come nuovo(-a); **that's nothing new** non è una novità; **what's new?** ci sono novità?; **are you new here?** sei nuovo di qui?; **I'm new to this job** sono nuovo del mestiere; **the idea was quite new to him** l'idea gli risultava nuova.

♦ **New Age** ADJ, N New Age (*f*) *inv*.

new·born [ˈnjuːˌbɔːn] ADJ neonato(-a); **newborn baby** neonato(-a).

♦ **new boy** N (*Scol*) nuovo scolaro.

♦ **new broom** N (*Brit*): **this firm needs a new broom** questa azienda ha bisogno di qualcuno che introduca dei cambiamenti; **a new broom sweeps clean** (*Proverb*) tutti sono bravi all'inizio.

new·comer [ˈnjuːˌkʌməʳ] N nuovo(-a) venuto(-a).

♦ **new-fangled** [ˈnjuːˌfæŋɡld] ADJ (*pej*) stramoderno(-a).

♦ **new-found** [ˈnjuːˌfaʊnd] ADJ nuovo(-a).

New·found·land [ˈnjuːfəndlənd] N Terranova.

♦ **new girl** N (*Scol*) nuova scolara.

♦ **New Guinea** N la Nuova Guinea.

♦ **new-laid** [ˈnjuːˌleɪd] ADJ (*egg*) fresco(-a).

new·ly [ˈnjuːlɪ] ADV (*recently*) appena, da poco, di recente; (*in a new way*) in modo nuovo; **newly made** appena fatto(-a).

♦ **newly-weds** [ˈnjuːlɪˌwɛdz] NPL sposini *mpl*, sposi *mpl* novelli.

♦ **new moon** N luna nuova.

new·ness [ˈnjuːnɪs] N novità.

news [njuːz] NSG (*gen, Press*) notizie *fpl*; (*report: on radio*) notiziario, giornale *m* radio; (: *on TV*) notiziario, telegiornale *m*; **a piece of** *or* **an item of news** una notizia; (*in newspaper*) un articolo; **have you heard the news?** hai saputo la notizia?; **have you heard the news about Maria?** hai saputo di Maria?; **have you any news of Maria/of her?** hai notizie di Maria/sue notizie?; **what's your news?** (ci sono) novità?; **what's the latest news about the earthquake?** si sa qualcosa di nuovo sul terremoto?; **is there any news?** ci sono notizie?; **good/bad news** buone/cattive notizie; **I've got news for you!** non sai l'ultima!; **this is news to me** questo mi giunge nuovo; **it's in the news** (*newspapers*) è su tutti i giornali; (*radio, TV*) è in tutti i notiziari; **home/foreign news** notizie dall'interno/dall'estero; **financial news** (*Press*) pagina economica e finanziaria; (*Radio, TV*) notiziario

economico.

♦ **news agency** N agenzia di stampa.

news·agent [ˈnjuːzˌeɪdʒənt] N (*Brit*) giornalaio(-a).

♦ **news bulletin** N (*Radio, TV*) notiziario.

news·cast [ˈnjuːzˌkɑːst] N (*esp Am Radio, TV*) notiziario.

news·caster [ˈnjuːzˌkɑːstəʳ] N (*Radio*) annunciatore(-trice); (*TV*) presentatore(-trice).

♦ **news conference** N (*Am*) conferenza *f* stampa *inv*.

news·dealer [ˈnjuːzˌdiːləʳ] N (*Am*) giornalaio(-a).

news·flash [ˈnjuːzˌflæʃ] N (notizia *f*) flash (*m*) *inv*.

♦ **news headlines** N titoli *mpl* delle principali notizie.

news·hound [ˈnjuːzˌhaʊnd] N (*esp Am fam*) reporter *m/f inv*.

news·letter [ˈnjuːzˌlɛtəʳ] N bollettino (*di ditta, associazione*).

news·man [ˈnjuːzˌmæn] N (*pl* **-men**) reporter *m inv*.

news·paper [ˈnjuːzˌpeɪpəʳ] N giornale *m*; **daily newspaper** quotidiano; **weekly newspaper** settimanale *m*.

news·paper·man [ˈnjuːzˌpeɪpəmən] N (*pl* **-men**) giornalista *m*.

news·print [ˈnjuːzˌprɪnt] N carta da giornale.

news·reader [ˈnjuːzˌriːdəʳ] N (*esp Brit*) = newscaster.

news·reel [ˈnjuːzˌriːl] N cinegiornale *m*.

news·room [ˈnjuːzˌrʊm] N redazione *f*.

♦ **news sheet** N notiziario, bollettino.

news·stand [ˈnjuːzˌstænd] N edicola.

news·worthy [ˈnjuːzˌwɜːðɪ] ADJ che vale la pena pubblicare.

newsy [ˈnjuːzɪ] ADJ (*fam*) ricco(-a) di notizie.

newt [njuːt] N tritone *m*.

♦ **New Testament** N: **the New Testament** il Nuovo Testamento.

♦ **new town** N (*Brit*) nuovo centro urbano (*creato con fondi pubblici*).

♦ **new wave** N new wave *f inv*.

♦ **New World** N: **the New World** il Nuovo Mondo.

♦ **New Year** ① N anno nuovo; **Happy New Year!** Buon anno!; **to wish sb a happy New Year** augurare buon anno a qn; **to bring in the New Year** brindare all'anno nuovo.

② ADJ (*party etc*) di Capodanno; (*resolution*) per l'anno nuovo.

♦ **New Year's Day** N Capodanno.

♦ **New Year's Eve** N la vigilia di Capodanno, la notte di San Silvestro.

♦ **New York** N New York *f*, Nuova York *f*; **New York State** stato di New York.

♦ **New Zea·land** [ˌnjuːˈziːlənd] N ① Nuova Zelanda.

② ADJ neozelandese.

♦ **New Zea·land·er** [ˌnjuːˈziːləndəʳ] N neozelandese *m/f*.

next [nɛkst] ① ADJ **a** (*immediately adjoining: house, street, room*) vicino(-a), accanto *inv*; (*immediately following: bus stop, turning: in future*) prossimo(-a); (: *in past*) successivo(-a), (subito) dopo; **"turn to the next page"** "vedi pagina seguente"; **the next size (up)** la misura più grande; **get off at the next stop** scendi alla prossima fermata; **he got off at the next stop** è sceso alla fermata successiva; **I arrived at 3 and Mary was next to arrive** io sono arrivato alle 3 e dopo di me è arrivata Mary; **it's the next door but one on the right** è la seconda porta a destra; **who's next?** a chi tocca?; **you're next** tocca a lei; **b** (*in time: day, week etc: in future*) prossimo(-a); (: *in past*) successivo(-a); **next time** la prossima volta; **next year** l'anno prossimo *or* venturo; **next month** il mese prossimo; **the next month** il mese dopo *or* successivo; **the week after next** fra due settimane; **(the) next time**

you come quando vieni la prossima volta, la prossima volta che vieni; **this time next year** in questo periodo fra un anno; **the next day** il giorno dopo, l'indomani; **the next morning** l'indomani mattina, la mattina dopo *or* seguente.

2 ADV **a** (*in time*) dopo, poi; **first he opened his letters and next he read the paper** prima ha aperto la corrispondenza e dopo *or* poi ha letto il giornale; **what will you do next?** e adesso che farai?; **when you next see him** quando lo vedi la prossima volta, la prossima volta che lo vedi; **when next I saw him** quando l'ho visto la volta dopo *or* una seconda volta; **when do we meet next?** quando ci rincontriamo?; **what comes next?** che cosa viene dopo?; **what next?** e poi?; (*expressing surprise etc*) e che altro mai?; **the next best thing would be ...** la migliore alternativa sarebbe...; **the next to last** il/la penultimo(-a)

b : **next to** (*nearly*) quasi, pressocché; **next to nothing** quasi niente; **we got it for next to nothing** non ci è costato quasi niente, l'abbiamo comprato per una sciocchezza; **there is next to no news** non si sa quasi niente.

3 PREP: **next to** (*beside*) di fianco a, accanto a; **his room is next to mine** la sua stanza è accanto alla mia; **I don't like wearing synthetics next to the skin** non mi piacciono le fibre sintetiche a contatto della pelle.

4 N prossimo(-a); **next please!** (avanti) il prossimo!; **the next to speak is Carla** Carla è la prossima a parlare.

♦ **next-door** [ˌnɛks'dɔːʳ] ADJ: **the next-door house** la casa accanto; **my next-door neighbour** il/la mio(-a) vicino(-a) di casa.

♦ **next door** 1 ADV accanto; **next door to us** accanto a noi, nella casa accanto; **the girl next door** la ragazza della porta accanto.

2 N la casa accanto; **from next door** della casa accanto.

♦ **next of kin** N parente *m/f* prossimo(-a).

NF [ˌɛn'ɛf] 1 N ABBR (*Brit Pol*: = *National Front*) *partito di estrema destra.*

2 ABBR (*Canada*)= *Newfoundland.*

NFL [ˌɛnɛf'ɛl] N ABBR (*Am*)= *National Football League.*

NG [ˌɛn'dʒiː] N ABBR (*Am*) = **National Guard.**

NGO [ˌɛndʒiː'əʊ] N ABBR (*Am*)= *non-governmental organization.*

NH ABBR (*Am Post*)= *New Hampshire.*

NHL [ˌɛneɪtʃ'ɛl] N ABBR (*Am*: = *National Hockey League*) ≈ F.I.H.P. *f* (= *Federazione Italiana Hockey e Pattinaggio*).

NHS [ˌɛneɪtʃ'ɛs] N ABBR = **National Health Service.**

NI ABBR **a** = **Northern Ireland b** (*Brit*) = **National Insurance.**

Ni·aga·ra Falls [naɪ'ægrə'fɔːls] NPL: **the Niagara Falls** le cascate del Niagara.

nib [nɪb] N (*of pen*) pennino.

nib·ble ['nɪbl] 1 VT (*also*: **nibble at**) **a** (*subj*: *mouse*) rosicchiare; (: *fish*) mordicchiare; (: *person*: *biscuit, nuts*) sgranocchiare; (: *bread, cheese*) sbocconcellare **b** (*fig*: *offer*) mostrarsi tentato(-a) da.

2 VI (*person*) mangiucchiare.

Nica·ra·gua [ˌnɪkə'rægjʊə] N Nicaragua *m.*

Nica·ra·guan [ˌnɪkə'rægjʊən] ADJ, N nicaraguense (*m/f*).

Nice [niːs] N Nizza.

nice [naɪs] ADJ (*comp* **-r**, *superl* **-st**) **a** (*gen*: *pleasant*) bello(-a), piacevole, gentile; (: *person*) simpatico(-a), piacevole; (: *taste, smell, meal*) buono(-a); (*attractive, pretty*) carino(-a), bello(-a); **he's a nice man** è una brava persona, è un uomo simpatico; **he was very nice about**

it è stato molto gentile; **be nice to him** sii gentile con lui; **how nice you look!** come stai bene!; **did you have a nice time?** ti sei divertito?; **it's nice here** si sta bene qui

b (*iro*) bello(-a); **that's a nice thing to say!** sono cose da dirsi, queste?; **you've got us into a nice mess!** ci hai messo in un bel pasticcio

c (*refined, polite*) gentile, garbato(-a); **he has nice manners** ha modi gentili *or* garbati; **nice girls don't go out at night on their own** le ragazze perbene non escono da sole la sera; **that's not nice** non sta bene

d (*intensifier*: *fam*) bello(-a) + *adj*; **he gets nice long holidays** le sue vacanze sono belle lunghe; **it's nice and warm here** è bello caldo qui, c'è un bel calduccio qui; **nice and early** di buon'ora

e (*frm*: *subtle*: *distinction*) sottile, fine.

♦ **nice-looking** ['naɪsˌlʊkɪŋ] ADJ bello(-a).

nice·ly ['naɪslɪ] ADV bene; (*kindly*) gentilmente; **that will do nicely** andrà benissimo; **he's getting on nicely in his new job** se la cava bene nel nuovo lavoro.

ni·cety ['naɪsɪtɪ] N (*of judgment*) accuratezza; **niceties** NPL particolari *mpl*, finezze *fpl*; **a question of some nicety** una questione piuttosto delicata; **to a nicety** alla perfezione.

niche [niːʃ] N (*Archit*) nicchia; (*Ecology*) nicchia ecologica; (*fig*): **to find a niche for o.s.** trovare una propria collocazione.

nick [nɪk] 1 N **a** (*in wood, blade*) tacca; (*in skin*) taglietto; (*in plate*) scheggiatura; **in the nick of time** appena in tempo

b (*fam*): **in good nick** decente, in buono stato

c (*Brit fam*: *prison*) galera; (: *police station*) centrale *f* (di polizia); **in the nick** in galera.

2 VT **a** (*see n*) intaccare; tagliare; scheggiare, scalfire; **to nick o.s.** farsi un taglietto

b (*fam*: *steal*) fregare

c (*Brit fam*: *arrest*) beccare; **to get nicked** farsi beccare.

nick·el ['nɪkl] N (*metal*) nichel *m*; (*Am*: *coin*) (moneta da) cinque centesimi *mpl* di dollaro.

♦ **nickel-plate** [nɪkl'pleɪt] VT nichelare.

♦ **nickel-plated** [nɪkl'pleɪtɪd] ADJ nichelato(-a).

nick·name ['nɪkˌneɪm] 1 N soprannome *m*; (*humorous, malicious*) nomignolo.

2 VT: **to nickname sb sth** soprannominare qn qc.

Nico·sia [ˌnɪkə'siːə] N Nicosia.

nico·tine ['nɪkəˌtiːn] N nicotina.

♦ **nicotine patch** N cerotto antifumo (a base di nicotina).

♦ **nicotine poisoning** N nicotinismo.

niece [niːs] N nipote *f* (di zii).

Nie·tzschean ['niːtʃɪən] ADJ nietzschiano(-a).

nif·ty ['nɪftɪ] ADJ (*comp* **-ier**, *superl* **-iest**) (*fam*: *car, jacket*) chic *inv*; (: *gadget, tool*) ingegnoso(-a); **that was a nifty piece of work** è stato un bel lavoretto.

Ni·ger ['naɪdʒə] N (*country, river*) il Niger *m.*

Ni·geria [naɪ'dʒɪərɪə] N la Nigeria.

Ni·gerian [naɪ'dʒɪərɪən] ADJ, N nigeriano(-a).

nig·gard·ly ['nɪgədlɪ] ADJ (*person*) tirchio(-a), spilorcio (-a); (*allowance, amount*) misero(-a).

nig·ger ['nɪgə'] N (*fam!*: *highly offensive*) negro(-a).

nig·gle ['nɪgl] 1 VT assillare.

2 VI fare il/la pignolo(-a).

nig·gling ['nɪglɪŋ] ADJ (*detail*) insignificante; (*doubt, pain*) persistente; (*person*) pignolo(-a).

nigh [naɪ] 1 ADV **a** (*close*) prossimo(-a), vicino(-a)

b : **well nigh** (*virtually*) praticamente; **it's well nigh**

impossible è praticamente impossibile.

[2] PREP: **nigh on** (*nearly*) quasi; **he is nigh on forty** ha quasi quarant'anni.

night [naɪt] [1] N notte *f*; (*evening*) sera; **good night!** buona notte!; **at night** di notte, la notte; **in the night** [OR] **during the night** durante la notte; **by night** di notte; **last night** la notte scorsa, ieri notte, stanotte; **Tuesday night** martedì notte, la notte di martedì, la notte fra martedì e mercoledì; (*evening*) martedì sera, la sera di martedì; **the night before** la notte prima; (*evening*) la sera prima; **the night before last** l'altro ieri notte; (*evening*) l'altro ieri sera; **11 o'clock at night** le 11 di sera; **the last 3 nights of** (*Theatre etc*) le 3 ultime serate *or* rappresentazioni di; **to have a night out** uscire la sera; **we had a lovely night out** abbiamo passato una bellissima serata fuori; **to spend the night** passare la notte; **I spent the night studying** ho passato la notte a studiare; **to have a good/bad night** dormire bene/male; **to have a late night** andare a letto tardi; **he's working nights** fa il turno di notte.

[2] ADJ (*work, nurse, train etc*) di notte; **night flight** volo notturno.

♦ **night-bird** ['naɪtˌbɜːd] N uccello notturno; (*fig*) nottambulo(-a).

night·cap ['naɪtˌkæp] N papalina, berretto da notte; (*drink*) *bicchierino prima di andare a letto.*

night·clothes ['naɪtˌkləʊðz] NPL (*pyjamas*) pigiama *m*; (*nightdress*) camicia da notte.

night·club ['naɪtˌklʌb] N locale *m* notturno, night(-club) *m inv.*

night·dress ['naɪtˌdrɛs] N camicia da notte.

night·fall ['naɪtˌfɔːl] N crepuscolo; **at nightfall** al calar della notte.

night·gown ['naɪtˌɡaʊn] N (*frm*) camicia da notte.

nightie ['naɪtɪ] N (*fam*) camicia da notte.

night·in·gale ['naɪtɪŋˌɡeɪl] N usignolo.

night·jar ['naɪtˌdʒɑː'] N (*Zool*) caprimulgo nostrano.

night·life ['naɪtˌlaɪf] N vita notturna.

♦ **night-light** ['naɪtˌlaɪt] N lumino da notte.

night·ly ['naɪtlɪ] [1] ADV ogni notte, tutte le notti; (*evening*) ogni sera, tutte le sere.

[2] ADJ di ogni notte, di tutte le notti; (*evening*) di ogni sera, di tutte le sere; (*by night*) notturno(-a).

night·mare ['naɪtˌmɛə'] N incubo.

night·mar·ish ['naɪtˌmɛərɪʃ] ADJ da incubo.

♦ **night owl** N (*fig*) nottambulo(-a).

♦ **night porter** N portiere *m* di notte.

♦ **night safe** N cassa continua.

♦ **night school** N scuola serale.

night·shade ['naɪtˌʃeɪd] N (*Bot*): **deadly nightshade** belladonna.

♦ **night shift** N turno di notte; **to be on night shift** fare il turno di notte, essere di notte.

night·shirt ['naɪtˌʃɜːt] N camicia da notte (*da uomo*).

♦ **night stick** N (*Am*) manganello.

♦ **night-time** ['naɪtˌtaɪm] N notte *f*; **at night-time** di notte, la notte.

♦ **night watchman** N (*pl* **-men**) guardiano notturno.

night·wear ['naɪtˌwɛə'] N indumenti *mpl* per la notte.

ni·hil·ism ['naɪɪˌlɪzəm] N nichilismo.

ni·hil·ist ['naɪɪlɪst] N nichilista *m/f*.

ni·hil·is·tic [ˌnaɪɪ'lɪstɪk] ADJ nichilista.

nil [nɪl] N nulla *m*; (*Sport*) zero.

Nile [naɪl] N: **the Nile** il Nilo.

nim·ble ['nɪmbl] ADJ (*comp* **-r**, *superl* **-st**) (*in moving*) agile;

(*mentally*) vivace, sveglio(-a).

nim·bly ['nɪmblɪ] ADV agilmente.

nim·bus ['nɪmbəs] N nembo.

nin·com·poop ['nɪŋkəmˌpuːp] N (*fam*) scemo(-a).

nine [naɪn] ADJ, N nove (*m*) *inv*; **nine times out of ten** (*fig*) nove volte su dieci; **they were dressed up to the nines** si erano messi in pompa magna *for usage see* **five.**

nine·pins ['naɪnˌpɪnz] NPL birilli *mpl*; **to go down like ninepins** cadere come birilli.

nine·teen [ˌnaɪn'tiːn] ADJ, N diciannove (*m*) *inv*; **to talk nineteen to the dozen** (*fam*) parlare come una mitragliatrice *for usage see* **five.**

nine·teenth [ˌnaɪn'tiːnθ] [1] ADJ diciannovesimo(-a).

[2] N (*in series*) diciannovesimo(-a); (*fraction*) diciannovesimo *for usage see* **fifth.**

nine·ti·eth ['naɪntɪθ] [1] ADJ novantesimo(-a).

[2] N (*in series*) novantesimo(-a); (*fraction*) novantesimo *for usage see* **fifth.**

nine·ty ['naɪntɪ] ADJ, N novanta (*m*) *inv for usage see* **fifty.**

nin·ny ['nɪnɪ] N (*fam*) sciocco(-a).

ninth [naɪnθ] [1] ADJ nono(-a).

[2] N (*in series*) nono(-a); (*fraction*) nono *for usage see* **fifth.**

nip¹ [nɪp] [1] N (*pinch*) pizzico; (*bite*) morso; **there's a nip in the air** l'aria è pungente.

[2] VT (*pinch*) pizzicare; (*bite*) morsicare; (*prune: bud, shoot*) spuntare; (*subj: cold: plant*) assiderare; (: *face*) pungere; **to nip sth in the bud** (*fig*) stroncare qc sul nascere.

[3] VI (*Brit fam*): **to nip inside** andar dentro un attimo; **to nip out/down/up** fare un salto fuori/giù/di sopra; **where has she nipped off to?** dov'è sparita?; **I nipped round to the shop** ho fatto un salto al negozio.

nip² [nɪp] N (*drink*) goccio, bicchierino.

nip·per ['nɪpə'] N (*Brit fam*) bambino(-a).

nip·ple ['nɪpl] N (*Anat*) capezzolo.

nip·py ['nɪpɪ] ADJ (*comp* **-ier**, *superl* **-iest**) (*fam*) **a** (*Brit: person, car*) svelto(-a); **be nippy about it!** sbrigati!, fa' alla svelta! **b** (*wind, weather*) pungente; **it's nippy** l'aria è pungente.

nit [nɪt] N **a** (*of louse*) lendine *m* **b** (*fam: idiot*) cretino(-a), scemo(-a).

♦ **nit-pick** ['nɪtˌpɪk] VI (*fam*) cercare il pelo nell'uovo.

nit-picking ['nɪtˌpɪkɪŋ] N (*fam*) il cercare il pelo nell'uovo.

ni·trate ['naɪtreɪt] N nitrato.

ni·tric ['naɪtrɪk] ADJ nitrico(-a).

ni·tri·fi·ca·tion [ˌnaɪtrɪfɪ'keɪʃən] N nitrificazione *f*.

ni·trite ['naɪtraɪt] N nitrito.

ni·tro·gen ['naɪtrədʒən] N azoto; **nitrogen cycle** ciclo dell'azoto.

ni·tro·glyc·er·ine [ˌnaɪtrəʊ'ɡlɪsəˌriːn], **ni·tro·glyc·er·in** [ˌnaɪtrəʊ'ɡlɪsərɪn] N nitroglicerina.

ni·trous ['naɪtrəs] ADJ nitroso(-a).

nitty-gritty ['nɪtɪ'ɡrɪtɪ] N (*fam*): **to get down to the nitty-gritty** venire al sodo.

nit·wit ['nɪtˌwɪt] N (*fam*) imbecille *m/f*, scemo(-a).

NJ ABBR (*Am Post*)= New Jersey.

NLF [ˌɛnɛl'ɛf] N ABBR (= *National Liberation Front*) ≈ F.L.N. *m* (= *Fronte di Liberazione Nazionale*).

NLQ [ˌɛnɛl'kjuː] ABBR (= *near letter quality*) stampa di qualità.

NLRB [ˌɛnɛlɑː'biː] N ABBR (*Am*: = *National Labor Relations Board*) *organismo per la tutela dei lavoratori.*

NM ABBR (*Am Post*)= New Mexico.

no [nəʊ]

1 ADV

a (*opposite of "yes"*) no

b (*emphatic*)

▷it is no *easy* task non è un'impresa facile

▷it is no *small* matter non è una cosa da poco

▷there is no *such* thing una cosa simile non esiste

▷in no *uncertain* terms in termini tutt'altro che ambigui

c (*in comparatives*)

▷there were no *fewer* than 100 people c'erano non meno di 100 persone

▷he wants to become prime minister, no *less*! vuole diventare nientemeno che primo ministro!

▷I can stand it no *longer* non ne posso più

▷I am no *taller* than you non sono più alto di te.

2 ADJ

a (*not any*) nessuno(-a);

▷there's no *denying* it non si può negarlo

▷"no *dogs*" "vietato l'accesso ai cani"

▷"no *entry*" "vietato l'accesso"

▷she has no *furniture* non ha mobili, non ha nessun mobile

▷it is of no *interest* to us non siamo interessati

▷I have no *money* non ho soldi

▷there is no *more* coffee non c'è più caffè

▷no *other* man nessun altro

▷"no *parking*" "divieto di sosta"

▷there is no *reason* to believe ... non c'è ragione di credere che...

▷"no *smoking*" "vietato fumare"

▷it's no *trouble* non c'è problema

▷no *two* houses are alike le case sono tutte diverse l'una dall'altra

▷no *two* people think alike non ci sono due persone che la pensino allo stesso modo

b (*quite other than*)

▷she's no *beauty* non è certo una bellezza

▷he's no *fool* è tutt'altro che stupido, non è affatto (uno) stupido

▷he's no *friend* of mine non è affatto un mio amico.

3 N (*pl* noes) no *m inv*

▷I won't take no for an answer non accetterò un rifiuto.

No., no. ABBR (*pl* Nos.) (= *number*) n. (= *numero*).

Noah ['nəʊə] N Noè *m*; Noah's ark l'arca di Noè.

nob [nɒb] N (*old fam*) persona altolocata.

nob·ble ['nɒbl] VT (*Brit fam*) **a** (*bribe: person*) comprare, corrompere **b** (*catch: thief*) beccare; (: *person to speak to*) bloccare, beccare **c** (*Racing*) impedire illegalmente *a un cane/cavallo di partecipare a una gara*.

Nobel prize ['nəʊbel'praɪz] N premio Nobel.

no·bil·ity [nəʊ'bɪlɪtɪ] N nobiltà.

no·ble ['nəʊbl] **1** ADJ (*comp* -r, *superl* -st) nobile; (*also iro*) generoso(-a); of noble birth di nobili natali. **2** N nobile *m/f*.

noble·man ['nəʊblmən] N (*pl* -men) nobile *m*, nobiluomo.

noble·woman ['nəʊbl,wʊmən] N (*pl* -women) nobile *f*, nobildonna.

no·bly ['nəʊblɪ] ADV (*selflessly*) generosamente.

no·body ['nəʊbədɪ] **1** PRON nessuno; I saw nobody non ho visto nessuno; nobody spoke nessuno ha parlato, non ha parlato nessuno; nobody else nessun altro/nessun'altra.

2 N: he's a nobody è una nullità.

♦ **no-claims bonus** [,nəʊ'kleɪmz ,bəʊnəs] N bonus malus *m inv*.

noc·tur·nal [nɒk'tɜːnl] ADJ notturno(-a).

noc·turne ['nɒktɜːn] N (*Mus*) notturno.

nod [nɒd] **1** N cenno del capo; to give sb a nod fare un cenno col capo a qn; (*answering yes*) accennare di sì a qn, fare di sì col capo a qn.

2 VT: to nod one's head fare di sì col capo; he nodded a greeting accennò un saluto col capo; they nodded their agreement accennarono di sì (col capo).

3 VI **a** fare un cenno col capo; (*say yes*) far segno di sì col capo, annuire; he nodded to me in a friendly way mi ha salutato cordialmente con un cenno del capo; we have a nodding acquaintance ci conosciamo solo di vista **b** (*doze*) ciondolare il capo (per il sonno); (*sleep*) sonnecchiare

▶ **nod off** VI + ADV appisolarsi, assopirsi.

nod·dle ['nɒdəl] N (*old fam*) zucca (*testa*); use your noddle! usa il cervello!

node [nəʊd] N (*Math, Bot*) nodo.

nod·ule ['nɒdjuːl] N nodulo.

♦ **no-fly zone** [,nəʊ'flaɪ,zəʊn] N zona di interdizione aerea.

♦ **no-go area** [,nəʊ'gəʊ,ɛərɪə] N zona proibita.

noise [nɔɪz] N (*sound*) rumore *m*; (*din*) rumore, chiasso, fracasso; (*Telec, Radio, TV*) disturbo, interferenza; to make a noise fare un rumore; stop making a noise! smettila di far rumore!; my wife's making noises about starting a family mia moglie sembra farmi capire che vuole avere un bambino; a big noise (*fam: person*) un pezzo grosso.

noise·less ['nɔɪzlɪs] ADJ silenzioso(-a).

noise·less·ly ['nɔɪzlɪslɪ] ADV senza far rumore, silenziosamente.

noisi·ly ['nɔɪzɪlɪ] ADV rumorosamente.

noisy ['nɔɪzɪ] ADJ (*comp* -ier, *superl* -iest) (*street, car*) rumoroso(-a); (*child, party*) rumoroso(-a), chiassoso (-a); stop being noisy! smettila di far rumore!

no·mad ['nəʊmæd] N nomade *m/f*.

no·mad·ic [nəʊ'mædɪk] ADJ nomade.

no·mad·ism ['nəʊmædɪzəm] N nomadismo.

♦ **no-man's-land** ['nəʊmænz,lænd] N terra di nessuno.

nom de plume [nɒmdə'pluːm] N (*Literature*) pseudonimo.

no·men·cla·ture [nəʊ'mɛnklətʃəʳ] N (*frm*) nomenclatura.

nomi·nal ['nɒmɪnl] ADJ (*Gram, Econ*) nominale; (*ostensible*) nominale, di nome.

nomi·nal·ly ['nɒmɪnəlɪ] ADV nominalmente.

nomi·nate ['nɒmɪ,neɪt] VT: to nominate sb (for sth) (*propose*) proporre qn come candidato (a qc); (*appoint*) nominare *or* designare qn (a qc).

nomi·na·tion [,nɒmɪ'neɪʃən] N (*see vb*) candidatura; nomina.

nomi·na·tive ['nɒmɪnətɪv] ADJ, N (*Gram*) nominativo(-a).

nomi·nee [,nɒmɪ'niː] N (*see vb*) candidato(-a); persona nominata.

non... [nɒn] PREF non...

non·ag·gres·sion [,nɒnə'grɛʃən] N non aggressione *f*.

nona·gon ['nɒnəgɒn] N nonagono.

♦ **non-alcoholic** ['nɒnælkə'hɒlɪk] ADJ analcolico(-a).

non·aligned [,nɒnə'laɪnd] ADJ non allineato(-a).

non·ar·ri·val [ˌnɒnə'raɪvəl] N mancato arrivo.

non·be·liev·er [ˌnɒnbɪ'liːvəʳ] N non credente m/f.

non·break·able ['nɒn'breɪkəbl] ADJ infrangibile.

nonce word ['nɒnsˌwɜːd] N parola coniata per l'occasione.

non·cha·lance ['nɒnʃələns] N disinvoltura, indifferenza.

non·cha·lant ['nɒnʃələnt] ADJ disinvolto(-a), indifferente, incurante.

non·cha·lant·ly ['nɒnʃələntlɪ] ADV con disinvoltura, con indifferenza.

non·com·bat·ant ['nɒn'kɒmbətənt] N militare m non combattente.

non·com·mis·sioned of·fic·er ['nɒnkə'mɪʃənd'ɒfɪsəʳ] N sottufficiale m.

non·com·mit·tal ['nɒnkə'mɪtl] ADJ (statement) non impegnativo(-a), evasivo(-a); (person) che non si compromette, evasivo(-a).

Non·con·form·ism ['nɒnkən'fɔːmɪzəm] N (Brit Rel) movimento protestante.

non·con·form·ism ['nɒnkən'fɔːmɪzəm] N anticonformismo.

Non·con·form·ist ['nɒnkən'fɔːmɪst] ADJ, N (Brit Rel) protestante non appartenente alla Chiesa Anglicana.

non·con·form·ist ['nɒnkən'fɔːmɪst] 1 ADJ anticonformista.

2 N anticonformista m/f.

non·con·tribu·tory [ˌnɒnkən'trɪbjʊtərɪ] ADJ: **noncontributory pension scheme** sistema di pensionamento con i contributi interamente a carico del datore di lavoro.

non·co·op·era·tion ['nɒnkəʊˌɒpə'reɪʃən] N non cooperazione f, non collaborazione f.

non·de·script ['nɒndɪˌskrɪpt] ADJ (person, clothes) qualunque inv; (colour) indefinito(-a).

none [nʌn] 1 PRON nessuno(-a), nemmeno uno(-a), neanche uno(-a); **none of them wants to go** nessuno di loro vuole andarci; **none of the machines is working** nessuna delle macchine funziona, non c'è neanche una macchina che funzioni; **I have none of the books** non ho nessuno dei libri; **I have none** non ne ho nemmeno uno; **none of this is yours** niente di questo è tuo; **none of this money** neanche un centesimo di questi soldi; **none of this wine** neanche una goccia di questo vino; **I have none left** non ne ho più; **any news? — none** ci sono novità? — niente or nessuna; **there's none left** non ce n'è più; **none of that!** basta!; **he would have none of it** non ne ha voluto sapere; **none at all** (nothing) proprio niente; (not one) nemmeno uno; **our host was none other than the president** il nostro ospite era nientemeno che il presidente.

2 ADV: **I was none too comfortable** non ero per niente a mio agio; **it's none too warm** non fa molto caldo; **and none too soon!** ed era ora!; **I like him none the worse for it** non per questo mi piace di meno; **he is none the worse for his experience** non sembra aver risentito di quell'esperienza.

non·en·tity [nɒn'ɛntɪtɪ] N persona insignificante, nullità f inv.

non·es·sen·tial ['nɒnɪ'sɛnʃəl] 1 ADJ non essenziale.

2: **nonessentials** NPL superfluo sg, cose fpl superflue.

none·the·less [ˌnʌnðə'lɛs] ADV nondimeno.

♦ **non·event** ['nɒnɪ'vɛnt] N delusione f; **the party turned out to be a non-event** la festa è stata deludente or una delusione.

non·ex·ecu·tive [ˌnɒnɪg'zɛkjʊtɪv] ADJ: **nonexecutive director** direttore m senza potere esecutivo.

non·ex·ist·ence [ˌnɒnɪg'zɪstəns] N inesistenza.

non·ex·ist·ent [ˌnɒnɪg'zɪstənt] ADJ inesistente.

non·fic·tion ['nɒn'fɪkʃən] N qualunque pubblicazione non di narrativa.

non·flam·mable ['nɒn'flæməbl] ADJ non infiammabile.

non·inter·ven·tion ['nɒnˌɪntə'vɛnʃən] N non intervento.

non·iron ['nɒn'aɪən] ADJ che non si stira.

non·mem·ber ['nɒn'mɛmbəʳ] N non socio(-a).

non·met·al ['nɒn'mɛtl] N (Chem) non metallo.

♦ **non·nuclear** ['nɒn'njuːklɪəʳ] ADJ (country) che non dispone di armi nucleari; **non-nuclear weapons** armi mpl convenzionali.

♦ **no·no** ['nəʊˌnəʊ] N: **it's a no-no!** (undesirable) è inaccettabile!; (forbidden) non si può fare!

non obst. ABBR (notwithstanding: = non obstante) nonostante.

♦ **no·nonsense** [ˌnəʊ'nɒnsɛns] ADJ che va al sodo.

non·par·ty ['nɒn'pɑːtɪ] ADJ (decision, vote) indipendente.

non·pay·ment ['nɒn'peɪmənt] N mancato pagamento.

non·plus ['nɒn'plʌs] (pt, pp **nonplussed**) VT sconcertare.

non·plussed ['nɒn'plʌst] ADJ sconcertato(-a).

non·pro·fes·sion·al ['nɒnprə'fɛʃənl] ADJ, N dilettante (m/f).

non·profit·making ['nɒn'prɒfɪtˌmeɪkɪŋ], (Am) **non-profit** ['nɒn'prɒfɪt] ADJ senza scopo di lucro.

non·resi·dent ['nɒn'rɛzɪdənt] N non residente m/f; (in hotel) ospite m/f di passaggio.

non·re·turn·able [ˌnɒnrɪ'tɜːnəbl] ADJ: **nonreturnable bottle** vuoto a perdere.

non·sense ['nɒnsəns] N sciocchezze fpl, assurdità fpl; **(what) nonsense!** che sciocchezze!, che assurdità!; **it is nonsense to say that ...** è un'assurdità or non ha senso dire che...; **to talk nonsense** dire sciocchezze or assurdità; **that's a piece of nonsense!** è una sciocchezza!; **to make (a) nonsense of sth** rendere assurdo qc; **he stands no nonsense** con lui non si scherza.

non·sen·si·cal [nɒn'sɛnsɪkəl] ADJ assurdo(-a), ridicolo(-a).

♦ **non se·qui·tur** [ˌnɒn'sɛkwɪtəʳ] N: **it is a non sequitur** è illogico.

non·shrink ['nɒn'ʃrɪŋk] ADJ (Brit) irrestringibile.

non·skid ['nɒn'skɪd], **non·slip** ['nɒn'slɪp] ADJ antisdrucciolo inv, antisdrucciolevole.

non·smok·er ['nɒn'sməʊkəʳ] N **a** (person) non fumatore (-trice); **I'm a nonsmoker** non fumo **b** (Rail) scompartimento per non fumatori.

non·smok·ing ['nɒn'sməʊkɪŋ] ADJ (person) che non fuma; (area, section) per non fumatori.

♦ **non·standard** ['nɒn'stændəd] ADJ (word, pronunciation) che non fa parte della lingua standard.

non·start·er [ˌnɒn'stɑːtəʳ] N: **it's a nonstarter** è fallito in partenza.

non·stick ['nɒn'stɪk] ADJ (saucepan) (con rivestimento) antiaderente.

non·stop ['nɒn'stɒp] 1 ADJ continuo(-a), senza sosta; (train, bus) diretto(-a), direttissimo(-a); (flight) diretto (-a), senza scalo; **nonstop entertainment** spettacolo continuo.

2 ADV ininterrottamente, senza sosta; (Rail) diretto; **I flew non-stop to New York** ho preso un volo diretto per New York.

non·tax·able ['nɒn'tæksəbl] ADJ: **non-taxable income** reddito non imponibile.

non-U [ˌnɒn'juː] ADJ ABBR (*Brit fam*)= *non-upper class*.

non·un·ion [ˌnɒn'juːnjən] ADJ (*workers, labour*) non appartenente al sindacato.

♦ **non-violence** ['nɒn'vaɪələns] N non violenza.

non·vio·lent ['nɒn'vaɪələnt] ADJ non violento(-a).

non·vola·tile [ˌnɒn'vɒlətaɪl] ADJ (*Comput*): **nonvolatile memory** memoria permanente.

non·voting [ˌnɒn'vəʊtɪŋ] ADJ: **non-voting shares** azioni *fpl* senza diritto di voto.

non·white [ˌnɒn'waɪt] 1 ADJ di colore.
2 N persona di colore.

noo·dles ['nuːdlz] NPL taglierini *mpl*, tagliatelle *fpl*; **egg noodles** pasta all'uovo.

nook [nʊk] N angolino; **we searched every nook and cranny** abbiamo frugato dappertutto *or* in ogni angolo.

noon [nuːn] N mezzogiorno; **at noon** a mezzogiorno.

noon·day ['nuːn,deɪ] (*old*) 1 ADJ (*meal, sun*) di mezzogiorno.
2 N: **at noonday** a mezzogiorno.

♦ **no-one** ['nəʊˌwʌn] PRON = **nobody**.

noose [nuːs] N (*loop*) nodo scorsoio, cappio; (*for animal trapping*) laccio; (*hangman's*) cappio; **to put one's head in the noose** (*fig*) scavarsi la fossa con le proprie mani.

nope [nəʊp] ADV (*fam*) no.

nor [nɔː'] 1 ADV see **neither**.
2 CONJ = **neither**.

Nor·dic ['nɔːdɪk] ADJ nordico(-a); **nordic skiing** sci *m* nordico.

Norf ABBR (*Brit*)= *Norfolk*.

norm [nɔːm] N norma.

nor·mal ['nɔːməl] 1 ADJ normale; **it was quite normal for him to object** era perfettamente normale che obiettasse; **it is perfectly normal to be left-handed** è perfettamente normale *or* naturale essere mancini.
2 N **a**: **to return to normal** tornare alla normalità; **above/below normal** al disopra/al disotto della norma **b** (*Math*) normale *f*.

nor·mal·ity [nɔː'mælɪtɪ] N normalità.

nor·mali·za·tion [ˌnɔːməlaɪ'zeɪʃən] N normalizzazione *f*.

nor·mal·ize ['nɔːmə,laɪz] VT normalizzare.

nor·mal·ly ['nɔːməlɪ] ADV normalmente.

Nor·man ['nɔːmən] N, ADJ normanno(-a).

Nor·man·dy ['nɔːməndɪ] N Normandia.

Norse [nɔːs] N lingua norrena.

north [nɔːθ] 1 N nord *m*, settentrione *m*; (**to the) north of** a nord di; **in the north of** nel nord di; **the wind is from the north** il vento soffia da nord; **to veer to the north** (*wind*) girare verso nord.
2 ADJ (*gen*) nord *inv*; (*wind*) del nord, settentrionale; (*coast*) settentrionale.
3 ADV verso nord; **to sail north** navigare verso nord; **the town lies north of the border** la città si trova a nord del confine; **a house facing north** una casa esposta a nord.

♦ **North Africa** N l'Africa del Nord.

♦ **North African** ADJ, N nordafricano(-a).

♦ **North America** N l'America del Nord.

♦ **North American** ADJ, N nordamericano(-a).

Northants [nɔː'θænts] ABBR (*Brit*)= *Northamptonshire*.

north·bound ['nɔːθ,baʊnd] ADJ (*traffic*) diretto(-a) a nord; (*carriageway*) nord *inv*.

♦ **north-country** ['nɔːθ,kʌntrɪ] ADJ del nord, settentrionale.

Northd ABBR (*Brit*)= *Northumberland*.

north·east [ˌnɔː'θiːst] 1 N nordest *m*.
2 ADJ di nordest.

3 ADV verso nordest.

north·easter·ly [ˌnɔː'θiːstəlɪ] ADJ (*wind*) che viene dal nordest; (*direction*) verso nordest.

north·eastern [ˌnɔː'θiːstən] ADJ di nordest.

nor·ther·ly ['nɔːðəlɪ] ADJ (*wind*) del nord; (*direction*) verso nord; **house with a northerly aspect** casa esposta a nord.

north·ern ['nɔːðən] ADJ (*region*) del nord, settentrionale; (*wall*) (esposto(-a) a) nord *inv*; (*coast*) settentrionale; **in northern Spain** nel nord della Spagna, nella Spagna settentrionale.

north·ern·er ['nɔːðənə'] N settentrionale *m/f*, abitante *m/f* del nord.

♦ **northern hemisphere** N: **the northern hemisphere** l'emisfero settentrionale *or* boreale.

♦ **Northern Ireland** N Irlanda del Nord.

♦ **northern lights** NPL: **the northern lights** l'aurora boreale.

north·ern·most ['nɔːðən,məʊst] ADJ (il/la) più a nord; **the northernmost town in Europe** la città più a nord dell'Europa.

♦ **north-northeast** [ˌnɔːθ,nɔː'θiːst] N nord-nordest *m*.

♦ **north-northwest** [ˌnɔːθ,nɔː'θwɛst] N nord-nordovest *m*.

♦ **North Pole** N: **the North Pole** il Polo Nord.

♦ **North Sea** N: **the North Sea** il mare del Nord.

♦ **North Sea gas** N gas del mare del Nord.

♦ **North Sea oil** N petrolio del mare del Nord.

♦ **North Star** N: **the North Star** la stella polare.

north·wards ['nɔːθwədz], **north·ward** ['nɔːθwəd] ADV verso nord.

north·west [ˌnɔː'θwɛst] 1 N nordovest *m*.
2 ADJ di nordovest.
3 ADV verso nordovest.

north·wester·ly [ˌnɔː'θwɛstəlɪ] ADJ (*wind*) che viene da nordovest; (*direction*) verso nordovest.

north·western [ˌnɔː'θwɛstən] ADJ di nordovest.

Nor·way ['nɔːˌweɪ] N Norvegia.

Nor·we·gian [nɔː'wiːdʒən] 1 ADJ norvegese.
2 N (*person*) norvegese *m/f*; (*language*) norvegese *m*.

Nos., nos. ABBR (= *numbers*) nn. (= *numeri*).

nose [nəʊz] 1 N naso; (*of animal, plane*) muso; **to speak through one's nose** parlare col naso; **to blow one's nose** soffiarsi il naso; **my nose is bleeding** perdo sangue dal naso; **nose drops** gocce *fpl* per il naso; **right under my nose** (*fig*) proprio sotto il naso; **to follow one's nose** andare a naso; **to pay through the nose (for sth)** (*fam*) pagare (qc) un occhio della testa; **to poke** *or* **stick one's nose into sth** (*fam*) ficcare *or* cacciare il naso in qc; **to turn up one's nose (at sth)** arricciare il naso (di fronte a qc); **to look down one's nose at** disprezzare; (*person*) guardare dall'alto in basso; **to have a (good) nose for** aver buon fiuto *or* buon naso per.
2 VI: **to nose (one's way)** avanzare cautamente; **the car nosed (its way) into the stream of traffic** l'auto si è infilata poco a poco nella corrente del traffico

► **nose about, nose around** VI + ADV curiosare

► **nose out** VT + ADV (*subj: dog, fig*) fiutare.

nose·bag ['nəʊz,bæg] N sacchetto per il foraggio.

nose·bleed ['nəʊz,bliːd] N emorragia nasale.

-nosed [nəʊzd] SUFF dal naso...; **red-nosed** dal naso rosso.

♦ **nose-dive** ['nəʊz,daɪv] 1 N (*Aer*) picchiata; (*fig*) calo vertiginoso.
2 VI (*see n*) scendere in picchiata; calare vertiginosamente.

nose·gay ['nəʊz‚geɪ] N (gen) mazzolino (di fiori); (at wedding) piccolo bouquet m inv.

nos·ey ['nəʊzɪ] ADJ = nosy.

♦ **nosey parker** N (Brit) = nosy parker.

nosh [nɒʃ] N (Brit fam) cibo.

♦ **nosh-up** ['nɒʃ‚ʌp] N (Brit fam) mangiata, abbuffata.

nos·tal·gia [nɒs'tældʒɪə] N nostalgia.

nos·tal·gic [nɒs'tældʒɪk] ADJ nostalgico(-a).

nos·tril ['nɒstrəl] N narice f; (of horse) frogia.

nosy, nos·ey ['nəʊzɪ] ADJ (comp -ier, superl -iest) (fam) curioso(-a); **don't be so nosy** non fare il ficcanaso; **she's a nosy girl** è una ficcanaso.

♦ **nosy parker, nosey parker** N (Brit fam) ficcanaso m/f.

not [nɒt] ADV non; **he is not here** non è qui, non c'è; **I haven't seen anybody** non ho visto nessuno; **it's too late, isn't it?** è troppo tardi, vero? or no?; **she will not** or **won't go** non ci andrà; **he asked me not to do it** mi ha chiesto di non farlo; **whether you go or not** che tu ci vada o no; **not that I don't like him** non che (lui) non mi piaccia; **big, not to say enormous** grosso, per non dire enorme; **why not?** perché no?; **I hope not** spero di no; **not at all** niente affatto, per niente; (after thanks) prego, s'immagini; **you must not** or **mustn't do this** non deve fare questo; **not one book** neanche un libro; **not me/you** etc io/tu etc no; **not yet** non ancora; see also **even**, **much**, **only** etc.

no·table ['nəʊtəbl] **1** ADJ (person) eminente; (event) notevole, degno(-a) di nota.

2 N notabile m, persona importante.

no·tably ['nəʊtəblɪ] ADV (noticeably) notevolmente; (in particular) in particolare.

no·ta·ry ['nəʊtərɪ] N (also: **notary public**) notaio.

no·ta·tion [nəʊ'teɪʃən] N notazione f.

notch [nɒtʃ] **1** N (in wood, blade) tacca; (in wheel, saw) dente m; (in belt) buco.

2 VT (stick, blade) intagliare, fare tacche in

▶ **notch up** VT + ADV (score, victory) marcare, segnare.

note [nəʊt] **1** N **a** (gen, Diplomacy) nota; **to take** or **make notes** prendere appunti; **Italian lecture notes** appunti mpl di italiano; **to take** or **make a note of sth** prendere nota di qc, prendere atto di qc; **I must make a note to buy some more** devo tenere a mente di comprarne di più; **to compare notes** (fig) scambiarsi le impressioni

b (informal letter) biglietto, due righe; **just a quick note to let you know ...** ti scrivo solo due righe per informarti...

c (Mus, of bird, fig) nota; **to play** or **sing a wrong note** prendere una stecca; **to strike the right/wrong note (with)** (fig) intonarsi (a)/stonare (con); **with a note of anxiety in his voice** con una nota di ansia nella voce

d (Comm) nota; (also: **banknote**) banconota, biglietto di banca; **delivery note** bolletta di consegna; **five-pound note** biglietto da cinque sterline

e (of person): **of note** eminente, importante

f (notice): **worthy of note** degno(-a) di nota.

2 VT (observe) notare, osservare; (also: **note down**) annotare, prendere nota di.

note·book ['nəʊt‚bʊk] N taccuino; (Scol) blocco per appunti; (for shorthand) bloc-notes m inv.

note·case ['nəʊt‚keɪs] N (Brit) portafoglio.

not·ed ['nəʊtɪd] ADJ (Brit): **noted (for)** celebre (per), famoso(-a) (per).

note·pad ['nəʊt‚pæd] N bloc-notes m inv, blocchetto.

note·paper ['nəʊt‚peɪpə'] N carta da lettere.

note·worthy ['nəʊt‚wɜ:ðɪ] ADJ degno(-a) di nota, impor-

tante.

noth·ing ['nʌθɪŋ] **1** N **a** niente m, nulla m; (Math, Sport) zero; **nothing happened** non è successo niente or nulla; **I've eaten nothing** non ho mangiato niente or nulla; **there is nothing to eat** non c'è niente or nulla da mangiare

b (in phrases): **as if nothing had happened** come se niente fosse; **nothing at all** proprio niente; **nothing else** nient'altro; **nothing much/new** etc niente di speciale/nuovo etc; **nothing but** nient'altro che; **she does nothing but sleep** non fa altro che dormire; **there is nothing for it but to go** non c'è altra scelta che andare; **there is nothing in it** (not true) non c'è niente di vero; (not interesting) non è per niente interessante; (nearly the same) non c'è una grande differenza; **there's nothing in it for us** non ci guadagniamo niente; **there's nothing to it!** (it's easy) è una cosa da niente!; **to have nothing on** (naked) non aver niente addosso; (not busy) non aver niente in programma; **for nothing** (free, unpaid) per niente, gratis; (in vain) per niente, inutilmente; (for no reason) senza ragione; **he is nothing if not careful** è soprattutto attento; **I can do nothing about it** non posso farci nulla; **to come to nothing** finire in nulla; **to say nothing of ...** per non parlare di...; **to think nothing of doing sth** non farsi nessun problema nel fare qc; **think nothing of it!** s'immagini!, si figuri!; **I can make nothing of it** non ci capisco niente; **a mere nothing** una cosa da nulla or da niente; **to whisper sweet nothings to sb** sussurrare tenerezze a qn; **nothing doing!** (fam) niente da fare!.

2 ADV per niente, niente affatto; **it was nothing like as expensive as we thought** era molto meno caro di quanto credessimo.

noth·ing·ness ['nʌθɪŋnɪs] N (non-existence) nulla m; (worthlessness, insignificance) nullità.

no·tice ['nəʊtɪs] **1** N **a** (intimation, warning) avviso; (period) preavviso; **without notice** senza preavviso; **advance** or **previous notice** preavviso; **a week's notice** una settimana di preavviso; **at short notice** con un breve preavviso; **at a moment's notice** immediatamente, all'istante; **until further notice** fino a nuovo avviso; **to give notice to** (to tenant) dare la disdetta a; (to landlord) dare il preavviso a; **to give sb notice** (Admin: inform) notificare a qn; (: sack) licenziare qn; **to give notice** OR **to hand in one's notice** (subj: employee) licenziarsi; **to give notice of sth** annunciare qc; **to give sb notice of sth** avvisare qn di qc

b (announcement) avviso; (Press) annuncio; (sign) cartello; (poster) manifesto, cartellone m; **to put a notice in the paper** mettere un annuncio sul giornale

c (Brit: review: of play etc) critica, recensione f

d (attention): **to bring sth to sb's notice** far notare qc a qn; **to take notice of sb/sth** notare qn/qc, fare caso a qn/qc; **to take no notice of sb/sth** non prestare attenzione a qn/qc; **he keeps waving at me — take no notice!** continua a farmi dei cenni — ignoralo!; **it has come to my notice that ...** sono venuto a sapere che...; **to escape** or **avoid notice** passare inosservato(-a); **it escaped my notice that ...** non ho notato che....

2 VT accorgersi di, notare; **he pretended not to notice us** ha fatto finta di non vederci; **I notice you have a new car** vedo che ha una macchina nuova.

no·tice·able ['nəʊtɪsəbl] ADJ (perceptible) percettibile; (obvious) evidente; (considerable) notevole; **the scar is hardly noticeable** la cicatrice si vede appena; **there has**

been a noticeable increase in prices c'è stato un notevole aumento dei prezzi.

no·tice·ably ['nəʊtɪsəblɪ] ADV (*perceptibly*) sensibilmente; (*obviously*) evidentemente; (*considerably*) notevolmente.

♦ **notice board** N (*Brit*) bacheca.

no·ti·fi·able ['nəʊtɪ,faɪəbəl] ADJ (*disease, crime*) che deve essere notificato(-a) *or* denunciato(-a) alle autorità.

no·ti·fi·ca·tion [,nəʊtɪfɪ'keɪʃən] N (*see vb*) notifica; denuncia; (*announcement*) annuncio.

no·ti·fy ['nəʊtɪ,faɪ] VT: **to notify sb of sth** informare *or* avvisare qn di qc; (*police*) denunciare qc a qn; **to notify sth to sb** notificare qc a qn; **you should notify the police that your car has been stolen** deve denunciare il furto della macchina alla polizia.

no·tion ['nəʊʃən] N **a** idea; (*concept*) nozione *f*; **to have no notion of time** non avere la nozione del tempo; **I haven't the slightest** *or* **foggiest notion** non ho la più pallida idea; **I have no notion of what you mean** non ho la più vaga idea di cosa tu voglia dire **b** : **notions** NPL (*Am: haberdashery*) merceria.

no·tion·al ['nəʊʃənəl] ADJ (*figure, amount, price*) simbolico (-a).

no·to·ri·ety [,nəʊtə'raɪɪtɪ] N notorietà.

no·to·ri·ous [nəʊ'tɔːrɪəs] ADJ (*thief, criminal, prison etc*) famigerato(-a); (*liar*) ben noto(-a); (*place, crime*) tristemente famoso(-a); **a town notorious for its fog** una città tristamente famosa per la nebbia.

no·to·ri·ous·ly [nəʊ'tɔːrɪəslɪ] ADV notoriamente.

Notts [nɒts] ABBR (*Brit*)= *Nottinghamshire*.

not·with·stand·ing [,nɒtwɪð'stændɪŋ] **1** PREP nonostante, malgrado.
2 CONJ: **international agreements notwithstanding ...** malgrado gli accordi internazionali ... .

nou·gat ['nuːɡɑː] N torrone *m*.

nought [nɔːt] N (*Math*) zero.

♦ **noughts and crosses** NSG (*Brit*) tris (*giocata segnando "x" e "o" su un quadrato con 9 caselle*).

noun [naʊn] N sostantivo, nome *m*.

nour·ish ['nʌrɪʃ] VT nutrire.

nour·ish·ing ['nʌrɪʃɪŋ] ADJ nutriente.

nour·ish·ment ['nʌrɪʃmənt] N nutrimento.

nous [naʊs] N (*Brit fam*) buonsenso; **to have the nous to do sth** avere il buonsenso di fare qc.

nou·veau riche [,nuːvəʊ'riːʃ] N (*pl* **nouveaux riches**) nuovo(-a) ricco(-a), arricchito(-a).

Nov. ABBR (= *November*) nov. (= *novembre*).

Nova Scotia ['nəʊvə'skəʊʃə] N Nuova Scozia.

nov·el ['nɒvəl] **1** ADJ originale, nuovo(-a) *after n*.
2 N (*Literature*) romanzo.

nov·el·ette [,nɒvə'lɛt] N (*usu pej*) romanzetto.

nov·el·ist ['nɒvəlɪst] N romanziere(-a).

nov·el·ty ['nɒvəltɪ] N **a** NO PL novità **b** (*Comm*) oggettino, ninnolo.

No·vem·ber [nəʊ'vɛmbəˈ] N novembre *m*; see also **July**.

no·vena [nəʊ'viːnə] N novena.

nov·ice ['nɒvɪs] N principiante *m/f*; (*Rel*) novizio(-a).

NOW [naʊ] N ABBR (*Am*: = *National Organization for Women*) ≈ U.D.I. *f* (= *Unione Donne Italiane*).

now [naʊ] **1** ADV **a** (*at present, these days*) adesso, ora; (*at that time*) allora; **right now** subito, immediatamente; **now is the time to do it** questo è il momento per farlo; **they won't be long now** ormai non tarderanno; **I saw her just now** l'ho vista proprio adesso; **that's the fashion just now** è la moda del momento; **I'll read it just now** lo

leggo subito; (*every*) **now and then** *or* **now and again** ogni tanto, di tanto in tanto; **it's now or never** ora o mai più

b (*with prep*): **between now and Monday** entro lunedì, da qui a lunedì; **I couldn't do it before now** non potevo farlo prima; **long before now** molto tempo fa; **by now** ormai; **the train should have arrived by now** il treno dovrebbe essere già arrivato; **in 3 days from now** fra 3 giorni; **from now on** d'ora in poi; **from now until then** da adesso fino a quel momento; **that's all for now** per ora basta; **until now** *or* **up to now** fino ad ora

c (*without temporal force*): **now (then)!** dunque!, allora!; **now then, no more quarrelling** ora *or* adesso basta con i litigi; **well now** vediamo, dunque; **well now, look who it is!** ma guarda un po' chi si vede!; **be careful now!** ma sta' attento!

2 CONJ: **now (that)** adesso che, ora che.

nowa·days ['naʊə,deɪz] ADV al giorno d'oggi, oggi, oggigiorno, oggidì; **nowadays I haven't got time to watch television** attualmente non ho il tempo per guardare la televisione.

no·where ['nəʊ,wɛəˈ] ADV in nessun posto *or* luogo, da nessuna parte; **I went nowhere** non sono andato in nessun posto *or* da nessuna parte; **nowhere in Italy** in nessuna parte d'Italia, da nessuna parte in Italia; **nowhere else** in nessun altro posto; **it/he is nowhere to be found** non si riesce a trovarlo da nessuna parte; **we're getting nowhere** non stiamo concludendo nulla; **that will get you nowhere** ciò non le servirà a nulla; **he appeared from nowhere** è saltato fuori da chissà dove; **Paul is nowhere near as tall as John** Paul non è neanche lontanamente alto come John; **it's nowhere near as good** non vale neanche la metà; **nowhere near enough** ben lontano dall'essere sufficiente.

♦ **no-win situation** [,nəʊwɪnsɪtjʊ'eɪʃən] N: **to be in a no-win situation** aver perso in partenza.

nowt [naʊt] N (*Brit dial*) = **nothing**.

nox·ious ['nɒkʃəs] ADJ nocivo(-a).

noz·zle ['nɒzl] N (*of hose, vacuum cleaner, syringe*) bocchetta, boccaglio; (*of fire extinguisher*) lancia.

NP [,ɛn'piː] N ABBR = **notary public**.

NS [,ɛn'ɛs] ABBR (*Canada*)= *Nova Scotia*.

NSC [,ɛnɛs'siː] N ABBR (*Am*) = **National Security Council**.

NSF [,ɛnɛs'ɛf] N ABBR (*Am*)= *National Science Foundation*.

NSPCC [,ɛnɛspiː,siː'siː] N ABBR (*Brit old*)= *National Society for the Prevention of Cruelty to Children*.

NSW ABBR (*Australia*)= *New South Wales*.

NT [,ɛn'tiː] N ABBR (= *New Testament*) N.T. (= *Nuovo Testamento*).

nth [ɛnθ] ADJ (*Math*): **to the nth power** *or* **degree** all'ennesima potenza; **for the nth time** (*fam*) per l'ennesima volta.

nu·ance ['njuːɑːns] N sfumatura.

nub [nʌb] N: **the nub of the matter** il nocciolo del problema.

nu·bile ['njuːbaɪl] ADJ nubile; (*attractive*) giovane e desiderabile.

nu·clear ['njuːklɪəˈ] ADJ nucleare; (*warfare*) atomico(-a).

♦ **nuclear disarmament** N disarmo nucleare.

♦ **nuclear family** N famiglia nucleare.

♦ **nuclear-free** ['njuːklɪəfriː] ADJ (*zone*) denuclearizzato (-a).

♦ **nuclear-free zone** [,njuːklɪəfriː'zəʊn] N zona denuclearizzata.

♦ **nuclear power** N energia nucleare, nucleare *m*.

♦ **nuclear-powered** [ˌnjuːklɪəˈpaʊəd] ADJ nucleare.
♦ **nuclear power station** N centrale *f* termonucleare.
♦ **nuclear reactor** N reattore *m* nucleare.
nu·cleic [njuːˈkliːɪk] ADJ nucleico(-a).
nu·cleon [ˈnjuːklɪɒn] N nucleone *m*.
nu·cleus [ˈnjuːklɪəs] N (*pl* nuclei [ˈnjuːklɪaɪ]) nucleo.
NUCPS [ˌɛnjuːsiːpiːˈɛs] N ABBR (*Brit*: = National Union of Civil and Public Servants) *sindacato nazionale del pubblico impiego.*
nude [njuːd] ① ADJ nudo(-a).
② N (*Art*) nudo; **in the nude** nudo(-a), tutto(-a) nudo (-a).
nudge [nʌdʒ] ① N gomitata.
② VT dare un colpetto col gomito a; **he nudged me out of the way** mi ha spinto via con una gomitata.
nud·ism [ˈnjuːdɪzəm] N nudismo.
nud·ist [ˈnjuːdɪst] ① ADJ (*colony*) nudista; (*camp, beach*) di nudisti.
② N nudista *m/f*.
nu·dity [ˈnjuːdɪtɪ] N nudità.
nug·get [ˈnʌgɪt] N pepita.
nui·sance [ˈnjuːsns] N (*state of affairs, thing*) fastidio, seccatura; (*person*) peste *f*; **what a nuisance!** che seccatura!; **it's a nuisance having to shave** doversi radere è una (gran) seccatura; **to make a nuisance of o.s.** rendersi insopportabile; **he's a nuisance** dà fastidio.
NUJ [ˌɛnjuːˈdʒeɪ] N ABBR (*Brit*: = National Union of Journalists) *sindacato nazionale dei giornalisti.*
nuke [njuːk] (*esp Am fam*) ① VT attaccare con armi atomiche.
② N bomba atomica.
null [nʌl] ADJ: **null and void** (*Law*) nullo(-a).
nul·li·fy [ˈnʌlɪˌfaɪ] VT annullare.
nul·lity [ˈnʌlɪtɪ] N nullità.
NUM [ˌɛnjuːˈɛm] N ABBR (*Brit*: = National Union of Mineworkers) *sindacato nazionale dei minatori.*
numb [nʌm] ① ADJ ⓐ (*fingers etc*) intorpidito(-a); **numb with cold** intirizzito(-a) (dal freddo); **my leg has gone numb** mi si è intorpidita una gamba
ⓑ (*fig*): **numb with** (*fear, grief*) paralizzato(-a) da, impietrito(-a) da.
② VT ⓐ intorpidire; **the cold numbs you as soon as you step outside** appena si esce si resta paralizzati dal freddo
ⓑ (*fig*) rendere insensibile; **she drinks to numb her grief** beve per attenuare il dolore.
num·ber [ˈnʌmbər] ① N ⓐ (*Math*) numero; (*figure*) cifra, numero; **in round numbers** in cifra tonda; **even/odd number** numero pari/dispari; **the Book of Numbers** (*Bible*) i Numeri
ⓑ (*quantity*) numero, quantità *f inv*; **a number of people** un certo numero di persone, diversa gente; **a fair number of** (*reasons, mistakes, people*) una buona quantità di; **on a number of occasions** diverse volte, in diverse occasioni; **any number of** una gran quantità di, moltissimi; **they were 15 in number** erano in 15; **times without number** tantissime volte; **one of their number** uno di loro
ⓒ (*of house etc*) numero; **at number 15** al (numero) 15; **his number's up!** (*fam*) è venuta la sua ora!; **to look after number one** (*fam*) fare solo i propri interessi; **he's my number two** è il mio vice
ⓓ (*issue: of magazine etc*) numero
ⓔ (*song, act etc*) numero; (*piece of music*) pezzo.
② VT ⓐ (*count, include*) contare; **to number sb among**

one's friends considerare qn un amico
ⓑ (*amount to*) ammontare a; **they numbered 10 in all** erano 10 in tutto
ⓒ (*assign number to*) numerare; **his days are numbered** (*fig*) ha i giorni contati.
num·bered ac·count [ˌnʌmbədəˈkaʊnt] N (*in bank*) conto numerato.
num·ber·ing [ˈnʌmbərɪŋ] N numerazione *f*.
num·ber·less [ˈnʌmbəlɪs] ADJ innumerevole, senza numero.
♦ **number plate** N (*Brit Aut*) targa.
♦ **Number Ten** N (*Brit*: 10 Downing Street) *residenza del Primo Ministro del Regno Unito.*
numb·ness [ˈnʌmnɪs] N intorpidimento; (*due to cold*) intirizzimento.
numb·skull [ˈnʌmˌskʌl] N (*fam*) imbecille *m/f*, idiota *m/f*.
nu·mera·cy [ˈnjuːmərəsɪ] N il saper far di conto.
nu·mer·al [ˈnjuːmərəl] N numero, cifra.
nu·mer·ate [ˈnjuːmərɪt] ADJ: **to be numerate** (*Brit*) saper far di conto.
nu·mera·tor [ˈnjuːməˌreɪtər] N numeratore *m*.
nu·meri·cal [njuːˈmɛrɪkəl] ADJ numerico(-a); **in numerical order** in ordine numerico.
nu·meri·cal·ly [njuːˈmɛrɪkəlɪ] ADV numericamente.
nu·mer·ous [ˈnjuːmərəs] ADJ numeroso(-a).
nu·mis·mat·ics [ˌnjuːmɪzˈmætɪks] NSG numismatica.
nun [nʌn] N suora, monaca.
nun·nery [ˈnʌnərɪ] N convento.
nup·tial [ˈnʌpʃəl] ADJ nuziale.
nurse [nɜːs] ① N ⓐ (*in hospital etc*) infermiere(-a); **student nurse** allievo(-a) infermiere(-a); **male nurse** infermiere *m*
ⓑ (*also*: **nursemaid**: *children's*) bambinaia.
② VT ⓐ (*patient*) assistere, curare; (*cold*) curare; **she nursed him back to health** è guarito grazie alle sue cure; **to nurse a cold** curarsi un raffreddore
ⓑ (*suckle: baby*) allattare, dare il latte a
ⓒ (*cradle*) cullare; (*fig: hope*) nutrire, cullare; (: *anger, grudge*) covare.
nurse·maid [ˈnɜːsˌmeɪd] N bambinaia.
nurse·ry [ˈnɜːsərɪ] N ⓐ (*room*) stanza dei bambini; (*institution*) asilo, nido ⓑ (*Agr*) vivaio.
♦ **nursery education** N istruzione *f* prescolastica.
♦ **nursery nurse** N (*Brit*) puericultrice *f*.
♦ **nursery rhyme** N filastrocca.
♦ **nursery school** N scuola materna, asilo infantile.
♦ **nursery slope** N (*Brit Skiing*) pista per principianti.
nurs·ing [ˈnɜːsɪŋ] ① N (*care of invalids*) assistenza; (*profession*) professione *f* di infermiere (*or* di infermiera); **she's going in for nursing** ha deciso di fare l'infermiera.
② ADJ ⓐ (*mother*) che allatta ⓑ (*of hospital*): **the nursing staff** gli infermieri, il personale infermieristico; **nursing auxiliary** infermiere(-a) non diplomato(-a).
♦ **nursing home** N casa di cura, clinica.
nur·ture [ˈnɜːtʃər] VT (*rear*) allevare con amore; (*feed*) nutrire.
NUT [ˌɛnjuːˈtiː] N ABBR (*Brit*: = National Union of Teachers) *sindacato nazionale degli insegnanti.*
nut [nʌt] ① N ⓐ (*Bot*) noce *f* (*or* nocciola *or* mandorla *etc*) (*no generic term in Italian*); **nuts** NPL frutta *sg* secca; **a bag of mixed nuts** un sacchetto di frutta secca mista
ⓑ (*Tech*) dado; (*Mountaineering*) nut *m inv*
ⓒ (*fam: head*) zucca; **he is off his nut** gli manca una rotella, è svitato
ⓓ (*fam: person*) pazzo(-a), matto(-a).

2 ADJ (*chocolate etc*) alle noci (*or* alla nocciola *or* alla mandorla *etc*); see also **nuts**.

nut·case ['nʌt‚keɪs] N (*fam*) matto(-a), pazzo(-a), pazzerello(-a).

nut·crackers ['nʌt‚krækəz] NPL schiaccianoci *m inv*.

nut·hatch ['nʌt‚hætʃ] N (*bird*) picchio muratore.

nut·house ['nʌt‚haʊs] N (*fam*) manicomio.

nut·meg ['nʌt‚mɛg] N noce *f* moscata.

nu·tria ['njuːtrɪə] N nutria.

nu·tri·ent ['njuːtrɪənt] 1 N sostanza nutritiva.

2 ADJ nutriente; **nutrient cycle** (*Geol*) ciclo pedogenetico.

nu·tri·tion [njuːˈtrɪʃən] N nutrizione *f*, alimentazione *f*.

nu·tri·tion·al [njuːˈtrɪʃənl] ADJ (*value*) nutritivo(-a).

nu·tri·tion·ist [njuːˈtrɪʃənɪst] N nutrizionista *m/f*.

nu·tri·tious [njuːˈtrɪʃəs], **nu·tri·tive** ['njuːtrɪtɪv] ADJ nutriente, nutritivo(-a).

nuts [nʌts] (*fam*) 1 ADJ matto(-a), pazzo(-a); **to be nuts about sb** essere pazzo(-a) di qn; **to be nuts about sth** andare matto(-a) per qc; **to go nuts** impazzire, dare i numeri.

2 EXCL (*nonsense*) col cavolo!

nut·shell ['nʌt‚ʃɛl] N guscio di noce (*or* nocciola *etc*) (*no*

generic term in Italian); **in a nutshell** in poche parole; **to put it in a nutshell** per farla breve.

nut·ter ['nʌtə'] N (*Brit fam*) matto(-a).

nut·ty ['nʌtɪ] ADJ (*comp* **-ier**, *superl* **-iest**) **a** (*flavour, taste*) di noce (*or* nocciola *or* mandorla *etc*); (*cake*) di frutta secca; (*chocolate*) alla nocciola *etc* **b** (*fam*) pazzo(-a), matto(-a).

nuz·zle ['nʌzl] VI: **to nuzzle up to** strofinare il muso contro.

NV ABBR (*Am*) = Nevada.

NWT [‚ɛndʌbljuːˈtiː] ABBR (*Canada*) = Northwest Territories.

NY [‚ɛnˈwaɪ] N ABBR (*Am Post*) = New York.

NYC [‚ɛnwaɪˈsiː] N ABBR (*Am Post*) = New York City.

ny·lon ['naɪlɒn] 1 N nailon *m*; **nylons** NPL calze *fpl* di nailon.

2 ADJ di nailon.

nymph [nɪmf] N ninfa.

nymph·et ['nɪmfɪt] N ninfetta.

nym·pho·ma·nia [‚nɪmfəʊˈmeɪnɪə] N ninfomania.

nym·pho·ma·ni·ac [‚nɪmfəʊˈmeɪnɪæk] ADJ, N ninfomane (*f*).

NYSE [‚ɛnwaɪɛsˈiː] N ABBR (*Am*) = New York Stock Exchange.

NZ ABBR = New Zealand.

O

O, o [əʊ] N **a** (*letter*) O, o *form inv*; **O for Oliver**, (*Am*) **O for Oboe** ≈ O come Otranto **b** (*number: Telec etc*) zero **c** (*Am Scol*: = *outstanding*) ≈ ottimo.

O, o [əʊ] EXCL (*liter*) oh!

oaf [əʊf] N zoticone(-a).

oaf·ish [ˈəʊfɪʃ] ADJ (*behaviour*) da zoticone(-a); **an oafish person** uno(-a) zoticone(-a).

oak [əʊk] **1** N quercia; **common oak** farnia; **English oak** rovere *m*; **red oak** quercia rossa.
2 ADJ di quercia.
♦ **oak apple** N galla di quercia.

oakum [ˈəʊkəm] N stoppa per calafataggio.

OAP [ˌəʊeɪˈpiː] N ABBR (*Brit*) = **old-age pensioner**.

oar [ɔː] N remo; **to put** *or* **shove one's oar in** (*fig fam*) impicciarsi.

oar·lock [ˈɔːˌlɒk] N (*Am*) scalmiera.

oars·man [ˈɔːzmən] N (*pl* **-men**) rematore *m*; (*Sport*) vogatore *m*.

oars·woman [ˈɔːzwʊmən] N (*pl* **-women**) rematrice *f*; (*Sport*) vogatrice *f*.

OAS [ˌəʊeɪˈɛs] N ABBR (= *Organization of American States*) O.S.A. *f* (= *Organizzazione degli Stati Americani*).

oasis [əʊˈeɪsɪs] N (*pl* **oases** [əʊˈeɪsiːz]) oasi *f inv*.

oat·cake [ˈəʊtˌkeɪk] N biscotto d'avena.

oath [əʊθ] N **a** (*solemn promise*) giuramento; **under** *or* **on oath** sotto giuramento; **to put sb on** *or* **under oath to do sth** far giurare a qn di fare qc; **to take the oath** giurare; **to swear on oath** *or* **on one's oath** giurare solennemente **b** (*swear word*) imprecazione *f*.

oat·meal [ˈəʊtmiːl] **1** N farina d'avena.
2 ADJ (*colour*) beige *inv*.

oats [əʊts] NPL avena.

OAU [ˌəʊeɪˈjuː] N ABBR (= *Organization of African Unity*) O.U.A. *f* (= *Organizzazione dell'Unità Africana*).

ob·du·ra·cy [ˈɒbdjʊrəsɪ] N (*frm*) caparbietà, pervicacia.

ob·du·rate [ˈɒbdjʊrɪt] (*frm*) ADJ (*unyielding*) irremovibile; (*stubborn*) caparbio(-a), pervicace; (*hard-hearted*) insensibile.

OBE [ˌəʊbiːˈiː] N ABBR (*Brit*: = *Order of the British Empire*) titolo onorifico.

obedi·ence [əˈbiːdɪəns] N ubbidienza; **in obedience to your orders** (*frm*) conformemente ai vostri ordini.

obedi·ent [əˈbiːdɪənt] ADJ ubbidiente; **to be obedient to sb/sth** ubbidire a qn/qc.

obedi·ent·ly [əˈbiːdɪəntlɪ] ADV docilmente.

ob·elisk [ˈɒbɪlɪsk] N obelisco.

obese [əʊˈbiːs] ADJ (*frm*) obeso(-a).

obesity [əʊˈbiːsɪtɪ] N (*frm*) obesità.

obey [əˈbeɪ] **1** VT (*person*) ubbidire a; (*instructions*) seguire; (*regulations*) osservare; **to obey one's conscience** seguire i dettami della propria coscienza.
2 VI ubbidire.

obi·tu·ary [əˈbɪtjʊərɪ] N necrologio.
♦ **obituary column** N colonna degli annunci mortuari.
♦ **obituary notice** N necrologio.

ob·ject[1] [ˈɒbdʒɪkt] N **a** (*gen*) oggetto; **she was an object of ridicule** era oggetto di scherno **b** (*aim*) scopo, intento, obiettivo; **with this object in view** *or* **in mind** in vista di questo scopo; **with the object of doing** al fine di fare; **what's the object of doing that?** a che serve farlo?; **expense is no object** non si bada a spese **c** (*Gram*) complemento; **direct/indirect object** complemento oggetto/indiretto.

ob·ject[2] [əbˈdʒɛkt] **1** VT: **to object that** obiettare che.
2 VI avere da obiettare su; **if you don't object** se non hai obiezioni; **to object to sb doing sth** disapprovare che qn faccia qc; **she objects to my behaviour** lei disapprova il mio comportamento; **do you object to my smoking?** la disturba se fumo?; **I object!** (*frm*) mi oppongo!

ob·jec·tion [əbˈdʒɛkʃən] N obiezione *f*; **to make** *or* **raise an objection** sollevare un'obiezione; **there is no objection to your going** non c'è alcuna obiezione alla tua partenza; **are there any objections?** ci sono obiezioni?; **have you any objection to my smoking?** la disturba se fumo?; **if you have no objection** se non hai nulla in contrario.

ob·jec·tion·able [əbˈdʒɛkʃnəbl] ADJ (*person*) antipatico (-a); (*conduct, method*) discutibile; (*language, attitude*) riprovevole; (*smell, colour*) sgradevole.

ob·jec·tive [əb'dʒɛktɪv] 1 ADJ a (*impartial*) obiettivo(-a). b (*Gram, Philosophy*) oggettivo(-a). 2 N (*aim*) obiettivo.

ob·jec·tive·ly [əb'dʒɛktɪvlɪ] ADV (*see adj*) obiettivamente; oggettivamente.

ob·jec·tiv·ity [ˌɒbdʒɛk'tɪvɪtɪ] N (*see adj*) obiettività; oggettività.

♦ **object lesson** N (*fig*): **object lesson (in)** dimostrazione *f* (di).

ob·jec·tor [əb'dʒɛktəʳ] N oppositore(-trice); **a conscientious objector** un obiettore di coscienza.

ob·jet d'art [ɔbʒedar] N oggetto artistico.

ob·li·gat·ed ['ɒblɪˌgeɪtɪd] ADJ (*Am, frm*): **to feel obligated to do sth** sentirsi in dovere di fare qc.

ob·li·ga·tion [ˌɒblɪ'geɪʃən] N (*duty*) obbligo; (*compulsion*) impegno; **"without obligation"** "senza impegno"; **to be under an obligation to sb/to do sth** essere in dovere verso qn/di fare qc; **I'm under no obligation to do it** non sono tenuto a farlo; **to meet one's obligations** rispettare i propri impegni; **to fail to meet one's obligations** venire meno ai propri impegni.

ob·liga·tory [ɒ'blɪgətərɪ] ADJ obbligatorio(-a), d'obbligo; **to make it obligatory for sb to do sth** imporre a qn l'obbligo di fare qc.

oblige [ə'blaɪdʒ] VT a (*compel*) obbligare, costringere; **to oblige sb to do sth** obbligare *or* costringere qn a fare qc; **to be obliged to do sth** essere obbligato(-a) *or* costretto (-a) a fare qc; **to feel obliged to do sth** sentirsi in dovere di fare qc. b (*do a favour to*) fare una cortesia a; **anything to oblige!** (*fam*) questo e altro!; **to be obliged to sb for sth** essere grato(-a) a qn per qc; **much obliged!** (*old*) molto grato!, obbligato!; **I am obliged to you for your help** ti sono grato per il tuo aiuto.

oblig·ing [ə'blaɪdʒɪŋ] ADJ gentile, servizievole; **it was very obliging of them** è stato molto gentile da parte loro.

oblig·ing·ly [ə'blaɪdʒɪŋlɪ] ADV cortesemente, gentilmente.

oblique [ə'bliːk] 1 ADJ (*angle*) obliquo(-a); (*fig: allusion*) indiretto(-a). 2 N (*Brit Typ*): **oblique (stroke)** barra.

oblique·ly [ə'bliːklɪ] ADV (*move*) obliquamente; (*mention, allude*) indirettamente.

oblit·erate [ə'blɪtəˌreɪt] VT cancellare completamente.

oblivi·on [ə'blɪvɪən] N oblio; **to fall** *or* **sink into oblivion** cadere nell'oblio.

oblivi·ous [ə'blɪvɪəs] ADJ: **oblivious of** *or* **to** ignaro(-a) di.

ob·long ['ɒblɒŋ] 1 ADJ oblungo(-a). 2 N rettangolo.

ob·nox·ious [əb'nɒkʃəs] ADJ (*person, behaviour*) detestabile, odioso(-a); (*fumes, smell*) pestifero(-a), pestilenziale.

o.b.o. [ˌəʊbiː'əʊ] ABBR (*Am: in classified ads*: = or best offer) o al miglior offerente.

oboe ['əʊbəʊ] N oboe *m*.

obo·ist ['əʊbəʊɪst] N oboista *m/f*.

ob·scene [əb'siːn] ADJ osceno(-a).

ob·scene·ly [əb'siːnlɪ] ADV oscenamente.

ob·scen·ity [əb'sɛnɪtɪ] N oscenità *f inv*.

ob·scu·rant·ism [ˌəbskjʊə'ræntɪzəm] N oscurantismo.

ob·scure [əb'skjʊəʳ] 1 ADJ (*comp* **-r**, *superl* **-st**) (*gen*) oscuro(-a); (*feeling, memory*) vago(-a). 2 VT (*darken*) oscurare; (*hide: sun*) coprire; (*issue, idea*) confondere.

ob·scure·ly [əb'skjʊəlɪ] ADV in modo oscuro.

ob·scu·rity [əb'skjʊərɪtɪ] N (*also fig*) oscurità *f inv*.

ob·se·qui·ous [əb'siːkwɪəs] ADJ (*pej*) ossequioso(-a).

ob·se·qui·ous·ly [əb'siːkwɪəslɪ] ADV (*pej*) ossequiosamente.

ob·serv·able [əb'zɜːvəbl] ADJ osservabile, riscontrabile; (*appreciable*) notevole.

ob·ser·vance [əb'zɜːvəns] N osservanza; **religious observances** pratiche *fpl* religiose.

ob·ser·vant [əb'zɜːvənt] ADJ (*watchful*) che ha spirito d'osservazione; **observant (of)** (*Rel, Law*) osservante (di).

ob·ser·va·tion [ˌɒbzə'veɪʃən] N a (*gen*) osservazione *f*; (*of the law*) osservanza; **the police are keeping him under observation** la polizia lo tiene sotto sorveglianza; **he is under observation in hospital** è in ospedale sotto osservazione; **powers of observation** spirito d'osservazione; **to escape observation** sfuggire alla sorveglianza. b (*remark*) osservazione *f*, commento.

ob·ser·va·tion·al [ˌɒbzə'veɪʃənl] ADJ (*frm: device*) per l'osservazione; (: *abilities, faculties*) di osservazione.

♦ **observation car** N (*Rail*) carrozza *f* belvedere *inv*.

♦ **observation post** N (*Mil*) osservatorio (militare).

♦ **observation tower** N torre *f* di osservazione.

ob·ser·va·tory [əb'zɜːvətrɪ] N osservatorio.

ob·serve [əb'zɜːv] VT osservare.

ob·serv·er [əb'zɜːvəʳ] N osservatore(-trice).

ob·sess [əb'sɛs] VT ossessionare; **to be obsessed by** *or* **with sb/sth** essere ossessionato(-a) da *or* con qn/qc.

ob·ses·sion [əb'sɛʃən] N ossessione *f*; **football is an obsession with him** è maniaco del calcio; **his obsession with her** la sua fissazione per lei; **his obsession about cleanliness** la sua mania della pulizia.

ob·ses·sive [əb'sɛsɪv] ADJ ossessivo(-a).

ob·ses·sive·ly [əb'sɛsɪvlɪ] ADV ossessivamente.

ob·sid·ian [ɒb'sɪdɪən] N ossidiana.

ob·so·les·cence ['ɒbsə'lɛsns] N obsolescenza; **built-in** *or* **planned obsolescence** (*Comm*) obsolescenza programmata.

ob·so·les·cent [ˌɒbsə'lɛsnt] ADJ obsolescente.

ob·so·lete ['ɒbsəˌliːt] ADJ obsoleto(-a), in disuso; (*word*) desueto(-a).

ob·sta·cle ['ɒbstəkl] N ostacolo; **to be an obstacle to sb/sth** essere di ostacolo a qn/qc; **to put an obstacle in the way of sb** ostacolare qn; **that is no obstacle to our doing it** questo non ci impedisce affatto di farlo.

♦ **obstacle race** N (*Sport*) corsa ad ostacoli.

ob·stet·ric [ɒb'stɛtrɪk], **ob·stet·rical** [ɒb'stɛtrɪkəl] ADJ ostetrico(-a).

ob·ste·tri·cian [ˌɒbstə'trɪʃən] N ostetrico.

ob·stet·rics [ɒb'stɛtrɪks] NSG ostetricia.

ob·sti·na·cy ['ɒbstɪnəsɪ] N ostinazione *f*.

ob·sti·nate ['ɒbstɪnɪt] ADJ (*gen*) ostinato(-a); (*resistance*) strenuo(-a); (*illness*) persistente; **as obstinate as a mule** testardo(-a) come un mulo.

ob·sti·nate·ly ['ɒbstɪnɪtlɪ] ADV ostinatamente.

ob·strep·er·ous [əb'strɛpərəs] ADJ turbolento(-a).

ob·struct [əb'strʌkt] VT (*block: pipe, artery*) ostruire; (: *traffic, road, Sport*) bloccare; (*hinder*) ostacolare; **you're obstructing my view** mi impedisci la visuale.

ob·struc·tion [əb'strʌkʃən] N (*sth which obstructs*) ostacolo; (: *in pipe, artery*) ostruzione *f*; **to cause an obstruction** (*in road*) bloccare la strada.

ob·struc·tion·ist [əb'strʌkʃənɪst] 1 ADJ ostruzionistico (-a). 2 N ostruzionista *m/f*.

ob·struc·tive [əb'strʌktɪv] ADJ che crea impedimenti;

stop being obstructive! smettila di fare ostruzionismo! **ob·tain** [əbˈteɪn] [1] VT (gen) ottenere; **to obtain sth (for o.s.)** (goods) procurarsi qc; **to obtain sth for sb** procurare qc a qn.

[2] VI (frm: circumstances, custom) esistere.

ob·tain·able [əbˈteɪnəbl] ADJ: **where is that obtainable?** dove si può trovare?

ob·trude [əbˈtruːd] (frm) [1] VI imporsi.

[2] VT imporre.

ob·tru·sive [əbˈtruːsɪv] ADJ (person) invadente, importuno(-a); (opinions) ostentato(-a); (smell) pungente; (building) che disturba la visuale.

ob·tru·sive·ly [əbˈtruːsɪvlɪ] ADV in modo invadente.

ob·tuse [əbˈtjuːs] ADJ (gen, Math) ottuso(-a); (remark) stolto(-a).

ob·tuse·ly [əbˈtjuːslɪ] ADV ottusamente.

ob·tuse·ness [əbˈtjuːsnɪs] N ottusità.

ob·verse [ˈɒbvɜːs] N (frm) opposto, inverso.

ob·vi·ate [ˈɒbvɪ.eɪt] (frm) VT (danger, objection) evitare; (necessity) ovviare a.

ob·vi·ous [ˈɒbvɪəs] ADJ (clear, perceptible) ovvio(-a), evidente; (unsubtle) scontato(-a), banale; **it's obvious that ...** è ovvio che...; **she's the obvious person for the job** è chiaramente la persona che ci vuole per quel lavoro; **the obvious thing to do is to leave** la cosa più logica da fare è andarsene; **try not to make it obvious that you're bored** cerca di non farti vedere annoiato.

ob·vi·ous·ly [ˈɒbvɪəslɪ] ADV ovviamente, evidentemente; **he was obviously not drunk** si vedeva che non era ubriaco; **he was not obviously drunk** non si vedeva che era ubriaco; **obviously!** certo!; **obviously not!** certo che no!

oca·ri·na [ˌɒkəˈriːnə] N ocarina.

oc·ca·sion [əˈkeɪʒən] [1] N **a** (point in time) occasione f, circostanza; **on occasion** di tanto in tanto; **on several occasions** in varie occasioni; **on that occasion** in quell'occasione, quella volta

b (special occasion) occasione f, avvenimento; **it was quite an occasion** è stato un avvenimento; **music written for the occasion** musica scritta per l'occasione; **on the occasion of** in occasione di; **to rise to the occasion** mostrarsi all'altezza della situazione

c (frm: reason) motivo, ragione f; **there was no occasion for it** non ce n'era motivo; **to have occasion to do sth** avere l'occasione di fare qc; **if you ever have occasion to be in London** se ti capita di essere a Londra.

[2] VT (frm) causare; (: remark) dare origine a.

oc·ca·sion·al [əˈkeɪʒənl] ADJ (gen) occasionale; (showers) sporadico(-a); **I like the occasional cigarette** ogni tanto mi piace fumare una sigaretta.

oc·ca·sion·al·ly [əˈkeɪʒnəlɪ] ADV ogni tanto; **very occasionally** molto raramente.

♦ **occasional table** N tavolino (che si usa saltuariamente).

oc·ci·den·tal [ˌɒksɪˈdɛntəl] ADJ (frm) occidentale.

oc·cipi·tal [ɒkˈsɪpɪtəl] ADJ: **occipital bone** osso occipitale.

oc·cult [ɒˈkʌlt] [1] ADJ occulto(-a).

[2] N: **the occult** l'occulto.

oc·cult·ism [ˈɒkʌlˌtɪzəm] N occultismo.

oc·cu·pan·cy [ˈɒkjʊpənsɪ] N (of house) occupazione f, presa di possesso; **to take up occupancy of a house** prendere possesso di una casa.

oc·cu·pant [ˈɒkjʊpənt] N (of house) inquilino(-a); (of boat, car) persona a bordo; (of job, post) titolare m/f.

oc·cu·pa·tion [ˌɒkjʊˈpeɪʃən] N **a** (job) mestiere m, professione f; (pastime) occupazione f; **he's a joiner by occupation** è falegname di mestiere

b (gen, Mil) occupazione f; **army of occupation** esercito d'occupazione; **the occupation of Paris** l'occupazione di Parigi; **the house is ready for occupation** la casa è pronta per essere abitata.

oc·cu·pa·tion·al [ˌɒkjʊˈpeɪʃənl] ADJ (group, disease) professionale; **occupational accident** infortunio sul lavoro.

♦ **occupational guidance** N (Brit) orientamento professionale.

♦ **occupational hazard** N rischio professionale.

♦ **occupational pension scheme** N sistema pensionistico a disposizione di una determinata categoria di lavoratori.

♦ **occupational therapy** N ergoterapia.

oc·cu·pi·er [ˈɒkjʊˌpaɪə'] N (of house) inquilino(-a); (of post) titolare m/f.

oc·cu·py [ˈɒkjʊˌpaɪ] VT occupare; **this job occupies all my time** questo lavoro occupa or prende tutto il mio tempo; **to be occupied with sth** essere preso(-a) da qc; **to be occupied in doing sth** essere occupato(-a) a fare qc; **she occupies herself by knitting** si tiene occupata lavorando a maglia; **to keep one's mind occupied** tenere la mente occupata.

oc·cur [əˈkɜː'] VI **a** (event) accadere; (difficulty, opportunity) presentarsi; (phenomenon) aver luogo; (error, word, plant) essere presente, trovarsi; **to occur again** ripetersi

b (come to mind): **to occur to sb** venire in mente a qn; **such an idea would never have occurred to her** una tale idea non le sarebbe mai venuta in mente.

oc·cur·rence [əˈkʌrəns] N evento; **an everyday occurrence** un fatto quotidiano; **this is a common occurrence** è una cosa che capita spesso.

ocean [ˈəʊʃən] N oceano; **oceans of** (fam) fiumi mpl di.

♦ **ocean bed** N fondale m oceanico.

♦ **ocean cruise** N crociera sull'oceano.

♦ **ocean-going** [ˈəʊʃənˌgəʊɪŋ] ADJ d'alto mare.

Oceania [ˌəʊʃɪˈɑːnɪə] N l'Oceania.

ocean·ic [ˌəʊʃɪˈænɪk] ADJ oceanico(-a).

♦ **ocean liner** N transatlantico.

ocean·og·ra·pher [ˌəʊʃəˈnɒgrəfə'] N oceanografo(-a).

ocean·og·raph·ic [ˌəʊʃənə'græfɪk] ADJ oceanografico(-a).

ocean·og·ra·phy [ˌəʊʃəˈnɒgrəfɪ] N oceanografia.

oc·elot [ˈɒsɪˌlɒt] N ocelot m inv.

ochre, (Am) **ocher** [ˈəʊkə'] [1] N ocra f inv.

[2] ADJ (color) ocra inv.

o'clock [əˈklɒk] ADV: **it is one o'clock** è l'una; **at 9 o'clock** alle 9; **at twelve o'clock** (midday) a mezzogiorno; (midnight) a mezzanotte.

OCR [ˌəʊsiːˈɑː'] N ABBR **a** = optical character reader **b** = optical character recognition.

Oct. ABBR (= October) ott. (= ottobre).

oc·ta·gon [ˈɒktəgən] N ottagono.

oc·tago·nal [ɒkˈtægənl] ADJ ottagonale.

oc·tane [ˈɒkteɪn] [1] N ottano.

[2] ADJ: **high-octane petrol**, (Am) **high-octane gas** benzina ad alto numero di ottani.

♦ **octane rating** N numero di ottani.

oc·tave [ˈɒktɪv] N (Mus) ottava.

oc·ta·vo [ɒkˈteɪvəʊ] N volume m in-ottavo.

oc·tet [ɒkˈtɛt] N ottetto.

Oc·to·ber [ɒkˈtəʊbə'] N ottobre m for usage see **July**.

oc·to·gen·ar·ian [ˌɒktəʊdʒɪˈnɛərɪən] N ottuagenario(-a).

oc·to·pus [ˈɒktəpəs] N (gen) polpo; (larger) piovra.

ocu·list [ˈɒkjʊlɪst] N oculista m/f.

odd [ɒd] ADJ (*comp* **-er**, *superl* **-est**) **a** (*strange*) strano(-a); **how odd!** che strano!; **he says some odd things** dice delle cose strane

b (*number*) dispari *inv*

c (*extra, left over*) in più; (*unpaired, sock*) spaiato(-a); **if you have an odd minute** se hai un momento libero; **the odd man** *or* **one out** l'eccezione *f*

d (*occasional*) occasionale; **at odd moments** in certi momenti; **he has written the odd article** ha scritto qualche articolo

e (*and more*): **30 odd** 30 e rotti, poco più di 30; see also **odds**.

odd·ball ['ɒd,bɔ:l] N, ADJ (*fam*) eccentrico(-a).

odd·ity ['ɒdɪtɪ] N **a** (*also*: **oddness**) stranezza, bizzarria

b (*person*) originale *m/f*.

♦ **odd-job man** [ɒd'dʒɒb'mæn] N (*pl* **-men**) tuttofare *m inv*.

♦ **odd jobs** NPL lavori *mpl* occasionali.

♦ **odd-looking** [ɒd'lʊkɪŋ] ADJ dall'aria strana.

odd·ly ['ɒdlɪ] ADV stranamente; **they are oddly similar** tra di loro c'è una strana somiglianza; **oddly enough you are right** stranamente hai ragione.

odd·ments ['ɒdmənts] NPL (*Brit Comm*) avanzi *mpl* di magazzino.

odd·ness ['ɒdnɪs] N = **oddity a.**

odds [ɒdz] NPL **a** (*Betting*) probabilità *fpl*; **the odds on the horse are 5 to 1** danno il cavallo 5 a 1; **short/long odds** alta/bassa probabilità; **the odds are in his favour** i pronostici sono a suo favore; **to fight against overwhelming odds** lottare contro enormi difficoltà; **to succeed against all the odds** riuscire contro ogni aspettativa; **the odds are that ...** è facile *or* probabile che...; **the odds are against his coming** è poco probabile che venga

b (*difference*): **what's the odds?** (*fam*) che differenza fa?, cosa cambia?; **it makes no odds** non fa differenza

c (*variance, strife*): **to be at odds with sb over sth** essere in disaccordo con qn su qc.

♦ **odds and ends** (*fam*) NPL (*assorted objects*) oggetti *mpl* vari; (*junk*) cianfrusaglie *fpl*; **I'll finish the last few odds and ends tomorrow** le ultime due o tre cosette le finisco domani.

♦ **odds-on** [ɒdz'ɒn] ADJ (*fam*) probabile; **it's odds-on that ...** è quasi certo che...; **odds-on favourite** (*Horseracing*) gran favorito(-a).

ode [əʊd] N ode *f.*

odi·ous ['əʊdɪəs] ADJ odioso(-a).

odium ['əʊdɪəm] N (*frm*) odio.

odom·eter [ɒ'dɒmɪtə'] N (*Aut*) odometro.

odor·ous ['əʊdərəs] ADJ (*liter*) odoroso(-a).

odour, (*Am*) **odor** ['əʊdə'] N odore *m*; **to be in bad odour with sb** (*fig*) essere malvisto(-a) da qn.

odour·less, (*Am*) **odor·less** ['əʊdəlɪs] ADJ inodore.

Odysseus [ə'di:sɪəs] N Ulisse.

od·ys·sey ['ɒdɪsɪ] N odissea.

OECD [,əʊi:si:'di:] N ABBR (= *Organization for Economic Cooperation and Development*) O.C.S.E. *f* (= *Organizzazione per la Cooperazione e lo Sviluppo Economico*).

Oedipus ['i:dɪpəs] N Edipo.

♦ **Oedipus complex** N (*Psych*) complesso di Edipo.

oesopha·gus, (*Am*) **esopha·gus** [i:'sɒfəgəs] N esofago.

oes·tro·gen, (*Am*) **es·tro·gen** ['i:strəʊdʒən] N estrogeno.

of [ɒv,əv] PREP **a** (*gen*) di; **the house of my uncle** la casa di mio zio; **the love of God** l'amore di Dio; **a friend of mine** un mio amico; **that was very kind of you** è stato molto carino da parte tua; **free of charge** gratis; **the 5th of July**

il 5 luglio; **loss of appetite** perdita dell'appetito; **south of Glasgow** a sud di Glasgow; **a quarter of 4** (*Am*: *time*) le 4 meno un quarto; **the City of New York** la città di New York; **a boy of 8** un ragazzo di 8 anni; **a man of great ability** un uomo di grande abilità; **that idiot of a minister** quell'idiota di ministro

b (*cause*) di, per; **of necessity** necessariamente, per necessità; **to die of pneumonia** morire di polmonite

c (*material*) di, in; **made of steel** (fatto(-a)) di *or* in acciaio

d (*concerning*) di; **what do you think of him?** cosa pensi di lui?; **what of it?** e allora?

e (*partitive*) di; **how much of this do you need?** quanto te ne serve?; **a kilo of flour** un chilo di farina; **a handful of coins** una manciata di monete; **there were four of us** eravamo in quattro; **four of us went** quattro di noi sono andati; **there were four of them** (*people*) erano in quattro; (*things*) ce n'erano quattro.

off [ɒf]

1 ADV

a (*distance, time*)

▷ **the game was/is three *days* off** la gara era dopo/è fra tre giorni

▷ **5 *km* off (the road)** a 5 km (dalla strada)

▷ **a place 2 *miles* off** un posto distante 2 miglia

▷ **it's a long *way* off** è molto lontano

b (*departure*)

▷ **I must *be* off** devo andare

▷ **off we *go*** via, partiamo

▷ **he's *gone* off to see the boss** è andato a parlare col capo

▷ **he's off *to* Paris tonight** parte per Parigi stasera

c (*removal*)

▷ **5% off** (*Comm*) sconto del 5%

▷ **a button *came* off** è venuto via un bottone

▷ **with his *hat* off** senza cappello

▷ **the *lid* was off** non c'era il coperchio

▷ **off *with* those wet clothes!** togliti quei vestiti bagnati!

d (*not at work*)

▷ **to take a *day* off** prendersi una giornata di vacanza

▷ **I'm off *on* Fridays** il venerdì non lavoro

▷ **he's off *sick*** è in malattia

e (*in phrases*): **off and on, on and off** di tanto in tanto

▷ **right** *or* **straight off** subito.

2 ADJ

a (*inoperative*): **to be off** (*machine, light, engine*) essere spento(-a); (*water, gas, tap*) essere chiuso(-a)

b (*cancelled*) sospeso(-a); (*Brit: not available: in restaurant*) finito(-a);

▷ **I'm afraid the *chicken* is off** purtroppo il pollo è finito

▷ **the *play* is off** la commedia è sospesa

▷ **the *wedding* is off** il matrimonio è saltato

c (*not fresh*) andato(-a) a male;

▷ **this *cheese* is off** questo formaggio è andato a male

▷ **that's a bit off, isn't it?** (*fig fam*) non è molto carino, vero?

d : **to be *badly* off** non essere benestante

▷ **you'd be *better* off staying where you are** faresti meglio a rimanere dove sei

▷ **how are you off *for* cash?** come stai a soldi?

▷ **to be *well* off** essere benestante

▷the less *well* off i meno abbienti

e: to have an off *day* (*fam*) avere una giornata no.

3 PREP

a (*indicating motion, removal*) da;

▷there *are* two buttons off my coat al mio cappotto mancano due bottoni

▷to *fall* off a cliff cadere da una scogliera

▷he *knocked* £20 off the price (*fam*) mi ha fatto uno sconto di 20 sterline

▷she *took* the picture off the wall tolse il quadro dalla parete

▷he *was* off work for three weeks è stato in malattia per tre settimane

b (*distant from*)

▷his flat is somewhere off *Baker Street* il suo appartamento è dalle parti di Baker Street

▷off the *coast* al largo della costa

▷height off the *ground* altezza dal suolo

▷it's just off the *M1* è appena fuori della M1

▷a house off the main *road* una casa poco lontana della strada principale

▷a street off the *square* una strada che parte dalla piazza

c

▷I've gone off fried *food* non mi piacciono più i fritti

▷I'm off *meat* non mangio più la carne.

of·fal ['ɒfəl] N frattaglie *fpl.*

off·beat [ˌɒf'biːt] ADJ (*fig*) originale, anticonvenzionale.

♦ **off-centre**, (*Am*) **off-center** [ˌɒf'sɛntər] ADJ storto(-a), fuori centro.

♦ **off-chance** ['ɒf.tʃɑːns] N: **on the off-chance of seeing him** nella vaga speranza di incontrarlo.

♦ **off-colour**, (*Am*) **off-color** [ˌɒf'kʌlər] ADJ a (*Brit: ill*) malato(-a), indisposto(-a); **to feel off-colour** sentirsi poco bene b (*joke, remark*) spinto(-a), osé *inv.*

♦ **off-duty** [ˌɒf'djuːtɪ] ADJ (*policeman*) non in servizio.

of·fence, (*Am*) **of·fense** [ə'fɛns] N a (*crime*) infrazione *f*, contravvenzione *f*, reato; **first offence** primo reato; **to commit an offence** commettere un reato; **it is an offence to** ... è vietato dalla legge... b (*moral*) offesa; **to give offence (to sb)** offendere (qn); **to take offence (at sth)** offendersi (per qc).

of·fend [ə'fɛnd] 1 VT (*person*) offendere; (*ears, eyes*) ferire; **it offends my sense of justice** è un'offesa al mio senso di giustizia; **to be offended (at)** offendersi (per).

2 VI: **to offend against** (*law, rule*) trasgredire, contravvenire a; (*God*) disubbidire a; (*common sense*) andare contro; (*good taste*) offendere.

of·fend·er [ə'fɛndər] N (*frm: criminal*) delinquente *m/f*; (*culprit*) reo(-a), colpevole *m/f.*

of·fend·ing [ə'fɛndɪŋ] ADJ (*often hum: word, object*) incriminato(-a).

of·fense [ə'fɛns] N (*Am*) = offence.

of·fen·sive [ə'fɛnsɪv] 1 ADJ a (*causing offence, unpleasant: behaviour, remark*) offensivo(-a); (: *person*) antipatico (-a); (: *smell, sight*) sgradevole; **to be offensive to sb** offendere qn b (*attacking*) offensivo(-a).

2 N (*Mil, Sport*) offensiva; **to go over to** *or* **go on** *or* **take the offensive** passare all'offensiva.

of·fen·sive·ly [ə'fɛnsɪvlɪ] ADV (*unpleasantly etc*) in modo offensivo.

of·fer ['ɒfər] 1 N (*gen*) offerta, proposta; **offer of marriage** proposta di matrimonio; **to make an offer for**

sth fare un'offerta per qc; **offers over £25** offerte dalle 25 sterline in su; **to be on offer** (*Comm*) essere in offerta (speciale).

2 VT (*gen*) offrire; (*apology*) presentare; (*comment, opinion*) dare; **to offer sth to sb** *or* **sb sth** offrire qc a qn; **to offer to do sth** offrirsi di fare qc; **to offer resistance** opporre resistenza.

of·fer·ing ['ɒfərɪŋ] N offerta.

of·fer·tory ['ɒfətərɪ] N (*Rel: part of service*) offertorio; (: *collection*) questua.

♦ **off-guard** [ˌɒf'gɑːd] ADJ: **to be taken off-guard** essere colto(-a) alla sopravvista.

off·hand ['ɒf'hænd] 1 ADJ (*casual*) disinvolto(-a); (*curt*) sgarbato(-a).

2 ADV: **I can't tell you offhand** non posso dirtelo su due piedi.

off·hand·ed·ly ['ɒf'hændɪdlɪ] ADV (*see adj*) con disinvoltura; sgarbatamente.

off·hand·ed·ness ['ɒf'hændɪdnɪs] N (*see adj*) disinvoltura; sgarbatezza.

of·fice ['ɒfɪs] 1 N a (*place*) ufficio; (: *of lawyer, doctor*) studio; **ticket office** biglietteria; **head office** sede *f* centrale

b (*public position*) ufficio, carica; (*duty, function*) incarico, compito; **to be in** *or* **to hold office** (*person*) essere in carica; (*political party*) essere al potere; **to come into office** OR **to take office** (*person*) assumere la carica; (*political party*) salire al potere

c: **through his good offices** con il suo prezioso aiuto; **through the offices of** grazie all'aiuto di

d (*Rel*) ufficio, funzione *f.* 2 ADJ (*staff*) d'ufficio; (*furniture*) da ufficio; (*supplies*) per ufficio.

♦ **office automation** N automazione *f* d'ufficio, burotica.

♦ **office bearer** N (*of club etc*) membro dell'amministrazione.

♦ **office block**, (*Am*) **office building** N complesso di uffici.

♦ **office boy** N fattorino.

♦ **office-holder** ['ɒfɪs,həʊldə'] N (*frm*) funzionario(-a).

♦ **office hours** NPL orario d'ufficio; (*Am Med*) orario delle visite.

♦ **office manager** N capoufficio *m/f.*

♦ **Office of Fair Trading** N (*Brit*) *organismo di tutela contro pratiche commerciali abusive.*

of·fic·er ['ɒfɪsə'] N a (*Mil, Naut, Aer*) ufficiale *m*; **officers' mess** mensa degli ufficiali b (*official*) funzionario; **police officer** agente *m* di polizia; **excuse me, officer** mi scusi, agente.

♦ **office work** N lavoro d'ufficio.

♦ **office worker** N impiegato(-a).

of·fi·cial [ə'fɪʃəl] 1 ADJ (*authorized*) ufficiale; (*formal*) ufficiale, formale; **to make official** (*position, agreement*) ufficializzare.

2 N (*civil servant*) funzionario, impiegato(-a) statale; (*of club, organization*) dirigente *m/f.*

of·fi·cial·dom [ə'fɪʃəldəm] N (*pej*) burocrazia.

of·fi·cial·ese [ə,fɪʃə'liːz] N (*pej*) burocratese *m.*

of·fi·cial·ly [ə'fɪʃəlɪ] ADV ufficialmente.

♦ **Official Receiver** N: **the Official Receiver** il curatore fallimentare.

of·fi·ci·ate [ə'fɪʃɪ,eɪt] VI (*Rel*) ufficiare; **to officiate as Mayor** esplicare le funzioni di sindaco; **to officiate at a marriage** celebrare un matrimonio.

of·fi·cious [ə'fɪʃəs] ADJ invadente.

of·fi·cious·ly [ə'fɪʃəslɪ] ADV con invadenza.

of·fi·cious·ness [ə'fɪʃəsnɪs] N invadenza.

of·fing ['ɒfɪŋ] N: **in the offing** (*fig*) in vista.

♦ **off-key** [,ɒf'kiː] ① ADJ stonato(-a).
② ADV fuori tono.

♦ **off-licence** ['ɒf,laɪsns] N (*Brit*) *negozio con speciale licenza per la vendita di vini e liquori.*

♦ **off-limits** [,ɒf'lɪmɪts] ADJ (*Am Mil*) vietato(-a) (al personale militare), off-limits *inv*; (: *not to be entered*) off-limits.

♦ **off-line** ['ɒf,laɪn] (*Comput*) ① ADJ off-line *inv*, fuori linea; (*switched off*) spento(-a).
② ADV: **to go off-line** andare off-line *or* fuori linea.

♦ **off-load** ['ɒf,ləʊd] VT scaricare.

♦ **off-peak** ['ɒf'piːk] ADJ (*time*) non di punta; (*ticket, heating*) a tariffa ridotta; (*tariff*) ridotto(-a).

♦ **off-piste** ['ɒf'piːst] (*Skiing*) ① N fuoripista *m*.
② ADV: **to ski off-piste** fare del fuoripista.

♦ **off-putting** ['ɒf,pʊtɪŋ] ADJ (*Brit fam: person, manner*) antipatico(-a), scostante; (*appearance*) sgradevole.

♦ **off-season** ['ɒf,siːzn] ① N: **the off-season** la bassa stagione.
② ADJ di bassa stagione *f*.

off·set ['ɒf,sɛt] (*vb: pt, pp* **offset**) ① VT bilanciare, compensare.
② N (*Typ*) offset *m inv*.

♦ **offset printing** N stampa in offset.

off·shoot ['ɒf,ʃuːt] N (*fig*) diramazione *f*; (*Bot*) germoglio.

off·shore ['ɒf'ʃɔː'] ADJ (*breeze*) di terra; (*island*) vicino(-a) alla costa; (*fishing*) costiero(-a); (*oil rig*) off-shore *inv*.

off·side ['ɒf'saɪd] ① ADJ **a** (*Sport*) in fuorigioco **b** (*Aut: right-hand drive*) destro(-a); (: *left-hand drive*) sinistro(-a).
② N (*Aut: see adj*) destra; sinistra.

off·spring ['ɒf,sprɪŋ] N (*pl inv: of person*) rampollo; (: *with pl sense*) prole *f*; (*of animal*) piccolo(-a); (: *with pl sense*) piccoli(-e).

off·stage [,ɒf'steɪdʒ] ADJ, ADV dietro le quinte.

♦ **off-the-cuff** [,ɒfðə'kʌf] ① ADV a braccio, improvvisando.
② ADJ (*speech*) a braccio, improvvisato(-a); (*remark*) spontaneo(-a).

♦ **off-the-job** ['ɒfðə'dʒɒb] ADJ (*course, training*) fuori sede *inv*.

♦ **off-the-peg** ['ɒfðə'pɛg], (*Am*) **off-the-rack** ['ɒfðə'ræk] ① ADJ (*clothes*) prêt-à-porter *inv*, confezionato(-a).
② ADV: **to buy a dress off-the-peg** comprare un abito confezionato.

♦ **off-the-record** [,ɒfðə'rɛkəd] ① ADJ ufficioso(-a).
② ADV in via ufficiosa.

♦ **off-white** ['ɒf,waɪt] ADJ bianco sporco *inv*.

Ofgas ['ɒfgæs] N (*Brit*: = *Office of Gas Supply*) *organo indipendente di controllo per la tutela degli utenti del gas.*

Oftel ['ɒftɛl] N (*Brit*: = *Office of Telecommunications*) *organo indipendente di controllo per la tutela degli utenti del telefono.*

of·ten ['ɒfən] ADV spesso; **as often as not** il più delle volte; **more often than not** quasi sempre; **every so often** (*of time*) una volta ogni tanto; (*of distance, spacing*) regolarmente, a intervalli regolari; **how often do you see him?** ogni quanto lo vedi?; **her behaviour is often disappointing** il suo comportamento è spesso deludente; **it's not often that I ask you to help me** non è che ti chieda spesso di aiutarmi.

Ofwat ['ɒfwɒt] N (*Brit*: = *Office of Water Services*) *in Inghilterra e Galles, organo indipendente di controllo per la tutela degli utenti dell'acqua.*

ogle ['əʊgl] VT mangiarsi con gli occhi.

ogre ['əʊgə'] N orco.

OH ABBR (*Am Post*)= *Ohio.*

oh [əʊ] EXCL oh!

OHMS [,əʊeɪtʃɛm'ɛs] ABBR (*Brit*: = *On His (or Her) Majesty's Service*) al servizio di Sua Maestà britannica.

oil [ɔɪl] ① N **a** (*Art, Aut, Culin*) olio; **fried in oil** fritto(-a) nell'olio **b** (*petroleum*) petrolio; (*for central heating*) nafta; **to pour oil on troubled waters** placare le acque.
② VT (*machine*) oliare, lubrificare; **to oil the wheels** (*fig*) appianare la difficoltà.
③ ADJ (*lamp, stove*) a olio.

♦ **oil-burning** ['ɔɪl,bɜːnɪŋ] ADJ (*lamp*) a petrolio.

oil·can ['ɔɪl,kæn] N oliatore *m*; (*for storing*) latta da olio.

♦ **oil change** N (*Aut*) cambio dell'olio.

♦ **oil·cloth** ['ɔɪl,klɒθ] N tela cerata.

♦ **oil colours** NPL colori *mpl* a olio.

oil·field ['ɔɪl,fiːld] N giacimento petrolifero.

♦ **oil filter** N (*Aut*) filtro dell'olio.

♦ **oil-fired** ['ɔɪl,faɪəd] ADJ a nafta.

♦ **oil gauge** N indicatore *m* del livello dell'olio.

♦ **oil industry** N industria petrolifera.

oili·ness ['ɔɪlɪnɪs] N (*of liquid, consistency*) oleosità; (*of hands, skin, also fig pej*) untuosità.

♦ **oil level** N livello dell'olio.

♦ **oil paint** N colore *m* a olio.

♦ **oil painting** N quadro a olio; **she's no oil painting** (*fam*) non è una bellezza.

♦ **oil refinery** N raffineria di petrolio.

♦ **oil rig** N derrick *m inv*; (*at sea*) piattaforma per trivellazioni subacquee.

oil·skin ['ɔɪl,skɪn] ① N tela cerata.
② ADJ (*hat, tablecloth*) di tela cerata.

oil·skins ['ɔɪl,skɪnz] NPL indumenti *mpl* di tela cerata.

♦ **oil slick** N chiazza di petrolio.

♦ **oil tanker** N petroliera.

♦ **oil well** N pozzo petrolifero.

oily ['ɔɪlɪ] ADJ (*comp* **-ier**, *superl* **-iest**) (*liquid, consistency*) oleoso(-a); (*hands*) unto(-a); (*fig pej*) untuoso(-a).

oint·ment ['ɔɪntmənt] N unguento.

OK ABBR (*Am Post*)= *Oklahoma.*

O.K., okay ['əʊ'keɪ] (*fam*) ① EXCL OK!, okay!, va bene!.
② ADJ: **the film was O.K.** il film non era male; **are you O.K. for money?** sei a posto coi soldi?; **it's O.K. with** *or* **by me** per me va bene; **is it O.K. with you if ...?** ti va bene se...?; **is it O.K.?** OR **are you O.K.?** tutto OK?; **did you hurt yourself? — no, I'm O.K.** ti sei fatto male? — no, sto bene; **is the car O.K.?** è a posto la macchina?; **that may have been O.K. last year** questo poteva forse andar bene l'anno scorso.
③ N: **to give sth one's O.K.** dare l'okay a qc.
④ VT (*pt, pp* **O.K.'d** *or* **okayed**) dare l'okay a, approvare.

oka·pi [əʊ'kɑːpɪ] N okapi *m inv*.

old [əʊld] ① ADJ (*comp* **-er**, *superl* **-est**) **a** (*gen*) vecchio (-a), anziano(-a); (*ancient*) antico(-a), vecchio(-a); **an old man** un vecchio; **old people** *or* **folk(s)** i vecchi, gli anziani; **to grow** *or* **get old(er)** invecchiare; **he's old for his years** è maturo per la sua età; **the old country** la madrepatria; **as old as the hills** vecchio(-a) come Matusalemme *or* come il cucco; **the old part of Glasgow** la zona vecchia di Glasgow; **an old friend of mine** un mio vecchio amico; **here's old Peter coming!** (*fam*) ecco

che arriva il vecchio Peter!; **she's a funny old thing** (*fam*) è un tipetto buffo; **we had a high old time** (*fam*) ci siamo divertiti un sacco; **any old thing will do** (*fam*) va bene qualsiasi cosa; **I say, old man** *or* **old boy!** (*old*) vecchio mio!; **my old man** (*fam*: *father*) il (mio) vecchio

b : **how old are you?** quanti anni hai?; **she is 8 years old** ha 8 anni; **an 8-year-old boy** un bambino di 8 anni; **she is 2 years older than you** ha 2 anni più di te; **older brother/sister** fratello/sorella maggiore; **my older brother** mio fratello maggiore; **the older generation** i vecchi; **he's old enough to look after himself** è grande abbastanza per sbrigarsela da solo; **to be old enough to vote** avere l'età per votare; **you're old enough to know better!** alla tua età dovresti avere più senno!; **when you're older** (*to child*) quando sarai grande; **if I were 20 years older** se avessi 20 anni di più

c (*former*) precedente; **my old school** la mia vecchia scuola; **in the old days** una volta, ai vecchi tempi; **it's not as good as our old one** non è buono come quello vecchio.

2 N **a** : **the old** NPL i vecchi, gli anziani

b : **of old** da tempo; **in days of old** nei tempi passati.

♦ **old age** N vecchiaia; **in one's old age** nella vecchiaia.

♦ **old-age pension** [ˌəʊldeɪdʒˈpenʃən] N pensione *f* di vecchiaia.

♦ **old-age pensioner** [ˌəʊldeɪdʒˈpenʃənəʳ] N (*Brit*) pensionato(-a).

♦ **old boy** N (*Scol*) ex alunno; (*fam*) vecchio.

old·en [ˈəʊldən] ADJ: **in the olden days** nei tempi antichi, nei giorni passati.

♦ **old English** N inglese *m* antico.

♦ **old-established** [ˈəʊldɪsˈtæblɪʃt] ADJ di vecchia data.

♦ **old-fashioned** [ˈəʊldˈfæʃnd] ADJ antiquato(-a), fuori moda; (*person*) all'antica.

♦ **old flame** N (*fam*) vecchia fiamma.

♦ **old girl** (*Brit*) N **a** (*former pupil*) ex alunna **b** (*old, woman*) vecchia.

♦ **old guard** N: **the old guard** la vecchia guardia.

♦ **old maid** N (*pej*) vecchia zitella.

♦ **old master** N (*artist*) *grande pittore europeo del periodo compreso tra il 16 e il 19 secolo*; (*painting*) *dipinto* (*di un grande pittore europeo dal 16 al 19 secolo*).

♦ **old people's home** N casa di riposo (per anziani).

♦ **old school tie** N (*pej*): **the old school tie** (*Brit*) *legame che resta tra ex compagni di studi che, arrivati a posizioni di potere, usano la propria influenza per aiutarsi a vicenda*.

♦ **old-style** [ˈəʊldˈstaɪl] ADJ (di) vecchio stampo *inv*.

♦ **Old Testament** N: **the Old Testament** il Vecchio Testamento.

♦ **old-time** [ˈəʊldˌtaɪm] ADJ di una volta.

♦ **old-timer** [ˌəʊldˈtaɪməʳ] N veterano(-a).

♦ **old wives' tale** N vecchia superstizione *f*.

♦ **Old World** N: **the Old World** il Vecchio mondo.

♦ **old-world** [ˈəʊldˈwɜːld] ADJ di vecchio stile, di vecchio stampo.

oleagi·nous [ˌəʊlɪˈædʒɪnəs] ADJ oleaginoso(-a), oleoso (-a).

olean·der [ˌəʊlɪˈændəʳ] N oleandro.

♦ **O-level** [ˈəʊˌlevl] N (*Brit: formerly*) *diploma di istruzione secondaria conseguito a 16 anni in Inghilterra e Galles, ora sostituito dal GCSE*.

oli·gar·chic [ˌɒlɪˈɡɑːkɪk] ADJ oligarchico(-a).

oli·gar·chy [ˈɒlɪˌɡɑːkɪ] N oligarchia.

ol·ive [ˈɒlɪv] **1** N (*fruit*) oliva; (*also*: **olive tree**) olivo.

2 ADJ (*skin*) olivastro(-a); (*also*: **olive-green**) verde oliva *inv*.

♦ **olive branch** N ramoscello d'olivo.

♦ **olive oil** N olio d'oliva.

Olym·pic [əʊˈlɪmpɪk] ADJ olimpico(-a).

♦ **Olympic Games** NPL: **the Olympic Games** i giochi *mpl* olimpici.

Olym·pics NPL: **the Olympics** le Olimpiadi *fpl*.

Olym·pus [əʊˈlɪmpəs] N (*Geog, Myth*) Olimpo.

OM [ˌəʊˈem] N ABBR (*Brit*: = *Order of Merit*) *titolo onorifico*.

Oman [əʊˈmɑːn] N l'Oman *m*.

om·buds·man [ˈɒmbʊdzmən] N (*pl* **-men**) difensore *m* civico.

ome·lette, ome·let [ˈɒmlɪt] N frittata, omelette *f inv*; **ham/cheese omelette** omelette al prosciutto/al formaggio.

omen [ˈəʊmən] N presagio, auspicio.

omi·nous [ˈɒmɪnəs] ADJ (*sign*) minaccioso(-a), infausto (-a); (*event*) di malaugurio; (*look, smile, silence*) sinistro (-a).

omi·nous·ly [ˈɒmɪnəslɪ] ADV minacciosamente.

omis·sion [əʊˈmɪʃən] N omissione *f*.

omit [əʊˈmɪt] VT omettere; **to omit to do sth** tralasciare *or* trascurare di fare qc.

om·ni·bus [ˈɒmnɪbəs] N (*old: bus*) autobus *m inv*; (*book*) raccolta; **omnibus edition** (*TV, Radio*) replica delle puntate precedenti.

om·nipo·tence [ɒmˈnɪpətəns] N onnipotenza.

om·nipo·tent [ɒmˈnɪpətənt] ADJ onnipotente.

om·ni·pres·ent [ˌɒmnɪˈprezənt] ADJ (*frm*) onnipresente.

om·nis·ci·ent [ɒmˈnɪsɪənt] ADJ onnisciente.

om·ni·vore [ˈɒmnɪˌvɔːʳ] N onnivoro.

om·niv·or·ous [ɒmˈnɪvərəs] ADJ onnivoro(-a).

ON ABBR (*Canada Post*)= Ontario.

on [ɒn]

1 PREP

a (*position*) su; (*on top of*) sopra;

▷**on the** *Continent* nell'Europa continentale

▷**with her hat on her** *head* col cappello in testa

▷**on the** *left* sulla *or* a sinistra

▷**I haven't any money on** *me* non ho soldi con me

▷**on** *page* 2 a pagina 2

▷**on the** *right* sulla *or* a destra

▷**the house is on the main** *road* la casa è sulla strada principale

▷**on the** *table* sul tavolo

▷**hanging on the** *wall* appeso(-a) al muro

b (*fig*)

▷**an** *attack* **on the government** un attacco al governo

▷**we did it on his** *authority* l'abbiamo fatto dietro sua autorizzazione

▷*based* **on fact** basato(-a) sui fatti

▷**he's away on** *business* è via per affari

▷**on** *Channel* 4 su Canale 4

▷**he is on the** *committee* fa parte della commissione

▷**on** *foot* a piedi

▷**he's on** *heroin* si fa di eroina

▷**to be on** *holiday* (*Brit*) essere in vacanza

▷**she** *lives* **on cheese** vive di formaggio

▷**the** *march* **on Rome** la marcia su Roma

▷**have it on** *me* offro io

▷**this round's on** *me* questo giro lo offro io

▷**on the** *plane* sull'*or* in aereo

▷he *played* it on the violin/piano l'ha suonato al violino/al pianoforte
▷on the *radio* alla radio
▷on the *telephone* al telefono
▷on the *television* alla televisione
▷on the *train* sul *or* in treno
▷prices are *up* on last year('s) i prezzi sono rincarati rispetto all'anno scorso
▷to be on *vacation* (*Am*) essere in vacanza
▷we're on irregular *verbs* stiamo facendo i verbi irregolari
▷he's on *£16,000* a year guadagna 16.000 sterline all'anno
c (*of time*)
▷on May *14th* il 14 maggio
▷on my *arrival* al mio arrivo
▷on a *day* like this in una giornata come questa
▷on *Friday* venerdì
▷a week on *Friday* venerdì a otto
▷on *Fridays* il *or* di venerdì
▷on *seeing* him nel vederlo, vedendolo
d (*about, concerning*) su, di;
▷a *book* on physics un libro di *or* sulla fisica
▷he *lectured* on Keats tenne un corso su Keats
▷have you *read* Purnell on Churchill? hai letto cosa scrive Purnell su Churchill?
▷while we're on the *subject* visto che siamo in argomento.
2 ADV
a (*covering*)
▷what's she *got* on? cosa indossa?
▷to *have* one's coat on avere indosso il cappotto
▷she *put* her boots on si mise gli stivali
▷*screw* the lid on tightly avvita il coperchio ben stretto
▷on *with* your coat! mettiti il cappotto!
b (*forward*)
▷*from* that day on da quel giorno in poi
▷it's *getting* on for ten o'clock sono quasi le dieci
▷it was *well* on in the evening era sera inoltrata
▷it was *well* on in May era maggio avanzato
▷they talked *well* on into the night continuarono a parlare fino a notte inoltrata
c (*continuation*): to *go* on, *walk* on, *carry* on continuare, proseguire
▷on and *off* ogni tanto
▷he *rambled* on and on continuava nei suoi discorsi sconclusionati
▷to *read* on continuare a leggere, proseguire nella lettura
▷and *so* on e così via
d (*in phrases*)
▷what are you on *about*? cosa vai dicendo?
▷my father's always on *at* me to get a job (*fam*) mio padre mi sta sempre addosso perché trovi un lavoro
▷the police are on *to* him la polizia lo tiene d'occhio.
3 ADJ
a (*functioning, in operation*: radio, light, oven) acceso (-a); (: *tap*) aperto(-a); (: *machine*) in moto; (: *brake*) inserito(-a);
▷when is this *film* on? quand'è che danno questo film?
▷there's a good *film* on at the cinema danno un buon film al cinema

▷the *meeting* is still on la riunione è ancora in corso
▷is the *meeting* still on tonight? è confermata la riunione di stasera?
▷the *programme* is on in a minute il programma inizia tra un minuto
▷sorry, I've got *something* on tonight mi spiace, stasera sono impegnato
b (*fam*): you're on! d'accordo!
▷that's not on! (*not acceptable*) non si fa così!; (*not possible*) non se ne parla neanche!

onan·ism ['əʊnə,nɪzəm] N onanismo.
ONC [,əʊɛn'siː] N ABBR (*Brit*: = *Ordinary National Certificate*) *diploma in materie tecniche a livello di maturità.*
once [wʌns] 1 ADV a (*on one occasion*) una volta; I've only met him once before prima d'ora l'ho incontrato una volta sola; once only solo una volta; once or twice un paio di volte; once again *or* once more ancora una volta; (every) once in a while (una volta) ogni tanto; once a week una volta alla settimana; once and for all una volta per tutte; just this once solo (per) questa volta; for once una volta tanto; it never once occurred to me non mi è mai venuto in mente
b (*formerly*) un tempo; I knew him once un tempo *or* in passato lo conoscevo; once upon a time there was ... c'era una volta...
c : at once (*immediately*) subito, immediatamente; (*simultaneously*) contemporaneamente, a un tempo; all at once (*suddenly*) tutt'a un tratto, improvvisamente; (*in one go*) tutto in una volta.
2 CONJ una volta che, quando, non appena; once he had finished he left una volta che *or* non appena ebbe finito andò via.
♦ **once-over** ['wʌns,əʊvəʳ] N (*fam*): to give sb/sth the once-over dare una sbirciata a qn/qc.
on·col·ogy [ɒŋ'kɒlədʒɪ] N (*Med*) oncologia.
on·coming ['ɒn,kʌmɪŋ] ADJ (*traffic*) in senso contrario.
OND [,əʊɛn'diː] N ABBR (*Brit*: = *Ordinary National Diploma*) *diploma in materie tecniche conseguito dopo un corso biennale.*

one [wʌn]
1 ADJ
a uno(-a);
▷one *day* un giorno
▷one cold winter's *day* una fredda giornata d'inverno
▷one *hundred* and fifty centocinquanta
▷the baby *is* one (year old) il bambino ha un anno
▷*it's* one (o'clock) è l'una
▷one *or two* people una o due persone, un paio di persone
▷for one *reason* or another per un motivo o per l'altro
▷*twenty*-one years ago ventun'anni fa
▷that's one *way* of doing it questo è uno dei modi per farlo
b (*sole*) unico(-a), solo(-a);
▷*his* one worry la sua unica *or* sola preoccupazione
▷*no* one man could do it nessuno potrebbe farlo da solo
▷one and *only* unico(-a)
▷the one and only Charlie Chaplin l'inimitabile

Charlie Chaplin
▷*the* one man who il solo *or* l'unico che
▷*the* one book which ... l'unico libro che...
[c] (*same*) stesso(-a);
▷they are one and the *same* person sono la stessa persona
▷it is one and the *same* thing è la stessa cosa
▷in *the* one car nella stessa macchina.
[2] N uno(-a);
▷one *after* the other uno(-a) dopo l'altro(-a)
▷one and *all* tutti
▷to be *at* one (with sb) andare d'accordo (con qn)
▷I *belted* him one (*fam*) gli ho mollato un cazzotto
▷to go one *better* than sb fare meglio di qn
▷one *by* one a uno(-a) a uno(-a)
▷I *for* one am not going per quanto mi riguarda non ci vado
▷to *have* one for the road bere il bicchiere della staffa
▷one *hundred* and one centouno
▷in ones and twos a piccoli gruppi
▷she's cook and housekeeper *in* one è contemporaneamente cuoca e governante
▷*twenty*-one ventuno
▷to be one *up* on sb essere avvantaggiato(-a) rispetto a qn.
[3] PRON
[a]: *this* one questo(-a)
▷*any* one of us chiunque *or* uno qualsiasi di noi
▷our *dear* ones i nostri cari
▷that's a *difficult* one quello è un osso duro
▷you're a *fine* one! (*fam*) sei un bel tipo!
▷he's a *great* one for chess va matto per gli scacchi
▷I'll have the *grey* one prenderò quello grigio
▷*have* you got one? ne hai uno?
▷what about this *little* one? cosa ne dici di questo piccolino?
▷the *little* ones i bambini, i piccoli
▷he is *not* one to protest non è il tipo che protesta
▷one or two *of* the books were damaged c'erano un paio di libri rovinati
▷one *of* them uno(-a) di loro
▷I lost one *of* them ne ho perso uno
▷one *or* two uno(-a) o due
▷*that* one quello(-a)
▷*the* one on the floor quello(-a) sul pavimento
▷*the* one who (*or* that *or* which) quello(-a) che
▷*the* ones who (*or* that *or* which) quelli(-e) che
▷*which* one do you want? quale vuoi?
[b]: one *another* l'un l'altro(-a)
▷they all *kissed* one another si baciarono tutti a vicenda
▷do you *see* one another much? vi vedete spesso?
[c] (*impersonal*)
▷to cut one's *finger* tagliarsi un dito
▷one never *knows* non si sa mai
▷one *must* eat bisogna mangiare
▷to express one's *opinion* esprimere la propria opinione.

♦ **one-armed** [ˌwʌn'ɑːmd] ADJ con un braccio solo.
♦ **one-armed bandit** N slot-machine *f inv.*
♦ **one-day excursion** [ˌwʌndeɪks'kɜːʃən] N (*Am*) biglietto giornaliero di andata e ritorno.

♦ **one-eyed** [ˌwʌn'aɪd] ADJ con un occhio solo.
♦ **one-horse** ['wʌnˌhɔːs] ADJ: **one-horse town** (*fam*) piccola città di provincia.
♦ **One-hundred share index** [ˌwʌnhʌndrədʃɛə'mdɛks] N *indice borsistico del Financial Times.*
♦ **one-legged** [ˌwʌn'legɪd] ADJ con una gamba sola.
♦ **one-man** ['wʌn'mæn] ADJ (*business*) gestito(-a) da una sola persona; (*art exhibition*) personale; (*boat*) a un posto; **one-man show** recital *m inv*; **she's a one-man woman** è tendenzialmente monogama, è una donna fedele.
♦ **one-man band** ['wʌnˌmæn'bænd] N (*Mus: person*) *suonatore ambulante con vari strumenti*; **it's a one-man band** (*fig fam*) c'è solo una persona a mandare avanti la baracca.
♦ **one-night** ['wʌnˌnaɪt] ADJ: **one-night stand** (*Theatre*) spettacolo unico; (*sexual*) avventura di una notte.
♦ **one-off** [ˌwʌn'ɒf] [1] N (*Brit fam*) fatto eccezionale. [2] ADJ eccezionale, più unico(-a) che raro(-a).
♦ **one-parent family** ['wʌnˌpɛərənt'fæmɪlɪ] N famiglia *f* monogenitore *inv.*
♦ **one-piece** ['wʌnˌpiːs] ADJ (*bathing suit*) intero(-a), monopezzo *inv.*
on·er·ous ['ɒnərəs] (*frm*) ADJ (*task, duty*) oneroso(-a); (*responsibility*) pesante.
one·self [wʌn'sɛlf] PERS PRON (*reflexive*) si; (*after prep*) se stesso(-a), sé; (*emphatic*) da sé; **to hurt oneself** farsi male; **to be by oneself** stare da solo(-a), stare per conto proprio; **to do sth by oneself** fare qc da solo(-a) *or* da sé; **to keep sth for oneself** tenere qc per sé; **to see for oneself** vedere con i propri occhi; **to say to oneself** dirsi; **to talk to oneself** parlare da solo *or* tra sé e sé.
♦ **one-shot** [ˌwʌn'ʃɒt] N (*Am*) = one-off.
♦ **one-sided** [ˌwʌn'saɪdd] ADJ (*decision, view*) unilaterale; (*judgment, account*) parziale; (*game, contest*) impari *inv.*
♦ **one-time** ['wʌnˌtaɪm] ADJ ex *inv.*
♦ **one-to-one** [ˌwʌntə'wʌn] ADJ (*correlation*) univoco(-a); (*relationship*) tra due persone; **teaching is on a one-to-one basis** l'insegnamento è organizzato in lezioni individuali.
♦ **one-track** ['wʌnˌtræk] ADJ: **to have a one-track mind** essere fissato(-a), avere la mente a senso unico.
♦ **one-upmanship** [ˌwʌn'ʌpmənʃɪp] N: **the art of one-upmanship** l'arte *f* di primeggiare.
♦ **one-way** ['wʌnˌweɪ] ADJ (*traffic, street*) a senso unico; (*ticket*) di sola andata.
on·go·ing ['ɒnˌgəʊɪŋ] ADJ (*in progress*) in corso; (*continuing*) che si sviluppa.
on·ion ['ʌnjən] N cipolla.
♦ **onion rings** NPL *rondelle di cipolla passate in pastella e fritte.*
♦ **onion soup** N zuppa di cipolle.
♦ **on-line** ['ɒnˌlaɪn] ADJ (*Comput*) on line *inv*, in linea; (: *switched on*) acceso(-a).
on·look·er ['ɒnˌlʊkə'] N astante *m/f*, spettatore(-trice).
only ['əʊnlɪ] [1] ADJ solo(-a), unico(-a); **it's the only one left** è l'unico rimasto; **your only hope is to hide** la tua unica speranza sta nel nasconderti; **you are the only one who can help us** sei l'unico che possa *or* che può aiutarci; **you are not the only one** non sei l'unico; **an only child** un(a) figlio(-a) unico(-a); **the only thing I don't like about it is** ... l'unica cosa che non mi va è....
[2] ADV solo, soltanto, solamente; **we have only five** ne abbiamo solo cinque; **only one choice** una sola possibilità, un'unica scelta; **only time will tell** chi vivrà vedrà;

I'm only the porter io sono solo il portinaio; I only touched it l'ho soltanto toccato; I only took one ne ho preso soltanto uno; only when I ... solo quando io...; not only A but also B non solo A ma anche B; I saw her only yesterday l'ho vista appena ieri; we can only hope non possiamo far altro che sperare; I'd be only too pleased to help sarei proprio felice di essere d'aiuto; it's only too true è proprio vero.

③ CONJ solo che, ma (purtroppo); I would come, only I'm very busy verrei volentieri, solo che sono molto occupato.

o.n.o. ABBR **= or nearest offer; see near.**

ono·mato·poeia [ˌɒnəʊmætəʊ'pi:ə] N onomatopea.

ono·mato·poe·ic [ˌɒnəʊmætəʊ'pi:ɪk] ADJ onomatopeico (-a).

on·rush ['ɒn,rʌʃ] N ondata.

on·set ['ɒn,sɛt] N (of winter) arrivo; (of illness, old age) inizio, principio.

on·shore ['ɒn'ʃɔ:'] ADJ (wind) di mare; (job) a terra.

on·slaught ['ɒn,slɔ:t] N (Mil, fig) attacco.

♦ **on-the-job** ['ɒnðə'dʒɒb] ADJ (course, training) in sede.

♦ **on-the-spot** ['ɒnðə'spɒt] ADJ (investigations) sul posto.

onto ['ɒntʊ] PREP su, sopra; he climbed onto the table è salito sopra il tavolo; to be onto sb (fam: suspect) scoprire qn; I'm onto something (fam) sono su una buona pista; to be onto a good thing (fam) trovare l'America; I'll get onto him about it gliene parlerò io.

on·tol·ogy [ɒn'tɒlədʒɪ] N (Philosophy) ontologia.

onus ['əʊnəs] N, NO PL onere m; the onus is upon him to prove it sta a lui dimostrarlo; to shift the onus for sth onto sb scaricare la responsabilità di qc su qn; the onus of proof is on the prosecution l'onere della prova spetta all'accusa.

on·ward ['ɒnwəd] ① ADJ in avanti.

② ADV (also: onwards) in avanti; from the 12th century onward(s) dal XII secolo in poi.

onyx ['ɒnɪks] N onice f.

oodles ['u:dəlz] N (old fam): oodles (of) un sacco (di).

oomph [ʊmf] N (fam) verve f inv.

oops [ʊps] EXCL ops! (esprime rincrescimento per un piccolo contrattempo).

oops-a-daisy! ['ʊpsə,deɪzɪ] EXCL oplà!

ooze [u:z] ① N melma.

② VI (water) filtrare; (gum, resin) trasudare; (pus) fuoriuscire.

③ VT: the wound oozed blood la ferita stillava sangue; he simply oozes confidence (pej) sprizza sicurezza da tutti i pori.

opa·city [əʊ'pæsɪtɪ] N opacità.

opal ['əʊpəl] N opale m or f.

opal·es·cence [ˌəʊpə'lɛsns] N opalescenza.

opal·ine ['əʊpə,laɪn] N opalina.

opaque [əʊ'peɪk] ADJ opaco(-a).

OPEC ['əʊpɛk] N ABBR (= Organization of Petroleum-Exporting Countries) O.P.E.C. f.

open ['əʊpən] ① ADJ ⓐ (gen) aperto(-a); (flower) aperto (-a), sbocciato(-a); wide open (door, window) spalancato (-a); half open OR slightly open socchiuso(-a); open at the neck col colletto sbottonato; to welcome with open arms accogliere a braccia aperte; to cut a sack open aprire un sacco con un taglio; to keep open house (fig) aprire la propria casa a tutti; open to the public on Mondays aperto(-a) al pubblico di lunedì

ⓑ (fig: letter) aperto(-a); (: water, channel) navigabile; (: cheque) in bianco; in the open air all'aria aperta; on

the open road su autostrada; road open to traffic strada aperta al traffico or transitabile; open to the elements/to attack esposto(-a) alle intemperie/all'attacco; open country aperta campagna; open ground (among trees) radura; (waste ground) terreno non edificato; the open sea il mare aperto; to lay o.s. open to criticism esporsi alle critiche; open to persuasion disposto(-a) a lasciarsi convincere; it is open to doubt whether ... è in dubbio se...

ⓒ (competition, scholarship) aperto(-a) a tutti; (meeting) pubblico(-a); (trial) a porte aperte; what choices are open to me? che scelta ho?; the post is still open il posto è sempre vacante; in open court (Law) a porte aperte

ⓓ (person, face) aperto(-a); (hatred, admiration) evidente, palese; (enemy) dichiarato(-a); it's an open secret that ... è il segreto di Pulcinella che...; in open revolt in aperta rivolta; to be open with sb essere franco(-a) con qn

ⓔ (undecided: question) aperto(-a); the race was still wide open la gara era ancora tutta da giocare; open verdict dichiarazione di morte per cause non accertate; open ticket biglietto aperto; to have an open mind (on sth) non avere ancora deciso (su qc); to leave the matter open lasciare la faccenda in sospeso.

② ⓐ N: out in the open (out of doors) fuori, all'aperto; (in the country) in campagna, all'aperto; their true feelings came into the open vennero a galla i loro veri sentimenti

ⓑ (Golf, Tennis): the Australian Open l'open m inv di Australia.

③ VT (gen) aprire; (legs) divaricare; to open sth wide spalancare qc; to open a road to traffic aprire al traffico una strada; to open a road through a forest aprire una strada nella foresta; to open Parliament aprire i lavori parlamentari; to open a bank account aprire un conto in banca; to open fire (Mil) aprire il fuoco; I didn't open my mouth non ho aperto bocca; to open one's heart to sb confidarsi con qn; to open one's mind to sth aprirsi con qc.

④ VI ⓐ (eyes, door, debate) aprirsi; (shop, bank, museum) aprire; the shops open at 9 i negozi aprono alle 9; to open onto or into dare su

ⓑ (begin: book, film) cominciare; (Cards, Chess) aprire; the play opens next Monday la prima della commedia è lunedì prossimo; the book opens with a long description il libro comincia con una lunga descrizione

▶ **open out** ① VT + ADV (unfold) aprire, spiegare.

② VI + ADV aprirsi, dischiudersi

▶ **open up** ① VT + ADV aprire; (blocked road) sgombrare; to open up a country for trade aprire il mercato di un paese.

② VI + ADV ⓐ (flower, shop) aprirsi

ⓑ (start shooting) aprire il fuoco.

♦ **open-air** [ˌəʊpn'ɛə'] ADJ all'aperto.

♦ **open-and-shut** [ˌəʊpnən'ʃʌt] ADJ: open-and-shut case caso di facile soluzione.

open·cast ['əʊpn,kɑ:st] ADJ: opencast mine/mining miniera/estrazione f a cielo aperto.

♦ **open day** N (Brit: in school, institution) giornata di apertura al pubblico.

♦ **open-ended** [ˌəʊpn'ɛndɪd] ADJ (question) aperto(-a); (discussion) senza conclusioni.

open·er ['əʊpnə'] N: bottle-opener apribottiglie m inv; (also: can opener or tin opener) apriscatole m inv.

♦ **open-handed** [ˌəʊpn'hændɪd] ADJ generoso(-a).

♦ **open-heart** ['əʊpn,hɑ:t] ADJ: **open-heart surgery** intervento *m* (chirurgico) a cuore aperto *inv*.

♦ **open-hearted** [,əʊpn'hɑ:tɪd] ADJ sincero(-a), franco (-a).

open·ing ['əʊpnɪŋ] ①ADJ (*gen*) d'apertura; (*ceremony, speech*) d'apertura, inaugurale.

② N **a** (*gap*) apertura; (: *in wall*) breccia

b (*beginning*) inizio; (*also*: **official opening**: *of factory, hospital*) inaugurazione *f*; (*first performance*: *of film, play*) prima (rappresentazione *f*)

c (*opportunity*) occasione *f*, possibilità *f inv*; (*post*) posto vacante; **to give one's opponent an opening** offrire il fianco all'avversario.

♦ **opening hours** NPL orario *msg* d'apertura.

♦ **opening night** N (*Theatre*) prima.

♦ **opening time** N (*Brit*) orario d'apertura (*dei pub*).

♦ **open learning** N *sistema educativo nel quale lo studente ha maggior controllo e gestione delle modalità di apprendimento.*

open·ly ['əʊpənlɪ] ADV apertamente.

♦ **open-minded** [,əʊpn'maɪndɪd] ADJ aperto(-a), dalla mentalità aperta.

♦ **open-mouthed** [,əʊpn'maʊðd] ADJ a bocca aperta.

♦ **open-necked** ['əʊpn,nɛkt] ADJ (*shirt, blouse*) col colletto slacciato *or* sbottonato.

open·ness ['əʊpnnɪs] N (*frankness*) franchezza, sincerità.

♦ **open-plan** ['əʊpn,plæn] ADJ senza pareti divisorie.

♦ **open prison** N *istituto di pena dove viene data maggiore libertà ai detenuti.*

♦ **open sandwich** N tartina.

♦ **open secret** N segreto di Pulcinella.

♦ **open shop** N (*Industry*) *impresa che assume anche operai non iscritti ai sindacati.*

♦ **Open University** N (*Brit*): **the Open University** *corsi universitari per corrispondenza con lezioni trasmesse alla radio e alla TV.*

op·era ['ɒpərə] N (*work*) opera (lirica); (*genre*) opera, (musica) lirica.

op·er·able ['ɒpərəbl] ADJ (*Med*) operabile.

♦ **opera glasses** NPL binocolo da teatro.

♦ **opera house** N teatro lirico *or* dell'opera, opera.

♦ **opera singer** N cantante *m/f* d'opera *or* lirico(-a).

op·er·ate ['ɒpə,reɪt] ① VT **a** (*machine, switchboard, brakes*) azionare, far funzionare; **a machine operated by electricity** una macchina funzionante a corrente (elettrica); **can you operate this tool?** sai usare questo strumento?

b (*company*) dirigere, gestire; (*service*) gestire; (*system, law*) applicare.

② VI **a** (*function*: *machine, mind*) funzionare

b (*drug, propaganda*) agire

c (*company, firm*) operare; (*bus, airport*) essere in funzione; (*person*) agire

d (*Med*) operare, intervenire (su); **to operate on sb** operare qn; **to be operated on** subire un'operazione *for* un intervento (chirurgico); **she was operated on for appendicitis** fu operata di appendicite.

op·er·at·ic [,ɒpə'rætɪk] ADJ operistico(-a), lirico(-a).

op·er·at·ing ['ɒpə,reɪtɪŋ] ADJ **a** (*Comm*: *costs*) di gestione, d'esercizio **b** (*Med*) operatorio(-a); (: *nurse*) di sala operatoria.

♦ **operating room** N (*Am*) = **operating theatre**.

♦ **operating system** N (*Comput*) sistema *m* operativo.

♦ **operating table** N (*Med*): **the operating table** il tavolo operatorio.

♦ **operating theatre** N (*Med*) sala operatoria.

op·era·tion [,ɒpə'reɪʃən] N **a** (*gen, Mil*) operazione *f*; (*Med*) operazione *f*, intervento (chirurgico); **to have an operation for appendicitis** essere operato(-a) di appendicite; **to undergo an operation** subire un'operazione *or* un intervento (chirurgico); **the company's operations during the year** le operazioni dell'azienda durante l'anno

b : **to be in operation** (*machine*) essere in funzione; (*plan, system*) essere in azione; (*law*) essere in vigore; **to come into operation** entrare in funzione (*or* in azione *etc*); **to bring** *or* **put into operation** mettere in funzione (*or* in azione); (*law*) far entrare in vigore.

op·era·tion·al [,ɒpə'reɪʃnl] ADJ (*relating to operations*) operativo(-a); (*Comm*) di gestione, d'esercizio; (*ready for use or action*) in attività, in funzione; **operational research** ricerca operativa; **when the service is fully operational** quando il servizio sarà completamente operante.

op·era·tive ['ɒpərətɪv] ① ADJ **a** (*law, measure*) in vigore, operativo(-a), operante; **the operative word** la parola chiave **b** (*Med*) operatorio(-a).

② N (*in factory*) operaio(-a).

op·era·tor ['ɒpə,reɪtə'] N (*of machine*) operatore(-trice); (*Telec*) centralinista *m/f*; **tour operator** operatore(-trice) turistico(-a); **a smooth operator** (*fam*) uno(-a) che ci sa fare.

oper·cu·lum [əʊ'pɜ:kjʊləm] N opercolo.

op·er·et·ta [,ɒpə'retə] N operetta.

oph·thal·mia [ɒf'θælmɪə] N oftalmia.

oph·thal·mic [ɒf'θælmɪk] ADJ oftalmico(-a).

oph·thal·molo·gist [,ɒfθæl'mɒlədʒɪst] N oculista *m/f*.

oph·thal·mol·ogy [,ɒfθæl'mɒlədʒɪ] N oculistica.

oph·thal·mo·scope [ɒf'θælmə,skəʊp] N oftalmoscopio.

opi·ate ['əʊpɪɪt] N oppiaceo.

opine [əʊ'paɪn] VT (*frm old*) opinare.

opin·ion [ə'pɪnjən] N (*belief, view*) opinione *f*, parere *m*; **public opinion** opinione pubblica; **in my opinion** secondo me, a mio avviso; **in the opinion of those who know** secondo gli esperti; **it's a matter of opinion** è discutibile *or* opinabile; **what is your opinion of him?** tu che cosa pensi di lui?; **to be of the opinion that ...** essere dell'opinione che..., ritenere che...; **to ask sb's opinion** chiedere il parere di qn, consultare qn; **to give one's opinion** dare il proprio parere; **to form an opinion of sb/sth** farsi un'opinione di qn/qc; **to have a high/poor opinion of sb** avere/non avere un'alta opinione di qn, stimare molto/poco qn; **to have a high opinion of o.s.** (*pej*) avere un'alta opinione di sé, credersi chissà chi; **to seek a second opinion** (*Med*) consultare un altro medico.

opin·ion·at·ed [ə'pɪnjə,neɪtɪd] ADJ dogmatico(-a).

♦ **opinion poll** N sondaggio di opinione.

opium ['əʊpɪəm] N oppio.

♦ **opium addict** N oppiomane *m/f*.

♦ **opium den** N fumeria d'oppio.

opos·sum [ə'pɒsəm] N opossum *m inv*.

op·po·nent [ə'pəʊnənt] N avversario(-a); (*in debate, discussion*) oppositore(-trice); **I have always been an opponent of privatization** sono sempre stato un accanito oppositore delle privatizzazioni.

op·por·tune ['ɒpə,tju:n] ADJ opportuno(-a); **to be opportune** capitare a proposito.

op·por·tune·ly ['ɒpə,tju:nlɪ] ADV opportunamente.

op·por·tune·ness ['ɒpə,tju:nnɪs] N opportunità.

op·por·tun·ism [ˌɒpə'tju:nɪzəm] N (*frm pej*) opportunismo.

op·por·tun·ist [ˌɒpə'tju:nɪst] N (*frm pej*) opportunista *m/f*.

op·por·tun·is·tic [ˌɒpətju'nɪstɪk] ADJ (*frm*) opportunistico (-a).

op·por·tu·nity [ˌɒpə'tju:nɪtɪ] N opportunità *f inv*, occasione *f*; **to have the opportunity to do** *or* **of doing** avere l'opportunità di fare; **to take the opportunity to do** *or* **of doing** cogliere l'occasione per fare; **at the earliest opportunity** appena possibile, alla prima occasione; **when I** (*or* **you** *etc*) **get the opportunity** quando capita l'occasione; **to miss one's opportunity** perdere l'occasione; **opportunities for promotion** possibilità *fpl* di carriera.

op·pose [ə'pəʊz] VT (*gen*) opporsi a; **she opposes my leaving** è contraria alla mia partenza.

op·posed [ə'pəʊzd] ADJ (*conflicting*: *ideas*) contrastante, opposto(-a); **to be opposed to** essere contrario(-a) a; **as opposed to** (*in contrast to*) in confronto a, rispetto a; (*instead of*) invece che *or* di; **how important is financial success, as opposed to job satisfaction?** quanto è importante il successo in termini economici rispetto alla soddisfazione che dà il lavoro?

op·pos·ing [ə'pəʊzɪŋ] ADJ (*tendencies, points of view*) opposto(-a); (*team*) avversario(-a).

op·po·site ['ɒpəzɪt] 1 ADV di fronte, dirimpetto; **they live directly opposite** abitano proprio di fronte.

2 PREP di fronte a; **opposite one another** l'uno(-a) di fronte all'altro(-a); **a house opposite the school** una casa di fronte alla scuola; **to play opposite sb** (*Theatre, Cine*) essere co-protagonista *m/f* insieme a qn.

3 ADJ (*house*) di fronte; (*end, direction, side*) opposto(-a); (*point of view*) opposto(-a), contrario(-a); **on the opposite side of the road** dall'altro lato della strada; **"see opposite page"** "vedere pagina a fronte".

4 N (*reverse*) contrario, opposto; (*of word*) contrario; **quite the opposite!** al contrario!; **she said just the opposite** lei ha detto esattamente il contrario.

♦ **opposite number** N omologo(-a), controparte *f*.

♦ **opposite sex** N: **the opposite sex** l'altro sesso.

op·po·si·tion [ˌɒpə'zɪʃən] N a (*resistance*) opposizione *f*; (*people opposing*) avversari *mpl*; **in opposition to** in contrasto con

b (*Brit Pol*): **the Opposition** l'opposizione *f*; **leader of the Opposition** leader *m/f inv* dell'opposizione; **to be in opposition** essere all'opposizione.

op·press [ə'prɛs] VT opprimere.

op·pres·sion [ə'prɛʃən] N oppressione *f*.

op·pres·sive [ə'prɛsɪv] ADJ (*regime, system*) oppressivo (-a); (*fig*: *heat, thought*) opprimente.

op·pres·sive·ly [ə'prɛsɪvlɪ] ADV (*see adj*) oppressivamente; in modo opprimente; **it was oppressively hot** faceva un caldo opprimente.

op·pres·sor [ə'prɛsə'] N oppressore *m*.

op·pro·brium [ə'prəʊbrɪəm] N (*frm*) vituperio.

opt [ɒpt] VI: **to opt for** optare per; **to opt to do** scegliere di fare, optare per fare

▶ **opt out (of)** VI + ADV (+ PREP) a (*of agreement, arrangement*) scegliere di non partecipare a; **I think I'll opt out of going** penso che non ci andrò; **we went to the match, but Fred opted out** noi siamo andati alla partita ma Fred non è venuto

b (*Brit*: *of NHS*) scegliere di non far più parte di.

op·ta·tive ['ɒptətɪv] 1 ADJ ottativo(-a).

2 N ottativo.

op·tic ['ɒptɪk] ADJ ottico(-a).

op·ti·cal ['ɒptɪkəl] ADJ ottico(-a).

♦ **optical character reader** N lettore *m* ottico di caratteri.

♦ **optical character recognition** N lettura ottica di caratteri.

♦ **optical fibre** N fibra ottica.

♦ **optical illusion** N illusione *f* ottica.

op·ti·cian [ɒp'tɪʃən] N (*also*: **ophthalmic optician**) optometrista *m/f*; (*also*: **dispensing optician**) ottico.

op·tics ['ɒptɪks] NSG ottica.

op·ti·mism ['ɒptɪˌmɪzəm] N ottimismo.

op·ti·mist ['ɒptɪmɪst] N ottimista *m/f*.

op·ti·mis·tic [ˌɒptɪ'mɪstɪk] ADJ (*attitude*) ottimistico(-a); (*person*) ottimista.

op·ti·mis·ti·cal·ly [ˌɒptɪ'mɪstɪklɪ] ADV ottimisticamente.

op·ti·mum ['ɒptɪməm] 1 ADJ ottimale.

2 N (*pl* **optimums** *or* **optima** ['ɒptɪmə]) optimum *m inv*, condizioni *fpl* ottimali.

op·tion ['ɒpʃən] N a (*choice*) scelta; **I have no option** non ho scelta; **she had no option but to leave** non poteva far altro che partire; **to keep one's options open** non precludersi alcuna possibilità; **imprisonment without the option of bail** (*Law*) carcerazione *f* senza possibilità di libertà provvisoria

b (*Comm*) opzione *f*; **with the option to buy** con opzione di acquisto

c (*Scol, Univ*) materia facoltativa.

op·tion·al ['ɒpʃənl] ADJ (*course, subject, ingredient*) facoltativo(-a); **optional extra** (*Comm*) optional *m inv*.

op·tom·etry [ɒp'tɒmɪtrɪ] N optometria.

opu·lence ['ɒpjʊləns] N opulenza.

opu·lent ['ɒpjʊlənt] ADJ opulento(-a).

opu·lent·ly ['ɒpjʊləntlɪ] ADV (*furnish etc*) con opulenza; (*live*) nell'opulenza.

opus ['əʊpəs] N (*pl* **opuses** *or* **opera** ['ɒpərə]) (*Mus*) opera.

OR ABBR (*Am Post*) = Oregon.

or [ɔ:'] CONJ (*gen*) o; **or rather** o meglio, o piuttosto; **or else** oppure, se no, altrimenti; **do it or else!** (*fam*) fallo, altrimenti...!; **20 or so** circa 20; **let me go or I'll scream!** lasciami andare o mi metto a urlare!; **without relatives or friends** senza né parenti né amici; **he can't read or write** non sa né leggere né scrivere; **he hasn't seen or heard anything** non ha (né) visto né sentito niente.

ora·cle ['ɒrəkl] N oracolo.

oral ['ɔ:rəl] 1 ADJ orale.

2 N (*examination*) (*esame m*) orale *m*.

oral·ly ['ɔ:rəlɪ] ADV oralmente; (*take medicine*) per via orale.

or·ange ['ɒrɪndʒ] 1 N (*fruit*) arancia; (*tree*) arancio; (*colour*) arancione *m*.

2 ADJ (*in colour*) arancione; (*juice, jelly*) d'arancia; (*marmalade*) di arance; (*cake*) all'arancia.

or·ange·ade [ˌɒrɪndʒ'eɪd] N aranciata.

♦ **orange blossom** N fiori *mpl* d'arancio.

Orange·man ['ɒrɪndʒmən] N (*pl* **-men**) *protestante militante dell'Irlanda del Nord*.

♦ **orange squash** N succo d'arancia (*da diluire con acqua*).

♦ **orange stick** N bastoncino d'arancio (*per manicure*).

orang-utan [ɔ:ˌræŋu:'tæn] N orango, orangutan *m inv*.

ora·tion [ɔ:'reɪʃən] N orazione *f*; **funeral oration** orazione funebre.

ora·tor ['ɒrətə'] N oratore(-trice).

ora·tori·cal [ˌɒrə'tɒrɪkəl] ADJ oratorio(-a).

ora·to·rio [ˌɒrəˈtɔːrɪəʊ] N (*Mus*) oratorio.
ora·tory[1] [ˈɒrətərɪ] N (*public speaking*) oratoria.
ora·tory[2] [ˈɒrətərɪ] N (*Rel*) oratorio.
orb [ɔːb] N ☐1☐ (*frm: sphere*) orbe *m*; (*liter: celestial body*) astro.
☐2☐ (*in regalia*) globo (*simbolo del potere reale e imperiale*).
or·bit [ˈɔːbɪt] ☐1☐ N orbita; **to be in/go into orbit (round)** essere/entrare in orbita (attorno a); **it's outside my orbit** (*fig*) non rientra nel mio campo.
☐2☐ VI (*satellite, astronaut*) orbitare.
☐3☐ VT (*earth, moon*) orbitare attorno a.
or·bit·al [ˈɔːbɪtəl] N (*also:* **orbital motorway**) raccordo anulare.
Or·cad·ian [ɔːˈkeɪdɪən] ☐1☐ ADJ delle Orcadi.
☐2☐ N abitante *m/f* delle Orcadi.
or·chard [ˈɔːtʃəd] N frutteto; **apple orchard** meleto.
or·ches·tra [ˈɔːkɪstrə] N orchestra; (*Am: seating*) platea.
or·ches·tral [ɔːˈkɛstrəl] ADJ (*music, style*) orchestrale; (*concert*) sinfonico(-a).
♦ **orchestra pit** N fossa dell'orchestra.
or·ches·trate [ˈɔːkɪstreɪt] VT (*Mus, fig*) orchestrare.
or·ches·tra·tion [ˌɔːkɪsˈtreɪʃən] N orchestrazione *f*.
or·chid [ˈɔːkɪd] N orchidea; **common spotted orchid** orchidea maculata.
or·dain [ɔːˈdeɪn] VT ☐a☐ (*decree*) decretare; **it was ordained that ...** (*fig*) era destino che... ☐b☐ (*Rel*) ordinare.
or·deal [ɔːˈdiːl] N esperienza traumatica.
or·der [ˈɔːdə] ☐1☐ N ☐a☐ (*sequence*) ordine *m*; **in alphabetical order** in ordine alfabetico; **in order of merit** in ordine di merito; **in order of size** in ordine di grandezza; **put these in the right order** mettili nell'ordine giusto; **to be in the wrong order** *or* **out of order** non essere in ordine; **she had no order in her life** aveva una vita disordinata; **in the order of things** nell'ordine delle cose
☐b☐ (*also:* **good order**) ordine *m*; **in order** (*room*) in ordine; (*documents*) in regola; **a machine in working order** un macchinario funzionante; **to be out of order** (*machine, toilets*) essere guasto(-a); (*telephone, lift*) essere fuori servizio
☐c☐ (*peace, control*) ordine *m*; **to keep order** mantenere l'ordine; **to keep children in order** tenere i bambini sotto controllo
☐d☐ (*command*) ordine *m*, comando; (*of court: for search, arrest*) mandato; (: *for payment of fine, maintenance*) ingiunzione *f*; **by order of** per ordine di; **on the orders of** agli ordini di; **to be under orders to do sth** avere l'ordine di fare qc; **to give sb orders to do sth** dare a qn l'ordine di fare qc; **to take orders from sb** prendere ordini da qn; **to obey orders** ubbidire agli ordini; **order of the day** ordine del giorno; **violence is the order of the day** (*fig*) la violenza è all'ordine del giorno
☐e☐ (*correct procedure: at meeting, Parliament*) procedura; **order (order)!** (*in Parliament*) ordine, signori!; **order in court!** silenzio!; **to call sb to order** richiamare qn all'ordine; **a point of order** una questione di procedura; **to be out of order** non (essere) regolamentare; **is it in order for me to go to Rome?** mi è permesso andare a Roma?
☐f☐ (*Comm*) ordinazione *f*, ordinativo; **to be on order** essere stato(-a) ordinato(-a); **to ask for a repeat order** chiedere che venga rinnovata un'ordinazione; **rush order** ordinazione urgente; **tall order** (*fig fam*) un'impresa ardua; **made to order** fatto(-a) su ordinazione, fatto(-a) su misura; **to place an order for sth with sb** fare un'ordinazione di qc a qn; **to the order of** (*Banking*)

all'ordine di; **payment order** (*social security*) mandato (di pagamento)
☐g☐ : **in order to do sth** per fare qc; **in order that** perché + *sub*, affinché + *sub*; **they cancelled their holiday in order to go to the wedding** hanno cancellato la vacanza per andare al matrimonio; **in order there should be no misunderstanding** affinché non ci siano equivoci
☐h☐ : **of** *or* **in the order of** (*approximately*) nell'ordine di; **his income is of the order of £40,000 per year** il suo reddito annuale è nell'ordine delle 40.000 sterline
☐i☐ (*of society, also Bio*) ordine *m*; **the lower orders** (*pej*) i ceti inferiori; **Benedictine Order** ordine benedettino; **holy orders** ordini (sacri); **to be in/take orders** (*Rel*) aver ricevuto/prendere gli ordini
☐2☐ VT ☐a☐ (*command*) ordinare; **to order sb to do sth** ordinare a qn di fare qc; **the referee ordered the player off the field** l'arbitro espulse il giocatore dal campo
☐b☐ (*put in order*) ordinare, fare ordine in, mettere in ordine
☐c☐ (*meal*) ordinare; (*goods*) ordinare, commissionare; (*taxi*) chiamare.
☐3☐ VI ordinare
▶ **order about**, **order around** VT + ADV comandare, dare ordini a.
♦ **order book** N copiacommissione *m inv*; **to have a full order book** avere molte ordinazioni.
or·dered [ˈɔːdəd] ADJ (*organized*) ordinato(-a).
♦ **order form** N modulo di ordinazione.
or·der·li·ness [ˈɔːdəlɪnɪs] N ordine *m*.
or·der·ly [ˈɔːdəlɪ] ☐1☐ ADJ (*person*) ordinato(-a); (*mind*) metodico(-a); (*room*) in ordine, ordinato(-a); (*meeting, crowd*) disciplinato(-a).
☐2☐ N (*Mil*) attendente *m*; (*Med*) inserviente *m*.
♦ **orderly room** N (*Mil*) fureria.
♦ **order number** N numero di commissione.
or·di·nal [ˈɔːdɪml] ☐1☐ ADJ (*number*) ordinale.
☐2☐ N (*numero*) ordinale *m*.
or·di·nance [ˈɔːdɪnəns] N (*frm*) ordinanza.
or·di·nari·ly [ˈɔːdɪnrɪlɪ] ADV normalmente, di solito.
or·di·nary [ˈɔːdɪnrɪ] ☐1☐ ADJ ☐a☐ (*usual*) abituale, solito(-a); **in the ordinary way** (*in the normal fashion*) nel solito modo; (*generally*) normalmente, di norma; **in ordinary use** usato(-a) normalmente
☐b☐ (*average*) comune, normale; (*pej*) mediocre, ordinario(-a); **the ordinary Italian** l'italiano qualunque; **the meal was very ordinary** il pranzo non era niente di speciale.
☐2☐ N: **out of the ordinary** diverso(-a) dal solito, fuori dell'ordinario.
♦ **ordinary degree** N corso di laurea di tre anni.
♦ **ordinary seaman** N (*Brit*) marinaio semplice.
♦ **ordinary shares** NPL (*Fin*) azioni *fpl* ordinarie.
or·di·nate [ˈɔːdɪnɪt] N ordinata.
or·di·na·tion [ˌɔːdɪˈneɪʃən] N (*Rel*) ordinazione *f*.
ord·nance [ˈɔːdnəns] (*Mil*) N (*guns*) artiglieria; (*supplies*) materiale *m* militare; **the ordnance** (*department*) il reparto di sussistenza.
♦ **Ordnance Survey map** N (*Brit*) ≈ carta topografica dell'Istituto Geografico Militare.
ore [ɔː] N minerale *m* grezzo; **copper ore** minerale grezzo di rame.
orega·no [ˌɒrɪˈɡɑːnəʊ] N origano.
Orestes [ɒˈrɛstiːz] N Oreste.
or·gan [ˈɔːɡən] N (*all senses*) organo.
or·gan·die, **or·gan·dy** [ˈɔːɡəndɪ] N (*Am*) organdì *m*.

♦ **organ-grinder** [ˈɔːgənˌgraɪndəʳ] N suonatore(-trice) di organetto.

or·gan·ic [ɔːˈgænɪk] ADJ **a** (*gen, also fig*) organico(-a) **b** (*free of chemicals*: *vegetables, food, farming*) biologico (-a); **organic restaurant** ristorante *m* macrobiotico.

or·gani·cal·ly [ɔːˈgænɪkəlɪ] ADV (*affect, develop*) organicamente; (*farm, cultivate*) biologicamente.

or·gan·ism [ˈɔːgəˌnɪzəm] N (*Bio*) organismo.

or·gan·ist [ˈɔːgənɪst] N organista *m/f*.

or·gani·za·tion [ˌɔːgənaɪˈzeɪʃən] N organizzazione *f*; **a charitable organization** un'organizzazione filantropica.

or·gani·za·tion·al [ˌɔːgənaɪˈzeɪʃənl] ADJ organizzativo (-a).

♦ **organization chart** N organigramma *m*.

or·gan·ize [ˈɔːgəˌnaɪz] VT organizzare; **to get organized** organizzarsi.

or·gan·ized [ˈɔːgəˌnaɪzd] ADJ organizzato(-a).

♦ **organized crime** N criminalità organizzata.

♦ **organized labour** N manodopera organizzata (in sindacati).

or·gan·iz·er [ˈɔːgəˌnaɪzəʳ] N organizzatore(-trice).

or·gan·iz·ing [ˈɔːgəˌnaɪzɪŋ] ADJ organizzativo(-a).

♦ **organ loft** N (*Mus*) tribuna dell'organo.

or·gasm [ˈɔːgæzəm] N orgasmo.

or·gas·mic [ɔːˈgæzmɪk] ADJ (*Med*) orgasmico(-a); (*fam*: *exciting*) eccitante.

orgy [ˈɔːdʒɪ] N (*also fig*) orgia.

Ori·ent [ˈɔːrɪənt] N: **the Orient** l'Oriente *m*.

ori·ent [ˈɔːrɪənt], **ori·en·tate** [ˈɔːrɪənˌteɪt] VT orientare; **to orient o.s.** orientarsi.

ori·en·tal [ˌɔːrɪˈentəl] [1] ADJ orientale.

[2] N: **Oriental** orientale *m/f*.

Ori·en·tal·ist [ˌɔːrɪˈentəlɪst] N orientalista *m/f*.

ori·en·ta·tion [ˌɔːrɪənˈteɪʃən] N orientamento.

ori·en·teer·ing [ˌɔːrɪənˈtɪərɪŋ] N (*sport*) gara di orientamento.

ori·fice [ˈɔrɪfɪs] N orifizio.

ori·ga·mi [ˌɒrɪˈgɑːmɪ] N origami *m inv*.

ori·gin [ˈɒrɪdʒɪn] N origine *f*; **country of origin** paese *m* d'origine; **to be of humble origin** *or* **have humble origins** essere di umili origini.

origi·nal [əˈrɪdʒɪnl] [1] ADJ (*gen*) originale; (*inhabitant, form, splendour*) originario(-a).

[2] N (*manuscript, painting etc*) originale *m*; (*garment*) modello originale; (*person*) originale *m/f*; **he reads Homer in the original** legge Omero in lingua originale.

origi·nal·ity [əˌrɪdʒɪˈnælɪtɪ] N originalità.

origi·nal·ly [əˈrɪdʒənəlɪ] ADV (*at first*) originariamente, all'inizio; (*in an original way*) originalmente.

♦ **original sin** N (*Rel*) peccato originale.

origi·nate [əˈrɪdʒɪˌneɪt] [1] VT dare origine a.

[2] VI: **to originate (from)** (*gen*) avere origine (da); (*suggestion, idea*) derivare (da); (*goods*) provenire (da); **to originate (in)** (*river*) nascere (in); (*custom*) avere origine (in).

origi·na·tor [əˈrɪdʒɪˌneɪtəʳ] N ideatore(-trice).

Orion [əˈraɪən] N (*Myth, Astron*) Orione *m*.

Ork·neys [ˈɔːknɪz] NPL: **the Orkneys, the Orkney Islands** le (isole) Orcadi *fpl*.

or·lon® [ˈɔːlɒn] N orlon ® *m inv*.

or·na·ment [*n* ˈɔːnəmənt; *vb* ˈɔːnəˌment] [1] N (*gen*) ornamento; (*vase, figurine*) soprammobile *m*; (*trinket*) ninnolo.

[2] VT ornare, decorare.

or·na·men·tal [ˌɔːnəˈmentl] ADJ ornamentale.

or·na·men·ta·tion [ˌɔːnəmenˈteɪʃən] N (*act*) ornamentazione *f*; (*ornaments*) decorazione *f*.

or·nate [ɔːˈneɪt] ADJ (*decor*) ricco(-a); (*style in writing*) ornato(-a).

or·ni·tho·logi·cal [ˌɔːnɪθəˈlɒdʒɪkəl] ADJ ornitologico(-a).

or·ni·tholo·gist [ˌɔːnɪˈθɒlədʒɪst] N ornitologo(-a).

or·ni·thol·ogy [ˌɔːnɪˈθɒlədʒɪ] N ornitologia.

oro·graph·ic [ˌɒrəʊˈgræfɪk] ADJ orografico(-a).

orog·ra·phy [ɒˈrɒgrəfɪ] N orografia.

or·phan [ˈɔːfən] [1] ADJ, N orfano(-a).

[2] VT: **to be orphaned** restare orfano(-a).

or·phan·age [ˈɔːfənɪdʒ] N orfanotrofio.

Orpheus [ˈɔːfɪəs] N Orfeo.

ortho·cen·tre, (*Am*) **ortho·cen·ter** [ˈɔːθəʊˌsentəʳ] N ortocentro.

ortho·don·tics [ˌɔːθəʊˈdɒntɪks] NSG ortodonzia.

ortho·dox [ˈɔːθəˌdɒks] ADJ ortodosso(-a).

ortho·doxy [ˈɔːθəˌdɒksɪ] N ortodossia.

or·thogo·nal [ɔːˈθɒgənəl] ADJ ortogonale.

or·thog·ra·phy [ɔːˈθɒgrəfɪ] N ortografia.

ortho·paedic, (*Am*) **ortho·pedic** [ˌɔːθəʊˈpiːdɪk] ADJ ortopedico(-a).

ortho·paedics, (*Am*) **ortho·pedics** [ˌɔːθəʊˈpiːdɪks] NSG ortopedia.

ortho·paedist, (*Am*) **ortho·pedist** [ˌɔːθəʊˈpiːdɪst] N ortopedico.

OS [ˌəʊˈes] ABBR (*Brit*) **a** (= *Ordnance Survey*) ≈ I.G.M. *m* (= *Istituto Geografico Militare*) **b** (*Naut*) = **ordinary seaman c** (*clothes*) = **outsize**.

O/S ABBR = **out of stock**.

Os·car [ˈɒskəʳ] N (*film award*) Oscar *m inv*.

os·cil·late [ˈɒsɪˌleɪt] VI oscillare.

os·cil·lat·ing [ˈɒsɪˌleɪtɪŋ] ADJ oscillante.

os·cil·la·tion [ˌɒsɪˈleɪʃən] N oscillazione *f*.

os·cil·la·tor [ˈɒsɪˌleɪtəʳ] N oscillatore *m*.

os·cil·lo·scope [ɒˈsɪləˌskəʊp] N oscilloscopio.

osier [ˈəʊzɪəʳ] N vinco.

Oslo [ˈɒzləʊ] N Oslo *f*.

os·mium [ˈɒzmɪəm] N osmio.

os·mo·sis [ɒzˈməʊsɪs] N osmosi *f*.

os·mot·ic [ɒzˈmɒtɪk] ADJ osmotico(-a).

os·prey [ˈɒspreɪ] N falco pescatore.

os·si·cle [ˈɒsɪkəl] N ossicino.

os·si·fi·ca·tion [ˌɒsɪfɪˈkeɪʃən] N ossificazione *f*; (*fig: of ideas*) fossilizzazione *f*.

os·si·fy [ˈɒsɪˌfaɪ] VI ossificarsi.

os·ten·sible [ɒsˈtensəbl] ADJ apparente; **ostensible reason** pretesto.

os·ten·sibly [ɒsˈtensəblɪ] ADV apparentemente.

os·ten·ta·tion [ˌɒstenˈteɪʃən] N ostentazione *f*.

os·ten·ta·tious [ˌɒstenˈteɪʃəs] ADJ (*lifestyle*) pretenzioso (-a); (*gesture, wealth*) ostentato(-a); **to be ostentatious about sth** ostentare qc.

os·ten·ta·tious·ly [ˌɒstenˈteɪʃəslɪ] ADV con ostentazione.

osteo... [ˈɒstɪəʊ] PREF osteo... .

os·teo·ar·thri·tis [ˌɒstɪəʊɑːˈθraɪtɪs] N osteoartrite *f*.

os·teo·my·eli·tis [ˌɒstɪəʊˌmaɪˈlaɪtɪs] N osteomielite *f*.

os·teo·path [ˈɒstɪəpæθ] N chiroterapista *m/f*.

os·teopa·thy [ˌɒstɪˈɒpəθɪ] N chiroterapia.

os·tra·cism [ˈɒstrəsɪzəm] N (*frm*) ostracismo.

os·tra·cize [ˈɒstrəsaɪz] VT (*frm*) ostracizzare.

os·trich [ˈɒstrɪtʃ] N struzzo.

OT ABBR (*Bible*: = *Old Testament*) V.T. *m* (= *Vecchio Testamento*).

OTB N ABBR (*Am*: = *off-track betting*) *puntate effettuate fuori dagli ippodromi.*

OTE ABBR (= *on-target earnings*) *stipendio (comprese le commissioni) obiettivo di un addetto alle vendite.*

oth·er ['ʌðəʳ] [1] ADJ altro(-a); **the other one** l'altro(-a); **other people** altri, altre persone *fpl*; **some other people have still to arrive** deve ancora arrivare altra gente; **the other day** l'altro giorno; **some other time** un'altra volta, un altro momento; **if there are no other questions** ... se non ci sono altre domande...; **some actor or other** un certo attore; **other people's property** la proprietà altrui. [2] PRON: **the other** l'altro(-a); **the others** gli altri/le altre; **one after the other** uno(-a) dopo l'altro(-a); **are there any others?** ce ne sono altri?; **one or other of them will come** o uno o l'altro verrà; **somebody or other** qualcuno (-a); **no other** (*nobody else*) nessun altro/nessun'altra; (*old*: *nothing else*) nient'altro. [3] ADV: **other (than)** (*differently*) diversamente (da); **he could not act other than as he did** non poteva agire diversamente (da come fece); **somewhere or other** da qualche parte. [4] PREP: **other (than)** (*except*) tranne (che); **nothing other than** nient'altro che; **she never discussed it with anyone other than David** non ne ha parlato con nessun altro a parte *or* all'infuori di David; **none other than** (*no less than*) nientemeno che; **the car was none other than Roberta's** la macchina era proprio di Roberta.

oth·er·ness ['ʌðənɪs] N diversità.

other·wise ['ʌðə‚waɪz] [1] ADV **a** (*in another way*) diversamente; **it cannot be otherwise** non può essere diversamente *or* altrimenti; **she was otherwise engaged** aveva già altri impegni; **except where otherwise stated** salvo indicazione contraria; **whether sold or otherwise** venduto o no **b** (*in other respects*) altrimenti, a parte ciò; **an otherwise good piece of work** un lavoro per il resto buono. [2] CONJ (*if not*) altrimenti, se no.

♦ **other-worldly** [‚ʌðə'wɜːldlɪ] ADJ (*person*) disinteressato (-a) alle cose materiali.

OTT [‚əʊtiː'tiː] ABBR (*fam*) = **over the top**; see **top**.

ot·ter ['ɒtəʳ] N lontra.

OU [‚əʊ'juː] N ABBR (*Brit*) = **Open University**.

ouch [aʊtʃ] EXCL ohi!, ahi!

ought[1] [ɔːt] N = **aught**.

ought[2] [ɔːt] (*pt* **ought**) MODAL AUX VB **a** (*moral obligation*): **I ought to do it** dovrei farlo; **one ought not to do it** non lo si dovrebbe fare; **this ought to have been corrected** questo avrebbe dovuto essere corretto **b** (*vague desirability*): **you ought to go and see it** dovresti andare a vederlo, faresti bene ad andarlo a vedere **c** (*probability*): **that ought to be enough** quello dovrebbe bastare; **he ought to have arrived by now** dovrebbe essere arrivato, ormai; **he ought to win** dovrebbe vincere.

ounce [aʊns] N oncia (= *28, 35 grammi; 16 in una libbra*).

our ['aʊəʳ] POSS ADJ il nostro/la nostra, i nostri/le nostre *pl*; **this is our house** questa è la nostra casa; **at our house** a casa nostra; **our brother** nostro fratello.

ours ['aʊəz] POSS PRON il/la nostro(-a), i/le nostri(-e) *pl*; **a friend of ours** un nostro amico; **theirs is red, ours is green** il loro è rosso, il nostro è verde; **this is ours** questo è (il) nostro.

our·selves [‚aʊə'sɛlvz] PERS PRON (*reflexive*) ci; (*emphatic, after preposition*) noi stessi(-e); **we did it (all) by our-** selves l'abbiamo fatto (tutto) da soli; see also **oneself**.

oust [aʊst] VT: **to oust sb from sth** spodestare qn da qc.

out [aʊt]
[1] ADV
a (*gen*) fuori;
▷**to be out and** *about* **again** (*Brit*) [OR] **to be out and** *around* **again** (*Am*) essere di nuovo in piedi
▷**the** *ball* **is out** (*Sport*) la palla è fuori
▷**out** *here* qui fuori
▷**they're out** *in* **the garden** sono fuori in giardino
▷**Mr Green** *is* **out** il signor Green non c'è *or* è uscito
▷**the** *journey* **out** l'andata
▷**to have a** *night* **out** passare una serata fuori
▷*speak* **out (loud)!** parla forte!
▷**out** *there* là fuori
▷**out** *with* **it!** sputa fuori!
▷**out!** (*Tennis*) fuori!
b (*indicating distance*)
▷**three days out** *from* **Plymouth** (*Naut*) a tre giorni di navigazione da Plymouth
▷**she's out** *in* **Kuwait** è via in Kuwait
▷**the boat was 10** *miles* **out** la barca era a 10 miglia dalla costa
▷**it carried us out** *to* **sea** ci portò al largo
c (*fig*): **to** *be* **out** (*person: unconscious*) essere privo(-a) di sensi; (: *on strike*) essere in sciopero; (: *out of game etc*) essere eliminato(-a); (*out of fashion*) essere out *inv or* passato(-a) di moda; (*have appeared: sun, moon*) splendere; (: *flowers*) sbocciare; (: *news, secret*) essere rivelato(-a); (: *book*) uscire; (*extinguished: fire, light, gas*) essere spento(-a);
▷**she is out and** *away* **the best** è di gran lunga la migliore
▷**it's the** *biggest* **swindle out** è la truffa più grossa che ci sia
▷**I was not** *far* **out** non mi sbagliavo di tanto
▷**he was out** *in* **his reckoning (by 5%)** si sbagliava nei suoi calcoli (del 5%)
▷**the** *tide* **is out** c'è bassa marea
▷**before the** *week* **was out** prima della fine della settimana
d: **to be out** *for* **sth** cercare qc, volere qc;
▷**he's out for** *all* **he can get** sta cercando di trarne il massimo profitto
▷**I'm only out for a good** *time* voglio solo divertirmi
e: **to be out** *to do* **sth** essere deciso(-a) a far qc, cercare di far qc;
▷**they're out** *to get* **me** mi danno la caccia
▷**he's out** *to make* **money** il suo unico scopo è quello di fare soldi.
[2]: **out of** PREP
a (*outside, beyond*) fuori;
▷**to be out of** *danger* essere fuori pericolo
▷**to** *disappear* **out of sight** sparire alla vista
▷**to** *feel* **out of it** (*fam*) sentirsi escluso(-a)
▷**to** *go* **out of the house** uscire di casa
▷**to** *look* **out of the window** guardare fuori dalla finestra
▷**to be out of** *sight* non essere visibile
▷**we're** *well* **out of it** (*fam*) per fortuna ne siamo fuori
b (*cause, motive*) per;
▷**out of** *curiosity* per curiosità

c (*origin, source*) da;
▷**to** *copy* **sth out of a book** copiare qc da un libro
▷**to** *drink* **sth out of a cup** bere qc da una tazza
▷**Blue Ribbon, by Black Rum out of** *Grenada* (*esp Horsebreeding*) Blue Ribbon, figlio di Black Rum e Grenada
▷**a box** *made* **out of wood** una scatola di *or* in legno
▷**it was like** *something* **out of a nightmare** era come in un incubo
▷**to** *take* **sth out of a drawer** prendere qc da un cassetto
d (*from among*) su;
▷*1* **out of every 3 smokers** 1 fumatore su 3
▷*9* **marks out of 10** 9 punti su 10
e (*without*) senza;
▷**to** *be* **out of sth** essere rimasto(-a) senza qc
▷**to be out of** *breath* essere senza fiato
▷**to be out of** *petrol* essere (rimasto(-a)) senza benzina
▷**it's out of** *stock* (*Comm*) non è disponibile.
3 N see **in 3**.
4 VT: **to out** *sb* rivelare pubblicamente l'omosessualità di qn.

out·age ['aʊtɪdʒ] N (*esp Am: power failure*) black-out *m inv*.
♦ **out-and-out** ['aʊtənd'aʊt] ADJ vero(-a) e proprio(-a).
out·back ['aʊtˌbæk] N (*in Australia*) entroterra *m*.
out·bid [ˌaʊt'bɪd] (*pt, pp* outbid) VT offrire di più di.
out·board ['aʊtˌbɔːd] ADJ, N: **outboard (motor)** (motore *m*) fuoribordo *inv*.
out·bound ['aʊtˌbaʊnd] ADJ: **outbound (for** *or* **from)** in partenza (per *or* da).
out·break ['aʊtˌbreɪk] N (*of war*) scoppio; (*of disease*) insorgenza; (*of food poisoning*) epidemia; (*of crime*) ondata; **at the outbreak of war** allo scoppio della guerra.
out·build·ing ['aʊtˌbɪldɪŋ] N costruzione *f* annessa.
out·burst ['aʊtˌbɜːst] N (*of anger*) scoppio; (*of applause*) scroscio.
out·cast ['aʊtˌkɑːst] N reietto(-a); (*socially*) emarginato (-a).
out·class [ˌaʊt'klɑːs] VT surclassare.
out·come ['aʊtˌkʌm] N esito, risultato.
out·crop ['aʊtˌkrɒp] N affioramento.
out·cry ['aʊtˌkraɪ] N protesta; **to raise an outcry about sth** protestare contro qc.
out·dat·ed [ˌaʊt'deɪtɪd] ADJ (*idea*) antiquato(-a), sorpassato(-a); (*custom, clothes*) fuori moda.
out·did [ˌaʊt'dɪd] PT of **outdo**.
out·distance [ˌaʊt'dɪstəns] VT distanziare.
out·do [ˌaʊt'duː] (*pt* outdid, *pp* outdone [ˌaʊt'dʌn]) VT: **to outdo sb (in)** superare qn (in); **he was not to be outdone** non voleva essere da meno.
out·door ['aʊtˌdɔːʳ] ADJ (*activity*) all'aperto; (*life*) all'aria aperta; (*swimming pool*) scoperto(-a); (*clothes*) pesante.
out·doors [ˌaʊt'dɔːz] 1 ADV (*go*) fuori; (*live, sleep*) all'aria aperta.
2 NSG: **the great outdoors** l'aria aperta.
out·er ['aʊtəʳ] ADJ esterno(-a); **outer suburbs** estrema periferia.
outer·most ['aʊtəˌməʊst] ADJ estremo(-a), più lontano (-a).
♦ **outer space** N spazio cosmico; **a creature from outer space** un/una extraterrestre *m/f*.

out·fit ['aʊtˌfɪt] N a (*clothes*) completo; (*for sports*) tenuta; (*for dressing up*) costume *m* b (*equipment*) attrezzatura c (*fam: organization*) organizzazione *f*.
out·fit·ter ['aʊtˌfɪtəʳ] N: **"(gent's) outfitters"** (*Brit*) "confezioni *mpl* da uomo"; **sports outfitter's** negozio di articoli sportivi.
out·flank [ˌaʊt'flæŋk] VT (*Mil*) aggirare; (*outdo*) prendere in contropiede.
out·flow ['aʊtˌfləʊ] N (*for liquid*) scarico.
out·fox [ˌaʊt'fɒks] VT superare in astuzia.
out·go·ing ['aʊtˌgəʊɪŋ] ADJ a (*president, tenant*) uscente; (*means of transport*) in partenza b (*character*) socievole, estroverso(-a).
out·go·ings ['aʊtˌgəʊɪŋz] NPL (*Brit: expenses*) spese *fpl*, uscite *fpl*.
out·grow [ˌaʊt'grəʊ] VT (*pt* outgrew [ˌaʊt'gruː], *pp* outgrown [ˌaʊt'grəʊn]) (*clothes*) diventare troppo grande per; (*habit, attitude*) perdere (col tempo).
out·growth ['aʊtˌgrəʊθ] N sviluppo.
out·house ['aʊtˌhaʊs] N = **outbuilding**.
out·ing ['aʊtɪŋ] N gita, escursione *f*.
out·land·ish [aʊt'lændɪʃ] ADJ (*dress, person*) bizzarro(-a).
out·last [ˌaʊt'lɑːst] VT sopravvivere a.
out·law ['aʊtˌlɔː] 1 N fuorilegge *m/f inv*.
2 VT (*person, practice*) bandire.
out·lay ['aʊtˌleɪ] N spesa.
out·let ['aʊtlɛt] 1 N (*for water, sewage*) scarico; (*for air*) sfogo; (*of river*) foce *f*; (*Comm*) mercato; (: *also:* **retail outlet**) punto *m* (di) vendita *inv*; (*Am Elec*) presa di corrente; (*fig: for emotion, talents*) (valvola di) sfogo.
2 ADJ (*Tech*) di scarico.
out·line ['aʊtˌlaɪn] 1 N (*of object*) contorno; (*of face, building*) profilo; (*summary, general idea*) abbozzo; **outlines** NPL aspetti *mpl* generali; **give me the broad outline(s)** spiegamelo a grandi linee.
2 VT (*theory, plan, idea*) abbozzare; (*book, event, facts*) descrivere a grandi linee; **to be outlined against sth** (*in silhouette*) stagliarsi contro qc.
out·live [ˌaʊt'lɪv] VT sopravvivere a.
out·look ['aʊtˌlʊk] N (*view*) vista, veduta; (*prospects*) prospettive *fpl*; (*opinion*) visione *f*, concezione *f*; **the outlook for next Saturday is sunny** si prevede bel tempo per sabato prossimo.
out·ly·ing ['aʊtˌlaɪɪŋ] ADJ (*distant*) fuori mano; (*outside town boundary*) periferico(-a).
out·ma·noeu·vre, (*Am*) **out·ma·neu·ver** [ˌaʊtmə'nuːvəʳ] VT (*Mil*) superare strategicamente; (*fig: rival, opposition*) surclassare.
out·mod·ed [ˌaʊt'məʊdɪd] ADJ = **outdated**.
out·num·ber [ˌaʊt'nʌmbəʳ] VT superare numericamente.
♦ **out-of-court** ['aʊtəv'kɔːt] 1 ADJ (*settlement*) extragiudiziale.
2 ADV (*settle*) senza ricorrere al tribunale.
♦ **out-of-date** [ˌaʊtəv'deɪt] ADJ (*passport, ticket*) scaduto (-a); (*theory, idea*) sorpassato(-a), superato(-a); (*custom*) antiquato(-a); (*clothes*) fuori moda.
♦ **out-of-doors** [ˌaʊtəv'dɔːz] ADV = **outdoors**.
♦ **out-of-pocket** [ˌaʊtəv'pɒkɪt] ADJ (*person*) a corto di soldi; **out-of-pocket expenses** spese *fpl* extra *inv*.
♦ **out-of-the-way** [ˌaʊtəvðə'weɪ] ADJ (*remote*) fuori mano; (*unusual*) insolito(-a).
♦ **out-of-work** [ˌaʊtəv'wɜːk] ADJ (*actor*) disoccupato(-a).
out·pace [ˌaʊt'peɪs] VT distanziare.
out·pa·tient ['aʊtˌpeɪʃənt] N paziente *m/f* esterno(-a); **outpatients' department** ambulatorio (*all'interno di un*

ospedale).

out·post ['aʊt,pəʊst] N (*Mil, fig*) avamposto.

out·pour·ing ['aʊt,pɔːrɪŋ] N (*fig*) torrente *m*.

out·put ['aʊt,pʊt] ⊡ N (*of machine, factory*) produzione *f*; (*of person*) rendimento; (*of computer*) output *m inv*, dati *mpl* in uscita; (*Elec*) erogazione *f*.
⊡ VT (*Comput*) emettere.

out·rage ['aʊt,reɪdʒ] ⊡ N (*wicked, violent deed*) atrocità *f inv*; (*emotion*) sdegno; **bomb outrage** attentato dinamitardo; **it caused a public outrage** ha provocato uno scandalo; **an outrage against good taste** un oltraggio al buon gusto; **an outrage against humanity** un crimine contro l'umanità; **it's an outrage!** è una vergogna!
⊡ VT offendere; **to be outraged by sth** essere scandalizzato(-a) da qc.

out·ra·geous [aʊt'reɪdʒəs] ADJ (*language, joke: offensive*) scioccante; (*price*) esorbitante; (*clothes*) stravagante; (*crime*) atroce; **it's outrageous that ...** è scandaloso che... .

out·ra·geous·ly [aʊt'reɪdʒəslɪ] ADV (*see adj*) in modo scioccante; in modo stravagante; in modo atroce; (*expensive*) terribilmente.

out·ran [,aʊt'ræn] PT of **outrun**.

out·rid·er ['aʊt,raɪdəʳ] N (*on motorcycle*) battistrada *m inv*.

out·right [*adv* ,aʊt'raɪt; *adj* 'aʊt,raɪt] ⊡ ADV (*kill*) sul colpo; (*win*) nettamente; (*own*) completamente; (*buy*) tutto(-a) in una volta; (*refuse, reject*) categoricamente.
⊡ ADJ (*winner, refusal*) netto(-a); (*liar, selfishness*) bell'e buono(-a).

out·run [,aʊt'rʌn] (*pt* **outran**, *pp* **outrun**) VT superare (nella corsa); (*fig*) superare.

out·sell [,aʊt'sɛl] VT (*product*): **to outsell sth** vendersi meglio di qc.

out·set ['aʊt,sɛt] N: **at the outset** all'inizio.

out·shine [,aʊt'ʃaɪn] (*pt, pp* **outshone** [,aʊt'ʃɒn]) VT (*fig*) eclissare.

out·side [,aʊt'saɪd] ⊡ ADV fuori, all'esterno; **to be/go outside** stare/andare fuori; **seen from outside** visto(-a) dall'esterno *or* da fuori.
⊡ PREP **a** fuori di, all'esterno di; **the car outside the house** la macchina fuori della casa; **he waited outside the door** aspettò fuori della porta; **outside the city** fuori (della) città; **don't go outside the garden** non uscire dal giardino
b (*not included in*) al di fuori di; **he has no interests outside his job** non ha altri interessi al di fuori del lavoro; **it's outside my experience** non ne ho una conoscenza diretta.
⊡ ADJ **a** (*exterior*) esterno(-a); **an outside seat** (*in bus, plane*) un posto vicino al corridoio; **outside contractor** appaltatore *m* esterno; **to get an outside opinion** chiedere un parere imparziale
b (*maximum: price*) massimo(-a), massimale
c (*remote, unlikely*): **an outside chance** una vaga possibilità.
⊡ N esterno, esteriore *m*; **to overtake on the outside** (*Aut*) ≈ sorpassare sulla sinistra; **judging from the outside** (*fig*) a giudicare dalle apparenze; **at the (very) outside** (*fig*) al massimo.

♦ **outside broadcast** N (*Radio, TV*) trasmissione *f* in esterni.

♦ **outside lane** N (*Aut*) ≈ corsia di sorpasso.

♦ **outside left** N (*Ftbl*) ala sinistra.

♦ **outside line** N (*Telec*) linea esterna.

out·sid·er [,aʊt'saɪdəʳ] N (*stranger*) estraneo(-a); (*in racing,*

contest) outsider *m/f inv*.

♦ **outside right** N (*Ftbl*) ala destra.

out·size ['aʊt,saɪz] ADJ (*gen*) gigante; (*clothes*) per taglie forti; **outsize department** reparto taglie forti.

out·sized ['aʊt,saɪzd] ADJ enorme, gigantesco(-a).

out·skirts ['aʊt,skɜːts] NPL (*of town*) sobborghi *mpl*, periferia *fsg*; (*of wood*) limitare *msg*, margine *msg*.

out·smart [,aʊt'smɑːt] VT superare in astuzia.

out·spo·ken [,aʊt'spəʊkən] ADJ franco(-a), senza peli sulla lingua (*fam*).

out·spo·ken·ly [,aʊt'spəʊkənlɪ] ADV (*support, condemn*) apertamente; **outspokenly in favour of** apertamente in favore di.

out·spo·ken·ness [,aʊt'spəʊkənnɪs] N il parlare franco.

out·spread ['aʊt,sprɛd] ADJ (*gen*) aperto(-a); (*wings*) spiegato(-a).

out·stand·ing [,aʊt'stændɪŋ] ADJ **a** (*exceptional*) eccezionale; (: *feature*) saliente
b (*not settled: bill*) non pagato(-a); (: *problem*) irrisolto(-a); **the work is still outstanding** il lavoro non è ancora stato finito; **your account is still outstanding** deve ancora saldare il conto.

out·stand·ing·ly [,aʊt'stændɪŋlɪ] ADV eccezionalmente.

out·stay [,aʊt'steɪ] VT: **to outstay sb** trattenersi più a lungo di qn; **to outstay one's welcome** abusare dell'ospitalità di qn.

out·stretched [,aʊt'strɛtʃt] ADJ (*body, legs*) disteso(-a), steso(-a); (*hand*) teso(-a); **with outstretched arms** a braccia aperte.

out·strip [,aʊt'strɪp] VT (*also fig*) superare.

♦ **out·tray** ['aʊt,treɪ] N *vassoio per la corrispondenza e gli ordini da evadere*.

out·vote [,aʊt'vəʊt] VT: **it was outvoted (by …)** fu respinto (con una maggioranza di...); **I wanted to go dancing but I was outvoted** volevo andare a ballare ma mi hanno messo in minoranza.

out·ward ['aʊtwəd] ADJ **a** (*movement*) verso l'esterno; **on the outward journey** durante il viaggio di andata **b** (*sign, appearances*) esteriore; **with an outward show of interest** mostrando un apparente interesse.

out·ward·ly ['aʊtwədlɪ] ADV (*on the surface*) esteriormente; (*apparently*) apparentemente.

out·wards, out·ward ['aʊtwəd(z)] ADV verso l'esterno; **outward bound** in partenza.

out·wash ['aʊt,wɒʃ] N depositi *mpl* fluvio-glaciali.

out·weigh [,aʊt'weɪ] VT avere maggior peso di.

out·wit [,aʊt'wɪt] VT essere più furbo(-a) di.

out·worn ['aʊtwɔːn] ADJ (*idea, expression*) trito(-a); (*custom*) sorpassato(-a).

ouzo ['uːzəʊ] N *liquore greco a base di anice*.

oval ['əʊvəl] ADJ, N ovale (*m*).

♦ **Oval Office** N *ufficio del Presidente degli Stati Uniti presso la Casa Bianca*.

ovar·ian [əʊ'vɛərɪən] ADJ ovarico(-a).

ova·ry ['əʊvərɪ] N (*Anat*) ovaia; (*Bot*) ovario.

ova·tion [əʊ'veɪʃən] N ovazione *f*.

oven ['ʌvn] N forno; **in the oven** al forno; **it's like an oven in there** è un forno lì dentro.

♦ **oven glove** N guanto da forno.

oven·proof ['ʌvn,pruːʃ] ADJ: **ovenproof dish** pirofila.

♦ **oven-ready** [,ʌvn'rɛdɪ] ADJ pronto(-a) da infornare.

oven·ware ['ʌvn,wɛəʳ] N pirofile *fpl*.

over ['əʊvəʳ] ⊡ ADV **a** (*across*): **over here** qui; **over there** laggiù, là; **over in France** in Francia; **he's over from France for a few days** è venuto dalla Francia per alcuni

giorni; **over against the wall** (lì *or* là) contro il muro; **the little boy went over to his mother** il bambino andò da sua madre; **to drive over to the other side of town** andare (in macchina) dall'altra parte della città; **can you come over tonight?** puoi venire da me (*or* noi) stasera?; **over to you!** (*TV, Radio*) a te (la linea) !; **now over to our Paris correspondent** diamo ora la linea al nostro corrispondente da Parigi; **to go over to the enemy** passare al nemico

b (*everywhere*): **the world over** in tutto il mondo; **I ache all over** mi fa male dappertutto; **I looked all over for you** ti ho cercato dappertutto; **that's him all over** è proprio da lui

c (*indicating movement from one side to another, from upright position*): **to turn sth over (and over)** girare (e rigirare) qc; **she hit me and over I went** mi ha colpito e sono caduto

d (*finished*) finito(-a); **the rain is over** la pioggia è cessata; **the danger was soon over** il pericolo cessò presto; **it's all over between us** tra noi è tutto finito

e (*again*): **to tell over and over** dire mille volte; **to start (all) over again** ricominciare da capo; **several times over** diverse volte

f (*excessively*) molto, troppo; **she's not over intelligent** (*Brit*) non è molto intelligente

g (*remaining*) rimasto(-a); **there are three over** ne sono rimasti tre; **is there any cake left over?** è rimasta della torta?

h (*more*): **persons of 21 and over** persone dai 21 anni in su

i (*esp in signalling and radio*): **over and out** passo e chiudo.

2 PREP **a** (*on top of, above*) su; **to spread a sheet over sth** stendere un lenzuolo su qc; **over my head** sopra la mia testa; **his speech went over my head** (*fig*) il suo discorso era troppo complicato per me; **he's over me** è un mio superiore; **to have an advantage over sb** avere un vantaggio su qn

b (*across*): **the pub over the road** il pub di fronte; **it's over the river** è al di là del fiume; **the bridge over the river** il ponte sul fiume; **the ball went over the wall** la palla andò al di là del muro; **over the page** alla pagina seguente

c (*everywhere in/on*): **all over the world** in tutto il mondo; **you've got mud all over your shoes** hai le scarpe tutte infangate

d (*more than*): **over 200** più di 200; **he must be over 60** deve aver superato i 60; **over and above normal requirements** oltre ai soliti requisiti; **an increase of 5% over last year's total** un aumento del 5% rispetto al totale dell'anno scorso

e (*during*) durante, nel corso di; **over the last few years** nel corso degli ultimi anni; **over the winter** durante l'inverno; **let's discuss it over dinner** discutiamone a cena; **how long will you be over it?** quanto tempo ti prenderà?

f (*means*): **I heard it over the radio** l'ho sentito alla radio

g (*about, concerning*): **they fell out over money** litigarono per una questione di denaro.

over... ['əʊvə'] PREF, E.G.: **overabundance** N sovrabbondanza; **overprotective** ADJ superprotettivo(-a).

over·abun·dant [,əʊvərə'bʌndənt] ADJ sovrabbondante.

over·act [,əʊvər'ækt] VI recitare con troppa enfasi.

over·ac·tive [,əʊvər'æktɪv] ADJ troppo attivo(-a); (*imagi-*

nation) sbrigliato(-a); **she's got an overactive thyroid** soffre di ipertiroidismo.

over·all [,əʊvər'ɔːl] **1** ADJ (*improvement*) generale; (*width, length*) totale; **overall dimensions** (*Aut*) ingombro; **overall placings** (*Sport*) classifica generale.
2 ADV nell'insieme, complessivamente.
3 N (*Brit*) camice *m*.
♦ **overall majority** N maggioranza assoluta.

over·alls ['əʊvərɔːlz] NPL tuta (da lavoro).

over·anx·ious [,əʊvər'æŋkʃəs] ADJ troppo ansioso(-a).

over·arch [,əʊvər'ɑːtʃ] VT formare un arco sopra.

over·ate [,əʊvər'eɪt] PT of **overeat**.

over·awe [,əʊvər'ɔː] VT intimidire.

over·bal·ance [,əʊvə'bæləns] **1** VI sbilanciarsi.
2 VT sbilanciare.

over·bear·ing [,əʊvə'bɛərɪŋ] ADJ autoritario(-a), prepotente.

over·board ['əʊvə,bɔːd] ADV (*Naut*) fuori bordo; **to fall overboard** cadere in mare; **man overboard!** uomo in mare!; **to go overboard for sth** (*fig*) impazzire per qc.

over·book [,əʊvə'bʊk] VI, VT *accettare troppe prenotazioni rispetto alla disponibilità di posti.*

over·bur·den [,əʊvə'bɜːdn] VT sovraccaricare.

over·came [,əʊvə'keɪm] PT of **overcome**.

over·capi·tal·ize [,əʊvə'kæpɪtə,laɪz] VT (*Fin*) sovraccapitalizzare.

over·cast ['əʊvə,kɑːst] ADJ nuvoloso(-a), coperto(-a).

over·cau·tious [,əʊvə'kɔːʃəs] ADJ troppo cauto(-a).

over·cau·tious·ness [,əʊvə'kɔːʃəsnɪs] N eccessiva cautela.

over·charge [,əʊvə'tʃɑːdʒ] VT **a** : **to overcharge sb for sth** far pagare troppo qc a qn **b** (*Elec*) sovraccaricare.

over·coat ['əʊvə,kəʊt] N (*light*) soprabito; (*heavy*) cappotto.

over·come [,əʊvə'kʌm] (*pt* **overcame**, *pp* **overcome**) VT (*enemies*) sopraffare; (*obstacle, difficulty*) superare; (*rage, temptation*) vincere; (*sb's doubts*) dissolvere; **to be overcome by the heat** essere sopraffatto(-a) dall'afa; **to be overcome by remorse** essere preso(-a) dal rimorso; **overcome with grief** sopraffatto(-a) dal dolore; **she was quite overcome by the occasion** era oltremodo emozionata per l'evento.

over·con·fi·dence [,əʊvə'kɒnfɪdəns] N eccessiva sicurezza (di sé), presunzione *f*.

over·con·fi·dent [,əʊvə'kɒnfɪdənt] ADJ troppo sicuro(-a) (di sé), presuntuoso(-a).

over·cook [,əʊvə'kʊk] VT far cuocere troppo.

over·crowd·ed [,əʊvə'kraʊdɪd] ADJ sovraffollato(-a).

over·crowd·ing [,əʊvə'kraʊdɪŋ] N (*in prison, housing*) sovraffollamento; (*in bus*) calca.

over·do [,əʊvə'duː] (*pt* **overdid** [,əʊvə'dɪd], *pp* **overdone**) VT **a** (*exaggerate*) esagerare; **don't overdo these exercises** cerca di non strafare con questi esercizi (di ginnastica); **to overdo it** *or* **things** (*work too hard*) lavorare troppo; (*convalescent*) affaticarsi troppo **b** (*cook too long*) (far) cuocere troppo.

over·done [,əʊvə'dʌn] **1** PP of **overdo**.
2 ADJ (*exaggerated*) esagerato(-a); (*overcooked*) troppo cotto(-a).

over·dose ['əʊvə,dəʊs] N overdose *f inv*.

over·draft ['əʊvə,drɑːft] N (*Fin*) scoperto (di conto); **to have an overdraft at the bank** avere il conto scoperto.

over·draw [,əʊvə'drɔː] (*pt* **overdrew** [,əʊvə'druː], *pp* **overdrawn** [,əʊvə'drɔːn]) VI avere il conto scoperto.

over·drawn [,əʊvə'drɔːn] ADJ (*account*) scoperto(-a); **to be**

overdrawn avere il conto scoperto; **I'm £200 overdrawn** sono in rosso di 200 sterline.

over·dress [ˌəʊvə'drɛs] VI vestirsi in modo troppo elegante; **don't you think you're a bit overdressed?** non pensi di essere un po' troppo elegante?

over·drive ['əʊvəˌdraɪv] N (Aut) overdrive m inv.

over·due [ˌəʊvə'dju:] ADJ (bill, rent) arretrato(-a); (library book) col prestito scaduto; (train, bus) in ritardo; (recognition) tardivo(-a); (fam: baby, period) in ritardo; **she's a week overdue** (pregnant woman) è in ritardo di una settimana (sulla data prevista del parto); **this work is 2 days overdue** questo lavoro andava consegnato 2 giorni fa; **that change was long overdue** quel cambiamento ci voleva da tempo.

over·eat [ˌəʊvər'i:t] (pt overate, pp overeaten) VI mangiare troppo.

over·eat·ing [ˌəʊvər'i:tɪŋ] N iperalimentazione f; **obesity is only partly caused by overeating** l'obesità è causata solo parzialmente dall'iperalimentazione.

over·em·pha·sis [ˌəʊvər'ɛmfəsɪs] N: **overemphasis on sth** importanza eccessiva data a qc.

over·em·pha·size [ˌəʊvər'ɛmfəˌsaɪz] VT dare troppa enfasi a; **to overemphasize the importance of sth** esagerare l'importanza di qc.

over·es·ti·mate [ˌəʊvər'ɛstɪˌmeɪt] VT (value, amount) sovrastimare; (fig: person, qualities) sopravvalutare.

over·es·ti·ma·tion [ˌəʊvərɛstɪ'meɪʃən] N sopravvalutazione f.

over·ex·cit·ed [ˌəʊvərɪk'saɪtɪd] ADJ sovraeccitato(-a).

over·ex·ert [ˌəʊvərɪg'zɜːt] VI: **to overexert o.s.** sovraffaticarsi.

over·ex·er·tion [ˌəʊvərɪg'zɜːʃən] N iperaffaticamento, surmenage m inv.

over·ex·pose [ˌəʊvərɪks'pəʊz] VT (Phot) sovraesporre.

over·feed [ˌəʊvə'fiːd] (pt, pp overfed [ˌəʊvə'fɛd]) VT sovralimentare.

over·feed·ing [ˌəʊvə'fiːdɪŋ] N sovralimentazione f.

over·flow [n 'əʊvəˌfləʊ; vb ˌəʊvə'fləʊ] **1** N (also: **overflow pipe**) troppopieno; (fig: people): **the overflow filled the courtyard** quelli che non riuscirono ad entrare si accalcarono nel cortile.
2 VI (gen) traboccare; (river) straripare; (people) riversarsi; **the theatre was overflowing with people** il teatro traboccava di gente.

over·fly [ˌəʊvə'flaɪ] (pt overflew [ˌəʊvə'fluː], pp overflown [ˌəʊvə'fləʊn]) VT sorvolare.

over·full [ˌəʊvə'fʊl] ADJ troppo pieno(-a).

over·gen·er·ous [ˌəʊvə'dʒɛnərəs] ADJ troppo generoso (-a).

over·grown ['əʊvə'grəʊn] ADJ (garden): **overgrown with weeds/ivy** coperto(-a) di erbacce/edera; **he's just an overgrown schoolboy** è proprio un bambinone.

over·hang [vb 'əʊvə'hæŋ; n 'əʊvəˌhæŋ] (vb: pt, pp overhung) **1** VT sporgere da.
2 VI sporgere.
3 N strapiombo.

over·hang·ing ['əʊvə'hæŋɪŋ] ADJ sporgente.

over·haul [n 'əʊvəˌhɔːl; vb ˌəʊvə'hɔːl] **1** N revisione f.
2 VT (service: machine) revisionare; (revise: system, method) rivedere.

over·head [adv ˌəʊvə'hɛd; adj 'əʊvəˌhɛd] **1** ADV in alto.
2 ADJ (railway) sopraelevato(-a); (cable) aereo(-a); **overhead shot** (Tennis) schiacciata; **overhead valve** (Aut) valvola in testa.
♦ **overhead projector** N lavagna luminosa.

over·heads ['əʊvəˌhɛdz] NPL (Brit) costi mpl di gestione.

over·hear [ˌəʊvə'hɪə'] (pt, pp overheard [ˌəʊvə'hɜːd]) VT (accidentally) sentire per caso; (deliberately) ascoltare; **she was overheard complaining** qualcuno l'ha sentita lamentarsi.

over·heat [ˌəʊvə'hiːt] **1** VI (engine, brakes) surriscaldarsi.
2 VT surriscaldare.

over·heat·ed [ˌəʊvə'hiːtɪd] ADJ (debate) surriscaldato(-a); (person: angry) arrabbiato(-a).

over·hung ['əʊvə'hʌŋ] PT, PP of **overhang**.

over·joyed [ˌəʊvə'dʒɔɪd] ADJ: **overjoyed (at)** pazzo(-a) di gioia (per).

over·kill ['əʊvəˌkɪl] N (Mil) potenziale m (nucleare) superiore al necessario; (fig) esagerazione f.

over·land ['əʊvəˌlænd] ADV, ADJ per via di terra.

over·lap [n 'əʊvəˌlæp; vb ˌəʊvə'læp] **1** N sovrapposizione f; (fig) coincidenza.
2 VI sovrapporsi; (fig) coincidere.
3 VT sovrapporre.

over·lay [ˌəʊvə'leɪ] (pt, pp overlaid [ˌəʊvə'leɪd]) VT ricoprire.

over·leaf [ˌəʊvə'liːf] ADV a tergo.

over·load [n 'əʊvəˌləʊd; vb ˌəʊvə'ləʊd] **1** N sovraccarico.
2 VT sovraccaricare.

over·look [ˌəʊvə'lʊk] VT **a** (subj: building) dare su; **our garden is not overlooked** nel nostro giardino nessuno ci può vedere **b** (not notice) lasciarsi sfuggire, trascurare; (tolerate) chiudere un occhio su, passare sopra a.

over·lord ['əʊvəˌlɔːd] N capo supremo.

over·ly ['əʊvəlɪ] ADV (old, Am) troppo.

over·manned [ˌəʊvə'mænd] ADJ: **to be overmanned** avere un'eccedenza di personale.

over·man·ning [ˌəʊvə'mænɪŋ] N esubero di manodopera.

over·much [ˌəʊvə'mʌtʃ] (frm) **1** ADV troppo.
2 ADJ troppo(-a).

over·night ['əʊvə'naɪt] **1** ADV (happen) durante la notte; (travel) di notte; (fig: quickly) da un giorno all'altro; **to stay overnight** fermarsi a dormire; **he stayed there overnight** ha passato la notte lì; **he'll be away overnight** passerà la notte fuori; **we can't solve this one overnight** non possiamo risolvere questo da un giorno all'altro.
2 ADJ (journey) di notte; (fig: success) istantaneo(-a), fulmineo(-a); **this'll mean an overnight stay at Calais** questo significa che dovremo passare la notte a Calais.
♦ **over·night bag** N borsa da viaggio.

over·paid [ˌəʊvə'peɪd] PT, PP of **overpay**.

over·par·ticu·lar [ˌəʊvəpə'tɪkjʊlə'] ADJ (on rules) pignolo (-a); **not to be overparticular about sth** (be indifferent) non badare molto or troppo a qc.

over·pass ['əʊvəˌpɑːs] N (Am) cavalcavia m inv.

over·pay [ˌəʊvə'peɪ] (pt, pp overpaid) VT strapagare; **to overpay sb by £50** pagare 50 sterline in più a qn.

over·pay·ment [ˌəʊvə'peɪmənt] N pagamento eccessivo.

over·play [ˌəʊvə'pleɪ] VT dare troppa importanza a; **to overplay one's hand** sopravvalutare la propria posizione.

over·popu·lated [ˌəʊvə'pɒpjʊˌleɪtɪd] ADJ sovrappopolato (-a).

over·popu·la·tion [ˌəʊvəˌpɒpjʊ'leɪʃən] N sovrappopolazione f.

over·pow·er [ˌəʊvə'paʊə'] VT sopraffare.

over·pow·er·ing [ˌəʊvə'paʊərɪŋ] ADJ (smell, heat) asfissiante, soffocante; (desire) irrefrenabile, irresistibile.

over·priced [ˌəʊvə'praɪst] ADJ (pej): **it's overpriced** costa

troppo per quello che è.

over·pro·duc·tion [ˌəʊvəprə'dʌkʃən] N sovrapproduzione f.

over·rate [ˌəʊvə'reɪt] VT sopravvalutare.

over·reach [ˌəʊvə'riːtʃ] VT: **to overreach o.s.** volere strafare.

over·react [ˌəʊvəri:'ækt] VI reagire in modo esagerato.

over·ride [ˌəʊvə'raɪd] (pt overrode [ˌəʊvə'rəʊd], pp overridden [ˌəʊvə'rɪdn]) VT (law) calpestare; (person) scavalcare; (decision) annullare; (sb's wishes, orders) non tener conto di; (Tech: cancel) annullare.

over·rid·ing [ˌəʊvə'raɪdɪŋ] ADJ (factor) preponderante; (importance) essenziale.

over·ripe [ˌəʊvə'raɪp] ADJ troppo maturo(-a).

over·rule [ˌəʊvə'ruːl] VT (person) prevalere su; (request, claim) respingere; (decision) annullare.

over·run [ˌəʊvə'rʌn] (pt overran [ˌəʊvə'ræn], pp overrun) 1 VT (Mil: country) invadere, occupare; (time limit) superare; **the town is overrun with tourists** la città è invasa dai turisti. 2 VI (meeting, event) protrarsi.

over·seas [ˌəʊvə'siːz] 1 ADV (abroad) all'estero; **visitors from overseas** visitatori stranieri. 2 ADJ (countries) d'oltremare; (foreign) straniero(-a); (: trade, market) estero(-a).

over·see [ˌəʊvə'siː] (pt oversaw [ˌəʊvə'sɔː], pp overseen [ˌəʊvə'siːn]) VT sorvegliare.

over·seer ['əʊvəˌsɪə] N sorvegliante m/f; (foreman) caposquadra m.

over·sell [ˌəʊvə'sɛl] VT (praise excessively) dare eccessivo valore a.

over·sexed [ˌəʊvə'sɛkst] ADJ (pej): **he's oversexed** pensa solo al sesso.

over·shad·ow [ˌəʊvə'ʃædəʊ] VT (fig) eclissare.

over·shoot [ˌəʊvə'ʃuːt] (pt, pp overshot [ˌəʊvə'ʃɒt]) VT (destination) superare.

over·sight ['əʊvəˌsaɪt] N (omission) svista; **due to an oversight** per una svista.

over·sim·pli·fi·ca·tion [ˌəʊvəˌsɪmplɪfɪ'keɪʃən] N eccessiva semplificazione f.

over·sim·pli·fy [ˌəʊvə'sɪmplɪˌfaɪ] VT semplificare troppo.

over·size(d) [ˌəʊvə'saɪz(d)] ADJ (gen) troppo grande; (class, family) troppo numeroso(-a).

over·sleep [ˌəʊvə'sliːp] (pt, pp overslept [ˌəʊvə'slɛpt]) VI non svegliarsi in tempo.

over·spend [ˌəʊvə'spɛnd] (pt, pp overspent [ˌəʊvə'spɛnt]) VI spendere troppo; **we have overspent by 5,000 dollars** abbiamo speso 5.000 dollari di troppo.

over·spill ['əʊvəˌspɪl] N (Brit: population) eccedenza di popolazione; **an overspill town** ≈ una città satellite.

over·staffed [ˌəʊvə'stɑːft] ADJ: **to be overstaffed** avere troppo personale.

over·staffing [ˌəʊvə'stɑːfɪŋ] N eccedenza di personale.

over·state [ˌəʊvə'steɪt] VT: **to overstate one's case** esagerare nel presentare le proprie ragioni.

over·state·ment [ˌəʊvə'steɪtmənt] N esagerazione f.

over·stay [ˌəʊvə'steɪ] VT: **to overstay one's welcome** trattenersi troppo a lungo (come ospite).

over·steer [ˌəʊvə'stɪə] VI (Aut) sovrasterzare.

over·step [ˌəʊvə'stɛp] VT: **to overstep the mark** superare ogni limite.

over·stock [ˌəʊvə'stɒk] VT sovrapprovvigionare, sovraimmagazzinare.

over·stretched [ˌəʊvə'strɛtʃt] ADJ (person) sovraccarico(-a); (resources, budget) arrivato(-a) al limite.

over·strike ['əʊvəˌstraɪk] 1 N (Typ) sovrapposizione f (di caratteri). 2 VT sovrapporre.

overt [əʊ'vɜːt] ADJ evidente, aperto(-a).

over·take [ˌəʊvə'teɪk] (pt overtook [ˌəʊvə'tʊk], pp overtaken [ˌəʊvə'teɪkən]) 1 VT (catch up) raggiungere; (pass) superare; **events have overtaken us** gli eventi ci hanno colto di sorpresa. 2 VI sorpassare.

over·tak·ing [ˌəʊvə'teɪkɪŋ] N (Aut) sorpasso; **"no overtaking"** "divieto di sorpasso".

over·tax [ˌəʊvə'tæks] VT (Fin) imporre tasse eccessive a; (fig: strength, patience) mettere a dura prova; **to overtax o.s.** abusare delle proprie forze.

over·throw [n 'əʊvəˌθrəʊ; vb ˌəʊvə'θrəʊ] (vb: pt overthrew [ˌəʊvə'θruː], pp overthrown [ˌəʊvə'θrəʊn]) 1 N (of government etc) rovesciamento. 2 VT (king, system, government) rovesciare.

over·time ['əʊvəˌtaɪm] N (lavoro) straordinario; **to do** or **work overtime** fare lo straordinario; **your imagination has been working overtime!** (fam) corri un po' troppo con la fantasia!

♦ **overtime ban** N rifiuto sindacale di fare gli straordinari.

over·tired [ˌəʊvə'taɪəd] ADJ stanchissimo(-a), sovraffaticato(-a).

overt·ly [əʊ'vɜːtlɪ] ADV apertamente.

over·tone ['əʊvəˌtəʊn] N a OFTEN PL (fig) sfumatura b (Mus): **overtones** NPL armoniche fpl superiori, ipertoni mpl.

over·ture ['əʊvəˌtjʊə] N a (Mus) ouverture f inv b : **to make overtures to sb** (fig: friendly) comportarsi amichevolmente verso qn; (: romantic) tentare un approccio con qn, fare delle avances a qn.

over·turn [ˌəʊvə'tɜːn] 1 VT (car, boat, chair) capovolgere, ribaltare; (government, regime) rovesciare; (Law: decision) annullare, cassare. 2 VI (car, boat) rovesciarsi, ribaltarsi.

over·use [ˌəʊvə'juːz] VT (chemicals, medication) fare uso eccessivo di.

over·value [ˌəʊvə'væljuː] VT sopravvalutare.

over·view ['əʊvəˌvjuː] N visione f d'insieme.

over·ween·ing [ˌəʊvə'wiːnɪŋ] ADJ (frm pej, pride, arrogance, ambition, self-confidence) smodato(-a), eccessivo(-a), smisurato(-a).

over·weight [ˌəʊvə'weɪt] ADJ: **to be overweight** (person) essere sovrappeso; (luggage) superare il peso consentito; **the parcel is a kilo overweight** il pacco pesa un chilo di troppo.

over·whelm [ˌəʊvə'wɛlm] VT (opponent, team) schiacciare; (with questions, requests, work) sommergere; **sorrow overwhelmed him** il dolore lo sopraffece; **overwhelmed by her kindness** confuso dalla sua gentilezza; **to be overwhelmed** (touched, impressed) rimanere colpito(-a); **we have been overwhelmed with offers of help** siamo stati sommersi da offerte di aiuto.

over·whelm·ing [ˌəʊvə'wɛlmɪŋ] ADJ (victory, majority) schiacciante; (defeat) pesante; (pressure, heat, desire, emotion) intenso(-a); **one's overwhelming impression is of heat** l'impressione dominante è quella di caldo.

over·whelm·ing·ly [ˌəʊvə'wɛlmɪŋlɪ] ADV (win) in modo schiacciante; (defeat) pesantemente; (vote) in massa.

over·work [ˌəʊvə'wɜːk] 1 N lavoro eccessivo. 2 VI lavorare troppo, strapazzarsi. 3 VT (staff, servants) far lavorare troppo.

over·write [ˌəʊvə'raɪt] VT (*Comput*) *cancellare informazioni scrivendoci sopra.*

over·wrought [ˌəʊvə'rɔːt] ADJ estremamente agitato(-a).

over·zeal·ous [ˌəʊvə'zɛləs] ADJ troppo zelante.

Ovid ['ɒvɪd] N Ovidio.

ovi·duct ['ɒvɪˌdʌkt] N ovidotto.

ovipa·rous [əʊ'vɪpərəs] ADJ oviparo(-a).

ovo·vi·vipa·rous [ˌəʊvəʊvaɪ'vɪpərəs] ADJ ovoviviparo(-a).

ovu·late ['ɒvjʊˌleɪt] VI ovulare.

ovu·la·tion [ˌɒvjʊ'leɪʃən] N ovulazione *f*.

ovule ['ɒvjuːl] N ovulo.

ovum ['əʊvəm] N (*pl* **ova** ['əʊvə]) ovocito.

owe [əʊ] VT (*gen*): **to owe sb sth, to owe sth to sb** dovere qc a qn; **to what do I owe the honour of your visit?** (*iro*) a che devo l'onore della visita?; **you owe it to yourself to come** è per te stesso che devi venire.

ow·ing ['əʊɪŋ] ADJ da pagare; **how much is owing to you now?** quanto ti devono (*or* devo *or* deve) adesso?

♦ **owing to** PREP a causa di; **owing to the bad weather** a causa del maltempo.

owl [aʊl] N (*small*) civetta; (*big*) gufo; **little owl** civetta notturna; **long-eared owl** gufo comune; **short-eared owl** gufo di palude.

owl·et ['aʊlɪt] N giovane gufo.

owl·ish ['aʊlɪʃ] ADJ da gufo.

owl·ish·ly ['aʊlɪʃlɪ] ADV con uno sguardo da gufo.

own [əʊn] 1 ADJ proprio(-a); **I made it with my own hands** l'ho fatto con le mie mani; **it's all my own money** sono tutti soldi miei; **the house has its own garage** la casa ha il suo garage.

2 PRON: **the house is her (very) own** la casa è di sua proprietà; **can I have it for my (very) own?** posso averlo tutto per me?; **he has a style all his own** ha uno stile tutto suo; **she has money of her own** è ricca di suo; **I'll give you a copy of your own** ti darò una copia tutta per te; **a room of my own** una camera tutta per me; **a place of one's own** una casa tutta per sé; **to come into one's own** mostrare le proprie qualità; **to be on one's own** stare per conto proprio; **from now on, you're on your own** (*fam*) d'ora in poi te la dovrai cavare da solo; **if I can get him on his own** se riesco a beccarlo da solo; **to do sth on one's own** (*unaided*) fare qualcosa da solo(-a); **I am so busy I have scarcely any time to call my own** sono così occupato che non ho tempo per me stesso; **without a chair to call my own** senza una sedia che possa chiamare mia; **to get one's own back** rendere pan per focaccia.

3 VT **a** (*possess*) possedere, essere proprietario(-a) di; **does anybody own this pen?** è di qualcuno questa penna?; **he acts as if he owns the place** si comporta come se fosse il padrone; **you don't own me!** non sei il mio padrone!

b (*old: admit*) ammettere.

4 VI (*Brit*): **to own to sth** ammettere qc; **to own to having**

done sth ammettere di aver fatto qc.

► **own up** VI + ADV: **to own up (to sth)** confessare (qc), ammettere (qc); **to own up to having done sth** ammettere di aver fatto qc.

♦ **own-brand** ['əʊnˌbrænd] ADJ: **our own-brand products** i prodotti *mpl* con il nostro marchio.

♦ **own brand** N (*Comm*) marchio proprio.

own·er ['əʊnə'] N proprietario(-a).

♦ **owner-occupier** [ˌəʊnər'ɒkjuˌpaɪə'] N proprietario(-a) della casa in cui abita.

own·er·ship ['əʊnəʃɪp] N proprietà; **it's under new ownership** ha un nuovo proprietario; **under his ownership the business flourished** nelle sue mani la ditta prosperava.

♦ **own goal** N (*Sport*, *fig*) autogol *m inv*, autorete *f*.

ox [ɒks] N (*pl* **oxen** ['ɒksən]) bue *m*.

oxa·lis [ɒk'sælɪs] N ossalide *f*.

ox·bow ['ɒksˌbəʊ] N (*also*: **oxbow lake**) *lago di meandro abbandonato*.

Ox·bridge ['ɒksˌbrɪdʒ] (*Brit*) 1 N *l'università di Oxford o di Cambridge (o entrambe)*.

2 ADJ (*education, accent, attitudes*) *di chi ha studiato a Oxford o Cambridge*.

ox·eye daisy ['ɒksˌaɪ'deɪzɪ] N margherita.

Ox·fam ['ɒksfæm] N ABBR (*Brit*: = *Oxford Committee for Famine Relief*) *organizzazione per aiuti al Terzo Mondo*.

oxi·da·tion [ˌɒksɪ'deɪʃən] N ossidazione *f*.

ox·ide ['ɒksaɪd] N ossido.

oxi·dize ['ɒksɪˌdaɪz] VI ossidare.

Oxon ABBR = *Oxfordshire*.

Oxon. ['ɒksən] ABBR (*Brit*: = *Oxoniensis*) *di Oxford University*.

oxo·nium [ɒk'səʊnɪəm]: **oxonium ion** N ione *m* ossonio.

ox·tail ['ɒksˌteɪl] N: **oxtail soup** zuppa di coda di bue.

oxy·acety·lene [ˌɒksɪə'setɪliːn] ADJ (*torch, burner*) ossiacetilenico(-a).

oxy·gen ['ɒksɪdʒən] N ossigeno.

oxy·gen·ate ['ɒksɪdʒɪˌneɪt] VT ossigenare.

oxy·gena·tion [ˌɒksɪdʒɪ'neɪʃən] N ossigenazione *f*.

♦ **oxygen mask** N maschera a ossigeno.

♦ **oxy·gen re-breather** ['ɒksɪdʒənˌriː'briːðə'] N (*Diving*) autorespiratore *m* ad ossigeno.

♦ **oxygen tent** N tenda a ossigeno.

oys·ter ['ɔɪstə'] N ostrica; **the world is your oyster** il mondo è tuo.

♦ **oyster bed** N banco di ostriche.

♦ **oyster-catcher** ['ɔɪstəˌkætʃə'] N beccaccia di mare.

♦ **oyster shell** N conchiglia di ostrica.

oz. ABBR = **ounce**.

ozone ['əʊzəʊn] N ozono.

♦ **ozone-friendly** [ˌəʊzəʊn'frɛndlɪ] ADJ che rispetta l'ozono.

♦ **ozone layer** N fascia d'ozono; **the hole in the ozone layer** il buco nell'ozono.

ozo·no·sphere [əʊ'zəʊnəˌsfɪə'] N ozonosfera.

P

P, p [pi:] N (*letter*) P, p *f or m inv*; **P for Peter** ≈ P come Padova; **mind your p's and q's!** bada a come parli!

p [pi:] ABBR (*Brit*) = **penny, pence**.

p. [pi:] ABBR (= *page*) p.

PA [pi:'eɪ] **1** N ABBR **a** = **personal assistant b** = **public address system**.

2 ABBR (*Am Post*)= *Pennsylvania*.

pa [pɑ:] N (*fam*) papà *m inv*, babbo.

p.a. ABBR = **per annum**.

pace [peɪs] **1** N **a** (*step*) passo; **30 paces away** a 30 passi di distanza; **to put sb through his paces** (*fig*) mettere qn alla prova

b (*speed*) passo, andatura; **at a good pace** (*walk*) di buon passo; (*work*) ad un buon ritmo; **at a slow pace** lentamente; **the pace of life** il ritmo di vita; **to keep pace with** (*person*) andare di pari passo con; (*fig: technology*) procedere di pari passo con; (: *events*) tenersi al corrente di; **to set the pace** (*running*) fare l'andatura; (*fig*) dare il la *or* il tono.

2 VT (*room*) andare su e giù per; **to pace sth off** *or* **out** misurare a passi qc.

3 VI: **to pace up and down** camminare su e giù *or* avanti e indietro.

pace·maker ['peɪsˌmeɪkə'] N **a** (*Med*) pacemaker *m inv* **b** (*Sport*) chi fa l'andatura, battistrada *m inv*.

pac·er ['peɪsə'] N (*Am Sport*) = **pacemaker** b.

pace·setter ['peɪsˌsetə'] N (*Am Sport*) = **pacemaker** b.

Pa·cif·ic [pə'sɪfɪk] **1** N: **the Pacific (Ocean)** il Pacifico, l'Oceano Pacifico.

2 ADJ del Pacifico.

pa·cif·ic [pə'sɪfɪk] ADJ (*frm*) pacifico(-a).

paci·fi·ca·tion [ˌpæsɪfɪ'keɪʃən] N pacificazione *f*.

paci·fi·er ['pæsɪˌfaɪə'] N (*Am fam: dummy*) succhiotto, ciuccio.

paci·fism ['pæsɪˌfɪzəm] N pacifismo.

paci·fist ['pæsɪfɪst] N pacifista *m/f*.

paci·fy ['pæsɪˌfaɪ] VT (*person*) calmare; (*country*) riportare la calma in, pacificare; (*fears*) placare; (*creditors*) ammansire.

pack [pæk] **1** N **a** (*packet*) pacco; (*Comm*) confezione *f*; (*of cotton, wool*) balla; (*Am: of cigarettes*) pacchetto; (*rucksack, Mil*) zaino; (*of cards*) mazzo; (*Rugby*) pacchetto; **a pack of lies** (*fig*) un mucchio *or* sacco di bugie

b (*of hounds*) muta; (*of wolves*) branco; (*of thieves*) banda; (*of fools*) massa.

2 VT **a** (*objects, goods*) imballare; **packed in dozens** (*Comm*) in confezioni da dodici; **to pack one's bags** fare le valigie *or* i bagagli; (*fig*) far fagotto; **I still have a few things to pack** ho ancora qualcosa da mettere in valigia

b (*cram full*): **to pack (with)** (*container*) riempire di; (*room, car*) stipare di; **can you pack two more into your car?** riesci a infilarci ancora due nella tua macchina?

c (*Comput*) comprimere, impaccare

d (*make firm: soil etc*) comprimere, pressare.

3 VI **a** (*do one's luggage*) fare le valigie *or* i bagagli; **to send sb packing** (*fam*) dare il benservito a qn

b (*people*): **to pack (into)** accalcarsi (in), pigiarsi (in); **packed like sardines** pigiati(-e) come sardine

▶ **pack away** VT + ADV riporre

▶ **pack in** (*Brit fam*)

1 VI + ADV (*break down: watch, car*) guastarsi.

2 VT + ADV mollare, piantare; **pack it in!** piantala!

▶ **pack off** VT + ADV: **to pack sb off to school/bed** spedire qn a scuola/letto

▶ **pack up** **1** VI + ADV (*person*) far fagotto; (*Brit fam: machine*) guastarsi.

2 VT + ADV **a** (*belongings, clothes*) mettere in una valigia; (*goods, presents*) imballare

b = **pack in** 2.

pack·age ['pækɪdʒ] **1** N (*parcel*) pacco; (*smaller*) pacchetto; (*fig: terms of agreement*) pacchetto.

2 VT (*Comm: goods*) confezionare.

♦ **package deal** N (*Comm*) offerta *f* tutto compreso *inv*.

♦ **package holiday** N (*Brit*) vacanza organizzata.

♦ **package tour** N (*Brit*) viaggio organizzato.

pack·ag·ing ['pækɪdʒɪŋ] N confezione *f*, imballo.

♦ **pack animal** N bestia da soma.

packed [pækt] ADJ (*crowded*) affollato(-a); **the place was packed** il posto era affollato.

♦ **packed lunch** N (*for walker*) pranzo al sacco; (*for traveller*) cestino da viaggio; **I always take a packed lunch to work** al lavoro mi porto sempre il pranzo da casa.

packed out ['pækt'aut] ADJ (*Brit fam*) strapieno(-a).

pack·er ['pækə'] N (*person*) imballatore(-trice); (*machine*) imballatrice *f*.

pack·et ['pækɪt] N (*gen*) pacchetto; (*of sweets, crisps*) sacchetto; (*of needles, seeds*) bustina; **to make a packet** (*fam*) fare un mucchio *or* un sacco di soldi; **that must have cost a packet** (*fam*) dev'essere costato un sacco di soldi.

♦ **packet switching** ['pækɪt'swɪtʃɪŋ] N (*Comput*) commutazione *f* di pacchetto.

♦ **pack ice** N banchisa, pack *m inv*.

pack·ing ['pækɪŋ] N **a** (*of luggage*): **to do one's packing** fare le valigie *or* i bagagli **b** (*material*) (materiale *m* da) imballaggio.

♦ **packing case** N cassa da imballaggio.

pact [pækt] N patto, trattato, accordo.

pad [pæd] [1] N **a** (*to prevent friction etc*) cuscinetto; (*Ftbl*) parastinco; (*Hockey*) gambiera; (*brake pad*) pastiglia; (*for ink*) tampone *m*

b (*writing pad*) blocco di carta da lettere; (*notepad*) bloc-notes *m inv*, blocchetto

c (*launch pad*) rampa di lancio

d (*of animal's foot*) cuscinetto

e (*fam: flat*) appartamentino.

[2] VT (*cushion, shoulders etc*) imbottire.

[3] VI: **to pad about/in** *etc* camminare/entrare *etc* a passi felpati

▶ **pad out** VT + ADV (*speech etc*) farcire.

pad·ded ['pædɪd] ADJ imbottito(-a).

♦ **padded cell** N cella con le pareti imbottite (*in carceri, ospedali psichiatrici*).

pad·ding ['pædɪŋ] N (*material*) imbottitura; (*fig: in speech, essay*) riempitivo.

pad·dle ['pædl] [1] N **a** (*oar*) pagaia; (*blade of wheel*) pala **b** : **to have a paddle** camminare nell'acqua bassa.

[2] VT (*boat*) fare andare a colpi di pagaia.

[3] VI **a** (*in boat*) pagaiare **b** (*walk in water*) sguazzare.

♦ **paddle boat**, (*Brit*) **paddle steamer** N battello a ruote.

pad·dling pool ['pædlɪŋ,pu:l] N piscina per bambini.

pad·dock ['pædək] N (*field*) recinto; (*of racecourse*) paddock *m inv*.

pad·dy ['pædɪ]: **paddy field** N risaia.

pad·lock ['pæd,lɒk] [1] N lucchetto.

[2] VT chiudere con il lucchetto.

pa·dre ['pɑːdrɪ] N **a** (*Mil, Naut*) cappellano **b** (*fam: clergyman*) padre *m*.

Pad·ua ['pædjuə] N Padova.

pae·di·at·ric, (*Am*) **pe·di·at·ric** [,pi:dɪ'ætrɪk] ADJ pediatrico(-a).

pae·dia·tri·cian, (*Am*) **pe·dia·tri·cian** [,pi:dɪə'trɪʃən] N pediatra *m/f*.

pae·di·at·rics, (*Am*) **pe·di·at·rics** [,pi:dɪ'ætrɪks] NSG pediatria.

pae·do·phile, (*Am*) **pe·do·phile** ['pi:dəʊ,faɪl] ADJ, N pedofilo(-a).

pagan ['peɪgən] ADJ, N pagano(-a).

page[1] [peɪdʒ] N (*of book etc*) pagina; **on page 2** a pagina 2; **on both sides of the page** su tutt'e due le facciate (del foglio).

page[2] [peɪdʒ] [1] (*also:* **pageboy:** *servant*) fattorino; (: *at wedding*) paggetto.

[2] VT: **to page sb** (far) chiamare qn.

pag·eant ['pædʒənt] N (*show*) spettacolo di rievocazione storica; (*procession*) corteo in costume.

pag·eant·ry ['pædʒəntrɪ] N sfarzo, pompa.

page·boy ['peɪdʒ,bɔɪ] N (*attendant*) paggio; (*hairstyle*) pettinatura alla paggetto.

pag·er ['peɪdʒə'] N cercapersone *m*.

♦ **page rate** N (*Press*) tariffa inserzioni per pagina.

pagi·nate ['pædʒɪ,neɪt] VT (*Typ*) impaginare; (*Comput*) paginare.

pagi·na·tion [,pædʒɪ'neɪʃən] N (*see vb*) impaginazione *f*; paginazione *f*.

pa·go·da [pə'gəʊdə] N pagoda.

paid [peɪd] [1] PT, PP of pay.

[2] ADJ (*work, official*) rimunerato(-a); **to put paid to sth** (*ruin*) metter fine a qc.

♦ **paid-up** ['peɪd,ʌp] ADJ, (*Am*) **paid-in** ['peɪd,ɪn] ADJ (*member*) che ha pagato la sua quota; (*share*) interamente pagato(-a); **paid-up capital** capitale *m* interamente versato.

pail [peɪl] N secchio.

pain [peɪn] [1] N **a** dolore *m*; **to cause pain to** (*physical*) provocare dolori a; (*mental*) far soffrire; **to be in pain** soffrire; **I have a pain in my leg** ho male *or* un dolore a una gamba; **he's a real pain (in the neck)** (*fam*) è un gran rompiscatole

b **pains** NPL (*efforts*) sforzi *mpl*; **and all I got for my pains was ...** e come ringraziamento ho avuto...; **to take pains over sth** mettercela tutta in qc; **to be at (great) pains to do sth** fare di tutto per fare qc

c (*penalty*): **on pain of death** sotto pena di morte.

[2] VT (*mentally*) addolorare, affliggere.

pained [peɪnd] ADJ: **a pained expression** un'aria seccata; **a pained silence** un silenzio amareggiato.

pain·ful ['peɪnfʊl] ADJ (*wound*) doloroso(-a); (*leg*) che fa male; (*task, sight, also fam*) penoso(-a); (*difficult*) difficile; **it is my painful duty to tell you that ...** purtroppo ho il dovere di informarla che...; **it was painful to watch** (*fam*) era penoso (a vedersi).

pain·ful·ly ['peɪnfəlɪ] ADV (*walk, breathe*) a fatica; (*thin*) penosamente; **the cut throbbed painfully** la ferita pulsava e faceva male; **it was painfully clear that ...** era fin troppo chiaro che... .

pain·kill·er ['peɪn,kɪlə'] N analgesico, antidolorifico.

pain·less ['peɪnlɪs] ADJ (*gen*) indolore; (*fig: exam*) non troppo difficile; (: *interview*) non spiacevole.

pain·less·ly ['peɪnlɪslɪ] ADV in modo indolore.

pains·tak·ing ['peɪnz,teɪkɪŋ] ADJ (*person*) coscienzioso(-a), diligente; (*work*) accurato(-a); (*accuracy*) minuzioso (-a).

pains·tak·ing·ly ['peɪnz,teɪkɪŋlɪ] ADV (*work*) accuratamente, diligentemente; (*research*) minuziosamente.

paint [peɪnt] [1] N (*Art*) colore *m*; (*for house etc*) tinta, vernice *f*; **a tin of paint** un barattolo di tinta *or* vernice; **a box of paints** una scatola di colori.

[2] VT (*house, also Art*) dipingere; (*door*) verniciare; **to paint sth blue/red** dipingere (*or* verniciare) qc di blu/rosso; **to paint the town red** (*fig*) far baldoria; **he's not as black as he's painted** è meno cattivo di quanto si dica in giro.

[3] VI dipingere; **to paint in oils** dipingere a olio.

paint·box ['peɪnt,bɒks] N scatola di colori.

paint·brush ['peɪnt,brʌʃ] N pennello.

paint·er[1] ['peɪntə'] N (*Art*) pittore(-trice); (*decorator*)

imbianchino(-a).

paint·er² ['peɪntə'] N (*Naut*) fune *f* d'ormeggio.

paint·ing ['peɪntɪŋ] N (*Art*: *picture*) dipinto, quadro; (: *activity*) pittura; (*decorating*: *of doors etc*) verniciatura; (: *of walls*) imbiancatura.

paint·pot ['peɪnt‚pɒt] N latta di tinta *or* vernice *f*.

♦ **paint stripper, paint remover** N prodotto sverniciante.

paint·work ['peɪnt‚wɜːk] N (*gen*) pittura; (*of car*) vernice *f*.

pair [pɛə'] ⟦1⟧ N (*of gloves, shoes etc*) paio; (*of people*) coppia; **a pair of scissors/trousers** un paio di forbici/ pantaloni; **arranged in pairs** disposti(-e) a due a due; **ordered pair** (*Math*) coppia ordinata.

⟦2⟧ VT accoppiare, appaiare

▶ **pair off** ⟦1⟧ VT + ADV trovar marito (*or* moglie) a.

⟦2⟧ VI + ADV: **to pair off (with sb)** fare coppia (con qn)

▶ **pair up** VI + ADV: **to pair up (with sb)** mettersi in coppia (con qn).

pais·ley ['peɪzlɪ] ADJ: **paisley pattern** disegno cachemire.

pa·jam·as [pə'dʒɑːməz] NPL (*Am*) = **pyjamas**.

Paki ['pækɪ] N (*Brit*) *termine spregiativo usato dagli inglesi per definire i pakistani*.

♦ **Paki-bashing** ['pækɪ‚bæʃɪŋ] N (*Brit fam*) *atti di violenza contro la minoranza pakistana*.

Pa·ki·stan [‚pɑːkɪs'tɑːn] N Pakistan *m*.

Pa·ki·stani [‚pɑːkɪs'tɑːnɪ] ADJ, N pakistano(-a).

PAL [pæl] N ABBR (*TV*: = *phase alternation line*) PAL *m*.

pal [pæl] N (*fam*) amico(-a)

▶ **pal up** VI + ADV (*fam*) far amicizia.

pal·ace ['pælɪs] N palazzo.

palae·on·tol·ogy,   (*Am*)   **pale·on·tol·ogy** [‚pælɪɒn'tɒlədʒɪ] N paleontologia.

pal·at·able ['pælətəbl] ADJ (*tasty*) gradevole (al palato); (*fig*) piacevole, gradevole.

pala·tal ['pælətl] ADJ palatale.

pal·ate ['pælɪt] N (*Anat, fig*) palato.

pa·la·tial [pə'leɪʃəl] ADJ sontuoso(-a), sfarzoso(-a).

pala·tine ['pælə‚taɪn] ADJ palatino(-a).

palaver [pə'lɑːvə'] N (*fam*: *fuss*) storie *fpl*; (: *talk*) tiritera.

pale¹ [peɪl] ⟦1⟧ ADJ (*comp* **-r**, *superl* **-st**) (*gen*) pallido(-a); (*colour*) chiaro(-a), pallido(-a); **pale blue** azzurro *or* blu pallido *inv*; **to grow** *or* **turn pale** diventare pallido(-a), impallidire.

⟦2⟧ VI impallidire; **to pale into insignificance (beside)** perdere d'importanza (nei confronti di).

pale² [peɪl] N: **to be beyond the pale** aver oltrepassato ogni limite.

pale·ly ['peɪllɪ] ADV pallidamente.

pale·ness ['peɪlnɪs] N pallore *m*.

Pal·es·tine ['pælɪ‚staɪn] N Palestina.

Pal·es·tin·ian [‚pæləs'tɪnɪən] ADJ, N palestinese (*m/f*).

pal·ette ['pælɪt] N tavolozza.

♦ **palette knife** N (*Art, Culin*) spatola di metallo.

palings ['peɪlɪŋz] NPL (*fence*) palizzata *fsg*; (*boards*) assi *fpl*.

pali·sade [‚pælɪseɪd] N palizzata.

pall¹ [pɔːl] N (*on coffin*) drappo funebre; (*of smoke*) coltre *f*, cappa.

pall² [pɔːl] VI: **to pall (on)** perdere il proprio fascino (per), diventare noioso(-a) (per).

pall·bearer ['pɔːl‚bɛərə'] N persona che porta la bara.

pal·let ['pælɪt] N (*for goods*) pallet *m inv*.

pal·lia·tive ['pælɪətɪv] N palliativo.

pal·lid ['pælɪd] ADJ pallido(-a), smorto(-a).

pal·lor ['pælə'] N pallore *m*.

pal·ly ['pælɪ] ADJ (*comp* **-ier**, *superl* **-iest**) (*fam*): **to be pally**

with sb essere molto amico (*or* amica) di qn.

palm¹ [pɑːm] N (*Bot*: *also*: **palm tree**) palma

▶ **palm off** VT + ADV: **to palm sth off on sb** (*fam*) rifilare qc a qn.

palm² [pɑːm] N (*Anat*) palma, palmo; **to read sb's palm** leggere la mano a qn; **to grease sb's palm** (*fig*) dare una bustarella a qn; **to have sb in the palm of one's hand** avere *or* tenere in pugno qn.

palm·ist ['pɑːmɪst] N chiromante *m/f*.

palm·is·try ['pɑːmɪstrɪ] N chiromanzia.

♦ **palm oil** N olio di palma.

♦ **Palm Sunday** N Domenica delle Palme.

pal·pable ['pælpəbl] ADJ (*lie, mistake*) palese, evidente.

pal·pably ['pælpəblɪ] ADV palesemente, evidentemente.

pal·pi·tate ['pælpɪ‚teɪt] VI palpitare.

pal·pi·ta·tion [‚pælpɪ'teɪʃən] N: **to have palpitations** avere le palpitazioni.

pal·sied ['pɔːlzɪd] ADJ paralitico(-a).

pal·try ['pɔːltrɪ] ADJ (*meagre*) irrisorio(-a); (*unworthy of consideration*) insignificante; **for a paltry £5** per la somma irrisoria di 5 sterline.

pam·pas ['pæmpəs] NPL pampas *fpl*.

pam·per ['pæmpə'] VT viziare, coccolare.

pam·phlet ['pæmflɪt] N (*informative brochure*) opuscolo, dépliant *m inv*; (*political, handed out in street*) volantino, manifestino.

Pan [pæn] N Pan.

pan [pæn] ⟦1⟧ N (*Culin*: *also*: **saucepan**) casseruola; (*frying pan*) padella; (*milk pan*) pentolino; (*of scales*) piatto; (*of lavatory*) tazza; **roasting pan** teglia per arrosti.

⟦2⟧ VT **a** (*gold etc*) passare al vaglio

b (*fam*: *play*) stroncare.

⟦3⟧ VI **a**: **to pan for gold** (lavare le sabbie aurifere per) cercare l'oro

b (*Cine*) fare una panoramica

▶ **pan out** VI + ADV (*develop*) andare; (*turn out well*) riuscire.

pan- [pæn] PREF pan... .

pana·cea [pænə'sɪə] N panacea.

pa·nache [pə'næʃ] N stile *m*.

♦ **Pan-African** ADJ panafricano(-a).

Pana·ma ['pænə‚mɑː] N Panama *f*.

pana·ma ['pænə‚mɑː] N (*also*: **panama hat**) (cappello di) panama *m inv*.

♦ **Panama Canal** N canale *m* di Panama.

Pana·ma·nian [‚pænə'meɪnɪən] ADJ, N panamense (*m/f*).

♦ **Pan-American** ['pænə'mɛrɪkən] ADJ panamericano (-a).

♦ **Pan-Asian** ['pæn'eɪʃən] ADJ panasiatico(-a).

pan·cake ['pæn‚keɪk] N frittella, crêpe *f inv*; **as flat as a pancake** (*fig*) piatto(-a) come una tavola.

♦ **Pancake Day** N (*Brit*) martedì *m* grasso.

♦ **pancake roll** N *crêpe ripiena di verdure alla cinese*.

pan·chro·mat·ic ['pænkrəʊ'mætɪk] ADJ pancromatico (-a).

pan·cre·as ['pæŋkrɪəs] N pancreas *m inv*.

pan·da ['pændə] N panda *m inv*.

♦ **panda car** N (*Brit*) auto *f* della polizia, ≈ pantera.

pan·dem·ic [pæn'dɛmɪk] ⟦1⟧ N (*frm, Med*) pandemia.

⟦2⟧ ADJ (*Med*) pandemico(-a).

pan·de·mo·nium [‚pændɪ'məʊnɪəm] N pandemonio.

pan·der ['pændə'] VI: **to pander to** (*person, whims*) assecondare; **to pander to sb's tastes** piegarsi ai gusti di qn.

Pandora's box [pæn‚dɔː'rəz'bɒks] N il vaso di Pandora.

pane [peɪn] N vetro.

pan·egyr·ic [‚pænɪ'dʒɪrɪk] N (*frm*) panegirico.

pan·el ['pænl] 1 N **a** (*gen*) pannello; (*of triptych*) tavola; (*of ceiling*) cassettone *m*; (*of instruments, switches*) quadro **b** (*Radio, TV: of judges*) giuria; (*of experts, researchers etc*) gruppo; (*in market research*) panel *m inv*. 2 VT (*wall, door*) rivestire di *or* con pannelli.

♦ **panel beater** N battilastra *m inv*.

♦ **panel discussion** N tavola rotonda.

♦ **panel game** N (*Brit*) quiz *m inv* a squadre.

pan·elled, (*Am*) **pan·eled** ['pænəld] ADJ (*door etc*) a pannelli.

panelling, (*Am*) **pan·el·ing** ['pænəlɪŋ] N rivestimento di *or* a pannelli.

pan·el·list, (*Am*) **pan·el·ist** ['pænəlɪst] N partecipante *m/f* (*al quiz, alla tavola rotonda etc*).

pang [pæŋ] N: **a pang of guilt/sadness** un senso di colpa/tristezza; **without a pang** senza rimpianti; **the pangs of hunger** i morsi della fame; **to feel pangs of remorse** essere torturato(-a) dal rimorso.

pan·han·dler ['pæn,hændlə'] N (*Am fam*) accattone(-a).

pan·ic ['pænɪk] 1 N panico; **to get into a panic about sth** farsi prendere dal panico per qc; **to throw into a panic** (*crowd*) seminare il panico tra; (*person*) gettare in uno stato di agitazione. 2 VI lasciarsi prendere dal panico; **don't panic!** non agitarti!

♦ **panic buying** ['pænɪk 'baɪŋ] N accaparramento (*di generi alimentari*).

pan·icky ['pænɪkɪ] ADJ (*person*) che si lascia prendere dal panico; (*report*) allarmista; (*decision*) dettato(-a) dal panico.

♦ **panic stations** N: **when he realized he'd lost the key it was panic stations** fu preso dal panico quando si accorse di aver perso la chiave.

♦ **panic-stricken** ['pænɪk,strɪkən] ADJ (*person*) preso(-a) dal panico, in preda al panico; (*look*) terrorizzato(-a).

pan·ni·er ['pænɪə'] N (*gen*) paniere *m*; (*on bicycle*) borsa; (*on animal*) bisaccia.

pano·ply ['pænəplɪ] N: **the whole panoply of** (*frm*) l'intera collezione di.

pano·ra·ma [,pænə'rɑːmə] N panorama *m*.

pano·ram·ic [,pænə'ræmɪk] ADJ panoramico(-a).

pano·rami·cal·ly [,pænə'ræmɪkəlɪ] ADV panoramicamente.

pan·pipes ['pæn,paɪps] NPL Flauto *msg* di Pan, siringa *fsg*.

pan·sy ['pænzɪ] N (*Bot*) viola del pensiero, pensée *f inv*; (*fam pej*) checca.

pant [pænt] VI ansimare, avere il fiatone; **he was panting for a drink** moriva dalla voglia di bere; **she panted up the stairs** salì le scale ansimando.

pan·tech·ni·con [pæn'teknɪkən] N (*Brit*) grosso furgone *m* per traslochi.

pan·theism ['pænθɪ,ɪzəm] N panteismo.

pan·theis·tic [,pænθɪ'ɪstɪk] ADJ panteistico(-a).

pan·the·on ['pænθɪən] N pantheon *m inv*.

pan·ther ['pænθə'] N pantera.

panties ['pæntɪz] NPL mutandine *fpl*.

pan·ti·hose ['pæntɪ,həʊz] N (*Am*) collant *m inv*.

pan·to ['pæntəʊ] N (*Brit fam*) = **pantomime a**.

pan·to·graph ['pæntə,grɑːf] N (*Rail, Tech*) pantografo.

pan·to·mime ['pæntə,maɪm] N **a** (*Brit: at Christmas*) spettacolo natalizio(*sulla falsariga delle favole per bambini*) **b** (*mime*) pantomima.

pan·try ['pæntrɪ] N dispensa.

pants [pænts] NPL (*Brit: underwear*) mutande *fpl*, slip *m inv*; (*Am: trousers*) pantaloni *mpl*, calzoni *mpl*; **to catch sb with his pants down** (*fam*) beccare qn in una situazione imbarazzante.

pant·suit ['pænt,suːt] N (*Am*) completo *m* pantalone *inv*.

pan·ty·hose ['pæntɪ,həʊz] N = **pantihose**.

pan·zer ['pænzə'] N panzer *m inv*.

pap [pæp] N (*pej: drivel*) stupidaggini *fpl*; (*food*) pappa.

pa·pa·cy ['peɪpəsɪ] N papato.

pa·pal ['peɪpəl] ADJ papale, pontificio(-a).

pa·pa·raz·zi [,pæpə'rætsɪ:] NPL paparazzi *mpl*.

pa·pa·ya [pə'paɪə] N papaia.

pa·per ['peɪpə'] 1 N **a** (*material*) carta; (*wallpaper*) carta da parati, tappezzeria; **a piece of paper** (*odd bit*) un pezzo di carta; (*sheet*) un foglio (di carta); **on paper** sulla carta; **to put sth down on paper** mettere qc per iscritto

 b (*exam questions*) prova scritta, scritto; (*lecture*) relazione *f*

 c (*newspaper*) giornale *m*; **the papers** i giornali; **it was in the papers** era su tutti giornali; **to write to the papers about sth** scrivere una lettera aperta *or* ai giornali su qc. 2 VT (*wall, room*) tappezzare.

 3 ADJ (*towel, cup*) di carta; (*industry*) cartario(-a), della carta; see also **papers**

▸ **paper over** VI + PREP: **to paper over the cracks** (*fig*) appianare le divergenze.

♦ **paper advance** N (*on printer*) avanzamento della carta.

paper·back ['peɪpə,bæk] N tascabile *m*, paperback *m inv*.

♦ **paperback edition** N edizione *f* economica.

♦ **paper bag** N sacchetto di carta.

paper·boy ['peɪpə,bɔɪ] N (*selling*) strillone *m*; (*delivering*) ragazzo che recapita i giornali.

♦ **paper chase** N (*game*) corsa campestre in cui i partecipanti seguono una scia di pezzetti di carta.

paper·clip ['peɪpə,klɪp] N graffetta, clip *f inv*.

♦ **paper-cutter** ['peɪpə,kʌtə'] N taglierina.

♦ **paper handkerchief** N fazzolettino di carta.

♦ **paper knife** N tagliacarte *m inv*.

♦ **paper mill** N cartiera.

♦ **paper money** N cartamoneta, moneta cartacea.

♦ **paper profit** N (*Fin*) utile *m* sulla carta.

♦ **paper round** N: **to do a paper round** recapitare i giornali a domicilio.

papers ['peɪpəz] NPL (*writings, documents*) carte *fpl*; (*identity papers*) documenti *mpl* (di riconoscimento); **old papers** scartoffie *fpl*; **Churchill's private papers** gli scritti *or* i documenti privati di Churchill.

♦ **paper shop** N giornalaio (*negozio*).

♦ **paper tiger** N tigre *f* di carta.

paper·weight ['peɪpə,weɪt] N fermacarte *m inv*.

paper·work ['peɪpə,wɜːk] N parte *f* amministrativa di un lavoro.

papier-mâché [,pæpjeɪ'mæʃeɪ] N cartapesta.

pa·pist ['peɪpɪst] N (*pej*) papista *m/f*.

pap·ri·ka ['pæprɪkə] N (*spice*) paprica; (*vegetable*) peperoncino rosso.

Pap test ['pæp,test], **Pap smear** N (*Med*) pap-test *m inv*.

par [pɑː'] N **a** (*equality of value*) parità, pari *f*; (*Fin: of shares*) valore *m* nominale; **to be on a par with sb/sth** essere allo stesso livello di qn/qc; **at/above/below par** (*Fin*) alla/sopra la/sotto la pari

 b (*average*): **to feel below** *or* **under** *or* **not up to par** (*ill*) non essere *or* non sentirsi in forma; **that's par for the course** (*fig*) è normale; **to be above/below par** (*gen, Golf*) essere al di sopra/al di sotto della norma.

para ['pærə] N (*fam*) parà *m inv*.

para·ble ['pærəbl] N parabola (Rel).
pa·rabo·la [pə'ræbələ] N parabola (Mat).
para·chute ['pærə,ʃuːt] ① N paracadute m inv.
② VT paracadutare.
③ VI (also: **parachute down**) paracadutarsi.
♦ **parachute jump** N lancio col paracadute.
para·chut·ist ['pærəʃuːtɪst] N paracadutista m/f.
pa·rade [pə'reɪd] ① N (procession) sfilata; (Mil: marchpast) parata; (: ceremony, inspection) rivista; **to be on parade** (Mil: marching) sfilare; (: for inspection) essere schierato (-a); **a fashion parade** (Brit) una sfilata di moda.
② VT (troops: in ceremonial order) schierare in parata; (: for a march) far sfilare; (placard etc) portare in giro or in corteo; (show off: learning, wealth, new clothes) fare sfoggio di, sfoggiare, ostentare.
③ VI (Mil: march) sfilare; (: in ceremonial order) schierarsi in parata; (boy scouts, demonstrators) marciare in corteo; **to parade about** or **around** (fam) pavoneggiarsi; **the strikers paraded through the town** gli scioperanti hanno attraversato la città in corteo.
♦ **parade ground** N piazza d'armi.
para·digm ['pærə,daɪm] N paradigma m.
para·dig·mat·ic [,pærədɪg'mætɪk] ADJ paradigmatico(-a).
para·dise ['pærə,daɪs] N paradiso.
para·dox ['pærə,dɒks] N paradosso.
para·doxi·cal [,pærə'dɒksɪkəl] ADJ paradossale.
para·doxi·cal·ly [,pærə'dɒksɪkəlɪ] ADV paradossalmente.
par·af·fin ['pærəfɪn], (Am) **par·af·fin oil** N cherosene m; **liquid paraffin** olio di paraffina.
♦ **paraffin heater** N (Brit) stufa al cherosene.
♦ **paraffin lamp** N (Brit) lampada al cherosene.
♦ **paraffin wax** N paraffina solida.
para·gon ['pærəgən] N: **paragon of virtue** modello di virtù.
para·graph ['pærəgrɑːf] N (gen) paragrafo; (in newspaper) trafiletto; **to begin a new paragraph** andare a capo.
Para·guay ['pærə,gwaɪ] N Paraguay m.
Para·guay·an [,pærə'gwaɪən] ADJ, N paraguaiano(-a).
para·keet ['pærəkiːt] N parrocchetto.
par·al·lel ['pærəlɛl] ① ADJ: **parallel (with, to)** parallelo(-a) (a); **the road runs parallel to the railway** la strada corre parallela alla ferrovia.
② N (Geom) parallela; (Geog) parallelo; (Horse-riding) largo; (fig) confronto, paragone m, parallelo; **to draw a parallel between** (fig) fare un parallelo fra.
③ VT (fig: equal) uguagliare; (: be similar to) essere analogo(-a) or parallelo(-a) a.
♦ **parallel bars** NPL parallele fpl.
par·al·lel·epi·ped [,pærə,lɛlə'paɪpɛd] N parallelepipedo.
par·al·lelo·gram [,pærə'lɛləʊ,græm] N parallelogramma m.
♦ **parallel turn** N (Skiing) curva a sci uniti.
pa·raly·sis [pə'ræləsɪs] N (pl **paralyses**) paralisi.
para·lyt·ic [,pærə'lɪtɪk] ADJ (Med: person) paralitico(-a); (: stroke) di paralisi; (Brit fam: drunk) ubriaco(-a) fradicio (-a).
para·lyze ['pærə,laɪz] VT (Med, fig) paralizzare; **paralyzed with fear** paralizzato(-a) dalla paura; **his leg is paralyzed** ha la gamba paralizzata.
para·medic [,pærə'mɛdɪk], **para·medi·cal** [,pærə'mɛdɪkəl] N paramedico.
para·medi·cal [,pærə'mɛdɪkəl] ADJ paramedico(-a).
pa·ram·eter [pə'ræmɪtə'] N parametro.
para·mili·tary [,pærə'mɪlɪtərɪ] ADJ paramilitare.
para·mount ['pærə,maʊnt] ADJ: **of paramount importance**

di capitale importanza.
para·noia [,pærə'nɔɪə] N paranoia.
para·noi·ac [,pærə'nɔɪɪk] ADJ paranoico(-a).
para·noid ['pærə,nɔɪd] ADJ (Psych) paranoico(-a); **para·noid (about)** (fig) ossessionato(-a) (da).
para·nor·mal [,pærə'nɔːməl] ① N: **the paranormal** i fenomeni paranormali.
② ADJ paranormale.
para·pet ['pærəpɪt] N parapetto.
para·pher·na·lia [,pærəfə'neɪlɪə] N armamentario.
para·phrase ['pærə,freɪz] ① N parafrasi f inv.
② VT parafrasare.
para·plegia [,pærə'pliːdʒə] N paraplegia.
para·plegic [,pærə'pliːdʒɪk] ADJ, N paraplegico(-a).
para·psy·chol·ogy [,pærəsaɪ'kɒlədʒɪ] N parapsicologia.
para·site ['pærə,saɪt] N parassita m.
para·sit·ic [,pærə'sɪtɪk], **para·siti·cal** [,pærə'sɪtɪkəl] ADJ (gen) parassita; (disease) parassitario(-a).
para·sit·ism ['pærəsaɪ,tɪzəm] N parassitismo.
para·sol [,pærə'sɒl] N parasole m inv.
para·trooper ['pærə,truːpə'] N (Mil) paracadutista m, parà m inv.
para·troops ['pærə,truːps] NPL paracadutisti mpl.
par·boil ['pɑː,bɔɪl] VT sbollentare.
par·cel ['pɑːsl] N (gen) pacchetto; (larger) pacco; (of land) appezzamento; (fig: of fools, liars) branco; (: of lies) mucchio
► **parcel out** VT + ADV (inheritance) dividere; (land) distribuire, spartire
► **parcel up** VT + ADV impacchettare, fare un pacco di.
♦ **parcel bomb** N (Brit) pacchetto esplosivo.
♦ **parcel office** N ufficio m spedizioni inv.
♦ **parcel post** N servizio pacchi.
parch [pɑːtʃ] VT riardere.
parched [pɑːtʃt] ADJ (land, garden) disseccato(-a), riarso (-a); (person) assetato(-a); **I'm parched!** (fam) muoio di sete!
parch·ment ['pɑːtʃmənt] N pergamena.
par·don ['pɑːdn] ① N perdono, scusa; (Rel) indulgenza; (Law) condono della pena, grazia; **general pardon** amnistia.
② VT (forgive) perdonare; (Law) graziare; **to pardon sb for sth/doing sth** perdonare qc a qn/qn per aver fatto qc.
③ EXCL (apologizing) mi scusi!; (not hearing) scusi?, come?, prego?; **(I beg your) pardon?**, (Am) **pardon me?** prego?
par·don·able ['pɑː,dnəbl] ADJ perdonabile.
par·don·ably ['pɑː,dnəblɪ] ADV comprensibilmente.
pare [pɛə'] VT (nails) tagliarsi; (fruit) sbucciare, pelare
► **pare down** VT + ADV (costs) ridurre, limitare.
par·ent ['pɛərənt] N padre m (or madre f); **his parents** i suoi genitori.
par·ent·age ['pɛərəntɪdʒ] N natali mpl; **of unknown parentage** di genitori sconosciuti.
pa·ren·tal [pə'rɛntl] ADJ dei genitori; (Bio) parentale.
♦ **parent company** N società f inv madre inv.
pa·ren·thesis [pə'rɛnθɪsɪs] N (pl **parentheses** [pə'rɛnθɪsiːz]) parentesi f inv; **in parentheses** fra parentesi.
par·en·theti·cal [,pærən'θɛtɪkəl] ADJ (clause) parentetico (-a); (statement) fra parentesi.
par·en·theti·cal·ly [,pærən'θɛtɪkəlɪ] ADV tra parentesi.
par·ent·hood ['pɛərənthʊd] N paternità (or maternità).
par·ent·ing ['pɛərəntɪŋ] N: **parenting is a full-time occupa-**

tion allevare i figli è un lavoro a tempo pieno; **young couples lacking parenting skills** giovani coppie che non riescono ad essere bravi genitori.

♦ **parent-teacher association** [ˌpɛərənt'tiːtʃəs͵səʊsɪ'eɪʃən] N ≈ consiglio di classe.

pa·resis [pə'riːsɪs] N paresi *f.*

par ex·cel·lence [ˌpɑːr'ɛksəlɑns] ADV per eccellenza.

pa·ri·ah [pə'raɪə] N (*frm*) paria *m inv.*

Par·is[1] ['pærɪs] N Parigi *f.*

Par·is[2] ['pærɪs] N (*Myth*) Paride.

par·ish ['pærɪʃ] 1 N (*Rel*) parrocchia; (*Brit*: civil) ≈ comune *m.*

2 ADJ (*church*) parrocchiale; (*hall*) parrocchiale *or* municipale.

♦ **parish council** N (*Brit*) ≈ consiglio comunale.

pa·rish·ion·er [pə'rɪʃənəʳ] N parrocchiano(-a).

♦ **parish priest** N parroco.

Pa·ris·ian [pə'rɪzɪən] 1 ADJ, N parigino(-a).

par·ity ['pærɪtɪ] N parità.

park [pɑːk] 1 N (*gen*) parco; (*public*) giardino pubblico.

2 VT (*Aut*) parcheggiare.

3 VI (*Aut*) parcheggiare, parcheggiarsi.

par·ka ['pɑːkə] N eskimo.

park·ing ['pɑːkɪŋ] 1 N (*act*) parcheggiare *m*; (*parking space*) parcheggio; **"no parking"** "sosta vietata".

2 ADJ (*space*) di parcheggio.

♦ **parking attendant** N custode *m/f* di posteggio, posteggiatore(-trice).

♦ **parking fine** N multa per sosta vietata.

♦ **parking lights** NPL luci *fpl* di posizione.

♦ **parking lot** N (*Am*) posteggio, parcheggio.

♦ **parking meter** N parchimetro.

♦ **parking offence**, (*Am*) **parking violation** N infrazione *f* al divieto di sosta.

♦ **parking place** N posto di parcheggio.

♦ **parking ticket** N multa per sosta vietata.

Parkinson's ['pɑːkɪnsənz] N (*also:* **Parkinson's disease**) morbo di Parkinson.

Parkinson's Law ['pɑːkɪnsənzˌlɔː] N legge *f* di Parkinson (*secondo la quale il tempo necessario a fare qualcosa tende ad allungarsi per riempire il tempo a disposizione*).

park·land ['pɑːkˌlænd] N parco.

park·way ['pɑːkˌweɪ] N (*Am*) viale *m.*

parky ['pɑːkɪ] ADJ (*comp* **-ier**, *superl* **-iest**) (*Brit fam*) freddino(-a).

par·lance ['pɑːləns] N: **in common/modern parlance** nel linguaggio comune/moderno.

par·ley ['pɑːlɪ] (*old*) 1 N colloquio.

2 VI conferire, parlamentare.

par·lia·ment ['pɑːləmənt] N parlamento; **to get into parliament** essere eletto(-a) al parlamento.

par·lia·men·tar·ian [ˌpɑːləmɛn'tɛərɪən] N parlamentare *m/f.*

par·lia·men·ta·ry [ˌpɑːlə'mɛntərɪ] ADJ parlamentare.

♦ **parliamentary secretary** N sottosegretario.

parlour, (*Am*) **par·lor** ['pɑːləʳ] N (*in house*) salotto; **ice-cream parlour** gelateria.

par·lous ['pɑːləs] ADJ (*old, liter*) periglioso(-a).

Par·me·san [ˌpɑːmɪ'zæn] N (*also:* **Parmesan cheese**) parmigiano.

Par·nas·sus [pɑː'næsəs] N (*Geog, Myth*) Parnaso.

pa·ro·chial [pə'rəʊkɪəl] ADJ (*of parish*) parrocchiale; (*fig pej*) provinciale, ristretto(-a).

pa·ro·chi·al·ly [pə'rəʊkɪəlɪ] ADV (*fig pej*) campanilistica-

mente.

paro·dy ['pærədɪ] 1 N parodia.

2 VT parodiare.

pa·role [pə'rəʊl] N (*Law*) libertà per buona condotta; **on parole** in libertà per buona condotta; **to break (one's) parole** *commettere un atto che ha per conseguenza la revoca della libertà per buona condotta.*

par·ox·ysm ['pærək͵sɪzəm] N (*Med*) parossismo; (*of laughter, coughing*) convulso; (*of grief, anger*) attacco.

par·quet ['pɑːkeɪ] N (*also:* **parquet floor**) parquet *m inv.*

par·rot ['pærət] N pappagallo.

♦ **parrot-fashion** ['pærət͵fæʃən] ADV (*learn*) a pappagallo, in modo pappagallesco.

par·ry ['pærɪ] VT (*blow*) parare; (*fig*: question) eludere.

parse [pɑːs] VT analizzare dal punto di vista grammaticale.

par·si·mo·ni·ous [ˌpɑːsɪ'məʊnɪəs] ADJ parsimonioso (-a).

par·si·mo·ni·ous·ly [ˌpɑːsɪ'məʊnɪəslɪ] ADV con parsimonia.

par·si·mo·ny ['pɑːsɪmənɪ] N parsimonia.

pars·ley ['pɑːslɪ] N prezzemolo.

♦ **parsley sauce** N besciamella con prezzemolo.

pars·nip ['pɑːsnɪp] N pastinaca.

par·son ['pɑːsn] N (*gen*) parroco, prete *m*; (*Church of England*) pastore *m.*

par·son·age ['pɑːsənɪdʒ] N canonica, casa parrocchiale.

♦ **parson's nose** N boccone *m* del prete.

part [pɑːt] 1 N a (*portion, fragment*) parte *f*; (*of serial*) episodio; **in part** in parte; **it was funny in parts** è stato divertente a tratti; **for the most part** nell'insieme, per lo più; **the greater part of it is done** il più è fatto; **for the better part of the day** per la maggior parte della giornata; **two parts of sand to one of cement** due parti di sabbia e una (parte) di cemento; **to be part and parcel of** essere parte integrante di

b (*Tech*: component) pezzo *or* parte *f* (di ricambio); (*Mus*) parte; **soprano part** la parte del soprano; **2-part song** canto a 2 voci; **moving part** parte meccanica

c (*role*: also Theatre) parte *f*, ruolo; **to take part in sth** prendere parte *or* partecipare a qc; **to have no part in sth** non aver nulla a che fare con qc; **to play a part in sth/doing sth** avere un certo ruolo in qc/nel fare qc; **to look the part** essere perfetto(-a) nella parte

d (*region*) parte *f*; **in these parts** da queste parti; **a lovely part of the country** una bella regione

e (*behalf, side*) parte *f*; **on his part** da parte sua; **to take sb's part** prendere le parti di qn, parteggiare per qn; **for my part** da parte mia, per quanto mi riguarda; **a mistake on the part of my brother** un errore da parte di mio fratello; **to take sth in good/bad part** prendere bene/male qc

f (*Am*: in hair) scriminatura, riga.

2 ADV (*partly*) in parte; **a part eaten apple** una mela mezza mangiata.

3 VT (*curtains, branches*) scostare; (*lovers*) dividere, separare; (*boxers*) separare; **to part one's hair** farsi la riga *or* la scriminatura (nei capelli).

4 VI (*boxers*) separarsi; (*curtains*) aprirsi; (*roads*) dividersi; (*rope*: break) spezzarsi, rompersi; (*friends, lovers*) lasciarsi; **to part (from sb)** separarsi (da qn); **they parted friends** si sono lasciati da buoni amici

▶ **part with** VI + PREP (*possessions*) separarsi da, disfarsi di; (*money*) sborsare; **I hate parting with it** mi dispiace disfarmene.

par·take [pɑːˈteɪk] (*pt* partook, *pp* partaken [pɑːˈteɪkən]) VI (*frm*) **a** : **to partake of sth** consumare qc, prendere qc **b** : **to partake in an activity** partecipare *or* prender parte ad una attività.

♦ **part exchange** N (*Brit*): **in part exchange** in pagamento parziale; **we will take your car in part exchange for a new one** detrarremo il valore della sua vecchia auto da quello della nuova.

par·tial [ˈpɑːʃəl] ADJ (*gen*) parziale; **to be in partial agreement** essere parzialmente *or* in parte d'accordo; **to be partial to sth** (*like*) avere un debole per qc.

par·tial·ity [ˌpɑːʃiˈælɪti] N **a** (*bias*): **partiality (towards)** parzialità (verso) **b** (*liking*): **partiality (for)** predilezione *f* (per), debole *m* (per).

par·tial·ly [ˈpɑːʃəli] ADV (*partly*) parzialmente, in parte.

par·tici·pant [pɑːˈtɪsɪpənt] N: **participant (in)** partecipante *m/f* (a).

par·tici·pate [pɑːˈtɪsɪˌpeɪt] VI: **to participate (in)** partecipare (a), prendere parte (a).

par·tici·pa·tion [pɑːˌtɪsɪˈpeɪʃən] N: **participation (in)** partecipazione *f* (a).

par·ti·ci·ple [pɑːˈtɪsɪpl] N participio; **past/present participle** participio passato/presente.

par·ti·cle [ˈpɑːtɪkl] N (*Gram, Phys*) particella; (*of dust*) granello; (*of food*) pezzettino; (*fig: of truth, sense*) briciolo.

par·ticu·lar [pəˈtɪkjʊləʳ] **1** ADJ **a** (*specific, special*) particolare; **that particular house/train** quella casa/quel treno in particolare; **to pay particular attention to** [OR] **to take particular care over** fare molta attenzione a; **in this particular case** in questo caso particolare; **for no particular reason** senza una ragione precisa *or* particolare; **she's a particular friend of mine** è una mia carissima amica **b** (*fastidious, fussy*) pignolo(-a), difficile; (*painstaking*) meticoloso(-a); **to be very particular about** essere molto pignolo (-a) su; **he's particular about his food** è molto difficile nel mangiare; **I'm not particular** per me va bene tutto.
2 N **a** (*detail*) particolare *m* **b** : **in particular** in particolare, particolarmente; **nothing in particular** nulla in *or* di particolare; see also **particulars**.

par·ticu·lar·ity [pəˌtɪkjʊˈlærɪti] N particolarità *f inv*; (*detail*) particolare *m*; (*fastidiousness*) pignoleria.

par·ticu·lar·ize [pəˈtɪkjʊləˌraɪz] VT, VI particolareggiare.

par·ticu·lar·ly [pəˈtɪkjʊləli] ADV (*especially*) particolarmente; **I particularly wanted it for tomorrow** lo volevo proprio per domani; **particularly since ...** soprattutto perché... .

par·ticu·lars [pəˈtɪkjʊləz] NPL (*information*) particolari *mpl*, dettagli *mpl*; (*personal details*) dati *mpl*; **full particulars** informazioni *fpl* complete.

part·ing [ˈpɑːtɪŋ] **1** ADJ (*kiss etc*) d'addio; **his parting words** le sue ultime parole; **parting shot** (*fig*) battuta finale; **and with this parting shot he left** e detto ciò se ne andò.
2 N **a** separazione *f*; **we have reached the parting of the ways** (*fig*) a questo punto le nostre strade si dividono **b** (*Brit: in hair*) scriminatura, riga.

par·ti·san [ˌpɑːtɪˈzæn] **1** ADJ (*gen*) fazioso(-a); (*fighter*) partigiano(-a); **partisan spirit** spirito di parte.
2 N (*fighter*) partigiano(-a).

par·ti·tion [pɑːˈtɪʃən] **1** N **a** (*wall*) parete *f* divisoria, tramezzo **b** (*of country*) suddivisione *f*, divisione *f*.

2 VT (*country etc*) suddividere, dividere
► **partition off** VT + ADV separare con una parete divisoria.

par·ti·tive [ˈpɑːtɪtɪv] **1** ADJ partitivo(-a).
2 N partitivo.

part·ly [ˈpɑːtli] ADV parzialmente, in parte.

part·ner [ˈpɑːtnəʳ] **1** N (*gen*) compagno(-a), partner *m/f inv*; (*Comm*) socio(-a); (*in crime*) complice *m/f*; (*Sport*) compagno(-a); (*at dance: male*) cavaliere *m*; (*: female*) dama.
2 VT (*Sport*) essere in coppia con; (*at dance*) accompagnare; (*in individual dance*) ballare con.

part·ner·ship [ˈpɑːtnəʃɪp] N (*gen*) associazione *f*; (*Comm*) società *f inv*; **to take sb into partnership** prendere qn come socio(-a); **to go into partnership (with)** [OR] **form a partnership (with)** mettersi in società (con), associarsi (a).

♦ **part of speech** N (*Gram*) parte del discorso.

par·took [pɑːˈtʊk] PT of **partake**.

♦ **part owner** N comproprietario(-a).

♦ **part payment** N acconto.

par·tridge [ˈpɑːtrɪdʒ] N pernice *f*.

♦ **part-time** [ˈpɑːtˈtaɪm] ADV, ADJ part-time *inv*.

♦ **part-timer** [ˌpɑːtˈtaɪməʳ] N (*also:* **part-time worker**) impiegato(-a) *or* lavoratore(-trice) part-time *inv*.

part·way [ˈpɑːtweɪ] ADV: **partway through sth** (*fam*) a metà di qc.

par·ty [ˈpɑːti] **1** N **a** (*Pol*) partito
b (*group*) gruppo; (*Mil, team*) squadra; **a party of travellers** una comitiva di viaggiatori
c (*celebration*) festa; **to have** *or* **give** *or* **throw a party** dare una festa *or* un party
d (*Law*) parte *f* (in causa); **the parties to a dispute** le parti in causa; **to be a party to a crime** essere coinvolto (-a) in un reato; **he refused to be a party to such an agreement** si è rifiutato di entrare in un accordo del genere.
2 ADJ (*leader*) del *or* di partito; (*dress, finery*) della festa.

par·ty·ing [ˈpɑːtiɪŋ] N (*fam*): **he loves partying** gli piace far baldoria.

♦ **party line** N **a** (*Pol*) linea del partito **b** (*Telec*) duplex *m inv*.

♦ **party piece** N (*Brit fam*): **to do one's party piece** esibirsi nel proprio pezzo forte per divertire gli altri.

♦ **party political broadcast** N *comunicato radiotelevisivo di propaganda*.

♦ **party politics** N (*Pol*) propaganda di partito.

♦ **party wall** N muro di confine *or* divisorio.

♦ **par value** [ˈpɑːˌvæljuː] N (*of share, bond*) valore *m* nominale.

par·venu [ˈpɑːvənˌjuː] N (*frm*) parvenu *m inv*.

pass [pɑːs] **1** N **a** (*permit*) lasciapassare *m inv*; (*for bus, train*) tesserino; (*Mil etc*) permesso.
b (*Geog: in mountains*) passo, gola, valico
c (*Sport*) passaggio
d (*in exams*) sufficienza; **to get a pass in German** prendere la sufficienza in tedesco
e : **things have come to a pretty pass** ecco a cosa siamo arrivati
f : **to make a pass at sb** (*fam*) fare delle proposte *or* delle avances a qn.
2 VT **a** (*move past*) passare, oltrepassare; (*in opposite direction*) incrociare; (*Aut: overtake*) sorpassare, superare; **they passed each other on the way** si sono incrociati per strada

b (*hand, give*) (*far*) passare; (*Sport: ball*) passare; **he passed his hand over his forehead** si passò la mano sulla fronte; **to pass a thread through a hole** far passare un filo attraverso un foro; **to pass sb sth** *or* **sth to sb** passare qc a qn

c (*Scol: exam*) superare, passare; (: *candidate*) promuovere

d (*approve: motion, plan*) approvare, votare

e (*spend: time*) passare, trascorrere; **we passed the weekend pleasantly** abbiamo trascorso *or* passato piacevolmente il fine settimana; **it passes the time** fa passare il tempo

f (*express: remark*) fare; (: *opinion*) esprimere; **to pass the time of day with sb** scambiarsi i (soliti) convenevoli.

3 VI **a** (*come, go*): **to pass (through)** passare (per); (*Aut: overtake*) sorpassare; **he passed by the cinema** è passato davanti al cinema; **to pass out of sight** sparire alla vista; **to pass into oblivion** cadere nell'oblio; **to pass into history** passare alla storia

b (*be accepted: behaviour*) essere accettabile; (: *plan*) essere approvato(-a); **she could pass for twenty-five** potrebbe passare per una venticinquenne; **what passes for art these days** quel che si definisce arte oggigiorno; **is this okay? — oh, it'll pass** questo va bene? — sì, può andare; **I decided to let it pass** ho deciso di lasciar correre

c (*time, day*) passare; **how time passes!** come passa il tempo!

d (*pain*) passare; (*memory, opportunity*) sfuggire

e (*in exam*) essere promosso(-a)

f (*happen*) accadere; **all that passed between them** tutto quello che c'è stato fra loro; **should it come to pass that …** (*frm*) dovesse accadere che…

g (*Cards*) passare

▶ **pass along** VT + ADV far passare

▶ **pass around** VT + ADV = **pass round**

▶ **pass away** VI + ADV (*euph: die*) mancare, spegnersi

▶ **pass back** VT + ADV (*object*) passare indietro; **I will now pass you back to the studio** (*Radio, TV*) e ora ridiamo la linea allo studio

▶ **pass by** [1] VI + ADV passare (di qui *or* lì).

[2] VT + ADV (*ignore*) ignorare, passar sopra a; **life has passed her by** non ha davvero vissuto

▶ **pass down** VT + ADV (*customs, inheritance*) tramandare, trasmettere

▶ **pass off** [1] VI + ADV (*happen*) svolgersi, andare; (*wear off: faintness, headache*) passare.

[2] VT + ADV: **to pass sb/sth off as** far passare qn/qc per

▶ **pass on** [1] VI + ADV (*euph: die*) spegnersi, mancare; (*proceed*): **to pass on (to)** passare (a).

[2] VT + ADV (*hand on*): **to pass on (to)** (*news, information, object*) passare (a); (*cold, illness*) attaccare *or* contagiare (a); (*benefits*) trasmettere (a); (*price rises*) riversare (su)

▶ **pass out** VI + ADV (*become unconscious*) svenire; (*Brit Mil*) uscire dall'accademia

▶ **pass over** [1] VI + ADV (*euph: die*) spirare.

[2] VT + ADV (*topic*) ignorare; (*employee, candidate*) non prendere in considerazione

▶ **pass round, pass around** VT + ADV (*bottle, photographs*) far girare; **could you pass the vegetables round?** potrebbe far passare la verdura?

▶ **pass through** [1] VI + ADV essere di passaggio.

[2] VT + ADV (*country, city*) passare per; (*hardships*) attraversare

▶ **pass up** VT + ADV (*opportunity*) lasciarsi sfuggire, perdere.

pass·able ['pɑːsəbl] ADJ **a** (*tolerable*) passabile; (*work*) accettabile

b (*road*) transitabile, praticabile; (*river*) attraversabile.

pass·ably ['pɑːsəblɪ] ADV (*tolerably*) discretamente, passabilmente.

pas·sage ['pæsɪdʒ] N **a** (*way through*) passaggio; (*corridor*) corridoio **b** (*Naut: voyage*) traversata; **to grant sb safe passage** garantire a qn di passare incolume **c** (*passing*) passare *m*; (: *of bill through parliament*) iter *m inv*; **with the passage of time** (*frm*) col passar del tempo **d** (*section: of book*) brano, passo; (*of music*) brano.

passage·way ['pæsɪdʒˌweɪ] N passaggio.

pass·book ['pɑːsˌbʊk] N libretto di risparmio.

♦ **pass degree** N laurea col minimo dei voti.

pas·sé ['pæseɪ] ADJ sorpassato(-a), fuori moda.

pas·sen·ger ['pæsɪndʒəʳ] [1] N (*in boat, plane, car*) passeggero(-a); (*on train*) viaggiatore(-trice), passeggero(-a).

[2] ADJ (*aircraft, liner*) di linea, passeggeri *inv*; (*train*) viaggiatori *inv*.

♦ **passenger list** N lista dei passeggeri.

♦ **passenger seat** N (*Aut*) posto di fianco al guidatore.

♦ **passenger traffic** N movimento passeggeri.

♦ **passer-by** ['pɑːsəˈbaɪ] N (*pl* passers-by) passante *m/f*.

pass·ing ['pɑːsɪŋ] [1] ADJ (*fleeting: fancy, thought*) passeggero(-a); (: *moment*) fuggevole; (*glance, remark*) di sfuggita; (*car, person*) di passaggio.

[2] N (*of customs, euph: death*) scomparsa; **with the passing of the years** col passar degli anni; **to mention sth in passing** accennare a qc di sfuggita.

♦ **passing-out parade** [ˌpɑːsɪŋˈaʊtpəˌreɪd] N (*Mil, Police*) parata finale.

♦ **passing place** N (*Aut*) piazzola (di sosta).

pas·sion ['pæʃən] N **a** passione *f*; **to have a passion for sth** aver la passione di qc, avere una passione per qc; **his passion for seafood** la sua passione per i frutti di mare; **his passion for accuracy** il suo amore per la precisione; **to get into a passion (about sth)** andare su tutte le furie (per qc) **b** (*Rel*): **the Passion** la Passione.

pas·sion·ate ['pæʃənɪt] ADJ (*embrace, speech*) appassionato(-a); (*temperament, person*) passionale; (*believer*) convinto(-a); (*desire*) ardente.

pas·sion·ate·ly ['pæʃənɪtlɪ] ADV (*embrace, speak*) appassionatamente; (*believe, desire*) ardentemente; **to be passionately fond of** adorare.

passion·flower ['pæʃənˌflaʊəʳ] N passiflora, fiore *m* della passione.

♦ **passion fruit** N frutto della passione.

♦ **Passion Play** N rappresentazione *f* della Passione di Cristo.

♦ **Passion Sunday** N domenica di Passione.

pas·sive ['pæsɪv] [1] ADJ (*gen, Gram*) passivo(-a).

[2] N passivo; **in the passive** al passivo.

pas·sive·ly ['pæsɪvlɪ] ADV passivamente.

pas·sive·ness ['pæsɪvnɪs], **pas·siv·ity** [pæ'sɪvɪtɪ] N passività.

♦ **passive smoking** N fumo passivo.

pass·key ['pɑːsˌkiː] N passe-partout *m inv*.

♦ **pass mark** N punteggio minimo (*per la promozione*).

Pass·over ['pɑːsˌəʊvəʳ] N Pasqua ebraica.

pass·port ['pɑːspɔːt] N passaporto; (*fig*): **passport (to)** chiave *f* (di).

♦ **passport control** N controllo *m* passaporti *inv*.

pass·word ['pɑːsˌwɜːd] N (also Comput) parola f d'ordine inv.

past [pɑːst] ① ADV: **to walk past, go past** passare; **to run** or **dash past** passare di corsa; **the days flew past** i giorni sono volati (via).

② PREP **a** (in place: in front of) davanti a; (: beyond) oltre, di là di, dopo; **I go past the school every day** passo davanti alla scuola ogni giorno; **it's just past the church** è appena oltre la chiesa

b (in time) passato(-a); **it's past midnight** è mezzanotte passata; **quarter/half past four** le quattro e un quarto/e mezzo; **at twenty past four** alle quattro e venti

c (beyond the limits of) al di là di, oltre; **it's past belief** è assolutamente incredibile; **I'm past caring** non me ne importa più nulla; **she's past forty** ha passato i quaranta; **to be past it** (fam: person) essere finito(-a); (: object) essere da buttar via; **I wouldn't put it past her to do it** (fam) non sarei affatto sorpreso se lo facesse.

③ ADJ (gen, Gram) passato(-a); (president, pupil) ex inv; **for some time past** da qualche tempo; **for the past few days** da qualche giorno, in questi ultimi giorni; **for the past 3 days** negli ultimi 3 giorni; **in past years** negli anni passati; **those days are past now** è passato quel tempo.

④ N passato; **in the past** in or nel passato; (Gram) al passato; **it's a thing of the past** è una cosa del passato.

pas·ta ['pæstə] N (Culin) pasta.

paste [peɪst] ① N **a** (substance, consistency) impasto; (glue) colla; **fish paste** pâté m inv di pesce **b** (gems) strass m inv.

② ADJ (jewellery) di strass.

③ VT (put glue on) spalmare di colla, collare; (fasten with glue) incollare; **to paste sth to the wall** appiccicare qc al muro.

paste·board ['peɪstˌbɔːd] N cartone m.

pas·tel ['pæstəl] ① N (crayon, drawing) pastello; (colour) colore m pastello inv.

② ADJ (colour) pastello inv; (drawing) a pastello.

♦ **paste-up** ['peɪstˌʌp] N collage m inv.

pas·teur·ize ['pæstəˌraɪz] VT pastorizzare.

pas·teur·ized ['pæstəˌraɪzd] ADJ pastorizzato(-a).

pas·tiche [pæ'stiːʃ] N (frm) pastiche m inv.

pas·tille ['pæstɪl] N pastiglia.

pas·time ['pɑːsˌtaɪm] N passatempo.

past·ing ['peɪstɪŋ] N (fam: thrashing) battuta, botte fpl.

♦ **past master** N: **to be a past master at** essere molto esperto(-a) in.

pas·tor ['pɑːstəʳ] N (Rel) pastore m.

pas·to·ral ['pɑːstərəl] ADJ (land) da pascolo; (scene, poetry, also Rel) pastorale.

♦ **past participle** N participio passato.

♦ **past perfect** N: **the past perfect** il piuccheperfetto, il trapassato (prossimo e remoto).

pas·try ['peɪstrɪ] N (dough) pasta (per rustici, dolci) (cake) pasta, pasticcino.

♦ **pastry board** N spianatoia.

♦ **pastry case** N base f di (or per) pasticcino.

♦ **pastry cook** N pasticciere(-a).

♦ **pastry cutter** N stampino per biscotti.

♦ **pastry fork** N forchetta da dolce.

♦ **pastry wheel** N rotella.

♦ **past tense** N passato; **in the past tense** al passato.

pas·ture ['pɑːstʃəʳ] N pascolo; **to put animals out to pasture** condurre gli animali al pascolo; **to move on to pastures new** (fig) cambiare aria.

♦ **pasture land** N pascolo.

pasty¹ ['pæstɪ] N (pie) sfogliatina salata ripiena di carne e patate.

pasty² ['peɪstɪ] ADJ (comp **-ier**, superl **-iest**) (complexion) smorto(-a).

pat¹ [pæt] ① N **a** (with hand) colpetto (affettuoso); (to animal) carezza; **to give sb/o.s. a pat on the back** (fig) congratularsi or compiacersi con qn/se stesso **b** (of butter) panetto.

② VT (hair, face etc) dare dei colpetti leggeri a; (dog) accarezzare; (sb's shoulder etc) dare un colpetto (affettuoso) su.

pat² [pæt] ADJ, ADV: **the answer came** or **was too pat** la risposta è stata troppo pronta; **he knows it (off) pat** OR (Am) **he has it down pat** lo conosce or sa a menadito.

patch [pætʃ] ① N (piece of cloth, material) toppa, pezza; (on tyre) toppa; (eye patch) benda; (area of colour, spot) macchia; (piece of land) appezzamento, pezzo; **a patch of blue sky** un pezzetto di cielo azzurro; **a vegetable patch** un orticello; **the team is going through a bad patch** la squadra sta attraversando un brutto periodo; **it's not a patch on the other one** (fam) non vale neanche la metà dell'altro.

② VT (garment, hole) rattoppare, mettere una pezza a

▸ **patch together** VT + ADV (cobble together: agreement, strategy) mettere insieme alla meglio; (article, report) raffazzonare

▸ **patch up** VT + ADV (clothes) rattoppare; (car, machine) riparare alla meglio; (quarrel) appianare; (marriage) rimettere in sesto.

patch·work ['pætʃˌwɜːk] ① N patchwork m inv; **a patchwork of fields** (fig) un mosaico di campi.

② ADJ (quilt) patchwork inv.

patchy ['pætʃɪ] ADJ (comp **-ier**, superl **-iest**) (performance etc) pieno(-a) di alti e bassi; (knowledge) incompleto (-a); (fog) a banchi; (colour) irregolare.

pate [peɪt] N: **a bald pate** una testa pelata.

pâté ['pæteɪ] N pâté m inv.

pat·en ['pætən] N patena.

pa·tent ['peɪtənt] ① ADJ (obvious) evidente, palese.

② N brevetto; **to take out a patent on sth** far brevettare qc.

③ VT brevettare.

♦ **patent leather** N vernice f (pellame).

pa·tent·ly ['peɪtəntlɪ] ADV palesemente.

♦ **patent medicine** N prodotto medicinale.

♦ **Patent Office** N: **the Patent Office** l'ufficio brevetti.

pa·ter·nal [pə'tɜːnl] ADJ paterno(-a).

pa·ter·nal·ism [pə'tɜːnəlɪzm] N paternalismo.

pa·ter·nal·ist [pə'tɜːnəlɪst], **pa·ter·nal·is·tic** [pəˌtɜːnə'lɪstɪk] ADJ paternalistico(-a).

pa·ter·nal·ly [pə'tɜːnəlɪ] ADV paternamente, in modo paterno.

pa·ter·nity [pə'tɜːnɪtɪ] N paternità.

♦ **paternity suit** N (Law) causa di riconoscimento della paternità.

path [pɑːθ] N (pl **paths** [pɑːðz]) **a** (gen) sentiero, viottolo; (in garden) vialetto; (fig) strada, via **b** (of river) corso; (of sun, missile, planet) traiettoria.

pa·thet·ic [pə'θɛtɪk] ADJ **a** (pitiful) patetico(-a), toccante **b** (very bad) penoso(-a), pietoso(-a).

pa·theti·cal·ly [pə'θɛtɪklɪ] ADV da far pena, da far pietà; **pathetically thin/weak** spaventosamente magro(-a)/debole; **a pathetically inadequate answer** una risposta da far cascar le braccia.

patho·gen ['pæθə,dʒɛn] N agente *m* patogeno.
patho·gen·ic [,pæθə'dʒɛnɪk] ADJ patogeno(-a).
patho·logi·cal [,pæθə'lɒdʒɪkəl] ADJ (*also fig*) patologico (-a).
pa·tholo·gist [pə'θɒlədʒɪst] N patologo(-a).
pa·thol·ogy [pə'θɒlədʒɪ] N patologia.
pa·thos ['peɪθɒs] N pathos *m inv*.
path·way ['pɑ:θ,weɪ] N sentiero, viottolo.
pa·tience ['peɪʃəns] N a pazienza; **to lose one's patience** spazientirsi; **to lose one's patience with sb/sth** perdere la pazienza con qn/qc; **he has no patience with children** non ha pazienza con i bambini b (*Brit Cards*) solitario; **to play patience** fare un solitario.
pa·tient ['peɪʃənt] 1 ADJ paziente; **to be patient with sb** essere paziente *or* aver pazienza con qn.
2 N (*Med*) paziente *m/f*, malato(-a).
pa·tient·ly ['peɪʃəntlɪ] ADV pazientemente.
pa·tio ['pætɪəʊ] N terrazza.
pa·tri·arch ['peɪtrɪ,ɑ:k] N patriarca *m*.
pa·tri·ar·chal [peɪtrɪ'ɑ:kəl] ADJ (*society, role*) patriarcale; (*man, figure*) dall'aspetto patriarcale.
pa·tri·cian [pə'trɪʃən] (*frm*) 1 ADJ (*family, looks, features*) aristocratico(-a).
2 N nobile *m/f*.
pa·tri·ot ['peɪtrɪət] N patriota *m/f*.
pat·ri·ot·ic [,pætrɪ'ɒtɪk] ADJ patriottico(-a).
pat·ri·oti·cal·ly [,pætrɪ'ɒtɪkəlɪ] ADV patriotticamente, con patriottismo.
pat·ri·ot·ism ['pætrɪə,tɪzəm] N patriottismo.
pa·trol [pə'trəʊl] 1 N a (*gen*) ronda, giro d'ispezione; (*by plane*) ricognizione *f*; (*by boat*) perlustrazione *f*; **to be on patrol** fare la ronda; essere in ricognizione; essere in perlustrazione b (*patrol unit*) pattuglia.
2 VT pattugliare.
3 VI fare la ronda; **to patrol up and down** andare avanti e indietro.
♦ **patrol boat** N guardacoste *m inv*.
♦ **patrol car** N autopattuglia (della polizia).
♦ **patrol leader** N capopattuglia *m*.
patrol·man [pə'trəʊlmən] N (*pl* -**men**) a (*Am*) agente *m* di polizia b (*Aut*) membro del personale del soccorso stradale.
♦ **patrol wagon** N (*Am*) (furgone *m*) cellulare.
pa·tron ['peɪtrən] N (*of artist*) mecenate *m/f*; (*of charity*) benefattore(-trice); (*of society*) patrono(-essa); (*of shop, hotel*) cliente *m/f* abituale; **patron of the arts** mecenate *m/f*.
pat·ron·age ['pætrənɪdʒ] N (*gen*) patrocinio; (*of shop etc*) frequentazione *f*; **under the patronage of** sotto l'alto patrocinio *or* patronato di; **patronage of the arts** mecenatismo.
pat·ron·ize ['pætrə,naɪz] VT a (*fig: treat condescendingly*) trattare con condiscendenza b (*shop*) essere cliente abituale di; (*cinema*) frequentare.
pat·ron·iz·ing ['pætrə,naɪzɪŋ] ADJ condiscendente.
pat·ron·iz·ing·ly ['pætrə,naɪzɪŋlɪ] ADV con condiscendenza.
♦ **patron saint** N patrono(-a).
pat·ro·nym·ic [,pætrə'nɪmɪk] ADJ, N patronimico(-a).
pat·ter¹ ['pætə'] N (*comedian's*) monologo; (*conjuror's*) chiacchiere *fpl*; (*sales talk*) discorsetto imbonitore.
pat·ter² ['pætə'] 1 N (*of feet*) scalpiccio; (*of rain*) picchiettio.
2 VI (*person*) trotterellare; (*rain*) picchiettare.
pat·tern ['pætən] 1 N a (*design*) motivo, disegno

b (*Sewing*) modello (di carta), cartamodello; (*fig*) modello; **pattern of events** sequenza degli avvenimenti; **behaviour patterns** tipi *mpl* di comportamento c (*sample*) campione *m*.
2 VT (*model*): **to pattern a dress on** fare un vestito sul modello di; **to pattern o.s. on sb/sth** prendere a modello qn/qc.
♦ **pattern book** N album *m inv* di modelli.
pat·terned ['pætənd] ADJ a disegni, a motivi; (*material*) fantasia *inv*.
pau·city ['pɔ:sɪtɪ] N (*frm*) scarsità.
paunch [pɔ:ntʃ] N pancia.
paunchy ['pɔ:ntʃɪ] ADJ (*comp* -**ier**, *superl* -**iest**) pancione (-a).
pau·per ['pɔ:pə'] N indigente *m/f*; **pauper's grave** fossa comune.
pau·per·ize ['pɔ:pə,raɪz] VT ridurre in miseria.
pause [pɔ:z] 1 N a (*gen*) pausa; (*Mus*) pausa; (: *sign*) corona; **there was a pause while** ... ci fu un momento di attesa mentre....
2 VI (*gen*) fermarsi un momento; (*in speech*) fare una pausa; **to pause for breath** fermarsi un attimo per riprendere fiato.
pave [peɪv] VT (*gen*) lastricare; (*road*) pavimentare, lastricare; **to pave the way for** (*fig: person*) spianare la strada a; (: *changes, reforms*) aprire la via a.
pave·ment ['peɪvmənt] N (*Brit*) marciapiede *m*; (*Am*) pavimentazione *f* stradale.
pa·vil·ion [pə'vɪlɪən] N (*gen*) padiglione *m*; (*Sport*) tribuna annessa ad un campo da cricket in cui sono anche alloggiati gli spogliatoi.
pav·ing ['peɪvɪŋ] N pavimentazione *f*.
♦ **paving stone** N lastra di pavimentazione.
paw [pɔ:] 1 N (*of animal, also fam: hand*) zampa.
2 VT a (*subj: animal*) dare una zampata a; **to paw the ground** (*also fig*) scalpitare b (*pej: sexually*) palpare, mettere le zampe addosso a.
pawn¹ [pɔ:n] N (*Chess*) pedone *m*; (*fig*) pedina; **to be sb's pawn** lasciarsi manovrare da qn.
pawn² [pɔ:n] 1 N: **in pawn** impegnato(-a) al monte di pietà; (*article pledged*) pegno; **to leave** *or* **put sth in pawn** impegnare qc.
2 VT impegnare, dare in pegno.
pawn·broker ['pɔ:n,brəʊkə'] N prestatore(-trice) su pegno.
pawn·shop ['pɔ:n,ʃɒp] N monte *m* di pietà.
pay [peɪ] (*vb: pt, pp* **paid**) 1 N (*gen*) paga; **to be in sb's pay** essere pagato(-a) da *or* essere al servizio di qn.
2 VT a (*gen*) pagare; (*debt, account*) saldare, pagare; **he paid him £10** gli ha dato 10 sterline; **I paid £15 for that record** quel disco l'ho pagato 15 sterline; **how much did you pay for it?** quanto l'hai pagato?; **to be** *or* **get paid on Fridays** prendere *or* riscuotere la paga il venerdì; **a badly paid worker** un(-a) lavoratore(-trice) mal pagato (-a); **that's what you're paid for** sei pagato per questo; **to pay one's way** (*to contribute one's share*) pagare la propria parte; (*to remain solvent: company*) coprire le spese; **to put paid to** (*plan, person*) rovinare; (*trip*) impedire; **to pay the penalty** (*fig*) pagare le conseguenze; **to pay dividends** (*Fin*) pagare dividendi; (*fig*) dare buoni frutti
b (*be profitable to: also fig*) convenire a; **it won't pay you to do that** non ti conviene farlo
c (*attention*) fare, prestare; (*homage*) rendere; (*respects*) porgere; see **visit**.

3 VI **a** pagare; **to pay in advance** pagare in anticipo; **don't worry, I'll pay** non preoccuparti, pagherò io; **they paid for her to go to Italy** le hanno pagato il viaggio in Italia

b (*be profitable*) rendere, convenire; **the business doesn't pay** l'attività non rende *or* non è redditizia; **it pays to be courteous** ci si guadagna sempre ad essere gentile; **it pays to advertise** far pubblicità conviene sempre; **crime doesn't pay** il delitto non paga

c (*fig: to suffer*) pagare; **she paid for it with her life** le è costato la vita, ha pagato con la vita; **I'll make you pay for this!** te la farò pagare!

▸ **pay back** VT + ADV

a restituire; **to pay sb back** rimborsare qn

b (*in revenge*) farla pagare a qn; **to pay sb back for doing sth** farla pagare a qn per aver fatto qc

▸ **pay down** VT + ADV versare un acconto di

▸ **pay for** VI + PREP pagare

▸ **pay in** VT + ADV versare, depositare

▸ **pay off** **1** VT + ADV **a** (*debts*) saldare; (*creditor*) pagare; (*mortgage*) estinguere; **to pay sth off in instalments** pagare qc a rate

b (*discharge*) licenziare.

2 VI + ADV (*scheme, ruse*) funzionare; (*patience, decision*) dare dei frutti

▸ **pay out** VT + ADV **a** (*money*) sborsare, tirar fuori; (*subj: cashier*) pagare

b (*rope*) far allentare

▸ **pay up** VT + ADV, VI + ADV saldare, pagare.

pay·able ['perəbl] ADJ pagabile; **to make a cheque payable to sb** intestare un assegno a (nome di) qn.

♦ **pay award** N aumento salariale.

♦ **pay-bed** ['perbed] N (*Brit*) *posto letto a pagamento in un ospedale pubblico.*

pay·day ['per,der] N giorno di paga.

♦ **pay desk** N cassa.

PAYE [,pi:erwar'i:] N ABBR (*Brit: = pay as you earn*) *sistema di pagamento delle imposte mediante trattenute sulle retribuzioni.*

payee [per'i:] N beneficiario(-a).

♦ **pay envelope** N (*Am*) = **pay packet.**

♦ **pay increase** N (*for individual*) aumento di stipendio; (*for group of workers*) aumento salariale.

pay·ing ['peɪɪŋ] ADJ (*business, scheme*) redditizio(-a).

♦ **paying guest** N ospite *m/f* pagante, pensionante *m/f*.

♦ **paying-in book** [,peɪɪŋ'mbuk] N (*Brit*) *carnet di distinte di versamento.*

♦ **paying-in slip** [,peɪɪŋ'ɪn,slɪp] N modulo di versamento.

pay·load ['per,ləud] N carico utile.

pay·master ['per,mɑːstəʳ] N (*Mil*) ufficiale *m* pagatore.

pay·ment ['permənt] N (*gen*) pagamento; (*of debt, account, interest*) saldo, pagamento; (*fig: reward*) ricompensa; **advance payment** (*part sum*) anticipo, acconto; (*total sum*) pagamento anticipato; **deferred payment** [OR] **payment by instalments** pagamento dilazionato *or* a rate; **payment in full** (pagamento a) saldo; **payment on account** acconto; **payment by results** ≈ premio di produzione; **in payment of** (*sum owed*) come saldo di; **in payment for** [OR] **as payment for** (*goods*) come pagamento di; (*help, efforts, kindness*) in cambio di, come ricompensa per; **on payment of £5** dietro pagamento di 5 sterline.

pay·off ['per,ɒf] N (*fam: payment*) saldo; (: *reward*) ricompensa; (: *retribution*) resa dei conti; (: *of joke*) finale *m*.

♦ **pay packet,** (*Am*) **pay envelope** N busta *f* paga *inv*.

pay·phone ['per,fəun], (*Am*) **pay station** N cabina telefonica.

♦ **pay rise** N = **pay increase.**

pay·roll ['per,rəul] N (*list*) lista del personale; (*money*) paga (di tutto il personale); (*employees*) personale *m*; **to be on a firm's payroll** far parte dell'organico di una ditta.

♦ **pay slip** N (*Brit*) busta *f* paga *inv*.

♦ **pay station** N (*Am*) = **payphone.**

PBS [,pi:bi:'ɛs] N ABBR (*Am*: = *Public Broadcasting Service*) *servizio che collabora alla realizzazione di programmi per la rete televisiva nazionale.*

PBX [,pi:bi:'ɛks] ABBR (*Telec*: = *private branch exchange*) *sistema telefonico con centralino.*

PC [,pi:'si:] **1** N ABBR **a** = **personal computer b** (*Brit*) = **police constable.**

2 ABBR (*Brit*) = **Privy Councillor.**

3 ADJ ABBR = **politically correct.**

pc [,pi:'si:] ABBR **a** (=*postcard*) CP (= *cartolina postale*) **b** = *per cent.*

p/c ABBR = *petty cash.*

pcm [,pi:si:'ɛm] ABBR = *per calendar month.*

PD [,pi:'di:] N ABBR (*Am*) = **Police Department.**

pd ABBR = *paid.*

pdq [,pi:di:'kju:] ADV ABBR (*fam*)= *pretty damn quick.*

PDSA [,pi:di:ɛs'er] N ABBR (*Brit*: = *People's Dispensary for Sick Animals*) *assistenza veterinaria pubblica.*

PDT [,pi:di:'ti:] ABBR (*Am*: = *Pacific Daylight Time*) *ora legale del Pacifico.*

PE [,pi:'i:] **1** N ABBR (= *physical education*) ed. fisica.

2 ABBR (*Canada*)= *Prince Edward Island.*

pea [pi:] N pisello; **green peas** pisellini *mpl*.

peace [pi:s] N (*gen*) pace *f*; **to be at peace with sb/sth** essere in pace con qn/qc; **he is at peace** (*euph: dead*) riposa in pace; **to make peace between** rappacificare; **to make one's peace with** fare la pace con; **peace of mind** tranquillità di spirito; **peace and quiet** pace e tranquillità; **to keep the peace** (*subj: policeman*) mantenere l'ordine pubblico; (: *citizen*) rispettare l'ordine pubblico; (*fig*) calmare le acque.

peace·able ['pi:səbl] ADJ pacifico(-a).

peace·ably ['pi:səblɪ] ADV in pace, pacificamente.

♦ **peace conference** N conferenza per la pace.

♦ **Peace Corps** NSG (*Am*) *organizzazione che invia giovani volontari in paesi sottosviluppati.*

peace·ful ['pi:sful] ADJ (*person, coexistence*) pacifico(-a); (*demonstration*) non violento(-a); (*period*) di pace; (*place, life, sleep*) tranquillo(-a).

peace·ful·ly ['pi:sfəlɪ] ADV (*coexist, reign*) in pace; (*demonstrate*) senza violenza; (*sleep, work, live*) tranquillamente.

peace·ful·ness ['pi:sfʊlnɪs] N tranquillità, pace *f*.

peace·keep·ing ['pi:s,ki:pɪŋ] **1** ADJ (*operation, force*) di pace.

2 N mantenimento della pace.

♦ **peace-loving** ['pi:s,lʌvɪŋ] ADJ pacifico(-a).

peace·maker ['pi:s,meɪkəʳ] N (*between nations*) mediatore (-trice) di pace; (*between individuals*) conciliatore(-trice) *m/f*.

♦ **peace offering** N (*fig*) dono in segno di riconciliazione.

♦ **peace pipe** N calumet *m inv* (della pace).

♦ **peace talks** NPL negoziati *mpl* per la pace.

peace·time ['pi:s,taɪm] N: **in peacetime** in tempo di pace.

♦ **peace treaty** N trattato di pace.

peach [pi:tʃ] **1** N **a** (*fruit*) pesca; (*tree*) pesco **b** (*fam*) : **she's a peach** è un amore.
2 ADJ (*blossom*) di pesco; (*colour*) (color) pesca *inv.*
♦ **peach melba** [ˈpi:tʃˈmɛlbə] N pesche *fpl* melba *inv.*
pea·cock [ˈpi:ˌkɒk] N pavone *m.*
♦ **peacock blue** ADJ, N azzurro pavone *(m) inv.*
♦ **pea green** ADJ, N verde pisello *(m) inv.*
pea·hen [ˈpi:ˌhɛn] N pavona, pavonessa.
peak [pi:k] **1** N (*of mountain*) vetta, cima; (*mountain itself*) picco; (*of roof etc*) cima; (*of cap*) visiera; (*on graph*) vertice *m*; (*fig: of power, career*) apice *m*, vertice; **to be at its peak** (*fame, career, empire*) essere all'apice; (*business*) essere nella fase culminante; (*traffic, demand*) aver raggiunto il livello massimo; **he was at the peak of fitness** era al massimo della forma fisica.
2 ADJ (*demand, production*) massimo(-a).
peaked [pi:kt] ADJ **a** (*cap*) con visiera **b** = **peaky.**
♦ **peak hours** NPL ore *fpl* di punta.
♦ **peak period** N periodo di punta.
♦ **peak rate** N tariffa ore di punta.
peaky [ˈpi:kɪ] ADJ (*comp* -**ier**, *superl* -**iest**) (*Brit fam*) sbattuto(-a); **I'm feeling a bit peaky** mi sento un po' giù.
peal [pi:l] **1** N (*sound of bells*) scampanio; **peal of thunder** fragore *m* di tuono; **peals of laughter** scoppi *mpl* di risa.
2 VT suonare (a distesa).
3 VI (*also:* **peal out:** *bell*) suonare (a distesa); (: *thunder*) rimbombare.
pea·nut [ˈpi:ˌnʌt] N arachide *f,* nocciolina americana; **to work for peanuts** (*fam*) lavorare per una miseria.
♦ **peanut butter** N burro di arachidi.
♦ **peanut oil** N olio di semi di arachide.
pear [pɛəʳ] N (*fruit*) pera; (*tree*) pero.
pearl [pɜ:l] **1** N perla; **pearl of wisdom** (*fig*) perla di saggezza; **to cast pearls before swine** (*fig*) gettare le perle ai porci.
2 ADJ (*necklace, brooch*) di perle; (*buttons*) di madreperla.
♦ **pearl barley** N orzo perlato.
♦ **pearl diver** N pescatore(-trice) di perle.
♦ **pearl oyster** N ostrica perlifera.
pearly [ˈpɜ:lɪ] ADJ (*comp* -**ier**, *superl* -**iest**) (*teeth*) come perle; (*buttons*) a perla; **pearly white** bianco perla *inv*; **the Pearly Gates** (*hum*) le porte del paradiso.
♦ **pear-shaped** [ˈpɛəˌʃeɪpt] ADJ a forma di pera; (*woman*) con le spalle strette e i fianchi larghi.
peas·ant [ˈpɛzənt] **1** N contadino(-a).
2 ADJ (*life*) dei contadini; (*societies*) contadino(-a); (*dress*) da contadino(-a).
♦ **peasant farmer** N contadino(-a).
pea·shooter [ˈpi:ˌʃu:təʳ] N cerbottana.
♦ **pea soup** N passato *or* crema di piselli.
peat [pi:t] N torba.
♦ **peat bog** N torbiera.
peaty [ˈpi:tɪ] ADJ (*comp* -**ier**, *superl* -**iest**) torboso(-a).
peb·ble [ˈpɛbl] N ciottolo; **you're not the only pebble on the beach** (*fam*) non ci sei mica solo tu.
♦ **pebble dash** N (*Brit*) intonaco a pinocchino.
peb·bly [ˈpɛblɪ] ADJ (*beach*) di ciottoli.
pe·can [pɪˈkæn] N pecan *m inv.*
pec·ca·dil·lo [ˌpɛkəˈdɪləʊ] N peccatuccio.
peck [pɛk] **1** N (*of bird*) beccata; (*fam: kiss*) bacetto; **to take a peck at** beccare.
2 VT (*subj: bird: grain*) beccare; (: *person*) dare una beccata a; (*hole*) fare a furia di beccate.
3 VI: **to peck at** (*subj: bird*) beccare; (: *person: food*)

mangiucchiare; **he pecked at his food** sbocconcellò il suo cibo.
peck·ing or·der [ˈpɛkɪŋˌɔ:dəʳ] N (*fig*) ordine *m* gerarchico.
peck·ish [ˈpɛkɪʃ] ADJ (*Brit fam*): **to feel a bit peckish** avere un languorino.
pec·tin [ˈpɛktɪn] N pectina.
pec·to·ral [ˈpɛktərəl] ADJ pettorale; **pectoral fins** pinne *fpl* ventrali.
pe·cu·li·ar [pɪˈkju:lɪəʳ] ADJ **a** (*strange: idea, smell*) strano (-a), curioso(-a) **b** (*particular: importance, qualities*) particolare; **peculiar to** caratteristico(-a) di, tipico(-a) di; **it is a phrase peculiar to him** è un modo di dire tutto suo.
pe·cu·li·ar·ity [pɪˌkju:lɪˈærɪtɪ] N peculiarità *f inv.*
pe·cu·liar·ly [pɪˈkju:lɪəlɪ] ADV **a** (*exceptionally*) particolarmente **b** (*strangely*) in un modo strano, in un modo curioso.
pe·cu·ni·ary [pɪˈkju:nɪərɪ] ADJ pecuniario(-a).
peda·gog·ic [ˌpɛdəˈgɒdʒɪk], **peda·gogi·cal** [ˌpɛdəˈgɒdʒɪkəl] ADJ pedagogico(-a).
peda·gogi·cal·ly [ˌpɛdəˈgɒdʒɪkəlɪ] ADV pedagogicamente.
peda·gogue [ˈpɛdəˌgɒg] N pedagogo(-a).
peda·go·gy [ˈpɛdəˌgɒgɪ] N pedagogia.
ped·al [ˈpɛdl] **1** N pedale *m.*
2 VI pedalare; **to pedal up/down** pedalare su per/giù per.
3 VT: **she pedalled her bicycle up the hill** salì la collina in bicicletta.
♦ **pedal bin** N (*Brit*) pattumiera a pedale.
♦ **pedal car** N automobilina a pedali.
peda·lo [ˈpɛdələʊ] N pedalò *m inv.*
ped·ant [ˈpɛdənt] N pedante *m/f.*
pe·dan·tic [pɪˈdæntɪk] ADJ pedante, pedantesco(-a).
pe·dan·ti·cal·ly [pɪˈdæntɪkəlɪ] ADV pedantemente, con pedanteria.
ped·ant·ry [ˈpɛdəntrɪ] N pedanteria.
ped·dle [ˈpɛdl] VT (*goods*) andare in giro a vendere; (*drugs*) spacciare; (*gossip*) mettere in giro.
ped·dler [ˈpɛdləʳ] N (*esp Am*) = **pedlar.**
ped·er·ast [ˈpɛdərˌæst] N pederasta *m.*
ped·er·as·ty [ˈpɛdərˌæstɪ] N pederastia.
ped·es·tal [ˈpɛdɪstl] N piedistallo; **to put sb on a pedestal** (*fig*) mettere qn su un piedistallo.
pe·des·trian [pɪˈdɛstrɪən] **1** N pedone *m.*
2 ADJ **a** (*pej: style, speech*) prosaico(-a), pedestre **b** (*access*) pedonale.
♦ **pedestrian crossing** N (*Brit*) passaggio pedonale.
pe·des·tri·an·ize [pɪˈdɛstrɪənaɪz] VT pedonalizzare.
♦ **pedestrian precinct** N (*Brit*) zona pedonale.
pe·di·at·ric *etc* [ˌpi:dɪˈætrɪk] = **paediatric** *etc.*
pedi·cel [ˈpɛdɪˌsɛl] N pedicello.
pedi·cure [ˈpɛdɪˌkjʊəʳ] N pedicure *m/f inv.*
pedi·gree [ˈpɛdɪˌgri:] **1** N (*of person*) discendenza, stirpe *f*; (*of animal*) pedigree *m inv.*
2 ADJ di razza (pura).
ped·lar [ˈpɛdləʳ] N venditore(-trice) ambulante; (*of drugs*) spacciatore(-trice).
pe·dom·eter [pɪˈdɒmɪtəʳ] N pedometro, contapassi *m inv.*
pe·dun·cle [pɪˈdʌŋkəl] N peduncolo.
pee [pi:] (*fam*) = **piss.**
peek [pi:k] **1** N sbirciatina; **to take** *or* **have a peek at** dare una sbirciatina a.
2 VI sbirciare.
peel [pi:l] **1** N (*gen*) buccia; (*of orange, lemon etc*) scorza, buccia.

2 VT (*fruit etc*) sbucciare; (*shrimps etc*) sgusciare; **to keep one's eyes peeled** (*fam*) stare all'erta.

3 VI (*wallpaper*) staccarsi; (*paint etc*) scrostarsi; (*skin*) squamarsi; (*person*) spellarsi

▶ **peel away** 1 VI + ADV (*skin*) squamarsi; (*paint*) scrostarsi; (*wallpaper*) staccarsi.

2 VT + ADV (*gen*) staccare; (*paint*) scrostare; (*wrapper*) togliere

▶ **peel back** VT + ADV togliere, levare.

▶ **peel off** 1 VT + ADV a = **peel away** 2
b (*clothes*) togliersi, sfilarsi.
2 VI + ADV = **peel away** 1

peel·er ['pi:lə'] N (*potato knife*) pelapatate *m inv*.

peel·ings ['pi:lɪŋz] NPL bucce *fpl.*

peep[1] [pi:p] 1 N (*of bird*) squittio; (*of chick*) pigolio; (*of whistle*) trillo; **we haven't heard a peep out of them** (*fam*) non hanno aperto bocca.

2 VI (*bird*) squittire; (*whistle*) trillare.

peep[2] [pi:p] 1 N (*Brit*: *look*) sbirciata, sguardo furtivo; **to take** *or* **have a peep (at sth)** dare una sbirciata (a qc).

2 VI: **to peep at sth** sbirciare qc

▶ **peep out** VI + ADV (*Brit*) far capolino; **the sun peeped out from behind the clouds** il sole fece capolino da dietro le nuvole.

peep·hole ['pi:p,həʊl] N spioncino.

Peep·ing Tom [,pi:pɪŋ'tɒm] N guardone *m*.

peep·show ['pi:p,ʃəʊ] N peep-show *m inv*.

peer[1] [pɪə'] N (*noble*) pari *m inv*; (*equal*) pari *m/f inv*, uguale *m/f.*

peer[2] [pɪə'] VI: **to peer at sth** aguzzare gli occhi per vedere qc; **to peer into a room** guardare in una stanza.

peer·age ['pɪərɪdʒ] N dignità di pari; **he was given a peerage** gli è stato conferito il titolo di pari.

peer·ess ['pɪərɪs] N *nobildonna che ha diritto al titolo di pari.*

♦ **peer group** N (*contemporaries*) gruppo di coetanei; (*from same social class, background*) persone *fpl* del proprio ambiente.

peer·less ['pɪəlɪs] ADJ (*frm*) impareggiabile, senza pari.

peeved [pi:vd] ADJ (*fam*) seccato(-a), stizzito(-a).

peev·ish ['pi:vɪʃ] ADJ scontroso(-a), stizzoso(-a).

peev·ish·ly ['pi:vɪʃlɪ] ADV stizzosamente.

pee·wit ['pi:,wɪt] N pavoncella.

peg [pɛg] 1 N (*for tent*) picchetto; (*Brit*: *also*: **clothes peg**) molletta; (*for coat, hat*) attaccapanni *m inv*; **to take sb down a peg (or two)** far abbassare la cresta a qn; **a peg on which to hang a theory** un pretesto per presentare una teoria.

2 VT (*clothes*) appendere con le mollette; (*groundsheet, tent*) fissare con i picchetti; (*fig*: *prices, wages*) fissare, stabilizzare

▶ **peg away** VI + ADV: **to peg away at sth** (*fam*) incaponirsi su qc

▶ **peg down** VT + ADV (*tent*) fissare con i picchetti

▶ **peg out** VI + ADV (*fam*: *die*) crepare, tirare le cuoia.

Pega·sus ['pɛgəsəs] N (*Myth, Astron*) Pegaso.

pe·jo·ra·tive [pɪ'dʒɒrɪtɪv] ADJ spregiativo(-a), peggiorativo(-a).

pe·jo·ra·tive·ly [pɪ'dʒɒrɪtɪvlɪ] ADV spregiativamente.

pe·kin·ese [,pi:kɪ'ni:z] N (*cane*) pechinese *m*.

Pe·king [pi:'kɪŋ], **Pekin** N = **Beijing**.

pe·lag·ic [pɛ'lædʒɪk] ADJ pelagico(-a).

pel·ar·go·nium [,pɛlə'gəʊnɪəm] N pelargonio.

peli·can ['pɛlɪkən] N pellicano.

♦ **pelican crossing** N (*Brit Aut*) attraversamento pedo-

nale con semaforo a controllo manuale.

pel·let ['pɛlɪt] N (*of paper, bread*) pallina; (*for gun*) pallino.

pell-mell ['pɛl'mɛl] ADV disordinatamente, alla rinfusa.

pel·met ['pɛlmɪt] N (*wooden*) cassonetto; (*cloth*) mantovana.

pelt[1] [pɛlt] 1 VT: **to pelt sb with sth** tirare qc addosso a qn; **to pelt sth with sth** colpire qc con qc; **they pelted him with questions** lo hanno tempestato *or* bombardato di domande.

2 VI a : **the rain is pelting (down)** (*fam*) piove a dirotto
b (*fam*: *go fast*): **she pelted across the road** ha attraversato sparata la strada.

pelt[2] [pɛlt] N (*of animal*) pelliccia, pelle *f*.

pel·vic ['pɛlvɪk] ADJ pelvico(-a).

pelvis ['pɛlvɪs] N bacino, pelvi *f inv*.

pen[1] [pɛn] 1 N (*for animals*) recinto, chiuso; (*playpen*) box *m inv*; (*Am fam*: *prison*) gattabuia.

2 VT (*also*: **pen in, pen up**) rinchiudere.

pen[2] [pɛn] 1 N (*gen*) penna; (*felt-tip pen*) pennarello; **to put pen to paper** prendere la penna in mano.

2 VT (*frm*) scrivere.

pe·nal ['pi:nl] ADJ (*gen*) penale; (*tax, fine*) oneroso(-a).

pe·nal·ize ['pi:nəlaɪz] VT a (*punish*) punire b (*Sport*) penalizzare c (*handicap*) handicappare.

♦ **penal servitude** N lavori *mpl* forzati.

pen·al·ty ['pɛnəltɪ] N a (*punishment*) pena; (*fig*: *disadvantage*) svantaggio; (*fine*) ammenda; **those who break the rules do so on penalty of dismissal** coloro che infrangono il regolamento verranno puniti con il licenziamento; **the penalty for not doing this is … se non si fa questo la punizione sarà…

b (*Sport*) penalità *f inv*; (*Ftbl*) (calcio di) rigore *m*.

♦ **penalty area**, **penalty box** N (*Brit Ftbl*) area di rigore.

♦ **penalty clause** N (*in contract*) penale *f*.

♦ **penalty goal** *m inv* su calcio di rigore.

♦ **penalty kick** N (*Ftbl*) calcio di rigore.

♦ **penalty shoot-out** [,pɛnəltɪ'ʃu:t,aʊt] N (*Ftbl*) rigori *mpl*; **to beat a team in a penalty shoot-out** battere una squadra ai rigori.

pen·ance ['pɛnəns] N penitenza; **to do penance for** fare la penitenza per.

♦ **pen-and-ink** [,pɛnənd'ɪŋk] ADJ: **pen-and-ink drawing** disegno a penna.

pence [pɛns] NPL of **penny**.

pen·chant ['pɒŋʃɒŋ] N (*frm*) debole *m*, penchant *m inv*.

pen·cil ['pɛnsl] 1 N matita.

2 ADJ (*drawing, line*) a matita

▶ **pencil in** VT + ADV (*note*) scrivere a matita; (*fig*: *date*) segnarsi provvisoriamente.

♦ **pencil case** N astuccio per matite.

♦ **pen·cil sharp·en·er** ['pɛnsl,ʃɑ:pnə'] N temperamatite *m inv*.

pen·dant ['pɛndənt] N pendaglio.

pend·ing ['pɛndɪŋ] 1 ADJ in sospeso.

2 PREP in attesa di; **pending the arrival of** in attesa dell'arrivo di.

pen·du·lum ['pɛndjʊləm] N pendolo.

pen·etrable ['pɛnɪtrəbl] ADJ penetrabile.

pen·etrate ['pɛnɪtreɪt] 1 VT (*gen, Mil*) penetrare in; (*infiltrate*) infiltrarsi in; (*understand*: *meaning, mystery*) penetrare; (: *truth*) afferrare.

2 VI (*go right through*) penetrare; **the significance of what he was saying finally penetrated** il significato delle sue parole fu finalmente chiaro.

pen·etrat·ing ['pɛnɪˌtreɪtɪŋ] ADJ (*look, sound*) penetrante;

(*question etc*) acuto(-a); (*person, mind etc*) perspicace.

pen·etrat·ing·ly ['pɛnɪˌtreɪtɪŋlɪ] ADV (*look, scream*) in modo penetrante.

pen·etra·tion [ˌpɛnɪ'treɪʃən] N penetrazione *f*.

pen·friend ['pɛnˌfrɛnd] N amico(-a) di penna.

pen·guin ['pɛŋgwɪn] N pinguino.

peni·cil·lin [ˌpɛnɪ'sɪlɪn] N penicillina.

pen·in·su·la [pɪ'nɪmsjʊlə] N penisola.

pe·nis ['piːnɪs] N pene *m*.

peni·tence ['pɛnɪtəns] N penitenza.

peni·tent ['pɛnɪtənt] [1] ADJ pentito(-a).
[2] N penitente *m/f*.

peni·ten·tial [ˌpɛnɪ'tɛnʃəl] ADJ (*frm: tone, look*) contrito (-a); (*psalm*) penitenziale.

peni·ten·tia·ry [ˌpɛnɪ'tɛnʃərɪ] N (*esp Am: prison*) penitenziario, carcere *m*.

peni·tent·ly ['pɛnɪtəntlɪ] ADV (*act, look*) con (un')aria contrita; (*say*) con tono pentito.

pen·knife ['pɛnˌnaɪf] N (*pl* **-knives** ['pɛnˌnaɪvz]) temperino.

♦ **pen name** N pseudonimo.

pen·nant ['pɛnənt] N bandierina.

pen·nies ['pɛnɪz] NPL of **penny**.

pen·ni·less ['pɛnɪlɪs] ADJ senza un soldo *or* una lira.

Pen·nines ['pɛnaɪnz] NPL: **the Pennines** i Pennini.

pen·ny ['pɛnɪ] N (*pl* **pennies** *or* **pence**) (*Brit*) penny *m inv*; (*Am*) centesimo; **in for a penny, in for a pound** abbiamo fatto trenta, facciamo trentuno; **I'm not a penny the wiser** continuo a capirci quanto prima; **she hasn't a penny to her name** non ha un soldo bucato; **he turns up like a bad penny** te lo ritrovi sempre tra i piedi; **a penny for your thoughts** a che pensi?; **and then the penny dropped!** (*fig*) improvvisamente ci sono arrivato!

♦ **penny-pinching** ['pɛnɪ'pɪntʃɪŋ] [1] N: **there should be no penny-pinching** non si dovrebbe stare a lesinare il centesimo.
[2] ADJ (*person*) taccagno(-a), spilorcio(-a).

♦ **pen pal** N (*fam*) amico(-a) di penna.

pen·pusher ['pɛnˌpʊʃəʳ] N (*pej*) scribacchino(-a).

pen·sion ['pɛnʃən] N pensione *f*

▶ **pension off** VT + ADV mandare in pensione.

pen·sion·able ['pɛnʃənəbl] ADJ pensionabile.

♦ **pension book** N (*Brit*) libretto della pensione.

pen·sion·er ['pɛnʃənəʳ] N pensionato(-a).

♦ **pension fund** N fondo pensioni.

♦ **pension scheme** N sistema *m* di pensionamento.

pen·sive ['pɛnsɪv] ADJ pensoso(-a).

pen·sive·ly ['pɛnsɪvlɪ] ADV pensosamente.

Pentagon ['pɛntəgən] N (*Am Pol*): **the Pentagon** il Pentagono.

pen·ta·gon ['pɛntəgən] N pentagono.

pen·tago·nal [pɛn'tægənl] ADJ pentagonale.

pen·tam·eter [pɛnt'æmɪtəʳ] N pentametro.

pen·tath·lon [pɛn'tæθlən] N pentathlon *m inv*.

Pen·tecost ['pɛntɪˌkɒst] N (*Rel*) Pentecoste *f*.

pent·house ['pɛntˌhaʊs] N attico.

pent-up [ˌpɛnt'ʌp] ADJ (*emotions, feelings*) represso(-a).

pe·nul·ti·mate [pɪ'nʌltɪmɪt] ADJ penultimo(-a).

pe·nu·ri·ous [pɪ'njʊərɪəs] ADJ (*frm*) indigente.

penu·ry ['pɛnjʊrɪ] N (*frm*) indigenza.

peo·ny ['pɪənɪ] N peonia.

peo·ple ['piːpl] [1] N **a** (*pl: persons*) persone *fpl*, gente *fsg*; **old people** i vecchi; **young people** i giovani; **some people** alcuni *mpl*, certa gente; **four/several people came** sono venute quattro/parecchie persone; **the room was full of people** la stanza era piena di gente;

what do you people think? e voi (altri) cosa ne pensate?; **some people are born lucky** c'è chi nasce con la camicia; **you of all people should ...** se c'è uno che dovrebbe... quello sei tu

  b (*pl: in general*) gente *fsg*; **many people think that ...** molti pensano che..., molta gente pensa che...; **people say that ...** si dice *or* la gente dice che...

  c (*pl: inhabitants*) abitanti *mpl*; **the people of London** i londinesi; **country people** la gente di campagna; **town people** la gente di città

  d (*pl: Pol: citizens*) popolo; (: *general public*) pubblico; **the people** il popolo; **people at large** il grande pubblico; **a man of the people** un uomo del popolo

  e (*pl: family*) famiglia *fsg*

  f (*sg: nation, race*) popolo, nazione *f*.
[2] VT: **to people (with)** popolare (con); **to be peopled with** essere popolato(-a) di.

PEP [pɛp] N ABBR (*Fin*) = **personal equity plan**.

pep [pɛp] N (*fam*) dinamismo, vitalità

▶ **pep up** VT + ADV (*person*) tirar su; (*party*) animare, vivacizzare; (*food*) rendere più gustoso(-a); (*drink*) correggere.

pep·per ['pɛpəʳ] [1] N **a** (*spice*) pepe *m*; **white/black pepper** pepe bianco/nero **b** (*vegetable*) peperone *m*.
[2] VT pepare; **to pepper an essay with quotations** (*fig*) infarcire un saggio di citazioni.

♦ **pepper-and-salt** [ˌpɛpərən'sɔːlt] ADJ (*hair*) brizzolato (-a), sale e pepe *inv*.

pepper·corn ['pɛpəˌkɔːn] N grano di pepe.

♦ **pepper mill** N macinapepe *m inv*.

pepper·mint ['pɛpəˌmɪnt] N (*Bot*) menta peperita; (*sweet*) caramella alla menta.

pep·pero·ni [ˌpɛpə'rəʊnɪ] N salsiccia piccante.

pepper·pot ['pɛpəˌpɒt] N pepaiola.

pep·pery ['pɛpərɪ] ADJ pepato(-a); (*fig*) irascibile.

♦ **pep pill** N stimolante *m*.

pep·sin ['pɛpsɪn] N pepsina.

♦ **pep talk** N (*fam*) discorso d'incoraggiamento.

pep·tic ['pɛptɪk] ADJ: **peptic ulcer** ulcera peptica.

pep·tide ['pɛptaɪd] N peptide *m*.

per [pɜː'] PREP per, a; **£7 per week/dozen** 7 sterline la *or* alla settimana/dozzina; **per day** al giorno; **per week** alla settimana; **per head** *or* **person** a testa, a *or* per persona; **per hour** all'ora, orario(-a); **per kilo** al *or* il chilo; **per pro** (*by proxy*) per procura; **as per your instructions** secondo le vostre istruzioni.

♦ **per annum** [ˌpər'ænəm] ADV all'anno.

per·bo·rate [pər'bɔːreɪt] N perborato.

per·cale [pə'keɪl] N percalle *m*.

♦ **per capita** [pə'kæpɪtə] ADJ, ADV pro capite (*inv*).

per·ceive [pə'siːv] VT (*sound, meaning, change*) percepire; (*person, object*) notare; (*realize*) accorgersi di.

♦ **per cent** [pə'sɛnt] [1] N per cento;
[2] ADV per cento **a 20 per cent discount** uno sconto del 20 per cento.

per·cent·age [pə'sɛntɪdʒ] N percentuale *f*; **as a percentage** in percentuale; **to get a percentage on all sales** avere una percentuale sulle vendite; **on a percentage basis** a percentuale.

♦ **percentage point** N punto percentuale.

per·cen·tile [pə'sɛntaɪl] N percentile *m*.

per·cep·tible [pə'sɛptəbl] ADJ percettibile.

per·cep·tibly [pə'sɛptɪblɪ] ADV visibilmente.

per·cep·tion [pə'sɛpʃən] N (*gen*) percezione *f*; (*sensitiveness*) sensibilità; (*insight*) perspicacia; **one's perception**

of a situation il proprio modo di vedere una situazione.

per·cep·tive [pə'sɛptɪv] ADJ (gen) perspicace; (analysis) acuto(-a).

per·cep·tive·ly [pə'sɛptɪvlɪ] ADV acutamente, con perspicacia.

perch¹ [pɜːtʃ] N (fish) pesce m persico.

perch² [pɜːtʃ] [1] N (of bird) pertica, posatoio; (in tree) ramo; (fig: for person etc) posto di vedetta.

[2] VT poggiare.

[3] VI (bird, person) appollaiarsi.

per·chance [pə'tʃɑːns] ADV (old: perhaps) forse.

per·co·late ['pɜːkə,leɪt] [1] VT filtrare; **percolated coffee** caffè filtrato.

[2] VI (water, coffee) passare, filtrare; (fig: news) filtrare.

per·co·la·tor ['pɜːkə,leɪtəʳ] N caffettiera a filtro.

per·cus·sion [pə'kʌʃən] N a percussione f b (Mus) percussioni fpl.

♦ **percussion instrument** N strumento a percussione.

per·cus·sion·ist [pə'kʌʃənɪst] N percussionista m/f.

per·egri·na·tion [pɛrɪɡrɪ'neɪʃən] N (frm) peregrinazione f.

per·egrine ['pɛrɪɡrɪn]: **peregrine falcon** N falco pellegrino.

per·emp·to·ri·ly [pə'rɛmptərɪlɪ] ADV perentoriamente.

per·emp·tory [pə'rɛmptərɪ] ADJ perentorio(-a).

per·en·nial [pə'rɛnɪəl] [1] ADJ perenne.

[2] N (Bot) pianta perenne.

per·en·ni·al·ly [pə'rɛnɪəlɪ] ADV perennemente.

per·fect [adj 'pɜːfɪkt; vb pə'fɛkt] [1] ADJ (gen, Gram) perfetto (-a); **it's a perfect day for skiing** è una giornata ideale per sciare; **he's a perfect stranger to me** mi è completamente sconosciuto.

[2] N (Gram: also: **perfect tense**) perfetto.

[3] VT perfezionare; (skill, technique) mettere a punto.

per·fect·ible [pə'fɛktɪbl] ADJ perfettibile.

per·fec·tion [pə'fɛkʃən] N perfezione f; **to perfection** a or alla perfezione.

per·fec·tion·ism [pə'fɛkʃə,nɪzm] N perfezionismo.

per·fec·tion·ist [pə'fɛkʃənɪst] N perfezionista m/f.

per·fect·ly ['pɜːfɪktlɪ] ADV (gen) perfettamente, alla perfezione; **she's perfectly lovely** è una bellezza; **I'm perfectly happy with the situation** sono completamente soddisfatta della situazione; **you know perfectly well** sai benissimo.

♦ **perfect pitch** N (Mus) intonazione f giusta.

per·fidi·ous [pɜː'fɪdɪəs] ADJ perfido(-a).

per·fidi·ous·ly [pɜː'fɪdɪəslɪ] ADV perfidamente.

per·fi·dy ['pɜːfɪdɪ] N perfidia.

per·fo·rate ['pɜːfə,reɪt] VT perforare; **perforated line** linea perforata.

♦ **per·fo·rat·ed ul·cer** ['pɜːfə,reɪtɪd'ʌlsəʳ] N (Med) ulcera perforata.

per·fo·ra·tion [,pɜːfə'reɪʃən] N (act) perforazione f; (in stamps) dentellatura; (hole) foro.

per·force [pə'fɔːs] ADV (old) per forza.

per·form [pə'fɔːm] [1] VT a (function, task) svolgere, eseguire; (duty) adempiere a; (miracles, experiments) fare, compiere; (ceremony) celebrare; **to perform an operation** (Med) operare

b (play, ballet, opera) rappresentare; (duet, symphony) eseguire, suonare; (acrobatics) fare.

[2] VI a (theatre company) dare una rappresentazione; (person) esibirsi

b (vehicle, machine, also fig: student) comportarsi; **if you want a car that performs really well** ... se volete una macchina che dia ottime prestazioni... .

per·for·mance [pə'fɔːməns] N a (see vt a) svolgimento; adempimento; celebrazione f; **in the performance of his duties** nell'adempimento dei suoi doveri

b (presentation: of play, opera) rappresentazione f; (: of film, ballet) spettacolo; (by actor, of a part) interpretazione f; **he gave a splendid performance** la sua interpretazione è stata magnifica; **a fine performance of the Ninth Symphony** un'ottima esecuzione della Nona sinfonia; **what a performance!** (fam) quante scene or storie!

c (effectiveness: of machine etc) prestazioni fpl; (: of company) rendimento; (: of racehorse, athlete) performance f inv; **the team put up a good performance** la squadra ha giocato una bella partita.

♦ **performance related pay** N retribuzione commensurata al rendimento.

per·form·er [pə'fɔːməʳ] N artista m/f.

per·form·ing [pə'fɔːmɪŋ] ADJ (animal) ammaestrato(-a); **a performing seal** una foca ammaestrata.

♦ **performing arts** NPL: **the performing arts** le arti fpl dello spettacolo.

per·fume [n 'pɜːfjuːm; vb pə'fjuːm] [1] N profumo.

[2] VT profumare.

per·fum·ery [pə'fjuːmərɪ] N profumeria.

per·func·to·ri·ly [pə'fʌŋktərɪlɪ] ADV (inspect, enquire) superficialmente; (agree, answer) senza convinzione; (greet, smile) meccanicamente.

per·func·tory [pə'fʌŋktərɪ] ADJ (inspection, inquiry) superficiale, pro forma inv; (nod) meccanico(-a).

per·go·la ['pɜːɡələ] N pergola.

per·haps [pə'hæps, præps] ADV forse; **perhaps so/not** forse sì/no, può darsi di sì/di no; **perhaps he'll come** magari or forse verrà, può darsi che venga.

peri·gla·cial [,pɛrɪ'ɡleɪʃəl] ADJ periglaciale.

per·il ['pɛrɪl] N pericolo; **at your peril** a tuo rischio e pericolo.

peri·lous ['pɛrɪləs] ADJ pericoloso(-a).

peri·lous·ly ['pɛrɪləslɪ] ADV pericolosamente; **they came perilously close to being caught** sono stati a un pelo dall'esser presi.

pe·rim·eter [pə'rɪmɪtəʳ] N perimetro.

♦ **perimeter wall** N muro di cinta.

pe·ri·od ['pɪərɪəd] [1] N a (length of time) periodo; (stage: in career, development etc) periodo, momento; (Am Ftbl) tempo; **for a period of three weeks** per un periodo di or per la durata di tre settimane; **at that period (of my life)** in quel periodo (della mia vita); **the holiday period** (Brit) il periodo delle vacanze; **the Victorian period** l'epoca or l'età vittoriana; **a painting of his early period** un dipinto del suo primo periodo

b (Scol) ora

c (Am: full stop) punto

d (menstruation) mestruazioni fpl.

[2] ADJ (costume) d'epoca.

♦ **period dress** N costume m d'epoca.

♦ **period furniture** N (genuine) mobili mpl d'epoca; (copy) mobili in stile.

pe·ri·od·ic [,pɪərɪ'ɒdɪk] ADJ periodico(-a).

pe·ri·odi·cal [,pɪərɪ'ɒdɪkəl] [1] ADJ periodico(-a).

[2] N periodico.

pe·ri·odi·cal·ly [,pɪərɪ'ɒdɪkəlɪ] ADV periodicamente.

♦ **periodic table** N (Chem): **the periodic table** la tavola periodica degli elementi.

♦ **period pains** NPL (Brit) dolori mpl mestruali.

♦ **period piece** N bell'esemplare m d'epoca.

peri·pa·tet·ic [ˌpɛrɪpəˈtɛtɪk] ADJ (*salesman*) ambulante; (*Brit: teacher*) *che insegna in varie scuole.*

pe·riph·er·al [pəˈrɪfərəl] [1] ADJ (*gen*) periferico(-a); (*interest*) marginale.
[2] N (*Comput*) unità *f inv* periferica.

pe·riph·ery [pəˈrɪfərɪ] N periferia.

peri·scope [ˈpɛrɪˌskəʊp] N periscopio.

per·ish [ˈpɛrɪʃ] VI (*person etc*) perire, morire; (*material*) deteriorarsi.

per·ish·able [ˈpɛrɪʃəbl] ADJ deperibile.

per·ish·ables [ˈpɛrɪʃəblz] NPL merci *fpl* deperibili.

per·ished [ˈpɛrɪʃt] ADJ (*fam: cold*) gelato(-a), intirizzito (-a).

per·ish·ing [ˈpɛrɪʃɪŋ] ADJ (*Brit fam*): **it's perishing (cold)** fa un freddo da morire.

peri·stal·sis [ˌpɛrɪˈstælsɪs] N peristalsi *f*.

peri·to·ni·tis [ˌpɛrɪtəˈnaɪtɪs] N peritonite *f*.

peri·win·kle[1] [ˈpɛrɪˌwɪŋkl] N (*Bot*) pervinca.

peri·win·kle[2] [ˈpɛrɪˌwɪŋkl] N (*Zool*) littorina.

per·jure [ˈpɜːdʒəʳ] VT: **to perjure o.s.** spergiurare; (*Law*) giurare il falso.

per·jury [ˈpɜːdʒərɪ] N (*breach of oath*) spergiuro; (*Law*) falso giuramento; **to commit perjury** spergiurare; (*Law*) giurare il falso.

perk [pɜːk] N (*fam*) vantaggio.

perki·ly [ˈpɜːkɪlɪ] ADV (*see adj*) con aria allegra, con tono allegro; vivacemente; con impertinenza.

perk up [1] VT + ADV (*cheer up*) tirar su di morale; **he tried to perk up her appetite** cercava di stimolarle l'appetito.
[2] VI + ADV (*cheer up*) tirarsi su di morale; (*show interest*) animarsi; **the dog's ears perked up** il cane drizzò le orecchie.

perky [ˈpɜːkɪ] ADJ (*comp* **-ier**, *superl* **-iest**) (*cheerful*) allegro (-a); (*bright*) vivace; (*cheeky*) impertinente.

perm [pɜːm] [1] N permanente *f*.
[2] VT: **to perm sb's hair** fare la permanente a qn; **to have one's hair permed** farsi fare la permanente.

per·ma·frost [ˈpɜːməˌfrɒst] N permafrost *m inv*.

per·ma·nence [ˈpɜːmənəns] N permanenza.

per·ma·nen·cy [ˈpɜːmənənsɪ] N **a** (*person*) figura sempre presente **b** (*job*) occupazione *f* fissa, lavoro fisso.

per·ma·nent [ˈpɜːmənənt] ADJ (*state, building, agreement*) permanente; (*job, position*) fisso(-a); (*dye, ink*) indelebile; **I'm not permanent here** non sono fisso qui; **permanent address** residenza fissa.

per·ma·nent·ly [ˈpɜːmənəntlɪ] ADV (*stay, leave*) definitivamente; **he is permanently drunk** è perennemente ubriaco.

♦ **permanent wave** N permanente *f*.

per·man·ga·nate [pɜːˈmæŋgənɪt] N permanganato.

per·me·abil·ity [ˌpɜːmɪəˈbɪlɪtɪ] N permeabilità.

per·me·able [ˈpɜːmɪəbl] ADJ permeabile; **selectively permeable** semipermeabile.

per·me·ate [ˈpɜːmɪˌeɪt] [1] VT (*gen*) filtrare attraverso; (*Tech*) permeare; (*subj: smell*) pervadere; (: *fig: ideas etc*) diffondersi in; **permeated with** impregnato(-a) di.
[2] VI filtrare; (*fig*) diffondersi.

per·mis·sible [pəˈmɪsɪbl] ADJ (*action*) permesso(-a); (*behaviour*) accettabile; (*attitude*) ammissibile, permissibile; **it is not permissible to do that** non è permesso farlo.

per·mis·sion [pəˈmɪʃən] N permesso; (*official*) autorizzazione *f*; **with your permission** se mi permette, con il suo permesso; **to give sb permission to do sth** dare a qn il permesso di fare qc.

per·mis·sive [pəˈmɪsɪv] ADJ (*parents, society*) permissivo (-a), tollerante.

per·mis·sive·ness [pəˈmɪsɪvnɪs] N permissività.

per·mit [*n* ˈpɜːmɪt; *vb* pəˈmɪt] [1] N (*gen*) autorizzazione *f* (scritta); (*for specific activity*) permesso; (*entrance pass*) lasciapassare *m*; **fishing permit** licenza di pesca; **building/export permit** permesso *or* licenza di costruzione/di esportazione.
[2] VT permettere; **to permit sb to do sth** permettere a qn di fare qc; **to permit sth to take place** permettere che qc avvenga.
[3] VI permettere; **to permit of** (*frm*) ammettere, consentire; **weather permitting** tempo permettendo.

per·mu·ta·tion [ˌpɜːmjuˈteɪʃən] N permutazione *f*.

per·ni·cious [pɜːˈnɪʃəs] ADJ nocivo(-a), dannoso(-a); (*Med*) pernicioso(-a).

per·nick·ety [pəˈnɪkətɪ] ADJ (*fam: person*) pignolo(-a); (: *job*) da certosino.

per·ox·ide [pəˈrɒksaɪd] N perossido.

♦ **peroxide blonde** N bionda ossigenata.

per·pen·dicu·lar [ˌpɜːpənˈdɪkjʊləʳ] [1] ADJ (*gen, Math*) perpendicolare; (*cliff*) a picco.
[2] N perpendicolare *f*.

per·pen·dicu·lar·ly [ˌpɜːpənˈdɪkjʊləlɪ] ADV perpendicolarmente.

per·pe·trate [ˈpɜːpɪˌtreɪt] VT perpetrare, commettere.

per·pe·tra·tor [ˈpɜːpɪˌtreɪtəʳ] N (*of crime*) autore(-trice).

per·pet·ual [pəˈpɛtjʊəl] ADJ (*gen, motion*) perpetuo(-a); (*ice, snow*) perenne; (*continuous: noise, complaining*) incessante, continuo(-a).

per·pet·ual·ly [pəˈpɛtjʊəlɪ] ADV eternamente, perennemente.

per·petu·ate [pəˈpɛtjʊˌeɪt] VT perpetuare.

per·pe·tu·ity [ˌpɜːpɪˈtjuːɪtɪ] N: **in perpetuity** in perpetuo.

per·plex [pəˈplɛks] VT lasciare perplesso(-a); **I was perplexed by his behaviour** il suo comportamento mi ha lasciato perplesso.

per·plexed [pəˈplɛkst] ADJ perplesso(-a).

per·plex·ed·ly [pəˈplɛksɪdlɪ] ADV con perplessità.

per·plex·ing [pəˈplɛksɪŋ] ADJ che lascia perplesso(-a).

per·plex·ity [pəˈplɛksɪtɪ] N perplessità.

per·qui·site [ˈpɜːkwɪzɪt] N (*frm*) = **perk**.

per·secute [ˈpɜːsɪkjuːt] VT perseguitare.

per·secu·tion [ˌpɜːsɪˈkjuːʃən] N persecuzione *f*.

♦ **persecution complex** N (*Psych*) mania di persecuzione.

per·secu·tor [ˈpɜːsɪkjuːtəʳ] N persecutore(-trice).

Persephone [pəˈsɛfənɪ] N Persefone *f*.

Perseus [ˈpɜːsjuːs] N Perseo.

per·sever·ance [ˌpɜːsɪˈvɪərəns] N perseveranza.

per·severe [ˌpɜːsɪˈvɪəʳ] VI perseverare.

per·sever·ing [ˌpɜːsɪˈvɪərɪŋ] ADJ perseverante, assiduo (-a).

per·sever·ing·ly [ˌpɜːsɪˈvɪərɪŋlɪ] ADV con perseveranza, assiduamente.

Per·sia [ˈpɜːʃə] N Persia.

Per·sian [ˈpɜːʃən] [1] ADJ persiano(-a).
[2] N **a** (*person*) persiano(-a) **b** (*language*) persiano.

♦ **Persian carpet** N tappeto persiano.

♦ **Persian cat** N (gatto) persiano.

♦ **Persian Gulf** N Golfo Persico.

♦ **Persian lamb** N (*animal*) karakul *m inv*; (*skin*) astrakan *m inv*.

per·sim·mon [pɜːˈsɪmən] N cachi *m inv*.

per·sist [pəˈsɪst] VI (*person*) persistere, ostinarsi; (*custom,*

rain) persistere, durare; **to persist in sth/in doing sth** ostinarsi in qc/a fare qc, persistere in qc/nel *or* a fare qc.

per·sis·tence [pə'sɪstəns] N (*tenacity*) perseveranza; (*obstinacy*) ostinazione *f*, persistenza; (*continued existence*) persistere *m*.

per·sis·tent [pə'sɪstənt] ADJ (*person, attempt, questions*) insistente, ostinato(-a); (*cough, pain, smell*) persistente; (*lateness, rain*) continuo(-a); **persistent offender** (*Law*) delinquente *m/f* abituale.

per·sis·tent·ly [pə'sɪstəntlɪ] ADV con insistenza; (*continuously*) continuamente.

per·snick·ety [pə'snɪkɪtɪ] ADJ (*Am*) = **pernickety**.

per·son ['pɜːsn] N **a** (*pl* **people** *or* (*frm*): **persons**) persona; **a person to person call** (*Telec*) una chiamata con preavviso

b (*pl* **persons**: *Gram, Law*) persona

c (*body, physical presence*) figura, personale *m*; (*appearance*) aspetto; **in person** di *or* in persona, personalmente; **in the person of my uncle** nella persona di mio zio; **on** *or* **about one's person** (*weapon*) su di sé; (*money*) con sé.

per·son·able ['pɜːsnəbl] ADJ di bell'aspetto, prestante.

per·son·age ['pɜːsnɪdʒ] N personaggio.

per·son·al ['pɜːsnl] ADJ (*gen, Gram*) personale; (*application*) (fatto(-a)) di persona; **personal belongings** oggetti d'uso personale; **a personal question** una domanda indiscreta; **a personal interview** un incontro privato; **for personal reasons** per motivi personali; **to make a personal appearance** apparire di persona; **to have personal knowledge of sth** conoscere qc per esperienza personale; **don't get personal!** non entriamo nel personale!; **one's personal habits** le proprie piccole manie; **"personal"** (*on letter*) "riservata", "personale".

♦ **personal allowance** N (*Tax*) quota non imponibile.

♦ **personal assistant** N segretario(-a) particolare.

♦ **personal call** N (*Brit Telec: person to person*) chiamata con preavviso; (: *private*) telefonata personale.

♦ **personal column** N colonna degli annunci personali, colonna dei piccoli annunci.

♦ **personal computer** N personal computer *m inv*.

♦ **personal details** NPL dati *mpl* personali.

♦ **personal equity plan** N *deposito a risparmio per investimento azionario con agevolazioni fiscali.*

♦ **personal identification number** N (*Comput, Banking*) numero di codice segreto.

per·son·al·ity [ˌpɜːsə'nælɪtɪ] N (*nature*) personalità *f inv*; (*famous person*) personalità, personaggio; **let's not indulge in personalities** lasciamo da parte i commenti personali.

♦ **personality cult** N culto della personalità.

per·son·al·ize ['pɜːsənəˌlaɪz] VT personalizzare.

per·son·al·ized ['pɜːsənəˌlaɪzd] ADJ personalizzato(-a).

♦ **personal loan** N credito *or* prestito personale, prestito privato.

per·son·al·ly ['pɜːsnəlɪ] ADV **a** (*for my part*) personalmente; **I feel personally responsible** mi sento personalmente responsabile; **personally I think that ...** personalmente penso che...; **don't take it too personally** non prenderla come un'offesa *or* una critica personale

b (*in person*) personalmente, di persona; **to hand sth over personally** consegnare qc di persona.

♦ **personal organizer** N (*book*) agenda; (*electronic*)

agenda elettronica.

♦ **personal property** N (*Law*) beni *mpl* personali.

♦ **personal stereo** N walkman ® *m inv*.

per·so·na non gra·ta [pɜː'səʊnənɒn'grɑːtə] N (*frm*) persona non grata.

per·soni·fi·ca·tion [pɜːˌsɒnɪfɪ'keɪʃən] N personificazione *f*.

per·soni·fy [pɜː'sɒnɪˌfaɪ] VT personificare.

per·son·nel [ˌpɜːsə'nɛl] N personale *m*.

♦ **personnel department** N ufficio del personale.

♦ **personnel management** N direzione *f* del personale.

♦ **personnel manager** N direttore(-trice) del personale.

♦ **personnel officer** N addetto(-a) all'ufficio del personale.

per·spec·tive [pə'spɛktɪv] N prospettiva; **to see** *or* **look at sth in perspective** (*fig*) vedere qc nella giusta prospettiva; **to get sth into perspective** ridimensionare qc.

per·spex® ['pɜːspɛks] N plexiglas ® *m*.

per·spi·ca·cious [ˌpɜːspɪ'keɪʃəs] ADJ (*frm*) perspicace.

per·spi·cac·ity [ˌpɜːspɪ'kæsɪtɪ] N (*frm*) perspicacia.

per·spi·ra·tion [ˌpɜːspə'reɪʃən] N traspirazione *f*, sudore *m*; **bathed in perspiration** in un bagno di sudore.

per·spire [pə'spaɪə'] VI traspirare, sudare.

per·suade [pə'sweɪd] VT persuadere; **to persuade sb of sth/that** persuadere qn di qc/che; **to persuade sb to do sth** persuadere qn a fare qc; **but they persuaded me not to** ma mi hanno persuaso a non farlo; **she is easily persuaded** si lascia facilmente persuadere *or* convincere; **I am persuaded that ...** (*frm*) sono persuaso *or* convinto che... +*sub*.

per·sua·sion [pə'sweɪʒən] N **a** (*persuading*) persuasione *f* **b** (*creed*) convinzione *f*, credo.

per·sua·sive [pə'sweɪsɪv] ADJ (*person*) convincente; (*argument*) persuasivo(-a), convincente.

per·sua·sive·ly [pə'sweɪsɪvlɪ] ADV in modo persuasivo.

per·sua·sive·ness [pə'sweɪsɪvnɪs] N (*of person, argument*) potere *m or* forza di convinzione.

pert [pɜːt] ADJ (*comp* **-er**, *superl* **-est**) (*girl, answer*) impertinente, sfacciato(-a); (*hat*) spiritoso(-a).

per·tain [pɜː'teɪn] VI (*frm*): **to pertain to** (*concern*) riferirsi a, riguardare; (*belong to*) appartenere a; **documents pertaining to the case** documenti relativi al caso.

per·ti·na·cious [ˌpɜːtɪ'neɪʃəs] ADJ ostinato(-a), pertinace.

per·ti·na·cious·ly [ˌpɜːtɪ'neɪʃəslɪ] ADV con ostinazione, con pertinacia.

per·ti·nac·ity [ˌpɜːtɪ'næsɪtɪ] N pertinacia.

per·ti·nence ['pɜːtɪnəns] N pertinenza.

per·ti·nent ['pɜːtɪnənt] ADJ pertinente.

per·ti·nent·ly ['pɜːtɪnəntlɪ] ADV in modo pertinente; **he very pertinently said that ...** disse molto a proposito che... .

pert·ly ['pɜːtlɪ] ADV (*reply, smile*) impudentemente.

per·turb [pə'tɜːb] VT turbare, agitare; **I was perturbed to learn that ...** fui sconvolto nello scoprire che... .

per·turb·ing [pə'tɜːbɪŋ] ADJ inquietante.

Peru [pə'ruː] N Perù *m*.

pe·rus·al [pə'ruːzəl] N lettura.

pe·ruse [pə'ruːz] VT leggere.

Pe·ru·vian [pə'ruːvɪən] ADJ, N peruviano(-a).

per·vade [pɜː'veɪd] VT (*subj: smell, feeling, atmosphere*) pervadere; (: *influence, ideas*) insinuarsi in, diffondersi in.

per·va·sive [pɜː'veɪsɪv] ADJ (*smell*) penetrante; (*influence*) dilagante; (*gloom, feelings, ideas*) diffuso(-a).

per·verse [pə'vɜːs] ADJ (*contrary*: *behaviour*) da bastian contrario; (*wicked*) cattivo(-a); (*desires*) perverso(-a); (*circumstances*) avverso(-a); **to be perverse** (*person*) essere un bastian contrario.

per·verse·ly [pə'vɜːslɪ] ADV (*see adj*) da bastian contrario; con cattiveria; perversamente.

per·ver·sion [pə'vɜːʃən] N (*Psych*) perversione *f*; (*of justice*, *truth*) travisamento, pervertimento.

per·ver·sity [pə'vɜːsɪtɪ] N (*wickedness*) perversità, malvagità; (*contrariness*) spirito di contraddizione.

per·vert [*vb* pə'vɜːt; *n* 'pɜːvɜːt] ① VT (*mind*) pervertire, corrompere; (*speech*, *truth etc*) travisare; **to pervert the course of justice** deviare il corso della giustizia.
② N pervertito(-a).

per·ver·ted [pə'vɜːtɪd] ADJ (*person*) pervertito(-a); (*behaviour*, *logic*, *imagination*) perverso(-a).

pesky ['pɛskɪ] ADJ (*comp* **-ier**, *superl* **-iest**) (*Am fam*) fastidioso(-a), noioso(-a).

pes·sa·ry ['pɛsərɪ] N pessario; (*contraceptive*) diaframma *m*.

pes·si·mism ['pɛsɪˌmɪzəm] N pessimismo.

pes·si·mist ['pɛsɪmɪst] N pessimista *m/f*.

pes·si·mis·tic [ˌpɛsɪ'mɪstɪk] ADJ (*attitude*, *forecast*) pessimistico(-a); (*person*) pessimista.

pes·si·mis·ti·cal·ly [ˌpɛsɪ'mɪstɪkəlɪ] ADV pessimisticamente.

pest [pɛst] N a (*Zool*) insetto (*or* animale *m*) nocivo b (*fig*: *person*) peste *f*; (: *thing*) rottura.

♦ **pest control** N disinfestazione *f*.

♦ **pest control officer** N funzionario responsabile della disinfestazione.

pes·ter ['pɛstəʳ] VT tormentare, molestare; **stop pestering me!** smettila di scocciarmi!

pes·ti·cide ['pɛstɪˌsaɪd] N pesticida *m*.

pes·ti·lence ['pɛstɪləns] N pestilenza.

pes·ti·lent ['pɛstɪlənt], **pes·ti·len·tial** [ˌpɛstɪ'lɛnʃəl] ADJ (*fam*: *exasperating*) pestifero(-a).

pes·tle ['pɛsl] N pestello.

pet [pɛt] ① N a (*animal*) animale *m* domestico; **my dad won't let me have any pets** il mio papà non mi lascia tenere (in casa) nessun animale
b (*favourite*) preferito(-a), favorito(-a), beniamino(-a); **come here pet** (*fam*) vieni qua tesoro.
② VT (*indulge*) coccolare; (*fondle*) accarezzare.
③ VI (*sexually*) pomiciare, fare il petting.
④ ADJ a (*monkey*) ammaestrato(-a); (*food*) per animali domestici; **we have a pet dog** abbiamo un cane; **pet mouse** topo addomesticato
b (*favourite*: *pupil*, *subject etc*) preferito(-a), prediletto(-a); **my pet aversion** la cosa che detesto di più.

pet·al ['pɛtl] N petalo.

pe·tard [pɪ'tɑːd]: **to be hoist with one's own petard** essere preso(-a) nelle proprie reti.

pe·ter ['piːtəʳ] VI: **to peter out** (*supply*) esaurirsi, estinguersi; (*stream*) perdersi; (*plan*) andare in fumo; (*interest*, *excitement*) svanire; (*conversation*) spegnersi; (*song*, *noise*) cessare; (*track*, *path*) finire.

peti·ole ['pɛtɪˌəʊl] N picciolo.

pe·tite [pə'tiːt] ADJ (*woman*) minuta e graziosa.

pe·ti·tion [pə'tɪʃən] ① N (*list of names*) petizione *f*; (*frm*: *request*) richiesta, istanza.
② VT (*person*) presentare una petizione a.
③ VI richiedere; **to petition for divorce** (*Law*) presentare un'istanza di divorzio.

♦ **pet name** N (*Brit*) nomignolo.

Petrarch ['pɛtrɑːk] N Petrarca *m*.

pet·ri·fied ['pɛtrɪˌfaɪd] ADJ terrorizzato(-a); **to be petrified (with fear)** restare impietrito(-a) (per la paura).

pet·ri·fy ['pɛtrɪˌfaɪ] ① VT (*fig*) terrorizzare.
② VI (*turn to stone*) pietrificarsi; (*frm*: *stagnate*) sclerotizzarsi.

pet·ro·chemi·cal [ˌpɛtrəʊ'kɛmɪkl] ① ADJ petrolchimico (-a).
② N prodotto petrolchimico.

pet·ro·dol·lar ['pɛtrəʊˌdɒləʳ] N petrodollaro.

pet·rol ['pɛtrəl] ① N (*Brit*) benzina; **high-octane petrol** (benzina) super *f inv*; **to be heavy on petrol** (*car*) bere molta benzina; **to run out of petrol** restare senza benzina.
② ADJ (*leak*, *stain*) di benzina.

♦ **petrol bomb** N (bottiglia *or* bomba) molotov *f inv*.

♦ **petrol can** N tanica per benzina.

♦ **petrol engine** N motore *m* a benzina.

pe·tro·leum [pɪ'trəʊlɪəm] N petrolio.

♦ **petroleum jelly** N vaselina.

♦ **petrol gauge** N spia della benzina.

♦ **petrol pump** N (*at garage*, *in car*) pompa della benzina.

♦ **petrol station** N stazione *f* di servizio *or* rifornimento.

♦ **petrol tank** N serbatoio della benzina.

♦ **pet shop** N negozio di animali domestici.

pet·ti·coat ['pɛtɪˌkəʊt] N (*full-length*) sottoveste *f*; (*waist*) sottogonna *f*.

pet·ti·fog·ging ['pɛtɪˌfɒgɪŋ] ADJ (*details*) insignificante; (*objections*) cavilloso(-a).

pet·ti·ly ['pɛtɪlɪ] ADV (*small-mindedly*) meschinamente.

pet·ti·ness ['pɛtnɪs] N (*small-mindedness*) meschinità *f inv*.

pet·ting ['pɛtɪŋ] N petting *m inv*.

pet·ty ['pɛtɪ] ADJ (*comp* **-ier**, *superl* **-iest**) a (*trivial*: *detail*, *complaint*) insignificante, di poca importanza b (*minor*: *official*) subalterno(-a) c (*small-minded*, *spiteful*) meschino(-a).

♦ **petty cash** N piccola cassa.

♦ **petty cash book** N primanota.

♦ **petty officer** N (*Naut*) sottufficiale *m* di marina.

petu·lance ['pɛtjʊləns] N irritabilità.

petu·lant ['pɛtjʊlənt] ADJ irritabile.

petu·lant·ly ['pɛtjʊləntlɪ] ADV con irritazione.

pew [pjuː] N (*in church*) banco; **take a pew!** (*fig fam*) accomodati!, siediti!

pew·ter ['pjuːtəʳ] N peltro.

PG [ˌpiː'dʒiː] N ABBR (*Cine*: = *parental guidance*) classificazione di film consentito ai minori solo se accompagnati.

PGA [ˌpiːdʒiː'eɪ] N ABBR (= *Professional Golfers' Association*) associazione dei giocatori di golf professionisti.

PH [ˌpiː'eɪtʃ] N ABBR (*Am Mil*) = **Purple Heart**.

pH [ˌpiː'eɪtʃ] N ABBR (*Chem*) pH *m*.

p&h [ˌpiːənd'eɪtʃ] N ABBR (*Am*: = *postage and handling*) affrancatura e trasporto.

PHA [ˌpiːeɪtʃ'eɪ] N ABBR (*Am*: = *Public Housing Administration*) amministrazione per l'edilizia pubblica.

Phaedra ['fiːdrə] N Fedra.

phal·lic ['fælɪk] ADJ fallico(-a).

phan·tom ['fæntəm] ① ADJ fantasma *inv*.
② N fantasma *m*.

Phar·aoh ['fɛərəʊ] N faraone *m*.

phar·ma·ceu·ti·cal [ˌfɑːmə'sjuːtɪkəl] ADJ farmaceutico (-a).

phar·ma·ceu·ti·cals [ˌfɑːmə'sjuːtɪkəlz] NPL prodotti *mpl* farmaceutici.

phar·ma·cist ['fɑːməsɪst] N farmacista *m/f*.

phar·ma·col·ogy [ˌfɑːməˈkɒlədʒɪ] N farmacologia.
phar·ma·cy [ˈfɑːməsɪ] N farmacia.
phar·yn·gi·tis [ˌfærɪnˈdʒaɪtɪs] N faringite f.
phar·ynx [ˈfærɪŋks] N faringe f.
phase [feɪz] [1] N fase f, periodo; **to be out of phase** (Tech, Elec) essere sfasato(-a) or fuori fase; **she's just going through a phase** sta attraversando un periodo difficile, le passerà.
　[2] VT (stagger) introdurre gradualmente; (coordinate) sincronizzare; **phased withdrawal** ritirata progressiva
▶ **phase in** VT + ADV introdurre gradualmente
▶ **phase out** VT + ADV eliminare gradualmente.
♦ **phase change** N (Chem) passaggio di stato; (Phys) cambiamento di fase.
Ph.D. [ˌpiːeɪtʃˈdiː] N ABBR **= Doctor of Philosophy.**
pheas·ant [ˈfeznt] N fagiano.
phe·no·bar·bi·tone [ˌfiːnəʊˈbɑːbɪˌtəʊn] N fenilbarbiturico, luminal® m.
phe·nol [ˈfiːnɒl] N fenolo.
phe·nom·enal [fɪˈnɒmɪnl] ADJ fenomenale.
phe·nom·enal·ly [fɪˈnɒmɪnəlɪ] ADV straordinariamente.
phe·nom·enon [fɪˈnɒmɪnən] N (pl phenomena [fɪˈnɒmɪnə]) fenomeno.
phe·no·type [ˈfiːnəʊˌtaɪp] N fenotipo.
phew [fjuː] EXCL (heat, tiredness) uff!; (relief, surprise) uh!
phial [ˈfaɪəl] N fiala.
Phidias [ˈfɪdɪæs] N Fidia m.
phi·lan·der [fɪˈlændəʳ] VI (pej): **to philander (with)** amoreggiare (con).
phi·lan·der·er [fɪˈlændərəʳ] N (pej) libertino.
phi·lan·der·ing [fɪˈlændərɪŋ] N (pej) libertinaggio.
phil·an·throp·ic [ˌfɪlənˈθrɒpɪk] ADJ filantropico(-a).
phil·an·thropi·cal·ly [ˌfɪlənˈθrɒpɪkəlɪ] ADV filantropicamente.
phi·lan·thro·pist [fɪˈlænθrəpɪst] N filantropo(-a).
phi·lan·thro·py [fɪˈlænθrəpɪ] N filantropia.
phi·lat·elist [fɪˈlætəlɪst] N filatelista m/f, filatelico(-a).
phi·lat·ely [fɪˈlætəlɪ] N filatelia.
phil·har·mon·ic [ˌfɪlhɑːˈmɒnɪk] ADJ filarmonico(-a).
Phil·ip·pines [ˈfɪlɪˌpiːnz] NPL: **the Philippines** le Filippine.
Phil·is·tine [ˈfɪlɪˌstaɪn] ADJ filisteo(-a).
Phil·is·tin·ism [ˈfɪlɪstɪˌnɪzəm] N mancanza di raffinatezza culturale.
philo·den·dron [ˌfɪləˈdɛndrən] N filodendro.
philo·logi·cal [ˌfɪləˈlɒdʒɪkəl] ADJ filologico(-a).
philo·logi·cal·ly [ˌfɪləˈlɒdʒɪkəlɪ] ADV filologicamente.
phi·lolo·gist [fɪˈlɒlədʒɪst] N filologo(-a).
phi·lol·ogy [fɪˈlɒlədʒɪ] N filologia.
phi·loso·pher [fɪˈlɒsəfəʳ] N filosofo(-a).
philo·sophi·cal [ˌfɪləˈsɒfɪkəl] ADJ (also fig) filosofico(-a); **he's been very philosophical about it** l'ha presa con molta filosofia.
philo·sophi·cal·ly [ˌfɪləˈsɒfɪkəlɪ] ADV filosoficamente.
phi·loso·phize [fɪˈlɒsəˌfaɪz] VI: **to philosophize (about** or **on)** filosofare (su).
phi·loso·phy [fɪˈlɒsəfɪ] N filosofia; **her philosophy of life** la sua massima or filosofia.
phle·bi·tis [flɪˈbaɪtɪs] N flebite f.
phlegm [flɛm] N flemma.
phleg·mat·ic [flɛɡˈmætɪk] ADJ flemmatico(-a).
phleg·mati·cal·ly [flɛɡˈmætɪkəlɪ] ADV flemmaticamente.
pho·bia [ˈfəʊbɪə] N fobia; **to have a phobia about sth** avere la fobia di qc.
pho·bic [ˈfəʊbɪk] ADJ [1]: **to be phobic about sth** avere una fobia per qc.

[2] N fobico(-a).
Phoebus [ˈfiːbəs] N Febo.
phoe·nix [ˈfiːnɪks] N fenice f.
phone [fəʊn] [1] N telefono; **to be on the phone** avere il telefono; (be calling) essere al telefono.
　[2] VT telefonare a.
　[3] VI telefonare
▶ **phone back** VT + ADV, VI + ADV richiamare
▶ **phone up** VT + ADV: **to phone sb up** dare un colpo di telefono a qn.
♦ **phone book** N guida del telefono, elenco telefonico.
♦ **phone booth** N cabina telefonica (in luogo pubblico).
♦ **phone box** N cabina telefonica (per strada).
♦ **phone call** N telefonata.
phone·card [ˈfəʊnˌkɑːd] N scheda telefonica.
♦ **phone-in** [ˈfəʊnˌɪn] N (Radio, TV) trasmissione con telefonate in diretta.
pho·neme [ˈfəʊniːm] N (Ling) fonema m.
♦ **phone tap·ping** [ˈfəʊnˌtæpɪŋ] N intercettazioni fpl telefoniche.
pho·net·ic [fəʊˈnɛtɪk] ADJ fonetico(-a).
pho·neti·cal·ly [fəˈnɛtɪkəlɪ] ADV foneticamente.
pho·neti·cian [ˌfəʊnɪˈtɪʃən], **pho·net·ist** [ˈfəʊnɪtɪst] N fonetista m/f.
pho·net·ics [fəʊˈnɛtɪks] NSG fonetica.
pho·ney [ˈfəʊnɪ] (fam) [1] ADJ (comp -ier, superl -iest) (gen) falso(-a), fasullo(-a); (accent) fasullo(-a).
　[2] N (person) venditore(-trice) di fumo, ciarlatano(-a).
pho·no·graph [ˈfəʊnəˌɡrɑːf] (old) N fonografo; (Am) giradischi m inv.
pho·no·logi·cal [ˌfəʊnəˈlɒdʒɪkəl] ADJ (Ling) fonologico (-a).
pho·nol·ogy [fəʊˈnɒlədʒɪ] N (Ling) fonologia.
pho·ny [ˈfəʊnɪ] (Am) **= phoney.**
phoo·ey [ˈfuːɪ] EXCL (fam: to express disbelief) ma dai!, ma va'!
phos·phate [ˈfɒsfeɪt] N fosfato.
phos·pho·res·cence [ˌfɒsfəˈrɛsns] N fosforescenza.
phos·pho·res·cent [ˌfɒsfəˈrɛsnt] ADJ fosforescente.
phos·phor·ic [fɒsˈfɒrɪk] ADJ fosforico(-a).
phos·pho·rus [ˈfɒsfərəs] N fosforo.
pho·to [ˈfəʊtəʊ] N foto f inv.
photo... [ˈfəʊtəʊ] PREF foto... .
photo·call [ˈfəʊtəʊˌkɔːl] N convocazione di fotoreporter a scopo pubblicitario.
photo·cell [ˈfəʊtəʊˌsɛl] N fotocellula.
photo·chemi·cal [ˌfəʊtəʊˈkɛmɪkəl] ADJ fotochimico(-a).
photo·copi·er [ˈfəʊtəʊˌkɒpɪəʳ] N fotocopiatrice f.
photo·copy [ˈfəʊtəʊˌkɒpɪ] [1] N fotocopia.
　[2] VT fotocopiare.
photo·copy·ing [ˈfəʊtəʊˌkɒpɪɪŋ] N fotocopiatura.
photo·elec·tric [ˌfəʊtəʊɪˈlɛktrɪk] ADJ fotoelettrico(-a).
♦ **photoelectric cell** N **= photocell.**
photo·elec·tric·ity [ˌfəʊtəʊɪlɛkˈtrɪsɪtɪ] N fotoelettricità.
♦ **photo finish** N (Sport) fotofinish m inv.
Photo·fit® [ˈfəʊtəʊˌfɪt] N photofit m inv.
photo·gen·ic [ˌfəʊtəʊˈdʒɛnɪk] ADJ fotogenico(-a).
photo·graph [ˈfəʊtəˌɡræf] [1] N fotografia; **to take a photograph of sb** fare una fotografia a or fotografare qn; **to take a photograph of sth** fotografare qc.
　[2] VT fotografare.
♦ **photograph album** N (new) album m inv per fotografie; (containing photos) album m inv delle fotografie.
pho·tog·ra·pher [fəˈtɒɡrəfəʳ] N fotografo(-a); **newspaper photographer** fotoreporter m/f inv; **street photographer**

fotografo di piazza; **he's a keen photographer** è appassionato di fotografia.

photo·graph·ic [ˌfəʊtə'græfɪk] ADJ fotografico(-a); **to have a photographic memory** avere una memoria fotografica.

photo·graphi·cal·ly [ˌfəʊtə'græfɪkəlɪ] ADV fotograficamente.

pho·tog·ra·phy [fə'tɒgrəfɪ] N fotografia.

photo·gra·vure [ˌfəʊtəʊgrə'vjʊə'] N fotoincisione *f*.

♦ **photo opportunity** N *opportunità di scattare delle foto ad un personaggio importante*.

photo·sen·si·tive [ˌfəʊtəʊ'sensɪtɪv] ADJ *(gen)* fotosensibile; *(lens)* fotocromatico(-a).

photo·stat® ['fəʊtəʊˌstæt] N = **photocopy**.

photo·syn·the·sis [ˌfəʊtəʊ'sɪnθəsɪs] N fotosintesi *f*.

photo·trop·ism [ˌfəʊtəʊ'trəʊpɪzəm] N fototropismo.

phras·al verb [ˌfreɪzəl'vɜːb] N *(Gram)* *verbo seguito da preposizione o avverbio*.

phrase [freɪz] ① N **a** *(Gram)* locuzione *f*; *(saying)* espressione *f*; **noun phrase** sintagma *m* nominale **b** *(Mus)* frase *f*.
② VT **a** *(thought)* esprimere; *(letter)* redigere **b** *(Mus)* dividere in frasi.

♦ **phrase book** N vocabolarietto.

phra·seol·ogy [ˌfreɪzɪ'ɒlədʒɪ] N fraseologia.

phras·ing ['freɪzɪŋ] N *(of thought, request, letter)* formulazione *f*; *(Mus)* fraseggio.

phre·nol·ogy [frɪ'nɒlədʒɪ] N frenologia.

phut [fʌt] ADV: **to go phut** *(fam)* andare in tilt; **the TV's gone phut** è saltata la tivù.

physi·cal ['fɪzɪkəl] ADJ **a** *(of the body)* fisico(-a) **b** *(world, object)* materiale; *(of physics)* fisico(-a); **physical change** reazione *f* fisica; **physical stocktaking** *(Comm)* inventario fisico; **it's a physical impossibility** è un'impossibilità materiale.

♦ **physical education** N educazione *f* fisica.

♦ **physical examination** N visita medica.

♦ **physical jerks** *(fam)*, **physical exercises** NPL ginnastica *fsg*.

physi·cal·ly ['fɪzɪkəlɪ] ADV fisicamente; **it's physically impossible** è materialmente impossibile.

♦ **physical sciences** NPL: **the physical sciences** le scienze fisiche.

phy·si·cian [fɪ'zɪʃən] N medico.

physi·cist ['fɪzɪsɪst] N fisico.

phys·ics ['fɪzɪks] NSG fisica.

physio ['fɪzɪəʊ] N *(fam: person)* fisioterapista *m/f*; *(: treatment)* fisioterapia.

physi·og·no·my [ˌfɪzɪ'ɒnəmɪ] N *(person's features, Geog etc)* fisionomia; *(art of judging character)* fisiognomia.

physio·logi·cal [ˌfɪzɪə'lɒdʒɪkəl] ADJ fisiologico(-a).

physio·logi·cal·ly [ˌfɪzɪə'lɒdʒɪkəlɪ] ADV fisiologicamente.

physi·olo·gist [ˌfɪzɪ'ɒlədʒɪst] N fisiologo(-a).

physi·ol·ogy [ˌfɪzɪ'ɒlədʒɪ] N fisiologia.

physio·thera·pist [ˌfɪzɪʊ'θerəpɪst] N fisioterapista *m/f*.

physio·thera·py [ˌfɪzɪʊ'θerəpɪ] N fisioterapia.

phy·sique [fɪ'ziːk] N fisico.

pi [paɪ] N *(Math)* pi greco *m*.

pia·nist ['pɪənɪst] N pianista *m/f*.

pia·no [pɪ:'ænəʊ] ① N piano(forte) *m*.
② ADJ *(lesson, teacher)* di piano(forte); *(concerto, stool)* per piano(forte).

♦ **piano accordion** N fisarmonica (a tastiera).

pia·no·la® [pɪə'nəʊlə] N pianola ®.

♦ **piano tuner** N accordatore(-trice) di pianoforti.

Pic·ar·dy ['pɪkədɪ] N Piccardia.

pica·resque [ˌpɪkə'resk] ADJ *(liter)* picaresco(-a).

pic·co·lo ['pɪkələʊ] N *(pl -s) (Mus)* ottavino.

pick [pɪk] ① N **a** *(also: pickaxe)* piccone *m*
b *(choice, right to choose)* scelta; **take your pick!** scegli quello che vuoi!, prendi quello che ti pare!; **it's the pick of the bunch** è il migliore di tutti.
② VT **a** *(choose)* scegliere; **to pick a winner** puntare sul vincente; *(fig)* fare un ottimo affare, imbroccarla giusta; **to pick one's way through** attraversare stando ben attento(-a) a dove mettere i piedi; **to pick a fight/ quarrel with sb** attaccar rissa/briga con qn
b *(flowers)* cogliere; *(fruit)* raccogliere
c *(scab, spot)* grattarsi; **to pick one's nose** mettersi le dita nel naso; **to pick one's teeth** pulirsi i denti con uno stuzzicadenti, stuzzicarsi i denti; **to pick a lock** far scattare una serratura; **to pick a bone** spolpare un osso; **I've got a bone to pick with you!** devo fare i conti con te; **to pick holes in sth** *(fig)* trovare i punti deboli in qc; **to pick sb's pocket** alleggerire qn del portafoglio; **to pick sb's brains** farsi dare dei suggerimenti da qn.
③ VI: **to pick and choose** scegliere con cura

► **pick at** VI + PREP *(food, meal)* mangiare contro voglia; *(scab)* grattarsi

► **pick off** VT + ADV
a *(remove: fluff)* togliere; *(: flower, leaf)* cogliere
b *(shoot)* abbattere (uno(-a) dopo l'altro(-a))

► **pick on** VI + PREP
a *(fam: harass)* avercela con, prendersela con
b *(single out)* beccare; **they always pick on him to do it** lo fanno sempre fare a lui

► **pick out** VT + ADV
a *(choose)* scegliere
b *(place: on map)* trovare; *(person: in crowd, photo)* individuare; *(: in identification parade)* identificare
c *(Mus)*: **to pick out a tune on the piano** trovare gli accordi di un motivo al piano

► **pick over** VT + ADV *(fruit, vegetables)* selezionare, scegliere; *(rice, lentils)* mondare

► **pick up** ① VT + ADV **a** *(lift: sth dropped)* raccogliere, raccattare; *(: sb fallen)* tirar su; **to pick o.s. up** rialzarsi; **to pick up a child** prendere in braccio un bambino; **to pick up the phone** alzare il ricevitore; **to pick up the bill** *(fig)* pagare (il conto); **to pick sb up for having made a mistake** riprendere qn per aver fatto uno sbaglio
b *(collect: goods, person)* passare a prendere; *(subj: bus etc)* far salire, caricare; *(rescue)* raccogliere; *(: from sea)* ripescare; *(arrest)* arrestare; **the car picked up speed** la macchina ha acquistato velocità *or* ha accelerato
c *(acquire: sale bargain)* trovare; *(: information, points in exam, germ)* prendere; *(learn: habit, ideas)* prendere; *(: skill, language, tricks)* imparare; **can you pick up some information while you're there?** puoi prendere delle informazioni mentre sei lì?; **he picked up a girl at the disco** *(fam)* ha rimorchiato una ragazza in discoteca
d *(Radio, TV, Telec)* captare.
② VI + ADV **a** *(improve: gen)* migliorare; *(: wages)* aumentare; *(: invalid, business)* riprendersi; *(: weather)* rimettersi
b *(continue)* continuare, riprendere; **to pick up where one left off** riprendere dal punto in cui ci si era fermati.

picka·back ['pɪkəˌbæk] N = **piggyback**.

pickaxe, *(Am)* **pick·ax** ['pɪkˌæks] N piccone *m*.

pick·er ['pɪkə'] N *(of fruit etc)* raccoglitore(-trice).

pick·et ['pɪkɪt] ① N **a** *(stake)* picchetto **b** *(striker, band of*

strikers) picchetto; (*Mil*: *sentry*) sentinella; (: *group*) picchetto.

2 VT picchettare.

3 VI picchettare.

♦ **picket duty** N: **to be on picket duty** (*Mil, Industry*) essere di picchetto.

♦ **picket fence** N steccato, palizzata.

♦ **picket line** N cordone *m* degli scioperanti.

pick·ings ['pɪkɪŋz] NPL (*profits*): **there are good pickings to be had here** qui si possono fare dei guadagni facili.

pick·le ['pɪkl] 1 N (*brine*) salamoia; (*vinegar*) aceto; **pickles** NPL (*preserved vegetables*) sottaceti *mpl*; **mixed pickles** giardiniera *fsg*; **to be in a pickle** (*fig fam*) essere in un guaio *or* pasticcio.

2 VT mettere sott'aceto; **pickled onions** cipolline *fpl* sott'aceto.

♦ **pick-me-up** ['pɪkmiːˌʌp] N (*fam*: *drink*) goccetto; (: *tonic*) tonico.

pick·pocket ['pɪkˌpɒkɪt] N borsaiolo(-a), borseggiatore(-trice).

♦ **pick-up** ['pɪkˌʌp] N **a** (*Brit*: *on record player*: *also*: **pick-up arm**) pick-up *m inv* **b** (*also*: **pick-up truck**) camioncino.

picky ['pɪkɪ] ADJ (*comp* **-ier**, *superl* **-iest**) (*fam pej*: *person*) difficile; **to be a picky eater** essere schizzinoso(-a) nel mangiare.

pic·nic ['pɪknɪk] (*vb*: *pt, pp* **picnicked**) 1 N picnic *m inv*; **to go on a picnic** andare a fare un picnic; **it was no picnic** (*fig fam*) non è stata una passeggiata.

2 VI fare un picnic.

♦ **picnic basket** N cestino per il picnic.

pic·nick·er ['pɪknɪkə'] N chi partecipa a un picnic.

pic·to·gram ['pɪktəˌgræm] N pittogramma *m*.

pic·to·rial [pɪk'tɔːrɪəl] ADJ (*magazine*) illustrato(-a); (*re-presentation*) pittoresco(-a); (*masterpiece*) di pittura; **a pictorial record of one's travels** una serie di immagini in ricordo dei propri viaggi.

pic·to·ri·al·ly [pɪk'tɔːrɪəlɪ] ADV (*record, express*) per immagini; (*describe*) pittorescamente.

pic·ture ['pɪktʃə'] 1 N **a** (*Art*: *painting*) quadro, pittura, dipinto; (: *drawing*) disegno; (: *portrait*) ritratto; (*photo*) fotografia; (*in book*) illustrazione *f*; **to take a picture of sb/sth** fare una foto a qn/di qc; **he looked the picture of health** sembrava il ritratto della salute; **you're the picture of your mother** sei (proprio) il ritratto di tua madre; **the garden is a picture in June** il giardino in giugno è uno spettacolo; **his face was a picture!** avresti dovuto vedere la sua faccia!; **to be in/out of the picture** essere/non essere coinvolto(-a)

b (*TV*) immagine *f*; **we get a good picture here** la ricezione qui è buona

c (*Cine*) film *m inv*; **to go to the pictures** (*esp Brit*) andare al cinema

d (*mental image*) immagine *f*, idea; **the other side of the picture** il rovescio della medaglia; **he painted a black picture of the future** ha dipinto il futuro a tinte fosche; **to get the picture** afferrare l'idea; **the overall picture** il quadro generale; **to put sb in the picture** mettere qn al corrente.

2 VT (*imagine*) immaginare; (*remember*) ricordare.

♦ **picture book** N libro illustrato.

♦ **picture frame** N cornice *f*.

♦ **picture gallery** N (*public*) pinacoteca; (*private*) galleria (d'arte).

♦ **picture postcard** N cartolina illustrata.

pic·tur·esque [ˌpɪktʃə'rɛsk] ADJ pittoresco(-a).

♦ **picture window** N finestra panoramica.

pid·dle ['pɪdl] (*Brit*) 1 VI (*fam*) fare pipì.

2 N: **to have a piddle** fare pipì.

pid·dling ['pɪdlɪŋ] ADJ (*fam*) insignificante.

pidg·in Eng·lish ['pɪdʒɪn 'ɪŋglɪʃ] N pidgin english *m inv*.

pie [paɪ] N (*of fruit*) torta; (*of fish, meat*) pasticcio in crosta; **as easy as pie** (*fam*) (facile) come bere un bicchier d'acqua; **that's pie in the sky** sono castelli in aria.

pie·bald ['paɪbɔːld] ADJ (*horse*) pezzato(-a).

piece [piːs] N **a** (*gen, also Chess*) pezzo; (*smaller*) pezzetto; (*of land*) appezzamento; (*fragment*) frammento; (*Draughts*) pedina; (*item*): **a piece of furniture/clothing/advice** un mobile/indumento/consiglio; **a piece of news/poetry** una notizia/poesia; **a piece of luck** un colpo di fortuna; **a 10p piece** (*Brit*) una moneta da 10 pence; **a six-piece band** un complesso di sei strumentisti; **a 21-piece tea set** ≈ un servizio da tè per 6 persone; **a piano piece** un pezzo *or* componimento per piano; **it is made all in one piece** è fatto in un pezzo solo; **in one piece** (*object*) intatto(-a); **to get back all in one piece** (*person*) tornare a casa incolume *or* sano(-a) e salvo(-a); **piece by piece** poco alla volta; **to be in pieces** (*taken apart*) essere smontato(-a); (*broken*) essere a pezzi; **to take sth to pieces** smontare qc; **to come** *or* **fall to pieces** sfasciarsi; **to smash sth to pieces** mandare in frantumi *or* in mille pezzi qc; **to go to pieces** (*fig*) crollare; **to say one's piece** dire la propria; **to give sb a piece of one's mind** dire a qn il fatto suo

b (*fam*): **she was a flighty piece** era una donna volubile

▶ **piece together** VT + ADV (*also fig*) ricostruire.

pièce de ré·sis·tance [pjɛsdəreˈzistɑ̃s] N cavallo di battaglia.

piece·meal ['piːsˌmiːl] 1 ADV poco alla volta.

2 ADJ (*approach, process*) graduale.

♦ **piece rate** N (*Industry*) tariffa a cottimo.

piece·work ['piːsˌwɜːk] N (*Industry*) (lavoro a) cottimo.

piece·worker ['piːsˌwɜːkə'] N (*Industry*) cottimista *m/f*.

♦ **pie chart** N areogramma *m*, grafico a torta.

pie·crust ['paɪˌkrʌst] N crosta di torta.

pied-à-terre [ˌpjeɪtɑːˈtɛə'] N pied-à-terre *m inv*.

♦ **pie dish** N terrina, tegame da forno.

Pied·mont ['piːdmɒnt] N Piemonte *m*.

♦ **pie-eyed** [ˌpaɪˈaɪd] ADJ (*fam*: *drunk*) sbronzo(-a).

pier [pɪə'] N pontile *m*; (*landing stage*) imbarcadero, pontile; (*of bridge*) pila.

pierce [pɪəs] VT (*gen*) bucare, forare; (*subj*: *cold, wind*) penetrare; (: *shriek, light*) squarciare; (: *arrow*) trafiggere; **to have one's ears pierced** farsi fare i buchi per gli orecchini.

pierc·ing ['pɪəsɪŋ] ADJ (*gen*) penetrante; (*cry*) lacerante, acuto(-a); (*wind, sarcasm*) pungente.

pi·etism ['paɪɪˌtɪzəm] N pietismo *m*.

pi·ety ['paɪətɪ] N pietà, devozione *f*.

pif·fle ['pɪfl] N (*Brit old fam*) sciocchezze *fpl*.

pif·fling ['pɪflɪŋ] (*fam*) ADJ insignificante.

pig [pɪg] N **a** maiale *m*, porco; **to buy a pig in a poke** (*fig*) fare un acquisto alla cieca *or* a scatola chiusa **b** (*fam*: *person*: *nasty*) stronzo(-a); (: *greedy, dirty*) porco, maiale *m*; **to make a pig of o.s.** mangiare (e bere) come un porco; see also **piggy in the middle**.

pi·geon ['pɪdʒən] N piccione *m*; **that's your pigeon** (*fig*) sono affari tuoi.

♦ **pigeon fancier** N colombicoltore(-trice).

pigeon·hole ['pɪdʒənˌhəʊl] 1 N (*also fig*) casella.

2 VT (*fig*) etichettare, catalogare.

♦ **pigeon loft** N piccionaia.

♦ **pigeon-toed** [ˈpɪdʒənˈtəʊd] ADJ: **to be pigeon-toed** camminare con i piedi in dentro.

pig·ery [ˈpɪɡərɪ] N allevamento di maiali.

piggy·back [ˈpɪɡɪˌbæk] N: **to give sb a piggyback** portare qn in groppa.

pig·gy bank [ˈpɪɡɪˌbæŋk] N salvadanaio.

pig·gy in the middle, pig in the middle N (*game*) ≈ palla prigioniera; **to be piggy in the middle** trovarsi fra due fuochi.

♦ **pig-headed** [pɪɡˈhɛdɪd] ADJ testardo(-a), cocciuto(-a).

♦ **pig-headedly** [ˌpɪɡˈhɛdɪdlɪ] ADV caparbiamente, con testardaggine.

♦ **pig-headedness** [ˌpɪɡˈhɛdɪdnɪs] N caparbietà, testar-daggine *f*.

♦ **pig in the mid·dle** N = **piggy in the middle**.

♦ **pig iron** N ghisa.

pig·let [ˈpɪɡlɪt] N maialino, porcellino.

pig·meat [ˈpɪɡˌmiːt] N = **pork**.

pig·ment [ˈpɪɡmənt] N pigmento.

pig·men·ta·tion [ˌpɪɡmənˈteɪʃən] N pigmentazione *f*.

pig·my [ˈpɪɡmɪ] N = **pygmy**.

pig·skin [ˈpɪɡˌskɪn] N cinghiale *m* (*pellame*).

pig·sty [ˈpɪɡˌstaɪ] N (*also fig*) porcile *m*.

pig·tail [ˈpɪɡˌteɪl] N (*plaited*) treccina; (*loose*) codino.

pike¹ [paɪk] N (*fish*) luccio.

pike² [paɪk] N (*spear*) picca.

pil·af(f) [ˈpɪlæf], **pilau** [pɪˈlaʊ] N pilaf *m inv*.

Pilate [ˈpaɪlət] N: **Pontius Pilate** Ponzio Pilato.

pilchard [ˈpɪltʃəd] N sardina.

pile¹ [paɪl] **1** N **a** (*heap: of books, records*) pila; (*less tidy*) mucchio, cumulo; **he put his things in a pile** ha ammucchiato le sue cose

b (*fam: large amount*) mucchio, sacco; **piles of** un mucchio di; **a pile of** una montagna di

c (*fam: fortune*) fortuna; **my brother made a pile selling videos** mio fratello ha fatto una barca di soldi vendendo video.

2 VT (*stack*) impilare; (*heap*) ammucchiare; **a table piled high with books** un tavolo coperto da pile di libri.

3 VI (*fam*): **pile in!** salta su!; **to pile into a car** stiparsi *or* ammucchiarsi in una macchina; **to pile on/off a bus** far ressa per salire sull'autobus/scendere dall'autobus

▶ **pile on** VT + ADV: **to pile on the pressure** (*fam*) fare pressione; **to pile it on** (*fam*) esagerare, drammatizzare; **to pile work on sb** caricare qn di lavoro.

▶ **pile up 1** VI + ADV (*also fig*) accumularsi, ammuc-chiarsi.

2 VT + ADV ammucchiare, accumulare

pile² [paɪl] N (*of carpet, cloth*) pelo.

pile³ [paɪl] N (*Constr*) palo.

piles [paɪlz] NPL (*Med*) emorroidi *fpl*.

♦ **pile-up** [ˈpaɪlˌʌp] N (*Aut fam*) tamponamento a catena.

pil·fer [ˈpɪlfə'] **1** VT rubacchiare.

2 VI fare dei furtarelli.

pil·fer·er [ˈpɪlfərə'] N ladruncolo(-a).

pil·fer·ing [ˈpɪlfərɪŋ] N furtarelli *mpl*.

pil·grim [ˈpɪlɡrɪm] N pellegrino(-a).

pil·grim·age [ˈpɪlɡrɪmɪdʒ] N pellegrinaggio; **to go on a pilgrimage** andare in pellegrinaggio.

pill [pɪl] N pillola; **to be on the pill** (*contraceptive*) prendere la pillola; **to sweeten** *or* **sugar the pill** (*fig*) indorare la pillola.

pil·lage [ˈpɪlɪdʒ] **1** VT saccheggiare.

2 VI darsi al saccheggio.

pil·lar [ˈpɪlə'] N (*round*) colonna; (*square*) pilastro; **a pillar of smoke** una colonna di fumo; **a pillar of the church** (*fig*) uno dei pilastri della chiesa; **to be driven from pillar to post** essere sballottato(-a) a destra e a manca.

♦ **pillar box** N (*Brit*) buca delle lettere (a colonnina).

♦ **pillar-box red** [ˌpɪləbɒksˈrɛd] N rosso fiammante.

♦ **Pillars of Hercules** N: **the Pillars of Hercules** (*Geog*) le Colonne d'Ercole.

pill·box [ˈpɪlbɒks] N (*Mil*) casamatta; (*for pills*) scatolina per pastiglie; (*also*: **pillbox hat**) toque *f inv*.

pil·lion [ˈpɪljən] **1** N sellino posteriore (*di moto*).

2 ADV: **to ride pillion** viaggiare dietro.

♦ **pillion passenger** N passeggero(-a) (*che viaggia sul sellino posteriore*).

pil·lo·ry [ˈpɪlərɪ] **1** N berlina.

2 VT (*fig*) mettere alla berlina.

pil·low [ˈpɪləʊ] N cuscino, guanciale *m*.

pillow·case [ˈpɪləʊˌkeɪs], **pillow·slip** [ˈpɪləʊˌslɪp] N federa.

♦ **pillow talk** N chiacchiere *fpl* fra le lenzuola.

pi·lot [ˈpaɪlət] **1** N (*Aer, Naut*) pilota *m/f*.

2 VT (*Aer, Naut*) pilotare; (*fig: guide*) guidare, dirigere.

3 ADJ (*scheme*) pilota *inv*.

♦ **pilot boat** N pilotina.

♦ **pilot certificate** N brevetto di pilota.

♦ **pilot light** N (*on cooker etc*) fiammella di sicurezza.

♦ **pilot study** N studio *m* pilota *inv*.

pi·men·to [pɪˈmɛntəʊ] N peperoncino.

pimp [pɪmp] N ruffiano, protettore.

pim·per·nel [ˈpɪmpəˌnɛl] N: **scarlet pimpernel** primula rossa.

pim·ple [ˈpɪmpl] N foruncolo.

pim·ply [ˈpɪmplɪ] ADJ (*comp* **-ier**, *superl* **-iest**) foruncoloso (-a).

PIN [pɪn] N ABBR = **personal identification number**.

pin [pɪn] **1** N (*gen, as ornament*) spillo; (*safety pin*) spillo di sicurezza; (*Tech*) perno; (*in grenade*) spoletta; (*Med*) chiodo; (*Elec: of plug*) spinotto; (*Bowling*) birillo; **as neat as a (new) pin** (*room*) lucido(-a) come uno specchio; (*person*) impeccabile; **you could have heard a pin drop** non si sentiva volare una mosca; **for two pins I'd have hit him!** (*fam*) per poco non l'avrei picchiato!.

2 VT **a** (*with drawing pin*) attaccare con una puntina; (*sewing*) attaccare con gli spilli

b (*fig*): **to pin sb against a wall** mettere qn con le spalle al muro; **to pin sb's arms to his sides** immobilizzare le braccia di qn contro i fianchi

▶ **pin down** VT + ADV **a** (*fasten or hold down*) immobilizzare

b (*fig*): **to pin sb down to a date** far fissare una data a qn; **to pin sb down to their promise** costringere qn a mantenere una promessa; **to pin sb down about his beliefs** far dire a qn quello che pensa; **there's something strange here but I can't quite pin it down** c'è qualcosa di strano qua ma non riesco a capire cos'è.

▶ **pin on 1** VT + PREP attaccare con uno spillo (*or* una puntina) a; **to pin one's hopes on sth** riporre le proprie speranze in qc; **to pin a crime on sb** (*fam*) addossare a qn la colpa di un delitto.

2 VT + ADV attaccare con uno spillo (*or* una puntina)

▶ **pin up** VT + ADV (*notice*) attaccare (al muro) con una puntina; (*hair*) appuntare con le forcine; (*hem*) appun-tare con gli spilli

pina·fore [ˈpɪnəˌfɔː'] N (*apron*) grembiule *m*.

♦ **pinafore dress** N scamiciato.

pin·ball [ˈpɪnˌbɔːl] N (*also*: **pinball machine**) flipper *m inv*.

pince-nez ['pæns‚neɪ] N pince-nez *m inv.*

pin·cers ['pɪnsəz] NPL (*of crab etc*) pinze *fpl,* chele *fpl;* (*tool*) tenaglie *fpl.*

pinch [pɪntʃ] ⊡ N **a** (*with fingers*) pizzicotto, pizzico; **to feel the pinch** (*fig*) trovarsi nelle ristrettezze; **at a pinch** (*fig*) se è proprio necessario; **if it comes to the pinch** se le cose si mettono male

b (*small quantity*) pizzico, presa; **to take sth with a pinch of salt** (*fig*) prendere qc con un grano di sale.

⊡ VT **a** (*with fingers*) pizzicare; **my shoes are pinching me** le scarpe mi vanno strette

b (*fam: steal*) fregare, grattare; (: *idea*) rubare

c (*fam: arrest*) pizzicare.

⊡ VI (*shoe*) essere (troppo) stretto(-a), stringere; **to pinch and scrape** fare economia (su tutto).

pinched ['pɪntʃt] ADJ (*face*) dai lineamenti tirati; **pinched with cold** raggrinzito(-a) dal freddo; **pinched with hunger** scavato(-a) dalla fame.

pin·cushion ['pɪn‚kʊʃn] N (cuscinetto) puntaspilli *m inv.*

pine¹ [paɪn] N (*also:* **pine tree**) pino.

pine² [paɪn] VI: **to pine for sb/sth** sentire tanto la mancanza di qn/qc

▶ **pine away** VI + ADV languire, deperire.

pine·apple ['paɪn‚æpl] N ananas *m inv.*

♦ **pine cone** N pigna.

♦ **pine needle** N ago di pino.

♦ **pine nut, pine kernel** N pinolo.

pine·wood ['paɪn‚wʊd] N (*grove of trees*) pineta; (*material*) (legno di) pino.

ping [pɪŋ] ⊡ N suono metallico; (*of bell*) tintinnio.

⊡ VI (*see n*) produrre un suono metallico; tintinnare.

ping-pong® ['pɪŋ‚pɒŋ] N ping-pong ® *m.*

pin·ion ['pɪnjən] N (*Tech*) pignone *m.*

pink¹ [pɪŋk] ⊡ N **a** (*colour*) rosa *m inv* **b** (*Bot*) garofano a piumino rosa **c** : **to be in the pink (of health)** essere in perfetta salute.

⊡ ADJ **a** (*colour*) rosa *inv*; **to turn** *or* **go pink** (*flush*) arrossire **b** (*Pol fam*) con tendenze di sinistra.

pink² [pɪŋk] VT (*Sewing*) dentellare.

pinkie ['pɪŋkɪ] N (*Scot fam, Am fam*) mignolo.

pink·ing shears ['pɪŋkɪŋ‚ʃɪəz], **pink·ing scissors** NPL forbici *fpl* a zigzag.

♦ **pin money** N (*Brit*) denaro per spese superflue; **most women work from economic necessity, not for pin-money** la maggior parte delle donne lavora per ragioni economiche, non per procurarsi il superfluo.

pin·na·cle ['pɪnəkl] N (*Archit*) pinnacolo; (*of rock*) guglia; (*top of mountain*) vetta, cima; (*fig*) apice *m,* vertice *m.*

pin·ny ['pɪnɪ] N (*fam*) grembiule *m.*

pin·point ['pɪn‚pɔɪnt] VT (*on map*) localizzare con esattezza; (*problem*) mettere a fuoco, individuare con esattezza.

pin·prick ['pɪn‚prɪk] N puntura di spillo.

♦ **pins and needles** NPL formicolio *msg.*

pin·stripe ['pɪn‚straɪp] ADJ: **pinstripe suit** (abito) gessato.

pint [paɪnt] N (*measure*) pinta (*Brit* = *0,568 litri; Am* = *0,4732 litri*); (*Brit fam: of beer*) ≈ boccale *m* di birra.

pin·ta ['paɪntə] N (*Brit fam*) pinta di latte.

♦ **pint-size** ['paɪnt‚saɪz], **pint-sized** ['paɪnt‚saɪzd] ADJ minuscolo(-a); **he's a pint-sized version of his father** è suo padre in versione ridotta.

♦ **pin-up** ['pɪn‚ʌp] N pin-up (girl) *f inv.*

pio·neer [‚paɪə'nɪə'] ⊡ N pioniere *m.*

⊡ VT (*technique, invention*) essere l'ideatore(-trice) di.

pio·neer·ing [‚paɪə'nɪərɪŋ] ADJ (*work, spirit*) pionieristico

(-a).

pi·ous ['paɪəs] ADJ pio(-a); (*pej*) bigotto(-a); **a pious hope** una vana speranza.

pi·ous·ly ['paɪəslɪ] ADV piamente, con devozione; (*pej*) in modo bigotto.

pip¹ [pɪp] N: **to give sb the pip** (*Brit fam*) far venire i nervi a qn.

pip² [pɪp] N (*seed*) seme *m;* (*on card*) seme *m;* (*on dice*) punto; (*Brit Mil fam: on uniform*) stelletta; (*on radar screen*) segnale *m;* **the pips** NPL (*Telec*) il segnale acustico; (*Radio*) il segnale orario.

pip³ [pɪp] VT (*Brit fam*): **to be pipped at the post** essere battuto(-a) sul traguardo.

pipe [paɪp] ⊡ N **a** (*tube*) tubo; **pipes** NPL (*piping*) tubatura *fsg,* conduttura *fsg*

b (*Mus: of organ*) canna; (: *wind instrument*) piffero; **pipes** NPL (*also:* **bagpipes**) cornamusa *fsg*

c (*smoker's*) pipa; **to smoke a pipe** fumare la pipa; **put that in your pipe and smoke it!** (*fam*) che ti piaccia o no, è così!.

⊡ VT **a** (*water, oil etc*) portare per mezzo di tubature

b (*Mus*) suonare (col piffero *or* con la cornamusa); (*speak or sing in high voice*) dire (*or* cantare) con un tono di voce acuto; **to pipe sb aboard** (*Naut*) accogliere qn a bordo al suono di una banda

c (*Culin*): **to pipe icing on a cake** decorare un dolce con la glassa

▶ **pipe down** VI + ADV (*fam*) fare silenzio.

▶ **pipe up** VI + ADV (*fam*) farsi sentire

♦ **pipe cleaner** N scovolino.

piped mu·sic ['paɪpt‚mjuːzɪk] N musica di sottofondo.

♦ **pipe dream** N sogno impossibile.

pipe·line ['paɪp‚laɪn] N (*gen*) conduttura; (*for oil*) oleodotto; (*for natural gas*) metanodotto; **it is in the pipeline** (*fig*) è in arrivo.

pip·er ['paɪpə'] N (*on bagpipes*) suonatore(-trice) di cornamusa.

♦ **pipe tobacco** N tabacco da pipa.

pi·pette [pɪ'pɛt] N pipetta.

pip·ing ['paɪpɪŋ] N (*tubing*) tubature *fpl;* (*Sewing*) cordoncino.

♦ **piping bag** N (*Culin*) tasca da pasticciere.

♦ **piping hot** ADJ (*food, water*) bollente.

pip·it ['pɪpɪt] N: **meadow pipit** prispola; **tree pipit** prispolone *m.*

pip·pin ['pɪpɪn] N renetta.

pi·quan·cy ['piːkənsɪ] N (*of food*) gusto piccante; (*of situation*) aspetto intrigante.

pi·quant ['piːkənt] ADJ (*sauce*) piccante; (*situation*) intrigante; **a piquant charm** un fascino strano.

pique [piːk] ⊡ N dispetto, picca.

⊡ VT indispettire.

pi·ra·cy ['paɪərəsɪ] N pirateria.

pi·ra·nha [pɪ'rɑːnjə] N piranha *m inv.*

pi·rate ['paɪrɪt] ⊡ N (*also fig*) pirata *m.*

⊡ VT (*product*) contraffare; (*idea*) impossessarsi di; (*record, video, book*) riprodurre abusivamente.

pi·rat·ed ['paɪrɪtɪd] ADJ (*book, record etc*) riprodotto(-a) abusivamente.

♦ **pirate radio** N radio *f inv* pirata.

pirou·ette [‚pɪru'ɛt] ⊡ N piroetta.

⊡ VI piroettare.

Pi·sces ['paɪsiːz] N Pesci *mpl;* **to be Pisces** essere dei Pesci.

♦ **piss** [pɪs] VI (*fam!*) pisciare (*fam!*)

▶ **piss about, piss around** VI + ADV (*fam!*) far caz-

zate (*fam!*)
► **piss down** VI + ADV (*fam: rain*) piovere a catinelle
► **piss off** (*fam!*) [1] VI + ADV: **piss off!** levati dalle palle! (*fam!*).
  [2] VT + ADV: **I'm pissed off with it** ne ho le palle piene (*fam!*)
pissed [pɪst] ADJ (*Brit fam!: drunk*) sbronzo(-a).
pis·ta·chio [pɪsˈtɑːʃɪəʊ] N pistacchio.
piste [piːst] N (*Skiing*) pista.
pis·tol [ˈpɪstl] N pistola.
♦ **pistol point** N: **at pistol point** sotto la minaccia della pistola.
♦ **pistol shot** N colpo di pistola.
pis·ton [ˈpɪstən] N (*gen*) stantuffo; (*Aut*) pistone *m*.
♦ **piston engine** N (*Aut*) motore *m* a pistoni.
♦ **piston ring** N (*Aut*) fascia elastica.
♦ **piston rod** N (*Aut*) biella.
pit¹ [pɪt] [1] N **a** (*hole in ground*) buca, fossa; (*on moon*) cratere *m*; (*coalmine*) miniera di carbone; (*quarry*) cava; (*to trap animals*) buca; **in the pit of one's stomach** alla bocca dello stomaco; **he works down the pit** lavora in miniera
  b (*Aut: in garage*) fossa; (: *Motor racing*) box *m inv*
  c (*Brit Theatre*) platea.
  [2] VT **a** (*subj: chickenpox*) butterare; (: *rust*) corrodere in più punti
  b : **to pit A against B** contrapporre A a B; **to pit one's wits against sb** misurarsi contro qn.
pit² [pɪt] N (*in fruit*) nocciolo, seme *m*.
pita·pat [ˈpɪtəˈpæt] ADV: **to go pitapat** (*heart*) palpitare; (*rain*) picchiettare.
pitch¹ [pɪtʃ] N (*tar*) pece *f*.
pitch² [pɪtʃ] [1] N **a** (*esp Brit Sport*) campo
  b (*angle, slope: of roof*) inclinazione *f*
  c (*Naut, Aer*) beccheggio
  d (*of note, voice, instrument*) intonazione *f*, altezza; (*fig: degree*) grado, punto; **I can't keep working at this pitch** non posso continuare a lavorare a questo ritmo; **at its (highest) pitch** al massimo, al colmo; **his anger reached such a pitch that ...** la sua furia raggiunse un punto tale che...
  e (*fam: also:* **sales pitch**) discorsetto imbonitore
  f (*Mountaineering*) tiro di corda
  g (*throw*) lancio.
  [2] VT **a** (*throw: ball, object*) lanciare; (: *hay*) sollevare col forcone; **he was pitched off his horse** fu sbalzato da cavallo *or* disarcionato
  b (*Mus: song*) intonare; (: *note*) dare; **she can't pitch a note properly** non riesce a prendere una nota giusta; **to pitch one's aspirations too high** mirare troppo in alto; **to pitch it too strong** (*fam*) esagerare, calcare troppo la mano
  c (*set up: tent*) piantare.
  [3] VI **a** (*fall*) cascare, cadere; **to pitch forward** essere catapultato(-a) in avanti
  b (*Naut, Aer*) beccheggiare
► **pitch in** VI + ADV (*fam*) darci dentro *or* sotto
► **pitch into** VI + PREP (*attack*) saltare addosso a; (*start: work, food*) attaccare, buttarsi su.
♦ **pitch-black** [ˌpɪtʃˈblæk] (*also:* **pitch-dark**) ADJ nero(-a) come la pece; **the room was pitch-black** nella stanza c'era un buio pesto.
pitched battle [ˌpɪtʃtˈbætl] N (*Mil, also fig*) battaglia campale.
pitch·er¹ [ˈpɪtʃəʳ] N (*jar*) brocca.

pitch·er² [ˈpɪtʃəʳ] N (*Baseball*) lanciatore *m*.
pitch·fork [ˈpɪtʃˌfɔːk] [1] N forcone *m*.
  [2] VT: **to pitchfork sb into a job** (*fig*) costringere qn ad accettare un lavoro di punto in bianco.
♦ **pitch pine** N pitch pine *m*.
pit·eous [ˈpɪtɪəs] ADJ pietoso(-a).
pit·eous·ly [ˈpɪtɪəslɪ] ADV pietosamente.
pit·fall [ˈpɪtˌfɔːl] N (*fig*) tranello, trappola.
pith [pɪθ] N (*of plant*) midollo; (*of oranges, lemons*) parte *f* bianca della scorza; (*fig: core: of argument*) nocciolo, essenza, succo; (: *force*) vigore *m*.
pit·head [ˈpɪtˌhɛd] N imbocco della miniera.
pithy [ˈpɪθɪ] ADJ (*comp* **-ier,** *superl* **-iest**) (*fig: argument*) vigoroso(-a); (: *remarks*) arguto(-a); (: *account*) conciso (-a).
piti·able [ˈpɪtɪəbl] ADJ pietoso(-a).
piti·ful [ˈpɪtɪfʊl] ADJ **a** (*sight, story*) pietoso(-a); (*person*) che fa pietà *or* compassione **b** (*pej: attempt*) pietoso (-a); (: *cowardice*) deplorevole; (: *sum*) miserabile.
piti·ful·ly [ˈpɪtɪfəlɪ] ADV (*gen*) pietosamente; (*thin etc*) da far pietà; **it's pitifully obvious** è penosamente chiaro.
piti·less [ˈpɪtɪlɪs] ADJ spietato(-a).
piti·less·ly [ˈpɪtɪlɪslɪ] ADV spietatamente, senza pietà.
pi·ton [ˈpiːtɒn] N chiodo.
♦ **pit pony** N *pony impiegato in una miniera*.
pit·tance [ˈpɪtəns] N miseria, somma miserabile.
pit·ted [ˈpɪtɪd] ADJ: **pitted with** (*potholes*) pieno(-a) di; (*chickenpox*) butterato(-a) da.
pitter-patter [ˈpɪtəˈpætəʳ] = **patter** 2.
pi·tui·tary [pɪˈtjuːɪtərɪ] N (*also:* **pituitary gland**) ghiandola pituitaria.
♦ **pit worker** N minatore *m*.
pity [ˈpɪtɪ] [1] N **a** compassione *f*, pietà; **to feel pity for sb** provare compassione per qn; **for pity's sake!** per amor del cielo!; (*pleading*) per pietà!; **to have** *or* **take pity on sb** aver pietà di qn
  b (*cause of regret*) peccato; **what a pity!** che peccato!; **more's the pity** purtroppo; **it is a pity that you can't come** è un peccato che tu non possa venire.
  [2] VT compatire, commiserare.
pity·ing [ˈpɪtɪɪŋ] ADJ compassionevole; (*with contempt*) di commiserazione.
pity·ing·ly [ˈpɪtɪɪŋlɪ] ADV (*see adj*) pietosamente; con aria (*or* tono) di commiserazione.
piv·ot [ˈpɪvət] [1] N (*Mil, Tech, fig*) perno.
  [2] VT imperniare.
  [3] VI girare su se stesso(-a).
piv·ot·al [ˈpɪvətl] ADJ essenziale, centrale.
pix·el [ˈpɪksəl] N (*Comput*) pixel *m inv*.
pixie [ˈpɪksɪ] N folletto.
piz·za [ˈpiːtsə] N pizza.
piz·zazz [pəˈzæz] N: **to have pizzazz** (*fam*) essere pieno(-a) di verve.
piz·zi·ca·to [ˌpɪtsɪˈkɑːtəʊ] ADV (*Mus*) pizzicato.
P&L ABBR (= *profit and loss*) P.P.
plac·ard [ˈplækɑːd] N cartello.
pla·cate [pləˈkeɪt] VT placare, calmare.
placa·tory [pləˈkeɪtərɪ] ADJ (*gesture, tone, words etc*) tranquillizzante, conciliante.
place [pleɪs] [1] N **a** (*in general*) posto; (*more formally*) luogo; **to take place** (*incident*) succedere, accadere; (*meeting*) aver luogo; **we came to a place where ...** siamo arrivati in un posto dove....; **from place to place** da un posto all'altro; **this is no place for you** questo non è un posto per te; **place of business** posto di lavoro; **place of**

worship/birth luogo di culto/nascita; **all over the place** dappertutto; **to go places** (*travel*) andare in giro (per il mondo); **he's going places** (*fig fam*) si sta facendo strada; **we're going places at last** (*fig fam*) finalmente abbiamo sfondato; **it's only a small place** (*town*) è solo un paesino; (*house*) è piccolina; **his place in the country** la sua villa in campagna; **come to our place** venite da noi *or* a casa nostra; **to put sth back in its place** rimettere qc al suo posto; **that remark was quite out of place** quell'osservazione era proprio fuori luogo; **I feel rather out of place here** qui mi sento un po' fuori posto; **this isn't the place to discuss politics!** questo non è il posto giusto per discutere di politica!; **to change places with sb** scambiarsi di posto con qn; **to take the place of sb/sth** sostituire qn/qc, prendere il posto di qn/qc; **in place of** al posto di, invece di

  b (*in street names*) via; **market place** piazza del mercato
  c (*in book*): **to find one's place** trovare la pagina giusta; **to lose one's place** perdere il segno
  d (*seat*) posto (a sedere); (*: at table*) posto (a tavola); (*: in restaurant*) coperto; **to lay an extra place for sb** aggiungere un posto a tavola per qn
  e (*job, vacancy in team, school*) posto; **he found a place for his nephew in the firm** ha trovato un posto a suo nipote nella ditta
  f (*social position*) posizione *f*, rango; **friends in high places** amici altolocati *or* nelle alte sfere; **to know one's place** (*fig*) sapere stare al proprio posto; **it is not my place to do it** non sta a me farlo; **to put sb in his place** (*fig*) mettere a posto qn, mettere qn al suo posto
  g (*in series, rank etc*): **in the first/second place** in primo/secondo luogo; **she took second place in the race** si è piazzata *or* è arrivata seconda nella gara; **she took second place in the exam** ha preso il secondo miglior voto all'esame; **A won, with B in second place** A ha vinto e B è finito secondo.
2 VT **a** (*put: gen*) posare, mettere; (*on wall*) mettere; **place it on the table** mettilo *or* posalo sul tavolo; **we should place no trust in that** non dovremmo farci nessun affidamento
  b (*situate: town*) situare; (*: person*) piazzare; **we are better placed than a month ago** siamo in una situazione migliore *or* siamo messi meglio di un mese fa; **awkwardly placed** (*shop*) piazzato(-a) male; (*fig: person*) messo(-a) male; (*: in embarassing situation*) in una posizione delicata
  c (*contract, bet*) fare; (*goods*) piazzare; **to place an order with sb (for)** fare un'ordinazione a qn (di); **to place a book with a publisher** trovare un editore per un libro; **to place sth in sb's hands** mettere qc nelle mani di qn; **we could place 200 men** possiamo procurare lavoro a 200 uomini
  d (*in exam, race etc*) classificare; **to be placed second** classificarsi *or* piazzarsi al secondo posto
  e (*recall, identify: person*) ricordarsi di; (*: face, accent*) riconoscere; **I can't place him** non riesco a ricordarmi dove l'ho visto.
pla·ce·bo [plə'si:bəʊ] N placebo *m inv*.
♦ **place card** N (*on table*) segnaposto.
♦ **place mat** N (*cork*) sottopiatto; (*linen*) tovaglietta.
place·ment ['pleɪsmənt] N (*in group, accommodation*) collocamento; (*of trainee*) stage *m inv*.
♦ **place name** N toponimo.
pla·cen·ta [plə'sɛntə] N placenta.
♦ **place setting** N coperto.

plac·id ['plæsɪd] ADJ placido(-a), calmo(-a).
pla·cid·ity [plə'sɪdɪtɪ] N placidità.
pla·cid·ly ['plæsɪdlɪ] ADV placidamente.
pla·gia·rism ['pleɪdʒjə‚rɪzəm] N plagio.
pla·gia·rist ['pleɪdʒjərɪst] N plagiario(-a).
pla·gia·rize ['pleɪdʒjə‚raɪz] VT plagiare.
plague [pleɪg] **1** N (*disease, also fig*) peste *f*; (*of rats, locusts*) invasione *f*; **to avoid sb/sth like the plague** evitare qn/qc come la peste.
  2 VT (*fig*) tormentare; **to plague sb with questions** assillare qn di domande.
plaice [pleɪs] N platessa, passera di mare.
plaid [plæd] N (*material*) tessuto scozzese; (*cloak*) plaid *m inv*; **a plaid shirt** una camicia scozzese.
plain [pleɪn] **1** ADJ (*comp -er, superl -est*) **a** (*clear, obvious*) chiaro(-a), palese, evidente; (*path, track*) ben segnato (-a); **it's as plain as a pikestaff** *or* **as the nose on your face** (*fam*) è chiaro come il sole; **you have made your feelings plain** ti sei spiegato benissimo; **to make sth plain to sb** far capire chiaramente qc a qn; **do I make myself plain?** mi sono spiegato?
  b (*outspoken, honest, frank*) franco(-a), aperto(-a), schietto(-a); **plain dealing** sincerità, franchezza; **in plain language** *or* **English** in parole povere; **I shall be plain with you** sarò franco con te
  c (*simple, with nothing added*) semplice; (*paper: unlined*) non rigato(-a); (*fabric: in one colour*) in tinta unita *inv*; (*without seasoning*) scondito(-a); **the plain truth** la pura verità; **he's a plain man** è un uomo semplice; **plain stitch** (*Knitting*) maglia a diritto; **it's just plain commonsense** (*fam*) è una questione di semplice buon senso; **to send sth under plain cover** spedire qc in busta riservata
  d (*not pretty*) insignificante, scialbo(-a).
2 ADV **a** (*fam: simply, completely*) semplicemente
  b (*clearly*): **I can't put it plainer than that** non potrei esprimermi più chiaramente.
3 N **a** (*Geog*) pianura
  b (*Knitting*) (maglia a) diritto.
♦ **plain chocolate** N cioccolato fondente.
♦ **plain clothes** NPL: **in plain clothes** in borghese.
♦ **plain flour** N farina.
plain·ly ['pleɪnlɪ] ADV (*clearly*) chiaramente; (*speak*) con franchezza, francamente; (*dress*) con semplicità, sobriamente.
plain·ness ['pleɪnnɪs] N (*simplicity*) semplicità; (*lack of beauty*) insignificanza.
♦ **plain sailing** N (*fam*): **it'll be plain sailing from now on** d'ora in poi andrà tutto liscio.
plain·song ['pleɪn‚sɒŋ] N canto piano.
♦ **plain speak·ing** [‚pleɪn'spi:kɪŋ] N **there has been some plain speaking between the two leaders** i due leader si sono parlati chiaro.
♦ **plain-spoken** [‚pleɪn'spəʊkən] ADJ (*person*) franco(-a), schietto(-a); (*criticism*) senza mezze parole.
plain·tiff ['pleɪntɪf] N (*Law*) attore(-trice).
plain·tive ['pleɪntɪv] ADJ (*voice, song*) lamentoso(-a); (*look*) struggente; **plaintive cry** lamento.
plain·tive·ly ['pleɪntɪvlɪ] ADV (*speak*) lamentosamente; (*look*) malinconicamente.
plait [plæt] **1** N treccia.
  2 VT (*raffia*) intrecciare; **to plait one's hair** farsi una treccia (*or* le trecce).
plan [plæn] **1** N **a** (*scheme*) piano, progetto; (*Pol, Econ*) piano; **plan of campaign** (*Mil, also fig*) piano di battaglia; **development plan** piano *or* progetto di sviluppo; **to**

draw up a plan fare *or* elaborare un programma; **if everything goes according to plan** se tutto va secondo le previsioni *or* il previsto; **to make plans** far programmi *or* progetti; **the best plan would be to** ... la cosa migliore sarebbe...; **have you got any plans for today?** che programmi hai per oggi?

b (*diagram, map*: *of building, town*) pianta; (: *for essay, speech*) schema *m*.

2 VT **a** (*arrange*: *robbery, holiday, campaign*) organizzare; (*economy, research*) pianificare; (*essay*) fare lo schema di; **to plan one's family** pianificare le nascite

b (*intend*) avere in progetto; **to plan to do** avere l'intenzione di fare; **how long do you plan to stay?** quanto conti di restare?

c (*design*) progettare; **a well-planned town** una città che ha un buon piano urbanistico.

3 VI: **to plan (for)** far piani *or* progetti (per); **one has to plan months ahead** bisogna cominciare a pensarci diversi mesi prima; **to plan on sth/on doing sth** contare su qc/di fare qc

▶ **plan out** VT + ADV organizzare nei particolari.

pla·nar ['pleɪnəʳ] ADJ planare.

plane[1] [pleɪn] N aereo.

plane[2] [pleɪn] **1** ADJ (*Geom*) piano(-a).

2 N **a** (*Art, Math*) piano **b** (*fig*) piano, livello.

plane[3] [pleɪn] **1** N (*tool*) pialla.

2 VT (*also*: **plane down**) piallare; **to plane sth smooth** levigare qc con la pialla.

plane[4] [pleɪn] N (*tree*) platano; **London plane** platano di Londra.

plane[5] [pleɪn] VI (*bird, glider, boat*) planare.

plan·et ['plænɪt] N pianeta *m*.

plan·etar·ium [ˌplænɪ'tɛərɪəm] N planetario.

plan·etary ['plænɪtərɪ] ADJ planetario(-a).

plani·sphere ['plænɪˌsfɪəʳ] N planisfero.

plank [plæŋk] N (*of wood*) tavola, asse *f*.

plank·ton ['plæŋktən] N plancton *m inv*.

planned economy [ˌplænd'kɒnəmɪ] N economia pianificata.

plan·ner ['plænəʳ] N (*Econ*) pianificatore(-trice); (*Industry*) progettista *m/f*; (*also*: **forward planner**) calendario.

plan·ning ['plænɪŋ] N (*Pol, Econ*) pianificazione *f*; (*Industry*) progettazione *f*.

♦ **planning committee** N (*in local government*) commissione *f* urbanistica.

♦ **planning permission** N (*Brit*) licenza edilizia.

plant [plɑːnt] **1** N **a** (*Bot*) pianta **b** (*no pl*: *machinery etc*) impianto; (*factory*) stabilimento.

2 VT **a** (*trees, seeds, flowers*) piantare; **to plant a field with corn** piantare *or* coltivare un terreno a grano **b** (*position*: *pole*) piantare, conficcare; (*bomb*) mettere; (*kiss*) stampare; **to plant an idea in sb's mind** ficcare *or* cacciare in testa un'idea a qn; **he planted himself right in her path** le si è piantato di fronte; **to plant sth on sb** (*fam*) nascondere qc su qn (*per incriminarlo*)

▶ **plant out** VT + ADV (*seedlings*) trapiantare.

plan·tain ['plæntɪn] N (*banana*) varietà di banana con la buccia verde.

plan·ta·tion [plæn'teɪʃən] N piantagione *f*.

plant·er ['plɑːntəʳ] N (*person*) piantatore(-trice); (*machine*) piantatrice *f*.

♦ **plant life** N flora.

♦ **plant pot** N vaso (per piante).

plaque [plæk] N (*on building*) placca, targa; (*on teeth*) placca batterica.

plas·ma ['plæzmə] N plasma *m*.

♦ **plasma proteins** NPL proteine *fpl* plasmatiche.

plas·ter ['plɑːstəʳ] **1** N **a** (*Constr*) intonaco **b** (*Med*) gesso; **with his leg in plaster** con la gamba ingessata **c** (*Brit*: *also*: **sticking plaster**) cerotto.

2 VT **a** (*Constr*) intonacare **b** (*fam*: *cover*) impiastricciare; **to be plastered with** (*mud*) essere impiastricciato(-a) di; **to plaster a wall with posters** tappezzare un muro di manifesti **c** (*Med*) ingessare.

plaster·board ['plɑːstəˌbɔːd] N lastra di cartongesso.

♦ **plaster cast** N (*Med*) ingessatura, gesso; (*model, statue*) modello in gesso.

plas·tered ['plɑːstəd] ADJ (*fam*: *drunk*) ubriaco(-a) fradicio (-a).

plas·ter·er ['plɑːstərəʳ] N intonacatore *m*.

♦ **plaster of Paris** N gesso.

plas·tic ['plæstɪk] **1** N plastica, materia plastica; **plastics** materie *fpl* plastiche.

2 ADJ **a** (*made of plastic*) di plastica **b** (*flexible*) plastico(-a); **plastic behaviour** (*Phys*) plasticità; **the plastic arts** le arti plastiche.

♦ **plastic bag** N sacchetto di plastica.

♦ **plastic bullet** N pallottola di plastica.

♦ **plastic explosive** N (esplosivo al) plastico.

plas·ti·cine® ['plæstɪsiːn] N plastilina ®.

plas·tic·ity [plæs'tɪsɪtɪ] N plasticità.

♦ **plastics industry** N industria delle materie plastiche.

♦ **plastic surgeon** N specialista *m/f* in chirurgia plastica *or* estetica.

♦ **plastic surgery** N chirurgia plastica, chirurgia estetica.

plate [pleɪt] **1** N **a** (*flat dish, plateful*) piatto; (*for church collection*) piatto delle elemosine; **to hand sb sth on a plate** (*fig fam*) offrire qc a qn su un piatto d'argento; **to have a lot on one's plate** (*fig fam*) avere un sacco di cose da fare

b : **gold/silver plate** vasellame *m* d'oro/d'argento; (*electroplated*) metallo placcato in oro/in argento **c** (*Phot*) lastra; (*Tech*) placca; (*on door*) targa, targhetta; (*Aut*: *number plate*) targa; (*on cooker*: *hot plate*) piastra **d** (*dental plate*) dentiera **e** (*book illustration*) tavola (fuori testo) **f** (*Geol*) zolla **g** (*sheet of metal*) lamiera **h** (*Typ*) cliché *m inv*.

2 VT (*gen*) placcare; (*with gold*) dorare; (*with silver*) argentare.

plat·eau ['plætəʊ] N (*pl* **plateaus** *or* **plateaux**) (*Geog*) altopiano.

plate·ful ['pleɪtfʊl] N piatto.

♦ **plate glass** N vetro piano.

plate·layer ['pleɪtˌleɪəʳ] N (*Brit Rail*) armatore *m*.

plate·let ['pleɪtlɪt] N (*Bio*) piastrina.

plat·en ['plætən] N (*of typewriter, printer etc*) rullo.

♦ **plate rack** N scolapiatti *m inv*.

♦ **plate warmer** N scaldapiatti *m inv*.

plat·form ['plætˌfɔːm] N (*Brit*: *on bus*) piattaforma; (*at meeting, for band, stage*) palco; (*Pol*: *manifesto*) piattaforma, programma *m* (di base); (*Rail*) marciapiede *m*, banchina; **the train leaves from platform 7** il treno parte dal binario 7.

♦ **platform shoe** N scarpa con la zeppa.

♦ **platform ticket** N (*Brit*) biglietto d'ingresso ai binari.
plat·ing ['pleɪtɪŋ] N (*gold/silver plating*) placcatura; (*chrome plating*) cromatura.
plati·num ['plætɪnəm] N platino.
♦ **platinum blond** ADJ: **a platinum blonde** una bionda platinata.
plati·tude ['plætɪtjuːd] N luogo comune, banalità *f inv*.
Plato ['pleɪtəʊ] N Platone *m*.
pla·ton·ic [plə'tɒnɪk] ADJ platonico(-a).
pla·toni·cal·ly [plə'tɒnɪkəlɪ] ADV platonicamente.
pla·toon [plə'tuːn] N (*Mil*) plotone *m*.
plat·ter ['plætəʳ] N piatto da portata.
plau·dits ['plɔːdɪts] NPL plauso *msg*.
plau·sibil·ity [ˌplɔːzə'bɪlɪtɪ] N (*of argument, story*) plausibilità; **he lacks plausibility** non è convincente.
plau·sible ['plɔːzəbl] ADJ (*argument, story*) plausibile, credibile; (*person*) convincente.
plau·sibly ['plɔːzəblɪ] ADV in modo convincente.
Plautus ['plɔːtəs] N Plauto.

play [pleɪ] ☐1 N **a** (*recreation*) gioco; **the children were at play** i bambini giocavano; **to do/say sth in play** fare/dire qc per scherzo; **a play on words** un gioco di parole
b (*Sport*) gioco; **play began at 3 o'clock** la partita è cominciata alle 3; **there was some good play in the first half** ci sono state delle belle azioni nel primo tempo; **to be in/out of play** (*ball*) essere in/fuori gioco
c (*Theatre*) opera teatrale; **radio/television play** commedia radiofonica/per la televisione
d (*Tech: movement, give*) gioco; **there's not enough play in the rope** la fune non ha abbastanza gioco
e (*fig phrases*): **to bring** *or* **call into play** (*plan*) mettere in azione; (*emotions*) esprimere; **to give full play to one's imagination** dare libero sfogo alla propria fantasia; **to make great play of sth** giocare molto su qc; **to make a play for sb** fare il filo a qn; **to make a play for sth** darsi da fare per ottenere qc; **the play of light on the water** i giochi di luce sull'acqua.
☐2 VT **a** (*match, card*) giocare; (*cards, chess, tennis*) giocare a; (*opponent*) giocare contro; (*chesspiece*) muovere; **to play a game of tennis** giocare una partita a tennis; **to play sb at chess** giocare contro qn a scacchi; **they played him in goal** l'hanno fatto giocare in porta; **don't play games with me** (*fam*) non prendermi in giro; **to play a trick on sb** fare uno scherzo a qn; **my eyes must be playing tricks on me** devo avere le traveggole; **to play the field** (*sexually*) darsi da fare in campo amoroso; **to play a fish** (*Angling*) stancare un pesce
b (*perform: role*) interpretare; (*: play*) rappresentare, dare; (*perform in: town*) esibirsi a, dare uno spettacolo (*or* una serie di spettacoli) a; **to play sth for laughs** interpretare qc in chiave comica
c (*instrument, piece of music*) suonare; (*record*) mettere; (*radio*) ascoltare
d (*direct: light, hose*) puntare, dirigere.
☐3 VI **a** (*gen*) giocare; **to play at tennis** giocare a tennis; **to go out to play** andar fuori a giocare; **to play with a stick** giocherellare con un bastone; **they're playing at soldiers** stanno giocando ai soldati; **to play with fire** (*fig*) scherzare col fuoco; **to play for money** giocare a soldi; **to play for time** (*fig*) cercare di guadagnar tempo; **to play into sb's hands** (*fig*) fare il gioco di qn; **to play safe** giocare sul sicuro; **to play hard to get** fare il/la prezioso(-a); **what are you playing at?** (*fam*) cosa cavolo stai facendo?; **he's just playing at it** non lo sta prendendo sul serio

b (*move about, form patterns*): **we watched the fountains playing** guardavamo i giochi d'acqua delle fontane; **the sun was playing on the water** il sole creava giochi di luce sull'acqua; **a smile played on his lips** un sorriso gli sfiorò le labbra
c (*Mus*) suonare; (*radio*) essere acceso(-a); **to play on the piano** suonare il piano
d (*Theatre, Cine*) recitare (una parte); **to play dead** (*fig*) fingere di essere morto(-a).
▶ **play about, play around** VI + ADV (*person*) divertirsi; **to play about** *or* **around with** (*fiddle with*) giocherellare con; (*idea*) accarezzare
▶ **play along** ☐1 VI + ADV: **to play along with** (*fig: person*) stare al gioco di; (*: plan, idea*) fingere di assecondare.
☐2 VT + ADV: **to play sb along** (*fig*) illudere qn
▶ **play around** VI = **play about**
▶ **play back** VT + ADV riascoltare, risentire
▶ **play down** VT + ADV minimizzare
▶ **play off** ☐1 VT + ADV: **to play X off against Y** mettere X e Y l'uno(-a) contro l'altro(-a).
☐2 VI + ADV (*Sport*) giocare lo spareggio
▶ **play on** ☐1 VI + ADV (*Sport*) continuare a giocare; (*Mus*) continuare a suonare.
☐2 VI + PREP (*sb's feelings, credulity*) giocare su; **to play on sb's nerves** dare sui nervi a qn
▶ **play out** VT + ADV (*enact*) mettere in atto
▶ **play through** VT + ADV (*piece*) suonare
▶ **play up** ☐1 VI + ADV **a** (*Brit fam: cause trouble: child, engine*) fare i capricci; (*: leg, ulcer*) farsi sentire
b (*fam: flatter*): **to play up to sb** arruffianarsi qn.
☐2 VT + ADV **a** (*fam: cause trouble to*): **to play sb up** (*subj: child*) combinarne di tutti i colori a qn; (*: leg*) fare male a qn
b (*exaggerate*) esagerare, gonfiare.
play·act ['pleɪˌækt] VI (*fig*) fare la commedia.
♦ **play-acting** ['pleɪˌæktɪŋ] N (*fig*): **it's only play-acting** è tutta una commedia.
play·back ['pleɪˌbæk] N playback *m inv*.
play·bill ['pleɪˌbɪl] N manifesto (di teatro), locandina.
play·boy ['pleɪˌbɔɪ] N playboy *m inv*.
played out ['pleɪd'aʊt] ADJ (*exhausted: person*) spossato(-a); (*: vein in mine*) esaurito(-a); (*: argument*) superato(-a).
play·er ['pleɪəʳ] N (*Sport*) giocatore(-trice); (*Mus*) musicista *m/f*; (*Theatre*) attore(-trice); **players of musical instruments** suonatori di strumenti musicali; **football player** calciatore(-trice); **piano player** pianista *m/f*.
play·fellow ['pleɪˌfɛləʊ] N = **playmate**.
play·ful ['pleɪfʊl] ADJ (*child, puppy*) giocherellone(-a); (*mood, smile, remark*) scherzoso(-a).
play·ful·ly ['pleɪfəlɪ] ADV giocosamente; (*remark, smile*) scherzosamente.
play·ful·ness ['pleɪfʊlnɪs] N (*of child, puppy*) carattere *m* giocoso; (*of remark, mood, smile*) scherzosità.
play·goer ['pleɪˌgəʊəʳ] N appassionato(-a) di teatro; **an actor well-loved by playgoers** un attore molto amato dal pubblico.
play·ground ['pleɪˌgraʊnd] N (*in school*) cortile *m* per la ricreazione; (*in park*) parco *m* giochi *inv*.
play·group ['pleɪˌgruːp] N ≈ asilo.
play·house ['pleɪˌhaʊs] N (*theatre*) teatro; (*for children*) casetta per i giochi.
play·ing ['pleɪɪŋ] N: **some fine playing** (*Mus*) dei passaggi ben eseguiti.

♦ **playing card** N carta da gioco.
♦ **playing field** N campo sportivo.
play·maker ['pleɪ,meɪkə'] N (*Sport*) playmaker *m/f inv.*
play·mate ['pleɪ,meɪt] N compagno(-a) di gioco.
♦ **play-off** ['pleɪ,ɒf] N (*Sport*) (partita di) spareggio, bella.
play·pen ['pleɪ,pɛn] N box *m inv* (*per bambini*).
play·room ['pleɪ,ruːm] N stanza dei giochi.
play·thing ['pleɪ,θɪŋ] N (*also fig*) giocattolo.
play·time ['pleɪ,taɪm] N (*Scol*) ricreazione *f.*
play·wright ['pleɪ,raɪt] N commediografo(-a), drammaturgo(-a).
plc, PLC [,piːɛl'siː] ABBR = **public limited company.**
plea [pliː] N **a** (*entreaty: for donations*) appello; (: *for leniency*) supplica; (*excuse*) scusa, pretesto; **on the plea of** con la scusa di **b** (*Law*): **to enter a plea of guilty** dichiararsi colpevole; **to put forward a plea of self-defence** invocare la legittima difesa.
♦ **plea bargaining** N (*Law*) patteggiamento (della pena).
plead [pliːd] (*pt, pp* **pleaded,** (*esp Am*) **pled**) **1** VT **a** : **to plead sb's case** (*Law*), **to plead sb's cause** (*fig*); perorare la causa di qn
b (*as excuse: ignorance*) addurre come (*or* a) pretesto; **to plead insanity** (*Law*) invocare l'infermità mentale.
2 VI **a** (*beg*): **to plead with sb (to do sth)** supplicare *or* implorare qn (di fare qc); **to plead for sth** (*beg for*) implorare qc; (*make speech in favour of*) parlare in favore di qc
b (*Law: lawyer*): **to plead for** perorare in favore di; **to plead guilty/not guilty** (*defendant*) dichiararsi colpevole/innocente.
plead·ing ['pliːdɪŋ] **1** N (*entreaties*) suppliche *fpl.*
2 ADJ supplichevole.
plead·ing·ly ['pliːdɪŋlɪ] ADV supplichevolmente.
pleas·ant ['plɛznt] ADJ (*gen*) piacevole, gradevole; (*surprise, news*) bello(-a); (*smell*) gradevole, buono(-a); (*people, smile*) simpatico(-a); (*weather*) bello(-a); **we had a pleasant time** ci siamo divertiti.
pleas·ant·ly ['plɛzntlɪ] ADV (*smile, greet*) cordialmente; **I am pleasantly surprised** sono piacevolmente sorpreso.
pleas·ant·ness ['plɛzntnɪs] N (*of person*) amabilità; (*of place*) amenità.
pleas·ant·ry ['plɛzntrɪ] N (*joke*) battuta di spirito, spiritosaggine *f*; (*polite remark*): **to exchange pleasantries** scambiarsi convenevoli.
please [pliːz] **1** EXCL per piacere, per favore; (**yes,) please** sì, grazie; **come in, please** entrate, prego; **please pass the salt** OR **pass the salt please** per piacere *or* per favore, mi passi il sale?; **my bill, please** il conto, per piacere; **please don't cry!** ti prego, non piangere!.
2 VI **a** : **if you please** (*frm: in request*) per piacere, per favore; **he wanted ten, if you please!** (*iro*) ne voleva dieci, figurati!; **he does as he pleases** fa come gli pare
b (*cause satisfaction*) far piacere, piacere; **anxious** *or* **eager to please** desideroso(-a) di piacere; **a gift that is sure to please** un dono sicuramente gradito.
3 VT (*give pleasure to*) far piacere a; (*satisfy*) accontentare; **I did it to please you** l'ho fatto per farti piacere; **there's no pleasing him** non c'è verso di accontentarlo; **to please o.s.** far come si vuole; **please yourself!** come vuoi!, come ti pare!
pleased [pliːzd] ADJ (*happy*) felice, lieto(-a); (*satisfied*) contento(-a), soddisfatto(-a); **to be pleased (about sth)** essere contento(-a) (di qc); **pleased to meet you!** piacere!; **I am not pleased at your decision** la tua decisione non mi ha fatto piacere; **to be pleased with**

sb/sth essere contento(-a) *or* soddisfatto(-a) di qn/qc; **to be pleased with o.s.** compiacersi, essere compiaciuto(-a) di sé; **we are pleased to inform you that ...** abbiamo il piacere di informarla che... .
pleas·ing ['pliːzɪŋ] ADJ (*person*) simpatico(-a); (*news, sight*) piacevole, che fa piacere.
pleas·ing·ly ['pliːzɪŋlɪ] ADV (*arranged, performed etc*) gradevolmente, in modo gradevole.
pleas·ur·able ['plɛʒərəbl] ADJ (molto) piacevole *or* gradevole.
pleas·ur·ably ['plɛʒərəblɪ] ADV (molto) gradevolmente; (*anticipate*) con piacere.
pleas·ure ['plɛʒə'] **1** N **a** (*satisfaction, happiness*) piacere *m*; **with pleasure** con piacere, volentieri; **it's a pleasure!** OR **my pleasure!** OR **the pleasure is mine!** (*frm: returning thanks*) prego!, il piacere è (tutto) mio!; **I have much pleasure in informing you that ...** sono lieto di informarla che...; **may I have the pleasure?** (*frm: at dance*) mi concede l'onore di questo ballo?; **Mr and Mrs Smith request the pleasure of your company** (*frm*) i Signori Smith gradirebbero averla come ospite
b (*source of pleasure*) piacere *m*; **all the pleasures of London** tutti i divertimenti di Londra; **is this trip for business or pleasure?** è un viaggio d'affari o di piacere?
c (*frm: will*) desiderio, volontà; **at sb's pleasure** secondo i desideri di qn; **we await your pleasure** (*Comm*) siamo a vostra disposizione; **to be detained during her Majesty's pleasure** (*Law*) *essere condannato ad una pena detentiva di durata illimitata (prevista per i reati più gravi).*
2 ADJ (*cruise*) di piacere.
♦ **pleasure boat** N battello da diporto.
♦ **pleasure-loving** ['plɛʒə,lʌvɪŋ] ADJ: **she's a pleasure-loving person** è amante dei piaceri.
♦ **pleasure steamer** N vapore *m* da diporto.
pleat [pliːt] **1** N piega.
2 VT pieghettare.
ple·beian [plɪ'biːən] ADJ, N plebeo(-a).
plebi·scite ['plɛbɪsɪt] N plebiscito; **to hold a plebiscite** fare un referendum.
plebs [plɛbz] NPL (*pej*) plebe *fsg.*
plec·trum ['plɛktrəm] N plettro.
pled [plɛd] (*esp Am*) PT, PP of **plead.**
pledge [plɛdʒ] **1** N (*promise*) promessa solenne; (*security, token*) pegno; **to be under a pledge of secrecy** aver promesso di mantenere il segreto; **as a pledge of** come pegno *or* testimonianza di; **to sign** *or* **take the pledge** (*hum fam*) promettere solennemente di non toccare alcolici.
2 VT **a** (*promise*): **to pledge sth/to do sth** promettere qc/di fare qc; **to pledge sb to secrecy** far promettere a qn di mantenere il segreto; **to pledge support for sb** impegnarsi a sostenere qn
b (*pawn*) impegnare.
ple·na·ry ['pliːnərɪ] ADJ plenario(-a); **in plenary session** in seduta plenaria.
pleni·po·ten·ti·ary [,plɛnɪpə'tɛnʃərɪ] **1** N plenipotenziario.
2 ADJ plenipotenziario(-a).
plen·ti·ful ['plɛntɪfʊl] ADJ abbondante; **to be in plentiful supply** abbondare, esserci in gran quantità.
plen·ty ['plɛntɪ] N **a** abbondanza; **in plenty** (*in large quantities*) in abbondanza; **land of plenty** paese *m* di cuccagna *or* di bengodi
b : **plenty of** (*lots of*) molto(-a), tanto(-a); (*enough*)

abbastanza; **he has plenty of friends** ha tanti amici; **I've got plenty** ne ho abbastanza; **there's plenty to go on** (*information*) ci sono indizi più che sufficienti; **we've got plenty of time** abbiamo un sacco di tempo.

pletho·ra ['plɛθərə] N pletora, sovrabbondanza.

pleu·ra ['plʊərə] N (*pl* **pleurae** ['plʊəri:]) pleura.

pleu·ral ['plʊərəl] ADJ pleurico(-a).

pleu·ri·sy ['plʊərɪsɪ] N pleurite *f*.

Plexi·glas® ['plɛksɪ,glɑ:s] N plexiglas ® *m*.

pli·abil·ity [,plaɪə'bɪlɪtɪ] N (*see adj*) flessibilità; malleabilità.

pli·able ['plaɪəbl], **pli·ant** ['plaɪənt] ADJ (*substance*) pieghevole, flessibile; (*fig: person*) malleabile.

pli·ers ['plaɪəz] NPL (*also:* **pair of pliers**) pinze *fpl*.

plight [plaɪt] N situazione *f* (critica); **the country's economic plight** le gravi condizioni economiche del paese.

plim·soll ['plɪmsəl] N (*Brit*) scarpa da tennis.

♦ **Plimsoll line** N (*Naut*) linea di immersione massima.

plinth [plɪnθ] N plinto.

Pliny ['plɪnɪ] N: **Pliny the Younger/the Elder** Plinio il Giovane/il Vecchio.

PLO [,pi:ɛl'əʊ] N ABBR (= *Palestine Liberation Organization*) OLP *f*.

plod [plɒd] VI: **to plod up/down** *etc* trascinarsi su per/giù per *etc*; **to plod away at sth** (*fig*) sgobbare su qc; **we must plod on** (*fig*) dobbiamo farci forza e tirare avanti.

plod·der ['plɒdə'] N sgobbone(-a).

plod·ding ['plɒdɪŋ] ADJ (*gait*) pesante; (*pace of work*) lento(-a) e pesante; (*fig: person*) che sgobba.

plonk[1] [plɒŋk] N (*Brit fam: wine*) vino ordinario.

plonk[2] [plɒŋk] [1] N (*sound*) tonfo.
[2] ADV: **plonk in the middle** nel bel mezzo.
[3] VT (*fam: also:* **plonk down**) appoggiare pesantemente; **to plonk o.s. down** lasciarsi cadere (di peso); **he plonked himself down on the sofa** è crollato sul sofà.

plop [plɒp] [1] N plop *m inv*.
[2] VI (*stone*) fare plop.

plo·sive ['pləʊsɪv] (*Phonetics*) [1] ADJ occlusivo(-a).
[2] N occlusiva.

plot[1] [plɒt] N (*of land*) appezzamento, lotto; **a vegetable plot** un orticello; **building plot** lotto edificabile.

plot[2] [plɒt] [1] N **a** (*conspiracy*) complotto, cospirazione *f*, congiura **b** (*of story, play*) intreccio, trama.
[2] VT **a** (*mark out: course, graph, diagram etc*) tracciare; **to plot one's position** (*Naut*) fare il punto **b** (*plan secretly*) complottare, cospirare, congiurare.
[3] VI complottare, congiurare.

plot·ter ['plɒtə'] N **a** (*conspirator*) cospiratore(-trice) **b** (*Naut, Comput*) plotter *m inv*.

plot·ting ['plɒtɪŋ] N (*conspiracy*) cospirazione *f*.

Plough [plaʊ] N (*Astron*): **the Plough** il Gran Carro.

plough, (*Am*) **plow** [plaʊ] [1] N aratro.
[2] VT (*field*) arare; (*furrow*) scavare; **to plough one's way through a book** (*fig*) leggere con fatica un libro.
[3] VI (*Agr*) arare; **the car ploughed into the wall** l'auto ha sfondato il muro

▶ **plough back** VT + ADV (*profits*) reinvestire

▶ **plough in** VT + ADV sotterrare arando

▶ **plough through** VI + PREP (*snow, mud*) procedere a fatica in; (*work*) procedere metodicamente in; (*speech*) leggere monotonamente; **he ploughed through a plate of spaghetti** macinò a fatica un piattone di spaghetti

▶ **plough up** VT + ADV (*field*) arare.

ploughing ['plaʊɪŋ], (*Am*) **plow·ing** N aratura.

plough·man, (*Am*) **plow·man** ['plaʊmən] N (*pl* **-men**)

aratore *m*.

♦ **ploughman's lunch** ['plaʊmənz 'lʌntʃ] N (*Brit*) semplice pasto a base di pane e formaggio.

plov·er ['plʌvə'] N piviere *m*; **ringed plover** corriere *m* grosso; **golden plover** piviere dorato.

plow [plaʊ] (*Am*) = **plough**.

plowing N (*Am*) = **ploughing**.

plowman N (*Am*) = **ploughman**.

ploy [plɔɪ] N stratagemma *m*, manovra.

pluck [plʌk] [1] N (*courage*) coraggio, fegato.
[2] VT (*fruit, flower*) cogliere; (*also:* **pluck out**) strappare; (*Mus: strings*) pizzicare; (: *guitar*) pizzicare le corde di; (*Culin: bird*) spennare; **to pluck one's eyebrows** depilarsi le sopracciglia; **to pluck up (one's) courage** farsi coraggio, armarsi di coraggio.
[3] VI: **to pluck at sb's sleeve** tirare qn per la manica.

plucki·ly ['plʌkɪlɪ] ADV coraggiosamente.

plucky ['plʌkɪ] ADJ (*comp* **-ier**, *superl* **-iest**) coraggioso(-a).

plug [plʌg] [1] N **a** (*of bath, basin, barrel, volcano*) tappo; (*for stopping a leak*) tampone *m*
b (*Elec*) spina; (*Aut: also:* **spark(ing) plug**) candela
c (*fam: piece of publicity*) pubblicità *f inv*, réclame *f inv*; **to give sb/sth a plug** fare pubblicità a qn/qc.
[2] VT **a** (*also:* **plug up**: *hole*) tappare; (*tooth*) otturare
b (*insert*) infilare, cacciare; **to plug a lead into a socket** inserire un filo (elettrico) in una presa di corrente
c (*fam: publicize*) fare pubblicità a; (: *push, put forward*) fare propaganda a

▶ **plug away** VI + ADV (*fam*): **to plug away (at sth)** sgobbare (su qc)

▶ **plug in** (*Elec*)
[1] VI + ADV collegarsi; **the TV plugs in behind the table** la presa per la TV è dietro il tavolo.
[2] VT + ADV (*appliance*) attaccare.

plug·hole ['plʌg,həʊl] N scarico; **it went down the plughole** è caduto nel buco del lavandino (or della vasca).

plum [plʌm] [1] N (*fruit*) prugna, susina; (*also:* **plum tree**) prugno, susino; **a real plum (of a job)** (*fig fam*) un lavoro favoloso.
[2] ADJ **a** (*tart, tree*) di prugne; (*plum-coloured*) (color) prugna *inv* **b** (*fig fam*): **a plum role** un ruolo ambito.

plum·age ['plu:mɪdʒ] N piume *fpl*, piumaggio.

plumb [plʌm] [1] N piombo.
[2] ADV (*fam*): **plumb in the middle** esattamente nel centro; **he's plumb stupid** (*Am fam*) è proprio stupido.
[3] VT scandagliare; (*sb's mind*) sondare; **to plumb the depths** scandagliare gli abissi; (*fig*) toccare il fondo

▶ **plumb in** VT + ADV (*washing machine*) collegare all'impianto idraulico.

♦ **plumb bob** N piombino.

plumb·er ['plʌmə'] N idraulico.

plumb·ing ['plʌmɪŋ] N (*craft*) lavoro *or* mestiere *m* di idraulico; (*piping*) impianto idraulico, tubature *fpl*.

♦ **plumb line** N (*builder's*) filo a piombo; (*Naut*) scandaglio.

plume [plu:m] N piuma, penna; (*on hat, helmet*) penna, pennacchio; **a plume of smoke** un pennacchio di fumo.

plumed [plu:md] ADJ (*helmet*) chiomato(-a).

plum·met ['plʌmɪt] VI (*bird*) calare a piombo; (*plane*) precipitare; (*temperature, price, sales*) calare bruscamente; (*spirits, morale*) calare a zero.

plum·my ['plʌmɪ] ADJ (*comp* **-ier**, *superl* **-iest**) **a** (*Brit: voice, accent*) (esageratamente) aristocratico(-a) **b** (*colour*) (color *m*) prugna *inv*.

plump [plʌmp] ADJ (*comp* **-er**, *superl* **-est**) (*person, chicken*) bene in carne; (*cheeks, face*) paffuto(-a); (*wallet, cushion*) (*bello(-a)*) gonfio(-a); (*arms, child, hands*) grassoccio (-a), grassottello(-a)
▶ **plump down** ① VT + ADV lasciar cadere di peso; **to plump sth (down) on** lasciar cadere qc di peso su.
② VI + ADV lasciarsi cadere di peso *or* di schianto
▶ **plump for** VI + PREP (*fam*) decidersi per.
▶ **plump up** VT + ADV (*cushion*) sprimacciare
plump·ness ['plʌmpnɪs] N (*of person, arms*) rotondità; (*of cheeks, face*) paffutezza.
♦ **plum pudding** N *specie di budino a base di farina, grasso di rognone, zucchero e frutta secca cotto a vapore.*
plun·der ['plʌndə'] ① N (*act*) saccheggio; (*loot*) bottino.
② VT (*gen*) saccheggiare; (*villagers*) depredare; (*objects*) far man bassa di.
plun·der·er ['plʌndərə'] N predone *m*, saccheggiatore(-trice).
plun·der·ing ['plʌndərɪŋ] ① ADJ saccheggiatore(-trice).
② N saccheggio.
plunge [plʌndʒ] ① N (*dive*) tuffo; (*fig: into debt, of currency*) caduta; **to take the plunge** (*fig*) buttarsi, saltare il fosso, fare il gran passo.
② VT **a** (*immerse*) immergere, tuffare; (*thrust: knife*) conficcare; (: *hand*) ficcare, tuffare; **to plunge a dagger into sb's chest** conficcare un pugnale nel petto di qn
b (*fig*): **to plunge a room into darkness** far piombare una stanza nel buio; **we were plunged into gloom by the news** la notizia ci ha gettato nella costernazione; **to plunge sb into debt** precipitare qn nei debiti.
③ VI **a** (*dive*) tuffarsi
b (*fall*) precipitare, cadere; **he plunged to his death** ha fatto una caduta mortale
c (*share prices, currency*) calare precipitosamente; **to plunge into debt** riempirsi di debiti
d (*fig: rush*): **he plunged into trade union activites** si buttò anima e corpo in attività sindacali; **to plunge heedlessly into danger** buttarsi allo sbaraglio.
plung·er ['plʌndʒə'] N (*for clearing drain*) sturalavandini *m inv*.
plung·ing ['plʌndʒɪŋ] ADJ (*neckline*) profondo(-a); (*back of dress*) profondamente scollato(-a).
plu·per·fect [ˌpluːˈpɜːfɪkt] N (*Gram*) piuccheperfetto.
plu·ral ['pluərəl] ① ADJ (*Gram: form*) plurale, del plurale; (: *noun, verb*) plurale, al plurale.
② N (*Gram*) plurale *m*; **in the plural** al plurale.
plu·ral·ism ['pluərəˌlɪzm] N pluralismo.
plu·ral·ist ['pluərəˌlɪst] ADJ pluralistico(-a).
plus [plʌs] ① PREP più.
② ADJ (*Math, Elec*) positivo(-a); **ten/twenty plus** più di dieci/venti; **you must be 20 plus** devi avere vent'anni compiuti; **a plus factor** (*fig*) un vantaggio.
③ N (*Math: plus sign*) più *m inv*; (*fig: advantage*) vantaggio.
♦ **plus fours** NPL calzoni *mpl* alla zuava.
plush [plʌʃ] ① N felpa.
② ADJ (*also:* **plushy:** *fam*) sontuoso(-a), lussuoso(-a).
Plutarch ['pluːtɑːk] N Plutarco.
Plu·to ['pluːtəʊ] N (*Astron, Myth*) Plutone *m*.
plu·toc·ra·cy [ˌpluːˈtɒkrəsɪ] N plutocrazia.
plu·to·crat ['pluːtəʊˌkræt] N plutocrate *m/f*.
plu·ton·ic [pluːˈtɒnɪk] ADJ plutonico(-a).
plu·to·nium [pluːˈtəʊnɪəm] N plutonio.
ply[1] [plaɪ] ① N (*of wool*) capo; (*of wood*) strato.

② ADJ: **three-ply wood** compensato a tre strati; **three-ply wool** lana a tre capi.
ply[2] [plaɪ] ① VT (*knitting needle, tool etc*) maneggiare; (*sea, river, route*) viaggiare regolarmente su; **to ply one's trade** esercitare il proprio mestiere; **to ply sb with questions** continuare a far domande a qn; **to ply sb with drink** continuare a offrir da bere a qn.
② VI: **to ply between** far la spola fra, fare servizio regolare fra; **to ply for hire** (*taxi*) andare avanti e indietro in attesa di clienti.
ply·wood ['plaɪˌwʊd] N (*legno*) compensato.
PM [ˌpiːˈɛm] N ABBR (*Brit fam*) = **Prime Minister**.
p.m. ['piːˈɛm] ADV ABBR (*in the afternoon*) del pomeriggio; (*in the evening*) di sera.
PMS [ˌpiːɛmˈɛs] N ABBR (= *premenstrual syndrome*) sindrome *f* premestruale.
PMT [ˌpiːɛmˈtiː] N ABBR (= *premenstrual tension*) sindrome *f* premestruale.
pneu·mat·ic [njuːˈmætɪk] ADJ pneumatico(-a); **pneumatic drill** martello pneumatico.
pneu·mo·nia [njuːˈməʊnɪə] N polmonite *f*.
pneu·mo·tho·rax [ˌnjuːməʊˈθɔːræks] N pneumotorace *m*.
PO [ˌpiːˈəʊ] ① N ABBR (= *Post Office*) ≈ PP.TT. *fpl*.
② ABBR (*Naut*) = **petty officer**.
p.o. [ˌpiːˈəʊ] ABBR = **postal order**.
POA [ˌpiːˈəʊˈeɪ] N ABBR (*Brit*: = *Prison Officers' Association*) ≈ sindacato degli agenti di custodia.
poach[1] [pəʊtʃ] VT (*Culin: fish*) cuocere in bianco; **poached egg** uovo affogato *or* in camicia.
poach[2] [pəʊtʃ] ① VT (*hunt: game*) cacciare di frodo; (*fish*) pescare di frodo; (*fig fam: steal*) soffiare, portar via.
② VI cacciare (*or* pescare) di frodo; **to poach on sb's preserves** (*fig*) invadere il campo di qn.
poach·er ['pəʊtʃə'] N (*of game*) bracconiere *m*.
poach·ing ['pəʊtʃɪŋ] N bracconaggio, caccia (*or* pesca) di frodo.
PO Box N ABBR (= *Post Office Box*) C.P. (= *casella postale*).
pock·et ['pɒkɪt] ① N (*in garment etc*) tasca; **breast pocket** taschino; **with his hands in his pockets** con le mani in tasca; **to have sb in one's pocket** (*fig*) tenere in pugno qn; **to have sth in one's pocket** (*fig*) avere qc (già) in tasca; **to be in pocket** guadagnarci; **to be out of pocket** rimetterci; **to line one's pockets** arricchirsi, fare i soldi; **to put one's hand in one's pocket** (*fig*) metter mano al portafoglio; **to go through sb's pockets** frugare le tasche di qn; **to live in each other's pockets** rimanere *or* essere sempre appiccicati; **pocket of resistance/warm air** sacca di resistenza/di aria calda.
② VT (*fig: gain, take*) intascare; **to pocket one's pride** (*fig*) metter da parte l'orgoglio.
③ ADJ (*edition, calculator*) tascabile.
pocket·book ['pɒkɪtˌbuk] N (*wallet*) portafoglio; (*notebook*) taccuino; (*Am: handbag*) borsetta ; (*paperback*) tascabile *m*.
pock·et·ful ['pɒkɪtfʊl] N tascata.
♦ **pocket handkerchief** N fazzoletto da taschino.
pocket·knife ['pɒkɪtnaɪf] N (*pl* **-knives**) temperino.
♦ **pocket money** N (*of child*) paghetta.
♦ **pocket-size**, **pocket-sized** ['pɒkɪtsaɪz(d)] ADJ (*book*) tascabile; (*garden*) piccolissimo(-a).
pock·marked ['pɒkˌmɑːkt] ADJ (*face*) butterato(-a); (*surface*) bucherellato(-a).
pod [pɒd] ① N baccello, guscio.
② VT sgusciare.
podgy ['pɒdʒɪ] ADJ (*comp* **-ier**, *superl* **-iest**) traccagnotto

po·dia·trist [pɒˈdiːətrɪst] N (*Am*) callista *m/f*, pedicure *m/f*.

po·dia·try [pɒˈdiːətrɪ] N (*Am*) mestiere *m* di callista.

po·dium [ˈpəʊdɪəm] N podio.

POE [ˌpiːəʊˈiː] ABBR = *port of entry*.

poem [ˈpəʊɪm] N poesia.

poet [ˈpəʊɪt] N poeta(-essa).

po·et·ess [ˈpəʊɪtɛs] N poetessa.

po·et·ic [pəʊˈɛtɪk] ADJ poetico(-a).

po·eti·cal·ly [pəʊˈɛtɪkəlɪ] ADV poeticamente.

po·eti·cize [pəʊˈɛtɪˌsaɪz] VT poeticizzare.

♦ **poetic justice** N: poetic justice! giustizia fatta!

♦ **poetic licence** N licenza poetica.

♦ **poet lau·reate** [ˌpəʊɪtˈlɔːrɪɪt] N (*Brit*) *poeta di corte nominato a vita*.

po·et·ry [ˈpəʊɪtrɪ] N poesia; **to write poetry** scrivere (delle) poesie.

♦ **poetry reading** N reading *m inv* di poesia.

POEU [ˌpiːəʊiːˈjuː] N ABBR (*Brit*: = *Post Office Engineering Union*) *sindacato del personale tecnico delle Poste*.

pog·rom [ˈpɒgrəm] N pogrom *m inv*.

poign·an·cy [ˈpɔɪnjənsɪ] N (*of grief*) intensità; **it was a moment of extraordinary poignancy** fu un attimo di grande commozione.

poign·ant [ˈpɔɪnjənt] ADJ commovente, toccante.

poign·ant·ly [ˈpɔɪnjəntlɪ] ADV (*feel*) intensamente; (*describe*) in modo toccante.

point [pɔɪnt] 1 N a (*dot, punctuation mark, Geom*) punto; (*decimal point*) virgola; **2 point 6 (2.6)** 2 virgola 6 (2,6)

b (*on scale, compass etc*) punto; **freezing point** punto di congelamento; **from all points of the compass** da tutte le parti del mondo; **up to a point** (*fig*) fino a un certo punto

c (*of needle, pencil, knife*) punta; **on points** (*Ballet*) sulle punte; **at the point of a gun/sword** sotto la minaccia di un fucile/una spada; **not to put too fine a point on it** (*fig*) parlando chiaro

d (*place*) punto; **the train stops at Carlisle and all points south** il treno ferma a Carlisle e in tutte le stazioni a sud di Carlisle; **point of contact** punto d'incontro; **point of departure** (*also fig*) punto di partenza; **at this point** (*spatially*) in questo punto; (*in time*) a questo punto; **from that point on** (*in time*) da quel momento in poi; (*in space*) da quel punto in poi; **to be on the point of doing sth** essere sul punto di *or* stare (proprio) per fare qc; **when it comes to the point** quando si arriva al dunque; **when it came to the point of leaving** quando giunse il momento di partire; **abrupt to the point of rudeness** brusco al punto di essere villano

e (*counting unit: Sport, in test, Stock Exchange*) punto; **to win on points** vincere ai punti; **the index is down 3 points** l'indice è sceso di 3 punti

f (*purpose*) scopo, motivo; (*matter*) questione *f*, argomento; (*main idea, important part: of argument, joke*) nocciolo; **there's no point in staying** è inutile *or* non ha senso restare; **I don't see** *or* **get the point** (*of joke*) mi sfugge; **I don't see the point of** *or* **in doing that** non vedo il motivo di farlo; **the point is that** ... il fatto è che...; **that's the whole point!** precisamente!, sta tutto lì!; **the point at issue** l'argomento in discussione *or* questione; **a 5-point plan** un piano articolato in 5 punti; **she described the process point by point** descrisse il processo punto per punto; **in point of fact** a dire il vero; **to be beside the point** non entrarci; **to get off the point** divagare; **to come** *or* **get to the point** venire al punto *or*

al dunque; **to keep** *or* **stick to the point** restare in argomento; **to make a point of doing sth** non mancare di fare qc; **to make a point** fare un'osservazione; **to make one's point** dimostrare la propria tesi; **I take your point** so che hai ragione; **to win one's point** averla vinta; **to stretch a point** fare uno strappo (alla regola) *or* un'eccezione; **his remarks were to the point** le sue osservazioni erano pertinenti *or* a proposito; **you've got a point there!** giusto!, hai ragione!; **I missed the point of that joke** non ho afferrato quella battuta; **you've missed the whole point!** non hai capito niente!; **a point of principle** una questione di principio

g (*characteristic*) caratteristica, qualità *f inv*; **good/bad points** lati positivi/negativi; **tact isn't one of his strong points** il tatto non è il suo forte; **what points should I look for?** a cosa devo stare attento?

h (*Brit Rail*): **points** NPL scambio *msg*

i (*Aut*): **points** NPL puntine *fpl*

j (*Brit Elec*: also: **power point**) presa (di corrente).

2 VT a (*aim, direct: gun, hosepipe etc*): **to point sth (at sb/sth)** puntare qc (contro *or* su qn/qc); **she pointed the car at the gap in the traffic** diresse la macchina verso un varco nel traffico; **to point one's finger at sb** indicare qn con il dito, additare; **to point one's toes** stendere il piede

b (*indicate, show*) indicare, mostrare; **to point the way** (*also fig*) indicare la strada *or* la direzione da seguire

c (*Constr*) riempire gli interstizi di.

3 VI a indicare (con il dito), additare; **to point at** *or* **to** *or* **towards sth/sb** indicare qc/qn

b (*indicate: signpost, hand*) indicare, segnare; **everything points to him being guilty** tutti gli indizi fanno pensare che sia colpevole; **it points (to the) north** (*compass needle*) segna *or* indica il nord; **this points to the fact that** ... questo fa pensare che...

▶ **point out** VT + ADV

a (*show*) additare, indicare

b (*mention*) far notare.

▶ **point up** VT + ADV sottolineare, mettere in evidenza.

♦ **point-blank** [ˌpɔɪntˈblæŋk] 1 ADJ (*shot, question*) a bruciapelo; (*refusal*) categorico(-a), secco(-a); **at point-blank range** a bruciapelo.

2 ADV (*fire*) a bruciapelo; (*refuse*) categoricamente.

♦ **point-by-point** [ˈpɔɪntˌbaɪˈpɔɪnt] ADJ (*analysis etc*) particolareggiato(-a).

♦ **point duty** N (*Brit: Police*) servizio di controllo del traffico; **to be on point duty** dirigere il traffico.

point·ed [ˈpɔɪntɪd] ADJ a (*sharp: stick, chin*) appuntito(-a), aguzzo(-a); (*beard*) a punta; (*roof*) aguzzo(-a); (*arch*) a sesto acuto b (*obvious in intention: remark, question*) pregno(-a) di significati; **in a pointed manner** in modo significativo.

point·ed·ly [ˈpɔɪntɪdlɪ] ADV (*look*) in modo significativo; (*say*) in un tono pieno di sottintesi.

point·er [ˈpɔɪntəʳ] N a (*indicator*) lancetta; (*stick*) bacchetta b (*dog*) pointer *m inv* c (*clue*) indizio; (*advice*) consiglio; **to give sb some pointers on** ... consigliare qn su...; **this is a pointer to the guilty man** questo è un indizio che ci aiuta ad identificare il colpevole.

point·ing [ˈpɔɪntɪŋ] N (*Constr*) fissaggio (con la malta).

point·less [ˈpɔɪntlɪs] ADJ (*suffering, existence, journey*) inutile, vano(-a); (*crime*) senza senso, gratuito(-a); (*remark*) superfluo(-a); (*story, joke*) senza capo né coda; **it is pointless to refuse** è inutile rifiutarsi.

point·less·ly ['pɔɪntlɪslɪ] ADV (*suffer, live, remark*) inutilmente, senza scopo; (*destroy, kill*) inutilmente, senza motivo.

point·less·ness ['pɔɪntlɪsnɪs] N (*gen*) inutilità, futilità; (*of crime*) gratuità.

♦ **point of no return** N: **to reach the point of no return** (*also fig*) arrivare a un punto da cui non è più possibile tornare indietro.

♦ **point of order** N (*in debate*) mozione *f* d'ordine.

♦ **point of reference** N punto di riferimento.

♦ **point of sale** N (*Comm*) punto di vendita.

♦ **point of view** N punto di vista.

points·man ['pɔɪnts,mæn] N (*pl* **-men**) (*Rail*) scambista *m*.

♦ **point-to-point** [,pɔɪntə'pɔɪnt] N *steeplechase per dilettanti*.

poise [pɔɪz] ① N (*carriage of head, body*) portamento; (*balance*) equilibrio; (*composure, dignity of manner*) padronanza di sé; (*calmness*) calma. ② VT (*balance*) mettere in equilibrio; (*hold balanced*) tenere in equilibrio.

poised [pɔɪzd] ADJ **a** (*suspended*) sospeso(-a); **her pen was poised over the paper** teneva la penna sospesa sul foglio; **poised on the brink of success/disaster** sull'orlo del successo/della rovina **b** (*ready*): **to be poised for sth/to do sth** essere pronto(-a) per/a fare qc; **they are poised to attack** *or* **for the attack** sono *or* si tengono pronti ad attaccare **c** (*self-possessed*) posato(-a).

poi·son ['pɔɪzn] ① N (*also fig*) veleno; **they hate each other like poison** si odiano a morte; **what's your poison?** (*fam*) cosa bevi?. ② VT **a** (*person, food*) avvelenare; (*air, atmosphere*) inquinare, avvelenare **b** (*fig*): **to poison sb's mind** corrompere qn; **to poison sb's mind against sb/sth** sobillare qn contro qn/qc.

poi·son·er ['pɔɪznə'] N avvelenatore(-trice).

♦ **poison gas** N gas *m inv* tossico.

poi·son·ing ['pɔɪznɪŋ] N (*also fig*) avvelenamento; **arsenic poisoning** avvelenamento da arsenico; **to die of poisoning** morire avvelenato(-a).

♦ **poison ivy** N edera del Canada.

poi·son·ous ['pɔɪznəs] ADJ **a** (*snake, plant*) velenoso(-a); (*fumes*) venefico(-a), tossico(-a) **b** (*fig: tongue*) velenoso(-a); (: *propaganda*) venefico(-a); (: *ideas, literature*) pernicioso(-a); (: *rumours, individual*) perfido(-a); (: *fam: coffee etc*) schifoso(-a).

♦ **poison-pen letter** [,pɔɪzən'pɛn,lɛtə'] N lettera (anonima) diffamatoria.

poke [pəʊk] ① N (*jab*) colpetto; (*with elbow*) gomitata; **to give the fire a poke** attizzare il fuoco. ② VT **a** (*jab with stick, finger etc*) dare un colpetto a; **to poke sb with one's umbrella** dare un colpetto con l'ombrello a qn; **you poked me in the eye** mi hai messo un dito nell'occhio; **to poke the fire** attizzare il fuoco **b** : **to poke fun at sb** (*mock*) prendere in giro qn **c** (*Am fam: punch*) dare un pugno a **d** (*thrust*) cacciare, ficcare; **to poke one's head out of the window** mettere la testa fuori dalla finestra; **to poke sth in(to) sth** spingere qc dentro qc **e** (*make by poking*): **to poke a hole in sth** fare un buco in qc (*con il dito, un bastone etc*). ③ VI: **to poke at** dare dei colpetti a

▶ **poke about, poke around** VI + ADV (*fam: in drawers, attic*) frugare, rovistare; (: *in shop*) curiosare

▶ **poke out** ① VI + ADV spuntar fuori, sporger fuori

② VT + ADV: **to poke sb's eye out** cavare un occhio a qn.

pok·er¹ ['pəʊkə'] N (*for fire*) attizzatoio.

pok·er² ['pəʊkə'] N (*Cards*) poker *m inv*.

♦ **poker-faced** ['pəʊkə,feɪst] ADJ dal viso impassibile.

poky, pok·ey ['pəʊkɪ] ADJ (*comp* **-ier**, *superl* **-iest**) (*pej*) angusto(-a).

Po·land ['pəʊlənd] N Polonia.

po·lar ['pəʊlə'] ADJ (*Elec, Geog*) polare.

♦ **polar bear** N orso(-a) bianco(-a).

po·lar·ity [pəʊ'lærɪtɪ] N polarità *f inv*.

po·lari·za·tion [,pəʊləraɪ'zeɪʃən] N polarizzazione *f*.

polarize ['pəʊlə,raɪz] (*also fig*) ① VT polarizzare. ② VI polarizzarsi.

Po·lar·oid® ['pəʊlə,rɔɪd] N **a** (*Polaroid photograph*) foto *f inv* polaroid ®; (*also*: **Polaroid camera**) (macchina fotografica) polaroid ® *f inv* **b** : **Polaroids** NPL (*also*: **Polaroid sunglasses**) occhiali *mpl* polaroid ® *inv* **c** (*material*) polaroid ® *m inv*.

Pole [pəʊl] N polacco(-a).

pole¹ [pəʊl] N (*gen*) palo; (*flagpole, for vaulting*) asta; (*of tent, fence*) paletto; (*for punting*) pertica; (*curtain pole*) bastone *m*; **up the pole** (*fig fam: mad*) fuori di testa; **to send** *or* **drive sb up the pole** (*infuriate*) far uscire dai gangheri qn.

pole² [pəʊl] N (*Elec, Geog, Astron*) polo; **poles apart** (*fig*) agli antipodi.

pole·axe, (*Am*) **pole·ax** ['pəʊl,æks] VT (*person*) atterrare, stendere.

pole·cat ['pəʊl,kæt] N (*Brit*) puzzola; (*Am*) moffetta.

po·lem·ic [pə'lɛmɪk] N polemica.

po·lemi·cal [pə'lɛmɪkəl] ADJ polemico(-a).

♦ **Pole Star** N stella polare.

♦ **pole vault** N salto con l'asta.

po·lice [pə'liːs] ① NPL (*organization*) polizia *fsg*; (*policemen*) poliziotti *mpl*; **the railway/river police** la polizia ferroviaria/fluviale; **a large number of police were hurt** molti poliziotti sono rimasti feriti; **the police have caught him** è stato preso dalla polizia; **extra police were brought in** sono state fatte intervenire forze di polizia supplementari; **to join the police** arruolarsi nella polizia. ② VT (*streets, city, frontier*) presidiare; (*fig: agreements, prices*) controllare; **to police a football match** presidiare lo stadio durante un incontro di calcio. ③ ADJ (*escort, protection*) di agenti di polizia.

♦ **police car** N macchina della polizia.

♦ **police constable** N (*Brit*) agente *m* di polizia.

♦ **police department** N (*Am*) dipartimento di polizia.

♦ **police dog** N cane *m* poliziotto *inv*.

♦ **police force** N corpo di polizia, polizia.

♦ **police inspector** N ispettore *m* di polizia.

police·man [pə'liːsmən] N (*pl* **-men**) poliziotto, agente *m* di polizia.

♦ **police officer** N (*man*) agente *m* di polizia; (*woman*) donna *f* poliziotto *inv*.

♦ **police record** N: **to have a police record** avere precedenti penali.

♦ **police state** N stato di polizia.

♦ **police station** N ≈ commissariato di Pubblica Sicurezza.

♦ **police superintendent** N ≈ commissario di Pubblica Sicurezza.

police·woman [pə'liːs,wʊmən] N (*pl* **-women**) donna *f* poliziotto *inv*.

poli·cy¹ ['pɒlɪsɪ] ① N (*gen*) politica; (*of newspaper, company*) linea di condotta, prassi *f inv*; **it is our policy to**

do that fa parte della nostra prassi *or* politica fare questo; **to follow a policy of** seguire una politica di; **the government's policies** la politica del governo; **foreign policy** politica estera; **it's a matter of policy** è una questione di principio; **it would be good/bad policy to do that** sarebbe una buona/cattiva politica fare questo. [2] ADJ (*discussion, statement*) sulla linea di condotta.

poli·cy² ['pɒlɪsɪ] N (*also:* **insurance policy**) polizza (d'assicurazione); **to take out a policy** fare *or* stipulare un'assicurazione.

♦ **policy holder** N assicurato(-a).

♦ **policy-making** ['pɒlɪsɪˌmeɪkɪŋ] N messa a punto di programmi.

po·lio ['pəʊlɪəʊ] N polio *f*; **polio victim** vittima *m/f* della polio.

po·lio·my·eli·tis ['pəʊlɪəʊˌmaɪə'laɪtɪs] N poliomielite *f*.

Po·lish ['pəʊlɪʃ] [1] ADJ polacco(-a). [2] N (*language*) polacco.

pol·ish ['pɒlɪʃ] [1] N **a** (*for shoes, car*) lucido; (*for furniture, floor*) cera **b** (*act*) lucidata; **to give sth a polish** dare una lucidata *or* lustrata a qc **c** (*shine*) lucido, lucentezza; **it has a very high polish** è molto lucido; **to put a polish on sth** far brillare qc **d** (*fig: of person*) raffinatezza; (*: of style, performance*) eleganza. [2] VT (*wood, leather*) lucidare; (*stones, glass*) levigare; (*style*) perfezionare, raffinare

▶ **polish off** VT + ADV (*food, drink*) far fuori; (*work, correspondence*) sbrigare

▶ **polish up** VT + ADV (*skill, ability*) perfezionare; (*shoes, metal objects*) lucidare, lustrare.

pol·ished ['pɒlɪʃt] ADJ (*surface*) lucidato(-a); (*stone*) levigato(-a); (*fig: person, manner, performer*) raffinato(-a); (*: performance*) impeccabile.

pol·ish·er ['pɒlɪʃə'] N (*machine*) levigatrice *f*; (*floor polisher*) lucidatrice *f*.

po·lite [pə'laɪt] ADJ (*comp* -**r**, *superl* -**st**) educato(-a); **it's not polite to do that** non è educato *or* buona educazione fare questo; **to be polite to sb/about sth** essere cortese con qn/riguardo a qc; **in polite society** nella buona società.

po·lite·ly [pə'laɪtlɪ] ADV educatamente, cortesemente.

po·lite·ness [pə'laɪtnɪs] N educazione *f*, cortesia.

poli·tic ['pɒlɪtɪk] ADJ (*frm*) prudente.

po·liti·cal [pə'lɪtɪkəl] ADJ politico(-a); **I'm not at all political** non mi interesso di politica; **political analyst** politologo(-a).

♦ **political asylum** N asilo politico.

po·liti·cal·ly [pə'lɪtɪkəlɪ] ADV politicamente.

♦ **politically correct** ADJ politicamente corretto(-a).

♦ **political science** N scienze *fpl* politiche.

poli·ti·cian [ˌpɒlɪ'tɪʃən] N politico.

po·liti·cize [pə'lɪtɪˌsaɪz] VT politicizzare.

poli·tick·ing ['pɒlɪˌtɪkɪŋ] N (*pej*) *il fare politica per vantaggio personale*.

poli·tics ['pɒlɪtɪks] N (*sg: career*) politica; (*: subject*) scienze *fpl* politiche; (*pl: views, policies*) tendenze *fpl*, idee *fpl* politiche; **to talk politics** parlare di politica; **to go into politics** darsi alla politica.

pol·ka ['pɒlkə] N (*dance*) polca.

♦ **polka dot** N pois *m inv*.

poll [pəʊl] [1] N **a** (*voting*) votazione *f*, votazioni *fpl*; (*election*) elezioni *fpl*; **to take a poll (on sth)** mettere (qc) ai voti; **they got 65% of the poll** hanno ottenuto il 65%

dei voti; **to go to the polls** (*voters*) andare alle urne; (*government*) indire le elezioni; **a defeat at the polls** una sconfitta alle elezioni **b** (*also:* **opinion poll**) sondaggio (d'opinione); **to conduct a poll** fare un sondaggio. [2] VT **a** (*votes*) ottenere **b** (*in opinion poll*) interrogare nel corso di un sondaggio.

pol·len ['pɒlən] N polline *m*.

♦ **pollen count** N *indice ufficiale della quantità di polline nell'aria*.

pol·li·nate ['pɒlɪˌneɪt] VT impollinare.

pol·li·na·tion [ˌpɒlɪ'neɪʃən] N impollinazione *f*.

pol·ling ['pəʊlɪŋ] N **a** (*Brit Pol*) votazioni *fpl*; **polling has been heavy** c'è stata un'alta percentuale di votanti **b** (*Comput*) interrogazione *f* ciclica, polling *m*.

♦ **polling booth** N (*Brit*) cabina elettorale.

♦ **polling day** N (*Brit*) giorno delle elezioni.

♦ **polling station** N (*Brit*) seggio *or* sezione *f* elettorale.

poll·ster ['pəʊlstə'] N chi esegue sondaggi d'opinione.

♦ **poll tax** N (*Brit fam*) *imposta locale sulla persona fisica (non più in vigore)*.

pol·lu·tant [pə'luːtənt] N sostanza inquinante.

pol·lute [pə'luːt] VT inquinare; (*fig*) inquinare, corrompere.

pol·lu·tion [pə'luːʃən] N (*see vb*) inquinamento; corruzione *f*.

Pollux ['pɒləks] N (*Myth, Astron*) Polluce *m*.

polo ['pəʊləʊ] N (*sport*) polo.

♦ **polo neck** [1] N (*collar*) collo alto; (*also:* **polo neck sweater**) dolcevita. [2] ADJ a collo alto.

pol·ter·geist ['pɒltəˌgaɪst] N poltergeist *m inv*.

poly ['pɒlɪ] N ABBR (*Brit*) = **polytechnic**.

poly... ['pɒlɪ] PREF poli...

poly·am·ide [ˌpɒlɪ'æmaɪd] N poliammide *f*.

poly·an·dry ['pɒlɪændrɪ] N poliandria.

poly·an·thus [ˌpɒlɪ'ænθəs] N *specie di primula*.

poly·chro·mat·ic [ˌpɒlɪkrəʊ'mætɪk] ADJ policromatico(-a).

poly·chro·my ['pɒlɪˌkrəʊmɪ] N policromia.

poly·es·ter [ˌpɒlɪ'ɛstə'] N poliestere *m*.

poly·eth·yl·ene [ˌpɒlɪ'ɛθɪˌliːn] N = **polythene**.

po·lyga·my [pɒ'lɪgəmɪ] N poligamia.

poly·glot ['pɒlɪˌglɒt] ADJ, N poliglotta (*m/f*).

poly·gon ['pɒlɪgən] N poligono.

po·lygo·nal [pɒ'lɪgənl] ADJ poligonale.

poly·graph ['pɒlɪˌgrɑːf] N macchina della verità.

poly·he·dral [ˌpɒlɪ'hiːdrəl] ADJ poliedrico(-a).

poly·he·dron [ˌpɒlɪ'hiːdrən] N poliedro.

poly·mer ['pɒlɪmə'] N polimero.

po·lym·eri·za·tion [pəˌlɪməraɪ'zeɪʃən] N polimerizzazione *f*.

Poly·nesia [ˌpɒlɪ'niːzɪə] N Polinesia.

Poly·nesian [ˌpɒlɪ'niːʒən] ADJ, N polinesiano(-a).

poly·no·mial [ˌpɒlɪ'nəʊmɪəl] N polinomio.

pol·yp ['pɒlɪp] N (*Zool, Med*) polipo.

poly·pep·tide [ˌpɒlɪ'pɛptaɪd] N polipeptide *m*.

Polyphemus [ˌpɒlɪ'fiːməs] N Polifemo.

poly·phon·ic [ˌpɒlɪ'fɒnɪk] ADJ (*Mus*) polifonico(-a).

po·lypho·ny [pə'lɪfənɪ] N (*Mus*) polifonia.

poly·pro·pyl·ene [ˌpɒlɪ'prəʊpɪˌliːn] N polipropilene *m*.

poly·semous [ˌpɒlɪ'siːməs] ADJ polisemico(-a).

poly·sty·rene [ˌpɒlɪ'staɪriːn] N polistirolo; **polystyrene chips** palline *fpl* di polistirolo.

poly·syl·lab·ic [ˌpɒlɪsɪˈlæbɪk] ADJ polisillabo(-a).

poly·syl·la·ble [ˈpɒlɪˌsɪləbl] N polisillabo.

poly·tech·nic [ˌpɒlɪˈtɛknɪk] N (Brit) istituto superiore ora inglobato nella struttura universitaria.

poly·theism [ˈpɒlɪθiːˌɪzəm] N politeismo.

poly·theis·tic [ˌpɒlɪθiːˈɪstɪk] ADJ politeistico(-a).

poly·thene [ˈpɒlɪˌθiːn] N (Brit) polietilene m, politene m.

♦ **polythene bag** N sacchetto di plastica.

poly·to·nal [ˌpɒlɪˈtəʊnəl] ADJ (Mus) politonale.

poly·un·satu·rat·ed [ˌpɒlɪʌnˈsætʃəˌreɪtɪd] ADJ (Chem, Culin) polinsaturo(-a).

poly·urethane [ˌpɒlɪˈjʊərɪˌθeɪn] N poliuretano.

pom·egran·ate [ˈpɒmɪˌgrænɪt] N (tree) melograno; (fruit) melagrana.

pom·mel [ˈpʌml] **1** N pomo.

2 VT = pummel.

pom·my [ˈpɒmɪ] ADJ, N termine leggermente spregiativo usato dagli australiani per definire gli inglesi.

pomp [pɒmp] N pompa, fasto; **pomp and circumstance** grande or magnifico apparato.

Pompey [ˈpɒmpɪ] N: **Pompey the Great** Pompeo Magno.

pom·pon [ˈpɒmpɒn], **pom·pom** [ˈpɒmpɒm] N (on hat) pompon m inv.

pom·pos·ity [pɒmˈpɒsɪtɪ] N pomposità.

pomp·ous [ˈpɒmpəs] ADJ (pej: speech, attitude) pomposo (-a); (: person) pieno(-a) di boria.

pomp·ous·ly [ˈpɒmpəslɪ] ADV pomposamente.

ponce [pɒns] (fam) **1** VI (pimp) fare il magnaccia.

2 N **a** (pimp) magnaccia m inv **b** (Brit pej: effeminate man) damerino.

pon·cho [ˈpɒntʃəʊ] N poncho m inv.

pond [pɒnd] N stagno; (in park) laghetto.

pon·der [ˈpɒndəʳ] **1** VT ponderare, riflettere su.

2 VI: **to ponder (on** or **upon)** riflettere (su), meditare (su).

pon·der·ous [ˈpɒndərəs] ADJ pesante, ponderoso(-a).

pon·der·ous·ly [ˈpɒndərəslɪ] ADV pesantemente, ponderosamente.

pong [pɒŋ] (Brit fam) **1** N puzzo.

2 VI puzzare.

pon·tiff [ˈpɒntɪf] N pontefice m.

pon·tifi·cal [pɒnˈtɪfɪkəl] ADJ pontificio(-a); (pej: speech, gesture, manner) pontificante.

pon·tifi·cate [pɒnˈtɪfɪˌkeɪt] VI: **to pontificate about** or **on** pontificare su.

pon·toon¹ [pɒnˈtuːn] N pontone m.

pon·toon² [pɒnˈtuːn] N (Cards) ventuno.

pony [ˈpəʊnɪ] N pony m inv.

pony·tail [ˈpəʊnɪˌteɪl] N (hairstyle) coda di cavallo.

♦ **pony trekking** N: **to go pony trekking** andare a fare un'escursione a cavallo.

poo·dle [ˈpuːdl] N barboncino.

poof [pʊf] N (Brit offensive) finocchio.

pooh [puː] EXCL puah!

♦ **pooh-pooh** [ˈpuːˈpuː] VT (fam) farsi beffe di.

pool¹ [puːl] N (of water, rain, blood) pozza; (of light) cerchio; (pond) stagno; (: artificial) vasca; (swimming pool) piscina; (in river) tonfano.

pool² [puːl] **1** N **a** (common fund) cassa comune; (at poker) piatto

b (supply, source: of money, goods, workers) riserva; (: of experience, ideas) fonte f; (: of experts) équipe f inv; (of cars) parco

c (game) biliardo

d (Comm: consortium) pool m inv; (Am: monopoly trust) trust m inv.

2 VT (money, resources) mettere insieme, mettere in un fondo comune; (efforts, knowledge) mettere insieme.

pool·room [ˈpuːlˌrʊm] N sala da biliardo.

pools [puːlz] NPL: **to do the (football) pools** ≈ giocare la schedina, ≈ giocare al totocalcio.

poor [pʊəʳ] **1** ADJ (comp **-er,** superl **-est)** (gen) povero(-a); (crop, light, visibility) scarso(-a); (effort, excuse) misero (-a); (memory, health, quality) cattivo(-a); **he's a poor loser** non sa perdere; **I'm a poor traveller** sopporto male i viaggi; **it has a poor chance of success** ha scarse possibilità di successo; **it's a poor thing when ...** è deplorevole che... + sub; **to be poor at maths** essere debole in matematica; **as poor as a church mouse** povero(-a) in canna; **you poor thing!** poverino!; **you poor fool!** povero scemo!.

2: **the poor** NPL i poveri.

♦ **poor box** N cassetta per i poveri.

poor·ly [ˈpʊəlɪ] **1** ADV (badly) male; **a poorly paid job** un lavoro mal retribuito; **a poorly furnished room** una stanza arredata squallidamente; **to be poorly off** non avere molti soldi.

2 ADJ (ill) indisposto(-a); **I'm a bit poorly today** oggi mi sento poco bene.

poor·ness [ˈpʊənɪs] N (lack of wealth) povertà; (of crop, light) scarsità; (of effort, excuse, accommodation) insufficienza, inadeguatezza; (of health) debolezza.

♦ **poor relation** N parente m/f povero(-a).

pop¹ [pɒp] **1** N **a** (sound) schiocco; **to go pop** schioccare

b (fam: drink) bevanda gasata.

2 VT **a** (balloon) far scoppiare; (cork) far saltare

b (fam: put) mettere; **I'll just pop my coat on** m'infilo il cappotto; **she popped her head out** (of the window) sporse fuori la testa; (from under the blankets) fece capolino; **to pop the question** (fig) fare la proposta di matrimonio.

3 VI **a** (balloon) scoppiare; (cork, buttons) saltare; (ears) sbloccarsi; (corn) scoppiettare

b (fam: go quickly): **she's just popped upstairs** è andata di sopra un attimo; **let's pop round to Joe's** facciamo un salto da Joe

▶ **pop in** VI + ADV (fam) fare un salto, entrare un attimo

▶ **pop off** VI + ADV (Brit fam) **a** (die) tirar le cuoia

b (leave) scappare

▶ **pop out** VI + ADV (person) fare un salto fuori; **to pop out to the shops** fare un salto ai negozi; **his eyes nearly popped out of his head** sgranò tanto d'occhi.

▶ **pop up** VI + ADV (fam) apparire.

pop² [pɒp] ABBR of popular **1** ADJ pop inv.

2 N (pop music) musica pop; **it's top of the pops** è in testa alla hit parade.

pop³ [pɒp] N (fam Am: dad) papà m inv.

♦ **pop art** N pop art f inv.

♦ **pop concert** N concerto m pop inv.

pop·corn [ˈpɒpˌkɔːn] N popcorn m inv.

pope [pəʊp] N: **the Pope** il Papa.

pop·ery [ˈpəʊpərɪ] N (pej) papismo.

pop·eyed [ˈpɒpˌaɪd] ADJ con gli occhi sbarrati.

pop·gun [ˈpɒpˌgʌn] N fucile m (or pistola) giocattolo inv (che spara tappi di sughero).

pop·ish [ˈpəʊpɪʃ] ADJ (pej) papistico(-a).

pop·lar [ˈpɒpləʳ] N pioppo; **black poplar** pioppo nero europeo.

pop·lin [ˈpɒplɪn] N popeline f.

pop·pa·dum, pop·pa·dom ['pɒpədəm] N *tipo di pane sottile e croccante, rotondo, tipico della cucina indiana.*
pop·per ['pɒpəʳ] N (*Brit*) (bottone *m*) automatico.
pop·pet ['pɒpɪt] N (*fam*) tesoro, amore *m*.
pop·py ['pɒpɪ] N papavero.
poppy·cock ['pɒpɪˌkɒk] N (*fam*) scempiaggini *fpl.*
♦ **Poppy Day** N (*Brit*) *giorno della commemorazione dei caduti delle due guerre mondiali.*
♦ **poppy seed** N seme *m* di papavero.
pop·sicle® ['pɒpsɪkl] N (*Am*) ghiacciolo.
popu·lace ['pɒpjʊlɪs] N popolo, popolino.
popu·lar ['pɒpjʊləʳ] ADJ `a` (*well-liked*): **to be popular (with)** (*person*) essere benvoluto(-a) *or* ben visto(-a) (da); (*decision*) essere gradito(-a) (a); (*product*) essere molto richiesto(-a) (da); **a popular song** una canzone di successo; **a popular colour** un colore che va di moda `b` (*for the layman*) popolare `c` (*widespread: theory, fallacy*) comune; (: *support*) popolare; **by popular request** a richiesta generale.
popu·lar·ity [ˌpɒpjʊˈlærɪtɪ] N popolarità.
popu·lar·ize ['pɒpjʊləˌraɪz] VT `a` (*make well-liked: person*) rendere popolare; (*make fashionable: product, fashion*) diffondere `b` (*make accessible to laymen*) rendere accessibile ai più, divulgare; (*science*) volgarizzare.
popu·lar·iz·er ['pɒpjʊləˌraɪzəʳ] N divulgatore(-trice).
popu·lar·ly ['pɒpjʊləlɪ] ADV comunemente.
popu·late ['pɒpjʊˌleɪt] VT popolare.
popu·la·tion [ˌpɒpjʊˈleɪʃən] N popolazione *f.*
♦ **population explosion** N boom *m inv* demografico.
♦ **population growth** N incremento demografico.
♦ **population pyramid** N piramide *f* d'età.
popu·lism ['pɒpjʊlɪzm] N (*frm*) populismo.
popu·list ['pɒpjʊlɪst] ADJ (*frm*) populistico(-a).
popu·lous ['pɒpjʊləs] ADJ popoloso(-a), densamente popolato(-a).
porce·lain ['pɔːsəlɪn] N porcellana; **a piece of porcelain** una porcellana.
porch [pɔːtʃ] N veranda; (*of church*) sagrato.
por·cu·pine ['pɔːkjʊˌpaɪn] N porcospino.
pore¹ [pɔːʳ] N (*Anat*) poro.
pore² [pɔːʳ] VI: **to pore over** (*map, problem*) studiare attentamente; (*book*) essere immerso(-a) in.
pork [pɔːk] N (carne *f* di) maiale *m.*
♦ **pork butcher** N ≈ salumiere *m.*
♦ **pork chop** N braciola di maiale.
♦ **pork pie** N pasticcio di maiale in crosta.
porn [pɔːn], **porno** ['pɔːnəʊ] (*fam*) `1` N porno *m inv*; **hard/soft porn** pornografia hard-core/soft-core. `2` ADJ (*film*) porno *inv.*
♦ **porn merchant** N commerciante *m/f* di pornografia.
por·no·graph·ic [ˌpɔːnəˈɡræfɪk] ADJ pornografico(-a).
por·no·graphi·cal·ly [ˌpɔːnəˈɡræfɪkəlɪ] ADV pornograficamente.
por·nog·ra·phy [pɔːˈnɒɡrəfɪ] N pornografia.
♦ **porn shop** N pornoshop *m inv.*
po·rous ['pɔːrəs] ADJ poroso(-a).
por·poise ['pɔːpəs] N focena.
por·ridge ['pɒrɪdʒ] N porridge *m.*
♦ **porridge oats** NPL fiocchi *mpl* d'avena.
port¹ [pɔːt] N (*harbour*) porto; (*town*) città *f inv* portuale; **naval/fishing port** porto militare/per pescherecci; **to come into port** entrare in porto; **any port in a storm** (*fig*) in tempo di tempesta ogni buco è porto.
port² [pɔːt] `1` N (*Naut, Aer: left side*) a babordo. `2` ADJ (*cabin*) di sinistra; **on the port side** a babordo.

port³ [pɔːt] N (*wine*) porto.
port⁴ [pɔːt] N (*Naut: access to hold*) portello; (*Comput*) porta.
port·able ['pɔːtəbl] ADJ portatile.
por·tal ['pɔːtl] N portale *m.*
♦ **port authorities** NPL capitaneria *fsg* di porto.
port·cul·lis [pɔːtˈkʌlɪs] N saracinesca.
por·tend [pɔːˈtɛnd] VT (*frm*) far presagire.
por·tent ['pɔːtɛnt] N presagio.
por·ten·tous [pɔːˈtɛntəs] ADJ (*frm: ominous*) funesto(-a); (: *grave*) solenne, grave; (*pompous*) pomposo(-a).
por·ter ['pɔːtəʳ] N (*of office etc*) portinaio(-a), portiere(-a); (*of hotel*) portiere(-a); (*Rail, Aer*) facchino, portabagagli *m inv*; (*Am Rail*) addetto ai vagoni letto.
por·ter·age ['pɔːtərɪdʒ] N facchinaggio.
porter·house ['pɔːtəˌhaʊs] N (*also:* **porterhouse steak**) lombata.
port·fo·lio [ˌpɔːtˈfəʊlɪəʊ] N (*case*) cartella; (*Fin, Pol: office*) portafoglio; (*of artist, designer etc*) portfolio *m inv*; **portfolio of shares** portafoglio *m inv* titoli.
port·hole ['pɔːtˌhəʊl] N oblò *m inv.*
por·ti·co ['pɔːtɪkəʊ] N (*pl* **porticos** *or* **porticoes**) portico.
por·tion ['pɔːʃən] N (*part, piece*) parte *f*; (*of food*) porzione *f*
▶ **portion out** VT + ADV distribuire.
port·ly ['pɔːtlɪ] ADJ (*comp* **-ier**, *superl* **-iest**) corpulento(-a).
port·man·teau [ˌpɔːtˈmæntəʊ] N baule *m* portabiti.
♦ **portmanteau word** N parola macedonia.
♦ **port of call** N (porto di) scalo.
por·trait ['pɔːtrɪt] N ritratto.
♦ **portrait gallery** N galleria di ritratti.
♦ **portrait painter** N ritrattista *m/f.*
por·trai·ture ['pɔːtrɪtʃəʳ] N (*Art*) ritrattistica.
por·tray [pɔːˈtreɪ] VT (*painter, writer, novel*) ritrarre; (*painting*) raffigurare; (*actor*) interpretare.
por·tray·al [pɔːˈtreɪəl] N (*see vb*) ritratto; rappresentazione *f*; interpretazione *f.*
Por·tu·gal ['pɔːtjʊɡəl] N Portogallo.
Por·tu·guese [ˌpɔːtjʊˈɡiːz] `1` ADJ portoghese. `2` N (*person: pl inv*) portoghese *m/f*; (*language*) portoghese *m.*
♦ **Portuguese man-of-war** [ˌpɔːtjʊˈɡiːzˌmænəvˈwɔːʳ] N (*jellyfish*) fisalia, caravella portoghese.
pose [pəʊz] `1` N posa; **to strike a pose** mettersi in posa; **it's only a pose** (*fig*) è tutta una posa. `2` VT `a` (*person*) mettere in posa `b` (*problem, difficulty*) porre, creare; (*question*) fare. `3` VI (*for artist, also fig: attitudinize*) posare; (*pretend to be*): **to pose as** atteggiarsi a, posare a; **to pose as a policeman** farsi passare per un poliziotto.
Poseidon [pɒˈsaɪdən] N Poseidone *m.*
pos·er ['pəʊzəʳ] (*fam*) N (*problem*) domanda difficile; (*pej: person*) posatore(-trice).
po·seur [pəʊˈzɜːʳ] N (*pej*) persona affettata.
posh [pɒʃ] (*fam*) `1` ADJ (*comp* **-er**, *superl* **-est**) (*people, neighbourhood, family*) per bene; (*car, hotel, clothes*) elegante. `2` ADV: **to talk posh** (*pej*) parlare in modo snob
▶ **posh up** (*fam*) VT + ADV (*decorate, improve*) abbellire; (*clean up*) pulire; **to posh o.s. up** agghindarsi.
pos·it ['pɒzɪt] VT (*frm*) postulare.
po·si·tion [pəˈzɪʃən] `1` N `a` (*gen*) posizione *f*; (*of furniture etc*) disposizione *f*; (*in class, league, job*) posizione, posto; **to be in/out of position** essere/non essere al proprio posto; **in an uncomfortable position** (*also fig*) in

una posizione scomoda; **in a reclining position** (*of chair*) reclinato(-a); (*of person*) semisdraiato(-a); **what position do you play?** (*Sport*) in che posizione giochi?; **he's lying in second position** si trova al secondo posto *or* in seconda posizione; **to jockey** *or* **manoeuvre for position** (*also fig*) dare l'assalto ai posti

b (*post*) posto, impiego; **to have a good position in a bank** avere un buon posto in banca; **a position of trust** un posto di fiducia

c (*fig: situation, standing*) posizione *f*; **a man in his position** un uomo nella sua posizione; **to be in a position to do sth** essere nella posizione di fare qc; **he's in no position to criticize** non sta proprio a lui criticare; **put yourself in my position** si metta al mio posto; **I am in an awkward position** sono in una posizione difficile

d (*fig: point of view, attitude*) posizione *f*; **to take up a position on sth** prendere posizione su qc; **what's your position on this?** qual è la tua posizione riguardo a questo?; **do I make my position clear?** sono stato sufficientemente chiaro?.

2 VT (*place in position: chairs, lamp*) sistemare; (: *model*) mettere in posa; (: *soldiers*) disporre; **I positioned myself to get the best view** mi sono piazzato in modo da poter vedere bene.

posi·tive ['pɒzɪtɪv] ADJ **a** (*gen, also Elec, Math, Phot*) positivo(-a); (*constructive: advice, help, criticism*) costruttivo(-a); **we look forward to a positive reply** (*Comm*) in attesa di una risposta favorevole

b (*definite: gen*) positivo(-a), preciso(-a); (: *improvement, increase*) deciso(-a); (: *proof*) inconfutabile; **are you sure? — yes, positive** sei sicuro? — sicurissimo; **to make a positive contribution to sth** dare un contributo effettivo a qc; **he's a positive nuisance** è un vero rompiscatole.

♦ **positive discrimination** N discriminazione *f* a favore di minoranze.

posi·tive·ly ['pɒzɪtɪvlɪ] ADV (*approach*) positivamente; (*decisively*) decisamente; (*effectively*) concretamente; (*fam: really, absolutely*) assolutamente; **to think positively** pensare in modo costruttivo; **this is positively the last time I'll do this** è decisamente l'ultima volta che lo faccio; **it looks positively frightening** fa decisamente paura.

posi·tiv·ism ['pɒzɪtɪvɪzm] N positivismo.

pos·se ['pɒsɪ] N (*Am*) gruppo armato di volontari.

pos·sess [pə'zɛs] VT possedere; **like one possessed** come un ossesso; **to be possessed by an idea** essere ossessionato(-a) da un'idea; **whatever can have possessed you?** cosa ti ha preso?

pos·ses·sion [pə'zɛʃən] N **a** (*ownership*) possesso; **in possession of** in possesso di; **house with vacant possession** casa libera subito; **to have sth in one's possession** avere qc in proprio possesso; **to get possession of** entrare in possesso di; **to take possession of sth** impossessarsi *or* impadronirsi di qc; **to take possession of a house** prendere possesso di una casa; **to get/have possession of the ball** (*Sport*) impossessarsi/essere in possesso della palla

b (*thing possessed*) bene *m*, avere *m*; **her most treasured possession** la cosa più cara che ha.

pos·ses·sive [pə'zɛsɪv] **1** ADJ (*gen, also Gram*) possessivo(-a); **an over-possessive wife** una moglie troppo possessiva; **to be possessive about sth/towards sb** essere possessivo(-a) nei confronti di qc/qn.

2 N (*Gram*) possessivo.

pos·ses·sive·ly [pə'zɛsɪvlɪ] ADV in modo possessivo.

pos·ses·sive·ness [pə'zɛsɪvnɪs] N possessività.

pos·ses·sor [pə'zɛsəʳ] N possessore *m*, proprietario(-a); **to be the proud possessor of sth** essere orgoglioso(-a) di possedere qc.

pos·sibil·ity [,pɒsə'bɪlɪtɪ] N possibilità *f inv*; **it's a distinct possibility** è molto probabile; **there is no possibility of his agreeing to it** non c'è la minima possibilità *or* probabilità che accetti; **there is some possibility of success** c'è qualche probabilità di successo *or* riuscita; **he's a possibility for the part** è uno dei candidati per la parte; **to foresee all the possibilities** prevedere tutte le eventualità; **to have possibilities** (*person*) avere delle (buone) possibilità; **your idea has possibilities** la tua idea ha delle buone possibilità di successo; **this job has possibilities** questo lavoro offre molte possibilità.

pos·sible ['pɒsəbl] **1** ADJ possibile; **it is possible that he'll come** può darsi che *or* è possibile che venga; **it is possible to do it** è possibile farlo, è fattibile; **it will be possible for you to leave early** potrai uscire prima; **as soon as possible** appena possibile, al più presto possibile; **as big as possible** il più grande possibile; **as far as possible** nei limiti del possibile; **if (at all) possible** se (appena è) possibile; **the best possible result** il miglior risultato possibile; **to make sth possible for sb** rendere qc possibile a qn; **what possible excuse can you have for your behaviour?** che giustificazione puoi trovare per il tuo comportamento?; **a possible candidate** un possibile candidato.

2 N: **a list of possibles for the job** una lista dei possibili candidati al posto; **he's a possible for Saturday's match** è uno dei possibili giocatori per la partita di sabato.

pos·sibly ['pɒsəblɪ] ADV **a**: **he did all he possibly could** ha fatto tutto il possibile; **as often as I possibly can** quanto più spesso posso; **how can I possibly?** come posso?; **I cannot possibly do it** non posso assolutamente *or* proprio farlo; **could you possibly...?** potresti...?; **if you possibly can** se le è possibile **b** (*perhaps*) forse.

pos·sum ['pɒsəm] N (*fam*) = opossum.

post... [pəʊst] PREF post...; **post-1980** dopo il 1980.

post¹ [pəʊst] **1** N (*pole*) palo; **starting/finishing post** (*for race*) palo di partenza/arrivo; **to be left at the post** rimanere indietro alla partenza; **to be pipped at the post** essere battuto(-a) sul filo del traguardo; (*fig*) perdere per un pelo.

2 VT **a** (*also:* **post up**, *notice, list*) affiggere

b (*announce*) annunciare; **to post sb/sth (as) missing** (*Mil*) dare qn/qc per disperso(-a).

post² [pəʊst] **1** N (*Brit: mail*) posta; **by post** per posta; **by return of post** a giro di posta; **to catch/miss the post** arrivare/non arrivare in tempo per la levata; **it's in the post** è stato spedito; **to take sth to the post** andare a spedire qc; **has the post come yet?** è già arrivata la posta?; **it went first post this morning** è partito stamattina con la prima posta.

2 VT **a** (*send*) spedire per posta, mandare per posta; (*Brit: put in mailbox*) impostare, imbucare

b (*inform*): **to keep sb posted** tenere qn al corrente.

post³ [pəʊst] **1** N **a** (*job*) posto; **to take up one's post** assumere la propria carica **b** (*Mil*) posto; **at one's post** al proprio posto.

2 VT **a** (*position: sentry*) piazzare **b** (*Brit: send, assign*) inviare; (: *Mil*) assegnare.

post·age ['pəʊstɪdʒ] N affrancatura; **"postage: 50p"** "spese di spedizione: 50 penny"; **postage due 40p**

soprattassa (*per affrancatura insufficiente*) di 40 penny.
♦ **postage stamp** N francobollo.
post·al ['pəʊstəl] ADJ (*service, charges*) postale; (*vote*) per posta; **postal worker** postelegrafonico(-a).
♦ **postal order** N vaglia *m inv* postale.
post·bag ['pəʊst,bæg] N (*Brit*) sacco postale, sacco della posta.
post·box ['pəʊst,bɒks] (*Brit*) N (*in street*) buca delle lettere; (*in entrance hall*) cassetta per le lettere.
post·card ['pəʊst,kɑːd] N cartolina (postale).
post·code ['pəʊst,kəʊd] N (*Brit*) codice *m* (di avviamento) postale.
post·date [,pəʊst'deɪt] VT (*cheque*) postdatare.
post·er ['pəʊstər] N (*for advertising*) manifesto, affisso; (*for decoration*) poster *m inv*.
poste res·tante [,pəʊst'rɛstãnt] N (*Brit*) fermo posta *m*.
pos·teri·or [pɒs'tɪərɪər] ① N (*hum*) deretano, didietro.
② ADJ (*Tech*) posteriore.
pos·ter·ity [pɒs'tɛrɪtɪ] N posterità.
♦ **poster paint** N tempera.
♦ **post-free** [,pəʊst'friː] ADJ, ADV franco di porto.
post·gradu·ate ['pəʊst'grædjʊɪt] ① ADJ (*studies, course*) successivo(-a) alla laurea.
② N *laureato che continua gli studi*.
post·haste [,pəʊst'heɪst] ADV in gran fretta.
post·hu·mous ['pɒstjʊməs] ADJ postumo(-a).
post·hu·mous·ly ['pɒstjʊməslɪ] ADV dopo la sua (loro *etc*) morte.
post·im·pres·sion·ism ['pəʊstɪm'prɛʃə,nɪzəm] N postimpressionismo.
postin·dus·trial [,pəʊstɪn'dʌstrɪəl] ADJ postindustriale.
post·ing ['pəʊstɪŋ] N (*Brit*) incarico.
post·man ['pəʊstmən] N (*pl* -**men**) (*Brit*) postino.
post·mark ['pəʊst,mɑːk] ① N bollo *or* timbro postale.
② VT timbrare; **it was postmarked Rome** il timbro postale era di Roma.
post·master ['pəʊst,mɑːstər] N direttore *m* di un ufficio postale.
♦ **postmaster general** N ≈ ministro delle Poste.
post·mistress ['pəʊst,mɪstrɪs] N direttrice *f* di un ufficio postale.
post·mor·tem [,pəʊst'mɔːtəm] N (*also*: **postmortem examination**) autopsia; (*fig*) analisi *f inv* a posteriori.
post·na·tal [,pəʊst'neɪtl] ADJ post-parto *inv*.
♦ **Post Office** N (*institution*): **the Post Office** ≈ le Poste e Telecomunicazioni.
♦ **post office** N (*place*) ufficio postale, posta.
♦ **post office box** N casella postale.
♦ **post office worker** N impiegato(-a) delle poste.
♦ **post-paid** ['pəʊst'peɪd] ADJ già affrancato(-a).
post·pone [,pəʊst'pəʊn] VT: **to postpone sth for a month/until Monday** rimandare *or* rinviare *or* posticipare qc di un mese/fino a lunedì.
post·pone·ment [,pəʊst'pəʊnmənt] N rinvio.
post·script ['pəʊs,skrɪpt] N poscritto.
pos·tu·late ['pɒstjʊ,leɪt] VT (*frm*) postulare.
pos·ture ['pɒstʃər] ① N posizione *f*; (*carriage*) portamento; (*pose*) posa, atteggiamento.
② VI (*pej*) mettersi in posa, posare.
post·war ['pəʊst'wɔː'] ADJ del dopoguerra; **the postwar period** il periodo postbellico *or* del dopoguerra.
posy ['pəʊzɪ] N mazzolino (di fiori).
pot [pɒt] ① N a (*for cooking*) pentola, casseruola; (*teapot*) teiera; (*coffeepot*) caffettiera; (*for jam*) vasetto, barattolo; (*piece of pottery*) ceramica; (*for plants*) vaso; **pots**

and pans pentole; **to go to pot** (*fam: plans, business*) andare in malora; (: *person*) lasciarsi andare
b (*potful*): **a pot of jam** un vasetto di marmellata; **a pot of tea for two, please** tè per due, per piacere
c : **pots of** (*fam*) un sacco di; **to have pots of money** avere quattrini a palate
d (*fam: marijuana*) erba.
② VT a (*plant*) mettere in un vaso, invasare; (*jam*) mettere nei vasetti
b (*shoot: pheasant, rabbit*) ammazzare
c (*Billiards*) mandare in buca *or* biglia.
pot·ash ['pɒt,æʃ] N potassa.
po·tas·sium [pə'tæsɪəm] N potassio.
♦ **po·tas·sium per·man·ga·nate** N permanganato di potassio.
po·ta·to [pə'teɪtəʊ] N (*pl* **potatoes**) patata.
♦ **potato crisps**, (*Am*) **potato chips** NPL patatine *fpl*.
♦ **potato flour** N fecola di patate.
♦ **potato peeler** N (*knife*) pelapatate *m inv*; (*machine*) pelapatate *m inv*.
pot·bel·lied ['pɒt,bɛlɪd] ADJ (*from overeating*) panciuto (-a); (*from malnutrition*) dal ventre gonfio.
pot·belly ['pɒt,bɛlɪ] N: **to have a potbelly** (*from overeating*) avere la pancia; (*from malnutrition*) avere il ventre gonfio.
pot·boiler ['pɒt,bɔɪlər] N (*pej: novel, musical*) opera commerciale.
pot·bound ['pɒt,baʊnd] ADJ: **this plant is potbound** il vaso è ormai troppo piccolo per questa pianta.
po·ten·cy ['pəʊtənsɪ] N (*see adj*) potenza; validità; (*of drink*) forza.
po·tent ['pəʊtənt] ADJ (*gen*) potente, forte; (*fig: argument, reason*) validissimo(-a).
po·ten·tate ['pəʊtən,teɪt] N potentato.
po·ten·tial [pəʊ'tɛnʃəl] ① ADJ potenziale.
② N a (*possibilities*) potenziale *m*; **to realize one's full potential** realizzarsi pienamente; **sales potential** potenziale di vendita; **to show potential** promettere bene; **to have potential** essere promettente
b (*Elec, Math, Phys*) potenziale *m*.
♦ **potential difference** N (*Math, Phys*) differenza di potenziale.
po·ten·tial·ly [pəʊ'tɛnʃəlɪ] ADV potenzialmente.
po·ten·til·la [,pəʊtən'tɪlə] N potentilla, cinquefoglie *m inv*.
po·ten·ti·om·eter [pə,tɛnʃɪ'ɒmɪtər] N (*Elec*) potenziometro.
pot·ful ['pɒtfʊl] N pentola (piena).
pot·herb ['pɒt,hɜːb] N erba aromatica.
♦ **pot holder** N (*Culin*) presina.
pot·hole ['pɒt,həʊl] N (*in road*) buca; (*Brit Geol*) marmitta.
pot·holer ['pɒt,həʊlər] N (*Brit*) speleologo(-a).
pot·hol·ing ['pɒt,həʊlɪŋ] N (*Brit*) esplorazione *f* speleologica; **to go potholing** fare una speleologia.
po·tion ['pəʊʃən] N pozione *f*, filtro.
pot·luck [,pɒt'lʌk] N: **to take potluck** (*for food*) mangiare quel che passa il convento; (*for other things*) tentare la sorte.
♦ **pot plant** N pianta in vaso.
pot·pour·ri [,pəʊ'pʊriː] N a (*flowers*) *miscuglio di petali essiccati per profumare un ambiente* b (*fig: of music, writing*) pot-pourri *m inv*.
♦ **pot roast** N (*Culin*) brasato.
♦ **pot scourer** N spugnetta abrasiva.
pot·sherd ['pɒt,ʃɜːd] N (*Archeol*) frammento di vaso.
♦ **pot shot** N: **to take a potshot at sth** sparare a casac-

cio contro qc.

pot·ted ['pɒtɪd] ADJ **a** (*fish, meat*) conservato(-a) in vaso; (*plant*) in vaso **b** (*fig: shortened*) condensato(-a).

pot·ter¹ ['pɒtə'] N ceramista *m/f*.

pot·ter² ['pɒtə'], (*Am*) **put·ter** ['pʌtə'] VI: **to potter round the shops** fare un tranquillo giretto per i negozi; **to potter round the house** sbrigare con calma le faccende di casa; **he likes pottering about in the garden** gli piace fare qualche lavoretto in giardino.

♦ **potter's wheel** N tornio (da vasaio).

pot·tery ['pɒtərɪ] **1** N (*workshop*) fabbrica *or* laboratorio di ceramiche; (*craft*) ceramica; (*pots*) ceramiche *fpl*; **a piece of pottery** una ceramica.

2 ADJ (*dish, jug*) di ceramica.

pot·ty¹ ['pɒtɪ] N (*fam*) vasino.

pot·ty² ['pɒtɪ] ADJ (*comp* **-ier**, *superl* **-iest**) (*Brit fam: mad*) matto(-a), tocco(-a); (*: idea*) balordo(-a); **you're driving me potty!** mi fai diventare matto!

♦ **potty-trained** ['pɒtɪ,treɪnd] ADJ che ha imparato a farla nel vasino.

pouch [paʊtʃ] N (*Anat, for tobacco*) borsa; (*for money*) borsellino; (*Zool*) marsupio.

pouf, pouffe [puːf] N **a** (*seat*) pouf *m inv* **b** (*Brit offensive*) = **poof**.

poul·ter·er ['pəʊltərə'] N (*Brit*) pollivendolo(-a).

poul·tice ['pəʊltɪs] N impiastro, cataplasma *m*.

poul·try ['pəʊltrɪ] N pollame *m*.

♦ **poultry farm** N azienda avicola.

♦ **poultry farmer** N pollicoltore(-trice).

♦ **poultry farming** N avicoltura.

pounce [paʊns] **1** N balzo.

2 VI (*cat, tiger*) balzare (sulla preda); (*bird*) piombare (sulla preda); **to pounce on sb/sth** (*animal*) balzare su qn/qc; (*bird*) piombare su qn/qc; (*person*) piombare *or* balzare su qn/qc; **she pounced on my offer of help** ha colto al volo la mia offerta di aiuto; **he pounced on my suggestion that ...** (*attack*) è saltato su quando ho proposto che... .

pound¹ [paʊnd] N **a** (*weight* = *453g, 16 ounces*) libbra; **sold by the pound** venduto(-a) alla libbra; **half a pound** mezza libbra **b** (*money* = *100 pence*) (lira) sterline; **one pound sterling** una sterlina; **a ten-pound note** una banconota da dieci sterline.

pound² [paʊnd] **1** VT (*hammer, strike: door, table, person*) picchiare; (*: piano*) pestare i tasti di; (*: typewriter*) battere sui tasti di; (*subj: sea, waves*) sbattere contro; (*: guns, bombs*) martellare; (*pulverize: drug, spices, nuts*) pestare, polverizzare; (*knead: dough*) lavorare; **to pound sth to pieces** fare a pezzi qc; **to pound sth to a pulp** ridurre qc in poltiglia.

2 VI **a** (*heart*) battere forte; (*drums*) rullare; (*sea*) sbattere; (*person*): **to pound at** *or* **on** dare dei gran colpi a *or* su; (*piano*) pestare i tasti di

b (*run, walk heavily*): **to pound in/out** entrare/uscire a passi pesanti.

pound³ [paʊnd] N (*enclosure: for dogs*) canile *m* municipale; (*: for cars*) deposito *m* auto *inv* (*per auto sottoposte a rimozione forzata*).

pound·ing ['paʊndɪŋ] N: **to take a pounding** (*team*) prendere una batosta; (*ship*) essere sbattuto(-a) violentemente dalle onde; (*town: in war*) venire duramente colpito(-a).

♦ **pound sterling** N lira sterlina.

pour [pɔː'] **1** VT versare; **to pour sth off** buttar via qc, versar fuori qc; **let me pour you a drink** lascia che ti versi

da bere; **to pour money into a project** investire molti soldi in un progetto.

2 VI **a** : **to come pouring in** (*water*) entrare a fiotti; (*letters*) arrivare a valanghe; (*cars, people*) affluire in gran quantità; **the sweat is pouring off you!** sei grondante di sudore!

b : **it's pouring (with rain)** sta piovendo a dirotto

▶ **pour away** VT + ADV buttar via

▶ **pour in** VI + ADV (*people*) entrare a frotte; **tourists are pouring in** i turisti stanno arrivando in massa; **the sunshine poured into the room** la luce del sole inondava la stanza

▶ **pour out** VT + ADV (*drink*) versare; (*dirty water*) buttar via; (*fig: feelings*) sfogare; (*: troubles*) sfogarsi parlando di; (*: story*) raccontare tutto d'un fiato; **she poured out her complaints** si lanciò in una serie di lamentele.

pour·ing ['pɔːrɪŋ] ADJ **a** (*rain*) torrenziale; **a pouring wet day** una giornata molto piovosa **b** (*custard*) liquido (-a).

pout [paʊt] **1** N broncio.

2 VI fare il broncio, mettere il muso.

pov·er·ty ['pɒvətɪ] N miseria, povertà; **poverty of resources** mancanza di risorse; **to live in poverty** vivere in miseria.

♦ **poverty line** N: **below the poverty line** sotto la soglia di povertà.

♦ **poverty-stricken** ['pɒvətɪ,strɪkən] ADJ (*gen*) poverissimo(-a); (*hum: hard up*) al verde.

♦ **poverty trap** N (*Econ*) *circolo vizioso nel quale, accettando un lavoro si perderebbe parte dell'assegno di disoccupazione.*

POW [,piːəʊ'dʌblju:] N ABBR = **prisoner of war**.

pow·der ['paʊdə'] **1** N (*gen*) polvere *f*; (*face powder*) cipria; (*medicine*) polverina.

2 VT **a** (*reduce to powder*) ridurre in polvere **b** (*apply powder to: face*) incipriarsi; **to powder one's body** mettersi il talco; **to powder one's nose** incipriarsi il naso; (*euph*) andare alla toilette.

♦ **powder compact** N portacipria *m inv*.

pow·dered ['paʊdəd] ADJ: **powdered milk** latte *m* in polvere; **powdered sugar** (*Am*) zucchero a velo.

♦ **powder keg** N (*fig: area*) polveriera; (*: situation*) situazione *f* esplosiva.

♦ **powder puff** N piumino della cipria.

♦ **powder room** N toilette *f inv* (*per signore*).

pow·dery ['paʊdərɪ] ADJ (*substance*) come polvere; (*surface*) impolverato(-a), polveroso(-a); (*snow*) farinoso(-a).

pow·er ['paʊə'] **1** N **a** (*physical strength, also fig*) forza; (*energy*) energia; (*force: of engine, blow, explosion*) potenza; (*: of sun*) intensità; (*electricity*) elettricità; **to cut off the power** (*Elec*) togliere la corrente; **the ship returned under its own power** la nave è tornata con i propri mezzi; **more power to your elbow!** (*fam*) dacci dentro!

b (*ability, capacity*) capacità *f inv*, potere *m*; (*faculty*) facoltà *f inv*; **mental powers** capacità *fpl* mentali; **it is beyond his power to save her** non può far nulla per salvarla; **to do all in one's power to help sb** fare tutto quello che si può per aiutare qn; **the power of speech** la facoltà *or* l'uso della parola; **powers of persuasion/ imagination** forza di persuasione/immaginazione

c (*Pol: authority*) potere *m*, autorità *f inv*; **the power of the Church** l'autorità della Chiesa; **that is beyond my power(s)** questo è al di là dei miei poteri; **to have power**

over sb aver potere su qn; **to have sb in one's power** avere qn in proprio potere; **to be in sb's power** essere in potere di qn; **to be in power** essere al potere; **to come to power** salire al potere; **the power behind the throne** l'eminenza grigia; **the world powers** le grandi potenze; **the powers that be** le autorità costituite; **the powers of darkness** or **evil** le forze del male

d (*Math*) potenza; **7 to the power (of) 3** 7 al cubo *or* alla terza

e (*fam*: *a lot of*): **it did me a power of good** mi ha fatto un bene enorme.

2 VT azionare; **plane powered by 4 jets** aereo azionato da 4 motori a reazione; **nuclear-powered submarine** sottomarino a propulsione atomica.

3 ADJ (*saw, also Elec*: *cable*) elettrico(-a); (*supply, consumption*) di energia elettrica.

pow·er·boat ['paʊə,bəʊt] N (*Brit*) motobarca, imbarcazione *f* a motore.

♦ **power cut** N (*Brit*) interruzione *f* or mancanza di corrente.

♦ **power drill** N trapano elettrico.

♦ **power-driven** ['paʊə,drɪvn] ADJ a motore; (*Elec*) elettrico(-a).

♦ **power failure** N guasto alla linea elettrica.

pow·er·ful ['paʊəfʊl] ADJ (*gen*) potente, forte; (*person*: *physically*) possente; (*film, actor, speech*) formidabile.

pow·er·ful·ly ['paʊəfəlɪ] ADV: **to be powerfully built** essere di costituzione robusta.

power·house ['paʊə,haʊs] N (*fig*: *person*) persona molto dinamica; **a powerhouse of ideas** una miniera di idee.

pow·er·less ['paʊəlɪs] ADJ impotente, senza potere.

pow·er·less·ly ['paʊəlɪslɪ] ADV con impotenza.

pow·er·less·ness ['paʊəlɪsnɪs] N impotenza.

♦ **power line** N linea elettrica.

♦ **power of attorney** N (*Law*) procura.

♦ **power pack** N (*Elec*) alimentatore.

♦ **power plant** N centrale *f* elettrica.

♦ **power point** N (*Elec*) presa di corrente.

♦ **power politics** NPL politica *fsg* della forza.

♦ **power-sharing** ['paʊə'ʃɛərɪŋ] N partecipazione *f* al potere.

♦ **power station** N centrale *f* elettrica.

♦ **power steering** N (*Aut*: *also*: **power-assisted steering**) servosterzo.

♦ **power structure** N gerarchia di poteri.

pow·wow ['paʊ,waʊ] N (*fam*) riunione *f*.

pox [pɒks] N: **the pox** (*fam*) il mal francese; *see also* **chickenpox**.

pp ['piː'piː] ABBR (= *per procurationem: by proxy*) p.p.; **pp J Smith** per il Signor J. Smith.

pp. ABBR (= *pages*) pp.

p&p [,piːənd'piː] N ABBR (*Brit*: = *postage and packing*) affrancatura ed imballaggio.

PPE [,piːpiː'iː] N ABBR (*Brit Univ*: = *philosophy, politics and economics*) corso di laurea.

PR [,piː'ɑ'] N ABBR **a** (= *public relations*) PR.

b = *proportional representation*.

prac·ti·cabil·ity [,præktɪkə'bɪlɪtɪ] N praticabilità, attuabilità.

prac·ti·cable ['præktɪkəbl] ADJ (*scheme*) praticabile, attuabile.

prac·ti·cal ['præktɪkəl] ADJ (*gen*) pratico(-a); **for all practical purposes** in pratica, agli effetti pratici; **he's very practical** è un tipo molto pratico.

prac·ti·cal·ity [,præktɪ'kælɪtɪ] N (*of person*) senso pratico;

(*of scheme, idea*) aspetto pratico; **practicalities** dettagli *mpl* pratici.

♦ **practical joke** N burla.

prac·ti·cal·ly ['præktɪklɪ] ADV **a** (*almost*) praticamente, quasi **b** : **practically based** (*education, training*) basato (-a) sulla pratica.

prac·tice ['præktɪs] **1** N **a** (*habit*) abitudine *f*, consuetudine *f*; **it's common practice** è d'uso; **it is not our practice to do that** generalmente non lo facciamo; **to make a practice of doing sth** avere l'abitudine di fare qc

b (*exercise*) esercizio; (*training*) allenamento; (*rehearsal*) prove *fpl*; **target practice** pratica di tiro; **piano practice** esercizi *mpl* al piano; **football practice** allenamento di calcio; **to be out of practice** esser fuori esercizio (*or* allenamento); **practice makes perfect** le cose si imparano a forza di pratica

c (*not theory*) pratica; **to put sth into practice** mettere qc in pratica

d (*of doctor, lawyer*): **to be in practice** esercitare la professione; **he has a small practice** (*doctor*) ha un numero ristretto di pazienti; (*lawyer*) ha un numero ristretto di clienti; **his practice is in Trieste** il suo studio è a Trieste; **to set up in practice as** cominciare ad esercitare la professione di.

2 VT, VI (*Am*) = **practise**.

♦ **practice match** N partita di allenamento.

prac·tise, (*Am*) **prac·tice** ['præktɪs] **1** VT **a** : **to practise patience/self-control** cercare di avere pazienza/ di controllarsi; **to practise charity** essere caritatevole; **to practise what one preaches** mettere in pratica ciò che si predica

b (*train o.s. at*: *piano*) esercitarsi a; (: *song*) esercitarsi per imparare; **to practise a shot** (*Golf, Tennis*) esercitarsi in un tiro; **to practise doing sth** esercitarsi a fare qc; **I practised my Italian on her** ho fatto pratica d'italiano con lei

c (*follow, exercise*: *profession*) esercitare; (: *sport, religion*) praticare; (: *method*) seguire, usare; (*custom*) seguire.

2 VI **a** (*in order to acquire skill*: *gen, Mus*) esercitarsi; (: *Sport*) allenarsi

b (*lawyer, doctor*) esercitare.

practised, (*Am*) **prac·ticed** ['præktɪst] ADJ (*person*) esperto(-a), provetto(-a); (*performance*) da virtuoso(-a); (*liar*) matricolato(-a); **with a practised eye** con occhio esperto.

practising, (*Am*) **prac·tic·ing** ['præktɪsɪŋ] ADJ (*lawyer*) che esercita (la professione); (*Jew, Catholic etc*) praticante; (*homosexual*) che è attivo(-a).

prac·ti·tion·er [præk'tɪʃənə'] N (*of an art*) professionista *m/f*; (*Med*) medico.

prag·mat·ic [præg'mætɪk] ADJ pragmatico(-a).

prag·ma·tism ['prægmə,tɪzəm] N pragmatismo.

Prague [prɑːg] N Praga.

prai·rie ['prɛərɪ] N prateria; **the prairies** le grandi praterie.

♦ **prairie dog** N cane *m* delle praterie.

♦ **prairie oyster** N (*Culin*) uovo all'ostrica.

praise [preɪz] **1** N elogio, lode *f*; **he spoke in praise of their achievements** ha elogiato i loro risultati; **I have nothing but praise for her** non posso che lodarla; **praise be to God!** sia lodato Iddio!; **praise be!** (*fam*) sia ringraziato il cielo!.

2 VT lodare, elogiare; (*God*) render lode a; **to praise sb for sth/for doing sth** lodare *or* elogiare qn per qc/per

aver fatto qc.

praise·worthy [ˈpreɪzˌwɜːðɪ] ADJ lodevole, degno(-a) di lode.

pra·line [ˈprɑːliːn] N pralina.

pram [præm] N (*Brit*) carrozzina.

prance [prɑːns] VI (*horse*) caracollare; (*person*: *proudly*) pavoneggiarsi; (: *gaily*) saltellare; **to prance in/out** entrare/uscire pavoneggiandosi (*or* saltellando).

prank [præŋk] N scherzetto, burla; **a childish prank** una birichinata; **to play a prank on sb** giocare un tiro a qn, fare uno scherzo a qn.

prank·ster [ˈpræŋkstəʳ] N burlone(-a).

prat [præt] N (*Brit fam!*) cretino(-a).

prate [preɪt] VI cicalare; **to prate on about sth** parlare a più non posso di qc.

prat·tle [ˈprætl] VI chiacchierare, cianciare.

prawn [prɔːn] N gambero, gamberetto.

♦ **prawn cocktail** N cocktail *m inv* di gamberetti.

prax·is [ˈpræksɪs] N (*frm*) prassi *f*.

pray [preɪ] VI (*say prayers*) pregare; **to pray to God** pregare Dio; **to pray for sb/sth** pregare per qn/qc; **to pray for forgiveness** implorare il perdono; **we are praying for good weather** preghiamo che faccia bello.

prayer [preəʳ] N preghiera; **to say one's prayers** dire *or* recitare le preghiere.

♦ **prayer beads** NPL corona *fsg* del rosario.

♦ **prayer book** N libro di preghiere.

♦ **prayer mat** N tappeto da preghiera (*usato dagli Islamici*).

♦ **prayer meeting** N incontro di preghiera.

♦ **prayer wheel** N mulino da preghiere (*nella religione buddista*).

pray·ing [ˈpreɪŋ] N preghiere *fpl*.

♦ **pray·ing man·tis** [ˌpreɪŋˈmæntɪs] N mantide *f* religiosa.

pre... [priː] PREF pre...; **pre-1970** prima del 1970.

preach [priːtʃ] **1** VT (*gen*) predicare; (*sermon*) fare.
2 VI predicare; **to preach at sb** far la predica a qn; **to preach to the converted** (*fig*) cercare di convincere chi è già convinto.

preach·er [ˈpriːtʃəʳ] N (*of sermon*) predicatore *m*; (*Am*: *minister*) pastore *m*.

pre·am·ble [priːˈæmbl] N preambolo.

pre·ar·range [ˌpriːəˈreɪndʒ] VT prestabilire.

pre·ar·ranged [ˌpriːəˈreɪndʒd] ADJ organizzato(-a) in anticipo.

pre·cari·ous [prɪˈkɛərɪəs] ADJ precario(-a).

pre·cari·ous·ly [prɪˈkɛərɪəslɪ] ADV precariamente.

pre·cari·ous·ness [prɪˈkɛərɪəsnɪs] N precarietà.

pre·cast [ˈpriːˌkɑːst] ADJ prefabbricato(-a).

pre·cau·tion [prɪˈkɔːʃən] N precauzione *f*; **as a precaution** per precauzione; **to take precautions** prendere precauzioni; **to take the precaution of doing** prendere la precauzione di fare.

pre·cau·tion·ary [prɪˈkɔːʃənərɪ] ADJ (*measure*) precauzionale.

pre·cede [prɪˈsiːd] VT (*in space, time*) precedere; **he preceded me as chairman of the Society** è stato il mio predecessore nella presidenza della Società.

prec·edence [ˈprɛsɪdəns] N (*in rank*) precedenza; (*in importance*) priorità; **to take precedence over sb/sth** avere la precedenza su qn/qc.

prec·edent [ˈprɛsɪdənt] N (*also Law*) precedente *m*; **without precedent** senza precedenti; **to establish** *or* **set a precedent** creare un precedente.

pre·ced·ing [prɪˈsiːdɪŋ] ADJ precedente.

pre·cept [ˈpriːsɛpt] N precetto.

pre·cinct [ˈpriːsɪŋkt] N **a** (*also*: **shopping precinct**) zona dei negozi (*chiusa al traffico automobilistico*) **b** (*of cathedral*) recinto; **precincts** NPL (*environs*) dintorni *mpl* **c** (*Am*: *district*) circoscrizione *f*.

pre·cious [ˈprɛʃəs] **1** ADJ prezioso(-a); **your precious dog** (*iro*) il tuo amatissimo cane.
2 ADV (*fam*): **precious little/few** ben poco/pochi.

♦ **precious stone** N pietra preziosa.

preci·pice [ˈprɛsɪpɪs] N precipizio; **on the edge of a precipice** sull'orlo del precipizio.

pre·cipi·tate [*adj, n* prɪˈsɪpɪtɪt; *vb* prɪˈsɪpɪteɪt] **1** ADJ (*hasty*) precipitoso(-a), affrettato(-a).
2 N (*Chem*) precipitato.
3 VT **a** (*bring on*: *crisis*) accelerare **b** (*Chem*) precipitare; (*Met*) far condensare.

pre·cipi·tate·ly [prɪˈsɪpɪtɪtlɪ] ADV precipitosamente.

pre·cipi·ta·tion [prɪˌsɪpɪˈteɪʃən] N precipitazione *f*.

pre·cipi·tous [prɪˈsɪpɪtəs] ADJ (*slope, path*) a precipizio; (*decision, action*) precipitoso(-a).

pre·cipi·tous·ly [prɪˈsɪpɪtəslɪ] ADV precipitosamente.

pré·cis [ˈpreɪsiː] N (*pl* précis) riassunto.

pre·cise [prɪˈsaɪs] ADJ (*gen*) preciso(-a); (*pej*: *over precise*) pignolo(-a), pedante; **there were 5, to be precise** ce n'erano 5, per essere precisi; **at that precise moment** in quel preciso istante; **he's very precise in everything he does** è sempre molto preciso in quello che fa; **a precise old lady** una vecchietta meticolosa.

pre·cise·ly [prɪˈsaɪslɪ] ADV con precisione; **at 4 o'clock precisely** [OR] **at precisely 4 o'clock** alle 4 precise *or* in punto; **what precisely is her job?** che lavoro fa esattamente?; **precisely!** precisamente!, proprio così!

pre·ci·sion [prɪˈsɪʒən] N precisione *f*.

♦ **precision bombing** N bombardamento di precisione.

♦ **precision instrument** N strumento di precisione.

pre·clude [prɪˈkluːd] (*frm*) VT (*possibility*) precludere, impedire; (*misunderstanding, doubt*) non lasciar adito a; **we are precluded from doing that** siamo impossibilitati a farlo; **to preclude sb from doing** impedire a qn di fare.

pre·co·cious [prɪˈkəʊʃəs] ADJ precoce.

pre·co·cious·ly [prɪˈkəʊʃəslɪ] ADV precocemente.

pre·co·cious·ness [prɪˈkəʊʃəsnɪs], **pre·coc·ity** [prɪˈkɒsɪtɪ] N precocità.

pre·con·ceived [ˌpriːkənˈsiːvd] ADJ (*idea*) preconcetto(-a).

pre·con·cep·tion [ˌpriːkənˈsɛpʃən] N preconcetto.

pre·con·di·tion [ˌpriːkənˈdɪʃən] N condizione *f* indispensabile.

pre·cooked [ˌpriːˈkʊkt] ADJ precotto(-a).

pre·cur·sor [ˌpriːˈkɜːsəʳ] N precursore *m*.

pre·date [ˌpriːˈdeɪt] VT (*precede*) precedere; (*put earlier date on*) retrodatare.

preda·tor [ˈprɛdətəʳ] N predatore(-trice).

preda·tory [ˈprɛdətərɪ] ADJ (*animal*) rapace, predatore(-trice); (*habits, army*) rapace; (*person, look*) avido(-a), cupido(-a).

pre·de·cease [ˌpriːdɪˈsiːs] VT morire prima di.

pre·de·ces·sor [ˈpriːdɪˌsɛsəʳ] N predecessore *m*.

pre·des·ti·na·tion [priːˌdɛstɪˈneɪʃən] N predestinazione *f*.

pre·des·tine [ˌpriːˈdɛstɪn] VT predestinare.

pre·de·ter·mine [ˌpriːdɪˈtɜːmɪn] VT predeterminare, determinare in anticipo.

pre·dica·ment [prɪˈdɪkəmənt] N situazione *f* difficile (*or* imbarazzante); **I'm in a bit of a predicament** sono in una

predi·cate [*n, adj* 'prɛdɪkɪt; *vb* 'prɛdɪˌkeɪt] ① N (*Gram*) predicato.
② ADJ (*Gram*) predicativo(-a).
③ VT **a** (*frm: imply*) asserire **b** (*frm: idea*): **to be predicated on sth** dipendere da qc.
pre·dica·tive [prɪ'dɪkətɪv] ADJ (*Gram*) predicativo(-a).
pre·dica·tive·ly [prɪ'dɪkətɪvlɪ] ADV (*Gram*) in funzione di predicato.
pre·dict [prɪ'dɪkt] VT predire.
pre·dict·able [prɪ'dɪktəbl] ADJ prevedibile.
pre·dict·ably [prɪ'dɪktəblɪ] ADV (*behave, react*) in modo prevedibile; **predictably she didn't turn up** come era da prevedere, non è arrivata.
pre·dic·tion [prɪ'dɪkʃən] N predizione *f*.
pre·di·gest·ed [ˌpriː'daɪdʒɛstɪd] ADJ (*pej*) predigerito(-a).
pre·di·lec·tion [ˌpriːdɪ'lɛkʃən] N predilezione *f*.
pre·dis·pose [ˌpriːdɪs'pəʊz] VT predisporre.
pre·dis·po·si·tion [ˌpriːdɪspə'zɪʃən] N predisposizione *f*.
pre·domi·nance [prɪ'dɒmɪnəns] N predominanza.
pre·domi·nant [prɪ'dɒmɪnənt] ADJ predominante.
pre·domi·nant·ly [prɪ'dɒmɪnəntlɪ] ADV prevalentemente, per lo più.
pre·domi·nate [prɪ'dɒmɪˌneɪt] VI predominare.
pre-eminence [ˌpriː'ɛmɪnəns] N preminenza.
pre-eminent [ˌpriː'ɛmɪnənt] ADJ eccezionale, preminente.
pre-eminently [ˌpriː'ɛmɪnəntlɪ] ADV soprattutto, preminentemente.
pre-empt [ˌpriː'ɛmpt] VT acquistare per diritto di prelazione; (*fig*) anticipare.
pre-emptive [ˌpriː'ɛmptɪv] ADJ: **pre-emptive strike** (*Mil*) azione *f* preventiva.
preen [priːn] VT **a** (*feathers*) lisciare (con il becco); **the bird was preening itself** l'uccello si stava lisciando le piume; **he was preening himself in front of the mirror** (*fig pej*) stava lisciandosi davanti allo specchio **b** : **to preen o.s. on sth/on doing sth** (*liter pej*) compiacersi di qc/di fare qc.
pre·es·tab·lish [ˌpriːɪs'tæblɪʃ] VT prestabilire.
pre·fab ['priːˌfæb] N (*fam*) casetta prefabbricata.
pre·fab·ri·ca·ted [ˌpriː'fæbrɪˌkeɪtɪd] ADJ prefabbricato(-a).
pref·ace ['prɛfɪs] N prefazione *f*; (*to speech*) introduzione *f*.
pre·fect ['priːfɛkt] N (*Brit: Scol*) *allievo delle classi superiori che è incaricato della disciplina e gode di alcuni privilegi*; (*Admin: in Italy, France*) prefetto.
pre·fec·ture ['priːfɛktjʊəʳ] N prefettura.
pre·fer [prɪ'fɜːʳ] VT **a** preferire; **to prefer coffee to tea** preferire il caffè al tè; **I prefer walking to going by car** preferisco camminare piuttosto che andare in macchina; **I prefer to stay home** preferisco restare a casa **b** (*Law: charges, complaint*) sporgere; (: *action*) intentare.
pref·er·able ['prɛfərəbl] ADJ preferibile.
pref·er·ably ['prɛfərəblɪ] ADV di preferenza, preferibilmente.
pref·er·ence ['prɛfərəns] N preferenza; **my preference is for ...** [OR] **I have a preference for ...** preferisco...; **in preference to sth** piuttosto che qc; **to give preference to sb/sth** dare la preferenza a qn/qc.
♦ **preference shares** NPL (*Brit Fin*) azioni *fpl* privilegiate.
pref·er·en·tial [ˌprɛfə'rɛnʃəl] ADJ preferenziale; preferen-

tial treatment trattamento di favore.
pre·ferred stock [prɪ'fɜːd'stɒk] NPL (*Am Fin*) = **preference shares**.
pre·fig·ure [priː'fɪgəʳ] VT (*Art*) prefigurare.
pre·fix ['priːfɪks] N (*Gram*) prefisso.
preg·nan·cy ['prɛgnənsɪ] N gravidanza.
♦ **pregnancy test** N test *m inv* (di gravidanza).
preg·nant ['prɛgnənt] ADJ (*woman*) incinta; (*animal*) gravida; (*liter: remark, pause*) significativo(-a); **3 months pregnant** incinta di 3 mesi; **pregnant with meaning** (*liter*) pregno(-a) di significato.
pre·heat [priː'hiːt] VT far riscaldare; **bake in a preheated oven at 250°** cucinare nel forno già riscaldato a 250°.
pre·hen·sile [prɪ'hɛnsaɪl] ADJ (*Zool*) prensile.
pre·his·tor·ic [ˌpriːhɪ'stɒrɪk] ADJ preistorico(-a).
pre·his·to·ry [ˌpriː'hɪstərɪ] N preistoria.
pre·in·dus·trial [ˌpriːɪn'dʌstrɪəl] ADJ preindustriale.
pre·judge [ˌpriː'dʒʌdʒ] VT farsi a priori un giudizio di.
preju·dice ['prɛdʒʊdɪs] ① N **a** (*biased opinion*) pregiudizio; (*collective noun*) pregiudizi *mpl*; **his prejudice against sb/sth** i suoi pregiudizi nei riguardi di qn/qc **b** (*Law: injury, detriment*) pregiudizio; **without prejudice to** (*frm*) senza pregiudicare.
② VT **a** (*bias*): **to prejudice sb in favour of/against** disporre bene/male qn verso **b** (*frm: injure*) pregiudicare, ledere, compromettere.
preju·diced ['prɛdʒʊdɪst] ADJ (*person*) pieno(-a) di pregiudizi, prevenuto(-a); (: *racially*) pieno(-a) di pregiudizi; (*view, opinion*) preconcetto(-a); **to be prejudiced against sb/sth** essere prevenuto(-a) contro qn/qc; **to be prejudiced in favour of sb/sth** essere ben disposto(-a) verso qn/qc.
preju·di·cial [ˌprɛdʒʊ'dɪʃəl] ADJ: **prejudicial (to)** pregiudizievole (per *or* a).
prel·ate ['prɛlɪt] N prelato.
pre·limi·naries [prɪ'lɪmɪnərɪz] NPL preliminari *mpl*.
pre·limi·nary [prɪ'lɪmɪnərɪ] ① ADJ preliminare.
② PREP: **preliminary to sth/doing sth** prima di qc/fare qc.
prel·ude ['prɛljuːd] N preludio.
pre·mari·tal [ˌpriː'mærɪtl] ADJ prematrimoniale.
prema·ture ['prɛməˌtjʊəʳ] ADJ (*baby, birth, decision*) prematuro(-a); (*arrival*) (molto) anticipato(-a); **you are being a little premature** sei un po' troppo precipitoso.
prema·ture·ly ['prɛməˌtjʊəlɪ] ADV prematuramente, prima del tempo.
pre·medi·tate [ˌpriː'mɛdɪteɪt] VT premeditare.
pre·medi·tat·ed [ˌpriː'mɛdɪteɪtɪd] ADJ premeditato(-a).
pre·medi·ta·tion [priːˌmɛdɪ'teɪʃən] N premeditazione *f*.
pre·men·stru·al [ˌpriː'mɛnstrʊəl] ADJ (*Med*) premestruale.
♦ **premenstrual tension, premenstrual syndrome** N (*Med*) sindrome *f* premestruale.
prem·ier ['prɛmɪəʳ] ① N (*Pol*) premier *m inv*, primo ministro.
② ADJ primo(-a).
premiere ['prɛmɪɛəʳ] N prima.
prem·ier·ship ['prɛmɪəʃɪp] N carica di premier.
prem·ise ['prɛmɪs] N (*hypothesis*) premessa.
prem·ises ['prɛmɪsɪz] NPL locale *msg*; **on the premises** sul posto; **he was asked to leave the premises** l'hanno invitato ad abbandonare il locale; **business premises** locali commerciali.
pre·mium ['priːmɪəm] N (*gen*) premio; (*additional charge*) maggiorazione *f*; **to sell at a premium** (*shares*) vendere sopra la pari; **to be at a premium** (*fig*) essere ricercatis-

simo(-a).

♦ **premium bond** N (*Brit*) *obbligazione emessa dal Tesoro britannico che non frutta interessi ma un premio periodico di denaro.*

♦ **premium deal** N (*Comm*) offerta speciale.

♦ **premium gasoline** N (*Am*) super *f*.

premo·ni·tion [ˌprɛːməˈnɪʃən] N presentimento, premonizione *f*.

pre·moni·tory [prɪˈmɒnɪtərɪ] ADJ (*frm*) premonitore(-trice).

pre·na·tal [ˌpriːˈneɪtl] ADJ prenatale.

pre·oc·cu·pa·tion [priːˌɒkjʊˈpeɪʃən] N preoccupazione *f*; **his preoccupation with death** la sua ossessione della morte.

pre·oc·cu·pied [ˌpriːˈɒkjʊpaɪd] ADJ (*absorbed*) assorto (-a).

pre·oc·cu·py [ˌpriːˈɒkjʊpaɪ] VT (*absorb*) assorbire; (*mind, thoughts*) occupare.

pre·or·dained [ˌpriːɔːˈdeɪnd] ADJ (*frm*) predestinato(-a).

prep [prɛp] (*fam Scol*) **1** N compiti *mpl*.
2 ADJ: **prep school = preparatory school**.

pre·pack [ˌpriːˈpæk], **pre·pack·age** [ˌpriːˈpækɪdʒ] VT preconfezionare.

pre·packed [ˌpriːˈpækt], **pre·pack·aged** ADJ preconfezionato(-a).

pre·paid [ˌpriːˈpeɪd] ADJ pagato(-a) in anticipo; (*envelope*) già affrancato(-a).

prepa·ra·tion [ˌprɛpəˈreɪʃən] N **a** (*preparing*) preparazione *f*; **in preparation for sth** in vista di qc; **to be in preparation** essere in (corso di) preparazione **b**: **preparations** NPL (*preparatory measures*) preparativi *mpl*; **to make preparations** fare i preparativi **c** (*Brit Scol*) compiti *mpl*.

pre·para·tory [prɪˈpærətərɪ] ADJ (*work*) preparatorio(-a); (*measure*) preliminare; **preparatory to sth/to doing sth** prima di qc/di fare qc.

♦ **preparatory school** N (*Brit*) *scuola privata di preparazione alla scuola superiore*; (*Am*) *scuola superiore privata di preparazione al college.*

pre·pare [prɪˈpɛəʳ] **1** VT preparare; **prepare yourself for a shock** preparati a uno shock; **to prepare the way for sth** preparare il terreno per qc; **to prepare to do sth** prepararsi a fare qc.
2 VI: **to prepare for** (*journey, party, sb's arrival*) fare dei preparativi per; (*exam, future*) prepararsi per; **to prepare for war** prepararsi alla guerra.

pre·pared [prɪˈpɛəd] ADJ **a** (*speech, answer*) preparato (-a) in anticipo; (*food*) pronto(-a)
b (*in state of readiness*) pronto(-a); **to be prepared for anything** essere pronto(-a) a tutto; **we were not prepared for this** questo ci ha colto alla sprovvista *or* non ce lo aspettavamo
c (*willing*): **to be prepared to help sb** essere disposto(-a) *or* pronto(-a) ad aiutare qn.

pre·par·ed·ness [prɪˈpɛərɪdnɪs] N preparazione *f*.

pre·pon·der·ance [prɪˈpɒndərəns] N preponderanza.

pre·pon·der·ant [prɪˈpɒndərənt] ADJ preponderante.

pre·pon·der·ant·ly [prɪˈpɒndərəntlɪ] ADV in modo preponderante.

prepo·si·tion [ˌprɛpəˈzɪʃən] N preposizione *f*.

pre·pos·sess·ing [ˌpriːpəˈzɛsɪŋ] ADJ attraente.

pre·pos·ter·ous [prɪˈpɒstərəs] ADJ ridicolo(-a), assurdo (-a).

pre·pos·ter·ous·ly [prɪˈpɒstərəslɪ] ADV ridicolmente, assurdamente.

♦ **Pre-Raphaelite** [priːˈræfəlaɪt] N, ADJ preraffaellita *(m/f)*.

pre·re·cord [ˌpriːrɪˈkɔːd] VT registrare in anticipo; **prerecorded broadcast** trasmissione *f* registrata; **prerecorded cassette** (musi)cassetta.

pre·requi·site [ˌpriːˈrɛkwɪzɪt] N prerequisito.

pre·roga·tive [prɪˈrɒɡətɪv] N prerogativa.

Pres·by·ter·ian [ˌprɛzbɪˈtɪərɪən] ADJ, N presbiteriano(-a).

Pres·by·teri·an·ism [ˌprɛzbɪˈtɪərɪəˌnɪzəm] N presbiterianesimo.

pres·by·tery [ˈprɛzbɪtərɪ] N presbiterio.

pre·school [ˈpriːˌskuːl] ADJ (*child*) in età prescolastica; (*age*) prescolastico(-a).

pres·ci·ence [ˈprɛsɪəns] N (*frm*) preveggenza.

pres·ci·ent [ˈprɛsɪənt] ADJ (*frm*) preveggente.

pre·scribe [prɪˈskraɪb] VT (*gen, Med*) prescrivere, ordinare; (*fig*) consigliare; **prescribed books** (*Scol, Univ*) testi *mpl* in programma.

pre·scrip·tion [prɪˈskrɪpʃən] N (*Med*) ricetta (medica); **to make up a prescription** OR (*Am*) **fill a prescription** preparare *or* fare una ricetta; **to make out a prescription for sb** fare una ricetta a qn; **only available on prescription** ottenibile solo dietro presentazione di ricetta medica.

♦ **prescription charges** NPL (*Brit*) ≈ ticket *m inv*.

pre·scrip·tive [prɪˈskrɪptɪv] ADJ normativo(-a).

pres·ence [ˈprɛzns] N presenza; **in the presence of** in presenza di, davanti a; **to make one's presence felt** far sentire la propria presenza.

♦ **presence of mind** N presenza di spirito.

pres·ent [*adj, n* ˈprɛznt; *vb* prɪˈzɛnt] **1** ADJ **a** (*in attendance*) presente; **to be present at** (*gen*) essere presente a; (*officially*) presenziare a; **those present** i presenti
b (*of the moment*) attuale; **in the present circumstances** date le circostanze attuali; **at the present moment** al momento attuale; **its present value** il suo valore attuale
c (*Gram*) presente.
2 N **a** (*present time*) presente *m*; (*Gram*) (tempo) presente *m*; **at present** al momento; **for the present** per il momento, per adesso, per ora; **up to the present** fino a questo momento, finora
b (*gift*) regalo; **I got this watch as a present** questo orologio mi è stato regalato; **to make sb a present of sth** regalare qc a qn.
3 VT **a** (*hand over: gen*) presentare; (*: prize, certificate*) consegnare; (*give as gift*) offrire (in omaggio); (*proof, evidence*) fornire; (*Law: case*) esporre; **to present sb with sth** OR **present sth to sb** fare dono di qc a qn; (*prize*) consegnare qc a qn; **to present arms** (*Mil*) presentare le armi; **to present o.s. for an interview** presentarsi per un colloquio
b (*offer: difficulty, problem, opportunity*) presentare; (*: features*) offrire
c (*put on: play, concert, film*) dare; (*TV, Radio: act as presenter of*) presentare; **to present the news** (*TV, Radio*) leggere le notizie; **presenting Jack Nicholson as ...** con Jack Nicholson nella parte di...
d (*frm: introduce*): **to present sb to sb** presentare qn a qn; **may I present Miss Clark?** permette che le presenti la signorina Clark?

pre·sent·able [prɪˈzɛntəbl] ADJ presentabile; **to make o.s. presentable** rendersi presentabile, mettersi in ordine.

pres·en·ta·tion [ˌprɛzənˈteɪʃən] N **a** (*act of presenting*) presentazione *f*; (*report*) relazione; (*Law: of case*) esposizione *f*; **on presentation of the voucher** dietro presentazione del buono; **to make a presentation of sth**

(*plan, report*) presentare

  b (*Radio, TV, Theatre*) rappresentazione *f*

  c (*of prizes etc*) consegna ufficiale; (*gift*) regalo, dono; **to make the presentation** fare la consegna ufficiale.

♦ **present-day** ['prɛznt,deɪ] ADJ attuale, d'oggigiorno, di oggi.

pre·sent·er [prɪ'zɛntə'] N (*Radio, TV*) presentatore(-trice).

pre·sen·ti·ment [prɪ'zɛntɪmənt] N presentimento.

pres·ent·ly ['prɛzntlɪ] ADV (*shortly*) tra poco, a momenti; (*esp Am: now*) adesso, ora.

♦ **present perfect** N (*Gram*) passato prossimo.

pres·er·va·tion [,prɛzə'veɪʃən] N conservazione *f*; (*of peace, one's dignity*) mantenimento.

♦ **preservation order** N (*on building, tree*) ordinanza per la salvaguardia (*di beni artistici e naturali*).

pre·serva·tive [prɪ'zɜ:vətɪv] N (*Culin*) conservante *m*.

pre·serve [prɪ'zɜ:v] **1** VT **a** (*maintain: traditions*) conservare, mantenere; (: *dignity, peace*) mantenere; (*keep intact: buildings, memory*) conservare

  b (*keep from decay*) preservare, proteggere; **well preserved** ben conservato(-a); **he is well preserved** (*hum*) si conserva bene

  c (*Culin*) conservare, mettere in conserva

  d (*keep from harm, save*) proteggere; **preserve me from that!** (che) Dio mi scampi!.

  2 N **a** (*domain*) dominio

  b (*reservation*) riserva

  c (*often pl: jam*) marmellata; (*bottled fruit*) frutta sciroppata.

preset [*vb* priː'sɛt; *adj* 'priːsɛt] **1** VT programmare.

  2 ADJ (*oven*) programmato(-a) (col timer).

pre·shrunk [,priː'ʃrʌŋk] ADJ (*fabric, garment*) irrestringibile.

pre·side [prɪ'zaɪd] VI: **to preside (at** *or* **over)** presiedere (a).

presi·den·cy ['prɛzɪdənsɪ] N (*Pol*) presidenza; (*Am: of company*) direzione *f*.

presi·dent ['prɛzɪdənt] N (*Pol*) presidente *m*; (*Am: of company*) direttore(-trice) generale.

♦ **president-elect** ['prɛzɪdəntɪ'lɛkt] N presidente *m* designato.

presi·den·tial [,prɛzɪ'dɛnʃəl] ADJ (*Pol*) presidenziale.

press [prɛs] **1** N **a** (*apparatus, machine: gen*) pressa; (: *for wine*) torchio

  b (*printing press*) torchio da stampa; (: *place*) tipografia; **to go to press** (*newspaper*) andare in macchina; **to be in the press** (*being printed*) essere in (corso di) stampa; (*in the newspapers*) essere sui giornali; **the press** (*newspapers*) la stampa, i giornali; **to get a good/bad press** avere una buona/cattiva stampa; **a member of the press** un rappresentante della stampa.

  2 VT **a** (*push: button*) premere, schiacciare; (: *doorbell*) suonare; (: *trigger*) premere; (*squeeze: grapes, olives*) pigiare; (: *flowers*) pressare; (: *hand*) stringere; **to press sb/sth to one's heart** stringersi qn/qc al petto *or* al cuore

  b (*iron*) stirare

  c (*urge, entreat*): **to press sb to do** *or* **into doing sth** fare pressione su qn affinché faccia qc; (*force*): **to press sth on sb** (*food, gift*) insistere perché qn accetti qc; (*one's opinions*) voler imporre qc su qn; (*insist on: attack*) rendere più pressante; (: *claim, demands*) insistere su *or* in; **to press sb for an answer** insistere perché qn risponda; **to be hard pressed** essere alle strette; **to press one's opponent** incalzare l'avversario; **to press**

home an advantage sfruttare al massimo un vantaggio; **to press the point** insistere sul punto; **to be pressed for time** aver poco tempo; **to be pressed for money** essere a corto di soldi; **to press sb into service** obbligare qn a lavorare; **to press sth into service** far uso di qc; **to press charges against sb** (*Law*) sporgere una denuncia contro qn.

  3 VI **a** (*in physical sense*) spingere, premere; **the people pressed round him** la gente gli si è accalcata intorno; **the crowd pressed towards the exit** la folla si accalcava all'uscita; **to press ahead** *or* **forward (with sth)** (*fig*) proseguire (in qc)

  b (*urge, agitate*): **to press for sth** fare pressioni per ottenere qc; **time presses** il tempo stringe

▶ **press down 1** VI + ADV: **to press down (on)** premere (su).

  2 VT + ADV premere

▶ **press on** VI + ADV continuare.

♦ **press agency** N agenzia di stampa.

♦ **press agent** N press agent *m/f*.

♦ **press box** N tribuna (della) stampa (*in manifestazioni sportive*).

♦ **press card** N tessera di giornalista.

♦ **press conference** N conferenza *f* stampa *inv*.

♦ **press corps** N: **the White House press corps** i giornalisti accreditati presso la Casa Bianca.

♦ **press cutting, press clipping** N ≈ ritaglio di giornale.

♦ **press gallery** N tribuna (della) stampa (*in tribunale, parlamento*).

♦ **press-gang** ['prɛs,gæŋ] VT: **to press-gang sb into doing sth** costringere qn a viva forza a fare qc.

press·ing ['prɛsɪŋ] **1** ADJ (*matter, problem*) urgente, pressante; (*request, invitation*) insistente, pressante; **he was very pressing** era molto insistente.

  2 N stiratura.

press·man ['prɛs,mæn] N (*pl* **-men**) giornalista *m*, cronista *m*.

press·mark ['prɛs,mɑːk] N (*on library book*) segnatura.

♦ **press officer** N addetto(-a) stampa.

♦ **press photographer** N fotoreporter *m/f inv*.

♦ **press release** N comunicato *m* stampa *inv*.

♦ **press report** N servizio giornalistico.

♦ **press reporter** N reporter *m/f inv*.

♦ **press stud** N (bottone *m*) automatico.

♦ **press-up** ['prɛs,ʌp] N (*Brit*) flessione *f* sulle braccia.

pres·sure ['prɛʃə'] **1** N **a** (*Phys, Tech, Met*) pressione *f*; **at full pressure** (*Tech*) al livello massimo di pressione

  b (*compulsion, influence*) pressione *f*, pressioni *fpl*; **he's under pressure from his wife to give up smoking** sua moglie fa pressione perché lui smetta di fumare; **to put pressure on sb** fare pressione su qn; **they are really putting the pressure on** ci (*or* vi etc) stanno assillando; **to use pressure to obtain sth** far pressione per ottenere qc; **to work under pressure** lavorare sotto pressione; **she's under a lot of pressure** è sotto un'enorme pressione; **the pressure of these events** la tensione creata da questi avvenimenti; **pressure of work prevented her from going** non è potuta andare per via del troppo lavoro.

  2 VT = **pressurize b**.

♦ **pressure cabin** N cabina pressurizzata.

♦ **pressure cooker** N pentola a pressione.

♦ **pressure gauge** N manometro.

♦ **pressure group** N (*Pol*) gruppo di pressione.

♦ **pressure plate** N (*Aut: of clutch*) spingidisco.

♦ **pressure point** N (*Med*) punto di compressione emostatica.

pres·suri·za·tion [ˌprɛʃərarˈzeɪʃən] N pressurizzazione *f*.

pres·sur·ize [ˈprɛʃəˌraɪz] VT **a** (*Tech*) pressurizzare **b** (*fig*): **to pressurize sb (into doing sth)** fare delle pressioni su qn (per costringerlo a fare qc).

pres·sur·ized [ˈprɛʃəˌraɪzd] ADJ pressurizzato(-a).

pres·tige [prɛsˈtiːʒ] N prestigio.

pres·tig·ious [prɛsˈtɪdʒəs] ADJ prestigioso(-a), di grande prestigio.

pre·stressed con·crete [ˈpriːˌstrɛstˈkɒnkriːt] ADJ cemento armato precompresso.

pre·sum·ably [prɪˈzjuːməblɪ] ADV: **presumably he did it** penso *or* presumo che l'abbia fatto.

pre·sume [prɪˈzjuːm] **1** VT **a** (*suppose*): **to presume (that)** supporre (che), presumere (che); **I presume she'll come** suppongo che verrà; **I presume he did it** suppongo che l'abbia fatto
b (*frm: venture*): **to presume to do sth** permettersi di fare qc.
2 VI (*frm: take liberties*) prendersi troppe libertà; **to presume on sb's friendship** approfittarsi dell'amicizia di qn.

pre·sump·tion [prɪˈzʌmpʃən] N **a** (*arrogance*) presunzione *f*; (*impudence*) audacia **b** (*thing presumed*) supposizione *f*; **there is a strong presumption that …** tutto fa supporre *or* presumere che… .

pre·sump·tu·ous [prɪˈzʌmptjʊəs] ADJ presuntuoso(-a).

pre·sump·tu·ous·ly [prɪˈzʌmptjʊəslɪ] ADV presuntuosamente.

pre·sup·pose [ˌpriːsəˈpəʊz] VT presupporre.

pre·sup·po·si·tion [ˌpriːsʌpəˈzɪʃən] N presupposto.

♦ **pre·tax** [ˈpriːˈtæks] ADJ al lordo d'imposta.

pre·tence, (*Am*) **pre·tense** [prɪˈtɛns] N **a** : **his pretence of innocence/sympathy** la sua finta *or* falsa innocenza/comprensione; **she is devoid of all pretence** non si nasconde dietro false apparenze; **to make a pretence of doing sth** far finta di fare qc; **it's all (a) pretence** è tutta una finta, è tutta scena
b (*claim*) pretesa
c (*pretext*) pretesto, scusa; **on** *or* **under the pretence of doing sth** con il pretesto *or* la scusa di fare qc; **under false pretences** con l'inganno.

pre·tend [prɪˈtɛnd] **1** VT **a** (*feign*): **to pretend illness/ignorance** fingersi malato(-a)/ignorante, far finta di essere malato(-a)/ignorante; **to pretend to do sth** far finta *or* fingere di fare qc; **she's pretending she can't hear us** fa finta di non sentirci; **he was pretending to be a lawyer** si spacciava per avvocato
b (*claim*): **to pretend to do/that** pretendere di fare/che + *sub*.
2 VI (*feign*) far finta, fingere; **she is only pretending** sta solo facendo finta.
3 ADJ (*fam: gun, money*) finto(-a).

pre·tend·ed [prɪˈtɛndɪd] ADJ falso(-a), finto(-a).

pre·tend·er [prɪˈtɛndəʳ] N (*to the throne*) pretendente *m/f*.

pre·tense [prɪˈtɛns] N (*Am*) = **pretence**.

pre·ten·sion [prɪˈtɛnʃən] N (*claim*) pretesa; **to have no pretensions to sth/to being sth** non avere la pretesa di avere qc/di essere qc.

pre·ten·tious [prɪˈtɛnʃəs] ADJ pretenzioso(-a).

pre·ten·tious·ly [prɪˈtɛnʃəslɪ] ADV pretenziosamente.

pre·ten·tious·ness [prɪˈtɛnʃəsnɪs] N pretenziosità.

pret·er·ite [ˈprɛtərɪt] N (tempo) passato, preterito.

pre·ter·natu·ral [ˌpriːtəˈnætʃrəl] ADJ (*frm*) soprannaturale.

pre·text [ˈpriːtɛkst] N pretesto; **on** *or* **under the pretext of doing sth** col pretesto di fare qc.

pret·ti·ly [ˈprɪtɪlɪ] ADV graziosamente.

pret·ty [ˈprɪtɪ] **1** ADJ (*comp* **-ier**, *superl* **-iest**) grazioso(-a), carino(-a); **he wasn't a pretty sight** non era bello da vedersi; **it'll cost you a pretty penny!** (*fam*) ti costerà una bella sommetta!.
2 ADV (*rather*) piuttosto; (*very*) molto; **pretty well** (*not badly*) piuttosto bene; **pretty nearly** (*almost*) quasi, praticamente; **it's pretty much the same** (*fam*) è praticamente uguale.

♦ **pretty-pretty** [ˈprɪtɪˈprɪtɪ] ADJ (*pej*) un po' troppo grazioso(-a).

pret·zel [ˈprɛtsl] N salatino.

pre·vail [prɪˈveɪl] VI **a** (*gain mastery*): **to prevail (against, over)** prevalere (su) **b** (*be current: fashion, belief etc*) essere diffuso(-a); **the conditions that prevail** le condizioni attuali **c** (*persuade*): **to prevail (up)on sb to do sth** convincere qn a fare qc, persuadere qn a fare qc.

pre·vail·ing [prɪˈveɪlɪŋ] ADJ (*conditions*) attuale; (*belief, customs, attitude*) predominante, prevalente; (*wind*) dominante.

preva·lence [ˈprɛvələns] N (*of crime, customs, attitude*) larga diffusione *f*; (*of conditions*) prevalere *m*.

preva·lent [ˈprɛvələnt] ADJ (*belief, disease, fashion etc*) diffuso(-a), comune, predominante; **the conditions which are prevalent in …** le condizioni esistenti in… .

pre·vari·cate [prɪˈværɪˌkeɪt] VI tergiversare.

pre·vari·ca·tion [prɪˌværɪˈkeɪʃən] N tergiversazione *f*.

pre·vent [prɪˈvɛnt] VT (*crime, accidents, fire*) prevenire; **to prevent sb/sth (from doing sth)** impedire a qn/qc (di fare qc); **to prevent sb's doing sth** (*frm*) impedire che qn faccia qc.

pre·vent·able [prɪˈvɛntəbl] ADJ che può essere prevenuto (-a), evitabile.

pre·ven·ta·tive [prɪˈvɛntətɪv] ADJ = **preventive**.

pre·ven·tion [prɪˈvɛnʃən] N prevenzione *f*; **the prevention of cruelty to animals** la protezione degli animali.

pre·ven·tive [prɪˈvɛntɪv] ADJ preventivo(-a).

pre·view [ˈpriːvjuː] N (*of film etc*) anteprima; **to give sb a preview of sth** (*fig*) dare a qn un'idea di qc.

pre·vi·ous [ˈpriːvɪəs] ADJ precedente; **the previous day** il giorno prima *or* precedente; **previous experience** precedente esperienza; **he has no previous experience in that field** non ha esperienza in quel campo; **I have a previous engagement** ho già (preso) un impegno; **on a previous occasion** in precedenza; **in a previous life** in un'altra vita; **to have no previous convictions** (*Law*) non aver precedenti penali; **to have 5 previous convictions** essere già stato(-a) condannato(-a) 5 volte.

pre·vi·ous·ly [ˈpriːvɪəslɪ] ADV (*before*) prima; (*in the past*) in precedenza; (*already*) già.

pre·war [ˈpriːˈwɔː] ADJ dell'anteguerra, anteguerra *inv*.

prey [preɪ] N (*also fig*) preda; **to be prey to** (*fig*) essere in preda a
▶ **prey on** VI + PREP (*subj: animals*) predare, far preda di; (: *person*) depredare; **to prey on sb's mind** ossessionare qn; **it was preying on his mind** gli rodeva la mente.

Priam [ˈpraɪəm] N Priamo.

pria·pism [ˈpraɪəˌpɪzəm] N priapismo.

price [praɪs] **1** N (*also fig*) prezzo; **to go up** *or* **rise in price** salire *or* aumentare di prezzo; **to go down** *or* **fall in price** scendere *or* calare di prezzo; **I got a good price for**

it me lo hanno pagato bene; **what is the price of that painting?** quanto costa quel quadro?; **at a reduced price** a prezzo ribassato; **we pay top prices for silver** offriamo ottimi prezzi per l'argento; **every man has his price** ogni uomo ha il suo prezzo; **the price of fame** il prezzo del successo; **it's a small price to pay for it** (*fig*) non è che un piccolo sacrificio; **to pay a high price for sth** (*also fig*) pagare caro qc; **peace at any price** pace ad ogni costo *or* costi quello che costi; **not at any price** per nessuna cosa al mondo; **he regained his freedom, but at a price** ha riconquistato la sua libertà, ma a caro prezzo

b (*value, valuation*) valore *m*; **to put a price on sth** valutare *or* stimare qc; **to put a price on sb's head** mettere una taglia sulla testa di qn; **what price his promises now?** a che valgono ora le sue promesse?; **you can't put a price on it** (*fig: friendship, loyalty*) è inestimabile

c (*Betting: odds*) quotazione *f*, quota.

2 VT (*fix price of*) fissare il prezzo di; (*put price label on*) prezzare, mettere il prezzo su; (*ask price of*) chiedere il prezzo di; **it was priced at £20** il prezzo era di 20 sterline; **it was priced too high/low** aveva un prezzo troppo alto/basso; **to be priced out of the market** (*article*) essere così caro(-a) da diventare invendibile; (*producer, nation*) non poter sostenere la concorrenza.

3 ADJ (*index*) dei prezzi; **prices and incomes policy** politica dei prezzi e dei salari.

♦ **price control** N calmiere *m* dei prezzi, controllo dei prezzi.

♦ **price cut** N ribasso.

♦ **price cutting** N riduzione *f* dei prezzi.

♦ **price-fixing** ['praɪsˌfɪksɪŋ] N controllo dei prezzi.

♦ **price freeze** N congelamento dei prezzi.

price·less ['praɪslɪs] ADJ (*jewels, necklace*) di valore inestimabile; (*fam: amusing*) impagabile, spassosissimo(-a); **friendship is priceless** l'amicizia è un bene inestimabile.

♦ **price limit** N limite *m* di prezzo.

♦ **price list** N listino (dei) prezzi.

♦ **price range** N gamma di prezzi; **it's within my price range** rientra nelle mie possibilità.

♦ **price tag** N cartellino del prezzo.

♦ **price war** N guerra dei prezzi.

pricey ['praɪsɪ] ADJ (*comp* **-ier**, *superl* **-iest**) (*Brit fam*) caruccio(-a).

prick [prɪk] **1** N **a** (*act, sensation*) puntura; (*mark*) buco; **pricks of conscience** rimorsi *mpl* di coscienza

b (*fam!: penis*) cazzo; (: *person*) testa di cazzo (*fam!*).

2 VT (*puncture: balloon, blister*) bucare; (*subj: thorn, needle*) pungere; (: *conscience*) rimordere; **to prick a hole in sth** fare un buco in qc; **to prick one's finger (with/on sth)** pungersi un dito (con/su qc)

► **prick out, prick off** VT + ADV (*seedlings*) trapiantare

► **prick up** VT + ADV: **to prick up one's ears** (*also fig*) drizzare le orecchie.

prick·ing ['prɪkɪŋ] N (*feeling*) prurito, pizzicore *m*; **to feel prickings of conscience** avere dei rimorsi di coscienza.

prick·le ['prɪkl] N **a** (*on plant, animal etc*) spina **b** (*sensation*) sensazione *f* di prurito, pizzicore *m*; (: *of fear*) brivido.

prick·ly ['prɪklɪ] ADJ (*comp* **-ier**, *superl* **-iest**) **a** (*plant*) spinoso(-a); (*animal*) pieno(-a) di spine; (*beard*) ispido (-a); (*wool*) che dà prurito **b** (*fig: person*) permaloso(-a); (: *subject*) spinoso(-a).

♦ **prickly heat** N (*Med*) sudamina.

♦ **prickly pear** N (*plant, fruit*) fico d'India.

pride [praɪd] **1** N **a** (*arrogance*) superbia, orgoglio; (*self-respect*) orgoglio, amor proprio; (*satisfaction*) fierezza; **false pride** falso orgoglio; **to take (a) pride in** (*appearance, punctuality*) tenere molto a; (*children, achievements*) essere orgoglioso(-a) di; **she takes (a) pride in arriving on time** ci tiene molto ad essere sempre puntuale; **his pride was hurt** fu ferito nell'orgoglio; **she is a (great) source of pride to him** è (molto) fiero *or* orgoglioso di lei; **her plants are her pride and joy** le sue piante sono il suo orgoglio *or* vanto; **to have pride of place** essere al primo posto

b (*of lions*) branco.

2 VT: **to pride o.s. on sth** essere orgoglioso(-a) di qc.

priest [priːst] N prete *m*, sacerdote *m*.

priest·ess ['priːstɪs] N sacerdotessa.

priest·hood ['priːstˌhud] N: **to enter the priesthood** farsi prete.

priest·ly ['priːstlɪ] ADJ sacerdotale.

prig [prɪg] N: **don't be such a prig!** non fare il(la) moralista!; **what a prig she is!** ma chi si crede di essere!

prig·gish ['prɪgɪʃ] ADJ (*person*) moralista; (*behaviour, attitude*) moraleggiante.

prig·gish·ness ['prɪgɪʃnɪs] N (*of person*) atteggiamento moraleggiante; **the priggishness of his behaviour** il suo atteggiamento moraleggiante; **the priggishness of his remarks** il suo tono moraleggiante.

prim [prɪm] ADJ (*comp* **-mer**, *superl* **-mest**) (*demure: person, dress*) per benino; (: *house, garden*) in cui nulla è fuori posto; (*manner, smile*) compassato(-a); (*prudish: also:* **prim and proper**) per benino.

pri·ma·cy ['praɪməsɪ] N (*frm*) suprema importanza.

pri·ma don·na ['priːməˈdɒnə] N primadonna; **she is a real prima donna** (*pej*) fa la primadonna.

pri·ma fa·cie [ˌpraɪməˈfeɪʃɪ] **1** ADV a prima vista.

2 ADJ (*assumption*) (a prima vista) legittimo(-a); (*evidence*) (a prima vista) convincente; **to have a prima facie case** (*Law*) presentare una causa in apparenza fondata.

pri·mal ['praɪml] ADJ (*origins, matter, world*) originario (-a); (*religion, music*) primitivo(-a); (*first in importance*) primario(-a).

pri·mari·ly ['praɪmərɪlɪ] ADV (*chiefly*) principalmente, essenzialmente.

pri·ma·ry ['praɪmərɪ] **1** ADJ (*chief, main: gen*) principale, primario(-a); **of primary importance** di primaria *or* fondamentale importanza.

2 N (*Am: election*) primarie *fpl*.

♦ **primary colour** N colore *m* fondamentale.

♦ **primary education** N istruzione *f* elementare *or* primaria.

♦ **primary products** NPL prodotti *mpl* del settore primario.

♦ **primary school** N (*Brit*) scuola elementare *or* primaria (*dai 5 agli 11 anni*).

♦ **primary sector** N settore *m* primario.

♦ **primary teacher** N insegnante *m/f* di scuola elementare, maestro(-a).

pri·mate [*sense a* 'praɪmeɪt, *sense b* 'praɪmɪt] N **a** (*Zool*) primate *m* **b** (*Rel*) primate *m*.

prime [praɪm] **1** ADJ **a** (*chief, major: gen*) principale, primario(-a), fondamentale; (: *cause, reason*) primo (-a), fondamentale; **of prime importance** della massima importanza

b (*excellent*: *example*) superbo(-a); (: *meat*) di prima scelta; **of prime quality** di prima scelta; **in prime condition** (*car, athlete*) in perfette condizioni; (*fruit*) in condizioni perfette.

2 N: **in the prime of life, in one's prime** nel fiore della vita; **to be past one's prime** non essere più quello(-a) di una volta.

3 VT (*wood*) preparare; (*gun*) innescare; (*pump*) adescare; (*fig*: *instruct*) istruire, mettere al corrente; **he arrived well primed** è arrivato ben preparato.

♦ **prime minister** N primo ministro.

♦ **prime mover** N primo motore *m*.

♦ **prime number** N (*Math*) numero primo.

prim·er ['praɪmə'] N **a** (*textbook*) testo elementare **b** (*paint*) vernice *f* base *inv*.

♦ **prime time** N (*Radio, TV*) fascia di massimo ascolto, prime time *m*.

pri·meval [praɪ'miːvəl] ADJ primordiale, primitivo(-a); **primeval forests** foreste originarie.

primi·tive ['prɪmɪtɪv] ADJ, N primitivo(-a).

prim·ly ['prɪmlɪ] ADV (*smile, behave*) da persona per benino.

prim·ness ['prɪmnɪs] N (*of person*) comportamento da persona per benino; (*of dress*) eccessiva modestia; (*of house, garden*) eccessivo ordine *m*; (*prudishness*) pudore *m* eccessivo.

pri·mor·dial [praɪ'mɔːdɪəl] ADJ primordiale.

prim·rose ['prɪm,rəʊz] **1** N (*Bot*) primula (gialla).

2 ADJ (*also*: **primrose yellow**) giallo canarino *inv*.

primu·la ['prɪmjʊlə] N (*Bot*) primula.

Pri·mus® ['praɪməs] N (*also*: **Primus stove**) fornello a petrolio.

prince [prɪns] N principe *m*; **Prince Charles** il principe Carlo.

♦ **prince charming** N il principe *m* azzurro.

♦ **prince consort** N principe *m* consorte.

prince·ly ['prɪnslɪ] ADJ (*also fig*) principesco(-a).

♦ **Prince of Wales** N il principe di Galles.

♦ **prince regent** N principe *m* reggente.

prin·cess [prɪn'sɛs] N principessa.

prin·ci·pal ['prɪnsɪpəl] **1** ADJ principale; **the principal violin** il primo violino.

2 N **a** (*of school, college*) preside *m/f*; (*in play*) protagonista *m/f*; (*in orchestra*) primo(-a) strumentista *m/f* **b** (*Fin*) capitale *m*.

prin·ci·pal·ity [,prɪnsɪ'pælɪtɪ] N principato.

prin·ci·pal·ly ['prɪnsɪpəlɪ] ADV principalmente.

♦ **principal parts** NPL (*Gram*) paradigma *msg*.

prin·ci·ple ['prɪnsəpl] N principio; **in principle** in linea di principio; **on principle** per principio; **it's a matter of principle** OR **it's the principle of the thing** è una questione di principio; **a man of principle** un uomo di saldi principi; **it's against my principles** è contrario ai miei principi; **to go back to first principles** (*fig*) tornare alle origini.

prin·ci·pled ['prɪnsɪpəld] ADJ (*person, position*) di principio; **I didn't know you were so high principled** non ti facevo uno di così elevati principi.

print [prɪnt] **1** N **a** (*mark, imprint*: *of foot, tyre, finger*) impronta

b (*typeface, characters*) caratteri *mpl*; (*printed matter*) stampa; **that book is in/out of print** quel libro è disponibile/esaurito; **to see o.s. in print** vedere il proprio nome stampato; **in small/large print** stampato (-a) a caratteri piccoli/grandi

c (*fabric*) (tessuto) stampato

d (*Art*) stampa; (*Phot*) fotografia.

2 VT **a** (*Typ, Textiles, Phot*) stampare; (*fig*: *on memory*) imprimere

b (*publish*) pubblicare, stampare

c (*write in block letters*) scrivere in stampatello

▶ **print out** VT + ADV (*Comput*) stampare.

print·able ['prɪntəbl] ADJ stampabile; **what he said is not printable!** (*hum*) ciò che ha detto non è ripetibile!

print·ed ['prɪntɪd] ADJ stampato(-a); **the power of the printed word** il potere di tutto ciò che è stampato.

♦ **printed circuit board** N circuito stampato.

♦ **printed matter** N stampe *fpl*.

print·er ['prɪntə'] N (*person*) tipografo(-a); (*machine*) stampante *m*; **at the printer's** (*book*) in tipografia; **printer's error** errore *m* di stampa; **printer's ink** inchiostro tipografico.

print·head ['prɪnt,hɛd] N (*Comput*) testina di stampa.

print·ing ['prɪntɪŋ] N **a** (*process, also Phot*) stampa **b** (*block writing*) stampatello; (*characters*) caratteri *mpl*; (*print*) stampa **c** (*number printed*) tiratura.

♦ **printing press** N pressa tipografica.

♦ **printing works** N tipografia, stamperia.

♦ **print-out** ['prɪnt,aʊt] N (*Comput*) tabulato, stampato.

♦ **print wheel** N margherita.

pri·or¹ ['praɪə'] **1** ADJ precedente; **without prior notice** senza preavviso; **to have a prior claim to sth** avere un diritto di precedenza su qc.

2 PREP: **prior to sth/to doing sth** prima di qc/di fare qc.

pri·or² ['praɪə'] N (*Rel*) priore *m*.

pri·or·ess ['praɪərɪs] N priora.

pri·or·ity [praɪ'ɒrɪtɪ] N priorità *f inv*, precedenza; **to have** *or* **take priority over sth** avere la precedenza su qc; **we must get our priorities right** dobbiamo decidere quali sono le cose più importanti per noi; **to treat sth as a priority** dare la precedenza a qc.

pri·ory ['praɪərɪ] N priorato.

prise, (*Am*) **prize** [praɪz] VT: **to prise sth open** aprire qc (forzando il coperchio); **to prise a lid up/off** aprire/togliere un coperchio facendo leva

▶ **prise out,** (*Am*) **prize out** VT + ADV: **to prise sth out (of sb)** (*secret*) tirar fuori qc (da qn).

prism ['prɪzəm] N (*Geom, Tech*) prisma *m*.

pris·mat·ic [prɪz'mætɪk] ADJ prismatico(-a).

pris·on ['prɪzn] **1** N prigione *f*, carcere *m*; **to be in prison** essere in prigione; **to go to prison for 5 years** essere condannato(-a) a 5 anni di carcere *or* di reclusione; **to send sb to prison for 2 years** condannare qn a 2 anni di reclusione.

2 ADJ (*system*) carcerario(-a); (*conditions, food*) nelle *or* delle prigioni.

♦ **prison camp** N campo di prigionia.

pris·on·er ['prɪznə'] N (*under arrest*) arrestato(-a); (*convicted*) detenuto(-a); (*Mil, fig*) prigioniero(-a); **the prisoner at the bar** l'accusato(-a), l'imputato(-a); **to take sb prisoner** far prigioniero(-a) qn.

♦ **prisoner of war** N prigioniero(-a) di guerra.

♦ **prisoner of war camp** N campo di prigionia.

♦ **prison life** N vita carceraria.

♦ **prison officer** N agente *m/f* di custodia.

pris·sy ['prɪsɪ] ADJ (*pej*) per benino.

pris·tine ['prɪstaɪn] ADJ (*unspoiled*) immacolato(-a), puro (-a); (*original*) originario(-a).

pri·va·cy ['prɪvəsɪ] N privacy *f*; **his desire for privacy** il suo desiderio di stare da solo; (*actor, popstar*) il suo deside-

rio di privacy; **in the privacy of one's own home** nell'intimità della propria casa; **in the strictest privacy** nella massima segretezza.

pri·vate ['praɪvɪt] **1** ADJ **a** (*not public: conversation, meeting, land*) privato(-a); (: *funeral, wedding*) in forma privata; (: *showing*) a inviti; (*confidential: letter*) personale; (: *agreement, information*) confidenziale; **"private"** (*on door*) "privato"; (*on envelope*) "riservata"; **this information must be kept private** quest'informazione deve rimanere strettamente confidenziale; **he is a very private person** è una persona molto riservata; **in (his) private life** nella vita privata; **private place** posto segreto; **private hearing** (*Law*) udienza a porte chiuse **b** (*for one person: car, house, secretary*) privato(-a), personale; (: *lessons*) privato(-a); (*personal: bank account, reasons*) personale; **a man of private means** un uomo che vive di rendita **c** (*not state-owned: company, army*) privato(-a); (: *doctor, nursing home*) non convenzionato(-a), privato(-a). **2** N **a** (*Mil*) soldato semplice **b** : **in private = privately** a, b.

♦ **private citizen** N privato (cittadino).
♦ **private detective, private investigator** N investigatore(-trice) *or* detective *m/f inv* privato(-a).
♦ **private enterprise** N l'iniziativa privata.
♦ **private eye** N (*Am fam*) investigatore(-trice) *or* detective *m/f inv* privato(-a).
♦ **private limited company** N società *f inv* a responsabilità limitata non quotata in borsa.

pri·vate·ly ['praɪvɪtlɪ] ADV **a** (*not publicly*) privatamente, in privato **b** (*secretly*) in privato; (*personally*) personalmente; (*within o.s.*) dentro di sé **c** (*unofficially*) a titolo personale.

♦ **private member** N (*Parliament*) deputato(-a) (*senza incarichi di governo*).
♦ **private member's bill** N (*Parliament*) progetto di legge ad iniziativa personale.
♦ **private parts** NPL (*euph*) parti *fpl* intime.
♦ **private practice** N (*Brit*) studio *or* ambulatorio privato; **to be in private practice** essere medico non convenzionato (con la mutua).
♦ **private property** N proprietà *f inv* privata.
♦ **private school** N scuola privata.
♦ **private sector** N: **the private sector** il settore privato.
♦ **private view** N (*Art*) vernissage *m inv*.

pri·va·tion [praɪ'veɪʃən] N **a** (*state*) privazione *f* **b** (*hardship*) privazioni *fpl*, stenti *mpl*.
pri·va·tize ['praɪvɪˌtaɪz] VT privatizzare.
priv·et ['prɪvɪt] N ligustro.
♦ **privet hedge** N siepe *f* di ligustro.

privi·lege ['prɪvɪlɪdʒ] **1** N privilegio; (*Parliament*) prerogativa; **I had the privilege of meeting her** ho avuto il privilegio *or* l'onore di incontrarla. **2** VT: **to be privileged to do sth** avere il privilegio *or* l'onore di fare qc.

privi·leged ['prɪvɪlɪdʒd] ADJ privilegiato(-a); **a privileged few** pochi privilegiati; **the privileged few** la minoranza dei privilegiati.

privy ['prɪvɪ] **1** ADJ: **to be privy to sth** essere a conoscenza *or* al corrente di qc. **2** N (*old: toilet*) gabinetto, ritirata.
♦ **Privy Council** N (*Brit*): **the Privy Council** il Consiglio della Corona.
♦ **Privy Councillor** N (*Brit*) Consigliere *m* della Corona.

prize¹ [praɪz] **1** N (*gen*) premio; **to win first prize** (*in game, race, lottery*) vincere il primo premio; (*Scol*) ottenere il

primo premio. **2** ADJ **a** (*awarded a prize*) premiato(-a); (*worthy of a prize*) eccellente; (*example*) perfetto(-a); **a prize idiot** (*fam*) un(-a) cretino(-a) patentato(-a) **b** (*awarded as a prize: cup, medal*) premio *inv* (*after n*). **3** VT (*honesty, friendship*) stimare, valutare; **he prizes his medals** è molto orgoglioso delle sue medaglie; **her most prized possession** il suo avere più prezioso; **a rare model, now much prized** un modello raro che oggi ha una valutazione molto alta.

prize² [praɪz] VT (*Am*) = **prise**.
♦ **prize draw** N estrazione *f* a premi *or* a premio.
♦ **prize fight** N (*Boxing*) incontro di pugilato fra professionisti.
♦ **prize fighter** N (*Am*) pugile *m* professionista.
♦ **prize fighting** N pugilato professionistico.
♦ **prize-giving** ['praɪzˌgɪvɪŋ] N premiazione *f*.
♦ **prize money** N soldi *mpl* del premio.

prize·winner ['praɪzˌwɪnə'] N (*in competition, lottery*) vincitore(-trice); (*Scol, in show*) premiato(-a).
prize·winning ['praɪzˌwɪnɪŋ] ADJ (*gen*) vincente; (*novel, essay*) premiato(-a).

pro- [prəʊ] PREF (*in favour of*) filo...; **pro-American** filoamericano(-a).
pro¹ [prəʊ] N: **the pros and cons** i pro e i contro.
pro² [prəʊ] N (*fam: Sport*) professionista *m/f*.
♦ **pro-active** [ˌprəʊ'æktɪv] ADJ: **to be pro-active** agire d'iniziativa.

prob·abil·ity [ˌprɒbə'bɪlɪtɪ] N probabilità *f inv*; **in all probability** con ogni probabilità.
prob·able ['prɒbəbl] ADJ probabile; **it is probable/hardly probable that...** è probabile/poco probabile che... + *sub*.
prob·ably ['prɒbəblɪ] ADV probabilmente.
pro·bate ['prəʊbɪt] N (*Law*) omologazione *f* (di un testamento).
pro·ba·tion [prə'beɪʃən] N: **to be on probation** (*Law*) essere in libertà vigilata; (*gen: in employment*) essere in prova, fare un periodo di prova; **to put sb on probation** (*Law*) sottoporre qn a libertà vigilata.
pro·ba·tion·ary [prə'beɪʃnərɪ] ADJ (*year, period*) di prova; (*teacher, nurse*) in prova; (*Law*) di libertà vigilata.
pro·ba·tion·er [prə'beɪʃnə'] N (*Law*) persona sottoposta a libertà vigilata; (*in employment*) persona in prova; (*novice*) novizio(-a).
♦ **probation officer** N (*Law*) *funzionario incaricato della sorveglianza delle persone sottoposte a libertà vigilata*.

probe [prəʊb] **1** N **a** (*Med, Space*) sonda **b** (*inquiry*) indagine *f*, investigazione *f*. **2** VT (*hole, crack*) tastare; (*Med*) esplorare, sondare; (*Space*) esplorare; (*also: probe into*) indagare su; **the policeman kept probing me** il poliziotto continuò a farmi domande.
prob·ing ['prəʊbɪŋ] ADJ (*look*) penetrante; (*question*) sottile; (*interrogation, study*) approfondito(-a).
pro·bity ['prəʊbɪtɪ] N probità, rettitudine *f*.
prob·lem ['prɒbləm] **1** N (*also Math*) problema *m*; **to have problems with the car** avere dei problemi con la macchina; **my son is a problem** mio figlio è un problema; **the housing problem** la crisi degli alloggi; **to have a drinking problem** avere il vizio del bere; **I had no problem in finding her** non mi è stato difficile trovarla; **what's the problem?** che cosa c'è?; **no problem!** ma certamente!, non c'è problema!; **it's not my problem** è un affare che non mi riguarda; **that's no problem for/to**

him per lui non è un problema.
[2] ADJ (*child, family*) difficile.

prob·lem·at·ic [ˌprɒblɪ'mætɪk], **prob·lem·at·ical** [ˌprɒblɪ'mætɪkəl] ADJ problematico(-a), dubbio(-a); **it is problematic whether** ... è in dubbio se... .

♦ **prob·lem page** N posta del cuore.

♦ **problem–solving** N risoluzione *f* di problemi.

pro·cedur·al [prə'si:djʊrəl] ADJ procedurale.

pro·cedure [prə'si:dʒəʳ] N (*Admin, Law*) procedura; **the usual procedure is to** ... la procedura normale *or* prassi è di...; **cashing a cheque is a simple procedure** riscuotere un assegno è un'operazione semplice.

pro·ceed [prə'si:d] [1] VI **a** (*move forward*) procedere; **let us proceed with caution** procediamo con cautela; **let us proceed to the next item** passiamo al prossimo punto; **things are proceeding according to plan** tutto procede *or* si svolge secondo i piani; **I am not sure how to proceed** non so bene come fare
b (*originate*): **to proceed from** (*sound*) provenire da; (*fear*) derivare da
c : **to proceed against sb** (*Law*) procedere contro qn.
[2] VT: **to proceed to do sth** cominciare *or* mettersi a fare qc.

pro·ceed·ing [prə'si:dɪŋ] N (*action, course of action*) modo d'agire.

proceedings ['prə'si:dɪŋz] NPL **a** (*events*) avvenimenti *mpl*; (*manoeuvres*) manovre *fpl*; (*function*) cerimonia *fsg*; (*meeting*) riunione *fsg*, seduta *fsg*; (*discussions*) dibattito *msg*
b (*esp Law: measures*) provvedimenti *mpl*, misure *fpl*; **to take proceedings (in order to do sth)** prendere i provvedimenti necessari (per fare qc); **to institute proceedings (against sb)** (*Law*) promuovere un'azione legale (contro qn)
c (*records: of learned society*) atti *mpl*, rendiconti *mpl*.

pro·ceeds ['prəʊsi:dz] NPL proventi *mpl*, ricavato *msg*.

pro·cess¹ ['prəʊsɛs] [1] N **a** processo; **the whole process** l'intera operazione; **in the process of restoring the picture he discovered** ... stava restaurando il quadro quando ha scoperto...; **in process of construction** (in corso di) costruzione; **the process of growing up** il processo della crescita; **we are in the process of moving to** ... stiamo per trasferirci a...
b (*specific method*) procedimento, sistema *m*, metodo; **the Bessemer process** il metodo Bessemer
c (*Law: action*) processo; (: *summons*) mandato di comparizione, citazione *f* in giudizio.
[2] VT (*Tech*) trattare; (*Phot*) sviluppare e stampare; (*Admin: application etc*) sbrigare; (*Comput*) elaborare.

pro·cess² [prə'sɛs] VI (*Brit frm: go in procession*) sfilare, procedere in corteo.

pro·cessed cheese [ˌprəʊsɛst'tʃi:z], (*Am*) **process cheese** N formaggio fuso.

pro·cess·ing ['prəʊsɛsɪŋ] N (*of data*) elaborazione *f*; (*of food*) trattamento; (*of film*) sviluppo e stampa; (*of application*) disbrigo.

pro·ces·sion [prə'sɛʃən] N (*of people, cars*) processione *f*, corteo; (*Rel*) processione; **funeral procession** corteo funebre.

♦ **pro–choice** ['prəʊ'tʃɔɪs] ADJ per la libertà di scelta di gravidanza.

pro·claim [prə'kleɪm] VT **a** (*gen*) proclamare, dichiarare; (*peace, public holiday*) dichiarare; **to proclaim sb king/that** proclamare qn re/che **b** (*fig: reveal*) dimostrare, rivelare.

proc·la·ma·tion [ˌprɒklə'meɪʃən] N proclama *m*, proclamazione *f*.

pro·cliv·ity [prə'klɪvɪtɪ] N (*frm*) tendenza, propensione *f*.

pro·cras·ti·nate [prəʊ'kræstɪˌneɪt] VI procrastinare.

pro·cras·ti·na·tion [prəʊˌkræstɪ'neɪʃən] N procrastinazione *f*.

pro·cre·ate ['prəʊkrɪˌeɪt] VI procreare.

pro·crea·tion [ˌprəʊkrɪ'eɪʃən] N procreazione *f*.

Procu·ra·tor Fis·cal ['prɒkjʊˌreɪtə'fɪskəl] N (*in Scotland*) ≈ procuratore *m*.

pro·cure [prə'kjʊəʳ] VT **a** procurare, ottenere; **to procure sb sth** [OR] **to procure sth for sb** procurare qc a qn, ottenere qc per qn; **I managed to procure a copy for myself** sono riuscito a procurarmene una copia **b** (*prostitute*) procurare.

pro·cure·ment [prə'kjʊəmənt] N (*of goods*) rifornimento, approvvigionamento.

pro·cur·er [prə'kjʊərəʳ] N (*Law*) prosseneta *m*, lenone *m*.

pro·cur·ing [prə'kjʊərɪŋ] N (*Law*) lenocinio.

prod [prɒd] [1] N (*push, jab*) colpetto; (*with elbow*) gomitata.
[2] VT (*jab: with stick, finger*) dare un colpetto a; **he prodded the page with his finger** ha puntato il dito sulla pagina; **he has to be prodded along** (*fig*) ha bisogno di essere pungolato.
[3] VI: **she prodded at the picture with a finger** ha puntato il dito sul quadro.

prodi·gal ['prɒdɪgəl] ADJ prodigo(-a).

prodi·gal·ity [ˌprɒdɪ'gælɪtɪ] N prodigalità.

pro·di·gious [prə'dɪdʒəs] ADJ prodigioso(-a), straordinario(-a).

pro·di·gious·ly [prə'dɪdʒəslɪ] ADV prodigiosamente.

prodi·gy ['prɒdɪdʒɪ] N prodigio; **child prodigy** [OR] **infant prodigy** bambino(-a) prodigio *inv*.

pro·drome ['prəʊˌdrəʊm] N (*Med*) prodromo.

pro·duce [*n* 'prɒdju:s; *vb* prə'dju:s] [1] N (*Agr*) prodotto; COLLECTIVE N prodotti *mpl*.
[2] VT **a** (*manufacture: gen*) produrre; (*create: book, essay*) scrivere; (: *work of art*) fare; (: *meal*) preparare; (: *ideas, profit*) dare; (: *give birth to*) partorire
b (*bring, show: gen*) tirar fuori; (: *tickets*) esibire, mostrare; (: *proof of identity*) produrre, fornire; **I can't suddenly produce £500!** da dove le tiro fuori 500 sterline?
c (*film*) produrre; (*play*) mettere in scena
d (*cause: gen*) causare, provocare; (: *results*) produrre; (: *interest*) suscitare; **this produced a stir** ha fatto sensazione.

pro·duc·er [prə'dju:səʳ] N (*Agr, Cine, TV, Theatre*) produttore(-trice).

prod·uct ['prɒdʌkt] N (*also Math*) prodotto; (*fig*) frutto.

pro·duc·tion [prə'dʌkʃən] N **a** (*manufacture*) produzione *f*; **to put into production** mettere in produzione; **to take out of production** togliere dalla produzione; **the country's steel production** la produzione siderurgica del paese
b (*showing*) presentazione *f*; (: *of documents*) produzione *f*; **on production of this ticket** dietro presentazione di questo biglietto
c (*of film, show*) produzione *f*; (*of play*) messa in scena; (*work produced*) realizzazione *f* teatrale (*or* cinematografica).

♦ **production agreement** N (*Am*) accordo sui tempi di produzione.

♦ **production control** N controllo di produzione.

♦ **production line** N catena di montaggio.

♦ **production manager** N direttore *m* di produzione, production manager *m/f inv.*

♦ **production overheads** NPL costi *mpl* indiretti di produzione.

pro·duc·tive [prə'dʌktɪv] ADJ (*gen*) produttivo(-a); (*meeting, discussion*) fruttuoso(-a); (*enterprise, business*) che rende; (*writer*) prolifico(-a); (*land, imagination*) fertile; **he had a very productive day** ha avuto una giornata molto soddisfacente.

prod·uc·tiv·ity [ˌprɒdʌk'tɪvɪtɪ] N produttività.

♦ **productivity agreement** N (*Brit*) accordo sui tempi di produzione.

♦ **productivity bonus** N premio di produzione.

pro·fane [prə'feɪn] ① ADJ **a** (*secular*) profano(-a) **b** (*irreverent*) irriverente; (: *language*) sacrilego(-a). ② VT profanare.

pro·fane·ly [prə'feɪnlɪ] ADV (*behave, speak*) in modo irriverente.

pro·fan·ity [prə'fænɪtɪ] N (*oath*) imprecazione *f*.

pro·fess [prə'fɛs] VT **a** (*faith, belief etc*) professare **b** (*claim*) dichiarare; **he professes extreme regret** si dichiara molto dispiaciuto; **I do not profess to be an expert** non pretendo di essere un esperto.

pro·fessed [prə'fɛst] ADJ (*Rel*) professo(-a); (*self-declared*) dichiarato(-a).

pro·fes·sion [prə'fɛʃən] N **a** (*gen*) professione *f*; **the professions** le professioni liberali; **by profession** di professione; **the medical profession** (*calling*) la professione medica; (*doctors collectively*) i medici **b** (*declaration*) dichiarazione *f*; **profession of faith** (*Rel*) professione *f* di fede.

pro·fes·sion·al [prə'fɛʃənl] ① ADJ **a** (*capacity*) professionale; (*diplomat, soldier*) di carriera; **a professional man** un professionista; **to take professional advice** consultare un esperto; **to be a professional singer** essere un(-a) cantante *m/f* professionista *or* di professione; **to turn** *or* **go professional** (*Sport*) passare al professionismo **b** (*competent, skilled: worker*) esperto(-a); (: *piece of work, approach*) da professionista; (: *attitude*) professionale; **it's not up to professional standards** non è da professionista. ② N professionista *m/f*.

pro·fes·sion·al·ism [prə'fɛʃnəˌlɪzəm] N professionismo.

pro·fes·sion·al·ly [prə'fɛʃnəlɪ] ADV (*play*) come professionista; (*sing*) per professione; (*expertly*) professionalmente, in modo professionale; **I only know him professionally** lo conosco solo per motivi di lavoro; **to be professionally qualified** essere abilitato(-a) alla professione.

pro·fes·sor [prə'fɛsəʳ] N (*Univ: Brit*) docente *m/f*; (: *Am: teacher*) professore(-essa).

prof·es·so·rial [ˌprɒfə'sɔːrɪəl] ADJ professorale.

pro·fes·sor·ship [prə'fɛsəʃɪp] N cattedra.

prof·fer ['prɒfəʳ] VT (*remark*) profferire; (*hand*) porgere; (*apologies*) porgere, presentare; (*advice*) fornire.

pro·fi·cien·cy [prə'fɪʃənsɪ] N competenza, abilità.

pro·fi·cient [prə'fɪʃənt] ADJ provetto(-a), competente.

pro·fi·cient·ly [prə'fɪʃəntlɪ] ADV abilmente.

pro·file ['prəʊfaɪl] N profilo; **in profile** di profilo; **to keep a low profile** (*fig*) cercare di non farsi notare troppo; **to maintain a high profile** mettersi in mostra; **low-profile tyre** (*Aut*) pneumatico a basso profilo.

prof·it ['prɒfɪt] ① N (*Comm*) profitto, utile *m*, guadagno;

(*fig*) profitto, vantaggio, beneficio; **profit and loss account** conto profitti e perdite; **to make a profit out of** *or* **on sth** ricavare un utile da qc; **to sell sth at a profit** vendere qc con un utile. ② VI: **to profit by** *or* **from sth** ricavare beneficio da qc.

prof·it·abil·ity [ˌprɒfɪtə'bɪlɪtɪ] N redditività.

prof·it·able ['prɒfɪtəbl] ADJ (*Comm*) remunerativo(-a), redditizio(-a); (*fig: beneficial: scheme*) vantaggioso(-a); (*meeting, visit*) fruttuoso(-a).

prof·it·ably ['prɒfɪtəblɪ] ADV (*Comm*) con profitto; (*fig*) vantaggiosamente; (: *spend time*) utilmente.

♦ **profit centre** N centro di profitto.

profi·teer [ˌprɒfɪ'tɪəʳ] ① VI speculare. ② N profittatore(-trice), speculatore(-trice).

profi·teer·ing [ˌprɒfɪ'tɪərɪŋ] N (*pej*) affarismo.

prof·it·less ['prɒfɪtlɪs] ADJ (*fig*) inutile.

♦ **profit-making** ['prɒfɪtˌmeɪkɪŋ] ADJ (*industry*) rimunerativo(-a).

♦ **profit margin** N margine *m* di profitto.

♦ **profit-sharing** ['prɒfɪtˌʃɛərɪŋ] N compartecipazione *f* agli utili.

♦ **profits tax** N (*Brit*) imposta sugli utili.

prof·li·ga·cy ['prɒflɪgəsɪ] N (*debauchery*) dissolutezza; (*extravagance*) grande prodigalità.

prof·li·gate ['prɒflɪgɪt] ADJ (*dissolute: behaviour, act*) dissipato(-a); (: *person*) dissoluto(-a); **he's very profligate with his money** è uno che sperpera i suoi soldi.

♦ **pro for·ma** ['prəʊ'fɔːmə] ADV: **pro forma invoice** fattura proforma.

pro·found [prə'faʊnd] ADJ profondo(-a).

pro·found·ly [prə'faʊndlɪ] ADV profondamente.

pro·fun·dity [prə'fʌndɪtɪ] N profondità.

pro·fuse [prə'fjuːs] ADJ (*tears, bleeding*) copioso(-a); (*vegetation*) abbondante; (*thanks, praise, apologies*) infinito(-a); **she was profuse in her thanks** si è profusa in ringraziamenti.

pro·fuse·ly [prə'fjuːslɪ] ADV (*sweat, bleed*) abbondantemente; (*praise*) con grande effusione; (*grow*) rigogliosamente; **he apologized profusely** si è profuso in scuse.

pro·fu·sion [prə'fjuːʒən] N profusione *f*, abbondanza; **in profusion** a profusione.

pro·geni·tor [prəʊ'dʒɛnɪtəʳ] N (*frm*) progenitore(-trice), antenato(-a).

prog·eny ['prɒdʒɪnɪ] N (*frm*) progenie *f*, discendenti *mpl*.

pro·ges·ter·one [prəʊ'dʒɛstəˌrəʊn] N progesterone *m*.

prog·no·sis [prɒg'nəʊsɪs] N (*pl* **prognoses** [prɒg'nəʊsiːz]) (*Med*) prognosi *f inv*.

prog·nos·ti·cate [prɒg'nɒstɪˌkeɪt] VT pronosticare, predire.

prog·nos·ti·ca·tion [prɒgˌnɒstɪ'keɪʃən] N pronostico.

program ['prəʊgræm] ① N (*Comput*) programma *m*. ② VT (*computer, machine*) programmare.

pro·gramme, (*Am*) **pro·gram** ['prəʊgræm] ① N (*gen, Pol*) programma *m*; (*Radio, TV: broadcast*) programma, trasmissione *f*; (: *station*) canale *m*; **what's the programme for today?** che cosa facciamo oggi?. ② VT (*arrange*) programmare, stabilire.

pro·grammed learn·ing [ˌprəʊgræmd'lɜːnɪŋ] N apprendimento graduale.

♦ **programme editor** N (*Radio, TV*) curatore(-trice) di un programma.

pro·gram·mer ['prəʊgræməʳ] N (*Comput*) programmatore(-trice).

♦ **programme seller** N (*Theatre*) venditore(-trice) di

programmi.

pro·gram·ming, (*Am*) **pro·gram·ing** ['prəʊgræmɪŋ] N (*Comput*) programmazione *f*.

♦ **programming language** N (*Comput*) linguaggio di programmazione.

pro·gress [*n* 'prəʊgrɛs; *vb* prəʊ'grɛs] ① N (*gen*) progresso, progressi *mpl*; **to make progress** (*gen*) fare progressi; (*walk forward*) avanzare; **the pupil is making good progress** l'allievo fa dei buoni progressi; **the work is making little progress** il lavoro procede lentamente; **the progress of events** il corso degli avvenimenti; **in progress** (*meeting, work etc*) in corso.

② VI **a** (*go forward*) avanzare, procedere **b** (*in time*) procedere; **as the match progressed** man mano che la partita procedeva **c** (*improve, make progress: person*) fare progressi; (: *investigation, studies*) progredire.

pro·gres·sion [prə'grɛʃən] N progresso; (*Math*) progressione *f*; **arithmetic/geometric progression** progressione aritmetica/geometrica.

pro·gres·sive [prə'grɛsɪv] ADJ **a** (*increasing: disease, taxation*) progressivo(-a) **b** (*favouring progress: idea, party*) progressista.

pro·gres·sive·ly [prə'grɛsɪvlɪ] ADV progressivamente, gradualmente.

♦ **progress report** N (*Med*) bollettino medico; (*Admin*) rendiconto dei lavori; (*Scol*) pagella, scheda di valutazione.

pro·hib·it [prə'hɪbɪt] VT **a** (*forbid*) proibire, vietare; **to prohibit sb from doing sth** vietare *or* proibire a qn di fare qc; **"smoking prohibited"** "vietato fumare" **b** (*prevent: thing*) impedire.

pro·hi·bi·tion [ˌprəʊɪ'bɪʃən] N proibizione *f*, divieto; **Prohibition** (*esp Am: of alcohol*) proibizionismo.

pro·hibi·tive [prə'hɪbɪtɪv] ADJ proibitivo(-a).

pro·hibi·tive·ly [prə'hɪbɪtɪvlɪ] ADV in modo proibitivo; **it's prohibitively expensive** il costo è proibitivo.

proj·ect [*n* 'prɒdʒɛkt; *vb* prə'dʒɛkt] ① N (*scheme, plan, venture*) progetto, piano; (*study*) progetto, lavoro di ricerca; (: *Scol, Univ*) ricerca, studio.

② VT (*film*) proiettare; (*voice*) spiegare; (*one's personality*) mettere in luce; (*visit*) progettare.

③ VI (*jut out*) sporgere in fuori.

proj·ect·ed [prə'dʒɛktɪd] ADJ (*predicted*) previsto(-a); (*planned*) progettato(-a).

pro·jec·tile [prə'dʒɛktaɪl] N proiettile *m*.

pro·jec·ting [prə'dʒɛktɪŋ] ADJ sporgente.

pro·jec·tion [prə'dʒɛkʃən] N **a** (*of films, figures*) proiezione *f* **b** (*forecast: of cost*) preventivo **c** (*overhang, protrusion*) sporgenza, prominenza.

pro·jec·tion·ist [prə'dʒɛkʃənɪst] N (*Cine*) proiezionista *m/f*.

♦ **projection room** N (*Cine*) cabina di proiezione.

pro·jec·tor [prə'dʒɛktə^r] N (*Cine*) proiettore *m*.

pro·lapse ['prəʊlæps] N (*Med*) prolasso.

pro·letar·ian [ˌprəʊlə'tɛərɪən] ADJ, N proletario(-a).

pro·letari·at [ˌprəʊlə'tɛərɪət] N proletariato.

♦ **pro-life** ['prəʊ'laɪf] ADJ per il diritto alla vita.

pro·lif·er·ate [prə'lɪfəˌreɪt] VI (*Bio, fig*) proliferare; (*animals*) prolificare.

pro·lif·era·tion [prəˌlɪfə'reɪʃən] N (*see vb*) proliferazione *f*; prolificazione *f*.

pro·lif·ic [prə'lɪfɪk] ADJ (*animal*) prolifico(-a); (*crop*) abbondante; (*writer*) fecondo(-a).

pro·lix ['prəʊlɪks] ADJ (*frm*) prolisso(-a).

prologue, (*Am*) **pro·log** ['prəʊlɒg] N prologo.

pro·long [prə'lɒŋ] VT prolungare.

pro·lon·ga·tion [ˌprəʊlɒŋ'geɪʃən] N prolungamento.

prom [prɒm] ① N ABBR **a** (*Brit fam*) = **promenade b** (*Brit fam*) = **promenade concert**.

② N (*Am*) ballo studentesco.

prom·enade [ˌprɒmɪ'nɑːd] ① N (*at seaside*) lungomare *m*.

② VI (*stroll*) passeggiare.

♦ **promenade concert** N (*Brit Mus*) concerto di musica classica (*che fa parte di una rassegna che si tiene ogni anno a Londra*).

♦ **promenade deck** N (*Naut*) ponte *m* di passeggio.

prom·enad·er [ˌprɒmɪ'nɑːdə^r] N (*Brit Mus*) spettatore(-trice) (*di un concerto*).

Prometheus [prə'miːθɪəs] N Prometeo.

promi·nence ['prɒmɪnəns] N (*of ridge*) prominenza; (*conspicuousness*) imponenza; (*of role*) importanza; **to come into prominence** (*person*) venire alla ribalta.

promi·nent ['prɒmɪnənt] ADJ **a** (*projecting: ridge*) prominente; (: *teeth*) sporgente; (: *cheekbones*) marcato(-a) **b** (*conspicuous*) che spicca; **put it in a prominent position** mettilo ben in vista **c** (*leading: role, feature*) di rilievo **d** (*well-known: personality*) molto in vista; **she is prominent in the field of …** è un'autorità nel campo di… .

promi·nent·ly ['prɒmɪnəntlɪ] ADV (*display, set*) ben in vista; **he figured prominently in the case** ha avuto una parte di primo piano nella faccenda.

promis·cu·ity [ˌprɒmɪs'kjuːɪtɪ] N (*sexual*) promiscuità.

pro·mis·cu·ous [prə'mɪskjʊəs] ADJ (*sexually*) promiscuo(-a).

pro·mis·cu·ous·ly [prə'mɪskjʊəslɪ] ADV (*behave*) promiscuamente, in modo promiscuo.

prom·ise ['prɒmɪs] ① N promessa; **to make sb a promise** fare una promessa a qn; **to keep one's promise** mantenere la propria promessa; **a young man of promise** un giovane promettente; **to show promise** promettere bene.

② VT promettere; **to promise (sb) to do sth** promettere (a qn) di fare qc; **to promise sb sth** [OR] **to promise sth to sb** promettere qc a qn; **to promise sb the earth** *or* **the moon** (*fig*) promettere a qn mari e monti; **to promise o.s. sth** promettere a se stesso(-a) qc.

③ VI: **I can't promise, but …** non te (*or* ve *etc*) lo prometto, ma…; **to promise well** promettere bene.

prom·is·ing ['prɒmɪsɪŋ] ADJ promettente; **it doesn't look promising** non sembra promettente; **the future is promising** il futuro promette bene.

prom·is·ing·ly ['prɒmɪsɪŋlɪ] ADV in modo promettente.

prom·is·sory note ['prɒmɪsərɪˌnəʊt] N pagherò *m inv*.

prom·on·tory ['prɒməntrɪ] N promontorio.

pro·mote [prə'məʊt] VT **a** (*in rank*): **to promote sb (from sth) to sth** promuovere qn (da qc) a qc; **the team was promoted to the second division** (*Brit Ftbl*) la squadra è stata promossa in serie B **b** (*encourage: trade, plan, concert, campaign*) promuovere; (: *product*) lanciare, reclamizzare.

pro·mot·er [prə'məʊtə^r] N (*gen*) promotore(-trice); (*of sporting event*) promoter *m inv*, organizzatore(-trice); (*of cause*) sostenitore(-trice).

pro·mo·tion [prə'məʊʃən] N (*gen*) promozione *f*; **to get promotion** ottenere la promozione.

pro·mo·tion·al [prə'məʊʃənl] ADJ promozionale.

prompt [prɒmpt] ① ADJ (*comp* -**er**, *superl* -**est**) (*action*) tempestivo(-a); (*delivery*) immediato(-a); (*payment*) pronto(-a), immediato(-a); **to be prompt to do sth** essere sollecito(-a) nel fare qc; **they're very prompt**

(*punctual*) sono molto puntuali. 2 ADV: **at 6 o'clock prompt** alle 6 in punto. 3 N a (*Theatre*) imbeccata b (*Comput*) prompt *m inv*. 4 VT a : **to prompt sb to do sth** spingere qn a fare qc; **it prompts the thought that ...** questo fa pensare che... b (*Theatre*) suggerire a.

prompt·er ['prɒmptə'] N (*Theatre*) suggeritore(-trice).

prompt·ing ['prɒmptɪŋ] N imbeccata, suggerimento.

prompt·ly ['prɒmptlɪ] ADV (*speedily*) prontamente; (*punctually*) puntualmente.

prompt·ness ['prɒmptnɪs] N (*speed*) prontezza, sollecitudine *f*; (*punctuality*) puntualità.

prone [prəʊn] ADJ a (*face down*) a faccia in giù, prono(-a) b (*liable*): **prone to** incline a, propenso(-a) a; **to be prone to illness** essere *or* andare soggetto(-a) a malattie; **she is prone to burst into tears if ...** scoppia facilmente in lacrime se... .

prong [prɒŋ] N (*of fork*) rebbio, dente *m*; **three-pronged** (*fork*) a tre rebbi *or* denti; (*attack*) su tre fronti, triplice.

pro·noun ['prəʊˌnaʊn] N pronome *m*.

pro·nounce [prə'naʊns] 1 VT a (*letter, word*) pronunciare b (*declare*) dichiarare; **they pronounced him unfit to drive** lo hanno dichiarato inabile alla guida; **to pronounce o.s. for/against sth** dichiararsi in favore di/contro qc; **to pronounce sentence** (*Law*) pronunziare la sentenza. 2 VI: **to pronounce in favour of/against sth** pronunciarsi in favore di/contro qc; **to pronounce on sth** pronunciarsi su qc.

pro·nounce·able [prə'naʊnsəbl] ADJ pronunciabile.

pro·nounced [prə'naʊnst] ADJ (*marked: improvement*) netto(-a), spiccato(-a); (: *views*) preciso(-a); **he has a pronounced limp** zoppica in modo molto pronunciato.

pro·nounce·ment [prə'naʊnsmənt] N dichiarazione *f*.

pron·to ['prɒntəʊ] ADV (*fam*) subito, immediatamente.

pro·nun·cia·tion [prəˌnʌnsɪ'eɪʃən] N pronuncia.

proof [pru:f] 1 N a (*evidence*) prova; (*Math*) dimostrazione *f*; **proof of identity** documento d'identità; **I have proof that he did it** ho le prove che è stato lui a farlo; **as** *or* **in proof of** come prova *or* testimonianza di; **to give** *or* **show proof of** dar prova di b (*test, trial*): **to put sth to the proof** mettere alla prova qc c (*Typ*) bozza, prova di stampa; (*Phot*) provino d (*of alcohol*): **70% proof** ≈ 40° (alcolici). 2 ADJ: **to be proof against** essere a prova di. 3 VT (*tent, anorak*) impermeabilizzare.

proof·read ['pru:fˌri:d] VT correggere le bozze di.

proof·reader ['pru:fˌri:də'] N correttore(-trice) di bozze.

proof·read·ing ['pru:fˌri:dɪŋ] N correzione *f* di bozze.

prop[1] [prɒp] 1 N sostegno, appoggio, puntello; (*fig*) sostegno. 2 VT (*also:* **prop up**) a (*rest, lean: ladder*) appoggiare; **to prop sth against** appoggiare qc contro *or* a b (*support*) sostenere, puntellare; (*fig*) tenere su, tenere in piedi.

prop[2] [prɒp] N (*Theatre fam*) (elemento del) materiale *m* di scena.

propa·gan·da [ˌprɒpə'gændə] 1 N propaganda. 2 ADJ (*campaign, leaflets*) propagandistico(-a).

propa·gan·dist [ˌprɒpə'gændɪst] 1 N (*pej*) persona che fa propaganda politica. 2 ADJ (*activities, literature*) di propaganda politica.

propa·gate ['prɒpəˌgeɪt] 1 VT propagare.

2 VI (*plants, theories*) propagarsi; (*birds*) riprodursi.

propa·ga·tion [ˌprɒpə'geɪʃən] N (*see vb*) propagazione *f*; riproduzione *f*.

pro·pane ['prəʊpeɪn] N propano.

pro·pel [prə'pɛl] VT spingere.

pro·pel·lant [prə'pɛlənt] N (*in rocket*) propellente *m*.

pro·pel·ler [prə'pɛlə'] N elica.

pro·pel·ling pen·cil [prəˌpɛlɪŋ'pɛnsl] N (*Brit*) portamina *m inv*.

pro·pen·sity [prə'pɛnsɪtɪ] N tendenza; **propensity (for)** propensione *f* (per).

prop·er ['prɒpə'] 1 ADJ a (*suitable, appropriate: clothes, tools*) adatto(-a), appropriato(-a); (*correct, right: order, way, method*) giusto(-a); (*seemly: behaviour, person*) decente, perbene; **the proper time** il momento adatto *or* giusto; **in the proper way** come si deve; **to go through the proper channels** (*Admin*) seguire la regolare procedura; **do as you think proper** fa'come ritieni opportuno; **it isn't proper to do that** non sta bene fare così; **to do the proper thing by sb** agire bene verso qn; **proper to** (*Chem, Philosophy*) proprio di b (*actual, authentic*) vero(-a) e proprio(-a); **physics proper** la fisica propriamente detta; **he isn't a proper doctor** non è un medico come si deve; **in the proper sense of the word** nel vero senso della parola; **in the city proper** nella città vera e propria c (*fam: real: lady, gentleman*) vero(-a), autentico(-a); (: *thorough: mess*) vero(-a), bello(-a); **it's a proper nuisance** è proprio una bella scocciatura. 2 ADV (*Brit fam: very*) proprio; **to talk proper** (*correctly*) parlare bene.

♦ **proper fraction** N (*Math*) frazione *f* propria.

prop·er·ly ['prɒpəlɪ] ADV a (*correctly: speak, write*) bene, come si deve; (: *use*) in modo giusto; **she very properly refused** ha giustamente rifiutato; **properly speaking** propriamente parlando b (*in seemly fashion*) correttamente, decentemente; **not properly dressed** vestito(-a) in maniera sconveniente c (*fam: really, thoroughly*) veramente.

♦ **proper noun** N nome *m* proprio.

prop·er·tied ['prɒpətɪd] ADJ: **a propertied man** un possidente.

prop·er·ty ['prɒpətɪ] N a (*quality*) proprietà *f inv*, caratteristica b (*possessions*) beni *mpl*; (*land, building, Chem*) proprietà *f inv*; **he owns property in Spain** ha delle proprietà in Spagna; **personal property** beni *mpl* mobili; **a man of property** un possidente; **is this your property?** è tuo?; **lost property** oggetti *mpl* smarriti c (*Theatre*) (elemento del) materiale *m* di scena.

♦ **property developer** N (*Brit*) costruttore *m* edile.

♦ **property man**, **property manager** N (*Theatre*) trovarobe *m inv*.

♦ **property owner** N proprietario(-a).

♦ **property tax** N imposta patrimoniale.

proph·ecy ['prɒfɪsɪ] N profezia.

proph·esy ['prɒfɪˌsaɪ] VT predire, profetizzare.

proph·et ['prɒfɪt] N profeta *m*.

proph·et·ess ['prɒfɪtɪs] N profetessa.

pro·phet·ic [prə'fɛtɪk] ADJ profetico(-a).

pro·pheti·cal·ly [prə'fɛtɪkəlɪ] ADV profeticamente.

prophy·lac·tic [ˌprɒfɪ'læktɪk] 1 ADJ (*Med*) profilattico (-a). 2 N profilattico.

pro·pi·ti·ate [prə'pɪʃɪˌeɪt] VT propiziarsi.

pro·pi·tia·tion [prə͵pɪʃɪ'eɪʃən] N propiziazione *f*.
pro·pi·tious [prə'pɪʃəs] ADJ propizio(-a).
pro·pi·tious·ly [prə'pɪʃəslɪ] ADV in modo propizio.
pro·po·nent [prə'pəʊnənt] N fautore(-trice).
pro·por·tion [prə'pɔːʃən] **1** N **a** (*ratio*) proporzione *f*, pro rata; **the proportion of boys to girls** la proporzione dei ragazzi rispetto alle ragazze; **to be in proportion** (*numbers*) essere proporzionali; **to be in/out of proportion (to one another)** essere proporzionati/sproporzionati (tra di loro); **to be in/out of proportion to** *or* **with sth** essere in proporzione/sproporzionato(-a) rispetto a qc; **to see sth in proportion** (*fig*) dare il giusto peso a qc; **sense of proportion** (*fig*) senso della misura
b (*part, amount, share*) parte *f*
c : **proportions** NPL (*size, dimensions*) proporzioni *fpl*.
2 VT proporzionare, commisurare; **well-proportioned** ben proporzionato(-a).
pro·por·tion·al [prə'pɔːʃənl] ADJ: **proportional (to)** proporzionale (a).
pro·por·tion·al·ly [prə'pɔːʃnəlɪ] ADV proporzionalmente.
♦ **proportional representation** N (*Pol*) rappresentanza proporzionale.
pro·por·tion·ate [prə'pɔːʃnɪt] ADJ: **proportionate (to)** proporzionato(-a) (a).
pro·po·sal [prə'pəʊzl] N (*offer*) offerta, proposta; (: *of marriage*) proposta di matrimonio; (*suggestion*): **proposal (for sth/to do sth)** proposta (di qc/di fare qc); (*plan*) progetto, proposta.
pro·pose [prə'pəʊz] **1** VT **a** proporre; **to propose doing sth** proporre di fare qc; **to propose that sth should be done** proporre che sia fatto qc; **I propose that we go by bus** propongo di andare con l'autobus; **to propose marriage to sb** fare una proposta di matrimonio a qn; **to propose sb for a job/as treasurer** proporre qn per un posto/come tesoriere; **to propose a toast to sb** proporre un brindisi a qn
b (*have in mind*): **to propose sth/to do** *or* **doing sth** proporsi qc/di fare qc.
2 VI (*offer marriage*) fare una proposta di matrimonio.
pro·pos·er [prə'pəʊzə'] N (*Brit: of motion*) proponente *m/f*.
propo·si·tion [͵prɒpə'zɪʃən] N **a** (*statement, Math, Logic*) proposizione *f* **b** (*proposal*) proposta; **to make sb a proposition** proporre qc a qn **c** (*person or thing to be dealt with*): **he's a tough proposition** è un osso duro; **that's a tough proposition** è un'impresa.
pro·pound [prə'paʊnd] VT (*idea, scheme, theory*) proporre, presentare; (*problem, question*) porre.
pro·pri·etary [prə'praɪətərɪ] ADJ (*Comm*): **proprietary article** prodotto con marchio depositato; **proprietary brand** marchio di fabbrica; **proprietary medicine** specialità farmaceutica; **proprietary name** nome depositato *or* registrato.
pro·pri·etor [prə'praɪətə'] N proprietario(-a).
pro·pri·etorial [prəpraɪə'tɔːrɪəl] (*frm*) ADJ **a** (*behaviour, attitude*) possessivo(-a) **b** (*duties, rights*) del proprietario.
pro·pri·ety [prə'praɪətɪ] N (*seemliness*) decoro, rispetto delle convenienze sociali; (*appropriateness*) convenienza; **the proprieties** le convenzioni sociali.
pro·pul·sion [prə'pʌlʃən] N: **jet propulsion** propulsione *f* a getto.
♦ **pro rata** ['prəʊ'rɑːtə] ADV in proporzione, pro rata.
pro·sa·ic [prəʊ'zeɪɪk] ADJ (*dull*) prosaico(-a), banale.

pro·sai·cal·ly [prəʊ'zeɪkəlɪ] ADV prosaicamente.
pro·scribe [prəʊs'kraɪb] VT proscrivere.
pro·scrip·tion [prəʊs'krɪpʃən] N proscrizione *f*.
prose [prəʊz] N prosa; (*Scol: translation*) traduzione *f* dalla lingua madre *or* madrelingua.
pros·ecute ['prɒsɪkjuːt] VT **a** (*Law*) intentare azione contro; **"trespassers will be prosecuted"** "i trasgressori saranno perseguiti a norma di legge" **b** (*frm: carry on: inquiry*) proseguire.
pros·ecut·ing at·tor·ney ['prɒsɪkjuːtɪŋə'tɜːnɪ] N (*Am*) ≈ procuratore *m*.
pros·ecu·tion [͵prɒsɪ'kjuːʃən] N (*Law: act, proceedings*) azione *f* giudiziaria; (*accusing side*) accusa; **witness for the prosecution** testimone per l'accusa; **the prosecution** ≈ il pubblico ministero.
pros·ecu·tor ['prɒsɪkjuːtə'] N (*Law*): **public prosecutor** ≈ procuratore *m* della Repubblica.
pros·elyt·ize ['prɒsɪlɪ͵taɪz] VI (*frm*) fare del proselitismo.
♦ **prose writer** N prosatore(-trice).
proso·dy ['prɒsədɪ] N prosodia.
pros·pect [*n* 'prɒspɛkt; *vb* prə'spɛkt] **1** N (*outlook*) vista; (*fig*) prospettiva; (: *hope*) speranza; (: *chance*) probabilità *f inv*; **future prospects** (*of person, country*) prospettive *fpl*; **it's a grim prospect** è una prospettiva poco allegra; **we are faced with the prospect of leaving** rischiamo di dovercene andare; **there's little prospect of its happening** ci sono poche probabilità che accada; **what have you got in prospect?** cos' hai in vista?; **there is every prospect of an early victory** tutto lascia prevedere una rapida vittoria; **what are his prospects?** che prospettiva ha?; **a job with no prospects** un lavoro che non offre nessuna prospettiva; **he is a good prospect for the team** è una speranza per la squadra; **to seem a good prospect** sembrare promettente.
2 VT esplorare.
3 VI: **to prospect for gold** cercare l'oro.
pros·pect·ing [prə'spɛktɪŋ] N (*Mining*) prospezione *f*.
pro·spec·tive [prə'spɛktɪv] ADJ (*buyer*) probabile; (*legislation, son-in-law*) futuro(-a).
pro·spec·tor [prə'spɛktə'] N prospettore *m*; **gold prospector** cercatore *m* d'oro.
pro·spec·tus [prə'spɛktəs] N prospetto.
pros·per ['prɒspə'] VI (*person*) raggiungere il benessere (economico); (*business, trade*) prosperare.
pros·per·ity [prɒs'pɛrɪtɪ] N benessere *m*, prosperità.
pros·per·ous ['prɒspərəs] ADJ (*industry*) prospero(-a), fiorente; (*businessman*) di successo.
pros·per·ous·ly ['prɒspərəslɪ] ADV in modo prospero; **to live prosperously** vivere agiatamente.
pros·ta·glan·din [͵prɒstə'glændɪn] N prostaglandina.
pros·tate ['prɒsteɪt] N (*also: prostate gland*) prostata, ghiandola prostatica.
pros·ti·tute ['prɒstɪ͵tjuːt] **1** N prostituta; **male prostitute** prostituto.
2 VT prostituire.
pros·ti·tu·tion [͵prɒstɪ'tjuːʃən] N prostituzione *f*.
pros·trate [*adj* 'prɒstreɪt; *vb* prɒ'streɪt] **1** ADJ bocconi *inv*; (*in respect, submission*) prosternato(-a), prostrato(-a); (*exhausted*): **prostrate (with)** prostrato(-a) (da).
2 VT: **to prostrate o.s.** (*before sb*) prostrarsi, prosternarsi; (*on the floor*) stendersi bocconi; (*fig*) abbattersi.
pros·tra·tion [prɒs'treɪʃən] N (*Med: exhaustion*) spossatezza.
pro·tago·nist [prəʊ'tægənɪst] N protagonista *m/f*.
pro·tect [prə'tɛkt] VT (*gen*) proteggere, salvaguardare;

(*from cold, heat*) riparare; (*interests, rights*) salvaguardare.

pro·tec·tion [prə'tɛkʃən] N **a** protezione *f*; (*against cold, wind*) riparo; **to be under sb's protection** essere sotto la protezione di qn **b** = **protection money.**

pro·tec·tion·ism [prə'tɛkʃə,nɪzəm] N protezionismo.

pro·tec·tion·ist [prə'tɛkʃənɪst] **1** ADJ protezionista. **2** N protezionista *m/f*.

♦ **protection money** N pizzo.

♦ **protection racket** N racket *m inv.*

pro·tec·tive [prə'tɛktɪv] ADJ (*gen*) protettivo(-a); **protective custody** (*Police*) protezione *f.*

pro·tec·tive·ly [prə'tɛktɪvlɪ] ADV (*say, act*) in modo protettivo.

pro·tec·tor [prə'tɛktə'] N protettore(-trice).

pro·tec·tor·ate [prə'tɛktərɪt] N protettorato.

pro·té·gé(e) ['prəʊtɪʒeɪ] N protetto(-a).

pro·tein ['prəʊtiːn] N proteina.

pro tem [prəʊ'tɛm] ADV ABBR (= *pro tempore: for the time being*) pro tempore.

pro·test [*n* 'prəʊtɛst; *vb* prə'tɛst] **1** N protesta; **to do sth under protest** fare qc protestando. **2** VT protestare. **3** VI: **to protest against/about** protestare contro/per; **to protest to sb** fare le proprie rimostranze a qn.

Prot·es·tant ['prɒtɪstənt] ADJ, N protestante (*m/f*).

Prot·es·tant·ism ['prɒtɪstən,tɪzəm] N protestantesimo.

pro·tes·ta·tion [,prɒtɛs'teɪʃən] N (*frm*) protesta.

pro·test·er, pro·tes·tor [prə'tɛstə'] N contestatore(-trice); (*in demonstration*) dimostrante *m/f.*

♦ **protest march** N marcia di protesta.

♦ **protest meeting** N manifestazione *f or* dimostrazione *f* di protesta.

proto·col ['prəʊtə,kɒl] N protocollo.

pro·ton ['prəʊtɒn] N protone *m.*

♦ **proton number** N numero protonico.

proto·plasm ['prəʊtəʊ,plæzəm] N protoplasma *m.*

proto·type ['prəʊtəʊ,taɪp] N prototipo.

pro·tract [prə'trækt] VT protrarre.

pro·tract·ed [prə'træktɪd] ADJ protratto(-a), prolungato(-a).

pro·trac·tor [prə'træktə'] N (*Geom*) goniometro.

pro·trude [prə'truːd] VI sporgere.

pro·trud·ing [prə'truːdɪŋ] ADJ sporgente.

pro·tu·ber·ance [prə'tjuːbərəns] N protuberanza, sporgenza.

pro·tu·ber·ant [prə'tjuːbərənt] ADJ (*eyes*) sporgente.

proud [praʊd] **1** ADJ (*comp* **-er,** *superl* **-est**) **a** (*person*) orgoglioso(-a), fiero(-a); (*pej: arrogant*) superbo(-a); **to be proud to do sth** essere fiero di fare qc; **he was as proud as a peacock** si è gonfiato come un tacchino; **that's nothing to be proud of!** non mi pare che sia il caso di vantarsene!
b (*splendid: ship*) superbo(-a), splendido(-a). **2** ADV: **to do sb proud** non far mancare nulla a qn; **to do o.s. proud** non farsi mancare nulla.

proud·ly ['praʊdlɪ] ADV (*see adj*) orgogliosamente, con fierezza; superbamente.

prove [pruːv] (*pt* **proved,** *pp* **proved** *or* **proven** ['pruːvən]) **1** VT **a** (*verify*) provare, dimostrare; **to prove sb innocent** provare *or* dimostrare l'innocenza di qn; **he was proved right in the end** alla fine i fatti gli hanno dato ragione. **b** (*put to the test: courage, usefulness etc*) dimostrare, mettere alla prova; **to prove o.s.** dar prova di sé

c (*turn out*): **to prove (to be) useful** rivelarsi utile; **to prove correct** risultare vero(-a); **if it proves (to be) otherwise** dovesse rivelarsi altrimenti. **2** VI = **vt c.**

prov·enance ['prɒvɪnəns] N (*frm*) provenienza, origine *f.*

Pro·vence [prɒ'vɑːns] N Provenza.

prov·erb ['prɒvɜːb] N proverbio.

pro·ver·bial [prə'vɜːbɪəl] ADJ proverbiale.

pro·ver·bi·al·ly [prə'vɜːbɪəlɪ] ADV proverbialmente.

pro·vide [prə'vaɪd] **1** VT **a** (*supply*) fornire; **it provides plenty of scope for development** offre molte possibilità di sviluppo; **to provide sb with sth** OR **provide sth for sb** fornire qc a qn; **to be provided with** essere dotato(-a) *or* munito(-a) di
b (*legislation*) prevedere. **2** VI: **the Lord will provide** Dio provvederà
▶ **provide for** VI + PREP **a** (*financially*) provvedere a; (: *in the future*) provvedere al futuro di
b : **the treaty does not provide for that** il trattato non lo contempla; **we have provided for that** vi abbiamo provveduto.

pro·vid·ed [prə'vaɪdɪd] CONJ: **provided (that)** sempre che + *sub*, a patto che + *sub*, purché + *sub*, a condizione che + *sub*.

provi·dence ['prɒvɪdəns] N provvidenza.

provi·den·tial [,prɒvɪ'dɛnʃəl] ADJ provvidenziale.

provi·den·tial·ly [,prɒvɪ'dɛnʃəlɪ] ADV provvidenzialmente.

pro·vid·ing [prə'vaɪdɪŋ] CONJ: **providing (that);** see **provided.**

prov·ince ['prɒvɪns] N provincia; **they live in the provinces** vivono in provincia; **it's not within my province** (*fig*) questo non rientra nel mio campo.

pro·vin·cial [prə'vɪnʃəl] **1** ADJ (*gen*) di provincia; (*pej*) provinciale. **2** N (*usu pej*) provincialotto(-a).

pro·vin·cial·ism [prə'vɪnʃə,lɪzəm] N (*pej*) provincialismo.

pro·vi·sion [prə'vɪʒən] N **a** (*supplying: of power, water*) fornitura; (: *of food*) approvvigionamento; (: *of hospitals, housing*) costruzione *f*
b (*supply*) provvista, riserva, rifornimento, scorta; **provisions** (*food*) provviste, scorte; **to get** *or* **lay in provisions** fare provviste; **provision of capital** (*Fin*) apporto di capitale
c (*preparation*): **to make provision for** (*one's family, future*) pensare a; (*journey*) fare i preparativi per
d (*stipulation*) disposizione *f*, clausola; **with the provision that** a condizione che; **there's no provision for this in the contract** il contratto non lo prevede.

Provisional ADJ, N (*Irish Pol*) provisional *m inv* (*membro dell'ala estremista dell'IRA*).

pro·vi·sion·al [prə'vɪʒənl] ADJ provvisorio(-a).

♦ **provisional licence** N (*Brit Aut*) ≈ foglio *m* rosa *inv.*

pro·vi·sion·al·ly [prə'vɪʒnəlɪ] ADV (*accept*) provvisoriamente; (*appoint*) a titolo provvisorio.

pro·vi·so [prə'vaɪzəʊ] N condizione *f*; **with the proviso that** a condizione che + *sub*, a patto che + *sub.*

pro·vi·sory [prə'vaɪzərɪ] ADJ (*provisional*) provvisorio(-a); (*Law*) condizionale.

Pro·vo ['prəʊvəʊ] N *membro dell'ala estremista dell'IRA.*

provo·ca·tion [,prɒvə'keɪʃən] N provocazione *f*; **she acted under provocation** ha agito così perché è stata provocata.

pro·voca·tive [prə'vɒkətɪv] ADJ (*causing anger*) provocatorio(-a); (*seductive*) provocante; (*thought-provoking*) stimolante.

pro·voca·tive·ly [prəˈvɒkətɪvlɪ] ADV (see adj) provocatoriamente, in modo provocatorio; in modo provocante; in modo stimolante.

pro·voke [prəˈvəʊk] VT (gen) provocare, incitare; **to provoke sb to sth/to do** or **into doing sth** spingere qn a qc/a fare qc.

pro·vok·ing [prəˈvəʊkɪŋ] ADJ irritante, esasperante.

prov·ost [ˈprɒvəst] N (Brit Univ) rettore m; (Scot) sindaco.

prow [praʊ] N prua.

prow·ess [ˈpraʊɪs] N (skill): **his prowess as a footballer** le sue capacità di calciatore.

prowl [praʊl] ① VI (also: **prowl about** or **around**) aggirarsi. ② N: **on the prowl** in cerca di preda.

prowl·er [ˈpraʊləʳ] N: **there was a prowler in the garden** c'era un tipo sospetto che si aggirava in giardino.

prox·im·ity [prɒkˈsɪmɪtɪ] N vicinanza, prossimità; **in the proximity of** in prossimità di.

proxy [ˈprɒksɪ] N (power) procura, delega; (person) mandatario(-a); **by proxy** per procura.

PRP [ˌpiːɑːˈpiː] N ABBR = performance related pay.

prude [pruːd] N puritano(-a), prude m/f.

pru·dence [ˈpruːdəns] N prudenza.

pru·dent [ˈpruːdənt] ADJ prudente.

pru·dent·ly [ˈpruːdəntlɪ] ADV prudentemente.

prud·ish [ˈpruːdɪʃ] ADJ puritano(-a), che si scandalizza facilmente.

prud·ish·ness [ˈpruːdɪʃnɪs] N puritanesimo.

prune¹ [pruːn] N (fruit) prugna (secca).

prune² [pruːn] VT (tree) potare.

prun·ing [ˈpruːnɪŋ] N potatura.

♦ **pruning knife** N falcetto.

♦ **pruning shears** NPL cesoie fpl, forbici fpl da giardiniere.

pru·ri·ence [ˈprʊərɪəns] N (unhealthy interest) curiosità morbosa, lascivia.

pru·ri·ent [ˈprʊərɪənt] ADJ (person) lascivo(-a); (interest) morboso(-a).

Prus·sia [ˈprʌʃə] N Prussia.

Prus·sian [ˈprʌʃən] ADJ, N prussiano(-a).

prus·sic acid [ˈprʌsɪkˈæsɪd] N acido prussico.

pry¹ [praɪ] VI essere troppo curioso(-a); **to pry into sb's affairs** cacciare il naso negli affari di qn.

pry² [praɪ] VT (Am) = prise.

pry·ing [ˈpraɪɪŋ] ADJ curioso(-a), indiscreto(-a).

ps. ABBR (= postscript) P.S.

psalm [sɑːm] N salmo.

psalm·ist [ˈsɑːmɪst] N salmista m.

psal·ter [ˈsɔːltəʳ] N salterio.

pseud [sjuːd] N (fam: poser) intellettualoide m/f.

pseu·do [ˈsjuːdəʊ] ADJ (fam) fasullo(-a), finto(-a).

pseudo... [ˈsjuːdəʊ] PREF pseudo... .

pseudo·bio·graph·ic, **pseudo·bio·graph·ical** [ˌsjuːdəʊˌbaɪəʊˈɡræfɪk(əl)] ADJ pseudobiografico(-a).

♦ **pseudo–intellectual** [ˌsjuːdəʊˌɪntɪˈlɛktjʊəl] ADJ, N pseudointellettuale (m/f).

pseudo·nym [ˈsjuːdəˌnɪm] N pseudonimo.

pseudo·sci·ence [ˈsjuːdəʊˌsaɪəns] N pseudoscienza.

pseudo·sci·en·tif·ic [ˌsjuːdəʊˌsaɪənˈtɪfɪk] ADJ pseudoscientifico(-a).

pso·ria·sis [sɒˈraɪəsɪs] N psoriasi f.

psyche [ˈsaɪkɪ] N (Psych) psiche f.

psychedel·ic [ˌsaɪkɪˈdɛlɪk] ADJ psichedelico(-a).

psy·chi·at·ric [ˌsaɪkɪˈætrɪk] ADJ (treatment, hospital) psichiatrico(-a); (disease, illness) mentale.

psy·chia·trist [saɪˈkaɪətrɪst] N psichiatra m/f.

psy·chia·try [saɪˈkaɪətrɪ] N psichiatria.

psy·chic [ˈsaɪkɪk] ADJ **a** (supernatural) metapsichico(-a), paranormale; (telepathic) che ha dei poteri telepatici; **you must be psychic!** (fam) devi essere un indovino! **b** (Psych) psichico(-a), della psiche.

psy·cho [ˈsaɪkəʊ] N (Am fam) folle m/f, psicopatico(-a).

psychoanalyse, (Am) **psycho·ana·lyze** [ˌsaɪkəʊˈænəˌlaɪz] VT psicanalizzare.

psy·cho·analy·sis [ˌsaɪkəʊəˈnælɪsɪs] N psicanalisi f inv.

psycho·ana·lyst [ˌsaɪkəʊˈænəlɪst] N psicanalista m/f.

psycho·ana·lyt·ic·al [ˈsaɪkəʊˌænəˈlɪtɪk(əl)] ADJ psicanalitico(-a).

psychoanalyze [ˌsaɪkəʊˈænəlaɪz] VT = psychoanalyse.

psycho·logi·cal [ˌsaɪkəˈlɒdʒɪkəl] ADJ psicologico(-a).

psycho·logi·cal·ly [ˌsaɪkəˈlɒdʒɪkəlɪ] ADV psicologicamente.

psy·cholo·gist [saɪˈkɒlədʒɪst] N psicologo(-a).

psy·chol·ogy [saɪˈkɒlədʒɪ] N psicologia.

psycho·path [ˈsaɪkəʊˌpæθ] N psicopatico(-a).

psycho·path·ic [ˌsaɪkəʊˈpæθɪk] ADJ psicopatico(-a).

psycho·physi·cal [ˌsaɪkəʊˈfɪzɪkəl] ADJ psicofisico(-a).

psycho·phys·ics [ˌsaɪkəʊˈfɪzɪks] NSG psicofisica.

psy·cho·sis [saɪˈkəʊsɪs] N (pl **psychoses** [saɪˈkəʊsiːz]) psicosi f inv.

psycho·so·mat·ic [ˌsaɪkəʊsəʊˈmætɪk] ADJ psicosomatico (-a).

psycho·thera·pist [ˌsaɪkəʊˈθɛrəpɪst] N psicoterapeuta m/f, psicoterapista m/f.

psycho·thera·py [ˌsaɪkəʊˈθɛrəpɪ] N psicoterapia.

psy·chot·ic [saɪˈkɒtɪk] ADJ, N psicotico(-a).

psych out VT + ADV (fam: frighten) intimidire.

psych up VT + ADV (fam): **to psych oneself up** caricarsi, prepararsi psicologicamente.

pt ABBR **a** = pint **b** = point.

PTA [ˌpiːtiːˈeɪ] N ABBR = parent-teacher association.

ptar·mi·gan [ˈtɑːmɪgən] N pernice f bianca.

ptero·dac·tyl [ˌtɛrəʊˈdæktɪl] N pterodattilo.

PTO [ˌpiːtiːˈəʊ] ABBR (= please turn over) v.r. (= vedi retro).

pub [pʌb] N (Brit) pub m inv.

♦ **pub-crawl** [ˈpʌbˌkrɔːl] N (Brit fam): **to go on a pub-crawl** fare il giro dei pub.

pu·ber·ty [ˈpjuːbətɪ] N pubertà.

pu·bes·cent [pjuːˈbɛsənt] ADJ (girl, boy) pubere, nell'età puberale; (age) puberale.

pu·bic [ˈpjuːbɪk] ADJ pubico(-a), del pube.

pu·bis [ˈpjuːbɪs] N pube m.

pub·lic [ˈpʌblɪk] ① ADJ (gen) pubblico(-a); (Comm: industry) statale; **in the public interest** nel pubblico interesse; **to be public knowledge** essere di pubblico dominio; **he's a public figure** OR **he's in public life** è un personaggio della vita pubblica; **this place is too public to discuss it** c'è troppa gente qui per poterne discutere; **to make sth public** render noto or di pubblico dominio qc; **to be in the public eye** essere una persona molto in vista; **her public support of** il suo aperto appoggio a; **to create more public awareness (of)** focalizzare l'attenzione del pubblico (su); **to go public** (Comm) immettere le azioni sul mercato. ② N: **the public** il pubblico; **in public** in pubblico; **the sporting/reading public** il pubblico sportivo/dei lettori.

♦ **public-address system** [ˌpʌblɪkəˈdrɛsˌsɪstəm] N impianto di amplificazione.

pub·li·can [ˈpʌblɪkən] N (Brit) gestore m (or proprietario) di un pub.

pub·li·ca·tion [ˌpʌblɪˈkeɪʃən] N pubblicazione f.

♦ **public company** N società *f inv* per azioni quotata in borsa.

♦ **public convenience** N (*Brit*) gabinetti *mpl* pubblici.

♦ **public enemy** N nemico *or* pericolo pubblico.

♦ **public holiday** N giorno festivo, festa nazionale.

♦ **public house** N (*Brit*) pub *m inv*.

pub·li·cist ['pʌblɪsɪst] N pubblicitario(-a).

pub·lic·ity [pʌb'lɪsɪtɪ] **1** N **a** pubblicità **b** (*Comm*: *advertising, advertisements*) pubblicità *f inv*, réclame *f inv*. **2** ADJ (*campaign, material, budget*) pubblicitario(-a); (*manager*) della pubblicità.

pub·li·cize ['pʌblɪ,saɪz] VT **a** (*make public*) far sapere in giro **b** (*advertise*) fare (della) pubblicità a, reclamizzare.

♦ **Public Lending Right** N *diritti d'autore sul prestito bibliotecario.*

♦ **public limited company** N ≈ società *f inv* a responsabilità limitata quotata in Borsa.

pub·lic·ly ['pʌblɪklɪ] ADV (*say, do etc*) pubblicamente; **a publicly-owned company** una società nazionalizzata.

♦ **public opinion** N opinione *f* pubblica.

♦ **public opinion poll** N sondaggio d'opinione.

♦ **public ownership** N: **to be taken into public ownership** essere statalizzato(-a).

♦ **public prosecutor** N (*Brit*) ≈ pubblico ministero; **public prosecutor's office** l'ufficio del pubblico ministero.

♦ **public relations** NPL relazioni *fpl* pubbliche.

♦ **public relations officer** N addetto(-a) alle pubbliche relazioni.

♦ **public school** N (*Brit*) scuola superiore privata; (*Am*) scuola statale.

♦ **public sector** N settore *m* pubblico.

♦ **public servant** N funzionario(-a) della pubblica amministrazione.

♦ **public service** N (*Civil Service*) amministrazione *f* pubblica.

♦ **public service vehicle** N (*Brit*) mezzo pubblico.

♦ **public speaking** N arte *f* oratoria.

♦ **public-spirited** [,pʌblɪk'spɪrɪtɪd] ADJ (*attitude*) che denota senso civico; (*act*) di civismo; (*person*) che ha senso civico.

♦ **public transport**, (*Am*) **public transportation** N mezzi *mpl* pubblici.

♦ **public utility** N servizio pubblico.

♦ **public works** NPL lavori *mpl* pubblici.

pub·lish ['pʌblɪʃ] VT pubblicare; **who publishes Moravia?** chi è l'editore di Moravia?; **"published weekly"** "edito settimanalmente", "pubblicato settimanalmente".

pub·lish·er ['pʌblɪʃə'] N (*person*) editore *m*; (*firm*) casa editrice.

pub·lish·ing ['pʌblɪʃɪŋ] N (*industry*) editoria, industria editoriale; (*of book*) pubblicazione *f*.

♦ **publishing company**, **publishing house** N casa *or* società editrice.

puce [pju:s] ADJ color pulce *inv*.

puck [pʌk] N (*Ice Hockey*) disco.

puck·er ['pʌkə'] VT (*also*: **pucker up**: *lips*) increspare; (: *brow*) aggrottare, corrugare; (: *Sewing*) increspare.

pud·ding ['pʊdɪŋ] N (*dessert*) dolce *m*, dessert *m inv*; (*steamed pudding*) *dolce cotto a bagnomaria a base di uova, burro, farina e latte*; **black pudding** [OR] (*Am*) **blood pudding** sanguinaccio; **rice pudding** budino di riso.

♦ **pudding basin** N terrina.

pud·dle ['pʌdl] N pozzanghera, pozza.

pu·er·ile ['pjʊəraɪl] ADJ puerile, infantile.

Puer·to Rico ['pwɜ:təʊ'ri:kəʊ] N Portorico.

puff [pʌf] **1** N **a** (*of breath*) soffio; (*of engine*) sbuffare *m*; (*of air, wind*) folata, soffio; (*of smoke*) sbuffo; (*of cigarette*) tiro, boccata; **I'm out of puff** (*fam*) sono senza fiato **b** (*powder puff*) piumino della cipria **c** (*Culin*): **cream puff** sfogliatina alla panna. **2** VT **a**: **to puff (out) smoke** *etc* mandar fuori fumo *etc* **b** (*also*: **puff out**: *sails, cheeks*) gonfiare; **his face was all puffed up** la sua faccia era tutta gonfia. **3** VI (*breathe heavily*) ansimare; (*blow*) soffiare; **the train puffed into the station** il treno entrò sbuffando in stazione; **to puff (away) at** *or* **on one's pipe** tirare boccate di fumo dalla pipa.

♦ **puff adder** N vipera del deserto.

puff·ball ['pʌf,bɔ:l] N (*mushroom*) vescia.

puffed ['pʌft] ADJ (*fam*: *out of breath*): **I'm puffed (out)** sono senza fiato.

puf·fin ['pʌfɪn] N pulcinella *m* di mare, puffino.

puffi·ness ['pʌfɪnɪs] N gonfiore *m*.

♦ **puff pastry**, (*Am*) **puff paste** N pasta sfoglia.

♦ **puff sleeves** NPL maniche *fpl* a sbuffo.

puffy ['pʌfɪ] ADJ (*comp* **-ier**, *superl* **-iest**) gonfio(-a).

pug [pʌg] N (*also*: **pug dog**) carlino.

pu·gi·lism ['pju:dʒɪ,lɪzəm] N (*frm*) pugilato, boxe *f*.

pu·gi·list ['pju:dʒɪlɪst] N (*frm*) pugile *m*.

pug·na·cious [pʌg'neɪʃəs] ADJ bellicoso(-a), battagliero(-a).

pug·na·cious·ly [pʌg'neɪʃəslɪ] ADV in modo battagliero.

pug·nac·ity [pʌg'næsɪtɪ] N combattività, bellicosità.

♦ **pug-nosed** [,pʌg'nəʊzd] ADJ dal naso rincagnato.

puke [pju:k] VI (*fam*) rigettare.

puk·ka ['pʌkə] ADJ (*fam*: *genuine*) originale, autentico(-a); (*excellent*) eccellente, di prim'ordine; **he's a pukka sahib** (*Brit*) è un vero gentleman.

pull [pʊl] **1** N **a** (*tug*) strattone *m*, tirata, strappo; (*of moon, magnet, the sea*) attrazione *f*; (*fig*: *attraction*: *of personality*) forza di attrazione; (: *of family ties*) forza; **I felt a pull at my sleeve** ho sentito qualcuno che mi tirava per la manica; **to give sth a pull** dare uno strattone a qc; **he has some pull with the manager** (*fam*: *influence*) ha dell'influenza sul direttore **b** (*at pipe*) boccata, tirata; (*at beer*) sorsata; **he took a pull at the bottle** ha bevuto un sorso dalla bottiglia **c** (*handle of drawer*) maniglia, pomolo; (*of bell*) cordone *m*. **2** VT **a** (*draw*: *cart*) tirare, trascinare; (: *curtains*) tirare; (: *fig*: *crowd*) attirare; **to pull a door shut/open** chiudere/aprire la porta tirandola **b** (*tug*: *handle, rope*) tirare; (*press*: *trigger*) premere; **to pull sb's hair** tirare i capelli a qn; **to pull to pieces** *or* **to bits** (*toy*) fare a pezzi; (*argument*) demolire; (*person, play*) stroncare; **to pull one's punches** (*Boxing*) risparmiare l'avversario; **she didn't pull any punches** (*fig*) non ha risparmiato nessun colpo; **to pull sb's leg** prendere in giro qn; **to pull strings (for sb)** muovere qualche pedina (per qn); **to pull one's weight** fare la propria parte, dare il proprio contributo; **to pull a face** fare una smorfia **c** (*extract, draw out*: *gen*) togliere; (: *gun, knife*) tirar fuori; (: *weeds*) strappare; (: *leeks, rhubarb*) raccogliere; (: *beer*) spillare; **to pull a gun on sb** estrarre una pistola e puntarla contro qn **d** (*tear*: *thread*) tirare; **to pull a muscle** farsi uno strappo

muscolare; **to pull a tendon** farsi uno stiramento **e** (*fam: carry out, do: robbery*) fare; **to pull a fast one on sb** combinarla a qn.

[3] VI **a** (*tug*) tirare; **to pull at sb's sleeve** tirare qn per la manica; **the car is pulling to the right** lo sterzo *or* la macchina tira a destra; **to pull at** *or* **on one's pipe** tirare boccate dalla pipa

b (*move*): **to pull for the shore** remare verso la riva; **the train pulled into/out of the station** il treno è entrato in/è partito dalla stazione; **he pulled alongside the kerb** ha accostato al marciapiede; **we pulled clear of the traffic** ci siamo lasciati il traffico alle spalle

▶ **pull about** VT + ADV (*handle roughly*: *object*) strapazzare; (: *person*) malmenare

▶ **pull along** VT + ADV trascinare; **to pull o.s. along** trascinarsi

▶ **pull apart** VT + ADV **a** (*pull to pieces*) smontare; (*break*) fare a pezzi, sfasciare; (*separate*) separare

b (*fig fam: search thoroughly*) frugare dappertutto in; (: *criticize: novel, theory*) demolire

▶ **pull away** [1] VT + ADV strappare via.

[2] VI + ADV (*move off: vehicle*) muoversi, partire; **to pull away from** (*kerb*) allontanarsi da; (*quay*) staccarsi da; (*platform*) muoversi da; (*subj: runner: competitors*) distanziare

▶ **pull back** [1] VT + ADV (*person, lever*) tirare indietro; (*curtains*) aprire.

[2] VI + ADV tirarsi indietro; (*Mil*) ritirarsi

▶ **pull down** VT + ADV

a (*gen*) tirar giù; (*opponent*) stendere a terra

b (*demolish: buildings*) demolire, buttar giù

▶ **pull in** [1] VT + ADV **a** (*rope, fishing line*) tirare su; (*Naut: sail*) cazzare; (*person: into car, room*) tirare dentro; (*stomach*) tirare in dentro

b (*rein in: horse*) trattenere

c (*attract: crowds*) attirare

d (*fam: take into custody*) mettere dentro; **the police pulled him in for questioning** la polizia l'ha fermato per interrogarlo.

[2] VI + ADV (*Aut: arrive*) arrivare; (: *stop*) fermarsi

▶ **pull off** VT + ADV **a** (*remove: wrapping paper*) strappare; (: *clothes, shoes, gloves*) levarsi, togliersi

b (*fam: succeed in: plan, attack etc*) portare a termine; **he didn't pull it off** non gli è riuscito il colpo

▶ **pull on** VT + ADV (*clothes*) mettersi

▶ **pull out** [1] VT + ADV **a** (*take out: tooth, splinter*) togliere; (: *gun, knife, person*) tirare fuori

b (*withdraw: troops, police*) (far) ritirare.

[2] VI + ADV **a** (*withdraw*) ritirarsi

b (*leave: train, car*) uscire; **he pulled out to overtake** si è spostato per sorpassare

▶ **pull over** [1] VT + ADV **a** (*box, table*): **pull it over here/there** tiralo in qua/in là; **pull it over to the window** tiralo vicino alla finestra

b (*topple*) far cascare, tirar giù.

[2] VI + ADV accostare

▶ **pull round** VI + ADV (*unconscious person*) rinvenire; (*sick person*) ristabilirsi.

▶ **pull through** [1] VT + ADV **a** tirare dall'altra parte

b (*fig*) aiutare a venirne fuori.

[2] VI + ADV (*fig*) cavarsela

▶ **pull together** [1] VT + ADV (*fig*): **to pull o.s. together** ricomporsi; **pull yourself together!** datti una mossa.

[2] VI + ADV (*make common effort*) cooperare, mettersi insieme

▶ **pull up** [1] VT + ADV **a** (*raise by pulling*) tirar su

b (*uproot: weeds*) sradicare

c (*stop: horse, car*) fermare

d (*scold*) riprendere.

[2] VI + ADV (*stop*) fermarsi

pul·let ['pʊlɪt] N pollastra, gallina giovane.

pul·ley ['pʊlɪ] N puleggia, carrucola.

Pull·man ['pʊlmən] N (*also*: **Pullman car**) pullman *m inv*.

♦ **pull-out** ['pʊl‚aʊt] [1] N inserto.

[2] ADJ staccabile.

pull·over ['pʊl‚əʊvə'] N pullover *m inv*.

pul·mo·nary ['pʌlmənərɪ] ADJ polmonare.

pulp [pʌlp] [1] N **a** (*for paper*) pasta (di legno *or* stracci etc); **to reduce sth to pulp** spappolare qc **b** (*of fruit, vegetable*) polpa **c** (*fiction*) romanzi di qualità scadente.

[2] VT (*fruit, vegetables*) spappolare; (*paper, book*) mandare al macero.

pul·pit ['pʊlpɪt] N pulpito.

pul·sar ['pʌlsə'] N pulsar *m or f inv*.

pul·sate [pʌl'seɪt] VI (*heart, blood*) pulsare; (*music*) vibrare.

pul·sat·ing [pʌl'seɪtɪŋ] ADJ pulsante.

pul·sa·tion [pʌl'seɪʃən] N pulsazione *f*.

pulse [pʌls] N (*Anat*) polso; (*Phys*) impulso; (*fig: of drums, music*) vibrazione *f*; **to feel** *or* **take sb's pulse** sentire *or* tastare il polso a qn.

♦ **pulse rate** N (*Med*) (numero di) pulsazioni *fpl*.

pulses ['pʌlsɪz] NPL (*Culin*) legumi *mpl* secchi.

pul·ver·ize ['pʌlvə‚raɪz] VT (*also fig*) polverizzare.

puma ['pju:mə] N puma *m inv*.

pum·ice ['pʌmɪs] N (*also*: **pumice stone**) (pietra) pomice *f*.

pum·mel ['pʌml] VT prendere a pugni.

pum·mel·ling ['pʌməlɪŋ] N scarica di pugni.

pump¹ [pʌmp] [1] N pompa; **petrol pump** distributore *m* (di benzina).

[2] VT **a** pompare; **to pump sth dry** prosciugare qc con una pompa; **to pump air into a tyre** gonfiare uno pneumatico; **to pump money into a project** immettere capitali in un progetto; **to pump sb for information** cercare di strappare delle informazioni a qn

b (*handle*) alzare e abbassare vigorosamente; **to pump sb's hand up and down** dare una vigorosa stretta di mano a qn

▶ **pump in** VT + ADV (*water*) far passare (con una pompa); (*foam into walls*) iniettare; (*fig: money*) immettere

▶ **pump out** VT + ADV pompare fuori; **to pump out sb's stomach** fare la lavanda gastrica a qn

▶ **pump up** VT + ADV (*tyre*) gonfiare.

pump² N (*sports shoe*) scarpa da ginnastica; (*dancing shoe*) scarpetta da ballo; (*slip-on shoe*) ballerina.

pump·kin ['pʌmpkɪn] N zucca.

♦ **pumpkin pie** N torta di zucca.

pump·kin·seed ['pʌmpkɪn‚si:d] N seme *m* di zucca.

pun [pʌn] N gioco di parole.

Punch [pʌntʃ] N Pulcinella *m*; **Punch and Judy show** spettacolo di burattini.

punch¹ [pʌntʃ] [1] N **a** (*for making holes*: *in metal, leather*) punzonatrice *f*; (: *in paper*) perforatore *m*; (: *in tickets*) pinza per forare; (*for stamping metal*) punzone *m*

b (*blow*) pugno; (*fig: vigour*) mordente *m*, forza.

[2] VT **a** (*with tool: gen*) punzonare; (: *ticket*) forare; **to punch a hole in sth** forare qc

b (*with fist*): **to punch sb/sth** dare un pugno a qn/qc; **to punch a ball** colpire una palla con un pugno; **to punch sb's nose** dare un pugno sul naso a qn

▶ **punch in** VI + ADV (*Am*) timbrare il cartellino (all'entrata)

▶ **punch out** VI + ADV (*Am*) timbrare il cartellino (all'uscita).

punch² [pʌntʃ] N (*drink*) punch *m inv*, ponce *m inv*.

punch·ball ['pʌntʃ,bɔːl] N punching ball *m inv*.

punch·bowl ['pʌntʃ,bəʊl] N grande coppa da punch.

♦ **punch-drunk** [,pʌntʃ'drʌŋk] ADJ (*Boxing*) groggy; (*fig: stupefied*) stordito(-a).

punched card [,pʌntʃt'kɑːd], (*esp Am*) **punch card** N (*Comput*) scheda perforata.

punch·ing bag ['pʌntʃɪŋ,bæg] N (*Am*) = **punchball.**

♦ **punch line** N (*of joke*) battuta finale; (*of story*) finale *m*.

♦ **punch-up** ['pʌntʃ,ʌp] N (*Brit fam*) scazzottata, rissa.

punchy ['pʌntʃɪ] ADJ (*comp* **-ier**, *superl* **-iest**) (*fam*) **a** (*prose, writing, article*) incisivo(-a) **b** (*punch-drunk: person*) stordito(-a).

punc·tili·ous [pʌŋk'tɪlɪəs] ADJ scrupoloso(-a), meticoloso (-a).

punc·tili·ous·ly [pʌŋk'tɪlɪəslɪ] ADV scrupolosamente, meticolosamente.

punc·tili·ous·ness [pʌŋk'tɪlɪəsnɪs] N scrupolosità, meticolosità.

punc·tu·al ['pʌŋktjʊəl] ADJ (*person*) puntuale; (*train*) in orario.

punc·tu·al·ity [,pʌŋktjʊ'ælɪtɪ] N puntualità.

punc·tu·al·ly ['pʌŋktjʊəlɪ] ADV (*see adj*) puntualmente; in orario; **it will start punctually at 6** comincerà alle 6 precise *or* in punto.

punc·tu·ate ['pʌŋktjʊ,eɪt] VT (*Gram*) mettere la punteggiatura a *or* in; **his speech was punctuated by bursts of applause** il suo discorso fu ripetutamente interrotto da scrosci di applausi.

punc·tua·tion [,pʌŋktjʊ'eɪʃən] N (*Gram*) punteggiatura, interpunzione *f*.

♦ **punctuation mark** N segno d'interpunzione.

punc·ture ['pʌŋktʃəʳ] ① N (*in tyre*) foratura; (*in balloon*) foratura, bucatura; (*in skin*) puntura; **I have a puncture** (*Aut*) ho forato (una gomma).

② VT bucare, forare.

③ VI bucarsi, forarsi.

pun·dit ['pʌndɪt] N (*iro*) esperto(-a), sapientone(-a).

pun·gen·cy ['pʌndʒənsɪ] N (*see adj*) asprezza; acredine *f*; sapore *m* piccante; causticità.

pun·gent ['pʌndʒənt] ADJ (*smell, taste*) pungente, aspro (-a); (*smoke*) acre; (*sauce*) piccante; (*remark, satire*) caustico(-a), mordace.

pun·gent·ly ['pʌndʒəntlɪ] ADV (*gen*) aspramente; (*seasoned*) in modo piccante; (*remark*) causticamente.

pun·ish ['pʌnɪʃ] VT **a** : **to punish sb for sth/for doing sth** punire qn per qc/per aver fatto qc **b** (*fig fam: car*) mettere a dura prova; (: *horse*) sfiancare; (: *opposition*) dare una bella batosta a; (: *meal, bottle of whisky*) far fuori.

pun·ish·able ['pʌnɪʃəbl] ADJ punibile.

pun·ish·ing ['pʌnɪʃɪŋ] ① ADJ (*fig: exhausting*) sfiancante.

② N punizione *f*.

pun·ish·ment ['pʌnɪʃmənt] N **a** (*punishing*) punizione *f*, castigo; (*penalty*) pena; **to take one's punishment** subire il castigo; **to make the punishment fit the crime** punire secondo il reato **b** (*fig fam*): **to take a lot of punishment** (*boxer*) incassare parecchi colpi; (*car*) essere messo(-a) a dura prova; (*furniture*) essere maltrattato(-a).

pu·ni·tive ['pjuːnɪtɪv] ADJ (*action, measures*) punitivo(-a).

Pun·ja·bi [pʌn'dʒɑːbɪ] ① N **a** abitante *m/f* or nativo(-a) del Punjab **b** (*language*) lingua parlata nel Punjab.

② ADJ del Punjab.

punk [pʌŋk] N **a** (*person: also:* **punk rocker**) punk *m/f inv*; (*music: also:* **punk rock**) musica punk, punk rock *m* **b** (*Am fam: hoodlum*) teppista *m*.

pun·net ['pʌnɪt] N cestello; **a punnet of strawberries** un cestino di fragole.

punt¹ [pʌnt] ① N (*boat*) barchino; (*Ftbl*) calcio al volo.

② VT (*boat*) spingere con la pertica; (*ball*) calciare al volo.

③ VI: **to go punting** andare in barchino.

punt² [pʌnt] N (*in Ireland*) sterlina irlandese.

punt·er ['pʌntəʳ] N (*Brit fam: gambler*) scommettitore(-trice); (: *customer*) cliente *m/f*.

puny ['pjuːnɪ] ADJ (*comp* **-ier**, *superl* **-iest**) (*person*) gracile, striminzito(-a); (*effort*) penoso(-a).

pup [pʌp] N (*dog*) cagnolino(-a), cucciolo(-a); (*seal*) cucciolo(-a).

pupa ['pjuːpə] N (*pl* **pupae** ['pjuːpiː]) pupa.

pu·pil¹ ['pjuːpl] N (*Scol*) allievo(-a), scolaro(-a).

pu·pil² ['pjuːpl] N (*Anat*) pupilla.

♦ **pupil power** N potere *m* studentesco.

pup·pet ['pʌpɪt] N (*glove puppet*) burattino; (*string puppet*) marionetta; (*fig*) burattino, fantoccio.

pup·pet·eer [pʌpɪ'tɪəʳ] N burattinaio(-a).

♦ **puppet government** N governo *m* fantoccio *inv*.

♦ **puppet show** N spettacolo di burattini (*or* di marionette).

pup·py ['pʌpɪ] N cucciolo(-a), cagnolino(-a).

♦ **puppy fat** N pinguedine *f* infantile.

♦ **puppy love** N infatuazione *f* giovanile.

pur·chase ['pɜːtʃɪs] ① N **a** (*act*) acquisto; (*thing purchased*) acquisto, compera **b** (*grip*) presa; **to get a purchase on** trovare un appoggio su.

② VT (*frm*) acquistare, comprare.

♦ **purchase order** N ordine *m* d'acquisto, ordinazione *f*.

♦ **purchase price** N prezzo d'acquisto.

pur·chas·er ['pɜːtʃɪsəʳ] N acquirente *m/f*, compratore(-trice).

♦ **purchase tax** N (*Brit*) imposta sugli acquisti.

pur·chas·ing pow·er ['pɜːtʃɪsɪŋ,paʊəʳ] N potere *m* d'acquisto.

pure [pjʊəʳ] ADJ (*comp* **-r**, *superl* **-st**) puro(-a); **the pure in heart** i puri di cuore; **as pure as the driven snow** innocente come un bambino; **a pure wool jumper** un golf di pura lana; **pure mathematics** matematica pura; **it's laziness pure and simple** è pura pigrizia; **by pure chance** per puro caso.

pure·bred ['pjʊə,bred] ADJ di razza pura.

pu·rée ['pjʊəreɪ] ① N purè *m inv*, purea.

② VT schiacciare, passare.

pure·ly ['pjʊəlɪ] ADV puramente.

pure·ness ['pjʊənɪs] N = **purity.**

pur·ga·tive ['pɜːgətɪv] ① N (*Med*) purgante *m*.

② ADJ purgativo(-a).

pur·ga·tory ['pɜːgətərɪ] N (*Rel, fig*) purgatorio.

purge [pɜːdʒ] ① N (*gen, Med*) purga; (*Pol*) epurazione *f*, purga.

② VT **a** (*Med*) purgare; (*Pol*): **to purge (of)** epurare (da); **to purge one's sins** espiare i propri peccati; **to purge o.s. of sth** liberarsi da qc **b** (*Law: offence, crime*) espiare.

pu·ri·fi·ca·tion [,pjʊərɪfɪ'keɪʃən] N (*see vb*) depurazione *f*; purificazione *f*.

pu·rifi·ca·tory [,pjʊərɪfɪ'keɪtərɪ] ADJ purificatorio(-a).

pu·ri·fi·er ['pjʊərɪ,faɪəʳ] N (*see vb*) depuratore *m*.

pu·ri·fy ['pjʊərɪ,faɪ] VT (*water, air*) depurare; (*person*)

purificare.

pur·ist ['pjʊərɪst] N purista *m/f.*

pu·ri·tan ['pjʊərɪtən] ADJ, N puritano(-a).

pu·ri·tani·cal [,pjʊərɪ'tænɪkəl] ADJ puritano(-a).

pu·ri·tan·ism ['pjʊərɪtən,ɪzəm] N puritanesimo.

pu·rity ['pjʊərɪtɪ] N purezza.

purl [pɜːl] ①N (maglia *or* punto a) rovescio. ②VT lavorare a rovescio.

pur·loin [pɜː'lɔɪn] VT (*frm*) sottrarre, rubare.

pur·ple ['pɜːpl] ①ADJ viola *inv*; **to go purple (in the face)** diventare paonazzo(-a), farsi di porpora. ②N (*colour*) viola *m inv*; (*Rel*): **the purple** la porpora.

♦ **Purple Heart** N (*Am*) *medaglia per ferite riportate in battaglia.*

♦ **purple heart** N (*fam*) pillola di amfetamina.

♦ **purple patch, purple passage** N brano ornato.

pur·port [*n* 'pɜːpət; *vb* pɜː'pɔːt] ①N significato, senso generale. ②VT: **to purport to be/do** pretendere di essere/fare.

pur·pose ['pɜːpəs] N ⓐ (*intention*) scopo, intenzione *f*; (*use*) uso; **she has a purpose in life** ha uno scopo nella vita; **for our purposes** per i nostri scopi; **for teaching purposes** per l'insegnamento; **for the purposes of this meeting** agli effetti di questa riunione; **for all practical purposes** a tutti gli effetti pratici, in pratica; **on purpose** di proposito, apposta; **for illustrative purposes** a titolo illustrativo; **to the purpose** a proposito, pertinente; **with the purpose of** con il proposito di; **to some purpose** con qualche risultato; **to no purpose** senza nessun risultato, inutilmente; **to good purpose** con buoni risultati ⓑ (*resolution, determination*): **sense of purpose** risolutezza.

♦ **purpose–built** ['pɜːpəs,bɪlt] ADJ (*Brit*) costruito(-a) appositamente.

pur·pose·ful ['pɜːpəsfʊl] ADJ deciso(-a), risoluto(-a).

pur·pose·ful·ly ['pɜːpəsfəlɪ] ADV con uno scopo preciso, deliberatamente.

pur·pose·ly ['pɜːpəslɪ] ADV di proposito, apposta.

purr [pɜːˀ] ①N (*of cat*) le fusa *fpl.* ②VI far le fusa.

purse [pɜːs] ①N (*for money*) borsellino, portamonete *m inv*; (*Am: handbag*) borsetta, borsa; (*esp Sport: prize*) montepremi *m inv.* ②VT: **to purse one's lips** increspare le labbra.

purs·er ['pɜːsəˀ] N (*Naut*) commissario di bordo.

♦ **purse snatch·er** ['pɜːs,snætʃəˀ] N (*Am*) scippatore *m.*

♦ **purse strings** NPL: **to hold the purse strings** (*fig*) tenere i cordoni della borsa.

pur·sue [pə'sjuː] VT ⓐ (*chase*) inseguire; (: *pleasures*) andare in cerca di; (*subj: bad luck*) perseguitare ⓑ (*carry on: studies*) proseguire; (: *career*) intraprendere; (: *inquiry, matter*) portare avanti; (: *plan*) andare avanti con.

pur·su·er [pə'sjuːəˀ] N inseguitore(-trice).

pur·suit [pə'sjuːt] N ⓐ (*chase*) inseguimento; (*fig: of pleasure, happiness, knowledge*) ricerca; **in (the) pursuit of sb** all'inseguimento di qn; **in (the) pursuit of sth** alla ricerca di qc; **with two policemen in hot pursuit** con due poliziotti alle calcagna ⓑ (*occupation*) attività *f inv*, occupazione *f*; (*pastime*) svago, passatempo; **scientific pursuits** ricerche *fpl* scientifiche.

pur·vey·or [pɜː'veɪəˀ] N (*frm*) fornitore(-trice).

pus [pʌs] N pus *m inv.*

push [pʊʃ] ①N ⓐ (*shove*) spinta, spintone *m*; **to give sb/sth a push** dare una spinta a qn/qc; **to give sb the push** (*Brit fam*) dare il benservito a qn ⓑ (*drive, aggression*) iniziativa, energia ⓒ (*effort*) grande sforzo; (*Mil: offensive*) offensiva ⓓ (*fam*): **at a push** in caso di necessità; **if *or* when it comes to the push** al momento critico. ②VT ⓐ (*shove, move by pushing*) spingere; (*press: button*) schiacciare, premere; **to push a door open/shut** aprire/ chiudere una porta con una spinta *or* spingendola; **he pushed it into my hands** me lo ha cacciato in mano; **the accident pushed everything else out of my mind** l'incidente mi ha fatto dimenticare tutto il resto ⓑ (*fig: press, advance: views*) imporre; (: *claim*) far valere; (: *product*) spingere le vendite di; (: *candidate*) appoggiare; **to push home an advantage** sfruttare a fondo un vantaggio; **to push home an attack** portare a conclusione un attacco; **to push drugs** spacciare droga; **don't push your luck!** (*fam*) non sfidare la fortuna! ⓒ (*fig: put pressure on*): **to push sb into doing sth** costringere qn a fare qc; **to push sb to do sth** spingere qn a fare qc; **don't push her too far** non esigere troppo da lei; **that's pushing it a bit** (*fam*) è un po' troppo; **to be pushed for time/money** essere a corto di tempo/soldi; **I'm hard pushed to understand how ...** mi riesce difficile capire come...; **I'm really pushed today** oggi non ho un minuto di tempo. ③VI spingere; **to push for** (*better pay, conditions*) fare pressione per ottenere; **to push past sb** spingere qn per passare; **to push into a room** entrare in una stanza facendosi largo; **"push"** (*on door*) "spingere"; (*on bell*) "suonare"

▶ **push about, push around** VT + ADV (*fig fam: bully*) fare il prepotente con

▶ **push ahead** VI + ADV: **to push ahead (with sth)** andare avanti (con qc)

▶ **push aside** VT + ADV spingere da parte, scostare; (*fig: suggestions*) scartare; (: *problems*) accantonare

▶ **push away** VT + ADV respingere

▶ **push back** VT + ADV (*blankets*) spingere via, buttare all'indietro; (*curtains*) aprire; (*lock of hair*) ricacciare all'indietro; (*enemy forces*) respingere

▶ **push down** ①VI + ADV: **to push down on** schiacciare, premere. ②VT + ADV (*switch, knob*) abbassare, tirare giù; (*knock over: fence, person*) buttare giù

▶ **push forward** ①VI + ADV (*Mil*) avanzare. ②VT + ADV spingere in avanti; **he tends to push himself forward** (*fig*) cerca sempre di mettersi in mostra

▶ **push in** ①VT + ADV ⓐ (*person*) spingere dentro; (*stick, rag: into hole*) ficcare dentro, cacciare dentro; **to push sb in(to) the water** spingere qn in acqua; **she pushed her way in** è entrata facendosi largo ⓑ (*break: door etc*) sfondare. ②VI + ADV introdursi a forza

▶ **push off** ①VT + ADV (*gen*) buttare giù; (*lid, top*) spingere via; **he pushed me off the wall** mi ha spinto giù dal muretto. ②VI + ADV ⓐ (*in boat*) prendere il largo ⓑ (*fam: leave*) filare, smammare

▶ **push on** ①VI + ADV (*with journey*) continuare; (*with job*) perseverare. ②VT + ADV (*fig: incite, urge on*) spronare, spingere

▶ **push out** VT + ADV (*car, person*) spingere fuori; (*cork*) far uscire

▶ **push over** VT + ADV **a** (*over cliff etc*) spingere giù; **to push sth over the edge** spingere qc oltre il bordo
  b (*knock over*) far cadere

▶ **push through** **1** VT + ADV **a** (*gen*) spingere dall'altra parte; **to push one's way through** farsi largo
  b (*force acceptance of: decision*) far accettare; (: *Parliament: bill*) riuscire a far votare.
  2 VI + ADV farsi strada, farsi largo; (*troops*) aprirsi un varco; **to push through a crowd** farsi largo *or* aprirsi un varco tra la folla

▶ **push to** VT + ADV (*door*) socchiudere

▶ **push up** VT + ADV **a** spingere in su
  b (*fig: raise, increase*) far salire.

♦ **push-bike** ['puʃˌbaɪk] N (*Brit*) bicicletta.

♦ **push-button** ['puʃˌbʌtn] ADJ a tastiera; **push-button warfare** guerra dei bottoni.

push·chair ['puʃˌtʃɛəʳ] N (*Brit*) passeggino.

push·er ['puʃəʳ] N (*fam*) **a** (*also:* **drug pusher**) spacciatore (-trice) (di droga) **b** (*ambitious person*) arrivista *m/f*.

push·ing ['puʃɪŋ] **1** PREP (*fam: almost*) quasi; **she is pushing 50** (*fam*) va per i 50.
  2 ADJ (*enterprising*) intraprendente; (*pej*) arrivista.

push·over ['puʃˌəʊvəʳ] N (*fam*): **it's a pushover** è un gioco da ragazzi; **she's a pushover** si lascia convincere facilmente.

♦ **push-up** ['puʃˌʌp] N (*Am*) flessione *f* sulle braccia.

pushy ['puʃɪ] ADJ (*comp* **-ier**, *superl* **-iest**) (*fam pej*) troppo intraprendente.

pu·sil·lani·mous [ˌpjuːsɪˈlænɪməs] ADJ pusillanime.

puss [pʊs], **pus·sy** ['pʊsɪ] N (*fam*) micio(-a).

pussy·cat ['pʊsɪˌkæt] N = **puss**.

pussy·foot ['pʊsɪˌfʊt] VI (*fam pej*) tentennare.

♦ **pussy willow** ['pʊsɪˌwɪləʊ] N salicone *m*.

put [pʊt] (*pt, pp* **put**) **1** VT **a** (*place*) mettere; posare, metter giù; **we put the children to bed** abbiamo messo a letto i bambini; **my brother put me on the train** mio fratello mi ha messo sul treno; **to put the ball in the net** mandare la palla in rete; **to put sth to one's ear** avvicinarsi qc all'orecchio; **she put her head on my shoulder** appoggiò la testa sulla mia spalla; **to put one's signature to sth** apporre la propria firma a qc; **to put a lot of time into sth** dedicare molto tempo a qc; **she has put a lot into her marriage** ha fatto molto per la riuscita del suo matrimonio; **to put money into a company** investire *or* mettere dei capitali in un'azienda; **to put money on a horse** scommettere su un cavallo
  b (*thrust, direct*) cacciare; **he put his finger right in my eye** mi ha cacciato un dito nell'occhio; **I put my fist through the window** sfondai la finestra con il pugno; **to put one's pen through sth** cancellare qc con un frego; **he put his head round the door** fece capolino dalla porta; **to put the shot** (*Sport*) lanciare il peso
  c (*cause to be*): **to put sb in a good/bad mood** mettere qn di buon/cattivo umore; **to put sb in charge of sth** incaricare qn di qc; **to put sb to a lot of trouble** dare un sacco da fare a qn; **I put her to answering the phone** le ho dato l'incarico di rispondere al telefono; **he put her to work immediately** l'ha messa subito al lavoro
  d (*express*) esprimere, dire; **let me put it another way** te lo spiego in un altro modo; **how shall I put it?** come dire?; **let me put it this way** diciamo così; **as Dante puts it** come dice Dante; **to put it bluntly** per parlar chiaro; **put it to him gently** diglielo senza spaventarlo; **to put sth into French** tradurre qc in francese; **to put the words to music** mettere in musica *or* musicare le parole

  e (*expound: case, problem*) esporre, presentare; **I put it to you that ...** io sostengo che...; **to put a question to sb** rivolgere una domanda a qn
  f (*estimate*) valutare, stimare; **what would you put it at?** quanto pensi che valga?; **I'd put his age at 40** direi che ha 40 anni.
  2 VI (*Naut*): **to put to sea** prendere il mare; **to put into port** entrare in porto.
  3 ADV: **to stay put** (*fam*) non muoversi

▶ **put about** **1** VT + ADV (*circulate: news, rumour*) mettere in giro.
  2 VI + ADV (*Naut*) virare di bordo, invertire la rotta

▶ **put across** VT + ADV **a** (*communicate: ideas, opinion*) comunicare, far capire; (: *new product*) propagandare; **she can't put herself across** non sa far valere le sue doti
  b (*fam: play trick*): **to put one across on sb** darla a bere a qn

▶ **put aside** VT + ADV **a** (*lay down: book, game*) mettere da una parte, posare
  b (*save*) mettere da parte; (*in shop*) tenere da parte
  c (*fig: abandon: idea, hope, doubt*) mettere da parte, dimenticare

▶ **put away** VT + ADV **a** (*clothes, toys, dishes*) mettere via, riporre
  b = **put aside b**
  c (*fam: consume: food, drink*) far fuori
  d (*fam: lock up in prison*) mettere dentro; (: *in mental hospital*) rinchiudere

▶ **put back** **1** VT + ADV **a** (*replace*) rimettere (a posto)
  b (*postpone*) rimandare, rinviare; (*slow down: production*) rallentare; (*set back: watch, clock*) mettere indietro; **this will put us back 10 years** questo ci farà tornare indietro di 10 anni; **you can't put the clock back** (*fig*) non si può tornare indietro.
  2 VI + ADV (*Naut*) rientrare (in porto)

▶ **put by** VT + ADV = **put aside a, b**

▶ **put down** **1** VT + ADV **a** (*set down*) mettere giù, posare; (*passenger*) far scendere; **I couldn't put that book down** (*fig*) non riuscivo a smettere di leggere quel libro
  b (*lower: umbrella*) chiudere; (: *car roof*) abbassare
  c (*crush: revolt*) reprimere; (: *gambling, prostitution*) abolire; (: *rumour*) mettere a tacere; (*humiliate*) mortificare
  d (*pay: deposit*) versare
  e (*destroy: pet*) abbattere
  f (*write down*) scrivere; **to put sth down in writing** mettere qc per iscritto; **put it down on my account** (*Comm*) me lo addebiti *or* metta in conto; **put me down for £15** segnami *or* mettimi in lista per 15 sterline; **he's put his son down for Harrow** ha iscritto suo figlio nella lista d'attesa per Harrow
  g (*classify*) considerare; **I'd put her down as about forty** le darei una quarantina d'anni; **I put him down as a troublemaker** lo considero un elemento disturbatore
  h (*attribute*): **to put sth down to sth** attribuire qc a qc.
  2 VI + ADV (*Aer*) atterrare

▶ **put forward** VT + ADV **a** (*propose: gen*) proporre; (: *theory*) avanzare; (: *opinion*) esprimere
  b (*advance: date, meeting, function*) anticipare; (: *clock*) mettere avanti

▶ **put in** **1** VT + ADV **a** (*place inside: drawer, bag*) metter dentro
  b (*insert: in book, speech*) aggiungere, inserire
  c (*interpose: remark*) fare; **she put in her piece** ha detto

la sua

d (*enter: application, complaint*) presentare; **to put in a plea of not guilty** (*Law*) dichiararsi innocente; **to put sb in for an exam** presentare qn a un esame; **to put sb in for an award** proporre qn per un premio

e (*install: central heating*) mettere, installare

f (*Pol: elect*) eleggere

g (*devote, expend: time*) passare, dedicare; **to put in a few extra hours** fare qualche ora in più; **to put in a good day's work** fare una bella giornata di lavoro.

2 VI + ADV (*Naut*) fare scalo

▶ **put in for** VI + ADV + PREP (*job*) far domanda per; (*promotion*) far domanda di

▶ **put off** VT + ADV **a** (*set down: passenger*) far scendere

b (*postpone, delay: match, decision*) rimandare, rinviare; (*: guest*) chiedere di rimandare la visita; **to put off doing sth** rimandare qc a più tardi; **to put sb off with an excuse** liberarsi di qn con una scusa

c (*discourage*) far passare la voglia a; **to put sb off their food** far passare a qc la voglia di mangiare

d (*repel: smell*) disgustare

e (*switch off*) spegnere

▶ **put on** VT + ADV **a** (*clothes, lipstick, shoes*) mettere, mettersi

b (*assume: accent, manner*) affettare; (*: airs*) darsi; (*fam: kid, have on: esp Am*) prendere in giro; **to put on airs** darsi delle arie; **to put on an innocent expression** assumere un'aria innocente; **she's just putting it on** sta solo facendo finta

c (*add, increase: speed, pressure*) aumentare; **to put on weight** aumentare di peso, ingrassare

d (*concert, exhibition*) allestire, organizzare; (*play*) mettere in scena; (*extra bus, train*) mettere in servizio

e (*on telephone*): **put me on to Mr Strong please** mi passi il signor Strong per favore

f (*switch on: light etc*) accendere; (*kettle, meal*) metter su; **to put on the brakes** frenare

g (*inform, indicate*): **to put sb on to sb/sth** indicare qn/qc a qn; **she put us on to you** è lei che ci ha detto di rivolgerci a te; **who put the police on to him?** chi lo ha segnalato alla polizia?; **what put you on to it?** cosa te lo ha fatto capire?

▶ **put out** **1** VT + ADV **a** (*place outside*) mettere fuori; **to put clothes out to dry** stendere la biancheria ad asciugare; **to be put out** (*asked to leave*) essere buttato (-a) fuori; **she couldn't put him out of her head** non riusciva a non pensare a lui

b (*stretch out: arm, foot, leg*) allungare; (*: one's hand*) porgere; (*tongue*) tirare fuori; (*push out: leaves etc*) spuntare; **to put one's head out of the window** metter fuori *or* sporgere la testa dalla finestra

c (*lay out in order*) disporre

d (*circulate: propaganda*) fare; (*: news*) annunciare; (*: rumour*) mettere in giro; (*bring out: new book*) pubblicare; (*: regulation*) emettere

e (*extinguish: fire, cigarette, light*) spegnere

f (*discontent, vex*) contrariare, seccare; **to be put out by sth/sb** essere contrariato(-a) da qn/qc

g (*inconvenience*): **to put o.s. out (for sb)** scomodarsi *or* disturbarsi per qn

h (*dislocate: shoulder, knee*) lussarsi; (*: back*) farsi uno strappo a

i (*subcontract*) subappaltare.

2 VI + ADV (*Naut*): **to put out to sea** prendere il largo; **to put out from Plymouth** partire da Plymouth

▶ **put over** VT + ADV = **put across**

▶ **put through** VT + ADV **a** (*complete: business, deal*) concludere; (*have accepted: reform, bill*) far approvare, far passare

b (*Telec: connect: caller*) mettere in comunicazione; (*call*) passare; **put me through to Miss Blair** mi passi la signorina Blair

▶ **put together** VT + ADV **a** mettere insieme, riunire; **she is worth more than all the others put together** vale più lei da sola che tutte le altre messe insieme

b (*assemble: furniture*) montare; (*: model*) fare; (*: essay*) comporre; (*: meal*) improvvisare; (*: evidence*) raccogliere; (*: team*) mettere insieme, formare

▶ **put up** **1** VT + ADV **a** (*raise, lift up: hand*) alzare; (*: umbrella*) aprire; (*: collar*) rialzare; (*hoist: flag, sail*) issare; **put 'em up!** (*fam: hands: in surrender*) arrenditi!; (*: in robbery*) mani in alto!; (*: fists: to fight*) forza, difenditi!

b (*fasten up*): **to put up (on)** attaccare (su), appendere (su); (*notice*) affiggere (su)

c (*erect: building, barrier, fence*) costruire, erigere; (*: tent*) montare

d (*send up: space probe, missile*) lanciare, mettere in orbita

e (*increase*) aumentare

f = **put forward a**

g (*offer*): **to put sth up for sale** mettere in vendita qc; **they put up a struggle** hanno opposto resistenza

h (*give accommodation to*) ospitare

i (*provide: money, funds*) fornire; (*: reward*) offrire

j (*incite*): **to put sb up to doing sth** istigare qn a fare qc.

2 VI + ADV **a** : **to put up (at)** (*at hotel*) alloggiare (in); (*: for the night*) pernottare (in)

b (*offer o.s.*): **to put up (for)** presentarsi come candidato(-a) (per)

▶ **put upon** VI + PREP: **to be put upon** (*imposed on*) farsi mettere sotto i piedi

▶ **put up with** VI + ADV + PREP sopportare; **she has a lot to put up with** ha un sacco di problemi.

pu·ta·tive ['pjuːtətɪv] ADJ (*frm*): **the putative father** il padre putativo.

pu·tre·fac·tion [ˌpjuːtrɪ'fækʃən] N putrefazione *f*.

pu·tre·fy ['pjuːtrɪˌfaɪ] VI putrefarsi.

pu·tre·fy·ing ['pjuːtrɪˌfaɪɪŋ] ADJ putrescente.

pu·trid ['pjuːtrɪd] ADJ putrido(-a); **to turn putrid** putrefarsi.

putsch [pʊtʃ] N putsch *m inv*, colpo di Stato.

putt [pʌt] **1** N (*Golf*) putting *m*.

2 VT (*ball*) colpire leggermente.

put·ter[1] ['pʌtəʳ] N (*Golf*) putter *m inv*.

put·ter[2] ['pʌtəʳ] VI (*Am*) = **potter**.

putt·ing ['pʌtɪŋ] N (*game*) un tipo di golf; **putting green** green *m inv*.

put·ty ['pʌtɪ] N (*for windows*) stucco, mastice *m* da vetrai; **to be putty in sb's hands** (*fig*) essere come la creta nelle mani di qn.

◆ **put-up** ['pʊtˌʌp] ADJ: **put-up job** (*fam*) montatura.

◆ **put-you-up** ['pʊtjuːˌʌp] N poltrona *f* (*or* divano *m*) letto *inv*.

puz·zle ['pʌzl] **1** N **a** (*game*) rompicapo; (*word game*) rebus *m inv*; (*crossword*) parole *fpl* incrociate, cruciverba *m inv*; (*riddle*) indovinello; (*jigsaw puzzle*) puzzle *m inv*

b (*mystery*) enigma *m*, mistero; **it's a puzzle to me how it happened** non so come sia successo, per me resta un enigma.

2 VT lasciar perplesso(-a)

▶ **puzzle out** VT + ADV (*problem*) risolvere; (*mystery, person, attitude*) capire; (*writing, instructions*) decifrare; (*answer, solution*) trovare; **I'm trying to puzzle out why** sto cercando di scoprire il perché

▶ **puzzle over, puzzle about** VT + ADV (*sb's actions*) cercare di capire; (*mystery, problem*) cercare di risolvere.

puz·zled ['pʌzld] ADJ perplesso(-a); **to be puzzled about sth** domandarsi il perché di qc.

puz·zle·ment ['pʌzlmənt] N perplessità.

puz·zler ['pʌzlə'] N mistero, enigma *m*.

puz·zling ['pʌzlɪŋ] ADJ (*question*) poco chiaro(-a); (*attitude, set of instructions*) incomprensibile.

PVC [ˌpiːviːˈsiː] N ABBR (= *polyvinyl chloride*) PVC.

p.w. [ˌpiːˈdʌblju:] ABBR = *per week*.

pyg·my ['pɪgmɪ] N pigmeo(-a).

py·ja·mas, (*Am*) **pa·jam·as** [pəˈdʒɑːməz] NPL pigiama *msg*; **a pair of pyjamas** un pigiama; **in one's pyjamas** in pigiama.

py·lon ['paɪlən] N pilone *m*.

pyra·mid ['pɪrəmɪd] N piramide *f*.

py·rami·dal [pɪˈræmɪdl] ADJ piramidale.

pyre ['paɪə'] N pira.

Pyr·enean [pɪrəˈniːən] ADJ pirenaico(-a), dei Pirenei.

Pyr·enees [pɪrəˈniːz] NPL: **the Pyrenees** i Pirenei.

Py·rex® ['paɪrɛks] N pirex ® *m inv*.

◆ **Pyrex dish** N pirofila.

pyro... ['paɪrəʊ] PREF piro... .

pyro·clasts [ˌpaɪrəʊˈklæsts] NPL materiali *mpl* piroclastici.

py·roly·sis [paɪˈrɒlɪsɪs] N pirolisi *f*.

pyro·ma·nia [ˌpaɪrəʊˈmeɪnɪə] N piromania.

pyro·ma·ni·ac [ˌpaɪrəʊˈmeɪnɪæk] N piromane *m/f*.

pyro·tech·nics [ˌpaɪrəʊˈtɛknɪks] N **a** (*sg: Phys*) pirotecnica **b** (*pl: fireworks display*) spettacolo *msg* pirotecnico.

Pythagoras [paɪˈθægərəs] N Pitagora *m*; **Pythagoras' theorem** teorema *m* di Pitagora.

py·thon ['paɪθən] N pitone *m*.

Q

Q, q [kju:] N (*letter*) Q, q *f or m inv*; **Q for Queen** ≈ Q come Quarto.

Qa·tar [kæ'tɑ:ʳ] N il Qatar *m*.

QC [ˌkju:'si:] N ABBR (*Brit*: = *Queen's Counsel*) *avvocato della Corona*.

QED [ˌkju:i:'di:] ABBR (= *quod erat demonstrandum*) q.e.d.

QM [ˌkju:'ɛm] N ABBR = **quartermaster**.

q.t. [kju:'ti:] N ABBR (*fam*)= *quiet*; **on the q.t.** di nascosto.

qty ABBR = **quantity**.

qua [kwɑ:] PREP (*frm*) in quanto.

quack¹ [kwæk] 1 N (*of duck*) qua qua *m inv*.
2 VI fare qua qua.

quack² [kwæk] N (*pej: bogus doctor*) ciarlatano(-a); (*hum: doctor*) dottore(-essa).

quad [kwɒd] N ABBR = **quadrangle b, quadruplet**.

Quad·ra·gesi·ma [ˌkwɒdrə'dʒɛsɪmə] N (*also:* **Quadragesima Sunday**) domenica di quadragesima.

quad·ran·gle ['kwɒdˌræŋgl] N **a** (*Math*) quadrangolo, quadrilatero **b** (*courtyard*) cortile *m* (*di collegio, scuola*).

quad·rant ['kwɒdrənt] N quadrante *m*.

quad·rat·ic [kwɒ'drætɪk] ADJ (*equation*) di secondo grado, quadratico(-a).

quad·ri·lat·er·al [ˌkwɒdrɪ'lætərəl] ADJ quadrilatero(-a).

quad·ri·no·mial [ˌkwɒdrɪ'nəʊmɪəl] N quadrinomio.

quad·ro·phon·ic [ˌkwɒdrə'fɒnɪk] ADJ quadrifonico(-a); **in quadrophonic sound** in quadrifonia.

quad·ru·ped ['kwɒdrʊˌpɛd] N quadrupede *m*.

quad·ru·ple ['kwɒdrʊpl] 1 ADJ quadruplo(-a), quadruplice.
2 VT quadruplicare.
3 VI quadruplicarsi.
4 N quadruplo.

quad·ru·plet [kwɒ'dru:plɪt] N uno(-a) di quattro gemelli.

quaff [kwɑ:f] VT (*old*) tracannare.

quag·mire ['kwæɡˌmaɪəʳ] N pantano; (*fig*) caos *m inv*.

quail¹ [kweɪl] N (*bird*) quaglia.

quail² [kweɪl] VI (*flinch*): **to quail at** *or* **before** perdersi d'animo davanti a.

quaint [kweɪnt] ADJ (*comp* **-er**, *superl* **-est**) (*odd*) strano(-a), bizzarro(-a); (*picturesque*) pittoresco(-a); (*old-fashioned*)

antiquato(-a) e pittoresco(-a).

quaint·ly ['kweɪntlɪ] ADV (*see adj*) in modo strano; in modo bizzarro; pittorescamente.

quake [kweɪk] 1 VI: **to quake (with)** tremare (di).
2 N (*earthquake*) terremoto.

Quak·er ['kweɪkəʳ] N quacchero(-a).

quali·fi·ca·tion [ˌkwɒlɪfɪ'keɪʃən] N **a** : **qualifications** NPL (*gen*) qualifiche *fpl*, requisiti *mpl*; (*paper qualifications*) titoli *mpl* di studio; **what are your qualifications?** quali sono le sue qualifiche?; (*paper qualifications*) quali sono i suoi titoli di studio?; **I've got a teaching qualification** sono abilitato *or* ho l'abilitazione all'insegnamento
b (*reservation*) riserva, restrizione *f*; **without qualification(s)** senza condizioni *or* riserve.

quali·fied ['kwɒlɪˌfaɪd] ADJ **a** (*engineer, doctor, teacher*) abilitato(-a); (*nurse*) diplomato(-a); **qualified for/to do** qualificato(-a) per/per fare; **he's not qualified for the job** non ha i requisiti necessari per questo lavoro
b (*support*) condizionato(-a); (*acceptance*) con riserva; **it was a qualified success** è stato un successo parziale; **the film has received qualified praise** il film non è stato accolto proprio favorevolmente.

quali·fi·er ['kwɒlɪˌfaɪəʳ] N (*Gram*) aggettivo qualificativo; (*Sport*) chi si è qualificato(-a).

quali·fy ['kwɒlɪˌfaɪ] 1 VT **a** (*make competent*) qualificare; **his experience in South Africa qualified him to speak on apartheid** la sua esperienza in Sudafrica lo autorizzava a parlare dell'apartheid
b (*modify*) modificare; (: *support, approval*) porre delle condizioni a
c (*Gram*) qualificare.
2 VI (*professionally*) abilitarsi, essere abilitato(-a); (*in competition*) qualificarsi; (*be eligible*) avere i requisiti necessari; **to qualify as an engineer** diventare un perito tecnico; (*with degree*) laurearsi in ingegneria; **to qualify for a job** avere i requisiti necessari per un lavoro; **he hardly qualifies as a major dramatist** non si può certamente definirlo un grande drammaturgo.

quali·fy·ing ['kwɒlɪˌfaɪɪŋ] ADJ (*Gram*) qualificativo(-a); (*exam*) di ammissione; (*round*) eliminatorio(-a).

quali·ta·tive ['kwɒlɪtətɪv] ADJ qualitativo(-a).

qual·ity ['kwɒlɪtɪ] [1] N qualità *f inv*; **of good quality** di buona qualità; **of poor quality** scadente.
[2] ADJ di qualità.

♦ **quality control** N controllo (di) qualità.

♦ **quality of life** N qualità *f inv* della vita.

♦ **quality papers** NPL, **quality press** N (*Brit*) stampa *fsg* d'informazione.

qualm [kwɑ:m] N (*often pl*: *fear*) apprensione *f*; (: *scruple*) scrupolo, esitazione *f*; **to have qualms about sth** avere degli scrupoli per qc.

quan·da·ry ['kwɒndərɪ] N: **to be in a quandary (about sth)** essere molto incerto(-a) (su qc).

quango ['kwæŋgəʊ] N ABBR (*Brit*: = *quasi-autonomous nongovernmental organization*) *organizzazione autonoma di nomina governativa, dotata di fondi, che agisce in vari settori (salute, scuola ecc).*

quan·ti·fi·able ['kwɒntɪfaɪəbl] ADJ quantificabile.

quan·ti·fy ['kwɒntɪˌfaɪ] VT quantificare.

quan·ti·ta·tive ['kwɒntɪtətɪv] ADJ quantitativo(-a).

quan·ti·ta·tive·ly ['kwɒntɪtətɪvlɪ] ADV quantitativamente.

quan·tity ['kwɒntɪtɪ] N quantità *f inv*; (*Comm*) quantità, quantitativo; **in quantity** in grande quantità.

♦ **quantity discount** N sconto sulla quantità.

♦ **quantity surveyor** N geometra *m* (*che valuta il costo del materiale e della manodopera necessari per una costruzione*).

quan·tum ['kwɒntəm] (*Phys*) [1] N quanto.
[2] ADJ (*number*) quantico(-a); (*mechanics*) quantistico (-a).

♦ **quantum leap** N (*fig*) enorme cambiamento.

♦ **quantum theory** N (*Phys*) teoria quantistica *or* dei quanti.

quar·an·tine ['kwɒrəntiːn] [1] N quarantena; **in quarantine** in quarantena.
[2] VT mettere in quarantena.

quark [kwɑːk] N (*Phys*) quark *m inv*.

quar·rel ['kwɒrəl] [1] N (*argument*) litigio, lite *f*; **to have a quarrel with sb** litigare con qn; **to pick a quarrel (with sb)** attaccar briga (con qn); **I've no quarrel with him** non ho niente contro di lui.
[2] VI: **to quarrel (with sb about *or* over sth)** litigare (con qn per qc); **they quarrelled about *or* over money** hanno litigato per i soldi; **I can't quarrel with that** non ho niente da ridire su questo.

quar·relling, (*Am*) **quar·rel·ing** ['kwɒrəlɪŋ] N litigi *mpl*.

quar·rel·some ['kwɒrəlsəm] ADJ litigioso(-a).

quar·ry¹ ['kwɒrɪ] N (*Hunting*, *fig*) preda.

quar·ry² ['kwɒrɪ] [1] N (*mine*) cava.
[2] VT cavare.

quarry·man ['kwɒrɪmən] N (*pl* -men) cavapietre *m inv*.

♦ **quarry-tiled** ['kwɒrɪˌtaɪld] ADJ (*floor*) di quadrelli.

quart [kwɔːt] N quarto di gallone (*Brit* = *1,136 litri; Am* = *0,964 litri*).

quar·ter ['kwɔːtə'] [1] N **a** (*fourth part*) quarto; (*of year*) trimestre *m*; **a quarter (of a pound) of tea** ≈ un etto di tè; **a quarter of a century** un quarto di secolo; **to divide sth into quarters** dividere qc in quattro (parti); **to pay by the quarter** pagare trimestralmente
b (*Am, Canada*: *25 cents*) quarto di dollaro, 25 centesimi
c (*time*): **a quarter of an hour** un quarto d'ora; **an hour and a quarter** un'ora e un quarto; **it's a quarter to *or* (*Am*) of 3** sono le 3 meno un quarto, manca un quarto alle 3; **it's a quarter past *or* (*Am*) after 3** sono le 3 e un

quarto
d (*district*) quartiere *m*
e (*direction*): **from all quarters** da tutte le parti *or* direzioni; **at close quarters** a distanza ravvicinata; **you won't get any help from that quarter** non otterrai nessun aiuto da quella parte
f : **quarters** NPL (*accommodation*) alloggio; (*Mil*) quartiere *m*; (: *temporary*) alloggiamento
g : **to give sb no quarter** essere implacabile verso qn.
[2] VT **a** (*divide into four*) dividere in quattro (parti)
b (*Mil*) alloggiare.

quarter·back ['kwɔːtəˌbæk] N (*American football*) quarterback *m inv*.

♦ **quarter-deck** ['kwɔːtəˌdɛk] N (*Naut*) cassero.

quarter·final ['kwɔːtəˌfaɪnl] N quarti *mpl* di finale.

quar·ter·ing ['kwɔːtərɪŋ] N (*Mil*) accantonamento.

quar·ter·ly ['kwɔːtəlɪ] [1] ADJ trimestrale.
[2] N periodico trimestrale.
[3] ADV trimestralmente.

quarter·master ['kwɔːtəˌmɑːstə'] N (*Mil*) furiere *m*; (*Naut*) timoniere *m*.

quar·tet, quar·tette [kwɔː'tɛt] N quartetto.

quar·tile ['kwɔːtaɪl] N quartile *m*.

quar·to ['kwɔːtəʊ] ADJ in quarto.

quartz [kwɔːts] [1] N quarzo.
[2] ADJ di quarzo; (*clock, watch*) al quarzo.

quartz·ite ['kwɔːtsaɪt] N quarzite *f*.

qua·sar ['kweɪzɑː'] N (*Astron*) quasar *f inv*.

quash [kwɒʃ] VT **a** (*reject*) respingere; (: *Law*: *sentence, conviction*) revocare, annullare **b** (*destroy*: *enemies, rebellion*) stroncare; (: *emotion*) reprimere.

quasi- ['kwɑːzɪ] PREF semi...; (*pej*) pseudo...; **quasi-official** ADJ semiufficiale; **quasi-religious** ADJ quasi religioso(-a); **quasi-revolutionary** ADJ, N pseudorivoluzionario(-a).

qua·ver ['kweɪvə'] [1] N (*when speaking*) tremolio; (*Brit Mus*: *note*) croma.
[2] VI (*voice*) tremare, tremolare.

qua·ver·ing ['kweɪvərɪŋ] ADJ (*voice*) tremulo(-a), tremolante.

quay [kiː] N molo, banchina.

quay·side ['kiːˌsaɪd] N banchina.

quea·si·ness ['kwiːzɪnɪs] N nausea.

quea·sy ['kwiːzɪ] ADJ (*comp* -ier, *superl* -iest) (*stomach*) nauseato(-a); **to feel queasy** avere la nausea.

Que·bec [kwɪ'bɛk] N il Quebec *m*.

queen [kwiːn] N regina; (*Cards, Chess*) regina, donna; **Queen Elizabeth** la regina Elisabetta.

♦ **queen bee** N ape *f* regina *inv*.

queen·ly ['kwiːnlɪ] ADJ regale, da regina.

♦ **queen mother** N regina madre.

♦ **Queen's speech** N (*Brit*): **the Queen's speech** *discorso redatto dal primo ministro e letto dalla regina in occasione della sessione d'apertura del parlamento.*

queer [kwɪə'] [1] ADJ (*comp* -er, *superl* -est) **a** (*odd*) strano(-a), curioso(-a), singolare; **he's a queer customer** è un tipo strano; **there's something queer going on here** qui c'è qualcosa che non va; **queer in the head** (*fam*) tocco(-a), picchiato(-a)
b (*ill*) strano(-a), non giusto(-a); **to feel queer** sentirsi poco bene
c (*fam offensive*: *homosexual*) omosessuale
d (*suspicious*) dubbio(-a), sospetto(-a).
[2] N (*old fam offensive*: *male homosexual*) finocchio.
[3] VT: **to queer sb's pitch** (*fam*) rovinare tutto a qn, rompere le uova nel paniere a qn.

♦ **queer-bashing** ['kwɪə‚bæʃɪŋ] N (*fam offensive*) *atti di violenza contro gli omosessuali.*

queer·ly ['kwɪəlɪ] ADV stranamente.

queer·ness ['kwɪənɪs] N stranezza.

quell [kwɛl] VT (*passion*) reprimere; (*fear*) dominare; (*rebellion*) soffocare; (*attempt*) sventare.

quench [kwɛntʃ] VT (*thirst*) togliere, levare; (*flames*) spegnere; **to quench one's thirst** dissetarsi.

queru·lous ['kwɛrʊləs] ADJ querulo(-a).

queru·lous·ly ['kwɛrʊləslɪ] ADV in tono querulo.

que·ry ['kwɪərɪ] **1** N (*question*) domanda; (*question mark*) punto interrogativo; (*fig: doubt*) interrogativo, dubbio.
2 VT **a** (*ask*): **to query sb about sth** rivolgere delle domande a qn riguardo a qc **b** (*doubt*) mettere in dubbio; (*disagree with, dispute*) sollevare (dei) dubbi su, contestare.

quest [kwɛst] N ricerca; **in quest of** alla ricerca di, in cerca di.

ques·tion ['kwɛstʃən] **1** N **a** (*enquiry*) domanda; **to ask sb a question** OR **put a question to sb** fare una domanda a qn
b (*matter, issue*) questione *f*, argomento; **it is an open question** ... resta da vedere se..., è una questione aperta se...; **the question is** ... il problema è...; **the person/night in question** la persona/la notte in questione; **it is a question of whether** ... si tratta di sapere se...; **it's a question of doing** ... si tratta di fare...; **that is not the question** non è questo il problema; **there is no question of outside help** non c'è nessuna possibilità di aiuto esterno; **there can be no question of your resigning** che lei dia le dimissioni non è nemmeno da prendersi in considerazione; **it's out of the question** è fuori discussione; **there's some question of closing the shop** c'è chi suggerisce di chiudere il negozio
c (*doubt*): **beyond** *or* **past question** fuori discussione *or* questione; **in question** in discussione, in dubbio; **there is no question about it** su questo non c'è (assolutamente) nessun dubbio; **to bring** *or* **call sth into question** mettere in dubbio qc.
2 VT **a** (*interrogate: person*) interrogare
b (*doubt*) mettere in dubbio, dubitare di; **I question whether it is worthwhile** mi domando se ne vale *or* valga la pena.

ques·tion·able ['kwɛstʃənəbl] ADJ discutibile.

ques·tion·er ['kwɛstʃənə'] N interrogante *m/f*.

ques·tion·ing ['kwɛstʃənɪŋ] **1** ADJ (*mind*) inquisitore(-trice), indagatore(-trice); (*expression*) interrogativo(-a).
2 N interrogatorio.

♦ **question mark** N punto interrogativo.

♦ **question master** N presentatore *m* (*di un quiz*).

ques·tion·naire [‚kwɛstʃə'nɛə'] N questionario.

queue [kju:] **1** N coda, fila; **to form a queue** mettersi in fila *or* in coda; **to stand in a queue** essere in fila *or* in coda, fare la fila *or* la coda; **to jump the queue** passare davanti agli altri (*in coda*).
2 VI (*also:* **queue up**) fare la fila, fare la coda.

quib·ble ['kwɪbl] **1** N cavillo, sottigliezza.
2 VI cavillare, sottilizzare.

quiche [ki:ʃ] N quiche *f inv*.

quick [kwɪk] **1** ADJ (*comp* **-er**, *superl* **-est**) (*fast: in motion*) veloce, rapido(-a); (*: in time*) svelto(-a), veloce; (*agile: reflexes*) pronto(-a); (*: in mind*) svelto(-a); **a quick temper** un temperamento irascibile; **the quickest method** il metodo più rapido; **a quick reply** una risposta pronta; **be quick about it!** fa' presto!, sbrigati!; **she was quick to**

see that ... ha visto subito che...; **to be quick to act** agire prontamente; **to be quick to take offence** essere permaloso(-a), offendersi subito; **do you fancy a quick one?** (*fam: drink*) andiamo a bere qualcosa?.
2 ADV in fretta, rapidamente; **come quick!** vieni subito!; **as quick as a flash** *or* **as lightning** veloce come un fulmine.
3 N: **to cut sb to the quick** pungere qn sul vivo.

quick·en ['kwɪkən] **1** VT affrettare, accelerare; (*fig: feelings*) stimolare; **to quicken one's pace** affrettare *or* allungare il passo.
2 VI: **the pace quickened** il ritmo divenne più veloce.

♦ **quick fix** N soluzione *f* tampone *inv*.

♦ **quick-freeze** [‚kwɪk'fri:z] VT sottoporre a congelamento rapido.

quickie ['kwɪkɪ] N (*fam*) cosa fatta velocemente; (*question*) domanda veloce; **do you fancy a quickie?** (*drink*) andiamo a bere qualcosa?

quick·lime ['kwɪk‚laɪm] N calce *f* viva.

quick·ly ['kwɪklɪ] ADV velocemente, rapidamente; **"certainly not" she said quickly** "certo che no" disse velocemente; **we must act quickly** dobbiamo agire tempestivamente.

quick·ness ['kwɪknɪs] N velocità, rapidità; (*of mind, intellect*) prontezza; (*of eye*) acutezza.

quick·sand ['kwɪk‚sænd] N sabbie *fpl* mobili.

quick·silver ['kwɪk‚sɪlvə'] N argento vivo, mercurio.

quick·step ['kwɪk‚stɛp] N (*dance*) quick step *m inv*.

♦ **quick-tempered** [‚kwɪk'tɛmpəd] ADJ che si arrabbia facilmente.

♦ **quick-witted** [‚kwɪk'wɪtɪd] ADJ sveglio(-a).

♦ **quick-wittedly** [‚kwɪk'wɪtɪdlɪ] ADV (*act, answer*) prontamente.

quid [kwɪd] N (*Brit fam: pl inv*) sterlina.

quid pro quo [‚kwɪdprəʊ'kwəʊ] N (*reciprocal exchange*) contraccambio; **his promotion was the quid pro quo for his support** venne promosso in cambio del suo appoggio.

qui·es·cent [kwɪ'ɛsənt] (*frm*) ADJ (*person: passive*) passivo (-a); (*: quiet*) tranquillo(-a); (*symptoms, disease, problem*) latente; **in a quiescent state** allo stato latente; **quiescent minorities** le minoranze per ora silenziose.

qui·et ['kwaɪət] **1** ADJ (*comp* **-er**, *superl* **-est**) **a** (*person: silent*) silenzioso(-a), tranquillo(-a); (*: reserved*) quieto (-a), taciturno(-a); (*: calm*) tranquillo(-a), calmo(-a); **be quiet!** OR **keep quiet!** silenzio!, sta' zitto!; (*when moving about*) non far rumore!, fa' piano!; **to keep sb quiet** tener tranquillo(-a) qn; **they paid him £1,000 to keep him quiet** gli hanno dato 1.000 sterline perché stesse zitto
b (*not noisy: engine*) silenzioso(-a); (*: music, voice, laugh*) sommesso(-a); (*: sound*) basso(-a), leggero(-a)
c (*not busy: day*) calmo(-a), tranquillo(-a); (*: place*) tranquillo(-a); **the shops/trains are always quiet on a Monday** i negozi/treni non sono mai affollati di lunedì; **business is quiet at this time of year** questa è la stagione morta
d (*discreet: manner*) dolce, garbato(-a); (*: colours*) tenue, smorzato(-a); (*: humour*) garbato(-a); (*private, intimate*) intimo(-a); **I'll have a quiet word with him** gli dirò due parole in privato; **to lead a quiet life** fare una vita tranquilla; **he managed to keep the whole thing quiet** è riuscito a tener segreta tutta la faccenda; **we had a quiet wedding** abbiamo avuto un matrimonio semplice.

[2] N (*silence*) silenzio; (*calm*) pace *f*, calma, tranquillità; **on the quiet** (*fam: act*) di nascosto; (: *tell*) in confidenza.
[3] VT (*Am*) = **quieten 1**.

qui·et·en ['kwaɪətən] [1] VT (*also:* **quieten down**) calmare, placare.
[2] VI (*also:* **quieten down**) calmarsi.

qui·et·ly ['kwaɪətlɪ] ADV (*softly, silently*) silenziosamente, senza far rumore; (*not loudly: speak, sing*) in modo sommesso; (*calmly*) tranquillamente, con calma; **to be quietly dressed** essere vestito(-a) in modo sobrio; **to be quietly situated** (*house*) trovarsi in un posto tranquillo; **let's get married quietly** sposiamoci con una cerimonia semplice; **he slipped off quietly to avoid being noticed** se n'è andato alla chetichella per non essere notato.

qui·et·ness ['kwaɪətnɪs] N (*silence*) silenzio; (*peacefulness*) tranquillità, calma, quiete *f*; (*softness: of voice, music*) dolcezza.

quill [kwɪl] N (*feather*) penna; (*pen*) penna d'oca; (*of porcupine*) aculeo.

quilt [kwɪlt] [1] N (*traditional*) trapunta; (*continental quilt*) piumino.
[2] VT trapuntare.

quilt·ed ['kwɪltɪd] ADJ trapuntato(-a).

quilt·ing ['kwɪltɪŋ] N (*material*) stoffa trapuntata; (*craft*) trapunto.

quin [kwɪn] N ABBR = **quintuplet**.

quince [kwɪns] N (*fruit*) (mela) cotogna; (*tree*) cotogno.
♦ **quince jelly** N cotognata.

qui·nine [kwɪ'niːn] N chinino.

quin·tes·sence [kwɪn'tɛsns] N (*frm*) quintessenza.

quin·tes·sen·tial [,kwɪntɪ'sɛnʃəl] ADJ (*frm*) per eccellenza; **the quintessential Renaissance man** l'uomo rinascimentale per eccellenza.

quin·tet, quin·tette [kwɪn'tɛt] N quintetto.

quin·tu·plet [kwɪn'tjuːplɪt] N uno(-a) di cinque gemelli.

quip [kwɪp] N battuta di spirito.

quire ['kwaɪəʳ] N ventesima parte di una risma; (*Bookbinding*) segnatura di 16 pagine.

quirk [kwɜːk] N (*oddity*) stranezza, bizzarria; **by some quirk of fate** per un capriccio della sorte.

quirky ['kwɜːkɪ] ADJ (*comp* **-ier**, *superl* **-iest**) stravagante, capriccioso(-a).

quis·ling ['kwɪzlɪŋ] N (*old*) collaborazionista *m/f*.

quit [kwɪt] (*vb: pt, pp* **quit** *or* **quitted**) [1] VT **a** (*cease: work*) lasciare, piantare; **to quit doing sth** smettere di fare qc; **quit stalling!** (*Am fam*) non tirarla per le lunghe!
b (*leave: place*) lasciare; **notice to quit** (*Brit*) preavviso (*dato all'inquilino*).
[2] VI (*resign*) dare le dimissioni, dimettersi; (*give up: in game*) abbandonare, mollare; (*accept defeat*) darsi per vinto(-a).
[3] ADJ: **quit of** sbarazzato(-a) di, liberato(-a) di.

quite [kwaɪt] ADV **a** (*rather*) abbastanza, piuttosto; **I quite like that idea** è un'idea che non mi dispiace; **quite a few of them** non pochi di loro; **quite a few people** un bel po'

di gente; **she's quite pretty** è piuttosto carina; **he's quite a good writer** è uno scrittore abbastanza bravo
b (*completely*) proprio, perfettamente; (*entirely*) completamente, del tutto; **quite new** proprio nuovo (-a); **quite (so)!** appunto!, proprio (così)!, precisamente!; **that's quite enough** è più che abbastanza, basta così; **that's not quite right** non è proprio esatto; **I can quite believe that** ... non faccio fatica a credere che...; **not quite as many as last time** non proprio così tanti come l'ultima volta; **I quite understand** capisco perfettamente.

Qui·to ['kiːtəʊ] N Quito *f*.

quits [kwɪts] ADV: **to be quits (with sb)** essere pari (con qn); **let's call it quits** adesso siamo pari.

quit·ter ['kwɪtəʳ] N rinunciatario(-a).

quiv·er¹ ['kwɪvəʳ] N (*for arrows*) faretra, turcasso.

quiv·er² ['kwɪvəʳ] VI (*person, voice, lips*): **to quiver (with)** tremare (per *or* da).

quix·ot·ic [kwɪk'sɒtɪk] ADJ (*frm*) donchisciottesco(-a).

quix·oti·cal·ly [kwɪk'sɒtɪkəlɪ] ADV (*frm*) alla don Chisciotte.

quiz [kwɪz] [1] N (*game*) quiz *m inv*.
[2] VT (*old*): **to quiz sb about** interrogare qn su.

quiz·master ['kwɪz,mɑːstəʳ] N (*TV, Radio*) presentatore *m* (*di quiz*).

quiz·zi·cal ['kwɪzɪkəl] ADJ (*glance*) interrogativo(-a) (e beffardo(-a)).

quiz·zi·cal·ly ['kwɪzɪkəlɪ] ADV con aria interrogativa (e beffarda).

quoit [kɔɪt] N anello (*per il gioco degli anelli*); **to play quoits** giocare agli anelli.

quor·um ['kwɔːrəm] N quorum *m inv*.

quo·ta ['kwəʊtə] N quota.

quo·ta·tion [kwəʊ'teɪʃən] N **a** (*words*) citazione *f* **b** (*estimate*) preventivo; (*of shares*) quotazione *f*.
♦ **quotation marks** NPL (*Typ*) virgolette *fpl*; **in quotation marks** tra virgolette.

quote [kwəʊt] [1] VT **a** (*words, author*) citare; **can you quote me an example?** puoi citarmi *or* farmi un esempio?
b (*Comm: sum, figure, price*) indicare, fissare; (*shares*) quotare; **to quote for a job** dare un preventivo per un lavoro; **the figure quoted for the repairs** il preventivo per le riparazioni.
[2] VI: **to quote from** citare; **and I quote** (*from text*) cito testualmente; (*sb's words*) riferisco *or* ripeto testualmente; **quote ...unquote** (*in dictation*) aprire le virgolette... chiudere le virgolette; (*in lecture, report*) cito... fine della citazione.
[3] N **a** = **quotation 1**
b : **quotes** NPL (*inverted commas*) virgolette *fpl*; **in quotes** tra virgolette.

quoth [kwəʊθ] VT: **quoth he** disse.

quo·tient ['kwəʊʃənt] N quoziente *m*.

R

R, r [ɑːʳ] N (*letter*) R, r *f or m inv*; **the three Rs** leggere, scrivere e far di conto; **R for Robert**, (*Am*) **R for Roger** ≈ R come Roma.

RA [,ɑːrˈeɪ] ① N ABBR (*Brit*)= *Royal Academy, Royal Academician.*

② ABBR = **rear admiral.**

RAAF [,ɑːreɪeɪˈɛf] N ABBR = *Royal Australian Air Force.*

Ra·bat [rəˈbɑːt] N Rabat *f.*

rab·bi [ˈræbaɪ] N rabbino.

rab·bit [ˈræbɪt] ① N coniglio; **doe rabbit** coniglia.

② VI: **to rabbit (on)** (*Brit fam*) blaterare.

♦ **rabbit hole** N tana di coniglio.

♦ **rabbit hutch** N conigliera.

rabble [ˈræbl] N confusione *f* di gente; **the rabble** (*pej*) il popolino, la plebaglia.

♦ **rabble-rouser** [ˈræbəlraʊzəʳ] N agitatore(-trice).

rab·id [ˈræbɪd] ADJ (*dog*) idrofobo(-a), rabbioso(-a); (*fig*: *furious*) arrabbiato(-a); (: *fanatical*) fanatico(-a).

ra·bies [ˈreɪbiːz] N rabbia, idrofobia.

♦ **rabies virus** N virus *m inv* rabbico.

RAC [,ɑːreɪˈsiː] N ABBR (*Brit*: = *Royal Automobile Club*) ≈ A.C.I. *m* (= *Automobile Club d'Italia*).

rac·coon [rəˈkuːn] N procione *m*, orsetto lavatore.

race¹ [reɪs] ① N (*competition, rush*) corsa; **the 100 metres race** la corsa sui 100 metri, i 100 metri (piani); **a race against time** una corsa contro il tempo; **the arms race** la corsa agli armamenti.

② VT **a** (*horse*) far gareggiare, far correre

b (*person*) correre contro, gareggiare contro; **I'll race you around the block** ti sfido a una corsa intorno all'isolato

c (*engine*) imballare.

③ VI **a** : **to race (against sb)** correre (contro qn)

b (*rush*) correre; **to race in/out** *etc* precipitarsi dentro/fuori *etc*; **he raced across the road** ha attraversato la strada di corsa

c (*pulse*) battere precipitosamente; (*engine*) imballarsi.

race² [reɪs] ① N razza; **the human race** l'umanità.

② ADJ (*hatred, riot*) razziale.

♦ **race car** N (*Am*) = **racing car.**

♦ **race car driver** N (*Am*) = **racing driver.**

race·course [ˈreɪsˌkɔːs] N ippodromo.

race·horse [ˈreɪsˌhɔːs] N cavallo da corsa.

♦ **race relations** NPL rapporti *mpl* fra le razze.

race·track [ˈreɪsˌtræk] N (*for horses, Aut*) pista.

ra·cial [ˈreɪʃəl] ADJ (*tension*) razziale; (*harmony, equality*) fra le razze.

♦ **racial discrimination** N discriminazione *f* razziale.

ra·cial·ism [ˈreɪʃəˌlɪzəm] N (*Brit old*) razzismo.

ra·cial·ist [ˈreɪʃəlɪst] ADJ, N razzista (*m/f*).

rac·ing [ˈreɪsɪŋ] ① N corsa; (*horse-racing*) corse *fpl.*

② ADJ (*cycle*) da corsa.

♦ **racing car** N (*Brit*) macchina da corsa.

♦ **racing driver** N (*Brit*) corridore *m* automobilista.

♦ **racing stables** NPL scuderia di cavalli da corsa.

♦ **racing yacht** N yacht *m inv* da competizione.

rac·ism [ˈreɪsɪzəm] N razzismo.

rac·ist [ˈreɪsɪst] ADJ, N razzista (*m/f*).

rack¹ [ræk] ① N **a** (*storage framework*) rastrelliera; (*for luggage*) rete *f* portabagagli *m inv*; (*for hats, coats*) appendiabiti *m inv*; (*in shops*) scaffale *m*; **magazine rack** portariviste *m inv*; **shoe rack** scarpiera; **toast rack** portatoast *m inv*

b (*for torture*) cavalletto.

② VT (*subj: pain, cough*) torturare, tormentare; **racked by remorse** roso(-a) dal rimorso; **to rack one's brains** scervellarsi

▶ **rack up** VT + ADV accumulare.

rack² [ræk] N: **to go to rack and ruin** (*building*) andare in rovina; (*business*) andare in malora *or* a catafascio; (*country*) andare a catafascio; (*person*) lasciarsi andare completamente.

♦ **rack-and-pinion** [,rækənˈpɪnjən] N (*Tech*) rocchetto *m* cremagliera *inv.*

rack·et¹ [ˈrækɪt] N (*for tennis*) racchetta.

rack·et² [ˈrækɪt] N **a** (*din*) baccano, fracasso **b** (*organised fraud*) traffico, racket *m inv*; (*swindle*) imbroglio, truffa; **he's on to quite a racket** (*fam*) gli sta andando bene con il suo giochetto.

rack·et·eer [,rækɪˈtɪəʳ] N (*esp Am*) trafficante *m/f.*

rack·et·eer·ing [ˌrækəˈtɪərɪŋ] N traffici *mpl.*
♦ **racket press** N (*Tennis*) tendiracchetta *m inv.*
rack·ing [rækɪŋ] ADJ (*pain*) atroce.
rac·on·teur [ˌrækɒnˈtɜː] N narratore(-trice).
ra·coon [rəˈkuːn] N = raccoon.
rac·quet [ˈrækɪt] N = racket[1].
racy [ˈreɪsɪ] ADJ (*comp* -ier, *superl* -iest) (*style*) spigliato(-a), brioso(-a); (*humour, talk*) un po' spinto(-a).
RADA [ˈrɑːdə] N ABBR (*Brit*)= Royal Academy of Dramatic Art.
ra·dar [ˈreɪdaː] ▢1 N radar *m inv.*
   ▢2 ADJ (*station, screen*) radar *inv.*
♦ **radar operator** N radarista *m/f.*
♦ **radar trap** N (*Aut*) multanova ® *m.*
ra·dial [ˈreɪdɪəl] ADJ (*also:* **radial-ply:** *tyre*) radiale.
ra·dian [ˈreɪdɪən] N radiante *m.*
ra·di·ance [ˈreɪdɪəns] N (*brilliance*) splendore *m*, fulgore *m*; (*fig*) radiosità.
ra·di·ant [ˈreɪdɪənt] ADJ (*Phys: heat*) radiante; (*light*) sfolgorante; (*fig*): **radiant (with)** raggiante (di).
ra·di·ant·ly [ˈreɪdɪəntlɪ] ADV (*smile*) radiosamente; **to be radiantly happy** essere raggiante di gioia.
ra·di·ate [ˈreɪdɪˌeɪt] ▢1 VT (*heat*) irraggiare, irradiare; (*fig: happiness*) irraggiare.
   ▢2 VI: **to radiate from** irraggiarsi da, irradiarsi da.
ra·dia·tion [ˌreɪdɪˈeɪʃən] N (*nuclear*) radiazione *f*; (*of heat*) irradiamento.
♦ **radiation sickness** N malattia da radiazioni.
♦ **radiation treatment** N (*Med*) radioterapia.
ra·dia·tor [ˈreɪdɪeɪtəʳ] N radiatore *m.*
♦ **radiator cap** N (*Aut*) tappo del radiatore.
♦ **radiator grill** N (*Aut*) mascherina, calandra.
radi·cal [ˈrædɪkəl] ▢1 ADJ radicale.
   ▢2 N **a** (*person*) radicale *m/f* **b** (*Math, Chem*) radicale *m.*
radi·cal·ism [ˈrædɪkəˌlɪzəm] N radicalismo.
radi·cal·ize [ˈrædɪkəlaɪz] VT (*frm*) radicalizzare.
radi·cal·ly [ˈrædɪkəlɪ] ADV radicalmente.
radi·cle [ˈrædɪkəl] N **a** (*Bot*) radichetta **b** (*Math, Chem*) = **radical b.**
ra·dii [ˈreɪdɪˌaɪ] NPL of **radius.**
ra·dio [ˈreɪdɪəʊ] ▢1 N (*Telec*) radio *f*; (*radio set*) radio *f inv*, apparecchio *m* radio *inv*; **by radio** per radio; **on the radio** alla radio.
   ▢2 VI: **to radio to sb** comunicare via radio con qn.
   ▢3 VT (*information*) trasmettere per radio; (*one's position*) comunicare via radio; (*person*) chiamare via radio.
   ▢4 ADJ (*programme*) radiofonico(-a); (*frequency*) radio *inv.*
radio... [ˈreɪdɪəʊ] PREF radio... .
radio·ac·tive [ˌreɪdɪəʊˈæktɪv] ADJ radioattivo(-a).
radio·ac·tiv·ity [ˌreɪdɪəʊækˈtɪvɪtɪ] N radioattività.
♦ **radio alarm** N radiosveglia.
♦ **radio announcer** N annunciatore(-trice) radiofonico (-a).
♦ **radio beacon** N radiofaro.
radio·bi·ol·ogy [ˌreɪdɪəʊbaɪˈɒlədʒɪ] N radiobiologia.
radio·car·bon [ˌreɪdɪəʊˈkɑːbən] N radiocarbonio.
♦ **radiocarbon dating** N prova del carbonio 14.
♦ **radio cassette** N radioriproduttore *m.*
♦ **radio cassette recorder** N radioregistratore *m.*
radio·com·mu·ni·ca·tion [ˌreɪdɪəʊkəˌmjuːnɪˈkeɪʃən] N radiocomunicazione *f.*
♦ **radio compass** N radiobussola.
♦ **radio-controlled** [ˌreɪdɪəʊkənˈtrəʊld] ADJ radiocomandato(-a), radioguidato(-a).
radio·elec·tric·ity [ˌreɪdɪəʊɪlekˈtrɪsɪtɪ] N radioelettricità.

radio·gram [ˈreɪdɪəʊˌgræm] N **a** (*combined radio and gramophone*) radiogrammofono **b** (*Med*) radiografia, radiogramma *m.*
ra·di·og·ra·pher [ˌreɪdɪˈɒɡrəfəʳ] N radiologo(-a) (*tecnico*).
ra·di·og·ra·phy [ˌreɪdɪˈɒɡrəfɪ] N radiografia.
radio·iso·tope [ˌreɪdɪəʊˈaɪsətəʊp] N radioisotopo.
♦ **radio link** N ponte *m* radio *inv.*
ra·di·olo·gist [ˌreɪdɪˈɒlədʒɪst] N radiologo(-a) (*medico*).
ra·di·ol·ogy [ˌreɪdɪˈɒlədʒɪ] N radiologia.
♦ **radio navigation** N navigazione *f* radioassistita.
♦ **radio operator** N operatore *m* radio *inv.*
ra·di·os·co·py [ˌreɪdɪˈɒskəpɪ] N radioscopia.
♦ **radio station** N stazione *f* radio *inv.*
♦ **radio taxi** N radiotaxi *m inv.*
radio·teleg·ra·phy [ˌreɪdɪəʊtɪˈlegrəfɪ] N radiotelegrafia.
radio·tele·phone [ˌreɪdɪəʊˈtelɪˌfəʊn] N radiotelefono.
♦ **radio telescope** N radiotelescopio.
radio·thera·pist [ˌreɪdɪəʊˈθerəpɪst] N radioterapista *m/f.*
radio·thera·py [ˌreɪdɪəʊˈθerəpɪ] N radioterapia.
♦ **radio wave** N radioonda.
rad·ish [ˈrædɪʃ] N ravanello.
ra·dium [ˈreɪdɪəm] N radio.
ra·dius [ˈreɪdɪəs] N (*pl* **radii** [ˈreɪdɪaɪ]) (*Math, fig*) raggio *m*; (*Anat*) radio; **within a radius of 50 miles** in un raggio di 50 miglia.
RAF [ˌɑːreɪˈɛf] N ABBR (*Brit*) = **Royal Air Force.**
raf·fia [ˈræfɪə] N rafia.
raff·ish [ˈræfɪʃ] ADJ (*liter*) dissipato(-a).
raf·fle [ˈræfl] ▢1 N lotteria, riffa.
   ▢2 VT (*object*) mettere in palio.
♦ **raffle ticket** N biglietto della lotteria *or* della riffa.
raft [rɑːft] N zattera.
raft·er [ˈrɑːftəʳ] N trave *f* (del tetto), puntone *m* (*Archit*).
rag[1] [ræg] N **a** (*piece of cloth*) straccio, cencio; **rags** NPL (*old clothes*) stracci *mpl*; **in rags** stracciato(-a); **dressed in rags** vestito(-a) di stracci; **to feel like a wet rag** (*fam*) sentirsi uno straccio **b** (*fam: newspaper*) giornalaccio.
rag[2] [ræg] ▢1 N (*practical joke*) scherzo; (*Univ: events*) *festa studentesca a scopo di beneficenza.*
   ▢2 VT (*Brit old: tease*) prendere in giro.
raga·muf·fin [ˈrægəˌmʌfɪn] N (*old*) monello(-a).
♦ **rag-and-bone man** [ˌrægəndˈbəʊnˌmæn] N (*pl* -men) straccivendolo.
rag·bag [ˈrægˌbæg] N (*fig: mixture*) guazzabuglio, accozzaglia.
♦ **rag doll** N bambola di pezza.
rage [reɪdʒ] ▢1 N **a** (*anger*) collera, furia; **to fly into a rage** andare *or* montare su tutte le furie; **to be in a rage** essere furioso(-a) *or* su tutte le furie **b** (*fashion, trend*) mania; **it's all the rage** fa furore.
   ▢2 VI (*person*) essere furioso(-a), andare su tutte le furie, infuriarsi; (*sea, fire, plague, wind*) infuriare.
rag·ged [ˈrægɪd] ADJ (*dress*) stracciato(-a); (*cuff*) logoro (-a); (*person*) lacero(-a), cencioso(-a); (*edge*) irregolare.
rag·ged·ly [ˈrægɪdlɪ] ADV **a**: **raggedly dressed** vestito(-a) di stracci **b** (*engine*): **to run raggedly** funzionare irregolarmente.
♦ **ragged robin** N (*Bot*) garofano di prato, fior *m* di cuculo.
rag·ing [ˈreɪdʒɪŋ] ADJ (*all senses*) furioso(-a); **in a raging temper** su tutte le furie; **I've got a raging thirst/ toothache** muoio di sete/dal mal di denti.
rag·lan [ˈræglən] ▢1 ADJ (*alla*) raglan *inv.*
   ▢2 N raglan *f.*
rag·man [ˈrægˌmæn] N (*pl* -men) = **rag-and-bone man.**

rag·tag ['ræg,tæg] (*pej*) ☐ N: **ragtag and bobtail** marmaglia.
☐ ADJ (*group, organization, collection*) di bassa lega; **a ragtag army** un'armata brancaleone.

rag·time ['ræg,taɪm] N ragtime *m inv*.

♦ **rag trade** N (*fam*): **the rag trade** (il settore *m* del) l'abbigliamento.

rag·wort ['ræg,wɜːt] N erba di San Giacomo.

raid [reɪd] ☐ N (*Mil*) incursione *f*; (*by police*) irruzione *f*; (*by bandits*) razzia; (*by criminals*) rapina.
☐ VT (*see n*) fare un'incursione in; fare irruzione in; fare razzia in; rapinare; **the boys raided the orchard** i ragazzi hanno saccheggiato il frutteto.

raid·er ['reɪdəʳ] N (*bandit*) bandito; (*bank raider etc*) rapinatore(-trice); (*plane*) aeroplano da incursione.

rail [reɪl] N **a** (*bar*) sbarra, traversa; (*banister*) corrimano; (*on bridge, balcony*) parapetto; (*of ship*) battagliola; **towel rail** portasciugamani *m inv*; **bath rail** maniglia del bagno **b** (*for train*) rotaia; **to go off the rails** (*train*) deragliare, uscire dal binario; (*fig: be confused*) uscire di carreggiata; (*: err*) sviarsi; **by rail** in treno, per ferrovia
▶ **rail off** VT + ADV recintare una ringhiera.

rail·card ['reɪl,kɑːd] N (*Brit*) tessera di riduzione ferroviaria.

rail·ing ['reɪlɪŋ] N (*also:* **railings**) ringhiera, inferriata.

rail·road ['reɪl,rəʊd] ☐ N (*Am*) = **railway**.
☐ VT (*fig*): **to railroad sb into doing sth** costringere velocemente qn a fare qc.

♦ **rail strike** N sciopero dei ferrovieri.

♦ **rail transport** N trasporto ferroviario.

rail·way ['reɪl,weɪ] ☐ N (*system*) ferrovia; (*track*) strada ferrata.
☐ ADJ (*bridge, timetable, network*) ferroviario(-a).

♦ **railway engine** N (*Brit*) locomotiva.

♦ **railway line** N (*Brit*) linea ferroviaria.

rail·way·man ['reɪl,weɪmən] N (*pl* **-men**) (*Brit*) ferroviere *m*.

♦ **railway station** N (*Brit*) stazione *f* ferroviaria.

♦ **rail workers** NPL ferrovieri *mpl*.

rain [reɪn] ☐ N pioggia; **in the rain** sotto la pioggia; **it looks like rain** per me si mette a piovere; **heavy/light rain** piogga forte/leggera; **come rain** or **shine** qualunque tempo faccia, col bello o col cattivo tempo; (*fig*) qualunque cosa succeda.
☐ VI piovere; **it's raining** piove; **it's raining cats and dogs** piove a catinelle; **it never rains but it pours** (*Proverb*) piove sempre sul bagnato; **to rain down (on sb)** (*blows*) piovere (addosso a qn)
▶ **rain off,** (*Am*) **rain out** VT + ADV: **the match has been rained off** l'incontro è stato sospeso per la pioggia.

rain·bow ['reɪn,bəʊ] N arcobaleno.

rain·check ['reɪn,tʃɛk] N: **I'll take a raincheck** (*Am fam*) sarà per un'altra volta.

rain·coat ['reɪn,kəʊt] N impermeabile *m*.

rain·drop ['reɪn,drɒp] N goccia di pioggia.

rain·fall ['reɪn,fɔːl] N (*amount*) piovosità, precipitazioni *fpl*.

rain·for·est ['reɪn,fɒrɪst] N foresta pluviale *or* equatoriale.

♦ **rain gauge** N pluviometro.

rain·proof ['reɪn,pruːf] ☐ ADJ impermeabile.
☐ VT impermeabilizzare.

rain·storm ['reɪn,stɔːm] N temporale *m*, pioggia torrenziale.

rain·water ['reɪn,wɔːtəʳ] N acqua piovana.

rainy ['reɪnɪ] ADJ (*comp* **-ier,** *superl* **-iest**) (*climate*) piovoso

(*-a*); (*season*) delle piogge; **rainy day** giorno piovoso; **to save** *or* **keep sth for a rainy day** (*fig*) mettere qc da parte per i tempi di magra.

raise [reɪz] ☐ VT **a** (*lift: gen*) sollevare, alzare; (*: shipwreck*) riportare alla superficie; (*: flag*) alzare, issare; (*: dust*) sollevare; (*fig: spirits, morale*) risollevare, tirar su; (*: to power, in rank*) elevare; (*Math*): **to raise to the third power** elevare alla terza potenza; **to raise o.s. up on one's elbows** sollevarsi sui gomiti; **he raised his hat to me** si è tolto il cappello per salutarmi; **to raise one's glass to sb/sth** brindare a qn/qc; **to raise one's voice** alzare la voce; **he didn't raise an eyebrow** non ha battuto ciglio; **to raise sb's hopes** accendere le speranze di qn; **to raise from the dead** risuscitare
b (*erect: building, statue*) erigere
c (*increase: salary, production*) aumentare; (*: price*) aumentare, alzare
d (*crop*) coltivare; (*bring up, breed: family, livestock*) allevare
e (*produce: question, objection*) sollevare; (*: problem*) porre; (*: doubts, suspicions*) far sorgere, far nascere; **to raise a laugh/a smile** far ridere/sorridere; **to raise hell** *or* **the roof** (*fam*) fare il diavolo a quattro
f (*get together: funds, army*) raccogliere; (*: taxes*) imporre; (*: money*) procurarsi; **to raise a loan** ottenere un prestito
g (*end: siege, embargo*) togliere.
☐ N (*Am: payrise*) aumento.

rai·sin ['reɪzən] N uvetta.

rai·son d'être [ˌreɪzõ:n'dɛɪtrə] N ragione *f* di vita.

Raj [rɑːdʒ] N: **the Raj** l'impero britannico (*in India*).

rajah ['rɑːdʒə] N ragià *m inv*.

rake¹ [reɪk] ☐ N (*tool*) rastrello.
☐ VT (*sand, leaves, soil*) rastrellare; (*strafe: ship, row of men*) spazzare
▶ **rake in** VT + ADV (*fam: money*) fare; **they raked in a profit of £1,000** ci hanno fatto un guadagno di 1.000 sterline
▶ **rake off** VT + ADV (*fam: share of profit*) intascare
▶ **rake out** VT + ADV (*fire*) spegnere facendo cadere la brace
▶ **rake over** VT + ADV (*fig*) rivangare
▶ **rake through** VI + PREP rovistare in, frugare in
▶ **rake up** VT + ADV (*subject, memories*) rivangare, riesumare.

rake² [reɪk] N (*old: dissolute man*) libertino.

raked [reɪkd] ADJ in pendenza.

♦ **rake-off** ['reɪk,ɒf] N (*fam: share of profit*) parte *f*, fetta.

rak·ish ['reɪkɪʃ] ADJ **a** (*person*) libertino(-a), dissoluto(-a) **b**: **at a rakish angle** (*hat*) sulle ventitré.

ral·ly ['rælɪ] ☐ N (*of troops, people, also Pol*) raduno, riunione *f*; (*Aut*) rally *m inv*; (*Tennis*) lungo scambio di colpi.
☐ VT (*troops, supporters*) riunire, radunare.
☐ VI (*troops, supporters*) riunirsi; (*revive, recover: patient, strength, share prices*) riprendersi
▶ **rally round** ☐ VI + ADV (*fig: cause*) far fronte comune.
☐ VI + PREP (*person needing help*) stringersi intorno a.

ral·ly·ing point ['rælɪŋ,pɔɪnt] N (*Pol, Mil*) punto di raduno.

RAM [ræm] N ABBR (*Comput: = random access memory*) RAM *f inv*.

ram [ræm] ☐ N (*Zool*) montone *m*, ariete *m*; (*Astrol, Mil*) ariete.
☐ VT **a**: **to ram (into)** (*pack tightly*) calcare (in), pigiare (in); (*push down*) ficcare (in); (*stick into*) conficcare; **to**

ram one's hat down on one's head calcarsi il cappello in testa; **they rammed their ideas down my throat** hanno cercato di imbottirmi la testa con le loro idee
b (*collide with: ship*) speronare; (: *car*) cozzare, sbattere contro; **the car rammed the lamppost** la macchina è andata a sbattere con il muso contro il lampione.

Rama·dan [ˌræməˈdɑːn] N (*Rel*) ramadan *m inv*.

ram·ble [ˈræmbl] **1** N (lunga) passeggiata; (*hike*) escursione *f*.
2 VI **a** (*walk*) gironzolare, vagare; (*hike*) fare escursioni **b** (*fig: in speech*) divagare, dilungarsi; **to ramble on** sproloquiare; **his mind has started to ramble** è un po' svanito.

ram·bler [ˈræmbləʳ] N **a** (*hiker*) escursionista *m/f* **b** (*Bot*) rosa rampicante.

ram·bling [ˈræmblɪŋ] ADJ (*plant*) rampicante; (*speech, book*) sconnesso(-a); (*house*) tutto(-a) nicchie e corridoi.

ram·bunc·tious [ræmˈbʌŋkʃəs] ADJ (*Am*) = **rumbustious**.

RAMC [ˌɑːreɪɛmˈsiː] N ABBR (*Brit*)= *Royal Army Medical Corps*.

rami·fi·ca·tion [ˌræmɪfɪˈkeɪʃən] N ramificazione *f*.

rami·fy [ˈræmɪˌfaɪ] VI (*tree, problem*) ramificare; (*system*) ramificarsi.

ramp [ræmp] N (*on road etc*) rampa; (*in garage*) ponte *m* idraulico; (*Aer*) scala d'imbarco; **"ramp"** (*Aut*) "fondo stradale in rifacimento".

ram·page [ræmˈpeɪdʒ] **1** N: **to go on the rampage** scatenarsi.
2 VI scatenarsi; **they went rampaging through the town** si sono scatenati in modo violento per la città.

ram·pant [ˈræmpənt] ADJ **a** (*fig: crime, disease*): **to be rampant** dilagare **b** (*Heraldry*) rampante.

ram·part [ˈræmpɑːt] N terrapieno, bastione *m*.

♦ **ram raid·ing** [ˈræmˌreɪdɪŋ] N *il rapinare un negozio o una banca sfondandone la vetrina con un'auto-ariete.*

ram·shack·le [ˈræmˌʃækl] ADJ (*house*) cadente, malandato(-a); (*car, table*) sgangherato(-a).

RAN [ˌɑːreɪˈɛn] N ABBR = *Royal Australian Navy*.

ran [ræn] PT of **run**.

ranch [rɑːntʃ] N ranch *m inv*.

ranch·er [ˈrɑːntʃəʳ] N (*owner*) proprietario di un ranch; (*ranch hand*) cowboy *m inv*.

ran·cid [ˈrænsɪd] ADJ rancido(-a); **to smell rancid** avere odore di rancido.

ran·cor·ous [ˈræŋkərəs] ADJ (*frm*) pieno(-a) di rancore.

ran·cour, (*Am*) **ran·cor** [ˈræŋkəʳ] N (*frm*) rancore *m*.

ran·dom [ˈrændəm] **1** ADJ (*arrangement*) casuale, fortuito (-a); (*selection, shot, killing*) a caso.
2 N: **at random** a caso, a casaccio.

♦ **random access** N (*Comput*) accesso casuale.

R and R [ˌɑːrənˈɑːʳ] N ABBR (*Am Mil*: = *rest and recreation*) ≈ permesso per militari.

randy [ˈrændɪ] ADJ (*comp* **-ier**, *superl* **-iest**) (*Brit fam*) arrapato(-a).

rang [ræŋ] PT of **ring**².

range [reɪndʒ] **1** N **a** (*distance attainable, scope: of gun, missile*) portata, gittata; (: *of ship, plane*) autonomia; **within (firing) range** a portata (di tiro); **out of (firing) range** fuori portata (di tiro); **at short/long range** a breve/lunga distanza; **range of vision** campo visivo **b** (*extent between limits: of temperature*) variazioni *fpl*; (: *of salaries, prices*) scala; (: *Mus: of instruments, voice*) gamma, estensione *f*; (*selection: of colours, feelings, speeds*) gamma; (: *of goods*) assortimento, gamma;

(*domain, sphere*) raggio, sfera; **the range of sb's mind** le capacità mentali di qn; **she has a wide range of interests** ha interessi molto vari; **price range** gamma di prezzi; **do you have anything else in this price range?** ha nient'altro più o meno a questo prezzo?
c (*row*) serie *f inv*, fila; (*of mountains*) catena
d (*Am Agr*) prateria
e (*also:* **shooting range**: *in open*) poligono di tiro; (: *at fair*) tiro a segno
f (*also:* **kitchen range**) cucina economica.
2 VT (*arrange, place*) disporre, allineare; **ranged left/ right** (*text*) allineato(-a) a destra/sinistra.
3 VI **a** (*mountains, discussion, search*) estendersi; (*numbers, opinions, results*) variare; **the discussion ranged over a wide number of topics** la discussione ha toccato vari argomenti
b (*roam*): **to range over** vagare per; **to range from ...to** andare da... a.

range·finder [ˈreɪndʒˌfaɪndəʳ] N telemetro.

rang·er [ˈreɪndʒəʳ] N (*also:* **forest ranger**) guardia forestale; (*Am: mounted policeman*) poliziotto a cavallo.

Ran·goon [ræŋˈguːn] N Rangoon *f*.

rank¹ [ræŋk] **1** N **a** (*row*) fila; **taxi rank** posteggio di taxi
b (*status: also Mil*) grado; **people of all ranks** gente *f sg* di tutti i ceti
c (*Mil*): **the ranks** la truppa; **he rose from the ranks** è venuto dalla gavetta; **to close ranks** (*Mil*) serrare le righe; (*fig*) serrare i ranghi; **to break rank(s)** rompere le righe; **I've joined the ranks of the unemployed** mi sono aggiunto alla massa dei disoccupati
d (*Math*) posizione *f*.
2 VT considerare, ritenere; **I rank him 6th** gli dò il sesto posto, lo metto al sesto posto.
3 VI: **to rank 4th** essere quarto(-a), essere al quarto posto; **to rank above sb** essere superiore a qn; (*Mil*) essere superiore in grado a qn; **he ranks among the best** è uno dei migliori.

rank² [ræŋk] ADJ **a** (*hypocrisy, injustice etc*) bello(-a) e buono(-a), vero(-a) e proprio(-a); (*traitor*) sporco(-a) **b** (*smell*) puzzolente, fetido(-a); (*fats*) rancido(-a) **c** (*frm: plants*) troppo rigoglioso(-a); **rank outsider** outsider *m/f inv*.

♦ **rank and file** N: **the rank and file** (*of political party*) la base.

rank·ing [ˈræŋkɪŋ] **1** N posizione *f*, posto (*in classifica*); **he holds the number two ranking** è in seconda posizione, è al secondo posto.
2 ADJ (*Am*): **ranking officer** ufficiale di grado più elevato.

ran·kle [ˈræŋkl] VI: **to rankle (with sb)** bruciare (a qn).

ran·sack [ˈrænsæk] VT (*drawer, room*) frugare, rovistare; (*town*) saccheggiare.

ran·som [ˈrænsəm] **1** N riscatto; **to hold sb to ransom** tenere in ostaggio qn (*per denaro*); (*fig*) tenere qc in scacco.
2 VT riscattare.

♦ **ransom demand** N richiesta di riscatto.

rant [rænt] VI (*pej*): **to rant (at sb)** inveire (contro qn).

rant·ing [ˈræntɪŋ] N (*pej*) invettiva.

rap [ræp] **1** N **a** (*noise*) colpetti *mpl*; (*at the door*) bussata; **there was a rap at the door** hanno bussato con un colpo secco alla porta; **to take the rap** (*fam*) pagare di persona
b (*Mus*) rap *m*.
2 VT (*window*) dare dei colpetti su; (*door*) bussare a; **to**

rap sb's knuckles dare un colpo secco sulle nocche di qn; (*fig*) dare una tirata d'orecchi a qn.

3 VI **a**: **to rap (at)** (*see vt*) dare dei colpetti (su); bussare (a)

b (*Am fam*: *talk*) chiacchierare

▶ **rap out** VT + ADV (*order*) dire bruscamente.

ra·pa·cious [rə'peɪʃəs] ADJ (*frm*) rapace.

ra·pa·cious·ly [rə'peɪʃəslɪ] ADV (*frm*) rapacemente.

ra·pa·city [rə'pæsɪtɪ] N (*frm*) rapacità.

rape[1] [reɪp] **1** N (*also Law*) stupro, violenza carnale.

2 VT violentare, stuprare.

rape[2] [reɪp] N (*Bot*) colza.

rape·seed oil ['reɪp,si:d'ɔɪl] N olio di colza.

Raphael ['ræfeɪəl] N (*Art*) Raffaello.

rap·id ['ræpɪd] ADJ rapido(-a).

ra·pid·ity [rə'pɪdɪtɪ] N rapidità.

rap·id·ly ['ræpɪdlɪ] ADV rapidamente.

rap·ids ['ræpɪdz] NPL (*in river*) rapide *fpl*.

ra·pi·er ['reɪpɪə'] N spadino.

rap·ist ['reɪpɪst] N violentatore *m*, stupratore *m*.

rap·port [ræ'pɔ:'] N intesa.

rap·proche·ment [ræprɔʃmɑ̃] N (*frm*): **rapprochment (with/of/between)** riavvicinamento (a/di/fra).

rapt [ræpt] ADJ (*person, face, expression*) rapito(-a); (*silence, attention*) profondo(-a); **to be rapt in contemplation** essere in estatica contemplazione.

rap·ture ['ræptʃə'] N (*liter*) estasi *f inv*; **to be in raptures over sth/sb** essere estasiato(-a) di fronte a qc/qn; **to go into raptures over sth/sb** andare in estasi per qc/qn.

rap·tur·ous ['ræptʃərəs] (*liter*) ADJ (*smile*) estatico(-a); (*welcome, praise, applause*) entusiastico(-a).

rap·tur·ous·ly ['ræptʃərəslɪ] (*liter*) ADV (*smile*) estaticamente; (*welcome, praise, applaud*) entusiasticamente.

rare [rɛə'] ADJ (*comp* **-r**, *superl* **-st**) **a** raro(-a); **in a rare moment of generosity** in un raro momento di generosità; **it is rare to find that** ... capita raramente *or* di rado che... + *sub* **b** (*air*) rarefatto(-a) **c** (*meat*) al sangue, poco cotto(-a).

rare·bit ['rɛəbɪt] N: **Welsh rarebit** toast *m inv* al formaggio fuso.

rar·efied ['rɛərɪ,faɪd] ADJ (*atmosphere, air*) rarefatto(-a); (*fig*) raffinato(-a).

rare·ly ['rɛəlɪ] ADV di rado, raramente.

rar·ing ['rɛərɪŋ] ADJ: **to be raring to go** (*fam*) non veder l'ora di cominciare.

rar·ity ['rɛərɪtɪ] N **a** (*also: **rareness**) rarità **b** (*rare thing*) rarità *f inv*.

ras·cal ['rɑ:skəl] N (*scoundrel*) mascalzone *m*; (*child*) birbante *m*.

ras·cal·ly ['rɑ:skəlɪ] ADJ briccone(-a).

rash[1] [ræʃ] ADJ avventato(-a).

rash[2] [ræʃ] N (*Med*: *gen*) eruzione *f*, sfogo *m*; (: *from food, allergy*) orticaria; **to come out in a rash** (*gen*) avere uno sfogo; **strawberries bring me out in a rash** le fragole mi fanno venire l'orticaria.

rash·er ['ræʃə'] N: **a rasher of bacon** una fettina di pancetta.

rash·ly ['ræʃlɪ] ADV avventatamente.

rash·ness ['ræʃnɪs] N avventatezza.

rasp [rɑ:sp] **1** N (*tool*) raspa, lima; (*sound*) stridio, suono stridulo.

2 VT (*file*) raspare, raschiare; (*speak*: *also*: **rasp out**) gracchiare.

rasp·berry ['rɑ:zbərɪ] **1** N (*fruit*) lampone *m*; **to blow a raspberry** (*fam*) fare una pernacchia.

2 ADJ (*jam*) di lamponi; (*ice cream, syrup*) di lampone.

♦ **raspberry bush** N lampone *m* (*pianta*).

rasp·ing ['rɑ:spɪŋ] ADJ stridulo(-a), stridente.

Ras·ta·far·ian [,ræstə'fɛərɪən] ADJ, N rastafariano(-a).

rat [ræt] **1** N ratto; **black rat** ratto comune; **brown rat** topo delle chiaviche; **you dirty rat!** (*fam*) brutta carogna!.

2 VI: **to rat on sb** (*fam*) fare una spiata *or* una soffiata su qn; **to rat on a deal** (*fam*) rimangiarsi la parola; **to smell a rat** subodorare qualcosa.

rat·able ['reɪtəbl] ADJ = **rateable**.

♦ **rat-catcher** ['ræt,kætʃə'] N *addetto alla derattizzazione*.

ratch·et ['rætʃɪt] N arpionismo.

♦ **ratchet wheel** N ruota dentata.

rate [reɪt] **1** N **a** (*ratio*) tasso, percentuale *f*; (*speed*) velocità *f inv*; **at a rate of 60 kph** alla velocità di 60 km all'ora; **at a great rate** [OR] **at a rate of knots** (*fam*) a tutta velocità; **rate of growth** tasso di crescita; **at a steady rate** a un ritmo costante; **birth/death rate** tasso *or* indice *m* di natalità/di mortalità; **failure rate** percentuale *f* dei bocciati; **rate of flow/consumption** flusso/consumo medio; **rate of reaction** (*Chem*) velocità *f inv* di reazione; **pulse rate** frequenza delle pulsazioni; **at this rate** di questo passo, con questo ritmo; **at any rate** in *or* ad ogni modo, comunque

b (*price, charge*) tariffa; (*Comm, Fin*) tasso; **at a rate of 5% per annum** al tasso (annuo) del 5%; **postage rates** tariffe postali; **insurance rates** premi *mpl* assicurativi; **rate of exchange** tasso di cambio; **rate of pay** compenso medio; **bank rate** tasso d'interesse bancario; see also **rates**.

2 VT (*evaluate, appraise*) valutare; **to rate sb/sth highly** stimare molto qn/qc; **how do you rate that film?** cosa pensi di quel film?; **I rate it as one of the best** lo considero uno fra i migliori.

3 VI: **it rates as one of the worst** è fra i peggiori; **to rate sb/sth among** annoverare qn/qc tra; **how does it rate among the critics?** che cosa ne hanno detto i critici?

rate·able, rat·able ['reɪtəbl] ADJ (*property*) soggetto(-a) a tassazione.

♦ **rat(e)able value** N (*Brit old*) valore *m* imponibile (*agli effetti delle imposte comunali*).

♦ **rate of return** N (*Fin*) tasso di rendimento.

rate·payer ['reɪt,peɪə'] N (*Brit old*) contribuente *m/f* (*di imposte comunali*).

rates ['reɪts] NPL (*Brit old*) imposte *fpl* comunali sugli immobili.

ra·ther ['rɑ:ðə'] **1** ADV **a** (*preference*) piuttosto; **rather than wait, she** ... piuttosto che aspettare, lei...; **I'd rather have this one than that** preferirei avere questo piuttosto che quello; **would you rather stay here?** preferisci rimanere qui?; **I'd rather you didn't come** preferirei che tu non venissi; **I'd rather not** preferirei di no; **I'd rather not come** preferirei non venire; **I would** *or* **I'd rather go** preferirei andare

b (*to a considerable degree*) piuttosto; (*somewhat*) abbastanza; (*to some extent*) un po'; **it's rather expensive** (*quite*) è piuttosto caro; (*excessively*) è un po' troppo caro; **there's rather a lot** ce n'è parecchio; **a rather difficult task** un compito piuttosto difficile; **I feel rather more happy today** oggi mi sento molto più contento; **it's rather a pity** è proprio *or* davvero un peccato

c: **or rather** (*more accurately*) anzi, per essere (più) precisi.

2 EXCL eccome!

rati·fi·ca·tion [ˌrætɪfɪˈkeɪʃən] N (frm) ratifica.

rati·fy [ˈrætɪˌfaɪ] VT (frm) ratificare.

rat·ing [ˈreɪtɪŋ] N a (assessment) valutazione f; **their popularity rating is at an all-time low** la loro popolarità ha raggiunto i minimi storici b (Naut) marinaio semplice.

rat·ings [ˈreɪtɪŋz] NPL (Radio, TV) indice msg di ascolto.

ra·tio [ˈreɪʃɪəʊ] N rapporto, proporzione f; **in the ratio of 2 to 1** in rapporto di 2 a 1.

ra·tion [ˈræʃən] 1 N razione f; **to be on ration** (food) essere razionato(-a); **to be on short rations** (person) essere a razioni ridotte.

2 VT (also: **ration out**) razionare; **to ration sb to sth** imporre a qn un limite di qc.

ra·tion·al [ˈræʃənl] ADJ (being) razionale; (Med: lucid) lucido(-a); (faculty, action, argument) razionale; (solution, explanation, reasoning) logico(-a), razionale.

ra·tion·ale [ˌræʃəˈnɑːl] N fondamento logico.

ra·tion·al·ism [ˈræʃənəˌlɪzəm] N razionalismo.

ra·tion·al·ist [ˈræʃnəlɪst] ADJ, N razionalista (m/f).

ra·tion·ali·za·tion [ˌræʃnəlaɪˈzeɪʃən] N razionalizzazione f.

ra·tion·al·ize [ˈræʃnəˌlaɪz] VT a (action, attitude) (cercare di) spiegare razionalmente b (reorganize: industry) razionalizzare c (Math) razionalizzare.

ra·tion·al·ly [ˈræʃnəlɪ] ADV (behave, speak, think) razionalmente.

♦ **ration book** N tessera annonaria.

ra·tion·ing [ˈræʃnɪŋ] N razionamento.

rat·pack [ˈrætˌpæk] N (Brit fam) stampa scandalistica.

♦ **rat poison** N veleno per topi.

♦ **rat race** N (pej) corsa al successo.

rat·tan [ræˈtæn] N malacca.

rat-tat-tat [ˈrætəˈtæt] N (on door) toc-toc m; (of machine gun) ta-ta-ta m.

rat·tle [ˈrætl] 1 N a (of train, car) rumore m di ferraglia; (of stone in tin, of windows) tintinnio; (of typewriter) ticchettio; (of hail, rain, bullets) crepitio; **a rattle of bottles/chains** un rumore di bottiglie/catene; **death rattle** rantolo

b (instrument: used by football fan) raganella; (: child's) sonaglio.

2 VT a (shake) agitare; (: moneybox) far tintinnare b (fam: person) innervosire; **to get rattled** innervosirsi.

3 VI (box, objects in box, machinery) far rumore; (bullets, hailstones) crepitare; (window) vibrare; **the train rattled over the crossing** il treno passò sferragliando al passaggio a livello

▶ **rattle off** VT + ADV (poem, speech) snocciolare

▶ **rattle on** VI + ADV blaterare.

rattle·snake [ˈrætlˌsneɪk] N crotalo, serpente m a sonagli.

♦ **rat-trap** [ˈrætˌtræp] N trappola per topi.

rat·ty [ˈrætɪ] ADJ (comp **-ier**, superl **-iest**) (Brit fam) incavolato(-a); **to get ratty** incavolarsi.

rau·cous [ˈrɔːkəs] ADJ (voice, person) rauco(-a); (laughter) sguaiato(-a).

rau·cous·ly [ˈrɔːkəslɪ] ADV (see adj) raucamente, con voce roca; sguaiatamente.

raun·chy [ˈrɔːntʃɪ] ADJ (comp **-ier**, superl **-iest**) (fam) sexy inv.

rav·age [ˈrævɪdʒ] VT (frm) devastare.

rav·ages [ˈrævɪdʒɪz] NPL (frm) danni mpl; **the ravages of time** le offese or ingiurie del tempo.

rave [reɪv] 1 VI (be delirious) delirare; (talk wildly) farneti-

care; (rant) infuriarsi, fare una sfuriata; (talk enthusiastically): **to rave (about)** andare in estasi (per).

2 N rave m inv.

3 ADJ (scene, culture, music) rave inv.

ra·ven [ˈreɪvn] N corvo (imperiale).

♦ **raven-haired** [ˌreɪvnˈhɛəd] ADJ (liter) dai capelli corvini.

rav·en·ous [ˈrævənəs] ADJ (person) affamato(-a); (appetite, animal) famelico(-a), vorace.

rav·en·ous·ly [ˈrævənəslɪ] ADV voracemente.

rav·er [ˈreɪvə] N (Brit fam) festaiolo(-a).

♦ **rave review** N (fam) critica entusiastica.

♦ **rave-up** [ˈreɪvʌp] N (Brit fam): **to have a rave-up** dare una grande festa.

ra·vine [rəˈviːn] N burrone m.

rav·ing [ˈreɪvɪŋ] ADJ: **raving lunatic** pazzo(-a) furioso(-a); **you must be raving mad!** sei matto da legare!

rav·ings [ˈreɪvɪŋz] NPL vaneggiamenti mpl.

ra·vio·li [ˌrævɪˈəʊlɪ] N ravioli mpl.

rav·ish [ˈrævɪʃ] VT a (liter: enchant, delight) estasiare, rapire b (old: rape) violentare; (: carry off) rapire.

rav·ish·ing [ˈrævɪʃɪŋ] ADJ (sight, beauty) incantevole.

rav·ish·ing·ly [ˈrævɪʃɪŋlɪ] ADV: **ravishingly beautiful** di incantevole bellezza.

raw [rɔː] 1 ADJ a (food) crudo(-a); (spirit) puro(-a); (silk, leather, cotton, ore) greggio(-a); (sugar) non raffinato (-a); **to get a raw deal** (fam: bad bargain) prendere un bidone; (: harsh treatment) venire trattato(-a) ingiustamente

b (wind, weather) gelido(-a)

c (wound: open) aperto(-a); (: sore) vivo(-a); (skin) screpolato(-a)

d (person: inexperienced) inesperto(-a); **he's still raw** è ancora un pivello or un novellino.

2 N: **it got him on the raw** (fig) lo ha punto sul vivo; **life in the raw** la vita così com'è.

Ra·wal·pin·di [rɔːlˈpɪndɪ] N Rawalpindi f.

raw-boned [ˌrɔːˈbəʊnd] ADJ scarno(-a).

raw·hide [ˈrɔːˌhaɪd] N a cuoio non conciato b (whip) frusta di cuoio.

Rawl·plug® [ˈrɔːlˌplʌg] N tassello.

♦ **raw material** N materia prima.

raw·ness [ˈrɔːnɪs] N a (of weather, wind) freddezza b (of skin) screpolature fpl c (lack of experience) inesperienza.

ray¹ [reɪ] N a raggio; (of hope) barlume m, raggio; **a ray of comfort** un po' di conforto b (Geom) semiretta.

ray² [reɪ] N (fish) razza.

ray·on [ˈreɪɒn] N raion m.

raze [reɪz] VT (also: **raze to the ground**) radere al suolo.

ra·zor [ˈreɪzə] N rasoio.

razor·bill [ˈreɪzəˌbɪl] N gazza marina.

♦ **razor blade** N lametta (da barba).

♦ **razor-sharp** [ˈreɪzəˈʃɑːp] ADJ (edge) tagliente come un rasoio; (mind) molto acuto(-a); (wit) tagliente.

♦ **razor shell** NPL cannolicchio.

razzle-dazzle [ˈræzlˈdæzl] N (Brit fam) brio; **to be/go on the razzle(-dazzle)** fare/andare a fare baldoria.

razz·ma·tazz [ˈræzməˈtæz] N (fam) clamore m.

R & B [ˌɑːrənˈbiː] N ABBR = rhythm and blues.

R.C. [ˌɑːˈsiː] ABBR = Roman Catholic.

RCAF [ˌɑːsiːeɪˈɛf] N ABBR = Royal Canadian Air Force.

RCMP [ˌɑːsiːɛmˈpiː] N ABBR = Royal Canadian Mounted Police.

RCN [ˌɑːsiːˈɛn] N ABBR = Royal Canadian Navy.

RD [ˌɑːˈdiː] ABBR (New Zealand Post) = rural delivery.

Rd ABBR = **road**.

R & D [ˌɑːrənˈdiː] N ABBR = **research and development.**

RDC [ˌɑːdiːˈsiː] N ABBR (*Brit*) = **rural district council.**

RE [ˌɑːˈriː] N ABBR a (*Brit Mil*: = *Royal Engineers*) ≈ G.M. (= *Genio Militare*) b = *religious education.*

re¹ [riː] PREP (*Comm*: *with regard to*) oggetto, con riferimento a.

re² [reɪ] N (*Mus*) re *m inv.*

re... [riː] PREF ri..., re...

re·ab·sorp·tion [ˌriːəbˈsɔːpʃən] N riassorbimento.

reach [riːtʃ] ① N a portata; **within (easy) reach** a portata di mano; **it's within easy reach by bus** lo si raggiunge facilmente in autobus; **out of reach** fuori portata
b (*of river*) tratto; **the upper reaches of the Thames** l'alto corso del Tamigi
c (*Naut*): **on a beam reach** al traverso; **on a broad reach** al gran lasco, al giardinetto; **on a close reach** al lasco.
② VT (*arrive at, attain*) arrivare a; (: *goal, limit, person*) raggiungere; **to reach a conclusion** arrivare ad una conclusione; **when the news reached my ears** quando mi è arrivata all'orecchio la notizia; **to reach a compromise** arrivare a *or* raggiungere un compromesso; **can I reach you at your hotel?** posso trovarla al suo albergo?; **to reach sb by phone** contattare qn per telefono.
③ VI a (*stretch out hand*: also: **reach down, reach over, reach across** etc) allungare una mano; **he reached (over) for the book** si è allungato per prendere il libro
b (*stretch: land etc*) estendersi; (: *wire, rope*) arrivare; (*voice, sound*) giungere.
▶ **reach out** VI + ADV: **to reach out for** stendere la mano per prendere.

re·act [riːˈækt] VI: **to react (against/to)** reagire (contro/a).

re·ac·tion [riːˈækʃən] N reazione *f*.

re·ac·tion·ary [riːˈækʃənrɪ] ADJ, N reazionario(-a).

re·ac·tive [riːˈæktɪv] ADJ reattivo(-a).

re·ac·tiv·ity [ˌriːækˈtɪvɪtɪ] N (*Chem*) reattività.

re·ac·tor [riːˈæktəʳ] N reattore *m*.

read [riːd] (*vb*: *pt, pp* read [rɛd]) ① VT a (*gen*) leggere; **to read o.s. to sleep** leggere per addormentarsi; **to take sth as read** (*fig*) dare qc per scontato; **to take the minutes as read** (*Admin*) passare subito all'ordine del giorno; **do you read me?** (*Telec*) mi ricevete?
b (*Univ*: *study*) studiare; **to read Chemistry** fare *or* studiare chimica
c (*interpret*: *dream, signal*) interpretare; (: *hand*) leggere; **she can read me like a book** mi legge nel cuore, per lei sono come un libro aperto; **to read sb's thoughts** leggere nel pensiero di qn; **to read between the lines** leggere tra le righe; **to read too much into sth** attribuire troppa importanza a qc.
② VI a leggere; **I read about him in the paper** ho letto qualcosa su di lui sul giornale; **I read about it in the paper** l'ho letto sul giornale; **to read to sb** leggere qualcosa a qn; **the book reads well** è un libro che si legge bene
b (*indicate*: *meter, clock*) segnare; **the inscription reads "To my son"** la dedica dice "A mio figlio".
③ N: **to have a quiet read** leggersi qualcosa in santa pace; **that book's a good read** quel libro è una buona lettura
▶ **read back** VT + ADV rileggere
▶ **read off** VT + ADV a (*without pause*) leggere tutto d'un fiato; **he read off the figures from the printout** (*at sight*) ha letto le cifre dal tabulato
b (*instrument readings*) leggere
▶ **read on** VI + ADV continuare a leggere

▶ **read out** VT + ADV leggere (ad alta voce)
▶ **read over** VT + ADV rileggere attentamente
▶ **read through** VT + ADV (*quickly*) dare una scorsa a; (*thoroughly*) leggere da cima a fondo
▶ **read up (on)** VT + ADV (+ PREP) studiare bene.

read·able [ˈriːdəbl] ADJ (*book*) che si legge volentieri; (*writing*) leggibile.

re·address [ˌriːəˈdrɛs] VT (*letter*) cambiare indirizzo a.

read·er [ˈriːdəʳ] N a lettore(-trice); **she's a great reader** adora leggere b (*Brit Univ*) ≈ (docente *m/f*) incaricato (-a) c (*book*) libro di lettura; (: *anthology*) antologia.

read·er·ship [ˈriːdəʃɪp] N (numero di) lettori *mpl*.

read·ily [ˈrɛdɪlɪ] ADV (*quickly*) prontamente; (*willingly*) volentieri; (*easily*) con facilità, facilmente.

readi·ness [ˈrɛdɪnɪs] N prontezza; **to be in readiness for** essere pronto(-a) per.

read·ing [ˈriːdɪŋ] N a (*gen*) lettura; (*of proofs*) correzione *f*; **I like reading** mi piace leggere
b (*interpretation*) interpretazione *f*; (*of original text, manuscript*) lezione *f*
c (*of thermometer etc*) lettura; **to take a reading** prendere *or* fare una lettura
d (*recital*: *of play, poem*) reading *m inv*; **to give a poetry reading** tenere un reading di poesia.
♦ **reading book** N libro di lettura.
♦ **reading glasses** NPL occhiali *mpl* per leggere.
♦ **reading knowledge** N: **to have a reading knowledge of Russian** essere capace di leggere il russo.
♦ **reading lamp** N lampada da scrivania.
♦ **reading matter** N qualcosa da leggere.
♦ **reading room** N sala di lettura.

re·adjust [ˌriːəˈdʒʌst] ① VT regolare (di nuovo).
② VI (*person*): **to readjust (to)** riadattarsi (a).

re·adjust·ment [ˌriːəˈdʒʌstmənt] N a (*to situation, change*) riadattamento; **a period of readjustment** un periodo di riadattamento b (*of mechanism*) regolazione *f*.

♦ **read only memory** N (*Comput*) memoria di sola lettura.

ready [ˈrɛdɪ] ① ADJ (*comp* **-ier**, *superl* **-iest**) pronto(-a); (*willing*) pronto(-a), disposto(-a); (*quick*) rapido(-a); (*available*) disponibile; **are you ready?** sei pronto?; **ready for use** pronto per l'uso; **ready for anything** pronto(-a) a tutto; **ready money** denaro contante, contanti *mpl*; **to be ready to do sth** essere pronto a fare qc; **to get ready to do** prepararsi a fare; **ready to serve** (*food*) già pronto; **to get sth ready** preparare qc; **ready, steady, go!** pronti, attenti, via!; **I'm ready for him!** lo sto aspettando!; **we were ready to give up there and then** eravamo sul punto di piantare lì tutto.
② N: **at the ready** (*Mil*) pronto(-a) (a far fuoco *or* sparare); (*fig*) (tutto(-a)) pronto(-a).
③ VT preparare.
♦ **ready cash** N contanti *mpl*.
♦ **ready-cooked** [ˌrɛdɪˈkʊkt] ADJ già cucinato(-a) *or* cotto (-a).
♦ **ready-made** [ˌrɛdɪˈmeɪd] ADJ (*clothes*) confezionato (-a); (*excuses, solution*) bell'e pronto(-a); (*ideas*) banale.
♦ **ready-mix** [ˌrɛdɪˈmɪks] N (*Culin*) miscela pronta; (*concrete*) calcestruzzo.
♦ **ready reck·on·er** [ˈrɛdɪˈrɛkənəʳ] N (*Brit*) prontuario di calcolo.
♦ **ready-to-wear** [ˌrɛdɪtəˈwɛəʳ] ADJ prêt-à-porter *inv.*

re·affirm [ˌriːəˈfɜːm] VT riaffermare.

re·agent [riːˈeɪdʒənt] N: **chemical reagent** reagente *m*

chimico.

real [rɪəl] **1** ADJ (*gen*) vero(-a); (*reason, motive*) reale, vero(-a); (*Philosophy*) reale; **in real life** nella realtà; **in real terms** (*Fin*) in termini effettivi; **real account** (*Fin: in ledger*) conto patrimoniale; **he's a real villain** è un vero mascalzone; **she has no real authority** in pratica non ha alcuna autorità; **once you've tasted the real thing** ... una volta provato l'originale....

2 ADV (*Am fam*) veramente, proprio.

3 N: **for real** (*fam*) per davvero, sul serio.

♦ **real ale** N *tipo di birra scura prodotta secondo il metodo tradizionale.*

♦ **real estate** N (*Am*) beni *mpl* immobili.

re·align·ment [ri:ə'laɪmmənt] N (*frm*): **realignment (of)** riallineamento (di).

re·al·ism ['rɪəˌlɪzəm] N (*also Art*) realismo.

re·al·ist ['rɪəlɪst] N realista *m/f*.

re·al·is·tic [rɪə'lɪstɪk] ADJ (*thing*) realistico(-a); (*person*) realista.

re·al·is·ti·cal·ly [ˌrɪə'lɪstɪkəlɪ] ADV realisticamente.

re·al·ity [ri:'ælɪtɪ] N realtà *f inv*; **in reality** in realtà, in effetti.

re·ali·za·tion [ˌrɪəlaɪ'zeɪʃən] N (*awareness*) presa di coscienza; (*frm: of hopes, plans, assets*) realizzazione *f*.

re·al·ize ['rɪəˌlaɪz] VT **a** (*become aware of*) rendersi conto di, accorgersi di; (*understand*) capire, realizzare; **I realize that** ... mi rendo conto *or* capisco che...; **she hadn't fully realized the gravity of the situation** non si era resa completamente conto della gravità della situazione; **without realizing it** senza rendersene conto, senza accorgersene; **he realized how/why** ha capito come/perché

b (*frm: hopes, ambitions, assets, project*) realizzare; (: *plan*) attuare, realizzare.

re·al·ly ['rɪəlɪ] ADV davvero, veramente; **I don't really know** a dire la verità non lo so; **he doesn't really speak Chinese, does he?** non parla cinese sul serio, vero?; **I really ought to go home** devo proprio andare a casa; **a really good party** una festa bellissima.

realm [rɛlm] N (*frm*) regno.

♦ **real number** N (*Maths*) numero reale.

♦ **real time** N (*Comput*) tempo reale.

re·al·tor ['rɪəltɔː'] N (*Am*) agente *m/f* immobiliare.

ream [ri:m] N risma; **reams** NPL (*fig fam*) pagine e pagine *fpl*.

reap [ri:p] VT mietere; (*fig: profit, benefit*) raccogliere.

reap·er ['ri:pə'] N (*person*) mietitore(-trice); (*machine*) mietitrice *f*.

re·appear [ˌri:ə'pɪə'] VI ricomparire, riapparire.

re·appear·ance [ˌri:ə'pɪərəns] N ricomparsa, riapparizione *f*.

re·apply [ˌri:ə'plaɪ] VI: **to reapply for** fare nuovamente domanda per.

re·apprais·al [ˌri:ə'preɪzəl] N riesame *m*.

rear¹ [rɪə'] **1** ADJ (*gen*) di dietro, posteriore; (*Aut: door, window, wheel*) posteriore.

2 N (*back part*) didietro, parte *f* posteriore; (*Anat fam: buttocks*) didietro, sedere *m*; (*Mil*) retroguardia; **in** *or* **at the rear (of)** dietro (a), didietro (a); **to bring up the rear** venire per ultimo; (*Mil*) formare la retroguardia.

rear² [rɪə'] **1** VT **a** (*raise: cattle, family*) allevare **b** (*one's head*) drizzare.

2 VI (*also: rear up: esp horse*) impennarsi.

♦ **rear admiral** N contrammiraglio.

♦ **rear-engined** [ˌrɪər'ɛndʒɪnd] ADJ (*Aut*) con motore

posteriore.

rear·guard ['rɪəgɑ:d] N (*Mil*) retroguardia.

♦ **rearguard action** N (*Mil*) azione *f* di retroguardia; (*fig*) azione *f* dilatoria.

re·arm [ˌri:'ɑ:m] **1** VT riarmare.

2 VI riarmarsi.

re·arma·ment [ˌri:'ɑ:məmənt] N riarmo.

rear·most ['rɪəˌməʊst] ADJ ultimo(-a).

re·arrange [ˌri:ə'reɪndʒ] VT (*objects*) ridisporre, riordinare; (*appointment*) fissare di nuovo.

re·arrange·ment [ˌri:ə'reɪndʒmənt] N (*see vt*) ridisposizione *f*; cambiamento.

♦ **rear-view mirror** ['rɪəˌvju:'mɪrə'] N (*Aut*) specchietto retrovisore.

rea·son ['ri:zn] **1** N **a** (*motive, cause*) ragione *f*, motivo; **the reason for/why** la ragione *or* il motivo di/per cui; **the reason (why) I'm late is** ... sono in ritardo perché...; **don't ask the reason why** non chiedere il perché; **for no reason** senza ragione; **she claims with good reason that she's underpaid** si lamenta, e a ragione, di essere sottopagata; **all the more reason why you should not sell it** ragione di più per non venderlo; **we have reason to believe that** ... abbiamo motivo di ritenere che...; **by reason of** a causa di

b (*faculty, good sense*) ragione *f*; **to lose one's reason** perdere la ragione; **to listen to reason** ascoltare (la voce della) ragione; **it stands to reason** è logico; **within reason** entro limiti ragionevoli, entro certi limiti.

2 VT: **to reason that** concludere che, fare il ragionamento che.

3 VI: **to reason (with sb)** far ragionare qn

▶ **reason out** VT + ADV: **to reason sth out** risolvere qc ragionandoci su.

rea·son·able ['ri:znəbl] ADJ (*person, price*) ragionevole; (*behaviour, decision*) sensato(-a); (*standard*) accettabile; **a perfectly reasonable thing to do** una cosa perfettamente sensata da farsi; **it is reasonable to conclude that** ... si può logicamente concludere che... .

rea·son·able·ness ['ri:znəblnɪs] N ragionevolezza.

rea·son·ably ['ri:znəblɪ] ADV (*fairly, quite*) abbastanza; (*in a reasonable way*) ragionevolmente; **a reasonably accurate report** una relazione abbastanza accurata; **one can reasonably suppose that** ... si può logicamente supporre che... .

rea·soned ['ri:znd] ADJ (*discussion, approach*) ragionato (-a); (*argument, opinion*) ponderato(-a).

rea·son·ing ['ri:znɪŋ] N ragionamento.

re·as·semble [ˌri:ə'sɛmbl] **1** VT (*machine*) rimontare, riassemblare.

2 VI (*reconvene*) tornare a riunirsi.

re·as·sert [ˌri:ə'sɜ:t] VT riaffermare.

re·as·sess [ˌri:ə'sɛs] VT (*situation*) riesaminare.

re·assur·ance [ˌri:ə'ʃʊərəns] N rassicurazione *f*.

re·assure [ˌri:ə'ʃʊə'] VT: **to reassure sb (of)** rassicurare qn (di *or* su).

re·assur·ing [ˌri:ə'ʃʊərɪŋ] ADJ rassicurante.

re·assur·ing·ly [ˌri:ə'ʃʊərɪŋlɪ] ADV in modo rassicurante.

re·awak·en [ˌri:ə'weɪkən] **1** VT risvegliare, ridestare.

2 VI risvegliarsi, ridestarsi.

re·awak·en·ing [ˌri:ə'weɪkənɪŋ] N risveglio.

re·bate ['ri:beɪt] N rimborso.

re·bel [*adj, n* 'rɛbl; *vb* rɪ'bɛl] **1** ADJ, N ribelle (*m/f*).

2 VI: **to rebel (against sb/sth)** ribellarsi (a qn/contro qc).

re·bel·lion [rɪ'bɛljən] N ribellione *f*.

re·bel·lious [rɪˈbɛljəs] ADJ ribelle.

re·bel·lious·ness [rɪˈbɛljəsnɪs] N spirito di ribellione.

re·birth [ˌriːˈbɜːθ] N rinascita.

re·bound [n ˈriːbaʊnd; vb rɪˈbaʊnd] 1 N: **on the rebound** per ripicca.

2 VI (ball) rimbalzare

▶ **rebound on** VI + PREP ricadere su, ritorcersi contro.

re·buff [rɪˈbʌf] 1 N secco rifiuto.

2 VT rifiutare, respingere.

re·build [ˌriːˈbɪld] (pt, pp **rebuilt** [ˌriːˈbɪlt]) VT ricostruire.

re·buke [rɪˈbjuːk] 1 N rimprovero.

2 VT rimproverare; **to rebuke sb for sth/for doing sth** rimproverare qn per qc/per aver fatto qc.

re·but [rɪˈbʌt] VT (frm) confutare.

re·but·tal [rɪˈbʌtl] N (frm) confutazione f.

re·cal·ci·trance [rɪˈkælsɪtrəns] N (frm) riluttanza.

re·cal·ci·trant [rɪˈkælsɪtrənt] ADJ (frm) riluttante.

re·call [rɪˈkɔːl] 1 N richiamo; **beyond recall** irrevocabile; **those days are gone beyond recall** quei tempi sono passati per sempre.

2 VT a (call back: gen, Comput) richiamare; (: parliament) riconvocare; (: past) far rivivere b (remember) ricordare, ricordarsi di.

re·cant [rɪˈkænt] (frm) 1 VT (religious belief) abiurare; (statement) ritrattare.

2 VI fare abiura.

re·cap[1] [ˈriːˌkæp] (fam) 1 N riepilogo.

2 VT, VI riepilogare, ricapitolare.

re·cap[2] [ˈriːˌkæp] N (Am: tyre) pneumatico rigenerato.

re·ca·pitu·late [ˌriːkəˈpɪtjʊˌleɪt] VT, VI riepilogare, ricapitolare.

re·ca·pitu·la·tion [ˈriːkəˌpɪtjʊˈleɪʃən] N (summary) ricapitolazione f.

re·cap·ture [ˈriːˈkæptʃəʳ] VT (prisoner etc) ricatturare; (town) riconquistare, riprendere; (memory, scene) ritrovare; (atmosphere) ricreare.

re·cast [ˌriːˈkɑːst] VT a (play, film) cambiare il cast di; (actor) dare una parte diversa a; (part) dare ad un altro attore b (rewrite: sentence) rimaneggiare.

recd ABBR = **received**.

re·cede [rɪˈsiːd] VI (tide, flood) abbassarsi; (view) allontanarsi; (danger, threat) diminuire.

re·ced·ing [rɪˈsiːdɪŋ] ADJ (forehead, chin) sfuggente; **he's got a receding hairline** è stempiato.

re·ceipt [rɪˈsiːt] N a (slip of paper) ricevuta b (frm esp Comm) ricevimento; **to acknowledge receipt of** accusare ricevuta di; **we are in receipt of ...** abbiamo ricevuto... c (money taken): **receipts** NPL incassi mpl, introiti mpl.

♦ **receipt book** N blocchetto delle ricevute.

re·ceiv·able [rɪˈsiːvəbl] ADJ (Comm) esigibile; (: owed) dovuto(-a).

re·ceive [rɪˈsiːv] VT (gen, Radio, TV) ricevere; (stolen goods) ricettare; **"received with thanks"** (Comm) "per quietanza"; **to receive sb into one's home** ricevere qn in casa; **the book was not well received** il libro non ha avuto or ricevuto un'accoglienza favorevole.

re·ceived [rɪˈsiːvd] ADJ (opinion) generalmente accettato (-a).

♦ **Received Pronunciation** N pronuncia standard (dell'inglese).

re·ceiv·er [rɪˈsiːvəʳ] N a (gen) persona che riceve qualcosa; (of letter) destinatario(-a); (of stolen goods) ricettatore(-trice); (**official**) **receiver** (liquidator) curatore m fallimentare b (Radio) apparecchio ricevente; (Telec) ricevitore m, cornetta (fam).

re·ceiv·er·ship [ˌrɪˈsiːvəʃɪp] N curatela; **to go into receivership** andare in amministrazione f controllata.

re·cent [ˈriːsnt] ADJ recente; **in recent memory** in tempi recenti; **in recent years** negli ultimi anni.

re·cent·ly [ˈriːsntlɪ] ADV di recente, recentemente, ultimamente; **as recently as 1990** soltanto nel 1990; **until recently** fino a poco tempo fa.

re·cep·ta·cle [rɪˈsɛptəkl] N (frm) recipiente m.

re·cep·tion [rɪˈsɛpʃən] N a (ceremony) ricevimento; (welcome) accoglienza; **to get a warm reception** avere or ricevere un'accoglienza calorosa b (desk: in hotel) reception f inv; (: in hospital, at doctor's) accettazione f; (: in large building, offices) portineria c (Radio, TV) ricezione f.

♦ **reception centre** N (Brit) centro di raccolta.

♦ **reception desk** N = **reception b**.

re·cep·tion·ist [rɪˈsɛpʃənɪst] N (in hotel, offices) receptionist m/f inv; (at doctor's) addetto(-a) alla ricezione, assistente m/f di studio.

re·cep·tive [rɪˈsɛptɪv] ADJ ricettivo(-a).

re·cep·tive·ness [rɪˈsɛptɪvnɪs], **re·cep·tiv·ity** [ˌriːsɛpˈtɪvɪtɪ] N ricettività.

re·cep·tor [rɪˈsɛptəʳ] N recettore m.

re·cess [rɪˈsɛs] N a (Law, Parliament: cessation of business) ferie fpl, vacanza; (Am Law: short break) sospensione f; (Scol: esp Am) intervallo b (for bed) rientranza; (for statue) nicchia; (fig: of mind) recesso.

re·ces·sion [rɪˈsɛʃən] N (Econ) recessione f.

re·ces·sive [rɪˈsɛsɪv] ADJ (Bio) recessivo(-a).

re·charge [riːˈtʃɑːdʒ] VT (battery) ricaricare.

re·charge·able [riːˈtʃɑːdʒəbl] ADJ (battery) ricaricabile.

re·cher·ché [rəˈʃɛəʃeɪ] ADJ ricercato(-a).

re·cidi·vism [rɪˈsɪdɪˌvɪzəm] N recidività.

re·cidi·vist [rɪˈsɪdɪvɪst] N recidivo(-a).

reci·pe [ˈrɛsɪpɪ] N (also fig) ricetta.

re·cipi·ent [rɪˈsɪpɪənt] N (of letter) destinatario(-a); (of cheque) beneficiario(-a); (of award) assegnatario(-a).

re·cip·ro·cal [rɪˈsɪprəkəl] ADJ reciproco(-a); **reciprocal trading** scambio commerciale.

re·cip·ro·cal·ly [rɪˈsɪprəkəlɪ] ADV reciprocamente.

re·cip·ro·cate [rɪˈsɪprəˌkeɪt] VT, VI ricambiare, contraccambiare.

reci·proc·ity [ˌrɛsɪˈprɒsətɪ] N reciprocità.

re·cit·al [rɪˈsaɪtl] N (Mus) recital m inv; (of poetry) recita; (account) resoconto.

reci·ta·tion [ˌrɛsɪˈteɪʃən] N recitazione f; **to give recitations from Shakespeare** recitare brani da Shakespeare.

re·cite [rɪˈsaɪt] 1 VT (poem) recitare; (facts, details) elencare, enumerare.

2 VI recitare.

reck·less [ˈrɛklɪs] ADJ (driver, driving, speed) spericolato (-a); (disregard, pursuit) incosciente; (action, decision) avventato(-a).

reck·less·ly [ˈrɛklɪslɪ] ADV (drive) in modo spericolato; (gamble, bet, plunge) avventatamente.

reck·less·ness [ˈrɛklɪsnɪs] N (of driving) spericolatezza; (of person, behaviour) incoscienza, avventatezza.

reck·on [ˈrɛkən] 1 VT (calculate) calcolare; (believe) pensare, credere; (judge) considerare, stimare; **I reckon him to be one of the best** lo considero uno dei migliori, per me è uno dei migliori; **I reckon (that) we'll be late** prevedo che saremo in ritardo.

2 VI contare, calcolare; **to reckon with sb** fare i conti con qn; **he is somebody to be reckoned with** è uno da non sottovalutare; **to reckon without sb/sth** non tener

conto di qn/qc; **to reckon without doing sth** non calcolare di fare qc

▶ **reckon in** VT + ADV considerare; **when everything is reckoned in ...** a conti fatti...

▶ **reckon on** VI + PREP (*bank on*) contare su; (*expect*) prevedere; **to reckon on doing sth** far conto di fare qc

▶ **reckon up** VT + ADV (*frm: cost, losses*) calcolare; **to reckon up the bill** fare il conto.

reck·on·ing ['rɛknɪŋ] N calcoli *mpl*, conti *mpl*; **to be out in one's reckoning** aver sbagliato *or* fatto male i propri conti; **the day of reckoning** (*fig*) il momento della resa dei conti.

re·claim [rɪ'kleɪm] VT (*baggage, waste materials*) ricuperare; (*money*) richiedere, reclamare; (*land*) bonificare.

rec·la·ma·tion [ˌrɛklə'meɪʃən] N (*of waste materials*) ricupero; (*of land*) bonifica.

re·cline [rɪ'klaɪm] VI (*person*) essere sdraiato(-a); **the seat reclines** il sedile è reclinabile *or* ribaltabile.

re·clin·ing [rɪ'klaɪnɪŋ] ADJ (*seat*) reclinabile, ribaltabile.

re·cluse [rɪ'klu:s] N recluso(-a), eremita *m*.

re·clu·sive [rɪ'klu:sɪv] ADJ (*frm*) recluso(-a); **to become reclusive** fare vita da recluso(-a), far vita appartata.

rec·og·ni·tion [ˌrɛkəg'nɪʃən] N riconoscimento; **in recognition of** in *or* come segno di riconoscimento per; **to gain recognition** ottenere un riconoscimento; **to change/change sth beyond recognition** diventare/rendere qc irriconoscibile; **transformed beyond recognition** irriconoscibile.

rec·og·niz·able ['rɛkəg,naɪzəbl] ADJ: **recognizable (by)** riconoscibile (a *or* da).

rec·og·niz·ably ['rɛkəg,naɪzəblɪ] ADV riconoscibilmente.

rec·og·nize ['rɛkəg,naɪz] VT (*all senses*) riconoscere; **to recognize (by/as)** riconoscere (a *or* da/come).

rec·og·nized ['rɛkəgnaɪzd] ADJ (*technique, authority*) riconosciuto(-a).

re·coil [rɪ'kɔɪl] ①VI **a** (*person: draw back*) tirarsi indietro; **to recoil (from) sth** indietreggiare (di fronte *or* davanti a) qc; **to recoil from doing sth** rifuggire dal fare qc **b** (*gun*) rinculare.

②N (*of gun*) rinculo.

rec·ol·lect [ˌrɛkə'lɛkt] VT rammentare, ricordare.

rec·ol·lec·tion [ˌrɛkə'lɛkʃən] N memoria, ricordo; **to the best of my recollection** per quello che mi ricordo.

rec·om·mend [ˌrɛkə'mɛnd] VT (*course of action*) consigliare; (*product, doctor*) raccomandare, consigliare; (*person: for job*) raccomandare; **I recommend that he sees a doctor** (*frm*) gli consiglierei di vedere un medico; **to recommend sb for sth** raccomandare qn per qc; **she has a lot to recommend her** ha molti elementi a suo favore.

rec·om·men·da·tion [ˌrɛkəmɛn'deɪʃən] N (*of person, product*) raccomandazione *f*; (*of course of action*) consiglio; **to do sth on sb's recommendation** fare qc su *or* dietro consiglio di qn.

rec·om·men·ded [ˌrɛkə'mɛndɪd] ADJ consigliato(-a); **highly recommended** vivamente consigliato(-a); **recommended retail price** prezzo (di vendita) consigliato.

rec·om·pense ['rɛkəmpɛns] ①N ricompensa; (*Law: for damage*) risarcimento.

②VT ricompensare; **to recompense sb (for sth)** (*Law*) risarcire qn (di qc).

rec·on·cil·able ['rɛkən,saɪləbl] ADJ: **reconcilable (with)** conciliabile (con).

rec·on·cile ['rɛkən,saɪl] VT (*persons*) riconciliare; (*theories, contradictions*) conciliare; **to become reconciled** (*people*)

riconciliarsi; **to reconcile o.s. to sth** rassegnarsi a qc.

rec·on·cilia·tion [ˌrɛkənsɪlɪ'eɪʃən] N (*of people*) riconciliazione *f*; (*of contradictions, attitudes*) conciliazione *f*.

re·con·dite [rɪ'kɒndaɪt] ADJ (*frm*) recondito(-a).

re·con·di·tion [ˌri:kən'dɪʃən] VT (*engine*) ricondizionare.

re·con·nais·sance [rɪ'kɒnɪsəns] N (*Mil*) ricognizione *f*.

♦ **reconnaissance flight** N volo di ricognizione.

re·con·noi·tre, (*Am*) **re·con·noi·ter** [ˌrɛkə'nɔɪtəʳ] (*Mil*) ①VT fare una ricognizione di.

②VI fare una ricognizione.

re·con·sid·er [ˌri:kən'sɪdəʳ] VT riconsiderare.

re·con·sid·era·tion [ˌri:kənˌsɪdə'reɪʃən] N riconsiderazione *f*.

re·con·sti·tute [ri:'kɒnstɪˌtju:t] VT ricostituire.

re·con·struct [ˌri:kən'strʌkt] VT ricostruire.

re·con·struc·tion [ˌri:kən'strʌkʃən] N ricostruzione *f*.

re·con·vene [ˌri:kən'vi:n] ①VT riconvocare.

②VI radunarsi.

re·con·ver·sion [ˌri:kən'vɜ:ʃən] N (*Fin*) riconversione *f*.

rec·ord [*n, adj* 'rɛkɔ:d; *vb* rɪ'kɔ:d] ①N **a** (*report, note*) rapporto; (*file*) pratica, dossier *m inv*; (*minutes: of meeting*) verbale *m*; (*Law*) registro; (*historical report*) documento; (*Comput*) record *m inv*, registrazione *f*; **record of attendance** registro delle presenze; **public records** archivi *mpl*; **there is no record of it** non c'è niente che lo possa comprovare; **to keep a record of sth** tener nota di qc; **just for the record** tanto per mettere le cose in chiaro; **he is on record as saying that ...** ha dichiarato pubblicamente che...; **it is on record that ...** è stato registrato che...; **to place** *or* **put sth on record** mettere qc agli atti; **he told me off the record** (*fam*) me l'ha detto ufficiosamente; **to set the record straight** mettere le cose in chiaro

b (*person's past in general*) precedenti *mpl*; (*as dossier*) resoconto; (*also*: **criminal record**) menzione *f* nel casellario giudiziale; **he has a clean record** ha la fedina penale pulita, non ha precedenti penali; **police records** schedario *msg* della polizia; **Italy's excellent record** i brillanti successi italiani; **the school has a poor record of exam passes** in quella scuola si registra una bassa percentuale di promozioni

c (*Sport*) record *m inv*, primato; **to beat** *or* **break a record** battere un record *or* un primato; **to hold the record (for sth)** detenere il primato (di qc)

d (*Mus*) disco.

②ADJ ATTR record *inv*; **in record time** a tempo di record.

③VT **a** (*set down*) registrare, prendere nota di; (*relate*) raccontare; **to record one's vote** votare

b (*Mus*) registrare, incidere; (*Comput*) registrare

c (*subj: thermometer*) registrare.

♦ **record-breaking** ['rɛkɔ:dˌbreɪkɪŋ] ADJ che batte tutti i record.

♦ **record card** ['rɛkɔ:dˌkɑ:d] N (*index card*) scheda.

♦ **record-changer** ['rɛkɔ:dˌtʃeɪndʒəʳ] N cambiadischi *m inv* automatico.

rec·ord·ed de·liv·ery let·ter [rɪkɔ:dɪdɪlɪvəriˌlɛtəʳ] N (*Brit Post*) lettera raccomandata.

re·cord·er [rɪ'kɔ:dəʳ] N **a** (*tape recorder*) registratore *m* **b** (*Mus*) flauto diritto *or* dolce **c** (*Law: in England and Wales*) avvocato che funge da giudice.

♦ **record holder** ['rɛkɔ:dˌhəʊldəʳ] N (*Sport*) primatista *m/f*, detentore(-trice) di (un) record.

re·cord·ing [rɪ'kɔ:dɪŋ] N (*of programme, song*) registrazione *f*.

♦ **recording session** N seduta di registrazione.

♦ **recording studio** N sala di registrazione.
♦ **record library** ['rɛkɔːd ˌlaɪbrərɪ] N discoteca (*raccolta*).
♦ **record player** ['rɛkɔːd ˌpleɪəʳ] N giradischi *m inv*.
♦ **record token** ['rɛkɔːdtəʊkən] N *buono per l'acquisto di dischi*.
re·count [rɪ'kaʊnt] VT (*narrate*) raccontare.
re-count [*n* 'riːˌkaʊnt; *vb* ˌriː'kaʊnt] ① N (*of votes*) nuovo conteggio.
② VT ricontare, rifare il conteggio di.
re·coup [rɪ'kuːp] VT ricuperare; **to recoup one's losses** ricuperare le perdite, rifarsi.
re·course [rɪ'kɔːs] N (*frm*): **to have recourse to** ricorrere a, far ricorso a.
re·cov·er [rɪ'kʌvəʳ] ① VT (*belongings, goods, wreck, lost time*) ricuperare; (*reclaim: money*) ottenere il rimborso di; (*Law: damages*) ottenere il risarcimento di; (*balance, appetite, health etc*) ritrovare, ricuperare; **to recover one's senses** riprendere i sensi; (*fig*) ritornare in sé.
② VI (*all senses*) riprendersi; (*from illness*) ristabilirsi.
re-cover [ˌriː'kʌvəʳ] VT (*chair, settee*) ricoprire.
re·cov·er·able [rɪ'kʌvərəbl] ADJ (*debt, loss*) ricuperabile.
re·cov·ery [rɪ'kʌvərɪ] N **a** (*see vt*) ricupero; rimborso; risarcimento **b** (*see vi*) ripresa; **to make a recovery** (*Med*) avere *or* fare un miglioramento; (*Sport, Fin*) avere una ripresa; **to be on the way to recovery** (*Med*) essere in via di guarigione; (*Sport, Fin*) essere in ripresa.
re·cre·ate [ˌriː'kreɪt] VT ricreare.
rec·rea·tion [*sense a* ˌrɛkrɪ'eɪʃən; *sense b* ˌriːkrɪ'eɪʃən] N **a** (*leisure*) ricreazione *f*. **b** (*restoration*) restaurazione *f*.
rec·rea·tion·al [ˌrɛkrɪ'eɪʃənəl] ADJ ricreativo(-a).
♦ **recreational drug** N *sostanza stupefacente usata a scopo ricreativo.*
♦ **recreational vehicle** N (*Am*) camper *m inv*.
♦ **recreation ground** N campo *m* giochi *inv*.
re·crimi·na·tion [rɪˌkrɪmɪ'neɪʃən] N recriminazione *f*.
re·cruit [rɪ'kruːt] ① N (*Mil*) recluta; (*new member: of club*) nuovo(-a) iscritto(-a); (: *of staff*) nuovo(-a) assunto(-a).
② VT (*staff, members, soldiers*) reclutare.
re·cruit·ing of·fice [rɪ'kruːtɪŋ ˌɒfɪs] N ufficio di reclutamento.
re·cruit·ment [rɪ'kruːtmənt] N reclutamento.
rec·tan·gle ['rɛkˌtæŋgl] N rettangolo.
rec·tan·gu·lar [rɛk'tæŋgjʊləʳ] ADJ rettangolare.
rec·ti·fi·er ['rɛktɪˌfaɪəʳ] N (*Elec*) raddrizzatore *m*.
rec·ti·fy ['rɛktɪˌfaɪ] VT (*error*) rettificare; (*omission*) riparare a.
rec·ti·lin·ear [ˌrɛktɪ'lɪnɪəʳ] ADJ rettilineo(-a); **rectilinear motion** moto rettilineo.
rec·ti·tude ['rɛktɪˌtjuːd] N (*frm*) rettitudine *f*.
rec·tor ['rɛktəʳ] N (*Rel*) parroco (*anglicano*); (*Univ*) rettore *m*; (*in Scottish universities*) *personalità eletta dagli studenti per rappresentarli*; (*of school*) preside *m/f*.
rec·tory ['rɛktərɪ] N casa parrocchiale (*anglicana*).
rec·tum ['rɛktəm] N (*Anat*) retto.
re·cum·bent [rɪ'kʌmbənt] ADJ (*frm*) giacente.
re·cu·per·ate [rɪ'kuːpəˌreɪt] ① VI (*Med*) ristabilirsi.
② VT (*losses*) ricuperare.
re·cu·pera·tion [rɪˌkuːpə'reɪʃən] N (*after illness*) convalescenza; (*of losses*) ricupero.
re·cu·pera·tive [rɪ'kuːpərətɪv] ADJ (*powers*) di ricupero.
re·cur [rɪ'kɜː'] VI (*pain, event, mistake*) ripetersi; (*idea, theme*) ricorrere, riapparire; (*difficulty, opportunity, symptoms*) ripresentarsi, ripetersi.
re·cur·rence [rɪ'kʌrəns] N (*of pain, dream, violence*) ripetersi *m*; (*of injury, problem*) ripresentarsi *m*; (*of disease,

symptoms*) ricomparsa; (*of idea, theme*) ricorrenza.
re·cur·rent [rɪ'kʌrənt] ADJ ricorrente.
re·cur·ring [rɪ'kɜːrɪŋ] ADJ (*Math*) periodico(-a).
re·cy·cle [ˌriː'saɪkl] VT riciclare.
red [rɛd] ① ADJ (*comp* -**der**, *superl* -**dest**) (*all senses*) rosso(-a); **to be red in the face** (*from physical effort*) essere tutto(-a) rosso(-a), avere il viso rosso; (*embarrassed*) essere rosso(-a) (in viso); **to roll out the red carpet (for sb)** (*fig*) accogliere qn in pompa magna; **it's like a red rag to a bull with him** è una cosa che gli fa vedere rosso.
② N (*colour*) rosso; (*Pol pej*) rosso(-a); **in the red** (*Fin: account*) in rosso, scoperto(-a); (: *firm*) in deficit, in rosso; **to see red** (*fig*) vedere rosso.
♦ **red alert** N allarme rosso.
♦ **red-blooded** [ˌrɛd'blʌdɪd] ADJ (*fam*) gagliardo(-a).
red·breast ['rɛdˌbrɛst] N (*bird*) pettirosso.
red·brick ['rɛdˌbrɪk] ADJ: **redbrick university** (*Brit*) *università istituita alla fine del secolo scorso.*
♦ **red carpet treatment** N trattamento d'onore.
♦ **Red Crescent** N: **the Red Crescent** la Mezzaluna Rossa.
♦ **Red Cross** N: **the Red Cross** la Croce Rossa.
red·cur·rant [ˌrɛd'kʌrənt] N ribes *m inv* rosso.
♦ **red deer** N, PL INV cervo(-a).
red·den ['rɛdn] ① VT arrossare, tingere di rosso.
② VI (*sky, leaves*) diventar rosso, tingersi di rosso; (*person*) arrossire.
red·dish ['rɛdɪʃ] ADJ rossiccio(-a), rossastro(-a); (*hair*) rossiccio(-a).
re·deco·rate [ˌriː'dɛkəˌreɪt] VT tinteggiare (e tappezzare) di nuovo.
re·deem [rɪ'diːm] VT (*Rel: sinner*) redimere; (*buy back: pawned goods*) disimpegnare, riscattare; (*Fin: debt, mortgage*) estinguere, ammortare; (*fulfil: promise*) mantenere; (: *obligation*) adempiere a; (*compensate for: fault*) compensare; **to redeem o.s.** farsi perdonare.
re·deem·able [rɪ'diːməbl] ADJ (*bonds, shares*) redimibile.
Re·deem·er [rɪ'diːməʳ] N Redentore *m*.
re·deem·ing [rɪ'diːmɪŋ] ADJ: **redeeming feature** unico aspetto positivo.
re·de·fine [ˌriːdɪ'faɪn] VT ridefinire.
re·demp·tion [rɪ'dɛmpʃən] N (*Rel*) redenzione *f*; **past** *or* **beyond redemption** irrecuperabile.
re·deploy [ˌriːdɪ'plɔɪ] VT (*troops: send elsewhere*) trasferire in un altro settore; (: *reorganize*) riorganizzare lo schieramento di; (*workers*) reimpiegare; (*resources*) ridistribuire.
re·deploy·ment [ˌriːdɪ'plɔɪmənt] N (*of resources*) ridistribuzione *f*.
re·deve·lop [riːdɪ'vɛləp] VT (*area*) ristrutturare.
re·devel·op·ment [ˌriːdɪ'vɛləpmənt] N (*of area*) ristrutturazione *f*.
♦ **red-eyed** [ˌrɛd'aɪd] ADJ con gli occhi rossi *or* arrossati.
♦ **red-faced** [ˌrɛd'feɪst] ADJ (*also fig*) rosso(-a) in viso.
♦ **red-haired** [ˌrɛd'hɛəd] ADJ con i *or* dai capelli rossi.
♦ **red-handed** [ˌrɛd'hændɪd] ADJ: **to catch sb red-handed** prendere qn con le mani nel sacco, cogliere qn in flagrante.
red·head ['rɛdˌhɛd] N (*person with red hair*) rosso(-a).
♦ **red herring** N (*fig*) falsa pista.
♦ **red-hot** [ˌrɛd'hɒt] ADJ arroventato(-a), rovente.
re·did [ˌriː'dɪd] PT of **redo**.
♦ **Red Indian** N (*offensive*) pellerossa *m/f*.
re·di·rect [ˌriːdaɪ'rɛkt] VT (*letter*) rispedire (*a un nuovo

indirizzo).

re·dis·count [ˌriː'dɪskaʊnt] VT (*Fin*) riscontare.

re·dis·trib·ute [ˌriːdɪs'trɪbjuːt] VT ridistribuire.

♦ **red-letter day** [ˌrɛd'lɛtəˌdeɪ] N giorno memorabile.

♦ **red light** N (*Aut*) (semaforo) rosso; **to go through a red light** passare col rosso.

♦ **red-light district** [ˌrɛd'laɪtˌdɪstrɪkt] N quartiere *m* a luce rossa.

♦ **red meat** N carne *f* rossa.

red·ness ['rɛdnɪs] N (*of skin*) rossore *m*; (*of hair, colour*) rosso.

re·do [ˌriː'duː] VT (*pt* redid, *pp* redone) rifare.

redo·lent ['rɛdəʊlənt] ADJ (*liter*): **redolent of** fragrante di, profumato(-a) di; (*fig*) evocativo(-a) di.

re·done [ˌriː'dʌn] PP of redo.

re·dou·ble [ˌriː'dʌbl] VT raddoppiare; **to redouble one's efforts** intensificare gli sforzi.

re·doubt·able [rɪ'daʊtəbl] ADJ (*frm*) formidabile, temibile.

re·dound [rɪ'daʊnd] VI: **to redound upon sb** riversarsi su qn; **to redound to sb's credit** tornare a credito di qn.

♦ **red pepper** N (*capsicum*) peperone *m*; (*cayenne pepper*) peperoncino rosso.

re·draft [*n* 'riːˌdrɑːft; *vb* ˌriː'drɑːft] ① N nuova stesura.

② VT stendere di nuovo, fare una nuova stesura di.

re·dress [rɪ'drɛs] (*frm*) ① N riparazione *f*.

② VT riparare; **to redress the balance** ristabilire l'equilibrio.

♦ **Red Sea** N: **the Red Sea** il mar Rosso.

red·shank ['rɛdˌʃæŋk] N (*Zool*) pettegola.

♦ **red shift** N (*Phys*) spostamento verso il rosso.

red·skin ['rɛdˌskɪn] N (*offensive*) pellerossa *m/f*.

♦ **red tape** N lungaggini *fpl* burocratiche.

♦ **red-throated diver** [ˌrɛdθrəʊtɪd'daɪvər] N tuffatore *m* stellato.

re·duce [rɪ'djuːs] ① VT ⓐ (*gen*) ridurre; (*prices, taxes*) abbassare, ridurre, diminuire; (*speed, voltage, expenses*, *Med*: *swelling*) ridurre, diminuire; (*temperature*) far diminuire, far scendere; **to reduce sth by/to** ridurre qc di/a; **"reduce speed now"** (*Aut*) "rallentare"; **to reduce sth to ashes** ridurre qc in cenere; **to reduce sb to silence/despair/tears** ridurre qn al silenzio/alla disperazione/in lacrime; **we were reduced to begging** eravamo ridotti all'elemosina; **reduced to nothing** ridotto(-a) a zero

ⓑ (*Mil*): **to reduce sb to the ranks** degradare qn a soldato semplice.

② VI (*slim*) dimagrire.

re·duced [rɪ'djuːst] ADJ (*decreased*) ridotto(-a); **at a reduced price** a prezzo ribassato *or* ridotto; **"greatly reduced prices"** "grandi ribassi"; **in reduced circumstances** nelle ristrettezze.

re·duc·tion [rɪ'dʌkʃən] N (*see vt a*) riduzione *f*; diminuzione *f*; **reductions for cash** sconto per (il pagamento in) contanti.

re·dun·dan·cy [rɪ'dʌndənsɪ] N (*Industry*) licenziamento (*per esubero di personale*); (*frm*: *profusion*) superfluità; (*Literature*) ridondanza; **compulsory redundancy** licenziamento (*per esubero*); **voluntary redundancy** *forma di cassa integrazione volontaria*.

♦ **redundancy payment** N (*Brit*) indennità *f inv* di licenziamento.

re·dun·dant [rɪ'dʌndənt] ADJ (*Brit*: *worker*) licenziato(-a)

(*per esubero di personale*); (*detail, object*) superfluo(-a); (*Literature*) ridondante; **to be made redundant** (*worker*) essere licenziato(-a) (*perché in esubero*).

red·wood ['rɛdˌwʊd] N sequoia.

reed [riːd] N (*Bot*) canna; (*Mus*: *in mouthpiece*) ancia; (: *instrument*) strumento a fiato munito di ancia.

re·educate [ˌriː'ɛdjʊˌkeɪt] VT rieducare.

reedy ['riːdɪ] ADJ (*comp* -ier, *superl* -iest) (*voice, instrument*) acuto(-a).

reef¹ [riːf] N (*Geog*) scogliera, banco di scogli; **coral reef** barriera corallina.

reef² [riːf] ① N terzarolo; **to take in a reef** (*Naut*) prendere una mano di terzaroli.

② VT terzarolare.

reef·er ['riːfər] N ⓐ (*jacket*) giacca da pescatore a doppiopetto ⓑ (*old fam*: *joint*) spinello.

♦ **reef knot** N nodo piano.

♦ **reef point** N (*Naut*) matafione *m*.

reek [riːk] VI: **to reek of sth** puzzare di qc.

reel [riːl] ① N ⓐ (*in fishing etc*) mulinello; (*cotton reel*) rocchetto, spoletta; (*Tech*) aspo; (*for tape recorder*) bobina; (*Phot*: *for small camera*) rotolino, rullino; (: *of cine film*) bobina, pizza

ⓑ (*dance*) *danza scozzese o irlandese molto vivace*.

② VI (*sway*) vacillare, barcollare; **my head is reeling** mi gira la testa.

③ VT (*Tech*) annaspare; (*wind up*) avvolgere

► **reel in** VT + ADV (*fish*) tirare su

► **reel off** VT + ADV snocciolare, sciorinare.

re-elect [ˌriːɪ'lɛkt] VT rieleggere.

re-election [ˌriːɪ'lɛkʃən] N rielezione *f*.

re-enact [ˌriːɪ'nækt] VT (*crime, scene*) ricostruire.

re-enter [ˌriː'ɛntər] ① VI rientrare; **to re-enter for an exam** ripresentarsi a un esame.

② VT rientrare in.

re-entry [ˌriː'ɛntrɪ] N rientro.

re-examine [ˌriːɪg'zæmɪn] VT (*person, proposal, evidence*) riesaminare; (*witness*) interrogare di nuovo.

re-export [ˌriːɪks'pɔːt] ① VT riesportare.

② N (*trading activity*) riesportazione *f*; (*goods*) merce *f* riesportata.

ref [rɛf] N ABBR (*Sport fam*: = referee) arbitro.

ref. ABBR (*Comm*) = reference.

re·fec·tory [rɪ'fɛktərɪ] N refettorio.

re·fer [rɪ'fɜːr] ① VT (*gen*): **to refer sth to** (*matter, decision*) sottoporre qc a qn, deferire qc a qn; **to refer sb to sth** richiamare l'attenzione di qn su qc; **he referred me to the manager** mi ha detto di rivolgermi al direttore; **"refer to drawer"** (*on cheque*) "rivolgersi al traente".

② VI: **to refer to** ⓐ (*relate to*) riferirsi a; **does that refer to me?** vale anche per me?

ⓑ (*allude to*: *directly*) fare riferimento a; (: *indirectly*) fare allusione *or* accenno a; **referring to your letter** (*Comm*) in riferimento alla Vostra lettera; **we will not refer to it again** non ne riparleremo più

ⓒ (*turn attention to, see*) consultare; (*consult*: *person*) rivolgersi a; **please refer to section 3** vedi sezione 3.

ref·eree [ˌrɛfə'riː] ① N ⓐ (*in dispute, Sport*) arbitro; (*Tennis*) giudice *m* di gara ⓑ (*Brit*: *for job application*) referenza; **to give sb as a referee** dare il nome di qn per referenze; **to be referee for sb** scrivere una lettera di referenze per qn.

② VT arbitrare.

ref·er·ence ['rɛfrəns] ① N ⓐ (*allusion*: *direct*) riferimento, menzione *f*; (: *indirect*) allusione *f*; (*relation, connection*)

rapporto; (*Comm*: *in letter*): **with reference to** in *or* con riferimento a; **without reference to any particular case** senza nessun riferimento specifico

b (*from book, list*) rimando; (*on letter*) numero di riferimento; (*on map*) coordinate *fpl*; **"please quote this reference"** (*Comm*) "si prega di far riferimento al numero di protocollo"

c (*testimonial*): **reference(s)** referenze *fpl*; **may I give you as a reference?** posso dare il suo nome per referenze?.

2 ADJ (*library*) di consultazione; (*point*) di riferimento.

♦ **reference book** N libro di consultazione.

♦ **reference library** N biblioteca per la consultazione.

♦ **reference number** N (*Comm*) numero di riferimento.

ref·er·en·dum [ˌrɛfəˈrɛndəm] N (*pl* **referendums** *or* **referenda** [ˌrɛfəˈrɛndə]) referendum *m inv.*

refer·ral [rɪˈfɜːrəl] N deferimento; (*Med*): **she got a referral to a specialist** l'hanno mandata da uno specialista.

re·fill [*n* ˈriːˌfɪl; *vb* ˌriːˈfɪl] N **1** N (*for pen etc*) ricambio.

2 VT (*gen*) riempire (di nuovo); (*pen, lighter*) ricaricare.

re·fine [rɪˈfaɪn] VT (*sugar, oil, tastes, style*) raffinare; (*design, technique, machine*) perfezionare

▶ **refine on, refine upon** VI + PREP perfezionare, migliorare.

re·fined [rɪˈfaɪnd] ADJ raffinato(-a).

re·fine·ment [rɪˈfaɪnmənt] N (*of person, language*) raffinatezza, finezza; (*in machine, system*) miglioramento.

re·fin·er [rɪˈfaɪnəʳ] N raffinatore *m.*

re·fin·ery [rɪˈfaɪnərɪ] N raffineria; **oil/sugar refinery** raffineria di petrolio/zucchero.

re·fit [*n* ˈriːˌfɪt; *vb* ˌriːˈfɪt] **1** N (*Naut*) raddobbo.

2 VT (*ship*) raddobbare.

re·flate [ˌriːˈfleɪt] VT (*Econ*) reflazionare.

re·fla·tion [ˌriːˈfleɪʃən] N (*Econ*) reflazione *f.*

re·fla·tion·ary [ˌriːˈfleɪʃənərɪ] ADJ (*Econ*: *programme*) reflazionistico(-a).

re·flect [rɪˈflɛkt] **1** VT **a** (*light, image, heat*) riflettere; (*fig*) rispecchiare; **to reflect credit on sb** fare onore a qn **b** (*think*): **to reflect that** riflettere sul fatto che.

2 VI **a** (*think, meditate*): **to reflect (on sth)** riflettere (su qc) **b** (*discredit*): **to reflect (up)on sb/sth** ripercuotersi su qn/qc.

re·flec·tion [rɪˈflɛkʃən] N **a** (*act*) riflessione *f*; (*in mirror etc*) riflesso **b** (*thought*) riflessione *f*; **on reflection** dopo aver riflettuto, pensandoci sopra **c** (*aspersion, doubt*) dubbio; **this is no reflection on your honesty** questa non è un'insinuazione sulla tua onestà **d** (*Math*) riflessione *f.*

re·flec·tive [rɪˌflɛktɪv] ADJ **a** (*pensive*) pensoso(-a) **b** (*indicative*): **to be reflective of** (*frm*) riflettere **c** (*light, surface*) riflettente **d** (*jacket, belt*) lucido(-a).

re·flec·tor [rɪˈflɛktəʳ] N (*Aut*: *also*: **rear reflector**) catarifrangente *m.*

re·flex [ˈriːflɛks] **1** N riflesso.

2 ADJ (*Math*) concavo(-a).

♦ **reflex action** N azione *f* riflessa.

♦ **reflex camera** N (*Phot*) reflex *f inv.*

re·flex·ive [rɪˈflɛksɪv] ADJ (*Gram*) riflessivo(-a).

re·float [ˌriːˈfləʊt] VT (*ship, business*) rimettere a galla.

re·for·est [riːˈfɒrɪst] VT rimboscare.

re·form [rɪˈfɔːm] **1** N riforma.

2 VT (*society, morals*) riformare; (*criminal*) rieducare, ricuperare socialmente; (*person's character*) correggere.

3 VI (*person*) emendarsi.

re·for·mat [ˌriːˈfɔːmæt] VT (*Comput*) riformattare.

Ref·or·ma·tion [ˌrɛfəˈmeɪʃən] N (*Rel*): **the Reformation** la Riforma.

re·forma·tory [rɪfɔːˈmətərɪ] N (*Am*) riformatorio.

re·formed [rɪˈfɔːmd] ADJ (*criminal*) rieducato(-a), ricuperato(-a) alla società; (*morals*) riformato(-a).

re·form·er [rɪˈfɔːməʳ] N riformatore(-trice).

re·form·ist [rɪˈfɔːmɪst] ADJ, N riformista (*m/f*).

re·fract [rɪˈfrækt] VT rifrangere.

re·frac·tion [rɪˈfrækʃən] N rifrazione *f.*

re·frac·tive [rɪˈfræktɪv] ADJ di *or* della rifrazione; **refractive constant** indice *m* di rifrazione costante.

re·frac·tory [rɪˈfræktərɪ] ADJ (*frm*) refrattario(-a).

re·frain¹ [rɪˈfreɪn] N (*Mus*) ritornello, refrain *m inv.*

re·frain² [rɪˈfreɪn] VI: **to refrain from sth/from doing sth** astenersi *or* trattenersi da qc/dal fare qc.

re·fresh [rɪˈfrɛʃ] VT (*subj*: *drink*) rinfrescare; (: *food, sleep, bath*) ristorare; (*fig*: *memory*) rinfrescare.

re·fresh·er course [rɪˈfrɛʃəˌkɔːs] N (*Brit*) corso di aggiornamento.

re·fresh·ing [rɪˈfrɛʃɪŋ] ADJ (*drink*) rinfrescante; (*sleep*) ristoratore(-trice); (*change*) piacevole; (*idea, point of view*) originale.

re·fresh·ment [rɪˈfrɛʃmənt] N (*eating, resting*) ristoro; **refreshments** NPL (*food and drink*) rinfreschi *mpl.*

♦ **refreshment room** N posto di ristoro.

re·frig·er·ate [rɪˈfrɪdʒəˌreɪt] VT refrigerare.

re·frig·era·tion [rɪˌfrɪdʒəˈreɪʃən] N refrigerazione *f.*

re·frig·era·tor [rɪˈfrɪdʒəˌreɪtəʳ] N frigorifero.

re·fu·el [ˌriːˈfjʊəl] **1** VI rifornirsi di carburante, fare rifornimento (di carburante).

2 VT rifornire di carburante.

re·fu·el·ling [ˌriːˈfjʊəlɪŋ] N rifornimento di carburante.

♦ **refuelling stop** N scalo tecnico.

ref·uge [ˈrɛfjuːdʒ] N (*shelter*) riparo; (*for climbers, battered wives, fig*) rifugio; **place of refuge** rifugio; **to take refuge in** (*also fig*) rifugiarsi in.

refu·gee [ˌrɛfjʊˈdʒiː] N rifugiato(-a), profugo(-a).

♦ **refugee camp** N campo *m* profughi *inv.*

re·fund [*n* ˈriːˌfʌnd; *vb* rɪˈfʌnd] **1** N rimborso.

2 VT rimborsare; **to refund sb's expenses** rimborsare qn.

re·fur·bish [ˌriːˈfɜːbɪʃ] VT (*frm*) rimettere a nuovo.

re·fur·nish [ˌriːˈfɜːnɪʃ] VT ammobiliare di nuovo.

re·fus·al [rɪˈfjuːzəl] N: **refusal (to do)** rifiuto (di *or* a fare); **to have first refusal on sth** avere il diritto d'opzione su qc.

re·fuse¹ [rɪˈfjuːz] **1** VT (*all senses*) rifiutare; **to refuse sb sth** rifiutare qc a qn; **to refuse to do sth** rifiutare *or* rifiutarsi di fare qc.

2 VI rifiutarsi; (*horse*) rifiutare (l'ostacolo).

ref·use² [ˈrɛfjuːs] N rifiuti *mpl*; **garden refuse** rifiuti del giardino.

♦ **refuse collection** [ˈrɛfjuːzkəˌlɛkʃən] N raccolta dei rifiuti.

♦ **refuse collector** [ˈrɛfjuːzkəˌlɛktəʳ] N netturbino.

♦ **refuse disposal** [ˈrɛfjuːzdɪspˌəʊzl] N smaltimento dei rifiuti.

♦ **refuse dump** [ˈrɛfjuːzˌdʌmp] N discarica (di rifiuti).

♦ **refuse lorry** [ˈrɛfjuːzˌlɒrɪ] N camion *m inv* della spazzatura.

re·fuse·nik [rɪˈfjuːznɪk] N (*old*) *ebreo a cui il governo sovietico impediva di lasciare il paese.*

refu·ta·tion [ˌrɛfjuːˈteɪʃən] N (*frm*) confutazione *f.*

re·fute [rɪˈfjuːt] VT (*frm*) confutare.

re·gain [rɪˈgeɪn] VT (*gen*) riguadagnare; (*balance, conscious-*

ness) riprendere; (*confidence*) riacquistare; (*health*) ricuperare; **to regain possession of sth** rientrare in possesso di qc; **to regain one's composure** ricomporsi.

re·gal ['riːgəl] ADJ (*bearing, manners*) regale; (*person*) dal portamento regale.

re·gale [rɪˈgeɪl] VT deliziare, intrattenere; **to regale sb with sth** intrattenere qn con qc.

re·ga·lia [rɪˈgeɪlɪə] N (*royal trappings*) insegne *fpl* reali; (*gen: insignia*) abiti *mpl* da cerimonia.

re·gal·ly ['riːgəlɪ] ADV regalmente.

re·gard [rɪˈgɑːd] **1** N **a** (*relation*): **in** *or* **with regard to** per quanto riguarda, riguardo a; **in this regard** (*frm*) a questo riguardo *or* proposito

b (*esteem, concern*) riguardo, stima; **out of regard for** per riguardo a; **to have a high regard for sb** OR **hold sb in high regard** aver molta stima per qn, tenere qn in grande considerazione; **he shows little regard for their feelings** dimostra scarsa considerazione per loro

c (*in messages*): **regards to Maria, please give my regards to Maria** salutami Maria, da' i miei saluti a Maria; (*as letter-ending*): **(kind) regards** cordiali saluti.

2 VT **a** (*consider*) considerare, stimare; **we don't regard it as necessary** non lo riteniamo necessario

b (*concern*) riguardare; **as regards ...** per quel che riguarda..., riguardo a... .

re·gard·ing [rɪˈgɑːdɪŋ] PREP riguardo a, per quanto riguarda.

re·gard·less [rɪˈgɑːdlɪs] **1** ADJ: **regardless of** (*heedless of*) senza preoccuparsi di; (*in spite of*) a dispetto di; **regardless of rank** senza distinzioni; **regardless of race** senza distinzioni di razza.

2 ADV (*fam*): **she did it regardless** l'ha fatto lo stesso.

re·gat·ta [rɪˈɡætə] N regata.

Re·gen·cy ['riːdʒənsɪ] **1** N: **the Regency** (*in England*) *la reggenza del principe di Galles, futuro Giorgio IV*; (*in France*) la Reggenza.

2 ADJ (*style*) reggenza *inv*; (*house, furniture*) (in) stile reggenza *inv*.

re·gen·cy ['riːdʒənsɪ] N reggenza.

re·gen·er·ate [rɪˈdʒɛnəˌreɪt] (*frm*) **1** VT (*Bio, fig: society*) rigenerare; (: *feelings, enthusiasm*) far rinascere.

2 VI (*see vt*) rigenerarsi; rinascere.

re·gen·era·tion [rɪˌdʒɛnəˈreɪʃən] N (*frm: of economy, society*) rigenerazione *f*; (: *of feelings, enthusiasm*) rinnovamento.

re·gen·era·tive [rɪˈdʒɛnərətɪv] ADJ (*frm: tissue*) rigenerativo(-a); (: *climate, air*) rigeneratore(-trice).

re·gent ['riːdʒənt] N reggente *m/f*.

reg·gae ['rɛɡeɪ] N (*Mus*) reggae *m*.

regi·cide ['rɛdʒɪˌsaɪd] N (*frm: crime*) regicidio; (: *person*) regicida *m/f*.

ré·gime [reɪˈʒiːm] N regime *m*.

regi·men ['rɛdʒɪˌmɛn] N (*frm*) regime *m*.

regi·ment [*n* 'rɛdʒɪmənt; *vb* 'rɛdʒɪˌmɛnt] **1** N (*Mil*) reggimento.

2 VT (*fig*) irreggimentare.

regi·men·tal [ˌrɛdʒɪˈmɛntl] ADJ reggimentale.

regi·men·ta·tion [ˌrɛdʒɪmɛnˈteɪʃən] N (*pej*) irreggimentazione *f*.

regi·men·ted ['rɛdʒɪˌmɛntɪd] ADJ (*pej: way of life, institution*) irregimentato(-a).

re·gion ['riːdʒən] N (*all senses*) regione *f*; **in the region of 40** (*fig*) circa 40, intorno a 40.

re·gion·al ['riːdʒənl] ADJ regionale; **regional development** (*Brit Admin*) sviluppo economico delle regioni; **regional**

development fund fondo per lo sviluppo regionale.

re·gion·al·ism ['riːdʒənəlɪzəm] N regionalismo.

re·gion·al·ly ['riːdʒənəlɪ] ADV (*vary*) da regione a regione; (*collaborate, manage*) regionalmente; (*based, organized*) a livello regionale.

reg·is·ter ['rɛdʒɪstə'] **1** N (*gen*) registro; (*of members*) elenco; **the register of births, marriages and deaths** l'anagrafe *f*.

2 VT **a** (*fact, birth, death*) registrare; (*vehicle*) immatricolare; (*trademark*) depositare; (*complaint, dissatisfaction*) sporgere; **to register a protest** presentare un esposto

b (*Post: letter*) assicurare; (*Rail: luggage*) spedire assicurato(-a)

c (*indicate: speed, temperature*) registrare, segnare; (: *dismay, disbelief, surprise*) dar segno di, mostrare.

3 VI **a** (*for class*) iscriversi; (*for work*) mettersi in lista per; (*at hotel*) firmare il registro; **to register with a doctor** mettersi nella lista di un medico come paziente; **to register for a course** iscriversi a un corso

b (*have impact, become clear*): **it didn't register (with me)** non me ne sono reso conto.

reg·is·tered ['rɛdʒɪstəd] ADJ **a** (*student, voter*) iscritto(-a); (*car*) immatricolato(-a); (*Comm: design*) depositato(-a); (*charity*) riconosciuto(-a) **b** (*Brit: letter, luggage*) assicurato(-a).

♦ **registered company** N società *f inv* iscritta all'Ufficio del Registro.

♦ **registered nurse** N (*Brit*) infermiere(-a) diplomato (-a).

♦ **registered office** N sede *f* legale.

♦ **registered trademark** N marchio registrato.

reg·is·trar [ˌrɛdʒɪsˈtrɑː'] N (*of births, deaths, marriages*) ufficiale *m* di stato civile; (*Univ*) direttore *m* amministrativo; (*Med*) *medico ospedaliero superiore ad un interno*; **Registrar of Companies** ≈ Ufficio del Registro.

reg·is·tra·tion [ˌrɛdʒɪsˈtreɪʃən] N (*gen*) registrazione *f*; (*of vehicle*) immatricolazione *f*; (*of voters, members*) iscrizione *f*; **during registration** (*Scol*) durante l'appello; **L-/M-** *etc* **registration** *dicitura su targhe automobilistiche che ne indica l'anno di fabbricazione*.

♦ **registration number** N (*Aut*) (numero di) targa.

reg·is·try ['rɛdʒɪstrɪ] N (*record office*) archivio; (*in university*) segreteria.

♦ **registry office** N (*Brit*) anagrafe *f*; **to get married in a registry office** ≈ sposarsi in municipio.

re·gress [rɪˈɡrɛs] VI (*frm*) regredire.

re·gres·sion [rɪˈɡrɛʃən] N (*frm*) regresso.

re·gres·sive [rɪˈɡrɛsɪv] ADJ (*frm*) regressivo(-a); **a regressive step** (*fig*) un passo indietro; **regressive tax** (*Econ*) imposta regressiva.

re·gret [rɪˈɡrɛt] **1** N **a** rimpianto, rammarico; **much to my regret** OR **to my great regret** con mio grande dispiacere; **I have no regrets** non ho rimpianti

b : **regrets** NPL (*excuses*) scuse *fpl*.

2 VT (*news, death*) essere dispiaciuto(-a) per, essere desolato(-a) per; **he is very ill, I regret to say** purtroppo è molto malato; **I regret that I will be unable to attend your party** (*frm*) mi rincresce (di) non poter venire alla vostra festa; **we regret to inform you that ...** (*frm*) siamo spiacenti di informarla che...; **I regret that I/he cannot help** mi rincresce (di) non poter aiutare/che lui non possa aiutare.

re·gret·ful [rɪˈɡrɛtfʊl] ADJ (*person*) spiacente, dispiaciuto (-a); (*look*) dispiaciuto(-a).

re·gret·ful·ly [rɪ'grɛtfəlɪ] ADV (*sadly*) con molto rimpianto, con rincrescimento; (*unwillingly*) a malincuore.

re·gret·table [rɪ'grɛtəbl] ADJ (*deplorable*) increscioso(-a), deplorevole; (*unfortunate*): **her absence is regrettable** ci rincresce che sia assente.

re·gret·tably [rɪ'grɛtəblɪ] ADV (*unfortunately*) purtroppo, sfortunatamente; **regrettably few** pochi, purtroppo.

re·group [,ri:'gru:p] ① VI raggrupparsi (di nuovo). ② VT raggruppare (di nuovo).

Regt ABBR = **regiment**.

regu·lar ['rɛgjʊlə'] ① ADJ a (*gen: shape, employment, army, verb*) regolare; **as regular as clockwork** (*person, event*) puntuale come un orologio; (*visits*) molto regolare; **at regular intervals** a intervalli regolari b (*habitual: visitor, client*) fisso(-a); (: *listener, reader*) fedele; (*Comm: size, price*) normale; **you need to take regular exercise** devi fare moto regolarmente c (*permissible: action, procedure*) corretto(-a) d (*fam: intensive*): **it's a regular nuisance** è una solenne scocciatura. ② N (*customer, client*) habitué m/f inv, cliente m/f abituale; (*Mil*) soldato regolare.

regu·lar·ity [,rɛgjʊ'lærɪtɪ] N regolarità.

regu·lar·ize ['rɛgjʊlə,raɪz] VT regolarizzare.

regu·lar·ly ['rɛgjʊləlɪ] ADV regolarmente.

regu·late ['rɛgjʊ,leɪt] VT regolare.

regu·la·tion [,rɛgjʊ'leɪʃən] ① N (*rule*) regolamento, regola; (*adjustment*) regolazione f. ② ADJ (*item, clothing*) di ordinanza.

regu·la·tor ['rɛgjʊleɪtə'] N (*Tech*) regolatore m.

re·gur·gi·tate [rɪgɜ:dʒɪ,teɪt] VT (*vomit*) rigurgitare; (*ideas, facts*) ripetere automaticamente.

re·ha·bili·tate [,ri:ə'bɪlɪ,teɪt] VT (*criminal, drug addict, invalid*) recuperare, reinserire.

re·ha·bi·li·ta·tion ['ri:ə,bɪlɪ'teɪʃən] N (*of offender, of disabled*) ricupero, reinserimento.

♦ **rehabilitation centre** N centro di ricupero.

re·hash [,ri:'hæʃ] (*pej*) ① N rimaneggiamento. ② VT rimaneggiare.

re·hears·al [rɪ'hɜ:səl] N prova; **dress rehearsal** prova generale.

re·hearse [rɪ'hɜ:s] VT (*Mus, Theatre*) provare; (: *one's part*) ripassare; (*what one is going to say*) ripetere.

re·house [,ri:'haʊz] VT rialloggiare.

reign [reɪn] ① N regno; **in the reign of** sotto *or* durante il regno di; **reign of terror** regno del terrore. ② VI (*also fig*) regnare; **the reigning champion** il campione in carica; **to reign supreme** (*champion*) non avere rivali; (*justice, peace etc*) regnare sovrano(-a).

reign·ing ['reɪnɪŋ] ADJ (*monarch*) regnante; (*champion*) in carica.

re·im·burse [,ri:ɪm'bɜ:s] VT: **to reimburse sb for sth** rimborsare qc a qn.

re·im·burse·ment [,ri:ɪm'bɜ:smənt] N rimborso.

rein [reɪn] N (*for horse*) redine f, briglia; **to keep a tight rein on sb** (*fig*) tenere a freno qn; **to give sb free rein** (*fig*) lasciare completa libertà a qn

▶ **rein back** VI + ADV indietreggiare

▶ **rein in** VT + ADV trattenere (tirando le briglie); (*expenditure*) limitare.

re·incar·nat·ed [ri:'ɪnkɑ:neɪtɪd] ADJ: **to be reincarnated (as)** reincarnarsi (in).

re·incar·na·tion [,ri:ɪnkɑ:'neɪʃən] N reincarnazione f.

rein·deer ['reɪn,dɪə'] N, PL INV renna.

re·inforce [,ri:ɪn'fɔ:s] VT (*army, material, structure*) rinforzare; (*fig: theory, belief*) rafforzare.

re·inforced con·crete [,ri:ɪnfɔ:st'kɒnkri:t] N cemento armato.

re·inforce·ment [,ri:ɪn'fɔ:smənt] N a (*action*) rinforzo, rafforzamento; (*thing*) rinforzo b (*Mil*): **reinforcements** NPL rinforzi mpl.

re·instate [,ri:ɪn'steɪt] VT (*employee, official*) reintegrare.

re·instate·ment [,ri:ɪn'steɪtmənt] N reintegrazione f.

re·invest [,ri:ɪn'vɛst] VT reimpiegare.

re·issue [,ri:'ɪʃju:] VT (*book*) fare una ristampa di, ristampare; (*record, film*) rimettere in circolazione, distribuire di nuovo.

re·it·er·ate [ri:'ɪtə,reɪt] VT (*frm*) ripetere, reiterare.

re·it·era·tion [ri:,ɪtə'reɪʃən] N (*frm*) reiterazione f.

re·ject [n 'ri:dʒɛkt; vb rɪ'dʒɛkt] ① N (*person, thing, also Comm*) scarto. ② VT (*offer etc*) rifiutare, respingere; (*applicant etc*) scartare, respingere; (*subj: body: food*) rifiutare; **the patient's body rejected the new organ** il paziente ha avuto una crisi di rigetto; **to feel rejected** sentirsi respinto(-a).

♦ **reject goods** NPL prodotti mpl di scarto.

re·jec·tion [rɪ'dʒɛkʃən] N (*of offer, applicant*) rifiuto; (*of new organ*) rigetto.

re·jig [,ri:'dʒɪg] VT a (*fam: rearrange, improve*) riorganizzare b (*factory etc*) riequipaggiare.

re·joice [rɪ'dʒɔɪs] VI (*frm*) rallegrarsi; **to rejoice in sth** godere di qc; **to rejoice (at *or* over)** provare diletto (in).

re·joic·ing [rɪ'dʒɔɪsɪŋ] (*liter*) N (*jubilation*) festeggiamenti mpl; **rejoicings** NPL (*festivities*) festività f inv.

re·join[1] [,ri:'dʒɔɪn] VT (*Mil: ship, regiment*) raggiungere; (*club, library*) iscriversi di nuovo a.

re·join[2] [rɪ'dʒɔɪn] VI (*frm: retort*) replicare.

re·join·der [rɪ'dʒɔɪndə'] N (*frm: retort*) replica.

re·ju·venate [rɪ'dʒu:vɪ,neɪt] VT (far) ringiovanire.

re·ju·vena·tion [rɪ,dʒu:vɪ'neɪʃən] N ringiovanimento.

re·kindle [,ri:'kɪndl] VT (*also fig*) riaccendere.

re·lapse [rɪ'læps] ① N (*Med*) ricaduta; **to have a relapse** avere una ricaduta. ② VI (*gen*): **to relapse (into)** ricadere (in); (*Med*) avere una ricaduta.

re·late [rɪ'leɪt] ① VT a (*tell: story*) raccontare, riferire b (*establish relation between*) collegare. ② VI: **to relate to** a (*connect*) riferirsi a b (*get on with*) stabilire un rapporto con.

re·lat·ed [rɪ'leɪtɪd] ADJ a (*connected: subject*) connesso(-a), collegato(-a); (: *substances, languages*) affine b (*attached by family: person*): **related to** imparentato(-a) con; **we are distantly related** siamo parenti alla lontana.

re·lat·ing [rɪ'leɪtɪŋ]: **relating to** PREP relativo(-a) a, che riguarda.

re·la·tion [rɪ'leɪʃən] N a (*relationship*) rapporto, relazione f; (*Math*) relazione; **to bear a relation to** corrispondere a; **in relation to** con riferimento a; **to have good relations with sb** essere in *or* avere buoni rapporti con qn; **diplomatic/international relations** rapporti diplomatici/internazionali; **sexual relations** rapporti sessuali b (*family: relative*) parente m/f; (: *kinship*) parentela; **what relation is she to you?** che legami di parentela ha con te?

re·la·tion·ship [rɪ'leɪʃənʃɪp] N a (*family ties*) legami mpl di parentela b (*connection: between two things*) rapporto, nesso; (: *with sb*) rapporti mpl; **to see a relationship**

between vedere un nesso fra; **to have a relationship with sb** (*sexual*) avere una relazione con qn; **they have a good relationship** vanno molto d'accordo.

rela·tive ['rɛlətɪv] [1] ADJ (*comparative, Gram*) relativo(-a); (*connected*): **relative to** legato(-a) a; **the relative merits of X and Y** i meriti rispettivi di X e Y.
  [2] N parente *m/f.*

rela·tive·ly ['rɛlətɪvlɪ] ADV relativamente; (*fairly, rather*) abbastanza.

rela·tiv·ity [ˌrɛlə'tɪvɪtɪ] N relatività.

re·lax [rɪ'læks] [1] VT (*muscles, person*) rilassare; (*restrictions*) diminuire; (*discipline*) allentare; **to relax one's hold on sth** allentare la presa di qc.
  [2] VI (*rest*) rilassarsi; (*amuse oneself*) svagarsi; (*slacken: sb's grip*) allentarsi; (*calm down*): **relax!** calma!; **his face relaxed into a smile** il suo viso si distese in un sorriso.

re·lax·ant [rɪ'læksənt] ADJ, N (*Med*) calmante (*m*).

re·laxa·tion [ˌriːlæk'seɪʃən] N (*rest*) relax *m*; (*of muscles*) rilassamento, rilasciamento; (*entertainment*) svago; **she plays the piano for relaxation** suona il piano per rilassarsi.

re·laxed [rɪ'lækst] ADJ (*muscles*) rilassato(-a), rilasciato (-a); (*person, mood*) disteso(-a), rilassato(-a).

re·lax·ing [rɪ'læksɪŋ] ADJ rilassante.

re·lay [*n* 'riːleɪ; *vb* rɪ'leɪ] [1] N **a** (*of workmen, horses*) ricambio; **to work in relays** lavorare a squadre (*dandosi il cambio*) **b** (*Radio, TV*) ripetitore *m*; (*Elec*) relé *m inv*; (*Sport: also:* **relay race**) (corsa a) staffetta.
  [2] VT (*Radio, TV*) ripetere; (*pass on: message*) passare, trasmettere.

re·lease [rɪ'liːs] [1] N **a** (*gen*) rilascio; (*from army*) congedo; (*from suffering, obligation*) liberazione *f*
  b (*of gas*) emissione *f*; (*of film, record*) uscita, distribuzione *f*; (*of book*) pubblicazione *f*; **on general release** (*film*) in distribuzione
  c (*record, film etc*): **new release** nuovo disco (*or* film *etc*); **his latest release** il suo ultimo disco (*or* film *etc*)
  d (*also:* **release switch**) disinnesto.
  [2] VT **a** (*let go*) lasciare andare, mollare; (:*bomb*) sganciare; (:*fig: tension*) allentare; **to release one's hold of** *or* **one's grip on sth** allentare la presa di qc
  b (*set free*) rilasciare; (: *Law*) rimettere in libertà; (: *from wreckage*) liberare; (: *from promise, vow*) sciogliere
  c (*issue: gas*) emettere; (: *book, record*) mettere in circolazione, fare uscire; (: *film*) distribuire; (: *statement*) rilasciare; (: *news*) rendere pubblico(-a)
  d (*Tech: catch, clasp, spring*) liberare; (*Phot: shutter*) far scattare; (*handbrake*) togliere; **to release the clutch** (*Aut*) staccare la frizione.

rel·egate ['rɛlɪˌgeɪt] VT (*demote*) relegare; (*Sport*) (far) retrocedere; **to be relegated** (*team*) essere retrocesso (-a).

rel·ega·tion [ˌrɛlɪ'geɪʃən] N (*see vb*) relegazione *f*; retrocessione *f*.

re·lent [rɪ'lɛnt] VI (*frm*) cedere.

re·lent·less [rɪ'lɛntlɪs] ADJ implacabile.

rel·evance ['rɛləvəns] N pertinenza; **relevance of sth to sth** rapporto tra qc e qc.

rel·evant ['rɛləvənt] ADJ: **relevant (to)** (*remark, fact*) pertinente (a); (*information, papers, chapter*) relativo(-a) (a); (*course of action*) adeguato(-a) (a).

re·li·abil·ity [rɪˌlaɪə'bɪlɪtɪ] N (*see adj*) attendibilità; affidabilità; capacità; sicurezza; (*of person*) serietà.

re·li·able [rɪ'laɪəbl] ADJ (*report, source*) attendibile; (*machine*) affidabile; (*person: trustworthy*) fidato(-a), che

dà affidamento; (: *capable*) capace; (*method*) sicuro(-a); **a reliable source of information** una fonte attendibile.

re·li·ably [rɪ'laɪəblɪ] ADV: **I am reliably informed that ...** so da fonti sicure che... .

re·li·ance [rɪ'laɪəns] N: **reliance (on)** dipendenza (da).

re·li·ant [rɪ'laɪənt] ADJ: **to be reliant on sth/sb** dipendere da qc/qn.

rel·ic ['rɛlɪk] N (*Rel*) reliquia; (*fig: of the past*) retaggio.

re·lief [rɪ'liːf] [1] N **a** (*from pain, anxiety*): **relief (from)** sollievo (a); **by way of light relief** come diversivo; **that's a relief!** che sollievo!
  b (*Mil: of besieged town*) liberazione *f*; (*help, supplies*) soccorsi *mpl*
  c (*also:* **tax relief**) sgravio fiscale
  d (*Art, Geog*) rilievo; **to throw sth into relief** (*fig*) mettere qc in evidenza *or* in risalto
  e (*of guard*) cambio.
  [2] ADJ (*bus*) supplementare; (*driver*) che dà il cambio a un collega; (*work, organization, troops*) di soccorso.

♦ **relief map** N carta in rilievo.

♦ **relief road** N (*Brit*) circonvallazione *f*.

re·lieve [rɪ'liːv] VT **a** (*pain, anxiety, boredom*) alleviare; (*person*) sollevare; (*bring help*) soccorrere; **I am relieved to hear you are better** sono sollevato dalla notizia che stai meglio; **to relieve sb of sth** (*load*) alleggerire qn di qc; (*anxiety*) sollevare qn da qc; (*duty*) esonerare qn da qc; **to relieve sb of his command** (*Mil*) esonerare qn dal comando; **to relieve one's anger** sfogare la propria rabbia; **to relieve congestion in sth** (*Med*) decongestionare qc; **to relieve o.s.** (*euph: go to lavatory*) fare i propri bisogni
  b (*take over from*) sostituire; (*replace, also Mil*) dare il cambio a; (*Mil: town*) liberare.

re·lieved [rɪ'liːvd] ADJ sollevato(-a); **to be relieved that ...** essere sollevato(-a) (dal fatto) che...; **I'm relieved to hear it** mi hai tolto un peso con questa notizia.

re·li·gion [rɪ'lɪdʒən] N religione *f.*

re·li·gious [rɪ'lɪdʒəs] ADJ (*gen*) religioso(-a); (*conscientious*) scrupoloso(-a).

♦ **religious education** N istruzione *f* religiosa.

re·li·gious·ly [rɪ'lɪdʒəslɪ] ADV (*see adj*) religiosamente; scrupolosamente.

re·line [ˌriː'laɪn] VT (*coat, jacket*) rifare la fodera a; (*brakes*) cambiare *or* sostituire le guarnizioni di.

re·lin·quish [rɪ'lɪŋkwɪʃ] VT (*frm: right, control, responsibility*) rinunciare a; (: *post*) lasciare, abbandonare; **to relinquish one's hold on sth** lasciare andare qc.

reli·quary ['rɛlɪkwərɪ] N reliquiario.

rel·ish ['rɛlɪʃ] [1] N **a**: **relish (for)** gusto (per); **to do sth with relish** fare qc con diletto **b** (*sauce*) condimento, salsa.
  [2] VT (*food, wine*) gustare; (*fig: like*): **I don't relish the idea** l'idea non è allettante; **he relishes the challenge** lo attrae la sfida.

re·live [ˌriː'lɪv] VT rivivere.

re·load [ˌriː'ləʊd] VT ricaricare.

re·load·ing [ˌriː'ləʊdɪŋ] N ricarica.

re·lo·cate [ˌriː'ləʊ'keɪt] [1] VT (*business*) trasferire.
  [2] VI: **to relocate to** trasferire la propria sede a.

re·luc·tance [rɪ'lʌktəns] N riluttanza.

re·luc·tant [rɪ'lʌktənt] ADJ (*person*) riluttante, restio(-a); (*praise, consent*) concesso(-a) a malincuore; **to be reluctant to do sth** essere restio(-a) a fare qc.

re·luc·tant·ly [rɪ'lʌktəntlɪ] ADV a malincuore, di mala voglia.

rely [rɪˈlaɪ] VI: **to rely on sb/sth** (*count on*) contare su qn/qc; (*be dependent on*) dipendere da qn/qc; **you can rely on my discretion** puoi fidarti della mia discrezione; **you can't rely on the trains** non si può fare affidamento sui treni; **she relies on him for financial support** dipende da lui finanziariamente.

re·main [rɪˈmeɪn] VI rimanere, restare; **it remains to be seen whether ...** resta da vedere se...; **it will remain in my memory** resterà sempre impresso nel mio ricordo; **the fact remains that ...** resta il fatto che...; **to remain faithful to sb** rimanere fedele a qn; **to remain silent** restare in silenzio; **to remain behind** restare indietro; **I remain, yours faithfully** (*Brit*: *in letters*) distinti saluti.

re·main·der [rɪˈmeɪndəʳ] N: **the remainder** (*amount, also Math*) il resto, l'avanzo; (*people*) i/le rimanenti *pl*; **remainders** NPL (*Comm*: *books*) remainder *mpl*; (: *other goods*) giacenze *fpl* di magazzino.

re·main·ing [rɪˈmeɪnɪŋ] ADJ che rimane; **the three remaining possibilities** le tre possibilità che restano *or* che rimangono.

re·mains [rɪˈmeɪnz] NPL (*gen*) resti *mpl*; (*of food*) avanzi *mpl*; **the remains of his fortune** ciò che restava del suo patrimonio.

re·make [ˈriːmeɪk] N (*Cine*) remake *m inv*.

re·mand [rɪˈmɑːnd] (*Law*) ①︎ N: **on remand** in custodia cautelare.

②︎ VT rinviare a giudizio; **to remand sb in custody** ordinare la custodia cautelare di qn.

♦ **remand home** N (*Brit*) riformatorio, casa di correzione.

re·mark [rɪˈmɑːk] ①︎ N osservazione *f*, commento; **worthy of remark** (*frm*) degno(-a) di nota.

②︎ VT (*say, notice*) osservare, notare.

③︎ VI: **to remark on sth** commentare qc.

re·mark·able [rɪˈmɑːkəbl] ADJ notevole.

re·mark·ably [rɪˈmɑːkəblɪ] ADV notevolmente.

re·mar·riage [ˌriːˈmærɪdʒ] N seconde (*or* terze) nozze *fpl*.

re·marry [ˌriːˈmærɪ] VI risposarsi.

re·medial [rɪˈmiːdɪəl] ADJ (*Med*) correttivo(-a); (*action*) atto(-a) a porre rimedio; (*school, teaching*) speciale; (*class, tuition*) di ricupero.

rem·edy [ˈrɛmədɪ] ①︎ N: **remedy (for)** rimedio (contro *or* per).

②︎ VT (*situation, problem, defect*) rimediare a; (*loss*) porre riparo a.

re·mem·ber [rɪˈmɛmbəʳ] VT ricordare, ricordarsi di; **I remember seeing it** ⎡OR⎤ **I remember having seen it** (mi) ricordo di averlo visto; **she remembered to do it** si è ricordata di farlo; **give me sth to remember you by** lasciami un tuo ricordo; **to remember sb in one's prayers** ricordare qn nelle proprie preghiere; **remember me to your wife and children!** saluta tua moglie e i bambini da parte mia!; **that's worth remembering** buono a sapersi.

re·mem·brance [rɪˈmɛmbrəns] N (*frm*) ricordo, memoria; **in remembrance of** in memoria di.

♦ **Remembrance Day** N *11 novembre, giorno della commemorazione dei caduti in guerra.*

♦ **Remembrance Sunday** N *la domenica più vicina all'11 novembre, giorno della commemorazione dei caduti in guerra.*

re·mind [rɪˈmaɪnd] VT ricordare, rammentare; **to remind sb of sth/to do sth** ricordare *or* rammentare qc a qn/di fare qc; **he reminds me of Brian** mi ricorda Brian; **that reminds me!** a proposito!

re·mind·er [rɪˈmaɪndəʳ] N **a** (*note*) promemoria *m inv*; (*Comm*: *letter*) (lettera di) sollecito; **as a reminder that** per ricordarsi che **b** (*memento*) ricordo.

remi·nisce [ˌrɛmɪˈnɪs] VI: **to reminisce (about)** abbandonarsi ai ricordi (di).

remi·nis·cence [ˌrɛmɪˈnɪsəns] N (*usu pl*) reminiscenza.

remi·nis·cent [ˌrɛmɪˈnɪsənt] ADJ: **reminiscent of** che ricorda, che fa venire in mente.

remi·nis·cent·ly [ˌrɛmɪˈnɪsəntlɪ] ADV (*smile*) in preda ai ricordi; **to talk reminiscently of** parlare nostalgicamente di.

re·miss [rɪˈmɪs] ADJ (*frm*) negligente; **it was remiss of me** è stata una negligenza da parte mia.

re·mis·sion [rɪˈmɪʃən] N (*gen, Rel, Med*) remissione *f*; (*Law*: *of debts, fee*) condono.

re·mit [rɪˈmɪt] VT (*frm*) **a** (*send*: *amount due*) rimettere **b** (*refer*: *decision*) rimettere **c** (*Rel*: *sins*) rimettere, perdonare; (*fee, penalty*) condonare.

re·mit·tal [rɪˈmɪtl] N (*Law*) rinvio.

re·mit·tance [rɪˈmɪtəns] N (*frm*) rimessa (di pagamento).

rem·nant [ˈrɛmnənt] N (*remainder*) resto; **remnants** NPL (*of food*) avanzi *mpl*; (*of cloth*) scampoli *mpl*.

♦ **remnant sale** N svendita di scampoli.

re·mod·el [ˌriːˈmɒdl] VT ristrutturare.

re·mon·strance [rɪˈmɒnstrəns] N (*frm*: *complaint*) rimostranza, protesta.

re·mon·strate [ˈrɛmənstreɪt] VI (*frm*) protestare; **to remonstrate with sb about sth** fare le proprie rimostranze a qn circa qc.

re·morse [rɪˈmɔːs] N rimorso; **without remorse** senza pietà.

re·morse·ful [rɪˈmɔːsful] ADJ pieno(-a) di rimorsi.

re·morse·ful·ly [rɪˈmɔːsfəlɪ] ADV con rimorso.

re·morse·less [rɪˈmɔːslɪs] ADJ (*person*) spietato(-a); (*wind, noise*) implacabile.

re·morse·less·ly [rɪˈmɔːslɪslɪ] ADV implacabilmente.

re·mote [rɪˈməʊt] ADJ (*comp* -r, *superl* -st) **a** (*place, period*) remoto(-a); (*ancestor*) lontano(-a); (*in concept*: *idea*) lontano(-a); (*person*: *aloof*) distante; (: *uninvolved*) distaccato(-a); (*Comput*) a distanza; **remote from the matter in hand** non pertinente alla questione **b** (*slight*: *possibility, resemblance*) vago(-a); **not the remotest idea/hope** neanche la più vaga idea/ speranza; **there is a remote possibility that ...** c'è una vaga possibilità che... +*sub*.

♦ **remote control** N (*TV*) telecomando.

♦ **remote-controlled** [rɪˌməʊtkənˈtrəʊld] ADJ telecomandato(-a).

re·mote·ly [rɪˈməʊtlɪ] ADV **a** (*distantly*) lontanamente, alla lontana; **remotely situated** in una posizione isolata **b** (*slightly*) vagamente.

re·mote·ness [rɪˈməʊtnɪs] N **a** (*of ancestor*) antichità; (*of place, period, concept*) lontananza; (*aloofness*) distacco **b** (*of possibility, resemblance*) vaghezza.

re·mould [ˈriːməʊld] N (*Brit*: *tyre*) pneumatico rigenerato.

re·mount [ˌriːˈmaʊnt] ①︎ VI (*on horse, on bicycle*) rimontare in sella. ②︎ VT: **to remount a horse/bicycle** rimontare a cavallo/in bicicletta.

re·mov·able [rɪˈmuːvəbl] ADJ (*detachable*) staccabile.

re·mov·al [rɪˈmuːvəl] N **a** (*of person*) allontanamento; (: *from post*) rimozione *f*, destituzione *f*; (*of problem*) allontanamento; (*of doubt, fear, obstacle, stain*) eliminazione *f*; (*Med*) asportazione *f* **b** (*move from house*) trasloco.

♦ **removal expenses** NPL spese *fpl* di trasloco.

♦ **removal man** N (*Brit*) addetto ai traslochi.

♦ **removal van** N (*Brit*) camion *m inv* per or dei traslochi.

re·move [rɪˈmuːv] 1 VT (*gen*) togliere, levare; (*person*) allontanare; (: *from post*) rimuovere; (*stain*) togliere, eliminare; (*problem*) allontanare; (*doubt, fear*) eliminare, dissipare; (*obstacle*) rimuovere, eliminare; (*Med*) asportare; **to remove from** togliere da, levare da; **to remove one's make-up** struccarsi; **first cousin once removed** cugino(-a) di secondo grado; **far removed from** (*fig*) ben lontano(-a) da.

2 VI traslocare; **to remove from London to the country** trasferirsi da Londra in campagna.

re·mov·er [rɪˈmuːvəʳ] N a (*removal man*) addetto ai traslochi; **removers** NPL (*Brit*: *firm*) ditta *fsg* or impresa *fsg* di traslochi b (*of stains*) smacchiatore *m*; (*of nail varnish*) solvente *m*; (*of paint, varnish*) sverniciatore *m*; **make-up remover** struccatore *m*.

re·mu·ner·ate [rɪˈmjuːnəˌreɪt] VT (*frm*) retribuire, rimunerare.

re·mu·nera·tion [rɪˌmjuːnəˈreɪʃən] N (*frm*) rimunerazione *f*.

re·mu·nera·tive [rɪˈmjuːnərətɪv] ADJ (*frm*) rimunerativo (-a).

Remus [ˈriːməs] N Remo.

Re·nais·sance [rɪˈneɪsɑːns] 1 N: **the Renaissance** il Rinascimento.

2 ADJ (*style*) (del) Rinascimento; (*palace, art*) rinascimentale, del Rinascimento.

re·nal [ˈriːnl] ADJ (*Med*) renale.

re·name [ˌriːˈneɪm] VT ribattezzare.

rend [rɛnd] VT (*pt, pp* rent) (*liter*) lacerare.

ren·der [ˈrɛndəʳ] VT a (*thanks, honour, service*) rendere; (*account*) presentare b (*make*) rendere; **this renders it impossible for me to leave** questo rende impossibile la mia partenza c (*interpret*: *sonata, role, play*) interpretare; (*translate*: *text*) tradurre d (*Culin*: *fat*) sciogliere.

ren·der·ing [ˈrɛndərɪŋ] N (*translation*) traduzione *f*; (*of song, role*) interpretazione *f*.

ren·dez·vous [ˈrɒndɪˌvuː] 1 N (*meeting*) appuntamento; (*meeting place*) punto or luogo di ritrovo.

2 VI ritrovarsi; (*spaceship*) effettuare un rendez-vous.

ren·di·tion [rɛnˈdɪʃən] N (*Mus*) interpretazione *f*.

ren·egade [ˈrɛnɪˌɡeɪd] N (*pej*) rinnegato(-a).

re·nege [rɪˈniːɡ], **re·negue** [rɪˈneɪɡ] VI (*frm*) mancare alla parola; **to renege on** (*agreement, deal*) venire meno a; (*promise*) mancare a, venire meno a.

re·new [rɪˈnjuː] VT (*gen*) rinnovare; (*negotiations, discussion, strength*) riprendere; **to renew one's acquaintance with sb** riprendere contatto con qn.

re·new·able [rɪˈnjuːəbl] ADJ rinnovabile.

re·new·al [rɪˈnjuːəl] N (*see vb*) rinnovo; ripresa.

re·newed [rɪˈnjuːd] ADJ rinnovato(-a).

ren·net [ˈrɛnɪt] N caglio.

re·nounce [rɪˈnaʊns] VT (*right, claim, title*) rinunciare a; (*violence, terrorism*) abbandonare; **to renounce one's faith** abiurare la fede.

reno·vate [ˈrɛnəʊˌveɪt] VT (*house*) rimettere a nuovo; (*furniture, building, art work*) restaurare.

reno·va·tion [ˌrɛnəʊˈveɪʃən] N (*see vb*) rimessa a nuovo; restauro.

re·nown [rɪˈnaʊn] N rinomanza, fama.

re·nowned [rɪˈnaʊnd] ADJ famoso(-a), rinomato(-a).

rent [rɛnt] 1 PT, PP of **rend**.

2 N (canone *m* di) affitto, pigione *f*.

3 VT a (*take for rent*: *house*) affittare, prendere in affitto;

(: *car, TV*) noleggiare, prendere a noleggio b (*also*: **rent out**) affittare, dare in affitto; (: *car, TV*) noleggiare, dare a noleggio.

rent·al [ˈrɛntl] N (*charge*: *on TV, telephone*) abbonamento; (: *on car*) nolo, noleggio.

♦ **rent book** N *libretto di ricevute dell'affitto*.

♦ **rent boy** N (*Brit fam*) giovane prostituto.

♦ **rent collector** N esattore *m* dell'affitto.

♦ **rent-free** [ˌrɛntˈfriː] 1 ADJ (*accommodation*) gratuito (-a).

2 ADV (*live*) senza pagare l'affitto.

♦ **rent rebate** N rimborso parziale dell'affitto.

re·nun·cia·tion [rɪˌnʌnsɪˈeɪʃən] N (*of right, claim, title*) rinuncia; (*of violence, terrorism*) abbandono; (*of faith*) abiura.

re·open [ˌriːˈəʊpən] 1 VT (*gen*) riaprire; (*discussion, hostilities*) riaprire, riprendere.

2 VI riaprirsi.

re·open·ing [ˌriːˈəʊpnɪŋ] N riapertura.

re·or·der [ˌriːˈɔːdəʳ] 1 N (*Comm*) riordino.

2 VT a (*goods, supplies*) ordinare di nuovo b (*reorganize*) riorganizzare; (*rearrange*) rimettere in ordine.

re·or·gani·za·tion [ˌriːˌɔːɡəˌnaɪˈzeɪʃən] N riorganizzazione *f*.

re·or·gan·ize [ˈriːˈɔːɡənaɪz] VT riorganizzare.

Rep ABBR (*Am Pol*) a = **representative** b = **republican**.

rep [rɛp] (*fam*) N a (*Comm*) rappresentante *m/f* b (*Theatre*) teatro di repertorio.

re·packing [ˌriːˈpækɪŋ] N reimballaggio.

re·paid [rɪˈpeɪd] PT, PP of **repay**.

re·paint [ˌriːˈpeɪnt] VT ridipingere.

re·pair [rɪˈpɛəʳ] 1 N riparazione *f*; **under repair** in riparazione; **in good repair** OR **in a good state of repair** in buono stato; **it is damaged beyond repair** è irrimediabilmente rovinato; **closed for repairs** chiuso(-a) per restauro.

2 VT (*car, shoes etc*) aggiustare, riparare; (*fig*: *wrong*) rimediare a.

re·pair·er [rɪˈpɛərəʳ] N riparatore(-trice).

♦ **repair kit** N attrezzatura per riparazioni.

♦ **repair man** N (*pl* **repair men**) riparatore *m*.

♦ **repair shop** N negozio di riparazioni; (*Aut*) officina.

repa·ra·tion [ˌrɛpəˈreɪʃən] N (*frm*) riparazione *f*; **to make reparation for sth** riparare a qc.

rep·ar·tee [ˌrɛpɑːˈtiː] N (*frm*) botta e risposta *m inv*.

re·past [rɪˈpɑːst] N (*frm*) pranzo.

re·pat·ri·ate [riːˈpætrɪˌeɪt] VT rimpatriare.

re·pat·ria·tion [riːˌpætrɪˈeɪʃən] N rimpatrio.

re·pay [riːˈpeɪ] VT (*pt, pp* repaid) (*money*) restituire; (*debt*) pagare; (*lender*) rimborsare, restituire i soldi a; (*sb's kindness etc*) ricambiare; **how can I ever repay you?** come potrò mai ricompensarti?

re·pay·able [riːˈpeɪəbl] ADJ rimborsabile.

re·pay·ment [riːˈpeɪmənt] N (*of money*) pagamento; (*of expenses*) rimborso; (*compensation*) ricompensa.

re·peal [rɪˈpiːl] 1 VT (*law*) abrogare; (*sentence*) annullare; (*decree*) revocare.

2 N (*see vb*) abrogazione *f*; annullamento; revoca.

re·peat [rɪˈpiːt] 1 VT (*gen*) ripetere; (*pattern*) riprodurre; (*promise, attack*) rinnovare; **don't repeat it to anybody** non riferirlo a nessuno; **this offer cannot be repeated** questa è un'offerta irripetibile; **to repeat an order** (*Comm*) rinnovare un'ordinazione; **in spite of repeated reminders** malgrado diversi or ripetuti solleciti.

2 VI ripetersi.

3 N ripetizione f; (Radio, TV) replica.

re·peat·ed·ly [rɪ'pi:tɪdlɪ] ADV ripetutamente.

♦ **repeat order** N (Comm): **to place a repeat order (for)** rinnovare l'ordinazione (di).

♦ **repeat performance** N (fig): **I don't want a repeat performance of that** non vorrei che questo si ripetesse.

♦ **repeat purchasing** N (Comm) riordino continuo.

re·pel [rɪ'pɛl] VT (frm: force back) respingere; (disgust) ripugnare a.

re·pel·lent [rɪ'pɛlənt] **1** ADJ (disgusting) ripugnante, repellente.

2 N: **insect repellent** insettifugo; **moth repellent** antitarmico.

re·pent [rɪ'pɛnt] VI (frm): **to repent (of)** pentirsi (di).

re·pent·ance [rɪ'pɛntəns] N (frm) pentimento.

re·pent·ant [rɪ'pɛntənt] ADJ (frm) pentito(-a).

re·per·cus·sions [ˌri:pə'kʌʃnz] NPL ripercussioni fpl.

rep·er·toire ['rɛpətwɑː'] N repertorio.

rep·er·tory ['rɛpətərɪ] **1** N (Theatre, fig: of jokes, songs) repertorio; **to act in repertory** far parte di una compagnia di repertorio.

♦ **repertory company** N compagnia di repertorio.

♦ **repertory theatre** N teatro di repertorio.

rep·eti·tion [ˌrɛpɪ'tɪʃən] N ripetizione f.

rep·eti·tious [ˌrɛpɪ'tɪʃəs] ADJ (frm: speech) pieno(-a) di ripetizioni.

repetitive [rɪ'pɛtɪtɪv] ADJ (work) ripetitivo(-a), monotono (-a); (movement) che si ripete.

♦ **repetitive strain injury** N (Med) lesione f da sforzo ripetuto.

re·phrase [ri:'freɪz] VT formulare in modo diverso.

re·place [rɪ'pleɪs] VT **a** (put back) rimettere (a posto); (: Telec: receiver) riattaccare **b** (get replacement for, take the place of): **to replace (by, with)** rimpiazzare (con), sostituire (con).

re·place·eable [rɪ'pleɪsəbl] ADJ sostituibile.

re·place·ment [rɪ'pleɪsmənt] N (substitute: thing) pezzo or parte f di ricambio; (: person) sostituto(-a); (act) sostituzione f.

♦ **replacement cost** N (Insurance) costo della sostituzione.

re·play [vb ˌri:'pleɪ; n 'ri:pleɪ] (Sport) **1** VT (match) ripetere.

2 VI ripetere l'incontro.

3 N (of match) partita ripetuta; (TV: playback) replay m inv; **to hold a replay** ripetere l'incontro.

re·plen·ish [rɪ'plɛnɪʃ] VT (frm: tank , glass) riempire (di nuovo); (: one's wardrobe) rifare; **to replenish one's supplies of sth** rifornirsi di qc.

re·plen·ish·ment [rɪ'plɛnɪʃmənt] N (frm: gen) rifornimento.

re·plete [rɪ'pli:t] ADJ (frm): **replete (with)** sazio(-a) (di).

re·ple·tion [rɪ'pli:ʃən] N (frm) sazietà.

rep·li·ca ['rɛplɪkə] N replica, copia.

rep·li·cate ['rɛplɪˌkeɪt] VT (frm) replicare.

re·ply [rɪ'plaɪ] **1** N risposta; **in reply** in risposta; **what did you say in reply?** cos'hai risposto?; **there's no reply** (Telec) non risponde (nessuno).

2 VT, VI rispondere.

♦ **reply coupon** N (Post) tagliando per la risposta.

♦ **reply-paid** [rɪ'plaɪˌpeɪd] ADJ: **reply-paid postcard** cartolina postale con risposta pagata.

re·port [rɪ'pɔ:t] **1** N **a** (account: written) rapporto, relazione f; (: spoken) resoconto; (Press, Radio, TV)

reportage m inv, servizio; (Brit Scol) pagella (scolastica); **annual report** (Comm) relazione annuale; **weather report** bollettino meteorologico; **to give a report on sth** fare una relazione or un rapporto su qc, fare un resoconto di qc; **to submit a progress report on sth/sb** fare un rapporto periodico su qc/qn; **I have heard a report that** ... ho sentito (dire) che...

b (frm: bang) detonazione f; (: shot) sparo.

2 VT (gen, Press, TV) riportare; (notify: accident, culprit) denunciare; (bring to notice: occurrence) segnalare; **it is reported from Berlin that** ... ci è stato riferito da Berlino che...; **what have you to report?** che cos'ha da riferire?; **to report progress** riferire sugli sviluppi della situazione; **to report one's findings** riferire sulle proprie conclusioni.

3 VI **a** : **to report (on)** fare un rapporto (su); (Press, Radio, TV) fare un reportage (su)

b (present oneself): **to report (to)** presentarsi (a); **to report for duty** presentarsi al lavoro; **to report sick** darsi malato(-a)

▶ **report back** VI + ADV **a** (come back) ritornare

b (make report) tornare a riferire.

♦ **report card** N (Am, Scot) pagella.

re·port·ed·ly [rɪ'pɔ:tɪdlɪ] ADV secondo le testimonianze; **it's reportedly the best restaurant in town** si dice che sia il miglior ristorante della città; **she is reportedly living in Spain** si dice che viva in Spagna.

re·port·ed speech [rɪpɔ:tɪd'spi:tʃ] N (Gram) discorso indiretto.

re·port·er [rɪ'pɔ:tə'] N (Press) cronista m/f, reporter m/f inv; (Radio) radiocronista m/f; (TV) telecronista m/f.

re·pose [rɪ'pəʊz] (frm) **1** N riposo; **in repose** in riposo.

2 VI riposare.

re·posi·tory [rɪ'pɒzɪtərɪ] N (of facts, information) miniera; (warehouse) deposito.

re·pos·sess [ˌri:pə'zɛs] VT (property) rientrare in possesso di.

re·pos·ses·sion or·der [ˌri:pə'zɛʃnˌɔ:də'] N (for house) ordine m di espropriazione.

rep·pot [ri:'pɒt] VT (plant) rinvasare.

rep·re·hend [ˌrɛprɪ'hɛnd] VT (frm) rimproverare, riprendere.

rep·re·hen·sible [ˌrɛprɪ'hɛnsɪbl] ADJ (frm) riprovevole.

rep·re·hen·sibly [ˌrɛprɪ'hɛnsəblɪ] ADV (frm) riprovevolmente, in modo riprovevole.

rep·re·sent [ˌrɛprɪ'zɛnt] VT (all senses) rappresentare.

rep·re·sen·ta·tion [ˌrɛprɪzɛn'teɪʃən] N **a** (Pol) rappresentanza; (portrayal) rappresentazione f **b** : **representations** NPL (frm: statements, protests) rimostranze fpl; **to make representations to sb** fare delle rimostranze a qn.

rep·re·sen·ta·tion·al [ˌrɛprɪzɛn'teɪʃənəl] ADJ (frm: art, painting) figurativo(-a).

rep·re·senta·tive [ˌrɛprɪ'zɛntətɪv] **1** ADJ: **representative (of)** rappresentativo(-a) (di).

2 N (gen) rappresentante m/f, delegato(-a); (Comm) rappresentante m/f (di commercio); (Am Pol): **Representative** deputato.

re·press [rɪ'prɛs] VT reprimere.

re·pressed [rɪ'prɛst] ADJ represso(-a).

re·pres·sion [rɪ'prɛʃən] N repressione f.

re·pres·sive [rɪ'prɛsɪv] ADJ repressivo(-a).

re·pres·sive·ly [rɪ'prɛsɪvlɪ] ADV in modo repressivo.

re·prieve [rɪ'pri:v] **1** N (Law: cancellation) commutazione f della pena capitale; (: postponement) sospensione f

dell'esecuzione della condanna; (*delay: also gen*) proroga.

[2] VT (*Law: for good*) rinviare l'esecuzione di; (: *for a time*) sospendere l'esecuzione di; (*grant a delay*) concedere una proroga a; (: *fig*) dare tregua a.

rep·ri·mand ['rɛprɪ,mɑːnd] [1] N rimprovero.

[2] VT redarguire, rimproverare.

re·print [*n* 'riː,prɪnt; *vb* ,riː'prɪnt] [1] N ristampa.

[2] VT ristampare.

re·pris·al [rɪ'praɪzəl] N: **reprisals** NPL rappresaglie *fpl*; **to take reprisals** fare delle rappresaglie; **as a reprisal for** come rappresaglia per.

re·proach [rɪ'prəʊtʃ] (*frm*) [1] N rimprovero; **above** or **beyond reproach** irreprensibile.

[2] VT: **to reproach sb with** or **for sth** rimproverare qc a qn; **to reproach sb with** or **for doing sth** rimproverare a qn di or per aver fatto qc; **don't reproach yourself for what happened** non devi sentirti in colpa per quello che è successo.

re·proach·ful [rɪ'prəʊtʃfʊl] ADJ (*look*) di rimprovero.

re·proach·ful·ly [rɪ'prəʊtʃfəlɪ] ADV con aria di rimprovero.

rep·ro·bate ['rɛprəʊ,beɪt] N (*hum*) canaglia.

re·pro·duce [,riːprə'djuːs] [1] VT riprodurre.

[2] VI riprodursi.

re·pro·duc·tion [,riːprə'dʌkʃən] N (*all senses*) riproduzione *f*.

♦ **reproduction furniture** N riproduzioni *fpl* di mobili antichi.

re·pro·duc·tive [,riːprə'dʌktɪv] ADJ riproduttore(-trice).

re·proof [rɪ'pruːf], **re·prov·al** [rɪ'pruːvəl] N (*frm*) riprovazione *f*.

re–proof [riː'pruːf] VT (*garment*) impermeabilizzare di nuovo.

re·prove [rɪ'pruːv] VT (*person*): **to reprove (for)** rimproverare (di or per), biasimare (per).

re·prov·ing [rɪ'pruːvɪŋ] ADJ (*frm: look, frown*) di rimprovero, di disapprovazione.

re·prov·ing·ly [rɪ'pruːvɪŋlɪ] ADV (*frm*) con aria di rimprovero.

rep·tile ['rɛptaɪl] N rettile *m*.

Repub. ABBR (*Am Pol*) = **republican**.

re·pub·lic [rɪ'pʌblɪk] N repubblica.

re·pub·li·can [rɪ'pʌblɪkən] ADJ, N repubblicano(-a).

re·pub·li·can·ism [rɪ'pʌblɪkə,nɪzəm] N repubblicanesimo.

re·pub·lish [,riː'pʌblɪʃ] VT ripubblicare.

re·pu·di·ate [rɪ'pjuːdɪ,eɪt] (*frm*) VT (*charge, offer of friendship*) respingere; (*debt, treaty*) disconoscere, rifiutarsi di onorare; (*one's wife*) ripudiare.

re·pu·dia·tion [rɪ,pjuːdɪ'eɪʃən] N (*frm*) ripudio.

re·pug·nance [rɪ'pʌgnəns] N ripugnanza.

re·pug·nant [rɪ'pʌgnənt] ADJ ripugnante; **to be repugnant to sb** ripugnare a qn.

re·pulse [rɪ'pʌls] VT respingere.

re·pul·sion [rɪ'pʌlʃən] N ripulsione *f*, ribrezzo.

re·pul·sive [rɪ'pʌlsɪv] ADJ ripugnante, ripulsivo(-a), ributtante.

re·pul·sive·ness [rɪ'pʌlsɪvnɪs] N (*ugliness*) aspetto ripugnante.

repu·table ['rɛpjʊtəbl] ADJ (*firm, supplier*) degno(-a) di fiducia, serio(-a); (*occupation*) rispettabile.

repu·ta·tion [,rɛpjʊ'teɪʃən] N reputazione *f*; **he has a reputation for being awkward** ha la fama di essere un tipo difficile; **to live up to one's reputation** non smen-

tirsi, non smentire la propria reputazione.

re·pute [rɪ'pjuːt] N (*frm*) reputazione *f*; **of (good) repute** (*person*) che ha una buona reputazione; (*place*) che ha un buon nome; **by repute** di fama.

re·put·ed [rɪ'pjuːtɪd] ADJ reputato(-a); **to be reputed to be rich/intelligent** essere ritenuto(-a) ricco(-a)/intelligente.

re·put·ed·ly [rɪ'pjuːtɪdlɪ] ADV (stando) a quel che si dice, secondo quanto si dice.

re·quest [rɪ'kwɛst] [1] N (*formal*) richiesta, domanda; **to make a request for sth** fare richiesta di qc; **at the request of** su richiesta di; **on** or **by request** a or su richiesta; **by popular request** a grande richiesta.

[2] VT: **to request sth from** or **of sb/sb to do sth** richiedere qc a qn/a qn di fare qc; "**you are requested not to smoke**" "si prega di non fumare".

♦ **request stop** N (*Brit: for bus*) fermata facoltativa or a richiesta.

requi·em ['rɛkwɪɛm] N requiem *m inv*.

♦ **requiem mass** N messa di requiem.

re·quire [rɪ'kwaɪəʳ] (*frm*) VT [a] (*subj: person*) aver bisogno di; (: *thing, action*) richiedere; **it requires careful thought** richiede un attento esame; **what qualifications are required?** che requisiti sono richiesti?; **if required** se necessario; **when required** quando è necessario [b] (*demand, order*): **to require sb to do sth/sth of sb** esigere che qn faccia qc/qc da qn; **to require that sth be done** esigere che qc sia fatto; **passengers are required to show their tickets** i passeggeri devono esibire i biglietti; **required by law** prescritto(-a) dalla legge.

re·quired [rɪ'kwaɪəd] ADJ (*qualifications, exams*) richiesto (-a); (*amount*) voluto(-a); **in the required time** nel tempo prescritto.

re·quire·ment [rɪ'kwaɪəmənt] N (*need*) esigenza; (*condition*) requisito, condizione *f* (richiesta); **to meet sb's requirements** soddisfare le esigenze di qn; **she meets all the requirements for the job** risponde a tutti i requisiti (necessari per il lavoro).

requi·site ['rɛkwɪzɪt] [1] N occorrente *m*, necessario; **toilet requisites** articoli *mpl* da bagno.

[2] ADJ (*frm*) necessario(-a), richiesto(-a).

requi·si·tion [,rɛkwɪ'zɪʃən] [1] N [a] (*Mil*) requisizione *f* [b] (*request for supply*) richiesta.

[2] VT (*see n*) requisire; richiedere.

rere·dos ['rɪədɒs] N (*Art*) dossale *m*.

re·route [,riː'ruːt] VT (*train*) deviare (il percorso di); **the train was rerouted through Blackpool** hanno fatto passare il treno per Blackpool.

♦ **re–run** [riː'rʌn] [1] N (*Cine, TV, Theatre*) replica.

[2] VT [a] (*film: at cinema*) ridare; (: *on TV*) trasmettere la replica di; (*Theatre*) rimettere in scena [b] (*race*) rifare.

re·sale ['riːseɪl] N rivendita.

♦ **resale price maintenance** N prezzo minimo di vendita imposto.

re·sat [,riː'sæt] PT, PP of **resit**.

re·scind [rɪ'sɪnd] VT (*law*) abrogare; (*contract*) rescindere; (*order*) annullare.

res·cue ['rɛskjuː] [1] N (*saving*) salvataggio; (*help*) soccorso; **to come/go to sb's rescue** venire/andare in aiuto a or di qn.

[2] VT salvare.

♦ **rescue attempt** N tentativo di salvataggio.

♦ **rescue operation** N operazione *f* di salvataggio.

♦ **rescue party** N squadra di salvataggio.

res·cu·er ['rɛskjʊəʳ] N soccorritore(-trice).

♦ **rescue team** N squadra di soccorso *or* di salvataggio.

re·search [rɪ'sɜːtʃ] ⟨1⟩ N ricerca, ricerche *fpl*; **a piece of research** un lavoro di ricerca; **to do research** fare ricerca.
⟨2⟩ VI: **to research (into sth)** fare ricerca (su qc).
⟨3⟩ VT documentarsi su; **a well researched book** un libro ben documentato.
⟨4⟩ ADJ (*centre, laboratory*) di ricerca.

♦ **research and development** N (*Industry*) ricerca e sviluppo.

re·search·er [rɪ'sɜːtʃə'] N ricercatore(-trice).

♦ **research establishment** N centro di ricerca.
♦ **research fellow** N (*Univ*) ricercatore(-trice).
♦ **research student** N studente(-essa) che fa della ricerca.
♦ **research work** N lavoro di ricerca, ricerche *fpl*.
♦ **research worker** N ricercatore(-trice).

re·sell [ˌriː'sel] VT rivendere.

re·sem·blance [rɪ'zembləns] N somiglianza; **to bear a strong resemblance to** somigliare moltissimo a.

re·sem·ble [rɪ'zembl] VT (as)somigliare a.

re·sent [rɪ'zent] VT risentirsi per; **I resent your remarks** le tue osservazioni mi offendono; **he resents my being here** è contrariato dalla mia presenza.

re·sent·ful [rɪ'zentfʊl] ADJ (*person*) pieno(-a) di risentimento; (*tone*) risentito(-a); **to be** *or* **feel resentful of sb** provare del risentimento per qn.

re·sent·ful·ly [rɪ'zentfəlɪ] ADV con risentimento.

re·sent·ment [rɪ'zentmənt] N risentimento.

res·er·va·tion [ˌrezə'veɪʃən] N ⟨a⟩ (*booking*) prenotazione *f*; **to make a reservation** prenotare, fare una prenotazione ⟨b⟩ (*doubt*) riserva; **without reservation** senza riserve; **with reservations** con le dovute riserve ⟨c⟩ (*area of land*) riserva; (*Brit Aut*: *also*: **central reservation**) spartitraffico *m inv.*

♦ **reservation desk** N (*Am*: *in hotel*) reception *f inv.*

re·serve [rɪ'zɜːv] ⟨1⟩ N ⟨a⟩ (*most senses*) riserva; (*hiding one's feelings*) riserbo; **keep/have in reserve** tenere/avere di riserva; **without reserve** senza riserve ⟨b⟩: **the reserves** NPL (*Mil*) le riserve.
⟨2⟩ VT ⟨a⟩ (*table, seat*) prenotare, riservare; (*set aside*) riservare; **to reserve one's strength** risparmiarsi le forze ⟨b⟩: **to reserve judgment (on)** (*fig*) riservarsi di decidere in merito (a); **to reserve the right to do** riservarsi il diritto di fare.

♦ **reserve currency** N (*Fin*) valuta di riserva.

re·served [rɪ'zɜːvd] ADJ (*booked*: *table, seat*) prenotato (-a), riservato(-a); (*shy*) riservato(-a).

♦ **reserve fund** N fondo di riserva.
♦ **reserve player** N (giocatore(-trice) di) riserva.
♦ **reserve price** N (*Brit*: *at auction*) prezzo minimo, prezzo *m* base *inv.*
♦ **reserve tank** N (*Aut*) serbatoio di riserva.
♦ **reserve team** N (*Brit Sport*) seconda squadra.

re·serv·ist [rɪ'zɜːvɪst] N (*Mil*) riservista *m.*

res·er·voir ['rezə.vwɑː'] N (*artificial lake*) bacino idrico; (*tank etc*) serbatoio.

reset [ˌriː'set] VT (*Comput*) azzerare.

re·set·tle [ˌriː'setl] ⟨1⟩ VT (*refugees*) far insediare; (*land*) ripopolare.
⟨2⟩ VI stabilirsi, insediarsi.

re·set·tle·ment [ˌriː'setlmənt] N (*see vt*) insediamento; ripopolamento.

re·shape [ˌriː'ʃeɪp] VT (*policy*) ristrutturare.

re·shuf·fle [ˌriː'ʃʌfl] N: **Cabinet reshuffle** (*Pol*) rimpasto

ministeriale.

re·side [rɪ'zaɪd] VI (*frm*) risiedere; (: *fig*: *power, authority*): **to reside in** *or* **with** essere nelle mani di.

resi·dence ['rezɪdəns] (*frm*) N (*gen*) residenza; (*stay*) permanenza, soggiorno; **"desirable residence for sale"** "abitazione signorile vendesi"; **to take up residence** prendere residenza; **in residence** (*queen*) in sede; **artist/ writer in residence** *artista/scrittore che insegna presso una scuola o università.*

♦ **residence permit** N (*Brit*) permesso di soggiorno.

resi·den·cy ['rezɪdənsɪ] N residenza.

resi·dent ['rezɪdənt] ⟨1⟩ N abitante *m/f*; (*of hotel*) cliente *m/f*; **local residents** abitanti della zona.
⟨2⟩ ADJ (*tutor, specialist*) interno(-a); (*population*) stabile; **to be resident in a town/in London** risiedere in una città/a Londra.

resi·den·tial [ˌrezɪ'denʃəl] ADJ (*area*) residenziale; **residential course** corso con pernottamento; **residential nurse** infermiere(-a) interno(-a).

re·sid·ual [rɪ'zɪdjʊəl] ADJ residuo(-a).

re·sidu·ary [rɪ'zɪdjʊərɪ] ADJ residuo(-a); **residuary legatee** (*Law*) legatario(-a) universale.

resi·due ['rezɪdjuː] N (*frm*) residuo, residui *mpl.*

re·sign [rɪ'zaɪn] ⟨1⟩ VT (*office, leadership*) lasciare; (*frm*: *claim*) rinunciare a; **to resign one's post** dimettersi; **to resign one's commission** (*Mil*) rassegnare le dimissioni; **to resign o.s. to (doing) sth** rassegnarsi a (fare) qc.
⟨2⟩ VI: **to resign (from)** dimettersi (da), dare le dimissioni (da).

res·ig·na·tion [ˌrezɪg'neɪʃən] N ⟨a⟩ (*from job*) dimissioni *fpl*; **to tender one's resignation** dare le dimissioni ⟨b⟩ (*mental state*) rassegnazione *f.*

re·signed [rɪ'zaɪnd] ADJ rassegnato(-a).

re·sign·ed·ly [rɪ'zaɪnɪdlɪ] ADV con rassegnazione.

re·sili·ence [rɪ'zɪlɪəns] N (*see adj*) elasticità; capacità di ripresa.

re·sili·ent [rɪ'zɪlɪənt] ADJ (*substance, material*) elastico(-a); (*fig*: *person*) che ha buone capacità di ripresa.

res·in ['rezɪn] N resina.

res·in·ous ['rezɪnəs] ADJ resinoso(-a).

re·sist [rɪ'zɪst] ⟨1⟩ VT (*attack*) resistere a; (*change*) opporsi a; **he couldn't resist taking a quick look** non ha resistito alla tentazione di dare un'occhiata.
⟨2⟩ VI resistere.

re·sist·ance [rɪ'zɪstəns] ⟨1⟩ N (*all senses*) resistenza; **to offer resistance (to)** opporre resistenza a; **to take the line of least resistance** scegliere la strada più facile.
⟨2⟩ ADJ (*fighter, movement*) della resistenza.

re·sist·ant [rɪ'zɪstənt] ADJ: **resistant (to)** resistente (a).

re·sit [*vb* ˌriː'sɪt; *n* 'riː.sɪt] (*vb*: *pt, pp* **resat**) ⟨1⟩ VT (*exam*) ripresentarsi a.
⟨2⟩ N: **when are the resits?** quando è la prossima sessione?; **I've got three resits** devo ripresentarmi a tre esami.

reso·lute ['rezəluːt] ADJ (*frm*) risoluto(-a).

reso·lute·ly ['rezəluːtlɪ] ADV (*frm*) risolutamente.

reso·lute·ness ['rezəluːtnɪs] N (*frm*) risolutezza.

reso·lu·tion [ˌrezə'luːʃən] N ⟨a⟩ (*determination*) risolutezza; (*resolve*) fermo proposito, risoluzione *f*; **to make a resolution** fare un proposito ⟨b⟩ (*of problem, Chem*) soluzione *f* ⟨c⟩ (*on screen, Pol*: *motion*) risoluzione *f.*

re·solve [rɪ'zɒlv] (*frm*) ⟨1⟩ N (*resoluteness*) risolutezza; **to make a resolve to do sth** risolversi a fare qc.
⟨2⟩ VT ⟨a⟩ (*sort out*) risolvere
⟨b⟩ (*decide*): **to resolve to do sth/that** decidere di fare

qc/che; **the committee resolved against appointing him** il comitato ha deliberato contro la sua nomina.

re·solved [rɪ'zɒlvd] ADJ risoluto(-a).

reso·nance ['rɛzənəns] *(frm)* N *(see adj)* risonanza; sonorità.

reso·nant ['rɛzənənt] *(frm)* ADJ *(sound)* risonante; *(voice)* sonoro(-a), risonante.

reso·nate ['rɛzə‚neɪt] *(frm)* VI *(voice, room)* risonare.

re·sort [rɪ'zɔːt] **1** N **a** *(recourse)* ricorso; *(thing resorted to)* risorsa; **without resort to force** senza ricorrere *or* far ricorso alla forza; **in the last resort** OR **as a last resort** come ultima risorsa

b *(place)* località *f inv*; **holiday resort** località di villeggiatura; **seaside/winter sports resort** stazione *f* balneare/di sport invernali.

2 VI: **to resort to** *(violence, treachery)* far ricorso a; **to resort to drink/stealing** *etc* mettersi *or* ridursi a bere/rubare *etc*.

re·sound [rɪ'zaʊnd] VI *(frm)*: **to resound (with)** risonare (di).

re·sound·ing [rɪ'zaʊndɪŋ] ADJ *(noise)* fragoroso(-a), risonante; *(victory, defeat)* clamoroso(-a).

re·sound·ing·ly [rɪ'zaʊndɪŋlɪ] ADV clamorosamente.

re·source [rɪ'sɔːs] N *(asset)* risorsa; **resources** NPL *(wealth)* mezzi *mpl*; **natural resources** risorse naturali.

re·source·ful [rɪ'sɔːsfʊl] ADJ *(person)* pieno(-a) di risorse, intraprendente.

re·source·ful·ly [rɪ'sɔːsfəlɪ] ADV ingegnosamente.

re·source·ful·ness [rɪ'sɔːsfʊlnɪs] N *(of person)* ingegnosità.

re·spect [rɪs'pɛkt] **1** N **a** *(gen)* rispetto; **respects** NPL *(regards)* ossequi *mpl*; **to have** *or* **show respect for** aver rispetto per; **out of respect for** per rispetto *or* riguardo a; **with due respect (for)** con tutto il rispetto (per); **with (all) due respect I think you're mistaken** con rispetto parlando, penso che si sbagli; **to pay one's respects to sb** *(frm)* rendere omaggio a qn

b *(point, detail)*: **in some respects** sotto certi aspetti; **I like the town except in one respect** la città mi piace salvo che per una cosa

c *(reference, regard)*: **in respect of** quanto a; **with respect to** per quanto riguarda.

2 VT rispettare.

re·spect·abil·ity [rɪs‚pɛktə'bɪlɪtɪ] N rispettabilità.

re·spect·able [rɪs'pɛktəbl] ADJ **a** *(decent)* rispettabile; **for perfectly respectable reasons** per motivi più che leciti; **in respectable society** nella società bene **b** *(quite big: amount, number)* considerevole; *(quite good: player, result)* niente male *inv*.

re·spect·ably [rɪs'pɛktəblɪ] ADV *(dress, behave)* perbene; *(quite well: perform, sing)* (piuttosto) bene.

re·spect·er [rɪs'pɛktə'] N: **he's no respecter of persons** non guarda in faccia a nessuno.

re·spect·ful [rɪs'pɛktfʊl] ADJ rispettoso(-a).

re·spect·ful·ly [rɪs'pɛktfəlɪ] ADV rispettosamente; **respectfully yours** *(in letter)* con rispetto.

re·spect·ing [rɪs'pɛktɪŋ] PREP riguardante, concernente.

re·spec·tive [rɪs'pɛktɪv] ADJ rispettivo(-a).

re·spec·tive·ly [rɪs'pɛktɪvlɪ] ADV rispettivamente.

res·pi·ra·tion [‚rɛspɪ'reɪʃən] N respirazione *f*.

res·pi·ra·tor ['rɛspəreɪtə'] N *(Med)* respiratore *m*; *(Mil)* maschera *f* antigas *inv*.

res·pira·tory [rɪs'paɪərətərɪ] ADJ respiratorio(-a).

re·spire [rɪs'paɪə'] VT *(frm)* VI respirare.

res·pite ['rɛspaɪt] N *(frm)* tregua, requie; **without respite** senza tregua *or* requie; **they gave us no respite** non ci hanno dato tregua.

re·splend·ent [rɪs'plɛndənt] ADJ *(frm)* risplendente.

re·spond [rɪ'spɒnd] VI rispondere; **to respond to treatment** *(Med)* reagire (bene) alla cura.

re·spond·ent [rɪ'spɒndənt] N *(Law)* convenuto(-a).

re·sponse [rɪ'spɒns] N *(answer)* risposta; *(reaction)* reazione *f*; **in response to** in risposta a.

re·spon·sibil·ity [rɪ‚spɒnsə'bɪlɪtɪ] N responsabilità *f inv*; **to place the responsibility for sth on sb** ritenere qn responsabile di qc; **on one's own responsibility** di propria iniziativa; **to take responsibility for sth/sb** assumersi *or* prendersi la responsabilità di qc/per qn; **that's his responsibility** è compito suo.

♦ **responsibility payment** N *premio per mansioni di responsabilità*.

re·spon·sible [rɪ'spɒnsəbl] ADJ responsabile; *(trustworthy)* fidato(-a); **to be responsible for sth** essere responsabile di qc; **to be responsible to sb (for sth)** dover rispondere a qn (di qc); **to hold sb responsible for** ritenere qn responsabile di; **it's a responsible job** è un posto di responsabilità.

re·spon·sibly [rɪ'spɒnsəblɪ] ADV responsabilmente.

re·spon·sive [rɪ'spɒnsɪv] ADJ *(audience, class, pupil)* che reagisce bene; *(to affection)* affettuoso(-a); *(to needs)*: **responsive to** sensibile a; **he has a very responsive nature** è un tipo molto aperto.

rest¹ [rɛst] **1** N **a** *(repose)* riposo; *(break)* pausa; (: *in walking)* sosta, tappa; **to come to rest** *(object)* fermarsi; **to have a good night's rest** farsi una buona *or* bella dormita; **at rest** *(not moving)* fermo(-a); *(euph: dead)* in pace; **to set sb's mind at rest** tranquillizzare qn

b *(Mus)* pausa

c *(support)* sostegno, supporto.

2 VT **a** *(animal, dough)* (far) riposare; **God rest his soul!** pace all'anima sua!; **to rest one's eyes** *or* **gaze on** posare lo sguardo su

b *(support: ladder, bicycle, head)*: **to rest on/against** appoggiare su/contro.

3 VI **a** *(repose)* riposarsi, riposare; **I feel quite rested** mi sento molto riposato; **may she rest in peace** riposi in pace; **we shall not rest until it is settled** non avremo pace finché la cosa non sarà sistemata

b *(remain)* stare; **it rests with him to decide** sta a lui decidere; **it doesn't rest with me** non dipende da me; **rest assured that …** stia tranquillo che…; **let the argument rest** there lascia le cose come stanno

c: **to rest on** *(perch)* posarsi su; *(be supported)* poggiare su, appoggiarsi su; *(Law: case)* basarsi su; **her head rested on my shoulder** il suo capo era appoggiato alla mia spalla; **a heavy responsibility rests on her** ha una grossa responsabilità sulle spalle.

rest² [rɛst] N *(remainder)*: **the rest** *(of money, substance)* il resto; *(of people, things)* gli altri/le altre *pl*; **the rest of them** gli altri; **the rest of us will go later** noialtri ci andiamo più tardi; **can you carry the rest?** porti tu quello che rimane?

re·start [‚riː'stɑːt] VT *(engine)* rimettere in marcia; *(work)* ricominciare.

re·state [riː'steɪt] VT *(frm: case, problem, reasons)* reiterare; (: *argument, theory)* enunciare nuovamente; **to restate one's position/one's opposition** riaffermare la propria posizione/la propria opinione.

res·tau·rant ['rɛstə‚rɒŋ] N ristorante *m*.

♦ **restaurant car** N *(Brit Rail)* vagone *m* ristorante.

♦ **restaurant owner** N proprietario(-a) di ristorante.
♦ **rest cure** N cura del riposo.
♦ **rest day** N giorno di riposo.
rest·ed ['rɛstɪd] ADJ riposato(-a); **to feel rested** sentirsi riposato(-a); **to look rested** avere un'aria riposata.
rest·ful ['rɛstfʊl] ADJ riposante.
♦ **rest home** N casa di riposo.
rest·ing place ['rɛstɪŋpleɪs] N **a** (gen) posto or luogo dove riposarsi **b** (grave) ultima dimora.
res·ti·tu·tion [ˌrɛstɪ'tjuːʃən] N (act) restituzione f; (reparation) riparazione f.
res·tive ['rɛstɪv] ADJ (person) irrequieto(-a), nervoso(-a), agitato(-a); (horse) restio(-a).
rest·less ['rɛstlɪs] ADJ (gen) irrequieto(-a), agitato(-a); (crowd etc) inquieto(-a); **to get restless** spazientirsi; **I had a restless night** ho passato una notte agitata; **if you're restless why not read for a while?** se non riesci a dormire perché non leggi per un po'?
rest·less·ly ['rɛstlɪslɪ] ADV (gen) irrequietamente; (fidget) nervosamente.
rest·less·ness ['rɛstlɪsnɪs] N (of person) irrequietezza; (of crowd) agitazione f, nervosismo.
re·stock [ˌriː'stɒk] VT rifornire.
res·to·ra·tion [ˌrɛstə'reɪʃən] N **a** (repair: of building, monument) restauro **b** (return: of land, property) restituzione f, riconsegna; (reintroduction: of law and order) ripristino; (: of confidence) ristabilimento; (History): **the Restoration** la Restaurazione.
re·stora·tive [rɪ'stɔːrətɪv] [1] ADJ (powers, effect) corroborante.
[2] N (tonic) ricostituente m; (hum: alcoholic drink) cordiale m.
re·store [rɪ'stɔːʳ] VT **a** (repair: building) restaurare **b** (give back: gen) restituire; (introduce again: confidence, custom, law and order) ripristinare; **restored to health** ristabilito (-a).
re·stor·er [rɪ'stɔːrəʳ] N (Art) restauratore(-trice).
♦ **rest period** N riposo.
re·strain [rɪ'streɪn] VT (feeling) contenere, frenare; (dog etc) tenere sotto controllo; **to restrain o.s.** controllarsi, trattenersi; **to restrain sb (from doing sth)** trattenere qn (dal fare qc).
re·strained [rɪ'streɪnd] ADJ (person, style etc) contenuto (-a), sobrio(-a); (manner) riservato(-a).
re·straint [rɪ'streɪnt] N **a** (check, control) limitazioni fpl, restrizioni fpl; **wage restraint** contenimento salariale **b** (constraint, moderation: of manner) ritegno, riservatezza; (self-control) autocontrollo; **without restraint** senza reticenze, liberamente.
re·strict [rɪ'strɪkt] VT limitare, restringere.
re·strict·ed [rɪ'strɪktɪd] ADJ (gen) limitato(-a); (by law) soggetto(-a) a restrizioni; **he has rather a restricted outlook** (fig) ha una visione piuttosto limitata delle cose.
♦ **restricted area** N (Brit Aut) zona con limitazione di velocità.
♦ **restricted zone** N (Mil) zona militare.
re·stric·tion [rɪ'strɪkʃən] N limitazione f, restrizione f; **to place restrictions on sth** imporre delle restrizioni su qc; **speed restriction** (Aut) limite m di velocità.
re·stric·tive [rɪ'strɪktɪv] ADJ restrittivo(-a).
♦ **restrictive practices** NPL (Industry) pratiche fpl restrittive di produzione.
♦ **rest room** N (Am) toilette f inv.
re·struc·ture [ˌriː'strʌktʃəʳ] VT ristrutturare.

re·struc·tur·ing [ˌriː'strʌktʃərɪŋ] N (also Econ) ristrutturazione f.
re·sult [rɪ'zʌlt] [1] N risultato; **as a result (of)** in or di conseguenza (a), in seguito (a); **as a result of the strike** ... in seguito allo sciopero...; **to get results** (fam: person) rendere; (: action) dare dei risultati.
[2] VI: **to result (from)** essere una conseguenza (di), essere causato(-a) (da); **to result in** avere come conseguenza; **if the police leave, disorder will result** se la polizia se ne andrà, ci saranno dei disordini; **the inquiry resulted in several dismissals** l'inchiesta ha portato a diversi licenziamenti.
re·sult·ant [rɪ'zʌltənt] [1] ADJ (frm)' risultante, conseguente.
[2] N (Phys, Math) risultante m/f.
re·sume [rɪ'zjuːm] [1] VT (start again) riprendere; **to resume one's seat** rimettersi a sedere.
[2] VI (class, meeting) riprendere.
ré·su·mé ['rezjuˌmeɪ] N **a** (summary) sommario **b** (Am: CV) curriculum vitae m inv.
re·sump·tion [rɪ'zʌmpʃən] N ripresa.
re·sur·face [ˌriː'sɜːfɪs] [1] VT (road) rifare il manto stradale di.
[2] VI (submarine) riaffiorare; (fig: problem) ripresentarsi; (fam: person) rispuntare.
re·sur·gence [rɪ'sɜːdʒəns] N (frm) rinascita.
re·sur·gent [rɪ'sɜːdʒənt] ADJ (frm) in fase di ripresa.
res·ur·rect [ˌrezə'rɛkt] VT risuscitare; (fig: ideas, fashion) riesumare.
Res·ur·rec·tion [ˌrezə'rɛkʃən] N (Rel): **the Resurrection** la Risurrezione.
res·ur·rec·tion [ˌrezə'rɛkʃən] N risurrezione f.
re·sus·ci·tate [rɪ'sʌsɪˌteɪt] VT (Med) rianimare.
re·sus·ci·ta·tion [rɪˌsʌsɪ'teɪʃən] N (frm) rianimazione f.
re·tail ['riːˌteɪl] [1] ADJ (price, trade) al dettaglio, al minuto.
[2] ADV al dettaglio, al minuto.
[3] VT (Comm) vendere al minuto or al dettaglio; (gossip) riferire.
[4] VI (Comm): **to retail at** essere in vendita al pubblico al prezzo di.
re·tail·er ['riːˌteɪləʳ] N dettagliante m/f, commerciante m/f al minuto or al dettaglio.
♦ **retail outlet** N punto di vendita al minuto or al dettaglio.
♦ **retail price** N prezzo al minuto or al dettaglio.
♦ **retail price index** N indice m dei prezzi al consumo.
re·tain [rɪ'teɪn] VT (hold) tenere; (keep) conservare, serbare; (remember) tenere a mente; (sign up: lawyer) impegnare (pagando una parte dell'onorario in anticipo).
re·tain·er [rɪ'teɪnəʳ] N **a** (fee) onorario (versato in anticipo) **b** (servant) servitore m.
re·take ['riːˌteɪk] (vb: pt retook, pp retaken) [1] VT **a** (city, hall) riprendere, riconquistare; (prisoner) ricatturare **b** (Cine) nuova ripresa; (scene) girare di nuovo **c** (exam) ridare.
[2] N **a** (exam) ≈ esame m di riparazione.
re·tali·ate [rɪ'tælɪˌeɪt] VI: **to retaliate (against sb/sth)** vendicarsi (contro qn/di qc).
re·talia·tion [rɪˌtælɪ'eɪʃən] N rappresaglie fpl; **by way of retaliation** OR **in retaliation** per rappresaglia; **in retaliation for** per vendicarsi di.
re·talia·tory [rɪ'tælɪətərɪ] ADJ di rappresaglia, di ritorsione.
re·tard [rɪ'tɑːd] VT ritardare.
re·tard·ed [rɪ'tɑːdɪd] ADJ (Med) ritardato(-a); **to be**

mentally retarded essere (un(a)) ritardato(-a) mentale.

retch [rɛtʃ] VI avere (dei) conati di vomito.

re·ten·tion [rɪˈtɛnʃən] N (frm: gen) conservazione f; (: of facts, faces, names) memorizzazione f; (Med) ritenzione f.

re·ten·tive [rɪˈtɛntɪv] ADJ (memory) ritentivo(-a).

re·think [ˌriːˈθɪŋk] VT ripensare.

reti·cence [ˈrɛtɪsəns] N reticenza.

reti·cent [ˈrɛtɪsənt] ADJ reticente, riservato(-a).

reti·na [ˈrɛtɪnə] N retina.

reti·nue [ˈrɛtɪˌnjuː] N seguito, scorta.

re·tire [rɪˈtaɪəʳ] 1 VI a (give up work) andare in pensione; (quit business) ritirarsi b (withdraw, go to bed, Sport) ritirarsi.

2 VT a (Fin: bill of exchange) ritirare b (person) mandare in pensione.

re·tired [rɪˈtaɪəd] ADJ a (no longer working) in pensione, pensionato(-a); **a retired person** un(a) pensionato(-a) b (liter: quiet, secluded) ritirato(-a), appartato(-a).

re·tire·ment [rɪˈtaɪəmənt] N: **to look forward to one's retirement** non vedere l'ora di andare in pensione; **on her retirement she hopes to ...** quando va in pensione spera di...; **early retirement** prepensionamento.

♦ **retirement age** N età del pensionamento.

re·tir·ing [rɪˈtaɪərɪŋ] ADJ a (frm: shy) riservato(-a) b (departing: chairman) uscente; (age) pensionabile.

re·tort [rɪˈtɔːt] 1 N a (answer) risposta (per le rime) b (Chem) storta.

2 VT (answer) ribattere.

3 VI rimbeccare, rispondere per le rime.

re·trace [rɪˈtreɪs] VT ripercorrere; (recall) ricostruire; **to retrace one's steps** (ri)tornare sui propri passi.

re·tract [rɪˈtrækt] 1 VT (statement) ritrattare; (draw in: claws) ritrarre; (: aerial) ritirare; (: wheels of plane) far rientrare.

2 VI (claws) ritrarsi; (aerial, wheels) rientrare.

re·tract·able [rɪˈtræktəbl] ADJ (undercarriage, nib) retrattile.

re·trac·tile [rɪˈtræktaɪl] ADJ (Zool) retrattile.

re·train [ˌriːˈtreɪn] 1 VT (worker) riqualificare.

2 VI riqualificarsi.

re·train·ing [ˌriːˈtreɪnɪŋ] N riqualificazione f.

re·tread [n ˈriːˌtrɛd; vb ˌriːˈtrɛd] 1 N gomma rigenerata.

2 VT (Aut: tyre) rigenerare.

re·treat [rɪˈtriːt] 1 N a (place) rifugio; (Rel) ritiro (spirituale); **a country retreat** una tranquilla casa in campagna; **to go into retreat** (Rel) andare in ritiro b (Mil) ritirata; **to be in retreat** essere in ritirata or rotta; **to beat a hasty retreat** (fig) battersela.

2 VI (Mil) ritirarsi, battere in ritirata; (flood) ritirarsi; (move back) ritrarsi.

re·trench [rɪˈtrɛntʃ] VI fare delle economie.

re·trench·ment [rɪˈtrɛntʃmənt] N riduzione f delle spese.

re·tri·al [ˌriːˈtraɪəl] N (Law) nuovo processo.

ret·ri·bu·tion [ˌrɛtrɪˈbjuːʃən] N castigo.

re·triev·able [rɪˈtriːvəbl] ADJ (see vb) ricuperabile; riconquistabile; rimediabile; richiamabile.

re·triev·al [rɪˈtriːvəl] N (Comput) richiamo; (see vb) ricupero; riconquista; rimedio, richiamo.

re·trieve [rɪˈtriːv] VT a (get back: object, money) ricuperare; (: honour, position) riconquistare; (set to rights: error, loss, situation) rimediare a b (Comput) richiamare.

re·triev·er [rɪˈtriːvəʳ] N cane m da riporto.

retro·ac·tive [ˌrɛtrəʊˈæktɪv] ADJ retroattivo(-a).

retro·ac·tive·ly [ˌrɛtrəʊˈæktɪvlɪ] ADV in modo retroattivo, retroattivamente.

retro·grade [ˈrɛtrəʊˌgreɪd] ADJ (frm): **a retrograde step** (fig) un passo (all')indietro.

retro·gress [ˌrɛtrəʊˈgrɛs] VI (frm) regredire.

retro·gres·sive [ˌrɛtrəʊˈgrɛsɪv] ADJ (frm: change) retrogrado(-a).

retro·rock·et [ˈrɛtrəʊˌrɒkɪt] N retrorazzo.

retro·spect [ˈrɛtrəʊˌspɛkt] N: **in retrospect** ripensandoci.

retro·spec·tive [ˌrɛtrəʊˈspɛktɪv] 1 ADJ (gen) retrospettivo(-a); (pay rise, Law) retroattivo(-a).

2 N (Art) retrospettiva.

retro·spec·tive·ly [ˌrɛtrəʊˈspɛktɪvlɪ] ADV retrospettivamente.

re·turn [rɪˈtɜːn] 1 N a (going, coming back) ritorno; (sending back) rinvio; (reappearance: of illness etc) ricomparsa; **on my return** al mio ritorno; **by return of post** a stretto giro di posta; **many happy returns (of the day)!** cento di questi giorni!

b (of thing borrowed, lost, stolen) restituzione f; (of money) rimborso; (Comm: of merchandise) reso

c (Fin: profit) profitto, guadagno; **to bring in a good return** or **good returns** fruttare or dare un buon guadagno

d (exchange): **in return (for)** in cambio (di)

e (declaration): **tax return** dichiarazione f dei redditi; **census/election returns** risultati mpl del censimento/delle elezioni

f (Brit: return ticket) (biglietto di) andata e ritorno

g (Sport) risposta; **return of serve** (Tennis) risposta al servizio.

2 VT a (give back) restituire, rendere; (bring back) riportare; (put back) rimettere; (send back) rinviare, mandare indietro; (: by post) rispedire; (Mil: gunfire) rispondere a; (favour, love, sb's visit) ricambiare; **"return to sender"** "rispedire al mittente"

b (Law): **to return a verdict of guilty/not guilty** pronunciare un verdetto di colpevolezza/di innocenza

c (Pol: elect) eleggere.

3 VI (go, come back) (ri)tornare; (illness, symptoms etc) ricomparire; **to return home** (ri)tornare a casa; **to return to** (room, office) (ri)tornare in; (school, work) (ri)tornare a; (subject, argument) (ri)tornare su.

4 ADJ (Brit: ticket, fare) di andata e ritorno; (journey, flight) di ritorno.

re·turn·able [rɪˈtɜːnəbl] ADJ: **returnable bottle** vuoto a rendere.

re·turn·er [rɪˈtɜːnəʳ] N (Brit) donna che ritorna a lavoro dopo la maternità.

re·turn·ing of·fic·er [rɪˌtɜːnɪŋ ˈɒfɪsəʳ] N (Brit Pol) funzionario addetto all'organizzazione e alla presentazione dei risultati delle elezioni in un distretto.

♦ **return key** N (on computer) tasto di ritorno (a margine).

♦ **return match** N (Sport) (partita di) ritorno.

♦ **return stroke** N (Tech) corsa di ritorno.

re·uni·fi·ca·tion [ˌriːjuːnɪfɪˈkeɪʃən] N riunificazione f.

re·union [rɪˈjuːnjən] N riunione f.

re·unite [ˌriːjuːˈnaɪt] 1 VT riunire.

2 VI riunirsi.

re·use [n riːˈjuːs; vt ˌriːˈjuːz] 1 N riutilizzazione f.

2 VT riusare, riutilizzare.

Rev, Revd. ABBR = Reverend.

rev [rɛv] (fam) 1 N (Aut) giro; **3,000 revs per minute** 3.000 giri al minuto; **to keep the revs up** tenere il motore su di giri.

2 VT (engine) mandare su di giri.

3 VI (*also:* **rev up**: *car*) andar su di giri, imballarsi; (: *driver*) tenere il motore su di giri.

re·valua·tion [ˌriːvæljʊˈeɪʃən] N rivalutazione *f*.

re·value [ˌriːˈvæljuː] VT rivalutare.

re·vamp [ˌriːˈvæmp] VT (*methods, system*) modernizzare; (*company, organization*) rinnovare; (*play*) rendere di nuovo attuale.

re·vanch·ism [rɪˈvæntʃɪzəm] N revanscismo.

♦ **rev counter** N (*Aut*) contagiri *m inv*.

re·veal [rɪˈviːl] VT (*make known*) rivelare, svelare; (*uncover*: *hidden object*) scoprire.

re·veal·ing [rɪˈviːlɪŋ] ADJ (*remarks, action*) rivelatore(-trice); (*dress*) scollato(-a).

re·veil·le [rɪˈvælɪ] N (*Mil*) sveglia.

rev·el [ˈrɛvl] VI far baldoria; **to revel in sth/in doing sth** godere di qc/nel fare qc.

rev·ela·tion [ˌrɛvəˈleɪʃən] N rivelazione *f*; **(the Book of the) Revelation** (*Bible*) l'Apocalisse *f*.

rev·el·ler, (*Am*) **rev·eler** [ˈrɛvlə'] N chi fa baldoria.

rev·el·ry [ˈrɛvlrɪ] N baldoria.

re·venge [rɪˈvɛndʒ] **1** N vendetta; (*in game etc*) rivincita; **to get one's revenge (for sth)** vendicarsi (di qc); **to take revenge on sb (for sth)** vendicarsi su qn (per qc).

2 VT vendicare; **to be revenged (on sb)** prendersi la rivincita (su qn); **to revenge o.s. (on sb)** vendicarsi (su qn).

re·venge·ful [rɪˈvɛndʒfʊl] ADJ vendicativo(-a).

rev·enue [ˈrɛvənjuː] N entrate *fpl*, reddito.

re·ver·ber·ate [rɪˈvɜːbəˌreɪt] VI (*frm: sound*) rimbombare; (: *fig*) ripercuotersi.

re·ver·bera·tion [rɪˌvɜːbəˈreɪʃən] (*frm*) N (*see vb*) rimbombo; ripercussione *f*.

re·vere [rɪˈvɪə'] VT (*frm*) venerare.

rev·er·ence [ˈrɛvərəns] **1** N venerazione *f*, riverenza.
2 VT venerare.

Rev·er·end [ˈrɛvərənd] ADJ (*in titles*) reverendo(-a).

rev·er·ent [ˈrɛvərənt] ADJ riverente.

rev·er·en·tial [ˌrɛvəˈrɛnʃəl] ADJ (*frm: awe, bow*) riverente.

rev·er·ent·ly [ˈrɛvərəntlɪ] ADV rispettosamente.

rev·erie [ˈrɛvərɪ] N fantasticheria.

re·ver·sal [rɪˈvɜːsəl] N (*of roles, tendencies*) inversione *f*; (*of situation, fortunes*) capovolgimento; (*of decision*) revoca; **the reversal of industrial decline** il risollevamento delle sorti dell'industria.

re·verse [rɪˈvɜːs] **1** ADJ (*order*) inverso(-a); (*direction*) opposto(-a); (*side*) altro(-a); **in reverse order** in ordine inverso.

2 N **a** (*opposite*): **the reverse** il contrario, l'opposto
b (*face: of coin, paper*) rovescio
c (*Aut*) retromarcia, marcia indietro; **to go into reverse** fare marcia indietro *or* retromarcia.

3 VT (*turn the other way round*) invertire; (*situation, position*) capovolgere, rovesciare; (*movement*) invertire la direzione di; (*garment*) rivoltare; (*Law*) cassare; **to reverse the charges** (*Brit Telec*) fare una telefonata a carico (del destinatario); **to reverse one's car** fare marcia indietro.

4 VI (*Brit Aut*) fare marcia indietro; **I reversed into the car behind** facendo retromarcia ho urtato la macchina di dietro.

re·versed charge call [rɪˌvɜːstʃɑːdʒˈkɔːl] N (*Brit Telec*) telefonata a carico (del destinatario).

♦ **reverse gear** N (*Aut*) marcia indietro.

♦ **reverse video** N (*Comput*) inversione *f* dei colori del video.

re·vers·ible [rɪˈvɜːsəbl] ADJ (*garment*) double-face *inv*; (*procedure*) reversibile.

re·vers·ing lights [rɪˈvɜːsɪŋˌlaɪts] NPL (*Brit Aut*) luci *fpl* di retromarcia.

re·ver·sion [rɪˈvɜːʃən] N (*return to previous state*) ritorno; (*Bio*) reversione *f*.

re·vert [rɪˈvɜːt] VI (*gen*): **to revert (to)** ritornare (a); **to revert to type** (*Bio*) ritornare allo stato primitivo; (*fig*) tornare alla propria natura.

re·view [rɪˈvjuː] **1** N **a** (*survey, taking stock*) revisione *f*; (*Mil: of troops*) rivista; (*critique*) critica, recensione *f*; **to come under review** essere preso(-a) in esame; **the play got good reviews** lo spettacolo ha ricevuto critiche favorevoli
b (*journal*) rivista, periodico.
2 VT (*take stock of*) fare una revisione di; (*situation*) fare il punto di; (*Mil: troops*) passare in rivista; (*book, play, film*) fare la recensione di.

♦ **review copy** N copia per la stampa.

re·view·er [rɪˈvjuː'] N recensore *m*; **book/film reviewer** critico letterario/cinematografico.

re·vile [rɪˈvaɪl] VT (*frm*) insultare.

re·vise [rɪˈvaɪz] **1** VT **a** (*look over: subject, notes*) ripassare
b (*alter: text*) emendare; (*decision, opinion*) modificare; **revised edition** edizione *f* riveduta e corretta.
2 VI (*for exams*) ripassare.

Re·vised Ver·sion [rɪˌvaɪzdˈvɜːʃən] N (*Brit: of Bible*): **the Revised Version** *la traduzione inglese della Bibbia effettuata nel 1884.*

re·vi·sion [rɪˈvɪʒən] N **a** (*before exam*) ripasso; (*of text*) revisione *f* **b** (*revised version*) versione *f* riveduta e corretta.

re·vi·sion·ism [rɪˈvɪʒəˌnɪzəm] N (*Pol*) revisionismo.

re·vi·sion·ist [rɪˈvɪʒənɪst] ADJ, N (*Pol*) revisionista (*m/f*).

re·vis·it [ˌriːˈvɪzɪt] VT rivisitare.

re·vi·tal·ize [ˌriːˈvaɪtəˌlaɪz] VT ravvivare.

re·viv·al [rɪˈvaɪvəl] N (*of person, business, play*) ripresa; (*of faith, religion*) risveglio; (*of custom, usage: restoration*) ripristino; (: *reappearance*) rinascita.

re·viv·al·ism [rɪˈvaɪvəˌlɪzəm] N (*Rel*) revivalismo.

re·viv·al·ist [rɪˈvaɪvəlɪst] N (*Rel*) revivalista *m/f*.

♦ **revival meeting** N (*Rel*) *incontro per il rinnovamento della fede religiosa.*

re·vive [rɪˈvaɪv] **1** VT (*person*) rianimare; (: *from faint*) far riprendere i sensi a; (*fig: spirits*) risollevare; (*old customs*) far tornare di moda, far rivivere; (*hopes, courage*) riaccendere; (*suspicions*) risvegliare, ridestare; (*Theatre: play*) riprendere.
2 VI (*person, business, trade, activity*) riprendersi, rianimarsi; (*hope, emotions*) riaccendersi, rinascere.

revo·ca·tion [ˌrɛvəˈkeɪʃən] (*frm*) N (*of law*) abrogazione *f*; (*of order, decision*) revoca.

re·voke [rɪˈvəʊk] (*frm*) VT (*law*) abrogare; (: *order, decision*) revocare.

re·volt [rɪˈvəʊlt] **1** N rivolta, ribellione *f*; **to be in open revolt** essere in aperta rivolta.
2 VT (*far*) rivoltare; **to be revolted by sth** provare disgusto per qc.
3 VI **a** (*rebel*): **to revolt (against sb/sth)** ribellarsi (a qn/qc) **b** (*feel disgust*): **to revolt at** *or* **against** rivoltarsi (a *or* di fronte a).

re·volt·ing [rɪˈvəʊltɪŋ] ADJ rivoltante, ripugnante.

re·volt·ing·ly [rɪˈvəʊltɪŋlɪ] ADV in modo rivoltante, disgustosamente.

revo·lu·tion [ˌrɛvəˈluːʃən] N (*movement, change, Pol*) rivo-

luzione *f*; (*of record, engine, wheel*) giro.

revo·lu·tion·ary [ˌrɛvəˈluːʃnərɪ] ADJ, N rivoluzionario(-a).

revo·lu·tion·ize [ˌrɛvəˈluːʃəˌnaɪz] VT rivoluzionare.

re·volve [rɪˈvɒlv] ① VT (*far*) girare.

② VI girare; **to revolve around sth** girare *or* ruotare intorno a qc; **the Earth revolves on its own axis** la Terra ruota intorno al proprio asse; **he thinks everything revolves round him** si crede il centro dell'universo.

re·volv·er [rɪˈvɒlvəʳ] N rivoltella.

re·volv·ing [rɪˈvɒlvɪŋ] ADJ girevole; **revolving light** (*on police car*) lampeggiatore *m*.

♦ **revolving credit** N (*Fin*) credito a termine rinnovabile automaticamente.

♦ **revolving door** N porta girevole.

re·vue [rɪˈvjuː] N (*Theatre*) rivista.

re·vul·sion [rɪˈvʌlʃən] N ripugnanza.

re·ward [rɪˈwɔːd] ① N ricompensa, premio; **as a reward for (doing) sth** in premio *or* come ricompensa per (aver fatto) qc.

② VT: **to reward (for)** ricompensare (per), premiare (per).

re·ward·ing [rɪˈwɔːdɪŋ] ADJ (*activity*) di grande soddisfazione, gratificante; (*book*) che vale la pena di leggere; **financially rewarding** conveniente dal punto di vista economico.

re·wind [ˌriːˈwaɪnd] VT **a** (*ball of wool etc*) riavvolgere, riarrotolare; (*tape, cassette*) far tornare indietro **b** (*clock, toy*) ricaricare.

re·wire [ˌriːˈwaɪəʳ] VT (*house*) rifare l'impianto elettrico di.

re·word [ˌriːˈwɜːd] VT formulare *or* esprimere con altre parole.

re·work [riːˈwɜːk] VT (*idea, novel*) modificare.

re·write [ˌriːˈraɪt] VT riscrivere.

Rey·kja·vik [ˈreɪkjəˌvɪk] N Reykjavik *f*.

RFD [ˌɑːrɛfˈdiː] ABBR (*Am Post*)= *rural free delivery*.

Rh ABBR (= *rhesus*) Rh.

rhap·sod·ic [ræpˈsɒdɪk] ADJ (*account, description, praise*) entusiastico(-a); (*Mus*) rapsodico(-a).

rhap·so·dize [ˈræpsəˌdaɪz] VI: **to rhapsodize (about)**, **rhapsodize (over)** parlare entusiasticamente (di).

rhap·so·dy [ˈræpsədɪ] N (*Mus*) rapsodia; **to go into rhapsodies over sth** (*fig*) andare in estasi per qc.

rheo·stat [ˈriəʊˌstæt] N (*Elec*) reostato.

rhe·sus [ˈriːsəs] N (*also:* **rhesus monkey**) reso.

♦ **rhesus factor** N (*Med*) fattore *m* Rh.

♦ **rhesus negative** ADJ (*Med*) Rh-negativo(-a).

♦ **rhesus positive** ADJ (*Med*) Rh-positivo(-a).

rheto·ric [ˈrɛtərɪk] N retorica.

rhe·tori·cal [rɪˈtɒrɪkəl] ADJ (*style, question*) retorico(-a).

rhe·tori·cal·ly [rɪˈtɒrɪkəlɪ] ADV (*ask, declaim*) in modo retorico.

rheu·mat·ic [ruːˈmætɪk] ADJ reumatico(-a).

♦ **rheumatic fever** N febbre *f* reumatica.

rheu·mat·ics [ruːˈmætɪks] NSG (*old*) reumatismi *mpl*.

rheu·ma·tism [ˈruːməˌtɪzəm] N reumatismo.

rheu·ma·toid ar·thri·tis [ˈruːmətɔɪdəːˈθraɪtɪs] N artrite *f* reumatoide.

Rhine [raɪn] N: **the Rhine** il Reno.

rhine·stone [ˈraɪnˌstəʊn] N strass *m inv*.

rhi·no [ˈraɪnəʊ] N (*fam*) rinoceronte *m*.

rhi·noc·er·os [raɪˈnɒsərəs] N rinoceronte *m*.

rhi·zome [ˈraɪzəʊm] N rizoma *m*.

Rhodes [rəʊdz] N Rodi *f*.

Rho·desia [rəʊˈdiːʃə] N la Rodesia.

Rho·desian [rəʊˈdiːʃən] ADJ, N Rodesiano(-a).

rho·do·den·dron [ˌrəʊdəˈdɛndrən] N rododendro.

rhom·bus [ˈrɒmbəs] N rombo.

Rhone [rəʊn] N: **the Rhone** il Rodano.

rhu·barb [ˈruːbɑːb] ① N rabarbaro.

② ADJ (*jam, pie, tart*) di rabarbaro.

rhyme [raɪm] ① N rima; (*verse*) poesia; **without rhyme or reason** senza capo né coda.

② VI: **to rhyme (with)** fare rima (con).

rhym·ing [ˈraɪmɪŋ] ADJ rimato(-a), in rima; **rhyming couplet** rima baciata.

♦ **rhyming slang** N *gergo Cockney che sostituisce una certa parola con altre che con questa fanno rima*.

rhythm [ˈrɪðəm] N ritmo.

rhyth·mic, **rhyth·mi·cal** [ˈrɪðmɪk(əl)] ADJ ritmico(-a).

rhyth·mi·cal·ly [ˈrɪðmɪkəlɪ] ADV ritmicamente.

♦ **rhythm method** N (*Med*): **the rhythm method** il metodo Ogino-Knauss.

RI [ˌɑːrˈaɪ] ① ABBR (*Am Post*)= *Rhode Island*.

② N ABBR (*Brit*)= *religious instruction*.

rib [rɪb] ① N (*Anat*) costola; (*Culin*) costata; (*of umbrella*) stecca; (*of leaf*) nervatura; (*Knitting*) costa; **to dig** *or* **poke sb in the ribs** dare una gomitata nelle costole a qn.

② VT (*fam: tease*) punzecchiare.

rib·ald [ˈrɪbəld] ADJ (*old: person*) sguaiato(-a); (: *joke*) licenzioso(-a).

rib·ald·ry [ˈrɪbəldrɪ] N (*old*) sguaiataggine *f*.

ribbed [rɪbd] ADJ (*Knitting*) a coste.

rib·bon [ˈrɪbən] N (*gen, of typewriter*) nastro; (*Mil*) nastrino; **to tear sth to ribbons** ridurre qc a brandelli; (*fig*) demolire qc.

♦ **ribbon development** N (*Brit*) *sviluppo urbano lineare sul bordo delle strade periferiche*.

♦ **rib cage** N (*Anat*) gabbia toracica.

ri·bo·fla·vin [ˌraɪbəʊˈfleɪvɪn] N (*Chem*) riboflavina.

rice [raɪs] N riso.

♦ **rice field** N risaia.

♦ **rice growing** N risicoltura.

♦ **rice paper** N (*for art*) carta di riso; (*Culin*) ≈ ostie *fpl*.

♦ **rice pudding** N budino di riso.

rich [rɪtʃ] ADJ (*comp* **-er**, *superl* **-est**) (*gen*) ricco(-a); (*food*) con molti grassi; (*colour*) intenso(-a); (*clothes*) sontuoso (-a); **it was lovely but rather rich** era buono ma un po' troppo sostanzioso; **that's rich!** (*fam iro*) questa sì che è bella!; **the rich** i ricchi; **to be rich in sth** essere ricco(-a) di qc; **to become** *or* **get** *or* **grow rich(er)** arricchirsi, diventar ricco(-a).

riches [ˈrɪtʃɪz] NPL ricchezze *fpl*.

rich·ly [ˈrɪtʃlɪ] ADV (*rewarded*) lautamente; (*endowed*) abbondantemente; (*dressed*) sontuosamente; (*deserved*) pienamente.

rich·ness [ˈrɪtʃnɪs] N (*see adj*) ricchezza; (*alto*) contenuto di grassi, intensità *f inv*; sontuosità *f inv*.

Richter scale [ˈrɪxtəʳ skeɪl] N: **the Richter scale** la scala Richter.

rick [rɪk] ① N covone *m*, pagliaio.

② VT (*Brit fam: one's neck, back*) farsi uno strappo muscolare a.

rick·ets [ˈrɪkɪts] NSG rachitismo.

rick·ety [ˈrɪkɪtɪ] ADJ (*furniture, structure*) traballante.

rick·shaw [ˈrɪkʃɔː] N risciò *m inv*.

rico·chet [ˈrɪkəˌʃeɪ] ① N rimbalzo.

② VI: **to ricochet (off)** rimbalzare (contro).

rid [rɪd] VT (*pt, pp* **rid** *or* **ridded**): **to rid sb/sth of** sbarazzare qn/qc di, liberare qn/qc da; **to get rid of sb/sth** OR **rid o.s. of sb/sth** sbarazzarsi *or* liberarsi di qn/qc.

rid·dance ['rɪdəns] N: **good riddance!** (*fam*) che liberazione!

rid·den ['rɪdn] PP of ride.

rid·dle¹ ['rɪdl] N (*puzzle*) indovinello; **to speak in riddles** parlare per enigmi.

rid·dle² ['rɪdl] ⟦1⟧ VT (*soil, coal*) setacciare, vagliare; (*fig*): **to riddle with** (*bullets*) crivellare di; **riddled with holes** bucherellato(-a); **the council was riddled with corruption** la corruzione dilagava nel consiglio.
⟦2⟧ N (*sieve*) setaccio, vaglio.

ride [raɪd] (*vb: pt* **rode,** *pp* **ridden**) ⟦1⟧ N (*on horse*) cavalcata; (*in car, on bike*) giro, corsa; (*esp Am: lift*) passaggio, strappo; **to go for a ride** (*on horse*) andare a fare una cavalcata; (*on bike*) andare a fare un giro; **it was a rough ride** è stato un viaggio scomodo; **he got** *or* **was given a rough ride** (*fig*) passò un momentaccio; **it's a 10-minute ride on the bus** ci vogliono 10 minuti in autobus; **he gave me a ride into town** (*in car*) mi ha dato un passaggio in città; **to take sb for a ride** (*in car, on horseback*) portare qn a fare un giro; (*fig: make fool of, swindle*) prendere in giro qn.
⟦2⟧ VT: **to ride a horse** andare a cavallo; (*subj: jockey*) montare un cavallo; **to ride a donkey/camel** cavalcare un asino/cammello; **to ride a bicycle** andare in bicicletta; **can you ride a bike?** sai andare in bicicletta?; **he rode his horse into town** è venuto in città a cavallo; **we rode 10 km yesterday** ieri abbiamo fatto 10 km a cavallo (*or* in bicicletta); **to ride a good race** fare un'ottima gara.
⟦3⟧ VI (*ride a horse*) andare a cavallo; (*go by car/bicycle etc*) andare in macchina/in bicicletta *etc*; **to ride along/ through** *etc* passare/attraversare *etc* a cavallo (*or* in macchina *etc*); **can you ride?** (*ride a horse*) sai andare a cavallo?, sai cavalcare?; **he's riding high at the moment** in questo momento è sulla cresta dell'onda; **to ride at anchor** (*ship*) essere all'ancora *or* alla fonda; **to let things ride** lasciare che le cose seguano il loro corso
► **ride out** VT + ADV (*Naut: storm*) sostenere; (*fig: difficult period*) superare; **to ride out the storm** (*fig*) mantenersi a galla
► **ride up** VI + ADV (*skirt, dress*) salire.

rid·er ['raɪdə'] N ⟦a⟧ (*horse rider*) uomo/donna a cavallo; (*: skilled man*) cavallerizzo; (*: skilled woman*) cavallerizza, amazzone *f*; (*jockey*) fantino(-a); (*cyclist*) ciclista *m/f*; (*motorcyclist*) motociclista *m/f* ⟦b⟧ (*addition to document*) clausola addizionale.

ridge [rɪdʒ] N (*of mountain, hill*) cresta; (*of chain of mountains*) crinale *m*; (*of roof*) colmo; (*in ploughed field*) porca; (*Met*): **ridge of high pressure** fascia di alta pressione.

ridge·pole ['rɪdʒpəʊl] N (*on tent*) asta di colmo.

♦ **ridge tent** N (tenda) canadese *f*.

ridi·cule ['rɪdɪkjuːl] ⟦1⟧ N ridicolo; **to hold sb/sth up to ridicule** mettere in ridicolo qn/qc.
⟦2⟧ VT ridicolizzare.

ri·dicu·lous [rɪ'dɪkjʊləs] ADJ ridicolo(-a); **to make o.s. (look) ridiculous** rendersi ridicolo(-a).

ri·dicu·lous·ly [rɪ'dɪkjʊləslɪ] ADV (*stupidly*) in modo ridicolo; (*disproportionately*) incredibilmente; **a ridiculously large/small amount** una quantità enorme/irrisoria.

ri·dicu·lous·ness [rɪ'dɪkjʊləsnɪs] N ridicolaggine *f*.

rid·ing ['raɪdɪŋ] N (*horse-riding*) equitazione *f*.

♦ **riding breeches** NPL pantaloni *mpl or* calzoni *mpl* da cavallerizzo.

♦ **riding crop, riding whip** N frustino.

♦ **riding habit** N amazzone *f*, abito da cavallerizza.

♦ **riding school** N scuola di equitazione.

rife [raɪf] ADJ (*frm*): **to be rife** (*corruption, disease*) dilagare; **to be rife with** abbondare di.

riff·raff ['rɪf,ræf] N gentaglia, canaglia.

ri·fle¹ ['raɪfl] VT (*house, till etc*) ripulire, svuotare
► **rifle through** VI + PREP frugare.

ri·fle² ['raɪfl] N fucile *m*, carabina.

♦ **rifle range** N (*Mil*) poligono di tiro; (*at fair*) tiro a segno.

rift [rɪft] N (*in family, between friends*) incrinatura; (*Pol: in party*) spaccatura; (*in rock, ground*) crepa, fessura; (*in clouds*) squarcio.

♦ **rift valley** N fossa tettonica.

rig [rɪg] ⟦1⟧ N (*oil rig*) impianto di trivellazione (per il petrolio); (*: offshore*) piattaforma petrolifera *or* di trivellazione.
⟦2⟧ VT ⟦a⟧ (*election, competition*) truccare; (*prices*) manipolare; (*also:* **rig up:** *equipment, device*) improvvisare, mettere su
⟦b⟧ (*boat*) armare
► **rig out** VT + ADV (*Brit*) attrezzare; (*pej*) abbigliare, agghindare; **to rig out (as/in)** vestire (da/in)
► **rig up** VT + ADV (*also fig*) improvvisare, mettere su.

rig·ging ['rɪgɪŋ] N (*Naut*) attrezzatura; **standing/running rigging** manovre *fpl* fisse/correnti.

right [raɪt] ⟦1⟧ ADJ ⟦a⟧ (*morally good*) retto(-a), onesto(-a); (*just*) giusto(-a); **it's not right to leave children alone in a house** non è ammissibile lasciare i bambini da soli a casa; **it's not right!** non è giusto!; **it is only right that ...** è più che giusto che...; **to do what is right** fare ciò che si crede giusto; **I thought it right to warn him** mi è sembrato giusto avvertirlo
⟦b⟧ (*suitable: person, clothes, time*) adatto(-a), appropriato(-a); **to choose the right moment for sth/to do sth** scegliere il momento giusto *or* adatto per qc/per fare qc; **that's the right attitude!** così va bene!; **to say the right thing** dire la cosa giusta; **you did the right thing** hai fatto bene; **what's the right thing to do?** qual è la cosa migliore da farsi?; **to know the right people** conoscere la gente giusta
⟦c⟧ (*correct: answer, solution etc*) giusto(-a), esatto(-a), corretto(-a); (*: size*) giusto(-a); **right first time!** hai azzeccato al primo colpo!; **to get sth right** far giusto qc; **I got every question right** ho risposto esattamente a tutte le domande; **let's get it right this time!** cerchiamo di farlo bene stavolta!; **to get one's facts right** sapere di che cosa si parla; **get your facts right!** non parlare se non sei sicuro di quello che dici!; **(yes,) that's right** sì, esatto; **the right road** la strada buona; **the right time** l'ora esatta; **to get on the right side of sb** (*fig*) entrare nelle grazie di qn; **to put a clock right** rimettere (all'ora esatta) un orologio; **to put a mistake right** (*Brit*) correggere un errore; **right you are!** *or* **right-oh!** (*fam*) va bene!
⟦d⟧: **to be right** (*person*) aver ragione; (*answer, behaviour*) essere giusto(-a) *or* corretto(-a); **you're quite right** *or* (*fam*) **you're dead right** hai proprio *or* perfettamente ragione; **you were right to come to me** hai fatto bene a venire da me
⟦e⟧ (*well, in order*): **to be/feel as right as rain** essere/ sentirsi completamente ristabilito(-a); **he is not quite right in the head** gli manca una rotella; **I don't feel quite right** non mi sento del tutto a posto; **all's right with the world** tutto va bene; **the stereo still isn't right** lo stereo ha ancora qualcosa che non va
⟦f⟧ (*not left*) destro(-a); **I'd give my right arm to know ...** darei un occhio per sapere...

g (*Math: angle*) retto(-a)

h (*fam: intensive*): **a right idiot** un perfetto idiota.

2 ADV **a** (*directly, exactly*): **right now** (*at this moment*) in questo momento, proprio adesso; (*immediately*) subito; **right away** subito; **right off** subito; (*at the first attempt*) al primo colpo; **right here** proprio qui; **she (just) went right on talking** ha continuato a parlare lo stesso; **right against the wall** proprio contro il muro; **right ahead** sempre diritto, proprio davanti; **right behind/in front of** proprio dietro/davanti a; **right before/after** subito prima/dopo; **right in the middle** proprio nel (bel) mezzo; (*of target*) in pieno centro; **right round sth** tutt'intorno a qc; **right at the end** proprio alla fine

b (*completely*) completamente; **to go right back to the beginning of sth** ricominciare qc da capo; **to go right to the end of sth** andare fino in fondo a qc; **to push sth right in** spingere qc fino in fondo; **to read a book right through** leggere un libro dall'inizio alla fine

c (*correctly*) giusto, bene; (*well*) bene; **if I remember right** se mi ricordo bene; **if everything goes right** se tutto va bene

d (*properly, fairly*) giustamente, con giustizia; **to treat sb right** trattare qn in modo giusto; **you did right not to go** hai fatto bene a non andarci

e (*not left*) a destra; **right, left and centre** (*fig*) da tutte le parti

f : **right, who's next?** bene, chi è il prossimo?; **right then, let's begin!** (va) bene allora, cominciamo!

g : **all right!** va bene!, d'accordo!; (*that's enough*) va bene!; **it's all right** (*don't worry*) va (tutto) bene; **it's all right for you!** già, facile per te!; **is it all right for me to go at 4?** va bene se me ne vado alle 4?; **I'm/I feel all right now** adesso sto/mi sento bene.

3 N **a** : **right and wrong** il bene e il male; **to be in the right** essere nel giusto; **to know right from wrong** distinguere il bene dal male; **I want to know the rights and wrongs of it** voglio sapere chi ha ragione e chi ha torto; **two wrongs don't make a right** due torti non fanno una ragione

b (*claim, authority*) diritto; **film rights** diritti *mpl* di riproduzione cinematografica; **to have a right to sth** aver diritto a qc; **you have a right to your own opinions** è tuo diritto pensarla come vuoi; **the right to be/say/do sth** il diritto di essere/dire/fare qc; **what right have you got to ...?** che diritto hai di...?; **by rights** di diritto; **to be within one's rights** avere tutti i diritti; **to own sth in one's own right** possedere qc per conto proprio; **she's a good actress in her own right** è una brava attrice anche per conto suo

c (*not left*) destra; (*Boxing: punch*) destro; **the Right** (*Pol*) la destra; **to the right (of)** sul lato destro (di); **on the right (of)** a destra (di)

d : **to set** *or* **put to rights** mettere a posto.

4 VT (*correct: balance*) ristabilire; (: *wrong, injustice*) riparare a; (*vehicle, vessel*) raddrizzare; **to right itself** (*vehicle, vessel*) raddrizzarsi; (*situation*) risolversi da solo *or* da sé.

5 EXCL bene!

♦ **right angle** N angolo retto; **at right angles (to)** ad angolo retto (con).

♦ **right-angled** ['raɪt,æŋgld] ADJ ad angolo retto; (*triangle*) rettangolo(-a).

right·eous ['raɪtʃəs] ADJ (*person*) virtuoso(-a), retto(-a); (*indignation, anger: moralistic*) un po' troppo virtuoso (-a); (: *justified*) giustificato(-a).

right·eous·ness ['raɪtʃəsnɪs] N rettitudine *f*, virtù.

right·ful ['raɪtfʊl] ADJ (*heir*) legittimo(-a).

right·ful·ly ['raɪtfəlɪ] ADV legittimamente, a buon diritto.

♦ **right-hand** ['raɪt,hænd] ADJ (*side*) destro(-a); **right-hand drive** (*Aut*) guida a destra.

♦ **right-handed** [,raɪt'hændɪd] ADJ (*person*) che usa *or* adopera la (mano) destra.

♦ **right-hander** [,raɪt'hændə'] N (*person*) chi usa *or* adopera la mano destra; (*blow*) destro.

♦ **right-hand man** N (*pl* **-men**) (*personal aide*) braccio destro.

♦ **right-hand side** N lato destro.

right·ist ['raɪtɪst] **1** N persona di destra.

2 ADJ di destra.

right·ly ['raɪtlɪ] ADV (*correctly*) correttamente; (*with reason*) a ragione, giustamente; **I don't rightly know** non so di preciso; **if I remember rightly** se mi ricordo bene; **rightly or wrongly** a torto o a ragione.

♦ **right-minded** [,raɪt'maɪndɪd], **right-thinking** ['raɪt,θɪŋkɪŋ] ADJ di buon senso, sensato(-a).

righto, right oh ['raɪt'əʊ] EXCL (*Brit fam*) OK.

♦ **right-of-centre** [raɪtɒf'sɛntə'] ADJ di centrodestra.

♦ **right of way** N (*across property*) diritto di accesso; (*Aut: precedence*) precedenza.

♦ **rights issue** N (*Stock Exchange*) emissione *f* di azioni riservate agli azionisti.

♦ **right wing** N: **the right wing** (*Pol*) la destra; (*Sport, Mil: position, person*) l'ala destra.

♦ **right-wing** [,raɪt'wɪŋ] ADJ (*Pol*) di destra.

♦ **right-winger** [,raɪt'wɪŋə'] N (*Pol*) uno(-a) di destra; (*Sport*) ala destra.

rig·id ['rɪdʒɪd] ADJ (*material*) rigido(-a); (*discipline, specifications, principle*) rigoroso(-a); (*rules*) severo(-a); (*pej: person, ideas*) inflessibile; **rigid with fear** impietrito(-a) dalla paura.

ri·gid·ity [rɪ'dʒɪdɪtɪ] N (*see adj*) rigidità; rigorosità; severità; inflessibilità.

rig·id·ly ['rɪdʒɪdlɪ] ADV (*strictly*) rigorosamente; (*inflexibly*) inflessibilmente; (*closely*) rigidamente; **to stand rigidly to attention** stare impalato(-a) sull'attenti.

rig·ma·role ['rɪgmə,rəʊl] N (*pej: speech*) storia, tiritera; (: *complicated procedure*) trafila.

ri·gor ['rɪgə'] N (*Am*) = **rigour**.

♦ **rig·or mor·tis** [,rɪgɔ:'mɔ:tɪs] N rigor mortis *m inv*.

rig·or·ous ['rɪgərəs] ADJ rigoroso(-a).

rig·or·ous·ly ['rɪgərəslɪ] ADV (*apply, test*) rigorosamente.

rig·our, (*Am*) **rig·or** ['rɪgə'] N rigore *m*.

rig·out ['rɪg,aʊt] N (*Brit fam old*) tenuta; **where are you going in that rigout?** dove vai conciato così?

rile [raɪl] VT (*fam*) irritare, seccare.

rim [rɪm] N (*of cup etc*) orlo; (*of wheel*) cerchione *m*; (*of spectacles*) montatura.

rim·less ['rɪmlɪs] ADJ (*spectacles*) senza montatura.

rimmed ['rɪmd] ADJ (*with colour*) bordato(-a).

rind [raɪnd] N (*of fruit*) buccia; (*of lemon*) scorza; (*of cheese*) crosta; (*of bacon*) cotenna.

ring[1] [rɪŋ] **1** N **a** (*gen*) anello; (*for napkin*) portatovagliolo; **wedding ring** fede *f*, (*of smoke*) spirale *f*; **the rings of Saturn** gli anelli di Saturno; **to run rings round sb** (*fig*) surclassare qn

b (*of people, objects*) cerchio; (*gang*) cricca, banda; (*of spies*) rete *f*; **they were sitting in a ring** erano seduti in circolo *or* in cerchio

c (*arena etc: Boxing*) ring *m inv*, quadrato; (: *at circus*) pista, arena.

②VT (*surround*) circondare, accerchiare; (*mark with ring*) fare un cerchietto intorno a.

ring² [rɪŋ] (*vb: pt* **rang**, *pp* **rung**) ① N **a** (*of bell*) trillo; (*of telephone*) squillo; (*tone of voice*) tono; **that has the ring of truth about it** questo ha l'aria d'essere vero

b (*Brit Telec*): **to give sb a ring** dare un colpo di telefono a qn.

②VT **a** (*bell, doorbell*) suonare; **to ring the changes** (*fig*) variare; **the name doesn't ring a bell (with me)** (*fig*) questo nome non mi dice niente

b (*Brit Telec*): **to ring sb (up)** telefonare a qn, dare un colpo di telefono a qn.

③VI **a** (*bell, telephone etc*) suonare; **to ring for sb/sth** (suonare il campanello per) chiamare qn/chiedere qc

b (*telephone*) telefonare

c (*words, voice*) risuonare; (*blast*) rimbombare; (*ears*) fischiare; **their laughter rang through the room** le loro risate risuonavano nella stanza; **my ears are still ringing from the blast** mi fischiano ancora le orecchie per via dell'esplosione; **to ring true/false** (*fig*) suonare vero(-a)/falso(-a)

▶ **ring around** VI + ADV = **ring round**

▶ **ring back** VT + ADV (*Brit Telec*) richiamare

▶ **ring in** VI + ADV (*Brit Telec*) telefonare

▶ **ring off** VI + ADV (*Brit Telec*) mettere giù, riattaccare

▶ **ring out** VI + ADV risuonare, riecheggiare

▶ **ring round** ① VI + ADV fare un giro di telefonate.

②VT + ADV: **to ring round one's friends** telefonare a tutti gli amici

▶ **ring up** VT + ADV = **ring²b**.

♦ **ring binder** N classificatore *m* ad anelli.

♦ **ring finger** N anulare *m*.

ring·ing [ˈrɪŋɪŋ] ① ADJ (*voice, tone*) sonoro(-a).

② N (*of church bells*) scampanio; (*of door bell*) scampanellata; (*of telephone*) squillo; (*in ears*) fischio, ronzio.

♦ **ringing tone** N (*Brit Telec*) segnale *m* di libero.

ring·leader [ˈrɪŋˌliːdəʳ] N (*of gang*) capobanda *m/f*.

ring·let [ˈrɪŋlɪt] N boccolo.

ring·master [ˈrɪŋˌmɑːstəʳ] N direttore *m* del circo.

♦ **ring road** N (*Brit*) circonvallazione *f*.

ring·side [ˈrɪŋˌsaɪd] ① N prima fila.

② ADJ in prima fila.

ring·worm [ˈrɪŋˌwɜːm] N tigna.

rink [rɪŋk] N (*for ice-skating*) pista di pattinaggio (su ghiaccio); (*for roller-skating*) pista di pattinaggio (a rotelle).

rinse [rɪns] ① N (ri)sciacquatura; (*quick*) (ri)sciacquata; (*hair-colouring*) cachet *m inv*; **to give sth a rinse** dare una sciacquata a qc.

②VT (ri)sciacquare; **to rinse (the soap off) one's hands** sciacquarsi le mani

▶ **rinse out** VT + ADV sciacquare; **to rinse out one's mouth** sciacquarsi la bocca.

Rio de Ja·nei·ro [ˌriːəʊdədʒəˈnɪərəʊ] N Rio de Janeiro *f*.

riot [ˈraɪət] ① N disordini *mpl*; **a riot of colour(s)** un'orgia di colori; **to put down a riot** sopprimere i disordini; **to read sb the riot act** (*fam*) dare una lavata di capo a qn; **to run riot** (*out of control*) scatenarsi.

②VI tumultuare, manifestare violentemente.

ri·ot·er [ˈraɪətəʳ] N dimostrante *m/f* (*durante dei disordini*).

♦ **riot gear** N (*Police*): **in riot gear** in tenuta *f* antisommossa *inv*.

ri·ot·ous [ˈraɪətəs] ADJ (*person, mob, party*) scatenato(-a); (*living*) sfrenato(-a); (*very funny*) che fa crepare dal ridere.

ri·ot·ous·ly [ˈraɪətəslɪ] ADV sfrenatamente; **riotously funny** che fa crepare dal ridere.

♦ **riot police** N ≈ la Celere.

RIP [ˌɑːraɪˈpiː] ABBR (= *rest in peace*) R.I.P.

rip [rɪp] ① N strappo.

②VT strappare; **to rip sth to pieces** stracciare in mille pezzi qc; **to rip open** strappare (per aprire).

③VI strapparsi; **to let rip** (*fig*) scatenarsi; **to let rip at sb** dirne di tutti di colori a qn

▶ **rip off** VT + ADV **a** strappare

b (*fam: overcharge*) pelare; (: *cheat*) fregare

▶ **rip up** VT + ADV stracciare.

rip·cord [ˈrɪpˌkɔːd] N (*Aer*) cavo di spiegamento.

ripe [raɪp] ADJ (*comp* **-r**, *superl* **-st**) (*gen, fruit*) maturo(-a); (*cheese*) stagionato(-a); **to be ripe for sth** (*fig*) essere pronto(-a) per qc; **to live to a ripe old age** vivere fino a una bella età.

rip·en [ˈraɪpən] ① VT maturare.

②VI maturarsi; (*cheese*) stagionarsi.

ripe·ness [ˈraɪpnɪs] N maturazione *f*.

♦ **rip-off** [ˈrɪpˌɒf] N (*fam*): **it's a rip-off!** è un furto!

ri·poste [rɪˈpɒst] (*liter*) ① N replica.

②VI replicare.

rip·per [ˈrɪpəʳ] N (*fam: murderer*) squartatore *m*; **Jack the Ripper** Jack lo squartatore.

rip·ple [ˈrɪpl] ① N (*of water*) ondulazione *f*; (*small wave*) increspatura; (*noise: of voices*) mormorio; (: *of laughter*) fremito.

②VT increspare.

③VI incresparsi.

♦ **ripple tank** N (*Phys*) serbatoio ad increspatura.

♦ **rip-roaring** [ˈrɪpˈrɔːrɪŋ] ADJ (*party, success*) travolgente.

rip·tide [ˈrɪpˌtaɪd] N corrente *f* di ritorno.

rise [raɪz] (*vb: pt* **rose**, *pp* **risen** [ˈrɪzn]) ① N **a** (*increase: in prices, wages, inflation*): **rise (in)** aumento (di); **to ask for a rise** chiedere un aumento

b (*of sun*) sorgere *m*; (*of theatre curtain*) alzarsi *m*; (*fig: ascendancy*) ascesa; **rise to power** ascesa al potere; **to take a rise out of sb** (*fam*) stuzzicare qn

c (*upward slope*) salita, pendio; (*small hill*) altura

d (*origin: of river*) sorgente *f*; **to give rise to** (*fig*) dar origine a.

②VI **a** (*get up*) alzarsi; (*fig: building*) sorgere; **to rise to one's feet** alzarsi in piedi; **the House rose** (*Parliament*) la seduta della Camera è stata tolta; **to rise to the occasion** dimostrarsi all'altezza della situazione

b (*go higher: sun*) sorgere, levarsi; (: *smoke*) alzarsi, levarsi; (: *dough, cake*) crescere (di volume), lievitare; (: *ground*) salire; (*fig: spirits*) sollevarsi; **the plane rose to 4,000 metres** l'aereo si è alzato a 4.000 metri; **to rise from the ranks** (*Mil*) venir su dalla gavetta; **to rise from nothing** venir su dal niente; **he rose to be President** ascese alla carica di Presidente; **to rise to the surface** (*also fig*) venire a galla, affiorare; **to rise above sth** (*fig*) essere al di sopra di qc; **to rise to a higher sum** offrire di più, fare un'offerta più alta

c (*increase: prices*) aumentare, rincarare; (*temperature, shares, numbers*) salire; (*wind, sea*) alzarsi; **his voice rose in anger** alzò la voce per la rabbia

d (*river*) nascere; (*water*) salire

▶ **rise up** VI + ADV (*rebel*) sollevarsi, insorgere.

ris·en [ˈrɪzn] PP of **rise**.

ris·er [ˈraɪzəʳ] N: **to be an early/late riser** essere mattiniero(-a)/alzarsi sempre tardi.

ris·ing [ˈraɪzɪŋ] ① ADJ **a** (*increasing: number*) sempre

crescente; (: *prices*) in aumento; (: *tide*) montante; (: *anger, alarm, doubt*) crescente **b** (*getting higher: sun, moon*) nascente, che sorge; (: *ground*) in salita; (*fig*: *promising*) promettente.

2 N (*uprising*) sommossa.

♦ **rising damp** N infiltrazioni *fpl* d'umidità (*dal sottosuolo*).

♦ **rising star** N (*also fig*) astro nascente.

risk [rɪsk] 1 N rischio; **fire/health/security risk** rischio d'incendio/per la salute/per la sicurezza; **to be a fire risk** essere una potenziale causa d'incendio; **there's not much risk of rain** non c'è pericolo che piova; **to take a risk** rischiare, correre un rischio; **to run the risk of sth** correre il rischio di qc; **it's not worth the risk** non vale la pena di correre il rischio; **at risk** in pericolo; **to put sth at risk** mettere a repentaglio qc; **he put his job at risk** ha rischiato di giocarsi il posto; **at one's own risk** a proprio rischio e pericolo; **at the risk of seeming stupid** a costo di sembrare stupido.

2 VT (*life, health, money*) rischiare, arrischiare; (*criticism, anger, defeat*) rischiare; **I'll risk it** ci proverò lo stesso; **to risk losing/being caught** rischiare di perdere/di esser preso(-a); **to risk one's neck** rischiare la pelle.

♦ **risk capital** N (*Fin*) capitale *m* di rischio.

riski·ness ['rɪskɪnɪs] N rischiosità.

risky ['rɪskɪ] ADJ (*comp* **-ier**, *superl* **-iest**) rischioso(-a).

ris·qué ['riːskeɪ] ADJ audace, spinto(-a), osé *inv*.

ris·sole ['rɪsəʊl] N (*Culin*) crocchetta.

rite [raɪt] N rito; (*Rel*): **the last rites** l'estrema unzione *fsg*; **rite of passage** rito di passaggio.

ritu·al ['rɪtjʊəl] ADJ, N rituale (*m*).

ritu·al·is·tic [ˌrɪtjʊə'lɪstɪk] ADJ (*ritual*) rituale; (*nonsense*) di rito.

ritu·al·ly ['rɪtjʊəlɪ] ADV ritualmente.

ri·val ['raɪvəl] 1 ADJ (*team*) rivale; (*firm*) concorrente; (*claim, attraction*) in concorrenza.

2 N (*see adj*) rivale *m/f*; concorrente *m/f*.

3 VT rivaleggiare con; **to rival sb/sth in** competere con qn/qc in.

ri·val·ry ['raɪvəlrɪ] N rivalità *f inv*; (*in business*) concorrenza.

riv·en ['rɪvən] ADJ (*old, frm*): **riven by** spaccato(-a) in due da.

riv·er ['rɪvəʳ] 1 N fiume *m*; **up/down river** a monte/valle; **the River Thames** il Tamigi.

2 ADJ (*port, police, basin, traffic*) fluviale.

river·bank ['rɪvəˌbæŋk] N sponda (del fiume), argine *m*.

river·bed ['rɪvəˌbed] N letto del fiume.

♦ **river fish** N pesce *m* d'acqua dolce.

♦ **river fishing** N pesca fluviale.

♦ **river head** N sorgente *f* (del fiume).

♦ **river horse** N (*fam*) ippopotamo.

river·side ['rɪvəˌsaɪd] 1 N: **by the riverside** la riva *or* la sponda (del fiume); **by the riverside** in riva al fiume; **along the riverside** lungo il fiume.

2 ADJ: **a riverside café** un bar sul fiume.

riv·et ['rɪvɪt] 1 N ribattino, rivetto.

2 VT rivettare; (*fig*: *attention*) attirare; (: *audience*) inchiodare.

riv·et·er ['rɪvɪtəʳ] N (*machine*) rivettatrice *f*.

riv·et·ing ['rɪvɪtɪŋ] ADJ (*gripping*) avvincente.

Rivi·era [ˌrɪvɪ'eərə] N: **the Italian Riviera** la Riviera; **the French Riviera** la Costa Azzurra.

rivu·let ['rɪvjʊlɪt] N (*frm*) rivolo.

Ri·yadh [rɪ'jɑːd] N Riad *f*.

RMT [ˌɑːrɛm'tiː] N ABBR (= *Rail, Maritime and Transport*) *sindacato degli autoferrotranvieri e dei marittimi*.

RN [ˌɑːr'ɛn] N ABBR **a** (*Brit*) = **Royal Navy b** (*Am*) = **registered nurse**.

RNA [ˌɑːrɛn'eɪ] N ABBR (*Biochemistry*: = *ribonucleic acid*) RNA.

RNLI [ˌɑːrɛn'ɛl'aɪ] N ABBR (*Brit*: = *Royal National Lifeboat Institution*) *associazione volontaria che organizza operazioni di salvataggio*.

RNZAF [ˌɑːrɛnzedeɪ'ɛf] N ABBR = *Royal New Zealand Air Force*.

RNZN [ˌɑːrɛnzed'ɛn] N ABBR = *Royal New Zealand Navy*.

road [rəʊd] 1 N (*route, fig*) strada, via; (*residential: Road*) via; **main road** strada principale; **A-/B-road** ≈ strada statale/secondaria; **country road** strada di campagna; **it takes 4 hours by road** sono 4 ore di macchina (*or in camion etc*); **just across the road (from)** proprio di fronte a; **to be off the road** (*car: for repairs*) essere in riparazione; (: *laid up*) essere fuori uso; **he shouldn't be allowed on the road** dovrebbero togliergli la patente; **that car shouldn't be allowed on the road** non dovrebbero lasciar circolare quella macchina; **to hold the road** (*Aut*) tenere la strada; **"road up"** "attenzione: lavori in corso"; **to be on the road** (*pop group*) essere in tournée; (*salesman*) viaggiare; **on the road to success** sulla via del successo; **to take to the road** (*tramp*) darsi al vagabondaggio; **to have one for the road** (*fam*) bere il bicchiere della staffa; **somewhere along the road** (*fig*) a un certo punto.

2 ADJ (*accident, sign*) stradale.

road·block ['rəʊdˌblɒk] N blocco stradale.

♦ **road haulage** N autotrasporti *mpl*.

♦ **road haulier** N autotrasportatore *m*.

road·hog ['rəʊdˌhɒg] N (*fam pej*) *automobilista che guida tenendosi al centro della strada così da impedire il sorpasso*.

road·house ['rəʊdˌhaʊs] N *posto di ristoro lungo la strada*.

♦ **road map** N carta stradale, carta automobilistica.

♦ **road racer, road rider** N (*Cycling*) stradista *m/f*.

road·roller ['rəʊdˌrəʊləʳ] N rullo compressore.

♦ **road safety** N sicurezza sulle strade.

♦ **road sense** N attitudine *f* alla guida; **to teach a child road sense** insegnare a un bambino a guardarsi dai pericoli della strada.

♦ **road show** N spettacolo di tournée.

road·side ['rəʊdˌsaɪd] N ciglio della strada; **by the roadside** a lato della strada.

♦ **road sign** N cartello stradale.

road·sweeper ['rəʊdˌswiːpəʳ] N (*Brit*: *person*) spazzino; (: *vehicle*) autospazzatrice *f*.

♦ **road test** N prova su strada.

♦ **road-test** ['rəʊdˌtest] VT provare su strada.

♦ **road transport** N autotrasporti *mpl*.

♦ **road user** N utente *m/f* della strada.

road·way ['rəʊdweɪ] N carreggiata.

♦ **road works** NPL lavori *mpl* stradali; (*on road sign*) "lavori in corso".

road·worthy ['rəʊdˌwɜːðɪ] ADJ (*vehicle*) in buono stato di marcia.

roam [rəʊm] 1 VT (*streets*) vagabondare per, gironzolare per, vagare per.

2 VI (*person*) vagabondare, errare, gironzolare; (*thoughts*) vagare.

roam·ing ['rəʊmɪŋ] ADJ vagabondo(-a).

roan [rəʊn] **1** ADJ roano(-a).
2 N (*horse*) roano.

roar [rɔː] **1** N (*of lion*) ruggito; (*of bull*) mugghio; (*of crowd*) urlo, tumulto; (*of waves*) fragore *m*; (*of wind, storm*) muggito; (*of thunder*) rimbombo; **with great roars of laughter** con fragorose risate.
2 VI (*lion*) ruggire; (*bull*) mugghiare; (*crowd, audience*) urlare, fare tumulto; (*wind, storm*) muggire; (*thunder*) rimbombare; (*guns*) tuonare; **to roar with laughter** ridere fragorosamente; **the lorry roared past** il camion passò rombando.

roar·ing [ˈrɔːrɪŋ] ADJ (*lion*) ruggente; (*bull*) mugghiante; (*crowd*) urlante; (*sea, thunder*) fragoroso(-a); **a roaring fire** un bel fuoco, una bella fiammata; **a roaring success** un successo strepitoso; **to do a roaring trade** fare affari d'oro; **roaring drunk** ubriaco(-a) fradicio(-a).

roast [rəʊst] **1** N arrosto.
2 ADJ arrosto *inv*.
3 VT (*meat*) arrostire; (*coffee*) tostare.
4 VI arrostire; **I'm roasting!** (*fam*) sto crepando dal caldo!
♦ **roast beef** N arrosto di manzo.

roast·ing [ˈrəʊstɪŋ] **1** ADJ **a** (*chicken*) da fare arrosto; (*pan*) per arrosti **b** (*fam*): **a roasting (hot) day** una giornata torrida.
2 N (*fam*): **to give sb a roasting** dare una lavata di capo a qn.

rob [rɒb] VT (*person*) derubare; (*with weapon*) rapinare; (*till, bank*) svaligiare; **to rob sb of sth** (*money*) derubare qn di qc; (*fig: happiness, right*) privare qn di qc; **I've been robbed!** mi hanno derubato!

rob·ber [ˈrɒbə] N ladro(-a); (*armed*) rapinatore(-trice).

rob·bery [ˈrɒbərɪ] N furto; (*armed robbery*) rapina; **robbery with violence** (*Law*) furto con aggressione; **it's daylight robbery!** (*fam*) (ma) è una rapina!

robe [rəʊb] N (*garment*) tunica; (*also*: **bathrobe**) accappatoio; (*also*: **robes**) abiti *mpl* da cerimonia; (*lawyer's, Univ*) toga.
2 VT (*frm*) vestire.

rob·in [ˈrɒbɪn] N pettirosso.

ro·bot [ˈrəʊbɒt] N robot *m inv*, automa *m*.

ro·bot·ics [rəʊˈbɒtɪks] NSG robotica.

ro·bust [rəʊˈbʌst] ADJ robusto(-a); (*material*) solido(-a).

rock [rɒk] **1** N **a** (*gen*) roccia; (*large stone, boulder*) roccia, masso; (*in sea*) scoglio; **the Rock of Gibraltar** la Rocca di Gibilterra; **on the rocks** (*drink*) con ghiaccio; **their marriage is on the rocks** il loro matrimonio sta naufragando
b : **stick of rock** (*Brit: sweet*) bastoncino di zucchero candito
c (*Mus*) rock *m*.
2 VT (*gently: cradle, boat*) far dondolare; (: *baby*) cullare; (*violently: boat*) sballottare; (*subj: earthquake*) squassare; (*fig: shake, startle*) sconvolgere, far tremare; **to rock the boat** (*fig fam*) piantare grane.
3 VI (*gently*) dondolare; (*violently*) oscillare.
♦ **rock and roll** N rock and roll *m*.
♦ **rock-bottom** [ˈrɒkˈbɒtəm] N (*fig*): **to reach** *or* **touch rock-bottom** (*person*) toccare il fondo; (*price*) raggiungere il livello più basso.
♦ **rock cake** N (*Brit: bun*) brutto ma buono.
♦ **rock climber** N rocciatore(-trice), scalatore(-trice).
♦ **rock climbing** N (*Sport*) roccia.
♦ **rock crystal** N cristallo di rocca.

rock·er [ˈrɒkə] N (*chair*) sedia a dondolo; **to be off one's**

rocker (*fam*) essere pazzo(-a).

rock·ery [ˈrɒkərɪ] N giardino roccioso.

rock·et[1] [ˈrɒkɪt] **1** N razzo; **to fire** *or* **send up a rocket** lanciare un razzo; **to give sb a rocket** (*fig fam*) fare un cicchetto a qn.
2 VI (*prices*) salire alle stelle.

rock·et[2] [ˈrɒkɪt] N (*Bot*) ruchetta, rucola.
♦ **rocket launcher** N lanciarazzi *m inv*.

rock·et·ry [ˈrɒkɪtrɪ] N (*science*) missilistica; (*rockets collectively*) missili *mpl*.
♦ **rock face** N parete ƒ di roccia.
♦ **rock fall** N caduta (di) massi.
♦ **rock garden** N = rockery.
♦ **rock-hard** [rɒkˈhɑːd] ADJ duro(-a) come la pietra.

rock·ing chair [ˈrɒkɪŋtʃɛə] N sedia a dondolo.

rock·ing horse [ˈrɒkɪŋhɔːs] N cavallo a dondolo.
♦ **rock plant** N pianta rupestre.
♦ **rock salmon** N blennio.
♦ **rock salt** N salgemma *m*.

rocky[1] [ˈrɒkɪ] ADJ (*comp* -**ier**, *superl* -**iest**) (*hill*) roccioso (-a); (*path*) sassoso(-a).

rocky[2] [ˈrɒkɪ] ADJ (*comp* -**ier**, *superl* -**iest**) (*shaky, unsteady*) malfermo(-a), traballante; (*fig: situation, marriage*) instabile.
♦ **Rocky Mountains** NPL: **the Rocky Mountains** le Montagne Rocciose.

ro·co·co [rəʊˈkəʊkəʊ] ADJ, N rococò *(m) inv*.

rod [rɒd] N (*wooden, plastic*) bacchetta; (*metallic, Tech*) asta, sbarra; (*fishing rod*) canna da pesca; (*curtain rod*) bastone *m*; **to rule with a rod of iron** comandare a bacchetta.

rode [rəʊd] PT of ride.

ro·dent [ˈrəʊdənt] N roditore *m*.

ro·deo [ˈrəʊdɪəʊ] N rodeo.

roe [rəʊ] N (*of fish*): **hard roe** uova *fpl* di pesce; **soft roe** latte *m* di pesce.

roe·buck [ˈrəʊˌbʌk] N capriolo maschio.
♦ **roe deer** [ˈrəʊˌdɪə] N (*species*) capriolo; (*female deer: pl inv*) capriolo femmina.

rogue [rəʊg] **1** N mascalzone *m*; **rogues' gallery** foto *fpl* di pregiudicati.
2 ADJ (*elephant*) solitario(-a).

ro·guish [ˈrəʊgɪʃ] ADJ (*look, smile*) malizioso(-a); (*child*) birichino(-a).

ro·guish·ly [ˈrəʊgɪʃlɪ] ADV (*smile, wink*) maliziosamente.

role [rəʊl] N ruolo.
♦ **role-model** [ˈrəʊlˌmɒdl] N modello (di comportamento).
♦ **role play**, **role playing** N il recitare un ruolo, role-playing *m inv*.
♦ **roll** [rəʊl] **1** N **a** (*of paper, wire*) rotolo; (*of hair*) chignon *m inv*; (*of banknotes*) mazzo; (*of film*) rullino; (*of cloth*) pezza, rotolo; (*of fat, flesh*) cuscinetto
b (*also*: **bread roll**) panino; **cheese roll** panino al formaggio
c (*list*) lista; **to have 500 pupils on the roll** avere 500 iscritti (alla scuola)
d (*sound: of thunder*) rombo; (*of drums*) rullio, rullo
e (*movement: of ship, plane*) rollio.
2 VT (*ball*) (far) rotolare; (*road, lawn, pitch*) cilindrare, rullare; (*cigarette*) rollare; (*also*: **roll out**: *pastry*) spianare, stendere; (*metal*) laminare; **roll the meatballs in breadcrumbs** passare le polpette nel pangrattato; **to roll one's eyes** roteare gli occhi; **to roll one's r's** arrotare la erre; **he can't roll his r's** ha la erre moscia.

3 VI **a** (*turn over*) rotolare; (*dog, horse*) rotolarsi; (*in pain*) contorcersi; **it rolled under the chair** è rotolato sotto la seggiola; **tears rolled down her cheeks** le lacrime le scendevano sulle guance; **they're rolling in money** *or* **they're rolling in it** (*fam*) sono ricchi sfondati **b** (*sound: thunder*) rombare; (: *drum*) rullare **c** (*ship*) rollare

▶ **roll about, roll around** VI + ADV (*ball, coin*) rotolare qua e là; (*person, dog*) rotolarsi; (*in pain*) contorcersi

▶ **roll away** VI + ADV (*ball*) rotolare (via); (*clouds, vehicle*) allontanarsi

▶ **roll back** VT + ADV arrotolare, togliere arrotolando

▶ **roll by** VI + ADV (*vehicle, years*) passare

▶ **roll in** VI + ADV (*money, letters*) continuare ad arrivare; (*fam: person*) arrivare

▶ **roll on** VI + ADV (*time*) passare; **roll on the holidays!** venite presto, vacanze!

▶ **roll out** VT + ADV (*pastry*) spianare; (*carpet, map*) srotolare, spiegare

▶ **roll over** VI + ADV (*object*) rotolare; (*person, animal*) (ri)girarsi, (ri)voltarsi

▶ **roll up** **1** VI + ADV **a** (*animal*): **to roll up into a ball** appallottolarsi **b** (*arrive*) arrivare; **roll up!** venite, venite!. **2** VT + ADV (*cloth, map, carpet*) arrotolare; (*sleeves*) rimboccare; **to roll o.s. up into a ball** raggomitolarsi.

♦ **roll call** N appello.

rolled gold [ˌrəʊld'gəʊld] **1** N oro laminato. **2** ADJ laminato(-a) oro *inv*.

roll·er ['rəʊlə*] N **a** (*gen*) rullo, cilindro; (*in metallurgy*) laminatoio; (*roadroller*) rullo compressore; (*castor*) rotella; (*for hair*) bigodino **b** (*wave*) cavallone *m*.

♦ **roller blind** N (*Brit*) avvolgibile *m*.

♦ **roller coaster** N montagne *fpl* russe.

roller·skate ['rəʊləˌskeɪt] VI pattinare a rotelle.

♦ **roller skates** NPL pattini *mpl* a rotelle.

♦ **roller skating** N pattinaggio a rotelle.

♦ **roller towel** N asciugamano a rullo.

rol·lick·ing ['rɒlɪkɪŋ] ADJ (*person*) incredibilmente esuberante; (*party*) allegro(-a) e chiassoso(-a); **to have a rollicking time** divertirsi pazzamente.

roll·ing ['rəʊlɪŋ] **1** ADJ (*waves, sea*) ondeggiante; (*countryside*) ondulato(-a).

♦ **rolling mill** N fabbrica di laminati.

♦ **rolling pin** N matterello.

♦ **rolling stock** N (*Rail*) materiale *m* rotabile.

♦ **rolling stone** N (*fig*) vagabondo(-a).

roll·neck ['rəʊlˌnɛk] **1** ADJ a dolce vita. **2** N dolcevita.

♦ **roll of honour** N (*Brit*) albo d'onore.

♦ **roll-on** ['rəʊlˌɒn] N (*corset*) panciera.

♦ **roll-on-roll-off** [ˌrəʊlɒnrəʊl'ɒf] ADJ (*Brit: ferry*) roll-on roll-off *inv*.

♦ **roll-over** ['rəʊl'əʊvə*] ADJ: **roll-over bar** roll-bar *m inv*.

♦ **roll-top** ['rəʊlˌtɒp] ADJ: **roll-top desk** scrittoio con alzata avvolgibile.

roly-poly ['rəʊlɪ'pəʊlɪ] N (*Brit Culin*) rotolo di pasta con ripieno di marmellata.

ROM [rɒm] N ABBR (*Comput*: = *read-only memory*) ROM *f inv*.

Ro·man ['rəʊmən] **1** ADJ romano(-a). **2** N (*person*) Romano(-a); (*Typ*): **roman** (carattere *m*) romano.

♦ **Roman alphabet** N: **the Roman alphabet** l'alfabeto latino.

♦ **Roman Catholic** ADJ, N cattolico(-a).

Ro·mance [rəʊ'mæns] ADJ (*language*) romanzo(-a).

ro·mance [rəʊ'mæns] N **a** (*love affair*) storia d'amore **b** (*romantic character*) fascino, romanticismo **c** (*love story*) romanzo *m* rosa *inv*; (*film*) film *m inv* d'amore; (*medieval*) romanzo (cavalleresco); (*Mus*) romanza.

Ro·man·esque [ˌrəʊmə'nɛsk] ADJ (*Archit*) romanico(-a).

Ro·ma·nia, Ru·ma·nia, Rou·ma·nia [rəʊ'meɪnɪə] N Romania.

Ro·ma·nian, Ru·ma·nian, Rou·ma·nian [rəʊ'meɪnɪən] **1** ADJ romeno(-a). **2** N (*person*) romeno(-a); (*language*) romeno.

Ro·man·ism ['rəʊməˌnɪzəm] N romanismo.

♦ **Roman nose** N naso aquilino.

♦ **Roman numerals** N numeri *mpl* romani.

ro·man·tic [rəʊ'mæntɪk] ADJ, N romantico(-a).

ro·man·ti·cal·ly [rəʊ'mæntɪkəlɪ] ADV romanticamente.

ro·man·ti·cism [rəʊ'mæntɪˌsɪzəm] N (*Art*) romanticismo.

ro·man·ti·cize [rəʊ'mæntɪˌsaɪz] VT romanzare.

Roma·ny ['rɒmənɪ] **1** ADJ zingaresco(-a). **2** N (*person*) zingaro(-a); (*language*) lingua degli zingari.

Rome [rəʊm] N Roma *f*; **the Church of Rome** la Chiesa Romana; **when in Rome (do as the Romans do)** paese che vai usanze che trovi.

romp [rɒmp] **1** N gioco chiassoso. **2** VI (*also: romp about: children, puppies*) giocare chiassosamente; **she romped through the examination** (*fig*) ha passato l'esame a occhi chiusi; **to romp home** (*horse*) vincere senza difficoltà, stravincere.

romp·ers ['rɒmpəz] NPL tutina, pagliaccetto.

Romulus ['rɒmjʊləs] N Romolo.

ron·do ['rɒndəʊ] N (*Mus*) rondò *m inv*.

roof [ruːf] **1** N tetto; (*of tunnel, cave*) volta; **roof of the mouth** palato; **to have a roof over one's head** avere un tetto sopra la testa; **we live under the same roof** viviamo sotto lo stesso tetto; **to go through the roof** (*fig: person*) andare su tutte le furie; (: *price*) salire alle stelle. **2** VT (*also: roof in, roof over*) mettere *or* fare il tetto a.

♦ **roof garden** N giardino pensile.

roof·ing ['ruːfɪŋ] N materiale *m* per copertura.

♦ **roof rack** N (*Aut*) portapacchi *m inv*, portabagagli *m inv*.

♦ **roof terrace** N tetto a terrazza.

roof·top ['ruːfˌtɒp] N tetto.

rook¹ [rʊk] **1** N (*bird*) corvo. **2** VT (*fam: swindle*) imbrogliare, truffare.

rook² [rʊk] N (*Chess*) torre *f*.

rook·ery ['rʊkərɪ] N colonia di corvi.

rookie ['rʊkɪ] N (*Mil fam*) burba.

room [rʊm] N **a** (*in house*) stanza, camera; (*in property adverts*) locale *m*, vano; (*bedroom, in hotel*) camera; (*large, public, in school*) sala; **rooms** NPL (*lodging*) alloggio *msg*; **"rooms to let"**, (*Am*) **"rooms for rent"** "si affittano camere"; **a 5-roomed house** una casa di 5 locali; **they've always lived in rooms** hanno sempre abitato in camere ammobiliate **b** (*space*) spazio, posto; **is there room for this?** c'è spazio per questo?, ci sta anche questo?; **is there room for me?** c'è posto per me?, ci sto anch'io?; **to make room for sb** far posto a qn; **standing room only** solo posti in piedi; **there is no room for doubt** non c'è nessuna possibilità di dubbio; **there is room for improvement** si potrebbe migliorare.

room·ful ['rʊmfʊl] N stanza piena.

room·ing house ['rʊmɪŋˌhaʊs] N (*Am*) casa con camere ammobiliate.

room·mate ['rʊm,meɪt] N compagno(-a) di stanza.
♦ **room service** N servizio in camera.
♦ **room temperature** N temperatura ambiente.
roomy ['rʊmɪ] ADJ (comp **-ier**, superl **-iest**) (flat, cupboard etc) spazioso(-a); (garment) ampio(-a).
roost [ru:st] [1] N posatoio; **to rule the roost** dettar legge.
   [2] VI appollaiarsi; **now the chickens are coming home to roost!** (fig) ora arriva il momento della resa dei conti!
roost·er ['ru:stə'] N gallo.
root [ru:t] [1] N (gen, Math) radice f; **repeated root** (Math) radice f multipla; **to pull up by the roots** sradicare; **to take root** (plant) attecchire, prendere; (idea) far presa; **the root of the problem is that** ... il problema deriva dal fatto che...; **to put down roots in a country** mettere radici in un paese.
   [2] VT (plant) far fare le radici a, far radicare; **to be rooted to the spot** (fig) rimanere inchiodato(-a) sul posto.
   [3] VI (Bot) attecchire, mettere radici
► **root about, root around** VI + ADV (fig) frugare, rovistare
► **root for** VI + PREP (Am fam) fare il tifo per
► **root out** VT + ADV (find) scovare, pescare; (remove) eradicare, estirpare
► **root up** VT + ADV sradicare.
♦ **root beer** N (Am) bibita dolce a base di estratti di erbe e radici.
♦ **root cause** N causa prima.
♦ **root crops** NPL tuberi mpl or radici fpl commestibili.
♦ **root hairs** NPL (Bot) peli mpl radicali.
root·less ['ru:tlɪs] ADJ (person) senza radici.
♦ **root nodules** NPL (Bot) noduli mpl radicali.
♦ **root word** N radice f.
rope [rəʊp] [1] N fune f, corda; (Naut) cima, cavo; **to give sb more rope** (fig) allentare le redini a qn; **to know/learn the ropes** (fig) conoscere/imparare i segreti or i trucchi del mestiere; **a rope of pearls** una lunga collana di perle; **a rope of climbers** una cordata di alpinisti.
   [2] VT legare (con una fune or una corda)
► **rope in** VT + ADV (fam fig): **to rope sb in to help** tirar dentro qn per aiutare
► **rope off** VT + ADV isolare con dei cordoni
► **rope up** VI + ADV (Mountaineering) legarsi in cordata.
♦ **rope ladder** N scala di corda.
ropy, ropey ['rəʊpɪ] ADJ (comp **-ier**, superl **-iest**) (fam) scadente; **to feel rop(e)y** (ill) sentirsi male.
ro·sary ['rəʊzərɪ] N **a** (Rel) rosario; **to say** or **recite the rosary** dire or recitare il rosario **b** (rose garden) roseto.
rose¹ [rəʊz] [1] N **a** (flower, colour) rosa; (also: **rose bush**) rosaio; **my life isn't all roses** (fam) la mia vita non è tutta rose e fiori **b** (on shower, watering can) bulbo (forato); (on ceiling) rosone m.
   [2] ADJ (rose-coloured) rosa inv.
rose² [rəʊz] PT of **rise**.
rosé ['rəʊzeɪ] N, ADJ rosé (m) inv.
rose·bay ['rəʊz,beɪ] N (Bot): **rosebay willowherb** camenerio, epilobio.
rose·bed ['rəʊz,bɛd] N rosaio, roseto.
rose·bud ['rəʊz,bʌd] N bocciolo di rosa.
♦ **rose-coloured** ['rəʊz,kʌləd] ADJ color rosa inv; **to see sth through rose-coloured spectacles** (fig) vedere tutto rosa.
♦ **rose garden** N roseto.
♦ **rose grower** N rosicoltore m.
rose-hip ['rəʊz,hɪp] N frutto della rosa canina.
rose·mary ['rəʊzmərɪ] N rosmarino.
♦ **rose quartz** N quarzo rosa.

♦ **rose-red** ['rəʊz'rɛd] ADJ vermiglio(-a).
ro·sette [rəʊ'zɛt] N (emblem, as prize) coccarda; (Archit) rosone m.
♦ **rose window** N rosone m (vetrata).
rose·wood ['rəʊz,wʊd] N palissandro.
ROSPA ['rɒspə] N ABBR (Brit: = Royal Society for the Prevention of Accidents) ≈ E.N.P.I. f (= Ente Nazionale Prevenzione Infortuni).
ros·ter ['rɒstə'] N = **rota**.
ros·trum ['rɒstrəm] N podio, tribuna.
rosy ['rəʊzɪ] ADJ (comp **-ier**, superl **-iest**) roseo(-a); **to paint a rosy picture of sth** (fig) dipingere qc a tinte rosa.
rot [rɒt] [1] N (decay) putrefazione f, marciume m; (fam: nonsense) fesserie fpl, stupidaggini fpl; **the rot has set in** (fig) le cose hanno cominciato a guastarsi; **to stop the rot** (Brit fig) salvare la situazione; **dry/wet rot** funghi parassiti del legno.
   [2] VT far marcire.
   [3] VI: **to rot (away)** marcire, imputridire.
Rota ['rəʊtə] N (Rel): **the Rota** il Tribunale della Sacra Rota.
rota ['rəʊtə] N tabella dei turni; **on a rota basis** a turno.
ro·ta·ry ['rəʊtərɪ] ADJ (movement) rotatorio(-a); (blades) rotante.
ro·tate [rəʊ'teɪt] [1] VT (revolve) far girare; (change round: crops, staff) avvicendare, fare la rotazione di.
   [2] VI (wheel, Earth) ruotare, girare; (staff etc) alternarsi, avvicendarsi.
ro·tat·ing [rəʊ'teɪtɪŋ] ADJ (revolving) rotante.
ro·ta·tion [rəʊ'teɪʃən] N rotazione f; **in rotation** a turno, in rotazione; **rotation of crops** rotazione f delle colture.
rote [rəʊt] N: **to learn sth by rote** imparare qc a memoria; **rote learning** l'imparare m a memoria.
ro·tor ['rəʊtə'] N rotore m.
♦ **rotor arm** N (Aut) spazzola rotante.
rot·ten ['rɒtn] ADJ **a** (fruit, eggs) marcio(-a); (meat) andato(-a) a male; (tooth) cariato(-a); (wood) marcio (-a), marcito(-a); (fig: morally) corrotto(-a), marcio(-a); **rotten to the core** completamente marcio(-a)
   b (fam: bad) schifoso(-a), brutto(-a); (action) vigliacco (-a); **what rotten luck!** che scalogna!; **what a rotten thing to do!** che vigliaccata!, che carognata!; **I feel rotten** (ill) mi sento da cani; (mean) mi sento un verme.
rot·ter ['rɒtə'] N (Brit old fam) mascalzone(-a).
rot·ting ['rɒtɪŋ] ADJ in putrefazione.
ro·tund [rəʊ'tʌnd] ADJ (frm: person) pingue; (: object) arrotondato(-a).
ro·tun·da [rəʊ'tʌndə] N rotonda.
rou·ble, (Am) ru·ble ['ru:bl] N rublo.
rouge [ru:ʒ] N belletto.
rough [rʌf] [1] ADJ (comp **-er**, superl **-est**) **a** (uneven: ground, road, path, edge) accidentato(-a); (not smooth: skin, cloth, surface, hands) ruvido(-a)
   b (voice) rauco(-a); (taste, wine) aspro(-a); (coarse, unrefined: person, manners, life) rozzo(-a); (harsh: person, game) violento(-a); (neighbourhood) poco raccomandabile, malfamato(-a); (sea crossing, weather) brutto(-a); **the sea is rough today** c'è mare grosso oggi; **I don't want any rough stuff!** (fam) niente risse!; **a rough customer** (fam) un duro; **to have a rough time (of it)** passare un periodaccio; **to give sb a rough time (of it)** rendere la vita dura a qn; **it's rough on him** che sfortuna per lui; **to feel rough** (Brit fam) sentirsi male
   c (calculation, figures) approssimativo(-a), approssimato(-a); (plan) sommario(-a); **rough work** [OR] **rough**

draft [OR] **rough copy** brutta copia; **rough sketch** schizzo; **rough estimate** approssimazione *f*; **at a rough guess** *or* **estimate** ad occhio e croce; **he's a rough diamond** sotto quei modi un po' grezzi si nasconde un cuore d'oro.
2 ADV: **to play rough** (*Sport*) giocare pesante; (*children*) fare dei giochi violenti; **to sleep rough** (*Brit*) dormire all'addiaccio; **to live rough** vivere in strada.
3 N **a** (*fam: person*) duro
  b : **to take the rough with the smooth** prendere le cose come vengono
  c (*Golf*) erba alta, macchia.
4 VT: **to rough it** (*fam*) far vita dura
▶ **rough out** VT + ADV (*draft, plan*) fare un abbozzo di, abbozzare
▶ **rough up** VT + ADV (*fam*): **to rough sb up** malmenare qn.
rough·age ['rʌfɪdʒ] N fibre *fpl*.
♦ **rough-and-ready** [ˌrʌfənd'rɛdɪ] ADJ rudimentale.
♦ **rough-and-tumble** [ˌrʌfən'tʌmbl] N zuffa.
rough·cast ['rʌfˌkɑːst] N intonaco grezzo.
rough·en ['rʌfn] VT (*a surface*) rendere ruvido(-a), irruvidire.
♦ **rough-hewn** [ˌrʌf'hjuːn] ADJ (*stone*) sgrossato(-a).
♦ **rough-house** ['rʌfˌhaʊs] N (*fam*) zuffa, baruffa.
♦ **rough justice** N giustizia sommaria.
rough·ly ['rʌflɪ] ADV **a** (*not gently: push, handle*) brutalmente; (: *speak, order*) bruscamente; **to treat sb/sth roughly** maltrattare qn/qc
  b (*not finely: make, sew*) grossolanamente; **to chop roughly** tagliare a pezzi grossi; **to sketch sth roughly** fare uno schizzo di qc
  c (*approximately*) grosso modo, approssimativamente, pressappoco; **roughly speaking** grosso modo, ad occhio e croce; **there were roughly 50 people** c'erano pressappoco 50 persone.
rough·neck ['rʌfˌnɛk] N (*Am fam*) duro, bestione *m*.
rough·ness ['rʌfnɪs] N (*of hands, surface*) ruvidità, ruvidezza; (*of person: abruptness*) modi *mpl* bruschi; (: *harshness*) durezza, brutalità; (*of sea*) violenza; (*of road*) cattive condizioni *fpl*; (*of terrain*) asprezza.
rough·shod ['rʌfˌʃɒd] ADV: **to ride roughshod over** (*person*) mettere sotto i piedi; (*objection*) non badare minimamente a.
♦ **rough-spoken** [ˌrʌf'spəʊkən] ADJ sboccato(-a).
rou·lette [ruːˈlɛt] N roulette *f inv*.
Rou·ma·nia *etc* [ruːˈmeɪnɪə] N = **Romania** *etc*.
round [raʊnd] **1** ADJ rotondo(-a); (*arms, body*) grassoccio (-a); (*cheeks*) paffuto(-a); **to have round shoulders** avere le spalle curve; **in round figures** in cifra tonda; **a round dozen** una dozzina completa.
2 ADV: **all round** [OR] **right round** tutt'intorno, tutt'in giro; **the wheels go round** le ruote girano; **all year round** (durante) tutto l'anno; **to ask sb round** invitare qn (a casa propria); **we were round at my sister's** eravamo da mia sorella; **I'll be round at 6 o'clock** ci sarò alle 6; **to take the long way round** fare il giro più lungo.
3 PREP intorno a, attorno a; **round the table** intorno alla tavola; **all round the house** (*inside*) dappertutto in casa; (*outside*) tutt'intorno alla casa; **she arrived round** (*about*) **noon** è arrivata verso mezzogiorno; **it's just round the corner** (*also fig*) è dietro l'angolo; **to look round a house/a town** visitare una casa/una città; **I've been round all the shops** ho fatto il giro di tutti i negozi; **round the clock** ininterrottamente, 24 ore su 24; **wrap a blanket round him** avvolgilo in una coperta.

4 N **a** (*circle*) cerchio, tondo; (*Brit: slice: of bread, meat*)fetta; **a round (of sandwiches)** due tramezzini
  b : **the daily round** (*fig*) la routine quotidiana
  c (*of watchman, postman, milkman*) giro; **I've got a paper round** consegno i giornali a domicilio; **the doctor's on his rounds** il dottore sta facendo il suo giro di visite; **to go the rounds** (*illness*) diffondersi; (*story*) passare di bocca in bocca, circolare
  d (*Boxing*) round *m inv*; (*Golf*) partita; (*Showjumping*) percorso; (*in tournament, competition*) incontro; **a round of talks** una serie di incontri; **in the first round of the elections** nella prima votazione; **a round of drinks** un giro di bevute; **it's my round** tocca a me offrire; **a round of ammunition** un colpo; **a round of applause** un applauso.
5 VT **a** (*make round: lips*) arrotondare; (: *edges*) smussare
  b (*go round: corner*) girare, voltare; (: *bend*) superare; (: *Naut*) doppiare
▶ **round off** VT + ADV (*speech, series, meal, evening*) finire in bellezza
▶ **round on** VI + PREP (*attacker, critic*) aggredire verbalmente
▶ **round up** VT + ADV **a** (*cattle*) radunare; (*friends etc*) riunire; (*criminals*) fare una retata di
  b (*figures*) arrotondare.
round·about ['raʊndəˌbaʊt] **1** ADJ (*route, means*) indiretto(-a); **I heard the news in a roundabout way** ho saputo la notizia per vie traverse; **to refer in a roundabout way to sth** accennare indirettamente a qc.
2 N (*Brit: at fair*) giostra; (: *Aut*) rotatoria.
round·ed ['raʊndɪd] ADJ (*shape*) arrotondato(-a); (*fig: sentence*) forbito(-a); (*style*) armonioso(-a).
round·ers ['raʊndəz] NPL (*Brit: game*) *gioco simile al baseball*.
♦ **round-eyed** [ˌraʊnd'aɪd] ADJ (*fig*) con gli occhi sbarrati.
♦ **round-faced** [ˌraʊnd'feɪst] ADJ dalla faccia tonda.
round·ly ['raʊndlɪ] ADV (*say, tell*) chiaro e tondo; (*condemn*) senza mezzi termini; **I cursed him roundly** gliene ho dette di tutti i colori.
♦ **round-necked** [ˌraʊnd'nɛkt] ADJ (*pullover*) a girocollo.
round·ness ['raʊndnɪs] N rotondità.
♦ **round robin** N petizione *f*.
♦ **round-shouldered** [ˌraʊnd'ʃəʊldəd] ADJ con le spalle curve.
rounds·man ['raʊndzmən] N (*pl* **-men**) (*Brit*) garzone *m* (*che esegue le consegne a domicilio*).
♦ **round trip** N (viaggio di) andata e ritorno.
round·up ['raʊndˌʌp] N (*of cattle, people*) raduno; (*of suspects*) retata; **a roundup of the latest news** un sommario *or* riepilogo delle ultime notizie.
rouse [raʊz] VT (*person: from sleep*) svegliare; (: *from apathy*) scuotere; (*interest, suspicion, admiration*) suscitare, destare; **to rouse sb to action** spronare qn ad agire; **to rouse sb to fury** far infuriare qn.
rous·ing ['raʊzɪŋ] ADJ (*cheer*) entusiasmante; (*welcome, applause*) entusiastico(-a); (*speech, song*) trascinante.
rout[1] [raʊt] **1** N (*defeat*) disfatta, rotta.
2 VT mettere in rotta, sbaragliare.
▶ **rout out** VT + ADV (*find*) scovare; (*force out*) (far) sloggiare.
rout[2] [raʊt] VI (*search*): **to rout about** frugare, rovistare.
route [ruːt] N (*gen*) itinerario; **shipping/air routes** rotte *fpl*

marittime/aeree; **bus route** percorso dell'autobus; **we're on the main bus route** abitiamo vicino alla linea dell'autobus; **the best route to London** la strada migliore per andare a Londra; **en route** per strada; **en route from ...to** viaggiando da... a; **en route for** in viaggio verso; "**all routes**" (*Aut*) "tutte le direzioni".

♦ **route map** N (*Brit: for journey*) cartina di itinerario; (*for trains*) pianta dei collegamenti.

rou·tine [ruː'tiːn] 1 N (*normal procedure*) ordinaria amministrazione *f*; (*study routine, work routine*) ritmo di lavoro; (*Theatre*) numero; (*Comput*) sottoprogramma *m*; **daily routine** routine *f*, tran tran *m*.

2 ADJ (*duties, work*) abituale; (*inspection, medical examination*) periodico(-a); (*questions*) di prammatica; **the meeting was just routine** si è trattato di un incontro di normale amministrazione; **routine procedure** prassi *f*.

rov·ing ['rəʊvɪŋ] ADJ (*person*) vagabondo(-a); (*life*) itinerante; **he has a roving eye** gli piace adocchiare le donne; **to have a roving commission** avere piena libertà d'azione *or* di manovra.

♦ **roving reporter** N reporter *m inv* volante.

row¹ [rəʊ] N (*line*) fila; (: *of plants*) fila, filare *m*; (*Knitting*) ferro; (*Math*) riga; **in a row** in fila; **in the front row** in prima fila; **for five days in a row** per cinque giorni di fila.

row² [rəʊ] 1 VT (*boat*) remare; **to row sb across a river** trasportare qn dall'altra parte di un fiume su una barca a remi.

2 VI remare; (*Sport*) vogare; **to go rowing** andare a fare una remata.

row³ [raʊ] 1 N (*noise*) baccano, fracasso; (*quarrel*) lite *f*, litigio; (*scolding*) sgridata; **to make a row** far baccano; **to have a row** litigare; **to get (into) a row** prendersi una sgridata; **to give sb a row** sgridare qn.

2 VI litigare.

ro·wan ['raʊən] N (*also:* **rowan tree**) sorbo.

row·boat ['rəʊ,bəʊt] N (*Am*) = **rowing boat**.

row·di·ness ['raʊdɪnɪs] N baccano; (*fighting*) zuffa.

row·dy ['raʊdɪ] 1 ADJ (*comp* **-ier**, *superl* **-iest**) (*noisy*) chiassoso(-a); (*rough*) turbolento(-a).

2 N teppista *m/f*.

row·dy·ism ['raʊdɪɪzəm] N teppismo.

row·er ['rəʊəʳ] N rematore(-trice); (*Sport*) vogatore(-trice).

row·ing ['rəʊɪŋ] N remare *m*; (*Sport*) canottaggio.

♦ **rowing boat** N (*Brit*) barca a remi.

♦ **rowing club** N circolo di canottaggio.

row·lock ['rɒlək] N scalmo.

roy·al ['rɔɪəl] 1 ADJ reale; **the royal household** la famiglia reale e il seguito; **the royal we** il pluralis maiestatis; **they gave us a royal welcome** ci hanno fatto un'accoglienza principesca.

2 N: **the Royals** (*fam*) i reali, la famiglia reale.

♦ **Royal Accademy** N (*Brit*) Accademia Reale d'Arte britannica (*fondata nel 1768*).

♦ **Royal Air Force** N (*Brit*) *areonautica militare britannica*.

♦ **royal blue** ADJ azzurro reale *inv*.

♦ **Royal Commission** N *commissione d'inchiesta di nomina reale*.

♦ **royal family** N: **the royal family** la famiglia reale.

♦ **royal icing** N (*Culin*) glassa reale.

roy·al·ist ['rɔɪəlɪst] N realista (*m/f*).

roy·al·ly ['rɔɪəlɪ] ADV da re.

♦ **Royal Navy** N (*Brit*) *marina militare britannica*.

roy·al·ty ['rɔɪəltɪ] N a (*people*) reali *mpl* b (*payment*:

also: **royalties**) diritti *mpl* d'autore; (*from oil well, to inventor*) royalty *f inv*.

RP [,ɑː'piː] N ABBR (*Brit:* = *received pronunciation*) pronuncia standard.

rpm [,ɑːpiː'ɛm] N ABBR a = **resale price maintenance** b (= *revolutions per minute*) giri/minuto.

RRP [,ɑːrɑː'piː] N ABBR (*Brit*) = **recommended retail price**.

RSA [,ɑːrɛs'eɪ] N ABBR (*Brit*) a = *Royal Society of Arts* b = *Royal Scottish Academy*.

RSI [,ɑːrɛs'aɪ] N ABBR (*Med:* = *repetitive strain injury*) lesione *f* da sforzo ripetuto.

RSPB [,ɑːrɛspiː'biː] N ABBR (*Brit:* = *Royal Society for the Protection of Birds*) ≈ L.I.P.U *f* (= *Lega Italiana Protezione Uccelli*).

RSPCA [,ɑːrɛspiːsiː'eɪ] N ABBR (*Brit:* = *Royal Society for the Prevention of Cruelty to Animals*) ≈ E.N.P.A. *m* (= *Ente Nazionale per la Protezione degli Animali*).

RSVP [,ɑːrɛsviː'piː] ABBR (= *répondez s'il vous plaît*) R.S.V.P.

RTA [,ɑːtiː'eɪ] N ABBR = *road traffic accident*.

Rt Hon. ABBR (*Brit:* = *Right Honourable*) ≈ On. (= *Onorevole*).

Rt Rev. ABBR (= *Right Reverend*) Rev.

rub [rʌb] 1 N (*with cloth*) fregata, strofinata; (*on person*) frizione *f*, massaggio; **to give sth a rub** (*furniture, mark*) strofinare qc; (*sore place*) massaggiare qc; **there's the rub!** (*liter*) qui sta il problema!.

2 VT sfregare, fregare, strofinare; **to rub one's hands together/one's nose** sfregarsi le mani/il naso; **to rub lotion into one's skin** frizionare la pelle con una lozione; **to rub sth dry** asciugare qc sfregando; **to rub a hole in sth** fare un buco in qc strofinando; **there is no need to rub my nose in it!** (*fig*) non c'è bisogno che continui a ricordarmelo!; **to rub shoulders with sb** (*fig*) venire a contatto con qn.

3 VI: **to rub against sth, rub on sth** strofinarsi contro *or* su qc

▶ **rub along** VI + ADV (*fam: two people*) andare d'accordo nonostante le difficoltà

▶ **rub away** VT + ADV togliere (sfregando)

▶ **rub down** VT + ADV a (*body*) strofinare, frizionare; (*horse*) strigliare

b (*door, wall*) levigare

▶ **rub in** VT + ADV (*ointment*) far penetrare (massaggiando *or* frizionando); (*cream, polish: into leather etc*) far penetrare (strofinando); **don't rub it in!** (*fam*) non rivoltare il coltello nella piaga!

▶ **rub off** 1 VI + ADV venire (*or* andare) via; **to rub off onto sth** restare attaccato(-a) a qc; **his opinions have rubbed off on me** ho finito col pensarla come lui.

2 VT + PREP (*writing*) cancellare; (*dirt*) togliere *or* levare (strofinando)

▶ **rub out** VT + ADV cancellare

▶ **rub up** VT + ADV (*silver, vase*) lucidare; **to rub sb up the wrong way**, (*Am*) **rub sb the wrong way** (*fig*) prendere qn per il verso sbagliato, lisciare qn contropelo.

rub·ber¹ ['rʌbəʳ] 1 N (*material*) gomma, caucciù *m*; (*eraser*) gomma (da cancellare).

2 ADJ (*ball, dinghy, gloves*) di gomma.

rub·ber² ['rʌbəʳ] N (*Bridge*) rubber *m inv*.

♦ **rubber band** N elastico.

♦ **rubber bullet** N pallottola di gomma.

♦ **rubber industry** N industria della gomma.

rub·ber·ized ['rʌbə,raɪzd] ADJ gommato(-a).

♦ **rubber plant** N ficus *m inv*.

♦ **rubber plantation** N piantagione *f* di gomma.

♦ **rubber ring** N (*for swimming*) ciambella.
♦ **rubber stamp** N timbro di gomma.
♦ **rubber-stamp** [ˌrʌbəˈstæmp] VT (*fig*) approvare senza discussione.
rub·bery [ˈrʌbərɪ] ADJ gommoso(-a).
rub·bing [ˈrʌbɪŋ] N sfregamento; (*Art*) rilievo (*ottenuto sfregando colore su un foglio sovrapposto*).
rub·bish [ˈrʌbɪʃ] **1** N (*waste material*) rifiuti *mpl*; (*household rubbish*) spazzatura, immondizia; (*nonsense*) sciocchezze *fpl*, fesserie *fpl*; (*worthless stuff*) cose *fpl* senza valore, robaccia; **children today eat a lot of rubbish** oggigiorno i bambini mangiano un sacco di porcherie; **the film was rubbish** il film non valeva niente; **what you've just said is rubbish** stai dicendo sciocchezze; **rubbish!** (*fam*) sciocchezze!, fesserie!.
2 VT (*fam*) sputtanare.
♦ **rubbish bin** N (*Brit*) pattumiera; (: *outside house*) bidone *m* (per la spazzatura).
♦ **rubbish collection** N raccolta dei rifiuti.
♦ **rubbish dump** N discarica (delle immondizie).
rub·bishy [ˈrʌbɪʃɪ] ADJ (*Brit fam*) scadente, che non vale niente.
rub·ble [ˈrʌbl] N detriti *mpl*; (*smaller*) pietrisco; (*of building*) macerie *fpl*; **the building was reduced to a heap of rubble** l'edificio era ridotto a un cumulo di macerie.
ru·bel·la [ruːˈbɛlə] N (*Med*) rosolia.
ru·ble [ˈruːbl] N (*Am*) = **rouble**.
ruby [ˈruːbɪ] **1** N rubino.
2 ADJ (*colour*) (color) rubino *inv*; (*lips*) rosso(-a); (*made of rubies: necklace, ring*) di rubini.
RUC [ˌɑːjuːˈsiː] N ABBR (*Brit*: = *Royal Ulster Constabulary*) *forze di polizia dell'Irlanda del Nord*.
ruck·sack [ˈrʌkˌsæk] N zaino.
ruck up [ˌrʌkˈʌp] VI + ADV (*skirt, coat*) fare le grinze.
ruc·tions [ˈrʌkʃənz] NPL (*fam*) putiferio *msg*, finimondo *msg*; **there will be ructions if** succederà il finimondo se.
rud·der [ˈrʌdə] N (*Naut*) timone *m*; (*Aer*) timone di direzione.
rud·dy¹ [ˈrʌdɪ] ADJ (*comp* **-ier**, *superl* **-iest**) (*complexion*) rubicondo(-a); (*sky*) rossastro(-a).
rud·dy² [ˈrʌdɪ] ADJ (*comp* **-ier**, *superl* **-iest**) (*Brit fam*) dannato(-a).
rude [ruːd] ADJ (*comp* **-r**, *superl* **-st**) **a** (*impolite*) villano(-a), maleducato(-a); (*indecent*) indecente, volgare; **to be rude to sb** essere maleducato con qn; **it's rude to talk with your mouth full** è cattiva educazione parlare con la bocca piena; **a rude word** una parolaccia
b : **a rude awakening** (*fig*) una doccia fredda; **to be in rude health** essere in ottima salute
c (*liter: primitive*) rudimentale.
rude·ly [ˈruːdlɪ] ADV **a** (*impolitely*) villanamente, maleducatamente; (*indecently*) indecentemente, volgarmente
b : **to be rudely awoken** (*fig*) tornare bruscamente alla realtà.
rude·ness [ˈruːdnɪs] N (*impoliteness*) villania, maleducazione *f*; (*indecency*) indecenza, volgarità.
ru·di·men·ta·ry [ˌruːdɪˈmɛntərɪ] ADJ rudimentale.
ru·di·ments [ˈruːdɪmənts] NPL: **the rudiments** i (primi) rudimenti *mpl*.
rue¹ [ruː] VT (*liter*) pentirsi amaramente di; **I rue the day that ...** maledico il giorno in cui... .
rue² [ruː] N (*Bot*) ruta.
rue·ful [ˈruːfʊl] ADJ (*liter*) mesto(-a).
rue·ful·ly [ˈruːfʊlɪ] ADV (*liter*) mestamente.
ruff [rʌf] N (*Dress*) gorgiera; (*Zool*) collare *m*.

ruf·fian [ˈrʌfɪən] N (*old*) manigoldo.
ruf·fle [ˈrʌfl] VT (*surface*) (far) increspare; (*hair, feathers*) arruffare, scompigliare; (*fig: person*) (far) agitare, turbare, (far) innervosire; **nothing ruffles him** non si scompone mai.
rug [rʌg] N (*floor mat*) tappeto; (*bedside rug*) scendiletto; (*travelling rug*) coperta (da viaggio); (*in tartan*) plaid *m inv*.
rug·by [ˈrʌgbɪ] **1** N rugby *m*.
2 ADJ (*team, player*) di rugby.
♦ **rugby league** N rugby a tredici.
rug·ged [ˈrʌgɪd] ADJ (*terrain*) accidentato(-a); (*coastline, mountains*) frastagliato(-a); (*character*) rude; (*features*) marcato(-a), duro(-a); (*landscape*) aspro(-a).
rug·ged·ness [ˈrʌgɪdnɪs] N (*of terrain, coastline, mountain*) asprezza, asperità; (*of character*) rudezza; (*of features*): **the ruggedness of his face** i lineamenti marcati del suo volto.
rug·ger [ˈrʌgə] N (*Brit fam*) = **rugby**.
ruin [ˈruːɪn] **1** N **a** rudere *m*; **ruins** NPL (*architectural remains*) rovine *fpl*; **in ruins** in rovina; **to fall into ruin** cadere in rovina **b** (*fig*) rovina.
2 VT rovinare.
ru·ina·tion [ˌruːɪˈneɪʃən] N rovina.
ruined [ˈruːɪnd] ADJ (*person*) rovinato(-a); (*castle*) in rovina.
ru·in·ous [ˈruːɪnəs] ADJ (*expensive*) costoso(-a).
ru·in·ous·ly [ˈruːɪnəslɪ] ADV: **ruinously expensive** costosissimo(-a).
rule [ruːl] **1** N **a** (*gen*) regola; (*regulation*) regola, regolamento; **the rules of the road** le norme della circolazione stradale; **rules and regulations** norme e regolamenti; **it's against the rules** è contro le regole *or* il regolamento; **as a rule** normalmente, di regola; **to make it a rule to do sth** essersi imposto(-a) la regola di fare qc; **by rule of thumb** a lume di naso
b (*dominion*): **under British rule** sotto il dominio britannico; **majority rule** (*Pol*) governo di maggioranza
c (*for measuring*) riga; **slide rule** regolo (calcolatore).
2 VT **a** (*govern: also:* **rule over**: *country*) governare; **he's ruled by his wife** è sua moglie che comanda
b (*subj: umpire, judge*): **to rule (that)** decretare (che), decidere (che)
c (*paper, page*) rigare.
3 VI **a** (*monarch*) regnare
b (*Law*): **to rule against/in favour of/on** pronunciarsi a sfavore di/in favore di/su
▶ **rule out** VT + ADV escludere; **murder cannot be ruled out** non si esclude che si tratti di omicidio.
♦ **rule book** N regolamento.
ruled [ruːld] ADJ (*paper*) vergato(-a), a righe.
♦ **rule of law** N (*frm*): **the rule of law** il principio di legalità.
rul·er [ˈruːlə] N **a** (*sovereign*) sovrano(-a); (*in a republic*) capo **b** (*for measuring*) righello, riga.
rul·ing [ˈruːlɪŋ] **1** ADJ (*passion, idea*) grande, dominante; (*party*) al potere; **the ruling classes** la classe dirigente.
2 N (*Law*) decisione *f*.
rum¹ [rʌm] N (*drink*) rum *m inv*.
rum² [rʌm] ADJ (*comp* **-mer**, *superl* **-mest**) (*Brit fam*) strambo(-a).
Ru·ma·nia etc [ruːˈmeɪnɪə] N = **Romania** etc.
rum·ble¹ [ˈrʌmbl] **1** N (*of traffic etc*) rombo; (*thunder*) brontolio.
2 VI (*thunder, cannon etc*) rimbombare; (*stomach*) bron-

tolare; (*pipe*) gorgogliare; **the train rumbled past** il treno passò sferragliando.

rum·ble² ['rʌmbl] VT (*Brit fam*) scoprire.

rum·bling ['rʌmblɪŋ] N (*of stomach, thunder, pipe*) brontolio; (*of traffic*) ronzio.

rum·bus·tious [rʌm'bʌstʃəs] ADJ (*person*): **to be rumbustious** essere un terremoto.

ru·mi·nant ['ruːmɪnənt] (*Zool*) [1] ADJ ruminante.
[2] N ruminante *m*.

ru·mi·nate ['ruːmɪneɪt] VI (*frm*) meditare.

ru·mi·na·tive ['ruːmɪnətɪv] ADJ (*liter*) meditativo(-a).

ru·mi·na·tive·ly ['ruːmɪnətɪvlɪ] ADV (*liter: nod, say*) con aria meditabonda.

rum·mage ['rʌmɪdʒ] VI: **to rummage (about** or **around)** rovistare, frugare; **to rummage about in sth/for sth** rovistare or frugare in qc/per trovare qc.

rum·my ['rʌmɪ] N ramino.

ru·mour, (*Am*) **ru·mor** ['ruːməʳ] [1] N voce *f*; **rumour has it that ...** corre voce che... + *sub*.
[2] VT: **it is rumoured that ...** si dice in giro che... + *sub*.

rump [rʌmp] N (*of horse*) groppa (posteriore), culatta; (*Culin*) scamone *m*.

rum·ple ['rʌmpl] VT (*clothes*) spiegazzare, sgualcire; (*hair*) arruffare, scompigliare.

♦ **rump steak** N bistecca di girello.

rum·pus ['rʌmpəs] N (*fam*) putiferio, casino; **to kick up a rumpus** scatenare un putiferio.

run [rʌn] (*vb: pt* **ran**, *pp* **run**) [1] VI **a** correre; (*flee*) scappare; **run and see** corri a vedere; **to run in/out** *etc* entrare/uscire *etc* di corsa; **to run for the bus** fare una corsa per prendere l'autobus; **to run to help sb** accorrere in aiuto di qn, correre ad aiutare qn; **don't come running to me when you've got problems** non correre da me quando avrai dei problemi; **we shall have to run for it** ci toccherà tagliare la corda; **he's running for the Presidency** si è presentato come candidato per la presidenza; **a rumour ran through the town that ...** si è sparsa la voce in città che...; **that tune keeps running through my head** continua a venirmi in mente quel motivetto; **it runs in the family** è un tratto di famiglia

b : **the train runs between Gatwick and Victoria** il treno fa servizio tra Gatwick e la stazione Victoria; **the bus runs every 20 minutes** c'è un autobus ogni 20 minuti

c (*function*) funzionare, andare; **leave the engine running** lascia il motore acceso; **to run on petrol/on diesel/off batteries** andare a benzina/a diesel/a batterie; **things did not run smoothly for him** (*fig*) le cose non gli sono andate molto bene

d (*extend: contract*) essere valido(-a); **it has another 5 years to run** vale per altri 5 anni; **the play ran for 2 years** lo spettacolo ha tenuto cartellone per 2 anni; **the cost ran to hundreds of pounds** alla fine la spesa è stata di centinaia di sterline; **their losses run into millions** hanno avuto una perdita di milioni

e (*river, tears, curtains, drawer*) scorrere; (*nose*) colare; (*eyes*) lacrimare; (*tap*) perdere; (*sore, abscess*) spurgare; (*melt: butter, icing*) fondere; (*colour, ink*) sbavare; (*colour: in washing*) stingere; **the tears ran down her cheeks** le lacrime le scorrevano sulle guance; **you left the tap running** hai lasciato il rubinetto aperto; **the river runs into the sea** il fiume sfocia nel mare; **the road runs into the square** la strada sbocca nella piazza; **the milk ran all over the floor** il latte si è sparso sul pavimento; **to run high** (*river, sea*) ingrossarsi; (*feelings*) inasprirsi; **his face was running with sweat** il sudore gli colava sul viso; **his**

blood ran cold gli si è gelato il sangue

f (*with adv or prep*): **to run across the road** attraversare di corsa la strada; **the road runs along the river** la strada corre lungo il fiume; **the road runs by our house** la strada passa davanti a casa nostra; **the path runs from our house to the station** il sentiero va da casa nostra fino alla stazione; **the car ran into the lamppost** la macchina è andata a sbattere contro il lampione; **he ran up to me** mi corse incontro; **she ran up the stairs** salì su per le scale di corsa.

[2] VT **a** correre; (*race*) partecipare a; **she ran a good race** ha fatto una buona gara; **the race is run over 4 km** la gara si svolge su un percorso di 4 km; **to let things run their course** lasciare che le cose seguano il loro corso; **to run a horse** far correre un cavallo

b (*move*): **to run sb into town** accompagnare or portare qn in città; **I'll run you to the station** ti porto io alla stazione; **to run the car into a lamppost** andare a sbattere con la macchina contro un lampione; **to run errands** andare a fare commissioni

c (*organize, manage: business, hotel*) dirigere, gestire; (*: country*) governare; (*: campaign*) organizzare; **are they running any trains today?** ci sono treni oggi?; **they ran an extra train** hanno messo un treno straordinario; **she runs everything** è lei che manda avanti tutto; **I want to run my own life** voglio essere io a gestire la mia vita

d (*operate: machine*) usare; **to run a program** (*Comput*) eseguire un programma; **we run two cars** abbiamo due macchine; **it's a very cheap car to run** è una macchina economica

e : **to be run off one's feet** doversi fare in quattro; **to run it close** or **fine** ridursi all'ultimo momento; **their win was a close run thing** hanno vinto per il rotto della cuffia; **to run a (high) temperature** avere la febbre (alta); **to run a risk** correre un rischio

f (*with adv or prep*): **to run one's eye over a letter** dare una scorsa a una lettera; **to run a fence round a field** costruire un recinto intorno a un campo; **to run a pipe through a wall** far passare un tubo attraverso un muro; **to run one's fingers through sb's hair** passare le dita fra i capelli di qn; **to run a comb through one's hair** darsi una pettinata; **to run water into the bath** far correre l'acqua nella vasca; **to run a bath for sb** preparare un bagno a qn.

[3] N **a** (*act of running*) corsa; **to go for a run** andare a correre; **at a run** di corsa; **to break into a run** mettersi a correre; **a prisoner on the run** un evaso; **he's on the run from the police** è ricercato dalla polizia; **to keep the enemy on the run** premere il nemico in fuga; **we've got them on the run now** adesso sono ridotti allo sbando; **he's on the run from his creditors** cerca di sfuggire ai creditori; **to make a run for it** scappare, tagliare la corda; **to give sb a run for his money** non darla vinta a qn prima del tempo; **she's had a good run** (*on death, retirement*) ha avuto il suo; **to have the run of sb's house** utilizzare la casa altrui come casa propria

b (*outing*) giro; **to go for a run in the car** fare un giro in macchina

c (*Rail*) percorso, tragitto; **it's a 10-minute bus run** è un tragitto di 10 minuti in autobus; **boats on the Calais run** navi che fanno il servizio per Calais

d (*sequence*) serie *f inv*; (*Cards*) scala; **a run of luck** un periodo di fortuna; **he's different from the common run of men** è fuori dall'ordinario; **it stands out from the general run of books** è un libro fuori dal comune; **the**

play **had a long run** lo spettacolo ha tenuto a lungo il cartellone; **in the long run** alla lunga; **in the short run** sulle prime
e (*Comm etc*): **there's been a run on ...** c'è stata una forte richiesta di...
f (*for animals*) recinto
g (*for skiing, bobsleighing*) pista
h (*in stocking, tights*) smagliatura
▶ **run about** VI + ADV correre (di) qua e (di) là
▶ **run across** VI + PREP (*meet, find*) incontrare per caso, imbattersi in
▶ **run along** VI + ADV correre, andare; **run along and play** su, vai a giocare
▶ **run away** VI + ADV **a** scappare di corsa, fuggire; **to run away from home** scappare di casa
b (*water*) scolare
▶ **run away with** VI + ADV + PREP scappare con; (*fig*) **he let his imagination run away with him** si lasciò trasportare dalla fantasia; **don't run away with the idea that ...** non credere che...
▶ **run down** ①VT + ADV **a** (*Aut*) investire, mettere sotto
b (*reduce: production*) ridurre gradualmente; (: *factory, shop*) rallentare l'attività di
c (*disparage*) parlar male di, denigrare
d (*battery*) scaricare
②VI + ADV (*battery, watch*) scaricarsi
▶ **run in** VT + ADV **a** (*car*) rodare, fare il rodaggio di
b (*fam: arrest*) mettere dentro
▶ **run into** VI + PREP (*meet: person*) incontrare per caso; (*difficulties, troubles etc*) incontrare, trovare; (*collide with*) andare a sbattere contro; **to run into debt** trovarsi nei debiti
▶ **run off** ①VI + ADV = **run away**.
②VT + ADV (*copies*) fare
▶ **run off with** VI + ADV + PREP = **run away with**
▶ **run on** VI + ADV **a** (*fam: person*) parlare senza tregua; (*talk, meeting*) protrarsi (oltre il previsto)
b (*Typ*) continuare senza andare a capo
▶ **run out** VI + ADV (*contract, lease*) scadere; (*food, money etc*) finire, esaurirsi; (*person*) uscire di corsa; (*liquid*) colare; **time is running out** ormai c'è poco tempo
▶ **run out of** VI + ADV + PREP non avere più; **I ran out of petrol**, (*Am*) **I ran out of gas** sono rimasto senza benzina
▶ **run out on** VI + ADV + PREP (*abandon*) piantare
▶ **run over** ①VI + ADV (*overflow*) traboccare.
②VI + PREP (*reread*) rileggere; (*recapitulate*) ricapitolare.
③VT + PREP (*Aut*) investire, mettere sotto
▶ **run through** VI + PREP **a** (*use up: fortune*) far fuori, dilapidare
b (*read quickly: notes etc*) dare un'occhiata a; (*list*) scorrere
c (*rehearse: play*) riprovare, ripetere; (*recapitulate*) ricapitolare
▶ **run to** VI + PREP (*be sufficient for*) essere sufficiente per; **my salary won't run to a car** col mio stipendio non posso permettermi una macchina
▶ **run up** VT + ADV **a** (*debt*) accumulare
b (*dress*) mettere insieme
▶ **run up against** VI + ADV + PREP (*person, problem*) imbattersi in; (*difficulties*) incontrare.
run·about ['rʌnəˌbaʊt] N (*car*) utilitaria.
run·around ['rʌnəˌraʊnd] N (*fam*): **to give sb the run-around** far girare a vuoto qn.

run·away ['rʌnəˌweɪ] ① ADJ (*slave, person*) in fuga; (*child*) scappato(-a) di casa; (*truck, train*) fuori controllo; (*horse*) imbizzarrito(-a); (*success, victory*) trascinante; **runaway inflation** inflazione *f* galoppante.
② N fuggitivo(-a), fuggiasco(-a).
♦ **run-down** ['rʌnˌdaʊn] ① ADJ (*person*) debilitato(-a); (*building*) fatiscente, in rovina.
② N **a** (*Brit: of industry*) riduzione *f* graduale dell'attività di **b**: **to give sb a run-down on sth** (*fam*) mettere qn al corrente di qc.
rung[1] [rʌŋ] N (*of ladder*) piolo; (*of chair*) traversa.
rung[2] [rʌŋ] PP of **ring**.
♦ **run-in** ['rʌnˌɪn] N (*fam*) scontro.
run·ner ['rʌnə'] N **a** (*athlete*) corridore *m*; (*horse*) partente *m* **b** (*of sledge, aircraft*) pattino; (*of skate*) lama; (*of car seat, drawer*) guida **c** (*hall carpet*) guida, passatoia **d** (*Bot*) stolone *m*.
♦ **runner bean** N (*Brit*) fagiolino.
♦ **runner-up** [ˌrʌnər'ʌp] N secondo(-a) arrivato(-a).
run·ning ['rʌnɪŋ] ① ADJ (*water*) corrente; (*tap*) che cola; (*sore*) che spurga; **a running stream** un corso d'acqua; **running battle** lotta continua; **to be in good running order** (*car*) essere in buone condizioni di marcia; **for the sixth time running** per la sesta volta di fila *or* di seguito.
② N (*of business, hotel*) gestione *f*, direzione *f*; (*of campaign*) organizzazione *f*; (*of machine*) funzionamento; (*of race*) corsa; **to be in/out of the running for sth** essere/non essere più in lizza per qc; **to make the running** (*Sport fig*) imporre il ritmo.
♦ **running board** N (*Aut*) predellino.
♦ **running commentary** N (*Radio*) radiocronaca; (*TV*) telecronaca.
♦ **running costs** NPL (*of business*) costi *mpl* d'esercizio; (*of car*) spese *fpl* di mantenimento.
♦ **running head** N (*Typ, Word processing*) testata, titolo corrente.
♦ **running mate** N (*Am Pol*) candidato(-a) alla vicepresidenza.
run·ny ['rʌnɪ] ADJ (*comp* -**ier**, *superl* -**iest**) (*butter*) sciolto (-a); (*sauce*) troppo liquido(-a); (*nose*) che cola, che gocciola.
♦ **run-off** ['rʌnˌɒf] N (*in contest, election*) ballottaggio finale; (*extra race*) spareggio.
♦ **run-of-the-mill** [ˌrʌnəvðə'mɪl] ADJ banale, solito(-a).
♦ **run-out** ['rʌnˌaʊt] N (*Horse-riding*) scarto.
runt [rʌnt] N (*Zool*): **the runt of the litter** (*puppy*) il cucciolo più piccolo della figliata; (*pej: person*) omuncolo.
♦ **run-through** ['rʌnˌθruː] N (*rehearsal*) prova generale.
♦ **run-up** ['rʌnˌʌp] N: **the run-up to Christmas** (*Brit*) il periodo che precede Natale.
run·way ['rʌnˌweɪ] N (*Aer*) pista.
ru·pee [ruːˈpiː] N rupia.
rup·ture ['rʌptʃə'] ① N rottura; (*Med: hernia*) ernia.
② VT (*blood vessel etc*) far scoppiare; **to rupture o.s.** farsi venire un'ernia.
ru·ral ['rʊərəl] ADJ (*gen*) rurale; (*scene*) campestre; (*life*) di campagna; **rural depopulation** deruralizzazione *f*.
♦ **rural district council** N (*Brit*) consiglio (amministrativo) di distretto rurale.
ruse [ruːz] N (*frm*) stratagemma *m*, astuzia.
rush[1] [rʌʃ] N (*Bot*) giunco.
rush[2] [rʌʃ] ① N **a** (*of people*) affollamento, ressa; **the Christmas rush** la ressa di Natale; **gold rush** corsa all'oro; **there was a rush to** *or* **for the door** tutti si

precipitarono verso la porta; **we've had a rush of orders** abbiamo avuto una valanga di ordinazioni

b (*hurry*) fretta, premura; **I'm in a rush (to do)** ho fretta *or* premura (di fare); **it was all done in a rush** è stato fatto tutto in gran fretta; **it got lost in the rush** nella fretta è andato perso; **what's all the rush about?** cos'è tutta questa fretta?; **is there any rush for this?** è urgente?; **we had a rush to get it ready in time** abbiamo dovuto affrettarci per prepararlo in tempo

c (*current*): **a rush of air** una corrente d'aria; **a rush of water** un flusso d'acqua.

2 VT **a** (*person*) far fretta *or* premura a; (*work, order*) fare in fretta; **to rush sth off** spedire con urgenza qc; **I hate being rushed** non mi piace che mi si faccia premura; **we were rushed off our feet** abbiamo dovuto correre come matti; **he was rushed (off) to hospital** lo hanno portato d'urgenza all'ospedale

b (*attack: town*) prendere d'assalto; (: *person*) precipitarsi contro; **the crowd rushed the barriers** la folla ha dato l'assalto ai cancelli.

3 VI (*person: run*) precipitarsi; (: *be in a hurry*) essere di corsa; (*car*) andare veloce; **don't rush at it, take it slowly** non farlo in fretta, prenditela con comodo; **to rush up/down** *etc* precipitarsi su/giù *etc*; **I rushed to her side** sono corso subito da lei; **I was rushing to finish it** mi affrettavo a finirlo

▶ **rush about, rush around** VI + ADV correre su e giù

▶ **rush out** 1 VT + ADV (*product*) immettere velocemente sul mercato; (*book*) pubblicare in tutta fretta.

2 VI + ADV precipitarsi fuori

▶ **rush over** VI + ADV: **to rush over (to sb/to do sth)** precipitarsi (da qn/a fare qc)

▶ **rush through** 1 VT + PREP (*meal*) mangiare in fretta; (*book*) dare una scorsa frettolosa a; (*work*) sbrigare frettolosamente; (*town*) attraversare in fretta.

2 VT + ADV (*Comm: order*) eseguire d'urgenza; (*supplies*) mandare d'urgenza

▶ **rush up** VI + ADV = **rush over**.

♦ **rush hour** N ora di punta; **the rush hour traffic** il traffico delle ore di punta.

♦ **rush job** N (*urgent*) lavoro urgente; (*botched, hurried*) lavoro fatto in fretta.

♦ **rush matting** N stuoia.

rusk [rʌsk] N fetta biscottata.

rus·set ['rʌsɪt] ADJ (*colour*) marrone rossiccio *inv*.

Rus·sia ['rʌʃə] N Russia.

Rus·sian ['rʌʃən] 1 ADJ russo(-a).

2 N (*person*) russo(-a); (*language*) russo.

♦ **Russian roulette** N roulette *f* russa.

rust [rʌst] 1 N ruggine *f*.

2 VI arrugginire, arrugginirsi.

3 VT (far) arrugginire.

♦ **rust-coloured** ['rʌst,kʌləd] ADJ (color) ruggine *inv*.

rustic ['rʌstɪk] 1 ADJ (*gen*) rustico(-a); (*scene*) campestre.

2 N (*pej*) cafone(-a).

rus·tle[1] ['rʌsl] 1 N fruscio.

2 VT (*paper*) far frusciare.

3 VI frusciare

▶ **rustle up** (*fam*) VT + ADV (*find*) ripescare; (: *money*) racimolare; (*meal*) rimediare, mettere insieme.

rus·tle[2] ['rʌsl] VT (*Am: cattle*) rubare.

rus·tler ['rʌslə'] N ladro di bestiame.

rus·tling[1] ['rʌslɪŋ] N (*noise*) fruscio.

rus·tling[2] ['rʌslɪŋ] N (*of cattle*) furto di bestiame.

rust·proof ['rʌst,pru:f], **rust-resistant** ['rʌstrɪ,zɪstənt] ADJ inattaccabile dalla ruggine.

rust·proofing ['rʌst,pru:fɪŋ] N trattamento antiruggine.

rusty ['rʌstɪ] ADJ (*comp* -**ier**, *superl* -**iest**) rugginoso(-a), arrugginito(-a); **my Greek is pretty rusty** (*fig*) il mio greco è molto arrugginito.

rut[1] [rʌt] N solco; **to get into a rut** (*fig*) fossilizzarsi; **to be in a rut** (*fig*) essersi fossilizzato(-a).

rut[2] (*Zool*) 1 N: **the rut** la fregola, il calore *m*.

2 VI andare in calore.

ru·ta·ba·ga [,ru:tə'beɪgə] N (*Am*) rapa svedese.

ruth·less ['ru:θlɪs] ADJ spietato(-a).

ruth·less·ly ['ru:θlɪslɪ] ADV spietatamente.

ruth·less·ness ['ru:θlɪsnɪs] N spietatezza.

rut·ted ['rʌtɪd] ADJ (*road, lane*) con solchi (delle ruote).

RV [,ɑː'vi:] N ABBR (= *revised version*) *versione riveduta della Bibbia anglicana*.

rye [raɪ] N segale *f*; (*Am: whisky*) whisky *m inv* di segale.

♦ **rye bread** N pane *m* di segale.

♦ **rye-grass** ['raɪ,grɑ:s] N loglio perenne.

S

S, s [ɛs] N (*letter*) S, s *for m inv*; **S for sugar** ≈ S come Savona.
S ABBR **a** (*on clothes*: = *small*) S **b** (= *south*) S **c** (*Scol*: = *satisfactory*) ≈ sufficiente.
S. (*pl* **SS.**) ABBR (= *Saint*) S., SS. *pl*.
SA ABBR = **South Africa, South America.**
Sab·bath ['sæbəθ], **Sab·bath Day** ['sæbəθ'deɪ] N (*Jewish*) sabato; (*Christian old*) domenica.
sab·bati·cal [sə'bætɪkəl] (*Univ*) ①N anno sabbatico; **to take a sabbatical** prendere un anno sabbatico.
②ADJ sabbatico(-a); **sabbatical year** anno sabbatico.
sa·ble ['seɪbl] ①N **a** (*animal, fur*) zibellino **b** (*liter: colour*) nero.
②ADJ (*fur*) di zibellino; (*brush*) di martora.
sabo·tage ['sæbə,tɑ:ʒ] ①N sabotaggio.
②VT sabotare.
sabo·teur [,sæbə'tɜ:'] N sabotatore(-trice).
sa·bre, (*Am*) **sa·ber** ['seɪbə'] N sciabola.
sac [sæk] N (*Anat*) sacco; **honey sac** cestella (del polline).
sac·cha·rine, (*Am*) **sac·cha·rin** ['sækərɪn] N saccarina.
sa·chet ['sæʃeɪ] N bustina.
sack[1] [sæk] ①N **a** (*bag*) sacco; **coal sack** sacco per il carbone; **sack of coal** sacco di carbone **b** (*fam*): **to get the sack** essere licenziato(-a); **to give sb the sack** licenziare qn **c** (*esp Am fam: bed*) letto.
②VT (*fam: dismiss*) licenziare.
sack[2] [sæk] ①N (*plundering*) saccheggio; **the sack of Rome** il sacco di Roma.
②VT (*plunder*) saccheggiare.
sack·cloth ['sæk,klɒθ] N tela di sacco; **sackcloth and ashes** (*Rel*) il sacco e la cenere; **to be in sackcloth and ashes** (*fig*) avere l'aria contrita.
♦ **sack dress** N vestito a sacco.
sack·ful ['sæk,fʊl] N sacco (pieno).
sack·ing ['sækɪŋ] N **a** (*cloth*) tela di sacco **b** (*fam: dismissal*) licenziamento.
sack·load ['sækləʊd] N sacco.
♦ **sack race** N corsa coi sacchi.
sac·ra·ment ['sækrəmənt] N sacramento; **the Blessed Sacrament** l'Eucaristia; **to receive the sacraments** ricevere i sacramenti.

sa·cred ['seɪkrɪd] ADJ (*holy*) sacro(-a); **sacred to the memory of** dedicato(-a) alla memoria di; **a sacred promise** (*fig*) una promessa solenne; **is nothing sacred?** non c'è più religione!
♦ **sacred cow** N (*fig: person*) intoccabile *m/f*; (: *institution*) caposaldo; (: *idea, belief*) dogma *m*.
♦ **Sacred Heart** N (*Rel*): **the Sacred Heart** il Sacro Cuore.
sac·ri·fice ['sækrɪˌfaɪs] ①N sacrificio; **to make sacrifices (for sb)** fare (dei) sacrifici (per qn).
②VT sacrificare.
sac·ri·fi·cial [,sækrɪ'fɪʃəl] ADJ (*act, altar*) sacrificale; (*lamb*) destinato(-a) al sacrificio.
sac·ri·lege ['sækrɪlɪdʒ] N sacrilegio.
sac·ri·legious [,sækrɪ'lɪdʒəs] ADJ sacrilego(-a).
sac·ris·tan ['sækrɪstən] N sagrestano.
sac·ris·ty ['sækrɪstɪ] N sagrestia.
sac·ro·sanct ['sækrəʊ,sæŋkt] ADJ sacrosanto(-a).
sad [sæd] ADJ (*comp* **-der**, *superl* **-dest**) **a** (*sorrowful, depressing*) triste; **to make sb sad** rattristare qn; **how sad!** che tristezza!; **sadder but wiser** maturato(-a) dall'esperienza **b** (*deplorable*) deplorevole; **sad but true** è triste ma è così; **it's a sad state of affairs when …** la situazione è proprio triste quando… .
sad·den ['sædn] VT rattristare.
sad·dle ['sædl] ①N (*of horse, also Culin*) sella; (*of bicycle*) sellino, sella; **in the saddle** in sella; **when he was in the saddle** (*fig*) quando aveva le redini (del potere); **saddle of lamb** sella d'agnello.
②VT (*horse: also:* **saddle up**) sellare; **to saddle sb with sth** (*fam: task, bill, name*) appioppare qc a qn; (: *responsibility*) accollare qc a qn; **I got saddled with him again** me lo sono dovuto sorbire di nuovo.
saddle·bag ['sædl,bæg] N bisaccia; (*on bicycle*) borsa.
sad·dler ['sædlə'] N sellaio.
sad·ism ['seɪdɪzəm] N sadismo.
sad·ist ['seɪdɪst] N sadico(-a).
sa·dis·tic [sə'dɪstɪk] ADJ sadico(-a), sadistico(-a).
sa·dis·ti·cal·ly [sə'dɪstɪkəlɪ] ADV sadisticamente, in modo sadico.
sad·ly ['sædlɪ] ADV (*unhappily*) tristemente; (*regrettably*)

sfortunatamente; **sadly lacking in** ... completamente privo(-a) di....

sad·ness ['sædnɪs] N tristezza.

sado·maso·chism [ˌseɪdəʊ'mæsəˌkɪzəm] N sadomasochismo.

sado·maso·chist [ˌseɪdəʊ'mæsəkɪst] N sadomasochista *m/f.*

sado·maso·chist·ic [ˌseɪdəʊmæsə'kɪstɪk] ADJ sadomasochistico(-a).

sae [ˌɛseɪ'i:] N ABBR (*Brit*) = **stamped addressed envelope**.

sa·fa·ri [sə'fɑ:rɪ] N safari *m inv*; **to be on safari** fare un safari.

♦ **safari park** N zoosafari *m inv.*

safe [seɪf] ADJ (*comp* **-r**, *superl* **-st**) **a** (*not in danger: person*) salvo(-a); (: *money, jewels, secret*) al sicuro; (*out of danger: person*) fuori pericolo; **safe and sound** sano(-a) e salvo(-a); **as safe as houses** sicurissimo(-a); **he didn't feel very safe up there** non si sentiva molto (al) sicuro lassù; **to be safe from** essere al sicuro da; **you'll be safe here** qui sarai al sicuro; **no woman is safe with you** (*hum*) non ti si può lasciare una donna vicino

b (*not dangerous: toy, beach, animal*) non pericoloso (-a); (: *ladder*) sicuro(-a); (*secure: hiding place, investment*) sicuro(-a); (*prudent: choice*) prudente; **that dog isn't safe with children** non si dovrebbe lasciare quel cane coi bambini; **(have a) safe journey!** buon viaggio!; **in safe hands** in buone mani; **just to be on the safe side** per andare sul sicuro, per precauzione, per non correre rischi; **better safe than sorry!** meglio essere prudenti!; **it's a safe bet** è praticamente certo; **it is safe to say that** ... si può affermare con sicurezza che...; **to play safe** giocare sul sicuro.

♦ **safe bet** N: **it's a safe bet** è una cosa sicura.

♦ **safe-breaker** ['seɪfˌbreɪkəʳ], (*Am*) **safe-cracker** ['seɪfˌkrækəʳ] N scassinatore(-trice).

♦ **safe-conduct** [ˌseɪf'kɒndʌkt] N salvacondotto.

♦ **safe-deposit** ['seɪfdɪˌpɒzɪt], **safety-deposit** ['seɪftɪdɪˌpɒzɪt] N (*vault*) caveau *m inv*; (*box*) cassetta di sicurezza.

safe·guard ['seɪfˌgɑ:d] **1** N salvaguardia.

2 VT salvaguardare.

♦ **safe haven** N zona sicura *or* protetta.

safe·keeping ['seɪf'ki:pɪŋ] N custodia; **I gave it to him for safekeeping** gliel'ho dato in custodia; **the key is in his safekeeping** gli è stata affidata la custodia della chiave.

safe·ly ['seɪflɪ] ADV (*securely*) al sicuro; (*without danger*) senza (correre) rischi, tranquillamente; (*without accident*): **to arrive safely** arrivare sano(-a) e salvo(-a); **I can safely say** ... posso tranquillamente asserire... .

safe·ness ['seɪfnɪs] N (*of construction, machine*) sicurezza.

♦ **safe passage** N passaggio sicuro.

♦ **safe period** N: **the safe period** (*fam: of menstrual cycle*) il periodo non fecondo.

♦ **safe seat** N (*Pol*) seggio sicuro.

♦ **safe sex** N sesso sicuro.

safe·ty ['seɪftɪ] **1** N sicurezza; **to reach safety** mettersi in salvo; **in a place of safety** al sicuro; **there's safety in numbers** l'unione fa la forza; **safety first!** la prudenza innanzitutto!; **for safety's sake** per (maggior) sicurezza.

2 ADJ (*device, measure, margin*) di sicurezza.

♦ **safety belt** N (*Aut, Aer*) cintura di sicurezza.

♦ **safety catch** N sicura.

♦ **safety curtain** N (*Theatre*) (sipario) spartifuoco.

♦ **safety-deposit** ['seɪftɪdɪˌpɒzɪt] N = **safe-deposit**.

♦ **safety glass** N cristallo di sicurezza.

♦ **safety lock** N chiusura *or* serratura di sicurezza.

♦ **safety match** N (fiammifero) svedese *m*.

♦ **safety net** N (*in circus*) rete *f* di protezione; (*fig: safeguard*) ancora di salvezza; **to slip through the social security safety net** (*fig*) scivolare attraverso le maglie dell'assistenza sociale.

♦ **safety pin** N spilla da balia *or* di sicurezza.

♦ **safety valve** N valvola di sicurezza.

saf·fron ['sæfrən] **1** N zafferano.

2 ADJ (*colour*) (color) zafferano *inv*.

sag [sæg] VI (*hang down: ceiling, awning, bed*) incurvarsi; (: *breasts*) afflosciarsi; (*slacken: rope*) allentarsi; (*fig: spirits*) deprimersi; **his knees sagged** gli hanno ceduto le ginocchia.

saga ['sɑ:gə] N saga.

sa·ga·cious [sə'geɪʃəs] ADJ sagace.

sa·ga·cious·ly [sə'geɪʃəslɪ] ADV sagacemente, in modo sagace.

sa·gac·ity [sə'gæsɪtɪ] N sagacia.

sage[1] [seɪdʒ] **1** ADJ (*liter*) saggio(-a).

2 N (*man*) saggio.

sage[2] [seɪdʒ] N (*herb*) salvia; **sage and onion stuffing** ripieno di salvia e cipolla.

♦ **sage green** ADJ, N verde salvia (*m*) *inv.*

sage·ly ['seɪdʒlɪ] ADV saggiamente.

sag·ging ['sægɪŋ] ADJ (*ceiling*) incurvato(-a); (*rope*) allentato(-a); (*breasts*) cadente; (*fig: spirits*) a terra.

Sag·it·ta·rius [ˌsædʒɪ'tɛərɪəs] N (*Astron, Astrol*) Sagittario; **to be Sagittarius** essere del Sagittario.

sago ['seɪgəʊ] N sagù *m inv.*

Sa·ha·ra [sə'hɑ:rə] N: **the Sahara (Desert)** il (deserto del) Sahara.

sa·hib ['sɑ:hɪb] N sahib *m inv.*

said [sɛd] **1** PT, PP of **say**.

2 ADJ (*aforementioned*): **the said** il/la suddetto(-a).

Sai·gon [saɪ'gɒn] N Saigon *f.*

sail [seɪl] **1** N (*of boat*) vela; (*of windmill*) pala; (*trip*): **to go for a sail** fare un giro in barca a vela; **to set sail** salpare; **under sail** a vela.

2 VT **a** (*ship*) condurre, governare

b (*travel over*): **to sail the Atlantic** attraversare l'Atlantico; **to sail the seas** solcare i mari.

3 VI **a** (*travel: ship*) navigare; (: *person*) viaggiare per mare; **to sail into harbour** entrare in porto; **the ship sailed into Naples** la nave è arrivata a Napoli; **to sail round the Cape** doppiare il Capo; **to sail away/back** *etc* allontanarsi/rientrare *etc* in barca; **they sailed into Genoa** sono entrati nel porto di Genova; **to sail round the world** fare il giro del mondo in barca a vela; **to sail close to the wind** (*fig*) tirare troppo la corda

b (*set off*) salpare; **the ship sails at 5 o'clock** la nave salpa alle 5

c (*Sport*) fare della vela

d (*fig: clouds*) veleggiare; (: *swan*) incedere maestosamente; **she sailed into the room** fece il suo ingresso solenne nella stanza; **the plate sailed over my head** il piatto è volato al di sopra della mia testa

▶ **sail through 1** VI + ADV (*fig*) farcela senza difficoltà.

2 VI + PREP (*fig*) fare qc senza difficoltà; (*pass: exam, driving text*) superare senza difficoltà.

sail·cloth ['seɪlˌklɒθ] N tela da vela.

sail·ing ['seɪlɪŋ] N (*sport*) vela; (*departure*) partenza; **(pleasure) sailing** navigazione *f* da diporto; **to go sailing** fare vela; **now it's all plain sailing** il resto è liscio come l'olio.

♦ **sailing boat**, (*Am*)**sail·boat** ['seɪlˌbəʊt] N barca a vela.

♦ **sailing dinghy** N deriva.

♦ **sailing ship** N veliero.

sail·maker ['seɪlˌmeɪkəʳ] N velaio; **sailmaker's (shop)** veleria.

sail·or ['seɪləʳ] N marinaio; **to be a bad sailor** soffrire il mal di mare.

♦ **sailor hat** N berretto da marinaio.

♦ **sailor suit** N divisa da marinaio; (*for children*) vestito alla marinara.

sail·plane ['seɪlˌpleɪn] N (*Aer*) veleggiatore *m*.

sain·foin ['sænfɔɪn] N fieno santo.

saint [seɪnt] N (*also fig*) santo(-a); **Saint John** San Giovanni; **Saint Mark's (Church)** (la chiesa di) San Marco.

♦ **Saint Bernard** [sənt'bɜ:nəd] N (*dog*) sanbernardo, San Bernardo.

saint·hood ['seɪnthʊd] N santità.

♦ **Saint John's wort** N (*Bot*) erba di San Giovanni.

saint·li·ness ['seɪntlɪnɪs] N santità.

saint·ly ['seɪntlɪ] ADJ (*comp* **-ier**, *superl* **-iest**) (*expression, life*) da santo(-a); **a saintly person** una santa persona.

♦ **saint's day** N *giorno dedicato a un santo*.

♦ **Saint Vitus's (dance)** [sənt'vaɪtəsɪz('dɑ:ns)] N (*Med*) ballo di San Vito.

sake [seɪk] N: **for the sake of sb/sth** per amor di qn/qc; **for my sake** per amor mio, per me; **for God's/for heaven's sake!** per amor di Dio!/del cielo!; **art for art's sake** l'arte per l'arte; **for your own sake** per te (stesso), per il tuo bene; **for pity's sake** per pietà; **for old times' sake** in ricordo del passato; **for argument's sake** [OR] **for the sake of argument** a titolo d'esempio.

sa·la·cious [sə'leɪʃəs] ADJ (*joke, remark*) salace; (*book, film*) scabroso(-a); (*look, smile*) lascivo(-a).

sa·la·cious·ness [sə'leɪʃəsnɪs] N (*see adj*) salacità; scabrosità; lascivia.

sal·ad ['sæləd] N insalata; **tomato salad** insalata di pomodori; **ham salad** prosciutto e insalata.

♦ **salad bowl** N insalatiera.

♦ **salad cream** N (*esp Brit*) *tipo di maionese con cui si condisce l'insalata*.

♦ **salad days** NPL (*liter*) anni *mpl* verdi; **in my salad days** quand'ero giovane e inesperto.

♦ **salad dressing** N condimento per l'insalata.

♦ **salad oil** N olio da tavola.

♦ **salad servers** NPL posate *fpl* da insalata.

♦ **salad spinner** N centrifuga scolaverdure.

sala·man·der ['sæləˌmændəʳ] N salamandra.

sa·la·mi [sə'lɑ:mɪ] N salame *m*.

sala·ried ['sælərɪd] ADJ (*person, post*) stipendiato(-a).

sala·ry ['sælərɪ] N stipendio.

♦ **salary earner** N stipendiato(-a).

♦ **salary range** N fascia salariale.

♦ **salary review** N revisione *f* degli stipendi.

♦ **salary scale** N scala salariale.

sale [seɪl] N **a** (*of article*) vendita; (*also:* **auction sale**) vendita all'asta; **"for sale"** (*one article*) "vendesi"; (*two or more articles*) "vendonsi"; **to put a house up for sale** mettere in vendita una casa; **to be on sale** essere in vendita **b** (*Comm: also:* **sales**) svendita, saldi *mpl*; **to be on sale** (*Am*) essere in saldi *or* in svendita; **she bought a dress in the sale(s)** ha comprato un vestito nei saldi; **the January sales** ≈ i saldi di fine anno.

sale·able, sal·able ['seɪləbl] ADJ vendibile.

♦ **sale and lease back** N (*Fin*) vendita con patto di

locazione.

♦ **sale of work** N vendita di beneficenza.

♦ **sale or return, sale and return** N conto a deposito; **on sale or return** [OR] **on a sale or return basis** in conto a deposito; **sale or return goods** merce *f* in conto a deposito.

♦ **sale price** N prezzo di liquidazione.

sale·room ['seɪlˌrʊm] N (*esp Brit*) sala di vendite all'asta.

♦ **sales analysis** N analisi *f inv* delle vendite.

♦ **sales assistant** N (*Brit*) commesso(-a).

♦ **sales budget** N bilancio preventivo delle vendite.

♦ **sales campaign** N campagna di vendita.

♦ **sales clerk** N (*Am*) commesso(-a).

♦ **sales conference** N riunione *f* marketing e vendite.

♦ **sales department** N reparto vendite.

♦ **sales drive** N campagna promozionale.

♦ **sales figures** N fatturato.

♦ **sales force** N forza di vendita.

♦ **sales forecast** N previsione *f* delle vendite.

sales·girl ['seɪlzˌgɜ:l] N commessa.

♦ **sales incentive** N incentivo sulle vendite.

♦ **sales inquiry** N richiesta d'offerta.

♦ **sales literature** N dépliant *mpl* illustrativi.

sales·man ['seɪlzmən] N (*pl* **-men**) (*representative*) rappresentante *m* di commercio; (*in shop*) commesso.

♦ **sales manager** N direttore *m* delle vendite.

sales·man·ship ['seɪlzmənʃɪp] N arte *f* del vendere.

♦ **sales manual** N manuale *m* di vendita.

sales·person ['seɪlzˌpɜ:sən] N (*in shop*) commesso(-a); (*representative*) rappresentante *m/f* di commercio.

♦ **sales promotion** N promozione *f* delle vendite.

♦ **sales prospect** N possibile cliente *m/f*.

♦ **sales quota** N quota stabilita di vendite.

♦ **sales resistance** N resistenza del consumatore all'acquisto.

♦ **sales revenue** N incassi *mpl* delle vendite.

sales·room ['seɪlzˌrʊm] N (*Am*) sala di vendite all'asta.

♦ **sales talk** N discorso imbonitore.

♦ **sales tax** N (*Am*) imposta sulle vendite.

♦ **sales territory** N zona di vendite.

♦ **sales volume** N volume *m* delle vendite.

sales·woman ['seɪlzˌwʊmən] N (*pl* **-women**) (*in shop*) commessa; (*representative*) rappresentante *f* di commercio.

sa·li·ent ['seɪlɪənt] ADJ (*frm*) saliente.

sa·line ['seɪlaɪn] ADJ salino(-a).

sa·li·va [sə'laɪvə] N saliva.

sali·vate ['sælɪˌveɪt] VI salivare.

sal·low ['sæləʊ] ADJ (*comp* **-er**, *superl* **-est**) (*complexion*) giallastro(-a).

sal·low·ness ['sæləʊnɪs] N colore *m* giallastro.

sal·ly ['sælɪ] N (*witty remark*) battuta

▶ **sally forth, sally out** VI + ADV (*old*) uscire di gran carriera.

salm·on ['sæmən] N salmone *m*; **salmon fishing** pesca del salmone; **salmon steak** trancio di salmone.

sal·mo·nel·la [ˌsælmə'nelə] N salmonella.

♦ **salmon pink** ADJ, N rosa salmone (*m*) *inv*.

♦ **salmon trout** N trota salmonata, trota di mare.

sa·lon ['sælɒn] N (*all senses*) salone *m*.

sa·loon [sə'lu:n] N **a** (*on ship*) sala, salone *m* **b** (*Brit: car*) berlina **c** (*Am: bar*) saloon *m inv*, bar *m inv*; (*Brit: also:* **saloon bar**) bar (*in pub, hotel*).

♦ **saloon car** N (*Brit Aut*) berlina; (*Am Rail*) vettura *or* carrozza salone.

Sal·op ['sæləp] N ABBR (*Brit*)= Shropshire.

sal·si·fy ['sælsɪfɪ] N (*Bot*) salsefica.

SALT [sɔ:lt] N ABBR (= *Strategic Arms Limitation Talks or Treaty*) S.A.L.T. *m*.

salt [sɔ:lt] ⊡ N sale *m*; **to rub salt into the wound** (*fig*) rigirare il coltello nella piaga; **not to be worth one's salt** non valere un granché; **he's the salt of the earth** è un brav'uomo; **an old salt** un lupo di mare; see also **salts**.

⊡ VT (*flavour*) salare; (*preserve*) conservare sotto sale.

⊡ ADJ (*water*) salato(-a); (*beef, meat*) salato(-a), sotto sale; (*mine*) di sale; (*spoon*) per il sale

▶ **salt away** VT + ADV (*fam*) mettere da parte.

salt·cellar ['sɔ:lt,sɛlə'], (*Am*) **salt shaker** N saliera.

♦ **salt flats** NPL saline *fpl*.

♦ **salt-free** [,sɔ:lt'fri:] ADJ senza sale.

salti·ness ['sɔ:ltɪnɪs] N (*of water*) salsedine *f*; (*of food*) sapore *m* salato.

♦ **salt lake** N lago salato.

salt·pan ['sɔ:lt,pæn] N (bacino di) salina.

salt·pe·tre, (*Am*) **salt·pe·ter** ['sɔ:lt,pi:tə'] N salnitro.

salts [sɔ:lts] NPL (*Med*) sali *mpl*.

♦ **salt shaker** N (*Am*) = **saltcellar**.

salt·water ['sɔ:lt,wɔ:tə'] ADJ (*fish*) di mare.

salty ['sɔ:ltɪ] ADJ (*comp* **-ier**, *superl* **-iest**) (*taste*) salato(-a); (*fig: humour, remark*) piccante.

sa·lu·bri·ous [sə'lu:brɪəs] (*frm*) ADJ salubre; (*fig: district*) raccomandabile.

salu·tary ['sæljʊtərɪ] ADJ salutare.

salu·ta·tion [,sælju'teɪʃən] N (*old, frm*) saluto.

sa·lute [sə'lu:t] ⊡ N (*Mil: with hand*) saluto; (: *with gunfire*) salva; **to take the salute** passare in rassegna le truppe.

⊡ VT (*Mil, fig*) salutare; **to salute the flag** salutare la bandiera.

sal·vage ['sælvɪdʒ] ⊡ N **a** (*saving: of ship etc*) salvataggio; (: *for re-use*) ricupero **b** (*things saved*) oggetti *mpl* salvati *or* ricuperati; (: *for re-use*) materiale *m* di ricupero **c** (*compensation*) compenso.

⊡ VT (*boat, cargo, goods*) ricuperare; (*fig*) salvare.

⊡ ADJ (*operation*) di salvataggio; (*goods*) di ricupero.

♦ **salvage vessel** N nave *f* di salvataggio.

sal·va·tion [sæl'veɪʃən] N salvezza.

♦ **Salvation Army** N: **the Salvation Army** l'Esercito della Salvezza.

sal·va·tion·ist, **Sal·va·tion·ist** [sæl'veɪʃənɪst] N salutista *m/f*.

salve [sælv] ⊡ VT: **to salve one's conscience** mettersi la coscienza in pace.

⊡ N balsamo.

sal·ver ['sælvə'] N vassoio (*d'argento o altro metallo*).

sal·vo ['sælvəʊ] N (*Mil*) salva; (*outburst: of applause*) scroscio.

Sa·mari·tan [sə'mærɪtən] N **a** : **the Good Samaritan** il buon Samaritano **b** : **the Samaritans** (*organisation*) ≈ Telefono Amico.

sam·ba ['sæmbə] N samba.

sam·bo ['sæmbəʊ] N (*offensive*) negro(-a).

same [seɪm] ⊡ ADJ stesso(-a), medesimo(-a); **the same book as/that** lo stesso libro di/che; **the same table as usual** il solito tavolo; **on the same day** lo stesso giorno; **the** *or* **that same day** il *or* quel giorno stesso; **at the same time** allo stesso tempo; **it comes to the same thing** è la stessa cosa; **in the same way** allo stesso modo; **to go the same way as sb** (*fig pej*) seguire le orme di qn.

⊡ PRON: **the same** (*sg*) lo(-a) stesso(-a); (*pl*) gli/le stessi(-e); **it's all the same to me** per me fa lo stesso; **just**

the same as usual come al solito; **same again, please** (*in pub*) un altro, per favore; **it was wrong but I did it all** *or* **just the same** non era giusto ma l'ho fatto lo stesso; **they're one and the same** (*person*) sono la stessa persona; (*thing*) sono la stessa cosa; **to do the same** fare la stessa cosa; **I'll do the same for you** farò altrettanto per te; **I would do the same again** rifarei quello che ho fatto; **to do the same as sb** fare come qn; **do the same as your father** fa' come tuo padre; **and the same to you!** altrettanto a te!; **I don't feel the same about it** non la vedo allo stesso modo; **I still feel the same about you** i miei sentimenti nei tuoi confronti non sono cambiati; **same here!** (*fam*) anch'io!

same·ness ['seɪmnɪs] N (*monotony*) monotonia.

samey ['seɪmɪ] ADJ (*Brit fam: unvaried*) tutto(-a) uguale.

sa·mo·sa [sə'məʊsə] N *triangolo di sfoglia ripieno di verdure o carne, fritto, specialità della cucina indiana*.

sam·ple ['sɑ:mpl] ⊡ N (*gen*) campione *m*; (*fig*) saggio; **to take a sample** prelevare un campione; **to take a blood sample** fare un prelievo di sangue; **free sample** campione omaggio.

⊡ VT (*food, wine*) assaggiare, degustare; (*fig: experience*) provare; (*Market Research: people*) usare come campione.

⊡ ADJ (*bottle*) campione *inv*; **sample line/verse** esempio; **sample selection** campioni *mpl*; **sample copy** copia di saggio; **sample survey** indagine *f* su campione.

sam·pler ['sɑ:mplə'] N (*Sewing*) saggio di ricamo; (*Mus*) *strumento elettronico per la campionatura di pezzi musicali*.

samu·rai ['sæmʊ,raɪ] N samurai *m inv*.

sana·to·rium [,sænə'tɔ:rɪəm] N (*pl* **sanatoria** *or* **sanatoriums** [,sænə'tɔ:rɪə]) **a** casa di cura; (*for tuberculosis*) sanatorio **b** (*Brit Scol*) ≈ infermeria.

sanc·ti·fy ['sæŋktɪ,faɪ] VT santificare.

sanc·ti·mo·ni·ous [,sæŋktɪ'məʊnɪəs] ADJ (*pej: person*) bigotto(-a), bacchettone(-a); (: *tone*) moraleggiante.

sanc·ti·mo·ni·ous·ly [,sæŋktɪ'məʊnɪəslɪ] ADV (*pej: say*) con tono moraleggiante.

sanc·tion ['sæŋkʃən] ⊡ N (*gen*) sanzione *f*; **to impose economic sanctions on** *or* **against** adottare sanzioni economiche contro.

⊡ VT sancire, sanzionare.

sanc·tity ['sæŋktɪtɪ] N (*of person, marriage*) santità; (*of oath, place*) sacralità.

sanc·tu·ary ['sæŋktjʊərɪ] N (*Rel*) santuario; (*fig, Pol: refuge*) asilo; (*for wildlife, birds*) riserva; **to seek sanctuary** cercare asilo.

sand [sænd] ⊡ N sabbia; see also **sands**.

⊡ VT **a** (*road*) cospargere di sabbia **b** (*also:* **sand down**: *wood*) levigare, smerigliare.

san·dal ['sændl] N sandalo.

sandal·wood ['sændl,wʊd] ⊡ N (*wood*) legno di sandalo; (*oil*) olio di sandalo.

⊡ ADJ (*soap, perfume*) al sandalo.

sand·bag ['sænd,bæg] ⊡ N sacchetto di sabbia.

⊡ VT (*protect*) proteggere con sacchetti di sabbia; (*hit*) colpire (con un sacchetto di sabbia).

sand·bank ['sænd,bæŋk] N banco di sabbia.

sand·blast ['sænd,blɑ:st] VT sabbiare.

sand·blast·er ['sænd,blɑ:stə'] N (*machine*) sabbiatrice *f*.

sand·box ['sænd,bɒks] N (*Am*) buca della sabbia (*per i giochi dei bambini*).

sand·boy ['sænd,bɔɪ] N: **(as) happy as a sandboy** contento (-a) come una Pasqua.

sand·castle ['sænd,kɑ:sl] N castello di sabbia.

♦ **sand dune** N duna.

♦ **sand eel** N anguilla della sabbia.

sand·er ['sændəʳ] N (*machine*) levigatrice *f*.

♦ **sand flea, sand hopper** N pulce *f* di mare.

sand·fly ['sænd,flaɪ] N pappataci *m inv*.

sand·man ['sænd,mæn] N: **the sandman** *personaggio fantastico che fa addormentare i bambini spargendo sabbia sui loro occhi.*

sand·paper ['sænd,peɪpəʳ] ① N carta vetrata. ② VT cartavetrare.

sand·piper ['sænd,paɪpəʳ] N (*also:* **common sandpiper**) piro piro piccolo.

sand·pit ['sænd,pɪt] N cava di sabbia; (*Brit: for children*) buca della sabbia (*per i giochi dei bambini*).

sands [sændz] NPL spiaggia *fsg*; **the sands of time** (*fig*) lo scorrere del tempo.

sand·shoe ['sænd,ʃu:] N scarpa di tela.

sand·stone ['sænd,stəʊn] N arenaria.

sand·storm ['sænd,stɔ:m] N tempesta di sabbia.

sand·wich ['sænwɪdʒ] ① N tramezzino, sandwich *m inv*; **cheese/ham sandwich** panino al formaggio/prosciutto. ② VT (*also:* **sandwich in:** *person, appointment etc*) infilare; **to be sandwiched between** essere incastrato(-a) fra.

♦ **sandwich bar** N snack bar *m inv*.

♦ **sandwich board** N cartello pubblicitario (*portato da uomo sandwich*).

♦ **sandwich cake** N torta farcita (*di marmellata o panna*).

♦ **sandwich course** N (*Brit*) corso che alterna lo studio a periodi di pratica presso aziende o fabbriche.

♦ **sandwich loaf** N pane *m* a cassetta.

♦ **sandwich man** N uomo *m* sandwich *inv*.

sandy ['sændɪ] ADJ (*comp* **-ier,** *superl* **-iest**) (*gen*) sabbioso (-a); (*colour*) color sabbia *inv*; (*hair*) biondo rossiccio *inv*.

sane [seɪn] ADJ (*comp* **-r,** *superl* **-st**) (*person*) sano(-a) di mente; (*judgment, outlook*) sensato(-a).

sane·ly ['seɪnlɪ] ADV (*act, speak*) in modo sensato.

sang [sæŋ] PT of **sing**.

sang·froid [,sɑ̃:ŋ'frwɑ:] N sangue *m* freddo.

san·gria [sæŋ'gri:ə] N sangria.

san·guine ['sæŋgwɪn] ADJ ottimista.

san·guine·ly ['sæŋgwɪnlɪ] ADV ottimisticamente.

San·hed·rin ['sænɪdrɪn] N sinedrio.

sani·ta·rium [,sænɪ'tɛərɪəm] N (*pl* **sanitaria** *or* **sanitariums** [,sænɪ'tɛərɪə]) (*Am*) = **sanatorium**.

sani·tary ['sænɪtərɪ] ADJ (*clean*) igienico(-a); (*system, arrangements, fittings*) sanitario(-a).

♦ **sanitary towel,** (*Am*) **sanitary napkin** N assorbente *m* (igienico).

sani·ta·tion [,sænɪ'teɪʃən] N (*plumbing: in house*) impianti *mpl* igienici; (: *in town*) fognature *fpl*; (*hygiene*) igiene *f*.

♦ **sanitation department** N (*Am*) ≈ assessorato alla nettezza urbana.

sani·tize ['sænɪ,taɪz] VT sanitizzare; (*fig: make inoffensive*) espurgare.

san·ity ['sænɪtɪ] N (*of person*) sanità mentale; (*of judgment*) buonsenso; **sanity prevailed** il buonsenso ha avuto la meglio.

sank [sæŋk] PT of **sink¹**.

San Ma·ri·no [,sænmə'ri:nəʊ] N San Marino *f*.

San·skrit [,sænskrɪt] N sanscrito.

Santa Claus [,sæntə'klɔ:z] N ≈ Babbo Natale.

San·tia·go [,sæntɪ'ɑ:gəʊ] N (*also:* **Santiago de Chile**) Santiago *f* (del Cile).

sap¹ [sæp] N (*of plants*) linfa.

sap² [sæp] VT (*strength*) fiaccare; (*confidence*) minare.

sap·ling ['sæplɪŋ] N alberello.

sa·poni·fi·ca·tion [sə,pɒnɪfɪ'keɪʃən] N saponificazione *f*.

sap·per ['sæpəʳ] N a (*Mil*) geniere *m* b : **the Sappers** (*Brit*) il Genio.

sap·phire ['sæfaɪəʳ] ① N zaffiro. ② ADJ (*necklace*) di zaffiri; (*colour*) blu zaffiro *inv*.

♦ **sapphire ring** N anello di zaffiri (*or* con uno zaffiro).

Sara·cen ['særəsn] N (*History*) saraceno(-a).

sar·casm ['sɑ:kæzəm] N sarcasmo.

sar·cas·tic [sɑ:'kæstɪk] ADJ sarcastico(-a); **to be sarcastic** fare del sarcasmo.

sar·cas·ti·cal·ly [sɑ:'kæstɪkəlɪ] ADV sarcasticamente, in modo sarcastico.

sar·copha·gus [sɑ:'kɒfəgəs] N (*pl* **sarcophaguses** *or* **sarcophagi**) sarcofago.

sar·dine [sɑ:'di:n] N sardina.

Sar·dinia [sɑ:'dɪnɪə] N la Sardegna.

Sar·din·ian [sɑ:'dɪnɪən] ADJ, N (*person*) sardo(-a).

sar·don·ic [sɑ:'dɒnɪk] ADJ sardonico(-a).

sar·doni·cal·ly [sɑ:'dɒnɪkəlɪ] ADV in modo sardonico, sardonicamente.

sari, saree ['sɑ:rɪ] N sari *m inv*.

sa·rong [sə'rɒŋ] N sarong *m inv*.

sar·to·rial [sɑ:'tɔ:rɪəl] ADJ (*frm*) sartoriale.

SAS [,ɛseɪ'ɛs] N ABBR (*Brit Mil:* = *Special Air Service*) *reparto dell'esercito britannico specializzato in operazioni segrete.*

SASE [,ɛseɪɛs'i:] N ABBR (*Am:* = *self-addressed stamped envelope*) *busta già affrancata e indirizzata a se stessi.*

sash¹ [sæʃ] N (*of dress*) fusciacca; (*on uniform*) fascia.

sash² [sæʃ] N (*also:* **window sash**) telaio.

♦ **sash window** N finestra a ghigliottina.

Sas·se·nach ['sæsənæk] N (*pej*) *termine usato dagli scozzesi per definire gli inglesi.*

SAT [,ɛseɪ'ti:] N ABBR (*Am*) = *Scholastic Aptitude Test*.

sat [sæt] PT, PP of **sit**.

Sat. ABBR = **Saturday**

Satan ['seɪtn] N Satana *m*.

sa·tan·ic [sə'tænɪk] ADJ satanico(-a).

satch·el ['sætʃəl] N cartella (*per la scuola*).

sa·ted ['seɪtɪd] ADJ (*frm*) sazio(-a).

sa·teen [sæ'ti:n] N rasatello.

sat·el·lite ['sætə,laɪt] ① N (*all senses*) satellite *m*. ② ADJ satellite *inv*.

♦ **satellite dish** N antenna parabolica.

♦ **satellite television** N televisione *f* via satellite.

♦ **satellite town** N città satellite *f inv*.

sa·ti·ate ['seɪʃɪ,eɪt] VT (*frm*) saziare.

sa·ti·ety [sə'taɪətɪ] N (*frm*) sazietà.

sat·in ['sætɪn] ① N raso, satin *m*. ② ADJ (*dress, blouse*) di raso *or* di satin; (*paper*) satinato (-a); **with a satin finish** satinato(-a).

sat·ire ['sætaɪəʳ] N: **satire (on)** satira (di, su).

sa·tiri·cal [sə'tɪrɪkəl] ADJ satirico(-a).

sa·tiri·cal·ly [sə'tɪrɪkəlɪ] ADV satiricamente.

sati·rist ['sætərɪst] N (*writer etc*) scrittore(-trice) satirico (-a); (*cartoonist*) caricaturista *m/f*.

sati·rize ['sætə,raɪz] VT satireggiare.

sat·is·fac·tion [,sætɪs'fækʃən] N (*gen*) soddisfazione *f*; (*of ambitions, hopes*) realizzazione *f*; **has it been done to your satisfaction?** ne è rimasto soddisfatto?; **it gives me great satisfaction to learn that ...** è con immenso piacere che apprendo che... .

sat·is·fac·to·ri·ly [,sætɪs'fæktərɪlɪ] ADV in modo soddisfa-

cente.

sat·is·fac·tory [ˌsætɪsˈfæktərɪ] ADJ soddisfacente; (*Scol*) sufficiente; **to bring sth to a satisfactory conclusion** concludere qc in modo soddisfacente.

sat·is·fied [ˈsætɪsˌfaɪd] ADJ (*person, voice, customer*) soddisfatto(-a); **I'm not satisfied with that** ciò non mi basta; **I am satisfied that** ... sono convinto *or* sicuro che... .

sat·is·fy [ˈsætɪsˌfaɪ] VT **a** (*make content*) soddisfare, contentare
b (*need, condition, creditor*) soddisfare; (*hunger*) calmare; **to satisfy the requirements** rispondere ai requisiti
c (*convince*): **to satisfy sb (that)** convincere qn (che); **to satisfy o.s. of sth** accertarsi di qc.

sat·is·fy·ing [ˈsætɪsˌfaɪɪŋ] ADJ (*gen*) soddisfacente; (*food, meal*) sostanzioso(-a).

sat·su·ma [ˌsætˈsuːmə] N satsuma, *tipo di mandarino*.

satu·rate [ˈsætʃəˌreɪt] VT: **to saturate (with)** (*soak*) inzuppare (di); (*Chem, fig*) saturare (di); **to saturate the market** (*Comm*) saturare il mercato.

satu·rat·ed [ˈsætʃəˌreɪtɪd] ADJ (*see vb*) inzuppato(-a); saturo(-a).

♦ **saturated fat** N grassi *mpl* saturi.

satu·ra·tion [ˌsætʃəˈreɪʃən] N saturazione *f.*

♦ **saturation bombing** N bombardamento a tappeto.

♦ **saturation point** N punto di saturazione; **to reach saturation point** (*Chem*) raggiungere il punto di saturazione; (*fig*) arrivare a saturazione.

Sat·ur·day [ˈsætədɪ] N sabato *for usage see* **Tuesday**.

Saturn [ˈsætɜːn] N (*Myth, Astron*) Saturno.

sat·ur·nine [ˈsætəˌnaɪn] ADJ (*liter*) malinconico(-a), taciturno(-a).

sa·tyr [ˈsætəʳ] N (*liter*) satiro.

sauce [sɔːs] N **a** (*containing meat, fish*) sugo; **tomato sauce** salsa di pomodoro **b** (*fam: impudence*) faccia tosta.

♦ **sauce boat** N salsiera.

sauce·pan [ˈsɔːspən] N pentola, casseruola.

sau·cer [ˈsɔːsəʳ] N piattino.

sau·ci·ly [ˈsɔːsɪlɪ] ADV (*see adj*) sfacciatamente; in modo provocante.

sau·ci·ness [ˈsɔːsɪnɪs] N sfacciataggine *f.*

saucy [ˈsɔːsɪ] ADJ (*comp* **-ier**, *superl* **-iest**) (*impertinent*) sfacciato(-a), impertinente; (*look*) provocante.

Sau·di Ara·bia [ˈsaʊdɪəˈreɪbɪə] N Arabia Saudita.

Sau·di Ara·bian [ˈsaʊdɪəˈreɪbɪən] ADJ, N (*also:* **Saudi**) saudita (*m/f*).

sau·er·kraut [ˈsaʊəˌkraʊt] N crauti *mpl.*

sau·na [ˈsɔːnə] N sauna.

saun·ter [ˈsɔːntəʳ] VI: **to saunter in/out** entrare/uscire con disinvoltura; **to saunter up and down** passeggiare su e giù.

sau·sage [ˈsɒsɪdʒ] N (*to be cooked*) salsiccia; (*salami etc*) salame *m.*

♦ **sausage dog** N (*Brit fam*) bassotto.

♦ **sausage meat** N carne macinata per salsicce.

♦ **sausage roll** N *involtino di pasta sfoglia ripieno di salsiccia.*

sau·té [ˈsaʊteɪ] **1** ADJ (*Culin: potatoes*) sauté *inv.*
2 VT (*potatoes, meat*) saltare; (*onions*) soffriggere.

sav·age [ˈsævɪdʒ] **1** ADJ **a** (*gen*) violento(-a); (*animal, murderer, attack*) feroce **b** (*primitive: custom, tribe*) selvaggio(-a).
2 N selvaggio(-a).
3 VT (*subj: dog*) sbranare; (*fig*) fare a pezzi, attaccare violentemente.

sav·age·ly [ˈsævɪdʒlɪ] ADV (*attack*) selvaggiamente; (*maul, criticize*) ferocemente.

sav·age·ry [ˈsævɪdʒrɪ] N ferocia.

sa·van·nah, sa·van·na [səˈvænə] N savana.

save[1] [seɪv] **1** VT **a** (*rescue: also Rel*): **to save (from)** salvare (da); **to save sb from falling** impedire a qn di cadere; **to save sb's life** salvare la vita a qn; **I couldn't do it to save my life** (*fig fam*) sono completamente negato per quello; **to save the situation** *or* **the day** salvare la situazione; **to save one's (own) skin** (*fam*) salvare la (propria) pelle; **to save face** salvare la faccia; **to save a goal** (*Ftbl*) parare un goal; **God save the Queen!** Dio salvi la Regina!
b (*put aside: money: also:* **save up**) risparmiare, mettere da parte; (*: food, newspapers*) conservare, tenere da parte; (*collect: stamps*) raccogliere; (*Comput*) memorizzare; **I saved you a piece of cake** ti ho tenuto da parte una fetta di dolce; **save me a seat** prendimi un posto; **to save sth till last** tenere qc per ultimo(-a)
c (*avoid using: money, effort*) risparmiare; **it saved us a lot of trouble/another journey** ci ha risparmiato una bella seccatura/un altro viaggio; **it will save me an hour** mi farà risparmiare un'ora; **to save time** ... per risparmiare *or* guadagnare tempo...; **save your breath** risparmia il fiato.
2 VI **a** (*also:* **save up**): **to save (for)** risparmiare (per)
b: **to save on time** risparmiare tempo; **to save on food/transport** risparmiare *or* economizzare sul vitto/trasporto.
3 N (*Sport*) parata.

save[2] [seɪv] PREP (*liter, old*) salvo, a eccezione di.

sav·eloy [ˈsævəlɔɪ] N cervellata.

sav·er [ˈseɪvəʳ] N risparmiatore(-trice).

sav·ing [ˈseɪvɪŋ] **1** N (*of time, money*): **saving of** *or* **in** risparmio di; **to make savings** fare economia.
2: **savings** NPL (*in bank*) risparmi *mpl*; **life savings** i risparmi di tutta una vita; **to live on** *or* **off one's savings** vivere dei propri risparmi.

♦ **saving grace** N: **her kindness is her saving grace** si salva grazie alla sua gentilezza.

♦ **savings account** N libretto di risparmio.

♦ **savings bank** N cassa di risparmio.

sav·iour, (*Am*) **sav·ior** [ˈseɪvjəʳ] N salvatore(-trice).

savoir-faire [ˈsævwɑːˈfɛəʳ] N (*frm*) savoir-faire *m inv.*

sa·vory [ˈseɪvərɪ] N **a** (*Bot*) satureia **b** (*Am*) = savoury.

sa·vour, (*Am*) **sa·vor** [ˈseɪvəʳ] **1** N sapore *m*, gusto.
2 VT (*also fig*) assaporare, gustare.
3 VI: **to savour of sth** sapere di qc.

sa·voury, (*Am*) **sa·vory** [ˈseɪvərɪ] **1** ADJ (*not sweet*) salato(-a); (*appetizing*) saporito(-a), appetitoso(-a); **savoury flan** *or* **tart** torta salata; **not very savoury** (*fig: district*) poco raccomandabile; (*: subject*) scabroso(-a).
2 N (*Culin*) piatto salato; (*: on toast*) crostino.

sav·vy [ˈsævɪ] N (*fam*) comprendonio.

saw[1] [sɔː] (*vb: pt* **sawed**, *pp* **sawed** *or* **sawn**) **1** N (*tool*) sega.
2 VT segare; **to saw sth up** fare a pezzi qc con la sega; **to saw sth off** segare via qc.
3 VI: **to saw through** segare.

saw[2] [sɔː] PT of **see**.

saw·dust [ˈsɔːˌdʌst] N segatura.

saw·mill [ˈsɔːˌmɪl] N segheria.

sawn [sɔːn] PP of **saw**[1].

♦ **sawn-off shotgun** [ˌsɔːnɒfˈʃɒtɡʌn], **sawed-off shotgun** [ˌsɒdɒfˈʃɒtɡʌn] N fucile *m* a canne mozze.

saxi·frage [ˈsæksɪˌfreɪdʒ] N sassifraga.

Sax·on ['sæksən] ADJ, N sassone *m/f*.

saxo·phone ['sæksə‚fəʊn] N sassofono.

sax·opho·nist [sæk'sɒfənɪst] N sassofonista *m/f*.

say [seɪ] (*vb: pt, pp* **said**) ① VT, VI **a** (*gen*) dire; (*subj: dial, gauge*) indicare; **he said (that) he'd do it** ha detto che l'avrebbe fatto; **she said (that) I was to give you this** mi ha detto di darti questo; **my watch says 3 o'clock** il mio orologio fa le 3; **the rules say that ...** il regolamento dice che...; **to say mass/a prayer** dire messa/una preghiera; **to say yes/no** dire di sì/di no; **to say yes/no to a proposal** accettare/rifiutare una proposta; **I wouldn't say no** (*Brit fam*) non mi dispiacerebbe; **to say goodbye/goodnight to sb** dire arrivederci/buonanotte a qn; **to say sth again** ripetere qc; **could you say that again?** potrebbe ripetere?; **say after me ...** ripetete con me...; **I've nothing more to say** non ho altro da dire; **I'll say more about it later** ne riparlerò più tardi; **let's say no more about it** non ne parliamo più; **I'd rather not say** preferisco non pronunciarmi; **I should say it's worth about £100** direi che vale sulle 100 sterline; **(let's) say it's worth £20** diciamo *or* ammettiamo che valga 20 sterline; **shall we say Tuesday?** facciamo martedì?; **will you take an offer of, say, £50?** accetta un'offerta di, diciamo, 50 sterline? **b** (*in phrases*): **that is to say** vale a dire, cioè; **to say nothing of** per non parlare di; **to say the least** a dir poco; **she hasn't much** *or* **has nothing to say for herself** (*by way of conversation*) non sa dire due parole; **what have you got to say for yourself?** (*by way of excuse*) qual è la tua giustificazione?; **that doesn't say much for him** non torna a suo credito; **it goes without saying (that)** va da sé (che); **there's no saying what he'll do** Dio solo sa cosa farà; **it's not for me to say** non sta a me dirlo; **what do** *or* **would you say to a walk?** che ne dici *or* diresti di una passeggiata?; **when all is said and done** in fin dei conti; **let's say that ...** mettiamo *or* diciamo che...; **it is said that ...** si dice che...+ *sub*; **they say that ...** dicono che...+ *sub*; **there is something** *or* **a lot to be said for it** ha i suoi lati positivi; **it must be said that ...** bisogna ammettere che...; **he is said to have ...** si dice che abbia...; **it is easier** *or* **sooner said than done** è più facile a dirsi che a farsi; **I say!** *or* (*Am*) **Say!** (*calling attention*) senta!, scusi!; (*in surprise, appreciation*) perbacco!; **I'll say!** (*fam*) eccome!; **I should say it is** *or* so! [OR] **you can say THAT again!** (*fam*) altrochè!; **you don't say!** (*fam: often iro*) ma va'!, ma che dici!; **you('ve) said it!** (*fam: emphatic*) l'hai detto!; **say no more!** (*fam: often hum*) non aggiungere altro!.

② N: **to have one's say** dire la propria; **to have a say/no say in the matter** avere/non avere voce in capitolo.

say·ing ['seɪɪŋ] N detto; **as the saying goes** come dice il proverbio.

♦ **say-so** ['seɪ‚səʊ] N (*fam: authority*): **to do sth on sb's say-so** fare qc col permesso di qn; **why should I believe it just on your say-so?** perché dovrei crederci, solo perché lo dici tu?

SBA [‚ɛsbiː'eɪ] N ABBR (*Am: = Small Business Administration*) *organismo ausiliario per piccole imprese.*

SC ABBR (*Am*) **a** = **supreme court b** (*Post*)= **South Carolina.**

s/c ABBR (*Brit*) = **self-contained.**

scab [skæb] N **a** (*Med*) crosta **b** (*fam pej: strikebreaker*) crumiro(-a).

scab·bard ['skæbəd] N fodero.

scab·by ['skæbɪ] ADJ (*comp* **-ier**, *superl* **-iest**) crostoso(-a).

sca·bies ['skeɪbiːz] N (*Med*) scabbia.

sca·bi·ous ['skeɪbɪəs] N (*Bot*): **field scabious** scabiosa.

scaf·fold ['skæfəld] N (*Constr*) impalcatura, ponteggio; (*for execution*) patibolo.

scaf·fold·ing ['skæfəldɪŋ] N impalcatura.

sca·lar ['skeɪlə'] (*Math, Phys*) ① ADJ scalare.

② N scalare *m*.

scala·wag ['skælə‚wæg] N (*Am*) = **scallywag.**

scald [skɔːld] ① N scottatura.

② VT (*gen*) scottare; (*Culin: milk*) sbollentare; (*sterilize*) sterilizzare.

scald·ing ['skɔːldɪŋ] ADJ: **scalding hot** bollente.

scale[1] [skeɪl] ① N (*of fish, reptile etc*) squama, scaglia; (*flake: of rust, chalk*) scaglia; (: *of skin*) squama.

② VT (*fish*) squamare.

scale[2] [skeɪl] ① N **a** (*on ruler, thermometer*) scala graduata; (*of model, map*) scala; **pay scale** scala salariale; **scale of charges** tariffario; **on a scale of 1 cm to 5 km** in scala di 1 a 500.000; **on a large scale** su vasta scala; **on a small scale** su scala ridotta; **small-scale model** modello in scala ridotta; **to draw sth to scale** disegnare qc in scala

b (*Mus*) scala; see also **scales.**

② VT (*wall, mountain*) scalare

▶ **scale down** VT + ADV ridurre proporzionalmente.

scaled-down ['skeɪld‚daʊn] ADJ su scala ridotta.

♦ **scale drawing** N disegno in scala.

♦ **scale factor** N (*Math*) fattore *m* di scala.

♦ **scale model** N modellino in scala.

sca·lene ['skeɪliːn] ADJ (*Geom*): **scalene triangle** triangolo scaleno.

scales [skeɪlz] NPL **a** : (**pair** *or* **set of**) **scales** bilancia; **he tips the scales at 70 kilos** pesa 70 chili; **to turn** *or* **tip the scales in sb's/sth's favour** far pendere la bilancia dalla parte di qn/qc; **to turn** *or* **tip the scales against sb** giocare a sfavore di qn; **the scales of justice** la bilancia della giustizia

b (*also:* **bathroom scales**) bilancia *f* pesapersone *inv*.

scal·lion ['skælɪən] N cipollotto; (*Am: shallot*) scalogno.

scal·lop ['skɒləp] N **a** (*Zool*) pettine *m* **b** (*Culin*) cappa santa **c** (*Sewing*) smerlo.

scal·loped ['skɒləpt] ADJ (*edge*) a smerlo; (*neck*) smerlato (-a).

♦ **scallop shell** N conchiglia di pettine.

scal·ly·wag ['skælɪ‚wæg] N (*fam*) briccone(-a).

scalp [skælp] ① N cuoio capelluto; (*as trophy*) scalpo.

② VT scotennare; (*Am: Stock Exchange*) speculare in Borsa.

scal·pel ['skælpəl] N bisturi *m inv*.

scalp·er ['skælpə'] N (*Am fam: of tickets*) bagarino.

scaly ['skeɪlɪ] ADJ (*comp* **-ier**, *superl* **-iest**) squamoso(-a).

scam [skæm] N (*fam*) truffa.

scamp[1] [skæmp] N (*fam: child*) peste *f*.

scamp[2] VT (*one's work*) fare in fretta e male.

scamp·er ['skæmpə'] VI + ADV (*child*): **to scamper about** scorrazzare; **to scamper in/out** *etc* entrare/uscire *etc* di corsa; **to scamper away** [OR] **scamper off** darsela a gambe.

scam·pi ['skæmpɪ] NPL scampi *mpl*.

scan [skæn] ① VT **a** (*inspect closely: horizon, sb's face, crowd*) scrutare; (: *newspaper*) leggere attentamente; **he scans the papers for European news** legge con attenzione i giornali alla ricerca di notizie dall'Europa

b (*glance at quickly*) dare un'occhiata a, scorrere

c (*machine*) leggere; (*Radar: sea bed*) scandagliare; (: *sky*) esplorare.

② VI (*Poetry*) scandire.

3 N (*Med*) ecografia.

scan·dal ['skændl] N **a** (*public furore, disgrace*) scandalo; **it's a scandal that** ... è uno scandalo *or* è scandaloso che...+ *sub* **b** (*gossip*) chiacchiere *fpl*, pettegolezzi *mpl*; **have you heard the latest scandal about ...?** hai sentito l'ultima su...?

scan·dal·ize ['skændə,laɪz] VT scandalizzare.

scandal·monger ['skændl,mʌŋgəʳ] N malalingua.

scan·dal·ous ['skændələs] ADJ scandaloso(-a).

scan·dal·ous·ly ['skændələslɪ] ADV scandalosamente, in modo scandaloso.

Scan·di·na·via [,skændɪ'neɪvɪə] N la Scandinavia.

Scan·di·na·vian [,skændɪ'neɪvɪən] ADJ, N scandinavo(-a).

scan·ner ['skænəʳ] N (*Radar, Med*) scanner *m inv*; (*for bar codes*) lettore *m* di codice a barre.

scan·sion ['skænʃən] N (*Literature*) scansione *f*.

scant [skænt] ADJ (*comp* **-er**, *superl* **-est**) scarso(-a); **with scant courtesy** poco cortesemente; **to pay scant attention to** prestare poca attenzione a; **they have scant respect for him** hanno scarsa considerazione per lui.

scanti·ly ['skæntɪlɪ] ADV: **scantily clad** *or* **dressed** succintamente vestito(-a).

scanti·ness ['skæntɪnɪs] N scarsezza; **the scantiness of her clothes** i suoi abiti succinti.

scanty ['skæntɪ] ADJ (*comp* **-ier**, *superl* **-iest**) (*meal etc*) scarso(-a); (*clothing*) succinto(-a); (*swimsuit*) ridotto(-a).

scape·goat ['skeɪp,gəʊt] N capro espiatorio.

scapu·la ['skæpjʊlə] N (*pl* **scapulas** *or* **scapulae**) (*Anat*) scapola.

scar¹ [skɑ:ʳ] **1** N (*Med*) cicatrice *f*; (*on face*) sfregio, cicatrice; (*fig: on landscape etc*) segno; **it left a deep scar on his mind** gli ha lasciato il segno.

2 VT (*gen*) lasciare delle cicatrici su; (*face*) sfregiare; (*fig*) segnare, lasciare il segno su; **scarred by acne** butterato (-a) dall'acne; **a battle-scarred town** una città segnata dalla guerra.

3 VI (*also*: **scar over**: *heal*) cicatrizzarsi.

scar² [skɑ:ʳ] N (*Geog*) rupe *f*.

scarce [skɛəs] ADJ (*comp* **-r**, *superl* **-st**) (*money, food, resources*) scarso(-a); (*copy, edition*) raro(-a); **to be scarce** scarseggiare; **to grow** *or* **become scarce** diventare raro(-a); **to make o.s. scarce** (*fig fam*) squagliarsela.

scarce·ly ['skɛəslɪ] ADV (*barely*) appena; **scarcely anybody** quasi nessuno; **scarcely ever** quasi mai; **I scarcely know what to say** non so proprio che dire; **I can scarcely believe it** faccio fatica a crederci; **I've scarcely seen him** l'ho visto raramente.

scar·city ['skɛəsɪtɪ], **scarce·ness** ['skɛəsnɪs] N (*of jobs, accommodation*) scarsezza, scarsità; (*of food*) penuria.

♦ **scarcity value** N: **this item has a certain scarcity value** questo oggetto ha un certo valore grazie alla sua rarità.

scare ['skɛəʳ] **1** N spavento, paura; **to cause a scare (amongst)** creare il panico (tra); **to give sb a scare** far prendere uno spavento a qn, mettere paura a qn.

2 VT spaventare, impaurire; **to scare sb to death** OR **scare sb stiff** (*fam*) spaventare qn a morte.

► **scare away, scare off** VT + ADV (*dog*) mettere in fuga; (*fig: subj: price*) far scappare; **the price scared him away** il prezzo l'ha scoraggiato.

scare·crow ['skɛəkrəʊ] N (*also fig*) spaventapasseri *m inv*.

scared [skɛəd] ADJ impaurito(-a), spaventato(-a); **to be scared (of)** aver paura (di); **to be scared to death** OR **be scared stiff** essere spaventato(-a) a morte; **to be scared out of one's wits** (*fam*) non capire più niente dalla paura.

scare·monger ['skɛə,mʌŋgəʳ] N allarmista *m/f*.

scare·monger·ing ['skɛə,mʌŋgərɪŋ] N allarmismo.

♦ **scare story** N notizie *fpl* allarmistiche.

scarf [skɑ:f] N (*pl* **scarfs** *or* **scarves**) **a** (*long*) sciarpa **b** (*also*: **headscarf**) foulard *m inv*.

scar·la·ti·na [,skɑ:lə'ti:nə] N (*Med*) scarlattina.

scar·let ['skɑ:lɪt] **1** N scarlatto.

2 ADJ scarlatto(-a).

♦ **scarlet fever** N scarlattina.

scarp [skɑ:p] N scarpata.

scarp·er ['skɑ:pəʳ] VI (*Brit fam*) darsela a gambe.

scarves [skɑ:vz] NPL of **scarf**.

scary ['skɛərɪ] ADJ (*comp* **-ier**, *superl* **-iest**) (*fam*) che fa paura.

scath·ing ['skeɪðɪŋ] ADJ (*remark, criticism*) aspro(-a); (*look*) sprezzante; **to be scathing about sth** essere molto critico(-a) nei confronti di qc.

scath·ing·ly ['skeɪðɪŋlɪ] ADV sprezzantemente, in modo sprezzante.

scat·ter ['skætəʳ] **1** VT **a** (*gen*) spargere; (*papers*) sparpagliare **b** (*disperse: crowd, clouds*) disperdere; (: *enemy*) mettere in fuga; **her relatives are scattered about the world** la sua famiglia è sparsa per il mondo.

2 VI (*crowd*) disperdersi.

scatter·brain ['skætə,breɪn] N (*fam*) sventato(-a), sbadato(-a).

scatter·brained ['skætə,breɪnd] ADJ (*fam*) sventato(-a), sbadato(-a).

♦ **scatter cushion** N cuscino (*decorativo*).

♦ **scatter diagram** N diagramma *m* di dispersione.

scat·tered ['skætəd] ADJ (*books, houses*) sparso(-a), sparpagliato(-a); (*population*) sparso(-a); **scattered showers** precipitazioni *fpl* sparse; **scattered with** (*strewn*) cosparso(-a) di.

scat·ty ['skætɪ] ADJ (*comp* **-ier**, *superl* **-iest**) (*Brit fam*) svitato(-a).

scav·enge ['skævɪndʒ] **1** VT (*food*) cercare; (*streets*) pulire.

2 VI (*hyenas, birds*) nutrirsi di carogne; **to scavenge (for)** (*person*) frugare tra i rifiuti (alla ricerca di).

scav·en·ger ['skævɪndʒəʳ] N (*animal*) insetto (*or animale m*) necrofago; (*person*) *chi fruga nei rifiuti alla ricerca di qualcosa*.

SCE [,ɛssi:'i:] N ABBR (= *Scottish Certificate of Education*) *diploma di scuola secondaria superiore*.

sce·nario [sɪ'nɑ:rɪəʊ] N scenario.

scene [si:n] N **a** (*gen, Theatre, Cine, TV*) scena; **indoor/ outdoor scenes** interni/esterni *mpl*; **the scene is set in a castle** la scena si svolge in un castello; **to set the scene** (*fig*) creare l'atmosfera; **behind the scenes** (*also fig*) dietro le quinte; **the political scene in Italy** il quadro politico in Italia; **the Punk scene** il mondo dei punk; **scenes of violence** scene di violenza; **to make a scene** (*fam: fuss*) fare una scenata

b (*of crime, accident*) luogo, scena; **at the scene of the crime** sul luogo *or* sulla scena del delitto; **she needs a change of scene** ha bisogno di cambiare aria; **to appear** *or* **come on the scene** (*also fig*) entrare in scena; **it's not my scene** (*fam*) non è il mio genere

c (*sight*) scena, spettacolo; (*view*) vista, spettacolo; **a scene of utter destruction** una scena di totale distruzione.

♦ **scene change** N (*Theatre*) cambio di scena.

♦ **scene painter** N scenografo(-a).

scen·ery ['si:nərɪ] N (*landscape*) paesaggio, panorama *m*;

(*Theatre*) scenario, scenari *mpl*.
♦ **scene shift·er** [ˈsiːnʃɪftəʳ] N (*Theatre*) macchinista *m* di scena.
sce·nic [ˈsiːnɪk] ADJ (*postcard, view*) pittoresco(-a); (*road, railway*) panoramico(-a).
scent [sɛnt] ① N **a** (*smell, perfume*) profumo **b** (*track*) tracce *fpl*, pista; **to follow/lose the scent** seguire/perdere le tracce *or* la pista; **to pick up the scent** fiutare le tracce; **to put** *or* **throw sb off the scent** (*fig*) far perdere le tracce a qn, sviare qn.
② VT **a** : **to scent (with)** (*make sth smell nice*) profumare (di *or* con) **b** (*smell*) fiutare.
scent·ed [ˈsɛntɪd] ADJ profumato(-a).
scep·ter [ˈsɛptəʳ] (*Am*) N = **sceptre**.
scep·tic, (*Am*) **skep·tic** [ˈskɛptɪk] N scettico(-a).
scep·ti·cal, (*Am*) **skep·ti·cal** [ˈskɛptɪkəl] ADJ: **sceptical (of** *or* **about)** scettico(-a) (su *or* circa).
scep·ti·cal·ly, (*Am*) **skep·ti·cal·ly** [ˈskɛptɪkəlɪ] ADV scetticamente.
scep·ti·cism, (*Am*) **skep·ti·cism** [ˈskɛptɪˌsɪzəm] N scetticismo.
scep·tre, (*Am*) **scep·ter** [ˈsɛptəʳ] N scettro.
sched·ule [ˈʃɛdjuːl, *Am* ˈskɛdjuːl] ① N **a** (*timetable: of work, visits, events*) programma *m*, tabella *or* ruolino di marcia; **the work is behind/ahead of schedule** il lavoro è in ritardo/in anticipo sul previsto; **on schedule** in orario; **we are working to a very tight schedule** il nostro programma di lavoro è molto intenso; **everything went according to schedule** tutto è andato secondo i piani *or* secondo il previsto
b (*list: of contents, goods*) lista; (*Customs, Tax etc*) tabella.
② VT (*date, time*) fissare, stabilire; (*visit, event*) programmare; **as scheduled** come stabilito; **scheduled flight** volo di linea; **the meeting is scheduled for 7.00** *or* **to begin at 7.00** la riunione è fissata per le 7; **this building is scheduled for demolition** questo edificio è destinato alla demolizione.
sched·uled [ˈʃɛdjuːld, *Am* ˈskɛdjuːld] ADJ (*date, time*) fissato(-a); (*meeting, event*) programmato(-a); (*programme*) in programma.
sche·ma [ˈskiːmə] N (*pl* **schemata**) (*frm*) schema.
sche·mat·ic [skɪˈmætɪk] ADJ schematico(-a).
sche·mati·cal·ly [skɪˈmætɪklɪ] ADV schematicamente.
scheme [skiːm] ① N **a** (*plan*) piano; (*method*) sistema *m*; **a scheme to rebuild** *or* **for rebuilding sth** un piano per la ricostruzione di qc; **a scheme of work** un piano *or* programma *m* di lavoro; **it's some crazy scheme of his** è una delle sue idee balzane
b (*dishonest plan, plot*): **scheme (to do** *or* **for doing sth/for sth**) piano (per fare qc/per qc)
c (*arrangement*) sistemazione *f*; **colour scheme** combinazione *f* di colori; **man's place in the scheme of things** (*fig*) il posto dell'uomo nell'ordine delle cose.
② VI: **to scheme (to do)** (*intrigue*) tramare (per fare), complottare (per fare).
schem·er [ˈskiːməʳ] N intrigante *m/f*.
schem·ing [ˈskiːmɪŋ] ① ADJ intrigante.
② N intrighi *mpl*, macchinazioni *fpl*.
schism [ˈsɪzəm, ˈskɪzəm] N scisma *m*.
schiz·oid [ˈskɪtsɔɪd] ADJ, N schizoide (*m/f*).
schizo·phre·nia [ˌskɪtsəʊˈfriːnjə] N schizofrenia.
schizo·phren·ic [ˌskɪtsəʊˈfrɛnɪk] ADJ, N schizofrenico(-a).
schmaltz, schmalz [ʃmɔːlts] N (*fam*) sdolcinatezza.
schmaltzy, schmalzy [ˈʃmɔːltsɪ] ADJ (*fam*) sdolcinato

(-a).
schnau·zer [ˈʃnaʊtsəʳ] N (*dog*) schnauzer *m inv*.
schol·ar [ˈskɒləʳ] N (*learned person*) erudito(-a), studioso (-a); **a famous Dickens scholar** un noto studioso di Dickens; **he's never been much of a scholar** non è mai stato portato per gli studi.
schol·ar·ly [ˈskɒləlɪ] ADJ dotto(-a), erudito(-a).
schol·ar·ship [ˈskɒləʃɪp] N **a** (*learning*) erudizione *f*, cultura **b** (*award, grant*) borsa di studio; **to win a scholarship** vincere una borsa di studio.
♦ **scholarship holder** N borsista *m/f*.
scho·las·tic [skəˈlæstɪk] ADJ scolastico(-a).
school¹ [skuːl] ① N **a** (*gen*) scuola; **to be at/go to school** frequentare la/andare a scuola; **to leave school** terminare gli studi; **school of motoring** scuola guida, autoscuola; **the Dutch school** (*Art*) la scuola olandese; **school of thought** corrente *f* di pensiero; **of the old school** (*fig*) di vecchio stampo
b (*Univ*) facoltà *f inv*; **medical/law school** facoltà di medicina/giurisprudenza; **art school** istituto d'arte; **she's at law school** studia legge; **School of Interpreters** Scuola Interpreti.
② VT (*animal*) addestrare; (*reaction, voice etc*) controllare; **he schooled himself in patience** *or* **to be patient** ha imparato ad essere paziente.
③ ADJ (*year, fees etc*) scolastico(-a); **during school hours** OR **in school time** durante l'orario scolastico.
school² [skuːl] N (*of fish*) banco.
♦ **school age** N età *f inv* scolare.
♦ **school attendance** N frequenza scolastica.
♦ **school attendance officer** N *funzionario addetto al controllo della frequenza scolastica*.
school·bag [ˈskuːlˌbæg] N cartella.
school·book [ˈskuːlˌbʊk] N libro scolastico, librò di scuola.
school·boy [ˈskuːlˌbɔɪ] N scolaro.
♦ **schoolboy slang** N gergo studentesco.
♦ **school bus** N scuolabus *m inv*.
school·child [ˈskuːlˌtʃaɪld] N (*pl* **-children**) scolaro(-a).
school·days [ˈskuːlˌdeɪz] NPL tempi *mpl* della scuola.
school·girl [ˈskuːlˌgɜːl] N scolara.
school·house [ˈskuːlˌhaʊs] N (*school building*) scuola (*edificio*); (*head teacher's house*) residenza del preside.
school·ing [ˈskuːlɪŋ] N istruzione *f*; **compulsory schooling** istruzione *f* obbligatoria, scuola dell'obbligo.
♦ **school-leaver** [ˈskuːlˌliːvəʳ] N (*Brit: about to leave*) ≈ maturando(-a); (: *having recently left*) ≈ neo-diplomato (-a).
♦ **school-leaving age** [ˌskuːlˈliːvɪŋˌeɪdʒ] N età *f* in cui termina l'obbligo scolastico.
school·marm [ˈskuːlˌmɑːm] N (*pej*) maestrina.
school·mar·mish [ˈskuːlˌmɑːmɪʃ] ADJ (*pej*) pedante.
school·master [ˈskuːlˌmɑːstəʳ] N (*in primary school*) maestro; (*in secondary school*) professore *m*.
school·mate [ˈskuːlˌmeɪt] N compagno(-a) di scuola.
school·mistress [ˈskuːlˌmɪstrɪs] N (*in primary school*) maestra; (*in secondary school*) professoressa.
♦ **school report** N (*Brit*) scheda di valutazione scolastica, pagella.
school·room [ˈskuːlˌrʊm] N aula.
school·teacher [ˈskuːlˌtiːtʃəʳ] N insegnante *m/f*.
school·teach·ing [ˈskuːlˌtiːtʃɪŋ] N insegnamento.
♦ **school uniform** N uniforme *f* scolastica.
school·work [ˈskuːlˌwɜːk] N studio.
school·yard [ˈskuːlˌjɑːd] N (*Am*) cortile *m* della scuola.

♦ **school year** N anno scolastico.

schoon·er ['sku:nə'] N **a** (*Naut*) schooner *m inv*, goletta **b** (*Brit*: *sherry glass*) bicchiere *m* da sherry; (*Am*: *beer glass*) boccale *m* da birra.

sci·ati·ca [saɪ'ætɪkə] N (*Med*) sciatica.

sci·ence ['saɪəns] **1** N scienza; (*Scol*) le materie scientifiche; **the sciences** le scienze; **the natural/social sciences** le scienze naturali/sociali.

2 ADJ (*teacher*, *exam*) di scienze; (*subject*, *equipment*, *laboratory*) scientifico(-a).

♦ **science faculty** N (*Univ*) facoltà *f inv* di scienze *fpl*.

♦ **science fiction** N fantascienza.

♦ **science park** N polo di ricerca scientifica applicata.

sci·en·tif·ic [ˌsaɪən'tɪfɪk] ADJ scientifico(-a).

sci·en·tifi·cal·ly [ˌsaɪən'tɪfɪkəlɪ] ADV scientificamente.

sci·en·tist ['saɪəntɪst] N scienziato(-a).

sci-fi ['saɪˌfaɪ] N ABBR (*fam*) = **science fiction**.

Scil·ly Isles ['sɪlɪˌaɪlz] NPL: **the Scilly Isles**, **the Scillies** le isole *fpl* Scilly.

scimi·tar ['sɪmɪtə'] N scimitarra.

scin·til·late ['sɪntɪˌleɪt] VI (*star*, *jewel*) brillare, scintillare; (*fig*: *person*) brillare.

scin·til·lat·ing ['sɪntɪˌleɪtɪŋ] ADJ (*jewels*, *chandelier*) scintillante; (*wit*, *conversation*, *company*) brillante.

scis·sors ['sɪzəz] NPL forbici *fpl*; **a pair of scissors** un paio di forbici.

♦ **scissors kick** N (*Ftbl*, *Swimming*) sforbiciata.

scle·ro·sis [sklɪ'rəʊsɪs] N (*Med*) sclerosi *f*.

scle·rot·ic [sklɪ'rɒtɪk] **1** ADJ (*Anat*) sclerale; (*Med*) sclerotico(-a); (*Bot*) scleroso(-a).

2 N sclera.

scoff [skɒf] **1** VI: **to scoff (at sb/sth)** (*mock*) farsi beffe (di qn/qc).

2 VT (*Brit fam*: *eat*) papparsi, spazzolare; **he scoffed the lot** si è pappato tutto, ha spazzolato tutto quello che c'era.

scold [skəʊld] VT: **to scold sb (for doing sth)** sgridare qn (per aver fatto qc).

scold·ing ['skəʊldɪŋ] N lavata di capo, sgridata.

scol·lop ['skɒləp] N = **scallop**.

scone [skɒn, skəʊn] N *tipo di focaccina da tè*.

scoop [sku:p] **1** N **a** (*for flour etc*) paletta; (*for ice cream*) cucchiaio dosatore; (*for water*) mestolo, ramaiolo

b (*also*: **scoopful**) palettata; cucchiaiata; mestolata; **three scoops of ice-cream** tre palline di gelato

c (*Press*) scoop *m inv*, colpo giornalistico; (*Comm*) affarone *m*.

2 VT (*Comm*: *market*) accaparrarsi; (: *profit*) intascare; (*Comm*, *Press*: *competitors*) battere sul tempo; (*Press*): **to scoop an exclusive (about)** accaparrarsi l'esclusiva (su)

▶ **scoop out** VT + ADV (*flour*, *water etc*) svuotare (con paletta, cucchiaio etc); (*hole*) scavare

▶ **scoop up** VT + ADV (*child*) sollevare (tra le braccia); (*books*) raccogliere.

scoot [sku:t] VI (*fam*): **to scoot in/out** entrare/uscire di corsa.

scoot·er ['sku:tə'] N scooter *m inv*; (*child's*) monopattino.

scope [skəʊp] N (*opportunity*: *for action*) possibilità *fpl*; (*range*: *of law*, *activity*) ambito; (*capacity*: *of person*) capacità *fpl*; (: *of plan*, *undertaking*) portata; **it's beyond the scope of a child's mind** è al di sopra delle capacità di un bambino; **it's well within his scope to ...** è perfettamente in grado di...; **there is plenty of scope for improvement** (*Brit*) ci sono notevoli possibilità di miglioramento; **it is within/beyond the scope of this**

book rientra/non rientra nei limiti di questo libro.

scorch [skɔ:tʃ] **1** N (*also*: **scorch mark**) bruciacchiatura.

2 VT (*fabric*) bruciacchiare; (*subj*: *sun*, *fire*: *earth*, *grass*) bruciare.

3 VI (*esp Brit fam*: *car*) andare a tutta velocità.

scorched earth policy [ˌskɔ:tʃt'ɜ:ˌpɒlɪsɪ] N tattica del fare terra bruciata.

scorch·er ['skɔ:tʃə'] N (*fam*: *hot day*) giornata torrida.

scorch·ing ['skɔ:tʃɪŋ] ADJ (*also*: **scorching hot**) rovente; (*day*) torrido(-a); (*sun*) che spacca le pietre; (*sand*) bollente; **it's scorching** fa un caldo pazzesco.

♦ **score** [skɔ:'] **1** N **a** (*Sport*, *Cards*) punteggio, punti *mpl*; **to keep (the) score** segnare i punti; **there's no score yet** (*Sport*) finora nessuno ha segnato (un punto); **there was no score in the match** (*Sport*) hanno finito zero a zero; **to know the score** (*fig fam*) sapere come stanno le cose; **to have an old score to settle with sb** (*fig*) avere un vecchio conto da saldare con qn

b (*account*) motivo, titolo; **on that score** a questo riguardo

c (*cut*, *mark*: *on wood*) scalfittura; (: *on leather*, *card*) incisione *f*

d (*Mus*: *of opera*) partitura, spartito; (: *of film*) colonna sonora

e (*twenty*): **a score** venti; **a score of people** una ventina di persone; **scores of people** (*fig*) un sacco di gente.

2 VT **a** (*goal*, *point*, *runs*) segnare; (*success*) ottenere; **to score 75% in an exam** prendere 75 su 100 a *or* in un esame; **to score a hit** (*Fencing*) fare una stoccata; (*Shooting*) centrare il bersaglio; **to score a hit with sth** (*fig*) far centro con qc; **to score a hit with sb** (*fig*) far colpo su qn

b (*cut*: *leather*, *wood*, *card*) incidere

c (*music*: *for piano etc*) comporre; (: *for film*) comporre la colonna sonora.

3 VI **a** (*Sport*: *footballer*) segnare; (: *player*) totalizzare; (: *keep score*) tenere il punteggio; **to score 6 out of 10** (*in exam*, *test*) prendere 6 su 10; **to score over sb** (*fig*) dare dei punti a qn

b (*fam!*: *have sex with*): **to score (with sb)** portarsi a letto qn

▶ **score off** VT + ADV **a** (*name*, *item on list*) cancellare, spuntare

b (*fig*: *in argument*): **to score points off sb** avere la meglio su qn

▶ **score out**, **score through** VT + ADV cancellare, cancellare (con un segno).

score·board ['skɔ:ˌbɔ:d] N tabellone *m* segnapunti *inv*.

score·card ['skɔ:ˌkɑ:d] N cartoncino *m* segnapunti *inv*.

score·line ['skɔ:lam] N (*Sport*) risultato.

scor·er ['skɔ:rə'] N (*keeping score*) segnapunti *m/f inv*; (*player*) marcatore(-trice).

scor·ing ['skɔ:rɪŋ] N (*Sport*) punteggio.

scorn ['skɔ:n] **1** N disprezzo, scherno; **to pour scorn on sb/sth** deridere qn/qc.

2 VT (*gen*) disprezzare; (*attempt*) ridicolizzare; (*advice*, *offer*) respingere con sdegno; **to scorn to tell a lie** (*frm*) rifiutarsi sdegnosamente di dire una bugia.

scorn·ful ['skɔ:nful] ADJ sprezzante; **to be scornful about sth** parlare con disprezzo di qc.

scorn·ful·ly ['skɔ:nfəlɪ] ADV sprezzantemente, in modo sprezzante.

Scor·pio ['skɔ:pɪəʊ] N (*Astron*, *Astrol*) Scorpione *m*; **to be Scorpio** essere dello Scorpione.

scor·pi·on ['skɔ:pɪən] N scorpione *m*.

Scot [skɒt] N scozzese *m/f*; **the Scots** gli scozzesi.

Scotch [skɒtʃ] N (*also:* **Scotch whisky**) scotch *m inv*.

scotch [skɒtʃ] VT (*attempt, plan*) bloccare; (*revolt, uprising*) stroncare; (*rumour, claim*) mettere a tacere.

♦ **Scotch broth** N (*Brit*) *minestra fatta con brodo di manzo o montone, verdure e orzo.*

♦ **Scotch egg** N (*Brit*) *uovo sodo ricoperto di salsiccia, impanato e fritto.*

♦ **Scotch mist** N nebbia densa accompagnata da pioggia.

♦ **Scotch tape**® N (*Am*) scotch ® *m*.

scot-free [ˌskɒtˈfriː] 1 ADJ: **to get off scot-free** (*unpunished*) farla franca; (*unhurt*) uscire illeso(-a).

Scot·land [ˈskɒtlənd] N la Scozia.

♦ **Scotland Yard** N Scotland Yard.

Scots [skɒts] ADJ scozzese.

Scots·man [ˈskɒtsmən] N (*pl* **-men**) scozzese *m*.

♦ **Scots pine** N pino silvestre.

Scots·woman [ˈskɒtsˌwʊmən] N (*pl* **-women**) scozzese *f*.

Scot·tish [ˈskɒtɪʃ] ADJ scozzese.

♦ **Scottish National Party** N: **the Scottish National Party** il partito nazionalista scozzese.

♦ **Scottish Office** N (*Brit Pol*): **the Scottish Office** il ministero degli Affari scozzesi.

scoun·drel [ˈskaʊndrəl] N (*old*) canaglia, furfante *m/f*; (*hum: child*) furfantello(-a), birba.

scour [ˈskaʊəʳ] VT **a** (*clean: pan, floor etc*) sfregare **b** (*search: area, countryside*) setacciare, perlustrare, battere palmo a palmo.

scour·er [ˈskaʊərəʳ] N (*pad*) paglietta.

scourge [skɜːdʒ] 1 N (*also fig*) flagello.
2 VT (*beat*) flagellare; (*fig: bedevil*) tormentare.

scour·ing pow·der [ˈskaʊərɪŋˌpaʊdəʳ] N detergente *m* in polvere.

scout [skaʊt] N (*Mil*) ricognitore (*persona*) *m*; (*boy*) boy-scout *m inv*.

▶ **scout around** VI + ADV andare alla ricerca.

scout·ing [ˈskaʊtɪŋ] N scoutismo.

scout·master [ˈskaʊtˌmɑːstəʳ] N capogruppo dei boy-scout.

scowl [skaʊl] 1 N espressione *f* accigliata; **with a scowl** con lo sguardo torvo.
2 VI accigliarsi; **to scowl at sb** guardare qn in malo modo.

Scrab·ble® [ˈskræbl] N Scarabeo ®.

scrab·ble [ˈskræbl] 1 VI (*claw*): **to scrabble (at)** raspare, grattare; **to scrabble about** *or* **around for sth** cercare a tastoni qc.

scrag·gy [ˈskrægɪ] ADJ (*comp* **-ier**, *superl* **-iest**) (*neck, limb*) scheletrico(-a); (*animal*) pelle e ossa *inv*.

scram [skræm] VI (*fam*) filare, filarsela.

scram·ble [ˈskræmbl] 1 VI **a** : **to scramble down/along** scendere/avanzare a fatica; **to scramble out** uscire in fretta; **to scramble for** (*coins, seats, job*) azzuffarsi per prendere; **he scrambled up (the hill)** si è inerpicato su (per la collina)
b (*Sport*): **to go scrambling** fare il motocross.
2 VT **a** (*Culin: eggs*) strapazzare
b (*Telec: message*) disturbare con interferenze.
3 N **a** (*rush*) corsa
b (*Sport: motorcycle meeting*) gara di motocross.

scram·bled eggs [ˌskræmbldˈɛgz] NPL uova *fpl* strapazzate.

scram·bler [ˈskræmbləʳ] N (*Telec*) *dispositivo per il disturbo di trasmissioni radio o telefoniche.*

scram·bling [ˈskræmblɪŋ] N motocross *m*.

scrap¹ [skræp] 1 N **a** (*small piece*) pezzo, pezzetto; (*fig: of truth*) briciolo; **a scrap of conversation** un frammento di conversazione; **there's not a scrap of proof** non c'è la benché minima prova; **it's not a scrap of use** non serve a un bel niente
b : **scraps** NPL (*left-overs*) avanzi *mpl*
c (*iron, gold*) scarti *mpl*; **to sell sth for scrap** vendere qc come rottame.
2 VT (*gen*) buttar via; (*ship, car*) demolire; (*fig: plan*) scartare.

scrap² [skræp] (*fam*) 1 N (*fight*) bisticcio, zuffa.
2 VI: **to scrap (with sb)** bisticciare *or* azzuffarsi (con qn).

scrap·book [ˈskræpˌbʊk] N album *m inv* per ritagli (*di giornali, fotografie etc*).

♦ **scrap dealer**, **scrap merchant** N rottamaio(-a), commerciante *m/f* in rottami.

scrape [skreɪp] 1 N **a** (*act*) raschiatura; (*sound*) stridio; (*mark*) graffio; (*on leg, elbow*) scorticatura, sbucciatura
b (*fig*) pasticcio, guaio; **to get into a scrape** mettersi nei pasticci *or* nei guai; **to get out of a scrape** tirarsi fuori dai pasticci *or* dai guai.
2 VT (*knee*) scorticare, sbucciare; (*clean: vegetables*) raschiare, grattare; (: *walls, woodwork*) raschiare; **the lorry scraped the wall** il camion ha strisciato il muro; **to scrape a living** sbarcare il lunario; **we managed to scrape enough money together** siamo riusciti a racimolare abbastanza soldi; **to scrape the bottom of the barrel** (*fig*) raschiare il fondo del barile.
3 VI (*make sound*) grattare; (*rub*): **to scrape (against)** strusciare (contro)

▶ **scrape along**, **scrape by** VI + ADV (*fam: manage*) cavarsela; (: *live*) tirare avanti

▶ **scrape off**, **scrape away** 1 VT + ADV grattare via, raschiare via.
2 VT + PREP grattare via

▶ **scrape through** 1 VI + ADV (*succeed*) farcela per un pelo, cavarsela.
2 VI + PREP (*exam*) passare per il rotto della cuffia.

scrap·er [ˈskreɪpəʳ] N raschietto.

scrap·heap [ˈskræpˌhiːp] N ammasso di rottami; **to throw on the scrapheap** (*fig*) mettere nel dimenticatoio.

♦ **scrap metal** N rottami *mpl*.

♦ **scrap paper** N (*for scribbling on*) (fogli *mpl* di) carta per appunti; (*for recycling*) carta da destinare al riciclo.

scrap·py [ˈskræpɪ] ADJ (*comp* **-ier**, *superl* **-iest**) (*essay etc*) senza capo né coda; (*knowledge, education*) lacunoso (-a); (*meal*) arrangiato(-a).

♦ **scrap yard** N deposito di rottami; (*for cars*) cimitero delle macchine.

scratch [skrætʃ] 1 N **a** (*mark*) graffio, graffiatura; **it's just a scratch** è solo un graffio; **without a scratch** (*unharmed*) illeso(-a), senza un graffio
b (*noise*): **I heard a scratch at the door** ho sentito grattare alla porta
c : **to start from scratch** (*fig*) cominciare *or* partire da zero; **his work wasn't** *or* **didn't come up to scratch** il suo lavoro non è stato all'altezza; **to keep sth up to scratch** mantenere qc al livello desiderato.
2 VT **a** (*gen*) graffiare; (*one's name*) incidere; **we've barely scratched the surface** (*fig: of problem, topic*) l'abbiamo appena sfiorato
b (*to relieve itch*) grattare; **he scratched his head** si è grattato la testa; **you scratch my back and I'll scratch yours** (*fig*) una mano lava l'altra

c (*cancel: meeting, game, Comput*) cancellare; (*cross off list: horse, competitor*) eliminare.

3 VI (*person, dog*) grattarsi; (*hens*) razzolare, raspare; (*pen*) raschiare; (*clothing*) pungere; **the dog scratched at the door** il cane raspava alla porta

▶ **scratch out** VT + ADV (*from list*) cancellare; **to scratch sb's eyes out** cavare gli occhi a qn.

♦ **scratch meal** N pranzo arrangiato.

♦ **scratch pad** N (*Am*) bloc-notes *m inv*.

♦ **scratch team** N squadra raccogliticcia.

scratchy ['skrætʃɪ] ADJ (*comp* **-ier**, *superl* **-iest**) (*fabric*) ruvido(-a); (*pen*) che raschia; (*record*) graffiato(-a).

scrawl [skrɔ:l] 1 N (*handwriting*) scrittura illeggibile; (*brief note*) messaggio scarabocchiato.

2 VT scarabocchiare.

3 VI scarabocchiare.

scrawny ['skrɔ:nɪ] ADJ (*comp* **-ier**, *superl* **-iest**) (*neck, limb*) scheletrico(-a); (*animal, person*) pelle e ossa *inv*.

scream [skri:m] 1 N (*of pain, fear*) grido, urlo; **screams of laughter** grasse risate *fpl*; **he let out a scream** cacciò un urlo; **it was a scream** (*fig fam*) era da crepar dal ridere; **he's a scream** (*fig fam*) è una sagoma, è uno spasso.

2 VT (*subj: person: abuse, insults*) urlare; (*subj: poster, headlines*) strombazzare.

3 VI gridare, urlare; **to scream at sb (to do sth)** gridare a qn (di fare qc); **to scream (out) with pain** gridare di *or* dal dolore; **to scream for help** gridare aiuto; **to scream with laughter** sbellicarsi dalle risa.

scream·ing·ly ['skri:mɪŋlɪ] ADV: **screamingly funny** spassosissimo(-a).

scree [skri:] N ghiaione *m*.

screech [skri:tʃ] 1 N (*of brakes, tyres*) stridio, stridore *m*; (*of owl*) strido; (*of person*) strillo; **a screech of laughter** una risata stridula.

2 VI (*person*) strillare; (*owl, brakes*) stridere.

♦ **screech owl** N gufo comune.

screeds [skri:dz] NPL (*fam*): **to write screeds** scrivere un romanzo (*iro*).

screen [skri:n] 1 N a (*in room*) paravento; (*for fire*) parafuoco; (*fig: of trees*) barriera; (: *of smoke*) cortina

b (*Cine, TV, Radar*) schermo; **stars of the big/small screen** divi(-e) del grande/piccolo schermo.

2 VT a : **to screen (from)** (*hide: from view, sight*) nascondere (da); (*protect*) schermire (da), riparare (da); **he screened his eyes (from the sun) with his hand** si schermiva gli occhi (dal sole) con la mano

b (*TV: film, programme*) mandare in onda; (*Cine: film*) dare al cinema; **his earlier films were only screened in France** i suoi primi film sono usciti solo in Francia

c (*sieve: coal*) setacciare; (*fig: person: for security*) passare al vaglio; (: *for job*) selezionare; (: *for illness*) fare uno screening.

♦ **screen editing** ['skri:n,edɪtɪŋ] N (*Comput*) editing *m inv* su schermo.

screen·ing ['skri:nɪŋ] N a (*of film*) proiezione *f*; (*TV*) messa in onda b (*also:* **medical screening**) screening *m inv* c (*for security*) controlli *mpl* (di sicurezza).

♦ **screen memory** N (*Psych*) ricordi *mpl* di copertura.

screen·play ['skri:n,pleɪ] N sceneggiatura.

♦ **screen test** N provino cinematografico.

♦ **screen writer** N sceneggiatore(-trice).

screw [skru:] 1 N a vite *f*; (*Brit old: of sweets*) cartoccio; **he's got a screw loose** (*fig fam*) gli manca una rotella; **to put the screws on sb** (*fig fam*) far pressione su qn

b (*propeller*) elica

c (*fam: prison officer*) secondino

d (*fam!: sexual intercourse*) chiavata (*fam!*).

2 VT a avvitare; **to screw sth to the wall** fissare qc al muro con viti; **to screw sth (up) tight** avvitare bene qc; **to screw money out of sb** (*fam*) far scucire soldi a qn; **to screw one's head round** storcere la testa; **to have one's head screwed on** avere la testa sulle spalle

b (*fam!: have sex with*) chiavare (*fam!*); **screw you!** va' a farti fottere!.

3 VI (*fam!: have sex*) chiavare (*fam!*)

▶ **screw off** 1 VI + ADV svitarsi.

2 VT + ADV svitare

▶ **screw together** 1 VI + ADV avvitarsi.

2 VT + ADV (*kit*) montare con viti; (*two pieces*) avvitare

▶ **screw up** VT + ADV a (*paper, material*) spiegazzare; **to screw up one's eyes** strizzare gli occhi; **to screw up one's face** fare una smorfia; **to screw up one's courage** (*fig*) armarsi di coraggio

b (*fam: ruin*) mandare all'aria; **he really screwed it up this time!** stavolta ha fatto davvero un casino!; **to screw sb up** (*fig fam*) incasinare qn; **to be screwed up (about sth)** (*fig fam*) essere incasinato(-a) (per qc).

screw·ball ['skru:,bɔ:l] (*fam: esp Am*) 1 N testa matta, svitato(-a)

1 ADJ mezzo matto(-a), svitato(-a).

screw·driver ['skru:,draɪvə'] N cacciavite *m inv*.

screwed-up [,skru:d'ʌp] ADJ (*fam*): **she's totally screwed-up** è nel pallone.

♦ **screw-top, screw-topped** ['skru:,tɒp(d)] ADJ con il tappo (*or* coperchio) a vite.

screwy ['skru:ɪ] ADJ (*comp* **-ier**, *superl* **-iest**) (*fam: mad*) strambo(-a), svitato(-a).

scrib·ble ['skrɪbl] 1 N scarabocchio.

2 VT scribacchiare, scarabocchiare; **to scribble sth down** scribacchiare qc.

3 VI scarabocchiare.

scrib·bler ['skrɪblə'] N (*pej*) scribacchino(-a).

scrib·bling ['skrɪblɪŋ] N scarabocchi *mpl*.

♦ **scribbling pad** N bloc-notes *m inv*.

scribe [skraɪb] N scriba *m*.

scrim·mage ['skrɪmɪdʒ] N tafferuglio.

scrimp [skrɪmp] VI: **to scrimp and save** risparmiare fino all'ultimo centesimo.

script [skrɪpt] N a (*Cine, Theatre*) copione *m*, sceneggiatura; (*Brit: answer paper*) elaborato; (*writing system*) caratteri *mpl*, sistema di scrittura b (*writing*) scrittura.

script·ed ['skrɪptɪd] ADJ (*Radio, TV*) preparato(-a).

scrip·tur·al ['skrɪptʃərəl] ADJ scritturale.

Scrip·ture ['skrɪptʃə'] N (*also:* **Holy Scripture**) Sacre Scritture *fpl*.

script·writer ['skrɪpt,raɪtə'] N sceneggiatore(-trice), soggettista *m/f*.

scroll [skrəʊl] 1 N (*roll of parchment*) rotolo (di pergamena); (*ancient manuscript*) papiro, pergamena; (*Archit*) voluta.

2 VT (*Comput: text*) far scorrere su video.

scro·tum ['skrəʊtəm] N (*pl* **scrota** *or* **scrotums**) scroto.

scrounge [skraʊndʒ] (*fam*) 1 N: **to be on the scrounge (for sth)** scroccare (qc); **here he comes, on the scrounge again** eccolo, il solito scroccone.

2 VT (*gen*) scroccare; **to scrounge sth off** *or* **from sb** scroccare qc a qn.

3 VI: **to scrounge on** *or* **off sb** vivere alle spalle di qn.

scroung·er ['skraʊndʒə'] N (*fam*) scroccone(-a); (*on society*) parassita *m*.

scrub¹ [skrʌb] N (*brushwood*) macchia.
scrub² [skrʌb] [1] N (*clean*) strofinata.
　[2] VT **a** (*clean*) strofinare con lo spazzolone; (*hands etc*) pulire con lo spazzolino; **to scrub sth clean** pulire qc strofinandolo(-a)
　b (*fam: cancel*) annullare; (: *holiday, plan*) cancellare
▶ **scrub down** VT + ADV (*room, wall*) pulire a fondo con lo spazzolone
▶ **scrub off** VT + ADV (*mark, stain*) togliere strofinando
▶ **scrub up** VI + ADV (*doctor etc*) lavarsi le mani.
scrub·ber¹ [ˈskrʌbəʳ] N (*also:* **pan-scrubber**) paglietta di ferro.
scrub·ber² [ˈskrʌbəʳ] N (*Brit, Aust fam pej*) puttanella (*fam!*)
scrubbing-brush [ˈskrʌbɪŋˌbrʌʃ] N spazzolone *m.*
scruff [skrʌf] N **a** : **by the scruff of the neck** per la collottola **b** (*fam: untidy person*) sciattone(-a).
scruffi·ness [ˈskrʌfɪnɪs] N (*of appearance, person, clothes*) trasandatezza, sciatteria.
scruffy [ˈskrʌfɪ] ADJ (*comp* **-ier,** *superl* **-iest**) (*person, clothes, appearance*) trasandato(-a), sciatto(-a); (*building*) squallido(-a); (*paintwork*) malandato(-a).
scrum [skrʌm], **scrum·mage** [ˈskrʌmɪdʒ] N (*Rugby*) mischia; **loose/set scrum** mischia aperta/chiusa.
♦ **scrum half** N mediano di mischia.
scrump·tious [ˈskrʌmpʃəs] ADJ (*fam: food, smell*) delizioso (-a).
scrunch [skrʌntʃ] = **crunch.**
scru·ple [ˈskruːpl] N scrupolo; **to have no scruples about doing sth** non avere scrupoli a fare qc.
scru·pu·lous [ˈskruːpjʊləs] ADJ scrupoloso(-a).
scru·pu·lous·ly [ˈskruːpjʊləslɪ] ADV scrupolosamente; **he tries to be scrupulously fair/honest** cerca di essere più imparziale/onesto che può.
scru·pu·lous·ness [ˈskruːpjʊləsnɪs] N scrupolosità.
scru·ti·nize [ˈskruːtɪˌnaɪz] VT (*work etc*) esaminare accuratamente; (*person's face*) scrutare; (*votes*) scrutinare.
scru·ti·ny [ˈskruːtɪnɪ] N esame *m* accurato; (*Pol: of votes*) scrutinio; **under the scrutiny of sb** sotto la sorveglianza di qn; **it does not stand up to scrutiny** non regge ad un esame accurato.
scu·ba [ˈskuːbə] N autorespiratore *m.*
♦ **scuba diving** N immersioni *fpl* subacquee (*con autorespiratore*).
scud [skʌd] VI: **clouds were scudding across the sky** (*liter*) le nuvole si rincorrevano nel cielo.
scuff [skʌf] VT (*shoes*) scorticare; (*floor*) segnare; (*feet*) strascicare.
scuf·fle [ˈskʌfl] [1] N tafferuglio, zuffa.
　[2] VI: **to scuffle (with sb)** venire alle mani *or* azzuffarsi (con qn).
scull [skʌl] [1] N bratto.
　[2] VI, VT vogare (a bratto).
scul·lery [ˈskʌlərɪ] N retrocucina *m or f inv.*
scul·ling [ˈskʌlɪŋ] N: **to go sculling** remare.
sculpt [skʌlpt] VT, VI scolpire.
sculp·tor [ˈskʌlptəʳ] N scultore *m.*
sculp·tress [ˈskʌlptrɪs] N scultrice *f.*
sculp·ture [ˈskʌlptʃəʳ] [1] N scultura.
　[2] VT, VI scolpire.
scum [skʌm] N (*on liquid*) schiuma; (*fig pej: people*) feccia; **the scum of the earth** la feccia della società; **to remove the scum (from sth)** schiumare (qc).
scup·per [ˈskʌpəʳ] VT (*Naut*) autoaffondare; (*Brit fig: plan*) far naufragare.

scurf [skɜːf] N forfora.
scur·ril·ity [skəˈrɪlɪtɪ] N (*frm*) scurrilità.
scur·ril·ous [ˈskʌrɪləs] ADJ (*remark*) scurrile; (*attack*) di bassa lega.
scur·ri·lous·ly [ˈskʌrɪləslɪ] ADV in modo scurrile.
scur·ry [ˈskʌrɪ] VI: **to scurry along/away** etc procedere/andarsene etc a tutta velocità.
scur·vy [ˈskɜːvɪ] N scorbuto.
scut·tle¹ [ˈskʌtl] [1] VT (*ship*) autoaffondare.
　[2] N **a** (*Naut*) portellino **b** (*also:* **coal scuttle**) secchio del carbone.
scut·tle² [ˈskʌtl] VI: **to scuttle away** *or* **off** filare via; **to scuttle in** entrare precipitosamente.
Scylla [ˈsɪlə] N Scilla.
scythe [saɪð] [1] N falce *f.*
　[2] VT falciare.
SD ABBR (*Am Post*)= *South Dakota.*
SDI [ˌɛsdiːˈaɪ] N ABBR (= *Strategic Defense Initiative*) programma di difesa strategica spaziale.
SDLP [ˌɛsdiːɛlˈpiː] N ABBR (*Brit Pol*)= *Social Democratic and Labour Party.*
SDP [ˌɛsdiːˈpiː] N ABBR (*Brit Pol*)= *Social Democratic Party.*
SE [ˌɛsˈiː] ABBR (= *South East(ern)*) SE.
sea [siː] [1] N mare *m*; **by** *or* **beside the sea** (*holiday*) al mare; (*village*) sul mare; **on the sea** (*boat*) sul mare, in mare; (*village, town*) sul mare; **to go by sea** andare per mare; **to go to sea** (*person*) diventare marinaio; **to put to sea** (*sailor*) uscire in mare; (*boat*) salpare; **to spend 3 years at sea** passare 3 anni in mare; **(out) at sea** al largo; **to look out to sea** guardare il mare; **heavy** *or* **rough sea(s)** mare grosso *or* agitato; **to be all at sea** (about *or* with sth) (*fig*) non capirci niente (di qc); **a sea of faces** (*fig*) una marea di gente.
　[2] ADJ (*salt*) marino(-a); (*fish, air*) di mare; (*route, transport, port*) marittimo(-a); (*battle, power*) navale.
♦ **sea anchor** N ancora galleggiante.
♦ **sea anemone** N anemone *m* di mare, attinia.
♦ **sea bathing** N bagni *mpl* di mare.
♦ **sea bed** N fondale *m* marino.
♦ **sea bird** N uccello marino.
sea·board [ˈsiːˌbɔːd] N litorale *m.*
sea·borne [ˈsiːˌbɔːn] ADJ via mare; **the arrival of seaborne reinforcements** l'arrivo di rinforzi via mare.
♦ **sea breeze** N brezza marina.
♦ **sea captain** N capitano di lungo corso (*nella marina mercantile*).
♦ **sea coast** N costa.
♦ **sea dog** N (*sometimes hum*) lupo di mare.
sea·farer [ˈsiːˌfɛərəʳ] N navigatore *m*, navigante *m.*
sea·faring [ˈsiːˌfɛərɪŋ] ADJ (*community*) marinaro(-a); (*life*) da marinaio.
♦ **sea floor** N fondo marino.
♦ **sea·floor spread·ing** [ˌsiːflɔːˈsprɛdɪŋ] N (*Geog*) espansione *f* del fondo marino.
sea·food [ˈsiːˌfuːd] N frutti *mpl* di mare.
♦ **sea front** N lungomare *m.*
sea·going [ˈsiːˌɡəʊɪŋ] ADJ (*nation*) marinaro(-a); (*ship*) d'alto mare.
♦ **sea-green** [ˌsiːˈɡriːn] ADJ verde mare *inv.*
sea·gull [ˈsiːˌɡʌl] N gabbiano.
♦ **sea horse** N cavalluccio marino.
seal¹ [siːl] N (*Zool*) foca.
seal² [siːl] [1] N (*gen*) sigillo; (*on parcel*) piombino; (*of door, lid*) chiusura ermetica; **to set one's seal to sth** [OR] **to give the** *or* **one's seal of approval to sth** dare il proprio

beneplacito a qc; **to set the seal on** (*bargain*) concludere; (*friendship*) suggellare.

2 VT **a** (*put seal on: document*) sigillare; (*close: envelope*) chiudere, incollare; (: *jar, tin*) chiudere ermeticamente; (*Culin: meat*) rosolare; **my lips are sealed** (*fig*) sarò una tomba

b (*decide: sb's fate*) segnare; (: *bargain*) concludere

► **seal off** VT + ADV (*close up: building, room*) sigillare; (*forbid entry to: area*) bloccare l'accesso a

► **seal up** VT + ADV (*parcel*) sigillare; (*jar, door*) chiudere ermeticamente.

♦ **sea lane** N linea marittima, rotta.

sealed-bid [ˌsiːldˈbɪd] ADJ (*Comm*): **sealed-bid tender** offerta in busta chiusa.

♦ **sea legs** NPL: **to find one's sea legs** abituarsi al mare.

seal·er ['siːlə'] N nave *f* per la caccia alle foche.

♦ **sea level** N livello del mare.

seal·ing ['siːlɪŋ] N (*seal hunting*) caccia alla foca.

seal·ing wax ['siːlɪŋˌwæks] N ceralacca.

♦ **sea lion** N leone *m* marino, otaria.

♦ **sea loch** N braccio di mare.

seal·skin ['siːlˌskɪn] N pelle *f* di foca.

seam [siːm] N **a** (*Sewing*) cucitura; (*Welding*) saldatura; **to come apart at the seams** scucirsi; **my dress is bursting at the seams** scoppio dentro questo vestito; **the hall was bursting at the seams** (*fig*) l'aula era piena zeppa **b** (*Geol: of coal*) filone *m*, vena.

sea·man ['siːmən] N (*pl* **-men**) marinaio.

sea·man·ship ['siːmənʃɪp] N tecnica di navigazione.

seam·less ['siːmlɪs] ADJ senza cucitura.

seam·stress ['sɛmstrɪs] N sarta.

seamy ['siːmɪ] ADJ (*comp* **-ier**, *superl* **-iest**) (*fam: district*) malfamato(-a); **the seamy side of life** gli aspetti più squallidi della vita.

se·ance, **sé·ance** ['seɪɑ̃ːns] N seduta spiritica.

♦ **sea pink** N (*Bot*) statice.

sea·plane ['siːˌpleɪn] N idrovolante *m*.

sea·port ['siːˌpɔːt] N porto di mare *or* marittimo.

sear [sɪə'] VT (*Culin: meat*) scottare; (*scorch*) bruciare.

search [sɜːtʃ] **1** N **a** (*for sth lost*) ricerca; **in search of** alla ricerca di; **to make a search for sb/sth** fare delle ricerche per trovare qn/qc

b (*of person, building etc*) perquisizione *f*; **to carry out a search of sth** (*subj: police, customs official*) eseguire una perquisizione di qc; (: *thief*) frugare in qc

c (*Comput*) ricerca; **"search and replace"** "ricerca e sostituzione".

2 VT **a**: **to search (for)** (*subj: police etc*) perquisire (alla ricerca di); (: *thief*) frugare (alla ricerca di); (*area, woods etc*) perlustrare *or* setacciare (alla ricerca di); **the police searched him for drugs** la polizia l'ha perquisito alla ricerca di droga; **search me!** (*fig fam*) e che ne so io?

b (*scan: records, documents, photograph*) esaminare minuziosamente; (: *notice-board, newspaper*) leggere attentamente; (: *Comput*) ricercare; (: *one's conscience*) interrogare; (: *one's memory*) frugare in; **he searched her face for some sign of affection** scrutava il suo viso in cerca di un segno di affetto.

3 VI **a** (*gen*) cercare; **to search after** *or* **for sb/sth** cercare qn/qc; **to search through** *or* **in sth for sth** frugare *or* rovistare qc alla ricerca di qc

b (*Comput*): **to search for** ricercare

► **search out** VT + ADV scovare; **the library eventually searched out the book I wanted** la biblioteca alla fine ha rintracciato il libro che cercavo.

search·er ['sɜːtʃə'] N chi cerca.

search·ing ['sɜːtʃɪŋ] ADJ (*look*) indagatore(-trice); (*examination*) minuzioso(-a); (*question*) pressante.

search·light ['sɜːtʃˌlaɪt] N riflettore *m*.

♦ **search party** N squadra di soccorso.

♦ **search warrant** N mandato di perquisizione.

sear·ing ['sɪərɪŋ] ADJ (*heat*) rovente; (*pain*) acuto(-a).

sea·scape ['siːˌskeɪp] N (*Art*) paesaggio marino.

sea·shell ['siːˌʃɛl] N conchiglia.

sea·shore ['siːˌʃɔː'] N riva del mare; **by the seashore** in riva al mare; **on the seashore** sulla riva del mare.

sea·sick ['siːˌsɪk] ADJ: **to be seasick** avere *or* soffrire il mal di mare.

sea·sick·ness ['siːˌsɪknɪs] N mal *m* di mare.

sea·side ['siːˌsaɪd] **1** N: **at the seaside** al mare; **to go to the seaside** andare al mare.

2 ADJ (*town*) di mare; (*holiday*) al mare.

♦ **seaside resort** N centro *or* stazione *f* balneare.

♦ **sea slug** N lumaca di mare.

sea·son ['siːzn] **1** N (*gen*) stagione *f*; **to be in/out of season** essere di/fuori stagione; **the Christmas season** il periodo natalizio; **"Season's Greetings"** "Buone Feste"; **the busy season** (*for shops*) il periodo di punta; (*for hotels etc*) l'alta stagione; **football/fishing season** stagione calcistica/della pesca; **the open season** (*Hunting*) la stagione della caccia; **it's against the law to hunt during the closed season** è proibito dalla legge andare a caccia quando la stagione è chiusa; **in season** (*Zool*) in calore.

2 VT **a** (*wood*) stagionare

b (*Culin*) condire.

sea·son·able ['siːznəbl] ADJ (*weather*) di stagione; (*advice*) opportuno(-a).

sea·son·al ['siːzənl] ADJ stagionale; **after seasonal adjustment** (*Econ*) dopo la destagionalizzazione.

sea·soned ['siːznd] ADJ (*wood*) stagionato(-a); (*fig: worker, troops*) con esperienza; (: *actor*) consumato(-a); **a seasoned campaigner** un(a) veterano(-a).

sea·son·ing ['siːznɪŋ] N condimento.

♦ **season ticket** N (*Theatre, Rail etc*) abbonamento.

seat [siːt] **1** N **a** (*chair*) sedia; (*in theatre etc*) posto; (*in bus, train, car etc*) posto, sedile *m*; (*on cycle*) sella, sellino; **are there any seats left?** ci sono posti?; **to take one's seat** prendere posto; **do take a seat** prego, si accomodi; **to take a back seat** (*fig*) restare in secondo piano

b (*Pol*) seggio; **to keep/lose one's seat** essere/non essere rieletto(-a); **to win four seats from the nationalists** strappare quattro seggi ai nazionalisti; **to take one's seat in the (House of) Commons** iniziare la propria carriera di parlamentare

c (*of chair*) sedile *m*; (*buttocks*) didietro; (*of trousers*) fondo

d (*centre: of government etc, of infection*) sede *f*; (: *of learning*) centro

e (*Horse-riding*) assetto.

2 VT **a** (*person etc*) far sedere; **to be seated** essere seduto(-a); **please be seated** accomodatevi per favore; **please remain seated** rimanete ai vostri posti per cortesia

b (*subj: hall, cinema etc*) essere fornito(-a) di posti a sedere per.

♦ **seat belt** N (*Aut, Aer*) cintura di sicurezza.

♦ **seat cover** N (*Aut*) coprisedile *m*.

-seater ['siːtə'] SUFF: **a three-seater settee** un divano a tre posti.

seat·ing ['si:tɪŋ] N posti *mpl* a sedere.
♦ **seating arrangements** NPL sistemazione *fsg* or disposizione *fsg* dei posti.
♦ **seating capacity** N posti *mpl* a sedere.
SEATO ['si:təʊ] N ABBR (= *South East Asia Treaty Organization*) S.E.A.T.O. *f.*
♦ **sea urchin** N riccio di mare.
♦ **sea wall** N diga marittima.
sea·wards ['si:wədz] ADV verso il mare.
♦ **sea water** N acqua di mare.
sea·way ['si:ˌweɪ] N rotta marittima.
sea·weed ['si:ˌwi:d] N alghe *fpl*; **a strand of seaweed** un'alga.
sea·worthiness ['si:ˌwɜ:ðmɪs] N idoneità alla navigazione.
sea·worthy ['si:ˌwɜ:ðɪ] ADJ idoneo(-a) alla navigazione.
se·ba·ceous [sɪ'beɪʃəs] ADJ sebaceo(-a).
se·bum ['si:bəm] N sebo.
SEC [ˌɛsi:'si:] N ABBR (*Am*: = *Securities and Exchange Commission*) *commissione di controllo sulle operazioni in Borsa.*
sec [sɛk] N (*fam*) attimo, secondo.
Sec. ABBR = *Secretary*.
sec. ABBR = **second**.
se·cant ['si:kənt] N secante *f.*
seca·teurs [ˌsɛkə'tɜ:z] NPL cesoie *fpl.*
se·cede [sɪ'si:d] VI (*frm*): **to secede (from)** staccarsi (da).
se·ces·sion [sɪ'sɛʃən] N (*frm*): **secession (from)** secessione *f* (da).
se·clud·ed [sɪ'klu:dɪd] ADJ (*house*) appartato(-a), isolato (-a); (*life*) ritirato(-a).
se·clu·sion [sɪ'klu:ʒən] N isolamento; **to live in seclusion** fare vita ritirata.
sec·ond¹ [*adj, adv, n, vt a* 'sɛkənd; *vt b* sɪ'kɒnd] ☐ ADJ secondo(-a); **he's a second Beethoven** è un nuovo Beethoven; **give him a second chance** dagli un'altra opportunità; **second floor** (*Brit*) secondo piano; (*Am*) primo piano; **in second gear** (*Aut*) in seconda; **to ask for a second opinion** (*Med*) chiedere un altro consulto; **second person** (*Gram*) seconda persona; **Charles the Second** Carlo II; **every second day/week** ogni due giorni/settimane; **to be second to none** non essere inferiore a nessuno; **to have second thoughts (about doing sth)** avere dei ripensamenti (quanto a fare qc); **we had second thoughts about it** ci abbiamo ripensato; **on second thoughts ...** ripensandoci meglio....
☐ ADV **a** (*in race, competition etc*) al secondo posto; **to come second** arrivare secondo(-a), piazzarsi al secondo posto; **it's the second largest fish I've ever caught** ho preso soltanto un pesce più grosso di questo, finora
b (*secondly*) in secondo luogo, secondo.
☐ N **a** (*Boxing, in duel*) secondo
b : **in second** (*Aut*) in seconda
c : **he came a good second** (*in race*) è arrivato secondo con un buon tempo; **he came a poor second** è arrivato secondo ma con notevole scarto
d (*Brit Univ*) ≈ laurea con punteggio discreto
e (*Comm: imperfect goods*): **seconds** NPL merce *fsg* di seconda scelta
f (*fam: second helping*): **seconds** NPL bis *m inv.*
☐ VT **a** (*motion, statement*) appoggiare; **I'll second that** (*fig*) l'appoggio, sono a favore
b (*Brit: employee*) distaccare.
sec·ond² ['sɛkənd] N (*in time, Geog, Math*) (minuto) secondo; **at that very second** (proprio) in quell'istante;

just a second! un attimo!; **it won't take a second** ci vuole un attimo.
sec·ond·ary ['sɛkəndərɪ] ADJ secondario(-a); **secondary sector** (*Industry*) settore *m* secondario.
♦ **secondary modern (school)** N (*Brit*) *scuola media superiore ad indirizzo tecnico, ora non più esistente.*
♦ **secondary picket** N picchetto di solidarietà.
♦ **secondary school** N scuola secondaria (*inferiore e superiore, per ragazzi dagli 11 ai 18 anni*).
♦ **second-best** [ˌsɛkənd'bɛst] ☐ N ripiego; **as a second-best** in mancanza di meglio.
☐ ADV: **to come off second-best** avere la peggio.
♦ **second childhood** N seconda infanzia.
♦ **second-class** [ˌsɛkənd'klɑ:s] ☐ ADJ **a** (*mail*) ordinario (-a); (*ticket, carriage*) di seconda classe **b** (*pej: goods, quality*) scadente.
☐ ADV: **to send sth second-class** spedire qc per posta ordinaria; **to travel second-class** viaggiare in seconda classe.
♦ **second-class citizen** N cittadino di serie B.
♦ **second cousin** N cugino(-a) di secondo grado.
sec·ond·er ['sɛkəndə'] N sostenitore(-trice).
♦ **second-guess** [ˌsɛkənd'gɛs] VT (*esp Am fam: predict*) anticipare; (: *after the event*) giudicare col senno di poi.
♦ **second-hand** [ˌsɛkənd'hænd] ☐ ADJ di seconda mano, usato(-a); **second-hand bookshop** negozio di libri usati.
☐ ADV: **to buy sth second-hand** comprare qc di seconda mano; **second-hand news** notizie *fpl* di seconda mano; **to hear sth second-hand** venire a sapere qc da terze persone.
♦ **second hand** N lancetta dei secondi.
♦ **second-in-command** [ˌsɛkəndɪnkə'mɑ:nd] N (*Mil*) comandante *m* in seconda; (*Admin*) aggiunto.
sec·ond·ly ['sɛkəndlɪ] ADV secondo, in secondo luogo, secondariamente.
se·cond·ment [sɪ'kɒndmənt] N (*Brit: of employee*) distaccamento.
♦ **second nature** N: **to be second nature to sb** essere naturale per qn; **it was second nature for him to help his friends** gli veniva naturale aiutare gli amici.
♦ **second-rate** [ˌsɛkənd'reɪt] ADJ di second'ordine, scadente.
♦ **second sight** N chiaroveggenza; **to have second sight** essere chiaroveggente.
♦ **Second World War** N: **the Second World War** la seconda guerra mondiale.
se·cre·cy ['si:krəsɪ] N segretezza; **there's no secrecy about ...** non si fa mistero di...; **in secrecy** in segreto, in tutta segretezza.
se·cret ['si:krɪt] ☐ ADJ segreto(-a); **to keep sth secret (from sb)** tenere qc nascosto (a qn); **keep it secret** che rimanga un segreto.
☐ N segreto; **to keep a secret** mantenere un segreto; **to let sb into a secret** mettere qn a parte di un segreto, confidare un segreto a qn; **to make no secret of sth** non far mistero di qc; **to do sth in secret** fare qc in segreto *or* segretamente.
♦ **secret agent** N agente *m* segreto.
sec·re·taire [ˌsɛkrɪ'tɛə'] N secrétaire *m inv.*
sec·re·tar·ial [ˌsɛkrə'tɛərɪəl] ADJ (*work*) di segreteria; (*college, course*) di segretariato.
sec·re·tari·at [ˌsɛkrə'tɛərɪət] N segretariato.
sec·re·tary ['sɛkrətrɪ] N segretario(-a).
♦ **secretary-general** [ˌsɛkrətrɪ'dʒɛnərəl] N segretario generale.

♦ **Secretary of State** N (*Brit*) ministro; (*Am*) segretario di Stato, ≈ ministro degli Esteri; **Secretary of State for Education** (*Brit*) ministro della Pubblica Istruzione.

se·crete [sɪ'kriːt] VT a (*Med, Anat, Bio*) secernere b (*frm: hide*) nascondere.

se·cre·tion [sɪ'kriːʃən] N secrezione *f*.

se·cre·tive ['siːkrətɪv] ADJ riservato(-a); **to be secretive about sth** essere riservato(-a) a proposito di qc.

se·cret·ly ['siːkrətlɪ] ADV in segreto, segretamente.

♦ **secret police** N: **the secret police** la polizia segreta.

♦ **Secret Service** N (*Am*): **the Secret Service** i servizi segreti.

sect [sɛkt] N setta.

sec·tar·ian [sɛk'tɛərɪən] ADJ settario(-a).

sec·tari·an·ism [sɛk'tɛərɪə,nɪzəm] N settarismo.

sec·tion ['sɛkʃən] 1 N a (*part: gen*) sezione *f*, parte *f*; (*of community, population*) settore *m*, fascia; (: *of town: esp Am*) quartiere *m*; (*of document, law etc*) articolo; (*of pipeline, road etc*) tratto; (*of machine, furniture*) pezzo; **the business section** (*Press*) la pagina economica
b (*department*) sezione *f*
c (*cut*) sezione *f*; **vertical section** sezione verticale, spaccato.
2 VT (*cut*) sezionare, dividere in sezioni.

sec·tion·al ['sɛkʃənl] ADJ a (*bookcase etc*) scomponibile, smontabile b (*interests*) settoriale c (*drawing etc*) in sezione.

sec·tor ['sɛktə'] N (*gen*) settore *m*; (*Geom*) settore *m* circolare.

secu·lar ['sɛkjʊlə'] ADJ (*authority, school*) laico(-a); (*writings, music*) profano(-a); (*clergy*) secolare.

secu·lar·ism ['sɛkjʊlə,rɪzəm] N secolarismo.

secu·lar·ize ['sɛkjʊlə,raɪz] VT secolarizzare.

se·cure [sɪ'kjʊə'] 1 ADJ (*comp* **-r,** *superl* **-st**) a (*firm: knot*) saldo(-a), sicuro(-a); (: *nail*) ben piantato(-a); (: *rope*) ben fissato(-a); (: *door*) ben chiuso(-a); (: *ladder, chair*) stabile; (: *hold*) saldo(-a); **to make sth secure** fissare bene qc
b (*safe: place, container*) sicuro(-a); (*certain: career, success*) assicurato(-a); (*victory*) certo(-a); **secure from** *or* **against sth** al sicuro da qc
c (*free from anxiety*) sicuro(-a), tranquillo(-a); **to rest secure in the knowledge that ...** stare tranquillo(-a) sapendo che....
2 VT a (*fix: rope*) assicurare; (: *door, window*) chiudere bene; (*tie up: person, animal*) legare
b (*make safe*): **to secure (from** *or* **against)** proteggere (da)
c (*frm: obtain: job, staff etc*) assicurarsi; **to secure sth for sb** procurare qc per *or* a qn
d (*Fin: loan*) garantire.

se·cured credi·tor [sɪ,kʊəd'krɛdɪtə'] N (*Fin*) creditore *m* privilegiato.

se·cure·ly [sɪ'kjʊəlɪ] ADV (*firmly*) saldamente, bene; (*safely*) in modo sicuro.

se·cu·rity [sɪ'kjʊərɪtɪ] N a (*safety, stability*) sicurezza; **job security** sicurezza dell'impiego; **security of tenure** garanzia di titolo *or* di godimento; (*in job*) garanzia del posto di lavoro; (*in property*): **they have security of tenure** non possono essere sfrattati fino al termine del contratto
b (*against theft etc*) misure *fpl* di sicurezza; **to increase/ tighten security** aumentare/intensificare la sorveglianza
c (*Fin: on loan*) garanzia; **to lend money on security** prestare denaro su *or* dietro garanzia
d (*Stock Exchange*): **securities** NPL titoli *mpl*.

♦ **security check** N controllo di sicurezza.

♦ **Security Council** N: **the Security Council** il Consiglio di Sicurezza.

♦ **security forces** NPL forze *fpl* dell'ordine.

♦ **security guard** N guardia giurata.

♦ **security leak** N fuga di notizie.

♦ **security police** NPL servizi *mpl* di sicurezza.

♦ **security risk** N *persona che costituisce una minaccia per la sicurezza dello stato*.

secy. ABBR = **secretary**.

se·dan [sɪ'dæn] N (*Am Aut*) berlina.

♦ **sedan chair** N (*Hist*) portantina.

se·date [sɪ'deɪt] 1 ADJ posato(-a), pacato(-a).
2 VT (*Med*) somministrare sedativi a.

se·date·ly [sɪ'deɪtlɪ] ADV in modo posato.

se·da·tion [sɪ'deɪʃən] N (*Med*): **to be under sedation** essere sotto l'effetto di sedativi.

seda·tive ['sɛdətɪv] 1 ADJ calmante, sedativo(-a).
2 N sedativo, calmante *m*.

sed·en·tary ['sɛdntrɪ] ADJ sedentario(-a).

sedi·ment ['sɛdɪmənt] N (*in liquids, boiler*) deposito, fondo; (*Geol*) sedimento.

sedi·men·tary [,sɛdɪ'mɛntərɪ] ADJ sedimentario(-a).

se·di·tion [sə'dɪʃən] N sedizione *f*.

se·di·tious [sə'dɪʃəs] ADJ sedizioso(-a).

se·di·tious·ly [sə'dɪʃəslɪ] ADV sediziosamente.

se·duce [sɪ'djuːs] VT sedurre.

se·duc·er [sɪ'djuːsə'] N seduttore(-trice).

se·duc·tion [sɪ'dʌkʃən] N seduzione *f*.

se·duc·tive [sɪ'dʌktɪv] ADJ (*gen*) seducente; (*dress*) sexy *inv*; (*offer*) allettante.

se·duc·tive·ly [sɪ'dʌktɪvlɪ] ADV in modo seducente.

sedu·lous ['sɛdjʊləs] ADJ (*frm*) diligente.

se·dum ['siːdəm] N (*Bot*) sedo.

see[1] [siː] (*pt* **saw**, *pp* **seen**) VT, VI a (*gen*) vedere; **I can't see him** non lo vedo; **I saw him writing the letter** l'ho visto scrivere *or* mentre scriveva la lettera; **I saw him write the letter** l'ho visto scrivere la lettera; **there was nobody to be seen** non c'era anima viva; **I can't see to read** non ci vedo abbastanza per leggere; **let me see** (*show me*) fammi vedere; (*let me think*) vediamo (un po'); **can you see your way to helping us?** (*fig*) puoi trovare il modo di aiutarci?; **to go and see sb** andare a trovare qn; **see you soon/later/tomorrow!** a presto/più tardi/domani!; **now see here!** (*in anger*) ma insomma!; **so I see** sì, vedo; **see for yourself!** guarda qua!; **as you can see** come vedi; **I must be seeing things** (*fam*) devo avere le allucinazioni *or* le traveggole; **I see in the paper that ...** vedo che sul giornale è scritto che...; **I see nothing wrong in it** non ci trovo niente di male; **I don't know what she sees in him** non so che cosa ci trova in lui; **(go and) see who it is** vai a vedere chi è, vedi chi è; **this car has seen better days** questa macchina ha conosciuto tempi migliori; **I never thought I'd see the day when ...** non avrei mai creduto che un giorno...
b (*understand, perceive*) vedere, capire; (: *joke*) afferrare; **to see the funny side of sth** vedere il lato comico di qc; **I see!** capisco!; **I don't** *or* **can't see how/why** *etc* ... non vedo come/perché *etc*...; **as far as I can see** da quanto posso vedere; **the way I see it** a parer mio, a mio giudizio
c (*accompany*) accompagnare; **to see sb to the door/ home** accompagnare qn alla porta/a casa

d (*ensure, check*) vedere, assicurarsi; **to see if ...** vedere se...+ *indic*; **to see that ...** vedere *or* badare che...+ *sub*; **see that he has all he needs** vedi che non gli manchi nulla; **I'll see that he gets it** farò in modo che lo riceva

e (*imagine*) vedere; **I can just see him as a teacher** lo vedo benissimo nei panni dell'insegnante; **I can't see myself as ...** non mi vedo come...; **I can't see him winning** non credo che lui vincerà

▶ **see about** VI + PREP **a** (*deal with*) occuparsi di

b (*consider*): **I'll see about it** ci penserò, vedrò; **we'll see about it** si vedrà; **we'll see about that!** (*iro*) vedremo!

▶ **see in** VT + ADV: **to see the New Year in** festeggiare l'Anno Nuovo

▶ **see off** VT + ADV salutare alla partenza

▶ **see out** VT + ADV (*person*) accompagnare alla porta; **I'll see myself out** (*fam*) non c'è bisogno che mi accompagni; **I'm afraid she won't see the week out** (*survive*) temo che non passerà la settimana

▶ **see over, see round** VI + PREP (*visit*) visitare

▶ **see through** 1 VI + PREP (*promises, behaviour*) non lasciarsi ingannare da; **I finally saw through him** finalmente ho capito che tipo è.

2 VT + ADV (*project, deal*) portare a termine; **we'll see him through** lo aiuteremo noi.

3 VT + PREP: **£100 will see him through the week** 100 sterline gli basteranno ad arrivare alla fine della settimana

▶ **see to** VI + PREP (*deal with*) occuparsi di; (: *work-load*) sbrigare; (*mend*) mettere a posto; **please see to it that you lock all doors** si assicuri di aver chiuso tutte le porte.

see² [si:] N (*Rel*) sede *f* vescovile; **the Holy See** la Santa Sede.

seed [si:d] 1 N **a** (*Bot*) seme *m*; (*for sowing*) semi *mpl*, semente *f*; **to go** *or* **run to seed** (*plant*) fare seme; **to go to seed** (*fig: person*) ridursi male

b (*fig: origin*): **the seeds of** il seme di, il germe di; **the seeds of discontent** il seme del malcontento

c (*Tennis: player*) testa di serie.

2 VT **a** (*lawn etc*) seminare

b (*remove the seed: raisins, grapes*) togliere i semi a

c (*Tennis*): **he was seeded fifth** è stato classificato quinta testa di serie.

3 VI fare seme.

4 ADJ (*potato, corn*) da semina.

seed·bed ['si:d‚bɛd] N semenzaio.

seed·less ['si:dlɪs] ADJ senza semi.

seed·ling ['si:dlɪŋ] N semenzale *m*.

♦ **seed pearls** NPL semenza *fsg*.

seedy ['si:dɪ] ADJ (*comp* **-ier,** *superl* **-iest**) (*fam: sordid, shabby*) squallido(-a); **I feel decidedly seedy today** non mi sento affatto bene oggi.

see·ing ['si:ɪŋ] CONJ: **seeing (that)** visto che.

seek [si:k] (*pt, pp* **sought**) 1 VT (*gen*): **to seek (sth/to do sth)** cercare (qc/di fare qc); **to seek shelter (from)** cercar riparo (da); **to seek one's fortune** cercar fortuna; **to seek advice/help from sb** chiedere consiglio/aiuto a qn.

2 VI: **to seek after, seek for** cercare

▶ **seek out** VT + ADV (*person*) andare a cercare.

seek·er ['si:kə'] N cercatore(-trice).

seem [si:m] VI sembrare, parere; **she seems capable** sembra (essere) in gamba; **he seemed to be in difficulty** sembrava (trovarsi) in difficoltà; **she seems to know you** sembra *or* pare che lei ti conosca; **she seems not to want**

to leave non dà segno di voler andar via; **I seemed to be sinking** mi sembrava di affondare; **I seem to have heard that before** questa mi pare di averla già sentita; **I can't seem to do it** a quanto pare non ci riesco; **how did he seem to you?** come ti è sembrato?; **it seems (that) ...** sembra *or* pare che...+ *sub*; **so it seems** così pare *or* sembra; **it seems not** pare di no; **it seems you're right** pare che tu abbia ragione; **it seems ages since ...** mi sembra una vita da quando...; **what seems to be the trouble?** cosa c'è che non va?; **there seems to be a mistake** ci dev'essere un errore, sembra *or* pare che ci sia un errore; **she died yesterday, it seems** pare che sia morta ieri; **I did what seemed best** ho fatto quello che sembrava più opportuno.

seem·ing ['si:mɪŋ] ADJ apparente.

seem·ing·ly ['si:mɪŋlɪ] ADV (*evidently*) a quanto pare; (*from appearances*) in apparenza, apparentemente.

seem·ly ['si:mlɪ] ADJ (*comp* **-ier,** *superl* **-iest**) (*frm: behaviour, language, dress*) decoroso(-a).

seen [si:n] PP of **see¹**.

seep [si:p] VI: **to seep (through/from/into)** filtrare (attraverso/da/in *or* dentro)

▶ **seep away** VI + ADV scolare a poco a poco

▶ **seep in** VI + ADV infiltrarsi

▶ **seep out** VI + ADV trapelare.

seep·age ['si:pɪdʒ] N infiltrazione *f*.

seer [sɪə'] N (*old, liter*) veggente *m/f*.

seer·sucker ['sɪə‚sʌkə'] N crespo di cotone a strisce.

see·saw ['si:‚sɔ:] 1 N altalena (a bilico).

2 VI (*fig*) oscillare.

seethe [si:ð] VI (*liquid*) ribollire, gorgogliare; (*street*): **to seethe (with)** brulicare (di); **to seethe** *or* **be seething with anger** schiumare *or* fremere di rabbia.

♦ **see-through** ['si:‚θru:] ADJ trasparente.

seg·ment [*n* 'sɛgmənt; *vb* ‚sɛg'mɛnt] 1 N (*section*) parte *f*; (*of orange*) spicchio; (*Geom*) segmento circolare; **line segment** (*Geom*) segmento.

2 VT segmentare.

seg·men·ta·tion [‚sɛgmɛn'teɪʃən] N segmentazione *f*.

seg·re·gate ['sɛgrɪ‚geɪt] VT: **to segregate (from)** separare (da), segregare (da).

seg·re·ga·ted ['sɛgrɪ‚geɪtɪd] ADJ (*Pol*) in cui vige la segregazione.

seg·re·ga·tion [‚sɛgrɪ'geɪʃən] N segregazione *f*.

seg·re·ga·tion·ist [‚sɛgrɪ'geɪʃnɪst] ADJ, N segregazionista (*m/f*).

Seine [sɛn] N: **the Seine** la Senna.

seis·mic ['saɪzmɪk] ADJ sismico(-a).

seis·mo·graph ['saɪzmə‚grɑ:f] N sismografo.

seis·mol·ogy [saɪz'mɒlədʒɪ] N sismologia.

seize [si:z] VT (*clutch, grasp*) afferrare; (*Mil, Law: person, territory, power*) prendere; (: *articles*) sequestrare; (*opportunity*) cogliere; **to seize hold of sth/sb** afferrare qc/qn; **he was seized with a fit of coughing** gli è venuto un accesso di tosse; **she was seized with fear/rage** è stata presa dalla paura/rabbia; **I was seized by the desire to laugh** mi è venuta una gran voglia di ridere

▶ **seize on, seize upon** VI + PREP (*chance, mistake*) non lasciarsi sfuggire; (*idea*) sfruttare prontamente

▶ **seize up** VI + ADV (*muscle, back*) bloccarsi; (*Tech: machine*) grippare.

sei·zure ['si:ʒə'] N **a** (*of goods*) sequestro, confisca; (*of land, city, ship*) presa **b** (*Med*) attacco.

sel·dom ['sɛldəm] ADV di rado, raramente.

se·lect [sɪˈlɛkt] **1** VT (*team, candidate*) scegliere, selezionare; (*book, gift etc*) scegliere; **selected works** opere *fpl* scelte.
2 ADJ (*hotel, restaurant*) chic *inv*; (*club*) esclusivo(-a); (*group*) ristretto(-a); (*audience*) scelto(-a); **a select few** pochi eletti *mpl*.

se·lec·tion [sɪˈlɛkʃən] N (*gen*) scelta; (*of goods etc*) scelta, selezione *f*; **selections from** (*Mus, Literature*) brani scelti da.

♦ **selection committee** N comitato di selezione.

se·lec·tive [sɪˈlɛktɪv] ADJ (*gen*) selettivo(-a).

se·lec·tively [sɪˈlɛktɪvlɪ] ADV (*used, applied*) in modo selettivo.

se·lec·tiv·ity [ˌsɪlɛkˈtɪvɪtɪ] N selettività.

se·lec·tor [sɪˈlɛktəʳ] N (*person*) selezionatore(-trice); (*Tech*) selettore *m*.

self [sɛlf] N (*pl* **selves**): **the self** l'io *m inv*; **my better self** la parte migliore di me stesso; **his true self** il suo vero io; **he's quite his old self again** è tornato quello di una volta.

self- [sɛlf] PREF auto... .

♦ **self-absorbed** [ˌsɛlfəbˈzɜːbd] ADJ egocentrico(-a).

♦ **self-addressed envelope** [ˌsɛlfəˈdrɛstˈɛnvələup] N busta col proprio nome e indirizzo.

♦ **self-adhesive** [ˌsɛlfədˈhiːsɪv] ADJ autoadesivo(-a).

♦ **self-adjusting** [ˌsɛlfəˈdʒʌstɪŋ] ADJ autoregolante.

♦ **self-appointed** [ˌsɛlfəˈpɔɪntɪd] ADJ (*usu pej*): **self-appointed leader** leader autonominatosi tale.

♦ **self-assertive** [ˌsɛlfəˈsɜːtɪv] ADJ che si fa valere.

♦ **self-assurance** [ˌsɛlfəˈʃuərəns] N sicurezza di sé.

♦ **self-assured** [ˌsɛlfəˈʃuəd] ADJ sicuro(-a) di sé.

♦ **self-catering** [ˌsɛlfˈkeɪtərɪŋ] ADJ (*Brit*): **self-catering apartment** appartamento indipendente (con cucina).

♦ **self-centred**, (*Am*) **self-centered** [ˌsɛlfˈsɛntəd] ADJ egocentrico(-a).

♦ **self-cleaning** [ˌsɛlfˈkliːnɪŋ] ADJ (*oven*) autopulente.

♦ **self-coloured**, (*Am*) **self-colored** [ˌsɛlfˈkʌləd] ADJ monocromatico(-a).

♦ **self-confessed** [ˌsɛlfkənˈfɛst] ADJ (*alcoholic, cheat*) dichiarato(-a); **he's a self-confessed thief/liar** ha ammesso di essere un ladro/bugiardo.

♦ **self-confidence** [ˌsɛlfˈkɒnfɪdəns] N fiducia in se (me, te *etc*) stesso(-a).

♦ **self-confident** [ˌsɛlfˈkɒnfɪdənt] ADJ sicuro(-a) di sé.

♦ **self-congratulation** [ˈsɛlfkənˌɡrætjuˈleɪʃən] N autocompiacimento.

♦ **self-conscious** [ˌsɛlfˈkɒnʃəs] ADJ a disagio, impacciato (-a).

♦ **self-consciousness** [ˌsɛlfˈkɒnʃəsnɪs] N disagio, imbarazzo.

♦ **self-contained** [ˌsɛlfkənˈteɪnd] ADJ (*Brit: flat*) indipendente.

♦ **self-contradictory** [ˌsɛlfkɒntrəˈdɪktərɪˌs] ADJ contraddittorio(-a).

♦ **self-control** [ˌsɛlfkənˈtrəul], **self-restraint** [ˌsɛlfrɪˈstreɪnt] N self-control *m inv*, autocontrollo, padronanza di sé.

♦ **self-controlled** [ˌsɛlfkənˈtrəuld] ADJ padrone(-a) di sé.

♦ **self-defeating** [ˌsɛlfdɪˈfiːtɪŋ] ADJ controproducente.

♦ **self-defence**, (*Am*) **self-defense** [ˌsɛlfdɪˈfɛns] N autodifesa; **to act in self-defence** (*Law*) agire per legittima difesa.

♦ **self-denial** [ˌsɛlfdɪˈnaɪəl] N abnegazione *f*, sacrificio.

♦ **self-determination** [ˌsɛlfdɪˌtɜːmɪˈneɪʃən] N autodeterminazione *f*.

♦ **self-discipline** [ˌsɛlfˈdɪsɪplɪn] N autodisciplina.

♦ **self-drive** [ˌsɛlfˈdraɪv] ADJ: **self-drive car** vettura da noleggio senza autista.

♦ **self-educated** [ˌsɛlfˈɛdjuˌkeɪtɪd] ADJ: **to be self-educated** essere un(a) autodidatta.

♦ **self-effacing** [ˌsɛlfɪˈfeɪsɪŋ] ADJ schivo(-a) e modesto (-a).

♦ **self-employed** [ˌsɛlfɪmˈplɔɪd] **1** ADJ (*worker*) autonomo(-a), che lavora in proprio.
2 NPL: **the self-employed** i lavoratori autonomi.

♦ **self-employment** [ˌsɛlfɪmˈplɔɪmənt] N lavoro autonomo.

♦ **self-esteem** [ˌsɛlfɪsˈtiːm] N stima di sé.

♦ **self-evident** [ˌsɛlfˈɛvɪdənt] ADJ evidente, lampante.

♦ **self-explanatory** [ˌsɛlfɪksˈplænətərɪ] ADJ ovvio(-a), che non ha bisogno di spiegazioni.

♦ **self-expression** [ˌsɛlfɪkˈsprɛʃən] N espressione *f* della propria personalità.

♦ **self-governing** [ˌsɛlfˈɡʌvənɪŋ] ADJ autonomo(-a).

♦ **self-government** [ˌsɛlfˈɡʌvənmənt] N autogoverno.

♦ **self-help** [ˌsɛlfˈhɛlp] N iniziativa individuale.

♦ **self-importance** [ˌsɛlfɪmˈpɔːtəns] N presunzione *f*, boria.

♦ **self-important** [ˌsɛlfɪmˈpɔːtənt] ADJ presuntuoso(-a), borioso(-a).

♦ **self-imposed** [ˌsɛlfɪmˈpəuzd] ADJ autoimposto(-a).

♦ **self-indulgence** [ˌsɛlfɪnˈdʌldʒəns] N indulgenza verso le proprie passioni.

♦ **self-indulgent** [ˌsɛlfɪnˈdʌldʒənt] ADJ indulgente verso le proprie passioni.

♦ **self-inflicted** [ˌsɛlfɪnˈflɪktɪd] ADJ: **self-inflicted wound** autolesione *f*; **your problems are self-inflicted** ti sei creato da solo i tuoi problemi.

♦ **self-interest** [ˌsɛlfˈɪntrɪst] N interesse *m* personale.

♦ **self-interested** [ˌsɛlfˈɪntrɪstɪd] ADJ egoistico(-a).

self·ish [ˈsɛlfɪʃ] ADJ egoista.

self·ish·ly [ˈsɛlfɪʃlɪ] ADV egoisticamente.

self·ish·ness [ˈsɛlfɪʃnɪs] N egoismo.

self·less [ˈsɛlfəs] ADJ altruista, altruistico(-a).

self·less·ly [ˈsɛlfəslɪ] ADV altruisticamente.

self·less·ness [ˈsɛlfəsnɪs] N altruismo.

♦ **self-made** [ˌsɛlfˈmeɪd] ADJ che si è fatto(-a) da sé.

♦ **self-made man** N self-made man *m inv*, uomo che si è fatto da sé.

♦ **self-opinionated** [ˌsɛlfəˈpɪnjəneɪtɪd] ADJ convinto(-a) di avere sempre ragione.

♦ **self-pity** [ˌsɛlfˈpɪtɪ] N autocommiserazione *f*.

♦ **self-portrait** [ˌsɛlfˈpɔːtrɪt] N autoritratto.

♦ **self-possessed** [ˌsɛlfpəˈzɛst] ADJ padrone(-a) di sé, composto(-a).

♦ **self-possession** [ˌsɛlfpəˈzɛʃən] N padronanza di sé.

♦ **self-preservation** [ˈsɛlfˌprɛzəˈveɪʃən] N istinto di conservazione.

♦ **self-raising** [ˌsɛlfˈreɪzɪŋ], (*Am*) **self-rising** [ˌsɛlfˈraɪzɪŋ] ADJ: **self-raising flour** *miscela di farina e lievito*.

♦ **self-reliant** [ˌsɛlfrɪˈlaɪənt] ADJ indipendente.

♦ **self-respect** [ˌsɛlfrɪsˈpɛkt] N dignità, amor proprio *m*.

♦ **self-respecting** [ˌsɛlfrɪsˈpɛktɪŋ] ADJ dignitoso(-a); **no self-respecting Englishman would do such a thing** nessun inglese che si rispetti farebbe una cosa simile.

♦ **self-restraint** [ˌsɛlfrɪˈstreɪnt] N = **self-control**.

♦ **self-righteous** [ˌsɛlfˈraɪtʃəs] ADJ (*pej*) presuntuoso(-a).

♦ **self-righteousness** [ˌsɛlfˈraɪtʃəsnɪs] N presunzione *f*.

♦ **self-rising** [ˌsɛlfˈraɪzɪŋ] ADJ (*Am*) = **self-raising**.

♦ **self-sacrifice** [ˌsɛlfˈsækrɪfaɪs] N abnegazione *f*.

♦ **self-sacrificing** [ˌsɛlfˈsækrɪfaɪsɪŋ] ADJ altruista.

♦ **self-same** [ˈsɛlfˌseɪm] ADJ stesso(-a).

♦ **self-satisfied** [ˌsɛlfˈsætɪsfaɪd] ADJ soddisfatto(-a) di sé.

♦ **self-sealing** [ˌsɛlfˈsiːlɪŋ] ADJ autosigillante.

♦ **self-seeking** [ˈsɛlfˈsiːkɪŋ] [1] ADJ egoista.
[2] N egoismo.

♦ **self-service** [ˌsɛlfˈsɜːvɪs] ADJ self-service *inv*.

♦ **self-starter** [ˌsɛlfˈstɑːtəʳ] N (*Aut*) motorino d'avviamento; (*fig: worker with initiative*) lavoratore(-trice) pieno(-a) d'iniziativa.

♦ **self-styled** [ˌsɛlfˈstaɪld] ADJ sedicente.

♦ **self-sufficiency** [ˌsɛlfsəˈfɪʃənsɪ] N autosufficienza.

♦ **self-sufficient** [ˌsɛlfsəˈfɪʃənt] ADJ autosufficiente.

♦ **self-supporting** [ˌsɛlfsəˈpɔːtɪŋ] ADJ economicamente indipendente.

♦ **self-taught** [ˌsɛlfˈtɔːt] ADJ autodidatta.

♦ **self-test** [ˌsɛlfˈtɛst] N (*Comput*) autotest *m inv*.

♦ **self-torture** [ˌsɛlfˈtɔːtʃəʳ], **self-torment** [ˌsɛlfˈtɔmɛnt] N il tormentarsi *m*.

♦ **self-willed** [ˌsɛlfˈwɪld] ADJ ostinato(-a).

♦ **self-winding** [ˌsɛlfˈwaɪndɪŋ] ADJ a carica automatica.

♦ **self-worship** [ˌsɛlfˈwɜːʃɪp] N narcisismo.

sell [sɛl] (*pt, pp* **sold**) [1] VT vendere; **to sell sth for £150** vendere qc per 150 sterline; **to sell sth at £10 per dozen** vendere qc a 10 sterline la dozzina; **to sell sth to sb** vendere qc a qn; **I was sold this in London** questo me l'hanno venduto a Londra; **to sell sb down the river** (*fig*) vendere qn; **to sell sb an idea** (*fig*) far accettare un'idea a qn; **to sell sb a pup** (*fig old*) imbrogliare qn; **to be sold on sb/sth** (*fam*) essere entusiasta di qn/qc; **he doesn't sell himself very well** non si sa vendere bene.
[2] VI essere in vendita; **they sell at** *or* **for 15p each** sono in vendita a 15p l'uno

▸ **sell off** VT + ADV (*stocks and shares, goods*) svendere, liquidare

▸ **sell out** [1] VI + ADV: **to sell out (to sb/sth)** (*Comm*) vendere (tutto) (a qn/qc); **to sell out to the enemy** (*fig*) passare al nemico.
[2] VT + ADV esaurire; **the tickets are all sold out** i biglietti sono esauriti; **we're** *or* **we've sold out of bread** il pane è tutto finito (*in negozio*)

▸ **sell up** [1] VI + ADV (*esp Brit*) vendere (tutto).
[2] VT + ADV vendere.

♦ **sell-by date** [ˈsɛlbaɪˌdeɪt] N data di scadenza.

sell·er [ˈsɛləʳ] N **a** venditore(-trice) **b** (*product*): **this item's a good seller** questo articolo (si) vende molto.

♦ **seller's market** N (*Fin*) mercato del venditore.

sell·ing [ˈsɛlɪŋ] N (*act, business*) vendita.

♦ **selling point** N (*Comm*) caratteristica che fa vendere bene un prodotto; (*fig: advantage*) vantaggio.

♦ **selling price** N prezzo di vendita.

sel·lo·tape® [ˈsɛləʊˌteɪp] (*Brit*) [1] N scotch ® *m inv*.
[2] VT attaccare con lo scotch.

sell·out [ˈsɛlˌaʊt] N **a** (*Theatre*): **it was a sellout** ha fatto registrare il tutto esaurito **b** (*betrayal: to enemy*) tradimento.

Selt·zer [ˈsɛltsəʳ] N seltz *m inv*.

sel·vage, **sel·vedge** [ˈsɛlvɪdʒ] N (*Sewing*) cimosa.

selves [sɛlvz] NPL of **self**.

se·man·tic [sɪˈmæntɪk] ADJ semantico(-a).

se·man·ti·cal·ly [sɪˈmæntɪkəlɪ] ADV semanticamente.

se·man·tics [sɪˈmæntɪks] NSG semantica.

sema·phore [ˈsɛməˌfɔːʳ] N **a** (*system*) segnalazioni *fpl* con bandierine **b** (*Rail: signal post*) semaforo ferroviario.

sem·blance [ˈsɛmbləns] N parvenza, apparenza.

se·men [ˈsiːmən] N seme *m*, sperma *m*.

se·mes·ter [sɪˈmɛstəʳ] N (*Am*) semestre *m*.

semi [ˈsɛmɪ] N (*Brit fam*) casetta a schiera.

semi- [ˈsɛmɪ] PREF semi-.

semi·auto·mat·ic [ˌsɛmɪˌɔːtəˈmætɪk] ADJ semiautomatico (-a).

semi·breve [ˈsɛmɪˌbriːv] N (*Brit Mus*) semibreve *f*.

semi·cir·cle [ˈsɛmɪˌsɜːkl] N semicerchio.

semi·cir·cu·lar [ˌsɛmɪˈsɜːkjʊləʳ] ADJ semicircolare.

semi·co·lon [ˌsɛmɪˈkəʊlən] N punto e virgola.

semi·con·duc·tor [ˌsɛmɪkənˈdʌktəʳ] N semiconduttore *m*.

semi·con·scious [ˌsɛmɪˈkɒnʃəs] ADJ parzialmente cosciente.

semi·dark·ness [ˌsɛmɪˈdɑːknɪs] N semioscurità.

semi·de·tached [ˌsɛmɪdɪˈtætʃt] ADJ: **semidetached house** casetta a schiera.

semi·fi·nal [ˌsɛmɪˈfaɪnl] N semifinale *f*.

semi·fi·nal·ist [ˌsɛmɪˈfaɪnəlɪst] N semifinalista *m/f*.

semi·nal [ˈsɛmɪnl] ADJ (*fig, book, film*) che ha fatto scuola.

semi·nar [ˈsɛmɪnɑːʳ] N (*Univ*) seminario.

semi·nar·ist [ˈsɛmɪnərɪst] N seminarista *m*.

semi·nary [ˈsɛmɪnərɪ] N (*Rel*) seminario.

semi·of·fi·cial [ˌsɛmɪəˈfɪʃəl] ADJ semiufficiale.

se·mio·logi·cal [ˌsɛmɪəˈlɒdʒɪkəl] ADJ semiologico(-a).

se·mi·ol·ogy [ˌsɛmɪˈɒlədʒɪ] N semiologia.

se·mi·ot·ics, **se·mei·ot·ics** [ˌsɛmɪˈɒtɪks] NSG (*Ling*) semiotica; (*Med*) semeiotica.

semi·precious [ˈsɛmɪˌprɛʃəs] ADJ semiprezioso(-a).

semi·qua·ver [ˈsɛmɪˌkweɪvəʳ] N (*Brit Mus*) semicroma.

semi·skilled [ˌsɛmɪˈskɪld] ADJ (*worker*) parzialmente qualificato(-a); (*work*) che richiede una specializzazione parziale.

♦ **semi-skimmed** [ˌsɛmɪˈskɪmd] ADJ parzialmente scremato(-a).

Se·mit·ic [sɪˈmɪtɪk] ADJ (*language*) semitico(-a); (*people*) semita.

semi·tone [ˈsɛmɪˌtəʊn] N (*Mus*) semitono.

semo·li·na [ˌsɛməˈliːnə] N semolino.

♦ **semolina pudding** N dolce *m* di semolino.

SEN [ˌɛsiːˈɛn] N ABBR (*Brit*: = *State Enrolled Nurse*) *infermiera diplomata (dopo corso biennale)*.

Sen., sen. ABBR **a** = **senator** **b** = **senior**.

sen·ate [ˈsɛnɪt] N (*Pol*) senato; (*Univ*) senato accademico.

sena·tor [ˈsɛnɪtəʳ] N (*Pol*) senatore(-trice).

sena·to·rial [ˌsɛnəˈtɔːrɪəl] ADJ (*frm*) senatoriale.

send [sɛnd] (*pt, pp* **sent**) VT **a** (*gen*) mandare; (*letter, telegram*) mandare, spedire; (*arrow, rocket, ball*) lanciare; **to send by post**, (*Am*) **send by mail** spedire per posta; **to send by telex/fax** mandare via telex/fax; **send word that ...** mandare a dire che...; **she sends (you) her love** ti saluta affettuosamente; **to send sb for sth** mandare qn a prendere qc; **to send sb to do sth** mandare qn a fare qc; **to send sb home** mandare qn a casa; (*from abroad*) rimpatriare qn; **to send sb to prison/bed/school** mandare qn in prigione/a letto/a scuola; **to send sb to sleep** (*bore*) far addormentare qn; **send sb into fits of laughter** far scoppiare dal ridere qn; **the explosion sent a cloud of dust into the air** l'esplosione ha sollevato una nuvola di polvere; **to send a shiver down sb's spine** far venire i brividi a qn; **to send sb flying** mandare qn a gambe all'aria; **to send sth flying** far volare via qc; **to send sb to Coventry** (*Brit*) dare l'ostracismo a qn
b (*cause to become*): **to send sb mad** far impazzire qn;

that really sends me (*fam old*) mi manda in visibilio

▶ **send away** VT + ADV (*person*) mandare; (: *get rid of*) mandare via

▶ **send away for, send off for** VI + ADV + PREP richiedere per posta, farsi spedire

▶ **send back** VT + ADV rimandare

▶ **send down** VT + ADV (*person, prices*) far scendere; (*Brit*: *student*) cacciare, mandar via; (*fam*: *imprison*) mandare in galera

▶ **send for** VI + PREP **a** (*doctor, police*) (mandare a) chiamare, far venire
   b (*by post*) ordinare per posta

▶ **send in** VT + ADV (*person*) far entrare; (*troops*) inviare; (*report, application, resignation*) presentare

▶ **send off** VT + ADV (*person*) mandare; (*letter, goods*) spedire; (*Ftbl*: *player*) espellere; **to send sb off to do sth** mandare qn a fare qc

▶ **send off for** VI + ADV + PREP = **send away for**

▶ **send on** VT + ADV (*Brit*: *letter*) inoltrare; (*luggage etc*: *in advance*) spedire in anticipo; (: *afterwards*) mandare, spedire

▶ **send out** **1** VI + ADV: **to send out for sth** mandare a prendere qc.
   2 VT + ADV **a** (*person*) mandar fuori; (*troops*) inviare
   b (*post: invitations*) mandare, spedire
   c (*emit: light, heat*) mandare, emanare; (: *signals*) emettere

▶ **send round** VT + ADV (*letter, document etc*) far circolare; **to send sb round (to sb)** mandare qn (da qn); **I'll send it round later** te lo farò pervenire più tardi

▶ **send up** VT + ADV **a** (*person, luggage*) mandar su; (*balloon, rocket, flare*) lanciare; (*smoke, dust*) sollevare; (*prices*) far salire
   b (*Brit fam: make fun of: person, book*) fare la parodia di.

send·er ['sɛndə'] N mittente *m/f.*

send·off ['sɛnd,ɒf] N: **to give sb a sendoff** festeggiare la partenza di qn.

◆ **send-up** ['sɛnd,ʌp] N (*Brit fam*) parodia.

Seneca ['sɛnɪkə] N Seneca *m.*

Sen·egal [,sɛnɪ'gɔːl] N il Senegal.

Sen·ega·lese [,sɛnɪgə'liːz] ADJ, N, PL INV senegalese (*m/f*).

se·nile ['siːnaɪl] ADJ senile; **I'm not senile yet!** non sono ancora rimbambito!

se·nil·ity [sɪ'nɪlɪtɪ] N senilità.

sen·ior ['siːnɪə'] **1** ADJ **a** (*in age*) maggiore, più anziano (-a); **she is 10 years senior to me** ha 10 anni più di me; **P. Jones senior** P. Jones senior *or* padre; **senior year** (*Am Univ, Scol*) ultimo anno di studi
   b (*of higher rank: employee, officer*) di grado superiore; (: *partner*) più anziano(-a); **he holds a senior position in the company** occupa una posizione di responsabilità nell'azienda; **he is senior to me in the firm** ha più anzianità di me nella ditta.
   2 N **a** (*in age*) persona più anziana; **he is my senior by 2 years** ha 2 anni più di me
   b (*Am Univ*) studente(-essa) dell'ultimo anno.

◆ **senior citizen** N (*euph: old person*) anziano(-a) (: *pensioner*) pensionato(-a).

◆ **senior high school** N (*Am*) ≈ liceo.

sen·ior·ity [,siːnɪ'ɒrɪtɪ] N (*in age, years of service*) anzianità; (*in rank*) superiorità.

sen·sa·tion [sɛn'seɪʃən] N **a** (*physical feeling, impression*) sensazione *f*; **he is completely without sensation in that leg** ha perso completamente la sensibilità della gamba
   b (*excitement*) sensazione *f*, scalpore *m*; **to be** *or* **cause a**

sensation fare sensazione, destare scalpore.

sen·sa·tion·al [sɛn'seɪʃənl] ADJ (*gen, also fam: marvellous*) sensazionale; (*newspaper*) sensazionalistico(-a); (*novel etc*) a sensazione; (*account, description*) a forti tinte.

sen·sa·tion·al·ism [sɛn'seɪʃnə,lɪzəm] N (*pej: of reporting*) sensazionalismo.

sen·sa·tion·al·ly [sɛn'seɪʃnəlɪ] ADV (*see adj*) sensazionalmente; a forti tinte.

sense [sɛns] **1** N **a** (*faculty*) senso; **a keen sense of smell/hearing** un olfatto/udito fine; **to come to one's senses** (*regain consciousness*) riprendere i sensi; **sixth sense** sesto senso; **senso of direction** senso di orientamento; **to lose all sense of time** perdere la nozione del tempo; **sense of humour** (senso dell') umorismo
   b (*feeling*) senso, sensazione *f*; **sense of duty/guilt** senso del dovere/di colpa; **a sense of well-being** una sensazione di benessere
   c (*also: common sense*) buonsenso; **he should have had more sense than to do it** avrebbe dovuto avere il buonsenso di non farlo; **there is no sense in (doing) that** non ha senso (farlo); **she had the sense to call the doctor** ha avuto il buonsenso di chiamare il medico; **to make sb see sense** far ragionare qn, far intendere ragione a qn
   d (*sanity*): **senses** NPL ragione *fsg*, senno *msg*; **to come to one's senses** (*become reasonable*) tornare in sé; **to bring sb to his senses** riportare qn alla ragione, far rinsavire qn; **to take leave of one's senses** perdere il lume *or* l'uso della ragione
   e (*meaning*) senso, significato; **it makes sense** ha senso; **it doesn't make sense** non ha senso; **I can't make (any) sense of this** non ci capisco niente; **in one** *or* **a sense** in un certo senso; **in every sense (of the word)** in tutti i sensi (del termine)
   f (*Math*) verso.
   2 VT (*presence, interest*) avvertire, intuire; (*danger*) sentire, percepire; **to sense that all is not well** sentire che c'è qualcosa che non va.

sense·less ['sɛnslɪs] ADJ **a** (*stupid: action*) insensato(-a); (: *idea*) assurdo(-a) **b** (*unconscious*) privo(-a) di sensi *or* di conoscenza.

sense·less·ly ['sɛnslɪslɪ] ADV in modo insensato.

sense·less·ness ['sɛnslɪsnɪs] N (*of person*) mancanza di buon senso; (*of action, idea*) insensatezza, assurdità.

sen·sibil·ities [,sɛnsɪ'bɪlɪtɪz] NPL (*frm*) suscettibilità *fsg.*

sen·sibil·ity [,sɛnsɪ'bɪlɪtɪ] N (*delicacy of feeling*) sensibilità *f inv* **b** (*sensitivity*) suscettibilità *f inv.*

sen·sible ['sɛnsəbl] ADJ **a** (*having good sense: person*) assennato(-a) **b** (*act, decision, choice*) sensato(-a), ragionevole; (*clothing, shoes*) pratico(-a); **it would be more sensible (to do)** avrebbe più senso (fare) **c** (*frm: noticeable*) sensibile, rilevante.

sen·sibly ['sɛnsəblɪ] ADV (*reasonably: behave, talk*) assennatamente, con molto buon senso.

sen·si·tive ['sɛnsɪtɪv] ADJ (*person, tooth, instrument, film*): **sensitive (to)** sensibile (a); (*delicate: skin, question*) delicato(-a); (*easily offended*) suscettibile; **he is very sensitive about it** è meglio non toccare quel tasto con lui.

sen·si·tiv·ity [,sɛnsɪ'tɪvɪtɪ] N (*see adj*) sensibilità; delicatezza; suscettibilità.

sen·si·tized ['sɛnsɪ,taɪzd] ADJ sensibilizzato(-a).

sen·sor ['sɛnsə'] N (*Tech*) sensore *m.*

sen·so·ry ['sɛnsərɪ] ADJ sensorio(-a).

sen·sual ['sɛnsjʊəl] ADJ (*gen*) sensuale; (*pleasures*) dei sensi.

sen·su·al·ity [ˌsɛnsjʊˈælɪtɪ] N sensualità.

sen·su·ous [ˈsɛnsjʊəs] ADJ sensuoso(-a).

sen·su·ous·ness [ˈsɛnsjʊəsnɪs] N l'essere sensuoso(-a).

sent [sɛnt] PT, PP of **send**.

sen·tence [ˈsɛntəns] ⬜1 N **a** (gen) frase f; (Gram) proposizione f; (: complex sentence) periodo

b (Law: verdict) sentenza; (: punishment) condanna; **to pass sentence on sb** condannare qn; (fig) giudicare qn; **sentence of death** condanna a morte; **under sentence of death** condannato(-a) a morte; **the judge gave him a 6-month sentence** il giudice lo ha condannato a 6 mesi di prigione.

⬜2 VT: **to sentence sb to death/to 5 years (in prison)** condannare qn a morte/a 5 anni (di prigione).

sen·ten·tious [sɛnˈtɛnʃəs] ADJ (frm) sentenzioso(-a).

sen·ten·tious·ly [sɛnˈtɛnʃəlɪ] ADV (frm) in modo sentenzioso.

sen·ti·ent [ˈsɛntɪənt] ADJ (frm: creature, being) sensibile, senziente.

sen·ti·ment [ˈsɛntɪmənt] N **a** (feeling) sentimento; (opinion) opinione f **b** (sentimentality) sentimentalismo.

sen·ti·ment·al [ˌsɛntɪˈmɛntl] ADJ (emotional) sentimentale; (pej: film, love story) troppo sentimentale; **I have a sentimental attachment to this pen** sono attaccato a questa penna per motivi sentimentali.

sen·ti·men·tal·ity [ˌsɛntɪmɛnˈtælɪtɪ] N (pej) sentimentalismo.

sen·ti·men·tal·ize [ˌsɛntɪˈmɛntəˌlaɪz] (frm pej) VT fare del sentimentalismo su.

sen·ti·men·tal·ly [ˌsɛntɪˈmɛntəlɪ] ADV sentimentalmente; (pej) con sentimentalismo.

♦ **sentimental value** N valore m affettivo.

sen·ti·nel [ˈsɛntɪnl] N (old) sentinella.

sen·try [ˈsɛntrɪ] N sentinella.

♦ **sentry box** N garitta.

♦ **sentry duty** N: **to be on sentry duty** essere di sentinella.

Seoul [səʊl] N Seul f.

sep·al [ˈsɛpəl] N sepalo.

sepa·rable [ˈsɛpərəbl] ADJ separabile.

sepa·rate [adj ˈsɛprɪt, vb ˈsɛpəˌreɪt] ⬜1 ADJ (gen) separato (-a); (organization, career) indipendente; (occasion, issue) diverso(-a); **they went their separate ways** (also fig) sono andati ognuno per la propria strada; **we sat at separate tables** ci siamo seduti a tavoli diversi; **it was discussed at a separate meeting** è stato discusso in un'altra riunione; **separate from** separato(-a) da; **under separate cover** (Comm) in plico a parte.

⬜2 VT (gen) separare, dividere; (divide up): **to separate into** dividere in; **to separate sth from sth** separare qc da qc; **he is separated from his wife, but not divorced** è separato dalla moglie ma non divorziato.

⬜3 VI (mixture, milk) separarsi; (married couple, boxers) separarsi, dividersi; (unmarried couple, friends) lasciarsi; see also **separates**.

sepa·rate·ly [ˈsɛprɪtlɪ] ADV separatamente.

sepa·rates [ˈsɛprɪts] NPL (clothes) coordinati mpl.

sepa·ra·tion [ˌsɛpəˈreɪʃən] N separazione f.

sepa·ra·tism [ˈsɛpərəˌtɪzəm] N separatismo.

sepa·ra·tist [ˈsɛpərətɪst] ADJ, N separatista (m/f).

se·pia [ˈsiːpjə] N nero di seppia.

Sept. ABBR (= September) sett., set.

Sep·tem·ber [sɛpˈtɛmbəʳ] N settembre m for usage see **July**.

sep·tic [ˈsɛptɪk] ADJ settico(-a); (wound) infetto(-a); **to go**

septic infettarsi.

sep·ti·cae·mia, (Am) **sep·ti·cemia** [ˌsɛptɪˈsiːmɪə] N setticemia.

♦ **septic tank** N fossa settica.

sep·tua·genar·ian [ˌsɛptjʊədʒɪˈnɛərɪən] N (frm) settuagenario(-a).

sepulchral [sɪˈpʌlkrəl] ADJ (liter: tone, gloom) sepolcrale.

sep·ul·chre, (Am) **sep·ul·cher** [ˈsɛpəlkəʳ] N (liter) sepolcro.

se·quel [ˈsiːkwəl] N (of film, book): **sequel (to)** seguito (di); (of event) conseguenza (di), strascico (di).

se·quence [ˈsiːkwəns] N **a** (order) successione f, ordine m; **in sequence** in ordine, di seguito; **sequence of tenses** (Gram) concordanza dei tempi **b** (series) serie f inv; (Mus, Cards, film sequence) sequenza.

se·quen·tial [sɪˈkwɛnʃəl] ADJ sequenziale; **sequential access** (Comput) accesso sequenziale.

se·ques·ter [sɪˈkwɛstəʳ] VT (Law: property) sequestrare, confiscare.

se·ques·tered [sɪˈkwɛstəd] ADJ **a** (liter: place) isolato(-a); (: life) ritirato(-a), appartato(-a) **b** (Law: property) sequestrato(-a).

se·ques·trate [sɪˈkwɛstreɪt] VT sequestrare, confiscare.

se·quin [ˈsiːkwɪn] N paillette f inv, lustrino.

ser·aph [ˈsɛrəf] N (pl **seraphs** or **seraphim**) serafino.

Serb [sɜːb] ADJ, N = **Serbian**.

Ser·bia [ˈsɜːbɪə] N Serbia.

Ser·bian [ˈsɜːbɪən] ⬜1 ADJ serbo(-a).

⬜2 N (person) serbo(-a); (language) serbo.

Serbo-Croat [ˌsɜːbəʊˈkrəʊæt] N (language) serbocroato.

ser·enade [ˌsɛrəˈneɪd] ⬜1 N serenata.

⬜2 VT fare la serenata a.

ser·en·dip·ity [ˌsɛrənˈdɪpɪtɪ] N (frm) serendipità.

se·rene [səˈriːn] ADJ (person, sky) sereno(-a); (sea) calmo (-a).

se·rene·ly [səˈriːnlɪ] ADV (smile, say) serenamente.

se·ren·ity [sɪˈrɛnɪtɪ] N serenità.

serf [sɜːf] N servo(-a) della gleba.

serf·dom [ˈsɜːfdəm] N servitù della gleba.

serge [sɜːdʒ] N serge f.

ser·geant [ˈsɑːdʒənt] N (Mil) sergente m; (Police) ≈ brigadiere m.

♦ **sergeant major** N (Mil) sergente m maggiore.

se·rial [ˈsɪərɪəl] ⬜1 N (in magazine) romanzo a puntate; (TV) teleromanzo a puntate, serial m inv televisivo; (Radio) commedia radiofonica a puntate.

⬜2 ADJ (Comput) seriale.

se·riali·za·tion [ˌsɪərɪəlaɪˈzeɪʃən] N (publishing in instalments) pubblicazione a puntate; (TV, Radio: adapting) adattamento e trasmissione a puntate; (: series of broadcasts): **a new serialization of a novel by Jane Austen** un nuovo teleromanzo a puntate tratto da un'opera di Jane Austen.

se·rial·ize [ˈsɪərɪəˌlaɪz] VT (Press) pubblicare a puntate; (TV/Radio) trasmettere a puntate.

♦ **serial killer** N serial-killer m/f inv.

♦ **serial number** N (of goods, machinery, banknotes etc) numero di serie.

se·ries [ˈsɪərɪz] N, PL INV (gen, Radio, TV) serie f inv; (set of books) collana.

♦ **series elements** NPL (Phys) elementi mpl in serie.

seri·graph [ˈsɛrɪˌgræf] N serigrafia (stampa).

se·rig·ra·phy [səˈrɪgrəfɪ] N serigrafia (metodo).

se·ri·ous [ˈsɪərɪəs] ADJ **a** (earnest) serio(-a); **to give serious thought to sth** considerare seriamente qc; **he's**

a serious student of jazz s'interessa seriamente di jazz; she's getting serious about him si sta innamorando sul serio di lui; are you serious (about it)? parli sul serio?; you can't be serious! stai scherzando!

 b (causing concern) serio(-a), grave; the patient's condition is serious il paziente versa in gravi condizioni.

se·ri·ous·ly ['sɪərɪəslɪ] ADV a (in earnest) seriamente; to take sth/sb seriously prendere qc/qn sul serio; seriously though ... scherzi a parte..., sul serio... b (wounded) gravemente; (worried) seriamente c (fam: extremely): he's seriously rich ha un casino di soldi.

se·ri·ous·ness ['sɪərɪəsnɪs] N (gen) serietà, gravità; (of error) gravità; in all seriousness in tutta sincerità.

ser·mon ['sɜːmən] N (in church) sermone m; (pej: lecture) predica.

ser·mon·ize ['sɜːmə,naɪz] VI (fig pej) fare la predica.

sero·thera·py [,sɪərəʊ'θɛrəpɪ] N sieroterapia.

ser·pent ['sɜːpənt] N (liter) serpente m.

ser·pen·tine ['sɜːpən,taɪn] N (liter: sinuous) sinuoso(-a).

ser·rat·ed [sɛ'reɪtɪd] ADJ seghettato(-a).

ser·ra·tion [sɛ'reɪʃən] N seghettatura.

ser·ried ['sɛrɪd] ADJ (liter) serrato(-a); in serried ranks in ranghi serrati.

se·rum ['sɪərəm] N siero.

serv·ant ['sɜːvənt] N (domestic) domestico(-a); (fig: of the public, one's country) servitore m.

serve [sɜːv] 1 VT a (work for: employer) servire; (: God, one's country) servire, essere al servizio di

 b (be used for or useful as): to serve (as) servire (da); that serves to explain ... così si spiega...; it serves a variety of purposes ha svariati usi; it serves my purpose fa al caso mio, serve al mio scopo; it serves its purpose serve allo scopo; it serves no useful purpose non serve a niente; it serves you right (fam) ben ti sta; his knowledge served him well la sua preparazione gli è tornata utile

 c (in shop, restaurant) servire; (food, meal, also Tennis) servire; to serve sb (with) sth servire qc a qn; are you being served? la stanno servendo?; this dish should be served hot è un piatto che va servito caldo; the power station serves the entire region la centrale elettrica alimenta l'intera regione; the railway line serves five cities la ferrovia serve cinque città

 d (complete): to serve an apprenticeship fare tirocinio; to serve a prison sentence scontare una condanna; he has served time (in prison) (fam) è stato in prigione; he has served his time (prisoner) ha scontato la sua condanna; (apprentice) ha finito il periodo di prova

 e (Law: summons, writ): to serve sth on sb notificare qc a qn; to serve a summons on sb (Criminal law) spiccare un mandato di comparizione contro qn.

 2 VI a (servant, soldier) prestare servizio; (shop assistant, waiter) servire; (Tennis) servire, battere; to serve on a committee/jury far parte di un comitato/una giuria; she served for 2 years as chairwoman è stata in carica come presidente per 2 anni

 b (be useful): to serve as/for/to do servire da/per/per fare.

 3 N (Tennis) servizio, battuta

▶ serve out, serve up VT + ADV (food) servire; (meal) servire in tavola.

serv·er ['sɜːvə'] N a (Rel) chierichetto; (Tennis) chi ha il servizio, battitore(-trice)

 b (piece of cutlery) posata di servizio; (tray) vassoio, piatto da portata.

ser·vice ['sɜːvɪs] 1 N a (gen, also Mil) servizio; to see

service (Mil) prestare servizio; military service servizio militare; at your service al suo (or vostro) servizio; to be of service (to sb) essere utile (a qn); to do sb a service fare un (gran) favore a qn; this old chair has seen a lot of service questa vecchia sedia ne ha viste tante; in service (domestic) a servizio; On Her (or His) Majesty's Service al servizio di Sua Maestà (Britannica); in the service of one's country al servizio della patria

 b (department, system) servizio; medical/social services servizi sanitari/sociali; the essential services i servizi primari; goods and services (Econ) beni mpl e servizi; the train service to London il servizio di treni per Londra; the number 13 bus service la linea del 13

 c : the Services (Mil) le Forze Armate

 d (Rel) funzione f; funeral service rito funebre; to hold a service celebrare una funzione

 e (maintenance work) revisione f (periodica); to put the car in for a service portare la macchina in officina per una revisione

 f (set of crockery) servizio; a tea/coffee/dinner service un servizio da tè/da caffè/da tavola

 g (on motorway): services NPL stazione fsg di servizio. h (Tennis etc) servizio, battuta.

 2 VT (car, washing machine) revisionare; (group, organization) dare assistenza a; (Fin: debt) pagare gli interessi su.

ser·vice·able ['sɜːvɪsəbl] ADJ (practical: clothes, shoes) pratico(-a); (usable, functioning) usabile.

♦ service area N (on motorway) area di servizio.

♦ service charge N (in restaurant) servizio.

♦ service court N (Tennis) rettangolo di battuta.

♦ service flat N (Brit) ≈ appartamento in un residence.

♦ service industries NPL settore msg terziario.

♦ service line N (Tennis) linea di battuta.

ser·vice·man ['sɜːvɪsmən] N (pl -men) militare m.

♦ service station N (Aut) stazione f di servizio.

ser·vi·cing ['sɜːvɪsɪŋ] N (of car) revisione f.

ser·vi·ette [,sɜːvɪ'ɛt] N (Brit) tovagliolo, salvietta.

♦ serviette ring N portatovagliolo.

ser·vile ['sɜːvaɪl] ADJ (pej) servile.

ser·vile·ly ['sɜːvaɪllɪ] ADV (pej) servilmente.

ser·vil·ity [sɜː'vɪlɪtɪ] N (pej) servilismo.

serv·ing ['sɜːvɪŋ] N (portion) porzione f; serving dish piatto da portata.

ser·vi·tude ['sɜːvɪtjuːd] N servitù f.

ser·vo·mecha·nism ['sɜːvəʊ,mɛkə,nɪzəm] N servomeccanismo.

sesa·me ['sɛsəmɪ] N a (plant) sesamo

 b (Arabian Nights): open sesame apriti sesamo; (fig): an open sesame to sth un biglietto d'ingresso per qc (fig).

♦ sesame oil N olio di sesamo.

♦ sesame seeds NPL (Culin) semi mpl di sesamo.

ses·sile ['sɛsaɪl] ADJ (Bot) sessile.

ses·sion ['sɛʃən] N a (sitting) seduta, sessione f; (meeting) riunione f; to be in session (parliament, court) essere in seduta; the court is now in session l'udienza è aperta; I had a long session with her (talk) ho avuto un lungo colloquio con lei; (work) ho avuto una lunga riunione di lavoro con lei

 b (esp Am, Scot Scol, Univ: year) anno scolastico (or accademico); (: term) trimestre m or quadrimestre m; the new parliamentary session begins in October l'attività parlamentare riprenderà a ottobre.

♦ session musician N musicista m/f di studio.

set [sɛt] (vb: pt, pp set) 1 N a (gen) serie f inv; (of kitchen

tools, saucepans) batteria; (*of books*) raccolta, collezione *f*; (*of dishes*) servizio; **a set of false teeth** una dentiera; **he still has a full set of teeth** ha ancora una dentatura completa; **a set of dining-room furniture** una camera da pranzo; **a chess/draughts set** un gioco di scacchi/ dama; **a painting/writing set** l'occorrente *m* per dipingere/per scrivere; **these articles are sold in sets** questi articoli si vendono in serie complete

  b (*Tennis*) set *m inv*

  c (*Math*) insieme *m*; **closed set** insieme chiuso; **empty set** insieme vuoto

  d (*Elec*) apparecchio; **television set** televisore *m*

  e (*Cine*) set *m inv*; (*Theatre*) scena

  f (*Hairdressing*) messa in piega

  g (*group: often pej*) cerchia; **the smart set** il bel mondo.

2 ADJ **a** (*unchanging: gen*) fisso(-a); (*smile*) artificiale; (*purpose*) definito(-a), preciso(-a); (*lunch*) a prezzo fisso; (*speech, talk*) preparato(-a); (*date, time*) preciso (-a), stabilito(-a); (*Scol: subjects*) obbligatorio(-a); (: *books*) in programma (per l'esame); **set in one's ways** abitudinario(-a); **set in one's opinions** rigido(-a nelle proprie convinzioni; **a set phrase** una frase fatta; **at a set time** a un'ora stabilita

  b (*determined*) deciso(-a); (*ready*) pronto(-a); **he is (dead) set on doing it** è deciso a farlo; **he is (dead) set on a new car** si è ficcato in testa di comprare una nuova macchina; **to be (dead) set against (doing) sth** essere assolutamente contrario(-a) a (fare) qc; **to be all set to do sth** essere pronto(-a) a fare qc; **the scene was set for ...** (*fig*) tutto era pronto per....

3 VT **a** (*place, put*) mettere; **a novel set in Rome** un romanzo ambientato a Roma; **to set a higher value on happiness than on wealth** dar più valore alla felicità che alla ricchezza; **to set the value of a ring at £500** valutare un anello 500 sterline; **to set sb free** liberare qn, mettere qn in libertà; **to set fire to sth** dare *or* appiccare fuoco a qc; **to set a dog on sb** aizzare un cane contro qn

  b (*arrange, adjust: clock, mechanism*) regolare; (: *alarm clock*) mettere, puntare; (: *trap*) mettere, tendere; (: *hair*) fissare, mettere in piega; (: *broken arm, leg: in plaster*) ingessare; (: *with splint*) mettere una stecca a; (: *type*) comporre; **to set a poem to music** mettere in musica una poesia

  c (*fix, establish: date, limit*) fissare, stabilire; (: *record*) stabilire; (: *fashion*) lanciare; (*dye, colour*) fissare; **to set course for** (*Naut*) far rotta per

  d (*gem*) montare

  e (*assign: task, homework*) dare, assegnare; **to set sb a problem** porre un problema a qn; **to set sb an exam in Italian** far fare un esame d'italiano a qn; **to set an exam in Italian** preparare il testo *or* le domande di un esame d'italiano

  f (*start, cause to start*): **to set sth going** mettere in moto qc; **it set me thinking** mi ha fatto pensare; **to set sb to work** mettere qn al lavoro; **to set to work** mettersi al lavoro.

4 VI **a** (*sun, moon*) tramontare

  b (*broken bone, limb*) saldarsi; (*jelly, jam*) rapprendersi; (*concrete, glue*) indurirsi, fare presa; (*fig: face*) irrigidirsi; see also **sail, table, example, heart**

▶ **set about** VI + PREP **a** (*task*): **to set about doing sth** intraprendere qc, mettersi a fare qc; **I don't know how to set about it** non so da che parte cominciare

  b (*attack*) assalire

▶ **set against** VT + PREP **a** (*make hostile to*): **to set sb**

against sb/sth mettere qn contro qn/qc

  b (*balance against*): **to set sth against sth** contrapporre qc a qc

▶ **set apart** VT + ADV (*object*) mettere da parte; (*fig: person*) distinguere

▶ **set aside** VT + ADV **a** (*book, work*) mettere via; (*money, time*) mettere da parte; (*differences, quarrels, principles*) accantonare; (*land*) mettere a riposo

  b (*reject: objection*) respingere; (: *will, judgement*) invalidare, annullare

▶ **set back** VT + ADV **a** (*clock*) mettere indietro; (*progress*) ritardare; **to set back the clock (by one hour)** mettere l'orologio indietro (di un'ora); **the strike has set us back 6 months** lo sciopero ci ha fatto perdere 6 mesi

  b : **a house set back from the road** una casa a una certa distanza dalla strada

  c (*fam: cost*): **it set me back £900** mi è costato la bellezza di 900 sterline

▶ **set down** VT + ADV **a** (*put down: object*) posare; (: *passenger*) lasciare, far scendere

  b (*record*) prendere nota di; **to set sth down in writing** *or* **on paper** mettere qc per iscritto *or* sulla carta

▶ **set forth** 1 VT + ADV (*frm: facts, reasons, arguments*) esporre.

  2 VI + ADV (*liter: set off*) mettersi in viaggio

▶ **set in** VI + ADV (*infection*) svilupparsi; (*complications*) intervenire; **the rain has set in for the day** ormai pioverà tutto il giorno; **before the rot sets in** prima che la situazione degeneri

▶ **set off** 1 VI + ADV (*leave*) mettersi in cammino, partire; **to set off on a journey (to)** mettersi in viaggio (per).

  2 VT + ADV **a** (*bomb*) far scoppiare *or* esplodere; (*mechanism, burglar alarm*) azionare; (*process, chain of events*) mettere in moto, scatenare

  b (*enhance*) mettere in risalto, far risaltare

▶ **set out** 1 VI + ADV: **to set out (for)** avviarsi (verso, a); **to set out (from)** partire (da); **to set out in search of sb/sth** mettersi alla ricerca di qn/qc; **to set out to do sth** proporsi di fare qc.

  2 VT + ADV (*goods etc, fig: reasons, ideas*) esporre, presentare; (*chess pieces*) schierare, disporre

▶ **set to** VI + ADV: **to set to (and do sth)** mettersi all'opera (e fare qc)

▶ **set up** 1 VI + ADV: **to set up (in business) as a baker/lawyer** aprire una panetteria/uno studio legale; **when did you set up in business?** quand'è che ti sei messo in proprio?.

  2 VT + ADV **a** (*place in position: chairs, stalls, road blocks*) disporre; (*tent*) rizzare, piantare; (*monument*) innalzare

  b (*start: firm, business etc*) avviare; (: *school, organization*) fondare; (: *fund*) costituire; (: *inquiry*) aprire; (: *infection*) provocare; (: *record*) stabilire; **to set up house** trovarsi una casa; **to set up camp** accamparsi; **to set up shop** mettersi in proprio; **to set sb up in business** avviare qn agli affari; **to set o.s. up as sth** (*fig*) pretendere di essere qc

▶ **set upon** VI + PREP (*attack*) assalire.

set·back ['sɛtˌbæk] N (*hitch*) contrattempo, inconveniente *m*; (*more serious*) momento di crisi; (*in health*) ricaduta.

♦ **set menu** N menù *m inv* fisso *or* turistico.

♦ **set piece** N (*Mus, Literature: part of work, piece of music*) brano famoso; (*in music competition*) brano obbligatorio; (*Sport*) tattica di gioco.

♦ **set-piece** ['sɛt,piːs] ADJ (*offensive, manoeuvre*) accurata-mente programmato(-a).

♦ **set square** N squadra da disegno.

set·tee [sɛ'tiː] N divano.

set·ter ['sɛtəʳ] N (*dog*) setter *m inv*.

♦ **set theory** N (*Math*) teoria degli insiemi, insiemistica.

set·ting ['sɛtɪŋ] N **a** (*of novel*) ambiente *m*, ambienta-zione *f*; (*scenery*) sfondo; (*of jewels*) montatura; **a house in a beautiful setting** una casa in una posizione meravigliosa **b** (*Mus*) adattamento (musicale) **c** (*of controls*) posizione *f* **d** (*of sun*) tramonto.

♦ **setting lotion** N fissatore *m* (*per messa in piega*).

set·tle¹ ['sɛtl] N cassapanca con schienale alto.

set·tle² ['sɛtl] **1** VT **a** (*place carefully*) sistemare; **to settle o.s.** OR **get settled** sistemarsi

b (*decide, finalize: details, date*) definire, concordare; (*pay: bill, account*) regolare, saldare; (*solve: problem*) risolvere; (: *difficulty*) appianare; (: *dispute, argument*) comporre; **to settle a case** *or* **claim out of court** definire una causa in via amichevole; **that's settled then** allora è deciso; **that settles it!** (*I've decided*) ecco, ho deciso!; (*indignant*) questo è il colmo!

c (*calm down: nerves*) distendere; (: *doubts*) dissipare; **to settle one's stomach** calmare il mal di stomaco

d (*colonize: land*) colonizzare

e (*Law*): **to settle sth on sb** intestare qc a qn.

2 VI **a** (*bird, insect*) posarsi; (*sediment, dust, snow*) depositarsi; (*building*) assestarsi; (*conditions, situation*) stabilizzarsi; (*weather*) mettersi al bello; (*emotions*) calmarsi; (*nerves*) distendersi; **to settle to sth** applicarsi a qc; **I couldn't settle to anything** non riuscivo a concentrarmi

b (*go to live: in town, country*) stabilirsi; (: *in new house*) sistemarsi, installarsi; (: *as colonist*) insediarsi; **to feel settled** (*in a place*) sentirsi a casa

c : **to settle with sb for the price of sth** concordare il prezzo di qc con qn; **can I settle with you later?** posso darti i soldi più tardi?; **to settle out of court** (*Law*) giungere a un accordo in via amichevole; **to settle on sth** (*choose*) decidere *or* optare per qc

▶ **settle down** VI + ADV (*person: in house, armchair etc*) sistemarsi; (: *become calmer*) calmarsi; (: *after wild youth*) mettere la testa a posto; (*situation*) sistemarsi, tornare alla normalità; **to settle down to work** mettersi a lavorare; **has he settled down in his new job?** si è adattato bene al nuovo lavoro?; **to get married and settle down** mettere su casa (e famiglia)

▶ **settle for** VI + PREP: **to settle for sth** accontentarsi di qc; **he settled for £100** ha accettato 100 sterline

▶ **settle in** VI + ADV (*in new house*) sistemarsi, installarsi; (*in new job, neighbourhood*) ambientarsi

▶ **settle up** VI + ADV: **to settle up (with sb)** saldare *or* regolare i conti (con qn).

set·tle·ment ['sɛtlmənt] N **a** (*of bill, debt*) pagamento, saldo; (*of question*) soluzione *f*; (*of dispute*) composi-zione *f*; **in settlement of our account** (*Comm*) a saldo del nostro conto

b (*agreement*) accordo

c (*village*) insediamento, comunità *f inv*; (*colony*) colo-nia.

set·tler ['sɛtləʳ] N colonizzatore(-trice).

♦ **set-to** ['sɛt'tuː] N (*fam: fight*) zuffa; (: *quarrel*) baruffa.

set-up ['sɛt,ʌp] N (*fam: situation*) situazione *f*.

♦ **setup costs** NPL (*Comm*) costi *mpl* d'impianto.

sev·en ['sɛvn] ADJ, N sette (*m*) *inv for usage see* **five**.

sev·en·teen [,sɛvn'tiːn] ADJ, N diciassette (*m*) *inv for usage see* **five**.

sev·en·teenth [,sɛvn'tiːnθ] **1** ADJ diciassettesimo(-a).

2 N (*in series*) diciassettesimo(-a); (*fraction*) diciassette-simo *for usage see* **fifth**.

sev·enth ['sɛvnθ] **1** ADJ settimo(-a).

2 N (*in series*) settimo(-a); (*fraction*) settimo *for usage see* **fifth**.

sev·en·ti·eth ['sɛvntɪθ] **1** ADJ settantesimo(-a).

2 N (*in series*) settantesimo(-a); (*fraction*) settantesimo *for usage see* **fifth**.

sev·en·ty ['sɛvntɪ] ADJ, N settanta (*m*) *inv for usage see* **fifty**.

sev·er ['sɛvəʳ] VT (*rope*) tagliare, recidere; (*limb*) staccare, mozzare; (*fig: relations*) troncare, rompere; (: *communi-cations*) interrompere.

sev·er·al ['sɛvrəl] **1** ADJ parecchi(-ie) *pl*, diversi(-e) *pl*; **several times** diverse volte.

2 PRON parecchi(-ie) *pl*, alcuni(-e) *pl*; **several of us** parecchi di noi, alcuni di noi.

sev·er·al·ly ['sɛvrəlɪ] ADV (*liter*) separatamente, indivi-dualmente.

sev·er·ance ['sɛvərəns] N (*frm: of relations*) rottura.

♦ **severance pay** N (*Industry*) indennità di licenzia-mento.

se·vere [sɪ'vɪəʳ] ADJ (*comp* **-r**, *superl* **-st**) (*problem, case, flooding, injuries*) grave; (*climate, winter, restrictions*) rigido(-a); (*frost, cold*) intenso(-a); (*punishment, person*) severo(-a); (*examination*) rigoroso(-a); (*damage*) ingente; (*blow, criticism*) duro(-a); (*pain, headache, pres-sure*) forte; (*symptoms*) acuto(-a); **to be severe (with sb)** essere severo(-a) (con qn); **a severe cold** un forte raffreddore.

se·vere·ly [sɪ'vɪəlɪ] ADV (*damage, affect, injure*) grave-mente; (*criticise, speak, strain*) duramente; (*punish, reprimand*) severamente; (*test*) rigorosamente; (*curtail, restrict, reduce*) seriamente; **to leave severely alone** (*object*) non toccare mai; (*person*) ignorare completa-mente; (*politics etc*) non interessarsi assolutamente a.

se·ver·ity [sɪ'vɛrɪtɪ] N (*gen*) gravità; (*of punishment*) seve-rità; (*of criticism*) durezza; (*of climate, weather*) rigore *m*; (*of damage*) ingenza; (*of pain*) intensità; (*of symptoms*) acutezza.

Seville [sə'vɪl] N Siviglia.

♦ **Seville orange** N arancia amara.

sew [səʊ] (*pt* **sewed**, *pp* **sewn** *or* **sewed**) VT, VI cucire; **to sew a button on sth** attaccare un bottone a qc

▶ **sew up** VT + ADV (*tear*) rammendare; (*wound*) ricucire; (*hem*) cucire; (*seam*) fare; **it's all sewn up** (*fig fam*) è tutto a posto.

sew·age ['sjuːɪdʒ] N acque *fpl* di scolo, liquami *mpl*.

♦ **sewage discharge** N scarico di liquami.

♦ **sewage farm** N impianto per il riciclaggio delle acque di scolo.

♦ **sewage works** N stabilimento per la depurazione dei liquami.

sew·er ['sjuəʳ] N fogna.

sew·er·age ['suːərɪdʒ] N rete *f* fognaria.

sew·ing ['səʊɪŋ] N (*skill, activity*) (il) cucire *m*; (*piece of work*) cucito; **I like sewing** mi piace cucire.

♦ **sewing basket** N cestino del cucito.

♦ **sewing cotton** N (filo) cucirino.

♦ **sewing machine** N macchina da cucire.

sewn [səʊn] PP of **sew**.

sex [sɛks] **1** N (*gender*) sesso; (*sexual intercourse*) rapporti *mpl* sessuali; **to have sex with sb** avere rapporti sessuali

con qn; **the opposite sex** l'altro sesso; **all he ever thinks about is sex** non pensa che al sesso *or* a quello. [2] ADJ (*discrimination*) sessuale.

♦ **sex act** N atto sessuale.

♦ **sex appeal** N sex appeal *m inv*.

♦ **sex education** N educazione *f* sessuale.

sex·ism ['sɛksɪzəm] N sessismo.

sex·ist ['sɛksɪst] N, ADJ sessista *(m/f)*.

sex·less ['sɛkslɪs] ADJ (*neuter*) asessuato(-a); (*incapable of sexual feeling*) frigido(-a); (*not sexually attractive*) per niente sensuale.

♦ **sex life** N vita sessuale.

♦ **sex link·age** ['sɛks,lɪŋkɪdʒ] N (*Genetics*) eredità *f inv* biologica legata al sesso.

♦ **sex maniac** N maniaco sessuale.

♦ **sex object** N oggetto sessuale; **to be treated as a sex object** (*woman*) essere trattata da donna oggetto; (*man*) essere trattato da uomo oggetto.

sex·olo·gist [sɛk'sɒlədʒɪst] N sessuologo(-a).

sex·ol·ogy [sɛk'sɒlədʒɪ] N sessuologia.

♦ **sex shop** N sex-shop *m inv*.

sex·tet [sɛks'tɛt] N sestetto.

sex·ton ['sɛkstən] N sagrestano.

sex·tup·let [sɛks'tjuːplɪt] N **a** uno(-a) di sei gemelli **b** (*Mus*) sestina.

sex·ual ['sɛksjʊəl] ADJ sessuale; **sexual assault** violenza carnale.

♦ **sexual harassment** N molestie *fpl* sessuali.

♦ **sexual intercourse** N rapporti *mpl* sessuali.

sexu·al·ity [,sɛksjʊˈælɪtɪ] N sessualità.

sex·ual·ly ['sɛksjʊəlɪ] ADV (*attract*) dal punto di vista sessuale; (*reproduce*) sessualmente.

♦ **sex urge** N pulsione *f* sessuale.

sexy ['sɛksɪ] ADJ (*comp* **-ier**, *superl* **-iest**) sexy *inv*, provocante.

Sey·chelles [seɪˈʃɛlz] NPL: **the Seychelles** le Seychelles.

SF [ɛsˈɛf] N ABBR = **science fiction**.

SG [,ɛsˈdʒiː] N ABBR (*Brit*: = *Solicitor General*) *assistente del Procuratore Generale*.

Sgt. ABBR = *sergeant*.

sh [ʃː] EXCL sss.

shab·bi·ness ['ʃæbɪnɪs] N (*of dress, person*) trasandatezza; (*of building*) squallore *m*; (*of treatment*) meschinità.

shab·by ['ʃæbɪ] ADJ (*comp* **-ier**, *superl* **-iest**) (*building*) malandato(-a), squallido(-a); (*clothes*) sciatto(-a); (*person: also*: **shabby-looking**) trasandato(-a); (*behaviour*) meschino(-a); **a shabby trick** un tiro mancino.

shack [ʃæk] [1] N capanno; (*in slum*) baracca. [2] VI: **to shack up with sb** (*fam*) convivere (con qn).

shack·le ['ʃækl] VT (*bind*) mettere i ferri *or* i ceppi a; (*fig: restrict*) ostacolare; see also **shackles**.

shackles ['ʃæklz] NPL ceppi *mpl*, ferri *mpl*; (*fig: constraints*) impacci *mpl*.

shade [ʃeɪd] [1] N **a** ombra; **in the shade** all'ombra; **to put in the shade** (*fig*) mettere in ombra, oscurare
b (*also*: **lampshade**) paralume *m*
c (*also*: **eyeshade**) visiera
d (*Am*: *window shade*) tapparella
e : **shades** NPL (*Am*: *sunglasses*) occhiali *mpl* da sole
f (*of colour*) tonalità *f inv*, sfumatura; (*fig: of meaning, opinion*) sfumatura; **several shades darker/lighter** di tonalità parecchio più scura/chiara; **this lipstick comes in several shades** questo rossetto è disponibile in diverse gradazioni di colore
g (*small quantity*): **just a shade more** un tantino di più; **a**

shade bigger un tantino più grande.
[2] VT (*from sun, light*) riparare; **to shade one's eyes from the sun** ripararsi gli occhi dal sole

▶ **shade in** VT + ADV (*drawing*) ombreggiare.

shad·ing ['ʃeɪdɪŋ] N **a** (*in drawing, painting*) ombreggiatura **b** (*gradation*) sfumatura.

shad·ow ['ʃædəʊ] [1] N ombra; **in shadow** in ombra, all'ombra; **in the shadow (of)** all'ombra (di); **without** *or* **beyond a shadow of a doubt** senz'ombra di dubbio; **to cast a shadow over** proiettare *or* fare ombra su; (*fig*) gettare un'ombra su, offuscare; **he's only a shadow of his former self** è diventato l'ombra di se stesso; **to have shadows under one's eyes** avere le occhiaie. [2] VT (*follow*) pedinare.

♦ **shadow boxing** N allenamento con l'ombra.

♦ **shadow cabinet** N (*Pol Brit*) governo *m* ombra *inv*; **the Shadow Foreign Secretary** il ministro degli Esteri del governo ombra.

shad·owy ['ʃædəʊɪ] ADJ (*form, figure*) indistinto(-a), vago (-a); (*place*) pieno(-a) di ombre.

shady ['ʃeɪdɪ] ADJ (*comp* **-ier**, *superl* **-iest**) (*place*) ombreggiato(-a); (*tree*) ombroso(-a); (*fig: person, deal*) losco(-a), equivoco(-a).

shaft [ʃɑːft] N **a** (*of arrow, spear*) asta; (*of tool*) manico; (*of cart etc*) stanga; (*Aut, Tech*) albero; **shaft of light/sunlight** raggio di luce/sole **b** (*of mine, lift etc*) pozzo; **ventilator shaft** condotto di ventilazione.

shag [ʃæg] [1] N **a** (*bird*) cormorano **b** (*tobacco*) trinciato forte.
[2] ADJ: **shag pile rug/carpet** tappeto folto/moquette *f inv* folta.
[3] VT (*Brit fam!*) scopare (*fam!*).

shagged [ʃægd], **shagged out** ADJ (*Brit fam!*) distrutto (-a), a pezzi.

shag·gy ['ʃægɪ] ADJ (*comp* **-ier**, *superl* **-iest**) (*mane, hair*) ispido(-a), arruffato(-a); (*dog*) a pelo lungo e arruffato.

♦ **shaggy dog story** N storiella interminabile senza capo né coda.

shah [ʃɑː] N scià *m inv*.

shake [ʃeɪk] (*vb: pt* **shook**, *pp* **shaken**) [1] N scossa, scrollata; **with a shake of her head** ... scuotendo *or* scrollando la testa *or* il capo...; **to give a rug a good shake** dare una bella sbattuta ad un tappeto; **he's no great shakes at swimming** (*fam*) nel nuoto non è che brilli; **in two shakes** (*fam*) in quattro e quattr'otto; **to have the shakes** avere la tremarella; **he gets the shakes when ...** gli viene la tremarella quando... .
[2] VT **a** (*person, object*) scuotere; (*building, windows*) far tremare; (*bottle, dice*) agitare; (*cocktail*) shakerare; **to shake one's fist at sb** minacciare qn col pugno; **to shake hands** stringersi la mano, darsi una stretta di mano; **to shake one's head** (*in refusal, dismay*) scuotere la testa
b (*harm: confidence, belief, opinion*) scuotere; (: *reputation*) minare; (*amaze, disturb*) scuotere, sconvolgere; **nothing will shake our resolve** niente ci smuoverà; **even torture did not shake him** nemmeno la tortura riuscì a farlo vacillare; **he needs to be shaken out of his apathy** bisogna scuoterlo dalla sua apatia.
[3] VI (*person, building, voice etc*) tremare; **to shake with fear/cold** tremare di paura/freddo; **to shake with laughter** essere scosso(-a) dalle risate; **the walls shook at the sound** il fragore ha fatto tremare i muri

▶ **shake down** [1] VT + ADV: **to shake down apples from a tree** scuotere un albero per far cadere le mele.
[2] VI + ADV (*fam: sleep*) dormire

▶ **shake off** VT + ADV (*raindrops, snow*) scrollarsi di dosso; (*dust*) scuotersi di dosso; (*fig: cold, cough*) sbarazzarsi di; (: *habit*) togliersi; (: *pursuer*) seminare

▶ **shake out** VT + ADV (*sail*) sciogliere; (*blanket etc*) scuotere; (*bag*) svuotare scuotendo

▶ **shake up** VT + ADV **a** (*bottle*) agitare; (*pillow*) sprimacciare

b (*upset: person*) sconvolgere, scuotere

c (*rouse, stir: person, company etc*) scuotere, dare una scossa salutare a.

shak·en ['ʃeɪkən] PP of **shake**.

shak·er ['ʃeɪkəʳ] N **a** (*also:* **cocktail shaker**) shaker *m inv* **b** (*also:* **salt shaker**) spargisale *m inv*, saliera.

Shake·spear·ean, Shake·spear·ian [ʃeɪks'pɪərɪən] ADJ shakespeariano(-a).

♦ **shake-up** ['ʃeɪk,ʌp] N (*fig*) cambiamento.

shaki·ly ['ʃeɪkɪlɪ] ADV (*reply*) con voce tremante; (*walk*) con passo malfermo; (*write*) con mano tremante.

shaky ['ʃeɪkɪ] ADJ (*comp* **-ier,** *superl* **-iest**) (*table, building*) traballante; (*trembling: voice*) tremulo(-a); (: *hands*) tremante; (: *handwriting*) tremolante; (*fig: health*) vacillante, malfermo(-a); (: *memory*) labile; (: *knowledge*) incerto(-a); (: *start*) incerto(-a); **I feel a bit shaky** mi gira un po' la testa; **my Spanish is rather shaky** il mio spagnolo lascia un po' a desiderare.

shale [ʃeɪl] N scisto.

shall [ʃæl] AUX VB **a** (*used to form 1st person in future tense and questions*): **I shall** *or* **I'll go tomorrow** ci andrò domani, ci vado domani; **shall I open the door or will you?** devo aprire io la porta o lo fai tu?; **shall we hear from you soon?** ci manderà presto sue notizie?; **I'll get some, shall I?** ne prendo un po', che ne dici?; **let's go out, shall we?** usciamo, vuoi?

b (*in commands, promises: emphatic*): **you shall pay for this!** questa la pagherai!; **it shall be done** sarà fatto; **but I wanted to see him – and so you shall** ma volevo vederlo! – lo vedrai!

shal·lot [ʃə'lɒt] N scalogno.

shal·low ['ʃæləʊ] **1** ADJ (*comp* **-er,** *superl* **-est**) (*water etc*) basso(-a), poco profondo(-a); (*dish*) piano(-a); (*breathing*) leggero(-a); (*fig: person*) superficiale, leggero (-a); (: *conversation*) futile, frivolo(-a).

2 : **shallows** NPL secche *fpl*.

shalt [ʃælt] (*old*) 2ND PERS SG of **shall**.

sham [ʃæm] **1** ADJ (*piety*) falso(-a); (*politeness*) finto(-a); (*elections*) fasullo(-a); (*battle, illness*) simulato(-a).

2 N **a** (*imposture*) messinscena, finta **b** (*person*) ciarlatano(-a), impostore *m*.

3 VT fingere, simulare; **to sham illness** fingersi malato (-a).

4 VI fingere, far finta; **he's just shamming** fa solo finta.

sham·an ['ʃæmən] N sciamano.

sham·ble ['ʃæmbl] VI: **to shamble in/out** *etc* entrare/ uscire *etc* trascinando i piedi.

sham·bles ['ʃæmblz] NSG (*scene of confusion*) macello, baraonda; **the area was (in) a shambles after the earthquake** dopo il terremoto la zona era nella distruzione più totale; **the economy is (in) a complete shambles** l'economia è nel caos più totale; **the place was (in) a shambles** c'era un macello; **the game was a shambles** la partita è stata un disastro.

sham·bo·lic [,ʃæm'bɒlɪk] ADJ (*Brit fam*) incasinato(-a).

shame [ʃeɪm] **1** N **a** (*feeling*) vergogna, pudore *m*; (*humiliation*) vergogna; **shame on you!** vergognati!, vergogna!; **to put sb/sth to shame** (*fig*) far sfigurare

qn/qc

b (*pity*): **it's a shame (that/to do)** è un peccato (che + *sub*/fare); **what a shame!** che peccato!.

2 VT (*make ashamed*) far vergognare; (*bring disgrace on*) disonorare; **to shame sb into doing sth** far vergognare qn a tal punto da fargli fare qc.

shame·faced ['ʃeɪm,feɪst] ADJ (*ashamed*) tutto(-a) vergognoso(-a); (*confused*) confuso(-a), timido(-a).

shame·fac·ed·ly ['ʃeɪm,feɪsɪdlɪ] ADV (*see adj*) vergognosamente; timidamente.

shame·fac·ed·ness ['ʃeɪm,feɪstɪdnɪs] N (*see adj*) aria vergognosa; timidezza.

shame·ful ['ʃeɪmfʊl] ADJ vergognoso(-a).

shame·less ['ʃeɪmlɪs] ADJ (*unashamed, brazen*) svergognato(-a), sfrontato(-a); (*immodest*) spudorato(-a).

shame·less·ly ['ʃeɪmlɪslɪ] ADV (*see adj*) sfrontatamente; spudoratamente.

shame·less·ness ['ʃeɪmlɪsnɪs] N (*see adj*) sfrontatezza; spudoratezza.

sham·my, cha·mois ['ʃæmɪ] N (*also:* **shammy leather**) pelle *f* di camoscio.

sham·poo [ʃæm'puː] **1** N (*for hair*) shampoo *m inv*; (*for carpet*) detersivo liquido; **shampoo and set** shampoo e messa in piega.

2 VT (*hair*) lavare (*con shampoo*); (*carpet*) lavare (*con detersivo liquido*); **to shampoo one's hair** farsi lo shampoo.

sham·rock ['ʃæm,rɒk] N trifoglio.

shan·dy ['ʃændɪ] N (*Brit*) birra con gazzosa.

shank [ʃæŋk] N (*of person*) stinco; (*of animal*) garretto; (*of tool*) manico.

shan't [ʃɑːnt] = **shall not**.

shan·tung [ʃæn'tʌŋ] N sciantung *m*.

shan·ty[1] ['ʃæntɪ] N (*also:* **sea shanty**) canzone *f* marinaresca.

shan·ty[2] ['ʃæntɪ] N baracca.

shanty·town ['ʃæntɪ,taʊn] N bidonville *f inv*, baraccopoli *f inv*.

SHAPE [ʃeɪp] N ABBR (= *Supreme Headquarters Allied Powers, Europe*) quartier *m* generale delle forze NATO in Europa.

shape [ʃeɪp] **1** N forma; **what shape is it?** di che forma è?, che forma ha?; **in the shape of a heart** a forma di cuore; **it is rectangular in shape** è di forma rettangolare; **his ears are a funny shape** le sue orecchie hanno una forma buffa; **in all shapes and sizes** d'ogni forma e dimensione, di tutti i tipi; **I can't bear gardening in any shape or form** detesto il giardinaggio di qualunque specie; **to take shape** prendere forma; **to take the shape of** prendere la forma di; **the news reached him in the shape of a telegram** ha ricevuto la notizia sotto forma di telegramma; **the shape of things to come** il volto del futuro; **to lose its shape** (*sweater etc*) sformarsi; **to be in good/poor shape** (*person*) essere in (ottima) forma/giù di forma; (*object*) essere in buone/cattive condizioni; **to knock** *or* **hammer sth into shape** dar forma a qc a colpi di martello; **to knock** *or* **lick into shape** (*fig: business etc*) rimettere in sesto; (: *plan, team*) mettere a punto; (: *athlete*) rimettere in forma; **to get o.s. into shape** rimettersi in forma; **a shape loomed up out of the fog** una forma indistinta emerse dalla nebbia.

2 VT (*clay, stone*) dar forma a; (*fig: ideas, character*) formare; (: *course of events*) determinare, condizionare.

3 VI (*fig: also:* **shape up**): **things are shaping (up) well** le cose si mettono bene; **he's shaping (up) nicely** sta

facendo dei progressi.

-shaped [ʃeɪpt] SUFF: **heart-shaped** a forma di cuore; **diamond-shaped** a forma di losanga.

shape·less [ʃeɪplɪs] ADJ informe, senza forma.

shape·less·ness [ʃeɪplɪsnɪs] N mancanza di forma.

shape·ly [ʃeɪplɪ] ADJ (comp -ier, superl -iest) (woman) ben fatto(-a).

shard [ʃɑːd] N (frm) coccio.

share [ʃɛəʳ] ① N a parte f; **to have a share in the profits** partecipare agli utili; **to have a share in sth** aver parte in qc; **he has a 50% share in a new business venture** è socio al 50% in una nuova impresa commerciale; **he had a share in it** (fig) c'è entrato anche lui; **to take a share in sth** partecipare a qc; **fair shares for all** parti giuste or uguali per tutti; **she's had more than her (fair) share of suffering** ha avuto la sua buona dose di sofferenze; **the minister came in for his share of criticism** il ministro ha avuto la sua parte di critiche; **to do one's (fair) share** fare la propria parte

b (Fin) azione f, titolo; **he has 500 shares in an oil company** possiede 500 azioni di una compagnia di petrolio; **ordinary/preference shares** azioni ordinarie/ privilegiate.

② VT a (also: **share out**) spartirsi; **to share (out) among** or **between** dividere tra; **the thieves shared (out) the money** i ladri si sono spartiti i soldi

b (use jointly): **to share (with)** dividere (con); **shall we share the last bottle of wine?** ci beviamo insieme l'ultima bottiglia di vino?; **shared line** (Telec) duplex m inv

c (fig: have in common) condividere, avere in comune; **she shares his love of gardening** hanno in comune la passione del giardinaggio.

③ VI: **children must learn to share** i bambini devono imparare a dividere ciò che hanno; **share and share alike** un po' per uno non fa male a nessuno; **to share in** (gen) partecipare a; (blame) prendersi la propria parte di.

♦ **share capital** N (Fin) capitale m azionario.

♦ **share certificate** N (Fin) certificato azionario.

share·holder [ʃɛəˌhəʊldəʳ] N azionista m/f.

♦ **share index** N (Fin) indice m azionario.

♦ **share issue** N (Fin) emissione f di azioni.

♦ **share-out** [ʃɛərˌaʊt] N spartizione f, ripartizione f.

♦ **share price** N (Fin) valore m azionario.

shark [ʃɑːk] N (fish) squalo, pescecane m; (fam: swindler) pirata m; (: a successful and rich one) pescecane m.

sharp [ʃɑːp] ① ADJ (comp -er, superl -est) a (edge, razor, knife) tagliente, affilato(-a); (point) acuminato(-a); (pencil) appuntito(-a); (needle, stone) aguzzo(-a); (angle) acuto(-a); (curve, bend) stretto(-a), a gomito; (features) spigoloso(-a); (nose, chin) affilato(-a), aguzzo(-a)

b (abrupt: change, halt) brusco(-a); (: descent) ripido (-a); (: rise, fall) improvviso(-a) e marcato(-a)

c (well-defined: outline) nitido(-a), netto(-a); (: contrast) spiccato(-a), marcato(-a); (TV: picture) chiaro(-a)

d (harsh: smell, taste) acuto(-a), aspro(-a); (: pain, cry) acuto(-a); (: blow) violento(-a); (: tone, voice) secco(-a), aspro(-a); (: wind, frost) penetrante, pungente; (: rebuke) aspro(-a); (: retort, tongue) tagliente, duro(-a); (: words) pungente; **to be sharp with sb** rimproverare aspramente qn

e (acute: eyesight, hearing, sense of smell) acuto(-a), fine; (: mind, intelligence) acuto(-a); (: person) sveglio(-a), svelto(-a)

f (Mus): **C sharp** do diesis.

② ADV a (Mus) in diesis

b : **at 5 o'clock sharp** alle 5 in punto; **turn sharp left** gira tutto a sinistra; **look sharp!** sbrigati!, spicciati!.

③ N (Mus) diesis m inv.

sharp·en [ʃɑːpən] VT a (tool, blade etc) affilare; (pencil) temperare

b (outline) mettere in risalto, far spiccare; (contrast, difference) sottolineare, evidenziare; (TV picture) mettere a fuoco; (conflict) intensificare; (desire, pain) acuire; (appetite) aguzzare, stuzzicare; **to sharpen one's wits** aguzzare l'ingegno.

sharp·en·er [ʃɑːpnəʳ] N (for pencils) temperamatite m inv; (for knives) affilacoltelli m inv.

♦ **sharp-eyed** [ˌʃɑːpˈaɪd], **sharp-sighted** [ˌʃɑːpˈsaɪtɪd] ADJ dalla vista acuta.

♦ **sharp-faced** [ˌʃɑːpˈfeɪst], **sharp-featured** [ˌʃɑːpˈfiːtʃəd] ADJ dal volto affilato.

sharp·ish [ʃɑːpɪʃ] ADV (Brit fam: quickly) subito.

sharp·ly [ʃɑːplɪ] ADV a (abruptly: turn, rise, stop) bruscamente b (clearly: stand out, contrast) nettamente c (harshly: criticize, retort) duramente, aspramente.

♦ **sharp practice** N pratiche fpl poco oneste.

sharp·shooter [ʃɑːpˌʃuːtəʳ] N tiratore m scelto.

♦ **sharp-sighted** [ˌʃɑːpˈsaɪtɪd] ADJ = **sharp-eyed**.

♦ **sharp-tempered** [ˌʃɑːpˈtɛmpəd] ADJ irascibile.

♦ **sharp-witted** [ˌʃɑːpˈwɪtɪd] ADJ sveglio(-a).

shat·ter [ʃætəʳ] ① VT (glass, window) frantumare, mandare in frantumi; (door) fracassare; (health) rovinare; (career) compromettere definitivamente; (nerves) mandare in pezzi; (self-confidence, hope) distruggere

② VI frantumarsi, andare in frantumi; **it shattered into a thousand pieces** è andato in mille pezzi.

shat·tered [ʃætəd] ADJ (grief-stricken) sconvolto(-a); (fam: exhausted) a pezzi, distrutto(-a).

shat·ter·ing [ʃætərɪŋ] ADJ (attack) schiacciante; (defeat, news) disastroso(-a); (experience) traumatico(-a); (day, journey) faticoso(-a); **it was a shattering blow to his hopes** è stato un colpo tremendo per le sue speranze.

shatter·proof [ʃætəˌpruːf] ADJ infrangibile.

shave [ʃeɪv] ① N: **to have a shave** farsi la barba; **to have a close shave** (fig) cavarsela per un pelo.

② VT (person, legs, head) radere, rasare; (wood) piallare; (fig: graze) sfiorare, rasentare; **to shave off one's beard** tagliarsi la barba.

③ VI (person) farsi la barba, radersi, sbarbarsi.

shav·en [ʃeɪvn] ADJ (head) rasato(-a), rapato(-a) (a zero).

shav·er [ʃeɪvəʳ] N (also: **electric shaver**) rasoio elettrico.

shav·ing [ʃeɪvɪŋ] N, GEN PL (of wood etc) truciolo.

♦ **shaving brush** N pennello da barba.

♦ **shaving cream** N crema da barba.

♦ **shaving soap** N sapone m da barba.

shawl [ʃɔːl] N scialle m.

she [ʃiː] ① PERS PRON a (used of people, animals) lei; **she has gone out** è uscita; **there she is** eccola; **SHE didn't do it** non è stata lei a farlo b (used of countries, cars, ships): **she does 0 to 60 in 10 seconds** ha un'accelerazione da 0 a 60 in 10 secondi.

② N: **it's a she** (animal, fam: baby) è una femmina.

sheaf [ʃiːf] N (pl **sheaves**) (Agr) covone m; (of papers) fascio.

shear [ʃɪəʳ] (pt **sheared**, pp **sheared** or **shorn**) VT (sheep) tosare

▶ **shear off** VI + ADV (break off) spezzarsi.

shear·er [ʃɪərəʳ] N (person) tosatore(-trice); (machine)

tosatrice *f*.

shear·ing [ˈʃɪərɪŋ] N tosatura.

shears [ʃɪəz] NPL (*for gardening*) cesoie *fpl*; (*for dress-making*) forbici *fpl*; (*for sheep*) forbici *fpl* da tosatore.

sheath [ʃiːθ] N (*gen*) guaina; (*for sword*) guaina, fodero; (*contraceptive*) preservativo.

sheathe [ʃiːð] VT ricoprire; (*sword*) rinfoderare.

♦ **sheath knife** N coltello con fodero.

sheaves [ʃiːvz] NPL of **sheaf**.

♦ **she-bear** [ˈʃiːˌbɛəʳ] N orsa.

she'd [ʃiːd] = **she had, she would**.

shed[1] [ʃɛd] (*pt, pp* **shed**) VT **a** (*get rid of: gen*) perdere; (: *clothes*) togliersi; (: *employees*) disfarsi di, licenziare **b** (*tears*) versare; (*blood*) spargere **c** (*send out: light, warmth*) diffondere; **to shed light on** (*problem, mystery*) far luce su.

shed[2] [ʃɛd] N (*in garden*) capanno; (*for bicycles*) rimessa; (*Industry, Rail*) capannone *m*; (*for cattle*) stalla.

♦ **she-elephant** [ˈʃiːˌɛlɪfənt] N elefantessa.

sheen [ʃiːn] N lucentezza.

sheep [ʃiːp] N, PL INV pecora; **to make sheep's eyes at sb** (*fig*) fare gli occhi dolci a qn.

sheep·dog [ˈʃiːpˌdɒg] N cane *m* (da) pastore.

♦ **sheep farm** N allevamento di pecore.

♦ **sheep farmer** N allevatore *m* di pecore.

♦ **sheep farming** N pastorizia.

sheep·fold [ˈʃiːpˌfəʊld] N ovile *m*.

sheep·ish [ˈʃiːpɪʃ] ADJ (*look, smile*) imbarazzato(-a), mortificato(-a).

sheep·ish·ly [ˈʃiːpɪʃlɪ] ADV (*look, smile*) in modo imbarazzato, con aria mortificata.

sheep·skin [ˈʃiːpˌskɪn] [1] N pelle *f* di pecora *or* di montone.

[2] ADJ (*gloves*) di montone.

♦ **sheepskin jacket** N (giacca di) montone *m*.

sheer[1] [ʃɪəʳ] [1] ADJ (*comp* **-er**, *superl* **-est**) **a** (*utter: madness, greed*) puro(-a); (: *waste of time*) totale; (: *necessity*) assoluto(-a); **that's sheer robbery!** è un furto bello e buono!; **the sheer impossibility of ...** l'assoluta impossibilità di...; **by sheer chance** [OR] **by a sheer accident** per puro caso *or* pura combinazione **b** (*transparent*) trasparente **c** (*precipitous*) a picco; **a sheer drop** uno strapiombo.

[2] ADV a picco, a perpendicolo.

sheer[2] [ʃɪəʳ] VI (*also*: **to sheer off**: *gen, Naut*) deviare.

sheet[1] [ʃiːt] N (*on bed*) lenzuolo; (*also*: **dust sheet**) telo; (*of paper, plastic*) foglio; (*of metal, glass, ice*) lastra; (*of water*) distesa; (*of flame*) muro

▶ **sheet down** VI + ADV (*rain*) piovere a dirotto.

sheet[2] [ʃiːt] N (*Naut*) scotta.

♦ **sheet anchor** N ancora di speranza *or* di riserva.

♦ **sheet feed** N (*on printer*) alimentazione *f* di fogli.

♦ **sheet lightning** N lampeggio diffuso.

♦ **sheet metal** N lamiera.

♦ **sheet music** N spartito (*non rilegato*).

sheik, sheikh [ʃeɪk] N sceicco.

sheik·dom, sheikh·dom [ˈʃeɪkdəm] N sceiccato.

shel·duck [ˈʃɛlˌdʌk] N volpoca (*femmina*).

shelf [ʃɛlf] N (*pl* **shelves**) **a** (*in cupboard, oven*) ripiano; (*fixed to wall*) mensola; **to be on the shelf** (*fig fam: woman*) essere zitella **b** (*in rock face, underwater*) piattaforma.

♦ **shelf life** N (*Comm*) durata di conservazione.

♦ **shelf mark** N (*in libraries*) collocazione *f*, segnatura.

♦ **shelf unit** N scaffalatura.

she'll [ʃiːl] = **she will, she shall**.

shell [ʃɛl] [1] N **a** (*of egg, nut, tortoise*) guscio; (*of oyster, mussel*) conchiglia; (*of lobster*) corazza, guscio; (*Phys*) guscio elettronico; **to come out of one's shell** (*fig*) uscire dal (proprio) guscio

b (*of building*) struttura, scheletro; (*of ship*) ossatura

c (*Mil*) granata.

[2] VT **a** (*nuts*) sgusciare; (*peas, beans*) sgranare

b (*Mil*) bombardare

▶ **shell out** (*fam*) [1] VI + ADV: **to shell out (for)** sganciare soldi (per).

[2] VT + ADV: **to shell out (for)** (*money*) sganciare (per).

shell·fire [ˈʃɛlˌfaɪəʳ] N bombardamento.

shell·fish [ˈʃɛlˌfɪʃ] N, PL INV (*crab etc*) crostaceo; (*mollusc*) mollusco; (*Culin*) frutti *mpl* di mare.

shell·ing [ˈʃɛlɪŋ] N bombardamento.

shell·proof [ˈʃɛlˌpruːf] ADJ a prova di bomba.

♦ **shell shock** N (*old*) psicosi traumatica (da bombardamento).

♦ **shell-shocked** [ˈʃɛlˌʃɒkt] ADJ **a** (*soldier*) traumatizzato(-a) da un bombardamento **b** (*stunned, dazed*) sotto shock.

shell·suit [ˈʃɛlˌsuːt] N tuta di acetato.

shel·ter [ˈʃɛltəʳ] [1] N **a** (*protection*) riparo; **under the shelter of** al riparo di; **to seek shelter (from)** cercare riparo (da *or* contro), ripararsi (da); **to take shelter (from)** mettersi al riparo (da)

b (*construction: on mountain etc*) rifugio; **bus shelter** pensilina; **air-raid shelter** rifugio antiaereo.

[2] VT **a** (*protect*): **to shelter (from)** riparare (da); (*from blame etc*) proteggere (da)

b (*give lodging to: homeless, criminal etc*) dare rifugio *or* asilo a.

[3] VI ripararsi, mettersi al riparo; **to shelter from the rain** ripararsi dalla pioggia; **to shelter under a tree** ripararsi sotto un albero.

shel·tered [ˈʃɛltəd] ADJ (*place*) riparato(-a); (*childhood*) sereno(-a), senza problemi; (*environment*) protetto(-a); **she has led a very sheltered life** è vissuta nella bambagia.

shelve [ʃɛlv] VT (*fig: postpone*) accantonare.

shelves [ʃɛlvz] NPL of **shelf**.

shelv·ing [ˈʃɛlvɪŋ] N scaffalature *fpl*.

shep·herd [ˈʃɛpəd] [1] N pastore *m*; **the Good Shepherd** (*Rel*) il buon Pastore.

[2] VT: **to shepherd sb in/out** accompagnare qn dentro/fuori; **she shepherded the children across the road** ha aiutato i bambini ad attraversare la strada.

shep·herd·ess [ˈʃɛpədɪs] N pastorella.

♦ **shepherd's pie** N (*Culin*) timballo di carne macinata e purè di patate.

sher·bet [ˈʃɜːbət] N (*Brit: powder*) polvere effervescente al gusto di frutta; (*Am: water ice*) sorbetto.

sher·iff [ˈʃɛrɪf] N sceriffo.

Sher·pa [ˈʃɜːpə] N sherpa *m inv*.

sher·ry [ˈʃɛrɪ] N sherry *m inv*.

she's [ʃiːz] = **she is, she has**.

Shet·land [ˈʃɛtlənd] N: **the Shetlands** [OR] **the Shetland Islands** le (isole) Shetland.

♦ **Shetland pony** N pony *m inv* delle Shetland.

♦ **Shetland wool** N (lana) Shetland.

shield [ʃiːld] [1] N (*armour*) scudo; (*on machine etc*) schermo (di protezione).

[2] VT: **to shield sb from sth** riparare qn da qc; **to shield sb with one's body** fare scudo a qn con il proprio corpo.

shift [ʃɪft] [1] N **a** (*change: in wind, opinion etc*) cambia-

mento; (*movement: of load*) spostamento; (*Comm: in demand*) variazione *f* (della domanda)

b (*period of work, group of workers*) turno; **to work in shifts** fare i turni (di lavoro); **to work on night/day shift** fare il turno di notte/di giorno

c (*old: expedient*) espediente *m*; **to make shift with/ without sth** arrangiarsi con/senza qc

d (*Am Aut: also:* **gear shift**) cambio.

2 VT (*gen*) spostare; (*sth stuck*) smuovere; (*dirt, stain*) togliere; (*employee*) trasferire; (*change: position etc*) cambiare; **to shift scenery** (*Theatre*) cambiare le scene; **to shift the blame on to sb** scaricare la colpa su qn.

3 VI **a** (*gen*) spostarsi; (*opinions*) mutare; (*change one's mind*) cambiare idea; **the wind has shifted to the south** il vento ha girato verso sud; **he shifted over to the door** si è avvicinato alla porta; **shift off the sofa!** togliti dal divano!; **shift up** *or* **over** *or* **along!** spostati!; **that car's certainly shifting** (*fam*) quella macchina va molto forte; **to shift into second gear** (*Aut*) innestare la seconda (marcia)

b: **to shift for o.s.** arrangiarsi da sé, cavarsela da solo(-a).

shifti·ly ['ʃɪftɪlɪ] ADV (*behave*) in modo equivoco, in modo losco; (*answer*) evasivamente.

shifti·ness ['ʃɪftɪnɪs] N (*of behaviour*) equivocità; (*of answer*) evasività.

shift·ing ['ʃɪftɪŋ] ADJ (*sand*) mobile; (*crowd*) in movimento; (*opinion, scene*) mutevole.

♦ **shifting cultivation** N agricoltura itinerante.

♦ **shift key** N (*on typewriter*) tasto delle maiuscole.

shift·less ['ʃɪftlɪs] ADJ: **a shiftless person** un(a) inetto(-a).

shift·less·ness ['ʃɪftlɪsnɪs] N inettitudine *f*.

♦ **shift work** N: **to do shift work** fare i turni.

shifty ['ʃɪftɪ] ADJ (*comp* **-ier,** *superl* **-iest**) (*person*) losco(-a), equivoco(-a); (*behaviour*) equivoco(-a); (*eyes*) sfuggente.

Shi·ite ['ʃiːaɪt] ADJ, N sciita *(m/f)*.

shil·ling ['ʃɪlɪŋ] N (*Brit*) scellino.

shilly·shally ['ʃɪlɪˌʃælɪ] VI (*fam*) tentennare, esitare; **don't shillyshally!** OR **stop shillyshallying!** deciditi una buona volta!

shim·mer ['ʃɪmə'] VI (*gen*) luccicare, scintillare; (*heat haze*) tremolare.

shim·mer·ing ['ʃɪmərɪŋ] ADJ (*gen*) luccicante, scintillante; (*haze*) tremolante; (*satin etc*) cangiante.

shin [ʃɪn] **1** N stinco.

2 VI: **to shin up a tree** arrampicarsi in cima a un albero.

shin·bone ['ʃɪnˌbəʊn] N tibia.

shin·dig ['ʃɪnˌdɪg] N (*fam*) festa indiavolata.

shin·dy ['ʃɪndɪ] N (*fam: noise*) gazzarra, casino; (: *brawl*) rissa; **to kick up a shindy** fare casino.

shine [ʃaɪn] **1** (*pt, pp* **shone**) VI (ri)splendere, brillare; **the light was shining in his eyes** aveva la luce negli occhi; **the light was shining under the door** si vedeva la luce sotto la porta; **the metal shone in the sun** il metallo risplendeva al sole; **her face shone with happiness** il suo viso splendeva di felicità; **her eyes shone with joy** i suoi occhi brillavano di gioia; **to shine at maths** (*fig*) brillare in matematica.

2 VT (*pt, pp* **shone** *or* **shined**) **a**: **shine the light** *or* **your torch over here** fai luce (con la pila) in questa direzione

b (*pt, pp* **shined**) (*polish*) lucidare, lustrare.

3 N (*of sun, metal*) lucentezza, splendore *m*; **to give sth a shine** dare una lucidata a qc; **those shoes have got a good shine** quelle scarpe luccicano; **to take the shine**

off sth far perdere il lucido a qc; (*fig*) offuscare qc; **to take a shine to sb** (*fig*) prendere qn in simpatia; **come rain or shine** ... qualunque tempo faccia..., col bello o col cattivo tempo... .

shin·gle ['ʃɪŋgl] N **a** (*on beach*) ciottoli *mpl* **b** (*on roof*) scandola **c** (*Am: signboard*) insegna.

shin·gles ['ʃɪŋglz] NSG (*Med*) fuoco di Sant'Antonio.

shin·gly ['ʃɪŋglɪ] ADJ (*beach*) ciottoloso(-a).

shin·ing ['ʃaɪnɪŋ] ADJ (*surface, hair*) lucente; (*light*) brillante; (*eyes*) splendente; **a shining example** (*fig*) un fulgido esempio.

shiny ['ʃaɪnɪ] ADJ (*comp* **-ier,** *superl* **-iest**) lucido(-a).

ship [ʃɪp] **1** N nave *f*; **Her** (*or* **His**) **Majesty's Ship Ark Royal** l'Ark Royal *f*; **on board ship** a bordo; **ship's company** equipaggio; **ship's papers** carte *fpl* di bordo; **ship's stores** riserve *fpl* di bordo.

2 VT **a** (*take on board: goods, water*) imbarcare; (: *oars*) tirare in barca

b (*transport: usu by ship*) spedire (*via mare*); **a new engine had to be shipped out to them** hanno dovuto spedire loro un motore nuovo.

ship·builder ['ʃɪpˌbɪldə'] N costruttore *m* navale.

ship·building ['ʃɪpˌbɪldɪŋ] N costruzione *f* navale.

♦ **ship chan·dler** ['ʃɪpˌtʃændlə'] N (*person*) fornitore *m* marittimo; (*company*) società *f inv* di forniture navali.

ship·load ['ʃɪpˌləʊd] N carico; (*fig fam*) marea.

ship·mate ['ʃɪpˌmeɪt] N compagno di bordo.

ship·ment ['ʃɪpmənt] N (*act*) spedizione *f*; (*quantity*) carico.

ship·owner ['ʃɪpˌəʊnə'] N armatore *m*.

ship·per ['ʃɪpə'] N spedizioniere *m* (marittimo).

ship·ping ['ʃɪpɪŋ] N (*ships*) imbarcazioni *fpl*; (*traffic*) navigazione *f*; **a danger to shipping** un pericolo per la navigazione.

♦ **shipping agent** N agente *m* marittimo.

♦ **shipping company, shipping line** N compagnia di navigazione.

♦ **shipping lane** N rotta (di navigazione).

ship·shape ['ʃɪpˌʃeɪp] ADJ in perfetto ordine.

♦ **ship-to-shore** [ˌʃɪptə'ʃɔː'] ADJ (*radio*) per le comunicazioni da bordo a terra.

ship·wreck ['ʃɪpˌrɛk] **1** N (*ship*) relitto; (*event*) naufragio.

2 VT: **to be shipwrecked** naufragare, fare naufragio.

ship·yard ['ʃɪpˌjɑːd] N cantiere *m* navale.

shire ['ʃaɪə'] N (*Brit*) contea.

shirk [ʃɜːk] **1** VT (*duty*) sottrarsi a, sfuggire a; (*issue*) ignorare; (*work*) scansare; **to shirk doing sth** evitare di fare qc.

2 VI fare lo(-a) scansafatiche.

shirk·er ['ʃɜːkə'] N scansafatiche *m/f inv*.

shirt [ʃɜːt] N (*man's*) camicia; (*woman's*) camicetta, camicia; **in one's shirt sleeves** in maniche di camicia; **to put one's shirt on sth** (*fig: Betting*) giocarsi anche la camicia su qc; **keep your shirt on!** (*fig fam*) non ti scaldare!

♦ **shirt front** N sparato.

shirty ['ʃɜːtɪ] ADJ (*comp* **-ier,** *superl* **-iest**) (*fam*): **he was pretty shirty about it** si è incavolato abbastanza per questa storia.

shit [ʃɪt] (*fam!*) **1** EXCL merda (*fam!*).

2 N (*excrement*) merda (*fam!*); (*rubbish*) porcheria; (*worthless person*) pezzo di merda (*fam!*); **to be in the shit** (*fig*) essere nella merda (*fam!*).

3 VI cacare.

shit·ty ['ʃɪtɪ] ADJ (*comp* **-tier,** *superl* **-tiest**) (*fam!*) di merda (*fam!*)

shiv·er[1] [ˈʃɪvəʳ] [1] N brivido; **it sends shivers down my spine** [OR] **it gives me the shivers** mi fa venire i brividi. [2] VI: **to shiver (with)** (*cold, fear*) rabbrividire (da), tremare (da).

shiv·er[2] [ˈʃɪvəʳ] (*liter*) [1] VT frantumare. [2] VI frantumarsi. [3] N (*of glass*) scheggia.

shiv·ery [ˈʃɪvərɪ] ADJ (*from cold*) che ha i brividi; (*from fear*) tremante; **I feel shivery** ho i brividi.

shoal [ʃəʊl] N (*of fish*) banco.

shock [ʃɒk] [1] N **a** (*Elec, of earthquake*) scossa; (*of explosion*) scossone *m*; (*of collision*) urto; **to get a shock** (*Elec*) prendere la scossa

b (*emotional*) shock *m inv*, colpo; **the shock was too much for him** non ha sopportato il colpo *or* lo shock; **it came as a shock to hear that …** è stato uno shock venire a sapere che…; **it may come as a shock to you, but …** per quanto possa sorprenderti…; **to give sb a shock** far venire un colpo a qn

c (*Med*) shock *m inv*; **to be suffering from shock** essere in stato di shock.

[2] VT (*affect emotionally, scandalize*) scioccare; **he is easily shocked** si scandalizza facilmente; **to shock sb out of his complacency** far perdere a qn un po' della propria boria.

[3] VI far scandalo, destare scalpore.

♦ **shock absorber** N (*Aut*) ammortizzatore *m*.

shock·er [ˈʃɒkəʳ] N (*fam*): **it was a real shocker** è stata una vera bomba.

shock·ing [ˈʃɒkɪŋ] ADJ (*appalling: news*) scioccante; (*: sight, crime*) agghiacciante; (*causing scandal: behaviour, film*) scandaloso(-a); (*: price*) sbalorditivo(-a); (*: waste*) vergognoso(-a); (*very bad: weather, handwriting*) orribile; (*: results*) disastroso(-a).

♦ **shocking pink** ADJ rosa shocking *inv*.

shock·proof [ˈʃɒkˌpruːf] ADJ antiurto *inv*.

♦ **shock reaction** N grande scalpore *m*.

♦ **shock tactics** NPL (*in war, struggle*) tattica *fsg* d'urto.

♦ **shock therapy, shock treatment** N (*Med*) trattamento con elettroshock.

♦ **shock troops** NPL truppe *fpl* d'assalto.

♦ **shock wave** N (*of explosion, earthquake*) onda d'urto; (*fig*): **shock waves** NPL impatto *msg*.

shod [ʃɒd] PT, PP of **shoe**.

shod·dy [ˈʃɒdɪ] ADJ (*comp* **-ier**, *superl* **-iest**) scadente.

shoe [ʃuː] (*vb: pt, pp* **shod**) [1] N **a** scarpa, calzatura; **I wouldn't like to be in his shoes** non vorrei essere nei suoi panni **b** (*horseshoe*) ferro di cavallo **c** (*also:* **brake shoe**) ganascia (del freno).

[2] VT (*horse*) ferrare.

shoe·brush [ˈʃuːˌbrʌʃ] N spazzola per le scarpe.

shoe·horn [ˈʃuːˌhɔːn] N calzante *m*, calzascarpe *m inv*.

shoe·lace [ˈʃuːˌleɪs] N laccio (di scarpa), stringa.

shoe·maker [ˈʃuːˌmeɪkəʳ] N calzolaio.

♦ **shoe polish** N lucido da *or* per scarpe.

♦ **shoe rack** N scarpiera.

♦ **shoe repairs** NPL calzoleria *fsg*.

shoe·shop [ˈʃuːˌʃɒp] N negozio di scarpe *or* di calzature.

shoe·string [ˈʃuːˌstrɪŋ] N (*Am*) stringa (di scarpa); **on a shoestring** (*fig: do sth*) con quattro soldi; (*: live*) contando il centesimo.

shoe·tree [ˈʃuːˌtriː] N forma per scarpe.

shone [ʃɒn] PT, PP of **shine**.

shoo [ʃuː] [1] EXCL sciò!, via!.

[2] VT (*also:* **shoo away, shoo off**) cacciare (via).

shook [ʃʊk] PT of **shake**.

shoot [ʃuːt] (*vb: pt, pp* **shot**) [1] VT **a** (*hit*) colpire, sparare a; (*hunt*) cacciare, andare a caccia di; (*execute*) fucilare; (*kill*) uccidere; **he was shot in the arm** gli hanno sparato al braccio; **to shoot o.s. in the foot** (*fig*) darsi la zappa sui piedi; **you'll get shot if you do that!** (*fig fam*) puoi rimetterci le penne!

b (*fire: bullet*) sparare; (*: arrow*) scoccare; (*: missile*) lanciare; **to shoot one's way out** farsi largo a colpi di pistola; **to shoot an arrow at sb** tirare una freccia contro qn; **to shoot dice** tirare i dadi

c (*direct: look, smile*) lanciare; **to shoot a question at sb** sparare una domanda a qn

d (*Cine: film, scene*) girare; (*: person, object*) riprendere

e (*pass quickly: rapids*) scendere.

[2] VI **a** : **to shoot (at sb/sth)** (*with gun*) sparare (a qn/qc); (*with bow*) tirare (su *or* contro qn/qc); **to shoot on sight** sparare a vista; **to shoot back** rispondere al fuoco; **to shoot at goal** (*Ftbl etc*) tirare in porta *or* a rete

b (*rush*): **to shoot in/out** entrare/uscire come una freccia; **to shoot across to** precipitarsi verso; **to shoot past sb** sfrecciare vicino a qn; **the pain shot up his leg** sentì una fitta lancinante alla gamba; **the bullet shot past his head** il colpo gli ha sfiorato la testa.

[3] N **a** (*Bot*) germoglio

b (*shooting party*) partita di caccia; (*competition*) gara di tiro; (*preserve*) riserva di caccia

c (*fig fam*): **the whole shoot** tutto, ogni cosa

▶ **shoot down** VT + ADV (*aeroplane*) abbattere; (*person*) uccidere; (*fig: person*) distruggere; (*: argument*) demolire

▶ **shoot out** [1] VT + ADV: **he shot out his arm and saved me** ha allungato prontamente il braccio e mi ha salvato; **to shoot it out** regolare una faccenda a colpi di pistola. [2] VI + ADV (*water*) sprizzare; (*flames*) divampare

▶ **shoot up** [1] VI + ADV **a** (*flames, rocket*) alzarsi; (*water*) scaturire con forza; (*price*) salire alle stelle

b : **he's shooting up** sta crescendo a vista d'occhio; **he has shot up** è cresciuto molto. [2] VT + ADV (*fam: heroin*) bucarsi.

shoot·ing [ˈʃuːtɪŋ] [1] N **a** (*shots*) spari *mpl*, colpi *mpl* d'arma da fuoco; (*continuous shooting*) sparatoria **b** (*act: murder*) uccisione *f* (a colpi d'arma da fuoco); (*: wounding*) ferimento **c** (*Cine*) riprese *fpl* **d** (*Hunting*) caccia.

[2] ADJ (*pain*) lancinante.

♦ **shooting gallery** N tiro a segno.

♦ **shooting match** N: **the whole shooting match** (*fig fam*) l'intera faccenda.

♦ **shooting range** N poligono di tiro.

♦ **shooting star** N stella cadente.

♦ **shooting stick** N *bastone da passeggio trasformabile in sgabello.*

shop [ʃɒp] [1] N **a** (*Comm*) negozio; **at the baker's shop** in panetteria; **to shut up shop** chiudere; (*fig*) chiudere bottega; **to talk shop** (*fig*) parlare di lavoro; **all over the shop** (*fig: fam*) dappertutto

b (*Industry: workshop*) officina; **repair shop** officina di riparazione.

[2] VI (*gen*) fare acquisti, fare compere; (*for food*) fare la spesa; **to go shopping** andare a fare lo shopping, andare a fare la spesa; **I was shopping for a dress** cercavo un vestito.

[3] VT (*fam: betray*) tradire

▶ **shop around** VI + ADV (*compare prices*) confrontare i prezzi; (*fig: weigh up alternatives*) confrontare diverse

possibilità.

shopa·holic [ˌʃɒpəˈhɒlɪk] N (fam) maniaco(-a) dello shopping.

♦ **shop assistant** N (Brit) commesso(-a).

♦ **shop floor** N (Industry): **the shop floor (workers)** le maestranze; **he works on the shop floor** è un operaio.

♦ **shop front** N (Brit) facciata di negozio.

♦ **shop girl** N commessa.

shop·keeper [ˈʃɒpˌkiːpəʳ] N negoziante m/f, bottegaio (-a).

shop·lift [ˈʃɒpˌlɪft] VI taccheggiare.

shop·lifter [ˈʃɒpˌlɪftəʳ] N taccheggiatore(-trice).

shop·lifting [ˈʃɒpˌlɪftɪŋ] N taccheggio.

shop·per [ˈʃɒpəʳ] N **a** (person) acquirente m/f **b** (bag) borsa per la spesa.

shop·ping [ˈʃɒpɪŋ] N (goods) acquisti mpl, compere fpl; (: food) spesa; **she loves shopping** adora lo shopping.

♦ **shopping bag** N borsa per la spesa.

♦ **shopping basket** N cestino della spesa, sporta.

♦ **shopping centre** N centro commerciale.

♦ **shopping list** N lista della spesa.

♦ **shopping precinct** N zona dei negozi (chiusa al traffico automobilistico).

shop·soiled [ˈʃɒpˌsɔɪld] ADJ sciupato(-a) (da lunga esposizione in vetrina).

♦ **shop steward** N (Brit: Industry) rappresentante m/f sindacale.

shop·walker [ˈʃɒpˌwɔːkəʳ] N (Brit) caporeparto m/f.

♦ **shop window** N vetrina.

♦ **shore** [ʃɔːʳ] VT: **to shore up** (tunnel, wall) puntellare; (fig) consolidare; (: prices) mantenere.

shore[1] [ʃɔːʳ] N (of sea) riva; (of lake) sponda, riva; (beach) spiaggia; (coast) costa; **on shore** a terra; **to go on shore** sbarcare; **the ship hugged the shore** la nave navigava sotto costa.

♦ **shore leave** N (Naut) franchigia.

shore·line [ˈʃɔːlaɪn] N litorale m.

shorn [ʃɔːn] **1** PP of **shear**.

2 ADJ **a** (grass) tosato(-a); (head) rasato(-a) **b** (fig): **shorn of** (power, glory) privato(-a) di.

short [ʃɔːt] **1** ADJ (comp -**er**, superl -**est**) **a** (in length, distance) corto(-a); (in time) breve; (person) basso(-a); **the days are getting shorter** le giornate si stanno accorciando; **to be short in the leg** (person) avere le gambe corte; (trousers) essere corti di gamba; **to win by a short head** (Racing) vincere di mezza testa or incollatura; **a short time ago** poco tempo fa; **time is getting short** il tempo stringe; **that was short and sweet** è stato sbrigativo; **to make short work of sb** (fig) sistemare qn; **to make short work of sth** (job) sbrigare qc; (cake, drink) far fuori qc

b (insufficient): **I'm £30 short** mi mancano 30 sterline; **to give short weight** or **short measure to sb** imbrogliare qn sul peso or sulla misura; **to be in short supply** scarseggiare; **to be short of sth** (money) essere a corto di qc; **I'm short of time** ho poco tempo; **short of breath** senza fiato, con il fiatone; **it's little short of madness** è pazzia bella e buona; **three miles short of home** a tre miglia da casa

c (concise) breve; **short and to the point** breve e conciso; **"Pat" is short for "Patricia"** "Pat" è il diminutivo di "Patricia"; **in short** in breve, a farla breve

d (reply, manner) secco(-a), brusco(-a); **to have a short temper** essere irascibile; **to be short with sb** essere brusco(-a) con qn.

2 ADV **a** (suddenly, abruptly): **to stop short** fermarsi di colpo; **I'd stop short of stealing** non arriverei mai a rubare; **he wouldn't stop short of murder** arriverebbe al punto di uccidere; **to pull up short** frenare bruscamente

b (insufficiently): **to run short of sth** rimanere senza qc; **we never went short (of anything) as children** da bambini non ci è mai mancato nulla; **to come** or **fall short of** (expectations) venire meno a; (needs) non soddisfare; **to sell sb short** (fig: belittle) sminuire qn, buttar giù qn; **to be taken** or **caught short** (fam) avere un bisognino urgente

c (except): **short of selling the house, what can we do?** non vedo cos'altro potremo fare, a parte vendere la casa; **I'll do anything short of...** farò tutto tranne che...; **nothing short of a miracle can save him** solo un miracolo potrebbe salvarlo.

3 N **a** (Elec) = **short circuit**

b (fam: drink) superalcolico

c (also: **short film**) cortometraggio; see also **shorts**.

4 VT, VI (Elec) = **short-circuit**.

short·age [ˈʃɔːtɪdʒ] N carenza, scarsità f inv; **the housing shortage** la crisi degli alloggi.

♦ **short back and sides** N (Brit) taglio di capelli corto sulla nuca e sulle tempie.

short·bread [ˈʃɔːtˌbrɛd] N frollino, biscotto di pasta frolla.

short·cake [ˈʃɔːtˌkeɪk] N (Am) torta di pasta frolla farcita con frutta e panna; (Brit) frollino.

♦ **short-change** [ˌʃɔːtˈtʃeɪndʒ] VT: **to short-change sb** imbrogliare qn sul resto; (fig) fregare qn.

♦ **short-circuit** [ˌʃɔːtˈsɜːkɪt] **1** VT (Elec) mettere in cortocircuito.

2 VI (Elec) fare cortocircuito.

♦ **short circuit** N (Elec) cortocircuito.

short·coming [ˌʃɔːtˈkʌmɪŋ] N difetto.

♦ **short crust pastry** N (Brit) = **short pastry**.

♦ **short cut** N scorciatoia.

short·en [ˈʃɔːtn] **1** VT (gen) accorciare.

2 VI accorciarsi.

short·en·ing [ˈʃɔːtnɪŋ] N (Culin) grasso (usato in pasticceria).

short·fall [ˈʃɔːtˌfɔːl] N (Fin) deficit sm inv; **there is a shortfall of £20,000** mancano 20.000 sterline.

short·hand [ˈʃɔːtˌhænd] N stenografia; **to take sth down in shorthand** stenografare qc.

♦ **short-handed** [ˈʃɔːtˈhændɪd] ADJ a corto di personale.

♦ **shorthand notebook** N bloc-notes m inv per stenografia.

♦ **shorthand typing** N stenodattilografia.

♦ **shorthand typist** N stenodattilografo(-a).

♦ **short-haul** [ˈʃɔːtˈhɔːl] ADJ a breve distanza.

♦ **short-list** [ˈʃɔːtˌlɪst] VT includere nella graduatoria finale; (Brit: for job) includere nella rosa dei candidati.

♦ **short list** N graduatoria finale; (Brit: for job) rosa dei candidati.

♦ **short-lived** [ˈʃɔːtˌlɪvd] ADJ (fig) di breve durata, effimero(-a).

short·ly [ˈʃɔːtlɪ] ADV **a** (soon) tra poco, tra breve; **shortly before/after** poco prima/dopo **b** (curtly) seccamente, bruscamente.

short·ness [ˈʃɔːtnɪs] N (of person) bassa statura; (of reply, manner) bruschezza; **shortness of temper** irascibiltà; **the shortness of her skirt** la sua gonna corta; **shortness**

of breath affanno.

♦ **short pastry, short crust pastry** N (*Brit*) pasta frolla.

♦ **short-range** [ˌʃɔːˈreɪndʒ] ADJ (*gun*) a gittata corta; (*aircraft*) a corto raggio d'azione; (*plan*) a breve termine; **the short-range weather forecast is for** ... il bollettino meteorologico per le prossime dodici ore prevede... .

shorts [ʃɔːts] NPL shorts *mpl*, calzoncini *mpl*.

♦ **short sight** N miopia.

♦ **short-sighted** [ˌʃɔːtˈsaɪtɪd] ADJ (*also fig*: *policy, decision*) miope.

♦ **short-sightedness** [ˌʃɔːtˈsaɪtɪdnɪs] N (*also fig*: *of policy, decision*) miopia.

♦ **short-staffed** [ˌʃɔːtˈstɑːft] ADJ a corto di personale.

♦ **short story** N racconto, novella.

♦ **short-tempered** [ˌʃɔːtˈtɛmpəd] ADJ (*in general*) irascibile; (*in a bad mood*) di cattivo umore.

♦ **short-term** [ˈʃɔːtˌtɜːm] ADJ a breve scadenza; (*solution*) di *or* a breve durata.

♦ **short term** N: **in the short term** nell'immediato futuro.

♦ **short time** N: **to work short time, be on short time** (*Industry*) essere *or* lavorare a orario ridotto.

♦ **short-wave** [ˈʃɔːtˌweɪv] ADJ (*radio*) a onde corte.

♦ **short wave** N (*Radio*) onde *fpl* corte.

shot [ʃɒt] ① N **a** (*from gun, also sound*) sparo, colpo d'arma da fuoco; (*shotgun pellets*) pallottole *fpl*; **to fire a shot at sb/sth** sparare un colpo a qn/qc; **a warning shot** un colpo di avvertimento; **good shot!** bel colpo!; **he was off like a shot** (*fig*) è partito come un razzo; **it was a shot in the dark** (*fig*) è stata un'ipotesi azzardata

b (*person*) tiratore(-trice); **he's a good/bad shot** è un buon/pessimo tiratore; **a big shot** (*fam*) un pezzo grosso *or* da novanta, un alto papavero

c (*Ftbl, Golf, Tennis etc*) tiro; (*throw*) lancio; **to put the shot** lanciare il peso; **a shot at goal** un tiro in porta; **good shot!** bel tiro!, bel lancio!

d (*attempt*) prova; (*turn to play*) turno; **to have a shot at sth/doing sth** provare a fare qc; **I'll have a shot at it** ci proverò

e (*injection*) puntura, iniezione *f*; (*of alcohol*) bicchierino; **the economy needs a shot in the arm** (*fig*) l'economia ha bisogno di una sferzata

f (*Phot*) foto *f inv*; (*Cine*) inquadratura.

② PT, PP of **shoot**: **to get shot of sb/sth** (*fam*) sbarazzarsi di qn/qc.

③ ADJ: **shot silk** seta cangiante; **shot with blue** screziato (-a) di blu.

shot·gun [ˈʃɒtˌɡʌn] N fucile *m* da caccia.

♦ **shotgun wedding** N (*fam*) matrimonio riparatore.

♦ **shot put** N: **the shot put** il lancio del peso.

should [ʃʊd] MODAL AUX VB **a** (*duty, advisability, desirability*): **all school buses should have seat belts** tutti gli autobus scolastici dovrebbero essere forniti di cinture di sicurezza; **I should go now** dovrei andare ora; **I should have been a doctor** avrei dovuto fare il medico; **you shouldn't do that** non dovresti farlo; **I should go if I were you** se fossi in te andrei; **I shouldn't if I were you** se fossi in te non lo farei; **how should I know?** e che ne so io?, e come faccio a saperlo?

b (*probability*): **he should pass his exams** dovrebbe superare gli esami; **they should have arrived by now** a quest'ora dovrebbero essere già arrivati; **he should be there now** dovrebbe essere arrivato ora; **this should be good** dovrebbe essere bello

c (*conditional uses*): **if they invited me I should go** *or* **I'd**

go se mi invitassero ci andrei; **I should like to** mi piacerebbe; **I should have liked to** mi sarebbe piaciuto; **I should think so!** mi pare!, direi!; **should he phone** ... (*frm*) se telefonasse..., se dovesse telefonare...; **who should I see but Maria!** e chi dovevo vedere se non Maria!

d (*remote form of shall in indirect speech*): **I told you I should be late** ti ho detto che avrei fatto tardi.

shoul·der [ˈʃəʊldəʳ] ① N **a** (*gen*) spalla; **to carry sth over one's shoulder** portare qc a spalla; **to cry on sb's shoulder** piangere sulla spalla di qn; **to look over one's shoulder** guardarsi alle spalle; **to look over sb's shoulder** guardare da dietro le spalle di qn; (*fig*) stare addosso a qn; **shoulder to shoulder** spalla a spalla; **to have broad shoulders** (*also fig*) avere le spalle larghe; **to put one's shoulder to the wheel** (*fig*) mettersi all'opera; **to rub shoulders with sb** (*fig*) frequentare qn; **to give sb the cold shoulder** (*fig*) trattare qn con freddezza; **he stands head and shoulders above everybody else** è di gran lunga superiore a tutti gli altri.

② VT (*fig*: *responsibilities etc*) accollarsi, addossarsi; **to shoulder sb aside** spingere qn da parte a spallate; **to shoulder one's way through the crowd** farsi largo a spallate tra la folla.

♦ **shoulder bag** N borsa a tracolla.

♦ **shoulder blade** N scapola.

♦ **shoulder-high** [ˈʃəʊldəˈhaɪ] ADV: **to carry sb shoulder-high** portare qn in trionfo.

♦ **shoulder-length** [ˈʃəʊldəˌlɛŋθ] ADJ (*hair*) (lungo(-a)) fino alle spalle.

♦ **shoulder pad** N spallina imbottita.

♦ **shoulder strap** N bretella, spallina.

shouldn't [ˈʃʊdnt] = **should not**.

shout [ʃaʊt] ① N (*gen*) urlo, grido; **a shout of laughter** una risata fragorosa; **to give sb a shout** dare una voce a qn.

② VT (*order, name*) gridare, urlare.

③ VI gridare, urlare; **to shout to sb to do sth** gridare a qn di fare qc; **to shout with pain** urlare per il *or* di dolore; **to shout for help** gridare aiuto; **to shout with laughter** scoppiare a ridere

▶ **shout at** VI + PREP gridare a, urlare a; **to shout at sb** (*angrily*) sgridare qn

▶ **shout down** VT + ADV: **they shouted him down** gridavano così forte che non si sentiva ciò che diceva

▶ **shout out** ① VI + ADV emettere un grido.

② VT + ADV gridare.

shout·ing [ˈʃaʊtɪŋ] N grida *fpl*, urla *fpl*; **it's all over bar the shouting** (*fig*) il più è fatto.

♦ **shouting match** N (*fam*) vivace scambio di opinioni.

shove [ʃʌv] ① N spintone *m*; **to give sb/sth a shove** dare uno spintone a qn/qc.

② VT (*gen*) spingere; (*thrust*) cacciare, ficcare; **he shoved me out of the way** mi ha spinto da parte in malo modo; **to shove in/out** *etc* spingere dentro/fuori *etc*; **he shoved his fist/stick into my face** mi ha minacciato con il pugno/bastone.

③ VI spingere; **he shoved (his way) through the crowd** si è fatto largo tra la folla a spintoni; **to shove past sb** passare davanti a qn con uno spintone

▶ **shove off** VI + ADV **a** (*fam*) sloggiare, smammare

b (*Naut*) prendere il largo

▶ **shove over, shove up** VI + ADV (*fam*) farsi più in là.

shov·el [ˈʃʌvl] ① N pala.

② VT (*coal, snow*) spalare; (*sth spilt*) raccogliere con una paletta; **he was shovelling food into his mouth** (*fig*) mangiava a quattro ganasce.

shov·el·er [ˈʃʌvlə] N (Zool) mestolone m.
shov·el·ful [ˈʃʌvlfʊl] N palata.
show [ʃəʊ] (vb: pt **showed**, pp **shown**) ⊡ N **a** (of feeling, emotion) manifestazione f; (of strength, goodwill) dimostrazione f, prova; (ostentation) mostra; **to ask for a show of hands** chiedere una votazione per alzata di mano
　b (exhibition: Art) mostra, esposizione f; (: Comm, Tech) salone m, fiera; (: Agr) fiera; **to be on show** essere esposto(-a); **the garden is a splendid show** il giardino offre uno spettacolo stupendo
　c (Theatre, Cine etc) spettacolo; (variety show) varietà m inv; **to go to a show** andare a vedere uno spettacolo; **on with the show!** (fig) andiamo avanti!; **good show!** (old fam) bene, bravo(-a)!; **the last show** (Theatre) l'ultima rappresentazione; (Cine) l'ultimo spettacolo; **she stole the show** tutti gli occhi erano puntati su di lei; **to put up a good show** (fam) difendersi bene; **to put up a poor show** (fam) essere una delusione; **it's a poor show when/if ...** (fam) siamo proprio ridotti male se...
　d (outward appearance, pretence) apparenza; **it's just for show** è solo per far scena; **to make a show of doing sth** far finta di fare qc; **to make a show of anger** far finta di essere arrabbiato(-a); **to make a show of resistance** accennare una qualche resistenza
　e (fam: organization) baracca; **who's running the show here?** chi è il padrone qui?; **this is my show** qui comando io.
　⊡ VT **a** (gen) mostrare; (film, slides) proiettare; (goods for sale, pictures) esporre; (animals) presentare ad una mostra; **he showed me his new car** mi ha mostrato la sua macchina nuova; **to show a film at Cannes** presentare un film a Cannes; **what's showing at the Odeon?** cosa danno all'Odeon?; **white shoes soon show the dirt** le scarpe bianche si sporcano in fretta; **don't show your face here again!** non farti mai più vedere da queste parti!; **to show one's hand** or **one's cards** scoprire le carte; (fig) mettere le carte in tavola; **I have nothing to show for it** non ho niente a dimostrazione dei miei sforzi; **I'll show him!** (fam) gli faccio vedere io!
　b (indicate) indicare, segnare; **as shown in the illustration** come da illustrazione; **the motorways are shown in black** le autostrade sono segnate in nero; **to show a profit/loss** (Comm) registrare un utile/una perdita
　c (reveal: interest, surprise) (di)mostrare, dar prova di; **her action showed intelligence** la sua azione ha dato prova di intelligenza; **her face showed her happiness/fear** le si leggeva la felicità/paura in viso; **the choice of dishes shows excellent taste** la scelta dei piatti rivela un ottimo gusto; **this shows him to be a coward** questo dimostra la sua vigliaccheria; **it just goes to show that ...** il che sta a dimostrare che...
　d (direct, conduct: person) accompagnare; **to show sb the way** indicare la strada a qn; **to show sb into a room** far entrare qn in una stanza; **to show sb to his seat/to the door** accompagnare qn al suo posto/alla porta; **to show sb the door** (fig) mettere qn alla porta; **to show sb round** or **over a house** far visitare or vedere la casa a qn; **to show sb in/out/up** far entrare/uscire/salire qn.
　⊡ VI (stain, emotion, underskirt) vedersi, essere visibile; **it doesn't show** non si vede; **don't worry, it won't show** sta' tranquillo, non si vedrà
　▶ **show off** ⊡ VI + ADV (pej) darsi delle arie, mettersi in mostra; **he's showing off again** ecco che ricomincia a darsi delle arie.

　⊡ VT + ADV (pej) mettere in mostra; (ability, one's figure) mostrare; (knowledge) ostentare; (subj: colour, dress: qualities, features) mettere in risalto, valorizzare
　▶ **show through** ⊡ VI + ADV vedersi.
　⊡ VI + PREP vedersi attraverso
　▶ **show up** ⊡ VI + ADV **a** (be visible: gen) risaltare; (: mistake) saltare all'occhio
　b (fam: arrive) farsi vivo(-a), farsi vedere.
　⊡ VT + ADV **a** (reveal: thief, fraud) smascherare; (: deception) mettere a nudo; **he was shown up as an impostor** è stato smascherato per l'impostore che era; **the bright lighting showed up her scars** la forte luce metteva in evidenza le sue cicatrici
　b (embarrass) far fare una figuraccia a.
　♦ **show business** [ˈʃəʊˌbɪznɪs], **show biz** [ˈʃəʊˌbɪz] (fam) N mondo dello spettacolo.
　show·case [ˈʃəʊˌkeɪs] N (cabinet) vetrina, bacheca; (fig) vetrina; **the tournament will be a showcase of European football** il torneo sarà la vetrina del calcio europeo.
　show·down [ˈʃəʊˌdaʊn] N regolamento di conti.
　show·er [ˈʃaʊə] ⊡ N **a** (of rain) rovescio; **a shower of hail** una grandinata; **a snow shower** una nevicata
　b (fig: of arrows, stones) pioggia; (: of blows) gragnuola, scarica; (: of bullets) scarica; (: of kisses, presents) valanga
　c (shower bath) doccia; **to have** or **take a shower** fare una doccia
　d (Am: party) festa di fidanzamento (in cui si fanno regali alla persona festeggiata).
　⊡ VT (fig): **to shower sb with** (gifts, abuse) coprire qn di; (blows) riempire qn di; (missiles) bersagliare qn con una pioggia di; **he was showered with invitations** è stato inondato di inviti.
　⊡ VI (take a shower) fare la doccia.
　♦ **shower cap** N cuffia da doccia.
　♦ **shower cubicle** N box m doccia inv.
　♦ **shower curtain** N tenda per doccia.
　shower·proof [ˈʃaʊəˌpruːf] ADJ impermeabile.
　♦ **shower unit** N blocco m doccia inv.
　show·ery [ˈʃaʊərɪ] ADJ (weather) con piogge intermittenti.
　show·girl [ˈʃəʊˌgɜːl] N show girl f inv.
　show·ground [ˈʃəʊˌgraʊnd] N area di esposizione.
　♦ **show house** N casa f tipo inv.
　show·ing [ˈʃəʊɪŋ] N (of film) proiezione f; (cinema session) spettacolo; **to make a poor showing in the opinion polls** avere un magro risultato al sondaggio d'opinione.
　♦ **showing off** N (pej) esibizionismo.
　show·jumping [ˈʃəʊˌdʒʌmpɪŋ] N concorso ippico (di salto ad ostacoli).
　show·man [ˈʃəʊmən] N (pl **-men**) (at fair, circus) impresario; **he's a great showman** (fig) fa sempre un po' l'attore.
　show·man·ship [ˈʃəʊmənˌʃɪp] N (fig) abilità or capacità di intrattenere il pubblico.
　shown [ʃəʊn] PP of **show**.
　♦ **show-off** [ˈʃəʊˌɒf] N (fam) esibizionista m/f.
　show·piece [ˈʃəʊˌpiːs] N (of exhibition) pezzo forte; **that hospital is a showpiece** quello è un ospedale modello.
　show·place [ˈʃəʊˌpleɪs] N: **the Lloyds Building is one of the showplaces of London** la sede dei Lloyds è una delle attrattive di Londra.
　show·room [ˈʃəʊˌrʊm] N (Comm) show-room m inv, salone m d'esposizione; (Art) sala d'esposizione.
　♦ **show stopper** N (fam) scena or numero etc che strappa gli applausi.
　♦ **show trial** N processo a scopo dimostrativo (spesso ideologico).

showy [ˈʃəʊɪ] ADJ (comp **-ier**, superl **-iest**) vistoso(-a), appariscente.

shrank [ʃræŋk] PT of **shrink**.

shrap·nel [ˈʃræpnl] N shrapnel *m inv*.

shred [ʃrɛd] **1** N, GEN PL (of cloth) brandello; (of paper) strisciolina; (fig: of truth, evidence) briciolo; **you haven't got a shred of evidence** non ne hai la benché minima prova; **in shreds** a brandelli; **to tear to shreds** fare a brandelli; (fig: argument) demolire.
2 VT (paper) stracciare, strappare; (mechanically) trinciare; (food: with grater) grattugiare; (: with knife) tagliuzzare, sminuzzare.

shred·der [ˈʃrɛdəʳ] N (for documents, papers) distruttore *m* di documenti.

shrew [ʃruː] N (Zool) toporagno; (fig pej: woman) strega.

shrewd [ʃruːd] ADJ (comp **-er**, superl **-est**) (person, assessment) acuto(-a), accorto(-a); (lawyer, businessman) scaltro(-a); (plan, look) astuto(-a); (guess) perspicace; **I have a shrewd idea that ...** mi sa tanto che... .

shrewd·ly [ˈʃruːdlɪ] ADV (act) con accortezza; (reason) con perspicacia; **to look at sb shrewdly** lanciare uno sguardo astuto a qn.

shrewd·ness [ˈʃruːdnɪs] N (see adj) acume *m*; accortezza; astuzia; perspicacia.

shrew·ish [ˈʃruːɪʃ] ADJ (pej: woman, wife) bisbetico(-a).

shriek [ʃriːk] **1** N strillo; **a shriek of pain** un grido di dolore; **shrieks of laughter** risate *fpl* stridule.
2 VI strillare; **to shriek at sb** strillare a qn; **to shriek with laughter** sbellicarsi dalle risa.
3 VT strillare.

shrift [ʃrɪft] N (fig): **to give sb short shrift** trattare qn in modo sbrigativo; **to get short shrift from sb** essere trattato(-a) in modo sbrigativo da qn.

shrike [ʃraɪk] N averla maggiore.

shrill [ʃrɪl] ADJ (comp **-er**, superl **-est**) (bell, sound) acuto (-a), penetrante; (laugh, voice) stridulo(-a); (demand, protest) insistente.

shrill·ness [ˈʃrɪlnɪs] N (of laugh, voice) suono stridulo.

shril·ly [ˈʃrɪlɪ] ADV in modo penetrante.

shrimp [ʃrɪmp] N (Zool) gamberetto; (fig: child) scricciolo.

shrine [ʃram] N (tomb) sepolcro; (place) santuario; (reliquary) reliquiario, teca.

shrink [ʃrɪŋk] (vb: pt **shrank**, pp **shrunk**) **1** VT (wool) far restringere.
2 VI **a** (clothes) restringersi, ritirarsi; (metal) contrarsi; (gums) ritirarsi; (piece of meat) ridursi; (area, person) rimpicciolirsi; **to shrink in the wash** restringersi con il lavaggio
b (also: **shrink away, shrink back**) ritrarsi, tirarsi indietro; **to shrink from doing sth** rifuggire dal fare qc; **he didn't shrink from telling her the truth** non ha esitato a dirle la verità.
3 N (fam pej) strizzacervelli *m/f inv*.

shrink·age [ˈʃrɪŋkɪdʒ] N (of clothes) restringimento; (Comm: in shops) perdite *fpl* (dovute a danno o taccheggio).

♦ **shrink-wrap** [ˌʃrɪŋkˈræp] VT cellofanare.

shriv·el [ˈʃrɪvl] (also: **shrivel up**) **1** VT (plant etc) far rinsecchire; (skin) far raggrinzire, far avvizzire.
2 VI (see vt) rinsecchirsi; raggrinzirsi, avvizzire.

shroud [ʃraʊd] **1** N (round corpse) sudario; (fig: of secrecy) alone *m*.
2 VT (fig): **shrouded in** (mist, darkness) circondato(-a) da; **shrouded in mystery** avvolto(-a) nel mistero.

Shrove Tuesday [ˌʃrəʊvˈtjuːzdɪ] N martedì *m inv* grasso.

shrub [ʃrʌb] N arbusto.

shrub·bery [ˈʃrʌbərɪ] N arbusti *mpl*.

shrug [ʃrʌg] **1** N alzata di spalle; **a shrug of indifference** un gesto d'indifferenza; **to give a shrug of contempt** alzare le spalle con disprezzo; **...he said with a shrug** ...disse alzando le spalle.
2 VT, VI: **to shrug (one's shoulders)** alzare le spalle, fare spallucce
▶ **shrug off** VT + ADV (danger) prendere sottogamba; (insult) ignorare, passare sopra a; (troubles) minimizzare; (cold, illness) sbarazzarsi di.

shrunk [ʃrʌŋk] PP of **shrink**.

shrunk·en [ˈʃrʌŋkən] ADJ (body) rinsecchito(-a).

shucks [ʃʌks] EXCL (Am fam): **shucks!** sciocchezze!

shud·der [ˈʃʌdəʳ] **1** VI (person): **to shudder (with)** rabbrividire (per or da); (machinery) vibrare; **the car shuddered to a halt** dopo vari sussulti la macchina si fermò; **I shudder to think!** rabbrividisco al solo pensiero!.
2 N (of person) brivido; (of machinery) vibrazione *f*; **to give a shudder** (person) rabbrividire; (car) sussultare.

shuf·fle [ˈʃʌfl] **1** N **a** passo strascicato **b** (Cards) mescolata, scozzata; **to give the cards a shuffle** dare una mescolata alle carte.
2 VT **a** (feet) strascicare **b** (mix up: cards) mescolare, scozzare; (: papers) mettere sottosopra.
3 VI (walk) strascicare i piedi; **to shuffle in/out** etc entrare/uscire etc con passo strascicato.

shun [ʃʌn] VT (person, work, publicity) evitare, sfuggire; (obligation) sottrarsi a.

shunt [ʃʌnt] **1** VT (Rail: direct) smistare; (: divert) deviare; (fig: from one place to another) spostare.
2 VI: **to shunt to and fro** fare la spola.

shunt·er [ˈʃʌntəʳ] N (Rail: engine) locomotiva da manovra.

shunt·ing [ˈʃʌntɪŋ] N (Rail) smistamento.

♦ **shunting yard** N fascio di smistamento.

shush [ʃuʃ] **1** EXCL zitto(-a)!.
2 VT (fam) zittire.

shut [ʃʌt] (pt, pp **shut**) **1** VT (gen) chiudere; **to shut the door in sb's face** sbattere la porta in faccia a qn; **to shut one's finger in the door** chiudersi un dito nella porta; **to shut sb in a room** rinchiudere qn in una stanza; **shut your mouth** or **face!** (fam!) chiudi il becco!.
2 VI (door, window) chiudersi; (shop, bank etc) chiudere.
3 ADJ chiuso(-a); **to keep one's mouth shut** tenere la bocca chiusa
▶ **shut away** VT + ADV (person, animal) rinchiudere, chiudere; (valuables) mettere al sicuro
▶ **shut down 1** VI + ADV (factory, shop) chiudere i battenti.
2 VT + ADV (factory, shop) chiudere; (machine) fermare; (nuclear reactor) ridurre al minimo
▶ **shut in** VT + ADV rinchiudere
▶ **shut off** VT + ADV **a** (stop: power) staccare; (: water) chiudere; (: engine) spegnere
b (isolate): **to shut off (from)** tagliar fuori (da), isolare (da)
▶ **shut out** VT + ADV (person, noise, cold) non far entrare; (block: view) impedire, bloccare; (: memory) scacciare; **to be shut out of the house** rimanere chiuso(-a) fuori casa
▶ **shut up 1** VI + ADV (fam: be quiet) star zitto(-a); **shut up!** stai zitto!.
2 VT + ADV **a** (factory, business, house) chiudere
b (person, animal) rinchiudere, chiudere; (valuables) mettere al sicuro
c (fam: silence) far stare zitto(-a).

shut·down [ˈʃʌtˌdaʊn] N chiusura.

♦ **shut-eye** [ˈʃʌtaɪ] N (*fam*) dormita; **to get some shut-eye** farsi una dormita.

♦ **shut-in** [ˌʃʌtˈɪn] ADJ (*feeling*) di soffocamento.

shut·ter [ˈʃʌtəʳ] N (*on window*) imposta; (*for shop*) battente *m*; (*Phot*) otturatore *m*; **shutter speed** tempo di apertura.

shut·tered [ˈʃʌtəd] ADJ con le imposte.

shut·tle [ˈʃʌtl] 1 N a (*of loom*) spola, navetta; (*of sewing machine*) spoletta
  b (*fig: plane etc*) navetta.
  2 VI (*subj: vehicle, person*) fare la spola.
  3 VT (*to and fro: passengers*) portare avanti e indietro; **I was/the papers were shuttled from one department to another** sono stato sballottato/la pratica è stata mandata da un ufficio all'altro.

shuttle·cock [ˈʃʌtlˌkɒk] N (*Badminton*) volano.

♦ **shuttle diplomacy** N *la gestione dei rapporti diplomatici caratterizzata da frequenti viaggi e incontri dei rappresentanti del governo.*

♦ **shuttle service** N servizio *m* navetta *inv.*

shy [ʃaɪ] 1 ADJ (*comp* -er, *superl* -est) timido(-a); (*unsociable*) schivo(-a); **to be shy of doing sth** esitare a fare qc; **don't be shy of asking for...** non esitare a chiedere...; **to fight shy of sth** tenersi alla larga da qc; **to fight shy of doing sth** cercare in tutti i modi di non fare qc.
  2 VI (*horse*): **to shy (at)** fare uno scarto (davanti a); **the horse shied at the noise** il cavallo ha fatto uno scarto quando ha sentito il rumore; **to shy away from sth** evitare qc; **to shy away from doing sth** (*fig*) rifuggire dal fare qc.
  3 VT (*old: throw*) scagliare.

shy·ly [ˈʃaɪlɪ] ADV timidamente.

shy·ness [ˈʃaɪnɪs] N timidezza.

shy·ster [ˈʃaɪstəʳ] N (*Am fam*) lestofante *m*; (*lawyer, politician*) filibustiere *m*.

SI [ˌɛsˈaɪ] N ABBR (= *Système International (d'unités)*) S.I. *m* (= *Sistema Internazionale (di unità di misura)*).

Siam [saɪˈæm] N il Siam.

Sia·mese [ˌsaɪəˈmiːz] 1 ADJ siamese.
  2 N (*person: pl inv*) siamese *m/f*; (*fam: cat*) siamese *m/f*; (*language*) siamese *m*.

♦ **Siamese cat** N gatto siamese.

♦ **Siamese twins** NPL fratelli *mpl* (*or* sorelle *fpl*) siamesi.

Si·beria [saɪˈbɪərɪə] N la Siberia.

sibi·lant [ˈsɪbɪlənt] 1 ADJ sibilante.
  2 N sibilante *f*.

sib·ling [ˈsɪblɪŋ] N (*frm*) fratello/sorella; **sibling rivalry** rivalità tra fratelli.

sib·yl [ˈsɪbɪl] N sibilla.

sic [sɪk] ADV: (**sic**) (sic).

Si·cil·ian [sɪˈsɪlɪən] ADJ, N siciliano(-a).

Sici·ly [ˈsɪsɪlɪ] N la Sicilia.

sick [sɪk] 1 ADJ (*comp* -er, *superl* -est) a (*ill*) malato(-a), ammalato(-a); **a sick person** un(a) malato(-a); **to fall** *or* **take sick** ammalarsi; **to be (off) sick** (*from work*) essere assente (per malattia); **to go sick** mettersi in malattia; **to be sick** (*vomiting*) vomitare, rimettere; **to feel sick** avere la nausea
  b (*fig: mind, imagination*) malato(-a); (: *humour*) macabro(-a); (: *joke*) di gusto macabro; **to be sick (and tired) of sb/sth** averne fin sopra i capelli di qn/qc; **to be sick to death of sb/sth** essere stufo(-a) marcio(-a) di qn/qc; **sick at heart** desolato(-a); **to be sick of the sight of sb/sth** non poterne più di qn/qc; **you make me sick!** mi fai schifo!.

  2 N a (*fam: vomit*) vomito
  b : **the sick** NPL i malati

▶ **sick up** VT + ADV (*fam*) vomitare, rimettere.

sick·bag [ˈsɪkˌbæg] N sacchetto (*da usarsi in caso di malessere*).

sick·bay [ˈsɪkˌbeɪ] N infermeria.

sick·bed [ˈsɪkˌbɛd] N letto di ammalato; **he rose from his sickbed to attend the meeting** fu costretto a lasciare il letto per partecipare alla riunione.

♦ **sick benefit** N = **sickness benefit**.

♦ **sick building syndrome** N *malattia causata dalla continua esposizione a ventilazione con sistemi di aria condizionata.*

sick·en [ˈsɪkn] 1 VT nauseare, stomacare; (*fig*) disgustare.
  2 VI sentirsi male, ammalarsi; **to sicken of sth** stufarsi di qc; **to be sickening for sth** (*cold, flu etc*) covare qc.

sick·en·ing [ˈsɪknɪŋ] ADJ (*smell, sight*) nauseante; (*fig: crime, waste, behaviour*) disgustoso(-a), rivoltante; (: *crash*) pauroso(-a); (*fam: annoying*) esasperante.

sick·en·ing·ly [ˈsɪknɪŋlɪ] ADV (*polite, cruel*) disgustosamente.

sick·le [ˈsɪkl] N falcetto; **hammer and sickle** falce e martello.

♦ **sick leave** N: **on sick leave** in congedo per motivi di salute *or* per malattia.

♦ **sickle-cell anaemia** [ˌsɪklsɛləˈniːmɪə] N anemia falciforme.

sick·li·ness [ˈsɪklɪnɪs] N (*of person*) salute *f* malferma; (*of cake, sweet*) sapore *m* stucchevole.

♦ **sick list** N: **on the sick list** sulla lista dei malati.

sick·ly [ˈsɪklɪ] ADJ (*comp* -ier, *superl* -iest) (*person*) malaticcio(-a); (*plant, animal*) malato(-a); (*smile*) stentato(-a); (*complexion*) giallastro(-a); (*taste, smell*) stomachevole; (*cake*) stucchevole; **sickly sweet** nauseante.

sick·ness [ˈsɪknɪs] N malattia; **there's a lot of sickness about** c'è molta gente malata; **wave of sickness** ondata di malessere.

♦ **sickness benefit** N indennità di malattia.

♦ **sick note** N certificato di malattia.

♦ **sick pay** N *salario erogato al dipendente in caso di malattia.*

sick·room [ˈsɪkˌrʊm] N stanza di malato.

side [saɪd] 1 N a (*of person, animal*) fianco; **side of beef** quarto di bue; **at** *or* **by sb's side** al fianco di qn, accanto a qn; **side by side** (*people*) fianco a fianco; (*objects*) uno(-a) accanto all'altro(-a)
  b (*edge: of box, square etc*) lato; (: *of buildings*) fianco, lato; (: *of boat, vehicle*) fiancata; (: *of ship*) murata, fianco; (: *of lake*) riva; (: *of road*) bordo, ciglio
  c (*face, surface: gen*) faccia; (: *of paper*) facciata; (: *of slice of bread*) lato; (*fig: aspect*) aspetto, lato; **the right/wrong side** il dritto/rovescio; **the other side of the coin** (*fig*) il rovescio della medaglia; **to hear both sides of the question** sentire tutt'e due le campane
  d (*part*) parte *f*; **from all sides** OR **from every side** da ogni parte; **from side to side** da una parte all'altra; **to move to one side** scostarsi, farsi *or* tirarsi da (una) parte; **to take sb on one side** prendere qn da parte *or* in disparte; **to put sth to** *or* **on one side (for sb)** mettere qc da parte (per qn); **on the mother's side** per parte di madre; **to be on the wrong/right side of 30** aver/non aver superato la trentina; **to get on the wrong/right side of sb** prendere qn per il verso sbagliato/giusto; **on this side of town** da questa parte della città; **it's a bit on the large side** è un po' abbondante; **to make a bit (of**

money) on the side (*fam*) farsi un po' di soldi extra

 e (*Sport*: *team*) squadra; (*Pol*: *faction*) parte *f*; **the other side** la parte avversaria; **God is on our side** Dio è con noi; **to be on sb's side** essere dalla parte di *or* con qn; **to be on the side of moderation** essere per la moderazione; **to have age/the law** *etc* **on one's side** avere l'età/la legge *etc* dalla propria (parte); **to pick** *or* **choose sides** formare le squadre; **to take sides** prendere posizione; **to take sides with sb** schierarsi con qn; **to let the side down** (*Sport*, *fig*) deludere le aspettative di qn.

 2 VI: **to side with sb** prendere le parti di qn, parteggiare per qn.

 3 ADJ (*door*, *entrance*) laterale; **a side issue** una questione secondaria

▶ **side against** VT + PREP schierarsi contro.

side·board ['saɪdˌbɔːd] N credenza.

side·boards ['saɪdˌbɔːdz], (*Am*) **side·burns** ['saɪdˌbɜːnz] NPL basette *fpl*.

side·car ['saɪdˌkɑːʳ] N sidecar *m inv*.

-sided [saɪdɪd] SUFF: **a seven-sided coin** una moneta ettagonale; **a many-sided problem** un problema complesso.

♦ **side dish** N contorno.

♦ **side drum** N (*Mus*) piccolo tamburo.

♦ **side effect** N effetto collaterale.

side·kick ['saɪdˌkɪk] N (*fam*: *esp Am*: *assistant*) braccio destro *m inv*; (: *friend*) amico(-a).

side·light ['saɪdˌlaɪt] N (*Aut*) luce *f* di posizione.

side·line ['saɪdˌlaɪn] N **a** (*Ftbl etc*) linea laterale **b** (*Comm*) attività *f inv* collaterale.

side·long ['saɪdˌlɒŋ] ADJ: **to give a sidelong glance at sth** guardare qc con la coda dell'occhio.

♦ **side plate** N piattino.

♦ **side road** N strada secondaria.

side·saddle ['saɪdˌsædl] ADV: **to ride sidesaddle** cavalcare all'amazzone.

side·show ['saɪdˌʃəʊ] N (*at fair*) attrazione *f*.

side·slip ['saɪdˌslɪp] (*Skiing*) **1** N derapata, dérapage *m inv*.

 2 VI derapare.

♦ **side-splitting** ['saɪdˌsplɪtɪŋ] ADJ (*fam*) da crepar dal ridere, esilarante.

side·step ['saɪdˌstɛp] **1** VT (*question*, *problem*) eludere, scansare.

 2 VI (*Boxing*) schivare.

side·step·ping ['saɪdˌstɛpɪŋ] N (*Skiing*) salita a scaletta.

♦ **side street** N traversa.

side·swipe ['saɪdˌswaɪp] N frecciata en passant; **to take a sideswipe at** lanciare una frecciata en passant a.

side·track ['saɪdˌtræk] VT (*person*) sviare, mettere fuori strada; **I got sidetracked** mi hanno distratto.

♦ **side view** N inquadratura di profilo.

side·walk ['saɪdˌwɔːk] N (*Am*: *pavement*) marciapiede *m*.

side·ways ['saɪdˌweɪz] **1** ADJ laterale; **to give a sideways glance at sth** guardare qc con la coda dell'occhio.

 2 ADV (*move*) di lato, di fianco; (*look*) con la coda dell'occhio.

side·winder ['saɪdˌwaɪndəʳ] N (*snake*) crotalo ceraste.

sid·ing ['saɪdɪŋ] N (*Rail*) binario di raccordo.

si·dle ['saɪdl] VI: **to sidle up to sb** avvicinarsi furtivamente a qn; **to sidle out/past** *etc* uscire/passare *etc* furtivamente.

SIDS [sɪdz] N = *sudden infant death syndrome* = **cot death**.

siege [siːdʒ] N assedio; **in a state of siege** in stato d'assedio; **to lay siege to** porre l'assedio a.

♦ **siege economy** N economia da stato d'assedio.

si·en·na [sɪˈɛnə] N (*colour*) terra di Siena.

Si·er·ra Leo·ne [sɪˈɛərəlɪˈəʊnɪ] N Sierra Leone *f*.

si·es·ta [sɪˈɛstə] N siesta; **to have a siesta** schiacciare un pisolino.

sieve [sɪv] **1** N (*for flour*) setaccio; (*for coal*, *soil*) crivello; **to have a memory like a sieve** (*fam*) avere una memoria che fa acqua, essere smemorato(-a).

 2 VT (*soil*, *flour etc*) setacciare, passare al setaccio; (*coal etc*) passare al crivello.

sift [sɪft] **1** VT (*flour*, *sand etc*) setacciare; (*coal etc*) passare al crivello; (*fig*: *evidence*) vagliare; **to sift out** (*truth etc*) separare.

 2 VI (*fig*): **to sift through** esaminare minuziosamente; (*statement*, *evidence*) vagliare accuratamente.

sigh [saɪ] **1** N (*of person*) sospiro; (*of wind*) sussurro; **Daphne heaved a sigh of relief** Daphne tirò un sospiro di sollievo.

 2 VI: **to sigh (with)** sospirare (di); **to sigh over** (*sth lost*) piangere su.

sigh·ing ['saɪɪŋ] N sospiri *mpl*; (*of wind*) sussurrio.

sight [saɪt] **1** N **a** (*faculty*, *act of seeing*) vista; **to have good/poor (eye)sight** avere la vista buona/cattiva; **at first sight** a prima vista; **I know her by sight** la conosco di vista; **payable at sight** (*Comm*) pagabile a vista; **to be within sight of** (*sea*) essere in vista di; (*victory*) essere vicino(-a) a; **the bus was still in sight** l'autobus si vedeva ancora; **the end is in sight** si intravvede la fine; **a solution is in sight** è in vista una soluzione; **to come into sight** (*thing*) profilarsi all'orizzonte; **Janice came into sight** abbiamo scorto Janice; **to catch sight of sth/sb** scorgere qc/qn; **keep out of my sight!** sparisci!; **don't let it out of your sight** non perderlo di vista; **when it's out of sight** quando non si vede più, quando non è più visibile; **out of sight out of mind** (*Proverb*) lontano dagli occhi lontano dal cuore; **to lose sight of sb/sth** perdere di vista qn/qc; **to hate the sight of sb/sth** non sopportare la vista di qn/qc

 b (*spectacle*) spettacolo; **to see the sights of Rome** vedere *or* visitare i monumenti di Roma; **it's not a pretty sight** non è uno spettacolo edificante; **you're a sight for sore eyes!** al solo vederti mi si allarga il cuore!; **you look a sight!** (*fam*) come sei conciato!; **it's a sight to be seen** è uno spettacolo da non perdere

 c (*on gun*: *often pl*) mirino; **in one's sights** sotto mira; **to set one's sights on sth/on doing sth** (*fig*) mirare a qc/a fare qc; **to set one's sights too high** (*fig*) mirare troppo in alto

 d (*fam*: *a great deal*) molto; **a sight more** molto di più; **it isn't finished by a long sight** è ben lungi dall'essere finito; **a sight too clever** fin troppo furbo(-a).

 2 VT (*rare animal*, *land*) avvistare; (*person*) scorgere.

sight·ed ['saɪtɪd] ADJ che ha il dono della vista; **partially sighted** parzialmente cieco(-a); **sighted people** i vedenti.

sight·ing ['saɪtɪŋ] N avvistamento; **several sightings have been reported** si è avuta notizia di diversi avvistamenti.

sight·less ['saɪtlɪs] ADJ (*person*) non vedente.

♦ **sight-read** ['saɪtˌriːd] VT, VI (*Mus*) suonare (*or* cantare) a prima vista.

sight·see·ing ['saɪtˌsiːɪŋ] N turismo; **to go sightseeing** OR **to do some sightseeing** (*gen*) fare un giro turistico; (*in town*) visitare la città.

sight·seer ['saɪtˌsiːəʳ] N turista *m/f*.

sig·ma ['sɪgmə] N sigma *m or f inv*.

sign [saɪn] **1** N **a** (*with hand etc*) segno, gesto; **to**

communicate **by signs** comunicare a gesti; **to make a sign to sb (to do sth)** far segno a qn (di fare qc); **to make the sign of the Cross** far(si) il segno della croce

b (*indication*) segno, indizio; **as a sign of** in segno di; **it's a sign of the times** è sintomo dei tempi che corrono; **it's a good/bad sign** è buon/brutto segno; **all the signs are that** ... tutto fa prevedere che...; **at the first** *or* **slightest sign of** al primo *or* al minimo segno di; **to show signs/no sign of doing sth** accennare/non accennare a fare qc; **there was no sign of him anywhere** non c'era traccia di lui da nessuna parte; **there was no sign of life in the village** nel paesino non c'era segno di vita

c (*also:* **road sign**) segnale *m*

d (*also:* **shop sign**) insegna; (*notice*) cartello, avviso

e (*written symbol*) segno; **plus/minus sign** segno del più/meno

f (*also:* **star sign**) segno zodiacale.

2 VT a (*letter, contract*) firmare; **to sign one's name** firmare, apporre la propria firma; **she signs herself B. Smith** si firma B. Smith

b (*Ftbl: player*) ingaggiare.

3 VI a (*with signature*) firmare; (*Ftbl*) firmare un contratto

b (*signal*): **to sign to sb to do sth** far segno a qn di fare qc

▶ **sign away** VT + ADV (*rights etc*) cedere (*con una firma*)

▶ **sign for** VI + PREP (*letter, goods*) firmare per l'accettazione di; (*football club, record company*) firmare un contratto con

▶ **sign in** VI + ADV (*in hotel*) firmare il registro (*all'arrivo*)

▶ **sign off** VI + ADV (*TV, Radio*) chiudere le trasmissioni

▶ **sign on** 1 VI + ADV (*as unemployed*) iscriversi all'ufficio di collocamento; (*Mil etc: enlist*) arruolarsi; (*as worker*) prendere servizio; (*enrol*): **to sign on for a course** iscriversi a un corso.

2 VT + ADV (*employees*) assumere; (*Mil: enlisted man*) arruolare

▶ **sign out** 1 VI + ADV (*in hotel*) firmare il registro (*alla partenza*).

2 VT + ADV (*book*) firmare il registro per il prestito di un libro

▶ **sign over** VT + ADV (*rights etc*): **to sign sth over to sb** cedere qc con scrittura legale a qn

▶ **sign up** 1 VI + ADV (*Mil: enlist*) arruolarsi; (*enrol: for course*) iscriversi.

2 VT + ADV (*employee*) assumere; (*Mil*) arruolare.

sig·nal ['sɪɡnl] 1 N: **signal (for)** segnale *m* (di); **at a prearranged signal** ad un segnale convenuto; **distress signal** segnale di soccorso; **traffic signals** semafori *mpl*; **railway signals** segnali *mpl* ferroviari; **the engaged signal** (*Telec*) il segnale di occupato; **the signal is very weak** (*TV*) la ricezione è molto debole.

2 ADJ (*frm: success, importance*) notevole.

3 VT a (*message*) comunicare per mezzo di segnali; **to signal a left/right turn** (*Aut*) segnalare una svolta a sinistra/destra; **to signal sb on/through** far segno a qn di avanzare/passare

b (*signify*) indicare.

4 VI (*gen*) segnalare; (*for help*) fare segnalazioni; **to signal to sb (to do sth)** far segno a qn (di fare qc).

♦ **signal box** N (*Rail*) cabina di manovra.

sig·nal·ly ['sɪɡnəlɪ] ADV (*fail, lack*) completamente.

signal·man ['sɪɡnlmən] N (*pl* **-men**) (*Rail*) deviatore *m*.

sig·na·tory ['sɪɡnətərɪ] N firmatario(-a).

sig·na·ture ['sɪɡnətʃə'] N a (*of person*) firma; **to put one's**

signature to sth firmare qc, apporre la propria firma a qc b (*Mus*): **key signature** segnatura in chiave; **time signature** indicazione *f* del tempo.

♦ **signature tune** N (*Brit*) sigla musicale.

sign·board ['saɪn,bɔːd] N cartello.

sig·net ['sɪɡnɪt] N sigillo.

♦ **signet ring** N anello con sigillo.

sig·nifi·cance [sɪɡ'nɪfɪkəns] N (*of remark*) significato; (*of event, speech*) importanza; **that is of no significance** ciò non ha importanza.

sig·nifi·cant [sɪɡ'nɪfɪkənt] ADJ (*discovery, change, event*) importante; (*increase, improvement, amount*) notevole; (*evidence*) significativo(-a); (*look, smile*) eloquente; **it is significant that** ... è significativo che... .

sig·nifi·cant·ly [sɪɡ'nɪfɪkəntlɪ] ADV (*smile*) in modo eloquente; (*improve, increase*) considerevolmente; **and, significantly,** ... e, fatto significativo, ...

sig·ni·fi·ca·tion [ˌsɪɡnɪfɪ'keɪʃən] N (*frm: of word*) significato.

sig·ni·fy ['sɪɡnɪ,faɪ] 1 VT (*mean*) significare; (*indicate*) indicare; (*make known*) manifestare, esprimere.

2 VI avere importanza.

♦ **sign language** N linguaggio dei muti.

sign·post ['saɪn,pəʊst] 1 N indicazione *f* or cartello stradale.

2 VT (*fig*) indicare, segnalare.

sign·post·ing ['saɪn,pəʊstɪŋ] N segnaletica.

Sikh [siːk] ADJ, N sikh (*m/f*) *inv*.

si·lage ['saɪlɪdʒ] N insilato.

si·lence ['saɪləns] 1 N silenzio; **silence!** silenzio!; **in (dead** *or* **complete) silence** in (totale *or* perfetto) silenzio; **there was silence on** *or* **about the subject** non si è parlato dell'argomento; **to pass over sth in silence** passare qc sotto silenzio.

2 VT (*person, critics*) ridurre al silenzio, far tacere; (*conscience*) mettere a tacere.

si·lenc·er ['saɪlənsə'] N (*Aut*) marmitta; (*on motorbike, gun*) silenziatore *m*.

si·lent ['saɪlənt] ADJ (*person*) silenzioso(-a); (*film, prayer etc*) muto(-a); **silent "h"** "h" muta; **to fall silent** tacere; **to keep** *or* **remain silent** tacere, stare zitto(-a).

si·lent·ly ['saɪləntlɪ] ADV (*noiselessly*) silenziosamente; (*without speaking*) in silenzio.

♦ **silent partner** N (*Am*) = **sleeping partner**.

sil·hou·ette [ˌsɪluː'ɛt] 1 N (*gen*) sagoma; (*drawing*) silhouette *f inv*.

2 VT: **to be silhouetted against** stagliarsi contro.

sili·ca ['sɪlɪkə] N silice *f*.

♦ **silica gel** N gel *m inv* di silice.

sili·con ['sɪlɪkən] N silicio.

♦ **silicon chip** N chip *m inv* al silicone.

sili·cone ['sɪlɪ,kəʊn] N silicone *m*.

sili·co·sis [ˌsɪlɪ'kəʊsɪs] N (*Med*) silicosi *f*.

silk [sɪlk] 1 N seta.

2 ADJ (*blouse, stockings*) di seta; (*industry*) della seta.

silk·en ['sɪlkən] (*liter*) ADJ (*dress, hair*) di seta; (*skin*) vellutato(-a); (*voice*) suadente, carezzevole.

♦ **silk factory** N setificio.

♦ **silk manufacturer** N fabbricante *m/f* di seta.

♦ **silk-screen** ['sɪlk,skriːn] N: **silk-screen printing** serigrafia.

silk·worm ['sɪlk,wɜːm] N baco da seta.

silky ['sɪlkɪ] ADJ (*comp* **-ier**, *superl* **-iest**) (*hair, dress*) di seta; (*skin*) vellutato(-a); (*voice*) suadente, carezzevole.

sill [sɪl] N a (*also:* **windowsill**) davanzale *m* b (*Aut*)

predellino **c** (*Geol*: *of corrie*) soglia.

sil·li·ness ['sɪlɪnɪs] N stupidità.

sil·ly ['sɪlɪ] ADJ (*comp* **-ier**, *superl* **-iest**) (*stupid*) sciocco(-a), stupido(-a); (*ridiculous*) ridicolo(-a); **don't be silly** non fare lo(-a) sciocco(-a), non essere stupido(-a); **to do something silly** fare una sciocchezza.

♦ **silly season** N: **the silly season** *periodo estivo in cui i giornali riportano notizie frivole perché l'attività parlamentare è sospesa.*

silo ['saɪləʊ] N silo.

silt [sɪlt] N limo

▶ **silt up** ① VI + ADV insabbiarsi.

　② VT + ADV ostruire.

sil·ver ['sɪlvə'] ① N **a** (*metal*) argento **b** (*silverware, cutlery*) argenteria **c** (*money*) *monete da 5, 10, 20 o 50 pence.*

　② ADJ (*ring, coin*) d'argento.

♦ **silver birch** N betulla argentata *or* bianca.

♦ **silver fir** N abete *m* bianco.

silver·fish ['sɪlvə‚fɪʃ] N INV pesciolino d'argento (*insetto*).

♦ **silver foil**, **silver paper** N carta argentata, (carta) stagnola.

♦ **silver gilt** N argento dorato.

♦ **silver-grey** [‚sɪlvə'greɪ] ADJ grigio argento *inv.*

♦ **silver-haired** [‚sɪlvə'hɛəd] ADJ dai capelli argentei.

♦ **silver jubilee** N venticinquesimo anniversario.

♦ **silver lining** N lato positivo; **every cloud has a silver lining** non tutto il male vien per nuocere.

♦ **silver paper** N = **silver foil**.

♦ **silver plate** N (*material*) argentatura; (*objects*) oggetti *mpl* placcati in argento.

♦ **silver-plated** [‚sɪlvə'pleɪtɪd] ADJ placcato(-a) in argento, argentato(-a).

♦ **silver screen** N: **the silver screen** il cinema (*attività*).

silver·side ['sɪlvə‚saɪd] N (*Culin*) culaccio di manzo.

silver·smith ['sɪlvə‚smɪθ] N argentiere *m.*

silver·ware ['sɪlvəwɛə'] N argenteria.

♦ **silver wedding** N nozze *fpl* d'argento.

sil·very ['sɪlvərɪ] ADJ (*colour*) argenteo(-a); (*hair*) argentato(-a); (*sound*) argentino(-a).

sima ['saɪmə] N (*Geol*) sima *m.*

sim·ian ['sɪmɪən] ADJ scimmiesco(-a).

simi·lar ['sɪmɪlə'] ADJ: **similar (to)** simile (a), dello stesso tipo (di); **similar in size** (*objects*) della stessa misura; (*people*) della stessa altezza; **...and similar products** ... e simili.

simi·lar·ity [‚sɪmɪ'lærɪtɪ] N (ras)somiglianza, similarità *f inv.*

simi·lar·ly ['sɪmɪləlɪ] ADV (*in a similar way*) allo stesso modo; (*as is similar*) così pure; **and similarly, ...** e allo stesso modo,... .

simi·ie ['sɪmɪlɪ] N similitudine *f*, paragone *m.*

sim·mer ['sɪmə'] ① VT cuocere a fuoco lento.

　② VI (*water*) sobbollire; (*food*) cuocere a fuoco lento; (*fig: revolt*) covare; **to simmer with rage** ribollire dalla rabbia

▶ **simmer down** VI + ADV (*fig fam*) calmarsi.

sim·per ['sɪmpə'] ① N sorriso affettato.

　② VI fare lo(-a) smorfioso(-a).

sim·per·ing ['sɪmpərɪŋ] ADJ lezioso(-a), smorfioso(-a).

sim·ple ['sɪmpl] ADJ (*comp* **-r**, *superl* **-est**) (*gen*) semplice; (*foolish*) sempliciotto(-a), sprovveduto(-a); **to make simple(r)** semplificare; **it's as simple as ABC** è come bere un bicchier d'acqua; **to make it simple for you ...** per semplificarti le cose...; **the simple truth** la pura

verità; **in simple terms** OR **in simple English** in parole povere; **for the simple reason that ...** per il semplice motivo che...; **a simple equation** (*Math*) equazione *f* di primo grado; **a simple Simon** un(a) sempliciotto(-a); **he's a bit simple** (*fam euph: mentally impaired*) è poco sveglio.

♦ **simple interest** N (*Fin*) interesse *m* semplice.

♦ **simple-minded** [‚sɪmpl'maɪndɪd] ADJ semplicione(-a).

♦ **simple-mindedness** [‚sɪmpl'maɪndɪdnɪs] N semplicioneria.

sim·ple·ton ['sɪmpltən] N (*old*) semplicione(-a), sempliciotto(-a).

sim·plic·ity [sɪm'plɪsɪtɪ] N semplicità.

sim·pli·fi·ca·tion [‚sɪmplɪfɪ'keɪʃən] N semplificazione *f.*

sim·pli·fy ['sɪmplɪ‚faɪ] VT semplificare.

sim·plis·tic [sɪm'plɪstɪk] ADJ (*pej: analysis, view*) semplicistico(-a).

simp·ly ['sɪmplɪ] ADV (*gen*) semplicemente; **I simply said that ...** ho semplicemente detto che...; **you simply MUST come!** devi assolutamente venire!; **a simply furnished room** una stanza arredata con semplicità.

simu·late ['sɪmjʊ‚leɪt] VT simulare.

simu·la·tion [‚sɪmjʊ'leɪʃən] N simulazione *f.*

simu·lat·or ['sɪmjʊ‚leɪtə'] N simulatore *m.*

sim·ul·ta·neity [‚sɪməltə'nɪətɪ] N simultaneità.

sim·ul·ta·neous [‚sɪməl'teɪnɪəs] ADJ simultaneo(-a).

♦ **simultaneous equations** NPL (*Math*) sistema *m* di equazioni.

sim·ul·ta·neous·ly [‚sɪməl'teɪnɪəslɪ] ADV simultaneamente, contemporaneamente; **simultaneously with** contemporaneamente a.

sin [sɪn] ① N peccato; **sins of omission** peccati di omissione; **mortal sin** peccato mortale; **it would be a sin to do that** (*Rel*) sarebbe peccato farlo; (*fig*) sarebbe un peccato farlo.

　② VI peccare.

Si·nai ['saɪnaɪ] N il Sinai.

since [sɪns] ① ADV da allora; **ever since** da allora (in poi); **(not) long since** da (non) molto (tempo).

　② PREP da; **since Monday** da lunedì; **(ever) since then/that ...** da allora....; **since leaving** da quando sono (*or* è *etc*) partito(-a); **how long is it since his last visit?** da quanto tempo non viene?.

　③ CONJ **a** (*time*) da quando; **(ever) since I arrived** (fin) da quando sono arrivato; **how long is it since you last saw him?** da quando non lo vedi?, quant'è che non lo vedi? **b** (*because*) siccome, dato che.

sin·cere [sɪn'sɪə'] ADJ sincero(-a).

sin·cere·ly [sɪn'sɪəlɪ] ADV sinceramente; **Yours sincerely** (*at end of letter*) Distinti saluti.

sin·cer·ity [sɪn'sɛrɪtɪ] N sincerità.

sine [saɪn] N (*Math*) seno.

si·necure ['saɪnɪkjʊə'] N sinecura *f.*

♦ **sine curve** N (*Math*) sinusoide *f.*

sin·ew ['sɪnju:] N (*tendon*) tendine *m*; **sinews** NPL (*muscles*) muscoli *mpl*; (*fig: strength*) forza.

sin·ewy ['sɪnjʊɪ] ADJ (*person*) muscoloso(-a); (*meat*) pieno(-a) di nervi.

sin·ful ['sɪnfʊl] ADJ (*Rel*) peccaminoso(-a); (*waste, act*) vergognoso(-a).

sin·ful·ly ['sɪnfəlɪ] ADV (*see adj*) in modo peccaminoso; vergognosamente.

sin·ful·ness ['sɪnfʊlnɪs] N (*Rel*: *of person, deeds*) peccaminosità.

sing [sɪŋ] (*pt* **sang**, *pp* **sung**) ① VT cantare; **to sing the tenor**

part cantare come tenore; **to sing sb's praises** (*fig*) cantare le lodi di qn; **to sing a child to sleep** cantare la ninna nanna a un bambino.

② VI (*person, bird*) cantare; (*ears, kettle, bullet*) fischiare; **to sing like a lark** cantare come un usignolo

▶ **sing out** VI + ADV (*fam: call*) chiamare.

Sin·ga·pore [ˌsɪŋgəˈpɔː] N Singapore *f*.

singe [sɪndʒ] VT bruciacchiare.

sing·er [ˈsɪŋəʳ] N cantante *m/f*.

Sin·gha·lese [ˌsɪŋəˈliːz] ADJ, N = **Sinhalese**.

sing·ing [ˈsɪŋɪŋ] ① N (*of person, bird*) canto; (*of kettle, bullet, in ears*) fischio.

② ADJ (*lessons, teacher*) di canto.

sin·gle [ˈsɪŋgl] ① ADJ **a** (*only one*) solo(-a), unico(-a) (*before n*); **a single tree in a garden** un solo albero in un giardino; **only on one single occasion** in una sola occasione; **he gave her a single rose** le ha dato una rosa; **I haven't a single moment to spare** non ho neanche un attimo di tempo; **not a single one was left** non ne è rimasto nemmeno uno; **she didn't see a single person** *or* **soul** non ha visto anima viva; **every single day** tutti i santi giorni

b (*not double*) unico(-a); (: *flower*) semplice; (: *ticket*) di (sola) andata; **down to single figures** (*inflation*) inferiore a dieci; **single spacing** (*Typ*) interlinea uno

c (*not married: man*) celibe, single *inv*; (: *woman*) nubile, single *inv*.

② N **a** (*Rail etc*) biglietto di (sola) andata

b (*record*): **a single** un 45 giri; see also **singles**

▶ **single out** VT + ADV (*choose*) scegliere; (*distinguish*) distinguere, isolare.

♦ **single bed** N letto a una piazza.

♦ **single-breasted** [ˈsɪŋglˌbrɛstɪd] ADJ (*jacket*) a un petto.

♦ **single cream** N (*Brit*) panna liquida (da cucina).

♦ **single-decker** [ˌsɪŋglˈdɛkəʳ] N (*Brit*) autobus *m inv* a un piano solo.

♦ **single-engined** [ˌsɪŋglˈɛndʒɪnd] ADJ monomotore.

♦ **Single European Market** N: **the Single European Market** il Mercato Unico.

♦ **single file** N: **in single file** in fila indiana.

♦ **single-handed** [ˌsɪŋglˈhændɪd] ① ADJ (*voyage*) solitario (-a); (*achievement*) fatto(-a) da solo(-a).

② ADV da solo(-a), senza aiuto.

♦ **single-minded** [ˌsɪŋglˈmaɪndɪd] ADJ (*person*) deciso(-a), tenace, risoluto(-a); (*ambition, attempt*) ostinato(-a); **to be single-minded about sth** concentrare tutte le proprie forze in qc.

♦ **single-mindedness** [ˌsɪŋglˈmaɪndɪdnɪs] N risolutezza.

sin·gle·ness [ˈsɪŋglnɪs] N: **singleness of purpose** tenacia.

♦ **single parent** N (*mother*) ragazza madre; (*father*) ragazzo padre.

♦ **single-parent** [ˈsɪŋglˈpɛərənt] ADJ: **the problems of single-parent families** i problemi delle famiglie con un solo genitore.

♦ **single-party** [ˈsɪŋglˈpɑːtɪ] ADJ (*Pol*) monopartitico(-a); **single-party system** monopartitismo.

♦ **single room** N camera singola.

singles [ˈsɪŋglz] NPL **a** (*Tennis*) singolo *msg* **b** (*Am: single people*) single *m/fpl*.

♦ **singles bar** N (*esp Am*) bar per single, *dove è possibile fare amicizia*.

♦ **single-seater** [ˌsɪŋglˈsiːtəʳ] ADJ: **single-seater aeroplane** aeroplano monoposto.

♦ **single-sex school** [ˌsɪŋglsɛksˈskuːl] ADJ (*for boys*) scuola maschile; (*for girls*) scuola femminile.

sin·glet [ˈsɪŋglɪt] N (*esp Brit*) canottiera.

sin·gle·ton [ˈsɪŋgltən] N (*Cards*) singleton *m inv*.

♦ **single-track** [ˈsɪŋglˌtræk] ADJ (*Rail*) a un solo binario.

sin·gly [ˈsɪŋglɪ] ADV singolarmente, uno(-a) a uno(-a).

sing·song [ˈsɪŋˌsɒŋ] ① ADJ (*tone*) cantilenante.

② N (*Brit fam*): **to have a singsong** farsi una cantata.

sin·gu·lar [ˈsɪŋgjʊləʳ] ① ADJ **a** (*Gram*) singolare **b** (*frm: extraordinary*) strano(-a), singolare.

② N (*Gram*) singolare *m*; **in the singular** al singolare; **in the feminine singular** al femminile singolare.

sin·gu·lar·ity [ˌsɪŋgjʊˈlærɪtɪ] N (*frm*) singolarità *f inv*.

sin·gu·lar·ly [ˈsɪŋgjʊlələ] ADV (*frm*) singolarmente.

Sin·ha·lese [ˌsɪnhəˈliːz] ADJ, N singalese (*m/f*).

sin·is·ter [ˈsɪnɪstəʳ] ADJ sinistro(-a).

sin·is·ter·ly [ˈsɪnɪstəlɪ] ADV sinistramente.

sink¹ [sɪŋk] (*pt* **sank**, *pp* **sunk**) ① VT **a** (*ship, object*) (far) affondare; (*fig: project*) far naufragare; (: *person*) distruggere; **to be sunk** (*fam*) essere nei guai; **I'm sunk without it** se non ce l'ho sono perso; **to be sunk in thought** essere immerso(-a) nei propri pensieri; **to be sunk in despair** essere assolutamente disperato(-a); **let's sink our differences** accantoniamo le divergenze

b (*mineshaft, well*) scavare; (*foundations*) gettare; (*stake*) piantare, conficcare; (*pipe etc*) interrare; **to sink the ball** (*Golf*) fare buca; **to sink money into an enterprise** investire denaro in un'impresa; **let's sink a few beers** (*Brit fam*) facciamoci un paio di birre.

② VI (*in water*) affondare; (*level of water, sun*) calare; (*ground*) cedere; (*value, voice*) abbassarsi; (*sales*) diminuire; **to sink to the bottom** (*ship*) colare a picco; **to sink to one's knees** cadere in ginocchio; **he sank into a chair/the mud** sprofondò in una poltrona/nel fango; **the water sank slowly into the ground** l'acqua è penetrata lentamente nel terreno; **she's sinking fast** (*dying*) deperisce rapidamente; **he has sunk in my estimation** è scaduto ai miei occhi; **he was left to sink or swim** (*fig*) fu lasciato a cavarsela da solo; **to sink like a stone** andar giù come un sasso; **to sink out of sight** scomparire alla vista; **the shares have** [OR] **the share price has sunk to 3 dollars** le azioni sono crollate a 3 dollari; **my heart** *or* **spirits sank** mi sentii venir meno

▶ **sink back** VI + ADV (*in chair*) accomodarsi bene; (*under water*) affondare di nuovo

▶ **sink down** VI + ADV: **to sink down onto a chair** lasciarsi cadere su una poltrona; **to sink down on one's knees** cadere in ginocchio; **to sink down out of sight** scomparire

▶ **sink in** VI + ADV (*person, car*) sprofondare; (*liquid: into ground, carpet*) penetrare; (*remark, explanation*) essere capito(-a); **it hasn't sunk in yet** (*fig*) non mi rendo (*or* si rende *etc*) ancora conto; **it took a long time to sink in** ci ho (*or* ha *etc*) messo molto a capirlo.

sink² [sɪŋk] N (*in kitchen*) lavello, acquaio; (*in bathroom*) lavandino.

sink·ing [ˈsɪŋkɪŋ] ① N (*shipwreck*) naufragio.

② ADJ: **a** *or* **that sinking feeling** una stretta allo stomaco; **I have a sinking feeling that things have gone wrong** ho il brutto presentimento che le cose siano andate male; **with sinking heart** con la morte nel cuore.

♦ **sinking fund** N (*Comm*) fondo d'ammortamento.

♦ **sink unit** N blocco *m* lavello *inv*.

sin·ner [ˈsɪnəʳ] N peccatore(-trice).

Sinn Féin [ˈʃɪnˈfeɪn] N Sinn Féin *m inv*, *braccio politico dei cattolici repubblicani*.

Sino... [ˈsaɪnəʊ] PREF: **Sino-Russian relations** i rapporti

Cina-Russia.

sinu·ous ['sɪnjʊəs] ADJ (*course, route*) sinuoso(-a), tortuoso(-a); (*dance, movement*) flessuoso(-a).

si·nus ['saɪnəs] N (*Anat*) seno, cavità *f inv.*

si·nusi·tis [ˌsaɪnə'saɪtɪs] N sinusite *f.*

si·nusoi·dal [ˌsaɪnə'sɔɪdəl] ADJ sinusoidale.

sip [sɪp] ① N sorso.
② VT sorseggiare, centellinare.

si·phon ['saɪfən] ① N sifone *m.*
② VT (*also:* **siphon off**: *liquid*) travasare (con un sifone); (*fig: funds, traffic*) deviare.

sir [sɜːʳ] N (*frm*) signore *m;* **yes, sir** sì, signore; (*Mil*) sissignore; **Dear Sir** (*in letter*) Egregio signor (+ *surname*); **Dear Sirs** Spettabile ditta; **Sir Winston Churchill** Sir Winston Churchill.

sire [saɪəʳ] ① VT (*Zool, old: child*) generare.
② N **a** (*old: to king*): **yes, sire** sì, maestà; (: *father*) padre *m* **b** (*Zool*) padre *m.*

si·ren ['saɪərən] N (*all senses*) sirena.

sir·loin ['sɜːˌlɔɪn] N (*of beef*) controfiletto.
♦ **sirloin steak** N bistecca di controfiletto.

si·roc·co [sɪrɒkəʊ] N scirocco.

si·sal ['saɪsəl] N sisal *f inv.*

sis·sy ['sɪsɪ] N (*fam pej*) femminuccia.

sis·ter ['sɪstəʳ] N **a** (*relation*) sorella **b** (*Med*) (infermiera *f*) caposala *inv* **c** (*Rel*) suora; **Sister Mary** Suor Maria.

sis·ter·hood ['sɪstəˌhʊd] N (*gen*) sorellanza; (*Rel*) congregazione *f* di suore.
♦ **sister-in-law** ['sɪstərɪnˌlɔː] N (*pl* **sisters-in-law**) cognata.

sis·ter·ly ['sɪstəlɪ] ADJ fraterno(-a), da sorella.
♦ **sister nations** NPL nazioni *fpl* sorelle.
♦ **sister organization** N organizzazione *f* affine.
♦ **sister ship** N nave *f* gemella.

Sisyphus ['sɪsɪfəs] N (*Myth*) Sisifo.

sit [sɪt] (*pt, pp* **sat**) ① VI **a** (*also:* **sit down**) sedersi, sedere; **sit!** (*to dog*) seduto!; **sit beside me** siediti accanto a me; **he just sits at home all day** sta a casa tutto il giorno senza far nulla; **this unit sits on top of that one** questo pezzo poggia su quello; **to sit still/straight** stare seduto (-a) fermo(-a)/dritto(-a); **to sit tight** (*wait patiently*) starsene seduto(-a); **to be sitting pretty** (*fig fam*) passarsela bene; **to sit on a committee** far parte di una commissione; **to sit for** (*a constituency*) rappresentare; **to sit in Parliament** sedere in Parlamento; **to sit for a painter/portrait** posare per un pittore/ritratto; **to sit for an examination** (*esp Brit*) dare *or* sostenere un esame; **to sit through** (*a film, play*) resistere fino alla fine di; **to sit over one's work** *or* **books** stare con la testa sui libri
b (*assembly, committee*) riunirsi, essere in seduta; **the committee is sitting now** il comitato è in riunione; **Parliament sits from November till June** i lavori parlamentari iniziano a novembre e terminano a giugno
c (*bird, insect*) posarsi; (*on eggs*) covare
d (*dress etc*) cadere; **that jacket sits well** quella giacca cade bene.
② VT **a** (*guest, child etc*) far sedere
b (*exam*) dare, sostenere
▶ **sit about, sit around** VI + ADV star seduto(-a) senza far nulla
▶ **sit back** VI + ADV (*in seat*) appoggiarsi allo schienale; (*doing nothing*) stare con le mani in mano
▶ **sit by** VI + ADV: **to sit by while sb does sth** starsene a guardare mentre qn fa qc
▶ **sit down** ① VI + ADV sedersi; **please sit down** prego, si

accomodi; **to be sitting down** essere seduto(-a).
② VT + ADV far sedere, far accomodare
▶ **sit in** VI + ADV **a** : **to sit in on a discussion** assistere ad una discussione; **to sit in for sb** (*as substitute*) fare le veci di qn, sostituire qn
b (*demonstrate*): **to sit in in a building** occupare un edificio
▶ **sit on** VI + PREP (*fig fam*) **a** (*keep secret: news, information*) tenere segreto(-a); (*delay taking action on: document, application*) tenere nel cassetto
b (*person: silence*) far tacere
▶ **sit out** VT + ADV (*dance etc*) non partecipare a, saltare; (*lecture, play*) restare fino alla fine di
▶ **sit up** ① VI + ADV **a** (*upright*) stare seduto(-a) diritto(-a); (*in bed*) tirarsi (su) a sedere; **to make sb sit up (and take notice)** (*fig*) far drizzare le orecchie a qn
b (*stay up late*) restare alzato(-a); **to sit up with** (*invalid*) passare la notte al capezzale di; **to sit up for sb** aspettare qn alzato(-a).
② VT + ADV (*baby, doll*) mettere a sedere, mettere seduto(-a).

si·tar [sɪ'tɑːʳ] N sitar *m inv.*

sit·com ['sɪtˌkɒm] N (*fam: Radio, TV*) situation comedy *f inv.*
♦ **sit-down** ['sɪtˌdaʊn] ① ADJ: **a sit-down strike** sciopero bianco (*con occupazione del posto di lavoro*); **a sit-down meal** un pranzo (a tavola).
② N (*fam*): **to have a sit-down** sedersi un momento.

site [saɪt] ① N **a** (*of town, building*) ubicazione *f*; (*Archeol*) località *f inv*; **the site of the accident** il luogo dell'incidente; **the site of the battle** il teatro della battaglia **b** (*Constr: also:* **building site**) cantiere *m* **c** (*also:* **camp site**) campeggio.
② VT collocare, situare; **a badly sited building** un edificio in una brutta posizione.
♦ **sit-in** ['sɪtˌɪn] N (*demonstration*) sit-in *m inv*; **to hold a sit-in** fare un sit-in.

sit·ing ['saɪtɪŋ] N ubicazione *f.*

sit·ter ['sɪtəʳ] N (*Art*) modello(-a); (*also:* **babysitter**) babysitter *m/f inv.*

sit·ting ['sɪtɪŋ] ① N (*of assembly, Parliament*) seduta; (*in canteen*) turno; (*for portrait*) seduta (di posa).
② ADJ: **in a sitting position** seduto(-a).
♦ **sitting duck, sitting target** N (*fig*) facile bersaglio.
♦ **sitting member** N (*Pol*) deputato in carica.
♦ **sitting room** N salotto, soggiorno.
♦ **sitting tenant** N (*Brit*) affittuario(-a), inquilino(-a).

situ·ate ['sɪtjʊˌeɪt] VT collocare, situare.

situ·ated ['sɪtjʊˌeɪtɪd] ADJ situato(-a); **well situated** (*house*) in una bella posizione; **how are you situated for money?** (*fig*) come stai a soldi?

situa·tion [ˌsɪtjʊ'eɪʃən] N (*position*) posizione *f*; (*fig*) situazione *f*; (*frm, old: job*) lavoro, impiego; **"situations vacant/wanted"** (*Brit*) "offerte *fpl*/domande *fpl* di impiego"; **to save the situation** salvare la situazione.
♦ **situation comedy** N (*TV, Radio, Theatre*) situation comedy *f inv.*
♦ **sit-up** ['sɪtˌʌp] N (*Gymnastics*): **to do sit-ups** passare dalla posizione supina a quella seduta.

six [sɪks] ① ADJ sei *inv.*
② N sei *m inv*; **to be (all) at sixes and sevens** (*fig: person, things*) essere sottosopra; **it's six of one and half a dozen of the other** (*fig*) se non è zuppa è pan bagnato, siamo lì *for usage see* **five.**
♦ **six-footer** [ˌsɪks'fʊtəʳ] N: **he's a six-footer** ≈ sarà alto due metri.

♦ **six-pack** ['sɪks,pæk] N confezione ƒ da sei (*di birra*).

six·pence ['sɪkspəns] N (*coin*) moneta da sei penny (*non più in circolazione legale*); (*value*) sei penny *mpl*.

♦ **six-shooter** ['sɪks,ʃu:tə'] N rivoltella a sei colpi.

six·teen [,sɪks'ti:n] [1] ADJ sedici *inv.*
[2] N sedici *m inv for usage see* **five**.

six·teenth [,sɪks'ti:nθ] [1] ADJ sedicesimo(-a).
[2] N (*in series*) sedicesimo(-a); (*fraction*) sedicesimo *for usage see* **fifth**.

sixth [sɪksθ] [1] ADJ sesto(-a).
[2] N (*in series*) sesto(-a); (*fraction*) sesto; **the upper/lower sixth** (*Brit Scol*) ≈ l'ultimo/il penultimo anno di scuola superiore *for usage see* **fifth**.

♦ **sixth form** N ≈ ultimo biennio delle superiori.

♦ **sixth-form college** ['sɪksθ,fɔ:m'kɒlɪdʒ] N (*Brit*) istituto *che offre corsi di preparazione all'esame di maturità*.

♦ **sixth-former** ['sɪksθ,fɔ:mə'] N (*Brit*) ≈ studente(-essa) dell'ultimo biennio delle superiori.

♦ **sixth sense** N sesto senso.

six·ti·eth ['sɪkstɪɪθ] [1] ADJ sessantesimo(-a).
[2] N (*in series*) sessantesimo(-a); (*fraction*) sessantesimo *for usage see* **fifth**.

six·ty ['sɪkstɪ] [1] ADJ sessanta *inv.*
[2] N sessanta *m inv for usage see* **fifty**.

♦ **sixty-four thousand dollar question** [,sɪkstɪfɔ:'θaʊsənd,dɒlə'kwɛstʃən] N: **that's the sixty-four thousand dollar question** (*fam*) questa è una domanda da mille punti.

size¹ [saɪz] N (*gen*) dimensioni *fpl*; (*fig: of problem, operation etc*) proporzioni *fpl*; (*of garments*) taglia, misura; (*of shoes*) numero, misura; (*of hat*) misura; **I take size 5 shoes** ≈ porto il 38 di scarpe; **I take size 14 in a dress** ≈ porto la 44 di vestiti; **what size (of) collar?** che misura di collo?; **what size are you?** [OR] **what size do you take?** che taglia porti?; **he's about your size** sarà più o meno come te; **it's the size of a brick/nut** sarà grande come un mattone/una noce; **I'd like the small/large size** (*of soap powder etc*) vorrei la confezione piccola/grande; (*of clothes*) vorrei la misura piccola/grande; **to try sth for size** misurare qc per vedere se è della taglia giusta; **to cut sth to size** tagliare qc nella misura desiderata *or* voluta; **to cut sb down to size** (*fig fam*) ridimensionare qn; **that's about the size of it** (*fig*) le cose stanno più o meno così

▶ **size up** VT + ADV (*person, problem*) valutare, farsi un'idea di.

size² [saɪz] [1] N (*for walls*) colla; (*for fabric*) appretto.
[2] VT (*wall*) dare una mano di colla a; (*fabric*) apprettare.

-size [saɪz], **-sized** [saɪzd] SUFF: **bite-size pieces** bocconcini *mpl*, pezzetti *mpl*.

size·able ['saɪzəbl] ADJ (*house, diamond*) abbastanza grande; (*sum, problem*) considerevole, notevole.

siz·zle ['sɪzl] VI sfrigolare.

siz·zler ['sɪzlə'] N (*fam*): **it's been a real sizzler today** ha fatto un caldo da morire, oggi.

SK ABBR (*Canada*)= *Saskatchewan*.

skate¹ [skeɪt] N (*pl inv: fish*) razza.

skate² [skeɪt] [1] N pattino; **to get one's skates on** (*fig: hurry up*) affrettarsi, sbrigarsi.
[2] VI pattinare; **to go skating** andare a pattinare; **to skate across/down** *etc* attraversare/scendere *etc* pattinando; **it went skating across the room** (*fig*) è scivolato lungo la stanza

▶ **skate over, skate around** VI + PREP (*problem, issue*) prendere alla leggera, prendere sottogamba.

skate·board ['skeɪt,bɔ:d] N skateboard *m inv.*

skat·er ['skeɪtə'] N pattinatore(-trice).

skat·ing ['skeɪtɪŋ] N pattinaggio; **figure skating** pattinaggio artistico.

♦ **skating rink** N pista di pattinaggio.

♦ **skating turn** N (*Skiing*) passo di pattinaggio.

skein [skeɪn] N (*of wool*) matassa.

skel·etal ['skɛlɪtl] ADJ (*Anat*) dello scheletro; (*like a skeleton*) scheletrico(-a).

skel·eton ['skɛlɪtn] [1] N (*of person*) scheletro; (*of building*) struttura, ossatura; (*of novel, report*) schema *m*; **a walking skeleton** (*fig*) uno scheletro ambulante; **the skeleton at the feast** (*fig*) il/la guastafeste; **skeleton in the cupboard** *or* **closet** (*fig*) scheletro nell'armadio.
[2] ADJ (*staff, service*) ridotto(-a).

♦ **skeleton key** N passe-partout *m inv.*

♦ **skeleton outline** N schema *m.*

skep·tic *etc* ['skɛptɪk] (*Am*) = **sceptic** *etc.*

sketch [skɛtʃ] [1] N **a** (*drawing*) schizzo, abbozzo; (*fig: rough draft: of ideas, plan*) abbozzo, schema *m*; (: *description*) schizzo
b (*Theatre etc*) sketch *m inv.*
[2] VT (*draw*) schizzare, abbozzare; (*fig: ideas, plan*) abbozzare; **to sketch a map for sb** fare una piantina per qn

▶ **sketch in** VT + ADV (*details*) inserire, aggiungere

▶ **sketch out** VT + ADV (*plan, situation*) descrivere a grandi linee.

sketch·book ['skɛtʃ,bʊk], **sketch·pad** ['skɛtʃ,pæd] N album *m inv or* blocco per schizzi.

sketchi·ly ['skɛtʃɪlɪ] ADV (*answer, understand*) in modo incompleto; (*plan, recall*) a grandi linee.

♦ **sketch map** N carta (geografica) muta.

sketchy ['skɛtʃɪ] ADJ (*comp* **-ier,** *superl* **-iest**) (*drawing, plan*) approssimato(-a); (*plans, knowledge*) vago(-a).

skew [skju:] [1] ADJ storto(-a); **skew distribution** (*Math*) distribuzione ƒ asimmetrica; **skew lines** (*Math*) rette *fpl* sghembe.
[2] VT: **to be skewed** essere inclinato(-a) *or* storto(-a).
[3] N (*Brit*): **on the skew** storto(-a), di traverso.

skew·er ['skjʊə'] [1] N (*for roasts*) spiedo; (*for kebabs*) spiedino.
[2] VT infilzare in uno spiedo.

skew-whiff ['skju:'wɪf] ADJ (*Brit fam*) a sghimbescio.

ski [ski:] [1] N sci *m inv.*
[2] VI sciare; **to ski down a slope** fare una discesa con gli sci; **to go skiing** andare a sciare.

♦ **ski binding** N attacco degli sci.

♦ **ski boot** N scarpone *m* da sci.

skid [skɪd] [1] N (*Aut*) slittamento; (: *sideways slip*) sbandamento; **to go into a skid** slittare; sbandare; **to get out of a skid** [OR] **to correct a skid** riprendere controllo del veicolo.
[2] VI (*Aut*) slittare; (: *slip sideways*) sbandare; (*person, object*) scivolare; **to skid into sth** (*car*) slittare e sbattere contro qc; (*person, object*) scivolare contro qc.

skid·lid ['skɪd,lɪd] N (*fam*) casco da motociclista.

♦ **skid mark** N (*Aut*) segno della frenata.

skid·proof ['skɪd,pru:f] ADJ antiscivolo *inv.*

ski·er ['ski:ə'] N sciatore(-trice).

skiff [skɪf] N (*boat*) skiff *m inv.*

ski·ing ['ski:ɪŋ] [1] N sci *m* (*sport*).
[2] ADJ (*holiday etc*) sciistico(-a).

♦ **ski instructor** N maestro(-a) di sci.

♦ **ski jump** N **a** trampolino **b** (*also:* **ski jumping**) salto

con gli sci.

skil·ful, (*Am*) **skill·ful** ['skɪlfʊl] ADJ abile.

skil·ful·ly, (*Am*) **skill·ful·ly** ['skɪlfəlɪ] ADV abilmente.

skil·ful·ness, (*Am*) **skill·ful·ness** ['skɪlfʊlnɪs] N (*of person, handiwork*) abilità.

♦ **ski lift** N impianto di risalita.

skill [skɪl] N **a** (*gen*) capacità *f inv*, abilità *f inv*; (*talent*) talento; **her skill in dealing with people** la sua abilità nel trattare con le persone; **his skill as a mechanic** la sua abilità come meccanico; **a writer of great skill** uno scrittore di grande talento; **to make use of sb's skills** sfruttare le capacità di qn **b** (*technique*) tecnica; **there's a certain skill to doing it** ci vuole una certa tecnica *or* arte nel farlo.

skilled [skɪld] ADJ **a** (*gen*) abile, esperto(-a) **b** (*job, work*) specializzato(-a); (*worker*) specializzato(-a), qualificato (-a).

skil·let ['skɪlɪt] N (*Am*) padella.

skill·ful ['skɪlfʊl] ADJ (*Am*) = **skilful**.

skill·fully ['skɪlfʊlɪ] ADJ (*Am*) = **skilfully**.

skill·ful·ness ['skɪlfʊlnɪs] N (*Am*) = **skilfulness**.

skim [skɪm] **1** VT **a** (*soup*) schiumare; (*milk*) scremare; **to skim the fat off the soup** schiumare il brodo; **to skim the cream off the milk** scremare il latte **b** (*stone*) far rimbalzare; (*subj: bird, plane*): **to skim the water/ground** sfiorare *or* rasentare l'acqua/il suolo. **2** VI: **to skim across** *or* **along** sfiorare; **the stone skimmed across the ice** il sasso rimbalzò sul ghiaccio; **to skim through a book** (*fig*) scorrere *or* dare una scorsa a un libro.

skimmed milk [ˌskɪmd'mɪlk] N latte *m* scremato.

♦ **ski mountaineering** N sci-alpinismo.

skimp [skɪmp] VI: **to skimp on** (*material etc*) risparmiare; (*work*) raffazzonare; (*refreshments*) lesinare.

skimpi·ly ['skɪmpɪlɪ] ADV (*dressed*) in modo succinto; (*provided*) insufficientemente.

skimpi·ness ['skɪmpɪnɪs] N (*of skirt*) scarsa ampiezza; (*of allowance*) esiguità; (*of meal*) frugalità.

skimpy ['skɪmpɪ] ADJ (*comp* **-ier,** *superl* **-iest**) (*skirt etc*) striminzito(-a), succinto(-a); (*hem*) piccolo(-a); (*allowance*) misero(-a); (*meal*) frugale.

skin [skɪn] **1** N **a** (*gen*) pelle *f*; (*of fruit, vegetable*) buccia; (*of boat, aircraft*) rivestimento; (*for duplicating*) matrice *f* per duplicatori; (*crust: on paint, milk pudding: thin*) pellicola; (: *thick*) crosta; **next to the skin** a contatto con la pelle; **to have a thick/thin skin** (*fig*) non essere/essere suscettibile; **by the skin of one's teeth** (*fig*) per un pelo; **wet** *or* **soaked to the skin** bagnato(-a) fino al midollo; **to be (all) skin and bone** (*fig*) essere pelle e ossa; **to get under sb's skin** (*fig*) dare sui nervi a qn; **I've got you under my skin** (*fig*) ti ho nella pelle; **it's no skin off my nose** (*fig fam: does not concern me*) non sono affari miei; (: *does not hurt me*) non mi costa niente **b** (*fam*) = **skinhead**. **2** VT (*animal*) spellare, scuoiare, scorticare; (*fruit etc*) sbucciare, pelare; **to skin one's knee/elbow** sbucciarsi *or* scorticarsi un ginocchio/gomito; **I'll skin him alive!** (*fig*) lo scortico vivo!; **keep your eyes skinned for a garage** tieni gli occhi aperti per un distributore.

♦ **skin cancer** N cancro alla pelle.

♦ **skin colour** N colore *m* della pelle.

♦ **skin cream** N crema (per il viso).

♦ **skin-deep** [ˌskɪn'diːp] ADJ (*also fig*) superficiale.

♦ **skin disease** N malattia della pelle, dermatosi *f inv*.

♦ **skin diver** N sub *m/f*.

♦ **skin diving** N nuoto subacqueo.

skin·flick ['skɪnˌflɪk] N (*fam*) film porno *inv*.

skin·flint ['skɪnˌflɪnt] N taccagno(-a), spilorcio(-a).

skin·ful ['skɪnfʊl] N (*fam*): **to have (had) a skinful** aver fatto il pieno.

♦ **skin graft** N innesto epidermico.

skin·head ['skɪnˌhɛd] N testa rasata, skinhead *m/f*.

skin·ny ['skɪnɪ] ADJ (*comp* **-ier,** *superl* **-iest**) (*usu pej: person*) magro(-a), gracile, mingherlino(-a); (*jumper*) striminzito(-a).

skint [skɪnt] ADJ (*Brit fam*): **to be skint** essere in bolletta, essere al verde.

♦ **skin test** N prova di reazione cutanea.

skin·tight ['skɪnˌtaɪt] ADJ aderente come una seconda pelle.

skip[1] [skɪp] **1** N saltello, balzo. **2** VI saltellare, salterellare; (*with rope*) saltare con la corda; **to skip in/out** *etc* entrare/uscire *etc* saltellando; **to skip off** (*fig*) tagliare la corda; **to skip over sth** (*fig*) sorvolare su qc; **to skip from one subject to another** saltare da un argomento a un altro. **3** VT (*fig: meal, lesson, page*) saltare; (: *school*) marinare, bigiare; **let's skip it!** (*fam*) sorvoliamo!

skip[2] [skɪp] N benna.

♦ **ski pants** NPL pantaloni *mpl* da sci.

♦ **ski pass** N ski-pass *m inv*.

ski·plane ['skiːˌpleɪn] N aeroplano munito di sci.

♦ **ski pole** N = **ski stick**.

skip·per ['skɪpə'] **1** N (*Sport, Naut*) capitano; (*in boat race*) skipper *m inv*. **2** VT (*boat*) essere al comando di; (*sports team*) capitanare.

skip·ping ['skɪpɪŋ] N salto della corda.

♦ **skipping rope** N (*Brit*) corda per saltare.

♦ **ski rack** N (*Aut*) portascì *m inv*.

♦ **ski resort** N località *f inv* *or* stazione *f* sciistica.

skir·mish ['skɜːmɪʃ] N scaramuccia.

skirt [skɜːt] **1** N gonna. **2** VT **a** (*road, path*) fiancheggiare, costeggiare **b** (*person: also: skirt around: town, table*) girare intorno a; (: *obstacle, difficulty*) aggirare; (: *argument, subject*) schivare.

♦ **skirt hanger** N reggigonne *m inv*.

skirt·ing ['skɜːtɪŋ], **skirt·ing board** N (*Brit*) zoccolo, battiscopa *m inv*.

♦ **ski run** N pista da sci.

♦ **ski school** N scuola di sci.

♦ **ski stick, ski pole** N racchetta da sci.

♦ **ski suit** N tuta da sci.

skit [skɪt] N (*Theatre*) sketch *m inv* satirico.

♦ **ski tow** N sciovia, ski-lift *m inv*.

skit·ter ['skɪtə'] VI: **to skitter around** *or* **about** (*bird, leaf*) svolazzare; (*dog*) scorrazzare.

skit·tish ['skɪtɪʃ] ADJ (*horse, person*) ombroso(-a).

skit·tle ['skɪtl] N birillo; **skittles** NPL (*game*) (gioco dei) birilli *mpl*; **to play skittles** giocare a birilli; **it isn't all beer and skittles** (*fam*) non è tutto rose e fiori.

skive [skaɪv] VI (*Brit fam*) fare il/la lavativo(-a); **to skive off** svignarsela, filarsela.

skiv·er ['skaɪvə'] N (*fam*) lavativo(-a), scansafatiche *m/f inv*.

skiv·vy ['skɪvɪ] N (*esp Brit fam pej*) sguattera.

skul·dug·gery, (*Am*) **skull·dug·gery** [skʌl'dʌgərɪ] N (*fam*) imbrogli *mpl*, manovre *fpl*.

skulk [skʌlk] VI (*also: skulk about*) aggirarsi furtivamente; **to skulk into/out of** entrare/uscire furtivamente.

skull [skʌl] N (*of live person*) cranio; (*of dead person*) teschio; (*fam: head*) testa, testona; **skull and crossbones** (*danger warning*) teschio; (*flag*) bandiera dei pirati.

skull·cap ['skʌl,kæp] N (*worn by Jews*) zucchetto; (*worn by Pope*) papalina.

skull·dug·gery [skʌl'dʌgərɪ] N (*Am*) = **skulduggery**.

skunk [skʌŋk] N (*Zool*) moffetta, puzzola; **you skunk!** (*fam*) farabutto!, carogna!

sky [skaɪ] N cielo; **to sleep under the open sky** dormire sotto le stelle *or* all'aperto; **to praise sb to the skies** portare alle stelle qn; **the sky's the limit** (*fig fam*) non ci sono limiti.

♦ **sky-blue** [,skaɪ'bluː] 1 N azzurro.
  2 ADJ azzurro(-a).

sky·div·er ['skaɪdaɪvə'] N paracadutista *m/f* acrobatico(-a).

♦ **sky-diving** ['skaɪ,daɪvɪŋ] N paracadutismo in caduta libera.

♦ **sky-high** [,skaɪ'haɪ] 1 ADV (*throw*) molto in alto; **to blow sth sky-high** far saltare in aria qc; **to blow a theory sky-high** confutare una teoria; **prices have gone sky-high** i prezzi sono saliti alle stelle.
  2 ADJ (*fam*) esorbitante.

sky·jack ['skaɪ,dʒæk] VT (*aircraft*) dirottare.

sky·jack·er ['skaɪ,dʒækə'] N pirata *m* dell'aria, dirottatore (-trice).

Sky·lab ['skaɪlæb] N laboratorio spaziale.

sky·lark ['skaɪ,laːk] 1 N (*bird*) allodola.
  2 VI (*fig fam*) fare il/la matto(-a).

sky·light ['skaɪ,laɪt] N lucernario.

sky·line ['skaɪlaɪn] N (*horizon*) orizzonte *m*; (*of city*) profilo.

sky·scraper ['skaɪ,skreɪpə'] N grattacielo.

sky·ward(s) ['skaɪwəd(z)] 1 ADJ (*glance*) al cielo; (*shot*) in aria.
  2 ADV (*look*) verso il cielo; (*shoot*) in aria.

sky·writing ['skaɪ,raɪtɪŋ] N pubblicità aerea.

slab [slæb] N (*of stone, metal*) lastra; (*of wood*) tavola; (*of chocolate*) tavoletta; (*of meat, cheese*) pezzo; (*fam: in mortuary*) tavolo anatomico.

slack [slæk] 1 ADJ (*comp* -er, *superl* -est) **a** (*not tight: rope, knot*) lento(-a), allentato(-a); (: *grip*) debole
  b (*lax: work*) trascurato(-a); (: *student, worker*) negligente; (*lazy*) pigro(-a), fiacco(-a); **to be slack about one's work** essere negligente nel proprio lavoro; **to grow slack** lasciarsi andare
  c (*Comm: market*) stagnante; (: *demand*) scarso(-a); (*period*) morto(-a); **business is slack** si fanno pochi affari; **the slack season** la bassa stagione.
  2 N **a** (*part of rope etc*): **to take up the slack in a rope** tendere una corda.
  b (*coal dust*) polvere *f* di carbone; see also **slacks**.
  3 VI (*fam*) fare il/la lavativo(-a).
  4 VT (*Naut: sail*) lascare
  ▶ **slack off** VI + ADV (*fam: activity etc*) ridursi, calare.

slack·en ['slækn] (*also:* **slacken off**) 1 VT (*rope, grip, reins, nut*) allentare; (*pressure*) diminuire; **to slacken speed** ridurre la velocità; **to slacken one's pace** rallentare il passo.
  2 VI (*gen*) allentarsi; (*pressure, speed, activity*) diminuire, rallentare; (*gale*) placarsi; (*trade*) calare, ridursi.

slack·er ['slækə'] N (*fam*) lavativo(-a), pelandrone(-a).

slack·ness ['slæknɪs] N (*of rope, cable*) mancanza di tensione; (*of person*) negligenza; (*of trade*) ristagno.

slacks [slæks] NPL pantaloni *mpl* casual *inv*.

slag [slæg] 1 N **a** (*waste: from coal mine, smelting*) scorie *fpl* **b** (*Brit fam offensive*) puttana.

  2 VT (*Brit fam*): **to slag sb/sth off** sputtanare qn/qc.

♦ **slag heap** N cumulo di scorie.

slain [sleɪn] 1 PP of **slay**.
  2 NPL (*liter*): **the slain** i caduti.

slake [sleɪk] VT (*liter: one's thirst*) spegnere.

sla·lom ['slaːləm] (*Sport*) 1 N slalom *m inv*; **special slalom** slalom speciale.
  2 VI fare lo slalom.

slam [slæm] 1 N **a** (*of door*) colpo
  b (*Bridge*) slam *m inv*; **grand slam** (*Cards, Sport*) grande slam.
  2 VT **a** (*door, lid*) sbattere; **to slam sth shut** chiudere qc sbattendolo(-a); **to slam down the phone** buttare giù la cornetta; **to slam sth (down) on the table** sbattere qc sul tavolo; **to slam on the brakes** frenare di colpo; **to slam the door in sb's face** sbattere la porta in faccia a qn
  b (*criticize*) stroncare.
  3 VI (*door, lid*) sbattere.

slam·mer ['slæmə'] N (*fam*): **the slammer** la gattabuia.

slan·der ['slaːndə'] 1 N calunnia; (*Law*) diffamazione *f*.
  2 VT calunniare; (*Law*) diffamare.

slan·der·ous ['slaːndərəs] ADJ calunnioso(-a); (*Law*) diffamatorio(-a).

slan·der·ous·ly ['slaːndərəslɪ] ADV calunniosamente.

slang [slæŋ] 1 N (*gen*) slang *m inv*, gergo; **school/army slang** gergo studentesco/militare; **to talk slang** parlare in gergo.
  2 ADJ (*word*) gergale.
  3 VT (*fam: insult, criticize*) dirne di tutti i colori a.

slang·ing match ['slæŋɪŋ,mætʃ] N (*Brit fam*) rissa verbale.

slangy ['slæŋɪ] ADJ (*comp* -ier, *superl* -iest) (*fam*) gergale.

slant [slaːnt] 1 N pendenza, inclinazione *f*; (*Geom*) apotema *m*; (*fig: point of view*) punto di vista, angolazione *f*; **to be on a slant** essere inclinato(-a); **to give a new slant on sth** presentare qc sotto una nuova angolazione; **to get a new slant on sth** vedere qc da un'altra angolazione.
  2 VT (*roof etc*) inclinare; **to slant a report** (*fig*) dare una versione distorta *or* tendenziosa dei fatti.
  3 VI essere inclinato(-a), pendere.

slant·ed ['slaːntɪd] ADJ (*programme, report*) tendenzioso(-a).

♦ **slant-eyed** ['slaːnt,aɪd] ADJ (*pej*) dagli occhi a mandorla.

slant·ing ['slaːntɪŋ] ADJ (*handwriting*) inclinato(-a); (*roof*) spiovente; (*line*) obliquo(-a); (*rain*) che cade di traverso.

slant·wise ['slaːnt,waɪz], **slant·ways** ['slaːnt,weɪz] ADJ, ADV di traverso.

slap [slæp] 1 N schiaffo, ceffone *m*; **a slap in the face** uno schiaffo; (*fig*) uno schiaffo morale; **a slap on the wrist** (*fig*) una tirata d'orecchi; **a slap on the back** una pacca sulla spalla.
  2 ADV (*fam*): **to run slap into** (*tree, lamppost*) colpire in pieno; (*person*) imbattersi in; **it fell slap in the middle** cadde proprio nel mezzo.
  3 VT **a** schiaffeggiare; **to slap a child's bottom** sculacciare un bambino; **to slap sb on the back** dare una pacca sulla spalla a qn; **to slap sb down** (*fig: child*) zittire; (: *opposition*) stroncare
  b: **he slapped the book on the table** ha sbattuto il libro sul tavolo; **slap a coat of paint on it** dagli una mano di vernice.
  4 VI: **to slap against** andare a sbattere contro; **the waves slapped against the pier** le onde si infrangevano sul molo.

♦ **slap-bang** [ˌslæpˈbæŋ] ADV (*esp Brit fam*): **he ran slap-bang into the door** ha preso in pieno la porta.

slap·dash [ˈslæpˌdæʃ], **slap·happy** [ˈslæpˌhæpɪ] ADJ (*person*) negligente; (*work*) raffazzonato(-a).

slap·head [ˈslæpˌhɛd] N (*Brit fam*) imbecille *m/f*.

slap·stick [ˈslæpˌstɪk] N (*also*: **slapstick comedy**) farsa grossolana.

♦ **slap-up** [ˈslæpˌʌp] ADJ (*Brit fam*): **a slap-up meal** un pasto coi fiocchi *or* da leccarsi i baffi.

slash [slæʃ] ① N **a** (*slit*) taglio; (: *in dress, skirt*) spacco; (*stroke: of sword, whip*) colpo **b** (*Typ: also*: **slash mark**) barra.
② VT (*with knife: gen*) tagliare, squarciare; (: *face, painting*) sfregiare; (*with whip, stick*) sferzare; (*fig: prices*) ridurre fortemente; **to slash one's wrists** tagliarsi le vene.

slat [slæt] N (*of wood*) stecca; (*of plastic*) lamina.

slate [sleɪt] ① N **a** (*rock*) ardesia; (*tile*) tegola (d'ardesia); (*writing tablet*) lavagnetta; **to wipe the slate clean** (*fig*) metterci una pietra sopra; **to put sth on sb's slate** mettere qc sul conto di qn **b** (*Am Pol*) lista di candidati.
② VT **a** (*roof*) coprire con tegole **b** (*fam: criticize*) criticare, stroncare.
③ ADJ di ardesia.

♦ **slate-blue** [ˌsleɪtˈbluː] ADJ blu ardesia *inv*.

♦ **slate-coloured** [ˈsleɪt ˌkʌləd] ADJ plumbeo(-a).

♦ **slate-grey** [ˌsleɪtˈgreɪ] ADJ grigio ardesia *inv*; (*sky, storm clouds*) plumbeo(-a).

slat·ted [ˈslætɪd] ADJ a stecche.

slat·tern [ˈslætən] N (*old pej*) sciattona.

slaugh·ter [ˈslɔːtəʳ] ① N (*of animals*) macellazione *f*; (*of people*) strage *f*, massacro, carneficina.
② VT (*animals*) macellare; (*people*) trucidare, massacrare; (*fig*) distruggere, massacrare.

slaughter·house [ˈslɔːtəˌhaʊs] N macello, mattatoio.

Slav [slɑːv] ADJ, N slavo(-a).

slave [sleɪv] ① N schiavo(-a); **to be a slave to sth** (*fig*) essere schiavo(-a) di qc; **to be a slave of habit** essere schiavo(-a) delle abitudini.
② VI: **to slave (away) at sth/at doing sth** sgobbare per qc/per fare qc.

♦ **slave-driver** [ˈsleɪvˌdraɪvəʳ] N sorvegliante *m* di schiavi; (*fig*) schiavista *m/f*.

♦ **slave labour** N lavoro fatto dagli schiavi; **we're just slave labour here** (*fig*) siamo solamente sfruttati qui dentro.

slav·er[1] [ˈslævəʳ] VI (*dribble*) sbavare.

slav·er[2] [ˈsleɪvəʳ] N (*person*) schiavista *m/f*.

slav·ery [ˈsleɪvərɪ] N (*condition*) schiavitù *f*; (*system*) schiavismo; **to reduce to slavery** schiavizzare.

♦ **slave trade** N tratta degli schiavi.

slav·ey [sleɪvɪ] N (*old fam*) serva.

slav·ish [ˈsleɪvɪʃ] ADJ (*pej: devotion*) servile; (: *imitation*) pedissequo(-a).

slav·ish·ly [ˈsleɪvɪʃlɪ] ADV (*see adj*) servilmente; pedissequamente.

Sla·von·ic [sləˈvɒnɪk], (*Am*) **Slav·ic** [ˈslɑːvɪk] ADJ, N slavo (-a).

slay [sleɪ] (*pt* **slew**, *pp* **slain**) VT (*liter: kill*) uccidere.

SLD [ˌɛsɛlˈdiː] N ABBR (*Brit*)= *Social and Liberal Democrats*.

sleaze [sliːz] (*fam*) N (*corruption*) corruzione *f*;(*sordidness*) sordidezza; **the sleaze factor** la questione morale.

slea·zy [ˈsliːzɪ] ADJ (*comp* **-ier**, *superl* **-iest**) squallido(-a), infimo(-a).

sledge [slɛdʒ] ① N (*also*: **sled**) slitta.
② VI: **to go sledging** andare in slitta; **to sledge down a hill** scendere in slitta giù per una collina.

sledge·hammer [ˈslɛdʒˌhæməʳ] N mazza.

sleek [sliːk] ① ADJ (*comp* **-er**, *superl* **-est**) (*shiny: hair, coat*) liscio(-a) e lucente; (*cat*) dal pelo lucido; (*person: in appearance*) azzimato(-a); (: *in manner*) untuoso(-a); (*car, boat*) elegante.
② VT: **to sleek one's hair down/back** lisciarsi i capelli.

sleek·ly [ˈsliːklɪ] ADV (*answer*) in modo untuoso.

sleep [sliːp] (*vb: pt, pp* **slept**) ① N sonno; **deep** *or* **sound sleep** sonno profondo; **to have a good night's sleep** farsi una bella dormita; **to drop off** *or* **go to sleep** addormentarsi; **to go to sleep** (*limb*) intorpidirsi; **to put to sleep** (*patient*) anestizzare; (*animal: euph: kill*) abbattere; **to talk in one's sleep** parlare nel sonno; **to walk in one's sleep** camminare nel sonno; (*as a habit*) essere sonnambulo(-a); **to send sb to sleep** (*bore*) far addormentare qn; **I shan't lose any sleep over it** (*fig*) non starò a perderci il sonno.
② VT: **we can sleep four** abbiamo quattro posti letto, possiamo alloggiare quattro persone.
③ VI dormire; **to sleep like a log** *or* **top** dormire della grossa *or* come un ghiro; **he was sleeping soundly** *or* **deeply** era profondamente addormentato; **to sleep lightly** avere il sonno leggero; **let's sleep on it** (*fig*) la notte porta consiglio, dormiamoci sopra; **sleep tight!** sogni d'oro!; **I slept through the storm/alarm clock** non ho sentito il temporale/la sveglia; **he slept at his mother's** ha dormito dalla mamma; **to sleep with sb** (*euph: have sex*) andare a letto con qn

► **sleep around** VI + ADV (*fam*) andare a letto con tutti

► **sleep in** VI + ADV (*lie late*) alzarsi tardi; (*oversleep*) dormire fino a tardi

► **sleep off** VT + ADV: **to sleep sth off** smaltire qc dormendo

► **sleep out** VI + ADV dormire all'aperto.

sleep·er [ˈsliːpəʳ] N **a** (*person*) dormiente *m/f*; **to be a heavy/light sleeper** avere il sonno pesante/leggero **b** (*Brit Rail: track*) traversina; (: *berth*) cuccetta; (: *coach*) vagone *m* letto *inv* **c** (*earring*) campanella.

sleepi·ly [ˈsliːpɪlɪ] ADV con aria assonnata.

sleepi·ness [ˈsliːpɪnɪs] N (*of person, village*) sonnolenza.

sleep·ing [ˈsliːpɪŋ] ADJ addormentato(-a); **the Sleeping Beauty** la Bella Addormentata nel bosco; **let sleeping dogs lie** (*Proverb*) non svegliare il can che dorme.

♦ **sleeping bag** N sacco a pelo.

♦ **sleeping car** N (*Rail*) vagone *m* letto *inv*.

♦ **sleeping partner** N (*Brit Comm*) socio inattivo.

♦ **sleeping pill** N sonnifero.

♦ **sleeping policeman** N (*esp Brit*) dosso artificiale (*per far diminuire la velocità*).

♦ **sleeping quarters** NPL dormitorio *msg*, camerata *fsg*.

♦ **sleeping sickness** N malattia del sonno.

sleep·less [ˈsliːplɪs] ADJ (*person*) insonne; (*night*) in bianco, insonne.

sleep·less·ly [ˈsliːplɪslɪ] ADV senza dormire.

sleep·less·ness [ˈsliːplɪsnɪs] N insonnia.

sleep·walk [ˈsliːpˌwɔːk] VI camminare nel sonno; (*as a habit*) essere sonnambulo(-a); **she sleepwalks** soffre di sonnambulismo, è sonnambula.

sleep·walk·er [ˈsliːpˌwɔːkəʳ] N sonnambulo(-a).

sleep·walk·ing [ˈsliːpˌwɔːkɪŋ] N sonnambulismo.

sleepy [ˈsliːpɪ] ADJ (*comp* **-ier**, *superl* **-iest**) (*person, voice, look*) assonnato(-a), sonnolento(-a); (*village*) addormentato(-a); **to be** *or* **feel sleepy** avere sonno.

sleepy·head [ˈsliːpɪˌhɛd] N (*fam*) dormiglione(-a); **go to**

bed, sleepyhead! va' a letto che stai dormendo in piedi!

sleet [sliːt] ① N nevischio.

② VI: **it was sleeting** nevischiava.

sleeve [sliːv] N (*of garment*) manica; (*of record*) copertina; **to roll up one's sleeves** rimboccarsi le maniche; **to have sth up one's sleeve** (*fig*) avere in serbo qc.

sleeve·board ['sliːv͵bɔːd] N stiramaniche *m inv*.

-sleeved [sliːvd] SUFF: **short/long-sleeved** con le maniche corte/lunghe.

sleeve·less ['sliːvlɪs] ADJ (*garment*) senza maniche.

sleigh [sleɪ] N slitta.

sleight [slaɪt] N: **sleight of hand** (*trick*) gioco di destrezza; (*fig*) trucchetto.

slen·der ['slɛndəʳ] ADJ (*person*) snello(-a), slanciato(-a); (*waist, neck, hand*) sottile; (*fig: resources, majority*) scarso (-a), esiguo(-a); (: *hope, chance*) piccolo(-a), scarso(-a).

slen·der·ness ['slɛndənɪs] N (*of person*) snellezza; (*of waist, neck, hand*) sottigliezza.

slept [slɛpt] PT, PP of **sleep**.

sleuth [sluːθ] N (*hum*) segugio.

slew[1] [sluː] PT of **slay**.

slew[2], (*Am*) **slue** [sluː] VI (*also:* **slew round**) rigirarsi.

slewed [sluːd] ADJ (*Brit old fam*) sbronzo(-a).

slice [slaɪs] ① N **a** (*of meat etc*) fetta; (*of lemon, cucumber*) fettina; **a slice of the profits** (*fig*) una fetta dei profitti; **a slice of life** (*fig*) uno scorcio di vita

  b (*tool*) paletta.

② VT (*meat etc*) affettare, tagliare a fette; (*rope etc*) tagliare di netto; (*Sport: ball*) tagliare; **to slice sth thickly/thinly** affettare qc grosso/sottile; **sliced loaf** *or* **bread** pane *m* a cassetta

▶ **slice off** VT + ADV tagliare (via)

▶ **slice through** VI + PREP tagliare di netto; (*fig: the air, waves*) fendere

▶ **slice up** VT + ADV affettare.

slic·er ['slaɪsəʳ] N affettatrice *f*.

slick [slɪk] ① ADJ (*comp* **-er**, *superl* **-est**) (*adroitly executed: show, performance*) brillante; (*pej: answer, excuse*) troppo pronto(-a); (: *person: glib*) dalla parlantina sciolta; (: *cunning*) scaltro(-a); (: *insincere*) untuoso(-a); **a slick character** un(a) dritto(-a).

② N (*also:* **oil slick**) chiazza di petrolio.

③ VT (*also:* **slick down:** *hair: with comb*) lisciare; (: *with haircream*) impomatare.

slick·ly [slɪklɪ] ADV (*answer*) abilmente, prontamente.

slid PT, PP of **slide**.

slide [slaɪd] (*vb: pt, pp* **slid**) ① N **a** (*action: on ice, mud etc*) scivolone *m*; (*fig: in temperature, profits*) caduta; **the slide in share prices** la caduta del prezzo delle azioni

  b (*in playground, swimming pool*) scivolo

  c (*landslide*) frana

  d (*Brit: also:* **hair slide**) fermacapelli *m inv*

  e (*also:* **microscope slide**) vetrino; (*Phot*) diapositiva.

② VI scivolare; **these drawers slide in and out easily** questi cassetti scorrono bene; **to slide down the banisters** scivolare giù per il corrimano; **to let things slide** (*fig*) trascurare tutto.

③ VT (*box, case*) far scivolare; (*bolt*) far scorrere; **he slid the gun from its holster** ha tirato la pistola fuori dalla custodia.

♦ **slide projector** N (*Phot*) proiettore *m* per diapositive.

♦ **slide rule** N (*Math*) regolo calcolatore.

♦ **slide show** N (*Phot*) proiezione *f* di diapositive.

slid·ing ['slaɪdɪŋ] ADJ (*part, seat*) mobile; (*door*) scorrevole; **sliding roof** (*Aut*) capotte *f* inv.

♦ **sliding scale** N (*Admin etc*) scala mobile.

slight [slaɪt] ① ADJ (*comp* **-er**, *superl* **-est**) **a** (*person: slim*) minuto(-a); (: *frail*) gracile, delicato(-a)

  b (*trivial: cold*) leggero(-a); (: *error*) piccolo(-a), insignificante; **a slight pain in the arm** un leggero dolore al braccio

  c (*small*) piccolo(-a), leggero(-a); **a slight improvement** un leggero miglioramento; **there's not the slightest possibility** non c'è la minima possibilità; **there's not the slightest danger** non c'è il benché minimo pericolo; **not in the slightest** per nulla, niente affatto.

② N offesa, affronto.

③ VT (*person*) snobbare, ignorare.

slight·ed ['slaɪtɪd] ADJ offeso(-a); **to feel slighted** sentirsi offeso(-a).

slight·ing ['slaɪtɪŋ] ADJ offensivo(-a).

slight·ing·ly ['slaɪtɪŋlɪ] ADV offensivamente.

slight·ly ['slaɪtlɪ] ADV **a** (*better, nervous*) leggermente; **I know her slightly** la conosco appena **b** : **slightly built** esile.

slim [slɪm] ① ADJ (*comp* **-mer**, *superl* **-mest**) **a** (*figure, person*) magro(-a), snello(-a); (*ankle, wrist, book*) sottile **b** (*fig: resources*) scarso(-a), magro(-a); (: *evidence*) insufficiente; (: *excuse*) magro(-a); (: *hope*) poco(-a); **his chances are pretty slim** le sue possibilità sono molto scarse.

② VI dimagrire, fare *or* seguire una dieta dimagrante.

slime [slaɪm] N (*mud*) melma; (*sticky substance*) sostanza viscida; (*of snail*) bava.

slimi·ness ['slaɪmɪnɪs] N (*also fig: of person*) viscidità.

slim·mer ['slɪməʳ] N chi è a dieta.

slim·ming ['slɪmɪŋ] ADJ (*diet, pills*) dimagrante; (*food*) ipocalorico(-a).

slim·ness ['slɪmnɪs] N (*goal of slimmer*) l'essere magro(-a); (*of ankle, wrist, book*) sottigliezza; (*fig: of resources*) scarsità, insufficienza.

slimy ['slaɪmɪ] ADJ (*comp* **-ier**, *superl* **-iest**) (*also fig: person*) viscido(-a); (*covered with mud*) melmoso(-a).

sling [slɪŋ] (*vb: pt, pp* **slung**) ① N (*weapon*) fionda; (*catapult*) catapulta; (*Med*) fascia a tracolla; (*Mountaineering*) anello di fettuccia; **to have one's arm in a sling** avere un braccio al collo.

② VT (*fam: throw*) scagliare; (*hang: hammock*) appendere; **to sling over** *or* **across one's shoulder** (*rifle, load*) mettere in spalla; (*coat, shawl*) buttarsi sulle spalle

▶ **sling out** VT + ADV (*fam: object*) buttare via; (: *person*) buttare fuori.

slink [slɪŋk] (*pt, pp* **slunk**) VI: **to slink away, slink off** svignarsela.

slinki·ly ['slɪŋkɪlɪ] ADV (*fam: dressed*) con abiti attillati.

slink·ing ['slɪŋkɪŋ] ADJ (*movement*) furtivo(-a).

slinky ['slɪŋkɪ] ADJ (*comp* **-ier**, *superl* **-iest**) (*fam: dress*) aderente, attillato(-a); (: *movement*) sinuoso(-a).

slip [slɪp] ① N **a** (*downward slide*) scivolata; (*trip*) scivolone *m*

  b (*also:* **landslip**) smottamento

  c (*mistake*) errore *m*, sbaglio; (*moral*) sbaglio; **a slip of the tongue** un lapsus linguae; **a slip of the pen** un lapsus calami; **a Freudian slip** un lapsus freudiano

  d (*petticoat*) sottoveste *f*

  e (*also:* **pillowslip**) federa

  f (*small receipt, bill*) scontrino; **a slip of paper** un foglietto; **pay slip** busta paga; **a slip of a girl** (*fig*) una ragazzina minuta

  g (*fam*): **to give sb the slip** seminare qn; see also **slips**.

2 VI **a** (*slide*) scivolare; **I slipped** sono scivolato; **my foot slipped** mi è scivolato un piede; **it slipped from** *or* **out of her hand** le sfuggì di mano; **to slip into bad habits** prendere delle cattive abitudini; **he let (it) slip that ...** si è lasciato sfuggire che...; **to let a chance slip through one's fingers** lasciarsi scappare un'occasione; **you're slipping!** (*fig fam*) perdi colpi!

  b (*move quickly*): **to slip into/out of** sgattaiolare dentro/fuori da; **to slip into a dress** infilarsi un vestito; **the months/years have slipped by** i mesi/gli anni sono passati.

  3 VT **a** (*slide*) far scivolare; **to slip a coin into a slot** infilare una moneta in una fessura; **to slip sb a tenner** allungare dieci sterline a qn; **to slip an arm round sb's waist** mettere il braccio attorno alla vita di qn; **to slip on/off a jumper** infilarsi/sfilarsi un maglione

  b (*escape*) sfuggire a; **the dog slipped its collar** il cane si liberò dal collare; **it slipped my memory** *or* **attention** *or* **mind** mi è sfuggito di mente

▶ **slip away, slip off** VI + ADV svignarsela

▶ **slip in** VT + ADV (*object*) far scivolare in (*or* dentro); (*reference, remark*) aggiungere en passant

▶ **slip out** VI + ADV (*thief*) svignarsela; (*guest*) andarsene alla chetichella; (*secret, word*) sfuggire; **to slip out to the shops** fare una scappatina per la spesa; **it slipped out that ...** è saltato fuori che...

▶ **slip up** VI + ADV (*fam*) sbagliarsi.

slip·case ['slɪpˌkeɪs] N (*of book*) custodia.

slip·cover ['slɪpˌkʌvəʳ] N (*Am*) fodera.

slip·knot ['slɪpˌnɒt] N nodo scorsoio.

♦ **slip-on** ['slɪpˌɒn] ADJ (*gen*) comodo(-a) da mettere; (*shoes*) senza allacciatura.

slip·over ['slɪpəʊvəʳ] N pullover *m inv* senza maniche.

slipped disc [ˌslɪpt'dɪsk] N (*Med*) ernia del disco.

slip·per ['slɪpəʳ] N pantofola.

slip·pery ['slɪpərɪ] ADJ sdrucciolevole, scivoloso(-a); (*fig pej: person*) viscido(-a); **it's slippery underfoot** il pavimento è scivoloso; **he's as slippery as they come** *or* **as an eel** è un tipo viscido.

slip·py ['slɪpɪ] ADJ (*comp* **-ier**, *superl* **-iest**) (*fam*) scivoloso (-a).

♦ **slip road** N (*Brit: to motorway*) rampa di accesso.

slip·shod ['slɪpˌʃɒd] ADJ sciatto(-a), trascurato(-a).

slip·stream ['slɪpˌstriːm] N (*Aer*) risucchio.

♦ **slip-up** ['slɪpˌʌp] N (*fam: mistake*) sbaglio.

slip·way ['slɪpˌweɪ] N (*Naut*) scalo.

slit [slɪt] (*vb: pt, pp* **slit**) 1 N (*opening*) fessura; (*cut*) taglio; (*tear*) strappo; (*in skirt*) spacco.

  2 VT tagliare; **to slit open** (*letter*) aprire; (*sack*) aprire con un taglio; **to slit sb's throat** tagliare la gola a qn.

slith·er ['slɪðəʳ] VI (*person*) scivolare; (*snake*) strisciare; **he was slithering about on the ice** avanzava slittando sul ghiaccio.

sliv·er ['slɪvəʳ] N (*of glass, wood*) scheggia; (*of cheese, sausage*) fettina.

slob [slɒb] N (*fam*) sciattone(-a).

slob·ber ['slɒbəʳ] VI (*pej*) sbavare

▶ **slobber over** VI + PREP sviolinare.

sloe [sləʊ] N (*tree*) pruno selvatico; (*fruit*) di prugnola.

♦ **sloe gin** N gin *m inv* alle prugnole.

slog [slɒg] 1 N faticata; **it's a hard slog to the top** è una faticaccia arrivare in cima.

  2 VI **a** (*work*) faticare, sgobbare; **to slog away at sth** sgobbare su qc **b** (*walk etc*): **to slog along** avanzare a fatica; **we slogged on for 8 kilometres** ci trascinammo per 8 chilometri.

  3 VT (*ball, opponent*) colpire con forza.

slo·gan ['sləʊgən] N slogan *m inv*.

slog·ger ['slɒgəʳ] N (*hard worker*) sgobbone(-a).

sloop [sluːp] N (*ship*) sloop *m inv*.

slop [slɒp] 1 VI (*also*: **slop over**) traboccare, versarsi; **the water was slopping about in the bucket** l'acqua quasi traboccava dal secchio.

  2 VT versare, rovesciare; see also **slops**.

slope [sləʊp] 1 N **a** (*gen, of hill*) pendio; (*side of hill*) versante *m*; (*of roof*) pendenza; (*of floor*) inclinazione *f*; **on the slopes of Mount Etna** alle falde *or* pendici dell'Etna; **the car got stuck on a slope** la macchina si è bloccata su una salita

  b (*also*: **ski slope**) pista (da sci).

  2 VI (*path, roof, handwriting*) essere inclinato(-a); **to slope up** essere in salita; **the garden slopes down to the stream** il giardino digrada verso il ruscello

▶ **slope off** VI + ADV (*fam*) filarsela, tagliare la corda.

slop·ing ['sləʊpɪŋ] ADJ inclinato(-a).

slop·pi·ly ['slɒpɪlɪ] ADV **a** (*carelessly*) con trascuratezza; **to dress sloppily** essere sciatto(-a) nel vestire **b** (*sentimentally*) in modo sdolcinato.

slop·pi·ness ['slɒpɪnɪs] N (*of work, appearance, dress*) sciatteria.

slop·py ['slɒpɪ] (*fam*) ADJ (*comp* **-ier**, *superl* **-iest**) **a** (*work*) trascurato(-a); (*appearance, dress*) trasandato(-a), sciatto(-a) **b** (*book, film, letter*) sdolcinato(-a) **c** (*food*) brodoso(-a).

♦ **sloppy joe** N (*fam*) maglione *m* informe.

slops [slɒps] NPL (*for animals*) pastone *m*; (*dirty water*) acqua sporca; (: *in teacup*) rimasugli *mpl*.

slosh [slɒʃ] (*fam*) 1 VT **a** (*liquid*) spargere; **to slosh some water over sth** gettare dell'acqua su qc **b** (*hit: person*) colpire.

  2 VI: **to slosh about in the puddles** sguazzare nelle pozzanghere.

sloshed [slɒʃt] ADJ (*fam: drunk*) sbronzo(-a); **to get sloshed** prendere una sbronza.

slot [slɒt] 1 N (*in machine etc*) fessura; (*groove*) scanalatura; (*fig: in timetable, Radio, TV*) spazio.

  2 VT (*object*) infilare; (*fig: activity, speech*) inserire.

  3 VI: **to slot (into)** inserirsi (in).

sloth [sləʊθ] N **a** (*frm: vice*) indolenza **b** (*Zool*) bradipo.

sloth·ful ['sləʊθfʊl] ADJ (*frm*) indolente.

sloth·ful·ness ['sləʊθfʊlnɪs] N (*frm*) indolenza.

♦ **slot machine** N (*for cigarettes, food*) distributore *m* automatico; (*for amusement*) slot-machine *f inv*.

♦ **slot meter** N contatore *m* a monete.

slouch [slaʊtʃ] 1 VI (*when walking*) camminare dinoccolato(-a); **don't slouch!** raddrizza la schiena!, non stare con la schiena curva!; **to slouch in/out** trascinarsi dentro/fuori; **she was slouched in the chair** era stravaccata nella poltrona.

  2 N: **to be no slouch at sth** (*fam*) cavarsela benino in qc

▶ **slouch about, slouch around** VI + ADV (*laze*) oziare.

slough off [ˌslʌf'ɒf] VT + ADV **a** (*subj: snake*): **to slough off its skin** mutare pelle **b** (*liter: abandon: habit*) abbandonare.

Slo·vak ['sləʊvæk] 1 ADJ slovacco(-a).

  2 N (*person*) slovacco(-a); (*language*) slovacco.

Slo·vakia [sləʊ'vækɪə] N Slovacchia.

Slo·vak·ian [sləʊ'vækɪən] ADJ, N = **Slovak**.

♦ **Slovak Republic** N: **the Slovak Republic** la repubblica slovacca.

Slo·vene ['sləυviːn] [1] ADJ sloveno(-a).

[2] N (person) sloveno(-a); (language) sloveno.

Slo·venia [sləυ'viːnɪə] N Slovenia.

Slo·venian [sləυ'viːnɪən] ADJ, N = **Slovene**.

slov·en·li·ness ['slʌvnlɪnɪs] N (of person) sciatteria; (of work) trascuratezza.

slov·en·ly ['slʌvnlɪ] ADJ (person) sciatto(-a), trasandato (-a); (work) trascurato(-a), poco accurato(-a).

slow [sləυ] (comp -er, superl -est) [1] ADJ **a** (gen) lento(-a); **at a slow speed** a bassa velocità; **she's a slow worker** lavora lentamente; **this car is slower than my old one** questa macchina è meno veloce di quella che avevo; **the slow lane** la corsia per il traffico lento; **to be slow to act/decide** essere lento(-a) ad agire/a decidere; **to be slow to anger** (liter) non arrabbiarsi facilmente

b (of clock): **to be slow** essere or andare indietro; **my watch is 20 minutes slow** il mio orologio è indietro di 20 minuti

c (person: stupid) lento(-a), tardo(-a); **slow to understand/notice** tardo(-a) a capire/notare; **he's a bit slow at maths** fa un po' di fatica in matematica

d (boring, dull: film, play) lento(-a); (: party) poco movimentato(-a); **life here is slow** qui la vita scorre lenta; **the game is very slow** il gioco è molto lento; **business is slow** (Comm) gli affari procedono a rilento

e (slowing down movement: pitch, track, surface) pesante; **bake for two hours in a slow oven** cuocere per due ore nel forno a bassa temperatura.

[2] ADV lentamente; **to go slow** (driver) andare piano; (in industrial dispute) attuare uno sciopero bianco; (be cautious) andare con i piedi di piombo; **"(go) slow"** "rallentare".

[3] VT (also: **slow down, slow up**: progress, machine) rallentare; (: person) far rallentare; (: pace of novel etc) rendere più lento(-a); **the interruptions have slowed us down** le interruzioni ci hanno fatto perdere tempo; **that car slows up the traffic** quella macchina fa rallentare il traffico.

[4] VI (also: **slow down, slow up**) rallentare; **production has slowed to almost nothing** la produzione si è ridotta a livelli minimi.

♦ **slow-acting** ['sləυˌæktɪŋ] ADJ che agisce lentamente, ad azione lenta.

slow·coach ['sləυˌkəυtʃ] N (fam: dawdler) lumaca; (: dullard) testone(-a).

slow·down ['sləυˌdaυn] N rallentamento.

slow·ly ['sləυlɪ] ADV lentamente; **to drive slowly** andare piano; **slowly but surely** a poco a poco ma in modo certo; **work is proceeding slowly but surely** il lavoro procede piano ma bene; **to go more slowly** rallentare.

♦ **slow motion** N: **in slow motion** al rallentatore.

♦ **slow-moving** ['sləυˌmuːvɪŋ] ADJ (vehicle, traffic) lento (-a).

slow·ness ['sləυnɪs] N lentezza.

slow·poke ['sləυˌpəυk] N (Am fam) = **slowcoach**.

♦ **slow-witted** [ˌsləυ'wɪtɪd] ADJ tardo(-a), ottuso(-a).

slow·worm ['sləυˌwɜːm] N orbettino.

sludge [slʌdʒ] N (mud, sediment) melma; (sewage) deposito di fognatura.

slue [sluː] (Am) N = slew².

slug [slʌg] [1] N (Zool) lumaca; (esp Am fam: bullet) pallottola; (fam: blow) colpo; (: large mouthful) sorsata; **a slug of whisky** (fam) un bicchierino di whisky.

[2] VT (fam: hit) colpire.

slug·gish ['slʌgɪʃ] ADJ (indolent) pigro(-a), fiacco(-a);

(slow-moving: river, engine, car) lento(-a); (: business, market, sales) stagnante, fiacco(-a); **the car is very sluggish** la macchina manca di ripresa.

slug·gish·ly ['slʌgɪʃlɪ] ADV (move) lentamente, pigramente.

slug·gish·ness ['slʌgɪʃnɪs] N (gen) lentezza; (of business, sales) stasi f, ristagno.

sluice [sluːs] [1] N (also: **sluicegate**) chiusa; (also: **sluiceway**) canale m di chiusa.

[2] VT: **to sluice down** or **out** lavare con abbondante acqua.

slum [slʌm] N (house) catapecchia, tugurio; **to live in the slums** vivere nei quartieri bassi.

♦ **slum area** N quartiere m povero.

slum·ber ['slʌmbəʳ] [1] N (often pl: liter) sonno.

[2] VI dormire (tranquillamente).

♦ **slum clearance** N (also: **slum clearance programme**) (programma m di) risanamento edilizio.

slum·my ['slʌmɪ] ADJ (buildings) povero(-a), squallido(-a); (appearance) misero(-a).

slump [slʌmp] [1] N (gen) caduta, crollo; (in production, sales) calo, crollo; (economic) crisi f inv, depressione f; **the slump in the price of copper** il crollo del prezzo del rame.

[2] VI **a** (price etc) cadere, crollare; (production, sales) calare, diminuire; (fig: morale etc) abbassarsi

b : **to slump into a chair** lasciarsi cadere su una sedia; **he was slumped over the wheel** era accasciato sul volante.

slung [slʌŋ] PT, PP of **sling**.

slunk [slʌŋk] PT, PP of **slink**.

slur [slɜːʳ] [1] N **a** (stigma) macchia; (insult) diffamazione f; **to cast a slur on sb** calunniare qn; **without wishing to cast a slur on his character, I think ...** senza per questo volerlo denigrare, penso che...

b (Mus) legatura.

[2] VT (word etc) farfugliare, pronunciare in modo inarticolato; (Mus) legare; **his speech was slurred** biascicava (perché ubriaco).

slurp [slɜːp] [1] VT, VI (fam) bere rumorosamente.

[2] N rumore fatto bevendo.

slurred [slɜːd] ADJ (speech) confuso(-a).

slurry ['slʌrɪ] N fanghiglia.

slush [slʌʃ] [1] N (melting snow) neve f sciolta, fanghiglia; (fam: literature etc) letteratura etc sdolcinata.

♦ **slush fund** N fondi mpl neri.

slushy ['slʌʃɪ] ADJ (comp -ier, superl -iest) (snow) sciolto (-a), fangoso(-a); (fam Brit: poetry) sdolcinato(-a).

slut [slʌt] (offensive) N (immoral) donnaccia, sgualdrina; (dirty, untidy) sciattona.

slut·tish ['slʌtɪʃ] ADJ (immoral: behaviour) immorale, dissoluto(-a); (dirty, untidy: appearance) sciatto(-a), disordinato(-a).

sly [slaɪ] [1] ADJ (comp -ier, superl -iest) (wily) astuto(-a), scaltro(-a); (secretive) furtivo(-a); (mischievous: trick) birbone(-a); (: smile) sornione(-a), malizioso(-a).

[2] N: **on the sly** di nascosto, di soppiatto.

sly·ly ['slaɪlɪ] ADV (see adj) astutamente, scaltramente; furtivamente; (smile, wink) maliziosamente.

sly·ness ['slaɪnɪs] N (wiliness) astuzia, scaltrezza; (mischievousness: of trick, smile) malizia.

S & M [ˌɛsən'ɛm] N ABBR = **sadomasochism**.

smack¹ [smæk] [1] N (slap: on buttocks) pacca; (: on face) schiaffo, ceffone m; (sound) colpo secco; (: of lips, whip) schiocco; **it was a smack in the eye for them** è stato uno

smacco *or* uno schiaffo morale per loro; **to give a child a smack** sculacciare un bambino; **to have a smack at doing sth** (*fig*) provare a fare qc.

2️⃣ VT (*child*) sculacciare; (*face*) schiaffeggiare; **she smacked the child's bottom** sculacciò il bambino; **to smack one's lips** schioccare le labbra.

3️⃣ ADV: **it fell smack in the middle** (*fam*) cadde giusto nel mezzo; **she ran smack into the door** andò a sbattere dritto contro la porta.

smack² [smæk] VI: **to smack of** (*fig*: *intrigue etc*) puzzare di.

smack³ [smæk] N (*also*: **fishing smack**) barca da pesca.

smack·er ['smækəʳ] N (*fam*: *kiss*) bacio; (: *Brit old*: *pound note*) sterlina; (: *Am*: *dollar bill*) dollaro.

smack·ing ['smækɪŋ] N sculacciata; **to give sb a smacking** sculacciare qn.

small [smɔːl] 1️⃣ ADJ (*comp* **-er**, *superl* **-est**) (*gen*: *in size, number*) piccolo(-a); (: *in height*) basso(-a); (*stock, supply, population*) scarso(-a); (*waist*) sottile; (*meal*) leggero(-a); (*letter*) minuscolo(-a); (*minor, unimportant*) da poco, insignificante; (: *increase, improvement*) piccolo(-a), leggero(-a); **when we were small** quando eravamo piccoli; **there was only a small audience** c'era poco pubblico; **this house makes the other one look small** questa casa fa sembrare piccola l'altra; **the smallest possible number of books** il minor numero di libri possibile; **the smallest details** i minimi dettagli; **to have a small appetite** avere poco *or* scarso appetito; **in a small voice** con un filo di voce; **to feel small** (*fig*) sentirsi umiliato(-a) *or* sminuito(-a); **to get** *or* **grow smaller** (*stain, town*) rimpicciolire; (*debt, organization, numbers*) ridursi; **to make smaller** (*amount, income*) ridurre; (*garden, object, garment*) rimpicciolire; **to have small hope of success** avere scarse speranze di successo; **to have small cause** *or* **reason to do sth** non avere molti motivi per fare qc; **to start in a small way** cominciare da poco; **a small shopkeeper** un(a) piccolo(-a) negoziante.

2️⃣ N a : **the small of the back** le reni.

b NPL: **smalls** (*fam*: *underwear*) biancheria intima.

♦ **small ad** N (*in newspaper*) annuncio economico.

♦ **small arms** NPL armi *fpl* leggere.

♦ **small business** N piccola impresa.

♦ **small change** N spiccioli *mpl*.

♦ **small fry** N: **he is small fry** è un pesce piccolo; **they are small fry** sono dei pesci piccoli.

small·holder ['smɔːlˌhəʊldəʳ] N (*Brit*) piccolo proprietario.

small·holding ['smɔːlˌhəʊldɪŋ] N (*Brit*) piccola tenuta.

♦ **small hours** NPL: **the small hours** le ore piccole; **in the small hours** alle ore piccole.

small·ish ['smɔːlɪʃ] ADJ piccolino(-a).

♦ **small-minded** [ˌsmɔːl'maɪndɪd] ADJ meschino(-a).

♦ **small-mindedness** [ˌsmɔːl'maɪndɪdnɪs] N meschinità.

small·ness ['smɔːlnɪs] N (*gen*) piccolezza; (*of person*) bassa statura; (*of income, sum*) scarsità.

small·pox ['smɔːlˌpɒks] N (*Med*) vaiolo.

♦ **small print** N caratteri *mpl* piccoli; (*in contract etc*) parte *f* scritta in piccolo.

♦ **small-scale** ['smɔːlˌskeɪl] ADJ (*map, model*) in scala ridotta; (*business, farming*) modesto(-a).

♦ **small screen** N: **the small screen** (*television*) il piccolo schermo.

♦ **small talk** N conversazione *f* mondana, chiacchiere *fpl*.

♦ **small-time** ['smɔːlˌtaɪm] ADJ (*fam*) da poco; **a small-time criminal** un delinquente di mezza tacca; **a small-time thief** un ladro di polli.

♦ **small-town** ['smɔːl'taʊn] ADJ (*pej*) provinciale.

smarmy ['smɑːmɪ] ADJ (*comp* **-ier**, *superl* **-iest**) (*Brit fam*) untuoso(-a), servile.

smart [smɑːt] 1️⃣ ADJ (*comp* **-er**, *superl* **-est**) **a** (*elegant*) elegante, chic *inv*; (*fashionable*) di moda; **the smart set** il bel mondo; **to look smart** essere elegante; **that's a smart car** è una bella macchina

b (*clever*) intelligente, brillante; (*quick-witted*) sveglio (-a), furbo(-a); **that was pretty smart of you!** che furbo!; **smart work by the police led to ...** una brillante operazione della polizia ha portato a...

c (*quick*: *pace, action*) svelto(-a), rapido(-a); **look smart about it!** sbrigati!, spicciati!.

2️⃣ VI **a** (*cut, graze etc*) bruciare; **my eyes are smarting** mi bruciano gli occhi

b (*fig*): **she's still smarting from his remarks** le bruciano ancora le sue osservazioni; **to smart under an insult/a reproof** soffrire per un insulto/un rimprovero.

3️⃣ N (*pain*) dolore *m* acuto.

♦ **smart aleck** ['smɑːtˌælɪk] N (*fam*) sapientone(-a), sputasentenze *m/f inv*.

smart·card ['smɑːtˌkɑːd] N (*Comput*) smart card *f inv*, carta intelligente.

smart·en ['smɑːtn] 1️⃣ VT (*also*: **smarten up**: *room, house etc*) abbellire, ravvivare; (: *child*) far bello(-a); (: *o.s.*) farsi bello(-a); **to smarten up one's ideas** darsi una mossa.

2️⃣ VI (*also*: **smarten up**) abbellirsi, farsi bello(-a).

smart·ly ['smɑːtlɪ] ADV (*elegantly*) elegantemente; (*cleverly*) con arguzia *or* intelligenza; (*quickly*: *walk*) velocemente; (: *answer*) con prontezza.

smart·ness ['smɑːtnɪs] N (*see adv*) eleganza; intelligenza; velocità; prontezza.

smarty ['smɑːtɪ] N (*fam*) = **smart aleck**.

smash [smæʃ] 1️⃣ N **a** (*sound*) fracasso

b (*also*: **smash-up**: *collision*) scontro; (*Tennis etc*) schiacciata, smash *m inv*; (*powerful blow*) pugno; (*Fin*) crollo; **he died in a car smash** è morto in un incidente automobilistico; **the smash of plates** il rumore di piatti rotti.

2️⃣ VT (*break*) rompere, fracassare; (*shatter*) infrangere, frantumare; (*beat*: *enemy, opponent*) schiacciare, annientare; (: *record*) polverizzare; (*wreck, also fig*) distruggere; (*Tennis etc*) schiacciare; **he smashed it against the wall** lo scagliò contro la parete; **we will smash this crime ring** distruggeremo quest'organizzazione criminale; **he smashed his way out of the building** uscì dall'edificio spaccando tutto quello che trovava davanti.

3️⃣ VI (*break*) rompersi, andare in frantumi; **the car smashed into the wall** la macchina si schiantò contro il muro

▸ **smash down** VT + ADV (*door*) abbattere

▸ **smash in** VT + ADV (*door, window*) abbattere; **to smash one's way in** entrare con la forza; **to smash sb's face in** (*fam*) spaccare la faccia a qn

▸ **smash up** VT + ADV (*car*) sfasciare; (*room*) distruggere.

♦ **smash-and-grab** [ˌsmæʃənd'græb] ADJ (*fam*): **smash-and-grab robbery** furto con scasso della vetrina.

smashed [smæʃt] ADJ **a** (*fam*: *drunk*) sbronzo(-a), partito (-a); (: *stoned*) fatto(-a) **b** (*wrecked*) fracassato(-a).

smash·er ['smæʃəʳ] N (*fam*): **she's a smasher** (*in appearance*) è una bomba; (*in character*) è fantastica.

♦ **smash-hit** [ˌsmæʃ'hɪt] N successone *m*.

smash·ing ['smæʃɪŋ] ADJ (*fam*) formidabile; **we had a smashing time** ci siamo divertiti come pazzi.

smat·ter·ing ['smætərɪŋ] N: **to have a smattering of** avere un'infarinatura di.

smear [smɪəʳ] [1] N (*smudge*) traccia; (*dirty mark, also fig*) macchia; (*insult*) calunnia; (*Med*) striscio.

[2] VT **a** (*butter etc*) spalmare; **to smear cream on one's hands** [OR] **smear one's hands with cream** spalmarsi le mani di crema

b (*make dirty*) sporcare; (*smudge: ink, paint*) sbavare; **the page was smeared** c'erano delle sbavature sulla pagina; **his hands were smeared with oil/ink** aveva le mani sporche di olio/inchiostro

c (*fig: libel*) calunniare, diffamare.

[3] VI (*paint, ink etc*) sbavare.

♦ **smear campaign** N campagna diffamatoria.

♦ **smear test** N (*Brit Med*) Pap-test *m inv*, striscio (*fam*).

smell [smɛl] (*vb: pt, pp* **smelled** *or* **smelt**) [1] N **a** (*sense of smell*) olfatto, odorato; (*of animal, fig*) fiuto; **to have a keen sense of smell** (*person*) avere l'olfatto sviluppato; (*animal*) avere un fiuto finissimo

b (*odour*) odore *m*; (: *pleasant*) profumo; (*stench*) puzza; **it has a nice smell** ha un buon odore; **there's a strong smell of gas here** qui c'è una forte puzza di gas.

[2] VT (*gas, cooking*) sentire odore di; (*flower*) annusare; **to smell something burning** sentire odore di bruciato; **to smell danger** (*fig*) fiutare un pericolo; **I smell a rat** (*fig*) qui gatta ci cova.

[3] VI (*pleasantly*) sapere, odorare; (*unpleasantly*) puzzare; **my fingers smell of garlic** ho le dita che puzzano di aglio; **it smells like chicken** odora di pollo; **it smells good** ha un buon odore; **it smells damp in here** c'è odore di umidità qui dentro; **his breath smells** gli puzza l'alito

▶ **smell out** VT + ADV **a** (*animal, prey, also fig*) fiutare

b : **your feet are smelling the room out!** i tuoi piedi appestano la stanza!

smell·ing salts ['smɛlɪŋ,sɔːlts] NPL sali *mpl*.

smelly ['smɛlɪ] ADJ (*comp* -ier, *superl* -iest) (*fam*) puzzolente; **it's smelly in here** qui c'è puzza.

smelt[1] [smɛlt] PT, PP of **smell**.

smelt[2] [smɛlt] VT (*ore*) fondere.

smel·ter ['smɛltəʳ] N fonderia.

smel·ting ['smɛltɪŋ] N fusione *f*.

♦ **smelting works** NPL fonderia.

smile [smaɪl] [1] N sorriso; **she said with a smile** disse sorridendo; **with a smile on one's lips** col sorriso sulle labbra; **to be all smiles** essere raggiante; **to give sb a smile** sorridere a qn; **I'll soon wipe the smile off your face!** ti faccio io passare la voglia di ridere!.

[2] VI sorridere; **to smile at sb/sth** sorridere a qn/qc; **to keep smiling** continuare a sorridere; (*fig*) conservare l'allegria; **fortune smiled on him** la fortuna gli arrise.

[3] VT: **he smiled his appreciation** sorrise in segno di apprezzamento.

smil·ing ['smaɪlɪŋ] ADJ sorridente.

smil·ing·ly ['smaɪlɪŋlɪ] ADV (*look, reply*) sorridendo.

smirk [smɜːk] [1] N (*self-satisfied*) sorriso compiaciuto; (*knowing*) sorrisetto furbo; (*affected*) sorriso affettato.

[2] VI (*see n*) sorridere compiaciuto(-a); fare un sorriso furbo; sorridere in modo affettato.

smite [smaɪt] (*pt* **smote**, *pp* **smitten**) VT (*old: strike*) colpire; (: *punish*) punire.

smith [smɪθ] N fabbro.

smith·er·eens [,smɪðə'riːnz] NPL: **to be smashed to smithereens** andare in frantumi *or* in mille pezzi.

smithy ['smɪðɪ] N fucina.

smit·ten ['smɪtn] [1] PP of **smite**.

[2] ADJ PRED: **to be smitten with** (*remorse, desire, fear*) essere preso(-a) da; (*idea*) entusiasmarsi per; **to be smitten (with sb)** avere una cotta (per qn); **to be smitten with flu** essere colpito(-a) dall'influenza.

smock [smɒk] N (*loose shirt*) camiciotto; (*blouse*) blusa; (*to protect clothing*) grembiule *m*.

smock·ing ['smɒkɪŋ] N ricamo a nido d'ape.

smog [smɒg] N smog *m inv*.

smoke [sməʊk] [1] N **a** fumo; **there's no smoke without fire** non c'è fumo senza arrosto; **to go up in smoke** (*house*) andare distrutto(-a) dalle fiamme; (*fig*) andare in fumo

b : **to have a smoke** (*cigarette, pipe*) fare una fumatina.

[2] VT **a** (*tobacco*) fumare

b (*bacon, fish, cheese*) affumicare.

[3] VI (*gen*) fumare; (*chimney*) fare fumo; **do you smoke?** fumi?

▶ **smoke out** VT + ADV (*insects etc*) snidare col fumo.

♦ **smoke bomb** N bomba fumogena, candelotto fumogeno.

smoked [sməʊkt] ADJ (*bacon, fish, etc*) affumicato(-a); **smoked glass** vetro fumé.

smoke·less fuel [,sməʊklɪs'fjʊəl] N combustibile *m* che non dà fumo.

smoke·less zone [,sməʊklɪs'zəʊn] N (*Brit*) *zona in cui sono vietati gli scarichi di fumo*.

smok·er ['sməʊkəʳ] N (*person*) fumatore(-trice), tabagista *m/f*; (*railway carriage*) carrozza (per) fumatori; **smoker's cough** tosse *f* da fumo.

♦ **smoke ring** N: **to blow smoke rings** fare anelli di fumo.

♦ **smoke screen** N (*Mil, fig*) cortina fumogena.

♦ **smoke shop** N (*Am*) tabaccheria.

♦ **smoke signal** N segnale *m* di fumo.

smoke·stack ['sməʊk,stæk] N ciminiera.

smok·ing ['sməʊkɪŋ] [1] ADJ fumante.

[2] N fumo; **"no smoking"** "vietato fumare"; **he's given up smoking** ha smesso di fumare; **smoking can damage your health** il fumo può danneggiare la salute.

♦ **smoking car**, **smoking compartment** N carrozza (per) fumatori.

♦ **smoking jacket** N giacca da camera.

smoky ['sməʊkɪ] ADJ (*comp* -ier, *superl* -iest) (*chimney, fire*) fumoso(-a), che fa fumo; (*room, atmosphere*) fumoso(-a), pieno(-a) di fumo; (*flavour*) affumicato(-a).

smol·der ['sməʊldəʳ] VI (*Am*) = **smoulder**.

smooch [smuːtʃ] VI (*fam*) sbaciucchiarsi, pomiciare.

smoochy ['smuːtʃɪ] ADJ (*comp* -ier, *superl* -iest) (*fam*) romantico(-a).

smooth [smuːð] [1] ADJ (*comp* -er, *superl* -est) **a** (*surface, skin*) liscio(-a); (*chin: hairless*) imberbe; (*sea*) liscio(-a), calmo(-a); **as smooth as silk** liscio(-a) come la seta

b (*in consistency: paste etc*) omogeneo(-a)

c (*movement, breathing, pulse*) regolare; (*landing, take-off, flight*) senza problemi; (*crossing, trip, life*) tranquillo(-a)

d (*not harsh: cigarette*) leggero(-a); (: *drink*) dal gusto morbido, amabile; (: *voice, sound*) carezzevole

e (*pej: person*) mellifluo(-a); **he's a smooth operator** (*fam*) ci sa fare; **he's a smooth talker** ha la parola facile.

[2] VT **a** (*also:* **smooth down**: *hair etc*) lisciare; **to smooth the way** *or* **path for sb** (*fig*) spianare la strada a qn

b (*stone, wood*) levigare; **to smooth away wrinkles** far sparire le rughe

c : **to smooth cream into one's face** massaggiarsi la

crema sul viso

▶ **smooth out** VT + ADV (*fabric, creases*) lisciare, spianare; (*fig: difficulties*) appianare

▶ **smooth over** VT + ADV: **to smooth things over** (*fig*) sistemare le cose.

smoothie, smoothy ['smu:ðɪ] N (*fam pej*): **to be a smoothie** essere anche troppo cortese e disinvolto(-a).

smooth·ly ['smu:ðlɪ] ADV (*easily*) liscio; (*gently*) dolcemente; (*move*) senza scosse; (*talk*) in modo mellifluo; **the engine is running smoothly** il motore non dà problemi; **everything went smoothly** tutto andò liscio.

smooth·ness ['smu:ðnɪs] N (*of stone, wood*) levigatezza; (*of skin*) morbidezza; (*of sauce*) omogeneità; (*of sea*) calma; (*of trip, life*) tranquillità; (*of manner*) mellifluità.

♦ **smooth-running** [ˌsmu:ð'rʌnɪŋ] ADJ (*engine*) che non perde colpi; (*business, project*) che va bene.

♦ **smooth-spoken** [ˌsmu:ð'spəʊkən], **smooth-tongued** [ˌsmu:ð'tʌŋd] ADJ mellifluo(-a).

smote [sməʊt] PT of **smite**.

smoth·er ['smʌðə'] VT **a** (*stifle*) soffocare **b** (*cover*) ricoprire; **to smother sb with kisses** ricoprire qn di baci; **fruit smothered in cream** frutta ricoperta di panna.

smoul·der, (*Am*) **smol·der** ['sməʊldə'] VI (*fire*) covare sotto la cenere; (*fig: passion etc*) covare.

smudge [smʌdʒ] ① N sbavatura, macchia.

② VT sporcare, imbrattare.

③ VI sbavare.

smug [smʌg] ADJ (*comp* **-ger**, *superl* **-gest**) compiaciuto (-a).

smug·gle ['smʌgl] VT (*tobacco, drugs*) contrabbandare; **to smuggle in/out** (*goods etc*) far entrare/uscire di contrabbando *or* clandestinamente; (*fig: person, letter etc*) far entrare/uscire di nascosto; **to smuggle sth past** *or* **through Customs** passare la dogana con qc senza dichiararlo.

smug·gler ['smʌglə'] N contrabbandiere(-a).

smug·gling ['smʌglɪŋ] N contrabbando.

smug·ly ['smʌglɪ] ADV con sufficienza, con compiacimento.

smug·ness ['smʌgnɪs] N (*of person, expression*) aria compiaciuta, aria di sufficienza.

smut [smʌt] N (*grain of soot*) granello di fuliggine; (*mark*) segno nero; (*in conversation etc*) sconcezze *fpl*.

smut·ty ['smʌtɪ] ADJ (*comp* **-ier**, *superl* **-iest**) (*crude*) osceno (-a), sconcio(-a); (*dirty*) sporco(-a), sudicio(-a).

snack [snæk] N spuntino; **to have a snack** fare uno spuntino.

♦ **snack bar** N snack-bar *m inv*, tavola calda (*or* fredda).

snaf·fle ['snæfl] N (*also:* **snaffle bit:** *for horse*) filetto.

sna·fu [snæ'fu:] ADJ (*Am fam*) incasinato(-a).

snag [snæg] ① N (*pulled thread*) filo tirato; (*difficulty*) intralcio, intoppo; **the snag is that** ... il guaio è che....; **what's the snag?** qual è il problema?; **to run into** *or* **hit a snag** incontrare una difficoltà, trovare un intoppo.

② VT (*jumper*) tirare un filo a; (*tights*) smagliare.

snail [sneɪl] N chiocciola; **at a snail's pace** a passo di lumaca.

snake [sneɪk] N serpente *m*, serpe *f*; **snake in the grass** (*fig*) traditore(-trice).

snake·bite ['sneɪkˌbaɪt] N morso di serpente.

♦ **snake charmer** N incantatore *m* di serpenti.

♦ **snakes and ladders** N ≈ gioco dell'oca.

snake·skin ['sneɪkˌskɪn] ① N pelle *f* di serpente.

② ADJ (*bag, shoes*) di serpente.

snap [snæp] ① N **a** (*sound, action: of sth breaking, closing*) colpo secco; (: *of fingers*) schiocco; **a cold snap** (*fam*) un'improvvisa ondata di freddo; **the dog made a snap at the biscuit** il cane ha cercato di afferrare il biscotto; **with a snap of one's fingers** schioccando le dita

b (*Cards*) rubamazzo

c (*fam: photo*) foto *f inv*.

② ADJ (*sudden: strike*) selvaggio(-a); (: *answer, judgement*) immediato(-a); (: *decision*) repentino(-a).

③ VT **a** (*break*) spezzare di netto

b (*fingers*) schioccare; **to snap one's fingers at sb/sth** (*fig*) infischiarsi di qn/qc; **to snap a box shut** chiudere una scatola di colpo

c : **"be quiet!"**, **she snapped** "sta' zitto!", sbottò

d (*Phot*) fotografare, scattare una foto a.

④ VI **a** (*break: elastic*) spezzarsi

b (*whip*) schioccare; **it snapped shut** si chiuse di scatto; **to snap back into place** scattare di nuovo a posto; **everything snapped into place** (*fig*) tutto fu chiaro

c : **to snap at sb** (*dog*) cercare di mordere qn; (*person*) rivolgersi a qn con tono brusco

▶ **snap off** VT + ADV rompere con un colpo secco; **to snap sb's head off** (*fig*) aggredire qn

▶ **snap out** ① VI + ADV: **snap out of it!** (*fam*) non lasciarti andare!. ② VT + ADV (*order etc*) dare bruscamente

▶ **snap up** VT + ADV afferrare; **to snap up a bargain** (*fig*) accaparrarsi un affare, non lasciarsi sfuggire un affare.

snap·dragon ['snæpˌdrægən] N bocca di leone.

♦ **snap fastener** N bottone *m* a pressione.

snap·pish ['snæpɪʃ] ADJ irritabile, bisbetico(-a).

snap·py ['snæpɪ] ADJ (*comp* **-ier**, *superl* **-iest**) (*fam: slogan, answer*) d'effetto; (: *way of speaking*) sbrigativo(-a); (: *smart*) elegante; **he's a snappy dresser** è un elegantone; **make it snappy!** (*fam*) sbrigati!

snap·shot ['snæpˌʃɒt] N (*Phot*) istantanea.

snare [snɛə'] ① N trappola.

② VT prendere in trappola, intrappolare.

snarl¹ [snɑ:l] ① N ringhio.

② VI: **to snarl (at sb)** ringhiare (a qn).

snarl² [snɑ:l] ① N (*in wool etc*) garbuglio.

② VT: **to get snarled up** (*wool, plans*) ingarbugliarsi; (*traffic*) intasarsi.

♦ **snarl-up** ['snɑ:lˌʌp] N (*of traffic*) intasamento.

snatch [snætʃ] ① N **a** (*act of snatching*): **to make a snatch at sth** cercare di afferrare qc

b (*fam: theft*) furto, rapina; (: *kidnapping*) rapimento; **there was a wages snatch** dei ladri hanno rubato le paghe

c (*snippet*) pezzo; **snatches of conversation** frammenti *mpl* di conversazione; **to sleep in snatches** dormire a intervalli.

② VT (*grab: object*) strappare con violenza; (: *opportunity*) cogliere; (: *few days, short break*) prendersi; (*steal, also fig: kiss, victory*) rubare; (*kidnap*) rapire; **to snatch a sandwich** buttar giù in fretta un panino; **to snatch some sleep** riuscire a dormire un po'; **to snatch a knife out of sb's hand** strappare di mano un coltello a qn.

③ VI: **don't snatch!** non strappare le cose di mano!; **to snatch at** (*object*) cercare di afferrare; (*opportunity*) cogliere al volo

▶ **snatch away** VT + ADV: **to snatch sth away from sb** strappare qc a qn

▶ **snatch up** VT + ADV raccogliere in fretta, afferrare.

snaz·zy ['snæzɪ] ADJ (*comp* **-ier**, *superl* **-iest**) (*fam: clothes*) sciccoso(-a).

sneak [sni:k] ① VT: **to sneak sth out of a place** portare

fuori qc di nascosto da un luogo; **to sneak a look at sth** dare una sbirciatina a qc; **to sneak a quick cigarette** fumarsi una sigaretta di nascosto.

2 VI **a** : **to sneak in/out** entrare/uscire di nascosto *or* di soppiatto; **to sneak away** *or* **off** allontanarsi di nascosto *or* di soppiatto, squagliarsela; **to sneak off with sth** portare via di soppiatto qc

b : **to sneak on sb** (*fam*) fare la spia a qn.

3 N (*fam: telltale*) spione(-a).

sneak·ers ['sni:kəz] NPL (*Am*) scarpe *fpl* da ginnastica.

sneak·ing ['sni:kɪŋ] ADJ (*dislike, preference*) segreto(-a); **I have a sneaking admiration for him** mio malgrado l'ammiro; **to have a sneaking feeling/suspicion that** ... avere la vaga impressione/il vago sospetto che... .

♦ **sneak preview** N anteprima non ufficiale.

♦ **sneak thief** N ladruncolo(-a).

sneaky ['sni:kɪ] ADJ (*comp* **-ier,** *superl* **-iest**) (*fam*) vile.

sneer [snɪəʳ] 1 N (*expression*) sogghigno, ghigno; (*remark*) commento sarcastico.

2 VI sogghignare; **to sneer at sb/sth** farsi beffe di qn/qc.

sneer·ing ['snɪərɪŋ] 1 ADJ (*smile, remark*) beffardo(-a).

2 N beffe *fpl*.

sneer·ing·ly ['snɪərɪŋlɪ] ADV sarcasticamente.

sneeze [sni:z] 1 N starnuto.

2 VI starnutire; **an offer not to be sneezed at** (*fig fam*) un'offerta su cui non si può sputare sopra.

snick·er ['snɪkəʳ] (*Am*) 1 VI ridacchiare.

2 N risatina.

snide [snaɪd] ADJ (*fam*) maligno(-a).

sniff [snɪf] 1 N (*sound*) annusata, fiutata; **to have a sniff of sth** annusare qc; **one sniff of this is enough to kill you** una annusata a questo e muori di sicuro; **he gave a sniff of contempt** ha arricciato il naso con disprezzo.

2 VT (*gen*) annusare, fiutare; (*glue, drug*) sniffare; (*inhalant*) fare inalazioni di.

3 VI (*person*) tirare su col naso; (: *in contempt*) arricciare il naso

▶ **sniff at** VI + PREP annusare; **it's not to be sniffed at** non è da disprezzare

▶ **sniff out** VT + ADV fiutare; (*fig*) fiutare, subodorare.

sniff·er dog ['snɪfə‚dɒg] N cane *m* poliziotto *inv* (*antidroga o antiterrorismo*).

snif·fle ['snɪfl] = **snuffle.**

snif·fy ['snɪfɪ] ADJ (*comp* **-ier,** *superl* **-iest**) (*fam: disdainful*) sprezzante.

snif·ter ['snɪftəʳ] N (*fam: of whisky etc*) cicchetto, goccetto.

snig·ger ['snɪgəʳ] (*pej*) 1 N risolino.

2 VI ridacchiare, ridere sotto i baffi; **to snigger at** ridere sotto i baffi per.

snig·ger·ing ['snɪgərɪŋ] (*pej*) N risatine *fpl*.

snip [snɪp] 1 N (*cut*) taglio; (*small piece*) ritaglio; (*Brit fam: bargain*) affare *m*, occasione *f*; **with a snip of the scissors** con un colpo di forbici.

2 VT tagliare; **to snip sth off** tagliare via qc.

snipe [snaɪp] 1 N, PL INV (*bird*) beccaccino.

2 VI: **to snipe at sb** sparare a qn da un nascondiglio; (*fig*) lanciare frecciatine a qn.

snip·er ['snaɪpəʳ] N franco tiratore *m*, cecchino.

snip·pet ['snɪpɪt] N (*of cloth, paper*) ritaglio; (*of information, conversation etc*) frammento.

snitch [snɪtʃ] (*fam*) 1 VI (*inform*): **to snitch on sb** fare la spia a qn.

2 VT (*steal*) sgraffignare.

sniv·el ['snɪvl] VI piagnucolare, frignare.

sniv·el·ler, (*Am*) **sniv·el·er** ['snɪvləʳ] N piagnucolone(-a),

frignone(-a).

sniv·el·ling, (*Am*) **sniv·el·ing** ['snɪvlɪŋ] ADJ piagnucoloso (-a).

snob [snɒb] N snob *m/f inv*; **he's an intellectual snob** è uno snob in fatto di cultura.

snob·bery ['snɒbərɪ] N snobismo.

snob·bish ['snɒbɪʃ] ADJ snob *inv*.

snob·bish·ness ['snɒbɪʃnɪs] N snobismo.

snob·by ['snɒbɪ] ADJ (*comp* **-ier,** *superl* **-iest**) (*fam*) = **snobbish.**

snog [snɒg] (*Brit fam*) 1 N pomiciata.

2 VI sbaciucchiarsi, pomiciare.

snook [snu:k] N (*Brit fam*): **to cock a snook at sb** fare marameo a qn, prendere in giro qn.

snook·er ['snu:kəʳ] 1 N ≈ (gioco del) biliardo.

2 VT: **to be properly snookered** (*fig fam*) essere in un bel casino.

snoop [snu:p] (*fam pej*) 1 N (*act*): **to have a snoop round** curiosare.

2 VI (*also:* **snoop about, snoop around**) curiosare; **to snoop into sb's affairs** ficcare il naso negli affari di qn; **to snoop on sb** spiare qn.

snoop·er ['snu:pəʳ] N ficcanaso *m/f*.

snooty ['snu:tɪ] ADJ (*comp* **-ier,** *superl* **-iest**) (*fam pej*) snob *inv*, borioso(-a), altezzoso(-a).

snooze [snu:z] 1 N sonnellino, pisolino; **to have a snooze** fare un sonnellino, schiacciare un pisolino.

2 VI sonnecchiare.

snore [snɔːʳ] 1 N: **to give a loud snore** russare sonoramente.

2 VI russare.

snor·ing ['snɔːrɪŋ] N il russare *m*.

snor·kel ['snɔːkl] 1 N (*of submarine*) presa d'aria; (*of swimmer*) respiratore *m* subacqueo, boccaglio.

2 VI: **to go snorkelling** nuotare con il boccaglio.

snort [snɔːt] 1 N sbuffata, sbuffo.

2 VI (*horse, person*) sbuffare; **to snort with laughter** soffocare dalle risate.

3 VT (*fam: drugs*) sniffare.

snort·er ['snɔːtəʳ] N (*Brit fam*) **a** : **a real snorter of a problem** un bel rompicapo **b** (*drink*) bicchierino, goccio.

snot [snɒt] N (*fam*) moccio.

snot·ty ['snɒtɪ] ADJ (*comp* **-ier,** *superl* **-iest**) (*fam*) moccioso (-a); (: *fig: snooty*) borioso(-a), altezzoso(-a).

snout [snaʊt] N (*of animal*) muso; (*of pig*) grugno.

snow [snəʊ] 1 N **a** neve *f*; (*also:* **snowfall**) nevicata; (*fam: cocaine*) neve **b** (*on TV screen*) effetto neve.

2 VT: **to be snowed in** *or* **up** essere isolato(-a) a causa della neve; **to be snowed under with work** essere sommerso(-a) di lavoro.

3 VI nevicare.

snow·ball ['snəʊ‚bɔːl] 1 N palla di neve.

2 VI (*fig: scheme, appeal*) crescere a vista d'occhio.

♦ **snowball fight** N: **to have a snowball fight** fare una battaglia a palle di neve.

♦ **snow blindness** N (*Med*) ambliopia da riflesso della neve.

snow·boot ['snəʊ‚bu:t] N doposcì *m inv*.

snow·bound ['snəʊ‚baʊnd] ADJ (*village*) isolato(-a) dalla neve; (*person, road*) bloccato(-a) dalla neve; (*countryside*) coperto(-a) di neve.

♦ **snow cannon** N (*Skiing*) cannone *m* per innevamento artificiale.

♦ **snow-capped** ['snəʊ‚kæpt] ADJ (*mountain*) incappuc-

ciato(-a) di neve; (*peak*) coperto(-a) di neve.

snow·cat ['snəʊˌkæt] N gatto delle nevi.

♦ **snow chains** NPL catene *fpl* da neve.

♦ **snow-covered** ['snəʊˌkʌvəd] ADJ coperto(-a) di neve.

snow·drift ['snəʊˌdrɪft] N cumulo di neve (*ammucchiato dal vento*).

snow·drop ['snəʊˌdrɒp] N bucaneve *m inv*.

snow·fall ['snəʊˌfɔːl] N (*fall of snow*) nevicata; (*amount that falls*) nevosità *f inv*.

snow·flake ['snəʊˌfleɪk] N fiocco di neve.

snow line N limite *m* delle nevi perenni.

snow·man ['snəʊˌmæn] N (*pl* -**men**) pupazzo di neve; **the abominable snowman** l'abominevole uomo delle nevi.

snow·mobile ['snəʊməˌbiːl] N = snowcat.

snow·plough, (*Am*) **snow·plow** ['snəʊˌplaʊ] N spazzaneve *m inv*.

♦ **snowplough turn** N (*Skiing*) curva a spazzaneve.

♦ **snow report** N (*Met*) bollettino della neve.

snow·shoe ['snəʊˌʃuː] N racchetta da neve.

snow·storm ['snəʊˌstɔːm] N tormenta, tempesta di neve.

♦ **Snow White** N Biancaneve *f*.

♦ **snow-white** [ˌsnəʊ'waɪt] ADJ candido(-a).

snowy ['snəʊɪ] ADJ (*comp* -**ier**, *superl* -**iest**) (*climate, region, day etc*) nevoso(-a); (*hills, roof*) innevato(-a); (*white as snow*) candido(-a), niveo(-a); **it's been very snowy recently** ha nevicato parecchio, ultimamente.

SNP [ˌɛsɛn'piː] N ABBR (*Brit Pol*: = *Scottish National Party*) *partito nazionalista scozzese*.

Snr ABBR (*Am*) = Senior.

snub [snʌb] [1] N affronto, offesa.

[2] VT (*person*) snobbare.

♦ **snub-nosed** [ˌsnʌb'nəʊzd] ADJ con il naso a patata *or* patatina.

snuff [snʌf] [1] N tabacco da fiuto; **to take snuff** fiutare tabacco.

[2] VT (*also*: snuff out: *candle*) spegnere; **to snuff it** (*Brit fam*) tirare le cuoia.

snuff·box ['snʌfˌbɒks] N tabacchiera.

snuf·fle ['snʌfl] [1] N: **I've got a snuffle** mi cola il naso; **I've got the snuffles** ho il raffreddore.

[2] VI tirare su col naso.

♦ **snuff movie** N (*fam*) *film porno dove una persona viene uccisa realmente*.

snug [snʌg] ADJ (*comp* -**ger**, *superl* -**gest**) (*cosy*: *room, house*) accogliente, comodo(-a); (*safe*: *harbour*) sicuro(-a); (*fitting closely*) attillato(-a); **warm and snug by the fire** accoccolato(-a) vicino al fuoco; **to be snug in bed** essere al calduccio nel letto; **it's a snug fit** è attillato(-a).

snug·gle ['snʌgl] VI: **to snuggle down in bed** rannicchiarsi nel letto; **to snuggle up to sb** stringersi a qn.

snug·ly ['snʌglɪ] ADV comodamente; **it fits snugly** (*object in pocket etc*) ci sta giusto(-a) giusto(-a); (*garment*) sta ben attillato(-a).

SO ABBR (*Banking*) = standing order.

----

so [səʊ]

[1] ADV

[a] (*in comparisons: before adjective and adverb*) così;

▷**so quickly** (*soon*) così presto; (*fast*) così in fretta

▷**it is so big** that ... è così grosso che...

▷**it was so much more difficult** than I expected era molto più difficile di quanto pensassi

▷**she's not so clever** as him lei non è intelligente come lui

▷**he's not so foolish** as I thought non è così scemo come pensavo

▷**I wish you weren't so clumsy** magari non fossi così maldestro

[b] (*very*) così;

▷**so much** tanto; (+ *noun*) tanto(-a);

▷**so many** tanti(-e)

▷**I love you so** (*much*) ti voglio tanto bene

▷**I'm so worried** sono così preoccupato

▷**I'm so glad to see you again** sono così felice rivederti

▷**I've got so much to do** ho tanto da fare

▷**I've got so much to do that** ... ho così tanto da fare che...

▷**thank you so much** grazie infinite *or* mille

[c] (*thus, in this way, likewise*) così, in questo modo;

▷**the article is so written as to** ... l'articolo è scritto in modo da...

▷**if so** se è così, quand'è così

▷**he likes things just so** vuole che tutto sia fatto a puntino

▷**I didn't do it — you DID so!** non l'ho fatto io — l'hai fatto tu eccome!

▷**so do I, so am I** etc anch'io

▷**he's wrong and so are you** lui si sbaglia e tu pure

▷**and so forth** OR **and so on** e così via

▷**so it is!** OR **so it does!** davvero!

▷**it so happens that** ... si dà il caso che... + *sub*

▷**while she was so doing** mentre lo stava facendo

▷**you should do it so** dovresti farlo così

▷**I hope so** lo spero

▷**I think so** penso di sì

▷**I'm afraid so** temo di sì

▷**so he says** così dice

▷**so to speak** per così dire

▷**don't worry so** non preoccuparti così tanto

▷**I told you so** te l'avevo detto io

▷**so saying he walked away** così dicendo se ne andò

▷**do so** fallo

[d] (*phrases*)

▷**she didn't so much as send me a birthday card** non mi ha neanche mandato un biglietto di auguri per il compleanno

▷**I haven't so much as a penny** non ho neanche una lira

▷**so much for her promises!** a fidarsi delle sue promesse!

▷**at so much per week** a un tot alla settimana

▷**ten or so** circa una decina

▷**just so!** OR **quite so!** esattamente!

▷**even so** comunque

▷**so long!** (*fam*) ciao!, ci vediamo!

▷**so far** finora, fin qui; (*in past*) fino ad allora.

[2] CONJ

[a] (*expressing purpose*): **so as to do sth** in modo *or* così da fare qc;

▷**we hurried so as not to be late** ci affrettammo per non fare tardi

▷**so (that)** perché + *sub*

▷**I brought it so that you could see it** l'ho portato perché tu lo vedessi

▷**so as to prevent cheating** così da evitare imbrogli

b (*expressing result*)

▷**it was raining and so we could not go out** pioveva e così non potemmo uscire;

▷**as her French improved so did her confidence** man mano che il suo francese migliorava acquistava più sicurezza

▷**so you see ...** così vedi...

c (*in questions, exclamations*)

▷**so you're Spanish?** e così sei spagnolo?

▷**so that's the reason!** allora è questo il motivo!, ecco perché!

▷**so there you are!** ah eccoti qua!

▷**so there!** (*fam*) ecco!

▷**so (what)?** (*fam*) e allora?, e con questo or ciò?

soak [səʊk] **1** VT **a** (*bread etc*) inzuppare; (*clothes*) mettere a mollo; **to get soaked (to the skin)** bagnarsi *or* infradiciarsi (fino alle ossa); **to be soaked through** essere (bagnato(-a)) fradicio(-a)

　b (*fam*): **to soak the rich** mungere i ricchi.

　2 VI (*clothes*) inzupparsi; **to leave to soak** (*garment*) lasciare in ammollo; (*dishes*) lasciare a bagno.

　3 N **a** (*in water*): **to have a long soak in the bath** restare a lungo a mollo nella vasca

　b (*fam: drunkard*) spugna

▶ **soak in** VI + ADV penetrare; **it took a long time to soak in** (*fig*) ci è voluto tanto prima che mi (*or* gli *etc*) entrasse in testa

▶ **soak up** VT + ADV (*liquid, knowledge*) assorbire; **to soak up the sunshine** (*fam*) crogiolarsi al sole.

soaking [ˈsəʊkɪŋ] ADJ (*also:* **soaking wet**) bagnato(-a) fradicio(-a).

◆ **so-and-so** [ˈsəʊənˌsəʊ] N (*somebody*) un(a) tale; **Mr/Mrs so-and-so** (*fam*) signor/signora tal dei tali; **he's a so-and-so!** (*fam*) che tipo odioso che è!

soap [səʊp] **1** N sapone *m*; (*also:* **cake of soap**) saponetta; (*TV fam*) telenovela, soap opera *f inv.*

　2 VT insaponare.

soap·box [ˈsəʊpˌbɒks] N palco improvvisato (*per orazioni pubbliche*).

soap·dish [ˈsəʊpˌdɪʃ] N portasapone *m inv.*

soap·flakes [ˈsəʊpˌfleɪks] NPL sapone *msg* in scaglie.

◆ **soap opera** N telenovela, soap opera *f inv.*

◆ **soap powder** N detersivo in polvere.

soap·suds [ˈsəʊpˌsʌdz] NPL saponata *fsg.*

soap·wort [ˈsəʊpˌwɜːt] N saponaria.

soapy [ˈsəʊpɪ] ADJ (*comp* **-ier**, *superl* **-iest**) (*covered in soap: person*) insaponato(-a); (*: water*) saponato(-a); (*like soap*) saponoso(-a); **to taste soapy** sapere di sapone.

soar [sɔː] VI **a** (*rise: bird*) librarsi; (*: plane, ball*) volare **b** (*fig: tower etc*) elevarsi, ergersi; (*: price, morale, spirits*) salire alle stelle; (*: ambitions, hopes*) aumentare notevolmente.

soar·ing [ˈsɔːrɪŋ] ADJ (*flight*) altissimo(-a); (*building*) slanciato(-a); (*prices*) alle stelle; (*hopes, imagination*) ardito(-a); **soaring inflation** inflazione *f* galoppante.

sob [sɒb] **1** N singhiozzo.

　2 VI singhiozzare.

　3 VT: **to sob one's heart out** piangere disperatamente.

s.o.b. [ˌɛsəʊˈbiː] N ABBR (*Am fam!:* = *son of a bitch*) figlio di puttana (*fam!*)

sob·bing [ˈsɒbɪŋ] **1** ADJ singhiozzante.

　2 N singhiozzi *mpl.*

so·ber [ˈsəʊbə] **1** ADJ **a** (*not drunk*) sobrio(-a); **to be far**

from sober non essere affatto sobrio(-a); **to be as sober as a judge** OR **be stone-cold sober** essere perfettamente sobrio(-a)

　b (*rational, sedate, dull: life, person, colour*) sobrio(-a); (*: opinion, statement, estimate*) ponderato(-a); (*: occasion*) solenne; **the sober truth** la verità pura e semplice; **in a sober mood** serio(-a).

　2 VT (*also:* **sober up**) far passare la sbornia a; (*fig*) calmare.

　3 VI (*also:* **sober up**) smaltire la sbornia; (*fig*) calmarsi; **her mother's rebuke had a sobering effect on her** il rimprovero di sua madre la fece pensare.

so·ber·ly [ˈsəʊbəlɪ] ADV in modo sobrio, sobriamente.

so·bri·ety [səʊˈbraɪətɪ] N **a** (*not being drunk*) sobrietà **b** (*seriousness, sedateness*) sobrietà, pacatezza.

◆ **sob story** N (*fam pej*) storia lacrimosa.

◆ **sob stuff** N (*fam: in film etc*) sentimentalismo.

Soc. ABBR (= *society*) Soc.

◆ **so-called** [ˌsəʊˈkɔːld] ADJ cosiddetto(-a).

soc·cer [ˈsɒkə] **1** N calcio.

　2 ADJ (*club, season, match*) calcistico(-a), di calcio.

◆ **soccer pitch** N campo di calcio.

◆ **soccer player** N calciatore *m.*

so·cia·bil·ity [ˌsəʊʃəˈbɪlɪtɪ] N (*of person*) socievolezza.

so·cia·ble [ˈsəʊʃəbl] ADJ (*person*) socievole, cordiale; (*evening, gathering*) amichevole, tra amici; **I don't feel very sociable** non ho molta voglia di vedere gente; **I'll have one drink, just to be sociable** berrò qualcosa, tanto per gradire.

so·cia·bly [ˈsəʊʃəblɪ] ADV (*behave*) in modo socievole; (*invite, say*) amichevolmente.

so·cial [ˈsəʊʃəl] **1** ADJ (*all senses*) sociale; **man is a social animal** l'uomo è un animale sociale *or* socievole.

　2 N festicciola.

◆ **social anthropology** N antropologia culturale.

◆ **social class** N classe *f* sociale.

◆ **social climber** N arrampicatore(-trice) sociale, arrivista *m/f.*

◆ **social club** N circolo.

◆ **social column** N (*Press*) cronaca mondana.

◆ **social democrat** N socialdemocratico(-a).

◆ **social disease** N malattia sociale.

◆ **social drinker** N: **to be a social drinker** bere solo in compagnia.

◆ **social insurance** N (*Am*) assicurazione *f* sociale.

so·cial·ism [ˈsəʊʃəˌlɪzəm] N socialismo.

so·cial·ist [ˈsəʊʃəlɪst] ADJ, N socialista (*m/f*).

so·cial·ite [ˈsəʊʃəˌlaɪt] N persona mondana.

so·ciali·za·tion [ˌsəʊʃəlaɪˈzeɪʃən] N (*Psych*) socializzazione *f.*

so·cial·ize [ˈsəʊʃəˌlaɪz] **1** VI (*be with people*) frequentare gente; (*make friends*) fare amicizia; (*chat*) chiacchierare; **he has to socialize a lot because he's a salesman** deve mantenere molti contatti a causa del suo lavoro di rappresentante; **to socialize with** socializzare con.

　2 VT (*Pol, Psych*) socializzare.

◆ **social life** N: **to have a good social life** avere un'intensa vita sociale.

so·cial·ly [ˈsəʊʃəlɪ] ADV (*gen*) socialmente, in società; **I know him socially** lo incontro in occasioni mondane.

◆ **social outcast** N emarginato(-a).

◆ **social science** N scienze *fpl* sociali.

◆ **social scientist** N specialista *m/f* in scienze sociali, sociologo(-a).

◆ **social security** N previdenza sociale; **to be on social**

security (*fam*) ricevere sussidi dalla previdenza sociale; **Department of Social Security** (*Brit*) ≈ Istituto di Previdenza Sociale.

♦ **social services** NPL servizi *mpl* sociali.

♦ **social studies** NPL scienze *fpl* sociali.

♦ **social welfare** N sicurezza sociale.

♦ **social work** N assistenza sociale.

♦ **social worker** N assistente *m/f* sociale.

so·ci·ety [sə'saɪətɪ] ☐1☐ N **a** (*social community*) società *f inv*; **to live in society** vivere in società; **he was a danger to society** era un pericolo pubblico

b (*club, organization*) società *f inv*, associazione *f*; **film society** cineclub *m inv*; **learned society** circolo culturale

c (*also:* **high society**) alta società; **polite society** società bene

d (*frm: company*) compagnia; **in the society of** in compagnia di; **I enjoyed his society** ho gradito la sua compagnia.

☐2☐ ADJ (*party, column*) mondano(-a).

♦ **Society of Friends** N: **the Society of Friends** i Quaccheri.

♦ **Society of Jesus** N Compagnia di Gesù.

♦ **society wedding** N matrimonio nell'alta società.

so·cio·eco·nom·ic [ˌsəʊsɪəʊˌiːkə'nɒmɪk] ADJ socioeconomico(-a).

so·cio·logi·cal [ˌsəʊsɪə'lɒdʒɪkəl] ADJ sociologico(-a).

so·ci·olo·gist [ˌsəʊsɪ'ɒlədʒɪst] N sociologo(-a).

so·ci·ol·ogy [ˌsəʊsɪ'ɒlədʒɪ] N sociologia.

so·cio·po·liti·cal [ˌsəʊsɪəʊpə'lɪtɪkəl] ADJ sociopolitico(-a).

sock[1] [sɒk] N (*short*) calzino; (*long*) calzettone *m*; (*of horse*) balzana; **to pull one's socks up** (*fig*) darsi una regolata; **put a sock in it!** (*Brit fam*) chiudi il becco!

sock[2] [sɒk] (*fam*) ☐1☐ N (*blow*) colpo, pugno; **to give sb a sock on the jaw** dare un pugno sul muso a qn.

☐2☐ VT colpire, picchiare; **come on, sock him one!** dai, suonagliele!

sock·et ['sɒkɪt] N (*of eye*) orbita; (*of joint*) cavità *f inv*; (*Elec: for plug*) presa (di corrente); (: *for light bulb*) portalampada *m inv*.

Socrates ['sɒkrə,tiːz] N Socrate *m*.

sod[1] [sɒd] N (*liter: of earth*) zolla erbosa.

sod[2] [sɒd] N (*Brit fam!*) stronzo(-a) (*fam!*); **you lazy sod!** pezzo di sfaticato!; **poor sod!** povero diavolo!

▶ **sod off** VI + ADV (*Brit fam!*): **sod off!** levati dalle palle! (*fam!*)

soda ['səʊdə] N **a** (*Chem*) soda **b** (*drink*) seltz *m inv*; **whisky and soda** whisky e soda **c** (*Am: also:* **soda pop**) gassosa.

♦ **soda fountain** N (*Am*) chiosco delle bibite.

♦ **soda siphon** N sifone *m* del seltz.

♦ **soda water** N acqua di seltz.

sod·den ['sɒdn] ADJ zuppo(-a).

sod·ding ['sɒdɪŋ] (*Brit fam!*) ☐1☐ ADJ: **that sodding dog!** quel cane del cazzo! (*fam!*).

☐2☐ ADV: **don't be so sodding stupid!** non fare il coglione! (*fam!*)

so·dium ['səʊdɪəm] N sodio.

♦ **sodium bicarbonate** N bicarbonato di sodio.

♦ **sodium chloride** N cloruro di sodio.

♦ **sodium hydroxide** N soda caustica.

♦ **sodium lamp** N lampada al sodio.

sodo·my ['sɒdəmɪ] N sodomia.

sofa ['səʊfə] N sofà *m inv*, divano.

So·fia ['səʊfɪə] N Sofia (*città*).

soft [sɒft] ADJ (*comp* **-er**, *superl* **-est**) **a** (*not hard, rough etc*:

gen) morbido(-a); (: *snow, ground*) soffice; (: *metal, stone*) tenero(-a); (: *cheese*) a pasta molle; (: *pej: muscles*) flaccido(-a)

b (*gentle, not harsh: breeze, rain, pressure*) leggero(-a); (: *colour*) delicato(-a); (: *light*) tenue; (: *look, smile, answer*) dolce; (: *heart*) tenero(-a); (: *life, option*) facile; (: *job*) non pesante; (: *teacher, parent*) indulgente; **you're too soft with him** sei troppo indulgente con lui; **to have a soft spot for sb** avere un debole per qn; **to be soft on sb** essere cotto(-a) di qn; **he has a soft time of it** lui se la passa bene

c (*not loud: sound, laugh, voice*) sommesso(-a); (: *steps, whisper*) leggero(-a); **the music is too soft** il volume della musica è troppo basso

d (*fam: person: no stamina*) smidollato(-a); (*stupid*): **to be soft (in the head)** essere un po' tocco(-a)

e (*Ling: consonant*) dolce.

soft·ball ['sɒft,bɔːl] N (*game*) softball *m inv*; (*ball*) palla da softball.

♦ **soft-boiled** ['sɒft,bɔɪld] ADJ (*egg*) alla coque.

♦ **soft currency** N moneta debole.

♦ **soft drink** N bibita analcolica.

♦ **soft drugs** NPL droghe *fpl* leggere.

sof·ten ['sɒfn] ☐1☐ VT (*gen*) ammorbidire; (*light*) attenuare; (*sound, impression*) attutire; (*colour, anger*) smorzare; (*resistance*) fiaccare; (*person: weaken*) addolcire; **he became softened by luxurious living** vivendo nel lusso si è rammollito; **to soften the blow** (*fig*) attutire il colpo.

☐2☐ (*see vt*) ammorbidirsi; attenuarsi; attutirsi; smorzarsi; fiaccarsi; (*person, character*) addolcirsi; **her heart softened** si intenerì

▶ **soften up** VT + ADV (*fam*): **to soften sb up** ammorbidire qn.

sof·ten·er ['sɒfnə'] N ammorbidente *m*.

♦ **soft fruit** N (*Brit*) ≈ frutti *mpl* di bosco.

♦ **soft furnishings** NPL (*Brit*) tessuti *mpl* d'arredo.

♦ **soft goods** NPL (*Comm*) tessili *mpl*.

♦ **soft-hearted** [ˌsɒft'hɑːtɪd] ADJ dal cuore tenero.

softie ['sɒftɪ] N = **softy**.

♦ **soft landing** N (*of spacecraft: on moon*) allunaggio morbido; (: *on earth*) atterraggio morbido; (*fig: easy answer*) soluzione *f* indolore.

soft·ly ['sɒftlɪ] ADV (*gen*) dolcemente; (*walk*) silenziosamente; (*gently: knock*) lievemente.

♦ **softly-softly** ['sɒftlɪ'sɒftlɪ] ADJ (*approach*) cauto(-a).

soft·ness ['sɒftnɪs] N (*of skin, bed, snow, leather*) morbidezza; (*of voice, manner, glance*) dolcezza; (*indulgence*) indulgenza.

♦ **soft option** N soluzione (più) facile.

♦ **soft palate** N palato molle.

♦ **soft-pedal** [ˌsɒft'pɛdl] VT (*fig*) minimizzare.

♦ **soft pedal** N (*on piano*) sordina.

♦ **soft porn** N pornografia soft-core.

♦ **soft sell** N persuasione *f* (indiretta) all'acquisto.

♦ **soft shoulder**, **soft verge** N (*Aut*) banchina non transitabile.

♦ **soft soap** N (*fam*) saponata, lusinghe *fpl*.

♦ **soft-soap** [ˌsɒft'səʊp] VT (*fam*) dare del sapone a, lusingare.

♦ **soft-spoken** ['sɒft,spəʊkən] ADJ dalla voce carezzevole.

♦ **soft target** N obiettivo civile (*e quindi facile da colpire*).

♦ **soft touch** N (*fam*): **to be a soft touch** lasciarsi mungere facilmente.

♦ **soft toy** N pupazzo di peluche.

♦ **soft verge** N (*Aut*) = **soft shoulder**.

soft·ware ['sɒft,wɛəʳ] N (*Comput*) software *m*.

♦ **software package** N (*Comput*) pacchetto di software.

♦ **soft water** N acqua non calcarea, acqua dolce.

soft·wood ['sɒft,wʊd] N legno dolce.

softy, softie ['sɒftɪ] N (*fam: weak*) pappamolle *m/f*; (: *tender-hearted*) tenerone(-a).

SOGAT ['səʊgæt] N ABBR (*Brit: = Society of Graphical and Allied Trades*) *sindacato dei lavoratori dell'industria della stampa*.

sog·gy ['sɒgɪ] ADJ (*comp* **-ier**, *superl* **-iest**) fradicio(-a), inzuppato(-a); (*bread, cake*) molle, pesante.

soh, so [səʊ] N (*Mus*) sol *m inv*.

soil [sɔɪl] [1] N (*earth*) terreno, terra, suolo; **chalky/poor soil** terreno calcareo/povero; **cover it with soil** coprilo di terra; **on British soil** sul suolo britannico; **the soil** (*fig: farmland*) la terra.
[2] VT (*dirty*) sporcare; (*fig: reputation, honour etc*) infangare, macchiare.

soiled [sɔɪld] ADJ sporco(-a), sudicio(-a).

so·journ ['sɒdʒɜːn] (*liter*) [1] N soggiorno.
[2] VI soggiornare.

sol·ace ['sɒlɪs] N consolazione *f*.

so·lar ['səʊləʳ] ADJ solare.

♦ **solar cell** N cellula solare.

so·lar·ium [səʊ'lɛərɪəm] N (*pl* **solariums** *or* **solaria** [səʊ'lɛərɪə]) solarium *m inv*.

♦ **solar panel** N pannello solare.

♦ **so·lar plex·us** [,səʊlə'plɛksəs] N (*Anat*) plesso solare.

♦ **solar power** N energia solare.

sold [səʊld] PT, PP *of* **sell**.

sol·der ['səʊldəʳ] [1] N lega per saldatura.
[2] VT saldare; **soldering iron** saldatore *m* (*attrezzo*).

sol·dier ['səʊldʒəʳ] [1] N soldato, militare *m*; **a girl soldier** una soldatessa; **toy soldier** soldatino; **an old soldier** (*also fig*) un veterano; **to play at soldiers** giocare alla guerra.
[2] VI fare il soldato
▶ **soldier on** VI + ADV perseverare.

sol·dier·ly ['səʊldʒəlɪ] ADJ (*behaviour, appearance*) da soldato.

sole¹ [səʊl] [1] N (*of foot*) pianta del piede; (*of shoe*) suola.
[2] VT risolare.

sole² [səʊl] N (*pl* **sole** *or* **soles**) (*fish*) sogliola.

sole³ [səʊl] ADJ **a** (*only*) unico(-a), solo(-a); **the sole reason** la sola *or* l'unica ragione **b** (*exclusive*) esclusivo (-a); **sole agent** agente *m or* rappresentante *m* esclusivo.

sol·ecism ['sɒlə,sɪzəm] N (*frm: in grammar*) solecismo; (: *in behaviour*) scorrettezza.

sole·ly ['səʊllɪ] ADV solamente, unicamente; **I will hold you solely responsible** ti considererò il solo responsabile.

sol·emn ['sɒləm] ADJ solenne.

so·lem·nity [sə'lɛmnɪtɪ] N solennità *f inv*.

sol·em·ni·za·tion [,sɒlɛmnaɪ'zeɪʃən] (*frm*) N solennizzazione *f*; (*of marriage*) celebrazione *f*.

sol·em·nize ['sɒləm,naɪz] (*frm*) VT solennizzare; (*marriage*) celebrare.

sol·emn·ly ['sɒləmlɪ] ADV solennemente.

so·lenoid ['səʊlɪ,nɔɪd] N (*Phys, Elec*) solenoide *m*.

♦ **sole trader** N commerciante *m/f* in proprio.

sol·fa ['sɒl'fɑː] N (*Mus*) solfeggio.

so·lic·it [sə'lɪsɪt] [1] VT (*frm: request*) richiedere, sollecitare.
[2] VI (*prostitute*) adescare.

so·lic·i·tor [sə'lɪsɪtəʳ] N (*Brit: in court*) ≈ avvocato(-essa); (:

for wills etc) ≈ notaio; (*Am*) rappresentante *m* legale (*di una città o un ministero*).

♦ **Solicitor General** N (*pl* **Solicitors General**) (*in GB*) ≈ sostituto procuratore *m* generale; (*in USA*) ≈ sottosegretario di stato al ministero di Grazia e Giustizia.

so·lici·tous [sə'lɪsɪtəs] ADJ (*frm: concerned, caring*) sollecito (-a); **solicitous (about** *or* **for)** preoccupato(-a) (per); **solicitous to please** ansioso(-a) di piacere.

so·lici·tude [sə'lɪsɪtjuːd] N (*frm*) sollecitudine *f*.

sol·id ['sɒlɪd] [1] ADJ (*gen*) solido(-a); (*not hollow*) pieno (-a); (*gold, wood*) massiccio(-a); (*crowd, row*) compatto (-a); (*line*) ininterrotto(-a); (*vote*) unanime; (*meal*) sostanzioso(-a); **to become solid** solidificarsi; **cut out of solid rock** scolpito(-a) nella roccia viva; **as solid as a rock** solido come una roccia; **to be frozen solid** essere completamente ghiacciato(-a); **we waited two solid hours** abbiamo aspettato due ore filate; **a man of solid build** un uomo di corporatura massiccia; **the street was packed solid with people** la strada era affollatissima; **a solid mass of colour** una massa uniforme di colore; **he's a good solid worker** è un lavoratore serio; **a solid argument** un argomento fondato *or* valido; **solid common sense** buon senso pratico; **the town is solid for Labour** nella città c'è una gran maggioranza laburista.
[2] N solido.

soli·dar·ity [,sɒlɪ'dærɪtɪ] N solidarietà.

♦ **solid fuel** N combustibile *m* solido.

♦ **solid geometry** N geometria solida.

♦ **solid ground** N: **to be on solid ground** essere su terraferma; (*fig*) muoversi su un terreno sicuro.

so·lidi·fi·ca·tion [sə,lɪdɪfɪ'keɪʃən] N solidificazione *f*.

so·lidi·fy [sə'lɪdɪ,faɪ] [1] VT solidificare.
[2] VI solidificarsi.

so·lid·ity [sə'lɪdɪtɪ] N solidità.

sol·id·ly ['sɒlɪdlɪ] ADV (*gen*) solidamente; **a solidly-built house** una casa costruita solidamente; **to work solidly** lavorare sodo; **to vote solidly for sb** votare all'unanimità per qn; **they are solidly behind him** lo appoggiano all'unanimità.

♦ **solid-state** ['sɒlɪd,steɪt] ADJ (*Elec*) a stato solido; **solid-state physics** fisica dei solidi.

so·lilo·quy [sə'lɪləkwɪ] N soliloquio.

sol·ip·sism ['sɒlɪp,sɪzəm] N solipsismo.

soli·taire [,sɒlɪ'tɛəʳ] N (*game, gem*) solitario.

soli·tary ['sɒlɪtərɪ] ADJ (*alone, secluded*) solitario(-a); (*sole: example, case*) solo(-a), unico(-a); **not a solitary one** neanche uno(-a).

♦ **solitary confinement** N: **to be in solitary confinement** essere in cella d'isolamento.

soli·tude ['sɒlɪtjuːd] N solitudine *f*.

solo ['səʊləʊ] [1] N (*pl* **solos**) (*Mus*) assolo; **a tenor solo** un assolo di tenore.
[2] ADJ: **solo flight** volo in solitario; **passage for solo violin** brano per violino solista.
[3] ADV (*Mus*): **to play** (*or* **sing**) **solo** fare un assolo; **to fly solo** volare in solitario.

so·lo·ist ['səʊləʊɪst] N solista *m/f*.

Solo·mon ['sɒləmən] N Salomone *m*.

♦ **Solomon Islands** NPL: **the Solomon Islands** le isole Salomone.

sol·stice ['sɒlstɪs] N solstizio.

sol·ubil·ity [,sɒljʊ'bɪlɪtɪ] N solubilità.

sol·uble ['sɒljʊbl] ADJ solubile.

so·lute [sɒ'ljuːt] N soluto.

so·lu·tion [sə'luːʃən] N soluzione *f*.

solv·able ['sɒlvəbəl] ADJ (*problem*) risolvibile.

solve [sɒlv] VT risolvere.

sol·ven·cy [ˈsɒlvənsɪ] N (*Fin*) solvibilità.

sol·vent [ˈsɒlvənt] **1** ADJ (*Fin*) solvibile; (*Chem*) solvente.

2 N (*Chem*) solvente *m*.

♦ **solvent abuse** N abuso di colle e solventi (*a scopo stupefacente*).

Som. ABBR (*Brit*)= Somerset.

So·ma·li [səʊˈmɑːlɪ] ADJ, N somalo(-a).

So·ma·lia [səʊˈmɑːlɪə] N la Somalia.

Somaliland [səʊˈmɑːlɪˌlænd] N paesi *mpl* del Corno d'Africa.

sombre, (*Am*) **som·ber** [ˈsɒmbə'] ADJ (*mood, person*) triste, tetro(-a); (*colour*) scuro(-a); **a sombre prospect** una triste prospettiva.

som·bre·ly, (*Am*) **som·ber·ly** [ˈsɒmbəlɪ] ADV (*reply, gaze etc*) tristemente; (*dressed*) di scuro; (*painted*) con colori scuri.

some [sʌm]

1 ADJ

a (*a certain amount or number of*): **some tea/water/ biscuits/girls** del tè/dell'acqua/dei biscotti/delle ragazze

▷**I have some books** ho qualche libro *or* alcuni libri

▷ **some children came** sono venuti dei bambini

▷**all I have left is some chocolate** mi è rimasto solo un po' di cioccolato

▷**have some more crisps** prendi ancora delle patatine

▷**there's some milk in the fridge** c'è del latte in frigo

▷**there were some people outside** c'era della gente fuori

▷**he asked me some questions about the accident** mi ha fatto qualche domanda *or* alcune domande *or* delle domande sull'incidente

▷**have some tea/ice-cream** prendi un po' di tè/gelato

▷**if you have some time to spare** se hai un po' di tempo a disposizione

b (*certain: in contrast*) certo(-a), alcuni(-e) *pl*;

▷**some people hate fish** certa gente odia il pesce

▷**some people say that ...** certa gente dice *or* alcuni dicono che...

▷**in some ways** per certi versi, in un certo senso

c (*vague, indeterminate*) un(a) certo(-a), qualche;

▷**some day** un giorno

▷**some day next week** un giorno della prossima settimana

▷**in some form or other** in una qualche forma

▷**some man was asking for you** un tale chiedeva di te

▷**at some place in Sweden** da qualche parte in Svezia

▷**some politician or other** un qualche uomo politico

▷**some other time!** sarà per un'altra volta!

d (*considerable amount of*)

▷**it took some courage to do that** ci è voluto un bel coraggio per farlo

▷**some days ago** parecchi giorni fa

▷**some distance away** abbastanza lontano

▷**at some length** a lungo

▷**after some time** dopo un po'

e (*emphatic: a few, a little*)

▷**that's SOME consolation!** questo è già qualcosa!

▷**there's still SOME petrol in the tank** c'è ancora un po' di benzina nel serbatoio

f (*fam: intensive*)

▷**that's some fish!** questo sì che è un pesce!

▷**it was some party** è stata una grande festa

▷**you're some help!** (*iro*) sei proprio un bell'aiuto!

2 PRON

a (*a certain number*) alcuni(-e) *pl*, certi(-e) *pl*;

▷**some of them are crazy** alcuni di loro sono pazzi

▷**I've got some** (*books etc*) ne ho alcuni; (*milk, money*) ne ho un po'

▷**some (of them) have been sold** alcuni sono stati venduti

▷**would you like some?** ne vorresti qualcuno?

▷**do take some** prendine qualcuno

▷**some went this way and some that** alcuni andarono di qua e altri di là

b (*a certain amount*) un po';

▷**could I have some of that cheese?** potrei avere un po' di quel formaggio?

▷**have some more** prendine ancora un po'

▷**have some!** prendine un po'!

▷**I've read some of the book** ho letto parte del libro

▷**some of what he said was true** parte di ciò che ha detto era vero

▷**some (of it) was left** ne è rimasto un po'.

3 ADV: **some 20 people** circa 20 persone.

some·body [ˈsʌmbədɪ] **1** PRON qualcuno; **there's somebody coming** sta arrivando qualcuno; **somebody knocked at the door** hanno bussato alla porta; **somebody else** qualcun altro; **somebody Italian** un italiano; **somebody told me so** me l'ha detto qualcuno; **somebody or other** qualcuno.

2 N: **to be somebody** essere qualcuno; **she thinks she's somebody** si crede importante.

some·day [ˈsʌmˌdeɪ] ADV uno di questi giorni, un giorno o l'altro.

some·how [ˈsʌmˌhaʊ] ADV **a** (*in some way*) in qualche modo, in un modo o nell'altro; **it must be done somehow or other** bene o male va fatto; **we managed it somehow** non so come, ma ce l'abbiamo fatta; **we'll manage somehow** in un modo o nell'altro ce la faremo **b** (*for some reason*) per un motivo o per l'altro; **it seems odd somehow** non so perché, ma mi sembra strano; **somehow I've never succeeded** chissà perché non ce l'ho mai fatta.

some·one [ˈsʌmˌwʌn] PRON = **somebody**.

some·place [ˈsʌmˌpleɪs] ADV (*Am*) = **somewhere**.

som·er·sault [ˈsʌməˌsɔːlt] **1** N (*by person*) capriola; (: *in air*) salto mortale; (*by car etc*) ribaltamento, cappottamento.

2 VI (*see n: also:* **turn a somersault**) fare una capriola; fare un salto mortale; cappottare, ribaltarsi.

some·thing [ˈsʌmˌθɪŋ] **1** PRON qualche cosa, qualcosa; **something nice** (*pretty*) qualcosa di carino; (*to eat*) qualcosa di buono; (*to do*) qualcosa di bello; **something interesting** qualcosa di interessante; **something to do** qualcosa da fare; **something else** altro, qualcos'altro; **something has happened** è successo qualcosa; **something of the kind** qualcosa del genere; **she said something or other about it** mi ha detto qualcosa a tale proposito; **he's a lecturer in something or other** è professore di non so che; **he's a doctor or something** è

dottore o qualcosa del genere; **there's something the matter** c'è qualcosa che non va; **to have something to live for** avere uno scopo nella vita; **there's something in what you say** c'è del vero in quello che dici; **will you have something to drink?** vuoi qualcosa da bere?; **he's called John something** si chiama John vattelappesca; **give her something for herself** regalale qualcosa di personale; **here's something for your trouble** eccoti qualcosa per il disturbo; **I hope to see something of you** spero di vederti qualche volta; **I think you may have something there** penso che tu abbia ragione; (*good idea*) mi sembra una buona idea, la tua; **there's something about him that ...** c'è qualcosa in lui che...; **she has a certain something** ha un certo non so che; **that's really something!** mica male!.

2 ADV **a** : **something over/under 200** un po' più/meno di 200; **something like 200** circa 200; **he's something like me** mi assomiglia un po'; **now that's something like a rose!** (*approving comment*) questa sì che è una rosa!

b : **it's something of a problem** è un bel problema; **he is something of a liar** è un bel pezzo di bugiardo; **he's something of a musician** è un musicista abbastanza bravo

c (*fam*): **the weather was something shocking** faceva un tempo da cani.

some·time ['sʌm,taɪm] **1** ADV un giorno, uno di questi giorni; **sometime last month** un giorno, il mese scorso; **sometime before tomorrow** prima di domani; **sometime next year** (nel corso del)l'anno prossimo; **sometime soon** presto, uno di questi giorni; **I'll finish it sometime** lo finirò uno di questi giorni; **sometime or (an)other it will have to be done** bisognerà farlo prima o poi.

2 ADJ (*frm: former*) ex.

some·times ['sʌm,taɪmz] ADV qualche volta, a volte.
some·what ['sʌm,wɒt] ADV piuttosto, alquanto.
some·where ['sʌm,wɛə] ADV **a** (*in space*) da qualche parte, in qualche posto; **somewhere else** da qualche altra parte; **I lost it somewhere** l'ho perso da qualche parte; **somewhere in Wales** da qualche parte nel Galles; **somewhere or other in Scotland** da qualche parte in Scozia; **now we're getting somewhere!** ora stiamo facendo dei passi in avanti

b (*approximately*) circa, all'incirca, più o meno; **he paid somewhere around £12** l'ha pagato circa 12 sterline; **he's somewhere in his fifties** è sulla cinquantina.

som·nam·bu·lism [sɒm'næmbjʊ,lɪzəm] N (*frm*) sonnambulismo.
som·nam·bu·list [sɒm'næmbjʊlɪst] N (*frm*) sonnambulo (-a).
som·no·lence ['sɒmnələns] N (*liter*) sonnolenza.
som·no·lent ['sɒmnələnt] ADJ (*liter*) sonnolento(-a).
son [sʌn] N figlio; **come here son** (*fam*) vieni qui figliolo; **the Son of God/of Man** (*Rel*) il Figlio di Dio/dell'uomo.
so·nar ['səʊnɑː] N sonar *m inv*.
so·na·ta [sə'nɑːtə] N sonata.
son et lu·mi·ère ['sɒneɪ'luːmɪ,ɛə] N (*Brit*) spettacolo "Suoni e Luci".
song [sɒŋ] N (*ballad etc*) canzone *f*; (*of birds*) canto; **give us a song!** cantaci una canzone!; **to burst into song** mettersi a cantare; **to make a great song and dance about sth** (*fig*) fare un sacco di storie per qc; **I got it for a song** (*fig*) l'ho avuto per quattro soldi.
song·bird ['sɒŋ,bɜːd] N uccello canoro.
♦ **song book** N canzoniere *m*.

♦ **song cycle** N ciclo di canzoni.
song·writer ['sɒŋ,raɪtə] N compositore(-trice) di canzoni.
son·ic ['sɒnɪk] ADJ sonico(-a); **sonic depth finder** ecoscandaglio.
♦ **sonic boom, sonic bang** N bang *m inv* sonico.
♦ **son-in-law** ['sʌnɪn,lɔː] N (*pl* **sons-in-law**) genero.
son·net ['sɒnɪt] N sonetto.
son·ny ['sʌnɪ] N (*fam*) figlio mio, ragazzo mio.
so·nor·ity [sə'nɒrɪtɪ] N (*frm*) sonorità *f inv*.
so·no·rous ['sɒnərəs] ADJ (*frm*) sonoro(-a).
so·no·rous·ly ['sɒnərəslɪ] ADV (*frm*) sonoramente.
soon [suːn] ADV **a** (*before long*) presto, fra poco; **come back soon!** torna presto!; **soon afterwards** poco dopo; **it will soon be summer** presto *or* fra poco sarà estate; **you would soon get lost** ti perderesti subito; **see you soon!** a presto!; **very/quite soon** molto/abbastanza presto; **he soon changed his mind** ha cambiato presto idea

b (*early*) presto; **how soon can you be ready?** fra quanto tempo sarai pronto?; **Friday is too soon** venerdì è troppo presto; **it's too soon to tell** è troppo presto per dirlo; **all too soon** fin troppo presto; **we were none too soon** siamo arrivati appena in tempo; **an hour too soon** con un'ora di anticipo

c (*with as*): **as soon as possible** prima possibile, il più presto possibile; **I'll do it as soon as I can** lo farò appena posso; **as soon as it was finished** appena finito

d (*expressing preference*): **I would as soon not go** preferirei non andarci; **I would as soon he didn't know** preferirei che non lo sapesse.
soon·er ['suːnə] ADV **a** (*of time*) prima; **sooner or later** prima o poi; **the sooner the better** prima è meglio è; **when are you leaving? — the sooner the better** quando parti? — prima parto meglio è; **no sooner had we left than ...** eravamo appena partiti, quando...; **no sooner said than done** detto fatto

b (*of preference*): **I'd** *or* **I would sooner not do it** preferirei non farlo; **I would sooner do something useful** preferirei fare qualcosa di utile; **I'd sooner die!** (*fam*) piuttosto morirei!
soot [sʊt] N fuliggine *f*.
soothe [suːð] VT (*gen*) calmare; (*pain, anxieties*) alleviare.
sooth·ing ['suːðɪŋ] ADJ (*ointment etc*) calmante; (*tone, words etc*) rassicurante; (*bath*) rilassante.
sooth·ing·ly ['suːðɪŋlɪ] ADV (*speak*) con tono rassicurante; (*stroke, caress*) in modo rassicurante.
sooty ['sʊtɪ] ADJ (*comp* **-ier**, *superl* **-iest**) fuligginoso(-a).
SOP [,ɛsəʊ'piː] N ABBR (*Banking*)= *standard operating procedure.*
sop [sɒp] N **a** (*concession*): **that's only a sop** è soltanto un contentino; **to give sb a sop** dare il contentino a qn; **as a sop to his pride** per lusingare il suo amor proprio **b** : **sops** NPL (*food*) pappette *fpl*
► **sop up** VT + ADV (*fam*) assorbire, bere.
so·phis·ti·cat·ed [sə'fɪstɪ,keɪtɪd] ADJ (*method, machine*) sofisticato(-a); (*person*) raffinato(-a), sofisticato(-a); (*clothes, room*) raffinato(-a); (*discussion*) sottile; (*mind, film*) complicato(-a).
so·phis·ti·ca·tion [sə,fɪstɪ'keɪʃən] N (*of method, machine*) complessità; (*of person, clothes etc*) raffinatezza; (*of argument etc*) sottigliezza.
soph·ist·ry ['səʊfɪstrɪ] N (*frm*) sofisma *m*.
Sophocles ['sɒfə,kliːz] N Sofocle *m*.
sopho·more ['sɒfə,mɔː] N (*Am*) *studente del secondo anno di scuola superiore o dell'università.*

sopo·rif·ic [ˌsɒpə'rɪfɪk] ADJ soporifero(-a).

sop·ping ['sɒpɪŋ] ADJ (also: **sopping wet**) bagnato(-a) fradicio(-a).

sop·py ['sɒpɪ] ADJ (comp **-ier**, superl **-iest**) (Brit fam: sentimental) sdolcinato(-a); (: silly) sciocco(-a).

so·pra·no [sə'prɑːnəʊ] ① N (pl **sopranos**) (Mus: singer) soprano m/f; (: voice) soprano m.
② ADJ di soprano.

sor·bet ['sɔːbɪt] N sorbetto.

sor·cer·er ['sɔːsərə'] N stregone m.

sor·cer·ess ['sɔːsərɪs] N maga, fattucchiera.

sor·cery ['sɔːsərɪ] N stregoneria.

sor·did ['sɔːdɪd] ADJ (place, room etc) sordido(-a); (deal, motive etc) meschino(-a), sordido(-a).

sor·did·ly ['sɔːdɪdlɪ] ADV (see adj) sordidamente; meschinamente.

sore [sɔː'] ① ADJ (comp **-r**, superl **-st**) a (painful) dolorante; **I feel sore all over** sono tutto indolenzito; **sore throat** mal m di gola; **my eyes are sore** OR **I have sore eyes** mi fanno male gli occhi; **he's like a bear with a sore head** (fig) è molto irascibile
b (fig): **it's a sore point** è un punto delicato; **to touch on a sore point** mettere il dito sulla piaga; **to feel sore about sth** (esp Am fam) essere molto seccato(-a) per qc; **don't get sore!** (esp Am fam) non te la prendere!.
② N (Med) piaga.

sore·ly ['sɔːlɪ] ADV (tempted) fortemente; (regretted) amaramente; **it is sorely needed** ce n'è un estremo bisogno; **she is sorely missed by her family** la sua famiglia sente molto la sua mancanza; **he has been sorely tried** (frm) è stato duramente provato.

sore·ness ['sɔːnɪs] N (painfulness) indolenzimento; (irritation) irritazione f.

sor·ghum ['sɔːgəm] N sorgo comune, saggina.

sor·rel ['sɒrəl] ① N a (Bot) acetosa b (horse) sauro; (colour) giallo bruno inv.
② ADJ (colour) giallo bruno inv.

sor·row ['sɒrəʊ] ① N dolore m; **her sorrow at the death of her son** il suo dolore per la morte del figlio; **more in sorrow than in anger** più con dolore che con rabbia.
② VI: **to sorrow over sth** (liter) addolorarsi per qc.

sor·row·ful ['sɒrəʊfʊl] ADJ addolorato(-a), triste.

sor·row·ful·ly ['sɒrəʊfəlɪ] ADV tristemente, con aria triste or desolata.

sor·row·ing ['sɒrəʊɪŋ] ADJ (liter) addolorato(-a), afflitto(-a).

sor·ry ['sɒrɪ] ADJ (comp **-ier**, superl **-iest**) a (in apologizing): **sorry!** scusa! (or scusi! or scusate!); **awfully sorry!** OR **so sorry!** OR **very sorry!** (more polite) scusa (or scusi or scusate) tanto!; **to be sorry** essere spiacente or desolato (-a); **to say sorry (to sb for sth)** chiedere scusa (a qn per qc); **to be sorry about sth** essere dispiaciuto(-a) or spiacente di qc; **I'm sorry about what happened last night** scusami per quello che è successo ieri sera; **I'm sorry, but you're wrong** scusa ma hai torto; **to be sorry to have to do sth** essere spiacente di dover fare qc
b (Brit: what did you say?): **sorry?** come, scusa?
c (regretful, sad) triste, addolorato(-a), desolato(-a); **I'm sorry to hear that** ... mi dispiace (sapere) che...; **I'm sorry to tell you that** ... mi dispiace dirti che...; **it was a failure, I'm sorry to say** purtroppo è stato un fiasco; **I can't say I'm sorry** non posso dire che mi dispiaccia; **you'll be sorry for this!** te ne pentirai!
d (pitying): **to be** or **feel sorry for sb** dispiacersi per qn; **to be** or **feel sorry for o.s.** compiangersi, piangersi

addosso
e (condition, tale) pietoso(-a); (sight, failure) triste; (excuse) misero(-a); **in a sorry state** in uno stato pietoso.

sort [sɔːt] ① N a (gen) specie f inv, genere m, tipo; (make: of coffee, car etc) tipo; **what sort do you want?** che tipo vuole?; **I know his sort** conosco il suo tipo; **books of all sorts** libri di ogni genere; **he's a painter of sorts** è, per così dire, un pittore; **of the worst sort** della peggior specie; **something of the sort** qualcosa del genere; **it's tea of a sort** è una specie di tè; **I'll do nothing of the sort!** nemmeno per sogno!; **behaviour of that sort** comportamento del genere; **it takes all sorts (to make a world)** il mondo è bello perché è vario
b : **sort of: what sort of car?** che tipo di macchina?; **what sort of man is he?** che tipo di uomo è?; **it's my sort of film** è il tipo di film che piace a me; **he's not the sort of man to say that** non è il tipo da dire cose del genere; **all sorts of dogs** cani di ogni tipo; **he's some sort of painter** è una specie di pittore; **it's a sort of dance** è una specie di danza; **and all that sort of thing** e così via; **what sort of an answer is that?** che razza di risposta è questa?; **that's the sort of person I am** io sono fatto così; **you know the sort of thing I mean** sai cosa voglio dire; **it's sort of awkward** (fam) è piuttosto difficile; **it's sort of yellow** (fam) è giallastro; **aren't you pleased? — sort of** (fam) non sei contento? — insomma; **I sort of thought that would happen** (fam) quasi me lo sentivo che sarebbe successo
c (person): **he's a good sort** è una brava persona; **he's not my sort** non è il mio tipo; **he's an odd sort** è un tipo strano
d : **to be out of sorts** (in a bad temper) avere la luna (storta or di traverso), non essere in vena; (unwell) non essere in forma.
② VT a (classify: documents, stamps) classificare; (put in order: papers, clothes) mettere in ordine; (: letters) smistare; (separate) separare, dividere
b (Comput) ordinare
▶ **sort out** VT + ADV a = **sort 2a**
b (straighten out: room) riordinare, sistemare; (: papers, one's ideas) riordinare; (solve: problem etc) risolvere; **have you managed to sort out what's happening?** sei riuscito a sapere cosa succede?; **things will sort themselves out** le cose si sistemeranno da sole; **we've got it sorted out now** la faccenda è risolta
c : **I'll sort him out!** (fam) lo sistemo io!

sor·tie ['sɔːtɪ] N (Aer, Mil) sortita.

sort·ing of·fice ['sɔːtɪŋˌɒfɪs] N (Post) ufficio di smistamento.

SOS [ˌɛsəʊ'ɛs] N S.O.S. m inv.

♦ **so-so** ['səʊsəʊ] ADJ, ADV (fam) così così.

sot [sɒt] N (old) ubriacone(-a).

souf·flé ['suːfleɪ] N soufflé m inv; **cheese soufflé** soufflé di formaggio.

♦ **soufflé dish** N stampo per soufflé.

sought [sɔːt] PT, PP of seek.

♦ **sought-after** ['sɔːtˌɑːftə'] ADJ richiesto(-a).

soul [səʊl] N a anima; **with all one's soul** con tutta l'anima; **All Souls' Day** il giorno dei morti; **God rest his soul** pace all'anima sua; **he's the soul of discretion** è la discrezione in persona
b (person) anima; **the ship sank with all souls** la nave affondò con tutti a bordo; **I didn't see a soul** non ho visto anima viva; **the poor soul had nowhere to sleep** il

poveraccio non aveva dove dormire

c (*also:* **soul music**) soul *m*.

♦ **soul-destroying** [ˈsəʊldɪˈstrɔɪŋ] ADJ (*fig: boring*) alienante; (: *depressing*) demoralizzante.

soul·ful [ˈsəʊlfʊl] ADJ (*gen*) pieno(-a) di sentimento; (*eyes, expression*) espressivo(-a).

soul·ful·ly [ˈsəʊlfəlɪ] ADV (*gaze*) in modo meditabondo.

soul·less [ˈsəʊllɪs] ADJ (*task, factory*) alienante; (*person*) senza cuore, crudele.

♦ **soul mate** N anima gemella.

♦ **soul-searching** [ˈsəʊlˌsɜːtʃɪŋ] N: **after much soul-searching** dopo un profondo esame di coscienza.

sound[1] [saʊnd] [1] N (*gen*) suono; (*of sea, breaking glass etc*) rumore *m*; (*volume of TV*) audio; **the speed of sound** la velocità del suono; **to the sound of the national anthem** al suono dell'inno nazionale; **not a sound was to be heard** non si sentiva volare una mosca; **a language with many consonant sounds** una lingua piena di consonanti; **I don't like the sound of it** (*fig: of film etc*) non mi dice niente; (: *of news*) è preoccupante.

[2] VT **a** (*alarm, bell, horn*) suonare; **to sound the retreat** (*Mil*) suonare la ritirata; **to sound a note of warning** (*fig*) dare un segnale d'allarme

b : **sound your "r"s more** pronuncia la r più chiaramente

c (*Med*): **to sound sb's chest** auscultare il torace di qn.

[3] VI **a** (*trumpet, bell, alarm*) suonare; (*voice, siren*) risuonare; **a cannon sounded a long way off** si sentì un colpo di cannone in lontananza

b : **it sounds hollow** dal rumore sembra vuoto; **he sounds Italian to me** da come parla mi sembra italiano; **it sounds like French** (*similar*) somiglia al francese; **it sounds better like that** suona meglio così; **that sounds like them arriving now** mi sembra di sentirli arrivare; **you sound like your mother** mi sembra di sentire parlare tua madre; **he sounded angry** (a giudicare) dalla voce sembrava arrabbiato

c (*seem*): **that sounds very odd** sembra molto strano; **how does it sound to you?** che te ne pare?; **that sounds like a good idea** sembra una buona idea; **she sounds like a nice girl** sembra una brava ragazza; **it sounds as if she won't be coming** ho l'impressione che non verrà

▶ **sound off** VI + ADV (*fam*): **to sound off (about)** (*give one's opinions*) fare dei grandi discorsi (su); (*boast*) vantarsi (di); (*grumble*) brontolare (per)

▶ **sound out** VT + ADV sondare.

sound[2] [saʊnd] [1] ADJ (*comp* **-er**, *superl* **-est**) **a** (*in good condition, healthy*) sano(-a); (: *structure, organization, investment*) solido(-a); **to be of sound mind** essere sano(-a) di mente; **as sound as a bell** (*person*) sano(-a) come un pesce; (*thing*) in perfette condizioni

b (*valid: argument, policy*) valido(-a); (: *move*) sensato (-a); (*dependable: person*) affidabile; **a sound conservative** un conservatore convinto; **he's sound on government policy** conosce molto bene la politica del governo

c (*thorough*): **to give sb a sound beating** picchiare qn di santa ragione

d (*sleep: deep, untroubled*) profondo(-a); **he's a sound sleeper** è uno che dorme sodo.

[2] ADV: **to be sound asleep** dormire sodo, dormire profondamente.

sound[3] [saʊnd] VT (*Naut*) scandagliare, sondare; **to sound sb out about sth** sondare le opinioni di qn su qc.

sound[4] [saʊnd] N (*Geog*) stretto.

♦ **sound archives** NPL (*Radio*) fonoteca.

♦ **sound barrier** N: **the sound barrier** la barriera *or* il muro del suono.

sound·bite [ˈsaʊndˌbaɪt] N frase *f* incisiva (*trasmessa per radio o per TV*).

♦ **sound effects** NPL effetti *mpl* sonori.

♦ **sound engineer** N tecnico del suono.

sound·ing [ˈsaʊndɪŋ] N (*Naut*) scandagliamento.

♦ **sounding board** N (*Mus*) tavola armonica; (*fig*) banco di prova.

sound·less [ˈsaʊndlɪs] ADJ silenzioso(-a).

sound·less·ly [ˈsaʊndlɪslɪ] ADV (*move etc*) silenziosamente.

sound·ly [ˈsaʊndlɪ] ADV (*build*) solidamente; (*argue*) giudiziosamente; (*invest*) saggiamente; **to beat sb soundly** (*thrash*) picchiare qn di santa ragione; (*defeat*) battere duramente qn; **to sleep soundly** dormire profondamente.

sound·ness [ˈsaʊndnɪs] N (*of body, mind*) sanità; (*of argument, judgment*) validità; (*of business, building*) solidità; (*solvency*) solvibilità.

sound·proof [ˈsaʊndˌpruːf] [1] ADJ insonorizzato(-a). [2] VT insonorizzare.

sound·proof·ed [ˈsaʊndˌpruːft] ADJ insonorizzato(-a).

sound·proofing [ˈsaʊndˌpruːfɪŋ] N insonorizzazione *f*.

♦ **sound system** N impianto *m* audio *inv*.

sound·track [ˈsaʊndˌtræk] N (*music*) colonna sonora; (*speech, noises*) sonoro.

♦ **sound wave** N (*Phys*) onda sonora.

soup [suːp] N minestra; (*thick*) zuppa; (*clear*) brodo; **vegetable soup** minestra di verdura; **to be in the soup** (*fam*) essere *or* trovarsi nei pasticci.

soup·çon [ˈsuːpsɒn] N (*frm, hum*) ombra.

♦ **soup course** N minestra.

souped-up [ˈsuːptˌʌp] ADJ (*fam: car/motorbike engine*) truccato(-a).

♦ **soup kitchen** N mensa dei poveri.

♦ **soup plate** N piatto fondo.

♦ **soup spoon** N cucchiaio da minestra.

♦ **soup tureen** N zuppiera.

soupy [ˈsuːpɪ] ADJ (*comp* **-ier**, *superl* **-iest**) **a** (*liquid, fog*) denso(-a) **b** (*Am fam: sentimental*) sdolcinato(-a).

sour [ˈsaʊə] ADJ (*comp* **-er**, *superl* **-est**) (*gen*) aspro(-a), agro(-a); (*milk, fig: person, remark*) acido(-a); (*smell*) acre; **whisky sour** cocktail di whisky al limone; **to go** *or* **turn sour** (*milk, wine*) inacidirsi; (*fig: relationship, plans*) guastarsi; **it was sour grapes on his part** (*fig*) ha fatto come la volpe con l'uva, è stata solo invidia da parte sua; **to be in a sour mood** (*fig*) essere di umore nero.

source [sɔːs] N (*of river*) sorgente *f*; (*fig: of problem, epidemic*) fonte *f*, origine *f*; **oranges are a source of vitamin C** le arance sono ricche di vitamina C; **I have it from a reliable source that** ... ho saputo da fonte sicura che... .

♦ **source language** N (*Ling*) lingua di partenza; (*Comput*) linguaggio di programmazione *or* assoluto.

♦ **sour cherry** N visciola.

♦ **sour(ed) cream** [ˈsaʊə(d)ˈkriːm] N (*Culin*) panna acida.

♦ **sour-faced** [ˈsaʊəˌfeɪsd] ADJ (*person*) dal viso arcigno.

sourly [ˈsaʊəlɪ] ADV (*remark, look*) aspramente.

sour·ness [ˈsaʊənɪs] N (*see adj*) asprezza; acidità; acredine *f*.

souse [saʊs] VT (*Culin: pickle*) marinare; (*plunge*) immergere; (*soak*) ammollare; **soused fish** (*Culin*) pesce *m* in

carpione; **to souse sth with water** inzuppare qc d'acqua.

south [saʊθ] [1] N sud *m*, meridione *m*, mezzogiorno; **(to the) south of** a sud di; **in the south of** nel sud di; **the wind is from the south** il vento soffia da sud *or* da mezzogiorno; **to veer to the south** (*wind*) girare verso sud; **the South of France** il sud della Francia, la Francia del sud *or* meridionale.

[2] ADJ (*gen*) sud *inv*; (*coast*) meridionale; (*wind*) del sud.

[3] ADV verso sud; **south of the border** a sud del confine; **to sail due south** andare direttamente verso sud; **to travel south** viaggiare verso sud; **this house faces south** questa casa è esposta a sud *or* a mezzogiorno.

♦ **South Africa** N il Sudafrica.

♦ **South African** ADJ, N sudafricano(-a).

♦ **South America** N il Sudamerica, l'America del sud.

♦ **South American** ADJ, N sudamericano(-a).

south·bound ['saʊθ,baʊnd] ADJ (*gen*) diretto(-a) a sud; (*carriageway*) sud *inv*.

♦ **south-east** [,saʊθ'i:st] [1] N sud-est *m*.

[2] ADJ (*wind*) di sud-est; (*counties etc*) sudorientale.

[3] ADV verso sud-est.

♦ **South-East Asia** N l'Asia sudorientale.

♦ **south-easterly** [,saʊθ'i:stəlɪ] ADJ (*wind*) che viene da sud-est; (*direction*) verso sud-est.

♦ **south-eastern** [,saʊθ'i:stən] ADJ di sudest, sudorientale.

south·er·ly ['sʌðəlɪ] ADJ (*wind*) del sud; (*direction*) verso sud; **house with a southerly aspect** casa esposta a sud.

south·ern ['sʌðən] ADJ (*region*) del sud, meridionale; (*coast*) meridionale; (*wall*) esposto(-a) a sud; **Southern Europe** l'Europa del sud *or* meridionale; **in southern Spain** nella Spagna del sud *or* meridionale, nel sud della Spagna.

south·ern·er ['sʌðənə'] N abitante *m/f* del sud.

♦ **southern hemisphere** N: **the southern hemisphere** l'emisfero australe.

south·ern·most ['sʌðən,məʊst] ADJ il/la più a sud.

♦ **South Pole** N: **the South Pole** il polo sud.

♦ **South Sea Islands** NPL: **the South Sea Islands** le isole dei Mari del Sud.

♦ **South Seas** NPL: **the South Seas** i Mari del Sud.

♦ **south-south-east** ['saʊθ,saʊθ'i:st] [1] N sud sud-est *m*.

[2] ADJ di sud sud-est.

[3] ADV verso sud sud-est.

♦ **south-south-west** ['saʊθ,saʊθ'wɛst] [1] N sud sud-ovest *m*.

[2] ADJ di sud sud-ovest.

[3] ADV verso sud sud-ovest.

♦ **South Vietnam** N Vietnam *m* del Sud.

south·ward(s) ['saʊθwəd(z)] [1] ADV verso sud.

[2] ADJ a sud.

♦ **south-west** [,saʊθ'wɛst] [1] N sud-ovest *m*.

[2] ADJ di sud-ovest.

[3] ADV verso sud-ovest.

♦ **south-westerly** [,saʊθ'wɛstəlɪ] ADJ (*wind*) che viene da sud-ovest; (*direction*) verso sud-ovest.

♦ **south-western** [,saʊθ'wɛstən] ADJ di sud-ovest.

sou·venir [,su:və'nɪə'] N souvenir *m inv*, ricordo.

sou·west·er [saʊ'wɛstə'] N cappello di cerata.

sov·er·eign ['sɒvrɪn] [1] ADJ (*gen*) sovrano(-a); **with sovereign contempt** (*fig*) con sommo disprezzo; **a sovereign remedy** (*old*) un rimedio infallibile.

[2] N (*monarch*) sovrano(-a); (*coin*) sovrana.

sov·er·eign·ty ['sɒvrəntɪ] N sovranità.

so·vi·et ['səʊvɪət] [1] N soviet *m inv*.

[2] ADJ sovietico(-a); **Soviet Russia** Russia Sovietica.

♦ **Soviet Union** N: **the Soviet Union** l'Unione *f* Sovietica.

sow[1] [səʊ] (*pt* **sowed**, *pp* **sown**) VT seminare; **to sow (the seeds of) doubt in sb's mind** far sorgere dei dubbi a qn; **to sow (the seeds of) discord** seminare zizzania.

sow[2] [saʊ] N scrofa.

sow·er ['səʊə'] N (*person*) seminatore(-trice); (*machine*) seminatrice *f*.

sow·ing ['səʊɪŋ] N semina.

sown [səʊn] PP of **sow** 1.

soya ['sɔɪə], (*Am*) **soy** [sɔɪ] N soia.

♦ **soya bean**, (*Am*) **soy bean** N seme *m* di soia.

♦ **soy(a) flour** N farina di soia.

soy sauce N salsa di soia.

soz·zled ['sɒzld] ADJ (*Brit fam*) sbronzo(-a); **to get sozzled** sbronzarsi.

spa [spɑ:] N (*resort*) stazione *f* termale, terme *fpl*; (*Am: also:* **health spa**) centro di cure estetiche.

space [speɪs] [1] N (*all senses*) spazio; **to stare into space** guardare nel vuoto; **to clear a space for sth** fare posto per qc; **to take up a lot of space** occupare molto spazio, ingombrare; **to buy space in a newspaper** comprare spazio pubblicitario su un giornale; **blank space** spazio in bianco; **answer in the space provided** scrivere le risposte negli appositi spazi; **in a confined space** in un luogo chiuso; **I couldn't find a space for my car** non sono riuscito a trovare un posto per la macchina; **in a short space of time** in un breve lasso di tempo; **(with)in the space of an hour/three generations** nell'arco di un'ora/di tre generazioni; **for the space of a fortnight** per un periodo di due settimane; **after a space of two hours** dopo un intervallo di due ore.

[2] VT (*also:* **space out**: *gen*) distanziare; (: *payments*) scaglionare, dilazionare; (: *type*) spaziare.

[3] ADJ (*research, capsule, probe etc*) spaziale.

♦ **space-age** ['speɪs,eɪdʒ] ADJ dell'era spaziale.

♦ **space age** N era spaziale.

♦ **space-bar** ['speɪs,bɑ:'] N (*on typewriter, computer*) barra spaziatrice.

space·craft ['speɪs,krɑ:ft] N, PL INV veicolo spaziale.

space·man ['speɪsmən] N (*pl* **-men**) astronauta *m*, cosmonauta *m*.

♦ **space-saving** ['speɪs,seɪvɪŋ] ADJ poco ingombrante.

space·ship ['speɪ,ʃɪp] N astronave *f*, navicella spaziale.

♦ **space shuttle** N *m inv*.

♦ **space station** N laboratorio spaziale.

space·suit ['speɪs,su:t] N tuta spaziale.

space·walk ['speɪs,wɔːk] N passeggiata spaziale.

space·woman ['speɪs,wʊmən] N (*pl* **-women**) astronauta *f*, cosmonauta *f*.

spac·ing ['speɪsɪŋ] N (*Typing etc*) spaziatura; **single/double spacing** spaziatura uno/due, spaziatura singola/doppia.

spa·cious ['speɪʃəs] ADJ spazioso(-a).

spa·cious·ness ['speɪʃəsnɪs] N spaziosità.

spade [speɪd] N **a** (*tool*) vanga; (*child's*) paletta; **to call a spade a spade** (*fig*) dire pane al pane (e vino al vino) **b** (*Cards*): **spades** NPL picche *fpl*; **the three of spades** il tre di picche; **to play spades** giocare picche; **to play a spade** giocare una carta di picche.

spade·ful ['speɪdfʊl] N vangata.

spade·work ['speɪd,wɜːk] N (*fig*) il grosso dei preparativi.

spa·ghet·ti [spə'gɛtɪ] N spaghetti *mpl*.

♦ **spaghetti western** N (*Cine*) western *m inv* all'italiana.

Spain [speɪn] N la Spagna.

span[1] [spæn] ①N (*of hand*) spanna; (*of bridge, arch, roof*) luce *f*, campata; (*of time*) periodo; **a short attention span** una limitata capacità di concentrazione.

②VT (*subj: bridge etc*) attraversare; **to span 3 decades** abbracciare un periodo di 30 anni; **his memory spanned 50 years** i suoi ricordi risalivano a 50 anni fa.

span[2] [spæn] PT of **spin**.

span·gle ['spæŋgl] ①VT far brillare.
②N paillette *f inv*.

Span·iard ['spænjəd] N spagnolo(-a).

span·iel ['spænjəl] N spaniel *m inv*.

Span·ish ['spænɪʃ] ①ADJ (*gen*) spagnolo(-a); (*teacher, lesson, book*) di spagnolo; **Spanish America** America latina.

②N a (*language*) spagnolo b : **the Spanish** NPL (*people*) gli Spagnoli.

♦ **Spanish omelette** N *frittata di patate*.

♦ **Spanish onion** N cipolla di Spagna.

spank [spæŋk] VT sculacciare.

spank·ing ['spæŋkɪŋ] ①N sculacciata.

②ADJ a (*breeze*) frizzante; (*pace*) svelto(-a) b (*fam: very*): **a spanking new car** una macchina nuova di zecca.

spanner ['spænə'] N (*Brit*) chiave *f* inglese; **adjustable spanner** chiave *f* a rullino; **to throw a spanner in the works** (*fig*) mettere il bastone tra le ruote.

spar[1] [spɑː'] N (*Naut*) asta, palo.

spar[2] [spɑː'] VI: **to spar with sb** (*Boxing*) allenarsi (con qn); (*argue*) discutere (con qn).

spare [spɛə'] ①ADJ a (*surplus*) in più, d'avanzo; (*reserve*) di riserva, di scorta; **I haven't enough spare cash to go on holiday** non mi avanzano soldi per andare in vacanza; **is there any string spare?** c'è rimasto un po' di spago?; **there are two going spare** (*Brit*) ce ne sono due in più; **to go spare** (*fam*) andare su tutte le furie
b (*person: lean*) asciutto(-a); **she's tall and spare** è alta e asciutta.

②N (*part*) pezzo di ricambio.

③VT a (*be grudging with*): **she spared no effort** *or* **pains in helping me** ha fatto tutto il possibile per aiutarmi; **to spare no expense** non badare a spese
b (*do without*) fare a meno di; **can you spare this for a moment?** puoi prestarmelo per un attimo?; **if you can spare it** se puoi farne a meno; **can you spare the time?** hai tempo?; **to spare a thought for** pensare a; **can you spare (me) £10?** puoi prestarmi 10 sterline?; **there is none to spare** ce n'è appena a sufficienza; **I've a few minutes to spare** ho un attimino di tempo; **I got to the station with 3 minutes to spare** sono arrivato alla stazione con 3 minuti di anticipo; **I had £1 to spare** mi avanzava 1 sterlina; **there is no time to spare** non c'è tempo da perdere
c (*refrain from hurting, using*) risparmiare; **to spare sb's feelings** avere riguardo per i sentimenti di qn; **she doesn't spare herself** non si risparmia
d (*save from need or trouble*): **to spare sb the trouble of doing sth** risparmiare a qn la fatica di fare qc; **spare me the details** risparmiami i particolari.

♦ **spare part** N pezzo di ricambio.

spare·rib ['spɛə.rɪb] N (*Culin*) costina di maiale.

♦ **spare room** N stanza degli ospiti.

♦ **spare time** N tempo libero.

♦ **spare tyre** N (*Aut*) gomma di scorta.

♦ **spare wheel** N (*Aut*) ruota di scorta.

spar·ing ['spɛərɪŋ] ADJ (*amount, use*) moderato(-a); **to be sparing of praise** essere avaro(-a) di lodi; **to be sparing with** essere parsimonioso(-a) con.

spar·ing·ly ['spɛərɪŋlɪ] ADV (*eat, live*) frugalmente; (*use, drink*) con moderazione, moderatamente.

spark [spɑːk] ①N (*from fire*) scintilla; (*fig*): **there wasn't a spark of life in the battery** la batteria non dava segni di vita; **he didn't show a spark of interest** non ha mostrato il benché minimo interesse; **bright spark** (*irə*) genio.

②VT (*also: spark off: debate, quarrel, revolt*) provocare; (: *interest*) suscitare.

spar·kle ['spɑːkl] ①N (*gen*) scintillio, sfavillio; (*fig: of person, conversation*) brio.

②VI (*flash, shine*) scintillare, sfavillare, luccicare; (: *eyes*) brillare, luccicare; (: *person, conversation*) brillare; (*wine*) frizzare, spumeggiare.

spar·kler ['spɑːklə'] N a bengala *m inv*, fuoco d'artificio
b (*fam: diamond*) brillante *m*.

spar·kling ['spɑːklɪŋ] ADJ (*gen*) scintillante, sfavillante; (*person, conversation*) brillante; (*wine*) frizzante.

♦ **spark plug**, **sparking plug** ['spɑːkɪŋ.plʌg] N (*Aut*) candela.

spar·ring match ['spɑːrɪŋ'mætʃ] N disputa amichevole.

spar·ring part·ner ['spɑːrɪŋ'pɑːtnə'] N sparring partner *m inv*; (*fig*) *interlocutore abituale in discussioni, dibattiti, tavole rotonde ecc.*

spar·row ['spærəu] N passero.

sparrow·hawk ['spærəu.hɔːk] N sparviero.

sparse [spɑːs] ADJ (*comp* **-r**, *superl* **-st**) (*vegetation, hair*) rado(-a); (*population*) scarso(-a).

sparse·ly ['spɑːslɪ] ADV poco, scarsamente.

Spar·ta ['spɑːtə] N Sparta.

Spar·tan, **spar·tan** ['spɑːtən] ADJ, N (*also fig*) spartano (-a).

spasm ['spæzəm] N (*Med*) spasmo; (*of coughing*) attacco, accesso; (*fig*) accesso; **there was a brief spasm of activity** c'è stato un momento di attività spasmodica.

spas·mod·ic [spæz'mɒdɪk] ADJ (*Med*) spasmodico(-a); (*fig: growth*) irregolare; **she made spasmodic attempts to give up smoking** ha tentato più volte di smettere di fumare.

spas·modi·cal·ly [spæz'mɒdɪkəlɪ] ADV (*fig: grow*) irregolarmente; (: *attempt, work*) in modo discontinuo.

spas·tic ['spæstɪk] ADJ, N (*offensive*) spastico(-a).

spat[1] [spæt] PT, PP of **spit**.

spat[2] [spæt] N (*Am*) battibecco.

spate [speɪt] N (*of letters, orders*) valanga; (*of words, abuse*) torrente *m*; (*of accidents*) gran numero; **to be in spate** (*river*) essere in piena.

spa·tial ['speɪʃəl] ADJ spaziale.

spat·ter ['spætə'] VT: **to spatter (with)** schizzare (di); **spattered with mud** inzaccherato(-a).

spatu·la ['spætjulə] N spatola.

spawn [spɔːn] ①N (*of fish, frogs*) uova *fpl*.
②VI deporre le uova.
③VT (*pej*) produrre.

spay [speɪ] VT sterilizzare.

speak [spiːk] (*vb: pt* **spoke**, *pp* **spoken**) ①VT (*words, lines*) dire; (*language*) parlare; **she speaks Italian** parla italiano; **to speak the truth** dire la verità; **to speak one's mind** dire quello che si pensa.

②VI a (*gen*) parlare; **to speak to sb** parlare a qn; (*converse with*) parlare con qn; **to speak about** (*or on or of*) **sth** parlare di qc; **to speak in a whisper** bisbigliare; **they haven't spoken to each other since they quarrelled**

da quando hanno litigato non si rivolgono la parola; **I'll speak to him about it** (*problem, idea*) gliene parlerò; (*his lateness etc*) glielo farò presente; **to speak at a conference/in a debate** intervenire *or* prendere la parola ad una conferenza/in un dibattito; **he's very well spoken of** tutti ne parlano bene; **I don't know him to speak to** lo conosco solo di vista; **so to speak** per così dire; **it's nothing to speak of** non è niente di speciale; **he has no money to speak of** non si può proprio dire che sia ricco; **speaking of holidays** a proposito di vacanze; **roughly speaking** grosso modo; **speaking for myself** per quel che mi riguarda; **speaking as a student myself, I ...** in qualità di studente, io...; **generally speaking** generalmente parlando

b (*Telec*): **speaking!** sono io!; **this is Peter speaking** sono Peter; **who's speaking?** chi parla?

▶ **speak for** VI + PREP: **to speak for sb** parlare a nome di qn; **speak for yourself!** (*fam*) parla per te!; **let her speak for herself** lascia che dica la sua opinione; **it speaks for itself** parla da sé; **that picture is already spoken for** (*in shop*) quel quadro è già stato venduto

▶ **speak up** VI + ADV

a (*raise voice*) parlare a voce alta; **speak up!** parli più forte!

b (*fig: also:* **speak out**) parlare apertamente; **to speak out against sth** dichiararsi pubblicamente contrario (-a) a qc; **to speak up for sb** parlare a favore di qn.

Speak·er ['spiːkəʳ] N (*Brit Parliament*): **the Speaker** ≈ il presidente della Camera dei deputati.

speak·er ['spiːkəʳ] N **a** (*gen*) chi parla; (*in discussion*) interlocutore(-trice); (*in public*) oratore(-trice); **he's a good/poor speaker** è un buon/pessimo oratore **b** (*of language*): **are you a Welsh speaker?** parla gallese? **c** (*also:* **loudspeaker**) altoparlante *m*.

speak·ing ['spiːkɪŋ] **1** ADJ parlante; **Italian-speaking people** persone che parlano italiano; **I am not on speaking terms with her** la conosco solo di vista; **they are not on speaking terms** (*after quarrel*) non si rivolgono la parola.

2 N (*skill*) arte *f* del parlare.

spear [spɪəʳ] N lancia.

spear·head ['spɪəˌhɛd] **1** N punta di lancia; (*Mil*) reparto d'assalto; (*fig*) avanguardie *mpl*.

2 VT (*attack etc*) condurre.

spear·mint ['spɪəmɪnt] N (*Bot etc*) menta verde.

spec [spɛk] N (*Brit fam*): **to buy sth on spec** comprare qc sperando di fare un affare; **I went to the theatre on spec** sono andato al teatro nella speranza di trovare un biglietto.

spe·cial ['spɛʃəl] **1** ADJ **a** (*specific*) particolare, speciale; **have you any special date in mind?** hai in mente una data particolare?; **I've no-one special in mind** non penso a nessuno in particolare

b (*exceptional: price, favour, legislation*) speciale; (*: powers*) straordinario(-a); (*particular: care, situation, attention*) particolare; **take special care!** siate particolarmente prudenti!; **to make a special effort** fare del proprio meglio; **this is a special day for me** è una giornata speciale per me; **you're extra special** (*fam*) sei veramente speciale; **to expect special treatment** aspettarsi un trattamento speciale; **nothing special** niente di speciale; **what's so special about her?** che cosa ha di tanto speciale?.

2 N (*train*) treno straordinario; (*newspaper*) edizione *f* straordinaria; **the chef's special** la specialità dello chef.

♦ **special agent** N agente *m* segreto.

♦ **Special Branch** N *servizi segreti in Gran Bretagna*.

♦ **special correspondent** N (*Press*) inviato speciale.

♦ **special delivery** N (*Post*): **by special delivery** per espresso.

♦ **special effects** NPL (*Cine*) effetti *mpl* speciali.

♦ **special feature** N (*Press*) servizio speciale.

spe·cial·ism ['spɛʃəlɪzəm] N (*subject, skill*) specialità *f inv*; (*specialization*) specializzazione *f*.

spe·cial·ist ['spɛʃəlɪst] **1** N specialista *m/f*; **a heart specialist** (*Med*) un cardiologo.

2 ADJ (*teacher*) specializzato(-a); (*dictionary*) specialistico(-a); (*knowledge, work*) da specialista.

spe·ci·al·ity [ˌspɛʃɪˈælɪtɪ], (*Am*) **spe·cial·ty** ['spɛʃəltɪ] N specialità *f inv*; **to make a speciality of sth** specializzarsi in qc.

spe·ciali·za·tion [ˌspɛʃəlaɪˈzeɪʃən] N specializzazione *f*.

spe·cial·ize ['spɛʃəˌlaɪz] VI: **to specialize (in)** specializzarsi (in).

spe·cial·ized ['spɛʃəˌlaɪzd] ADJ (*work*) specialistico(-a); (*staff, worker*) specializzato(-a).

spe·cial·ly ['spɛʃəlɪ] ADV (*specifically*) specialmente; (*on purpose*) apposta; (*particularly*) particolarmente.

♦ **special offer** N (*Comm*) offerta speciale.

spe·cial·ty ['spɛʃəltɪ] N (*Am*) = **speciality**.

spe·cies ['spiːʃiːz] N, PL INV specie *f inv*.

spe·cif·ic [spəˈsɪfɪk] ADJ **a** (*example, order etc*) preciso(-a); (*meaning*) specifico(-a); **he was very specific about that** è stato molto chiaro in proposito; **to be specific** to avere un legame specifico con **b** (*Bio, Phys, Chem, Med*) specifico(-a); see also **specifics**.

spe·cifi·cal·ly [spəˈsɪfɪkəlɪ] ADV (*explicitly: state, warn*) chiaramente, esplicitamente; (*especially: design, intend*) appositamente.

speci·fi·ca·tion [ˌspɛsɪfɪˈkeɪən] N **a** (*gen*) specificazione *f* **b** : **specifications** (*of car, machine*) dati *mpl* caratteristici; (*for building*) dettagli *mpl*; **the parts do not meet our specification** i pezzi non sono conformi alle nostre specifiche.

♦ **specific gravity** N (*Phys*) peso specifico.

spec·if·ics [spəˈsɪfɪks] NPL: **the specifics** i dettagli, i particolari.

speci·fy ['spɛsɪˌfaɪ] VT specificare, precisare; **unless otherwise specified** salvo indicazioni contrarie.

speci·men ['spɛsɪmɪn] N (*sample: gen*) campione *m*; (*: of rock, species*) esemplare *m*; **he's an odd specimen** (*fig*) è un tipo strano.

♦ **specimen page** N (*Typ*) prova di stampa.

♦ **specimen signature** N firma depositata.

spe·cious ['spiːʃəs] ADJ (*frm*) specioso(-a).

speck [spɛk] N (*of dust, dirt*) granello; (*of ink, paint etc*) macchiolina, puntino; **it was just a speck on the horizon** era solo un puntino all'orizzonte.

speck·led ['spɛkld] ADJ maculato(-a).

specs [spɛks] NPL (*fam*) occhiali *mpl*.

spec·ta·cle ['spɛktəkl] N spettacolo; **to make a spectacle of o.s.** (*fig*) coprirsi di ridicolo; see also **spectacles**.

♦ **spectacle case** N (*Brit*) custodia degli occhiali.

spec·ta·cles ['spɛktəklz] NPL (*Brit*) occhiali *mpl*.

spec·tacu·lar [spɛkˈtækjʊləʳ] **1** ADJ (*gen*) spettacolare; (*view*) favoloso(-a).

2 N (*Cine, TV*) kolossal *m*, film *m inv etc* spettacolare.

spec·tacu·lar·ly [spɛkˈtækjʊləlɪ] ADV in modo spettacolare.

spec·ta·tor [spɛkˈteɪtəʳ] N spettatore(-trice).

◆ **spectator sport** N sport *m inv* come spettacolo *inv*; **football is Britain's most popular spectator sport** in Gran Bretagna il calcio è lo sport più seguito dal pubblico.

spec·tra ['spɛktrə] NPL of **spectrum**.

spec·tral ['spɛktrəl] ADJ (*liter: ghostly*) spettrale.

spec·tre, (*Am*) **spec·ter** ['spɛktəʳ] N spettro.

spec·trum ['spɛktrəm] N (*pl* **spectra**) (*Phys*) spettro; (*fig*) gamma.

specu·late ['spɛkjʊˌleɪt] [1] VI (*Fin*) speculare; (*wonder*): **to speculate (about or on sth/whether)** chiedersi (qc/se); **I can only speculate** posso solo fare congetture. [2] VT: **to speculate that ...** ipotizzare che... .

specu·la·tion [ˌspɛkjʊˈleɪʃən] N (*guessing*) congetture *fpl*; (*Fin*) speculazione *f*.

specu·la·tive ['spɛkjʊlətɪv] ADJ (*Philosophy, Fin*) speculativo(-a); (*expression*) indagatore(-trice).

specu·la·tor ['spɛkjʊˌleɪtəʳ] N (*Fin*) speculatore(-trice).

sped [spɛd] PT, PP of **speed**.

speech [spiːtʃ] N **a** (*faculty*) parola; (*manner of speaking*) parlata, modo di parlare; **to lose the power of speech** perdere l'uso della parola; **freedom of speech** libertà di parola **b** (*language*) linguaggio; **children's speech** il linguaggio dei bambini **c** (*formal talk*) discorso, intervento; **to make a speech** fare un discorso **d** (*Brit Gram*): **direct/indirect speech** discorso diretto/indiretto.

◆ **speech day** N (*Brit Scol*) giorno della premiazione.

speechi·fy ['spiːtʃɪˌfaɪ] VI (*pej*): **to speechify (about)** sproloquiare (su).

◆ **speech impediment** N difetto di pronuncia.

speech·less ['spiːtʃlɪs] ADJ senza parole, ammutolito(-a).

speech·less·ly ['spiːtʃlɪslɪ] ADV: **I watched speechlessly** rimasi a guardare senza riuscire a proferire parola.

speech·mak·ing ['spiːtʃˌmeɪkɪŋ] N (*slightly pej*) discorsi *mpl* d'occasione.

◆ **speech organ** N organo vocale.

◆ **speech therapist** N logopedista *m/f*, logoterapista *m/f*.

◆ **speech therapy** N logoterapia.

◆ **speech training** N corso di dizione.

speed [spiːd] [1] N **a** (*rate of movement*) velocità; (*rapidity, haste*) rapidità; (*promptness*) prontezza; **at speed** (*Brit*) velocemente; **at full speed** OR **at top speed** a tutta velocità; **at a speed of 70 km/h** a una velocità di 70 km all'ora; **the speed of light/sound** la velocità della luce/del suono; **what speed were you doing?** (*Aut*) a che velocità andavi?; **to pick up or gather speed** (*car*) acquistare velocità; (*project, work*) procedere più speditamente; **the speed of his reactions** la sua prontezza di riflessi; **shorthand/typing speeds** numero di parole al minuto in stenografia/dattilografia **b** (*Aut, Tech: gear*) marcia; **a five-speed gearbox** un cambio a cinque marce. **c** (*Phot: of film*) sensibilità; (: *of shutter*) tempo di apertura. [2] VI **a** (*pt, pp* **sped**): **to speed along** (*car, work*) procedere velocemente; **to speed away or off** (*car, person*) sfrecciare via; **the years sped by** gli anni sono volati **b** (*pt, pp* **speeded**) (*Aut: exceed speed limit*) andare a velocità eccessiva

▶ **speed up** (*pt, pp* **speeded up**) [1] VI + ADV (*gen*) andare più veloce; (*Aut*) accelerare;

(*walker/worker/train etc*) camminare/lavorare/viaggiare più veloce; (*engine, machine*) girare più veloce; (*production*) accelerare. [2] VT + ADV accelerare.

speed·boat ['spiːdˌbəʊt] N motoscafo.

◆ **speed cop** N (*fam*) agente *m* della stradale.

speedi·ly ['spiːdɪlɪ] ADV (*see adj*) velocemente, rapidamente; prontamente.

speed·ing ['spiːdɪŋ] N (*Aut*) eccesso di velocità.

◆ **speed limit** N limite *m* di velocità; **to exceed the speed limit** superare il limite di velocità.

◆ **speed merchant** N (*fam*) amante *m/f* della velocità.

speed·om·eter [spɪˈdɒmɪtəʳ] N tachimetro.

◆ **speed restriction** N limite *m* di velocità.

◆ **speed trap** N (*Aut*) *tratto di strada sul quale la polizia controlla la velocità dei veicoli.*

speed·way ['spiːdˌweɪ] N: **speedway racing** corsa motociclistica su pista.

speedy ['spiːdɪ] ADJ (*comp* **-ier**, *superl* **-iest**) (*gen*) veloce, rapido(-a); (*reply*) pronto(-a).

spe·leolo·gist [ˌspiːlɪˈɒlədʒɪst] N speleologo(-a).

spell[1] [spɛl] (*pt, pp* **spelled** *or* **spelt**) VT: **how do you spell your name?** come si scrive il tuo nome?; **can you spell it for me?** me lo puoi dettare lettera per lettera?; **c-a-t spells "cat"** c-a-t formano la parola "cat"; **I can't spell** faccio errori di ortografia; **it spells disaster for us** (*fig*) significa la nostra rovina

▶ **spell out** VT + ADV (*fig*): **to spell sth out for sb** spiegare qc a qn per filo e per segno.

spell[2] [spɛl] N (*also:* **magic spell**) incantesimo; (*words*) formula magica; **an evil spell** una stregoneria; **to cast or put a spell on sb** fare un incantesimo a qn; (*fig*) stregare qn; **to fall under sb's spell** (*fig*) subire il fascino di qn; **to break the spell** (*also fig*) rompere l'incantesimo.

spell[3] [spɛl] N (*period of time*) periodo; **cold spell** periodo di freddo; **to do a spell of duty** fare un turno; **they're going through a bad spell** stanno attraversando un brutto periodo.

spell·bind·ing ['spɛlˌbaɪndɪŋ] ADJ affascinante.

spell·bound ['spɛlˌbaʊnd] ADJ incantato(-a), affascinato(-a); **to hold sb spellbound** affascinare qn.

spell·er ['spɛləʳ] N **a** (*person*): **to be a bad/good speller** fare/non fare errori di ortografia **b** (*Am: book*) sillabario.

spell·ing ['spɛlɪŋ] N ortografia.

◆ **spelling mistake** N errore *m* di ortografia.

spelt [spɛlt] PT, PP of **spell**[1].

spend [spɛnd] (*pt, pp* **spent**) VT **a** (*money*) spendere; **to spend money on sb/sth** spendere soldi per qn/qc; **without spending a penny** senza spendere una lira; **to go to spend a penny** (*Brit fam euph*) ≈ andare a fare una telefonata (*fig fam*) **b** (*pass*) passare, trascorrere; **he spends his time sleeping** passa il tempo dormendo **c** (*devote*): **to spend time/money/effort on sth** dedicare tempo/soldi/energie a qc; **I spent 2 hours writing that letter** ho passato 2 ore a scrivere quella lettera.

spend·er ['spɛndəʳ] N: **to be a big spender** avere le mani bucate.

spend·ing ['spɛndɪŋ] N spesa; **government spending** spesa pubblica.

◆ **spending money** N denaro per le piccole spese.

◆ **spending power** N potere *m* d'acquisto.

spend·thrift ['spɛndˌθrɪft] [1] ADJ spendereccio(-a). [2] N spendaccione(-a).

spent [spɛnt] ① PT, PP of **spend**.
② ADJ (*cartridge, bullets, match*) usato(-a); (*supplies*) esaurito(-a); **he's a spent force** è un uomo finito.

sperm [spɜːm] N (*Bio*) sperma *m*.

sper·ma·to·zo·on [ˌspɜːmətəʊˈzəʊɒn] N (*pl* **spermatozoa** [ˌspɜːmətəʊˈzəʊə]) spermatozoo.

♦ **sperm bank** N banca dello sperma.

sper·mi·ci·dal [ˌspɜːmɪˈsaɪdəl] ADJ spermicida.

sper·mi·cide [ˈspɜːmɪˌsaɪd] N spermicida *m*.

♦ **sperm whale** N capodoglio.

spew [spjuː] ① VT (*also:* **spew out**: *smoke, pollution*) emettere.
② VI **a** (*subj: smoke, pollution*) fuoriuscire **b** (*also:* **to spew up**: *fam: vomit*) rigettare.

sphere [sfɪəʳ] N (*gen*) sfera; **his sphere of interest** la sua sfera d'interessi; **his sphere of activity** il suo campo di attività; **within a limited sphere** in un ambito molto ristretto; **sphere of influence** sfera d'influenza; **that's outside my sphere** non rientra nelle mie competenze.

spheri·cal [ˈsfɛrɪkəl] ADJ sferico(-a).

sphinx [sfɪŋks] N (*also fig*) sfinge *f*.

spice [spaɪs] ① N (*Culin*) droga, spezia; (*fig*) sapore *m*; **mixed spice(s)** spezie miste; **variety is the spice of life** la varietà dà sapore alla vita.
② VT (*Culin*) condire (con spezie), aromatizzare; **a highly spiced account** un racconto molto gustoso.

♦ **spice rack** N mensolina *f* portaspezie *inv*.

spick-and-span [ˌspɪkənˈspæn] ADJ pulito(-a) come uno specchio.

spicy [ˈspaɪsɪ] ADJ (*comp* **-ier**, *superl* **-iest**) (*Culin, fig*) piccante.

spi·der [ˈspaɪdəʳ] N ragno; (*tool*) chiave *f* a croce; **spider's web** ragnatela.

♦ **spider crab** N grancevola.

♦ **spider elastic** N (*Aut*) elastico *m* fermabagagli *inv*.

♦ **spider monkey** N scimmia *f* ragno *inv*.

spi·dery [ˈspaɪdərɪ] ADJ (*handwriting*) angoloso(-a).

spiel [ʃpiːl] N (*fam*) tiritera.

spike [spaɪk] ① N **a** (*point*) punta; (*on shoe*) chiodo; **rocky spike** (*Mountaineering*) spuntone *m* **b** : **spikes** NPL (*Sport*) scarpe *fpl* chiodate **c** (*Elec*) punta (di corrente).
② VT (*fig*): **to spike sb's guns** rompere le uova nel paniere a qn; **a spiked drink** (*fam*) una bevanda corretta.

♦ **spike heel** N (*Am*) tacco a spillo.

spiky [ˈspaɪkɪ] ADJ (*comp* **-ier**, *superl* **-iest**) (*bush, branch*) spinoso(-a); (*animal*) ricoperto(-a) di aculei; (*fig: person*) spigoloso(-a).

spill [spɪl] (*pt, pp* **spilled** *or* **spilt** [spɪlt]) ① VT (*gen*) rovesciare, versare; (*blood*) spargere; **to spill the beans** (*fam*) spiattellare tutto, vuotare il sacco.
② VI rovesciarsi, versarsi
► **spill out** ① VI + ADV uscire fuori; (*fall out*) cadere fuori; **the audience spilt out of the cinema** gli spettatori si riversarono fuori dal cinema.
② VT + ADV (*contents etc*) rovesciare; (*fig: story*) rivelare
► **spill over** VI + ADV: **to spill over (into)** (*liquid*) versarsi (in); (*crowd*) riversarsi (in).

spill·age [ˈspɪlɪdʒ] N (*event*) fuoriuscita; (*substance*) sostanza fuoriuscita.

spin [spɪn] (*vb: pt* **spun** *or* **span**, *pp* **spun**) ① N **a** (*revolution*) giro; **to give a wheel a spin** far girare una ruota; **to give sth a long/short spin** (*in washing machine*) fare una centrifuga completa/ridotta; **to be in a flat spin** (*fam*) essere in preda al panico; **to go into a flat spin**

lasciarsi prendere dal panico
b (*on ball*) effetto; **to put a spin on a ball** imprimere l'effetto a una palla
c (*Aer*): **to go into a spin** discendere in avvitamento; (*Aut*) fare un testa-coda
d (*ride*): **to go for a spin** fare un giretto.
② VT **a** (*turn: wheel*) far girare; (*Brit: clothes*) mettere nella centrifuga; (*ball*) imprimere l'effetto a; **to spin a coin** (*Brit*) lanciare in aria una moneta
b (*cotton, wool*) filare; (*subj: spider*) tessere; **to spin a yarn** (*fig*) imbastire una storia.
③ VI **a** filare
b (*revolve: person*) girarsi; (: *ball*) ruotare; (: *wheel*) girare; **to spin round and round** girare su se stesso(-a); **the car spun out of control** la macchina ha sbandato e ha girato su se stessa; **to send sb spinning** mandare qn a gambe all'aria; **it makes my head spin** mi fa girare la testa
► **spin out** VT + ADV (*fam: visit, holiday*) prolungare; (: *speech, food*) far durare.

spi·na bi·fi·da [ˌspaɪnəˈbɪfɪdə] N spina bifida.

spin·ach [ˈspɪnɪdʒ] N spinaci *mpl*.

spi·nal [ˈspaɪnl] ADJ spinale; **spinal injury** lesione *f* alla spina dorsale.

♦ **spinal column** N colonna vertebrale, spina dorsale.

♦ **spinal cord** N midollo spinale.

spin·dle [ˈspɪndl] N (*Tech*) perno, asse *m*; (*for spinning*) fuso.

spin·dly [ˈspɪndlɪ] ADJ (*comp* **-ier**, *superl* **-iest**) (*legs, arms, plant*) stecchito(-a).

♦ **spin doctor** N (*Pol*) *pierre addetto alla difesa di provvedimenti impopolari con interviste, interventi in TV ecc.*

♦ **spin-dry** [ˌspɪnˈdraɪ] VT strizzare con la centrifuga.

♦ **spin-dryer** [ˌspɪnˈdraɪəʳ] N (*Brit*) centrifuga.

spine [spaɪn] N (*Anat*) spina dorsale; (*Zool*) aculeo; (*Bot*) spina; (*of book*) dorso; (*of mountain range*) cresta.

♦ **spine-chiller** [ˈspaɪnˌtʃɪləʳ] N (*film, book etc*) thriller *m inv*.

♦ **spine-chilling** [ˈspaɪnˌtʃɪlɪŋ] ADJ agghiacciante.

spine·less [ˈspaɪnlɪs] ADJ (*fig*) smidollato(-a); (*animal*) invertebrato(-a).

spin·na·ker [ˈspɪnəkəʳ] N (*Naut*) spinnaker *m inv*.

spin·ner [ˈspɪnəʳ] N (*of thread, yarn*) tessitore(-trice); (*Fishing*) cucchiaino; (*fam: spin-dryer*) centrifuga.

spin·ney [ˈspɪnɪ] N boschetto.

spin·ning [ˈspɪnɪŋ] N filatura.

♦ **spinning mill** N filanda.

♦ **spinning top** N trottola.

♦ **spinning wheel** N filatoio.

♦ **spin-off** [ˈspɪnˌɒf] N (*Tech, Industry*) applicazione *f* secondaria; (*product*) prodotto secondario; **this TV series is a spin-off from the famous film** questa serie televisiva è ispirata al famoso film.

spin·ster [ˈspɪnstəʳ] N (*old*) zitella.

spiny [ˈspaɪnɪ] ADJ coperto(-a) di spine.

spi·ral [ˈspaɪərəl] ① ADJ a spirale.
② N spirale *f*; **the inflationary spiral** la spirale dell'inflazione.
③ VI (*prices*) salire vertiginosamente; **to spiral up/down** (*also Aer*) salire/scendere a spirale.

♦ **spiral staircase** N scala a chiocciola.

spire [ˈspaɪəʳ] N guglia.

spir·it [ˈspɪrɪt] N **a** (*soul*) spirito; **I'll be with you in spirit** ti sarò vicino col pensiero; **one of the greatest spirits of the age** uno dei più grandi personaggi dell'epoca; **one**

of the leading spirits in the party uno dei principali animatori del partito

b (*ghost, supernatural being*) spirito; **Holy Spirit** Spirito Santo

c (*courage*) coraggio; (*energy*) energia; (*vitality*) brio, vitalità

d (*attitude etc*) spirito; **community spirit** [OR] **public spirit** senso civico; **in a spirit of optimism** con un atteggiamento ottimista; **to enter into the spirit of sth** entrare nello spirito di qc; **that's the spirit!** (*fam*) bravo!, così va bene!; **the spirit of the law** lo spirito della legge; **to take sth in the right/wrong spirit** prendere qc bene/male

e : **spirits** NPL (*state of mind*): **high spirits** buon umore *m*; **to be in low spirits** essere giù di morale; **we kept our spirits up by singing** ci siamo tenuti su di morale cantando; **my spirits rose somewhat** mi sono tirato un po' su

f : **spirits** NPL (*alcohol*) liquori *mpl*; **raw spirits** alcol *m* puro

g (*Chem*) spirito, alcol *m inv*

▶ **spirit away, spirit off** VT + ADV far sparire misteriosamente.

spir·it·ed ['spɪrɪtɪd] ADJ (*horse*) focoso(-a); (*conversation*) animato(-a); (*person, attack etc*) energico(-a); (*description*) vivace, vigoroso(-a); **he gave a spirited performance** (*Mus, Theatre*) ha dato una brillante interpretazione.

♦ **spirit lamp** N lampada a spirito.

♦ **spirit level** N livella a bolla d'aria.

spir·itu·al ['spɪrɪtjʊəl] [1] ADJ spirituale.

[2] N (*Mus*) spiritual *m inv*.

spir·itu·al·ism ['spɪrɪtjʊə‚lɪzəm] N (*occult*) spiritismo.

spir·itu·al·ist ['spɪrɪtjʊəlɪst] N (*Rel*) spiritualista *m/f*.

spir·itu·al·ity [‚spɪrɪtjʊ'ælɪtɪ] N spiritualità.

spir·itu·al·ly ['spɪrɪtjʊəlɪ] ADV spiritualmente.

spit[1] [spɪt] N (*Culin: for roasting*) spiedo; (*of land*) lingua di terra.

spit[2] [spɪt] (*vb: pt, pp* **spat**) [1] N (*spittle*) sputo; (*saliva*) saliva; **a bit of spit and polish** (*fam*) una bella lucidata; **to be the dead spit of sb** (*fam*) essere il ritratto sputato di qn.

[2] VT sputare.

[3] VI: **to spit (at)** sputare (addosso a); (*cat*) soffiare (contro); **to spit on the ground** sputare per terra; **it is spitting with rain** sta piovigginando

▶ **spit out** VT + ADV (*sparks*) sprigionare; (*fat*) schizzare; **spit it out!** (*fam: say it*) sputa il rospo!

spite [spaɪt] [1] N **a** (*ill will*) dispetto; **to do sth out of (or from) spite** fare qc per dispetto

b : **in spite of** (*despite*) nonostante, malgrado; **in spite of the fact that** malgrado *or* nonostante (il fatto che) + *sub*; **she laughed in spite of herself** ha riso suo malgrado.

[2] VT far dispetto a.

spite·ful ['spaɪtfʊl] ADJ (*person, behaviour*) dispettoso(-a); (*tongue, remark*) maligno(-a), velenoso(-a).

spite·ful·ly ['spaɪtfəlɪ] ADV (*see adj*) dispettosamente; malignamente.

spit·fire ['spɪt‚faɪəʳ] N: **she's a real spitfire** è una persona molto irascibile.

spit·roast ['spɪt‚rəʊst] VT cuocere allo spiedo.

spit·ting ['spɪtɪŋ] [1] N: **"spitting prohibited"** "vietato sputare".

[2] ADJ: **to be the spitting image of sb** essere il ritratto sputato di qn.

spit·tle ['spɪtl] N (*ejected*) sputo; (*dribbled*) saliva; (*of*

animal) bava.

spit·toon [spɪ'tuːn] N sputacchiera.

spiv [spɪv] N (*Brit fam*) imbroglione *m*.

splash [splæʃ] [1] N (*sound*) tonfo; (*series of splashes*) sciabordio; (*mark*) spruzzo, macchia; (*fig: of colour, light*) chiazza; **to make a splash** (*fig*) far furore.

[2] VT schizzare; **to splash sb with water** schizzare qn d'acqua; **to splash sth over sb** schizzare qc addosso a qn; **to splash one's face with water** spruzzarsi acqua sul viso; **to splash paint on the floor** schizzare il pavimento di vernice; **the story was splashed across the front page** (*fam*) la notizia è stata sbattuta in prima pagina.

[3] VI (*liquid, mud etc*) schizzare; (*person, animal in water*: *also*: **splash about**) sguazzare; **to splash across a stream** guadare un ruscello; **to splash into the water** (*stone*) cadere nell'acqua con un tonfo

▶ **splash down** VI + ADV ammarare

▶ **splash out** VI + ADV (*fam*) fare spese folli

▶ **splash up** VI + ADV schizzare; **the waves splashed up against the rocks** le onde s'infrangevano sugli scogli.

splash·back ['splæʃ‚bæk] N (*at sink etc*) pannello di protezione (contro gli spruzzi).

splash·down ['splæʃ‚daʊn] N ammaraggio.

splat·ter ['splætəʳ] [1] VI schizzare; **mud had splattered onto our shoes** avevamo le scarpe inzaccherate di fango.

[2] VT (*liquid*) schizzare; (*food*) spiaccicare; **an apron splattered with blood** un grembiule schizzato di sangue.

[3] N (*sound*): **the splatter of rain on the windows** il tamburellare della pioggia sui vetri.

splay [spleɪ] VI: **splayed fingers** dita allargate.

spleen [spliːn] N (*Anat*) milza; **to vent one's spleen** (*fig*) sfogarsi.

splen·did ['splendɪd] ADJ (*ceremony, clothes*) splendido (-a), magnifico(-a); (*idea, example*) eccellente, ottimo (-a); **that's splendid!** magnifico!, fantastico!

splen·did·ly ['splendɪdlɪ] ADV splendidamente, magnificamente.

splen·dif·er·ous [splen'dɪfərəs] ADJ (*old, hum*) magnifico (-a), splendido(-a).

splen·dour, (*Am*) **splen·dor** ['splendəʳ] N splendore *m*, magnificenza.

splice [splaɪs] VT (*rope, film*) giuntare; (*wood*) calettare.

splint [splɪnt] N (*Med*) stecca; **to put sb's arm in splints** steccare il braccio di qn.

splin·ter ['splɪntəʳ] [1] N scheggia.

[2] VI (*wood, glass*) scheggiarsi; (*fig: party*) staccarsi, scindersi.

[3] VT (*wood, glass*) scheggiare; (*fig: party*) scindere.

♦ **splinter group** N gruppo scissionista.

split [splɪt] (*vb: pt, pp* **split**) [1] N **a** (*in ground, wall, rock*) fessura, crepa; (*in wood*) spacco; (*in garment, fabric*) strappo

b (*fig: division, quarrel*) scissione *f*, spaccatura; **there are fears of a split in the party** si teme una scissione nel partito

c : **to do the splits** fare la spaccata

d (*cake etc*): **jam split** tortina farcita di marmellata; **banana split** banana-split *f inv*.

[2] VT **a** (*cleave*) spaccare; (*tear*) strappare; **to split the atom** scindere l'atomo; **to split sth open** aprire qc spaccandolo(-a); **he split his head open** si è spaccato la testa; **to split sth down the middle** (*also fig*) spaccare qc a metà; **to split hairs** (*fig*) spaccare il capello in quattro;

to split one's sides laughing (*fig*) ridere a crepapelle

b (*divide: also fig*) dividere, spartire; **to split sth into three parts** dividere qc in tre; **to split the profit five ways** dividere il guadagno in cinque parti; **to split the difference** (*agree price*) incontrarsi a metà strada; (*fig*) accettare una soluzione di compromesso.

3 VI **a** (*wood, stone*) spaccarsi; (*cloth*) strapparsi; (*fig: party, church*) spaccarsi, dividersi; **to split open** spaccarsi; **my head is splitting** mi scoppia la testa

b (*fam: tell tales*): **don't you split on me to the police!** non provarti a denunciarmi alla polizia!

▶ **split off** **1** VI + ADV (*also fig*) staccarsi, separarsi.

2 VT + ADV (*also fig*) staccare, separare

▶ **split up** **1** VI + ADV (*stone etc*) spaccarsi; (*ship on rocks*) schiantarsi; (*crowd*) disperdersi; (: *into groups*) dividersi; (*meeting*) sciogliersi; (*partners*) separarsi; (*couple*) separarsi, rompere; (*friends*) rompere.

2 VT + ADV (*stone etc*) dividere; (*crowd*) disperdere; (*partners*) separare.

♦ **split infinitive** N (*Gram*) *infinito in cui un avverbio divide il 'to' dal verbo.*

♦ **split-level** ['splɪt,lɛvl] ADJ (*house*) a piani sfalsati.

♦ **split peas** NPL piselli *mpl* secchi spaccati.

♦ **split personality** N sdoppiamento della personalità.

♦ **split screen** N (*Cine, TV, Comput*) schermo diviso.

♦ **split-screen** ['splɪt'skri:n] ADJ (*Cine, TV, Comput: technique, facility*) di schermo diviso.

♦ **split second** N frazione *f* di secondo.

♦ **split shifts** NPL (*Industry*) turni *mpl* articolati.

split·ting ['splɪtɪŋ] ADJ: **a splitting headache** un terribile mal di testa.

♦ **split-up** ['splɪt,ʌp] N (*of married couple*) separazione *f*; (*of friends, political group*) rottura.

splodge [splɒdʒ], **splotch** [splɒtʃ] N macchia.

splurge [splɜːdʒ] (*fam*) **1** VI fare una follia; **to splurge on sth** fare una follia comprando qc.

2 VT: **to splurge one's money (on sth)** fare una follia (comprando qc).

3 N (*spending spree*) spese *fpl* folli; **to go on** *or* **have a splurge** darsi alle spese folli.

splut·ter ['splʌtə] VI (*person: spit*) sputacchiare; (: *stutter*) farfugliare; (*fire*) crepitare; (*fat*) schizzare; (*engine*) scoppiettare.

spoil [spɔɪl] (*pt, pp* **spoiled** *or* **spoilt**) **1** VT **a** (*ruin, detract from*) rovinare, sciupare; (*ballot paper*) annullare, invalidare; **don't spoil our fun** non fare il guastafeste; **to spoil one's appetite** guastarsi l'appetito

b (*child*) viziare.

2 VI **a** (*food*) guastarsi, andare a male; (: *while cooking*) rovinarsi

b : **to be spoiling for a fight** morire dalla voglia di litigare.

spoil·er ['spɔɪlə] N (*Aut, Aer*) spoiler *m inv*.

spoils [spɔɪlz] NPL: **the spoils** il bottino *msg*.

spoil·sport ['spɔɪl,spɔːt] N (*fam*) guastafeste *m/f inv*.

spoilt [spɔɪlt] **1** PT, PP of **spoil**.

2 ADJ (*child*) viziato(-a); (*meal*) rovinato(-a); (*ballot paper*) nullo(-a).

spoke[1] [spəʊk] N raggio; **to put a spoke in sb's wheel** mettere i bastoni fra le ruote a qn.

spoke[2] [spəʊk] PT of **speak**.

spo·ken ['spəʊkən] PP of **speak**.

spokes·man ['spəʊksmən] N (*pl* **-men**) portavoce *m inv*.

spokes·person ['spəʊks,pɜːsən] N portavoce *m/f inv*.

spokes·woman ['spəʊks,wʊmən] N (*pl* **-women**) porta-

voce *f inv*.

sponge [spʌndʒ] **1** N spugna; (*Culin: also:* **sponge cake**) pan *m* di Spagna; **to throw in the sponge** (*fig*) gettare la spugna.

2 VT (*wash*) lavare con una spugna; **to sponge a stain off** pulire una macchia con una spugna.

3 VI (*fam: scrounge*) scroccare; **to sponge off** *or* **on sb** vivere alle spalle di qn.

▶ **sponge down** VT + ADV lavare con una spugna.

♦ **sponge bag** N (*Brit*) nécessaire *m inv*.

♦ **sponge cake** N (*Culin*) = **sponge 1**.

spong·er ['spʌndʒə] N (*fam*) scroccone(-a); (*pej*) parassita *m inv*.

spon·gy ['spʌndʒɪ] ADJ (*comp* **-ier**, *superl* **-iest**) spugnoso (-a).

spon·sor ['spɒnsə] **1** N (*of enterprise, bill, for fund raising*) promotore(-trice); (*for loan*) garante *m/f*; (*of member*) socio(-a) garante; (*Radio, TV, Sport etc*) sponsor *m inv*; (*godparent*) padrino/madrina.

2 VT (*enterprise etc*) promuovere, patrocinare; (*borrower, member of club*) garantire; (*Pol: Parliamentary bill*) presentare; (*Radio, TV, Sport etc*) sponsorizzare; (*as godparents*) tenere a battesimo; **I sponsored him at 20p a mile** (*in fund-raising race*) mi sono impegnato a donare 20 penny per ogni miglio.

spon·sor·ship ['spɒnsə,ʃɪp] N (*financial backing*) promozione *f*; (*of arts, events*) sponsorizzazione *f*; (*of candidate*) sostegno.

spon·ta·neity [,spɒntə'neɪətɪ] N spontaneità.

spon·ta·neous [spɒn'teɪnɪəs] ADJ spontaneo(-a).

♦ **spontaneous combustion** N autocombustione *f*.

spon·ta·neous·ly [spɒn'teɪnɪəslɪ] ADV spontaneamente.

spoof [spuːf] N (*fam*) parodia.

spook [spuːk] N (*fam*) fantasma *m*, spettro.

spooky ['spuːkɪ] ADJ (*comp* **-ier**, *superl* **-iest**) (*fam*) sinistro (-a).

spool [spuːl] N (*Phot, on sewing machine, on fishing line*) bobina; (*spool of thread*) rocchetto di filo.

spoon [spuːn] **1** N cucchiaio; **to be born with a silver spoon in one's mouth** essere nato(-a) con la camicia.

2 VT: **to spoon out** (*sauce, cream*) servire con il cucchiaio; **to spoon sth into a plate** versare qc in un piatto con il cucchiaio.

spoon·bill ['spuːn,bɪl] N (*Zool*) spatola.

spoon·er·ism ['spuːnə,rɪzəm] N *papera consistente nello scambio delle iniziali di due parole.*

♦ **spoon-feed** ['spuːn,fiːd] (*pt, pp* **spoon-fed** ['spuːn,fɛd]) VT imboccare; (*fig*) scodellare la pappa a.

spoon·ful ['spuːnfʊl] N cucchiaiata.

spoor [spʊə] N traccia, pista.

spo·rad·ic [spə'rædɪk] ADJ (*attempts, gunfire*) sporadico (-a); (*work*) discontinuo(-a).

spo·radi·cal·ly [spə'rædɪkəlɪ] ADV (*attempt, fire*) sporadicamente; (*work*) saltuariamente; (*function*) in modo discontinuo.

spore [spɔː] N spora.

spor·ran ['spɒrən] N *borsello agganciato alla cintura del kilt, indossato con il tradizionale costume scozzese.*

sport [spɔːt] **1** N **a** sport *m inv*; **indoor/outdoor sports** sport al chiuso/all'aria aperta; **to be good at sport** riuscire bene nello sport; **sports** NPL (*meeting*) gare *fpl* **b** (*amusement*) divertimento **c** (*fam: person*) persona di spirito; **be a sport!** sii buono!.

2 VT sfoggiare.

sport·ing ['spɔːtɪŋ] ADJ (*event, behaviour, attitude*) sportivo

(-a); **there's a sporting chance that** c'è una buona probabilità che + sub; **to give sb a sporting chance** dare a qn una possibilità (di vincere).

sport·ing·ly ['spɔ:tɪŋlɪ] ADV sportivamente.

♦ **sports car** N automobile f sportiva.

♦ **sports ground** N campo sportivo.

♦ **sports jacket**, (Am) **sport jacket** N giacca sportiva.

sports·man ['spɔ:tsmən] N (pl **-men**) sportivo.

sportsmanlike ['spɔ:tsmən‚laɪk] ADJ sportivo(-a); **in a sportsmanlike fashion** sportivamente.

sports·man·ship ['spɔ:tsmən‚ʃɪp] N spirito sportivo.

♦ **sports page** N pagina sportiva.

sports·wear ['spɔ:ts‚wɛə'] N abbigliamento sportivo.

sports·woman ['spɔ:ts‚wʊmən] N (pl **-women**) sportiva.

sporty ['spɔ:tɪ] ADJ (comp **-ier**, superl **-iest**) (fam) sportivo (-a).

spot [spɒt] **1** N **a** (dot) puntino; (on dress) pois m inv, pallino; (stain, also fig) macchia; **a material with blue spots** una stoffa a pallini o pois blu; **to knock spots off sb** (fig fam) dare dei punti a qn; **to have spots before one's eyes** vedere dei puntini

  b (pimple) foruncolo; **to break** or **come out in spots** coprirsi di foruncoli

  c (place) posto; **a pleasant spot** un bel posto; **to have a tender spot on the arm** avere un punto dolorante nel braccio; **the reporter was on the spot** il reporter era sul posto; **the firemen were on the spot in 3 minutes** i pompieri sono arrivati sul posto in 3 minuti; **an on-the-spot broadcast** una trasmissione in diretta; **to do sth on the spot** fare qc immediatamente or lì per lì; **to be in a (tight) spot** (fig) essere nei guai or nei pasticci; **to put sb in a spot** or **on the spot** (fig) mettere in difficoltà qn; **that's my weak spot** (fig) è il mio punto debole

  d (Brit fam: small amount): **a spot of** un po' di; (: of milk, wine etc) un goccio di; **just a spot, thanks** solo un goccio, grazie; **we had a spot of rain yesterday** c'è stata qualche goccia di pioggia ieri; **would you like a spot of lunch?** vuoi mangiare un boccone?; **to have a spot of bother** avere noie

  e (Radio, Theatre, TV: in show) numero; (Radio, TV: advertisement) spot m inv (pubblicitario)

  f (fam: also: **spotlight**) faretto.

  2 VT **a** (speckle): **to spot (with)** macchiare (di)

  b (notice, see: mistake, person in a crowd) notare; (: car, person in the distance) scorgere; (recognize: winner) indovinare; (: talent, sb's ability) scoprire; (: bargain) riconoscere.

♦ **spot check** N controllo casuale.

spot·less ['spɒtlɪs] ADJ pulitissimo(-a), immacolato(-a); (fig: reputation) senza macchia; (: character) retto(-a).

spot·less·ly ['spɒtlɪslɪ] ADV: **spotlessly clean** pulitissimo (-a).

spot·light ['spɒt‚laɪt] N (lamp) spot m inv, faro; (beam) fascio luminoso; (Aut) faro, riflettore m; **in the spotlight** sotto la luce dei riflettori; (fig) al centro dell'attenzione; **to turn the spotlight on sb/sth** (fig) mettere in risalto qn/qc, richiamare l'attenzione su qn/qc.

spot·lit ['spɒtlɪt] ADJ (stage, building) illuminato(-a) dai riflettori.

♦ **spot-on** ['spɒt'ɒn] ADJ (Brit) esatto(-a).

♦ **spot price** N (Comm) prezzo per contanti.

♦ **spot remover** N smacchiatore m.

spot·ted ['spɒtɪd] ADJ (material) a pois, a pallini; (animal) maculato(-a); **spotted with** punteggiato(-a) di.

spot·ty ['spɒtɪ] ADJ (comp **-ier**, superl **-iest**) (fam) foruncoloso(-a).

spouse [spaʊs] N (frm) coniuge m/f.

spout [spaʊt] **1** N (of teapot) becco, beccuccio; (of guttering) scarico; (for tap) cannella; (column of water) getto, zampillo; **those figures are completely up the spout** (fam) quei dati sono completamente sballati.

  2 VT (water) gettare; (lava) eruttare; (smoke) emettere; (fam pej: poetry) declamare.

  3 VI (liquid) zampillare.

sprain [spreɪn] **1** N slogatura, storta, distorsione f; (of muscle) strappo muscolare.

  2 VT (muscle) stirarsi; **to sprain one's wrist/ankle** slogarsi un polso/una caviglia.

sprang [spræŋ] PT of **spring**.

sprat [spræt] N (fish) spratto.

sprawl [sprɔ:l] **1** VI (person: sit, lie) stravaccarsi; (: fall) cadere scompostamente; (town) estendersi in modo incontrollato; (plant) crescere disordinatamente; **her handwriting sprawled all over the page** la sua scrittura copriva tutta la pagina; **to send sb sprawling** mandare qn a gambe all'aria.

  2 N: **urban sprawl** sviluppo urbanistico incontrollato, espansione f urbana tentacolare; **a sprawl of buildings lay below them** un gruppo di edifici si estendeva disordinatamente dinanzi ai loro occhi.

sprawl·ing ['sprɔ:lɪŋ] ADJ (person) sdraiato(-a); (: in armchair) stravaccato(-a); (handwriting) disordinato(-a); (city) tentacolare.

spray¹ [spreɪ] **1** N **a** (from hosepipe) getto; (from wet road) schizzi mpl; (of sea, fountain) spruzzi mpl; (from atomizer, aerosol) spruzzo

  b (aerosol, atomizer) spray m inv, bomboletta; (: of perfume) vaporizzatore m; (: for paint, garden) spruzzatore m, nebulizzatore m; (Med) spray.

  2 VT (gen) spruzzare; (crops) irrorare; **to spray sth/sb with water** spruzzare qc/qn d'acqua; **to spray sth/sb with bullets** sparare una scarica di proiettili contro qc/qn.

  3 ADJ (deodorant) spray inv; (gun, paint) a spruzzo.

spray² [spreɪ] N (of greenery) ramoscello; (of flowers) mazzolino; (brooch) spilla a forma di ramoscello.

♦ **spray can** N bombola f spray inv.

spray·er ['spreɪə'] N = **spray 1 b**.

spray·ing ma·chine ['spreɪɪŋ mə‚ʃi:n] N (Agr) irroratrice f.

spread [spred] (vb: pt, pp **spread**) **1** N **a** (of fire, infection) propagazione f; (of idea, knowledge) diffusione f; (of crime) il dilagare; **the spread of nuclear weapons** la proliferazione delle armi nucleari

  b (extent: of bridge) ampiezza; (: of wings, arch) apertura

  c (range: of prices, figures, marks) gamma; (: on graph, scale) distribuzione f; **middle-age spread** pancetta

  d (fam: feast) banchetto

  e (also: **bedspread**) copriletto

  f (for bread): **anchovy spread** ≈ pasta d'acciughe; **cheese spread** formaggio da spalmare

  g (Press, Typ: two pages) doppia pagina; (: across columns) articolo a più colonne.

  2 VT **a** (open or lay out: also: **spread out**: wings, sails etc) spiegare; (: cloth) stendere; (: fingers) distendere; (: arms) allargare, spalancare; **to spread a map out on the table** spiegare una cartina sul tavolo; **to spread one's wings** (fig) spiccare il volo

  b (butter, cream etc) spalmare; **to spread cream on one's face** spalmarsi la crema sul viso

c (*distribute*: *also*: **spread out**: *sand, fertilizer*): **to spread sth on sth** cospargere qc di qc; (: *goods, objects*) disporre; (: *cards, toys*) spargere; (: *soldiers*) scaglionare; (: *payments*) rateizzare, scaglionare; (: *resources*) distribuire; **repayments will be spread over 18 months** i pagamenti saranno scaglionati lungo un periodo di 18 mesi

d (*disseminate*: *germs, disease*) propagare, diffondere; (: *knowledge, panic etc*) diffondere; (: *news*) spargere, diffondere.

3 VI (*news, rumour etc*) diffondersi, propagarsi, spargersi; (*pain, fire, flood etc*) estendersi; (*milk etc*) spargersi; (*disease, weeds*) propagarsi; **to spread into sth** estendersi fino a qc; **margarine spreads better than butter** la margarina si spalma meglio del burro

▶ **spread out** **1** VI + ADV (*view, valley*) stendersi; (*soldiers, police*) disporsi.

2 VT + ADV = **spread 2a and 2c**.

♦ **spread-eagled** [ˌsprɛdˈiːgld] ADJ: **to be** *or* **lie spread-eagled** essere disteso(-a) a gambe e braccia aperte.

spread·sheet [ˈsprɛdˌʃiːt] N (*Comput*) foglio elettronico.

spree [spriː] N (*fam*): **to go on a spending spree** fare spese folli; **to go on a spree** darsi alla pazza gioia, fare baldoria.

sprig [sprɪg] N ramoscello.

spright·ly [ˈspraɪtlɪ] ADJ (*comp* **-ier**, *superl* **-iest**) vivace; **a sprightly old man** un vecchietto arzillo.

spring [sprɪŋ] (*vb*: *pt* **sprang**, *pp* **sprung**) **1** N **a** (*season*) primavera; **in spring** OR **in the spring** in primavera; **spring is in the air** c'è aria di primavera

b (*coiled metal, also Tech*) molla

c : **springs** NPL (*Aut*) sospensioni *fpl*, balestre *fpl*

d (*of water*) sorgente *f*; **hot spring** sorgente termale

e (*leap*) salto, balzo; **in one spring** in un salto

f (*bounciness*) elasticità; **to walk with a spring in one's step** camminare con passo elastico.

2 VT (*trap, lock etc*) far scattare; **to spring a leak** (*pipe etc*) cominciare a perdere; **the boat has sprung a leak** s'è aperta una falla nella barca; **he sprang a question on me** (*fig*) mi ha fatto una domanda a bruciapelo; **to spring a surprise on sb** fare una sorpresa a qn; **he sprang the news on me** mi ha sorpreso con quella notizia; **he sprang it on me** mi ha preso alla sprovvista.

3 VI **a** (*leap*) saltare, balzare; **to spring aside/forward** balzare da una parte/in avanti; **to spring back** saltare *or* scattare all'indietro; **the door sprang open** la porta si aprì di scatto; **where on earth did you spring from?** (*fam*) da dove spunti?; **to spring into the air** fare un balzo in aria; **to spring into action** entrare rapidamente in azione; **to spring to one's feet** scattare in piedi; **to spring to mind** venire in mente

b (*originate*: *gen*) sorgere; (: *tears*) sgorgare.

4 ADJ **a** (*of season*) di primavera, primaverile

b (*with springs*: *mattress*) a molle

▶ **spring up** VI + ADV (*person*) saltar su; (*plant, weeds, building*) spuntare; (*problem, obstacle*) presentarsi; (*wind, storm*) alzarsi, levarsi; (*doubt, friendship, rumour*) nascere.

♦ **spring binder** N (*file*) raccoglitore *m* a molla.

spring·board [ˈsprɪŋˌbɔːd] N trampolino.

spring·bok [ˈsprɪŋˌbɒk] N (*Zool*) antidorcade *f*.

♦ **spring-clean** [ˌsprɪŋˈkliːn] VI fare le pulizie di primavera.

♦ **spring-cleaning** [ˌsprɪŋˈkliːnɪŋ] N pulizie *fpl* di primavera.

spring·like [ˈsprɪŋˌlaɪk] ADJ (*day, weather*) primaverile.

♦ **spring onion** N (*Brit*) cipollina.

♦ **spring-release** [ˈsprɪŋrɪˌliːs] ADJ a cerniera; **spring-release tin** (*Culin*) stampo a cerniera.

♦ **spring roll** N involtino primavera, *involtino fritto farcito di verdure o carne, specialità cinese*.

spring·time [ˈsprɪŋˌtaɪm] N primavera.

springy [ˈsprɪŋɪ] ADJ (*comp* **-ier**, *superl* **-iest**) (*gen*) elastico (-a); (*carpet, turf*) morbido(-a); (*mattress*) molleggiato (-a).

sprin·kle [ˈsprɪŋkl] VT: **to sprinkle with** (*gen*) cospargere di; (*water*) spruzzare di; **they are sprinkled about here and there** sono sparsi un po' dovunque; **to sprinkle water** *etc* **on** spruzzare dell'acqua *etc* su; **to sprinkle sugar** *etc* **on** OR **sprinkle with sugar** *etc* spolverizzare di zucchero *etc*.

sprin·kler [ˈsprɪŋklə'] N (*for lawn etc*) irrigatore *m*; (*for fire-fighting*) sprinkler *m inv*.

sprin·kling [ˈsprɪŋklɪŋ] N (*of water, snow*) spruzzatina; (*of salt, sugar*) pizzico; **there was a sprinkling of young people** c'era qualche giovane.

sprint [sprɪnt] **1** N (*in race*) sprint *m inv*, scatto; (*dash*) corsa; **the 200-metres sprint** i 200 metri piani.

2 VI (*in race*) scattare, sprintare; (*dash*: *for bus etc*) fare una corsa.

sprint·er [ˈsprɪntə'] N (*Sport*) velocista *m/f*.

sprite [spraɪt] N elfo, folletto.

spritz·er [ˈsprɪtsə'] N spritz *m inv*.

sprock·et [ˈsprɒkɪt] N (*on printer, bicycle*) dente *m*, rocchetto.

sprout [spraʊt] **1** N (*from bulb, seeds*) germoglio; see also **sprouts**.

2 VT (*leaves, shoots*) mettere, produrre; **to sprout a moustache** farsi crescere i baffi.

3 VI germogliare; **skyscrapers are sprouting up everywhere** i grattacieli spuntano dappertutto.

sprouts [spraʊts] NPL (*also*: **Brussels sprouts**) cavoletti *mpl* di Bruxelles.

spruce¹ [spruːs] N (*Bot*) abete *m*; **Norway spruce** abete norvegese *or* rosso.

spruce² [spruːs] ADJ (*outfit*) elegante; (*lawn*) curato(-a); (*person*) azzimato(-a).

▶ **spruce up** VT + ADV (*tidy*) mettere in ordine; (*smarten up*: *room etc*) abbellire; **to spruce o.s. up** farsi bello(-a); **all spruced up** tutto(-a) azzimato(-a) *or* agghindato(-a).

sprung [sprʌŋ] **1** PP of **spring**.

2 ADJ (*seat, mattress*) a molle; **interior-sprung mattress** materasso a molle.

spry [spraɪ] ADJ (*comp* **-er**, *superl* **-est**) vivace, sveglio(-a), arzillo(-a).

SPUC [spʌk] N ABBR (= *Society for the Protection of Unborn Children*) *associazione anti-abortista*.

spud [spʌd] N (*fam*: *potato*) patata.

spun [spʌn] PT, PP of **spin**.

spunk [spʌŋk] N (*fam*): **she's got spunk** ha fegato.

spur [spɜː'] **1** N (*also Geog*) sperone *m*; (*fig*) sprone *m*; **on the spur of the moment** su due piedi, d'impulso.

2 VT (*also*: **spur on**: *horse, fig*) spronare; **to spur sb on to do sth** spronare qn a fare qc.

spurge [spɜːdʒ] N euforbia.

spu·ri·ous [ˈspjʊərɪəs] ADJ (*gen*) falso(-a); (*affection, interest*) falso(-a), simulato(-a).

spurn [spɜːn] VT respingere, sdegnare.

spurt [spɜːt] **1** N (*of water, steam etc*) getto; (*of speed, energy, anger*) scatto; **to put on a spurt** (*runner*) fare uno

scatto; (*fig: in work etc*) affrettarsi, sbrigarsi.

2 VI (*gush: also:* **spurt out**) sgorgare.

sput·nik ['spʊtnɪk] N sputnik *m inv.*

sput·ter ['spʌtə'] VI = **splutter.**

spy [spaɪ] 1 N spia; **police spy** informatore(-trice) (della polizia).

2 VT (*catch sight of*) scorgere.

3 VI spiare; **to spy on sb** spiare qn.

4 ADJ (*film, story*) di spionaggio

▶ **spy out** VT + ADV: **to spy out the land** (*fig*) tastare il terreno.

spy·glass ['spaɪˌglɑːs] N cannocchiale *m.*

spy·hole ['spaɪˌhəʊl] N spioncino.

spy·ing ['spaɪɪŋ] N spionaggio.

Sq. ABBR (= *Square: in address*) P.zza.

sq. ABBR (*Math*) of **square.**

squab·ble ['skwɒbl] 1 N battibecco.

2 VI: **to squabble (over** *or* **about)** bisticciarsi (per).

squab·bling ['skwɒblɪŋ] N bisticci *mpl*; **stop that squabbling, you two!** smettetela di bisticciare voi due!

squad [skwɒd] N (*Mil*) drappello, plotone *m*; (*of police, workmen etc*) squadra; **flying squad** (*Police*) (squadra) volante *f*, (squadra) mobile *f*; **the England World Cup squad was named today** (*Ftbl*) oggi è stata annunciata la formazione inglese convocata per i mondiali.

♦ **squad car** N (*Brit Police*) automobile *f* della polizia.

squad·die ['skwɒdɪ] N (*Brit Mil fam*) burba.

squad·ron ['skwɒdrən] N (*Mil*) squadrone *m*; (*Aer, Naut*) squadriglia.

squal·id ['skwɒlɪd] ADJ squallido(-a), sordido(-a).

squall [skwɔːl] 1 N (*Met*) bufera, burrasca.

2 VI (*baby*) strillare, urlare.

squal·ling ['skwɔːlɪŋ] ADJ (*baby*) che strilla, urlante.

squal·or ['skwɒlə'] N squallore *m.*

squan·der ['skwɒndə'] VT (*money*) sperperare, dissipare, scialacquare; (*time, opportunity*) sprecare, perdere.

square [skwɛə'] 1 N a (*gen*) quadrato; (*instrument*) squadra; (*check on material*) quadro; **with red and blue squares** a quadri rossi e blu; **to cut into squares** tagliare in (pezzi) quadrati; **we're back to square one** (*fig*) siamo al punto di partenza

b (*in town*) piazza; (*Am: block of houses*) isolato; **the town square** la piazza principale

c (*Math*) quadrato; **16 is the square of 4** 16 è il quadrato di 4

d (*fam: old-fashioned person*) matusa *m inv*; **he's a real square** è proprio un matusa.

2 ADJ a (*in shape*) quadrato(-a); **he's a square peg in a round hole in that job** non è tagliato per quel lavoro

b (*Math*) quadrato(-a); **1 square metre** 1 metro quadrato; **it is less than a centimetre square** misura meno di un centimetro per lato; **2 metres square** di 2 metri per 2

c : **a square meal** un pasto sostanzioso

d (*fair, honest*) onesto(-a), retto(-a); **to give sb a square deal** trattare qn onestamente; **I'll be square with you** sarò franco con te

e (*even: accounts, figures*) in ordine; **to get one's accounts square** mettere in ordine i propri conti; **to get square with sb** (*also fig*) regolare i conti con qn; **now we're all square** (*fig*) adesso siamo pari

f (*fam: old-fashioned: person*) all'antica; (: *idea*) sorpassato(-a); (: *style*) fuori moda.

3 ADV: **square in the middle** esattamente *or* proprio nel centro; **to look sb square in the eye** guardare qn diritto

negli occhi.

4 VT a (*make square: stone, timber*) squadrare; (: *shape*) rendere quadrato(-a); **to square one's shoulders** raddrizzare le spalle

b (*settle etc: accounts, books*) far quadrare; (: *debts*) saldare, regolare; **can you square it with your conscience?** riesci a conciliarlo con la tua coscienza?; **I'll square it with him** (*fam*) sistemo io le cose con lui

c (*Math*) elevare al quadrato; **2 squared is 4** 2 al quadrato fa 4.

5 VI (*agree*) accordarsi; **to square with** quadrare con

▶ **square off** VT + ADV (*wood, edges*) squadrare

▶ **square up** VI + ADV a (*Brit: settle*) saldare; **to square up with sb** regolare i conti con qn

b : **to square up (to)** (*opponent*) affrontare; (*fig: difficulties*) far fronte a.

♦ **square-bashing** ['skwɛəˌbæʃɪŋ] N (*Brit Mil fam*) esercitazioni *fpl.*

♦ **square bracket** N (*Typ*) parentesi *f inv* quadra.

♦ **square-built** ['skwɛə'bɪlt] ADJ (*squat: person*) tarchiato(-a), tozzo(-a).

♦ **square dance** N (*esp Am*) quadriglia.

square·ly ['skwɛəlɪ] ADV a (*directly*) direttamente; **to place sth squarely in the middle of the table** mettere qc proprio in mezzo al tavolo; **to face sth squarely** affrontare qc con coraggio b (*honestly, fairly*) onestamente; **to deal squarely with sb** trattare qn onestamente.

♦ **square root** N radice *f* quadrata.

squash¹ [skwɒʃ] 1 N a (*Brit: drink*): **orange/lemon squash** ≈ sciroppo di arancia/limone

b (*crowd*) ressa, calca.

2 VT a (*squeeze*) schiacciare; **can you squash two more in?** (*passengers*) puoi farne entrare altri due?; **to be squashed together** essere schiacciati(-e) l'uno(-a) contro l'altro(-a)

b (*fig: argument*) soffocare; (: *opposition*) mettere a tacere; (: *person*) umiliare, schiacciare.

3 VI: **to squash in** riuscire a entrare; **to squash up to make room for sb** stringersi per fare posto a qn.

squash² [skwɒʃ] N (*vegetable*) zucca.

squash³ [skwɒʃ] N (*Sport*) squash *m.*

♦ **squash ball** N pallina da squash.

♦ **squash court** N campo da squash.

♦ **squash racket** N racchetta da squash.

squashy ['skwɒʃɪ] ADJ (*fruit*) molle; (*cushion etc*) morbido(-a).

squat [skwɒt] 1 ADJ (*comp* **-ter,** *superl* **-test**) (*person*) tarchiato(-a), tozzo(-a); (*building, shape etc*) tozzo(-a).

2 VI a (*also:* **squat down**) accovacciarsi, acquattarsi b (*on property*) occupare abusivamente; **to squat in a house** occupare abusivamente una casa.

3 N (*fam: house*) casa occupata.

squat·ter ['skwɒtə'] N occupante *m/f* abusivo(-a).

squaw [skwɔː] N squaw *f inv.*

squawk [skwɔːk] 1 N strido rauco.

2 VI (*parrot, baby, person*) strillare; (*fam: complain*) lamentarsi.

squeak [skwiːk] 1 N (*of hinge, wheel etc*) cigolio; (*of shoes*) scricchiolio; (*of mouse etc*) squittio; **a squeak of surprise** un gridolino di sorpresa; **I don't want to hear a squeak out of you!** non voglio sentire una parola!

2 VI (*see n*) cigolare; scricchiolare; squittire; emettere un gridolino.

squeaky ['skwiːkɪ] ADJ (*comp* **-ier,** *superl* **-iest**) (*hinge, wheel*) cigolante; (*shoes*) scricchiolante; **squeaky clean**

(*hair*) splendente; (*fig*: *very clean*: *office, home*) tirato(-a) a specchio; (: *person*: *irreproachable*) dall'immagine cristallina.

squeal [skwi:l] **1** N (*gen*) strillo; (*of tyres, brakes*) stridore *m*; **a squeal of laughter** una risatina.

2 VI (*see n*) strillare; stridere; (*fam*: *inform*): **to squeal (on sb)** fare una soffiata (a qn).

squeam·ish ['skwi:mɪʃ] ADJ (*easily nauseated*) facilmente impressionabile; **I was too squeamish to look** mi faceva troppa impressione guardare.

squeam·ish·ness ['skwi:mɪʃnɪs] N impressionabilità.

squeeze [skwi:z] **1** N (*pressure*) pressione *f*; (*of hand*) stretta; (*crush, crowd*) ressa, calca; **credit squeeze** (*Fin*) stretta creditizia; **to give sb's hand a squeeze** dare una lieve stretta di mano a qn; **it was a tight squeeze to get through** c'era appena il posto per passare; **we're in a tight squeeze** (*fig fam*) ci troviamo in difficoltà; **a squeeze of lemon** una spruzzata di limone; **give me a squeeze of toothpaste** dammi un po' di dentifricio; **to put the squeeze on sb** far pressione su qn.

2 VT (*gen*) premere; (*sponge*) strizzare; (*lemon etc*) spremere; (*hand, arm*) stringere; **to squeeze the juice out of a lemon** spremere un limone; **to squeeze toothpaste out of a tube** spremere il dentifricio da un tubetto; **to squeeze clothes into a case** pigiare i vestiti in una valigia; **to squeeze information out of sb** strappare delle informazioni a qn; **can you squeeze two more in?** riesci a farcene entrare altri due?.

3 VI: **to squeeze past/under sth** passare vicino/sotto a qc con difficoltà; **to squeeze in** infilarsi; **to squeeze through a hole** passare a forza attraverso un buco; **to squeeze through the crowd** riuscire ad aprirsi un varco tra la folla

▶ **squeeze out** VT + ADV spremere.

squeez·er ['skwi:zə'] N: **lemon squeezer** spremiagrumi *m inv*.

squelch [skwɛltʃ] VI: **to squelch in/out** *etc* entrare/uscire sguazzando.

squib [skwɪb] N petardo.

squid [skwɪd] N calamaro.

squig·gle ['skwɪgl] **1** N scarabocchio.

2 VI scarabocchiare.

squint [skwɪnt] **1** N (*Med*) strabismo; (*sidelong look*) occhiata, sbirciata; **to have a squint** (*Med*) essere strabico(-a); **let's have a squint** (*fam*) diamo un'occhiata.

2 VI (*Med*) essere strabico(-a); **to squint at sth** guardare qc di traverso; (*quickly*) sbirciare qc; **he squinted in the sunlight** la luce del sole gli faceva strizzare gli occhi.

squire ['skwaɪə'] N (*old*: *landowner*) possidente *m*.

squirm [skwɜ:m] VI contorcersi; **to squirm with embarrassment** sentirsi morire dall'imbarazzo.

squir·rel ['skwɪrəl] N scoiattolo; **red squirrel** scoiattolo eurasiatico; **grey squirrel** scoiattolo grigio.

squirt [skwɜ:t] **1** N (*of water*) schizzo; (*of detergent, perfume*) spruzzo.

2 VT spruzzare.

3 VI schizzare.

Sr ABBR = **senior, sister** c.

Sri Lan·ka ['srɪ'læŋkə] N lo Sri Lanka.

Sri Lan·kan ['srɪ'læŋkən] **1** ADJ dello Sri Lanka.

2 N abitante *m/f or* nativo(-a) dello Sri Lanka.

SRN [,ɛsɑːr'ɛn] N ABBR (*Brit*: = *State Registered Nurse*) infermiera diplomata (*dopo corso triennale*).

SS [,ɛs'ɛs] ABBR = **steamship**.

SSA [,ɛsɛs'eɪ] N ABBR (*Am*: = *Social Security Administration*) ≈ Previdenza Sociale.

ST [,ɛs'tiː] ABBR (*Am*) = **Standard Time**.

St ABBR = **Saint**.

St. ABBR = **Street**.

stab [stæb] **1** N **a** (*with knife*) coltellata; (*with dagger*) pugnalata; (*of pain*) fitta; **a stab in the back** (*also fig*) una pugnalata alla schiena; **he felt a stab of remorse** gli rimordeva la coscienza

b (*fam*: *try*): **to have a stab at (doing) sth** provare a fare qc.

2 VT (*with dagger*) pugnalare; (*with knife*) accoltellare; **to stab sb to death** uccidere qn a coltellate; **to stab sb in the back** (*also fig*) pugnalare qn alla schiena; **he was stabbed through the heart** fu pugnalato al cuore.

stab·bing ['stæbɪŋ] **1** N: **there's been a stabbing** c'è stato un accoltellamento.

2 ADJ (*pain, ache*) lancinante.

sta·bil·ity [stə'bɪlɪtɪ] N (*structural, political, economic*) stabilità; (*mental, emotional*) equilibrio; (*of family, relationship*) solidità.

sta·bi·li·za·tion [,steɪbəlaɪ'zeɪʃən] N stabilizzazione *f*.

sta·bi·lize ['steɪbəˌlaɪz] **1** VT stabilizzare; **stabilizing jacket** (*Skin diving*) giubbetto equilibratore.

2 VI stabilizzarsi.

sta·bi·li·zer ['steɪbəˌlaɪzə'] N (*Aer, Naut*) stabilizzatore *m*.

sta·ble¹ ['steɪbl] ADJ (*comp* **-r**, *superl* **-st**) (*government, economy*) stabile; (*relationship*) solido(-a), stabile; (*person*: *emotionally, mentally*) equilibrato(-a); **the patient is stable** (*Med*) le condizioni del paziente sono stazionarie.

sta·ble² ['steɪbl] **1** N (*building*) stalla; (*establishment*) scuderia; **riding stables** maneggio.

2 VT (*keep in stable*) tenere in una stalla.

stable·boy ['steɪblˌbɔɪ], **stable·lad** ['steɪblˌlæd] N garzone *m* di stalla.

♦ **stab wound** N ferita da taglio.

stac·ca·to [stə'kɑːtəʊ] (*Mus*) **1** ADV in staccato.

2 ADJ staccato(-a); (*sound*) scandito(-a).

stack [stæk] **1** N **a** (*pile*) pila, catasta; (*Brit fam*) mucchio, sacco; **there's stacks of time to finish it** abbiamo un sacco di tempo per finirlo

b (*also*: **chimney stack**) comignolo; (: *of factory*) ciminiera

c (*Geog*) faraglione *m*.

2 VT (*books, boxes*) impilare, accatastare; (*chairs*) mettere l'uno(-a) sopra l'altro(-a); (*aircraft*) tenere a quote assegnate (*in attesa dell'atterraggio*); **the cards are stacked against us** (*fig*) tutto è contro di noi.

stack·er ['stækə'] N (*on printer*) casella di ricezione.

sta·dium ['steɪdɪəm] N stadio.

staff [stɑːf] **1** N **a** (*personnel*: *gen*) personale *m*; (: *servants*) personale di servizio; (*Mil*) Stato Maggiore; **the administrative staff** il personale amministrativo; **the teaching staff** il corpo insegnante; **to be on the staff** far parte del personale *or* dell'organico; **a staff of 15** un personale *or* organico di 15 persone; **to join the staff** entrare a far parte del personale; **"staff only"** "passaggio di servizio"

b (*old*: *stick*) bastone *m*; (*Rel*) bastone pastorale; (*of flag*) asta

c (*Mus*: *also*: **stave**) pentagramma *m*, rigo.

2 VT fornire di personale; **to be staffed by Asians/women** avere un personale asiatico/costituito da donne; **to be well staffed** essere ben fornito(-a) di

personale.

staff·ing ['stɑːfɪŋ] ① N dotazione *f* di personale.
② ADJ: **staffing problems** problemi *mpl* di personale.
♦ **staff meeting** N riunione *f* del personale; (*Scol*) riunione dei professori.
♦ **staff nurse** N (*Brit*) infermiere(-a).
♦ **staff officer** N (*Mil*) ufficiale *m* di Stato Maggiore.
♦ **staff room** N sala dei professori.
Staffs ABBR (*Brit*) = *Staffordshire*.
stag [stæg] N (*Zool*) cervo; (*Brit Stock Exchange*) rialzista *m/f* su nuove emissioni.
♦ **stag beetle** N cervo volante.
stage [steɪdʒ] ① N **a** (*period, section: of process, development*) fase *f*, stadio; (: *of journey*) tappa; (: *of rocket*) stadio; **in stages** (*travel, work etc*) a tappe; **in** *or* **by easy stages** a piccole tappe; **in the early/final stages** negli stadi iniziali/finali; **at this stage in the negotiations** in questa fase dei negoziati; **to go through a difficult stage** attraversare un periodo difficile
  b (*platform*) palco; (: *in theatre*) palcoscenico; **the stage** (*profession*) il teatro; **to go on the stage** entrare in scena; (*become an actor*) fare del teatro.
  ② VT (*play*) mettere in scena, rappresentare; (*arrange: welcome, demonstration*) organizzare; (*fake: accident*) simulare; **to stage a scene** allestire una scena; (*fig*) fare una sceneggiata; **to stage a quick recovery** riprendersi subito; **to stage a comeback** fare ritorno.
stage·coach ['steɪdʒˌkəʊtʃ] N diligenza.
stage·craft ['steɪdʒˌkrɑːft] N tecnica teatrale.
♦ **stage direction** N (*in text*) didascalie *fpl*.
♦ **stage director** N regista *m/f* teatrale.
♦ **stage door** N ingresso degli artisti.
♦ **stage fright** N panico prima di andare in scena; **to get stage fright** essere assalito(-a) dal panico prima di andare in scena.
stage·hand ['steɪdʒˌhænd] N (*Theatre*) macchinista *m*.
♦ **stage-manage** ['steɪdʒˌmænɪdʒ] VT (*event, confrontation*) montare, inscenare; (: *pej*) orchestrare.
♦ **stage manager** N direttore(-trice) di scena.
♦ **stage name** N nome *m* d'arte.
♦ **stage-struck** ['steɪdʒˌstrʌk] ADJ: **to be stage-struck** essere preso(-a) dal fuoco sacro del teatro.
♦ **stage whisper** N (*fig*) sussurro perfettamente udibile.
stag·ey ['steɪdʒɪ] ADJ = **stagy**.
stag·fla·tion [stæg'fleɪʃən] N stagflazione *f*.
stag·ger ['stægəʳ] ① VT **a** (*amaze: person*) sbalordire **b** (*holidays, payments, hours*) scaglionare; (*objects*) disporre a intervalli.
  ② VI barcollare; **to stagger along/in/out** avanzare/entrare/uscire barcollando; **he staggered to the door** andò verso la porta barcollando.
stag·gered ['stægəd] ADJ **a** (*amazed*) sbalordito(-a), stupefatto(-a) **b** (*hours, holidays etc*) scaglionato(-a); **staggered working hours** orario di lavoro scaglionato *or* diversificato.
stag·ger·ing ['stægərɪŋ] ADJ (*amazing*) sbalorditivo(-a), incredibile.
stag·ing post ['steɪdʒɪŋˌpəʊst] N tappa obbligata.
stag·nant ['stægnənt] ADJ stagnante.
stag·nate [stæg'neɪt] VI (*water*) stagnare; (*fig: economy*) ristagnare; (: *person*) vegetare; (: *mind*) intorpidirsi.
stag·na·tion [stæg'neɪʃən] N (*of water, economy*) ristagno, stagnazione *f*; (*of mind*) intorpidimento.
♦ **stag night**, **stag party** N festa di addio al celibato.
stagy, **stagey** ['steɪdʒɪ] ADJ (*comp* **-ier**, *superl* **-iest**) (*pej*)

teatrale.
staid [steɪd] ADJ (*comp* **-er**, *superl* **-est**) compassato(-a).
staid·ness ['steɪdnɪs] N eccessiva posatezza.
stain [steɪn] ① N **a** (*also fig*) macchia; **grease stain** macchia di grasso **b** (*dye*) colorante *m*.
  ② VT **a** (*also fig*) macchiare; **to stain with** macchiare di **b** (*wood*) tingere; (: *glass*) colorare.
  ③ VI macchiarsi.
♦ **stained glass** [ˌsteɪnd'glɑːs] N vetro colorato.
♦ **stained-glass window** [ˌsteɪndglɑːs'wɪndəʊ] N vetrata colorata.
stain·less ['steɪnlɪs] ADJ (*steel*) inossidabile.
♦ **stain remover** N smacchiatore *m*.
stair [stɛəʳ] N (*single step*) scalino, gradino; (*whole flight: usu pl*) scala; **he fell down the stairs** è caduto (giù) per le scale; **on the stairs** per le *or* sulle scale.
♦ **stair carpet** N guida.
stair·case ['stɛəˌkeɪs], **stair·way** ['stɛəˌweɪ] N scala.
♦ **stair rod** N asta metallica per fissare la guida.
stair·well ['stɛəˌwɛl] N tromba delle scale.
stake [steɪk] ① N **a** (*share*) interesse *m*; (*bet*) puntata, scommessa; **to be at stake** essere in gioco; **to have a stake in sth** avere un interesse in qc
  b (*for fence, tree*) palo; (*for plant*) bastoncino
  c (*for execution*): **to be burnt at the stake** essere bruciato(-a) sul rogo.
  ② VT **a** (*bet*): **to stake (on)** scommettere (su); **I'd stake my reputation on it** ci giocherei la reputazione
  b (*also:* **stake out**: *area*) delimitare con paletti; (*also:* **stake up**: *plant*) legare a un bastoncino; **to stake a claim (to sth)** rivendicare (qc).
stake·out ['steɪkaʊt] N (*esp Am Police*) sorveglianza.
stal·ac·tite ['stæləkˌtaɪt] N stalattite *f*.
stal·ag·mite ['stæləgˌmaɪt] N stalagmite *f*.
stale [steɪl] ADJ (*comp* **-r**, *superl* **-st**) (*food: gen*) stantio(-a); (: *bread*) stantio(-a), raffermo(-a); (: *beer*) svaporato(-a); (*air*) viziato(-a); (*news, joke*) vecchio(-a) come il cucco, trito(-a); (*Law: claim*) caduto(-a) in prescrizione, prescritto(-a); **I'm getting stale** non ho più entusiasmo.
stale·mate ['steɪlˌmeɪt] N (*Chess*) stallo; (*fig*) punto morto; **to reach stalemate** (*fig*) arrivare a un punto morto.
stale·ness ['steɪlnɪs] N (*of food*) mancanza di freschezza; (*of air*) pesantezza.
Sta·lin·ism ['stɑːlɪˌnɪzəm] N stalinismo.
Sta·lin·ist ['stɑːlɪnɪst] N stalinista *m/f*.
stalk[1] [stɔːk] ① VT (*animal, person*) inseguire.
  ② VI: **to stalk in/out** *etc* entrare/uscire *etc* impettito(-a); **she stalked out of the room angrily** uscì furiosa dalla stanza.
stalk[2] [stɔːk] N (*Bot*) gambo, stelo; (*of cabbage*) torsolo; (*of fruit*) picciolo.
stall [stɔːl] ① N **a** (*Agr: stable*) stalla, box *m inv*; (*Brit: in market*) bancarella, banco; (*at exhibition, fair*) stand *m inv*; **a newspaper/flower stall** chiosco del giornalaio/del fioraio
  b (*Theatre*): **the stalls** la platea
  c (*Aer*) stallo.
  ② VT (*plane*) far andare in stallo; **he stalled the car** gli si è spento il motore.
  ③ VI **a** (*car, engine*) bloccarsi; (*plane*) andare in stallo
  b (*fig: delay*): **to stall for time** prendere tempo, temporeggiare; **stop stalling!** smettila di menare il can per l'aia!
stall·holder ['stɔːlˌhəʊldəʳ] N (*Brit*) bancarellista *m/f*.
stal·lion ['stæljən] N stallone *m*.

stal·wart ['stɔ:lwət] [1] ADJ (*person*: *in spirit*) prode, coraggioso(-a); (*party member*) fidato(-a); (*supporter, opponent*) risoluto(-a), deciso(-a).
[2] N prode *m*, persona coraggiosa.

sta·men ['steɪmɛn] N stame *m*.

stami·na ['stæmɪnə] N resistenza; **he's got stamina** ha molta resistenza.

stam·mer ['stæmə'] [1] N balbuzie *f*.
[2] VI, VT balbettare.

stam·mer·er ['stæmərə'] N balbuziente *m/f*.

stamp [stæmp] [1] N **a** (*also*: **postage stamp**) francobollo; (*also*: **trading stamp**) bollino premio, ≈ marchetta
b (*rubber stamp*) timbro; (*mark*) bollo; **it bears the stamp of genius** porta l'impronta del genio
c: **with an angry stamp of her foot** battendo il piede per terra con rabbia.
[2] VT **a**: **to stamp one's feet** battere i piedi; (*in anger*) pestare i piedi; **to stamp the ground** (*person*) pestare i piedi per terra; (*horse*) scalpitare
b (*letter*) affrancare
c (*mark with rubber stamp*) timbrare, bollare; (*emboss*) imprimere su; **they stamped my passport at the border** mi hanno timbrato il passaporto al confine.
[3] VI (*single movement*) battere il piede per terra; **to stamp in/out** entrare/uscire infuriato(-a); **ouch, you stamped on my foot!** ahi, mi hai pestato un piede!
▶ **stamp out** VT + ADV (*fire*) estinguere; (*crime*) eliminare; (*opposition*) soffocare.
♦ **stamp album** N (*new*) album *m inv* per francobolli; (*containing stamps*) album *m inv* di francobolli.
♦ **stamp collecting** N filatelia.
♦ **stamp collection** N collezione *f* di francobolli.
♦ **stamp collector** N collezionista *m/f* di francobolli.
♦ **stamp dealer** N commerciante *m/f* di francobolli da collezione, filatelico(-a).
♦ **stamp duty** N (*Brit*) bollo.

stamped addressed envelope ['stæmptəd,rɛst-'ɛnvələʊp] N busta affrancata per la risposta.

stam·pede [stæm'pi:d] [1] N (*of cattle*) fuga precipitosa; (*of people*) fuggi fuggi *m inv*; **there was a sudden stampede for the door** ci fu un fuggi fuggi verso la porta.
[2] VT (*cattle*) far scappare; **to stampede sb into doing sth** (*pej*) spingere qn a fare qc senza dargli il tempo di riflettere.
[3] VI (*cattle*) fuggire precipitosamente; (*fig*) precipitarsi.

stamp·ing ground ['stæmpɪŋ'graʊnd] N: **to be sb's (old) stamping ground** essere il ritrovo (favorito) di qn.
♦ **stamp machine** N distributore *m* automatico di francobolli.

stance [stæns] N **a** (*way of standing*) posizione *f* **b** (*attitude*) presa di posizione *f*.

stand [stænd] (*vb*: *pt, pp* **stood**) [1] N **a** (*booth*) chiosco; (*market stall*) banco, bancarella; (*at exhibition, fair*) stand *m inv*; (*raised area*: *also*: **bandstand**) palco; (: *Sport*) tribuna; (: *Am Law*: *also*: **witness stand**) banco; **a music stand** un leggio; **he kicked the ball into the stand** con un calcio ha tirato la palla in tribuna
b (*position, also fig*) posizione *f*; (*resistance*) resistenza; **to take (up) one's stand at the door** prendere il proprio posto vicino alla porta; **to take a stand on an issue** prendere posizione su un problema; **to make a stand against sth** (*Mil, fig*) opporre resistenza contro qc
c (*also*: **taxi stand**) posteggio di taxi.

[2] VT **a** (*place*) mettere, porre; **to stand sth against a wall** appoggiare qc a un muro; **to stand sth on end** mettere qc in piedi
b (*withstand, bear*: *weight*) reggere a, resistere, sopportare; **it won't stand serious examination** non reggerà ad un esame accurato; **the troops stood heavy bombardment** le truppe hanno sopportato pesanti bombardamenti; **the company will have to stand the loss** la ditta dovrà sostenere la perdita; **to stand the cost of** sobbarcarsi le spese di
c (*tolerate*) sopportare; **I can't stand him** non lo sopporto; **I can't stand the sight of him** non lo posso vedere; **I can't stand it any longer!** non ce la faccio più!; **I can't stand waiting for people** non sopporto aspettare la gente
d (*fam*: *treat*): **to stand sb a drink/meal** offrire da bere/un pranzo a qn
e (*phrases*): **to stand guard** *or* **watch** (*Mil*) essere di guardia *or* sentinella; **to stand guard over** (*Mil, fig*) fare la guardia a.
[3] VI **a** (*be upright*) stare in piedi; (*stay standing*) restare in piedi; (*get up*) alzarsi; **I had to stand** sono dovuto restare in piedi; **he could hardly stand** si reggeva a malapena; **the woman standing over there** la donna in piedi laggiù; **don't just stand there - help me!** non stare lì impalato - aiutami!; **the house is still standing** la casa è ancora in piedi; **they stood talking for hours** restarono a parlare per delle ore; **they kept us standing about** *or* **around for ages** ci hanno fatto aspettare in piedi per ore; **to stand on sb's foot** pestare il piede a qn; **to stand in sb's way** intralciare il passaggio a qn; **I won't stand in your way** (*fig*) non ti sarò d'ostacolo; **nothing stands in our way** la via è libera; **that was all that stood between him and ...** era tutto ciò che si frapponeva fra lui e...; **nothing stands between us** non c'è niente che ci separi; **to be left standing** (*building*) essere rimasto(-a) in piedi; (*fig*: *competitor*) essere bruciato(-a) in partenza; **it made my hair stand on end** mi ha fatto rizzare i capelli; **to stand still** stare fermo(-a) (in piedi); **to stand fast** tener duro; **to stand on one's own two feet** (*fig*) cavarsela da solo(-a); **to stand on one's head/hands** fare la verticale in appoggio/la verticale; **he could do the job standing on his head** potrebbe fare quel lavoro a occhi chiusi; **to stand a (good) chance of** avere una (buona) possibilità di; **to stand on the brakes** (*Aut*) frenare di colpo; **to stand on one's dignity** stare sulle sue
b: **he stands over 6 feet** è alto più di 2m; **the tower stands 50m high** la torre è alta 50m
c (*be situated*: *building, tree*) trovarsi, stare; **the car stands outside all year round** la macchina sta fuori tutto l'anno
d (*Culin*): **to leave to stand** (*tea*) lasciare in infusione; (*batter*) (lasciar) riposare; **my objection still stands** la mia obiezione è ancora valida; **to let sth stand as it is** lasciare qc così com'è; **the theory stands or falls on this** è questo il presupposto su cui si basa la teoria; **it stands to reason that ...** è logico che...
e (*fig*: *be placed*) stare; **to stand accused of** essere accusato(-a) di; **how do things stand?** come stanno le cose?; **as things stand** stando così le cose; **to stand at** (*thermometer, clock*) indicare, segnare; (*offer, price, sales*) ammontare a; (*score*) essere
f (*Pol*): **to stand as a candidate** candidarsi; **to stand in an election** candidarsi ad un'elezione; **to stand for Parliament** candidarsi al Parlamento

g (*Naut*): **to stand out to sea** stare al largo
▶ **stand aside** VI + ADV farsi da parte, scostarsi
▶ **stand back** VI + ADV tirarsi indietro; (*building: be placed further back*): **to stand back from** essere arretrato(-a) rispetto a
▶ **stand by** ⓵ VI + ADV (*be onlooker*) stare là (a non far niente); (*be ready*) tenersi pronto(-a); **stand by for further news** tenetevi pronti a ricevere altre notizie.
⓶ VI + PREP (*person*) rimanere vicino(-a) a; (*promise*) mantenere; (*opinion*) sostenere
▶ **stand down** VI + ADV (*withdraw*) ritirarsi; (*Mil*) smontare di guardia; (*Law*) lasciare il banco dei testimoni; **to stand down in favour of** (*fig*) farsi da parte a favore di
▶ **stand for** VI + PREP **a** (*represent: principle, honesty*) rappresentare; (: *subj: initials*) indicare, stare per
b (*tolerate*) tollerare, sopportare; **I won't stand for that** non tollero una cosa del genere
c (*Pol*) = **stand 3f**
▶ **stand in** VI + ADV: **to stand in for sb** sostituire qn
▶ **stand out** VI + ADV **a** (*be noticeable: veins, eyes*) sporgere; (: *colours*) risaltare, spiccare; (: *person*) distinguersi; (: *mountains*) stagliarsi; **it stands out a mile!** si vede lontano un miglio!
b (*be firm, hold out*) resistere, tener duro; **to stand out against sth** opporsi fermamente a qc; **to stand out for sth** rivendicare qc, insistere su qc
▶ **stand over** ⓵ VI + ADV (*items for discussion*) rimanere in sospeso.
⓶ VT + PREP (*person*) stare adosso a
▶ **stand to** VI + ADV (*Mil*) tenersi pronto(-a)
▶ **stand up** ⓵ VI + ADV (*rise*) alzarsi in piedi; (*be standing*) stare in piedi; (*fig: argument*) reggersi.
⓶ VT + ADV (*fam: girlfriend, boyfriend*): **she stood me up** non è venuta all'appuntamento
▶ **stand up for** VI + ADV + PREP difendere; **to stand up for sb/sth** difendere qn/qc; **to stand up for o.s.** difendersi
▶ **stand up to** VI + ADV + PREP tenere testa a, resistere a; **to stand up to sb** tenere testa a qn, affrontare qn con coraggio; **it stands up to hard wear** è resistente (all'uso).
♦ **stand-alone** [ˌstændə'ləʊn] ADJ (*Comput*) a sé stante, indipendente; **stand-alone word processor** elaboratore *m* di testi indipendente.
stand·ard ['stændəd] ⓵ N **a** (*norm*) standard *m inv*; (*intellectual standard*) livello culturale; **the gold standard** (*Fin*) il tallone aureo; **to be or come up to standard** rispondere ai requisiti; **to set a high standard** dare il buon esempio; **at first-year university standard** a livello del primo anno d'università; **of (a) high/low standard** di alto/basso livello; **below or not up to standard** (*work*) mediocre
b (*moral: usu pl*) scala di valori; **moral standards** valori *mpl* morali; **to accept sb's standards** accettare la scala di valori di qn; **to apply a double standard** avere due pesi e due misure
c (*flag*) insegna; (*Mil*) stendardo.
⓶ ADJ (*size, quality*) standard *inv*; (*reference book*) classico(-a).
♦ **standard-bearer** ['stændədˌbɛərəʳ] N (*Mil, fig*) portabandiera *m/f*.
♦ **standard English** N inglese *m* standard.
stand·ard·i·za·tion [ˌstændədaɪ'zeɪʃən] N standardizzazione *f*.
stand·ard·ize ['stændədaɪz] VT standardizzare.
♦ **standard lamp** N (*Brit*) lampada a stelo.

♦ **standard model** N modello di serie.
♦ **standard of living** N tenore *m or* standard *m inv* di vita.
♦ **standard practice** N procedura normale; **it's standard practice to do so** è d'ordinaria amministrazione fare così; **to become standard practice** diventare normale.
♦ **standard rate** N (*Fin: of income tax*) aliquota di base.
♦ **standard time** N ora ufficiale.
♦ **stand-by** ['stændˌbaɪ] N **a** (*person*) riserva; **have you got a stand-by, should that fail?** ha qualcosa che lo rimpiazzi nel caso che non funzioni?; **to be on stand-by** (*gen*) tenersi pronto(-a); (*doctor*) essere di guardia **b** (*also:* **stand-by ticket**) biglietto *m* stand-by *inv*.
♦ **stand-by generator** N generatore *m* d'emergenza.
♦ **stand-by passenger** N (*Aer*) passeggero(-a) in lista d'attesa.
♦ **stand-by ticket** N (*Aer*) biglietto *m* stand-by *inv*.
♦ **stand-in** ['stændˌɪn] N sostituto(-a); (*Cine*) controfigura.
stand·ing ['stændɪŋ] ⓵ ADJ **a** (*passenger*) in piedi; (*upright: corn*) non mietuto(-a); **he was given a standing ovation** tutti si alzarono per applaudirlo; **standing start** partenza da fermo; **standing waves** (*Phys*) onde *fpl* stazionarie
b (*permanent: rule*) fisso(-a); (: *army*) regolare; (*grievance*) continuo(-a); **it's a standing joke** è diventato proverbiale.
⓶ N **a** (*social position*) rango, condizione *f*, posizione *f*; (*repute*) reputazione *f*; **financial standing** standing *m*; **a man of some standing** un uomo di una certa importanza; **what is his standing locally?** che reputazione ha da queste parti?
b (*duration*): **of 6 months' standing** che dura da 6 mesi; **of long standing** di lunga data.
♦ **standing committee** N commissione *f* permanente.
♦ **standing order** N **a** (*Brit: at bank*) ordine *m* permanente (di pagamento) **b**: **standing orders** NPL (*Mil, Parliament*) regolamento.
♦ **standing room** N posto in piedi.
♦ **standing stone** N menhir *m inv*.
♦ **stand-off** ['stændˌɒf] N (*stalemate*) situazione *f* di stallo.
stand·off·ish [ˌstænd'ɒfɪʃ] ADJ (*fam pej*) scostante, freddo (-a).
stand·off·ish·ly [ˌstænd'ɒfɪʃlɪ] ADV (*fam pej*) in modo scostante, con freddezza.
stand·pat ['stænd'pæt] ADJ (*Am*) irremovibile.
stand·pipe ['stændˌpaɪp] N fontanella.
stand·point ['stændˌpɔɪnt] N punto di vista.
stand·still ['stændˌstɪl] N: **to bring a car to a standstill** fermare una macchina; **to be at a standstill** (*vehicle*) essere fermo(-a); (*industry etc*) ristagnare, essere paralizzato(-a); **to come to a standstill** (*vehicle*) fermarsi; (*industry etc*) rimanere paralizzato(-a); (*production*) arrestarsi; (*talks, negotiations*) giungere a un punto morto.
♦ **stand-to** ['stænd'tuː] N (*Mil: order*): **to give the stand-to** dare l'allerta.
♦ **stand-up** ['stændˌʌp] ADJ (*fight, argument*) accanito(-a); (*meal*) in piedi; **stand-up comedian** ≈ comico da cabaret.
stank [stæŋk] PT of **stink**.
stan·za ['stænzə] N stanza (*Poesia*).
sta·ple[1] ['steɪpl] ⓵ N (*for papers*) punto metallico.
⓶ VT (*also:* **staple together**) cucire con punti metallici.
sta·ple[2] ['steɪpl] ⓵ ADJ (*diet, food, products*) base *inv*; (*crop,*

industry) principale.

[2] N (*chief product*) prodotto principale; (*of diet*) alimento principale.

♦ **staple extractor** N levapunti *m inv.*

♦ **staple gun** N pistola *f* sparachiodi *inv.*

sta·pler ['steɪplə'], **sta·pling ma·chine** ['steɪplɪŋmə,ʃiːn] N cucitrice *f.*

star [stɑː'] [1] N **a** (*gen*) stella; (*Mil*) stelletta; (*Typ etc*) asterisco; **four-star hotel** albergo a quattro stelle; **3-star petrol** (*Brit*) ≈ benzina normale; **4-star petrol** (*Brit*) ≈ (benzina) super *f*, **born under a lucky star** nato(-a) sotto una buona stella; **the stars** (*horoscope*) le stelle; **you can thank your lucky stars that ...** puoi ringraziare la tua buona stella che...+ *sub*; **to see stars** (*fig*) vedere le stelle **b** (*celebrity*) divo(-a); (*actress only*) stella.

[2] VT (*Cine etc*) essere interpretato(-a) da; **a film starring Greta Garbo** un film con Greta Garbo.

[3] VI (*Cine etc*): **to star in a film** essere il (*or* la) protagonista di un film; **he starred as Othello** ha interpretato il ruolo di Otello.

♦ **star attraction** N (*in show*) numero principale; (*in museum*) l'attrazione *f* principale.

star·board ['stɑːbəd] N tribordo; **on the starboard side** a dritta, a tribordo.

starch [stɑːtʃ] [1] N amido.

[2] VT inamidare.

starched [stɑːtʃt] ADJ (*collar*) inamidato(-a).

♦ **starch-reduced** [,stɑːtʃrɪ'djuːsd] ADJ (*bread etc*) povero (-a) d'amido.

starchy ['stɑːtʃɪ] ADJ (*comp* **-ier**, *superl* **-iest**) (*food*) ricco (-a) di amido.

star·dom ['stɑːdəm] N celebrità.

stare [stɛə'] [1] N sguardo fisso; **a vacant stare** uno sguardo assente.

[2] VT: **it's staring you in the face** (*obvious*) salta agli occhi; (*very near*) ce l'hai sotto il naso.

[3] VI: **to stare at sb/sth** fissare qn/qc; **to stare into space** fissare il vuoto; **to stare at sb in surprise** fissare qn con aria sorpresa; **it's rude to stare** non sta bene fissare la gente

▶ **stare out** VT + ADV (*fissare fino a*) fare abbassare gli occhi a.

star·fish ['stɑː,fɪʃ] N stella di mare.

star·gaz·ing ['stɑː,geɪzɪŋ] N (*fig*): **to be stargazing** avere la testa nelle nuvole.

stark [stɑːk] [1] ADJ (*comp* **-er**, *superl* **-est**) (*outline*) aspro (-a); (*landscape*) desolato(-a); (*simplicity, colour*) austero (-a); (*contrast*) forte; (*reality, poverty, truth*) crudo(-a).

[2] ADV: **stark staring** *or* **raving mad** matto(-a) da legare; **stark naked** nudo(-a) come un verme.

stark·ers ['stɑːkəz] ADJ (*Brit fam*) nudo(-a) come un verme.

star·let ['stɑːlɪt] N (*Cine*) stellina.

star·light ['stɑː,laɪt] N: **in the starlight** alla luce delle stelle.

star·ling ['stɑːlɪŋ] N storno.

star·lit ['stɑː,lɪt] ADJ stellato(-a).

♦ **star part** N ruolo principale.

♦ **star player** N giocatore(-trice) di prima grandezza.

star·ry ['stɑːrɪ] ADJ (*comp* **-ier**, *superl* **-iest**) stellato(-a).

♦ **starry-eyed** [,stɑːrɪ'aɪd] ADJ (*idealistic, gullible*) ingenuo (-a); (*from wonder*) meravigliato(-a); (*from love*) perdutamente innamorato(-a).

♦ **Stars and Stripes** NPL: **the Stars and Stripes** la bandiera a stelle e strisce.

♦ **star sign** N segno zodiacale.

♦ **star-studded** ['stɑː,stʌdɪd] ADJ: **a star-studded cast** un cast di attori famosi.

start [stɑːt] [1] N **a** (*beginning*) inizio; (*in race*) partenza; (: *starting line*) linea di partenza; (*Mountaineering*) attacco; **at the start** all'inizio; **the start of the school year** l'inizio dell'anno scolastico; **from the start** dall'inizio; **for a start** tanto per cominciare; **to get off to a good** *or* **flying start** cominciare bene; **to make an early start** partire di buon'ora; **to make a fresh (*or* new) start in life** ricominciare daccapo *or* da zero **b** (*advantage*) vantaggio; **the thieves had 3 hours' start** i ladri avevano 3 ore di vantaggio; **to give sb a 5-minute start** dare un vantaggio di 5 minuti a qn **c** (*sudden movement*) sussulto, sobbalzo; **to give a start** trasalire; **to give sb a start** far trasalire qn; **to wake with a start** svegliarsi di soprassalto.

[2] VT **a** (*begin: gen*) cominciare, iniziare; (: *bottle*) aprire; (: *habit*) prendere; **to start doing sth** *or* **to do sth** iniziare a fare qc; **to start negotiations** avviare i negoziati; **he started life as a labourer** ha cominciato come operaio **b** (*cause to begin or happen: conversation, discussion*) iniziare; (: *quarrel*) cominciare, provocare; (: *rumour*) mettere in giro; (: *series of events, policy*) dare l'avvio a; (: *reform*) avviare; (: *fashion*) lanciare; (*found: business, newspaper*) fondare, creare; (*car, engine*) mettere in moto, avviare; **to start a fire** provocare un incendio; **to start a race** dare il via a una gara; **you started it!** hai cominciato tu!; **don't start anything!** non cominciare!; **don't start him on that!** non toccare quest'argomento in sua presenza!; **we'd like to start a family** ci piacerebbe avere un bambino subito.

[3] VI **a** (*begin: gen*) cominciare; (: *rumour*) nascere; (*on journey*) partire, mettersi in viaggio; (*car, engine*) mettersi in moto, partire; **starting from Tuesday** a partire da martedì; **to start on a task** cominciare un lavoro; **to start at the beginning** cominciare dall'inizio; **it started (off) well/badly** è cominciato bene/male; **she started (off) down the street** s'incamminò giù per la strada; **what shall we start (off) with?** con che cosa cominciamo?; **she started (off) as a nanny** ha cominciato come bambinaia; **to start (off) with ...** (*firstly*) per prima cosa...; (*at the beginning*) all'inizio...; **he started (off) by saying (that) ...** cominciò col dire che... **b** (*in fright*): **to start (at)** trasalire (a), sobbalzare (a); **his eyes were starting out of his head** aveva gli occhi fuori dalle orbite

▶ **start off** [1] VI + ADV (*leave*) partire; *see also* **start 3a**.

[2] VT + ADV causare, far nascere; **to start sb off** (*on complaints, story etc*) far cominciare qn; (*give initial help*) aiutare qn a cominciare; **that was enough to start him off** è bastato questo a dargli il via

▶ **start out** VI + ADV (*begin journey*) partire; (*fig*): **to start out as** cominciare come; **to start out to do sth** cominciare con l'intenzione di fare qc

▶ **start over** VI + ADV (*Am*) ricominciare

▶ **start up** [1] VI + ADV (*engine*) mettersi in moto; (*driver*) mettere in moto; (*music*) cominciare.

[2] VT + ADV (*car, engine*) mettere in moto, avviare.

start·er ['stɑːtə'] N **a** (*Brit Culin*): **as a starter** come *or* per antipasto; **for starters** (*fig*) per cominciare **b** (*Aut etc: motor*) motorino d'avviamento; (*on machine*) pulsante *m* d'accensione **c** (*Sport: judge*) starter *m inv*; (: *competitor*) concorrente *m/f*; **he was a late starter** (*child*) ha comin-

ciato tardi a leggere e a scrivere.

start·ing [ˈstɑːtɪŋ] ADJ di partenza.

♦ **starting handle** N (*Brit*) manovella d'avviamento.

♦ **starting point** N punto di partenza.

♦ **starting post** N palo di partenza.

♦ **starting price** N (*Horse-racing*) ultima quotazione.

star·tle [ˈstɑːtl] VT far trasalire, spaventare.

star·tling [ˈstɑːtlɪŋ] ADJ (*surprising*) sorprendente, sbalorditivo(-a); (*alarming*) impressionante.

♦ **star turn** N (*Theatre, fig: person*) vedette *f inv*; (*act*) attrazione *f* principale.

star·va·tion [stɑːˈveɪʃən] N inedia, fame *f*; **to die of starvation** morire d'inedia; **it might be fuel starvation** (*Tech*) potrebbe essere un problema di alimentazione del carburante.

♦ **starvation diet** N dieta da fame.

♦ **starvation wages** NPL salario *msg* da fame.

starve [stɑːv] [1] VT far patire la fame a, affamare; **to starve sb to death** far morire qn di fame; **to starve o.s.** lasciarsi morire di fame; **to starve sb into submission** prendere qn per fame; **to be starved of affection** soffrire per mancanza di affetto.

[2] VI (*lack food*) soffrire la fame; **to starve (to death)** morire di fame; **I'm starving!** (*fam*) sto morendo di fame!

starv·ing [ˈstɑːvɪŋ] ADJ affamato(-a).

stash [stæʃ] VT (*fam*): **to stash sth away** nascondere qc.

state [steɪt] [1] N a (*condition*) stato, condizione *f*; **state of emergency** stato di emergenza; **state of mind** stato d'animo; **state of war** stato di guerra; **to be in a bad/good state** essere in cattivo/buono stato; **he's not in a (fit) state to do it** non è in condizioni di farlo; **he arrived home in a shocking state** è arrivato a casa ridotto proprio male

b (*anxiety*) agitazione *f*; **now don't get into a state** non ti agitare

c (*pomp*): **in state** in pompa; **to lie in state** essere esposto(-a) solennemente

d (*Pol*): **the State** lo Stato.

[2] VT (*gen*) dichiarare, affermare; (*time, place*) decidere, fissare; (*conditions*) indicare; (*case, problem, theory, facts*) esporre; **as stated above** come indicato sopra; **state your name and address** fornisca nome e indirizzo; **cheques must state the amount clearly** gli assegni debbono indicare chiaramente la somma.

[3] ADJ (*business*) di stato; (*control*) statale; (*security*) dello stato; **the State line** (*Am*) il confine (tra due stati); **to pay a state visit to a country** andare in visita ufficiale in un paese.

♦ **state banquet** N banchetto ufficiale.

♦ **state-controlled** [ˌsteɪtkənˈtrəʊld] ADJ parastatale.

stat·ed [ˈsteɪtɪd] ADJ stabilito(-a), fissato(-a); **within stated limits** entro i limiti stabiliti.

♦ **State Department** N (*Am*): **the State Department** il Dipartimento di Stato, ≈ Ministero degli Esteri.

♦ **state education** N (*Brit*) istruzione *f* pubblica *or* statale.

state·less [ˈsteɪtlɪs] ADJ apolide; **a stateless person** un(a) apolide.

state·li·ness [ˈsteɪtlɪnɪs] N maestosità.

state·ly [ˈsteɪtlɪ] ADJ (*comp* **-ier**, *superl* **-iest**) maestoso(-a).

♦ **stately home** N (*Brit*) residenza nobiliare (*d'interesse storico e artistico*).

state·ment [ˈsteɪtmənt] N (*gen*) dichiarazione *f*; (*of views, facts*) esposizione *f*; (*Law*) deposizione *f*; (*Fin*) rendi-

conto; **statement of account** OR **bank statement** estratto conto; **official statement** comunicato ufficiale; **to make a statement** rilasciare una dichiarazione; (*Law*) fare una deposizione.

♦ **state of affairs** N circostanze *fpl*, situazione *f*.

♦ **state of the art** [1] ADJ (*equipment*) dell'ultima generazione.

[2] N: **the state of the art** l'ultima generazione.

♦ **state-owned** [ˈsteɪtˈəʊnd] ADJ statale, pubblico(-a).

state·room [ˈsteɪtˌrʊm] N (*in palace*) salone *m* di rappresentanza; (*on ship*) cabina.

States [steɪts] NPL: **the States** (*USA*) gli Stati *mpl* Uniti.

♦ **state school** N (*Brit*) scuola statale.

states·man [ˈsteɪtsmən] N (*pl* **-men**) statista *m*.

states·man·like [ˈsteɪtsmənˌlaɪk] ADJ da statista.

states·man·ship [ˈsteɪtsmənʃɪp] N abilità *f inv* politica.

♦ **state-subsidized** [ˌsteɪtˈsʌbsɪˌdaɪzd] ADJ sovvenzionato(-a) dallo stato.

♦ **state trooper** N (*Am*) agente *m* di polizia.

stat·ic [ˈstætɪk] [1] ADJ statico(-a); **static electricity** elettricità statica.

[2] N a (*Radio, TV*) scariche *fpl* b : **statics** NSG (*Phys*) statica.

sta·tion [ˈsteɪʃən] [1] N a (*gen, Rail*) stazione *f*; (*also*: **fire station**) caserma (dei pompieri); (*also*: **police station**) commissariato (di Pubblica Sicurezza), questura, caserma (dei Carabinieri); (*esp Mil: post*) base *f*; **action stations** posti *mpl* di combattimento

b (*Radio*) stazione *f*

c (*social position*) condizione *f* sociale, rango; **to have ideas above one's station** montarsi la testa.

[2] VT (*Mil: troops, sentry*) stanziare; (*fig*) piazzare; **to be stationed in** (*Mil*) essere di stanza in; **to station o.s. by the door** piazzarsi sulla porta.

[3] ADJ (*Rail: staff, bookstall*) della stazione.

sta·tion·ary [ˈsteɪʃənərɪ] ADJ (*gen*) fermo(-a), immobile; (*vehicle*) in sosta; (*temperature, condition*) stazionario (-a); (*not movable*) fisso(-a); **to remain stationary** rimanere fermo(-a); **stationary point** (*Math*) punto di stazionarietà.

sta·tion·er [ˈsteɪʃənəʳ] N cartolaio(-a); **stationer's shop** cartoleria.

sta·tion·ery [ˈsteɪʃənərɪ] N articoli *mpl* di cancelleria; (*writing paper*) carta da lettere.

♦ **station master** N (*Rail*) capostazione *m*.

♦ **station wagon** N (*Am Aut*) station-wagon *f*, familiare *f*.

sta·tis·tic [stəˈtɪstɪk] N statistica; see also **statistics**.

sta·tis·ti·cal [stəˈtɪstɪkəl] ADJ statistico(-a).

sta·tis·ti·cal·ly [stəˈtɪstɪkəlɪ] ADV statisticamente.

stat·is·ti·cian [ˌstætɪsˈtɪʃən] N esperto(-a) di statistica.

sta·tis·tics [stəˈtɪstɪks] [1] NSG (*science*) statistica.

[2] NPL (*numbers*) statistiche *fpl*.

statu·ary [ˈstætjʊərɪ] N (*frm: technique, statues*) statuaria.

statue [ˈstætjuː] N statua.

statu·esque [ˌstætjʊˈɛsk] ADJ (*woman*) statuario(-a).

statu·ette [ˌstætjʊˈɛt] N statuetta.

stat·ure [ˈstætʃəʳ] N a (*build*) statura; **to be of short stature** essere basso(-a) *or* di bassa statura b (*fig*) importanza; **a woman of considerable intellectual stature** una donna di grande levatura.

sta·tus [ˈsteɪtəs] N (*of person: legal, marital*) stato; (: *economic, official etc*) posizione *f*; (*of agreement etc*) validità; (*prestige*) prestigio; **social status** status *m inv*.

♦ **status quo** N: **the status quo** lo statu quo.

♦ **status symbol** N status symbol *m inv*.

stat·ute ['stætjuːt] N (*law*) legge *f*, statuto.

♦ **statute book** N codice *m*.

statu·tory ['stætjʊtərɪ] ADJ (*right, wage, control etc*) stabilito(-a) dalla legge; (*offence*) legalmente punibile; **statutory meeting** (*Comm*) assemblea ordinaria.

staunch[1] [stɔːntʃ] ADJ (*comp* -er, *superl* -est) (*supporter, friend*) fedele, leale; (*believer, Christian*) convinto(-a).

staunch[2] [stɔːntʃ] VT (*flow*) arrestare; (*blood*) tamponare.

staunch·ly ['stɔːntʃlɪ] ADV (*defend, support*) fedelmente; (*deny, refuse*) recisamente; **they moved to a staunchly Republican area** si trasferirono in una zona ultrarepubblicana.

stave [steɪv] N (*Mus*) = **staff 1 c**

▶ **stave in** VT + ADV (*pt, pp* **stove in**)sfondare

▶ **stave off** VT + ADV (*pt, pp* **staved off**) (*crisis, threat, illness*) evitare; (*attack*) respingere; (: *temporarily*) allontanare.

stay [steɪ] [1] N a (*period of time*) soggiorno, permanenza; (*in hospital*) degenza; **a stay of ten days** [OR] **a ten-day stay** un soggiorno di dieci giorni

  b (*Law*): **stay of execution** sospensione *f* dell'esecuzione di una sentenza.

[2] VI a (*remain in a place or situation*) rimanere, restare; (*spend some time*) fermarsi, soggiornare; (*reside, visit*: *in hotel*) alloggiare, stare; (: *with friends*) stare; **you stay right there** stai fermo dove sei; **to stay to dinner** rimanere a cena; **how long can you stay?** quanto ti fermi?; **to stay with friends** stare con degli amici; **to stay the night** passare la notte; **to stay overnight with friends** passare la notte a casa di amici; **camcorders are here to stay** le videocamere non sono un fenomeno temporaneo

  b (*continue, remain*: *with adj*) rimanere; **if it stays fine** se il tempo si mantiene bello; **to stay put** non muoversi.

[3] VT a (*last out*): **to stay the course** (*also fig*) resistere fino alla fine

  b (*punishment*) sospendere; (*spread of disease, flow*) fermare; **to stay sb's hand** fermare la mano a qn.

▶ **stay away** VI + ADV: **to stay away from** (*person*) stare lontano da; (*school, party etc*) non andare a; **to stay away for** (*period of time*) stare via per

▶ **stay behind** VI + ADV (*after school, work etc*) fermarsi, trattenersi; (*not to go*) non andare

▶ **stay down** VI + ADV (*downstairs*) rimanere giù, rimanere di sotto; (*crouching, lying*) rimanere a terra; (*under water*) rimanere sott'acqua

▶ **stay in** VI + ADV (*person*) rimanere a casa, non uscire; (*screw*) tenere

▶ **stay on** VI + ADV rimanere, restare; **he stayed on as manager** è rimasto in carica come direttore

▶ **stay out** VI + ADV (*overnight, outside*) rimanere fuori, restare fuori; (*strikers*) continuare lo sciopero; **to stay out late** stare fuori fino a tardi; **to stay out of trouble** tenersi fuori dai pasticci; **you stay out of this!** non ti immischiare!

▶ **stay over** VI + ADV fermarsi

▶ **stay up** VI + ADV (*trousers, tent*) tenersi su; (*person*: *wait up*) rimanere alzato(-a) *or* in piedi; **to stay up late** fare tardi.

♦ **stay-at-home** ['steɪət,həʊm] N tipo(-a) casalingo(-a).

stay·er ['steɪəʳ] N (*in race*) persona (*or* cavallo *etc*) che ha resistenza; (*fig*) chi tiene duro, chi non si dà per vinto(-a).

stay·ing pow·er ['steɪɪŋ,paʊəʳ] N capacità di resistenza.

STD [,esti:'di:] N ABBR a = **subscriber trunk dialling** b (= *sexually transmitted disease*) malattia venerea.

stead [stɛd] N: **to stand sb in good stead** essere utile a qn; **in sb's stead** (*Brit*) al posto di qn.

stead·fast ['stɛdfəst] ADJ costante, risoluto(-a).

stead·fast·ly ['stɛdfəstlɪ] ADV fermamente.

stead·fast·ness ['stɛdfəstnɪs] N (*of spirit, character*) costanza, risolutezza; (*of resolution*) fermezza.

steadi·ly ['stɛdɪlɪ] ADV (*walk*) con passo sicuro; (*speak*) con tono risoluto; (*improve, decrease*) gradualmente; (*rain*) di continuo; **it is getting steadily worse** continua a peggiorare; **to gaze steadily at sb** guardare qn senza distogliere lo sguardo; **to work steadily** lavorare senza interruzione *or* costantemente.

steady ['stɛdɪ] [1] ADJ (*comp* -ier, *superl* -iest) (*not wobbling*: *gen*) fermo(-a), stabile; (: *voice, gaze*) sicuro(-a); (: *nerves*) saldo(-a); (*not fluctuating*: *prices, sales*) stabile; (*regular*: *temperature, demand, improvement*) costante; (*reliable*: *person, character*) serio(-a); (*boyfriend, girlfriend*) fisso(-a); **a steady job** un lavoro *or* impiego fisso; **a steady hand** una mano ferma; **we were going at a steady 70 km/h** andavamo a una velocità costante di 70 km l'ora.

[2] ADV: **steady!** calma!, piano!; **they are going steady** (*old fam*) fanno coppia fissa, stanno insieme.

[3] VT stabilizzare; (*wobbling object*) tenere fermo(-a); (*nervous person*) calmare; **to steady o.s.** reggersi, tenersi in equilibrio; **she smokes to steady her nerves** fuma per calmarsi; **to have a steadying influence on sb** rendere più calmo(-a) qn.

steak [steɪk] N (*beef*) carne *f* di manzo; (*piece of beef, pork etc*) bistecca; **a cod steak** un trancio di merluzzo; **steak and kidney pie** *pasticcio di carne e rognoni di manzo in pasta sfoglia*.

♦ **steak hammer** N batticarne *m inv*.

steak·house ['steɪk,haʊs] N *ristorante specializzato in bistecche*.

♦ **steak knife** N coltello a lama seghettata (da bistecca).

steal [stiːl] (*pt* **stole**, *pp* **stolen**) [1] VT (*also fig*) rubare; **to steal money/an idea from sb** rubare denaro/un'idea a qn; **to steal a glance at sb** dare un'occhiata furtiva a qn; **to steal a march on sb** battere qn sul tempo.

[2] VI a (*thieve*) rubare

  b (*move quietly*): **to steal in/out** *etc* entrare/uscire *etc* furtivamente; **to steal up on sb** avvicinarsi furtivamente a qn

▶ **steal away, steal off** VI + ADV svignarsela, andarsene alla chetichella.

steal·ing ['stiːlɪŋ] N furto.

stealth [stɛlθ] N: **by stealth** furtivamente, di nascosto.

stealthi·ly ['stɛlθɪlɪ] ADV furtivamente.

stealthy ['stɛlθɪ] ADJ (*comp* -ier, *superl* -iest) furtivo(-a).

steam [stiːm] [1] N vapore *m*; **to get up steam** (*train, ship*) aumentare la pressione; (*worker, project*) mettersi in moto; **to let off steam** (*fig*) sfogarsi; **under one's own steam** (*fig*) da solo, con i propri mezzi; **to run out of steam** (*fig*: *person*) non farcela più; (: *project, movement*) perdere vigore; **full steam ahead!** (*Naut*) avanti tutta!; **to go full steam ahead** (*fig*) andare a tutto vapore.

[2] VT (*Culin*) cuocere a vapore; **to steam open an envelope** aprire una busta con il vapore.

[3] VI a (*give off steam*: *liquid, food etc*) fumare

  b : **the ship steamed into harbour** la nave entrò nel porto; **to steam along** filare; **to steam away** (*ship*) partire; (*fig*: *person, car*) partire a tutto gas

▶ **steam up** VI + ADV (*window*) appannarsi; **to get steamed up about sth** (*fig*) andare in bestia per qc.

steam·boat ['sti:m,bəʊt] N nave ƒ a vapore; (small) vaporetto.

♦ **steam-driven** ['sti:m,drɪvn] ADJ a vapore.

♦ **steam engine** N (Rail) locomotiva a vapore.

steam·er ['sti:mə'] N (steamship) nave ƒ a vapore, piroscafo; (Culin) pentola per cottura a vapore.

♦ **steam iron** N ferro a vapore.

steam·roller ['sti:m,rəʊlə'] N rullo compressore.

steam·ship ['sti:m,ʃɪp] N piroscafo, nave ƒ a vapore.

steamy ['sti:mɪ] ADJ (comp -ier, superl -iest) (room) pieno (-a) di vapore; (window) appannato(-a); (atmosphere, heat) umido(-a); (fam: book, film, play) erotico(-a).

stea·rin, stea·rine ['stɪərɪn] N stearina.

steed [sti:d] N (liter) corsiero, destriero.

steel [sti:l] [1] N acciaio; **nerves of steel** nervi mpl di acciaio.

[2] VT: **to steel one's heart against** corazzarsi contro; **to steel o.s. for sth/to do sth** armarsi di coraggio per affrontare qc/per fare qc.

[3] ADJ (knife, tool) d'acciaio.

♦ **steel band** N banda di strumenti metallici a percussione (tipica delle Antille).

♦ **steel helmet** N casco di protezione.

♦ **steel mill** N acciaieria.

♦ **steel-plated** [,sti:l'pleɪtɪd] ADJ rivestito(-a) d'acciaio.

♦ **steel wool** N lana d'acciaio.

steel·worker ['sti:l,wɜ:kə'] N operaio(-a) di acciaieria.

steel·works ['sti:l,wɜ:ks] N, PL INV acciaieria.

steely ['sti:lɪ] ADJ (comp -ier, superl -iest) (determination) inflessibile; (gaze) duro(-a); (eyes) freddo(-a) come l'acciaio; **steely grey** color piombo inv.

steel·yard ['sti:l,jɑ:d] N stadera.

steep¹ [sti:p] ADJ (comp -er, superl -est) (gen) ripido(-a); (cliff) scosceso(-a); (increase, drop) drastico(-a); (fig fam: price) alto(-a); (: demands) eccessivo(-a); (: story) inverosimile; **it's a bit steep!** (fig fam) è un po' troppo!

steep² [sti:p] VT (washing): **to steep (in)** mettere a bagno (in); (Culin) lasciare in infusione; **a town steeped in history** (fig) una città impregnata di storia; **steeped in prejudice** pieno(-a) di pregiudizi.

stee·ple ['sti:pl] N campanile m.

steeple·chase ['sti:plt,ʃeɪs] N corsa ad ostacoli, steeplechase m inv.

steeple·jack ['sti:pl,dʒæk] N chi ripara campanili e ciminiere.

steep·ly ['sti:plɪ] ADV ripidamente; **to rise/fall steeply** (road, hill) salire/scendere ripidamente; (fig: prices) aumentare/diminuire vertiginosamente.

steep·ness ['sti:pnɪs] N (of hill etc) ripidezza.

steer¹ [stɪə'] [1] VT a (car) guidare; (fig: conversation, person) dirigere, condurre; (ship, boat) dirigere b (handle controls of: ship) governare; (: boat) portare.

[2] VI (in car) sterzare; (on ship) dirigere; **to steer towards** or **for sth** dirigersi verso qc; **to steer clear of sb/sth** (fig) tenersi alla larga da qn/qc.

steer² [stɪə'] N (animal) manzo.

steer·ing ['stɪərɪŋ] N (Aut) sterzo; **power steering** servosterzo.

♦ **steering column** N (Aut) piantone m dello sterzo.

♦ **steering committee** N (Amm) comitato direttivo.

♦ **steering lock** N (Aut) bloccasterzo.

♦ **steering wheel** N (Aut) volante m, sterzo.

stel·lar ['stɛlə'] ADJ (frm, also fig) stellare.

stem [stɛm] [1] N (of plant) gambo, stelo; (of fruit, leaf) gambo, picciolo; (of glass) stelo; (of word) radice ƒ.

[2] VT (check, stop) frenare, arrestare; (river) arginare, contenere; (disease) contenere; **to stem the tide of events** arrestare il corso degli eventi

► **stem from** VI + ADV derivare da.

stench [stɛntʃ] N puzzo, fetore m.

sten·cil ['stɛnsl] [1] N (for lettering etc) stampino; (in typing) matrice ƒ.

[2] VT stampinare.

ste·nog·ra·pher [stɛ'nɒɡrəfə'] N (Am) stenografo(-a).

ste·nog·ra·phy [stɛ'nɒɡrəfɪ] N (Am) stenografia.

ste·no·sis [stɪ'nəʊsɪs] N stenosi ƒ.

sten·to·rian [stɛn'tɔ:rɪən] ADJ (frm: voice) stentoreo(-a).

step [stɛp] [1] N a (movement) passo; (fig: move) mossa, passo; **to take a step back/forward** fare un passo indietro/avanti; **it's a great step forward** (fig) è un gran passo avanti; **a step in the right direction** (fig) un passo nella direzione giusta; **step by step** un passo dietro l'altro; (fig) poco a poco; **to be in/out of step with** (also fig) stare/non stare al passo con; **to keep in step (with)** (also fig) mantenersi al passo (con); **to watch one's step** guardare dove si mettono i piedi; (fig) fare attenzione

b (measure) misura; **to take steps to solve a problem** prendere le misure necessarie per risolvere un problema

c (stair) gradino, scalino; (of ladder) piolo; (of vehicle) predellino; (fig: in scale) gradino; **steps** NPL (stairs) scala ƒsg; (: outside building) scalinata ƒsg; **folding steps** [OR] **pair of steps** scala a libretto; **a step up in his career** (fig) un passo avanti nella carriera.

[2] VI fare un passo, andare; **to step aside** farsi da parte, scansarsi; **to step inside** entrare; **she stepped out of the car** uscì dalla macchina; **to step back** tirarsi indietro; **step this way, please!** da questa parte, per favore!; **to step over sth** scavalcare qc; **to step off the pavement** scendere dal marciapiede; **to step on sth** calpestare qc; **step on it!** (fam) muoviti!; **to step out of line** (fig) sgarrare

► **step down** VI + ADV scendere; (fig: resign): **to step down (in favour of sb)** dimettersi or dare le dimissioni (a favore di qn)

► **step forward** VI + ADV fare un passo avanti; (fig: volunteer) farsi avanti

► **step in** VI + ADV entrare, fare il proprio ingresso; (fig) intromettersi

► **step up** VT + ADV (production) aumentare; (efforts, campaign) intensificare; **to step up work on sth** accelerare i lavori per qc.

♦ **step aerobics** NPL step msg.

step·brother ['stɛp,brʌðə'] N fratellastro.

step·child ['stɛp,tʃaɪld] N (pl -children) figliastro(-a).

step·daughter ['stɛp,dɔ:tə'] N figliastra.

step·father ['stɛp,fɑ:ðə'] N patrigno.

step·ladder ['stɛp,lædə'] N scala a libretto.

step·mother ['stɛp,mʌðə'] N matrigna.

♦ **step-parent** ['stɛp,pɛərənt] N (stepfather) patrigno; (stepmother) matrigna.

steppe [stɛp] N steppa.

step·ping stone ['stɛpɪŋ,stəʊn] N pietra di un guado; (fig): **stepping stone (to)** trampolino di lancio (verso).

Step Reebok® [,stɛp'ri:bɒk] N = step aerobics.

step·sister ['stɛp,sɪstə'] N sorellastra.

step·son ['stɛp,sʌn] N figliastro.

ste·reo ['stɛrɪəʊ] [1] N (hi-fi equipment) stereo m inv; (sound) stereofonia; **in stereo** in stereofonia.

[2] ADJ stereofonico(-a), stereo inv.

ste·reo·phon·ic [ˌstɛrɪə'fɒnɪk] ADJ stereofonico(-a).

ste·reo·scope ['stɛrɪəˌskəʊp] N stereoscopio.

ste·reo·scop·ic [ˌstɛrɪə'skɒpɪk] ADJ stereoscopico(-a).

ste·reo·type ['stɛrɪəˌtaɪp] N stereotipo.

ster·ile ['stɛraɪl] ADJ sterile.

ste·ril·ity [stɛ'rɪlɪtɪ] N sterilità.

steri·li·za·tion [ˌstɛrɪlaɪ'zeɪʃən] N sterilizzazione f.

steri·lize ['stɛrɪˌlaɪz] VT sterilizzare.

ster·ling ['stɜ:lɪŋ] ① N (Fin) sterlina.
② ADJ **a** (silver) al titolo di 925/1000, di buona lega; (Econ): **pound sterling** lira sterlina **b** (fig): **of sterling qualities** di gran pregio; **he is of sterling character** è una persona fidata.
♦ **sterling area** N (Fin) area della sterlina.

stern¹ [stɜ:n] ADJ (comp -er, superl -est) (discipline) rigido (-a); (person, warning) severo(-a); **I thought he was made of sterner stuff** pensavo fosse più forte.

stern² [stɜ:n] N (Naut) poppa.

stern·ly ['stɜ:nlɪ] ADV (warn, glare) severamente.

stern·ness ['stɜ:nnɪs] N (of discipline) rigidità, rigore m; (of person, warning, voice) severità.

ster·num ['stɜ:nəm] N (Anat) sterno.

ster·oid ['stɛrɔɪd] N steroide m.

ster·to·rous ['stɜ:tərəs] ADJ (frm: breathing) stertoroso(-a).

stet [stɛt] N (Typ) vive.

stetho·scope ['stɛθəˌskəʊp] N stetoscopio.

stet·son° ['stɛtsən] N lobbia.

ste·vedore ['sti:vɪˌdɔ:'] N scaricatore m di porto.

stew [stju:] ① N **a** (Culin) stufato **b** (fig): **to be in a stew (about sth)** essere agitato(-a) (per qc); **to get into a stew (about sth)** mettersi in agitazione (per qc).
② VT (meat) stufare, cuocere in umido; **stewed fruit** frutta cotta.
③ VI (tea) diventare troppo forte; **to let sb stew in his own juice** (fig) lasciar cuocere qn nel suo brodo.

stew·ard ['stju:əd] N (Aer, Naut, Rail) steward m inv; (on estate) fattore m; (in club) dispensiere m; (butler) maggiordomo; (shop steward) rappresentante m/f sindacale.

stew·ard·ess ['stjʊədɛs] N (Aer, Naut) hostess f inv.

stew·ard·ship ['stjʊədˌʃɪp] N (frm: supervision, care) amministrazione f.

stew·ing steak ['stju:ɪŋˌsteɪk], (Am) **stew meat** N carne f di manzo per stufato.

stg ABBR = sterling.

stick [stɪk] (vb: pt, pp stuck) ① N (gen) bastone m; (twig) ramoscello; (support for plants) asticella, bastoncino; (of celery, rhubarb) gambo; (of shaving soap) stick m inv; (of dynamite) candelotto; **to wave the big stick** (fig) fare il/la prepotente; **to get hold of the wrong end of the stick** (fig) fraintendere; **a few sticks of furniture** pochi mobili mpl sgangherati; **to live in the sticks** (fam) abitare a casa del diavolo; **to give sb stick** (fig) fare un cicchetto a qn.
② VT **a** (with glue etc) incollare; **to stick two things together** incollare due cose; **he was sticking stamps into his album** attaccava i francobolli nell'album; **she stuck the envelope down** incollò la busta
b (thrust, poke: hand etc) ficcare; (sth pointed: pin, needle) conficcare, piantare; **he stuck his hand in his pocket** ficcò una mano in tasca; **to stick a knife into sb** accoltellare qn
c (fam: place, put) mettere; **stick it in your case** mettilo or ficcalo nella borsa
d (fam: tolerate) sopportare; **I can't stick it any longer** non ne posso più

e : **to be stuck** (door, window) essere bloccato(-a); (knife, screw) essere incastrato(-a); **it's stuck in my throat** mi si è conficcato in gola; **to be stuck with sb/sth** (fam) doversi sorbire qn/qc, dover sopportare qn/qc; **I'm stuck in bed** sono inchiodato a letto; **I'm stuck at home all day** sono bloccato a casa tutto il giorno.
③ VI (glue, sticky object etc) attaccarsi, appiccicarsi; (food, sauce) attaccarsi; (get jammed: door, lift) bloccarsi; (: lock) incepparsi; (in mud etc) impantanarsi; (sth pointed) conficcarsi; **it stuck to the wall** è rimasto attaccato al muro; **the nickname seems to have stuck** (fam) sembra che il soprannome gli (or le etc) sia rimasto; **to stick to sb's wheel** (Cycling) incollarsi alla ruota di qn; **it stuck in my mind** mi è rimasto in mente; **she will stick at nothing to get what she wants** è capace di tutto per ottenere quello che vuole; **just stick at it and I'm sure you'll manage it** non mollare e sono sicuro che riuscirai a farlo
► **stick around** VI + ADV (fam) restare, rimanere, fermarsi
► **stick by** VI + PREP (stand by) stare vicino(-a); **we'll all stick by you** (support you) siamo tutti con te
► **stick in** VT + ADV (knife) affondare; (pin, needle etc) appuntare; (photo in album etc) incollare, attaccare; **to get stuck in** (fam) impegnarsi seriamente; **I stuck in a few quotations from Shakespeare** ho inserito qua e là delle citazioni di Shakespeare
► **stick on** VT + ADV (stamp, label) incollare
► **stick out** ① VI + ADV **a** (protrude) sporgere; (be noticeable) spiccare; **his teeth stick out** ha i denti sporgenti; **his ears stick out** ha le orecchie a sventola; **to stick out like a sore thumb** essere un pugno nell'occhio
b : **to stick out for sth** battersi per qc.
② VT + ADV (tongue) tirar fuori; (arm) allungare; (head) sporgere; **to stick it out** (fam) tener duro; (one's word, promise) mantenere; (principles) tener fede a; (text) rimanere fedele a; (facts) attenersi a; **decide what you're going to do, then stick to it** decidi il da farsi e poi fallo
► **stick together** VI + ADV (people) restare uniti; (things) attaccarsi
► **stick up** ① VI + ADV (protrude) rimanere diritto(-a); **to stick up out of the water** uscire dall'acqua.
② VT + ADV **a** (fam: raise: hand) alzare; (: rob) rapinare; **stick 'em up!** mani in alto!
b (notice) affiggere
► **stick up for** VI + ADV + PREP difendere; **to stick up for sb/sth** (fam) battersi per qn/qc
► **stick with** VI + PREP (carry on with) attenersi a; **I'll stick with the job for another few months** continuerò a fare questo lavoro per qualche altro mese.

stick·er ['stɪkə'] N (label) etichetta; (on car etc) adesivo.

sticki·ness ['stɪkɪnɪs] N (of pastry) collosità f inv; (of mud) vischiosità f inv; (fam: of situation) difficoltà f inv.

stick·ing plas·ter ['stɪkɪŋˌplɑ:stə'] N cerotto adesivo.

stick·ing point ['stɪkɪŋˌpɔɪnt] N (fig) punto di stallo, impasse f inv.

♦ **stick insect** N insetto stecco.

♦ **stick-in-the-mud** ['stɪkɪnðəˌmʌd] N (fam) retrogrado (-a).

stickle·back ['stɪklˌbæk] N spinarello.

stick·ler ['stɪklə'] N: **to be a stickler for** essere esigente in fatto di, essere pignolo(-a) su.

♦ **stick-on** ['stɪkˌɒn] ADJ (label) adesivo(-a).

♦ **stick pin** N (Am) fermacravatta m inv.

♦ **stick shift** N (Am Aut) cambio manuale.

♦ **stick-up** ['stɪkˌʌp] N (fam) rapina a mano armata.

sticky ['stɪkɪ] ADJ (comp **-ier**, superl **-iest**) appiccicoso(-a), vischioso(-a); (label) adesivo(-a); (fam: situation) difficile, imbarazzante; **he was a bit sticky about lending me the money** ha fatto un sacco di storie per prestarmi i soldi; **to come to a sticky end** (fam) fare una brutta fine; **sticky tape** nastro adesivo; **you're on a sticky wicket there** (fam) sei proprio nelle peste.

stiff [stɪf] ADJ (comp **-er**, superl **-est**) **a** (gen) rigido(-a); (starched: shirt) inamidato(-a); (brush) duro(-a); (dough) compatto(-a), sodo(-a); (arm, joint) rigido(-a), indolenzito(-a); (muscle) legato(-a); **to have a stiff neck/back** avere il torcicollo/mal di schiena; **to be** or **feel stiff** essere or sentirsi indolenzito(-a); **the door's stiff** la porta si apre (or si chiude) con difficoltà; **as stiff as a ramrod** or **a poker** dritto(-a) come un palo; **to keep a stiff upper lip** (Brit fig) restare impassibile

b (fig: climb, examination, test) arduo(-a), difficile; (: competition, breeze, drink) forte; (: resistance) tenace; (punishment) severo(-a); (price, fine) salato(-a); (manner, smile, reception) freddo(-a); **that's a bit stiff!** (fam) è un po' troppo!; **it was a stiff price to pay** (fig) l'hanno pagata cara; **bored stiff** annoiato(-a) a morte.

stiff·en ['stɪfn] **1** VT (legs etc) irrigidire; (with starch) inamidare; (fig: resistance etc) rafforzare.
2 VI (person, manner) irrigidirsi; (determination) rafforzarsi; (morale) risollevarsi.

stiff·ly ['stɪflɪ] ADV (walk, move) rigidamente; (smile, bow) freddamente.

♦ **stiff-necked** ['stɪf'nɛkt] ADJ (pej) ostinato(-a), cocciuto (-a).

stiff·ness ['stɪfnɪs] N (gen) rigidità; (of punishment) durezza; (of climb) difficoltà; (of back etc) indolenzimento; (of manner) freddezza; (of resolution) fermezza.

sti·fle ['staɪfl] **1** VT (yawn, sob, anger) soffocare; (desire, smile) reprimere; (revolt, opposition) stroncare.
2 VI soffocare.

sti·fled ['staɪfld] ADJ soffocato(-a).

sti·fling ['staɪflɪŋ] ADJ (heat) soffocante; **it's stifling in here** qui non si respira.

stig·ma ['stɪgmə] N stigma m.

stig·ma·ta [stɪg'mɑːtə] NPL (Rel) stigmate fpl.

stig·ma·tize ['stɪgmətaɪz] VT stigmatizzare.

stile [staɪl] N (per scavalcare una siepe).

sti·let·to [stɪ'lɛtəʊ] N (knife) stiletto; (shoe) scarpa con tacco a spillo.

♦ **stiletto heel** N tacco a spillo.

still[1] [stɪl] ADV **a** (up to now) ancora; **she's still in bed** è ancora a letto; **it's past midnight and he still hasn't arrived** è mezzanotte passata e non è ancora arrivato; **she still doesn't believe me** ancora non mi crede
b (with comp: even) ancora; **still better** OR **better still** meglio ancora
c (nevertheless) tuttavia, nonostante ciò; **still, it was worth it** però, ne valeva la pena; **she's still your sister** è pur sempre tua sorella.

still[2] [stɪl] **1** ADJ (comp **-er**, superl **-est**) (motionless) fermo(-a), immobile; (quiet) tranquillo(-a), silenzioso (-a); (orange juice) non gassato(-a); **still mineral water** acqua minerale naturale; **still waters run deep** (Proverb) le acque chete rovinano i ponti.
2 N **a**: **in the still of the night** nel silenzio della notte
b (Cine) fotogramma m.
3 ADV: **to stand still, sit still** stare fermo(-a); **to hold still** tenersi fermo(-a); **keep still!** stai fermo!

still[3] [stɪl] N (for alcohol) alambicco; (: place) distilleria.

still·birth ['stɪl,bɜːθ] N bambino(-a) nato(-a) morto(-a).

still·born ['stɪl,bɔːn] ADJ nato(-a) morto(-a).

♦ **still life** N (Art) natura morta.

still·ness ['stɪlnɪs] N immobilità; (quietness) silenzio, tranquillità.

stilt [stɪlt] N trampolo; (pile) palo; **to walk on stilts** camminare sui trampoli.

stilt·ed ['stɪltɪd] ADJ (style) artificioso(-a); (way of speaking) formale; (translation) poco naturale.

stimu·lant ['stɪmjʊlənt] N stimolante m.

stimu·late ['stɪmjʊˌleɪt] VT stimolare; **to stimulate sb to do sth** stimolare qn a fare qc.

stimu·lat·ing ['stɪmjʊˌleɪtɪŋ] ADJ stimolante.

stimu·la·tion [ˌstɪmjʊˈleɪʃən] N stimolazione f.

stimu·lus ['stɪmjʊləs] N (pl **stimuli** ['stɪmjʊlaɪ]) stimolo; **it gave trade a new stimulus** ha dato un nuovo impulso al commercio; **under the stimulus of** stimolato(-a) da.

sting [stɪŋ] (vb: pt, pp **stung**) **1** N (Zool) pungiglione m; (Bot) pelo urticante; (pain, mark) puntura; (of iodine, antiseptic) bruciore m; **to take the sting out of sth** (fig) rendere qc meno pungente; **but there was a sting in the tail** (fig) ma c'era una spiacevole sorpresa.
2 VT **a** (subj: insect, nettle) pungere; (: jellyfish) pizzicare; (: iodine) bruciare; (: cold wind) tagliare; (fig: remark, criticism) pungere sul vivo; **he was stung into action** fu spronato all'azione; **she was stung by remorse** fu presa dal rimorso
b (fam): **they stung me for £40** mi hanno scucito 40 sterline.
3 VI (iodine etc) bruciare; (remark, criticism) ferire; **my eyes are stinging** mi bruciano gli occhi.

stin·gi·ly ['stɪndʒɪlɪ] ADV (pej: spend) con parsimonia; (: behave) da avaro(-a); **they rewarded him rather stingily** gli hanno dato una ben magra ricompensa.

stin·gi·ness ['stɪndʒɪnɪs] N (pej: of person) avarizia, tirchieria; (: of gift, contribution) esiguità.

sting·ray ['stɪŋreɪ] N (fish) pastinaca.

stin·gy ['stɪndʒɪ] ADJ (comp **-ier**, superl **-iest**) (pej: person) avaro(-a), tirchio(-a), spilorcio(-a), taccagno(-a); (: gift etc) misero(-a); **to be stingy with** (one's praise, money) essere avaro(-a) di; (food) razionare.

stink [stɪŋk] (vb: pt **stank**, pp **stunk**) **1** N puzza, fetore m; **to raise** or **kick up a stink** (fig fam) scatenare un putiferio, piantare un casino.
2 VI: **to stink (of)** puzzare (di); **it stinks in here** che puzza c'è qui; **it stinks to high heaven** puzza tremendamente; **the whole thing stinks** (fig fam) tutta la faccenda puzza.
3 VT (also: **stink out**: room) appestare.

♦ **stink bomb** N fialetta puzzolente.

stink·er ['stɪŋkə'] N (fam: person) carogna, fetente m/f; **this problem is a stinker** questo problema è una bella rogna; **he wrote her a real stinker** gliene ha scritte di tutti i colori.

stink·horn ['stɪŋk,hɔːn] N (fungus) satirione m.

stink·ing ['stɪŋkɪŋ] **1** ADJ: **a stinking cold** un raffreddore tremendo; **what stinking weather!** che tempo da cani!.
2 ADV: **stinking rich** ricco(-a) sfondato(-a).

stint [stɪnt] **1** N: **to do one's stint (at sth)** fare la propria parte (di qc); **I do a stint in the pool every day** faccio una nuotata in piscina ogni giorno; **to do a stint at the wheel** (Aut) fare il proprio turno al volante.
2 VT: **he did not stint his praises** non è stato avaro di complimenti; **don't stint yourself!** (iro) non farti mancare niente!

sti·pend ['staɪpɛnd] N congrua.

sti·pen·di·ary [staɪˈpɛndɪərɪ] ADJ: **stipendiary magistrate** magistrato stipendiato.

stip·pled [ˈstɪpəld] ADJ punteggiato(-a).

stipu·late [ˈstɪpjʊˌleɪt] VT: **to stipulate (that)** stabilire (che).

stipu·la·tion [ˌstɪpjʊˈleɪʃən] N stipulazione *f*; **on the stipulation that** a condizione che + *sub.*

stir [stɜːʳ] 1 N a: **to give sth a stir** mescolare qc
  b (*fig*) agitazione *f*, scalpore *m*; **to cause a stir** fare scalpore.
  2 VT a (*liquid etc*) mescolare; (*fire*) attizzare
  b (*move*) muovere, agitare; **she didn't stir a finger** non ha mosso un dito; **the breeze stirred the leaves** la brezza muoveva le foglie
  c (*fig: emotions, interest*) risvegliare; (: *person*) commuovere; (: *imagination, curiosity*) eccitare, stimolare; **to stir sb to do sth** incitare qn a fare qc; **come on, stir yourself!** forza, muoviti!.
  3 VI (*move*) muoversi; **he never stirred from the spot** non si è mosso

▶ **stir in** VT + PREP aggiungere mescolando

▶ **stir up** VT + ADV (*memories*) risvegliare; (*hatred, revolt*) fomentare; (*trouble*) provocare; **he's always trying to stir things up** cerca sempre di creare problemi.

♦ **stir-fry** [ˈstɜːˌfraɪ] 1 VT saltare in padella.
  2 N pietanza al salto.

stir·rer [ˈstɜːrəʳ] N (*Brit fam*) piantagrane *m/f*.

stir·ring [ˈstɜːrɪŋ] ADJ (*exciting*) entusiasmante; (*moving*) commovente.

stir·rup [ˈstɪrəp] N staffa.

♦ **stirrup leather** N staffile *m*.

stitch [stɪtʃ] 1 N (*Sewing*) punto; (*Med*) punto (di sutura); (*Knitting*) maglia, punto; (*pain in side*) fitta (al fianco); **to put a few stitches in sth** mettere due punti a qc; **a stitch in time saves nine** (*Proverb*) un punto in tempo ne salva cento; **to put stitches in a wound** cucire una ferita; **she hadn't a stitch on** era completamente nuda; **we were in stitches** (*fam*) ridevamo a crepapelle.
  2 VT (*Sewing*) cucire; (*Med*) suturare, cucire; **to stitch up a hem/wound** cucire un orlo/una ferita

▶ **stitch down** VT + ADV cucire

▶ **stitch on** VT + ADV (*button etc*) attaccare; (*button that's come off*) riattaccare.

stitch·ing [ˈstɪtʃɪŋ] N cucitura.

stoat [stəʊt] N ermellino.

stock¹ [stɒk] 1 N a (*supply, store*) provvista, scorta; (*in bank: of money*) riserva; (*Comm*) stock *m inv*; **out of stock** esaurito(-a); **to have sth in stock** avere qc in magazzino, avere disponibilità di qc; **to take stock** (*Comm*) fare l'inventario; **to take stock (of the situation)** fare il punto della situazione; **to lay in a stock of** fare una scorta di
  b (*Agr: also:* **livestock**) bestiame *m*
  c (*Culin*) brodo
  d (*Rail: also:* **rolling stock**) materiale *m* rotabile
  e (*Fin: company's capital*) capitale *m* azionario; (: *investor's shares*) titoli *mpl*, azioni *fpl*; **stocks and shares** valori *mpl* di borsa; **government stock** titoli di Stato
  f (*descent, origin*) stirpe *f*
  g: **to be on the stocks** (*ship*) essere in cantiere; (*fig: piece of work*) essere in lavorazione; **the stocks** NPL (*History: for punishment*) la gogna.
  2 VT (*Comm: goods*) tenere, avere, vendere; (*supply: shop, library, freezer, cupboard*) rifornire; (: *lake, river*) ripopolare; (: *farm*) fornire di bestiame; (: *shelves*) riempire; **a well-stocked shop/library** un negozio/una biblioteca ben fornito(-a).
  3 ADJ (*Comm: size*) standard *inv*; (*fig: response, arguments, excuse*) solito(-a), consueto(-a); (: *greeting*) usuale

▶ **stock up** VI + ADV: **to stock up (on)** rifornirsi (di), fare provvista (di).

stock² [stɒk] N (*Bot*) violacciocca.

stock·ade [stɒˈkeɪd] N palizzata.

stock·breeder [ˈstɒkˌbriːdəʳ] N allevatore(-trice) di bestiame.

stock·breeding [ˈstɒkˌbriːdɪŋ] N allevamento di bestiame.

stock·broker [ˈstɒkˌbrəʊkəʳ] N agente *m* di cambio.

♦ **stock car** N (*Sport*) stock-car *m inv.*

♦ **stock control** N gestione *f* magazzino.

♦ **stock cube** N (*Brit Culin*) dado (da brodo).

♦ **stock exchange** N (*Fin*) borsa valori.

stock·holder [ˈstɒkˌhəʊldəʳ] N (*Fin*) azionista *m/f.*

Stock·holm [ˈstɒkhəʊm] N Stoccolma.

stock·ing [ˈstɒkɪŋ] 1 N calza (*da donna*).
  2 ADJ: **in one's stocking(ed) feet** senza scarpe.

♦ **stocking mask** N calza di nylon (*di bandito mascherato*).

♦ **stocking stitch** N (*Knitting*) maglia rasata.

♦ **stock-in-trade** [ˌstɒkɪnˈtreɪd] N (*goods*) merce *f* a magazzino; (*tools etc*) strumenti *mpl* di lavoro; (*fig*) ferri *mpl* del mestiere; **it's his stock-in-trade** è la sua specialità.

stock·ist [ˈstɒkɪst] N (*Brit*) fornitore *m.*

♦ **stock level** N livello di magazzino.

♦ **stock market** N (*Brit Fin*) mercato azionario.

♦ **stock phrase** N frase *f* fatta, cliché *m inv.*

stock·pile [ˈstɒkˌpaɪl] 1 N riserva, scorta.
  2 VT accumulare riserve di.

stock·pot [ˈstɒkˌpɒt] N (*Culin*) pentola per brodo.

stock·room [ˈstɒkˌruːm] N magazzino.

♦ **stock-still** [ˌstɒkˈstɪl] ADV: **to be** or **stand stock-still** stare immobile; (*from shock, horror*) restare impietrito(-a).

stock·taking [ˈstɒkˌteɪkɪŋ] N (*Brit Comm*) inventario.

♦ **stock turnover** N ricambio del magazzino.

stocky [ˈstɒkɪ] ADJ (*comp* -**ier**, *superl* -**iest**) tarchiato(-a), tozzo(-a).

stodge [stɒdʒ] N (*fam*) cibo pesante.

stodgy [ˈstɒdʒɪ] ADJ (*comp* -**ier**, *superl* -**iest**) (*food, book*) pesante, indigesto(-a); (: *person*) pesante.

sto·ic [ˈstəʊɪk] N stoico(-a).

stoi·cal [ˈstəʊɪkəl] ADJ stoico(-a).

stoi·cal·ly [ˈstəʊɪkəlɪ] ADV stoicamente.

stoi·chi·om·etry [ˌstɔɪkɪˈɒmɪtrɪ] N stechiometria.

stoi·cism [ˈstəʊɪsɪzəm] N stoicismo.

stoke [stəʊk] VT (*also:* **stoke up**: *fire*) attizzare; (: *furnace*) alimentare.

stok·er [ˈstəʊkəʳ] N fuochista *m.*

stole¹ [stəʊl] N stola.

stole² [stəʊl] PT of **steal.**

stol·en [ˈstəʊlən] PP of **steal.**

stol·id [ˈstɒlɪd] ADJ flemmatico(-a).

sto·lid·ity [stɒˈlɪdɪtɪ] N flemma.

stol·id·ly [ˈstɒlɪdlɪ] ADV flemmaticamente.

sto·lon [ˈstəʊlən] N (*Bot, Zool*) stolone *m.*

stom·ach [ˈstʌmək] 1 N (*gen*) stomaco; (*abdomen*) ventre *m*; **it turns my stomach** mi rivolta lo stomaco; **they have no stomach for a fight** (*fig*) non hanno il fegato di battersi.

2 VT (*fig fam*) sopportare, digerire.
♦ **stomach ache** N mal *m* di stomaco.
♦ **stomach pump** N lavanda gastrica.
♦ **stomach trouble** N disturbi *mpl* gastrici.
♦ **stomach ulcer** N ulcera gastrica.
stomp [stɒmp] VI: **to stomp in/out** *etc* entrare/uscire *etc* con passo pesante.
stone [stəʊn] 1 N a (*material*) pietra; (*single pebble, rock*) sasso, ciottolo; (*also:* **gemstone**) pietra preziosa, gemma; (*of fruit*) nocciolo; (*Med*) calcolo; (*also:* **gravestone**) lastra tombale, lapide *f*; **to turn to stone** (*vt*) pietrificare; (*vi*) rimanere pietrificato(-a); **within a stone's throw of the station** a due passi dalla stazione, ad un tiro di schioppo dalla stazione; **to leave no stone unturned** non lasciare nulla d'intentato
  b (*Brit*: *weight*: *pl gen inv*) ≈ 6,348 kg.
2 ADJ (*wall*) di pietra.
3 VT a (*person*) scagliare pietre contro; **to stone sb to death** lapidare qn
  b (*fruit*) snocciolare.
♦ **Stone Age** N: **the Stone Age** l'età della pietra.
stone·chat ['stəʊnˌtʃæt] N saltimpalo.
♦ **stone-cold** ['stəʊn'kəʊld] 1 ADJ ghiacciato(-a).
2 ADV: **stone-cold sober** perfettamente sobrio(-a).
stone·cutter ['stəʊnˌkʌtə'] N (*person*) scalpellino; (*machine*) mola.
stoned [stəʊnd] ADJ PRED (*fam: drunk, on drugs*) fatto(-a).
♦ **stone-dead** [ˌstəʊn'dɛd] ADJ morto(-a) stecchito(-a).
♦ **stone-deaf** [ˌstəʊn'dɛf] ADJ sordo(-a) come una campana.
stone·ground ['stəʊngraʊnd] ADJ (*flour, wheat*) macinato (-a) con la mola.
stone·mason ['stəʊnˌmeɪsn] N scalpellino.
stone·wall [ˌstəʊn'wɔ:l] 1 VI (*fig*) fare ostruzionismo.
2 VT ostacolare.
stone·ware ['stəʊnˌwɛə'] N articoli *mpl* di grès.
stone·work ['stəʊnˌwɜ:k] N lavoro in muratura.
stoni·ly ['stəʊnɪlɪ] ADV (*fig*: *glance, reply*) freddamente.
stony ['stəʊnɪ] ADJ (*comp* **-ier**, *superl* **-iest**) (*ground*) sassoso (-a); (*beach*) pieno(-a) di ciottoli; (*fig*: *glance, silence*) freddo(-a); **a stony heart** un cuore di pietra.
♦ **stony-broke** [ˌstəʊnɪ'brəʊk] ADJ (*fam*): **to be stony-broke** essere al verde, *or* in bolletta.
♦ **stony-faced** [ˌstəʊnɪ'feɪst] ADJ dal volto impassibile.
stood [stʊd] PT, PP of **stand**.
stooge [stu:dʒ] N (*fam: minion*) tirapiedi *m/f*; (*Theatre*) spalla.
stool [stu:l] N (*seat*) sgabello; **to fall between two stools** (*fig*) fare come l'asino di Buridano.
♦ **stool pigeon** N (*fam*) informatore(-trice).
stoop [stu:p] 1 N: **to have a stoop** avere la schiena curva; **to walk with a stoop** camminare curvo(-a).
2 VI a (*bend*: *also:* **stoop down**) chinarsi, curvarsi, abbassarsi; (*have a stoop*) essere curvo(-a) b (*fig*): **to stoop to sth/doing sth** abbassarsi a qc/a fare qc; **I wouldn't stoop so low!** non mi abbasserei a tanto!
stoop·ing ['stu:pɪŋ] ADJ curvo(-a).
stop [stɒp] 1 N a (*halt*) arresto; (*break, pause*) pausa; (: *overnight*) sosta; **a 20 minute stop for coffee** una pausa di 20 minuti per il caffè; **without a stop** senza fermarsi; **to come to a stop** (*traffic, production*) arrestarsi; (*work*) fermarsi; **to bring to a stop** (*traffic, production*) paralizzare; (*work*) fermare; **to make a stop** (*bus*) fare una fermata; (*train*) fermarsi; (*plane, ship*) fare scalo; **to put a stop to sth** mettere fine a qc

  b (*stopping place: for bus etc*) fermata
  c (*Typ: also:* **full stop**) punto; (*in telegrams*) stop *m inv*
  d (*Mus: on organ*) registro; (: *on trombone etc*) chiave *f*; **to pull out all the stops** (*fig*) mettercela tutta.
2 VT a (*arrest movement of: runaway, engine, car*) fermare, bloccare; (: *blow, punch*) parare
  b (*put an end to: gen*) mettere fine a; (: *noise*) far cessare; (: *pain*) far passare; (: *production: permanently*) arrestare; (: *temporarily*) interrompere, sospendere; **she drew the curtains to stop the light coming in** tirò le tende per impedire che entrasse la luce; **rain stopped play** la partita è stata sospesa a causa del maltempo
  c (*prevent*) impedire; **to stop sb (from) doing sth** impedire a qn di fare qc; **to stop sth (from) happening** impedire che qc succeda; **can't you stop him?** non puoi fermarlo?; **to stop o.s. (from doing sth)** trattenersi (dal fare qc); **I managed to stop myself in time** sono riuscito a fermarmi in tempo
  d (*cease*) smettere; **to stop doing sth** smettere di fare qc; **I'm trying to stop smoking** sto cercando di smettere di fumare; **stop it!** smettila!; **I just can't stop it** (*help it*) proprio non riesco a smetterla
  e (*suspend: payments, wages*) sospendere; (: *subscription*) cancellare; (: *leave*) revocare; (: *cheque*) bloccare; **to stop £30 from sb's wages** trattenere 30 sterline dallo stipendio di qn
  f (*also:* **stop up**: *block: hole*) bloccare, otturare; (: *leak, flow of blood*) arrestare, fermare; **to stop one's ears** tapparsi *or* turarsi le orecchie.
3 VI a (*stop moving, pause: gen*) fermarsi; (*cease: gen*) cessare; (*machine, production*) arrestarsi; (*play, concert, speaker*) finire; **stop!** fermo!; **stop, thief!** al ladro!; **without stopping** senza fermarsi; **to stop in one's tracks** OR **stop dead** fermarsi di colpo; **to stop at nothing (to do sth)** non fermarsi davanti a niente (pur di fare qc); **to know where to stop** (*fig*) avere il senso della misura
  b (*fam: stay*): **to stop (at/with)** fermarsi (a/da); **I'm not stopping** non mi fermo
► **stop away** VI + ADV (*fam*) stare via
► **stop by** VI + ADV (*fam*) passare, fare un salto
► **stop in** VI + ADV rimanere a casa
► **stop off** VI + ADV fermarsi, sostare brevemente
► **stop over** VI + ADV: **to stop over (in)** fermarsi (a), fare una sosta (a); (*Aer*) fare scalo (a)
► **stop up** 1 VT + ADV = **stop 2a**.
2 VI + ADV (*fam*) stare alzato(-a).
stop·cock ['stɒpˌkɒk] N rubinetto di arresto.
stop·gap ['stɒpgæp] 1 N (*person*) supplente, sostituto (-a) temporaneo(-a); (*measure*) palliativo.
2 ADJ (*measures, solution*) tampone *inv*, sostitutivo(-a).
stop·light ['stɒpˌlaɪt] N (*traffic light*) (semaforo) rosso.
stop·over ['stɒpˌəʊvə'] N sosta; (*Aer*) scalo intermedio.
stop·page ['stɒpɪdʒ] N (*in pipe etc*) ostruzione *f*; (*of work*) interruzione *f*; (*strike*) interruzione *f* del lavoro; (*from wages*) detrazione *f*, trattenuta.
stop·per ['stɒpə'] N tappo.
stop·ping ['stɒpɪŋ] 1 N (*gen*) arresto; (*fam: in tooth*) otturazione *f*.
2 ADJ: **stopping place** (*lay-by*) piazzola di sosta; **we found a good stopping place** abbiamo trovato un bel posto per fare una sosta; **stopping train** ≈ (treno) locale *m*.
♦ **stop press** N ultimissime *fpl*.
♦ **stop sign** N (*Aut*) (segnale *m* di) stop *m inv*.
stop·watch ['stɒpˌwɒtʃ] N cronometro.

stor·age ['stɔːrɪdʒ] [1] N (*of goods, fuel*) immagazzinamento; (*of heat, electricity*) accumulazione *f*; (*of documents*) conservazione *f*; (*Comput*) memoria; **to put sth into storage** immagazzinare qc; **the cupboards provide ample storage** gli armadi offrono ampio spazio per tenere la roba.
♦ **storage battery** N accumulatore *m*.
♦ **storage capacity** N (*Comput*) capacità *f inv* di memoria.
♦ **storage charges** NPL magazzinaggio *msg*.
♦ **storage heater** N (*Brit*) radiatore *m* elettrico che accumula calore.
♦ **storage space** N: **we haven't got much storage space** non abbiamo molto spazio per riporre la roba.
♦ **storage tank** N (*for rainwater, oil*) cisterna.
store [stɔː*] [1] N **a** (*stock*) provvista, scorta, riserva; (*fig: of knowledge etc*) bagaglio; **stores** NPL (*food*) provviste *fpl*, scorte *fpl*, rifornimenti *mpl*; **to lay in a store of sth** fare provvista di qc; **in store** di riserva, come provvista; **who knows what is in store for us** chissà cosa ci riserva il futuro; **to set great/little store by sth** dare molta/poca importanza a qc
  b (*also:* **storehouse, storeroom**: *depot*) deposito; **to put one's furniture in(to) store** mettere i mobili in un deposito
  c (*Am: shop*) negozio; (*Brit: also:* **department store**) grande magazzino.
  [2] VT **a** (*also:* **store up**: *food, fuel, goods*) fare provvista di; (: *heat, electricity*) accumulare; (: *documents*) conservare
  b (*also:* **store away**: *food, fuel*) mettere da parte; (: *grain, goods*) immagazzinare; (: *information: in memory*) immagazzinare; (: *in filing system*) schedare
► **store up** VT + ADV conservare.
store·front [ˌstɔːˈfrʌnt] N (*Am*) facciata di negozio.
store·house ['stɔːˌhaʊs] N magazzino, deposito.
store·keeper ['stɔːˌkiːpə*] N (*Am: shopkeeper*) negoziante *m/f*.
store·room ['stɔːˌrʊm] N deposito; (*for food*) dispensa.
♦ **stores requisition** N (*Admin*) richiesta di materiale a magazzino.
sto·rey, (*Am*) **sto·ry** ['stɔːrɪ] N piano; **a 9-stor(e)y building** un edificio a 9 piani.
stork [stɔːk] N cicogna.
storks·bill ['stɔːksˌbɪl] N (*Bot*) becco di gru.
storm [stɔːm] [1] N **a** (*Met*) tempesta, (: *at sea*) burrasca, tempesta; (: *thunderstorm*) temporale *m*; (*fig: of applause*) scroscio; (: *of abuse*) torrente *m*; (: *of protests*) uragano; (: *of weeping, tears*) mare *m*; (: *of uproar*) scompiglio; **it caused a storm** (*fig*) ha creato scompiglio; **a storm in a teacup** (*fig*) una tempesta in un bicchier d'acqua
  b (*Mil*): **to take a town by storm** prendere d'assalto una città; **the play took Paris by storm** (*fig*) la commedia ha trionfato a Parigi.
  [2] VT (*Mil*) prendere d'assalto.
  [3] VI (*wind, rain*) infuriare; (*person*): **to storm in/out** entrare/uscire come una furia; **she stormed up the stairs** si è precipitata di sopra furiosa; **"get out!" she stormed** "fuori!" urlò.
  [4] ADJ (*signal, warning*) di burrasca.
storm·bound ['stɔːmbaʊnd] ADJ (*ship, plane, passengers*) bloccato(-a) dal maltempo.
♦ **storm cloud** N nube *f* temporalesca; **there are storm clouds on the horizon** (*fig*) c'è aria di burrasca.

♦ **storm door** N controporta.
stormi·ly ['stɔːmɪlɪ] ADV burrascosamente.
♦ **storm jib** N (*Naut: sail*) tormentina.
♦ **storm pet·rel** ['stɔːmˌpɛtrəl] N procellaria.
♦ **storm troops** NPL (*Mil: gen*) truppe *fpl* d'assalto; (: *Nazi*) reparti *mpl* d'assalto.
♦ **storm window** N controfinestra.
stormy ['stɔːmɪ] ADJ (*comp* **-ier**, *superl* **-iest**) (*also fig*) burrascoso(-a), tempestoso(-a).
sto·ry[1] ['stɔːrɪ] N **a** (*account, lie*) storia; (*of book, film*) trama; (*tale, Literature*) racconto; **short story** (*Literature*) novella; **that's not the whole story** non è tutto; **it's the same old story** è sempre la solita storia; **to cut a long story short** per farla breve; **but that's another story** ma questa è un'altra storia; **that's the story of my life!** (*fam*) per me va sempre a finire così!; **to tell stories** (*fam: lies*) raccontare storie
  b (*Press*) articolo; **he covered the story of the earthquake** ha fatto il servizio sul terremoto.
sto·ry[2] ['stɔːrɪ] N (*Am*) = **storey**.
story·book ['stɔːrɪˌbʊk] N libro di racconti.
♦ **story line** N trama.
story·teller ['stɔːrɪˌtɛlə*] N **a** narratore(-trice); **he's a good storyteller** è uno che sa raccontare bene le storie
  b (*fam: liar*) bugiardo(-a).
stout [staʊt] [1] ADJ (*comp* **-er**, *superl* **-est**) (*sturdy: stick, shoes etc*) robusto(-a), solido(-a); (*fat: person*) corpulento(-a), robusto(-a); (*determined: supporter, resistance*) tenace; (: *refusal*) deciso(-a); (*brave*) coraggioso(-a); **with stout hearts** coraggiosamente, valorosamente; **a stout fellow** (*old fig*) un tipo in gamba.
  [2] N (*beer*) birra scura.
♦ **stout-hearted** [ˌstaʊtˈhɑːtɪd] ADJ (*liter*) coraggioso(-a), valoroso(-a).
stout·ly ['staʊtlɪ] ADV (*defend, resist, fight*) valorosamente; (*deny*) categoricamente; (*believe, maintain*) fermamente.
stout·ness ['staʊtnɪs] N (*of person*) corpulenza; (*of stick, shoes*) robustezza.
stove[1] [stəʊv] N **a** (*for heating*) stufa **b** (*for cooking*) cucina; (: *small*) fornelletto; **gas/electric stove** cucina a gas/elettrica.
stove[2] [stəʊv]: **stove in** PT, PP of **stave in**.
stow [stəʊ] VT (*Naut: cargo*) stivare
► **stow away** [1] VT + ADV mettere via.
  [2] VI + ADV imbarcarsi clandestinamente.
stow·away ['stəʊəˌweɪ] N passeggero(-a) clandestino(-a).
strad·dle ['strædl] VT (*subj: person: stream*) stare a gambe divaricate su; (: *chair*) stare a cavalcioni di; (: *horse*) stare in groppa a; (*subj: bridge: stream*) essere sospeso (-a) sopra; (*subj: town: border*) essere a cavallo di.
Stradi·var·ius [ˌstrædɪˈvɛərɪəs] N stradivario.
strafe [strɑːf] VT mitragliare.
strag·gle ['strægl] VI (*lag behind*) rimanere indietro; (*spread untidily*) estendersi disordinatamente; **to straggle in/out** entrare/uscire uno ad uno.
strag·gler ['stræglə*] N chi rimane indietro.
strag·gling ['stræglɪŋ], **strag·gly** ['stræglɪ] ADJ (*village*) sparso(-a); (*hair*) scarmigliato(-a); (*line*) irregolare; (*plant*) che cresce in modo disordinato.
straight [streɪt] [1] ADJ (*comp* **-er**, *superl* **-est**) **a** (*gen*) diritto(-a); (*hair*) liscio(-a); (*Geom*) retto(-a); (*posture*) eretto(-a); **the picture isn't straight** il quadro non è diritto; **to be (all) straight** (*tidy*) essere a posto, essere sistemato(-a); (*clarified*) essere chiaro(-a); **let's get this**

straight mettiamo le cose in chiaro; **to put straight** (*picture*) raddrizzare; (*hat, tie*) aggiustare; (*house, room, accounts*) mettere in ordine; **to put things** *or* **matters straight** chiarire le cose; **he soon put me straight** mi ha corretto immediatamente; **I couldn't keep a straight face** OR **I couldn't keep my face straight** non riuscivo a stare serio

b (*continuous, direct*) diritto(-a); **ten straight wins** dieci vittorie di fila

c (*honest, frank: person*) onesto(-a); (: *answer*) franco (-a); (: *denial*) netto(-a); **straight speaking** OR **straight talking** franchezza; **I'll be straight with you** sarò franco con te

d (*plain, uncomplicated*) semplice; (*drink*) liscio(-a); (*Theatre: part, play*) serio(-a); (*person: conventional*) normale; (: *heterosexual*) etero *inv*.

2 ADV **a** (*in a straight line: gen*) dritto; **to go straight up/down** andare dritto su/giù; **it's straight across the road from us** è proprio di fronte a noi; **straight ahead** avanti dritto; **to go straight on** andare dritto; **to go straight** (*fig*) rigare dritto

b (*directly, without diversion*) direttamente, diritto; **I went straight home** sono andato direttamente a casa; **to come straight to the point** venire al sodo

c (*immediately*) subito, immediatamente; **straight away** OR **straight off** subito

d (*frankly*) chiaramente, francamente; **straight out** chiaro e tondo.

3 N (*on racecourse*) dirittura d'arrivo; (*Rail*) rettilineo; **to cut sth on the straight** tagliare qc in drittofilo; **to keep to the straight and narrow** (*fig*) seguire la retta via.

straight·away [ˌstreɪtəˈweɪ] ADV subito.

straight·edge [ˈstreɪtˌɛdʒ] N (*Carpentry*) regolo.

straight·en [ˈstreɪtn] **1** VT (*sth bent: also:* **straighten out**) raddrizzare; (*hair*) stirare; (*tablecloth, tie*) aggiustare; (*tidy: also:* **straighten up**) mettere in ordine; (*fig: problem: also:* **straighten out**) spianare, risolvere; **to straighten things out** mettere le cose a posto; **to straighten one's shoulders** raddrizzarsi; **straighten your shoulders!** stai su dritto!.

2 VI (*person: also:* **straighten (o.s.) up**) raddrizzarsi.

♦ **straight-faced** [ˌstreɪtˈfeɪst] **1** ADJ serio(-a).

2 ADV con espressione seria.

straight·forward [ˌstreɪtˈfɔːwəd] ADJ (*honest, frank*) franco(-a), diretto(-a); (*simple*) semplice.

straight·forward·ly [ˌstreɪtˈfɔːwədlɪ] ADV (*behave*) onestamente; (*answer*) francamente; **to proceed straightforwardly** procedere senza intoppi.

straight·forward·ness [ˌstreɪtˈfɔːwədnɪs] N (*of reply*) franchezza, schiettezza; (*of behaviour*) onestà.

straight·laced [ˌstreɪtˈleɪst] = **strait-laced**.

strain¹ [streɪn] **1** N **a** (*Tech: on rope*) tensione *f*; (: *on beam*) sollecitazione *f*; (*on person: physical*) sforzo; (: *mental*) tensione *f*; (: *tiredness*) fatica; **to take the strain off sth** ridurre la tensione di (*or* la sollecitazione su) qc; **the bridge is showing signs of strain** il ponte mostra segni di deformazione; **the rope broke under the strain** la corda si è spezzata a causa della tensione; **she's under a lot of strain** è molto tesa, è sotto pressione; **I can't stand the strain** non resisto, non ce la faccio più; **the strains of modern life** il logorio della vita moderna; **to put a great strain on** (*marriage, friendship*) mettere a dura prova; (*person, savings, budget*) pesare molto su

b (*Med: sprain*) strappo

c : **to the strains of** (*Mus*) sulle note di; **he continued in**

that strain (*fig*) e continuò su questo tono.

2 VT **a** (*stretch*) tendere, tirare

b (*put strain on*) sottoporre a sforzo; (: *fig: relationship, marriage*) mettere a dura prova; (: *resources etc*) gravare su; (: *meaning*) forzare; (*Med: back, muscle, ligament*) farsi uno stiramento a; (: *eyes, heart*) affaticare; **don't strain yourself!** (*also iro*) non affaticarti troppo!; **to strain the truth** deformare la verità; **to strain every nerve to do sth** fare ogni sforzo per fare qc; **to strain one's voice** sforzare la voce; **to strain one's ears** aguzzare le orecchie; **to strain (one's eyes) to see sth** aguzzare la vista per vedere qc

c (*soup*) passare; (*tea*) filtrare; (*vegetables, pasta*) scolare.

3 VI: **to strain at sth** (*push/pull*) spingere/tirare qc con tutte le forze; **to strain against** (*ropes, bars*) far forza contro

▶ **strain off** VT + ADV (*liquid*) togliere.

strain² [streɪn] N (*breed*) razza; (*lineage*) stirpe *f*; (*of virus*) tipo; (*streak, trace*) tendenza.

strained [streɪnd] ADJ (*muscle*) stirato(-a); (*arm, ankle*) slogato(-a); (*heart, eyes*) affaticato(-a); (*laugh, smile etc*) forzato(-a); (*relations*) teso(-a); (*liquid*) filtrato(-a); (*solid food*) passato(-a).

strain·er [ˈstreɪnəʳ] N (*Culin*) passino, colino.

strait [streɪt] N (*Geog*) stretto; **the Straits of Dover** lo stretto di Dover; **to be in dire straits** (*fig*) essere nei guai.

strait·ened [ˈstreɪtnd] ADJ: **to be in straitened circumstances** (*frm*) vivere nelle ristrettezze.

strait·jacket [ˈstreɪtˌdʒækɪt] N camicia di forza.

♦ **strait-laced** [ˌstreɪtˈleɪst] ADJ puritano(-a).

strand [strænd] N (*of thread, pearls*) filo; (*of hair*) ciocca.

strand·ed [ˈstrændɪd] ADJ: **to be (left) stranded** (*ship, fish*) essere arenato(-a); (*person: without transport*) essere lasciato(-a) a piedi; (: *without money etc*) trovarsi nei guai; **to leave sb stranded** lasciare qn nei guai.

strange [streɪndʒ] ADJ (*comp* **-r**, *superl* **-st**) **a** (*odd*) strano (-a), bizzarro(-a); **it is strange that ...** è strano che...; **strange as it may seem ...** per quanto possa sembrare strano...; **I felt rather strange** mi sono sentito strano

b (*unknown, unfamiliar*) sconosciuto(-a); **you'll feel rather strange at first** all'inizio ti sentirai un po' spaesato; **to wake up in a strange bed** svegliarsi in un letto che non è il proprio; **the work is strange to him** non è pratico di questo lavoro.

strange·ly [ˈstreɪndʒlɪ] ADV stranamente; **strangely (enough), I've never met him** stranamente, non l'ho mai incontrato.

stran·ger [ˈstreɪndʒəʳ] N (*unknown person*) sconosciuto (-a); (*from another place*) forestiero(-a), estraneo(-a); **I'm a stranger here** non sono del posto; **he's a complete stranger to me** non lo conosco affatto, per me è un perfetto sconosciuto; **I'm no stranger to Rome** conosco Roma.

stran·gle [ˈstræŋgl] VT strangolare, strozzare.

strangle·hold [ˈstræŋglˌhəʊld] N (*Wrestling*) presa di gola; **to have a stranglehold on sb/sth** (*fig*) tenere qn/qc in pugno.

stran·gler [ˈstræŋgləʳ] N strangolatore(-trice).

stran·gling [ˈstræŋglɪŋ] N strangolamento.

stran·gu·la·tion [ˌstræŋgjʊˈleɪʃən] N strangolamento.

strap [stræp] **1** N (*of watch, shoes*) cinturino; (*for suitcase*) cinghia; (*in bus etc*) maniglia a pendaglio; (*also:* **shoulder strap**: *of bra*) bretella, spallina; (: *of bag*) tracolla; **to give sb the strap** punire qn con la cinghia.

2 VT **a** (*fasten*): **to strap down, strap in, strap on, strap up** legare; **to strap sb in** (*in car, plane*) allacciare la cintura di sicurezza a qn

b (*Med*: *also*: **strap up**) fasciare.

strap·hanger ['stræp,hæŋəˀ] N chi viaggia in piedi (*su mezzi pubblici reggendosi a un sostegno*).

strap·less ['stræplɪs] ADJ (*bra, dress*) senza spalline.

strapped ['stræpt] ADJ: **strapped for cash** a corto di soldi; **financially strapped** messo(-a) male finanziariamente.

strap·ping ['stræpɪŋ] ADJ (*person*) robusto(-a), ben piantato(-a).

Stras·bourg ['stræzbɜːg] N Strasburgo f.

stra·ta ['strɑːtə] NPL of **stratum**.

strata·gem ['strætɪdʒəm] N stratagemma m.

stra·tegic [strə'tiːdʒɪk] ADJ (*anche fig*) strategico(-a).

stra·tegi·cal·ly [strə'tiːdʒɪkəlɪ] ADV strategicamente.

strat·egist ['strætɪdʒɪst] N stratega m.

strat·egy ['strætɪdʒɪ] N (*also fig*) strategia.

strati·fi·ca·tion [,strætɪfɪ'keɪʃən] N stratificazione f.

strati·fied ['strætɪfaɪd] ADJ stratificato(-a).

strato·sphere ['strætəʊ,sfɪəˀ] N stratosfera.

stra·tum ['strɑːtəm] N (*pl* **strata**) (*also fig*) strato.

stra·tus ['streɪtəs] N (*pl* **strati** ['streɪtaɪ]) (*Met*) strato.

straw [strɔː] N paglia; (*drinking straw*) cannuccia; **that's the last straw!** questa è la goccia che fa traboccare il vaso!

straw·berry ['strɔːbərɪ] **1** N fragola; **wild strawberry** fragolina di bosco.

2 ADJ (*jam, tart*) di fragole; (*ice cream*) alla fragola.

♦ **strawberry mark** N voglia di fragola.

♦ **straw-coloured** ['strɔː,kʌləd] ADJ color paglia *inv*.

♦ **straw hat** N cappello di paglia, paglietta.

♦ **straw poll** N sondaggio d'opinione (*su un campione scelto a caso*).

stray [streɪ] **1** ADJ (*dog, cat*) randagio(-a); (*person, cow, sheep*) smarrito(-a); **he was killed by a stray bullet** è stato ucciso da un proiettile vagante; **a few stray cars** qualche rara macchina.

2 N (*animal*) randagio m.

3 VI (*animal*: *get lost*) smarrirsi, perdersi; (*wander*: *person*) allontanarsi, staccarsi dal gruppo; (: *speaker*) divagare; (: *thoughts*) vagare; **some cows strayed into the garden** delle mucche hanno sconfinato nel giardino; **to stray into enemy territory** ritrovarsi in territorio nemico.

streak [striːk] **1** N (*line*) striscia, riga; (*of mineral*) filone m, vena; **he had streaks of grey in his hair** aveva delle ciocche di capelli grigi; **to have streaks in one's hair** avere le mèches; **like a streak of lightning** come un fulmine; **to have a streak of madness** avere una vena di pazzia; **he had a cruel streak (in him)** c'era un che di crudele in lui; **lucky streak** periodo di fortuna; **a winning/losing streak** un periodo fortunato/sfortunato.

2 VT rigare, screziare, striare; **streaked with** (*tears*) rigato(-a) di; (*subj*: *sky*) striato(-a) di; (: *clothes*) macchiato(-a) di.

3 VI (*move quickly*): **to streak away/across/past** allontanarsi/attraversare/passare come un fulmine; (*run naked*) fare lo streaking.

streak·er ['striːkəˀ] N streaker m/f.

streak·ing ['striːkɪŋ] N streaking m *inv*.

streaky ['striːkɪ] ADJ (*colour, window, sky*) striato(-a); (*rock*) venato(-a), screziato(-a).

♦ **streaky bacon** N (*Brit*) ≈ pancetta.

stream [striːm] **1** N (*brook*) ruscello; (*current*) corrente f;

(*flow*: *of liquid, people, words*) fiume m; (: *of cars*) colonna; (: *of air*) soffio; (: *of light*) fascio; **against the stream** controcorrente; **an unbroken stream of cars** un fiume ininterrotto di macchine; **divided into three streams** (*Scol*) diviso in tre gruppi di diverso livello; **the B stream** (*Scol*) il gruppo di secondo livello; **to come on stream** (*oilwell, production line*) entrare in attività.

2 VT **a** (*water etc*) scendere a fiumi; **his nose streamed blood** grondava sangue dal naso

b (*Scol*) dividere in gruppi di diverso livello (*di rendimento e abilità*).

3 VI (*liquid*) scorrere; (*cars, people*) riversarsi; **her eyes were streaming** (*because of smoke*) le lacrimavano gli occhi; **her cheeks were streaming with tears** le lacrime le rigavano il volto; **cars kept streaming past me** fiumi di macchine continuavano a passarmi davanti; **to stream in/out** *etc* entrare/uscire *etc* a fiotti.

stream·er ['striːməˀ] N (*of paper, at parties etc*) stella filante.

♦ **stream feed** N (*on photocopier etc*) alimentazione f continua.

stream·ing ['striːmɪŋ] **1** N (*Scol*) suddivisione degli studenti in livelli (*di rendimento e abilità*).

2 ADJ: **I've got a streaming cold** ho il naso che cola per il raffreddore.

stream·line ['striːm,laɪn] VT dare una linea aerodinamica a; (*fig*) razionalizzare, snellire.

stream·lined ['striːm,laɪnd] ADJ (*see vb*) aerodinamico(-a); razionalizzato(-a), snellito(-a).

street [striːt] N strada, via; **the back streets** le strade secondarie; **to be on the streets** (*homeless*) essere senza tetto; (*as prostitute*) battere il marciapiede; **it's right up my street** (*fig*: *job*) è proprio quello che fa per me, è il mio forte; **to be streets ahead of sb** (*fam*) essere di gran lunga superiore a qn.

street·car ['striːt,kɑːˀ] N (*Am*) tram m *inv*.

♦ **street cleaner**, **street sweeper** N spazzino(-a), netturbino(-a).

♦ **street cred** N (*fam*) *credibilità presso i giovani*.

♦ **street door** N porta, portone m.

♦ **street lamp** N lampione m.

♦ **street lighting** N illuminazione f stradale.

♦ **street map**, **street plan** N pianta (della città), stradario.

♦ **street market** N mercato rionale.

♦ **street musician** N suonatore(-trice) ambulante.

♦ **street sweeper** N = **street cleaner**.

♦ **street theatre** N teatro di piazza.

♦ **street urchin** N scugnizzo(-a).

♦ **street value** N (*of drug*) valore m di mercato.

street·walker ['striːt,wɔːkəˀ] N passeggiatrice f.

street·wise ['striːt,waɪz] ADJ (*fam*) scafato(-a).

strength [strɛŋθ] N **a** (*gen, fig*) forza; (*of wall, nail, wood etc*) solidità; (*of rope*) resistenza; (*of chemical solution*) concentrazione f; (*of wine*) gradazione f alcolica; **you'll soon get your strength back** presto ti rimetterai in forze; **his strength failed him** gli sono mancate le forze; **strength of character/mind** forza di carattere/d'animo; **strength of purpose** risolutezza; **on the strength of** sulla base di, in virtù di; **to go from strength to strength** andare di bene in meglio

b (*Mil etc*) effettivo; **below/at full strength** con gli effettivi ridotti/al completo; **to come in strength** (*fig*) venire in gran numero.

strength·en ['strɛŋθən] **1** VT (*person, muscles*) irrobu-

stire; (*wall, building*) rinforzare; (*economy, currency*) consolidare; (*desire, determination*) rafforzare.

2 VI (*economy, currency*) consolidarsi; (*wind*) aumentare di intensità; (*desire, determination*) rafforzarsi.

strength·en·ing ['strɛŋθənɪŋ] N (*of structure*) rinforzo; (*of economy, currency*) consolidamento; (*of desire, determination*) rafforzamento.

strenu·ous ['strɛnjʊəs] ADJ (*denial, attempt*) energico(-a), vigoroso(-a); (*game, match, day*) faticoso(-a); (*opposition, efforts, resistance*) accanito(-a); **you mustn't do anything too strenuous** non devi fare troppi sforzi.

strenu·ous·ly ['strɛnjʊəslɪ] ADV (*deny*) energicamente; (*attempt, exercise, play*) con impegno; (*resist, oppose, attempt*) accanitamente.

stress [strɛs] 1 N **a** (*Tech*) sforzo; (*force, pressure*) pressione *f*; (*psychological etc: strain*) tensione *f*, stress *m*; **to be under stress** essere stressato(-a); (*fig*) essere sotto pressione; **in times of stress** in momenti di grande tensione; **the stresses and strains of modern life** il logorio *or* lo stress della vita moderna

b (*emphasis*) enfasi *f*; (*Ling, Poetry*) accento; **to lay great stress on sth** dare grande importanza a qc.

2 VT (*emphasize*) sottolineare, mettere in rilievo.

stressed [strɛst] ADJ (*syllable*) accentato(-a).

stress·ful ['strɛsfʊl] ADJ (*job*) difficile, stressante.

♦ **stress mark** N accento.

stretch [strɛtʃ] 1 N **a** (*distance*) tratto; (*expanse*) distesa; (*of time*) periodo; **for a long stretch it runs between ...** per un lungo *or* bel tratto passa fra...; **for three days at a stretch** per tre giorni di seguito *or* di fila; **he's done a five-year stretch** (*fam: in prison*) è stato dentro cinque anni

b (*elasticity*) elasticità; **to have a stretch** (*person*) stiracchiarsi; **to be at full stretch** lavorare a tutta forza; **by no stretch of the imagination** in nessun modo.

2 VT **a** (*pull out: elastic*) tendere, tirare; (*make larger: pullover, shoes*) allargare; (*spread on ground etc*) stendere; **to stretch (between)** (*rope etc*) tendere (fra); **to stretch one's legs** sgranchirsi le gambe; **to stretch o.s.** (*after sleep etc*) stiracchiarsi

b (*money, resources, meal*) far bastare

c (*meaning*) forzare; (*truth*) esagerare; **to stretch a point** fare uno strappo alla regola

d (*athlete, student etc*) far sforzare al massimo; **to be fully stretched** essere impegnato(-a) a fondo; **to stretch o.s.** mettercela tutta, impegnarsi a fondo.

3 VI **a** (*reach, extend: area of land*) **to stretch to** *or* **as far as** estendersi fino a; (*: meeting*) **to stretch (into)** prolungarsi (fino a); (*reach: rope, power, influence*) **to stretch (to)** andare (fino a); (*be enough: money, food*) bastare (per)

b (*stretch one's limbs*) stirarsi, stiracchiarsi; **I stretched across for the book** mi sono allungato per prendere il libro

c (*be elastic*) essere elastico(-a); (*become larger: clothes, shoes*) allargarsi.

4 ADJ (*fabric, trousers*) elasticizzato(-a)

▶ **stretch out** 1 VI + ADV (*person*) allungarsi; (*: lie down*) stendersi; (*countryside etc*) estendersi, stendersi; **to stretch out for sth** allungare la mano per prendere qc; **a life of unrelieved monotony stretched out before him** lo aspettava una vita di terribile monotonia.

2 VT + ADV (*arm, leg*) allungare, tendere; (*net, blanket*) distendere, stendere; (*rope*) stendere.

stretch·er ['strɛtʃə'] N (*Med*) barella.

♦ **stretcher-bearer** ['strɛtʃə,bɛərə'] N barelliere *m*.

♦ **stretcher case** N ferito(-a) che dev'essere trasportato (-a) in barella.

♦ **stretch marks** NPL smagliature *fpl*.

stretchy ['strɛtʃɪ] ADJ (*comp* **-ier**, *superl* **-iest**) (*fabric*) elastico(-a).

strew [struː] (*pt* **strewed**, *pp* **strewed** *or* **strewn** ['struːn]) VT (*scatter: sand, straw, wreckage*) spargere; (*cover*): **to strew (with)** ricoprire (di); **to strew one's things about the room** disseminare la roba in giro per la stanza.

strewn [struːn] ADJ: **strewn with** cosparso(-a) di.

stria·tion [straɪˈeɪʃən] N striatura; (*Geol*) striatura glaciale.

strick·en ['strɪkən] 1 (*old*) PP of **strike**.

2 ADJ (*distressed, upset*) colpito(-a); (*wounded*) ferito (-a); (*damaged: ship etc*) in avaria; (*: city*) colpito(-a); **grief stricken** affranto(-a); **she was stricken with remorse** fu presa dal rimorso.

strict [strɪkt] ADJ (*comp* **-er**, *superl* **-est**) **a** (*stern, severe: person, principles, views*) severo(-a), rigido(-a); (*: order, rule*) rigoroso(-a); (*: supervision*) stretto(-a); (*: discipline, ban*) rigido(-a)

b (*precise: meaning, accuracy*) preciso(-a); (*absolute: secrecy, truth*) assoluto(-a); (*: time limit*) tassativo(-a); **in the strict sense of the word** nel senso stretto della parola; **in strict confidence** in assoluta confidenza.

strict·ly ['strɪktlɪ] ADV (*see adj*) severamente; rigorosamente; strettamente; rigidamente; precisamente; assolutamente; tassativamente; **she was strictly brought up** ha ricevuto un'educazione rigida; **strictly confidential** strettamente confidenziale; **it is strictly forbidden** è severamente proibito; **strictly speaking** a rigor di termini; **strictly between ourselves ...** detto fra noi... .

strict·ness ['strɪktnɪs] N (*of person*) severità.

stric·ture ['strɪktʃə'] N (*usu pl: frm: criticism*) critica.

stride [straɪd] (*vb: pt* **strode**, *pp* **stridden** ['strɪdn]) 1 N passo, falcata; **to get into one's stride** (*fig*) trovare il ritmo giusto; **to take sth in one's stride** (*fig: changes etc*) prendere con tranquillità; (*: exam*) sostenere senza grossi problemi; **to make great strides** (*fig*) fare passi da gigante.

2 VI: **to stride in/out** *etc* entrare/uscire a grandi passi; **to stride along** camminare a grandi passi; **to stride up and down** camminare avanti e indietro.

stri·dent ['straɪdənt] ADJ (*sound*) stridente, stridulo(-a); (*voice*) stridulo(-a); (*protest*) energico(-a).

strife [straɪf] N conflitto; **industrial strife** lotte *fpl* sindacali.

strike [straɪk] (*vb: pt, pp* **struck**) 1 N **a** (*by workers*) sciopero; **to go on** *or* **come out on strike** entrare in sciopero; **to call a strike** organizzare uno sciopero

b (*Mil: also:* **air strike**) incursione *f* aerea

c (*discovery: of oil, gold*) scoperta; **to make a strike** scoprire un giacimento

d (*Baseball, Bowling*) strike *m inv*.

2 VT **a** (*hit: gen*) colpire; **to strike a blow at sb** sferrare un colpo a qn; **who struck the first blow?** chi ha colpito per primo?; **to strike a blow for freedom** spezzare una lancia in favore della libertà; **to strike a man when he's down** (*fig*) uccidere un uomo morto; **the president was struck by two bullets** il presidente è stato colpito da due pallottole; **the clock struck nine o'clock** l'orologio ha suonato le nove; **to be struck by lightning** essere colpito(-a) da un fulmine; **panic struck** preso(-a) dal panico; **to strike sth out of sb's hand** far cadere qc di

mano a qn

b (*collide with*) urtare, sbattere contro; (: *rocks etc*) sbattere contro, cozzare contro; **she struck her head against the wall** ha battuto la testa contro il muro; **a ghastly sight struck our eyes** una scena orribile si presentò ai nostri occhi; **disaster struck us** siamo stati colpiti da una sciagura

c (*produce, make*: *coin, medal*) coniare; (: *agreement, deal*) concludere; (: *a light, match*) accendere; (: *sparks*) far sprizzare; **to strike an attitude** assumere un atteggiamento; **to strike a balance** (*fig*) trovare il giusto mezzo; **to be struck dumb** ammutolire; **to strike terror into sb's heart** terrorizzare qn

d (*occur to*) colpire; **the thought** *or* **it strikes me that ...** mi viene in mente che...; **it strikes me as being most unlikely** mi sembra molto improbabile; **how does it strike you?** che te ne pare?, che ne pensi?; **I'm not much struck with him** non mi ha fatto una buona impressione

e (*find*: *gold, oil*) trovare; **he struck it rich** (*fig*) ha fatto fortuna, ha trovato l'America

f (*pp*: *also* **stricken**) (*remove, cross out*): **to strike: (from)** cancellare (da).

3 VI **a** (*workers*) scioperare; **to strike for higher wages** scioperare per rivendicazioni salariali

b (*clock*) rintoccare, suonare

c (*attack*: *Mil etc*) attaccare, sferrare un attacco; (: *tiger*) aggredire la preda; (: *snake*) mordere; (: *disease, disaster*) colpire, abbattersi; **now is the time to strike** questo è il momento di agire; **it strikes at our very existence** minaccia di distruggerci; **to strike at** (*person, evil*) colpire; **to strike at the root of a problem** intervenire alla radice di un problema

d : **to strike on an idea** avere un'idea.

4 ADJ (*pay, committee*) di sciopero

► **strike back** VI + ADV (*Mil*) fare rappresaglie; (*fig*) reagire
► **strike down** VT + ADV (*subj*: *illness etc*: *incapacitate*) colpire; (: *kill*) uccidere; **he was struck down in his prime** è morto nel fiore degli anni
► **strike off** **1** VT + ADV (*from list*) cancellare; (: *doctor*) radiare.

2 VT + PREP (*name off list*) depennare.
3 VI + ADV: **he struck off across the fields** ha tagliato per i campi
► **strike out** **1** VT + ADV (*cross out*) depennare.

2 VI + ADV **a** (*hit out*): **to strike out (at)** tirare colpi (a), dare botte (a)

b (*set out*): **to strike out (for)** dirigersi (verso); **to strike out across country** tagliare per la campagna; **to strike out on one's own** (*fig*: *in business*) mettersi in proprio
► **strike up** **1** VT + ADV **a** (*friendship*) fare; **to strike up a conversation** attaccare discorso

b (*tune*) attaccare.
2 VI + ADV (*band*) attaccare.

strike·bound ['straɪkˌbaʊnd] ADJ (*factory*) paralizzato(-a) da uno sciopero.

strike·breaker ['straɪkˌbreɪkə'] N crumiro(-a).

strike·breaking ['straɪkˌbreɪkɪŋ] N: **he was accused of strikebreaking** l'hanno tacciato di crumiraggio.

♦ **strike force** N (*Mil, Aer*) distaccamento aereo.

strik·er ['straɪkə'] N (*in industry*) scioperante *m/f*; (*Sport*) attaccante *m/f*.

strik·ing ['straɪkɪŋ] ADJ (*arresting*: *picture, dress, colour*) che colpisce; (: *person*) che fa colpo; (*obvious*: *contrast, resemblance*) evidente, lampante; (*shocking*: *change, sight*) impressionante; **to be within striking distance of**

sth (*Mil*) essere a portata di tiro da qc; (*fig*) essere a un tiro di schioppo da qc.

strik·ing·ly ['straɪkɪŋlɪ] ADV (*different, original*) totalmente; (*pretty, handsome*) straordinariamente.

Strim·mer® ['strɪmə'] N tagliabordi *m inv.*

string [strɪŋ] (*vb*: *pt, pp* **strung**) **1** N **a** (*cord*) spago; (*of puppet*) filo; (*plait*: *of onions*) treccia; (*row*: *of beads*) filo; (: *of vehicles, people*) fila; (: *of excuses*) sfilza, serie *f inv*; (*Comput, Linguistics*) stringa, sequenza; **to pull strings for sb** raccomandare qn; **to get a job by pulling strings** ottenere un lavoro a forza di raccomandazioni; **with no strings attached** (*fig*) senza legami, senza obblighi

b (*on musical instrument, racket*) corda; **the strings** (*Mus*) gli archi; **to have more than one string to one's bow** (*fig*) avere molte frecce al proprio arco.

2 VT **a** (*pearls*) infilare; (*lights, decorations*) appendere; (*rope*): **to string across/between** tendere attraverso/tra

b (*violin, bow*) incordare; (*tennis racket*) mettere le corde a; **he can't even string two sentences together** non sa mettere insieme due parole

► **string along** VT + ADV (*fam*) menare per il naso
► **string out** VT + ADV: **to be strung out behind sb/along sth** formare una fila dietro a qn/lungo qc
► **string up** VT + ADV (*object*) appendere a una corda; (*fam*: *hang*) appendere (per il collo); **to be strung up about sth** (*fig*) essere teso(-a) per qc.

♦ **string bean** N fagiolino.

stringed in·str·ument [ˌstrɪŋdˈɪnstrʊmənt] N (*Mus*) strumento a corda.

strin·gen·cy ['strɪndʒənsɪ] N rigore *m.*

strin·gent ['strɪndʒənt] ADJ (*measures, economies, tests*) rigoroso(-a); **stringent rules** regolamento *msg* stretto.

string·ing ['strɪŋɪŋ] N (*Tennis*) accordatura.

♦ **string instrument** N = **stringed instrument**.

string·pulling ['strɪŋˌpʊlɪŋ] N: **to do some stringpulling for sb** raccomandare qn.

♦ **string quartet** N quartetto d'archi.

♦ **string vest** N canottiera a rete.

stringy ['strɪŋɪ] ADJ (*comp* **-ier**, *superl* **-iest**) (*meat, celery*) filaccioso(-a); (*cooked cheese*) filante; (*plant, hair*) lungo (-a) e rado(-a).

strip [strɪp] **1** N **a** (*gen*) striscia; (*of metal*) nastro; (*Aer*) pista; **comic strip** fumetto; **to tear a strip off sb** (*fig fam*) dare una lavata di capo a qn

b (*Sport*: *clothes*) divisa; **wearing the Celtic strip** con la divisa del Celtic.

2 VT **a** (*person, plants, bushes*) spogliare; (*bed*) disfare; (*house*) vuotare, svuotare; (*wallpaper*) staccare; (*paint*) togliere; (*furniture, woodwork*) sverniciare; **to strip from** staccare (*or* togliere) da; **to strip sb/sth of sth** spogliare qn/qc di qc; **he was stripped of his rank** (*Mil*) è stato degradato

b (*Tech*: *also*: **strip down**: *engine*) smontare.
3 VI (*undress*) spogliarsi, svestirsi; (*do striptease*) fare lo spogliarello; **to strip to the waist** spogliarsi fino alla cintola

► **strip off** VI + ADV spogliarsi.

♦ **strip cartoon** N fumetto.

♦ **strip club** N (*Brit*) locale *m* di spogliarelli.

stripe [straɪp] N **a** riga, striscia; **white with green stripes** bianco(-a) a strisce verdi **b** (*Mil*) gallone *m.*

striped [straɪpt] ADJ a strisce, a righe.

♦ **strip joint** N (*Am fam*) = **strip club**.

♦ **strip light** N (*Brit*) tubo al neon.

♦ **strip lighting** N illuminazione *f* al neon.

strip·ling ['strɪplɪŋ] N (*esp hum*) giovanotto.

strip·per ['strɪpəʳ] N (*also:* **paint stripper**) sverniciatore *m*; (*striptease*) spogliarellista *m/f.*

♦ **strip poker** N strip-poker *m.*

♦ **strip-search** [ˌstrɪp'sɜ:tʃ] ⒈ VT: **to strip-search sb** perquisire qn facendolo(-a) spogliare. ⒉ N perquisizione *f (facendo spogliare il perquisito).*

♦ **strip show** N spettacolo di spogliarello.

strip·tease ['strɪpˌti:z] N spogliarello.

stripy ['straɪpɪ] ADJ (*comp* **-ier**, *superl* **-iest**) (*shirt*) a righe.

strive [straɪv] (*pt* **strove**, *pp* **striven** ['strɪvn]) VI sforzarsi; **strive as he might** per quanto si sforzasse; **to strive after** *or* **for sth** lottare per ottenere qc; **to strive to do sth** sforzarsi di fare qc, fare ogni sforzo per fare qc.

strobe [strəʊb], **strobe light** N luce *f* stroboscopica.

strode [strəʊd] PT of **stride**.

stroke [strəʊk] ⒈ N **a** (*blow*) colpo; **at a stroke** ⒪ⓡ **at one stroke** d'un solo colpo

  b (*caress*) carezza

  c (*Med*) colpo apoplettico

  d (*of pen*) tratto; (*of brush*) pennellata

  e (*Cricket, Golf*) colpo; (*Rowing*) vogata, remata; (*Swimming: single movement*) bracciata; (: *style*) nuoto; **butterfly stroke** nuoto a farfalla; **he hasn't done a stroke (of work)** non ha fatto un bel niente; **a stroke of genius** un lampo di genio; **a stroke of luck** un colpo di fortuna; **to put sb off his stroke** (*Sport*) far perdere il ritmo a qn; (*fig*) far perdere la concentrazione a qn

  f (*of bell, clock*) rintocco; **on the stroke of 12** allo scoccare delle 12

  g (*of piston*) corsa; **two-stroke engine** motore *m* a due tempi.

⒉ VT (*cat, sb's hair*) accarezzare.

stroll [strəʊl] ⒈ N passeggiata, giretto; **to go for a stroll** ⒪ⓡ **have** *or* **take a stroll** andare a fare un giretto *or* due passi. ⒉ VI andare a spasso; **to stroll around** *or* **through** gironzolare per; **to stroll in/out** *etc* entrare/uscire *etc* tranquillamente.

stroll·er ['strəʊləʳ] N (*Am: pushchair*) passeggino.

strong [strɒŋ] ⒈ ADJ (*comp* **-er**, *superl* **-est**) (*gen*) forte; (*sturdy: table, shoes, fabric*) solido(-a), resistente; (*candidate*) che ha buone possibilità; (*protest, letter, measures*) energico(-a); (*concentrated, intense: bleach, acid*) concentrato(-a); (*marked, pronounced: characteristic*) marcato(-a); (: *accent*) marcato(-a), forte; **as strong as a horse** *or* **an ox** (*powerful*) forte come un toro; (*healthy*) sano(-a) come un pesce; **he's never been very strong** è sempre stato di salute cagionevole; **there's a strong possibility that ...** ci sono buone possibilità che...; **there are strong indications that ...** tutto sembra indicare che...; **to have a strong stomach** avere uno stomaco di ferro; **I have strong feelings on the matter** ho molto a cuore quel problema; **to be a strong believer in** credere fermamente in; **strong language** (*swearing*) linguaggio volgare; (*frank and critical*) linguaggio incisivo; **he's not very strong on grammar** non è molto forte in grammatica; **geography was never my strong point** la geografia non è mai stata il mio forte; **they are 20 strong** sono in 20.

⒉ ADV: **to be going strong** (*company, business*) andare a gonfie vele; (*song, singer*) andare forte, avere successo; (*old person*) essere attivo(-a).

♦ **strong-arm** ['strɒŋˌɑ:m] ADJ (*pej: methods*) brutale; **strong-arm tactics** le maniere forti.

strong·box ['strɒŋˌbɒks] N cassaforte *f.*

♦ **strong drink** N alcolici *mpl.*

strong·hold ['strɒŋˌhəʊld] N fortezza; **the last stronghold of ...** (*fig*) l'ultima roccaforte di... .

strong·ly ['strɒŋlɪ] ADV (*made, built*) solidamente; (*tempted, influenced*) fortemente; (*remind*) moltissimo; (*protest, support, argue*) energicamente; (*believe*) fermamente; (*feel*) profondamente, intensamente; **to feel strongly about sth** avere molto a cuore qc; **she strongly resembles her mother** somiglia molto a sua madre; **it smells strongly of garlic** ha un forte odore di aglio; **a strongly-worded letter** una lettera dura.

strong·man ['strɒŋˌmæn] N (*pl* **-men**) (*circus performer*) maciste *m.*

♦ **strong-minded** [ˌstrɒŋ'maɪndɪd] ADJ deciso(-a), risoluto(-a).

♦ **strong-mindedly** [ˌstrɒŋ'maɪndɪdlɪ] ADV fermamente, con decisione, con risolutezza.

strong·room ['strɒŋˌrʊm] N camera blindata.

♦ **strong verb** (*Gram*) N verbo forte.

♦ **strong-willed** [ˌstrɒŋ'wɪld] ADJ prepotente.

stron·tium ['strɒntɪəm] N stronzio.

strop·py ['strɒpɪ] ADJ (*comp* **-ier**, *superl* **-iest**) (*Brit fam*) indisponente, scontroso(-a); **to get stroppy** mettersi a fare il/la difficile.

strove [strəʊv] PT of **strive**.

struck [strʌk] PT, PP of **strike**.

struc·tur·al ['strʌktʃərəl] ADJ strutturale; **structural formula** (*Chem*) formula di struttura.

struc·tur·al·ism ['strʌktʃərəˌlɪzəm] N strutturalismo.

struc·tur·al·ist ['strʌktʃərəlɪst] ⒈ ADJ strutturalistico(-a). ⒉ N strutturalista *m/f.*

struc·tur·al·ly ['strʌktʃərəlɪ] ADV strutturalmente.

struc·ture ['strʌktʃəʳ] ⒈ N (*gen, Chem, of building*) struttura; (*building itself*) costruzione *f*, fabbricato. ⒉ VT (*essay, argument*) strutturare.

strug·gle ['strʌgl] ⒈ N (*fight*) lotta; (*effort*) sforzo; **he lost his glasses in the struggle** ha perso gli occhiali nella zuffa; **a power struggle** una lotta per il potere; **the struggle for survival** la lotta per la sopravvivenza; **without a struggle** (*surrender*) senza opporre resistenza; (*without difficulty*) senza problemi; **to have a struggle to do sth** avere dei problemi a fare qc. ⒉ VI (*physically*) lottare; **to struggle with sth/sb** lottare con qc/qn; **to struggle to one's feet** alzarsi con sforzo; **to struggle through the crowd** avanzare a fatica tra la folla. ⒊ VT: **to struggle to do sth** lottare per fare qc; **to struggle to make ends meet** faticare a sbarcare il lunario

▶ **struggle on** VI + ADV (*fighting*) continuare a lottare; (*walking*) avanzare a fatica; (*living*) tirare avanti

▶ **struggle through** VI + ADV (*fig*): **they managed to struggle through** sono riusciti a farcela.

strug·gling ['strʌglɪŋ] ADJ (*artist, actor etc*) che lotta per affermarsi.

strum [strʌm] VT (*guitar*) strimpellare.

strung [strʌŋ] PT, PP of **string**; see also **highly**.

strut[1] [strʌt] VI: **to strut about** *or* **around** pavoneggiarsi; **he strutted past** mi passò davanti impettito; **to strut into a room** entrare impettito(-a) in una stanza.

strut[2] [strʌt] N (*beam*) supporto, sostegno.

strych·nine ['strɪkni:n] N stricnina.

stub [stʌb] ⒈ N (*of cigarette, pencil*) mozzicone *m*; (*of candle*) moccolo; (*of cheque, receipt, ticket*) matrice *f*, talloncino. ⒉ VT: **to stub one's toe (on sth)** urtare

or sbattere il dito del piede (contro qc)

▶ **stub out** VT + ADV: **to stub out a cigarette** spegnere una sigaretta.

stub·ble ['stʌbl] N (*in field*) stoppia; (*on chin*) barba di due giorni.

stub·born ['stʌbən] ADJ (*gen*) ostinato(-a); (*person*) cocciuto(-a), testardo(-a).

stub·born·ly ['stʌbənlɪ] ADV ostinatamente, cocciutamente.

stub·born·ness ['stʌbənnɪs] N testardaggine *f*, ostinazione *f*.

stub·by ['stʌbɪ] ADJ tozzo(-a).

stuc·co ['stʌkəʊ] N stucco.

stuck [stʌk] ☐1 PT, PP of **stick**.

☐2 ADJ **a** (*jammed*) bloccato(-a); **to get stuck** bloccarsi **b** (*stumped*): **I'm stuck** (*fam: with crossword, puzzle*) non riesco ad andare avanti; **to be stuck for an answer** non sapere cosa rispondere; **he's never stuck for an answer** ha sempre la risposta pronta.

♦ **stuck-up** [,stʌk'ʌp] ADJ (*fam*) presuntuoso(-a), arrogante.

stud[1] [stʌd] ☐1 N (*in road*) chiodo; (*of football boots*) tacchetto; (*decorative*) borchia; (*also:* **collar stud, shirt stud**) bottoncino.

☐2 VT: **studded with** (*fig*) ornato(-a) di, tempestato(-a) di; **studded tyre** pneumatico chiodato.

stud[2] [stʌd] N (*stud farm*) scuderia di allevamento; (*also:* **stud horse**) stallone *m*.

stud·book ['stʌd,bʊk] N registro di allevamento.

stu·dent ['stju:dənt] ☐1 N (*Scol, Univ*) studente(-essa); (*of human nature etc*) studioso(-a); **a law/medical student** uno(-a) studente(-essa) di legge/di medicina.

☐2 ADJ (*life, unrest*) studentesco(-a); (*attitudes, opinions*) degli studenti; (*canteen*) scolastico(-a).

♦ **student driver** N (*Am*) conducente *m/f* principiante.

stu·dent·ship ['stju:dənt,ʃɪp] N borsa di studio.

♦ **students' union** N (*Brit: association*) associazione *f* universitaria; (*: building*) sede *f* dell'associazione universitaria.

♦ **student teacher** N *studente che fa il tirocinio di insegnamento.*

stud·ied ['stʌdɪd] ADJ (*calm, simplicity*) studiato(-a), calcolato(-a); (*insult*) premeditato(-a), intenzionale; (*pose, style*) affettato(-a).

stu·dio ['stju:dɪəʊ] N (*TV, Radio, Cine, of artist*) studio; (*also:* **recording studio**) sala di registrazione.

♦ **studio audience** N (*TV, Radio*) pubblico in sala.

♦ **studio couch** N divano *m* letto *inv*.

♦ **studio flat**, (*Am*) **studio apartment** N monolocale *m*.

♦ **studio portrait** N fotoritratto.

stu·di·ous ['stju:dɪəs] ADJ (*person*) studioso(-a); (*attention to detail*) accurato(-a).

stu·di·ous·ly ['stju:dɪəslɪ] ADV (*see adj*) studiosamente; accuratamente; (*deliberately*) studiatamente, deliberatamente.

stu·di·ous·ness ['stju:dɪəsnɪs] N amore *m* per lo studio.

study ['stʌdɪ] ☐1 N (*activity, room*) studio; **to make a study of sth** fare uno studio su qc; **his face was a study!** (*fig*) ha fatto una faccia!; **it repays closer study** vale la pena di studiarlo a fondo.

☐2 VT (*gen*) studiare; (*examine: evidence, painting*) esaminare, studiare.

☐3 VI studiare; **she's studying to be a doctor** studia medicina; **to study under sb** (*Univ*) essere uno degli

studenti di qn; (*subj: artist, composer*) essere allievo(-a) di qn; **to study for an exam** prepararsi a un esame.

stuff [stʌf] ☐1 N **a** (*substance*) roba; **there is some good stuff in that book** ci sono delle buone cose in quel libro; **it's dangerous stuff** è roba pericolosa; **do you call this stuff beer?** questa robaccia la chiami birra?; **I can't read his stuff** non riesco a leggere quello che scrive; **he's the stuff that heroes are made of** ha la stoffa dell'eroe

b (*possessions, equipment*) cose *fpl*, roba; **she leaves her stuff scattered about** lascia la sua roba sparsa in giro

c (*fam: nonsense*): **all that stuff about her leaving** tutte quelle storie sulla sua partenza; **stuff and nonsense!** sciocchezze!

d (*fam*): **to do one's stuff** fare la propria parte; **go on, do your stuff!** forza, fai quello che devi fare!; **he certainly knows his stuff** sa il fatto suo.

☐2 VT (*fill*) riempire; (*: Culin*) farcire; (*: animal: for exhibition*) impagliare; **to stuff (with)** (*container*) riempire (di); (*cushion, toy*) imbottire (di); **to stuff into** (*stow: contents*) ficcare (in); **he stuffed it into his pocket** se lo ficcò in tasca; **my nose is stuffed up** ho il naso chiuso; **get stuffed!** (*offensive*) va' a quel paese!; **stuffed shirt** (*fam*) pallone *m* gonfiato; **to stuff o.s. (with food)** rimpinzarsi, strafogarsi.

stuffi·ly ['stʌfɪlɪ] ADV (*say*) con tono di disapprovazione.

stuffi·ness ['stʌfɪnɪs] N **a** (*in room*) odore *m* di chiuso **b** (*of person*) ristrettezza di idee; (*of ideas*) arretratezza.

stuff·ing ['stʌfɪŋ] N (*in cushion etc*) imbottitura; (*Culin*) farcia, ripieno; **to knock the stuffing out of sb** (*subj: boxer, blow*) mettere al tappeto qn.

stuffy ['stʌfɪ] ADJ (*comp* -**ier**, *superl* -**iest**) **a** (*room*) mal ventilato(-a), senz'aria; **it's terribly stuffy in here** qui non si respira; **it smells stuffy** c'è odore di chiuso **b** (*ideas*) antiquato(-a), arretrato(-a); (*person*) all'antica.

stul·ti·fy ['stʌltɪ,faɪ] VT (*frm*) istupidire.

stum·ble ['stʌmbl] VI inciampare; (*in speech*) incespicare; **to stumble against sth** inciampare contro qc; **to stumble in/out** entrare/uscire barcollando; **to stumble on** *or* **across sth** (*fig: secret*) scoprire per caso; (*: photo etc*) trovare per caso.

stum·bling block ['stʌmblɪŋ,blɒk] N ostacolo, scoglio.

stump [stʌmp] ☐1 N (*of limb*) moncone *m*; (*of pencil, tail*) mozzicone *m*; (*of tree*) troncone *m*; (*of tooth*) pezzo; (*Cricket*) paletto (*della porta*).

☐2 VT (*perplex*) sconcertare, lasciare perplesso(-a); **to be stumped for an answer** essere incapace di rispondere.

☐3 VI: **to stump in/out** *etc* entrare/uscire *etc* con passo pesante

▶ **stump up** ☐1 VT + ADV (*fam*) sganciare, sborsare.

☐2 VI + ADV (*fam*) sborsare i soldi, sganciare i soldi.

stumpy ['stʌmpɪ] ADJ (*person*) tarchiato(-a).

stun [stʌn] VT (*subj: blow*) stordire, tramortire; (*fig: amaze*) sbalordire, stupefare; **the news stunned everybody** la notizia sbalordì tutti.

stung [stʌŋ] PT, PP of **sting**.

stunk [stʌŋk] PP of **stink**.

stunned [stʌnd] ADJ (*by blow*) stordito(-a); (*fig*) sbalordito (-a); **in stunned silence** ammutolito(-a).

stun·ner ['stʌnə'] N (*fam*): **she's a stunner** è uno schianto.

stun·ning ['stʌnɪŋ] ADJ (*news etc*) sbalorditivo(-a), stupefacente; (*dress, girl etc*) fantastico(-a), splendido(-a).

stunt[1] [stʌnt] N (*Aer, for film etc*) acrobazia; (*Comm*) trovata pubblicitaria; **it's just a stunt to get your money** è tutto un trucco per farti tirar fuori i soldi.

stunt[2] [stʌnt] VT (*tree, person*) arrestare la crescita *or* lo

sviluppo di; (*growth*) arrestare.

stunt·ed ['stʌntɪd] ADJ (*tree*) striminzito(-a); (*person*)
rachitico(-a).

stunt·man ['stʌntˌmæn] N (*pl* **-men**) stuntman *m inv*,
cascatore *m*.

♦ **stunt woman** N (*pl* **stunt women**) stuntwoman *f inv*.

stu·pefac·tion [ˌstjuːpɪˈfækʃən] N stupefazione *f*, stupore
m.

stu·pefy ['stjuːpɪˌfaɪ] VT (*subj: tiredness, alcohol*) stordire,
istupidire; (*fig: astound*) stupire, sbalordire.

stu·pefy·ing ['stjuːpɪˌfaɪɪŋ] ADJ (*news*) sbalorditivo(-a),
stupefacente; (*boredom*) che stupidisce.

stu·pen·dous [stjuːˈpɛndəs] ADJ (*fam: film, holiday etc*)
stupendo(-a), fantastico(-a); (: *price*) altissimo(-a);
(: *mistake*) enorme.

stu·pen·dous·ly [stjuːˈpɛndəslɪ] ADV stupendamente,
fantasticamente; **a stupendously high price** un prezzo
incredibilmente alto.

stu·pid ['stjuːpɪd] ADJ (*gen*) stupido(-a); (*person*) stupido
(-a), sciocco(-a); (: *from sleep, drink*) intontito(-a), istu-
pidito(-a); **that was stupid of you** [OR] **that was a stupid
thing to do** hai fatto una stupidaggine; **he drank himself
stupid last night** era ubriaco fradicio ieri sera.

stu·pid·ity [stjuːˈpɪdɪtɪ] N stupidità *f inv*.

stu·pid·ly ['stjuːpɪdlɪ] ADV (*smile, say*) stupidamente; **I
stupidly forgot to lock the door** mi sono stupidamente
dimenticato di chiudere la porta a chiave.

stu·por ['stjuːpəʳ] N (*from heat, alcohol*) intontimento,
stordimento.

stur·di·ly ['stɜːdɪlɪ] ADV (*built, supported*) solidamente; (*fig:
refuse*) energicamente, risolutamente.

stur·di·ness ['stɜːdɪnɪs] N (*see adj*) robustezza; solidità;
risolutezza.

stur·dy ['stɜːdɪ] ADJ (*comp* **-ier**, *superl* **-iest**) (*person, tree*)
robusto(-a), forte; (*boat, material*) resistente, solido(-a);
(*fig: supporter*) accanito(-a); (: *refusal*) risoluto(-a).

stur·geon ['stɜːdʒən] N storione *m*.

stut·ter ['stʌtəʳ] [1] N balbuzie *f*; **he has a bad stutter** ha
una balbuzie pronunciata.
[2] VI, VT balbettare.

stut·ter·er ['stʌtərəʳ] N balbuziente *m/f*.

stut·ter·ing ['stʌtərɪŋ] N balbuzie *f*.

Stutt·gart ['stʊtgɑːt] N Stoccarda.

sty[1] [staɪ] N (*for pigs*) porcile *m*.

sty[2], **stye** [staɪ] N (*Med*) orzaiolo.

style [staɪl] N **a** (*gen*) stile *m*; **in the Renaissance style** in
stile rinascimentale; **that's the style!** così va bene!
b (*of dress etc*) modello, linea; (*also:* **hair style**) pettinatura; (: *more elaborate*) acconciatura; **in the latest style**
all'ultima moda; **something in this style** qualcosa di
questo tipo
c (*elegance: of person, car, film*) classe *f*, stile *m*; **to dress
with style** vestire con un certo stile; **she has style** ha
classe *or* stile; **to live in style** avere un elevato tenore di
vita; **to do things in style** fare le cose in grande stile
d (*Bot*) stilo.

sty·li ['staɪlaɪ] NPL of **stylus**.

styl·ing ['staɪlɪŋ] N (*Hairdressing*) taglio.

styl·ish ['staɪlɪʃ] ADJ (*person*) di classe; (*car, district, furniture*) elegante; (*film*) raffinato(-a).

styl·ish·ly ['staɪlɪʃlɪ] ADV (*dress, live, travel*) con stile, con
classe.

styl·ish·ness ['staɪlɪʃnɪs] N stile *m*, classe *f*.

styl·ist ['staɪlɪst] N: **hair stylist** parrucchiere(-a).

sty·lis·tic [staɪˈlɪstɪk] ADJ stilistico(-a).

sty·lis·tics [staɪˈlɪstɪks] NSG stilistica.

styl·ized ['staɪlaɪzd] ADJ stilizzato(-a).

sty·lus ['staɪləs] N (*pl* **styli**) (*of record player*) puntina; (*pen*)
stilo.

sty·mie ['staɪmɪ] VT (*fam*) ostacolare.

styp·tic ['stɪptɪk] ADJ emostatico(-a); **styptic pencil** matita
emostatica.

Styro·foam® ['staɪrəˌfəʊm] (*Am*) [1] N polistirene.
[2] ADJ (*cup*) di polistirene.

Styx [stɪks] N (*Myth*): **the Styx** lo Stige.

suave [swɑːv] ADJ (*person, manners*) mellifluo(-a);
(*question, suggestion*) insinuante.

suave·ly ['swɑːvlɪ] ADV (*see adj*) mellifluamente; in
maniera insinuante.

suav·ity ['swɑːvɪtɪ], **suave·ness** ['swɑːvnɪs] N (*see adj*)
mellifluità; fare *m* insinuante.

sub [sʌb] N ABBR **a** = **submarine b** = **subscription**.

sub... [sʌb] PREF sub..., sotto... .

sub·al·tern ['sʌbltən] N (*Mil*) subalterno.

sub·atom·ic [ˌsʌbəˈtɒmɪk] ADJ subatomico(-a).

sub·com·mit·tee ['sʌbkəˌmɪtɪ] N sottocommissione *f*.

sub·con·scious [ˌsʌbˈkɒnʃəs] [1] ADJ subcosciente.
[2] N: **the subconscious** il subcosciente, il subconscio.

sub·con·scious·ly [ˌsʌbˈkɒnʃəslɪ] ADV inconsciamente.

sub·con·ti·nent [ˌsʌbˈkɒntɪnənt] N: **the (Indian) subconti-
nent** il subcontinente (indiano).

sub·con·tract [*n* ˌsʌbˈkɒntrækt; *vb* ˌsʌbkənˈtrækt] [1] N
subappalto.
[2] VT subappaltare.

sub·con·trac·tor [ˌsʌbkənˈtræktəʳ] N subappaltatore(-
trice).

sub·cul·ture ['sʌbˌkʌltʃəʳ] N sottocultura.

sub·di·vide [ˌsʌbdɪˈvaɪd] VT suddividere.

sub·di·vi·sion ['sʌbdɪˌvɪʒən] N suddivisione *f*.

sub·due [səbˈdjuː] VT (*enemy*) sottomettere; (*children*) far
star buono(-a); (*high spirits*) smorzare; (*passions etc*)
controllare.

sub·dued [səbˈdjuːd] ADJ (*person: downcast*) giù di morale;
(*emotions*) contenuto(-a); (*voice, tone*) sommesso(-a);
(*colours*) tenue; (*lighting*) soffuso(-a); **he's rather
subdued these days** ultimamente non è allegro come al
solito.

sub·edit [ˌsʌbˈɛdɪt] VT (*book, article*) revisionare.

sub·edi·tor [ˌsʌbˈɛdɪtəʳ] N redattore(-trice) aggiunto(-a).

sub·group ['sʌbˌgruːp] N sottogruppo.

sub·head·ing ['sʌbˌhɛdɪŋ] N sottotitolo.

sub·hu·man [ˌsʌbˈhjuːmən] ADJ subumano(-a).

sub·ject [*n, adj* 'sʌbdʒɪkt; *vb* səbˈdʒɛkt] [1] N **a** (*topic: gen*)
argomento, soggetto; (*Scol*) materia; **let's keep to the
subject** non divaghiamo; **let's drop the subject**
lasciamo perdere; **(while we're) on the subject of money** ... a proposito di soldi...; **to change the subject**
cambiare discorso
b (*Gram*) soggetto
c (*Pol: of country*) cittadino(-a); (: *of sovereign*) suddito
(-a).
[2] ADJ **a** : **subject to** (*liable to: law, tax, disease, delays*)
soggetto(-a) a; **subject to doing that** (*conditional upon*) a
condizione di fare *or* che si faccia ciò; **subject to
confirmation in writing** a condizione di ricevere
conferma per iscritto; **these prices are subject to
change without notice** questi prezzi sono suscettibili di
modifiche senza preavviso; **subject to contract** (*Comm*)
fino a stipulazione del contratto
b (*people, nation*) assoggettato(-a), sottomesso(-a).

3 VT: **to subject sb to sth** sottoporre qn a qc; **to subject o.s. to ridicule/criticism** esporsi al ridicolo/alle critiche; **she was subjected to severe criticism** è stata duramente criticata.

♦ **subject heading** N (*Library*) titolo.

♦ **subject index** N (*Library*) indice *m* per argomenti.

sub·jec·tion [səb'dʒɛkʃən] N (*state*): **subjection (to)** sottomissione *f* (a), soggezione *f* (a); **to hold a people in subjection** tenere un popolo in servitù.

sub·jec·tive [səb'dʒɛktɪv] ADJ soggettivo(-a).

sub·jec·tive·ly [səb'dʒɛktɪvlɪ] ADV soggettivamente.

♦ **subject matter** N argomento.

sub ju·di·ce [ˌsʌb'juːdɪsɪ] (*Law*) sub iudice.

sub·ju·gate [ˈsʌbdʒʊˌgeɪt] VT sottomettere, soggiogare.

sub·junc·tive [səb'dʒʌŋktɪv] (*Gram*) 1 ADJ congiuntivo (-a).

2 N congiuntivo; **in the subjunctive** al congiuntivo.

sub·let [ˌsʌb'lɛt] VT, VI (*pt, pp* **sublet**) subaffittare.

sub·lieu·ten·ant [ˌsʌblɛf'tɛnənt] N (*Naut*) sottotenente *m* di vascello.

sub·li·mate [ˈsʌblɪˌmeɪt] VT (*Psych*) sublimare.

sub·li·ma·tion [ˌsʌblɪ'meɪʃən] N (*Psych*) sublimazione *f*.

sub·lime [sə'blaɪm] 1 ADJ (*beauty, emotion, achievement*) sublime; (*indifference, contempt*) supremo(-a).

2 N **sublime** *m*; **from the sublime to the ridiculous** dal sublime al grottesco.

3 VT (*Chem*) sublimare.

sub·lime·ly [sə'blaɪmlɪ] ADV (*happy, beautiful*) immensamente; (*indifferent*) sommamente.

sub·limi·nal [ˌsʌb'lɪmɪnl] ADJ subliminale.

sub·limi·nal·ly [ˌsʌb'lɪmɪnlɪ] ADV in modo subliminale.

sub·machine gun [ˌsʌbmə'ʃiːnˌgʌn] N mitra *m inv*.

sub·ma·rine [ˈsʌbməˌriːn] 1 N sottomarino, sommergibile *m*. 2 ADJ (*frm*) sottomarino(-a).

sub·merge [səb'mɜːdʒ] 1 VT (*flood*) sommergere; (*plunge*): **to submerge (in)** immergere (in).

2 VI (*submarine*) immergersi.

sub·mer·sion [səb'mɜːʃən] N (*see vt*) sommersione *f*; immersione *f*.

sub·mis·sion [səb'mɪʃən] N sottomissione *f*; (*to committee etc*) richiesta, domanda.

sub·mis·sive [səb'mɪsɪv] ADJ sottomesso(-a), remissivo (-a).

sub·mis·sive·ly [səb'mɪsɪvlɪ] ADV in modo sottomesso, in modo remissivo.

sub·mis·sive·ness [səb'mɪsɪvnɪs] N sottomissione *f*, remissività.

sub·mit [səb'mɪt] 1 VT (*proposal, claim*) presentare; **I submit that ...** propongo che....

2 VI (*give in*): **to submit to** (*pressure, threats*) cedere a; (*sb's will*) sottomettersi a.

sub·nor·mal [ˌsʌb'nɔːməl] ADJ subnormale.

sub·or·di·nate [*adj, n* sə'bɔːdnɪt; *vb* sə'bɔːdɪˌneɪt] 1 ADJ (*rank, officer*) subalterno(-a); **subordinate clause** (*Gram*) proposizione *f* subordinata.

2 N subalterno(-a), subordinato(-a).

3 VT: **to subordinate (to)** subordinare (a); **subordinating conjunction** (*Gram*) congiunzione *f* subordinativa.

sub·or·di·na·tion [səˌbɔːdɪ'neɪʃən] N subordinazione *f*.

sub·orn [sə'bɔːn] VT (*Law: witness*) subornare.

sub·plot [ˈsʌbˌplɒt] N vicenda secondaria.

sub·poe·na [səb'piːnə] (*Law*) 1 N citazione *f*, mandato di comparizione.

2 VT citare in giudizio.

♦ **sub-post office** [sʌb'pəʊstˌɒfɪs] N ufficio postale secondario.

sub·rou·tine [ˈsʌbruːˌtiːn] N (*Comput*) sottoprogramma *m*.

sub·scribe [səb'skraɪb] 1 VI: **to subscribe to** (*magazine etc*) abbonarsi a; (*fund*) sottoscrivere; (*opinion*) condividere, approvare; **to subscribe for** (*shares*) sottoscrivere.

2 VT (*money*) devolvere.

sub·scrib·er [səb'skraɪbəʳ] N (*to magazine, telephone*): **subscriber (to)** abbonato(-a) (a).

♦ **subscriber trunk dialling** N teleselezione *f*.

sub·script [ˈsʌbˌskrɪpt] N (*Typ*) deponente *m*.

sub·scrip·tion [səb'skrɪpʃən] N (*to magazine etc*) abbonamento; (*membership fee*) quota d'iscrizione; (*for shares*) sottoscrizione *f*; **to take out a subscription to** abbonarsi a.

sub·sec·tion [ˈsʌbˌsɛkʃən] N sottosezione *f*.

sub·se·quent [ˈsʌbsɪkwənt] ADJ (*later*) successivo(-a); (*further*) ulteriore; **subsequent to** in seguito a.

sub·se·quent·ly [ˈsʌbsɪkwəntlɪ] ADV successivamente, in seguito.

sub·ser·vi·ence [səb'sɜːvɪəns] N: **subservience (to)** sottomissione *f* (a).

sub·ser·vi·ent [səb'sɜːvɪənt] ADJ: **subservient (to)** sottomesso(-a) (a).

sub·set [ˈsʌbˌsɛt] N (*Math*) sottoinsieme *m*.

sub·side [səb'saɪd] VI (*flood*) calare, decrescere; (*road, land*) cedere, avvallarsi; (*wind, anger*) calmarsi, placarsi.

sub·sid·ence [səb'saɪdəns] N (*of land etc*) cedimento, avvallamento; (*of waters etc*) abbassamento.

sub·sidi·ari·ty [səbˌsɪdɪ'ærɪtɪ] N (*Pol*) *principio del decentramento del potere*.

sub·sidi·ary [səb'sɪdɪərɪ] 1 ADJ (*company*) consociato(-a); (*role etc*) secondario(-a); (*Brit Univ: subject*) complementare; **subsidiary cone** (*Geol*) cono vulcanico secondario.

2 N (*Comm*) filiale *f*; (*Univ*) materia complementare.

sub·si·dize [ˈsʌbsɪˌdaɪz] VT sovvenzionare.

sub·si·dy [ˈsʌbsɪdɪ] N sovvenzione *f*, sussidio.

sub·sist [səb'sɪst] VI: **to subsist on sth** vivere di qc.

sub·sist·ence [səb'sɪstəns] N sopravvivenza; **means of subsistence** mezzi *mpl* di sussistenza.

♦ **subsistence allowance** N indennità *f inv* di trasferta.

♦ **subsistence level** N livello minimo di vita.

♦ **subsistence wage** N salario appena sufficiente per vivere.

sub·soil [ˈsʌbˌsɔɪl] N sottosuolo.

sub·son·ic [ˌsʌb'sɒnɪk] ADJ subsonico(-a).

sub·spe·cies [ˈsʌbˌspiːʃiːz] N, PL INV sottospecie *f inv*.

sub·stance [ˈsʌbstəns] N (*gen*) sostanza; **to lack substance** (*argument*) essere debole; (*accusation*) essere privo(-a) di fondamento; (*film, book*) essere scarso(-a) di contenuto; **a man of substance** un uomo benestante; **in substance** sostanzialmente, fondamentalmente.

♦ **substance abuse** N abuso di sostanze tossiche.

sub·stand·ard [ˌsʌb'stændəd] ADJ (*goods*) scadente; (*housing*) di qualità scadente.

sub·stan·tial [səb'stænʃəl] ADJ **a** (*considerable: amount, progress*) notevole, considerevole; (: *majority, proportion*) largo(-a), grande; (: *difference*) sostanziale; (*solid: building, table*) solido(-a); (: *meal*) sostanzioso(-a); (*wealthy: landowner, businessman*) ricco(-a) **b** (*frm: real*) reale.

sub·stan·tial·ly [səb'stænʃəlɪ] ADV **a** (*considerably*) notevolmente; **substantially bigger** molto più grande; **substantially different** notevolmente diverso(-a) **b** (*in essence*) sostanzialmente **c** (*solidly: built*) solidamente.

sub·stan·ti·ate [səb'stænʃɪˌeɪt] VT comprovare.

sub·stan·tive ['sʌbstəntɪv] [1] ADJ (*frm: issues, measures*) sostanziale; (*Gram*) sostantivo(-a).

[2] N (*Gram*) sostantivo.

sub·sti·tute ['sʌbstɪˌtjuːt] [1] N (*person*) sostituto(-a); (*teacher*) supplente *m/f*; (*thing*) surrogato; **coffee substi-tute** surrogato di caffè; **there's no substitute for butter** non c'è niente di meglio del burro.

[2] VT: **to substitute sb/sth (for)** sostituire qn/qc (con *or* a).

[3] VI: **to substitute for sb** sostituire qn.

sub·sti·tu·tion [ˌsʌbstɪ'tjuːʃən] N (*gen*) sostituzione *f*; (*in school*) supplenza.

♦ **substitution reaction** N (*Chem*) reazione *f* di sostitu-zione.

sub·stra·tum [sʌb'strɑːtəm] N (*pl* **substrata** [sʌb'strɑːtə]) (*Geol, fig*) sostrato.

sub·struc·ture ['sʌbˌstrʌktʃəʳ] N sottostruttura.

sub·sume [səb'sjuːm] VT: **to subsume within/under** (*frm*) includere in, inglobare in.

sub·ten·ant [ˌsʌb'tɛnənt] N subaffittuario(-a).

sub·tend [səb'tɛnd] VT (*Geom*) sottendere.

sub·ter·fuge ['sʌbtəfjuːdʒ] N sotterfugio.

sub·ter·ra·nean [ˌsʌbtə'reɪnɪən] ADJ sotterraneo(-a).

sub·ti·tle ['sʌbˌtaɪtl] N (*Cine*) sottotitolo.

sub·tle ['sʌtl] ADJ (*gen*) sottile; (*flavour, perfume*) delicato (-a).

sub·tle·ty ['sʌtltɪ] N (*see adj*) sottigliezza; delicatezza.

sub·tly ['sʌtlɪ] ADV (*see adj*) sottilmente; delicatamente.

sub·to·tal [ˌsʌb'təʊtl] N totale *m* parziale.

sub·tract [səb'trækt] VT sottrarre.

sub·trac·tion [səb'trækʃən] N sottrazione *f*.

sub·urb ['sʌbɜːb] N sobborgo; **to live in the suburbs** vivere in periferia.

sub·ur·ban [sə'bɜːbən] ADJ suburbano(-a), periferico(-a).

sub·ur·ban·ite [sə'bɜːbəˌnaɪt] N abitante *m/f* dei sobbor-ghi.

sub·ur·bia [sə'bɜːbɪə] N periferia, sobborghi *mpl*.

sub·ver·sion [səb'vɜːʃən] N sovversione *f*.

sub·ver·sive [səb'vɜːsɪv] ADJ, N sovversivo(-a).

sub·vert [səb'vɜːt] VT sovvertire.

sub·way ['sʌbˌweɪ] N (*Brit: underpass*) sottopassaggio; (*Am: underground*) metropolitana.

sub·zero [ˌsʌb'zɪərəʊ] ADJ: **subzero temperatures** tempe-rature *fpl* sotto zero.

suc·ceed [sək'siːd] [1] VI a (*be successful: gen*) riuscire, avere successo; **to succeed in life/business** avere successo nella vita/negli affari; **to succeed in doing sth** riuscire a fare qc

b (*follow*): **to succeed (to)** succedere (a).

[2] VT (*monarch*) succedere a; **to succeed sb in a post** succedere a qn in un posto.

suc·ceed·ing [sək'siːdɪŋ] ADJ (*following: in past*) successivo (-a), seguente; (: *in future*) futuro(-a); **succeeding gen-erations** generazioni *fpl* future; **each succeeding year brought ...** ogni anno che passava recava...; **each succeeding year will bring further wealth** con ogni anno che passa aumenterà la ricchezza.

suc·cess [sək'sɛs] N (*gen*) successo, riuscita; **she was a great success** ha avuto un grande successo; **without success** senza successo *or* risultato; **to make a success of sth** riuscire bene in qc; **to meet with success** avere successo.

suc·cess·ful [sək'sɛsfʊl] ADJ (*person: in attempt*) che ha successo; (: *in life*) affermato(-a), di successo; (*attempt,*

plan, venture) riuscito(-a), coronato(-a) da successo; (*play, film*) di successo; (*business*) prospero(-a); **to be successful in doing sth** riuscire a fare qc.

suc·cess·ful·ly [sək'sɛsfəlɪ] ADV con successo.

suc·ces·sion [sək'sɛʃən] N a (*series*) serie *f inv*; **in succes-sion** di seguito; **in quick succession** in rapida successione b (*to post etc*) successione *f*.

suc·ces·sive [sək'sɛsɪv] ADJ (*days, months*) consecutivo (-a); (*generations*) successivo(-a); **on three successive days** per tre giorni consecutivi *or* di seguito; **each successive failure** ogni nuovo insuccesso.

suc·ces·sive·ly [sək'sɛsɪvlɪ] ADV successivamente.

suc·ces·sor [sək'sɛsəʳ] N (*in office*) successore *m*; (*heir*) erede *m/f*.

♦ **success story** N successo.

suc·cinct [sək'sɪŋkt] ADJ succinto(-a), breve.

suc·cinct·ly [sək'sɪŋktlɪ] ADV succintamente.

suc·cour, (*Am*) **suc·cor** ['sʌkəʳ] (*frm, liter*) [1] N soccorso; **to provide succo(u)r to** prestare soccorso a.

[2] VT soccorrere, aiutare.

suc·cu·lence ['sʌkjʊləns] N succulenza.

suc·cu·lent ['sʌkjʊlənt] [1] ADJ (*tasty*) succulento(-a).

[2] N (*Bot*): **succulents** piante *fpl* grasse.

suc·cumb [sə'kʌm] VI: **to succumb to** (*temptation, illness*) soccombere a; (*entreaties, charms*) cedere a.

such [sʌtʃ] [1] PREDETERMINER, DETERMINER a (*of this/that sort*) tale, del genere; **such a book** un tale libro, un libro del genere; **such books** tali libri, libri del genere; **did you ever hear of such a thing?** hai mai sentito una cosa del genere?; **there's no such thing** non esiste; **there's no such thing as a unicorn** gli unicorni non esistono; **there's no such place in Italy** non c'è un posto del genere in Italia; **such was his answer** questa è stata la sua risposta; **such is life** così è la vita; **I said no such thing** non ho detto niente del genere; **in such cases** in casi del genere; **we had such a case last year** si è avuto un caso del genere l'anno scorso; **some such idea** un'idea del genere; **it was such as to/that** era tale da/che; **this is my car such as it is** questa è la mia macchina, se così si può chiamare

b (*so much, so great*) tale, tanto(-a); **he's not such a fool as you think** non è così scemo come pensi; **I had such a fright** ho preso un tale spavento; **such courage** tanto coraggio; **I was in such a hurry** avevo una tale fretta; **I was in such a hurry that ...** avevo così tanta fretta che...; **such a lot of** talmente, così tanto(-a); **making such a noise that** facendo un rumore tale che; **a noise such as** to un rumore tale da

c (*so very*) talmente, così; **such good food** cibo così buono; **such good books** libri così buoni; **such a clever girl** una ragazza così intelligente; **it's such a long time since we saw each other** è da tanto tempo che non ci vediamo; **such a long time ago** tanto tempo fa; **I haven't had such good tea for ages** erano secoli che non bevevo un tè così buono; **such a long trip** un viaggio così lungo

d : **such as** (*introducing examples*) come; **such a man as you** *or* **a man such as you** un uomo come te; **such writers as Updike** *or* **writers such as Updike** scrittori come Updike; **books such as these** libri come questi; **such as?** per esempio?; **have you got such a thing as a torch?** hai una pila per caso?.

[2] PRON a (*this, that, those*): **such as wish to go** chi desidera andare; **but such is not the case** ma non è questo caso; **and such (like)** e così via; **I haven't many, but I'll give you such as I have** non ne ho molti, ma ti

darò tutti quelli che ho

b : **as such** (*in that capacity*) come tale, in quanto tale; (*in itself*) di per sé; **and as such he was promoted** e come tale fu promosso; **there's no garden as such** non c'è un vero e proprio giardino; **doctors as such are ...** i medici in quanto tali sono...; **the work as such is poorly paid** il lavoro di per sé non è pagato bene.

♦ **such-and-such** ['sʌtʃ ən ˌsʌtʃ] [1] ADJ tale; **they live in such-and-such street** abitano nella tale strada.

[2] N: **Mr such-and-such** il signor tal dei tali.

such·like ['sʌtʃ laɪk] (*fam*) [1] ADJ simile, di tal genere; **sheep and suchlike animals** pecore *fpl* e animali *mpl* del genere.

[2] PRON: **and suchlike** e così via.

suck [sʌk] [1] VT (*gen*) succhiare; (*subj: baby*) poppare, succhiare; (: *pump, machine*) aspirare; **to suck one's thumb** succhiarsi il dito; **to suck sth through a straw** bere qc con la cannuccia; **to suck an orange dry** succhiare tutto il succo di un'arancia; **to suck dry** (*fig: person: of money*) ripulire; (: *of energy*) esaurire.

[2] VI (*baby*) succhiare, poppare; **to suck at sth** succhiare qc

▶ **suck down** VT + ADV (*subj: current, mud*) inghiottire, risucchiare

▶ **suck in** VT + ADV (*subj: machine, dust, air etc*) aspirare; **to suck one's cheeks in** succhiarsi le guance

▶ **suck out** VT + ADV succhiare, far uscire succhiando

▶ **suck up** [1] VT + ADV (*dust, liquid etc*) aspirare.

[2] VI + ADV (*fam*): **to suck up to sb** leccare i piedi a qn.

suck·er ['sʌkəʳ] N (*fam: person*) babbeo(-a), citrullo(-a), gonzo(-a); (*Zool, Tech*) ventosa; (*Bot*) pollone *m*; (*Am: lollipop*) lecca lecca *m inv*; **he's a sucker for flattery** (*fam*) non sa resistere ai complimenti.

suck·le ['sʌkl] VT allattare.

su·crose ['suːkrəʊz] N saccarosio.

suc·tion ['sʌkʃən] N (*Tech*) aspirazione *f*.

♦ **suction pump** N pompa aspirante.

Su·dan [suːˈdɑːn] N il Sudan.

Su·da·nese [ˌsuːdəˈniːz] ADJ, N, PL INV sudanese (*m/f*).

sud·den ['sʌdn] ADJ improvviso(-a); **this is so sudden!** non me l'aspettavo!; **all of a sudden** all'improvviso, improvvisamente.

♦ **sudden-death** [ˌsʌdnˈdɛθ] N **a** (*also:* **sudden-death playoff:** *in football*) rigori *mpl* a oltranza; (*in American football*) tempo supplementare (*in cui vince la prima squadra che segna* **b** (*Golf*): **sudden-death hole** *buca supplementare per decidere la vittoria.*

sud·den·ly ['sʌdnlɪ] ADV improvvisamente, all'improvviso.

sud·den·ness ['sʌdnnɪs] N: **the suddenness of his death/departure** la sua morte/partenza improvvisa.

suds [sʌdz] NPL (*lather*) schiuma *fsg*; (*soapy water*) saponata *fsg*.

sue [suː] [1] VT: **to sue sb for libel/damages** *etc* citare qn per diffamazione/danni *etc*.

[2] VI: **to sue (for)** intentare causa (per); **to sue for divorce** intentare causa di divorzio.

suede [sweɪd] [1] N pelle *f* scamosciata.

[2] ADJ scamosciato(-a).

suet ['suɪt] N grasso di rognone.

Suez ['suːɪz] N Suez *f*.

♦ **Suez Canal** N: **the Suez Canal** il canale di Suez.

Suff. ABBR (*Brit*)= *Suffolk*.

suf·fer ['sʌfəʳ] [1] VT **a** (*hardship, hunger*) soffrire, patire; (*pain*) provare; (*undergo: loss, setback*) subire; **to suffer**

pangs of hunger provare i morsi della fame

b (*tolerate: opposition, rudeness*) sopportare, tollerare; **she doesn't suffer fools gladly** non sopporta proprio gli stupidi.

[2] VI (*physically*) soffrire; (*be adversely affected: town*) subire danni; (: *regiment*) subire perdite; **to suffer from** (*rheumatism, headaches, deafness*) soffrire di; (*malnutrition, the cold*) soffrire; (*a cold, influenza, bad memory*) avere; **she suffers from a limp** zoppica; **she was suffering from shock** era sotto shock; **to suffer from the effects of alcohol/a fall** risentire degli effetti dell'alcol/di una caduta; **the house is suffering from neglect** la casa è in stato di abbandono; **your health will suffer** la tua salute ne risentirà; **to suffer for one's sins** scontare i propri peccati; **you'll suffer for it!** la pagherai!

suf·fer·ance ['sʌfərəns] N: **he was only there on sufferance** lì era più che altro sopportato.

suf·fer·er ['sʌfərəʳ] N (*Med*): **sufferer (from)** malato(-a) (di); **diabetes sufferers** i diabetici.

suf·fer·ing ['sʌfərɪŋ] N (*pain, grief*) sofferenza; (*hardship, deprivation*) privazione *f*.

suf·fice [səˈfaɪs] (*frm*) [1] VI bastare, essere sufficiente.

[2] VT: **suffice it to say ...** basti dire che... .

suf·fi·cien·cy [səˈfɪʃənsɪ] N (*frm*) quantità sufficiente; **to have a sufficiency of paper** avere abbastanza carta.

suf·fi·cient [səˈfɪʃənt] ADJ: **sufficient (for)** sufficiente (per); **that's sufficient** basta così; **do you have sufficient money?** hai abbastanza soldi?

suf·fi·cient·ly [səˈfɪʃəntlɪ] ADV sufficientemente, abbastanza; **sufficiently large** (*quantity*) sufficiente; (*number*) abbastanza grande; **she is sufficiently intelligent to understand** è abbastanza *or* sufficientemente intelligente per capire.

suf·fix ['sʌfɪks] N suffisso.

suf·fo·cate ['sʌfəkeɪt] VT, VI soffocare, asfissiare.

suf·fo·cat·ing ['sʌfəkeɪtɪŋ] ADJ (*heat, atmosphere*) soffocante, opprimente.

suf·fo·ca·tion [ˌsʌfəˈkeɪʃən] N soffocazione *f*, soffocamento; (*Med*) asfissia; **to die from suffocation** morire per asfissia.

suf·frage ['sʌfrɪdʒ] N suffragio.

suf·fra·gette [ˌsʌfrəˈdʒɛt] N suffragetta.

suf·fuse [səˈfjuːz] VT (*frm*): **to suffuse (with)** (*colour*) tingere (di); **her face was suffused with joy** la gioia si dipingeva sul suo volto; **the room was suffused with light** nella stanza c'era una luce soffusa.

sug·ar ['ʃʊgəʳ] [1] N zucchero.

[2] VT (*tea etc*) zuccherare; **to sugar the pill** (*fig*) indorare la pillola.

♦ **sugar basin, sugar bowl** N zuccheriera.

♦ **sugar beet** N barbabietola da zucchero.

♦ **sugar cane** N canna da zucchero.

♦ **sugar-coated** [ˈʃʊgəˌkəʊtɪd] ADJ ricoperto(-a) di zucchero.

♦ **sugar daddy** N (*fam*) vecchio amante *m* danaroso.

sug·ared [ˈʃʊgəd] ADJ: **sugared almonds** confetti *mpl* alla mandorla.

♦ **sugar-free** [ˈʃʊgəˌfriː], **sug·ar·less** [ˈʃʊgəlɪs] ADJ senza zucchero.

♦ **sugar loaf** N pan *m* di zucchero.

♦ **sugar lump** N zolletta di zucchero.

♦ **sugar maple** N acero canadese.

♦ **sugar plantation** N piantagione *f* di canne da zucchero.

♦ **sugar refinery** N raffineria di zucchero.

♦ **sugar tongs** NPL mollette *fpl* da zucchero.

sug·ary [ˈʃugərɪ] ADJ (*food etc*) zuccherato(-a), zuccherino (-a); (*fig: sentimental*) sdolcinato(-a), stucchevole.

sug·gest [səˈdʒɛst] VT (*gen*) suggerire, proporre; (*evoke*) indicare, far pensare a; **to suggest doing sth** proporre *or* suggerire di fare qc; **it was you who suggested coming** sei stato tu a voler venire; **he suggested (that) they should come too** ha proposto *or* suggerito che venissero anche loro; **this suggests that ...** questo fa pensare *or* indica che...; **what are you trying to suggest?** cosa stai cercando di insinuare?; **nothing suggests itself** non mi viene in mente niente; **what do you suggest I do?** cosa mi suggerisci di fare?

sug·gest·ible [səˈdʒɛstɪbəl] ADJ (*person*) suggestionabile, influenzabile.

sug·ges·tion [səˈdʒɛstʃən] N **a** suggerimento, proposta; **if I may make** *or* **offer a suggestion** se mi è concesso avanzare una proposta; **my suggestion is that ...** propongo *or* suggerisco che...; **at sb's suggestion** su *or* dietro suggerimento di qn; **there's no suggestion that** non c'è niente che indichi *or* che faccia pensare a
  b (*trace*): **a suggestion of** un'idea di.

sug·ges·tive [səˈdʒɛstɪv] ADJ **a** (*remark*) spinto(-a); (*look*) indecente **b** (*evocative*): **to be suggestive of** far pensare a, evocare.

sui·cid·al [ˌsʊɪˈsaɪdl] ADJ suicida; (*fig*) fatale, disastroso (-a).

sui·cide [ˈsʊɪsaɪd] N **a** (*also fig*) suicidio; **to attempt suicide** tentare il suicidio; **to commit suicide** suicidarsi **b** (*person*) suicida *m/f*.

♦ **suicide attempt, suicide bid** N tentato suicidio.

♦ **suicide pact** N patto suicida.

suit [suːt] **1** N **a** (*for man*) abito; (*for woman*) tailleur *m inv*; (*for bathing*) costume *m*; (*astronaut's*) tuta; **a suit of armour** un'armatura
  b (*lawsuit*) causa; **to bring a suit against sb** intentare causa a qn
  c (*Cards*) colore *m*, seme *m*; **to follow suit** (*fig*) fare altrettanto.
  2 VT **a** (*adapt*): **to suit (to)** adattare (a); **to suit one's language to one's audience** usare un linguaggio adatto a chi ascolta; **to suit the action to the word** mettere in pratica le proprie parole; **to be suited to sth** (*suitable for*) essere adatto(-a) a qc; **they are well suited (to each other)** stanno bene insieme
  b (*be acceptable: time, day*) andare bene a; (: *food, climate*) fare per; (: *clothes, colour*) stare bene a; **that suits me (down to the ground)** per me va benissimo; **it doesn't suit me to leave now** non mi va di partire ora; **the post suited her perfectly** il lavoro faceva proprio per lei
  c (*please*) contentare; **suit yourself whether you do it or not** se vuoi farlo fallo, se no lascia perdere; **suit yourself!** fa' come ti pare!

suit·abil·ity [ˌsuːtəˈbɪlɪtɪ] N (*for job*) idoneità; **I doubt the suitability of this book for children** dubito che sia un libro adatto ai bambini.

suit·able [ˈsuːtəbl] ADJ (*gen*) adatto(-a); **I haven't anything suitable to wear** non ho niente di adatto da mettermi; **the most suitable man for the job** l'uomo più adatto a questo lavoro; **we found somebody suitable** abbiamo trovato la persona adatta; **the film is not suitable for children** non è un film adatto ai bambini; **would tomorrow be suitable?** andrebbe bene domani?

suit·ably [ˈsuːtəblɪ] ADV (*dress*) in modo adatto; (*thank*) adeguatamente; **he was suitably impressed** ha giustamente ricevuto un'impressione favorevole; **to reply suitably** dare una risposta adeguata.

suit·case [ˈsuːtˌkeɪs] N valigia.

suite [swiːt] N (*of rooms*) appartamento; (: *in hotel*) suite *f inv*; (*Mus*) suite *f inv*; (*furniture*): **dining room suite** arredo *or* mobilia per la sala da pranzo; **a bathroom suite** i sanitari e gli arredi per il bagno; **a bedroom suite** una camera da letto; **a three-piece suite** un divano e due poltrone.

suit·ing [ˈsuːtɪŋ] N (*material*) tessuto per abiti da uomo.

suit·or [ˈsuːtə] N corteggiatore *m*, spasimante *m*.

sul·fate [ˈsʌlfeɪt] N (*Am*) = **sulphate**.

sul·fur *etc* [ˈsʌlfə] (*Am*) = **sulphur** *etc*.

sulk [sʌlk] **1** VI tenere il broncio *or* il muso.
  2 N: **to have the sulks** tenere il broncio *or* il muso.

sulki·ly [ˈsʌlkɪlɪ] ADV con aria imbronciata.

sulki·ness [ˈsʌlkɪnɪs] N musoneria.

sulky [ˈsʌlkɪ] ADJ (*comp* **-ier**, *superl* **-iest**) imbronciato(-a).

sul·len [ˈsʌlən] ADJ indisponente; (*sky*) cupo(-a); **to have a sullen face** avere il viso imbronciato.

sul·len·ly [ˈsʌlənlɪ] ADV in modo indisponente.

sul·len·ness [ˈsʌlənnɪs] N (*see adj*) l'essere indisponente; l'essere cupo(-a).

sul·ly [ˈsʌlɪ] VT (*frm*) macchiare.

sul·phate [ˈsʌlfeɪt] N solfato; **copper sulphate** solfato di rame.

sul·phide [ˈsʌlfaɪd] N solfuro.

sul·phite [ˈsʌlfaɪt] N solfito.

sul·phona·mide [sʌlˈfɒnəˌmaɪd] N sulfamidico.

sul·phur [ˈsʌlfə] N zolfo.

♦ **sulphur dioxide** N anidride *f* solforosa, biossido di zolfo.

sul·phu·ric [sʌlˈfjʊərɪk] ADJ: **sulphuric acid** acido solforico.

sul·phur·ous [ˈsʌlfərəs] ADJ solforoso(-a); **sulphurous acid** acido solforoso.

sul·tan [ˈsʌltən] N sultano.

sul·tana [sʌlˈtɑːnə] N (*fruit*) (uva) sultanina.

sul·try [ˈsʌltrɪ] ADJ (*weather*) afoso(-a), opprimente; (*woman, character*) ardente, sensuale.

sum [sʌm] N (*piece of arithmetic*) somma, addizione *f*; (*amount of money*) somma; **the sum of 6 and 4 is 10** 6 più 4 fa 10; **that is the sum (total) of his achievements** questo è tutto quello che ha fatto

▶ **sum up** **1** VT + ADV (*review*) riassumere, ricapitolare; (*evaluate rapidly*) valutare, giudicare; **to sum up an argument** riassumere una discussione; **she quickly summed him up** capì subito che tipo era; **he summed up the situation quickly** valutò subito la situazione.
  2 VI + ADV riassumere; **to sum up ...** per riassumere..., riassumendo... .

Su·ma·tra [sʊˈmɑːtrə] N Sumatra.

sum·ma [ˈsʊmɑː] N summa.

sum·mari·ly [ˈsʌmərɪlɪ] ADV sommariamente.

sum·ma·rize [ˈsʌməˌraɪz] VT riassumere, riepilogare.

sum·mary [ˈsʌmərɪ] **1** N riassunto.
  2 ADJ (*dismissal, treatment, justice*) sommario(-a); (*perusal*) sbrigativo(-a).

sum·mat [ˈsʌmət] PRON (*Brit dial*) qualcosa.

sum·ma·tion [sʌˈmeɪʃən] N (*frm: summary*) sommario; (: *total*) somma, totale *m*.

sum·mer [ˈsʌmə] **1** N estate *f*; **in (the) summer** d'estate; **in the summer of 1995** nell'estate del 1995; **last/next summer** l'estate scorsa/prossima.

2 ADJ (gen) estivo(-a), d'estate.
♦ **summer camp** N (Am) colonia estiva.
summer·house ['sʌmə,haʊs] N (in garden) padiglione m.
♦ **summer lightning** N temporale m estivo.
♦ **summer school** N corsi mpl estivi.
♦ **summer solstice** N solstizio d'estate.
summer·time ['sʌmə,taɪm] N (season) stagione f estiva, estate f.
♦ **summer time** N (Brit: daylight saving time) ora legale.
sum·mery ['sʌmərɪ] ADJ estivo(-a).
summing-up [,sʌmɪŋ'ʌp] N (Law) ricapitolazione f del processo (fatta dal giudice alla giuria).
sum·mit ['sʌmɪt] N cima, vetta, sommità f inv; (fig) culmine m; (Pol) vertice m, summit m inv.
♦ **summit conference** N incontro al vertice.
sum·mon ['sʌmən] VT (meeting) convocare; (aid, doctor, servant etc) chiamare; (Law): **to summon a witness** citare un testimone
▶ **summon up** VT + ADV (courage, interest) trovare; **to summon up all one's courage** farsi coraggio, armarsi di coraggio; **to summon up all one's strength** fare appello a tutte le proprie forze; **I couldn't summon up the courage to tell him** non ho trovato il coraggio di dirglielo.
sum·mons ['sʌmənz] 1 N (pl -es) (Law) citazione f, mandato di comparizione; **to serve a summons on sb** notificare una citazione a qn.
2 VT citare (in giudizio).
sumo ['suːməʊ], **sumo wrestling** N sumo m inv.
sump [sʌmp] N (Aut) coppa dell'olio, carter m inv.
sump·tu·ous ['sʌmptjʊəs] ADJ sontuoso(-a).
sump·tu·ous·ly ['sʌmptjʊəslɪ] ADV sontuosamente.
sump·tu·ous·ness ['sʌmptjʊəsnɪs] N sontuosità.
sun [sʌn] 1 N sole m; **to get up with the sun** alzarsi allo spuntar del sole; **the sun is in my eyes** ho il sole negli occhi; **in the sun** al sole; **you've caught the sun!** come sei abbronzato!; **a place in the sun** (also fig) un posto al sole; **they have everything under the sun** hanno tutto ciò che possono desiderare; **there's nothing new under the sun** non c'è niente di nuovo sotto il sole.
2 VT: **to sun o.s.** godersi il sole.
Sun. ABBR = Sunday.
sun·bathe ['sʌn,beɪð] VI prendere il sole.
sun·bather ['sʌn,beɪðə'] N chi prende il sole.
sun·bathing ['sʌn,beɪðɪŋ] N bagni mpl di sole; **to go sunbathing on the beach** andare a prendere il sole sulla spiaggia.
sun·beam ['sʌn,biːm] N raggio di sole.
sun·bed ['sʌn,bɛd] N lettino solare.
sun·blind ['sʌn,blaɪnd] N tenda da sole.
sun·burn ['sʌn,bɜːn] N (painful) scottatura; (tan) abbronzatura.
sun·burnt, sun·burned ['sʌn,bɜːnt] ADJ (tanned) abbronzato(-a); (painfully) scottato(-a).
♦ **sun cream** N crema solare.
sun·dae ['sʌndeɪ] N coppa di gelato guarnita.
Sun·day ['sʌndɪ] N domenica; **he'll never do it in a month of Sundays** non ci riuscirà mai e poi mai for usage see **Tuesday.**
♦ **Sunday best** N abito della domenica.
♦ **Sunday paper** N giornale m della domenica.
♦ **Sunday school** N ≈ scuola di catechismo.
sun·deck ['sʌn,dɛk] N ponte m scoperto.
sun·dial ['sʌn,daɪəl] N meridiana.
sun·down ['sʌn,daʊn] N (esp Am) tramonto.
♦ **sun-drenched** ['sʌn,drɛntʃt] ADJ inondato(-a) dal sole.

♦ **sun-dried** ['sʌn,draɪd] ADJ essiccato(-a) al sole; **sun-dried tomatoes** pomodori mpl secchi.
sun·dry ['sʌndrɪ] 1 ADJ vari(e), diversi(e); **all and sundry** tutti quanti.
2: **sundries** NPL (items) varie fpl; (Comm) articoli mpl vari.
sun·flower ['sʌn,flaʊə'] N girasole m.
♦ **sunflower oil** N olio di semi di girasole.
♦ **sunflower seeds** NPL semi mpl di girasole.
sung [sʌŋ] PP of **sing.**
sun·glasses ['sʌn,glɑːsɪz] NPL occhiali mpl da sole.
sun·hat ['sʌn,hæt] N cappello (per proteggersi dal sole).
sunk [sʌŋk] PP of **sink.**
sunk·en ['sʌŋkən] ADJ (ship) affondato(-a); (eyes, cheeks) infossato(-a); (bath) incassato(-a).
♦ **sun·lamp** ['sʌn,læmp] N lampada a raggi UVA.
sun·less ['sʌnlɪs] ADJ senza sole.
sun·light ['sʌn,laɪt] N (luce f del) sole m; **in the sunlight** alla luce del sole.
sun·lit ['sʌn,lɪt] ADJ illuminato(-a) dal sole.
sun·ny ['sʌnɪ] ADJ (comp -ier, superl -iest) **a** (place, room etc) assolato(-a), soleggiato(-a); (day) di sole; **it is sunny** c'è il sole; **the outlook is sunny** (Met) si prevede il sole **b** (fig: person, disposition) allegro(-a); (: smile) radioso(-a).
sun·rise ['sʌn,raɪz] N: **at sunrise** allo spuntar del sole.
sun·roof ['sʌn,ruːf] N (on building) tetto a terrazzo; (Aut) tettuccio apribile.
sun·screen ['sʌn,skriːn] N (protective ingredient) filtro solare; (cream, lotion) crema (or lozione f) solare protettiva.
sun·set ['sʌn,sɛt] N tramonto.
sun·shade ['sʌn,ʃeɪd] N (portable) parasole m inv; (for eyes) visiera; (in car) aletta parasole; (awning) tenda da sole.
sun·shine ['sʌn,ʃaɪn] N (luce f del) sole m; **hours of sunshine** (Met) ore fpl di sole; **she's a little ray of sunshine** (iro) è una dolce creatura.
sun·specs ['sʌn,spɛks] NPL (fam) occhiali mpl da sole.
sun·spot ['sʌn,spɒt] N (Astron) macchia solare.
sun·stroke ['sʌn,strəʊk] N colpo di sole, insolazione f.
sun·suit ['sʌn,suːt] N prendisole m inv.
sun·tan ['sʌn,tæn] N abbronzatura, tintarella.
♦ **suntan cream** N crema solare.
sun·tanned ['sʌn,tænd] ADJ abbronzato(-a).
♦ **suntan oil** N olio solare.
sun·trap ['sʌn,træp] N angolo molto assolato.
♦ **sun umbrella** N ombrellone m.
sun·up ['sʌnʌp] N (fam) alba; **to work sunup to sundown** lavorare dall'alba al tramonto.
su·per ['suːpə'] ADJ (fam) fantastico(-a), splendido(-a); **we had a super time** ci siamo divertiti da morire.
super... ['suːpə'] PREF super..., sovra..., iper...; **supersensitive** ipersensibile.
supera·bun·dance [,suːpərə,bʌndəns] N sovrabbondanza.
super·an·nu·at·ed [,suːpər'ænjʊ,eɪtɪd] (frm) ADJ (old-fashioned) démodé inv, passato(-a) di moda; (antiquated) antiquato(-a).
super·an·nua·tion [,suːpər,ænjʊ'eɪʃən] N (pension) pensione f; (contribution) contributi mpl pensionistici.
su·perb [suː'pɜːb] ADJ (quality) superbo(-a); (control, confidence) magnifico(-a).
su·perb·ly [suː'pɜːblɪ] ADV (see adj) superbamente; magnificamente.
♦ **Super Bowl** N (American football) super bowl m inv.
super·charged ['suːpə,tʃɑːdʒd] ADJ (Aut) sovralimentato

(-a).

super·char·ger [ˈsuːpəˌtʃɑːdʒəʳ] N compressore m.

super·cili·ous [ˌsuːpəˈsɪlɪəs] ADJ (frm) altezzoso(-a), sprezzante.

super·cili·ous·ly [ˌsuːpəˈsɪlɪəslɪ] ADV (frm) altezzosamente, sprezzantemente.

super·cili·ous·ness [ˌsuːpəˈsɪlɪəsnɪs] N (frm) alterigia.

super·con·duc·tiv·ity [ˈsuːpəˌkɒndʌkˈtɪvɪtɪ] N superconduttività.

super·con·duc·tor [ˌsuːpəkɒnˈdʌktəʳ] N superconduttore m.

super·ego [ˌsuːpərˈiːgəu] N (Psych) super-ego m inv, super-io m inv.

super·fi·cial [ˌsuːpəˈfɪʃəl] ADJ superficiale.

super·fi·ci·al·ity [ˌsuːpəfɪʃɪˈælɪtɪ] N superficialità.

super·fi·cial·ly [ˌsuːpəˈfɪʃəlɪ] ADV superficialmente.

super·flu·ity [ˌsuːpəˈfluːɪtɪ] N sovrabbondanza.

super·flu·ous [suːˈpɜːfluəs] ADJ superfluo(-a); **he felt rather superfluous** si sentì di troppo.

super·flu·ous·ly [suːˈpɜːfluəslɪ] ADV inutilmente.

super·glue [ˈsuːpəˌgluː] N colla a presa rapida.

super·grass [ˈsuːpəˌgrɑːs] N pentito(-a).

super·high·way [ˈsuːpəˌhaɪweɪ] N (Am) autostrada; **the information superhighway** l'autostrada telematica.

super·hu·man [ˌsuːpəˈhjuːmən] ADJ sovrumano(-a).

super·im·pose [ˌsuːpərɪmˈpəuz] VT: **to superimpose (on)** sovrapporre (a).

super·in·tend [ˌsuːpərɪnˈtɛnd] VT (work, shop, department) dirigere, soprintendere; (exam) sorvegliare, vigilare; (production) controllare; (counting of votes) presiedere a.

super·in·ten·dent [ˌsuːpərɪnˈtɛndənt] N soprintendente m/f, direttore(-trice); (Police) ≈ commissario (capo) di Pubblica Sicurezza.

su·peri·or [suˈpɪərɪəʳ] 1 ADJ (gen): **superior to** superiore a; (Comm: goods, quality) di prim'ordine, superiore; (smug: person) che fa il/la superiore; (: smile, air) di superiorità; (: remark) altezzoso(-a); **superior number** (Typ) esponente m; **he felt rather superior** si sentì importante.
2 N (in rank) superiore m/f; **Mother Superior** (Rel) (madre f) superiora.

su·peri·or·ity [suˌpɪərɪˈɒrɪtɪ] N superiorità.

♦ **superiority complex** N (fam) complesso di superiorità.

super·la·tive [suˈpɜːlətɪv] 1 ADJ (superb: quality, achievement) eccellente; (: indifference) sommo(-a); (Gram) superlativo.
2 N (Gram) superlativo; **to talk in superlatives** fare largo uso di superlativi nel parlare.

super·la·tive·ly [suˈpɜːlətɪvlɪ] ADV (good, intelligent) estremamente; (play, perform) superlativamente; **to be superlatively fit** essere in ottima forma.

super·man [ˈsuːpəˌmæn] N (pl -men) superuomo.

super·mar·ket [ˈsuːpəˌmɑːkɪt] N supermercato.

super·model [ˈsuːpəˌmɒdəl] N top model m/f inv.

super·natu·ral [ˌsuːpəˈnætʃərəl] ADJ, N soprannaturale (m).

super·nova [ˌsuːpəˈnəuvə] N supernova.

super·nu·mer·ary [ˌsuːpəˈnjuːmərərɪ] ADJ, N soprannumerario(-a).

super·pow·er [ˈsuːpəˌpauəʳ] N (Pol) superpotenza.

super·satu·rat·ed [ˌsuːpəˈsætʃəˌreɪtɪd] ADJ (solution) soprassaturo(-a).

super·script [ˈsuːpəˌskrɪpt] N esponente m.

super·sede [ˌsuːpəˈsiːd] VT sostituire, soppiantare; a

superseded method un metodo sorpassato.

super·son·ic [ˌsuːpəˈsɒnɪk] ADJ supersonico(-a).

super·star [ˈsuːpəstɑːʳ] N superstar f inv.

super·sti·tion [ˌsuːpəˈstɪʃən] N superstizione f.

super·sti·tious [ˌsuːpəˈstɪʃəs] ADJ superstizioso(-a).

super·sti·tious·ly [ˌsuːpəˈstɪʃəslɪ] ADV superstiziosamente.

super·store [ˈsuːpəˌstɔːʳ] N (Brit) ipermercato.

super·struc·ture [ˈsuːpəˌstrʌktʃəʳ] N sovrastruttura.

super·tank·er [ˈsuːpəˌtæŋkəʳ] N superpetroliera.

super·tax [ˈsuːpəˌtæks] N sopratassa.

super·vise [ˈsuːpəˌvaɪz] VT (person) sorvegliare, vigilare; (work, organization, research) soprintendere a.

super·vi·sion [ˌsuːpəˈvɪʒən] N (of activity, process) supervisione f; (of person) sorveglianza; **under medical supervision** sotto controllo medico.

super·vi·sor [ˈsuːpəˌvaɪzəʳ] N sorvegliante m/f, soprintendente m/f, supervisore m; (Univ) relatore(-trice); (in shop) capocommesso(-a).

super·vi·sory [ˈsuːpəˌvaɪzərɪ] ADJ di sorveglianza, di vigilanza.

su·pine [ˈsuːpaɪn] ADJ supino(-a).

sup·per [ˈsʌpəʳ] N (evening meal) cena; (late-night snack) spuntino; **to have supper** cenare.

sup·plant [səˈplɑːnt] VT soppiantare.

sup·ple [ˈsʌpl] ADJ (comp -r, superl -st) elastico(-a), flessibile; (person) agile.

sup·plement [n ˈsʌplɪmənt; vb ˌsʌplɪˈmɛnt] 1 N (also Press) supplemento.
2 VT (diet etc) integrare; (income) arrotondare; (information) completare.

sup·plemen·ta·ry [ˌsʌplɪˈmɛntərɪ] ADJ supplementare.

sup·ple·ness [ˈsʌplnɪs] N (see adj) elasticità, flessibilità; agilità.

sup·pli·cant [ˈsʌplɪkənt] N (frm) supplice m/f.

sup·pli·ca·tion [ˌsʌplɪˈkeɪʃən] N (frm) supplica.

supplier [səˈplaɪəʳ] N (Comm) fornitore(-trice).

sup·ply¹ [səˈplaɪ] 1 N (delivery) fornitura; (stock) provvista; (Tech) alimentazione f; **the electricity/water/gas supply** l'erogazione f di corrente/d'acqua/di gas; **to cut off the water supply** tagliare l'acqua; **the supply of fuel to the engine** l'afflusso di carburante al motore; **supply and demand** (Econ) domanda e offerta; **to be in short supply** scarseggiare, essere scarso(-a); **supplies** NPL (food) viveri mpl; (Mil) approvvigionamenti mpl, rifornimenti mpl; (: food only) sussistenza; **medical supplies** materiale msg sanitario; **office supplies** forniture fpl per ufficio.
2 VT (goods, materials, information etc) fornire; (fill: need, want) soddisfare; **to supply sth (with sth)** (system, machine) alimentare qc (con qc); **to supply sb (with sth)** (with goods) fornire a qn qc, rifornire qn di qc; (Mil) approvvigionare qn (di qc); **she supplied us with the necessary evidence** ci ha fornito le prove necessarie; **most towns are supplied with electricity** quasi tutte le città sono dotate di elettricità; **who will supply their needs?** chi farà fronte ai loro bisogni?.
3 ADJ (ship, train) di rifornimento.

sup·ply² [ˈsʌplɪ] ADV (bend) agilmente.

♦ **supply teacher** N (Brit) supplente m/f.

sup·port [səˈpɔːt] 1 N (gen) sostegno, appoggio; (object) sostegno, supporto; **she was a great support to me** mi è stata di grande conforto; **moral support** aiuto morale; **he has no visible means of support** non è ben chiaro come si mantenga; **to speak in support of a candidate**

parlare a favore di un candidato; **to lean on sb for support** (*also fig*) appoggiarsi a qn; **they stopped work in support (of)** hanno interrotto l'attività lavorativa per solidarietà (con); **our support comes from the workers** sono gli operai ad appoggiarci; **there's a great deal of support for his views** le sue opinioni sono ampiamente condivise.

[2] VT (*gen*) sostenere, sorreggere; (*fig: person: emotionally*) sostenere; (: *financially*) mantenere; (: *proposal, project*) appoggiare; (: *Sport: team*) tifare per; (: *corroborate: evidence*) confermare, convalidare; **to support o.s.** (*financially*) mantenersi; **all that is necessary to support life** tutto ciò che rende possibile l'esistenza di una forma di vita.

sup·port·er [sə'pɔːtəʳ] N (*of proposal, project*) sostenitore (-trice); (*Pol etc*) sostenitore(-trice), fautore(-trice); (*Sport*) tifoso(-a).

sup·port·ing [sə'pɔːtɪŋ] ADJ **a** (*Theatre, Cine: role, actor, actress*) non protagonista **b** (*wall*) sostegno.

sup·port·ive [sə'pɔːtɪv] ADJ **a** (*person*): **to be very supportive (towards sb)** dare il proprio appoggio (a qn); (*emotionally*) essere di grande conforto (per qn); **I have a supportive family/husband** la mia famiglia/mio marito mi appoggia **b** (*gesture, effort*) di aiuto.

sup·pose [sə'pəʊz] VT **a** (*assume, believe*): **I suppose she'll come** suppongo che verrà; **I don't suppose she'll come** non credo che venga; **I suppose she won't come** penso che non verrà; **I suppose so/not** credo di sì/di no; **I don't suppose so** non credo; **you're going to accept, I suppose?** accetti, immagino?; **I don't suppose you could lend me £10?** [OR] **I suppose you couldn't lend me £10?** non potresti per caso prestarmi 10 sterline?; **he's supposed to be an expert** dicono che sia un esperto, passa per un esperto

b (*assume as hypothesis*) supporre + *sub*, mettere + *sub*; **let us suppose that ...** supponiamo che..., mettiamo che...; **but just suppose he's right** ma supponi *or* metti che abbia ragione; **even supposing (that) it were true** anche nel caso (che) fosse vero; **always supposing (that) he comes** ammesso e non concesso che venga; **suppose** *or* **supposing it rains, what shall we do?** metti che piova, cosa facciamo?; **suppose she doesn't come?** e se non venisse?

c (*in passive: ought*): **to be supposed to do sth** essere tenuto(-a) a fare qc; **you're not supposed to do that** non bisogna farlo

d (*in imperative: I suggest*): **suppose you do it now?** e se lo facessi adesso?; **suppose we change the subject?** e se parlassimo d'altro?

e (*presuppose*) presupporre.

sup·posed [sə'pəʊzd] ADJ (*presumed*) presunto(-a); (*so-called*) cosiddetto(-a).

sup·pos·ed·ly [sə'pəʊzɪdlɪ] ADV (*presumably*) presumibilmente; (*seemingly*) apparentemente.

sup·pos·ing [sə'pəʊzɪŋ] CONJ se, ammesso che + *sub*.

sup·po·si·tion [ˌsʌpə'zɪʃən] N (*frm*) supposizione *f*, ipotesi *f inv*; **on the supposition that ...** partendo dal presupposto che...+ *sub*.

sup·pos·i·tory [sə'pɒzɪtərɪ] N suppositorio.

sup·press [sə'prɛs] VT (*emotion, revolt*) reprimere, soffocare; (*scandal*) mettere a tacere, soffocare; (*yawn, smile*) trattenere; (*publication*) sopprimere; (*news, the truth*) tacere; (*evidence*) occultare.

sup·pres·sion [sə'prɛʃən] N (*of emotions etc*) repressione *f*; (*of scandal*) soffocamento; (*of truth*) il tacere; (*of evidence*) occultamento; (*of publication*) soppressione *f*.

sup·pres·sor [sə'prɛsəʳ] N (*Elec*) soppressore *m*.

sup·pu·rate ['sʌpjʊˌreɪt] VI suppurare.

supra·na·tion·al [ˌsuːprə'næʃənl] ADJ sopranazionale.

su·prema·cy [sʊ'prɛməsɪ] N supremazia.

su·preme [sʊ'priːm] ADJ (*in authority*) supremo(-a); (*very great*) sommo(-a), massimo(-a); **with supreme indifference** con somma indifferenza; **the supreme sacrifice** il sacrificio supremo; **to reign supreme** (*fig*) dominare.

♦ **Supreme Court** N (*Am*): **the Supreme Court** la corte suprema.

su·preme·ly [sʊ'priːmlɪ] ADV estremamente, sommamente.

su·pre·mo [sʊ'priːməʊ] N (*Brit fam*) grande capo.

Supt ABBR (*Police*) = **superintendent**.

sur·charge ['sɜːˌtʃɑːdʒ] [1] N (*gen*) supplemento, sovrapprezzo; (*tax*) soprattassa.

[2] VT far pagare un sovrapprezzo (*or* una soprattassa).

surd [sɜːd] N (*Math*) espressione *f* irrazionale.

sure [ʃʊəʳ] [1] ADJ (*comp* **-r**, *superl* **-st**) (*gen*) sicuro(-a); (*definite, convinced*) sicuro(-a), certo(-a); **it's sure to rain** pioverà di sicuro; **I'm sure it's going to rain** sono sicuro che pioverà; **I'm not sure how/why/when** non so bene come/perché/quando; **be sure to tell me if you see him** mi raccomando, dimmi se lo vedi; **to be sure of sth** essere sicuro(-a) di qc; **to be sure of o.s.** essere sicuro(-a) di sé; **to be sure of one's facts** essere sicuro(-a) dei fatti; **you can be sure of a good time there** puoi essere sicuro che ti divertirai; **to make sure of sth** assicurarsi di qc; **be** *or* **make sure you do it right** bada di farlo bene; **I'll find out for sure** vedrò di accertarmene; **I think I locked up, but I'll just make sure** credo di aver chiuso a chiave, ma voglio assicurarmene; **just to make sure** per sicurezza; **do you know for sure?** ne sei proprio sicuro?; **she'll leave, for sure** senza dubbio partirà; **I'm sure I don't know** [OR] **I don't know, I'm sure** che vuoi che ne sappia io?; **he's a sure thing for president** ha la presidenza assicurata.

[2] ADV: **is that O.K.? — sure!** va bene? — certo! *or* sicuro!; **that sure is pretty** [OR] (*Am*) **that's sure pretty** è veramente *or* davvero carino; **sure enough!** (*of course*) sicuro!, senz'altro!; **sure enough** (*predictably*) infatti; **as sure as fate** ovviamente; **as sure as eggs is eggs** [OR] **as sure as I'm standing here** è com'è vero Dio.

♦ **sure-fire** ['ʃʊəˌfaɪəʳ] ADJ (*fam: winner, success*) sicuro (-a).

♦ **sure-footed** [ˌʃʊə'fʊtɪd] ADJ dal passo sicuro.

sure·ly ['ʃʊəlɪ] ADV (*certainly*) certamente, sicuramente; **surely we've met before?** ma non ci siamo già incontrati?; **surely you don't mean that!** non parlerai sul serio!; **surely not!** ma non è possibile!

sure·ness ['ʃʊənɪs] N (*of aim, footing*) sicurezza; (*positiveness*) certezza.

sure·ty ['ʃʊərətɪ] N cauzione *f*; **to go** *or* **stand surety for sb** farsi garante per qn.

surf [sɜːf] N (*waves*) cavalloni *mpl*; (*foam*) spuma.

sur·face ['sɜːfɪs] [1] N (*gen*) superficie *f*; (*of road*) piano stradale; **on the surface it seems that ...** (*fig*) superficialmente sembra che...; **we've only scratched the surface** (*fig: of argument, work*) abbiamo appena iniziato.

[2] VT (*road*) asfaltare.

[3] VI (*submarine etc*) risalire in superficie; (*fig: person: after absence*) farsi vivo(-a); (: *from bed*) emergere; **he**

surfaces in London occasionally ogni tanto si fa vedere a Londra.
[4] ADJ (Mil, Naut) di superficie.
♦ **surface area** N superficie f.
♦ **surface mail** N posta ordinaria.
♦ **sur·face run-off** [ˌsɜːfɪsˈrʌndf] N (Geog) acque fpl superficiali.
♦ **surface tension** N (Phys) tensione f di superficie.
♦ **surface-to-air missile** [ˌsɜːfɪstuˌɛəˈmɪsaɪl] N missile m terra aria inv.
♦ **surface-to-surface** [ˌsɜːfɪstəˈsɜːfɪs] ADJ (Mil) superficie-superficie inv.
surf·board ['sɜːfˌbɔːd] N surf m inv.
sur·feit ['sɜːfɪt] N (frm) sovrabbondanza.
surf·er ['sɜːfəʳ] N surfista m/f.
surf·ing ['sɜːfɪŋ], **surf·riding** ['sɜːfˌraɪdɪŋ] N surfing m inv, surf m inv; **to go surfing** fare surf.
surge [sɜːdʒ] [1] N (of sea, sympathy) ondata; (of people) marea; (Elec) sovratensione f transitoria; **a surge of anger** un impeto di rabbia.
[2] VI (water, people) riversarsi; (waves) sollevarsi; (Elec: power) aumentare improvvisamente; **to surge into/over sth** riversarsi in/su qc; **to surge forward** buttarsi avanti; **to surge round sb/sth** accalcarsi intorno a qn/qc; **the blood surged to her cheeks** il sangue le affluì al viso.
sur·geon ['sɜːdʒən] N chirurgo.
♦ **Surgeon General** N (Am): **the Surgeon General** ≈ il ministro della Sanità.
sur·gery ['sɜːdʒərɪ] N (art) chirurgia; (operation) intervento chirurgico; (Brit Med: consulting room) ambulatorio; (: session) visita ambulatoriale; (Brit: of MP) incontri mpl con gli elettori; **to undergo surgery** subire un intervento chirurgico.
♦ **surgery hours** NPL (Brit) orario di visita.
sur·gi·cal ['sɜːdʒɪkəl] ADJ chirurgico(-a); **surgical cotton** cotone m idrofilo; **surgical dressing** medicazione f.
sur·gi·cal·ly ['sɜːdʒɪkəlɪ] ADV chirurgicamente.
♦ **surgical spirit** N (Brit) alcol denaturato.
surg·ing ['sɜːdʒɪŋ] ADJ (crowd, waves) impetuoso(-a).
sur·li·ness ['sɜːlɪnɪs] N scontrosità.
sur·ly ['sɜːlɪ] ADJ (comp -ier, superl -iest) burbero(-a), scontroso(-a).
sur·mise [n 'sɜːmaɪz or sɜːˈmaɪz; vb sɜːˈmaɪz] [1] N congettura.
[2] VT supporre, congetturare; **I surmised as much** me lo immaginavo.
sur·mount [sɜːˈmaunt] VT (difficulty) sormontare.
sur·mount·able [sɜːˈmauntəbl] ADJ sormontabile.
sur·name ['sɜːˌneɪm] N cognome m.
sur·pass [sɜːˈpɑːs] VT (expectations, person) superare; **it surpassed all his hopes** è andata meglio di quanto sperasse.
sur·plice ['sɜːplɪs] N (Rel) cotta.
sur·plus ['sɜːpləs] [1] N (Fin, Comm) surplus m inv; **to have a surplus of sth** avere qc in eccedenza; **labour surplus** eccedenza di manodopera.
[2] ADJ eccedente, d'avanzo; (Fin, Comm) di sovrappiù, in eccedenza; **surplus stock** merce f in sovrappiù; **it is surplus to our requirements** eccede i nostri bisogni.
sur·prise [səˈpraɪz] [1] N (gen) sorpresa; (astonishment) stupore m, sorpresa; **it came as quite a surprise to me** fu una grande sorpresa per me; **a look of surprise** uno sguardo di sorpresa; **much to my surprise** [OR] **to my great surprise** con mia grande sorpresa; **to take by surprise** (person) cogliere di sorpresa; (Mil: town, fort)

attaccare di sorpresa; **to give sb a surprise** fare una sorpresa a qn.
[2] VT (astonish) sorprendere, stupire; (catch unawares) sorprendere, cogliere di sorpresa; **he was surprised to learn that** ... fu sorpreso di sapere che...; **I'm surprised at you!** mi meraviglio di te!; **he surprised me into accepting** ho accettato perché colto alla sprovvista; **I wouldn't be surprised if he accepts** non mi sorprenderebbe se accettasse; **don't be surprised if he comes** non ti meravigliare se viene.
[3] ADJ (present, visit) inaspettato(-a); (attack) di sorpresa.
sur·pris·ing [səˈpraɪzɪŋ] ADJ sorprendente.
sur·pris·ing·ly [səˈpraɪzɪŋlɪ] ADV (good, bad) sorprendentemente; (somewhat) surprisingly, **he agreed** cosa (alquanto) sorprendente, ha accettato; **not surprisingly he refused** come c'era da aspettarsi ha rifiutato.
sur·re·al [səˈrɪəl] ADJ (unreal) surreale; (strange) bizzarro (-a).
sur·re·al·ism [səˈrɪəˌlɪzəm] N surrealismo.
sur·re·al·ist [səˈrɪəlɪst] ADJ, N surrealista (m/f).
sur·re·al·is·tic [səˌrɪəˈlɪstɪk] ADJ surreale; (Art) surrealistico(-a).
sur·ren·der [səˈrɛndəʳ] [1] N resa, capitolazione f; **no surrender!** non ci arrendiamo!.
[2] VT (gen, Mil): **to surrender (to)** consegnare (a); (lease) cedere; (claim, right) rinunciare a; (hope) abbandonare; (insurance policy) riscattare.
[3] VI: **to surrender (to)** arrendersi (a).
♦ **surrender value** N (Insurance) valore m di riscatto.
sur·rep·ti·tious [ˌsʌrəpˈtɪʃəs] ADJ furtivo(-a).
sur·rep·ti·tious·ly [ˌsʌrəpˈtɪʃəslɪ] ADV furtivamente.
sur·ro·gate ['sʌrəgɪt] [1] N (Brit: substitute) surrogato.
[2] ADJ surrogato(-a).
♦ **surrogate mother** N madre f biologica.
sur·round [səˈraund] [1] VT circondare; (Mil) accerchiare; **a town surrounded by hills** una città circondata da colline.
[2] N bordo.
sur·round·ing [səˈraundɪŋ] ADJ circostante; **the surrounding hills** le colline circostanti.
sur·round·ings [səˈraundɪŋz] NPL (of place) dintorni mpl; (environment) ambiente msg; **in beautiful surroundings** (house, hotel) in una bella posizione.
sur·tax ['sɜːˌtæks] N soprattassa.
sur·veil·lance [sɜːˈveɪləns] N sorveglianza; **under surveillance** sotto sorveglianza.
sur·vey [n 'sɜːveɪ; vb sɜːˈveɪ] [1] N **a** (comprehensive view: of situation, developments) quadro generale
b (inquiry, study) indagine f, studio; **a survey of public opinion** un sondaggio d'opinione; **to carry out a survey of** fare un'indagine di
c (Surveying: of building) perizia; (: of land) rilevamento; (: of country) rilevamento topografico.
[2] VT **a** (look at) guardare; (: prospects, trends) passare in rassegna
b (examine) studiare, esaminare; **the book surveys events up to 1992** il libro esamina gli eventi fino al 1992
c (Surveying: building) fare una perizia di; (: land) fare il rilevamento di; (: country) fare il rilevamento topografico di.
sur·vey·ing [səˈveɪɪŋ] N (of land) agrimensura.
sur·vey·or [səˈveɪəʳ] N (of buildings) perito; (of land) agrimensore m.

♦ **survey ship** N *nave utilizzata per rilevamenti idrografici.*

sur·viv·al [səˈvaɪvəl] N (*act*) sopravvivenza; (*relic*) retaggio; **the survival of the fittest** (*Bio*) la selezione naturale; **in the business world it's a case of the survival of the fittest** nel mondo degli affari vige la legge della giungla.

♦ **survival course** N corso di sopravvivenza.

♦ **survival kit** N equipaggiamento di prima necessità.

sur·vive [səˈvaɪv] **1** VI (*gen*) sopravvivere; (*fig: in job etc*) durare; **you'll survive!** stai tranquillo che non morirai!. **2** VT sopravvivere a

▶ **survive on** VI + PREP sopravvivere con; **my salary's only just enough to survive on** col mio stipendio riesco a malapena a sopravvivere.

sur·vi·vor [səˈvaɪvə] N superstite *m/f*, sopravvissuto(-a).

sus·cep·tibil·ity [səˌsɛptəˈbɪlɪtɪ] N suscettibilità *f inv*; (*Med*) predisposizione *f*.

sus·cep·tible [səˈsɛptəbl] ADJ **a** : **to be susceptible to** (*infection, illness*) essere predisposto(-a) a, soggetto(-a) a; (*persuasion, flattery*) essere sensibile a **b** (*impressionable*) (facilmente) impressionabile **c** : **susceptible of change** (*frm*) suscettibile di cambiamenti.

sus·pect [*adj, n* ˈsʌspɛkt; *vb* səˈspɛkt] **1** ADJ sospetto(-a). **2** N persona sospetta. **3** VT (*person*): **to suspect (of)** sospettare (di); (*think likely*): **to suspect that** sospettare che + *sub*, supporre che + *sub*; **to suspect sb of a crime** sospettare qn di un delitto; **I suspect his motives** non mi convince; **I suspect that he is the author** immagino che sia lui l'autore; **he suspects nothing** non sospetta niente.

sus·pect·ed [səˈspɛktɪd] ADJ presunto(-a); **to have a suspected fracture** avere una sospetta frattura.

sus·pend [səˈspɛnd] VT (*gen*) sospendere; **it was suspended from the ceiling/between two posts** era appeso al soffitto/sospeso tra due pali; **he was suspended for cheating** è stato sospeso perché aveva imbrogliato.

sus·pend·ed ani·ma·tion [səˌspɛndɪdæniˈmeɪʃən] N interruzione *f* delle funzioni vitali.

sus·pend·ed sen·tence [səˌspɛndɪdˈsɛntəns] N (*Law*) (condanna) condizionale *f*.

sus·pend·er [səˈspɛndə] N (*for stocking*) giarrettiera (di reggicalze); see also **suspenders**.

♦ **suspender belt** N (*Brit*) reggicalze *m inv*.

sus·pend·ers [səˈspɛndəz] NPL (*Brit*) giarrettiere *fpl*; (*Am: braces*) bretelle *fpl*.

sus·pense [səˈspɛns] N incertezza, apprensione *f*; (*in film, book*) suspense *f*; **we waited in suspense** attendevamo ansiosamente; **the suspense is killing me!** muoio dalla curiosità!; **to keep sb in suspense** tenere qn in sospeso.

♦ **suspense account** N (*in ledger*) voce *f* in sospeso; (*Comm*) conto in sospeso.

sus·pen·sion [səˈspɛnʃən] N (*gen, Aut*) sospensione *f*; (*of driving licence*) ritiro temporaneo.

♦ **suspension bridge** N ponte *m* sospeso.

♦ **suspension points** NPL (*Gram*) puntini *mpl* di sospensione.

sus·pi·cion [səˈspɪʃən] N **a** (*suspicious belief*) sospetto; (*lack of trust*) diffidenza; **I had no suspicion that ...** non avevo il benché minimo sospetto che... + *sub*; **my suspicion is that ...** ho il sospetto che...+ *sub*; **arrested on suspicion of murder** arrestato(-a) per sospetto omicidio; **to be under suspicion** essere sospettato(-a); **above suspicion** al di sopra di ogni sospetto; **I had my suspicions about him** non mi ha mai convinto troppo **b** (*hint: of danger, scandal*) segno; (: *of garlic*) punta.

sus·pi·cious [səˈspɪʃəs] ADJ (*causing suspicion*) sospetto (-a); (*feeling suspicion*): **suspicious (of)** sospettoso(-a) (di), diffidente (di); **to be suspicious of** *or* **about sb/sth** nutrire dei sospetti nei riguardi di qn/qc; **that made him suspicious** questo lo ha insospettito; **a suspicious character** un(a) tipo(-a) sospetto(-a).

sus·pi·cious·ly [səˈspɪʃəslɪ] ADV (*look etc*) con sospetto; (*behave etc*) in modo sospetto; **it looks suspiciously like measles** ha tutta l'aria di essere morbillo.

suss [sʌs] VT (*Brit fam*): **I've sussed it/him out** ho capito come stanno le cose/che tipo è.

sus·tain [səsˈteɪn] VT **a** (*weight*) sostenere, sopportare; (*body, life*) mantenere; (*Mus: note*) tenere; (*effort, role, pretence*) sostenere; **"objection sustained"** (*Am Law*) "obiezione accolta" **b** (*receive: damage, loss etc*) subire, soffrire.

sus·tain·able [səsˈteɪnəbl] ADJ che può essere mantenuto (-a).

sus·tained [səsˈteɪnd] ADJ (*effort etc*) prolungato(-a).

sus·tain·ing [səsˈteɪnɪŋ] ADJ (*food*) nutriente.

sus·te·nance [ˈsʌstɪnəns] N (*food*) nutrimento; (*livelihood*) mezzi *mpl* di sussistenza *or* di sostentamento; **there's not much sustenance in it** non è molto nutriente.

su·ture [ˈsuːtʃə] N (*Med*) sutura.

SW ABBR **a** (= *southwest(ern)*) SO (= *sud ovest*) **b** (*Radio*: = *short wave*) OC *fpl* (= *onde corte*).

swab [swɒb] **1** N (*Med: for cleaning wound, for specimen*) tampone *m*. **2** VT (*Naut: also*: **swab down**) redazzare.

swad·dle [ˈswɒdl] VT (*in bandages*) fasciare, bendare; (*in blanket*) avvolgere; (*baby*) fasciare.

swag [swæg] N (*fam*) malloppo.

swag·ger [ˈswæɡə] **1** N andatura spavalda. **2** VI pavoneggiarsi; **to swagger in** entrare pavoneggiandosi.

swag·ger·ing [ˈswæɡərɪŋ] **1** ADJ (*gait*) spavaldo(-a); (*gesture*) da fanfarone(-a); **a swaggering fellow** un fanfarone. **2** N fanfaronate *fpl*.

swal·low[1] [ˈswɒləʊ] **1** N (*act*) deglutizione *f*; (*of food*) boccone *m*; (*of drink*) sorso. **2** VT (*food, drink*) inghiottire, mandar giù, ingoiare; (*fig: suppress: anger, resentment*) inghiottire; (: *believe, story*) bere; **to swallow one's pride** mettere il proprio orgoglio sotto i piedi; **that's hard to swallow** è difficile crederci; **they swallowed it whole!** (*story*) se la sono bevuta in pieno!. **3** VI inghiottire; (*fig*): **he swallowed hard and said ...** con l'emozione che gli serrava la gola ha detto...

▶ **swallow up** VT + ADV (*fig*) inghiottire; **they were soon swallowed up in the darkness** furono presto inghiottiti dalle tenebre; **I wished the ground would open and swallow me up** avrei voluto sprofondare.

swal·low[2] [ˈswɒləʊ] N rondine *f*.

♦ **swallow dive** N (*Swimming*) tuffo ad angelo.

♦ **swallow hole** N (*Geol*) inghiottitoio.

swam [swæm] PT of **swim**.

swamp [swɒmp] **1** N palude *f*, pantano. **2** VT (*flood*) inondare, allagare; (: *boat etc*) sommergere; **to swamp (with)** (*fig*) sommergere (di).

swamp·land [ˈswɒmpˌlænd] N palude *f*, zona paludosa.

swampy [ˈswɒmpɪ] ADJ paludoso(-a).

swan [swɒn] **1** N cigno. **2** VI (*fam*): **to swan around** fare la bella vita; **he swanned off to New York** se n'è andato bellamente a New York.

swank [swæŋk] (*fam*) ⚊1⚊ N **a** (*vanity, boastfulness*) ostentazione *f*; **he does it for swank** lo fa per mettersi in mostra **b** (*person*) spaccone(-a).

⚊2⚊ VI (*fam: show off*) mettersi in mostra; (: *talk boastfully*) fare lo(-a) spaccone(-a); **to swank about sth** vantarsi di qc.

swanky ['swæŋkɪ] ADJ (*comp* **-ier**, *superl* **-iest**) (*fam: person*) pieno(-a) di sé; (: *car etc*) vistoso(-a).

♦ **swan's-down** ['swɒnz‚daʊn] N piumino (di cigno).

♦ **swan song** N (*fig*) canto del cigno.

swap [swɒp] ⚊1⚊ N (*exchange*) scambio.

⚊2⚊ VT (*cars, stamps etc*) scambiare; **to swap sth for sth else** scambiare qc con qualcos'altro; **to swap places with sb** cambiare di posto con qn.

⚊3⚊ VI fare uno scambio

▶ **swap over, swap round** VT + ADV: **to swap sth over** *or* **round** cambiare di posto qc; **you can swap them over** li puoi cambiare di posto.

SWAPO ['swɑːpəʊ] N ABBR = *South-West Africa People's Organization*.

swarm[1] [swɔːm] ⚊1⚊ N (*of bees, flying insects*) sciame *m*; (*of crawling insects*) schiera, esercito; (*fig: of tourists etc*) sciame *m*, frotta, stuolo; **swarm of ants** formicaio; **in swarms** (*fig*) a frotte.

⚊2⚊ VI (*bees*) sciamare; **to swarm about** (*crawling insects, people*) brulicare; **to swarm in/out** *etc* entrare/uscire *etc* a frotte; **to swarm with** (*people, insects*) brulicare di.

swarm[2] [swɔːm] VI: **to swarm up a tree/rope** arrampicarsi su un albero/su per una corda.

swarthi·ness ['swɔːðɪnɪs] N (*of person*) carnagione *f* scura; (*of complexion*) colore *m* scuro.

swarthy ['swɔːðɪ] ADJ (*comp* **-ier**, *superl* **-iest**) (*person*) di carnagione scura; (*skin*) scuro(-a).

swash [swɒʃ] N (*sound*) sciabordio.

swash·buck·ling ['swɒʃ‚bʌklɪŋ] ADJ (*role, hero*) spericolato(-a); (*film, novel*) di cappa e spada.

swas·ti·ka ['swɒstɪkə] N svastica, croce *f* uncinata.

SWAT [swɒt] N ABBR (*Am.: = Special Weapons and Tactics*) *corpo speciale di polizia*; **a SWAT team** ≈ un reparto di teste di cuoio.

swat [swɒt] ⚊1⚊ VT (*fly*) schiacciare.

⚊2⚊ N (*Brit: also:* **fly swat**) acchiappamosche *m inv.*

swathe[1] [sweɪð], **swath** [swɔːθ] N (*pl* **swathes** *or* **swaths** [swɔːðz]) (*of grass etc*) falciata.

swathe[2] [sweɪð] VT: **to swathe in** (*bandages, blankets*) avvolgere in.

swat·ter ['swɒtə'] N (*also:* **fly swatter**) acchiappamosche *m inv.*

sway [sweɪ] ⚊1⚊ N **a** (*movement: gen*) ondeggiamento; (*of boat*) dondolio, rollio

b (*rule, power*): **sway (over)** influenza (su); **to hold sway over sb** dominare qn.

⚊2⚊ VI (*tree, hanging object*) ondeggiare; (*bridge, building, train*) oscillare; (*person*) barcollare; **the train swayed from side to side** il treno oscillava violentemente.

⚊3⚊ VT **a** (*move*) far oscillare; **to sway one's hips** ancheggiare

b (*influence*) influenzare; **these factors finally swayed me** questi fattori hanno finito per influenzarmi.

Swa·zi·land ['swɑːzɪ‚lænd] N lo Swaziland.

swear [sweə'] (*pt* **swore**, *pp* **sworn**) ⚊1⚊ VT (*gen*) giurare; **to swear an oath** prestare giuramento; **I swear it!** lo giuro!; **I swear (that) I did not steal it** giuro che non l'ho rubato, giuro di non averlo rubato; **to swear to do sth** promettere di fare qc; **I could have sworn that was Louise** avrei

giurato che fosse Louise; **to swear sb to secrecy** far giurare a qn di mantenere il segreto.

⚊2⚊ VI **a** (*solemnly: witness etc*) giurare; **to swear on the Bible** giurare sulla Bibbia; **to swear to the truth of sth** giurare che qc è vero; **I can't swear to it** non posso giurarlo

b (*use swearwords*): **to swear (at sb)** bestemmiare *or* imprecare (contro qn), dire parolacce (a qn); **to swear like a trooper** bestemmiare come uno scaricatore di porto

▶ **swear by** VI + PREP (*fam*): **my mother swears by hot baths for backache** mia madre dice che non c'è rimedio migliore di un bagno caldo contro il mal di schiena

▶ **swear in** VT + ADV (*jury, witness, president*) prestare giuramento.

swear·word ['sweə‚wɜːd] N parolaccia; (*curse*) bestemmia.

sweat [swet] ⚊1⚊ N sudore *m*; **by the sweat of one's brow** con il sudore della fronte; **to get in** *or* **into a sweat about sth** (*fam*) farsi prendere dal panico per qc; **in a sweat** in un bagno di sudore; **to be in a cold sweat** (*also: fig*) avere i sudori freddi; **it was a real sweat!** è stata una faticaccia!; **no sweat!** (*fam*) non ci sono problemi!.

⚊2⚊ VI (*person*) sudare; (*walls*) trasudare; (*fam: work hard*): **to sweat (over sth)** sudare (su qc); **to sweat like a pig** essere in un bagno di sudore, sudare sette camicie.

⚊3⚊ VT: **to sweat blood** (*fig: work hard*) sudare sangue; (: *be anxious*) sudare freddo; **to sweat it out** (*fig fam*) armarsi di pazienza.

sweat·band ['swet‚bænd] N (*Sport*) fascia (elastica) (*per assorbire il sudore: da polso o da fronte*).

sweat·er ['swetə'] N maglione *m*.

♦ **sweat gland** N ghiandola sudoripara.

sweat·ing ['swetɪŋ] N (*of person*) sudorazione *f*; (*of wall etc*) trasudazione *f*.

sweat·shirt ['swet‚ʃɜːt] N felpa.

sweat·shop ['swet‚ʃɒp] N *azienda o fabbrica in cui i dipendenti sono sfruttati*.

sweaty ['swetɪ] ADJ (*comp* **-ier**, *superl* **-iest**) (*gen*) sudato(-a), sudaticcio(-a); (*smell*) di sudore.

Swede [swiːd] N svedese *m/f*.

swede [swiːd] N (*Brit: vegetable*) rapa svedese.

Swe·den ['swiːdn] N la Svezia.

Swe·dish ['swiːdɪʃ] ⚊1⚊ ADJ svedese.

⚊2⚊ N (*language*) svedese *m*.

sweep [swiːp] (*vb: pt, pp* **swept**) ⚊1⚊ N **a** (*of room*) scopata, spazzata; (*of chimney*) pulita

b (*also:* **chimney sweep**) spazzacamino

c (*range*) portata; (*movement: of arm*) ampio gesto; (: *of scythe, sword*) sciabolata; (: *of beam, searchlight*) fascio luminoso; (*curve: of road, hills etc*) curva; (*expanse: of countryside*) distesa; **a wide sweep of country** una vasta distesa di campi.

⚊2⚊ VT **a** (*stairs, floor*) scopare, spazzare; (*chimney*) pulire; (*dust, snow*) spazzare; **to sweep (out) a room** scopare una stanza; **to sweep a problem under the carpet** (*fig*) accantonare un problema

b (*move over: subj: waves, wind*) spazzare; (: *searchlight*) perlustrare; (: *disease*) dilagare in; (: *fashion, craze*) invadere; **to sweep the sea for mines** dragare il mare; **to sweep the horizon** (*with eyes, binoculars*) scrutare l'orizzonte; **to sweep the board** (*fig*) fare tabula rasa

c (*remove with sweeping movement*) spazzar via; **to be swept overboard** essere spazzato(-a) fuori bordo; **the crowd swept him along** fu trascinato dalla folla; **he**

swept her off her feet (*fig*) l'ha conquistata.

3 VI **a** (*with broom*) scopare, spazzare

b (*move*): **to sweep in/out/along** entrare/uscire/procedere maestosamente; **to sweep past sb** sfrecciare davanti a qn; **the hurricane swept through the city** l'uragano infuriava sulla città; **panic swept through the crowd** la folla fu assalita dal panico; **he swept past in a sports car** è passato sfrecciando alla guida di un'auto sportiva; **the mountains sweep down to the coast** le montagne digradano maestose fino al mare

▶ **sweep aside** VT + ADV spingere di lato; (*fig*: *objections*) scartare

▶ **sweep away** VT + ADV (*dust, rubbish*) spazzar via; (*subj*: *crowd, current*) trascinare via

▶ **sweep up** **1** VI + ADV spazzare.

2 VT + ADV (*leaves, rubbish*) raccogliere; (*pick up*: *books etc*) acchiappare.

sweep·er ['swiːpə'] N **a** (*worker*) spazzino(-a) **b** (*machine*) spazzatrice *f* **c** (*Brit Ftbl*) libero.

sweep·ing ['swiːpɪŋ] ADJ (*gesture*) ampio(-a); (*statement etc*) generico(-a); (*changes, reforms*) radicale, ampio (-a).

sweep·stake ['swiːpˌsteɪk] N lotteria (*spesso abbinata alle corse dei cavalli*).

sweet [swiːt] **1** ADJ (*comp* -**er**, *superl* -**est**) **a** (*taste*) dolce; **this coffee is too sweet** questo caffè è troppo dolce; **I love sweet things** adoro i dolci

b (*fresh, pleasant: smell, perfume, sound*) dolce; (: *breath*) fresco(-a); (*fig*: *success*) piacevole; (: *revenge*) dolce; **the sweet smell of success** il profumo del successo; **it was sweet to his ear** era musica per le sue orecchie

c (*charming: person*) carino(-a), dolce; (: *smile, character*) dolce; (: *appearance, village, kitten*) grazioso(-a), carino(-a); **that's very sweet of you** è molto carino da parte tua; **what a sweet little dress!** che vestitino grazioso!; **he carried on in his own sweet way** (*iro*) ha continuato (a fare) come gli pareva.

2 ADV: **to smell/taste sweet** avere un odore/sapore dolce.

3 N (*Brit*: *toffee etc*) caramella; (: *dessert*) dolce *m*.

♦ **sweet-and-sour** [ˌswiːtəndˈsauə'] ADJ agrodolce.

sweet·breads ['swiːtˌbrɛdz] NPL animelle *fpl*.

♦ **sweet chestnut** N (*Bot*) castagno.

♦ **sweet corn** N mais *m*.

sweet·en ['swiːtn] VT (*tea etc*) zuccherare; (*air*) profumare; (*fig*: *temper*) addolcire; (: *task*) rendere più piacevole; (*also*: **sweeten up**: *person*) ingraziarsi; (: *child*) tenere buono(-a).

sweet·en·er ['swiːtnə'] N (*Culin*) dolcificante *m*; (*fam*: *bribe*) zuccherino, contentino.

sweet·en·ing ['swiːtnɪŋ] N (*substance*) dolcificante *m*.

sweet·heart ['swiːtˌhɑːt] N innamorato(-a); **yes, sweetheart** sì, tesoro.

sweetie ['swiːtɪ] N (*fam*: *toffee etc*) caramella; (: *person*) tesoro.

sweet·ly ['swiːtlɪ] ADV (*gen*) dolcemente, con dolcezza; **the engine is running sweetly** il motore non dà problemi.

♦ **sweet-natured** [ˌswiːtˈneɪtʃəd] ADJ di indole buona.

sweet·ness ['swiːtnɪs] N (*gen*) dolcezza; (*of taste*) sapore *m* dolce; (*of breath*) freschezza; **now all is sweetness and light** adesso tutti sono felici e contenti.

♦ **sweet nothings** NPL: **to whisper sweet nothings in sb's ear** sussurrare paroline dolci a qn.

♦ **sweet pea** N pisello odoroso.

♦ **sweet pepper** N peperone *m*.

♦ **sweet potato** N patata americana *or* dolce.

♦ **sweet shop** N (*Brit*) negozio di dolciumi.

♦ **sweet-smelling** ['swiːtˌsmɛlɪŋ] ADJ profumato(-a).

♦ **sweet-tempered** [ˌswiːtˈtɛmpəd] ADJ: **to be sweet-tempered** avere un carattere dolce.

♦ **sweet tooth** N: **to have a sweet tooth** avere un debole per i dolci, essere goloso(-a) di dolci.

♦ **sweet william** N (*flower*) garofano a mazzetti.

swell [swɛl] (*vb*: *pt* **swelled**, *pp* **swollen**) **1** N (*of sea*) mare *m* lungo.

2 ADJ (*Am*: *fine, good*) eccezionale, favoloso(-a); **that's just swell** perfetto.

3 VI (*ankle, eye etc*: *also*: **swell up**) gonfiarsi; (*sails*) prendere il vento; (*in size, number*) aumentare; (*sound, music*) diventare più forte; (*river etc*) ingrossarsi; **to swell with pride** gonfiarsi d'orgoglio; **the cheers swelled to a roar** gli applausi si tramutarono in un boato.

4 VT (*numbers, sales etc*) far aumentare; (*sails*) gonfiare; (*river*) ingrossare.

♦ **swell-headed** [ˌswɛlˈhɛdɪd] ADJ (*fam*) borioso(-a), pieno(-a) di sé.

swell·ing ['swɛlɪŋ] N (*Med*) gonfiore *m*, tumefazione *f*.

swel·ter ['swɛltə'] VI soffocare, morire di caldo.

swel·ter·ing ['swɛltərɪŋ] ADJ soffocante, afoso(-a); **I'm sweltering** sto soffocando.

swept [swɛpt] PT, PP of **sweep**.

swerve [swɜːv] **1** N deviazione *f*; (*in car*) sterzata.

2 VI deviare bruscamente; (*in car*) sterzare; (*in ship*) virare; (*boxer*) scartare; **nothing will make him swerve from his aims** niente lo distoglierà dai suoi propositi.

swift [swɪft] **1** ADJ (*comp* -**er**, *superl* -**est**) (*movement*) rapido(-a), repentino(-a); (*runner*) veloce; (*reply, reaction*) pronto(-a).

2 N (*bird*) rondone *m*.

swift·ly ['swɪftlɪ] ADV rapidamente, repentinamente; velocemente; prontamente.

swift·ness ['swɪftnɪs] N (*see adj*) rapidità, repentinità; velocità; prontezza.

swig [swɪg] (*fam*) **1** N (*drink*) sorsata; **he took a swig at his bottle** ha bevuto un lungo sorso dalla bottiglia.

2 VT tracannare.

swill [swɪl] **1** N (*also pej*) broda.

2 VT **a** (*clean*: *also*: **swill out**) risciacquare **b** (*fam*: *drink*: *beer etc*) tracannare.

swim [swɪm] (*vb*: *pt* **swam**, *pp* **swum**) **1** N **a** nuotata; **it's a long swim back to the shore** è una bella nuotata fino alla spiaggia; **to go for a swim** andare a fare una nuotata; **to have a swim** fare una nuotata

b (*fam*): **to be in the swim** essere al corrente.

2 VT (*river etc*) attraversare a nuoto; (*distance*) nuotare per; **to swim the crawl** nuotare a crawl; **to swim a length** fare una vasca; **she can't swim a stroke** non sa nuotare.

3 VI (*gen*) nuotare; (*as sport*) fare nuoto; **to go swimming** andare a nuotare; **to swim across a river** attraversare un fiume a nuoto; **my head is swimming** (*fig*) mi gira la testa; **the meat was swimming in gravy** la carne galleggiava nel sugo; **eyes swimming with tears** occhi inondati di lacrime.

♦ **swim bladder** N (*Zool*) vescica natatoria.

swim·mer ['swɪmə'] N nuotatore(-trice).

swim·ming ['swɪmɪŋ] N nuoto.

♦ **swimming baths** NPL (*Brit*) piscina pubblica.

♦ **swimming cap** N cuffia.

♦ **swimming costume** N (*Brit*) costume *m* da bagno.

♦ **swimming gala** N gara di nuoto.

swim·ming·ly ['swɪmɪŋlɪ] ADV (*smoothly*): **everything went swimmingly** tutto è andato liscio come l'olio.

♦ **swimming pool** N piscina.

♦ **swimming trunks** NPL calzoncini *mpl* da bagno.

swim·suit ['swɪm,suːt] N costume *m* da bagno (*da donna*).

swin·dle ['swɪndl] [1] N truffa.

[2] VT imbrogliare, truffare; **to swindle sb out of sth** estorcere qc a qn con l'inganno.

swin·dler ['swɪndlə'] N imbroglione(-a), truffatore(-trice).

swine [swaɪn] N **a** (*fig fam*: *person*) porco (*fam*); **you swine!** brutto porco! **b** (*pl inv*: *old*: *pig*) maiale *m*.

swing [swɪŋ] (*vb*: *pt*, *pp* **swung**) [1] N **a** (*of pendulum, needle*) oscillazione *f*; (*distance*) arco; **to take a swing at sb** mollare un pugno a qn

b (*seat for swinging*) altalena; **to have a swing** andare sull'altalena; **it's swings and roundabouts** (*fig*) che ci vuoi fare, le cose a volte vanno bene, a volte vanno male

c (*Pol*: *in attitudes, opinions, support*): **there was a swing towards/away from Labour** c'è stato un aumento/una diminuzione di voti per i Laburisti; **a sudden swing in public opinion** un improvviso cambiamento dell'opinione pubblica; **a swing to the left** una svolta a sinistra

d (*Boxing, Golf*) swing *m inv*

e (*rhythm*) ritmo; **to get into the swing of things** entrare nel pieno delle cose; **to be in full swing** essere in pieno corso; **the party went with a swing** la festa è stata una bomba

f (*also*: *swing music*) swing *m*.

[2] VT **a** (*pendulum*) far oscillare; (*person on swing, in hammock*) dondolare, spingere; (*arms, legs*) dondolare, ciondolare; **to swing the door open** spalancare la porta

b (*wield*: *axe, sword*) brandire, roteare; **he swung the case up onto his shoulder** si è messo la valigia sulla spalla; **he swung himself over the wall** si è lanciato al di là del muro; **she swung the car round** girò di colpo la macchina

c (*influence*: *opinion, decision*) influenzare; **she managed to swing it so that we could all go** (*fam*) è riuscita a fare in modo che ci potessimo andare tutti; **what swung it for me was ...** ciò che mi ha fatto decidere è stato....

[3] VI dondolare, oscillare; (*on swing, hammock*) dondolarsi; (*arms, legs*) ciondolare; **to swing to and fro** dondolare avanti e indietro; **the door swung open** la porta si spalancò; **the door swung shut** la porta si chiuse sbattendo; **he'll swing for it** (*fam*) lo impiccheranno; **the road swings south** la strada prende la direzione sud; **he swung round** si voltò bruscamente; **the car swung into the square** la macchina svoltò bruscamente nella piazza; **to swing to the right** (*fig Pol*) svoltare a destra; **to swing into action** entrare in azione.

♦ **swing bridge** N ponte *m* girevole.

♦ **swing door** N porta a vento.

swinge·ing ['swɪndʒɪŋ] ADJ (*cuts*) drastico(-a); (*attack, blow*) violento(-a); (*defeat, majority*) schiacciante; (*taxation*) forte; (*price increase*) enorme.

swing·er ['swɪŋə'] N (*old*): **he's a swinger** (*sexually*) è un farfallone; (*socially*) è un festaiolo.

swing·ing ['swɪŋɪŋ] ADJ (*step*) cadenzato(-a), ritmico(-a); (*rhythm, music*) trascinante; **swinging door** (*Am*) porta a vento.

♦ **swing-wing** ['swɪŋ,wɪŋ] ADJ (*Aer*) a geometria variabile.

swipe [swaɪp] [1] N: **to take a swipe at sb** dare uno schiaffo

a qn.

[2] VT **a** (*hit*: *ball, person*) colpire **b** (*fam*: *steal*) fregare, sgraffignare **c** (*credit card*) far passare nell'apposita macchinetta.

[3] VI: **to swipe at sb/sth** tentare di colpire qn/qc.

swirl [swɜːl] [1] N (*movement*) turbinio, turbine *m*, mulinello; (*of cream etc*) ricciolo.

[2] VI turbinare, far mulinello.

swish [swɪʃ] [1] N (*sound*: *of whip*) schiocco; (: *of skirts, grass*) fruscio.

[2] ADJ (*fam*: *smart*) all'ultimo grido, alla moda.

[3] VT (*whip*) schioccare; (*skirt*) far frusciare; (*tail*) agitare.

[4] VI (*whip*) schioccare; (*skirts, grass*) frusciare.

Swiss [swɪs] [1] ADJ svizzero(-a).

[2] N, PL INV svizzero(-a).

♦ **Swiss French** ADJ svizzero(-a) francese.

♦ **Swiss German** ADJ svizzero(-a) tedesco(-a).

♦ **swiss roll** N (*Culin*) rotolo (*di pan di Spagna*) *farcito di marmellata.*

switch [swɪtʃ] [1] N **a** (*Elec etc*) interruttore *m*

b (*Rail*: *points*) scambio

c (*change*) cambiamento, mutamento; (*exchange*) scambio; **a rapid switch of plan** un improvviso cambiamento di programma

d (*stick*) bacchetta; **riding switch** frustino.

[2] VT **a** (*change*: *plans, jobs*) cambiare; (: *allegiance*): **to switch (to)** spostare (a); (: *conversation*) spostare (su)

b (*exchange*) scambiarsi; (*transpose*: *also*: **switch round, switch over**) scambiare; (: *two objects*) invertire; **I switched hats with him** OR **we switched hats** ci siamo scambiati i cappelli

c (*TV, Radio*: *programme*) cambiare; **to switch the TV to another channel** cambiare canale; **to switch the radio to another programme** cambiare stazione; **to switch the heater to high** regolare la stufa al massimo

d (*Rail*) deviare.

[3] VI (*also*: **switch over**) passare; **he switched to another topic** è passato a un altro argomento; **he has switched to Labour** è passato al partito laburista

► **switch back** [1] VI + ADV (*gen*) ritornare; (*TV, Radio*): **to switch back to the other programme** rimettere l'altro programma, ritornare all'altro programma; **he switched back to being calm** è tornato alla calma.

[2] VT + ADV: **can you switch the heater back to "low"?** puoi rimettere la stufa al minimo?; **to switch the light back on/off** riaccendere/rispegnere la luce

► **switch off** [1] VT + ADV (*Elec, TV, Aut*) spegnere.

[2] VI + ADV (*Elec, TV, Aut*) spegnersi da solo(-a); (*fig fam*: *not listen*) smettere di ascoltare.

► **switch on** [1] VT + ADV (*Elec, TV etc*) accendere; (*water supply*) aprire; (*machine, Aut*) mettere in moto, avviare; (: *ignition*) inserire; **to switch on the charm** diventare tutto(-a) gentile.

[2] VI + ADV (*heater, oven*) accendersi da solo(-a).

switch·back ['swɪtʃ,bæk] N (*Brit*: *roller coaster*) montagne *fpl* russe.

switch·blade ['swɪtʃ,bleɪd] N (*also*: **switchblade knife**) coltello a scatto.

switch·board ['swɪtʃ,bɔːd] N centralino.

♦ **switchboard operator** N centralinista *m/f*.

switch·over ['swɪtʃ,əʊvə'] N passaggio; **the switchover to the metric system** l'adozione *f* del sistema metrico decimale.

Swit·zer·land ['swɪtsələnd] N la Svizzera.

swiv·el ['swɪvl] [1] N perno.

2 VI (*also:* **swivel round**) girarsi.
swol·len ['swəʊlən] 1 PP of **swell**.

2 ADJ (*ankle, finger, stomach*) gonfio(-a); (*river*) in piena; her eyes were swollen with tears aveva gli occhi gonfi di pianto; you'll give him a swollen head (*fig*) gli farai montare la testa.

♦ **swollen-headed** ['swəʊlən'hɛdɪd] ADJ (*Brit pej*) borioso (-a), pieno(-a) di sé.

swoon [swu:n] (*old*) 1 N svenimento.

2 VI svenire; to swoon over sb (*fig*) morire dietro a qn.

swoop [swu:p] 1 N (*of bird etc*) picchiata; (*by police*): swoop (on) incursione *f* (in); in one fell swoop in un colpo solo.

2 VI (*bird: also:* **swoop down**) scendere in picchiata; (*police*): to swoop (on) fare un'incursione (in); the plane swooped low over the village l'aereo è sceso in picchiata sul villaggio.

swop [swɒp] N, VT = **swap**.

sword [sɔ:d] N spada.

♦ **sword dance** N danza delle spade.

sword·fish ['sɔ:d,fɪʃ] N pesce *m* spada *inv.*

sword·play ['sɔ:d,pleɪ] N (*technique*) abilità nel maneggiare la spada; (*fighting*) combattimento con la spada.

swords·man ['sɔ:dzmən] N (*pl* **-men**) spadaccino.

swords·man·ship ['sɔ:dzmən,ʃɪp] N abilità con la spada.

swore [swɔ:ʳ] PT of **swear**.

sworn [swɔ:n] 1 PP of **swear**.

2 ADJ (*enemy*) giurato(-a); (*friend*) per la pelle; (*ally*) fedele; (*testimony*) giurato(-a), fatto(-a) sotto giuramento.

swot [swɒt] 1 VT (*fam*) sgobbare su; to swot up (on) one's maths ripassare tutta la matematica.

2 VI sgobbare; to swot for an exam sgobbare per un esame.

3 N (*pej*) sgobbone(-a), secchione(-a).

swum [swʌm] PP of **swim**.

swung [swʌŋ] PT, PP of **swing**.

syca·more ['sɪkəmɔ:ʳ] N sicomoro.

syco·phant ['sɪkəfənt] N adulatore(-trice).

syco·phan·tic [,sɪkə'fæntɪk] ADJ (*frm*) ossequioso(-a), adulatore(-trice).

Syd·ney ['sɪdnɪ] N Sydney *f.*

syl·lab·ic [sɪ'læbɪk] ADJ sillabico(-a).

syl·la·ble ['sɪləbl] N sillaba.

syl·la·bub ['sɪlə,bʌb] N (*Culin: dessert*) ≈ zabaione *m.*

syl·la·bus ['sɪləbəs] N (*Scol, Univ*) programma *m*; on the syllabus in programma d'esame.

syl·lo·gism ['sɪlə,dʒɪzəm] N sillogismo.

sylph [sɪlf] N silfo.

sylph·like ['sɪlf,laɪk] ADJ (*woman*) snella; (*figure*) da silfide.

sym·bio·sis [,sɪmbɪ'əʊsɪs] N simbiosi *f inv.*

sym·bi·ot·ic [,sɪmbɪ'ɒtɪk] ADJ (*frm: relationship*) simbiotico (-a).

sym·bol ['sɪmbəl] N simbolo.

sym·bol·ic [sɪm'bɒlɪk], **sym·boli·cal** [sɪm'bɒlɪkəl] ADJ simbolico(-a); to be symbolic of sth simboleggiare qc.

sym·boli·cal·ly [sɪm'bɒlɪkəlɪ] ADV emblematicamente, simbolicamente.

sym·bol·ism ['sɪmbə,lɪzəm] N simbolismo.

sym·boli·za·tion [,sɪmbəlaɪ'zeɪʃən] N simbolizzazione *f.*

sym·bol·ize ['sɪmbə,laɪz] VT simboleggiare.

sym·met·ri·cal [sɪ'mɛtrɪkəl] ADJ simmetrico(-a).

sym·met·ri·cal·ly [sɪ'mɛtrɪkəlɪ] ADV simmetricamente.

sym·me·try ['sɪmɪtrɪ] N simmetria; line symmetry simmetria rispetto a una retta; rotational symmetry simmetria

rotazionale.

sym·pa·thet·ic [,sɪmpə'θɛtɪk] ADJ (*showing pity*) compassionevole; (*kind, understanding*) comprensivo(-a); they were sympathetic but could not help sono stati molto comprensivi ma non hanno potuto aiutare; to be sympathetic to a cause (*well-disposed*) simpatizzare per una causa; to be sympathetic towards (*person*) essere comprensivo(-a) nei confronti di.

sym·pa·theti·cal·ly [,sɪmpə'θɛtɪkəlɪ] ADV (*see adj*) in modo compassionevole; con comprensione.

sym·pa·thize ['sɪmpə,θaɪz] VI: to sympathize (with sb) (*feel pity*) partecipare al dolore (di qn); (*understand*) capire (qn); I sympathize with you in your grief ti sono molto vicino nel dolore; I sympathize with what you say, but ... capisco quello che vuoi dire, ma... .

sym·pa·thiz·er ['sɪmpə,θaɪzəʳ] N (*fig: esp Pol*): sympathizer (with) simpatizzante *m/f* (di).

sym·pa·thy ['sɪmpəθɪ] N a (*pity, compassion*) compassione *f*; you have my deepest sympathy *or* sympathies hai tutta la mia comprensione; you won't get any sympathy from me! non venire a piangere da me!; with our deepest sympathy con le nostre più sincere condoglianze; a letter of sympathy una lettera di cordoglio b (*understanding*) comprensione *f*; (*fellow-feeling, agreement*) solidarietà; I am in sympathy with your suggestions mi trovo d'accordo con i tuoi suggerimenti; to strike in sympathy with sb scioperare per solidarietà con qn.

sym·phon·ic [sɪm'fɒnɪk] ADJ sinfonico(-a).

sym·pho·ny ['sɪmfənɪ] N sinfonia.

♦ **symphony orchestra** N orchestra sinfonica.

sym·po·sium [sɪm'pəʊzɪəm] N (*pl* **symposia**) simposio.

symp·tom ['sɪmptəm] N sintomo.

symp·to·mat·ic [,sɪmptə'mætɪk] ADJ: symptomatic (of) sintomatico(-a) (di).

syna·gogue ['sɪnə,gɒg] N sinagoga.

syn·apse ['saɪnæps] N sinapsi *f.*

sync [sɪŋk] N (*Tech*): in/out of sync in/fuori sincronia; everything is out of sync (*fig*) è tutto sballato(-a).

syn·chro·mesh [,sɪŋkrəʊ'mɛʃ] N cambio sincronizzato.

syn·chro·ni·za·tion [,sɪŋkrənaɪ'zeɪʃən] N sincronizzazione *f.*

syn·chro·nize ['sɪŋkrə,naɪz] 1 VT sincronizzare.

2 VI: to synchronize with essere in sincronia con.

syn·chro·nized swim·ming ['sɪŋkrə,naɪzd'swɪmɪŋ] N nuoto sincronizzato.

syn·cline ['sɪŋklaɪn] N sinclinale *f.*

syn·co·pate ['sɪŋkə,peɪt] VT sincopare.

syn·co·pa·tion [,sɪŋkə'peɪʃən] N (*Mus*) sincope *f.*

syn·di·cate [*n* 'sɪndɪkɪt; *vb* 'sɪndɪ,keɪt] 1 N (*Comm etc*) sindacato; (*Press*) agenzia di stampa.

2 VT (*Press*) vendere tramite agenzia di stampa.

syn·drome ['sɪndrəʊm] N sindrome *f.*

syn·er·esis [sɪ'nɪərɪsɪs] N (*Gram*) crasi *f.*

syn·od ['sɪnəd] N sinodo.

syno·nym ['sɪnənɪm] N sinonimo.

syn·ony·mous [sɪ'nɒnɪməs] ADJ: synonymous (with) sinonimo(-a) (di).

syn·ony·my [sɪ'nɒnəmɪ] N sinonimia.

syn·op·sis [sɪ'nɒpsɪs] N (*pl* **synopses** [sɪ'nɒpsi:z]) (*of plot*) trama.

syn·tac·tic [sɪn'tæktɪk], **syntactical** [sɪn'tæktɪk(əl)] ADJ sintattico(-a).

syn·tax ['sɪntæks] N sintassi *f inv.*

syn·the·sis ['sɪnθəsɪs] N (*pl* **syntheses** ['sɪnθəsi:z]) sintesi *f*

inv.

syn·the·size ['sɪnθəˌsaɪz] VT sintetizzare.

syn·the·siz·er ['sɪnθəˌsaɪzə'] N (*Mus*) sintetizzatore *m.*

syn·thet·ic [sɪn'θɛtɪk] ⊡ ADJ (*fabric etc*) sintetico(-a).

⊡ N prodotto sintetico; (*Textiles*) fibra sintetica.

syphi·lis ['sɪfɪlɪs] N sifilide *f.*

syphi·lit·ic [ˌsɪfɪ'lɪtɪk] ADJ, N sifilitico(-a).

sy·phon ['saɪfən] N, VB = **siphon**.

Syria ['sɪrɪə] N la Siria.

Syr·ian ['sɪrɪən] ADJ, N siriano(-a).

sy·ringe [sɪ'rɪndʒ] ⊡ N siringa.

⊡ VT (*Med*) siringare.

syr·up ['sɪrəp] N sciroppo; **golden syrup** (*Brit*) melassa raffinata.

syr·upy ['sɪrəpɪ] ADJ (*also fig*) sciropposo(-a).

sys·tem ['sɪstəm] N (*method*) sistema *m*; (*network*) rete *f*; (*Anat*) apparato; **it was quite a shock to his system** è stato uno shock per il suo organismo; **to get sth out of one's system** (*fig*) sfogarsi.

sys·tem·at·ic [ˌsɪstə'mætɪk] ADJ sistematico(-a).

sys·tem·ati·cal·ly [ˌsɪstə'mætɪkəɪ] ADV sistematicamente.

sys·tema·ti·za·tion [ˌsɪstəmətar'zeɪʃən] N sistematizzazione *f.*

sys·tema·tize ['sɪstəməˌtaɪz] VT sistematizzare.

♦ **systems analyst** N analista *m/f* di sistemi.

♦ **systems disk** N (*Comput*) disco del sistema.

sys·to·le ['sɪstəlɪ] N sistole *f.*

T

T, t [tiː] N (*letter*) T, t *m or f inv*; **T for Tommy** ≈ T come Taranto; **it fits you to a T** (*fam*) ti sta a pennello; **that's him to a T** (*fam*) è proprio lui.

TA [ˌtiːˈeɪ] N ABBR (*Brit*) = **Territorial Army**.

ta [tɑː] EXCL (*Brit fam*) grazie!

tab [tæb] [1] N ABBR = **tabulator**.

[2] N (*label*) etichetta; (*flap on garment*) cartellino; (*Am fam: bill*) conto; **to keep tabs on sb/sth** (*fig fam*) tenere d'occhio qn/qc; **to pick up the tab** (*Am fam*) pagare il conto.

tab·by [ˈtæbɪ] N (*also:* **tabby cat**) (gatto(-a)) soriano(-a), gatto(-a) tigrato(-a).

tab·er·nac·le [ˈtæbəˌnækl] N tabernacolo.

ta·ble [ˈteɪbl] [1] N **a** tavolo; (*for meals*) tavola; (*also:* **coffee table**) tavolino; **card table** tavolino da gioco; **to lay** *or* **set the table** apparecchiare *or* preparare la tavola; **to clear the table** sparecchiare; **at table** a tavola; **the entire table was in fits of laughter** l'intera tavolata moriva dalle risate; **to drink sb under the table** battere qn nel bere; **to turn the tables on sb** (*fig*) rovesciare la situazione a danno di qn

b (*Math, Chem: illustration*) tavola; (*chart*) tabella; **table of contents** indice *m*; **league table** (*Ftbl, Rugby*) classifica.

[2] VT (*bill, motion: Brit: propose*) presentare; (*: Am: postpone*) rinviare.

tab·leau [ˈtæbləʊ] N (*pl* **tableaux**) (*Theatre*) quadro vivente.

table·cloth [ˈteɪblˌklɒθ] N tovaglia.

♦ **table d'hôte** [ˌtɑːblˈdəʊt] [1] N pasto a prezzo fisso.
[2] ADJ (*meal*) a prezzo fisso.

♦ **table football** N calcetto, calcio-balilla *m*.

♦ **table lamp** N lampada da tavolo.

table·land [ˈteɪblˌlænd] N tavolato, altopiano.

♦ **table manners** NPL maniere *fpl* a tavola.

table·mat [ˈteɪblˌmæt] N tovaglietta.

♦ **table napkin** N tovagliolo.

♦ **table salt** N sale *m* fino *or* da tavola.

table·spoon [ˈteɪblˌspuːn] N cucchiaio da portata *or* da tavola; (*also:* **tablespoonful:** *as measurement*)

cucchiaiata.

tab·let [ˈtæblɪt] N (*inscribed stone*) lapide *f*, targa; (*Med*) compressa; (*: for sucking*) pastiglia; (*for writing*) blocco; **tablet of soap** (*Brit*) saponetta.

♦ **table talk** N conversazione *f* a tavola.

♦ **table tennis** N tennis *m* da tavolo, ping-pong ® *m*.

♦ **table tennis player** N giocatore(-trice) di ping-pong.

♦ **table top** N piano del tavolo.

table·ware [ˈteɪblˌwɛəʳ] N servizi *mpl* da tavola.

♦ **table wine** N vino da tavola.

tab·loid [ˈtæblɔɪd] N (*newspaper*) tabloid *m inv*.

♦ **tabloid press** N: **the tabloid press** i tabloid.

ta·boo [təˈbuː] ADJ, N tabù (*m*) *inv*.

tabu·lar [ˈtæbjʊləʳ] ADJ (*frm*) tabellare; **in tabular form** sotto forma di tabella.

tabu·late [ˈtæbjʊˌleɪt] VT (*data, figures*) disporre in tabelle, tabulare.

tabu·la·tion [ˌtæbjʊˈleɪʃən] N tabulazione *f*.

tabu·la·tor [ˈtæbjʊˌleɪtəʳ] N tabulatore *m*.

tacho·graph [ˈtækəˌɡrɑːf] N tachigrafo.

ta·chom·eter [tæˈkɒmɪtəʳ] N tachimetro.

tac·it [ˈtæsɪt] ADJ tacito(-a).

tac·it·ly [ˈtæsɪtlɪ] ADV tacitamente.

taci·turn [ˈtæsɪˌtɜːn] ADJ taciturno(-a).

taci·tur·nity [ˌtæsɪˈtɜːnɪtɪ] N l'essere taciturno, carattere *m* taciturno.

Tacitus [ˈtæsɪtəs] N (*History, Literature*) Tacito.

tack [tæk] [1] N **a** (*nail*) bulletta; (*: for upholstery*) borchia; (*Am fam: also:* **thumbtack**) puntina da disegno; **to get down to brass tacks** venire al sodo

b (*Naut: course*) bordo; **to be on the port/starboard tack** avere le mura a sinistra/dritta; **to change tack** virare di bordo; (*fig*) cambiare linea di condotta; **to be on the right/wrong tack** (*fig*) essere sulla buona strada/sulla strada sbagliata; **to try a different tack** (*fig*) prendere le cose per un altro verso

c (*stitch*) punto d'imbastitura

d (*for horse*) selleria, equipaggiamento.

[2] VT **a** (*nail*) imbullettare

b (*Sewing*) imbastire; (*fig: add*): **to tack sth on to (the**

end of) sth (*of letter, book*) aggiungere qc alla fine di qc. $\boxed{3}$ VI (*Naut: change direction*) virare di bordo (in prua); (*go zigzag*) bordeggiare.

tack·ing ['tækɪŋ] N **a** (*Sewing*) imbastitura **b** (*Naut*) virata.

tack·le ['tækl] $\boxed{1}$ N **a** (*lifting gear*) paranco **b** (*equipment: esp for sport*) attrezzatura, equipaggiamento
  c (*Ftbl*) contrasto; (*Rugby*) placcaggio.
  $\boxed{2}$ VT (*Ftbl*) contrastare; (*Rugby*) placcare; (*thief, intruder*) agguantare; (*fig: person, problem, job*) affrontare; **I'll tackle him about it at once** affronterò subito la cosa con lui.

♦ **tack room** N selleria.

tacky ['tækɪ] ADJ (*comp* **-ier**, *superl* **-iest**) (*sticky*) appiccicoso(-a), appiccicaticcio(-a); (: *of paint, glue*) ancora bagnato(-a), non ancora asciutto(-a); (*fam: shabby*) scadente; (: *tasteless*) di cattivo gusto.

tact [tækt] N tatto.

tact·ful ['tæktful] ADJ (*person*) pieno(-a) di tatto; (*remark, reply*) discreto(-a); **to be tactful** avere tatto.

tact·ful·ly ['tæktfəlɪ] ADV con tatto, con discrezione.

tac·tic ['tæktɪk] N tattica; see also **tactics**.

tac·ti·cal ['tæktɪkəl] ADJ tattico(-a).

tac·ti·cal·ly ['tæktɪkəlɪ] ADV tatticamente.

♦ **tactical voting** N voto tattico.

tac·ti·cian [tæk'tɪʃən] N (*Mil, fig*) stratega *m/f*.

tac·tics ['tæktɪks] N, NPL tattica; **strong-arm tactics** le maniere forti.

tac·tile ['tæktaɪl] ADJ tattile.

tact·less ['tæktlɪs] ADJ (*person*) privo(-a) di tatto, che manca di tatto; (*remark*) indelicato(-a).

tact·less·ly ['tæktlɪslɪ] ADV senza tatto.

tad·pole ['tædpəʊl] N girino.

taf·fe·ta ['tæfɪtə] N taffettà *m inv*.

taf·fy ['tæfɪ] N (*Am*) caramella *f* mou *inv*.

tag [tæg] N **a** (*label*) etichetta; (*metal point*) puntale *m*; **price/name tag** etichetta del prezzo/con il nome **b** (*game*) chiapparello

▶ **tag along** VI + ADV andare (*or* venire); **do you mind if I tag along?** ti dispiace se vengo anch'io?; **to tag along behind sb** andare (*or* venire) dietro a qn

▶ **tag on** VT + ADV: **to tag sth on (to the end of sth)** aggiungere qc (alla fine di qc).

Ta·hi·ti [tɑːˈhiːtɪ] N Tahiti *f*.

tail [teɪl] $\boxed{1}$ N (*gen*) coda; (*of shirt*) estremità inferiore; **to put a tail on sb** (*fig fam*) far pedinare qn; **he was right on my tail** mi stava alle calcagna; **to turn tail** voltare la schiena; **he went off with his tail between his legs** (*fig*) se ne è andato con la coda fra le gambe; see also **head, tails**.
  $\boxed{2}$ VT (*fam: follow: suspect*) pedinare, seguire

▶ **tail away, tail off** VI + ADV (*in size, quality*) diminuire gradatamente.

tail·back ['teɪlˌbæk] N (*Brit Aut*) coda.

♦ **tail coat** N frac *m inv*, marsina.

♦ **tail end** N (*of party, meeting*) fine *f*; (*of train, procession*) coda; **to be at the tail end of the procession/queue** essere in coda alla processione/in fondo alla coda.

♦ **tail flap** N (*Aer*) timone *m* di profondità.

tail·gate ['teɪlˌgeɪt] N (*Aut*) portellone *m* posteriore.

♦ **tail light** N (*Aut*) fanalino di coda; (*Rail*) luce *f* di coda.

tai·lor ['teɪlə'] $\boxed{1}$ N sarto; **tailor's dummy** manichino (da sarto); **tailor's (shop)** sartoria (da uomo).

$\boxed{2}$ VT (*suit*) confezionare; (*fig*:): **to tailor sth (to)** adattare qc (alle esigenze di).

tai·lored ['teɪləd] ADJ (*suit, dress*) attillato(-a).

tail·or·ing ['teɪlərɪŋ] N (*cut*) taglio.

♦ **tailor-made** ['teɪləˈmeɪd] ADJ (*also fig*) fatto(-a) su misura; (*fig*): **it's tailor-made for you** è fatto apposta per te.

tail·plane ['teɪlˌpleɪn] N (*Aer*) stabilizzatore *m*.

tails [teɪlz] N **a** SG (*of coin*) testa; **heads or tails** testa o croce **b** PL (*Dress*) frac *m inv*, marsina.

tail·spin ['teɪlˌspɪn] N (*Aer*) vite *f* di coda.

tail·wind ['teɪlˌwɪnd] N vento in coda.

taint [teɪnt] $\boxed{1}$ N (*fig*) macchia; **the taint of madness** il marchio della pazzia.
  $\boxed{2}$ VT (*meat, food*) far avariare; (*fig: reputation*) infangare.

taint·ed ['teɪntɪd] ADJ (*food*) avariato(-a), guasto(-a), andato(-a) a male; (*water, air*) contaminato(-a); (*fig: system*) inquinato(-a); (: *reputation*) infangato(-a).

Tai·wan [taɪˈwɑːn] N la Repubblica di Taiwan.

Ta·jiki·stan [tɑːˌdʒɪkɪˈstɑːn] N il Tagikistan.

take [teɪk] (*vb: pt* **took**, *pp* **taken**) $\boxed{1}$ VT **a** (*gen*) prendere; (*remove, steal*) portar via; **let me take your coat** posso prenderti il cappotto?; **to take sb's hand** prendere qn per mano; **to take sb's arm** appoggiarsi al braccio di qn; **to take sb by the throat** afferrare qn alla gola; **he must be taken alive** dev'essere preso vivo; **to take the train** prendere il treno; **take the first on the left** prenda la prima a sinistra; **he hasn't taken any food for four days** non mangia nulla da quattro giorni; **to take notes** prendere appunti; **take 6 from 9** (*Math*) 9 meno 6; **he took £5 off the price** ha fatto uno sconto di 5 sterline; **to take a trick** (*Cards*) fare una presa; **"to be taken three times a day"** (*Med*) "da prendersi tre volte al dì"; **to take cold/fright** prendere freddo/paura; **to be taken ill** avere un malore
  b (*bring, carry*) portare; (*accompany*) accompagnare; **I took the children with me** ho portato i bambini con me; **to take for a walk** (*child, dog*) portare a fare una passeggiata
  c (*require: effort, courage*) volerci, occorrere; (*Gram*) prendere, reggere; **it took me two hours to do it** $\boxed{\text{OR}}$ **I took two hours to do it** mi ci sono volute due ore per farlo; **it won't take long** non ci vorrà molto tempo; **she's got what it takes to do the job** ha i requisiti necessari per quel lavoro; **it takes a brave man to do that** ci vuole del coraggio per farlo; **it takes a lot of time/courage** occorre *or* ci vuole molto tempo/coraggio; **that will take some explaining** non sarà facile da spiegare; **it takes some believing** bisogna fare uno sforzo per crederci
  d (*accept, receive*) accettare; (*obtain, win: prize*) vincere, ottenere; (: *1st place*) conquistare; (*Comm: money*) incassare; **he didn't take my advice** non mi ha ascoltato; **how did he take the news?** come ha preso la notizia?; **please take a seat** prego, si sieda; **is this seat taken?** è occupato (questo posto)?; **it's worth taking a chance** vale la pena di correre il rischio; **it's £50, take it or leave it** sono 50 sterline, prendere o lasciare; **can you take it from here?** (*handing over task*) puoi andare avanti tu?; **you must take us as you find us** devi prenderci per quel che siamo
  e (*have room or capacity for: passengers*) contenere; (*support: subj: bridge*) avere una portata di; (: *chair*) tenere; **the hall will take 200 people** nel salone c'è posto per 200 persone; **the bus takes 60 passengers**

l'autobus porta 60 persone; **it will take at least five litres** contiene almeno cinque litri

f (*conduct*: *meeting*) condurre; (: *church service*) officiare; (*teach, study*: *course*) fare; (*exam, test*) fare, sostenere; **the professor is taking the French course himself** sarà il professore stesso a fare *or* tenere il corso di francese; **I only took Russian for one year** ho fatto russo solo per un anno; **I took the driving test** ho fatto *or* sostenuto l'esame di guida

g (*understand, assume*) pensare; (*consider*: *case, example*) prendere; **how old do you take him to be?** quanti anni pensi che abbia?; **I took him for a doctor** l'ho preso per un dottore; **I took him to be foreign** l'ho preso per uno straniero; **I take it that ...** suppongo che...; **may I take it that ...?** allora posso star certo che...?; **take it from me!** credimi!; **take D.H. Lawrence, for example** prendete D.H. Lawrence, per esempio

h (*put up with, tolerate*: *climate, alcohol*) sopportare; **she can't take the heat** non sopporta il caldo; **I can't take any more!** non ce la faccio più!; **I won't take no for an answer** non accetterò una risposta negativa *or* un rifiuto

i (*negotiate*: *bend*) prendere; (: *fence*) saltare

j (*attracted*): **to be taken with sb/sth** essere tutto(-a) preso(-a) da qn/qc; **I'm quite taken with the idea** l'idea non mi dispiace per niente

k (*as function verb*: *see other element*): **to take a photograph** fare una fotografia; **to take a bath/shower** fare un bagno/una doccia; **take your time!** calma!; **it took me by surprise** mi ha colto di sorpresa.

2 VI (*dye, fire*) prendere; (*injection*) fare effetto; (*plant, cutting*) attecchire.

3 N (*Cine*) ripresa

▶ **take after** VI + PREP assomigliare a

▶ **take against** VI + PREP prendere in antipatia

▶ **take along** VT + ADV portare

▶ **take apart** VT + ADV (*clock, machine*) smontare; (*fig fam*: *criticize*) demolire

▶ **take aside** VT + ADV prendere in disparte

▶ **take away** 1 VI + ADV: **to take away from sth** danneggiare qc; **his bad temper took away from the pleasure of our party** ci ha guastato un po' la festa con il suo cattivo umore.

2 VT + ADV **a** (*subtract*): **to take away (from)** sottrarre (da)

b (*remove*: *person, thing, privilege*) togliere; (*carry away, lead away*) portar via; **we took him away on holiday** l'abbiamo portato in vacanza; **pizzas to take away** pizze *fpl* da asporto

▶ **take back** VT + ADV **a** (*get back, reclaim*) riprendere; (*retract*: *statement, promise*) ritirare

b (*return*: *book, goods, person*) riportare; **can you take him back home?** puoi riaccompagnarlo a casa?; **it takes me back to my childhood** (*fig*) mi ha fatto tornare alla mia infanzia

▶ **take down** VT + ADV **a** (*curtains, picture, vase from shelf*) tirare giù

b (*dismantle*: *scaffolding*) smontare; (: *building*) demolire

c (*write down*: *notes, address*) prendere; (: *letter*) scrivere

▶ **take in** VT + ADV **a** (*bring in*: *object, harvest*) portare dentro; (: *person*) far entrare; (: *lodger*) prendere, ospitare; (: *orphan*) accogliere; (: *stray dog*) raccogliere

b (*receive*: *money*) incassare; (: *laundry, sewing*) prendere a domicilio

c (*Sewing*) stringere

d (*include, cover*) coprire; (*prices*) includere, comprendere; **we took in Florence on the way** abbiamo visitato anche Firenze durante il viaggio

e (*grasp, understand*: *meaning, complex subject*) capire; (: *situation*) rendersi conto di; (: *impressions, sights*) assimilare; (: *visually*: *surroundings, people, area*) prendere nota con uno sguardo; **he took the situation in at a glance** ha afferrato subito la situazione

f (*deceive, cheat*) imbrogliare, abbindolare; **to be taken in by appearances** farsi ingannare dalle apparenze

▶ **take off** 1 VI + ADV **a** (*plane, passengers*) decollare; (*high jumper*) spiccare un salto.

2 VT + ADV **a** (*remove*: *clothes*) togliere *or* togliersi; (: *price tag, lid, item from menu*) togliere; (: *leg, limb*) amputare; (*cancel*: *train*) sopprimere

b (*deduct*: *from bill, price*): **she took 50p off** ha fatto 50 penny di sconto

c (*lead away*: *person, object*) portare; **she was taken off to the hospital** è stata portata all'ospedale; **to take o.s. off** andarsene

d (*imitate*) imitare.

3 VT + PREP **a** (*remove*: *clothes, price tag, lid*) togliere da; (: *item from menu*) cancellare da; (*cancel*: *train*) togliere da; **to take sb off sth** (*remove from duty, job*) allontanare qn da qc; **they took him off the Financial Page** (*journalist*) gli hanno tolto la pagina economica

b (*deduct*: *from bill, price*): **he took 5% off the price for me** mi ha fatto uno sconto del 5% sul prezzo

▶ **take on** 1 VI + ADV **a** (*old fam*: *become upset*) prendersela

b (*song, fashion*) fare presa.

2 VT + ADV **a** (*work*) accettare, intraprendere; (*responsibility*) prendersi, addossarsi; (*bet, challenger*) affrontare

b (*worker, fig*: *qualities, form*) assumere; (*cargo, passengers*) caricare; **her face took on a wistful expression** sul suo volto si era dipinta un'espressione malinconica

▶ **take out** VT + ADV **a** (*bring, carry out*) portare fuori; **he took the dog out for a walk** ha portato il cane a passeggio; **can I take you out to lunch?** posso invitarti a pranzo fuori?

b (*extract*: *appendix, tooth*) togliere; (*remove*: *stain*) rimuovere, togliere; (*pull out*: *from pocket, drawer*): **to take sth out of sth** tirare fuori qc da qc, estrarre qc da qc

c (*insurance, patent, licence*) prendere, ottenere, procurarsi

d : **to take sb out of himself** far distrarre qn; **redecorating a house takes it out of you** è spossante ridipingere una casa; **don't take it out on me!** non prendertela con me!

▶ **take over** 1 VI + ADV (*dictator, political party*) prendere il potere; **to take over from sb** prendere le consegne da qn, subentrare a qn.

2 VT + ADV (*debts, business*) rilevare; (*company*) assumere il controllo di; **to take over sb's job** subentrare a qn nel lavoro; **the tourists have taken over Florence** (*fig*) i turisti hanno preso d'assalto Firenze

▶ **take to** VI + PREP **a** (*develop liking for*: *person*) prendere in simpatia; (: *games, surroundings, activity*) prendere gusto a; **I just can't take to my friend's husband** il marito della mia amica non riesce proprio a piacermi; **she didn't take kindly to the idea** l'idea non le è piaciuta per niente

b (*form habit of*): **to take to sth** darsi a qc; **to take to doing sth** prendere *or* cominciare a fare qc

c (*escape to*) fuggire verso; **to take to one's bed** mettersi a letto

▶ **take up** 1 VI + ADV; **to take up with sb** fare amicizia con qn; **she took up with bad company** si è messa a frequentare cattive compagnie.

2 VT + ADV **a** (*raise, lift*) raccogliere; (: *subj*: *bus*) prendere; (: *carpet, floorboards*) sollevare; (: *road*) spaccare; (: *dress, hem*) accorciare

b (*lead, carry upstairs*) portare su

c (*continue*) riprendere

d (*occupy*: *time, attention*) assorbire; (: *space*) occupare; **it will take up the whole of our Sunday** ci porterà via tutta la domenica; **he's very taken up with his work** è molto preso dal suo lavoro; **he's very taken up with her** non fa che pensare a lei

e (*absorb*: *liquids*) assorbire

f (*raise question of*: *matter, point*) affrontare

g (*start*: *job, duties*) cominciare; (: *hobby, sport*): **to take up painting/golf/photography** cominciare a dipingere/giocare a golf/fare fotografie; **to take up a career as** intraprendere la carriera di

h (*accept*: *offer, challenge*) accettare; **I'll take you up on your offer** accetto la tua offerta

i (*adopt*: *cause, case, person*) appoggiare

▶ **take upon** VT + PREP: **to take sth upon o.s.** prendersi la responsabilità di qc; **to take it upon o.s. to do sth** prendersi la responsabilità di fare qc.

♦ **take·away** ['teɪkə,wəɪ] (*Brit*) 1 N (*shop*) ≈ rosticceria; (*meal*) piatto pronto (*da asporto*).

2 ADJ (*food*) da asporto, da portar via.

♦ **take–home pay** ['teɪkhəʊm,peɪ] N stipendio netto.

tak·en ['teɪkən] PP of **take**.

♦ **take·off** ['teɪk,ɒf] N **a** (*Aer*) decollo; (*Horse-riding*) battuta **b** (*fam*: *imitation*) imitazione *f*.

take·out ['teɪk,aʊt] ADJ (*Am*) = **takeaway**.

take·over ['teɪk,əʊvə'] N (*Comm*) assorbimento.

♦ **takeover bid** N offerta di assorbimento.

tak·er ['teɪkə'] N: **drug-takers** drogati *mpl*; **at £100 he found few takers** per 100 sterline ha trovato pochi acquirenti; **his suggestion found no takers** la sua proposta non è stata accolta.

tak·ing ['teɪkɪŋ] ADJ (*attractive*) accattivante.

tak·ings ['teɪkɪŋz] NPL (*Fin*) introiti *mpl*, entrate *fpl*; (*at show*) incasso.

talc [tælk], **tal·cum pow·der** ['tælkəm,paʊdə'] N talco.

tale [teɪl] N (*gen*) storia; (*story*) racconto; (*legend*) leggenda; (*pej*) fandonia; **to tell tales** (*inform*) fare la spia; (*lies*) dire bugie; **he told us the tale of his escape** ci ha raccontato la storia della sua fuga.

tal·ent ['tælənt] N **a** (*skill*) talento; **he has a talent for languages** è portato per le lingue, ha facilità nell'apprendere le lingue; **there isn't much musical talent in this town** non ci sono molti grandi talenti musicali in questa città; **there's not much talent about tonight** (*Brit fam*: *attractive people*) non c'è nessuno di decente in giro stasera

b (*Bible*) talento.

tal·ent·ed ['tæləntɪd] ADJ di talento.

♦ **talent scout** N talent scout *m/f inv*.

tal·is·man ['tælɪzmən] N talismano.

talk [tɔ:k] 1 N **a** (*conversation*) conversazione *f*; (*chat*) chiacchierata; (*speech*) discorso; (*interview*) discussione *f*; **talks** NPL (*Pol*) colloqui *mpl*; **I must have a talk with you** devo parlarti

b (*lecture*) conferenza; **to give a talk** tenere una conferenza; **he will give us a talk on ...** ci parlerà di...; **to give a talk on the radio** parlare alla radio

c (*gossip*) dicerie *fpl*, chiacchiere *fpl*; **the talk was all about the wedding** non si faceva che parlare del matrimonio; **there has been a lot of talk about him** si è molto parlato di lui; **she's the talk of the town** è sulla bocca di tutti; **it's just talk** sono solo chiacchiere.

2 VI (*gen*) parlare; (*discuss*) discutere; (*chatter*) chiacchierare; **to talk about** parlare di; (*converse*) discorrere *or* conversare di; **to talk to/with sb about** *or* **of sth** parlare a/con qn di qc; **to talk to o.s.** parlare da solo; **try to keep him talking** cerca di farlo parlare; **to get o.s. talked about** far parlare di sé; **it's all right for you to talk!** parli bene tu!; **look who's talking!** senti chi parla!, parli proprio tu!; **now you're talking!** questo sì che è parlare!; **he talks too much** (*talkative*) parla troppo; (*indiscreet*) non sa tenere la bocca chiusa; **they are talking of going to Sicily** pensano di andare in Sicilia; **who were you talking to?** con chi stavi parlando?; **he knows what he's talking about** lui sì che se ne intende; **talking of films, have you seen ...?** a proposito di film, hai visto...?.

3 VT (*a language, slang*) parlare; **they were talking Arabic** parlavano arabo; **to talk business** parlare di affari; **to talk shop** parlare del lavoro *or* degli affari; **to talk nonsense** dire stupidaggini; **to talk sb into doing sth** persuadere *or* convincere qn a fare qc; **to talk sb out of doing sth** dissuadere qn dal fare qc

▶ **talk back** VI + ADV: **to talk back (to sb)** rispondere impertinentemente (a qn)

▶ **talk down** 1 VI + ADV: **to talk down to sb** parlare a qn con condiscendenza.

2 VT + ADV: **to talk a plane** (*or* pilot) **down** guidare l'atterraggio dalla torre di controllo

▶ **talk out** VT + ADV: **to talk things out** mettere le cose in chiaro discutendone

▶ **talk over** VT + ADV discutere; **I'll have to talk it over with my wife** devo parlarne con mia moglie

▶ **talk round** 1 VT + ADV: **to talk sb round** convincere qn.

2 VI + PREP (*subject, problem*) girare intorno a.

talka·tive ['tɔ:kətɪv] ADJ loquace, ciarliero(-a).

talked-of ['tɔ:kt,ɒv] ADJ: **a much talked-of event** un avvenimento di cui si parla molto.

talk·er ['tɔ:kə'] N parlatore(-trice); (*pej*) chiacchierone (-a).

talkie ['tɔ:kɪ] N (*Cine*: *old fam*): **with the advent of the talkie** con l'avvento del sonoro.

talk·ing ['tɔ:kɪŋ] 1 ADJ (*doll, bird*) parlante.

2 N parlare *m*; **I'll do the talking** parlo io; **she does all the talking** è lei che tiene in piedi la conversazione.

♦ **talking book** N audiolibro.

♦ **talking point** N argomento di conversazione.

♦ **talking-to** ['tɔ:kɪŋ,tu:] N (*fam*): **to give sb a good talking-to** fare una bella paternale a qn.

♦ **talk show** N (*Am*: *TV, Radio*) talk show *m inv*.

tall [tɔ:l] ADJ (*comp* -er, *superl* -est) alto(-a); **how tall are you?** quanto sei alto?; **I'm 6 feet tall** ≈ sono alto 1 metro 80; **that's a tall order!** è una bella pretesa!

tall·boy ['tɔ:l,bɔɪ] N (*Brit*) cassettone *m* alto.

tall·ness ['tɔ:lnɪs] N altezza.

tal·low ['tæləʊ] N sego.

♦ **tall story** N (*Brit*) storia incredibile.

tal·ly ['tælɪ] 1 N (*count*) conto, conteggio; (*running total*) totale *m*; (*score*) punteggio; **to keep a tally of sth** tener il conto di qc.

2 VI: **to tally (with)** corrispondere (a).

Tal·mud ['tælmʊd] N Talmud *m*.

tal·on ['tælən] N artiglio.

tama·rind ['tæmərɪnd] N tamarindo.

tama·risk ['tæmərɪsk] N tamerice *f*, tamarisco.

tam·bou·rine [ˌtæmbə'ri:n] N tamburello.

tame [teɪm] 1 ADJ (*comp* **-r**, *superl* **-st**) (*animal*) addomesticato(-a); (*fig: person*) docile; (: *story, style*) scialbo(-a), insipido(-a); (: *book, performance*) banale.

2 VT (*wild creature*) addomesticare; (*lion, tiger, passion*) domare.

tame·ly ['teɪmlɪ] ADV (*agree*) docilmente.

Tam·il ['tæmɪl] 1 ADJ tamil *inv*.

2 N (*person*) tamil *m/f*; (*language*) tamil *m*.

tam·ing ['teɪmɪŋ] N (*gen*) addomesticamento; "The Taming of the Shrew" "La Bisbetica Domata".

Tampax® ['tæmpæks] N, PL INV Tampax ® *m inv*.

tam·per ['tæmpəʳ] VI: **to tamper with** manomettere; **someone had tampered with the brakes** qualcuno aveva manomesso i freni.

tam·pon ['tæmpɒn] N tampone *m*.

tan [tæn] 1 N (*also:* **suntan**) abbronzatura; (*colour*) color *m* marrone chiaro; **to get a tan** abbronzarsi.

2 ADJ marrone chiaro *inv*.

3 VI abbronzarsi.

4 VT (*person, skin*) abbronzare; (*leather*) conciare; **to tan sb's hide** (*fam*) darle a qn.

tan·dem ['tændəm] 1 N (*bicycle*) tandem *m inv*.

2 ADV: **in tandem** in tandem.

tan·doori [tæn'dʊərɪ] ADJ *nella cucina indiana, detto di carni o verdure cucinate allo spiedo in particolari forni*.

tang [tæŋ] N (*taste*) sapore *m* forte; (*smell*) odore *m* penetrante.

tan·gent ['tændʒənt] N (*Geom*) tangente *f*; **to go off at a tangent** (*fig*) partire per la tangente.

tan·gen·tial [ˌtæn'dʒɛnʃəl] ADJ (*frm*) marginale.

tan·ge·rine [ˌtændʒə'ri:n] N *specie di mandarino*.

tan·gible ['tændʒəbl] ADJ (*proof, results*) tangibile; (*difference*) sostanziale; **tangible assets** patrimonio reale.

tan·gibly ['tændʒəblɪ] ADV (*see adj*) in modo tangibile; sostanzialmente.

Tan·gier [tæn'dʒɪəʳ] N Tangeri *f*.

tan·gle ['tæŋgl] 1 N (*of wool, wire*) groviglio; (*in hair*) nodo; (*fig: muddle*) confusione *f*; **to get into a tangle** (*gen*) aggrovigliarsi; (*hair*) arruffarsi; (*person*) combinare un pasticcio.

2 VT (*also:* **tangle up**) aggrovigliare; (*hair*) arruffare.

3 VI aggrovigliarsi; (*hair*) ingarbugliarsi; **to tangle with sb** (*fig fam*) azzuffarsi con qn.

tan·gled ['tæŋgəld] ADJ (*string, wires, hair*) aggrovigliato (-a); (*fig: situation, negotiations*) ingarbugliato(-a).

tan·go ['tæŋgəʊ] N tango.

tangy ['tæŋɪ] ADJ (*comp* **-ier**, *superl* **-iest**) (*flavour, taste, smell*) aspro(-a).

tank [tæŋk] N a (*container: for gas, petrol*) serbatoio; (: *for rainwater*) cisterna; (: *for processing*) vasca; (: *for fish*) acquario; **fuel tank** serbatoio del carburante b (*Mil*) carro armato.

tank·ard ['tæŋkəd] N boccale *m* (con coperchio).

tanked-up [ˌtæŋkt'ʌp] ADJ (*Brit fam*): **to be tanked-up** essere sbronzo(-a).

tank·er ['tæŋkəʳ] N (*ship: for oil*) petroliera; (: *for water*) nave *f* cisterna *inv*; (*aircraft*) aereocisterna; (*lorry*) autocisterna, autobotte *f*.

tank·ful ['tæŋkfʊl] N: **a tankful of water** una cisterna

(piena) d'acqua; **to pay for a tankful of petrol** (*for car*) pagare per un pieno (di benzina).

tanned [tænd] ADJ abbronzato(-a).

tan·ner ['tænəʳ] N (*person*) conciatore(-trice).

tan·nery ['tænərɪ] N conceria.

tan·nin ['tænɪn] N tannino.

tan·ning ['tænɪŋ] N a (*by sun*) abbronzatura; (*of leather*) conciatura b (*fam: beating*) botte *fpl*.

Tan·noy® ['tænɔɪ] N (*Brit*) altoparlante *m*; **over the Tannoy** con l'altoparlante.

tan·ta·lize ['tæntəˌlaɪz] VT tormentare.

tan·ta·liz·ing ['tæntəˌlaɪzɪŋ] ADJ (*food*) stuzzicante; (*idea, offer*) allettante.

tan·ta·liz·ing·ly ['tæntəˌlaɪzɪŋlɪ] ADV in modo allettante; **we were tantalizingly close to victory** eravamo così vicino alla vittoria.

tan·ta·mount ['tæntəˌmaʊnt] ADJ: **to be tantamount to** equivalere a.

tan·trum ['tæntrəm] N accesso di collera; **to throw a tantrum** fare le bizze.

Tan·za·nia [ˌtænzə'nɪə] N la Tanzania.

Tan·za·nian [ˌtænzə'nɪən] ADJ, N tanzaniano(-a).

tap¹ [tæp] 1 N (*Brit: on sink*) rubinetto; **on tap** (*beer*) alla spina; (*fig: resources*) a disposizione.

2 VT (*barrel*) spillare; (*telephone*) mettere sotto controllo; (*telephone conversation*) intercettare; (*resources*) sfruttare, utilizzare.

tap² [tæp] 1 N (*gentle blow*) colpetto; **there was a tap on the door** hanno bussato leggermente alla porta.

2 VT (*pat, knock*) picchiare leggermente su, dare un colpetto a; **I tapped him on the shoulder** gli ho dato un colpetto sulla spalla; **to tap one's foot** (*impatiently*) battere il piede; (*in time to music*) segnare il tempo con il piede; **to tap out a message in Morse** trasmettere un messaggio in Morse.

3 VI (*knock*) bussare; (*rain*) picchiettare.

♦ **tap-dancer** ['tæpˌdɑːnsəʳ] N ballerino(-a) di tip tap.

♦ **tap dancing** N tip tap *m*.

tape [teɪp] 1 N (*gen, Sport, for recording*) nastro; (*also:* **magnetic tape**) nastro (magnetico); (*Sewing*) fettuccia; **on tape** (*song*) su nastro; **to break the tape** (*Sport*) tagliare la linea del traguardo.

2 VT (*record*) registrare (su nastro); (*also:* **tape up**) legare con un nastro; **I've got him taped** (*Brit fam*) ho capito il tipo.

♦ **tape deck** N piastra di registrazione.

♦ **tape library** N nastroteca.

♦ **tape measure** N metro a nastro.

ta·per ['teɪpəʳ] 1 N (*waxed spill*) cerino; (*thin candle*) candelina.

2 VI (*also:* **taper off**) assottigliarsi; (*trousers*) restringersi.

♦ **tape-record** ['teɪprɪˌkɔːd] VT registrare (su nastro).

♦ **tape recorder** N registratore *m* (a nastro).

♦ **tape recording** N registrazione *f*.

ta·pered ['teɪpəd] ADJ (*trouser leg, stick*) affusolato(-a).

ta·per·ing ['teɪpərɪŋ] ADJ (*fingers*) affusolato(-a).

tap·es·try ['tæpɪstrɪ] N (*object*) arazzo, tappezzeria; (*art*) mezzo punto.

tape·worm ['teɪpˌwɜːm] N tenia, verme *m* solitario.

tapio·ca [ˌtæpɪ'əʊkə] N tapioca.

ta·pir ['teɪpəʳ] N tapiro.

tap·pet ['tæpɪt] N punteria.

tap·root ['tæpˌruːt] N radice *f* principale.

♦ **tap water** N (*Brit*) acqua del rubinetto.

tar [tɑ:ʳ] [1] N catrame *m*; **low-/middle-tar cigarettes** sigarette a basso/medio contenuto di catrame.
[2] VT (*road*) incatramare; **he's tarred with the same brush** (*fig*) è della stessa razza.

ta·ran·tu·la [təˈræntjʊlə] N tarantola.

tar·dy [ˈtɑ:dɪ] ADJ (*comp* **-ier**, *superl* **-iest**) (*slow*) lento(-a); (*later than expected*) tardivo(-a), tardo(-a); (*Am: late: person*) in ritardo.

tare [tɛəʳ] N (*Comm*) tara.

tar·get [ˈtɑ:gɪt] N (*gen: objective*) obiettivo; (*Mil, Archery*) bersaglio; (*fig*) obiettivo, bersaglio; **she has been the target of criticism** è stata fatta oggetto *or* bersaglio di critiche; **the targets for production in 1990** gli obiettivi della produzione per il 1990; **to be on target** (*project*) essere nei tempi (di lavorazione).
♦ **target practice** N (esercitazioni *fpl* di) tiro al bersaglio.

tar·iff [ˈtærɪf] N (*price list*) tariffa; (*tax*) tariffa doganale, dazio.
♦ **tariff barrier** N barriera tariffaria.

tar·mac® [ˈtɑ:mæk] [1] N (*Brit: on road*) macadam *m* al catrame; (*runway*): **the tarmac** la pista.
[2] VT (*Brit*) macadamizzare con il catrame.

tar·nish [ˈtɑ:nɪʃ] [1] VT ossidare, annerire; (*fig: reputation*) infangare, macchiare.
[2] VI ossidarsi, annerirsi.

ta·rot [ˈtærəʊ] N tarocco.
♦ **tarot cards** NPL tarocchi *mpl*.

tar·pau·lin [tɑ:ˈpɔ:lɪn] N (*waterproof cover*) (tela) incerata.

tar·ra·gon [ˈtærəgən] N dragoncello.

tar·ry¹ [ˈtærɪ] VI (*old, liter*) **a** (*linger*) trattenersi **b** (*delay*) tardare.

tar·ry² [ˈtærɪ] ADJ (*road*) incatramato(-a); (*tar-stained*) macchiato(-a) di catrame.

tart¹ [tɑ:t] ADJ (*fruit, flavour*) aspro(-a), agro(-a); (*fig: remark*) caustico(-a)
▶ **tart up** VT + ADV (*Brit fam*) agghindare; **to tart o.s. up** [OR] **get tarted up** farsi bello(-a); (*pej*) agghindarsi.

tart² [tɑ:t] N **a** (*Brit Culin: large*) crostata; (: *individual*) crostatina **b** (*fam offensive: woman*) puttana (*fam!*)

tar·tan [ˈtɑ:tən] [1] N tartan *m inv*, tessuto scozzese.
[2] ADJ di tessuto scozzese.
♦ **tartan rug** N coperta di tessuto scozzese.

tar·tar¹ [ˈtɑ:təʳ] N (*on teeth*) tartaro; **cream of tartar** cremortartaro.

tar·tar² [ˈtɑ:təʳ] N (*fig*) despota *m*.
♦ **tartar sauce** N salsa tartara.

tart·ly [ˈtɑ:tlɪ] ADV (*remark*) causticamente.

tart·ness [ˈtɑ:tnɪs] N (*of fruit*) asprezza, agro; (*of remark*) asprezza, causticità *f inv*.

task [tɑ:sk] N compito; **to take sb to task (for sth)** richiamare qn all'ordine (per qc), rimproverare qn (per qc).
♦ **task force** N (*Mil, Police*) unità *f inv* operativa, task force *f inv*.

task·master [ˈtɑ:sk͵mɑ:stəʳ] N: **he's a hard taskmaster** è un vero tiranno.

Tas·ma·nia [tæzˈmeɪnɪə] N la Tasmania.

tas·sel [ˈtæsəl] N nappa, fiocco.

tas·selled [ˈtæsəld] ADJ guarnito(-a) di nappe.

taste [teɪst] [1] N (*gen*) gusto; (*flavour*) sapore *m*, gusto; (*fig: glimpse, idea*) idea; **the soup had an odd taste** la minestra aveva un sapore un po' strano; **to have a taste of sth** assaggiare qc; **may I have a taste?** posso assaggiare?; **have a taste of everything!** assaggia un po' di

tutto!; **to have a taste for sth** avere un'inclinazione per qc; **he acquired a taste for sports cars** gli è preso il gusto delle macchine sportive; **it's not to my taste** non è di mio gusto; **to be in bad** *or* **poor taste** essere di cattivo gusto; **"sweeten to taste"** (*Culin*) "zuccherare a piacere".
[2] VT **a** gustare; (*sample*) assaggiare; **just taste this** assaggiane un pochino
b (*notice flavour of*) sentire il sapore di; **you can taste the garlic (in it)** (ci) si sente il sapore dell'aglio
c (*fig: experience*) assaporare; **once he had tasted power** una volta assaporato il gusto del potere.
[3] VI: **to taste of** (*fish, garlic*) sapere di, avere sapore di; **it tastes good/bad** ha un buon/cattivo sapore; **what does it taste like?** che sapore *or* gusto ha?; **rabbit tastes quite like chicken** il coniglio ha un gusto molto simile a quello del pollo.
♦ **taste bud** N papilla gustativa.

taste·ful [ˈteɪstfʊl] ADJ di (buon) gusto.

taste·ful·ly [ˈteɪstfəlɪ] ADV con gusto.

taste·less [ˈteɪstlɪs] ADJ (*food*) insipido(-a); (*decor, joke, remark*) di cattivo gusto.

taste·less·ly [ˈteɪstlɪslɪ] ADV senza gusto.

tast·er [ˈteɪstəʳ] N assaggiatore(-trice).

tasty [ˈteɪstɪ] ADJ (*comp* **-ier**, *superl* **-iest**) (*food*) saporito (-a), gustoso(-a); (*dish, meal*) succulento(-a).

tat [tæt] N **a** (*Brit fam pej*) ciarpame *m* **b** see **tit²**.

ta-ta [ˈtæˈtɑ:] EXCL (*Brit fam: goodbye*) ciao!

tat·tered [ˈtætəd] ADJ sbrindellato(-a).

tat·ters [ˈtætəz] NPL stracci *mpl*; **in tatters** a brandelli, sbrindellato(-a).

tat·tle [ˈtætl] [1] VI spettegolare.
[2] N chiacchiere *fpl*, pettegolezzi *mpl*.

tat·too¹ [təˈtu:] [1] N (*on skin*) tatuaggio.
[2] VT tatuare.

tat·too² [təˈtu:] N (*Mil: signal*) ritirata; (: *show*) parata militare.

tat·too·ist [tæˈtu:ɪst] N tatuatore(-trice).

tat·ty [ˈtætɪ] ADJ (*comp* **-ier**, *superl* **-iest**) (*Brit fam: shabby*) malandato(-a), malridotto(-a); (: *paint*) scrostato(-a).

taught [tɔ:t] PT, PP of **teach**.

taunt [tɔ:nt] [1] N scherno.
[2] VT: **to taunt sb (with)** schernire qn (per).

taunt·ing [ˈtɔ:ntɪŋ] [1] ADJ beffardo(-a).
[2] N frasi *fpl* di scherno.

Tau·rus [ˈtɔ:rəs] N (*Astron, Astrol*) Toro; **to be Taurus** essere del Toro.

taut [tɔ:t] ADJ (*comp* **-er**, *superl* **-est**) (*also fig*) teso(-a).

taut·en [ˈtɔ:tən] VI tendersi.

tau·to·logi·cal [͵tɔ:təˈlɒdʒɪkəl] ADJ tautologico(-a).

tau·tol·ogy [tɔ:ˈtɒlədʒɪ] N tautologia.

tav·ern [ˈtævən] N (*old*) taverna.

taw·dry [ˈtɔ:drɪ] ADJ (*comp* **-ier**, *superl* **-iest**) pacchiano(-a).

taw·ny [ˈtɔ:nɪ] ADJ (*comp* **-ier**, *superl* **-iest**) fulvo(-a).
♦ **tawny owl** N allocco.

tax [tæks] [1] N (*on income*) imposta, tasse *fpl* (*fam*); (*on goods, services*) tassa; **before/after tax** al lordo/netto delle imposte (*or* delle tasse); **free of tax** esente da imposte; esentasse *inv*; **a third of my wages goes in tax** un terzo del mio stipendio se ne va in tasse; **how much tax do you pay?** quanto paghi di tasse?; **to put a tax on sth** mettere una tassa su qc.
[2] VT **a** (*Fin: people, salary, goods*) tassare; **tobacco and petrol are heavily taxed** le tasse sul tabacco e sulla benzina sono altissime

b (*fig*: *resources*) gravare su; **to tax sb's patience** mettere alla prova la pazienza di qn
c (*fig*: *accuse*): **to tax sb with sth/with doing sth** accusare qn di qc/di aver fatto qc.
3 ADJ fiscale, delle tasse; **for tax purposes** per motivi fiscali.
tax·able ['tæksəbl] ADJ imponibile.
♦ **tax allowance** N detrazione *f* d'imposta.
taxa·tion [tæk'seɪʃən] N (*act*) tassazione *f*; (*taxes*) imposte *fpl*, tasse *fpl*; **system of taxation** sistema *m* fiscale.
♦ **tax avoidance** N elusione *f* fiscale.
♦ **tax collector** N esattore *m* delle imposte.
♦ **tax-deductible** [ˌtæksdɪ'dʌktɪbəl] ADJ detraibile dalle imposte.
♦ **tax disc** N (*Brit Aut*) ≈ bollo.
♦ **tax evasion** N evasione *f* fiscale.
♦ **tax exemption** N esenzione *f* fiscale.
♦ **tax exile** N *chi ripara all'estero per evadere le imposte*.
♦ **tax-free** [ˌtæks'friː] 1 ADJ esente da imposte, esentasse *inv*.
2 ADV senza pagare tasse.
♦ **tax haven** N paradiso fiscale.
taxi ['tæksɪ] 1 N taxi *m inv*.
2 VI (*Aer*) rullare.
taxi·cab ['tæksɪ'kæb] N taxi *m inv*.
taxi·der·mist ['tæksɪ'dɜːmɪst] N tassidermista *m/f*.
taxi·der·my ['tæksɪ'dɜːmɪ] N tassidermia.
♦ **taxi driver** N tassista *m/f*.
taxi·ing ['tæksɪɪŋ] N (*Aer*) rullaggio.
taxi·meter ['tæksɪˌmiːtəʳ] N tassametro.
tax·ing ['tæksɪŋ] ADJ oneroso(-a).
♦ **tax inspector** N ispettore *m* delle tasse.
♦ **taxi rank**, (*Am*) **taxi stand** N posteggio dei taxi.
taxi·way ['tæksɪˌweɪ] N (*Aer*) pista di rullaggio.
tax·man ['tæks,mæn] N (*pl* **-men**) (*Brit fam*): **the taxman** il fisco.
tax·ono·my [tæk'sɒnəmɪ] N tassonomia.
tax·payer ['tæks,peɪəʳ] N contribuente *m/f*.
♦ **tax rebate** N rimborso fiscale.
♦ **tax relief** N sgravio fiscale.
♦ **tax return** N dichiarazione *f* dei redditi.
♦ **tax shelter** N *espediente legale per pagare meno tasse*.
♦ **tax system** N sistema *m* fiscale.
♦ **tax year** N anno fiscale.
TB [ˌtiː'biː] N ABBR (= *tuberculosis*) TBC *f*.
♦ **T-bone steak** [ˌtiː'bəʊn'steɪk] N (*also*: **T-bone**) bistecca alla fiorentina.
tbs. N ABBR = **tablespoonful**.
TD [ˌtiː'diː] N ABBR (*Am*) **a** = **Treasury Department b** (*American football*) = **touchdown**.
tea [tiː] 1 N **a** (*beverage*) tè *m inv*; **I made a pot of tea** ho fatto un po' di tè; **tea with lemon** tè al limone; **it's just my cup of tea!** (*fig*) è proprio quello che fa per me! **b** (*Brit*: *main evening meal*) cena; (: *also*: **afternoon tea**) tè *m inv*; **we're invited to tea at the Browns'** siamo stati invitati per il tè dai Brown.
2 ADJ di tè, del tè.
♦ **tea bag** N bustina di tè.
♦ **tea break** N (*Brit*) pausa sul lavoro (*per bere un tè, un caffè*).
♦ **tea caddy** N barattolo per il tè.
tea·cake ['tiːˌkeɪk] N (*Brit*) *panino dolce all'uvetta*.
♦ **teacart** ['tiːˌkɑːt] N (*Am*) = **tea trolley**.
teach [tiːtʃ] (*pt, pp* **taught**) 1 VT insegnare; **I teach English** insegno inglese; **to teach sb sth** OR **teach sth to sb**

insegnare qc a qn; **to teach sb (how) to do sth** insegnare a qn come si fa qc; **I taught him (how) to write** gli ho insegnato a scrivere; **it taught him a lesson** (*fig*) gli è servito da lezione; **I'll teach you to leave the gas on!** ti faccio vedere io cosa ti succede quando lasci il gas aperto!.
2 VI insegnare; **his wife teaches in our school** sua moglie insegna nella nostra scuola.
teach·er ['tiːtʃəʳ] N (*gen*) insegnante *m/f*; (*in secondary school*) professore(-essa); (*in primary school*) maestro (-a); **French teacher** insegnante di francese.
♦ **teacher's pet** N (*fam pej*) beniamino dell'insegnante.
♦ **teacher training college** N (*for primary schools*) ≈ istituto magistrale; (*for secondary schools*) *scuola universitaria per l'abilitazione all'insegnamento*.
♦ **tea chest** N cassa per il tè.
♦ **teach-in** ['tiːtʃ,ɪn] N seminario.
teach·ing ['tiːtʃɪŋ] N (*gen*) insegnamento; **she went into teaching 10 years ago** ha incominciato a insegnare 10 anni fa; **the teaching profession** l'insegnamento.
♦ **teaching aids** NPL sussidi *mpl* didattici.
♦ **teaching hospital** N clinica universitaria.
♦ **teaching practice** N (*Brit*) *periodo di tirocinio per insegnanti*.
♦ **teaching staff** N (*Brit*) corpo insegnante *or* docente, insegnanti *mpl*.
♦ **tea cloth** N (*for dishes*) strofinaccio; (*Brit*: *for trolley, tray*) tovaglietta da tè.
♦ **tea cosy** N copriteiera *m inv*.
tea·cup ['tiːˌkʌp] N tazza da tè.
teak [tiːk] N teak *m*.
teal [tiːl] N, PL INV alzavola.
♦ **tea leaves** NPL foglie *fpl* di tè.
team [tiːm] N (*of people*) équipe *f inv*; (: *Sport*) squadra; (*of animals*) tiro; **home team** squadra di casa.
▶ **team up** VI + ADV: **to team up (with)** mettersi insieme (a).
♦ **team games** NPL giochi *mpl* di squadra.
♦ **team-mate** ['tiːmˌmeɪt] N compagno(-a) di squadra.
♦ **team spirit** N (*cooperativeness*) spirito di collaborazione; (*Sport*) spirito di squadra.
team·ster ['tiːmstəʳ] N (*Am*) camionista *m*.
♦ **team teaching** N team-teaching *m*.
team·work ['tiːmˌwɜːk] N lavoro d'équipe; (*Sport*) lavoro di squadra.
♦ **tea party** N tè *m inv* (*ricevimento*).
♦ **tea plate** N piattino da frutta.
tea·pot ['tiːpɒt] N teiera.
tear[1] [tɛəʳ] (*vb*: *pt* **tore**, *pp* **torn**) 1 N (*rip, hole*) strappo; **your shirt has a tear in it** hai uno strappo nella camicia, hai la camicia strappata.
2 VT (*gen*) strappare; **torn by remorse** tormentato(-a) dal rimorso; **torn by war** (*fig*) devastato(-a) dalla guerra; **torn by his emotions** combattuto(-a); **he was torn between going and staying** era combattuto tra andare e restare; **to tear to pieces** *or* **to bits** *or* **to shreds** (*also fig*) fare a pezzi *or* a brandelli; **to tear a muscle** strapparsi un muscolo; **to tear a hole in** (*shirt*) fare un buco in; (*argument*) dimostrare che fa acqua; **to tear a letter** *or* **an envelope open** aprire una busta strappandola; **that's torn it!** (*Brit fam*) sono fregato! (*or* siamo fregati! *etc*).
3 VI (*be ripped*) strapparsi; (*subj*: *person, animal*): **to tear at sth** strappare qc
▶ **tear along** 1 VI + ADV (*rush*) correre all'impazzata.
2 VI + PREP correre per
▶ **tear apart** VT + ADV (*also fig*) distruggere

▶ **tear away** VT + ADV: **to tear o.s. away (from sth)** (*fig*) staccarsi (da qc)

▶ **tear down** VT + ADV (*flag, poster*) tirare giù; (*building*) demolire

▶ **tear into** VI + PREP (*fam*): **to tear into sb** criticare ferocemente qn

▶ **tear loose** ① VT + ADV **a** : **to tear o.s. loose** liberarsi (con uno strattone)
b : **to tear sth loose** strappare via qc.
② VI + ADV liberarsi (con uno strattone)

▶ **tear off** ① VT + ADV (*wrapping*) strappare; (*perforated section*) staccare; (*roof*) portare via.
② VT + PREP (*piece of material*) strappare da

▶ **tear out** ① VT + ADV (*sheet of paper, cheque*) staccare; **to tear one's hair out** strapparsi i capelli.
② VI + ADV correre fuori

▶ **tear up** VT + ADV **a** (*also fig*) strappare; (*agreement*) annullare
b (*plant, stake*) sradicare; (*sheet of paper*) strappare.

tear² [tɪəʳ] N lacrima; **to be close to tears** stare per piangere; **to burst into tears** scoppiare in lacrime; **to bring tears to sb's eyes** far venire le lacrime agli occhi a qn.

tear·away ['tɛərə‚weɪ] N (*Brit fam*) ragazzaccio.

tear·drop ['tɪə‚drɒp] N lacrima.

tear·ful ['tɪəful] ADJ (*face*) coperto(-a) di lacrime; (*voice*) piangente; (*person*) in lacrime; **she looked a bit tearful** sembrava che stesse per piangere.

tear·ful·ly ['tɪəfəlɪ] ADV con le lacrime agli occhi.

♦ **tear gas** ['tɪə‚gæs] N gas *m* lacrimogeno.

tear·ing ['tɛərɪŋ] ADJ: **to be in a tearing hurry** avere una fretta terribile.

♦ **tear-jerker** ['tɪə‚dʒɜːkəʳ] N (*fam*): **the film/story is a real tear-jerker** è veramente un film/una storia strappalacrime.

tea·room ['tiː‚rʊm] N sala da tè.

♦ **tear-stained** ['tɪə‚steɪnd] ADJ rigato(-a) di lacrime.

tease [tiːz] ① N (*person*) burlone(-a).
② VT (*playfully*) stuzzicare; (: *make fun of*) prendere in giro, canzonare; (*cruelly*) tormentare

▶ **tease out** VT + ADV **a** (*tangle, knots*) sbrogliare; **to tease the tangles** *or* **knots out of one's hair** sbrogliarsi i capelli
b : **to tease information out of sb** cavare delle informazioni a qn.

tea·sel ['tiːzl] N (*Bot*) cardo dei lanaioli; (*Tech*) cardo.

teas·er ['tiːzəʳ] N (*fam: problem*) rompicapo.

♦ **tea service, tea set** N servizio da tè.

tea·shop ['tiː‚ʃɒp] N (*Brit*) sala da tè.

tea·sing ['tiːzɪŋ] ① N burle *fpl*, beffe *fpl*.
② ADJ canzonatorio(-a).

Teas·maid® ['tiːz‚meɪd] N *macchinetta per fare il tè.*

tea·spoon ['tiː‚spuːn] N (*also:* **teaspoonful:** *as measurement*) cucchiaino da tè.

♦ **tea strainer** N colino per il tè.

teat [tiːt] N (*of bottle*) tettarella; (*of animal*) capezzolo.

tea·time ['tiː‚taɪm] N ora del tè.

♦ **tea towel** N (*Brit*) strofinaccio (per i piatti).

♦ **tea tray** N vassoio da tè.

♦ **tea trolley** N (*Brit*) carrello da tè.

♦ **tea urn** N bollitore *m* per il tè.

tech [tɛk] N ABBR **a** (*Brit fam*) = **technical college b** (*fam*) = **technology.**

tech·ni·cal ['tɛknɪkəl] ADJ (*process, word*) tecnico(-a); **this book is too technical for me** questo libro è troppo tecnico *or* specifico per me; **technical expert** tecnico

specializzato; **technical offence** (*Law*) infrazione *f.*

♦ **technical college** N (*Brit*) ≈ istituto tecnico.

tech·ni·cal·ity [‚tɛknɪ'kælɪtɪ] N (*quality*) tecnicità *f inv*; (*detail*) dettaglio tecnico; **on a legal technicality** grazie a un cavillo legale; **I don't understand all the technicalities** non riesco a capire tutti i dettagli tecnici.

tech·ni·cal·ly ['tɛknɪkəlɪ] ADV (*gen*) dal punto di vista tecnico; (*in theory*) tecnicamente, in teoria.

tech·ni·cian [tɛk'nɪʃən] N tecnico(-a).

Tech·ni·col·or® ['tɛknɪ‚kʌləʳ] ① N Technicolor ® *m.*
② ADJ (*fam*) in technicolor; **a Technicolor sunset** un tramonto in technicolor.

tech·nique [tɛk'niːk] N tecnica.

tech·no ['tɛknəʊ] N (*Mus*) techno *f inv.*

tech·no·crat ['tɛknəʊ‚kræt] N tecnocrate *m/f.*

tech·no·logi·cal [‚tɛknə'lɒdʒɪkəl] ADJ tecnologico(-a).

tech·nolo·gist [tɛk'nɒlədʒɪst] N tecnologo(-a).

tech·nol·ogy [tɛk'nɒlədʒɪ] N tecnologia.

tec·ton·ics [tɛk'tɒnɪks] NSG tettonica.

ted·dy bear ['tɛdɪ‚bɛəʳ] N (*also:* **teddy**) orsacchiotto.

ted·dy boy ['tɛdɪ‚bɔɪ] N (*Brit*) teddy boy *m inv.*

te·di·ous ['tiːdɪəs] ADJ noioso(-a), tedioso(-a).

te·di·ous·ly ['tiːdɪəslɪ] ADV noiosamente; **tediously long** insopportabilmente lungo(-a).

te·di·ous·ness ['tiːdɪəsnɪs], **te·dium** ['tiːdɪəm] N noia, tedio.

tee [tiː] N (*Golf*) tee *m inv*

▶ **tee off** VI + ADV (*Golf*) cominciare la partita.

teem [tiːm] VI **a** brulicare, abbondare; **to teem with** brulicare di **b** : **it's teeming (with rain)** piove a dirotto.

teen·age ['tiːn‚eɪdʒ] ADJ (*problems*) da adolescente; (*rebelliousness*) adolescenziale; (*fashions*) per teenager, per giovani; **teenage boy/girl** adolescente *m/f.*

teen·ager ['tiːn‚eɪdʒəʳ] N adolescente *m/f*, teenager *m/f inv.*

teens [tiːnz] NPL: **he is still in his teens** è ancora un adolescente.

tee·ny ['tiːnɪ] ADJ (*comp* **-ier**, *superl* **-iest**) (*fam*) piccolino (-a), piccino(-a).

tee-shirt ['tiː‚ʃɜːt] N = **T-shirt.**

tee·ter ['tiːtəʳ] VI barcollare, vacillare; **to teeter on the edge** *or* **brink of** vacillare sull'orlo di.

teeth [tiːθ] NPL of **tooth.**

teethe [tiːð] VI mettere i denti.

teeth·ing ['tiːðɪŋ] N dentizione *f.*

♦ **teething ring** N dentaruolo.

♦ **teething troubles** NPL (*fig*) difficoltà *fpl* iniziali.

tee·to·tal ['tiː'təʊtl] ADJ astemio(-a).

tee·to·tal·ler, (*Am*) **tee·to·tal·er** ['tiː'təʊtləʳ] N (*person*) astemio(-a).

TEFL ['tɛfl] N ABBR = *Teaching of English as a Foreign Language.*

Tef·lon® ['tɛflɒn] N Teflon ® *m.*

Te·he·ran [tɛə'rɑːn] N Teheran *f.*

tel. ABBR (= *telephone*) tel.

Tel Aviv ['tɛlə'viːv] N Tel Aviv *f.*

tele... ['tɛlɪ] PREF tele... .

tele·cast ['tɛlɪ‚kɑːst] ① N trasmissione *f* televisiva.
② VT, VI teletrasmettere.

tele·com·mu·ni·ca·tions ['tɛlɪkə‚mjuːnɪ'keɪʃənz] NPL telecomunicazioni *fpl.*

tele·gram ['tɛlɪ‚græm] N telegramma *m.*

tele·graph ['tɛlɪ‚grɑːf] ① N (*apparatus*) telegrafo; (*message*) telegramma *m*; **by telegraph** via telegrafo.
② VT trasmettere per telegrafo, telegrafare.

tele·graph·ic [‚tɛlɪ'græfɪk] ADJ telegrafico(-a).

te·leg·ra·phist [tɪ'lɛgrəfɪst] N telegrafista *m/f*.

♦ **telegraph pole**, **telegraph post** N (*Brit*) palo del telegrafo.

♦ **telegraph wire** N filo del telegrafo.

te·leg·ra·phy [tɪ'lɛgrəfɪ] N telegrafia.

Te·lema·chus [tə'lɛməkəs] N Telemaco.

te·lem·eter ['tɛlɪˌmiːtə'] N telemetro.

tele·ol·ogy [ˌtɛlɪ'ɒlədʒɪ] N teleologia.

tele·path·ic [ˌtɛlɪ'pæθɪk] ADJ telepatico(-a).

te·lepa·thy [tɪ'lɛpəθɪ] N telepatia.

tele·phone ['tɛlɪˌfəʊn] 1 N telefono; **by telephone** telefonicamente; **to have a telephone** avere il telefono; **to be on the telephone** (*Brit: subscriber*) avere il telefono; (*be speaking*) essere al telefono; **I've just been on the telephone to my mother** ho appena parlato al telefono con mia madre. 2 VI telefonare. 3 VT (*person*) telefonare a; (*message*) telefonare.

♦ **telephone box**, (*Am*) **telephone booth** N cabina telefonica.

♦ **telephone call** N telefonata.

♦ **telephone directory**, **telephone book** N guida del telefono, elenco telefonico.

♦ **telephone exchange** N centralino (telefonico).

♦ **telephone kiosk** N (*Brit*) cabina telefonica.

♦ **telephone line** N linea telefonica.

♦ **telephone message** N messaggio (telefonico).

♦ **telephone meter** N contascatti *m inv*.

♦ **telephone number** N numero di telefono.

♦ **telephone operator** N centralinista *m/f*.

♦ **telephone poll** N (*Am*) palo del telegrafo.

♦ **telephone selling** N (*Comm*) vendita per telefono.

♦ **tele·phone tap·ping** ['tɛlɪfəʊnˌtæpɪŋ] N intercettazione *f* telefonica.

tele·phon·ic [ˌtɛlɪ'fɒnɪk] ADJ telefonico(-a).

te·lepho·nist [tɪ'lɛfənɪst] N (*Brit*) telefonista *m/f*.

tele·photo lens [ˌtɛlɪfəʊtəʊ'lɛnz] N teleobiettivo.

tele·print·er ['tɛlɪˌprɪntə'] N telescrivente *f*.

Tele·prompt·er® ['tɛlɪˌprɒmptə'] N (*Am*) gobbo.

tele·sales ['tɛlɪˌseɪlz] N vendita per telefono.

tele·scope ['tɛlɪˌskəʊp] 1 N telescopio. 2 VI chiudersi a telescopio; (*fig: vehicles*) accartocciarsi.

tele·scop·ic [ˌtɛlɪs'kɒpɪk] ADJ telescopico(-a); (*umbrella*) pieghevole.

♦ **telescopic lens** N (*Phot*) teleobiettivo.

♦ **telescopic sight** N (*on gun*) collimatore *m*.

Tele·text® ['tɛlɪˌtɛkst] N (*system*) teletext *m inv*; (*in Italy*) televideo.

tele·thon ['tɛlɪˌθɒn] N Telethon *m inv*, *maratona televisiva.*

tele·type® ['tɛlɪˌtaɪp] N (*Am*) = **teleprinter**.

tele·view·er ['tɛlɪˌvjuːə'] N telespettatore(-trice).

tele·vise ['tɛlɪˌvaɪz] VT trasmettere per televisione, teletrasmettere.

tele·vi·sion ['tɛlɪˌvɪʒən] 1 N (*broadcasts, broadcasting industry*) televisione *f*; (*also:* **television set**) televisore *m*, televisione; **to watch television** guardare la televisione; **on television** alla televisione. 2 ADJ televisivo(-a).

♦ **television licence** N (*Brit*) abbonamento alla televisione.

♦ **television programme**, (*Am*) **television program** N programma *m* televisivo.

♦ **television set** N televisore *m*, televisione *f*.

tel·ex ['tɛlɛks] 1 N telex *m inv*. 2 VI mandare un telex. 3 VT (*message*) trasmettere per telex; **to telex sb (about sth)** informare qn via telex (di qc).

tell [tɛl] (*pt, pp* told) 1 VT **a** (*gen*) dire; (*story, adventure*: *relate*) raccontare; (*secret*) svelare; **to tell sb sth** dire qc a qn; **to tell sb about sth** dire a qn di qc, raccontare qc a qn; **I have been told that ...** mi è stato detto che...; **I am glad to tell you that ...** (*frm*) ho il piacere di comunicarle che...; **I cannot tell you how pleased I am** non so come esprimere la mia felicità; **so much happened that I can't begin to tell you** sono successe tante cose che non saprei da dove incominciare a raccontarti; **(I'll) tell you what ...** so io che cosa fare...; **I told you so!** OR **didn't I tell you so?** te l'avevo (pur) detto!; **I was furious, I can tell you** ti dirò che ero furioso; **let me tell you** credimi; **you're telling me!** (*fam*) a me lo dici!, lo vieni a dire a me!; **don't tell me you can't do it!** non starmi a raccontare che non sei capace!; **tell me another!** (*fam*) raccontala giusta!; **to tell the time** leggere l'ora; **can you tell me the time?** puoi dirmi l'ora?; **to tell the future/sb's fortune** predire il futuro/il futuro a qn

b (*order, instruct*): **to tell sb to do sth** dire a qn di fare qc; **do as you are told!** fai come ti si dice!; **he won't be told** non dà ascolto

c (*indicate*: *subj*: *sign, dial*): **to tell sb sth** indicare qc a qn; **there was a sign telling us which way to go** c'era un cartello che ci indicava la strada

d (*know, be sure of*) sapere; **how can you tell what he'll do?** come fai a prevedere cosa farà?; **there's no telling what may happen** non si può prevedere cosa succederà; **you can tell he's unhappy** si vede che è infelice

e (*distinguish*): **to tell sth from** distinguere qc da; **to tell right from wrong** distinguere il bene dal male; **I couldn't tell them apart** non riuscivo a distinguerli

f : **400 all told** 400 in tutto.

2 VI **a** (*talk*) parlare; (*fam: sneak, tell secrets*) fare la spia; **to tell (of)** parlare (di); **more than words can tell** più di quanto non riescano ad esprimere le parole; **that would be telling!** non te lo dico!

b (*know, be certain*) sapere; **I can't tell** non saprei dire; **who can tell?** chi lo può dire?; **there is no telling** non si sa; **you never can tell** non si può mai dire

c (*have effect*) farsi sentire, avere effetto; **to tell against sb** ritorcersi contro qn; **the strain is beginning to tell** la fatica incomincia a farsi sentire; **their lack of fitness began to tell** incominciavano a risentire della mancanza di forma

► **tell off** VT + ADV (*fam*): **to tell sb off (for sth/for doing sth)** sgridare qn (per qc/per aver fatto qc)

► **tell on** VI + PREP (*fam: inform against*) denunciare.

tell·er ['tɛlə'] N **a** (*of story*) narratore(-trice) **b** (*person: in bank*) cassiere(-a); (: *at election*) scrutatore(-trice).

tell·ing ['tɛlɪŋ] ADJ (*effective: blow*) efficace; (*significant: figures, remark, detail*) rivelatore(-trice).

♦ **telling-off** ['tɛlɪŋˌɒf] N (*fam*): **to give sb a telling-off** dare a qn una lavata di testa.

tell·tale ['tɛlˌteɪl] 1 ADJ (*sign*) rivelatore(-trice). 2 N (*fam pej, person*) spione(-a), pettegolo(-a).

tel·lu·ric [tɛ'lʊərɪk] ADJ (*frm*) tellurico(-a).

tel·ly ['tɛlɪ] N ABBR = *television*; (*Brit fam*) tele *f inv*; **on the telly** alla tele.

te·mer·ity [tɪ'mɛrɪtɪ] N (*frm*) audacia, temerarietà *f inv*.

temp [tɛmp] (*Brit fam*) 1 N ABBR (= *temporary*) impiegato (-a) temporaneo(-a) *or* straordinario(-a). 2 VI lavorare come impiegato(-a) temporaneo(-a) *or*

straordinario(-a).

tem·per ['tɛmpəʳ] **1** N (*nature*) temperamento, carattere *m*, indole *f*; (*mood*) umore *m*; (*fit of anger*) collera; **she has a sweet temper** è dolce per temperamento *or* di indole; **to be in a temper** essere in collera; **to be in a good/bad temper** essere di buon/cattivo umore; **to keep one's temper** restare calmo(-a); **to lose one's temper** perdere le staffe, andare in collera; **in a fit of temper** in un accesso d'ira; **to fly into a temper** andare su tutte le furie; **mind your temper!** OR **temper, temper!** cerca di controllarti!, calma, calma!.

2 VT (*moderate*) moderare; (*soften: metal*) temprare.

tem·pera·ment ['tɛmpərəmənt] N (*nature*) temperamento, carattere *m*, indole *f*; (*moodiness*) umore *m* variabile.

tem·pera·men·tal [ˌtɛmpərə'mɛntl] ADJ **a** (*moody: person*) capriccioso(-a); (: *fig: machine*) che fa i capricci **b** (*caused by one's nature*) innato(-a).

tem·per·ance ['tɛmpərəns] N (*frm: self-control*) moderazione *f*; (*in drinking*) temperanza nel bere; (*teetotalism*) astinenza dal bere.

♦ **temperance hotel** N albergo dove non si vendono alcolici.

♦ **temperance society** N lega antialcolica.

tem·per·ate ['tɛmpərɪt] ADJ (*climate, zone*) temperato(-a); (*frm: language, response*) moderato(-a).

tem·pera·ture ['tɛmprɪtʃəʳ] N temperatura; **to have** *or* **run a temperature** avere la febbre.

tem·pered ['tɛmpəd] ADJ (*steel*) temprato(-a).

tem·per·ing ['tɛmpərɪŋ] N (*of metal*) tempera.

tem·pest ['tɛmpɪst] N (*liter*) tempesta.

tem·pes·tu·ous [tɛm'pɛstjʊəs] ADJ (*relationship, meeting*) burrascoso(-a).

tem·pi ['tɛmpi:] NPL of **tempo**.

Tem·plar ['tɛmpləʳ] N (*Rel, History: also:* **Knight Templar**) templare *m*.

template, (*Am*) **templet** ['tɛmplɪt] N sagoma.

tem·ple ['tɛmpl] N **a** (*Rel*) tempio **b** (*Anat*) tempia.

tem·po ['tɛmpəʊ] N (*pl* **tempi** ['tɛmpi:]) (*Mus*) tempo; (*fig: of life*) ritmo; **the busy tempo of city life** il ritmo veloce della vita di città.

tem·po·ral ['tɛmpərəl] ADJ temporale.

tem·po·rari·ly ['tɛmpərərɪlɪ] ADV temporaneamente.

tem·po·rary ['tɛmpərərɪ] ADJ (*gen*) provvisorio(-a); (*powers, relief, improvement, job*) temporaneo(-a); (*worker*) avventizio(-a); **a temporary illness** una malattia passeggera; **temporary secretary** segretario(-a) temporaneo(-a) *or* straordinario(-a); **temporary teacher** supplente *m/f*.

tem·po·rize ['tɛmpəˌraɪz] VI (*delay deliberately*) temporeggiare; (*compromise*) adeguarsi, adattarsi (alle circostanze).

tempt [tɛmpt] VT (*person*) tentare; **to be tempted to do sth** essere tentato(-a) di fare qc; **can I tempt you with another cake?** posso tentarti con un altro dolce?; **to tempt Providence** *or* **fate** sfidare il destino; **to tempt sb into doing** indurre qn a fare.

temp·ta·tion [tɛmp'teɪʃən] N tentazione *f*; **there is always a temptation to …** si ha sempre la tentazione di…; **I couldn't resist the temptation** non sono riuscito a resistere alla tentazione.

tempt·er ['tɛmptəʳ] N tentatore(-trice).

tempt·ing ['tɛmptɪŋ] ADJ (*offer*) allettante; (*food*) appetitoso(-a).

tempt·ing·ly ['tɛmptɪŋlɪ] ADV in modo allettante.

tempt·ress ['tɛmptrɪs] N tentatrice *f*, seduttrice *f*.

ten [tɛn] **1** ADJ dieci *inv*.

2 N dieci *m inv*; **tens of thousands** decine di migliaia; **ten to one he'll be late** (*fam*) dieci a uno che arriva tardi; **they're ten a penny** (*fam*) ce ne sono a bizzeffe *for usage see* **five**.

ten·able ['tɛnəbl] ADJ sostenibile.

te·na·cious [tɪ'neɪʃəs] ADJ tenace.

te·na·cious·ly [tɪ'neɪʃəslɪ] ADV tenacemente.

te·nac·ity [tɪ'næsɪtɪ] N tenacia.

ten·an·cy ['tɛnənsɪ] N (*use of rented property*) locazione *f*, conduzione *f*; **to have a 5 year tenancy** avere un contratto d'affitto di 5 anni; **during his tenancy** durante il periodo in cui abitava lì.

ten·ant ['tɛnənt] N inquilino(-a).

tend¹ [tɛnd] VI tendere; **to tend to do sth** tendere a fare qc; **that tends to be the case with young people** questa è la tendenza tra i giovani; **to tend to** *or* **towards sth** (*colour*) tendere a; (*characteristic*) propendere per qc.

tend² [tɛnd] VT (*sick person*) prendersi cura di; (*cattle, machine*) badare a, occuparsi di.

ten·den·cy ['tɛndənsɪ] N tendenza; **to have a tendency to do sth** avere la tendenza a fare qc.

ten·den·tious [tɛn'dɛnʃəs] ADJ tendenzioso(-a).

ten·den·tious·ly [tɛn'dɛnʃəslɪ] ADV tendenziosamente.

ten·der¹ ['tɛndəʳ] ADJ **a** tenero(-a); **to bid sb a tender farewell** salutare qn con tenerezza **b** (*sore: part of body*) sensibile, dolente; (*fig: subject*) delicato(-a); **tender to the touch** sensibile al tatto.

ten·der² ['tɛndəʳ] **1 a** (*Comm*) offerta; **to make a tender (for)** OR **put in a tender (for)** fare un'offerta (per); **to put work out to tender** (*Brit*) dare lavoro in appalto **b** (*Fin*): **to be legal tender** essere in corso legale.

2 VT presentare, offrire; **to tender one's resignation** (*frm*) rassegnare le proprie dimissioni.

3 VI (*Comm*): **to tender (for)** fare un'offerta (per), concorrere a un appalto (per).

ten·der³ ['tɛndəʳ] N (*Rail, Naut*) tender *m inv*.

♦ **tender-hearted** [ˌtɛndə'hɑːtɪd] ADJ dal cuore tenero, sensibile.

ten·der·ize ['tɛndəˌraɪz] VT (*Culin*) far intenerire.

tender·loin ['tɛndəˌlɔɪn] N filetto di maiale.

ten·der·ly ['tɛndəlɪ] ADV (*affectionately*) teneramente.

ten·der·ness ['tɛndənɪs] N (*see adj*) tenerezza; sensibilità *f inv*.

ten·don ['tɛndən] N tendine *m*.

ten·dril ['tɛndrɪl] N viticcio.

ten·ement ['tɛnɪmənt] N casamento.

♦ **tenement block** N isolato.

Ten·erife [ˌtɛnə'riːf] N Tenerife *f*.

ten·et ['tɛnət] N principio.

ten·ner ['tɛnəʳ] N (*Brit fam*) (banconota da) dieci sterline *fpl*.

ten·nis ['tɛnɪs] **1** N tennis *m*.

2 ADJ da tennis.

♦ **tennis ball** N palla da tennis.

♦ **tennis club** N tennis club *m inv*.

♦ **tennis court** N campo da tennis.

♦ **tennis elbow** N (*Med*) gomito del tennista.

♦ **tennis match** N partita di tennis.

♦ **tennis player** N tennista *m/f*.

♦ **tennis racket** N racchetta da tennis.

♦ **tennis shoes** NPL scarpe *fpl* da tennis.

ten·or ['tɛnəʳ] **1** ADJ (*voice*) tenorile; (*part*) del tenore; (*instrument*) tenore *inv*.

2 N (*Mus, frm: of speech, discussion*) tenore *m*.

ten·pin bowl·ing [ˌtɛnpɪnˈbəʊlɪŋ] N (*Brit*) bowling *m*.

tense[1] [tɛns] N (*Gram*) tempo; **in the present tense** al presente.

tense[2] [tɛns] 1 ADJ (*comp* **-r**, *superl* **-st**) teso(-a); **tense with fear** teso(-a) per la paura.

2 VT (*tighten: muscles*) tendere.

tensed up [ˈtɛnsdˈʌp] ADJ teso(-a).

tense·ly [ˈtɛnslɪ] ADV nervosamente.

tense·ness [ˈtɛnsnɪs] N tensione *f*.

ten·sion [ˈtɛnʃən] N tensione *f*.

tent [tɛnt] 1 N tenda.

2 ADJ da tenda.

ten·ta·cle [ˈtɛntəkl] N tentacolo.

ten·ta·tive [ˈtɛntətɪv] ADJ (*hesitant: person*) esitante, incerto(-a); (*provisional: conclusion, arrangement*) provvisorio(-a).

ten·ta·tive·ly [ˈtɛntətɪvlɪ] ADV (*see adj*) con esitazione; provvisoriamente.

tenter·hooks [ˈtɛntəˌhʊks] NPL: **to be on tenterhooks** essere sulle spine; **to keep sb on tenterhooks** tenere qn sulle spine.

tenth [tɛnθ] 1 ADJ decimo(-a).

2 N (*in series*) decimo(-a); (*fraction*) decimo *m for usage see* **fifth**.

♦ **tent peg** N picchetto (da tenda).

♦ **tent pole** N palo da tenda, montante *m*.

tenu·ous [ˈtɛnjʊəs] ADJ (*thread*) tenue; (*argument*) debole.

ten·ure [ˈtɛnjʊəʳ] N (*of land*) possesso; (*of office*) incarico; **to have tenure** (*guaranteed employment*) essere di ruolo.

tep·id [ˈtɛpɪd] ADJ (*also fig*) tiepido(-a).

Ter. ABBR = **terrace**.

ter·cen·te·nary [ˌtɜːsɛnˈtiːnərɪ] N terzo centenario.

term [tɜːm] 1 N **a** (*limit*) termine *m*; (*period*) periodo; **in the short term** a breve scadenza; **in the long term** a lungo andare; **during his term of office** durante il suo incarico; **term of imprisonment** periodo di detenzione *or* prigionia; **to serve a 3-year term of imprisonment** scontare 3 anni di carcere

b (*Scol*) trimestre *m*; (*Law*) sessione *f*; **the autumn/spring/summer term** il primo/secondo/terzo trimestre

c (*word, expression*) termine *m*, vocabolo; **to tell sb sth in no uncertain terms** dire qc chiaro e tondo a qn, dire qc a qn senza mezzi termini; **in terms of ...** in termini di...

d : **terms** NPL (*conditions*) condizioni *fpl*; (*Comm*) prezzi *mpl*, tariffe *fpl*; **terms of employment** condizioni di impiego; **terms of reference** termini *mpl* (stabiliti); **"easy terms"** (*Comm*) "facilitazioni di pagamento"; **reduced terms for pensioners** agevolazioni *fpl* per i pensionati; **on one's own terms** a modo proprio; **to come to terms with** (*person*) arrivare a un accordo con; (*problem*) affrontare; **to come to terms with a situation** accettare una situazione; **not on any terms** a nessuna condizione

e : **terms** NPL (*relations*): **to be on good terms with** avere buoni rapporti con; **not to be on speaking terms with sb** non rivolgere la parola a qc.

2 VT (*name*) definire.

♦ **term exams** NPL esami *mpl* di fine trimestre.

ter·mi·nal [ˈtɜːmɪnəl] 1 ADJ (*patient*) incurabile, terminale; (*disease*) letale; (*stages*) finale, terminale, conclusivo(-a).

2 N **a** (*Elec, Comput*) terminale *m* **b** (*of bus*) capolinea *m*; (*of train*) stazione *f* terminale; (*Aer depot: for oil,*

containers) terminal *m inv*.

ter·mi·nal·ly [ˈtɜːmɪnəlɪ] ADV: **the terminally ill** i malati terminali.

ter·mi·nate [ˈtɜːmɪˌneɪt] 1 VT terminare, mettere fine a; (*contract*) rescindere.

2 VI (*contract*) terminare, concludersi; (*train, bus*) finire; **to terminate in** finire in *or* con.

ter·mi·na·tion [ˌtɜːmɪˈneɪʃən] N fine *f*; (*of contract*) rescissione *f*; **termination of pregnancy** (*Brit Med*) interruzione *f* di gravidanza.

ter·mi·nol·ogy [ˌtɜːmɪˈnɒlədʒɪ] N terminologia.

ter·mi·nus [ˈtɜːmɪnəs] N (*pl* **termini** [ˈtɜːmɪnaɪ]) (*of bus*) capolinea *m*; (*of train*) stazione *f* terminale; (*building: Rail*) stazione *f* di testa.

ter·mite [ˈtɜːmaɪt] N termite *f*.

♦ **term paper** N (*Am Univ*) *saggio scritto da consegnare a fine trimestre*.

term·time [ˈtɜːmˌtaɪm] N: **in termtime** durante il trimestre.

Terr., Ter. ABBR = **terrace**.

ter·race [ˈtɛrəs] N **a** (*patio, verandah*) terrazza, terrazzo **b** (*Brit: row of houses*) fila di case a schiera **c** : **the terraces** NPL (*Brit Sport*) le gradinate.

ter·raced [ˈtɛrɪst] ADJ (*layered: hillside, garden*) terrazzato (-a), a terrazze; (*in a row: house, cottage*) a schiera.

ter·racing [ˈtɛrəsɪŋ] N (*Agr*) terrazzamento; (*Brit Sport*): **the terracing** le gradinate.

ter·ra·cot·ta [ˌtɛrəˈkɒtə] N terracotta.

ter·rain [təˈreɪn] N terreno.

ter·res·trial [tɪˈrɛstrɪəl] ADJ terrestre.

ter·ri·ble [ˈtɛrəbl] ADJ (*gen*) terribile, tremendo(-a); (*play, film*) orrendo(-a); (*performance, report*) pessimo(-a); (*weather*) bruttissimo(-a); **to be terrible at sth** essere un disastro in qc.

ter·ri·bly [ˈtɛrəblɪ] ADV (*very*) tremendamente, terribilmente; (*very badly: play, sing*) malissimo.

ter·ri·er [ˈtɛrɪəʳ] N terrier *m inv*.

ter·rif·ic [təˈrɪfɪk] ADJ (*fam: very good: performance, book, news*) fantastico(-a), stupendo(-a), formidabile, eccezionale; (*extreme: heat, speed, noise, anxiety*) spaventoso(-a); (: *amount, scare*) enorme; (*terrifying*) terrificante, impressionante.

ter·ri·fy [ˈtɛrɪˌfaɪ] VT terrorizzare; **to be terrified** essere atterrito(-a); **to be terrified of** avere il terrore folle di.

ter·ri·fy·ing [ˈtɛrɪˌfaɪɪŋ] ADJ terrificante.

ter·ri·fy·ing·ly [ˈtɛrɪˌfaɪɪŋlɪ] ADV paurosamente, spaventosamente.

ter·rine [tɛˈriːn] N (*for pâté*) terrina.

ter·ri·to·rial [ˌtɛrɪˈtɔːrɪəl] 1 ADJ territoriale.

2 N: **Territorial** (*Brit: soldier*) soldato della milizia territoriale.

♦ **Territorial Army** N (*Brit*) Milizia Territoriale.

♦ **territorial waters** NPL acque *fpl* territoriali.

ter·ri·tory [ˈtɛrɪtərɪ] N territorio.

ter·ror [ˈtɛrəʳ] N (*fear*) terrore *m*; (*fam: child*) peste *f*; **to live in terror of sth** vivere nel terrore di qc; **she's a terror on the roads** al volante è un pericolo pubblico; **you little terror!** piccola peste!

ter·ror·ism [ˈtɛrəˌrɪzəm] N terrorismo.

ter·ror·ist [ˈtɛrərɪst] ADJ, N terrorista (*m/f*).

ter·ror·ize [ˈtɛrəˌraɪz] VT terrorizzare.

♦ **terror-stricken** [ˈtɛrəˌstrɪkən] ADJ terrorizzato(-a), atterrito(-a).

ter·ry [ˈtɛrɪ] N (*also: terry towelling*) (tessuto di) spugna.

terse [tɜːs] ADJ (*comp* **-r**, *superl* **-st**) (*style*) conciso(-a);

(*reply*) laconico(-a).

terse·ly ['tɜːslɪ] ADV (*see adj*) concisamente; laconicamente.

terse·ness ['tɜːsnɪs] N (*see adj*) concisione *f*; laconicità *f inv*.

ter·tiary ['tɜːʃərɪ] ADJ (*gen*) terziario(-a); **tertiary education** (*Brit*) educazione *f* superiore post-scolastica; **tertiary sector** (*Industry*) settore *m* terziario.

Tery·lene® ['tɛrəˌliːn] N terital ® *m*, terilene ® *m*.

TESL ['tɛsl] N ABBR = *Teaching of English as a Second Language*.

TESSA ['tɛsə] N ABBR (*Brit*: = *Tax Exempt Special Savings Account*) *deposito a risparmio esente da tasse*.

test [tɛst] ☐1 N (*trial, check*) prova; (: *of goods in factory*) controllo, collaudo; (: *of machinery*) collaudo; (*Med*) analisi *f inv*, esame *m*; (*Chem*) analisi; (*exam: of intelligence*) test *m inv*; (: *Scol: written*) compito in classe; (: *oral*) interrogazione *f*; (*Aut: also:* **driving test**) esame *m* di guida; **a weekly Italian test** un compito in classe di italiano alla settimana; **to do tests on sth** fare delle prove su qc; **to put sth to the test** mettere qc alla prova; **it has stood the test of time** ha resistito alla prova del tempo.

☐2 VT (*gen*) provare, controllare; (*try, ascertain the worth of*) mettere alla prova; (*machine*) collaudare; (*Chem*) analizzare; (*blood, urine*) fare le analisi di; (*new drug*) sperimentare; (*Psych*) fare un test psicologico a; **to have one's eyes** *etc* **tested** farsi controllare la vista *etc*; **to test sb's patience** mettere alla prova la pazienza di qn; **to test sb in mathematics** esaminare *or* interrogare qn in matematica; **to test sb for sth** fare delle analisi a qn per qc; **to test sth for sth** analizzare qc alla ricerca di qc.

☐3 VI: **to test (for)** fare ricerche (per trovare); **testing, testing ...** (*Telec*) prova, prova....

☐4 ADJ di collaudo.

tes·ta·ment ['tɛstəmənt] N testamento; **the Old/New Testament** (*Rel*) il Vecchio/Nuovo Testamento.

♦ **test ban** N (*also:* **nuclear test ban**) divieto dei test nucleari.

♦ **test bore** N (*for oil*) sondaggio.

♦ **test card** N (*TV*) monoscopio.

♦ **test case** N (*Law, fig*) caso che costituisce un precedente.

♦ **test drive** N prova su strada.

♦ **test-drive** ['tɛstˌdraɪv] (*pt* **test-drove** ['tɛstˌdrəʊv], *pp* **test-driven** ['tɛstˌdrɪvn]) VT provare su strada.

tes·tes ['tɛstiːz] NPL of **testis**.

♦ **test flight** N (*Aer*) volo di prova *or* collaudo.

tes·ti·cle ['tɛstɪkl] N testicolo.

tes·ti·fy ['tɛstɪˌfaɪ] VI (*Law*) testimoniare, deporre; **to testify in favour** (*Brit*) *or* **favor** (*Am*) **of/against sb** testimoniare a favore di/contro qn; **to testify to sth** (*Law*) testimoniare qc; (*prove*) comprovare *or* dimostrare qc; (*be sign of*) essere una prova di qc.

testi·ly ['tɛstɪlɪ] ADV (*behave*) con impazienza; (*speak*) con irritazione, con un tono irritato.

tes·ti·mo·nial [ˌtɛstɪˈməʊnɪəl] N **a** (*Brit: reference*) referenze *fpl*, benservito **b** (*gift*) tributo di riconoscimento, testimonianza di stima.

tes·ti·mo·ny ['tɛstɪmənɪ] N (*Law*) testimonianza, deposizione *f*.

test·ing ['tɛstɪŋ] ADJ (*difficult: time*) duro(-a).

♦ **testing ground** N terreno di prova.

tes·tis ['tɛstɪs] N (*pl* **testes**) (*frm*) testicolo.

♦ **test match** N (*Cricket, Rugby*) partita internazionale.

tes·tos·ter·one [tɛˈstɒstəˌrəʊn] N testosterone *m*.

♦ **test paper** N (*Chem*) carta reattiva; (*Scol*) prova (scritta).

♦ **test pilot** N pilota *m* collaudatore.

♦ **test tube** N (*Chem*) provetta.

♦ **test-tube baby** [ˌtɛsttjuːbˈbeɪbɪ] N bambino(-a) in provetta.

tes·ty ['tɛstɪ] ADJ (*comp* **-ier**, *superl* **-iest**) (*impatient: person*) irritabile; (: *remark*) stizzoso(-a).

teta·nus ['tɛtənəs] N tetano.

tetchy ['tɛtʃɪ] ADJ (*comp* **-ier**, *superl* **-iest**) irritabile, irascibile.

teth·er ['tɛðə'] ☐1 N laccio; **to be at the end of one's tether** (*fig*) non poterne più.

☐2 VT (*animal*) legare.

text [tɛkst] N testo.

text·book ['tɛkstˌbʊk] N libro di testo.

tex·tile ['tɛkstaɪl] ☐1 ADJ tessile; **textile industry** industria tessile.

☐2 N tessuto; **textiles** NPL (*industry*) industria tessile; (*materials*) tessuti *mpl*.

tex·tu·al ['tɛkstjʊəl] ADJ (*error, differences*) di testo; (*criticism*) testuale, basato(-a) sul testo.

tex·ture ['tɛkstʃə'] N (*gen*) consistenza; (*of soil*) struttura; **the material has a rough texture** la stoffa è ruvida al tatto; **the smooth texture of her skin** la sua pelle liscia.

TGIF [ˌtiːdʒiːaɪˈɛf] EXCL, ABBR (*fam*) = *thank God it's Friday*.

TGWU [ˌtiːdʒiːdʌbljuːˈjuː] N ABBR (*Brit*: = *Transport and General Workers' Union*) *sindacato degli operai dei trasporti e non specializzati*.

Thai [taɪ] ☐1 ADJ tailandese.

☐2 N (*person*) tailandese *m/f*; (*language*) tailandese *m*.

Thai·land ['taɪˌlænd] N la Tailandia.

tha·lido·mide® [θəˈlɪdəʊˌmaɪd] N talidomide ® *m*.

Thames [tɛmz] N: **the Thames** il Tamigi.

than [ðæn; *weak form* ðən] CONJ che; (*with numerals, pronouns, proper names*) di; **you have more than me/Mary/ten** ne hai più di me/Mary/dieci; **she has more apples than pears** ha più mele che pere; **more than ever** più che mai; **she is older than you think** è più vecchia di quanto tu (non) creda; **it was a better play than we expected** la commedia è stata migliore di quanto (non) pensassimo; **they have more money than we have** hanno più soldi di noi; **it is better to phone than to write** è meglio telefonare che scrivere; **more/less than 90** più/meno di 90; **more than once** più di una volta; **more often than not** il più delle volte; **I'd die rather than admit I'm wrong** piuttosto che ammettere di aver torto morirei; **no sooner did he leave than the phone rang** non appena uscì il telefono suonò; **you know her better than I do** la conosci meglio di me *or* di quanto non la conosca io.

thank [θæŋk] VT: **to thank sb (for sth/for doing sth)** ringraziare qn (per qc/per aver fatto qc); **thank you (very much)** grazie (mille), tante grazie; **no thank you** no grazie; **to have only o.s. to thank for sth** dovere ringraziare se stesso per qc; **I have John to thank for getting me the job** devo ringraziare John per avermi trovato il lavoro; **I know who to thank!** (*iro*) so io chi devo ringraziare!; **thank heavens/God!** grazie al cielo/a Dio!; *see also* **thanks**.

thank·ful ['θæŋkfʊl] ADJ: **thankful (to sb for sth)** grato(-a) *or* riconoscente (a qn per qc); **let us be thankful that it's over** ringraziamo il cielo che è tutto finito; **thankful for/that ...** (*relieved*) sollevato(-a) da/dal fatto che....

thank·ful·ly ['θæŋkfəlɪ] ADV (*gratefully*) con riconoscenza; (*with relief*) con sollievo; **thankfully there were few victims** grazie al cielo ci sono state poche vittime.

thank·less ['θæŋklɪs] ADJ (*unrewarding*: *task*) ingrato(-a).

thanks [θæŋks] [1] NPL ringraziamenti *mpl*, grazie *m inv*; **thanks to** grazie a; **that's all the thanks I get!** bel ringraziamento!; **thanks to you ...** (*also iro*) grazie a te...; **it's all thanks to** (*also iro*) è tutto merito di; **it's small or no thanks to you that ...** non è certo per merito tuo se...; **thanks be to God** rendiamo grazie a Dio.

[2] EXCL grazie!; **(very) many thanks** grazie mille.

thanks·giving ['θæŋks,gɪvɪŋ] N ringraziamento.

♦ **Thanksgiving Day** N (*Am: also:* **Thanksgiving**) giorno del ringraziamento.

thank·you ['θæŋk,ju:] [1] N ringraziamento.

[2] ADJ: **a thankyou letter/card** una lettera/un biglietto di ringraziamento.

---

that [ðæt; *weak form* ðət]

[1] DEM ADJ (*pl* **those**) quel (quell', quello) *m*, quella (quell') *f*; (*as opposed to "this"*) quello(-a) là;

▷**that** *book* quel libro

▷**what about that** *cheque*? e quel famoso assegno?

▷**that wretched** *dog*! quel cagnaccio!

▷**that** *man* quell'uomo

▷**I only met her that** *once* l'ho incontrata solo quella volta

▷**that** *one* **over there** quello là

▷**it's not this picture but that** *one* **I like** non mi piace questo quadro ma quello là

▷**that crazy** *son* **of yours** quel pazzo di tuo figlio

▷**that** *woman* quella donna.

[2] DEM PRON (*pl* **those**) ciò; (*as opposed to 'this'*) quello (-a);

▷*after* **that** dopo

▷**and** *after* **that he left** dopodiché uscì

▷*at* **that, she ...** con ciò lei...

▷**and they were late** *at* **that** e per di più erano in ritardo

▷**if it** *comes to* **that** se è per quello

▷**that's my** *house* quella è la mia casa

▷**I prefer this** *to* **that** preferisco questo a quello

▷**£5? — it must have cost** *more than* **that** 5 sterline? — dev'essere costato di più

▷**that** *is* **(to say), ...** cioè..., vale a dire...

▷**that's** *Joe* quello è Joe

▷**do it** *like* **that** fallo così

▷**how do you** *like* **that?** (*iro*) niente male, ti pare?

▷**that's** *odd*! che strano!

▷**that's** *that*! punto e basta!

▷**you can't go and that's** *that*! non puoi andare e basta!

▷**that's** *true* è proprio vero

▷*what* **is that?** che cos'è quello?

▷**that's** *what* **he said** questo è ciò che ha detto

▷*who* **is that?** chi è quello?

▷*with* **that, she ...** con ciò lei...

▷**is that** *you*? sei tu?

[3] DEM ADV così;

▷**he was that** *angry* (*fam*) tanto era arrabbiato

▷**cheer up, it isn't that** *bad* coraggio, non va poi così male

▷**that** *high* così alto(-a), alto(-a) così

▷**it's about that** *high* è alto circa così

▷**I didn't know he was that** *ill* non sapevo che fosse così malato

▷**that** *many* così tanti(-e)

▷**that** *much* così tanto(-a)

▷**this one isn't that** *much* **more difficult** questo non è poi tanto più difficile

▷**I can't work that** *much* non posso lavorare così tanto.

[4] REL PRON

[a] che, il/la quale; (*indirect*) cui;

▷*all* **(that) I have** tutto ciò che ho

▷**the** *book* **(that) I read** il libro che ho letto

▷**the** *box* **(that) I put it in** la scatola in cui l'ho messo

▷**the** *house* **(that) we're speaking of** la casa di cui stiamo parlando

▷**the** *man* **(that) I saw** l'uomo che ho visto

▷**the** *man* **(that) I gave it to** l'uomo (a) cui l'ho dato

▷*not* **that I know of** non che io sappia

▷**the** *people* **(that) I spoke to** le persone con cui *or* con le quali ho parlato

[b] (*of time: when*) in cui;

▷**on the** *day* **that he came** il giorno in cui *or* quando venne

▷**the** *evening/winter* **that** la sera/l'inverno in cui.

[5] CONJ che;

▷**I** *believe* **that he exists** credo che esista

▷*not* **that I want to, of course** non che lo voglia, naturalmente

▷*oh* **that I could ...** oh se potessi...

▷**he** *said* **that ...** disse che...

▷**that he** *should* **behave like this is incredible** è incredibile che si sia comportato così

▷*so* **that** [OR] **in order that** affinché + *sub*, perché + *sub*.

---

thatch [θætʃ] [1] N (*on roof*) copertura di paglia (*or* frasche).

[2] VT coprire con paglia (*or* frasche).

thatched [θætʃt] ADJ (*roof*) di paglia (*or* frasche); (*cottage*) con il tetto di paglia (*or* frasche).

Thatch·er·ism ['θætʃə,rɪzəm] N thatcherismo.

thaw [θɔ:] [1] N disgelo; (*fig: easing up*) distensione *f*.

[2] VT (*also:* **thaw out**: *food*) (fare) scongelare.

[3] VI (*weather*) sgelare; (*ice*) sciogliersi; (*also:* **thaw out**: *frozen food, cold toes*) scongelarsi; (*fig: person*) aprirsi; (: *relations*) distendersi; **it's thawing** sta sgelando.

---

the [ði:; *weak form* ðə]

[1] DEF ART

[a] il (lo, l') *m*, la (l') *f*, i (gli) *mpl*, le *fpl*;

▷**in this age of the** *computer* **...** in quest'era di computer...

▷**she was the** *elder* era la maggiore delle due

▷**did you see the** *photographs*? hai visto le fotografie?

▷**to play the** *piano* suonare il piano

▷**if it is within the realms of the** *possible* se è umanamente possibile

▷**the** *rich* **and the** *poor* i ricchi e i poveri

▷**do you know the** *Smiths*? conosci gli Smith?

▷**could you pass me the** *sugar*? mi passi lo zucchero?

▷**it's on the** *table* è sulla tavola

▷**I haven't the** *time* non ho il tempo

▷**it was the *year* of the student riots** quello era l'anno delle manifestazioni studentesche

b (*distributive*)

▷**1,600 lire to the *dollar*** 1.600 lire per un dollaro

▷**eggs are usually sold by the *dozen*** di solito le uova si vendono alla dozzina

▷**this car does 30 miles to the *gallon*** ≈ questa macchina fa 11 chilometri con un litro

▷**paid by the *hour*** pagato(-a) a ore

c (*emphatic*)

▷**he's THE *man* for the job** è proprio l'uomo adatto al lavoro

d (*in titles*)

▷**Richard the *Second*** Riccardo II

▷**Ivan the *Terrible*** Ivan il terribile.

2 ADV

▷**she looks all the *better* for it** adesso ha un aspetto molto più sano

▷**the *more* he works the *more* he earns** più lavora più guadagna

▷**(all) the *more* so because ...** soprattutto perché...

▷**the *sooner* the *better*** prima è, meglio è.

theatre, (*Am*) **theater** ['θɪətə'] N teatro; **to go to the theatre** andare a teatro; **operating theatre** sala operatoria; **lecture theatre** auditorium *m inv*; **theatre of war** teatro di guerra.

♦**theatre company**, (*Am*) **theater company** N compagnia teatrale.

theatre-goer, (*Am*) **theater·goer** ['θɪətə,gəʊə'] N habitué *m/f inv* del teatro, frequentatore(-trice) abituale di teatri.

the·at·ri·cal [θɪ'ætrɪkəl] ADJ (*also fig*) teatrale.

Thebes [θiːbz] NSG Tebe *f*.

thee [ðiː] PRON (*old, poet*) ti.

theft [θeft] N furto.

their [ðeə'] POSS ADJ il/la loro, i/le loro *pl*.

theirs [ðeəz] POSS PRON il/la loro, i/le loro *pl*; **this car is theirs** questa macchina è loro; **a friend of theirs** un loro amico.

the·ism ['θiːɪzəm] N teismo.

them [ðem, *weak form* ðəm] PERS PRON PL a (*direct*: *unstressed*: *people*) li/le; (: *stressed*: *people*) loro; (: *things*) essi(-e); **I watched them** li ho guardati *or* le ho guardate; **he knows THEM** conosce LORO; **if I were them** se io fossi in loro; **it's them!** eccoli!

b (*indirect*: *people*) loro(*after verb*), gli (*fam*); (: *things*) essi(-e); **she gave them the money** ha dato loro i soldi, gli ha dato i soldi (*fam*)

c (*after prep*: *people*) loro; (: *things*) essi(-e); **I'm thinking of them** penso a loro; **as for them** quanto a loro (*or* a questi); **both of them** tutt'e due; **several of them** parecchi (di loro *or* di essi); **give me a few of them** dammene un po' *or* qualcuno; **I don't like either of them** non mi piace nessuno dei due; **none of them would do it** nessuno (di loro) lo voleva fare; **that was very good of them** è stato molto gentile da parte loro.

the·mat·ic [θiː'mætɪk] ADJ (*frm*: *approach, treatment, arrangement*) per temi; (*Art, Mus, Literature, Ling*) tematico(-a).

theme [θiːm] N (*of speech, argument*) tema *m*, argomento; (*Mus*) tema.

♦**theme park** N parco a tema.

♦**theme song** N (*of musical, film*) motivo conduttore;

(*Am*: *signature tune*) sigla musicale.

♦**theme tune** N tema *m* musicale.

them·selves [ðəm'selvz] PERS PRON PL (*reflexive*) si; (*emphatic*) loro stessi(-e); (*after prep*) se stessi(-e); **between themselves** tra (di) loro; **they did it (all) by themselves** hanno fatto tutto da soli; see also **oneself**.

then [ðen] 1 ADV a (*at that time*) allora; **it was then that ...** fu allora che...; **before/since then** prima di/da allora; **until then** fino ad allora; **from then on** da allora in poi; **by then** allora; **then and there** all'istante

b (*afterwards, next*) poi, dopo; **what happened then?** e poi cos'è successo?; **and then what?** e poi?, e allora?

c (*in that case*) allora, dunque; **what do you want me to do then?** allora cosa vuoi che faccia?; **well then** dunque; **and *or* but then again** ma del resto; **I like it, but then I'm biased** mi piace, ma del resto non sono del tutto imparziale; **it would be awkward at work, and then there's the family** sarebbe difficile al lavoro, e poi c'è la famiglia.

2 ADJ: **the then president** l'allora presidente *or* il presidente di allora.

thence [ðens] ADV (*frm*: *from that place*) di lì *or* là; (*therefore*) quindi, perciò.

thence·forth ['ðens'fɔ,θ] ADV (*frm*) da allora in poi.

theo·cen·tric [,θiə'sentrɪk] ADJ teocentrico(-a).

the·oc·ra·cy [θi'ɒkrəsɪ] N (*Pol*) teocrazia.

the·odo·lite [θi'ɒdə,laɪt] N teodolite *m*.

theo·lo·gian [θɪə'ləʊdʒən] N teologo(-a).

theo·logi·cal [θɪə'lɒdʒɪkəl] ADJ teologico(-a).

♦**theological virtues** NPL virtù *fpl* teologali.

the·ol·ogy [θɪ'ɒlədʒɪ] N teologia.

theo·rem ['θɪərəm] N (*Math*) teorema *m*.

theo·ret·ical [θɪə'retɪkəl], **theoretic** [θɪə'retɪk] ADJ (*Science*) teoretico(-a); (*possibility*) teorico(-a).

theo·reti·cal·ly [θɪə'retɪkəlɪ] ADV in linea teorica; **theoretically possible** teoricamente possibile.

theo·reti·cian [,θɪərɪ'tɪʃən] N teorico(-a).

theo·rist ['θɪərɪst] N teorico(-a).

theo·rize ['θɪə,raɪz] VI: **to theorize (about)** teorizzare (su).

theo·ry ['θɪərɪ] N (*statement, hypothesis*) teoria; **in theory** in teoria.

thera·peu·tic [,θerə'pjuːtɪk] ADJ terapeutico(-a).

thera·peu·tics [,θerə'pjuːtɪks] NSG terapeutica.

thera·pist ['θerəpɪst] N terapista *m/f*.

thera·py ['θerəpɪ] N terapia.

there [ðeə']

1 ADV

a (*at that place*) lì *or* là;

▷**he's not *all* there** (*fam*) gli manca un venerdì

▷**_back_ there** là dietro

▷**_down_ there** laggiù

▷**to _go_ there and back** andarci e ritornare

▷**_in_ there** là dentro

▷**we _left_ there** ce ne andammo

▷**_on_ there** lassù

▷**_over_ there** là

▷**_put_ it there** mettilo lì *or* là

▷**we _shall be_ there at 8** saremo lì alle 8

▷**we _shall be_ there for sure** ci saremo di sicuro

▷**_through_ there** di là

▷**he _went_ there** ci è andato

b (*to draw attention to sb/sth*)

▷**there _he is_!** eccolo (là)!

▷*mind* out there! attenzione!
▷*that man* there quell'uomo là
▷**there's** *the bus* ecco l'autobus
▷**there** *we differ* su questo non siamo d'accordo
▷*you* there! ehilà!
▷**there** *you are*! eccoti!; (*I told you so*) visto?
▷**there** *you are wrong* in questo hai torto
▷**there** *you go again* eccoti di nuovo
[c]: **there** *is* c'è
▷**there** *are* ci sono
▷**there** *has been* ... c'è stato...
▷**there** *is* no wine left non c'è più vino
▷**there** *might be* time forse c'è tempo
▷**there** *might be* room forse c'è posto
▷**there** *was* laughter at this al che ci fu uno scoppio di risa
▷**there** *were* 10 of them erano in 10
▷**there** *will be* 8 people for dinner tonight ci saranno 8 persone a cena stasera.
[2] EXCL: **there, there, don't cry** su, su, non piangere.

there·abouts [ˈðɛərəˌbaʊts] ADV (*place*) nei pressi, nei dintorni, da quelle parti; (*amount*) giù di lì, all'incirca.
there·after [ˌðɛərˈɑːftəʳ] ADV (*past*) da allora in poi; (*future*) in seguito.
there·by [ˌðɛəˈbaɪ] ADV con ciò.
there·fore [ˈðɛəˌfɔːʳ] ADV perciò, quindi; **it isn't therefore any better** per questo non è meglio.
there·in [ˌðɛərˈɪn] ADV (*old, liter*) ivi; **and therein lies** ... ed in ciò sta la causa di... .
there's [ðɛəz] ADV [a] = there is [b] = there has.
there·upon [ˌðɛərʌˈpɒn] ADV (*at that point*) a quel punto; (*frm: on that subject*) in merito.
therm [θɜːm] N ≈ 1.055 056 × 10⁸ joule (*unità termica usata in Gran Bretagna*).
ther·mal [ˈθɜːməl] ADJ (*currents, spring*) termale; (*underwear*) termico(-a); (*paper*) termosensibile.
♦ **thermal power station** N centrale *f* termoelettrica.
♦ **thermal printer** N stampante *f* termica.
thermo... [ˈθɜːməʊ] PREF termo... .
ther·mo·dy·nam·ic [ˌθɜːməʊdaɪˈnæmɪk] ADJ termodinamico(-a).
ther·mo·dy·nam·ics [ˌθɜːməʊdaɪˈnæmɪks] NSG termodinamica.
ther·mom·eter [θəˈmɒmɪtəʳ] N termometro.
ther·mo·nu·clear [ˌθɜːməʊˈnjuːklɪəʳ] ADJ termonucleare.
ther·mo·plas·tic [ˌθɜːməʊˈplæstɪk] ADJ termoplastico(-a).
Ther·mos® [ˈθɜːmɒs] N (*also:* **Thermos flask** *or* **bottle**) thermos ® *m inv*.
ther·mo·set·ting [ˌθɜːməʊˈsɛtɪŋ] ADJ termoindurente.
ther·mo·stat [ˈθɜːməˌstæt] N termostato.
ther·mo·stat·ic [ˌθɜːməˈstætɪk] ADJ termostatico(-a).
♦ **thermostatic temperature control** N termoregolazione *f*.
the·sau·rus [θɪˈsɔːrəs] N dizionario dei sinonimi.
these [ðiːz] (*pl of* **this**) [1] DEM ADJ questi(-e); (*as opposed to "those"*) questi(-e) (qui); **these ones over here** questi qui; **how are you getting on these days?** come ti va di questi tempi?.
[2] DEM PRON questi(-e).
Theseus [ˈθiːsɪəs] N Teseo.
the·sis [ˈθiːsɪs] N (*pl* **theses** [ˈθiːsiːz]) tesi *f inv*.
they [ðeɪ] PERS PRON PL [a] (*gen*) essi(-e); (*people only*) loro; **they have gone** sono partiti (*or* partite); **there they are**

eccoli (*or* eccole) là; THEY **know nothing about it** LORO non ne sanno nulla [b] (*people in general*) si; **they say that** ... (*it is said that*) si dice che... .
they'd [ðeɪd] [a] = they would [b] = they had.
they'll [ðeɪl] [a] = they will [b] = they shall.
they're [ðɛəʳ] = they are.
they've [ðeɪv] = they have.
thick [θɪk] [1] ADJ (*comp* **-er**, *superl* **-est**) [a] (*gen*) grosso(-a); (*wall, layer, line*) spesso(-a); (*hair*) folto(-a); (*soup, paint, smoke*) denso(-a); (*fog, vegetation*) fitto(-a); (*crowd*) compatto(-a); (*strong: accent*) marcato(-a); **it's 20 cm thick** ha uno spessore di 20 cm; **the furniture was thick with dust** sui mobili c'era la polvere di mesi; **the air was thick with exhaust fumes** l'aria era satura di gas di scarico; **the leaves were thick on the ground** sul terreno c'era una spessa coltre di foglie; **they're thick as thieves** (*fig fam*) sono amici per la pelle
[b] (*fam: stupid*) ottuso(-a), lento(-a); **he's as thick as two short planks** (*Brit*) è proprio duro di comprendonio.
[2] ADV: **to spread sth thick** spalmare uno spesso strato di qc; **to cut sth thick** tagliare qc a fette grosse; **thick and fast** senza tregua; **to lay it on (a bit) thick** (*fig fam: exaggerate*) calcare un po' la mano.
[3] N: **in the thick of** (*activity, situation, event*) nel mezzo di; **in the thick of battle** nel mezzo della battaglia; **he likes to be in the thick of things** gli piace buttarsi nella mischia; **through thick and thin** nella buona e nella cattiva sorte.
thick·en [ˈθɪkən] [1] VT (*gen*) ispessire; (*sauce*) rendere più denso(-a).
[2] VI (*gen*) ispessirsi; (*grow denser: forest, jungle*) infittirsi; **the plot thickens** (*fig*) il mistero s'infittisce.
thick·en·er [ˈθɪkənəʳ] N addensante *m*.
thick·et [ˈθɪkɪt] N boscaglia.
thick·headed [ˌθɪkˈhɛdɪd] ADJ (*fam*) ottuso(-a), tonto(-a).
♦ **thick-lipped** [ˌθɪkˈlɪpt] ADJ dalle labbra grosse.
thick·ly [ˈθɪklɪ] ADV (*spread*) a strati spessi; (*cut*) a fette grosse; (*populated*) densamente; **the snow fell thickly** la neve cadeva fitta fitta; **a thickly-wooded slope** un pendio molto boscoso.
thick·ness [ˈθɪknɪs] N (*gen*) spessore *m*; (*of fog*) densità *f inv*; (*of hair*) foltezza.
♦ **thickness gauge** N spessimetro.
thick·set [ˌθɪkˈsɛt] ADJ (*person*) tarchiato(-a), tozzo(-a).
♦ **thick-skinned** [ˌθɪkˈskɪnd] ADJ (*fig: insensitive*) insensibile, coriaceo(-a).
thief [θiːf] N (*pl* **thieves** [θiːvz]) ladro(-a); **stop thief!** al ladro!
thieve [θiːv] VI rubare.
thiev·ing [ˈθiːvɪŋ] [1] ADJ ladro(-a); **you thieving scoundrel!** brutto ladruncolo!.
[2] N furti *mpl*.
thigh [θaɪ] N coscia.
thigh·bone [ˈθaɪˌbəʊn] N femore *m*.
thim·ble [ˈθɪmbl] N ditale *m*.
thin [θɪn] [1] ADJ (*comp* **-ner**, *superl* **-nest**) (*gen*) sottile; (*paper, glass*) fine; (*blanket, parcel, coat, fog*) leggero(-a); (*soup, paint, honey*) poco denso(-a); (*vegetation, hair, crowd*) rado(-a); (*population*) scarso(-a); (*person*) esile, magro(-a); (*crop, excuse, argument*) magro(-a); **at 20,000 metres the air is thin** a 20.000 metri l'aria è molto rarefatta; **the crowd seemed suddenly thinner** improvvisamente la folla sembrò essersi diradata; **he's as thin as a rake** è magro come un chiodo; **to vanish into thin air** volatilizzarsi; **doctors are thin on the ground at**

the moment i dottori scarseggiano in questo periodo. ② ADV: **to spread sth thin** spalmare uno strato sottile di qc; **to cut sth thin** tagliare qc a fette sottili.

③ VT (*also:* **thin down**: *sauce, paint*) diluire; (*also:* **thin out**: *trees, plants, hair*) sfoltire.

④ VI (*fog*) diradarsi; (*also:* **thin out**: *crowd*) disperdersi; **his hair is thinning** sta perdendo i capelli.

thine [ðaɪn] POSS PRON (*old, poet*) il/la tuo(-a).

thing [θɪŋ] N **a** cosa; (*object*) oggetto; (*contraption*) aggeggio; **a thing of beauty** una bella cosa, un bell'oggetto; **things of value** oggetti di valore; **what's that thing?** cos'è quell'affare?; **the main thing is to keep calm** la cosa più importante è mantenere la calma; **the first thing to do is (to) check the facts** la prima cosa da fare è controllare i fatti; **the best thing would be to ...** la cosa migliore sarebbe...; **for one thing** in primo luogo, tanto per cominciare; **what with one thing and another** tra una cosa e l'altra; **if it's not one thing it's the other** se non è una è l'altra; **it's neither one thing nor the other** non è né carne né pesce; **first thing (in the morning)** come *or* per prima cosa (di mattina); **last thing (at night)** come *or* per ultima cosa (di sera); **it's a good thing that he left** è stato un bene che se ne sia andato; **it was a close** *or* **near thing** ce l'ha fatta per un pelo; **it's the (very) thing** è proprio quello che ci vuole; **the thing is ...** il fatto è che...; **it's just one of those things** sono cose che capitano; **what a thing to say!** cosa dici mai!; **how are things (with you)?** come (ti) va?; **things are going badly** le cose vanno male; **things aren't what they used to be** non è più come una volta; **not a thing to say/to wear** niente da dire/da mettersi; **I haven't done a thing about it yet** non ho ancora fatto niente; **he knows a thing or two** la sa lunga; **to make a mess of things** farla grossa, combinare un casino; **you did the right thing** (*fam*) hai fatto la cosa migliore; **to make a (big) thing out of sth** (*fam*) fare una tragedia di qc

b : **things** NPL (*belongings, clothes, equipment*) roba *sg*, cose *fpl*; **take your wet things off** togliti quella roba bagnata di dosso; **the tea things** le cose per il tè; **take your things and go!** prendi la tua roba e vattene!

c : **to do one's own thing** (*fam*) fare quello che si vuole; **she's got a thing about mice** è terrorizzata dai topi; **he's got a thing about brunettes** ha un debole per le brune; **the latest thing in hats** l'ultimo grido in fatto di cappelli

d (*creature*): **poor thing** poveretto(-a); **what a sweet little thing!** che carino!

thingu·ma·bob [ˈθɪŋəmɪˌbɒb], **thinga·ma·jig** [ˈθɪŋə-mɪˌdʒɪg], **thingum·my** [ˈθɪŋəmɪ] N (*fam*) coso, cosa.

thingy [ˈθɪŋɪ] N (*fam: person, thing*) coso(-a).

think [θɪŋk] (*vb: pt, pp* thought) ① VI (*gen*): **to think of** *or* **about sth** pensare a qc; (*more carefully*) riflettere su qc; **to think of** *or* **about doing sth** pensare di fare qc; **to act without thinking** agire senza riflettere *or* pensare; **think before you reply** rifletti *or* pensa prima di rispondere; **think carefully** pensaci bene; **think again!** rifletti!, pensaci su!; **just think!** ma pensa un po'!; **let me think** fammi pensare; **let's think** pensiamoci un attimo; **to think twice before doing sth** pensare due volte prima di fare qc; **to think straight** concentrarsi; **to think aloud** pensare ad alta voce; **to think for o.s.** pensare con la propria testa; see also **think about**, **think of**.

② VT **a** (*use one's brain, have ideas*) pensare; (*imagine*) pensare, immaginare; **I can't think what he can want** non riesco ad immaginare che cosa possa volere; **did you think to bring a corkscrew?** hai pensato a portare

un cavatappi?; **I thought I might go swimming** ho pensato che potrei andare a nuotare; **think what you've done** pensa a ciò che hai fatto; **think what we could do** pensa che cosa potremmo fare; **to think evil thoughts** avere cattivi pensieri

b (*believe, consider*): **to think (that ...)** pensare (che...), credere (che...); **we all thought him a fool** pensavamo tutti che fosse un cretino; **I don't think it likely** penso che sia improbabile; **who'd have thought it possible?** chi l'avrebbe mai pensato?; **I don't think it can be done** non penso che si possa fare; **I think (that) you're wrong** penso che tu abbia torto; **I thought as much** lo sapevo io; **I think so** penso *or* credo di sì; **I should think so too!** lo credo bene!; **what do you think?** che cosa ne pensi?; **who do you think you are?** ma chi credi di essere?; **what do you think I should do?** cosa pensi che dovrei fare?; **what do you think you're doing?** ma cosa stai facendo?; **anyone would have thought she was dying!** sembrava che stesse per morire!.

③ N: **to have a think about sth** riflettere su qc; **I'd like to have a think about it** vorrei pensarci su; **you've got another think coming!** (*fam*) ti sbagli!, hai capito male!

▸ **think about** VI + PREP (*remember*) pensare a; (*consider*) pensare di; **I'll think about it** ci penserò; **what are you thinking about?** a cosa stai pensando?; **what were you thinking about!** che cosa ti è saltato in mente!; see also **think 1**

▸ **think back** VI + ADV: **to think back (to)** ripensare (a), riandare con la mente (a)

▸ **think of** VI + PREP **a** (*remember: names*) ricordare; **you can't think of everything** non ci si può ricordare di tutto, non si può pensare a tutto; **I'll be thinking of you** ti penserò

b (*consider, reckon*) pensare di; **to think of doing sth** pensare di fare qc; **I thought of going to Spain** pensavo di andare in Spagna; **he never thinks of other people's feelings** non si cura mai dei sentimenti degli altri; **think of the expense** pensa a quanto costa; **what do you think of him?** che cosa pensi di lui?; **what do you think of it?** che cosa ne pensi?; **I told him what I thought of him** gli ho detto ciò che pensavo di lui; **I wouldn't think of such a thing!** non mi sognerei mai di fare una cosa simile!; **to think highly of sb** stimare qn; **to think well of** avere una buona opinione di; **I didn't think much of it** non mi è piaciuto molto, non mi ha convinto

c (*devise: plan*) escogitare; (: *solution*) trovare; **what will he think of next?** una ne fa e cento ne pensa!; see also **think 1**

▸ **think out** VT + ADV (*plan*) elaborare; (*solution*) trovare; **this needs thinking out** bisogna pensarci su

▸ **think over** VT + ADV: **to think sth over** riflettere su qc; **I'd like to think things over** vorrei pensarci su

▸ **think through** VT + ADV: **to think sth through** riflettere a fondo su qc

▸ **think up** VT + ADV (*idea, solution*) escogitare, ideare.

think·able [ˈθɪŋkəbl] ADJ: **it isn't thinkable that ...** è impensabile che... + *sub*.

think·er [ˈθɪŋkə'] N pensatore(-trice).

think·ing [ˈθɪŋkɪŋ] ① ADJ: **to any thinking person** a ogni persona ragionevole; **to put on one's thinking cap** (*fam*) mettersi a pensare.

② N pensiero; **to my (way of) thinking** a mio parere; **I've done some thinking about it** ci ho pensato un po' sopra.

♦ **think tank** N gruppo di esperti.

♦ **thin-lipped** [ˌθɪnˈlɪpt] ADJ dalle labbra sottili; **he was**

thin-lipped with rage stringeva i denti dalla rabbia.

thin·ly [ˈθɪnlɪ] ADV (*spread*) in uno strato sottile; (*cut*) a fette sottili; (*scantily: dressed*) scarsamente; (*disguised*) malamente.

thin·ner [ˈθɪnəʳ] ⊡ COMP of **thin 1**.
⊡ N solvente *m*.

thin·ness [ˈθɪnnɪs] N (*gen*) sottigliezza; (*of person*) magrezza; (*of hair*) radezza; (*of soup*) eccessiva liquidità; (*of excuse*) debolezza.

♦ **thin-skinned** [ˌθɪnˈskɪnd] ADJ (*fig: person*) permaloso (-a).

third [θɜːd] ⊡ ADJ terzo(-a); **third time lucky!** questa è la volta buona!.
⊡ N **a** (*in series*) terzo(-a); (*fraction*) terzo, terza parte *f* *for usage see* **fifth b** (*Brit Scol: degree*) *laurea col minimo dei voti*.

♦ **third-class** [ˌθɜːdˈklɑːs] ADJ di terza classe.

♦ **third degree** N: **to give sb the third degree** (*fam: interrogation*) fare il terzo grado a qn.

♦ **third-degree burns** [ˌθɜːddɪɡriːˈbɜːnz] NPL ustioni *fpl* di terzo grado.

third·ly [ˈθɜːdlɪ] ADV in terzo luogo, terzo.

♦ **third party** N (*Law*) terzo.

♦ **third party insurance** N (*Brit*) assicurazione *f* contro terzi.

♦ **third person** N (*Gram*) terza persona.

♦ **third-rate** [ˌθɜːdˈreɪt] ADJ (di qualità) scadente, di terz'ordine.

♦ **Third World** N: **the Third World** il Terzo Mondo.

♦ **third-world** [ˌθɜːdˈwɜːld] ADJ del terzo mondo.

thirst [θɜːst] ⊡ N sete *f*; **thirst for knowledge** sete di conoscenza.
⊡ VI: **to thirst for** (*fig*) essere assetato(-a) di.

thirsty [ˈθɜːstɪ] ADJ (*comp* **-ier**, *superl* **-iest**) (*person*) assetato(-a), che ha sete; (*hum: work*) che fa venire sete; **to be thirsty** aver sete.

thir·teen [ˌθɜːˈtiːn] ADJ, N tredici (*m*) *inv for usage see* **five**.

thir·teenth [ˌθɜːˈtiːnθ] ⊡ ADJ tredicesimo(-a).
⊡ N (*in series*) tredicesimo(-a); (*fraction*) tredicesimo *for usage see* **fifth**.

thir·ti·eth [ˈθɜːtɪɪθ] ⊡ ADJ trentesimo(-a).
⊡ N (*in series*) trentesimo(-a); (*fraction*) trentesimo *for usage see* **fifth**.

thir·ty [ˈθɜːtɪ] ADJ, N trenta (*m*) *inv for usage see* **fifty**.

this [ðɪs]
⊡ DEM ADJ (*pl* **these**) questo(-a); (*as opposed to "that"*) questo(-a) (qui);
▷ **this book** questo libro
▷ **this man** quest'uomo
▷ **this one** here questo qui
▷ **it's not that picture but this one I like** non è quel quadro che mi piace, ma questo qui
▷ **this time** questa volta
▷ **this time next week** a quest'ora la settimana prossima
▷ **this time last year** l'anno scorso in questo periodo
▷ **this way** (*in this direction*) da questa parte; (*in this fashion*) così
▷ **this woman** questa donna.
⊡ DEM PRON (*pl* **these**) questo(-a); (*as opposed to 'that'*) questo(-a) (qui);
▷ **what's all this I hear about you leaving?** mi hanno detto che te ne vai, è vero?

▷ **this is April** è aprile
▷ **this is Friday** è venerdì
▷ **do it like this** fallo così
▷ **it was like this** è successo *or* è andata così
▷ **this is Mr Brown** (*in introductions, in photo*) questo è il signor Brown; (*on telephone*) sono il signor Brown
▷ **they were talking of this and that** stavano parlando del più e del meno
▷ **I prefer this to that** preferisco questo a quello
▷ **what is this?** che cos'è questo?
▷ **this is what he said** questo è ciò che ha detto
▷ **this is where I live** io abito qui
▷ **who is this?** chi è questo?
▷ **and with this he left** e con ciò se ne andò
▷ **what with this and that I was busy all week** tra una cosa e l'altra non ho avuto un momento libero questa settimana
▷ **where did you find this?** dove l'hai trovato?
⊡ DEM ADV
▷ **this far** fino qui
▷ **this high** alto(-a) così, così alto(-a)
▷ **it's about this high** è alto circa così.

this·tle [ˈθɪsl] N cardo.

thistle·down [ˈθɪslˌdaʊn] N pappo del cardo.

thith·er [ˈðɪðəʳ] ADV (*old, liter*) là, laggiù.

tho' [ðəʊ] ABBR = **though**.

thong [θɒŋ] N laccio *or* cinghia di cuoio.

tho·rac·ic [θɔːˈræsɪk] ADJ (*Med*) toracico(-a).

thor·ax [ˈθɔːræks] N torace *m*.

thorn [θɔːn] N spina; **you're a thorn in my side** *or* **flesh** (*fig*) sei la mia spina nel fianco *or* la mia croce.

thorny [ˈθɔːnɪ] ADJ (*comp* **-ier**, *superl* **-iest**) irto(-a) di spine; (*fig: tricky*) spinoso(-a), scabroso(-a).

thor·ough [ˈθʌrə] ADJ (*work, worker*) preciso(-a), accurato (-a); (*search*) minuzioso(-a); (*examination, knowledge, research*) approfondito(-a); (*cleaning*) a fondo; (*complete: attr only: idiot, scoundrel*) vero(-a); **she has a thorough knowledge of the subject** ha una profonda conoscenza in materia; **he's a thorough rascal** è una canaglia matricolata, è un vero mascalzone.

thorough·bred [ˈθʌrəˌbred] ADJ, N (*horse*) purosangue (*m/f*) *inv*.

thorough·fare [ˈθʌrəˌfɛəʳ] N strada transitabile; **"no thoroughfare"** (*Brit*) "divieto di transito".

thorough·going [ˈθʌrəˌɡəʊɪŋ] ADJ (*examination, search*) accurato(-a), minuzioso(-a); (*analysis*) approfondito (-a); (*reform*) totale; **he's a thoroughgoing idiot** è un perfetto idiota.

thor·ough·ly [ˈθʌrəlɪ] ADV **a** (*with vb: agree*) completamente; (: *understand*) perfettamente; (: *search, clean*) accuratamente, minuziosamente, a fondo; **she thoroughly agreed** fu completamente d'accordo **b** (*with adj: very*) assolutamente; **thoroughly clean** completamente pulito(-a); **a thoroughly unpleasant person** una persona assolutamente antipatica.

thor·ough·ness [ˈθʌrənɪs] N precisione *f*.

those [ðəʊz] (*pl of* **that**) ⊡ DEM ADJ quei (quegli) *mpl*, quelle *fpl*; (*as opposed to "these"*) quelli(-e) (là).
⊡ DEM PRON quelli(-e); (*as opposed to 'these'*) quelli(-e) (là); **those of you who were here yesterday** quelli di voi che erano qua ieri; **those of us who fought in the war** noi che abbiamo combattuto la guerra.

thou [ðaʊ] PRON (*old, poet*) tu.

though [ðəʊ] **1** CONJ benché + sub, sebbene + sub; **though it was raining** benché piovesse; **even though** anche se; **strange though it may appear** per quanto strano possa sembrare.

2 ADV tuttavia, comunque; **it's not so easy, though** tuttavia non è così facile.

thought [θɔːt] **1** PT, PP of **think**.

2 N (reflection, mental activity) pensiero; (idea) idea; (opinion) opinione f; (intention) intenzione f; **to be lost** or **deep in thought** essere assorto(-a) or perso(-a) nei propri pensieri; **after much thought** dopo molti ripensamenti; **I've just had a thought** mi è appena venuta un'idea; **that's a thought!** che bell'idea!; **I shudder at the very thought of it** rabbrividisco solo al pensiero; **to collect one's thoughts** raccogliere le proprie idee; **my thoughts were elsewhere** avevo la testa altrove; **with no thought for o.s.** senza pensare a se stesso; **to give sth some thought** prendere qc in considerazione, riflettere su qc; **it's the thought that counts** è il pensiero che conta.

thought·ful ['θɔːtfʊl] ADJ **a** (pensive) pensieroso(-a), pensoso(-a); (serious: book) ragionato(-a); (: remark) ponderato(-a) **b** (considerate) gentile, premuroso(-a); **how thoughtful of you!** che pensiero gentile!

thought·ful·ly ['θɔːtfəlɪ] ADV **a** (pensively) con aria pensierosa; **he looked at me thoughtfully** mi ha guardato pensieroso **b** (considerately) gentilmente.

thought·ful·ness ['θɔːtfʊlnɪs] N (pensiveness) pensosità f inv, pensierosità f inv; (kindness) gentilezza.

thought·less ['θɔːtlɪs] ADJ (person, remark, words) sconsiderato(-a); (: behaviour) scortese; **thoughtless of the consequences** senza pensare alle conseguenze.

thought·less·ly ['θɔːtlɪslɪ] ADV (see adj) sconsideratamente; scortesemente.

thought·less·ness ['θɔːtlɪsnɪs] N (of remark) sconsideratezza; (of behaviour) negligenza, trascuratezza.

♦ **thought-provoking** ['θɔːtprəˌvəʊkɪŋ] ADJ che dà da pensare, stimolante.

thou·sand ['θaʊzənd] **1** ADJ mille.

2 N mille m inv; **one/two/five thousand** mille/duemila/ cinquemila; **a thousand and one/two** mille e uno/due; **about a thousand** circa un migliaio; **in their thousands** OR **by the thousand** a migliaia; **thousands of** migliaia fpl di.

thou·sandth ['θaʊzəndθ] **1** ADJ millesimo(-a).

2 N (in classification) millesimo(-a); (fraction) millesimo.

thrash [θræʃ] **1** VT (gen) percuotere, picchiare; (with whip) frustare; (with stick) bastonare; (Sport fam: defeat) dare una batosta a, battere.

2 VI (also: **thrash about, thrash around**) agitarsi, dibattersi

▸ **thrash out** VT + ADV (problem, difficulty: discuss) sviscerare; (: solve) risolvere; (plan) mettere a punto con difficoltà.

thrash·ing ['θræʃɪŋ] N: **to give sb a thrashing** (beat) picchiare qn di santa ragione; (Sport fam: defeat) dare una batosta a qn.

thread [θrɛd] **1** N **a** filo; **cotton/nylon thread** filo di cotone/di nailon; **to hang by a thread** (fig) essere appeso a un filo; **to lose the thread (of what one is saying)** perdere il filo (del discorso); **to pick up the thread again** (fig) riprendere il filo **b** (of screw) filettatura, filetto.

2 VT (needle, beads) infilare; **to thread one's way through a crowd** infilarsi or farsi largo tra una folla; to

thread one's way between infilarsi tra.

thread·bare ['θrɛdˌbɛəʳ] ADJ (coat, blanket) logoro(-a), consumato(-a), liso(-a); (fig: argument) trito(-a).

threat [θrɛt] N minaccia; **to be a threat to sb/sth** costituire una minaccia per qn/qc; **to be under threat of** (closure, extinction) rischiare; (exposure) essere minacciato(-a) di.

threat·en ['θrɛtn] **1** VT minacciare; **to threaten sb with sth** minacciare qn di qc; **to threaten to do sth** minacciare di fare qc.

2 VI (storm) minacciare.

threat·en·ing ['θrɛtnɪŋ] ADJ minaccioso(-a).

threat·en·ing·ly ['θrɛtnɪŋlɪ] ADV minacciosamente.

three [θriː] **1** ADJ tre inv.

2 N tre m inv; **the best of three** (Sport) partita, rivincita e bella for usage see **five**.

♦ **three-D, 3-D** [ˌθriː'diː] **1** ADJ (also: **three-dimensional**) tridimensionale.

2 N: **to be in three-D** essere tridimensionale.

♦ **three-dimensional** [ˌθriːdaɪ'mɛnʃənl] ADJ tridimensionale.

♦ **three-legged** [ˌθriː'lɛgɪd] ADJ (table, stool) a tre gambe.

♦ **three-legged race** N corsa a coppie (con due gambe legate insieme).

♦ **three-piece suit** [ˌθriːpiːs'suːt] N completo (con gilè), tre pezzi m inv.

♦ **three-piece suite** [ˌθriːpiːs'swiːt] N salotto comprendente un divano e due poltrone.

♦ **three-pin plug** [ˌθriːpɪn'plʌg] N spina a tre spinotti.

♦ **three-ply** [ˌθriː'plaɪ] ADJ (wood) a tre strati; (wool) a tre capi, a tre fili.

♦ **three-point turn** [ˌθriːpɔɪnt'tɜːn] N (Aut) inversione a U (eseguita in tre manovre).

♦ **three-quarter** [ˌθriː'kwɔːtəʳ] N (Rugby) trequarti m inv.

♦ **three-quarters** [ˌθriː'kwɔːtəz] NPL tre quarti mpl; **three-quarters full** pieno per tre quarti.

♦ **three Rs** N: **the three Rs** leggere, scrivere e far di conto.

three·some ['θriːsəm] N (people) terzetto.

♦ **three-wheeler** [ˌθriː'wiːləʳ] N (car) veicolo a tre ruote; (tricycle) triciclo.

thresh [θrɛʃ] VT (corn) trebbiare.

thresh·ing ma·chine ['θrɛʃɪŋməˌʃiːn] N trebbiatrice f, trebbia.

thresh·old ['θrɛʃhəʊld] N (also fig) soglia; **to be on the threshold of** (fig) essere sulla soglia di.

♦ **threshold agreement** N (Econ) ≈ scala mobile.

♦ **threshold population** N (Econ) soglia di popolazione.

threw [θruː] PT of **throw**.

thrice [θraɪs] ADV (frm, liter) tre volte.

thrift [θrɪft], **thrifti·ness** ['θrɪftɪnɪs] N parsimonia.

thrifty ['θrɪftɪ] ADJ (comp -ier, superl -iest) parsimonioso (-a).

thrill [θrɪl] **1** N (of fear) brivido; (of pleasure, joy) fremito; **it gave me a great thrill** è stata un'esperienza emozionante.

2 VT (with fear) far rabbrividire; (with pleasure) entusiasmare; (audience) elettrizzare; **I was thrilled to get your letter** la tua lettera mi ha fatto veramente piacere.

3 VI tremare; **to thrill at** or **to sth** fremere (di gioia) a qc.

thrill·er ['θrɪləʳ] N thriller m inv.

thrill·ing ['θrɪlɪŋ] ADJ (book, play) pieno(-a) di suspense; (news, discovery) entusiasmante.

thrive [θraɪv] VI (be healthy: person, animal) crescere or svilupparsi bene; (: plant) crescere rigoglioso(-a); (fig:

business) prosperare; **he thrives on it** gli fa bene, ne gode; **children thrive on milk** il latte è ottimo per i bambini; **she thrives on hard work** il lavoro le fa bene; **business is thriving** il commercio prospera.

thriv·ing ['θraɪvɪŋ] ADJ (*industry, community*) fiorente.

throat [θrəʊt] N gola; **to clear one's throat** schiarirsi la gola; **to have a sore throat** avere (il) mal di gola; **to stick in sb's throat** (*fig*) restare in gola a qn.

throaty ['θrəʊtɪ] ADJ (*comp* **-ier,** *superl* **-iest**) (*voice*) roco (-a).

throb [θrɒb] ☐ N (*of heart*) palpito, battito; (*of pain*) fitta; (*of music*) battito; (*of engine*) vibrazione *f*; (*of drum*) rullio.

☐ VI (*heart*) palpitare, battere forte; (*wound*) pulsare; (*engine*) vibrare; **my head is throbbing** mi martellano le tempie; **throbbing with life** (*fig*: *town*) pieno(-a) di vita.

throes [θrəʊz] NPL: **in the throes of** alle prese con; **in the throes of death** in agonia; **in the throes of war** dilaniato (-a) dalla guerra.

throm·bo·sis [θrɒm'bəʊsɪs] N trombosi *f inv*; **coronary thrombosis** trombosi coronarica.

throne [θrəʊn] N trono; **to ascend to the throne** salire al trono; **the heir to the throne** l'erede *m/f* al trono.

throng [θrɒŋ] ☐ N moltitudine *f*.

☐ VT affollare.

☐ VI affollarsi.

throt·tle ['θrɒtl] ☐ N (*on motorcycle*) (manopola del) gas; (*valve*) valvola a farfalla; (*on motorboats*) (manetta del) gas; **to go at full throttle** andare a tutto gas.

☐ VT (*strangle*) strangolare, strozzare.

☐ VI: **to throttle back** *or* **down** togliere il gas.

through [θruː] ☐ PREP a (*place*) attraverso; **to look through a telescope** guardare attraverso un telescopio; **to look through the window** (*look out*) guardare dalla finestra; (*look in*) guardare dentro; **to walk through the woods** camminare per *or* attraversare i boschi; **he shot her through the head** le ha sparato in testa; **to go through** (*house, garden, wood*) attraversare; **to go through one's pockets** frugarsi le tasche; **to go through sb's papers** scartabellare le carte di qn

b (*time, process*) per, durante; **all** *or* **right through the night** per tutta la notte; **he won't live through the night** non supererà la notte; **(from) Monday through Friday** (*Am*) da lunedì a venerdì; **to go through a bad/good period** attraversare un brutto momento/un periodo felice; **I am halfway through the book** sono a metà libro

c (*owing to*) a causa di; (*by means of*) per, per mezzo di; (*thanks to*) grazie a; **through lack of resources** per mancanza di mezzi; **through the post** per posta; **he got the job through them** ha avuto quel posto grazie a loro; **it was through you that we were late** è colpa tua se siamo arrivati tardi; **I heard it through my sister** l'ho saputo da mia sorella.

☐ ADV a (*place*): **to let sb through** lasciar passare qn; **the soldiers didn't let us through** i soldati non ci hanno lasciato passare; **please go through into the dining room** prego, entrate in sala da pranzo; **does this train go through to London?** va direttamente a Londra questo treno?; **the nail went right through** il chiodo è passato da parte a parte; **I am wet through** sono bagnato fino al midollo; **my coat is wet through** ho il cappotto inzuppato; **he is through to the finals** ce l'ha fatta a entrare in finale; **the wood has rotted through** il legno è completamente marcio

b (*Brit Telec*): **to get through** ottenere la comunica-

zione; **to put sb through** passare la linea a qn; **to put sb through to sb** passare qn a qn; **you're through!** è in linea!

c (*time, process*): **the party lasted right through until morning** la festa è andata avanti fino al mattino; **I read the book right through** ho letto il libro da cima a fondo

d : **through and through** fino in fondo.

☐ ADJ a (*attr*: *traffic*) di passaggio; (*ticket, train, passage*) diretto(-a); **"no through road"** (*sign*: *Brit*) "strada senza uscita"; **"no through traffic"** (*sign*: *Am*) "divieto d'accesso"

b (*finished*): **to be through** avere finito; **we'll be through at 7** avremo finito per le sette; **I'm through with my girlfriend** ho chiuso con la mia ragazza; **I'm not through with you yet** con te non ho ancora finito; **you're through!** sei finito!

through·out [θruː'aʊt] ☐ PREP a (*place*) in tutto(-a), dappertutto in; **throughout Italy** in tutta l'Italia

b (*time, process*) per *or* durante tutto(-a); **throughout last summer** per tutta l'estate scorsa

☐ ADV a (*everywhere*) dappertutto; **the house is carpeted throughout** c'è la moquette dappertutto in casa

b (*the whole time*) dal principio alla fine, sempre.

through·put ['θruː‚pʊt] N (*of goods, materials*) materiale *m* in lavorazione; (*Comput*) volume *m* di dati immessi.

through·way, thru·way ['θruː‚weɪ] N (*Am*) autostrada a pagamento.

throve [θrəʊv] PT of **thrive.**

♦ **throw** [θrəʊ] (*vb*: *pt* **threw,** *pp* **thrown**) ☐ N (*gen*) tiro; (*Sport*) lancio; (*in judo, wrestling*) atterramento.

☐ VT (*gen, fig*) lanciare, tirare, gettare; (*ball, javelin, hammer*) lanciare; (*dice*) gettare; (*horserider*) disarcionare, gettare a terra; (*judo opponent*) atterrare, mettere al tappeto; (*pottery*) tornire, formare al tornio; (*fig fam*: *disconcert*) sconcertare, disorientare; **to throw a ball 200 metres** lanciare una palla a duecento metri; **to throw a coat round one's shoulders** buttarsi un cappotto sulle spalle; **to throw a switch** (*Elec*) azionare una leva; **he was thrown from his horse** fu disarcionato; **to throw a party** dare una festa; **to throw open** (*doors, windows*) spalancare; (*house, gardens*) aprire al pubblico; (*competition, race*) aprire a tutti; **to throw o.s. off a cliff/into a river** gettarsi da una scogliera/in un fiume; **to throw o.s. at sb** (*rush at*) gettarsi *or* scagliarsi su qn; (*fig*) buttarsi su qn; **to throw o.s. into one's work** buttarsi a capofitto nel lavoro; **to throw o.s. at sb's feet** gettarsi ai piedi di qn; **to throw o.s. on sb's mercy** rimettersi alla pietà di qn

▶ **throw about, throw around** VT + ADV (*litter*) spargere; **to throw money about** *or* **around** sperperare il denaro; **to throw one's weight about** *or* **around** far pesare la propria presenza

▶ **throw away** VT + ADV (*rubbish, old things*) gettare *or* buttare via; (*chance, money, time*) sprecare, gettare *or* buttare via

▶ **throw back** VT + ADV a (*return*: *ball*) rinviare

b (*head, hair*) buttare all'indietro; (*shoulders*) raddrizzare; **she was thrown back on her own resources** (*fig*) se l'è dovuta cavare da sola

▶ **throw down** VT + ADV (*object*) gettare giù; (*weapons*) deporre; **to throw o.s. down** gettarsi a terra; **to throw down the gauntlet** (*fig*) gettare il guanto

▶ **throw in** VT + ADV (*Sport*: *ball*) rimettere in gioco; (*add, include*) aggiungere; (*say casually*: *remark*) buttar lì

▶ **throw on** VT + ADV (*clothes*) buttarsi addosso; (*coal*)

aggiungere

▶ **throw off** 1 VT + ADV (*get rid of*) sbarazzarsi di, liberarsi di; (*escape: pursuers, dogs*) sbarazzarsi di, seminare.

2 VT + PREP: **to throw sb off the trail** mettere qn fuori pista

▶ **throw out** VT + ADV **a** (*rubbish, person*) buttar fuori; (*fig: proposal*) respingere

b (*offer: idea, suggestion*) lanciare

c (*calculation, prediction*) far sballare

▶ **throw over** VT + ADV (*person*) piantare

▶ **throw together** VT + ADV (*clothes*) raccattare; (*meal*) raffazzonare; (*essay*) buttar giù; (*people*) fare incontrare

▶ **throw up** 1 VI + ADV (*fam: vomit*) vomitare.

2 VT + ADV (*ball*) lanciare in aria; **she threw up her hands in despair** ha alzato le braccia al cielo per la disperazione.

throw·away ['θrəʊəˌweɪ] ADJ (*disposable: product*) da buttar via, usa e getta; (*casual: remark*) buttato(-a) lì.

throw·back ['θrəʊˌbæk] N: **it's a throwback to** (*fig*) ciò risale a.

throw·er ['θrəʊə'] N lanciatore(-trice).

♦ **throw-in** ['θrəʊˌɪn] N (*Ftbl*) rimessa in gioco.

thrown [θrəʊn] PP of **throw**.

thru [θruː] PREP, ADV (*Am*) = **through**.

thrush[1] [θrʌʃ] N (*bird*) tordo.

thrush[2] [θrʌʃ] N (*Med: esp in children*) mughetto; (: *Brit: in women*) candida.

thrust [θrʌst] (*vb: pt, pp* **thrust**) 1 N (*push*) spintone *m*; (*Aer, Space*) spinta; (*Mil: offensive*) attacco, offensiva; **forward thrust** spinta propulsiva.

2 VT (*push*) spingere con forza; (*push in: finger, stick, dagger*) conficcare; **he thrust a book into my hands** mi ha cacciato un libro tra le mani; **she thrust her head out of the window** ha sporto la testa dalla finestra; **to thrust o.s. upon sb** (*fig*) imporre la propria presenza a qn; **they thrust the job on me** (*fig*) mi hanno costretto ad accettare il lavoro; **I thrust my way through the crowd** mi sono fatto largo tra la folla; **to thrust sb/sth aside** spingere qn/qc da una parte; **to thrust an idea aside** scartare un'idea.

thrust·ing ['θrʌstɪŋ] ADJ (*troppo*) intraprendente.

thru·way ['θruːˌweɪ] N = **throughway**.

Thucydides [θuːˈsɪdɪˌdiːz] N (*History, Literature*) Tucidide *m*.

thud [θʌd] 1 N tonfo.

2 VI: **to thud to the ground** cadere a terra con un tonfo; **to thud against the wall** colpire il muro con un tonfo.

thug [θʌg] N teppista *m/f*, delinquente *m/f*.

thug·gery ['θʌgərɪ] N brutalità *f inv*, violenza.

thumb [θʌm] 1 N (*Anat*) pollice *m*; **to be under sb's thumb** (*fig*) essere succube di qn; **to be all thumbs** (*fig fam*) essere maldestro(-a); **to give sb/sth the thumbs up** (*fam: sign*) far segno di essere d'accordo con qn/qc; (: *approve*) dare l'okay a qn/qc; **to give sth the thumbs down** (*fam*) disapprovare *or* bocciare qc.

2 VT (*book*) sfogliare; **to thumb a lift** *or* **a ride** (*fam*) fare l'autostop; **to thumb one's nose at sb** fare marameo a qn; **to thumb one's nose at sb/sth** (*fig fam*) beffarsi di qn/qc.

3 VI: **to thumb through a book/magazine** sfogliare un libro/una rivista.

♦ **thumb index** N indice *m* a rubrica.

thumb·nail ['θʌmneɪl] N unghia del pollice.

♦ **thumbnail sketch** N descrizione *f* breve.

thumb·screw ['θʌmˌskruː] N (*instrument of torture*) strumento di tortura con cui si schiacciano i pollici; (*Tech*) vite *f* con testa ad alette.

thumb·tack ['θʌmˌtæk] N (*Am*) puntina da disegno.

thump [θʌmp] 1 N (*blow*) forte colpo; (*noise of fall*) tonfo; **it came down with a thump** è caduto con un tonfo.

2 VT (*hit hard: person*) picchiare; (: *door*) picchiare su; (: *table*) battere su.

3 VI (*person: on door, table*) picchiare, battere; (: *move heavily*) camminare pesantemente; (*pound: heart*) battere forte

▶ **thump out** VT + ADV (*tune*) suonare pestando sui tasti.

thump·ing ['θʌmpɪŋ] (*Brit fam*) 1 ADJ: **a thumping headache** un mal di testa martellante.

2 ADV: **it's a thumping great book** è un libro enorme.

thun·der ['θʌndə'] 1 N (*Met*) tuono; (*of hooves, traffic*) fragore *m*; **with a face like thunder** nero(-a) *or* scuro(-a) in volto.

2 VI (*Met, voice, fig*) tuonare; **the guns thundered in the distance** i cannoni tuonavano in lontananza; **to thunder by** *or* **past** (*train*) passare rombando *or* con un rombo; **he thundered at him to stop** gli urlò di fermarsi.

thunder·bolt ['θʌndəˌbəʊlt] N fulmine *m*.

thunder·clap ['θʌndəˌklæp] N rombo di tuono.

thunder·cloud ['θʌndəˌklaʊd] N nube *f* temporalesca; (*fig*) nube minacciosa.

thun·der·ing ['θʌndərɪŋ] 1 ADJ **a**: **in a thundering rage/fury** in preda a una rabbia/furia tremenda; **in a thundering temper** d'umore collerico **b** (*Brit old fam: success, nuisance*) enorme.

2 ADV (*Brit old fam*): **thundering great** fenomenale.

thun·der·ous ['θʌndərəs] ADJ (*applause*) fragoroso(-a).

thunder·storm ['θʌndəˌstɔːm] N temporale *m*.

thunder·struck ['θʌndəˌstrʌk] ADJ (*fig*) sbigottito(-a).

thun·dery ['θʌndərɪ] ADJ (*weather*) minaccioso(-a), da temporale, temporalesco(-a).

Thurs., Thur. ABBR = **Thursday**.

Thurs·day ['θɜːzdɪ] N giovedì *m inv for usage see* **Tuesday**.

thus [ðʌs] ADV (*frm: in this way*) così; (*as a result*) perciò; **thus far** fino ad ora.

thwack [θwæk] 1 N (*blow*) colpo; (*noise*) schiocco.

2 VT colpire.

thwart [θwɔːt] VT ostacolare, contrastare.

thy [ðaɪ] POSS ADJ (*old, poet*) il/la tuo(-a).

thyme [taɪm] N timo.

thy·roid ['θaɪrɔɪd] N (*also:* **thyroid gland**) tiroide *f*.

ti [tiː] N (*Mus*) si *m inv*.

ti·ara [tɪˈɑːrə] N (*woman's*) diadema *m*; (*of pope*) tiara.

Ti·ber ['taɪbə'] N: **the Tiber** il Tevere.

Ti·bet [tɪˈbɛt] N il Tibet.

Ti·bet·an [tɪˈbɛtən] 1 ADJ tibetano(-a).

2 N (*person*) tibetano(-a); (*language*) tibetano.

tibia ['tɪbɪə] N tibia.

tic [tɪk] N (*Med*) tic *m inv*.

tick[1] [tɪk] 1 N **a** (*sound: of clock*) tic tac *m inv*

b (*Brit fam: moment*) secondo, attimo; **I shan't be a tick** ci metto un secondo

c (*Brit: mark*) segno, spunta; **to put a tick against sth** fare un segno a fianco di qc.

2 VT spuntare; **to tick the right answer** segnare la risposta giusta; *see also* **tick off**.

3 VI (*clock*) ticchettare, fare tic tac; **I can't understand what makes him tick** (*fig*) non riesco a capire come ragioni

▶ **tick away, tick by** VI + ADV (*hours, minutes*) scorrere

▶ **tick off** VT + ADV **a** (*Brit*: *from a list*) spuntare; (: *fam*: *scold*) sgridare

b (*Am fam*: *annoy*) seccare, infastidire

▶ **tick over** VI + ADV (*Brit*: *engine*) andare al minimo; (: *business, organization*) segnare il passo.

tick² [tɪk] N (*Zool*) zecca.

tick³ [tɪk] N (*Brit fam*: *credit*): **to buy sth on tick** comprare qc a credito.

tick·er ['tɪkə'] N (*fam*: *watch*) orologio; (: *heart*) cuore *m*.

♦ **ticker tape** N nastro di telescrivente; (*Am*: *in parades*) stelle *fpl* filanti.

tick·et ['tɪkɪt] **1** N (*gen*) biglietto; (*for library*) tessera; (*Comm*: *label on goods*) cartellino, etichetta; (: *from cash register*) scontrino; (*Am Pol*) lista dei candidati; **to get a (parking) ticket** (*Aut*) prendere una multa (per sosta vietata); **return ticket**, (*Am*) **round-trip ticket** biglietto di andata e ritorno; **open/closed ticket** (*Aer*) biglietto aperto/chiuso; **admission is by ticket only** si ammettono solo le persone munite di biglietto; **that's the ticket!** (*fig fam*) è quel che ci voleva!.

2 VT (*label*: *goods*) etichettare.

3 ADJ di biglietti.

♦ **ticket agency** N (*Theatre*) agenzia di vendita di biglietti.

♦ **ticket collector** N bigliettaio.

♦ **ticket holder** N persona munita di biglietto.

♦ **ticket inspector** N controllore *m*.

♦ **ticket office** N biglietteria.

♦ **ticket tout** N (*Brit*) bagarino.

tick·ing¹ ['tɪkɪŋ] N (*of clock, watch*) ticchettio.

tick·ing² ['tɪkɪŋ] N (*material*) tela da materassi.

♦ **ticking-off** [,tɪkɪŋ'ɒf] N (*Brit fam*): **to give sb a ticking-off** dare a qn una lavata di testa, sgridare qn.

tick·le ['tɪkl] **1** VT (*person*) fare il solletico a; (*fig*: *palate*) stuzzicare; (: *amuse*) divertire, far ridere; **it tickled his fancy** stuzzicava la sua fantasia; **to be tickled pink** (*fam*) andare in brodo di giuggiole.

2 VI: **it tickles** mi (*or* gli *etc*) fa il solletico.

3 N solletico; **to give sb a tickle** fare il solletico a qn.

tick·ling ['tɪklɪŋ] **1** N solletico.

2 ADJ (*sensation*) di solletico; (*cough*) che provoca una sensazione di irritazione in gola.

tick·lish ['tɪklɪʃ], **tick·ly** ['tɪklɪ] ADJ (*fam*: *easily tickled*: *person*) che soffre il solletico; (*which tickles*: *blanket*) che provoca prurito; (: *cough*) che provoca una sensazione di irritazione in gola; (*fig*: *touchy*: *person*) permaloso (-a); (: *delicate*: *situation, problem*) delicato(-a).

tick·tock ['tɪk,tɒk] N tic tac *m inv.*

tid·al ['taɪdl] ADJ (*flow*) di marea; (*river, estuary*) soggetto (-a) alla marea; **tidal range** escursione *f* di marea.

♦ **tidal wave** N onda di marea; (*fig*: *of protest, enthusiasm*) ondata.

tid·bit ['tɪd,bɪt] N (*Am*) = titbit.

tid·dler ['tɪdlə'] N (*Brit fam*: *small fish*) pesciolino; (: *child*) bambinetto(-a).

tid·dly ['tɪdlɪ] ADJ (*comp* -ier, *superl* -iest) (*Brit fam*: *drunk*) brillo(-a).

tiddly·winks ['tɪdlɪ,wɪŋks] NSG gioco della pulce.

tide [taɪd] **1** N marea; (*fig*: *of emotion*) ondata; (: *of events*) corso; **the tide of public opinion** l'orientamento dell'opinione pubblica; **high/low tide** alta/bassa marea; **the tide has turned** la marea è cambiata; (*fig*) c'è stato un cambiamento (di tendenze); **to go with the tide** (*fig*) seguire la corrente; **to swim against the tide** (*fig*) andare controcorrente.

2 VT: **to tide sb over** *or* **through (until)** aiutare qn a tirare avanti (fino a); **can you lend me £10 to tide me over until Friday?** mi puoi prestare 10 sterline per tirare avanti fino a venerdì?

tide·mark ['taɪd,mɑːk] N linea di marea.

ti·di·ly ['taɪdɪlɪ] ADV in modo ordinato; **to arrange tidily** sistemare; **to dress tidily** vestirsi per benino.

ti·di·ness ['taɪdɪnɪs] N ordine *m*.

tid·ings ['taɪdɪŋz] NPL (*old*) notizie *fpl*.

tidy ['taɪdɪ] **1** ADJ (*comp* -ier, *superl* -iest) (*gen*) ordinato (-a), in ordine; (*hair, dress*) in ordine, curato(-a), a posto; (*room*) lindo(-a); (*work*) accurato(-a); (*drawing*) pulito(-a); (*person*: *in appearance*) curato(-a); (: *in character*) ordinato(-a); (*mind*) organizzato(-a); **a tidy sum** (*fam*) una bella sommetta.

2 VT (*also*: **tidy up**: *room, toys*) mettere in ordine, riordinare; (: *one's hair*) ravviarsi

▶ **tidy away** VT + ADV mettere via

▶ **tidy out** VT + ADV mettere in ordine

▶ **tidy up** **1** VI + ADV fare ordine.

2 VT + ADV = **tidy 2**; **to tidy o.s. up** rassettarsi.

♦ **tidy-out** ['taɪdɪ,aʊt], **tidy-up** ['taɪdɪ,ʌp] N: **to have a tidy-out (of)** (*fam*) dare una ripulita (a).

tie [taɪ] **1** N **a** (*Brit*: *also*: **necktie**) cravatta; (*cord, ribbon, string*) legaccio; (*fig*: *bond*) legame *m*; **black/white tie** (*on invitation*) smoking/abito di rigore; **the children are a tie** i bambini legano; **ties of friendship** legami d'amicizia; **family ties** legami familiari

b (*Sport*: *draw*) pareggio; (: *match in series*) incontro; (*Pol*) parità *f inv* di voti; **the match ended in a tie** l'incontro è finito con un pareggio; **cup tie** (*Brit Sport*: *match*) incontro di coppa

c (*Am Rail*) traversina.

2 VT (*gen, fig*) legare; (*ribbon*) annodare; (*also*: **tie up**: *shoe*) allacciare, allacciarsi; **to tie sth in a bow** annodare qc; **to tie a knot (in sth)** fare un nodo (a qc); **to get tied in knots** (*also fig fam*) ingarbugliarsi; **to tie a necktie** fare il nodo a una cravatta; **my job ties me to London** il mio lavoro mi tiene a Londra; **his hands are tied** (*fig*) ha le mani legate.

3 VI **a** (*dress, shoes*) allacciarsi

b (*Sport*: *draw*) pareggiare

▶ **tie back** VT + ADV (*curtains*) fissare; **to tie back one's hair** farsi la coda (di cavallo)

▶ **tie down** VT + ADV assicurare, fissare con una corda; (*fig*): **to tie sb down to sth** costringere qn ad accettare qc; **to tie sb down to a promise/a price/a time** costringere qn a mantenere una promessa/ad accettare un prezzo/a venire a una certa ora; **to be tied down to sth** (*promise, date*) essere vincolato(-a) da qc; **to be tied down** (*restricted*) essere legato(-a) mani e piedi

▶ **tie in** **1** VI + ADV: **to tie in (with)** (*correspond*) corrispondere (a); (*be connected*) avere legami (con).

2 VT + ADV: **to tie in (with)** (*meeting, visit*) far coincidere (con); (*findings*) far combaciare (con)

▶ **tie on** VT + ADV (*Brit*: *label*) attaccare

▶ **tie together** VT + ADV legare (insieme)

▶ **tie up** **1** VI + ADV (*Naut*) ormeggiare.

2 VT + ADV (*person, parcel*) legare; (*boat*) ormeggiare; (*fig*: *capital*) impegnare; (: *business deal*) concludere; (: *connect*) ricollegare; **to be tied up (with sb/sth)** (*busy*) essere occupato(-a) *or* impegnato(-a) (con qn/a fare qc); **the traffic was tied up by the accident** il traffico è rimasto bloccato per l'incidente.

♦ **tie-breaker** ['taɪ,breɪkə'], **tie-break** ['taɪ,breɪk] N

(*Tennis*) tie-break *m inv*; (*in quiz*) spareggio.
♦ **tie-in** [ˈtaɪˌɪn] N (*Comm: link*) legame *m*.
♦ **tie-on** [ˈtaɪˌɒn] ADJ (*Brit: label*) volante.
tie·pin [ˈtaɪˌpɪn] N (*Brit*) fermacravatta *m inv*.
tier [tɪəʳ] N (*in theatre*) fila; (*in stadium*) gradinata; (*layer*) strato; (*of cake*) piano; **to arrange in tiers** disporre in file (*or* in strati).
♦ **tie rack** N portacravatte *m inv*.
Tier·ra del Fue·go [tɪˌɛrədɛlˈfweɪgəʊ] N Terra del Fuoco.
♦ **tie tack** N (*Am*) fermacravatta *m inv*.
♦ **tie-up** [ˈtaɪˌʌp] N (*connection*) legame *m*.
tiff [tɪf] N battibecco; **a lover's tiff** un battibecco tra innamorati.
ti·ger [ˈtaɪgəʳ] N tigre *f*.
tight [taɪt] **1** ADJ **a** (*gen, clothes, budget, bend*) stretto(-a); (*rope*) teso(-a), tirato(-a); (*usu pred: firmly fixed, hard to move*) duro(-a); (*strict: control, discipline*) severo(-a), fermo(-a); (*Brit fam: mean*) tirchio(-a); **it's a tight fit** è un po' stretto; **to be in a tight spot** (*fig fam*) essere in una situazione difficile; **space is a bit tight** siamo un po' stretti; **money is a bit tight** siamo un po' a corto di denaro; **to keep a tight hold of sth** tenere qc stretto; **to keep a tight hold on the reins** (*fig*) tenere le redini in pugno
b (*fam: drunk*) sbronzo(-a); **to get tight** sbronzarsi.
2 ADV (*hold*) stretto(-a); (*close*) ermeticamente; (*grasp*) saldamente; (*squeeze*) fortemente; **to be packed tight** (*suitcase*) essere pieno(-a) zeppo(-a); (*people*) essere pigiati; **screw it up tight!** avvitalo stretto!; **pull the door tight!** chiudi bene la porta!; **to hold sb tight** tenere stretto(-a) qn; **everybody hold tight!** tenetevi stretti!; **the room was packed tight with people** la stanza era piena zeppa di persone; **to sleep tight** (*soundly*) dormire sodo.
tight·en [ˈtaɪtn] **1** VT (*also:* **tighten up**: *gen*) stringere; (: *rope*) tendere; (: *regulation*) rendere più severo(-a); (: *control*) intensificare; **to tighten one's belt** (*fig*) tirare la cinghia.
2 VI (*also:* **tighten up**) stringersi; (*rope*) tendersi; (*grasp*) farsi più stretto(-a)
▶ **tighten up 1** VI + ADV **a** = **tighten 2**
b : **to tighten up on sth** rendere qc più severo(-a).
2 VT + ADV = **tighten 1**.
♦ **tight-fisted** [ˌtaɪtˈfɪstɪd] ADJ (*fam*) avaro(-a), tirchio(-a).
♦ **tight-fitting** [ˌtaɪtˈfɪtɪŋ] ADJ (*garment*) attillato(-a); (*lid*) ermetico(-a).
tight·knit [ˌtaɪtˈnɪt] ADJ (*family*) unito(-a); (*programme, schedule*) intenso(-a).
♦ **tight-lipped** [ˌtaɪtˈlɪpt] ADJ: **to be tight-lipped** (*silent*) essere reticente; (*angry*) tenere le labbra serrate.
tight·ly [ˈtaɪtlɪ] ADV (*grasp*) bene, saldamente.
tight·ness [ˈtaɪtnɪs] N (*of lid, screw*) resistenza; (*of discipline*) rigore *m*; (*of regulations*) rigidità *f inv*; **you should have seen the tightness of her trousers!** avresti dovuto vedere com'erano stretti i suoi pantaloni!; **I can feel a tightness in my chest** ho un senso di oppressione al torace.
tight·rope [ˈtaɪtˌrəʊp] N corda (da acrobata).
♦ **tightrope walker** N funambolo(-a).
tights [taɪts] NPL (*Brit*) collant *m inv*.
tight·wad [ˈtaɪtˌwɒd] N (*Am fam pej*) tirchione(-a).
ti·gress [ˈtaɪgrɪs] N tigre *f*(femmina).
tile [taɪl] **1** N (*on roof*) tegola; (*on floor, wall*) mattonella, piastrella; **a night on the tiles** (*Brit fam*) una notte brava.
2 VT (*roof*) rivestire di tegole; (*floor, bathroom*) piastrel-

lare.
tiled [taɪld] ADJ (*floor, wall, bathroom*) a mattonelle, a piastrelle; (*roof*) rivestito(-a) di tegole.
till[1] [tɪl] PREP = **until**.
till[2] [tɪl] N (*for money*) cassa, registratore *m* di cassa.
till[3] [tɪl] VT (*land*) coltivare.
till·er [ˈtɪləʳ] N (*Naut*) barra del timone.
tilt [tɪlt] **1** N **a** (*slope*) pendio; **to wear one's hat at a tilt** portare il cappello sulle ventitré
b (*fam*): **(at) full tilt** a tutta velocità.
2 VT inclinare, far pendere; **tilt it this way/the other way** inclinalo da questa/quella parte; **he tilted his chair back** ha inclinato la sedia indietro.
3 VI inclinarsi, pendere; **to tilt to one side** inclinarsi da una parte; **he tilted back in his chair** si è inclinato indietro con la sedia.
tim·ber [ˈtɪmbəʳ] **1** N (*material*) legname *m*; (*trees*) alberi *mpl* da legname; **timber!** cade!.
2 ADJ (*roof, cabin*) di legno.
tim·bered [ˈtɪmbəd] ADJ (*house*) rivestito(-a) di legno.
♦ **timber merchant** N (*Brit*) commerciante *m/f* di legname.
timber·yard [ˈtɪmbəˌjɑːd] N (*Brit*) deposito *m* legname *inv*.
tim·bre [ˈtɪmbəʳ] N timbro.
time [taɪm] N **1** (*gen*) **a** tempo; **time and space** il tempo e lo spazio; **how time flies** come vola il tempo!; **only time will tell** si saprà solo col tempo; **time is on our side** il tempo è dalla nostra; **all in good time** senza fretta; **to have (the) time (to do sth)** avere il tempo (di fare qc); **to find the time for reading** trovare il tempo per leggere; **I've no time for them** (*too busy*) non ho tempo da perdere con loro; (*contemptuous*) non li posso soffrire; **I've no time for it** (*fig*) non ho tempo da perdere con cose del genere; **he lost no time in doing it** l'ha fatto subito senza perdere tempo; **it takes time to ...** ci vuole tempo per...; **to take one's time** prenderla con calma; **time is money** (*Proverb*) il tempo è denaro; **he'll do it in his own (good) time** (*without being hurried*) lo farà quando ha (un minuto di) tempo; **he'll do it in his own time** (*out of working hours*) lo farà nel suo tempo libero; **my time is my own** dispongo del mio tempo
b (*period of time*) tempo; **a long time** molto tempo; **a long time ago** molto tempo fa; **in a short time she will have left** fra poco sarà partita; **in a short time they were all gone** nel giro di poco tempo se ne erano andati tutti; **a short time after** poco tempo dopo; **for a time** per un po' di tempo; **have you been here all this time?** sei stato qui tutto questo tempo?; **for the time being** per il momento; **in no time** in un attimo; **in a week's time** fra una settimana
c (*moment*) momento; (*period*) periodo; **any time** in qualsiasi momento; **come any time you like** vieni quando vuoi; **any time now** da un momento all'altro; **at that time** allora, a quel tempo; **at the present time** al momento, adesso; **at this time of the year** in questo periodo dell'anno; **(by) this time next year** in questo periodo l'anno prossimo; **by the time he arrived** quando è arrivato; **at the same time** (*simultaneously*) contemporaneamente; **but at the same time, I have to admit ...** tuttavia devo ammettere...; **at the same time** allo stesso momento in cui; **at times** a volte; **at all times** in ogni momento, sempre; **from time to time** di tanto in tanto; **now is the time to go to Venice** questo è il periodo *or* momento giusto per andare a Venezia; **the time has come to leave** è arrivato il momento *or* l'ora di

partire; **this is no time for jokes** non è il momento di scherzare; **this is neither the time nor the place to discuss it** non è né il luogo né il momento adatto per discuterne

d (*by clock*) ora; **what time do you make it?** che ora fai?; **have you got the (right) time?** hai l'ora (esatta)?; **what's the time?** [OR] **what time is it?** che ora è?, che ore sono?; **in time** (*soon enough*) in tempo; (*after some time*) col tempo; **to arrive (just) in time for dinner** arrivare (appena) in tempo per cena; **on time** (*person*) puntuale; (*train*) in orario; **it's time for the news** (*on radio*) c'è il giornale radio; (*on television*) c'è il telegiornale; **time's up!** è (l')ora!; **to be 30 minutes behind/ahead of time** avere 30 minuti di ritardo/anticipo; **about time too!** era anche ora!; **it was about time you had a haircut** era proprio ora che ti tagliassi i capelli

e (*era: often pl*) era; (*period*) periodo, epoca; **in modern times** nell'era moderna; **in Elizabethan times** nel periodo elisabettiano; **in my time** ai miei tempi; **during my time at HarperCollins** quando ero alla HarperCollins; **it was before my time** non ero ancora nata; **times were hard** erano tempi duri; **in times to come** nel tempo a venire; **to be ahead of one's time** precorrere i tempi; **to be behind the times** essere rimasto(-a) indietro

f (*experience*): **to have a good time** divertirsi; **to have a bad** *or* **rough time (of it)** passarsela male; **they had a hard time of it** è stata dura per loro

g (*occasion*) volta; **three times** tre volte; **this/next time** questa/la prossima volta; **the last time I did it** l'ultima volta che l'ho fatto; **time after time** [OR] **time and again** mille volte; **many's the time** ... più di una volta...; **I remember the time when** ... ricordo ancora quando...; **for weeks at a time** per settimane; **to carry 3 boxes at a time** portare 3 scatole per volta

h (*Mus, Mil*) tempo; **to play/march in time** suonare/marciare a tempo; **to keep time** andare a tempo; **to be out of time** essere *or* andare fuori tempo

i (*Math*): **4 times 3 is 12** 4 per *or* volte 3 fa 12; **3 times as fast (as)** [OR] **3 times faster (than)** 3 volte più veloce (di).

2 VT **a** (*schedule*) programmare; (: *measure duration of*) calcolare la durata di; (*choose time of: joke, request*): **to time sth well/badly** scegliere il momento più/meno opportuno per qc, fare qc al momento giusto/sbagliato; **the footballer timed his shot perfectly** il giocatore ha calcolato il tiro alla perfezione; **the bomb was timed to explode 5 minutes later** la bomba era stata regolata in modo da esplodere 5 minuti più tardi

b (*with stopwatch*) cronometrare; **to time an egg** controllare il tempo per la cottura di un uovo; **to time o.s.** prendere i propri tempi.

♦ **time and motion expert** N esperto nei tempi e nelle fasi di produzione.

♦ **time and motion study** N analisi *f inv* dei tempi e delle fasi di produzione.

♦ **time bomb** N bomba a orologeria.

time-card ['taɪmˌkɑːd] N cartellino (di presenza).

♦ **time clock** N (*Industry*) orologio marcatempo.

♦ **time-consuming** ['taɪmkənˌsjuːmɪŋ] ADJ che richiede molto tempo.

♦ **time difference** N differenza di fuso orario.

♦ **time exposure** N (*Phot*) posa lunga.

♦ **time frame** N tempi *mpl*.

♦ **time-honoured**, (*Am*) **time-honored** ['taɪmˌɒnəd] ADJ consacrato(-a) dal tempo.

time-keeper ['taɪmˌkiːpəʳ] N (*Sport*) cronometrista *m/f*;

he's a good timekeeper è sempre puntuale; **my old watch is a good timekeeper** il mio vecchio orologio non perde un secondo.

♦ **time lag** N (*between events*) intervallo (di tempo); (*in travel*) differenza di fuso orario.

time-less ['taɪmlɪs] ADJ (*frm: unchanging*) senza tempo; (: *unending*) eterno(-a), infinito(-a).

♦ **time limit** N limite *m* di tempo; **to set a time limit** fissare un limite di tempo.

time-li-ness ['taɪmlɪnɪs] N (*see adj*) tempestività *f inv*; opportunità *f inv*.

time-ly ['taɪmlɪ] ADJ tempestivo(-a); (*opportune*) opportuno(-a).

♦ **time off** N tempo libero.

♦ **time out** N **a** (*Sport*) time out *m inv* **b** (*fam*): **to take time out** assentarsi (*da lavoro, attività*).

time-piece ['taɪmˌpiːs] N (*old, frm*) orologio.

tim-er ['taɪməʳ] N (*in kitchen*) contaminuti *m inv*; (*hourglass*) clessidra; (*Tech*) timer *m inv*, temporizzatore *m inv*.

♦ **time-saving** ['taɪmˌseɪvɪŋ] ADJ che fa risparmiare tempo.

♦ **time scale** N tempi *mpl* d'esecuzione.

time-server ['taɪmˌsɜːvəʳ] N (*pej*) **a** (*changing opinions*) banderuola (*fig*) **b** (*in job*) chi fa il minimo indispensabile aspettando di andare in pensione.

♦ **time-share** ['taɪmˌʃɛəʳ] **1** ADJ (*holiday home*) in multiproprietà.

2 N (*property*) casa in multiproprietà; (*system*) multiproprietà *f inv*.

♦ **time shar-ing** ['taɪmˌʃɛərɪŋ] N **a** (*Comput*) time sharing *m inv*, ripartizione *f* del tempo **b** (*of property*) multiproprietà *f inv*.

♦ **time sheet** N foglio di presenza.

♦ **time signal** N segnale *m* orario.

♦ **time signature** N (*Mus*) indicazione *f* del tempo.

♦ **time switch** N interruttore *m* a tempo.

time-table ['taɪmˌteɪbl] N (*for trains*) orario; (*programme of events*) programma *m*.

time-worn ['taɪmˌwɔːn] ADJ (*hackneyed: phrase, idea, excuse*) trito(-a) e ritrito(-a).

♦ **time zone** N fuso orario.

tim-id ['tɪmɪd] ADJ (*shy*) timido(-a); (*easily scared*) timoroso(-a), pauroso(-a).

ti-mid-ity [tɪˈmɪdɪtɪ] N timidezza.

tim-id-ly ['tɪmɪdlɪ] ADV timidamente.

tim-ing ['taɪmɪŋ] N (*of tennis player, cricketer*) coordinazione *f*; (*of musician*) tempismo; (*of comedian*) tempestività *f inv*; (*of demonstration, elections*) momento; (*of engine*) messa in fase; (*of race, industrial process*) cronometraggio; **that was good/bad timing** hai (*or* ha *etc*) scelto il momento opportuno/sbagliato; **that was perfect timing!** che tempismo!

♦ **timing device** N (*on bomb*) timer *m inv*.

tim-or-ous ['tɪmərəs] ADJ timoroso(-a).

tim-pa-ni ['tɪmpənɪ] NPL (*Mus*) timpani *mpl*.

tim-pa-nist ['tɪmpənɪst] N timpanista *m/f*.

tin [tɪn] **1** N **a** (*metal*) stagno; (*also: tin plate*) latta **b** (*Brit: can*) barattolo *or* scatola (di latta); (: *for baking*) teglia; **a tin of paint** un barattolo di vernice.

2 VT (*Brit*) inscatolare.

♦ **tin can** N (*empty*) barattolo *or* scatola (di latta).

tin-der ['tɪndəʳ] N esca.

tin-foil ['tɪnˌfɔɪl] N (*carta*) stagnola.

tinge [tɪndʒ] **1** N (*of colour, fig*) punta, sfumatura; **her hair had a tinge of red in it** i suoi capelli avevano dei riflessi

rossi.

[2] VT: **to be tinged with** avere una punta *or* sfumatura di.

tin·gle ['tɪŋgl] [1] N (*of skin*) formicolio; (*thrill*) fremito.

[2] VI (*cheeks, skin: from cold*) pungere, pizzicare; (: *from bad circulation*) formicolare; **a tingling sensation** un formicolio; **to tingle with excitement** fremere dall'eccitazione.

♦ **tin hat** N (*fam*) elmetto.

♦ **tink·er** ['tɪŋkəʳ] N stagnino ambulante

▸ **tinker with** VI + PREP, **tinker about with** VI + ADV + PREP (*play*) trastullarsi con; (*repair*) armeggiare intorno a, cercare di riparare.

tin·kle ['tɪŋkl] [1] N [a] (*of bell*) tintinnio; (*Brit fam*): **give me a tinkle** dammi un colpetto di telefono [b] (*fam: act of urinating*) pipì *fig.*

[2] VI (*bell*) tintinnare.

tin·kling ['tɪŋklɪŋ] [1] ADJ (*sound*) tintinnante, argentino (-a).

[2] N tintinnio.

♦ **tin mine** N miniera di stagno.

tinned [tɪnd] ADJ (*Brit: food*) in scatola.

tin·ni·tus [tɪ'naɪtəs] N (*Med*) ronzio auricolare.

tin·ny ['tɪnɪ] ADJ (*comp* -**ier**, *superl* -**iest**) (*metallic: sound*) metallico(-a); (*pej: car, machine*) che sembra di latta.

♦ **tin-opener** ['tɪn‿əʊpnəʳ] N (*Brit*) apriscatole *m inv.*

♦ **Tin Pan Alley** N (*fam*) il mondo della musica.

tin·plate ['tɪn‿pleɪt] N latta.

tin·pot ['tɪn‿pɒt] ADJ (*Brit fam: dictator, government*) da due soldi.

tin·sel ['tɪnsəl] N decorazioni *fpl* natalizie (*argentate*).

♦ **tin soldier** N soldatino di latta.

tint [tɪnt] [1] N (*gen*) sfumatura; (*colour*) tinta; (*for hair*) shampoo *m inv* colorante.

[2] VT (*hair*) fare uno shampoo colorante a.

tint·ed ['tɪntɪd] ADJ (*hair*) tinto(-a); (*spectacles, glass*) colorato(-a); **tinted windows** (*Aut*) cristalli *mpl* fumé *inv.*

♦ **tin whistle** N (*Mus*) zufolo.

tiny ['taɪnɪ] ADJ (*comp* -**ier**, *superl* -**iest**) minuscolo(-a).

tip¹ [tɪp] N (*end*) punta; (*peak*) cima, vetta; (*of stick, umbrella: protective*) puntale *m*; **it's on the tip of my tongue** (*fig*) ce l'ho sulla punta della lingua; **it was just the tip of the iceberg** (*fig*) era solo la punta dell'iceberg

▸ **tip off** VT + ADV (*inform*) fare una soffiata a

▸ **tip up** [1] VI + ADV ribaltarsi.

[2] VT + ADV inclinare.

tip² [tɪp] [1] N [a] (*gratuity*) mancia

[b] (*hint*) suggerimento; (*advice*) consiglio; (: *for horse race*) cavallo; **I'll give you a tip** ti darò un consiglio.

[2] VT [a] (*porter, waiter*) dare la mancia a; **I tipped him £1** gli ho dato una mancia di 1 sterlina, gli ho dato 1 sterlina di mancia

[b] (*predict: winner*) pronosticare; (: *horse*) dare vincente; **he is being tipped for the job** secondo i pronostici dovrebbe avere il posto.

tip³ [tɪp] [1] N (*Brit: for rubbish*) discarica, immondezzaio; (: *for coal waste*) discarica.

[2] VT (*tilt*) inclinare; (*empty: also:* **tip out**) svuotare, scaricare; (*overturn: also:* **tip over**) rovesciare, capovolgere; **to tip sb off his seat** far cadere qn dalla sedia; **to tip away the dishwater** svuotare l'acqua dei piatti; **to tip back a chair** inclinare una sedia all'indietro; **he tipped out the contents of the box** ha rovesciato il contenuto della scatola; **to tip over a glass of wine** rovesciare un bicchiere di vino; **to tip the balance** far pendere la bilancia da una parte.

[3] VI (*incline*) pendere, essere inclinato(-a); (*also:* **tip over**) rovesciarsi.

♦ **tip-off** ['tɪp‿ɒf] N (*information*) soffiata.

tipped [tɪpt] ADJ (*Brit: cigarette*) col filtro; **steel-tipped** con la punta d'acciaio.

tip·per ['tɪpəʳ] N (*truck*) autocarro a cassone ribaltabile.

Tipp-Ex® ['tɪpɛks] N (*Brit*) liquido correttore.

tip·ping ['tɪpɪŋ] N: **"no tipping"** "divieto di scarico".

tip·ple ['tɪpl] (*fam*) [1] N drink *m inv* preferito: **to have a tipple** bere un bicchierino.

[2] VI sbevazzare.

tip·pler ['tɪpləʳ] N (*fam*) beone(-a).

tip·ster ['tɪpstəʳ] N (*Racing*) *chi vende informazioni sulle corse e altre manifestazioni oggetto di scommesse.*

tip·sy ['tɪpsɪ] ADJ (*comp* -**ier**, *superl* -**iest**) brillo(-a).

tip·toe ['tɪp‿təʊ] [1] N: **to walk on tiptoe** camminare in punta di piedi.

[2] VI camminare in punta di piedi.

tip·top [‿tɪp'tɒp] ADJ: **in tiptop condition** in ottime condizioni.

TIR [‿tiːɑɪ'ɑːʳ] ABBR (= *transport internationaux routiers*) T.I.R.

ti·rade [taɪ'reɪd] N filippica.

tire¹ ['taɪəʳ] [1] VT (*exhaust*) stancare.

[2] VI stancarsi; **to tire of sb/sth** stancarsi di qn/qc

▸ **tire out** VT + ADV sfinire, spossare.

tire² ['taɪəʳ] N (*Am*) = **tyre.**

tired ['taɪəd] ADJ [a] stanco(-a); **to be/feel/look tired** essere/sentirsi/sembrare stanco(-a); **to be tired of sb/sth** essere stanco(-a) *or* stufo(-a) di qn/qc; **to get** *or* **grow tired of doing sth** stancarsi di fare qc [b] (*fig: cliché*) trito(-a) e ritrito(-a); (*fig: shabby*) consunto(-a).

tired·ly ['taɪədlɪ] ADV stancamente.

tired·ness ['taɪədnɪs] N stanchezza.

tire·less ['taɪəlɪs] ADJ instancabile.

tire·less·ly ['taɪəlɪslɪ] ADV instancabilmente.

tire·some ['taɪəsəm] ADJ (*job, person*) noioso(-a); (*situation*) seccante; **how tiresome!** che seccatura!

tir·ing ['taɪərɪŋ] ADJ faticoso(-a).

tis·sue ['tɪʃuː] N [a] (*thin paper*) velina; (*paper handkerchief*) fazzolettino di carta [b] (*Anat*) tessuto [c] (*fig*): **to weave a tissue of lies** ordire tutta una serie di menzogne.

♦ **tissue paper** N carta velina.

tit¹ [tɪt] N (*bird: also:* **titmouse**) cincia.

tit² [tɪt] N [a] (*fam: breast*) tetta [b] (*Brit fam*): **to get on sb's tits** rompere le palle a qn (*fam*); (: *person*) cretino(-a).

tit³ [tɪt] N: **to give tit for tat** rendere pan per focaccia.

Ti·tan ['taɪtən] N Titano(-a).

ti·tan·ic [taɪ'tænɪk] ADJ titanico(-a).

ti·ta·nium [tɪ'teɪnɪəm] N titanio.

tit·bit ['tɪt‿bɪt], (*Am*) **tid·bit** ['tɪd‿bɪt] N (*of food*) bocconcino, leccornia; (*fig: of news, information, gossip*) notizia ghiotta.

titchy ['tɪtʃɪ] ADJ (*comp* -**ier**, *superl* -**iest**) (*Brit fam*) minuscolo(-a).

tithe [taɪð] N decima.

tit·il·late ['tɪtɪ‿leɪt] VT (*sexually*) titillare.

titi·vate ['tɪtɪ‿veɪt] VT agghindare.

ti·tle ['taɪtl] N [a] (*gen*) titolo; **to hold a title** detenere un titolo [b] (*Law: right*): **title (to)** diritto (a).

ti·tled ['taɪtld] ADJ (*person*) titolato(-a).

♦ **title deed** N (*Law*) atto di proprietà.

♦ **title holder** N (*Sport*) detentore(-trice) del titolo.

♦ **title page** N frontespizio.

♦ **title role** N (*Theatre, Cine*) ruolo *or* parte *f* principale.

ti·tra·tion [taɪ'treɪʃən] N titolazione *f.*

tit·ter ['tɪtə'] ① N risatina nervosa.
② VI ridere nervosamente, ridacchiare.
tittle-tattle ['tɪtl,tætl] (fam) ① N pettegolezzi mpl, chiacchiere fpl.
② VI pettegolare.
titu·lar ['tɪtjʊlə'] ADJ (in name only) nominale.
tiz·zy ['tɪzɪ] N (fam): **to be in/get into a tizzy (about sth)** essere/mettersi in agitazione (per qc).
♦ **T-junction** ['ti:,dʒʌŋkʃən] N (Brit) incrocio a T.
TM [,ti:'ɛm] N ABBR a (= transcendental meditation) M.T. f b (Comm) = **trademark**.
TN ABBR (Am Post)= Tennessee.
TNT [,ti:ɛn'ti:] N ABBR (= trinitrotoluene) T.N.T. m.

to [tu:; weak form tə] PREP
1
a (direction: gen) a; (: towards) verso; (: to a country) in; (: to sb's house, office, shop) da;
▷ **have you ever been to India?** sei mai stata in India?
▷ **to go to the doctor's** andare dal dottore
▷ **to go to France** andare in Francia
▷ **to the left** a sinistra
▷ **a letter to his wife** una lettera a sua moglie
▷ **to go to Paris** andare a Parigi
▷ **to go to Peter's** andare da Peter
▷ **to go to Portugal** andare in Portogallo
▷ **to the right** a destra
▷ **the road to Edinburgh** la strada per Edimburgo
▷ **to go to school** andare a scuola
▷ **to go to the station** andare alla stazione
b (next to, with position) a;
▷ **with one's back to the wall** con le spalle al muro
▷ **the door is to the left (of)** la porta è a sinistra (di)
▷ **at right angles to sth** ad angolo retto con qc
c (as far as) fino a;
▷ **to count to 10** contare fino a dieci
▷ **to some extent** fino a un certo punto, in parte
▷ **from here to London** da qui (fino) a Londra
▷ **from 40 to 50 people** da 40 a 50 persone
▷ **to be wet to the skin** essere bagnato(-a) fino al midollo
d (with expressions of time) a;
▷ **it's twenty-five to 3** mancano venticinque minuti alle 3, sono le 2 e trentacinque
e (expressing indirect object) a;
▷ **it belongs to him** gli appartiene, è suo
▷ **to drink to sb** bere a qn or alla salute di qn
▷ **to give sth to sb** dare qc a qn
▷ **give it to me** dammelo
▷ **the key to the front door** la chiave della porta d'ingresso
▷ **to be kind to sb** essere gentile con qn
▷ **a monument to the fallen** un monumento ai caduti
▷ **the man I sold it to** [OR] (frm) **the man to whom I sold it** l'uomo (a) cui l'ho venduto
▷ **a solution to the problem** una soluzione al problema
f (in relation to) (in confronto) a;
▷ **A is to B as C is to D** A sta a B come C sta a D
▷ **30 miles to the gallon** ≈ 11 chilometri con un litro
▷ **5 apples to the kilo** 5 mele in un chilo
▷ **10 inhabitants to the square kilometre** 10 abitanti per chilometro quadrato
▷ **that's nothing to what is to come** non è nulla in

confronto a ciò che ancora deve venire
▷ **superior to the others** superiore agli altri
▷ **three goals to two** tre reti a due
g (about)
▷ **that's all there is to it** questo è tutto, è tutto qui
▷ **what do you say to this?** che cosa ne pensi?
h (according to) secondo;
▷ **to the best of my recollection** per quanto mi ricordi io
▷ **we danced to the music of ...** abbiamo ballato con la musica di...
▷ **to my way of thinking** secondo il mio modo di pensare, a mio parere
i (purpose, result)
▷ **to come to sb's aid** venire in aiuto a qn
▷ **to sentence sb to death** condannare qn a morte
▷ **to my great surprise** con mia grande sorpresa.
2 PARTICLE (with verb)
a (simple infinitive)
▷ **to go/eat** andare/mangiare
b (following another verb)
▷ **to start to cry** incominciare or mettersi a piangere
▷ **to try to do** cercare di fare
▷ **to want to do** voler fare
c (purpose, result) per;
▷ **he did it to help you** l'ha fatto per aiutarti
▷ **he came to see you** è venuto per vederti
d (with ellipsis of verb)
▷ **you ought to** dovresti (farlo)
▷ **I don't want to** non voglio (farlo)
e (equivalent to relative clause) da;
▷ **I have things to do** ho (delle cose) da fare
▷ **he's not the sort to do that** non è il tipo da fare una cosa del genere
▷ **now is the time to do it** è ora di farlo
▷ **he has a lot to lose** rischia grosso
▷ **he has nothing to lose** non ha nulla da perdere
f (after adjective etc)
▷ **the first to go** il/la primo(-a) ad andarsene
▷ **hard to believe** difficile da credere
▷ **too old to ...** troppo vecchio(-a) per...
▷ **ready to go** pronto(-a) a partire
▷ **too young to ...** troppo giovane per....
3 ADV
a
▷ **to go to and fro** andare e tornare
▷ **to pull/push the door to** (closed) accostare la porta
b: **to come to** (recover consciousness) riprendere conoscenza.

toad [təʊd] N rospo.
♦ **toad-in-the-hole** [,təʊdɪnðə'həʊl] N (Brit Culin) salsicce coperte di pastella e cotte nel forno.
toad·stool ['təʊd,stu:l] N fungo velenoso.
toady ['təʊdɪ] (pej) ① N leccapiedi m/f inv.
② VI: **to toady to sb** leccare i piedi a qn.
toast [təʊst] ① N a (bread) pane m tostato; **a piece or slice of toast** una fetta di pane tostato or abbrustolito b (drink, speech) brindisi m inv; **to propose/drink a toast to sb** proporre (di fare)/fare un brindisi a qn; **the toast of the town/nation** (fig) il vanto della città/nazione.
② VT a (bread) tostare, abbrustolire b (drink to) brindare a.

toast·ed ['təʊstɪd] ADJ tostato(-a).

toast·er ['təʊstə'] N tostapane *m inv*.

toast·master ['təʊst,mɑːstə'] N direttore *m* dei brindisi.

♦ **toast rack** ['təʊst,ræk] N portatoast *m inv*.

to·bac·co [tə'bækəʊ] N tabacco; **pipe tobacco** tabacco da pipa.

to·bac·co·nist [tə'bækənɪst] N (*Brit*) tabaccaio(-a); **tobacconist's (shop)** tabaccheria.

♦ **tobacco pouch** N borsa per il tabacco.

To·ba·go [tə'beɪgəʊ] N see **Trinidad**.

to·bog·gan [tə'bɒgən] [1] N toboga *m inv*, slittino; (*child's*) slitta, slittino.

[2] VI andare in slittino.

to·day [tə'deɪ] [1] ADV oggi; (*these days*) al giorno d'oggi, oggigiorno; **a week from today** [OR] **a week today** [OR] **today week** (*Brit*) oggi a otto; **a fortnight today** (*Brit*) [OR] (*Am*) **two weeks from today** quindici giorni a oggi; **what day is it today?** che giorno è oggi?; **what date is it today?** quanti ne abbiamo oggi?; **today is the 4th of March** (oggi) è il 4 (di) marzo.

[2] N (*also fig*) oggi *m inv*; **writers of today** gli scrittori d'oggi; **today's paper** il giornale di oggi.

tod·dle ['tɒdl] VI (*child*): **to toddle in/out** *etc* entrare/uscire *etc* a passettini; (*fam*: *adult*): **he toddled off** se n'è andato camminando tranquillamente.

tod·dler ['tɒdlə'] N (*small child*) bambino(-a) che impara a camminare.

tod·dy ['tɒdɪ] N: **hot toddy** grog *m inv*.

♦ **to-do** [tə'duː] N (*fam*: *fuss*): **to cause a to-do** fare delle storie.

toe [təʊ] [1] N (*Anat*) dito del piede; (*of shoe*) punta; **big toe** alluce *m*; **little toe** mignolino; **to keep sb on his toes** (*fig*) tenere qn sull'attenti.

[2] VT: **to toe the line** (*fig*: *conform*) conformarsi alle regole, stare in riga.

♦ **toe·cap** ['təʊ,kæp] N mascherina.

♦ **toe·clip** ['təʊ,klɪp] N (*Cycling*) puntapiedi *m inv*.

TOEFL ['təʊfl] N ABBR = *Test(ing) of English as a Foreign Language*.

♦ **toe·hold** ['təʊ,həʊld] N punto d'appoggio.

♦ **toe·nail** ['təʊ,neɪl] N unghia del piede.

♦ **toe·piece** ['təʊ,piːs] N (*Skiing*) puntale *m*.

toff [tɒf] N (*Brit old fam*) gran signore(-a).

tof·fee ['tɒfɪ] N caramella *f* mou *inv*; **he can't sing for toffee** (*Brit fam*) come cantante non vale una cicca.

♦ **toffee apple** N (*Brit*) mela caramellata.

♦ **toffee-nosed** ['tɒfɪ,nəʊzd] ADJ (*Brit fam pej*) con la puzza sotto il naso.

tofu ['təʊ,fuː] N tofu *m*, *caglio di latte di soia non fermentato*.

toga ['təʊgə] N toga.

to·geth·er [tə'geðə'] ADV a (*gen*) insieme; **together with** insieme a; **all together** tutti insieme; **they were both in it together** (*pej*) vi erano implicati entrambi; **we're in this together** siamo nella stessa barca; **to bring the two sides together** far mettere d'accordo le due parti; **to gather together** radunarsi; **to put a meal together** mettere insieme un pranzo *or* una cena b (*simultaneously*) insieme, contemporaneamente, allo stesso tempo; (*continuously*) di seguito.

to·geth·er·ness [tə'geðənɪs] N (*closeness*) intimità *f inv*.

togged out ['tɒgd'aʊt] ADJ: **to be togged out in sth** essere abbigliato(-a) con qc; **to be togged out to do sth** essere abbigliato(-a) di tutto punto per fare qc.

tog·gle ['tɒgl] N (*on coat*) olivetta.

♦ **toggle switch** N deviatore *m* a comando manuale; (*Comput*) tasto bistabile.

Togo ['təʊgəʊ] N il Togo.

togs [tɒgz] NPL (*fam*: *clothes*) vestiti *mpl*.

toil [tɔɪl] [1] N duro lavoro, fatica.

[2] VI lavorare sodo, faticare; **to toil away at sth** lavorare duramente su qc; **to toil up a hill** arrancare su per una collina.

toi·let ['tɔɪlɪt] [1] N a (*Brit*: *lavatory*) gabinetto; **to go to the toilet** andare al gabinetto *or* al bagno; **she's in the toilet** è in gabinetto *or* in bagno b (*old*: *dressing, washing*) toilette *f*; **she was at her toilet** si stava facendo la toilette.

[2] ADJ (*soap*) da toilette.

♦ **toilet bag** N (*Brit*) nécessaire *m inv* da toilette.

♦ **toilet bowl** N vaso *or* tazza del gabinetto.

♦ **toilet paper** N carta igienica.

toi·let·ries ['tɔɪlɪtrɪz] NPL articoli *mpl* da toilette.

♦ **toilet roll** N (*Brit*) rotolo di carta igienica.

♦ **toilet-train** ['tɔɪlɪt,treɪn] VT: **to toilet-train a child** insegnare ad un bambino ad usare il vasino.

♦ **toilet water** N acqua di colonia.

♦ **to-ing and fro-ing** [,tuː:ɪŋən'frəʊɪŋ] N (*pl* **to-ings and fro-ings**) (*Brit*) andirivieni *m inv*.

to·ken ['təʊkən] [1] N a (*Brit*: *voucher*) buono; **record token** buono *m* disco *inv* b (*metal disc*) gettone *m* c (*sign, symbol*) segno; **by the same token** (*fig*) per lo stesso motivo.

[2] ADJ (*fee, strike*) simbolico(-a); (*resistance, gesture*) formale.

to·ken·ism ['təʊkə,nɪzəm] N concessione *f* pro forma *inv*.

To·kyo ['təʊkjəʊ] N Tokyo *f*.

told [təʊld] PT, PP of **tell**.

tol·er·able ['tɒlərəbl] ADJ a (*bearable*) sopportabile, tollerabile b (*fairly good*) passabile, discreto(-a).

tol·er·ably ['tɒlərəblɪ] ADV (*good, comfortable*) abbastanza.

tol·er·ance ['tɒlərəns] N (*of pain, hardship*) sopportazione *f*; (*of behaviour, Med, Tech*) tolleranza.

tol·er·ant ['tɒlərənt] ADJ: **tolerant (of)** tollerante (nei confronti di).

tol·er·ant·ly ['tɒlərəntlɪ] ADV con tolleranza.

tol·er·ate ['tɒlə,reɪt] VT (*gen, Med, Tech*) tollerare, sopportare.

tol·era·tion [,tɒlə'reɪʃən] N tolleranza.

toll[1] [təʊl] [1] N a (*on road*) pedaggio b (*losses, casualties*): **the death toll on the roads** il numero di vittime sulle strade; **the severe winter has taken its toll on the crops** l'inverno rigido ha colpito duramente il raccolto.

[2] ADJ (*road, bridge*) a pedaggio.

toll[2] [təʊl] [1] VT, VI (*bell*) suonare lentamente e solennemente.

[2] N (*of bell*) rintocco.

toll·bridge ['təʊl,brɪdʒ] N ponte *m* a pedaggio.

♦ **toll call** N (*Am Telec*) (telefonata) interurbana.

♦ **toll-free** [,təʊl'friː] (*Am*) [1] ADJ senza addebito, gratuito (-a); **toll-free number** ≈ numero verde.

[2] ADV gratuitamente.

Tom [tɒm] N: **any Tom, Dick or Harry** chiunque, il primo venuto.

tom [tɒm] N (*fam*) micio.

to·ma·to [tə'mɑːtəʊ, *Am* tə'meɪtəʊ] [1] N (*pl* **tomatoes**) pomodoro.

[2] ADJ (*juice, sauce*) di pomodoro.

♦ **tomato paste** N concentrato di pomodoro.

tomb [tuːm] N tomba.

tom·bo·la [tɒm'bəʊlə] N (*Brit*) tombola.
tom·boy ['tɒm,bɔɪ] N maschiaccio.
tomb·stone ['tu:m,stəʊn] N pietra tombale.
tom·cat ['tɒm,kæt] N gatto maschio.
tome [təʊm] N tomo; (*hum*) librone *m*.
tom·fool·ery [,tɒm'fu:lərɪ] N sciocchezze *fpl*.
tom·my gun ['tɒmɪ,ɡʌn] N (*fam*) fucile *m* mitragliatore.
to·mor·row [tə'mɒrəʊ] [1] ADV (*also fig*) domani; **tomor-row morning** domani mattina; **a week from tomorrow** [OR] **a week tomorrow** (*Brit*) domani a otto.
[2] N domani *m inv*; **tomorrow is Sunday** domani è domenica; **the day after tomorrow** dopodomani; **tomorrow's paper** il giornale di domani; **tomorrow is another day** (*fig*) domani è un altro giorno.
tom·tom ['tɒm,tɒm] N tamtam *m inv*.
ton [tʌn] N (*weight*) tonnellata (*Brit* = 1016 *kg*; *Am* = 907 *kg*); (*metric ton*) tonnellata; (*Naut*: *also*: **register ton**) tonnellata di stazza (*2.83 cu.m*; *100 cu.ft*); (: *also*: **displacement ton**) tonnellata inglese; **this suitcase weighs a ton** (*fam*) questa valigia pesa una tonnellata; **tons of sth** (*fam*) un mucchio *or* sacco di qc.
to·nal ['təʊnl] ADJ tonale.
tone [təʊn] [1] N (*gen*) tono; (*of colour*) tonalità *f inv*; (*of musical instrument*) timbro; (*dialling* (*Brit*) *or* **dial** (*Am*) **tone** (*Telec*) segnale *m* di libero; **to praise sb in ringing tones** (*fig*) portare qn alle stelle; **they were speaking in low tones** parlavano a voce bassa; **two tones of red** due tonalità di rosso; **to raise/lower the tone of sth** migliorare/abbassare il tono di qc.
[2] VI (*also*: **tone in**: *colours*) intonarsi
► **tone down** VT + ADV (*moderate*: *colour, sound*) attenuare; (*fig*: *language, criticism*) moderare
► **tone up** VT + ADV (*muscles*) tonificare.
♦ **tone control** N (*on radio, hi-fi*) tasto (per la regolazione) del tono.
♦ **tone-deaf** [,təʊn'dɛf] ADJ stonato(-a), completamente privo(-a) di orecchio (musicale).
tone·less ['təʊnlɪs] ADJ (*voce*) inespressivo(-a).
tone·less·ly ['təʊnlɪslɪ] ADV in modo inespressivo.
ton·er ['təʊnə'] N (*for photocopier*) colorante *m* organico, toner *m inv*.
Tonga Is·lands ['tɒŋɡə,aɪləndz] NPL, **Tonga** N le (isole *fpl*) Tonga.
tongs [tɒŋz] NPL (*for coal*) molle *fpl*, tenaglie *fpl*; (*for sugar, in laboratory*) pinza.
tongue [tʌŋ] N **a** (*gen*) lingua; (*of shoe*) linguetta; (*of bell*) battaglio; **have you lost your tongue?** hai perso la lingua?; **hold your tongue!** chiudi quella bocca!; **to put out one's tongue (at sb)** mostrare la lingua (a qn); **to say sth tongue in cheek** (*fig*) dire qc ironicamente; **I can't get my tongue round it** (*fig*) non riesco a pronunziarlo **b** (*frm, liter*: *language*) lingua.
♦ **tongue-tied** ['tʌŋ,taɪd] ADJ (*fig*) muto(-a); **he was tongue-tied with embarrassment** l'imbarazzo lo ha fatto ammutolire.
♦ **tongue-twister** ['tʌŋ,twɪstə'] N scioglilingua *m inv*.
ton·ic ['tɒnɪk] [1] N **a** (*Med*) ricostituente *m*; (*also*: **skin tonic**) tonico; **fresh air is the best tonic when you have a headache** l'aria fresca è il miglior rimedio per il mal di testa; **this will be a tonic to her** questo la tirerà su **b** (*also*: **tonic water**) acqua tonica **c** (*Mus*) nota tonica.
[2] ADJ (*all senses*) tonico(-a); **tonic solfa** (*Mus*) solfeggio.
to·night [tə'naɪt] ADV, N (*this evening*) questa sera, stasera; (*this night*) questa notte, stanotte; **I'll see you tonight** ci vediamo stasera; **tonight's TV programmes** (*Brit*) or

programs (*Am*) i programmi della serata.
ton·nage ['tʌnɪdʒ] N (*Naut*) tonnellaggio, stazza.
tonne [tʌn] N (*Brit*: *metric ton*) tonnellata.
ton·sil ['tɒnsl] N tonsilla; **to have one's tonsils out** farsi operare di tonsille.
ton·sil·lec·to·my [,tɒnsɪ'lɛktəmɪ] N tonsillectomia.
ton·sil·li·tis [,tɒnsɪ'laɪtɪs] N tonsillite *f*; **to have tonsillitis** avere la tonsillite.
too [tu:] ADV **a** (*excessively*) troppo; **it's too sweet** è troppo dolce; **it's too sweet for me to drink** non lo bevo, è troppo dolce per me; **it's too heavy for me** è troppo pesante per me; **it's too heavy for me to lift** non riesco a sollevarlo, è troppo pesante per me; **it's too good to be true** è troppo bello per essere vero; **I'm not too sure about that** non ne sono troppo sicuro; **too much** troppo(-a); **too many** troppi(-e); **too bad!** (*unsympathetic*) tanto peggio!; (*expressing regret*) che peccato!
b (*also*) anche; (*moreover*) per di più; **I went too** ci sono andato anch'io; **I speak French and Japanese too** parlo il francese e (anche) il giapponese; **not only that, he's blind too!** non solo, ma è anche cieco!; **he's famous, intelligent and rich too** è famoso, intelligente e per di più anche ricco.
took [tʊk] PT of **take**.
tool [tu:l] [1] N **a** (*gen, Tech*) attrezzo, utensile *m*, arnese *m*; (**set of**) **tools** (set *m inv* di) attrezzi; **the tools of one's trade** i ferri del mestiere **b** (*fig*: *person*) strumento; **he was a mere tool in their hands** non era che uno strumento *or* un fantoccio nelle loro mani.
[2] VT lavorare con un attrezzo.
tool·bag ['tu:l,bæɡ] N borsa degli attrezzi.
♦ **tool box** N cassetta degli attrezzi.
tooled [tu:ld] ADJ (*silver*) cesellato(-a); (*leather*) goffrato (-a).
♦ **tool kit** N kit *m inv* di attrezzi.
♦ **tool-maker** ['tu:l,meɪkə'] N chi fabbrica attrezzi.
tool·shed ['tu:l,ʃed] N capanno degli attrezzi.
toot [tu:t] [1] N colpo di clacson.
[2] VT: **to toot one's horn** suonare il clacson.
[3] VI suonare; (*with car horn*) suonare il clacson.
tooth [tu:θ] N (*pl* teeth) (*Anat, Tech*) dente *m*; **to clean one's teeth** lavarsi i denti; **to have a tooth out** [OR] (*Am*) **to have a tooth pulled** farsi togliere un dente; **to have a sweet tooth** essere ghiotto(-a) di dolci; **long in the tooth** (*fam*: *old*) vecchiotto(-a); **to be fed up to the (back) teeth with sb/sth** (*fam*) averne fin sopra i capelli di qn/qc; **to get one's teeth into** (*fig*: *work*) impegnarsi a fondo in; (: *subject*) immergersi in; **armed to the teeth** armato(-a) fino ai denti; **to fight tooth and nail** combattere con le unghie e con i denti; **it sets my teeth on edge** mi fa venire i brividi; **by the skin of one's teeth** per il rotto della cuffia; **in the teeth of great opposition** malgrado la forte opposizione.
tooth·ache ['tu:θ,eɪk] N mal *m* di denti; **to have toothache** avere il mal di denti.
tooth·brush ['tu:θ,brʌʃ] N spazzolino da denti.
tooth·comb ['tu:θ,kəʊm] N: **to go through sth with a fine toothcomb** passare qc al setaccio.
tooth·less ['tu:θlɪs] ADJ sdentato(-a).
tooth·paste ['tu:θ,peɪst] N dentifricio.
tooth·pick ['tu:θ,pɪk] N stuzzicadenti *m inv*.
tooth powder N dentifricio in polvere.
toothy ['tu:θɪ] ADJ (*comp* -ier, *superl* -iest) (*fam*) che ha una dentatura cavallina; **to give sb a toothy smile** fare a qn un sorriso a trentadue denti.

toot·sie ['tutsɪ] N (fam) **a** (toe) ditino; (foot) piedino **b** (Am old) tesoro; (woman) bella ragazza; **hi, tootsie** ciao bella.

top[1] [tɒp] [1] N **a** (highest point: of mountain, page, ladder) cima; (: of list, table, queue) testa; (: of career) apice m; **at the top of the hill** sulla cima della collina; **at the top of the stairs/page/street** in cima alle scale/alla pagina/ alla strada; **at the top of the table** a capotavola; **to be top of the charts** essere in testa alla hit-parade; **Liverpool is at the top of the league** (Sport) il Liverpool è in testa alla classifica; **from top to bottom** (fig) da cima a fondo; **from top to toe** dalla testa ai piedi; **from the top** dall'alto; **from the top of the hill** dalla cima della collina; **on top** sopra; **on top of** in cima a, sopra; (Brit: in addition to) oltre a; **to fall on top of sb** cadere addosso a qn; **he's going thin on top** (fam) sta incominciando a perdere i capelli; **to reach the top** (fig: of career) raggiungere l'apice; **the men at the top** (fig) quelli che sono al potere **b** (surface) superficie f; (of box, cupboard, table) sopra m inv, parte f superiore; (roof: of car) tetto; (upper part: of bus) piano superiore; **the top of the table needs wiping** bisogna pulire la superficie or il piano della tavola; **oil comes to the top** l'olio sale alla superficie; **seats on top!** (Brit: in double-decker bus) ci sono posti di sopra!; **the top of the milk** (Brit) la panna **c** (Dress: blouse) camicia; (: T-shirt) maglietta; (of pyjamas) giacca **d** (lid: of bottle) tappo; (: of box, jar) coperchio; (of pen) tappo, cappuccio **e** (also: **top gear**): **to change into top** mettere la quarta (or quinta) **f** (in phrases): **on top of (all) that** per di più, inoltre; **it's just one thing on top of another** è una cosa dietro a un'altra; **to be/feel on top of the world** (fam) essere/ sentirsi al settimo cielo; **to be/get on top of things** (fig) dominare/cominciare a dominare la situazione; **things are getting on top of me** (fam) mi sta precipitando tutto addosso; **to come out on top** (fig) uscire vincitore (-trice); **I can't tell you off the top of my head** a mente non te lo posso dire; **at the top of one's voice** (fig) a squarciagola; **over the top** (Brit fam: behaviour) eccessivo(-a); **to go over the top** (Brit fam) esagerare. [2] ADJ **a** (highest: floor, step) ultimo(-a); (: shelf, drawer) (ultimo(-a)) in alto; (: price) più alto(-a); (: in rank) primo(-a); **at top speed** a tutta velocità; **top gear** la marcia più alta, quarta (or quinta); **the top men in the party** i dirigenti del partito; **a top job** un posto di prestigio; **she's top dog at work** (fig fam) è il grande capo sul lavoro **b** (best) migliore; **to get top marks** (Brit) avere i voti migliori; **to come top of the class** avere i voti più alti di tutta la classe, risultare il/la migliore della classe; **he came top in maths** ha avuto i voti migliori in matematica; **the top twenty** (Mus) i venti migliori dischi (della settimana); **to be on top form** (fam) sentirsi veramente in forma; **a top surgeon** un grande chirurgo **c** (last: layer) ultimo(-a); **the top coat (of paint)** l'ultima mano (di pittura); **she is in the top class at school** sta facendo l'ultimo anno di scuola. [3] VT **a** sormontare; **a church topped by a steeple** una chiesa sovrastata da un campanile; **to top a cake with cream** coprire una torta di panna **b** (be first in) essere in testa a; **to top the bill** (Theatre) avere il primo posto sul cartellone

c (exceed) superare; **and to top it all ...** (fig) e come se non bastasse; **profits topped £50,000 last year** i profitti hanno superato le 50.000 sterline l'anno scorso **d** (vegetables, fruit) tagliare le punte a; **to top and tail fruit** tagliare le punte e i gambi alla frutta
► **top off** VT + ADV (finish): **to top off with** concludere con; **we topped off the dinner with a toast to the happy couple** abbiamo concluso il pranzo con un brindisi in onore della coppia festeggiata
► **top up** VT + ADV riempire; **to top sb's glass up** riempire il bicchiere a qn, dare ancora da bere a qn; **to top up a battery** fare un rabbocco alla batteria

top[2] [tɒp] N (toy) trottola; **to sleep like a top** dormire come un ghiro.

to·paz ['təʊpæz] N topazio.

♦ **top-class** [ˌtɒp'klɑːs] ADJ di prim'ordine.

top·coat ['tɒpˌkəʊt] N (old: overcoat) soprabito.

♦ **top-flight** [ˌtɒp'flaɪt] ADJ di primaria importanza.

♦ **top floor** N ultimo piano.

♦ **top hat** N cilindro.

♦ **top-heavy** [ˌtɒp'hɛvɪ] ADJ (structure) con la parte superiore troppo pesante; **this company is top-heavy** (fig) ci sono troppi dirigenti in questa società.

to·pi·ary ['təʊpɪərɪ] N arte f topiaria.

top·ic ['tɒpɪk] N (of conversation) argomento; (of essay) soggetto.

topi·cal ['tɒpɪkəl] ADJ d'attualità; **a highly topical question** un argomento di grande attualità.

topi·cal·ity [ˌtɒpɪ'kælɪtɪ] N attualità f inv.

top·knot ['tɒpnɒt] N crocchia.

♦ **top·less** ['tɒplɪs] [1] ADJ (bather) a seno scoperto; **topless swimsuit** topless m inv. [2] ADV (sunbathe) in topless.

♦ **top-level** [ˌtɒp'lɛvl] ADJ (talks) ad alto livello.

top·most ['tɒpˌməʊst] ADJ il/la più alto(-a).

♦ **top-notch** [ˌtɒp'nɒtʃ] ADJ (fam: player, performer) di razza; (: school, car) eccellente.

to·pog·ra·pher [tə'pɒgrəfə'] N topografo(-a).

to·pog·ra·phy [tə'pɒgrəfɪ] N topografia.

to·pol·ogy [tə'pɒlədʒɪ] N topologia.

to·pony·my [tə'pɒnɪmɪ] N toponimia.

top·per ['tɒpə'] N (fam) cilindro.

top·ping ['tɒpɪŋ] N (Culin) guarnizione f.

top·ple ['tɒpl] [1] VT (fig: overthrow) far cadere, rovesciare. [2] VI cadere, rovesciarsi
► **topple over** [1] VI + ADV cadere. [2] VI + PREP cadere da; **he toppled over a cliff** è caduto da una scogliera.

♦ **top-ranking** [ˌtɒp'ræŋkɪŋ] ADJ di massimo grado.

TOPS [tɒps] N ABBR (Brit: = Training Opportunities Scheme) corsi di avviamento professionale per chi ha più di 19 anni.

♦ **top-secret** [ˌtɒp'siːkrɪt] ADJ segretissimo(-a).

♦ **top-security** [ˌtɒpsɪ'kjʊərɪtɪ] ADJ (Brit) di massima sicurezza.

top·side ['tɒpˌsaɪd] N **a** (Brit Culin) girello **b** (Naut): **topsides** NPL opera morta.

top·soil ['tɒpˌsɔɪl] N strato superficiale del terreno.

top·spin ['tɒpˌspɪn] N (Tennis) effetto topspin.

topsy-turvy [ˌtɒpsɪ'tɜːvɪ] ADJ, ADV sottosopra (inv).

♦ **top-up** ['tɒpˌʌp] N (Brit fam: refill): **would you like a top-up?** vuoi che ti riempia la tazza (or il bicchiere etc)?

♦ **top-up loan** N (Brit) prestito integrativo.

To·rah ['təʊrə] N: **the Torah** il Torà.

torch [tɔːtʃ] N (Brit: electric) torcia elettrica, lampadina

tascabile; (*flaming*) torcia, fiaccola; **to carry a torch for sb** (*fig*) essere innamorato(-a) cotto(-a) di qn.

torch·light ['tɔːtʃˌlaɪt] N: **by torchlight** al lume di una fiaccola; **torchlight procession** fiaccolata.

tore [tɔː'] PT of **tear**[1].

torea·dor ['tɒrɪəˌdɔː'] N toreador *m inv*.

tor·ment [n 'tɔːmɛnt; *vb* tɔː'mɛnt] **1** N tormento, tortura; **to be in torment** (*also fig*) soffrire le pene dell'inferno.

2 VT (*hurt*) tormentare; (*fig: annoy*) molestare, infastidire; **she was tormented by doubts** era tormentata *or* assillata dai dubbi.

tor·men·tor [tɔː'mɛntə'] N tormentatore(-trice).

torn [tɔːn] PP of **tear**[1].

tor·na·do [tɔː'neɪdəʊ] N (*pl* **tornadoes**) tornado.

tor·pe·do [tɔː'piːdəʊ] **1** N (*pl* **torpedoes**) siluro.

2 VT silurare.

♦ **torpedo boat** N motosilurante *f*.

tor·pid ['tɔːpɪd] ADJ (*frm*) intorpidito(-a).

tor·por ['tɔːpə'] N (*frm*) torpore *m*.

torque [tɔːk] N (*Phys*) coppia di torsione.

♦ **torque wrench** N chiave *f* torsiometrica *or* tarata.

tor·rent ['tɒrənt] N (*also fig*) torrente *m*; **we got caught in a torrent of rain** una pioggia torrenziale ci ha sorpresi.

tor·ren·tial [tɒ'rɛnʃəl] ADJ torrenziale.

tor·rid ['tɒrɪd] ADJ (*liter*) torrido(-a); (*fig*) denso(-a) di passione.

tor·sion ['tɔːʃən] N torsione *f*.

tor·so ['tɔːsəʊ] N (*Anat*) torso; (*Sculpture*) busto.

tor·til·la [tɔː'tiːə] N tortilla *f inv*.

tor·toise ['tɔːtəs] N tartaruga.

tortoise·shell ['tɔːtəsˌʃɛl] **1** N guscio di tartaruga.

2 ADJ di tartaruga.

tor·tu·ous ['tɔːtjʊəs] ADJ tortuoso(-a).

tor·tu·ous·ly ['tɔːtjʊəslɪ] ADV contortamente.

tor·ture ['tɔːtʃə'] **1** N tortura; **it was sheer torture!** (*fig*) è stata una vera tortura!.

2 VT torturare; (*fig*) tormentare.

tor·tur·er ['tɔːtʃərə'] N torturatore(-trice).

Tory ['tɔːrɪ] **1** ADJ tory *inv*, conservatore(-trice).

2 N tory *m/f inv*, conservatore(-trice).

toss [tɒs] **1** N **a** (*movement: of head*) scrollata; **to take a toss** (*from horse*) fare una caduta

b (*of coin*) lancio; **to win/lose the toss** vincere/perdere a testa e croce; (*Sport*) vincere/perdere il sorteggio; **it's pointless to argue the toss** (*Brit fam*) è inutile stare a discutere.

2 VT **a** (*repeatedly*) muovere bruscamente, scuotere; **the boat was tossed by the waves** l'imbarcazione era sballottata dalle onde

b (*throw: ball*) lanciare, gettare; (: *head*) scuotere; (*subj: horse: head*) tirare su; (: *mane*) agitare; (: *rider*) disarcionare; (*subj: bull*) lanciare in aria; **to toss sth to sb** lanciare qc a qn; **to toss salad** mescolare l'insalata; **to toss a pancake** far saltare una crêpe; **to toss a coin** lanciare in aria una moneta, fare a testa o croce; **I'll toss you for it** ce lo giochiamo a testa e croce.

3 VI **a** (*also:* **toss about, toss around**) agitarsi; (: *boat*) rollare e beccheggiare; **to toss (in one's sleep)** OR **toss and turn** (*in bed*) agitarsi nel sonno, girarsi e rigirarsi

b (*also:* **toss up**) tirare a sorte, fare a testa e croce; **we tossed (up) for the last piece of cake** abbiamo fatto a testa e croce per l'ultima fetta di torta

▶ **toss off** **1** VT + ADV **a** (*drink*) buttare giù; (*book, letter*) sfornare

b (*Brit fam!: masturbate*) fare una sega a (*fam!*); **to toss o.s. off** farsi una sega (*fam!*).

2 VI + ADV (*Brit fam!: masturbate*) farsi una sega (*fam!*)

♦ **toss-up** ['tɒsˌʌp] N (*fig fam*): **it was a toss-up who would get there first** avevano tutti le stesse probabilità di arrivare per primo.

tot [tɒt] N **a** (*child*) bimbetto(-a), bimbo(-a) **b** (*Brit: drink*) bicchierino; **a tot of rum** un bicchierino di rum

▶ **tot up** VT + ADV (*Brit: figures*) sommare.

to·tal ['təʊtl] **1** ADJ (*complete, utter*) totale, completo(-a); (*sum*) globale; **the total losses amount to ...** il totale delle perdite ammonta a...; **a total failure** un vero fiasco, un assoluto disastro; **he was in total ignorance of the fact that ...** non sapeva assolutamente che....

2 N totale *m*; **grand total** somma globale; **in total** in tutto.

3 VT (*also:* **total up**: *add*) sommare; (: *amount to*) ammontare a.

to·tali·tar·ian [ˌtəʊtælɪ'tɛərɪən] ADJ totalitario(-a).

to·tali·tari·an·ism [ˌtəʊtælɪ'tɛərɪəˌnɪzəm] N totalitarismo.

to·tal·ity [təʊ'tælɪtɪ] N totalità *f inv*.

to·tal·ly ['təʊtəlɪ] ADV completamente.

tote[1] [təʊt] N (*Brit fam: Racing*) totalizzatore *m*.

tote[2] [təʊt] VT (*fam*) trascinare; **to tote a gun** portare con sé il fucile.

♦ **tote bag** N sporta.

to·tem ['təʊtəm] N totem *m inv*.

♦ **totem pole** N totem *m inv*.

tot·ter ['tɒtə'] VI (*person*) camminare barcollando, barcollare; (*object, government*) vacillare; **to totter in/out** *etc* entrare/uscire *etc* barcollando.

tou·can ['tuːkən] N tucano.

touch [tʌtʃ] **1** N **a** (*sense*) tatto; (*act of touching*) contatto; **rough to the touch** ruvido(-a) al tatto; **by touch** al tatto; **at the slightest touch** al minimo contatto; **the touch of her hand** il tocco della sua mano; **a pianist with a delicate touch** un pianista dal tocco raffinato; **the personal touch** una nota personale; **it has a touch of genius** è quasi geniale; **to lose one's touch** (*fig*) perdere la mano; (: *with people*) perdere il proprio fascino; **to put the finishing touches to sth** dare gli ultimi ritocchi a qc

b (*small amount: of milk*) goccio; (: *of colour, paint*) tocco; (: *of frost*) leggero strato; **a touch of irony** una punta *or* un pizzico d'ironia; **to have a touch of flu** avere una leggera influenza

c (*contact*) contatto; **to be in touch with sb** essere in contatto con qn; **to get in touch with sb** mettersi in contatto con qn; **I'll be in touch** mi farò sentire; **you can get in touch with me here** mi puoi rintracciare qui; **to keep in touch with sb** mantenere i rapporti con qn; **to lose touch** (*friends*) perdersi di vista; **to lose touch with sb** perdere di vista qn; **to be out of touch with events** essere tagliato(-a) fuori

d (*Brit: Ftbl, Rugby*): **the ball is in touch** la palla è fuori gioco.

2 VT **a** (*gen*) toccare; (*brush lightly*: *fig: topic, problem*) sfiorare; **she touched his arm** gli ha toccato il braccio; **his hair touches his shoulders** i capelli gli sfiorano le spalle; **touch wood!** tocchiamo ferro!; **to touch sb for £5** (*fam*) chiedere 5 sterline in prestito a qn

b (*neg phrases*): **I never touch gin** non tocco mai il gin; **you haven't touched your cheese** non hai neppure toccato il formaggio; **if you admit nothing, they can't touch you** (*fig*) se non confessi non ti possono toccare

c (*move*) commuovere; (*affect*) riguardare; **I am touched by your offer** la tua offerta mi commuove; **she**

was touched by his gift fu commossa dal suo regalo; **it touches all our lives** riguarda tutti noi, ci tocca tutti
▣ **d** (*compare*) uguagliare; **nobody can touch them for quality** per quanto riguarda la qualità non li batte nessuno; **no artist in the country can touch him** non c'è artista nel paese che lo possa uguagliare.
▣ **3** VI (*hands*) toccarsi; (*property, gardens*) confinare; **our hands touched** le nostre mani si sono sfiorate; **"do not touch"** "non toccare"
▶ **touch down** ▣ VT + ADV (*Rugby: score*): **to touch the ball down** segnare una meta.
▣ **2** VI + ADV **a** (*on land*) atterrare; (*on sea*) ammarare; (*on moon*) allunare
  b (*Rugby: score*) segnare una meta
▶ **touch off** VT + ADV (*argument, riot*) provocare
▶ **touch on** VI + PREP (*topic, subject*) sfiorare, accennare a
▶ **touch up** VT + ADV **a** (*improve*) ritoccare
  b (*fam: sexually*) mettere le mani addosso a.
♦ **touch-and-go** [ˌtʌtʃən'gəu] ADJ incerto(-a); **it's touch-and-go whether ...** è incerto se...; **it was touch-and-go with the sick man** il malato era tra la vita e la morte.
touch·down ['tʌtʃˌdaun] N (*on land*) atterraggio; (*on sea*) ammaraggio; (*on moon*) allunaggio; (*Rugby*) meta.
tou·ché [tu:'ʃeɪ] EXCL toccato!
touched [tʌtʃt] ADJ (*moved*) commosso(-a); (*fam: crazy*) tocco(-a), toccato(-a).
touchi·ness ['tʌtʃmɪs] N permalosità *f inv*, suscettibilità *f inv*.
touch·ing ['tʌtʃɪŋ] ADJ commovente.
touch·ing·ly ['tʌtʃɪŋlɪ] ADV in modo toccante, in modo commovente.
touch·line ['tʌtʃˌlaɪn] N (*Ftbl*) linea laterale; (*Rugby*) linea di touche.
♦ **touch-sensitive** [ˌtʌtʃ'sɛnsɪtɪv] ADJ sensibile al tatto.
touch·stone ['tʌtʃˌstəun] N pietra di paragone.
♦ **touch-type** ['tʌtʃˌtaɪp] VI dattilografare (*senza guardare i tasti*).
touchy ['tʌtʃɪ] ADJ (*comp* **-ier**, *superl* **-iest**) (*person*) permaloso(-a), suscettibile; (*subject*) delicato(-a); **he's touchy about his weight** è molto suscettibile quando si parla del suo peso.
tough [tʌf] ▣ **1** ADJ (*comp* **-er**, *superl* **-est**) **a** (*substance, fabric*) resistente, duro(-a); (*conditions, regulations*) duro(-a); (*meat*) duro(-a), tiglioso(-a); (*journey*) faticoso(-a), duro(-a); (*task, problem, situation*) difficile; (*fig: resistance*) tenace; (: *fight*) accanito(-a); **as tough as old boots** duro(-a) come una suola di scarpa; **tough opposition** opposizione tenace
  b (*person: hardy, resilient*) robusto(-a), resistente; (: *mentally strong*) resistente, tenace; (: *hard: in character*) inflessibile; (: *rough*) violento(-a), brutale; **they got tough with the workers** hanno adottato una politica inflessibile con i lavoratori; **he's a tough man to deal with** è un tipo difficile; **a tough guy** un duro; **he's a tough customer** (*fam*) è un osso duro
  c (*fam: unfortunate*): **but it was tough on the others** ma è stata una sfortuna per gli altri; **if you can't get here on time, that's your tough luck!** (*unsympathetic*) se non ce la fai ad arrivare in orario, peggio per te!.
▣ **2** N (*fam: gangster, lout*) delinquente *m/f*.
tough·en ['tʌfn] VT (*also:* **toughen up**: *substance*) rinforzare, rendere più resistente; (: *metal*) indurire; (: *person*) rendere più forte.
tough·ness ['tʌfnɪs] N (*see adj*) **a** resistenza; durezza; difficoltà *f inv*; accanimento **b** resistenza; tenacia;

inflessibilità *f inv*; violenza.
tou·pee ['tu:peɪ] N toupet *m inv*, parrucchino.
tour ['tuəʳ] ▣ **1** N (*gen*) giro; (*of building, exhibition, town*) visita; (*by performers, team*) tournée *f inv*; **package tour** viaggio organizzato; **a round the world tour** un giro del mondo; **to go on a tour of** (*region, country*) fare il giro di; (*museum, castle*) visitare; **to go on a walking/cycling tour of Tuscany** fare il giro della Toscana a piedi/in bicicletta; **on tour** (*Theatre*) in tournée; **to go on tour** andare in tournée; **tour of inspection** giro d'ispezione.
▣ **2** VT (*subj: tourists*) fare un giro di, fare un viaggio in; (: *performers, team*) fare una tournée in.
▣ **3** VI (*also:* **to go touring**) andare a fare un viaggio.
tour de force ['tuədə'fɔ:s] N tour de force *m inv*.
tour·ing ['tuərɪŋ] N viaggi *mpl* turistici.
♦ **touring company** N (*Theatre*) compagnia in tournée.
tour·ism ['tuərɪzəm] N turismo.
tour·ist ['tuərɪst] ▣ **1** N turista *m/f*.
▣ **2** ADJ (*attraction, season*) turistico(-a); **the tourist trade** il turismo.
▣ **3** ADV (*travel*) in classe turistica.
♦ **tourist agency** N agenzia di viaggi e turismo.
♦ **tourist class** N (*Aer*) classe *f* turistica.
♦ **tourist office** N ufficio turistico.
tour·isty ['tuərɪstɪ] ADJ (*pej*) turistico(-a).
tour·na·ment ['tuənəmənt] N torneo; **tennis tournament** torneo di tennis.
tour·ni·quet ['tuənɪˌkeɪ] N (*Med*) laccio emostatico, pinza emostatica.
♦ **tour operator** N (*Brit*) operatore *m* turistico.
tou·sled ['tauzld] ADJ (*hair*) arruffato(-a); (*bedclothes*) sottosopra *inv*.
tout [taut] ▣ **1** N (*for hotels*) procacciatore *m* di clienti; (*Brit: also:* **ticket tout**) bagarino; (*Racing*) portaquote *m inv*.
▣ **2** VI: **to tout for business** raccogliere ordinazioni; (*for hotels*) procacciare clienti.
▣ **3** VT: **to tout sth (around)** (*Brit*) cercare di (ri)vendere qc.
tow [təu] ▣ **1** N rimorchio; **to give sb a tow** (*Aut*) rimorchiare qn; **to be on tow** essere a rimorchio; **"on tow"** [OR] (*Am*) **"in tow"** "veicolo rimorchiato"; **he arrived with a friend in tow** (*fig: fam*) si è portato dietro un amico.
▣ **2** VT (*boat, car, caravan*) rimorchiare; **to tow a car away** portar via una macchina con il carro attrezzi.
to·wards [tə'wɔ:dz], **to·ward** [tə'wɔ:d] PREP (*gen*) verso; (*of attitude*) nei confronti di, verso; (*of purpose*) per; **we walked towards the sea** ci siamo incamminati verso il mare; **the government is moving towards disaster** il governo si avvia al disastro; **towards noon/the end of the year** verso mezzogiorno/la fine dell'anno; **your attitude towards him** il tuo atteggiamento nei suoi confronti *or* verso di lui; **to feel friendly towards sb** provare un sentimento d'amicizia per qn; **to save towards sth** risparmiare per comprare qc; **half my salary goes towards paying the rent** metà del mio stipendio se ne va per l'affitto *or* in affitto.
♦ **tow·bar** ['təuˌbɑ:'] N barra di rimorchio.
♦ **tow·boat** ['təuˌbəut] N rimorchiatore *m*.
tow·el ['tauəl] ▣ **1** N (*also:* **hand towel**) asciugamano; (*also:* **bath towel**) telo da bagno; (*also:* **tea towel**, **dishtowel**) strofinaccio; **to throw in the towel** (*fig*) gettare la spugna.
▣ **2** VT: **to towel o.s. dry** asciugarsi con un asciugamano.
tow·el·ling ['tauəlɪŋ] N (*fabric*) (tessuto di) spugna.

♦ **towel rail**, **towel rack** N portasciugamano.

tow·er ['tauə'] [1] N (*of castle, church*) torre *f*; **he was a tower of strength to me** mi ha dato un grande appoggio.
[2] VI (*building, mountain*) innalzarsi; **to tower above** or **over sb/sth** sovrastare qn/qc.

♦ **tower block** N (*Brit*) palazzone *m*.

tow·er·ing ['tauərɪŋ] ADJ (*building, figure*) imponente, altissimo(-a); **in a towering rage** (*fig*) in preda a un violento accesso d'ira.

♦ **Tower of London** N: **the Tower of London** la Torre di Londra.

tow·line ['təu,laɪn] N (cavo da) rimorchio.

town [taun] [1] N città *f inv*; **to live in a town** vivere in città; **to be out of town** essere fuori città; **in (the) town** in città; **to go (in) to town** andare in città or in centro; **to go out on the town** (*fam*) uscire a far baldoria; **to go to town on sth** (*fig fam*) fare qc in grande.
[2] ADJ (*centre*) della città; (*life*) di città; (*house*) in città.

♦ **town centre** N (*Brit*) centro (città).

♦ **town clerk** N segretario comunale.

♦ **town council** N (*Brit*) consiglio comunale.

♦ **town cri·er** [,taun'kraɪə'] N (*Brit*) banditore(-trice).

♦ **town hall** N ≈ municipio.

townie ['taonɪ] N (*Brit fam*) persona di città.

♦ **town plan** N pianta della città.

♦ **town planner** N (*Brit*) urbanista *m/f*.

♦ **town planning** N (*Brit: action*) pianificazione *f* urbana; (: *study*) urbanistica.

town·ship ['taonʃɪp] N township *f inv*.

towns·people ['taonz,pi:pl] NPL cittadinanza, cittadini *mpl*.

tow·path ['təu,pɑ:θ] N alzaia.

tow·rope ['təu,rəup] N (cavo da) rimorchio.

♦ **tow truck** N (*Am*) carro *m* attrezzi *inv*.

tox·aemia, (*Am*) **tox·emia** [tɒk'si:mɪə] N tossiemia.

tox·ic ['tɒksɪk] ADJ tossico(-a).

toxi·colo·gist [,tɒksɪ'kɒlədʒɪst] N tossicologo(-a).

toxi·col·ogy [,tɒksɪ'kɒlədʒɪ] N tossicologia.

tox·in ['tɒksɪn] N tossina.

toy [tɔɪ] [1] N giocattolo.
[2] ADJ (*train, house*) in miniatura; (*gun*) giocattolo *inv*
▶ **toy with** VI + PREP **a** (*play with: object*) giocherellare con; (: *food*) trastullarsi con; (: *affections*) giocare con **b** (*consider: idea*) accarezzare.

toy·box ['tɔɪ,bɒks] N baule *m* per i giocattoli.

♦ **toy boy** N (*Brit fam fig*) uomo-giocattolo.

♦ **toy car** N automobilina, modellino.

♦ **toy poodle** N barboncino nano.

toy·shop ['tɔɪ,ʃɒp] N negozio di giocattoli.

♦ **toy soldier** N soldatino.

trace¹ [treɪs] [1] N (*sign*) traccia; **there was no trace of it** non ne restava traccia; **to vanish without trace** sparire senza lasciar traccia; **I've lost all trace of them** ho completamente perso le loro tracce; **the postmortem revealed traces of poison in the blood** l'autopsia ha rivelato tracce di veleno nel sangue.
[2] VT **a** (*draw*) tracciare; (: *with tracing paper*) ricalcare **b** (*follow*) seguire (le tracce di); (*find, locate*) rintracciare; **I cannot trace any reference to the matter** non riesco a rintracciare alcun riferimento alla faccenda
▶ **trace back** VT + ADV: **they traced the weapon back to here** hanno stabilito che l'arma proviene da qui; **to trace back one's family to** rintracciare le origini della propria famiglia fino a.

trace² [treɪs] N (*of harness*) tirella; **to kick over the traces** (*Brit fig*) sfuggire al controllo.

♦ **trace element** N oligoelemento.

trac·ery ['treɪsərɪ] N (*of frost*) disegno.

tra·chea [trə'kɪə] N (*Anat*) trachea.

tra·cheal [trə'kɪəl] ADJ tracheale.

trac·ing pa·per ['treɪsɪŋ,peɪpə'] N carta da ricalco.

track [træk] [1] N **a** (*mark: of person, animal*) orma, traccia, impronta; (: *of vehicle*) solco; (: *of ship*) scia; **to be on sb's track** essere sulle tracce di qn; **to follow in sb's tracks** (*also: fig*) seguire le orme di qn; **to keep track of** (*fig: person*) seguire le tracce di; (: *keep in touch with*) restare in contatto con; (: *event*) essere al corrente di; **to lose track of** (*fig: person*) perdere le tracce di; (: *lose contact with*) perdere di vista; (: *event*) non essere al corrente di; **to lose track of an argument** perdere il filo del discorso; **to make tracks (for)** (*fig fam*) avviarsi (a or verso).
b (*path*) sentiero; (: *of comet, rocket*) traiettoria; (: *of suspect, animal*) pista, tracce *fpl*; **to be on the right track** (*fig*) essere sulla buona strada; **to be on the wrong track** (*fig*) essere fuori strada; **to throw sb off the track** (*fig*) mettere qn fuori strada
c (*Sport*) pista
d (*Rail*) binario, rotaie *fpl*; **on the right/wrong side of the tracks** (*Am fam*) nei quartieri alti/poveri della città
e (*Mus: on tape*) pista; **a 4-track tape** un nastro a 4 piste; **the first track on the record/tape** il primo pezzo del disco/nastro
f (*Comput*) pista.
[2] VT (*person, animal*) seguire le tracce di
▶ **track down** VT + ADV (*locate: person*) snidare; (: *prey*) scovare; (: *sth lost*) rintracciare.

track·er dog ['trækə,dɒg] N (*Brit*) cane *m* poliziotto *inv*.

♦ **track events** NPL (*Sport*) gare *fpl* di atletica (*su pista*).

track·ing sta·tion ['trækɪŋ,steɪʃən] N (*Space*) osservatorio spaziale.

♦ **track meet** N (*Am*) meeting *m inv* di atletica.

♦ **track race** N prova su pista.

♦ **track record** N: **to have a good track record** (*fig*) avere un buon curriculum.

track·suit ['træk,su:t] N tuta sportiva or da ginnastica.

tract¹ [trækt] N **a** (*area*) distesa **b** (*Anat*): **respiratory tract** apparato respiratorio.

tract² [trækt] N (*pamphlet*) trattatello, libretto, opuscolo.

trac·table ['træktəbl] ADJ (*person*) accomodante; (*animal*) docile.

trac·tion ['trækʃən] N trazione *f*.

♦ **traction engine** N trattrice *f*.

trac·tor ['træktə'] N trattore *m*.

tractor·feed ['træktə,fi:d] N (*on printer*) trascinamento a trattore.

trade [treɪd] [1] N **a** (*commerce*) commercio; (*business*) affari *mpl*; **to do trade with sb** fare affari con qn, essere in rapporti commerciali con qn; **foreign trade** commercio estero; **to do a brisk** or **roaring trade** fare affari d'oro; **Department of Trade and Industry** (*Brit*), **Department of Trade** (*Am*) ≈ Ministero del Commercio
b (*industry*) industria, settore *m*; **he's in the cotton/building trade** è nell'industria cotoniera/edilizia; **the book trade** l'editoria
c (*profession*) mestiere *m*; **he's a butcher by trade** di mestiere fa il macellaio; **tailoring is a useful trade** quello del sarto è un mestiere utile; **to sell to the trade** vendere all'ingrosso.
[2] VT (*fig: swap sth for sth*) barattare; **he traded his tennis**

racquet for a football ha barattato la sua racchetta da tennis con un pallone.

3 VI: **to trade with sb** fare affari con qn, intrattenere rapporti commerciali con qn.

4 ADJ (*association, route*) commerciale

▶ **trade in** 1 VT + ADV (*old car*) cedere in permuta, dare in pagamento parziale.

2 VI + PREP commerciare in

▶ **trade on** VI + PREP (*pej*) approfittare di, sfruttare.

♦ **trade agreement** N accordo commerciale.

♦ **trade barrier** N barriera commerciale.

♦ **trade deficit** N bilancio commerciale in deficit.

♦ **Trade Descriptions Act** N (*Brit*) legge *f* a tutela del consumatore.

♦ **trade discount** N sconto sul listino (*fatto al commerciante*).

♦ **trade fair** N fiera campionaria.

♦ **trade-in** ['treɪd‚ɪn] N a : **to take as a trade-in** accettare in permuta b (*car*) *macchina ceduta a parziale pagamento di una nuova*.

♦ **trade-in price** N prezzo di permuta.

♦ **trade-in value** N valore *m* di permuta.

trade·mark ['treɪd‚mɑːk] N (*Comm*) marchio di fabbrica; (*fig*) marchio; **registered trademark** marchio registrato.

♦ **trade mission** N missione *f* commerciale.

♦ **trade name** N (*of product*) nome *m* depositato, marca; (*of a company*) ragione *f* sociale.

♦ **trade-off** ['treɪd‚ɒf] N (*exchange*) scambio; (*balancing*) compromesso.

♦ **trade press** N stampa del settore commerciale.

♦ **trade price** N prezzo all'ingrosso.

trad·er ['treɪdə'] N commerciante *m/f*.

♦ **trade reference** N *referenze commerciali sulla solvibilità di un'azienda*.

♦ **trade route** N rotta commerciale.

♦ **trade secret** N segreto commerciale.

trades·man ['treɪdzmən] N (*pl* **-men**) fornitore *m*; (*shopkeeper*) negoziante *m*; **tradesman's entrance** ingresso per i fornitori *or* di servizio.

♦ **trade union**, (*Brit*) **trades union** 1 N sindacato.

2 ADJ (*official*) sindacale; **trade-union dues** quota di associazione al sindacato.

♦ **trade un·ion·ism** [‚treɪd'juːnjə‚nɪzəm], **trades un·ion·ism** [‚treɪdz'juːnjə‚nɪzəm] N (*Brit*) sindacalismo.

♦ **trade unionist**, (*Brit*) **trades unionist** N sindacalista *m/f*.

♦ **trade wind** N aliseo.

trad·ing ['treɪdɪŋ] 1 ADJ (*port, centre*) commerciale; (*nation*) che vive di commercio.

2 N commercio.

♦ **trading estate** N (*Brit*) zona industriale.

♦ **trading post** N stazione *f* commerciale.

♦ **trading stamp** N bollino premio.

tra·di·tion [trə'dɪʃən] N tradizione *f*; **traditions** NPL tradizioni, usanze *fpl*.

tra·di·tion·al [trə'dɪʃənl] ADJ tradizionale.

tra·di·tion·al·ism [trə'dɪʃnə‚lɪzəm] N tradizionalismo.

tra·di·tion·al·ist [trə'dɪʃnəlɪst] ADJ, N tradizionalista (*m/f*).

tra·di·tion·al·ly [trə'dɪʃnəlɪ] ADV per tradizione.

tra·duce [trə'djuːs] VT (*frm*) calunniare, diffamare.

traf·fic ['træfɪk] (*vb: pt, pp* **trafficked**) 1 N traffico; **rail traffic** traffico ferroviario; **the traffic is heavy during the rush hour** il traffico è molto intenso nelle ore di punta; **closed to heavy traffic** (*Aut*) divieto di transito per gli automezzi pesanti; **drug traffic** traffico di droga.

2 VI: **to traffic in** (*pej: liquor, drugs*) trafficare in.

3 ADJ (*Aut: regulations*) stradale.

♦ **traffic calming** N *uso di accorgimenti per rallentare il traffico in zone abitate*.

♦ **traffic circle** N (*Am*) isola rotatoria.

♦ **traffic island** N salvagente *m*, isola *f* spartitraffico *inv*.

♦ **traffic jam** N ingorgo (del traffico); **a 5-mile traffic jam** una coda di 5 miglia.

traf·fick·er ['træfɪkə'] N trafficante *m/f*.

♦ **traffic lights** NPL semaforo.

♦ **traffic offence** N (*Brit*) infrazione *f* al codice stradale.

♦ **traffic sign** N cartello stradale.

♦ **traffic violation** N (*Am*) = **traffic offence**.

♦ **traffic warden** N (*Brit*) ≈ vigile *m* (urbano).

trag·edy ['trædʒɪdɪ] N (*gen, Theatre*) tragedia; **it is a tragedy that** ... è una vera disgrazia che... .

trag·ic ['trædʒɪk] ADJ tragico(-a); **tragic actor** attore *m* tragico.

tragi·cal·ly ['trædʒɪkəlɪ] ADV tragicamente.

tragi·com·edy [‚trædʒɪ'kɒmɪdɪ] N tragicommedia.

tragi·com·ic [‚trædʒɪ'kɒmɪk] ADJ tragicomico(-a).

♦ **trail** [treɪl] 1 N a (*of dust, smoke*) scia; **the hurricane left a trail of destruction** l'uragano non ha lasciato altro che distruzione dietro di sé

b (*track*) orma; (*tracks*) pista, tracce *fpl*; **to be on sb's trail** essere sulle orme di qn

c (*path*) sentiero; (*Skiing*) pista da fondo.

2 VT a (*drag*) trascinare, strascicare; **don't trail mud into the house** non portare fango in casa

b (*track: animal*) seguire le orme di; (: *person*) pedinare, seguire.

3 VI a (*object*) strisciare; (*plant*) arrampicarsi; (*dress*) strusciare; **to trail by 2 goals** (*Sport*) essere in svantaggio di 2 goal

b (*wearily: also: trail along*) trascinarsi

▶ **trail away, trail off** VI + ADV (*sound*) affievolirsi; (*interest, voice*) spegnersi a poco a poco

▶ **trail behind** VI + ADV essere al traino

▶ **trail off** VI + ADV = **trail away**.

trail·blazer ['treɪl‚bleɪzə'] N pioniere(-a).

trail·er ['treɪlə'] N a (*Aut*) rimorchio; (*for horses*) van *m inv*; (*Am: caravan*) roulotte *f inv* b (*Cine*) trailer *m inv*.

♦ **trailer truck** N (*Am*) autoarticolato.

train [treɪn] 1 N a (*Rail*) treno; **to go by train** andare in *or* col treno; **to travel by train** viaggiare in treno; **in** *or* **on the train** in treno, sul treno; **to take the 3.00 train** prendere il treno delle 3; **to change trains** cambiare treno

b (*line: of animals, vehicles*) fila; (*entourage*) seguito; (*of admirers*) codazzo

c (*Brit: series*): **train of events** serie *f inv* di avvenimenti a catena; **my train of thought** il filo dei miei pensieri; **the earthquake brought great suffering in its train** il terremoto ha portato con sé disgrazie e sofferenze

d (*of dress*) strascico, coda.

2 VT a (*instruct*) istruire; (*apprentice, doctor*) formare; (*Mil*) addestrare; (*sportsman*) allenare; (*mind, memory*) far esercitare; (*animal*) addestrare, ammaestrare; **to train sb to do sth** preparare qn a fare qc

b : **to train on** (*direct: gun*) puntare qc contro; (: *camera, telescope*) puntare (a *or* verso).

3 VI a (*learn a skill*) fare pratica, fare tirocinio; **to train as** *or* **to be a lawyer** fare pratica come avvocato; **where did you train?** dove hai fatto pratica *or* tirocinio?

b (*Sport*): **to train (for)** allenarsi (per).

♦ **train attendant** N (*Am*) addetto(-a) ai vagoni letto.

train·bearer ['treɪnˌbɛərə'] N damigella; (*little boy*) paggio.

trained [treɪnd] ADJ (*accountant, nurse*) diplomato(-a), qualificato(-a); (*teacher*) abilitato(-a) all'insegnamento; (*Sport: athlete, horse*) allenato(-a); (*animal*) addestrato(-a), ammaestrato(-a); **well-trained** (*child, dog*) ben educato(-a); **I've got him well-trained** (*hum*) l'ho addomesticato per bene.

trainee [treɪ'ni:] ① N (*gen, in trade*) apprendista *m/f*; (*for profession*) tirocinante *m/f*; **she's a management trainee** sta facendo tirocinio come dirigente.

② ADJ: **he's a trainee teacher** sta facendo tirocinio come insegnante; **to be a trainee chef** fare il tirocinio come chef.

train·er ['treɪnə'] N **a** (*Sport*) allenatore(-trice); (*of circus animals*) domatore(-trice); (*of dogs*) addestratore (-trice) **b** (*Brit: shoe*) scarpa da ginnastica.

train·ing ['treɪnɪŋ] ① N (*in job*) pratica, tirocinio; (*for job*) formazione *f*; (*Mil*) addestramento; (*Sport*) allenamento; **to be in training** (*for race, event*) essere in allenamento; (*fit*) essere in forma; **to be out of training** essere fuori allenamento *or* forma.

② ADJ (*scheme, centre: for job*) di formazione professionale; (*Sport*) di allenamento.

♦ **training college** N istituto professionale.

♦ **training course** N corso di formazione professionale.

♦ **training shoe** N (*Brit*) scarpa da ginnastica.

♦ **train service** N collegamento ferroviario.

♦ **train set** N trenino elettrico.

♦ **train-spotting** ['treɪnˌspɒtɪŋ] N: **to go train-spotting** andare a osservare i treni.

traipse [treɪps] ① VI (*fam*): **to traipse around** trascinarsi in giro.

② N: **a long traipse** una camminata sfiancante.

trait [treɪt] N caratteristica, tratto.

trai·tor ['treɪtə'] N traditore(-trice); **to turn traitor** passare al nemico.

tra·jec·tory [trə'dʒɛktərɪ] N traiettoria.

tram [træm], **tram·car** ['træmˌkɑː'] N (*Brit*) tram *m inv*.

tram·line ['træmˌlaɪn] N linea tranviaria.

tram·lines ['træmˌlaɪnz] NPL (*Brit*) **a** rotaie *fpl* del tram **b** (*Tennis*) corridoio.

tram·mel ['træməl] VT (*frm, liter*) intralciare.

tram·mels ['træməlz] NPL (*frm, liter*) legami *mpl*, vincoli *mpl*.

tramp [træmp] ① N **a** (*sound of feet*) rumore *m* pesante (di passi)

b (*long walk*) camminata; **to go for a tramp in the hills** andare a fare una camminata sui colli

c (*person*) vagabondo(-a); **she's a tramp** (*fam pej*) è una sgualdrina.

② VT (*walk through: town, streets*) percorrere a piedi; **to tramp the streets looking for sth** battere le strade in cerca di qc.

③ VI camminare con passo pesante; **the soldiers tramped past** i soldati sono passati marciando pesantemente; **he tramped up to the door** si è avvicinato con passi pesanti alla porta.

tram·ple ['træmpl] VT: **to trample (underfoot)** (*crush*) calpestare; **to trample sth into the ground** calpestare qc

▶ **trample on** VI + PREP calpestare; **to trample on sb's feelings** (*fig*) calpestare i sentimenti di qn.

tram·po·line ['træmpəlɪn] N trampolino.

tram·way ['træmweɪ] N (*Brit*) tranvia.

trance [trɑːns] N trance *f inv*; (*Med*) catalessi *f inv*; **to go into a trance** cadere in trance.

tran·quil ['træŋkwɪl] ADJ tranquillo(-a).

tran·quil·lity, (*Am*) **tran·quil·ity** [træŋ'kwɪlɪtɪ] N tranquillità *f inv*.

tran·quil·lize, (*Am*) **tran·quil·ize** ['træŋkwɪˌlaɪz] VT (*Med*) calmare con un tranquillante.

tran·quil·lizer, (*Am*) **tran·quil·iz·er** ['træŋkwɪˌlaɪzə'] N (*Med*) tranquillante *m*.

trans... [trænz] PREF trans... .

trans·act [træn'zækt] VT (*business*) trattare.

trans·ac·tion [træn'zækʃən] N (*business*) trattativa; (*in bank*) operazione *f*, transazione *f*; **transactions** NPL (*minutes*) atti *mpl*; **cash transaction** operazione in contanti.

trans·at·lan·tic [ˌtrænzət'læntɪk] ADJ transatlantico(-a).

trans·cend [træn'sɛnd] VT (*frm: go beyond*) trascendere, superare.

trans·cend·ent [træn'sɛndənt] ADJ (*frm*) trascendente.

tran·scen·den·tal [ˌtrænsɛn'dɛntl] ADJ (*frm*) trascendentale.

♦ **transcendental meditation** N meditazione *f* trascendentale.

tran·scribe [træn'skraɪb] VT trascrivere.

tran·script ['trænskrɪpt] N trascrizione *f*.

tran·scrip·tion [træn'skrɪpʃən] N trascrizione *f*.

trans·duc·er [trænz'djuːsə'] N trasduttore *m*.

tran·sect [træn'sɛkt] VT tagliare trasversalmente.

tran·sept ['trænsɛpt] N (*Archit*) transetto.

trans·fer [n 'trænsfɜː'; vb træns'fɜː'] ① N **a** (*gen*) trasferimento; (*Pol: of power*) passaggio; (*Law*) cessione *f*; (*Ftbl*) cessione (*or* acquisto); **by bank transfer** tramite trasferimento bancario

b (*picture, design: stick-on*) decalcomania, autoadesivo.

② VT **a** (*move*): **to transfer (from/to)** trasferire (da/a); (*Sport*): **to be transferred (from/to)** essere ceduto(-a) (da/a); **to transfer one's affections/ambitions to sb** trasferire i propri sentimenti/le proprie ambizioni su qn; **to transfer money from one account to another** trasferire il denaro da un conto su un altro; **to transfer sth to sb's name** mettere qc a nome di qn; **to make a transferred charge call** (*Brit*) fare una chiamata a carico del destinatario

b (*picture, design*) decalcare.

③ VI (*gen*) trasferirsi, passare; **she transferred from History to Classics** (*Univ*) è passata da Storia a Lettere Antiche.

trans·fer·able [træns'fɜːrəbl] ADJ trasferibile; **not transferable** non cedibile, personale.

trans·fer·ence ['trænsfərəns] N (*frm*) trasferimento; (*Psych*) transfert *m inv*.

trans·figu·ra·tion [ˌtrænsfɪgə'reɪʃən] N (*liter, Rel*) trasfigurazione *f*.

trans·fig·ure [træns'fɪgə'] VT (*liter*) trasfigurare.

trans·fix [træns'fɪks] VT trafiggere; (*fig*): **transfixed with fear** paralizzato(-a) dalla paura.

trans·form [træns'fɔːm] VT trasformare.

trans·for·ma·tion [ˌtrænsfə'meɪʃən] N trasformazione *f*.

trans·for·ma·tion·al [ˌtrænsfə'meɪʃənl] ADJ (*Ling*) trasformazionale.

trans·form·er [træns'fɔːmə'] N (*Elec*) trasformatore *m*.

trans·fu·sion [træns'fjuːʒən] N trasfusione *f*; **to give sb a blood transfusion** praticare una trasfusione di sangue a qn.

trans·gress [trænsˈgrɛs] (*frm*) ① VI (*sin*) peccare.
② VT (*violate: moral law*) infrangere, trasgredire.
trans·gress·or [trænsˈgrɛsəʳ] N (*frm*) trasgressore/trasgreditrice.
tran·ship [trænˈʃɪp] VT = **transship**.
tran·si·ence [ˈtrænzɪəns] N (*frm*) transitorietà.
tran·si·ent [ˈtrænzɪənt] ADJ transitorio(-a), fugace.
tran·sis·tor [trænˈzɪstəʳ] N (*Elec*) transistor *m inv*.
tran·sis·tor·ized [trænˈzɪstəˌraɪzd] ADJ (*circuit*) transistorizzato(-a).
♦ **transistor radio** N (radio *f inv* a) transistor *m inv*.
trans·it [ˈtrænzɪt] N transito; **in transit** in transito; **their luggage was lost in transit** il loro bagaglio è stato smarrito durante il trasferimento.
♦ **transit camp** N campo (di raccolta) profughi.
tran·si·tion [trænˈzɪʃən] N transizione *f*, passaggio; **transition period** periodo di transizione.
tran·si·tion·al [trænˈzɪʃnl] ADJ (*period, government*) di transizione; (*measures*) transitorio(-a).
tran·si·tive [ˈtrænzɪtɪv] ADJ (*Gram*) transitivo(-a).
♦ **transit lounge** N (*Aer*) sala di transito.
tran·si·tory [ˈtrænzɪtərɪ] ADJ transitorio(-a).
♦ **transit passenger** N passeggero in transito.
♦ **transit visa** N visto di transito.
trans·lat·able [trænzˈleɪtəbl] ADJ traducibile.
trans·late [trænzˈleɪt] ① VT: **to translate (from/into)** tradurre (da/in); **it is translated as** si traduce con.
② VI tradurre; **it won't translate** è intraducibile.
trans·la·tion [trænzˈleɪʃən] N (*of text*) traduzione *f*; (*Scol: as opposed to prose*) versione *f*; (*Geom*) traslazione *f*.
trans·la·tor [trænzˈleɪtəʳ] N traduttore(-trice).
trans·lit·er·ate [trænzˈlɪtəˌreɪt] VT traslitterare.
trans·lit·era·tion [ˌtrænzlɪtəˈreɪʃən] N traslitterazione *f*.
trans·lu·cence [trænzˈluːsns] N traslucidità *f inv*.
trans·lu·cent [trænzˈluːsnt] ADJ traslucido(-a).
trans·mis·sion [trænzˈmɪʃən] N (*Aut, TV, Radio*) trasmissione *f*.
♦ **transmission cable** N (*Aut*) flessibile *m* di trasmissione.
♦ **transmission shaft** N (*Aut*) albero di trasmissione.
trans·mit [trænzˈmɪt] VT (*illness, programme, message*) trasmettere.
trans·mit·ter [trænzˈmɪtəʳ] N (*TV, Radio, Telec*) trasmettitore *m*.
trans·mit·ting [trænzˈmɪtɪŋ] ADJ (*TV, Radio, Telec*) trasmittente; **transmitting set** radiotrasmettitore *m*; **transmitting station** emittente *f*.
trans·mute [trænzˈmjuːt] VT (*frm*): **to transmute (into)** tramutare (in).
tran·som [ˈtrænsəm] N traversa.
trans·par·en·cy [trænsˈpærənsɪ] N trasparenza; (*Phot*) diapositiva.
trans·par·ent [trænsˈpærənt] ADJ trasparente; **a transparent lie** (*fig*) una menzogna palese.
tran·spi·ra·tion [ˌtrænspɪˈreɪʃən] N traspirazione *f*.
tran·spire [trænsˈpaɪəʳ] VI **a** (*Bot, Physiology*) traspirare **b** (*frm: become known*): **it finally transpired that ...** alla fine si è venuto a sapere che... **c** (*incorrect use: happen*) succedere.
trans·plant [*vb* trænsˈplɑːnt; *n* ˈtrænsˌplɑːnt] ① VT (*also Med*) trapiantare.
② N (*Med*) trapianto; **to have a heart transplant** subire un trapianto cardiaco.
trans·port [*n* ˈtrænspɔːt; *vb, adj* trænsˈpɔːt] ① N **a** (*gen*) trasporto; (*vehicle*) mezzo di trasporto; **public transport**

mezzi *mpl* pubblici; **Department of Transport** (*Brit*) Ministero dei Trasporti; **I haven't got any transport** non ho un mezzo
 b (*fig: of delight, rage*) trasporto; **to go into transports of joy** esultare dalla gioia.
② VT **a** trasportare; (*History: convicts*) deportare
 b (*fig*): **transported with delight** deliziato(-a); **transported with joy** estasiato(-a).
③ ADJ (*system, costs*) di trasporto.
trans·por·ta·tion [ˌtrænspɔːˈteɪʃən] N **a** trasporto; (*vehicle*) mezzo di trasporto **b** (*History: of convicts*) deportazione *f*; **Department of Transportation** (*Am*) Ministero dei Trasporti.
♦ **transport café** N (*Brit*) trattoria per camionisti.
trans·port·er [trænsˈpɔːtəʳ] N autotreno.
trans·pose [trænsˈpəʊz] VT **a** (*frm: words*) trasporre **b** (*Mus*) trasportare.
trans·po·si·tion [ˌtrænspəˈzɪʃən] N (*frm*) trasposizione *f*.
trans·sexu·al [trænzˈsɛksjʊəl] N, ADJ transessuale (*m/f*) *inv*.
trans·ship [trænsˈʃɪp] VT trasbordare.
tran·sub·stan·tia·tion [ˈtrænsəbˌstænʃɪˈeɪʃən] N (*Rel*) transustanziazione *f*.
trans·ver·sal [trænzˈvɜːsəl] (*Geom*) ① ADJ trasversale.
② N retta trasversale.
trans·verse [ˈtrænzvɜːs] ADJ trasversale.
trans·ves·tite [trænzˈvestaɪt] N travestito(-a).
trap [træp] ① N **a** (*snare, trick*) trappola; **to set** *or* **lay a trap (for sb)** tendere una trappola (a qn); **he was caught in his own trap** si è fregato con le sue stesse mani
 b (*fam: mouth*) boccaccia; **shut your trap!** (*fam*) chiudi quella boccaccia!
 c (*carriage*) calesse *m*.
② VT **a** prendere in trappola, intrappolare; **to trap sb into saying sth** far raccontare qc a qn con un trucco
 b (*immobilize*) bloccare; (: *in wreckage*) intrappolare, bloccare; **the miners are trapped** i minatori sono rimasti intrappolati; **to trap one's finger in the door** chiudersi il dito nella porta; **to trap the ball** (*Ftbl*) stoppare la palla.
♦ **trap door** N botola.
tra·peze [trəˈpiːz] N (*di circo*) trapezio.
♦ **trapeze artist** N trapezista *m/f*.
tra·pezium [trəˈpiːzɪəm] N (*Geom*) trapezio.
trap·per [ˈtræpəʳ] N cacciatore *m* di animali da pelliccia.
trap·pings [ˈtræpɪŋz] NPL (*of public office*) bardatura, ornamenti *mpl*; (*fig: of success*) segni *mpl* esteriori.
Trap·pist [ˈtræpɪst] ① ADJ trappista *m*.
② N trappista *m*.
trash [træʃ] N (*Am: rubbish*) rifiuti *mpl*, spazzatura; (*pej: goods*) ciarpame *m*; (*fig: nonsense*) sciocchezze *fpl*, stupidaggini *fpl*; **the book is trash** il libro è una schifezza; **they're just trash** (*fam pej: people*) sono dei pezzenti.
trash·can [ˈtræʃˌkæn] N (*Am*) secchio della spazzatura.
trashy [ˈtræʃɪ] ADJ (*comp* **-ier**, *superl* **-iest**) (*fam: book, film*) scadente.
trau·ma [ˈtrɔːmə] N trauma *m*.
trau·mat·ic [trɔːˈmætɪk] ADJ (*Med*) traumatico(-a); (*Psych, fig*) traumatizzante, traumatico(-a).
trav·el [ˈtrævl] ① N il viaggiare, viaggi *mpl*; **travel is easier now** viaggiare è più facile al giorno d'oggi; **when are you off on your travels?** quando parti per uno dei tuoi viaggi?; **if you meet him on your travels** (*fig*) se lo incontri in uno dei tuoi giri.
② VI **a** viaggiare; (*make a journey*) fare un viaggio; **we**

shall be travelling in France faremo un viaggio in Francia; **to travel round the world** fare un viaggio intorno al mondo; **to travel by car** viaggiare in macchina; **they have travelled a lot** hanno viaggiato molto; **they have travelled a long way** sono venuti da lontano; **to travel light** viaggiare con poco bagaglio; **this wine doesn't travel well** questo vino non resiste agli spostamenti

b (go at a speed) viaggiare, andare; **it travels at 50 km/h** fa 50 km/h; **light travels at a speed of ...** la velocità della luce è di...; **news travels fast** le notizie si diffondono molto velocemente

c (Tech: move) spostarsi; **it travels along this wire** si sposta lungo questo filo

d (Comm) fare il/la rappresentante (di commercio); **he travels in furs** fa il rappresentante di pellicce.

3 VT (road, distance) percorrere, fare; **this is a much travelled road** questa è una strada di grande traffico.

♦ **travel agency** N agenzia (di) viaggi.

♦ **travel agent** N agente m di viaggio.

trav·el·at·or ['trævə‚leɪtəʳ] N (Brit) tapis roulant m inv.

♦ **travel brochure** N dépliant m inv di viaggi.

trav·el·ler, (Am) **trav·el·er** ['trævləʳ] N (gen) viaggiatore (-trice); (Comm) commesso viaggiatore; (Brit: gypsy) zingaro(-a); **my fellow travellers** i miei compagni di viaggio.

♦ **traveller's cheque**, (Am) **traveler's check** N traveller's cheque m inv.

trav·el·ling, (Am) **trav·el·ing** ['trævlɪŋ] **1** ADJ (circus, exhibition) itinerante; (expenses, allowance) di viaggio; (bag, rug, clock) da viaggio.

2 N viaggi mpl.

♦ **travelling salesman**, (Am) **traveling salesman** N commesso viaggiatore.

trav·elogue ['trævəlɒg] N (book) diario di viaggio; (film) documentario di viaggio; (talk) conferenza su un viaggio.

♦ **travel-sick** ['trævl‚sɪk] ADJ: **to get travel-sick** soffrire di mal d'auto.

♦ **travel sickness** N (in car) mal m d'auto; (in plane) mal d'aria; (in boat) mal di mare.

trav·erse ['trævɜ:s] (frm) **1** N (line) linea trasversale; (crossbeam) traversa; (Mountaineering) traversata.

2 VT traversare, attraversare; (Mountaineering) traversare.

3 VI (Mountaineering) fare una traversata.

trav·es·ty ['trævɪstɪ] N parodia; **his trial was a travesty of justice** il suo processo è stato una farsa.

trav·ol·at·or ['trævə‚leɪtəʳ] N (Brit) tapis roulant m inv.

trawl [trɔ:l] **1** N (net) rete f a strascico.

2 VI: **to trawl (for sth)** pescare (qc) con rete a strascico.

trawl·er ['trɔ:ləʳ] N peschereccio (per la pesca a strascico).

trawl·ing ['trɔ:lɪŋ] N pesca a strascico.

tray [treɪ] N (for carrying) vassoio; (filing tray) vassoio per la corrispondenza.

treach·er·ous ['trɛtʃərəs] ADJ (disloyal: person, act) sleale; (smile) traditore(-trice); (answer) infido(-a); (fig: surface, ground, tide) pericoloso(-a); **road conditions today are treacherous** oggi il fondo stradale è pericoloso.

treach·er·ous·ly ['trɛtʃərəslɪ] ADV (act) slealmente; (speak) con falsità; **the roads are treacherously icy** il fondo stradale è infido or pericoloso con questo ghiaccio.

treach·ery ['trɛtʃərɪ] N slealtà f inv; **an act of treachery** un

tradimento.

trea·cle ['tri:kl] N (Brit) melassa.

trea·cly ['tri:klɪ] ADJ (substance) sciropposo(-a); (fig: voice) melato(-a).

tread [trɛd] (vb: pt **trod**, pp **trodden**) **1** N **a** (footsteps) passo; (sound) rumore m di passi; **to walk with (a) heavy tread** avere un'andatura pesante

b (of stair) pedata; (of tyre) battistrada m inv.

2 VT (ground) calpestare; (path) percorrere; (grapes) pigiare; **to tread water** tenersi a galla verticalmente (muovendo solo le gambe); **don't tread mud into the carpet** non infangare il tappeto; **he trod his cigarette end into the mud** ha schiacciato il mozzicone della sigaretta nel fango; **to tread a dangerous path** (fig) battere un sentiero pericoloso.

3 VI (walk) camminare; **to tread on sth** calpestare qc; **to tread on sb's toes** (also fig) pestare i piedi a qn; **we must tread very carefully** or **warily** dobbiamo muoverci con molta cautela

► **tread on** VI + PREP calpestare.

trea·dle ['trɛdl] N pedale m.

tread·mill ['trɛd‚mɪl] N (fig): **to go back to the treadmill** tornare alla solita routine.

♦ **tread pattern** N (of tyre) disegno.

treas. ABBR = **treasurer**.

trea·son ['tri:zn] N tradimento.

trea·son·able ['tri:zənəbl] ADJ proditorio(-a).

treas·ure ['trɛʒəʳ] **1** N (no pl: gold, jewels) tesori mpl; (valuable object, fig: person) tesoro; **our cleaner is a real treasure** la nostra donna delle pulizie è una vera rarità.

2 VT (value: friendship) apprezzare molto, tenere in gran conto; (keep: valuables) custodire gelosamente; (: memory) fare tesoro di.

♦ **treasure house** N: **a treasure house of knowledge** (fig) un pozzo di scienza.

♦ **treasure hunt** N caccia al tesoro.

treas·ur·er ['trɛʒərəʳ] N tesoriere(-a).

♦ **treasure trove** N reperto archeologico di proprietà dello Stato.

treas·ury ['trɛʒərɪ] N **a** tesoreria; **the Treasury** (Brit), **the Treasury Department** (Am) ≈ il Ministero del Tesoro **b** (fig) pozzo.

♦ **treasury bill** N ≈ buono del tesoro.

treat [tri:t] **1** N (pleasure) piacere m; (present) sorpresa, sorpresina; **it was a treat** mi (or ci etc) ha fatto veramente piacere; **as a special birthday treat they took me to the theatre** mi hanno fatto una piacevole sorpresa per il compleanno portandomi a teatro; **to give sb a treat** fare una sorpresa a qn; **to have a treat in store** avere una sorpresa in serbo; **this is my treat** offro io.

2 VT **a** (gen, Tech) trattare; **to treat sb like a child** trattare qn come se fosse un bambino

b (consider) considerare; **to treat sth as a joke** considerare qc uno scherzo; **we treat all applications in the order in which we receive them** prendiamo in considerazione le domande nell'ordine in cui ci arrivano

c (give, buy for sb): **to treat sb to sth** offrire qc a qn; **I'll treat you** offro io; **he treated himself to a new jacket** si è concesso il lusso di una giacca nuova

d (patient, illness) curare; **he was treated with antibiotics/for bronchitis** è stato sottoposto a un trattamento di antibiotici/per la bronchite.

trea·tise ['tri:tɪz] N trattato.

treat·ment ['tri:tmənt] N **a** trattamento; **to give sb**

preferential treatment fare un trattamento di favore a qn; **he got good/bad treatment** è stato trattato bene/male; **our treatment of foreigners** il modo in cui trattiamo gli stranieri

  b (*Med*: *of illness*) cura; (: *of wound*) medicazione *f*; **to give sb medical treatment for sth** curare qc a qn; **to have treatment for sth** farsi curare qc.

trea·ty ['triːtɪ] N trattato, patto; **to sell a house by private treaty** (*agreement*) vendere una casa con un accordo privato.

tre·ble ['trɛbl] ⨩1⨩ ADV (*3 times*) tre volte.

  ⨩2⨩ ADJ **a** triplo(-a), triplice **b** (*Mus*: *voice, part*) da soprano; (: *note, instrument*) alto(-a).

  ⨩3⨩ N **a** (*Mus*) soprano *m/f*; (*also*: **boy treble**) voce *f* bianca **b** (*Horse-riding*) doppia gabbia.

  ⨩4⨩ VT triplicare.

  ⨩5⨩ VI triplicarsi.

♦ **treble clef** N chiave *f* di violino.

tree [triː] N **a** (*Bot*) albero; (*fig*): **to be at the top of the tree** essere all'apice **b** (*also*: **shoetree**) tendiscarpe *m inv*.

♦ **tree diagram** N (*Math*) diagramma *m* ad albero.

♦ **tree house** N capanna costruita su un albero.

♦ **tree line** N limite *m* della vegetazione ad alto fusto.

♦ **tree-lined** ['triːˌlaɪnd] ADJ fiancheggiato(-a) da alberi.

♦ **tree of heaven** N albero del paradiso.

tree·top ['triːˌtɒp] N cima di un albero.

♦ **tree trunk** N tronco d'albero.

tre·foil ['trɛfɔɪl] N (*Bot*) trifoglio; (*Archit*) decorazione *f* a trifoglio.

trek [trɛk] ⨩1⨩ N (*hike*) spedizione *f*; (*fam*: *tiring walk*) camminata sfiancante.

  ⨩2⨩ VI (*hike*) fare una camminata lunga e faticosa; (*as holiday*) fare dell'escursionismo; (*fam*) trascinarsi.

trel·lis ['trɛlɪs] N graticcio; (*arched*) pergola.

trem·ble ['trɛmbl] ⨩1⨩ N (*of fear*) tremito; (*of passion, excitement*) fremito; **to be all of a tremble** (*fam*) tremare dalla testa ai piedi, tremare come una foglia.

  ⨩2⨩ VI tremare; (*machine*) vibrare; **to tremble with** tremare per; **to tremble at the thought of sth** tremare al pensiero di qc.

trem·bling ['trɛmblɪŋ] ⨩1⨩ ADJ tremante.

  ⨩2⨩ N tremore *m*, tremito.

tre·men·dous [trəˈmɛndəs] ADJ (*enormous: difference, pleasure*) enorme; (*dreadful: storm, blow*) tremendo(-a); (: *speed*) spaventoso(-a), folle; (*terrific: success*) strepitoso(-a); (*fam*: *excellent*) fantastico(-a), formidabile, meraviglioso(-a).

tre·men·dous·ly [trəˈmɛndəslɪ] ADV incredibilmente; **he enjoyed it tremendously** gli è piaciuto da morire.

trem·or ['trɛmə'] N (*of fear, shock*) tremito, tremore *m*; (*of excitement*) fremito; (*also*: **earth tremor**) scossa di terremoto, scossa sismica; **it sent tremors down my spine** mi ha fatto venire i brividi.

tremu·lous ['trɛmjʊləs] ADJ (*liter*: *trembling*) tremulo(-a); (: *timid*) timido(-a).

tremu·lous·ly ['trɛmjʊləslɪ] ADV (*liter*: *speak*) con voce tremula; (: *smile*) timidamente.

trench [trɛntʃ] N (*gen*) fosso; (*Mil*) trincea.

trench·ant ['trɛntʃənt] ADJ tagliente.

♦ **trench coat** N trench *m inv*.

♦ **trench warfare** N guerra di trincea.

trend [trɛnd] N (*tendency*) tendenza; (*of events*) andamento, corso; (*of prices, coastline*) andamento; (*fashion*) moda; **to set a trend** lanciare una moda; **to set the**

trend essere all'avanguardia; **trend towards sth/away from sth** tendenza a qc/ad allontanarsi da qc; **there is a trend towards doing sth/away from doing sth** si tende a fare qc/a non fare qc.

trend·set·ter ['trɛndˌsɛtə'] N (*fam*) persona che detta la moda.

trendy ['trɛndɪ] ADJ (*comp* **-ier**, *superl* **-iest**) (*Brit fam*: *person, idea*) à la page; (: *clothes, night club*) trendy.

trepi·da·tion [ˌtrɛpɪˈdeɪʃən] N (*frm*) trepidazione *f*.

tres·pass ['trɛspəs] ⨩1⨩ VI: **to trespass (on)** (*on land*) entrare abusivamente (in); (*fig*: *on time, hospitality*) abusare (di); **"no trespassing"** "proprietà privata", "vietato l'accesso".

  ⨩2⨩ N (*on land*) transito abusivo.

tres·pass·er ['trɛspəsə'] N (*Bible, Law*) trasgressore *m*; **"trespassers will be prosecuted"** "vietato l'accesso - i trasgressori saranno puniti secondo i termini di legge".

tress [trɛs] N (*liter*) ciocca di capelli.

tres·tle ['trɛsl] N cavalletto.

♦ **trestle table** N tavola su cavalletti.

tri... [traɪ] PREF tri... .

tri·al ['traɪəl] ⨩1⨩ N **a** (*gen*) giudizio; (*proceedings*) processo; **trial by jury** processo penale con giuria; **to be on trial (for a crime)** essere sotto processo (per un reato); **to bring sb to trial (for a crime)** portare qn in giudizio (per un reato); **to go on trial** OR **to stand trial** essere processato(-a); **to be sent for trial** essere rinviato(-a) a giudizio

  b (*test: gen*) prova; (: *of drugs*) sperimentazione *f*; (: *of machine*) collaudo; **trials** NPL (*Athletics*) prove *fpl* di qualificazione; (*Ftbl*) prova di selezione; **horse trials** concorso ippico; **a trial of strength** una prova di forza; **by trial and error** per tentativi; **to be on trial** (*drug*) essere in via di sperimentazione; (*machine*) essere al collaudo; **to give sb a trial** (*for job*) far fare una prova a qn

  c (*hardship*) prova, difficoltà *f inv*; (*worry*) cruccio; **it was a great trial** è stata una dura prova; **that child is a great trial to them** quel bambino è una continua preoccupazione per loro; **the trials and tribulations of life** le tribolazioni della vita.

  ⨩2⨩ ADJ (*flight, order, period*) di prova; **trial offer** offerta di lancio; **on a trial basis** in prova.

♦ **trial balance** N (*Comm*) bilancio di verifica.

♦ **trial run** N periodo di prova.

tri·an·gle ['traɪˌæŋgl] N (*Math, Mus*) triangolo.

tri·an·gu·lar [traɪˈæŋgjʊlə'] ADJ triangolare.

tri·ath·lon [traɪˈæθlɒn] N triathlon *m inv*.

trib·al ['traɪbəl] ADJ tribale; (*warfare*) fra tribù.

trib·al·ism ['traɪbəlɪzəm] N (*Anthropology, Sociol*) organizzazione *f* tribale; (*pej*) tribalismo.

tribe [traɪb] N tribù *f inv*.

tribes·man ['traɪbzmən] N (*pl* **-men**) membro della tribù.

tribu·la·tion [ˌtrɪbjʊˈleɪʃən] N (*frm*) tribolazione *f*.

tri·bu·nal [traɪˈbjuːnl] N tribunale *m*; **tribunal of inquiry** commissione *f* d'inchiesta.

tribu·tary ['trɪbjʊtərɪ] N (*river*) affluente *m*, tributario.

trib·ute ['trɪbjuːt] N tributo, omaggio; **to pay tribute to sb/sth** rendere omaggio a qn/qc; **floral tribute** omaggio floreale.

trice [traɪs] N: **in a trice** (*Brit fam*) in un batter d'occhio, in un attimo.

tri·ceps ['traɪsɛps] N, PL INV tricipite *m*.

trick [trɪk] ⨩1⨩ N **a** (*joke, hoax*) scherzo, tiro; (*ruse, catch, special knack*) trucco; (*clever act*) stratagemma *m*; **to**

play a trick on sb giocare un tiro a qn; dirty or mean trick scherzo di cattivo gusto; there must be a trick in it ci deve essere sotto qualche cosa; he's up to his old tricks again è tornato ai suoi vecchi trucchetti; there's a trick to opening this door c'è un trucco per aprire questa porta; it's a trick of the light è un effetto ottico; he knows all the tricks of the trade conosce tutti i trucchi del mestiere

b (habit) mania; he has a trick of turning up when least expected ha il dono di spuntare quando uno meno se l'aspetta

c (Cards) presa; (also: conjuring trick) gioco di prestigio; that should do the trick (fam) vedrai che funziona; he doesn't miss a trick (fig) non gliene scappa mai una.

2 VT (deceive) ingannare, imbrogliare; (swindle) imbrogliare; I've been tricked! mi hanno imbrogliato!; to trick sb into doing sth convincere qn a fare qc con l'inganno; to trick sb out of sth fregare qc a qn.

trick·ery ['trɪkərɪ] N inganno.

trick·le ['trɪkl] **1** N (of liquid) rivolo; (in drops) gocciolio; (fig): we've had only a trickle of customers abbiamo avuto solo pochi clienti; there was a steady trickle of orders gli ordini erano pochi ma regolari.

2 VI (liquid) gocciolare; (ball) rotolare lentamente; to trickle in (orders, money) arrivare a poco a poco; to trickle in/out (people) entrare/uscire alla spicciolata.

♦ **trick photography** N fotografia truccata.

♦ **trick question** N domanda f trabocchetto inv.

trick·ster ['trɪkstə'] N imbroglione(-a).

tricky ['trɪkɪ] ADJ (comp -ier, superl -iest) (situation, problem) difficile; (job, task) delicato(-a); (person: sly) astuto(-a).

tri·col·our, (Am) **tri·col·or** ['trɪkələ'] N tricolore m.

tri·cy·cle ['traɪsɪkl] N triciclo.

tried [traɪd] **1** PT, PP of try.

2 ADJ: tried and tested sperimentato(-a).

tri·er ['traɪə'] N: to be a trier essere perseverante.

tri·fle ['traɪfl] N **a** (unimportant thing) cosa di poco valore, sciocchezza; he worries about trifles si preoccupa per niente; it's a trifle difficult è piuttosto difficile; a trifle long un po' lungo(-a)

b (Brit Culin) ≈ zuppa inglese

▶ **trifle with** VI + PREP prendere alla leggera; he's not a person to be trifled with non è una persona da prendere alla leggera; to trifle with sb's affections giocare con i sentimenti di qn.

tri·fling ['traɪflɪŋ] ADJ insignificante.

trig·ger ['trɪgə'] **1** N (of gun, machine) grilletto; to pull the trigger premere il grilletto.

2 VT (also: trigger off: event) provocare, scatenare.

♦ **trigger-happy** ['trɪgə,hæpɪ] ADJ (fam) dalla pistola facile.

trigo·no·met·ric [,trɪgənə'mɛtrɪk] ADJ trigonometrico(-a).

trigo·nom·etry [,trɪgə'nɒmɪtrɪ] N trigonometria.

trike [traɪk] N (fam) triciclo.

tri·lat·er·al [,traɪ'lætərəl] ADJ trilaterale.

tril·by ['trɪlbɪ] N (Brit: also: trilby hat) cappello di feltro.

trill [trɪl] N (of bird, Mus) trillo.

tril·lion ['trɪljən] N **a** (Am) mille miliardi mpl; (Brit) trilione m **b**: trillions (of) milioni mpl (di).

tril·ogy ['trɪlədʒɪ] N trilogia.

trim [trɪm] **1** ADJ (comp -mer, superl -mest) curato(-a), ordinato(-a); (house, garden) ben tenuto(-a); (figure) snello(-a).

2 N **a**: in good trim (car) in buone condizioni; (person) in forma; to keep in (good) trim mantenersi in forma

b (haircut) spuntata, regolata; to have a trim farsi spuntare i capelli

c (embellishment) finiture fpl; (decoration) applicazioni fpl; (on car) guarnizioni fpl; car with grey interior trim macchina con gli interni grigi.

3 VT **a** (cut: hedge, beard, edges) regolare tagliando; (: hair) spuntare

b : to trim (with) (decorate: Christmas tree) decorare (con); to trim sth with sth (edge) mettere un bordo di qc a qc

c (Naut: sail) orientare

▶ **trim off** **1** VT + ADV tagliare via.

2 VT + PREP: to trim sth off sth tagliare via qc da qc.

tri·ma·ran ['traɪmə,ræn] N trimarano.

trim·ming ['trɪmɪŋ] N (edging) bordura; **trimmings** NPL (embellishments) decorazioni fpl; (extras) accessori mpl; (Culin) guarnizione f; (cuttings) ritagli mpl; turkey with all the trimmings tacchino con contorno e tutto il resto.

Trini·dad and To·ba·go [,trɪnɪdædəntə'beɪgəʊ] N Trinidad e Tobago f.

Trini·ty ['trɪnɪtɪ] N: the Trinity la Trinità.

♦ **Trinity Sunday** N festa della santissima Trinità.

trin·ket ['trɪŋkɪt] N (piece of jewellery) ciondolo; (ornament) ninnolo, gingillo.

trio ['triːəʊ] N trio.

trip [trɪp] **1** N **a** viaggio; (outing) gita; (excursion) escursione f; (away) on a trip in viaggio; to take a trip fare un viaggio; she does 3 trips to Milan a week va a Milano 3 volte alla settimana; I've made 2 trips to the shops already sono già andata 2 volte a far la spesa

b (Drugs slang) trip m inv, viaggio

c (stumble) passo falso.

2 VI **a** (stumble) inciampare

b : to trip along or go tripping along (skip) andare saltellando; (move lightly) camminare con passo leggero.

3 VT = trip up².

▶ **trip over** **1** VI + ADV inciampare.

2 VI + PREP inciampare in

▶ **trip up** **1** VI + ADV inciampare; (fig: make a mistake) fare un passo falso.

2 VT + ADV far inciampare, fare lo sgambetto a.

tri·par·tite [,traɪ'pɑːtaɪt] ADJ (agreement) tripartito(-a); (talks) a tre.

tripe [traɪp] N (Culin) trippa; (fam pej: rubbish) sciocchezze fpl, fesserie fpl.

tri·ple ['trɪpl] **1** ADJ triplo(-a).

2 ADV: triple the distance/the speed tre volte più lontano/più veloce.

3 VT triplicare.

4 VI triplicarsi.

♦ **Triple Alliance** N: the Triple Alliance la Triplice Alleanza.

♦ **triple jump** N salto triplo.

tri·plets ['trɪplɪts] NPL: she's just had triplets ha appena avuto tre gemelli or un parto trigemino.

trip·li·cate ['trɪplɪkɪt] N: in triplicate in triplice copia.

tri·pod ['traɪpɒd] N treppiede m.

Tripo·li ['trɪpəlɪ] N Tripoli f.

trip·per ['trɪpə'] N (Brit) gitante m/f.

trip·tych ['trɪptɪk] N trittico.

trip·wire ['trɪp,waɪə'] N filo in tensione che fa scattare una trappola, un allarme ecc.

tri·syl·la·ble [,traɪ'sɪləbl] N trisillabo.

trite [traɪt] ADJ (*remark*) banale; (*story, idea*) trito(-a) e ritrito(-a).

Triton ['traɪtən] N Tritone *m*.

tri·umph ['traɪʌmf] ⊡ N (*success*) successo; (*sense of triumph*) trionfo; (*victory*): **triumph (over)** trionfo (su), vittoria (su); **in triumph** in trionfo.
⊡ VI: **to triumph (over)** trionfare (su).

tri·um·phal [traɪ'ʌmfəl] ADJ trionfale.

tri·um·phant [traɪ'ʌmfənt] ADJ (*jubilant*) trionfante; (: *homecoming*) trionfale; (*victorious*) vittorioso(-a).

tri·um·phant·ly [traɪ'ʌmfəntlɪ] ADV (*march, carry*) in trionfo; (*announce*) con tono trionfante.

tri·um·vi·rate [traɪ'ʌmvɪrɪt] NSG OR PL (*frm*) triunvirato.

trivia ['trɪvɪə] NPL banalità *fpl*.

triv·ial ['trɪvɪəl] ADJ (*matter*) futile; (*excuse, comment*) banale; (*amount*) irrisorio(-a); (*mistake*) di poco conto.

trivi·al·ity [ˌtrɪvɪ'ælɪtɪ] N frivolezza; (*trivial detail*) futilità *f inv*.

trivi·al·ize ['trɪvɪəˌlaɪz] VT sminuire.

trod [trɒd] PT of **tread**.

trod·den ['trɒdn] PP of **tread**.

trog·lo·dyte ['trɒgləˌdaɪt] N (*frm*) troglodita *m/f*.

troi·ka ['trɔɪkə] N troica.

Tro·jan ['trəʊdʒən] ADJ, N troiano(-a).

troll [trəʊl] N troll *m inv*.

trol·ley ['trɒlɪ] N (*Brit: in station, supermarket, also:* **tea trolley**) carrello; (: *in hospital*) lettiga.

♦ **trolley bus** N filobus *m inv*.

trol·lop ['trɒləp] N (*old offensive*) sgualdrina.

trom·bone [trɒm'bəʊn] N trombone *m*.

troop [tru:p] ⊡ N (*gen, of scouts*) gruppo; (*Mil*) squadrone *m*; **troops** NPL (*Mil*) truppe *fpl*.
⊡ VI (*walk*): **to troop in/past/off** *etc* entrare/passare/andarsene *etc* in gruppo; **trooping the colour** (*Brit*) cerimonia del saluto alla bandiera.

♦ **troop carrier** N **a** (*plane*) aereo per il trasporto (di) truppe **b** (*Naut*) = **troopship**.

troop·er ['tru:pəʳ] N (*Mil*) soldato di cavalleria; (*Am: policeman*) ≈ poliziotto, *agente della polizia di uno stato*; **to swear like a trooper** bestemmiare come un turco.

troop·ship ['tru:pˌʃɪp] N nave *f* per il trasporto (di) truppe.

tro·phy ['trəʊfɪ] N trofeo.

trop·ic ['trɒpɪk] N tropico; **the tropics** i tropici; **Tropic of Cancer/Capricorn** tropico del Cancro/Capricorno.

tropi·cal ['trɒpɪkəl] ADJ tropicale; **tropical rain forest** foresta pluviale equatoriale.

trot [trɒt] ⊡ N **a** (*pace*) trotto; **sitting/rising trot** (*Horse-riding*) trotto seduto/sollevato; **to break into a trot** (*horse, rider*) partire al trotto; (*person*) mettersi a camminare di buon passo; **to go for a trot** (*on horse*) andare a fare una trottata
b (*Brit, fam*): **on the trot** di fila, uno(-a) dopo l'altro(-a); **three weeks on the trot** tre settimane di fila; **to be on the trot** (*fam*) essere sempre in movimento; **the baby keeps her on the trot** il bambino non le concede un attimo di tregua
c: **the trots** (*fam: diarrhoea*) la cacarella.
⊡ VI (*horse, rider*) andare al trotto, trottare; (*person*): **to trot in/past** *etc* entrare/passare *etc* di corsa

▶ **trot out** VT + ADV (*excuse, reason*) tirar fuori; (*names, facts*) recitare di fila.

trot·ter ['trɒtəʳ] N **a** (*horse*) trottatore *m* **b** (*Culin*): **pig's trotter** zampone *m*.

trou·ble ['trʌbl] ⊡ N **a** (*problems*) problemi *mpl*, difficoltà *fpl*; (: *as result of doing wrong*) guai *mpl*, pasticci *mpl*; (: *with sth mechanical*) noie *fpl*; (*unrest, fighting*) agitazione *f*, disordine *m*; **troubles** NPL disordini, conflitti *mpl*; **to have trouble doing sth** avere delle difficoltà a fare qc; **to be in trouble** (*having problems*) avere qualche problema *or* difficoltà; (*for doing wrong*) essere nei guai; **to get into trouble** cacciarsi nei guai; **to get sb into trouble** mettere *or* cacciare qn nei guai; **to help sb out of trouble** aiutare qn a tirarsi fuori dai guai; **what's the trouble?** cosa c'è che non va?; **the trouble is ...** c'è che...; il guaio è che...; **don't go looking for trouble** non andare in cerca di guai; **engine trouble** noie al motore; **stomach trouble** disturbi *mpl* gastrici; **heart/back trouble** disturbi al cuore/di schiena
b (*bother, effort*) sforzo; (*worry*) preoccupazione *f*; **it's no trouble** (*offering help*) non è un problema; **it's no trouble!** (*accepting thanks*) di niente!; **it's not worth the trouble** non vale la pena; **to go to (all) the trouble of doing sth** ⊡ **take the trouble to do sth** darsi la pena di fare qc.
⊡ VT **a** (*worry*) preoccupare; **my eyes have been troubling me** ho avuto dei disturbi agli occhi
b (*bother, be nuisance to*) disturbare; **I'm sorry to trouble you** mi dispiace disturbarla; **I shan't trouble you with all the details** non starò ad annoiarla con tutti i particolari; **please don't trouble yourself** non si disturbi
c (+ *infin*: *make the effort*): **to trouble to do sth** darsi la pena di fare qc.

trou·bled ['trʌbld] ADJ (*person, expression*) preoccupato (-a), inquieto(-a); (*period*) travagliato(-a); (*epoch, life*) agitato(-a), difficile.

♦ **trouble-free** [ˌtrʌbl'fri:] ADJ (*life, car, trip*) senza problemi; (*area, factory*) tranquillo(-a); (*demonstration*) pacifico(-a).

trouble·maker ['trʌblˌmeɪkəʳ] N elemento disturbatore, agitatore(-trice).

trouble·shooter ['trʌblˌʃu:təʳ] N (*Tech*) esperto(-a) (*chiamato in casi di emergenza*); (*Pol*) mediatore(-trice); (*in conflict*) conciliatore *m*.

trou·ble·some ['trʌblsəm] ADJ (*person*) molesto(-a), importuno(-a); (*headache*) fastidioso(-a); (*dispute, problem*) difficile, seccante.

♦ **trouble spot** N zona calda.

trou·bling ['trʌblɪŋ] ADJ (*thought*) preoccupante; **these are troubling times** questi sono tempi difficili.

trough [trɒf] N **a** (*also:* **feeding trough**) mangiatoia, trogolo; (*also:* **drinking trough**) abbeveratoio; (*channel*) canale *m* **b** (*between waves*) cavo; (*on graph*) punto più basso; (*Met*): **trough of low pressure** area di bassa pressione, depressione *f*.

trounce [traʊns] VT (*beat*) picchiare; (*defeat*) battere.

troupe [tru:p] N (*Theatre*) compagnia, troupe *f inv*.

♦ **trouser hanger** N (*Brit*) reggipantaloni *m inv*.

♦ **trouser press** N (*Brit*) stiracalzoni *m inv*.

trou·sers ['traʊzəz] NPL (*Brit*) pantaloni *mpl*, calzoni *mpl*; **short trousers** calzoncini *mpl*; **she wears the trousers** (*fig*) è lei che porta i calzoni.

♦ **trouser suit** N (*Brit*) completo *m* pantalone *inv*, tailleur *m inv* pantalone *inv*.

trous·seau ['tru:səʊ] N corredo da sposa.

trout [traʊt] ⊡ N, PL INV trota.
⊡ ADJ: **trout fishing** pesca della trota.

trow·el ['traʊəl] N (*for garden*) paletta da giardiniere; (*builder's*) cazzuola.

Troy [trɔɪ] N Troia.

tru·an·cy ['truənsɪ] N (Scol) assenze fpl ingiustificate.

tru·ant ['truənt] N (Scol): **to play truant** marinare la scuola.

truce [tru:s] N tregua; **to call a truce** dichiarare una tregua.

truck[1] [trʌk] N **a** (Brit: Rail: wagon) carro m merci inv (aperto) **b** (esp Am: lorry) camion m inv, autocarro **c** (for luggage) carrello m portabagagli inv.

truck[2] [trʌk] N: **to have no truck with sb** non volere avere a che fare con qn.

♦ **truck driver** (Am) **truck·er** ['trʌkə'] N camionista m/f.

truck·ing ['trʌkɪŋ] N (Am) autotrasporto, trasporto su gomma.

♦ **trucking company** N (Am) impresa di trasporti.

truck·le ['trʌkəl] VI: **to truckle to sb** strisciare davanti a qn.

truck·load ['trʌk‚ləʊd] N carico (di camion).

trucu·lence ['trʌkjʊləns] N aggressività f inv, brutalità f inv.

trucu·lent ['trʌkjʊlənt] ADJ aggressivo(-a), brutale.

trucu·lent·ly ['trʌkjʊləntlɪ] ADV con aggressività, brutalmente.

trudge [trʌdʒ] VI: **to trudge up/down/along** etc trascinarsi pesantemente su/giù/lungo etc; **to trudge round the town** girare la città in lungo e in largo.

true [tru:] **1** ADJ (comp **-r**, superl **-st**) **a** (not fiction: story) vero(-a); (accurate, correct: statement, description) preciso(-a), esatto(-a), accurato(-a); (: portrait, likeness) fedele; **to come true** avverarsi; **the same holds true of** or **for** ... lo stesso vale per...; **too true!** fin troppo vero!; **true, but** ... sì, ma...

b (real, genuine: emotion, interest) sincero(-a), vero(-a); **true love** vero amore; **to behave like a true Englishman** comportarsi da vero inglese; **in the truest sense of the word** nel vero senso della parola

c (wall, beam) a piombo; (wheel) centrato(-a)

d (faithful: friend) fedele; **to be true to sb/sth** essere fedele a qn/qc; **to be true to one's word** tenere fede alla parola data; **true to life** verosimile; **to run true to type** essere fedele alla propria immagine.

2 N: **to be out of true** (wall, beam) non essere a piombo; (wheel) non essere centrato(-a).

♦ **true-blue** [‚tru:'blu:] ADJ (fam: loyal) fedele, leale.

♦ **true north** N nord m inv.

truf·fle ['trʌfl] N tartufo.

tru·ism ['tru:ɪzəm] N verità f inv lapalissiana.

tru·ly ['tru:lɪ] ADV (genuinely: believe, love) veramente, sinceramente; (faithfully: serve, love, reflect) fedelmente; (emphatic: very) veramente, davvero; **well and truly** per bene; **yours truly** (in letter-writing) distinti saluti.

trump [trʌmp] **1** N (Cards) atout m inv; **hearts are trumps** l'atout è di cuori; **to turn up trumps** (fig) fare miracoli.

2 VT (Cards) tagliare, prendere con l'atout.

♦ **trump card** N atout m inv; (fig) asso nella manica.

trumped-up [‚trʌmpt'ʌp] ADJ (charge) inventato(-a), falso (-a).

trum·pet ['trʌmpɪt] **1** N tromba; **a trumpet player** (Jazz) un(-a) trombettista.

2 VI (elephant) barrire.

trum·pet·er ['trʌmpɪtə'] N suonatore m di tromba; (Mil) trombettiere m.

trun·cate [trʌŋ'keɪt] VT (report, speech) tagliare.

trun·cat·ed [trʌŋ'keɪtɪd] ADJ (Geom) tronco(-a).

trun·cheon ['trʌntʃən] N manganello, sfollagente m inv.

trun·dle ['trʌndl] **1** VT (push, pull): **to trundle along** far rotolare (a fatica).

2 VI (cart) avanzare lentamente.

trunk [trʌŋk] N (of tree, person) tronco; (of elephant) proboscide f; (piece of luggage) baule m; (Am Aut: boot of car) bagagliaio; see also **trunks**.

♦ **trunk call** N (Brit: old Telec) (telefonata) interurbana.

♦ **trunk line** N (Rail, Telec) linea principale.

♦ **trunk road** N (Brit) strada principale.

trunks [trʌŋks] NPL: **(swimming** or **bathing) trunks** calzoncini mpl da bagno.

truss [trʌs] **1** VT (also: **truss up**) legare stretto; (Culin) legare.

2 N (Med) cinto erniario.

trust [trʌst] **1** N **a** : **trust (in)** fiducia (in); **to put one's trust in sb** riporre la propria fiducia in qn; **to put one's trust in sth** riporre le proprie speranze in qc; **to be in a position of trust** ricoprire un incarico di fiducia; **you'll have to take it on trust** devi credermi sulla parola

b (charge): **to leave sth in sb's trust** affidare qc a qn or alle cure di qn

c (Law, Fin) amministrazione f fiduciaria; **in trust** in amministrazione fiduciaria

d (Comm: also: **trust company**) trust m inv.

2 VT **a** (have faith, confidence in) avere fiducia in, fidarsi di; (rely on) fare affidamento su, contare su; **to trust sth to sb/trust sb with sth** (entrust) affidare qc a qn; **I wouldn't trust him an inch** non mi fiderei proprio di lui; **trust you!** (fam) ci avrei scommesso!

b (hope): **to trust (that ...)** sperare (che...).

3 VI (have faith): **to trust in** credere in; **to trust to luck/fate** (rely) affidarsi alla fortuna/al destino.

trust·ed ['trʌstɪd] ADJ (friend, adviser) fidato(-a).

trus·tee [trʌs'ti:] **1** N (Law) amministratore(-trice) fiduciario(-a); (of school, institution) amministratore(-trice).

♦ **Trustee Savings Bank** N (Brit) ≈ cassa di risparmio.

trust·ful ['trʌstfʊl], **trust·ing** ['trʌstɪŋ] ADJ fiducioso(-a).

trust·ful·ly ['trʌstfəlɪ], **trust·ing·ly** ['trʌstɪŋlɪ] ADV fiduciosamente, con fiducia.

♦ **trust fund** N fondo fiduciario.

trust·worthi·ness ['trʌst‚wɜːðɪnɪs] N (of person) affidabilità f inv; (of statement) attendibilità f inv.

trust·worthy ['trʌst‚wɜːðɪ] ADJ (person) fidato(-a), degno (-a) di fiducia; (source of news) attendibile.

trusty ['trʌstɪ] ADJ (comp **-ier**, superl **-iest**) (hum) fidato(-a).

truth [tru:θ] N verità f inv; **to tell the truth** dire la verità; **to tell (you) the truth** [OR] **truth to tell** a dire il vero or la verità; **the truth of the matter is that** ... la verità è che...; **the truth hurts** la verità fa male; **there is some truth in what he says** c'è del vero in ciò che dice; **there isn't a word of truth in it** non c'è nulla di vero; **truth will out** la verità viene sempre a galla.

♦ **truth drug** N siero della verità.

truth·ful ['tru:θfʊl] ADJ (account) veritiero(-a), esatto(-a); (person) sincero(-a).

truth·ful·ly ['tru:θfəlɪ] ADV sinceramente.

truth·ful·ness ['tru:θfʊlnɪs] N (of account) veridicità f inv; (of person) sincerità f inv.

♦ **truth serum** N = **truth drug**.

try [traɪ] **1** N **a** (attempt) tentativo, prova; **to give sth a try** provare qc; **why don't you give the exam a try?** perché non provi a fare l'esame?; **to have a try (at doing sth)** provare (a fare qc); **it's worth a try** vale la pena di tentare

b (Rugby) meta.

2 VT **a** (usu + infin): **to try to do sth** (attempt) provare a

fare qc; (*seek*) cercare di fare qc; **to try one's (very) best**
or **one's (very) hardest** mettercela tutta
b (*sample, experiment with*: *method, car, food*) provare;
why not try him for the job? perché non gli fai fare una
prova?; **try pressing that switch** prova a schiacciare
quell'interruttore
c (*test*: *strength, vehicle, machine*) verificare, collaudare;
(*tax, strain*: *patience, person*) mettere alla prova; (: *eyes*)
affaticare; **to try one's hand at sth** (*fig*) cimentarsi in qc
d (*Law*): **to try sb (for sth)** processare qn (per qc).
3 VI (*attempt*) provare; **try again!** provaci ancora!
▶ **try for** VI + PREP mirare a
▶ **try on** VT + ADV **a** (*clothes, shoes*) provare
   b (*Brit fam*): **to try it on (with sb)** cercare di farla (a qn)
▶ **try out** VT + ADV (*test*: *sth new, different*) provare;
(*employee*) far fare una prova a; **to try sth out on sb** far
provare qc a qn.
try·ing ['traɪɪŋ] ADJ (*tiring*: *situation, time*) difficile, duro
(-a); (: *day, experience*) logorante, pesante; (*tiresome*:
person) noioso(-a), seccante; (: *child*) insopportabile; **to**
have a trying time passare un periodo difficile.
tryp·sin ['trɪpsɪn] N tripsina.
tsar [zɑːʳ] N zar *m inv*.
tsa·ri·na [zɑːˈriːnə] N zarina.
tsar·ist, tzar·ist, czar·ist ['zɑːrɪst] ADJ, N zarista *(m/f)*.
tset·se fly ['tsɛtsɪˌflaɪ] N mosca *f* tse-tse *inv.*
♦ **T-shirt** ['tiːˌʃɜːt] N maglietta.
♦ **T-square** ['tiːˌskwɛəʳ] N riga a T.
TT [ˌtiːˈtiː] **1** ADJ ABBR (*Brit*: *fam*) = **teetotal**.
   2 ABBR (*Am Post*)= *Trust Territory*.
tub [tʌb] N (*for washing clothes*) tinozza, mastello; (*for*
flowers) vasca; (*for ice cream*) vaschetta; (: *individual*)
coppetta; (*fam*: *also*: **bathtub**) vasca da bagno.
tuba ['tjuːbə] N tuba.
tub·by ['tʌbɪ] ADJ (*comp* **-ier**, *superl* **-iest**) (*fam*) grassoccio
(-a).
tube [tjuːb] **1** N **a** (*pipe*) tubo; (*of toothpaste, paint*)
tubetto; (*Anat*) tuba; (*for tyre*) camera d'aria **b** (*Brit*:
London Underground) metrò *m inv*, metropolitana **c** : **the**
tube (*Am fam*: *television*) la tele.
   2 ADJ (*Brit*) del metrò; **tube station** stazione *f* del metrò.
tube·less ['tjuːblɪs] ADJ (*tyre*) senza camera d'aria.
tu·ber ['tjuːbəʳ] N (*Bot*) tubero.
tu·ber·cu·lar [tjʊˈbɜːkjʊləʳ] ADJ tubercolare.
tu·ber·cu·lo·sis [tjʊˌbɜːkjʊˈləʊsɪs] N tubercolosi *f*.
tub·ing ['tjuːbɪŋ] N tubi *mpl*, tubazione *f*; **a piece of tubing**
un tubo.
tubu·lar ['tjuːbjʊləʳ] ADJ tubolare.
TUC [ˌtiːjuːˈsiː] N ABBR (*Brit*: = *Trades Union Congress*)
confederazione *f* dei sindacati (britannici).
tuck [tʌk] **1** N (*Sewing*) pince *f inv*, piega.
   2 VT (*put*) infilare, mettere, cacciare; **she tucked a**
blanket round him lo ha avvolto in una coperta.
   3 VI: **to tuck into a meal** (*Brit fam*) lanciarsi sul pasto
▶ **tuck away** VT + ADV (*put away*) riporre in un luogo
sicuro; (*hide*) nascondere; **she has her money safely**
tucked away ha messo i soldi in un posto sicuro
▶ **tuck in** **1** VI + ADV (*Brit fam*: *eat*) mangiare con grande
appetito, abbuffarsi.
   2 VT + ADV (*blankets*) rimboccare; (*shirt*) mettere dentro;
to tuck sb in rimboccare le coperte a qn
▶ **tuck up** VT + ADV (*skirt, sleeves*) tirare su; **to tuck sb up**
rimboccare le coperte a qn.
♦ **tuck box** N (*Brit Scol*: *old*) scatola di dolciumi (*mandata*
da casa).

♦ **tuck shop** N (*Brit Scol*: *old*) negozio di pasticceria (*in o*
vicino ad una scuola).
Tue., Tues. ABBR = *Tuesday.*
Tues·day ['tjuːzdɪ] N martedì *m inv*; **(the date) today is**
Tuesday 23 March oggi è martedì 23 marzo; **on**
Tuesday martedì; **on Tuesdays** di martedì; **every**
Tuesday tutti i martedì; **every other Tuesday** ogni due
martedì; **last/next Tuesday** martedì scorso/prossimo;
Tuesday next martedì prossimo; **the following Tuesday**
(*in past*) il martedì successivo; (*in future*) il martedì
dopo; **the Tuesday before last** martedì di due settimane fa; **the Tuesday after next** non questo martedì
ma il prossimo; **a week/fortnight** (*Brit*) **on Tuesday** OR
Tuesday week/fortnight (*Brit*) martedì fra una setti-
mana/quindici giorni; **Tuesday morning/lunchtime/**
afternoon/evening martedì mattina/all'ora di pranzo/
pomeriggio/sera; **Tuesday night** martedì sera; (*over-*
night) martedì notte; **the Tuesday film** (*TV*) il film del
martedì; **Tuesday's newspaper** il giornale di martedì.
tuft [tʌft] N (*of hair*) ciuffo, ciocca; (*of grass*) ciuffo.
tug [tʌg] **1** N **a** (*pull*) strattone *m*; **to give sth a (good) tug**
dare uno strattone a qc **b** (*ship*: *also*: **tugboat**) rimorchiatore *m*.
   2 VT (*pull*) tirare con forza.
   3 VI: **to tug (at)** dare uno strattone (a).
♦ **tug-of-love** [ˌtʌgəvˈlʌv] N (*Brit fam*) contesa per la
custodia dei figli; **tug-of-love children** *bambini coinvolti*
nella contesa per la custodia.
♦ **tug-of-war** [ˌtʌgəvˈwɔːʳ] N (*Sport*) tiro alla fune; (*fig*)
braccio di ferro.
tui·tion [tjʊˈɪʃən] N (*Brit*: *lessons*) lezioni *fpl*; (*Am*: *fees*)
tasse *fpl* scolastiche (*or* universitarie).
tu·lip ['tjuːlɪp] N tulipano.
tulle [tjuːl] N tulle *m*.
tum·ble ['tʌmbl] **1** N (*fall*) ruzzolone *m*, capitombolo; **to**
have a tumble OR **take a tumble** fare un ruzzolone *or*
capitombolo.
   2 VI **a** (*fall*) ruzzolare, capitombolare, fare un capitombolo; (*somersault*) fare capriole; **to tumble**
downstairs ruzzolare giù dalle scale
   b (*rush*): **to tumble into/out of bed** buttarsi a/cadere
giù dal letto; **the children tumbled out of the room/the**
car i bambini si sono precipitati fuori dalla stanza/
dalla macchina
   c (*suddenly understand*): **to tumble to sth** (*Brit fam*)
realizzare qc.
   3 VT far cadere
▶ **tumble over** VI + ADV ruzzolare.
tumble·down ['tʌmblˌdaʊn] ADJ cadente, diroccato(-a).
♦ **tumble dryer** N (*Brit*) asciugatrice *f*.
tum·bler ['tʌmbləʳ] N (*glass*) bicchiere *m* (senza stelo).
tum·brel, tum·bril ['tʌmbrəl] N *carretta su cui si traspor-*
tavano i condannati alla ghigliottina durante la
Rivoluzione francese.
tum·my ['tʌmɪ] N (*fam*) pancia.
tummy·ache ['tʌmɪˌeɪk] N (*fam*) mal *m* di pancia.
tumour, (*Am*) **tu·mor** ['tjuːməʳ] N tumore *m*.
tu·mult ['tjuːmʌlt] N tumulto.
tu·mul·tu·ous [tjuːˈmʌltjʊəs] ADJ tumultuoso(-a).
tuna ['tjuːnə] N, PL INV (*also*: **tuna fish**) tonno.
tun·dra ['tʌndrə] N tundra.
tune [tjuːn] **1** N **a** (*melody*) melodia, aria; **he gave us a**
tune ci ha suonato qualcosa; **to change one's tune** (*fig*)
cambiare tono; **to the tune of** (*fig*: *amount*) per la

modesta somma di

b : **in tune** (*instrument*) accordato(-a); (*person*) intonato (-a); **out of tune** (*instrument*) scordato(-a); (*person*) stonato(-a); **to sing in tune** cantare senza stonare; **to sing out of tune** stonare; **in tune with** (*fig*) in accordo con.

2 VT (*Mus*) accordare; (*Aut: engine*) mettere a punto; (*Radio, TV*) regolare.

3 VI (*Mus: also:* **tune up**) accordare lo strumento

▶ **tune in** VI + ADV (*Radio, TV*): **to tune in (to)** sintonizzarsi (su).

tune·ful ['tju:nfʊl] ADJ melodioso(-a).

tune·ful·ly ['tju:nfəlɪ] ADV melodiosamente.

tune·less ['tju:nlɪs] ADJ poco melodioso(-a).

tune·less·ly ['tju:nlɪslɪ] ADV (*sing*) con voce stonata.

tun·er ['tju:nəʳ] N **a** (*Radio: control*) sintonizzatore *m*, tuner *m inv* **b** (*also:* **piano tuner**) accordatore(-trice) di pianoforte.

♦ **tuner amplifier** N amplificatore *m* di sintonia.

tung·sten ['tʌŋstən] N tungsteno.

tu·nic ['tju:nɪk] N tunica.

tun·ing ['tju:nɪŋ] N (*Mus*) accordatura; (*Aut*) messa a punto; (*Radio, TV*) sintonizzazione *f*.

♦ **tuning fork** N diapason *m inv*.

Tu·nis ['tju:nɪs] N Tunisi *f*.

Tu·ni·sia [tju:'nɪzɪə] N la Tunisia.

Tu·ni·sian [tju:'nɪzɪən] ADJ, N tunisino(-a).

tun·nel ['tʌnl] **1** N (*gen*) galleria, tunnel *m inv*; (*Min*) galleria; **the Mont Blanc tunnel** il traforo del Monte Bianco.

2 VT: **to tunnel one's way out** aprirsi un passaggio scavando; **to tunnel a passage** scavare un passaggio.

3 VI scavare una galleria.

♦ **tunnel vision** N (*Med*) riduzione *f* del campo visivo; (*fig*) visuale *f* ristretta.

tun·ny ['tʌnɪ] N (*Brit*) = **tuna**.

tup·pence ['tʌpəns] N (*Brit fam*) = **twopence**.

tur·ban ['tɜ:bən] N turbante *m*.

tur·bid ['tɜ:bɪd] ADJ (*liquid, fig: situation*) torbido(-a); (*smoke, fog*) denso(-a).

tur·bine ['tɜ:baɪn] N turbina.

tur·bo ['tɜ:bəʊ] N turbo *m inv*.

turbo... ['tɜ:bəʊ] PREF turbo...; **turbo(-charged) engine** motore *m* turbo *inv*.

tur·bo·jet [,tɜ:bəʊ'dʒɛt] N turbogetto, turboreattore *m*.

tur·bo·prop [,tɜ:bəʊ'prɒp] N turboelica *m inv*.

tur·bot ['tɜ:bət] N, PL INV rombo gigante.

tur·bu·lence ['tɜ:bjʊləns] N turbolenza.

tur·bu·lent ['tɜ:bjʊlənt] ADJ turbolento(-a); (*sea*) agitato (-a).

turd [tɜ:d] N (*fam!: faeces, person*) stronzo (*fam!*)

tu·reen [tə'ri:n] N zuppiera.

turf [tɜ:f] **1** N (*pl* **turfs** *or* **turves**) (*grass*) tappeto erboso; (*one piece*) zolla erbosa; **the turf** (*horse racing*) l'ippica, le corse ippiche; (*racetrack*) l'ippodromo.

2 VT (*also:* **turf over**) ricoprire di zolle erbose

▶ **turf out** VT + ADV (*Brit fam*) buttar fuori.

♦ **turf accountant** N (*Brit*) allibratore *m*.

tur·gid ['tɜ:dʒɪd] ADJ (*liter: prose, speech*) ampolloso(-a), pomposo(-a).

Tu·rin [tjʊə'rɪn] N Torino *f*.

Turk [tɜ:k] N turco(-a).

Tur·key ['tɜ:kɪ] N la Turchia.

tur·key ['tɜ:kɪ] N tacchino.

Turk·ish ['tɜ:kɪʃ] **1** ADJ turco(-a).

2 N (*language*) turco.

♦ **Turkish bath** N bagno turco.

♦ **Turkish delight** N *gelatine ricoperte di zucchero a velo*.

tur·mer·ic ['tɜ:mərɪk] N curcuma.

tur·moil ['tɜ:mɔɪl] N confusione *f*, tumulto; **to be in a turmoil** essere in uno stato di confusione.

turn [tɜ:n] **1** N **a** (*rotation*) giro; **to give sth a turn** girare qc; **done to a turn** (*Culin*) cotto a puntino

b (*change of direction: in road*) curva; **"no left turn"** "divieto di svolta a sinistra"; **to take a left turn** (*Aut*) girare a sinistra; **take the next left turn** prendi la prossima a sinistra; **a road full of twists and turns** una strada a zigzag *or* tutta a curve; **to take a turn in the park** fare un giro nel parco; **at the turn of the year/century** alla fine dell'anno/del secolo; **at every turn** (*fig*) a ogni piè sospinto; **things took a new turn** (*fig*) le cose hanno preso una nuova piega; **to take a turn for the better** (*situation, events*) volgere al meglio; (*patient, health*) migliorare; **to take a turn for the worse** (*situation, events*) volgere al peggio; (*patient, health*) peggiorare; **an odd turn of mind** una strana disposizione mentale; **turn of phrase** modo di esprimersi

c (*Med*) attacco, crisi *f inv*; **he had a bad turn last night** la scorsa notte ha avuto una crisi *or* un peggioramento; **the news gave me quite a turn** (*fam*) la notizia mi ha fatto prendere un bello spavento

d (*in series*) turno; **by turns** a turno; **in turn** a sua volta; **hot and cold by turns** ora caldo ora freddo; **and he, in turn, said ...** e lui, a sua volta, ha detto...; **they spoke in turn** hanno parlato a turno; **to take turns at (doing) sth** [OR] **take it in turn(s) to do sth** fare qc a turno; **to take/wait/miss one's turn** fare/aspettare/saltare il proprio turno; **it's my turn** è il mio turno, tocca me; **whose turn is it?** a chi tocca?; **your turn will come** verrà anche il tuo momento; **to take turn and turn about** fare i turni; **to take turns at the wheel** fare i turni al volante; **to take a turn at the wheel** fare un turno al volante; **to speak out of turn** (*fig*) parlare a sproposito

e (*performance*) numero; **to do a comedy turn** fare un numero comico

f (*action*): **to do sb a good turn** rendere un servizio a qn; **to do sb a bad turn** fare un brutto tiro a qn; **his good turn for the day** la sua buona azione quotidiana; **one good turn deserves another** una mano lava l'altra.

2 VT **a** (*wheel, handle*) girare; (: *mechanically*) far girare; **turn the key in the lock** gira la chiave nella toppa

b (*also:* **turn over:** *record, mattress, steak*) girare, voltare, rivoltare; **to turn one's ankle** storcersi una caviglia; **it turns my stomach** mi fa rivoltare lo stomaco

c (*direct: car, object*) voltare; (: *attention*) rivolgere; (: *gun, telescope*) puntare; **the fireman turned the hose on the building** il pompiere ha puntato l'idrante verso l'edificio; **to turn a gun on sb** puntare la pistola contro qn; **to turn one's back on sb** (*also fig*) voltare le spalle a qn; **to turn one's back on the past** tagliare i ponti col passato; **as soon as his back is turned** non appena volta le spalle; **power/success turned his head** il potere/il successo gli ha dato alla testa; **without turning a hair** senza battere ciglio; **to turn the other cheek** (*fig*) porgere l'altra guancia; **he turned his hand to cookery** si è dato alla cucina; **to turn the tables on sb** (*fig*) capovolgere la situazione a danno di qn; **they turned him against us** ce l'hanno messo contro

d (*go past, round*) girare, voltare; **the car turned the**

corner la macchina ha voltato l'angolo; **to have turned the corner** (*fig*) aver superato la fase critica; **he's turned 50** ha passato i 50; **it's turned four o'clock** sono le quattro passate

e (*change*): **to turn sb/sth into sth** trasformare qn/qc in qc; **to turn iron into gold** trasformare il ferro in oro; **to turn a book into a film** fare un film da un libro; **it turned him into a bitter man** lo ha reso un uomo pieno d'amarezza; **the shock turned her hair white** le sono venuti i capelli bianchi dallo shock; **the heat has turned the milk** il caldo ha fatto andare a male il latte

f (*shape: wood, metal*) tornire; **to turn wood on a lathe** lavorare il legno con il tornio; **a well-turned phrase** un'espressione molto elegante; **a well-turned ankle** una caviglia ben tornita.

3 VI **a** (*rotate*) girare; (*change direction: person*) girarsi, voltarsi; (: *vehicle*) girare, svoltare; (: *ship*) virare; (: *wind, tide, weather*) cambiare; (*reverse direction*) girarsi indietro; **my head is turning** (*fig*) mi gira la testa; **everything turns on his decision** (*fig*) tutto dipende dalla sua decisione; **to turn and go back** girare *or* girarsi e tornare indietro; **to turn left/right** (*Aut*) girare a sinistra/destra; **the car turned into a lane** la macchina ha svoltato in una stradina; **to wait for the weather to turn** aspettare che il tempo cambi; **he turned to me and smiled** si è girato verso di me e mi ha sorriso; **to turn to sb for help** rivolgersi a qn per un aiuto; **she has no-one to turn to** non ha nessuno cui potersi rivolgere; **he turned to politics** si è messo in politica, si è dato alla politica; **he turned to drink** si è dato al bere; **I don't know which way to turn** (*fig*) non so dove sbattere la testa; **the conversation turned to religion** la conversazione passò alla religione

b (*become*) diventare; (*change*): **to turn into sth** trasformarsi in qc, cambiare in qc; **the milk has turned** il latte è andato a male; **to turn nasty** diventare cattivo(-a); **he turned into a cynic** è diventato cinico; **they turned communist** sono diventati comunisti; **a singer turned songwriter** un cantante divenuto autore

▶ **turn about, turn around** VI + ADV girarsi indietro
▶ **turn against** VI + PREP: **to turn against sb** mettersi contro qn
▶ **turn aside** VI + ADV girarsi *or* voltarsi dall'altra parte
▶ **turn away** 1 VI + ADV girarsi *or* voltarsi dall'altra parte; **he turned away from the awful sight** ha distolto lo sguardo da quel tremendo spettacolo.

2 VT + ADV **a** (*move: eyes*) distogliere; (: *head*) girare dall'altra parte; (: *gun*) spostare
b (*reject: person*) mandar via; (: *business*) rifiutare
▶ **turn back** 1 VI + ADV **a** (*on journey*) ritornare, tornare indietro
b (*in book*) ritornare.
2 VT + ADV **a** (*fold: bedclothes*) ripiegare
b (*send back*) far tornare indietro; **to turn back the clock 20 years** ritornare indietro di 20 anni; **it's no use trying to turn the clock back** è inutile tornare sui propri passi
▶ **turn down** VT + ADV **a** (*fold: bedclothes, collar, page*) ripiegare
b (*reduce: gas, heat, volume*) abbassare
c (*refuse: offer*) rifiutare; (*candidate*) scartare
▶ **turn in** 1 VI + ADV **a** : **to turn in (to)** girare (in); **she turned in at the house** ha girato per entrare nella casa
b (*fam: go to bed*) andare a letto.
2 VT + ADV **a** (*hand over*) consegnare; **to turn sb in**

consegnare qn alla polizia
b (*fold*) voltare in dentro
▶ **turn off** 1 VI + ADV **a** (*from road*) girare, voltare
b (*appliance, machine*) spegnersi.
2 VT + ADV **a** (*light, radio, machine*) spegnere; (*tap*) chiudere
b (*fam: person: also sexually*) fare schifo a
▶ **turn on** 1 VI + ADV (*appliance*) accendersi.
2 VT + ADV **a** (*light, radio, electricity*) accendere; (*tap*) aprire; (*engine*) avviare
b (*fam: person: also sexually*) eccitare
▶ **turn out** 1 VI + ADV **a** (*appear, attend: troops, doctor*) presentarsi; **to turn out for a meeting** presentarsi a un'assemblea
b (*prove to be*) rivelarsi; **it turned out to be true** è risultato essere vero; **things will turn out all right** andrà tutto bene; **how did the cake turn out?** come è venuta la torta?; **it turned out that** ... si è scoperto che....
2 VT + ADV **a** (*light, appliance, gas*) chiudere, spegnere
b (*produce: goods*) produrre; (: *novel, good pupils*) creare; **to be well turned out** (*fig*) essere ben vestito(-a)
c (*empty: pockets*) vuotare; (*tip out: cake*) capovolgere
d (*clean out: room*) dare una bella pulita a
e (*expel: tenant, employee*) mandar via
f (*guard, police*) far uscire
▶ **turn over** 1 VI + ADV **a** (*person*) girarsi; (*car*) capovolgersi; (*engine*) girare; **my stomach turned over** mi si è rivoltato lo stomaco; **she turned over onto her back** si è girata sulla schiena
b (*in reading*) girare *or* voltare la pagina; (*in letter*): **please turn over** segue.
2 VT + ADV **a** (*page, mattress, card*) girare; (*patient*) far girare; **to turn sth over in one's mind** riflettere a lungo *or* rimurginare su qualcosa
b (*hand over: object, person*) consegnare
▶ **turn round** 1 VI + ADV **a** (*person*) girarsi; (*vehicle*) girare
b (*rotate*) girare; **to turn round and round** girare su se stesso(-a).
2 VT + ADV girare
▶ **turn up** 1 VI + ADV **a** (*lost object*) saltar fuori; (*person*) arrivare, presentarsi; **something will turn up** salterà fuori qualcosa; **we waited but she didn't turn up** abbiamo aspettato ma non si è fatta vedere
b (*point towards*) essere rivolto(-a) all'insù; **his nose turns up** ha il naso all'insù.
2 VT + ADV **a** (*collar, sleeve, hem*) alzare, tirare su; **to turn up one's nose at sth** (*fig*) arricciare il naso davanti a qc
b (*heat, gas, radio*) alzare
c (*find*) scoprire.

turn·about ['tɜːnəˌbaʊt], **turn·around** ['tɜːnəˌraʊnd] N (*fig*) voltafaccia *m inv*, dietrofront *m inv.*
turn·coat ['tɜːnˌkəʊt] N voltagabbana *m/f inv.*
♦ **turned-up** [ˌtɜːnd'ʌp] ADJ (*nose*) all'insù.
turn·ing ['tɜːnɪŋ] N (*side road*) strada laterale; (*fork*) biforcazione *f*; (*bend*) curva; **the first turning on the right** la prima a destra.
♦ **turning circle**, (*Am*) **turning radius** N diametro di sterzata.
♦ **turning point** N (*fig*) svolta decisiva; (*Math*) punto di ondulazione.
tur·nip ['tɜːnɪp] N rapa.
turn·off ['tɜːnˌɒf] N (*in road*) strada laterale.
turn·out ['tɜːnˌaʊt] N **a** (*attendance*) presenza, affluenza; **there was a poor turnout** la partecipazione è stata molto scarsa **b** (*clean*) ripulita.

turn·over ['tɜːn‚əʊvə'] N **a** (*Comm*: *amount of money*) giro d'affari; (: *of goods*) smercio; **these goods have a rapid turnover** di questi prodotti c'è grande smercio; **there is a extremely high turnover in staff** c'è un ricambio molto rapido di personale **b** (*Culin*): **apple turnover** ≈ sfogliatella alle mele.

turn·pike ['tɜːn‚paɪk] N (*Am Aut*) autostrada (a pagamento).

turn·stile ['tɜːn‚staɪl] N cancelletto girevole, tornella.

turn·table ['tɜːn‚teɪbl] N (*of record player*) piatto; (*for trains*) piattaforma girevole.

♦ **turn-up** ['tɜːn‚ʌp] N **a** (*Brit*: *of trousers*) risvolto **b** : **that was a turn-up for the books** (*Brit fam*) è stato un colpo di scena.

tur·pen·tine ['tɜːpən‚taɪn] N trementina; **turpentine substitute** acquaragia.

tur·pi·tude ['tɜːpɪ‚tjuːd] N (*frm*) turpitudine *f.*

turps [tɜːps] N ABBR (*Brit fam*) = **turpentine.**

tur·quoise ['tɜːkwɔɪz] **1** N (*stone, colour*) turchese *m.*
2 ADJ (*ring, earrings*) di turchesi; (*colour*) (color) turchese *inv.*

tur·ret ['tʌrɪt] N torretta.

tur·tle ['tɜːtl] **1** N testuggine *f,* tartaruga acquatica; **to turn turtle** (*boat*) scuffiare.
2 ADJ (*soup*) di tartaruga.

turtle·dove ['tɜːtl‚dʌv] N tortora.

turtle·neck ['tɜːtl‚nɛk] N (*also:* **turtleneck sweater**) maglione *m* con il collo alto.

Tus·can ['tʌskən] **1** ADJ toscano(-a).
2 N (*person*) toscano(-a); (*dialect*) toscano.

Tus·ca·ny ['tʌskənɪ] N la Toscana.

tusk [tʌsk] N zanna.

tus·sle ['tʌsl] **1** N baruffa, mischia; **to have a tussle with** fare baruffa con.
2 VI: **to tussle (with sb for sth)** far baruffa (con qn per qc).

tus·sock ['tʌsək] N ciuffo d'erba.

tut [tʌt] (*also:* **tut-tut**) **1** EXCL non si fa così!.
2 VI *far schioccare la lingua in segno di disapprovazione.*

tu·telage ['tjuːtɪlɪdʒ] N (*frm*) tutela; **under sb's tutelage** sotto la tutela di qn.

tu·tor ['tjuːtə'] **1** N (*private teacher*) insegnante *m/f* privato (-a); (*living with family*) precettore *m*; (*Brit Univ*) docente *m/f* (*responsabile di un gruppo*).
2 VT: **to tutor sb in Italian** dare lezioni private d'italiano a qn.

tu·to·rial [tjuː'tɔːrɪəl] N (*Univ*) seminario, esercitazione *f* (*di un gruppo limitato*).

tutu ['tuːtuː] N tutù *m inv.*

tux·edo [tʌk'siːdəʊ] N (*Am*) smoking *m inv.*

TV [‚tiː'viː] N ABBR (= *television*) TV *f inv,* tivù *f inv.*

♦ **TV dinner** N *pasto veloce da mangiare davanti alla TV.*

twad·dle ['twɒdl] N (*fam*) scemenze *fpl.*

twain [tweɪn] N (*old, poetic*): **the twain** i (*or* le) due; **and never the twain shall meet** e mai i (*or* le) due si incontreranno.

twang [twæŋ] **1** N (*of wire, bow*) suono acuto; (*of instrument*) suono vibrante; (*of voice*) accento nasale; **to speak with a twang** parlare con voce nasale.
2 VT (*guitar*) pizzicare le corde di.
3 VI vibrare.

tweak [twiːk] **1** N: **to give sb's nose/ear a tweak** dare un pizzicotto sul naso/una tirata d'orecchie a qn.
2 VT (*nose*) pizzicare; (*ear, hair*) tirare.

twee [twiː] ADJ (*Brit fam pej*: *person*) affettato(-a); (: *decor*) lezioso(-a).

tweed [twiːd] N (*cloth*) tweed *m*; **tweeds** NPL (*suit*) abito di tweed.

tweet [twiːt] VI cinguettare.

tweet·er ['twiːtə'] N (*Stereo*) tweeter *m inv.*

twee·zers ['twiːzəz] NPL pinzette *fpl.*

twelfth [twelfθ] **1** ADJ dodicesimo(-a).
2 N (*in series*) dodicesimo(-a); (*fraction*) dodicesimo *for usage see* **fifth.**

♦ **Twelfth Night** N la notte dell'Epifania.

twelve [twelv] ADJ, N dodici (*m*) *inv*; **at twelve** alle dodici, a mezzogiorno; (*midnight*) a mezzanotte *for usage see* **five.**

twen·ti·eth ['twentɪθ] **1** ADJ ventesimo(-a).
2 N (*in series*) ventesimo(-a); (*fraction*) ventesimo *for usage see* **fifth.**

twen·ty ['twentɪ] **1** ADJ venti *inv.*
2 N venti *m inv for usage see* **fifty.**

♦ **twenty-first** [‚twentɪ'fɜːst] N (*Brit fam*: *birthday*) il ventunesimo compleanno; (: *birthday party*): **I'm having my twenty-first on Saturday** sabato faccio una festa per il mio ventunesimo compleanno.

twerp [twɜːp] N (*fam*) idiota *m/f.*

twice [twaɪs] ADV due volte; **twice as much** OR **twice as many** il doppio, due volte tanto; **I have twice as many cigarettes as you** ho il doppio delle sigarette che hai tu; **there's twice as much wine here as beer** qui c'è vino in quantità due volte superiori alla birra; **twice a week** due volte alla settimana; **she is twice your age** ha il doppio dei tuoi anni; **twice as big** due volte più grande.

twid·dle ['twɪdl] VT, VI: **to twiddle (with) sth** giocherellare con qc; **to twiddle one's thumbs** (*fig*) girarsi i pollici.

twig[1] [twɪg] N ramoscello.

twig[2] [twɪg] VT, VI (*fam*) capire.

twi·light ['twaɪ‚laɪt] N (*evening, also fig*) crepuscolo; (*morning*) alba; **at twilight** al crepuscolo, all'alba; **in the twilight** nella penombra.

twi·lit ['twaɪ‚lɪt] ADJ **a** (*sky*) crepuscolare; (*place*) tetro(-a) **b** (*fig: shadowy*) nebuloso(-a).

twill [twɪl] N (*fabric*) twill *m*, spigato.

twin [twɪn] **1** ADJ gemello(-a); **twin lead** (*Elec*) piattina.
2 N gemello(-a).
3 VT: **to twin one town with another** fare il gemellaggio di una città con un'altra.

♦ **twin beds** NPL letti *mpl* gemelli.

♦ **twin-carburettor** [‚twɪnkɑːbjuːˈrɛtə'] ADJ a doppio carburatore.

twine [twaɪn] **1** N cordicella, spago.
2 VT intrecciare.
3 VI (*plant*) attorcigliarsi.

♦ **twin-engined** [‚twɪn'ɛndʒɪnd] ADJ a due motori; **twin-engined aircraft** bimotore *m.*

twinge [twɪndʒ] N (*of pain*) fitta; **a twinge of regret/sadness/conscience** una punta di rimpianto/tristezza/rimorso; **I've been having twinges of conscience** ho i rimorsi di coscienza.

twin·kle ['twɪŋkl] **1** N scintillio; **he had a twinkle in his eye** gli brillavano gli occhi.
2 VI scintillare; (*eyes*) brillare.

twin·kling ['twɪŋklɪŋ] N scintillio; **in the twinkling of an eye** in un batter d'occhio.

♦ **twin room** N (*also:* **twin-bedded room**) stanza a due letti.

♦ **twin-set** ['twɪn‚sɛt] N (*Brit*) completo di golf e cardigan.

♦ **twin town** N città *f inv* gemellata.
twirl [twɜ:l] **1** N (*of body*) piroetta; (*in writing*) ghirigoro.
  2 VT (*also:* **twirl round**) far roteare; (: *knob*) far girare; (: *moustache*) arricciare.
  3 VI (*also:* **twirl round**) volteggiare, roteare.
twist [twɪst] **1** N **a** (*in wire, flex*) piega; (*of tobacco*) treccia; (*of paper*) cartoccio; (*of lemon*) scorzetta
  b (*twisting action*) torsione *f*; **to give sth a twist** far girare qc; **to give one's ankle/wrist a twist** OR **twist one's ankle/wrist** (*Med*) slogarsi la caviglia/il polso; **with a quick twist of the wrist** con un rapido movimento del polso
  c (*bend*) svolta, piega; (*fig: in story*) sviluppo imprevisto; **a road full of twists and turns** una strada a zigzag *or* tutta a curve; **the plot has an unexpected twist** la trama ha uno sviluppo inatteso; **to go round the twist** (*Brit fam*) ammattire, impazzire
  d : **the twist** (*dance*) il twist; **to do the twist** ballare il twist.
  2 VT (*wrench out of shape*) far piegare, deformare; (*fig: sense, words*) travisare, distorcere; (*turn*) girare; (*unscrew*) svitare; (*weave: also:* **twist together**) intrecciare; (*roll around*) arrotolare; **to twist (round)** (*coil*) attorcigliare (intorno a); **his face was twisted with pain** il suo volto era contratto dal dolore; **to twistle one's ankle/neck/wrist** (*Med*) slogarsi la caviglia/il collo/il polso; **to twistle sb's arm** (*fig*) forzare qn.
  3 VI **a** (*rope*) attorcigliarsi; (*road*) snodarsi; **the road twisted and turned** la strada procedeva a zigzag
  b (*dance*) ballare il twist
▶ **twist off** VT + ADV svitare
▶ **twist round** **1** VI + ADV (*person*) girarsi, voltarsi; (*thing*) arrotolarsi; (*road*) serpeggiare.
  2 VT + ADV (*words*) travisare.
  3 VT + PREP: **to twist sth round sth** mettere qc intorno a qc, avvolgere qc in qc; **to twist sb round one's little finger** (*fam*) rigirare qn.
twist·ed ['twɪstɪd] ADJ (*wire, rope*) attorcigliato(-a); (*ankle, wrist*) slogato(-a); (*fig: logic, mind*) contorto(-a).
twist·er ['twɪstə'] N (*fam*) **a** (*cheat*) imbroglione(-a) **b** (*Am: tornado*) tornado.
twist·ing ['twɪstɪŋ] **1** ADJ (*path*) serpeggiante.
  2 N (*of body*) torsioni *fpl*; (*of meaning*) travisamento.
twit [twɪt] N (*fam*) cretino(-a).
twitch [twɪtʃ] **1** N (*slight pull*) tiratina; (*nervous*) tic *m inv*; **to give sth a twitch** dare una tiratina a qc.
  2 VI (*hands, face, muscles*) contrarsi; (*person: in particular situation*) agitarsi; (: *habitually*) avere un tic; (*tail, ears*) drizzarsi; (*nose*) muoversi.
  3 VT (*rope, sleeve*) tirare; **he twitched the letter out of her hand** le sfilò la lettera dalle mani; **the dog twitched its ears** il cane drizzò le orecchie; **the rabbit twitched its nose** il coniglio arricciò il naso.
twitchy ['twɪtʃɪ] ADJ (*comp* -**ier**, *superl* -**iest**) (*fam*) nervosetto(-a).
twit·ter ['twɪtə'] **1** N (*of bird*) cinguettio; **to be all of a twitter** OR **be in a twitter** (*fam*) essere in grande agitazione.
  2 VI (*bird*) cinguettare; (*person*) cicalare.
two [tu:] **1** ADJ due *inv.*
  2 N due *m inv*; **to break sth in two** spezzare qc in due; **two by two** OR **in twos** a due a due; **to arrive in twos and threes** arrivare alla spicciolata; **to put two and two together** (*fig*) fare uno più uno, trarre le conclusioni; **that makes two of us** e così siamo in due *for usage see*

five.
♦ **two-bit** ['tu:ˌbɪt] ADJ (*esp Am fam pej*) da quattro soldi.
♦ **two-dimensional** [ˌtu:dɪ'mɛnʃənəl] ADJ **a** (*Geom*) bidimensionale **b** (*pej: superficial: characters*) senza spessore.
♦ **two-door** [ˌtu:'dɔ:'] ADJ (*car*) a due porte.
♦ **two-edged** [ˌtu:'ɛdʒd] ADJ (*also fig*) a doppio taglio.
♦ **two-faced** [ˌtu:'feɪst] ADJ (*fig pej: person*) doppio(-a), falso(-a).
two·fold ['tu:ˌfəʊld] **1** ADV: **to increase twofold** aumentare del doppio.
  2 ADJ (*increase*) doppio(-a); (*reply*) in due punti.
♦ **two-handed** [ˌtu:'hændɪd] ADJ (*Tennis*): **two-handed grip** impugnatura a due mani.
♦ **two-legged** [ˌtu:'lɛgd] ADJ a due gambe, bipede.
♦ **two-party** ['tu:ˌpɑ:tɪ] ADJ (*Pol*) bipartitico(-a).
two·pence ['tʌpəns] N (*Brit: amount*) due penny; (: *coin*) moneta da due penny.
♦ **two-phase** ['tu:ˌfeɪz] ADJ (*Elec*) bifase.
♦ **two-piece** ['tu:ˌpi:s] **1** ADJ a due pezzi.
  2 N (*also:* **two-piece suit**) due pezzi *m inv*; (*also:* **two-piece swimsuit**) (costume *m* da bagno a) due pezzi *m inv*.
♦ **two-ply** ['tu:ˌplaɪ] ADJ (*wool*) a due capi.
♦ **two-seater** [ˌtu:'si:tə'] N (*car*) macchina a due posti; (*plane*) biposto.
two·some ['tu:səm] N (*people*) coppia; **to go out in a twosome** uscire in coppia.
♦ **two-stroke** ['tu:ˌstrəʊk] **1** N (*engine*) due tempi *m inv*.
  2 ADJ a due tempi.
♦ **two-time** ['tu:ˌtaɪm] VT (*fam*) fare le corna a.
♦ **two-tone** ['tu:ˌtəʊn] ADJ (*colour*) bicolore.
♦ **two-way** ['tu:ˌweɪ] ADJ (*street*) a doppio senso; (*traffic*) a doppio senso di circolazione; **two-way radio** radio *f inv* ricetrasmittente.
♦ **two-wheeler** [ˌtu:'wi:lə'] N bicicletta.
TX ABBR (*Am Post*)= *Texas.*
ty·coon [taɪ'ku:n] N: (**business**) **tycoon** magnate *m.*
tym·pa·num ['tɪmpənəm] N (*Anat, Archit*) timpano.
type [taɪp] **1** N **a** (*gen, Bio*) tipo; (*sort*) genere *m*, tipo; (*model*) modello; (*make: of tea, machine*) marca; **what type do you want?** che tipo vuole?; **what type of person is he?** che tipo è?; **he's not my type** non è il mio tipo; **it's my type of film** è il mio genere di film; **he's a pleasant type** è un tipo piacevole
  b (*Typ: one letter*) carattere *m* (tipografico); (: *letters collectively*) caratteri (tipografici), tipi *mpl*; **in bold/italic type** in grassetto/corsivo.
  2 VT **a** (*also:* **type out**, **type up**: *letter*) battere (a macchina), dattilografare
  b (*disease*) classificare.
  3 VI dattilografare, battere a macchina.
type·cast ['taɪpˌkɑ:st] VT (*pt, pp* **typecast**) (*Cine, Theatre*) far sempre fare la stessa parte a.
♦ **type-cast** ['taɪpˌkɑ:st] ADJ (*actor*) a ruolo fisso.
type·face ['taɪpˌfeɪs] N carattere *m* (tipografico).
type·script ['taɪpˌskrɪpt] N dattiloscritto.
type·set ['taɪpˌsɛt] VT comporre.
type·set·ter ['taɪpˌsɛtə'] N compositore *m.*
type·set·ting ['taɪpˌsɛtɪŋ] N composizione *f.*
type·writ·er ['taɪpˌraɪtə'] N macchina da scrivere.
type·writ·ing ['taɪpˌraɪtɪŋ] N dattilografia.
type·writ·ten ['taɪpˌrɪtn] ADJ dattiloscritto(-a), battuto (-a) a macchina.
ty·phoid ['taɪfɔɪd] N febbre *f* tifoidea.
ty·phoon [taɪ'fu:n] N tifone *m.*

ty·phus ['taɪfəs] N tifo.

typi·cal ['tɪpɪkəl] ADJ tipico(-a); **a typical case/example** un caso/esempio tipico; **the typical Spaniard** il tipico spagnolo, lo spagnolo tipo; **(isn't that just) typical!** tipico!; **that's typical of her!** questo è tipico di lei!

typi·cal·ly ['tɪpɪkəlɪ] ADV tipicamente; **typically, he arrived home late** come al solito è arrivato a casa tardi.

typi·fy ['tɪpɪˌfaɪ] VT (thing) essere tipico(-a) di, caratterizzare; (person) impersonare.

typ·ing ['taɪpɪŋ] **1** N (skill) dattilografia; **have you finished that typing?** hai finito quelle cose che dovevi battere a macchina?.

2 ADJ (lesson) di dattilografia; (paper) per macchina da scrivere.

♦ **typing pool** N ufficio m dattilografia inv.

typ·ist ['taɪpɪst] N dattilografo(-a).

typo ['taɪpəʊ] N ABBR (fam: = typographical error) refuso.

ty·pog·ra·pher [taɪ'pɒgrəfəʳ] N tipografo(-a).

ty·po·graph·ical [ˌtaɪpə'græfɪkəl], **ty·po·graph·ic** [ˌtaɪpə'græfɪk] ADJ tipografico(-a).

ty·pog·ra·phy [taɪ'pɒgrəfɪ] N tipografia.

ty·pol·ogy [taɪ'pɒlədʒɪ] N tipologia.

ty·ran·nical [tɪ'rænɪkəl], **ty·ran·nic** [tɪ'rænɪk] ADJ tirannico(-a).

ty·ran·ni·cal·ly [tɪ'rænɪkəlɪ] ADV tirannicamente.

tyr·an·nize ['tɪrəˌnaɪz] **1** VT tiranneggiare.

2 VI: **to tyrannize over sb** tiranneggiare qn.

tyr·an·ny ['tɪrənɪ] N tirannia.

ty·rant ['taɪərənt] N tiranno.

tyre, (Am) **tire** ['taɪəʳ] N (Aut) gomma, pneumatico.

♦ **tyre gauge**, (Am) **tire gauge** N manometro (per pneumatici).

♦ **tyre pressure**, (Am) **tire pressure** N pressione f (dei pneumatici).

tyro, tiro ['taɪrəʊ] N (Brit old frm) principiante m/f.

Ty·rol [tɪ'rəʊl] N: **the Tyrol** il Tirolo.

Ty·ro·lean [ˌtɪrəʊ'liːən], **Tyro·lese** [ˌtɪrə'liːz] ADJ, N tirolese (m/f).

Tyrrhenian Sea [tɪˌriːnɪən'siː] N: **the Tyrrhenian Sea** il mar Tirreno.

tzar [zɑːʳ] N = **tsar**.

tzar·ist ['zɑːrɪst] ADJ, N zarista m/f.

tzet·ze fly ['tsɛtsɪˌflaɪ] N = **tsetse fly**.

U

U, u [juː] N (*letter*) U, u *f or m inv*; **U for Uncle** ≈ U come Udine.

U [juː] N ABBR (*Brit Cine*: = *universal*) per tutti.

UAE [ˌjuːeɪˈiː] N ABBR (= *United Arab Emirates*) E.A.U. (= *Emirati Arabi Uniti*).

UAW [ˌjuːeɪˈdʌblju:] N ABBR (*Am*: = *United Automobile Workers*) *sindacato dei lavoratori del settore automobilistico*.

UB40 [ˌjuːbiːˈfɔːtɪ] N ABBR (*Brit*: = *unemployment benefit form 40*) *modulo per la richiesta del sussidio di disoccupazione*.

♦ **U-bend** [ˈjuːˌbɛnd] N (*in pipe*) gomito.

ubiqui·tous [juːˈbɪkwɪtəs] ADJ (*frm*) onnipresente.

ubiquity [juːˈbɪkwɪtɪ] N (*frm*) onnipresenza, ubiquità.

♦ **U-boat** [ˈjuːˌbəʊt] N sottomarino tedesco.

UCCA [ˈʌkə] N ABBR (*Brit*: = *Universities Central Council on Admissions*) *organo centrale di coordinamento per le ammissioni all'Università*.

UDA [ˌjuːdiːˈeɪ] N ABBR (*Brit*: = *Ulster Defence Association*) *organizzazione paramilitare protestante dell'Irlanda del nord*.

UDC [ˌjuːdiːˈsiː] N ABBR (*Brit*)= *Urban District Council*.

ud·der [ˈʌdəʳ] N mammella (*di animale*).

UDI [ˌjuːdiːˈaɪ] ABBR (*Brit Pol*)= *unilateral declaration of independence*.

UDR [ˌjuːdiːˈɑːʳ] N ABBR (*Brit*: = *Ulster Defence Regiment*) *reggimento dell'esercito britannico in Irlanda del Nord*.

UEFA [juːˈeɪfə] N ABBR (= *Union of European Football Association*) U.E.F.A. *f*.

UFO [ˌjuːɛfˈəʊ] N ABBR (= *unidentified flying object*) ufo *m inv*.

Ugan·da [juːˈgændə] N l'Uganda.

Ugan·dan [juːˈgændən] ADJ, N ugandese (*m/f*).

UGC [ˌjuːdʒiːˈsiː] N ABBR (*Brit*: = *University Grants Committee*) *organo che autorizza sovvenzioni alle università*.

ugh [ɜːh] EXCL puah!

ug·li·ness [ˈʌglɪnɪs] N bruttezza.

ugly [ˈʌglɪ] ADJ (*comp* -**ier**, *superl* -**iest**) **a** (*not pretty*) brutto(-a); **as ugly as sin** brutto(-a) come la fame **b** (*nasty*: *situation, incident*) brutto(-a); (: *rumour*) inquietante; (: *mood, look*) minaccioso(-a); (: *crime, sight*) ripugnante; (: *vice*) osceno(-a); **an ugly customer** (*fam*) un brutto tipo.

♦ **ugly duckling** N brutto anatroccolo.

UHF [ˌjuːeɪtʃˈɛf] N ABBR (= *ultra-high frequency*) UHF *f*.

UHT [ˌjuːeɪtʃˈtiː] ADJ ABBR = *ultra-heat treated*; **UHT milk** latte *m* UHT *inv*.

UK [ˌjuːˈkeɪ] N ABBR = *United Kingdom*; **the UK** il Regno Unito.

Ukraine [juːˈkreɪn] N l'Ucraina.

Ukrainian [juːˈkreɪnɪən] **1** ADJ ucraino(-a).
2 N ucraino(-a); (*language*) ucraino.

ul·cer [ˈʌlsəʳ] N (*gen*) ulcera, ulcerazione *f*; (**stomach**) **ulcer** ulcera gastrica; **mouth ulcer** afta.

ul·cer·at·ed [ˈʌlsəˌreɪtɪd] ADJ ulcerato(-a).

ulna [ˈʌlnə] N (*Anat*) ulna.

Ul·ster [ˈʌlstəʳ] N l'Ulster *m*.

ul·te·ri·or [ʌlˈtɪərɪəʳ] ADJ recondito(-a); **ulterior motive** secondo fine *m*.

ul·ti·ma·ta [ˌʌltɪˈmeɪtə] (*frm*) NPL of **ultimatum**.

ul·ti·mate [ˈʌltɪmɪt] **1** ADJ **a** (*final*: *result, outcome*) finale; (: *conclusion*) definitivo(-a); (: *destination*) ultimo(-a) **b** (*greatest*: *insult*) massimo(-a); (: *authority*) supremo(-a), massimo(-a); **the ultimate deterrent** (*Mil*) il mezzo di dissuasione risolutivo **c** (*principle, cause*) fondamentale.
2 N: **the ultimate in luxury** il non plus ultra del lusso.

ul·ti·mate·ly [ˈʌltɪmɪtlɪ] ADV (*in the end, eventually*) in fin dei conti, in definitiva; (*in the last analysis*) in ultima analisi; (*at last*) alla fine; **to be ultimately responsible for sth** dover rispondere per primi di qc.

ul·ti·ma·tum [ˌʌltɪˈmeɪtəm] N (*pl* **ultimatums** *or* **ultimata** [ˌʌltɪˈmeɪtə]) (*Mil, fig*) ultimatum *m inv*; **to issue an ultimatum to** dare l'ultimatum a.

ultra... [ˈʌltrə] PREF ultra... .

ultra·con·ser·va·tive [ˌʌltrəkənˈsɜːvətɪv] ADJ ultraconservatore(-trice), reazionario(-a).

ultra·ma·rine [ˌʌltrəməˈriːn] **1** ADJ oltremarino(-a).
2 N oltremarino.

ultra·mod·ern [ˌʌltrəˈmɒdən] ADJ ultramoderno(-a).

ultra·sen·si·tive [ˌʌltrəˈsɛnsɪtɪv] ADJ (*equipment*) ultrasensibile; (*skin, issue*) delicatissimo(-a).

ultra·son·ic [ˌʌltrəˈsɒnɪk] ADJ ultrasonico(-a).

ultra·sound [ˌʌltrəˈsaʊnd] N (Med) ecografia.

ultra·vio·let [ˌʌltrəˈvaɪəlɪt] ADJ ultravioletto(-a).

Ulysses [ˈjuːlɪˌsiːz] N Ulisse m.

um·ber [ˈʌmbəʳ] (frm) **1** N terra di Siena.
2 ADJ color terra di Siena.

um·bili·cal [ˌʌmbɪˈlaɪkəl] ADJ ombelicale.
♦ **umbilical cord** N cordone m ombelicale.

um·brage [ˈʌmbrɪdʒ] N: **to take umbrage (at sth)** adombrarsi (a or per qc), risentirsi (di or per qc).

um·brel·la [ʌmˈbrɛlə] N ombrello; **under the umbrella of** (fig) sotto l'egida di; **an umbrella organization** una organizzazione a cui fanno capo diverse altre.
♦ **umbrella pine** N pino domestico.
♦ **umbrella stand** N portaombrelli m inv.

um·laut [ˈumlaʊt] N (Ling) umlaut m inv.

um·pire [ˈʌmpaɪəʳ] **1** N arbitro.
2 VI arbitrare.
3 VT arbitrare.

ump·teen [ˈʌmptiːn] ADJ (fam) non so quanti(-e), innumerevole; **umpteen times** centomila volte fpl.

ump·teenth [ˈʌmptiːnθ] ADJ (fam) ennesimo(-a); **for the umpteenth time** per l'ennesima volta.

UMW [ˌjuːɛmˈdʌblju:] N ABBR (= United Mineworkers of America) sindacato dei minatori americani.

UN [juːˈɛn] N ABBR = United Nations; **the UN** le Nazioni Unite, l'ONU f.

un·abashed [ˌʌnəˈbæʃt] ADJ imperterrito(-a).

un·abat·ed [ˌʌnəˈbeɪtɪd] ADJ (energy, enthusiasm) costante, inesauribile; **to be** or **continue unabated** (storm, wind) non accennare a diminuire; (fighting) senza tregua.

un·able [ʌnˈeɪbl] ADJ: **to be unable to do sth** (not to know how to) non saper fare qc, non essere capace di fare qc; (not to have it in one's power to) non poter fare qc, essere nell'impossibilità di fare qc.

un·abridged [ˌʌnəˈbrɪdʒd] ADJ integrale.

un·ac·cep·table [ˌʌnəkˈsɛptəbl] ADJ (proposal, behaviour) inaccettabile; (price) impossibile; **it's unacceptable that** è inammissibile che + sub.

un·ac·com·pa·nied [ˌʌnəˈkʌmpənɪd] ADJ (child, person) non accompagnato(-a); (luggage) incustodito(-a); (singing, song) senza accompagnamento; (violin) solo (-a).

un·ac·count·able [ˌʌnəˈkaʊntəbl] ADJ (inexplicable) inspiegabile; (not answerable) non responsabile.

un·ac·count·ably [ˌʌnəˈkaʊntəblɪ] ADV (inexplicably) inesplicabilmente, inspiegabilmente.

un·ac·count·ed [ˌʌnəˈkaʊntɪd] ADJ: **unaccounted for** mancante; **two passengers are unaccounted for** due passeggeri mancano all'appello.

un·ac·cus·tomed [ˌʌnəˈkʌstəmd] ADJ **a** (unused to): **to be unaccustomed to sth/to doing** non essere abituato(-a) a qc/a fare **b** (unwonted) insolito(-a); **with unaccustomed zeal** con insolito zelo.

un·ac·knowl·edged [ˌʌnəkˈnɒlɪdʒd] ADJ **a** (disregarded, not recognized) non riconosciuto(-a) **b** (ignored): **unacknowledged, he sat down in silence** ignorato da tutti i presenti, si sedette in silenzio.

un·ac·quaint·ed [ˌʌnəˈkweɪntɪd] ADJ: **to be unacquainted with** (facts) ignorare, non essere al corrente di; (poverty) non aver mai conosciuto.

un·adorned [ˌʌnəˈdɔːnd] ADJ disadorno(-a).

un·adul·ter·at·ed [ˌʌnəˈdʌltəˌreɪtɪd] ADJ (water, nonsense) puro(-a); (wine) non sofisticato(-a).

un·af·fect·ed [ˌʌnəˈfɛktɪd] ADJ **a** (sincere) naturale, spon-

taneo(-a); (manner, voice) non affettato(-a); (gratitude) sincero(-a) **b** (unchanged): **to be unaffected by** non essere toccato(-a) da; **she was wholly unaffected by the news** la notizia non le ha fatto né caldo né freddo.

un·af·fect·ed·ly [ˌʌnəˈfɛktɪdlɪ] ADV senza affettazione.

un·afraid [ˌʌnəˈfreɪd] ADJ: **to be unafraid** non aver paura.

un·aid·ed [ʌnˈeɪdɪd] **1** ADV senza aiuto.
2 ADJ: **by his own unaided efforts** con le sue sole forze, senza l'aiuto di nessuno.

un·al·loyed [ˌʌnəˈlɔɪd] ADJ (liter: bliss, pleasure) purissimo (-a).

un·al·ter·able [ʌnˈɒltərəbl] ADJ inalterabile.

un·al·tered [ʌnˈɒltəd] ADJ inalterato(-a).

un·am·bigu·ous [ˌʌnæmˈbɪgjʊəs] ADJ non ambiguo(-a), inequivocabile.

un·am·bigu·ous·ly [ˌʌnæmˈbɪgjʊəslɪ] ADV in modo chiaro, inequivocabilmente.

un·am·bi·tious [ˌʌnæmˈbɪʃəs] ADJ (person) poco ambizioso(-a); (plan) senza pretese.

un-American [ˌʌnəˈmɛrɪkən] ADJ (anti-American) antiamericano(-a); (uncharacteristic of America) poco americano(-a).

una·nim·ity [juːnəˈnɪmɪtɪ] N unanimità.

unani·mous [juːˈnænɪməs] ADJ unanime.

unani·mous·ly [juːˈnænɪməslɪ] ADV all'unanimità.

un·an·nounced [ˌʌnəˈnaʊnst] **1** ADJ inatteso(-a).
2 ADV (arrive) senza preavviso.

un·an·swer·able [ʌnˈɑːnsərəbl] ADJ (case, argument) irrefutabile; (question) senza risposta.

un·an·swered [ʌnˈɑːnsəd] ADJ (question, letter) senza risposta; (criticism) non contestato(-a).

un·ap·peal·ing [ˌʌnəˈpiːlɪŋ] ADJ poco attraente.

un·ap·pe·tiz·ing [ʌnˈæpɪˌtaɪzɪŋ] ADJ poco appetitoso(-a).

un·ap·pre·cia·tive [ˌʌnəˈpriːʃɪətɪv] ADJ che non sa apprezzare; **an unappreciative audience** un pubblico indifferente.

un·ap·proach·able [ˌʌnəˈprəʊtʃəbl] ADJ (person) inavvicinabile, inabbordabile.

un·ar·gu·able [ˌʌnˈɑːgjʊəbl] ADJ indiscutibile, incontestabile.

un·ar·gu·ably [ˌʌnˈɑːgjʊəblɪ] ADV indiscutibilmente, incontestabilmente.

un·armed [ʌnˈɑːmd] ADJ (person) disarmato(-a).
♦ **unarmed combat** N lotta senz'armi.

un·ashamed [ˌʌnəˈʃeɪmd] ADJ (brazen) sfrontato(-a), sfacciato(-a); **she was quite unashamed about it** non se ne vergognava minimamente.

un·asham·ed·ly [ˌʌnəˈʃeɪmɪdlɪ] ˌADV sfacciatamente, sfrontatamente.

un·asked [ʌnˈɑːskt] **1** ADJ (question) non posto(-a), non formulato(-a).
2 ADV: **to do sth unasked** fare qc spontaneamente.

un·as·sail·able [ˌʌnəˈseɪləbl] ADJ (fortress) imprendibile; (position, reputation) inattaccabile.

un·as·sist·ed [ˌʌnəˈsɪstɪd] ADJ senza nessun aiuto.

un·as·sum·ing [ˌʌnəˈsjuːmɪŋ] ADJ modesto(-a), senza pretese.

un·at·tached [ˌʌnəˈtætʃt] ADJ (part) staccato(-a); (not married) libero(-a), senza legami; (independent) indipendente, sciolto(-a).

un·at·tain·able [ˌʌnəˈteɪnəbl] ADJ irraggiungibile.

un·at·tend·ed [ˌʌnəˈtɛndɪd] ADJ (not looked after: luggage) incustodito(-a); (: patient, baby) solo(-a), senza sorveglianza.

un·at·trac·tive [ˌʌnəˈtræktɪv] ADJ (person) poco attraente;

(*offer*) poco allettante; (*place*) privo(-a) di attrattiva.

un·author·ized [ʌnˈɔːθəˌraɪzd] ADJ non autorizzato(-a).

un·avail·able [ˌʌnəˈveɪləbl] ADJ (*article, room, book*) non disponibile; (*person*) impegnato(-a).

un·avail·ing [ˌʌnəˈveɪlɪŋ] ADJ (*liter: effort*) vano(-a), inutile.

un·avoid·able [ˌʌnəˈvɔɪdəbl] ADJ inevitabile.

un·avoid·ably [ˌʌnəˈvɔɪdəblɪ] ADV (*detained*) per cause di forza maggiore.

un·aware [ˌʌnəˈwɛəʳ] ADJ: **to be unaware of sth/that** ... non rendersi conto di *or* ignorare qc/che... .

un·awares [ˌʌnəˈwɛəz] ADV: **to catch** *or* **take sb unawares** prendere qn alla sprovvista.

un·bal·ance [ʌnˈbæləns] VT alterare l'equilibrio di.

un·bal·anced [ˌʌnˈbælənst] ADJ non equilibrato(-a); (*mentally*) squilibrato(-a).

un·bear·able [ʌnˈbɛərəbl] ADJ insopportabile.

un·bear·ably [ʌnˈbɛərəblɪ] ADV insopportabilmente.

un·beat·able [ʌnˈbiːtəbl] ADJ imbattibile.

un·beat·en [ˌʌnˈbiːtn] ADJ (*team, army*) imbattuto(-a); (*record*) insuperato(-a).

un·be·com·ing [ˌʌnbɪˈkʌmɪŋ] ADJ (*liter: unseemly: conduct, behaviour*) sconveniente; (: *unflattering: garment*) che non dona.

un·be·known [ˌʌnbɪˈnəʊn], **un·be·knownst** [ˌʌnbɪˈnəʊnst] ADV (*old*): **unbeknown to** all'insaputa di; **unbeknown to me** a mia insaputa.

un·be·lief [ˌʌnbɪˈliːf] N incredulità.

un·be·liev·able [ˌʌnbɪˈliːvəbl] ADJ incredibile; **it's unbelievable that** ... è incredibile che...+ *sub*.

un·be·liev·ably [ˌʌnbɪˈliːvəblɪ] ADV incredibilmente.

un·be·liev·er [ˌʌnbɪˈliːvəʳ] N non credente *m/f*.

un·be·liev·ing [ˌʌnbɪˈliːvɪŋ] ADJ incredulo(-a).

un·be·liev·ing·ly [ˌʌnbɪˈliːvɪŋlɪ] ADV con aria incredula; **he looked at me unbelievingly** mi ha guardato incredulo.

un·bend [ʌnˈbɛnd] (*pt, pp* **unbent** [ˌʌnˈbɛnt]) ⬜1 VT (*pipe, wire*) raddrizzare.

⬜2 VI (*fig: person*) distendersi, rilassarsi.

un·bend·ing [ʌnˈbɛndɪŋ] ADJ (*fig*) inflessibile, rigido(-a).

un·bi·ased, unbiassed [ʌnˈbaɪəst] ADJ obiettivo(-a), imparziale.

un·bid·den [ʌnˈbɪdn] ADJ (*liter*): **he did it unbidden** lo ha fatto senza che nessuno glielo avesse chiesto; **he came in unbidden** è entrato senza essere stato invitato.

un·blem·ished [ʌnˈblɛmɪʃt] ADJ senza macchia.

un·blink·ing [ʌnˈblɪŋkɪŋ] ADJ (*person*) impassibile; **he looked at me with unblinking eyes** mi guardò senza batter ciglio.

un·block [ʌnˈblɒk] VT (*pipe*) sbloccare.

un·blush·ing [ʌnˈblʌʃɪŋ] ADJ inverecondo(-a).

un·bolt [ʌnˈbəʊlt] VT levare il catenaccio a.

un·born [ʌnˈbɔːn] ADJ non ancora nato(-a).

un·bound·ed [ʌnˈbaʊndɪd] ADJ sconfinato(-a), senza limite.

un·break·able [ʌnˈbreɪkəbl] ADJ infrangibile.

un·bri·dled [ʌnˈbraɪdld] ADJ (*lust, ambition*) sfrenato(-a).

un·bro·ken [ʌnˈbrəʊkən] ADJ **a** (*intact*) intatto(-a), intero (-a); **his spirit remained unbroken** ha conservato un animo indomito **b** (*continuous: sleep, silence*) ininterrotto(-a); (*line of descent*) diretto(-a) **c** (*record*) insuperato(-a) **d** (*horse*) non domato(-a).

un·buck·le [ʌnˈbʌkl] VT slacciare.

un·bur·den [ʌnˈbɜːdn] VT: **to unburden o.s. to sb** sfogarsi con qn.

un·business·like [ʌnˈbɪznɪsˌlaɪk] ADJ (*shopkeeper*) che non ha il senso degli affari; (*transaction*) irregolare; (*fig:*

person) poco efficiente.

un·but·ton [ʌnˈbʌtn] VT sbottonare.

uncalled-for [ˌʌnˈkɔːldfɔːʳ] ADJ (*remark*) fuori luogo *inv*; (*action*) ingiustificato(-a).

un·can·ni·ly [ʌnˈkænɪlɪ] ADV straordinariamente, incredibilmente.

un·can·ny [ʌnˈkænɪ] ADJ (*comp* **-ier**, *superl* **-iest**) (*knack, resemblance*) sconcertante; (*sound, silence*) strano(-a), inquietante.

uncared-for [ʌnˈkɛədfɔːʳ] ADJ (*child, garden*) trascurato (-a); (*nails*) non curato(-a).

un·car·ing [ʌnˈkɛərɪŋ] ADJ indifferente, insensibile.

un·ceas·ing [ʌnˈsiːsɪŋ] ADJ incessante.

un·ceas·ing·ly [ʌnˈsiːsɪŋlɪ] ADV incessantemente, senza sosta.

un·cer·emo·ni·ous [ˌʌnsɛrɪˈməʊnɪəs] ADJ (*abrupt, rude*) brusco(-a); **in unceremonious haste** in modo sbrigativo.

un·cer·emo·ni·ous·ly [ˌʌnsɛrɪˈməʊnɪəslɪ] ADV senza tante cerimonie.

un·cer·tain [ʌnˈsɜːtn] ADJ (*person, future, result*) incerto (-a); (*aims*) vago(-a); (*temper*) instabile; **I'm uncertain about what to do** sono incerto sul da farsi; **it is uncertain whether** non è sicuro se; **he is uncertain whether** non sa bene se; **in no uncertain terms** chiaro e tondo, senza mezzi termini.

un·cer·tain·ly [ʌnˈsɜːtnlɪ] ADV (*say*) senza troppa convinzione, con aria incerta; (*move*) con passo incerto.

un·cer·tain·ty [ʌnˈsɜːtntɪ] N (*of situation*) incertezza; (*confusion*) dubbi *mpl*; **the uncertainties of this life** le incognite della vita.

un·chal·lenge·able [ʌnˈtʃælɪndʒəbl] ADJ incontestabile.

un·chal·lenged [ˌʌnˈtʃælɪndʒd] ADJ (*gen, Law*) incontestato(-a); **to go unchallenged** non venire contestato(-a), non trovare opposizione; **to let a remark go unchallenged** lasciar passare un'osservazione senza replicare.

un·changed [ˌʌnˈtʃeɪndʒd] ADJ (*plans, situation*) immutato (-a), invariato(-a); **he's completely unchanged** non è cambiato minimamente.

un·chang·ing [ʌnˈtʃeɪndʒɪŋ] ADJ che resta immutato(-a).

un·char·ac·ter·is·tic [ˌʌnˌkærəktəˈrɪstɪk] ADJ (*generosity, behaviour*) insolito(-a); **that's uncharacteristic of him** non è (una cosa) da lui.

un·chari·table [ʌnˈtʃærɪtəbl] ADJ (*attitude*) poco generoso (-a), duro(-a); (*remark*) cattivo(-a).

un·chart·ed [ʌnˈtʃɑːtɪd] ADJ inesplorato(-a).

un·checked [ʌnˈtʃɛkt] ADJ **a** (*unrestrained: anger*) incontrollato(-a); **to go unchecked** (*abuse, violence*) rimanere incontrollato(-a); (*virus, inflation*) dilagare; **to advance unchecked** (*army*) avanzare senza incontrare opposizione **b** (*not verified: facts*) non controllato(-a), non verificato(-a); (*typescript*) non corretto(-a).

un·chris·tian [ʌnˈkrɪstjən] ADJ poco cristiano(-a).

un·civ·il [ʌnˈsɪvəl] ADJ scortese, maleducato(-a).

un·civi·lized [ʌnˈsɪvɪˌlaɪzd] ADJ (*tribe, people*) selvaggio (-a); (*behaviour, conditions*) incivile, barbaro(-a).

un·claimed [ʌnˈkleɪmd] ADJ (*prize, social security benefit*) non ritirato(-a); (*property*) non reclamato(-a).

un·clas·si·fied [ʌnˈklæsɪˌfaɪd] ADJ **a** (*not secret: documents, information*) accessibile al pubblico **b** (*items, papers, road*) non classificato(-a); (*Brit: football results*) non classificato(-a) per campionato.

un·cle [ˈʌŋkl] N zio.

un·clean [ʌnˈkliːn] ADJ sporco(-a); (*fig, Rel*) immondo(-a).

un·clear [ʌnˈklɪəʳ] ADJ non chiaro(-a); **I'm still unclear about what I'm supposed to do** non ho ancora ben

capito cosa dovrei fare.

♦ **Uncle Tom** N (*pej*) *termine spregiativo usato per definire una persona di colore troppo servile con i bianchi.*

un·climbed [ʌn'klaɪmd] ADJ (*mountain*) vergine.

un·cloud·ed [ʌn'klaʊdɪd] ADJ senza nuvole; (*fig: mind, judgement*) lucido(-a); (: *happiness*) senza una nube.

un·clut·tered [ˌʌn'klʌtəd] ADJ (*room*) privo(-a) di oggetti superflui; (*view*) non ostruito(-a).

un·coil [ʌn'kɔɪl] ① VT srotolare.
② VI srotolarsi.

un·col·lect·ed [ˌʌnkə'lɛktɪd] ADJ (*luggage, prize*) non ritirato(-a); (*rubbish*) non portato(-a) via; (*tax*) non riscosso(-a).

un·combed [ʌn'kəʊmd] ADJ spettinato(-a).

un·com·fort·able [ʌn'kʌmfətəbl] ADJ **a** (*person, chair*) scomodo(-a); (*afternoon*) poco piacevole; (*situation*) sgradevole; **to have an uncomfortable time** passare un brutto quarto d'ora; **to make life uncomfortable for sb** rendere la vita difficile a qn
b (*uneasy, embarrassed*) a disagio, non a proprio agio; **to make sb feel uncomfortable** mettere qn a disagio; **I had an uncomfortable feeling that** ... ho avuto la sgradevole sensazione che... .

un·com·fort·ably [ʌn'kʌmfətəblɪ] ADV **a** (*sit*) scomodamente; (*dressed*) in modo poco pratico; (*hot*) eccessivamente **b** (*uneasily: say*) con voce inquieta; (: *think*) con inquietudine; **uncomfortably close** a una vicinanza preoccupante.

un·com·mit·ted [ˌʌnkə'mɪtɪd] ADJ (*attitude, country*) neutrale; **to be uncommitted** (*person*) non essere impegnato(-a); **to remain uncommitted to** (*policy, party*) non dare la propria adesione a.

un·com·mon [ʌn'kɒmən] ADJ **a** (*unusual*) insolito(-a); (*rare*) non comune, raro(-a); **it's not uncommon that** non è raro che + *sub* **b** (*outstanding*) fuori dal comune.

un·com·mon·ly [ʌn'kɒmənlɪ] ADV (*hot*) insolitamente; **not uncommonly** non di rado; **it was uncommonly kind of you** è stato squisito da parte sua; **to be uncommonly gifted** avere delle doti fuori del comune.

un·com·mu·ni·ca·tive [ˌʌnkə'mjuːnɪkətɪv] ADJ poco comunicativo(-a).

un·com·plain·ing [ˌʌnkəm'pleɪnɪŋ] ADJ che non si lamenta.

un·com·plain·ing·ly [ˌʌnkəm'pleɪnɪŋlɪ] ADV senza lamentarsi.

un·com·pli·cat·ed [ʌn'kɒmplɪˌkeɪtɪd] ADJ semplice, poco complicato(-a).

un·com·pli·men·ta·ry [ˌʌnkɒmplɪ'mɛntərɪ] ADJ poco gentile.

un·com·pre·hend·ing [ʌnˌkɒmprɪ'hɛndɪŋ] ADJ (*baffled*) perplesso(-a).

un·com·pre·hend·ing·ly [ʌnˌkɒmprɪ'hɛndɪŋlɪ] ADV in modo perplesso.

un·com·pro·mis·ing [ʌn'kɒmprəˌmaɪzɪŋ] ADJ (*honesty, dedication*) assoluto(-a); (*attitude*) intransigente.

un·con·cealed [ˌʌnkən'siːld] ADJ non dissimulato(-a).

un·con·cerned [ˌʌnkən'sɜːnd] ADJ (*unworried*) tranquillo (-a); **to be unconcerned about** non darsi pensiero di, non preoccuparsi di *or* per.

un·con·cern·ed·ly [ˌʌnkən'sɜːnɪdlɪ] ADV con indifferenza.

un·con·di·tion·al [ˌʌnkən'dɪʃənl] ADJ (*surrender, refusal*) incondizionato(-a); (*freedom*) assoluto(-a).

un·con·di·tion·al·ly [ˌʌnkən'dɪʃnəlɪ] ADV incondizionatamente, senza condizioni.

un·con·firmed [ˌʌnkən'fɜːmd] ADJ non confermato(-a).

un·con·gen·ial [ˌʌnkən'dʒiːnɪəl] ADJ (*person*) poco simpatico(-a); (*surroundings, work*) poco piacevole.

un·con·nect·ed [ˌʌnkə'nɛktɪd] ADJ **a** (*unrelated*) senza connessione, senza rapporto; **to be unconnected with** essere estraneo(-a) a **b** (*incoherent*) sconnesso(-a).

un·con·scion·able [ʌn'kɒnʃənəbl] ADJ (*liter*) **a** (*excessive*) eccessivo(-a); **to be an unconscionable time doing sth** impiegare un tempo eccessivo a fare qc **b** (*unprincipled: liar*) spregiudicato(-a).

un·con·scious [ʌn'kɒnʃəs] ① ADJ **a** (*Med*) privo(-a) di sensi, svenuto(-a); **to fall unconscious** svenire, cadere (a terra) privo(-a) di sensi; **to knock sb unconscious** far perdere i sensi a qn con un colpo
b (*unaware*): **unconscious (of)** inconsapevole (di), ignaro(-a) (di)
c (*unintentional*: *action, desire*) inconscio(-a).
② N (*Psych*): **the unconscious** l'inconscio.

un·con·scious·ly [ʌn'kɒnʃəslɪ] ADV inconsciamente, senza rendersi conto.

un·con·sti·tu·tion·al [ˌʌnkɒnstɪ'tjuːʃənl] ADJ (*frm*) anticostituzionale.

un·con·sti·tu·tion·al·ity [ˌʌnkɒnstɪˌtjuːʃə'nælɪtɪ] N (*frm*) anticostituzionalità.

un·con·sti·tu·tion·al·ly [ʌnˌkɒnstɪ'tjuːʃnəlɪ] ADV (*frm*) anticostituzionalmente.

un·con·test·ed [ˌʌnkən'tɛstɪd] ADJ (*champion*) incontestato(-a); (*Pol: seat, election*) non disputato(-a).

un·con·trol·lable [ˌʌnkən'trəʊləbl] ADJ (*desire, epidemic*) incontrollabile; (*child*) indisciplinato(-a); (*laughter*) irrefrenabile; (*temper, reaction*) incontrollato(-a).

un·con·trol·lably [ˌʌnkən'trəʊləblɪ] ADV: **to laugh uncontrollably** ridere senza potersi fermare; **the car skidded uncontrollably** la macchina ha slittato e ne ho (*or* hai *etc*) perso il controllo.

un·con·trolled [ˌʌnkən'trəʊld] ADJ (*laughter, weeping*) irrefrenabile; (*child, dog*) scatenato(-a); (*inflation, price rises*) incontenibile.

un·con·ven·tion·al [ˌʌnkən'vɛnʃənl] ADJ poco convenzionale.

un·con·vinced [ˌʌnkən'vɪnst] ADJ: **to be** *or* **remain unconvinced** non essere convinto(-a).

un·con·vinc·ing [ˌʌnkən'vɪnsɪŋ] ADJ non convincente, poco persuasivo(-a).

un·con·vinc·ing·ly [ˌʌnkən'vɪnsɪŋlɪ] ADV in modo poco convincente.

un·cooked [ʌn'kʊkt] ADJ crudo(-a).

un·co·op·era·tive [ˌʌnkəʊ'ɒpərətɪv] ADJ restio(-a) a collaborare.

un·co·ordi·nat·ed, unco-ordinated [ˌʌnkəʊ'ɔːdɪˌneɪtɪd] ADJ (*person, movements, efforts*) scoordinato(-a).

un·cork [ʌn'kɔːk] VT stappare.

un·cor·robo·rat·ed [ˌʌnkə'rɒbəˌreɪtɪd] ADJ (*evidence, confession*) non convalidato(-a).

un·cou·ple [ʌn'kʌpl] VT sganciare.

un·couth [ʌn'kuːθ] ADJ (*old*) maleducato(-a), rozzo(-a), villano(-a).

un·cov·er [ʌn'kʌvəʳ] VT **a** (*find out*) scoprire; (: *scandal*) portare alla luce **b** (*remove coverings of*) scoprire; (: *drain*) scoperchiare.

un·criti·cal [ʌn'krɪtɪkəl] ADJ (*pej: reader, admirer*) poco critico(-a); (: *approach, attitude*) acritico(-a); **to be uncritical of** avere poco senso critico nei confronti di.

un·crossed [ʌn'krɒst] ADJ (*cheque*) non sbarrato(-a).

un·crush·able [ʌn'krʌʃəbl] ADJ (*material*) ingualcibile.

unc·tion ['ʌŋkʃən] N: **extreme unction** (*Rel*) estrema unzione *f*.

unc·tu·ous ['ʌŋktjʊəs] ADJ (*liter*) untuoso(-a).

un·cul·ti·vat·ed [ʌn'kʌltɪˌveɪtɪd] ADJ incolto(-a).

un·cul·tured [ʌn'kʌltʃəd] ADJ (*person*) senza cultura, ignorante; (*mind*) poco raffinato(-a).

un·curl [ʌn'kɜ:l] VT (*gen*) srotolare; (*one's fingers*) distendere.

un·dam·aged [ʌn'dæmɪdʒd] ADJ (*goods*) in buono stato; (*fig: reputation*) intatto(-a).

un·dat·ed [ʌn'deɪtɪd] ADJ senza data.

un·daunt·ed [ʌn'dɔ:ntɪd] ADJ: **undaunted by** per nulla intimidito(-a) da; **to carry on undaunted** continuare imperterrito(-a).

un·de·cid·ed [ˌʌndɪ'saɪdɪd] ADJ (*person*) indeciso(-a), incerto(-a); (*matter*) irrisolto(-a); **we are still undecided whether to go** siamo ancora indecisi se andare o meno.

un·de·feat·ed [ˌʌndɪ'fi:tɪd] ADJ imbattuto(-a).

un·de·fined [ˌʌndɪ'faɪnd] ADJ (*idea*) non ben definito(-a); (*number, quantity*) indefinito(-a); (*feeling*) vago(-a).

un·de·liv·ered [ˌʌndɪ'lɪvəd] ADJ non recapitato(-a); **if undelivered return to sender** in caso di mancato recapito rispedire al mittente.

un·de·mand·ing [ˌʌndɪ'mændɪŋ] ADJ (*job, task, book, programme*) poco impegnativo(-a); (*person*) poco esigente.

un·demo·crat·ic [ˌʌndɛməʊ'krætɪk] ADJ antidemocratico (-a).

un·de·mon·stra·tive [ˌʌndɪ'mɒnstrətɪv] ADJ riservato(-a), poco espansivo(-a).

un·de·ni·able [ˌʌndɪ'naɪəbl] ADJ innegabile, indiscutibile, fuori discussione.

un·de·ni·ably [ˌʌndɪ'naɪəblɪ] ADV innegabilmente, indiscutibilmente.

un·der ['ʌndər] ⟦1⟧ PREP **a** (*beneath*) sotto; **under the table** sotto il tavolo; **from under the bed** da sotto il letto; **it's under there** sta lì sotto; **under water** sott'acqua

b (*less than*) meno di; (: *in rank, scale*) al di sotto di; **in under 2 hours** in meno di 2 ore; **people under 50 (years old)** gente al di sotto dei 50 (anni)

c (*fig: sb's leadership, sign of zodiac, letter in catalogue*) sotto; **under anaesthetic** sotto anestesia; **under discussion/repair/construction** in discussione/riparazione/costruzione; **to study under sb** studiare con qn *or* sotto la guida di qn; **under the circumstances** date le circostanze; **under the Romans** sotto i Romani; **under a false name** sotto falso nome; **he has 30 workers under him** ha 30 operai sotto di sé

d (*according to*) secondo; **under the new law** secondo quanto previsto dalla nuova legge.

⟦2⟧ ADV **a** (*beneath: position*) sotto; (: *direction*) sotto, di sotto; **to be under** (*under anaesthetic*) essere sotto anestesia

b (*less*) al di sotto, meno; **girls of 14 and under** ragazze dai 14 anni in giù.

under... ['ʌndər] PREF **a** (*in rank*) sotto..., aiuto; (*in age*): **the under-15s** i ragazzi al di sotto dei 15 anni; **under-gardener** aiuto giardiniere *m* **b** (*insufficiently*) sotto...; **underprepared** poco preparato(-a); **undercooked** poco cotto(-a).

under·achieve [ˌʌndərə'tʃi:v] VI non dare il meglio di sé.

under·achiev·er [ˌʌndərə'tʃi:vər] N chi non dà il meglio di sé.

♦ **under-age** [ˌʌndər'eɪdʒ] ADJ minorenne.

under·arm ['ʌndərˌɑ:m] ⟦1⟧ ADV (*throw*) da sotto in su.
⟦2⟧ ADJ (*temperature*) ascellare; (*deodorant*) per le ascelle; (*bowling*) da sotto in su; **underarm hair** i peli delle ascelle; **underarm serve** (*Tennis*) servizio dal basso verso l'alto.

under·belly ['ʌndəˌbɛlɪ] N (*Anat*) basso ventre *m*; (*fig*) punto debole; **the soft underbelly** il ventre molle.

under·capi·tal·ized [ˌʌndə'kæpɪtəˌlaɪzd] ADJ (*Fin*) carente di capitali.

under·carriage ['ʌndəˌkærɪdʒ] N (*Brit Aer*) carrello (d'atterraggio).

under·charge [ˌʌndə'tʃɑ:dʒ] VT far pagare di meno a.

under·class ['ʌndəˌklɑ:s] N sottoproletariato.

under·clothes ['ʌndəˌkləʊðz] NPL biancheria *fsg* intima.

under·coat ['ʌndəˌkəʊt] N (*of paint*) mano *f* di fondo.

under·cover [ˌʌndə'kʌvər] ADJ (*agent*) segreto(-a); (*meeting*) clandestino(-a).

under·cur·rent ['ʌndəˌkʌrənt] N corrente *f* sottomarina; (*fig*) vena nascosta.

under·cut [ˌʌndə'kʌt] (*pt, pp* **undercut**) VT (*Comm*) vendere a minor prezzo di.

under·de·vel·oped [ˌʌndədɪ'vɛləpt] ADJ (*country*) sotto-sviluppato(-a); (*baby, muscles, photo*) non ben sviluppato(-a).

under·dog ['ʌndəˌdɒg] N: **the underdog** (*in fight, contest*) il/la più debole; (*in society*) l'oppresso(-a); (*in family, organization*) l'ultima ruota del carro.

under·done [ˌʌndə'dʌn] ADJ (*Culin: food*) poco cotto(-a); (: *steak*) al sangue.

under·dressed [ˌʌndə'drɛst] ADJ non vestito(-a) in modo adeguato.

under·em·ployed [ˌʌndərɪm'plɔɪd] ADJ sottoccupato(-a).

♦ **under-employment** [ˌʌndərɪm'plɔɪmənt] N sottoccupazione *f*.

under·es·ti·mate [ˌʌndər'ɛstɪˌmeɪt] VT sottovalutare.

under·es·ti·ma·tion [ˌʌndərɛstɪ'meɪʃən] N (*also:* **underestimate**) sottovalutazione *f*.

under·ex·posed [ˌʌndərɪks'pəʊzd] ADJ (*Phot*) sottoesposto(-a).

under·ex·po·sure [ˌʌndərɪk'spəʊʒər] N (*Phot*) sottoesposizione *f*.

under·fed [ˌʌndə'fɛd] ADJ malnutrito(-a).

under·felt ['ʌndəˌfɛlt] N *feltro su cui poggia la moquette*.

♦ **under-financed** [ˌʌndə'faɪnænst] ADJ senza fondi sufficienti.

under·floor heat·ing [ˌʌndəflɔ:'hi:tɪŋ] N riscaldamento a pavimento.

under·foot [ˌʌndə'fʊt] ADV sotto i piedi, per terra; **to trample underfoot** (*also fig*) calpestare; **the children are always getting underfoot** i bambini sono sempre tra i piedi.

♦ **under-funded** [ˌʌndə'fʌndɪd] ADJ insufficientemente sovvenzionato(-a).

under·gar·ment ['ʌndəˌgɑ:mənt] N indumento intimo.

under·go [ˌʌndə'gəʊ] (*pt* **underwent**, *pp* **undergone** [ˌʌndə'gɒn]) VT sottoporsi a, subire; **to undergo changes** essere sottoposto(-a) a modifiche; **the car is under-going repairs** la macchina è in riparazione.

under·gradu·ate [ˌʌndə'grædjʊɪt] ⟦1⟧ N (*also:* **undergrad**) studente(-essa) universitario(-a).
⟦2⟧ ADJ (*opinion, attitudes*) degli studenti; **undergraduate courses** corsi *mpl* di laurea.

under·ground [*adj* 'ʌndəˌgraʊnd; *adv* ˌʌndə'graʊnd] ⟦1⟧ ADJ (*passage, cave, railway*) sotterraneo(-a); (*fig: political movement, press*) clandestino(-a); (: *Art, Cine*) under-

ground *inv.*

2 ADV sottoterra; (*fig*) clandestinamente; **to go underground** (*fig*) entrare in clandestinità.

3 N **a** (*Brit Rail*): **the Underground** la metropolitana; **to go by underground** *or* **on the underground** andare in *or* con la metropolitana

b (*Mil, Pol*): **the underground** il movimento clandestino, la resistenza; (*Art*) la controcultura, l'underground *m*.

under·growth ['ʌndəˌgrəʊθ] N sottobosco.

under·hand [ˌʌndə'hænd], **under·hand·ed** [ˌʌndə'hændɪd] ADJ (*method*) equivoco(-a), poco pulito(-a); (*trick*) subdolo(-a), mancino(-a).

under·in·sured [ˌʌndərɪn'ʃʊəd] ADJ sottoassicurato(-a).

under·lay ['ʌndəˌleɪ] N = **underfelt**.

under·lie [ˌʌndə'laɪ] (*pt* **underlay** [ˌʌndə'leɪ], *pp* **underlain** [ˌʌndə'leɪn]) VT essere alla base di; **an underlying nervousness** un nervosismo di fondo; **the underlying cause** il motivo di fondo.

under·line [ˌʌndə'laɪn] VT (*also fig*) sottolineare.

under·ling ['ʌndəlɪŋ] N (*pej*) galoppino, tirapiedi *m inv*.

under·manned [ˌʌndə'mænd] ADJ carente di personale.

under·men·tioned [ˌʌndə'menʃənd] ADJ (riportato(-a)) qui sotto *or* qui di seguito.

under·mine [ˌʌndə'maɪn] VT (*fig*) minare; (: *authority*) pregiudicare.

under·neath [ˌʌndə'niːθ] **1** PREP sotto, al di sotto di.

2 ADV sotto, di sotto.

3 N: **the underneath** la parte di sotto.

under·nour·ished [ˌʌndə'nʌrɪʃt] ADJ denutrito(-a).

under·nour·ish·ment [ˌʌndə'nʌrɪʃmənt] N sottoalimentazione *f*, denutrizione *f*.

under·paid [ˌʌndə'peɪd] **1** PT, PP of **underpay**.

2 ADJ mal pagato(-a), sottopagato(-a).

under·pants ['ʌndəˌpænts] NPL (*Brit*) mutande *fpl* da uomo; (*Am*) mutande *fpl* da donna.

under·pass ['ʌndəˌpɑːs] N (*for cars*) sottopassaggio; (*for pedestrians*) sottopassaggio pedonale.

under·pay [ˌʌndə'peɪ] (*pt, pp* **underpaid**) VT pagare male, sottopagare.

under·pin [ˌʌndə'pɪn] VT (*Archit*) puntellare; (*fig: argument, case*) corroborare.

under·play [ˌʌndə'pleɪ] VT minimizzare; **to underplay a role** (*Theatre*) recitare una parte con misura.

under·popu·lat·ed [ˌʌndə'pɒpjʊˌleɪtɪd] ADJ scarsamente popolato(-a), sottopopolato(-a).

under·price [ˌʌndə'praɪs] VT vendere sottoprezzo.

under·priced [ˌʌndə'praɪst] ADJ (*product*) in vendita a un prezzo inferiore al dovuto.

under·privi·leged [ˌʌndə'prɪvɪlɪdʒd] ADJ svantaggiato(-a); **the underprivileged** i diseredati *mpl*.

under·rate [ˌʌndə'reɪt] VT sottovalutare.

under·score [ˌʌndə'skɔː'] VT sottolineare.

under·seal ['ʌndəˌsiːl] VT (*Aut*) trattare con antiruggine.

under·sec·re·tary [ˌʌndə'sekrətrɪ] N sottosegretario.

under·sell [ˌʌndə'sel] (*pt, pp* **undersold**) VT (*competitors*) vendere a prezzi più bassi di; (*fig*) non valorizzare a sufficienza.

under·sexed [ˌʌndə'sekst] ADJ con scarsa libido.

under·shirt ['ʌndəˌʃɜːt] N (*Am*) maglietta, canottiera.

under·shorts ['ʌndəˌʃɔːts] NPL (*Am*) mutande *fpl* da uomo.

under·side ['ʌndəˌsaɪd] N parte *f* di sotto.

under·signed ['ʌndəˌsaɪnd] ADJ, N sottoscritto(-a); **I the undersigned** io sottoscritto.

under·sized [ˌʌndə'saɪzd] ADJ (*pej*) troppo piccolo(-a).

under·skirt ['ʌndəˌskɜːt] N sottogonna.

under·sold [ˌʌndə'səʊld] PT, PP of **undersell**.

under·staffed [ˌʌndə'stɑːft] ADJ a corto di personale.

under·stand [ˌʌndə'stænd] (*pt, pp* **understood**) **1** VT **a** (*gen*) capire; **to make o.s. understood** farsi capire; **I can't understand a word of it** non ci capisco un'acca; **I don't understand why** ... non capisco perché...; **she understands children** capisce i bambini; **we understand one another** ci capiamo (tra di noi); **he doesn't understand how I feel** non mi capisce quello che provo; **I can understand his wanting to go** posso ben capire il suo desiderio di andarsene; **is that understood?** è chiaro?; **I wish it to be understood that** ... vorrei che fosse chiaro che...; **understood!** (*agreed*) intesi!

b (*believe*) credere; **we understood we were to be paid** a quanto avevamo capito dovevamo essere pagati; **I understand you have been absent** mi risulta che lei è stato assente; **it's understood that** ... resta inteso che...; **he let it be understood that he was leaving** ha dato a intendere che stava per partire; **she is understood to be ill** pare che stia poco bene.

2 VI capire; **I quite understand** capisco benissimo, s'immagini; **she was, I understand, a Catholic** era, se non sbaglio, cattolica.

under·stand·able [ˌʌndə'stændəbl] ADJ comprensibile.

under·stand·ably [ˌʌndə'stændəblɪ] ADV comprensibilmente.

under·stand·ing [ˌʌndə'stændɪŋ] **1** ADJ (*person*) comprensivo(-a); (*smile*) indulgente.

2 N **a** (*intelligence*) comprensione *f*; **his understanding of the situation is that** ... il modo in cui vede la situazione è che...; **it was my understanding that** ... quello che ho capito io era che...+ *sub*

b (*sympathy*) simpatia, comprensione *f*

c (*agreement*) accordo, intesa; **to come to an understanding with sb** giungere ad un accordo con qn; **on the understanding that he pays** a patto che *or* a condizione che paghi lui.

under·state [ˌʌndə'steɪt] VT minimizzare, sminuire.

under·state·ment ['ʌndəˌsteɪtmənt] N understatement *m inv*; **that's an understatement!** a dir poco!

under·stood [ˌʌndə'stʊd] **1** PT, PP of **understand**.

2 ADJ inteso(-a); (*implied*) sottinteso(-a).

under·study ['ʌndəˌstʌdɪ] **1** N (*Theatre*) doppio.

2 VT sostituire.

under·take [ˌʌndə'teɪk] (*pt* **undertook**, *pp* **undertaken** [ˌʌndə'teɪkən]) VT (*task*) intraprendere; (*responsibility*) assumersi; **to undertake to do sth** impegnarsi a fare qc.

under·tak·er ['ʌndəˌteɪkə'] N impresario di pompe funebri.

under·tak·ing [ˌʌndə'teɪkɪŋ] N **a** (*task*) impresa; **it is quite an undertaking!** è una bella impresa! **b** (*promise*) promessa, assicurazione *f*; **to give an undertaking that** ... dare la propria parola che... .

under·things ['ʌndəˌθɪŋz] NPL (*fam*) biancheria *fsg* intima.

under·tone ['ʌndəˌtəʊn] N **a** (*low voice*) tono sommesso; **in an undertone** a mezza voce, sottovoce, a voce bassa

b : **undertones** NPL (*comic, religious*) sfumature *fpl*.

under·took [ˌʌndə'tʊk] PT of **undertake**.

under·tow ['ʌndəˌtəʊ] N (*of wave*) corrente *f* di risacca; (*undercurrent*) risucchio.

under·used [ˌʌndə'juːzd] ADJ (*resources, facilities*) poco sfruttato(-a).

under·value [ˌʌndə'væljuː] VT (*person, contribution*) svalu-

tare, sottovalutare; (*Comm, Fin*) deprezzare, svalutare.

under·vest ['ʌndəˌvɛst] N (*Brit*) maglietta intima.

under·wa·ter [ˌʌndə'wɔːtəʳ] **1** ADJ (*swimming, photography*) subacqueo(-a); (*exploration*) sottomarino(-a). **2** ADV sott'acqua.

under·way [ˌʌndə'weɪ] ADJ: **to be underway** essere in corso.

under·wear ['ʌndəˌwɛəʳ] N biancheria intima.

under·weight [ˌʌndə'weɪt] ADJ (*person*) sottopeso *inv*; (*thing*) al di sotto del giusto peso.

under·went [ˌʌndə'wɛnt] PT of **undergo**.

under·world ['ʌndəˌwɜːld] N: **the underworld** (*criminal*) la malavita; (*hell*) gli inferi *mpl*.

under·write ['ʌndəˌraɪt] (*pt* **underwrote** ['ʌndəˌrəʊt], *pp* **underwritten** ['ʌndəˌrɪtn]) VT (*Fin*) sottoscrivere; (*Insurance*) assicurare.

under·writ·er ['ʌndəˌraɪtəʳ] N (*Insurance*) assicuratore(-trice); (*Fin*) sottoscrittore(-trice).

un·de·served [ˌʌndɪ'zɜːvd] ADJ immeritato(-a).

un·des·erved·ly [ˌʌndɪ'zɜːvɪdlɪ] ADV (*rewarded*) immeritatamente; (*punished*) ingiustamente.

un·de·serv·ing [ˌʌndɪ'zɜːvɪŋ] ADJ: **to be undeserving of** non meritare, non essere degno(-a) di.

un·de·sir·able [ˌʌndɪ'zaɪərəbl] **1** ADJ (*effects*) indesiderato(-a); (*behaviour, habits, friendship*) discutibile. **2** N persona indesiderabile.

un·de·tect·ed [ˌʌndɪ'tɛktɪd] ADJ: **to go undetected** passare inosservato(-a).

un·de·vel·oped [ˌʌndɪ'vɛləpt] ADJ (*land, resources*) non sfruttato(-a).

un·did [ʌn'dɪd] PT of **undo**.

un·dies ['ʌndɪz] NPL (*fam*) biancheria *fsg* intima (*da donna*).

un·dig·ni·fied [ʌn'dɪgnɪˌfaɪd] ADJ (*person*) senza dignità, poco dignitoso(-a); (*manner, action*) indecoroso(-a), sconveniente.

un·di·lut·ed [ˌʌndaɪ'luːtɪd] ADJ (*concentrated*) non diluito (-a); (*fig: bliss, love*) totale, assoluto(-a).

un·dip·lo·matic [ˌʌndɪplə'mætɪk] ADJ poco diplomatico (-a).

un·dis·cern·ing [ˌʌndɪ'sɜːnɪŋ] ADJ (*reader*) poco selettivo (-a); (*critic*) di scarso acume.

un·dis·charged [ˌʌndɪs'tʃɑːdʒd] ADJ (*debt*) non pagato (-a); (*bankrupt*) non riabilitato(-a).

un·dis·ci·plined [ʌn'dɪsɪplɪnd] ADJ indisciplinato(-a).

un·dis·cov·ered [ˌʌndɪs'kʌvəd] ADJ (*area*) inesplorato(-a); (*work of art*) ignoto(-a).

un·dis·crimi·nat·ing [ˌʌndɪs'krɪmɪˌneɪtɪŋ] ADJ (*choice*) indiscriminato(-a); (*person*) che non fa discriminazioni; (*taste*) non selettivo(-a).

un·dis·guised [ˌʌndɪs'gaɪzd] ADJ (*dislike, amusement*) palese.

un·dis·mayed [ˌʌndɪs'meɪd] ADJ (*liter*): **to be undismayed at** non lasciarsi impressionare da.

un·dis·put·ed [ˌʌndɪs'pjuːtɪd] ADJ incontrastato(-a), indiscusso(-a).

un·dis·tin·guished [ˌʌndɪs'tɪŋgwɪʃt] ADJ (*pej: person*) qualunque, mediocre; (*: career, design, performance*) mediocre; **an undistinguished poet** un poetucolo; **an undistinguished wine** un vino qualsiasi.

un·dis·turbed [ˌʌndɪs'tɜːbd] ADJ **a** (*sleep*) tranquillo(-a); **to work undisturbed** lavorare in pace; **to leave sth undisturbed** lasciare qc così com'è **b** (*unworried*): **undisturbed (by)** indifferente (a); **the Prime Minister is undisturbed by rising inflation** l'aumento dell'inflazione non turba minimamente il primo ministro.

un·di·vid·ed [ˌʌndɪ'vaɪdɪd] ADJ: **I want your undivided attention** esigo (da voi) la massima attenzione.

undo [ʌn'duː] (*pt* **undid**, *pp* **undone**) VT **a** (*unfasten: button*) sbottonare; (*: shoelaces*) slacciare; (*: knot*) sciogliere; (*: parcel*) aprire; (*: knitting*) disfare **b** (*reverse: action, wrong*) riparare (a); (*spoil*) rovinare.

un·do·ing [ʌn'duːɪŋ] N rovina.

un·done [ʌn'dʌn] **1** PP of **undo**. **2** ADJ (*unfastened: button*) sbottonato(-a); **to come undone** slacciarsi; **to leave undone** (*shirt*) lasciare aperto(-a) *or* sbottonato(-a); (*job*) non fare, lasciare da fare.

un·doubt·ed [ʌn'daʊtɪd] ADJ indubbio(-a).

un·doubt·ed·ly [ʌn'daʊtɪdlɪ] ADV indubbiamente, senza dubbio.

un·dreamed [ʌn'driːmd], **un·dreamt** [ʌn'drɛmt] ADJ: **undreamed of** mai sognato(-a).

un·dress [ʌn'drɛs] **1** VT spogliare. **2** VI (*also:* **get undressed**) spogliarsi, svestirsi.

un·drink·able [ʌn'drɪŋkəbl] ADJ (*unpalatable*) imbevibile; (*polluted*) non potabile.

un·due [ʌn'djuː] ADJ eccessivo(-a).

un·du·lat·ing ['ʌndjʊˌleɪtɪŋ] ADJ (*surface*) ondulato(-a); (*countryside*) collinoso(-a); (*sea*) ondeggiante.

un·du·ly [ʌn'djuːlɪ] ADV troppo, eccessivamente.

un·dy·ing [ʌn'daɪɪŋ] ADJ (*liter: fame, glory*) imperituro(-a); (*: love*) eterno(-a).

un·earned [ʌn'ɜːnd] ADJ (*praise, respect*) immeritato(-a).
♦ **unearned income** N reddito non da lavoro.

un·earth [ʌn'ɜːθ] VT dissotterrare; (*fig: secret*) scoprire; (*: object*) scovare; (*: evidence*) portare alla luce.

un·earth·ly [ʌn'ɜːθlɪ] ADJ (*eerie: brightness*) innaturale; (*: noise, sound*) spettrale; **unearthly hour** (*fam*) ora impossibile.

un·ease [ʌn'iːz] N (*nervousness*) disagio; (*tension*) tensione *f*.

un·easi·ly [ʌn'iːzɪlɪ] ADV (*sleep*) male; (*glance, look*) con apprensione; **to be uneasily balanced** essere in equilibrio precario; **she glanced uneasily at him** gli lanciò uno sguardo inquieto.

un·easi·ness [ʌn'iːzɪnɪs] N disagio.

un·easy [ʌn'iːzɪ] ADJ (*person: worried*) inquieto(-a), preoccupato(-a), agitato(-a); (*: ill at ease*) a disagio; (*calm, peace*) precario(-a); (*night, sleep*) agitato(-a); (*silence*) imbarazzato(-a); **to feel uneasy about doing sth** non sentirsela di fare qc; **to become uneasy about sb/sth** cominciare a preoccuparsi per qn/qc; **to have an uneasy conscience** non avere la coscienza a posto.

un·eat·en [ʌn'iːtn] ADJ (*breakfast, lunch*) non mangiato (-a); (*food, sandwiches*) avanzato(-a); **she left the steak uneaten** non ha nemmeno toccato la bistecca.

un·eco·nom·ic [ˌʌniːkə'nɒmɪk] ADJ (*wasteful: method, process*) antieconomico(-a); (*unprofitable*) poco redditizio(-a).

un·eco·nomi·cal [ˌʌniːkə'nɒmɪkəl] ADJ (*car, machine*) poco economico(-a); (*use*) dispendioso(-a).

un·edu·cat·ed [ʌn'ɛdjʊˌkeɪtɪd] ADJ (*person*) senza istruzione, incolto(-a); (*speech*) popolare.

un·emo·tion·al [ˌʌnɪ'məʊʃənl] ADJ (*person*) freddo(-a), impassibile; (*account*) distaccato(-a).

un·emo·tion·al·ly [ˌʌnɪ'məʊʃnəlɪ] ADV (*see adj*) impassibilmente, in modo distaccato.

un·em·ploy·able [ˌʌnɪm'plɔɪəbl] ADJ non adatto(-a) a nessun lavoro.

un·em·ployed [ˌʌnɪm'plɔɪd] **1** ADJ disoccupato(-a),

senza lavoro.

2 NPL: **the unemployed** i disoccupati.

un·em·ploy·ment [ˌʌnɪm'plɔɪmənt] N disoccupazione *f.*

♦ **unemployment benefit**, (*Am*) **unemployment compensation** N sussidio di disoccupazione.

un·end·ing [ʌn'ɛndɪŋ] ADJ interminabile, senza fine.

un·en·dur·able [ˌʌnɪn'djʊərəbl] ADJ (*frm*) insopportabile.

un·en·ter·pris·ing [ʌn'ɛntəˌpraɪzɪŋ] ADJ poco intraprendente.

un·en·thu·si·as·tic [ˌʌnɪnˌθuːzɪ'æstɪk] ADJ poco entusiasta.

un·en·thu·si·as·ti·cal·ly [ˌʌnɪnˌθuːzɪ'æstɪkəlɪ] ADV senza entusiasmo.

un·en·vi·able [ʌn'ɛnvɪəbl] ADJ poco invidiabile.

un·equal [ʌn'iːkwəl] ADJ (*length, objects*) disuguale; (*amounts*) diverso(-a); (*division of labour*) ineguale; **to be unequal to a task** (*frm*) non essere all'altezza di un compito.

un·equalled, (*Am*) **un·equaled** [ʌn'iːkwəld] ADJ senza pari, insuperato(-a).

un·equivo·cal [ˌʌnɪ'kwɪvəkəl] ADJ (*answer*) inequivocabile; (*person*) esplicito(-a), chiaro(-a).

un·equivo·cal·ly [ˌʌnɪ'kwɪvəkəlɪ] ADV inequivocabilmente.

un·err·ing [ʌn'ɜːrɪŋ] ADJ (*aim, taste, instinct*) infallibile.

UNESCO [juː'nɛskəʊ] N ABBR (= *United Nations Educational, Scientific and Cultural Organization*) U.N.E.S.C.O. *f.*

un·ethi·cal [ʌn'ɛθɪkəl] ADJ (*methods*) moralmente inaccettabile; (*doctor's behaviour*) contrario(-a) all'etica professionale.

un·even [ʌn'iːvən] ADJ (*heartbeat, work, quality, performance*) irregolare; (*thickness*) ineguale; (*ground*) disuguale, accidentato(-a).

un·even·ly [ʌn'iːvənlɪ] ADV (*distributed, spread*) in modo irregolare.

un·even·ness [ʌn'iːvənnɪs] N irregolarità.

un·event·ful [ˌʌnɪ'vɛntfʊl] ADJ senza sorprese, tranquillo (-a).

un·ex·cep·tion·able [ˌʌnɪk'sɛpʃnəbl] (*frm*) ADJ (*behaviour*) irreprensibile; (*style*) ineccepibile; (*speech*) inappuntabile.

un·ex·cep·tion·al [ˌʌnɪk'sɛpʃənl] ADJ che non ha niente d'eccezionale.

un·ex·cit·ing [ˌʌnɪk'saɪtɪŋ] ADJ (*news*) poco emozionante; (*film, evening*) poco interessante; (*person*) scialbo(-a).

un·ex·pec·ted [ˌʌnɪks'pɛktɪd] ADJ inatteso(-a), imprevisto (-a).

un·ex·pect·ed·ly [ˌʌnɪks'pɛktɪdlɪ] ADV (*happen*) inaspettatamente; (*die*) improvvisamente, inaspettatamente; (*arrive*) senza preavviso.

un·ex·plained [ˌʌnɪks'pleɪnd] ADJ inspiegato(-a).

un·ex·plod·ed [ˌʌnɪks'pləʊdɪd] ADJ inesploso(-a).

un·ex·posed [ˌʌnɪks'pəʊzd] ADJ (*film*) vergine.

un·ex·pressed [ˌʌnɪks'prɛst] ADJ inespresso(-a).

un·ex·pur·gat·ed [ʌn'ɛkspɜːˌgeɪtɪd] ADJ (*text, version*) integrale.

un·fail·ing [ʌn'feɪlɪŋ] ADJ (*frm: remedy*) sicuro(-a), infallibile; (: *humour, supply, energy*) inesauribile; (: *zeal, courage*) senza riserve.

un·fail·ing·ly [ʌn'feɪlɪŋlɪ] ADV immancabilmente, senza fallo.

un·fair [ʌn'fɛəʳ] ADJ (*comp* **-er**, *superl* **-est**) (*person, decision, criticism*) ingiusto(-a); (*means, tactics*) sleale; (*competition*) scorretto(-a); **it's unfair that ...** non è giusto che... + *sub*; **to be unfair to sb** essere ingiusto(-a) verso qn.

♦ **unfair dismissal** N (*Industry*) licenziamento ingiustificato.

un·fair·ly [ʌn'fɛəlɪ] ADV (*treat, criticize*) ingiustamente; (*play*) scorrettamente.

un·fair·ness [ʌn'fɛənɪs] N (*see adj*) ingiustizia; slealtà; scorrettezza.

un·faith·ful [ʌn'feɪθfʊl] ADJ: **unfaithful (to sb)** infedele (a qn).

un·fa·mil·iar [ˌʌnfə'mɪljəʳ] ADJ (*subject*) sconosciuto(-a); (*experience*) insolito(-a); (*surroundings*) estraneo(-a); **to be unfamiliar with sth** non essere pratico(-a) di qc, non avere familiarità con qc.

un·fash·ion·able [ʌn'fæʃnəbl] ADJ (*clothes*) fuori moda; (*district*) non alla moda; **these trousers are unfashionable** questi pantaloni sono fuori moda *or* non vanno più.

un·fas·ten [ʌn'fɑːsn] VT (*buttons, seatbelt*) slacciare; (*scarf, rope*) sciogliere; (*gate*) aprire.

un·fath·om·able [ʌn'fæðəməbl] ADJ (*depths, mystery*) insondabile, imperscrutabile; (*person*) impenetrabile.

un·fa·vour·able, (*Am*) **un·fa·vor·able** [ʌn'feɪvərəbl] ADJ (*circumstances, climate*) sfavorevole; (*report, impression*) negativo(-a).

un·fa·vour·ably, (*Am*) **un·fa·vor·ably** [ʌn'feɪvərəblɪ] ADV (*judge, see*) in senso sfavorevole; (*speak, review*) sfavorevolmente; **to look unfavourably upon** vedere di mal occhio.

un·feel·ing [ʌn'fiːlɪŋ] ADJ insensibile, duro(-a).

un·femi·nine [ʌn'fɛmɪnɪn] ADJ poco femminile.

un·fet·tered [ʌn'fɛtəd] ADJ: **unfettered (by)** senza restrizioni (da parte di).

un·fin·ished [ʌn'fɪnɪʃt] ADJ (*task*) non finito(-a); (*letter*) da finire; (*business*) in sospeso; (*symphony*) incompiuto (-a); **I have some unfinished business to attend to** ho un affare in sospeso da regolare.

un·fit [ʌn'fɪt] ADJ (*unsuitable*): **unfit for** inadatto(-a) a; (*Sport: injured*) non in grado di giocare (*or* correre); (*out of training*) non in forma; **unfit for habitation** inabitabile; **to be unfit to do sth** non essere in grado di fare qc; **unfit for military service** inabile (al servizio militare).

un·flag·ging [ʌn'flægɪŋ] ADJ instancabile.

un·flap·pable [ʌn'flæpəbl] ADJ calmo(-a), composto(-a).

un·flat·ter·ing [ʌn'flætərɪŋ] ADJ (*dress, hairstyle*) che non dona; (*portrait, light*) poco lusinghiero(-a).

un·flinch·ing [ʌn'flɪntʃɪŋ] ADJ risoluto(-a), che non indietreggia.

un·fo·cused, **un·fo·cussed** [ʌn'fəʊkəst] ADJ (*camera*) non a fuoco; (*gaze, eyes*) perso(-a) nel vuoto; (*aims, desire*) vago(-a).

un·fold [ʌn'fəʊld] 1 VT (*newspaper, map, wings*) spiegare, aprire; (*arms*) distendere; (*fig: plan, idea*) esporre; (: *secret*) svelare. 2 VI (*flower*) schiudersi; (*fig: view*) spiegarsi; (: *story*) svolgersi.

un·fore·see·able [ˌʌnfɔː'siːəbl] ADJ imprevedibile.

un·fore·seen [ˌʌnfɔː'siːn] ADJ imprevisto(-a).

un·for·get·table [ˌʌnfə'gɛtəbl] ADJ indimenticabile.

un·for·giv·able [ˌʌnfə'gɪvəbl] ADJ imperdonabile.

un·for·giv·ably [ˌʌnfə'gɪvəblɪ] ADV imperdonabilmente.

un·for·giv·ing [ˌʌnfə'gɪvɪŋ] ADJ implacabile, irremovibile.

un·for·mat·ted [ʌn'fɔːmætɪd] ADJ (*disk, text*) non formattato(-a).

un·formed [ʌn'fɔːmd] ADJ (*clay*) informe, senza forma; (*character*) non ancora formato(-a); (*ideas*) non definito(-a).

un·for·tu·nate [ʌn'fɔːtʃnɪt] 1 ADJ (*deserving of pity*)

povero(-a); (*unlucky*) sfortunato(-a); (*unsuitable, regrettable*: *event, remark*) infelice; (*habit*) deplorevole; **it is most unfortunate that he left** ci rincresce molto che se ne sia andato.

[2] N sfortunato(-a), sventurato(-a).

un·for·tu·nate·ly [ʌnˈfɔːtʃnɪtlɪ] ADV purtroppo, sfortunatamente; **an unfortunately worded speech** un discorso infelice.

un·found·ed [ʌnˈfaʊndɪd] ADJ infondato(-a), senza fondamento.

un·freeze [ʌnˈfriːz] (*pt* **unfroze** [ʌnˈfrəʊz], *pp* **unfrozen** [ʌnˈfrəʊzn]) VT (*thaw*) sgelare; (*assets, bank account*) scongelare, sbloccare.

un·fre·quent·ed [ʌnfrɪˈkwɛntɪd] ADJ poco frequentato (-a).

un·friend·ly [ʌnˈfrɛndlɪ] ADJ (*comp* **-ier**, *superl* **-iest**) (*person*): **unfriendly (to)** scostante (con), antipatico(-a) (con); (*attitude, reception*) ostile, poco amichevole; (*remark*) scortese.

un·ful·filled [ˌʌnfʊlˈfɪld] ADJ **a** (*ambition*) non realizzato (-a); (*prophecy*) che non si è avverato(-a); (*desire*) insoddisfatto(-a); (*promise*) non mantenuto(-a); (*terms of contract*) non rispettato(-a) **b** (*person*) frustrato(-a).

un·furl [ʌnˈfɜːl] VT (*flag, banner*) spiegare.

un·fur·nished [ʌnˈfɜːnɪʃt] ADJ non ammobiliato(-a).

un·gain·ly [ʌnˈgeɪnlɪ] ADJ sgraziato(-a), goffo(-a).

un·gen·er·ous [ʌnˈdʒɛnərəs] ADJ (*frm: miserly, uncharitable*) poco generoso(-a).

un·get·at·able [ˌʌngɛtˈætəbl] ADJ (*fam*) inaccessibile.

un·god·ly [ʌnˈgɒdlɪ] ADJ (*person, language, action*) empio (-a); (*fam*): **at an ungodly hour** a un'ora allucinante.

un·gov·ern·able [ʌnˈgʌvənəbl] ADJ (*country*) ingovernabile; (*passion*) incontrollabile.

un·gra·cious [ʌnˈgreɪʃəs] ADJ sgarbato(-a), scortese.

un·gra·cious·ly [ʌnˈgreɪʃəslɪ] ADV sgarbatamente, scortesemente.

un·gram·mati·cal [ˌʌngrəˈmætɪkəl] ADJ sgrammaticato (-a), scorretto(-a).

un·grate·ful [ʌnˈgreɪtfʊl] ADJ ingrato(-a).

un·grate·ful·ly [ʌnˈgreɪtfəlɪ] ADV in modo ingrato, senza riconoscenza.

un·grudg·ing [ʌnˈgrʌdʒɪŋ] ADJ (*help*) dato(-a) volentieri; (*praise*) sincero(-a).

un·guard·ed [ʌnˈgɑːdɪd] ADJ **a** (*Mil*) indifeso(-a), sguarnito(-a) **b** (*fig: careless*) imprudente; **in an unguarded moment** in un momento di distrazione.

un·ham·pered [ʌnˈhæmpəd] ADJ: **unhampered by** libero (-a) da, non ostacolato(-a) da.

un·hap·pi·ly [ʌnˈhæpɪlɪ] ADV (*miserably*) tristemente, con aria infelice; (*unfortunately*) purtroppo, sfortunatamente; **she was unhappily married** non era felice con suo marito.

un·hap·pi·ness [ʌnˈhæpɪnɪs] N infelicità.

un·hap·py [ʌnˈhæpɪ] ADJ (*comp* **-ier**, *superl* **-iest**) **a** (*sad*) infelice; **an unhappy state of affairs** una situazione spiacevole

b (*not pleased*) scontento(-a); (*uneasy, worried*) preoccupato(-a), inquieto(-a); **unhappy with** (*arrangements*) insoddisfatto(-a) di; **to be unhappy about sth/doing sth** non essere contento(-a) di qc/di fare qc

c (*unfortunate: remark, choice*) infelice; (: *coincidence*) sfortunato(-a).

un·harmed [ʌnˈhɑːmd] ADJ (*person*) illeso(-a), sano(-a) e salvo(-a), incolume; (*thing*) intatto(-a).

UNHCR [juːɛneɪtʃsiːˈɑːʳ] N ABBR (= *United Nations High*

Commission for Refugees) Alto Commissariato delle Nazioni Unite per Rifugiati.

un·healthy [ʌnˈhɛlθɪ] ADJ (*comp* **-ier**, *superl* **-iest**) (*person*) malaticcio(-a), poco sano(-a); (*climate, place, complexion*) malsano(-a); (*curiosity, interest*) morboso(-a).

unheard-of [ʌnˈhɜːdɒv] ADJ (*unprecedented*) inaudito(-a), senza precedenti; (*outrageous*) dell'altro mondo.

un·heed·ed [ʌnˈhiːdɪd] ADJ: **the warning went unheeded** l'avvertimento fu ignorato.

un·help·ful [ʌnˈhɛlpfʊl] ADJ (*person*) poco disponibile, di scarso aiuto; (*remark, advice*) di scarso aiuto.

un·hesi·tat·ing [ʌnˈhɛzɪˌteɪtɪŋ] ADJ (*reply, offer*) pronto (-a), immediato(-a); (*loyalty, faith*) che non vacilla; **she was unhesitating in her support** non ha esitato a darmi (*or* dargli *etc*) il suo appoggio.

un·hesi·tat·ing·ly [ʌnˈhɛzɪˌteɪtɪŋlɪ] ADV senza esitazione.

un·hin·dered [ʌnˈhɪndəd] ADJ (*progress*) senza ostacoli; (*movement*) senza impedimenti; **to be unhindered by moral scruples** agire senza farsi scrupoli.

un·hinge [ʌnˈhɪndʒ] VT (*door*) scardinare; (*fig: mind*) sconvolgere; (: *person*) far perdere la ragione a.

un·ho·ly [ʌnˈhəʊlɪ] ADJ profano(-a); **at an unholy hour** (*fam*) ad un'ora indecente; **an unholy alliance** una coalizione *f* paradossale.

un·hook [ʌnˈhʊk] VT (*remove: picture*) staccare; (: *trailer*) sganciare; (*undo: gate*) aprire; (: *dress*) slacciare.

unhoped-for [ˌʌnˈhəʊptfɔːʳ] ADJ insperato(-a).

un·hur·ried [ʌnˈhʌrɪd] ADJ (*person, steps*) tranquillo(-a); **after a little unhurried reflection** dopo averci pensato con calma.

un·hur·ried·ly [ʌnˈhʌrɪdlɪ] ADV senza fretta, con comodo.

un·hurt [ʌnˈhɜːt] ADJ incolume, illeso(-a).

un·hy·gien·ic [ˌʌnhaɪˈdʒiːnɪk] ADJ (*conditions*) non igienico (-a); (*surroundings*) insalubre.

UNICEF [ˈjuːnɪˌsɛf] N ABBR (= *United Nations International Children's Emergency Fund*) U.N.I.C.E.F. *f*.

uni·corn [ˈjuːnɪˌkɔːn] N unicorno.

un·iden·ti·fi·able [ˌʌnaɪdɛntɪˈfaɪəbl] ADJ non identificabile.

un·iden·ti·fied [ˌʌnaɪˈdɛntɪˌfaɪd] ADJ non identificato(-a).

♦ **unidentified flying object** N oggetto volante non identificato.

uni·di·rec·tion·al [ˌjuːnɪdɪˈrɛkʃənl] ADJ unidirezionale.

uni·fi·ca·tion [ˌjuːnɪfɪˈkeɪʃən] N unificazione *f*.

uni·form [ˈjuːnɪˌfɔːm] [1] N (*Mil, school*) uniforme *f*, divisa; **in full uniform** in alta uniforme; **in uniform** in divisa; **out of uniform** in borghese.

[2] ADJ (*colour, acceleration*) uniforme.

uni·formed [ˈjuːnɪˌfɔːmd] ADJ (*police*) in divisa.

uni·form·ity [ˌjuːnɪˈfɔːmɪtɪ] N uniformità.

uni·form·ly [ˈjuːnɪˌfɔːmlɪ] ADV uniformemente.

uni·fy [ˈjuːnɪˌfaɪ] VT (*country*) unire; (*different parts, systems*) unificare.

uni·lat·er·al [ˌjuːnɪˈlætərəl] ADJ unilaterale.

uni·lat·er·al·ly [ˌjuːnɪˈlætərəlɪ] ADV unilateralmente.

un·im·agi·nable [ˌʌnɪˈmædʒnəbl] ADJ inimmaginabile, inconcepibile.

un·im·agi·na·tive [ˌʌnɪˈmædʒnətɪv] ADJ privo(-a) di fantasia.

un·im·agi·na·tive·ly [ˌʌnɪˈmædʒnətɪvlɪ] ADV senza fantasia.

un·im·paired [ˌʌnɪmˈpɛəd] ADJ (*health, mental powers*) buono(-a) come prima; (*quality*) non danneggiato(-a).

un·im·peach·able [ˌʌnɪmˈpiːtʃəbl] ADJ (*honesty, character*) irreprensibile; (*conduct*) incensurabile; (*witness*) al di

sopra di ogni sospetto.

un·im·ped·ed [ˌʌnɪm'piːdɪd] [1] ADJ (*development, access, growth*) senza impedimenti *or* costrizioni.

[2] ADV (*proceed, continue*) senza impacci.

un·im·por·tant [ˌʌnɪm'pɔːtənt] ADJ (*matter*) senza importanza, di scarsa importanza; (*detail*) trascurabile.

un·im·pressed [ˌʌnɪm'prɛst] ADJ (*unmoved*) niente affatto colpito(-a), indifferente; (*unconvinced*) niente affatto convinto(-a).

un·im·pres·sive [ˌʌnɪm'prɛsɪv] ADJ (*person, sight*) che lascia indifferente; (*amount*) insignificante; (*achievement, result*) poco notevole; (*argument, performance*) poco convincente.

un·in·formed [ˌʌnɪn'fɔːmd] ADJ (*person*) non informato (-a), non al corrente; (*opinion, guess*) non fondato(-a) sulla conoscenza dei fatti.

un·in·hab·it·able [ˌʌnɪn'hæbɪtəbl] ADJ inabitabile.

un·in·hab·it·ed [ˌʌnɪn'hæbɪtɪd] ADJ (*house*) disabitato(-a); (*island*) deserto(-a).

un·in·hib·it·ed [ˌʌnɪn'hɪbɪtɪd] ADJ (*person, behaviour*) disinibito(-a), senza inibizioni; (*emotion, laughter*) sfrenato(-a).

un·ini·ti·at·ed [ˈʌnɪ'ɪʃɪˌeɪtɪd] [1] ADJ non iniziato(-a). [2] NPL: **the uninitiated** i profani.

un·in·jured [ʌn'ɪndʒəd] ADJ (*person*) incolume; (*reputation*) salvo(-a).

un·in·spired [ˌʌnɪn'spaɪəd] ADJ (*poem, performance*) privo (-a) d'ispirazione, piatto(-a); **he was uninspired by the essay topic** l'argomento del tema non l'ha ispirato.

un·in·spir·ing [ˌʌnɪn'spaɪərɪŋ] ADJ banale.

un·in·tel·li·gent [ˌʌnɪn'tɛlɪdʒənt] ADJ poco intelligente.

un·in·tel·li·gible [ˌʌnɪn'tɛlɪdʒəbl] ADJ incomprensibile, inintelligibile.

un·in·tend·ed [ˌʌnɪn'tɛndɪd] ADJ non voluto(-a); **it was quite unintended** non l'ho (*or* l'ha *etc*) fatto apposta.

un·in·ten·tion·al [ˌʌnɪn'tɛnʃənl] ADJ involontario(-a).

un·in·ten·tion·al·ly [ˌʌnɪn'tɛnʃnəlɪ] ADV senza volerlo, involontariamente.

un·in·ter·est·ed [ʌn'ɪntrɪstɪd] ADJ (*person, attitude*) indifferente; **to be uninterested in politics** non interessarsi di politica.

un·in·ter·est·ing [ʌn'ɪntrɪstɪŋ] ADJ (*person*) poco interessante; (*book, offer*) privo(-a) d'interesse.

un·in·ter·rupt·ed [ˌʌnɪntə'rʌptɪd] ADJ (*line, series*) ininterrotto(-a); (*work*) senza interruzioni; **to have an uninterrupted night's sleep** dormire una notte di filato.

un·in·ter·rupt·ed·ly [ˌʌnɪntə'rʌptɪdlɪ] ADV ininterrottamente.

un·in·vit·ed [ˌʌnɪn'vaɪtɪd] ADJ (*guest*) non invitato(-a); (*criticism, attention*) non richiesto(-a); **to arrive uninvited (at sb's house)** piovere in casa (a qn); **to help o.s. to sth uninvited** servirsi di qc senza chiedere il permesso.

un·in·vit·ing [ˌʌnɪn'vaɪtɪŋ] ADJ (*place, food*) poco invitante; (*offer*) poco allettante.

Un·ion ['juːnjən] N: **the Union** (*Am*) gli stati dell'Unione; (*Brit*) *unificazione della Gran Bretagna e dell'Irlanda del Nord dal 1920*.

un·ion ['juːnjən] [1] N **a** (*also:* **trade union**) sindacato **b** (*gen, also Pol*) unione *f* **c** (*club, society*) associazione *f*, circolo.

[2] ADJ (*leader, movement*) sindacale.

♦ **union-bashing** ['juːnjənˌbæʃɪŋ] N (*Brit fam*) propaganda antisindacale.

♦ **union card** N tessera del sindacato.

Un·ion·ist ['juːnjənɪst] N (*Pol: in Northern Ireland*) unionista

m/f.

un·ion·ist ['juːnjənɪst] N = **trade unionist.**

un·ion·ize ['juːnjəˌnaɪz] VT sindacalizzare, organizzare in sindacato.

♦ **Union Jack** N *bandiera nazionale britannica*.

♦ **Union of Soviet Socialist Republics** N Unione *f* delle Repubbliche Socialiste Sovietiche.

♦ **union shop** N *stabilimento in cui tutti gli operai sono tenuti ad aderire ad un sindacato*.

unique [juː'niːk] ADJ unico(-a).

unique·ly [juː'niːklɪ] ADV (*talented*) eccezionalmente; (*confined*) unicamente; **this is a uniquely western phenomenon** è un fenomeno limitato al mondo occidentale.

unique·ness [juː'niːknɪs] N singolarità, unicità.

uni·sex ['juːnɪˌsɛks] ADJ unisex *inv*.

Uni·son ['juːnɪzn] N (*Brit*) *sindacato generale dei funzionari pubblici e degli operatori sanitari*.

uni·son ['juːnɪzn] N: **in unison** (*Mus, fig*) all'unisono.

unit ['juːnɪt] N **a** (*gen, Elec, Math, Mil*) unità *f inv*; **monetary/linguistic unit** unità monetaria/linguistica; **unit of length** unità di lunghezza

b (*division, section*) reparto; (*of furniture*) elemento (componibile); (*team, squad*) squadra; **production unit** reparto *m* produzione *inv*; **the basic social unit** il nucleo sociale di base; **research unit** (*personnel*) équipe *f inv*; (*building*) sede *f* di ricerca.

♦ **unit cost** N (*Industry*) costo unitario.

unite [juː'naɪt] [1] VT (*join: parts, pieces*) unire; (*unify: parts of country*) unificare.

[2] VI (*join*) unirsi; (*companies*) fondersi; **to unite with sb/in doing** *or* **to do sth** unirsi a qn/per fare qc.

unit·ed [juː'naɪtɪd] ADJ (*family, people*) unito(-a); (*effort*) unitario(-a); (*efforts*) comune, congiunto(-a).

♦ **United Arab Emirates** NPL: **the United Arab Emirates** gli Emirati Arabi Uniti.

♦ **United Kingdom** N: **the United Kingdom** il Regno Unito.

♦ **United Nations** N: **the United Nations** le Nazioni Unite, l'Organizzazione *f* delle Nazioni Unite.

♦ **United States** N: **the United States (of America)** gli Stati Uniti (d'America).

♦ **unit price** N (*Industry*) prezzo unitario.

♦ **unit trust** N (*Brit Fin*) fondo d'investimento.

unity ['juːnɪtɪ] N (*in party, country*) unità; (*of members, individuals*) unione *f*; **in unity** in armonia, in pieno accordo.

Univ. ABBR = **university.**

uni·ver·sal [ˌjuːnɪ'vɜːsəl] ADJ (*phenomenon, disapproval*) generale; (*language, values*) universale; **a universal favourite** un(-a) gran favorito(-a).

♦ **universal joint, universal coupling** N (*Tech*) giunto cardanico.

uni·ver·sal·ly [ˌjuːnɪ'vɜːsəlɪ] ADV (*known*) universalmente; (*accepted*) all'unanimità.

uni·verse ['juːnɪˌvɜːs] N: **the universe** l'universo.

uni·ver·sity [ˌjuːnɪ'vɜːsɪtɪ] [1] N università *f inv*; **Oxford University** l'Università di Oxford; **to be at/go to university** essere/andare all'università.

[2] ADJ (*student, professor, education*) universitario(-a).

♦ **university degree** N (diploma *m* di) laurea.

♦ **university year** N anno accademico.

un·just [ʌn'dʒʌst] ADJ ingiusto(-a); **to be unjust to sb** essere ingiusto(-a) con *or* verso qn.

un·jus·ti·fi·able [ʌn'dʒʌstɪˌfaɪəbl] ADJ ingiustificabile.

un·jus·ti·fi·ably [ʌnˈdʒʌstɪˌfaɪəblɪ] ADV senza motivo.
un·jus·ti·fied [ʌnˈdʒʌstɪˌfaɪd] ADJ (remark) ingiustificato
(-a), immotivato(-a); (suspicion) infondato(-a); (Typ:
text) non giustificato(-a).
un·just·ly [ʌnˈdʒʌstlɪ] ADV ingiustamente.
un·kempt [ʌnˈkɛmpt] ADJ (hair) scarmigliato(-a), spetti-
nato(-a); (appearance) trasandato(-a).
un·kind [ʌnˈkaɪnd] ADJ (comp -er, superl -est) (person,
remark) poco gentile, scortese; (: stronger) villano(-a);
(fate, blow) crudele; **the sun can be unkind to delicate
skins** il sole può far male alle pelli delicate.
un·kind·ly [ʌnˈkaɪndlɪ] ADV (speak) in modo sgarbato;
(treat) male; **don't take it unkindly if ...** non te la
prendere se... .
un·kind·ness [ʌnˈkaɪndnɪs] N sgarbatezza; (stronger)
cattiveria.
un·know·able [ʌnˈnəʊəbl] ADJ inconoscibile.
un·know·ing [ʌnˈnəʊɪŋ] ADJ inconsapevole, ignaro(-a).
un·know·ing·ly [ʌnˈnəʊɪŋlɪ] ADV senza accorgersene,
senza saperlo.
un·known [ʌnˈnəʊn] 1 ADJ sconosciuto(-a), ignoto(-a);
the murderer is as yet unknown ancora non si sa chi sia
l'assassino; **it's unknown for her to get to work on time**
quando mai è arrivata al lavoro in orario?; **unknown
quantity** (Math, fig) incognita; **his intentions are
unknown to me** non conosco le sue intenzioni; **a
substance unknown to scientists** una sostanza ignota
agli scienziati.
2 ADV: **unknown to me** a mia insaputa; **unknown to them
he was nearby** era nelle vicinanze, a loro insaputa.
3 N a (person) sconosciuto(-a)
b (Math) incognita; **the unknown** l'ignoto.
♦ **Unknown Soldier, Unknown Warrior** N: the
Unknown Soldier il Milite Ignoto.
un·lad·en [ʌnˈleɪdn] ADJ (ship, weight) a vuoto.
un·lady·like [ʌnˈleɪdɪˌlaɪk] ADJ (pej) non da signora
(perbene); **it's unladylike to swear** una vera signora non
dice le parolacce.
un·law·ful [ʌnˈlɔːfʊl] ADJ illecito(-a), illegale.
un·law·ful·ly [ʌnˈlɔːfəlɪ] ADV illegalmente.
un·lead·ed [ʌnˈlɛdɪd] N (also: unleaded petrol) benzina
senza piombo.
un·leash [ʌnˈliːʃ] VT (dog) sguinzagliare; (fig) scatenare.
un·leav·ened [ʌnˈlɛvnd] ADJ (bread) azzimo(-a), non
lievitato(-a).
un·less [ʌnˈlɛs] CONJ a meno che non + sub, se non + indic, a
meno di + infin; **we won't get there on time unless we
leave earlier** non arriveremo in tempo a meno che
partire prima or a meno che non partiamo prima;
unless otherwise stated salvo indicazione contraria;
unless I am mistaken se non mi sbaglio.
un·li·censed [ˌʌnˈlaɪsənst] ADJ (vehicle) senza bollo; (Brit:
hotel, restaurant) senza licenza per la vendita di alcolici.
un·like [ˌʌnˈlaɪk] 1 ADJ diverso(-a), dissimile; **that photo
is quite unlike her** quella foto non le somiglia affatto;
it's quite unlike him to do that non è da lui fare una cosa
simile.
2 PREP a differenza di, contrariamente a; **I, unlike
others ...** diversamente dagli or a differenza degli altri,
io...;
un·like·li·hood [ʌnˈlaɪklɪhʊd], **un·like·li·ness**
[ʌnˈlaɪklɪnɪs] N improbabilità.
un·like·ly [ʌnˈlaɪklɪ] ADJ (comp -ier, superl -iest) (happening)
improbabile; (explanation) inverosimile; **in the unlikely
event that it does happen ...** dovesse succedere, cosa

assai improbabile...; **it is unlikely that he will come** OR he
is unlikely to come è poco probabile che venga.
un·lim·it·ed [ʌnˈlɪmɪtɪd] ADJ (time, power) illimitato(-a);
(wealth) smisurato(-a).
un·lined [ʌnˈlaɪnd] ADJ (paper) senza righe; (garment)
senza fodera, sfoderato(-a).
un·list·ed [ʌnˈlɪstɪd] ADJ (item) non elencato(-a); (Stock
Exchange: share) non quotato(-a); (Am Telec) non sull'e-
lenco del telefono.
un·lit [ʌnˈlɪt] ADJ (lamp) spento(-a); (room) senza luce;
(road) non illuminato(-a).
un·load [ʌnˈləʊd] 1 VT a scaricare b (fam: get rid of): **to
unload onto sb** (problem, children) scaricare su qn.
2 VI scaricare.
un·load·ing [ʌnˈləʊdɪŋ] N scarico.
un·lock [ʌnˈlɒk] VT aprire; **she left the door unlocked** non
ha chiuso la porta a chiave.
unlooked-for [ˌʌnˈlʊktfɔː'] ADJ inaspettato(-a), inatteso
(-a).
un·loose [ʌnˈluːs], **un·loos·en** [ʌnˈluːsn] VT (hair) sciogliere; (knot) slegare, sciogliere.
un·lov·able [ʌnˈlʌvəbl] ADJ antipatico(-a).
un·loved [ʌnˈlʌvd] ADJ non amato(-a); **to feel unloved**
sentirsi non amato(-a).
un·lucki·ly [ʌnˈlʌkɪlɪ] ADV purtroppo, sfortunatamente;
unluckily for her per sua sfortuna.
un·lucky [ʌnˈlʌkɪ] ADJ (comp -ier, superl -iest) (person, day)
sfortunato(-a); (decision) infausto(-a), infelice; (number,
object) che porta sfortuna or male, di malaugurio; **she
was unlucky enough to meet him** ha avuto la sfortuna di
incontrarlo; **to be unlucky** (person) essere sfortunato
(-a), non avere fortuna; **it's unlucky to walk under a
ladder** porta sfortuna or male passare sotto una scala.
un·made [ʌnˈmeɪd] ADJ (bed) disfatto(-a).
un·man·age·able [ʌnˈmænɪdʒəbl] ADJ (unwieldy: tool, vehicle) poco maneggevole; (: parcel, size) ingombrante;
(uncontrollable: teenage child) difficile; (: hair) ribelle; (:
situation) difficile da gestire.
un·manned [ˌʌnˈmænd] ADJ (spacecraft) senza equipaggio.
un·man·ner·ly [ʌnˈmænəlɪ] ADJ maleducato(-a), scortese.
un·marked [ʌnˈmɑːkt] ADJ (unstained) pulito(-a), senza
macchie; (unblemished: face, body) senza rughe; (without
marking: linen) senza cifre; (: banknote) non segnato(-a);
(uncorrected: essay) non corretto(-a); **unmarked police
car** auto f civetta inv.
un·mar·ried [ʌnˈmærɪd] ADJ (man) celibe, non sposato;
(woman) nubile, non sposata.
♦ **unmarried mother** N ragazza f madre inv.
un·mask [ʌnˈmɑːsk] VT (fig) smascherare.
un·matched [ʌnˈmætʃt] ADJ senza pari, impareggiabile.
un·men·tion·able [ʌnˈmɛnʃnəbl] ADJ (topic) tabù inv;
(vice, disease) innominabile; (word) irripetibile.
un·mer·ci·ful [ʌnˈmɜːsɪfʊl] ADJ spietato(-a).
un·mer·ci·fully [ʌnˈmɜːsɪfəlɪ] ADV (tease, bully) senza
pietà.
un·mind·ful [ʌnˈmaɪndfʊl] ADJ: **to be unmindful of** (frm)
essere incurante di.
un·mis·tak·able, un·mis·take·able [ˌʌnmɪsˈteɪkəbl] ADJ
(person, sound) inconfondibile; (displeasure, meaning)
indubbio(-a), lampante.
un·mis·tak·ably, un·mis·take·ably [ˌʌnmɪsˈteɪkəblɪ] ADV
senza timore di sbagliarsi, inconfondibilmente; **unmistakably clear** inequivocabilmente chiaro(-a).
un·miti·gat·ed [ʌnˈmɪtɪˌgeɪtɪd] ADJ (disaster, nonsense)

totale, completo(-a); (*criminal, scoundrel*) incallito(-a).

un·mo·ti·vat·ed [ʌn'məʊtɪˌveɪtɪd] ADJ immotivato(-a).

un·moved [ʌn'muːvd] ADJ: **unmoved (by)** indifferente (a).

un·mu·si·cal [ʌn'mjuːzɪkəl] ADJ (*sound*) disarmonico(-a); (*person*) che non ha orecchio.

un·named [ʌn'neɪmd] ADJ (*fear, object*) senza nome; (*donor, author*) anonimo(-a).

un·natu·ral [ʌn'nætʃrəl] ADJ (*gen*) innaturale; (*affected*) affettato(-a); (*abnormal*) non normale; **it's unnatural for him to behave like that** non è da lui comportarsi così.

un·natu·ral·ly [ʌn'nætʃrəlɪ] ADV in modo innaturale; **the house was unnaturally silent** la casa era stranamente silenziosa; **not unnaturally she was worried** è comprensibile che fosse preoccupata.

un·nec·es·sari·ly [ʌn'nɛsɪsərɪlɪ] ADV (*worry, suffer*) inutilmente; (*large, long, difficult*) eccessivamente.

un·nec·es·sary [ʌn'nɛsɪsərɪ] ADJ (*superfluous*) non necessario(-a), superfluo(-a); (*useless*) inutile; **it was unnecessary to be rude!** non c'era bisogno di essere sgarbato!; **it's unnecessary for you to attend** non è necessario che tu intervenga.

un·nerve [ʌn'nɜːv] VT (*subj: accident*) sgomentare; (: *hostile attitude*) bloccare; (*experience*) far sentire disagio.

unnerving [ʌn'nɜːvɪŋ] ADJ inquietante.

un·no·ticed [ʌn'nəʊtɪst] ADJ: **to go** *or* **pass unnoticed** passare inosservato(-a).

un·num·bered [ʌn'nʌmbəd] ADJ (*without a number: house*) senza numero, non numerato(-a); (*frm: innumerable*) innumerevole.

UNO [ˌjuːɛn'əʊ] N ABBR (= *United Nations Organization*) O.N.U. *f*.

un·ob·jec·tion·able [ˌʌnəb'dʒɛkʃnəbl] ADJ (*person*) ammodo *inv*; (*conduct*) ineccepibile.

un·ob·serv·ant [ˌʌnəb'zɜːvənt] ADJ: **to be unobservant** non avere spirito di osservazione.

un·ob·served [ˌʌnəb'zɜːvd] ADJ inosservato(-a); **to go unobserved** passare inosservato(-a).

un·ob·struct·ed [ˌʌnəb'strʌktɪd] ADJ (*vision*) libero(-a); (*road*) sgombro(-a); (*pipe*) non ostruito(-a), non bloccato(-a); **an unobstructed view** un'ampia visuale.

un·ob·tain·able [ˌʌnəb'teɪnəbl] ADJ (*food, materials*) introvabile; **this number is unobtainable** (*Telec*) è impossibile ottenere questo numero.

un·ob·tru·sive [ˌʌnəb'truːsɪv] ADJ discreto(-a).

un·ob·tru·sive·ly [ˌʌnəb'truːsɪvlɪ] ADV (*discreetly*) con discrezione.

un·oc·cu·pied [ʌn'ɒkjʊˌpaɪd] ADJ (*house*) vuoto(-a); (*seat, table, also Mil: zone*) libero(-a), non occupato(-a); (*person: not busy*) libero(-a), senza impegni.

un·of·fi·cial [ˌʌnə'fɪʃəl] ADJ (*visit*) privato(-a), non ufficiale; (*unconfirmed: report, news*) ufficioso(-a); **in an unofficial capacity** in veste ufficiosa; **unofficial strike** sciopero a sorpresa *or* selvaggio.

un·of·fi·cial·ly [ˌʌnə'fɪʃəlɪ] ADV ufficiosamente.

un·opened [ʌn'əʊpənd] ADJ (*letter*) chiuso(-a); (*present*) ancora incartato(-a); (*bottle, tin*) non aperto(-a).

un·op·posed [ˌʌnə'pəʊzd] ADJ (*enter, be elected*) senza incontrare opposizione; **the motion was unopposed by the committee** il comitato non si è opposto alla mozione.

un·or·gan·ized [ʌn'ɔːgəˌnaɪzd] ADJ (*person*) disorganizzato(-a); (*essay, life*) mal organizzato(-a).

un·origi·nal [ˌʌnə'rɪdʒɪnəl] ADJ poco originale, privo(-a) di originalità.

un·ortho·dox [ʌn'ɔːθəˌdɒks] ADJ poco ortodosso(-a).

un·os·ten·ta·tious [ˌʌnɒstən'teɪʃəs] ADJ modesto(-a), semplice.

un·pack [ʌn'pæk] **1** VT (*suitcases*) disfare; (*belongings*) sballare.
2 VI disfare le valige *or* i bagagli.

un·paid [ʌn'peɪd] ADJ (*bill, debt*) da pagare; (*holiday*) non pagato(-a); (*work*) non retribuito(-a).

un·pal·at·able [ʌn'pælətəbl] ADJ (*food*) immangiabile; (*drink*) imbevibile; (*fig: truth*) sgradevole.

un·par·al·leled [ʌn'pærəˌlɛld] ADJ senza pari, impareggiabile.

un·par·don·able [ʌn'pɑːdnəbl] ADJ imperdonabile.

un·par·lia·men·ta·ry [ˌʌnpɑːləˈmɛntərɪ] ADJ (*Brit*: *language, behaviour*) non consono(-a) alla sede parlamentare.

un·pat·ri·ot·ic [ˌʌnpætrɪˈɒtɪk] ADJ (*person*) poco patriottico(-a); (*speech, attitude*) antipatriottico(-a).

un·per·turbed [ˌʌnpə'tɜːbd] ADJ imperturbato(-a), imperterrito(-a); **unperturbed by sth** per nulla scosso(-a) da qc.

un·pick [ʌn'pɪk] VT (*seam*) disfare; (*stitches*) togliere.

un·pin [ʌn'pɪn] VT (*dress*) togliere gli spilli a; (*hair*) togliere le forcine a; (*notice*) staccare.

un·planned [ʌn'plænd] ADJ (*visit*) imprevisto(-a); (*baby, pregnancy*) non previsto(-a).

un·pleas·ant [ʌn'plɛznt] ADJ (*smell, task*) sgradevole, spiacevole; (*person, remark*) antipatico(-a); (*day, experience*) brutto(-a); **to be unpleasant to sb** essere villano(-a) con qn.

un·pleas·ant·ly [ʌn'plɛzntlɪ] ADV in modo poco piacevole; **the room smelt unpleasantly of fish** c'era un odore sgradevole di pesce nella stanza; **it was unpleasantly close to the truth** era spiacevolmente vicino al vero; **it's unpleasantly hot in here** qui dentro fa troppo caldo, per i miei gusti.

un·pleas·ant·ness [ʌn'plɛzntnɪs] N (*bad feeling, quarrelling*) tensioni *fpl*; (*nastiness: of smell, event*) sgradevolezza; (: *of person*) antipatia.

un·plug [ʌn'plʌg] VT staccare (la spina di).

un·pol·ished [ʌn'pɒlɪʃt] ADJ (*shoes, furniture*) non lucidato(-a); (*diamond*) grezzo(-a); (*manners, person*) rozzo(-a).

un·pol·lut·ed [ˌʌnpə'luːtɪd] ADJ non inquinato(-a).

un·popu·lar [ʌn'pɒpjʊlə] ADJ (*gen*) impopolare; **to be unpopular with sb** (*person, law*) non riscuotere l'approvazione di qn; **to make o.s. unpopular (with)** rendersi antipatico(-a) (a); (*subj: politician*) alienarsi le simpatie (di); **I'm unpopular with the boss at the moment** non sono nelle grazie del capo in questo momento; **he's unpopular with the rest of the class** è mal visto dal resto della classe.

un·popu·lar·ity [ˌʌnpɒpjʊ'lærɪtɪ] N impopolarità.

un·prec·edent·ed [ʌn'prɛsɪdəntɪd] ADJ senza precedenti.

un·pre·dict·able [ˌʌnprɪ'dɪktəbl] ADJ imprevedibile.

un·preju·diced [ʌn'prɛdʒʊdɪst] ADJ (*not biased*) obiettivo(-a), imparziale; (*having no prejudices*) senza pregiudizi.

un·pre·pared [ˌʌnprɪ'pɛəd] ADJ (*person*) impreparato(-a); (*speech*) improvvisato(-a); **it caught me unprepared** mi ha trovato impreparato; **he was unprepared for her reaction** la sua reazione lo colse alla sprovvista.

un·pre·pos·sess·ing [ˌʌnpriːpə'zɛsɪŋ] ADJ poco attraente.

un·pre·ten·tious [ˌʌnprɪ'tɛnʃəs] ADJ senza pretese.

un·prin·ci·pled [ʌn'prɪnsɪpld] ADJ senza scrupoli.

un·print·able [ʌn'prɪntəbl] ADJ non pubblicabile; (*fig: word, remark*) irripetibile.

un·pro·duc·tive [ˌʌnprə'dʌktɪv] ADJ improduttivo(-a); (*discussion*) sterile.

un·pro·fes·sion·al [ˌʌnprə'fɛʃənl] ADJ: **unprofessional conduct** scorrettezza professionale.

un·prof·it·able [ʌn'prɒfɪtəbl] ADJ (*financially*) non redditizio(-a); (: *job, deal*) poco lucrativo(-a); (*fig*) infruttuoso(-a), poco produttivo(-a); **an unprofitable afternoon** un pomeriggio poco produttivo.

UNPROFOR [ʌn'prəʊfɔ:'] N ABBR (= *United Nations Protection Force*) U.N.P.R.O.F.O.R. *m*.

un·prom·is·ing [ʌn'prɒmɪsɪŋ] ADJ poco promettente.

un·pro·nounce·able [ˌʌnprə'naʊnsəbl] ADJ impronunciabile.

un·pro·tect·ed [ˌʌnprə'tɛktɪd] ADJ (*town*) indifeso(-a); (*house*) esposto(-a), non riparato(-a); (*sex*) non protetto(-a).

un·pro·voked [ˌʌnprə'vəʊkt] ADJ (*attack*) non provocato (-a); (*unpleasant remark*) ingiustificato(-a).

un·pub·lished [ʌn'pʌblɪʃt] ADJ inedito(-a).

un·pun·ished [ʌn'pʌnɪʃt] ADJ: **to go unpunished** restare impunito(-a).

un·quali·fied [ʌn'kwɒlɪˌfaɪd] ADJ **a** (*worker*) non qualificato(-a); (*in professions*) non diplomato(-a), non abilitato(-a); (*applicant*) senza i requisiti necessari **b** (*absolute*: *assent, denial*) incondizionato(-a); (: *admiration*) senza riserve; (: *success, disaster*) completo(-a), assoluto(-a).

un·ques·tion·able [ʌn'kwɛstʃənəbl] ADJ (*fact*) incontestabile, indiscutibile; (*honesty*) indiscusso(-a).

un·ques·tion·ably [ʌn'kwɛstʃənəblɪ] ADV indiscutibilmente.

un·ques·tioned [ʌn'kwɛstʃənd] ADJ (*popularity, virtue*) indiscusso(-a); (*statement*) incontestato(-a).

un·ques·tion·ing [ʌn'kwɛstʃənɪŋ] ADJ (*obedience, acceptance*) cieco(-a).

un·rav·el [ʌn'rævəl] **1** VT (*knitting*) disfare; (*wool*) dipanare, districare; (*threads*) sfilare, sbrogliare; (*fig*: *mystery*) risolvere; (: *plot*) venire a capo di.
2 VI (*knitting*) disfarsi; (*threads*) sbrogliarsi.

un·read [ʌn'rɛd] ADJ non letto(-a); **a pile of unread magazines** una pila di riviste non lette; **I returned the book unread** ho restituito il libro senza leggerlo.

un·read·able [ʌn'ri:dəbl] ADJ illeggibile.

un·ready [ʌn'rɛdɪ] ADJ impreparato(-a).

un·real [ʌn'rɪəl] ADJ irreale.

un·re·al·is·tic [ˌʌnrɪə'lɪstɪk] ADJ (*idea*) illusorio(-a); (*estimate*) non realistico(-a); **you're being unrealistic if you think ...** ti fai delle illusioni se credi... .

un·re·al·ity [ˌʌnrɪ'ælɪtɪ] N irrealtà.

un·rea·son·able [ʌn'ri:znəbl] ADJ (*person, idea, behaviour*) irragionevole; (*price, time*) irragionevole, assurdo(-a); **it is unreasonable to expect that ...** è un po' troppo aspettarsi che...+ *sub*; **he makes unreasonable demands on me** pretende troppo da me; **he was most unreasonable about it** non ha voluto sentire ragioni.

un·rea·son·ably [ʌn'ri:znəblɪ] ADV (*behave*) irragionevolmente; (*demand*) eccessivamente; **not unreasonably** a ragione.

un·rea·son·ing [ʌn'ri:znɪŋ] ADJ irragionevole.

un·rec·og·niz·able [ʌn'rɛkəgˌnaɪzəbl] ADJ irriconoscibile.

un·rec·og·nized [ʌn'rɛkəgˌnaɪzd] ADJ (*talent, genius*) misconosciuto(-a); (*Pol*: *regime*) non riconosciuto(-a) ufficialmente; **he walked along the street unrecognized by passers-by** ha camminato per la strada senza che nessuno lo riconoscesse.

un·re·cord·ed [ˌʌnrɪ'kɔ:dɪd] ADJ non documentato(-a), non registrato(-a).

un·re·fined [ˌʌnrɪ'faɪnd] ADJ (*petroleum*) greggio(-a); (*sugar*) non raffinato(-a); (*person, manners*: *coarse*) rozzo(-a).

un·re·hearsed [ˌʌnrɪ'hɜ:st] ADJ (*Theatre*) improvvisato (-a); (*spontaneous*) imprevisto(-a).

un·re·lat·ed [ˌʌnrɪ'leɪtɪd] ADJ: **unrelated (to)** (*unconnected*) senza nesso or rapporto (con); (*by family*) non imparentato(-a) (con), senza legami di parentela (con).

un·re·lent·ing [ˌʌnrɪ'lɛntɪŋ] ADJ (*rain, heat*) incessante; (*activity*) senza tregua; (*attack*) che non dà tregua; (*hatred*) irriducibile, implacabile; (*person*) spietato(-a).

un·re·li·abil·ity [ˌʌnrɪlaɪə'bɪlɪtɪ] N scarsa affidabilità.

un·re·li·able [ˌʌnrɪ'laɪəbl] ADJ (*person*) su cui non si può contare or fare affidamento; (*source*) inattendibile; (*firm*) poco serio(-a); (*car, machine*) che non dà affidamento.

un·re·lieved [ˌʌnrɪ'li:vd] ADJ (*pain, gloom*) costante; (*anguish, depression*) totale; (*boredom*) mortale; (*monotony*) ininterrotto(-a); (*colour*) uniforme.

un·re·mark·able [ˌʌnrɪ'mɑ:kəbl] ADJ mediocre.

un·re·mark·ed [ˌʌnrɪ'mɑ:kt] ADJ: **to go** or **remain unremarked** passare inosservato(-a).

un·re·mit·ting [ˌʌnrɪ'mɪtɪŋ] ADJ (*activity*) senza sosta, incessante; (*efforts, demands*) costante; (*hatred*) irriducibile, implacabile.

un·re·peat·able [ˌʌnrɪ'pi:təbl] ADJ irripetibile.

un·re·pent·ant [ˌʌnrɪ'pɛntənt] ADJ (*sinner*) impenitente; (*believer, supporter*) irriducibile; **to be unrepentant about sth** non mostrare un'ombra di rimorso per qc.

un·rep·re·senta·tive [ˌʌnrɛprɪ'zɛntətɪv] ADJ (*untypical*) atipico(-a), poco rappresentativo(-a).

un·rep·re·sent·ed [ˌʌnˌrɛprɪ'zɛntɪd] ADJ non rappresentato(-a).

un·re·quit·ed [ˌʌnrɪ'kwaɪtɪd] ADJ (*liter*: *love*) non ricambiato(-a), non corrisposto(-a).

un·re·served [ˌʌnrɪ'zɜ:vd] ADJ **a** (*seat*) non prenotato (-a), non riservato(-a) **b** (*approval, admiration*) senza riserve.

un·re·serv·ed·ly [ˌʌnrɪ'zɜ:vɪdlɪ] ADV (*without reservation*) senza riserve; (*frankly*) francamente.

un·re·solved [ˌʌnrɪ'zɒlvd] ADJ (*frm*: *difficulty, problem, issue*) irrisolto(-a).

un·re·spon·sive ['ʌnrɪs'pɒnsɪv] ADJ che non reagisce; **unresponsive to** insensibile a.

un·rest [ʌn'rɛst] N (*disturbances*) agitazioni *fpl*.

un·re·strained [ˌʌnrɪ'streɪnd] ADJ sfrenato(-a).

un·re·strain·ed·ly [ˌʌnrɪ'streɪnɪdlɪ] ADV sfrenatamente.

un·re·strict·ed [ˌʌnrɪ'strɪktɪd] ADJ senza una regolamentazione; (*power, time*) illimitato(-a); (*access, parking*) libero(-a).

un·re·ward·ed [ˌʌnrɪ'wɔ:dɪd] ADJ non ricompensato(-a); **to go unrewarded** rimanere senza ricompensa.

un·re·ward·ing [ˌʌnrɪ'wɔ:dɪŋ] ADJ (*job*) ingrato(-a), senza soddisfazioni; (: *financially*) poco remunerativo(-a).

un·ripe [ʌn'raɪp] ADJ non maturo(-a).

un·ri·valled, (*Am*) **un·ri·valed** [ʌn'raɪvəld] ADJ senza pari; **to be unrivalled** non avere or non temere rivali.

un·roll [ʌn'rəʊl] **1** VT srotolare.
2 VI srotolarsi.

un·ro·man·tic [ˌʌnrə'mæntɪk] ADJ poco romantico(-a).

un·ruf·fled [ʌn'rʌfld] ADJ (*person*) imperturbato(-a); (*hair*) a posto; (*water*) senza un'increspatura.

un·ruled [ʌn'ru:ld] ADJ (*paper*) senza righe.

un·ru·ly [ʌn'ruːlɪ] ADJ (*comp* **-ier**, *superl* **-iest**) (*behaviour*) indisciplinato(-a); (*child*, *mob*) turbolento(-a); (*hair*) ribelle.

un·sad·dle [ʌn'sædl] VT (*horse*) dissellare; (*rider*) disarcionare.

un·safe [ʌn'seɪf] ADJ (*machine*, *car*, *wiring*) pericoloso(-a); (*method*) poco sicuro(-a), rischioso(-a); **unsafe to drink** non potabile; **unsafe to eat** non commestibile; **to feel unsafe** non sentirsi sicuro(-a).

un·said [ʌn'sɛd] ADJ non detto(-a), taciuto(-a); **consider it unsaid** come non detto; **to leave sth unsaid** passare qc sotto silenzio; **it would have been better left unsaid** sarebbe stato meglio non dirlo; **much was left unsaid** molte cose sono rimaste non dette.

un·sale·able, (*Am*) **un·sal·able** [ʌn'seɪləbl] ADJ invendibile.

un·sat·is·fac·tory [ˌʌnsætɪs'fæktərɪ] ADJ (*result*) poco soddisfacente; (*profits*) al di sotto delle aspettative; (*piece of work*, *hotel room*) che lascia a desiderare; (*on school report*) insufficiente.

un·sat·is·fied [ʌn'sætɪsˌfaɪd] ADJ (*desire*, *need*) non appagato(-a); (*not fulfilled*: *person*) insoddisfatto(-a); (*not convinced*): **unsatisfied (with)** poco convinto(-a) (di).

un·sat·is·fy·ing [ʌn'sætɪsˌfaɪɪŋ] ADJ (*result*, *work*) insoddisfacente, poco soddisfacente; (*meal*) che non soddisfa.

un·satu·rat·ed [ʌn'sætʃəˌreɪtɪd] ADJ (*fat*) insaturo(-a).

un·sa·voury, (*Am*) **un·sa·vory** [ʌn'seɪvərɪ] ADJ (*character*, *business*, *activity*) equivoco(-a), losco(-a); (*place*, *district*, *reputation*) poco raccomandabile; (*appearance*) sgradevole.

un·scathed [ʌn'skeɪðd] ADJ senza un graffio, incolume; (*fig*) indenne.

un·sched·uled [ʌn'ʃɛdjuːld, *Am* ʌn'skɛdjuːld] ADJ (*announcement*, *landing*, *stop*) non programmato(-a), imprevisto(-a).

un·sci·en·tif·ic [ˌʌnsaɪən'tɪfɪk] ADJ poco scientifico(-a).

un·screw [ʌn'skruː] ☐1 VT svitare.
☐2 VI svitarsi.

un·script·ed [ʌn'skrɪptɪd] ADJ (*Radio*, *TV*) improvvisato (-a).

un·scru·pu·lous [ʌn'skruːpjʊləs] ADJ (*person*) senza scrupoli, privo(-a) di scrupoli; (*means*) disonesto(-a).

un·scru·pu·lous·ly [ʌn'skruːpjʊləslɪ] ADV senza scrupoli.

un·scru·pu·lous·ness [ʌn'skruːpjʊləsnɪs] N mancanza di scrupoli.

un·sea·son·able [ʌn'siːznəbl] ADJ (*weather*) non tipico (-a) della stagione.

un·sea·soned [ʌn'siːznd] ADJ (*food*) scondito(-a); (*timber*) non stagionato(-a); (*fig*: *inexperienced*) inesperto(-a).

un·seat [ʌn'siːt] VT (*rider*) disarcionare; (*fig*: *official*) spodestare; (: *Members of Parliament*) far perdere il seggio a.

un·secured [ˌʌnsɪ'kjʊəd] ADJ: **unsecured creditor** creditore *m* non privilegiato.

un·seed·ed [ʌn'siːdɪd] ADJ (*Sport*) che non è una testa di serie.

un·seem·ly [ʌn'siːmlɪ] ADJ (*pej*) sconveniente, indecoroso (-a).

un·seen [ʌn'siːn] ☐1 ADJ (*person*) inosservato(-a); (*danger*) nascosto(-a); (*Scol*: *translation*) all'impronta.
☐2 N (*Scol*) traduzione *f* all'impronta.

un·self·con·scious [ˌʌnsɛlf'kɒnʃəs] ADJ disinvolto(-a).

un·self·ish [ʌn'sɛlfɪʃ] ADJ (*person*) altruista; (*act*) disinteressato(-a).

un·self·ish·ly [ʌn'sɛlfɪʃlɪ] ADV con altruismo, generosa-

mente.

un·self·ish·ness [ʌn'sɛlfɪʃnɪs] N (*of person*) altruismo; (*of act*) generosità.

un·ser·vice·able [ʌn'sɜː'vɪsəbl] ADJ inservibile.

un·set·tle [ʌn'sɛtl] VT (*stomach*, *plans*) scombussolare; (*person*) disorientare.

un·set·tled [ʌn'sɛtld] ADJ (*weather*, *market*, *situation*) instabile, variabile; (*person*: *restless*) irrequieto(-a); (: *itinerant*) nomade; (*frm*: *question*, *issue*) non risolto(-a); **to feel unsettled** sentirsi turbato(-a) *or* scombussolato (-a).

un·set·tling [ʌn'sɛtlɪŋ] ADJ inquietante; **the news had an unsettling effect on me** la notizia mi ha scombussolato.

un·shak·able, **un·shake·able** [ʌn'ʃeɪkəbl] ADJ irremovibile.

un·shak·en [ʌn'ʃeɪkən] ADJ (*person*) nient'affatto scosso (-a), risoluto(-a); (*resolve*) saldo(-a) come prima.

un·shav·en [ʌn'ʃeɪvn] ADJ non rasato(-a).

un·shock·able [ʌn'ʃɒkəbl] ADJ: **he is unshockable** niente lo scandalizza.

un·shrink·able [ʌn'ʃrɪŋkəbl] ADJ irrestringibile.

un·sight·ly [ʌn'saɪtlɪ] ADJ (*unattractive*) sgradevole a vedersi; (*ugly*) brutto(-a).

un·sink·able [ʌn'sɪŋkəbl] ADJ inaffondabile.

un·skilled [ʌn'skɪld] ADJ (*worker*, *manpower*) non specializzato(-a).

un·so·ciable [ʌn'səʊʃəbl] ADJ (*pej*: *person*) poco socievole; **he's very unsociable** è un orso.

un·so·cial [ʌn'səʊʃəl] ADJ: **unsocial hours** orario *msg* sconveniente.

un·sold [ʌn'səʊld] ADJ invenduto(-a).

un·so·lic·it·ed [ˌʌnsə'lɪsɪtɪd] ADJ non richiesto(-a).

un·solved [ʌn'sɒlvd] ADJ non risolto(-a).

un·so·phis·ti·cat·ed [ˌʌnsə'fɪstɪˌkeɪtɪd] ADJ (*person*, *dress*, *habits*) semplice; (*machine*) primitivo(-a), rudimentale.

un·sound [ʌn'saʊnd] ADJ (*health*) debole, cagionevole; (*in construction*: *floor*, *foundations*) malsicuro(-a); (*argument*) che non regge; (*opinion*) poco fondato(-a); (*policy*, *advice*) poco sensato(-a); (*judgment*, *investment*) poco sicuro(-a); (*business*) poco solido(-a); **of unsound mind** (*Law*) non in pieno possesso delle proprie facoltà mentali.

un·spar·ing [ʌn'spɛərɪŋ] ADJ (*generous*): **to be unsparing of** *or* **in** non risparmiare; (*criticism*) spietato(-a).

un·spar·ing·ly [ʌn'spɛərɪŋlɪ] ADV (*generously*) generosamente; (*unmercifully*) spietatamente.

un·speak·able [ʌn'spiːkəbl] ADJ (*behaviour*, *crime*) abominevole; (*pain*, *joy*) indicibile, indescrivibile.

un·speak·ably [ʌn'spiːkəblɪ] ADV indicibilmente.

un·speci·fied [ʌn'spɛsɪfaɪd] ADJ imprecisato(-a).

un·spoiled [ʌn'spɔɪld], **un·spoilt** [ʌn'spɔɪlt] ADJ (*countryside*, *beauty*) non deturpato(-a); (*child*) non viziato(-a); (*person*) genuino(-a).

un·spo·ken [ʌn'spəʊkən] ADJ (*words*) non detto(-a); (*thoughts*) non espresso(-a); (*agreement*, *approval*) tacito (-a).

un·sport·ing [ʌn'spɔːtɪŋ] ADJ (*pej*) poco sportivo(-a).

un·sta·ble [ʌn'steɪbl] ADJ (*structure*, *situation*, *Chem*, *Phys*) instabile; (*person*) squilibrato(-a).

un·stamped [ʌn'stæmpt] ADJ (*letter*) non affrancato(-a).

un·steadi·ly [ˌʌn'stɛdɪlɪ] ADV in modo incerto.

un·steady [ʌn'stɛdɪ] ADJ (*ladder*, *foothold*) instabile, malsicuro(-a); (*hand*, *voice*) tremante; (*economy*) vacillante; **to be unsteady on one's feet** non reggersi bene sulle gambe.

un·stint·ing [ʌnˈstɪntɪŋ] ADJ (*support*) incondizionato(-a); (*generosity*) illimitato(-a); (*praise*) senza riserve.

un·stop·pable [ʌnˈstɒpəbl] ADJ inarrestabile.

un·stressed [ʌnˈstrest] ADJ (*syllable*) non accentato(-a).

un·stuck [ʌnˈstʌk] ADJ: **to come unstuck** (*label*) staccarsi, scollarsi; (*fam: plan*) andare a monte, fallire; (: *person*) fare fiasco.

un·sub·stan·ti·at·ed [ˌʌnsəbˈstænʃɪˌeɪtɪd] ADJ (*rumour, accusation*) infondato(-a).

un·suc·cess·ful [ˌʌnsəkˈsesfʊl] ADJ (*gen*) che non ha successo; (*writer*) fallito(-a); (*businessman*) di scarso successo; **to be unsuccessful** (*play, book, actor*) non avere successo; (*idea*) non avere fortuna; (*attempt, marriage, negotiation*) non riuscire, fallire; (*application*) avere esito negativo; **to be unsuccessful in an exam** non superare un esame; **to be unsuccessful in an attempt to do sth** fallire nel tentativo di fare qc.

un·suc·cess·ful·ly [ˌʌnsəkˈsesfəlɪ] ADV senza successo.

un·suit·able [ʌnˈsuːtəbl] ADJ: **unsuitable (for)** (*clothes, colour*) non adatto(-a) (a), inadatto(-a) (a); (*moment*) inopportuno(-a) (a *or* per); **this film is unsuitable for children** non è un film adatto ai bambini; **unsuitable for children under 15** sconsigliabile ai minori di 15 anni; **he's unsuitable for the post** non è la persona adatta per quell'impiego; **the post is unsuitable for him** quel posto non fa per lui.

un·suit·ed [ʌnˈsuːtɪd] ADJ: **to be unsuited for** *or* **to** non essere fatto(-a) per.

un·sul·lied [ʌnˈsʌlɪd] ADJ (*liter: reputation*) immacolato (-a).

un·sung [ʌnˈsʌŋ] ADJ: **an unsung hero** un eroe misconosciuto.

un·sup·port·ed [ˌʌnsəˈpɔːtɪd] ADJ (*claim*) senza fondamento; (*theory*) non dimostrato(-a); (*mother*) senza aiuti finanziari.

un·sure [ʌnˈʃʊə] ADJ: **unsure of, unsure about** incerto(-a) su; **to be unsure of o.s.** essere un(-a) insicuro(-a).

un·sur·passed [ˌʌnsəˈpɑːst] ADJ insuperato(-a).

un·sus·pect·ed [ˌʌnsəsˈpektɪd] ADJ insospettato(-a).

un·sus·pect·ing [ˌʌnsəsˈpektɪŋ] ADJ (*gen*) che non sospetta nulla; (*public*) ignaro(-a).

un·sweet·ened [ʌnˈswiːtnd] ADJ (*tea*) senza zucchero; (*fruit juice*) non zuccherato(-a).

un·swerv·ing [ʌnˈswɜːvɪŋ] ADJ (*loyalty, devotion*) ferreo (-a), incrollabile.

un·sym·pa·thet·ic [ˌʌnsɪmpəˈθetɪk] ADJ (*attitude*) poco incoraggiante; (*person: not understanding*) poco comprensivo(-a); (: *disagreeable*) antipatico(-a); (*response*) gelido(-a); **to be unsympathetic to a cause** non appoggiare una causa.

un·sys·tem·at·ic [ˌʌnsɪstɪˈmætɪk] ADJ poco sistematico (-a).

un·tan·gle [ʌnˈtæŋgl] VT (*knots, wool*) sbrogliare.

un·tapped [ʌnˈtæpt] ADJ (*resources*) non sfruttato(-a).

un·taxed [ʌnˈtækst] ADJ (*goods*) esente da imposte; (*income*) non imponibile.

un·teach·able [ʌnˈtiːtʃəbl] ADJ (*person*) a cui è impossibile insegnare; (*subject*) impossibile da insegnare.

un·ten·able [ʌnˈtenəbl] ADJ (*position*) insostenibile.

un·test·ed [ʌnˈtestɪd] ADJ (*theory*) non sperimentato(-a); (*new product, method*) non collaudato(-a).

un·think·able [ʌnˈθɪŋkəbl] ADJ impensabile, inconcepibile.

un·think·ing [ʌnˈθɪŋkɪŋ] ADJ (*remark*) sconsiderato(-a).

un·think·ing·ly [ʌnˈθɪŋkɪŋlɪ] ADV senza pensare.

un·ti·di·ly [ʌnˈtaɪdɪlɪ] ADV: **to dress untidily** non aver cura nel vestirsi; **to write/work untidily** scrivere/lavorare in modo disordinato.

un·ti·di·ness [ʌnˈtaɪdɪnɪs] N (*of dress, person*) trascuratezza, sciatteria; (*of room*) disordine *m*.

un·ti·dy [ʌnˈtaɪdɪ] ADJ (*comp* -**ier**, *superl* -**iest**) (*person, room, writing*) disordinato(-a).

un·tie [ʌnˈtaɪ] VT (*parcel*) disfare; (*knot, shoelaces*) sciogliere; (*hands, person, dog*) slegare.

un·til [ʌnˈtɪl] **1** PREP fino a; (*after negative*) prima di; **until now** finora; **until then** fino ad allora; **until such time as I decide otherwise** fino a quando non cambio idea; **from morning until night** dalla mattina alla sera; **until his arrival** fino al suo arrivo; **I didn't know anything about it until 10 minutes ago** non ne sapevo niente fino a 10 minuti fa.

2 CONJ finché (non), fino a quando; **I won't see her until I return** non la vedrò fino al mio ritorno; **wait until I get back** aspetta finché torno; **he did nothing until I told him** non ha mosso un dito finché non gliel'ho detto; **we had a lovely view from here until they built the factory** qui si godeva une bella vista fino a quando non hanno costruito la fabbrica.

un·time·ly [ʌnˈtaɪmlɪ] ADJ (*death, end*) prematuro(-a); (*remark*) fuori luogo, inopportuno(-a); **to come to an untimely end** (*person*) morire prematuramente; (*project*) naufragare anzitempo.

un·tir·ing [ʌnˈtaɪərɪŋ] ADJ instancabile, indefesso(-a).

un·tir·ing·ly [ʌnˈtaɪərɪŋlɪ] ADV instancabilmente.

un·told [ʌnˈtəʊld] ADJ (*loss, wealth*) incalcolabile; (*misery*) indicibile, indescrivibile; (*story, secret*) mai rivelato(-a).

un·touch·able [ʌnˈtʌtʃəbl] **1** N (*in India*) paria *m inv*, intoccabile *m/f*.

2 ADJ intoccabile.

un·touched [ʌnˈtʌtʃt] ADJ **a** (*unchanged*) così com'era; (*unaffected*) non toccato(-a); **she left her breakfast untouched** non ha nemmeno toccato la colazione; **untouched by human hand** manipolato(-a) a distanza **b** (*safe: person*) incolume; **the thieves left our cases untouched** i ladri non hanno toccato le nostre valigie **c** (*unmoved*): **untouched by her pleas** insensibile alle sue preghiere.

un·to·ward [ˌʌntəˈwɔːd] ADJ (*frm*) increscioso(-a).

un·trained [ʌnˈtreɪnd] ADJ (*worker, teacher*) privo(-a) di formazione professionale; (*troops*) privo(-a) di addestramento; **to the untrained eye/ear** ad un occhio inesperto/orrechio non esercitato.

un·tram·melled, (*Am*) **un·tram·meled** [ʌnˈtræməld] ADJ (*liter*) senza vincoli.

un·trans·lat·able [ˌʌntrænzˈleɪtəbl] ADJ intraducibile.

un·treat·ed [ʌnˈtriːtɪd] ADJ (*illness, patient*) non curato(-a); (*sewage, water*) non depurato(-a); (*wood*) non trattato (-a).

un·tried [ʌnˈtraɪd] ADJ (*method*) non collaudato(-a); (*person*) non messo(-a) alla prova; (*Law: criminal*) non processato(-a); (: *case*) non portato(-a) in tribunale.

un·trou·bled [ʌnˈtrʌbld] ADJ calmo(-a); **untroubled by the thought of** per niente preoccupato(-a) al pensiero di.

un·true [ʌnˈtruː] ADJ (*statement*) falso(-a), non vero(-a).

un·trust·wor·thy [ʌnˈtrʌst͵wɜːðɪ] ADJ (*person*) di cui non ci si può fidare; (*source*) inattendibile, non degno(-a) di fede.

un·truth [ʌnˈtruːθ] N (*pl* **untruths** [ʌnˈtruːðz]) falsità *f inv*.

un·truth·ful [ʌnˈtruːθfʊl] ADJ falso(-a), menzognero(-a).

un·truth·ful·ly [ʌnˈtruːθfəlɪ] ADV falsamente.

un·us·able [ʌn'juːzəbl] ADJ inservibile, inutilizzabile.

un·used[1] [ʌn'juːzd] ADJ (*new*) mai usato(-a), nuovo(-a); (*not made use of*) non usato(-a), non utilizzato(-a).

un·used[2] [ʌn'juːst] ADJ: **to be unused to sth/to doing sth** non essere abituato(-a) a qc/a fare qc.

un·usual [ʌn'juːʒʊəl] ADJ (*uncommon*) insolito(-a); (*exceptional*: *event, talent*) non comune, raro(-a); **it's unusual for him to be late** è strano che arrivi in ritardo; **that's unusual for her** che strano, non è da lei; **isn't it unusual!** che originale!

un·usu·al·ly [ʌn'juːʒʊəlɪ] ADV (*unaccustomedly*) insolitamente; (*exceptionally*: *tall, gifted*) eccezionalmente; **most unusually, she was late** fatto molto strano, era in ritardo.

un·ut·ter·able [ʌn'ʌtərəbl] ADJ (*liter*: *joy, boredom*) indicibile.

un·var·ied [ʌn'vɛərɪd] ADJ (*routine*) invariato(-a); (*diet*) monotono(-a).

un·var·nished [ʌn'vɑːnɪʃt] ADJ (*wood*) non verniciato(-a); (*fig*: *truth*) nudo(-a) e crudo(-a); (: *account*) senza fronzoli.

un·vary·ing [ʌn'vɛərɪŋ] ADJ immutabile.

un·veil [ʌn'veɪl] VT (*plan*) svelare; (*monument*) scoprire, inaugurare.

un·veil·ing [ʌn'veɪlɪŋ] N (*ceremony*) scoprimento.

un·ven·ti·lat·ed [ʌn'vɛntɪ,leɪtɪd] ADJ non ventilato(-a).

un·voiced [ʌn'vɔɪst] ADJ (*consonant*) sordo(-a); (*opinion*) inespresso(-a).

un·waged [ʌn'weɪdʒd] (*Brit*) [1] ADJ non retribuito(-a). [2] NPL: **the unwaged** i non salariati.

un·want·ed [ʌn'wɒntɪd] ADJ (*person, effect*) non desiderato(-a); (*clothes*) smesso(-a); **to feel unwanted** sentirsi respinto(-a).

un·war·rant·ed [ʌn'wɒrəntɪd] ADJ ingiustificato(-a).

un·wary [ʌn'wɛərɪ] ADJ incauto(-a).

un·wa·ver·ing [ʌn'weɪvərɪŋ] ADJ (*support, faith*) incrollabile, fermo(-a).

un·wel·come [ʌn'wɛlkəm] ADJ (*guest, news*) non gradito(-a); (*development*) sgradito(-a); **to feel unwelcome** sentire che la propria presenza non è gradita.

un·well [ʌn'wɛl] ADJ indisposto(-a); **to feel unwell** non sentirsi bene.

un·whole·some [ʌn'həʊlsəm] ADJ (*food*) non genuino(-a); (*climate, smell*) malsano(-a); (*thoughts, influence*) cattivo(-a).

un·wieldy [ʌn'wiːldɪ] ADJ poco maneggevole.

un·will·ing [ʌn'wɪlɪŋ] ADJ riluttante; **to be unwilling to do sth** non essere disposto(-a) a fare qc, non voler fare qc; **he was unwilling to admit he was wrong** non voleva ammettere di aver torto.

un·will·ing·ly [ʌn'wɪlɪŋlɪ] ADV controvoglia, malvolentieri, di malavoglia.

un·wind [ʌn'waɪnd] (*pt, pp* **unwound**) [1] VT srotolare, svolgere. [2] VI srotolarsi; (*fam*: *relax*) distendersi, rilassarsi.

un·wise [ʌn'waɪz] ADJ (*decision, act*) avventato(-a); **it was unwise of you to do that** è stato imprudente da parte tua farlo.

un·wise·ly [ʌn'waɪzlɪ] ADV imprudentemente; **she unwisely decided to take the job** ha deciso, poco saggiamente, di accettare il lavoro.

un·wit·ting [ʌn'wɪtɪŋ] ADJ (*cause*) involontario(-a); (*victim*) inconsapevole; (*insult*) non intenzionale, non voluto(-a).

un·wit·ting·ly [ʌn'wɪtɪŋlɪ] ADV senza volerlo; **quite unwit-**tingly in tutta innocenza.

un·wont·ed [ʌn'wəʊntɪd] ADJ (*frm*) inconsueto(-a).

un·work·able [ʌn'wɜːkəbl] ADJ (*plan*) inattuabile.

un·world·ly [ʌn'wɜːldlɪ] ADJ poco materialista.

un·wor·thy [ʌn'wɜːðɪ] ADJ (*undeserving*) non degno(-a); (*ignoble*) indegno(-a); **to be unworthy of sth/to do sth** non essere degno(-a) di qc/di fare qc.

un·wound [ʌn'waʊnd] PT, PP of **unwind**.

un·wrap [ʌn'ræp] VT (*present*) aprire, scartare; (*parcel*) disfare.

un·writ·ten [ʌn'rɪtn] ADJ (*agreement*) tacito(-a); **it is an unwritten law that ...** la norma vuole che... .

un·yield·ing [ʌn'jiːldɪŋ] ADJ (*person*) inflessibile; (*material*) rigido(-a), duro(-a).

un·zip [ʌn'zɪp] VT aprire (la chiusura lampo di).

up [ʌp]
[1] ADV
[a] (*upwards, higher*) su, in alto;
▷ **up** *above* su in alto, al di sopra
▷ **to be up** *among* **the leaders** essere tra i primi
▷ **he's been up** *and down* **all evening** non è stato fermo un momento, stasera
▷ **to walk up** *and down* camminare su e giù
▷ **to jump up** *and down* saltellare
▷ **she's still a bit up** *and down* (*sick person*) ancora non si è ripresa del tutto
▷ **my office is five** *floors* **up** il mio ufficio è al quinto piano
▷ **to stop** *halfway* **up** fermarsi a metà salita
▷ **a bit** *higher* **up** un po' più su *or* in alto
▷ **up** *in* **the sky/mountains** su nel cielo/in montagna
▷ **they've got the** *road* **up** la strada è interrotta
▷ **"this** *side* **up"** "alto"
▷ **the** *sun* **is up** è sorto il sole
▷ **up** *there* lassù
▷ **to** *throw* **sth up in the air** gettare qc in aria
▷ **he goes up** *to* **Oxford next year** va a Oxford l'anno prossimo
▷ **to be up** *with* **the leaders** essere tra i primi
▷ **up** *with* **Leeds United!** viva il Leeds United!, forza Leeds United!
[b] (*installed, built*): **to be** up (*building*) essere terminato(-a); (*tent*) essere piantato(-a); (*shutters*) essere sollevato(-a); (*wallpaper*) essere su; (*picture*) essere appeso(-a); (*notice*) essere esposto(-a)
[c] (*out of bed*): **to be** up essersi alzato(-a)
▷ **to be up and** *about again* essere di nuovo in piedi
▷ **to be up** *early* alzarsi presto
▷ **to be up** *late* (*at night*) fare tardi
[d] (*in price, value*): **to be** up (**by**) essere andato(-a) su (di); (*standard, level*): **to be** up essere salito(-a)
▷ **we are 3** *goals* **up** abbiamo un vantaggio di 3 gol, vinciamo per 3 gol
▷ *prices* **are up on last year** i prezzi sono più alti dell'anno scorso
[e] (*finished*)
▷ **it's** *all* **up with her** (*fam*) per lei è finita
▷ **the** *lease* **is up** il contratto d'affitto è scaduto
▷ **his** *leave* **is up** il suo congedo è scaduto
▷ *time's* **up** il tempo è scaduto
▷ **when the** *year* **was up** finito l'anno
[f] (*upwards*): **from £20 up** dalle 20 sterline in su

g (*in or towards the north*) su;
▷he's up **for** the day è qui per la giornata
▷she's up **from** **Birmingham** è arrivata da Birmingham
▷up *in* Scotland su in Scozia
▷up *North* su al Nord
▷to live/go up *North* vivere/andare su al Nord
h (*Brit: knowledgeable*)
▷I'm not very *well* up **on** what's going on non sono molto al corrente di ciò che sta succedendo
▷he's *well* up **in** or **on** politics è informatissimo sulla politica
i (*fam: wrong*)
▷there's *something* up with him/with the TV (lui)/la TV ha qualcosa che non va
▷what's up? cosa c'è che non va?
▷what's up with him? che ha?, che gli prende?
j: up **to** (*as far as*) fino a;
▷up **to** here fin qui, fino a qui
▷up **to** now finora
▷up **to** £100 fino a 100 sterline
k: *what* is he up **to**? (*fam pej: doing*) cosa sta combinando?;
▷he's up **to** *no good* OR he's up **to** *something* sta architettando qualcosa
l: up **to** (*equal to*) all'altezza di;
▷he is not up **to** *it* non ne è capace
▷I don't feel up **to** *it* non me la sento
▷the book isn't up **to** *much* (*fam*) il libro non vale un granché
m
▷it's up **to** you to decide (*depends on*) sta *or* tocca a te decidere
▷I'd go, but it's up **to** you io ci andrei, ma dipende da te
n
▷to be up *against* opposition (*faced with*) trovarsi di fronte una forte opposizione
▷you don't know what you're up *against* non sai a cosa vai incontro
▷he's really up *against* it sta in un bell'impiccio.
2 PREP: to *go* up (*stairs*) salire; (*hill*) salire su per; (*river*) risalire;
▷to travel up *and down* the country viaggiare su e giù per il paese
▷*further* up the page più su nella stessa pagina
▷*halfway* up the stairs a metà scala
▷it's up that *road* è su per quella strada
▷he went off up the *road* se n'è andato su per la strada
▷he pointed up the *street* ha indicato in fondo alla strada
▷to be up a *tree* essere su un albero.
3 N: ups *and downs* (*in life, career*) alti e bassi *mpl*;
▷the road is full of ups *and downs* la strada è molto accidentata
▷he's on the up *and up* le cose gli vanno di bene in meglio.
4 ADJ (*train, line*) per la città.
5 VI (*fam*)
▷she upped and left ha preso e se n'è andata
▷he upped and punched him gli ha mollato un pugno.
6 VT (*fam: price*) alzare.

♦ **up-and-coming** [ˌʌpəndˈkʌmɪŋ] ADJ promettente.
♦ **up-and-down** [ˌʌpənˈdaʊn] ADJ (*movement*) (in) su e giù; (*business, progress*) con molti alti e bassi.
♦ **up-and-under** [ˌʌpəndˈʌndəˈ] N (*Rugby*) calcio al volo.
up·beat [ˈʌpˌbiːt] **1** N (*Mus*) tempo in levare; (*positive trend*) tendenza al rialzo.
  2 ADJ (*fam*) ottimistico(-a).
up·braid [ʌpˈbreɪd] VT (*frm*) rimproverare.
up·bring·ing [ˈʌpˌbrɪŋɪŋ] N educazione *f*.
up·coming [ˌʌpˈkʌmɪŋ] ADJ imminente, prossimo(-a).
up·country [ʌpˈkʌntrɪ] ADV (*be*) all'interno; (*go*) verso l'interno.
up·date [ʌpˈdeɪt] VT aggiornare.
up·end [ʌpˈɛnd] VT (*box*) mettere in piedi; (*fig: system*) rovesciare.
♦ **up-front** [ˌʌpˈfrʌnt] (*fam*) **1** ADJ franco(-a), aperto(-a); **upfront payment** pagamento immediato.
  2 ADV (*pay*) in anticipo.
up·grade [ʌpˈgreɪd] VT (*employee*) promuovere, avanzare di grado; (*job*) rivalutare; (*Comput*) far passare a potenza superiore; (*goods*) migliorare la qualità di.
up·heav·al [ʌpˈhiːvəl] N (*disturbance*) scompiglio; (*Pol*) sconvolgimento; (*Geol*) sollevamento.
up·held [ʌpˈhɛld] PT, PP of **uphold**.
up·hill [ˌʌpˈhɪl] **1** ADV: to go uphill andare in salita, salire.
  2 ADJ in salita, in su; (*fig: task, battle*) arduo(-a); **uphill ski** sci *m inv* a monte; **it's uphill all the way** è tutta salita; (*fig*) è una continua lotta.
up·hold [ʌpˈhəʊld] (*pt, pp* **upheld**) VT (*frm: law, principle*) difendere; (: *decision, verdict*) confermare.
up·hol·ster [ʌpˈhəʊlstəˈ] VT (*cover*) tappezzare, ricoprire; (*pad*) imbottire; **to be well upholstered** (*fig hum*) essere bene in carne.
up·hol·ster·er [ʌpˈhəʊlstərəˈ] N tappezziere(-a).
up·hol·stery [ʌpˈhəʊlstərɪ] N tappezzeria.
up·keep [ˈʌpˌkiːp] N manutenzione *f*.
up·lands [ˈʌpləndz] NPL regioni *fpl* montagnose.
up·lift [ʌpˈlɪft] VT (*spiritually*) elevare, esaltare; (*materially*) sollevare, tirar su.
♦ **up-market** [ˌʌpˈmɑːkɪt] ADJ (*product*) che si rivolge ad una fascia di mercato superiore; (*restaurant*) elegante.
upon [əˈpɒn] PREP = **on 1**.
up·per [ˈʌpəˈ] **1** ADJ **a** (*jaw, lip*) superiore; (*storey*) superiore, di sopra; **the upper reaches of the Po** l'alto Po
  b (*in importance, rank*) superiore, più alto(-a), più elevato(-a); **the upper school** gli ultimi anni di scuola superiore; **the upper income bracket** la fascia di reddito più alto; **the upper middle class** l'alta borghesia.
  2 N (*of shoe*) tomaia; **to be on one's uppers** (*fig fam*) non avere il becco d'un quattrino.
♦ **Upper Chamber** N (*Pol*): **the Upper Chamber** la Camera Alta.
♦ **upper-class** [ˌʌpəˈklɑːs] ADJ (*district*) signorile; (*people*) dell'alta borghesia; (*accent*) aristocratico(-a); (*attitude*) snob *inv*.
♦ **upper classes** NPL: **the upper classes** i ceti più elevati.
♦ **upper crust** N: **the upper crust** (*fam*) l'aristocrazia.
upper·cut [ˈʌpəˌkʌt] N (*Boxing*) uppercut *m inv*, montante *m*.
♦ **upper hand** N: **to have the upper hand** prendere il sopravvento.
♦ **Upper House** N: **the Upper House** (*in Britain*) la Camera Alta, la Camera dei Lords; (*in US etc*) il Senato.
upper·most [ˈʌpəˌməʊst] ADJ (*thought*) dominante; (*eche-*

lon) più alto(-a), più elevato(-a); **it was uppermost in my mind** è stata la mia prima preoccupazione.

♦ **Upper Volta** N: **the Upper Volta** l'Alto Volta *m*.

up·pish [ˈʌpɪʃ] ADJ (*Brit fam*) con la puzza al *or* sotto il naso; **to get uppish** darsi importanza.

up·pi·ty [ˈʌpɪtɪ] (*fam*) ADJ **a** (*hard to control*): **to get uppity** alzare la cresta **b** = **uppish**.

up·right [ˈʌpˌraɪt] **1** ADJ **a** (*posture*) ritto(-a), eretto(-a); (*post*) verticale **b** (*fig*) retto(-a), onesto(-a).

2 ADV dritto(-a); **to stand upright** (*person*) stare dritto (-a); (*object*) essere in posizione verticale.

3 N **a** (*post*) supporto verticale; (*of door, window*) montante *m* **b** (*piano*) pianoforte *m* verticale *or* a mezza coda.

up·ris·ing [ˈʌpˌraɪzɪŋ] N rivolta, insurrezione *f*.

up·roar [ˈʌpˌrɔːʳ] N trambusto, clamore *m*; **the whole place was in uproar** c'era un gran baccano.

up·roari·ous [ʌpˈrɔːrɪəs] ADJ (*group, meeting*) chiassoso (-a); (*laughter*) fragoroso(-a); (*welcome*) entusiastico (-a); (*very funny: joke, mistake*) esilarante.

up·roari·ous·ly [ʌpˈrɔːrɪəslɪ] ADV (*see adj*) chiassosamente; fragorosamente; entusiasticamente; **he is uproariously funny** è (un tipo) spassosissimo.

up·root [ʌpˈruːt] VT sradicare.

up·set [*vb, adj* ʌpˈsɛt; *n* ˈʌpˌsɛt] (*vb: pt, pp* upset) **1** VT **a** (*container, contents*) rovesciare; (*boat*) capovolgere, rovesciare; (*fig: plan, schedule*) scombussolare. **b** (*emotionally: disturb*) turbare; (*stronger*) sconvolgere; (: *offend*) offendere; (: *annoy*) contrariare, seccare; **don't upset yourself** non te la prendere **c** (*make ill: person*) far star male; (: *stomach*) scombussolare.

2 ADJ **a** (*emotionally: disturbed*) turbato(-a); (*stronger*) sconvolto(-a); (: *offended*) offeso(-a); (: *annoyed*) contrariato(-a), seccato(-a); **to get upset** (*distressed*) lasciarsi turbare *or* sconvolgere; (*offended*) offendersi; (*annoyed*) seccarsi; **don't get upset** non te la prendere **b** : **I have an upset stomach** ho lo stomaco in disordine *or* scombussolato.

3 N **a** (*disturbance: in plans etc*) contrattempo, contrarietà *f inv*; (*emotional*) dispiacere *m* **b** : **to have a stomach upset** (*Brit*) avere disturbi di stomaco.

♦ **upset price** N (*Am, Scot*) prezzo di riserva.

up·set·ting [ʌpˈsɛtɪŋ] ADJ (*distressing*) sconvolgente; (*disturbing*) scioccante.

up·shot [ˈʌpˌʃɒt] N (*result*) risultato; **the upshot of it all was that** … la conclusione è stata che…. .

up·side down [ˌʌpsaɪdˈdaʊn] **1** ADV (*person*) a testa in giù; (*object*) alla rovescia, sottosopra; **to turn upside down** capovolgere; (*mattress*) rivoltare; (*fig*) mettere sottosopra *or* a soqquadro.

2 ADJ (*person*) a testa in giù; (*object*) capovolto(-a); **the room was upside down** (*in disorder*) la stanza era tutta sottosopra *or* a soqquadro.

up·stage [ˌʌpˈsteɪdʒ] VT: **to upstage sb** rubare la scena a qn.

up·stairs [*adv, n* ˌʌpˈstɛəz; *adj* ˈʌpstɛəz] **1** ADV di sopra; **to go upstairs** andare di sopra; **the people upstairs** quelli di sopra.

2 N: **the upstairs** il piano di sopra.

3 ADJ (*room*) al piano di sopra.

up·stand·ing [ʌpˈstændɪŋ] ADJ (*honourable*) retto(-a); (*strong*) aitante.

up·start [ˈʌpˌstɑːt] N (*pej: in society*) parvenu *m inv*; (*in*

organization, hierarchy) ultimo(-a) arrivato(-a) che si dà arie d'importanza.

up·stream [ˌʌpˈstriːm] ADV (*be*) a monte; (*swim*) controcorrente; **to sail upstream** risalire la corrente.

up·surge [ˈʌpˌsɜːdʒ] N (*of enthusiasm*) ondata; (*of prices, inflation*) impennata, improvviso aumento.

up·swing [ˈʌpswɪŋ] N: **upswing (in sth)** ripresa (in qc).

up·take [ˈʌpˌteɪk] N (*fam*): **slow on the uptake** duro(-a) di comprendonio; **to be quick on the uptake** capire le cose al volo.

up·thrust [ˈʌpˌθrʌst] N (*gen, Phys*) spinta verso l'alto; (*Geol*) sollevamento.

up·tight [ʌpˈtaɪt] ADJ (*fam*) teso(-a), nervoso(-a).

♦ **up-to-date** [ˌʌptəˈdeɪt] ADJ (*figures, edition*) aggiornato (-a); (*person*) ben informato(-a), aggiornato(-a); (*ideas*) attuale, al passo coi tempi; (*clothes*) alla moda; **to bring sb up-to-date (on sth)** aggiornare qn (su qc).

♦ **up-to-the-minute** [ˌʌptəðəˈmɪnɪt] ADJ (*fashionable*: *dress, person*) all'ultimissima moda; (: *style*) attuale; (*latest*: *information*) dell'ultimo minuto.

up·town [ˌʌpˈtaʊn] (*Am*) **1** ADV (*walk, drive*) verso i quartieri residenziali; (*live*) in un quartiere residenziale.

2 ADJ dei quartieri residenziali.

up·turn [ˈʌpˌtɜːn] N (*fig: improvement*) ripresa; (*in value of currency*) rialzo; (*in luck*) svolta favorevole.

up·turned [ʌpˈtɜːnd] ADJ (*box*) capovolto(-a), rovesciato (-a); (*nose*) all'insù.

up·ward [ˈʌpwəd] **1** ADJ (*movement*) verso l'alto, in su; (*curve*) ascendente; **upward tendency** (*Fin*) tendenza al rialzo.

2 ADV (*also*: **upwards**) **a** in su, verso l'alto; **to lie face upward** giacere supino(-a) **b** (*with numbers*): **from the age of 13 upwards** dai 13 anni in su; **upwards of 500** 500 e più.

upwardly-mobile [ˌʌpwədlɪˈməʊbaɪl] N: **to be upwardly-mobile** salire nella scala sociale.

Ural Mountains [jʊərəlˈmaʊntɪnz] NPL: **the Ural Mountains** (*also*: **the Urals**) gli Urali, i Monti Urali.

ura·nium [jʊəˈreɪnɪəm] N uranio.

Ura·nus [jʊəˈreɪnəs] N (*Myth, Astron*) Urano.

ur·ban [ˈɜːbən] ADJ urbano(-a); **urban sprawl** sviluppo urbanistico incontrollato, espansione *f* urbana tentacolare.

ur·bane [ɜːˈbeɪn] ADJ urbano(-a), civile.

ur·bani·za·tion [ˌɜːbənaɪˈzeɪʃən] N urbanizzazione *f*.

ur·chin [ˈɜːtʃɪn] N monello(-a).

Urdu [ˈɜːduː] N urdu *m*.

urea [ˈjʊərɪə] N urea.

ureter [jʊəˈriːtəʳ] N (*Anat*) uretere *m*.

urethra [jʊəˈriːθrə] N (*Anat*) uretra.

urge [ɜːdʒ] **1** N impulso, stimolo, voglia; **to feel an urge to do sth** sentire l'impulso di fare qc.

2 VT **a** (*try to persuade*) esortare; **to urge sb to do sth** esortare qn a fare qc; **he urged me to visit the Uffizi** mi ha raccomandato vivamente di visitare gli Uffizi; **he needed no urging** non si è fatto pregare

b (*frm: advocate: measure*) fare pressioni per; (: *caution, acceptance*) raccomandare vivamente; **to urge that** insistere che + *sub*; **to urge sth on** *or* **upon sb** sottolineare a qn l'importanza di qc

▶ **urge on** VT + ADV (*also fig*) incitare, spronare.

ur·gen·cy [ˈɜːdʒənsɪ] N (*of case, need*) urgenza; (*of tone of voice, pleas*) insistenza; **it is a matter of urgency** è una questione della massima urgenza.

ur·gent ['ɜːdʒənt] ADJ **a** (*message, need*) urgente **b** (*earnest, persistent: plea*) pressante; (: *tone*) insistente, incalzante.

ur·gent·ly ['ɜːdʒəntlɪ] ADV (*see adj*) d'urgenza, urgentemente; in modo pressante, con insistenza.

uri·nal [jʊˈraɪnl] N (*building*) vespasiano; (*vessel*) orinale *m.*

uri·nary ['jʊərɪnərɪ] ADJ urinario(-a).

uri·nate ['jʊərɪˌneɪt] VI orinare.

urine ['jʊərɪn] N orina.

urn [ɜːn] N **a** (*vase*) urna **b** (*also:* **tea urn, coffee urn**) *capace contenitore provvisto di cannella per tè, caffè (specialmente nelle mense).*

Uru·guay ['jʊərəˌgwaɪ] N l'Uruguay *m.*

Uru·guay·an [ˌjʊərəˈgwaɪən] ADJ, N uruguaiano(-a).

US [ˌjuːˈɛs] N ABBR = **United States**.

us [ʌs] PERS PRON PL **a** (*direct, indirect*) ci; (*stressed, after prep, in comparatives*) noi; **they saw us** ci hanno visto; **they're older than us** sono più vecchi di noi; **we had some suitcases with us** avevamo con noi delle valigie; **let's go** andiamo; **us Scots** noialtri Scozzesi **b** (*fam: me*): **give us a kiss** dammi un bacino.

USA [ˌjuːɛsˈeɪ] N ABBR **a** (*Geog: = United States of America*) U.S.A. *mpl* **b** (*Mil*)= *United States Army*.

us·able ['juːzəbl] ADJ utilizzabile, usabile.

USAF [ˌjuːɛseɪˈɛf] N ABBR = *United States Air Force*.

us·age ['juːzɪdʒ] N **a** (*Ling: use, way of using*) uso; **to be in common usage** essere nell'uso comune **b** (*custom*) usanza, uso **c** (*treatment, handling, use*) uso; (*of energy*) utilizzo; **it's had some rough usage** è stato un po' bistrattato.

USDAW [ˌjuːɛsdiːeɪˈdʌbljuː] N ABBR (*Brit: = Union of Shop, Distributive and Allied Workers*) *sindacato dei dipendenti di negozi, reti di distribuzione e simili.*

use [*n* juːs; *vb* juːz] **1** N **a** (*gen*) uso, utilizzazione *f*, impiego; **a new use for old tyres** un nuovo modo di utilizzare vecchi copertoni; **directions for use** istruzioni *fpl* per l'uso; **for the use of the blind** ad uso dei non vedenti; **for use in case of emergency** da usarsi in caso di emergenza; **ready for use** pronto(-a) per l'uso; **to make use of sth** far uso di qc, utilizzare qc; **in use** in uso; **out of use** fuori uso; **is your old radio still in use?** funziona ancora la tua vecchia radio?; **to be in daily use** venire adoperato(-a) quotidianamente; **to be no longer in use** non essere più usato(-a); **it's gone** *or* **fallen out of use** non lo si usa più; **for one's own use** per uso personale; **fit for use** che si può ancora usare; **to make good use of sth** OR **put sth to good use** far buon uso di qc; **to find a use for sth** trovare il modo di utilizzare qc; **we have no further use for this** questo non ci serve più **b** (*usefulness*): **to be of use** essere utile, servire; **it's (of) no use** non serve, è inutile; **it's no use!** niente da fare!; **it's no use discussing it further** non serve a niente continuare a discuterne; **what's the use of all this?** a che serve tutto ciò?; **she's no use as a teacher** non vale niente come insegnante **c** (*ability or right to use*): **to lose the use of one's legs** perdere l'uso delle gambe; **I've got the use of the car this evening** stasera posso prendere la macchina. **2** VT **a** (*gen*) usare; **to use force** usare la forza; **"to be used only in emergencies"** "da usare solo in caso d'emergenza"; **to use sth as a hammer** usare qc come martello; **what's this used for?** a che serve?; **I could use a drink** (*fam*) non mi dispiacerebbe bere qualcosa; **this room could use some paint** (*fam*) una passata di vernice

non farebbe male a questa stanza; **use your head** *or* **brains!** usa la testa *or* il cervello!; **use your eyes!** apri gli occhi!

b (*make use of, exploit: influence*) servirsi di, adoperare; (: *opportunity*) sfruttare, approfittare di

c (*use up, consume*) consumare; (*finish*); (*supplies*) usare, utilizzare

d (*old liter: treat*) trattare.

3 AUX VB: **I used to go there every day** ci andavo ogni giorno, ero solito(-a) andarci ogni giorno; **she used to do it** era solita farlo, lo faceva (una volta); **things are not what they used to be** non è più come una volta

▶ **use up** VT + ADV (*strength*) usare; (*left-overs*) utilizzare; (*supplies*) dare fondo a; (*petrol, paper, money*) finire.

used¹ [juːzd] ADJ (*secondhand: clothing*) usato(-a); (: *car*) di seconda mano, d'occasione, usato(-a); (*dirty: glass, napkin*) (già) usato(-a).

used² [juːst] ADJ: **to be used to sth** essere abituato(-a) a qc; **to be used to doing sth** essere abituato(-a) a *or* avere l'abitudine di fare qc; **to get used to** abituarsi a, fare l'abitudine a.

use·ful ['juːsfʊl] ADJ **a** (*gen*) utile; **he's a useful man to know** è una conoscenza utile; **that's a useful thing to know** buono a sapersi; **it is very useful to be able to drive** saper guidare è molto utile; **to make o.s. useful** rendersi utile; **to come in useful** fare comodo, tornare utile

b (*fam: capable: player*) bravino(-a); **he is useful with a gun** sa maneggiare il fucile.

use·ful·ly ['juːsfəlɪ] ADV utilmente.

use·ful·ness ['juːsfʊlnɪs] N utilità.

use·less ['juːslɪs] ADJ **a** (*no good: remedy*) inefficace; (: *advice*) inutile; (*unusable: object*) inservibile; **he's useless as a forward** come centravanti non vale niente; **you are useless!** sei un inetto!

b (*pointless*) inutile; **it's useless arguing with him** non serve a niente *or* è inutile discutere con lui.

user ['juːzə'] N (*of public service, dictionary*) utente *m/f*; (*of petrol, gas*) consumatore(-trice); **car users** automobilisti *mpl*; **library users** lettori *mpl*; **drug users** drogati *mpl*.

♦ **user-friendly** [ˌjuːzəˈfrɛndlɪ] ADJ (*machine, Comput*) di facile uso.

♦ **U-shaped** ['juːˌʃeɪpt] ADJ ad U.

ush·er ['ʌʃə'] **1** N (*Law*) usciere *m*; (*in theatre, cinema*) maschera; (*at wedding*) *valletto che accompagna gli ospiti ai loro posti.*

2 VT: **to usher sb in** far entrare qn; **it ushered in a new era** (*fig*) ha inaugurato una nuova era.

ush·er·ette [ˌʌʃəˈrɛt] N (*in cinema*) mascherina.

USIA [ˌjuːɛsarˈeɪ] N ABBR = *United States Information Agency*.

USM [ˌjuːɛsˈɛm] N ABBR = *United States Mint; United States Mail*.

USN [ˌjuːɛsˈɛn] N ABBR = *United States Navy*.

USPHS [ˌjuːɛspiːeɪtʃˈɛs] N ABBR = *United States Public Health Service*.

USPO [ˌjuːɛspiːˈəʊ] N ABBR = *United States Post Office*.

USS [ˌjuːɛsˈɛs] ABBR = *United States Ship (or Steamer)*.

USSR [ˌjuːɛsɛsˈɑː'] N ABBR (= *Union of Soviet Socialist Republics*) U.R.S.S. *f.*

usu. ABBR = **usually**.

usu·al ['juːʒʊəl] **1** ADJ (*gen*) solito(-a); **as usual** come al solito, come d'abitudine; **more than usual** più del solito; **at the usual time** alla solita ora; **earlier than usual** prima del solito; **as is usual on these occasions** come vuole la tradizione; **as is usual with this type of housing** come sempre in questo genere di alloggi; **he's not his**

usual self di solito non è così; **he'll soon be his usual self again** tornerà presto ad essere quello di sempre; **"business as usual"** "l'ufficio (*or* il negozio *etc*) è aperto al pubblico"; **it's not usual for her to be late** non è sua abitudine arrivare in ritardo.

2 N: **the usual, please!** (*fam: drink*) il solito, per favore!

usu·al·ly ['ju:ʒʊəlɪ] ADV di solito; **to be more than usually careful** fare ancora più attenzione del solito.

usu·rer ['ju:ʒərəʳ] N (*old*) usuraio(-a).

usurp [ju:'zɜ:p] VT usurpare.

usurp·er [ju:'zɜ:pəʳ] N usurpatore(-trice).

usu·ry ['ju:ʒʊrɪ] N (*frm old*) usura.

UT ABBR (*Am Post*)= *Utah.*

uten·sil [ju:'tɛnsl] N utensile *m*.

uter·us ['ju:tərəs] N utero.

utili·tar·ian [ˌju:tɪlɪ'tɛərɪən] ADJ **a** (*Philosophy*) utilitarista, utilitaristico(-a) **b** (*furniture*) funzionale.

util·ity [ju:'tɪlɪtɪ] N (*usefulness*) utilità; (*also:* **public utility**) servizio pubblico.

♦ **utility room** N *locale adibito alla stiratura dei panni ecc.*

uti·li·za·tion [ˌju:tɪlaɪ'zeɪʃən] N utilizzazione *f*.

uti·lize ['ju:tɪˌlaɪz] VT (*frm: facilities, resources*) utilizzare; (: *talent, opportunity*) sfruttare.

ut·most ['ʌtˌməʊst] 1 ADJ **a** (*greatest: simplicity, caution*) massimo(-a); (: *danger*) estremo(-a); **with the utmost speed** a tutta velocità; **of the utmost importance** della massima importanza; **it is of the utmost importance that ...** è estremamente importante che...+ *sub* **b** (*furthest: limits*) estremo(-a).

2 N: **to do one's utmost (to do sth)** fare tutto il possibile (per fare qc); **to the utmost of one's ability** al limite delle proprie capacità.

uto·pia [ju:'təʊpɪə] N utopia.

uto·pian [ju:'təʊpɪən] ADJ utopico(-a).

ut·ter[1] ['ʌtəʳ] ADJ (*disaster, silence*) totale, assoluto(-a); (*madness*) puro(-a); (*fool*) perfetto(-a); **that's utter nonsense** sono tutte sciocchezze.

ut·ter[2] ['ʌtəʳ] VT (*groan, sigh*) emettere; (*cry, insult*) lanciare; (*word*) pronunciare, proferire; **she never uttered a word** non ha fiatato.

ut·ter·ance ['ʌtərəns] N (*remark, statement*) parole *fpl*; (*expression*) espressione *f*.

ut·ter·ly ['ʌtəlɪ] ADV completamente, del tutto.

utter·most ['ʌtəˌməʊst] = **utmost.**

♦ **U-turn** ['ju:ˌtɜ:n] N inversione *f* a U; (*fig*) voltafaccia *m inv*, cambiamento di rotta, dietro-front *m inv*.

Uzbekistan [ˌʊzbɛkɪ'stɑ:n] N l'Uzbekistan *m*.

V

V, v [vi:] N (letter) V, v f or m inv; **V for Victor** ≈ V come Venezia.

V ABBR (= volt) V.

V. ABBR **a** (= verse) v **b** (= vide) v (= vedi) **c** = **versus.**

VA [,vi:'eɪ] ABBR (Am Post)= Virginia.

vac [væk] N (Brit fam) = **vacation.**

va·can·cy ['veɪkənsɪ] N **a** (job) posto (vacante); **have you any vacancies?** avete bisogno di personale?; "**vacancy for a secretary**" "segretaria cercasi" **b** (in boarding house etc) stanza libera; "**no vacancies**" "completo" **c** (emptiness) vuoto.

va·cant ['veɪkənt] ADJ **a** (seat, room) libero(-a); (property, house) vuoto(-a), libero(-a); (post) vacante; **vacant lot** terreno non occupato; (for sale) terreno in vendita **b** (look, expression) vuoto(-a), vacuo(-a), assente.

va·cant·ly ['veɪkəntlɪ] ADV con sguardo assente; **to gaze vacantly into space** guardare nel vuoto.

va·cate [və'keɪt] VT (house, seat, room) lasciare libero(-a); (post) lasciare, dare le dimissioni da.

va·ca·tion [və'keɪʃən] N (esp Am) vacanza, ferie fpl; (Univ) vacanze fpl; **on vacation** in vacanza, in ferie; **to take a vacation** prendere una vacanza, prendere le ferie.

♦ **vacation course** N corso estivo.

vac·ci·nate ['væksɪ,neɪt] VT vaccinare.

vac·ci·na·tion [,væksɪ'neɪʃən] N vaccinazione f.

vac·cine ['væksi:n] N vaccino; **polio vaccine** vaccino antipolio.

vac·il·late ['væsɪ,leɪt] VI (frm): **to vacillate (between)** oscillare (tra).

vacu·ous ['vækjʊəs] ADJ (look, expression) vacuo(-a); (comment) stupido(-a), insulso(-a).

vacuum ['vækjʊm] N (also fig) vuoto; **in a vacuum** (fig) in assoluto isolamento.

♦ **vacuum cleaner** N aspirapolvere m inv.

♦ **vacuum flask,** (Am) **vacuum bottle** N termos m inv.

♦ **vacuum-packed** ['vækjʊm,pækt] ADJ confezionato(-a) sottovuoto inv.

vade me·cum ['vɑ:dɪ'meɪkʊm] N (liter) vademecum m inv.

vaga·bond ['vægə,bɒnd] N vagabondo(-a), barbone(-a).

va·gary ['veɪgərɪ] N (usu pl) capriccio.

va·gi·na [və'dʒaɪnə] N vagina.

vagi·nal [və'dʒaɪnəl] ADJ vaginale.

va·gran·cy ['veɪgrənsɪ] N vagabondaggio.

va·grant ['veɪgrənt] N vagabondo(-a), barbone(-a).

vague [veɪg] ADJ (comp **-r,** superl **-st**) (gen) vago(-a); (directions, description) impreciso(-a), confuso(-a); (indistinct: memory) sfocato(-a); (person: absent-minded) distratto(-a); **I have a vague idea that ...** ho la vaga impressione che...; **I haven't the vaguest idea** non ho la minima or più pallida idea; **the vague outline of a ship** la sagoma indistinta or confusa di una nave; **a vague look** uno sguardo assente or vuoto.

vague·ly ['veɪglɪ] ADV vagamente.

vague·ness ['veɪgnɪs] N (of outline) indeterminatezza; (of meaning) vaghezza; (of person) distrazione f.

vain [veɪn] ADJ (comp **-er,** superl **-est**) **a** (attempt, hope) vano(-a), inutile; **in vain** invano, inutilmente; **all our efforts were in vain** tutti i nostri sforzi sono stati inutili **b** (person) vanitoso(-a).

vain·ly ['veɪnlɪ] ADV (see adj) invano; vanitosamente.

val·ance ['væləns] N volant m inv, balza.

val·edic·tion [,vælɪ'dɪkʃən] N (frm) discorso di commiato.

val·edic·tory [,vælɪ'dɪktərɪ] ADJ (frm) di commiato.

va·len·cy ['veɪlənsɪ], (Am) **va·lence** ['veɪləns] N (Chem) valenza.

val·en·tine ['vælən,taɪn] N (card) biglietto di auguri per San Valentino; (sweetheart) innamorato(-a).

va·lerian [və'lɪərɪən] N valeriana.

val·et ['væleɪ] N cameriere m personale.

♦ **valet parking** N servizio di parcheggio (offerto da albergo ecc ai clienti).

♦ **valet service** N (for car) servizio completo di lavaggio; (for clothes) servizio di lavanderia.

val·iant ['væljənt] ADJ (liter) coraggioso(-a), valoroso(-a); **a valiant knight** un prode cavaliere.

val·iant·ly ['væljəntlɪ] ADV (liter) coraggiosamente.

val·id ['vælɪd] ADJ (ticket, document, excuse) valido(-a); (claim, objection) giustificato(-a).

vali·date ['vælɪ,deɪt] VT (contract, document) convalidare; (argument, claim) comprovare.

va·lid·ity [vəˈlɪdɪtɪ] N (of document) validità; (of argument) fondatezza, validità.

va·lise [vəˈliːz] N (old) borsa da viaggio.

Va·lium® [ˈvælɪəm] N Valium ® m inv.

Val·kyrie [vælˈkɪərɪ] N valchiria.

val·ley [ˈvælɪ] N valle f.

val·or·ous [ˈvælərəs] ADJ (liter) valoroso(-a).

val·our [ˈvælə], (Am) **val·or** N (liter) valore m (coraggio).

valu·able [ˈvæljʊəbl] ADJ (contribution, time) prezioso(-a); (painting, object) di valore, costoso(-a).

valuables [ˈvæljʊəblz] NPL preziosi mpl, oggetti mpl di valore.

valu·a·tion [ˌvæljʊˈeɪʃən] N (of monetary worth) valutazione f; (of quality) valutazione, stima; **what is your valuation of him?** che opinione ti sei fatto di lui?

value [ˈvæljuː] [1] N a (worth) valore m; (usefulness) utilità; **to lose (in) value** (currency) svalutarsi; (property) perdere (di) valore; **to gain (in) value** (currency) guadagnare; (property) aumentare di valore; **of no value** di nessun valore, senza valore; **to be of great value to sb** avere molta importanza per qn; **it has been of no value to him** non gli è servito a nulla; **you get good value (for money) in that shop** si compra bene in quel negozio; **this dress is good value (for money)** questo abito ha un buon prezzo
b : **values** NPL (principles) valori mpl.
[2] VT (financially) valutare, stimare; (friendship, independence etc) tenere a, apprezzare; **it is valued at £80** è valutato 80 sterline.

♦ **value add·ed tax** [ˌvæljuːædɪdˈtæks] N (Brit) imposta sul valore aggiunto.

val·ued [ˈvæljuːd] ADJ (appreciated) stimato(-a), apprezzato(-a), tenuto(-a) in grande considerazione.

♦ **value judgment** N giudizio di valore.

value·less [ˈvæljʊlɪs] ADJ privo(-a) di valore.

valu·er [ˈvæljʊə] N stimatore(-trice).

valve [vælv] N (all senses) valvola.

vam·pire [ˈvæmpaɪə] N vampiro.

♦ **vampire bat** N (Zool) vampiro.

van¹ [væn] N (Aut: small) furgoncino; (: for furniture) furgone m; (Rail) vagone m.

van² [væn] N: **in the van** all'avanguardia.

va·na·dium [vəˈneɪdɪəm] N vanadio.

V and A [ˌviːəndˈeɪ] N ABBR (Brit)= Victoria and Albert Museum.

van·dal [ˈvændəl] N vandalo.

van·dal·ism [ˈvændəˌlɪzəm] N vandalismo.

van·dal·ize [ˈvændəˌlaɪz] VT vandalizzare.

vane [veɪn] N (also: **weathervane**) segnavento.

van·guard [ˈvænˌɡɑːd] N avanguardia; **to be in the vanguard of progress** essere all'avanguardia del progresso; **to be in the vanguard of a movement** essere le avanguardie fpl di un movimento.

va·nil·la [vəˈnɪlə] [1] N vaniglia.
[2] ADJ (ice cream) alla vaniglia; (essence) di vaniglia.

van·ish [ˈvænɪʃ] VI svanire; **to vanish into thin air** svanire nel nulla, volatilizzarsi.

♦ **van·ish·ing cream** [ˈvænɪʃɪŋˌkriːm] N base f per il trucco.

♦ **van·ish·ing point** [ˈvænɪʃɪŋˌpɔɪnt] N punto di fuga.

van·ity [ˈvænɪtɪ] N vanità f inv.

♦ **vanity case** N beauty case m inv.

♦ **vanity mirror** N (Aut) specchietto di cortesia.

♦ **vanity unit** N elemento da bagno con lavandino incorporato.

van·quish [ˈvæŋkwɪʃ] VT (liter) sconfiggere.

van·tage [ˈvɑːntɪdʒ] N (also: **advantage:** Tennis) vantaggio.

♦ **vantage point** N punto d'osservazione f (favorevole).

vap·id [ˈvæpɪd] ADJ (liter) scipito(-a), scialbo(-a).

va·por·ize [ˈveɪpəˌraɪz] [1] VT vaporizzare.
[2] VI vaporizzarsi.

va·pour, (Am) **va·por** [ˈveɪpə] N vapore m.

♦ **vapour trail** N (Aer) scia.

vari·abil·ity [ˌvɛərɪəˈbɪlɪtɪ] N variabilità.

vari·able [ˈvɛərɪəbl] [1] ADJ (output, performance) non costante; (weather, wind) variabile; (mood) mutevole.
[2] N (Math) variabile f.

vari·ance [ˈvɛərɪəns] N a : **to be at variance (with sb over sth)** essere in disaccordo (con qn per qc); **to be at variance (with sth)** (facts, statements) essere in contraddizione (con qc) b (Math) varianza.

vari·ant [ˈvɛərɪənt] [1] N variante f.
[2] ADJ diverso(-a).

vari·ation [ˌvɛərɪˈeɪʃən] N (of amount, quality, also Mus) variazione f; (in opinion) cambiamento.

vari·cose veins [ˌværɪkəʊsˈveɪnz] NPL varici fpl, vene fpl varicose.

var·ied [ˈvɛərɪd] ADJ (types, sizes, qualities) vario(-a), diverso(-a); (life) movimentato(-a); (diet) diversificato(-a).

varie·gat·ed [ˈvɛərɪˌɡeɪtɪd] ADJ variegato(-a).

va·ri·ety [vəˈraɪətɪ] N (type) varietà f inv, tipo; (range, diversity) molteplicità, varietà; **in a wide** or **large variety of colours** in una vasta gamma di colori; **for a variety of reasons** per una serie di motivi; **for variety** per variare.

♦ **variety artist** N artista m/f di varietà.

♦ **variety show** N spettacolo di varietà.

vari·ous [ˈvɛərɪəs] ADJ (several) diverso(-a), vario(-a); (different) diverso(-a), differente; **at various times** (different) in momenti diversi or differenti; **various times** (several) diverse or varie volte; **we went our various ways home** ognuno è tornato a casa per la sua strada.

vari·ous·ly [ˈvɛərɪəslɪ] ADV in modo vario, variamente.

var·nish [ˈvɑːnɪʃ] [1] N (for wood) vernice f trasparente; (for nails) smalto.
[2] VT (wood) verniciare; (nails) smaltare; **to varnish one's nails** smaltarsi le unghie

▶ **varnish over** VT + ADV: **to varnish over sth** (event, fact) mascherare qc.

vary [ˈvɛərɪ] [1] VT variare.
[2] VI a (change): **to vary (with** or **according to)** variare (con or a seconda di) b (deviate): **to vary (from)** discostarsi (da); **the temperature/her mood varies** la temperatura/il suo umore è variabile; **these items vary in price** questi articoli si differenziano per il prezzo.

vary·ing [ˈvɛərɪŋ] ADJ variabile, che varia; **with varying degrees of success** con più o meno successo.

vas·cu·lar [ˈvæskjʊlə] ADJ (system) vascolare; **vascular bundle** (Bot) fascio vascolare.

vase [vɑːz, Am veɪs] N vaso.

vas·ec·to·my [væˈsɛktəmɪ] N vasectomia.

vas·eline® [ˈvæsɪˌliːn] N vaselina ®.

vaso·con·stric·tor [ˌveɪzəʊkənˈstrɪktə] N vasocostrittore m.

vaso·di·la·tor [ˌveɪzəʊdaɪˈleɪtə] N vasodilatatore m.

vast [vɑːst] ADJ (comp **-er**, superl **-est**) (territory, expanse) vasto(-a); (sum, amount) ingente; (difference, improvement) enorme; **at vast expense** con enorme dispendio di capitale.

vast·ly [ˈvɑːstlɪ] ADV (grateful, rich) enormemente; **vastly**

superior to di gran lunga superiore a; **he's vastly mistaken if** ... sbaglia di grosso se...; **a vastly overrated player** un giocatore incredibilmente sopravvalutato.

vast·ness ['vɑːstnɪs] N (*of territory*) vastità, immensità; **the vastness of his wealth** la vastità delle sue ricchezze.

VAT ['viːeɪtiː, væt] N ABBR (*Brit*: = *value added tax*) I.V.A. *f*.

vat [væt] N (*for wine, dye*) tino.

Vati·can ['vætɪkən] N: **the Vatican** il Vaticano.

♦ **Vatican council** N concilio vaticano.

vat·man ['vætmən] N (*Brit fam*): **the vatman** (*inspector*) l'ispettore *m* dell'IVA; (*Inland Revenue*) il fisco.

vau·de·ville ['vəʊdəvɪl] N (*esp Am*) vaudeville *m*.

vault[1] [vɔːlt] N (*Archit*) volta; (*of bank*) caveau *m inv*; (*tomb*) cripta, tomba; **family vault** cappella di famiglia.

vault[2] [vɔːlt] VT, VI: **to vault (over) sth** saltare qc con un balzo.

vault·ed ['vɔːltɪd] ADJ a volta.

vaunt·ed ['vɔːntɪd] ADJ: **much vaunted** tanto celebrato (-a).

VC [ˌviːˈsiː] N ABBR **a** (*Brit*: = *Victoria Cross*) *medaglia al valore* **b** = **vice-chairman**.

VCR [ˌviːsiːˈɑːʳ] N ABBR = **video cassette recorder**.

VD [ˌviːˈdiː] N ABBR = **venereal disease**.

VDU [ˌviːdiːˈjuː] N ABBR = **visual display unit**.

veal [viːl] N (*carne f* di) vitello.

vec·tor ['vɛktəʳ] N (*Math, Phys, Bio*) vettore *m*.

veer [vɪəʳ] VI (*ship, car*) virare; (*wind*) girare; **wind veering westerly at times** vento con tendenza a provenire da occidente; **the country has veered to the left** il paese ha fatto una svolta a sinistra; **the conversation veered round to politics** la conversazione si è spostata sulla politica.

veg [vɛdʒ] N ABBR (*Brit fam*) = *vegetable(s)*.

ve·gan ['viːgən] N vegetaliano(-a).

veg·eburg·er, veg·gie·burg·er ['vɛdʒɪˌbɜːgəʳ] N hamburger *m inv* vegetariano.

veg·eta·ble ['vɛdʒɪtəbl] [1] **a** verdura; **vegetables** NPL (*in restaurant*) ≈ contorno *msg* (di verdure); **would you like some vegetables?** desidera un contorno di verdure?; (*at home*) vuoi un po' di verdura? **b** (*generic term: plant*) vegetale *m*.

[2] ADJ (*oil, wax*) vegetale; (*soup*) di verdura.

♦ **vegetable garden** N orto.

♦ **vegetable knife** N coltello per pelare le verdure.

♦ **vegetable marrow** N (*Am*) zucca.

♦ **vegetable rack** N carrello *m inv* portaverdure.

veg·etar·ian [ˌvɛdʒɪˈtɛərɪən] ADJ, N vegetariano(-a).

veg·etari·an·ism [ˌvɛdʒɪˈtɛərɪəˌnɪzəm] N vegetarianismo.

veg·etate ['vɛdʒɪˌteɪt] VI vegetare.

veg·eta·tion [ˌvɛdʒɪˈteɪʃən] N vegetazione *f*.

veg·eta·tive ['vɛdʒɪtətɪv] ADJ (*also Bot*) vegetativo(-a).

veg·gie ['vɛdʒɪ] N, ADJ (*fam*) vegetariano(-a).

veg·gie·burg·er ['vɛdʒɪˌbɜːgəʳ] N = **vegeburger**.

ve·he·mence ['viːɪməns] N veemenza.

ve·he·ment ['viːɪmənt] ADJ (*speech, passions*) veemente, violento(-a); (*attack*) vigoroso(-a); (*dislike, hatred*) profondo(-a); **there was vehement opposition** ci fu una dura opposizione.

ve·he·ment·ly ['viːɪməntlɪ] ADV con veemenza.

ve·hi·cle ['viːɪkl] N veicolo; (*fig*) mezzo.

ve·hicu·lar [vɪˈhɪkjʊləʳ] ADJ (*frm*): **"no vehicular traffic"** "chiuso al traffico di veicoli".

veil [veɪl] [1] N velo; **to take the veil** (*Rel*) prendere il velo; **under a veil of secrecy** protetto(-a) da una cortina di segretezza.

[2] VT velare, coprire con un velo; **the town was veiled in mist** la città era avvolta dalla nebbia.

veiled [veɪld] ADJ (*also fig*) velato(-a).

vein [veɪn] N (*in body, stone, also fig*) vena; (*Bot: on leaf*) nervatura; **in melancholy vein** d'umore *m* malinconico; **in a different vein** in un tenore *m* diverso.

veined [veɪnd] ADJ (*hand*) venoso(-a); (*leaf*) nervoso(-a).

Vel·cro® ['vɛlkrəʊ] N velcro ®.

veld, veldt [vɛlt] N: **the veld** l'altopiano sudafricano.

vel·lum ['vɛləm] N (*writing paper*) pergamena.

ve·loc·ity [vɪˈlɒsɪtɪ] N velocità *f inv*.

ve·lour(s) [vəˈlʊəʳ] N velours *m inv*.

vel·vet ['vɛlvɪt] [1] N velluto.

[2] ADJ (*skirt, curtain*) di velluto.

vel·vet·een [ˌvɛlvɪˈtiːn] N vellutino.

vel·vety ['vɛlvɪtɪ] ADJ vellutato(-a).

ve·nal ['viːnl] ADJ (*frm*) venale.

ve·nal·ity [viːˈnælɪtɪ] N venalità.

ven·det·ta [vɛnˈdɛtə] N vendetta, faida.

vend·ing ma·chine ['vɛndɪŋməˌʃiːn] N distributore *m* automatico.

ven·dor ['vɛndɔːʳ] N venditore(-trice); **street vendor** venditore ambulante.

ve·neer [vəˈnɪəʳ] N impiallacciatura; (*fig*) parvenza, vernice *f*.

ven·er·able ['vɛnərəbl] ADJ venerabile; (*old man, appearance*) venerando(-a).

ven·er·ate ['vɛnəˌreɪt] VT (*frm*) venerare.

ven·era·tion [ˌvɛnəˈreɪʃən] N venerazione *f*.

ve·nereal [vɪˈnɪərɪəl] ADJ venereo(-a).

♦ **venereal disease** N malattia venerea.

Ve·netian [vɪˈniːʃən] ADJ, N veneziano(-a).

♦ **Venetian blind** N veneziana.

♦ **Venetian glass** N vetro di Murano.

Ven·ezue·la [ˌvɛnɪˈzweɪlə] N Venezuela *m*.

Ven·ezue·lan [ˌvɛnɪˈzweɪlən] ADJ, N venezuelano(-a).

venge·ance ['vɛndʒəns] N vendetta; **to take vengeance on sb** vendicarsi su qn; **with a vengeance** (*fig*) a più non posso.

venge·ful ['vɛndʒfʊl] ADJ (*liter*) vendicativo(-a).

ve·nial ['viːnɪəl] ADJ (*Rel, frm: sin*) veniale.

Ven·ice ['vɛnɪs] N Venezia.

veni·son ['vɛnɪsən] N carne *f* di cervo.

ven·om ['vɛnəm] N (*also fig*) veleno.

ven·om·ous ['vɛnəməs] ADJ (*also fig*) velenoso(-a).

vent [vɛnt] [1] N (*Tech: airhole*) presa d'aria; (*of jacket*) spacco; **to give vent to one's anger** sfogare la propria rabbia.

[2] VT: **to vent one's anger (on sb/sth)** scaricare *or* sfogare la propria rabbia (su qn/qc).

ven·ti·late ['vɛntɪˌleɪt] VT ventilare, arieggiare.

ven·ti·la·tion [ˌvɛntɪˈleɪʃən] N aerazione *f*, ventilazione *f*.

♦ **ventilation shaft** N condotto di aerazione.

ven·ti·la·tor ['vɛntɪˌleɪtəʳ] N ventilatore *m*.

ven·tri·cle ['vɛntrɪkəl] N (*Anat*) ventricolo.

ven·trilo·quism [vɛnˈtrɪləˌkwɪzəm] N ventriloquio.

ven·trilo·quist [vɛnˈtrɪləkwɪst] N ventriloquo(-a).

ven·ture ['vɛntʃə] [1] N impresa; **a business venture** un'iniziativa commerciale; **a new venture in publishing** una nuova iniziativa editoriale.

[2] VT (*money, reputation, life*) rischiare; (*opinion, guess*) azzardare; **to venture to do sth** azzardarsi a fare qc; **if I may venture an opinion** se posso azzardare *or* arrischiare un parere; **nothing ventured, nothing gained** chi non risica non rosica.

3 VI: **to venture on sth** avventurarsi in qc; **to venture out (of doors)** arrischiarsi ad uscire (di casa).

♦ **venture capital** N (*Fin*) capitale *m* a rischio.

venue ['vɛnjuː] N luogo (designato) (*per concerto, incontro sportivo, convegno*).

Venus ['viːnəs] N (*Astron, Myth*) Venere *f*.

ve·rac·ity [vəˈræsɪtɪ] N (*frm*) veridicità.

ve·ran·da, ve·ran·dah [vəˈrændə] N veranda.

verb [vɜːb] N verbo.

ver·bal ['vɜːbəl] ADJ verbale.

ver·bal·ize ['vɜːbəlaɪz] **1** VT (*feelings, emotions, ideas*) esprimere, tradurre in parole.
2 VI esprimersi.

ver·bal·ly ['vɜːbəlɪ] ADV a voce, verbalmente.

ver·ba·tim [vɜːˈbeɪtɪm] ADV, ADJ parola per parola.

ver·bi·age ['vɜːbɪdʒ] N (*frm pej*) verbalismo.

ver·bose [vɜːˈbəʊs] ADJ verboso(-a), prolisso(-a).

ver·bose·ly [vɜːˈbəʊslɪ] ADV verbosamente.

ver·bos·ity [vɜːˈbɒsɪtɪ] N verbosità.

ver·dant ['vɜːdənt] ADJ (*liter*) verdeggiante.

ver·dict ['vɜːdɪkt] N (*Law*) verdetto, sentenza; (*opinion*) giudizio, parere *m*; **verdict of guilty/not guilty** verdetto di colpevolezza/non colpevolezza; **his verdict on the wine was unfavourable** ha dato un giudizio sfavorevole sul vino.

ver·di·gris ['vɜːdɪɡrɪs] N verderame *m*.

verge [vɜːdʒ] N (*of road*) bordo, margine *m*; (*fig*) orlo; "**soft verges**" (*Brit*) "banchina cedevole"; **to be on the verge of** (*disaster*) essere sull'orlo di; (*a discovery*) essere alle soglie di; **she was on the verge of tears** stava quasi per piangere; **to be on the verge of doing sth** essere sul punto di fare qc.
▶ **verge on** VI + PREP rasentare.

ver·ger ['vɜːdʒəʳ] N (*Rel*) sagrestano.

veri·fi·able ['vɛrɪfaɪəbl] ADJ verificabile.

veri·fi·ca·tion [ˌvɛrɪfɪˈkeɪʃən] N verifica, accertamento.

veri·fy ['vɛrɪfaɪ] VT (*check*) verificare, controllare; (*confirm the truth of*) confermare.

veri·si·mili·tude [ˌvɛrɪsɪˈmɪlɪˌtjuːd] N (*frm*) verosimiglianza.

veri·table ['vɛrɪtəbl] ADJ vero(-a).

ver·mil·ion [vəˈmɪljən] **1** ADJ vermiglio(-a).
2 N vermiglio.

ver·min ['vɜːmɪn] NPL animali *mpl* nocivi; (*fig pej*) parassiti *mpl*.

ver·mi·nous ['vɜːmɪnəs] ADJ infestato(-a) dai parassiti.

ver·mouth ['vɜːməθ] N vermut *m inv*.

ver·nacu·lar [vəˈnækjʊləʳ] **1** N vernacolo.
2 ADJ vernacolare.

ver·ni·er ['vɜːnɪəʳ] N (*Tech: rule*) verniero.

ve·roni·ca [vəˈrɒnɪkə] N (*Bot*) veronica.

ver·ru·ca [vəˈruːkə] N verruca.

ver·sa·tile ['vɜːsəˌtaɪl] ADJ (*person*) versatile; (*machine, tool*) multiusi *inv*.

ver·sa·til·ity [ˌvɜːsəˈtɪlɪtɪ] N (*of person*) versatilità.

verse [vɜːs] N **a** (*of poem*) verso; (: *stanza*) strofa; (*of Bible*) versetto **b** (*no pl: poetry*) poesia, versi *mpl*; **in verse** in versi.

versed [vɜːst] ADJ: **to be well versed in sth** essere molto versato(-a) in qc.

ver·sion ['vɜːʃən] N versione *f*.

ver·sus ['vɜːsəs] PREP (*Law, Sport, gen*) contro.

ver·te·bra ['vɜːtɪbrə] N (*pl* **vertebrae** ['vɜːtɪbriː]) vertebra.

ver·te·bral ['vɜːtɪbrəl] ADJ vertebrale.

ver·te·brate ['vɜːtɪbrɪt] **1** ADJ vertebrato(-a).

2 N vertebrato.

ver·tex ['vɜːtɛks] N (*pl* **vertices** ['vɜːtɪsiːz]) vertice *m*.

ver·ti·cal ['vɜːtɪkəl] **1** ADJ (*gen*) verticale, perpendicolare; (*cliff*) a picco; **vertical takeoff** (*Aer*) decollo verticale.
2 N verticale *f*.

ver·ti·cal·ly ['vɜːtɪkəlɪ] ADV verticalmente.

ver·tigi·nous [vɜːˈtɪdʒɪnəs] ADJ (*frm: cliff, descent, view*) che dà le vertigini.

ver·ti·go ['vɜːtɪɡəʊ] N vertigine *f*; **to suffer from vertigo** soffrire di vertigini.

verve [vɜːv] N (*of person*) verve *f*, brio; (*of painting, writing*) vivacità.

very ['vɛrɪ] **1** ADV **a** (*extremely*) molto, tanto; **very happy** molto felice, felicissimo(-a); **it's very cold** fa molto freddo; **very well** molto bene; **very little** molto poco; **very much** molto, tanto; (*stronger*) moltissimo, tantissimo; **very much younger** molto più giovane; **are you tired? — (yes,) very** sei stanco? — (sì,) tanto; **he's so very poor** è poverissimo
b (*absolutely*): **the very first** il/la primissimo(-a), proprio il/la primo(-a); **the very last** l'ultimissimo(-a), proprio l'ultimo(-a); **the very latest design** l'ultimissimo modello; **they are the very best of friends** sono grandissimi amici; **to wish sb the very best of luck** augurare a qn ogni fortuna; **at the very most** al massimo; **at the very least** come minimo, almeno; **at the very latest** al più tardi; **he won't come until 9 o'clock, at the very earliest** non arriverà prima delle 9, al più presto; **the very same hat** lo stesso identico cappello; **it's my very own** è proprio mio.
2 ADJ **a** (*precise*) stesso(-a); **that very day** quello stesso giorno; **his very words** le sue stesse parole; **her very words were …** le sue parole testuali furono…; **he's the very man we want** è proprio l'uomo che cercavamo; **the very book which** proprio il libro che; **the very thing!** proprio quel che ci vuole!
b (*mere*) solo(-a); **the very thought (of it) alarms me** il solo pensiero mi spaventa, sono spaventato solo al pensiero; **the very idea!** neanche per sogno!
c (*extreme*): **at the very bottom/top** proprio in fondo/in cima; **at the very end** proprio alla fine; **to the very end** fino alla fine; **in the very depths of the jungle** nel cuore della giungla.

♦ **very high frequency** N (*Radio*) altissima frequenza.

ves·pers ['vɛspəz] NPL (*Rel*) vespro.

ves·sel ['vɛsl] N (*ship*) vascello, nave *f*; (*container*) recipiente *m*; (*Anat*) vaso.

vest[1] [vɛst] N (*Brit: with sleeves*) maglia intima; (: *sleeveless*) canottiera; (*Am: waistcoat*) panciotto, gilè *m inv*.

vest[2] [vɛst] VT (*frm*): **to vest sb with sth** investire qn di qc; **to vest powers/authority in sb** conferire poteri/autorità a qn.

vest·ed in·te·rest [ˌvɛstɪdˈɪntrɪst] N: **to have a vested interest in doing sth** avere un interesse personale nel fare qc; **vested interests** NPL (*Comm*) diritti *mpl* acquisiti.

ves·ti·bule ['vɛstɪbjuːl] N atrio, vestibolo.

ves·tige ['vɛstɪdʒ] N vestigio; **the last vestiges of** le ultime vestigia di.

ves·tig·ial [vɛˈstɪdʒɪəl] ADJ **a** (*Bio: organ*) vestigiale, rudimentale **b** (*frm: remaining*): **vestigial traces of** tracce residue di.

vest·ment ['vɛstmənt] N (*Rel*) paramento liturgico.

♦ **vest pocket** N (*Am*) taschino.

ves·try ['vɛstrɪ] N sagrestia.

Ve·su·vi·us [vɪˈsuːvɪəs] N Vesuvio.

vet¹ [vɛt] **1** N (*esp Brit*) veterinario.
2 VT (*text*) rivedere; (*person, application*) esaminare minuziosamente; **to vet sb for a job** informarsi su qn prima di offrirgli un posto.

vet² [vɛt] N ABBR (*esp Am*) = **veteran** 2.

vet·er·an ['vɛtərən] **1** ADJ: **veteran soldier** veterano; **a veteran teacher** un(-a) veterano(-a) dell'insegnamento; **she's a veteran campaigner for** ... lotta da sempre per....
2 N (*also:* **war veteran**) reduce *m*.

♦ **veteran car** N (*Brit*) auto *f inv* d'epoca (*anteriore al 1919*).

vet·eri·nar·ian [ˌvɛtərɪˈnɛərɪən] N (*Am*) = **veterinary surgeon**.

vet·eri·nary ['vɛtərɪnərɪ] ADJ veterinario(-a).

♦ **veterinary surgeon** N (*Brit*) veterinario.

veto ['viːtəʊ] **1** N (*pl* **vetoes**) veto; **to use** *or* **exercise one's veto** esercitare il proprio diritto di veto; **to put a veto on** (op)porre il veto a.
2 VT (op)porre il veto a.

vet·ting ['vɛtɪŋ] N (*also:* **positive vetting:** *Brit*) *indagine per accertare l'idoneità di un aspirante ad una carica ufficiale.*

vex [vɛks] VT irritare, contrariare.

vexa·tion [vɛkˈseɪʃən] N (*state*) irritazione *f*; (*problem*) contrarietà *f inv*, cruccio.

vexa·tious [vɛkˈseɪʃəs], **vex·ing** ['vɛksɪŋ] ADJ irritante, fastidioso(-a).

vexed [vɛkst] ADJ **a** irritato(-a); **to be/get vexed (with sb about sth)** essere irritato(-a)/irritarsi (con qn per qc) **b** (*question*) controverso(-a), dibattuto(-a).

vex·ing ['vɛksɪŋ] ADJ **a** (*annoying*) = **vexatious b** (*puzzling*) sconcertante.

VG [ˌviːˈdʒiː] ABBR (*Brit Scol:* = *very good*) ottimo.

VHF [ˌviːeɪtʃˈɛf] N ABBR (= *very high frequency*) VHF *f*.

VI ABBR (*Am Post*)= **Virgin Islands**.

via [ˈvaɪə] PREP (*by way of: place*) via; (: *person*) attraverso, tramite; (*by means of*) tramite, attraverso, per mezzo di.

vi·abil·ity [ˌvaɪəˈbɪlɪtɪ] N attuabilità.

vi·able ['vaɪəbl] ADJ (*proposal*) attuabile, fattibile; (*foetus*) in grado di sopravvivere.

via·duct ['vaɪəˌdʌkt] N viadotto.

vial ['vaɪəl] N fiala.

vibes [vaɪbz] NPL (*fam*) **a** (*vibrations*) atmosfera; **I got good vibes** l'impressione è stata buona **b** (*Mus*) = **vibraphone**.

vi·bran·cy ['vaɪbrənsɪ] N vitalità.

vi·brant ['vaɪbrənt] ADJ (*sound*) vibrante; (*colour*) vivace, vivo(-a); **to be vibrant with life** sprizzare vita da tutti i pori.

vi·bra·phone ['vaɪbrəˌfəʊn] N vibrafono.

vi·brate [vaɪˈbreɪt] VI: **to vibrate (with)** (*quiver*) vibrare (per); (*resound*) risuonare (di); (*footsteps*) risuonare.

vi·bra·tion [vaɪˈbreɪʃən] N vibrazione *f*.

vi·bra·tor [vaɪˈbreɪtə] N (*for massage*) vibromassaggiatore *m* (elettrico); (*sex toy*) vibratore *m*.

vic·ar ['vɪkə] N (*Church of England*) pastore *m*; (*Roman Catholic*) vicario.

vic·ar·age ['vɪkərɪdʒ] N canonica (*anglicana*).

vi·cari·ous [vɪˈkɛərɪəs] ADJ: **to get vicarious pleasure out of sth** trarre piacere indirettamente da qc.

vice- [vaɪs] PREF vice... .

vice¹ [vaɪs] N vizio.

vice² [vaɪs] N (*tool*) morsa.

♦ **vice-chairman** [ˌvaɪsˈtʃeəmən] N (*pl* **-men**) vicepresi-

dente *m*.

♦ **vice-chancellor** [ˌvaɪsˈtʃɑːnsələ] N (*Brit Univ*) rettore *m* (*eletto, non onorario*).

♦ **vice-consul** [ˌvaɪsˈkɒnsəl] N viceconsole *m*.

♦ **vice-presidency** [ˌvaɪsˈprɛzɪdənsɪ] N vicepresidenza.

♦ **vice-president** [ˌvaɪsˈprɛzɪdənt] N vicepresidente *m*.

vice·roy ['vaɪsrɔɪ] N viceré *m inv*.

♦ **vice squad** N (squadra del) buon costume *f*.

♦ **vice ver·sa** [ˌvaɪsɪˈvɜːsə] ADV viceversa.

vi·cin·ity [vɪˈsɪnɪtɪ] N vicinanze *fpl*.

vi·cious ['vɪʃəs] ADJ (*attack*) brutale; (*blow, kick*) dato(-a) con cattiveria, violento(-a); (*animal*) cattivo(-a); (*remark, criticism*) crudele; (*glare*) malevolo(-a), d'odio; (*tongue*) velenoso(-a); **a vicious habit** un vizio.

♦ **vicious circle** N circolo vizioso.

vi·cious·ly ['vɪʃəslɪ] ADV (*fight*) ferocemente; (*hit*) con cattiveria; (*speak*) malignamente; (*glare*) con odio, velenosamente.

vi·cious·ness ['vɪʃəsnɪs] N (*of behaviour*) brutalità, ferocia; (*of remark, criticism*) cattiveria, malignità.

vi·cis·si·tudes [vɪˈsɪsɪtjuːdz] NPL (*frm*) vicissitudini *fpl*.

vic·tim ['vɪktɪm] N vittima; **to be the victim of** essere la vittima di; **to fall victim to** (*fig: desire, sb's charms*) essere vittima di.

vic·timi·za·tion [ˌvɪktɪmaɪˈzeɪʃən] N persecuzione *f*; **to be the subject of victimization by sb** essere oggetto di persecuzione da parte di qn.

vic·tim·ize ['vɪktɪˌmaɪz] VT perseguitare qn.

vic·tor ['vɪktə] N (*in sport, battle*) vincitore(-trice).

Vic·to·rian [vɪkˈtɔːrɪən] ADJ, N vittoriano(-a).

Vic·to·ri·ana [vɪkˌtɔːrɪˈɑːnə] NPL *oggetti d'antiquariato dell'epoca vittoriana.*

vic·to·ri·ous [vɪkˈtɔːrɪəs] ADJ (*gen*) vittorioso(-a); (*shout*) di vittoria, trionfante.

vic·to·ry ['vɪktərɪ] N vittoria; **to win a victory over sb** riportare una vittoria su qn.

vict·uals ['vɪtlz] NPL (*old*) vettovaglie *fpl*.

vi·cu·ña [vɪˈkjuːnjə] N vigogna.

vide ['vaɪdɪ] IMPERS VB vedi.

video ['vɪdɪəʊ] N (*fam*) video *m inv*.

♦ **video camera** N videocamera.

♦ **video cassette** N videocassetta.

♦ **video (cassette) recorder** N videoregistratore *m*.

video·disk ['vɪdɪəʊˌdɪsk] N videodisco.

♦ **video game** N videogioco.

♦ **video nasty** N (*fam*) horror-film *m inv* (*a sfondo pornografico*).

video·phone ['vɪdɪəʊˌfəʊn] N videotelefono.

♦ **video recorder** N videoregistratore *m*.

♦ **video recording** N videoregistrazione *f*.

video·tape ['vɪdɪəʊˌteɪp] VT registrare su videocassetta.

♦ **video tape** N videocassetta.

vie [vaɪ] VI: **to vie (with sb) for sth** competere (con qn) per qc; **to vie with one another for sth** contendersi qc.

Vi·en·na [vɪˈɛnə] N Vienna.

Vi·et·nam, Viet Nam [ˌvjɛtˈnæm] N Vietnam *m*.

Vi·et·nam·ese [ˌvjɛtnəˈmiːz] **1** ADJ vietnamita *inv*.
2 N (*person*) vietnamita *m/f*; (*language*) vietnamita *m*.

view [vjuː] **1** N **a** (*sight*) vista; (*panorama*) veduta; **a splendid view of the river** una splendida veduta del fiume; **50 views of Venice** 50 vedute di Venezia; **you'll get a better view from here** da qui vedrai meglio; **back/front view of the house** la casa vista da dietro/davanti; **to be in** *or* **within view (of sth)** essere in vista (di qc); **the house is within view of the sea** la casa ha la vista

sul mare; **to come into** or **within view** arrivare in vista; **the city suddenly came into view** la città apparve all'improvviso; **in full view of sb** sotto gli occhi di qn; **hidden from view** nascosto(-a) alla vista; **on view** (*house*) in visione; (*exhibit*) in esposizione; **an overall view of the situation** (*survey*) una visione globale della situazione **b** (*opinion*) punto di vista, opinione *f*; **in my view** a mio parere, a mio avviso; **to take** or **hold the view that** ... essere dell'opinione che...; **to take a dim** or **poor view of sth** accogliere male qc **c** (*consideration*): **in view of the fact that** ... visto che..., considerato che...; **in view of this,** ... visto ciò... **d** (*intention*): **to have in view** avere in mente; **to keep sth in view** non perdere qc di vista; **with this in view** a questo scopo; **with a view to doing sth** con l'intenzione di fare qc. [2] VT (*house*) vedere; (*television*) guardare; (*situation*) considerare; **how does the government view it?** che cosa ne pensa il governo?

View·data® ['vju:ˌdeɪtə] N (*Brit*) *sistema di televideo.*

view·er ['vju:əʳ] N [a] (*TV*) telespettatore(-trice) [b] (*for slides*) visore *m*.

view·finder ['vju:ˌfaɪndəʳ] N (*Phot*) mirino.

view·point ['vju:ˌpɔɪnt] N (*on hill*) posizione *f*; (*fig*) punto di vista.

vig·il ['vɪdʒɪl] N veglia; **to keep vigil** vegliare.

vigi·lance ['vɪdʒɪləns] N vigilanza.

vigi·lant ['vɪdʒɪlənt] ADJ vigile.

vigi·lan·te [ˌvɪdʒɪˈlæntɪ] N vigilante *m/f* (*privato cittadino*).

vi·gnette [vɪˈnjet] N (*description*) quadretto; (*illustration in book*) illustrazione *f*; (*Art, Phot*) ritratto a mezzo busto su sfondo sfumato.

vig·or·ous ['vɪgərəs] ADJ (*handshake, speech, protest*) vigoroso(-a), energico(-a); (*character*) vitale; (*plant*) forte.

vig·or·ous·ly ['vɪgərəslɪ] ADV (*move, grow*) con vigore; (*speak, protest*) vigorosamente.

vig·our, (*Am*) **vig·or** ['vɪgəʳ] N vigore *m*.

Vi·king ['vaɪkɪŋ] ADJ, N vichingo(-a).

vile [vaɪl] ADJ (*horrible*) orrendo(-a); (*very bad*: *temper*) pessimo(-a); (: *smell*) disgustoso(-a); **what a vile trick!** che scherzo meschino!; **a vile habit** un vizio detestabile.

vili·fi·ca·tion [ˌvɪlɪfɪˈkeɪʃən] N (*frm*) diffamazione *f*.

vili·fy ['vɪlɪˌfaɪ] VT (*frm*) diffamare.

vil·la ['vɪlə] N villa.

vil·lage ['vɪlɪdʒ] [1] N paese *m*, villaggio. [2] ADJ (*of a village, villages*) di paese; (*local*) del paese; **a village inn** una locanda di paese; **the village inn** la locanda del paese; **the village idiot** lo scemo del villaggio.

♦ **village green** N *spazio verde al centro del paese.*

vil·lag·er ['vɪlɪdʒəʳ] N abitante *m/f* di paese, paesano(-a).

vil·lain ['vɪlən] N mascalzone *m*; (*hum*: *rascal*) briccone (-a); (*scoundrel*) canaglia; (*in novel, film*) cattivo; (*fam*: *criminal*) delinquente *m*.

vil·lain·ous ['vɪlənəs] ADJ scellerato(-a), infame.

vil·lainy ['vɪlənɪ] N scelleratezza.

vim [vɪm] N (*fam*) energia.

vinai·grette [ˌvɪneɪˈɡret] N vinaigrette *f inv*.

vin·di·cate ['vɪndɪˌkeɪt] VT (*assertion, claim*) provare la fondatezza di, confermare; **he was finally vindicated** fu alla fine provato che aveva ragione.

vin·di·ca·tion [ˌvɪndɪˈkeɪʃən] N giustificazione *f*; **in vindi·cation of** a conferma di.

vin·dic·tive [vɪnˈdɪktɪv] ADJ vendicativo(-a); **to feel vindic·tive towards sb** volersi vendicare di qn.

vin·dic·tive·ly [vɪnˈdɪktɪvlɪ] ADV vendicativamente.

vine [vaɪn] N (*grapevine*) vite *f*; (*climbing plant*) rampicante *m*.

vin·egar ['vɪnɪɡəʳ] N aceto.

vin·egary ['vɪnɪɡərɪ] ADJ (*wine, taste, smell*) che sa d'aceto; (*person*) acido(-a).

vine·grower ['vaɪnˌɡrəʊəʳ] N viticoltore *m*.

♦ **vine-growing** ['vaɪnˌɡrəʊɪŋ] [1] ADJ viticolo(-a). [2] N viticoltura.

vine·yard ['vɪnjəd] N vigna, vigneto.

vin·tage ['vɪntɪdʒ] N (*harvest*) vendemmia; (*season*) periodo della vendemmia; (*year*) annata; **what vintage is this wine?** di che annata è questo vino?; **the 1980 vintage** il vino del 1980.

♦ **vintage car** N auto *f inv* d'epoca.

♦ **vintage wine** N vino d'annata.

♦ **vintage year** N: **it has been a vintage year for plays** è stata una buona annata per il teatro.

vint·ner ['vɪntnəʳ] N (*retailer*) vinaio(-a); (*wholesaler*) commerciante *m/f* di vini.

vi·nyl ['vaɪnɪl] N vinile *m*.

vio·la[1] [vɪˈəʊlə] N (*Mus*) viola.

vio·la[2] [vɪˈəʊlə] N (*Bot*) viola.

vio·late ['vaɪəˌleɪt] VT violare.

vio·la·tion [ˌvaɪəˈleɪʃən] N violazione *f*; **in violation of sth** in contravvenzione *f inv* a qc.

vio·lence ['vaɪələns] N violenza; (*Pol*) incidenti *mpl* violenti; **outbreaks of violence** episodi di violenza; **acts of violence** atti di violenza; **robbery with violence** rapina a mano armata; **to do violence to sth** (*fig*) fare violenza a qc.

vio·lent ['vaɪələnt] ADJ (*gen*) violento(-a); **to die a violent death** morire di morte violenta; **a violent temper** un temperamento violento; **to be in a violent temper** essere furioso(-a); **a violent dislike of sb/sth** una violenta avversione per qn/qc; **by violent means** con l'uso della forza.

vio·lent·ly ['vaɪələntlɪ] ADV (*attack, react*) in modo violento, violentemente; (*severely*: *sick, angry*) terribilmente; **to fall violently in love with sb** innamorarsi follemente di qn.

vio·let ['vaɪəlɪt] [1] N (*Bot*) violetta; (*colour*) violetto. [2] ADJ violetto(-a).

vio·lin [ˌvaɪəˈlɪn] [1] N violino. [2] ADJ (*case, concerto*) per violino.

vio·lin·ist [ˌvaɪəˈlɪnɪst] N violinista *m/f*.

VIP [ˌviːaɪˈpiː] N ABBR (= *very important person*) Vip *m/f inv*.

vi·per ['vaɪpəʳ] N (*Zool, also fig*) vipera.

vi·ra·go [vɪˈrɑːɡəʊ] N (*frm pej*) virago *f*.

vi·ral ['vaɪərəl] ADJ virale.

Virgil ['vɜːdʒɪl] N Virgilio.

vir·gin ['vɜːdʒɪn] [1] N vergine *f*; **she/he is a virgin** lei/lui è vergine; **the Virgin** (*Mary*) la Beata Vergine. [2] ADJ (*fig*: *forest, soil*) vergine *inv*; **virgin snow** neve fresca.

vir·gin·al ['vɜːdʒɪnəl] [1] ADJ [a] (*chaste*) verginale [b] (*pristine*) immacolato(-a). [2] N (*Mus*) spinetta.

Vir·ginia creep·er [vəˌdʒɪnjəˈkriːpəʳ] N vite *f* del Canada.

vir·gin·ity [vɜːˈdʒɪnɪtɪ] N verginità.

Vir·go ['vɜːɡəʊ] N (*Astron, Astrol*) Vergine *f*; **to be Virgo** essere della Vergine.

vir·ile ['vɪraɪl] ADJ virile.

vi·ril·ity [vɪˈrɪlɪtɪ] N virilità.

vir·tual ['vɜːtjʊəl] ADJ effettivo(-a), vero(-a); (*Comput,*

Phys) virtuale; **the virtual leader** il capo all'atto pratico; **the strike led to the virtual closure of the dock** lo sciopero ha praticamente portato alla chiusura del porto; **it was a virtual defeat** di fatto è stata una sconfitta; **it's a virtual impossibility** è praticamente impossibile.

vir·tu·al·ly ['vɜ:tjʊəlɪ] ADV (*in effect*) di fatto; (*to all intents and purposes*) praticamente; **she virtually runs the business** di fatto è lei che gestisce l'azienda; **it is virtually impossible to do anything** è praticamente impossibile fare qualcosa.

♦ **virtual reality** N (*Comput*) realtà *f* virtuale.

vir·tue ['vɜ:tju:] N (*goodness*) virtù *f inv*; (*advantage*) pregio, vantaggio; **it has the virtue of simplicity** *or* **of being simple** ha il pregio di essere semplice; **I see no virtue in doing that** non vedo nessun vantaggio nel farlo; **to make a virtue of necessity** fare di necessità virtù; **by virtue of** in virtù di, grazie a.

vir·tu·os·i·ty [ˌvɜ:tjʊˈɒsɪtɪ] N virtuosismo.

vir·tuo·so [ˌvɜ:tjʊˈəʊzəʊ] N virtuoso(-a).

vir·tu·ous ['vɜ:tjʊəs] ADJ virtuoso(-a).

viru·lence ['vɪrʊləns] N (*frm*) virulenza.

viru·lent ['vɪrʊlənt] ADJ (*frm*) virulento(-a).

vi·rus ['vaɪərəs] N virus *m inv*.

visa ['vi:zə] N visto.

vis-à-vis [ˌvi:zəˈvi:] PREP rispetto a, in confronto a, nei riguardi di.

vis·cer·al ['vɪsərəl] ADJ (*liter*) viscerale.

vis·cose ['vɪskəʊs] N viscosa.

vis·cos·i·ty [vɪsˈkɒsɪtɪ] N viscosità.

vis·count ['vaɪkaʊnt] N visconte *m*.

vis·cous ['vɪskəs] ADJ viscoso(-a).

vise [vaɪs] N (*Am*) = **vice**[1].

vis·ibil·i·ty [ˌvɪzɪˈbɪlɪtɪ] N visibilità.

vis·ible ['vɪzəbl] ADJ a visibile; **visible to the naked eye** che si può vedere ad occhio nudo; **to become visible** apparire b (*obvious*) evidente; **visible exports/imports** esportazioni *fpl*/importazioni *fpl* visibili.

vis·ibly ['vɪzəblɪ] ADV visibilmente.

Visi·goth ['vɪzɪˌgɒθ] N Visigoto.

vi·sion ['vɪʒən] N a (*eyesight*) vista, capacità visiva b (*imagination, foresight, apparition*) visione *f*; **a man of vision** un uomo lungimirante *or* che vede lontano; **my vision of the future** la mia visione del futuro; **to see visions** avere le visioni; **I had visions of having to walk home** già mi vedevo dover andare a casa a piedi.

vi·sion·ary ['vɪʒənərɪ] [1] N visionario(-a).
[2] ADJ lungimirante; (*dreamlike*) irreale.

♦ **vision defect** N difetto della vista.

vis·it ['vɪzɪt] [1] N visita; (*stay*) soggiorno; **to go on a visit to** (*person*) andare in visita da; (*place*) andare a visitare; **to pay a visit to** (*person*) fare una visita a; (*place*) andare a visitare; **on a private/official visit** in visita privata/ufficiale.
[2] VT a (*person*) andare a trovare; (*frm*) andare in visita da; (*place: go and see*) visitare; (: *inspect*) ispezionare b (*stay with: person*) essere ospite di

▶ **visit with** VI + PREP (*Am*) chiacchierare con.

vis·ita·tion [ˌvɪzɪˈteɪʃən] N a (*frm: by official*) visita; (: *by bishop*) visita pastorale b (*hum*): **a visitation (from sb)** una visita inopportuna (da parte di qn) c (*Rel*): **the Visitation of the Blessed Virgin Mary** la Visitazione della Beata Vergine d (*frm: calamity*) punizione *f* divina.

vis·it·ing ['vɪzɪtɪŋ] ADJ (*speaker, professor, team*) ospite.

♦ **visiting card** N biglietto da visita.

♦ **visiting hours** NPL orario *msg* delle visite.

visi·tor ['vɪzɪtə'] N (*guest*) ospite *m/f*; (*tourist*) turista *m/f*; (*in hospital, at zoo, exhibition*) visitatore(-trice); **visitors to the town** i visitatori della città; **you've got a visitor** (*in hospital, at home*) c'è una visita per te.

♦ **visitors' book** N (*in hotel*) registro dei clienti; (*in museum*) registro dei visitatori.

vi·sor ['vaɪzə'] N (*on helmet*) visiera; (*Aut*) aletta parasole.

VISTA ['vɪstə] N ABBR (= *Volunteers in Service to America*) *volontariato in zone depresse degli Stati Uniti*.

vis·ta ['vɪstə] N (*view*) vista; (*fig*) prospettiva.

vis·ual ['vɪzjʊəl] ADJ visivo(-a).

♦ **visual aid** N sussidio visivo.

♦ **visual arts** NPL: **the visual arts** le arti figurative.

♦ **visual display unit** N (*Comput*) videoterminale *m*, unità *f inv* di visualizzazione *f*.

visu·al·ize ['vɪzjʊəˌlaɪz] VT (*imagine*) immaginare, immaginarsi; (*foresee*) prevedere; **to visualize sb doing sth** immaginare qn che fa qc.

visu·al·ly ['vɪzjʊəlɪ] ADV: **visually handicapped** (*blind*) non vedente; (*visually impaired*) videoleso(-a); **visually the film was good** sul piano dell'immagine il film era buono; **visually appealing** piacevole a vedersi.

vi·tal ['vaɪtl] ADJ a (*gen*) vitale; (*error*) fatale; **of vital importance (to sb/sth)** di vitale importanza (per qn/qc); **it is vital that** è essenziale che b (*lively*) pieno(-a) di vitalità.

vi·tal·i·ty [vaɪˈtælɪtɪ] N vitalità; **his performance lacked vitality** la sua esecuzione mancava di brio.

vi·tal·ly ['vaɪtlɪ] ADV: **vitally important** di vitale importanza; **vitally urgent** estremamente urgente.

♦ **vital statistics** NPL (*of population*) statistica *fsg* demografica; (*fam: woman's*) misure *fpl*.

vita·min ['vɪtəmɪn] N vitamina; **with added vitamins** vitaminizzato(-a).

♦ **vitamin deficiency** N carenza vitaminica, avitaminosi *f*.

♦ **vitamin tablet** N (confetto di) vitamina.

vi·ti·ate ['vɪʃɪˌeɪt] VT (*frm: all senses*) viziare.

vit·re·ous ['vɪtrɪəs] ADJ (*china, enamel*) vetrificato(-a); (*rock*) vetroso(-a).

vit·ri·fy ['vɪtrɪˌfaɪ] VT vetrificare.

vit·ri·ol ['vɪtrɪɒl] N (*Chem*) vetriolo; (*fig*) veleno.

vit·ri·ol·ic [ˌvɪtrɪˈɒlɪk] ADJ (*fig*) al vetriolo.

vi·tu·pera·tive [vɪˈtju:pərətɪv] ADJ (*frm: person*) offensivo (-a); (: *speech*) ingiurioso(-a).

viva ['vaɪvə] N (*also*: **viva voce**) (esame *m*) orale *m*.

vi·va·cious [vɪˈveɪʃəs] ADJ vivace, pieno(-a) di brio.

vi·vac·i·ty [vɪˈvæsɪtɪ] N vivacità.

viv·id ['vɪvɪd] ADJ (*colour*) vivo(-a), vivido(-a); (*dream, recollection, expression on face*) chiaro(-a); (*description, memory*) vivido(-a); **a vivid imagination** una fervida immaginazione.

viv·id·ly ['vɪvɪdlɪ] ADV (*describe*) in modo vivido; (*remember*) chiaramente.

viv·id·ness ['vɪvɪdnɪs] N (*of colour, description*) vivacità; (*of impression, recollection*) chiarezza.

vivi·sec·tion [ˌvɪvɪˈsekʃən] N vivisezione *f*.

vix·en ['vɪksn] N volpe *f* femmina; (*pej: woman*) vipera.

viz ABBR (= *videlicet: namely*) cioè.

vi·zier [vɪˈzɪə'] N visir *m inv*.

VLF [ˌvi:elˈef] N ABBR (= *very low frequency*) V.L.F. (= *bassissima frequenza*).

♦ **V-neck** ['vi:ˌnek] N maglione *m* con scollo a V.

♦ **V-necked** [ˌviːˈnɛkt] ADJ con scollo a V.

VOA [ˌviːəʊˈeɪ] N ABBR (= *Voice of America*) voce *f* dell'America (*alla radio*).

vo·cabu·lary [vəʊˈkæbjʊlərɪ] N (*gen*) vocabolario; (*in textbook*) vocabolario, dizionario; **we have to learn all the new vocabulary** dobbiamo imparare tutti i vocaboli nuovi.

vo·cal [ˈvəʊkəl] ADJ **a** (*gen*) vocale **b** (*fig: vociferous*) pronto(-a) a esprimere la propria opinione.

♦ **vocal chords** NPL corde *fpl* vocali.

vo·cal·ic [vəʊˈkælɪk] ADJ vocalico(-a).

vo·cal·ist [ˈvəʊkəlɪst] N cantante *m/f* (*in un gruppo*).

vo·cal·ize [ˈvəʊkəˌlaɪz] VT (*Ling*) vocalizzare; (*frm: opinions etc*) esprimere, dar voce a.

vo·cals [ˈvəʊkəlz] NPL: **lead vocals** voce *fsg* solista; **backing vocals** accompagnamento vocale.

vo·ca·tion [vəʊˈkeɪʃən] N vocazione *f*; **to have a vocation for teaching** avere la vocazione dell'insegnamento.

vo·ca·tion·al [vəʊˈkeɪʃənl] ADJ (*training*) professionale.

♦ **vocational guidance** N orientamento professionale.

voca·tive [ˈvɒkətɪv] **1** ADJ vocativo(-a). **2** N vocativo.

vo·cif·er·ous [vəʊˈsɪfərəs] ADJ rumoroso(-a).

vod·ka [ˈvɒdkə] N vodka *f inv*.

vogue [vəʊg] N (*fashion*) moda; (*popularity*) voga; **to be in vogue** OR **be the vogue** essere di moda, essere in voga.

voice [vɔɪs] **1** N (*gen, Gram*) voce *f*; **to lose one's voice** perdere la voce; **she is in fine voice again** ha riacquistato la sua bella voce; **in a loud/soft voice** a voce alta/bassa; **at the top of one's voice** a tutta voce, con quanta voce si ha in gola *or* in corpo; **with one voice** all'unisono; **to have a voice in the matter** aver voce in capitolo; **to give voice to** esprimere. **2** VT (*feelings, opinions*) esprimere.

voice·less [ˈvɔɪslɪs] ADJ (*Ling*) sordo(-a); (*mute*) muto(-a).

♦ **voice-over** [ˈvɔɪsˌəʊvəʳ] N (*TV, Cine*) voce *f* fuori campo *inv*.

void [vɔɪd] **1** ADJ (*frm: Law*) nullo(-a); (*empty*) vuoto(-a); **void of** privo(-a) di; **to make** *or* **render a contract void** invalidare un contratto. **2** N vuoto; **to fill the void** colmare il vuoto.

voile [vɔɪl] N voile *m*.

vol. ABBR (= *volume*) vol.

vola·tile [ˈvɒləˌtaɪl] ADJ (*Chem*) volatile; (*fig: situation*) esplosivo(-a); (: *character*) volubile.

vol-au-vent [ˈvɒləˌvɒŋ] N vol-au-vent *m inv*.

vol·can·ic [vɒlˈkænɪk] ADJ vulcanico(-a).

vol·ca·no [vɒlˈkeɪnəʊ] N (*pl* **volcanoes**) vulcano.

vole [vəʊl] N: **field vole** topo campagnolo comune; **water vole** topo arvicola.

vo·li·tion [vəˈlɪʃən] N: **of one's own volition** di propria volontà.

vol·ley [ˈvɒlɪ] N (*of shots, stones, insults*) raffica, scarica; (*of gunfire*) salva; (*Tennis*) volée *f inv*, volata.

volley·ball [ˈvɒlɪˌbɔːl] N pallavolo *f*.

volt [vəʊlt] N volt *m inv*.

volt·age [ˈvəʊltɪdʒ] N tensione *f*, voltaggio; **high/low voltage** alta/bassa tensione.

♦ **voltage regulator** N regolatore *m* di tensione.

volte [ˈvɒltɪ] N (*Horse-riding*) volta.

volte-face [ˈvɒltˈfɑːs] N voltafaccia *m inv*.

volt·me·ter [ˈvəʊltˌmiːtəʳ] N voltimetro.

vol·uble [ˈvɒljʊbl] ADJ loquace.

vol·ume [ˈvɒljuːm] N **a** (*book*) volume *m*; **volume one/two** primo/secondo volume **b** (*size, sound*) volume *m*; (*of*

tank) capacità *f inv* **c** : **to speak volumes** (*express a great deal*) dire tutto; **his expression spoke volumes** la sua espressione lasciava capire tutto; **it speaks volumes for his charm** la dice lunga sul suo fascino.

♦ **volume control** N (*Radio, TV*) regolatore *m or* manopola del volume.

♦ **volume discount** N (*Comm*) vantaggio sul volume di vendita.

volu·met·ric [ˌvɒljʊˈmɛtrɪk] ADJ volumetrico(-a).

vo·lu·mi·nous [vəˈluːmɪnəs] ADJ voluminoso(-a); (*writer*) prolifico(-a); (*notes*) abbondante.

vol·un·tari·ly [ˈvɒləntərɪlɪ] ADV spontaneamente, volontariamente.

vol·un·tary [ˈvɒləntərɪ] ADJ (*statement, confession*) spontaneo(-a); (*attendance*) facoltativo(-a); (*unpaid: contribution, work, worker*) volontario(-a).

♦ **voluntary liquidation** N (*Comm*) liquidazione *f* volontaria.

vol·un·teer [ˌvɒlənˈtɪəʳ] **1** N (*Mil, gen*) volontario(-a). **2** VT (*one's help, services, suggestion*) offrire spontaneamente; (*information*) fornire; **no-one volunteered an answer** nessuno si è offerto di rispondere; **he rarely volunteers his opinion** è raro che esprima la propria opinione spontaneamente. **3** VI (*for a task*) offrirsi come volontario(-a), offrirsi spontaneamente; (*Mil*) arruolarsi volontario(-a); **to volunteer to do sth** offrirsi spontaneamente di fare qc. **4** ADJ (*forces, helpers*) volontario(-a); (*corps*) di volontari.

vo·lup·tu·ous [vəˈlʌptjʊəs] ADJ (*pleasure, sensation*) voluttuoso(-a); (*lips, figure*) sensuale.

vo·lup·tu·ous·ness [vəˈlʌptjʊəsnɪs] N voluttuosità, sensualità.

vom·it [ˈvɒmɪt] **1** N vomito. **2** VT, VI vomitare.

vom·it·ing [ˈvɒmɪtɪŋ] N vomito.

voo·doo [ˈvuːduː] N vudù *m*.

vo·ra·cious [vəˈreɪʃəs] ADJ (*appetite*) smisurato(-a); (*reader*) avido(-a).

vo·ra·cious·ly [vəˈreɪʃəslɪ] ADV (*eat*) voracemente; (*read*) avidamente.

vo·rac·ity [vɒˈræsɪtɪ] N voracità.

vor·tex [ˈvɔːtɛks] N (*pl* **vortices** [ˈvɔːtɪsiːz]) (*frm: whirl*) vortice *m*; (*fig*) turbine *m*.

vote [vəʊt] **1** N voto; (*ballot, election*) votazione *f*; **vote for/against** voto a favore/contrario; **to put sth to the vote** OR **to take a vote on sth** mettere qc ai voti; **as the 1979 vote showed** com'è risultato dalle votazioni del 1979; **the Labour vote has decreased** il partito laburista ha perso voti. **2** VT (*gen*) votare; (*sum of money*) votare a favore di; **the bill was voted through parliament** la proposta di legge è stata approvata dal parlamento; **he was voted secretary** è stato eletto segretario; **to vote a proposal down** respingere una proposta. **3** VI: **to vote (for sb/sth)** votare (per qn/qc); **to vote on sth** mettere qc ai voti; **to vote Labour/Conservative** votare laburista/conservatore; **to vote to do sth** scegliere di fare qc; **to vote against/in favour of sth** votare a favore di/contro qc; **I vote we turn back** (*fam*) io propongo di tornare indietro
▶ **vote down** VT + ADV bocciare ai voti
▶ **vote in** VT + ADV eleggere
▶ **vote out** VT + ADV: **to vote sb out** votare a sfavore della rielezione di qn.

♦ **vote of confidence** N (*Pol*) voto di fiducia.

♦ **vote of no confidence** N (*Pol*) voto di sfiducia; **to pass a vote of no confidence** dare il voto di sfiducia.

♦ **vote of thanks** N discorso di ringraziamento.

vot·er ['vəʊtəˢ] N elettore(-trice).

vot·ing ['vəʊtɪŋ] N votazione *f*, voto.

♦ **voting booth** N cabina elettorale.

♦ **voting paper** N (*Brit*) scheda elettorale.

♦ **voting right** N (*of shareholder*) diritto di voto.

vo·tive ['vəʊtɪv] ADJ (*offering*) votivo(-a).

vouch [vaʊtʃ] VI: **to vouch for sth** garantire qc; **to vouch for sb** garantire per qn.

vouch·er ['vaʊtʃəˢ] N buono, tagliando, coupon *m inv*; **travel voucher** voucher *m inv*.

vouch·safe [ˌvaʊtʃ'seɪf] VT (*liter, frm*): **to vouchsafe sth (to sb)** (*reply, help*) accordare qc (a qn); (*peace*) garantire qc (a qn).

vow [vaʊ] ⬚1 N voto; **to take** or **make a vow to do sth** fare voto di fare qc; **to take one's vows** (*Rel*) prendere i voti. ⬚2 VT (*obedience, allegiance*) giurare; **to vow to do sth/ that** giurare di fare qc/che.

vow·el ['vaʊəl] N vocale *f*.

♦ **vowel sound** N suono vocalico.

voy·age ['vɔɪdʒ] N viaggio per mare; **the voyage out/back** il viaggio di andata/di ritorno.

voy·ag·er ['vɔɪədʒəˢ] N viaggiatore(-trice).

vo·yeur [vwɑːˈjɜːˢ] N guardone(-a), voyeur *m inv*.

vo·yeur·ism [vwɑːˈjɜːrɪzəm] N voyeurismo.

VP [ˌviːˈpiː] N ABBR (= *vice-president*) V.P.

VS ABBR = **versus**.

♦ **V-sign** ['viːˌsaɪn] N: **to give (sb) the V-sign** (*for victory*) fare il segno di vittoria; (*Brit: as insult*) ≈ fare le corna.

VSO [ˌviːɛsˈəʊ] N ABBR (*Brit*: = *Voluntary Service Overseas*) *servizio volontario in paesi sottosviluppati*.

VT ABBR (*Am Post*) = *Vermont*.

Vulcan ['vʌlkən] N Vulcano.

vul·cani·za·tion [ˌvʌlkənaɪˈzeɪʃən] N vulcanizzazione *f*.

vul·can·ize ['vʌlkəˌnaɪz] VT vulcanizzare.

vul·gar ['vʌlgəˢ] ADJ (*gen, pej*) volgare.

♦ **vulgar fraction** N (*Math*) frazione *f* ordinaria.

vul·gar·ity [vʌlˈgærɪtɪ] N volgarità.

♦ **vulgar Latin** N latino volgare.

Vul·gate ['vʌlgeɪt] N (*Bible*): **the Vulgate** la Vulgata.

vul·ner·abil·ity [ˌvʌlnərəˈbɪlɪtɪ] N vulnerabilità.

vul·ner·able ['vʌlnərəbl] ADJ (*person*) vulnerabile; (*position*) esposto(-a).

vul·ture ['vʌltʃəˢ] N avvoltoio.

W

W, w ['dʌblju:] N (letter) W, w f or m inv; **W for William** ≈ W come Washington.

W ABBR a (= West) O b (Elec: = watt) W.

WA ABBR a (Am Post)= Washington b (Australia Post)= Western Australia.

wacky, whacky ['wækɪ] ADJ (comp -ier, superl -iest) (fam) pazzoide.

wad [wɒd] N (of cloth) tampone m; (of chewing gum, putty) pallina; (of cotton wool) batuffolo; (of papers, banknotes) fascio.

wad·ding ['wɒdɪŋ] N imbottitura.

wad·dle ['wɒdl] VI camminare come una papera; **to waddle in/out** etc entrare/uscire etc camminando come una papera.

wade [weɪd] [1] VI: **to wade through** (water, mud) camminare in; (long grass, corn) farsi strada attraverso; (fig: book) leggere con fatica; **to wade ashore** raggiungere a piedi la riva; **to wade into sb** (fig) scagliarsi su qn; **he waded in and helped us** (fig) si rimboccò le maniche e ci aiutò.
[2] VT (river) guadare.

wad·er ['weɪdə'] N (bird) trampoliere m; (boot) stivale m da pesca.

wadi ['wɒdɪ] N uadi m inv.

wa·fer ['weɪfə'] N (Culin, Elec) wafer m inv; (with ice cream) cialda; (Rel) ostia.

♦ **wafer-thin** [ˌweɪfə'θɪn] ADJ sottilissimo(-a).

waf·fle ['wɒfl] [1] N (Culin) cialda; (fam: talk) chiacchiere fpl, ciance fpl.
[2] VI (fam: also: **waffle on**) cianciare, chiacchierare; (in exam, essay) chiacchierare molto e dire poco.

♦ **waffle iron** N stampo per cialde.

waft [wɑ:ft] [1] VT (sound, scent) portare.
[2] VI diffondersi.

wag[1] [wæg] [1] N: **with a wag of its tail** dimenando la coda.
[2] VT: **the dog wagged its tail** il cane scodinzolò; **to wag one's finger at sb** fare un cenno di rimprovero a qn scuotendo il dito.
[3] VI (tail) dimenarsi; **that'll set the tongues wagging** (fig) farà scatenare le malelingue; **his tongue never stops wagging** (fig) non sta mai zitto.

wag[2] [wæg] N (joker) burlone(-a).

wage [weɪdʒ] [1] N (often pl) paga; **a day's wages** un giorno di paga; **she gets a good wage** è pagata bene; **minimum wage** minimo salariale.
[2] VT (campaign) intraprendere; **to wage war** fare la guerra.
[3] ADJ (demand, negotiations) salariale.

♦ **wage claim** N rivendicazione f salariale.

♦ **wage differential** N differenziali mpl salariali.

♦ **wage earn·er** ['weɪdʒ,ɜ:nə'] N salariato(-a); **the family wage earner** il sostegno economico della famiglia.

♦ **wage freeze** N blocco dei salari.

♦ **wage packet** N (Brit) busta f paga inv.

wa·ger ['weɪdʒə'] [1] N: **wager (on)** scommessa (su).
[2] VT (sum of money): **to wager (on)** puntare (su), scommettere (su); **to wager that ...** scommettere che... .

♦ **wage rise** N aumento di stipendio.

♦ **wages clerk** N contabile m/f.

wag·gle ['wægl] [1] N: **with a waggle of her hips** ancheggiando; **with a waggle of its tail** scodinzolando.
[2] VT (tail) dimenare, agitare; **to waggle one's hips** ancheggiare.
[3] VI dimenarsi, agitarsi.

wag·on, wag·gon ['wægən] N (horse-drawn) carro; (truck) camion m inv; (Rail) vagone m merci inv; (trolley) carrello; **he's on the wagon again!** (fam) ha nuovamente smesso di bere!

wag·on·er, wag·gon·er ['wægənə'] N carrettiere m.

wagon·load, wag·gon·load ['wægən,ləʊd] N (on train) carico; (on cart) carrettata.

♦ **wagon train** N (Am History) carovana di carri.

wag·tail ['wæg,teɪl] N (Zool) ballerina; **grey wagtail** ballerina gialla.

waif [weɪf] N bambino(-a) abbandonato(-a); (slight person) creatura gracile; **waifs and strays** trovatelli mpl.

wail [weɪl] [1] N (of suffering) gemito; (of baby) vagito; (of siren) urlo; (of wind) ululato; **a wail of protest** un urlo di protesta.
[2] VI (see n) gemere; vagire; urlare; ululare.

wail·ing ['weɪlɪŋ] N (of suffering) gemito; (of baby) vagito; (of siren) urlo; (of wind) ululato.

wain·scot·ing, wain·scot·ting ['weɪnskətɪŋ] N perlinatura.

waist [weɪst] N (Anat, of dress) vita; (fig: narrow part: of violin) strozzatura; **stripped to the waist** nudo(-a) fino alla cintura, a torso nudo; **to be up to one's waist in mud** essere nel fango fino alla vita.

waist·band ['weɪst,bænd] N cintura.

waist·coat ['weɪs,kəʊt] N panciotto, gilè m inv.

♦ **waist–deep** [,weɪst'diːp] 1 ADV fino alla cintura, fino alla vita.
2 ADJ alto(-a) fino alla cintura, alto(-a) fino alla vita.

waist·ed ['weɪstɪd] ADJ (dress) segnato(-a) in vita; **high-/low-waisted** a vita alta/bassa.

waist·line ['weɪst,lam] N vita; **to watch one's waistline** badare alla linea.

♦ **waist measurement, waist size** N punto m or giro m vita inv.

wait [weɪt] 1 N: **wait (for)** attesa (di); **to have a long wait** aspettare a lungo; **a 2-hour wait** un'attesa di 2 ore; **to lie in wait (for sb)** tendere un agguato (a qn).
2 VT a (turn, chance) aspettare, attendere
b (Am: delay: dinner etc) ritardare.
3 VI a : **to wait (for sb/sth)** aspettare (qn/qc); **to wait for sb to do sth** aspettare che qn faccia qc; **wait a moment!** (aspetta) un momento!; **wait and see!** aspetta e vedrai!; **we'll have to wait and see** dobbiamo vedere come vanno le cose; **just you wait!** ti faccio vedere io!; **just you wait till your father comes home!** vedrai quando torna tuo padre!; **wait till you're older** aspetta di essere cresciuto(-a); **to keep sb waiting** far aspettare qn; **"repairs while you wait"** "riparazioni lampo"; **I can't wait to see his face** non vedo l'ora di vedere che faccia farà; **I can hardly wait!** non vedo l'ora!; **that was worth waiting for** valeva la pena aspettare tanto
b (as servant): **to wait at table** servire a tavola
▶ **wait about, wait around** VI + ADV restare ad aspettare
▶ **wait behind** VI + ADV trattenersi
▶ **wait in** VI + ADV restare a casa ad aspettare
▶ **wait on** VI + PREP servire; **to wait on sb hand and foot** servire qn in tutto e per tutto
▶ **wait up** VI + ADV restare alzato(-a) (ad aspettare); **don't wait up for me** non rimanere alzato ad aspettarmi
▶ **wait upon** VI + PREP (old: visit) presentare i propri rispetti a.

wait·er ['weɪtəʳ] N cameriere m.

wait·ing ['weɪtɪŋ] N attesa; (Brit Aut): **"no waiting"** "divieto di sosta".

♦ **waiting game** N: **to play a waiting game** temporeggiare.

♦ **waiting list** N lista d'attesa.

♦ **waiting room** N sala d'attesa or d'aspetto.

wait·ress ['weɪtrɪs] N cameriera.

waive [weɪv] VT (claim) rinunciare a; (rule, age limit) non tener conto di.

waiv·er ['weɪvəʳ] N rinuncia.

wake¹ [weɪk] N (of ship) scia; **in the wake of** sulla scia di; **to follow in sb's wake** (fig) camminare dietro a qn; **it left a trail of destruction in its wake** ha lasciato dietro di sé una scia di distruzione.

wake² [weɪk] N (over corpse) veglia funebre.

wake³ [weɪk] (pt woke or waked, pp woken or waked) 1 VI (also: **wake up**) svegliarsi, destarsi; **wake up!** (also fig) svegliati!; **there's enough noise to wake the dead!** c'è un

baccano del diavolo!; **to wake up to sth** (fig) rendersi conto di qc.
2 VT (also: **wake up**) svegliare; (memories, desires) risvegliare; **to wake sb (up) to sth** (fig) aprire gli occhi a qn su qc; **to wake one's ideas up** (fam) darsi una mossa.

wake·ful ['weɪkfʊl] ADJ (person, night) insonne.

wak·en ['weɪkən] VT, VI = **wake³**.

wak·ing ['weɪkɪŋ] ADJ: **in my waking hours** quando sono sveglio(-a).

Wales [weɪlz] N Galles m.

walk [wɔːk] 1 N a (stroll, ramble) passeggiata; (path, place to walk) percorso, sentiero; **to take sb/one's dog for a walk** portare qn/il cane a spasso; **to go for a walk** (short) fare quattro passi or un giretto; (long) fare una passeggiata; **it's only a 10-minute walk from here** ci vogliono solo 10 minuti a piedi da qui; **there's a nice walk by the river** c'è una bella passeggiata lungo il fiume; **from all walks of life** (fig) con ogni tipo di esperienza
b (gait) passo, andatura, camminata; **at a walk** (of person, horse) al passo; **he has an odd sort of walk** ha una camminata tutta particolare.
2 VT a (distance) percorrere a piedi; **we walked 40 kilometres yesterday** ieri abbiamo percorso 40 chilometri a piedi; **to walk the streets** vagare per le strade; (prostitute) battere il marciapiede; **you can walk it in a few minutes** puoi arrivarci a piedi in pochi minuti; **he walked it** (fig) è stato uno scherzo per lui
b (cause to walk: invalid) aiutare a camminare; (lead: dog) portare a spasso; (: horse) portare; **I'll walk you home** ti accompagno a casa; **to walk sb into the ground** or **off their feet** far stancare qn a furia di camminare.
3 VI (gen) camminare; (for pleasure, exercise) passeggiare; (not drive or ride) andare a piedi; **to walk in one's sleep** camminare nel sonno; (habitually) essere sonnambulo(-a); **can your little boy walk yet?** tuo figlio sa già camminare?; **walk a little with me** accompagnami per un pezzo; **to walk up and down (the room)** camminare su e giù (per la stanza); **we had to walk** siamo dovuti andare a piedi; **to walk home** andare a casa a piedi; **we were out walking in the hills** stavamo passeggiando in collina; **to walk into sth** (bump into) andare a sbattere contro qc; (fig: fall into: trap) cadere in qc
▶ **walk about, walk around** 1 VI + ADV camminare; **I've been walking about all afternoon** sono stato in giro tutto il pomeriggio.
2 VI + PREP: **to walk about the room** camminare per la stanza; **to walk about the town** gironzolare per la città
▶ **walk across** VI + PREP attraversare
▶ **walk away** VI + ADV allontanarsi (a piedi), andare via; (fig: unhurt) uscire illeso(-a); **to walk away with sth** (fig: win easily) vincere facilmente qc
▶ **walk away from** VI + ADV + PREP a (pej: job, marriage, relationship) mollare, piantare
b : **to walk away from an accident** uscire incolume da un incidente
▶ **walk in** VI + ADV entrare
▶ **walk off** 1 VI + ADV = **walk away**.
2 VT + ADV (lunch) smaltire; (headache) farsi passare camminando
▶ **walk off with** VI + ADV + PREP (fam): **to walk off with sth** (steal) andarsene con qc; (win: prize, bargain) assicurarsi qc con facilità
▶ **walk on** VI + ADV (go on walking) continuare a camminare; (Theatre) fare la comparsa
▶ **walk out** VI + ADV (go out) uscire; (as protest) uscire

in segno di protesta; (*strike*) scendere in sciopero; **to walk out of a meeting** abbandonare una riunione in segno di protesta; **to walk out on sb** piantare in asso qn; **he walked out on his wife** ha lasciato la moglie

▶ **walk over** VI + PREP (*defeat*) schiacciare; **to walk all over sb** (*dominate*) mettere i piedi in testa a qn

▶ **walk up** VI + ADV (*approach*): **to walk up (to)** avvicinarsi (a); **walk up, walk up!** (*at fair*) avanti!

walk·about ['wɔːkə,baʊt] N: **to go (on a) walkabout** *avere incontri informali col pubblico durante una visita ufficiale.*

walk·er ['wɔːkəʳ] N (*person*) camminatore(-trice); (*for babies*) girello; **he's a good walker** gli piace camminare; **he's a slow walker** ha il passo lento.

walkie-talkie [,wɔːkɪ'tɔːkɪ] N walkie-talkie *m inv.*

♦ **walk-in** ['wɔːk,ɪn] ADJ: **walk-in cupboard** stanzino.

walk·ing ['wɔːkɪŋ] 1 N camminare *m*; **to do a lot of walking** camminare molto.

2 ADJ: **it's within walking distance** ci si arriva a piedi; **he's a walking encyclopaedia** è un'enciclopedia ambulante; **the walking wounded** i feriti in grado di camminare; **walking boots** pedule *fpl*; **walking tour** (*of a city*) giro a piedi; **a walking tour of the hills** una lunga gita a piedi sulle colline.

♦ **walking holiday** N vacanza fatta di lunghe camminate.

♦ **walking shoes** NPL scarpe *fpl* da passeggio.

♦ **walking stick** N bastone *m* da passeggio.

Walk·man® ['wɔːkmən] N walkman ® *m inv.*

♦ **walk-on** ['wɔːk,ɒn] ADJ (*Theatre: part*) da comparsa.

walk·out ['wɔːk,aʊt] N (*from conference*) abbandono; (*strike*) sciopero selvaggio *or* a sorpresa; **to stage a walkout** (*from conference*) ritirarsi in segno di protesta; (*from work*) scendere in sciopero.

walk·over ['wɔːk,əʊvəʳ] N (*Sport*) vittoria facile; **the exam was a walkover** l'esame è stato una vera passeggiata.

♦ **walk-up** ['wɔːk,ʌp] N (*Am*) casa senza ascensore.

walk·way ['wɔːk,weɪ] N passaggio pedonale.

wall [wɔːl] 1 N (*internal, of tunnel, cave*) muro, parete *f*; (*outside*) muro; (*Anat*) parete; (*of tyre*) fianco; (*fig: of smoke*) cortina; **the Berlin Wall** il muro di Berlino; **the Great Wall of China** la Grande Muraglia Cinese; **the city walls** le mura della città; **it drives me up the wall** (*fam*) mi fa uscire dai gangheri; **to go to the wall** (*fig: firm*) andare a rotoli *or* in rovina; **walls have ears** (*fam*) anche i muri hanno orecchi.

2 ADJ (*clock*) a muro.

▶ **wall in** VT + ADV (*garden etc*) circondare con un muro

▶ **wall off** VT + ADV (*area of land*) recingere con un muro

▶ **wall up** VT + ADV (*entrance etc*) murare.

wal·la·by ['wɒləbɪ] N wallaby *m inv.*

♦ **wall bars** NPL (*Sport*) spalliera *fsg.*

♦ **wall cupboard** N pensile *m.*

walled [wɔːld] ADJ (*city*) fortificato(-a); (*house, garden*) cinto(-a) da mura.

wal·let ['wɒlɪt] N portafoglio.

wall·flower ['wɔːl,flaʊəʳ] N violaciocca (gialla); (*fig*): **to be a wallflower** fare (da) tappezzeria.

♦ **wall hanging** N tappezzeria.

♦ **wall light** N applique *f inv.*

♦ **wall map** N carta murale.

Wal·loon [wɒ'luːn] 1 ADJ vallone.

2 N (*person*) vallone *m/f*; (*language*) vallone *m.*

wal·lop ['wɒləp] (*fam*) 1 N (*blow*) cazzotto; (*sound*): **with a wallop** con un tonfo.

2 VT (*fam: person*) suonarle a; **to wallop the table** battere il pugno sul tavolo.

wal·lop·ing ['wɒləpɪŋ] (*fam*) 1 N: **to give sb a walloping** suonarle a qn.

2 ADJ (*also*: **walloping great**) enorme.

wal·low ['wɒləʊ] VI: **to wallow (in)** (*in water, mud*) rotolarsi (in); (*in bath*) sguazzare (in); **to wallow in one's grief** crogiolarsi nel proprio dolore; **to wallow in luxury** nuotare nell'oro.

wall·paper ['wɔːl,peɪpəʳ] N carta da parati, tappezzeria.

♦ **Wall Street** N Wall Street *f.*

♦ **wall-to-wall** [,wɔːltə'wɔːl] ADJ: **wall-to-wall carpeting** moquette *f.*

wal·ly ['wɒlɪ] N (*fam*) scemo(-a).

wal·nut ['wɔːl,nʌt] 1 N (*nut*) noce *f*; (*tree, wood*) noce *m.*

2 ADJ (*furniture*) di noce; (*cake*) di noci.

wal·rus ['wɔːlrəs] N tricheco.

waltz [wɔːlts] 1 N valzer *m inv.*

2 VI ballare il valzer; **to waltz in/out** *etc* (*confidently*) entrare/uscire *etc* con fare sicuro; (*cheekily*) entrare/uscire *etc* con fare spavaldo.

wan [wɒn] ADJ (*gen*) pallido(-a); (*look, person*) triste.

wand [wɒnd] N (*also*: **magic wand**) bacchetta magica; (*of usher*) mazza.

wan·der ['wɒndəʳ] 1 N: **to go for a wander around the shops/the town** fare un giro per i negozi/in città.

2 VI (*person*) gironzolare, girare senza meta; (*river, road*) serpeggiare; (*stray: from path*) allontanarsi; (: *thoughts, eyes*) vagare; **to wander back/out** *etc* tornare indietro/uscire *etc* con calma; **don't go wandering off** non allontanarti; **to wander from** *or* **off the point** divagare; **to let one's mind** *or* **attention wander** distrarsi.

3 VT (*streets, hills*) girovagare per; **to wander the world** girare il mondo.

wan·der·er ['wɒndərəʳ] N giramondo *m/f inv.*

wan·der·ing ['wɒndərɪŋ] 1 ADJ (*tribe*) nomade; (*minstrel, actor*) girovago(-a); (*path, river*) tortuoso(-a); (*mind*) distratto(-a).

2: **wanderings** NPL peregrinazioni *fpl*, vagabondaggi *mpl.*

♦ **wandering Jew** N **a** (*Bot*) miseria **b**: **the Wandering Jew** l'ebreo errante.

wan·der·lust ['wɒndə,lʌst] N sete *f* di viaggi.

wane [weɪn] 1 VI (*moon*) calare; (*fig*) declinare, scemare.

2 N: **to be on the wane** = **to wane.**

wan·gle ['wæŋgl] (*fam*) 1 N astuzia.

2 VT (*job, ticket*) rimediare *or* procurare (con l'astuzia); (*days off*) ottenere (con l'astuzia); **he wangled his way in** è riuscito ad entrare con un sotterfugio.

wan·gler ['wæŋgləʳ] N (*fam*) furbacchione(-a).

wan·gling ['wæŋglɪŋ] N (*fam*) astuzia.

wan·ing ['weɪnɪŋ] ADJ (*moon*) calante; (*fig: power, influence, strength*) in declino.

wank [wæŋk] VI (*fam!*) farsi una sega (*fam!*)

wank·er ['wæŋkəʳ] N (*fam!*) testa di cazzo (*fam!*), coglione (*fam!*)

wan·ly ['wɒnlɪ] ADV tristemente.

want [wɒnt] 1 N **a** (*lack*): **want (of)** mancanza (di); **for want of** per mancanza di; **for want of anything better to do** non avendo nulla di meglio da fare; **it wasn't for want of trying** non si può dire che non ci abbia (*or* abbiamo *etc*) provato

b (*poverty*) miseria, povertà; **to be in want** essere in miseria

c (*need*) bisogno; **to be in want of sth** avere bisogno di

qc; **it fills a long-felt want** soddisfa un bisogno che si sentiva da tempo

d (*requirements*): **wants** NPL esigenze *fpl*; **my wants are few** ho poche esigenze.

2 VT **a** (*gen*) volere; (*wish, desire*) volere, desiderare; **to want to do sth** voler fare qc; **to want sb to do sth** volere che qn faccia qc; **I want you to tell me** voglio che tu mi dica; **I want it done now** voglio che sia fatto subito; **what do you want with me?** cosa vuoi da me?; **you've got him where you want him** (*fig*) ce l'hai in pugno; **you don't want much!** (*iro*) ti accontenti di poco!; **she wants £5,000 for the car** vuole or chiede 5.000 sterline per la macchina; **I don't want you interfering!** non voglio che tu ti intrometta!; **I know when I'm not wanted** so quando non si mi vuole; **you're wanted on the phone** ti vogliono al telefono; **I don't want to** non ne ho voglia; **"cook wanted"** "cercasi cuoco"; **he is wanted for murder** è ricercato per omicidio; **to want sb** (*sexually*) desiderare qn

b (*need, require*: subj: *person*) avere bisogno di; (: *task*) richiedere; (*ought*) dovere; **you want to see a doctor** dovresti andare dal dottore; **that's the last thing I want!** (*fam*) è l'ultima cosa che vorrei!; **it's just what we wanted!** (*fam*) è proprio quello che ci voleva!; **you want a screwdriver to do that** ti ci vuole un cacciavite per farlo; **it only wanted the parents to come in ...** bastava solo che i genitori entrassero...; **you want your head seeing to** tu hai bisogno di uno psicanalista.

3 VI (*lack*): **to want (for)** mancare (di); **she doesn't want for friends** gli amici non le mancano; **they want for nothing** a loro non manca nulla

► **want out** VI + ADV (*fam*) volerne uscire.

♦ **want ads** NPL (*Am*) annunci *mpl* economici.

want·ing ['wɒntɪŋ] ADJ: **to be wanting (in)** mancare (di); **humour is completely wanting in his work** la sua opera manca totalmente di senso dell'umorismo; **he is wanting in confidence** non è abbastanza sicuro di sé; **he was tried and found wanting** lo hanno messo alla prova e non è risultato all'altezza.

wan·ton ['wɒntən] ADJ (*wilful*) gratuito(-a), ingiustificato (-a); (*shameless*: *woman*) scostumato(-a).

wan·ton·ly ['wɒntənlɪ] ADV (*see adj*) gratuitamente, ingiustificatamente; in modo scostumato.

war [wɔːʳ] **1** N guerra; (*fig*): **war (on** or **against)** lotta (contro); **to be at/go to war (with)** essere/entrare in guerra (con); **to make war (on)** fare guerra (a); **a war of words** una guerra verbale; **to have been in the wars** (*fig hum*) essere malridotto(-a).

2 VI: **to war (with)** guerreggiare (con), far guerra (a).

3 ADJ (*wound, crime, bride*) di guerra.

war·ble ['wɔːbl] **1** N (*of bird*) trillo.

2 VI (*bird*) trillare; (*person*) gorgheggiare.

war·bler ['wɔːbləʳ] N uccello canoro; **reed warbler** cannaiola comune; **sedge warbler** forapaglie *m inv* comune; **willow warbler** lui *m inv* grosso.

war·bling ['wɔːblɪŋ] N (*of bird*) trillo, gorgheggio.

♦ **war correspondent** N corrispondente *m/f* di guerra.

♦ **war cry** N grido di guerra.

ward [wɔːd] N **a** (*in hospital*) corsia, reparto **b** (*Law*) pupillo(-a); **ward of court** minore *m/f* sotto tutela (giudiziaria) **c** (*Pol*) collegio (elettorale).

► **ward off** VT + ADV (*blow, attack*) parare, schivare; (*attacker*) respingere; (*danger, depression*) scongiurare.

♦ **war dance** N danza di guerra.

war·den ['wɔːdn] N (*of institution*) direttore(-trice); (*of park, game reserve*) guardiano(-a).

war·der ['wɔːdəʳ] N guardia carceraria.

war·dress ['wɔːdrɪs] N guardia carceraria (*donna*).

ward·robe ['wɔːdrəub] N (*cupboard*) guardaroba *m inv*, armadio; (*clothes*) guardaroba; (*Theatre*) costumi *mpl*.

♦ **wardrobe mistress** N costumista.

ward·room ['wɔːd,rʊm] N (*Naut*) quadrato (di poppa).

ware·house ['wɛə,haʊs] N deposito, magazzino.

ware·house·man ['wɛə,haʊsmən] N (*pl* **-men**) magazziniere *m*.

ware·hous·ing ['wɛə,haʊzɪŋ] N magazzinaggio.

wares [wɛəz] NPL merci *fpl*.

war·fare ['wɔː,fɛəʳ] N (*fighting*) guerra, lotta; (*technique*) arte *f* bellica.

♦ **war footing** N: **on a war footing** sul piede di guerra.

♦ **war game** N war game *m inv.*

war·head ['wɔː,hɛd] N (*Mil*) testata.

war·horse ['wɔː,hɔːs] N (*fig*): **old warhorse** veterano.

wari·ly ['wɛərɪlɪ] ADV cautamente, con prudenza.

wari·ness ['wɛərɪnɪs] N cautela, prudenza.

war·like ['wɔːˌlaɪk] ADJ battagliero(-a), bellicoso(-a).

warm [wɔːm] **1** ADJ (*comp* **-er**, *superl* **-est**) **a** (*gen*) caldo(-a); **I'm warm** OR **I feel warm** ho caldo; **it's warm today** oggi fa caldo; **it's warm work** è un lavoro che ti fa sudare; **come and get warm** vieni a scaldarti; **keep yourself warm!** non prendere freddo!; **it keeps me warm** mi tiene caldo; **to keep sth warm** tenere qc in caldo; **am I getting warm?** (*fig*: *in game*) fuocherello?

b (*fig*: *colour*) caldo(-a); (: *thanks, congratulations, apologies*) sentito(-a); (: *welcome, applause*) caloroso(-a); (: *person, greeting*) cordiale; (: *heart*) d'oro; (: *supporter*) convinto(-a); **with my warmest thanks** con i miei più sentiti ringraziamenti.

2 VT (*gen*) scaldare; **to warm o.s. by the fire** scaldarsi vicino al fuoco; **it warmed my heart** mi ha fatto tanto piacere.

3 VI (*food, water*) scaldarsi; **he warmed to his subject** si appassionò all'argomento; **I** or **my heart warmed to him** mi è entrato in simpatia

► **warm up** **1** VI + ADV (*person*) scaldarsi, scaldarsi i muscoli; (*fig*: *party*) animarsi.

2 VT + ADV (*food*) scaldare, riscaldare; (*engine*) scaldare; (*fig*: *party, audience*) animare.

♦ **warm-blooded** [ˌwɔːmˈblʌdɪd] ADJ (*animal*) a sangue caldo.

♦ **war memorial** N monumento ai caduti.

♦ **warm front** N (*Met*) fronte *m* caldo.

♦ **warm-hearted** [ˌwɔːmˈhɑːtɪd] ADJ cordiale, affettuoso (-a).

♦ **warm·ing pan** ['wɔːmɪŋ,pæn] N scaldaletto.

warm·ly ['wɔːmlɪ] ADV (*recommend*) caldamente; (*welcome, thank, applaud*) calorosamente; **to dress warmly** portare indumenti pesanti.

war·monger ['wɔːˌmʌŋgəʳ] N guerrafondaio.

war·monger·ing ['wɔːˌmʌŋgərɪŋ] N bellicismo.

warmth [wɔːmθ] N calore *m*; (*fig*) calore, calorosità.

♦ **warm-up** ['wɔːmˌʌp] N (*Sport*) riscaldamento.

warn [wɔːn] VT: **to warn (of** or **about)** avvertire (di), avvisare (di); **to warn sb not to do sth** or **against doing sth** avvertire qn di non fare qc; **you have been warned!** sei avvisato!; **to warn sb off** or **against sth** mettere qn in guardia contro qc.

warn·ing ['wɔːnɪŋ] N (*gen*) avvertimento, ammonimento;

(*by police, judge*) diffida; (*advance notice*): **warning (of)** preavviso (di); **to give sb a warning that** avvertire qn che; **to give sb due/a few days' warning** avvertire qn a tempo debito/con qualche giorno di anticipo; **without (any) warning** senza preavviso; **let this be a warning to you!** che ti serva da ammonimento!; **gale warning** (*Met*) avviso di burrasca.

♦ **warning device** N dispositivo d'allarme.

♦ **warning light** N spia luminosa.

♦ **warning shot** N: **to fire a warning shot** sparare (in aria) un colpo di avvertimento.

♦ **warning triangle** N (*Aut*) triangolo.

warp [wɔːp] ☐ N (*in weaving*) ordito; (*of wood*) curvatura, deformazione *f*.

☐ VT (*wood*) deformare, curvare; (*fig: mind, personality, judgment*) influenzare negativamente.

☐ VI (*wood*) deformarsi, curvarsi.

warp·age [ˈwɔːpɪdʒ] N (*Textiles*) orditura.

♦ **war paint** N pitture *fpl* di guerra (*dei pellirosse*).

war·path [ˈwɔːˌpɑːθ] N: **to be on the warpath** (*fig*) essere sul sentiero di guerra.

warped [wɔːpt] ADJ (*wood*) curvo(-a); (*fig: character, sense of humour etc*) contorto(-a).

war·plane [ˈwɔːˌpleɪn] N aereo militare.

war·rant [ˈwɒrənt] ☐ N ⓐ (*Law: to arrest*) mandato di cattura; (: *to search*) mandato di perquisizione; (*for travel etc*) buono; **there is a warrant out for his arrest** è stato emesso un mandato di cattura nei suoi confronti ⓑ (*justification*) giustificazione *f*.

☐ VT ⓐ (*justify, merit*) giustificare; **nothing warrants such an assumption** nulla giustifica questa ipotesi ⓑ (*guarantee*) garantire; **I'll warrant you he'll be back soon** ti assicuro *or* garantisco che sarà di ritorno presto.

war·rant·ed [ˈwɒrəntɪd] ADJ (*action, remark*) giustificato (-a); (*Comm: goods*) garantito(-a).

♦ **warrant officer** N (*Mil*) sottufficiale *m*.

war·ran·ty [ˈwɒrəntɪ] N (*Comm*) garanzia; **under warranty** in garanzia.

war·ren [ˈwɒrən] N (*also:* **rabbit warren**) tana; (*fig*) alveare *m*; **a warren of little streets** un dedalo di stradine.

war·ring [ˈwɔːrɪŋ] ADJ (*interests etc*) opposto(-a), in lotta; (*nations*) in guerra.

war·ri·or [ˈwɒrɪəʳ] N guerriero(-a).

War·saw [ˈwɔːsɔː] N Varsavia.

♦ **Warsaw Pact** N: **the Warsaw Pact** il patto di Varsavia.

war·ship [ˈwɔːˌʃɪp] N nave *f* da guerra.

wart [wɔːt] N (*Med*) porro, verruca.

wart·hog [ˈwɔːtˌhɒg] N facocero.

war·time [ˈwɔːˌtaɪm] ☐ N: **in wartime** in tempo di guerra.

☐ ADJ (*regulations, rationing etc*) di guerra.

wary [ˈwɛərɪ] ADJ (*comp* **-ier**, *superl* **-iest**) (*gen*) prudente; (*manner*) cauto(-a); **to be wary (of)** essere diffidente (di); **to keep a wary eye on sth** tenere d'occhio qc; **to be wary about** *or* **of doing sth** andare cauto(-a) nel fare qc.

was [wɒz] 1ST, 3RD PERS SG PT OF **be**.

wash [wɒʃ] ☐ N ⓐ (*act of washing*) lavata; **to have a wash** darsi una lavata, lavarsi; **to give sth a wash** dare una lavata a qc, lavare qc; **it needs a wash** ha bisogno di essere lavato; **your jeans are in the wash** i tuoi jeans sono a lavare; **it ran in the wash** si è stinto nel lavaggio; **it'll all come out in the wash** (*fig: work out*) tutto si sistemerà ⓑ (*of ship*) scia ⓒ (*Art*) lavatura.

☐ VT ⓐ (*gen*) lavare; **to wash o.s.** lavarsi; **to wash one's hands/hair** lavarsi le mani/i capelli; **to wash one's hands of sth** (*fig*) lavarsene le mani (di qc) ⓑ (*lap: sea, waves*) bagnare, lambire; **an island washed by a blue sea** un'isola bagnata da un mare azzurro ⓒ (*sweep, carry: sea*) portare, trascinare; **he was washed overboard** fu trascinato in mare dalle onde.

☐ VI ⓐ (*have a wash*) lavarsi; (*do the washing*) fare il bucato; **man-made fabrics usually wash well** di solito i tessuti sintetici si lavano facilmente; **I'll wash if you'll wipe** (*dishes*) io lavo i piatti se tu li asciughi; **that excuse won't wash!** (*fam*) quella scusa non regge! ⓑ (*sea*): **to wash against sth** frangersi contro qc; **to wash over sth** infrangersi su qc

▶ **wash away** VT + ADV (*mark*) togliere lavando; (*subj: river etc*) trascinare via; (*fig: sins etc*) cancellare

▶ **wash down** VT + ADV (*walls, car*) lavare; (*pill, food*) mandar giù (*con acqua etc*)

▶ **wash off** ☐ VI + ADV andare via con il lavaggio.

☐ VT + ADV (*dirt*) togliere (lavando)

▶ **wash through** VT + ADV dare una lavata a

▶ **wash up** ☐ VI + ADV (*Brit: do dishes*) lavare i piatti; (*Am: have a wash*) darsi una lavata, lavarsi.

☐ VT + ADV ⓐ (*Brit: dishes*) lavare, rigovernare ⓑ (*subj: sea etc*) portare, trascinare ⓒ: **to be all washed up** (*fig: fam*) essere finito(-a)

▶ **wash out** VT + ADV (*stain*) togliere (lavando); (*bottle, paintbrush*) sciacquare.

wash·able [ˈwɒʃəbl] ADJ lavabile.

wash·basin [ˈwɒʃˌbeɪsn], **wash·bowl** [ˈwɒʃˌbəʊl] N lavabo, lavandino.

wash·cloth [ˈwɒʃˌklɒθ] N (*Am*) pezzuola (per lavarsi).

wash·day [ˈwɒʃˌdeɪ] N giorno di bucato.

washed-out [ˈwɒʃtˈaʊt] ADJ (*faded: colour*) slavato(-a), sbiadito(-a); (*tired: person*) sfinito(-a), distrutto(-a); *see also* **wash out**.

wash·er [ˈwɒʃəʳ] N ⓐ (*Tech*) rondella ⓑ (*washing machine*) lavatrice *f*.

♦ **wash-hand basin** [ˈwɒʃhændˌbeɪsn] N (*Brit old*) lavabo, lavandino.

♦ **wash house** N lavanderia.

wash·ing [ˈwɒʃɪŋ] N ⓐ (*act*) lavaggio; (: *of clothes*) bucato ⓑ (*clothes themselves*) bucato; **dirty washing** biancheria da lavare.

♦ **washing line** N (*Brit*) corda del bucato.

♦ **washing machine** N lavatrice *f*.

♦ **washing powder** N (*Brit*) detersivo in polvere per bucato.

♦ **washing soda** N soda.

Wash·ing·ton [ˈwɒʃɪŋtən] N Washington *f*.

♦ **washing-up** [ˌwɒʃɪŋˈʌp] N (*dishes*) piatti *mpl* sporchi; **to do the washing-up** lavare i piatti, rigovernare.

♦ **washing-up bowl** N catino, bacinella.

♦ **washing-up liquid** N (*Brit*) detersivo liquido per i piatti.

♦ **wash leather** N pelle *f* di daino.

♦ **wash-out** [ˈwɒʃˌaʊt] N (*fam: plan, party, person*) disastro.

wash·room [ˈwɒʃˌrʊm] N bagno, gabinetto.

wash·stand [ˈwɒʃˌstænd] N lavamano *m inv*.

wash·tub [ˈwɒʃˌtʌb] N tinozza per il bucato.

wasn't [ˈwɒznt] = **was not**.

WASP, Wasp N ABBR (*Am: = White Anglo-Saxon Protestant*) W.A.S.P. *m* (= *bianco protestante anglosassone*).

wasp [wɒsp] N vespa; **wasp's nest** nido di vespe.

wasp·ish ['wɒspɪʃ] ADJ (*character*) litigioso(-a); (*comment*) pungente.

wasp·ish·ly ['wɒspɪʃlɪ] ADV (*comment*) astiosamente.

Wassermann ['wæsəmən] N (*Med*): **Wassermann test** (reazione *f*) wassermann *f inv*.

wast·age ['weɪstɪdʒ] N (*gen*) spreco; (*of time, Comm*: *through pilfering*) perdita; (*in manufacturing*) scarti *mpl*; (*amount wasted*) scarto; **natural wastage** normale diminuzione *f* del personale.

waste [weɪst] 1 ADJ (*material*) di scarto; (*food*) avanzato (-a); (*land, ground*: *in city*) abbandonato(-a), desolato (-a); (: *in country*) incolto(-a); **to lay waste** devastare.
2 N a (*gen*) spreco; (*of time*) perdita; **it's a waste of money** è uno spreco di denaro; **it's a waste of effort** è fatica sprecata; **it's a waste of breath** è fiato sprecato; **it's a waste of time doing that** è tempo sprecato; **to go to waste** andare sprecato(-a)
b (*waste material*: *industrial, chemical etc*) scorie *fpl*; (*rubbish*) spazzatura, immondizia, rifiuti *mpl*; **nuclear waste** scorie *mpl* radioattive
c (*land*: *often pl*) distesa desolata; **desert waste** landa desertica.
3 VT (*gen*) sprecare; (*time, opportunity*) perdere, sprecare; **you didn't waste much time finding a replacement!** (*iro*) non hai perso tempo a rimpiazzarmi!; **he's wasted in that job** è sprecato in quel lavoro; **sarcasm is wasted on him** non afferra il sarcasmo; **to waste one's breath** sprecare (il) fiato; **waste not, want not** (*Proverb*) chi risparmia guadagna
▸ **waste away** VI + ADV deperire, consumarsi.

waste·basket ['weɪstˌbɑːskɪt] N (*Am*) = **wastepaper basket**.

waste·bin ['weɪstˌbɪn] N (*basket*) cestino per la cartaccia; (*in kitchen*) pattumiera.

wast·ed ['weɪstɪd] ADJ a (*efforts*) sprecato(-a), inutile b (*face*: *from disease, starvation*) scarno(-a); (*limbs*: *from disease*) atrofizzato(-a).

♦ **waste disposal** N smaltimento dei rifiuti.

♦ **waste disposal unit** N tritarifiuti *m inv*.

waste·ful ['weɪstful] ADJ (*person*) sprecone(-a); (*process*) dispendioso(-a); **to be wasteful with** *or* **of sth** sprecare qc.

waste·ful·ly ['weɪstfəlɪ] ADV: **to spend wastefully** fare degli sprechi nello spendere; **to use sth wastefully** non utilizzare al meglio qc.

waste·ful·ness ['weɪstfulnɪs] N (*of person*) prodigalità; (*of process*) spreco, dispendio.

♦ **waste ground** N (*Brit*) terreno incolto *or* abbandonato.

waste·land ['weɪstˌlænd] N terra desolata.

waste·paper ['weɪstˌpeɪpəʳ] N cartaccia.

♦ **wastepaper basket** N cestino per la cartaccia.

♦ **waste pipe** N tubo di scarico.

♦ **waste products** N (*Industry*) materiali *mpl* di scarto; (*from body*) materiali *mpl* di rifiuto.

wast·er ['weɪstəʳ] N (*good-for-nothing*) perdigiorno *m/f*; (*spendthrift*) sprecone(-a).

wast·ing ['weɪstɪŋ] ADJ: **wasting disease** deperimento organico.

wast·rel ['weɪstrəl] N (*layabout*) perdigiorno *m/f*; (*spendthrift*) spendaccione(-a), sprecone(-a).

watch[1] [wɒtʃ] N (*also*: **wrist watch**) orologio (da polso); **it's 10 o'clock by my watch** il mio orologio fa le 10.

watch[2] [wɒtʃ] 1 N a (*act of watching*) sorveglianza; **to be on the watch for** (*danger, person*) stare in guardia

contro; (*vehicle*) stare all'erta per l'arrivo di; (*bargain*) essere a caccia di; **to keep watch over** (*prisoner*) sorvegliare; (*patient*) vigilare; **to keep a close watch on sb/sth** sorvegliare da vicino qn/qc; **to keep watch for sb/sth** stare all'erta per qn/qc
b (*period of duty*) guardia; (*Naut*) quarto; (*sentry*) sentinella; **officer of the watch** (*Naut*) ufficiale *m* di quarto; **to be on watch** (*Naut*) essere di guardia.
2 VT a (*guard*: *gen*) tener d'occhio
b (*observe*: *gen*) guardare; (*subj*: *police*) tenere d'occhio, sorvegliare; (*monitor*: *case*) seguire; **to watch sb do(ing) sth** osservare qn mentre fa qc; **you can't do that! — just you watch (me)!** non puoi farlo! — e come no, sta' a vedere!; **to watch one's chance** aspettare il momento propizio; **to watch the time** controllare l'ora; **a new actor to be watched** un nuovo attore molto promettente *or* da seguire
c (*be careful with*) stare attento(-a) a; **to watch one's language** moderare i termini, badare a come si parla; **watch it!** attento!; **watch how you drive/what you're doing** fai attenzione a come guidi/quel che fai; **watch your head** attento alla testa; **we shall have to watch our spending** dovremo limitare le spese; **to watch the clock** (*fig*) tenere d'occhio l'orologio; **to watch sb's interests** badare agli interessi di qn.
3 VI (*observe*) guardare; (*keep guard*) fare *or* montare la guardia; (*pay attention*) stare attento(-a); (*at bedside*) vegliare; **to watch for sb/sth** aspettare qn/qc; **the doctors are watching for any deterioration in his condition** i medici lo tengono sotto osservazione nell'eventualità che le sue condizioni peggiorino
▸ **watch out** VI + ADV fare attenzione *f*, stare attento(-a); **to watch out for** (*keep watch*) fare attenzione a; (*be on the alert*) stare attento(-a) a; **watch out!** (*also threatening*) attento!, occhio!
▸ **watch over** VI + PREP sorvegliare.

watch·band ['wɒtʃˌbænd] N (*Am*) cinturino dell'orologio.

♦ **watch chain** N catena dell'orologio.

watch·dog ['wɒtʃˌdɒg] 1 N cane *m* da guardia; (*fig*) sorvegliante *m/f*.
2 ADJ di controllo; **a watchdog committee** un comitato di controllo.

watch·er ['wɒtʃəʳ] N (*observer*) osservatore(-trice); (*spectator*) spettatore(-trice).

watch·ful ['wɒtʃful] ADJ: **to be watchful for sth** stare attento a qc; **to keep a watchful eye on sb** guardare con occhio vigile qn; **under the watchful eye of** sotto lo sguardo vigile di.

watch·ful·ness ['wɒtʃfulnɪs] N attenzione *f*, vigilanza.

watch·maker ['wɒtʃˌmeɪkəʳ] N orologiaio(-a).

watch·making ['wɒtʃˌmeɪkɪŋ] N orologeria (*arte*).

watch·man ['wɒtʃmən] N (*pl* -**men**) guardiano.

watch·strap ['wɒtʃˌstræp] N cinturino dell'orologio.

watch·tower ['wɒtʃˌtaʊəʳ] N torre *f* di guardia.

watch·word ['wɒtʃˌwɜːd] N parola d'ordine.

wa·ter ['wɔːtəʳ] 1 N (*gen*) acqua; **fresh/salt water** acqua dolce/salata; **"hot and cold water in all rooms"** "acqua corrente calda e fredda in tutte le camere"; **I'd like a drink of water** vorrei un bicchier d'acqua; **the High Street is under water** la strada principale è inondata; **to turn on the water** aprire il rubinetto dell'acqua; **to spend money like water** spendere e spandere, avere le mani bucate; **a lot of water has flowed under the bridge since then** (*fig*) da allora è passata molta acqua sotto i ponti; **that theory won't hold water** (*fig*) quella teoria fa

acqua; **to pour cold water on sth** (*fig*) mostrarsi poco entusiasta di qc; **it's like water off a duck's back** (*fig*) è come parlare al muro; **the waters of the Tiber** le acque del Tevere; **British waters** acque *fpl* (territoriali) britanniche; **to take the waters** fare la cura delle acque (termali); **the waters** (*in pregnancy*) le acque; **to pass water** orinare; **water on the brain** (*Med*) idrocefalia; **water on the knee** (*Med*) sinovite *f*.

2 VT (*garden, plant*) annaffiare; (*horses, cattle*) abbeverare; (*wine*) annacquare.

3 VI (*eyes*) lacrimare; **to make sb's mouth water** far venire l'acquolina in bocca a qn.

4 ADJ (*pressure, supply*) dell'acqua; (*purifier, power*) idrico(-a).

► **water down** VT + ADV (*milk, wine*) diluire; (*fig: claim*) moderare, attenuare; (: *report, article*) edulcorare.

♦ **water bed** N materasso ad acqua.

♦ **water biscuit** N cracker *m inv*.

♦ **water blister** N vescica.

water·borne [ˈwɔːtəˌbɔːn] ADJ (*disease*) trasmesso(-a) con l'acqua.

♦ **water bottle** N (*for drinking*) borraccia; (*for heat*) borsa dell'acqua calda.

♦ **water buffalo** N bufalo indiano.

♦ **water cannon** N idrante *m*.

♦ **water chestnut** N castagna d'acqua.

♦ **water closet** N (*Brit: frm*) water closet *m inv*.

water·colour, (*Am*) **water·color** [ˈwɔːtəˌkʌləʳ] N (*picture*) acquerello; (*paints*): **watercolours** NPL acquerelli *mpl*.

♦ **water-cooled** [ˈwɔːtəˌkuːld] ADJ raffreddato(-a) ad acqua.

♦ **water cooler** N impianto di raffreddamento ad acqua.

water·course [ˈwɔːtəˌkɔːs] N corso d'acqua.

water·cress [ˈwɔːtəˌkrɛs] N crescione *m*.

♦ **wa·ter di·vin·er** [ˈwɔːtədɪˌvaɪnəʳ] N rabdomante *m/f*.

wa·tered [ˈwɔːtəd] ADJ (*silk*) damascato(-a).

water·fall [ˈwɔːtəˌfɔːl] N cascata.

water·fowl [ˈwɔːtəˌfaʊl] N, PL INV uccello acquatico.

water·front [ˈwɔːtəˌfrʌnt] N (*seafront*) lungomare *m*; (*at docks*) banchina, fronte *m* del porto.

♦ **water gauge** N indicatore *m* del livello dell'acqua.

♦ **water heater** N scaldabagno, scaldaacqua *m inv*.

♦ **water hole** N pozza d'acqua.

♦ **water ice** N (*Brit Culin*) sorbetto.

wa·ter·ing [ˈwɔːtərɪŋ] N (*of plants*) annaffiatura; (*of field, region*) irrigazione *f*; (*of animals*) abbeveraggio.

♦ **watering can** N annaffiatoio.

♦ **watering hole** N a = **water hole** b (*hum*) bar *m inv*.

♦ **water jump** N (*Horse-riding*) riviera.

♦ **water level** N livello dell'acqua; (*of flood*) livello delle acque.

♦ **water lily** N ninfea.

water·line [ˈwɔːtəˌlaɪn] N (*Naut*) linea di galleggiamento.

water·logged [ˈwɔːtəˌlɒgd] ADJ (*ground etc*) impregnato (-a) *or* imbevuto(-a) d'acqua; (*fields, football pitch*) allagato(-a); (*shoes*) inzuppato(-a).

Wa·ter·loo [ˌwɔːtəˈluː] N: **to meet one's Waterloo** (*fig*) subire una disfatta.

♦ **water main** N conduttura dell'acqua.

water·mark [ˈwɔːtəˌmɑːk] N (*in paper*) filigrana; (*left by tide*) segno della marea.

♦ **water meadow** N acquitrino.

water·melon [ˈwɔːtəˌmɛlən] N anguria, cocomero.

♦ **water mill** N mulino ad acqua.

♦ **water pistol** N pistola ad acqua.

♦ **water polo** N pallanuoto *f*.

water·proof [ˈwɔːtəˌpruːf] 1 ADJ impermeabile.

2 N impermeabile *m*.

3 VT impermeabilizzare.

water·proof·ing [ˈwɔːtəˌpruːfɪŋ] N impermeabilizzazione *f*.

♦ **water rat** N topo d'acqua.

♦ **water rate** N canone *m* per la fornitura dell'acqua.

♦ **water-repellent** [ˈwɔːtərɪˌpɛlənt] ADJ idrorepellente.

♦ **water-resistant** [ˈwɔːtərɪˌzɪstənt] ADJ (*fabric*) impermeabile; (*sun lotion*) resistente all'acqua.

water·shed [ˈwɔːtəˌʃɛd] N (*Geog, also fig*) spartiacque *m inv*.

water·side [ˈwɔːtəˌsaɪd] 1 N lungomare.

2 ADJ sul lungomare.

♦ **water-ski** [ˈwɔːtəˌskiː] VI praticare lo sci d'acqua *or* acquatico.

♦ **water-skiing** [ˈwɔːtəˌskiːɪŋ] N sci *m* d'acqua *or* acquatico.

♦ **water softener** N addolcitore *m* d'acqua; (*substance*) anti-calcare *m*.

♦ **water-soluble** [ˌwɔːtəˈsɒljʊbl] ADJ idrosolubile, solubile in acqua.

water·spout [ˈwɔːtəˌspaʊt] N (*pipe, channel*) pluviale *m*; (*Met*) tromba d'acqua.

♦ **water table** N livello idrostatico.

♦ **water tank** N serbatoio *or* cisterna d'acqua.

water·tight [ˈwɔːtəˌtaɪt] ADJ (*compartment, seal*) stagno (-a); (*fig: excuse, argument*) inattaccabile.

♦ **water torture** N tortura della goccia (d'acqua).

♦ **water tower** N serbatoio a torre.

♦ **water vapour** N vapore *m* acqueo.

water·way [ˈwɔːtəˌweɪ] N corso d'acqua navigabile.

water·wheel [ˈwɔːtəˌwiːl] N ruota idraulica.

♦ **water wings** NPL braccioli *mpl* salvagente.

water·works [ˈwɔːtəˌwɜːks] 1 NSG (*place*) impianto idrico.

2 (*fig fam*) NPL: **to turn on the waterworks** piangere come una fontana; **to have trouble with one's waterworks** avere dei problemi alla vescica.

wa·tery [ˈwɔːtəri] ADJ (*tea, soup*) acquoso(-a); (*coffee*) lungo(-a); (*pale: sun, colour*) slavato(-a), pallido(-a); (*eyes*) umido(-a); **to go to a watery grave** perire tra i flutti.

watt [wɒt] N watt *m inv*.

watt·age [ˈwɒtɪdʒ] N potenza in watt.

wat·tle [ˈwɒtl] N a (*woven sticks*) graticcio b (*on turkey*) bargiglio.

♦ **wattle and daub** N: **houses of wattle and daub** case di paglia e fango.

wave [weɪv] 1 N a (*gen, Phys, Radio*) onda; (*in hair, on surface*) ondulazione *f*; (*fig: of enthusiasm, strikes etc*) ondata; **in waves** a ondate; **short/medium/long wave** (*Radio*) onde *fpl* corte/medie/lunghe; **the new wave** (*Cine*) la nouvelle vague; (*Mus*) la new wave

b (*greeting*) cenno di saluto; (*signal*) gesto, cenno; **to give sb a wave** salutare qn con la mano; **with a wave of his hand** con un cenno della mano.

2 VT a (*brandish: flag, banner, handkerchief*) sventolare; (: *stick, umbrella*) agitare; (*beckon, motion*) far segno a; **he waved the ticket under my nose** mi sventolò il biglietto sotto il naso; **to wave sb goodbye** OR **wave goodbye to sb** fare un cenno d'addio a qn; **she waved a greeting to the crowd** salutò la folla con un cenno della mano; **he waved us over to the best table** ci indicò il tavolo

migliore con un cenno della mano
b (*hair*) ondulare.
3 VI **a** (*person*) gesticolare; **to wave to** or **at sb** fare un cenno a qn
b (*flag, branches etc*) ondeggiare, sventolare
c (*hair*) essere mosso(-a) or ondulato(-a).
► **wave about, wave around** VT + ADV (*object*) agitare; **to wave one's arms about** (*in talking*) gesticolare
► **wave aside, wave away** VT + ADV (*person*): **to wave sb aside** fare cenno a qn di spostarsi; (*fig: suggestion, objection*) respingere, rifiutare
► **wave down** VT + ADV: **to wave sb/a car down** far segno a qn/a un'auto di fermarsi
► **wave off** VT + ADV: **to wave sb off** salutare qn
► **wave on** VT + ADV (*subj: policeman*) fare segno di avanzare a.
wave·band ['weɪvˌbænd] N (*Radio*) gamma di lunghezza d'onda.
wave·length ['weɪvˌlɛŋθ] N (*Phys, Radio*) lunghezza d'onda; **we're not on the same wavelength** (*fig*) non siamo sulla stessa lunghezza d'onda.
wa·ver ['weɪvəʳ] VI (*flame, needle etc*) oscillare; (*voice*) tremare; (*fig: hesitate*): **to waver (between)** tentennare, titubare; **she's beginning to waver** comincia a vacillare.
wa·ver·ing ['weɪvərɪŋ] **1** ADJ (*flame*) tremolante; (*needle*) oscillante; (*voice*) tremulo(-a); (*voters, support*) tentennante.
2 N (*of flame*) tremolio; (*of needle*) oscillazione *f*; (*of voice*) tremito; (*fig: hesitation*) tentennamento, titubanza.
wavy ['weɪvɪ] ADJ (*comp* **-ier**, *superl* **-iest**) (*hair, surface*) ondulato(-a); (*line*) ondeggiante, sinuoso(-a).
wax[1] [wæks] **1** N cera; (*for skis*) sciolina; (*in ear*) cerume *m.*
2 ADJ di cera.
3 VT (*furniture, car*) dare la cera a; (*skis*) sciolinare.
wax[2] [wæks] VI (*moon*) crescere; **to wax enthusiastic** diventare entusiasta; **to wax eloquent about sth** diventare infervorato(-a) nel parlare di qc.
wax·en ['wæksən] ADJ (*of wax*) di cera; (*fig: pale*) cereo(-a).
♦ **wax paper, waxed paper** N carta oleata.
wax·wing ['wæksˌwɪŋ] N beccofrusone *m.*
wax·work ['wæksˌwɜːk] N (*model*) statua di cera.
wax·works ['wæksˌwɜːks] NSG OR PL museo delle cere.
waxy ['wæksɪ] ADJ (*comp* **-ier**, *superl* **-iest**) (*fig: complexion*) cereo(-a).
way [weɪ] **1** N **a** (*road, lane*) strada; (*path, access*) passaggio; (*in street names*) via; **private/public way** strada privata/pubblica; **the way across the fields** il sentiero attraverso i campi; **the Appian Way** la via Appia; **across** or **over the way** di fronte
b (*route*) strada; **the Way of the Cross** (*Rel*) la via crucis; **to ask one's way to the station** chiedere la strada per la stazione; **can you tell me the way to the station?** mi sa indicare la strada per la stazione?; **the way back** la via del ritorno; **we came a back way** siamo arrivati per strade secondarie; **she went by way of Birmingham** è andata passando per Birmingham; **to go the wrong way** andare dalla parte sbagliata; **to lose one's way** perdere la strada, perdersi; **the way in** l'entrata, l'ingresso; **the way out** l'uscita; **to find one's way into a building** riuscire a entrare in un edificio; **don't bother, I'll find my own way out** non si scomodi, troverò l'uscita; **to find a way out of a problem** trovare una via d'uscita a un problema; **to take the easy way out** scegliere la solu-

zione più facile; **on the way** (*en route*) per strada; (*expected*) in arrivo; **on the way to work** andando a lavorare; **you pass it on your way home** ci passi davanti andando a casa; **he's on his way to becoming an alcoholic** è sulla strada dell'alcolismo; **to be on one's way** essere in cammino or sulla strada; **economic recovery is on the way** siamo sulla strada della ripresa economica; **I'm on my way** sto arrivando; **it's time we were on our way** è ora di andare; **all the way (here/home)** per tutta la strada (venendo qui/andando a casa); **I'm with you all the way** (*fig fam*) sono assolutamente d'accordo con te; **to make one's (own) way home** andare a casa (da solo(-a)); **I know my way about town** sono pratico della città; **to lead the way** fare strada; (*fig*) essere all'avanguardia; **I don't want to take you out of your way** non voglio farti deviare; **the village is rather out of the way** il villaggio è abbastanza fuori mano; **that's nothing out of the way these days** non è nulla di eccezionale al giorno d'oggi; **to go out of one's way to help sb** farsi in quattro per aiutare qn; **can you see your way (clear) to helping me tomorrow?** pensi di potermi aiutare domani?; **to go one's own way** (*fig*) fare di testa propria; **to make one's way in the world** farsi strada nel mondo; **he worked his way up in the company** si è fatto strada nella ditta; **the company isn't paying its way** la ditta non rende più; **he put me in the way of some good contracts** mi ha procurato dei buoni contratti
c (*space sb wants to go through*) strada; **to be** or **get in the** or **sb's way** essere d'intralcio or d'impiccio a qn; **am I in your way?** (*of sb watching sth*) ti tolgo la visuale?; **to stand in sb's way** intralciare il passaggio a qn; (*fig*) essere d'ostacolo a qn; **"give way"** (*Brit Aut*) "dare la precedenza"; **to stand in the way of progress** ostacolare il progresso; **to get out of the** or **sb's way** lasciare passare qn; **to keep out of sb's way** evitare qn, stare alla larga da qn; **to move sth out of the way** togliere di torno qc; **as soon as I've got this essay out of the way** appena mi sono liberato di questo tema; **keep those matches out of his way** tieni lontano da lui quei fiammiferi; **to push/elbow one's way through the crowd** farsi strada a spinte/gomitate tra la folla; **he lied his way out of it** se l'è cavata mentendo; **he crawled/limped his way to the gate** andò a carponi/zoppicando verso il cancello; **to make way (for sb/sth)** far strada (a qn/qc); (*fig*) lasciare il posto or fare largo (a qn/qc); **to leave the way open for further talks** lasciare aperta la possibilità di ulteriori colloqui
d (*direction*) direzione *f*, parte *f*; **which way? — this way** da che parte? — da questa (parte), in quale direzione? — per di qua; **come this way** vieni da questa parte; **this way for ...** da questa parte per...; **which way did he go?** da che parte è andato?; **which way do we go from here?** da che parte dobbiamo andare da qui?; (*fig*) cosa facciamo adesso?; **are you going my way?** fai la strada che faccio io?; **everything is going my way** (*fig*) mi sta andando tutto liscio; **this way and that** di qua e di là; **down our way** dalle nostre parti; **she didn't know which way to look** non sapeva da che parte guardare; **put it the right way up** (*Brit*) mettilo in piedi dalla parte giusta; **to be the wrong way round** essere al contrario; **to look the other way** (*fig*) guardare dall'altra parte; **to be in a fair way to doing sth** essere sulla strada giusta per fare qc; **to split sth three ways** dividere qc in tre
e (*indicating distance, motion, progress*): **to come a long way** (*also fig*) fare molta strada; **it's a long way away** è

molto lontano da qui; **a little way along the road** un po' più avanti lungo la strada; **she'll go a long way** (*fig*) farà molta strada; **we've come a long way since those days** abbiamo fatto molta strada da allora; **it should go a long way towards convincing him** dovrebbe contribuire molto a convincerlo; **to be under way** (*work, project*) essere in corso; **to get under way** avviarsi; **the job is now well under way** il lavoro ora è ben avviato

f (*means*) mezzo, modo; (*manner*) modo; **the British way of life** lo stile di vita britannico; **there are ways and means** il modo per farlo si trova; **we'll find a way of doing it** troveremo un modo per farlo; **the only way of doing it** l'unico modo per farlo; **there are no two ways about it** non ci sono dubbi; **he has his own way of doing it** ha un modo tutto suo per farlo; **I'll do it (in) my own way** lo farò a modo mio; **they've had it all their own way too long** hanno fatto per troppo tempo a modo loro; **to get one's own way** averla vinta; **I will help in every way possible** aiuterò in tutti i modi possibili; **he helped in a small way** ha aiutato un pochino; **in no way** OR **not in any way** per nulla; **no way!** (*fam*) neanche per sogno!; **there's no way I'll do it** non lo farò per nessun motivo al mondo; **do it this way** fallo in questo modo *or* così; **in this way** così, in questo modo; **it was this way ...** è stato così...; **(in) one way or another** in un modo o nell'altro; **in a way** in un certo senso; **in some ways** in un certo senso, sotto certi aspetti; **in many ways** per molti versi; **to my way of thinking** a mio modo di vedere; **either way I can't help you** non ti posso aiutare in nessun caso; **to go on in the same old way** continuare nel modo di sempre; **the way things are** come stanno le cose; **in the ordinary way (of things)** normalmente

g (*habit*) abitudine *f*; (*manner*) modo di fare; **the ways of the Spaniards** i costumi degli Spagnoli; **foreign ways** abitudini *fpl* forestiere; **he has his little ways** ha le sue piccole abitudini; **it's not my way** non è mia abitudine fare così; **he has a way with people** ci sa fare con la gente; **he has a way with him** ci sa fare; **to get into/out of the way of doing sth** prendere/perdere l'abitudine di fare qc

h (*state*): **things are in a bad way** le cose si mettono male; **he's in a bad way** è ridotto male; **to be in the family way** (*fam*) aspettare un bambino

i (*with "by"*): **by the way** a proposito; **but that's just by the way** ma questo è tra parentesi; **by way of a warning** come avvertimento; **she's by way of being an artist** è una specie di artista.

2 ADV (*fam*): **it happened way back** è successo molto tempo fa; **way back in 1900** nel lontano 1900; **it's way out in Nevada** è nel lontano Nevada; **he was way out in his estimate** la sua valutazione era decisamente errata.

way·bill ['weɪˌbɪl] N (*Comm*) bolla di accompagnamento.

way·farer ['weɪˌfɛərə'] N (*old*) viandante *m/f*.

way·faring ['weɪˌfɛərɪŋ] **1** ADJ (*old: man, gipsy*) vaga-bondo(-a).

2 N vagabondaggi *mpl*.

way·lay [weɪˈleɪ] (*pt, pp* **waylaid**) VT (*old*) intercettare; **I got waylaid** (*fig*) ho avuto un contrattempo.

♦ **way-out** [ˌweɪˈaʊt] ADJ (*fam*) eccentrico(-a).

way·side ['weɪˌsaɪd] **1** N bordo della strada; **along the wayside** OR **by the wayside** sul ciglio della strada; **to fall by the wayside** (*fig*) perdersi lungo la strada.

2 ADJ (*flowers, café*) sul bordo della strada.

♦ **way station** N (*Am Rail*) stazione *f* secondaria; (*fig*) tappa.

way·ward ['weɪwəd] ADJ (*self-willed*) ribelle, capriccioso (-a).

WC [ˌdʌbljuːˈsiː] N ABBR (*Brit*: = *water closet*) W.C. *m inv.*

WCC [ˌdʌbljuːsiːˈsiː] N ABBR (= *World Council of Churches*) *Consiglio Ecumenico delle Chiese.*

we [wiː] PERS PRON PL noi; **we understand** abbiamo capito; (*stressed*) noi sì che abbiamo capito; **here we are** eccoci; **we Italians** noi *or* noialtri italiani; **as we say in Florence ...** come si dice a Firenze...; **we all make mistakes** tutti possiamo sbagliare.

weak [wiːk] ADJ (*comp* -**er**, *superl* -**est**) (*gen*) debole; (*tea, coffee*) leggero(-a); (*health*) precario(-a); (*excuse, effort*) inefficace; **to grow weak(er)** = **to weaken** 2; **a weak chin** un mento sfuggente; **to have weak eyes** *or* **eyesight** avere la vista debole; **her French is weak** OR **she is weak at French** è scarsa in francese; **weak in the head** (*fam*) tocco(-a), toccato(-a); **to go weak at the knees** (*with excitement, hunger etc*) avere le gambe che fanno giacomo giacomo; **the weak link in the chain** l'anello debole della catena; **weak verb** verbo debole.

weak·en ['wiːkən] **1** VT (*gen*) indebolire; (*grip*) allentare; (*influence*) diminuire; (*solution, mixture*) diluire; **this fact weakens your case** questo fatto sminuisce il tuo argomento.

2 VI (*gen*) indebolirsi; (*grip*) allentarsi; (*influence*) diminuire; (*give way*) cedere; **we must not weaken now** non dobbiamo cedere proprio ora.

weak·en·ing ['wiːkənɪŋ] N (*gen*) indebolimento; (*of grip*) allentamento; (*of influence*) diminuzione *f*.

♦ **weak-kneed** [ˌwiːkˈniːd] ADJ (*fig*) debole, codardo(-a).

weak·ling ['wiːklɪŋ] N (*physically*) mingherlino(-a); (*morally*) smidollato(-a).

weak·ly ['wiːklɪ] **1** ADJ deboluccio(-a), gracile.

2 ADV debolmente.

♦ **weak-minded** [ˌwiːkˈmaɪndɪd] ADJ debole di carattere.

weak·ness ['wiːknɪs] N debolezza; **chocolate is one of my weaknesses** il cioccolato è una delle mie passioni; **to have a weakness for sth** avere un debole per qc.

♦ **weak-willed** [ˌwiːkˈwɪld] ADJ debole.

weal [wiːl] N (*welt*) piaga.

wealth [wɛlθ] N (*money, resources*) ricchezza, ricchezze *fpl*; (*fig: abundance*): **wealth (of)** dovizia *or* abbondanza (di).

♦ **wealth tax** N imposta sul patrimonio.

wealthy ['wɛlθɪ] ADJ (*comp* -**ier**, *superl* -**iest**) ricco(-a).

wean [wiːn] VT (*baby*) svezzare; **to wean sb (away) from alcohol** far perdere a qn il vizio del bere.

weap·on ['wɛpən] N arma.

wea·pon·ry ['wɛpənrɪ] N armamenti *mpl*.

wear [wɛə'] (*vb: pt* **wore**, *pp* **worn**) **1** N **a** (*use*) uso; **shoes for everyday wear** scarpe da mettere tutti i giorni; **there's still a lot of wear in these** (*shoes, carpets, tyres*) sono ancora in buono stato; **I've had a lot of wear out of this jacket** porto questa giacca da anni; **to stand up to a lot of wear** durare a lungo

b (*deterioration through use*) logoramento, logorio; **wear and tear** usura; **fair wear and tear** (*Comm*) normale usura; **the wear on the engine** l'usura del motore; **she looks the worse for wear** (*old, exhausted*) sembra sciupata; (*hung-over*) ha l'aria distrutta

c (*clothing*) abbigliamento; **children's wear** confezioni *fpl* per bambini; **sports/baby wear** abbigliamento sportivo/per neonati; **summer wear** abiti *mpl* estivi; **evening wear** abiti *npl* da sera.

2 VT **a** (*spectacles, necklace, beard*) portare; (*clothes*)

portare, indossare; (*look, smile*) avere; **to wear make-up** truccarsi; **she wasn't wearing any make-up** non era truccata; **she wore her blue dress** portava il vestito blu; **I have nothing to wear to the dinner** non ho niente da mettermi per la cena; **to wear one's hair long** portare i capelli lunghi; **he wore a big smile** sfoderò un gran sorriso

b (*damage through use*) consumare, logorare; **I always manage to wear my jumpers at the elbow** i miei maglioni sono sempre consumati nei gomiti; **they have worn a path across the lawn** hanno formato un sentiero nel prato a forza di camminarci sopra; **to wear a hole in sth** bucare qc a furia di usarlo(-a); **the rocks had been worn smooth** le rocce erano state levigate dal tempo

c (*fam: believe, tolerate*) bere; **he won't wear that** questa non la beve.

③ VI **a** (*last*) durare; **she has worn well** porta bene i suoi anni; **that theory has worn well** quella teoria è ancora valida

b (*become worn: shoes, inscription etc*) consumarsi; (*: rocks*) levigarsi; **the edges have worn smooth** gli spigoli si sono smussati; **that excuse is wearing a bit thin** quella scusa non regge più

▶ **wear away** ① VT + ADV (*rock, pattern etc*) consumare. ② VI + ADV consumarsi

▶ **wear down** ① VT + ADV (*heel, tyre tread etc*) consumare; (*fig: opposition etc*) fiaccare; (*: strength*) esaurire; **to wear down sb's patience** far perdere la pazienza a qn. ② VI + ADV (*heels, tyre tread*) consumarsi

▶ **wear off** VI + ADV (*plating, paint etc*) consumarsi; (*pain, excitement etc*) diminuire; (*anaesthetic*) perdere efficacia; **after a while the novelty wore off** dopo un po' non era più una novità

▶ **wear on** VI + ADV avanzare, passare; **as the evening wore on** nel corso della serata

▶ **wear out** ① VT + ADV consumare, logorare; (*fig: exhaust*) stancare; (*: patience*) far perdere; **to be worn out** essere consumato(-a); (*fig: person*) essere estenuato(-a) *or* distrutto(-a). ② VI + ADV (*shoes, carpet etc*) consumarsi; **his strength wore out** era spossato; **her patience wore out** ha perso la pazienza

▶ **wear through** ① VT + ADV consumare. ② VI + ADV consumarsi.

wear·able ['wɛərəbl] ADJ indossabile.

wear·er ['wɛərəʳ] N: **the wearers of the blue coats** quelli che portano il cappotto blu; **will the wearer of the red jacket come forward?** si prega la persona che indossa la giacca rossa di venire avanti.

wea·ri·ly ['wɪərɪlɪ] ADV stancamente.

wea·ri·ness ['wɪərɪnɪs] N stanchezza.

wear·ing ['wɛərɪŋ] ADJ (*tiring*) stancante, logorante.

wea·ri·some ['wɪərɪsəm] ADJ (*tiring*) estenuante; (*boring*) noioso(-a).

wea·ry ['wɪərɪ] ① ADJ (*comp* **-ier**, *superl* **-iest**) (*tired*) stanco(-a), affaticato(-a); (*dispirited*) stanco(-a), abbattuto(-a); (*tiring: wait, day*) estenuante; **to be weary of sb/sth** essere stanco(-a) di qn/qc; **five weary miles** cinque lunghe miglia. ② VT stancare. ③ VI: **to weary of sb/sth** stancarsi di qn/qc.

wea·sel ['wiːzl] N (*Zool*) donnola.

weath·er ['wɛðəʳ] ① N tempo; **in this weather** con questo tempo; **what's the weather like?** che tempo fa?; **it gets left outside in all weathers** rimane fuori con qualsiasi

tempo; **to be under the weather** (*fig: ill*) sentirsi poco bene; **to make heavy weather of sth** far sembrare qc più difficile di quello che sia.

② VT **a** (*wood*) stagionare

b : **to weather the storm** (*ship*) resistere alla tempesta; (*fig*) superare le difficoltà.

③ VI (*rocks*) logorarsi; (*wood*) stagionare.

④ ADJ (*bureau, ship, chart, station*) meteorologico(-a).

♦ **weather-beaten** ['wɛðəˌbiːtn] ADJ (*rocks, building*) logorato(-a) dalle intemperie; (*person, skin*) segnato(-a) dal tempo.

weather·board ['wɛðəˌbɔːd] N tavola di copertura.

weather·boarding ['wɛðəˌbɔːdɪŋ] N rivestimento con tavole di copertura.

♦ **weather-bound** ['wɛðəˌbaʊnd] ADJ bloccato(-a) dalle intemperie.

weather·cock ['wɛðəˌkɒk] N banderuola.

weath·ered ['wɛðəd] ADJ (*skin, rocks*) segnato(-a) dalle intemperie; (*wood*) stagionato(-a).

♦ **weather eye** N: **to keep a weather eye on sth** (*fig*) tener d'occhio qc.

♦ **weather forecast** N previsioni *fpl* del tempo.

♦ **weather forecaster** N meteorologo(-a).

weath·er·ing ['wɛðərɪŋ] N (*of rocks*) degradazione *f* meteorica.

weather·man ['wɛðəˌmæn] N (*pl* **-men**) meteorologo.

weather·proof ['wɛðəˌpruːf] ADJ (*garment*) impermeabile.

♦ **weather report** N bollettino meteorologico.

♦ **weather situation** N condizioni *fpl* metereologiche.

weather·vane ['wɛðəˌveɪn] N = **weathercock**.

weave [wiːv] (*pp: pt* **wove**, *pp* **woven**) ① N trama.

② VT (*threads, basket*) intrecciare; (*fabric*) tessere; **he wove these details into the story** ha intrecciato nella storia questi dettagli; **he wove a story round these experiences** ha intessuto una storia attorno a queste esperienze.

③ VI (*pt, pp* **weaved**) tessere; (*fig: move in and out*) zigzagare; **to weave in and out of the traffic** zigzagare nel traffico.

weav·er ['wiːvəʳ] N tessitore(-trice).

weav·ing ['wiːvɪŋ] N tessitura.

web [wɛb] N (*of spider*) ragnatela, tela; (*between toes*) membrana interdigitale; (*fig*) insieme *m*; **it was a web of lies** era un castello di menzogne.

webbed [wɛbd] ADJ: **webbed foot** piede *m* palmato.

web·bing ['wɛbɪŋ] N (*on chair*) cinghie *fpl*.

♦ **web-footed** [ˌwɛbˈfʊtɪd] ADJ palmipede, dai piedi palmati.

we'd [wiːd] = **we had**, **we would**.

wed [wɛd] ① VT sposare; **to be wedded to one's job/an idea** essere consacrato(-a) al proprio lavoro/a un'idea. ② VI sposarsi. ③ N: **the newly-weds** gli sposi novelli.

Wed. ABBR = **Wednesday**.

wed·ded ['wɛdɪd] ADJ (*wife, husband*) legittimo(-a); (*bliss, life*) coniugale.

wed·ding ['wɛdɪŋ] ① N matrimonio, nozze *fpl*; **silver/ golden** *etc* **wedding** nozze *fpl* d'argento/d'oro *etc*; **to have a church wedding** sposarsi in chiesa. ② ADJ (*cake, dress, reception*) nuziale.

♦ **wedding anniversary** N anniversario di matrimonio.

♦ **wedding breakfast** N (*old*) pranzo nuziale.

♦ **wedding day** N giorno delle nozze *or* del matrimonio.

♦ **wedding dress** N abito da sposa.

♦ **wedding invitation** N partecipazione *f* di nozze.
♦ **wedding night** N prima notte di nozze.
♦ **wedding present** N regalo di nozze.
♦ **wedding ring** N fede *f*, vera.
wedge [wɛdʒ] **1** N (*under door*) zeppa; (*for splitting sth*) cuneo; (*piece: of cheese, cake*) fetta; **it's the thin end of the wedge** (*fig*) è l'inizio della fine; **to drive a wedge between two people** intaccare il rapporto tra due persone.
2 VT mettere una zeppa sotto *or* in; **to wedge a door open** tenere aperta una porta con un fermo; **the car was wedged between two lorries** la macchina era incastrata tra due camion.
♦ **wedge-heeled shoes** [ˌwɛdʒhiːldˈʃuːz] NPL scarpe *fpl* con la zeppa.
♦ **wedge-shaped** ['wɛdʒˌʃeɪpt] ADJ a forma di cuneo.
wed·lock ['wɛdlɒk] N (*old*) vincolo matrimoniale.
Wednes·day ['wɛnzdɪ] N mercoledì *m inv for usage see* **Tuesday.**
wee [wiː] ADJ (*comp* -**er**, *superl* -**est**) (*Scot fam*) piccolo(-a); **a wee bit** uno zinzino.
weed [wiːd] **1** N (*plant*) erbaccia; (*weak person*) tipo(-a) allampanato(-a).
2 VT (*flower bed*) diserbare.
3 VI strappare le erbacce
▶ **weed out** VT + ADV (*fig*) eliminare.
weed·ing ['wiːdɪŋ] N diserbatura.
♦ **weed-killer** ['wiːdˌkɪləʳ] N diserbante *m*, erbicida *m*.
weedy ['wiːdɪ] ADJ (*comp* -**ier**, *superl* -**iest**) (*fam: person*) allampanato(-a).
week [wiːk] N settimana; **once/twice a week** una volta/due volte alla settimana; **this week** questa settimana; **next/last week** la settimana prossima/scorsa; **in the middle of the week** a metà settimana; **a week today** oggi a otto, una settimana a oggi; **2 weeks ago** 2 settimane fa; **in 2 weeks' time** fra 2 settimane, fra 15 giorni; **Tuesday week** [OR] **a week on Tuesday** martedì a otto; **to take 3 weeks' holiday** prendere 3 settimane di ferie; **the week ending January 3rd** ≈ la prima settimana di gennaio; **a 35-hour week** una settimana lavorativa di 35 ore; **week in, week out** [OR] **week after week** settimana dopo settimana; **every other week** una settimana sì e una no, a settimane alterne; **to knock sb into the middle of next week** (*fam*) darle di santa ragione a qn.
week·day ['wiːkˌdeɪ] N giorno feriale; (*Comm*) giornata lavorativa; **on weekdays** durante la settimana, nei giorni feriali.
week·end [ˌwiːkˈɛnd] **1** N week-end *m inv*, fine settimana *m or f inv*; **a long weekend** un fine settimana lungo (*che include il venerdì o il lunedì*); **at the weekend** durante il fine settimana; **at weekends** al weekend *or* fine settimana; **to go away for the weekend** andare via per il weekend *or* il fine settimana.
2 ADJ (*cottage*) per il fine settimana; (*visit*) di fine settimana.
♦ **weekend case** N borsa da viaggio.
week·ly ['wiːklɪ] **1** ADJ settimanale.
2 ADV settimanalmente, ogni settimana; **£45 weekly** 45 sterline alla settimana.
3 N (*magazine*) settimanale *m*.
wee·ny, wee·ney ['wiːnɪ], (*Am*) **ween·sie** ['wiːnzɪ] ADJ (*comp* -**ier**, *superl* -**iest**) (*fam*) minimo(-a); **a weeny bit more** ancora un pochino.
weep [wiːp] (*vb: pt, pp* **wept**) **1** VT (*tears*) versare, piangere.

2 VI piangere; (*Med, wound etc*) essudare; **to weep for sb** piangere per qn; **to weep bitterly** piangere amaramente; **I could have wept!** mi sarei messo a piangere!.
3 N: **to have a good weep** farsi un bel pianto.
weep·ing ['wiːpɪŋ] N pianto.
♦ **weeping willow** N salice *m* piangente.
weepy ['wiːpɪ] **1** ADJ piagnucoloso(-a).
2 N (*fam: film*) film *m* strappalacrime *inv*.
wee·vil ['wiːvl] N (*Zool*) tonchio.
wee-wee ['wiːwiː] (*fam*) **1** N pipì *f inv*.
2 VI fare la pipì.
weft [wɛft] N (*Textiles*) trama.
weigh [weɪ] **1** VT **a** (*also fig*) pesare; **it weighs a ton** (*also fig*) pesa una tonnellata; **to weigh sth in one's hand** soppesare qc; **to weigh sth in one's mind** soppesare mentalmente qc; **to weigh the pros and cons** valutare i pro e i contro
b : **to weigh anchor** (*Naut*) salpare, levare l'ancora.
2 VI (*fig: be a worry*): **to weigh on sb** pesare su qn; **to weigh with sb** avere importanza *or* contare per qn; **it weighs on her mind** la preoccupa; **that didn't weigh with him** quello per lui non aveva importanza
▶ **weigh down** VT + ADV (*branches*) piegare; (*person: with worry*) opprimere; **to be weighed down by sth** curvarsi sotto il peso di qc; **to be weighed down with sorrows** essere oppresso(-a) dai dispiaceri
▶ **weigh in** VI + ADV (*Sport*) pesarsi (prima di una gara); **he weighed in at 60 kilos** al controllo del peso era 60 chili
▶ **weigh out** VT + ADV (*goods*) pesare
▶ **weigh up** VT + ADV (*alternatives, situation*) pesare, valutare.
weigh·bridge ['weɪˌbrɪdʒ] N bascula.
♦ **weigh-in** ['weɪˌɪn] N (*Sport*) pesata.
weigh·ing ['weɪɪŋ] N pesatura.
♦ **weighing machine** N bilancia *f* pesapersone *inv*.
weight [weɪt] **1** N **a** (*gen, fig*) peso; **sold by weight** venduto(-a) a peso; **it** (*or* **he** *etc*) **is worth its** (*or* **his** *etc*) **weight in gold** vale tanto oro quanto pesa; **to put on/lose weight** ingrassare/dimagrire; **to carry weight** (*fig*) avere peso; **these are arguments of some weight** questi sono argomenti di un certo peso; **that's a weight off my mind** mi sono tolto un peso; **they won by sheer weight of numbers** hanno vinto solo per superiorità numerica; **to chuck** *or* **throw one's weight about** (*fam*) fare il/la prepotente; **he doesn't pull his weight** non lavora quanto dovrebbe
b (*for scales etc*) peso; **weights and measures** pesi e misure.
2 VT (*also:* **weight down**) mettere dei pesi su.
♦ **weight belt** N (*Diving*) cintura dei pesi.
weight·ed ['weɪtɪd] ADJ: **to be weighted in favour of/against** essere nettamente a favore di/contro.
weight·ing ['weɪtɪŋ] N indennità *f inv* speciale (*per carovita etc*).
weight·less ['weɪtlɪs] ADJ senza peso.
weight·less·ness ['weɪtlɪsnɪs] N assenza di peso.
weight·lifter ['weɪtˌlɪftəʳ] N pesista *m/f*.
weight·lifting ['weɪtˌlɪftɪŋ] N sollevamento pesi, pesistica.
♦ **weight training** N: **to do weight training** allenarsi con i pesi.
weighty ['weɪtɪ] ADJ (*comp* -**ier**, *superl* -**iest**) (*fig: problems, duties, considerations*) importante.
weir [wɪəʳ] N sbarramento.
weird [wɪəd] ADJ (*comp* -**er**, *superl* -**est**) strano(-a),

bizzarro(-a).

weird·ly ['wɪədlɪ] ADV stranamente.

weird·ness ['wɪədnɪs] N stranezza.

weir·do ['wɪədəʊ] N (fam) tipo(-a) allucinante.

welch [wɛlʃ] VI = **welsh**.

wel·come ['wɛlkəm] ① ADJ (gen) gradito(-a); **welcome!** benvenuto(-a)!; **welcome to Britain!** benvenuti in Gran Bretagna!; **to be welcome** (person) essere il/la benvenuto(-a); **welcome back!** bentornato(-a)!; **you will always be welcome here** qui sarai sempre il benvenuto; **to make sb welcome** accogliere bene qn; **you're welcome** (after thanks) prego; **you're welcome to try** prova pure; **you're welcome to (borrow) it** prendilo pure; **it's a welcome change** è un piacevole cambiamento.

② N accoglienza, benvenuto; **a cold/warm welcome** un'accoglienza fredda/calorosa; **to bid sb welcome** dare il benvenuto a qn; **the crowd gave him an enthusiastic welcome** la folla lo accolse con entusiasmo; **what sort of a welcome will this product get?** che accoglienza avrà questo prodotto?.

③ VT accogliere, ricevere; (also: **bid welcome**) dare il benvenuto a; (fig: change, suggestion, development) rallegrarsi di; (: criticism) accettare di buon grado; **I'd welcome your help** gradirei il tuo aiuto; **we welcome this step** siamo lieti di questa iniziativa; **he didn't welcome the suggestion** non ha gradito il suggerimento.

wel·com·ing ['wɛlkəmɪŋ] ADJ accogliente.

weld [wɛld] ① VT saldare.

② N saldatura.

weld·en ['wɛldən] (Skiing) ① N serpentina.

② VI fare la serpentina.

weld·er ['wɛldə'] N (person) saldatore m.

weld·ing ['wɛldɪŋ] N saldatura.

♦ **welding torch** N cannello per saldatura.

wel·fare ['wɛl,fɛə'] ① N a (gen) bene m; (comfort) benessere m; **the nation's welfare** il bene della nazione; **spiritual welfare** benessere spirituale; **to look after sb's welfare** preoccuparsi di qn; **child welfare** protezione f dell'infanzia

b (social aid etc) assistenza sociale; **they were living off welfare** vivevano del sussidio dello stato.

② ADJ (aid, organization) di assistenza sociale.

♦ **welfare centre** N centro di assistenza sociale.

♦ **welfare state** N: **the welfare state** lo stato assistenziale.

♦ **welfare work** N assistenza sociale.

♦ **welfare worker** N assistente m/f sociale.

we'll [wi:l] = **we will, we shall**.

well- [wɛl] PREF bene.

well¹ [wɛl] ① N (for water etc) pozzo; (of stairs) tromba; (of lift) gabbia. ② VI (tears, emotions) sgorgare

▶ **well up** VI + ADV (tears, emotions) sgorgare.

well² [wɛl] (comp **better**, superl **best**) ① ADV a (gen) bene; **very well** benissimo; **she plays the flute very well** suona molto bene il flauto; **he did as well as he could** ha fatto come meglio poteva; **to do well (in sth)** andare bene (in qc); **to be doing well** stare bene; **you did well to come** hai fatto bene a venire; **he did well to come tenth** anche arrivare decimo è stato per lui un buon risultato; **well done!** ben fatto!, bravo(-a)!; **to think well of sb** avere una buona opinione di qn; **to be well in with sb** essere in buoni rapporti con qn; **to do well by sb** trattare bene qn; **it was well worth it** ne valeva certo la pena; **you're well out of it** è un bene che tu ne sia uscito; **well and truly** completamente; **well over a thousand** molto or

ben più di mille; **all** or **only too well** anche troppo bene; **and well I know it!** è proprio vero!; **he's well away** (fam: drunk) è completamente andato

b (probably, reasonably): **we might just as well have ...** tanto valeva...; **she cried, as well she might** piangeva a buon diritto; **one might well ask why ...** ci si potrebbe ben chiedere perché...; **you may well ask!** buona domanda!; **you might as well tell me** potresti anche dirmelo; **I might** or **may as well come** quasi quasi vengo; **I couldn't very well leave** non potevo andarmene così

c : **as well** (in addition) anche; **she sings, as well as playing the piano** oltre a suonare il piano, canta; **X as well as Y** sia X che Y.

② ADJ a (healthy): **to be well** stare bene; **get well soon!** guarisci presto!; **I don't feel well** non mi sento bene

b (acceptable, satisfactory) buono(-a); **all is not well** non va tutto bene; **that's all very well, but ...** va benissimo, ma..., d'accordo, ma...; **well and good bene**; **it would be as well to ask** sarebbe bene chiedere; **it's just as well we asked** abbiamo fatto bene a chiedere.

③ EXCL (gen) bene; (resignation, hesitation) beh; **well, as I was saying ...** dunque, come stavo dicendo...; **well, well, well!** ma guarda un po'!; **very well then** va bene, molto bene; **very well, if that's the way you want it** (unenthusiastic) va bene, se questo è quello che vuoi; **well I never!** ma no!, ma non mi dire!; **well there you are then!** ecco, hai visto!.

④ N: **to wish sb well** augurare ogni bene a qn; (in exam, new job) augurare a qn di riuscire.

♦ **well-advised** [,wɛləd'vaɪzd] ADJ (action, decision) saggio (-a).

♦ **well-appointed** [,wɛlə'pɔɪntɪd] ADJ (flat, hotel etc) ben attrezzato(-a), ben equipaggiato(-a).

♦ **well-balanced** [,wɛl'bælənst] ADJ equilibrato(-a).

♦ **well-behaved** [,wɛlbɪ'heɪvd] ADJ (child) che si comporta bene, beneducato(-a).

♦ **well-being** [,wɛl'bi:ɪŋ] N benessere m.

♦ **well-bred** [,wɛl'brɛd] ADJ educato(-a), beneducato(-a).

♦ **well-brought-up** [,wɛlbrɔ:t'ʌp] ADJ ben educato(-a).

♦ **well-built** [,wɛl'bɪlt] ADJ (person) ben fatto(-a); (house) ben costruito(-a).

♦ **well-chosen** [,wɛl'tʃəʊzn] ADJ (remarks, words) ben scelto(-a), appropriato(-a).

♦ **well-connected** [,wɛlkə'nɛktɪd] ADJ: **to be well-connected** avere amicizie influenti.

♦ **well-developed** [,wɛldɪ'vɛləpt] ADJ ben sviluppato(-a).

♦ **well-disposed** [,wɛldɪ'spəʊzd] ADJ: **well-disposed to(wards)** ben disposto(-a) verso.

♦ **well-dressed** [,wɛl'drɛst] ADJ ben vestito(-a), vestito (-a) bene.

♦ **well-earned** [,wɛl'ɜ:nd] ADJ (rest) meritato(-a).

♦ **well-educated** [,wɛl'ɛdjʊ,keɪtɪd] ADJ colto(-a), istruito (-a).

♦ **well-fed** [,wɛl'fɛd] ADJ ben nutrito(-a).

♦ **well-founded** [,wɛl'faʊndɪd] ADJ ben fondato(-a).

♦ **well-groomed** [,wɛl'gru:md] ADJ (person) curato(-a) (nel vestire); (horse) ben strigliato(-a); (dog) ben tenuto (-a).

♦ **well-grounded** [,wɛl'graʊndɪd] ADJ ben fondato(-a).

♦ **well-heeled** [,wɛl'hi:ld] ADJ (fam: wealthy) agiato(-a), facoltoso(-a).

wel·lies ['wɛlɪz] NPL (fam) = **wellingtons**.

♦ **well-informed** [,wɛlɪn'fɔ:md] ADJ (knowledgeable) informato(-a); (having knowledge of) ben informato(-a).

Wel·ling·ton ['wɛlɪŋtən] N (city) Wellington f.

wel·ling·tons [ˈwɛlɪŋtənz] NPL (*also:* **wellington boots**) stivali *mpl* di gomma.

♦ **well-intentioned** [ˌwɛlɪnˈtɛnʃənd] ADJ benintenzionato(-a).

♦ **well-judged** [ˌwɛlˈdʒʌdʒd] ADJ (*aim, shot*) ben calcolato (-a); (*remark*) ben ponderato(-a); (*estimate*) giusto(-a).

♦ **well-kept** [ˌwɛlˈkɛpt] ADJ (*house, grounds*) ben tenuto (-a); (*secret*) ben custodito(-a); (*hair, hands*) ben curato (-a).

♦ **well-known** [ˌwɛlˈnəʊn] ADJ noto(-a), famoso(-a).

♦ **well-liked** [ˌwɛlˈlaɪkt] ADJ (*person*) benvoluto(-a); (*film, book*) di successo, gradito(-a).

♦ **well-lined** [ˌwɛlˈlaɪnd] ADJ (*fam*): **to have well-lined pockets** avere il portafoglio ben fornito; **to have a well-lined stomach** avere la pancia piena.

♦ **well-made** [ˌwɛlˈmeɪd] ADJ ben fatto(-a).

♦ **well-mannered** [ˌwɛlˈmænəd] ADJ (*person*) beneducato (-a); (*remark*) cortese.

♦ **well-meaning** [ˌwɛlˈmiːnɪŋ] ADJ (*person*) spinto(-a) da buone intenzioni.

♦ **well-meant** [ˌwɛlˈmɛnt] ADJ (*remark, act*) dettato(-a) dalle migliori intenzioni.

♦ **well-nigh** [ˌwɛlˈnaɪ] ADV: **well-nigh impossible** quasi impossibile.

♦ **well-off** [ˌwɛlˈɒf] 1 ADJ (*rich*) benestante, danaroso (-a); **you're well-off without him** puoi fare tranquillamente a meno di lui; **you don't know when you're well-off** non sai quanto sei fortunato. 2 NPL: **the well-off** i benestanti; see also **better-off**.

♦ **well-oiled** [ˌwɛlˈɔɪld] ADJ (*fam: drunk*) sbronzo(-a).

♦ **well-preserved** [ˌwɛlprɪˈzɜːvd] ADJ (*person*): **to be well-preserved** portare bene i propri anni.

♦ **well-read** [ˌwɛlˈrɛd] ADJ colto(-a).

♦ **well-spent** [ˌwɛlˈspɛnt] ADJ (*money*) ben speso(-a); **that was time well-spent** non è stata una perdita di tempo.

♦ **well-spoken** [ˌwɛlˈspəʊkən] ADJ che parla bene.

♦ **well-stacked** [ˌwɛlˈstækt] ADJ (*fam: woman*) ben carrozzata.

♦ **well-stocked** [ˌwɛlˈstɒkt] ADJ (*shop, larder*) ben fornito (-a); (*river*) pescoso(-a).

♦ **well-thought-of** [ˌwɛlˈθɔːtɒv] ADJ rispettato(-a); (*person*) benvoluto(-a).

♦ **well-thought-out** [ˈwɛlˌθɔːtˈaʊt] ADJ (*plan*) ben ponderato(-a).

♦ **well-thumbed** [ˌwɛlˈθʌmd] ADJ (*book, magazine*) consumato(-a) dall'uso.

♦ **well-timed** [ˌwɛlˈtaɪmd] ADJ opportuno(-a), tempestivo (-a).

♦ **well-to-do** [ˌwɛltəˈduː] ADJ abbiente, benestante.

♦ **well-tried** [ˌwɛlˈtraɪd] ADJ sperimentato(-a).

♦ **well-wisher** [ˈwɛlˌwɪʃə'] N ammiratore(-trice); **letters from well-wishers** lettere *fpl* di incoraggiamento.

♦ **well-woman clinic** [wɛlˈwʊmənˌklɪnɪk] N ≈ consultorio (familiare).

♦ **well-worn** [ˌwɛlˈwɔːn] ADJ (*path*) molto battuto(-a); (*carpet, clothes*) logoro(-a), liso(-a); (*fig: phrase*) trito(-a) e ritrito(-a).

Welsh [wɛlʃ] 1 ADJ gallese; **the Welsh Office** (*Pol*) il ministero degli Affari gallesi. 2 N **a** : **the Welsh** NPL i gallesi **b** (*language*) gallese *m*.

welsh [wɛlʃ] VI (*fam*): **to welsh on** (*promise*) venir meno a; (*debt*) non pagare.

♦ **Welsh dresser** N *credenza con alzata a ripiani.*

Welsh·man [ˈwɛlʃmən] N (*pl* -men) gallese *m*.

Welsh rare·bit [ˌwɛlʃˈrɛəbɪt], **Welsh rabbit** N crostino al formaggio.

Welsh·woman [ˈwɛlʃˌwʊmən] N (*pl* -women) gallese *f*.

welt [wɛlt] N (*bruise*) livido.

wel·ter [ˈwɛltə'] N massa, mucchio.

wel·ter·weight [ˈwɛltəˌweɪt] N peso welter *m inv*.

wench [wɛntʃ] 1 N (*old, liter*) ragazzotta; **a serving wench** una servetta. 2 VI (*old*) andare a donne.

wend [wɛnd] VT (*frm*): **to wend one's way home** incamminarsi verso casa.

went [wɛnt] PT of **go**.

wept [wɛpt] PT, PP of **weep**.

we're [wɪə'] = **we are**.

were [wɜː'] 2ND PERS SG, PL PT of **be**.

weren't [wɜːnt] = **were not**.

were·wolf [ˈwɪəˌwʊlf] N (*pl* -wolves) licantropo, lupo mannaro (*fam*).

west [wɛst] 1 N ovest *m*, ponente *m*, occidente *m*; **the wind is in** *or* **from the west** il vento viene da ovest *or* da ponente *or* da occidente; **(to the) west of** a ovest di; **in the west of** nella parte occidentale di; **the West** (*Pol*) l'Occidente *m*. 2 ADJ (*gen*) ovest *inv*; (*part, coast*) occidentale; (*wind*) di ponente. 3 ADV verso ovest; **to sail west** navigare verso ovest; **a house facing west** una casa esposta a ovest.

west·bound [ˈwɛstˌbaʊnd] ADJ (*traffic*) diretto(-a) a ovest; (*carriageway*) ovest *inv*.

♦ **West Country** N: **the West Country** il sud-ovest dell'Inghilterra.

west·er·ly [ˈwɛstəlɪ] ADJ (*wind*) di ponente; **in a westerly direction** verso ovest.

west·ern [ˈwɛstən] 1 ADJ (*also Pol*) occidentale, dell'ovest; **in Western France/Europe** nella Francia/nell'Europa occidentale. 2 N (*film*) western *m inv*; (*novel*) romanzo *m* western *inv*.

west·ern·er [ˈwɛstənə'] N occidentale *m/f*.

west·erni·za·tion [ˌwɛstənaɪˈzeɪʃən] N occidentalizzazione *f*.

west·ern·ize [ˈwɛstəˌnaɪz] VT occidentalizzare.

west·ern·ized [ˈwɛstəˌnaɪzd] ADJ occidentalizzato(-a).

west·ern·most [ˈwɛstənˌməʊst] ADJ il/la più occidentale; **the westernmost stretches of the desert** le distese più occidentali del deserto.

♦ **West German** ADJ, N tedesco(-a) occidentale.

♦ **West Germany** N Germania Occidentale.

♦ **West Indian** 1 ADJ delle Indie Occidentali. 2 N abitante *m/f* (*or* originario(-a)) delle Indie Occidentali.

♦ **West Indies** NPL: **the West Indies** le Indie Occidentali.

West·min·ster [ˈwɛstˌmɪnstə'] N il parlamento (britannico).

west·ward [ˈwɛstwəd] 1 ADJ (*direction*) ovest *inv*. 2 ADV (*also:* **westwards**) a ovest, verso ovest.

wet [wɛt] 1 ADJ (*comp* -ter, *superl* -test) **a** bagnato(-a); (*damp*) umido(-a); (*soaked*) fradicio(-a); (*paint, varnish, ink*) fresco(-a); **in wet clothes** coi vestiti bagnati; **to get wet** bagnarsi; **to be wet through** *or* **wet to the skin** essere fradicio(-a) fino alle ossa; **he's still wet behind the ears** (*fig*) ha ancora il latte alla bocca **b** (*rainy*) piovoso(-a); **a wet day** una giornata piovosa **c** (*fam pej: person*) smidollato(-a). 2 N **a** (*moisture*) umidità; (*rain*) pioggia; **it got left out in the wet** l'hanno lasciato fuori sotto la pioggia **b** (*fam pej: person*) smidollato(-a). 3 VT bagnare; **to wet the bed** bagnare il letto; **to wet**

one's pants *or* o.s. farsela addosso.

♦ **wet blanket** N (*fig*) guastafeste *m/f inv*; **what a wet blanket you are!** (*fam*) che pesante che sei!

wet·ness ['wɛtnɪs] N umidità.

♦ **wet nurse** N balia.

♦ **wet suit** N muta (*da subacqueo*).

we've [wiːv] = **we have**.

whack [wæk] **1** N **a** (*blow*) (forte) colpo **b** (*fam: attempt*): **to have a whack at sth/at doing sth** provare qc/a fare qc, tentare qc/di fare qc **c** (*fam: share*) parte *f*, fetta. **2** VT (*person*) dare un ceffone a; (*ball*) colpire con forza; (*fam: defeat*) dare una batosta a.

whacked [wækt] ADJ (*fam: exhausted*) sfinito(-a), stremato(-a).

whack·ing ['wækɪŋ] **1** ADJ (*fam: also*: **whacking great**) enorme. **2** N (*spanking*) sculacciata; (*fig*) batosta.

whacky ['wækɪ] = **wacky**.

whale [weɪl] N (*Zool*) balena; **we had a whale of a time** (*fam*) ci siamo divertiti da matti.

whale·bone ['weɪlˌbəʊn] N (*in corset*) stecca di balena.

♦ **whale oil** N olio di balena.

whal·er ['weɪləʳ] N (*person*) baleniere *m*; (*ship*) baleniera.

whal·ing ['weɪlɪŋ] N caccia alla balena.

♦ **whaling fleet** N flotta baleniera.

♦ **whaling industry** N industria baleniera.

♦ **whaling ship, whaling vessel** N (nave *f*) baleniera.

wham [wæm] EXCL (*fam*) bang.

wharf [wɔːf] N (*pl* **wharfs** *or* **wharves** [wɔːvz]) banchina.

wharf·age ['wɔːfɪdʒ] N diritti *mpl* di ormeggio.

what [wɒt]
1 ADJ che, quale;
▷**to what extent?** fino a che punto?
▷**buy what food you like** compra il cibo che vuoi
▷**what a fool I was!** che sciocco sono stato!
▷**what good would that do?** a che può servire?
▷**what little I had** il poco che avevo
▷**what a mess!** che disordine!
▷**what a nuisance!** che seccatura!
▷**for what reason?** per quale motivo?
▷**what time is it?** che ore sono?
▷**in what way did it strike you as odd?** in che cosa esattamente ti è sembrato strano?
2 PRON
a (*interrogative*) che cosa, cosa, che;
▷**what were you talking about?** di cosa stavate parlando?
▷**what is his address?** qual è il suo indirizzo?
▷**he asked me what she had said** mi ha chiesto che cosa avesse detto lei
▷**what is it** (*or he etc*) **called?** come si chiama?
▷**what will it cost?** quanto sarà *or* costerà?
▷**what are you doing?** che *or* (che) cosa fai?
▷**what are you doing that for?** perché lo fai?
▷**what is that tool for?** a che *or* a cosa serve quello strumento?
▷**what's happening?** che *or* (che) cosa succede?
▷**it's what?** come?, cosa?
▷**I don't know what to do** non so cosa fare
▷**what's the weather like?** che tempo fa?
▷**what's in there?** cosa c'è lì dentro?
▷**what is it now?** che c'è ora?
▷**tell me what you're thinking about** dimmi a cosa

stai pensando
▷**tell us what you're laughing at** dicci perché stai ridendo
▷**what is the Italian for "book"?** come si dice "book" in italiano?
▷**what do you want now?** che cosa vuoi adesso?
▷**I wonder what he'll do now** mi chiedo cosa farà adesso
b (*relative*) ciò che, quello che;
▷**I saw what you did** ho visto quello che hai fatto
▷**is that what happened?** è andata così?
▷**it's just what I wanted** è proprio ciò che volevo
▷**I know what, let's go to the cinema** sai cosa facciamo? - andiamo al cinema
▷**say what you like** di' quello che vuoi
▷**she's not what she was** non è più quella di una volta
▷**I tell you what, why not come back later?** sai cosa ti dico? perché non torniamo più tardi?
▷**what I want is a cup of tea** ciò che voglio adesso è una tazza di tè
▷**I saw what was on the table** ho visto quello che c'era sul tavolo
▷**he knows what's what** (*fam*) sa come stanno le cose
▷**I'll show her what's what!** le farò vedere io!
c
▷**what about me?** e io?
▷**what about doing ...?** cosa ne diresti di fare...
▷**what about a drink?** beviamo qualcosa?
▷**what about going to the cinema?** e se andassimo al cinema?
▷**...and what have you** (*fam*) ... e roba del genere
▷**you know John — yes, what about him?** conosci John — sì, perché?
▷**what about it?** (*what do you think*) cosa ne pensi?
▷**what about that money you owe me?** e quei soldi che mi devi?
▷**and what's more** e per di più
▷**...and what not** (*fam*) ... e così via
▷**so what** e allora?
▷**what with one thing and another** tra una cosa e l'altra.
3 EXCL (*disbelieving*) cosa?!, come?!;
▷**what, no coffee!** come, non c'è caffè?!

what-d'ye-call-her ['wɒtdtʃə'kɔːləʳ], **what's-her-name** ['wɒtsəneɪm] N (*fam*) cosa... come si chiama.

what-d'ye-call-him ['wɒtdtʃə'kɔːlɪm], **whats-his-name** ['wɒtsɪzneɪm] N (*fam*) coso(-a).

what-d'ye-call it ['wɒtdtʃə'kɔːlˌɪt], **what·sit** ['wɒtsɪt], **what's-its-name** ['wɒtsɪtsneɪm] N (*fam*) coso, aggeggio.

what·ev·er [wɒt'evəʳ] **1** PRON **a** (*anything that*) (tutto) ciò che, (tutto) quello che; (*no matter what*) qualsiasi *or* qualunque cosa + *sub*; **do whatever you want** fa' quello *or* ciò che vuoi; **do whatever is necessary** fai qualunque cosa sia necessaria; **whatever happens** qualsiasi *or* qualunque cosa succeda; **whatever it costs** costi quello che costi; **or whatever they're called** o come caspita si chiamano
b (*emphatic*): **whatever do you mean?** cosa vorresti dire?; **whatever did you do that for?** perché mai l'hai fatto?.
2 ADJ, ADV (*any*): **whatever book you choose** qualsiasi *or* qualunque libro tu scelga; (*all*): **give me whatever money you've got** dammi i soldi che hai; **nothing**

whatever proprio niente; **it's no use whatever** non serve proprio a nulla; **no reason whatever** *or* **whatsoever** nessuna ragione al mondo.

what·so·ev·er [ˌwɒtsəʊ'ɛvəʳ] = **whatever.**

wheat [wiːt] N grano, frumento.

wheat·ear ['wiːt.ɪəʳ] N (*Zool*) culbianco.

wheat·en ['wiːtn] ADJ di frumento, di grano.

wheat·germ ['wiːt.dʒɜːm] N germe *m* di grano.

wheat·meal ['wiːt.miːl] N *tipo di farina integrale di frumento.*

whee·dle ['wiːdl] VT: **to wheedle sb into doing sth** convincere qn a fare qc con lusinghe; **to wheedle sth out of sb** (*favour etc*) ottenere qc da qn con lusinghe; (*secret, name*) farsi dire qc da qn con lusinghe.

whee·dling ['wiːdlɪŋ] ① ADJ (*voice, tone*) suadente.
② N lusinghe *fpl.*

wheel [wiːl] ① N (*gen*) ruota; (*also:* **steering wheel**) volante *m*; (*Naut*) timone *m*; (*also:* **potter's wheel**) tornio da vasaio; (*also:* **spinning wheel**) filatoio; **at the wheel** (*Aut*) al volante; (*Naut*) al timone; **this car is a four-wheel drive** questa è una macchina a quattro ruote motrici; **to take the wheel** prendere il volante; (*Naut*) prendere il timone; **the wheel of fortune** la ruota della fortuna; **the wheels of government** gli ingranaggi dello stato; **there are wheels within wheels** (*fig*) è più complesso di quello che sembra; **to put one's shoulder to the wheel** (*fig*) darci dentro; **the wheel has come** *or* **turned full circle** (*fig*) la fortuna è girata.
② VT (*push: bicycle, pram etc*) spingere; **we wheeled it over to the window** l'abbiamo spinto verso la finestra.
③ VI (*birds*) roteare; **to wheel left** (*Mil*) fare una conversione a sinistra; **to wheel round** (*person*) girarsi sui tacchi, voltarsi; **to wheel and deal** (*fam*) trafficare.

wheel·bar·row ['wiːl.bærəʊ] N carriola.

wheel·base ['wiːl.beɪs] N (*Aut*) interasse *m*, passo.

wheel·chair ['wiːl.tʃɛəʳ] N sedia a rotelle.

♦ **wheel clamp** N (*Aut*) ceppo *m* bloccaruote *inv.*

wheeled [wiːld] ADJ a ruote; **a three-wheeled car** un'auto a tre ruote.

wheeler-dealer ['wiːlə.diːləʳ] N trafficone(-a).

wheel·house ['wiːl.haʊs] N (*Naut*) timoneria.

♦ **wheelie-bin** ['wɪːlɪ.bɪn] N (*Brit*) bidone *m* (della spazzatura) a rotelle.

wheel·ing ['wiːlɪŋ] N: **wheeling and dealing** traffici *mpl.*

wheel·wright ['wiːl.raɪt] N carradore *m.*

wheeze [wiːz] ① VI ansimare.
② N respiro affannoso.

wheezy ['wiːzɪ] ADJ (*comp* **-ier**, *superl* **-iest**) (*person*) chi respira con affanno; (*breath*) sibilante.

whelk [wɛlk] N (*Zool*) buccino.

whelp [wɛlp] N cucciolo.

---

when [wɛn]
① ADV quando;
▷**when did it *happen?*** quando è successo?
▷**I *know* when it happened** lo so io quando è successo
▷*say* **when!** (*pouring drinks*) dimmi (quando) basta
▷*since* **when do you like Indian food?** da quando (in qua) ti piace la cucina indiana?
② CONJ
a (*at, during or after the time that*) quando;
▷**when I *came in*** quando sono entrato

▷**be careful when you *cross* the road** *or* **when *crossing* the road** stai attento quando attraversi la strada
▷*even* **when** anche quando
▷**when it's *finished*, it will measure …** quando sarà finito misurerà…
▷**when you've *read* it** quando l'hai *or* avrai letto
▷*why* **walk when you can take a bus?** perché camminare se puoi andare in autobus?
b (*the time that*)
▷**she told me *about* when she was in Milan** mi parlò di quando era a Milano
▷*that* **was when I needed you** era allora che avevo bisogno di te
▷*that's* **when the train arrives** il treno arriva a quell'ora
c (*relative: in, on or at which*) in cui;
▷**on the *day* when** il giorno in cui
▷**one *day* when it was raining** un giorno che pioveva
▷**at the very *moment* when …** proprio quando…
▷**during the *time* when she lived abroad** nel periodo in cui viveva all'estero
▷**in the *winter* when …** nell'inverno in cui…
d (*whereas, although*) mentre, sebbene;
▷**you call the policy rigid, when in fact it is very flexible** la definisci rigida, mentre in realtà è una politica molto flessibile.

---

whence [wɛns] ADV (*liter: from where*) da dove.

when·ever [wɛn'ɛvəʳ] ① CONJ **a** (*rel: at whatever time*) quando, in qualsiasi momento + *sub*; (*every time that*) quando, ogni volta che; **come whenever you like** vieni quando vuoi; **leave whenever it suits you** parti quando ti fa comodo *or* in qualsiasi momento ti faccia comodo; **I go whenever I can** ci vado quando posso; **whenever you see one of those, stop** fermati quando ne vedi uno **b** (*in questions*): **whenever did I say that?** quando mai l'ho detto?.
② ADV: **tomorrow or whenever** domani o in un altro momento; **last week or whenever** la settimana scorsa o non so più quando.

where [wɛəʳ] ① ADV dove; **where are you from?** di dove sei?; **where am I?** dove sono?; **where are you going (to)?** dove stai andando?; **where have you come from?** da dove sei venuto?; **did he tell you where he was going?** ti ha detto dove andava?; **where should we be if …?** dove saremmo se…?.
② CONJ **a** (*gen*) dove; **there's a cinema where the butcher's used to be** dove una volta c'era la macelleria ora c'è un cinema; **where possible** quando è possibile, se possibile; **from where I'm standing it looks fine** da dove sono, mi sembra vada bene; **so that's where they've got to!** ecco dove erano finiti!; **this is where we found it** è qui che l'abbiamo trovato; **that's where we got to in the last lesson** è qui che siamo arrivati nell'ultima lezione; **that's just where you're wrong!** è proprio lì che ti sbagli!; **sometimes a teacher will be listened to, where a parent might not** qualche volta si è più disposti ad ascoltare un insegnante che un genitore
b (*rel: in, on, at which*) dove, in (*or* da, su *etc*) cui; **the town where we come from** la città da cui veniamo; **the house where I was born** la casa in cui sono nato; **the hill where the heather grows** la collina dove *or* su cui cresce l'erica.

where·abouts ['wɛərə‚baʊts] 1 ADV dove; **whereabouts did you say you lived?** da che parte hai detto che abiti?. 2 NPL: **to know sb's whereabouts** sapere dove si trova qn.

where·as [wɛər'æz] CONJ (*while on the other hand*) mentre; (*Law*) considerato che.

where·by [wɛə'baɪ] ADV (*frm*) per cui.

where·fore ['wɛə‚fɔː] N see **why 3**.

where·in [wɛər'ɪn] ADV (*frm*) dove.

where·upon [‚wɛərə'pɒn] ADV (*frm*) al che, dopo di che.

wher·ev·er [wɛər'ɛvə'] 1 CONJ dovunque + *sub*; **wherever you go I'll go too** dovunque tu vada andrò anch'io; **wherever they went they were cheered** venivano acclamati dovunque andassero; **Udine, wherever that is** un posto che non so dove sia ma che si chiama Udine; **sit wherever you like** siediti dove vuoi. 2 ADV **a**: **in Naples, Florence, or wherever** a Napoli, Firenze o in qualche altro posto **b** (*in questions*) dove; **wherever did he put it?** dove (mai) l'ha messo?

where·with·al ['wɛəwɪð‚ɔːl] N: **the wherewithal (to do sth)** i mezzi *mpl* (per fare qc).

whet [wɛt] VT (*tool*) affilare; (*appetite, curiosity*) stuzzicare.

wheth·er ['wɛðə'] CONJ (*if*) se; (*no matter whether*) che + *sub*; **whether you want to or not** che tu voglia o no; **whether it's sunny or not** che ci sia il sole o no; **I am not certain whether he'll come (or not)** non so con certezza se verrà (o no), non sono sicuro che venga; **whether they come or not** che vengano o meno; **I don't know whether you know** ... non so se lo sai...; **I doubt whether that's true** dubito che sia vero; **I don't know whether to accept or not** non so se accettare o no; **it's doubtful whether** è poco probabile che.

whet·stone ['wɛt‚stəʊn] N cote *f.*

whew [hwjuː] EXCL uuh!

whey [weɪ] N siero.

---

which [wɪtʃ]
1 ADJ
a (*interrogative*) quale;
▷**which *book* do you want?** quale libro vuoi?
▷**she didn't say which *books* she wanted** non ha detto quali libri voleva
▷**which *books* are yours?** quali sono i tuoi libri?
▷**tell me which *one* you want** dimmi quale vuoi
▷**which *one* of you?** chi di voi?
▷**which *one/ones* do you want?** quale/quali vuoi?
▷**which *way* did she go?** da che parte è andata?
b
▷**in which *case*** nel qual caso
▷**he lived in Italy for a year, during which *time*** ... ha vissuto in Italia per un anno, periodo in cui...
▷**by which *time*** e a quel punto.
2 PRON
a (*interrogative: the one or ones that*) quale;
▷**I *know* which I'd rather have** io lo so quale preferirei
▷**I don't *mind* which** non mi importa quale
▷**which *of* these are yours?** quali di questi sono tuoi?
▷**which *of* your sisters?** quale delle tue sorelle?
▷**which *of* you?** chi di voi?
▷**which do you *want*?** quale vuoi?
▷**I can't tell which is *which*** non riesco a distinguere l'uno dall'altro

b (*relative: that*) che; (*indirect*) cui, il/la quale;
▷**the book *about* which** il libro del quale *or* di cui
▷***after* which** dopo di che
▷**the apple (which) you ate** la mela che hai mangiato
▷**the apple which is on the table** la mela che è sul tavolo
▷**the hotel *at* which we stayed** l'albergo in cui abbiamo soggiornato
▷***from* which one can deduce** ... dal che si può dedurre...
▷**he said he was there, which *is* true** ha detto che c'era, il che è vero
▷**the *meeting* (which) we attended** la riunione a cui abbiamo partecipato
▷**the chair *on* which** la sedia sulla quale *or* su cui
▷**you're late, which *reminds* me** ... sei in ritardo, il che mi fa venire in mente...
▷**it rained a lot, which *upset* her** ha piovuto tanto e ciò l'ha irritata.

---

which·ever [wɪtʃ'ɛvə'] 1 ADJ (*that one which*) quello(-a) che; (*no matter which*) qualsiasi + *sub*, qualunque + *sub*; **take whichever one you prefer** prendi quello che preferisci; **take whichever book you prefer** prendi il libro che preferisci; **whichever book you take** qualsiasi libro tu prenda; **you can choose whichever system you want** puoi scegliere il sistema che vuoi; **whichever system you have there are difficulties** qualsiasi sistema tu abbia ci sono delle difficoltà; **whichever way you look at it** da qualunque punto di vista lo si consideri. 2 PRON (*the one which*) quello(-a) che; (*no matter which one*) qualsiasi + *sub*, qualunque + *sub*; **whichever of the methods you choose** qualsiasi *or* qualunque metodo tu scelga; **choose whichever you like** scegli quello che ti piace.

whiff [wɪf] N (*of gas, sth unpleasant*) zaffata; (*of sea air, perfume*) odore *m*; **to catch a whiff of sth** sentire l'odore di qc; **a few whiffs of this could knock you out** se annusi un po' di questo svieni.

while [waɪl] 1 N **a**: **a while** un po' (di tempo); **for a little while** per un po'; **for a long while** per un bel po', a lungo; **after a while** dopo un po'; **for a while** per un po', per un certo periodo; **in a while** tra poco; **once in a while** ogni tanto, una volta ogni tanto; **it will be a good while before he gets here** gli ci vorrà un bel po' (di tempo) per arrivare qui; **a little while ago** poco fa; **in between whiles** nel frattempo; **all the while** tutto il tempo **b**: **we'll make it worth your while** faremo in modo che non ti penta; **it might be worth your while to** ... forse ti converrebbe.... 2 CONJ **a** (*during the time that*) mentre; (*as long as*) finché, mentre; **while this was happening** mentre avveniva questo; **she fell asleep while reading** si addormentò mentre stava leggendo; **it won't happen while I'm here** non accadrà finché sono qui io **b** (*although*) benché + *sub*, sebbene + *sub*, anche se; **while I agree with what you have said** benché sia d'accordo *or* anche se sono d'accordo con ciò che hai detto **c** (*whereas*) mentre; **I enjoy sport, while he prefers reading** a me piace lo sport, mentre lui preferisce la lettura
▶ **while away** VT + ADV (*time, hours*) far passare.
♦ **while-you-wait** [‚waɪljuː'weɪt] ADJ: **"while-you-wait shoe repairs"** "riparazioni lampo" (*di scarpe*).

whilst [waɪlst] CONJ = while[2].

whim [wɪm] N capriccio; **a passing whim** una passione momentanea; **as the whim takes me** come mi gira.

whim·per ['wɪmpə'] **1** N (of person) gemito; (: whine) piagnucolio; (of dog) mugolio.
2 VI (see n) gemere; piagnucolare; mugolare.

whim·per·ing ['wɪmpərɪŋ] **1** N (of person) gemiti mpl, piagnucolio; (of dog) mugolio.
2 ADJ (see n) gemente, piagnucoloso(-a); mugolante.

whim·si·cal ['wɪmzɪkəl] ADJ (person) particolare; (look) curioso(-a); (idea, story) fantasioso(-a); **a whimsical smile** uno strano sorrisetto.

whim·si·cal·ly ['wɪmzɪkəlɪ] ADV (describe) in modo fantastico; (smile, look) curiosamente.

whin [wɪn] N (Bot) ginestrone m.

whin·chat ['wɪn,tʃæt] N (Zool) staccino.

whine [waɪn] **1** N (of dog) guaito; (of child) piagnucolio; (of engine) sibilo; (of bullet) fischio.
2 VI (dog) guaire; (child) piagnucolare; (engine) sibilare; (bullet) fischiare; (fig fam: complain) piagnucolare, lamentarsi; **don't come whining to me about it** non venire a piangere da me.

whinge [wɪndʒ] VI: **whinge about** (fam pej): **to whinge (about)** frignare (per), lamentarsi (di).

whin·ing ['waɪnɪŋ] **1** N (of dog) guaito; (of child) piagnucolio; (of engine) sibilo; (fam: complaining) lamentele fpl.
2 ADJ (dog) che guaisce; (child) piagnucoloso(-a); (engine) sibilante.

whin·ny ['wɪnɪ] **1** VI nitrire.
2 N nitrito.

whip [wɪp] **1** N **a** frusta; (also: **riding whip**) frustino
b (Parliament: person) capogruppo; **three-line whip** ordine m tassativo di votare
c (Culin) mousse f inv.
2 VT **a** frustare, fustigare; (Culin: cream etc) montare
b (fam: move quickly): **he whipped the book off the table** tolse rapidamente il libro dal tavolo; **they whipped her into hospital** la portarono d'urgenza all'ospedale; **he whipped a gun out of his pocket** estrasse fulmineamente una pistola dalla tasca; **the car whipped round the corner** la macchina svoltò l'angolo a gran velocità.
3 VI: **to whip along/away** etc fare una corsa; **she whipped round when she heard me** si voltò di scatto quando mi sentì
▶ **whip up** VT + ADV (cream) montare, sbattere; (fam: meal) improvvisare; (: stir up: support, feeling) suscitare.
♦ **whip hand** N: **to have the whip hand (over sb)** avere il predominio (su qn).

whip·lash ['wɪp,læʃ] N (blow from whip) frustata; (Med: also: **whiplash injury**) colpo di frusta.

whipped cream [,wɪpt'kriːm] N panna montata.

whip·per·snap·per ['wɪpə,snæpə'] N (also: **young whippersnapper**) piccolo(-a) impertinente.

whip·pet ['wɪpɪt] N piccolo levriero inglese.

whip·ping ['wɪpɪŋ] N: **to give sb a whipping** dare delle frustate fpl a qn.
♦ **whipping boy** N (fig) capro espiatorio.
♦ **whipping cream** N panna da montare.
♦ **whip-round** ['wɪp,raʊnd] N (Brit fam) colletta; **to have a whip-round for sb** fare una colletta per qn.

whip·stitch ['wɪp,stɪtʃ] N sopraggitto.

whirl [wɜːl] **1** N (spin) vortice m, turbinio; (of dust, water etc) turbine m; (of cream) ricciolo; **my head is in a whirl** mi gira la testa; **the social whirl** il vortice della vita mondana; **let's give it a whirl** (fam) facciamo un tenta-

tivo.
2 VT (also: **whirl round**: dance partner) far roteare, far volteggiare; **the wind whirled the leaves** il vento ha sollevato le foglie in un vortice; **he whirled us round the town** ci ha fatto visitare la città a tutta velocità or in un baleno; **he whirled us off to the theatre** ci trascinò con sé al teatro.
3 VI (also: **whirl round**: wheel, merry-go-round) girare; (: dancers) volteggiare; (: leaves, dust) sollevarsi in un vortice; **the countryside whirled past us** la campagna sfrecciava accanto a noi; **the dancers whirled past us** i danzatori passarono accanto a noi volteggiando; **my head was whirling** mi girava la testa.

whirl·pool ['wɜːl,puːl] N mulinello, vortice m.

whirl·wind ['wɜːl,wɪnd] **1** N tromba d'aria, turbine m.
2 ADJ (romance etc) travolgente.

whirr, whir [wɜː'] **1** N (of insect wings, machine) ronzio.
2 VI ronzare.

whisk [wɪsk] **1** N (Culin: also: **hand whisk**) frusta, frullino a mano; (: also: **electric whisk**) frullino elettrico; **with a whisk of its tail** con un colpo di coda.
2 VT **a** (Culin) frullare, sbattere; (: egg whites) montare a neve
b : **whisk the eggs into the mixture** incorporare le uova all'impasto mescolando energicamente; **the horse whisked the flies away with its tail** il cavallo scacciava le mosche con la coda; **the waiter whisked the dishes away** il cameriere tolse in fretta i piatti; **they whisked him off to a meeting** lo trascinarono di gran fretta a una riunione.

whisk·ers ['wɪskəz] NPL (also: **side whiskers**) basette fpl; (beard) barba; (moustache, of animal) baffi mpl.

whis·ky, (Am) whis·key ['wɪskɪ] N whisky m inv; **a whisky and soda** un whisky e soda.

whis·per ['wɪspə'] **1** N **a** (gen) sussurro, bisbiglio; (of leaves) fruscio, stormire m; **to speak in a whisper** bisbigliare **b** (rumour) voce f.
2 VT bisbigliare, sussurrare; **to whisper sth to sb** bisbigliare qc a qn.
3 VI (gen) bisbigliare; (leaves) frusciare, stormire; **to whisper to sb** bisbigliare a qn.

whis·per·ing ['wɪspərɪŋ] N bisbiglio; (of leaves) fruscio; **there's been a lot of whispering about her** sono corse parecchie voci sul suo conto.
♦ **whispering campaign** N campagna diffamatoria.
♦ **whispering gallery** N galleria acustica.

whist [wɪst] N whist m.
♦ **whist drive** N torneo di whist.

whis·tle ['wɪsl] **1** N (sound) fischio; (instrument) fischietto; **the referee blew his whistle** l'arbitro fischiò; **the police searched him, but he was as clean as a whistle** la polizia lo ha perquisito ma lui era pulito; **the handle broke off as clean as a whistle** il manico si è staccato di netto; **to blow the whistle on** (inform on) fare una soffiata su.
2 VT: **to whistle a tune** fischiettare un motivetto.
3 VI (gen) fischiare; (in low tone) fischiettare; **he whistled for a taxi** fischiò per fermare un taxi; **the referee whistled for a foul** l'arbitro fischiò un fallo; **the bullet whistled past my ear** la pallottola mi fischiò vicino all'orecchio; **he's whistling in the dark** (fig) lo fa (or dice) per darsi coraggio; **he can whistle for it!** (fig fam) se lo può sognare!
▶ **whistle up** VT + ADV (taxi, dog) fare un fischio a.
♦ **whistle-stop** ['wɪsl,stɒp] ADJ: **whistle-stop tour** (Pol)

visita *f* lampo *inv* (*in una città nel corso di una campagna elettorale*).

Whit [wɪt] (*fam*) ①N Pentecoste *f*.
② ADJ (*holiday, weekend*) di Pentecoste.

whit [wɪt] N: **not a whit** neanche un po'; **not a whit of truth** neanche un briciolo di verità; **the place hasn't changed a whit** il posto non è cambiato affatto *or* per nulla.

white [waɪt] ① ADJ (*comp* **-er**, *superl* **-est**) (*gen*) bianco(-a), candido(-a); **to turn** *or* **go white** (*person*) sbiancare; (*hair*) diventare bianco(-a); **a white man** un bianco; **a white Christmas** un Natale con la neve; **the great white hope** (*fig*) la promessa numero uno; **to be as white as a sheet** essere bianco(-a) come un cencio; **as white as snow** niveo(-a), bianco *or* candido come la neve; **white with fear** pallido(-a) dalla paura; **it washes the clothes whiter than white** lava più bianco del bianco.
② N **a** (*colour, of eyes*) bianco; (*of egg*) bianco, albume *m*; **the whites** (*washing*) i capi bianchi; **tennis whites** completo *msg* da tennis; **dressed in white** vestito(-a) di bianco; **her dress was a dazzling white** il suo abito era di un bianco abbagliante
b (*person*) bianco(-a).

white·bait ['waɪtˌbeɪt] N bianchetti *mpl*.
white·beam ['waɪtˌbiːm] N sorbo comune.
♦ **white coffee** N (*Brit*) caffè *m inv* con latte.
♦ **white-collar** ['waɪtˌkɒlə'] ADJ: **white-collar job** lavoro impiegatizio.
♦ **white-collar worker** N impiegato(-a), colletto bianco.
♦ **white elephant** N (*fam*) cattedrale *f* nel deserto.
♦ **white-faced** [ˌwaɪt'feɪst] ADJ pallido(-a), bianco(-a).
♦ **white flag** N bandiera bianca.
♦ **white goods** NPL (*appliances*) elettrodomestici *mpl*; (*linen*) biancheria *fsg* per la casa.
♦ **white-haired** [ˌwaɪt'hɛəd] ADJ canuto(-a), dai capelli bianchi.
White·hall ['waɪtˌhɔːl] N (*street*) *strada londinese dove hanno sede i ministeri del governo inglese*; (*British Government*) il governo inglese.
♦ **white horse** N (*on wave*) cresta di spuma (dell'onda).
♦ **white-hot** [ˌwaɪt'hɒt] ADJ (*metal*) incandescente.
♦ **White House** N (*Am*): **the White House** la Casa Bianca.
♦ **white lead** N biacca.
♦ **white lie** N bugia pietosa, bugia innocua.
♦ **white meat** N carni *fpl* bianche.
whit·en ['waɪtn] VT (*shoes*) dare il bianchetto a.
white·ness ['waɪtnɪs] N (*gen*) bianco; (*of skin*) candore *m*; (*pallor*) biancore *m*.
whit·en·ing ['waɪtnɪŋ] N (*substance*) bianchetto.
♦ **white noise** N (*Radio, TV*) sibilo (per interferenza).
White·out® ['waɪtˌaʊt] N bianchetto.
white·out ['waɪtˌaʊt] N (*Met*): **there is a whiteout** tutto è coperto di neve.
♦ **white paper** N (*Pol*) ≈ libro bianco.
♦ **white pepper** N pepe *m* bianco.
♦ **white sale** N fiera del bianco.
♦ **white sauce** N besciamella.
♦ **white spirit** N acquaragia (sintetica).
white·thorn ['waɪtˌθɔːn] N biancospino.
white·wash ['waɪtˌwɒʃ] ①N (bianco di) calce *f*.
② VT (*wall*) imbiancare (con la calce); (*fig: person, sb's faults*) coprire; (: *motives*) dissimulare; (: *event, episode*) sminuire.
♦ **white wedding** N matrimonio in bianco.
♦ **white wine** N vino bianco.

whith·er ['wɪðə'] ADV (*liter*) dove.
whit·ing ['waɪtɪŋ] N INV (*fish*) merlango.
whit·ish ['waɪtɪʃ] ADJ biancastro(-a), bianchiccio(-a).
whit·low ['wɪtləʊ] N patereccio.
♦ **Whit Monday** N lunedì *m inv* di Pentecoste.
Whit·sun ['wɪtsən] N (*also:* **Whitsuntide**) Pentecoste *f*; (*week*) settimana di Pentecoste.
♦ **Whit Sunday** N Pentecoste *f*.
whit·tle ['wɪtl] VT (*wood*) intagliare
▶ **whittle away** VT + ADV (*fig*) ridurre
▶ **whittle down** VT + ADV (*fig*) ridurre, tagliare.
whiz, whizz [wɪz] VI (*motorbike, sledge etc*) sfrecciare; (*bullet*) sibilare; **to whiz through the air** sfrecciare; **cars were whizzing past** le macchine passavano sfrecciando.
♦ **whiz kid** N (*fam*) mago(-a).
WHO [ˌdʌbljuːeɪtʃ'əʊ] N ABBR (= *World Health Organization*) O.M.S. *f* (= *Organizzazione Mondiale della Sanità*).

who [huː] PRON
ⓐ (*interrogative:* si può anche usare al posto di "whom" nella lingua parlata) chi;
▷**who should it be but Graham!** chi poteva essere se non Graham!
▷**who's the book by?** chi è l'autore del libro?
▷**who are you looking for?** chi stai cercando?
▷**who is it?** chi è?
▷**I know who it was** io so chi è stato
▷**who's there?** chi è?
▷**who does she think she is?** (*fam*) chi si crede di essere?
▷**you'll soon find out who's who** presto li conoscerai
ⓑ (*relative*) che;
▷**my cousin who lives in New York** mio cugino che vive a New York
▷**those who can swim** quelli che sanno nuotare, chi sa nuotare.

whoa [wəʊ] EXCL (*also:* **whoa there**) altolà!
who'd [huːd] = **who would, who had**.
who·dun·it, who·dun·nit [huːˈdʌnɪt] N (*fam*) (romanzo) giallo.
who·ever [huːˈɛvə'] PRON **a** (*the person that, anyone that*) chiunque + *sub*, chi; (*no matter who*) chiunque + *sub*; **whoever said that was an idiot** chiunque l'abbia detto *or* chi l'ha detto è un idiota; **whoever finds it** chiunque lo trovi; **ask whoever you like** chiedi a chiunque; **it won't be easy, whoever does it** non sarà facile, chiunque lo faccia; **whoever she marries** chiunque lei sposi
b (*in questions*) chi (mai); **whoever told you that?** chi (mai) te l'ha detto?
whole [həʊl] ① ADJ **a** (*entire:* + *sg n*) intero(-a), tutto(-a); (: + *pl n*) intero(-a); **with my whole heart** con tutto il mio cuore; **a whole lot of things** una gran quantità di cose, moltissime cose; **a whole lot of people** moltissima gente; **a whole lot better** molto meglio; **the whole lot** tutto; **the whole lot (of them)** tutti(-e); **3 whole days** 3 giorni interi; **the whole day** tutto il giorno, il giorno intero; **I read the whole book** ho letto tutto il libro *or* il libro per intero; **the whole world** tutto il mondo, il mondo intero; **whole villages were destroyed** interi paesi furono distrutti; **is that the whole truth?** è tutta la verità?; **but the whole purpose** *or* **point was to ...** ma lo scopo era proprio di...

b (*intact, unbroken*) intero(-a); (: *series, set*) completo (-a); **to swallow sth whole** mandar giù qc intero(-a); (*fig*): **he swallowed it whole** l'ha bevuta tutta; **to our surprise he came back whole** con nostra sorpresa tornò sano e salvo.

2 N **a** (*all*): **the whole of the film** tutto il film, il film intero; **the whole of the sum** la somma intera, l'intera somma; **the whole of the time** tutto il tempo; **the whole of Italy** tutta l'Italia, l'Italia intera; **the whole of the town** la città intera, tutta la città; **as a whole** nell'insieme, nel suo insieme; **on the whole** nel complesso

b (*entire unit*) tutto; **they make a whole** formano un tutto; **two halves make a whole** due metà fanno un intero.

whole·food ['həʊlˌfuːd] **1** N: **wholefoods** alimenti *mpl* integrali.

2 ADJ: **wholefood diet** dieta a base di prodotti integrali.

whole·hearted [ˌhəʊl'hɑːtɪd] ADJ (*approval, agreement*) incondizionato(-a), totale; (*thanks, congratulations*) sentito(-a), sincero(-a); **to be wholehearted in sth** fare qc di tutto cuore.

whole·heart·ed·ly [ˌhəʊl'hɑːtɪdlɪ] ADV (*approve, agree*) incondizionatamente; (*thank, congratulate*) sentitamente, di tutto cuore; (*do, work, play*) con impegno, mettendoci l'anima.

whole·meal ['həʊlˌmiːl] ADJ (*Brit: flour, bread*) integrale.

♦ **whole milk** N latte *m* intero.

♦ **whole note** N (*Am Mus*) semibreve *f*.

♦ **whole number** N numero intero.

whole·sale ['həʊlseɪl] **1** ADJ (*prices, trade*) all'ingrosso; (*fig: slaughter, destruction*) in massa, totale; (*acceptance*) in blocco; (*modification*) su vasta scala; **his work came in for wholesale criticism** il suo lavoro è stato criticato in blocco.

2 ADV (*see adj*) all'ingrosso; in massa; in blocco; su vasta scala.

3 N commercio *or* vendita all'ingrosso.

whole·sal·er ['həʊlˌseɪlə'] N grossista *m/f*.

whole·some ['həʊlsəm] ADJ (*gen*) sano(-a); (*climate*) salubre.

whole·wheat ['həʊlˌwiːt] ADJ (*Am*) = **wholemeal**.

who'll [huːl] = **who will**.

whol·ly ['həʊlɪ] ADV completamente, del tutto.

---

whom [huːm] PRON
a (*spesso sostituito da "who" nella lingua parlata: interrogative*) chi;
▷ **from whom did you receive it?** da chi l'hai ricevuto?
▷ **whom did you see?** chi hai visto?
b (*relative: direct object*) che, prep + il/la quale; (: *indirect*) cui;
▷ **the man whom I saw** l'uomo che ho visto
▷ **three policemen, none of whom wore a helmet** tre poliziotti, nessuno dei quali portava il casco
▷ **those to whom I spoke** le persone con le quali ho parlato
▷ **the lady with whom I was talking** la signora con cui stavo parlando.

---

whoop [huːp] **1** N grido.

2 VI gridare; (*Med: when coughing*) tossire in modo convulso.

3 VT: **to whoop it up** (*fam*) fare baldoria.

whoo·pee [wʊ'piː] **1** EXCL urrà!, evviva!.

2 N: **to make whoopee** (*fam*) fare baldoria.

whoop·ing cough ['huːpɪŋˌkɒf] N pertosse *f*, tosse *f* asinina (*or* canina *or* cavallina).

whoops [wuːps] EXCL (*also*: **whoops-a-daisy!**: *avoiding fall etc*) ops!

whoosh [wuːʃ] N: **it came out with a whoosh** (*sauce, water*) è uscito(-a) di getto; (*air*) è uscito(-a) con un sibilo.

whop·per ['wɒpə'] N (*fam: large thing*) cosa enorme; (: *lie*) balla.

whop·ping ['wɒpɪŋ] ADJ (*fam: also:* **whopping great**) enorme.

whore [hɔː'] N (*pej*) puttana.

whore·house ['hɔːˌhaʊs] N (*old*) bordello.

whorl [wɜːl] N (*of shell*) voluta.

who's [huːz] = **who is, who has**.

---

whose [huːz]
1 POSS PRON di chi;
▷ **whose *is* this?** di chi è questo?
▷ **I *know* whose it is** io lo so di chi è.
2 POSS ADJ
a (*interrogative*) di chi;
▷ **whose *daughter* are you?** di chi sei figlia?
▷ **whose *fault* was it?** di chi era la colpa?
▷ **whose *hat* is this?** di chi è questo cappello?
▷ **whose *pencil* have you taken?** di chi è la matita che hai preso?
b (*relative*) il/la cui;
▷ **the *girl* whose sister you were speaking to** la ragazza alla cui sorella stavi parlando
▷ **the *man* whose wife I was talking to** l'uomo alla cui moglie stavo parlando
▷ **the *man* whose son you rescued** l'uomo di cui hai salvato il figlio
▷ ***those* whose passports I have** quelli di cui ho il passaporto
▷ **the *woman* whose car was stolen** la donna la cui macchina è stata rubata

---

♦ **Who's Who** N chi è *m inv*.

who've [huːv] = **who have**.

why [waɪ] **1** ADV, CONJ perché; **why is he always late?** perché è sempre in ritardo?; **I wonder why he said that** mi chiedo perché l'abbia detto; **why not do it now?** perché non farlo adesso?; **why don't you come too?** perché non vieni anche tu?; **there's no reason why ...** non c'è motivo per cui ...+ *sub*; **why (ever) not?** perché no?; **so that's why he did it!** ecco perché l'ha fatto!.

2 EXCL (*surprise*) guarda guarda!, ma guarda un po'!; (*remonstrating*) ma via!; (*explaining*) ebbene!; **why, it's you!** guarda guarda, *or* ah sei tu!; **why, it's obvious!** ma via, è ovvio!.

3 N: **the whys and (the) wherefores** le ragioni *or* i motivi; **the why and the how** il perché e il percome.

WI **1** N ABBR (*Brit:* = *Women's Institute*) circolo *femminile*.

2 ABBR **a** (*Geog*) = **West Indies b** (*Am Post*)= **Wisconsin**.

wick [wɪk] N stoppino, lucignolo.

wick·ed ['wɪkɪd] ADJ (*person, remark, smile*) cattivo(-a), malvagio(-a); (: *mischievous*) malizioso(-a); (*satire*) sferzante; (*system, policy*) iniquo(-a); (*fam: price, weather etc*) allucinante; **she has a wicked temper** ha un caratteraccio; **that was a wicked thing to do** è stata una

cattiveria; **a wicked blow** un brutto colpo; **a wicked sense of humour** un senso dell'umorismo un po' malizioso.

wick·ed·ly ['wɪkɪdlɪ] ADV (*remark, smile, behave*) perfidamente, con cattiveria; (*roguishly*) maliziosamente; **wickedly expensive** terribilmente costoso; **a wickedly humorous play** una commedia maliziosamente spiritosa.

wick·ed·ness ['wɪkɪdnɪs] N (*see adj*) cattiveria, malvagità; malizia; iniquità.

wick·er ['wɪkə'] ① N vimini *mpl.*
② ADJ di vimini.

wicker·work ['wɪkə,wɜːk] N oggetti *mpl* di vimini.

wick·et ['wɪkɪt] (*Cricket*) N porta.

♦ **wicket keeper** N (*Cricket*) ≈ portiere *m.*

wide [waɪd] ① ADJ (*comp* **-er**, *superl* **-est**) (*gen*) largo(-a); (*publicity, margin*) ampio(-a); (*ocean, desert, region*) vasto(-a); (*fig: considerable: variety, choice*) grande, ampio(-a), vasto(-a); **it is 3 metres wide** è largo 3 metri; **his wide knowledge of the subject** la sua vasta conoscenza dell'argomento; **in the whole wide world** nel mondo intero, in tutto il mondo; **the wide screen** il grande schermo.
② ADV (*aim, fall*) lontano dal bersaglio; **set wide apart** (*houses, eyes*) ben distanziato(-a); (*legs*) divaricato(-a); **to be wide open** (*door*) essere spalancato(-a); **to open wide** spalancare; **to shoot wide** tirare a vuoto *or* fuori bersaglio; **the ball went wide** la palla ha mancato il bersaglio; **to be wide open to criticism/attack** essere esposto(-a) alle critiche/agli attacchi.

♦ **wide-angle lens** [,waɪdæŋgl'lɛnz] N grandangolare *m.*

♦ **wide-awake** [,waɪdə'weɪk] ADJ completamente sveglio (-a); (*fig*) sveglio(-a).

♦ **wide-eyed** [,waɪd'aɪd] ADJ con gli occhi spalancati.

wide·ly ['waɪdlɪ] ADV (*distributed, scattered*) ampiamente, largamente; (*read etc*) molto; (*travel*) in lungo e in largo; (*differing*) molto, profondamente; (*popularly, by many people*) generalmente; **to be widely read** (*author*) essere molto letto(-a); (*reader*) essere molto colto(-a); **it is widely believed that** è una credenza diffusa che; **widely-held opinions** opinioni molto diffuse; **to be widely spaced** (*houses, trees*) essere molto distanziati(-e).

wid·en ['waɪdn] ① VT (*also fig*) ampliare, allargare.
② VI (*also*: **widen out**) ampliarsi.

wide·ness ['waɪdnɪs] N (*see adj*) larghezza; vastità; ampiezza.

♦ **wide open** ADJ (*door*) spalancato(-a); (*defences*) vulnerabile; (*outcome*) aperto(-a).

♦ **wide-ranging** [,waɪd'reɪndʒɪŋ] ADJ (*survey, report*) vasto (-a); (*interests*) svariato(-a).

wide·spread ['waɪd,sprɛd] ADJ (*disease, belief*) molto diffuso(-a); **there is widespread fear that ...** c'è una paura diffusa che... .

widg·eon ['wɪdʒən] = **wigeon.**

wid·ow ['wɪdəʊ] ① N vedova; **to be left a widow** restare vedova; **she is a golf widow** (*hum*) è una vedova del gioco del golf; **widow's peak** attaccatura dei capelli a forma di V (sulla fronte).
② VT: **to be widowed** restare vedovo(-a).

wid·owed ['wɪdəʊd] ADJ (*che è rimasto(-a)*) vedovo(-a); **his widowed mother** sua madre (rimasta) vedova.

wid·ow·er ['wɪdəʊə'] N vedovo.

wid·ow·hood ['wɪdəʊhʊd] N vedovanza.

width [wɪdθ] N (*see adj*) larghezza; ampiezza; (*of fabric*) altezza; **it's 7 metres in width** è largo 7 metri.

width·ways ['wɪdθ,weɪz], **width·wise** ['wɪdθ,waɪz] ADV trasversalmente.

wield [wiːld] VT (*sword, axe*) maneggiare; (: *brandish*) brandire; (*power, influence*) esercitare.

wife [waɪf] N (*pl* **wives**) moglie *f*; **the wife** (*fam*) la padrona; **it's just an old wives' tale** è solo una superstizione.

wife·ly ['waɪflɪ] ADJ coniugale, di moglie.

♦ **wife-swapping** ['waɪf,swɒpɪŋ] N scambio delle mogli.

wig [wɪg] N parrucca.

wig·eon ['wɪdʒən] N (*Zool*) fischione *m.*

wig·ging ['wɪgɪŋ] N (*Brit fam old*) lavata di capo.

wig·gle ['wɪgl] ① N: **with a wiggle of her hips** ancheggiando.
② VT (*fingers, loose tooth*) muovere; **to wiggle one's hips** ancheggiare.
③ VI (*person*) dimenarsi, agitarsi; (*worm*) agitarsi, muoversi; (*tooth, loose screw*) tentennàre.

wig·gly ['wɪglɪ] ADJ (*line*) ondulato(-a), sinuoso(-a).

wig·wam ['wɪg,wæm] N wigwam *m inv.*

wild [waɪld] ① ADJ (*comp* **-er**, *superl* **-est**) **a** (*not domesticated*: *animal, plant*) selvatico(-a); (*horse*) brado(-a); (*countryside*) selvaggio(-a); **in its wild state** allo stato selvatico; **to grow wild** (*plant*) crescere incolto(-a); **wild horses wouldn't make me tell you** (*fig*) non riuscirai a cavarmelo neanche con la forza; **to sow one's wild oats** (*fig*) correre la cavallina
b (*rough*: *wind, weather*) violento(-a); (*sea, night*) tempestoso(-a)
c (*unrestrained, disorderly*: *child*) turbolento(-a); (*appearance, look*) selvaggio(-a); (*eyes*) sbarrato(-a); (*hair*) incolto(-a); **to lead a wild life** fare una vita sregolata; **to run wild** (*children*) scatenarsi
d (*fam*: *angry*) fuori di sé; **wild with indignation** fuori di sé dall'indignazione; **it makes me wild** mi manda su tutte le furie
e (*fam*: *enthusiastic*): **to be wild about** andare pazzo(-a) per; **to be wild with joy** essere fuori di sé dalla gioia; **I'm not wild about the idea** non è che l'idea mi faccia impazzire; **to go wild (with)** non stare più in sé (da); **the audience went wild** la folla andò in delirio
f (*rash, extravagant*: *idea*) folle; (: *laughter*) sguaiato(-a); (*erratic*: *shot, guess*) azzardato(-a); **it's a wild exaggeration** è una grossa esagerazione; **you've let your imagination run wild** hai lavorato troppo di fantasia
② N: **the wild** la natura; **to live out in the wilds** (*hum*) vivere a casa del diavolo.

♦ **wild card** N (*Comput*) wild card *m inv.*

wild·cat ['waɪld,kæt] N gatto(-a) selvatico(-a).

♦ **wildcat strike** N sciopero (a gatto) selvaggio.

♦ **wild cherry** N (*tree*) ciliegio dolce; (*fruit*) ciliegia dolce.

wil·de·beest ['wɪldɪ,biːst] N gnu *m inv.*

wil·der·ness ['wɪldənɪs] N (*gen*) deserto; (*neglected garden*) giungla.

wild·fire ['waɪld,faɪə'] N: **to spread like wildfire** diffondersi a macchia d'olio.

wild·fowl ['waɪld,faʊl] NPL selvaggina *fsg* di penna.

♦ **wild goat** N capra selvatica.

♦ **wild-goose chase** [,waɪld'guːs,tʃeɪs] N (*fig*): **to be on a wild-goose chase** seguire una pista falsa.

wild·life ['waɪld,laɪf] ① N natura, flora e fauna.
② ADJ (*sanctuary, reserve*) naturale.

wild·ly ['waɪldlɪ] ADV (*gen*) violentemente; (*behave*) in modo sfrenato; (*talk*) fervorosamente; (*rush around*) come un(a) pazzo(-a); (*exaggerate*) largamente; (*applaud, cheer*) freneticamente; **to guess wildly** tirare a

indovinare; **wildly happy/enthusiastic** terribilmente felice/entusiasta; **her heart was beating wildly** il cuore le batteva forte.

wild·ness ['waɪldnɪs] N (*gen*) violenza; (*of countryside, scenery*) aspetto selvaggio; (*of the weather*) avversità; **the wildness of his appearance** il suo aspetto selvaggio; **the wildness of her imagination** la sua fervida immaginazione.

♦ **Wild West** N: **the Wild West** il far West.

wiles [waɪlz] NPL astuzie *fpl*.

wil·ful, (*Am*) **will·ful** ['wɪlfʊl] ADJ (*deliberate*: *act*) intenzionale, premeditato(-a); (*self-willed*) testardo(-a), ostinato(-a).

wil·ful·ly, (*Am*) **will·ful·ly** ['wɪlfəlɪ] ADV (*see adj*) intenzionalmente, premeditatamente; testardamente.

wil·ful·ness ['wɪlfʊlnɪs] N testardaggine *f*.

---

will[1] [wɪl] (*pt* **would**)

1 MODAL AUX VB

a (*forming future tense*)

▷**will you** *be* **there?** ci sarai?

▷**he will** *come* verrà

▷**will you** *do* **it? — yes, I will/no, I won't** lo farai? — sì (lo farò)/no (non lo farò)

▷**I will** *finish* **it tomorrow** lo finirò domani

▷**I will** *have finished* **it by tomorrow** lo finirò entro domani

▷**you won't** *lose* **it, will you?** non lo perderai, vero?

b (*in conjectures*)

▷**he will** *or* **he'll** *be* **there by now** dovrebbe essere arrivato ormai

▷**that will** *be* **the postman** sarà il postino

c (*in commands, requests, offers*)

▷**will you** *be quiet*! vuoi fare silenzio?

▷**will you** *come*? vieni?

▷**won't you** *come* **with us?** non vuoi venire con noi?

▷**will you** *have* **a cup of tea?** vorresti una tazza di tè?

▷**will you** *help* **me?** mi puoi aiutare?

▷**I won't go — oh yes you will, my lad!** non ci andrò — oh sì che ci andrai, ragazzo mio!

▷**I will not** *or* **won't** *put up* **with it!** non intendo tollerarlo!

▷**will you** *sit down* (*politely*) prego, si accomodi (*angrily*) vuoi metterti seduto!

d (*expressing habits, persistence, capability*)

▷**the car will** *do* **100 mph** la macchina fa 100 miglia all'ora

▷**accidents will** *happen* gli incidenti possono capitare

▷**he will often** *sit* **there for hours** spesso rimane seduto lì per ore

▷**the car won't** *start* la macchina non parte

▷**he WILL** *fidget*! e continua a muoversi!

2 VI (*wish*) volere;

▷**(just)** *as* **you will!** come vuoi!

▷**say** *what* **you will** di' quello che vuoi.

---

will[2] [wɪl] **1** N **a** volontà; **to have a will of one's own** avere una volontà indipendente; **to do sth of one's own free will** fare qc di propria volontà; **the will to win/live** la voglia di vincere/vivere; **against sb's will** contro la volontà *or* il volere di qn; **at will** a volontà; **to work with a will** lavorare di buona lena; **with the best will in the world** con tutta la più buona volontà del mondo; **where there's a will there's a way** volere è potere

b (*testament*) testamento; **the last will and testament of** le ultime volontà di; **to make a will** fare testamento.

2 VT **a** (*urge on by willpower*): **to will sb to do sth** pregare (tra sé) perché qn faccia qc; **he willed himself to stay awake** si costrinse a restare sveglio; **he willed himself to go on** andò avanti con un grande sforzo di volontà

b (*leave in one's will*): **to will sth to sb** lasciare qc a qn in eredità.

wil·lie, wil·ly ['wɪlɪ] N (*Brit fam*) pisello (*fig*).

wil·lies ['wɪlɪz] NPL (*fam*): **it gives me the willies** mi fa venire i brividi.

will·ing ['wɪlɪŋ] **1** ADJ **a** (*obedience, help*) spontaneo(-a); (*helper, worker*) volenteroso(-a); **he's very willing** è pieno di buona volontà; **there were plenty of willing hands** erano tutti disposti a dare una mano

b : **to be willing (to do sth)** essere disposto(-a) (a fare qc); **he wasn't very willing to help me** non aveva una gran voglia di aiutarmi; **God willing** se Dio vuole.

2 N: **to show willing** mostrarsi disponibile.

will·ing·ly ['wɪlɪŋlɪ] ADV volentieri.

will·ing·ness ['wɪlɪŋnɪs] N disponibilità, buona volontà; **I don't doubt her willingness** non metto in dubbio la sua buona volontà.

will-o'-the-wisp [ˌwɪləðə'wɪsp] N (*also fig*) fuoco fatuo.

wil·low ['wɪləʊ] N (*also:* **willow tree**) salice *m*; **white willow** salice bianco.

wil·low·herb ['wɪləʊˌhɜːb] N epilobio.

♦ **willow pattern** N motivo cinese (*in blu su ceramica bianca*).

wil·lowy ['wɪləʊɪ] ADJ slanciato(-a).

will·power ['wɪlˌpaʊə] N forza di volontà.

wil·ly ['wɪlɪ] = **willie**.

willy-nilly [ˌwɪlɪ'nɪlɪ] ADV volente o nolente.

wilt [wɪlt] VI (*flower*) appassire; (*fig: person*) crollare; (: *effort, enthusiasm*) diminuire.

Wilts [wɪlts] ABBR (*Brit*) = **Wiltshire**.

wily ['waɪlɪ] ADJ (*comp* **-ier**, *superl* **-iest**) astuto(-a), furbo (-a); **he's a wily old devil** *or* **bird** *or* **fox** (*fam*) è una vecchia volpe, è un furbo matricolato *or* di tre cotte.

wimp [wɪmp] N (*fam*) pappamolle *m/f*.

wim·ple ['wɪmpl] N soggolo.

win [wɪn] (*vb: pt, pp* **won**) **1** N (*in sports etc*) vittoria; **their fifth win in a row** la quinta vittoria consecutiva.

2 VT (*battle, race, cup, prize*) vincere; (*victory*) conquistare, aggiudicarsi; (*sympathy, popularity, support, friendship*) conquistare, ottenere; (*person*) accattivarsi, conquistare; (*contract*) aggiudicarsi; **I won £20 from him** gli ho vinto 20 sterline; **to win sb's favour/heart** conquistare il favore/cuore di qn; **she won it at tennis** l'ha vinto a tennis; **it won him first prize** gli ha valso il primo premio; **to win the day** (*Mil, fig*) avere il soppravvento.

3 VI vincere; **O.K., you win** (*fam*) va bene, ti do ragione

▶ **win back** VT + ADV riconquistare

▶ **win over, win round** VT + ADV convincere; **we won him over to our point of view** l'abbiamo convinto ad accettare il nostro punto di vista

▶ **win out, win through** VI + ADV uscirne vittorioso(-a).

wince [wɪns] **1** N: **to give a wince** rabbrividire; (*grimace*) smorfia.

2 VI rabbrividire; (*grimace*) fare una smorfia (*di dolore*); **he winced at the thought** rabbrividì al pensiero.

win·cey·ette [ˌwɪnsɪ'ɛt] N cotone *m* felpato.

winch [wɪntʃ] [1] N argano, verricello.

[2] VT: **to winch up/down** sollevare/abbassare con un argano.

wind¹ [wɪnd] [1] N **a** vento; **high wind** vento forte; **the wind is in the west** il vento viene da ponente; **into** or **against the wind** controvento; **to go like the wind** filare come il vento; **to run before the wind** (Naut) andare con il vento in poppa; **there's something in the wind** (fig) c'è qualcosa nell'aria; **to get wind of sth** venire a sapere qc; **to get** or **have the wind up** (fam) agitarsi; **to take the wind out of sb's sails** smontare qn, spegnere l'entusiasmo di qn; **to sail close to the wind** (fig) spingere le cose troppo in là; (act almost illegally) rasentare l'illegalità; (risk causing offence) rischiare di offendere; **to throw caution to the winds** gettare la prudenza alle ortiche

b (flatulence) flatulenza; **to break wind** fare aria; (fam): **to bring up wind** (baby) fare il ruttino

c (breath) respiro, fiato; **to get one's wind back** or **one's second wind** riprendere fiato; **to be short of wind** essere senza fiato

d (Mus): **the wind(s)** i fiati mpl.

[2] VT: **to wind sb** (with punch etc) mozzare il fiato a qn; **to wind a baby** far fare il ruttino a un bambino.

wind² [waɪnd] (pt, pp **wound**) [1] VT **a** (roll, coil) avvolgere, arrotolare; **to wind sth into a ball** aggomitolare qc

b (clock, watch, toy) caricare.

[2] VI (also: **wind its way**: river, path) serpeggiare; (procession) snodarsi

▶ **wind back** VT + ADV (tape) riavvolgere

▶ **wind down** [1] VT + ADV (car window) abbassare; (fig: production, business) diminuire.

[2] VI + ADV rilassarsi, distendersi

▶ **wind forward** VT + ADV (tape) mandare avanti

▶ **wind in** VT + ADV (fishing line) riavvolgere

▶ **wind on** VT + ADV (film, tape) far avanzare

▶ **wind up** [1] VT + ADV **a** (car window) alzare; (clock, toy) caricare; **to wind sb up** (fig fam: annoy) far venire i nervi a or innervosire qn; (: kid, trick) prendere in giro qn

b (close: meeting, debate) concludere, chiudere; (: company) chiudere.

[2] VI + ADV (meeting, debate) concludersi; (fam: end up) finire; **we wound up in Rome** siamo finiti a Roma.

wind·bag [ˈwɪndˌbæg] N (fam: person) trombone m.

wind·blown [ˈwɪndˌbləʊn] ADJ (hair, trees) agitato(-a) dal vento; (hills, balconies etc) battuto(-a) dal vento.

wind·break [ˈwɪndˌbreɪk] N frangivento.

Wind·breaker® [ˈwɪndˌbreɪkəʳ] N (Am) = **windcheater**.

wind·cheater [ˈwɪndˌtʃiːtəʳ] N giacca a vento.

wind·er [ˈwaɪndəʳ] N (Brit: on watch) corona di carica; (Aut: also: **window winder**) manovella f alzacristalli inv.

♦ **wind erosion** N erosione f del vento.

wind·fall [ˈwɪndˌfɔːl] N (apple etc) frutto fatto cadere dal vento; (fig) colpo di fortuna.

♦ **wind gauge** N anemometro.

wind·ing [ˈwaɪndɪŋ] ADJ (road, path) serpeggiante, tortuoso(-a); (staircase) a chiocciola.

♦ **wind instrument** N (Mus) strumento a fiato.

wind·lass [ˈwɪndləs] N argano, verricello.

wind·less [ˈwɪndlɪs] ADJ senza vento.

wind·mill [ˈwɪndˌmɪl] N mulino a vento.

win·dow [ˈwɪndəʊ] N (gen, Comput) finestra; (of car, train) finestrino; (also: **window pane**) vetro; (also: **stained glass window**) vetrata; (also: **shop window**) vetrina; (of booking office etc) sportello; (in envelope) finestrella; **to break a window** rompere un vetro; **to clean the windows** pulire i vetri; **to look out of the window** guardare fuori della finestra; **"do not lean out of the window"** "vietato sporgersi dal finestrino".

♦ **window box** N cassetta per i fiori (da tenere sul davanzale).

♦ **window cleaner** N lavavetri m/f.

♦ **window dresser** N (Comm) vetrinista m/f.

♦ **window dressing** N (Comm) vetrinistica; (fig) fumo negli occhi.

♦ **window envelope** N busta a finestra.

♦ **window frame** N telaio di finestra.

♦ **window ledge** N davanzale m.

♦ **window pane** N vetro.

♦ **window sash** N telaio di finestra.

♦ **window seat** N (in house) panchetta fissa vicino alla finestra; (in train etc) posto vicino al finestrino.

window-shopping [ˈwɪndəʊˌʃɒpɪŋ] N: **to go window-shopping** andare a vedere le vetrine.

window-sill [ˈwɪndəʊˌsɪl] N davanzale m.

wind·pipe [ˈwɪndˌpaɪp] N (Anat) trachea.

♦ **wind power** N energia eolica.

wind·proof [ˈwɪndˌpruːf] ADJ a prova di vento.

wind·screen [ˈwɪndskriːn], (Am) **wind·shield** [ˈwɪndʃiːld] N parabrezza m inv.

♦ **windscreen washer** N lavacristallo.

♦ **windscreen wiper** N tergicristallo.

wind·sock [ˈwɪndˌsɒk] N manica a vento.

wind·surfer [ˈwɪndˌsɜːfəʳ] N (person) windsurfista m/f; (board) windsurf m inv.

wind·surfing [ˈwɪndˌsɜːfɪŋ] N windsurf m inv (l'attività); **to go windsurfing** fare del windsurf.

wind·swept [ˈwɪndˌswɛpt] ADJ (landscape) ventoso(-a); (square) spazzato(-a) dal vento; (person) scompigliato(-a) per il vento.

♦ **wind tunnel** [ˈwɪndˌtʌnəl] N galleria aerodinamica or del vento.

wind·ward [ˈwɪndwəd] (Naut) [1] ADJ, ADV sopravvento inv.

[2] N lato sopravvento; **to windward** sopravvento.

windy [ˈwɪndɪ] ADJ (comp **-ier**, superl **-iest**) **a** ventoso(-a); **it's windy** c'è vento **b** (fam old: afraid, nervous): **windy (about)** teso(-a) (per), nervoso(-a) (per).

wine [waɪn] [1] N vino.

[2] VT: **to wine and dine sb** offrire un ottimo pranzo a qn.

[3] ADJ (bottle) da vino; (vinegar) di vino.

♦ **wine bar** N enoteca (per degustazione).

♦ **wine cellar** N cantina.

♦ **wine cooler** N secchiello del ghiaccio (per vino o champagne).

wine·glass [ˈwaɪnˌglɑːs] N bicchiere m da vino.

♦ **wine list** N lista or carta dei vini.

♦ **wine merchant** N commerciante m di vini.

wine·press [ˈwaɪnˌprɛs] N torchio.

wine·skin [ˈwaɪnˌskɪn] N otre m.

♦ **wine tast·ing** [ˈwaɪnˌteɪstɪŋ] N degustazione f di vini.

♦ **wine waiter** N sommelier m inv.

wing [wɪŋ] N **a** (gen, also Sport, Archit, Pol) ala; (Brit Aut) fiancata; **to take sb under one's wing** prendere qn sotto le proprie ali; **the left wing of the Conservative Party** la sinistra del Partito Conservatore **b**: **the wings** NPL (Theatre) le quinte.

winged [wɪŋd] ADJ alato(-a).

wing·er [ˈwɪŋəʳ] N (Sport) ala.

wing·less [ˈwɪŋlɪs] ADJ (insect etc) privo(-a) di ali.

♦ **wing mirror** N (Brit) specchietto laterale esterno.

♦ **wing nut** N galletto.

wing·span ['wɪŋ͵spæn], **wing·spread** ['wɪŋ͵sprɛd] N apertura alare, apertura d'ali.

♦ **wing tip** N punta dell'ala.

wink [wɪŋk] 1 N (blink) strizzata d'occhi; (meaningful) occhiolino, strizzatina d'occhi; **to give sb a wink** ammiccare or fare l'occhiolino a qn; **in a wink** in un batter d'occhio; **I didn't sleep a wink** non ho chiuso occhio.

2 VI (meaningfully): **to wink (at sb)** fare l'occhiolino (a qn), ammiccare (a qn); (blink) strizzare gli occhi; (light, star etc) baluginare.

wink·ing ['wɪŋkɪŋ] 1 ADJ (light, star) baluginante.

2 N: **it's as easy as winking** è un gioco da bambini.

win·kle ['wɪŋkl] 1 N litorina.

2 VT: **to winkle a secret out of sb** carpire un segreto a qn.

win·ner ['wɪnəʳ] N (gen) vincitore(-trice); **to pick a winner** (horse) scegliere il cavallo vincente; (gen) fare un affare; **it's a winner!** (fam) è un successone!; (likely to be a success) è un successo garantito!

win·ning ['wɪnɪŋ] ADJ **a** (gen) vincente; (hit, shot, goal) decisivo(-a) **b** (charming) affascinante; **a winning smile** un sorriso accattivante; see also **winnings**.

♦ **winning post** N traguardo.

win·nings ['wɪnɪŋz] NPL vincita fsg.

win·now ['wɪnəʊ] VT (grain) vagliare, mondare.

win·some ['wɪnsəm] ADJ accattivante.

win·ter ['wɪntəʳ] 1 N inverno; **in winter** d'inverno, in inverno; **the winter of 1981** l'inverno del 1981; **it's winter** è inverno.

2 ADJ (clothes, weather, day) invernale, d'inverno.

♦ **winter cherry** N alchechengi m inv.

♦ **winter sports** NPL sport mpl invernali.

winter·time ['wɪntə͵taɪm] N inverno, stagione f invernale.

win·try, win·tery ['wɪntrɪ] ADJ invernale; (fig: look) freddo (-a).

wipe [waɪp] 1 N pulita, passata; **to give sth a wipe** dare una pulita or una passata a qc.

2 VT (gen) pulire; (blackboard, tape) cancellare; **to wipe one's eyes** asciugarsi gli occhi; **to wipe one's nose** soffiarsi il naso; **to wipe one's feet** or **shoes** pulirsi i piedi; **to wipe one's bottom** pulirsi il sedere; **to wipe the dishes** asciugare i piatti; **to wipe sth dry** asciugare qc; **to wipe the floor with sb** (fig fam) schiacciare qn

► **wipe away** VT + ADV (marks) togliere; (tears) asciugare

► **wipe down** VT + ADV pulire

► **wipe off** VT + ADV cancellare; (stains) togliere (strofinando)

► **wipe out** VT + ADV **a** (erase: writing, memory) cancellare; (: debt) liquidare

b (destroy: town, race, enemy) annientare

► **wipe up** 1 VI + ADV (dry dishes) asciugare i piatti.

2 VT + ADV asciugare.

wip·er ['waɪpəʳ] N (Aut) tergicristallo; **intermittent wiper** tergicristallo (a funzionamento) intermittente.

♦ **wiper arm** N braccio del tergicristallo.

wire ['waɪəʳ] 1 N **a** filo di ferro; (Elec) filo (elettrico); **to get one's wires crossed** (fam) fraintendere

b (telegram) telegramma m.

2 VT **a** (Elec: house) fare l'impianto elettrico di; (circuit) installare; (: also: **wire up**: two pieces of equipment) collegare, allacciare; **to wire a room for sound** installare un impianto di sonorizzazione in una stanza

b (Telec) telegrafare

c : **to wire sth to sth** (tie) attaccare qc a qc con un filo.

♦ **wire brush** N spazzola metallica.

♦ **wire cutters** NPL tronchese msg or fsg.

wired [waɪəd] ADJ **a** (clothing, material) rinforzato(-a) (con filo metallico) **b** (palce: fitted with alarm) collegato(-a) ad un sistema di allarme; (: bugged) avere dei microfoni nascosti.

wire·less ['waɪəlɪs] (old) 1 N (Brit) radio f; (also: **wireless set**) (apparecchio m) radio f inv; **on the wireless** per radio.

2 ADJ (station, programme) radiofonico(-a).

♦ **wireless operator** N operatore m radio inv.

♦ **wire netting** N rete f metallica.

wire·pulling ['waɪə͵pʊlɪŋ] N (esp Am fam) maneggi mpl, intrighi mpl.

♦ **wire service** N (Am) = **news agency**.

♦ **wire-tapping** ['waɪə͵tæpɪŋ] N intercettazione f telefonica.

♦ **wire wool** N lana d'acciaio.

wir·ing ['waɪərɪŋ] N (Elec) impianto elettrico.

wiry ['waɪərɪ] ADJ (comp **-ier**, superl **-iest**) (person) asciutto (-a) e muscoloso(-a); (hair) ispido(-a).

wis·dom ['wɪzdəm] N (of person) saggezza; (of remark, action) opportunità.

♦ **wisdom tooth** N dente m del giudizio.

wise¹ [waɪz] ADJ (comp **-r**, superl **-st**) (gen, person) saggio (-a); (: learned) sapiente; (prudent: advice, remark) prudente; **a wise man** un saggio; **the Three Wise Men** i Re Magi; **to be wise after the event** giudicare con il senno di poi; **it was wise of you not to do that** sei stato saggio a non farlo; **I'm none the wiser** ne so quanto prima; **to get wise to sb/sth** (fam) aprire gli occhi su qn/qc; **to put sb wise to sb/sth** (fam) mettere qn al corrente di qn/qc

► **wise up** VI + ADV (esp Am fam): **to wise up to** aprire gli occhi su; **wise up!** svegliati!

wise² [waɪz] 1 N (old): **in no wise** affatto, in nessun modo; **in this wise** in tal guisa.

2 ADV ENDING: **workwise** per quel che riguarda il lavoro; **how are we foodwise?** come stiamo a cibo?

wise·crack ['waɪz͵kræk] N (fam) battuta, spiritosaggine f.

♦ **wise guy** N (fam) sapientone(-a), sputasentenze m/f inv.

wise·ly ['waɪzlɪ] ADV (decide) saggiamente; (nod, smile) con aria saggia.

wish [wɪʃ] 1 N **a** (desire) desiderio; (specific desire) richiesta; **I had no wish to upset you** non avevo nessuna intenzione di farti star male; **to go against sb's wishes** andare contro il volere di qn; **I'll grant you three wishes** ti concedo di esprimere tre desideri; **you shall have your wish** realizzerai il tuo desiderio; **to make a wish** esprimere un desiderio

b : **best wishes** (in greetings) tanti auguri; (in letter) cordiali saluti; **give her my best wishes** le porga i miei più cordiali saluti; **with best wishes** con i migliori auguri.

2 VT **a** (want) volere, desiderare; **to wish sb to do sth** volere che qn faccia qc; **to wish to do sth** voler fare qc; **I wish he'd shut up** (fam) magari chiudesse il becco; **I wish I'd gone too** vorrei esserci andato anch'io; **I wish I could!** mi piacerebbe!, magari!

b (foist): **to wish sth on sb** appioppare or affibbiare qn a qn; **to wish sth on sb** rifilare qc a qn

c (bid, express) augurare; **to wish sb goodbye** dire arrivederci a qn; **to wish sb good luck/a happy Christmas** augurare a qn buona fortuna/buon Natale; **to wish sb well** augurare ogni bene a qn; **to wish sb ill** voler del

male a qn.

3 vi: **to wish for sth** desiderare qc; **she has everything she could wish for** ha tutto ciò che desidera; **what more could you wish for?** cosa vuoi di più?

wish·bone [ˈwɪʃˌbəʊn] N (*of turkey, chicken etc*) forcella.

wish·ful [ˈwɪʃfʊl] ADJ: **it's just wishful thinking** è solo un'illusione.

wishy-washy [ˈwɪʃɪˌwɒʃɪ] ADJ (*fam: colour*) slavato(-a); (: *person, argument, ideas*) insulso(-a).

wisp [wɪsp] N (*of straw, smoke*) filo; (*of hair*) ciuffetto.

wispy [ˈwɪspɪ] ADJ (*hair*) fine, sottile; (*clouds*) vaporoso(-a).

wis·te·ria [wɪsˈtɪərɪə] N glicine m.

wist·ful [ˈwɪstfʊl] ADJ (*look, smile*) pieno(-a) di rammarico; (: *nostalgic*) nostalgico(-a).

wist·ful·ly [ˈwɪstfəlɪ] ADV (*see adj*) con rammarico; nostalgicamente.

wit [wɪt] N **a** (*understanding*: *gen pl*) intelligenza; **native wit** buon senso; **to be at one's wits' end** avere esaurito tutte le risorse, non sapere più che fare; **to have** *or* **keep one's wits about one** avere presenza di spirito; **use your wits!** usa il cervello!; **to live by one's wits** vivere di espedienti; **to collect one's wits** rimettersi in sesto; **to be frightened** *or* **scared out of one's wits** essere spaventato(-a) a morte

b (*humour, wittiness*) spirito, arguzia

c (*person*) persona arguta, bello spirito

d (*namely*): **to wit** cioè.

witch [wɪtʃ] N strega.

witch·craft [ˈwɪtʃˌkrɑːft] N stregoneria.

♦ **witch doctor** N stregone m.

witch hazel, wych-hazel [ˈwɪtʃˌheɪzl] N (*Bot*) amamelide ƒ; (*astringent*) tonico astringente a base di amamelide.

♦ **witch-hunt** [ˈwɪtʃˌhʌnt] N caccia alle streghe.

---

with [wɪð, wɪθ] PREP

a (*gen*) con;

▷**she mixed the sugar with the *eggs*** mischiò lo zucchero con le uova

▷**she stayed with *friends*** è stata a casa di amici

▷**to stay overnight with *friends*** passare la notte da amici

▷**I was with *him*** ero con lui

▷**he had no money with *him*** non aveva denaro con sé

▷**to be with *it*** (*fam: up-to-date*) essere à la page

▷**to rise with the *sun*** alzarsi all'alba

▷**she just wasn't with *us*** (*fig*) era completamente assente

▷**I'm with *you*** (*fig: I understand*) ti seguo

b (*descriptive*) con;

▷**the fellow with the *big beard*** il tipo con la *or* dalla barba folta

▷**the man with the *grey hat*** l'uomo dal *or* con il cappello grigio

▷**a room with a *view*** una camera con vista (sul mare etc)

c (*manner, means, cause*) con;

▷**red with *anger*** rosso(-a) dalla *or* per la rabbia

▷**to cut wood with an *axe*** tagliare la legna con l'ascia

▷**to shake with *fear*** tremare di paura

▷**she's gone down with *flu*** ha preso l'influenza

▷**in bed with *measles*** a letto con il morbillo

▷**white with *snow*** bianco(-a) a causa della neve

▷**covered with *snow*** coperto(-a) di neve

▷**to walk with a *stick*** camminare con l'aiuto di un

bastone

▷**with *tears* in her eyes** con le lacrime agli occhi

▷**with *that*, he left** con ciò se ne andò

▷**with *time*** col tempo

d (*concerning, in the case of*)

▷**she's *good* with children** ci sa fare con i bambini

▷**you must be *patient* with her** devi avere pazienza con lei

▷**how are *things* with you?** (*fam*) come te la passi?

▷**the *trouble* with Harry is that ...** il guaio con Harry è che...

e (*in proportion*) a seconda di;

▷**it varies with the *time* of year** varia a seconda della stagione

f (*in spite of*) nonostante;

▷**with *all* his faults I still like him** nonostante i suoi difetti mi piace ancora.

---

with·draw [wɪθˈdrɔː] (*pt* **withdrew**, *pp* **withdrawn**) **1** vt: **to withdraw (from)** (*gen*) ritirare (da); (*money from bank*) prelevare (da); **he withdrew his remarks** ha ritirato quanto aveva detto.

2 vi: **to withdraw from** (*gen*) ritirarsi da; (*move away*) allontanarsi da; **to withdraw in sb's favour** ritirarsi a favore di qn; **to withdraw to a new position** (*Mil*) arretrare su una nuova posizione; **to withdraw into o.s.** chiudersi in se stesso(-a).

with·draw·al [wɪθˈdrɔːəl] N (*gen*) ritiro; (*of money*) prelievo; (*of army*) ritiro; (*Med*) sindrome ƒ da astinenza.

♦ **withdrawal symptoms** NPL crisi ƒsg di astinenza.

with·drawn [wɪθˈdrɔːn] **1** PP of **withdraw**.

2 ADJ chiuso(-a) in se stesso(-a).

with·drew [wɪθˈdruː] PT of **withdraw**.

with·er [ˈwɪðəʳ] **1** vt far appassire.

2 vi (*plant*) appassire; (*limb*) atrofizzarsi; (*fig*: *love, passion*) spegnersi; (: *beauty*) sfiorire.

with·ered [ˈwɪðəd] ADJ (*plant*) appassito(-a), vizzo(-a); (*skin*) avvizzito(-a); (*limb*) atrofizzato(-a); **a withered old woman** una vecchietta grinzosa.

with·er·ing [ˈwɪðərɪŋ] ADJ (*tone, look, remark*) raggelante.

with·ers [ˈwɪðəz] NPL garrese *msg* (*di cavallo*).

with·hold [wɪðˈhəʊld] (*pt, pp* **withheld**) vt (*money from pay etc*) trattenere; (*truth, news*) nascondere; (*refuse: consent*) non concedere, negare; **to withhold from** (*permission*) rifiutare a; (*information*) nascondere a; **I'm withholding my rent until the roof is repaired** non pagherò l'affitto finché il tetto non sarà stato riparato.

with·in [wɪðˈɪn] **1** PREP **a** (*inside*) dentro; **a voice within me said ...** una vocina dentro di me disse...; **to be within the law** restare nei limiti della legalità; **to live within one's income** vivere secondo i propri mezzi; **within sight of** in vista di

b (*less than*): **we were within 100 metres of the summit** eravamo a meno di 100 metri dalla vetta; **within a mile of** entro un miglio da; **within a year of her death** meno di un anno prima della (*or* dopo la) sua morte; **correct to within a millimetre** preciso(-a) al millimetro; **within an hour** entro un'ora; **within an hour from now** da qui a un'ora; **he returned within the week** è tornato prima della fine della settimana.

2 ADV: **"car for sale - apply within"** "auto in vendita - rivolgersi all'interno".

with·out [wɪðˈaʊt] PREP senza; **he did it without telling me** l'ha fatto senza dirmelo; **he came without a coat/any**

money è venuto senza cappotto/soldi; **without a coat or hat** senza cappotto né cappello; **the bus left without me** l'autobus è partito senza di me; **he is without friends** non ha amici; **to be quite without shame** non avere un minimo di pudore; **without anybody knowing** senza che nessuno lo sappia; **to go** or **do without sth** fare a meno di qc.

with·stand [wɪθ'stænd] (pt, pp **withstood** [wɪθ'stud]) VT resistere a.

wit·less ['wɪtlɪs] ADJ (pej) stupido(-a); **to scare sb witless** spaventare qn a morte; **to be scared witless** essere spaventato(-a) a morte.

wit·ness ['wɪtnɪs] [1] N **a** (person) testimone m/f; **witness for the prosecution/defence** testimone a carico/discarico; **to call sb as a witness** chiamare qn a testimoniare **b** (evidence) testimonianza; **to bear witness to sth** (subj: person) testimoniare qc; (: thing, result) provare qc.
[2] VT **a** (event, crime) essere testimone di; (change, improvement) constatare **b** (attest by signature: document) autenticare.
[3] VI (testify) testimoniare; **to witness to sth/having seen sth** testimoniare qc/di aver visto qc.

♦ **witness box**, (Am) **witness stand** N banco dei testimoni.

wit·ti·cism ['wɪtɪˌsɪzəm] N arguzia.

wit·ti·ly ['wɪtɪlɪ] ADV argutamente.

wit·ting·ly ['wɪtɪŋlɪ] ADV (frm) deliberatamente, intenzionalmente.

wit·ty ['wɪtɪ] ADJ (comp **-ier**, superl **-iest**) arguto(-a), spiritoso(-a).

wives [waɪvz] NPL of **wife**.

wiz·ard ['wɪzəd] N mago, stregone m; (fig) mago; **he's a financial wizard** è un mago della finanza; **he's a wizard at maths** è un genio matematico.

wiz·ard·ry ['wɪzədrɪ] N magia.

wiz·ened ['wɪznd] ADJ raggrinzito(-a).

wk ABBR = **week**.

WO [ˌdʌbljuː'əʊ] N ABBR = **warrant officer**.

wob·ble ['wɒbl] [1] N: **to have a wobble** (chair) traballare; **she had a wobble in her voice** le tremava la voce.
[2] VI (table, chair, wheel, cyclist) traballare; (dancer, acrobat) vacillare; (compass needle) oscillare; (hand, voice) tremare.

wob·bly ['wɒblɪ] ADJ (comp **-ier**, superl **-iest**) (hand, voice) tremante; (table, chair) traballante; (object about to fall) che oscilla pericolosamente; (wheel) che ha troppo gioco; **to feel wobbly** (person) sentirsi debole.

wodge [wɒdʒ] N (Brit fam): **a wodge of** un grosso pezzo di.

woe [wəʊ] N (liter, hum) dolore m; **woe is me!** me tapino(-a)!; **woe betide him who ...** guai a chi...; **a tale of woe** una triste storia.

woe·be·gone ['wəʊbɪˌɡɒn] ADJ triste.

woe·ful ['wəʊful] ADJ (sad) triste; (deplorable) deplorevole, vergognoso(-a).

woe·ful·ly ['wəʊfəlɪ] ADV (sadly: sigh, say etc) tristemente; (deplorably: inadequate etc) deplorabilmente.

wog [wɒɡ] N (offensive) termine offensivo riferito a pesona di colore.

wok [wɒk] N wok m inv, padella concava usata nella cucina cinese.

woke [wəʊk] PT of **wake³**.

wok·en ['wəʊkən] PP of **wake³**.

wold [wəʊld] N altopiano.

wolf [wʊlf] [1] N (pl **wolves** [wʊlvz]) **a** lupo; (fig): **a wolf in**

sheep's clothing un lupo in veste di agnello; **to keep the wolf from the door** sbarcare il lunario; **to cry wolf** gridare al lupo **b** (fig fam: womanizer) mandrillo, drago.
[2] VT (also: **wolf down**) divorare.

wolf·hound ['wʊlf,haʊnd] N cane m lupo.

wolf·ish ['wʊlfɪʃ] ADJ (features, appetite) da lupo; (fig: grin, ideas) feroce.

♦ **wolf whistle** N: **he gave her a wolf whistle** le ha fischiato dietro.

wol·ver·ine ['wʊlvəˌriːn] N ghiottone m.

wolves [wʊlvz] NPL of **wolf**.

wom·an ['wʊmən] N (pl **women**) donna; **young woman** giovane donna; **come along, young woman!** su, signorina!; **I have a woman who comes in to do the cleaning** ho una donna che viene a fare le pulizie; **woman of the world** donna di mondo; **the little woman** (hum: wife) la mogliettina; **the woman in his life** la donna della sua vita; **women's page** (Press) rubrica femminile.

♦ **woman doctor** N dottoressa.

♦ **woman driver** N guidatrice f.

♦ **woman friend** N amica.

♦ **woman-hater** ['wʊmən,heɪtəʳ] N misogino.

wom·an·hood ['wʊmən,hʊd] N femminilità; **to reach womanhood** diventare donna.

wom·an·ize ['wʊmənaɪz] VI correre dietro alle donne.

wom·an·iz·er ['wʊmənaɪzəʳ] N donnaiolo.

wom·an·iz·ing ['wʊmənaɪzɪŋ] N avventure fpl con le donne.

wom·an·kind ['wʊmən,kaɪnd] N (frm) le donne.

wom·an·like ['wʊmən,laɪk] ADJ (features) femminile; (behaviour) da donna.

wom·an·li·ness ['wʊmənlɪnɪs] N femminilità.

wom·an·ly ['wʊmənlɪ] ADJ femminile; **womanly behaviour** comportamento da donna.

♦ **woman teacher** N insegnante f.

womb [wuːm] N (Anat) grembo.

wom·bat ['wɒmbæt] N vombato orsino.

wom·en ['wɪmɪn] NPL of **woman**.

women·folk ['wɪmɪn,fəʊk] NPL donne fpl.

♦ **wom·en's lib·ber** [ˌwɪmɪnz'lɪbəʳ] N (fam) femminista.

♦ **Women's Liberation** ['wɪmɪnzˌlɪbə'reɪʃən] N (also: **Women's Lib**) Movimento per la Liberazione della Donna.

♦ **women's movement** N: **the women's movement** il movimento per la liberazione della donna.

won [wʌn] PT, PP of **win**.

won·der ['wʌndəʳ] [1] N **a** (feeling) meraviglia, stupore m; **in wonder** con stupore; **lost in wonder** stupefatto(-a)
b (object or cause of wonder) miracolo, portento; **the wonders of science** i miracoli della scienza; **the Seven Wonders of the World** le sette meraviglie del mondo; **it is no** or **little** or **small wonder that he left** c'è poco or non c'è da meravigliarsi che sia partito; **the wonder of it was that ...** la cosa incredibile or sorprendente era che...; **to do** or **work wonders** fare miracoli; **no wonder!** non mi meraviglio!; **no wonder he got upset** non mi stupisce che si sia arrabbiato.
[2] VT chiedersi, domandarsi; **I wonder whether** or **if ...** mi chiedo se...; **I was wondering if you could give me a lift** mi chiedevo se potessi darmi un passaggio; **I wonder where/how/when** mi chiedo dove/come/quando.
[3] VI **a** (ask o.s., speculate): **to wonder about** pensare di; **I was wondering about going out for dinner** pensavo di andare fuori a cena, magari; **does she know about it? —**

I **wonder** lo sa? — è quello che mi chiedo anch'io
 b (*be surprised*) stupirsi, meravigliarsi; **to wonder at sth** stupirsi di qc.

won·der·ful ['wʌndəfʊl] ADJ meraviglioso(-a), stupendo (-a).

won·der·ful·ly ['wʌndəfəlɪ] ADV (*with adjective*) meravigliosamente; (*with verb*) a meraviglia.

won·der·ing ['wʌndərɪŋ] ADJ stupito(-a), stupefatto(-a).

wonder·land ['wʌndə‚lænd] N paese *m* delle meraviglie.

won·der·ment ['wʌndəmənt] N stupore *m*, meraviglia.

won·ky ['wɒŋkɪ] ADJ (*comp* **-ier**, *superl* **-iest**) (*Brit fam*: *chair*, *table*) traballante; **to go wonky** (*TV picture*, *machine*) fare i capricci.

won't [wəʊnt] PT, PT = will not.

wont [wəʊnt] N: **as is his/her wont** com'è solito(-a) fare.

woo [wu:] VT corteggiare; (*fig*: *voters*, *audience*) cercare di conquistare.

wood [wʊd] 1 N a (*material*) legno; (*timber*) legname *m*; **touch wood!**, (*Am*) **knock on wood!** tocca ferro!; **aged in the wood** invecchiato(-a) in botti di legno
 b (*forest*) bosco; **woods** NPL boschi *mpl*; **we're not out of the wood yet** (*fig*) non ne siamo ancora usciti completamente; **he can't see the wood for the trees** (*fig*) si perde nei dettagli
 c (*Golf*) mazza di legno; (*Bowls*) boccia.
 2 ADJ a (*made of wood*) di legno
 b (*living etc in a wood*) di bosco, silvestre.

♦ **wood anemone** N anemone *m* dei boschi.

wood·bine ['wʊd‚baɪn] N (*honeysuckle*) caprifoglio.

wood·carving ['wʊd‚kɑ:vɪŋ] N scultura in legno.

wood·chuck ['wʊd‚tʃʌk] N marmotta americana.

wood·cock ['wʊd‚kɒk] N beccaccia.

wood·craft ['wʊd‚krɑ:ft] N conoscenza dei boschi.

wood·cut ['wʊd‚kʌt] N incisione *f* su legno.

wood·cut·ter ['wʊd‚kʌtəʳ] N tagliaboschi *m inv*.

wood·ed ['wʊdɪd] ADJ coperto(-a) di boschi, boscoso(-a); **thickly/sparsely wooded** a bosco fitto/rado.

wood·en ['wʊdn] ADJ a (*made of wood*) di legno b (*fig*: *movements*, *manner*) impacciato(-a), rigido(-a); (: *face*, *stare*) inespressivo(-a); (: *personality*) goffo(-a); **to give a wooden performance** (*actor*) recitare in maniera impacciata.

♦ **wood engraving** N (*Art*) incisione *f* su legno.

wood·land ['wʊdlənd] 1 N zona boscosa.
 2 ADJ di bosco, silvestre.

wood·louse ['wʊd‚laʊs] N (*Zool*) onisco.

wood·pecker ['wʊd‚pɛkəʳ] N picchio.

♦ **wood pigeon** N colombaccio.

wood·pile ['wʊd‚paɪl] N catasta di legna.

♦ **wood pulp** N pasta di legno.

♦ **wood shavings** NPL trucioli *mpl* di legno.

wood·shed ['wʊd‚ʃɛd] N legnaia.

woods·man ['wʊdzmən] N (*pl* **-men**) (*lumberjack*) tagliaboschi *m inv*; (*forester*) guardaboschi *m inv*.

wood·wind ['wʊd‚wɪnd] NPL (*Mus*): **the woodwind** i legni *mpl*.

wood·work ['wʊd‚wɜ:k] N a (*craft*, *subject*) falegnameria
 b (*wooden parts of room*) parti *fpl* in legno.

wood·worm ['wʊd‚wɜ:m] N tarlo; **to have woodworm** essere tarlato(-a).

woody ['wʊdɪ] ADJ (*stem*, *plant etc*) ligneo(-a).

woof¹ [wʊf] 1 N (*of dog*) bau bau *m*.
 2 VI abbaiare; **woof, woof!** bau bau!

woof² [wʊf] N (*Textiles*) trama.

woof·er ['wʊfəʳ] N woofer *m inv*.

wool [wʊl] 1 N lana; **all wool** OR **pure wool** pura lana; **pure new wool** pura lana vergine; **knitting wool** lana per lavorare a maglia; **a ball of wool** un gomitolo di lana; **to pull the wool over sb's eyes** (*fam*) gettare fumo negli occhi a qn.
 2 ADJ (*dress*) di lana; (*shop*) di lane, di filati; (*trade*, *industry*) della lana.

wool·gather·ing ['wʊl‚gæðərɪŋ] N (*fig*): **to be woolgathering** avere la testa fra le nuvole.

wool·len, (*Am*) **wool·en** ['wʊlən] 1 ADJ (*cloth*, *dress*) di lana; (*industry*) della lana.
 2 : **woollens** NPL indumenti *mpl* di lana.

wool·ly, (*Am*) **wooly** ['wʊlɪ] 1 ADJ (*comp* **-ier**, *superl* **-iest**) (*jumper etc*) di lana; (*fig*: *clouds*) come batuffoli; (: *ideas*) confuso(-a), vago(-a); (: *essay*, *book*) sul vago.
 2 N (*fam*) indumento di lana.

woozy ['wu:zɪ] ADJ (*comp* **-ier**, *superl* **-iest**) (*fam*) stordito (-a), intontito(-a).

word [wɜ:d] 1 N a (*gen*) parola; **what's the word for "pen" in Italian?** come si dice "pen" in italiano?; **what does this word mean?** cosa vuol dire questa parola?; **words** NPL (*of song*) parole *fpl*, testo; **in the words of Dante** come disse Dante; **word for word** parola per parola, testualmente; **words per minute** parole al minuto; **to put sth into words** esprimere qc a parole; **silly isn't the word for it!** sciocco non è la parola esatta!; **words fail me** non ho parole; **in a word** in una parola; **in other words** in altre parole, in altri termini; **not in so many words** non esplicitamente; **those were her very words** quelle furono le sue testuali parole; **the last word in** l'ultima novità in fatto di; **to have the last word** avere l'ultima parola; **to give sb a word of warning** dare a qn un piccolo avvertimento; **I can't get a word out of him** non riesco a cavargli una parola di bocca; **by word of mouth** con il passaparola; **to take the words out of sb's mouth** rubare le parole di bocca a qn; **don't put words into my mouth!** non mettermi parole in bocca!; **to have a word with sb** fare un discorsetto a qn; **could I have a word with you?** posso parlarti un attimo?; **to put in a (good) word for sb** mettere una buona parola per qn; **without a word** senza una parola; **don't say** or **breathe a word about it** non farne parola; **to have words with sb** (*quarrel with*) venire a parole con qn
 b (*news*) notizia, notizie *fpl*; **is there any word from Peter yet?** non ci sono ancora notizie da parte di Peter?; **word came from headquarters that ...** il quartiere generale ci ha fatto sapere che...; **to bring/send word of sth to sb** portare/dare la notizia di qc a qn; **to leave word (with sb, for sb) that ...** lasciare detto (a qn) che...; **word of command** ordine *m*; **to give the word to do sth** dare l'ordine di fare qc
 c (*promise*) parola; **word of honour** parola d'onore; **he is a man of his word** è un uomo di parola; **to be as good as one's word** OR **keep one's word** essere di parola, tenere fede alla parola data; **to break one's word** mancare di parola; **to give sb one's word (that ...)** dare a qn la propria parola (che...); **I've only got your word for it** devo fidarmi di quello che dici tu; **to take sb at his word** prendere qn in parola; **I'll take your word for it** ti credo sulla parola
 d (*gospel*): **the Word** il Verbo, la parola di Dio; **to preach the Word** predicare la buona novella.
 2 VT (*document*, *protest*) formulare.

♦ **word-blind** ['wɜ:d‚blaɪnd] ADJ dislessico(-a).

♦ **word blindness** N dislessia.

word·book ['wɜːd͵bʊk] N vocabolario.

♦ **word game** N gioco con le parole.

wordi·ness ['wɜːdmɪs] N verbosità.

word·ing ['wɜːdɪŋ] N (of contract, document) formulazione f; **to change the wording** formulare diversamente.

♦ **word list** N lemmario.

♦ **word order** N ordine m delle parole.

♦ **word-perfect** [͵wɜːd'pɜːfɪkt] ADJ (speech etc) imparato (-a) a memoria; **to be word-perfect** (actor) sapere a memoria la parte.

word·play ['wɜːd͵pleɪ] N gioco di parole.

♦ **word processing** N word processing m inv.

♦ **word processor** N (machine) word processor m inv.

♦ **word wrap** N (Comput) ritorno a margine m automatico.

wordy ['wɜːdɪ] ADJ (comp **-ier**, superl **-iest**) verboso(-a), prolisso(-a).

wore [wɔː] PT of **wear**.

work [wɜːk] [1] N **a** (gen) lavoro; **it's hard work** è un lavoro duro; **to be at work (on sth)** lavorare (a qc); **men at work** lavori in corso; **it's all in a day's work** è una cosa di ordinaria amministrazione; **to get on with one's work** continuare il proprio lavoro; **the forces at work** gli elementi che influiscono; **work on the new school has begun** sono cominciati i lavori per la nuova scuola; **a good piece of work** un buon lavoro; **to set sb to work doing sth** mettere qn a fare qc; **to set to work (on)** [OR] **start work (on)** mettersi al lavoro (a); **I'm trying to get some work done** sto cercando di lavorare; **to make short** or **quick work of** (sth) sbrigare in fretta; (fig fam: sb) sistemare subito

b (employment, job) lavoro; **to go to work** andare al lavoro; **he's at work today** oggi è al lavoro; **to look for work** cercare lavoro; **to be out of work** essere disoccupato(-a); **to be in work** avere un lavoro; **to put** or **throw sb out of work** licenziare qn; **he's off work this week** questa settimana non lavora; **he hasn't done a day's work in his life** non ha mai lavorato in vita sua

c (product: of writer, musician, scholar) opera; **his life's work** il lavoro di tutta la sua vita; **he sells a lot of his work** vende molti dei suoi lavori; **good works** opere fpl buone; **work of art/reference** opera d'arte/di consultazione; **the works of Dickens** le opere di Dickens; **he's a nasty piece of work** (fig) è un tipaccio; see also **works**.

[2] VT **a** (students, employees) far lavorare; **to work o.s. to death** ammazzarsi di lavoro

b (operate) azionare; **can you work the photocopier?** sai usare la fotocopiatrice?; **it is worked by electricity** va a corrente

c (miracle) fare; (change) operare; **to work wonders** fare miracoli; **she managed to work her promotion** è riuscita a garantirsi la promozione; **they worked it so that she could come** (fam) hanno fatto in modo che potesse venire; **to work sth into a speech** far scivolare qc in un discorso; **to work one's passage on a ship** pagarsi il viaggio su una nave lavorando (a bordo della stessa); **to work one's way through college** lavorare per pagarsi gli studi; **to work one's way along sth** avanzare lentamente lungo qc; **to work one's hands free** riuscire a liberarsi le mani; **to work sth loose** far smollare qc; **to work one's way through a book** leggersi pazientemente un libro; **he worked his way up from the factory floor** ha cominciato come umile operaio; **to work one's way up to the top of a company** farsi strada fino al vertice di una società; **to work o.s. into a rage** andare in bestia

d (shape: metal, dough, clay, wood) lavorare; (exploit: mine) sfruttare; (: land) coltivare; (Sewing: design) ricamare; **worked by hand** lavorato(-a) a mano.

[3] VI **a** lavorare; **to work towards/for sth** lavorare in vista di/per qc; **to work hard** lavorare sodo; **to work at** or **on sth** (essay, project) lavorare su qc; **she's working at her desk** sta lavorando alla scrivania; **to work to rule** (Industry) fare uno sciopero bianco; **to work like a Trojan** lavorare come un(a) pazzo(-a)

b (machine, plan, brain) funzionare; (drug, medicine) fare effetto; **to get sth working** far funzionare qc; **it works off the mains** funziona a corrente; **it works both ways** (fig) funziona nei due sensi

c (mouth, face, jaws) contrarsi

d (move gradually) muoversi pian piano; **to work loose** (screw) allentarsi; **he worked slowly along the cliff** avanzava lentamente lungo la scogliera; **to work round to a question** formulare una domanda dopo averci girato intorno

▶ **work in** [1] VI + ADV (arrangement) inserirsi.

[2] VT + ADV (reference) inserire, infilare

▶ **work off** VT + ADV (fat) eliminare; (annoyance, tension) sfogare; (debt) pagare lavorando

▶ **work on** VI + PREP **a** (task, novel) lavorare a; **he's working on the car** sta facendo dei lavori alla macchina; **the police are working on the case** la polizia sta facendo indagini sul caso

b (principle, assumption) basarsi su; **we've no clues to work on** non abbiamo indizi su cui basarci; **we're working on the principle that ...** partiamo dal presupposto che... +sub

c (persuade, influence): **to work on sb** lavorarsi qn

▶ **work out** [1] VI + ADV **a** (problem) risolversi

b (amount to): **the cost worked out at £50** il costo ammontava a 50 sterline; **it works out at £100** fa 100 sterline

c (succeed: plan, marriage) riuscire, funzionare; **I hope it all works out for you** spero che ti vada tutto bene; **things aren't working out as planned** le cose non stanno andando come previsto

d (Sport) allenarsi.

[2] VT + ADV **a** (problem, calculation) risolvere; **I can't work out the percentage** non riesco a calcolare la percentuale; **things will work themselves out** tutto si sistemerà

b (devise: plan, details) mettere a punto

c (understand: behaviour) capire

d (exhaust: resources) esaurire

▶ **work over** VT + ADV (fam) pestare

▶ **work up** VT + ADV **a** (develop: trade) sviluppare; **to work up an appetite** farsi venire appetito; **to work up enthusiasm for sth** entusiasmarsi per qc

b : **to work sb up into a temper/fury** far arrabbiare/infuriare qn

▶ **work up to** VI + ADV + PREP (point, climax) preparare il terreno a.

work·able ['wɜːkəbl] ADJ (plan) fattibile; (solution) realizzabile; (land) coltivabile; (mine) sfruttabile.

worka·day ['wɜːkə͵deɪ] ADJ niente di speciale.

worka·hol·ic [͵wɜːkə'hɒlɪk] N stacanovista m/f, maniaco (-a) del lavoro.

work·bag ['wɜːk͵bæg] N borsa da lavoro.

♦ **work basket** N cestino da lavoro.

work·bench ['wɜːk͵bɛntʃ] N banco da lavoro.

work·book ['wɜːk͵bʊk] N quaderno per esercizi.

work·box ['wɜːkˌbɒks] N (for sewing) cofanetto da lavoro.

work·day ['wɜːkˌdeɪ] N (Am) giorno lavorativo or feriale.

worked up [ˌwɜːkt'ʌp] ADJ: **to get worked up** andare su tutte le furie; **don't get all worked up!** non agitarti tanto!

work·er ['wɜːkə'] N (gen, Agr) lavoratore(-trice); (esp Industry) operaio(-a); **he's a poor worker** non lavora bene; **office worker** impiegato(-a); **management and workers** il padronato e i lavoratori.

♦ **worker-priest** [ˌwɜːkə'priːst] N prete m operaio.

♦ **work force** N forza f lavoro inv.

work·horse ['wɜːkˌhɔːs] N cavallo da lavoro; (fig: person) lavoratore(-trice) indefesso(-a).

work·house ['wɜːkˌhaʊs] N (Brit History) ospizio (in cui i ricoverati lavoravano).

♦ **work·in** ['wɜːkˌɪn] N (Brit) *forma di protesta in cui gli operai occupano e continuano a lavorare in una fabbrica o azienda minacciata di chiusura.*

work·ing ['wɜːkɪŋ] ADJ (day) feriale; (week) lavorativo(-a); (tools, conditions, lunch) di lavoro; (clothes) da lavoro; (mother) che lavora; (partner) attivo(-a); **an 8-hour working day** una giornata lavorativa di 8 ore; **working knowledge** conoscenza pratica; **in working order** funzionante; see also **workings**.

♦ **working capital** N (Comm) capitale m d'esercizio.

♦ **working class** N classe f operaia or lavoratrice.

♦ **working-class** [ˌwɜːkɪŋ'klɑːs] ADJ: **to be working-class** appartenere alla classe operaia; **to come from a working-class background** venire da una famiglia di operai.

♦ **working man** N lavoratore m, operaio.

♦ **working model** N modello operativo.

♦ **working party** N (Brit) commissione f d'inchiesta.

work·ings ['wɜːkɪŋz] NPL **a** (way sth works) funzionamento msg; **the workings of his mind** i meccanismi della sua mente **b** (of quarry) scavi mpl.

♦ **work-in-progress** [ˌwɜːkɪn'prəʊgrɛs] (Comm) N (value) valore m del manufatto in lavorazione.

work·load ['wɜːkˌləʊd] N carico di lavoro.

work·man ['wɜːkmən] N (pl -men) operaio.

work·man·like ['wɜːkmənˌlaɪk] ADJ (attitude) professionale; (work) ben fatto(-a).

work·man·ship ['wɜːkmənˌʃɪp] N (of worker) abilità professionale; (of thing) fattura.

work·mate ['wɜːkˌmeɪt] N collega m/f di lavoro.

work·out ['wɜːkˌaʊt] N (Sport) allenamento.

♦ **work permit** N permesso di lavoro.

work·room ['wɜːkˌrʊm] N laboratorio.

works [wɜːks] N (Brit) **a** NPL (of machine, clock) meccanismo; (Admin) opere fpl; (Mil) opere, fortificazioni fpl; **road works** lavori stradali; **to give sb the works** (fam: treat harshly) dare una strigliata a qn **b** PL INV (factory etc) fabbrica, stabilimento; **works outing** gita aziendale.

♦ **works council** N consiglio aziendale.

♦ **work sharing** N *divisione di un posto di lavoro tra due o più persone con relativa divisione di stipendio.*

♦ **work sheet** N scheda; (Comput) foglio col programma di lavoro.

work·shop ['wɜːkˌʃɒp] N officina; (fig): **a music workshop** un seminario di musica.

work·shy ['wɜːkˌʃaɪ] ADJ pigro(-a), indolente.

♦ **work station** N stazione f di lavoro.

♦ **work study** N studio di organizzazione del lavoro.

♦ **work surface** N piano di lavoro.

work·top ['wɜːkˌtɒp] N piano di lavoro.

♦ **work-to-rule** [ˌwɜːktə'ruːl] N (Brit) sciopero bianco.

world [wɜːld] ① N **a** (gen) mondo; **in the world** al mondo; **all over the world** in tutto il mondo; **to be on top of the world** essere al settimo cielo; **it's a small world!** com'è piccolo il mondo!; **alone in the world** solo(-a) al mondo; **it's not the end of the world!** (fam) non è la fine del mondo!; **to live in a world of one's own** vivere in un mondo tutto proprio; **the business world** il mondo degli affari; **the world we live in** il mondo in cui viviamo; **to come** or **go down** [OR] **go up** or **rise in the world** scendere/salire nella scala sociale; **to come into the world** venire al mondo; **the next world** l'aldilà m inv; **to have the best of both worlds** avere un doppio vantaggio; **it's out of this world!** (fam) è la fine del mondo!; **he's not long for this world** non gli rimane molto da vivere **b** (phrases): **I wouldn't do it for the world** or **for anything in the world** non lo farei per niente al mondo; **what in the world is he doing?** che caspita sta facendo?; **to think the world of sb** pensare un gran bene di qn; **there's a world of difference between ...** c'è un abisso tra...; **to do sb a world of good** fare un gran bene a qn; **the world and his wife** un miliardo di persone; **they're worlds apart** non hanno niente in comune; **she looked for all the world as if she was dead** sembrava proprio che fosse morta; **the world's worst cook** la cuoca peggiore che possa esistere

② ADJ (tour, power) mondiale; (record) del mondo, mondiale.

♦ **world champion** N campione(-essa) mondiale.

♦ **world-class** ['wɜːld'klɑːs] ADJ (sportsman, player) di livello internazionale.

♦ **World Cup** N (Ftbl): **the World Cup** il campionato mondiale or i mondiali mpl di calcio.

♦ **World Fair** N (Comm): **the World Fair** la fiera mondiale.

♦ **world-famous** [ˌwɜːld'feɪməs] ADJ di fama mondiale.

♦ **World Health Organization** N: **the World Health Organization** l'Organizzazione f Mondiale della Sanità.

world·ly ['wɜːldlɪ] ADJ (comp -ier, superl -iest) (matters, person) mondano(-a); (attitude, pleasures) materiale.

worldly-wise [ˌwɜːldlɪ'waɪz] ADJ di mondo.

♦ **world music** N musica etnica, world music f inv.

♦ **World Series** N (Am Baseball): **the World Series** torneo di spareggio al termine del campionato di baseball.

♦ **World War I** N la prima guerra mondiale.

♦ **World War II** N la seconda guerra mondiale.

♦ **world-weary** ['wɜːld'wɪərɪ] ADJ stanco(-a) della vita.

♦ **world-wide** [ˌwɜːld'waɪd] ADJ mondiale, universale.

worm [wɜːm] ① N (Zool, also person: pej) verme m; **to have worms** (Med) avere i vermi; **the worm will turn** (Proverb) anche la pazienza ha un limite; **a can of worms** (fam) un vespaio; **you worm!** (fam) verme!.

② VT **a** : **to worm one's way through a crowd** insinuarsi tra la folla; **to worm one's way into a group** infiltrarsi in un gruppo; **to worm one's way into sb's confidence** riuscire a conquistare la fiducia di qn **b** : **to worm a secret out of sb** carpire un segreto a qn.

worm·cast ['wɜːmˌkɑːst] N *mucchietto di terra scavata da un verme.*

♦ **worm-eaten** ['wɜːmˌiːtn] ADJ (apple) bacato(-a); (wood) tarlato(-a).

worm·wood ['wɜːmˌwʊd] N (Bot) assenzio.

wormy ['wɜːmɪ] ADJ (comp -ier, superl -iest) (fruit) bacato(-a); (furniture) tarlato(-a).

worn [wɔːn] ① PP of **wear**.

② ADJ (carpet, tyre) consumato(-a), logoro(-a); (person) stanco(-a), sfinito(-a).

♦ **worn-out** [ˌwɔːnˈaʊt] ADJ (*thing*) consunto(-a), logoro (-a); (*person*) sfinito(-a).

wor·ried [ˈwʌrɪd] ADJ preoccupato(-a); **to be worried about sth** essere preoccupato per qc; **to be worried sick** (*fam*) essere preoccupatissimo(-a); **to be worried to death about sth/sb** (*fam*) essere molto ansioso(-a) per qc/qn.

wor·ried·ly [ˈwʌrɪdlɪ] ADV (*say, look about etc*) ansiosamente.

wor·rier [ˈwʌrɪəʳ] N ansioso(-a).

wor·ri·some [ˈwʌrɪsəm] ADJ **a** (*causing worry*) preoccupante **b** (*worried*) ansioso(-a).

wor·ry [ˈwʌrɪ] ⟨1⟩ N preoccupazione *f*; **what's your worry?** cosa ti preoccupa?; **to cause sb a lot of worry** creare un sacco di preoccupazioni a qn; **that's the least of my worries** questa è l'ultima cosa di cui mi preoccupo.

⟨2⟩ VT **a** (*cause concern*) preoccupare; **to worry o.s. sick (about** *or* **over sth)** preoccuparsi da morire (per qc); **don't worry yourself** *or* **your head about it** non fartene un pensiero

b (*bother*) disturbare, importunare

c (*subj: dog: bone*) azzannare; (: *sheep*) inseguire e attaccare.

⟨3⟩ VI: **to worry about** *or* **over sth/sb** preoccuparsi di qc/per qn

▶ **worry at** VI + PREP **a** (*gnaw*) rosicchiare

b (*try to deal with*): **to worry at sth** scervellarsi su qc.

wor·ry·ing [ˈwʌrɪɪŋ] ADJ (*problem*) preoccupante; **it's a worrying time for her** è un brutto momento per lei; **she's not the worrying kind** non è il tipo che si preoccupa.

worse [wɜːs] ⟨1⟩ ADJ (*comp of* bad) peggiore; **worse than** peggio *or* peggiore di; **the situation is worse than we expected** la situazione è peggiore di quanto ci aspettassimo; **it's worse than ever** è peggio che mai; **it could have been worse!** poteva andare peggio!; **he was the worse for drink** (*fam*) aveva un po' bevuto; **he is none the worse for it** non ha avuto brutte conseguenze; **to get worse** OR **grow worse** peggiorare; **it gets worse and worse** va peggiorando (sempre di più); **so much the worse for you!** tanto peggio per te!; **I've got to work this weekend, worse luck** devo lavorare questo fine settimana, sfortunatamente.

⟨2⟩ ADV (*comp of* badly) peggio; **she's behaving worse than ever** si comporta peggio che mai; **I don't think any the worse of you** non per questo ti stimo meno; **I won't think any the worse of you (for having done)** non ti stimerò di meno (per aver fatto); **you might do worse than (to) marry him** sposare lui non è il male peggiore.

⟨3⟩ N peggio; **a change for the worse** un cambiamento in peggio, un peggioramento; **worse followed** a questo seguì il peggio; **there is worse to come** il peggio deve ancora venire.

wors·en [ˈwɜːsn] ⟨1⟩ VT (*health, situation*) peggiorare; (*chances*) diminuire.

⟨2⟩ VI peggiorare.

♦ **worse off** ADJ più povero(-a); (*fig*): **you'll be worse off this way** così sarà peggio per te; **he is now worse off than before** ora è in condizioni economiche peggiori di prima.

wor·ship [ˈwɜːʃɪp] ⟨1⟩ N **a** (*adoration*) adorazione *f*, culto; (*also:* **organized worship**) culto; **place of worship** (*Rel*) luogo di culto

b (*Brit: in titles*): **Your Worship** (*to judge*) Vostro Onore; (*to mayor*) signor sindaco.

⟨2⟩ VT adorare, venerare; **she worships her children** (*fig*) adora i suoi bambini; **he worships the ground she treads on** bacia la terra su cui lei cammina.

⟨3⟩ VI (*Rel*) assistere alle funzioni.

wor·ship·per [ˈwɜːʃɪpəʳ] N adoratore(-trice); (*in church*) fedele *m/f*, devoto(-a).

worst [wɜːst] ⟨1⟩ ADJ (*superl of* bad) il/la peggiore; **it was the worst possible time** era il momento peggiore *or* meno opportuno; **the worst film of the three** il peggiore fra i tre film; **the worst pupil in the school** il peggior alunno della scuola; **one of his worst efforts** una delle sue prove peggiori.

⟨2⟩ ADV (superl of badly) peggio; **he sings worst of all** canta peggio di tutti; **to come off worst** (*in fight, argument*) avere la peggio.

⟨3⟩ N peggio *m or f*; (*of crisis, storm*) culmine *m*; **at (the) worst** alla peggio, per male che vada; **the worst of it is that …** il peggio è che...; **the worst is yet to come** il peggio deve ancora venire; **if the worst comes to the worst** nel peggiore dei casi; **to get the worst of an argument** avere la peggio in una discussione; **he brings out the worst in me** risveglia in me gli istinti peggiori; **we're over** *or* **past the worst of it now** il peggio è passato, ora; **do your worst!** sono pronto al peggio!

♦ **worst-case** [ˌwɜːstˈkeɪs] ADJ: **the worst-case scenario** la peggiore delle ipotesi.

wor·sted [ˈwʊstɪd] N (*cloth*) pettinato(-a); **wool worsted** lana pettinata.

worth [wɜːθ] ⟨1⟩ ADJ: **to be worth** valere; **how much is it worth?** quanto vale?; **it's worth £5** vale 5 sterline; **it's worth a great deal** vale molto; **it's worth a great deal to me** (*sentimentally*) ha un gran valore per me; **he is worth his weight in gold** vale tanto oro quanto pesa; **I'll tell you this for what it's worth** ti dico questo, per quello che può valere; **what's it worth to you?** che valore ha per te?; **to run for all one is worth** correre a gambe levate; **it hardly seemed worth mentioning** non mi sembrava abbastanza importante da parlarne; **it's well worth the effort/expense** vale lo sforzo/la spesa; **it's not worth the paper it's written on** non vale nemmeno la carta su cui è scritto; **it's worth it** ne vale la pena; **it's not worth it** OR **it's not worth the trouble** non ne vale la pena; **it's more than my life is worth** non oserei mai; **is it worth doing?** vale la pena di farlo?.

⟨2⟩ N valore *m*; **50 pence worth of apples** 50 pence di mele; **he had no chance to show his true worth** non ebbe occasione di mostrare quanto valeva.

worth·less [ˈwɜːθlɪs] ADJ (*effort, action, attempt*) inutile; (*assurance, guarantee, object*) senza valore, di nessun valore; **a worthless individual** un individuo spregevole.

worth·while [ˌwɜːθˈwaɪl] ADJ (*gen*) che vale la pena; (*book, film*) che merita; (*life, work, activity*) utile; (*contribution*) valido(-a); (*cause*) lodevole; **a worthwhile trip** un viaggio che vale la pena di fare; **a worthwhile book** un libro che vale la pena leggere.

wor·thy [ˈwɜːðɪ] ⟨1⟩ ADJ (*comp* -ier, *superl* -iest) (*gen*) degno(-a); (*cause, aim, motive*) lodevole; **worthy of** degno di; **worthy of note** *or* **mention** degno di nota.

⟨2⟩ N (*hum*) personalità *f inv*.

would [wʊd] MODAL AUX VB

conditional of **will**

a (*conditional tense*)

▷**she would** *come* verrebbe

▷**if you asked him he would** *do* **it** se tu glielo chiedessi lo farebbe

▷**he would** *have come* sarebbe venuto

▷**if you had asked him he would** *have done* **it** se tu gliel'avessi chiesto l'avrebbe fatto

▷**you'd** *think* **she had enough to worry about** si direbbe che abbia già abbastanza preoccupazioni

b (*in indirect speech*)

▷**I** *said* **I would do it** ho detto che l'avrei fatto

c (*emphatic*)

▷**you would** *be* **the one to forget!** è proprio da te dimenticartelo!

▷**it** WOULD *have* **to snow today!** doveva proprio nevicare oggi!

▷**you** WOULD *say* **that, wouldn't you!** e ti pareva! sapevo che avresti detto così!

d (*insistence*)

▷**she wouldn't** *behave* non ha voluto comportarsi bene

▷**I told her not to but she would** *do* **it** le avevo detto di non farlo ma lei l'ha voluto fare a tutti i costi

e (*conjecture*)

▷**what would this** *be*? questo cosa sarebbe?

▷**it would** *have been* **about midnight** sarà stato verso mezzanotte

▷**it would** *seem* **so** sembrerebbe proprio di sì

f (*wish*)

▷**what would you** *have* **me do?** cosa desideri che faccia?

▷**would (that) it** *were* **not so!** (*old liter*) magari non fosse così!

g (*in offers, invitations, requests*)

▷**would you** *ask* **him to come in?** lo faccia entrare per cortesia

▷**would you** *care* **for some tea?** gradiresti del tè?

▷**would you** *close* **the door, please** chiuda la porta per favore

▷**would you** *like* **a biscuit?** gradisce un biscotto?

h (*habit*)

▷**he would** *go* **there on Mondays** ci andava il lunedì

▷**he would** *paint* **it each year** era solito dipingerlo ogni anno.

would-be ['wʊd‚bi:] ADJ: **a would-be poet/politician** un aspirante poeta/politico.

wouldn't ['wʊdnt] **= would not.**

wound[1] [wu:nd] ① N ferita; **leg/bullet wound** ferita alla gamba/di proiettile.

② VT (*also fig*) ferire.

wound[2] [waʊnd] PT, PP of **wind**[2].

wound·ed ['wu:ndɪd] ① ADJ (*also fig*) ferito(-a); **a wounded man** un ferito.

② NPL: **the wounded** i feriti.

wound·ing ['wu:ndɪŋ] ADJ (*blow, remark*) che lascia il segno.

wound up [‚waʊnd'ʌp] ADJ teso(-a).

wove [wəʊv] PT of **weave**.

wo·ven ['wəʊvən] PP of **weave**.

wow [waʊ] EXCL (*fam*) wow!

WP [‚dʌblju:'pi:] ① ABBR (*Brit fam*: = *weather permitting*) tempo permettendo.

② N ABBR **= word processing, word processor.**

WPC [‚dʌblju:pi:'si:] N (*Brit*: = *woman police constable*)

donna *f* poliziotto *inv*, agente *f* di polizia femminile.

wpm ABBR **= words per minute; see word.**

WRAC [‚dʌblju:ɑ:reɪ'si:] N ABBR (*Brit*: = *Women's Royal Army Corps*) ausiliarie dell'esercito.

WRAF [‚dʌblju:ɑ:reɪ'ɛf] N ABBR (*Brit*: = *Women's Royal Air Force*) ausiliarie dell'aeronautica militare.

wraith [reɪθ] N spettro.

wran·gle ['ræŋgl] ① N litigio, alterco.

② VI: **to wrangle (about** *or* **over)** litigare (su).

wrap [ræp] ① N (*shawl*) scialle *m*; (*housecoat*) vestaglia; (*rug*) coperta; (*cape*) mantellina; **still under wraps** (*fig*: *plan, scheme*) ancora segreto(-a).

② VT (*also:* **wrap up**) avvolgere, incartare; **the scheme is wrapped in secrecy** il piano è avvolto nel mistero

▶ **wrap up** ① VT + ADV **a** (*gen*) avvolgere; (*parcel*) incartare; (*child*) coprire bene; **she wrapped it up a bit, but what she meant was ...** ci ha girato un po' intorno, ma intendeva dire che...

b (*fam*: *finalize*) concludere; **I think that (just) about wraps it up** direi che questo è tutto ciò che c'è da dire

c : **to be wrapped up in sb/sth** essere completamente preso(-a) da qn/qc; **she's wrapped up in herself** non pensa che a se stessa.

② VI + ADV **a** (*dress warmly*) coprirsi (bene)

b (*fam*: *be quiet*): **wrap up!** chiudi il becco!

wrap·over ['ræp‚əʊvə'] ADJ (*skirt*) a portafoglio.

wrap·per ['ræpə'] N (*on chocolate*) carta; (*postal*) fascetta; (*of book*) foderina, copertina.

wrap·ping ['ræpɪŋ] N (*for chocolate, parcel*) carta.

♦ **wrapping paper** N (*brown*) carta da pacchi; (*for gift*) carta da regali.

wrath [rɒθ] N (*liter*) ira, collera.

wreak [ri:k] VT (*destruction, havoc*) portare, causare; **to wreak vengeance on** vendicarsi su.

wreath [ri:θ] N (*pl* **wreaths** [ri:ðz]) (*of flowers*) ghirlanda; (*at funeral*) corona; (*of smoke*) anello; (*mist*) corona.

wreathed [ri:ðd] ADJ: **a face wreathed in smiles** un volto raggiante; **wreathed in mist** avvolto(-a) nella nebbia.

wreck [rɛk] ① N (*of ship, scheme etc*) naufragio; (*ship itself*) relitto; (*fig*: *old car etc*) rottame *m*; (: *building*) rudere *m*; **I'm a wreck** [OR] **I feel a wreck** sono distrutto(-a).

② VT (*gen*) distruggere, rovinare; (*ship*) far naufragare; (*train*) far deragliare; (*house*) demolire; (*health*) rovinare; **to be wrecked** (*Naut*) fare naufragio.

wreck·age ['rɛkɪdʒ] N (*of ship*) relitto; (*of car etc*) rottami *mpl*; (*of building*) macerie *fpl*.

wreck·er ['rɛkə'] N (*Naut*: *salvager*) addetto al ricupero di relitti; (*Am*: *breaker, salvager*) demolitore *m*; (: *breakdown van*) carro *m* attrezzi *inv*.

WREN [rɛn] N ABBR (*Brit*) *membro del WRNS*.

wren [rɛn] N scricciolo.

wrench [rɛntʃ] ① N **a** (*tug*) strattone *m*; **to give sth a wrench** dare uno strattone a qc

b (*tool*) chiave *f*

c (*fig*) strazio.

② VT **a** : **to wrench sth (away) from** *or* **off sb** strappare qc a qn; **he wrenched it out of my hands** me lo ha strappato di mano; **she wrenched herself free** si liberò con uno strattone; **to wrench a door open** aprire bruscamente una porta

b (*Med*) slogare, storcere.

wrest [rɛst] VT: **to wrest sth from sb** strappare qc a qn.

wres·tle ['rɛsl] ① N: **to have a wrestle with sb** fare la lotta con qn.

② VI **a** lottare, fare la lotta; (*Sport*) praticare la lotta

libera **b** (*fig*): **to wrestle with** (*one's conscience, device, machine*) lottare con; (*temptation, sins*) lottare contro.

wres·tler ['rɛslə'] N (*Sport*) lottatore(-trice).

wres·tling ['rɛslɪŋ] N (*Sport*) lotta libera; (*also*: **all-in wrestling**: *Brit*) catch *m*.

♦ **wrestling match** N incontro di lotta libera.

wretch [rɛtʃ] N disgraziato(-a), sciagurato(-a); **little wretch!** (*often hum*) birbante!

wretch·ed ['rɛtʃɪd] ADJ **a** (*house, conditions*) misero(-a), disgraziato(-a); (*life*) gramo(-a); (*pittance*) misero(-a); (*unhappy, depressed*) infelice, triste; **I feel wretched** (*fam*: *ill*) sto malissimo
b (*fam*: *very bad*: *weather, behaviour*) pessimo(-a), atroce; (*holiday*) orrendo(-a), orribile; (*results*) pessimo (-a); (*child*) pestifero(-a); **I feel wretched about it** (*fam*: *conscience-stricken*) mi sento un verme; **what wretched luck!** (*fam*) che scalogna!; **where's that wretched dog?** (*fam*) dov'è quel maledetto cane?

wretch·ed·ly ['rɛtʃɪdlɪ] ADV (*live*) miseramente; (*say, weep*) tristemente; (*pay*) male; (*treat, behave, perform*) in modo atroce.

wretch·ed·ness ['rɛtʃɪdnɪs] N (*of life, conditions, pay*) miseria; (*unhappiness*) infelicità; (*of behaviour, weather*) meschinità.

wrick, rick [rɪk] VT: **to wrick one's ankle** slogarsi la caviglia; **to wrick one's neck** farsi uno strappo (muscolare) al collo.

wrig·gle ['rɪgl] ① VT (*toes, fingers*) muovere; **to wriggle one's way through** (*tunnel*) attraversare strisciando; (*undergrowth*) strisciare in.
② VI (*also*: **wriggle about** *or* **around**) agitarsi, dimenarsi; (*fish*: *on hook*) contorcersi; **to wriggle along/down** avanzare/scendere strisciando; **to wriggle free** liberarsi contorcendosi; **to wriggle through a hole** contorcersi per passare attraverso un buco; **he managed to wriggle out of it** (*fig*) se l'è cavata con un espediente.
③ N contorsione *f*.

wrig·gly ['rɪglɪ] ADJ (*comp* **-ier**, *superl* **-iest**) che si dimena.

wring [rɪŋ] (*pt, pp* **wrung**) VT **a** (*also*: **wring out**: *wet clothes*) strizzare **b** (*twist*) torcere; **I'll wring your neck!** (*fam*) ti torco il collo!; **she wrung my hand** mi strinse forte la mano; **to wring one's hands** (*fig*: *in distress*) torcersi le mani; **to wring sb's heart** (*fig*) stringere il cuore a qn **c** (*also*: **wring out**: *confession, truth, money*) estorcere.

wring·er ['rɪŋə'] N strizzatoio (manuale).

wring·ing ['rɪŋɪŋ] ADJ (*also*: **wringing wet**) bagnato(-a) fradicio(-a).

wrin·kle ['rɪŋkl] ① N (*on face, skin*) ruga; (*in stockings, paper etc*) grinza.
② VT (*fabric*) stropicciare; (*nose*) arricciare; (*flat surface, skin*) corrugare, raggrinzire.
③ VI (*see vt*) stropicciarsi; arricciarsi; corrugarsi, raggrinzirsi.

wrin·kled ['rɪŋkld], **wrin·kly** ['rɪŋklɪ] ADJ (*fabric, paper*) stropicciato(-a); (*nose*) arricciato(-a); (*surface*) corrugato(-a), increspato(-a); (*skin*) rugoso(-a).

wrist [rɪst] N polso.

wrist·band ['rɪst,bænd] N (*of shirt*) polsino; (*of watch*) cinturino.

♦ **wrist loop** N (*Mountaineering*) dragona.

wrist·watch ['rɪst,wɒtʃ] N orologio da polso.

writ [rɪt] N (*Law*) mandato; **to issue a writ against sb** [OR] **serve a writ on sb** notificare un mandato di comparizione a qn.

write [raɪt] (*pt* **wrote**, *pp* **written**) ① VT scrivere; (*list*) compilare; (*certificate*) redigere; **she wrote that she'd arrive soon** scrisse che sarebbe arrivata presto; **to write sb a letter** scrivere una lettera a qn; **he's just written another novel** ha appena scritto un altro romanzo; **how is his name written?** come si scrive il suo nome?; **she wrote three pages** ha scritto tre pagine; **his guilt was written all over his face** gli si leggeva in faccia che era colpevole.
② VI scrivere; **to write to sb** scrivere a qn; **it's nothing to write home about** (*fam*) non è niente di speciale; **I'll write for the catalogue** scriverò per farmi mandare il catalogo; **to write for a paper** scrivere per un giornale

▶ **write away** VI + ADV: **to write away for** (*information*) richiedere per posta; (*goods*) ordinare per posta

▶ **write back** VI + ADV rispondere (*con una lettera*)

▶ **write down** VT + ADV (*make a note of*) segnare, annotare; (*put in writing*) mettere per iscritto

▶ **write in** ① VT + ADV inserire.
② VI + ADV scrivere; **to write in for sth** scrivere per richiedere qc

▶ **write into** VT + PREP includere in, scrivere in

▶ **write off** ① VI + ADV = **write away**.
② VT + ADV (*debt*) estinguere; (*scheme*) porre un termine a; (*smash up*: *car*) distruggere; **he was written off as useless** (*fig*) fu deciso che era un incompetente punto e basta

▶ **write out** VT + ADV (*gen*) scrivere; (*list, form*) compilare; (*cheque*) fare; (*copy*: *essay*) ricopiare

▶ **write up** VT + ADV (*notes, diary*) aggiornare; (*write report on*: *developments etc*) mettere per iscritto; **she wrote the play up in the Glasgow Herald** ha scritto una recensione della commedia sul Glasgow Herald.

♦ **write-off** ['raɪt,ɒf] N (*Comm*) perdita; (*fig*: *car etc*) rottame *m*; **the car is a write-off** la macchina è ridotta ad un rottame.

♦ **write-protect** [,raɪtprə'tɛkt] VT (*Comput*) proteggere contro scrittura.

writ·er ['raɪtə'] N (*of letter, report*) autore(-trice); (*as profession*) scrittore(-trice); **to be a good/poor writer** scrivere/non scrivere bene; **he's a thriller writer** è un autore di gialli; **he's a writer of novels** è un romanziere; **writer's cramp** crampo dello scrivano.

♦ **write-up** ['raɪt,ʌp] N (*review*) recensione *f*.

writhe [raɪð] VI contorcersi; **to writhe with embarrassment** morire di vergogna.

writ·ing ['raɪtɪŋ] N (*art*) scrivere *m*; (*sth written*) scritto; (*handwriting*) scrittura; **writings** NPL (*author's works*) opera *fsg*; **to put sth in writing** mettere qc per iscritto; **in my own writing** scritto di mio pugno; **Aubrey's biographical writings** gli scritti biografici di Aubrey; **writing is my profession** faccio lo scrittore di professione; **writing is just a hobby with me** scrivere è solo un hobby per me; **the writing on the wall** (*fig*) il presagio della rovina.

♦ **writing case** N nécessaire *m inv* per la corrispondenza.

♦ **writing desk** N scrivania.

♦ **writing pad** N (*for letters*) blocco di carta da lettere; (*for notes*) bloc notes *m inv*.

♦ **writing paper** N carta da lettere.

♦ **writing table** N scrittoio.

writ·ten ['rɪtn] ① PP of **write**.
② ADJ scritto(-a).

♦ **written word** N: **the written word** la parola scritta.

WRNS [,dʌblju:ɑ:rɛn'ɛs] N ABBR (*Brit*: = *Women's Royal Naval Service*) ausiliarie della marina militare.

wrong [rɒŋ] ① ADJ **a** (*morally*) sbagliato(-a), riprovevole;

(*unfair*) ingiusto(-a), sbagliato(-a); (*wicked*) cattivo(-a); **it's wrong to steal, stealing is wrong** non si deve rubare; **you were wrong to do that** hai sbagliato a fare così; **what's wrong with a drink now and again?** che c'è di male nel bere un bicchierino ogni tanto?

b (*incorrect*) sbagliato(-a), errato(-a); **to be wrong** (*answer*) essere sbagliato(-a); (*in doing, saying*) avere torto; **I was wrong in thinking that** ... avevo torto a pensare che...; **you are wrong about that** ti sbagli

c (*improper, not sought, not wanted*) sbagliato(-a), inadatto(-a); **to say/do the wrong thing** dire/fare qc che non va

d (*amiss*): **is anything** *or* **something wrong?** c'è qualcosa che non va?; **what's wrong (with you)?** che cos'hai?, cosa c'è che non va?; **there's nothing wrong** va tutto bene; **there is something wrong with my lights** le luci non funzionano bene; **what's wrong with your arm?** cos'hai al braccio?; **what's wrong with the car?** cos'ha la macchina che non va?; **to be wrong in the head** (*fam*) essere un po' tocco(-a).

2 ADV (*spell, pronounce*) in modo sbagliato, erroneamente; **you're doing it all wrong** stai sbagliando tutto; **you did wrong to do it** hai fatto male agendo così; **to get sth wrong** sbagliare qc; **don't get me wrong** (*fam*) non fraintendermi; **to go wrong** (*on route*) sbagliare strada; (*in calculation*) sbagliarsi, commettere un errore; (*morally*) prendere una cattiva strada; (*plan etc*) andare male, fallire; **something went wrong with the brakes** è successo qualcosa ai freni; **you can't go wrong** non puoi sbagliarti; **you won't go far wrong if you follow his advice** non rischi più di tanto a seguire il suo consiglio.

3 N **a** (*evil*) male *m*; **to do wrong** far (del) male; **he can do no wrong in her eyes** ai suoi occhi lui è perfetto

b (*unjust act*) torto; **to do sb a wrong** fare un torto a qn; **to be in the wrong** avere torto; **to put sb in the wrong** mettere qn dalla parte del torto; **to right a wrong** riparare a un torto; **to suffer a wrong** subire un torto.

4 VT fare (un) torto a.

wrong·doer ['rɒŋˌduːəʳ] N malfattore(-trice).

wrong·doing ['rɒŋˌduːɪŋ] N malefatta, misfatto.

♦ **wrong-foot** ['rɒŋˌfʊt] VT (*Ftbl, also fig*) prendere in contropiede.

wrong·ful ['rɒŋfʊl] ADJ (*unjust: accusation*) ingiusto(-a); (*unlawful: arrest, imprisonment*) illegale, illecito(-a); **wrongful dismissal** licenziamento ingiustificato.

wrong·ful·ly ['rɒŋfəlɪ] ADV (*see adj*) ingiustamente; illegalmente.

♦ **wrong-headed** [ˌrɒŋ'hɛdɪd] ADJ (*stubborn*) ostinato (-a); (*mistaken*) sbagliato(-a).

wrong·ly ['rɒŋlɪ] ADV (*answer, do, count*) erroneamente; (*treat*) ingiustamente; (*accuse, dismiss*) a torto.

♦ **wrong number** N: **you have the wrong number** (*Telec*) ha sbagliato numero.

♦ **wrong side** N (*of cloth*) rovescio.

wrote [rəʊt] PT of **write**.

wrought [rɔːt] **1** (*old, liter*) **a** PT, PP of **work b** : **great changes have been wrought** sono avvenuti dei grandi cambiamenti.

2 ADJ (*silver*) lavorato(-a); (*iron*) battuto(-a).

♦ **wrought-iron** [ˌrɔːt'aɪən] ADJ di ferro battuto.

♦ **wrought-up** [ˌrɔːt'ʌp] ADJ: **to be wrought-up** essere teso(-a).

wrung [rʌŋ] PT, PP of **wring**.

WRVS [ˌdʌbljuːɑːrviːˈɛs] N ABBR (*Brit*: = *Women's Royal Voluntary Service*) *ausiliarie al servizio della collettività*.

wry [raɪ] ADJ beffardo(-a); **to make a wry face** fare una smorfia.

wry·ly ['raɪlɪ] ADV beffardamente.

wt. ABBR = **weight**.

WV ABBR (*Am Post*)= *West Virginia*.

WY ABBR (*Am Post*)= *Wyoming*.

WYSIWYG ABBR (*Comput*)= *what you see is what you get*.

X

X, x [ɛks] N (*letter, Math*) X, x *for m inv*; **X for Xmas** ≈ X come Xeres; **if you have x dollars a year** se hai x dollari all'anno; **x marks the spot** il punto è segnato con una croce.
- ♦ **X-certificate** [ˌɛksəˈtɪfɪkət] ADJ (*Brit Cine*) vietato ai minori di 18 anni (*secondo un sistema di censura non più in uso*).
- ♦ **X-chromosome** [ˈɛksˈkrəʊməsəʊm] N cromosoma *m* X.
- **xen·on** [ˈzɛnɒn] N (*Chem*) xeno.
- **xeno·phobe** [ˈzɛnəˌfəʊb] N (*frm*) xenofobo(-a).
- **xeno·pho·bia** [ˌzɛnəˈfəʊbɪə] N (*frm*) xenofobia.
- **xeno·phobic** [ˌzɛnəˈfəʊbɪk] ADJ (*frm*) xenofobo(-a), xenofobico(-a).
- **Xenophon** [ˈzɛnəfən] N Senofonte *m*.
- **Xer·ox®** [ˈzɪərɒks] 1 VT fotocopiare.

2 N (*also:* **Xerox machine**) fotocopiatrice *f*; (*photocopy*) fotocopia.
- **Xerxes** [ˈzɜːksiːz] N Serse *m*.
- **XL** [ˌɛksˈɛl] ABBR (= *extra large*) XL.
- **Xmas** [ˈɛksməs, ˈkrɪsməs] N = **Christmas**.
- ♦ **X-rated** [ˌɛksˈreɪtɪd] ADJ (*Am: film*) ≈ vietato ai minori di 18 anni.
- ♦ **X-ray** [ˈɛksˌreɪ] 1 N (*ray*) raggio X; (*photograph*) radiografia; **to have an X-ray** farsi fare una radiografia.
  2 VT radiografare.
  3 ADJ (*examination*) radiografico(-a).
- ♦ **X-ray picture** N lastra.
- **xy·lem** [ˈzaɪləm] N (*Bot*) xilema *m*.
- **xy·lo·phone** [ˈzaɪləˌfəʊn] N xilofono.

Y

Y, y [waɪ] N (*letter*) Y, y *f or m inv*; **Y for Yellow**, (*Am*) **Y for Yoke** ≈ Y come Yacht.

yacht [jɒt] N yacht *m inv*, panfilo da diporto.

♦ **yacht club** N yacht club *m inv*, circolo nautico.

yacht·ing [ˈjɒtɪŋ] N yachting *m*, navigazione *f* da diporto.

yachts·man [ˈjɒtsmən] N (*pl* **-men**) yachtsman *m inv*.

yachts·woman [ˈjɒtsˌwʊmən] N (*pl* **-women**) yachtswoman *f inv*.

yak¹ [jæk] N (*Zool*) yak *m inv*.

yak² [jæk] (*fam*) ① VI cicalare, cianciare.

② N cicaleccio.

yam [jæm] N (*plant, tuber*) igname *m*; (*sweet potato*) patata dolce.

Yank [jæŋk], **Yan·kee** [ˈjæŋkɪ] (*fam often pej*) ① N yankee *m/f inv*.

② ADJ yankee *inv*.

yank [jæŋk] ① N strattone *m*.

② VT tirare, dare uno strattone a; **to yank a nail out** strappare via un chiodo.

yap [jæp] (*of dog*) ① N guaito.

② VI (*dog*) guaire.

yap·ping [ˈjæpɪŋ] ① ADJ (*dog*) che guaisce.

② N guaiti *mpl*.

Yard [jɑːd] N (*Brit fam*): **the Yard** Scotland Yard *m inv*.

yard¹ [jɑːd] N **a** (*measure*) iarda (91,44 cm), yard *f inv*; **to sell sth by the yard** ≈ vendere qc al metro; **yards of** (*fig*) chilometri di

b (*Naut*) pennone *m*.

yard² [jɑːd] N (*courtyard, farmyard*) cortile *m*; (*Am: garden*) giardino; (*worksite*) cantiere *m*; (*for storage*) deposito; **builder's yard** deposito di materiale da costruzione; **back yard** (*Brit*) cortile sul retro; (*Am*) giardino sul retro.

yard·age [ˈjɑːdɪdʒ] N ≈ metraggio.

yard·arm [ˈjɑːdɑːm] N (*Naut*) varea.

yard·stick [ˈjɑːdstɪk] N (*fig*) metro, criterio.

yarn [jɑːn] N **a** (*wool, thread*) filato **b** (*tale*) storia, racconto; **to spin sb a yarn** raccontare a qn una grossa balla.

yash·mak [ˈjæʃmæk] N velo (*indossato dalle donne musul-* mane).

yawn [jɔːn] ① N sbadiglio; **to give a yawn** fare uno sbadiglio.

② VI sbadigliare; (*fig: hole, chasm*) aprirsi; **"yes", she yawned** "sì", disse con uno sbadiglio.

③ VT: **to yawn one's head off** non riuscire a smettere di sbadigliare.

yawn·ing [ˈjɔːnɪŋ] ADJ (*fig: gap, abyss*) spalancato(-a).

♦ **Y-chromosome** [ˈwaɪˌkrəʊməsəʊm] N cromosoma *m* Y.

yd(s). ABBR of **yard(s)**.

ye¹ [jiː] PRON (*old*) = **you** (*pl*).

ye² [jiː] DEF ART (*old: on shop signs*) = **the**.

yea [jeɪ] (*old*) ① ADV (*yes*) sì.

② N: **to count the yeas and the nays** (*votes*) contare i sì e i no.

yeah [jɛə] ADV (*fam*) sì.

year [jɪəʳ] N **a** (*gen*) anno; **this year** quest'anno; **every year** tutti gli anni, ogni anno; **all (the) year round** (per) tutto l'anno; **year in, year out** anno dopo anno; **year by year** OR **from year to year** col passar degli anni; **years and years ago** tanti anni fa; **from one year to the next** da un anno all'altro; **three times a year** tre volte all'anno; **in the year 1869** nell'anno 1869, nel 1869; **in the year of grace** nell'anno di grazia; **last year** l'anno scorso; **next year** (*looking to future*) l'anno prossimo *or* venturo; **the next year** (*in past time*) l'anno seguente *or* successivo; **he got 10 years** (*in prison*) si è beccato 10 anni; **it takes years** ci vogliono anni; **I met him a year last January** a gennaio fa un anno che l'ho conosciuto; **a year tomorrow** domani tra un anno; **I haven't seen her for years** non la vedo da anni, sono anni che non la vedo; **over the years** con gli anni; **she's three years old** ha tre anni; **she's in her fiftieth year** compierà cinquant'anni; **it's taken years off her** l'ha ringiovanita; **a** *or* **per year** all'anno

b (*Scol, Univ*) anno; **he's in the second year** è al secondo anno; **he was in my year at university** frequentavamo lo stesso anno di università

c (*of wine*) annata

d (*age*): **old/young for one's years** vecchio/giovane per

i suoi anni *or* per la sua età; **from her earliest years** fin dall'infanzia, fin dalla più tenera età; **he's getting on in years** ha i suoi anni ormai.

year·book ['jɪə‚bʊk] N annuario.

year·ling ['jɪəlɪŋ] N (*racehorse*) yearling *m inv.*

year·long ['jɪə'lɒŋ] ADJ di un anno.

year·ly ['jɪəlɪ] 1 ADJ annuale; **twice-yearly** semestrale.

2 ADV annualmente; **three times yearly** tre volte all'anno.

yearn [jɜ:n] VI: **to yearn for sb/sth** desiderare ardentemente qn/qc; **to yearn to do sth** struggersi dal desiderio di fare qc.

yearn·ing ['jɜ:nɪŋ] 1 ADJ (*desire*) intenso(-a); (*look, tone*) desideroso(-a), bramoso(-a).

2 N: **yearning (for)** desiderio struggente (di).

yearn·ing·ly ['jɜ:nɪŋlɪ] ADV con smania, con desiderio.

♦ **year-round** [‚jɪə'raʊnd] ADJ che dura tutto l'anno; **a year-round swimming pool** una piscina aperta tutto l'anno.

yeast [ji:st] N lievito; **dried yeast** lievito disidratato (*or* in polvere).

yeasty ['ji:stɪ] ADJ (*comp* -ier, *superl* -iest) (*smell, flavour*) di lievito.

yell [jɛl] 1 N urlo; **to give a yell** or **let out a yell** lanciare un urlo; **a yell of laughter** una fragorosa risata.

2 VI urlare.

3 VT (*order, name*) urlare.

yell·ing ['jɛlɪŋ] 1 ADJ urlante.

2 N urla *fpl.*

yel·low ['jɛləʊ] 1 ADJ (*comp* -er, *superl* -est) **a** (*colour*) giallo(-a); **to go** *or* **turn yellow** (*person*) diventare giallo (-a); (*leaf, paper*) ingiallire **b** (*fam pej: cowardly*) fifone (-a).

2 N (*colour*) giallo; (*of an egg*) rosso.

3 VI ingiallire.

♦ **yellow fever** N febbre *f* gialla.

yellow·hammer ['jɛləʊ‚hæmə'] N (*Zool*) zigolo giallo.

yel·low·ish ['jɛləʊɪʃ] ADJ giallastro(-a), giallognolo(-a).

♦ **Yellow Pages®** NPL (*Telec*): **the Yellow Pages** le pagine gialle ®.

♦ **Yellow Sea** N: **the Yellow Sea** il mar Giallo.

yelp [jɛlp] 1 N (*of dog*) guaito; (*of person*) strillo.

2 VI (*see n*) guaire, strillare.

yelp·ing ['jɛlpɪŋ] 1 ADJ (*dog*) che guaisce.

2 N guaiti *mpl.*

Yem·en ['jɛmən] N Yemen *m.*

Yem·eni ['jɛmənɪ] ADJ, N yemenita (*m/f*).

yen¹ [jɛn] N (*currency*) yen *m inv.*

yen² [jɛn] N (*fam*): **to have a yen to do sth** avere una gran voglia di fare qc.

yeo·man ['jəʊmən] N (*pl* -men) (*Brit old*) piccolo proprietario terriero.

♦ **Yeoman of the Guard** N Guardiano della Torre di Londra.

yep [jɛp] ADV (*fam*) = **yes**.

yes [jɛs] 1 ADV sì; **to say yes (to)** dire di sì (a); **don't you want any? — yes (I do)!** non ne vuoi? — ma sì!; **yes yes, but what if it doesn't?** sì, va bene, ma se non lo fa?.

2 N sì *m inv.*

♦ **yes man** N (*pej*) yes-man *m inv.*

yes·ter·day ['jɛstə‚deɪ] 1 ADV ieri; **yesterday morning/ evening** ieri mattina/sera; **the day before yesterday** l'altro ieri; **a week yesterday** (*past*) una settimana fa, ieri; **late yesterday** ieri in serata; **it rained all (day)**

yesterday ieri è piovuto tutto il giorno; **the great men of yesterday** i grandi uomini del passato.

2 N ieri *m inv.*

yes·ter·year ['jɛstə‚jɪə'] N (*old, liter*) il tempo andato.

yet [jɛt] 1 ADV **a** (*already, up to now, so far*) già; (*now, by now*) ancora; **I wonder if he's come yet** mi chiedo se non sia già arrivato; **not yet** non ancora; **he hasn't come yet** non è ancora arrivato; **it is not finished yet** non è ancora finito; **I needn't go (just) yet** non è ancora il momento di andare; **don't go (just) yet** non andare già via; **this is his best film yet** finora questo è il suo film migliore; **as yet** per ora, finora

b (*still*) ancora; **he may come yet** or **he may yet come** può ancora arrivare; **that question is yet to be decided** quella questione è ancora da decidere; **I'll do it yet!** prima o poi ce la farò!

c (*in addition, even*): **yet again** di nuovo; **yet another/ more** ancora un altro/più; **yet once more** ancora una volta; **a few days yet** ancora qualche giorno

d (*frm*): **nor yet** tanto meno; **I do not like him, nor yet his sister** lui non mi piace, e tanto meno sua sorella.

2 CONJ ma, tuttavia; **and yet** eppure, tuttavia; **it was funny, yet sad at the same time** era buffo e triste nel contempo; **and yet I enjoyed it** e tuttavia mi è piaciuto.

yeti ['jɛtɪ] N yeti *m inv.*

yew [ju:] N (*also:* **yew tree**) tasso.

Y-fronts® ['waɪ‚frʌnts] NPL mutande *fpl* da uomo (*con apertura davanti*).

YHA [‚waɪeɪtʃ'eɪ] N ABBR (*Brit*: = *Youth Hostels Association*) associazione degli ostelli della gioventù.

Yid·dish ['jɪdɪʃ] ADJ, N yiddish (*m*) *inv.*

yield [ji:ld] 1 N (*of land, mine*) resa; (*of investment*) rendita; (*of crops*) raccolto; **a yield of 5%** un profitto del 5%.

2 VT **a** (*produce: harvest, dividend*) fruttare; (*: results*) fornire, produrre; (*: information, opportunity*) fornire

b (*surrender*) cedere.

3 VI (*surrender*): **to yield (to)** cedere (a), arrendersi (a); (*break, collapse*) cedere; (*Am Aut*) dare la precedenza; **to yield to temptation** cedere alla tentazione

▶ **yield up** VT + ADV (*liter: secret*) svelare, rivelare.

yield·ing ['ji:ldɪŋ] ADJ (*person*) arrendevole; (*ground, surface*) cedevole.

yip·pee [jɪ'pi:] EXCL (*fam*) hurrà!

YMCA [‚waɪɛmsi:'eɪ] N ABBR (= *Young Men's Christian Association*) Y.M.C.A. *f.*

yob ['jɒb], **yob·bo** ['jɒbəʊ] N (*Brit fam*) teppista *m/f.*

yo·del ['jəʊdl] 1 VI fare lo jodel.

2 N jodel *m inv.*

yoga ['jəʊgə] N yoga *m inv.*

yo·ghurt, yo·ghourt, yo·gurt ['jɒgət] N yogurt *m inv.*

yoke [jəʊk] 1 N **a** (*of oxen, also fig*) giogo; **under the yoke of** (*fig*) sotto il giogo di **b** (*on dress*) sprone *m.*

2 VT (*also:* **yoke together**: *oxen*) aggiogare.

yo·kel ['jəʊkəl] N zotico(-a), villano(-a).

yolk [jəʊk] N tuorlo, rosso (d'uovo).

yomp [jɒmp] VI (*Brit Mil fam*) percorrere un terreno accidentato.

yon·der ['jɒndə'] ADV (*old*): **(over) yonder** laggiù, là.

yonks [jɒnks] ADV (*Brit fam*): **I haven't seen her for yonks** è un secolo che non la vedo.

Yorks [yɔ:ks] ABBR (*Brit*) = Yorkshire.

York·shire pud·ding ['jɔ:kʃə'pʊdɪŋ] N *tipo di bignè salato, cotto in forno, che accompagna il tradizionale arrosto della domenica in Gran Bretagna.*

you [juː] PERS PRON
a (*subject*: *singular*) tu; (: *plural*) voi; (: *singular*: *polite form*) lei; (: *plural*: *very formal*) loro;
▷**you** *and I* **will go** tu ed io andiamo
▷**you angel!** sei un angelo!
▷**you** *are* **very kind** è molto gentile da parte tua (*or sua etc*)
▷*here* **you are!** eccoti!
▷**that dress just** *isn't* **you** quel vestito proprio non ti si addice
▷**you** *Italians* voi *or* voialtri italiani
▷**if I** *was or were* **you** se fossi in te (*or lei etc*)
b (*see a*) (*object*: *direct*) ti; la; vi; loro (*after verb*); (: *indirect*) ti; le; vi; loro (*after verb*);
▷**I'll** *phone* **you later** ti chiamo più tardi/la chiamerò più tardi/vi chiamerò più tardi/chiamerò loro più tardi
▷**I'll** *see* **you tomorrow** ci vediamo domani
▷**I gave it** *to* **you** te l'ho dato; gliel'ho dato; ve l'ho dato; l'ho dato loro
c (*see a*) (*stressed, after preposition, in comparisons*) te; lei; voi; loro;
▷**it's** *for* **you** è per te (*or lei etc*)
▷**she's younger** *than* **you** è più giovane di te (*or lei etc*)
▷**I** *told* **you to do it** ho detto a TE (*or* LEI *etc*) di farlo
d (*impersonal*: *one*) si;
▷**you** *can't* **do that!** non si fanno queste cose!
▷**fresh air** *does* **you good** l'aria fresca fa bene
▷**you** *know* **who/what** sappiamo chi/cosa
▷**you** *never* **can tell** non si sa mai
▷**you** *never* **know** non si sa mai.

you'd [juːd] = **you would, you had.**
you'll [juːl] = **you will, you shall.**
young [jʌŋ] **1** ADJ (*comp* **-er**, *superl* **-est**) (*gen*) giovane; (*vegetables*) novello(-a); (*offender*) minorenne; **a young man** un giovanotto; **a young lady** una signorina; **they have a young family** hanno dei bambini piccoli; **in my young days** quand'ero giovane; **she's not so young as she was** non è più tanto giovane; **the younger son** il figlio minore; **he is two years younger than her** ha due anni meno di lei; **if I were 15 years younger** se avessi 15 anni di meno; **you're only young once** si è giovani una volta sola; **she's young at heart** è giovane di spirito; **he looks young for his age** sembra più giovane di quanto sia in realtà; **the night is young** la notte è appena cominciata; **to grow** *or* **get younger** ringiovanire; **the younger generation** la nuova generazione.
2 NPL (*of animals*) piccoli *mpl*, prole *fsg*; **the young** (*young people*) i giovani.
young·ish [ˈjʌŋɪʃ] ADJ abbastanza giovane.
young·ster [ˈjʌŋstəʳ] N (*child*) bambino(-a); (*young person*) giovane *m/f*.
your [jʊəʳ] POSS ADJ **a** SG il/la tuo(-a); PL i/le tuoi/tue; (*sg*: *polite form*) il/la suo(-a); PL i/le suoi/sue; PL il/la vostro(-a); PL i/le vostri(-e); (*sg*: *polite*: *very formal*) il/la loro; (: *pl*) i/le loro; **your house** la tua (*or* sua *etc*) casa; **your brother** tuo (*or* suo *etc*) fratello
b (*impersonal*: *one's*): **it's bad for your health** danneggia la salute; **your average Italian** l'italiano medio.
you're [jʊəʳ] = **you are.**
yours [jʊəz] POSS PRON, SG il/la tuo(-a); PL i/le tuoi/tue; PL

il/la vostro(-a); PL i/le vostri(-e); (*sg*: *polite form*) il/la suo(-a);(: *pl*) i/le suoi/sue; (*pl*: *very formal*) il/la loro; PL i/le loro; **yours is red, mine is green** il tuo (*or* suo *etc*) è rosso, il mio è verde; **this is yours** questo è il tuo (*or* suo *etc*); **a friend of yours** un tuo (*or* suo *etc*) amico; **yours faithfully/sincerely** (*in letters*) distinti/cordiali saluti; **what's yours?** (*fam*: *drink*) tu che prendi?
your·self [jəˈsɛlf] PERS PRON (*pl* **yourselves** [jəˈsɛlvz]) **a** (*reflexive*: *sg*) ti; (: *pl*) vi; (*sg*: *polite*) si; (*pl*: *very formal*) si; **have you hurt yourself?** ti sei (*or* si è) fatto male?; **have you hurt yourselves?** vi siete (*or* si sono) fatti male?
b (*emphatic*: *sg*) tu stesso(-a); (: *pl*) voi stessi(-e); (*sg*: *polite*) lei stesso(-a); (*pl*: *very formal*) loro stessi(-e); **you yourself told me** me l'hai detto proprio tu, tu stesso me l'hai detto
c (*after prep*) te, te stesso(-a); (: *polite*) lei, lei stesso(-a); (: *pl*) voi, voi stessi(-e); (: *very formal*) loro, loro stessi (-e); **(all) by yourself** (tutto) da solo
d (*impersonal*: *reflexive*) se stessi; (: *emphatic*) se stessi; (: *after prep*) sé, se stessi; see also **oneself**.
youth [juːθ] N **a** giovinezza, gioventù *f*; **in early youth** nella prima giovinezza; **in my youth** da giovane, quando ero giovane **b** (*pl* **youths** [juːðz]) (*boy*) ragazzo, giovane *m* **c** PL (*young people*) giovani *mpl*; **the youth of today** i giovani di oggi.
♦ **youth club** N circolo giovanile.
youth·ful [ˈjuːθfʊl] ADJ (*air, figure, manner*) giovanile; (*mistakes*) di gioventù.
youth·ful·ness [ˈjuːθfʊlnɪs] N giovinezza; **youthfulness of appearance** aspetto giovanile.
♦ **youth hostel** N ostello della gioventù.
♦ **youth leader** N animatore(-trice) (di circolo giovanile).
♦ **youth movement** N movimento giovanile.
you've [juːv] = **you have.**
yowl [jaʊl] **1** N (*of dog, person*) latrato; (*of cat*) miagolio.
2 VI (*see n*) latrare; miagolare.
yo-yo [ˈjəʊjəʊ] N yo-yo *m inv*.
yr ABBR = **year.**
♦ **Y-shaped** [ˈwaɪˌʃeɪpt] ADJ a forma di ipsilon.
YT [ˌwaɪˈtiː] ABBR (*Canada*)= **Yukon Territory**.
YTS [ˌwaɪtiːˈɛs] N ABBR (*Brit*: = *Youth Training Scheme*) *programma di tirocinio per giovani tramite sovvenzioni al datore di lavoro.*
yucky, yuk·ky [ˈjʌkɪ] ADJ (*fam*) schifoso(-a).
Yu·go·slav [ˌjuːgəʊˈslɑːv] ADJ, N jugoslavo(-a).
Yu·go·sla·via [ˌjuːgəʊˈslɑːvɪə] N Jugoslavia; **the former Yugoslavia** l'ex Jugoslavia.
Yu·go·sla·vian [ˌjuːgəʊˈslɑːvɪən] ADJ, N jugoslavo(-a).
yuk [jʌk] EXCL (*fam*) puh!, puah!
yuk·ky [ˈjʌkɪ] ADJ = **yucky.**
yule [juːl] N = **Yuletide.**
♦ **yule log** N (*cake*) tronchetto di Natale; (*piece of wood*) *ceppo nel caminetto a Natale.*
Yule·tide [ˈjuːlˌtaɪd] N (*old*) periodo natalizio.
yum·my [ˈjʌmɪ] ADJ (*comp* **-ier**, *superl* **-iest**) (*fam*: *food*) delizioso(-a), squisito(-a).
♦ **yum-yum** [ˌjʌmˈjʌm] EXCL gnam gnam!
yup·pie [ˈjʌpɪ] N yuppie *m/f inv*.
YWCA [ˌwaɪdʌbljuːsiːˈeɪ] N ABBR (= *Young Women's Christian Association*) *organizzazione che mette a disposizione ostelli per donne.*

Z

Z ABBR (*atomic number*) Z.

Z, z [zɛd, *Am* zi:] N (*letter*) Z, z *for m inv*; **Z for Zebra** ≈ Z come Zara.

Za·ire [zɑːˈiːəʳ] N lo Zaire *m*.

Zam·bia [ˈzæmbɪə] N lo Zambia *m*.

Zam·bian [ˈzæmbɪən] ADJ, N zambiano(-a).

zany [ˈzeɪnɪ] ADJ (*comp* **-ier**, *superl* **-iest**) (*fam*) pazzoide, un po' pazzo(-a).

zap [zæp] VT (*fam: destroy*) far fuori; (*Comput*) cancellare; (*TV*) fare lo zapping.

zeal [ziːl] N (*fervour*) zelo; (*enthusiasm*) entusiasmo; **zeal for** ansia di.

zeal·ot [ˈzɛlət] N zelota *m/f*.

zeal·ous [ˈzɛləs] ADJ (*supporter, believer, worker*) zelante.

zeal·ous·ly [ˈzɛləslɪ] ADV (*support*) con zelo, in modo zelante.

zeb·ra [ˈziːbrə] N zebra.

♦ **zebra crossing** N (*Brit*) strisce *fpl* (pedonali), zebre *fpl*.

zed [zɛd], (*Am*) **zee** [ziː] N (*letter name*) zeta *m or f inv*.

Zen [zɛn] N Zen *m inv*.

zen·ith [ˈzɛnɪθ] N (*liter: of civilization*) culmine *m*; (*of career*) apice *m*; (*Astron*) zenit *m inv*.

zeph·yr [ˈzɛfəʳ] N (*liter*) zefiro.

zep·pe·lin [ˈzɛpəlɪn] N zeppelin *m inv*.

zero [ˈzɪərəʊ] 1 N zero; **5 below zero** 5 sotto zero. 2 ADJ (*altitude, gravity*) zero *inv*; (*fam: interest, hope*) nullo(-a)

▶ **zero in on** VI + ADV + PREP (*target*) essere puntato(-a) su; (*problem, subject*) concentrarsi su.

♦ **zero hour** N ora zero.

♦ **zero option** N (*Pol*) opzione *f* zero.

♦ **zero-rated** [ˌzɪərəʊˈreɪtɪd] ADJ (*Brit Comm*) ad aliquota zero.

zest [zɛst] N **a** (*enthusiasm*): **zest (for)** gusto (per), entusiasmo (per); (*fig: spice*) sapore *m*; **zest for living** gioia di vivere **b** (*Culin: of orange, lemon*) buccia.

zest·ful [ˈzɛstfʊl] ADJ entusiasta.

Zeus [zjuːs] N Zeus *m*.

zib·et [ˈzɪbɪt] N zibetto.

zig·zag [ˈzɪɡˌzæɡ] 1 N zigzag *m inv*.

2 VI zigzagare; **to zigzag across/down/up** attraversare/scendere/salire a zigzag.

3 ADJ a zigzag.

Zim·ba·bwe [zɪmˈbɑːbwɪ] N lo Zimbabwe.

Zim·ba·bwean [zɪmˈbɑːbwɪən] ADJ dello Zimbabwe.

Zim·mer® [ˈzɪməʳ] N (*also:* **Zimmer frame**: *Brit*) deambulatore *m*.

zinc [zɪŋk] 1 N zinco. 2 ADJ di zinco.

zing [zɪŋ] N (*fam*) verve *f inv*.

Zi·on·ism [ˈzaɪəˌnɪzəm] N sionismo.

Zi·on·ist [ˈzaɪənɪst] 1 ADJ sionistico(-a). 2 N sionista *m/f*.

zip [zɪp] 1 N **a** (*Brit: also:* **zip fastener**) cerniera (lampo), zip *m inv* **b** (*fam: energy*) energia, forza; **put a bit of zip into it** mettici un po' di entusiasmo.

2 VT: **to zip up** chiudere la cerniera di; **zipped pockets** (*with zips*) tasche con cerniera; (*zipped up*) tasche con la cerniera chiusa; **he zipped the bag open/closed** ha aperto/chiuso la cerniera della borsa.

3 VI: **to zip past** sfrecciare davanti; **to zip along to the shops** fare una corsa per comprare qc.

♦ **zip code** N (*Am Post*) codice *m* di avviamento postale.

zip·per [ˈzɪpəʳ] N (*Am*) = **zip 1a**.

zip·py [ˈzɪpɪ] ADJ (*fam*) scattante.

zir·con [ˈzɜːkən] N zircone *m*.

zith·er [ˈzɪðəʳ] N cetra.

zo·di·ac [ˈzəʊdɪæk] N zodiaco.

zom·bie [ˈzɒmbɪ] N zombie *m/f inv*; **like a zombie** come uno zombie.

zon·al [ˈzəʊnl] ADJ zonale.

zone [zəʊn] 1 N zona; **danger zone** zona pericolosa; **war zone** zona di guerra. 2 VT zonizzare.

zon·ing [ˈzəʊnɪŋ] N zonizzazione *f*.

zonked [zɒŋkt] ADJ (*fam: exhausted*) distrutto(-a).

zoo [zuː] N zoo *m inv*, giardino zoologico.

♦ **zoo keeper** N guardiano di zoo.

zoo·logi·cal [ˌzəʊəˈlɒdʒɪkəl] ADJ zoologico(-a).

♦ **zoological garden** N (*frm*) giardino zoologico.

zo·olo·gist [zəʊˈɒlədʒɪst] N zoologo(-a).

zo·ol·ogy [zəʊˈɒlədʒɪ] N zoologia.

zoom [zu:m] ⒈ N (*sound*) rombo.

⒉ VI (*go fast*): **to zoom off** sfrecciare via; **he zoomed past at 120 mph** ci sfrecciò accanto a 120 miglia all'ora

▶ **zoom in** VI + ADV (*Phot, Cine*): **to zoom in (on sb/sth)**

zumare (su qn/qc)

▶ **zoom out** VI + ADV allargare l'immagine.

♦ **zoom lens** N zoom *m inv*.

zoo·tech·nics [ˌzəʊəˈtɛknɪks] NSG zootecnia.

zuc·chi·ni [zuːˈkiːnɪ] N, PL INV (*Am*) zucchina.

Zulu [ˈzuːluː] ADJ, N zulù *(m/f) inv*.

Zü·rich [ˈzjʊərɪk] N Zurigo *f*.

LANGUAGE IN USE

LINGUA E FUNZIONI

LINGUA E FUNZIONI LANGUAGE IN USE

INTRODUCTION

One of the chief aims of foreign language learners is to be able to express themselves naturally and correctly, and in a way which is appropriate to the particular situation. A bilingual dictionary is an invaluable tool, of course, providing translations for all the words needed to construct sentences in the other language. The fact remains, however – and teachers and experts in the field frequently point this out – that putting one's ideas into another language is apt to be an awkward and frustrating process, resulting in clumsy constructions and a distorted version of what one wants to say.

It is for this reason that we have added a further resource, to be used alongside the dictionary itself.

As can be seen from the index we have identified various key functions that language can perform. Hundreds of examples, with translations, have been grouped according to the function they exemplify. Particular attention has been paid to such concepts as obligation, possibility and permission, which are expressed very differently in Italian. All functions, however, present their own problems, depending on the particular context, the particular person addressed, and linguistic conventions.

As well as examples of spoken language, this section also contains useful examples of private and business letters, job applications, and CVs, together with announcements of engagements, marriages and deaths, and invitations to parties.

There is a particularly detailed section relating to essay writing, where you will find extended examples demonstrating techniques for structuring, developing and concluding a reasoned argument. The translations here are inevitably less literal than they have to be in a dictionary, and serve to illustrate that an utterance in one language cannot always be adequately rendered by a word for word translation.

Where appropriate the examples are graded according to whether they are neutral or emphatic, or according to register, under such headings as *formal, informal, more directly, less directly* and so on. Guidance on such matters is useful, indeed often indispensable, if one is to express oneself appropriately in the foreign language.

INTRODUZIONE

Uno dei principali obiettivi di chi impara una lingua straniera è quello di riuscire ad esprimersi in quella lingua in modo naturale, corretto ed adeguato alla situazione. Il dizionario bilingue è uno strumento prezioso e, se fatto bene, consente di trovare le traduzioni per tutte le parole che ci servono a costruire frasi e periodi in una lingua che non è la nostra. Va detto però che, come affermano numerosi docenti ed esperti, il passaggio, di necessità "frazionato", dalla propria lingua all'espressione in una lingua straniera può portare a distorcerne significati e costruzioni, con risultati non del tutto soddisfacenti.

Per questo motivo abbiamo voluto creare questa sezione che proponiamo come uno strumento complementare al dizionario bilingue.

Come si può vedere nell'indice abbiamo identificato quelle che riteniamo **funzioni** importanti dell'espressione linguistica e raccolto centinaia di esempi che abbiamo tradotto e raggruppato a seconda della funzione espressa. In particolare ci siamo voluti soffermare su concetti quali l'obbligo, la possibilità e il permesso che, per l'uso dei verbi modali inglesi, risultano particolarmente ostici dal punto di vista sintattico e lessicale. Ogni funzione, comunque, presenta problemi intrinseci legati al contesto, alle convenzioni linguistiche e la destinatario del messaggio.

La sezione comprende non solo esempi d conversazione tratti da contesti reali, ancora una volta utilizzando i corpora elettronici di lingua a nostra disposizione, ma anche esempi di lettere commerciali, lettere personali, domande di impiego, curriculum vitae e poi partecipazioni di nozze, inviti a battesimo e così via. Particolarmente approfondito è il capitolo sulla dissertazione, con esempi articolati ed esaustivi che illustrano come strutturare, sviluppare e concludere un argomento, e dove le traduzioni, di necessità meno letterali di quanto debbano essere in un dizionario, fanno luce sui complessi meccanismi di corrispondenza tra le due lingue.

Quando è stato ritenuto utile, le frasi sono state proposte in una successione di intensità e registro linguistico introdotta da titoletti quali *formale, informale, in modo più diretto, meno diretto* e così via, indicazioni preziose e spesso cruciali per la corretta espressione nella lingua straniera.

1 Suggerimenti

1.1 Per dare suggerimenti

You might like to think it over before giving me your decision — *forse preferiresti...*
If you were to give me the negative, **I could** get copies made — *se vuoi... potrei...*
You could help me clear out my office, **if you don't mind** — *potresti... se non ti dispiace*
We could stop off in Venice for a day or two, **if you like** — *potremmo... se vuoi...*
I've got an idea - **let's organize** a surprise birthday party for Megan! — *... organizziamo...*
My idea was to tour the area by car — *pensavo di...*
If you've no objection(s), I'll ask them round for dinner on Sunday — *se non hai obiezioni...,*
If I were you, I'd be very careful — *se fossi in te...*
If you ask me, you'd better take some extra cash — *secondo me faresti meglio a...*
I'd be very careful not to commit myself at this stage — *mi guarderei bene dal...*
I would recommend (that) you discuss it with him before making a decision — *ti suggerisco di...*
It could be in your interest to have a word with the owner first — *sarebbe meglio per te se...*
There's a lot to be said for living alone — *... presenta un sacco di vantaggi*

In modo meno diretto

Say you were to approach the problem from a different angle — *mettiamo che...*
In these circumstances, **it might be better to** wait — *... sarebbe meglio...*
It might be a good thing o **a good idea to** warn her about this — *forse sarebbe il caso di...*
Perhaps it might be as well to look now at the debate and prepare our own feasibility study — *forse dovremmo...*
Perhaps you should take up birdwatching — *forse dovresti...*
If I may make a suggestion, a longer hemline might suit you better — *se mi è permesso un suggerimento...*
If I may be permitted to remind you of one of the golden rules of journalism: try not to split infinitives — *se mi è concesso farti presente...*
If I might be permitted to suggest something, installing bigger windows would make the office much brighter — *se mi è concesso dare un suggerimento...*

In modo diretto

I suggest that you go to bed and try to sleep — *ti consiglio di...*
I'd like to suggest that you seriously consider taking a long holiday — *ti consiglierei di...*
We propose that half the fee be paid in advance, and half on completion of the job — *proponiamo che...*
Because she is basically rather a serious child, **it is quite important that** you develop her sense of fun and adventure — *... è molto importante che...*
I am convinced that this would be a dangerous step to take — *sono sicura che...*
I cannot put it too strongly: **you really must** see a doctor — *... devi assolutamente*

Facendo una domanda

How do you fancy a holiday in Australia? — *che ne diresti di...*
I was thinking of using this opportunity to meet some chess players. **How about it?** — *... che ne dici?*
What would you say to a trip up to town next week? — *che ne diresti di...*
Would you like to go away on a second honeymoon? — *ti piacerebbe...*
What if you try ignoring her and see if that stops her complaining? — *e se...*
What you need is a change of scene. **Why not** go on a cruise or to a resort? — *... perché non...*
Suppose o **Supposing** you left the kids with your mother and came out with me? — *e se...*
How would you feel about taking a calcium supplement? — *che ne pensi di...*
Have you ever thought of starting up a magazine of your own? — *hai mai pensato di...*
Would you care to have lunch with me? — *posso invitarla a pranzare con me?*

1.2 Per chiedere un'idea a qualcuno

What would you do if you were me? — *cosa faresti se fossi in me?*
Have you any idea how I should go about it to get the best results? — *hai idea di come dovrei...*
I've no idea what to call our pet snake: **have you any suggestions?** — *... cosa suggerisci?*
I can only afford to buy one of them: **which do you suggest?** — *... quale mi consigli?*
I wonder if you could suggest where we might go for a few days? — *potresti suggerirmi...*
I'm a bit doubtful about where to start — *non so bene...*

2 Consigli

2.1 Per chiedere un consiglio

I'd like o **I'd appreciate your advice on** personal pensions

I'd be grateful if you could advise me on how to approach this problem

What would you advise me to do in the circumstances?

Would you advise me to seek promotion within this firm or apply for another job?

Do you think I ought to tell the truth if he asks me where I've been?

Would an apple tree grow in this situation? If not, **what would you recommend**?

How would you go about it **if you were me** o What would you do **if you were me**?

gradirei qualche consiglio su...

vi sarei grato se poteste darmi un consiglio su...

cosa mi consiglierebbe di fare...

secondo lei, dovrei...

pensi che dovrei...

... cosa mi consiglia?

... al mio posto...

2.2 Per dare un consiglio

In modo indiretto

It might be wise o **sensible** o **It might be a good idea to** consult a specialist

It might be better to think the whole thing over before making any decisions

You'd be as well to state your position at the outset, so there is no mistake

You would be well-advised to invest in a pair of sunglasses if you're going to Morocco

You'd be ill-advised to have any dealings with this firm

It would certainly be advisable to book a table

It is in your interest to keep your dog under control if you don't want it to be reported

Do be sure to read the small print before you sign anything

Try to avoid putting her back up; she'll only make your life a misery

Whatever you do, don't drink the local schnapps

sarebbe opportuno...

sarebbe meglio...

faresti bene a...

faresti bene a...

sarebbe un errore...

si consiglia di...

è nel suo interesse...

ti raccomando di...

cerca di evitare di...

ma soprattutto, non...

In modo diretto

I think you ought to o **should** seek professional advice

I would urge you to reconsider selling the property

I would advise you to pay up promptly before they take you to court

I would strongly advise you to reconsider this decision

My advice would be to have nothing to do with them

Take my advice and don't rush into anything

I would advise against calling in the police unless they threaten you with violence

I'd be very careful not to commit myself at this stage

If you ask me, you'd better smarten up your ideas if you want to get ahead

In your shoes o **If I were you**, I'd be thinking about moving on

If you want my opinion, I'd go by air to save time

If you want my advice, I'd steer well clear of them

Might I be allowed to offer a little advice? - talk it over with a solicitor before you go any further

penso che dovresti...

le raccomando vivamente di...

le consiglierei di...

le consiglio caldamente di...

ti consiglierei di...

segui il mio consiglio...

ti sconsiglio di...

starei molto attento a non...

secondo me, faresti meglio...

se fossi in te...

se vuoi sapere come la penso, io al posto tuo...

se vuoi un consiglio...

mi permette di darle un consiglio?...

2.3 Per dare un avvertimento

It's really none of my business but **I don't think** you should get involved...

A word of caution: watch what you say to him if you want it to remain a secret

I should warn you that he's not an easy customer to deal with

Take care not to burn your fingers, as caramel sticks and continues to burn

Make sure that o **Mind that** o **See that you don't** say anything they might find offensive

I'd think twice about sharing a flat with the likes of him

It would be sheer madness to attempt to drive without your glasses

You risk a long delay in Amsterdam **if** you come back by that route

io non penso che...

un consiglio:...

ti avverto che...

fai attenzione a non...

soprattutto non...

ci penserei su due volte prima di...

sarebbe una vera follia...

rischi... se...

3 Offerte

I would be delighted to help out, if I may

It would give me great pleasure to invite your mother to dinner on Saturday

We would like to offer you the post of Sales Director

I hope you will not be offended if I offer a contribution towards your expenses

Do let me know if I can help in any way

If we can be of any further assistance, **please do not hesitate to** contact us

Usando una domanda diretta

May o **Can I offer you** a drink?

Could I give you a hand with your luggage?

Would you like me to find out more about it for you?

Would you allow me to pay for dinner, at least?

Is there anything I can do to help you find suitable accommodation?

Shall I pick you up from work on Friday afternoon?

What if I were to call for you in the car?

Say we were to offer you a 10% increase plus a company car, how would that sound?

sarei ben felice di...

mi farebbe molto piacere...

siamo onorati di offrirle...

spero di non offenderla, ma vorrei offrire...

mi faccia sapere se posso ...

se possiamo... non esitate a...

posso offrirti...

posso...

vuole che...

mi permette di...

posso far qualcosa per...

vuoi che...

e se...

mettiamo che...

4 Richieste

Would you please drop by on your way home and pick up the papers you left here?

Could you please try to keep the noise down while I'm studying?

Would you mind looking after Hannah for a couple of hours tomorrow?

Could I ask you to watch out for anything suspicious in my absence?

In comunicazioni scritte

I should be grateful if you could confirm whether it would be possible to increase my credit limit to £5000

We should be glad to receive your reply by return of post

We would ask you not to use the telephone for long-distance calls

You are requested to park at the rear of the building

We look forward to receiving confirmation of your order within 14 days

Kindly inform us if you require alternative arrangements to be made

puoi (per piacere)...

potresti per cortesia...

ti dispiacerebbe...

posso chiederti di...

vi sarei estremamente grato se poteste...

gradiremmo...

siete pregati di non...

siete pregati di...

restiamo in attesa di...

vogliate gentilmente farci sapere se...

In modo più indiretto

I would rather you didn't breathe a word to anyone about this

I would appreciate it if you could let me have copies of the best photographs

I was hoping that you might find time to visit your grandmother

I wonder whether you could spare a few pounds till I get to the bank?

I hope you don't mind if I borrow your exercise bike for half an hour

It would be very helpful o **useful if you could** have everything ready a week in advance

If it's not too much trouble, would you pop my suit into the dry cleaners on your way past?

You won't forget to lock up before you leave, will you?

preferirei che voi non...

vi sarei grato se poteste...

speravo che tu potessi...

chissà se potresti...

spero non ti dispiaccia se ...

ci sarebbe di grande aiuto se poteste...

se non ti è di troppo disturbo, puoi...

non dimenticarti di...

5 Paragoni

The streets, though wide for China, are narrow **in comparison with** English ones	... paragonate a...
Some of the claims that are made about his status simply cannot be defended **if you compare** him **with** other writers	... se lo si paragona a...
I visited France to **compare and contrast** what was being done there and here	... vedere e paragonare...
It is interesting to note **the similarities and the differences between** the two approaches	... le somiglianze e le differenze fra...
In contrast to the opulent Kirov, the Northern Ballet is a modest company	in confronto a...
The loss of power because of the lower octane rating of paraffin **as opposed to** petrol is about fifteen per cent	... a differenza di...
Unlike other loan repayments, those to the IMF cannot simply be rescheduled	a differenza di...
The quality of the paintings is disappointing **beside** that of the sculpture section	... vicino a...
If we set the actual cost **against** our estimate, we can see how inaccurate our forecast was	se si paragona... con...
Whereas burglars often used to make off only with video recorders, they now also tend to empty the fridge	mentre...
Property rights are conferred on both tenants and home owners; **the former** are common, **the latter** are private	i primi..., i secondi...
It's (something) **like** my car **but** o **only** it's much faster	assomiglia un po' a... ma o solo...

Per dire che qualcosa è migliore

Orwell was, indeed, **far superior to** him intellectually	... di gran lunga superiore a...
St Petersburg **has the edge over** Moscow and other central cities in the availability of some foods	... è leggermente superiore a...
Michela was astute beyond her years and altogether **in a class of her own**	... unica nel suo genere

Per dire che qualcosa è peggiore

Matthew's piano playing **is not a patch on** his little sister's	... non vale neanche la metà di...or ... è ben peggio di...
The chair he sat in **was nowhere near as** comfortable as the one for clients	... era ben lontana dall'essere...
Ella doesn't rate anything that **doesn't measure up to** Shakespeare or, at the very least, Tennessee Williams	... che non regga il confronto con...
The sad truth was that **he was never in the same class as** his friend	... non è mai stato alla pari di...
The opposition **is no match for** the government, with its massive majority	... non è in grado di tenere testa a...
Her brash charms **don't bear comparison with** Marlene's sultry sex appeal	... non si può paragonare a...
Commercially-made ice-cream **is far inferior to** the home-made variety	... è di gran lunga inferiore a...

Per paragonare cose simili

The new system of computer control for traffic lights costs **much the same as** conventional traffic lights but reduces traffic delays by 13%	... praticamente quanto...
When it comes to performance, **there's not much to choose between** o **there's not much difference between** them	... non c'è molta differenza fra...
Chick brought the drums from the back of the band down to the front as an instrument **of equal value** o **equal in value to** the horns and piano	... di valore uguale a...
The impact could have been **equivalent to** explosion of 250 of the biggest hydrogen bombs	... equivalente a...
English literature written by the people of ex-colonies should be regarded as being **on a par with** the writings of native-born English people	... alla pari con...
In Kleinian analysis, the psychoanalyst's role **corresponds to** that of mother	... corrisponde a...
The immune system **can be likened to** o **compared to** a very complicated electronic network with switches and feedback circuits	... può essere paragonato a...
There was a close resemblance between her **and** her son	c'era una notevole somiglianza fra... e...
It's swings and roundabouts - what you win in one round, you lose in another	a conti fatti il risultato non cambia...

Per paragonare cose diverse

In Portsmouth we have a specialist naval history library with a national reputation. **You cannot compare** that **with** a branch library in a suburb	... non si può paragonare... a
Important as these are locally, **they cannot compare with** the international significance of those superb cliffs	... non possono essere paragonate a...
There's no comparison between Waddle now **and** Waddle three years ago	non c'è confronto fra... e...
Experts claim **there is no correlation between** the complexity of a fraud **and** the value of the return	... non c'è alcuna correlazione fra... e...
His books **have little in common with** those approved by the Communist Party	... hanno ben poco in comune con...
The modern army, in fact, **bears little resemblance to** the army of 1940	... assomiglia ben poco a...

6 Opinioni

6.1 Per chiedere l'opinione di qualcuno

What do you think of the new Managing Director? — *cosa ne pensi di...*

What is your opinion on women's rights? — *qual è la tua opinione...*

What are your thoughts on the way forward? — *hai qualche idea su...*

What is your attitude to people who say there is no such thing as sexual inequality? — *cosa ne pensi di...*

What are your own feelings about the way the case was handled? — *cosa ne pensi di come...*

How do you see the next stage developing? — *come prevedi che...*

How do you view an event like the Birmingham show in terms of the cultural life of the city? — *come valuti...*

I would value your opinion on how best to set this all up — *mi piacerebbe avere la tua opinione su...*

I'd be interested to know what your reaction is to the latest report on food additives — *sarei interessato...*

6.2 Per esprimere la propria opinione

In my opinion, eight years as President is enough, and sometimes too much, for any man to serve in that capacity — *a mio avviso...*

As I see it, everything depended on Karlov being permitted to go to Finland — *secondo me...*

I feel that there is an epidemic of fear about cancer which is not helped by the regular flow of publicity about the large numbers of people who die of it — *ho la sensazione che...*

Personally, I believe the best way to change a government is through the electoral process — *personalmente trovo che...*

It seems to me that the successful designer leads the public — *mi sembra che...*

I am under the impression that he is essentially a man of peace — *ho l'impressione che...*

I have an idea that you and Nivelle are going to do something very effective in the course of three weeks — *ho l'idea che...*

I am of the opinion that the rules should be looked at and refined — *sono dell'opinione che...*

I'm convinced that we all need a new vision of the future — *sono convinto che...*

I daresay there are so many names that you get them mixed up once in a while — *..., immagino*

We're prepared to prosecute the company, which to my mind has committed a criminal offence — *siamo pronti a...*

Most parts of the black market activity, **from my point of view**, is not, strictly speaking, illegal — *..., dal mio punto di vista,...*

As far as I'm concerned, Barnes had it coming to him — *per me,...*

It's a matter of mutual accommodation, nothing more. **That's my view of the matter** — *... questo è il mio punto di vista*

It is our belief that to be proactive is more positive than being reactive — *è nostra convinzione...*

If you ask me, there's something a bit odd going on — *se vuoi sapere cosa ne penso...*

If you want my opinion, if you don't do it soon, you'll lose the opportunity altogether and you'll be sorry — *se vuoi il mio parere...*

6.3 Per rispondere senza esprimere un'opinione

Would I say she had been a help? **It depends** what you mean by help — *... dipende da...*

It could be seen as a triumph for capitalism but **it depends on your point of view** — *... è una questione di punti di vista*

It's hard o **difficult to say** whether I identify with the hippy culture or not — *è difficile dire...*

I'm not in a position to comment on whether the director's accusations are well-founded — *non sono in grado di...*

I'd prefer not to comment on operational decisions taken by the service in the past — *preferirei non esprimere un giudizio su...*

I'd rather not commit myself at this stage — *peferirei non impegnarmi...*

I don't have any strong feelings about which of the two companies we decide to use for the job — *non ho alcuna preferenza su...*

This isn't something **I've given much thought to** — *... su cui abbia riflettuto seriamente*

I know nothing about the workings of the female mind — *ignoro completamente...*

7 Gusti e preferenze

7.1 Per chiedere a qualcuno cosa preferisca

Would you like to visit the castle, while you are here?   *ti piacerebbe...*
How would you feel about asking Simon to join us?   *cosa ne pensi di...*
What do you like doing best when you're on holiday?   *cosa ti piace fare più di tutto...*
What's your favourite way to relax at the end of a hectic day?   *tu cosa fai...*
Which of the two proposed options **do you prefer**?   *quale... preferisci?*
We could either go to Rome or stay in Florence - **which would you rather do**?   *... cosa preferisci fare?*

7.2 Per parlare di ciò che piace

I'm very keen on gardening   *mi piace moltissimo...*
I'm very fond of white geraniums and blue petunias   *mi piacciono particolarmente...*
I really enjoy a good game of squash after work   *mi piace moltissimo...*
There's nothing I like more than a quiet night in with a good book   *niente mi piace di più che...*
I have a weakness for rich chocolate gateaux   *ho un debole per...*
I have a soft spot for the rich peaty flavours of Islay malt   *ho un debole per...*

7.3 Per parlare di ciò che non piace

Acting **isn't really my thing** - I'm better at singing   *... non è il mio forte...*
Watching football on television **isn't my favourite pastime**   *... non è il mio passatempo preferito*
Some people might find it funny but **it's not my kind of** humour   *... non è il mio tipo di...*
I enjoy playing golf, although American-style greens - fast and full of bumps - **are not my cup of tea**   *... non siano esattamente il mio genere*
Sitting for hours on motorways **is not my idea of fun**   *non trovo per niente divertente...*
The idea of walking home from here at 10 or 11 o'clock at night **doesn't appeal to me**   *... non mi sorride affatto*
I've gone off the idea of cycling round Holland   *mi è passata la voglia di...*
I am not enthusiastic about growing plants directly in greenhouse soil because of the risk of soil diseases   *non mi convince molto l'idea di...*
I'm not keen on seafood   *non vado pazza per...*
I don't like the fact that he always gets away with not helping out in the kitchen   *non mi piace il fatto che...*
I dislike laziness since I'm such an energetic person myself   *non mi piace per niente...*
There's nothing I dislike more than having to go to work in the dark   *non c'è niente che odi di più...*
I have a particular aversion to the religious indoctrination of schoolchildren   *ho una particolare avversione per...*
What **I hate most** is waiting in queues for buses   *odio al massimo...*
I can't stand o **can't bear the thought of** seeing him   *non sopporto l'idea di...*
I find it intolerable that people like him should have so much power   *trovo intollerabile che...*

7.4 Per dire cosa si preferisce

I'd prefer to o **I'd rather** wait until I have enough money to go by air   *preferirei...*
I'd prefer not to o **I'd rather not** talk about it just now   *preferirei non...*
I'd prefer you to o **I'd rather** you put your comments in writing   *preferirei che tu...*
I'd prefer you not to o **I'd rather you didn't** invite him   *preferirei che tu non...*
I like the blue curtains **better than** o **I prefer** the blue curtains to the red ones   *mi piacciono di più...*

7.5 Per dire che qualcosa ci è indifferente

I don't mind at all - let's do whatever is easiest   *non importa...*
I have no particular preference   *non ho delle preferenze particolari*
It's all the same to me whether he comes or not   *per me è uguale se...*
I don't feel strongly about the issue of privatization   *non sono molto interessato a...*
It doesn't matter which method you choose to use as long as the end result is acceptable   *non ha importanza...*
It makes no odds whether you have a million pounds or nothing, we won't judge you on your wealth   *non cambia nulla...*
I really don't care what you tell her as long as you tell her something   *non m'interessa...*

8   Intenzioni e desideri

8.1   Per chiedere a qualcuno cosa intenda fare

Do you intend to o **mean to** o **Will you** take the job?	*hai intenzione di...*
What flight **do you mean to** o **intend to** take?	*intendi...*
Did you mean to o **intend to** tell him about it, or did it just slip out?	*avevi l'intenzione di...*
What do you intend to do o **What are your intentions**?	*cosa pensi di fare?*
What do you propose to do with the money?	*cosa conti di fare...*
What did you have in mind for the rest of the programme?	*cosa avevi in mente...*
Have you anyone in mind for the job?	*hai qualcuno in mente...*

8.2   Per esprimere le proprie intenzioni

We're toying with the idea of releasing a compilation album of some of the bands we've worked with	*stiamo meditando di...*
I'm thinking of retiring next year	*sto pensando di...*
I'm hoping to go and see her when I'm in Paris	*spero di...*
What **I have in mind** is **to** start a small software business	*ho in mente di...*
I studied history, **with a view to** becoming a politician	*... per...*
We bought the land **in order to** o **for the purpose of** farming it	*... per...*
We plan to move o **We are planning** on moving next year	*contiamo di...*
Our aim in o **Our object** in buying the company is to provide jobs	*il nostro obiettivo...*
I aim to reach Africa in three months	*conto di...*

In modo più convinto

I am going to o **I intend to** sell the car as soon as possible	*ho l'intenzione di...*
I went to London, **intending to** visit her o **with the intention of** visiting her, but she was away on business	*... con l'idea di...*
I have made up my mind to o **I have decided** to go to Japan	*ho deciso...*
We have every intention of winning a sixth successive championship	*abbiamo tutta l'intenzione di...*
I have set my sights on recapturing the title	*miro a...*
My overriding ambition is to overthrow the President	*il mio più grande desiderio...*
I resolved to do everything in my power to bring the affair to a satisfactory conclusion	*ho deciso di...*

8.3   Per dire ciò che non si ha intenzione di fare

I don't mean to offend you, but could you take your shoes off before you come in?	*non voglio...*
I don't intend to pay unless he completes the job	*non intendo pagare...*
I have no intention of accepting the post	*non ho alcuna intenzione di...*
We are not thinking of advertising this post at the moment	*non stiamo pensando di...*
We do not envisage making changes at this late stage	*non prevediamo di...*

8.4   Per dire cosa piacerebbe fare

I'd like to see the Sistine Chapel some day	*mi piacerebbe...*
I want to work abroad when I leave college	*voglio...*
We want her to be an architect when she grows up	*vogliamo...*
I'm keen to see more students take up zoology	*vorrei vedere...*

Con più entusiasmo

I desperately want to leave and make my fortune in Paris	*muoio dalla voglia di...*
I'm dying to go to Australia but I can't afford it	*muoio dalla voglia di...*
My ambition is to go straight from being an enfant terrible to a grande dame	*la mia massima aspirazione...*
I insist on speaking to the manager	*insisto...*

8.5   Per dire quello che non si vuole fare

I would prefer not to o **I would rather not** have to speak to her about this	*preferirei non...*
I wouldn't want to have to change my plans just because of her	*non vorrei...*
I don't want to o **I have no wish to** o **I have no desire to** take the credit for something I didn't do	*non voglio o desidero...*
I refuse to be patronized by the likes of her	*mi rifiuto di...*

9 Permesso

9.1 Per chiedere l'autorizzazione a fare qualcosa

Can I o **Could I** borrow your car this afternoon?	*posso o potrei...*
Can I have the go-ahead to order the supplies?	*mi date l'autorizzazione a...*
Are we allowed to say what we're up to or is it top secret at the moment?	*siamo autorizzati a...*
Would it be all right if I arrived on Monday instead of Tuesday?	*andrebbe bene se...*
Would it be possible for us to leave the car in your garage for a week?	*potremmo...*
We leave tomorrow. **Is that all right by you?**	*... ti va bene?*
Do you mind if I come to the meeting next week?	*ti dispiace se...*
Would it bother you if I invited him?	*ti dispiace se...*
Would you let me come into partnership with you?	*mi permettete di...*
Would you have any objection to sailing at once?	*avresti delle obiezioni a...*
With your permission, I'd like to ask some questions	*se mi permette, mi piacerebbe...*

In modo più indiretto

Is there any chance of borrowing your boat while we're at the lake?	*c'è qualche speranza di...*
I wonder if I could possibly use your telephone?	*potrei forse...*
Might I be permitted to suggest the following ideas?	*posso permettermi di...*
May I be allowed to set the record straight?	*mi è concesso di...*

9.2 Come concedere il permesso

You can have anything you want	*puoi...*
You are allowed to visit the museum, as long as you apply in writing to the Curator first	*è permesso...*
It's all right by me if you want to skip the Cathedral visit	*non ho problemi se...*
You have my permission to be absent for that week	*siete autorizzati a...*
There's nothing against her go**ing** there with us	*niente le impedisce di...*
The Crown **was agreeable to** hav**ing** the case called on March 23	*... ha acconsentito a...*
I do not mind if my letter is forwarded to the lady concerned	*non ho niente in contrario se...*
You have been authorised to use all necessary force to protect relief supply routes	*siete autorizzati a...*
We should be happy to allow you to inspect the papers here	*vi autorizziamo volentieri a...*

In modo più deciso

If you need to keep your secret, **of course you must** keep it	*... devi ovviamente...*
By all means charge a reasonable consultation fee	*non esitate a...*
I have no objection at all to your quoting me in your article	*non ho niente in contrario se...*
We would be delighted to have you	*saremo felicissimi di...*

9.3 Per negare il permesso

You can't o **you mustn't** go anywhere near the research lab	*non potete...*
I don't want you to see that Milner again	*non voglio che tu...*
I'd rather you didn't give them my name	*preferirei che tu non...*
I wouldn't want you to be asking around about them too much	*preferirei che tu non...*
You're not allowed to leave the ship until relieved	*non siete autorizzati a...*
I've been forbidden to swim for the moment	*mi hanno proibito di...*
I've been forbidden alcohol by my doctor	*... mi ha proibito...*
I couldn't possibly allow you to pay for all this	*non posso assolutamente lasciarti...*
You must not enter the premises without the owners' authority	*non è permesso...*
We cannot allow the marriage to take place	*non possiamo permettere che...*

In modo formale

I absolutely forbid you to take part in any further search	*ti proibisco assolutamente di...*
You are forbidden to contact my children	*le proibisco di...*
Smoking **is strictly forbidden** at all times	*... è assolutamente vietato...*
It is strictly forbidden to carry weapons in this country	*è fatto divieto di...*
We regret that it is not possible for you to visit the castle at the moment, owing to the building works	*purtroppo non potete...*

10   Obbligo

10.1   Per dire che si è obbligati a fare qualcosa

Go and see Pompeii - **it's a must!**	... *non te la puoi perdere!*
You need to be very good, **no two ways about it**	... *non c'è scelta*
You've got to o **You have to** be back before midnight	*devi...*
You need to o **You must** have an address in Prague before you can apply for the job	*devi...*
I have no choice: this is how **I must** live and I cannot do otherwise	*devo...*
He was forced to ask his family for a loan	*fu obbligato a...*
Jews **are obliged to** accept the divine origin of the Law	*è fatto obbligo a... di...*
A degree **is indispensable** for future entrants to the profession	... *è indispensabile...*
Party membership **is an essential prerequisite of** a successful career	... *è un prerequisito essenziale per...*
It is essential to know what the career options are before choosing a course of study	*è essenziale...*
A dog collar **is a requirement of law**	... *è obbligatorio per legge*
Wearing the kilt **is compulsory** for all those taking part	... *è obbligatorio...*
One cannot admit defeat, **one is driven to** keep on trying	... *si è costretti a...*
We have no alternative but to fight	*non abbiamo altra scelta che...*
Three passport photos **are required**	*sono necessarie...*
Soldiers **must not fail to** take arms against those who are in front of them	... *devono assolutamente...*
You will go directly to the headmaster's office and wait for me there	*vai...*

10.2   Per sapere se si ha l'obbligo di fare qualcosa

Do I have to o **Have I got to** be home by midnight?	*devo...*
Does one have o **need to** book in advance?	*si deve...*
Is it necessary to look at the problem across the continent?	*è necessario...*
Ought I to tell my colleagues?	*dovrei...*
Should I tell my boyfriend about my fantasy about painting his face and dressing him in my petticoat?	*dovrei...*
Am I meant to o **Am I expected to** o **Am I supposed to** fill in this bit of the form?	*devo...*

10.3   Per dire che non si è obbligati a fare qualcosa

I don't have to o **I haven't got to** be home so early now the nights are lighter	*non devo...*
You don't have to o **You needn't** go there if you don't want to	*non sei obbligato a...*
You are not obliged to o **You are under no obligation to** invite him	*non sei obbligato a...*
It is not necessary to o **It is not compulsory to** o **It is not obligatory to** have a letter of acceptance but it does help	*non è necessario o obbligatorio...*
The Inland Revenue **does not expect you to** pay the assessed amount	... *non esige che si...*

10.4   Per dire quello che non è permesso fare

On no account must you be persuaded to give up the cause	*in nessun caso devi...*
You are not allowed to sit the exam more than three times	*non si può...*
Smoking **is not allowed** in the dining room	*non è permesso...*
You mustn't show this document to any unauthorised person	*non devi...*
These are tasks **you cannot** ignore, delegate or bungle	... *che non si possono...*
You're not supposed to o **You're not meant to** use this room unless you are a club member	*non siete autorizzati a...*

In modo più formale

It is forbidden to bring cameras into the gallery	*è proibito o vietato...*
I forbid you to return there	*ti proibisco di...*
You are forbidden to talk to anyone while the case is being heard	*vi è proibito o vietato...*
Smoking **is forbidden** o **is prohibited** o **is not permitted** in the dining room	... *è proibito o vietato...*

11.1   Per dire che si è d'accordo

I fully agree with you o **I totally agree with you** on this point	*sono del tutto d'accordo con te...*
We are in complete agreement on this	*siamo completamente d'accordo*
I entirely take your point about the extra vehicles needed	*capisco perfettamente quello che pensi di...*
I think **we see completely eye to eye** on this issue	*... la vediamo esattamente allo stesso modo*
I feel that **his comments are quite correct**	*... le sue osservazioni siano esatte*
I talked it over with the chairman and **we are both of the same mind**	*... siamo dello stesso avviso*
You're quite right in pointing at the distribution system as the main problem	*hai ragione a...*
We have been thinking along the same lines	*la pensiamo allo stesso modo*
We share your views on the proposed expansion of the site	*condividiamo il vostro punto di vista...*
My own experience certainly bears out o **confirms** what you say	*... è confermato dalla mia esperienza personale*
Our opinion coincides with yours on all the important points	*le nostre opinioni coincidono...*
It's true that you had the original idea but many other people worked on it	*è vero che...*
As you have quite rightly pointed out, we still have to convince management	*come tu hai giustamente fatto notare...*
I have to concede that the results are quite eye-catching	*devo dare atto che...*
I have no objection to this being done	*non ho obiezioni a...*
We do not object to paying our share	*non abbiamo obiezioni a...*
I agree up to a point	*sono d'accordo fino ad un certo punto*

In modo informale

Go for a drink instead of working late? **Sounds good to me!**	*... buona idea!*
That's a lovely thought!	*ma che pensiero gentile!*
I'm all for encouraging a youth section in video clubs such as ours	*ci sto a...*
I couldn't agree with you more	*sono perfettamente d'accordo con te*

In modo più formale

I am delighted to endorse wholeheartedly your campaign	*sono ben lieto di dare il mio completo appoggio a...*
Our conclusions are entirely consistent with your findings	*le nostre conclusioni confermano...*
Independent statistics **corroborate** those of your researcher	*... corroborano...*
We applaud the group's decision to stand firm on this point	*approviamo...*

11.2   Per esprimere l'accordo con quanto proposto

This certainly **seems the right way to go about it**	*... sembra il modo giusto di procedere*
I will certainly give my backing to such a scheme	*non mancherò di dare il mio appoggio a...*
We certainly welcome this development in Stirling	*siamo lieti di...*

In modo più informale

It's a great idea/I like the sound of that	*è un'ottima idea*
I'll go along with Ted's proposal that we open the club up to women	*sono d'accordo con...*

In modo più formale

This solution **is most acceptable to us**	*... ci trova d'accordo*
The proposed scheme **meets with our approval**	*... ha la nostra approvazione*
This is a proposal **which deserves our wholehearted support**	*... che merita tutto il nostro sostegno*
I shall do my best **to fall in with** her wishes	*... conformarmi a...*
We assent to o **We give our assent to** your plan to develop the site	*diamo il nostro assenso a...*

11.3   Per dire che si è d'accordo con quanto chiesto

Of course **I'll be happy to** organise it for you	*sarò lieto di...*
I'll do as you suggest and send him the documents	*seguirò il vostro consiglio...*
There's no problem about getting tickets for him	*non è un problema...*
His promise **gives the go-ahead for** British businessmen to open up trade	*... dà il via a...*

In modo più formale

Reputable builders **will not object to** this reasonable request	*... non faranno obiezioni a...*
We should be delighted to cooperate with you in this enterprise	*saremmo lieti di...*
The army stated **it would comply** with the ceasefire if the other side did	*... rispetterà ...*

12 Dissenso

12.1 Per esprimere dissenso

There must be some mistake - **it can't possibly** cost as much as that	... non è possibile che...
I'm afraid (that) your doctor **is quite wrong** if he has told you that vasectomies cannot be reversed	... si sbaglia...
You're wrong in thinking that I haven't understood	sbagli a credere che...
The article **is mistaken in** claiming that debating the subject is a desperate waste of public money	... sbaglia nel...
The report **diverges from the facts** as I know them	... non corrisponde ai fatti...
Surveys **do not bear out** Mrs Fraser's assumption that these people will return to church at a later date	... non comprovano...
I cannot agree with you on this	non sono d'accordo con te su...
We cannot accept the view that R and D spending or rather the lack of it explains the decline of Britain	non condividiamo affatto l'opinione secondo la quale...
To say we should forget about it, no **I cannot go along with that**	... non sono per niente d'accordo
We must agree to differ on this one	rassegnamoci al fatto che le nostre idee divergono su questo punto
I think **it might be better if you thought it over again**	... sarebbe meglio se voi riconsideraste la questione
I'm afraid I think **the whole thing sounds rather unlikely**	... tutto ciò sembra poco probabile

Con più convinzione

This is most emphatically not the case	non è assolutamente così
I entirely reject his contentions	respingo assolutamente...
We explicitly reject the implication in your letter	respingiamo categoricamente...
I totally disagree with the previous two callers	non sono per niente d'accordo con...
This is your view of the events: **it is certainly not mine**	... non è certamente la mia
I cannot support you on this matter	non posso darti il mio appoggio...
Surely you can't believe that he'd do such a thing?	ovviamente non crederai che...

12.2 Per dire che non si è d'accordo con quanto proposto

Con decisione

I'm dead against this idea	sono assolutamente contrario a...
Right idea, wrong approach	l'idea è buona, la tattica è sbagliata
I will not hear of such a thing	non voglio neanche sentir parlare di...
It is not feasible to change the schedule at this late stage	non è possibile...
This **is not a viable alternative**	... non è fattibile
Running down the street shouting "Eureka" has emotional appeal but **is the wrong approach**	... ma non è così che si fa

Con minore decisione

I'm not too keen on o **don't think much of this idea**	non mi piace tanto...
This doesn't seem to be the right way of dealing with the problem	non ci sembra il modo giusto di...
While we are grateful for the suggestion, **we are unfortunately unable to** implement this change	... siamo spiacenti di non poter...
I regret that I am not in a position to accept your kind offer	sono desolato di non poter...

12.3 Per dire che non si intende fare qualcosa

I wouldn't dream of doing a thing like that	non mi sognerei neanche di...
I'm sorry but **I just can't** do it	... mi è semplicemente impossibile
I cannot in all conscience leave those kids in that atmosphere	in tutta coscienza non posso...

Con maggiore decisione

This is quite out of the question for the time being	è fuori discussione...
I won't agree to o **I can't agree to** any plan that involves your brother	mi oppongo a...
I refuse point blank to have anything to do with this affair	mi rifiuto categoricamente di...

... e in modo formale

I am afraid I must refuse	mi dispiace ma devo rifiutare
I cannot possibly comply with this request	non posso assolutamente soddisfare...
It is unfortunately impracticable for us to commit ourselves at this stage	sfortunatamente ci è impossibile...
In view of the proposed timescale, **I must reluctantly decline to** take part	... mi trovo purtroppo costretto a declinare dal...

13 Approvazione

13.1 Come approvare un'affermazione

I couldn't agree (with you) more	*sono interamente del vostro avviso*
I couldn't have put it better myself	*io stesso non avrei saputo esprimerlo meglio*

We must oppose terrorism, whatever its source. - **Hear, hear!** — *... bravo!*
I endorse his feelings regarding the condition of the Simpson memorial — *condivido...*

13.2 Come approvare una proposta

We recognize the merits of this scheme — *riconosciamo i vantaggi di...*
This project **is worthy of our attention** — *... merita la nostra attenzione*
We view your proposal to extend the site **favourably** — *consideriamo favorevolmente...*
There are considerable advantages in this alternative method you propose — *... comporta notevoli vantaggi*
Any game which is as clearly enjoyable as this **meets with my approval** — *... incontra tutta la mia approvazione*
Skinner's plan **deserves our total support** o **our wholehearted approval** — *... merita tutto il nostro sostegno*
I shall certainly give it my backing — *darò sicuramente il mio appoggio*
Thank you for sending the draft agenda: **I like the look of it very much** — *... mi pare vada benissimo*
We are all very enthusiastic about o **very keen on** his latest proposals — *accogliamo con entusiasmo...*
This is just the sort of thing I wanted — *è esattamente quello che volevo*
This is exactly what I had in mind — *è proprio ciò che avevo in mente*
It's just the job! — *è proprio quello che ci vuole!*

13.3 Come approvare un'idea

You're quite right to wait before making such an important decision — *hai perfettamente ragione a...*
I entirely approve of the idea — *approvo totalmente...*
I'd certainly go along with that! — *sono completamente d'accordo!*
I'm very much in favour of that sort of thing — *sono completamente favorevole a...*
What an excellent idea! — *che magnifica idea!*

13.4 Come approvare ciò che si è fatto

I applaud Noble's perceptive analysis of the problems — *lodo...*
I have a very high opinion of their new teaching methods — *ho un'altissima opinione di...*
I have a very high regard for the work of the Crown Prosecution Service — *tengo in grande considerazione...*
I think very highly of the people who have been leading thus far — *ho una grande stima per...*
I certainly admire his courage in telling her exactly what he thought of her — *di sicuro ammiro...*
I must congratulate you on the professional way you handled the situation — *mi voglio congratulare con lei per...*
I entirely appreciate the enormous risk they all took — *mi rendo benissimo conto di...*
I can thoroughly recommend the event to field sports enthusiasts — *raccomando vivamente...*

14 Disapprovazione

This doesn't seem to be the right way of going about it — *non mi sembra il modo migliore di...*
I don't think much of what this government has done so far — *non ho una grande opinione di...*
I can't say I'm pleased about what has happened — *non posso dire di essere soddisfatto di...*

As always, Britain **takes a dim view of sex** — *... vede di malocchio...*
We have a low opinion of o **poor opinion of** opportunists like him — *non abbiamo gran rispetto per...*
They **should not have** refused to give her the money — *non avrebbero dovuto...*
He was quite wrong to repeat what I said about her — *ha avuto torto...*
I cannot approve of o **support** any sort of testing on live animals — *... non possono avere la mia approvazione o il mio sostegno*

We are opposed to all forms of professional malpractice — *siamo contrari a...*
We condemn anything which could have the effect of damaging race relations — *condanniamo...*
I must object to the tag 'soft porn actress' — *non posso accettare...*
I'm very unhappy about your (idea of) going off to Turkey on your own — *non mi piace affatto...*
I'm fed up with having to wait so long for payments to be made — *sono stufo di...*
I've had (just) about enough of this whole supermodel thing — *comincio ad averne abbastanza di...*
I can't bear o **stand** people who smoke in restaurants — *non sopporto...*
I strongly disapprove of such behaviour — *disapprovo totalmente...*
How dare he say that! — *come osa...*

15 Scuse

15.1 Come scusarsi

I'm really sorry, Steve, **but** we won't be able to come on Saturday	*mi dispiace molto... ma...*
I'm sorry I have to say this to you but you're not as good a risk as you were	*mi dispiace doverglielo dire...*
I'm sorry that your time has been wasted	*mi dispiace che...*
Apologies if I seemed obsessed with private woes last night	*scusa se...*
I must apologize for what happened. The man responsible has been disciplined	*vi prego di accettare le mie scuse per...*
I owe you an apology. I didn't think you knew what you were talking about	*ti devo delle scuse...*
Please accept our apologies if this has caused you any inconvenience	*vi preghiamo di accettare le nostre scuse...*
Sorry, Nanna. **I didn't mean to** upset you	*... non volevo...*
The general back-pedalled, saying that **he had had no intention of** offend**ing** the German government	*... non aveva alcuna intenzione di...*
Please forgive me for feel**ing** sorry for myself	*vi prego di perdonarmi se...*
Do forgive me for be**ing** a little abrupt	*vogliate scusarmi se...*

15.2 Ammettendo di essere responsabile

I admit I submitted the second gun for inspection, in the knowledge that you had used my own for the killing	*ammetto di...*
I have no excuse for what happened. I was in love with Duncan, yes, but I did not realise to what lengths I would go to to keep him	*non ho scusanti per...*
It is my fault that our marriage is on the rocks	*è colpa mia se...*
The Government **is not entirely to blame but neither is it innocent**	*... non è completamente colpevole, ma neanche completamente innocente*
I should never have let him rush out of the house in anger	*non avrei mai dovuto...*
Oh, but **if only I hadn't** made Freddy try to get my bag back!	*... se solo non avessi...*
I hate to admit that the old man was right, but **I made a stupid mistake**	*... ho fatto uno stupido errore*
My mistake was in fail**ing** to push my concerns and convictions as hard as I could have done	*il mio errore è stato quello di...*
My mistake was to arrive wearing a jacket and neat black polo-neck jumper In December and January the markets raced ahead, and I missed out on that.	*ho commesso l'errore di...*
That was my mistake	*mea culpa!*

15.3 Per dire che si è dispiaciuti

I'm very upset about her decision but when only one partner wants to make an effort you're fighting a losing battle	*... mi addolora molto...*
It's just a bit of a shame that, on close inspection, the main vocalists look like Whitney Houston and Lionel Richie	*... è un po' un peccato che...*
I feel awful but I couldn't stand by and watch him make a fool of himself, someone had to tell him to shut up	*mi spiace moltissimo...*
I'm afraid I can't help you very much	*purtroppo non posso...*
It is a pity that my profession can make a lot of money out of the misfortunes of others	*è triste...*
It is unfortunate that the matter should have come to a head when the Western allies may be on the brink of military engagement	*è un peccato che...*
David and I **very much regret that** we have been unable to reach a working agreement for the future	*... siamo estremamente dispiaciuti di...*
The accused **bitterly regrets** this incident and it won't happen again	*... è terribilmente dispiaciuto di...*
We regret to inform you that the post of Editor has now been filled	*ci dispiace doverla informare che...*

15.4 Declinando la propria responsabilità

I didn't do it on purpose, it just happened	*non l'ho fatto apposta...*
Excuse me, but **I was under the impression that** these books were for women	*... mi era sembrato di capire che...*
We are simply trying to protect the interests of our horses and owners	*stiamo semplicemente tentando di...*
I know how this hurt you but **I had no choice.** I had to put David's life above all else	*... non ho avuto scelta...*
We were obliged to accept their conditions	*siamo stati obbligati a...*
We are unhappy with 1.5%, but **we have no alternative but to** accept	*... non possiamo far altro che...*
I must ask you to accept my assurance that **I had nothing to do with** the placing of any advertisement	*... non ho avuto niente a che fare con...*
A Charlton spokesman assured Sheffield supporters that it **was a genuine error** and **there was no intention** to mislead them	*... si è trattato solo di un errore... non c'era affatto l'intenzione di...*

11 North Street
Barnton
BN7 2BT

19th August 1994

The Personnel Director,
Messrs. J. M. Kenyon Ltd.,
Firebrick House,
Clifton,
MC45 6RB

Dear Sir or Madam,

With reference to your advertisement in today's <u>Guardian</u>, I wish to apply for the post of systems analyst.

I enclose my curriculum vitae. Please do not hesitate to contact me if you require any further details.

Yours faithfully,

Rosalind A Williamson

CURRICULUM VITAE

Name:	Rosalind Anna WILLIAMSON
Address:	11 North Street, Barnton, BN7 2BT, England
Telephone:	Barnton (0294) 476230
Date of Birth:	6.5.1969
Marital Status:	Single
Nationality:	British
Qualifications:	B.A. 2nd class Honours degree in Italian with French, University of Newby, England (June 1991)
	A-levels: Italian (A), French (B), English (D) (1987)
	O-Levels in 9 subjects. (1985)
Present Post:	Assistant Personnel Officer, Metal Company plc, Barnton (since January 1993)
Previous Employment	Nov. 1991 - Jan. 1992: Personnel trainee Metal Company plc.
	Oct. 1987 - June 1991: Student, University of Newby

Skills, Interests and Experience: fluent Italian & French; adequate German; some Russian; car owner and driver (clean licence); riding & sailing.

The following have agreed to provide references:

Ms. Alice Bluegown, Personnel Manager, Metal Company plc, Barnton, NB4 3K1

Dr. I.O. Sono, Department of Italian, University of Newby, Newby, SR13 2RR

16.1 Come iniziare la lettera

In reply to your advertisement for a Trainee Manager in today's Guardian/ in the Independent of 30 November 1994, I would be grateful if you would send me further details of the post, along with an application form

I wish to apply for the post of bilingual correspondent, as advertised in this week's Euronews

I would like to work in Britain in my summer vacation

I am writing to ask if there is any possibility of work in your company

in riferimento al vostro annuncio...

vorrei sottoporre la mia candidatura per il posto di...

mi piacerebbe lavorare...

vi sarei grato se voleste farmi sapere se ci sono possibilità di impiego...

16.2 Come presentare le precedenti esperienze di lavoro

I have three **years' experience of** office work/this kind of work

I can use a word processor

As well as speaking fluent English, **I have a working knowledge of** German and **a reading knowledge of** Swedish.

I have **good commercial Italian**

I am currently working in this field/a related field

As you will see from my CV, I have worked abroad before

Although I have no experience of this type of work, **I have** had other jobs and can supply references

My current salary is ... per annum with pay

ho... anni di esperienza...

ho buona conoscenza PC

...ho una buona conoscenza del... e sono in grado dileggere...

Ho una buona conoscenza dell'italiano commerciale

attualmente lavoro...

come risulta dal mio CV...

sebbene non abbia previa esperienza di... ho tuttavia...

la mia remunerazione attuale è...

16.3 Per spiegare le proprie motivazioni

I would like to work in Britain for six months before starting university

I would like to make better use of my languages

I am keen to work in public relations/banking

I feel my experience would be of value to your company

mi piacerebbe lavorare in...

mi piacerebbe sfruttare meglio...

desidero inserirmi nel campo di...

penso che la mia esperienza possa essere utile...

16.4 Come concludere la lettera

I will be available from the end of April

I am available for interview at any time

I would be glad to supply further details

Please do not hesitate to contact me for further information

Please do not contact my current employers

I enclose a s.a.e./an international reply coupon

sono disponibile a partire da...

mi tengo a vostra disposizione per un eventuale colloquio

sarò lieto di fornirvi ulteriori informazioni

non esitate a contattarmi...

vi sarei estremamente riconoscente se evitaste di contattare il mio attuale datore di lavoro

accludo...

16.5 Per accettare o rifiutare un'offerta di lavoro

Thank you for your letter of 20 March. **I will be pleased to attend for interview** at your Manchester offices on Thursday 7 April at 10am

I would like to confirm my acceptance of the post of Marketing Executive, commencing 2 February

I would be delighted to accept this post. However, would it be possible to postpone my starting date until 8 May?

Having given your offer much careful thought, **I regret that I am unable to accept**

... sarò onorata di incontrarvi per un colloquio...

desidero comunicarvi che sono lieto di accettare...

sono onorato di accettare la posizione. Tuttavia...

... sono infinitamente spiacente di non poter accettare

16.6 Per chiedere e dare referenze

In my application for the position of German lecturer, I have been asked for two referees and **I wondered whether you would mind if I gave your name** as one of them

Ms Lee has applied for the post of Marketing Executive with our company. **We would be grateful if you would let us know whether you would recommend her for the position**

Your reply will be treated in the strictest confidence

... le sarei estremamente riconoscente se mi autorizzasse a fare il suo nominativo...

... le saremo riconoscenti se volesse farci pervenire la sua opinione in proposito

la sua risposta verrà trattata con la massima riservatezza

17.1   La corrispondenza commerciale

James & Hedgehopper Limited
MASTER CUTLERS
Railway Arcade, Harley SG16 4BD
Tel: Harley (0123) 99876

29th January, 1995

Dr. T. Armitage
65 Middlewich Street,
Addenborough,
AG3 9LL

Dear Sir,

   Thank you for your letter of 22nd January. We still stock the type of knife
that you are looking for, and are pleased to enclose our catalogue and price list.
We would draw your attention to the discount prices which are operative until
12th March on this range of goods.

   Yours faithfully
for JAMES & HEDGEHOPPER LTD

William Osgood.

William Osgood
Managing Director

Smith, Jones & Robertson Limited
RAINWEAR MANUFACTURERS
Block 39, Newtown Industrial Estate, Newtown SV7 3QS Tel: 0965 477366

Our ref: SAL/35/IM
12th August 1994
Your Ref: JCB/JO

Messrs. Kidsfunwear Ltd.,
3 High Street,
Barnton, BN17 2EJ

For the attention of Mr. J. Brown

Dear Sir,

   Thank you for your enquiry about our children's
rainwear. We have pleasure in enclosing our latest catalogue
and current price list, and would draw your attention
particularly to our SUNFLOWER range. We are prepared to
offer the usual discount on these items, and we look forward
to receiving your order.

Yours faithfully

Ian MacIntosh.

Ian MacIntosh
Sales Department

Come richiedere informazioni e come rispondere

We see o **note** from your advertisement in the latest edition of the Healthy Holiday Guide that your are offering salmon fishing holidays in Scotland, and **would be grateful if you would send us** full details of prices and dates available between 14 July and 30 August

abbiamo appreso da... e vi saremmo estremamente grati se poteste inviarci...

I read about the Association for Improvements in the Maternity Services in your journal and would be very interested to learn more about your activities. **Please send me details of** membership

ho appreso dell'esistenza di ... e vi sarei estremamente grata se poteste inviarmi informazioni più precise circa...

In response to your enquiry of 8 March, **we have pleasure in enclosing** full details on our activity holidays in Cumbria, **together with** our price list, which is valid until January 1996

a seguito della vostra lettera del... ci pregiamo includere... e...

Thank you for your enquiry about the Association for the Conservation of Energy (ACE). **I have enclosed** a leaflet on our background, **as well as** a list of the issues we regularly campaign on. **Should you wish** to join ACE, a membership application form is also enclosed

vi ringraziamo della vostra richiesta di informazioni circa... accludo... con... nel caso in cui vogliate...

Ordinazioni e come rispondere

We would like to place an order for the following items:

desideriamo ordinare...

Please find enclosed our order no. 3011 for ...

alla presente si acclude l'ordinativo n...

The enclosed order is based on your current price list

la fattura acclusa...

I wish to order a can of "Buzz off!" wasp repellent **and enclose a cheque for** £2.50

vorrei ordinare... e accludo un assegno di...

Thank you for your order of 16 June, which will be despatched within 30 days

vi ringraziamo del vostro ordinativo in data...

We acknowledge receipt of your order no. 3570 and advise that the goods will be despatched within 7 working days

con la presente accusiamo ricevuta del vostro ordinativo n... .

We regret that the goods you ordered are temporarily out of stock

siamo desolati di comunicarvi che le merci da voi ordinate sono momentaneamente esaurite

Please allow 28 days for delivery

vi comunichiamo che saranno necessari 28 giorni per la consegna

La consegna

Our delivery time is 60 days from receipt of order

i nostri tempi di consegna sono di...

We await confirmation of your order

attendiamo conferma del vostro ordinativo

We confirm that the goods were despatched on 4 July

vi diamo conferma che la merce è stata spedita in data...

We cannot accept responsibility for goods damaged in transit

non possiamo accettare alcuna responsabilità per quanto riguarda...

Reclami

We have not yet received the items ordered on 22 January

non abbiamo ancora ricevuto...

We wish to draw your attention to an error in the consignment

desideriamo segnalarvi...

Unfortunately, the goods were damaged in transit

purtroppo...

The goods received differ significantly from the description in your catalogue

gli articoli ricevuti non corrispondono alla descrizione che appare nel vostro catalogo

If the goods are not received by 20 October, **we shall have to cancel our order**

... ci troveremo purtroppo costretti ad annullare il nostro ordine

Pagamento

The total amount payable/outstanding is ...

la cifra da regolare ammonta a...

We would be grateful if you would attend to this account immediately

vi saremmo estremamente grati se...

Please remit payment by return

vogliate farci pervenire il saldo a stretto giro di posta

Full payment/the balance **is due within** 14 working days from receipt of goods...

è dovuto entro...

We enclose a cheque for ... **in settlement of your invoice no.** 2003L/58

con la presente vi inviamo... a regolamento della vostra fattura n....

We must point out an error in your account and **would be grateful if you would adjust your invoice** accordingly

... vi saremmo estremamente riconoscenti se voleste rettificare la vostra fattura...

This mistake was due to an accounting error, and **we enclose a credit note for** the sum involved

... vi preghiamo di accettare un buono di credito per...

Thank you for your cheque for ... in settlement of our invoice. **We look forward to doing further business with you in the near future**

vi ringraziamo dell'assegno dell'ammontare di ... e ci teniamo a vostra disposizione per ulteriori ordinativi

17

17.2 La corrispondenza generale

11 South Street
BARCOMBE
BN7 2BT

14th March 1994

Dear Betty,

It seems such a long time since we last met and caught up with each other's news. However, I'm writing to say that Peter and I plan to take our holiday this summer in the Lake District, and we'll be driving past Preston on the M.6 some time during the morning of Friday, July 23rd. Will you be at home then? Perhaps we could call in? It would be lovely to see you and Alan again and to get news of Janie and Mark. Do let me know whether Friday, 23rd is convenient. We would expect to arrive at your place around 11 a.m. or so, and hope very much to see you then.

With love from

Susan.

65 Middlewich Street
ADDENBOROUGH
AG3 9LL

23rd January, 1995

Mr. J. Hedgehopper,
Hedgehoppers Knives Ltd.,
Railway Arcade
HARLEY

Dear Mr. Hedgehopper,

Some years ago I bought a SHARPCUTTER penknife from you, and, as you know, it has been invaluable to me. Unfortunately, however, I have now lost it, and wonder if you still stock this range? If so, I should be grateful if you would let me have details of the various types of knife you make, and of their prices.

Yours sincerely,

Thomas Armitage

Thomas Armitage

Come iniziare una lettera

Per scrivere a qualcuno che si conosce

Thank you *or* **Thanks for your letter**, which arrived yesterday
It was good *o* **nice** *o* **lovely to hear from you**

It's such a long time since we were last in touch that I felt I must write a few lines just to say hello

I'm sorry I haven't written for so long, and hope you will forgive me; I've had a lot of work recently and ...
This is a difficult letter for me to write, and I hope you will understand how I feel

Per scrivere ad un'organizzazione

I am writing to ask whether you (have in) stock a book entitled ...
Please send me ... I enclose a cheque for ...
I think I may have left a beige raincoat in your office. **Would you kindly let me know whether** it has been found
I would like to know whether you still have any vacancies

Per concludere una lettera (prima dei saluti) ad un conoscente

Gerald joins me in sending very best wishes to you all
Irene sends her kindest regards

Please remember me to your wife - I hope she is well
If there is anything else I can do, **please don't hesitate to get in touch** again
I look forward to hearing from you

Ad un amico

Say hello to Martin for me
Give my warmest regards to Vincent
Carmela asks me to give you her best wishes

Do write when you have a minute
Hoping to hear from you before too long

Ad un amico intimo

Rhona **sends her love**/Raimond **sends his love**
Liliana **sends her love to you both**
Give my love to Lucy and Kenny, and tell them how much I miss them
Jodie and Carla **send you a big hug**

grazie della lettera...
mi ha fatto molto piacere ricevere tue notizie
è un sacco di tempo che non mi faccio viva e mi sento proprio in dovere di mandarvi due righe
mi dispiace di non aver scritto prima...
non è facile per me scrivere questa lettera...

vi scrivo per sapere se...
vi prego di inviarmi...
... vi sarei estremamente grata se poteste farmi sapere se...
... gradirei sapere se...

Gerald si unisce a me nell'inviarvi...
Irene si unisce a me nel trasmettervi i suoi più cordiali saluti
fai pervenire i miei più cari saluti...
... non esitate a contattarmi...
attendo con impazienza la vostra lettera

di ciao a Martin da parte mia
cari saluti a Vincent
Carmela mi incarica di trasmettervi i suoi saluti

scrivi...
aspetto con impazienza una risposta

... ti abbraccia
... vi abbraccia entrambi
un abbraccio...
un abbraccio forte forte da...

17.3   Per organizzare un viaggio

Come chiedere informazioni e prenotare

Please send me details of your prices
Please advise availability of dates between 1 August and 30 September
Please let me know by return of post if you have one single room with bath/shower, full/half board, for the week commencing 3 October
I would like to book bed-and-breakfast accommodation

vi sarei grato se poteste inviarmi...
vi prego di comunicarmi se...
vi sarei grato se poteste farmi sapere a stretto giro di posta se...
vorrei prenotare...

Per confermare o annullare una prenotazione

Please consider this a firm booking and hold the room until I arrive, however late in the evening
Please confirm the following by fax: one single room with shower for the nights of 20-23 October 1995
We expect to arrive in the early evening, unless something unforeseen happens
I am afraid I must ask you to alter my booking from 25 August to 3 September. I hope this will not cause too much inconvenience
Owing to unforeseen circumstances, **I am afraid (that) I must cancel the booking** made with you for the week beginning 5 September

vi prego di confermare la mia prenotazione...
vi sarei grato se voleste confermare via fax:...
pensiamo di arrivare...
purtroppo mi trovo costretto a chiedervi di...
... mi trovo costretto a disdire la prenotazione...

18 Ringraziamenti

Please accept our sincere thanks for all your help and support
I am writing to thank you *o* **to say thank you for** your help
Your advice and understanding **were much appreciated**

i miei più sentiti ringraziamenti per...
scrivo per ringraziarvi di...
vi sono molto riconoscente per...

In modo informale

Just a line to say **thanks for** the lovely book which arrived today
(Would you) please thank him from me
I can't thank you enough for finding my watch

... per ringraziare del...
ringrazialo da parte mia
non so come ringraziarti di...

Da parte di un gruppo

Thank you on behalf of the Society for all your support
We send our heartfelt thanks to you both

grazie a nome di...
i nostri più vivi ringraziamenti a...

A un gruppo

A big thank you to everyone involved in the show this year
We must express our appreciation to the University of Durham Research
  Committee for providing a grant which made this undertaking possible
I should like to extend my grateful thanks to all the volunteers who helped
  make it such an enjoyable event
My debts of gratitude also extend to colleagues on this side of the Atlantic

tante grazie a..
*siamo estremamente riconoscenti
  a...*
*vorrei estendere i miei ringraziamenti
  a...*
tutta la mia gratitudine anche a...

19 Auguri

I hope you have a nice holiday/a safe and pleasant journey/a successful trip
With love and best wishes for ...
(Do) give my best wishes to your mother **for** ...

Len **joins me in sending you all our very best wishes for** ...

spero che facciate...
i miei più sinceri auguri di...
*trasmetti i miei più sinceri auguri a...
  per...*
*... si unisce a me nel tramettervi i
  nostri più cari auguri di...*

Per Natale

Merry Christmas and a happy New Year
With season's greetings and very best wishes from
May I send you all our very best wishes for 1995

Buon Natale e Felice Anno Nuovo
Auguri di Buone Feste da
*i nostri migliori auguri per un felice
  1995*

Per un compleanno

All our love and best wishes on your 21st **birthday**, from Mum, Dad, Kerry
  and the cats
**This is to send you our fondest love and very best wishes on your
  eighteenth birthday.**
Many happy returns from Aunt Alison and Uncle Paul
Wishing you a happy birthday for next Wednesday. See you at the party,
  love Melanie

*tanti cari auguri per il tuo...
  compleanno...*
*affettuosissimi auguri in occasione
  del tuo diciottesimo compleanno.*
Cento di questi giorni...
*ti auguro di trascorrere un felice
  compleanno mercoledì prossimo...*

Auguri di pronta guarigione

Sorry (to hear) you're ill - **get well soon!**
I was very sorry to learn that you were ill, and **send you my best wishes for
  a speedy recovery**

... guarisci presto!
*... le invio i miei più sinceri auguri di
  pronta guarigione*

Per augurare buona fortuna

I thought I'd drop you a line **to send you best wishes for your** ...
Good luck for your ... . I hope things go well for you on Friday
Sorry to hear you didn't get the job - **better luck next time!**

Sorry you're leaving us. **Good luck in** your future career

... per augurarti buona fortuna per...
in bocca al lupo per...
*... spero che tu sia più fortunato la
  prossima volta!*
... buona fortuna in...

Per congratularsi con qualcuno di persona

You're doing a great job! **Good for you!** Keep it up!
You're pregnant? **Congratulations!** When is the baby due?
You've finished the job already? **Well done!**

... bravo!...
... congratulazioni!...
... bravo!

In comunicazioni scritte

We all send you our love and congratulations on such an excellent result

*le nostre più sentite congratulazioni
  per...*

20 Partecipazioni, inviti e risposte

20.1 Partecipazioni

Come annunciare la nascita e come rispondere

Julia Archer **gave birth to** a healthy 6lb 5oz baby son, Andrew, last Monday

Lisa **had** a baby boy, 7lb 5oz, last Saturday. **Mother and baby are both doing well**

Graham and Susan Anderson (nee McDonald) **are delighted to announce the birth of** a daughter, Laura Anne, on 11th October, 1994

Congratulations (to you both) on the birth of your son, and best wishes to Alexander for good health and happiness throughout his life

We were delighted to hear about the birth of Stephanie, and send our very best wishes to all of you

... annuncia la nascita di...

... ha avuto... Sia la mamma che il bimbo stanno bene

... sono lieti di annunciare la nascita di...

... sentite congratulazioni per la nascita di...

abbiamo ricevuto con gioia l'annuncio della nascita di...

Come annunciare il fidanzamento e come rispondere

Ad amici e parenti

I'm sure you'll be delighted to learn that Harry and I **got engaged** last Saturday

I'm happy to be able to tell you that James and Valerie **have** at last **become engaged**

sono sicura che sarai felice di sapere che... ci siamo fidanzati...

è con grande gioia che ti comunico che... si sono fidanzati...

sul giornale

It is with much pleasure that the engagement is announced between Michael, younger son of Professor and Mrs Perkins, Fintry, **and** Jennifer, only daughter of Dr and Mrs Campbell, Hucknall

Mr and Mrs Levison **have much pleasure in announcing the engagement of** their daughter Marie **to** Mr David Hood, Canada

Congratulations to you both on your engagement, and very best wishes for a long and happy life together

I was delighted to hear of your engagement, and wish you both all the best for your future together

siamo lieti di annunciare il fidanzamento fra ... e ...

... sono lieti di annunciare il fidanzamento di ... con ...

felicitazioni ad entrambi in occasione del vostro fidanzamento...

abbiamo appreso con grande gioia del vostro fidanzamento...

Come annunciare il matrimonio e come rispondere

Ad amici e parenti

Louise and Peter **have decided to get married** on the 4th June

I'm getting married in June, to a wonderful man named Lester Thompson

... hanno deciso di sposarsi...

mi sposerò...

In modo formale

Mr and Mrs William Morris **are delighted to announce the marriage of** their daughter Sarah to Mr. Jack Bond

Congratulations on your marriage, and best wishes to you both

We were delighted to hear about your daughter's marriage to Iain, and wish them both all the best for your future life together

... sono lieti di annunciare il matrimonio di...

congratulazioni...

abbiamo appreso con grande gioia del matrimonio di vostra figlia con...

Come annunciare un lutto e come rispondere

In una lettera ad amici o parenti

It is with great sadness that I have to tell you that Joe's father **passed away** three weeks ago

My husband **died suddenly** last year

con grande dolore ti annuncio che ... è mancato...

... è improvvisamente mancato

sul giornale

Suddenly (*o* **Peacefully**), at home, in Newcastle-upon-Tyne, on Saturday 2nd July, 1994, Alan, aged 77 years, **beloved husband of** Helen and **loving father of** Matthew

Mavis Ann, wife of the late Gavin Birch, **passed away peacefully** in the Western Infirmary on 4th October 1994, aged 64 years. **No flowers, please**

I was terribly upset to hear of Jim's death, and am writing to send you **all warmest love and deepest sympathy**

My husband and I **were greatly saddened to learn of the passing of** Dr Smith, and send (*o* offer) you and your family our most sincere condolences

è improvvisamente mancato ... ne danno il triste annuncio la moglie... e il figlio...

... è serenamente mancata ... niente fiori ma opere di bene

... le nostre più sentite condoglianze

abbiamo appreso con immenso dolore della scomparsa di ...

Per comunicare che si è cambiato indirizzo

Our new address as of 4 May 1995 **will be** 1 Acacia Road, Barnton BN7 2BT

... il nostro nuovo indirizzo ... sarà...

20.2 Inviti

Gli inviti ufficiali e come rispondere

Annunci di matrimonio

Mr and Mrs James Waller **request the pleasure of your company at the marriage of** their daughter Tamsin to Mr Richard Hanbury
... hanno il piacere di invitarvi al matrimonio di ...

The Chairman and Governors of Hertford College, Oxford **request the pleasure of the company of** Miss Charlotte Young and partner **at a dinner** to mark the anniversary of the founding of the College
... hanno l'onore di invitare... alla cerimonia...

Margaret and Gary Small **request the pleasure of your company at a reception** (o **dinner**) to celebrate their Silver Wedding, on Saturday 12th November, 1995
... hanno il piacere di invitarvi alla cerimonia...

We thank you for your kind invitation to the marriage of your daughter Annabel on 20th November, **and have much pleasure in accepting**
vi ringraziamo infinitamente del vostro gentile invito al ... al quale saremo onorati di partecipare

We regret that we are unable to accept your invitation to the marriage of your daughter on 6th May
siamo infinitamente spiacenti di non poter accettare il vostro gentile invito a...

Inviti vari

We are celebrating Rosemary's engagement to David by holding a dinner dance at the Central Hotel on Friday 11th February, 1994, **and very much hope that you will be able to join us**
festeggeremo il fidanzamento di Rosemary e David... e ci auguriamo di tutto cuore che possiate unirvi a noi

We are giving a dinner party next Saturday, **and would be delighted if you and your wife could come**
saremmo onorati della vostra presenza al ricevimento che si terrà...

I am planning a party for my nephew - **hope you'll be able to make it**
ho in programma di organizzare una festa ... e spero che possiate venire

I'm having a party next week for my 18th - **come along, and bring a friend**
farò una festa... vieni e porta qualcuno

Inviti a teatro, cena ecc. e come rispondere

Why don't you come down for a weekend and let us show you Sussex?
perché non venite a trovarci...

Would you be interested in com**ing** with us to the theatre next Friday?
ti piacerebbe...

Would you and Gordon **like to come** to dinner next Saturday?
perché tu e... non venite...

Would you be free for lunch next Tuesday?
sei libera per...

Perhaps we could meet for coffee some time next week?
che ne dici di...

Come accettare

I'd love to meet up with you tomorrow, it will be such fun
sarei contentissima di...

It was good of you to invite me, I've been longing to do something like this for ages
è stato molto gentile da parte tua invitarmi...

Thank you for your invitation to dinner - **I look forward to it very much**
ti ringrazio del cortese invito... non vedo l'ora!

Come scusarsi di non poter intervenire

I'd love to come, but I'm afraid I'm already going out that night
mi piacerebbe moltissimo venire, ma purtroppo...

I'm terribly sorry, but I won't be able to come to your party
sono terribilmente spiacente, ma purtroppo non potrò venire...

I wish I could come, but unfortunately I have something else on
mi piacerebbe moltissimo venire, ma purtroppo...

Unfortunately, it's out of the question for the moment
sfortunatamente è impossibile...

It was very kind of you to invite me to your dinner party next Saturday. **Unfortunately I will not be able to accept**
... sfortunatamente non posso accettare

Much to our regret, we are not able to accept
siamo estremamente spiacenti di non poter accettare

Per dire che non si è sicuri

I'm not sure what I'm doing that night, but I'll let you know by Friday
non sono sicura di...

It all depends on whether I can get a sitter for Rosie at short notice
dipende tutto se...

I'm afraid I can't really make any definite plans until I know when Alex will be able to take her holidays
purtroppo non posso prendere impegni...

It looks as if we might be going abroad with Jack's company in August so **I'd rather not commit myself** to a holiday yet
... per il momento preferisco non prendere impegni...

21   La Dissertazione

21.1   La struttura in generale

Per introdurre un concetto

In modo impersonale

It is often said *o* **asserted** *o* **claimed that** the informing 'grass' is named after the song Whispering Grass, but the tag long predates the ditty	*si afferma da più parti...*
It is a truism *o* **a commonplace that** American accents, place-names and slang are infinitely more glamorous and than their British counterparts	*è un luogo comune dire che...*
It is undeniably true that Gormley helped to turn his members into far more sophisticated workers	*è innegabile che...*
It is a well-known fact that in this age of technology, it is computer screens which are responsible for many illnesses	*è un fatto ben noto che...*
It is sometimes forgotten that much Christian doctrine comes from Judaism	*talvolta si dimentica che...*
It would be naïve to suppose that these 50-year-old arrangements can survive	*sarebbe da ingenui credere...*
It would hardly be an exaggeration to say that the friendship of both of them with Britten was among the most creative in the composer's life	*si potrebbe dire, senza timore di esagerare, che...*
It is hard to open a newspaper nowadays without reading that TV will destroy reading and that electronic technology has made the written word obsolete	*al giorno d'oggi non si può aprire un giornale senza leggere che...*
First of all, it is important to try to understand some of the systems and processes involved in order to create a healthier body	*prima di tutto, è importante cercare di capire...*
It is in the nature of classics in sociological theory **to** make broad generalizations about such things as societal evolution	*è nella natura stessa di...*
It is often the case that early interests lead on to a career	*è spesso vero che...*

In modo soggettivo

By way of introduction, let me briefly review the background to this question	*per iniziare, permettetemi di...*
I'd like to start with a sweeping statement which can be easily challenged	*comincerei con...*
Before going specifically into the issue of criminal law and legal punishment, **I wish first to summarize** how Gewirth derives his principles of justice	*prima di addentrarmi nei dettagli di... vorrei riassumere innanzitutto...*
Let us look at what self-respect in your job actually means.	*esaminiamo...*
What we are mainly concerned with here is the conflict between what the hero says and what he actually does	*ci occupiamo qui di...*
We live in a world in which the word 'equality' is liberally bandied about in connection with colour, creed, race, and gender	*viviamo in un mondo in cui...*

Per esporre un concetto o un problema

The concept of controlling harmful insects by genetic means isn't new	*l'idea di...*
The idea of getting rich without too much effort has universal appeal	*l'idea di...*
The question of whether Hamlet was really insane has occupied critics for generations	*... si sono posti la domanda "Amleto era veramente pazzo?"*
Why they were successful where their predecessors had failed **is a question that has been much debated**	*... è un tema che è stato spesso dibattuto*
One of the most striking features *o* **aspects of this issue** *o* **topic** *o* **question is** the way (in which) it arouses strong emotions	*uno degli aspetti più interessanti di questo problema è...*
There are a number of issues on which China and Britain openly disagree	*c'è tutta una serie di questioni...*

Come introdurre delle generalizzazioni

People working outside the home **tend to believe** parenting is an easy option	*coloro che... sono portati a credere che...*
There's always **a tendency for people to** exaggerate your place in the world	*... la tendenza da parte della gente a...*
Many gardeners **have a tendency to** anthropomorphise plants	*hanno la tendenza a...*
Fate **has a propensity to** behave in the same way to people of similar natures	*... tende a...*
Viewed psychologically, it seems **we all have the propensity for such** traits	*... tutti abbiamo una propensione per...*
For the (vast) majority of people, literature is a subject which is studied at school but which has no relevance to life as they know it	*per una vasta maggioranza...*
For most of us, the alternative to extreme old age is worse	*per molti di noi...*

History provides **numerous examples** *o* **instances of** misguided national heroes
... numerosi esempi di...
We commonly think of people as isolated individuals but, in fact, few of us
ever spend more than an hour or two of our waking hours alone
normalmente si pensa a...

Per mettere a fuoco un particolare aspetto

The Meters' work with Lee Dorsey **in particular** merits closer inspection
... in particolare...
One particular issue raised by Narayan was, suppose Grant at the time of his
conviction was old enough to be hanged, what would have happened?
un problema particolare...
A more specific point relates to using the instrument given in Figure 6.6 as a way
of challenging our hidden assumptions about the realities of the outside world
un aspetto più specifico...
More specifically, Pilger accuses Western governments of continuing to
supply weapons and training to the Khmer Rouge
più precisamente...

21.2   Per presentare un argomento

In apertura

First of all, let us consider the advantages of urban life
cominciano con l'esaminare...
Let us begin with an examination of the social aspects of this question
iniziamo con un esame di...
The first thing that needs to be said is that the author gives a biased view
per prima cosa va detto che...
What should be established at the very outset is that we are dealing here
with a practical rather than philosophical issue
la prima constatazione che si impone
è che...

Per dire di cosa si vuole /non si vuole parlare

In the next section, **I will pursue the question of** whether the expansion of
the Dutch prison system and population can be explained by Box's theory
... svilupperò il problema di...
I will then deal with the question of whether or not the requirements for
practical discourse are compatible with criminal procedure
tratterò quindi il problema di...
We must distinguish between the psychic and the spiritual, and **we shall see
how** the subtle level of consciousness is the basis for the spiritual level
... vedremo come...
I will confine myself to giving an account of certain decisive facts in my
'militant' career with Sartre
mi limiterò a...
We will not concern ourselves here with the Christian legend of St James
in questa sede non ci occuperemo
di...

Let us now consider to what extent the present municipal tribunals differ
from the former popular tribunals in the above-mentioned points
consideriamo per ora...
Let us now look at the ideal types of corporatism that neo-corporatist
theorists developed to clarify the concept
esaminiamo ora...

La presentazione del problema

The main issue under discussion is how the party should re-define itself if
it is to play any future role in Hungarian politics
il problema principale è...
A second, related problem is that business ethics has mostly concerned
itself with grand theorising
un altro problema, strettamente
connesso al primo, è...
The basic issue at stake is this: is research to be judged by its value in
generating new ideas for their own sakes?
essenzialmente questo è il problema
che ci si pone:...
An important aspect of Milton's imagery **is** the play of light and shade
un aspetto importante di... è...
It is worth mentioning here that when this was first translated, the opening
reference to Heidegger was entirely deleted
è utile o vale la pena di ricordare qui
che...

Per analizzare più da vicino i fatti citati

In their joint statement the two presidents use tough language to condemn
Iraqi behaviour but **is there any real substance in** what's been agreed?
... c'è qualcosa di concreto in...
This is a question which **merits close(r) examination**
... merita un (più) attento esame
The unity of the two separate German states **raises fundamental questions
for** Germany's neighbours and for European security as a whole
... solleva questioni fondamentali
per...
The pathetic failure to protect our fellow Europeans in Bosnia **raises
fundamental questions on** the role of the armed forces
... pone una questione di fondo...
This raises once again the question of whether a government's right to
secrecy should override the public's right to know
ciò solleva ancora una volta la
questione circa...

This poses the question whether it is possible for equity capital to be cheap (abundant) and portfolio capital to be expensive (scarce) simultaneously

ci si chiede quindi se...

Analisi dei problemi

It is interesting to consider why this scheme has been so successful
è interessante esaminare perché...

On the question of whether civil disobedience is likely to help end the war, Chomsky is deliberately diffident
in merito alla questione se...

We are often faced with the choice between our sense of duty **and** our own personal inclinations
siamo spesso costretti ad una scelta fra... e...

When we speak of realism in music, **we do not at all have in mind** the illustrative bases of music
quando si parla di..., non si pensa affatto a...

It is reasonable to assume that most people living in industrialized societies are to some extent contaminated by environmental poisons
si può presumere con una certa sicurezza che...

Come motivare una teoria

An argument in support of this approach **is that** it produces results
a favore di... c'è da dire che...

In support of his theory, Dr Gold notes that most oil contains higher-than-atmospheric concentrations of helium-3
a sostegno della sua teoria...

This is the most telling argument in favour of extending the right to vote
questo è l'argomento più convincente a favore di...

The second reason for advocating this course of action **is that** it benefits the community at large
un'altra ragione per sostenere la validità di... è che...

The third, more fundamental, reason for look**ing** to the future **is that** even the angriest investors realise they need a successful market
il terzo e più importante motivo, per... è che...

Despite communism's demise, confidence in capitalism seems at a post-war low. **The fundamental reason for** this contradiction seems to me quite simple
... il motivo fondamentale di...

21.3   Come presentare la tesi opposta

Come confutare una tesi

In actual fact, the idea of there being a rupture between a so-called old criminology and an emergent new criminology is somewhat misleading
in realtà...

In order to argue this, I will show that Wyeth's **position is**, in actual fact, **untenable**
il punto di vista di... è indifendibile

It is claimed, however, that the strict 'Leboyer method' is not essential for a less traumatic birth experience
tuttavia si afferma...

This need not mean that we are destined to suffer for ever. **Indeed, the opposite may be true**
questo non vuol dire necessariamente che... può essere vero l'esatto contrario

Many observers, though, **find it difficult to share his opinion that** it could mean the end of the Tamil Tigers
... non condividono la sua opinione che...

On the other hand, there is a competing principle in psychotherapy that should be taken into consideration
d'altro canto...

The judgement made **may well be true but** the evidence given to sustain it is unlikely to convince the sceptical
potrebbe essere giusto, ma...

Regulatory reform **is all very well, but** it is pointless if the rules are not enforced
è ottima, ma...

The case against the use of drugs in sport rests primarily on the argument that ... **This argument is weak, for two reasons**
... questa tesi ha due punti deboli

According to one theory, the ancestors of vampire bats were fruit-eating bats. But **this idea** o **argument does not hold water**
... questo ragionamento fa acqua da tutte le parti

The idea of 'peripheralization' **does not stand up to** historical scrutiny
... non regge a...

This view does not stand up if we examine the known facts about John
questa tesi non regge...

The trouble with the idea that social relations are the outcome of past actions is not that it is wrong, but rather that it is uninformative
la difficoltà con il concetto che...

The difficulty with this view is that he bases the principle on a false premise
il punto debole di questa tesi è che...

The snag with such speculations is that too much turns on one man or event
il guaio con...

But removing healthy ovaries, especially before the time of the menopause, **is entirely unjustified in my opinion**
... secondo me è totalmente ingiustificato

Come proporre un'alternativa

Another approach may be to develop substances capable of blocking the effects of the insect's immune system
un altro approccio potrebbe essere quello di...

Another way of looking at that claim is to note that Olson's 'explanations' require little knowledge of the society or situation in question — *ci si può accostare al problema da un'angolatura diversa, notando che...*

However, the other side of the coin is the fact that an improved self-image really can lead to prosperity — *comunque, il rovescio della medaglia...*

It is more accurate to speak of a plurality of new criminologies rather than of a single new criminology — *sarebbe più accurato parlare di...*

Paradoxical though it may seem, computer models of mind can be positively humanising — *per quanto possa sembrare paradossale...*

21.4 Per introdurre la sintesi

Come valutare i pro e i contro

How can we reconcile these two apparently contradictory viewpoints? — *come è possibile conciliare...*
Could it be that some kind of synthesis is possible? — *sarebbe possibile fare una sintesi?*
On balance, making money honestly is more profitable than making it dishonestly — *tutto sommato...*
Since such vitamins are more expensive, one has to weigh up the pros and cons — *... si devono considerare i pro e i contro*
We need to look at the pros and cons of normative theory as employed by Gewirth and Phillips — *dobbiamo considerare i pro e i contro di...*
The benefits of partnership in a giant trading market will almost certainly outweigh the disadvantages — *i vantaggi di... superanno gli svantaggi*
The two perspectives are not mutually exclusive — *i due punti di vista non sono poi così inconciliabili*

Come optare per una tesi

Dr Meaden's theory, backed by careful observation and documentary evidence from previous centuries, is the most convincing explanation — *... è la spiegazione più convincente*
The truth o fact of the matter is that in a free society you can't turn every home into a fortress — *la verità è che...*
But the truth is that Father Christmas has a rather mixed origin and one that goes back many centuries — *... la verità è che...*
This is an exercise that on paper might not seem to be quite in harmony, but in actual fact this is not the position — *... in realtà...*
When all is said and done, it must be acknowledged that a purely theoretical approach to social issues is sterile — *a conti fatti dobbiamo riconoscere che...*

Per ricapitolare

In this chapter, I have demonstrated o shown that the Cuban alternative has been undergoing considerable transformations — *... ho dimostrato che...*
This shows how, in the final analysis, adhering to a particular theory on crime is at best a matter of reasoned choice — *ciò mostra che...*
The overall picture shows that prison sentences were relatively frequent, but not particularly severe — *la visione d'insieme mostra che...*
To recap o To sum up, then, (we may conclude that) there are in effect two possible solutions to this problem — *ricapitolando, si può concludere che...*
To sum up this chapter I will offer two examples of a treatment process — *riassumendo questo capitolo...*
To summarize, we have seen that the old staple industries in Britain had been hit after the First World War by a deteriorating competitive position — *in breve...*
Habermas's argument, in a nutshell, is as follows — *... in poche parole...*
But the key to the whole argument concerning the occult is a single extraordinary paragraph — *... il punto focale di tutta la questione... è...*
To round off this section on slugs, gardeners may be interested to hear that there are three species of predatory slugs in the British Isles — *per concludere questa sezione...*

Per concludere

From all this it follows that it is impossible to extend those kinds of security measures to all potential targets of terrorism — *da tutto ciò ne consegue che...*
This, of course, leads to the logical conclusion that those who actually produce do have a claim to the results of their efforts — *ci porta logicamente a concludere che...*

There is only one logical conclusion we can reach, which is that we ask our customers what is the reality that they perceive in our marketing programme — *c'è una sola conclusione logica...*

The inescapable conclusion is that the criminal justice system does not simply reflect the reality of crime; it helps create the reality we see — *non ci resta altro che concludere che...*

We must conclude that there is no solution to the problem of defining crime — *si deve concludere che...*

In conclusion, the simple punishment model of deterrence is highly unsatisfactory without a nuclear monopoly — *per concludere...*

The upshot of all this, is that this treatment is not likely to be readily available — *come risultato si ha che...*

So it would appear that ESP is not necessarily limited to the right hemisphere of the brain — *sembrerebbe dunque che...*

This only goes to show that a good man is hard to find, be he Black or White — *questa è un'ulteriore prova che...*

The lesson to be learned is that the past, especially a past lived in impotence, can be enslaving — *l'insegnamento che si può trarre è che...*

At the end of the day, the only way the drugs problem will be beaten is when people are encouraged not to take them — *in fin dei conti...*

Ultimately, then, these critics are significant and democracy in America cannot be appreciated without understanding this work — *in definitiva, quindi...*

21.5   Come strutturare un paragrafo

Per aggiungere ulteriori informazioni

In addition, there is evidence that the author does not really empathize with his hero — *inoltre...*

This award-winning writer, **in addition to being** a critic, biographer and poet, has written 26 crime novels — *... oltre ad essere...*

But this is only part of the picture. **Added to this** are fears that a major price increase would cause riots — *... oltre a ciò...*

An added complication **is** that the characters are not aware of their relationship to one another — *un'altra... è...*

Also, there is the question of language. We were in fact doing training in both Swahili and Masai, which is the local language — *inoltre...*

The question also arises as to how this idea can be put into practice — *si pone inoltre la questione di...*

Politicians, **as well as** academics and educationalists, tend to feel strongly about the way in which history is taught — *... così come...*

But, **over and above that**, each list contains fictitious names or addresses — *... oltre a ciò...*

Furthermore, ozone is, like carbon dioxide, a greenhouse gas, trapping solar radiation at the Earth's surface — *inoltre...*

Per fare dei paragoni

Compared with the heroine, Alison is an insipid character — *paragonata a...*

In comparison with the Czech Republic, Bulgarian culture is less westernized — *se la si paragona con...*

This is a high percentage for the English Midlands but low **by comparison with** some other parts of Britain — *a paragone di...*

On the one hand, there is no longer a Warsaw Pact threat. **On the other (hand)**, the positive changes could have negative side-effects — *da un lato... dall'altro...*

Similarly, a good historian is not obsessed by dates — *analogamente...*

There can only be one total at the bottom of a column of figures and **likewise** only one solution to any problem — *... ugualmente...*

What others say of us will translate into reality. **Equally**, what we affirm as true of ourselves will likewise come true — *... allo stesso modo...*

There will now be a seminal change in the way we are regarded by our partners, and, **by the same token**, the way we regard them — *... per la stessa ragione...*

There is a fundamental difference between adequate nutrient intake **and** optimum nutrient intake — *c'è una fondamentale differenza fra... e...*

Per collegare vari punti

First of all o **Firstly**, I would like to outline the benefits of the system — *prima di tutto...*

In music we are concerned **first and foremost** with the practical application of controlled sounds relating to the human psyche — *... in primo luogo...*

In order to understand the conflict between the two nations, **it is first of all necessary to** know something of the history of the area — *per capire... è necessario prima di tutto...*

Secondly, it might be simpler to develop chemical or even nuclear warheads for a large shell than for a missile   *in secondo luogo...*

In the first/second/third place, the objectives of privatization were contradictory   *in primo, secondo, terzo luogo...*

Finally there is the argument that castrating a dog will give it a nasty streak   *in ultimo...*

Per esprimere un punto di vista personale

In my opinion, the government is underestimating the scale of the epidemic   *a mio parere...*

My personal opinion is that the argument lacks depth   *sono del parere che...*

This is a popular view, but **speaking personally**, I cannot follow its logic   *personalmente...*

Personally, I think that no one can appreciate 'ethnicity' more than Black or African people themselves   *personalmente...*

For my part, I cannot agree with the leadership on this question   *da parte mia...*

My own view is that what largely determines the use of non-national workers are economic factors rather than political ones   *trovo che...*

In my view, it only perpetuates the very problem that it sets out to address   *secondo me...*

Although the author argues the case for patriotism, **I feel that** he does not do it with any great personal conviction   *... penso che...*

I believe that people do understand that there can be no quick fix for Britain's economic problems   *credo che...*

It seems to me that what we have is a political problem that needs to be solved at a political level   *mi sembra che...*

I would maintain that we have made a significant effort to ensure that the results are made public   *desidero sostenere che...*

Per introdurre il punto di vista di qualcun altro

He claims o **maintains that** intelligence is conditioned by upbringing   *sostiene che...*

Bukharin **asserts that** all great revolutions are accompanied by destructive internal conflict   *... afferma che...*

The NATO communique **states that** some form of nuclear deterrent will continue to be needed for the foreseeable future   *... afferma che...*

What he is saying is that the time of the old, highly structured political party is over   *ciò che sostiene è che...*

His admirers **would have us believe that** watching this film is more like attending a church service than having a night at the pictures   *... vorrebbero farci credere...*

According to the report, the continued use of torture creates a climate favourable to violence   *secondo...*

Per introdurre un esempio

To take another example: many thousands of people have been condemned to a life of sickness and pain because   *... prendiamo un altro esempio...*

Let us consider, **for example** o **for instance**, the problems faced by immigrants arriving in a strange country   *... per esempio...*

His meteoric rise **is the most striking example yet of** voters' disillusionment with the record of the previous government   *... è l'esempio migliore di...*

The case of Henry Howey Robson **serves to illustrate** the courage exhibited by young men in the face of battle   *... serve bene ad illustrare...*

Just consider, **by way of illustration**, the difference in amounts accumulated if interest is paid gross, rather than having tax deducted   *... per esempio...*

A case in point is the decision to lift the ban on contacts with the republic   *un esempio tipico è...*

Take the case of the soldier returning from war. He finds no words adequate to convey his experience of being under fire   *prendiamo il caso di...*

As the Prime Minister **remarked** recently, the Channel Tunnel will greatly benefit the whole of the European Community   *come... ha fatto notare...*

21.6   I meccanismi di un dibattito

Per esprimere una supposizione

They are alleged to have telephoned the president to put pressure on him. And **that could be interpreted as** trying to gain an unconstitutional political advantage   *... potrebbe essere interpretato...*

Retail sales in Britain rose sharply last month. This was higher than expected and **could be taken to mean that** inflationary pressures remain strong — *... farebbe supporre che...*

For the usage of these types of drugs, **it might well be prudent to** actually see if people have this metabolic defect or not — *... sarebbe senza dubbio più prudente...*

These substances do not remain effective for very long. This is **possibly** because they work against the insects' natural instinct to feed — *... forse...*

Marilyn Monroe had become a definite security risk and **it is not beyond the bounds of possibility that** murder may have been considered — *... non è impossibile che...*

As to marriage, I am somewhat reassured by Mr Fraser's assertion, as **this leads one to suppose that** on that subject he is in full agreement with Catholic teaching — *... ciò ci porta a supporre...*

It is **probably** the case that all long heavy ships are vulnerable — *... probabilmente...*

After hearing nothing from the taxman for so long, most people **might reasonably assume** their tax affairs were in order — *... è giustamente portata a credere...*

One could be forgiven for thinking that because the substances are 'chemicals', they'd be easy to study — *è comprensibile che si pensi che...*

Thus, **I venture to suggest that** very often when 'visions' are mentioned in the literature of occultism, self-created visualizations are meant — *... mi permetto di dire che...*

Per esprimere una certezza

It is clear that any risk to the human foetus is very low — *è chiaro che...*

Whatever may be said about individual works, the early poetry as a whole is **indisputably** a poetry of longing — *... indiscutibilmente...*

Yet, **undeniably**, this act of making it a comprehensible story does remove it one degree further from reality — *... innegabilmente...*

There can be no doubt that the Earth underwent a dramatic cooling which destroyed their environment and life style — *non c'è dubbio alcuno che...*

It is undoubtedly true that over the years there has been a much greater emphasis on safer sex — *è senza dubbio vero che...*

As we all know, adultery is far from uncommon, particularly in springtime and particularly among people in the prime of life — *come tutti ben sappiamo...*

One thing is certain: no one can claim that ESP has never helped make money — *una cosa è certa:...*

It is (quite) certain that unless peace can be brought to this troubled land, no amount of aid will solve the long term problems of the people — *è assodato che...*

Per esprimere il dubbio

It is doubtful whether, in the present repressive climate, anyone would be brave or foolish enough to demonstrate publicly — *ci sono forti dubbi che...*

It remains to be seen whether the security forces will try to intervene, given the huge numbers of demonstrators involved — *resta da vedere se...*

Once in a while I think about all that textbook Nietzsche **and I wonder whether** anyone ever truly understood a word of it — *... e mi chiedo se...*

I have (a few) reservations about the book — *ho delle riserve su...*

Since it spans a spectrum of ideologies, **it is by no means certain that** it will stay together — *... non è affatto certo che...*

It is questionable whether media coverage of terrorist organizations actually affects terrorism — *non si sa se...*

This raises the whole question of exactly when in a high-tech society men and women should retire — *ciò solleva la questione di sapere...*

The crisis **sets a question mark against** the Prime Minister's stated commitment to intervention — *... rimette in questione...*

Both these claims **are true up to a point** and they need to be made. But they are limited in their significance — *... sono vere fino ad un certo punto...*

Per esprimere che si è d'accordo (vedi anche 11. Accordo)

I agree wholeheartedly with the opinion, recently given on television, that smacking should be outlawed — *sono completamente d'accordo con...*

One must acknowledge that China's history will make change more painful — *si deve prendere atto che...*

It cannot be denied that there are similarities between these two views — *è innegabile che...*

Courtney - **rightly in my view** - is strongly critical of the snobbery and elitism that is all too evident in these circles — *... giustamente, a mio avviso...*

Preaching was considered an important activity, **and rightly so** in a country with a high illiteracy rate

... *a buon diritto...*

Per esprimere il dissenso (vedi anche 12. Dissenso)

I must disagree with with Gordon's article on criminality: it is dangerous to suggest that to be a criminal one must look like a criminal
non sono d'accordo con...

He is seen not a lovable failure but rather, a difficult man who succeeded.
It is hard to agree
... *è difficile trovarsi d'accordo*

As a former teacher **I find it hard to believe that** there is no link at all between screen violence and violence on the streets
... *mi riesce difficile credere che...*

The strength of their feelings **is scarcely credible**
... *è poco credibile*

Steele's claim to have been the first to discover the phenomenon **defies credibility**
... *non è credibile*

Nevertheless, **I remain unconvinced by** Milton
... *non mi ha affatto convinto*

Many do not believe that water contains anything remotely dangerous. Sadly, **this is far from the truth**
... *si è molto lontano dalla verità*

To say that everyone requires the same amount of a vitamin is as stupid as saying we all have blonde hair and blue eyes. **It simply isn't true**
... *è completamente errato*

His remarks were not only offensive to ethnic minorities but **totally inaccurate**
... *completamente errati*

Stomach ulcers are often associated with good living and a fast-moving lifestyle. **(But) in reality** there is no evidence to support this theory
... *ma in realtà...*

This version of a political economy **does not stand up to close scrutiny**
... *non regge ad un più attento esame*

Per enfatizzare

Nowadays, there is **clearly** less stigma attached to unmarried and single mothers
... *chiaramente...*

Evidence shows that ..., so once again **the facts speak for themselves**
... *i fatti parlano da sé*

Few will argue with the principle that such a fund should be set up
non si vuole mettere in dubbio l'idea che...

Hyams **supports this claim** by looking at sentences produced by young children learning German
... *corrobora questa affermazione...*

This issue **underlines** the dangers of continuing to finance science in this way
... *sottolinea...*

The most important thing is to reach agreement from all sides
la cosa più importante è...

Perhaps **the most important aspect of** cognition is the ability to manipulate symbols
... *l'aspetto più importante di...*

Per mettere in evidenza un concetto

It would be impossible to exaggerate the importance of these two volumes for anyone with a serious interest in the development of Black gospel music
non si può sottolineare abbastanza l'importanza di...

The symbolic importance of Jerusalem for both Palestinians and Jews is almost **impossible to overemphasize**
è impossibile trascurare...

It is important to be clear that Jesus does not identify himself with Yahweh but with the servant of Yahweh
è importante chiarire che...

It is significant that Mandalay seems to have become the central focus in this debate
è significativo che...

It should not be forgotten that many of those now in exile were close to the centre of power until only one year ago
non dobbiamo dimenticare che...

It should be stressed that the only way pet owners could possibly contract such a condition from their pets is by eating them
va sottolineato che...

There is a very important point here and that is that the accused claims that he was with Ms Martins all evening on the night of the crime
c'è da sottolineare un aspetto molto importante qui ed è che...

At the beginning of his book Mr Cviic **makes a telling point**. The Balkan peoples, he notes, are for the first time ...
... *fa un'osservazione rivelatrice...*

Suspicion is **the chief feature of** Britain's attitude to European theatre
... *è la caratteristica principale di...*

In order to focus attention on Hobson's distinctive contributions to macroeconomics, these wider issues are neglected here
poiché si vuole attirare l'attenzione...

These statements **are interesting in that** they illustrate different views
... *sono interessanti poiché...*

22.1   Per ottenere un numero

Could you get me Newhaven 465786, please.
(four-six-five-seven-eight-six)
You'll have to look up the number in the directory.
You should get the number from International Directory
    Enquiries.
Would you give me Directory Enquiries, please?
Can you give me the number of the Decapex company, of
    54 Broad Street, Newham.
It's not in the book.
They're ex-directory *(Brit)*. // They're unlisted *(Am)*.
What is the code for Exeter?
Can I dial direct to Colombia?
You omit the '0' when dialling England from Italy.
How do I make an outside call? // What do I dial for an
    outside line?

22.2   Diversi tipi di telefonate

It's a local call.
It's a long-distance call from Worthing.
I want to make an international call.
I want to make a reverse charge call *o* a transferred
    charge call to a London number *(Brit)*. // I want to call a
    London number collect *(Am)*.
I'd like to make a personal call *(Brit)* *o* a person-to-person
    call *(Am)* to Joseph Broadway on Jamestown 123456.
I want to make an ADC call to Bournemouth.
I'd like to make a credit card call to Berlin.
What do I dial to get the speaking clock?
I'd like an alarm call for 7.30 tomorrow morning.

22.3   Risponde l'operatore

Number, please.
What number do you want? // What number are you
    calling? // What number are you dialling?
Where are you calling from?
Would you repeat the number, please?
You can dial the number direct.
Replace the receiver and dial again.
There's a Mr Sandy Campbell calling you from Canberra
    and wishes you to pay for the call. Will you accept it?
Can Mr Williams take a personal call *(Brit)*? // Can Mr
    Williams take a person-to-person call *(Am)*?
Go ahead, caller.
(Directory Enquiries) There's no listing under that name.
There's no reply from 45 77 57 84.
I'll try to reconnect you.
Hold the line, caller.
All lines to Bristol are engaged - please try later.
It's a card phone.
I'm trying it for you now.
It's ringing. // Ringing for you now.
The line is engaged *(Brit)*. // The line is busy *(Am)*.

22.4   Quando l'abbonato risponde

Could I have extension 516? // Can you give me extension
    516?
Is that Mr Lambert's phone?
Could I speak to Mr Swinton, please? // I'd like to speak to
    Mr Swinton, please. // Is Mr Swinton there?
Could you put me through to Dr Henderson, please?
Who's speaking?
I'll try again later.

I'll call back in half an hour.
Could I leave my number for her to call me back?
I'm ringing from a callbox *(Brit)*. // I'm calling from a pay
    station *(Am)*.
I'm phoning from England.
Would you ask him to ring me when he gets back?

22.5   Risponde il centralino/la centralinista

Queen's Hotel, can I help you?
Who is calling, please?
Who shall I say is calling?
Do you know his extension number?
I am connecting you now. // I'm putting you through now.
I'm putting you through now to Mrs Thomas.
I have a call from Tokyo for Mrs Thomas.
I've got Miss Martin on the line for you.
Miss Paxton is calling you from Paris.
Dr Craig is talking on the other line.
Sorry to keep you waiting.
There's no reply.
You're through to our Sales Department.

22.6   Messaggi registrati

British Telecom: **The number you have dialled has not
    been recognized. Please check and call again**.
British Telecom: **This number has now been changed.
    Please ring 465322**.
British Telecom: **Operator dial 100. Directory enquiries
    dial 192**
British Telecom: **The mobile you have dialled is
    switched off**.(cellulare)
British Telecom: **Sorry we are unable to connect your
    call**.(cellulare)
Non si riesce a prendere la linea.
British Telecom: **All Greenock 5 figure numbers have
    been changed by prefixing them with 7. Please
    redial using the national code followed by the new 6
    figure number. B.T has not charged you for this call**.
Tutti i numeri telefonici a cinque cifre di Greenock sono
    stati modificati con l'aggiunta del prefisso 7. Vi
    preghiamo di formare nuovamente il numero usando il
    prefisso 0475 seguito dal nuovo numero a sei cifre.
    Questo servizio è gratuito.

22.7   Per rispondere al telefono

Hallo, this is Anne speaking.
(Is that Anne?) Speaking.
Would you like to leave a message?
Can I take a message for him?
This is a recorded message.
Please speak after the tone.

22.8   In caso di difficoltà

I can't get through (at all).
The number is not ringing.
I'm getting 'number unobtainable'. // I'm getting the
    'number unobtainable' signal.
Their phone is out of order.
We were cut off.
I must have dialled the wrong number.
We've got a crossed line.
I've called them several times with no reply.
I got the wrong extension.
This is a very bad line.

23.1   Giving suggestions

Non sarebbe una cattiva idea chiedergli un parere.	*it might not be a bad idea to ...*
Si potrebbe, per esempio, rivedere la prima parte.	*we could think of ...*
Sarebbe opportuno inviargli immediatamente il dossier.	*it would be as well to ...*
Sarebbe un'ottima idea visitare la mostra di scultura moderna.	*it would be an excellent idea to ...*
Mi permetterei di suggerire una data diversa.	*I'd like to suggest ...*
Mi permette di darle un consiglio? Mi sembra che...	*may I make a suggestion? ...*
Se posso permettermi di dare un consiglio, io qui includerei una piantina.	*if I might suggest something ...*
Vorremmo sottoporle alcune proposte.	*we should like to put to you ...*
Nulla vi impedisce di chiedere un aumento.	*there is nothing to prevent you from ...*
Le ricordo che il direttore attende una sua risposta.	*may I remind you that ...*
Sarebbe preferibile distribuire a tutti una copia del documento.	*it would be better to ...*
Sarebbe meglio informare i suoi genitori.	*it might be better to ...*
Forse sarebbe il caso di rielaborare completamente il testo della conferenza.	*perhaps we should ...*
Basterebbe che tu dilazionassi la scadenza.	*you only need to ...*
Allo stato attuale **non ci resta che** aspettare.	*...we can only ...*
Se non le è di troppo disturbo, mi potrebbe rispedire l'originale del documento?	*if it wouldn't be too much trouble ...*
Sarei molto lieto di partecipare alla fase preliminare.	*I'd be very happy to ...*
Non devi assolutamente dimenticarti di fargli notare che...	*you mustn't forget to ...*
Si potrebbe adottare un altro metodo.	*we could ...*
Potresti andarci domani.	*you could ...*
Queste sono le mie proposte: per prima cosa un'indagine di mercato, poi...	*here are my suggestions: ...*
Sarebbe nel tuo interesse cambiare banca.	*you'd do better to ...*
Faresti meglio ad andare in vacanza a settembre.	*you'd be better off going ...*
È urgentissimo e **dovresti** cercare di finirlo per domani.	*...you ought to ...*
Se fossi in te *or* **al tuo posto** *or* **personalmente** non ci andrei.	*if I were you ...*
A mio avviso non dovresti rifiutare.	*in my view ...*
Ti consiglio di prendere le dovute precauzioni.	*I advise you to ...*
Se lei è d'accordo la richiamo domani.	*if you agree, I'll call you back ...*
Propongo di parlargliene immediatamente.	*I suggest that ...*
Proponiamo di pagarvi metà adesso e metà a fine lavoro.	*we propose ...*
Ti consiglierei di prenderti una lunga vacanza	*I'd advise you to ...*

Using direct questions

E se andassimo a cena fuori stasera?	*what about going ...*
Che ne dici di andare a Londra questo week-end?	*how about ...*
Hai mai pensato di iscriverti all'Università?	*have you (ever) thought of ...*
Perché non ti iscrivi ad una palestra?	*why don't you ...*
Sei mai stato tentato dall'idea di lasciarlo? *or* **Non ti è mai venuta la tentazione di** lasciarlo?	*haven't you ever been tempted by the idea of ...*

23.2   Asking for advice

Cosa faresti al posto mio?	*what would you do if you were me?*
Che fare?	*what shall we do?*
Forse lei potrebbe suggerire una soluzione più soddisfacente per tutti	*perhaps you could suggest a solution...*
Per quale delle due proposte opteresti?	*which of the two suggestions would you go for?*
Non vedo altra soluzione, e tu?	*I don't see what else we can do, do you?*

24 Advice

24.1 Asking for advice

Vorrei qualche consiglio sulle possibilità di carriera al termine del corso.
I'd like some advice ...

Ho bisogno di un consiglio: secondo te è meglio comprare una macchina nuova o una usata?
I need some advice: ...

Date le circostanze, **cosa mi consigli di fare?**
...what would you advise me to do?

Cosa faresti al mio posto?
what would you do in my place?

Le sarei estremamente grata se potesse darmi un consiglio sul modo migliore di...
I should be very grateful if you would advise me as to ...

Vorrei la tua opinione a proposito di...
I'd like your opinion on ...

24.2 Giving advice

Personalmente, trovo che dovresti insistere.
personally, I think you should ...

Se vuoi il mio consiglio, interrompi questa relazione.
my advice would be to ...

Se mi permetti di darti un consiglio faresti meglio a non andarci.
if I can offer a piece of advice, you'd do better ...

Ti raccomando la massima discrezione.
please keep this absolutely confidential

Ti sconsiglio vivamente di prendere il treno.
I (strongly) advise you not to ...

Al tuo posto or **Se fossi in te**, me ne andrei immediatamente.
if I were you ...

A mio avviso, dovresti rivolgerti ad uno specialista.
in my opinion, you should ...

Mi permetta di suggerirle Oslo quale sede migliore per...
may I suggest ...

Si sconsiglia un uso eccessivo di antibiotici.
it is inadvisable to ...

Sarebbe opportuno ottenere prima di tutto la sua autorizzazione.
it would be wise to ...

E soprattutto non credere ad una parola di quello che dice.
whatever you do ...

Prenditi una vacanza, è **la cosa migliore che tu possa fare**.
...it's the best thing you could do

Hai tutto l'interesse a fare tutto il possibile per...
you would be best to ...

Sbagli a non pretendere di essere pagato per le ore extra.
you'd be wrong not to ...

Hai avuto torto a fidarti di lui.
you were wrong to ...

Sarebbe una buona idea anticipare l'incontro.
it might be a good idea to ...

More tentatively

Non vedo perché tu non debba dirglielo.
there is no reason why you shouldn't ...

Hai mai pensato ad un corso di informatica?
have you ever thought of ...

Ci sembra avventato rischiare dei capitali in questa impresa.
it seems rash to us to ...

Forse potreste spiegarglielo di persona.
perhaps you could ...

Mi domando se non sarebbe meglio attendere ancora qualche giorno.
I wonder if it wouldn't ...

Non sarebbe mica una cattiva idea comprarne due dozzine
it wouldn't at all be a bad idea to ...

24.3 Warning someone about something

Sarebbe opportuno spedirgliene una copia, **così non se ne dimentica**.
you'd be as well to ... or else he will forget ...

Diffidate di tutti quelli senza una tessera di riconoscimento.
beware of ...

Sarebbe pura follia mettersi in viaggio il 15 di agosto.
it would be madness to ...

L'avverto che se il vestito non sarà pronto, non salderò il conto.
I warn you that ...

Correte il rischio di perdere tutti i vostri risparmi.
you are running the risk of ...

Ti troverai nei guai se non inizi subito a studiare.
you'll be in trouble if ...

Un consiglio: smettila di fare commenti saccenti.
let me give you a word of warning: ...

Ti avverto che comincio ad averne abbastanza delle tue continue assenze.
I warn you that ...

E non venirti poi a lamentare che il tuo nome non è stato incluso nell'elenco!
don't come to me complaining that ...

25   Offers

Sarebbe più che un piacere farvi visitare il museo domani.   *it would be a great pleasure to ...*
Mi chiedo se non sarebbe meglio se lo facessi io.   *I wonder if it wouldn't be better ...*
Se lo desidera, potremmo venire con lei.   *we could ... if you like ...*
Se vuole, le posso mandare un'altra segretaria.   *I can ..., if you like ...*
Mi permetta almeno di pagare le spese del telefono!   *at least let me ...*
Andrò **volentieri** a tener compagnia alla nonna, in caso voi non poteste.   *I'll gladly ...*
Siamo lieti di offrirle il posto di segretaria.   *we should like to offer you ...*
Non esiti a chiedermi ulteriori spiegazioni, se necessario.   *don't hesitate to ask me ...*
Provvederò io a farla avvisare in tempo.   *I'll see to it that ...*
Sono pronto ad occuparmi io di tutto.   *I'm ready to ...*
Sono lieto di mettermi a sua completa disposizione.   *I would be happy to ...*

Using questions

Mi permette di accompagnarla a visitare il reparto vendite?   *may I ...*
Posso aiutarti a finirlo?   *can I ...*
Mi permette di presentarla al direttore?   *may I ...*
Vuole che l'aiuti ad archiviare le pratiche?   *would you like me to ...*
Perché non lascia a noi l'intera organizzazione del viaggio?   *why not leave to us ...*
Vuole che prenoti io l'hotel?   *would you like me to ...*
E se venissi io a far da baby sitter domani sera?   *shall I come to ...*
Cosa ne dite se ci andassi io?   *what would you say to ...*
Che ne direste di organizzare una cena per gli ex allievi?   *how about ...*

26   Requests

Può, per cortesia, far sì che ci sia un'auto ad attendermi all'aeroporto?   *could you ...*
Le spiacerebbe occuparsi lei delle prenotazioni?   *would you mind ...*
Vorrei sapere se la banca è aperta il sabato mattina.   *I'd like to ...*
Conto su di lei affinchè l'assegno venga spedito in tempo.   *I'm counting on you to ...*
Preferirei che non ne facesse parola.   *I would rather you ...*
Le spiace fare una fotocopia?   *would you mind ...*
Potrebbe gentilmente spedirmene due copie?   *would you kindly ...*
Siete tenuti a presentare il bilancio prima del 12.   *you are requested to ...*
Può, per cortesia, comunicarmi la data della sua partenza?   *would you kindly ...*
Mi sarebbe di enorme aiuto se potesse sostituirmi la prossima settimana.   *it would be most helpful if ...*

More formally

Sarei lieto se fosse così gentile da confermarmi la data e l'ora del suo arrivo.   *would you please be kind enough to ...*

Mi trovo costretto a ribadirle che si deve rivolgere al direttore in persona.   *I must insist that ...*
Sono costretta a chiederle di non trattenere più il personale oltre le 18.   *I must ask you not to ...*
Le sarei molto grato se potesse riservare due sale per la conferenza.   *I should be grateful if you would ...*
Le sarei veramente grato se non ne facesse parola con gli altri colleghi.   *I should be most grateful if you didn't ...*

Vi saremmo grati se poteste regolare immediatamente la fattura.   *we should be grateful if you would ...*

27 Comparisons

In confronto ai or **A confronto dei** supermercati, i negozi rionali sono spesso più cari.	*in comparison with ...*
Sì, può essere, ma **a paragone del** suo primo romanzo, questo è decisamente un'opera minore.	*...compared with ...*
Paragonata a Londra, Roma è decisamente più piccola.	*if you compare it with ...*
È stato spesso paragonato al nostro Pasolini.	*he has often been compared to ...*
In paragone, è meno caro d'agosto	*comparatively ...*
Quest'articolo è **molto più** interessante **di** quello che ho letto ieri.	*...(much) more ... than ...*
Le vendite sono aumentate considerevolmente **rispetto all**'anno scorso.	*...in comparison with ...*
Negli ultimi anni è diventato **sempre più** difficile/ **sempre meno** facile affittare un alloggio in centro a prezzi accessibili.	*...more and more ... /...less and less ...*
La casa nuova è **molto simile** all'altra, **ma più piccola.**	*...is very like ... but (very much) smaller*
Ricorda vagamente un tempio greco.	*it is somewhat reminiscent of ...*
I loro due stili **non si assomigliano affatto**.	*...are not at all alike*
I romanzi sono entrambi ambientati in Sicilia nel '700, ma **le somiglianze finiscono qui.**	*...there the likeness ends*
Questa casa ha il giardino, **mentre tutte le altre** hanno solo un cortiletto.	*...whereas all the others ...*
Sono molto simili, ma l'appartamento che abbiamo visto prima ha un bagno più grande.	*they are very similar, but ...*
Quello che lo distingue dagli altri scrittori neorealisti è l'interesse per...	*what distinguishes him from ...*

Comparing favourably

Questo vino è **nettamente superiore all**'altro.	*...far superior to ...*
Non c'è confronto: lui è molto più simpatico.	*there is no comparison: he's much nicer*

Comparing unfavourably

Il film è **molto meno interessante del** libro da cui è stato tratto.	*...is far less interesting than ...*
La qualità di questo tessuto è **decisamente inferiore**.	*...is certainly inferior*
L'ultimo romanzo **non regge al** or **il confronto** con i precedenti.	*...doesn't bear comparison with ...*
La qualità della sua produzione poetica è **di gran lunga inferiore a** quella dei romanzi.	*...is not nearly as good as ...*

Comparing similar things

Le due case **sono molto simili**.	*...are very similar ...*
Corrisponde a 6 intere settimane di lavoro.	*it is the equivalent of ...*
I due quadri **sono di valore equivalente**.	*...are equal in value*
Non vedo alcuna differenza fra i due metodi.	*I cannot see any difference between ...*
Il valore degli immobili è crollato e **lo stesso vale** per i terreni.	*...the same is true of ...*

Comparing dissimilar things

Non c'è assolutamente confronto fra i due candidati.	*there is simply no comparison between ...*
È certamente **difficile stabilire un confronto fra** i due.	*it is ...difficult to draw a comparison between ...*
Non è proprio possibile paragonare due opere così diverse.	*one just cannot compare ...*
Non ci sono punti in comune: questo è un brano letterario, l'altro un'analisi filologica del testo.	*there are no points of comparison ...*

28.1 Asking for somebody's opinion

Che ne pensi del suo comportamento? — *what do you think of ...*
Mi puoi dire qual è la tua opinione in proposito? — *can you give me your opinion ...*
A vostro avviso *or* **Secondo voi** sarebbe meglio dare più libertà ai giovani? — *in your opinion ...*
Qual è la vostra opinione sulle TV private? — *what is your attitude to ...*
Potreste dirmi la vostra opinione personale su questi cambiamenti? — *can you tell me what your own feelings are about ...*

Mi piacerebbe sapere cosa ne pensate del programma del festival. — *I'd like to know what you think of ...*
Ho saputo che il progetto è stato bocciato: **mi farebbe piacere sapere qual è stata la vostra reazione**. — *...I would like to know your reaction to the decision*

28.2 Expressing your opinion

Penso/credo di aver seguito alla lettera le tue istruzioni. — *I think/believe that ...*
Presumo/suppongo/immagino che tu sappia già di cosa si tratta. — *I presume/suppose/immagine that ...*
Credo che la loro proposta sia stata accolta favorevolmente. — *I believe that ...*
Ho la sensazione che non sia stato dato abbastanza spazio alla creatività del bambino. — *my feeling is that ...*
A mio avviso credo si possa fare di meglio. — *in my view ...*
Secondo me *or* **Per me** non la si doveva lasciare da sola in casa. — *in my opinion ...*
Personalmente *or* **Per quel che mi concerne** si è già tardato fin troppo. — *personally, I think that ...*
A mio parere il Governo dovrebbe intervenire immediatamente. — *my own view is that ...*
Da quanto vedo non si può rimediare in altro modo. — *as far as I can see ...*
Ho l'impressione che i suoi genitori lo trascurino un po'. — *I have the impression that ...*
Ripensandoci mi sembra meglio non rispondere. — *on second thoughts, we'd better ...*
Sono persuaso che finiranno per mettersi d'accordo. — *I'm sure that ...*
Sono convinto che questa sia l'unica soluzione possibile. — *it is my belief that ...*
Ho la sensazione che stia per andarsene. — *I've got a feeling that ...*
Devo dire che i risultati mi paiono proprio scadenti. — *I must say that ...*
Ho paura che sia ormai troppo tardi. — *I fear it may be ...*
Se volete la mia opinione, è pura follia assumersi tali responsabilità. — *if you want my opinion ...*
Non posso fare a meno di pensare che l'abbia fatto deliberatamente. — *I can't help thinking that ...*
È indispensabile una selezione più severa: o **almeno questa è la mia posizione** a riguardo. — *...at least, this is what I feel*
Con tutto il rispetto, mi sembra che questa sia la soluzione meno soddisfacente. — *with all due respect, I feel that ...*
Se posso esprimere un parere personale, il sistema di classificazione recentemente introdotto creerà solo dei problemi. — *if I may express my opinion ...*

28.3 Replying without giving an opinion

È difficile dire, allo stadio attuale, quali saranno le reazioni del pubblico. — *it is difficult to tell ...*
Preferirei non pronunciarmi su una questione così delicata. — *I'd rather not commit myself ...*
È difficile dare un giudizio conclusivo. — *it is difficult to give a final opinion*
Devo ammettere di **non avere alcuna idea** in proposito. — *... I have no particular views ...*
Non ci ho mai riflettuto seriamente. // Non mi sono mai posto la questione. — *I've never really thought about it*
Non sta a me fare delle critiche. — *it's not for me to ...*
Tutto dipende da quello che si intende con... — *it all depends on what you mean by ...*

29 Likes, dislikes and preferences

29.1 Asking people what they like

Ti piacerebbe ricominciare a giocare a tennis?	*would you like to ...*
Ti piace lavorare con lui?	*do you like ...*
Ti piacerebbe visitare il Museo Egizio quando vieni a Torino?	*would you like to ...*
Quale ti piace di più: il piano o il violino?	*which do you prefer ...*
Può farmi sapere quali sono le sue preferenze?	*could you let me know what or which ones you prefer?*
Sarei lieto di avere la vostra opinione sulla scelta dei materiali.	*I'd be glad to have your opinion ...*

29.2 Saying what you like

Il concerto **mi è piaciuto moltissimo**.	*I enjoyed ... very much*
Occuparmi del giardino **mi dà grandissima soddisfazione**.	*I really enjoy ...*
La cosa che mi piace di più è andare in montagna con gli amici.	*my greatest pleasure is ...*
Mi piace che la gente sia puntuale.	*I like people to ...*
La sua interpretazione di Amleto **non mi è spiaciuta**.	*I quite liked ...*
... **ma più di tutto mi piace** una serata tranquilla con pochi amici.	*...but what I like better than anything else is ...*
Secondo me non c'è niente che stia al pari di un concerto di Debussy.	*for me, there's nothing to compare with ...*

29.3 Saying what you dislike

Se c'è una cosa che odio è aspettare l'autobus sotto la pioggia.	*if there's one thing I hate, it's ...*
Odio cordialmente quelli che si danno troppe arie.	*I really hate ...*
Il suo comportamento **non mi piace per niente**.	*I don't like ... at all*
Non mi piace affatto lavorare in queste condizioni.	*I don't enjoy ...*
Trovo molto difficile parlare in pubblico.	*I find it hard to ...*
Non sopporto proprio quelli che arrivano costantemente in ritardo.	*I just can't bear ...*
Mi è stato subito antipatico.	*I took an instant dislike to him*
Non è niente di speciale, non so perché tutti ne vadano matti.	*it's nothing special ...*

29.4 Saying what you prefer

Preferisco le pesche **alle** albicocche. // **Preferisco** andare in aereo **piuttosto** che in macchina.	*I prefer ... to ...*
Leggere è probabilmente il mio passatempo **preferito**.	*...favourite ...*
Se non ti dispiace, **preferisco** prendere il più grande.	*I would prefer to ...*
Preferirei se partissi immediatamente.	*I'd rather you ...*
Se non c'è in rosso nella mia taglia, **piuttosto prendo** quello verde.	*I'll have ...instead*
Sarebbe meglio comprare un tavolo rotondo.	*It would be better to ...*
Per me venerdì **andrebbe meglio**.	*...would suit me better*
Preferirei che non pronunciassi il suo nome in mia presenza.	*I'd as soon you didn't ...*
Hanno una spiccata predilezione per il teatro giapponese.	*they have a marked preference for ...*

29.5 Expressing indifference

Credimi, **che tu venga o no per me è** *or* **fa proprio lo stesso**.	*...I really don't mind whether you come or not.*
A dir la verità, **non ho alcuna preferenza**.	*...I have no particular preference.*
Fai tu/fa come vuoi: a me piacciono entrambe	*you choose: ...*
Non ha la minima importanza.	*it's of no importance whatsoever*
È un genere che **non mi interessa assolutamente** *or* che **mi lascia totalmente indifferente**.	*...doesn't interest me in the slightest*

30.1   Asking what someone intends or wants

Che cosa conti di fare? // Cosa intendi fare? // Cosa pensi di fare?   *what do you intend to do?*
Ci farebbe molto piacere conoscere le vostre intenzioni.   *it would be good to know what your intentions are.*

Perché non ti iscrivi a un corso di danza classica?   *why don't you ...*
Cosa speri di ottenere comportandoti così?   *what are you hoping to ...*
Sarebbe meglio comunicare le vostre intenzioni a tutti i membri.   *it would be better if you were to communicate your intentions to ...*

Vogliamo sapere cosa i nostri clienti si aspettano di trovare nei supermercati.   *we want to know what our customers expect to find ...*

30.2   Talking about intentions

Ho intenzione di sostituire tutte le piastrelle in cucina.   *I'm going to ...*
Avevo in mente di andare ad un concerto.   *what I wanted to do was to ...*
Aveva programmato di andare ad almeno due delle conferenze.   *he had planned to ...*
Avevo l'intenzione di parlargliene, ma poi me ne sono dimenticata.   *I was going to speak to him about it ...*

L'avevo preso in prestito **con l'intenzione di** fare delle fotocopie, ma poi non ho avuto tempo.   *...intending to ...*
Progettavo di ristrutturare il fienile.   *I was planning to ...*

With more determination

Voglio dimagrire di almeno quattro chili.   *I want to ...*
Voglio che l'ingresso sia finito prima di Natale.   *I want ...*
Desidero farvelo pervenire immediatamente.   *I want ...*
Ho deciso di invitare tutto il parentado per Natale.   *I have decided to ...*
È fermamente deciso a fare il giro del mondo su quel ridicolo barchino.   *he is determined to ...*
Ha preso la ferma decisione di fare 5 ore di straordinario ogni settimana.   *she made up her mind to ...*
Voglio che tutti ne siano a conoscenza.   *I want everyone to be ...*
Non se ne parla neanche di vendere la macchina.   *there is no question of ...*
Sono assolutamente contrario a concedere ulteriori dilazioni.   *I am dead against ...*

More enthusiastically

Muoio dalla voglia di vederlo.   *I'm dying to ...*
Desidero ardentemente andare in Australia, ma non posso permettermelo.   *I'd really love to ...*

30.3   Saying what you would like

Vorrei due biglietti per domani sera, ma temo che sia tutto esaurito.   *I'd like (to have) ...*
Vorrei andare al cinema.   *I'd like to ...*
Vorrei esprimere tutta la mia riconoscenza a coloro che hanno collaborato.   *I'd like to ...*
Avrei voluto congratularmi di persona.   *I should have liked to ...*
Se solo avessi avuto un po' più di tempo!   *if only I had ...*
C'è da sperare che tutto vada secondo i piani.   *it is to be hoped that ...*
Sarebbe auspicabile che intervenissero tutti i membri.   *it is to be hoped that ...*
Soprattutto **mi auguro che** si trovi una rapida soluzione.   *...my hope is that ...*

30.4   Saying what you don't want to do

Preferirei non doverglielo dire io.   *I'd rather not have to ...*
Non voglio dover cambiare i miei piani solo per lei.   *I don't want to have to ...*
Mi rifiuto di subire le sue continue prepotenze.   *I refuse ...*
Non ho la minima *or* **alcuna intenzione di** consultarlo.   *I have no intention of ...*

31 Permission

31.1 Asking for permission

Potrei essere trasferito ad un altro dipartimento?	*could I ...*
Spero non la secchi troppo inserire questi piccoli cambiamenti.	*I hope it won't be too much bother to ...*
Se non crea troppi problemi, mi piacerebbe partecipare a questa fase.	*I'd like to ... if it is no trouble*
Mi permette di usare il suo computer, per un attimo?	*would you allow me to ...*
Avete delle obiezioni se mi assento *or* **Avreste delle obiezioni se mi** assentassi per un'altra settimana?	*would you have any objection to my ...*
Sarebbe così gentile da prestarmi il suo programma?	*would you be kind enough to ...*
È permesso *or* **Si possono** fare telefonate personali?	*are you allowed to ...*
Sarebbe mica possibile avere una stanza più grande?	*would it be at all possible to ...*

31.2 Giving permission

Se volete **potete** comprarne uno nuovo.	*...you may ...*
Acconsento ben volentieri ad una vostra partenza per il Canada.	*I'm quite ready to give you permission to ...*
Vi do il mio permesso ad uscire due ore prima.	*I give you my permission to...*
Ma certamente, fate come vi pare più opportuno.	*by all means, do ...*
Vi autorizzo ben volentieri a parlargliene.// Ma è **naturale che siete autorizzati a** dirglielo.	*I certainly authorise you to ...*

31.3 Having permission

Ho avuto l'autorizzazione a saldare il conto in tre versamenti.	*I have been given permission to ...*
Mi ha detto che, se avessi voluto, avrei potuto assentarmi un'ora o due.	*he said I could ... if I wanted to*
Sono autorizzato a firmare gli assegni in sua vece.	*I am authorised to ...*
Gli lasciano bere il caffè anche se ha solo 3 anni.	*they let him ...*
Solo i genitori **possono** firmare le giustificazioni.	*...can ...*
In questo tipo di calcolo è **tollerato un errore del 3%**.	*...3% error is allowable*

31.4 Refusing permission

Non potete iscrivervi a più di cinque corsi.	*you can't ...*
Non avete la mia autorizzazione a *or* **Non vi permetto di** spedirgli questa foto.	*I will not allow you to ...*
Preferirei che non ci andaste.	*I'd rather you didn't ...*
Mi rifiuto categoricamente di autorizzarti a cambiare il testo. // **Mi oppongo assolutamente ad** ogni cambiamento nel testo.	*I absolutely refuse to allow you to ...*
Mi è stato proibito di fumare.	*I have been forbidden to ...*
Il dottore mi ha proibito tutti i grassi.	*my doctor has banned ...*
È categoricamente contrario ad un mio colloquio con il direttore.	*he is totally against my ...*
Mi dispiace, ma non posso acconsentire a concedervi un altro permesso.	*I am sorry, but I cannot agree to ...*
Mi dispiace doverla deludere, ma la sua proposta è stata respinta.	*I'm sorry to have to disappoint you ...*
Le proibisco categoricamente di contattare la concorrenza.	*I absolutely forbid you to ...*
È contro il regolamento consultare il catalogo generale.	*it is against the rules to ...*
È assolutamente vietato l'uso del telefono per comunicazioni personali.	*...is strictly prohibited*
Non vi è consentito utilizzare la mensa se non fate parte del personale.	*you are not allowed to ...*

32 Obligation

32.1 Saying what someone must do

Devi assolutamente mostrarti più tollerante.	*you really must ...*
Tutti i prelevamenti oltre i 10 milioni **devono essere** autorizzati dal direttore.	*...must be ...*
È mio dovere informarvi che l'ufficio sarà chiuso per inventario.	*I have to ...*
Dovete assolutamente presentargli le vostre scuse.	*you absolutely must ...*
Non si può accedere all'Università **senza** un titolo di scuola media superiore.	*you cannot ... without ...*
Lo sciopero mi **costringe a** rimandare la partenza di un giorno.	*the strike means I have to ...*
Dovete trovarvi un avvocato.	*you have got to ...*
Si è trovata costretta a fermarsi altre due ore.	*she found herself having to ...*
Si è visto costretto a chiedere l'intervento del direttore.	*he found himself forced to ...*
È obbligatorio versare l'intera somma prima della fine dell'anno.	*the whole sum is payable ...*
Non ne avevo alcuna intenzione, ma mi **hanno costretto** or **sono stato costretto**.	*I was made to ...*
Mi trovo costretto, ancora una volta, **a** chiedere un prestito.	*I find myself forced to ...*
È indispensabile segnalare or **È indispensabile che** segnaliate l'incidente entro 24 ore.	*it is essential to or that ...*
Per ottenere questo documento **ci si può** solo or **ci si deve** rivolgere al Consolato.	*in order to ... you have to ...*
Non ho potuto far altro or **non mi è rimasto altro che accettare**.	*I had no choice but to accept*
Mi è stato dato l'incarico di organizzare il corso.	*I have been given the task of...*
Esigiamo or **Si esige** che **i candidati abbiano** delle solide basi in algebra.	*candidates must have ...*
È stato disposto che le istruzioni per l'uso appaiano sulla confezione.	*it is laid down that ...*

32.2 Enquiring if one is obliged to do something

È indispensabile or **Dobbiamo** or **Si deve avere** l'invito?	*is it necessary to ...*
Devo proprio andarci oggi?	*do I really have to ...*

32.3 Saying what someone is not obliged to do

Non c'è bisogno di prenotare così in anticipo.	*there is no need to ...*
Nessuno vi obbliga or **non siete obbligati a** mangiare in mensa.	*you don't have to ...*
Non voglio mica costringervi a dirmi di che si tratta!	*I have no desire to force you to ...*
Non è obbligatorio essere muniti di un documento di identità.	*it is not necessary to ...*
Non è necessario or **non è indispensabile** confermare la prenotazione.	*it is not necessary to ...*
Non vale la pena tradurre tutto il capitolo.	*it isn't worth ...*
È inutile chiedergli un parere.	*there is no point in ...*
Non siete tenuti a dirgli di che si tratta.	*you don't have to ...*
Si è sentito obbligato a dare le dimissioni.	*he thought he had to ...*

32.4 Saying what someone must not do

Non si può sostenere l'esame più di tre volte.	*one is not allowed to ...*
È vietato parcheggiare davanti alla Questura.	*it is forbidden to ...*
Non bisogna impedire ai bambini di farsi degli amici.	*one must not ...*
Non puoi assentarti per più di due mesi.	*you cannot ...*
Non si può richiedere la carta d'identità **se non si** risiede nel Comune.	*you cannot ... unless you...*
Non ti permetto di usare questo linguaggio con me.	*I will not allow you to ...*
Non possiamo tollerare un tale comportamento in classe.	*we cannot allow ...*
Mi raccomando, non parlargliene.	*whatever you do, don't ...*
Ti proibisco or **Non ti permetto di** andarci da solo.	*I forbid you to ...*
È vietato usare il flash.	*It is forbidden to use ...*
È vietato fumare in sala.	*smoking is forbidden*

33 Agreement

33.1 Agreeing with a statement

Siamo dello stesso avviso su questo punto.// **Condividiamo la vostra posizione** su questo punto.	*we agree with you on ...*
Sono interamente d'accordo con te.	*I entirely agree with ...*
Come te, sono dell'avviso che si dovrebbe rimandare a domani.	*like you, I believe that ...*
Hai perfettamente ragione or **Hai tutte le ragioni a** voler chiarire la faccenda.	*you are quite right to ...*
Come avete giustamente fatto notare, è **vero che** non sono state vagliate tutte le possibilità.	*...it is true that ...*
Devo ammettere che non è uno stupido.	*I admit that ...*
Sono d'accordo con te **che** la situazione è molto delicata.	*I agree ... that ...*
Capisco or **Comprendo fin troppo bene** le sue incertezze.	*I fully understand ...*
Devo concederti di aver mancato di tatto.	*I grant you that ...*
Senza dubbio hai ragione quando dici che è più facile, ma...	*you are probably right when you say ...*

33.2 Agreeing to a proposal

Sono d'accordo sul fatto che dovreste cercare di parlargli alla prima occasione.	*I agree that you should ...*
Abbiamo preso visione del documento e ci **affrettiamo a concedervi la nostra autorizzazione**.	*...we give you our agreement without hesitation*
Siamo d'accordo a modificare il regolamento.	*we agree to ...*
Sono d'accordo con quello che voi avete proposto.	*I agree with what ...*
A grandi linee accetto le vostre proposte.	*I am broadly in agreement with ...*
Sono d'accordo, come lei aveva suggerito, **che dovremmo** rivolgerci ad un esperto.	*I agree ... we should ...*
Siamo d'accordo a concedervi una dilazione.	*we agree to ...*
Penso che tu abbia ragione ad indicare il mese di settembre come il più adatto per...	*I think you are right to ...*
Ho saputo che hai ritirato la tua candidatura e **non posso che darti ragione**.	*...I can only feel you did right*
D'accordo, ne discuteremo di persona.	*all right ...*
Sembrerebbe esattamente quello di cui abbiamo bisogno, ma purtroppo è troppo caro.	*it seems just what we need, but ...*

More informally

Che ne dici di andare per un aperitivo invece di fare straordinario? **Buona idea!**	*...sounds good to me!*
È una magnifica idea!	*It's a great idea!*
Due settimane in montagna? **Mi sembra una buona idea.**	*...I'd go for that*

More formally

Sono onorato di dare il mio più completo sostegno alla vostra iniziativa.	*I'm delighted to endorse wholeheartedly ...*
Le nostre conclusioni **vanno a corroborare** la vostra tesi.	*...corroborate ...*
Lo schema **incontra la nostra più completa approvazione**.	*...meets with our entire approval*
Farò del mio meglio per adeguarmi alle esigenze del resto del team.	*I'll do my best to ...*
Sono lieto di darle tutto il mio sostegno in questa impresa.	*I am happy to give you my full support ...*
Non mancherò di appoggiare la vostra proposta.	*I shall certainly support ...*

33.3 Agreeing to a request

Come mi avete richiesto, lascerò libero l'appartamento il primo di settembre.	*as you asked me to ...*
Vi assicuro che **seguirò le vostre istruzioni alla lettera**.	*...I shall follow your instructions to the letter*
Non mancherò di seguire i vostri consigli nella preparazione del programma.	*I shall certainly follow your advice about ...*
Cercheremo di attenerci alle vostre preferenze nella scelta dei materiali.	*we shall try to meet your preferences ...*
Abbiamo preso nota dei vostri suggerimenti.	*we have noted ...*
Mi va benissimo incontrarci alle 5.	*it suits me perfectly ...*
Sarò felicissimo di mettermi a vostra completa disposizione.	*I shall be delighted to...*

34.1 Disagreeing with what someone has said

È sbagliato dire che non si è impegnato a fondo.	*it is wrong to say ...*
Non è vero che mi hai visto al ristorante, non ci sono mai stato.	*it isn't true that ...*
Non sono d'accordo con te.	*I don't agree with you*
Sbagli se credi che sia stata io.	*you are wrong ...*
La differenza è irrilevante, **ma si è pur sempre trattato di un errore.**	*...but there has still been a mistake*
Hai torto *or* **Sbagli a** credere che l'abbia fatto apposta.	*you are wrong to ...*
Penso che tu abbia fatto male a dirglielo.	*I think you were wrong to ...*
Non condivido il vostro punto di vista.	*I don't share your opinion*
Mi è impossibile accettare il vostro punto di vista.	*I cannot accept ...*
Nego categoricamente di aver fatto pressioni su di lui.	*I categorically deny ...*
Non capisco come possiate andare in vacanza nelle attuali circostanze.	*I can't understand how ...*
Non voglio offenderti, ma **io la vedo in modo totalmente diverso**.	*...I see things quite differently*
Mi dispiace contraddirti *or* **doverti contraddire, ma** l'ho visto coi miei occhi.	*I am sorry to have to contradict you, but ...*

34.2 Disagreeing with what someone proposes

In questa fase è **impossibile** *or* **non è più possibile** apportare dei cambiamenti.	*it's impossible to ...*
Non sono d'accordo si debba annullare la riunione.	*I don't agree we should ...*
Ci opponiamo con fermezza all'apertura di un altro supermercato.	*we are totally opposed to ...*
Mi rifiuto di andarci.	*I refuse to ...*
Se sta pensando di dare le dimissioni sappia che **porrò il veto**.	*...I shall veto it*
Credo purtroppo di non poter approvare la vostra proposta.	*I'm afraid I can't accept ...*
Mi dispiace non poter appoggiare la vostra richiesta.	*I am sorry I cannot support ...*
È stato molto gentile da parte vostra offrire di aiutarmi, ma **credo di potercela fare** da sola.	*...I think I can manage ...*
Siamo sinceramente spiaciuti di non poter accettare la vostra gentile offerta.	*we are very sorry we cannot accept your kind offer*

34.3 Refusing a request

Mi è veramente impossibile *or* **Non posso proprio farlo** prima di martedì.	*I cannot possibly do it ...*
Sfortunatamente non posso fissare un appuntamento con il vostro rappresentante.	*unfortunately I cannot ...*
A causa della mole di lavoro, **mi è difficile** al momento iniziare la sua pratica.	*it is difficult for me to ...*
L'argomento è troppo delicato e **la mia posizione non mi permette** di farne parola con nessuno.	*...in my position I cannot ..*
Ci dispiace non poter mandare avanti il progetto.	*we are sorry we cannot go ahead with ...*
Siamo spiacenti di informarvi che non potremo applicare i soliti termini di consegna.	*we regret to have to inform you that we cannot ...*

More assertively

È fuori questione che debba essere **io ad** occuparmene. // **Non se ne parla neanche che sia io** ad occuparmene.	*it is out of the question for me to ...*
Mi rifiuto assolutamente di lavorare in queste condizioni.	*I totally refuse to ...*
Non accetterò mai di lavorare con lui.	*I will never agree to ...*

35 Approval

Sono totalmente d'accordo con te.	I couldn't agree (with you) more
Non avrei potuto esprimermi meglio.	I couldn't have put it better myself
Dobbiamo opporci al terrorismo! **Bravo!**	...hear, hear!
Condivido pienamente la sua posizione.	I fully endorse ...
Questa è un'idea eccellente!	what an excellent idea!
Siamo favorevoli a dei cambiamenti.	we are in favour of ...
Hai fatto bene ad andarci subito.	you did right to ...
Penso che tu abbia ragione or **penso che tu non abbia torto a** chiedergli una spiegazione.	I think you are right to ...
Trovo che faccia bene a voler approfondire la sua cultura generale.	I approve of his ...
Ho apprezzato moltissimo la vostra gentile offerta.	I greatly appreciated ...
Mi è piaciuta moltissimo la coreografia.	I very much liked ...

More formally

Accettiamo la vostra proposta a grandi linee, ma restiamo in attesa di ulteriori dettagli.	we accept ...
Approviamo la vostra decisione di rimandare la riunione.	we agree with your decision to ...
L'autore **giustamente** ha voluto **sottolineare** l'importanza di questo periodo.	...rightly emphasizes ...
Non si può far altro che ammirare la chiarezza con cui ha presentato i fatti.	one can but admire ...
Approviamo senza riserve tutte le vostre iniziative.	we unreservedly approve ...
Accogliamo l'iniziativa **con grande entusiasmo**.	we welcome wholeheartedly ...
Quello che è stato detto finora **ci ha fatto un'impressione molto favorevole**.	we are very favourably impressed by ...
L'iniziativa **ha tutto il nostro appoggio**.	we declare our full support for ...

36 Disapproval

Non sono d'accordo sulla proposta di apportare dei cambiamenti al programma.	I do not support ...
Do la colpa a te.	I blame you
Non avrebbe dovuto iniziare così presto.	he shouldn't have ...
Avresti piuttosto dovuto suggerirgli or **Avresti fatto meglio a** suggerirgli di partire prima.	you would have done better to ...
Penso che abbia avuto torto a fare così.	I think he was wrong to ...
Non ho apprezzato per niente come si è svolto il dibattito.	I didn't think much of the way ...
È un'idea **che disapprovo totalmente**.	...which I am profoundly unhappy about
È veramente deplorevole che ci sia stato un tale ritardo nella spedizione.	it is most unfortunate that ...
Non posso fare a meno di esprimere il mio disappunto circa la mancanza di conclusioni in una relazione peraltro eccellente.	I feel compelled to express my disappointment ...
Mi trovo costretto ad esprimere tutta la mia disapprovazione a proposito della cifra astronomica sprecata in questo progetto.	I feel bound to express my disapproval ...
Non sono disposto a tollerare or **Non ammetto** un altro ritardo.	I cannot tolerate ...
Non riesco a capire come si sia potuto ignorare così a lungo questo problema. // **Mi sembra veramente incomprensibile come** abbiano potuto ignorare così a lungo questo problema.	I can't understand how ...
Sono stato profondamente deluso dai risultati del secondo quadrimestre.	I was deeply disappointed by ...
Sono decisamente contrario alla vivisezione.	I am totally against ...
Con quale diritto si sono permessi di apportare delle modifiche così importanti senza la mia autorizzazione?	what right did they have to ...

37 Apologies

37.1 Apologizing

Scusa se non ti ho chiamato ieri.	*I'm sorry I ...*
Mi scuso di non averle potuto telefonare l'altra settimana.	*I am sorry I ...*
Vi prego di scusarmi di non essermi messo in contatto prima.	*please accept my apologies for ...*
La prego di scusarmi per non averglielo chiesto prima.	*do forgive me for ...*
Imperdonabile da parte mia!	*it's unforgivable of me!*
È un vero peccato che non possiate venire.	*it is a real pity that ...*
Mi dispiace moltissimo, ma non posso venire venerdì prossimo.	*I am very sorry but ...*
Sfortunatamente mi è impossibile *or* **mi trovo nell'impossibilità** di accettare l'invito.	*unfortunately I cannot ...*
È colpa mia: mi sono completamente dimenticata di spedirgliela.	*it is my fault:...*

More formally

Non posso far altro che rinnovarle ancora una volta le mie scuse.	*I can only say once again how sorry I am*
Ci teniamo a porgerle le nostre scuse per quanto è avvenuto.	*we must apologise for ...*
Vi prego di scusare il ritardo con cui vi rispondo.	*I must ask you to forgive ...*
Siamo desolati di non poter pubblicare il suo articolo.	*we are very sorry not to ...*
Siamo profondamente dispiaciuti degli inconvenienti causati.	*we greatly regret ...*
Siamo veramente rammaricati per questo increscioso malinteso.	*we are very sorry about ...*
Mi dispiace informarla che purtroppo la sua domanda è scaduta.	*I must regretfully inform you that ...*
Mi dispiace doverla informare che la sua candidatura non ha incontrato l'appoggio previsto.	*I must regretfully inform you that ...*
Mi rincresce di non poter presenziare a questo seminario a causa di un impegno precedente.	*I regret that I cannot ...*

37.2 Admitting responsibility

Riconosco di aver sbagliato a dargli il tuo numero di telefono.	*I realise I was wrong ...*
Non è arrivato **per un errore da parte nostra**.	*...because of a mistake on our part*
Sono io il responsabile di questo malinteso.	*it's I who am responsible for ...*
Ammetto *or* **Riconosco di** essere stato tentato molte volte di dirglielo.	*I admit that I ...*
Mi assumo la responsabilità di quanto avvenuto.	*I accept full responsibility for ...*

37.3 Expressing regret

Tentatively, or suggesting explanation

Solo ora mi rendo conto che **non avrei mai dovuto** dirglielo.	*I should never have ...*
Se solo non mi avesse vista!	*if only ...*
Sono sicuro che comprenderete i motivi della mia scelta.	*I am sure you will understand ...*
Purtroppo me ne sono completamente dimenticato.	*unfortunately ...*
Non volevo preoccuparti con quanto è avvenuto mentre eri in vacanza.	*I didn't want to worry you with ...*
Non avevo intenzione di andarmene, ma sono stata costretta.	*I didn't mean to ...*
So bene che non è la soluzione migliore, ma **ho dovuto** prendere una decisione lì per lì.	*I had to ...*
Ho creduto di far bene ad avvertirlo, ma non è servito a niente.	*I thought I was doing right ...*
Non ho potuto far altrimenti *or* **nient'altro**.	*I couldn't do anything else*

37.4 Disclaiming responsibility

Ti giuro che **non l'ho fatto apposto**!	*...I didn't do it on purpose*
Spero che tu mi creda quando ti dico che **sono stato obbligato ad** accettare.	*...I had no choice but to ...*
Spero che vi rendiate conto che non sono responsabile di questo ritardo.	*you will understand, I hope, that I am not responsible for ...*
Ti assicuro che **io non c'entro** *or* **non ho niente a che fare con** questa faccenda	*...is nothing to do with me*

PAOLA ROSSOTTI
VIA SAN FRANCESCO 28
TORINO

C.O.G.E.A.T SpA
Ufficio Personale
Via Dante 88
Milano

Torino, 14 ottobre 1993

con riferimento all'annuncio apparso su "Il Commercio e l'Industria" del 12 ottobre gradirei venisse presa in considerazione la mia candidatura per il posto di segretaria del Direttore Amministrativo presso la Vostra società.

Alla presente allego copia del mio Curriculum Vitae ove troverete le informazioni relative ai titoli di studio conseguiti ed alla mia precedente esperienza lavorativa.

In attesa di un cortese riscontro da parte vostra, porgo i miei più distinti saluti.

Paola Rossotti

Paola Rossotti

CURRICULUM VITAE

Nome	Silvana
Cognome	MARCONINI
Luogo e data di nascita	Torino, 3 marzo 1965
Domicilio attuale	via San Francesco 28, Torino
Numero telefonico	7536832
Curriculum scolastico	Maturità conseguita nel luglio 1983 presso il liceo classico Gioberti con la votazione finale di 60/60
	Dal 1983 al 1987 frequenta la facoltà di Economia e Commercio presso l'Università di Torino e consegue la laurea in data 6 aprile 1988 con la votazione finale di 110 e lode.
Corsi postuniversitari	Master in Business Administration (MBA) conseguito presso la London Business School nel 1990.
Impiego attuale	Dal 1992 al 1994 lavora presso la società L.O.G.I a Torino in qualità di EDP manager - coordina un'équipe di 10 persone; è responsabile di tutto il settore informatico

Motivazione per il cambio di lavoro

Desidera arricchire la propria professionalità con lavori sempre più stimolanti

Esperienze di lavoro precedenti

Dal 1988 al 1989	Programmatore presso la società Fornasetti in un'équipe di 6 persone
Dal 1989 al 1992	Analista programmatore presso la società Inteltel in qualità di responsabile dei DSS
Referenze:	dott. Zanda

Via Cristoforo Colombo 39	
Torino	dott. Cena
Tel: 68 12 04	Viale Bruno Buozzi 19
	Tel: 87 11 93

38.1 Starting your letter

In riferimento all'annuncio apparso oggi in "La Settimana" vi sarei grato se potete fornirmi maggiori dettagli e spedirmi il modulo di domanda.
in reply to your advertisement ...

Vi sarei estremamente grato se voleste considerare il mio nominativo in relazione all'annuncio apparso ieri in "il Corriere della Sera".
I wish to apply ...

È mio vivo desiderio lavorare in Italia durante le vacanze estive e vi sarei estremamente riconoscente se poteste farmi sapere se ci sono possibilità d'impiego presso la vostra ditta.
I would very much like to work in ...

38.2 Detailing your experience

Ho tre **anni di esperienza quale** segretaria, con buona conoscenza PC.
I have ...years' experience of working as a ...

Parlo l'inglese correntemente, ho una buona conoscenza del tedesco e sono in grado di leggere lo svedese.
as well as speaking fluent English, I have a working knowledge of German and a reading knowledge of Swedish.

Sebbene non abbia previa esperienza in questo settore, **ho** tuttavia lavorato durante le vacanze estive e, a richiesta, potrei fornirvi le referenze dei miei precedenti datori di lavoro.
although I do not have experience in ..., I have ...

La remunerazione annua attuale è di L..., incluse 4 settimane all'anno di ferie retribuite.
my current salary is ...

38.3 Giving your reasons for applying

Quest'offerta mi interessa vivamente poiché **sono ansiosa di inserirmi** nel campo dell'editoria.
...I am keen to work in ...

È mia intenzione lavorare in Italia **per migliorare la conoscenza** della lingua ed arricchire la mia esperienza nel settore alberghiero.
...to improve my knowledge ...

38.4 Closing the letter

Sono disponibile a partire alla fine di aprile.
I will be available from ...

38.5 Accepting and refusing

Vi ringrazio della vostra in data 19 marzo e vi comunico che **sarò onorata di incontrarvi per un colloquio** presso gli uffici della vostra sede in via Roma 7, il 12 ottobre alle ore 15.
...I will be pleased to attend for interview ...

38.6 Asking for and giving a reference

Mi è stato richiesto di includere due referenze nella mia domanda e **vi sarei estremamente riconoscente se mi autorizzaste a fare il vostro nominativo**.
...I would be very grateful if you would permit me to give your name

Ho fatto domanda come cameriera presso l'hotel 'Le due palme' a Santa Margherita e poiché devo allegare due referenze **vi sarei estremamente grata se voleste fornirne una.**
...I would be most grateful if you would be ready to give me one

La signorina Grazia Conti ha presentato domanda come receptionist presso il nostro hotel e ha fornito il vostro nominativo come referenza. **Vi saremo perciò estremamente grati se poteste farci pervenire la vostra valutazione sul suo operato presso la vostra ditta.**
...we would be most grateful if you would give us your assessment of her

La vostra risposta verrà trattata con la massima riservatezza.
your reply will be treated in the strictest confidence

Vi prego di comunicarci da quanto tempo conoscete la signorina Paola Bogliotti, quale ruolo ha ricoperto presso di voi e la vostra opinione sulle sue capacità nello svolgere il lavoro per il quale ha presentato domanda.
please could you let us know how long you have known Miss Paola Bogliotti, in what capacity, and whether in your opinion she is suitable for the post she has applied for

Sono lieto di raccomandare la signora Amalia Dossi **quale** segretaria; durante il periodo in cui ha lavorato presso la nostra ditta si è sempre dimostrata un'eccellente impiegata, degna di tutta la nostra fiducia.
I am happy to recommend ...for the position of ...

Il signor Conti ha lavorato presso la nostra ditta per 11 anni, durante i quali **si è sempre dimostrato un impiegato modello, completamente affidabile e dotato di un notevole senso di responsabilità.**
...he has always been a model employee - reliable at all times and extremely responsible

L'Arte Orafa

Gioielli antichi e moderni

Via S. Francesco 18, 10104 Vercelli

La Pulce
Piazza 4 Novembre 26
Cuneo

Ref/1200/Ma
Oggetto: invio documentazione

26 gennaio 1995

Spett.Ditta,

vi ringraziamo della vostra in data 20 ottobre contenente richiesta di informazioni concernente i nostri articoli. Siamo lieti di inviarvi il catalogo completo e il listino prezzi. Cogliamo l'occasione per segnalarvi la nuova serie natalizia al momento oggetto di una vantaggiosa offerta di lancio.

Restiamo a vostra completa disposizione per ulteriori informazioni e vi preghiamo di accettare i nostri più distinti saluti.

Il direttore commerciale

Paolo Morelli

dott. Paolo Morelli

Allegato n. 1:
documentazione completa

IL LAMPADARIO

via Milano 14, 44031 Pavia

Pavia, 15 giugno 1995

Sig. Carlo Marini
viale Cavour 12
44023 Cuneo

Gentile sig. Marini,

La ringrazio della sua lettera del 21 maggio.

Devo purtroppo confermarle che l'articolo da lei richiesto è attualmente esaurito. Mi permetto di inviarle il nostro nuovo catalogo augurandomi che lei potrà trovare tra i nuovi modelli un articolo di suo gradimento.

Colgo l'occasione per invitarla a visitare la mostra dei nuovi articoli che si terrà presso il nostro negozio di via Milano in data 21 giugno 1995.

Ringraziandola nuovamente per il suo interesse,

Distinti saluti

Marta Pollini

Marta Pollini
servizio clienti

Enquiries

Abbiamo appreso dal vostro annuncio nell'ultimo numero di "..." che la vostra ditta produce una vasta gamma di articoli da campeggio. **Vi saremo estremamente grati se poteste inviarci** un catalogo dei vostri articoli, inclusivo del listino prezzi, di eventuali offerte di sconto e dei tempi di consegna.

we would be grateful if you would send us ...

... and replies

A seguito della vostra lettera ci pregiamo includere il catalogo dei nostri articoli **e** il listino prezzi, valido fino al 31 marzo.

in response to your enquiry, we have pleasure in enclosing ... together with ...

Vi ringraziamo della vostra richiesta di informazioni del 16 giugno e siamo lieti di potervi offrire le seguenti condizioni:

thank you for your enquiry of ...

Questa offerta è **valida solo se ci farete pervenire una conferma prima del** 31 gennaio prossimo.

...subject to your firm acceptance by ...

Orders

Vogliate inviarci immediatamente i seguenti articoli nelle taglie e quantità sottoelencate...

please send us ...

Questo ordinativo è basato sul vostro listino prezzi, presupponendo l'usuale sconto del 10% per acquisti all'ingrosso.

the enclosed order ...

... and replies

Vi ringraziamo del vostro ordinativo in data 16 maggio a cui daremo seguito il più presto possibile.

thank you for your order of ...

Ci occorreranno circa 3 settimane per dar seguito al vostro ordinativo.

please allow 3 weeks for ...

Deliveries

I nostri termini di consegna sono di due mesi dalla data di ricevimento dell'ordinativo.

our delivery time is ...

Siamo in attesa di vostre istruzioni per quanto riguarda la consegna.

we await your instructions ...

La merce vi è stata spedita per ferrovia **il** 4 luglio.

the goods were despatched... on ...

Complaining

Non abbiamo ancora ricevuto gli articoli di cui al nostro ordinativo in data 26 agosto, n. 6496.

we have not yet received ...

Siamo costretti a segnalarvi un errore nel lotto ricevuto in data 3 febbraio.

we wish to draw your attention to an error ...

Purtroppo le merci sono state danneggiate durante il trasporto.

unfortunately ...

Siamo estremamente desolati nell'apprendere che **la qualità della merce era insoddisfacente** e siamo ben lieti di sostituire gli articoli in questione.

...the goods were unsatisfactory ...

Payment

Alla presente accludiamo la fattura n. 64321.

we enclose ...

Il totale ammonta a ... Vi saremmo grati se voleste saldarlo tempestivamente.

the total amount payable or outstanding is ...

Con la presente vi inviamo l'assegno di L.... **relativo alla vostra fattura** n. 678/94.

we enclose ...in settlement of your invoice no. ...

Vi ringraziamo del vostro assegno di... relativo alla nostra fattura N... **e ci teniamo a vostra disposizione per eventuali ulteriori ordinativi da parte vostra**.

thank you for your cheque for .... we look forward to doing further business with you in the near future.

Torino, 10 dicembre 1994

Carissimi Carlo e Francesca,

sono secoli che non ci si vede e così ho pensato di scrivervi per sentire cosa ne pensavate di venire da noi per qualche giorno. Abbiamo un sacco di cose da raccontarci e si potrebbe anche approfittare dell'occasione per fare un po' i turisti. Siccome le vacanze di Natale si stanno avvicinando che ne direste dei giorni fra S. Stefano e Capodanno? Fateci sapere qualcosa al più presto.

Non preoccupatevi per i bambini: naturalmente saranno i benvenuti!

Nella speranza di rivedervi presto, vi inviamo i nostri più affettuosi saluti.

Elena e Piercarlo

CARLA BOINOTTI
Via San Carlo 18
10100 Torino

Torino, 16 agosto 1995

Spett. Ditta,

qualche anno fa ho acquistato presso il vostro negozio un servizio da caffè in porcellana di Limoges, modello "Trianon".

Ho purtroppo rotto due tazzine e poiché vorrei sostituirle gradirei sapere se il modello è ancora in produzione. In caso di risposta affermativa, gradirei ricevere il vostro listino prezzi insieme alle modalità di consegna.

Ringraziandovi in anticipo, invio distinti saluti.

Carla B

Carla Boinotti

Standard formulae

Used when the person is not personally known to you

Opening
Gentile signore,
Gentile signora,
Gentile Signora/Signor Paolozzi,

Closing
Distinti saluti
La prego di accettare distinti saluti
Cordiali saluti

Used for acquaintances and friends

Fairly informal: "tu" form could be used

Opening
Caro Patrizio,
Cara Silvia,
Cari Claudio e Paola,

Closing
Cari saluti
Cordialmente
Saluti

Used for close friends and family

Opening
Caro Franco,
Carissima zia Carla,
Mio cara Giovanni,
Mia cara Ingrid
Carissimi nonni,

Closing
Ti abbraccio affettuosamente
Tante belle cose e tutti
Bacioni
Un abbraccio
A presto

Writing to a firm or an institution
Spett. Ditta,

To a person in an important position

Opening
Al Magnifico Rettore dell'Università di Torino,
Al Chiarissimo professore...
Sua eccellenza onorevole...

Closing
Gradisca i sensi della più viva stima
Con rispettosa cordialità
Rispettosamente suo

Starting a letter

Writing to someone you know

Sono stata molto contenta di ricevere tue notizie.	*it was very good to hear from you*
Mi dispiace moltissimo di non averti scritto prima e spero mi vorrai perdonare; ultimamente sono stata impegnatissima con il lavoro e...	*I'm sorry I haven't written for so long,...*
Non ci sentiamo da così tanto tempo che mi sento proprio in dovere di scrivervi almeno due righe per...	*it's such a long time since we were in touch that I felt I had to write a few lines just to ...*
Non so come cominciare questa lettera e spero che comprendiate il mio imbarazzo.	*this is a difficult letter for me to write ...*

Writing to an organization

Vi sarei estremamente riconoscente se poteste controllare nel vostro catalogo...	*I would be most grateful if you could ...*
Vi prego di inviarmi... Accludo un assegno dell'ammontare di L....	*Please send me ...*
Credo di aver dimenticato un impermeabile beige nella stanza del vostro hotel ove ho soggiornato per una settimana. **Vi sarei estremamente grata se poteste controllare** se è stato rinvenuto.	*...would you kindly let me know if ...*
Sono molto interessata ai vostri corsi estivi e **vorrei sapere se** vi sono ancora dei posti per...	*...I would like to know whether ...*

Ending a letter

To an acquaintance

Pietro si unisce a me nell'inviarvi cari saluti.	*Pietro joins me in sending ...*
(Fate pervenire) i miei più cordiali saluti anche a Marco	*give my kindest regards to Marco*

Giovanna vi manda cari saluti *or* **vi abbraccia**

Giovanna sends her kindest regards
  or her love

Ti prego di far pervenire i miei saluti alla mamma.
E mi raccomando non esitate a scrivermi se posso esservi di aiuto

please remember me to ...
don't hesitate to get in touch ...

To a friend

Caterina mi ha incaricato di trasmettervi cari saluti.

Caterina asks me to give you her
  best wishes

Saluta Sandra da parte mia.
Scrivimi quando hai un minuto di tempo libero.
E non dimenticatevi di **darci vostre notizie** di quando in quando.
Attendo con impazienza la tua risposta.

say hello to Sandra for me
do write ...
do let us have your news ...
hoping to hear from you soon

To a close friend

Abbraccia Mariella **da parte mia** e dille che sento molto la sua mancanza.
Un caro abbraccio a tutte e due da Maria.

give my love to ...
Maria sends her love to you both

39.3   Travel plans

Enquiring about and booking accommodation

Vi sarei grato se poteste inviarmi il vostro tariffario/listino prezzi.
Vorrei prenotare una camera con prima colazione.

please send me ...
I would like to book bed-and-
  breakfast accommodation with you

Vorrei prenotare una (camera) matrimoniale *or* **doppia per me e mia moglie e una con lettini gemelli per i bambini,** entrambi al di sotto dei 12 anni.

I wish to book one double room for
  my wife and myself and one twin-
  bedded room for our chidren ...

Confirming and cancelling a booking

Vogliate confermare per cortesia, a stretto giro di posta, la disponibilità di una camera singola con doccia, pensione completa per una settimana ad iniziare dal 24 giugno.
Vi prego di comunicarmi l'ammontare del deposito necessario per la prenotazione.
Vi prego di confermare la mia prenotazione e di tenermi la camera fino a tardi se necessario.
Purtroppo sono costretto a chiedervi di cambiare la prenotazione dal 25 agosto al 3 settembre.
Per ragioni indipendenti dalla mia volontà **sono costretto ad annullare la prenotazione** per una settimana, ad iniziare dal 5 settembre.
Vorrei prenotare una piazzola per un camper e una tenda (due adulti e due bambini) dal 15 giugno al 7 luglio incluso.

please let me know by return of post
  if you have ...
would you please let me know what
  deposit you require on this booking
please consider this a firm booking ...
I am afraid I must ask you to alter my
  booking ...
I am afraid (that) I have to cancel the
  booking ...
I wish to reserve a site for a caravan
  and a tent ...

40 Thanks

Un grazie ad entrambi per il vostro gentile pensiero.	*thank you both for your kind thought*
Scrivo per ringraziarvi di tutto cuore dei magnifici fiori che mi sono arrivati proprio oggi.	*I am writing to thank you most warmly for ...*
Non so come ringraziarvi per il vostro aiuto...	*I don't know how to thank you for ...*
Io e mio marito **vi siamo estremamente riconoscenti per** i vostri preziosi consigli.	*...are exceedingly grateful to you for ...*
È stato veramente gentile da parte vostra scrivere dopo...	*it was really very kind of you to ...*
Ringrazialo da parte mia per quello che ha fatto.	*give him my thanks for ...*
Vi ringrazio di avermi fatto pervenire il nuovo indirizzo.	*thank you for letting me have ...*
Grazie per aver dedicato tutto quel tempo ad aiutarmi a correggere la tesi.	*thank you for ...*

On behalf of a group

A nome dell'intero comitato ci tengo **ad esprimere la nostra gratitudine per** il sostegno dimostratoci durante i recenti avvenimenti.	*I am writing on behalf of ...to express our gratitude to you for ...*

To a group

Vi prego di trasmettere tutti i miei ringraziamenti ai vostri colleghi.	*please give my warmest thanks to your colleagues*
Vi prego di accettare i nostri più vivi ringraziamenti per il vostro contributo alla raccolta dei fondi.	*I would ask you to accept our most sincere thanks for ...*

41 Best Wishes

I migliori auguri di... da...	*with all good wishes for ... from ...*
Cari auguri di...	*with love and best wishes for ...*
Vogliate accettare i nostri più cordiali auguri per...	*please accept our best wishes for ...*

Season's Greetings

Buon Natale e felice Anno Nuovo da...	*Merry Christmas and Happy New Year from ...*
Auguri di Buone Feste da...	*Season's greetings from ...*

Birthday greetings

Buon compleanno da...	*happy birthday from ...*
Tanti auguri di buon compleanno	*best wishes for a happy birthday*
I nostri più sinceri auguri in occasione dei tuoi 18 anni.	*our very best wishes on your 18th birthday*
Cento di questi giorni!	*Many happy returns (of the day)*

Get well wishes

I miei più sentiti auguri per una pronta guarigione.	*very best wishes for a speedy recovery*

Wishing someone success

Le auguro tutto il successo che giustamente merita nella sua nuova carriera.	*I wish you every success in your new career.*

Giving congratulations

Verbally

Congratulazioni!	*Congratulations!*
Bravo!	*Well done!*

In writing

Mi felicito *or* **Mi congratulo con lei per** i brillanti risultati conseguiti al termine del corso di laurea.	*congratulations on...*
Permettete di offrirvi le mie più sentite congratulazioni per la vostra promozione.	*allow me to congratulate you on ...*

42 Announcements, invitations and replies

42.1 Announcements

Announcing a birth

in writing

Paolo e Giovanna Carlotti **sono lieti di annunciare la nascita della** piccola Francesca.

...*are happy to announce the birth of* ...

Francesco **annuncia con mamma e papà la nascita del fratellino** Carlo.

...*joins Mummy and Daddy in announcing the birth of his little brother* ...

To a friend

Abbiamo la grande gioia di annunciarvi la nascita della piccola Carlotta. Tutto è andato bene e la bimba è un vero amore!

we are delighted to tell you that we've had a little girl ...

And responding

Inviamo le nostre più sentite congratulazioni per la nascita della piccola Maria.

we send you our warmest congratulations on the birth of ...

Abbiamo ricevuto con immensa gioia l'annuncio della nascita del piccolo Fulvio. Congratulazioni e auguri di ogni felicità a tutti voi. Nella speranza di rivedervi presto, un caro abbraccio da Ruggero e Donatella

we are delighted to learn of the birth of ...

Announcing an engagement

in writing

Speranza e Fulvio Carretta **annunciano il fidanzamento della** loro figlia Carolina con Aldo Benotti.

...*are happpy to announce the engagement of* ...

And responding

Abbiamo appreso con immensa gioia del vostro fidanzamento e vi inviamo i nostri più sinceri auguri.

we were delighted to hear of your engagement and send you our warmest good wishes

Announcing a marriage

in writing

Paolo Rossi e Laura Torasso **annunciano il loro matrimonio che verrà celebrato** il giorno 3 dicembre alle ore 11 nella chiesa di San Giovanni. Paolo Rossi via del Carmelo, 18 Laura Torasso, vicolo Sant'Antonio 1.

...*are happy to announce their marriage, which will take place* ...

42.2 Invitations

Invitation to a wedding

Paolo e Ortensia **riceveranno amici e parenti** alle ore 13 presso l'hotel "la Colomba" via Fortezza 18 Pianezza R.S.V.P.

...*request the pleasure of your company afterwards at* ...*(on card inside wedding invitation)*

And responding

Ci congratuliamo con voi per la felice notizia e saremo ben lieti di partecipare alla cerimonia.

congratulations on your good news - we have great pleasure in accepting your invitation to the wedding

Ci congratuliamo con voi per la felice notizia ma **purtroppo a causa di improrogabili impegni siamo estremamente spiacenti di non poter partecipare alla cerimonia.**

....*to our great regret a previous engagement makes it impossible for us to accept your invitation to the wedding*

Ci congratuliamo con voi e **vi inviamo i nostri più sinceri auguri per un sereno futuro insieme.**
Sincere felicitazioni.
Con i nostri più sinceri auguri.
Carissimi auguri di ogni felicità alla cara Francesca in occasione del suo matrimonio.

....*our best wishes for happiness in your future life together*
warmest congratulations
with our very best wishes
best wishes for every happiness to dear Francesca on the occasion of her marriage

formal invitations

"il circolo" via Balduzzi 33 **ha l'onore di invitarLa** il 6 dicembre alle ore 18 **al** cocktail che si terrà in occasione della presentazione del primo volume della "Architettura: nuovi itinerari"

...*has pleasure in inviting you to* ...

I signori Dossi **saranno onorati di averla quale ospite** mercoledi 18 dicembre alle ore 20.

...request the pleasure of your company on ...

...and replies

Vi ringrazio del cortese invito a presenziare al lancio della vostra nuova collana al quale **sarò onoratissimo di intervenire/ma purtroppo non potrò intervenire** a causa di impegni precedenti.

thanks... and accepts with pleasure/but regrets that she cannot accept

informal invitations

Per festeggiare il fidanzamento di Ortensia e Filippo **organizzeremo un cocktail** al hotel "Principi di Piemonte" il 22 Ottobre dalle ore 20 **e saremo estremamente onorati se poteste intervenire**.

... we are holding a cocktail party ... and will be delighted if you could be with us

Michela e Giovanni **verranno a cena** da noi venerdì e **saremo felicissimi se anche voi poteste essere dei nostri**.

...are coming to lunch ... and we would be delighted if you could join us

Che ne diresti di passare la giornata a Santa Margherita?

would you like to spend the day ...

Quando sarete di passaggio a Torino dateci un colpo di telefono: **sarebbe bello ritrovarsi per una cena**.

when you are in ... it would be lovely if we could have dinner together

Abbiamo in programma di trascorre il mese di luglio a Cortina **e saremo onorati di ospitarvi** per qualche giorno.

we plan to spend July... and would be delighted to welcome you ...

... and replies

Un grazie per il vostro gentile invito: **sarò dei vostri!**

thank you for your very kind invitation I'm looking forward very much to being with you

Pensavamo di trascorrere la settimana delle vacanze pasquali a Porretta Terme **e vi telefoneremo per organizzare di vederci**.

we are thinking of spending Easter week... and we'll give you a ring to arrange a meeting.

Ci ha fatto un enorme piacere ricevere il vostro invito a trascorrere qualche giorno da voi e **contiamo di raggiungervi per un fine settimana il** 31 luglio.

we were so pleased to have your invitation... we hope to come for the weekend of...

Ti accompagnerò al Regio **con grande piacere. Ti ringrazio sentitamente per aver pensato a me**.

I'd love to go with you to ... Thank you so much for thinking of me

Purtroppo non potrò partecipare martedi prossimo alla vostra serata a causa di precedenti ed improrogabili impegni.

Unfortunately a previous engagement makes it impossible for me to accept your invitation for next Tuesday

Mi piacerebbe moltissimo venire da voi per un fine settimana ma purtroppo per le date da voi indicate sono già impegnata.

I'd love to spend a weekend with you ... but I can't manage any of the dates you suggest unfortunately

Purtroppo non potrò liberarmi prima della fine di dicembre: **che ne direste di spostare ad allora il nostro incontro?**

Unfortunately I won't be free until ... shall we put off our meeting until then?

Announcing a death

in a newspaper

È mancato all'affetto dei suoi cari Carlo Bonuzzi. **Ne danno il triste annuncio** la moglie Marisa con le adorate figlie Paola e Luisa. **I funerali si svolgeranno** nella parrocchia di Santa Maria in Santena venerdì 6 dicembre alle ore 10. **La salma verrà tumulata nella tomba di famiglia** a Chieri.

the death is announced of ... he leaves ... the funeral will take place ... burial will be in the family tomb ...

Con immenso dolore diamo il triste annuncio che la nostra cara mamma ci ha lasciate il 3 dicembre dopo una breve malattia.

we announce with deep sorrow the death of our beloved mother on 3 December after a short illness

And responding

Irene e Cesare Fava **partecipano al vostro profondo dolore e vi porgono le loro più sentite condoglianze**.

...join with you in your grief and offer their most sincere condolences

È con profondo dolore che apprendiamo della morte del vostro caro papà. Ci stringiamo a voi con affetto in quest'ora dolorosa.

we were greatly saddened to learn of the death of your dear father. We send you our warmest love and sympathy in your loss

Announcing a change of address

Vi prego di voler prender nota che **il nostro nuovo indirizzo** a partire dal 3 novembre **sarà** il seguente:...

...our new address ... will be ...

43 Essay writing

43.1 The broad outline of the essay

Introductory remarks

Al giorno d'oggi molti concordano nel sostenere **che** la disoccupazione minaccia la struttura stessa della società; **sta di fatto** che talune misure, suggerite da più parti, **implicano** a loro volta dei cambiamenti fondamentali, **tali da farci domandare se**, in certi casi, il rimedio non sia peggiore del male.
it is generally agreed today that ...however ...imply ...this leads us to wonder whether ...

"L'automobile, un lusso indispensabile". Ecco **un'affermazione che sentiamo spesso** a proposito della moderna società dei consumi. **Conviene dunque esaminare** quale sia il ruolo attualmente ricoperto dall'auto.
...such a remark is often heard ...let us therefore take a closer look at ...

Ancora una volta si tratta di sapere se valga la pena sacrificare un'intera comunità in nome del mero profitto.
once more the question arises ...

Non passa una settimana senza che si legga un articolo sul problema della disoccupazione: **una volta** è per sottolineare il ruolo dell'imprenditoria privata, **un'altra** è per criticare quello della scuola.
hardly a week goes by without ...sometimes ...sometimes ...

Queste posizioni così contraddittorie mettono ancora una volta in discussione il ruolo della famiglia nella società moderna.
this clash of opinions... calls once again into question ...

Un problema ricorrente al giorno d'oggi è quello del risanamento del debito pubblico.
one recurring problem today is ...

Non si può negare il fatto che la televisione abbia influenzato profondamente la nostra percezione della vita politica.
it cannot be denied that ...

Sarebbe da ingenui credere che i politici agiscano sempre disinteressatamente.
it would be naïve to believe that ...

Non si sta certo esagerando quando si dice che gli incidenti sul lavoro gravino pesantemente sul bilancio.
it is by no means an exaggeration to say that ...

Viviamo *or* **si vive in un mondo in cui** la pace è costantemente minacciata.
we live in a world where ...

Il corso della storia ci offre numerosi esempi di artisti misconosciuti in vita ed esaltati nelle epoche successive.
history offers us numerous example of ...

Non si può aprire un giornale senza trovare un ennesimo esempio di violenza.
it is impossible to open a newspaper without finding some new example of ...

43.2 Developing the argument

La prima constatazione da farsi è che l'argomento trattato dall'autore è poco conosciuto al pubblico.
the first thing to be said is that ...

Prendiamo come punto di partenza il ruolo che il governo ha giocato nell'elaborazione di questo programma.
let us begin with ...

Sarà utile esaminare il modo in cui l'autore ha definito i suoi personaggi nel primo capitolo.
it would be useful to consider ...

In primo luogo conviene esaminare l'affermazione secondo cui lo sport è un dovere.
let us first of all look at ...

Secondo l'autore la vita di provincia soffoca lo sviluppo culturale del personaggio ed **egli ritorna più volte su questo concetto**.
the author would have us believe that ... he repeatedly returns to this idea

Se cerchiamo di analizzare le cause dell'insoddisfazione degli insegnanti, **per prima cosa dobbiamo riconoscere** il ruolo giocato dagli incessanti cambiamenti partiti dall'alto, senza un consenso più ampio.
if we set out to analyse ... we must first acknowledge ...

Un tale atteggiamento merita di essere analizzato più da vicino; sarà bene dunque inserirlo in un contesto storico.
such an attitude deserves closer attention, ...

L'aspetto più significativo consiste purtroppo nella totale mancanza di coerenza.
the most significant feature is ...

Questa affermazione può parere azzardata, ma **solleva nondimeno una questione essenziale**, quella del rapporto fra arte e morale.
this assertion ... it however raises a fundamental question ...

Permettetemi ancora una volta di ribadire i fatti: le piogge acide distruggono ogni anno una considerevole parte dei boschi europei.
let me state the facts once more: ...

La prima domanda che ci si pone è di sapere quali motivi l'abbiano spinta ad agire così.
the first question that arises is ...

43.3 The other side of the argument

Dopo aver analizzato la successione degli eventi, **passiamo ora ad esaminare** lo stile.
...let us now consider ...

Poiché lo studio dell'ambiente non può darci delle risposte soddisfacenti su questo punto, **dobbiamo cercare quali altri fattori** possano aver contribuito a creare tale squilibrio.
...we need to look for other factors which ...

L'autore ha un bel da insistere sull'importanza della relazione fra l'eroina e il maestro: non riesce tuttavia ad essere pienamente convincente.
despite the author's efforts to stress ...

È necessario a questo punto affrontare la questione della censura televisiva.
we must now consider ...

Procediamo/andiamo ora ad analizzare i personaggi.
now we come to ...

Ed è questa una ragione sufficiente per invocare il ritorno della pena di morte?
is this really a good enough reason for ...

Passiamo ora ad un altro aspetto del problema, vale a dire le conseguenze che queste misure avranno sull'occupazione femminile.
let us now turn our attention to ...

Avendo stabilito che l'eroe non è spinto dal desiderio di vendetta, esaminiamo ora più da vicino la scena in cui si trova in presenza del padre.
...let us take a closer look at ...

Sarebbe interessante andare a vedere se si riscontra lo stesso fenomeno anche in altri paesi.
it would be interesting to see whether ...

È perfettamente giustificabile affermare che l'autore si è espresso con sincerità.
it is quite reasonable to suppose that ...

Ci si può accostare al problema da un'angolatura completamente diversa e considerare la portata politica di queste misure.
the problem could also be approached from another angle, by ...

Secondo l'autore la forma è più importante del contenuto, ma naturalmente si può ugualmente affermare l'esatto contrario.
for the author ... but of course one may equally well hold the opposite to be true

Siamo dunque autorizzati ad affermare che i difensori dei diritti degli animali siano diventati i profeti di una nuova moralità?
is it then reasonable to claim that ...

C'è un secondo aspetto che non può essere trascurato ed è il modo in cui i più giovani, così come gli anziani, sono particolarmente trascurati nella nostra società.
there is a second consideration which cannot be ignored, namely the way ...

43.4 The balanced view

Dopo un'attenta analisi dobbiamo comunque far notare che è la rapidità dei cambiamenti che potrebbe essere il fattore più importante.
when everything has been taken into account, it must nonetheless be pointed out that ...

Si deve comunque riconoscere che un intervento del Governo è a questo punto indispensabile.
it must however be recognised that ...

Dobbiamo tener conto anche di un terzo fattore.
we must allow for a third factor

Infine ci si deve domandare se l'interesse dell'opera non risieda invece nello studio della struttura sociale.
.finally we must ask ourselves if ...

La posizione dell'autore è più complessa di quanto non appaia a prima vista.
...is more complex ...

Dovremmo forse spingerci oltre e chiederci se il risvolto psicologico non sia, in ultima analisi, il tema centrale del testo.
we should perhaps go further and ask whether ...

In conclusion

Alla fine di questa complessa analisi che cosa si può concludere?
...what conclusions may be drawn?

Gli incidenti a cui abbiamo accennato precedentemente dimostrano chiaramente che i regolamenti non sono stati rispettati.
...which have been discussed earlier ...prove that ...

Sembrerebbe dunque che nel suo romanzo, l'autore non sia interessato al contesto sociale ed infatti tutta la sua attenzione si concentra sull'analisi psicologica.
it would seem clear that ... in point of fact ...

Tutto va a dimostrare che il carcere non fa altro che sfornare criminali.
all the evidence indicates that ...

Come valutare le attività di questi primi mesi del nuovo governo?
...how should we assess the performance of ...

Da quello che si è detto prima, si direbbe che l'autore si nasconda dietro i suoi personaggi femminili.
our previous discussion would seem to suggest that ...

In definitiva il nostro più grande problema è la mancanza di immaginazione.
all in all ...

Sembra che l'opinione pubblica sia sempre più cosciente del rischio nucleare.
it would appear then that ...

Questi dunque sono i principali mezzi espressivi utilizzati dall'autore.
these then are ...

43.5 Constructing a paragraph

ordering various elements within it

Si possono citare *or* invocare vari argomenti a questo proposito.
at this point, several arguments could be mentioned ...

Più fattori hanno contribuito al successo del prodotto: come prima cosa il direttore ha ottenuto una licenza di fabbricazione dal Giappone, quindi si è organizzata una vivace campagna pubblicitaria e in ultimo si è lanciata una nuova gamma di accessori.
several factors contributed to ...first ...then ...and lastly ...

Chi sono i poveri al giorno d'oggi? Be', **da una parte** or **da un lato** ci sono quelli che nascono poveri, **dall'altra** or **dall'altro** quelli che lo diventano. — *on the one hand ...and on the other ...*

I primi hanno analizzato gli aspetti sociali, **i secondi** si sono fatti carico delle implicazioni economiche. — *the first ...the second ... or the former ...the latter ...)*

Ciò è dovuto essenzialmente a tre fattori: il primo ... — *this is basically due to three factors: first ...*

La scuola è oggetto di critiche continue **così come** l'assistenza sanitaria. — *...as is ...*

Così come gli studenti si interrogano sull'utilità dei loro studi, **allo stesso modo gli insegnanti** si interrogano sul loro ruolo di educatori. — *just as students ...so also teachers ...*

Stabilito quanto sopra vorremmo far presente il deterioramento subito dalla merce. — *in view of the point made above ...*

Prima di affrontare la questione dello stile, **vorrei soffermarmi brevemente sulla** scelta delle metafore. — *let us look briefly at ...*

Senza entrare troppo nei dettagli, or **Senza soffermarci troppo sui dettagli ci terrei** a sottolineare l'importanza del suo intervento. — *without going into too much detail, we should ...*

Come vedremo in seguito più dettagliatamente, sono soprattutto i personaggi secondari a far progredire l'azione. — *as we shall see in greater detail later ...*

Non si può dissociare questo fattore dal complesso quadro descritto in precedenza. — *this factor cannot be separated from ...*

Si riprende qui un'idea già esposta in precedenza. — *here we touch again on an idea dealt with earlier*

Ritorneremo ancora su questo punto, tuttavia vogliamo già qui segnalare la totale assenza di emozioni in questo passaggio. — *we shall return to this later, but ...*

Ma per ritornare all'argomento che più ci sta a cuore or **interessa**, ... — *but to return to the topic which interests us most, ...*

Adding, enumerating etc

In più c'è da dire che il progetto è straordinariamente ben congegnato. — *moreover ...*

Inoltre, vogliamo far notare che gli operai sono stati sottopagati. — *we must also remember that ...*

Esamineremo le origini del problema e **anche** talune delle soluzioni che ci sono state suggerite. — *...as well as ... or ...in addition to ...*

Si devono includere anche le persone anziane nella statistica? **Oppure** si devono escludere i giovani e quelli che non risiedono nel Comune? **O ancora** si deve analizzare un campione più ampio? — *or ...or finally ...*

Varie categorie sono state completamente ignorate, **particolarmente** or **principalmente** le segretarie e le centraliniste. — *...in particular ...*

Si conoscono bene **i problemi della scuola** e **del** mondo del lavoro, **problemi** esacerbati quando si tratta delle minoranze etniche. — *...problems of schooling, of ..., problems which are ...*

Dal partito comunista **all'**estrema destra, **tutti si sono trovati d'accordo** nel condannare questo ennesimo atto di terrorismo. — *from ...to ... all are agreed ...*

Medici, chirurghi, anestesisti, infermieri: **tutti sono** ugualmente indispensabili. — *doctors, surgeons ...they are all ...*

A questo si deve aggiungere una notevole attenzione ai dettagli. — *added to that, ...*

Per quanto riguarda i personaggi secondari, **anch'essi sono** straordinariamente rappresentati. — *as far as the ...are concerned, they to are ...*

Per quanto concerne l'inquinamento chimico dobbiamo riconoscere che si tratta di un problema gravissimo. — *as far as ...is concerned or as for the matter of ...*

E per quanto riguarda le trasmissioni destinate ai giovanissimi, non sempre la qualità viene al primo posto. — *as for the ...*

Allo stesso modo potremmo inferire che lo stile manca totalmente di originalità. — *similarly ...*

Introducing one's own point of view

A mio avviso or **Secondo me** or **Per quanto mi concerne** questo è il miglior capitolo del libro. — *in my view or as far as I am concerned ...*

Per quanto mi riguarda or **Da parte mia** non c'è stato alcun ripensamento. — *as far as I am concerned or for my part ...*

Personalmente quello che mi ha colpito di più è stata la reazione del giudice. — *personally, what I found most striking was ...*

Se mi è permesso di esprimere un'opinione in proposito, mi sembra che l'autore si sia avventurato su un terreno minato. — *if I may be permitted to give my opinion ..*

Sono dell'opinione che la televisione abbia un effettto nefasto sulla formazione dei bambini. — *I maintain that ...or it is my view that ...*

L'autore afferma, **a pieno titolo secondo me**, che queste sono attitudini disfattiste. — *...and rightly, in my opinion ...*

Introducing someone else's point of view

Secondo l'autore il principale motivo del crimine è la gelosia. — *according to the author ...*

Come viene spesso sottolineato dagli esperti, l'importante è inventare nuove soluzioni. — *as the experts often stress ...*

Il bilancio del ministro rispetta, **secondo lui** or **stando a lui**, le normative CEE. — *...he says ...*

Dice/afferma/crede/dichiara che questo sistema presenterà numerosi problemi in futuro. — *he says/thinks/believes/declares that ...*

L'autore attira la nostra attenzione su/ci ricorda/ci segnala la necessità di apportare dei cambiamenti. — *the author draws our attention to/reminds us of/points out ...*

Insiste sul fatto che/sostiene/afferma che sono state le rivalità intestine ad indebolire l'organizzazione. — *he emphasizes/maintains/claims/ that ...*

Gli esperti **pretendono che** sia possibile/**vogliono farci credere che** sia possibile imparare le lingue senza alcun sforzo. — *...claim or would have us believe that ...*

Secondo la versione ufficiale dei fatti, gli arrestati sarebbero solo qualche decina. — *according to the official version of the facts ...*

Introducing an example

Prendiamo il caso dell'invio di armamenti in paesi dalla situazione politica instabile. — *consider the case of ...*

Basta citare ad esempio i documentari a sfondo educativo. — *one need only instance ...*

Basta un solo esempio a segnalare l'importanza di questa ristrutturazione. — *a single example will suffice to show ...*

Uno degli esempi più eclatanti si trova nel terzo capitolo. — *one of the most striking examples ...*

In questo caso, ad esempio, mille operai, di cui il 10% donne, rischiano di perdere il posto. — *...In this case, for example, ...*

Introducing a quotation or source

Secondo gli autori della relazione "l'importante non è sfamare l'Africa, è partecipare al suo rimboschimento la vera risposta." — *according to ...*

Conclude/dichiara/osserva/ La Fontaine 'Il più forte ha sempre ragione' — *...concludes/declares/observes ...*

Come ha fatto notare il presidente 'la crescita economica dipende dagli investimenti' — *as the president has pointed out ...*

Il Foscolo **scrive**:... — *...writes: ...*

... riprende l'idea (di)... — *takes up the same theme ...*

A dirla con... — *in the words of ...*

In un articolo pubblicato recentemente in "..." troviamo la seguente affermazione **a firma di**... — *in a recent article in ... from the pen of ...*

43.6   The mechanics of the argument

Introducing a fact

È vero che i lavori sono cominciati. — *it is true that ...*

Si constata or **si osserva** un consistente miglioramento. — *...is noticeable*

È stato notato che la CEE non ha dato il suo assenso. — *it was noted that ...*

È or **si tratta di** una questione semplicistica. — *it is a ...*

Il nuovo programma è **stato fatto oggetto di** violentissime critiche. — *...has been a target for ...*

Non dobbiamo perdere di vista i fatti: l'inquinamento del Reno si è fatto inquietante e... — *we must not lose sight of the facts: ...*

Man mano che ci si inoltra nella lettura dell'opera si aprono nuove prospettive. — *as one reads on, new perspectives open up*

L'autore racconta delle numerose superstizioni concernenti piante e animali. — *the author details ...*

Indicating a supposition

Siamo pienamente autorizzati a supporre che questa sarà la soluzione adottata. — *one might justifiably suppose that ...*

È probabile che la loro reazione venga conosciuta fra poco. — *it is probable that ...*

Viene qui citata la possibilità di un nuovo vertice. — *the possibility of ... is mentioned here*

Ci potrebbe essere un'altra spiegazione. — *there could be ...*

Supponiamo che diventi obbligatorio usare la benzina senza piombo: gli automobilisti dovranno adeguarsi a... — *let us suppose that ...*

Il rifiuto **fa pensare** or **lascia pensare che** i fondi necessari non siano stati raccolti in tempo. — *...leads one to think that ...*

Non è impossibile che ci sia un'esplosione. — *it is not impossible that ...*

Questo spiegherebbe l'abbassamento delle temperature in febbraio. — *this would explain ...*

Si presuppone che l'autore fosse a conoscenza dei fatti. — *one may assume that ...*

Expressing a certainty

È chiaro che or è **evidente che** questa scoperta costituisce un gran passo avanti. — *it is clear that ...*

Il suo secondo romanzo è **senza dubbio** il migliore. — *...is indisputably or undeniably ...*

Tutto fa credere or **pensare che** vincerà lei.
everything leads one to the conclusion that ...

Senza dubbio ha del talento. / **Non c'è alcun dubbio che** abbia del talento.
there can be no doubt that ...

Tutti sono d'accordo nel criticare i suoi metodi.
everyone agrees in criticising ...

È chiaro che gli avvenimenti hanno preso una brutta piega.
it is clear that ...

Come tutti sanno la camomilla è un rimedio sicuro contro l'insonnia.
as everyone knows ...

Indicating doubt or uncertainty

Sembra che abbia cercato di contattarli.
it would seem that ...

È possibile or **può essere** or **può darsi che** non se ne sia accorto.
it is possible that ...

Forse alla gente piacerà di più questo tipo di trasmissione.
perhaps people will prefer ...

Sarebbe forse preferibile risparmiare più elettricità.
it might be preferable to ...

Potrebbe trattarsi di or **essere** un nuovo virus.
it could be ...

Questo potrebbe spiegare il ritardo con cui ci è giunta la notizia.
this could explain ...

Questo rimette in dubbio la validità delle statistiche.
this again calls into question ...

È difficile credere che sia stata presa una tale decisione.
It is difficult to believe that ...

Conceding a point

Si sa come ridurre l'inquinamento, **tuttavia** spesso è una questione di costi.
...however ...

Sebbene i personaggi siano descritti con cura, mancano di autenticità.
although ...

Lo stile è interessante **seppure** appesantito da un uso eccessivo di figure retoriche.
...albeit ...

Fino ad un certo punto hanno ragione, però...
they are right up to a point, but ...

Sono d'accordo con l'autore su molti punti, tuttavia ho ancora qualche riserva.
I agree with the author on many points, but ...

Ovviamente or **sicuramente** la riduzione della velocità limiterà il numero degli incidenti, **ma** si creeranno altri problemi.
of course... but ...

Secondo lei è finito: **resta comunque il fatto che** si devono ancora mettere a punto numerosi dettagli.
... the fact remains that ...

Per quanto grande sia la sua bravura di regista, resta tuttavia il fatto che la storia è totalmente implausibile.
no matter how talented he is ...

Non si può negare che l'introduzione dei robot abbia ridotto il numero degli impiegati, ma...
it cannot be denied that ...

Senza dubbio la pubblicità aumenta le vendite, ma costa anche parecchio.
...undoubtedly ...

Senza arrivare a dire che le donne siano sfruttate sul lavoro, **bisogna riconoscere tuttavia che** le difficoltà da loro incontrate siano ancora numerose.
...it must nonetheless be recognized that ...

Pur ammettendo or **riconoscendo** che i nuovi quartieri siano serviti ad alloggiare migliaia di senzatetto, **ci si deve render conto che** le condizioni di vita sono spesso intollerabili.
while recognising ...one must also accept that ...

Senza dubbio la solitudine è uno dei mali della società moderna, **ma** sono spesso gli individui stessi a crearne le condizioni.
undeniably ...but ...

Il minimo che si può dire è che almeno ha fatto un'offerta disinteressata.
the least one can say is that ...

Emphasizing particular points

Per sottolineare la complessità del problema l'autore si addentra nella descrizione dei risvolti sociali.
in order to emphasize ...

Sarà bene precisare che si tratta di un metodo ancora largamente usato.
we should make it quite clear that ...

Questa decisione **mette in luce** l'ignoranza e i pregiudizi di cui è afflitto.
...highlights ...

Non dimentichiamoci che le donne vivono nel complesso più a lungo degli uomini.
let us not forget that ...

Si deve insistere sul fatto che nessuno ne era a conoscenza.
we must make it absolutely clear that ...

È quest'incidente **che** ha iniziato la rivolta.
it was this ...which ...

Se non se ne è ancora occupata è **per indifferenza e non per mancanza di tempo.**
it is lack of interest rather than lack of time that has prevented her from ...

Non solo si è opposto alla riduzione del budget, **ma** ha chiesto ulteriori finanziamenti.
not only did he ...but ...

Questo non significa che il libro sia poco valido, si vuole **piuttosto** sottolineare che l'autore è ancora immaturo.
this does not mean that ..., but rather ...

L'ambizione, **ecco che cosa** lo distingue dagli altri.
...that is what ...

Lungi dal trasformarci in deficienti, la televisione ci informa e diverte.
far from turning us into ...

La disoccupazione sta aumentando e **il fenomeno è aggravato dall'**inerzia governativa.
...the problem is worsened by ...

Ci sono numerose inesattezze, **ma la cosa più grave è che** l'intera cronologia è errata.
...but the worst thing is that ...

È una legge ingiusta, **oggi più che mai**, con l'evoluzione che c'è stata nella protezione dei diritti del malato. — *...now more than ever that ...*

Moderating a statement

Senza voler criticare i suoi metodi, ho l'impressione che avrebbe potuto scegliere una soluzione più economica. — *without wishing to criticize ...*

L'autore ha ragione **nel complesso**, ma certi dettagli meritano di essere rivisti. — *...by and large ...*

Sarebbe auspicabile chiarire insieme alcuni punti. — *here we might usefully attempt to clarify certain points*

Senza voler dare troppa importanza ai dettagli, si impone tuttavia una revisione. — *without laying too much emphasis on details ...*

Sarebbe ingiusto rimproverargli la sua inesperienza. — *it would be unfair to ...*

Sarebbe di cattivo gusto chiedergli i particolari. — *it would be churlish to ...*

Indicating agreement

Molti lo trovano orribile **e, in effetti**, *or* **effettivamente**, è un pugno in un occhio. — *...and indeed ...*

Si deve ammettere che ci sono stati dei miglioramenti. — *one must admit that ...*

La sua descrizione dei fatti è **esatta in ogni dettaglio**. — *...is correct in every detail*

La spiegazione che ci ha dato è **pienamente convincente** *or* **ci ha pienamente convinto.** — *...is wholly convincing*

Non possiamo far altro che inchinarci di fronte alla sua rettitudine. — *we can only pay tribute to his integrity*

Come suggerito dall'autore *or* **Come suggerisce l'autore**, si dovrebbero proseguire le ricerche. — *as the author suggests ...*

Effettivamente **tutto sembrerebbe far pensare ad** un incidente di eccezionale gravità. — *everything would seem to point to ...*

È evidente *or* **chiaro che** si tratta di un metodo efficace. — *it is clear that ...*

Indicating disagreement

È impossibile accettare il suo punto di vista. — *it is impossible to accept ...*

È un suggerimento che non merita neanche di essere preso in esame. — *it is a suggestion which doesn't merit a moment's consideration*

Gli abitanti hanno **protestato contro** la costruzione del ponte. — *...protested against ...*

Questi fatti contraddicono *or* **sono in contraddizione** con la versione ufficiale. — *these facts contradict ...*

Non se ne parla neanche di andare a nuove elezioni. — *there can be no question of ...*

Sono costretto **ad esprimere qualche riserva / a sollevare delle obiezioni**. — *...to express some reservations/to raise some objections*

Il ministro **ha negato la tesi secondo cui** la medicina preventiva sia, in ultima analisi, la più economica. — *...took issue with the claim that ...*

A tutti i critici della pubblicità, **possiamo rispondere** *or* **si può rispondere che** si tratta di un nuovo genere artistico. — *...one can reply that ...*

È una tesi discutibile. — *this is a questionable view •*

L'autore commette un grave errore inducendoci a pensare che sia stato raggiunto un accordo. — *the author makes a grave mistake in ...*

Sebbene sia molto valido, **non condivido il punto di vista dell'autore**. — *...I do not share the author's point of view*

Anche se ha ragione su questo punto, sta di fatto che non è arrivato ad alcuna conclusione. — *even if he is right ...*

Si è ancora molto lontani dalla verità nel dire che ci sono state 2000 vittime. — *it is nowhere near the truth to say ...*

Indicating approval

Non è difficile capire come un simile atteggiamento abbia trovato molti consensi. — *one can well understand how ...*

Effettivamente la soluzione migliore sarebbe restaurarlo. — *the best solution would certainly be to ...*

Basta leggere le prime righe per essere immediatamente trasportati nella Venezia del '700. — *you have only to read the opening lines to be ...*

Hanno avuto ragione nell'includere nello studio anche i minorenni. — *they were right to ...*

L'autore **sottolinea a ragione** *or* **giustamente** questo punto. — *...rightly emphasizes ...*

Era ora che qualcuno prendesse le difese degli anziani. — *it was certainly high time that ...*

Finalmente un'opera che tratta dei problemi delle lavoratrici part-time. — *at last, a work which deals with ...*

Indicating disapproval

È un peccato che l'autore non sia presente. — *it is a pity that ...*

Sarebbe un peccato se un'opera di tale portata non venisse tradotta. — *it would be a pity if ...*

Sfortunatamente è un'opera di limitatissimo interesse. — *unfortunately ...*

Sorprende la rapidità con cui le riforme sono state applicate. — *one may well be surprised at ...*

È difficile immaginare come gli allievi ne possano beneficiare. — *it is difficult to see how ...*

Tutti **hanno criticato** or **condannato** aspramente il progetto di una nuova autostrada.

...have condemned ...

Si accusa il Governo or **si rimprovera al Governo di** non aver agito in tempo.

there are complaints that the government ...

Making a correction

In realtà non è di questo che sto parlando.

in (actual) fact ...

Non è questione di soldi, **ma piuttosto è** la volontà di intervenire tempestivamente che è mancata.

it is not a question of..., but rather of ...

Sei molto lontano dalla verità: in realtà ...

you are very far from the truth: in fact ...

Ad un'analisi più attenta le sue critiche **non sembrano per niente giustificate.**

On closer examination...do not seem to be at all justified

Sono critiche senza alcun fondamento.

These criticisms are quite without foundation

Indicating the reason for something

È dovuto ad un malinteso.

this arises from ...

Questo è il motivo per cui ci è impossibile terminare in tempo.

it is for this reason that...

Il castello sarà restaurato: **in effetti rappresenta** uno dei migliori esempi di architettura del XVI secolo.

...indeed, it is ...

Non ci si può basare su queste cifre, **visto che** i dati di partenza sono così approssimativi.

...given that ...

Se è stato accettato è **certamente perchè** sono sono state fatte delle pressioni.

...it is undoubtedly because ...

Questo spiega or **spiegherebbe** il calo delle vendite in febbraio.

this would explain ...

L'autore **lascia intendere che** il vero motivo sia un altro.

...suggests that ...

Setting out the consequences of something

La decisione **ha avuto conseguenze fatali**.

...had fatal consequences

I recenti licenziamenti **hanno avuto la conseguenza** or **l'effetto di** creare un diffuso malcontento.

...have led to ...

Si può dunque concludere or **dedurre che** l'autore non sia completamente d'accordo con un tale concetto dell'autorità.

one is led to the conclusion that ...

Era molto scontento delle condizioni e **questo è il motivo per cui** si è licenziato.

...this is why ...

Ed ecco perchè la famiglia occupa una posizione centrale nel suo romanzo.

...and that is why ...

La sospensione del servizio **avrà come conseguenza** or **risultato** un aumento del traffico automobilistico.

...will result in ...

I posti verranno ridotti di un terzo, **il che implica** or **significa** il licenziamento di tre impiegati.

...which means ...

Il personaggio principale non appare in questo capitolo, **con il risultato che** le figure secondarie occupano una posizione primaria.

...and as a consequence ...

Si è rifiutato di dare una spiegazione, il **che sembra confermare la sua colpevolezza**.

...which seems to confirm his guilt

Contrasting or comparing

Alcuni dicono che la produzione di energia sia essenziale allo sviluppo, **altri sostengono** che sia già eccessiva.

some say ...others declare ...

Mentre alcuni sono certi del declino dei servizi sociali, **altri,** al contrario, sbandierano i risultati positivi recentemente conseguiti.

while some people ... others ...

È molto meglio del suo rivale./ **Lo sorpassa di gran lunga**.

he is far better than ...

Questa, **in confronto al** suo primo romanzo, è un'opera molto più raffinata.

...compared with ...

Fra questi due libri **non c'è alcun confronto**.

...there is no comparison

44   The telephone

44.1   Getting a number

Vorrei il 46 57 86, per favore.
(quarantasei cinquantasette ottantasei or quattro sei cinque sette otto sei)
Deve cercare il numero sull'elenco telefonico.
Può avere il numero tramite il servizio informazioni internazionali.
Mi può passare il servizio informazioni, per favore?
Vorrei il numero della ditta Decapex, via Manzoni 20, Vercelli.
Il numero non è sull'elenco
Mi spiace, il loro numero è fuori elenco.
Qual è il prefisso di Livorno?
Posso telefonare in Colombia direttamente or senza passare per il centralino?
Se chiama l'Inghilterra dall'Italia deve omettere lo '0' iniziale.
Cosa devo fare per ottenere la linea esterna?

44.2   Different types of calls

È una telefonata or chiamata urbana.
È una telefonata or chiamata interurbana da Foggia.
Vorrei telefonare all'estero. // Vorrei fare una telefonata internazionale.
Vorrei fare una telefonata a carico del destinatario.
Vorrei fare una telefonata con preavviso di chiamata al signor Sergio Pozzi, numero 26 85 77 08.
Vorrei fare una telefonata con indicazione di durata a Messina.
Vorrei telefonare pagando con la carta di credito.
Qual è il numero per avere l'ora esatta?
Vorrei la sveglia telefonica alle 7.30 domani mattina.

44.3   The operator speaks

Che numero desidera?
Che numero vuole? // Che numero sta facendo?
Da dove chiama?
Mi ripete il numero, per favore?
Può chiamare questo numero direttamente.
Riaggranci il ricevitore e rifaccia il numero.
C'è una telefonata a suo carico dal signor Baresi ad Amsterdam. Accetta la chiamata?
C'è una telefonata con preavviso di chiamata per il signor Williams. È lì?
Prego, è in linea.
(Servizio Informazioni) Non c'è nessun abbonato con questo nome.
Il 45 77 57 84 non risponde.
Provo a ridarle la linea.
Attenda in linea, prego.
Al momento tutte le linee per la Francia sono occupate. Riprovi più tardi.
È un telefono a scheda.
Sto cercando di darle la linea.
Sta suonando.
La linea è occupata.

44.4   When your number answers

Mi può passare l'interno 516, per favore?
Parla il signor Lamberti?
Vorrei parlare con il signor Matta, per favore. // C'è il signor Matta, per favore?
Mi può passare il dottor Asselle, per cortesia?
Chi parla?

Richiamerò più tardi.
Richiamerò tra una mezz'ora.
Potrei lasciare il numero e farmi richiamare?
Sto telefonando da una cabina. // Sto chiamando da una cabina telefonica.
Sto telefonando or chiamando dall'Inghilterra.
Potrebbe chiedergli di chiamarmi quando rientra?
Le dispiace chiamare lei quel numero per me?

44.5   The switchboard operator speaks

Pronto, Hotel Rex, desidera?
Chi parla, per cortesia?
Chi devo annunciare?
Sa il numero dell'interno?
Glielo passo.
Le passo la signora Marelli.
C'è una telefonata in linea da Tokyo per la signora Marelli.
C'è la signorina Martini in linea.
La signora Bottaro è in linea da Parigi per lei.
Il dottor Cassini è sull'altra linea.
Rimanga in linea, per favore.
Non risponde nessuno.
Il Servizio Vendite è in linea.

44.6   Recorded messages

Telecom Italia: Informazione gratuita. **Il numero selezionato da voi è inesistente.**
Telecom Italia: **La numerazione da lei formulata è inesistente. La preghiamo di consultare l'elenco abbonati.**
Telecom Italia: servizio gratuito. **L'utente da lei chiamato ha cambiato numero. Attenda in linea senza riaggranciare poiché stiamo inoltrando automaticamente la sua chiamata al nuovo numero 45 63 02. Per le prossime comunicazioni la preghiamo di utilizzare la nuova numerazione. Grazie.**
Telecom Italia: **Servizio 12 (dodici). Risponde l'operatore numero 56.**
Telecom Italia: **informazione gratuita. Il terminale potrebbe essere spento.** (for mobile phones)

44.7   Answering the telephone

Pronto, sono Anna.
(Anna?) Sì, sono io.
Vuole lasciare un messaggio?
C'è un messaggio per lui?
Non chiuda. // Non riaggranci.
Metta giù e la richiamo io.
Questo è un messaggio registrato.
Lasciate un messaggio dopo il segnale acustico.

44.8   When in trouble

Non riesco a prendere la linea.
Non mi dà nessun segnale.
Mi dà solo il segnale 'non c'è nessun abbonato al numero da lei richiesto'.
Il loro apparecchio è fuori servizio.
È caduta la linea.
Devo aver fatto un numero sbagliato.
C'è un'interferenza sulla linea.
Ho chiamato diverse volte ma non ho avuto risposta.
Mi ha dato un numero sbagliato.
Mi hanno dato l'interno sbagliato.
La linea è molto disturbata.

A

A, a [a] SF O M INV (*lettera*) A, a; **A come Ancona** ≈ A for Andrew (*Brit*), ≈ A for Able (*Am*); **dall'a alla zeta** from A to Z.

A [a] ABBR **a** = **autostrada; sull'A1** ≈ on the M1 (*Brit*) **b** (= *altezza*) h **c** (= *area*) A.

---

a [a] PREP

---
a+il=al, a+lo=allo, a+l'=all', a+la=alla, a+i=ai, a+gli=agli, a+le=alle
---

a (*complemento di termine*) to (*spesso omesso*);
▷ *dare* qc a qn to give sth to sb, give sb sth
▷ **ho dato un giocattolo a Sandro** I gave Sandro a toy, I gave a toy to Sandro
b (*stato in luogo: posizione*) at; (: *in*) in; (: *su*) on;
▷ *abitare* **a Milano/al terzo piano** to live in Milan/on the third floor
▷ **è a 10** *chilometri* **da qui** it's 10 kilometres from here
▷ *essere* **a scuola/a casa/al cinema** to be at school/at home/at the cinema
▷ *lavora* **alle poste/alle ferrovie** he works at the Post Office/on the railways
▷ **alla** *radio* on the radio
▷ **alla** *televisione* on television
c (*moto a luogo*) to;
▷ *andare* **a casa/a Roma/al mare** to go home/to Rome/to the seaside
d (*tempo*) at; (*epoca, stagione*) in; (*fino a*) to, till, until;
▷ **alle** *3* at 3 o'clock
▷ **all'***alba* at dawn
▷ **a 18** *anni* **si diventa maggiorenni** at 18 you come of age
▷ **dalle** *3* **alle** *5* from 3 to *o* till 5 (o'clock)
▷ **a** *domani*! see you tomorrow!
▷ **tornerà a** *giorni* he'll be back in a few days
▷ **a** *lunedì*! see you on Monday!
▷ **a** *maggio* in May
▷ **a** *mezzanotte* at midnight
▷ **tornerà a** *minuti* he'll be back in a few minutes
▷ **a** *Natale* at Christmas
▷ **a** *primavera* in spring
e (*mezzo, modo*) on, by, with;
▷ **andare a** *cavallo* to go on horseback
▷ **bistecca ai** *ferri* grilled steak
▷ **bistecca alla** *fiorentina* T-bone steak
▷ **fatto a** *mano* made by hand, handmade
▷ **scrivere qc a** *matita* to write sth in pencil *o* with a pencil
▷ **alla** *milanese* Milanese-style, in the Milanese fashion
▷ **una barca a** *motore* a motorboat
▷ **andare a** *piedi* to go on foot
▷ **gonna a** *pieghe* pleated skirt
▷ **pasta al** *pomodoro* pasta with *o* in tomato sauce
▷ **gonna a** *righe* striped skirt
▷ **entrare a** *uno* **a** *uno* to come in one by one
f (*rapporto*) by, per; (*con prezzi*) at;
▷ **essere pagato a** *giornata* to be paid by the day
▷ **vendere qc a** *5.000 lire* **il chilo** to sell sth at 5,000 lire a *o* per kilo
▷ **prendo 3 milioni al** *mese* I get 3 million lire a *o* per month
▷ **viaggiare a** *100 km* **all'***ora* to travel at 100 km an *o* per hour
▷ **essere pagato a** *ore* to be paid by the hour
g (*scopo, fine*) for, to;
▷ **restare a** *cena* to stay for *o* to dinner.

AA SIGLA = *Alto Adige.*
A.A.S.T. [a'a'ɛsse'ti] SIGLA F = **Azienda Autonoma di Soggiorno e Turismo.**
AA.VV. ABBR = *autori vari.*
ab. ABBR = **abitante.**
abaco, chi ['abako] SM (*Archit, Mat*) abacus.
abate [a'bate] SM abbot.
abat-jour [a'ba'ʒur] SM INV bedside lamp.

abbacchiato, a [abbakˈkjato] AGG (*fam*) down, depressed; **ha un'aria abbacchiata** he's looking a bit down.

abbacinare [abbatʃiˈnare] VT to dazzle.

abbacinato, a [abbatʃiˈnato] AGG dazzled, blinded.

abbagliante [abbaʎˈʎante] ☐1 AGG dazzling; **fare uso dei fari abbaglianti** to have one's headlights on full (*Brit*) *o* high (*Am*) beam.
☐2 SM, GEN PL (*Aut*): **accendere gli abbaglianti** to put one's headlights on full (*Brit*) *o* high (*Am*) beam.

abbagliare [abbaʎˈʎare] VT (*anche fig*) to dazzle; (*illudere*) to delude; **non lasciarti abbagliare** don't let yourself be taken in.

abbaglio, gli [abˈbaʎʎo] SM blunder; **prendere un abbaglio** to blunder, make a blunder.

abbaiare [abbaˈjare] VI: **abbaiare (a)** to bark (at); (*fig*: *gridare rabbiosamente*) to bawl (at).

abbaino [abbaˈino] SM (*finestra*) dormer window; (*soffitta*) attic room.

abbandonare [abbandoˈnare] ☐1 VT **a** (*gen*) to abandon; (*famiglia, paese*) to abandon, desert; **abbandonare qn a se stesso** to leave sb to his (*o* her) own devices; **il coraggio lo abbandonò** his courage deserted him; **abbandonare la nave** (*anche fig*) to abandon ship; **abbandonare il campo** (*Mil, fig*) to retreat
b (*trascurare*: *casa, lavoro*) to neglect
c (*rinunciare a*) to give up; (: *studi, progetto, speranza*) to abandon, give up; **abbandonare la gara** to withdraw from the race
d (*lasciare andare*: *redini*) to slacken; **abbandonò la testa sul cuscino** he let his head fall back on the pillow.
☐2 **abbandonarsi** VR to let o.s. go; **si abbandonò sul divano** he sank onto the couch; **abbandonarsi a qc** (*ricordi, passioni*) to give o.s. up to sth; **abbandonarsi a qn** (*affidarsi*) to put o.s. in sb's hands.

abbandonato, a [abbandoˈnato] AGG **a** (*casa*) deserted; (*miniera*) disused **b** (*trascurato*: *terreno, podere*) neglected **c** (*bambino*) abandoned.

abbandono [abbanˈdono] SM **a** (*di famiglia, paese*) desertion, abandonment ▶ **abbandono del tetto coniugale** (*Dir*) desertion
b (*trascuratezza*) neglect; **in abbandono** (*edificio, giardino*) neglected; **lasciare qc in stato di abbandono** to neglect sth
c (*rinuncia*: *di progetto*) abandonment, dropping, giving up
d (*Sport*) withdrawal; **vincere per abbandono dell'avversario** to win by default
e (*rilassamento, cedimento*) abandon; **momenti di abbandono** moments of abandon.

abbarbicarsi [abbarbiˈkarsi] VIP: **abbarbicarsi (a)** (*anche fig*) to cling (to).

abbassamento [abbassaˈmento] SM lowering; (*di pressione, livello dell'acqua*) fall; (*di prezzi*) reduction; ▶ **abbassamento di temperatura** drop in temperature.

abbassare [abbasˈsare] ☐1 VT **a** to lower; (*leva*) to press down; (*finestrino della macchina*) to wind down; (*finestrino del treno, tapparella*) to pull down; **abbassare le armi** (*Mil*) to lay down one's arms; **abbassò la testa per la vergogna** he hung his head in shame; **abbassare la guardia** (*Sport, fig*) to drop one's guard
b (*volume, radio, TV*) to turn down; (*voce*) to lower
c (*diminuire*: *prezzi*) to reduce, bring down
d (*luce*) to dim; (*fari*) to dip (*Brit*), dim (*Am*)

e (*Geom*: *perpendicolare*) to drop.
☐2 **abbassarsi** VR (*chinarsi*) to bend down, stoop; (: *per evitare*) to duck; (*fig*: *umiliarsi*) to demean o.s.; **abbassarsi a fare qc** to lower o.s. to do sth.
☐3 **abbassarsi** VIP **a** (*temperatura, prezzi*) to drop, fall; (*marea*) to go out, fall; (*livello*) to go down; (*sipario*) to fall
b (*peggiorare*: *vista*) to deteriorate.

abbasso [abˈbasso] ESCL: **abbasso il re!** down with the king!

abbastanza [abbasˈtantsa] AVV **a** (*a sufficienza*) enough; **non mangia abbastanza** he doesn't eat enough; **non ho abbastanza tempo/denaro** I don't have *o* haven't got enough *o* sufficient time/money; **hai trovato una casa abbastanza grande per la tua famiglia?** have you found a big enough house for your family?; **non ho abbastanza denaro per comprarlo** I don't have enough money to buy it; **averne abbastanza di qn/qc** to have had enough of sb/sth, be fed up with sb/sth
b (*alquanto*) quite, rather, fairly; **un vino abbastanza dolce** quite a sweet wine, a fairly sweet wine; **ti piace il film? — sì, abbastanza** are you enjoying the film? — yes, quite *o* it's o.k.

abbattere [abˈbattere] ☐1 VT **a** (*edificio, muro, ostacolo*) to knock down; (*albero*) to fell, cut down; (*sogg*: *vento*) to bring down; (*aereo*) to shoot down; (*porta*) to break down; (*fig*: *governo*) to overthrow
b (*uccidere*: *persona, selvaggina*) to shoot; (: *bestie da macello*) to slaughter; (: *cane, cavallo*) to destroy, put down
c (*prostrare*: *sogg*: *malattia, disgrazia*) to lay low; **non lasciarti abbattere** don't be disheartened, don't let it get you down.
☐2 **abbattersi** VIP **a** (*cadere*): **abbattersi al suolo** to fall to the ground
b (*colpire*): **abbattersi su** (*sogg*: *maltempo*) to beat down on; (: *disgrazia*) to hit, strike
c (*avvilirsi*) to lose heart.

abbattimento [abbattiˈmento] SM **a** (*di albero*) felling; (*di muro*) knocking down; (*di casa*) demolition; (*di aereo*) shooting down (*Brit*), downing (*Am*); (*di animali*: *a caccia*) shooting; (: *al macello*) slaughter **b** (*prostrazione*: *fisica*) exhaustion; (: *morale*) despondency.

abbattuto, a [abbatˈtuto] AGG despondent, depressed.

abbazia [abbatˈtsia] SF abbey.

abbecedario, ri [abbetʃeˈdarjo] SM ABC book.

abbellimento [abbelliˈmento] SM **a** (*ornamento*) embellishment **b** (*Mus*) embellishment, grace note.

abbellire [abbelˈlire] ☐1 VT to make (more) attractive; (*racconto*) to embellish.
☐2 **abbellirsi** VIP to become more attractive.

abbeveraggio, gi [abbeveˈraddʒo] SM (*di animali*) watering.

abbeverare [abbeveˈrare] ☐1 VT to water.
☐2 **abbeverarsi** VR to drink.

abbeverata [abbeveˈrata] SF (*atto*) watering; (*luogo*) watering place.

abbeveratoio, oi [abbeveraˈtojo] SM drinking trough.

abbi, abbia, abbiamo, abbiano, abbiate VB vedi avere.

abbiccì [abbitˈtʃi] SM INV (*alfabeto*) ABC, alphabet; (*fig*) ABC, rudiments *pl*; (*abbecedario, sillabario*) ABC book; **l'abbiccì del fai da te** the abc of do-it-yourself.

abbiente [abˈbjɛnte] ☐1 AGG well-to-do, well-off.
☐2: **gli abbienti** SMPL the well-to-do; **gli abbienti e i non**

abbienti the haves and the have-nots.

abbietto *ecc* [ab'bjetto] AGG = **abietto** *ecc.*

abbiezione [abbjet'tsjone] SF = **abiezione**.

abbigliamento [abbiʎʎa'mento] SM (*modo di vestire*) clothes *pl*; (*vestiario*) clothing; **capo di abbigliamento** article of clothing; **abbigliamento maschile/femminile** menswear/ladieswear; **industria dell'abbigliamento** clothing industry, fashion business.

abbigliare [abbiʎ'ʎare] ① VT (*aiutare a vestire*) to dress; (*agghindare*) to dress up.

② **abbigliarsi** VR to dress.

abbinamento [abbina'mento] SM (*vedi vb*) combination; linking; matching.

abbinare [abbi'nare] VT: **abbinare (con** *o* **a)** (*gen*) to combine (with); (*nomi*) to link (with); (*colori ecc*) to match (with).

abbinata [abbi'nata] SF = **accoppiata**.

abbindolamento [abbindola'mento] SM (*fig*) trick.

abbindolare [abbindo'lare] VT (*fig*) to trick, take in, cheat; **si è fatto abbindolare** he was done.

abbisognare [abbizoɲ'ɲare] VI **a** (*aus* essere) (*essere necessario*): **chiedi ciò che ti abbisogna** ask for what you need; **mi abbisogna il tuo aiuto** I need your help **b** (*aus* avere) (*aver bisogno*): **abbisognare di** to need; **abbisognare di denaro/di consigli** to need (some) money/advice.

abboccamento [abbokka'mento] SM **a** (*colloquio*) preliminary meeting **b** (*Tecn: di tubi*) connection.

abboccare [abbok'kare] ① VI (*aus* avere) (*pesce*) to bite; (*fig: farsi raggirare*) to swallow the bait; **abboccare all'amo** (*anche fig*) to rise to the bait.

② VT (*Tecn: tubi, condutture*) to connect, join (up).

abboccato, a [abbok'kato] AGG (*vino*) medium sweet.

abboffarsi *ecc* [abbof'farsi] = **abbuffarsi** *ecc.*

abbonamento [abbona'mento] SM **a** : **abbonamento (a)** (*rivista*) subscription (to); (*teatro, trasporti*) season ticket (for); **abbonamento settimanale/mensile** (*a teatro, trasporti*) weekly/monthly ticket; **fare l'abbonamento (a qc)** to take out a subscription (to sth), to buy a season ticket (for sth); **in abbonamento** for subscribers only, for season ticket holders only **b** (*al telefono*) rental; **abbonamento alla radio/alla televisione** radio/television licence.

abbonare¹ [abbo'nare] VT (*cifra*) to deduct; (*fig: perdonare*) to forgive.

abbonare² [abbo'nare] ① VT: **abbonare qn (a qc)** (*rivista*) to take out a subscription for sb (to sth); (*teatro, trasporti*) to buy sb a season ticket (for sth); (*televisione ecc*) to get *o* buy a licence (for sth) for sb.

② **abbonarsi** VR: **abbonarsi (a)** (*rivista*) to subscribe (to); (*teatro, trasporti*) to buy a season ticket (for); **abbonarsi al telefono** to have a telephone installed *o* put in; **abbonarsi alla radio/alla televisione** to get *o* buy a radio/television licence.

abbonato, a [abbo'nato] ① AGG: **essere abbonato** (*a rivista*) to be a subscriber; (*a teatro, trasporti*) to be a season ticket holder; (*alla televisione ecc*) to be a licence holder; (*fig: abituato*): **viene a cena da noi ogni settimana: ormai c'è abbonato!** he comes to our house for dinner every week: it's part of his routine!.

② SM/F (*vedi* abbonare²) subscriber; season ticket holder; licence holder; **abbonato al telefono** telephone subscriber; **elenco degli abbonati** telephone directory.

abbondante [abbon'dante] AGG **a** (*gen*) abundant, plen-

tiful; (*misure*) generous; (*nevicata*) heavy **b** (*abito: troppo grande*) too big, on the large side; (: *ampio*) loose-fitting.

abbondantemente [abbondante'mente] AVV: **ha piovuto abbondantemente** it rained heavily; **abbiamo mangiato abbondantemente** we had plenty to eat; **ci hanno rifornito abbondantemente di carta** they gave us an ample supply of paper.

abbondanza [abbon'dantsa] SF **a** (*gran quantità*) abundance; **ci sono pere in abbondanza** there are plenty of pears, there is an abundance of pears **b** (*ricchezza*) plenty; **vivere nell'abbondanza** to live in plenty.

abbondare [abbon'dare] VI **a** (*aus* essere) to abound, be plentiful **b** (*aus* avere): **abbondare di** to be full of, abound in; **abbondare in** *o* **di cortesie** to be extremely polite.

abbordabile [abbor'dabile] AGG (*persona*) approachable; (*prezzo*) affordable.

abbordare [abbor'dare] VT **a** (*Naut*) to go alongside; (: *nave nemica*) to board **b** (*curva, salita*) to take **c** (*persona*) to accost; (*questione, argomento*) to tackle.

abbottonare [abbotto'nare] ① VT to button (up), do up; **abbottonarsi il cappotto** to button (up) one's coat.

② **abbottonarsi** VR (*fig fam: diventare riservato*) to clam up.

abbottonato, a [abbotto'nato] AGG (*camicia ecc*) buttoned (up); (*fig*) buttoned up.

abbottonatura [abbottona'tura] SF buttons *pl*; **questo cappotto ha l'abbottonatura da uomo/da donna** this coat buttons on the man's/woman's side.

abbozzare [abbot'tsare] VT **a** (*scultura*) to rough-hew; (*disegno*) to sketch, outline; (*romanzo*) to sketch out **b** (*fig: idea, progetto*) to outline; (: *contratto*) to draft; **abbozzare un sorriso** to give a faint smile *o* a hint of a smile; **abbozzare un saluto** (*con la mano*) to half wave; (*con un cenno del capo*) to half nod.

abbozzo [ab'bottso] SM **a** (*di scultura, disegno*) sketch, outline; (*di libro*) rough outline **b** (*di progetto*) outline; (*di contratto*) draft; (*fig: accenno*) hint; **un abbozzo di sorriso** the ghost of a smile.

abbracciare [abbrat'tʃare] ① VT **a** (*persona*) to embrace, hug; **ti abbraccio** (*in una lettera*) lots of love **b** (*professione*) to take up; (*fede*) to embrace **c** (*includere*) to include; **abbracciare qc con lo sguardo** to take sth in at a glance; **la sua opera abbraccia due secoli di storia** his work covers two hundred years of history.

② **abbracciarsi** VR (*uso reciproco*) to hug *o* embrace (one another).

abbraccio, ci [ab'brattʃo] SM embrace, hug; **un abbraccio** (*in lettera, cartolina*) love.

abbrancare [abbran'kare] ① VT to grasp, seize; **abbrancare per il colletto qn** to seize hold of sb by the collar.

② **abbrancarsi** VR: **abbrancarsi a qc** to grab hold of sth.

abbreviare [abbre'vjare] VT (*gen*) to shorten; (*parola*) to abbreviate, shorten.

abbreviazione [abbrevjat'tsjone] SF (*vedi vb*) shortening; abbreviation.

abbrivio, vi [ab'brivjo] SM (*Naut*) headway; **prendere l'abbrivio** (*fig: iniziare*) to get under way ►**abbrivio residuo** residual thrust.

abbronzante [abbron'dzante] ① AGG (*prodotto*) suntan *attr*, sun *attr*.

② SM (*crema*) suntan cream; (*olio*) suntan oil.

abbronzare [abbron'dzare] **1** VT (*pelle*) to tan; (*metalli*) to bronze.

2 **abbronzarsi** VIP to get a tan; **stare ad abbronzarsi** to sunbathe.

abbronzato, a [abbron'dzato] AGG (sun)tanned.

abbronzatura [abbrondza'tura] SF (sun)tan.

abbrustolire [abbrusto'lire] **1** VT (*pane*) to toast; (*semi, caffè*) to roast.

2 **abbrustolirsi** VIP: **abbrustolirsi al sole** (*fig*) to soak up the sun.

abbrutimento [abbruti'mento] SM degradation.

abbrutire [abbru'tire] **1** VT (*degradare*) to degrade; **essere abbrutito dall'alcol** to be ruined by drink; **la guerra abbrutisce l'uomo** war brutalizes people.

2 **abbrutirsi** VIP to be degraded, be brutalized.

abbuffarsi [abbuf'farsi] VR (*fam*): **abbuffarsi (di qc)** to stuff o.s. (with sth).

abbuffata [abbuf'fata] SF (*fam*) nosh-up, blow-out; (*fig*) binge; **farsi un'abbuffata** to stuff o.s.

abbuiare [abbu'jare] **1** VB IMPERS (*aus* **essere**) to get dark.

2 **abbuiarsi** VIP (*farsi buio*) to grow dark; (*fig: espressione, volto*) to darken.

abbuonare [abbwo'nare] VT = **abbonare**[1].

abbuono [ab'bwɔno] SM **a** (*Comm*) discount **b** (*Ippica*) handicap.

abdicare [abdi'kare] VI **a** (*al trono*): **abdicare (a)** to abdicate (from); (*rinunciare*): **abdicare a** to renounce, to give up; **abdicare a una carica** to give up a position **b** (*venir meno a: responsabilità, dovere*) to abdicate.

abdicatario, ria, ri, rie [abdika'tarjo] AGG abdicating.

abdicazione [abdikat'tsjone] SF abdication.

Abele [a'bele] SM Abel.

aberrante [aber'rante] AGG aberrant.

aberrazione [aberrat'tsjone] SF aberration.

abetaia [abe'taja] SF fir wood.

abete [a'bete] SM (*albero*) fir (tree); (*legno*) fir ▶ **abete bianco** silver fir ▶ **abete rosso** spruce.

abiettamente [abjetta'mente] AVV despicably.

abietto, a [a'bjetto] AGG (*spregevole: persona, azione*) despicable, vile; (*squallido: condizioni*) abject, appalling.

abiezione [abjet'tsjone] SF (*vedi agg*) vileness; abjectness.

abigeato [abidʒe'ato] SM (*Dir*) rustling.

abile ['abile] AGG **a** (*capace*) skilful, able; **essere abile in qc** to be good at sth; **abile chirurgo/artigiano** skilful surgeon/craftsman

b (*accorto*) clever; (*astuto*) shrewd; **un'abile mossa** a good *o* clever move; **un abile uomo d'affari** a shrewd businessman

c (*idoneo*): **abile (a qc/a fare qc)** fit (for sth/to do sth); **abile al servizio militare** fit for military service.

abilità [abili'ta] SF INV **a** (*capacità*) ability; (*destrezza*) skill; **abilità nel fare qc** ability to do sth; **una grande abilità nella guida** great skill in driving **b** (*accortezza*) cleverness; (*astuzia*) shrewdness.

abilitante [abili'tante] AGG qualifying; **corsi abilitanti** (*Scol*) ≈ teacher training *sg*.

abilitare [abili'tare] VT: **abilitare qn a qc/a fare qc** to qualify sb for sth/to do sth; **è stato abilitato all'insegnamento** he has qualified as a teacher.

abilitato, a [abili'tato] **1** AGG **a** (*qualificato*) qualified **b** (*Telec*) which has an outside line.

2 SM/F qualified person; **solo gli abilitati possono partecipare** only those with the required qualifications may take part.

abilitazione [abilitat'tsjone] SF qualification; **esame di abilitazione** qualifying exam; **conseguire l'abilitazione** to qualify.

abilmente [abil'mente] AVV (*vedi agg*) skilfully; cleverly.

abissale [abis'sale] AGG abysmal; (*fig: senza limiti: ignoranza*) profound; **Mario è di un'ignoranza abissale!** Mario is a total ignoramus.

abissino, a [abis'sino] AGG, SM/F Abyssinian.

abisso [a'bisso] SM (*anche fig*) abyss, gulf; **tra noi c'è un abisso** we are poles apart; **essere sull'orlo dell'abisso** to be on the brink of ruin; **è un abisso di ignoranza** he is utterly ignorant.

abitabile [abi'tabile] AGG habitable.

abitabilità [abitabili'ta] SF INV: **licenza** *o* **autorizzazione di abitabilità** *document stating that a property is fit for habitation*.

abitacolo [abi'takolo] SM (*di aereo*) cockpit; (*di macchina*) inside; (*di camion*) (driver's) cab.

abitante [abi'tante] SM/F (*di città, paese*) inhabitant; (*di casa*) occupant.

abitare [abi'tare] **1** VI (*aus* **avere**): **abitare in, a** to live (in); **abitare in campagna/a Roma/all'estero** to live in the country/in Rome/abroad; **abita al numero 10** she lives at number 10.

2 VT (*casa*) to live in, dwell in (*letter*); (*luogo*) to inhabit.

abitato, a [abi'tato] **1** AGG (*casa, appartamento*) occupied, inhabited.

2 SM (*anche:* **centro abitato**) built-up area.

abitazione [abitat'tsjone] SF (*casa*) house, residence (*frm*).

abito ['abito] SM **a** (*da donna*) dress; (*da uomo*) suit; **in abito da cerimonia** in formal dress; **"è gradito l'abito scuro"** "dress formal"; **in abito da sera** in evening dress; **abito da sposa** wedding dress

b (*vestiti*): **abiti** SMPL clothes, dress *no pl*; **abiti civili** civilian clothes *pl*, civvies *pl* (*fam*)

c (*disposizione*): **abito mentale** way of thinking

d (*Rel*) habit; **l'abito non fa il monaco** (*Proverbio*) you can't tell a book by its cover, you can't judge by appearances.

abituale [abitu'ale] AGG usual; (*cliente, frequentatore*) regular.

abitualmente [abitual'mente] AVV usually, normally.

abituare [abitu'are] **1** VT: **abituare qn (a qc/a fare qc)** to accustom sb to sth/to doing sth, get sb used to sth/to doing sth.

2 **abituarsi** VR: **abituarsi a qc/a fare qc** to get used to *o* accustomed *o* to sth/to doing sth, accustom o.s. to sth/to doing sth (*frm*); **adesso mi ci sono abituato** I'm used to it now.

abitudinario, ria, ri, rie [abitudi'narjo] **1** AGG of fixed habits.

2 SM/F creature of habit.

abitudine [abi'tudine] SF habit; **aver l'abitudine di fare qc** to be in the habit of doing sth; **prendere/perdere l'abitudine di fare qc** to get into/out of the habit of doing sth; **per abitudine** from *o* out of habit; **come d'abitudine** as usual; **d'abitudine** usually; **buona** *o* **bella/cattiva** *o* **brutta abitudine** good/bad habit; **ci ho fatto l'abitudine** I've got used to it.

abiura [a'bjura] SF (*Rel*) abjuration.

abiurare [abju'rare] VT (*Rel*) to abjure; (*principi*) to renounce.

ablativo [abla'tivo] SM, AGG ablative.

abluzione [ablut'tsjone] SF (*Rel*) ablution.

abnegazione [abnegat'tsjone] SF (self-)abnegation, self-denial; **con abnegazione** selflessly.

abnorme [ab'nɔrme] AGG (*enorme*) extraordinary; (*anormale*) abnormal.

abolire [abo'lire] VT to abolish; (*Dir*) to repeal; **abbiamo abolito lo zucchero dalla nostra dieta** we have eliminated sugar from our diet; **abolire una legge/tassa** to abolish a law/tax.

abolizione [abolit'tsjone] SF abolition.

abomaso [abo'mazo] SM (*Zool*) abomasum.

abominevole [abomi'nevole] AGG abominable.

aborigeno, a [abo'ridʒeno] ① AGG aboriginal.

  ② SM/F aboriginal, aborigine ▶ **aborigeno australiano** Aborigine.

aborrire [abor'rire] VT to abhor, loathe.

abortire [abor'tire] VI **a** (*aus* **avere**) (*Med*) to abort; (: *accidentalmente*) to have a miscarriage, miscarry; (: *volontariamente*) to have an abortion **b** (*aus* **essere**) (*fig: progetto ecc*) to fail, come to nothing, miscarry (*frm*); (*Inform*) to abort.

abortista, i, e [abor'tista] ① AGG pro-choice, pro-abortion.

  ② SM/F pro-choicer.

aborto [a'bɔrto] SM **a** (*provocato*) abortion; (*spontaneo*) miscarriage ▶ **aborto clandestino** backstreet abortion **b** (*feto*) aborted foetus; (*fig*) freak; **è un aborto di quadro** (*fig*) it's a ghastly painting.

abracadabra [abraka'dabra] SM INV abracadabra.

Abramo [a'bramo] SM Abraham.

abrasione [abra'zjone] SF abrasion.

abrasivo, a [abra'zivo] AGG, SM abrasive.

abrogare [abro'gare] VT (*legge*) to repeal, abrogate (*frm*).

abrogazione [abrogat'tsjone] SF repeal, abrogation (*frm*).

abruzzese [abrut'tsese] ① AGG of *o* from the Abruzzi.

  ② SM/F inhabitant *o* native of the Abruzzi.

Abruzzo [a'bruttso] SM: **l'Abruzzo** the Abruzzi.

abside ['abside] SF apse.

Abu Dhabi [abu'dabi] SF Abu Dhabi.

abulia [abu'lia] SF (*Psic*) abulia; (*fig*) lethargy.

abulico, a, ci, che [a'buliko] AGG (*vedi sf*) abulic; lethargic.

abusare [abu'zare] VI (*aus* **avere**): **abusare di** (*fare uso eccessivo*: *di pazienza, cortesia*) to take advantage of; (: *di alcol, stupefacenti*) to abuse; (*fare uso indebito* : *di potere, autorità, fiducia*) to abuse; (*sessualmente*) to rape.

abusivamente [abuziva'mente] AVV without authorization, unlawfully, illegally; **occupare abusivamente una casa** to squat.

abusivismo [abuzi'vizmo] SM (*anche:* **abusivismo edilizio**) unlawful building, building without planning permission (*Brit*).

abusivo, a [abu'zivo] AGG unauthorized; **edilizia abusiva** unauthorized building; **occupante abusivo** (*di una casa*) squatter; **taxi abusivo** unlicensed taxi.

abuso [a'buzo] SM **a** (*uso eccessivo*) excessive use; (*uso improprio*) abuse, misuse; **abuso di medicinali** drug abuse; **fare abuso di** (*stupefacenti, medicine*) to abuse; **abuso di potere** abuse of power **b** (*violenza*) abuse; **abusi sessuali sui minori** child abuse.

a.C. ABBR (= *avanti Cristo*) BC.

acacia, cie [a'katʃa] SF acacia.

acaro ['akaro] SM (*Zool*) mite ▶ **acaro della scabbia** itch mite.

acca ['akka] SF letter H; **non capire un'acca** not to understand a thing; **non sai un'acca di latino** you don't know a thing about Latin.

accadde ecc VB vedi **accadere**.

accademia [akka'dɛmja] SF (*scuola: d'arte, militare*) academy; (*società*) learned society; **accademia di Belle Arti** art school.

accademicamente [akkademika'mente] AVV (*vedi agg*) academically; academically, pedantically.

accademico, a, ci, che [akka'dɛmiko] ① AGG academic; (*fig: pedante*) academic, pedantic; **anno accademico** academic year.

  ② SM/F academician.

accademismo [akkade'mizmo] SM academicism.

accadere [akka'dere] VB IRREG (*aus* **essere**) ① VB IMPERS to happen; **mi è accaduto di incontrarlo** I happened to meet him.

  ② VI to happen, occur.

accaduto [akka'duto] SM event; **raccontare l'accaduto** to describe what happened; **in seguito all'accaduto** following what happened.

accalappiacani [akkalappja'kani] SM INV dog-catcher.

accalappiare [akkalap'pjare] VT (*animali*) to catch; (*fig: persona*) to trick, dupe.

accalcare [akkal'kare] VT, **accalcarsi** VIP to crowd, throng; **i tifosi accalcavano lo stadio** OR **i tifosi si accalcavano nello stadio** the fans crowded *o* thronged the stadium.

accaldarsi [akkal'darsi] VIP to get hot; **era tutto accaldato dopo la corsa** he was boiling hot after the race.

accalorarsi [akkalo'rarsi] VR (*infervorarsi*) to become worked up, get excited.

accampamento [akkampa'mento] SM (*Mil, di zingari ecc*) camp, encampment; **togliere/porre l'accampamento** to strike/pitch camp.

accampare [akkam'pare] ① VT **a** (*Mil*) to encamp **b** (*fig: diritti*) to assert; (: *pretese*) to advance; **accampare scuse** to make excuses.

  ② **accamparsi** VR (*Mil*) to pitch camp; (*fare campeggio*) to camp; (*sistemarsi alla meglio*) to bed down.

accanimento [akkani'mento] SM (*odio, furia*) fury; (*tenacia*) tenacity, perseverance; **con accanimento** (*furiosamente*) furiously; (*tenacemente*) assiduously; **lavorare con accanimento** to work extremely hard.

accanirsi [akka'nirsi] VIP **a** (*infierire*): **accanirsi (contro)** to rage (against) **b** (*ostinarsi*): **accanirsi a** *o* **nel fare qc** to persist in doing sth; **accanirsi nello studio** to study very hard.

accanitamente [akkanita'mente] AVV (*vedi agg*) fiercely; assiduously.

accanito, a [akka'nito] AGG (*odio*) fierce; (*lavoratore*) assiduous; (*giocatore*) inveterate; (*tifoso, sostenitore*) keen; **fumatore accanito** chain smoker.

accanto [ak'kanto] ① AVV nearby, near; **abito qui accanto** (*di fianco*) I live next door; (*vicino*) I live near here; **la casa accanto** the house next door.

  ②: **accanto a** PREP next to, beside; **accanto alla porta** by the door.

accantonamento¹ [akkantona'mento] SM (*di progetto, idea*) shelving.

accantonamento² [akkantona'mento] SM (*Mil*) quartering.

accantonare [akkanto'nare] VT (*progetto, idea, problema*) to shelve; (*argomento*) to leave aside; (*denaro, viveri*) to

put aside, set aside.

accaparramento [akkaparra'mento] SM (*Comm*) buying up.

accaparrare [akkapar'rare] VT **a** (*Comm*) to buy up **b** (*assicurare con caparra*) to pay a deposit on, secure (by deposit) **c** : **accaparrarsi qc** (*simpatia, voti*) to secure sth (for o.s.); **accaparrarsi il mercato** to corner the market; **accaparrarsi il posto migliore** to grab the best seat.

accapigliarsi [akkapiʎ'ʎarsi] VR (*uso reciproco*) to come to blows; (*fig*) to squabble.

accappatoio, oi [akkappa'tojo] SM (*da bagno*) bathrobe; (*da spiaggia*) beach robe.

accapponare [akkappo'nare] VI (*aus* **essere**), **accapponarsi** VIP: **mi si è accapponata la pelle** I came out in goosepimples *o* gooseflesh; **uno spettacolo da far accapponare la pelle** a sight to make your flesh creep.

accarezzare [akkaret'tsare] VT **a** to caress; (*in modo spinto*) to fondle; (*animali, capelli*) to stroke; **accarezzarsi il mento** to stroke one's chin **b** (*fig*: *idea,progetto*) to toy with.

accartocciare [akkartot'tʃare] **1** VT (*carta*) to roll up, screw up.

2 accartocciarsi VIP (*foglie*) to curl up.

accartocciato, a [akkartot'tʃato] AGG (*vedi vb*) rolled up, curled up.

accasarsi [akka'sarsi] VR (*sposarsi*) to get married; (*metter su casa*) to set up house.

accasciarsi [akkaʃ'ʃarsi] VIP to collapse; (*fig*: *deprimersi*) to lose heart; **accasciarsi su una sedia** to collapse into a chair.

accatastare [akkatas'tare] VT to stack, pile.

accattonaggio [akkatto'naddʒo] SM begging.

accattone, a [akkat'tone] SM/F beggar.

accavallare [akkaval'lare] **1** VT (*gambe*) to cross.

2 accavallarsi VIP (*sovrapporsi*: *muscolo, nervo*): **mi si è accavallato un tendine** I've pulled a tendon; (*fig*: *avvenimenti*) to overlap; (*addensarsi*: *pensieri, nubi*) to gather.

accecante [attʃe'kante] AGG (*abbagliante*) blinding, dazzling.

accecare [attʃe'kare] **1** VT to blind; (*abbagliare*) to dazzle.

2 accecarsi VIP to become *o* go blind.

accedere [at'tʃɛdere] VI IRREG: **accedere a a** (*aus* **essere**) (*luogo*) to enter; (*scuola*: *essere ammesso*) to enter, be admitted to **b** (*aus* **avere**) (*avere accesso a*: *notizia, fonte*) to gain access to **c** (*acconsentire*: *richiesta*) to accede to.

accelerare [attʃele'rare] **1** VI (*aus* **avere**) to accelerate, speed up.

2 VT to speed up; **accelerare il passo** to quicken one's pace.

accelerato, a [attʃele'rato] **1** AGG (*rapido*) quick, rapid; **tempo/ritmo accelerato** fast tempo/rhythm.

2 SM (*treno*: *ant*) local train, stopping train.

acceleratore [attʃelera'tore] SM (*Aut*) accelerator.

accelerazione [attʃelerat'tsjone] SF acceleration.

accendere [at'tʃɛndere] VB IRREG **1** VT **a** (*fiammifero, candela, sigaretta, fuoco*) to light; **accendere il camino** to light the fire; **mi fa accendere?** do you have a light? **b** (*radio, televisione, luce, lampada*) to switch *o* turn on; (*gas*) to light; (*Aut*: *motore*) to switch on **c** (*fig*: *speranza, desiderio*) to arouse **d** (*Fin*: *conto*) to open; (: *ipoteca*) to raise; **accendere un debito** to take out a loan.

2 accendersi VIP **a** (*fuoco*) to start; (*legna*) to catch fire; (*riscaldamento*) to come on; (*luce*) to come *o* go on

b (*fig*: *di sentimenti*): **accendersi di gioia** (*occhi, volto*) to light up with joy; **accendersi in volto** (*per la vergogna*) to go red

c (*fig*: *disputa*) to flare up.

accendigas [attʃendi'gas] SM INV gas lighter (*for cooker ecc*).

accendino [attʃen'dino] SM (cigarette) lighter; **accendino a gas/elettronico** gas/electronic lighter.

accendisigari [attʃendi'sigari] SM INV (cigarette) lighter.

accennare [attʃen'nare] **1** VT **a** (*indicare*) to indicate, point out; **le accennai la porta** I showed her the door

b (*abbozzare*): **accennare un saluto** (*con la mano*) to make as if to wave; (*col capo*) to half nod; **accennare un sorriso** to half smile

c (*citare*) to mention; **mi ha accennato qualcosa a proposito del suo progetto** he mentioned something to me about his project

d (*canzone, melodia*: *al piano*) to pick out; (: *canticchiando*) to hum.

2 VI (*aus* **avere**) **a** (*far cenno*): **mi accennò di star zitto** he signalled to me to keep quiet

b (*far atto di*): **accennare a fare qc** to show signs of doing sth; **accennò ad alzarsi, ma poi si trattenne** he made as if to get up but then stopped; **accenna a piovere** it looks as if it's going to rain

c : **accennare a** (*menzionare*) to mention; (*alludere a*) to hint at; **ha accennato al fatto che vuole partire** he mentioned that he wants to leave.

accenno [at'tʃenno] SM (*menzione, allusione, abbozzo*) hint; (*segno premonitore*) sign; **non ha fatto accenno all'accaduto** he made no mention of what had happened; **con un accenno di sorriso** with a hint of a smile.

accensione [attʃen'sjone] SF **a** (*Aut*) ignition **b** (*di fiammifero, candela, sigaretta, fuoco*) lighting **c** (*di radio, televisione, luce, lampada*) switching *o* turning on; (*di gas*) lighting, turning on **d** (*Fin*: *di conto*) opening; (: *di ipoteca*) raising; (: *di debito*) contracting.

accentare [attʃen'tare] VT (*scrivendo*) to put an accent on; (*parlando*) to stress; **gli articoli non sono accentati** there is no (written) accent on the articles.

accentazione [attʃentat'tsjone] SF (*vedi vb*) marking with an accent; stressing.

accento [at'tʃɛnto] SM **a** (*pronuncia*) accent; **parla con un accento straniero** he speaks with a foreign accent

b (*Fonetica*) accent, stress; (*fig*) stress, emphasis; **mettere l'accento su qc** to stress sth

c (*segno grafico*) accent; **accento grave/acuto/circonflesso** grave/acute/circumflex accent

d (*inflessione*) tone (of voice); **un breve accento di tristezza** a slight note of sadness.

accentramento [attʃentra'mento] SM (*Amm*) centralization.

accentrare [attʃen'trare] VT (*potere ecc*) to centralize; (*fig*: *interesse, sguardi*) to attract, draw.

accentratore, trice [attʃentra'tore] AGG (*persona*) unwilling to delegate; **politica accentratrice** policy of centralization; **governo accentratore** centralizing government.

accentuare [attʃentu'are] **1** VT **a** (*mettere in rilievo*) to emphasize, accentuate **b** (*sillaba, parola*) to stress, emphasize.

2 accentuarsi VIP (*tendenza*) to become more marked *o* pronounced *o* noticeable; (*crisi*) to become worse.

accerchiare [attʃer'kjare] VT to encircle, surround.

accertamento [attʃertaˈmento] SM (*verifica*) check; (: *Fisco*) assessment; (*Dir*) investigation; (*Med*) examination; **essere in corso di accertamento** to be under investigation; **fare un accertamento** (*Fisco*) to carry out an inspection.

accertare [attʃerˈtare] ⓵ VT **a** (*verificare*) to verify, check **b** (*Fisco: reddito*) to assess. ⓶ **accertarsi** VR: **accertarsi di qc/che** to make sure of sth/that, ascertain sth/that.

acceso, a [atˈtʃeso] ⓵ PP di **accendere**. ⓶ AGG **a** (*fuoco, lampada*) lit; (*luce, televisore, gas*) on; (*Fin*) open **b** (*intenso: colore*) bright, vivid; (*infervorato: discussione, parole*) heated; **acceso di** (*ira, entusiasmo ecc*) burning with.

accessibile [attʃesˈsibile] AGG (*luogo*) accessible; (*persona*) approachable; (*prezzo*) affordable; **accessibile a tutti** (*prezzo, articolo*) within everyone's means, affordable; (*concetto, materia*) within the reach of everyone.

accessibilità [attʃessibiliˈta] SF accessibility; **data l'accessibilità del prezzo...** given that the price is reasonable ....

accesso [atˈtʃesso] SM **a** (*gen, Inform*) access; **vietato l'accesso** no entry, no admittance; **di facile accesso** (*luogo*) (easily) accessible; **avere accesso a** to have access to; **dare accesso a** (*sogg: porta, scala*) to lead to; (: *corso*) to lead to, open the door to; (: *qualifica*) to open the door to; **tempo di accesso** (*Inform*) access time ► **accesso casuale** random access ► **accesso sequenziale** sequential access ► **accesso seriale** serial access **b** (*impulso violento: di rabbia, gelosia, Med: di tosse*) fit; (: *di febbre*) attack, bout **c** (*TV*): **programmi dell'accesso** educational programmes.

accessoriato, a [attʃessoˈrjato] AGG (*Aut*) (fitted) with accessories.

accessorio, ria, ri, rie [attʃesˈsɔrjo] ⓵ AGG secondary, of secondary importance. ⓶ SM (*Aut, Moda ecc*) accessory.

accessorista, i [attʃessoˈrista] SM (*Aut*) car-accessory dealer.

accetta [atˈtʃetta] SF hatchet; **fatto con l'accetta** (*fig: lavoro ecc*) clumsily done; **tagliato con l'accetta** (*dal carattere grossolano*) uncouth; (*dai lineamenti marcati*) craggy.

accettabile [attʃetˈtabile] AGG acceptable.

accettare [attʃetˈtare] VT (*gen, Comm*) to accept; (*proposta*) to agree to, accept; **accettare di fare qc** to agree to do sth; **accettare qn come socio** to accept sb as a member.

accettazione [attʃettatˈtsjone] SF **a** (*gen*) acceptance ► **accettazione bancaria** bank acceptance **b** (*di albergo, ospedale ecc*) reception ► **accettazione bagagli** (*Aer*) check-in (desk).

accetto, a [atˈtʃetto] AGG: **bene/male accetto** welcome/unwelcome; **ben accetto a tutti** (*persona*) well-liked by everybody.

accezione [attʃetˈtsjone] SF meaning, sense.

acchiappamosche [akkjappaˈmoske] SM INV (fly) swatter.

acchiappare [akkjapˈpare] VT (*prendere, catturare*) to catch; (*afferrare*) to seize.

acchito [akˈkito] SM: **di primo acchito** at first.

acciaccato, a [attʃakˈkato] AGG **a** (*persona*) full of aches and pains **b** (*abito, cappello*) crushed; (*macchina*) battered.

acciacco, chi [atˈtʃakko] SM ailment; **acciacchi** SMPL aches and pains.

acciaieria [attʃajeˈria] SF steelworks *sg*.

acciaio, ai [atˈtʃajo] SM steel; **d'acciaio** (*trave*) steel *attr*, of steel; (*fig: uomo, nervi*) of steel ► **acciaio al carbonio** carbon steel ► **acciaio inossidabile** stainless steel.

accidentale [attʃidenˈtale] AGG accidental; **in circostanze accidentali** accidentally.

accidentalità [attʃidentaliˈta] SF fortuity, chance nature.

accidentalmente [attʃidentalˈmente] AVV (*per caso*) by chance; (*non deliberatamente*) accidentally, by accident.

accidentato, a [attʃidenˈtato] AGG (*terreno*) uneven, rough; (*strada*) bumpy, uneven.

accidente [attʃiˈdɛnte] SM **a** (*gen, Filosofia*) accident; (*disgrazia*) mishap **b** (*fam: colpo apoplettico*) stroke; (: *fig*) fit, shock; **quando ho visto il conto mi è venuto un accidente!** I had a fit when I saw the bill!; **mandare un accidente a qn** to curse sb **c** (*fig: niente*): **non vale un accidente** it's not worth a damn; **non capisco un accidente** it's as clear as mud to me.

accidenti [attʃiˈdɛnti] ESCL (*fam: per rabbia*) damn (it)!; (: *per meraviglia*) good heavens!; **accidenti a lui!** damn him!; **ma che accidenti vuole?** what on earth does he want?

accidia [atˈtʃidja] SF sloth; (*Rel*) accidie.

accigliato, a [attʃiʎˈʎato] AGG frowning.

accingersi [atˈtʃindʒersi] VR IRREG: **accingersi a fare** to be all set to do.

accinto, a [atˈtʃinto] PP di **accingersi**.

acciottolato [attʃottoˈlato] SM cobblestones *pl*.

acciuffare [attʃufˈfare] VT to seize, catch.

acciuga, ghe [atˈtʃuga] SF anchovy; **magro come un'acciuga** as thin as a rake; **stretti come acciughe** packed like sardines.

acclamare [akklaˈmare] ⓵ VT **a** (*applaudire*) to cheer, applaud **b** (*eleggere*) to acclaim. ⓶ VI (*aus avere*): **acclamare a** to cheer, applaud.

acclamazione [akklamatˈtsjone] SF (*vedi vb*) applause; acclamation.

acclimatare [akklimaˈtare] ⓵ VT to acclimatize. ⓶ **acclimatarsi** VR to become acclimatized.

acclimatazione [akklimatatˈtsjone] SF acclimatization.

accludere [akˈkludere] VT IRREG: **accludere (a)** to enclose (with).

accluso, a [akˈkluzo] ⓵ PP di **accludere**. ⓶ AGG enclosed; **qui accluso è...** please find enclosed ....

accoccolarsi [akkokkoˈlarsi] VR to crouch (down).

accodarsi [akkoˈdarsi] VR to follow, tag along (behind).

accogliente [akkoʎˈʎɛnte] AGG (*atmosfera*) welcoming, friendly; (*stanza*) pleasant, cosy.

accoglienza [akkoʎˈʎɛntsa] SF welcome, reception; **fare una buona accoglienza a qn** to welcome sb; **fare una cattiva accoglienza a qn** to give sb a cool reception.

accogliere [akˈkɔʎʎere] VT IRREG **a** (*persona: ricevere*) to receive; (: *calorosamente*) to welcome; (*sogg: sala, stadio*) to accommodate, hold; **questa sala può accogliere 600 persone** this hall can hold *o* accommodate 600 people **b** (*notizia*) to receive **c** (*richiesta*) to agree to, accept.

accoglimento [akkoʎʎiˈmento] SM (*di proposta*) acceptance; (*di richiesta*) granting.

accolgo *ecc* [akˈkɔlgo] VB vedi **accogliere**.

accollare [akkolˈlare] VT (*fig*): **accollare qc a qn** (*spesa, responsabilità, obbligo*) to force sth on sb; **accollarsi qc** to

take sth upon o.s., shoulder sth.

accollato, a [akkol'lato] AGG (*vestito*) high-necked; (*scarpa*) ankle-high.

accolsi *ecc* [ak'kɔlsi] VB vedi **accogliere.**

accolta [ak'kɔlta] SF (*letter*) assembly, gathering; (*pegg*) bunch.

accoltellamento [akkoltella'mento] SM stabbing, knifing.

accoltellare [akkoltel'lare] ⊡ VT to knife, stab.

⊠ **accoltellarsi** VR (*uso reciproco*) to attack each other with knives.

accolto, a [ak'kɔlto] PP di **accogliere.**

accomandante [akkoman'dante] AGG (*Dir*): **socio accomandante** limited partner.

accomandatario, ria, ri, rie [akkomanda'tarjo] AGG (*Dir*): **socio accomandatario** active partner.

accomandita [akko'mandita] SF (*Dir*): **(società in) accomandita** limited partnership.

accomiatare [akkomja'tare] ⊡ VT to dismiss.

⊠ **accomiatarsi** VR: **accomiatarsi (da)** to take one's leave (of), say goodbye (to).

accomodamento [akkomoda'mento] SM (*accordo*) arrangement, agreement.

accomodante [akkomo'dante] AGG accommodating.

accomodare [akkomo'dare] ⊡ VT **a** (*riparare*) to fix, repair, mend

b (*sistemare*) to arrange; (: *fig: questione, lite*) to settle.

⊠ **accomodarsi** VIP: **le cose col tempo si accomoderanno** things will get sorted out in time.

⊡ **accomodarsi** VR **a** (*sedersi*) to sit down; **si accomodi!** (*venga avanti*) come in!; (*mi segua*) this way please!; (*si sieda*) please take a seat!

b (*uso reciproco: accordarsi*): **accomodarsi (con qn su qc)** to come to an agreement (with sb on sth).

accompagnamento [akkompaɲɲa'mento] SM **a** (*Mus*) accompaniment; **senza accompagnamento** unaccompanied **b** (*Comm*): **lettera di accompagnamento** accompanying letter **c** (*Dir*): **indennità di accompagnamento** attendance allowance.

accompagnare [akkompaɲ'ɲare] ⊡ VT **a** (*gen*) to accompany, come *o* go with; (*Mus*) to accompany; **accompagnare qn a casa** to see sb home; **ti accompagno** I'll come with you; **accompagnare qn alla porta** to show sb out; **accompagnare qn al piano** to accompany sb on the piano; **accompagnare un regalo con un biglietto** to put in *o* send a card with a present

b (*fig: seguire*) to follow; **accompagnare qn con lo sguardo** to follow sb with one's eyes; **accompagnare la porta** to close the door gently; **accompagnare il colpo** (*Tennis*) to follow through.

⊠ **accompagnarsi** VIP (*armonizzarsi*) to go well together; **accompagnarsi a** (*colori*) to go with, match; (*cibi*) to go with.

⊡ **accompagnarsi** VR (*frequentare*): **accompagnarsi a qn** to associate with sb.

accompagnatore, trice [akkompaɲɲa'tore] SM/F **a** companion, escort ▶**accompagnatore turistico** courier **b** (*Mus*) accompanist **c** (*Sport*) team manager.

accomunare [akkomu'nare] VT **a** (*persone*) to unite, join; **molti interessi ci accomunano** we have many interests in common; **non voglio che mi si accomuni a lui** I don't want to be associated with him **b** (*ricchezze, idee*) to pool, share.

acconciatura [akkontʃa'tura] SF (*pettinatura*) hairstyle; (*ornamento*) headdress.

accondiscendente [akkondiʃʃen'dɛnte] AGG affable.

accondiscendere [akkondiʃ'ʃendere] VI IRREG (*aus avere*): **accondiscendere a** to agree to, consent to.

accondisceso, a [akkondiʃ'ʃeso] PP di **accondiscendere.**

acconsentire [akkonsen'tire] VI (*aus avere*): **acconsentire (a)** to agree (to), consent (to); **chi tace acconsente** (*Proverbio*) silence means consent.

accontentare [akkonten'tare] ⊡ VT to satisfy; **cercare di accontentare tutti** to try to please everybody.

⊠ **accontentarsi** VIP: **accontentarsi (di)** to content o.s. (with); (*essere soddisfatto*) to be content (with), be satisfied (with); **chi si accontenta gode** (*Proverbio*) well pleased is well served.

acconto [ak'konto] SM (*sullo stipendio*) advance; (*caparra*) deposit, part payment; **pagare una somma in acconto** to pay a sum of money as a deposit ▶**acconto di dividendo** (*Fin*) interim dividend.

accoppiamento [akkoppja'mento] SM (*vedi vb*) pairing off; mating; coupling, connecting (up).

accoppiare [akkop'pjare] ⊡ VT **a** (*persone, cose*) to pair off; **essere ben accoppiati** to be well matched, go well together **b** (*animali*) to mate **c** (*Tecn*) to couple, connect (up).

⊠ **accoppiarsi** VR (*animali*) to mate; (*persone: formare una coppia*) to pair off.

accoppiata [akkòp'pjata] SF (*Ippica, anche fig*) each-way bet; **un'accoppiata vincente** a winning combination.

accoppiatore [akkoppja'tore] SM (*Tecn*) coupler ▶**accoppiatore acustico** (*Inform*) acoustic coupler.

accoramento [akkora'mento] SM distress; **nel vedere il suo accoramento fui commosso** when I saw how heartbroken he was I was filled with pity.

accoratamente [akkorata'mente] AVV heartbrokenly.

accorato, a [akko'rato] AGG heartfelt.

accorciare [akkor'tʃare] ⊡ VT to shorten; **far accorciare una gonna** to have a skirt shortened.

⊠ **accorciarsi** VIP (*giornate*) to grow *o* get shorter.

accordare [akkor'dare] ⊡ VT **a** (*concedere*): **accordare qc a qn** to grant sb sth *o* sth to sb

b (*Mus*) to tune

c (*Gramm*): **accordare qc (con qc)** to make sth agree (with sth).

⊠ **accordarsi** VR (*uso reciproco: mettersi d'accordo*): **accordarsi (con qn su** *o* **per qc)** to agree (on sth with sb).

⊡ **accordarsi** VIP (*intonarsi: sogg: colore*): **accordarsi (con qc)** to match (sth).

accordata [akkor'data] SF (*Mus*): **dare un'accordata a** to tune up.

accordatore, trice [akkorda'tore] SM/F piano tuner.

accordatura [akkorda'tura] SF (*Mus*) tuning.

accordo [ak'kɔrdo] SM ⊡ **a** (*gen, Gramm*) agreement; (*armonia*) harmony; **andare d'accordo (con qn)** to get on well (with sb); **vanno d'accordo** they get on well together; **essere d'accordo** to agree, be in agreement; **mettersi d'accordo (con qn)** to agree *o* come to an agreement (with sb); **d'accordo!** agreed!, all right!, O.K.! (*fam*); **sono d'accordissimo** I quite agree; **decidere di comune accordo di fare qc** to make a joint decision to do sth; **prendere accordi con** to reach an agreement with

b (*Mus*) chord; **conosci gli accordi di quella canzone?** can you play that song?.

⊠ ▶**accordo commerciale** trade agreement ▶**accordo di esclusiva** exclusive agency agreement

▶**Accordo generale sulle tariffe doganali ed il commercio** General Agreement on Tariffs and Trade.

accorgersi [akˈkɔrdʒersi] VIP IRREG: **accorgersi di** (*notare*) to notice; (*capire*) to realize; **accorgersi che** to notice (o realize) that.

accorgimento [akkɔrdʒiˈmento] SM **a** (*espediente*) trick, device **b** (*astuzia*) shrewdness *no pl*.

accorrere [akˈkorrere] VI IRREG (*aus* **essere**): **accorrere (a)** to rush up (to), hurry (to), run up (to); **la gente accorreva da tutte le parti** people rushed up from all directions; **accorrere in aiuto di qn** to rush to sb's aid.

accorsi [akˈkɔrsi] VB **a** vedi **accorgersi b** vedi **accorrere**.

accorso, a [akˈkorso] PP di **accorrere**.

accortamente [akkortaˈmente] AVV (*con avvedutezza*) wisely, sensibly; (*con astuzia*) shrewdly.

accortezza [akkorˈtettsa] SF (*avvedutezza*) good sense; (*astuzia*) shrewdness.

accorto, a [akˈkɔrto] ① PP di **accorgersi**.
② AGG shrewd, alert; **stare accorto** to be on one's guard.

accostamento [akkostaˈmento] SM (*di colori ecc*) combination.

accostare [akkosˈtare] ① VT **a** : **accostare qc a qc** (*mettere vicino*: *oggetto*) to move sth near sth; (: *colori, stili*) to match sth with sth; (*appoggiare*: *scala*) to lean sth against sth; **accosta la sedia al tavolo** move your chair nearer the table; **ha accostato la tazza alle labbra** he put the cup to his lips
  b (*avvicinare*: *persona*) to approach, come up to
  c (*socchiudere*: *persiane*) to half-close; (: *porta*) to push (o pull) to; **lasciare la porta accostata** to leave the door ajar.
② VI (*aus* **avere**) **a** : **accostare (a)** (*Aut*) to draw up (at); (*Naut*) to come alongside
  b (*Naut*: *modificare la rotta*) to alter course.
③ **accostarsi** VR: **a** (*andare o venire vicino*): **accostarsi (a)** to approach, go (o come) nearer; **accostarsi a qc/qn** (*Aut*) to draw up at sth/next to sb; (*Naut*) to come alongside
  b (*fig*: *abbracciare*: *fede, religione*): **accostarsi a** to turn to; (: *idee politiche*) to come to agree with
  c (*somigliare*): **accostarsi a** to be like, resemble.

accovacciarsi [akkovatˈtʃarsi] VR to crouch (down).

accozzaglia [akkotˈtsaʎʎa] SF (*pegg*: *di persone*) odd assortment; (: *di oggetti, colori, idee*) jumble, hotchpotch.

accrebbi *ecc* [akˈkrebbi] VB vedi **accrescere**.

accreditare [akkrediˈtare] ① VT **a** (*Comm, Fin*): **accreditare qc a** *o* **a favore di qn** to credit sb with sth; **accreditare su un conto** to credit to an account
  b (*convalidare*) to confirm; (: *voce*) to substantiate; (: *notizia*) to confirm the truth of
  c (*diplomatico*) to accredit.
② **accreditarsi** VIP (*teoria ecc*) to gain ground *o* credence.

accreditato, a [akkrediˈtato] AGG (*diplomatico, giornalista*) accredited; (*notizie*) confirmed.

accredito [akˈkredito] SM (*Comm, Fin*: *atto*) crediting; (: *effetto*) credit.

accrescere [akˈkreʃʃere] VB IRREG ① VT to increase.
② **accrescersi** VIP to grow, increase.

accrescimento [akkreʃʃiˈmento] SM increase, growth.

accrescitivo, a [akkreʃʃiˈtivo] AGG, SM (*Gramm*) augmentative.

accresciuto, a [akkreʃˈʃuto] PP di **accrescere**.

accucciarsi [akkutˈtʃarsi] VR (*cane*) to lie down; (*persona*) to crouch down.

accudire [akkuˈdire] ① VI (*aus* **avere**): **accudire a** to attend to.
② VT to look after.

acculturarsi [akkultuˈrarsi] VIP (*Sociol*) to integrate, become integrated.

acculturazione [akkulturatˈtsjone] SF (*Sociol*) acculturation, integration.

accumulare [akkumuˈlare] ① VT (*gen*) to accumulate; (*energia*) to store; **il treno ha accumulato un ritardo di 3 ore** the train is running 3 hours late; **accumulare degli arretrati** to have backpay due *o* owing.
② **accumularsi** VIP to accumulate; (*Fin*) to accrue.

accumulatore [akkumulaˈtore] SM (*Elettr*) accumulator, (storage) battery.

accumulazione [akkumulatˈtsjone] SF (*vedi vb*) accumulation; storage.

accumulo [akˈkumulo] SM accumulation.

accuratamente [akkurataˈmente] AVV carefully, thoroughly.

accuratezza [akkuraˈtettsa] SF (*precisione*) accuracy; (*diligenza*) care, thoroughness.

accurato, a [akkuˈrato] AGG (*preciso*) accurate; (*diligente*) careful, thorough.

accusa [akˈkuza] SF (*gen*) accusation; (*Dir*) charge; **fare** *o* **muovere un'accusa a qn** to make an accusation against sb; **l'accusa** [OR] **la pubblica accusa** (*Dir*) the prosecution; **mettere qn sotto accusa** (*Dir*) to indict sb; **in stato di accusa** (*Dir*) committed for trial.

accusabile [akkuˈzabile] AGG (*Dir*) chargeable.

•**accusare** [akkuˈzare] VT **a** (*incolpare*): **accusare qn di (fare) qc** to accuse sb of (doing) sth; **accusare qn/qc di qc** (*biasimare*) to blame sb/sth for sth; **accusare qn di qc** (*Dir*) to charge sb with sth
  b (*sentire*: *dolore*) to feel; (*mostrare*): **accusare la fatica** to show signs of exhaustion; **ha accusato il colpo** (*fig*) you could see that he had felt the blow
  c (*Comm*): **accusare ricevuta (di)** to acknowledge receipt (of).

accusativo [akkuzaˈtivo] AGG, SM (*Gramm*) accusative.

accusato, a [akkuˈzato] SM/F accused.

accusatore, trice [akkuzaˈtore] ① AGG accusing.
② SM/F accuser; (*Dir*) prosecutor.

acerbo, a [aˈtʃɛrbo] AGG (*non maturo*: *frutto*) unripe; (: *fig*: *bellezza*) adolescent; (: *persona*) very young.

acero [ˈatʃero] SM maple ▶ **acero campestre** field maple.

acerrimamente [atʃerrimaˈmente] AVV very fiercely.

acerrimo, a [aˈtʃɛrrimo] AGG bitter.

acetato [atʃeˈtato] SM acetate.

acetilene [atʃetiˈlɛne] SM acetylene, ethyne.

aceto [aˈtʃeto] SM vinegar; **sotto aceto** pickled; **mettere sotto aceto** to pickle.

acetone [atʃeˈtone] SM (*Chim*) acetone; (*per unghie*) nail varnish remover.

acetosa [atʃeˈtosa] SF (*Bot*) sorrel.

acetosella [atʃetoˈsɛlla] SF (*Bot*) wood sorrel.

Achille [aˈkille] SM Achilles.

A.C.I. [ˈatʃi] SIGLA M (= *Automobile Club d'Italia*) ≈ AA (*Brit*), ≈ AAA (*Am*).

acidamente [atʃidaˈmente] AVV (*rispondere*) acidly, tartly.

acidificare [atʃidifiˈkare] VT, VI (*aus* **essere**) to acidify.

acidificazione [atʃidifikatˈtsjone] SF acidification.

acidità [atʃidiˈta] SF INV (*vedi agg*) acidity, sourness, tart-

ness ► **acidità (di stomaco)** heartburn.

acido, a ['atʃido] [1] AGG (*anche fig*) acid, sour, tart; (*Chim*) acid; **giallo/verde acido** acid yellow/green.

[2] SM acid; **sapere di acido** to taste sour.

[3] ► **acido acetico** acetic acid ► **acido acetilsalicilico** acetylsalicylic acid ► **acido cloridrico** hydrogen chloride ► **acido lisergico** lysergic acid ► **acido muriatico** hydrochloric acid ► **acido solfidrico** ⸱ hydrogen sulphide ► **acido solforoso** sulphurous acid.

acidulo, a [a'tʃidulo] AGG slightly sour, slightly acid.

acino ['atʃino] SM: **acino (d'uva)** grape.

aclassista, i, e [aklas'sista] AGG (*Pol*) classless.

A.C.L.I. ['akli] SIGLA FPL (= *Associazioni Cristiane dei Lavoratori Italiani*) Catholic Association of Italian Workers.

acme ['akme] SF acme, peak; (*Med*) crisis.

acne ['akne] SF (*anche:* **acne giovanile**) acne.

ACNUR ['aknur] SIGLA M (= *Alto Commissariato delle Nazioni Unite per i Rifugiati*) UNHCR (*United Nations High Commission for Refugees*).

acqua ['akkwa] SF [1] **a** (*gen*) water; (*pioggia*) rain; **le acque** SFPL (*Med*) the waters; **prendere l'acqua** to get caught in the rain, get wet; **far la cura delle acque** to go to a spa

b (*fraseologia*): **acqua, acqua!** (*in giochi*) you're cold!; **acqua in bocca!** mum's the word!; **(all')acqua e sapone** (*faccia, ragazza: senza trucco*) without makeup; (: *semplice*) natural; **buttare acqua sul fuoco** to pour oil on troubled waters; **è sempre stata un'acqua cheta** she has always seemed a quiet one; **fare acqua (da tutte le parti)** (*situazione, posizione*) to be shaky; **la sua versione dei fatti fa acqua da tutte le parti** his version of what happened won't hold water; **essere con** *o* **avere l'acqua alla gola** to be snowed under; **tirare acqua al proprio mulino** to feather one's own nest; **è acqua passata** that's (ancient) history; **è passata molta acqua sotto i ponti** a lot of water has flowed under the bridge; **trovarsi** *o* **navigare in cattive acque** to be in deep water.

[2] ► **acqua di calce** limewater ► **acqua di colonia** eau de Cologne, cologne ► **acqua corrente** running water ► **acqua distillata** distilled water ► **acqua dolce** fresh water ► **acqua di mare** sea water ► **acqua minerale** mineral water ► **acqua ossigenata** hydrogen peroxide ► **acqua pesante** (*Fis*) heavy water ► **acqua piovana** rain water ► **acqua potabile** drinking water ► **acqua ragia** = **acquaragia** ► **acqua di rose** rose water; **all'acqua di rose** mild ► **acqua del rubinetto** tap water ► **acqua salata** salt water ► **acqua santa** = **acquasanta** ► **acqua sorgiva** *o* **di sorgente** spring water ► **acqua tonica** tonic water ► **acque superficiali** (*Geog*) surface runoff *sg* ► **acque territoriali** territorial waters *pl*.

acquaforte [akkwa'fɔrte] SF (*pl* **acqueforti**) etching.

acquaio, ai [ak'kwajo] SM (kitchen) sink.

acquamarina [akkwama'rina] SF (*pietra, colore*) aquamarine.

acquaplano [akkwa'plano] SM aquaplane.

acquaragia [akkwa'radʒa] SF turpentine.

acquarello [akkwa'rɛllo] SM = **acquerello**.

acquario, ri [ak'kwarjo] SM **a** (*vasca per pesci, edificio*) aquarium **b** (*Astrol*): **Acquario** Aquarius; **essere dell'Acquario** to be Aquarius *o* (an) Aquarian.

acquartierare [akkwartje'rare] VT, **acquartierarsi** VR (*Mil*) to quarter.

acquasanta [akkwa'santa] SF holy water.

acquasantiera [akkwasan'tjɛra] SF holy water font.

acquatico, a, ci, che [ak'kwatiko] AGG aquatic; (*sport, sci*) water *attr*; **uccello acquatico** waterfowl.

acquattarsi [akkwat'tarsi] VR to crouch (down).

acquavite [akkwa'vite] SF (*pl* **acquaviti** *o* **acqueviti**) spirit.

acquazzone [akkwat'tsone] SM downpour.

acquedotto [akkwe'dotto] SM (*conduttura*) aqueduct; (*intero sistema*) water system.

acqueo, a ['akkweo] AGG: **vapore acqueo** water vapour (*Brit*) *o* vapor (*Am*); **umore acqueo** aqueous humour (*Brit*) *o* humor (*Am*).

acquerellista, i, e [akkwerel'lista] SM/F watercolourist (*Brit*) *o* watercolorist (*Am*).

acquerello [akkwe'rɛllo] SM (*tecnica*) watercolours (*Brit*), watercolors (*Am*); (*opera*) watercolour (*Brit*), watercolor (*Am*).

acquerugiola [akkwe'rudʒola] SF drizzle.

acquiescente [akkwjeʃ'ʃɛnte] AGG acquiescent.

acquiescenza [akkwjeʃ'ʃɛntsa] SF acquiescence.

acquietare [akkwje'tare] [1] VT (*dolore*) to ease; (*desiderio, fame*) to appease.

[2] **acquietarsi** VIP to calm down.

acquifero, a [ak'kwifero] AGG (*Geol*) aquiferous, water-bearing; **falda acquifera** aquifer.

acquirente [akkwi'rɛnte] SM/F buyer.

acquisire [akkwi'zire] VT (*diritto, proprietà*) to acquire; (*qualità, cognizione*) to acquire, gain.

acquisitivo, a [akkwizi'tivo] AGG (*Dir*): **contratto acquisitivo** purchase contract.

acquisito, a [akkwi'zito] AGG acquired; **diritto acquisito** acquired right.

acquisizione [akkwizit'tsjone] SF acquisition.

acquistare [akkwis'tare] [1] VT **a** (*casa, mobili*) to buy, purchase; (*beni, diritti*) to acquire; **acquistare a rate** to buy on hire purchase; **acquistare in contanti** to buy for cash **b** (*fig: esperienza, pratica ecc*) to gain; **acquistare terreno** to gain ground.

[2] VI (*aus* **avere**) to improve; **acquistare in bellezza** to become more beautiful; **ha acquistato in salute** his health has improved.

acquisto [ak'kwisto] SM purchase; **andare a fare acquisti** to go shopping; **fare molti acquisti** to buy a lot of things; **fare un buon/cattivo acquisto** (*anche fig*) to get a good/bad buy; **ecco il nostro ultimo acquisto** (*persona*) here is our latest recruit; **campagna acquisti** (*Sport*) transfer season; **potere d'acquisto** (*Econ*) buying power ► **acquisto d'impulso** impulse buying ► **acquisto rateale** instalment purchase, hire purchase (*Brit*).

acquitrino [akkwi'trino] SM bog, marsh.

acquitrinoso, a [akkwitri'noso] AGG boggy, marshy.

acquolina [akkwo'lina] SF: **far venire l'acquolina in bocca a qn** to make sb's mouth water; **ho l'acquolina in bocca** OR mi viene l'acquolina in bocca my mouth is watering.

acquoso, a [ak'kwoso] AGG watery; **soluzione acquosa** aqueous solution.

acre ['akre] AGG (*sapore, odore*) acrid, pungent; (*fig: polemica*) bitter; (: *critica*) harsh, biting.

acredine [a'krɛdine] SF (*fig*) bitterness.

acrilico, a, ci, che [a'kriliko] AGG, SM acrylic.

acrimonia [akri'mɔnja] SF acrimony.

acritico, a, ci, che [a'kritiko] AGG uncritical.

acrobata, i, e [a'krɔbata] SM/F acrobat.

acrobatica [akro'batika] SF acrobatics *sg*.

acrobaticamente [akrobatika'mente] AVV acrobatically.

acrobatico, a, ci, che [akro'batiko] AGG (*ginnastica*) acrobatic; (*Aer*) aerobatic.

acrobazia [akrobat'tsia] SF **a** (*ginnica*) acrobatic feat; **fare acrobazie** (*anche fig*) to perform acrobatics **b** (*aerea*) aerobatic feat; **acrobazie aeree** aerobatics.

acronimo [a'krɔnimo] SM acronym.

acropoli [a'krɔpoli] SF INV: **l'Acropoli** the Acropolis.

acuire [aku'ire] ① VT to sharpen; (*desiderio*) to increase.

② **acuirsi** VIP (*gen*) to increase; (*crisi, dissidio*) to worsen.

aculeo [a'kuleo] SM (*di riccio, istrice, pianta*) prickle; (*di vespa, ape*) sting.

acume [a'kume] SM perspicacity; **con grande acume** with great shrewdness.

acuminato, a [akumi'nato] AGG sharp.

acustica [a'kustika] SF (*scienza*) acoustics *sg*; (*di ambiente*) acoustics *pl*.

acusticamente [akustika'mente] AVV acoustically.

acustico, a, ci, che [a'kustiko] AGG acoustic; **apparecchio acustico** hearing aid; **cornetto acustico** ear trumpet.

acutamente [akuta'mente] AVV (*osservare, rilevare*) acutely, sharply.

acutezza [aku'tettsa] SF (*vedi agg*) acuteness; keenness; intensity; sharpness; shrillness; (*Mus*) high pitch.

acutizzare [akutid'dzare] ① VT to intensify.

② **acutizzarsi** VIP (*crisi, malattia*) to become worse, worsen.

acuto, a [a'kuto] AGG ① **a** (*Mat, Med, Gramm*) acute; (*vista, udito, senso dell'umorismo*) keen; (*desiderio, fastidio, sofferenza*) intense; (*mente, osservazione, dolore*) sharp, acute **b** (*suono, voce*) shrill, high-pitched, piercing; (*Mus*) high.

② SM (*Mus*) high note.

ad [ad] PREP (*davanti a vocale*) = **a**.

A.D. [a'di] SIGLA F (*Pol*) = **Alleanza Democratica**.

adagiare [ada'dʒare] ① VT to lay *o* set down carefully.

② **adagiarsi** VR (*mettersi comodo*) to make o.s. comfortable; (*sdraiarsi*) to lie down, stretch out; **si è adagiato (nell'ozio)** (*fig*) he sat back idly.

adagio[1] [a'dadʒo] AVV (*lentamente*) slowly; (*con cura*) with care, gently; **vacci adagio con la birra!** go easy on the beer!; **adagio!** easy does it!; **adagio adagio** gradually.

adagio[2], **gi** [a'dadʒo] SM **a** (*Mus*) adagio **b** (*proverbio*) adage, saying.

adamitico, a, ci, che [ada'mitiko] AGG: **in costume adamitico** in one's birthday suit.

Adamo [a'damo] SM Adam.

adattabile [adat'tabile] AGG (*persona*) adaptable.

adattabilità [adattabili'ta] SF adaptability.

adattamento [adatta'mento] SM (*Bio, Med, di romanzo*) adaptation; (*di stanza, edificio*) conversion; **avere spirito di adattamento** to be adaptable.

adattare [adat'tare] ① VT (*gen*): **adattare qc (a)** to adapt sth (to); (*camera*) to convert sth (into); **si era fatta adattare il cappotto della madre** she had her mother's coat altered to fit her.

② **adattarsi** VR **a** (*adeguarsi*): **adattarsi (a)** (*ambiente, situazione, tempi*) to adapt (to); **si adatta facilmente** she adapts easily, she's very adaptable

b (*accontentarsi*): **adattarsi a qc/a fare qc** to make the best of sth/of doing sth; **dobbiamo adattarci** we'll have to make the best of it.

③ **adattarsi** VIP (*addirsi*): **adattarsi a** to be suitable for.

adattatore [adatta'tore] SM (*Elettr*) adapter, adaptor.

adatto, a [a'datto] AGG: **adatto (a)** (*giusto*) right (for); (*appropriato*) suitable (for); **è la persona più adatta per** *o* **a fare questo lavoro** he is the most suitable person for this job *o* to do this job.

addebitare [addebi'tare] VT: **addebitare qc a qn** to debit sb with sth; (*fig: incolpare*) to blame sb for sth; **addebitare qc in conto a qn** (*Comm*) to debit sb's account with sth.

addebito [ad'debito] SM **a** (*Comm*) debit **b** (*imputazione*) blame; **muovere (un) addebito di qc a qn** to accuse sb of sth.

addenda [ad'dɛnda] SMPL addenda.

addendo [ad'dɛndo] SM (*Mat*) addend.

addensamento [addensa'mento] SM (*vedi vb*) thickening; gathering.

addensante [adden'sante] SM (*Chim*) thickener.

addensare [adden'sare] ① VT to thicken.

② **addensarsi** VIP (*nebbia*) to get thicker; (*nuvole, folla*) to gather; (*salsa, sugo*) to thicken.

addentare [adden'tare] VT (*panino*) to bite into.

addentrarsi [adden'trarsi] VIP: **addentrarsi in** (*posto*) to penetrate, go into; (*fig: problema*) to go (deeply) into.

addentro [ad'dentro] AVV (*fig*): **essere (molto) addentro a** *o* **in qc** to be well up on sth, be well-versed in sth.

addestrabile [addes'trabile] AGG that can be trained.

addestramento [addestra'mento] SM (*gen*) training; (*Mil*) drill; (*Equitazione: specialità*) dressage ▶**addestramento professionale** vocational training.

addestrare [addes'trare] ① VT: **addestrare qn/qc a** *o* **per qc** to train sb/sth for sth; **quel cane è stato addestrato alla guardia** that dog has been trained as a watchdog.

② **addestrarsi** VR: **addestrarsi (a** *o* **in qc)** to train (in sth), practise (*Brit*) *o* practice (*Am*) sth.

addetto, a [ad'detto] ① PP di **addirsi**.

② AGG: **addetto a** (*persona*) employed on, in charge of; (*oggetto*) intended for.

③ SM/F **a** : **addetto al telex** telex operator; **addetti alle pulizie** cleaning staff; "**vietato l'ingresso ai non addetti ai lavori**" "authorized personnel only"; **gli addetti ai lavori** (*fig*) those in the know ▶**addetto stampa** press officer

b (*Diplomazia*) attaché ▶**addetto commerciale** commercial attaché ▶**addetto militare** military attaché.

addì [ad'di] AVV (*Amm*): **addì 31 luglio 1997** on (the) 31st (of) July 1997, on July 31st 1997.

addiaccio [ad'djattʃo] SM: **all'addiaccio** (*Mil*) without shelter; **dormire all'addiaccio** to sleep in the open.

addietro [ad'djetro] AVV (*letter: nel passato, prima*) before, ago; **l'aveva conosciuto anni addietro** she'd met him years before.

addio [ad'dio] ① ESCL goodbye, farewell (*old*); **dire addio a qn/qc** (*anche fig*) to say goodbye to sb/sth; **se arrivano i bambini, addio pace!** if the children turn up, that'll be the end of our peace and quiet!.

② SM goodbye, farewell; **serata d'addio** (*Teatro*) farewell performance ▶**addio al celibato** stag night.

addirittura [addirit'tura] AVV (*perfino*) even; **addirittura?!** really!; **il suo comportamento è addirittura ridicolo** his behaviour is downright ridiculous.

addirsi [ad'dirsi] VIP IRREG E DIF: **addirsi a** to suit, be suitable for; **questo comportamento non si addice a un padre di famiglia** such behaviour doesn't suit a man with a family.

Addis Abeba [ad'dis a'beba] SF Addis Ababa.

additare [addi'tare] VT to point out; (*fig*) to expose.

additivo, a [addi'tivo] AGG, SM additive.

addivenire [addive'nire] VI IRREG (*aus* **essere**): **addivenire a** to come to.

addizionale [addittsjo'nale] ☐1☐ AGG additional.

☐2☐ SF (*anche:* **imposta addizionale**) surtax.

addizionare [addittsjo'nare] VT (*Mat*) to add (up); **addizionare qc a qc** to add sth to sth.

addizionatrice [addittsjona'tritʃe] SF adding machine.

addizione [addit'tsjone] SF (*Mat, Chim*) addition; **fare un'addizione** to do a sum.

addobbare [addob'bare] ☐1☐ VT **a** (*chiesa, sala, vetrina*) to decorate; **addobbare a festa** to deck out **b** (*scherz: persona*) to put on one's glad rags.

☐2☐ **addobbarsi** VR (*scherz*) to dress up.

addobbo [ad'dɔbbo] SM decoration; **addobbi natalizi** Christmas decorations.

addolcire [addol'tʃire] ☐1☐ VT **a** (*caffè, bevanda*) to sweeten **b** (*fig: mitigare: brutta notizia, carattere*) to soften; (*: calmare*) to soothe, calm **c** (*Tecn: acqua*) to soften; (*: acciaio*) to temper.

☐2☐ **addolcirsi** VIP (*fig: carattere, persona*) to mellow, soften.

addolcitore [addoltʃi'tore] SM water softener (*device*).

addolorare [addolo'rare] ☐1☐ VT to grieve, sadden.

☐2☐ **addolorarsi** VIP: **addolorarsi (per)** to be saddened (by).

Addolorata [addolo'rata] SF (*Rel*): **l'Addolorata** Our Lady of Sorrows.

addolorato, a [addolo'rato] AGG upset, distressed.

addome [ad'dɔme] SM abdomen.

addomesticabile [addomesti'kabile] AGG which can be tamed; **poco addomesticabile** difficult to tame.

addomesticamento [addomestika'mento] SM taming.

addomesticare [addomesti'kare] VT (*anche fig*) to tame; **è riuscita ad addomesticare il marito** she's managed to make her husband more civilized.

addomesticato, a [addomesti'kato] AGG tame.

addominale [addomi'nale] ☐1☐ AGG abdominal.

☐2☐ SM (*anche:* **muscolo addominale**) stomach muscle.

☐3☐ SMPL: **fare un po' di addominali** to do exercises for the stomach muscles.

addormentare [addormen'tare] ☐1☐ VT (*anche fig*): **(far) addormentare** to send to sleep.

☐2☐ **addormentarsi** VIP to go to sleep, fall asleep; **mi si è addormentato un piede** my foot has gone to sleep.

addormentato, a [addormen'tato] AGG sleeping, asleep; (*fig: tardo*) stupid, dopey.

addossare [addos'sare] ☐1☐ VT **a** (*appoggiare*): **addossare qc a qc** to lean sth against sth

b (*attribuire*): **addossare la colpa/la responsabilità di qc a qn** to lay the blame/the responsibility for sth on sb; **si addossò la colpa** he took the blame.

☐2☐ **addossarsi** VR (*appoggiarsi*): **addossarsi a** to stand against; **stava addossato al muro** he was leaning against the wall; **si sono addossati gli uni agli altri** they crowded together.

addosso [ad'dɔsso] ☐1☐ AVV (*sulla persona*) on; **mettersi addosso il cappotto** to put one's coat on; **addosso non ho molti soldi** I don't have much money on me; **ho una tale sfortuna addosso** I've had such a run of bad luck.

☐2☐: **addosso a** PREP (*sopra*) on; (*molto vicino*) right next to; **gli ombrelloni sono praticamente uno addosso all'altro**

the beach umbrellas are practically on top of each other; **andare (*o* venire) addosso a** (*Aut: altra macchina*) to run into; (*: pedone*) to run over; **mettere gli occhi addosso a qn/qc** to take quite a fancy to sb/sth; **mettere le mani addosso a qn** (*picchiare*) to hit sb, lay hands on sb; (*catturare*) to seize sb; (*molestare*) to touch sb up; **dare addosso a qn** (*fig*) to attack sb; **il mio capo mi sta addosso** my boss is breathing down my neck.

addotto, a [ad'dotto] PP di **addurre**.

adduco *ecc* [ad'duko] VB vedi **addurre**.

addurre [ad'durre] VT IRREG **a** (*Dir: fatti, prove, ragioni*) to produce **b** (*citare: esempi, scuse, argomenti, fatti*) to advance, put forward.

addussi *ecc* [ad'dussi] VB vedi **addurre**.

Ade ['ade] SM Hades.

adeguamento [adegwa'mento] SM adjustment.

adeguare [ade'gware] ☐1☐ VT: **adeguare qc (a)** (*stipendio*) to adjust sth (to); (*produzione, struttura*) to bring into line (with).

☐2☐ **adeguarsi** VR (*conformarsi*): **adeguarsi (a)** to adapt (to).

adeguatamente [adegwata'mente] AVV (*pagare*) adequately, properly; (*rispondere*) satisfactorily; (*comportarsi*) properly.

adeguatezza [adegwa'tettsa] SF (*vedi agg*) adequacy; suitability; fairness.

adeguato, a [ade'gwato] AGG: **adeguato (a)** (*proporzionato*) adequate (to); (*adatto*) suitable (for); (*equo*) fair.

adempiere [a'dempjere] VT, VI (*aus* **avere**): **adempiere (a)** (*dovere, promessa*) to carry out, fulfil (*Brit*), fulfill (*Am*); (*ordine*) to carry out.

adempimento [adempi'mento] SM (*di dovere, ordine*) carrying out; (*di promessa*) fulfilment (*Brit*), fulfillment (*Am*); **nell'adempimento del proprio dovere** in the performance of one's duty.

adempire [adem'pire] VT = **adempiere**.

Aden ['aden] SF Aden; **il golfo di Aden** the Gulf of Aden.

adenoidi [ade'nɔidi] SFPL adenoids.

adenoma, i [ade'nɔma] SM adenoma.

adepto, a [a'dɛpto] SM/F disciple, follower.

aderente [ade'rɛnte] ☐1☐ AGG **a** (*abiti*) tight-fitting **b** (*fig: fedele*): **una traduzione aderente al testo originale** a translation faithful to the original.

☐2☐ SM/F: **aderente (a)** follower (of), supporter (of).

aderenza [ade'rɛntsa] SF **a** (*gen, Med*) adhesion; (*Aut: di ruota*) grip **b** (*fig: conoscenze*): **aderenze** SFPL connections, contacts.

aderire [ade'rire] VI (*aus* **avere**): **aderire (a)** **a** (*stare attaccato*) to adhere (to), stick (to); **aderire alla strada** (*Aut*) to grip the road **b** (*partito*) to join; (*idea*) to support **c** (*richiesta*) to agree to.

adescamento [adeska'mento] SM (*Dir*) soliciting; (*lusinga*) enticement.

adescare [ades'kare] VT **a** (*Dir*) to solicit; (*attirare*) to lure, entice **b** (*Tecn: pompa*) to prime.

adesione [ade'zjone] SF **a** (*iscrizione: a partito*) joining; (*assenso*) agreement, acceptance; (*appoggio*) support; **dare/rifiutare la propria adesione ad un'iniziativa** to give one's support to/to refuse to support a proposal **b** (*Fis*) adhesion.

adesività [adezivi'ta] SF adhesiveness.

adesivo, a [ade'zivo] AGG, SM adhesive.

adesso [a'dɛsso] AVV (*ora*) now; (*poco fa*) just now; (*fra poco*) any moment now; **da adesso in poi** from now on;

per adesso for the moment, for now.
ad hoc [a'dɔk] AVV, AGG INV ad hoc.
ad honorem [ado'nɔrem] AGG INV: **laurea ad honorem** honorary degree.
adiacente [adja'tʃɛnte] AGG adjacent, adjoining; **adiacente a** adjacent to.
adiacenze [adja'tʃɛntse] SFPL vicinity *sg*, environs.
adibire [adi'bire] VT: **adibire qc a** to use sth as; **questo edificio è adibito a deposito merci** this building is used as a goods depot.
Adige ['adidʒe] SM: **l'Adige** the Adige.
adipe ['adipe] SM (adipose) fat.
adiposità [adiposi'ta] SF adiposity.
adiposo, a [adi'poso] AGG (*Anat*) adipose.
adirarsi [adi'rarsi] VIP: **adirarsi (con qn per qc)** to get angry (with sb over sth).
adirato, a [adi'rato] AGG angry.
adire [a'dire] VT (*Dir*): **adire le vie legali** to institute *o* commence legal proceedings; **adire un'eredità** to take legal possession of an inheritance.
adito ['adito] SM: **dare adito a** (*sospetti*) to give rise to.
adocchiare [adok'kjare] VT (*scorgere*) to catch sight of; (*desiderare*) to have one's eye on.
adolescente [adoleʃ'ʃɛnte] 1 AGG adolescent.
  2 SM/F adolescent, teenager.
adolescenza [adoleʃ'ʃɛntsa] SF adolescence.
adolescenziale [adoleʃʃen'tsjale] AGG of adolescence.
adombrare [adom'brare] 1 VT (*fig*: *celare*) to veil, conceal.
  2 **adombrarsi** VIP (*cavallo*) to shy; (*persona*: *offendersi*) to be offended; (: *insospettirsi*) to grow suspicious.
Adone [a'done] SM Adonis; **un adone** (*fig*) an Adonis.
adoperare [adope'rare] 1 VT to use.
  2 **adoperarsi** VR: **adoperarsi (per** *o* **per fare qc)** to make every effort (to do sth), strive (to do sth); **adoperarsi in favore di qn** to do one's best for sb.
adorabile [ado'rabile] AGG adorable.
adorabilmente [adorabil'mente] AVV adorably.
adorare [ado'rare] VT (*gen*) to adore; (*Rel*) to adore, worship.
adorazione [adorat'tsjone] SF (*gen*) adoration; (*Rel*) worship, adoration.
adornare [ador'nare] 1 VT (*anche fig*): **adornare (di** *o* **con)** to adorn (with).
  2 **adornarsi** VR: **adornarsi (di** *o* **con)** to adorn o.s. (with).
adorno, a [a'dorno] AGG: **adorno (di)** adorned (with).
adottare [adot'tare] VT (*gen*) to adopt; (*libro di testo*) to choose, select; (*decisione, provvedimenti*) to pass.
adottivo, a [adot'tivo] AGG (*genitori*) adoptive; (*figlio, patria*) adopted.
adozione [adot'tsjone] SF (*vedi vb*) adoption; selection; **si rende necessaria l'adozione di misure di sicurezza** security measures will have to be adopted.
adrenalina [adrena'lina] SF adrenaline, epinephrine (*Am*).
adrenalinico, a, ci, che [adrena'liniko] AGG (*fig: vivace, eccitato*) charged-up.
adriatico, a, ci, che [adri'atiko] 1 AGG Adriatic.
  2 SM: **l'Adriatico** the Adriatic.
adulare [adu'lare] VT to flatter.
adulatore, trice [adula'tore] SM/F flatterer.
adulatorio, ria, ri, rie [adula'tɔrjo] AGG flattering.
adulazione [adulat'tsjone] SF flattery.

adulterare [adulte'rare] VT to adulterate; (*fig: informazione*) to distort.
adulterio, ri [adul'tɛrjo] SM adultery.
adultero, a [a'dultero] 1 AGG adulterous.
  2 SM/F adulterer/adulteress.
adulto, a [a'dulto] 1 AGG adult; (*fig*) mature.
  2 SM/F adult, grown-up.
adunanza [adu'nantsa] SF meeting, assembly.
adunare [adu'nare] VT, **adunarsi** VIP to assemble, gather.
adunata [adu'nata] SF (*Mil*) muster, parade.
adunco, a, chi, che [a'dunko] AGG hooked.
aerare [ae'rare] VT (*arieggiare*) to ventilate; **"aerare il locale prima di soggiornarvi"** "ventilate the room before use".
aerazione [aerat'tsjone] SF **a** ventilation **b** (*Tecn*) aeration.
aereo, a [a'ɛreo] 1 AGG **a** (*gen, Aer, Posta*) air *attr*; (*navigazione, fotografia*) aerial; (*linea elettrica*) overhead *attr*
  b (*Bot: radice*) aerial.
  2 SM (*anche:* **aeroplano**) plane ►**aereo da caccia** fighter (plane) ►**aereo da guerra** warplane ►**aereo di linea** airliner ►**aereo a reazione** jet (plane) ►**aereo da trasporto merci** cargo plane ►**aereo da turismo** light aircraft *inv*.
aerobica [ae'rɔbika] SF aerobics *sg*.
aerobio, bi [ae'rɔbjo] SM aerobe.
aerobus ['aerobus] SM INV airbus.
aerodinamica [aerodi'namika] SF aerodynamics *sg*.
aerodinamico, a, ci, che [aerodi'namiko] AGG (*Fis*) aerodynamic; (*affusolato*) streamlined.
aerofagia [aerofa'dʒia] SF aerophagia.
aerofotografia [aerofotogra'fia] SF aerial photography.
aerogramma, i [aero'gramma] SM aerogramme, air letter.
aeromobile [aero'mɔbile] SM aircraft *inv*, airliner.
aeromodellismo [aeromodel'lizmo] SM aircraft modelling.
aeromodello [aeromo'dɛllo] SM model aircraft.
aeronauta, i [aero'nauta] SM pilot.
aeronautica [aero'nautika] SF (*scienza*) aeronautics *sg* ►**aeronautica civile** civil aviation ►**aeronautica militare** air force.
aeronautico, a, ci, che [aero'nautiko] AGG aeronautical.
aeronavale [aerona'vale] AGG (*forze, manovre*) air and sea *attr*.
aeroplano [aero'plano] SM (aero)plane (*Brit*), (air)plane (*Am*).
aeroporto [aero'pɔrto] SM airport.
aeroportuale [aeroportu'ale] AGG airport *attr*.
aerorimessa [aerori'messa] SF hangar.
aeroscalo [aeros'kalo] SM airstrip.
aerosol [aero'sɔl] SM INV aerosol.
aerospaziale [aerospat'tsjale] AGG aerospace.
aerostatico, a, ci, che [aeros'tatiko] AGG aerostatic; **pallone aerostatico** air balloon.
aerostato [ae'rɔstato] SM aerostat.
aerostazione [aerostat'tsjone] SF airport (buildings).
aerotaxi [aero'taksi] SM INV air taxi.
aerovia [aero'via] SF airway.
A.F. 1 SIGLA (= *alta frequenza*) HF.
  2 ABBR (*Amm*) = **assegni familiari**.
afa ['afa] SF closeness; **c'è un'afa terribile** it's terribly close.

affabile [af'fabile] AGG friendly.

affabilità [affabili'ta] SF affability.

affabilmente [affabil'mente] AVV affably.

affaccendarsi [affattʃen'darsi] VR: **affaccendarsi a fare qc** to be busy doing sth, bustle about doing sth; **si affaccendava intorno ai fornelli** she was busy at the stove.

affaccendato, a [affattʃen'dato] AGG busy.

affacciarsi [affat'tʃarsi] ① VR (*sporgersi*): **affacciarsi (a)** to appear (at); **affacciarsi alla vita** (*bambino*) to come into the world; **un dubbio gli si affacciò alla mente** a sudden doubt came into his mind.

② VIP (*guardare*): **affacciarsi su** OR **il balcone si affaccia sulla piazza** the balcony looks (out) onto the square.

affamato, a [affa'mato] AGG starving, hungry; **affamato d'affetto** starved of affection.

affannare [affan'nare] ① VT to leave breathless.

② **affannarsi** VR (*preoccuparsi*): **affannarsi (per)** to worry (about), get worked up (about); (*sforzarsi*): **affannarsi a fare qc** to do one's utmost to do sth, hurry *o* race to do sth; **è inutile che ti affanni a trovar scuse** don't waste your breath looking for excuses.

affanno [af'fanno] SM **a** breathlessness; **ho fatto le scale a piedi e mi è venuto l'affanno** I got out of breath going up the stairs, I was panting after walking up the stairs **b** (*preoccupazione*) worry.

affannosamente [affannosa'mente] AVV (*respirare*) with difficulty; (*freneticamente*) anxiously.

affannoso, a [affan'noso] AGG (*respiro*) laboured; (*fig*: *ricerca*: *di oggetto, regalo*) frantic; (: *della verità*) painstaking.

affare [af'fare] SM **a** (*faccenda*) matter, affair; (*Dir*) case; **è stato un brutto affare** it was a nasty business; **questo non è affar tuo** this is none of your business; **sono affari miei** that's my business; **bada agli affari tuoi!** OR **fatti gli affari tuoi!** mind your own business!; **affare di cuore** love affair; **affare di Stato** (*Pol, anche fig*) affair of state **b** (*Comm*: *transazione*) piece of business, (business) deal; (*occasione*) bargain; **affare fatto!** done!, it's a deal!; **concludere un affare** to conclude a (business) deal; **hai fatto un (buon) affare** you got a bargain **c** (*fam*: *coso*) thing; **come funziona quest'affare?** how does this thing work?

d : **affari** SMPL (*gen, Pol*) affairs; (*commercio*) business *sg*; **è qua per affari** he's here on business; **uomo d'affari** businessman; **ministro degli Affari Esteri** Foreign Secretary (*Brit*), Secretary of State (*Am*).

affarista, i, e [affa'rista] SM/F shrewd businessman/businesswoman; (*pegg*) profiteer, unscrupulous businessman/businesswoman.

affascinante [affaʃʃi'nante] AGG (*uomo, donna*) terribly attractive; (*argomento, libro*) fascinating.

affascinare [affaʃʃi'nare] VT (*ammaliare*) to bewitch, enchant; (*sedurre*) to charm, fascinate.

affastellare [affastel'lare] VT (*rami*) to tie up in bundles.

affaticamento [affatika'mento] SM tiredness.

affaticare [affati'kare] ① VT to tire.

② **affaticarsi** VR (*stancarsi*) to get tired; **affaticarsi a fare qc** to tire o.s. out doing sth.

affaticato, a [affati'kato] AGG tired.

affatto [af'fatto] AVV (*interamente*) completely; **non...affatto** not ...at all; **non mi piace affatto** I don't like it at all; **non sei affatto divertente** you're not at all funny; **niente affatto!** not at all!

affermare [affer'mare] ① VT (*dichiarare*) to declare; (*diritti*) to assert; **afferma di essere innocente** he maintains that he is innocent; **affermò col capo** he nodded in agreement.

② **affermarsi** VR (*imporsi*) to make o.s. *o* one's name known.

affermativamente [affermativa'mente] AVV in the affirmative, affirmatively.

affermativo, a [afferma'tivo] AGG affirmative; **dare una risposta affermativa** to say yes.

affermato, a [affer'mato] AGG established, well-known.

affermazione [affermat'tsjone] SF **a** (*dichiarazione*) statement; (*di diritti, verità*) assertion **b** (*successo*) achievement; **una grande affermazione degli azzurri** a great triumph for the Italian team.

afferrare [affer'rare] ① VT (*prendere*) to seize, grasp; (*fig*: *idea*) to grasp, get; **afferrare un'occasione** to seize an opportunity; **non ho afferrato quello che hai detto** (*sentito*) I didn't get *o* catch what you said; (*capito*) I didn't understand what you said.

② **afferrarsi** VR: **afferrarsi a** to cling to.

Aff. Est. ABBR = *Affari Esteri*.

affettare¹ [affet'tare] VT (*tagliare a fette*) to slice.

affettare² [affet'tare] VT (*ostentare*) to affect.

affettato¹, a [affet'tato] ① AGG sliced.

② SM (sliced) cold meat (*ham ecc*).

affettato², a [affet'tato] AGG (*lezioso*) affected.

affettatrice [affetta'tritʃe] SF meat slicer.

affettazione [affettat'tsjone] SF affectation.

affettivamente [affettiva'mente] AVV: **essere affettivamente legato a** (*città, oggetto*) to be (sentimentally) attached to.

affettivo, a [affet'tivo] AGG (*vita*) emotional; **la sfera affettiva** the area of feelings and emotions; **la vita affettiva** personal relationships; **una collanina con un valore puramente affettivo** a little necklace only of sentimental value.

affetto¹ [af'fetto] SM **a** (*sentimento*) affection; **con affetto** (*nelle lettere*) with love, affectionately yours **b** (*persona, cosa*) object of affection; **gli affetti familiari** one's nearest and dearest.

affetto², a [af'fetto] AGG: **essere affetto da** to suffer from.

affettuosamente [affettuosa'mente] AVV affectionately; **(ti saluto) affettuosamente, Roberta** (*nelle lettere*) love Roberta.

affettuosità [affettuosi'ta] SF INV **a** affection **b** : **affettuosità** SFPL (*manifestazioni*) demonstrations of affection.

affettuoso, a [affettu'oso] AGG affectionate; **un saluto** *o* **un abbraccio affettuoso, Roberta** (*nelle lettere*) love Roberta.

affezionarsi [affettsjo'narsi] VIP: **affezionarsi a** to grow fond of.

affezionatamente [affettsjonata'mente] AVV affectionately.

affezionato, a [affettsjo'nato] AGG **a** : **affezionato a** fond of; (*attaccato*) attached to **b** (*abituale*: *cliente*) regular.

affezione [affet'tsjone] SF **a** (*Med*) ailment, disorder **b** (*affetto*) affection.

affiancare [affjan'kare] ① VT **a** (*mettere a fianco*: *due oggetti*) to place side by side; **affiancare qc a qc** (*un oggetto a un altro*) to put sth beside *o* next to sth **b** (*Mil*) to flank **c** (*fig*: *sostenere*) to support.

② **affiancarsi** VR: **affiancarsi a qn** to stand beside sb.

affiatamento [affjata'mento] SM team spirit; **c'è molto affiatamento fra di loro** (*giocatori, colleghi*) they make a good team.

affiatarsi [affja'tarsi] VR to work well together; **sono molto affiatati** (*coppia*) they make a good couple; (*giocatori*) they play well together.

affiatato, a [asffja'tato] AGG: **essere affiatati** to get on; **formano una squadra affiatata** they make a good team.

affibbiare [affib'bjare] VT **a** (*appioppare*): **affibbiare qc a qn** (*soprannome, colpa*) to pin sth on sb; (*compito sgradevole*) to saddle sb with sth; **affibbiare uno schiaffo a qn to slap sb in the face b** (*allacciare*) to buckle, do up.

affidabile [affi'dabile] AGG (*persona, macchina*) reliable.

affidabilità [affidabili'ta] SF reliability.

affidamento [affida'mento] SM **a** (*fiducia*) trust, confidence; (*garanzia*) assurance; **dare affidamento** to seem reliable; **fare affidamento su qn/qc** to rely o count on sb/sth; **quel tipo lì non mi dà nessun affidamento** I don't trust that chap at all **b** (*Dir: di bambino*) fostering; **avere/dare in affidamento** to foster; **bambini in affidamento** foster children.

affidare [affi'dare] 1 VT: **affidare qn/qc a qn** to entrust sb/sth to sb; **affidare un incarico a qn** to entrust sb with a task. 2 **affidarsi** VR: **affidarsi a** to place one's trust in; **mi affido alla tua discrezione** I rely on your discretion.

affidatario, ria, ri, rie [affida'tario] AGG foster *attr.*

affievolire [affjevo'lire] 1 VT (*forze*) to weaken; (*suoni*) to make faint. 2 **affievolirsi** VIP (*suoni*) to grow faint; (*passione, affetto*) to fade, grow less.

affiggere [af'fiddʒere] VT IRREG to stick up.

affilacoltelli [affilakol'tɛlli] SM INV knife-sharpener.

affilare [affi'lare] 1 VT to sharpen. 2 **affilarsi** VIP (*viso, naso*) to get thinner.

affilato, a [affi'lato] AGG (*gen*) sharp; (*volto, naso*) thin.

affiliare [affi'ljare] 1 VT (*aggregare*) to affiliate. 2 **affiliarsi** VR: **affiliarsi (a qc)** to join (sth), become a member (of sth).

affiliato, a [affi'ljato] SM/F (*membro*) affiliated member.

affiliazione [affiljat'tsjone] SF affiliation.

affinare [affi'nare] VT (*Tecn, fig: gusto*) to refine; (: *ingegno*) to sharpen.

affinché [affin'ke] CONG (+ *congiunt*) in order that, so that.

affine [af'fine] 1 AGG similar. 2 SM/F **a** (*di coniuge*) in-law **b** (*prodotto dello stesso tipo*) similar product; **sapone e affini** soap and allied products.

affinità [affini'ta] SF INV affinity.

affioramento [affjora'mento] SM **a** (*Naut*) surfacing **b** (*Geol*) outcrop.

affiorare [affjo'rare] VI (*aus essere*) **a** (*venire in superficie*) to appear on the surface; **affiorare alla o in superficie** to come to the surface; **affiorare da** to emerge from **b** (*fig: indizi*) to come to light.

affissi *ecc* [af'fissi] VB vedi **affiggere**.

affissione [affis'sjone] SF billposting; **"divieto di affissione"** "stick no bills".

affisso, a [af'fisso] 1 PP di **affiggere**. 2 SM **a** (*avviso*) notice; (*manifesto*) poster, bill **b** (*Gramm*) affix.

affittacamere [affitta'kamere] SM/F INV landlord/landlady; **fare l'affittacamere** to take in lodgers.

affittare [affit'tare] VT **a** (*dare in affitto: casa*) to rent (out), let; (: *macchina*) to hire (out) (*Brit*), rent (out); **"affittasi"**

"to let" **b** (*prendere in affitto: casa*) to rent; (: *macchina*) to hire (*Brit*), rent.

affitto [af'fitto] SM **a** (*vedi vb*) renting; hiring; **dare in affitto** to rent (out), let; to hire (out); **prendere in affitto** to rent; to hire; **contratto d'affitto** lease **b** (*prezzo*) rent.

affittuario, ri [affittu'arjo] SM tenant.

affliggere [af'fliddʒere] VB IRREG 1 VT **a** (*sogg: malattia*) to trouble; (: *notizia*) to grieve, distress; (: *persona: con lamentele*) to torment; **i dolori reumatici la affliggono da tempo** she has been troubled with rheumatics for years. 2 **affliggersi** VIP: **affliggersi (per)** (*rattristarsi*) to grieve (over); (*preoccuparsi*) to worry (over).

afflissi *ecc* [af'flissi] VB vedi **affliggere**.

afflitto, a [af'flitto] 1 PP di **affliggere**. 2 AGG: **aver l'aria afflitta** to look miserable. 3 SM/F: **gli afflitti** SMPL the afflicted.

afflizione [afflit'tsjone] SF distress, torment.

afflosciarsi [affloʃ'ʃarsi] VIP **a** (*perdere tensione: vela, tenda*) to become limp; (: *pelle*) to become flabby, sag; (*sgonfiarsi: palloncino*) to go down **b** (*accasciarsi: persona*) to collapse, go limp.

affluente [afflu'ɛnte] SM (*Geog*) tributary.

affluenza [afflu'ɛntsa] SF (*di persone, merci*) influx; (*di liquidi*) flow; (*degli elettori*) turnout.

affluire [afflu'ire] VI (*aus essere*) **a** (*liquidi*) to flow **b** (*persone, merci*) to pour in; **affluire in** to pour into.

afflusso [af'flusso] SM (*di gente, prodotti*) influx; (*di liquidi*) flow.

affogare [affo'gare] 1 VI (*aus essere*) (*anche fig*) to drown; **affogare in un bicchier d'acqua** to be unable to cope with the slightest difficulty. 2 VT (*gen, fig*) to drown; **affogare i dispiaceri nell'alcol** to drown one's sorrows in drink. 3 **affogarsi** VR to drown o.s.

affogato, a [affo'gato] 1 AGG **a** drowned; **è morta affogata** she drowned **b** (*Culin: uova*) poached. 2 SM: **un affogato al caffè** coffee with ice cream.

affollamento [affolla'mento] SM **a** crowding **b** (*folla*) crowd.

affollare [affol'lare] 1 VT (*gen, fig*) to crowd. 2 **affollarsi** VIP (*gen, fig*) to crowd; **affollarsi intorno a qn/qc** to crowd around sb/sth.

affollato, a [affol'lato] AGG: **affollato (di)** crowded (with).

affondamento [affonda'mento] SM (*di nave*) sinking; (*di ancora*) dropping.

affondare [affon'dare] 1 VT **a** (*mandare a fondo: nave*) to sink; (: *ancora*) to drop **b** (*immergere*): **affondare in qc** to sink into sth; **affondare le mani in tasca** to plunge one's hands into one's pockets. 2 VI (*aus essere*) **a** (*andare a fondo*) to sink **b** (*penetrare*): **affondare in qc** to sink into sth.

affondata [affon'data] SF (*Aer*) dive.

affondo [af'fondo] SM (*Scherma*) lunge; **fare un affondo** to lunge.

affossamento [affossa'mento] SM (*avvallamento*) hollow.

affossare [affos'sare] VT (*respingere: proposta, progetto*) to ditch.

affrancare [affran'kare] 1 VT **a** (*con francobolli*) to stamp; **affrancare (a macchina)** to frank (*Brit*), meter (*Am*) **b** (*liberare: schiavo, popolo*) to liberate, free; (*beni, proprietà*) to redeem. 2 **affrancarsi** VR (*da schiavitù, passione, debiti*) to free o.s.

affrancatrice [affranka'tritʃe] SF franking machine (*Brit*), postage meter (*Am*).

affrancatura [affranka'tura] SF (*valore*) postage; (*operazione*) stamping, franking (*Brit*), metering (*Am*); **affrancatura a carico del destinatario** postage paid (*Brit*), post-paid (*Am*).

affranto, a [af'franto] AGG (*dallo sconforto, dal dolore*): **affranto (da)** overcome (with).

affresco, schi [af'fresko] SM fresco.

affrettare [affret'tare] ① VT (*lavoro, operazione*) to speed up; (*partenza*) to bring forward; **affrettare il passo** to quicken one's pace. ② **affrettarsi** VR (*sbrigarsi*) to hurry up; **affrettarsi a fare qc** to hurry o hasten to do sth.

affrettatamente [affrettata'mente] AVV hurriedly, hastily, in a hurry.

affrettato, a [affret'tato] AGG **a** (*veloce: passo, ritmo*) quick, fast **b** (*frettoloso: decisione*) hurried, hasty; (: *lavoro*) rushed.

affrontare [affron'tare] ① VT (*nemico, pericolo*) to face, confront; (*situazione*) to face up to; (*questione*) to deal with, tackle; (*Equitazione: ostacolo*) to negotiate; **affrontare una spesa** to meet an expense. ② **affrontarsi** VR (*uso reciproco: scontrarsi*) to confront each other.

affronto [af'fronto] SM affront; **fare un affronto a qn** to insult sb.

affumicare [affumi'kare] VT **a** (*riempire di fumo*) to fill with smoke **b** (*annerire*) to blacken with smoke **c** (*alimenti*) to smoke.

affumicato, a [affumi'kato] AGG (*salmone, prosciutto*) smoked; (*lenti*) tinted.

affusolare [affuso'lare] VT to taper.

affusolato, a [affuso'lato] AGG tapering.

afgano, a, afghano, a [af'gano] AGG, SM/F Afghan.

Afghanistan [af'ganistan] SM: **l'Afghanistan** Afghanistan.

a.f.m. ABBR (*Comm*: = *a fine mese*) e.o.m. (= *end of month*).

afono, a ['afono] AGG voiceless.

aforisma, i [afo'rizma] SM aphorism.

afosità [afosi'ta] SF closeness.

afoso, a [a'foso] AGG close.

Africa ['afrika] SF: **l'Africa** Africa.

africano, a [afri'kano] AGG, SM/F African.

afrikaans [afri'ka:ns] SM INV (*lingua*) Afrikaans.

afrikander [æfri'kændə] SM/F INV Afrikaner.

afroamericano, a [afroameri'kano] AGG Afro-American.

afroasiatico, a, ci, che [afroa'zjatiko] AGG Afro-Asian.

afrodisiaco, a, ci, che [afrodi'ziako] AGG, SM aphrodisiac.

Afrodite [afro'dite] SF Aphrodite.

afta ['afta] SF (*Med*) aphtha.

AG SIGLA = *Agrigento*.

Agamennone [aga'mennone] SM Agamemnon.

agar-agar ['agar'agar] SM INV agar-agar.

agata ['agata] SF agate.

agave ['agave] SF (*Bot*) agave.

agenda [a'dʒɛnda] SF **a** (*taccuino*) diary ▶**agenda elettronica** personal organizer ▶ **agenda tascabile** pocket diary ▶ **agenda da tavolo** desk diary **b** (*in una riunione*) agenda.

agente [a'dʒɛnte] ① SM **a** (*Polizia*) policeman, police officer
b (*incaricato*) agent, representative
c (*Chim, Med, Meteor*) agent; **resistente agli agenti atmosferici** weather-resistant. ② ▶**agente di cambio** stockbroker ▶**agente di custodia** prison officer ▶**agente immobiliare** estate agent (*Brit*), realtor (*Am*) ▶**agente marittimo** shipping agent ▶**agente di polizia** o **di Pubblica Sicurezza** police officer ▶**agente provocatore** agent provocateur ▶**agente segreto** secret agent ▶**agente teatrale** theatrical agent ▶**agente di vendita** sales agent.

agenzia [adʒen'tsia] ① SF **a** (*impresa*) agency **b** (*succursale*) branch office. ② ▶**agenzia di collocamento** employment agency ▶**agenzia immobiliare** estate agent's (office) (*Brit*), real estate office (*Am*) ▶**agenzia d'informazioni** news agency ▶**Agenzia Internazionale per l'Energia Atomica** International Atomic Energy Agency ▶**agenzia matrimoniale** marriage bureau ▶**agenzia pubblicitaria** advertising agency ▶**agenzia di stampa** press agency ▶**agenzia di viaggi** travel agency.

agevolare [adʒevo'lare] VT **a** (*facilitare: compito, operazione*): **agevolare qc (a qn)** to make sth easier (for sb), facilitate sth (for sb) **b** (*aiutare*): **agevolare qn (in qc)** to help sb (with sth).

agevolazione [adʒevolat'tsjone] SF (*facilitazione economica*): **concedere delle agevolazioni** to give special terms ▶**agevolazione di pagamento** payment on easy terms ▶**agevolazioni creditizie** credit facilities ▶**agevolazioni fiscali** tax relief.

agevole [a'dʒevole] AGG (*salita, compito*) easy; (*strada*) smooth.

agevolmente [adʒevol'mente] AVV easily.

agganciare [aggan'tʃare] VT (*unire con un gancio*) to hook; (*ricevitore del telefono*) to hang up; (*Ferr: vagone, vettura*) to couple; (*fig: persona*) to catch.

aggancio, ci [ag'gantʃo] SM **a** (*Tecn*) coupling **b** (*fig: conoscenza*) contact.

aggeggio, gi [ad'dʒeddʒo] SM (*fam*) thingy.

aggettivale [addʒetti'vale] AGG adjectival.

aggettivato, a [addʒetti'vato] AGG: **sostantivo aggettivato** noun used as an adjective.

aggettivazione [addʒettivat'tsjone] SF adjectival use.

aggettivo [addʒet'tivo] SM adjective.

agghiacciante [aggjat'tʃante] AGG chilling.

agghiacciare [aggjat'tʃare] ① VT: **agghiacciare qn** OR **agghiacciare il sangue a qn** to make sb's blood run cold. ② **agghiacciarsi** VIP: **mi si è agghiacciato il sangue** my blood ran cold.

agghindarsi [aggin'darsi] VR to dress o.s. up.

agghindato, a [aggin'dato] AGG dressed up.

aggio, gi ['addʒo] SM (*Fin*) premium.

aggiogare [addʒo'gare] VT (*buoi*) to yoke; (*popolo*) to subjugate.

aggiornamento [addʒorna'mento] SM (*vedi vb*) updating; revision; postponement, adjournment; **corso di aggiornamento** refresher course.

aggiornare [addʒor'nare] ① VT **a** (*testo*) to update; (: *rivedere*) to revise; (*persona*) to bring up-to-date; **mi piace tenermi aggiornato (su ciò che succede)** I like to keep up to date with what's happening; **tienimi aggiornato!** keep me posted!
b (*rimandare*): **aggiornare (a)** to postpone (till), put off (till); (: *Dir*) to adjourn (till). ② **aggiornarsi** VR: **aggiornarsi (su qc)** to bring (o keep) o.s. up to date (about sth).

aggiornato, a [addʒor'nato] AGG up-to-date.

aggiotaggio, gi [addʒo'taddʒo] SM (*Econ*) rigging the market.

aggirare [addʒi'rare] ⟦1⟧ VT (*andare intorno a*) to go round; **aggirare un ostacolo/problema** (*fig*) to get round an obstacle/problem.

⟦2⟧ **aggirarsi** VIP **a** : **aggirarsi in** *o* **per** (*girare qua e là*) to go about, wander about; (: *tipo sospetto*) to hang about **b** (*approssimarsi*): **il prezzo s'aggira sul milione** the price is around the million mark.

aggiudicare [addʒudi'kare] VT (*premio, merito*): **aggiudicare qc a qn** to award sb sth, award sth to sb; (*all'asta*) to knock sth down to sb; **aggiudicato!** (*all'asta*) gone!; **si è aggiudicato il primo posto** he won first place.

aggiungere [ad'dʒundʒere] VB IRREG ⟦1⟧ VT to add.

⟦2⟧ **aggiungersi** VIP: **aggiungersi a** to add to.

aggiunsi ecc [ad'dʒunsi] VB vedi **aggiungere**.

aggiunta [ad'dʒunta] SF addition; **in aggiunta...** what's more ... .

aggiunto, a [ad'dʒunto] ⟦1⟧ PP di **aggiungere**.

⟦2⟧ AGG (*Amm: aiuto*) assistant *attr*; (: *sostituto*) stand-in; **sindaco aggiunto** deputy mayor.

⟦3⟧ SM (*Amm*) assistant.

aggiustare [addʒus'tare] ⟦1⟧ VT **a** (*riparare*) to repair, mend **b** (*adattare: vestito*) to alter; (*regolare: tiro, mira*) to adjust; **aggiustarsi la cravatta/gli occhiali** to adjust one's tie/glasses; **gli aggiustò un manrovescio** he gave him a backhander **c** (*fig: sistemare: lite, conti*) to settle; **ti aggiusto io!** I'll fix you!.

⟦2⟧ **aggiustarsi** VR **a** (*uso reciproco: accordarsi*) to come to an agreement; (*per soldi*) to settle (up) **b** (*arrangiarsi*): **mi aggiusterò sul divano** the sofa will be fine.

agglomerato [agglome'rato] SM **a** (*di rocce*) agglomerate, conglomerate ▶ **agglomerato urbano** built-up area **b** (*Tecn*) agglomeration ▶ **agglomerato di legno** chipboard.

aggomitolare [aggomito'lare] VT to wind.

aggradare [aggra'dare] VI DIF (*letter*): **se vi aggrada** if you so desire *o* wish.

aggrapparsi [aggrap'parsi] VR (*anche fig*): **aggrapparsi (a)** to cling (to).

aggravamento [aggrava'mento] SM worsening; **c'è stato un aggravamento** there has been a turn for the worse.

aggravante [aggra'vante] (*Dir*) ⟦1⟧ AGG aggravating.

⟦2⟧ SF aggravation.

aggravare [aggra'vare] ⟦1⟧ VT (*peggiorare*) to worsen; (*accrescere*) to increase.

⟦2⟧ **aggravarsi** VIP (*situazione, malato*) to get worse.

aggravio, vi [ag'gravjo] SM: **aggravio fiscale** tax increase.

aggraziatamente [aggrattsjata'mente] AVV (*muoversi*) gracefully.

aggraziato, a [aggrat'tsjato] AGG (*movimenti*) graceful; (*lineamenti*) pretty; (*modi*) gracious.

aggredire [aggre'dire] VT to attack.

aggregare [aggre'gare] ⟦1⟧ VT: **aggregare qn a qc** to include sb in sth; (*a un club*) to admit sb to sth.

⟦2⟧ **aggregarsi** VR: **aggregarsi (a)** to join; (*a un club*) to become a member of.

⟦3⟧ **aggregarsi** VIP (*Geol, Bio*) to aggregate.

aggregato, a [aggre'gato] ⟦1⟧ AGG (*associato*) associated; **socio aggregato** associate member; **aggregato a un reparto** attached to a section.

⟦2⟧ SM (*gen, Bot, Geol*) aggregate ▶ **aggregato urbano** built-up area.

aggregazione [aggregat'tsjone] SF (*gen, Fis, Chim*) aggregation.

aggressione [aggres'sjone] SF **a** (*contro una persona*) attack, assault ▶ **aggressione a mano armata** armed assault **b** (*Mil, Pol: contro un paese*) aggression; **patto di non aggressione** non-aggression pact **c** (*fig: a volto, capelli, monumento*) attack.

aggressivamente [aggressiva'mente] AVV aggressively.

aggressività [aggressivi'ta] SF aggressiveness.

aggressivo, a [aggres'sivo] AGG aggressive.

aggressore [aggres'sore] ⟦1⟧ SM (*persona*) attacker; (*Pol*) aggressor.

⟦2⟧ AGG (*stato, esercito*) aggressor *attr*.

aggrottare [aggrot'tare] VT: **aggrottare le sopracciglia/la fronte** to frown.

aggrovigliare [aggroviʎ'ʎare] ⟦1⟧ VT (*fili, matassa*) to (en)tangle; **aggrovigliare la matassa** (*fig*) to complicate things.

⟦2⟧ **aggrovigliarsi** VIP to become tangled; (*fig*) to become complicated.

agguantare [aggwan'tare] VT to catch (hold of), seize.

agguato [ag'gwato] SM **a** (*insidia*) trap; **tendere un agguato a qn** to set a trap for sb; **cadere in un agguato** to fall into a trap **b** (*appostamento*) ambush; **stare** *o* **essere in agguato** to lie in ambush.

agguerrito, a [aggwer'rito] AGG (*sostenitore, nemico*) fierce.

aghiforme [agi'forme] AGG needle-shaped.

agiatamente [adʒata'mente] AVV (*vivere*) comfortably.

agiatezza [adʒa'tettsa] SF prosperity; **vivere nell'agiatezza** to live in comfort.

agiato, a [a'dʒato] AGG (*vita, condizione*) comfortable, easy; (*persona, famiglia*) well-off, well-to-do.

agibile [a'dʒibile] AGG (*luogo pubblico*) conforming to required standards; **la strada non è agibile** the road is impassable.

agibilità [adʒibili'ta] SF (*di locale, luogo pubblico*) conformity to standards.

agile ['adʒile] AGG agile, nimble.

agilità [adʒili'ta] SF agility, nimbleness.

agilmente [adʒil'mente] AVV with agility, nimbly.

agio, gi ['adʒo] SM **a** ease, comfort; **sentirsi/trovarsi a proprio agio** to feel/be at one's ease; **mettersi a proprio agio** to make o.s. at home *o* comfortable **b** (*opportunità*): **dare agio a qn di fare qc** to give sb the chance of doing sth **c** : **agi** SMPL comforts; **vivere negli agi** to live in comfort.

agire [a'dʒire] VI **a** (*gen*) to act; (*comportarsi*) to behave; **bisogna agire immediatamente** we must act *o* take action at once; **ha agito male verso i colleghi** he behaved badly towards his colleagues; **non mi piace il suo modo di agire** I don't like the way he goes about things; **agire su qn/qc** to act on sb/sth **b** (*esercitare un'azione*) to work, function; **la leva agisce sul cambio** the lever operates the gear; **una medicina che agisce rapidamente** a medicine which acts *o* takes effect quickly **c** (*Dir*): **agire contro qn** to take (legal) action against sb, start proceedings against sb.

agitare [adʒi'tare] ⟦1⟧ VT **a** (*liquido, bottiglia*) to shake; (*mano, fazzoletto*) to wave; **"agitare prima dell'uso"** "shake well before use"; **il vento agitava i rami** the wind was shaking the branches **b** (*fig: incitare*) to incite; (: *turbare*) to trouble, disturb.

2 **agitarsi** VIP **a** (*rami*) to sway; (*bambino*) to fidget; (*mare*) to get rough; (*dubbio, pensiero*) to stir; (*folla*) to become restless; **agitarsi nel sonno** to toss and turn in one's sleep
b (*turbarsi*) to get worked up, get upset; (*eccitarsi*) to get excited
c (*Pol*) to agitate.

agitato, a [adʒi'tato] AGG **a** (*malato*) restless; (*bambino*) fidgety; (*mare*) rough **b** (*persona*: *turbato*) worried, upset; (: *eccitato*) excited.

agitatore, trice [adʒita'tore] SM/F (*Pol*) agitator.

agitazione [adʒitat'tsjone] SF **a** (*inquietudine*) agitation; **essere in uno stato di agitazione** to be worked up; **mettersi in agitazione** to get worked up; **mettere in agitazione qn** to upset *o* distress sb **b** (*Pol*) agitation, unrest; **entrare in agitazione** to take industrial action.

agit-prop ['adʒit'prɔp] SM/F INV agitprop.

agli ['aʎʎi] PREP + ART vedi **a**.

aglio, gli ['aʎʎo] SM garlic.

agnellino [aɲɲel'lino] SM **a** (*piccolo*) baby lamb **b** (*pelliccia*): **agnellino di Persia** Persian Lamb **c** (*fig*: *persona*): **è (buono come) un agnellino** he's (as quiet as) a lamb.

agnello [aɲ'ɲɛllo] SM lamb; **Agnello di Dio** (*Rel*) Lamb of God.

agnosticismo [aɲɲosti'tʃismo] SM agnosticism.

agnostico, a, ci, che [aɲ'ɲɔstiko] AGG, SM/F agnostic.

ago, aghi ['ago] SM (*gen*) needle; (*della bilancia*) pointer; **lavoro ad ago** needlework; **è come cercare un ago in un pagliaio** it's like looking for a needle in a haystack ►**ago da calza** knitting needle ►**ago magnetico** magnetic needle.

agonia [ago'nia] SF **a** (*Med*) death throes *pl*; **entrare in agonia** to be close to death; **è stata una lunga agonia** it was a slow death **b** (*fig*) agony.

agonismo [ago'nizmo] SM competitiveness.

agonisticamente [agonistika'mente] AVV competitively.

agonistico, a, ci, che [ago'nistiko] AGG (*Sport fig*) competitive.

agonizzante [agonid'dzante] AGG dying.

agonizzare [agonid'dzare] VI (*aus* **avere**) (*malato*) to be dying; (*fig*: *civiltà*) to decline.

agopuntore, trice [agopun'tore] SM/F acupuncturist.

agopuntura [agopun'tura] SF acupuncture.

agorafobia [agorafo'bia] SF agoraphobia.

agorafobo, a [ago'rafobo] AGG agoraphobic.

agostiniano, a [agosti'njano] AGG, SM/F (*Rel*) Augustinian.

agosto [a'gosto] SM August *per fraseologia vedi* **luglio**.

agraria [a'grarja] SF agriculture.

agrario, ria, ri, rie [a'grarjo] **1** AGG (*scuola, scienza*) agricultural; (*leggi*) agrarian; **riforma agraria** land reform.
2 SM landowner.

agricolo, a [a'grikolo] AGG (*gen*) agricultural; (*lavoratori, prodotti, macchine*) farm *attr*; (*popolazione*) farming.

agricoltore [agrikol'tore] SM farmer.

agricoltura [agrikol'tura] SF agriculture ►**agricoltura biologica** organic farming ►**agricoltura intensiva** intensive farming.

agrifoglio, gli [agri'fɔʎʎo] SM holly.

agrimensore [agrimen'sore] SM land surveyor.

agrimensura [agrimen'sura] SF land surveying.

agrimonia [agri'mɔnja] SF agrimony.

agriturismo [agritu'rizmo] SM farm holidays *pl*.

agrituristico, a, ci, che [agritu'ristiko] AGG farm holiday *attr*.

agro, a ['agro] AGG bitter, sharp.

agrodolce [agro'doltʃe] **1** AGG (*sapore*) bittersweet; (*salsa*) sweet-and-sour.
2 SM (*Culin*) sweet and sour sauce.

agronomia [agrono'mia] SF agronomy.

agronomo, a [a'grɔnomo] SM/F agronomist.

agrostide [a'grɔstide] SF bent (grass).

agrume [a'grume] SM (*spesso al pl*: *pianta*) citrus; (: *frutto*) citrus fruit.

agrumeto [agru'meto] SM citrus grove.

aguzzare [agut'tsare] VT to sharpen; **aguzzare la vista** *o* **gli occhi** to strain to see; **aguzzare le orecchie** to prick up one's ears; **aguzzare l'ingegno** to sharpen one's wits; **il bisogno aguzza l'ingegno** (*Proverbio*) necessity is the mother of invention.

aguzzino, a [agud'dzino] SM/F jailer; (*fig*) tyrant.

aguzzo, a [a'guttso] AGG sharp.

ah [a] ESCL ah!, oh!; **ah si?** really?

ahi ['ai] ESCL (*dolore*) ouch!

ahimè [ai'mɛ] ESCL (*spec letter*) alas!

ai ['ai] PREP + ART vedi **a**.

Aia ['aja] SF: **L'Aia** The Hague.

aia ['aja] SF (*cortile*) farmyard; (*per battere il grano*) threshing floor.

Aiace [a'jatʃe] SM Ajax.

A.I.D.D.A. [a'idda] SIGLA F (= *Associazione Imprenditrici Donne Dirigenti d'Azienda*) *association of women entrepreneurs and managers*.

AIDS [eidz] SIGLA M O F AIDS.

A.I.E. ['aiɛ] SIGLA F (= *Associazione Italiana degli Editori*) *publishers' association*.

A.I.E.A. [a'jɛa] SIGLA F (= *Agenzia Internazionale per l'Energia Atomica*) IAEA.

A.I.E.D. ['ajɛd] SIGLA F (= *Associazione Italiana Educazione Demografica*) ≈ FPA (= *Family Planning Association*).

aiola [a'jɔla] SF = **aiuola**.

A.I.P.I. [a'ipi] SIGLA F (= *Associazione Italiana Protezione Infanzia*) ≈ NSPCC (= *National Society for the Protection of Children*).

airbag ['ɛəbæg] SM INV air bag.

AIRC [airk] SIGLA F = *associazione italiana per la ricerca sul cancro*.

airone [ai'rone] SM heron ►**airone bianco** great white egret.

air-terminal ['ɛə,təːminl] SM INV air terminal.

aitante [ai'tante] AGG robust.

aiuola [a'jwɔla] SF flower bed; **"non calpestare le aiuole"** "keep off the flower beds" ►**aiuola spartitraffico** (*Aut*) traffic island.

aiutante [aju'tante] SM/F **a** (*nel lavoro*) assistant; **fare da aiutante a qn** to be sb's assistant **b** (*Mil*) adjutant ►**aiutante di campo** aide-de-camp **c** (*Naut*) master-at-arms ►**aiutante di bandiera** flag lieutenant.

aiutare [aju'tare] **1** VT to help; (*assistere*) to assist; **aiutare qn (a fare qc)** to help sb (to do sth); **aiutare la digestione** to aid (the) digestion.
2 **aiutarsi** VR **a** to help o.s.; **aiutati, che Dio ti aiuta** God helps those who help themselves **b** (*uso reciproco*) to help one another.

aiuto [a'juto] **1** SM **a** (*soccorso*) help, assistance, aid; **prestare** *o* **dare aiuto a qn** to help sb; **venire in aiuto di qn** to help sb, come to sb's assistance *o* aid; **essere di**

aiuto (a qn) to be a help (to sb); **mi è stata di grande aiuto** she has been a great help to me; **chiedere aiuto a qn** to ask sb for help; **correre in aiuto di qn** to rush to sb's assistance

b (*aiutante, assistente*) assistant ▶**aiuto contabile** junior accountant ▶**aiuto giardiniere** under gardener ▶**aiuto regista** assistant director.

2 ESCL help!

aizzare [ait'tsare] VT **a** (*cani*): **aizzare contro qn** to set on sb **b** (*folla*) to incite; (*contendenti*) to urge on.

AL SIGLA = *Alessandria*.

al [al] PREP + ART vedi **a**.

a.l. ABBR = *anno luce*.

ala ['ala] SF (*pl* **ali**) (*gen*) wing; (*di cappello*) brim; (*di mulino*) sail; **ala destra/sinistra** (*Sport*) right/left wing(er); **fare ala** to make way; **avere le ali ai piedi** to have wings; **mettere le ali** (*fig*) to spread one's wings; **prendere qn sotto le proprie ali** (*fig*) to take sb under one's wing.

alabastro [ala'bastro] SM alabaster.

alacre ['alakre] AGG (*persona*) eager; (*mente, fantasia*) lively.

alacremente [alakre'mente] AVV promptly.

alacrità [alakri'ta] SF promptness, speed.

alamaro [ala'maro] SM (*abbottonatura*) frog; **alamari** SMPL frogging *sg*.

alambicco, chi [alam'bikko] SM still (*Chim*).

alano [a'lano] SM Great Dane.

alare[1] [a'lare] AGG wing *attr*.

alare[2] [a'lare] SM (*di camino*) firedog, andiron.

Alaska [a'laska] SF: **l'Alaska** Alaska.

alato, a [a'lato] AGG winged.

alba ['alba] SF dawn; **all'alba** at dawn, at daybreak; **spunta l'alba** dawn is breaking; **alzarsi all'alba** to get up at dawn.

albanese [alba'nese] AGG, SM/F, SM Albanian.

Albania [alba'nia] SF: **l'Albania** Albania.

albatro ['albatro] SM, **albatros** ['albatros] SM INV albatross.

albeggiare [albed'dʒare] VB IMPERS (*aus* **essere**) to dawn; **comincia ad albeggiare** day is dawning; **albeggiava quando arrivò a casa** day was breaking when he arrived home.

alberato, a [albe'rato] AGG (*viale, piazza*) lined with trees, tree-lined.

alberatura [albera'tura] SF (*Naut*) masts *pl*.

albergare [alber'gare] 1 VT (*letter: sentimenti*) to harbour. 2 VI (*aus* **avere**) (*letter*) to dwell.

albergatore, trice [alberga'tore] SM/F (*proprietario*) hotel owner, hotelier; (*gestore*) hotel manager/manageress.

alberghiero, a [alber'gjɛro] AGG hotel *attr*.

albergo, ghi [al'bɛrgo] SM hotel ▶**albergo diurno** *public toilets with washing and shaving facilities* ecc.

albero ['albero] 1 SM **a** (*pianta*) tree ▶**albero da frutto** fruit tree ▶**albero genealogico** family tree ▶**albero di Natale** Christmas tree

b (*Naut*) mast ▶**albero maestro** mainmast

c (*Tecn*) shaft ▶**albero a camme** *o* **della distribuzione** camshaft ▶**albero motore** *o* **a gomiti** crankshaft ▶**albero di trasmissione** transmission shaft.

albicocca, che [albi'kɔkka] SF apricot.

albicocco, chi [albi'kɔkko] SM apricot tree.

albino, a [al'bino] AGG, SM/F (*Bio*) albino.

albo ['albo] SM (*registro professionale*) register; (*Amm: bacheca*) notice board; (*fascicolo illustrato*) album; **radiare dall'albo** to strike off.

albori [al'bori] SMPL (*letter*) dawn *sg*.

album ['album] SM INV (*libro, disco*) album ▶**album da disegno** sketch book; **album per francobolli/fotografie** stamp/photo album.

albume [al'bume] SM egg white, albumen (*termine tecn*).

albumina [albu'mina] SF albumin.

alcali ['alkali] SM INV alkali.

alcalino, a [alka'lino] AGG alkaline.

alce ['altʃe] SM elk, moose.

alcelafo [al'tʃelafo] SM hartebeest.

alchechengi [alke'kɛndʒi] SM INV winter cherry.

alchimia [alki'mia] SF alchemy.

alchimista, i, e [alki'mista] SM/F alchemist.

alchino [al'kino] SM alkyne.

alcol ['alkol] SM INV (*gen, Chim*) alcohol ▶**alcol denaturato** methylated spirits *pl* (*Brit*), wood alcohol (*Am*) ▶**alcol etilico** ethyl alcohol, ethanol ▶**alcol metilico** methyl alcohol.

alcolicità [alkolitʃi'ta] SF alcoholic strength.

alcolico, a, ci, che [al'kɔliko] 1 AGG alcoholic. 2 SM alcohol; **non bevo alcolici** I don't drink.

alcolimetro [alko'limetro] SM Breathalyzer ®.

alcolismo [alko'lizmo] SM alcoholism.

alcolista, i, e [alko'lista] SM/F alcoholic.

alcolizzato, a [alkolid'dzato] AGG, SM/F alcoholic.

alcoltest [alkol'tɛst] SM INV Breathalyzer ®.

alcool *ecc* ['alkool] SM INV = **alcol** *ecc*.

alcova [al'kɔva] SF alcove.

alcuno, a [al'kuno] 1 AGG (*dav sm:* **alcun** + *consonante, vocale*, **alcuno** + s *impura, gn, pn, ps, x, z; dav sf:* **alcuna** + *consonante*, **alcun'** + *vocale*) **a** (*nessuno*): **non… alcuno** no, not any; **non c'è alcuna fretta** there's no hurry, there isn't any hurry; **senza alcun riguardo** without any consideration

b : **alcuni(e)** some, a few.

2 : **alcuni(e)** PRON PL some, a few.

aldilà [aldi'la] SM: **l'aldilà** the next life, the after-life.

aleatorio, ria, ri, rie [alea'tɔrjo] AGG (*incerto*) uncertain.

aleggiare [aled'dʒare] VI (*aus* **avere**) (*fig: profumo, sospetto*) to be in the air.

alesatura [aleza'tura] SF boring.

Alessandria [ales'sandria] SF (*anche:* **Alessandria d'Egitto**) Alexandria.

alessia [ales'sia] SF alexia (*Med*), word blindness.

aletta [a'letta] SF (*Tecn, Zool*) fin; (*Aer*) tab.

alettone [alet'tone] SM (*Aer*) aileron; (*Aut*) spoiler.

Aleutine [aleu'tine] SFPL: **le isole Aleutine** the Aleutian Islands.

alfa ['alfa] AGG INV, SM O F INV alpha.

alfabeticamente [alfabetika'mente] AVV alphabetically, in alphabetical order.

alfabetico, a, ci, che [alfa'bɛtiko] AGG alphabetical.

alfabetizzare [alfabetid'dzare] VT (*popolazione*) to make literate.

alfabetizzazione [alfabetiddzat'tsjone] SF (*leggere e scrivere*) literacy; **corso di alfabetizzazione informatica** introductory computing course.

alfabeto [alfa'bɛto] SM alphabet ▶**alfabeto fonetico** phonetic alphabet ▶**alfabeto Morse** Morse code.

alfanumerico, a, ci, che [alfanu'mɛriko] AGG alphanumeric.

alfiere [al'fjɛre] SM (*Mil*) standard-bearer; (*Scacchi*) bishop.

alfine [al'fine] AVV finally, in the end.

alga, ghe ['alga] SF strand of seaweed, alga (*Bot*); **alghe** SFPL seaweed *sg*, algae (*Bot*).

algebra ['aldʒebra] SF algebra; **questo per me è algebra** (*fig*) this is Greek to me.

Algeri [al'dʒeri] SF Algiers.

Algeria [aldʒe'ria] SF: **l'Algeria** Algeria.

algerino, a [aldʒe'rino] AGG, SM/F Algerian.

algoritmo [algo'ritmo] SM algorithm.

A.L.I. ['ali] SIGLA F (= *Associazione Librai Italiani*) *booksellers' association*.

aliante [ali'ante] SM (*Aer*) glider.

alias ['aljas] AVV alias.

alibi ['alibi] SM INV alibi.

alice [a'litʃe] SF anchovy.

alienante [alje'nante] AGG alienating.

alienare [alje'nare] **1** VT (*gen*) to alienate; (*Dir: trasferire*) to transfer; **alienarsi un amico** to alienate a friend. **2 alienarsi** VR: **alienarsi (da)** to cut o.s. off (from).

alienato, a [alje'nato] **1** AGG (*gen*) alienated; (*Dir*) transferred; (*pazzo*) insane. **2** SM/F lunatic, insane person.

alienazione [aljenat'tsjone] SF (*gen*) alienation; (*Dir*) transfer ▶ **alienazione mentale** (*Psic*) insanity.

alieno, a [a'ljɛno] **1** AGG: **alieno (da)** opposed (to), averse (to). **2** SM/F alien.

alimentare¹ [alimen'tare] AGG food *attr*; **generi alimentari** foodstuffs; **regime alimentare** diet.

alimentare² [alimen'tare] **1** VT **a** (*Tecn*) to feed, supply; (: *stufa*) to add fuel to; (: *caldaia*) to stoke; (: *fuoco*) to stoke up **b** (*fig: tener vivo*) to keep alive **c** (*nutrire*) to nourish, feed. **2 alimentarsi** VR: **alimentarsi di** to live o feed on.

alimentari [alimen'tari] **1** SMPL foodstuffs. **2** SM (*anche:* **negozio di alimentari**) grocer's shop.

alimentarista, i, e [alimenta'rista] SM/F dietician.

alimentatore [alimenta'tore] SM **a** (*Tecn, Elettr*) feeder **b** (*operaio*) stoker.

alimentazione [alimentat'tsjone] SF **a** (*nutrizione*) nutrition; (*cibi*) diet; **alimentazione equilibrata/priva di grassi** balanced/low fat diet **b** (*Tecn*) feeding; (: *di caldaia*) stoking **c** (*Inform: di carta*) feed ▶ **alimentazione a fogli singoli** sheet feed ▶ **alimentazione a modulo continuo** stream feed.

alimento [ali'mento] SM **a** (*cibo*) food; **contenitore per alimenti** food container **b** (*Dir*): **alimenti** SMPL alimony.

aliquota [a'likwota] SF **a** (*Mat*) aliquot **b** (*Fin*) rate ▶ **aliquota d'imposta** (*Fisco*) tax rate ▶ **aliquota minima** (*Fisco*) basic rate.

aliscafo [alis'kafo] SM hydrofoil.

aliseo [ali'zɛo] SM (*Geog*) trade wind.

alitare [ali'tare] VI (*aus* **avere**) (*persona*) to breathe; (*vento*) to blow gently.

alito ['alito] SM (*anche fig*) breath; **avere l'alito cattivo** to have bad breath; **non c'è un alito di vento** there isn't a breath of wind.

all' [all] PREP + ART vedi **a**.

all. ABBR (= *allegato*) enc.

alla ['alla] PREP + ART vedi **a**.

allacciamento [allattʃa'mento] SM (*Tecn*) connection; **far fare l'allacciamento dell'acqua/del gas** to have the water/gas connected.

allacciare [allat'tʃare] VT **a** (*cintura, mantello, cerniera*) to fasten, do up; (*scarpe*) to lace (up), tie; **allacciare** o **allacciarsi la cintura di sicurezza** to fasten one's seat belt; **allacciarsi il cappotto** to fasten one's coat; **allacciare due funi** to join two ropes together **b** (*Tecn: luce, gas, telefono*) to connect; (*due località*) to link **c** (*fig: rapporti*) to start.

allacciatura [allattʃa'tura] SF fastening.

allagamento [allaga'mento] SM (*atto*) flooding *no pl*; (*effetto*) flood.

allagare [alla'gare] VT, **allagarsi** VIP to flood.

allampanato, a [allampa'nato] AGG lanky.

allargare [allar'gare] **1** VT **a** (*passaggio*) to widen; (*buco*) to enlarge; (*vestito*) to let out; (*scarpe nuove*) to break in; (*fig: orizzonti*) to widen, broaden **b** (*aprire: braccia*) to open. **2** VI (*aus* **avere**) (*Aut*): **allargare in curva** to take a bend wide. **3 allargarsi** VIP (*gen*) to widen; (*scarpe, pantaloni*) to lose its shape; (*espandersi: problema, fenomeno*) to spread; **si sentì allargare il cuore** he felt his heart swell.

allarmante [allar'mante] AGG alarming, very worrying.

allarmare [allar'mare] **1** VT to alarm. **2 allarmarsi** VIP to become alarmed.

allarme [al'larme] SM (*gen*) alarm; **dare l'allarme** to give o sound the alarm; **essere in allarme per qc** to be alarmed about sth; **mettere qn in allarme** to alarm sb ▶ **allarme aereo** air-raid warning ▶ **allarme rosso** red alert.

allarmismo [allar'mizmo] SM scaremongering.

allarmista, i, e [allar'mista] SM/F alarmist, scaremonger.

allarmisticamente [allarmistika'mente] AVV in an alarmist way.

allarmistico, a, ci, che [allar'mistiko] AGG alarmist.

allascare [allas'kare] VT (*Naut: vela*) to slacken.

allattamento [allatta'mento] SM (*vedi vb*) (breast-)feeding; suckling ▶ **allattamento artificiale** bottle-feeding ▶ **allattamento naturale** breast-feeding.

allattare [allat'tare] VT (*sogg: donna*) to (breast-)feed; (: *animale*) to suckle; **allattare artificialmente** to bottle-feed.

alle ['alle] PREP + ART vedi **a**.

alleanza [alle'antsa] SF alliance ▶ **Alleanza Democratica** (*Pol*) *moderate centre-left party* ▶ **Alleanza Nazionale** (*Pol*) *party on the far right*.

alleare [alle'are] **1** VT to unite. **2 allearsi** VR to form an alliance; **allearsi** o **con qn/qc** to become allied with sb/sth; **l'Italia e la Germania si allearono contro la Francia** Italy and Germany joined forces against France.

alleato, a [alle'ato] **1** AGG allied. **2** SM/F ally; **gli Alleati** SMPL the Allies.

alleg. ABBR (= *allegato*) encl.

allegare [alle'gare] VT **a** (*in una lettera*): **allegare (a)** to enclose (with); **alleghiamo alla presente una fotocopia** we enclose herewith a photocopy **b** (*gen, Dir: addurre*) to adduce, put forward **c** (*denti*) to set on edge.

allegato, a [alle'gato] **1** AGG enclosed. **2** SM enclosure; **in allegato** enclosed; **in allegato Vi inviamo...** please find enclosed ... .

alleggerimento [alleddʒeri'mento] SM (*gen*) lightening; (*di sofferenza, coscienza*) easing; (*di tasse*) reduction.

alleggerire [alleddʒe'rire] VT **a** (*rendere più leggero*) to lighten, make lighter; (*fig: responsabilità*) to lighten; (: *sofferenza*) to relieve, lessen, alleviate; (: *lavoro, tasse*)

to reduce; (: *coscienza*) to ease; **lo hanno alleggerito del portafoglio** (*scherz*) he's had his wallet pinched **b** (*Sci*) to unweight.

allegoria [allego'ria] SF allegory.

allegoricamente [allegorika'mente] AVV allegorically.

allegorico, a, ci, che [alle'goriko] AGG allegorical.

allegramente [allegra'mente] AVV (*gen*) cheerfully; (*arredato*) brightly.

allegria [alle'gria] SF cheerfulness, gaiety; **mettere allegria a qn** to cheer sb up; **su, un po' di allegria!** come on, cheer up!; **tutte queste luci colorate fanno allegria** all these coloured lights make things more cheerful *o* brighten the place up.

allegro, a [al'legro] ⬚1⬚ AGG **a** (*persona*) cheerful; (*colore*) bright; (*musica*) lively; **c'è poco da stare allegri** things are pretty grim, there's not much to be cheerful about **b** (*un po' brillo*) merry, tipsy. ⬚2⬚ SM (*Mus*) allegro.

allele [al'lɛle] SM (*Bio*) allele.

alleluia [alle'luja] SM INV, ESCL hallelujah.

allenamento [allena'mento] SM training; **essere fuori allenamento** (*anche fig*) to be out of training.

allenare [alle'nare] VT, **allenarsi** VR to train.

allenatore, trice [allena'tore] SM/F trainer, coach.

allentamento [allenta'mento] SM (*fig*) relaxing.

allentare [allen'tare] ⬚1⬚ VT **a** (*nodo, cintura, vite*) to loosen; **allentare le redini** (*anche fig*) to slacken the reins; **allentare il passo** to slacken one's pace **b** (*diminuire: disciplina*) to relax. ⬚2⬚ **allentarsi** VIP (*nodo, stringhe*) to loosen, become loose; (*ingranaggio, vite*) to loosen, work loose.

allergia, gie [aller'dʒia] SF allergy.

allergico, a, ci, che [al'lɛrdʒiko] AGG: **allergico (a)** allergic (to).

allertare [aller'tare] VT to alert.

allestimento [allesti'mento] SM preparation, setting up; **in allestimento** in preparation.

allestire [alles'tire] VT **a** (*spettacolo, mostra, fiera*) to organize, stage; (*vetrina*) to dress; (*cena*) to prepare **b** (*esercito, nave*) to equip.

allettante [allet'tante] AGG attractive.

allettare [allet'tare] VT to attract, entice; **l'idea non mi alletta** the idea doesn't appeal to me.

allevamento [alleva'mento] SM **a** (*di animali*) breeding, rearing; **pollo d'allevamento** battery hen **b** (*luogo*) (stock) farm; (: *per cavalli*) stud farm; (: *per cani*) kennels *pl.*

allevare [alle'vare] VT (*animali*) to breed, rear; (*bambini*) to bring up; **allevato male** (*bambino*) badly brought up.

allevatore, trice [alleva'tore] SM/F breeder.

alleviare [alle'vjare] VT (*pene, stanchezza*) to alleviate, relieve.

allibire [alli'bire] VI (*aus essere*) (*dallo stupore*) to be appalled; (*dalla paura*) to go white.

allibito, a [alli'bito] AGG (*vedi vi*) appalled; white.

allibratore [allibra'tore] SM bookmaker.

allietare [allje'tare] ⬚1⬚ VT to delight, gladden. ⬚2⬚ **allietarsi** VIP to be delighted, rejoice.

allievo, a [al'ljɛvo] SM/F pupil, student ▶ **allievo ufficiale** (*Mil*) cadet.

alligatore [alliga'tore] SM alligator.

allineamento [allinea'mento] SM alignment.

allineare [alline'are] ⬚1⬚ VT (*persone, cose*) to line up; (*Tip*) to align; (*Mil*) to draw up in lines; (*fig: economia, salari*) to adjust. ⬚2⬚ **allinearsi** VR (*anche Mil*) to line up; **allinearsi a** *o* **con** (*conformarsi*) to go along with.

allineato, a [alline'ato] AGG aligned, in line; **testo allineato/non allineato** justified/unjustified text; **paesi non allineati** (*Pol*) non-aligned countries.

allo ['allo] PREP + ART vedi **a**.

allocare [allo'kare] VT to allocate.

allocco, a, chi, che [al'lokko] ⬚1⬚ SM (*Zool*) tawny owl. ⬚2⬚ SM/F fool.

allocuzione [allokut'tsjone] SF address.

allodola [al'lɔdola] SF (sky)lark.

alloggiare [allod'dʒare] ⬚1⬚ VI (*aus avere*): **alloggiare (in)** to stay (at); **sono alloggiato al Ritz** I'm staying at the Ritz. ⬚2⬚ VT to accommodate, put up.

alloggio, gi [al'lɔddʒo] SM **a** (*abitazione provvisoria*) accommodation (*Brit*), accommodations (*Am*); **vitto e alloggio** board and lodging **b** (*appartamento*) flat (*Brit*), apartment (*Am*); **la crisi degli alloggi** the housing problem; **cercare alloggio** to look for somewhere to live.

allontanamento [allontana'mento] SM (*gen*) separation; (*affettivo*) estrangement; (*di funzionario*) removal; (*di studente*) exclusion, expulsion; **c'è stato un graduale allontanamento fra i 2 paesi** relations between the 2 countries have grown cooler.

allontanare [allonta'nare] ⬚1⬚ VT **a** (*persona*) to take away; (*oggetto*) to move away, take away; (*fig: affetti, amici*) to alienate; **allontanare una poltrona dal fuoco** to move an armchair away from the fire; **la polizia fece allontanare i passanti** the police moved on the bystanders; **la maestra ha allontanato Maria da Roberto** the teacher has separated Maria and Roberto
b (*mandare via*) to send away, send off; (*licenziare*) to dismiss
c (*fig: pericolo*) to avert; (: *sospetti*) to divert. ⬚2⬚ **allontanarsi** VR: **allontanarsi (da)** to go away (from); (*fig: possibilità*) to grow more remote; **c'eravamo allontanati troppo** we had wandered too far; **allontanarsi da qn** to wander away from sb; (*fig*) to grow away from sb.

allora [al'lora] AVV **a** (*in quel momento*) then, at that moment; (*a quel tempo*) then, in those days, at that time; **la gente di allora** people then *o* in those days; **da allora in poi** since then, from then on
b (*in questo caso*) then, in that case, so; (*dunque*) well then, so; **hai paura? - allora dillo!** are you frightened? - (well) then, say so!; **allora vieni?** well (then), are you coming?; **e allora?** (*che fare?*) what now?; (*e con ciò?*) so what?

allorché [allor'ke] CONG (*letter*) when, as soon as.

alloro [al'lɔro] SM laurel; **riposare** *o* **dormire sugli allori** to rest on one's laurels.

allotropo [al'lɔtropo] SM allotrope.

alluce ['allutʃe] SM big toe.

allucinante [allutʃi'nante] AGG (*scena, spettacolo*) awful, terrifying; (*fam: incredibile*) amazing.

allucinare [allutʃi'nare] VT (*abbagliare*) to dazzle; (*dare allucinazioni*) to cause to hallucinate; (*fig: impressionare fortemente*) to shock.

allucinato, a [allutʃi'nato] ⬚1⬚ AGG (*persona*) suffering from hallucinations; (: *fig*) shocked; (*sguardo*) staring. ⬚2⬚ SM/F: **sguardo da allucinato** staring eyes.

allucinazione [allutʃinat'tsjone] SF hallucination; **avere le allucinazioni** (*anche fig*) to hallucinate.

allucinogeno, a [allutʃi'nɔdʒeno] [1] AGG hallucinogenic, mind-expanding. [2] SM hallucinogen.

alludere [al'ludere] VI IRREG (*aus* avere): **alludere a** to allude to, hint at.

alluminio [allu'minjo] SM aluminium (*Brit*), aluminum (*Am*).

allunaggio, gi [allu'naddʒo] SM moon landing.

allunare [allu'nare] VI (*aus* essere) to land on the moon.

allungabile [allun'gabile] AGG extendable.

allungare [allun'gare] [1] VT **a** (*rendere più lungo*) to lengthen; **allungare il passo** to quicken one's step; **allungare la strada** to take the long way round

b (*tendere*) to stretch out; **allungare le gambe** to stretch one's legs; **allungare le orecchie/il collo** to strain one's ears/crane one's neck; **allungare le mani** (*rubare*) to pick pockets; (*picchiare*) to become violent; **non allungare le mani sulla mia ragazza** keep your hands off my girlfriend

c (*fam: dare*) to pass, hand; **mi allunghi il sale per favore?** could you pass me the salt please?; **gli allungò uno schiaffo** he gave him a slap

d (*diluire*) to dilute, water down.

[2] **allungarsi** VIP (*diventare più lungo*) to grow *o* get longer; (: *ombre*) to lengthen; (: *pianta*) to grow taller; (: *vestito, maglione*) to stretch.

[3] **allungarsi** VR (*stendersi*) to stretch out.

allungato, a [allun'gato] AGG (*Equitazione*): **passo/trotto allungato** extended walk/trot.

allusi *ecc* [al'luzi] VB *vedi* **alludere**.

allusione [allu'zjone] SF: **allusione (a)** allusion (to), hint (at).

allusivamente [alluziva'mente] AVV allusively.

allusivo, a [allu'zivo] AGG allusive.

alluso [al'luzo] PP *di* **alludere**.

alluvionale [alluvjo'nale] AGG alluvial; **materiale alluvionale** alluvium.

alluvionato, a [alluvjo'nato] [1] AGG (*regione, città*) flooded. [2] SM/F flood victim.

alluvione [allu'vjone] SF flood.

almanacco, chi [alma'nakko] SM almanac.

almeno [al'meno] [1] AVV at least. [2] CONG: **(se) almeno** if only; **(se) almeno piovesse!** if only it would rain!

alogeno, a [a'lɔdʒeno] [1] AGG (*luce, lampada*) halogen *attr*. [2] SF (*lampada*) halogen lamp. [3] SM (*Chim*) halogen.

alone [a'lone] SM (*di sole, luna*) halo; (*di fiamma, lampada*) glow; (*di macchia*) ring; **un alone di mistero** an aura *o* air of mystery.

alpaca ['alpaka] SM INV alpaca.

alpe ['alpe] SF (*letter: montagna*) alp; (*pascolo*) mountain pasture.

alpeggio, gi [al'peddʒo] SM mountain pasture.

alpestre [al'pɛstre] AGG (*delle Alpi*) alpine; (*montuoso*) mountainous.

Alpi ['alpi] SFPL: **le Alpi** the Alps.

alpinismo [alpi'nizmo] SM mountaineering, climbing.

alpinista, i, e [alpi'nista] SM/F mountaineer, climber.

alpino, a [al'pino] [1] AGG (*montano*) alpine, mountain *attr*; (*delle Alpi*) Alpine. [2] SM (*Mil*): **gli alpini** *Italian Alpine troops*.

alquanto, a [al'kwanto] [1] AGG INDEF a certain amount of, some; **alquanti(e)** quite a few, several.

[2] PRON INDEF PL: **alquanti(e)** quite a few, several. [3] AVV rather, somewhat.

Alsazia [al'sattsja] SF Alsace.

alsaziano, a [alsat'tsjano] AGG, SM/F, SM Alsatian.

alt [alt] [1] ESCL halt!, stop!. [2] SM: **dare l'alt** to call a halt.

altalena [alta'lena] SF (*a funi*) swing; (*a bilico, anche fig*) seesaw; **un'altalena di fortuna e disgrazie** a series of ups and downs.

altamente [alta'mente] AVV (*specializzato, qualificato*) highly; (*seccato, scocciato*) extremely; **me ne frego altamente** I don't give a damn.

altare [al'tare] SM altar ▶ **altare maggiore** high altar.

altarino [alta'rino] SM (*scherz*): **scoprire gli altarini** to reveal one's guilty secrets.

alteramente [altera'mente] AVV proudly.

alterare [alte'rare] [1] VT **a** (*fatti, verità*) to distort; (*registro*) to falsify; (*qualità, colore*) to affect, impair; (*alimenti*) to adulterate **b** (*piani*) to alter, change; (*persona*) to irritate.

[2] **alterarsi** VIP **a** (*alimenti*) to go bad *o* off; (*vino*) to spoil **b** (*irritarsi*) to get angry, lose one's temper.

alterazione [alterat'tsjone] SF (*vedi vt*) distortion; falsification; impairment; adulteration; alteration, change; **alterazione del polso** change in the pulse rate.

altercare [alter'kare] VI (*aus* avere) to argue, quarrel.

alterco, chi [al'tɛrko] SM row, altercation.

alter ego [alte'rɛgo] SM INV alter ego.

alternamente [alterna'mente] AVV alternately.

alternanza [alter'nantsa] SF alternation; (*Agr*) rotation.

alternare [alter'nare] [1] VT (*avvicendare*): **alternare qc a *o* con qc** to alternate sth with sth; (*Agr*) to rotate.

[2] **alternarsi** VR: **alternarsi (a *o* con)** to alternate (with).

alternatamente [alternata'mente] AVV = **alternamente**.

alternativa [alterna'tiva] SF alternative; **non abbiamo alternativa** we have no alternative; **in alternativa** as an alternative.

alternativo, a [alterna'tivo] AGG (*energia, medicina ecc*) alternative.

alternato, a [alter'nato] AGG alternate; (*Elettr*) alternating.

alternatore [alterna'tore] SM alternator.

alterno, a [al'tɛrno] AGG (*gen*) alternate; (*mutevole: fortuna, vicenda*) changing; **a giorni alterni** every other day, on alternate days; **circolazione a targhe alterne** (*Aut*) *anti-pollution measure whereby, on days with an even date, only cars whose numberplate ends in an even number may be on the road, while on days with an odd date, only cars whose numberplate ends in an odd number may be on the road.*

altero, a [al'tero] AGG proud.

altezza [al'tettsa] SF **a** (*di edificio, persona*) height; (*quota*) height, altitude; (*di suono*) pitch; (*di acqua, pozzo*) depth; (*di tessuto*) width; (*fig: d'animo*) greatness; **altezza sul mare** height above sea level; **da un'altezza di 2000 metri** from a height of 2000 metres; **essere all'altezza di una situazione** (*fig*) to be equal to a situation; **non sono all'altezza** (*fig*) I'm not up to it

b (*Geom*) perpendicular height; (: *linea*) perpendicular; (*Astron*) elevation, altitude

c (*prossimità*): **all'altezza della farmacia** near the chemist's; **all'altezza di Capo Horn** off Cape Horn

d (*titolo*) highness; **Sua Altezza** Your Highness.

altezzosamente [altettsosa'mente] AVV haughtily, arrogantly.

altezzosità [altettsosi'ta] SF haughtiness, arrogance.
altezzoso, a [altet'tsoso] AGG haughty, arrogant.
alticcio, cia, ci, ce [al'tittʃo] AGG tipsy.
altimetro [al'timetro] SM altimeter.
altipiano [alti'pjano] SM = altopiano.
altisonante [altiso'nante] AGG high-sounding, pompous.
Altissimo [al'tissimo] SM: **l'Altissimo** the Most High.
altitudine [alti'tudine] SF altitude.
alto, a ['alto] **1** AGG **a** (gen) high, tall; **un muro alto 10 metri** a wall 10 metres high; **è alto 1 metro e 80** ≈ he's 6 foot (tall); **andare a testa alta** (fig) to carry one's head high
b (suono: elevato) high(-pitched); (: forte) loud; **ad alta voce** out loud, aloud
c (fig: elevato: carica, dignitario) high; (: sentimenti, pensieri) lofty, noble; **avere un'alta opinione di sé** to have a high opinion of o.s.
d (profondo: acqua) deep; **a notte alta** in the dead of night; **siamo in alto mare** (fig) we still have a long way to go
e (Geog): **l'alta Italia** Northern Italy; **l'alto Po** the upper reaches of the Po
f (largo: tessuto) wide.
2 SM (parte superiore) top (part); **mani in alto!** hands up!; **guardare in alto** to look up; **là in alto** up there; **dall'alto** (fig) from on high; **dall'alto di** from the top of; **dall'alto in** o **al basso** up and down; **guardare dall'alto in basso qn** (fig) to look down on sb; **(degli) alti e bassi** ups and downs.
3 AVV (volare) high; **"alto"** (su casse di imballaggio) "this side up".
4 ▶ **alta fedeltà** high fidelity, hi-fi ▶ **alta moda** haute couture ▶ **alta società** high society ▶ **alta stagione** high o peak season ▶ **alto comando** (Mil) high command ▶ **alto commissario** high commissioner ▶ **l'Alto Medioevo** the Early Middle Ages.
altoatesino, a [altoate'zino] **1** AGG of o from the Alto Adige.
2 SM/F inhabitant o native of the Alto Adige.
altoforno [alto'forno] SM blast furnace.
altolà [alto'la] **1** ESCL (Mil) halt!.
2 SM INV: **gli hanno dato l'altolà** they ordered him to stop.
altolocato, a [altolo'kato] AGG of high rank, highly placed; **amicizie altolocate** friends in high places.
altoparlante [altopar'lante] SM (loud)speaker.
altopiano [alto'pjano] SM (pl altipiani) upland plain, plateau ▶ **altopiano basaltico** lava plateau.
altresì [altre'si] AVV (letter) also.
altrettanto, a [altret'tanto] **1** AGG as much; **altrettanti(e)** as many; **ho altrettanta fiducia in te** I have as much o the same confidence in you.
2 PRON as much; **altrettanti(e)** as many; **domani dovrò comprarne altrettanto** I'll have to buy as much o the same tomorrow; **sono 2 mesi che cerco lavoro, e temo che ne passeranno altrettanti prima di trovarlo** I have been looking for work for 2 months now, and I'm afraid it'll be as long again before I find any; **se n'è andato ed io ho fatto altrettanto** he left and so did I o and I followed suit; **tanti auguri! — grazie, altrettanto** all the best! — thank you, the same to you.
3 AVV equally; **lui è altrettanto bravo** he is equally clever, he is just as clever.
altri ['altri] PRON PERS SG (qualcun altro) someone else; (: in frasi negative) anyone else; **né tu né altri potrà convincermi** neither you nor anyone else is going to persuade me; **non si tocca la roba d'altri** you shouldn't touch other people's things.
altrimenti [altri'menti] AVV **a** (in caso contrario) otherwise, or else **b** (in modo diverso) differently.

altro, a ['altro]
1 AGG INDEF
a (diverso) other, different;
▷**questa è un'altra cosa** that's another o a different thing
▷**erano altri tempi** things were different then
b (supplementare) other;
▷**prendi un altro cioccolatino** have another chocolate
▷**gli altri allievi usciranno più tardi** the other pupils o the rest of the pupils will come out later
c (opposto) other;
▷**dall'altra parte della strada** on the other o opposite side of the street
▷**d'altra parte** on the other hand
d (nel tempo)
▷**domani l'altro** the day after tomorrow
▷**l'altro giorno** the other day
▷**l'altro ieri** the day before yesterday
▷**quest'altro mese** next month
e
▷**chi/dove/chiunque altro** who/where/anybody else
▷**noi altri** = noialtri
▷**voi altri** = voialtri.
2 PRON INDEF
a (persona, cosa diversa o supplementare): **un altro/un'altra** another (one)
▷**altri(e)** others; (persone) others, other people
▷**prendine un altro** take another one
▷**se non lo fai tu lo farà un altro** if you don't do it someone else will
▷**da un giorno all'altro** (improvvisamente) from one day to the next; (presto) any day now
▷**aiutarsi l'un l'altro** to help one another o each other
b (opposizione): **l'altro(a)** the other (one)
▷**gli altri/ le altre** the others
▷**l'uno e l'altro** both (of them)
▷**o l'uno o l'altro** either (of them)
▷**né l'uno né l'altro** neither (of them)
▷**non questo, l'altro** not this one, the other one
c (sostantivato: solo maschile) something else; (in espressioni interrogative) anything else;
▷**non faccio che studiare** I do nothing but study, all I do is study
▷**non ho altro da dire** I have nothing else to say, I don't have anything else to say
▷**desidera altro?** (would you like) anything else?
▷**gli dirò questo ed altro!** I'll tell him this and more besides!
▷**ci mancherebbe altro!** that's all we need!
▷**più che altro** above all
▷**se non altro** at least
▷**tra l'altro** among other things
▷**sei contento? — tutt'altro!** are you pleased? — far from it! o anything but!
▷**ci vuole altro per spaventarmi!** it takes a lot more (than this) to frighten me!

altroché [altro'ke] ESCL certainly!, and how!

altronde [al'tronde] AVV: **d'altronde** on the other hand.

altrove [al'trove] AVV elsewhere, somewhere else.

altrui [al'trui] AGG INV other people's, others'; **la roba altrui** other people's things *pl.*

altruismo [altru'izmo] SM altruism.

altruista, i, e [altru'ista] ⊡ AGG altruistic.
⊡ SM/F altruist.

altruisticamente [altruistika'mente] AVV altruistically.

altruistico, a, ci, che [altru'istiko] AGG altruistic.

altura [al'tura] SF **a** (*rialto*) height, high ground **b** (*Naut*): **d'altura** deep-sea.

alunno, a [a'lunno] SM/F pupil.

alveare [alve'are] SM (bee)hive.

alveo ['alveo] SM riverbed.

alveolo [al'vɛolo] SM alveolus.

alzabandiera [altsaban'djɛra] SM INV (*Mil*): **l'alzabandiera** the raising of the flag.

alzacristallo [altsakris'tallo] SM (*Aut*) window winder (*Brit*), window roller (*Am*) ►**alzacristalli elettrici** electric windows.

alzare [al'tsare] ⊡ VT **a** (*gen*) to raise; (*peso*) to lift; **alzare gli occhi** *o* **lo sguardo** to raise one's eyes; **lo sciopero fece alzare i prezzi** the strike caused an increase in prices
b (*issare: bandiera, vela*) to hoist
c (*costruire*) to build, erect
d (*fraseologia*): **alzare le carte** to cut the cards; **non ha alzato nemmeno un dito per aiutarmi** he didn't lift a finger to help me; **alzare il gomito** to drink too much; **alzare le mani su qn** to lay hands on sb; **alzare le spalle** to shrug one's shoulders; **alzare i tacchi** to take to one's heels.
⊡ **alzarsi** VR (*persona*) to rise, get up; **alzarsi (in piedi)** to stand up, get to one's feet; **alzarsi da tavola** to get up from the table; **alzarsi col piede sbagliato** to get out of bed on the wrong side.
⊡ **alzarsi** VIP **a** (*sorgere: sole, luna*) to rise; (: *vento*) to rise, get up
b (*aumentare: temperatura*) to rise; (*fiamma*) to leap up.

alzata [al'tsata] SF **a** (*vedi vb*) raising; lifting; **un'alzata di spalle** a shrug; **un'alzata d'ingegno** a flash of genius; **votare per alzata di mano** to vote by show of hands **b** (*di mobile*) upper part, top **c** (*per dolci*) cakestand.

alzato, a [al'tsato] ⊡ AGG (*braccio*) raised; (*persona: in piedi*) up; **stare alzato tutta la notte** to stay up all night.
⊡ SM (*Archit*) elevation.

alzavola [al'tsavola] SF teal.

A.M. [a'ɛmme] SIGLA F (= *Aeronautica Militare*) ≈ RAF.

amabile [a'mabile] AGG **a** (*persona, conversazione*) pleasant, amiable **b** (*vino*) sweet.

amabilità [amabili'ta] SF INV pleasantness, amiability.

amabilmente [amabil'mente] AVV pleasantly, amiably.

amaca, che [a'maka] SF hammock.

amalgama, i [a'malgama] SM (*Chim*) amalgam; (*fig*) amalgam, mixture.

amalgamare [amalga'mare] ⊡ VT to amalgamate, combine; (*impastare*) to mix.
⊡ **amalgamarsi** VIP (*sostanze*) to amalgamate, combine; (*Culin*) to mix; (*fig: gruppo, squadra*) to become unified.

amante [a'mante] ⊡ AGG (*appassionato*): **amante di** fond of, keen on.
⊡ SM/F lover; (*extraconiugale: uomo*) lover; (: *donna*) lover, mistress.

amaramente [amara'mente] AVV bitterly.

amaranto [ama'ranto] ⊡ SM (*Bot*) love-lies-bleeding.
⊡ AGG INV: **color amaranto** reddish purple.

amare [a'mare] ⊡ VT (*provare affetto*) to love; (: *amante, marito, moglie*) to love, be in love with; (*amico, musica, sport*) to be fond of, love; **noi amiamo la musica classica** we love *o* enjoy *o* are fond of classical music; **amare fare qc** to like *o* love doing *o* to do sth; **farsi amare da qn** to win sb's love.
⊡ **amarsi** VR (*uso reciproco*) to be in love, love each other.

amareggiare [amared'dʒare] ⊡ VT to embitter; **amareggiarsi la vita** to make one's life a misery.
⊡ **amareggiarsi** VR to get upset.

amareggiato, a [amared'dʒato] AGG embittered.

amarena [ama'rɛna] SF (sour) black cherry.

amaretto [ama'retto] SM (*biscotto*) amaretto biscuit; (*liquore*) amaretto liqueur.

amarezza [ama'rettsa] SF bitterness; **le amarezze della vita** life's disappointments.

amarico, a [a'mariko] ⊡ AGG Amharic.
⊡ SM/F (*abitante*) Amhara.
⊡ SM (*lingua*) Amharic.

amaro, a [a'maro] ⊡ AGG (*sapore, fig*) bitter; (*caffè*) without sugar; (*spiacevole*) unpleasant, bitter; (*triste*) unhappy; (*doloroso*) painful; **avere la bocca amara** to have a bitter taste in one's mouth.
⊡ SM **a** (*liquore*) bitters *pl*
b (*gusto*) bitter taste; (*fig: tristezza, dolore*) bitterness; **mi ha lasciato l'amaro in bocca** it left a bitter taste in my mouth.

amarognolo, a [ama'roɲɲolo] AGG slightly bitter.

amato, a [a'mato] ⊡ AGG beloved, loved, dear.
⊡ SM/F loved one.

amatore, trice [ama'tore] SM/F **a** (*amante*) lover **b** (*appassionato*) lover; (*intenditore: di vini ecc*) connoisseur; **pezzo da amatore** collector's item **c** (*dilettante*) amateur.

amazzone [a'maddzone] SF **a** (*Mitol*) Amazon; **il Rio delle Amazzoni** (*Geog*) the (river) Amazon **b** (*cavallerizza*) horsewoman; (*abito*) riding habit; **cavalcare all'amazzone** to ride sidesaddle.

Amazzonia [amad'dzɔnja] SF Amazonia.

amazzoniano, a [amaddzo'njano] AGG Amazonian.

amazzonico, a, ci, che [amad'dzɔniko] AGG (*gen*) Amazonian; (*giungla, bacino*) Amazon *attr*.

ambasceria [ambaʃʃe'ria] SF embassy.

ambasciata [ambaʃ'ʃata] SF embassy; (*messaggio*) message.

ambasciatore, trice [ambaʃʃa'tore] SM/F ambassador; **ambasciator non porta pena!** don't take it out on me (*o* him *ecc*)!

ambedue [ambe'due] ⊡ AGG INV both; **ambedue i ragazzi** both boys.
⊡ PRON INV both.

ambidestro, a [ambi'dɛstro] AGG ambidextrous.

ambientale [ambjen'tale] AGG (*temperatura*) ambient *attr*; (*problemi, tutela*) environmental.

ambientalismo [ambjenta'lizmo] SM environmentalism.

ambientalista, i, e [ambjenta'lista] ⊡ AGG environmental.
⊡ SM/F environmentalist.

ambientamento [ambjenta'mento] SM (*in luogo, lavoro*): **periodo di ambientamento** settling-in period.

ambientare [ambjen'tare] ① VT (*film, racconto*) to set.
② **ambientarsi** VR to get used to one's surroundings, settle down.

ambientazione [ambjentat'tsjone] SF (*di film, racconto*) setting.

ambiente [am'bjɛnte] ① SM **a** environment; **negli ambienti politici** in political circles **b** (*stanza*) room.
② AGG INV: **temperatura ambiente** room temperature.

ambiguamente [ambigua'mente] AVV ambiguously.

ambiguità [ambigui'ta] SF INV ambiguity.

ambiguo, a [am'biguo] AGG ambiguous; (*persona*) shady.

ambio ['ambjo] SM (*Equitazione*) amble.

ambire [am'bire] VT, VI (*aus avere*): **ambire a** to aspire to; **un premio molto ambito** a much sought-after prize.

ambito ['ambito] SM area; (*tecnico, specialistico*) field; (*fig*: *cerchia*) sphere, circle.

ambivalente [ambiva'lɛnte] AGG (*termini*) with two possible interpretations.

ambivalenza [ambiva'lɛntsa] SF ambivalence.

ambizione [ambit'tsjone] SF ambition.

ambizioso, a [ambit'tsjoso] AGG ambitious.

ambo ['ambo] ① AGG (*pl m* **ambo** *o* **ambi**, *pl f* **ambo** *o* **ambe**) both; **da ambo** *o* **ambe le parti** from *o* on both sides.
② SM (*al gioco*) double.

ambosessi [ambo'sɛssi] AGG INV of either sex, male or female.

ambra ['ambra] SF amber ► **ambra grigia** ambergris.

ambrosia [am'brɔzja] SF ambrosia.

ambulante [ambu'lante] ① AGG travelling, itinerant; (*biblioteca*) mobile; **sei un'enciclopedia ambulante!** you're a walking encyclopaedia!.
② SM pedlar.

ambulanza [ambu'lantsa] SF (*veicolo*) ambulance; (*Mil*) field hospital.

ambulatoriale [ambulato'rjale] AGG (*Med*) outpatients *attr*; **operazione ambulatoriale** operation in a doctor's surgery; **visita ambulatoriale** visit to the doctor's surgery (*Brit*) *o* office (*Am*).

ambulatorio, ri [ambula'torjo] SM (*di medico*) surgery (*Brit*), doctor's office (*Am*); (*di ospedale*) outpatients' department.

A.M.D.I. ['amdi] SIGLA F = *Associazione Medici Dentisti Italiani*.

A.M.E. ['ame] SIGLA M = *Accordo Monetario Europeo*.

ameba [a'mɛba] SF amoeba (*Brit*), ameba (*Am*).

amebiasi [ame'biazi] SF (*Med*) amoebiasis.

amen ['amen] ① ESCL (*Rel*) amen; **e allora amen!** (*fam*) alright, alright.
② SM: **in un amen** in the twinkling of an eye.

amenità [ameni'ta] SF INV **a** (*di luogo, pensieri*) pleasantness *no pl* **b** (*facezia*) pleasantry.

ameno, a [a'mɛno] AGG **a** (*luogo, lettura, pensieri*) pleasant, agreeable **b** (*faceto*: *tipo, discorso*) droll, amusing.

America [a'mɛrika] SF: **l'America** America ► **l'America latina** Latin America ► **l'America del sud** South America.

americanata [amerika'nata] SF (*pegg*): **le Olimpiadi sono state una vera americanata** the Olympics were a typical American extravaganza; **gli piacciono le americanate** he likes everything that's typically American.

americanismo [amerika'nizmo] SM (*espressione*) Americanism; (*ammirazione*) love of America.

americanizzare [amerikanid'dzare] ① VT to americanize.
② **americanizzarsi** VIP to become americanized.

americano, a [ameri'kano] ① AGG American; **confronto all'americana** identity parade; **servizio all'americana** table mats.
② SM/F American.

ametista [ame'tista] SF amethyst.

amfetamina [anfeta'mina] SF amphetamine.

amianto [a'mjanto] SM asbestos.

amichevole [ami'kevole] ① AGG (*anche Sport*) friendly; **in via amichevole** amicably.
② SF (*Sport*) friendly match.

amichevolmente [amikevol'mente] AVV in a friendly way.

amicizia [ami'tʃittsja] SF **a** (*rapporto*) friendship; **fare amicizia con qn** to make friends with sb; **un'affettuosa amicizia** (*euf*: *relazione sentimentale*) a close friendship
b : **amicizie** SFPL (*amici*) friends; **ha molte amicizie influenti** she has a lot of influential friends *o* friends in high places.

amico, a, ci, che [a'miko] ① AGG friendly.
② SM/F **a** friend; **amico del cuore** best friend; **amico intimo** close friend; **un amico d'infanzia** a childhood friend; **Michela e le sue amiche** Michela and her (girl)friends; **sono amici per la pelle** they're great pals; **farsi qn amico** to make friends with sb; **senza amici** friendless; **un mio amico avvocato** a lawyer friend of mine
b (*euf*: *amante*) friend, man friend/lady friend
c (*appassionato*) lover, enthusiast; **amico degli animali** animal lover; **club degli amici della musica** music club.

amido ['amido] SM starch.

amilasi [ami'lazi] SF amylase.

amletico, a, ci, che [am'lɛtiko] AGG: **dubbio amletico** paralyzing doubt.

ammaccare [ammak'kare] ① VT (*auto, pentola, cappello*) to dent; (*frutta, parte del corpo*) to bruise.
② **ammaccarsi** VIP (*vedi vt*) to get dented; bruise.

ammaccatura [ammakka'tura] SF (*segno*: *su auto ecc*) dent; (: *su parte del corpo*) bruise.

ammaestrare [ammaes'trare] VT (*addestrare*) to teach; (: *animali*) to train; (: *scherz fig*: *persona*) tame; **orso/cavallo ammaestrato** performing bear/horse.

ammainabandiera [ammainaban'djera] SM INV (*Mil*): **l'ammainabandiera** the lowering of the flag.

ammainare [ammai'nare] VT (*vela, bandiera*) to lower, haul down.

ammalarsi [amma'larsi] VIP to fall *o* become ill.

ammalato, a [amma'lato] ① AGG ill, unwell, sick.
② SM/F sick person; (*paziente*) patient.

ammaliare [amma'ljare] VT (*con sortilegio*) to bewitch; (*fig*) to bewitch, enchant, charm.

ammaliatore, trice [ammalja'tore] ① SM/F (*uomo*) charmer; (*donna*) enchantress.
② AGG bewitching, charming.

ammanco, chi [am'manko] SM (*Amm, Econ*) deficit; **c'è stato un ammanco di cassa di 30 sterline** the till was £30 short.

ammanettare [ammanet'tare] VT to handcuff.

ammanicato, a [ammani'kato], **ammanigliato, a** [ammaniʎ'ʎato] AGG (*fam*) well-connected, with friends in high places.

ammansire [amman'sire] VT (*animale*) to tame; (*fig*: *persona*) to calm (down).

ammantarsi [amman'tarsi] ① VR (*persona*) to wrap o.s.; (:

fig): **ammantarsi di virtù** to pretend virtue.

2 VIP: **ammantarsi di** (*prato*: *di fiori*) to be carpeted with; (*cielo*: *di stelle*) to be studded with.

ammantato, a [amman'tato] AGG: **ammantato di neve** with a mantle of snow.

ammaraggio, gi [amma'raddʒo] SM (*vedi vb*) (sea) landing; splashdown.

ammarare [amma'rare] VI (*aus* **essere**) (*aereo*) to make a sea landing; (*astronave*) to splash down.

ammassare [ammas'sare] **1** VT (*cose*, *fig*: *ricchezze*) to pile up, accumulate, amass; (*persone*) to pack.

2 **ammassarsi** VIP (*cose*) to pile up, accumulate; (*persone*) to crowd; **la gente si era ammassata sull'autobus** people were crammed together on the bus.

ammasso [am'masso] SM (*cumulo*) pile, heap; (*Econ*) stockpile; **portare all'ammasso** (*grano, olio*) to stockpile.

ammattire [ammat'tire] VI (*aus* **essere**) (*anche fig*) to go mad, be driven mad.

ammazzacaffè [ammattsakaf'fe] SM INV (*fam*) *brandy* ecc *after a meal*.

ammazzare [ammat'tsare] **1** VT (*uccidere*) to kill; (*fig*: *affaticare*) to exhaust, wear out; **ammazzare il tempo** to kill time.

2 **ammazzarsi** VR (*uso reciproco*) to kill e.o.; (*suicidarsi*) to kill o.s, commit suicide; **ammazzarsi di lavoro** to kill o.s. with work, work o.s. to death.

3 **ammazzarsi** VIP (*rimanere ucciso*) to die, be killed.

ammenda [am'mɛnda] SF **a** (*Dir, Sport*) fine **b** (*riparazione*): **fare ammenda di qc** to make amends for sth.

ammesso, a [am'messo] PP di **ammettere**.

ammettere [am'mettere] VT IRREG **a** (*far entrare*: *visitatore*) to admit, let in, allow in; (*accettare*: *nuovo socio*, *studente*) to admit; **ammettere qn in un club** to admit sb to a club; **essere ammesso agli esami orali** to be admitted to *o* to be allowed to do the oral exams **b** (*riconoscere*: *colpa, errore, fatto*) to admit, acknowledge **c** (*supporre*) to suppose, assume; **ammettiamo che sia vero** let us suppose *o* assume that it's true; **ammesso (e non concesso) che** (just) assuming that **d** (*tollerare*: *scuse, comportamento*) to accept; (*permettere*) to allow; **non ammetto che si bestemmi** I will not tolerate swearing.

ammezzato [ammed'dzato] SM (*anche:* **piano ammezzato**) mezzanine, entresol.

ammiccare [ammik'kare] VI (*aus* **avere**): **ammiccare (a)** to wink (at).

amministrare [amminis'trare] VT **a** (*ditta*) to manage, run; (*patrimonio*) to administer; (*stato*) to run, govern **b** (*Rel, Dir*) to administer.

amministrativamente [amministrativa'mente] AVV administratively.

amministrativo, a [amministra'tivo] AGG administrative.

amministratore [amministra'tore] SM (*Amm*) administrator; (*di stabile*) manager of flats ►**amministratore aggiunto** associate director ►**amministratore delegato** managing director, chief executive (*Am*) ►**amministratore fiduciario** trustee ►**amministratore unico** sole director.

amministrazione [amministrat'tsjone] SF (*vedi vb*) management, running; administration; government; **consiglio d'amministrazione** board of directors ►**amministrazione controllata** temporary receiver-ship ►**amministrazione fiduciaria** trusteeship ►**amministrazione pubblica** public administration, ≈ civil service ►**amministrazione straordinaria** *control by a government-appointed administrator* ►**amministrazioni locali** local government.

amminoacido [ammino'atʃido] SM amino acid.

ammiraglia [ammi'raʎʎa] SF flagship.

ammiragliato [ammiraʎ'ʎato] SM (*ufficio*) admiralship; (*consesso, sede*) admiralty.

ammiraglio, gli [ammi'raʎʎo] SM admiral.

ammirare [ammi'rare] VT to admire.

ammiratore, trice [ammira'tore] SM/F admirer.

ammirazione [ammirat'tsjone] SF admiration.

ammirevole [ammi'revole] AGG admirable.

ammirevolmente [ammirevol'mente] AVV admirably.

ammisi ecc [am'mizi] VB vedi **ammettere**.

ammissibile [ammis'sibile] AGG (*comportamento*) acceptable; (*Dir: testimonianza*) admissible.

ammissione [ammis'sjone] SF **a** (*a club*) admission, entry; (*a scuola*) entrance, acceptance; **esame d'ammissione** entrance exam **b** (*di colpa, errore*) admission.

Amm.ne ABBR = **amministrazione**.

ammobiliare [ammobi'ljare] VT to furnish.

ammobiliato, a [ammobi'ljato] AGG (*camera, appartamento*) furnished.

ammodernare [ammoder'nare] VT to modernize.

ammodo, a modo [am'mɔdo] **1** AVV (*per bene*) well, properly.

2 AGG INV respectable, nice.

ammogliare [ammoʎ'ʎare] **1** VT to find a wife for.

2 **ammogliarsi** VR to marry, take a wife (*old*).

ammollo [am'mɔllo] SM soaking; **mettere/lasciare i panni in ammollo** to leave the clothes to soak.

ammoniaca [ammo'niaka] SF ammonia.

ammoniacato, a [ammonia'kato] **1** AGG containing ammonia.

2 SM ammoniate.

ammonimento [ammoni'mento] SM (*rimprovero*) reprimand, admonishment; (*lezione*) lesson, warning.

ammonio, ni [am'mɔnjo] **1** SM ammonium; **idrossido di ammonio** ammonium hydroxide.

2 AGG INV: **ione ammonio** ammonium ion.

ammonire [ammo'nire] VT **a** (*rimproverare*) to admonish, reprimand; (*avvertire*) to warn **b** (*Dir*) to caution; (*Calcio*) to book.

ammonitivo, a [ammoni'tivo] AGG warning.

ammonito, a [ammo'nito] SM/F (*gen*) person who has been warned; (*Calcio*) booked player.

ammonizione [ammonit'tsjone] SF **a** (*monito*) warning; (*rimprovero*) reprimand **b** (*Dir*) caution; (*Calcio*) booking.

ammontare [ammon'tare] **1** VI (*aus* **essere**): **ammontare a** to amount to, add up to.

2 SM (*somma*) (total) amount.

ammonticchiare [ammontik'kjare] VT to pile up, heap up.

ammorbare [ammor'bare] VT **a** (*diffondere malattia*) to infect **b** (*sogg*: *odore*) to foul; **un tanfo tremendo ammorbava l'aria** a terrible stench poisoned the air.

ammorbidente [ammorbi'dɛnte] SM fabric softener.

ammorbidire [ammorbi'dire] **1** VT to soften.

2 **ammorbidirsi** VIP to soften; **ammorbidirsi con l'età** (*fig*) to mellow with age.

ammortamento [ammorta'mento] SM (*Fin: estinzione di debito*) redemption, amortization; (: *in bilancio*) depre-

ciation ▶ **ammortamento fiscale** capital allowance.

ammortare [ammor'tare] VT (*Fin*: *debito*) to pay off, redeem; (: *spese d'impianto*) to write off.

ammortizzamento [ammortiddza'mento] SM **a** (*Fin*) = ammortamento **b** (*Aut*) cushioning.

ammortizzare [ammortid'dzare] VT **a** (*Fin*: *debito*) to pay off, redeem; (: *spese d'impianto*) to write off **b** (*Aut*, *Tecn*: *attutire*) to cushion, absorb.

ammortizzatore [ammortiddza'tore] SM (*Aut*, *Tecn*) shock absorber ▶ **ammortizzatori sociali** *measures to cushion the effects of unemployment*.

Amm.re ABBR = **amministratore**.

ammucchiare [ammuk'kjare] [1] VT (*disporre in mucchio*) to heap, pile up; (: *denaro*) to pile up, accumulate.

[2] **ammucchiarsi** VIP (*cose*) to pile up, accumulate; (*persone*) to crowd.

ammuffire [ammuf'fire] VI (*aus* **essere**) to go *o* grow mouldy (*Brit*) *o* moldy (*Am*); (*fig*: *persona*) to moulder, languish.

ammuffito, a [ammuf'fito] AGG mouldy; (*fig*) fossilized.

ammutinamento [ammutina'mento] SM mutiny.

ammutinarsi [ammuti'narsi] VIP to mutiny.

ammutinato, a [ammuti'nato] [1] AGG mutinous.

[2] SM mutineer.

ammutolire [ammuto'lire] VI (*aus* **essere**) to be struck dumb.

amnesia [amne'zia] SF amnesia.

amnio, ni ['amnjo] SM amnion.

amniocentesi [amnjo'tʃɛntezi] SF INV amniocentesis.

amniotico, a, ci, che [am'njɔtiko] AGG amniotic; **liquido amniotico** amniotic fluid.

amnistia [amnis'tia] SF amnesty.

amnistiare [amnis'tjare] VT to amnesty, grant an amnesty to.

•**amo** ['amo] SM (*Pesca*) (fish) hook; (*fig*) bait; **l'abbiamo preso all'amo** (*fig*) he's swallowed the bait; **gettare l'amo** to cast one's line; (*fig*) to lay bait.

amorale [amo'rale] AGG amoral.

amoralità [amorali'ta] SF amorality.

amore [a'more] SM **a** (*affetto*) love, affection; (*sessuale*) love; **il suo amore per lui/per le piante** her love for him/of plants; **fare qc con amore** to do sth with loving care; **fare l'amore** *o* **all'amore (con qn)** to make love (with sb); **mi ha raccontato tutto dei suoi amori** he told me all about his love affairs

b (*persona*) love; **vieni, amore** come here, darling *o* love; **il tuo bambino è un amore** your baby is a darling **c** (*fraseologia*): **per amore di** for the sake of; **per l'amor di Dio!** for God's sake!; **per amore o per forza** willy-nilly; **andare d'amore e d'accordo con qn** to get on like a house on fire with sb; **che amore di vestito!** what a lovely dress! ▶ **amore libero** free love ▶ **amore di sé** egoism, selfishness ▶ **amor proprio** self-esteem, pride.

amoreggiamento [amoreddʒa'mento] SM flirting.

amoreggiare [amored'dʒare] VI (*aus* **avere**) to flirt.

amorevole [amo'revole] AGG loving, affectionate.

amorfo, a [a'mɔrfo] AGG amorphous; (*fig*: *persona*) colourless; **ma come sei amorfo!** how apathetic you are!

amorino [amo'rino] SM cupid.

amorosamente [amorosa'mente] AVV lovingly.

amoroso, a [amo'roso] [1] AGG (*affettuoso*) loving, affectionate; (*d'amore*: *sguardo*) amorous; (: *poesia, lettera, relazione*) love *attr*.

[2] SM/F (*fam*) sweetheart.

amperaggio, gi [ampe'raddʒo] SM amperage.

ampere [ã'pɛr] SM INV (*Elettr*) amp(ère).

amperometro [ampe'rɔmetro] SM ammeter.

ampiamente [ampja'mente] AVV (*trattare, discutere*) fully.

ampiezza [am'pjettsa] SF **a** (*di sala*) (large) size; (*di gonna*) fullness; (*fig*: *di fenomeno*) scale; **ampiezza di vedute** broad-mindedness **b** (*Fis*) amplitude, range; (*Geom*) size; (*Mus*) range.

ampio, pia, pi, pie ['ampjo] AGG **a** (*vasto*: *spazio, sala*) spacious; (: *strada, corridoio*) wide, broad; **di ampio respiro** (*fig*: *ricerca, articolo*) wide-ranging; **di ampie vedute** broad-minded **b** (*largo*: *vestito*) loose; (: *gonna*) full **c** (*abbondante*: *garanzie*) ample.

amplesso [am'plɛsso] SM (*sessuale*) intercourse.

ampliamento [amplia'mento] SM (*di strada*) widening; (*di aeroporto*) expansion; (*fig*) broadening.

ampliare [ampli'are] [1] VT (*allargare*) to widen; (*fig*: *discorso*) to enlarge (up)on; (: *raggio di azione*) to widen; **ampliare le proprie cognizioni** to widen one's knowledge.

[2] **ampliarsi** VIP to grow, increase.

amplificare [amplifi'kare] VT (*suono*) to amplify; (*fig*: *sensazione*) to increase; (: *pregi*) to extol.

amplificatore [amplifika'tore] SM (*Tecn, Mus*) amplifier.

amplificazione [amplifikat'tsjone] SF amplification.

ampolla [am'polla] SF **a** (*per olio, aceto*) cruet **b** (*Chim*) round-bottom flask.

ampollina [ampol'lina] SF (*Rel*) ampulla.

ampollosamente [ampollosa'mente] AVV bombastically.

ampollosità [ampollosi'ta] SF INV bombast.

ampolloso, a [ampol'loso] AGG bombastic.

amputare [ampu'tare] VT (*Med*) to amputate; (*fig*: *testo, scritto*) to cut.

amputazione [amputat'tsjone] SF amputation.

Amsterdam ['amsterdam] SF Amsterdam.

amuleto [amu'lɛto] SM lucky charm.

AN SIGLA = *Ancona*.

A.N. SIGLA F (*Pol*) = **Alleanza Nazionale**.

A.N.A. ['ana] SIGLA F (= *Associazione Nazionale Alpini*) *Italian association of alpine soldiers*.

A.N.A.A.O. [a'nao] SIGLA F (= *Associazione Nazionale Aiuti e Assistenti Ospedalieri*) *national union of Italian hospital doctors*.

anabbagliante [anabbaʎ'ʎante] (*Aut*) [1] AGG dipped (*Brit*), dimmed (*Am*).

[2] SM dipped (*Brit*) *o* dimmed (*Am*) headlight.

anabolismo [anabo'lizmo] SM anabolism.

anaconda [ana'kɔnda] SM INV anaconda.

anacronismo [anakro'nizmo] SM anachronism.

anacronisticamente [anakronistika'mente] AVV anachronistically.

anacronistico, a, ci, che [anakro'nistiko] AGG anachronistic.

anaerobio, bi [anae'rɔbjo] SM anaerobe.

anafilattico, a, ci, che [anafi'lattiko] AGG (*Med*): **shock anafilattico** toxic shock syndrome.

anagrafe [a'nagrafe] SF (*Amm*: *registro*) register of births, marriages and deaths; (: *ufficio*) registry *o* register office (*Brit*), office of vital statistics (*Am*) ▶ **anagrafe tributaria** *central tax records*.

anagraficamente [anagrafika'mente] AVV according to public records.

anagrafico, a, ci, che [ana'grafiko] AGG (*Amm*): **dati**

anagrafici personal data o records; **luogo di residenza anagrafica** place of residence.

anagramma, i [ana'gramma] SM anagram.

analcolico, a, ci, che [anal'kɔliko] [1] AGG non-alcoholic; **bevanda analcolica** non-alcoholic drink; **bibita analcolica** soft drink.

[2] SM non-alcoholic aperitif.

anale [a'nale] AGG anal.

analfabeta, i, e [analfa'bɛta] AGG, SM/F illiterate.

analfabetismo [analfabe'tizmo] SM illiteracy.

analgesico [anal'dʒεziko] SM painkiller, analgesic.

analisi [a'nalizi] SF INV **a** (gen) analysis; (di orina, sangue) test; **all'analisi dei fatti** on examining the facts; **in ultima analisi** all in all, in the final analysis; **sono in analisi da 5 anni** (Psic) I've been in analysis for the past 5 years ▶ **analisi dei costi** cost analysis ▶ **analisi di mercato** market analysis ▶ **analisi dei sistemi** systems analysis ▶ **analisi delle vendite** sales analysis

b (Gramm): **analisi grammaticale** parsing; **analisi logica** sentence analysis.

analista, i, e [ana'lista] SM/F (Chim, Med, Inform) analyst; (Psic) (psycho)analyst ▶ **analista finanziario** financial analyst ▶ **analista di sistemi** systems analyst.

analiticamente [analitika'mente] AVV analytically.

analitico, a, ci, che [ana'litiko] AGG analytic(al); **indice analitico** index.

analizzare [analid'dzare] VT (gen) to analyse (Brit), analyze (Am); (sangue, orina) to test, analyse; (Gramm: frase) to parse; (poesia, testo) to give a commentary on.

anallergico, a, ci, che [anal'lɛrdʒiko] AGG (Med) hypoallergenic.

analogamente [analoga'mente] AVV similarly, in a similar way.

analogia, gie [analo'dʒia] SF analogy; **per analogia (con)** by analogy (with).

analogicamente [analodʒika'mente] AVV analogically, by analogy.

analogico, a, ci, che [ana'lɔdʒiko] AGG analogical; (calcolatore, orologio) analog(ue).

analogo, a, ghi, ghe [a'nalogo] AGG: **analogo (a)** analogous (to), similar (to).

ananas ['ananas] SM INV pineapple.

anarchia [anar'kia] SF anarchy.

anarchico, a, ci, che [a'narkiko] [1] AGG anarchistic; (disordinato) anarchic(al).

[2] SM/F anarchist.

anarchismo SM anarchism.

A.N.A.S. ['anas] SIGLA F (= Azienda Nazionale Autonoma delle Strade) national roads department.

anatema, i [ana'tɛma] SM (Rel) anathema; **scagliare** o **gettare l'anatema contro** to anathematize.

anatomia [anato'mia] SF (gen) anatomy; (analisi) analysis.

anatomicamente [anatomika'mente] AVV anatomically.

anatomico, a, ci, che [ana'tɔmiko] AGG anatomical; **sedile anatomico** contoured o anatomical seat.

anatomizzare [anatomid'dzare] VT to anatomize.

anatra ['anatra] SF duck ▶ **anatra selvatica** mallard.

anatroccolo [ana'trɔkkolo] SM duckling.

anca, che ['anka] SF (di persona) hip; (di animale) haunch.

A.N.C.A. ['anka] SIGLA F (= Associazione Nazionale Cooperative Agricole) ≈ NFU (= National Farmers Union).

A.N.C.C. [a'ɛnnetʃi'tʃi] SIGLA F = Associazione Nazionale Carabinieri.

A.N.C.E. ['antʃe] SIGLA F (= Associazione Nazionale Costrut-

tori Edili) national association of builders.

ancestrale [antʃes'trale] AGG ancestral.

anche ['anke] CONG **a** (pure) also, too; **e va anche a Roma** and he's going to Rome too, and he's also going to Rome; **parla inglese e anche italiano** he speaks English and Italian too o as well; **vengo anch'io!** I'm coming too!; **gli ho parlato ieri — anch'io** I spoke to him yesterday — so did I; **anche oggi non potrò venire** I won't be able to come today either; **potrebbe anche cambiare idea, ma...** he may change his mind, but ...

b (perfino) even; **anche se** even if; **anche volendo, non finiremmo in tempo** however much we wanted to, we wouldn't finish in time.

ancheggiare [anked'dʒare] VI (aus avere) to wiggle (one's hips).

anchilosato, a [ankilo'zato] AGG stiff.

A.N.C.I. ['antʃi] SIGLA F (= Associazione Nazionale dei Comuni Italiani) national confederation of local authorities.

ancia, ce ['antʃa] SF (Mus) reed.

anconetano, a [ankone'tano] [1] AGG of o from Ancona.

[2] SM/F inhabitant o native of Ancona.

ancora¹ ['ankora] SF (Naut, fig) anchor; **gettare/levare l'ancora** to cast/weigh anchor; ▶ **ancora galleggiante** sea anchor ▶ **ancora di salvezza** (fig) last hope.

ancora² [an'kora] [1] AVV **a** (tuttora) still; **è ancora innamorato di lei** he's still in love with her; **ancora oggi** still today

b (di nuovo) again; **ancora tu!** (not) you again!; **sei andato ancora a Parigi da allora?** have you been back to Paris since then?

c : **non ancora** not yet; **il direttore non è ancora qui** the manager isn't here yet

d (più) (some) more; **ancora un po'** a little more; **vuoi ancora zucchero?** would you like some more sugar?; **ne vorrei ancora** I'd like some more; **prendi ancora un biscotto** have another biscuit; **ci sono ancora caramelle?** are there any sweets left?; **cosa vuoi ancora?** what else do you want?; **ancora per una settimana** for another week, for one week more; **ancora una volta** once more, once again; **ancora un po' e finivamo in acqua** we almost ended up in the water.

[2] CONG (nei comparativi) even, still; **ancora di più/meno** even more/less; **ancora meglio/peggio** even o still better/worse; **ancora altrettanto** as much again; **oggi fa ancora più freddo** it's even colder today.

ancoraggio, gi [anko'raddʒo] SM anchorage; **tassa d'ancoraggio** anchorage dues pl.

ancorare [anko'rare] VT, **ancorarsi** VR (anche fig) to anchor.

A.N.C.R. [ankr] SIGLA F (= Associazione Nazionale Combattenti e Reduci) servicemen's and ex-servicemen's association.

Andalusia [andalu'zia] SF: **l'Andalusia** Andalusia.

andaluso, a [anda'luzo] AGG, SM/F Andalusian.

andamento [anda'mento] SM (di malattia) course; (della Borsa, del mercato) trend; (del lavoro) progress.

andante [an'dante] [1] SM (Mus) andante.

[2] AGG (corrente) current; (di poco pregio) cheap, second-rate.

andare [an'dare]
[1] VI IRREG (aus essere)
a (gen) to go;

▷**andare** in *bicicletta* to cycle
▷**andare** a *casa* to go home
▷**andare** a *cavallo* to ride
▷*dove* va (messa) questa vite? where does this screw go?
▷**andare** a *letto* to go to bed
▷**andare** *lontano* (anche fig) to go far
▷**andare** in *macchina* to drive
▷**andare** a *male* to go bad
▷**andare** per i 50 (età) to be getting on for 50
▷**andare** in città a *piedi* to walk to town
▷**andare** a *Roma* to go to Rome
▷**andrò** all'*università* l'anno prossimo I'm going to university next year
▷**vado** e *vengo* I'll be back in a minute
▷**andare** e *venire* to come and go
b (essere)
▷se non vado *errato* if I'm not mistaken
▷va *fatto* entro oggi it's got to be done today
▷**andare** *fiero* di qc/qn to be proud of sth/sb
▷*ne* va della nostra vita our lives are at stake
▷**vado** *pazzo* per la pizza I'm crazy about pizza, I adore pizza
▷la situazione va *peggiorando* the situation is getting worse
▷**andare** *perduto* to go missing
▷non va *trascurato* il fatto che... we shouldn't forget o overlook the fact that ...
▷va sempre *vestita* di rosso she always wears red
c (salute, situazione): come va? — bene grazie how are you? — fine thanks
▷va *bene* (d'accordo) all right, O.K (fam)
▷ti è andata *bene* you got away with it
▷**andare** di *bene* in meglio to get better and better
▷*com'è* andata? how did it go?
▷*come* va (la salute)? — va bene how are you? — I'm fine
▷*come* va la scuola? how's school?
▷*come* vai a scuola? how are you getting on at school?
d (funzionare) to work;
▷la macchina va a *benzina* the car runs on petrol
▷non riesco a *far* andare la macchina I can't start the car
▷la lavatrice *non* va the washing machine won't work
e: andare *a* qn (calzare: scarpe, vestito) to fit sb; (essere gradito): quest'idea non mi va I don't like this idea
▷questi jeans *non* mi vanno più these jeans don't fit me any more
▷*ti* va il cioccolato? do you like chocolate?
▷*ti* va di andare al cinema? do you feel like going to the cinema?
▷*ti* va (bene) se ci vediamo alle 5? is it ok if we meet at 5?
f (essere venduto) to sell; (essere di moda) to be fashionable;
▷un modello che va molto a style that sells well
g (+ infinito)
▷**andare** a *pescare* to go fishing
▷**andare** a *prendere* qc/qn to go and get sth/sb
▷**andare** a *sciare* to go skiing
▷**andare** a *vestirsi* to go and get dressed

h (fraseologia)
▷va *là* che ti conosco bene come off it, I know you too well
▷vai a quel *paese*! (fam) get lost!
▷vada *per* una birra ok, I'll have a beer
▷chi va *piano* va sano e va lontano (Proverbio) slow and steady wins the race
▷va da *sé* (è naturale) it goes without saying
▷per questa *volta* vada let's say no more about it this time
▷andiamo! let's go!; (coraggio!) come on!
i: *andarsene* to go away
▷me ne vado I'm off, I'm going
▷se ne sono andati they've gone
j (+ avverbio, preposizione) vedi **fuori**, **via** ecc.
2 SM
▷a *lungo* andare in time, in the long run
▷con l'andar del *tempo* with the passing of time
▷racconta storie a *tutto* andare she's forever talking rubbish
▷**andare** e *venire* coming and going.

andata [an'data] SF (viaggio) outward journey; all'andata c'era brutto tempo on the outward journey there was bad weather; biglietto di sola andata single (Brit) o one-way ticket; biglietto di andata e ritorno return (Brit) o round-trip (Am) ticket; partita/girone di andata (Sport) first leg/first half of the season.
andatura [anda'tura] SF **a** (modo di camminare) gait, walk **b** (Sport) pace; imporre l'andatura to set the pace **c** (Naut) tack.
andazzo [an'dattso] SM (pegg): con o di questo andazzo, finiremo male the way things are going, we'll finish up in a mess; le cose hanno preso un brutto andazzo things have taken a turn for the worse.
Ande ['ande] SFPL: le Ande the Andes.
andino, a [an'dino] AGG Andean.
andirivieni [andiri'vjeni] SM INV coming and going.
Andorra [an'dorra] SF Andorra.
andrò ecc [an'drɔ] VB vedi **andare**.
androceo [andro'tʃɛo] SM (Bot) androecium.
androgino, a [an'drɔdʒino] **1** AGG androgynous. **2** SM hermaphrodite, androgyne.
Andromaca [an'drɔmaka] SF Andromache.
Andromeda [an'drɔmeda] SF Andromeda.
androne [an'drone] SM entrance hall.
aneddoto [a'nɛddoto] SM anecdote.
anelare [ane'lare] VI (aus avere): anelare a qc/a fare qc to long o yearn for sth/to do sth.
anelito [a'nɛlito] SM (letter): anelito (di) longing (for), yearning (for).
anellidi [a'nɛllidi] SMPL (Zool) annelids.
anello [a'nɛllo] SM (gen, fig) ring; (di catena) link; ad anello ring-shaped; anello di fidanzamento/nuziale engagement/wedding ring; anello di congiunzione/mancante (fig) connecting/missing link.
anemia [ane'mia] SF anaemia (Brit), anemia (Am) ▶ anemia falciforme sickle-cell anaemia.
anemico, a, ci, che [a'nɛmiko] **1** AGG anaemic (Brit), anemic (Am). **2** SM/F an(a)emic person.
anemometro [ane'mɔmetro] SM wind gauge.
anemone [a'nɛmone] SM anemone ▶ anemone di bosco

wood anemone ▶**anemone di mare** sea anemone.

anestesia [aneste'zia] SF anaesthesia (*Brit*), anesthesia (*Am*); **sotto anestesia** under anaesthetic, under anaesthesia ▶**anestesia locale** local anaesthetic ▶**anestesia totale** general anaesthetic.

anestesista, i, e [aneste'zista] SM/F anaesthetist (*Brit*), anesthetist (*Am*).

anestetico, a, ci, che [anes'tɛtiko] AGG, SM anaesthetic (*Brit*), anesthetic (*Am*).

anestetizzare [anestetid'dzare] VT to anaesthetize (*Brit*), anesthetize (*Am*).

anfetamina [anfeta'mina] SF amphetamine.

anfetaminico, a, ci, che [anfeta'miniko] AGG (*fig*) hyper (*fam*).

anfibio, bia, bi, bie [an'fibjo] [1] AGG amphibious. [2] SM **a** (*Zool*) amphibian; (*veicolo*) amphibious **b** : **anfibi** SMPL (*scarpe*) heavy-duty boots.

anfiteatro [anfite'atro] SM amphitheatre (*Brit*), amphitheater (*Am*).

anfitrione [anfitri'one] SM (*letter*) host.

anfora ['anfora] SF amphora.

anfotero, a [an'fɔtero] AGG (*Chim*) amphoteric.

anfratto [an'fratto] SM cleft.

angariare [anga'rjare] VT to vex.

angelica [an'dʒelika] SF (*Bot*) angelica.

angelicamente [andʒelika'mente] AVV like an angel, angelically.

angelico, a, ci, che [an'dʒeliko] AGG angelic(al).

angelo ['andʒelo] SM angel; **fabbricante d'angeli** (*euf*) backstreet abortionist ▶**angelo custode** guardian angel.

Angelus ['andʒelus] SM (*Rel*) Angelus.

angheria [ange'ria] SF vexation.

angina [an'dʒina] SF (*tonsillite*) tonsillitis ▶**angina pectoris** angina (pectoris).

angioino, a [andʒo'ino] AGG, SM/F Angevin.

angioma, i [an'dʒɔma] SM (*Med*) angioma.

anglicanesimo [anglika'nezimo] SM anglicanism.

anglicano, a [angli'kano] AGG, SM/F Anglican.

anglicismo [angli'tʃizmo] SM anglicism.

anglicizzare [anglitʃid'dzare] [1] VT to anglicize. [2] **anglicizzarsi** VR to become anglicized.

anglista, i, e [an'glista] SM/F anglicist.

anglofilo, a [an'glɔfilo] [1] AGG anglophilic, anglophile. [2] SM/F anglophile.

anglosassone [anglo'sassone] AGG, SM/F Anglo-Saxon.

Angola [an'gɔla] SF: **l'Angola** Angola.

angolano, a [ango'lano] AGG, SM/F Angolan.

angolare¹ [ango'lare] AGG (*gen, Geom*) angular; **mobile angolare** corner unit; **pietra angolare** (*Archit, fig*) cornerstone.

angolare² [ango'lare] VT (*Calcio, Tennis, Cine*) to angle.

angolazione [angolat'tsjone] SF (*Fot, Cine, TV, fig*) angle; **visto da questa angolazione** seen from this angle.

angolo ['angolo] SM **a** (*di stanza, tavolo, strada, bocca*) corner; **fare angolo con** (*strada*) to run into; **sull'** o **all'angolo della strada** on o at the corner of the street; **faccio un salto al negozio all'angolo** I'm just popping out to the corner shop; **dietro l'angolo** (*anche fig*) round the corner; **abito in Via Cairoli angolo Via Bersaglio** I live on the corner of Via Cairoli and Via Bersaglio; **ho scoperto degli angoli di Londra che non conoscevo** I've discovered some out-of-the-way bits of London I never knew before; **starsene in un angolo** to stay all by one's self; **non startene sempre in un angolo, vieni con noi** don't stay on your own all the time, come with us ▶**angolo cottura** (*di appartamento*) kitchen area **b** (*Geom*) angle ▶**angolo retto/acuto/ottuso** right/acute/obtuse angle.

angoloso, a [ango'loso] AGG (*oggetto*) angular; (*volto, corpo*) angular, bony.

angora ['angora] SF: **lana d'angora** angora.

angoscia [an'gɔʃʃa] SF (*gen, Psic*) anguish *no pl*.

angosciare [angoʃ'ʃare] [1] VT to cause anguish to; **la scena mi ha angosciato** I was very upset by what I saw; **il pensiero della morte mi angoscia** the thought of dying terrifies me. [2] **angosciarsi** VIP: **angosciarsi (per)** (*preoccuparsi*) to become anxious (about); (*provare angoscia*) to get upset (about o over).

angosciatamente [angoʃʃata'mente] AVV with anguish.

angosciato, a [angoʃ'ʃato] AGG upset, distressed.

angosciosamente [angoʃʃosa'mente] AVV with anguish.

angoscioso, a [angoʃ'ʃoso] AGG (*scena, situazione*) distressing, harrowing; (*attesa*) agonizing.

anguilla [an'gwilla] SF eel.

anguria [an'gurja] SF watermelon.

angustia [an'gustja] SF (*letter*) **a** (*di spazio*) lack of space **b** (*povertà*) poverty, want; **vive in angustia** he lives in straitened circumstances **c** (*ansia*) anguish, distress.

angustiare [angus'tjare] [1] VT to torment, distress. [2] **angustiarsi** VIP: **angustiarsi (per)** to become distressed (about).

angusto, a [an'gusto] AGG (*stanza, letto*) narrow; (*fig*: *pensiero*) mean, petty; (: *mente*) narrow.

anice ['anitʃe] SM **a** (*Bot*: *pianta*) anise; (: *frutto*) aniseed **b** (*liquore*) anisette.

anidride [ani'dride] SF (*Chim*) ▶**anidride carbonica** carbon dioxide ▶**anidride solforosa** sulphur dioxide.

anidro, a ['anidro] AGG anhydrous.

anilina [ani'lina] SF aniline.

anima ['anima] SF **a** (*gen*) soul; **volere un bene dell'anima a qn** to be extremely fond of sb; **con tutta l'anima** with all one's heart; **mettere l'anima in qc/nel fare qc** to put one's heart into sth/into doing sth; **vendere l'anima (al diavolo)** to sell one's soul (to the devil); **anima e corpo** body and soul, wholeheartedly; **rompere l'anima a qn** to drive sb mad; **mi hai rotto l'anima** I've had enough of you; **il nonno buon'anima...** Grandfather, God rest his soul ...; **la buon'anima di Mario** (*defunto*) the dear departed Mario **b** (*persona*) soul; (*abitante*) inhabitant; **il paese conta 1000 anime** the town has 1000 inhabitants; **un'anima in pena** (*anche fig*) a tormented soul; **anima gemella** soul mate; **l'anima della festa** the life and soul of the party; **non c'era neanche un'anima** there wasn't a soul; **non c'era anima viva** there wasn't a living soul.

animale [ani'male] [1] SM (*gen, fig*) animal. [2] AGG animal.

animalesco, a, schi, sche [anima'lesko] AGG (*gesto, atteggiamento*) animal-like.

animalista, i, e [anima'lista] [1] AGG animal rights *attr*. [2] SM/F animal rights activist.

animare [ani'mare] [1] VT **a** (*dare vita a*) to animate; (*serata, conversazione*) to liven up, enliven; **la gioia le animava il volto** her face shone with joy **b** (*sogg*: *sentimento*) to drive, impel; **era animato dal desiderio di libertà** he was driven by the desire for

freedom
c (*incoraggiare: persona, commercio*) to encourage.
2 animarsi VIP (*persona, oggetto, strada*) to come to life; (*festa*) to liven up, become animated; (*scaldarsi: conversazione, persona*) to become animated.
animatamente [animata'mente] AVV (*parlare*) animatedly.
animato, a [ani'mato] AGG **a** (*vivace: strada*) lively, busy; (: *conversazione*) lively, animated **b** (*vivo*) animate.
animatore, trice [anima'tore] **1** AGG (*principio*) guiding; (*forza*) driving.
2 SM/F (*turistico, di festa, gruppo*) organizer; (*di spettacolo*) compère; (*Cine*) animator; **è sempre lui l'animatore della festa** he's always the life and soul of the party.
animazione [animat'tsjone] SF (*eccitazione*) excitement; (*vivacità*) liveliness; (*di città, strada*) bustle; (*Cine*) animation ▶**animazione teatrale** amateur dramatics.
animismo [ani'mizmo] SM animism.
animo ['animo] SM **a** (*mente*) mind; (*disposizione*) character, disposition; **stato d'animo** state of mind; **avere in animo di fare qc** to have a mind to do sth, intend to do sth; **mettersi l'animo in pace** to set one's mind at rest; **fare qc di buon/mal animo** to do sth willingly/unwillingly
b (*coraggio*) courage; **perdersi d'animo** to lose heart; **fare animo a qn** to cheer sb up; **farsi animo** to pluck up courage; **fatti animo!** [OR] **animo!** cheer up!
animosamente [animosa'mente] AVV with animosity.
animosità [animosi'ta] SF animosity.
anione [a'njone] SM anion.
anisetta [ani'zetta] SF anisette.
anitra ['anitra] SF = **anatra**.
Ankara ['ankara] SF Ankara.
A.N.M. [a'ɛnne'ɛmme] SIGLA F (= *Associazione Nazionale dei Magistrati*) *national association of magistrates*.
A.N.M.I. [a'ɛnne'ɛmme'i] SIGLA F (= *Associazione Nazionale Marinai d'Italia*) *national association of seamen*.
A.N.M.I.G. ['anmig] SIGLA F (= *Associazione Nazionale fra Mutilati e Invalidi di Guerra*) *national association for disabled ex-servicemen*.
annacquare [annak'kware] VT to dilute; (*vino*) to water down.
annacquato, a [annak'kwato] AGG (*vedi vt*) watered down; diluted.
annaffiare [annaf'fjare] VT (*fiori, piante*) to water.
annaffiatoio, oi [annaffja'tojo] SM watering can.
annali [an'nali] SMPL annals.
annaspare [annas'pare] VI (*aus* avere) (*nell'acqua*) to flounder; (*fig: nel buio, nell'incertezza*) to grope.
annata [an'nata] SF (*gen*) year; (*di vino*) vintage, year; (*importo annuo*) annual amount; **vino di annata** vintage wine.
annebbiare [anneb'bjare] **1** VT (*gen, fig*) to cloud.
2 annebbiarsi VIP to become foggy; (*vista*) to become blurred.
annegamento [annega'mento] SM drowning; **è morto per annegamento** he drowned.
annegare [anne'gare] **1** VI (*aus* essere) to drown.
2 VT to drown; **annegare i dispiaceri nel vino** to drown one's sorrows.
3 annegarsi VR to drown o.s.
annegato, a [anne'gato] SM/F drowned man/woman.
annerire [anne'rire] **1** VT to blacken.
2 VI (*aus* essere), **annerirsi** VIP to go o become black.

annessione [annes'sjone] SF (*Pol*) annexation.
annesso, a [an'nɛsso] **1** PP di **annettere**.
2 AGG (*attaccato: gen*) attached; (: *Pol*) annexed.
3 SMPL: **fra annessi e connessi**... what with one thing and another ...; ... **e tutti gli annessi e connessi** ...and so on and so forth; **mi occupo del nuovo progetto con tutti gli annessi e connessi** I'm working on the new project and everything relating to it.
annettere [an'nɛttere] VT IRREG (*Pol*) to annexe (*Brit*), annex (*Am*); (*accludere*) to attach.
Annibale [an'nibale] SM Hannibal.
annichilire [anniki'lire], **annichilare** [anniki'lare] VT to annihilate; (*fig*) to devastate.
annidarsi [anni'darsi] **1** VR (*uccello*) to nest; (*fig: persona*) to hide. **2** VIP (*paura, dubbio, invidia*) to take root.
annientamento [annjenta'mento] SM annihilation, destruction.
annientare [annjen'tare] VT to annihilate, destroy.
anniversario, ri [anniver'sarjo] SM anniversary.
anno ['anno] **1** SM **a** year; **anno per** o **dopo anno** year after year; **è aperto tutto l'anno** it's open all year round; **uno studente del primo anno** a first year student; **gli anni Venti** the Twenties; **un anno di affitto** a year's rent; **sono anni che non ti vedo** it's been ages since I last saw you, I haven't seen you for ages o years; **correva l'anno di grazia ...** it was in the year of grace ...; **Buon Anno!** Happy New Year!; **gli anni di piombo** *the Seventies in Italy, a time of terrorist outrages*
b (*età*): **quanti anni hai?** — **ho 40 anni** how old are you? — I'm 40; **quando compi gli anni?** when is your birthday?; **un bambino di 6 anni** a 6-year-old child; **porta bene gli anni** she doesn't look her age; **porta male gli anni** she looks older than she is.
2 ▶**anno accademico** academic year ▶**anno bisestile** leap year ▶**anno commerciale** business year ▶**anno finanziario** financial year ▶**anno giudiziario** legal year ▶**anno luce** (*Astron*) light year ▶**anno sabbatico** sabbatical year ▶**anno santo** (*Rel*) holy year.
annodare [anno'dare] **1** VT (*lacci*) to tie; (*cravatta*) to knot, tie; (*fune, corda*) to knot; (*due corde*) to knot o tie together; **annodarsi la cravatta** to tie o knot one's tie
2 ,**annodarsi** VIP to become o get knotted o tangled.
annoiare [anno'jare] **1** (*tediare*) to bore.
2 annoiarsi VIP to get bored; **annoiarsi di qc/di fare qc** to be bored with sth/with doing sth.
annoiato, a [anno'jato] AGG bored.
annonario, ria, ri, rie [anno'narjo] AGG: **tessera annonaria** ration book.
annoso, a [an'noso] AGG (*questione, problema*) age-old.
annotare [anno'tare] VT **a** (*scrivere*) to note, note down (*Brit*), take down **b** (*commentare: testo*) to annotate.
annotazione [annotat'tsjone] SF **a** (*appunto*) note **b** (*di testo*) annotation.
annottare [annot'tare] VB IMPERS (*aus* essere): **annotta** night is falling.
annoverare [annove'rare] VT to number.
annuale [annu'ale] AGG (*gen*) annual, yearly; (*pianta*) annual.
annualmente [annual'mente] AVV annually, yearly.
annuario, ri [annu'arjo] SM (*gen*) annual publication; (*di scuola ecc*) yearbook.
annuire [annu'ire] VI (*aus* avere) (*assentire: anche:* **annuire col capo**) to nod.

annullamento [annulla'mento] SM (*vedi vb*) cancellation; annulment; quashing; destruction.

annullare [annul'lare] 1 VT a (*francobollo, ordine, contratto*) to cancel; (*Dir: testamento, matrimonio*) to annul; (: *sentenza*) to quash; (*partita, risultati*) to declare void b (*distruggere*) to destroy. 2 **annullarsi** VR: **annullarsi (a vicenda)** to cancel each other out.

annullo [an'nullo] SM (*Amm*) cancelling.

annunciare [annun'tʃare] VT (*gen*) to announce; (*predire*) to foretell; (*essere segno di*) to be a sign of; **annunciare una brutta notizia a qn** to break bad news to sb; **il barometro annuncia pioggia** the barometer is indicating rain; **entrò senza farsi annunciare** he came in unannounced.

annunciatore, trice [annuntʃa'tore] SM/F (*Radio, TV*) announcer.

Annunciazione [annuntʃat'tsjone] SF (*Rel*): **l'Annunciazione** the Annunciation.

annuncio, ci [an'nuntʃo] SM (*gen*) announcement; (*presagio*) sign; **mettere un annuncio sul giornale** to place *o* put an advert(isement) in the newspaper ▶ **annunci economici** classified ad(vertisement)s, small ads ▶ **annunci mortuari** (*colonna*) death announcements ▶ **annuncio pubblicitario** advertisement.

annuo, a ['annuo] AGG annual, yearly.

annusare [annu'sare] VT (*anche fig*) to smell; (*cane*) to smell, sniff; **annusare tabacco** to take snuff.

annuvolamento [annuvola'mento] SM clouding (over).

annuvolare [annuvo'lare] 1 VT to cloud. 2 **annuvolarsi** VIP to become cloudy, cloud over.

ano ['ano] SM anus.

anodizzare [anodid'dzare] VT to anodize.

anodo ['anodo] SM anode.

anomalia [anoma'lia] SF (*gen*) anomaly; (*Med*) abnormality; **anomalia di funzionamento** (*Tecn*) technical fault.

anomalo, a [a'nɔmalo] AGG anomalous.

anonima [a'nonima] SF: **l'Anonima sequestri** *kidnapping gang*.

anonimamente [anonima'mente] AVV anonymously.

anonimato [anoni'mato] SM anonymity; **conservare l'anonimato** to remain anonymous.

anonimo, a [a'nɔnimo] 1 AGG anonymous; **un tipo anonimo** (*banale*) a colourless (*Brit*) *o* colorless (*Am*) character. 2 SM/F (*persona*) unknown person; (*pittore, autore ecc*) anonymous painter (*o* writer *ecc*).

anoressia [anores'sia] SF anorexia ▶ **anoressia nervosa** anorexia nervosa.

anoressico, a, ci, che [ano'ressiko] AGG anorexic.

anormale [anor'male] 1 AGG abnormal. 2 SM/F mentally retarded person, subnormal person.

anormalità [anormali'ta] SF INV abnormality.

A.N.P.A. ['anpa] SIGLA F (= *Agenzia nazionale di protezione ambientale*) EPA.

ansa ['ansa] SF (*curva*) loop, bend; (*di vaso*) handle; (*Anat*) loop.

A.N.S.A. ['ansa] SIGLA F (= *Agenzia Nazionale Stampa Associata*) *national press agency*.

ansante [an'sante] AGG out of breath, panting.

ansia ['ansja] SF anxiety; **stare** *o* **essere in ansia (per qn/qc)** to be anxious (about sb/sth); **con ansia** anxiously.

ansietà [ansje'ta] SF INV anxiety.

ansimare [ansi'mare] VI (*aus* **avere**) to pant, gasp for breath; (*respirare pesantemente*) to breathe heavily.

ansiosamente [ansjosa'mente] AVV (*gen*) anxiously; (*con desiderio*) eagerly.

ansioso, a [an'sjoso] AGG (*agitato*) anxious; (*desideroso*): **ansioso di fare qc** anxious *o* eager to do sth.

anta ['anta] SF (*di armadio*) door; (*di finestra*) shutter.

antagonismo [antago'nizmo] SM antagonism.

antagonista, i, e [antago'nista] 1 SM/F antagonist. 2 AGG antagonistic.

antagonistico, a, ci, che [antago'nistiko] AGG antagonistic.

antartico, a, ci, che [an'tartiko] 1 AGG Antarctic. 2 SM: **l'Antartico** the Antarctic.

Antartide [an'tartide] SF: **l'Antartide** Antarctica.

ante... ['ante] PREF pre..., ante... .

antebellico, a, ci, che [ante'bɛlliko] AGG prewar *attr*.

antecedente [antetʃe'dɛnte] 1 AGG previous, preceding. 2 SM a (*Gramm, Filosofia*) antecedent b (*antefatto*): **gli antecedenti** previous history *sg*.

antefatto [ante'fatto] SM prior event; **gli antefatti dell'incidente** the events leading up to the accident, what happened before the accident.

anteguerra [ante'gwɛrra] 1 SM prewar period; **dell'anteguerra** prewar. 2 AGG INV prewar; (*scherz*) ancient.

ante litteram ['ante 'litteram] AGG INV ahead of one's time.

antenato [ante'nato] SM ancestor, forefather.

antenna [an'tenna] SF (*Zool*) antenna, feeler; (*Radio, TV*) aerial; **(d)rizzare le antenne** (*fig*) to prick up one's ears ▶ **antenna parabolica** (satellite) dish.

anteporre [ante'porre] VT IRREG: **anteporre qc a qc** to place *o* put sth before sth.

anteposto, a [ante'posto] PP di **anteporre**.

anteprima [ante'prima] SF (*Teatro, Cine*) preview; **presentare qc in anteprima** to preview sth; **comunichiamo in anteprima la notizia di...** we are bringing you advance news of ... .

antera [an'tɛra] SF (*Bot*) anther.

anteriore [ante'rjore] AGG a (*tempo*) previous, preceding b (*spazio*) front *attr*; **zampe anteriori** forelegs.

anteriormente [anterjor'mente] AVV a (*prima*) previously, before, earlier; **anteriormente a** prior to b (*davanti*) in front.

antesignano [antesiɲ'ɲano] SM forerunner; (*Storia*) standard-bearer.

anti... ['anti] PREF a (*contro*) anti... b (*prima*) ante... .

antiaderente [antiade'rɛnte] AGG non-stick.

antiaereo, a [antia'ɛreo] AGG anti-aircraft *attr*.

antiallergico, a, ci, che [antial'lɛrdʒiko] AGG, SM hypoallergenic.

antiatomico, a, ci, che [antia'tɔmiko] AGG anti-nuclear; **rifugio antiatomico** fallout shelter.

antibiotico, a, ci, che [antibi'ɔtiko] AGG, SM antibiotic.

antibloccaggio [antiblok'kaddʒo] AGG INV (*Aut*): **sistema antibloccaggio** anti-lock brake.

anticaglia [anti'kaʎʎa] SF junk *no pl*.

anticamente [antika'mente] AVV formerly.

anticamera [anti'kamera] SF (*ingresso*) hall; (*sala d'attesa*) antechamber, anteroom; **fare anticamera** to be kept waiting; **non mi passerebbe neanche per l'anticamera del cervello** it wouldn't even cross my mind.

anticarie [anti'karje] AGG INV which fights tooth decay.

anticarro [anti'karro] AGG INV antitank.

antichità [antiki'ta] SF INV a antiquity b: **antichità** SFPL

antiques; **negozio di antichità** antique shop.

anticiclone [antitʃi'klone] SM anticyclone.

anticiclonico, a, ci, che [antitʃi'klɔniko] AGG anticyclonic; **zona anticiclonica** anticyclone area.

anticima [anti'tʃima] SF (Alpinismo) foresummit, subsidiary summit.

anticipare [antitʃi'pare] 1 VT a (spostare prima nel tempo) to bring forward; **anticipare un incontro di 3 giorni** to bring a meeting forward 3 days; **anticipare i tempi** (accelerare) to speed things up; (precorrere) to be ahead of one's time

b (precedere: reazione, risposta) to anticipate; **anticipare qn nel fare qc** to do sth before sb; **mi ha anticipato** he did it before me; **anticipare la palla/l'avversario** (Sport) to keep ahead of the ball/one's opponent

c (sorpresa, notizia) to reveal

d (pagare) to pay in advance; (prestare) to lend.

2 VI (aus avere) to come early, arrive early; **anticipare di un'ora** to come o arrive an hour earlier.

anticipatamente [antitʃipata'mente] AVV (arrivare) earlier than expected; (pagare) in advance.

anticipato, a [antitʃi'pato] AGG (prima del previsto) early; **pagamento anticipato** payment in advance.

anticipazione [antitʃipat'tsjone] SF a (spostamento) bringing forward

b (di notizia) anticipation; (: pronostico) forecast; **vi diamo delle anticipazioni sui risultati** we have advance news for you on the results; **è difficile fare delle anticipazioni sull'esito della partita** it's difficult to predict the result of the match

c (di denaro) advance ▶ **anticipazione bancaria** bank loan.

anticipo [an'titʃipo] SM (gen, Fin) advance; **con due giorni di anticipo** two days in advance; **arrivare in anticipo** to arrive early o ahead of time; **avvertire qn in anticipo** to warn sb in advance o beforehand; **gli ho dato un anticipo sullo stipendio** I gave him an advance on his salary; **con un sensibile anticipo** well in advance.

anticlan [anti'klan] AGG INV (magistrato, processo) anti-mafia.

anticlericale [antikleri'kale] AGG, SM/F anticlerical.

antico, a, chi, che [an'tiko] 1 AGG a (vecchio: mobile, quadro) antique; (: manoscritto) ancient; **all'antica** old-fashioned b (dell'antichità) ancient.

2: **gli antichi** SMPL the ancients.

anticoagulante [antikoagu'lante] AGG, SM anticoagulant.

anticoncezionale [antikontʃettsjo'nale] AGG, SM contraceptive.

anticonformismo [antikonfor'mizmo] SM unconventionality.

anticonformista, i, e [antikonfor'mista] 1 AGG unconventional.

2 SM/F unconventional person.

anticonformistico, a, ci, che [antikonfor'mistiko] AGG nonconformist.

anticongelante [antikondʒe'lante] AGG, SM antifreeze.

anticongiunturale [antikondʒuntu'rale] AGG (Econ): **misure anticongiunturali** measures to remedy the economic situation; **soluzione anticongiunturale** solution to the (unfavourable) economic situation.

anticorpo [anti'kɔrpo] SM antibody.

anticostituzionale [antikostituttsjo'nale] AGG unconstitutional.

anticostituzionalità [antikostituttsjonali'ta] SF INV unconstitutionality.

anticostituzionalmente [anticostituttsjonal'mente] AVV unconstitutionally.

anticristo [anti'kristo] SM Antichrist.

anticrittogamico, a, ci, che [antikritto'gamiko] 1 AGG fungicidal.

2 SM fungicide.

antidemocratico, a, ci, che [antidemo'kratiko] AGG undemocratic.

antidiluviano, a [antidilu'vjano] AGG (fig: antiquato) ancient, antediluvian.

antidivo, a [anti'divo] SM/F: **essere un antidivo** to rebel against the star system.

antidoping ['anti'doupiŋ] SM INV (Sport) dope test.

antidorcade [anti'dɔrkade] SF (Zool) springbok.

antidoto [an'tidoto] SM antidote.

antidroga [anti'drɔga] AGG INV anti-drugs attr.

antieconomico, a, ci, che [antieko'nɔmiko] AGG uneconomic(al).

antiemorragico, a, ci, che [antiemor'radʒiko] AGG, SM haemostatic.

antieroe [antie'rɔe] SM antihero.

antiestetico, a, ci, che [anties'tɛtiko] AGG unsightly.

antifascismo [antifaʃ'ʃizmo] SM antifascism.

antifascista, i, e [antifaʃ'ʃista] AGG, SM/F antifascist.

antifona [an'tifona] SF (Mus, Rel) antiphon; **capire l'antifona** (fig) to take the hint.

antifurto [anti'furto] AGG INV, SM INV alarm.

antigas [anti'gas] AGG INV: **maschera antigas** gas mask.

antigelo [anti'dʒelo] 1 AGG INV antifreeze; 2 SM INV (per motore) antifreeze; (per cristalli) de-icer.

antigene [an'tidʒene] SM antigen.

antigienico, a, ci, che [anti'dʒeniko] AGG unhygienic.

Antigone [an'tigone] SF Antigone.

Antille [an'tille] SFPL: **le Antille** the Antilles.

antilope [an'tilope] SF antelope.

antimafia [anti'mafja] AGG INV anti-Mafia attr.

antimateria [antima'tɛrja] SF antimatter.

antimilitarismo [antimilita'rizmo] SM antimilitarism.

antimilitarista, i, e [antimilita'rista] AGG, SM/F antimilitarist.

antimilitaristico, a, ci, che [antimilita'ristiko] AGG antimilitarist.

antimonio [anti'mɔnjo] SM antimony.

antincendio [antin'tʃɛndjo] AGG INV fire attr.

antinebbia [anti'nebbja] SM INV (Aut: anche: **faro antinebbia**) fog light.

antinevralgico, a, ci, che [antine'vraldʒiko] 1 AGG painkilling. 2 SM painkiller.

antinfluenzale [antinfluen'tsale] 1 AGG anti-flu attr. 2 SM flu remedy.

antiorario, ria, ri, rie [antio'rarjo] AGG anticlockwise (Brit), counterclockwise (Am); **in senso antiorario** in an anticlockwise o counterclockwise direction.

antipastiera [antipas'tjɛra] SF hors d'oeuvre tray.

antipasto [anti'pasto] SM hors d'oeuvre, starter.

antipatia [antipa'tia] SF antipathy, dislike; **prendere in antipatia** to take a dislike to.

antipatico, a, ci, che [anti'patiko] 1 AGG unpleasant, disagreeable.

2 SM/F unpleasant person; (rompiscatole) nuisance.

antipiega [anti'pjɛga] AGG INV (tessuto, vestito) crease-resistant, non-crease.

antipiretico, a, ci, che [antipi'rɛtiko] AGG, SM antipyretic.

antipodi [an'tipodi] SMPL: **gli antipodi** the antipodes; **essere agli antipodi** (*fig*) to be poles apart.

antipolio [anti'pɔljo] SF INV (*anche:* **vaccino antipolio**) polio vaccine.

antiquariato [antikwa'rjato] SM (*cose antiche*) antiques *pl*; (*Comm*) antique trade; **negozio di antiquariato** antique shop; **un pezzo d'antiquariato** an antique.

antiquario, ri [anti'kwarjo] SM antique dealer; **negozio di antiquario** antique shop.

antiquato, a [anti'kwato] AGG antiquated, old-fashioned.

antiriciclaggio [antiritʃi'kladdʒo] AGG INV (*attività, operazioni*) anti-laundering.

antiriflesso [antiri'flesso] AGG INV (*schermo, lenti*) non-glare *attr*.

antiruggine [anti'ruddʒine] [1] AGG INV anti-rust *attr*. [2] SM INV rust preventer.

antisdrucciolo [antiz'druttʃolo] AGG INV non-slip.

antisemita, i, e [antise'mita] [1] AGG anti-semitic. [2] SM/F anti-semite.

antisemitismo [antisemi'tizmo] SM anti-semitism.

antisettico, a, ci, che [anti'settiko] AGG, SM antiseptic.

antispastico, a, ci, che [antis'pastiko] AGG, SM antispasmodic.

antistaminico, a, ci, che [antista'miniko] AGG, SM antihistamine.

antistante [antis'tante] AGG opposite.

antiterrorismo [antiterro'rizmo] [1] SM antiterrorism, anti-terrorist measures *pl*. [2] AGG INV antiterrorist *attr*.

antiterrorista, i, e [antiterro'rista] AGG antiterrorist *attr*.

antitesi [an'titezi] SF INV antithesis.

antitetanico, a, ci, che [antite'taniko] [1] AGG (*siero, iniezione*) tetanus *attr*. [2] SF: **l'antitetanica** tetanus injection *o* jab (*fam*).

antitetico, a, ci, che [anti'tɛtiko] AGG antithetical.

antivigilia [antivi'dʒilja] SF: **l'antivigilia di Natale/Capodanno** the day before Christmas Eve/New Year's Eve.

antologia, gie [antolo'dʒia] SF anthology.

antologico, a, ci, che [anto'lɔdʒiko] AGG anthological.

antonomasia [antono'mazja] SF antonomasia; **per antonomasia** par excellence.

antracite [antra'tʃite] SF anthracite.

antro ['antro] SM cave, cavern.

antropofago, a, gi, ghe [antro'pɔfago] [1] AGG cannibal *attr*. [2] SM cannibal.

antropologia [antropolo'dʒia] SF anthropology ▸ **antropologia criminale** criminology.

antropologico, a, ci, che [antropo'lɔdʒiko] AGG anthropological.

antropologo, a, gi, ghe [antro'pɔlogo] SM/F anthropologist.

antropomorfo, a [antropo'mɔrfo] AGG anthropomorphic.

anulare [anu'lare] [1] AGG ring *attr*; **raccordo anulare** (*Aut*) ring road. [2] SM (*Anat*) ring finger.

Anversa [an'vɛrsa] SF Antwerp.

anzi ['antsi] AVV **a** (*avversativo*) on the contrary **b** (*rafforzativo*) or rather, or better still.

anzianità [antsjani'ta] SF INV (*età avanzata*) old age; (*Amm*) seniority ▸ **anzianità di servizio** length of service.

anziano, a [an'tsjano] [1] AGG (*vecchio*) elderly, old; (*socio*) senior. [2] SM/F senior citizen (*euf*), old person; (*di associazione*) senior member.

anziché [antsi'ke] CONG rather than.

anzitempo [antsi'tɛmpo] AVV (*in anticipo*) early; **morire anzitempo** to die before one's time.

anzitutto [antsi'tutto] AVV first of all.

AO SIGLA = *Aosta*.

aoristo [ao'risto] SM (*Gramm*) aorist.

aorta [a'ɔrta] SF aorta.

aostano, a [aos'tano] [1] AGG of *o* from Aosta. [2] SM/F inhabitant *o* native of Aosta.

AP SIGLA = *Ascoli Piceno*.

apartheid [a'parteit] SM INV (*Pol*) apartheid.

apartitico, a, ci, che [apar'titiko] AGG (*Pol*) non-party *attr*.

apatia [apa'tia] SF apathy.

apaticamente [apatika'mente] AVV apathetically.

apatico, a, ci, che [a'patiko] AGG apathetic.

a.p.c. ABBR = **a pronta cassa**; *vedi* **pronto**.

ape ['ape] SF bee ▸ **ape regina** queen bee.

aperitivo [aperi'tivo] SM aperitif.

apertamente [aperta'mente] AVV openly.

aperto, a [a'pɛrto] [1] PP di **aprire**. [2] AGG (*gen, fig*) open; (*rubinetto*) on, running; (*gas*) on; **di mentalità aperta** open-minded; **lasciare la macchina aperta** to leave the car unlocked; **a cuore aperto** (*intervento*) open heart *attr*, (*fig*) frankly, sincerely; **a bocca aperta** open-mouthed; **rimanere a bocca aperta** (*fig*) to be taken aback; **sognare ad occhi aperti** to daydream; **all'aria aperta** in the open air. [3] SM: **all'aperto** outdoors; (*cinema, piscina*) open-air *attr*; (*giochi, vacanze*) outdoor *attr*.

apertura [aper'tura] SF **a** (*gen, Carte*) opening; (*Pol*) opening up; (*Fot*) aperture; **in apertura di** at the beginning of; **movimento di apertura** (*Tennis*) backswing ▸ **apertura di credito** (*Comm*) granting of credit **b** (*ampiezza*) width, spread ▸ **apertura alare** wing span ▸ **apertura mentale** open-mindedness.

A.P.I. ['api] SIGLA F = *Associazione Piccole e Medie Industrie*.

apice ['apitʃe] SM peak, summit; (*fig*) height, peak; **essere all'apice del successo** to be at the height *o* peak of one's success.

apicoltore, trice [apikol'tore] SM/F beekeeper.

apicoltura [apikol'tura] SF beekeeping.

apnea [ap'nɛa] SF: **immergersi in apnea** to dive without breathing apparatus.

apocalisse [apoka'lisse] SF (*Rel*): **l'Apocalisse** (the book of) Revelation, the Apocalypse; (*fig*) apocalypse.

apocalittico, a, ci, che [apoka'littiko] AGG apocalyptic.

apocrifo, a [a'pɔkrifo] AGG apocryphal.

apogeo [apo'dʒɛo] SM (*Astron*) apogee; (*fig: culmine*) zenith, apogee.

apolide [a'pɔlide] (*Pol*) [1] AGG stateless. [2] SM/F stateless person.

apolitico, a, ci, che [apo'litiko] AGG (*neutrale*) non-political; (*indifferente*) apolitical.

Apollo [a'pɔllo] SM Apollo.

apologia, gie [apolo'dʒia] SF (*frm*) apologia; **fare l'apologia di** to extol the virtues of; **accusare qn di apologia di reato** (*Dir*) to accuse sb of attempting to defend criminal acts.

apoplessia [apoples'sia] SF (*Med*) apoplexy.

apoplettico, a, ci, che [apo'plɛttiko] AGG apoplectic; **colpo apoplettico** apoplectic fit.

apostata, i, e [a'pɔstata] SM/F apostate.

a posteriori [a poste'rjɔri] [1] AGG INV after the event (*dopo sostantivo*). [2] AVV looking back.

apostolato [aposto'lato] SM (*Rel*) apostolate; **fare opera di apostolato** (*anche fig*) to spread the word.

apostolico, a, ci, che [apos'tɔliko] AGG apostolic.

apostolo [a'pɔstolo] SM apostle.

apostrofare[1] [apostro'fare] VT (*parola*) to write with an apostrophe.

apostrofare[2] [apostro'fare] VT (*persona*) to address indignantly.

apostrofo [a'pɔstrofo] SM (*segno*) apostrophe.

apoteosi [apote'ɔzi] SF INV apotheosis.

app. ABBR (= *appendice*) app.

appagamento [appaga'mento] SM (*vedi vb*) satisfaction; fulfilment.

appagare [appa'gare] [1] VT (*gen*) to satisfy; (*desiderio*) to fulfil; (*fame*) to satisfy; (*sete*) to quench.
[2] **appagarsi** VR: **appagarsi di** to be satisfied with.

appagato, a [appa'gato] AGG satisfied.

appaiare [appa'jare] VT (*oggetti*) to pair; (*animali*) to match, couple.

appaio *ecc* [ap'pajo] VB vedi **apparire**.

Appalachi [appa'laki] SMPL: **i Monti Appalachi** the Appalachian Mountains.

appallottolare [appallotto'lare] [1] VT (*carta, foglio*) to screw into a ball.
[2] **appallottolarsi** VR (*gatto*) to roll up into a ball.

appaltare [appal'tare] VT (*dare in appalto*) to put out to contract; (*prendere in appalto*) to undertake on contract.

appaltatore, trice [appalta'tore] [1] SM contractor.
[2] AGG contracting.

appalto [ap'palto] SM contract; **dare in appalto** to put out to contract; **prendere in appalto** to take on a contract for; **gara di appalto** invitation to tender.

appannaggio, gi [appan'naddʒo] SM (*Pol: compenso*) annuity; (*fig*) prerogative.

appannare [appan'nare] [1] VT (*vetro*) to steam up, mist up; (*metallo*) to tarnish; (*vista*) to blur.
[2] **appannarsi** VIP (*vedi vt*) to steam up, mist up; to tarnish; (*vista: offuscarsi*) to blur; (: *affievolirsi*) to grow dim.

apparato [appa'rato] SM **a** (*impianto*) equipment, machinery ▶**apparato burocratico** bureaucratic machinery ▶**apparato scenico** (*Teatro*) set **b** (*Anat, Bio*) apparatus ▶**apparato circolatorio** circulatory system **c** (*sfoggio*) display, pomp.

apparecchiare [apparek'kjare] VT: **apparecchiare (la tavola)** to set *o* lay the table.

apparecchiatura [apparekkja'tura] SF (*Tecn: impianto*) equipment *no pl*; (: *macchina*) machine, device.

apparecchio, chi [appa'rekkjo] SM **a** (*gen*) instrument, device, piece of equipment; (*per denti*) brace ▶**apparecchio acustico** hearing aid ▶**apparecchio telefonico** telephone **b** (*Radio, TV*) set **c** (*Aer*) aircraft *inv*.

apparente [appa'rɛnte] AGG apparent.

apparentemente [apparente'mente] AVV apparently.

apparenza [appa'rɛntsa] SF **a** (*aspetto*) appearance; **l'apparenza inganna** appearances can be deceptive; **in** *o* **all'apparenza** to all appearances, seemingly
b : **apparenze** SFPL (*convenienze sociali*) appearances; **badare alle apparenze** to care about appearances; **salvare le apparenze** to keep up appearances; **giudicare dalle apparenze** to judge by appearances.

apparire [appa'rire] VI IRREG (*aus* **essere**) **a** (*mostrarsi*) to appear; **apparire in sogno** to appear in a dream; **l'uomo**

gli apparve davanti all'improvviso the man suddenly appeared in front of *o* before him
b (*essere evidente*): **apparire (chiaro)** to seem clear; **dalle indagini è apparso chiaro il suo coinvolgimento** the enquiries clearly demonstrate his involvement
c (*sembrare*) to seem, appear; **appare che... it appears** *o* turns out that ...; **apparve sorpreso di vedermi** he seemed surprised to see me.

appariscente [appariʃ'ʃɛnte] AGG (*vestito*) showy; (*colore*) gaudy, garish; (*bellezza*) striking.

apparizione [apparit'tsjone] SF (*comparsa*) appearance; (*fantasma*) apparition.

apparso, a [ap'parso] PP di **apparire**.

appartamento [apparta'mento] SM flat (*Brit*), apartment (*Am*).

appartarsi [appar'tarsi] VR to withdraw.

appartato, a [appar'tato] AGG (*luogo*) secluded.

appartenente [apparte'nɛnte] [1] AGG: **appartenente a** belonging to.
[2] SM/F: **appartenente (a)** member (of).

appartenenza [apparte'nɛntsa] SF: **appartenenza (a)** (*gen*) belonging (to); (*a un partito, club*) membership (of).

appartenere [apparte'nere] VI IRREG (*aus* **essere** *o* **avere**): **appartenere a a** (*chiesa, fede*) to belong to; (*club, partito*) to be a member of **b** (*essere di proprietà*) to belong to; **mi appartiene di diritto** it belongs to me by right.

apparvi *ecc* [ap'parvi] VB vedi **apparire**.

appassimento [appassi'mento] SM withering.

appassionante [appassjo'nante] AGG thrilling, exciting.

appassionare [appassjo'nare] [1] VT to grip, fascinate.
[2] **appassionarsi** VIP: **appassionarsi a qc** to develop a passion for sth, get very interested in sth.

appassionatamente [appassjonata'mente] AVV (*amare, credere*) passionately; (*lavorare*) enthusiastically.

appassionato, a [appassjo'nato] [1] AGG **a** (*entusiasta*): **appassionato (di)** keen (on) **b** (*passionale*) passionate.
[2] SM/F enthusiast.

appassire [appas'sire] VI (*aus* **essere**) (*pianta*) to wither; (*fig: bellezza, speranze*) to fade.

appellare [appel'lare] [1] VI (*aus* **avere**) (*Dir*): **appellare (contro)** to appeal (against).
[2] **appellarsi** VIP **a** : **appellarsi a** (*rivolgersi*) to appeal to; **mi appello alla vostra generosità** I appeal to your generosity **b** (*Dir*): **appellarsi contro** to appeal against; **si è appellato contro la sentenza** he appealed against the sentence.

appellativo [appella'tivo] SM name.

appello [ap'pɛllo] SM **a** (*chiamata per nome*) roll-call; **fare l'appello** (*Scol*) to call the register; (*Mil*) to call the roll **b** (*Univ: sessione d'esame*) exam session **c** (*Dir*) appeal; **corte d'appello** court of appeal **d** (*invocazione*) appeal; **fare appello a** (*anche fig*) to call upon, appeal to.

appena [ap'pena] [1] AVV (*a stento*) hardly, scarcely; (*solamente, da poco*) just; **ci si vede appena** you can hardly see; **sono appena le 9** it's only just 9 o'clock; **sarà alto appena appena un metro e 80** he is certainly no more than 6 foot tall.
[2] CONG as soon as; **appena possibile** as soon as possible; **(non) appena (furono) arrivati...** as soon as they had arrived ...; **appena... che** *o* **quando** no sooner ...than; **era appena tornato quando è dovuto ripartire** no sooner *o* scarcely had he returned than he had to leave again; **non appena ho finito, vado** I'll leave the

moment I've finished.

appendere [ap'pɛndere] VB IRREG **1** VT: **appendere (a)** to hang (on *o* up).

2 appendersi VR: **appendersi a qc** to hang on to sth.

appendiabiti [appendi'abiti] SM INV hook, peg; (*mobile*) hall stand (*Brit*), hall tree (*Am*).

appendice [appen'ditʃe] SF (*Anat, di libro*) appendix; **romanzo d'appendice** popular serial (*formerly appearing in newspapers*).

appendicite [appendi'tʃite] SF appendicitis.

appendino [appen'dino] SM (coat) hook.

Appennini [appen'nini] SMPL: **gli Appennini** the Apennines.

appenninico, a, ci, che [appen'niniko] AGG Apennine.

appesantire [appesan'tire] **1** VT (*anche fig*) to weigh down; (*atmosfera*) to make strained; **quella torta mi ha appesantito lo stomaco** that cake is lying on my stomach.

2 appesantirsi VIP (*gen*) to grow heavier; (*ingrassare*) to put on weight; (*fig: atmosfera, situazione*) to become strained.

appeso, a [ap'peso] PP di **appendere**.

appestare [appes'tare] VT (*Med*) to infect with plague; (: *contagiare*) to infect; (*aria, stanza*) to make stink; **il fumo delle sigarette ha appestato la stanza** the cigarette smoke made the room stink.

appestato, a [appes'tato] AGG (*Med*) infected with the plague; (: *contagioso*) infected; (*aria*) stinking.

appetibile [appe'tibile] AGG (*cibo*) appetizing; (*lavoro, ragazza*) attractive.

appetibilità [appetibili'ta] SF (*vedi agg*) appetizing nature; attractiveness.

appetito [appe'tito] SM **a** (*gen*) appetite; **avere appetito** to have an appetite; **non ho appetito** I'm not hungry; **perdere l'appetito** to lose one's appetite; **buon appetito!** enjoy your meal! (*said by waiter*), **bon appétit!** (*said by fellow diner*); **stuzzicare l'appetito** (*anche fig*) to whet one's appetite

b (*istinti*): **appetiti** SMPL instincts; **soddisfare/frenare i propri appetiti** satisfy/curb one's instincts *o* appetite.

appetitoso, a [appeti'toso] AGG (*cibo*) appetizing; (*fig*) attractive, desirable.

appezzamento [appettsa'mento] SM (*anche:* **appezzamento di terreno**) plot, piece of ground.

appianamento [appjana'mento] SM (*vedi vt*) levelling; settlement; ironing out.

appianare [appja'nare] **1** VT (*terreno*) to flatten, level; (*fig: contesa, lite*) to settle; (*difficoltà*) to iron out, smooth away.

2 appianarsi VIP (*divergenze*) to be ironed out.

appiattire [appjat'tire] **1** VT to flatten; (*fig: rendere monotono*) to make dull, make boring.

2 appiattirsi VR (*farsi piatto: persona, animale*) to flatten o.s.; **si appiattì al** *o* **contro il muro** he flattened himself against the wall; **appiattirsi al suolo** to lie flat on the ground.

3 appiattirsi VIP (*diventare piatto: oggetto*) to become flatter; (*fig*) to become dull.

appiccare [appik'kare] VT: **appiccare il fuoco a qc** to set fire to sth, set sth on fire.

appiccicare [appittʃi'kare] **1** VT: **appiccicare (a** *o* **su)** to stick (on); **appiccicare un soprannome a qn** (*fig: appioppare*) to pin a nickname on sb; **questa colla non appiccica bene** this glue doesn't stick very well.

2 appiccicarsi VR: **appiccicarsi (a)** to stick (to); (*fig: persona*) to cling (to).

appiccicaticcio, cia, ci, ce [apittʃika'tittʃo] AGG sticky.

appiccicoso, a [appittʃi'koso] AGG sticky; (*fig: persona*): **essere appiccicoso** to cling like a leech.

appiedato, a [appje'dato] AGG: **rimanere appiedato** to be left without means of transport.

appieno [ap'pjeno] AVV fully.

appigliarsi [appiʎ'ʎarsi] VR: **appigliarsi a** to grasp, seize (hold of), take hold of; (*fig: scusa, pretesto*) to cling to; **non appigliarti a quella scusa** don't try that as an excuse.

appiglio, gli [ap'piʎʎo] SM (hand)hold; (*fig: pretesto*) pretext, excuse.

appiombo [ap'pjombo] **1** SM perpendicularity; (*di muro*) plumb.

2 AVV (*anche:* **a piombo**) perpendicularly.

appioppare [appjop'pare] VT: **appioppare qc a qn** (*nomignolo*) to pin on sb; (*compito difficile*) to saddle sb with sth; **gli ha appioppato un pugno sul muso** he punched him in the face.

appisolarsi [appizo'larsi] VIP to doze off.

applaudire [applau'dire] **1** VI (*aus avere*): **applaudire (a)** to applaud, clap; (*fig*) to applaud.

2 VT (*anche fig*) to applaud.

applaudito, a [applau'dito] AGG famous, celebrated.

applauso [ap'plauzo] SM applause *no pl*; **un applauso** a round of applause.

applicabile [appli'kabile] AGG: **applicabile (a)** applicable (to).

applicabilità [applikabili'ta] SF applicability.

applicare [appli'kare] **1** VT (*gen*) to apply; (*cucire*) to sew on; **applicare la mente a qc** to apply one's mind to sth; **(fare) applicare una legge/un regolamento** to enforce a law/a regulation; **applicare una tassa** to impose a tax.

2 applicarsi VR: **applicarsi (a** *o* **in)** to apply o.s. (to).

applicato, a [appli'kato] **1** AGG (*arte, scienze*) applied.

2 SM/F (*Amm*) clerk.

applicatore [applika'tore] SM applicator.

applicazione [applikat'tsjone] SF **a** (*gen*) application; (*di legge, norma*) enforcement

b (*su stoffa*) appliqué.

applique [a'plik] SF INV wall light.

appoggiare [appod'dʒare] **1** VT **a** (*posare*): **appoggiare qc su qc** to put sth (down) on sth, lay sth (down) on sth

b (*mettere contro*): **appoggiare qc a qc** to lean *o* rest sth against sth

c (*sostenere: idea, candidato*) to support, back.

2 VI (*aus avere*): **appoggiare su** to rest on.

3 appoggiarsi VR: **appoggiarsi a** *o* **su** (*reggersi*) to lean against; (*fig*) to rely on *o* upon.

appoggiatesta [appoddʒa'tɛsta] SM INV headrest.

appoggiato, a [appod'dʒato] AGG (*Ling*): **consonante appoggiata** consonant joined with another.

appoggio, gi [ap'pɔddʒo] SM (*gen, fig*) support; (*Alpinismo*) press hold; **appoggio morale** moral support; **ho un appoggio importante al ministero** I have an important contact in the ministry.

appollaiarsi [appolla'jarsi] VR (*anche fig*) to perch; **se ne stava appollaiato sullo sgabello** he was perched on the stool.

appongo *ecc* [ap'pongo] VB vedi **apporre**.

apporre [ap'porre] VT IRREG (*firma*) to append; (*sigillo, nome*) to affix.

apportare [appor'tare] VT (*novità, cambiamento*) to bring (about); **apportare (delle) modifiche a** to modify.

apporto [ap'porto] SM (*gen, Fin*) contribution; **dare il proprio apporto a qc** to make one's contribution to sth.

apposi *ecc* [ap'posi] VB vedi **apporre**.

appositamente [appozita'mente] AVV (*apposta*) on purpose; (*specialmente*) specially.

appositivo, a [appozi'tivo] AGG (*Gramm*) appositional.

apposito, a [ap'pozito] AGG (*adatto*) appropriate, proper; (*fatto appositamente*) special.

apposizione [appozit'tsjone] SF (*Gramm*) apposition.

apposta [ap'posta] AVV (*intenzionalmente*) on purpose, intentionally, deliberately; (*proprio*) specially; **scusa, non l'ho fatto apposta** I'm sorry, I didn't do it on purpose; **neanche a farlo apposta,...** by sheer coincidence, ...; **sono venuto apposta per (vedere) te** I came here specially for you/to see you.

appostamento [apposta'mento] SM (*agguato*) ambush; (*Mil*) post.

appostare [appos'tare] [1] VT (*Mil*) to post, station. [2] **appostarsi** VR to lie in wait.

apposto, a [ap'posto] PP di **apporre**.

apprendere [ap'prɛndere] VT IRREG (*imparare*) to learn; (*venire a sapere*) to learn, find out; **hai appreso la notizia?** have you heard the news?

apprendimento [apprendi'mento] SM learning.

apprendista, i, e [appren'dista] SM/F apprentice.

apprendistato [apprendis'tato] SM apprenticeship; **fare l'apprendistato** to serve one's apprenticeship.

apprensione [appren'sjone] SF apprehension; **essere in uno stato di apprensione** to be anxious; **non stare in apprensione** don't worry.

apprensivamente [apprensiva'mente] AVV apprehensively, anxiously.

apprensivo, a [appren'sivo] AGG apprehensive, anxious.

appreso, a [ap'preso] PP di **apprendere**.

appresso [ap'prɛsso] [1] AVV (*vicino*) nearby, close up; (*con sé*) with me (*o* you *ecc*); (*dietro*) behind me (*o* you *ecc*); **me lo porto sempre appresso** I always carry it with me; **stammi appresso** stay *o* keep close to me. [2] PREP: **appresso a** near, close to; **andare appresso a qn** to go after sb, follow sb. [3] AGG INV (*dopo*): **il giorno appresso** the next day, the day after.

apprestare [appres'tare] [1] VT to prepare, get ready. [2] **apprestarsi** VR: **apprestarsi a fare qc** to prepare *o* get ready to do sth.

appretto [ap'prɛtto] SM starch.

apprezzabile [appret'tsabile] AGG (*notevole*) noteworthy, significant; (*percepibile*) appreciable; **è un'opera apprezzabile da tutti** it is a work which everybody can enjoy.

apprezzamento [apprettsa'mento] SM **a** appreciation **b** (*commento*) comment; **fare apprezzamenti su** to make comments about, pass comment on.

apprezzare [appret'tsare] VT to appreciate.

approccio, ci [ap'prɔttʃo] SM approach.

approdare [appro'dare] VI (*aus essere o* avere) (*Naut*) to land; **approdare a** (*fig*) to arrive at; **non approderà a nulla** (*piano, progetto*) it won't come to anything; (*persona*) he won't achieve anything.

approdo [ap'prɔdo] SM (*Naut: l'approdare*) landing; (*luogo*) landing place.

approfittare [approfit'tare] VI (*aus* avere): **approfittare di** (*persona, situazione ecc*) to take advantage of; **dovresti approfittare dell'occasione** you should make the most of the opportunity.

approfondimento [approfondi'mento] SM deepening; **per l'approfondimento di questo argomento si consulti...** for a thorough examination of this subject consult ... .

approfondire [approfon'dire] [1] VT (*fossa*) to deepen, make deeper; (*fig: conoscenza*) to deepen, increase; (*argomento*) to go into, study in depth; **approfondire un problema** to go into a problem in more depth. [2] **approfondirsi** VIP (*gen, fig*) to deepen.

approfonditamente [approfondita'mente] AVV thoroughly.

approfondito, a [approfon'dito] AGG (*esame, studio, conoscenza*) thorough, detailed.

approntare [appron'tare] VT to prepare, get ready.

appropriarsi [appro'prjarsi] VIP: **appropriarsi di qc** to appropriate sth; **appropriarsi indebitamente di** to embezzle.

appropriato, a [appro'prjato] AGG appropriate, suitable.

appropriazione [approprjat'tsjone] SF appropriation ▸ **appropriazione indebita** (*Dir*) embezzlement, misappropriation.

approssimare [approssi'mare] [1] VT (*cifra*): **approssimare per eccesso/per difetto** to round up/down. [2] **approssimarsi** VR (*frm*) to approach, draw near.

approssimativamente [approssimativa'mente] AVV roughly, approximately.

approssimativo, a [approssima'tivo] AGG (*calcolo*) rough, approximate; (*numero*) approximate; **è stato molto approssimativo nel darmi informazioni** the information he gave me was very vague.

approssimazione [approssimat'tsjone] SF approximation; **per approssimazione** approximately, roughly.

approvabile [appro'vabile] AGG that can be approved.

approvare [appro'vare] VT **a** (*comportamento, decisione, azione*) to approve of **b** (*candidato, legge*) to pass; (*mozione*) to approve.

approvazione [approvat'tsjone] SF (*vedi vb*) approval; passing.

approvvigionamento [approvvidʒona'mento] SM **a** (*atto*) supplying **b** (*provviste*): **approvvigionamenti** SMPL supplies.

approvvigionare [approvvidʒo'nare] [1] VT: **approvvigionare (di)** to supply (with). [2] **approvvigionarsi** VR (*fare provviste*): **approvvigionarsi (di)** to stock up (with).

appuntamento [appunta'mento] SM (*d'affari, dal medico*) appointment; (*con amici, amoroso*) date; **darsi appuntamento** to arrange to meet (one another); **il medico mi ha dato un appuntamento per venerdì** the doctor gave me an appointment for Friday.

appuntare[1] [appun'tare] [1] VT **a** (*fissare: con spillo: foglio ecc*) to pin (on); (: *due cose tra loro*) to pin (together); (: *piega dei pantaloni ecc*) to pin **b** (*puntare: dito*) to point; (: *sguardo*) to fix, rivet. [2] **appuntarsi** VIP (*interesse, attenzione*): **appuntarsi su** to be focussed on.

appuntare[2] [appun'tare] VT (*annotare*) to note down, take note of.

appuntato [appun'tato] SM (*Carabinieri*) corporal.

appuntino [appun'tino] AVV (*anche:* **a puntino**) perfectly; **cotto appuntino** cooked to perfection.

appuntire [appun'tire] VT to sharpen.

appuntito, a [appun'tito] AGG (*lama, lancia*) pointed; (*matita*) sharp.

appunto¹ [ap'punto] SM **a** (*nota*) note; **prendere appunti** to take notes **b** (*rimprovero*) reproach; **fare/muovere un appunto a qn** to find fault with sb.

appunto² [ap'punto] AVV (*precisamente, proprio*) exactly, just; **dicevo appunto ieri** I was just saying yesterday; **si parlava (per l')appunto di questo** we were talking about that very thing; **stavo appunto per chiederti di venire** I was (actually) just going to ask you to come; **per l'appunto!** OR **appunto!** exactly!

appurare [appu'rare] 1 VT (*verificare*) to check, verify; (*: verità*) to ascertain.

2 **appurarsi** VR: **appurarsi di qc/che** to make sure of sth/that, check sth/that.

apribottiglie [apribot'tiʎʎe] SM INV bottle-opener.

aprile [a'prile] SM April; **pesce d'aprile!** April Fool!; **aprile dolce dormire** (*Proverbio*) April slumbers *per fraseologia vedi* **luglio**.

a priori [a pri'ɔri] AVV, AGG a priori.

aprioristicamente [aprioristika'mente] AVV a priori.

aprioristico, a, ci, che [aprio'ristiko] AGG a priori.

apripista [apri'pista] SM/F INV (*Sci*) trailmaker.

aprire [a'prire] VB IRREG 1 VT **a** (*gen*) to open; (*porta chiusa a chiave*) to unlock; (*camicia*) to undo, unfasten; (*ali, anche fig*) to spread; **va' ad aprire (la porta)** go and open *o* answer the door; **non ha aperto bocca** he didn't say a word, he didn't open his mouth; **tutto ciò mi ha aperto gli occhi** all that was an eye-opener to me; **apri bene gli orecchi** listen carefully; **aprirsi un varco tra la folla** to cut one's way through the crowd

b (*acqua, rubinetto*) to turn on; (*gas*) to turn on, switch on

c (*istituire: negozio, club, conto*) to open; (*inchiesta*) to open, set up; (*strada*) to build; **aprire bottega** to open shop

d (*dare inizio: anno, stagione*) to start, open; (*lista*) to head; (*processione*) to lead; **aprire (il gioco)** (*Carte*) to open play; **aprire il fuoco** to open fire; **aprire le ostilità** (*Mil*) to begin hostilities; **aprire una sessione** (*Inform*) to log on

e (*Dir: testamento*) to read.

2 VI (*aus* **avere**) to open; **la banca apre alle otto** the bank opens at eight.

3 **aprirsi** VIP **a** (*gen*) to open; (*fiore*) to open (up); **la finestra si apre sulla piazza** the window looks onto the square; **la porta dev'essersi aperta** the door must have come open; **quest'abito si apre sul davanti** this dress opens at the front; **la vita che le si apre davanti** the life which is opening in front of *o* before her; **mi si aprì davanti la vista del mare** the sea appeared before me; **davanti a quella scena le si è aperto il cuore** (*commuoversi*) she was moved by the scene before her; (*rallegrarsi*) the scene gladdened her heart; **apriti cielo!** heaven forbid!; (*cominciare*) to start, open.

4 **aprirsi** VR (*confidarsi*): **aprirsi (con qn)** to open one's heart (to sb), confide (in sb).

apriscatole [apris'katole] SM INV tin (*Brit*) *o* can opener.

A.P.T. [api'ti] SIGLA F (= *Azienda di Promozione Turistica*) tourist board.

AQ SIGLA = *L'Aquila*.

aquaplaning ['aekwəpleiniŋ] SM INV (*Aut*): **andare** *o* **entrare in aquaplaning** to aquaplane.

aquario, ri [a'kwarjo] SM = **acquario**.

aquila ['akwila] SF eagle; **sei un'aquila!** (*anche iro*) you're a genius! ▶ **aquila reale** golden eagle.

aquilegia, gie [akwi'lɛdʒa] SF (*Bot*) columbine, aquilegia.

aquilino, a [akwi'lino] AGG aquiline; **naso aquilino** aquiline nose.

aquilone [akwi'lone] SM **a** (*giocattolo*) kite **b** (*vento*) north wind.

AR SIGLA = *Arezzo*.

Ara ['ara] SF (*Zool: pappagallo*) macaw.

ara¹ ['ara] SF (*letter: altare*) altar.

ara² ['ara] SF (*unità di misura*) are (= *one hundred square metres*).

arabesco, schi [ara'besko] SM arabesque.

Arabia Saudita [a'rabja sau'dita] SF: **l'Arabia Saudita** Saudi Arabia.

arabico, a, ci, che [a'rabiko] AGG Arabic; **il deserto arabico** the Arabian desert; **la penisola arabica** the Arabian peninsula.

arabile [a'rabile] AGG arable.

arabo, a ['arabo] 1 AGG (*popolo, paesi*) Arab; (*lingua, arte*) Arabic, Arab; **numeri arabi** Arabic numerals.

2 SM/F (*persona*) Arab.

3 SM (*lingua*) Arabic; **questo per me è arabo** (*fig*) it's all Greek to me, it sounds like double Dutch to me (*Brit*); **ma parlo arabo?** (*fig*) don't you understand English?

arachide [a'rakide] SF peanut, groundnut; **olio di semi di arachide** peanut oil.

Aragona [ara'gona] SF Aragon.

aragosta [ara'gosta] 1 SF lobster.

2 AGG INV: **color aragosta** bright orange.

araldica [a'raldika] SF heraldry.

araldo [a'raldo] SM herald.

aramaico, a, ci, che [ara'maiko] AGG, SM Aramaic.

aranceto [aran'tʃeto] SM orange grove.

arancia, ce [a'rantʃa] SF orange.

aranciata [aran'tʃata] SF orangeade ▶ **aranciata amara** bitter orange (drink).

arancio, ci [a'rantʃo] 1 SM orange tree; (*colore*) orange; **arancio amaro** Seville orange; **fiori di arancio** orange blossom *sg*.

2 AGG INV (*colore*) orange.

arancione [aran'tʃone] 1 AGG INV, SM bright orange.

2 SM/F (*fam*): **gli arancioni** the Hare Krishna people.

arare [a'rare] 1 VT to plough (*Brit*), plow (*Am*).

2 VI (*aus* **avere**) (*Naut: ancora*) to drag.

aratore [ara'tore] SM ploughman (*Brit*), plowman (*Am*).

aratro [a'ratro] SM plough (*Brit*), plow (*Am*).

aratura [ara'tura] SF ploughing (*Brit*), plowing (*Am*).

araucaria [arau'karja] SF (*Bot*) monkey puzzle (tree).

arazzo [a'rattso] SM tapestry.

arbitraggio, gi [arbi'traddʒo] SM **a** (*Sport*) refereeing; (*: Tennis, Cricket*) umpiring **b** (*Dir*) arbitration **c** (*Econ*) arbitrage.

arbitrare [arbi'trare] VT (*Sport*) to referee; (*: Tennis, Cricket*) to umpire; (*Dir*) to arbitrate.

arbitrariamente [arbitrarja'mente] AVV arbitrarily.

arbitrario, ria, rie [arbi'trarjo] AGG arbitrary.

arbitrato [arbi'trato] SM (*Sport, Dir*) arbitration.

arbitrio, rii [ar'bitrjo] SM **a** (*capacità, potere*) will; (*atto*) arbitrary act; **libero arbitrio** free will; **prendersi l'arbitrio di fare qc** to take the liberty of doing sth **b** (*sopruso*): **commettere un arbitrio** to act unlawfully.

arbitro ['arbitro] SM **a** (*Sport*) referee; (: *Cricket, Tennis*) umpire **b** (*di contese*) arbitrator; (*fig*): **un arbitro di eleganza** an arbiter of fashion.

arboreo, a [ar'bɔreo] AGG: **piante arboree** trees; **fusto arboreo** woody stem.

arboscello [arboʃ'ʃɛllo] SM sapling.

arbustivo, a [arbus'tivo] AGG shrub-like.

arbusto [ar'busto] SM shrub.

arca ['arka] SF ark; **l'Arca di Noè** Noah's Ark.

arcade ['arkade] SM/F Arcadian.

Arcadia [ar'kadja] SF Arcadia.

arcadico, a, ci, che [ar'kadiko] AGG Arcadian.

arcaico, a, ci, che [ar'kaiko] AGG archaic.

arcaismo [arka'izmo] SM archaism.

arcangelo [ar'kandʒelo] SM archangel.

arcano, a [ar'kano] ☐1 AGG arcane. ☐2 SM mystery.

arcata [ar'kata] SF (*Anat*) arch.

archeggio, gi [ar'keddʒo] SM (*Mus*) bowing.

archeologia [arkeolo'dʒia] SF arch(a)eology.

archeologico, a, ci, che [arkeo'lɔdʒiko] AGG arch(a)e-ological.

archeologo, a, gi, ghe [arke'ɔlogo] SM/F arch(a)eologist.

archetipo [ar'kɛtipo] SM archetype.

archetto [ar'ketto] SM (*Mus*) bow.

archibugio, gi [arki'budʒo] SM (*Storia*) arquebus.

Archimede [arki'mɛde] SM Archimedes.

architettare [arkitet'tare] VT (*ideare*) to devise; (*macchinare*) to plan, concoct.

architetto [arki'tetto] SM architect.

architettonicamente [arkitettonika'mente] AVV architec-turally.

architettonico, a, ci, che [arkitet'tɔniko] AGG architec-tural.

architettura [arkitet'tura] SF architecture ▶ **architettura del paesaggio** landscaping.

architrave [arki'trave] SM architrave.

archiviare [arki'vjare] VT (*documenti*) to file; (*Dir*) to dismiss; **per questa volta archiviamo la faccenda** (*passiamoci sopra*) let's forget about it this time.

archiviazione [arkivjat'tsjone] SF (*vedi vb*) filing; dismis-sal.

archivio, vi [ar'kivjo] SM (*insieme di documenti, luogo*) archives *pl*; (*mobile*) filing cabinet; (*Inform*) file ▶ **archivio principale** (*Inform*) master file ▶ **archivio di riserva** (*Inform*) back-up file.

archivista, i, e [arki'vista] SM/F (*Amm*) archivist; (*in ufficio*) filing clerk.

A.R.C.I. ['artʃi] SIGLA F = *Associazione Ricreativa Culturale Italiana*.

arciduca, chi [artʃi'duka] SM archduke.

arciere [ar'tʃɛre] SM archer.

arcigno, a [ar'tʃiɲɲo] AGG (*espressione*) frowning, grim; (*persona*) severe.

arcione [ar'tʃone] SM saddlebow; **montare in arcione** to get into the saddle.

Arcip. ABBR = **arcipelago**.

arcipelago, ghi [artʃi'pɛlago] SM archipelago.

arciprete [artʃi'prɛte] SM archpriest.

arcivescovado [artʃivesko'vado] SM (*sede*) archbishop's palace.

arcivescovile [artʃivesko'vile] AGG of an archbishop (*o* archbishops); **palazzo arcivescovile** archbishop's palace.

arcivescovo [artʃi'veskovo] SM archbishop.

arco, chi ['arko] SM **a** (*arma, Mus*) bow; **strumento ad arco** string(ed) instrument; **archi** SMPL (*Mus*) strings **b** (*Geom*) arc; (*Archit, forma*) arch; **ad arco** arched ▶ **arco costituzionale** *parties formulating Italy's post-war constitution* ▶ **arco trionfale** triumphal arch **c** (*lasso di tempo*) space; **nell'arco di 3 settimane** within the space of 3 weeks; **la somma verrà pagata in un arco di 6 mesi** the sum will be paid over a period of 6 months.

arcobaleno [arkoba'leno] SM rainbow.

arcolaio, ai [arko'lajo] SM wool-winder, skein-winder.

arcuare [arku'are] VT (*schiena*) to arch; (*bastone*) to bend.

arcuato, a [arku'ato] AGG (*gen*) curved, bent; (*sopracciglia*) arched; **dalle gambe arcuate** bow-legged.

ardente [ar'dɛnte] AGG (*sole, fuoco*) blazing, burning; (*sguardo*) passionate; (*ammiratore*) ardent; (*passione*) ardent, burning; (*preghiera, desiderio*) fervent.

ardentemente [ardente'mente] AVV (*desiderare, sperare*) fervently, passionately.

ardere ['ardere] VB IRREG ☐1 VT (*anche fig*) to burn; **legna da ardere** firewood.
☐2 VI (*aus* essere) to burn; **ardere di passione/dalla curiosità** to burn with passion/curiosity; **ardere d'amore** to burn with love.

ardesia [ar'dɛzja] SF (*minerale*) slate; (*colore*) slate-grey.

ardimento [ardi'mento] SM daring.

ardimentoso, a [ardimen'toso] AGG daring, bold.

ardire [ar'dire] ☐1 VI DIF (*aus* avere): **ardire (di) fare qc** to dare (to) do sth.
☐2 SM (*audacia*) daring, boldness; (*impudenza*) impu-dence.

arditamente [ardita'mente] AVV (*vedi agg*) bravely; dar-ingly; impertinently.

ardito, a [ar'dito] AGG (*coraggioso*) brave, daring; (*temera-rio*) daring; (*impertinente*) impertinent, bold; **impresa ardita** risky undertaking; **scollatura ardita** daring neckline.

ardore [ar'dore] SM (*calore intenso*) (blazing) heat; (*fig: passione*) ardour; (: *fervore*) fervour, eagerness.

arduo, a ['arduo] AGG (*impresa*) arduous, difficult; (*problema*) difficult; (*salita*) steep.

area ['area] SF **a** (*gen, Geom*) area; **nell'area dei partiti di sinistra** among the parties of the left **b** (*Edil*) land, ground ▶ **area di attesa** (*Aer*) holding position ▶ **area convocazione gruppi** (*Aer*) meeting point ▶ **area edificabile** building land ▶ **area di meta** (*Rugby*) in-goal area ▶ **area della porta** (*Calcio*) goal area ▶ **area di rigore** (*Calcio*) penalty area ▶ **area di servizio** (*Aut*) service area.

arena [a'rɛna] SF **a** (*gen, fig*) arena; (*per corride*) bullring **b** (*letter: sabbia*) sand.

arenaria [are'narja] SF sandstone.

arenario, ria, ri, rie [are'narjo] AGG (*rocce, pietra*) sand-stone *attr*.

arenarsi [are'narsi] VIP (*Naut*) to run aground; (*fig: trattative*) to come to a standstill; **la mia pratica si è arenata** my file is gathering dust.

arenicola [are'nikola] SF (*Bot*) lugworm.

arenile [are'nile] SM strand.

areola [a'rɛola] SF (*Anat*) areola.

areoplano [areo'plano] SM = **aeroplano**.

aretino, a [are'tino] ☐1 AGG *o* from Arezzo.
☐2 SM/F inhabitant *o* native of Arezzo.

argano ['argano] SM winch; (*Naut*) capstan.

argentare [ardʒen'tare] VT to silver-plate.

argentato, a [ardʒen'tato] AGG silver-plated; (*colore*) silver, silvery; (*capelli*) silver(-grey).

argenteo, a [ar'dʒɛnteo] AGG silver, silvery.

argenteria [ardʒente'ria] SF (*oggetti*) silverware, silver; (*fabbrica*) silverware factory.

argentiere [ardʒen'tjɛre] SM silversmith.

Argentina [ardʒen'tina] SF: l'Argentina Argentina.

argentina [ardʒen'tina] SF (*maglietta*) crewneck sweater.

argentino[1], a [ardʒen'tino] AGG (*voce*) silvery.

argentino[2], a [ardʒen'tino] SM/F, AGG (*dell'Argentina*) Argentinian.

argento [ar'dʒɛnto] SM a silver; piatto d'argento silver dish; capelli d'argento silver(-grey) hair; avere l'argento vivo addosso (*fig*) to be fidgety ▶ argento dorato silver gilt ▶ argento vivo (*Chim*) quicksilver b : argenti SMPL (*argenteria*) silverware sg, silver sg.

argilla [ar'dʒilla] SF clay.

argilloso, a [ardʒil'loso] AGG (*contenente argilla*) clayey; (*simile ad argilla*) clay-like.

arginare [ardʒi'nare] VT (*fiume, acque*) to embank; (: *con diga*) to dyke up; (*fig: inflazione, corruzione*) to check; (: *spese*) to limit; arginare la piena to stem the flow of water; arginare l'avanzata nemica to check the enemy advance.

argine ['ardʒine] SM (*di fiume*) embankment, bank; rompere gli argini to break the banks; porre un argine a (*fig*) to check, hold back.

argo ['argo] SM (*Chim*) argon.

argomentare [argomen'tare] VI (*aus avere*): argomentare (su *o* di qc) to argue (about sth).

argomentazione [argomentat'tsjone] SF argument.

argomento [argo'mento] SM a (*tema*) subject; argomento di conversazione topic of conversation; qual è l'argomento del film/del libro? what is the film/book about?; cambiare argomento to change the subject; visto che siamo entrati in argomento... since we're on the subject ...; tornare sull'argomento to bring the matter up again b (*argomentazione*) argument; addurre/confutare un argomento to put forward/refute an argument.

argonauta, i [argo'nauta] SM Argonaut.

arguire [argu'ire] VT to deduce, infer.

argutamente [arguta'mente] AVV (*con spirito*) wittily; (*con prontezza*) quick-wittedly.

arguto, a [ar'guto] AGG (*battuta, conversazione*) witty; (*persona*) quick-witted; (*sguardo*) sharp, keen.

arguzia [ar'guttsja] SF (*spirito*) wit; (*battuta*) witty remark.

aria[1] ['arja] SF a (*gen*) air; aria di mare/montagna sea/mountain air; all'aria (aperta) in the open (air); vivere all'aria aperta to live an outdoor life; mettere le lenzuola all'aria to air the sheets; cambiare l'aria in una stanza to air a room; è meglio cambiare aria (*fig fam: andarsene*) we'd better make ourselves scarce; esco a prendere una boccata d'aria I'm going out for a breath of (fresh) air; manca l'aria it's stuffy; che aria tira? (*fig: atmosfera*) what's the atmosphere like?; c'è aria di burrasca (*anche fig*) there's a storm brewing; vivere *o* campare d'aria to live on thin air; aria! (*fam: vattene*) out of the way!, move! ▶ aria compressa compressed air ▶ aria condizionata air conditioning b : andare all'aria (*piano, progetto*) to come to nothing; buttare *o* mandare all'aria (*progetto, piano*) to ruin, upset; buttare all'aria qc (*mettere a soqquadro*) to turn

sth upside-down; discorsi a mezz'aria vague remarks; ha la testa per aria he's got his head in the clouds; lasciare tutto per aria (*in disordine*) to leave everything in a mess; sta sempre con la pancia all'aria he's always lazing about.

aria[2] ['arja] SF a (*espressione, aspetto*) look, air; (*modi*) manner, air; hai l'aria così stanca oggi you look so tired today; quel ragazzo ha l'aria intelligente that boy looks *o* seems intelligent; ha l'aria della persona onesta he looks (like) *o* seems (to be) an honest person; ha l'aria di voler piovere it looks like *o* as if it's going to rain; ha un'aria di famiglia there is a family likeness; cos'è quell'aria da funerale? what are you looking so gloomy about? b : arie SFPL airs (and graces); darsi delle arie to put on airs.

aria[3] ['arja] SF (*Mus: di opera*) aria; (: *di canzonetta*) tune.

Ariadne [a'rjadne] SF Ariadne.

arianesimo [arja'nezimo] SM Arianism.

ariano[1], a [a'rjano] AGG, SM/F (*Rel: eretico*) Arian.

ariano[2], a [a'rjano] AGG, SM/F (*Nazismo, Linguistica*) Aryan.

aridamente [arida'mente] AVV (*fig*) insensitively.

aridità [aridi'ta] SF aridity, dryness; (*fig*) lack of feeling.

arido, a ['arido] AGG (*suolo, regione*) arid; (*clima*) dry; (*fig: persona*) insensitive; cuore arido heart of stone.

arieggiare [arjed'dʒare] VT a (*stanza, abiti*) to air b (*imitare*) to imitate.

ariete [a'rjɛte] SM a (*Zool*) ram b (*Astrol*): Ariete Aries; essere dell'Ariete to be Aries c (*Storia, Mil*) battering ram.

arietta [a'rjetta] SF (*brezza*) breeze; (*Mus*) arietta.

aringa, ghe [a'ringa] SF herring ▶ aringa affumicata smoked herring, kipper ▶ aringa marinata pickled herring.

arioso, a [a'rjoso] AGG (*ambiente, stanza*) airy; (*Mus*) ariose.

arista ['arista] SF (*Culin*) chine of pork for roasting.

aristocraticamente [aristokratika'mente] AVV aristocratically.

aristocratico, a, ci, che [aristo'kratiko] [1] AGG (*gen, fig*) aristocratic. [2] SM/F aristocrat.

aristocrazia [aristokrat'tsia] SF aristocracy.

Aristofane [ari'stɔfane] SM Aristophanes.

Aristotele [ari'stɔtele] SM Aristotle.

aristotelico, a, ci, che [aristo'tɛliko] AGG Aristotelian.

aritmetica [arit'mɛtika] SF arithmetic.

aritmetico, a, ci, che [arit'mɛtiko] AGG arithmetical.

aritmia [arit'mia] SF (*anche: aritmia cardiaca*) arrhythmia.

arlecchino [arlek'kino] SM (*Teatro*) harlequin.

arma, i ['arma] SF a (*anche fig*) weapon; battersi all'arma bianca to fight with blades; all'armi! to arms!; passare qn per le armi to execute sb; arma a doppio taglio (*fig*) double-edged weapon; combattere ad armi pari (*anche fig*) to fight on equal terms; deporre le armi (*anche fig*) to lay down one's arms; essere alle prime armi (*fig*) to be a novice; prendere armi e bagagli e partire (*fig*) to pack up and go ▶ arma da fuoco firearm ▶ armi atomiche atomic weapons ▶ armi biologiche biological weapons b (*corpo dell'esercito*) arm, force; (*dei carabinieri*) force c (*servizio militare*): essere sotto le armi to be in the army *o* in the forces; andare sotto le armi to join the army *o* forces; chiamare alle armi to call up (*Brit*), draft

(*Am*).

armadillo [arma'dillo] SM armadillo.

armadio, di [ar'madjo] SM (*gen*) cupboard, closet (*Am*); (*per abiti*) wardrobe ▶**armadio a muro** built-in cupboard.

armaiolo [arma'jɔlo] SM **a** (*fabbricante*) armourer; (: *di armi da fuoco*) gunsmith **b** (*venditore*) arms dealer.

armamentario, ri [armamen'tarjo] SM (*attrezzatura*) equipment, tools *pl*; (*scherz*) paraphernalia.

armamento [arma'mento] SM **a** (*armi: di soldato*) arms *pl*, weapons *pl*; (: *di nazione*): **armamenti** SMPL arms, armaments; **la corsa agli armamenti** the arms race; **società di armamenti** shipowning company **b** (*azione: di nazione*) armament; (*Naut*) fitting out, equipping; (: *provvedere di uomini*) manning.

armare [ar'mare] ① VT **a** (*persona, nazione, fortezza*) to arm; (*arma da fuoco*) to cock **b** (*Naut*) to equip, fit out; (: *di uomini*) to man **c** (*Edil*) to prop up, shore up. ② **armarsi** VR (*Mil*) to take up arms: **armarsi di** (*anche fig*) to arm o.s. (with).

armata [ar'mata] SF (*esercito*) army; (*flotta*) fleet; **corpo d'armata** army corps *pl o sg*.

armato, a [ar'mato] ① AGG **a** : **armato (di)** (*anche fig*) armed (with); **armato fino ai denti** armed to the teeth; **sono partiti armati di tutto punto** they set off equipped for anything; **rapina a mano armata** armed robbery **b** (*Tecn: cemento, volta*) reinforced. ② SM (*soldato*) soldier.

armatore, trice [arma'tore] ① AGG shipping *attr*. ② SM shipowner.

armatura [arma'tura] SF **a** (*corazza*) (suit of) armour *no pl* (*Brit*), armor *no pl* (*Am*) **b** (*struttura di sostegno*) framework; (*impalcatura*) scaffolding **c** (*Elettr: di cavo*) sheath; (: *di condensatore*) plate.

armeggiare [armed'dʒare] VI (*aus* avere) (*affaccendarsi*): **armeggiare (intorno a qc)** to mess about (with sth).

Armenia [ar'mɛnja] SF: **l'Armenia** Armenia.

armeno, a [ar'mɛno] AGG, SM/F, SM Armenian.

armento [ar'mento] SM herd.

armeria [arme'ria] SF (*deposito*) armoury (*Brit*), armory (*Am*); (*negozio*) gun shop; (*collezione*) collection of arms.

armistizio, zi [armis'tittsjo] SM armistice.

armonia [armo'nia] SF (*concordia, Mus*) harmony; (*conformità*) agreement; **vivere in armonia con qn** to live in harmony with sb, get on very well with sb.

armonica, che [ar'mɔnika] SF **a** (*strumento*) harmonica ▶**armonica a bocca** mouth organ **b** (*Mus, Fis*) harmonic ▶**armoniche superiori** overtones.

armonico, a, ci, che [ar'mɔniko] AGG **a** (*Mus*) harmonic; **cassa armonica** sound box **b** (*ben proporzionato*) harmonious.

armoniosamente [armonjosa'mente] AVV harmoniously.

armonioso, a [armo'njoso] AGG (*voce*) melodious; (*suono*) harmonious; (*lingua*) musical; (*movimenti*) graceful; (*corpo*) well-proportioned.

armonizzare [armonid'dzare] ① VT (*Mus*) to harmonize; (*fig: colori*) to match. ② VI (*aus* avere): **armonizzare (con)** to harmonize (with); to match.

arnese [ar'nese] SM **a** (*strumento, utensile*) tool, implement; **arnesi da giardino/falegname** gardening/carpenter's tools **b** (*oggetto qualsiasi*) gadget, thing **c** : **essere male in arnese** (*vestito male*) to be poorly o

badly dressed; (*di salute malferma*) to be in poor health; (*di condizioni economiche*) to be hard up.

arnia ['arnja] SF (bee)hive.

aroma, i [a'rɔma] SM **a** (*odore*) aroma **b** (*erbe*): **aromi** SMPL herbs (and spices); **aromi naturali/artificiali** natural/artificial flavouring *sg* (*Brit*) o flavoring *sg* (*Am*).

aromaterapia [aromatera'pia] SF aromatherapy.

aromaticità [aromatitʃi'ta] SF INV aromatic quality.

aromatico, a, ci, che [aro'matiko] AGG aromatic; (*cibo*) spicy; **erbe aromatiche** herbs.

aromatizzare [aromatid'dzare] VT flavour (*Brit*), flavor (*Am*).

arpa ['arpa] SF harp.

arpeggiare [arped'dʒare] VI (*aus* avere) (*suonare l'arpa*) to play the harp; (*fare arpeggi*) to play arpeggios.

arpeggio, gi [ar'peddʒo] SM arpeggio.

arpia [ar'pia] SF (*Mitol*) Harpy; (*fig*) harpy.

arpionare [arpjo'nare] VT to harpoon.

arpione [ar'pjone] SM (*Pesca*) harpoon; (*uncino, Alpinismo*) hook; (*cardine*) hinge.

arrabattarsi [arrabat'tarsi] VIP: **arrabattarsi per fare qc** to do all one can to do sth, strive to do sth.

arrabbiare [arrab'bjare] ① VI (*aus* essere) **a** (*cane*) to be affected with rabies **b** (*persona*): **far arrabbiare** to make sb angry. ② **arrabbiarsi** VIP to get angry, fly into a rage.

arrabbiato, a [arrab'bjato] AGG **a** (*cane*) rabid, with rabies **b** (*persona*) angry; **un giocatore arrabbiato** (*fig: entusiasta*) a keen player.

arrabbiatura [arrabbja'tura] SF: **prendersi un'arrabbiatura (per qc)** to become furious (over sth).

arraffare [arraf'fare] VT to snatch, seize; (*rubare*) to pinch.

arrampicarsi [arrampi'karsi] VIP to climb (up); **arrampicarsi sul tetto** to climb (up) onto the roof; **arrampicarsi sugli specchi** o **sui vetri** (*fig*) to clutch at straws.

arrampicata [arrampi'kata] SF climb ▶**arrampicata libera** free climbing.

arrampicatore, trice [arrampika'tore] SM/F (*gen, Sport*) climber ▶**arrampicatore sociale** (*fig*) social climber.

arrancare [arran'kare] VI (*aus* avere) to limp, hobble; (*fig*) to struggle along.

arrangiamento [arrandʒa'mento] SM (*Mus*) arrangement.

arrangiare [arran'dʒare] ① VT (*gen, Mus*) to arrange; **abbiamo arrangiato un pranzo alla bell'e meglio** we've rustled up some lunch; **ti arrangio io!** (*fam*) I'll fix you!, I'll sort you out!. ② **arrangiarsi** VIP (*cavarsela*) to get by o along, manage; **con l'arte di arrangiarsi si risolve tutto** with a bit of ingenuity you can sort anything out; **arrangiati un po' tu!** (*fam*) sort it out for yourself!

arrangiatore, trice [arrandʒa'tore] SM/F (*Mus*) arranger.

arrapante [arra'pante] AGG (*fam: sessualmente eccitante*) sexually arousing.

arrapare [arra'pare] ① VT (*eccitare sessualmente*) to make randy (*Brit*), make horny. ② **arraparsi** VR to get randy (*Brit*), get horny.

arrapato, a [arra'pato] AGG (*fam*) randy (*Brit*), horny.

arrecare [arre'kare] VT (*causare*) to cause; **arrecare danni/disturbo** to do damage/cause trouble.

arredamento [arreda'mento] SM **a** (*azione*) furnishing; (*mobilia*) furniture **b** (*arte*) interior design.

arredare [arre'dare] VT to furnish.

arredatore, trice [arreda'tore] SM/F interior designer.

arredo [ar'rɛdo] SM furnishings *pl*; **per l'arredo della vostra casa...** to furnish your home ... ▶**arredi sacri** religious ornaments ▶**arredo urbano** street furniture.

arrembaggio, gi [arrem'baddʒo] SM (*Naut*) boarding; **si buttarono all'arrembaggio dei posti migliori** (*fig*) there was a mad scramble for the best seats.

arrendersi [ar'rɛndersi] VIP IRREG (*persona*): **arrendersi (a)** (*polizia, nemico*) to give o.s. up (to), surrender (to); **arrendersi all'evidenza (dei fatti)** to accept *o* yield to the evidence.

arrendevole [arren'devole] AGG (*persona*) yielding, compliant.

arrendevolezza [arrendevo'lettsa] SF compliancy.

arrendevolmente [arrendevol'mente] AVV compliantly.

arreso, a [ar'reso] PP di **arrendersi**.

arrestare [arres'tare] ① VT (*Dir*) to arrest; (*fermare*) to stop, halt.
② **arrestarsi** VR to stop.

arrestato, a [arres'tato] SM/F person under arrest.

arresto [ar'rɛsto] SM **a** (*Dir*) arrest; **mandato d'arresto** warrant of arrest *o* arrest warrant; **essere in stato di arresto** to be under arrest; **la dichiaro in arresto** I'm putting you under arrest; **essere/mettere agli arresti** (*Mil*) to be/place under arrest ▶**arresti domiciliari** house arrest
b (*azione*) stopping; (*sosta, pausa*) interruption; (*Comm: nella produzione*) stoppage; **aspettate l'arresto del treno** wait until the train stops *o* comes to a stop; **segnale d'arresto** stop sign; **il gioco ha avuto una battuta d'arresto** the game was interrupted; **le discussioni fra i due partiti subirono un arresto** discussions between the two parties came to a standstill ▶**arresto cardiaco** (*Med*) cardiac arrest.

arretramento [arretra'mento] SM (*gen*) moving back; (*Mil: in battaglia*) falling back.

arretrare [arre'trare] ① VI (*aus* **essere**) to move back, withdraw; **arretrare davanti** *o* **di fronte a qc** (*fig*) to shrink from sth.
② VT to move back.

arretratezza [arretra'tettsa] SF backwardness.

arretrato, a [arre'trato] ① AGG **a** (*paese, zona*) backward **b** (*numero di giornale, pagamento, interesse*) back *attr*; **ho un sacco di lavoro arretrato da finire** I've got a huge backlog of work to finish.
② SM **a**: **essere in arretrato con qc** to be behind with sth **b**: **arretrati** SMPL arrears; **gli arretrati dello stipendio** back pay *sg*.

arricchimento [arrikki'mento] SM (*anche fig*) enrichment.

arricchire [arrik'kire] ① VT to make rich; **arricchire qc di** *o* **con qc** (*fig*) to enrich sth with sth.
② **arricchirsi** VIP (*persona*) to grow *o* become *o* get rich; (*collezione*): **arricchirsi di** to be enriched with.

arricchito, a [arrik'kito] SM/F nouveau riche.

arricciaburro [arrittʃa'burro] SM INV butter curler.

arricciacapelli [arrittʃaka'pelli] SM INV curling tongs *pl*.

arricciare [arrit'tʃare] ① VT (*capelli, baffi*) to curl; **arricciare il naso** (*fig*) to turn up one's nose.
② **arricciarsi** VIP to become curly.

arridere [ar'ridere] VI IRREG (*aus* **avere**) (*fortuna, successo*): **arridere a qn** to smile on sb.

arringa [ar'ringa] SF (*gen*) (formal) address; (*Dir*) address by counsel.

arringare [arrin'gare] VT to address.

arrischiare [arris'kjare] ① VT (*parola, giudizio*) to venture, hazard.
② **arrischiarsi** VR: **arrischiarsi (a fare qc)** to venture (to do sth), dare (to do sth).

arrischiato, a [arris'kjato] AGG (*pericoloso: impresa, speculazione*) risky; (*avventato: giudizio, ipotesi*) rash.

arriso, a [ar'riso] PP di **arridere**.

arrivare [arri'vare] VI (*aus* **essere**) **a** (*essere a destinazione*) to arrive; (*avvicinarsi*) to come; (*raggiungere*): **arrivare a** to reach, arrive at, get to; **arrivare a casa** to arrive *o* get *o* reach home; **arrivare a Roma/in Italia** to arrive in Rome/in Italy; **mi è arrivato un pacco dall'Italia** a parcel has arrived for me from Italy, I've had a parcel from Italy; **arrivare a destinazione** to arrive at *o* reach one's destination; **arrivare allo scopo** to reach one's goal; **arrivare al potere** to come to power; **arrivare primo** (*in un luogo*) to be the first to arrive; (*in classifica*) to come (in) first; **non credevo arrivasse a tanto** *o* **a quel punto** I didn't think he'd go that far; **arrivo!** (I'm) coming!; **siamo arrivati** we're here; **per fare arrivare la corrente alla macchina** in order to connect the machine up to the electricity supply; **l'acqua mi arrivava alle ginocchia** the water came up to my knees; **la notizia è arrivata fino a lui** the news (even) reached him; **non ci arrivo** (*a prendere qc*) I can't reach it; (*a capire qc*) I can't understand it, I don't get it; **a questo siamo arrivati!** so this is what we've come to!; **il mio stipendio non arriva ai due milioni di lire** my salary doesn't reach the two million lire mark; **dove ti arriva la gonna?** how long is the skirt on you?; **se non la smetti ti arriva uno schiaffo** (*fam*) if you don't stop it *o* leave off you'll get a smack; **chi tardi arriva male alloggia** (*Proverbio*) the early bird catches the worm
b (*riuscire*): **arrivare a fare qc** to manage to do sth, succeed in doing sth; **non arriverò mai a capirlo** I'll never understand him; **non arriverà a niente** he'll never get anywhere, he'll never achieve anything; **non ci arrivo da solo** I can't do it on my own.

arrivato, a [arri'vato] ① AGG **a** (*persona di successo*) successful **b**: **ben arrivato!** welcome!.
② SM/F **a** (*persona di successo*): **essere un arrivato** to have made it **b**: **nuovo arrivato** newcomer; **l'ultimo arrivato** the last to arrive.

arrivederci [arrive'dertʃi] ESCL goodbye!; **arrivederci a domani!** see you tomorrow!

arrivederla [arrive'derla] ESCL goodbye!

arrivismo [arri'vizmo] SM social climbing.

arrivista, i, e [arri'vista] SM/F social climber.

arrivistico, a, ci, che [arri'vistiko] AGG: **avere manie arrivistiche** to be pushy.

arrivo [ar'rivo] SM **a** arrival; **al mio arrivo** on my arrival; **telefonami al tuo arrivo in Italia** phone me when you arrive in *o* get to Italy; **il treno è in arrivo al binario 7** the train is arriving *o* coming in at platform 7; **arrivi e partenze** arrivals and departures
b (*Sport*) finish, finishing line
c (*Comm*): **questi sono gli ultimi arrivi** these have just come in; **ci sono nuovi arrivi?** has anything new come in?

arroccare [arrok'kare] ① VT (*Scacchi*) to castle.
② **arroccarsi** VR: **arroccarsi in qc** (*fig*) to shelter behind sth.

arrogante [arro'gante] AGG arrogant.

arrogantemente [arrogante'mente] AVV arrogantly.

arroganza [arro'gantsa] SF arrogance.

arrogare [arro'gare] VT: **arrogarsi il diritto di fare qc** to assume the right to do sth; **arrogarsi il merito di qc** to claim credit for sth.

arrossamento [arrossa'mento] SM reddening.

arrossare [arros'sare] 1 VT (*occhi, pelle*) to redden, make red.

2 **arrossarsi** VIP to go *o* turn red.

arrossire [arros'sire] VI (*aus* **essere**): **arrossire (di, per)** (*vergogna, imbarazzo*) to blush (with); (*piacere*) to flush (with); **arrossire fino alle orecchie** to go *o* turn bright red, blush to the roots of one's hair.

arrostimento [arrosti'mento] SM (*vedi vb*) roasting; grilling.

arrostire [arros'tire] 1 VT (*al forno*) to roast; (*ai ferri, alla griglia*) to grill; **sotto un sole che arrostiva** under a blazing sun.

2 **arrostirsi** VIP: **arrostirsi al sole** to soak up *o* roast in the sun.

arrosto [ar'rɔsto] 1 AGG INV (*vedi vb*) roast; grilled.

2 SM roast ►**arrosto arrotolato** stuffed rolled veal ►**arrosto di manzo** roast beef.

3 AVV: **fare *o* cuocere arrosto** (*vedi vb*) to roast; to grill; **pollo da fare arrosto** roasting chicken.

arrotare [arro'tare] VT **a** (*lame, coltelli*) to sharpen; (*denti*) to grind **b**: **arrotare la erre** to roll one's r's **c** (*investire con un veicolo*) to run over.

arrotino [arro'tino] SM knife-grinder.

arrotolare [arroto'lare] VT (*stoffa, sigaretta*) to roll; (*carta*) to roll up.

arrotondare [arroton'dare] VT (*cifra*) to round up; (*forma, oggetto*) to (make) round; (*fig: stipendio*) to supplement.

arrotondato, a [arroton'dato] AGG rounded.

arrovellare [arrovel'lare] 1 VT: **arrovellarsi il cervello** to rack one's brains.

2 **arrovellarsi** VR: **arrovellarsi (per qc)** to rack one's brains (about sth).

arroventare [arroven'tare] 1 VT to make red hot.

2 **arroventarsi** VIP to become red hot.

arroventato, a [arroven'tato] AGG red-hot.

arruffare [arruf'fare] 1 VT to ruffle; (*fili*) to tangle.

2 **arruffarsi** VIP to become tousled.

arruffato, a [arruf'fato] AGG (*capelli, pelo*) tousled, ruffled; (*piume*) ruffled.

arruffianare [arruffja'nare] (*fam*) 1 VT: **arruffianarsi qn** to lick *o* suck up to sb.

2 VIP: **arruffianarsi con qn** to lick *o* suck up to sb.

arrugginire [arruddʒi'nire] 1 VI (*aus* **essere**) to rust, get rusty.

2 VT to rust.

3 **arrugginirsi** VIP (*metallo*) to rust, get rusty; (*fig: atleta, memoria*) to become rusty.

arrugginito, a [arruddʒi'nito] AGG (*anche fig*) rusty.

arruolamento [arrwola'mento] SM enlistment.

arruolare [arrwo'lare] 1 VT to enlist.

2 **arruolarsi** VR to enlist; **arruolarsi volontario** to join up, enlist.

arsenale [arse'nale] SM (*cantiere navale*) dockyard; (*di armi*) arsenal; **si è portato dietro un arsenale** he had everything but the kitchen sink with him, he brought everything but the kitchen sink.

arsenico [ar'sɛniko] SM arsenic.

arsi *ecc* ['arsi] VB vedi **ardere**.

arso, a ['arso] 1 PP di **ardere**.

2 AGG (*bruciato*) burnt; (*arido*) dry.

arsura [ar'sura] SF **a** (*siccità*) drought; (*sete*) thirst **b** (*calore: del sole*) burning heat; (: *di febbre*) burning.

art. ABBR (= *articolo*) art.

arte ['arte] SF **a** (*gen*) art; (*abilità*) skill; (*mestiere, attività*) craft; **opera d'arte** work of art; **con arte** skilfully; **a regola d'arte** (*fig*) perfectly; **avere l'arte di fare qc** to have the knack of doing sth; **senz'arte né parte** penniless and jobless ►**arti figurative** visual arts

b (*Storia*) guild; **l'arte della lana** the woollen guild; **arti e mestieri** arts and crafts.

artefatto, a [arte'fatto] AGG (*stile, modi*) artificial.

artefice [ar'tefitʃe] SM/F (*autore*) author; **il sommo artefice** (*Dio*) the supreme Architect.

Artemide [ar'tɛmide] SF Artemis.

arteria [ar'tɛrja] SF (*Anat, fig*) artery.

arteriosclerosi [arterjoskle'rɔzi] SF arteriosclerosis (*Med*), hardening of the arteries.

arteriosclerotico, a, ci, che [arterjoskle'rɔtiko] AGG (*Med*) suffering from hardening of the arteries; (*fig scherz*) senile.

arterioso, a [arte'rjoso] AGG (*Anat*) arterial.

artesiano, a [arte'zjano] AGG: **pozzo artesiano** artesian well.

artico, a, ci, che ['artiko] 1 AGG Arctic; **il Circolo polare artico** the Arctic Circle; **l'Oceano artico** the Arctic Ocean.

2 SM: **l'Artico** the Arctic.

articolare[1] [artiko'lare] AGG (*Anat*) articular, of the joints.

articolare[2] [artiko'lare] 1 VT **a** (*muovere: giunture*) to move **b** (*pronunciare: parole*) to articulate **c** (*suddividere: discorso, periodo*) to split (up), divide; **ha articolato bene la sua relazione** his presentation was well organized.

2 **articolarsi** VIP (*discorso, progetto*): **articolarsi in** to be divided into.

articolato, a [artiko'lato] AGG **a** (*snodato*) articulated **b** (*linguaggio*) articulate; **un ragionamento ben articolato** a clear and well developed argument **c** (*Gramm*): **preposizione articolata** preposition combined with the definite article.

articolazione [artikolat'tsjone] SF **a** (*Anat, Tecn*) joint **b** (*di voce, concetto*) articulation.

articolo [ar'tikolo] SM **a** (*Gramm*) article **b** (*di giornale, legge, regolamento*) article ►**articolo di fede** (*Rel*) article of faith ►**articolo di fondo** (*Stampa*) editorial, leader, leading article **c** (*Comm*) item, article; **quel suo amico è un bell'articolo** (*fig*) that friend of his is a real character ►**articoli di cancelleria** stationery ►**articoli casalinghi** kitchenware ►**articoli di lusso** luxury goods ►**articoli di marca** branded *o* brand-name goods ►**articoli da regalo** gifts ► **articolo civetta** loss leader.

Artide ['artide] SM: **l'Artide** the Arctic.

artificiale [artifi'tʃale] AGG (*gen*) artificial; (*allegria*) forced, unnatural.

artificialmente [artifitʃal'mente] AVV (*vedi agg*) artificially; unnaturally.

artificiere [artifi'tʃɛre] SM (*Mil*) artificer; (: *per disinnescare bombe*) bomb disposal expert.

artificio, ci [arti'fitʃo] SM (*espediente*) trick; (*ricerca di effetto*) artificiality; **fuochi d'artificio** fireworks.

artificioso, a [artifi'tʃoso] AGG (*comportamento*) unnatural; (*argomento*) forced.

artigianale [artidʒa'nale] AGG craft *attr*; **produzione arti-**

gianale production by craftsmen; **lavoro artigianale** craftsmanship; **è un pezzo artigianale** it was made by a craftsman.

artigianalmente [artidʒanal'mente] AVV by craftsmen.

artigianato [artidʒa'nato] SM **a** (*arte*) craft; **corso di artigianato** arts and crafts course **b** (*prodotti*) arts and crafts *pl* **c** (*categoria*) artisans *pl*, craftsmen *pl*.

artigiano, a [arti'dʒano] [1] AGG craft *attr*. [2] SM/F craftsman/craftswoman, artisan.

artigliere [artiʎ'ʎɛre] SM artilleryman.

artiglieria [artiʎʎe'ria] SF artillery; **tiro di artiglieria** artillery fire.

artiglio, gli [ar'tiʎʎo] SM (*di felini*) claw; (*di rapaci*) talon; **sfoderare gli artigli** (*fig*) to show one's claws; **cadere negli artigli di qn** (*fig*) to fall into sb's clutches.

artista, i, e [ar'tista] SM/F (*pittore, scultore ecc*) artist; (*di spettacolo, circo*) artiste; **un lavoro da artista** (*fig*) a professional piece of work ▶ **artista di varietà** variety artist.

artisticamente [artistika'mente] AVV artistically.

artistico, a, ci, che [ar'tistiko] AGG artistic.

arto ['arto] SM limb.

artrite [ar'trite] SF arthritis.

artritico, a, ci, che [ar'tritiko] AGG, SM/F arthritic.

artropodi [ar'trɔpodi] SMPL arthropods *pl*.

artrosi [ar'trɔzi] SF INV osteoarthritis.

Artù [ar'tu] SM: **re Artù** King Arthur.

arvicola [ar'vikola] SF (*Zool*) water vole.

arzigogolare [ardzigogo'lare] VI (*aus avere*) (*fantasticare*) to daydream; (*cavillare*) to quibble.

arzigogolato, a [ardzigogo'lato] AGG tortuous.

arzigogolo [ardzi'gɔgolo] SM tortuous expression.

arzillo, a [ar'dzillo] AGG lively, sprightly.

Asburgo [az'burgo] SM INV: **gli Asburgo** the House of Hapsburg, the Hapsburgs.

asce ['aʃʃe] SFPL di **ascia**.

ascella [aʃ'ʃɛlla] SF (*Anat*) armpit.

ascellare [aʃʃel'lare] AGG underarm *attr*.

ascendente [aʃʃen'dɛnte] [1] AGG (*moto, piano*) ascending, upward; (*Mus: scala*) ascending. [2] SM **a** (*influenza*): **ascendente (su)** ascendancy (over) **b** (*Astrol*) ascendant **c** (*antenato*) ancestor.

ascendenza [aʃʃen'dɛntsa] SF ancestry.

ascendere [aʃ'ʃendere] VI IRREG (*aus essere*) (*frm*): **ascendere al trono** to ascend the throne; **ascendere a grandi onori** to rise to great honours.

ascensionale [aʃʃensjo'nale] AGG (*forza, moto*) upward; **velocità ascensionale** (*Aer*) rate of climb.

ascensione [aʃʃen'sjone] SF **a** (*Alpinismo*) ascent, climb; (*Aer*) ascent **b** (*Rel*): **l'Ascensione** the Ascension **c**: **(isola dell')Ascensione** Ascension Island.

ascensore [aʃʃen'sore] SM lift (*Brit*), elevator (*Am*).

ascesa [aʃ'ʃesa] SF (*gen*) ascent, climb; (*fig: al trono*) accession; (: *al potere, successo*) rise.

ascesi [aʃ'ʃɛzi] SF asceticism.

asceso, a [aʃ'ʃeso] PP di **ascendere**.

ascesso [aʃ'ʃɛsso] SM abscess.

asceta, i [aʃ'ʃɛta] SM/F ascetic.

ascetico, a, ci, che [aʃ'ʃɛtiko] AGG ascetic(al).

ascetismo [aʃʃe'tizmo] SM asceticism.

ascia, sce ['aʃʃa] SF axe; (*più piccola*) hatchet.

ascissa [aʃ'ʃissa] SF (*Mat*) x-axis.

asciugacapelli [aʃʃugaka'pelli] SM INV hair dryer.

asciugamano [aʃʃuga'mano] SM towel ▶ **asciugamano da bagno** bath towel.

asciugare [aʃʃu'gare] [1] VT (*gen*) to dry; (*sudore*) to wipe; **asciugare i piatti** to wipe *o* dry the dishes; **asciugarsi le mani/le lacrime** to dry one's hands/one's eyes. [2] **asciugarsi** VIP (*panni*) to dry; **asciugarsi al sole** to dry in the sun. [3] **asciugarsi** VR (*persona*) to dry o.s.; **asciugarsi al sole** to dry off in the sun.

asciugatoio, oi [aʃʃuga'tojo] SM = **essiccatoio**.

asciugatrice [aʃʃuga'tritʃe] SF spin-dryer ▶ **asciugatrice a centrifuga** tumble dryer.

asciuttezza [aʃʃut'tettsa] SF (*vedi agg*) dryness; leanness; curtness.

asciutto, a [aʃ'ʃutto] [1] AGG (*gen, fig*) dry; (*magro: viso, corpo ecc*) lean; (*brusco: risposta*) curt; **rimanere *o* restare a bocca asciutta** (*fig*) to be disappointed. [2] SM: **tenere all'asciutto** to keep in a dry place; **rimanere *o* restare all'asciutto** (*fig*) to be broke; **sono rimasto all'asciutto, puoi prestarmi 50.000 lire?** I haven't got a bean, can you lend me 50,000 lire?

ascolano, a [asko'lano] [1] AGG of *o* from Ascoli. [2] SM/F inhabitant *o* native of Ascoli.

ascoltare [askol'tare] VT (*persona, musica, radio, discorso ecc*) to listen to; **ascoltare qn parlare/cantare** to listen to sb talk/sing; **ascoltare qn con un orecchio solo** to half listen to sb; **ascoltare il consiglio di qn** to listen to *o* heed sb's advice; **ascoltare la messa/una lezione** to attend Mass/a class; **ascoltare un testimone** (*Dir*) to hear a witness.

ascoltatore, trice [askolta'tore] SM/F listener.

ascolto [as'kolto] SM **a** (*Radio*) reception; (*gen, programma*): **essere *o* stare in ascolto (di qc)** to be listening (to sth); **mettersi in ascolto (di qc)** to listen (to sth); **indice di ascolto** (*TV, Radio*) audience rating **b** (*attenzione*): **dare *o* prestare ascolto a qn/ai consigli di qn** to listen to *o* heed sb/sb's advice; **non presterai ascolto a queste chiacchiere** you won't take any notice of *o* you won't listen to these rumours, will you?

AS. COM. ['askom] SIGLA F (= *Associazione Commercianti*) *association of merchants and shopkeepers.*

ascorbico, a, ci, che [as'kɔrbiko] AGG: **acido ascorbico** ascorbic acid.

ascritto, a [as'kritto] PP di **ascrivere**.

ascrivere [as'krivere] VT IRREG **a** (*attribuire*): **ascrivere qc a qn** to attribute sth to sb; **ascrivere qc a merito di qn** to give sb credit for sth **b** (*annoverare*): **ascrivere (tra)** to number (among).

asessuale [asessu'ale] AGG (*Bio*) asexual.

asessuato, a [asessu'ato] AGG asexual.

asettico, a, ci, che [a'sɛttiko] AGG aseptic.

asfaltare [asfal'tare] VT to asphalt.

asfalto [as'falto] SM asphalt.

asfissia [asfis'sia] SF asphyxia, asphyxiation.

asfissiante [asfis'sjante] AGG (*gas*) asphyxiant, asphyxiating; (*fig: calore, ambiente*) stifling, suffocating; (: *persona*) tiresome.

asfissiare [asfis'sjare] [1] VT to asphyxiate, suffocate; (*fig: opprimere*) to stifle; (*fig: infastidire*) to get on sb's nerves; **asfissiare (con il gas)** to gas; **è morto asfissiato** he died of suffocation; **la sta asfissiando con la sua gelosia** he's stifling her with his jealousy. [2] VI (*aus essere*) to suffocate, asphyxiate. [3] **asfissiarsi** VR to suffocate o.s.; **asfissiarsi col gas** to gas o.s.

Asia ['azja] SF: **l'Asia** Asia.

asiatico, a, ci, che [a'zjatiko] [1] AGG Asian, Asiatic.
[2] SM/F Asian, Asiatic.
[3] SF (Med) Asian flu.

asilo [a'zilo] SM **a** : **asilo (infantile)** nursery (school) ▶**asilo nido** day nursery (for children aged 0 to 3), crèche **b** (rifugio) shelter, refuge; (Pol) asylum; **diritto di asilo** right of asylum; **dare/chiedere asilo** to grant/seek political asylum.

asimmetria [asimme'tria] SF asymmetry.

asimmetricamente [asimmetrika'mente] AVV asymmetrically.

asimmetrico, a, ci, che [asim'mɛtriko] AGG asymmetric (al).

asina ['asina] SF she-ass.

asinello [asi'nɛllo] SM (little) donkey.

asinino, a [asi'nino] AGG: **tosse asinina** whooping cough.

asino ['asino] SM (Zool) donkey, ass; (fig) fool, ass; (: scolaro) dunce; **a dorso d'asino** on the back of a donkey; **qui casca l'asino!** there's the rub!

asma ['azma] SF asthma.

asmatico, a, ci, che [az'matiko] AGG, SM/F asthmatic.

asociale [aso'tʃale] [1] AGG antisocial; (chiuso) unsociable.
[2] SM/F unsociable person.

asocialità [asotʃali'ta] SF antisocial behaviour.

asola ['azola] SF buttonhole.

asparago, gi [as'parago] SM asparagus; **un mazzo di asparagi** a bunch of asparagus.

aspergere [as'pɛrdʒere] VT IRREG: **aspergere (di** o **con)** to sprinkle (with).

asperità [asperi'ta] SF INV (di terreno, roccia) roughness no pl, ruggedness no pl; (fig) harshness no pl; **le asperità della vita** the trials of life.

aspersi ecc [as'pɛrsi] VB vedi **aspergere**.

aspersione [asper'sjone] SF (anche Rel) sprinkling.

asperso, a [as'pɛrso] PP di **aspergere**.

aspersorio, ri [asper'sɔrjo] SM aspersorium.

aspettare [aspet'tare] VT **a** (attendere) to wait for, await (frm); **aspettiamo che arrivi** let's wait for him to come; **aspetta un po'** wait a second o moment, hold on; **aspetta a giudicare!** wait and see!; **aspetta la fine** (di film ecc) to wait until the end; **aspettare conferma** (Comm) to await confirmation; **aspettare un bambino** (essere incinta) to be expecting (a baby); **è mezz'ora che ti aspetto** I've been waiting for you for half an hour; **fare aspettare qn** to keep sb waiting; **farsi aspettare** to keep people waiting; **aspetta e spera!** that'll be the day!; **chi la fa, l'aspetti!** (Proverbio) it'll all come home to roost **b** (essere in serbo: notizia, evento ecc) to be in store for, lie ahead of; **non sapeva che cosa lo aspettasse** he didn't know what was in store for him o lay ahead of him
c : **aspettarsi qc** to expect sth; **non mi aspettavo che partisse** I didn't expect him to leave; **quando meno te l'aspetti** when you least expect it; **me l'aspettavo!** I thought as much!

aspettativa [aspetta'tiva] SF **a** (previsione, speranza) expectation; **contro ogni mia aspettativa** against all my expectations ...; **inferiore/superiore all'aspettativa** worse/better than expected; **corrispondere alle/deludere le aspettative di qn** to come up to/fall short of sb's expectations; **superare ogni aspettativa** to exceed o go beyond all expectations
b (Amm): **chiedere l'aspettativa** to ask for o put in for

leave; **essere/mettersi in aspettativa** to be on/take leave (of absence).

aspetto [as'pɛtto] SM **a** (apparenza) appearance, look; **un uomo di bell'aspetto** a good-looking man; **all'aspetto** o **a giudicare dall'aspetto, pare una persona onesta** as far as we can tell, he seems an honest person; **avere l'aspetto di** to look like **b** (di questione ecc) aspect, side; **sotto un certo aspetto** in some ways.

aspic [as'pik] SM INV: **aspic di pollo** chicken in aspic.

aspide ['aspide] SM asp.

aspidistra [aspi'distra] SF (Bot) aspidistra.

aspirante [aspi'rante] [1] AGG **a** (Tecn) suction attr **b** (attore, artista ecc) aspiring.
[2] SM/F (a un titolo) aspirant; (candidato) candidate.

aspirapolvere [aspira'polvere] SM INV vacuum cleaner, hoover ®; **passare l'aspirapolvere** to vacuum, hoover.

aspirare [aspi'rare] [1] VT **a** (fumo) to inhale; (aria, profumo) to breathe in **b** (Tecn) to suck (up) **c** (Fonetica) to aspirate.
[2] VI (aus avere) (anelare): **aspirare a qc/a fare qc** to aspire to sth/to do sth.

aspiratore [aspira'tore] SM (di aria, gas) extractor fan; (di liquidi) aspirator, extractor.

aspirazione [aspirat'tsjone] SF **a** (Tecn) suction **b** (anelito) aspiration; (ambizione) ambition **c** (Fonetica) aspiration.

aspirina® [aspi'rina] SF aspirin.

asportare [aspor'tare] VT to take away; (Med) to remove.

asportazione [asportat'tsjone] SF (anche Med) removal.

asporto [as'porto] SM: **da asporto** (gelato, pizza) take-away.

aspramente [aspra'mente] AVV (rimproverare) harshly.

asprezza [as'prettsa] SF INV (vedi agg) sourness; sharpness; pungency; rugged nature; severity; harshness, roughness; strictness.

asprigno, a [as'priɲɲo] AGG rather sour.

aspro, a ['aspro] AGG **a** (agrumi) sour; (vino) sharp; (odore) pungent, acrid; (paesaggio) rugged; (clima) severe, harsh **b** (fig: voce, giudizio) harsh, rough; (: disciplina, regime) strict **c** (Fonetica): **"s" aspra** unvoiced "s".

Ass. ABBR **a** = **assicurazione b** = **assicurata c** = **assegno**.

assaggiare [assad'dʒare] VT (pietanza, bevanda) to taste, try; **fammi assaggiare** let me have a taste; **gli hanno fatto assaggiare la frusta** (fig) they gave him a taste of the whip.

assaggiatore, trice [assaddʒa'tore] SM/F taster.

assaggini [assad'dʒini] SMPL (Culin) selection of first courses.

assaggio, gi [as'saddʒo] SM (prova, degustazione) tasting, sampling; (piccola quantità) taste; (campione) sample.

assai [as'sai] AVV (molto) a lot, much; (: con agg) very; **è assai più giovane di me** she is very much o a lot younger than me; **sono assai contento del risultato** I'm very pleased with the result; **m'importa assai di lui!** what do I care about him!

assalgo ecc [as'salgo] VB vedi **assalire**.

assalire [assa'lire] VT IRREG to attack, assail; (fig) to assail; **assalire a parole** to attack verbally.

assalitore, trice [assali'tore] SM/F attacker, assailant.

assaltare [assal'tare] VT (Mil) to storm; (banca) to raid; (treno, diligenza) to hold up.

assalto [as'salto] SM **a** (Mil) attack, assault; **truppe d'assalto** assault troops; **d'assalto** (fig: editoria, giornali-

sta ecc) aggressive **b** (*rapina*) raid; **prendere d'assalto** (*fig: negozio, treno*) to storm; (: *personalità*) to besiege.

assaporare [assapo'rare] VT (*anche fig*) to savour (*Brit*), savor (*Am*).

assassinare [assassi'nare] VT (*gen*) to murder; (*Pol*) to assassinate.

assassinio, nii [assas'sinjo] SM murder; (*politico*) assassination.

assassino, a [assas'sino] ① SM/F murderer; (*Pol*) assassin. ② AGG (*mania, tendenza*) murderous; (*seducente: sguardo, occhiata*) seductive.

asse[1] ['asse] SF (*di legno*) board ▶**asse di equilibrio** (*Ginnastica*) beam ▶**asse del gabinetto** lavatory seat ▶**asse da stiro** ironing board.

asse[2] ['asse] SM (*Geom*) axis; (*Tecn*) axle; **l'asse terrestre** the earth's axis; **l'asse Roma-Berlino** (*alleanza*) the Rome-Berlin axis.

assecondare [assekon'dare] VT: **assecondare qn (in qc)** to go along with sb (in sth); **assecondare i desideri di qn** to go along with sb's wishes; **assecondare i capricci di qn** to give in to sb's whims.

assediante [asse'djante] SM/F besieger.

assediare [asse'djare] VT (*anche fig*) to besiege.

assediato, a [asse'djato] ① AGG (*anche fig*) besieged. ②: **gli assediati** SMPL people under siege.

assedio, di [as'sɛdjo] SM (*anche fig*) siege; **porre in stato di assedio** to lay siege to; **cingere d'assedio** to besiege.

assegnamento [asseɲɲa'mento] SM: **fare assegnamento su** to rely on.

assegnare [asseɲ'ɲare] VT: **assegnare (a)** (*gen*) to assign (to); (*premio, borsa di studio*) to award (to); (*somma*) to allocate (to), allot (to).

assegnatario, ria, ri, rie [asseɲɲa'tarjo] SM/F (*Dir*) assignee; **l'assegnatario del premio** the person awarded the prize.

assegnazione [asseɲɲat'tsjone] SF (*di casa, somma*) allocation; (*di carica*) assignment; (*di premio, borsa di studio*) awarding.

assegno [as'seɲɲo] SM **a** (*Comm*): **contro assegno** cash on delivery
b (*somma integrativa*): **assegni familiari** ≈ child benefit *sg* ▶**assegno di studio** ≈ study grant
c (*Fin*): **assegno (bancario)** cheque (*Brit*), check (*Am*); **un assegno per** *o* **di 500.000 lire** a cheque for 500,000 lire ▶**assegno in bianco** blank cheque ▶**assegno circolare** bank draft ▶**"assegno non trasferibile"** "account payee only" ▶**assegno post-datato** post-dated cheque ▶**assegno sbarrato** crossed cheque ▶**assegno a vuoto** dud cheque.

assemblaggio, gi [assem'bladdʒo] SM (*Industria*) assembly; (*Inform*) assembling.

assemblare [assem'blare] VT (*Industria, Inform, anche fig*) to assemble.

assemblatore [assembla'tore] ① SM assembly worker. ② AGG (*Inform*): **programma assemblatore** assembler.

assemblea [assem'blɛa] SF (*gen*) assembly; (*raduno, adunanza*) meeting ▶**assemblea generale** general meeting.

assembleare [assemble'are] AGG (*decisione, riunione*) of the meeting, of the assembly.

assembramento [assembra'mento] SM (public) gathering; **divieto di assembramento** ban on public meetings.

assembrarsi [assem'brarsi] VIP to gather.

assennatamente [assennata'mente] AVV sensibly, wisely.

assennatezza [assenna'tettsa] SF good sense, wisdom.

assennato, a [assen'nato] AGG sensible, wise.

assenso [as'sɛnso] SM approval, assent; (*Dir*) consent; **dare/negare il proprio assenso** give/not give *o* withold one's consent.

assentarsi [assen'tarsi] VIP (*gen*) to go out; **il direttore dovrà assentarsi per un paio di giorni** the manager will be away for a couple of days; **si assenta spesso dal lavoro** he is frequently absent from work.

assente [as'sɛnte] ① AGG **a**: **assente (da)** (*gen*) away (from); (*malato, scolaro*) absent (from); **il direttore è momentaneamente assente** the manager is out at the moment
b (*espressione, sguardo*) vacant, faraway; **avere lo sguardo assente** to look miles away.
② SM/F absentee; **quanti assenti ci sono oggi?** how many people are absent today?; **non sparlare degli assenti** you shouldn't talk behind people's backs; **il grande assente alla riunione** the most notable absentee at the meeting.

assenteismo [assente'izmo] SM absenteeism.

assenteista, i, e [assente'ista] SM/F (*dal lavoro*) absentee; **è un assenteista** he is often absent.

assentire [assen'tire] VI (*aus* avere): **assentire (a)** to agree (to), assent (to).

assenza [as'sɛntsa] SF absence; **in assenza di** in the absence of; **non ho fatto nessuna assenza a scuola/in ufficio** I haven't missed a day at school/at the office; **quanto durerà la sua assenza?** how long will he be away for?

assenzio, zi [as'sɛntsjo] SM **a** (*Bot*) wormwood **b** (*liquore*) absinthe.

asserire [asse'rire] VT to maintain, assert; **ha asserito di avere ragione** he maintained (that) he was right.

asserragliarsi [asserraʎ'ʎarsi] VR: **asserragliarsi (in)** to barricade o.s. (in).

assertore, trice [asser'tore] SM/F supporter, upholder.

asservimento [asservi'mento] SM (*azione*) enslavement; (*stato, anche fig*): **asservimento (a)** slavery (to), subservience (to).

asservire [asser'vire] ① VT to enslave; (*fig: animo, passioni*) to subdue.
② **asservirsi** VR: **asservirsi (a)** to submit (to).

asserzione [asser'tsjone] SF assertion.

assessorato [assesso'rato] SM (*carica*) councillorship ▶**assessorato alla cultura** *local authority arts and entertainment department.*

assessore [asses'sore] SM councillor.

assestamento [assesta'mento] SM (*gen, Geol, Edil*) settlement; **essere in via di assestamento** (*terreno*) to be settling; **la situazione è in via di assestamento** things are settling down.

assestare [asses'tare] ① VT (*gen, Geol*) to settle; **assestare un colpo a qn** to deal sb a blow; **assestare la mira** to adjust one's aim.
② **assestarsi** VIP (*situazione ecc*) to settle down; (*terreno*) to settle.

assestato, a [asses'tato] AGG: **un colpo ben assestato** a well-aimed blow.

assetato, a [asse'tato] AGG thirsty; **assetato di** (*fig*) thirsting for; **assetato di potere** greedy for power; **assetato di sangue** bloodthirsty.

assetto [as'sɛtto] SM **a** (*ordine*) order, arrangement; **dare**

un assetto nuovo a qc to (re)arrange sth; **in assetto di guerra** ready for war **b** (*Aer, Naut*) trim; (*Aut*) balance; (*Equitazione*) seat; **assetto delle ruote** (*Aut*) (wheel) alignment; **assetto territoriale** country planning.

assiale [as'sjale] AGG axial.

assicurare [assiku'rare] 1 VT **a** (*Assicurazione: vita, casa*) to insure; (*lettera, pacco*) to register

b (*garantire*) assure; **assicurare l'avvenire ai figli** to secure the children's future; **assicurarsi qc** to secure o ensure sth for o.s.; **assicurarsi un lavoro** to get a job for o.s; **assicurare qn alla giustizia** (*arrestare*) to arrest sb **c** (*per tranquillizzare*): **assicurare qn che** to assure sb that; **te l'assicuro!** I assure you!

d (*fermare, legare*): **assicurare (a)** to secure (to); (*Alpinismo*) to belay.

2 **assicurarsi** VR **a** (*Assicurazione*): **assicurarsi (contro qc)** to insure o.s. (against sth)

b (*accertarsi*): **assicurarsi di/che** to make sure of/that **c** (*legarsi*): **assicurarsi (a)** to fasten o.s. (to), tie o.s. (to).

assicurata [assiku'rata] SF registered letter.

assicurativo, a [assikura'tivo] AGG insurance *attr*.

assicurato, a [assiku'rato] 1 AGG insured.

2 SM/F policy holder.

assicuratore, trice [assikura'tore] 1 AGG insurance *attr*; **società assicuratrice** insurance company.

2 SM/F insurance agent.

assicurazione [assikurat'tsjone] SF **a** (*conferma, garanzia*) assurance

b (*contratto*) insurance (policy) ▶**assicurazione contro furti** theft insurance ▶**assicurazione contro incendi** fire insurance ▶**assicurazione contro terzi** third party insurance ▶**assicurazione multi-rischio** comprehensive insurance ▶**assicurazione sulla vita** life insurance

c (*Alpinismo*) belaying.

assideramento [assidera'mento] SM (*Med*) exposure.

assiderare [asside'rare] 1 VT to freeze; **questo freddo mi sta assiderando** (*fig*) I'm chilled to the bone.

2 **assiderarsi** VIP to freeze; **morire assiderato** to die of exposure.

assiduamente [assidua'mente] AVV (*vedi agg*) assiduously; regularly.

assiduità [assidui'ta] SF (*vedi agg*) assiduity; regularity; **assiduità alle lezioni** (*Scol*) regular attendance at classes; **viene a trovarmi con assiduità** he comes to see me frequently.

assiduo, a [as'siduo] AGG (*cure, studio, applicazione*) assiduous; (*visitatore, lettore*) regular.

assieme [as'sjɛme] 1 AVV (*insieme*) together.

2 PREP: **assieme a** (together) with.

assillante [assil'lante] AGG (*dubbio, pensiero*) nagging; (*creditore*) pestering.

assillare [assil'lare] VT (*sogg: dubbio, pensiero, persona*) to nag at; (: *creditore*) to hound.

assillo [as'sillo] SM **a** (*pensiero tormentoso*) nagging worry, worrying thought; **aver l'assillo di qc** to be constantly worrying about sth **b** (*Zool*) horsefly, gadfly.

assimilabile [assimi'labile] AGG (*sostanza*) easily assimilated; (: *cibo*) digestible.

assimilare [assimi'lare] VT (*anche fig*) to assimilate.

assimilazione [assimilat'tsjone] SF assimilation.

assiolo [assi'ɔlo] SM horned owl.

assioma [as'sjɔma] SM axiom.

assiomatico, a, ci, che [assjo'matiko] AGG axiomatic.

assise [as'size] SFPL (*Dir*): **la Corte d'Assise** ≈ the crown court (*Brit*).

assistente [assis'tɛnte] SM/F (*gen*) assistant ▶**assistente ai lavori** supervisor ▶**assistente di polizia** inspector ▶**assistente sanitario** health worker ▶**assistente sociale** social worker ▶**assistente universitario** ≈ (assistant) lecturer ▶**assistente di volo** (*Aer*) flight attendant.

assistenza [assis'tɛntsa] SF (*aiuto*) assistance; **dare** o **prestare assistenza a qn** to assist sb, give assistance to sb; **fare opera di assistenza** to help out ▶**assistenza legale** legal aid ▶**assistenza ospedaliera** free hospital treatment ▶**assistenza sanitaria** health service ▶**assistenza sociale** social security ▶**assistenza tecnica** after-sales service ▶**assistenza a terra** (*Aer*) ground handling.

assistenziale [assisten'tsjale] AGG (*ente, organizzazione*) welfare *attr*; (*opera*) charitable.

assistenzialismo [assistentsja'lizmo] SM (*pegg*) excessive state aid.

assistere [as'sistere] VB IRREG 1 VI (*aus avere*): **assistere a** (*essere presente*) to be present at, attend; (*incidente, scena*) to witness; (*sorvegliare: lavori, esami*) to supervise.

2 VT (*aiutare*) to assist; (*malato*) to look after; (: *curare*) to treat.

assistito, a [assis'tito] 1 PP di **assistere**.

2 SM/F (*di medico*) patient; (*di avvocato, ente assistenziale*) client.

asso ['asso] SM **a** (*carta, dado*) ace; **asso di picche/cuori ecc** ace of spades/hearts *ecc*; **avere un** o **l'asso nella manica** (*fig*) to have an ace up one's sleeve; **piantare qn in asso** to leave sb in the lurch **b** (*campione*) ace; **asso del volante** ace driver.

associare [asso'tʃare] 1 VT **a** (*idee, parole, fatti*): **associare (a)** to associate (with); **il suo nome è stato associato alla Mafia** his name has been linked with the Mafia

b: **associare qn a** (*ad un circolo*) to make sb a member of; (*ad una ditta*) to take sb into partnership in; **associare qn alle carceri** to take sb to prison.

2 **associarsi** VR **a**: **associarsi con qn** (*in una ditta*) to enter into partnership with sb

b: **associarsi a** (*circolo*) to join, become a member of; (*dolori, gioie, lutto*) to share in.

associativo, a [assotʃa'tivo] AGG **a** (*Mat*) associative **b**: **quota associativa** (*a club ecc*) enrolment fee.

associato, a [asso'tʃato] 1 AGG **a**: **professore associato** ≈ senior lecturer (*Brit*), ≈ associate professor (*Am*) **b** (*di associazione*) associate.

2 SM/F (*socio*) member.

associazione [assotʃat'tsjone] SF **a** (*gen, Pol, Sport ecc*) association ▶**associazione a** o **per delinquere** (*Dir*) criminal association ▶**associazione di categoria** trade association ▶**Associazione Europea di Libero Scambio** European Free Trade Association ▶**associazione in partecipazione** (*Comm*) joint venture

b (*di idee*) association; **per associazione di idee** by association of ideas.

assodare [asso'dare] 1 VT **a** (*accertare: fatti, verità*) to ascertain **b** (*muro, posizione*) to strengthen.

2 **assodarsi** VIP (*sostanza*) to harden.

assodato, a [asso'dato] AGG well-founded.
assoggettamento [assoddʒetta'mento] SM subjection.
assoggettare [assoddʒet'tare] [1] VT (*persone*) to subjugate; (*fig*: *passioni, istinti*) to curb.
[2] **assoggettarsi** VR: **assoggettarsi a** to submit to; (*adattarsi*) to adapt to.
assolato, a [asso'lato] AGG sunny.
assoldare [assol'dare] VT (*sicario*) to hire; (*spia*) to recruit.
assolo [as'solo] SM (*Mus*) solo.
assolsi *ecc* [as'solsi] VB vedi **assolvere**.
assolto, a [as'solto] PP di **assolvere**.
assolutamente [assoluta'mente] AVV absolutely; **devo assolutamente andare** I've simply got to go; **assolutamente no** certainly not.
assolutismo [assolu'tizmo] SM absolutism.
assoluto, a [asso'luto] [1] AGG (*gen, Pol, Gramm*) absolute; **in caso di assoluta necessità** if absolutely essential; **è in assoluto il più bravo** he is without doubt o altogether the best.
[2] SM (*Filosofia*): **l'assoluto** the absolute.
assoluzione [assolut'tsjone] SF (*Rel*) absolution; (*Dir*) acquittal; **dare l'assoluzione a qn** to give sb absolution; **concedere l'assoluzione a qn** to acquit sb.
assolvere [as'solvere] VT IRREG **a**: **assolvere qn (da)** (*Rel*) to absolve sb (from); (*Dir*) to acquit sb (of) **b** (*adempiere*: *mansioni, compiti*) to carry out, perform; **assolvere il proprio dovere** to perform one's duty.
assomigliare [assomiʎ'ʎare] [1] VI (*aus* **essere** o **avere**): **assomigliare a** to resemble, look like; **assomiglia a suo padre** he looks like his father.
[2] **assomigliarsi** VR (*uso reciproco*) to be alike, resemble each other; **si assomigliano come due gocce d'acqua** they are as like as two peas (in a pod).
assommare [assom'mare] [1] VT to combine.
[2] VI (*aus* **essere**) (*ammontare*): **assommare a** to amount to, come to.
assonanza [asso'nantsa] SF assonance.
assone [as'sone] SM (*Anat*) axon.
assonnato, a [asson'nato] AGG sleepy; **hai l'aria assonnata** you look sleepy.
assonometria [assonome'tria] SF (*Mat*) axonometry.
assopimento [assopi'mento] SM doziness, sleepiness.
assopire [asso'pire] [1] VT **a**: **far assopire** to make drowsy **b** (*dolore*) to soothe.
[2] **assopirsi** VIP to doze off.
assorbente [assor'bɛnte] [1] AGG absorbent; **carta assorbente** blotting paper.
[2] SM: **assorbente (igienico)** sanitary towel ▶ **assorbente interno** tampon.
assorbimento [assorbi'mento] SM (*Chim, Fis*) absorption; (*Bot*) uptake.
assorbire [assor'bire] VT (*liquidi*) to absorb, soak up; (*suono*) to absorb; (*tempo, attenzione*) to take up, occupy; (*cultura, influenza*) to assimilate, absorb.
assordante [assor'dante] AGG (*rumore, musica*) deafening.
assordare [assor'dare] VT to deafen.
assortimento [assorti'mento] SM assortment, variety.
assortire [assor'tire] VT (*combinare*) to combine; (: *colori*) to match; (*disporre*) to arrange.
assortito, a [assor'tito] AGG **a** (*combinato*: *persone, cose, colori*): **bene/male assortito** well/badly matched **b** (*antipasti, cioccolatini*) assorted.
assorto, a [as'sorto] AGG: **essere assorto in qc** to be engrossed in sth.

assottigliare [assottiʎ'ʎare] [1] VT **a** (*affilare*) to sharpen **b** (*ridurre*: *spessore*) to make thinner, thin (down); (: *provviste*) to reduce; (: *caviglie*) to slim; (: *girovita*) to reduce, slim down.
[2] **assottigliarsi** VIP (*provviste*) to dwindle; (*caviglie, girovita*) to slim down.
assuefare [assue'fare] VB IRREG [1] VT: **assuefare a** to get used to, accustom to.
[2] **assuefarsi** VR: **assuefarsi a** to become o get accustomed o used to; (*droga*) to become addicted to.
assuefatto, a [assue'fatto] PP di **assuefare**.
assuefazione [assuefat'tsjone] SF (*Med*) addiction; **questo medicinale non dà assuefazione** this drug is not habit-forming.
assumere [as'sumere] VT IRREG **a** (*impiegato*) to take on, engage, employ **b** (*atteggiamento, espressione*) to assume, put on; (*comando, potere*) to assume, take over; (*incarico*) to take up; **assumersi il compito di fare qc** to take on the job of doing sth; **si è assunto ogni responsabilità** he's taken responsability for everything; **assumere informazioni su qn/qc** to make enquiries about sb/sth **c** (*supporre*) to assume; **assumendo (come ipotesi) che...** assuming that ... **d** (*droga*) to take **e** (*innalzare a dignità*) to raise.
assunsi *ecc* [as'sunsi] VB vedi **assumere**.
assunto, a [as'sunto] [1] PP di **assumere**.
[2] SM (*Filosofia*) proposition.
assunzione [assun'tsjone] SF **a** (*di impiegati*) employment, engagement; **ci sono state poche assunzioni** few people have been taken on; **il problema delle assunzioni** the employment problem **b** (*Rel*): **l'Assunzione** the Assumption.
assurdamente [assurda'mente] AVV absurdly.
assurdità [assurdi'ta] SF INV absurdity; **che assurdità!** how absurd!; **dire delle assurdità** to talk nonsense.
assurdo, a [as'surdo] AGG absurd.
asta ['asta] SF **a** (*palo*) pole; **bandiera a mezz'asta** flag at half-mast **b** (*di occhiali*) arm (*Brit*), stem (*Am*); (*di compasso, bilancia*) arm; (*Sci: di skilift*) bar **c** (*Comm*) auction; **mettere all'asta** to put up for auction; **vendere all'asta** to auction off; **vendita all'asta** auction sale ▶ **asta fallimentare** bankruptcy sale **d** (*nella scrittura*) stroke.
astante [as'tante] SM/F bystander.
astanteria [astante'ria] SF casualty department.
astemio, mia, mi, mie [as'tɛmjo] [1] AGG teetotal.
[2] SM/F teetotaller.
astenersi [aste'nersi] VR IRREG: **astenersi (dal fare qc/da qc)** to abstain o refrain (from doing sth/from sth); **astenersi dal dire** to refrain from saying; **astenersi dal bere/dal fumo** to keep off drink/cigarettes; **astenersi (dal voto)** (*Pol*) to abstain.
astensione [asten'sjone] SF abstention.
astensionismo [astensjo'nizmo] SM (*Pol*) abstentionism.
astensionista, i, e [astensjo'nista] SM/F (*Pol*) abstentionist.
asterisco, schi [aste'risko] SM asterisk.
asteroide [aste'rɔide] SM asteroid.
astice ['astitʃe] SM lobster.
astigiano, a [asti'dʒano] [1] AGG of o from Asti.
[2] SM/F inhabitant o native of Asti.

astigmatico, a, ci, che [astig'matiko] [1] AGG astigmatic.
[2] SM/F person suffering from astigmatism.

astigmatismo [astigma'tizmo] SM astigmatism.

astinenza [asti'nɛntsa] SF abstinence; **fare astinenza (da)** (*Rel*) to abstain (from); **essere in crisi di astinenza** (*di droga*) to suffer from withdrawal symptoms.

astio ['astjo] SM: **astio (contro)** rancour (against), resentment (towards); **portare astio a qn** to bear sb a grudge.

astiosamente [astjosa'mente] AVV resentfully.

astiosità [astjosi'ta] SF INV rancour, resentment.

astioso, a [as'tjoso] AGG resentful.

astore [as'tore] SM (*Zool*) goshawk.

astrakan ['astrakan] SM INV astrakhan.

astrale [as'trale] AGG astral; **influsso astrale** (*Astrol*) influence of the planets.

astrarre [as'trarre] VB IRREG [1] VT: **astrarre (da)** to abstract (from).
[2] **astrarsi** VR: **astrarsi da** to cut o.s. off from.

astrattamente [astratta'mente] AVV in the abstract.

astrattezza [astrat'tettsa] SF abstract nature.

astrattismo [astrat'tizmo] SM (*Arte*) abstract art.

astratto, a [as'tratto] [1] PP di **astrarre**.
[2] AGG, SM abstract; **in astratto** in the abstract.

astrazione [astrat'tsjone] SF abstraction.

astringente [astrin'dʒɛnte] AGG, SM astringent.

astro ['astro] SM (*Astron*, *fig*) star; (*Bot*) aster; **un astro nascente del cinema italiano** a rising star of Italian cinema.

astrofisica [astro'fizika] SF astrophysics *sg*.

astrologia [astrolo'dʒia] SF astrology.

astrologico, a, ci, che [astro'lɔdʒiko] AGG astrological.

astrologo, a, gi, ghe [as'trɔlogo] SM/F astrologer.

astronauta, i, e [astro'nauta] SM/F astronaut.

astronautica [astro'nautika] SF astronautics *sg*.

astronautico, a, ci, che [astro'nautiko] AGG astronautical.

astronave [astro'nave] SF spaceship.

astronomia [astrono'mia] SF astronomy.

astronomico, a, ci, che [astro'nɔmiko] AGG (*anche fig*) astronomic(al).

astronomo, a [as'trɔnomo] SM/F astronomer.

astruso, a [as'truzo] AGG (*discorso, ragionamento*) abstruse.

astuccio, ci [as'tuttʃo] SM (*per gioielli*) box, case; (*per compasso, matite*) case.

astutamente [astuta'mente] AVV astutely, shrewdly.

astuto, a [as'tuto] AGG astute, shrewd, cunning; **astuto come una volpe** cunning as a fox.

astuzia [as'tuttsja] SF (*qualità*) astuteness, shrewdness, cunning; (*azione*) trick.

AT SIGLA = *Asti*.

A.T. ABBR (= *alta tensione*) HT.

ATA ['ata] SIGLA F (= *Associazione Turistica Albergatori*) *Italian association of hoteliers*.

atavico, a, ci, che [a'taviko] AGG primitive, atavistic (*frm*).

atavismo [ata'vizmo] SM atavism.

ateismo [ate'izmo] SM atheism.

ateistico, a, ci, che [ate'istiko] AGG atheistic.

atelier [atə'lje] SM INV (*sartoria*) fashion house; (*studio*) studio; (*laboratorio*) workshop.

atemporale [atempo'rale] AGG atemporal.

Atena [a'tena] SF Athena.

Atene [a'tene] SF Athens.

ateneo [ate'nɛo] SM university.

ateniese [ate'njese] AGG, SM/F Athenian.

ateo, a ['ateo] [1] AGG atheistic.
[2] SM/F atheist.

atipico, a, ci, che [a'tipiko] AGG atypical.

Atlante [a'tlante] SM (*Mitol*) Atlas; **la catena di Atlante** the Atlas Mountains *pl*.

atlante [a'tlante] SM (*libro, Anat*) atlas.

atlantico, a, ci, che [a'tlantiko] [1] AGG Atlantic.
[2] SM: **l'(Oceano) Atlantico** the Atlantic (Ocean).

atleta, i, e [a'tlɛta] SM/F athlete.

atletica [a'tlɛtika] SF athletics *sg* ▶ **atletica leggera** track and field events *pl* ▶ **atletica pesante** weightlifting and wrestling.

atleticamente [atletika'mente] AVV athletically.

atletico, a, ci, che [a'tlɛtiko] AGG athletic.

ATM [ati'ɛmme] SIGLA F (= *Azienda Tranviaria Municipale*) *municipal bus corporation*.

atmosfera [atmos'fɛra] SF (*anche fig*) atmosphere.

atmosferico, a, ci, che [atmos'fɛriko] AGG atmospheric.

atollo [a'tɔllo] SM atoll.

atomico, a, ci, che [a'tɔmiko] AGG atomic; (*nucleare*) nuclear; **numero atomico** atomic number; **bomba atomica** atom bomb; **guerra atomica** nuclear war.

atomistica [ato'mistika] SF (*Chim*) atomic theory.

atomistico, ci [ato'mistiko] SM (*Filosofia*) atomist.

atomizzatore [atomiddza'tore] SM (*di acqua, lacca*) spray; (*di profumo*) atomizer.

atomo ['atomo] SM atom.

atono, a ['atono] AGG (*Fonetica*) unstressed.

atrio, ri ['atrjo] SM (*di albergo*) entrance hall, lobby; (*di stazione, aeroporto*) concourse; (*Storia, Anat*) atrium.

atroce [a'trotʃe] AGG (*delitto*) atrocious; (*sofferenza, destino*) terrible, dreadful; (*dolore*) excruciating; (*tempo*) ghastly, dreadful; **fa un freddo atroce** it's dreadfully cold; **in modo atroce** dreadfully; **ho l'atroce dubbio che...** I have the horrible feeling that ... .

atrocemente [atrotʃe'mente] AVV (*soffrire*) atrociously; (*seviziato, ucciso*) savagely.

atrocità [atrotʃi'ta] SF INV (*caratteristica*) atrocity, atrociousness; (*azione*) atrocity.

atrofia [atro'fia] SF atrophy.

atrofico, a, ci, che [a'trɔfiko] AGG atrophic.

atrofizzare [atrofid'dzare] VT, **atrofizzarsi** VIP to atrophy.

attaccabottoni [attakkabot'toni] SM/F INV (*fam*): **è un tremendo attaccabottoni** he'll latch onto anyone.

attaccabrighe [attakka'brige] SM/F INV quarrelsome person.

attaccamento [attakka'mento] SM (*a tradizioni ecc*) attachment; (*a persona, famiglia*) affection.

attaccante [attak'kante] SM/F (*Calcio*) forward.

attaccapanni [attakka'panni] SM INV (*su parete*) hook, peg; (*mobile*) hall stand.

attaccare [attak'kare] [1] VT **a** (*far aderire*) to attach; (*incollare: manifesto*) to stick up; (: *francobollo*) to stick (on); (*cucire*) to sew (on); (*legare*) to tie (up); (*appendere: quadro*) to hang (up)
b (*Mil, Sport, fig*) to attack
c (*cominciare: discorso, lite*) to start, begin; **attaccare discorso con qn** to start a conversation with sb
d (*contagiare, anche fig*) to affect; **ha attaccato il morbillo a sua cugina** he's given his cousin the measles.
[2] VI (*aus avere*) **a** (*incollare*) to stick
b (*aver successo*): **la nuova moda non attacca** the new fashion isn't catching on; **con me non attacca!** it doesn't

work with me!, that won't work with me!

c (*cominciare*) to start, begin; **attaccare a suonare** to strike up; **ha attaccato con una delle sue lamentele** *o* **a lamentarsi** he started whingeing.

3 **attaccarsi** VIP **a** : **attaccarsi (a)** (*appiccicarsi*) to stick (to); (*aggrapparsi*: *anche fig*) to cling (to); **le pagine si sono attaccate** the pages have stuck together; **attaccati alla corda!** hold on tight to the rope!; **è inutile che ti attacchi a dei pretesti** there's no point (in) making excuses; **attaccarsi alla bottiglia** (*fig*) to take to the bottle; **il sugo si è attaccato** the sauce has stuck

b (*affezionarsi*): **attaccarsi a** to become attached to

c (*trasmettersi per contagio*) to be contagious.

attaccaticcio, cia, ci, ce [attakka'tittʃo] 1 SM: **sapere d'attaccaticcio** to taste burnt.

2 AGG sticky; **è una persona attaccaticcia** (*fig*) he (*o* she) is a very clingy person.

attaccatura [attakka'tura] SF (*di manica*) join
▶ **attaccatura dei capelli** hairline.

attaccatutto° [attakka'tutto] SM INV superglue.

attacco, chi [at'takko] SM **a** (*Mil, Sport, anche fig*) attack; (*giocatori*) forward line, forwards *pl*; (*Alpinismo*) start; **giocare in attacco** to play an attacking game

b (*Med*) fit; **un attacco di tosse** a coughing fit; **un attacco epilettico** an epileptic fit

c (*Sci*) binding; **attacchi di sicurezza** safety bindings

d (*Tecn*) connection; (*Elettr*) socket.

attaché [ata'ʃe] SM INV (*Amm*) attaché.

attanagliare [attanaʎ'ʎare] VT (*anche fig*) to grip; **attanagliato dalla paura** gripped by fear.

attardarsi [attar'darsi] VIP to linger; **attardarsi a fare qc** (*fermarsi*) to stop to do sth; (*stare più a lungo*) to stay behind to do sth; **dev'essersi attardato in ufficio** he must have stayed on *o* behind at the office.

attecchire [attek'kire] VI (*aus avere*) (*pianta*) to take root; (*fig*) to catch on.

atteggiamento [atteddʒa'mento] SM (*disposizione mentale*) attitude; (*aria*) air; (*del corpo*) pose; **atteggiamento dimesso** unassuming attitude; **perché hai avuto quell'atteggiamento strano quando l'abbiamo incontrato?** why did you act so strangely when we met him?; **è tutto un atteggiamento il suo** it's all an act with him.

atteggiare [atted'dʒare] 1 VT: **atteggiare il viso a compassione** to assume a sympathetic expression.

2 **atteggiarsi** VR: **atteggiarsi ad artista** to play *o* act the artist.

attempato, a [attem'pato] AGG elderly.

attendarsi [atten'darsi] VIP to camp, pitch one's tent.

attendente [atten'dɛnte] SM (*Mil*) orderly, batman.

attendere [at'tɛndere] VB IRREG 1 VT (*aspettare*) to wait for, await (*frm*); **attendo l'arrivo di mio fratello** I'm waiting for my brother to arrive; **attenda in linea** hold the line, please.

2 VI (*aus avere*): **attendere a** (*dedicarsi*) to attend to.

attendibile [atten'dibile] AGG (*scusa, storia*) credible; (*fonte, testimone, notizia*) reliable; (*persona*) trustworthy.

attendibilità [attendibili'ta] SF (*vedi agg*) credibility; reliability; trustworthiness.

attenersi [atte'nersi] VR IRREG: **attenersi a** (*istruzioni, regolamento*) to keep to, stick to.

attentamente [attenta'mente] AVV (*con attenzione*) attentively; (*con cura*) carefully.

attentare [atten'tare] VI (*aus avere*): **attentare a** (*libertà, diritti*) to attack; **attentare alla vita di qn** to make an attempt on sb's life.

attentato [atten'tato] SM (*a libertà, onore*) attack; (*contro persona*) assassination attempt; **un attentato terroristico** a terrorist attack; **commettere un attentato contro qn** *o* **alla vita di qn** to make an attempt on sb's life.

attentatore, trice [attenta'tore] SM/F attacker.

attenti [at'tɛnti] 1 ESCL (*Mil*) attention!.

2 SM: **mettersi/stare sull'attenti** to come to/stand at attention.

attento, a [at'tɛnto] AGG **a** (*che presta attenzione*) attentive; **avere lo sguardo attento** to watch attentively **b** (*avviso di pericolo*): **attento!** (be) careful!, look *o* watch out!; **attenti al cane** beware of the dog; **stai attento!** (*non distrarti*) pay attention!; (*stai in guardia*) be careful! **c** (*accurato*: *esame, ricerca*) careful, thorough.

attenuante [attenu'ante] (*Dir*) 1 AGG: **circostanze attenuanti** extenuating circumstances.

2 SF extenuating *o* mitigating circumstance; **concedere le attenuanti (generiche/specifiche)** to make allowances for the (general/particular) extenuating circumstances.

attenuare [attenu'are] 1 VT (*dolore*) to ease, alleviate; (*rumore*) to reduce, deaden; (*colpo*) to soften; (*Dir: colpa*) to mitigate. 2 **attenuarsi** VIP to ease, abate.

attenuazione [attenuat'tsjone] SF (*vedi vb*) easing, alleviation; reduction; softening; mitigation.

attenzione [atten'tsjone] 1 ESCL watch out!, (be) careful!

2 SF **a** (*gen*) attention; (*cura*) care; **con attenzione** (*ascoltare*) carefully, attentively; (*esaminare*) carefully, closely; **attenzione al gradino** mind the step; **fare** *o* **prestare attenzione** (*stare in guardia*) to be careful; (*ascoltare, guardare*) to pay attention; **alla cortese attenzione di** (*Comm*) for the attention of

b : **attenzioni** SFPL (*gentilezze*) attentions; **avere mille attenzioni per qn** OR **coprire qn di attenzioni** to lavish attentions on sb.

atterraggio, gi [atter'raddʒo] SM landing; **all'atterraggio** on landing; **essere in fase di atterraggio** to be coming in to land ▶ **atterraggio di fortuna** emergency landing.

atterrare [atter'rare] 1 VI (*aus avere o essere*) (*aereo, persona*) to land.

2 VT (*avversario*) to floor, bring down.

atterrire [atter'rire] VB DIF 1 VT to terrify.

2 **atterrirsi** VIP to become terrified.

atterrito, a [atter'rito] AGG terrified.

attesa [at'tesa] SF wait; **l'attesa durò a lungo** it was a long wait; **essere in attesa di qc** to be waiting for sth; **è in attesa del terzo figlio** she is expecting her third baby; **in attesa di una vostra risposta** (*Comm*) awaiting your reply; **restiamo in attesa di Vostre ulteriori notizie** (*Comm*) we look forward to hearing (further) from you.

attesi ecc [at'tesi] VB vedi **attendere**.

atteso, a [at'teso] 1 PP di **attendere**.

2 AGG long-awaited.

attestare [attes'tare] VT: **attestare qc/che** to testify to sth/(to the fact) that.

attestato [attes'tato] SM (*certificato*) certificate; **quest'attestato certifica che** this document testifies to the fact that.

attestazione [attestat'tsjone] SF (*certificato*) certificate; (*dichiarazione*) statement.

Attica ['attika] SF Attica.

attico[1], a, ci, che ['attiko] AGG (*Storia*) Attic.

attico², **ci** ['attiko] SM (*soffitta*) attic; (*di lusso*) penthouse.

attiguità [attigui'ta] SF adjacency.

attiguo, a [at'tiguo] AGG (*contiguo*) adjoining; (*adiacente*) adjacent; **il suo appartamento è attiguo al nostro** his flat is next to ours.

Attila ['attila] SM Attila.

attillato, a [attil'lato] AGG (*vestito*) skin-tight, close-fitting.

attimo ['attimo] SM moment; **un attimo, per favore** just a moment, please; **un attimo di pazienza!** wait a moment!; **fra un attimo** in a minute *o* moment; **un attimo fa** a moment ago; **ci metto un attimo** I'll just be a minute; **in un attimo** in a moment; **attimo per attimo** moment by moment.

attinente [atti'nɛnte] AGG: **attinente a** relating to, concerning.

attinenza [atti'nɛntsa] SF connection.

attingere [at'tindʒere] VT IRREG: **attingere a** *o* **da** (*acqua*) to draw from; (*denaro, risorse*) to draw on, obtain from; **attingere informazioni a una fonte sicura** to obtain information from a reliable source.

attinia [at'tinja] SF (*Bot*) actinia.

attinto, a [at'tinto] PP di **attingere**.

attirare [atti'rare] VT (*attenzione, persona*) to attract; **l'idea mi attira** the idea appeals to me; **attirarsi delle critiche** to incur criticism.

attitudinale [attitudi'nale] AGG: **test attitudinale** aptitude test.

attitudine [atti'tudine] SF (*disposizione*) aptitude; **avere attitudine per qc** to have a flair for sth.

attivamente [attiva'mente] AVV actively; **partecipare attivamente a qc** to play an active part in sth.

attivare [atti'vare] VT (*motore, azienda*) to start; (*dispositivo, mina*) to activate; **attivare la circolazione** (*Med*) to stimulate the circulation.

attivismo [atti'vizmo] SM activism.

attivista, i, e [atti'vista] SM/F activist.

attivistico, a, ci, che [atti'vistiko] AGG activist.

attività [attivi'ta] SF INV **a** (*gen*) activity; **essere/entrare in attività** to be/become active **b** (*Comm: azienda*) business; **le attività e passività di un'azienda** the assets and liabilities of a business ▸ **attività liquide** liquid assets.

attivo, a [at'tivo] **1** AGG (*gen, Gramm*) active; (*Comm*) profit-making; **bilancio attivo** credit balance; **un'azienda attiva** a going concern.

2 SM (*Comm*) assets *pl*; **in attivo** in credit; **chiudere in attivo** to show a profit; **avere qc al proprio attivo** (*fig*) to have sth to one's credit.

attizzare [attit'tsare] VT (*fuoco*) to poke (up); (*fig: passioni, odi*) to stir up.

attizzatoio, oi [attittsa'tojo] SM poker.

atto¹ ['atto] SM **a** (*azione, gesto*) action, deed, act; **atto eroico** heroic feat; **essere in atto** to be under way; **cogliere** *o* **sorprendere qn nell'atto di fare qc** to catch sb in the act of doing sth; **all'atto pratico** in practice; **mettere in atto qc** to put into action *o* practice; **fare (l')atto di fare qc** to make as if to do sth ▸ **atti osceni (in luogo pubblico)** (*Dir*) indecent exposure (*o* obscene behaviour)

b (*dimostrazione*): **atto di fede/affetto** *ecc* act of faith/friendship *ecc*; **dare atto a qn di qc** to give sb credit for sth; **prendere atto di qc** to take note of sth

c (*Dir: documento*) document; (*del parlamento*) act; (*notarile*) deed; **atti** SMPL (*di congresso ecc*) proceedings;

(*di processo*) records; **mettere agli atti** to put on record ▸ **atto di morte** death certificate ▸ **atto di nascita** birth certificate ▸ **atto di proprietà** title deed ▸ **atto pubblico** official document ▸ **atto di vendita** bill of sale

d (*Teatro*) act; **una commedia in 3 atti** a three-act play ▸ **atto unico** one-act play.

atto², a ['atto] AGG: **atto a** a fit for, capable of; **atto alle armi** fit for military service; **atto a proseguire gli studi** capable of going on with one's studies.

attonito, a [at'tɔnito] AGG astonished, amazed, dumbfounded.

attorcigliare [attortʃiʎ'ʎare] **1** VT to twist.

2 attorcigliarsi VIP **a** to twist; **le funi si sono attorcigliate** the cords have got twisted.

3 attorcigliarsi VR (*serpente*) to coil.

attore, trice [at'tore] SM/F actor/actress; (*Dir*) plaintiff.

attorniare [attor'njare] **1** VT (*circondare*) to surround.

2 attorniarsi VR: **attorniarsi di** to surround o.s. with.

attorno [at'torno] **1** AVV around; **è entrato e si è guardato attorno** he came in and looked around *o* about him; **tutt'attorno** all around; **d'attorno = di torno**.

2 PREP: **attorno a** around, round; **stare attorno a qn** to hang round sb; **attorno al fuoco** around *o* round the fire.

attraccare [attrak'kare] VT, VI (*aus* essere *o* avere) (*Naut*) to dock, berth.

attracco, chi [at'trakko] SM (*Naut: manovra*) docking, berthing; (*: luogo*) berth.

attrae *ecc* [at'trae] VB vedi **attrarre**.

attraente [attra'ɛnte] AGG (*gen*) attractive; **dai modi attraenti** charming; **una prospettiva ben poco attraente** not a particularly attractive *o* exciting prospect.

attraggo *ecc* [at'traggo] VB vedi **attrarre**.

attrarre [at'trarre] VT IRREG (*anche fig*) to attract; **l'attrasse a sé** he drew her into his arms.

attrassi *ecc* [at'trassi] VB vedi **attrarre**.

attrattiva [attrat'tiva] SF **a** (*fascino*) attraction, charm; **esercitare una grande** *o* **forte attrattiva su qn** to hold a great attraction for sb; **dotato di grande attrattiva** charming **b** (*cosa attraente*): **attrattive** SFPL attractions; **una località che offre molte attrattive per i giovani** a town with a lot to offer to young people.

attratto, a [at'tratto] PP di **attrarre**.

attraversamento [attraversa'mento] SM crossing ▸ **attraversamento pedonale** pedestrian crossing.

attraversare [attraver'sare] VT (*strada, fiume, ponte*) to cross; (*bosco, città, periodo*) to go through; (*sogg: fiume*) to run through; **attraversare la strada di corsa** to rush across the road; **attraversare il fiume a nuoto** to swim across the river; **attraversare il ponte correndo** to run across the bridge; **il fiume attraversa la città** the river passes through the town; **attraversare un brutto periodo** to go through a bad patch; **la pallottola gli ha attraversato il braccio** the bullet went straight through his arm.

attraverso [attra'vɛrso] PREP **a** (*gen*) through; **abbiamo camminato attraverso i campi** we walked through the fields; **ha ottenuto il lavoro attraverso suo zio** he got the job through his uncle

b (*da una parte all'altra*) across; **ha nuotato attraverso il fiume** he swam across the river

c (*di tempo*) over, through; **attraverso i secoli** over *o*

through the centuries.

attrazione [attrat'tsjone] SF **a** (gen, Fis) attraction; **esercitare una grande attrazione su qc** to hold a great attraction for sb; **provare attrazione per qn** to feel attracted to sb; **uno spettacolo di grande attrazione** a very entertaining show **b** (di circo, luna park) attraction.

attrezzare [attret'tsare] VT (gen) to equip; (nave) to rig.

attrezzato, a [attret'tsato] AGG (laboratorio, studio) having the necessary equipment, fully equipped.

attrezzatura [attrettsa'tura] SF equipment no pl; (di nave) rigging ▶**attrezzature sportive** sports facilities ▶**attrezzature per uffici** office equipment.

attrezzista, i, e [attret'tsista] SM/F (Atletica) gymnast; (Teatro) propman, property man.

attrezzistica [attret'tsistika] SF gymnastics sg.

attrezzistico, a, ci, che [attret'tsistiko] AGG: **ginnastica attrezzistica** gymnastics sg.

attrezzo [at'trettso] SM tool, implement; **gli attrezzi** SMPL (Atletica) the apparatus sg.

attribuibile [attribu'ibile] AGG: **attribuibile a** attributable to.

attribuire [attribu'ire] VT: **attribuire qc a qn** (gen) to attribute sth to sb; (premio) to give o award sth to sb; **non attribuirmi colpe che non ho** don't blame me for things I didn't do; **va attribuito a lui il merito di tale successo** he should be given the credit for this success; **attribuirsi il merito di qc** to take the credit for sth; **il dipinto è stato attribuito a Picasso** the painting has been attributed to Picasso.

attributo [attri'buto] SM (gen, Gramm) attribute; **gli attributi maschili** (scherz) the male attributes.

attribuzione [attribut'tsjone] SF (vedi vb) attribution; awarding.

attrice [at'tritʃe] SF vedi **attore**.

attrito [at'trito] SM (anche fig) friction.

attuabile [attu'abile] AGG feasible.

attuabilità [attuabili'ta] SF feasibility.

attuale [attu'ale] AGG (presente) present; (di attualità) topical; (che è in atto) current; **al momento attuale** at the present moment; **lo stato attuale dell'economia** the present state of the economy; **le leggi attuali** the current legislation; **un problema attuale** a current problem; **il suo attuale ragazzo** her current boyfriend; **è un filosofo ancora attuale** his philosophy is still relevant today; **il marrone è molto attuale** (di moda) brown is very fashionable.

attualità [attuali'ta] SF INV **a** (di argomento) topicality; **un problema di grande attualità** a very topical question; **argomento d'attualità** topical subject **b** (avvenimenti) current affairs pl; **notizie d'attualità** the news sg, **settimanale d'attualità** (weekly) news magazine.

attualizzare [attualid'dzare] VT to focus attention on.

attualmente [attual'mente] AVV at the moment, at present.

attuare [attu'are] **1** VT to carry out.
2 **attuarsi** VIP to be realized.

attuazione [attuat'tsjone] SF carrying out; **di facile/difficile attuazione** easy/difficult to carry out; **l'attuazione del progetto sembra impossibile** it seems an impossible plan to carry out.

attutimento [attuti'mento] SM (di suono) deadening; (di colpo, caduta) cushioning.

attutire [attu'tire] **1** VT (colpo, caduta) to cushion; (suono) to deaden; (dolore) to ease, reduce.

2 **attutirsi** VIP (suono) to die down; (dolore) to ease.

A.U. ABBR = **allievo ufficiale**.

audace [au'datʃe] AGG **a** (coraggioso: persona) daring, audacious; (: impresa) daring, bold **b** (ipotesi) daring; (proposta) suggestive; (provocante: scollatura) daring; (sfacciato) impudent, bold.

audacemente [audatʃe'mente] AVV daringly.

audacia [au'datʃa] SF (vedi agg) daring, audacity; boldness; impudence; **tutti hanno notato l'audacia del suo vestito** everyone noticed her daring dress.

audio ['audjo] SM INV (TV, Radio, Cine) sound.

audiocassetta [audjokas'setta] SF (audio) cassette.

audioleso, a [audjo'lezo] SM/F person who is hard of hearing.

audiolibro [au'djolibro] SM talking book.

audiovisivo, a [audjovi'zivo] AGG audiovisual; **sussidi audiovisivi** audiovisual aids.

auditorio, ri [audi'torjo], **auditorium** [audi'torjum] SM auditorium.

audizione [audit'tsjone] SF hearing; (Mus) audition.

auge ['audʒe] SF: **essere in auge** to be at the top.

augurale [augu'rale] AGG: **messaggio augurale** greeting.

augurare [augu'rare] VT (buon viaggio, buonanotte ecc) to wish; **gli augurò di guarire presto** he wished him a speedy recovery; **augurarsi qc/che succeda qc** to hope for sth/that sth will happen; **me lo auguro** I hope so; **mi auguro di no/sì** I hope not/so.

augurio, ri [au'gurjo] SM **a** greeting; **auguri di Natale/ Pasqua** Christmas/Easter greetings; **biglietto di auguri** greetings card; **fare gli auguri a qn** to give sb one's best wishes, wish sb all the best; **tanti auguri!** best wishes!, all the best!; (di compleanno) happy birthday!; (buona fortuna) good luck!; **auguri di pronta guarigione!** get well soon!

b (presagio): **essere di cattivo/di buon augurio** to be ominous/a good omen.

augusto, a [au'gusto] AGG (letter) august.

aula ['aula] SF (di scuola) classroom; (di università) lecture room o theatre; (di tribunale) courtroom; (di Parlamento ecc) chamber; **silenzio in aula!** (Dir) silence in court! ▶**aula bunker** high security court for Mafia trials ▶**aula magna** main hall.

aulicamente [aulika'mente] AVV (scrivere) in a highly stylized way.

aulico, a, ci, che ['auliko] AGG (tono) dignified; (stile) refined.

aumentare [aumen'tare] **1** VT (prezzo) to increase, put up; (stipendi) to increase, raise.
2 VI (aus essere) (gen) to increase; (prezzi) to go up, rise, increase; (livello) to rise; (qualità) to improve; **aumentare di peso** (persona) to put on weight; **la produzione è aumentata del 50%** production has increased by 50%.

aumento [au'mento] SM: **aumento (di)** increase (in), rise (in); **un imprevisto aumento delle nascite** an unexpected rise in the birth rate; **ottenere un aumento (di stipendio)** to get a rise; **essere in aumento** (gen) to be rising, be going up; (qualità) to be improving.

au pair [o'pɛr] SF INV au pair (girl).

aura ['aura] SF (Med, fig) aura; (letter: venticello) light breeze.

aureo, a ['aureo] AGG (di oro) gold attr; (fig: colore, periodo) golden.

aureola [au'rɛola] SF (Rel, Astron) halo.

auricolare [auriko'lare] **1** AGG auricular, ear attr; **padi-**

glione auricolare external ear.
[2] SM (*Radio*) earphone.
aurifero, a [au'rifero] AGG gold *attr*.
aurora [au'rɔra] SF (*anche fig*) dawn.
auscultare [auskul'tare] VT (*Med*) to auscultate.
ausiliare [auzi'ljare] AGG, SM (*gen, Gramm*) auxiliary.
ausiliaria [auzi'ljarja] SF (*Mil*) *member of Women's Army Auxiliary Corps*.
ausiliario, ria, ri, rie [auzi'ljarjo] AGG, SM/F auxiliary.
ausilio [au'ziljo] SM aid; **con l'ausilio di** with the aid of.
auspicabile [auspi'kabile] AGG desirable; **è auspicabile che** it is to be hoped that.
auspicare [auspi'kare] VT to hope for; **ci si auspica che** it is hoped that.
auspicio, ci [aus'pitʃo] SM **a** (*presagio*) omen; **essere di buon auspicio** to be a good omen, augur well **b** (*aiuto,protezione*) auspices *pl*; **sotto gli auspici di** under the auspices of.
austeramente [austera'mente] AVV austerely; **vivere austeramente** to lead an austere life.
austerità [austeri'ta] SF (*gen, Econ*) austerity.
austerity [ɔs'teriti] SF INV (*Econ*) austerity.
austero, a [aus'tɛro] AGG (*persona, vita*) austere; (*disciplina*) strict.
Australasia [austra'lazja] SF: **l'Australasia** Australasia.
australe [aus'trale] AGG southern.
Australia [aus'tralja] SF: **l'Australia** Australia.
australiano, a [austra'ljano] AGG, SM/F Australian.
Austria ['austria] SF: **l'Austria** Austria.
austriaco, a, ci, che [aus'triako] AGG, SM/F Austrian.
austroungarico, a, ci, che [austroun'gariko] AGG Austro-Hungarian.
autarchia [autar'kia] SF (*Econ*) autarky; (*Pol*) autarchy.
autarchico, a, ci, che [au'tarkiko] AGG (*sistema*) self-sufficient, autarkic; (*prodotto*) home *attr*, home-produced.
aut aut ['aut 'aut] SM INV ultimatum; **dare un aut aut** to give *o* issue *o* deliver an ultimatum.
autentica, che [au'tɛntika] SF authentication.
autenticamente [autentika'mente] AVV authentically, genuinely.
autenticare [autenti'kare] VT to authenticate.
autenticità [autentitʃi'ta] SF authenticity.
autentico, a, ci, che [au'tɛntiko] AGG (*quadro, firma*) authentic, genuine; (*notizia, sentimento, fatto*) true; **è un autentico cretino** he's an absolute fool.
autismo [au'tizmo] SM (*Psic*) autism; **essere affetto da autismo** to be autistic.
autista, i, e [au'tista] SM/F driver; (*personale*) chauffeur; **auto con autista** chauffeur-driven car.
autistico, a [au'tistiko] AGG (*Psic*) autistic.
auto ['auto] SF INV (motor) car, automobile (*Am*) ▶**auto blu** official car ▶**auto da corsa** racing car (*Brit*), race car (*Am*).
auto... ['auto] PREF **a** self-, auto... **b** (*Aut*) car *attr*.
autoadesivo, a [autoade'zivo] [1] AGG self-adhesive.
[2] SM sticker.
autoambulanza [autoambu'lantsa] SF ambulance.
autoanalisi SF (*Psic*) self-analysis.
autoarticolato [autoartiko'lato] SM articulated lorry (*Brit*), semi (trailer) (*Am*).
autoassicurazione [autoassikurat'tsjone] SF (*Dir*) self-insurance; (*Alpinismo*) self belay, self-belaying system.
autoavvolgente [autoavvol'dʒɛnte] AGG: **tendina autoav-**

volgente roller blind; **cintura di sicurezza autoavvolgente** (*Aut*) inertia-reel seat-belt.
autobiografia [autobiogra'fia] SF autobiography.
autobiografico, a, ci, che [autobio'grafiko] AGG autobiographic(al).
autoblinda [auto'blinda] SF INV armoured (*Brit*) *o* armored (*Am*) car.
autobomba [auto'bomba] SF INV car carrying a . bomb; **l'autobomba si trovava a pochi metri** the car bomb was a few metres away.
autobotte [auto'botte] SF tanker.
autobus ['autobus] SM INV bus ▶**autobus a due piani** double-decker bus.
autocarro [auto'karro] SM lorry (*Brit*), truck.
autocertificazione [autotʃertifikat'tsjone] SF self-declaration.
autocisterna [autotʃis'tɛrna] SF tanker.
autoclave [auto'klave] SF autoclave.
autocolonna [autoko'lonna] SF convoy.
autocombustione [autokombus'tjone] SF spontaneous combustion.
autocommiserazione [autokommizerat'tsjone] SF self-pity.
autocompiacimento [autokompjatʃi'mento] SM self-satisfaction.
autocontrollo [autokon'trollo] SM self-control.
autocopiante [autoko'pjante] AGG: **carta autocopiante** carbonless paper.
autocrate [au'tokrate] SM autocrat.
autocratico, a, ci, che [auto'kratiko] AGG autocratic.
autocrazia [autokrat'tsia] SF autocracy.
autocritica, che [auto'kritika] SF self-criticism.
autocritico, a, ci, che [auto'kritiko] AGG self-critical.
autoctono, a [au'tɔktono] AGG, SM/F native.
autodemolizione [autodemolit'tsjone] SF breaker's yard (*Brit*), junk yard (*Am*).
autodeterminazione [autodeterminat'tsjone] SF self-determination.
autodidatta, i, e [autodi'datta] SM/F self-taught person, autodidact (*frm*); **è un autodidatta** he is self-taught.
autodidattico, a, ci, che [autodi'dattiko] AGG teach-yourself *attr*.
autodifesa [autodi'fesa] SF self-defence.
autodisciplina [autodiʃʃi'plina] SF self-discipline.
autodromo [au'tɔdromo] SM motor racing track.
autoferrotranviario, ria, ri, rie [autoferrotran'vjarjo] AGG public transport *attr*.
autofilotranviario, ria, ri, rie [autofilotran'vjarjo] AGG bus, trolley and tram *attr*.
autofurgone [autofur'gone] SM van.
autogeno, a [au'tɔdʒeno] AGG **a**: **saldatura autogena** welding **b**: **training autogeno** autogenic training, autogenics.
autogestione [autodʒes'tjone] SF worker management.
autogestito, a [autodʒes'tito] AGG (*fabbrica*) under worker management.
autogol [auto'gɔl] SM INV (*Calcio, anche fig*) own goal.
autogoverno [autogo'vɛrno] SM self-government.
autografo, a [au'tɔgrafo] AGG, SM autograph.
autogrill [auto'gril] SM INV motorway café (*Brit*), roadside restaurant (*Am*).
autoimmunità [autoimmuni'ta] SF autoimmunity.
autolavaggio, gi [autola'vaddʒo] SM (*Aut*) car wash ▶**autolavaggio automatico** (automatic) car wash.

autolesionismo [autolezjo'nizmo] SM self-destruction; (*fisicamente*) self-mutilation.

autolesionista, i, e [autolezjo'nista] AGG self-destructive.

autolettiga, ghe [autolet'tiga] SF ambulance.

autolinea [auto'linea] SF bus service.

automa, i [au'tɔma] SM (*anche fig*) automaton.

automaticamente [automatika'mente] AVV automatically.

automatico, a, ci, che [auto'matiko] [1] AGG automatic; **selezione automatica** (*Telec*) direct dialling, subscriber trunk dialling.
[2] SM (*bottone*) press stud, snap fastener.
[3] SF: **(pistola) automatica** automatic (pistol).

automatismo [automa'tizmo] SM (*Tecn: metodo*) automation; (*: congegno*) mechanism; (*Psic*) automatism.

automatizzare [automatid'dzare] VT to automate.

automazione [automat'tsjone] SF automation ▶**automazione delle procedure d'ufficio** office automation.

automedicazione [automedikat'tjone] SF: **medicinale di automedicazione** self-medication.

automezzo [auto'mɛddzo] SM motor vehicle.

automobile [auto'mɔbile] SF (*motor*) car, automobile (*Am*); **viaggiare in automobile** to travel by car.

automobilina [automobi'lina] SF (*toy*) car.

automobilismo [automobi'lizmo] SM (*gen*) motoring; (*Sport*) motor racing.

automobilista, i, e [automobi'lista] SM/F motorist.

automobilistico, a, ci, che [automobi'listiko] AGG (*industria, assicurazione, incidente*) car *attr*, automobile *attr* (*Am*); (*sport*) motor *attr*.

automotrice [automo'tritʃe] SF railcar.

autonoleggio, gi [autono'leddʒo] SM car hire (*Brit*), car rental.

autonomamente [autonoma'mente] AVV independently, autonomously.

autonomia [autono'mia] SF (*Pol*) autonomy; (*fig: di idee, comportamento*) independence; (*Tecn: di macchine, motori*) range ▶**autonomia di volo** (*Aer*) flight range.

autonomista, i, e [autono'mista] AGG, SM/F (*Pol*) autonomist.

autonomo, a [au'tɔnomo] [1] AGG (*Pol*) autonomous; (*sindacato, pensiero*) independent; **lavoro autonomo** self-employment.
[2]: **autonomi** SMPL *independent trade union members*.

autoparcheggio, gi [autopar'keddʒo] SM car park (*Brit*), parking lot (*Am*).

autoparco, chi [auto'parko] SM (*insieme di automezzi*) transport fleet; (*parcheggio*) car park (*Brit*), parking lot (*Am*).

autopilota, i [autopi'lɔta] SM (*Aer*) autopilot.

autopista [auto'pista] SF fairground race track.

autopompa [auto'pompa] SF fire engine.

autopsia [autop'sia] SF autopsy, post-mortem (examination).

autopubblica, che [auto'pubblika] SF taxi.

autopulente [autopu'lɛnte] AGG (*forno*) self-cleaning.

autopullman [auto'pulman] SM INV (*di linea*) bus; (*per gite turistiche*) coach.

autoradio [auto'radjo] SF INV (*apparecchio*) car radio; (*autoveicolo*) radio car.

autoraduno [autora'duno] SM (*Sport*) motor racing meeting.

autore, trice [au'tore] SM/F (*gen, scrittore*) author; (*di pittura*) painter; (*di scultura*) sculptor; (*di musica*) composer; **l'autore del delitto/del furto** the person who committed the crime/the robbery; **quadro d'autore** painting by a famous artist; **diritti d'autore** copyright *sg*; (*compenso*) royalties.

autoregolamentazione [autoregolamentat'tsjone] SF self-regulation.

autorespiratore [autorespira'tore] SM (*sub*) breathing apparatus ▶**autorespiratore ad aria** aqualung ▶**autorespiratore ad ossigeno** oxygen re-breather.

autorevole [auto'revole] AGG (*giudizio*) authoritative; (*fonte*) reliable; (*influente: persona*) influential.

autorevolezza [autorevo'lettsa] SF authority.

autorevolmente [autorevol'mente] AVV authoritatively, with authority.

autorilevazione [autorilevat'tsjone] SF (*Inform*): **autorilevazione di errori** automatic error detection.

autorimessa [autori'messa] SF garage.

autorità [autori'ta] SF INV **a** (*potere*) authority; **agire d'autorità** to act with authority, have the authority to act; **esercitare la propria autorità su qn** to exercise one's authority over sb
b (*Amm: governo, ente*): **l'autorità** [OR] **le autorità** the authorities *pl*; **le autorità competenti** the relevant authorities; **erano presenti tutte le autorità** all the public services were represented
c (*esperto*) authority, expert; **è una vera autorità in questo campo** he's a real expert in this field
d (*prestigio*) repute.

autoritariamente [autoritarja'mente] AVV in an authoritarian way.

autoritario, ria, ri, rie [autori'tarjo] AGG (*sistema, persona*) authoritarian.

autoritarismo [autorita'rizmo] SM authoritarianism.

autoritratto [autori'tratto] SM self-portrait.

autorizzare [autorid'dzare] VT to give permission for, to authorize; **autorizzare qn a fare qc** to give sb permission to do sth; **"vietato l'accesso al personale non autorizzato"** "authorized personnel only".

autorizzazione [autoriddzat'tsjone] SF (*permesso*) authorization, permission; (*documento*) permit ▶**autorizzazione a procedere** (*Dir*) authorization to proceed.

autosalone [autosa'lone] SM car showroom.

autoscatto [autos'katto] SM (*Fot*) self-timer.

autoscontro [autos'kontro] SM dodgem car (*Brit*), bumper car (*Am*).

autoscuola [autos'kwɔla] SF driving school.

autosnodato [autozno'dato] SM articulated vehicle.

autostazione [autostat'tsjone] SF (*Aut*) service station; (*di corriere*) bus station.

autostop [autos'tɔp] SM hitchhiking; **fare l'autostop** to hitchhike; **è andato a Parigi in** *o* **con l'autostop** he hitchhiked to Paris.

autostoppista, i, e [autostop'pista] SM/F hitchhiker.

autostrada [autos'trada] SF motorway (*Brit*), highway (*Am*).

autostradale [autostra'dale] AGG motorway *attr*.

autosufficiente [autosuffi'tʃɛnte] AGG self-sufficient.

autosufficienza [autosuffi'tʃɛntsa] SF self-sufficiency.

autosuggestionarsi [autosuddʒestjo'narsi] VR to get o.s. into a state.

autosuggestione [autosuddʒes'tjone] SF (*Psic*) autosuggestion.

autotassazione [autotassat'tsjone] SF *tax system where people assess themselves.*

autotrasportatore [autotrasporta'tore] SM road haulier.

autotrasporto [autotras'porto] SM (*di persone*) road transport; (*di merci*) road haulage.

autotreno [auto'trɛno] SM lorry with trailer (*Brit*), trailer truck (*Am*).

autovaccino [autovat'tʃino] SM autogenous vaccine.

autoveicolo [autove'ikolo] SM motor vehicle.

autovettura [autovet'tura] SF (motor) car.

autunnale [autun'nale] AGG (*di autunno*) autumn *attr*, fall *attr* (*Am*); (*da autunno*) autumnal.

autunno [au'tunno] SM autumn, fall (*Am*); **l'autunno della vita** the autumn of life *o* one's years.

AV SIGLA = *Avellino*.

a/v ABBR (*Comm*) = **a vista**; vedi **vista**.

avallare [aval'lare] VT (*Fin*) to guarantee; (*sostenere*) to back; (*confermare*) to confirm.

avallo [a'vallo] SM (*Fin*) guarantee.

avambraccio, ci [avam'brattʃo] SM forearm.

avamposto [avam'posto] SM (*Mil*) outpost.

Avana [a'vana] SF: **l'Avana** Havana.

avana [a'vana] **1** SM INV (*sigaro*) Havana (cigar); (*colore*) tobacco-coloured.
2 AGG (*colore*) tobacco-brown.

avance [a'vãs] SF (*pl* avances): **fare delle avances a qn** to make advances to sb.

avanguardia [avan'gwardja] SF **a** (*Mil*, *fig*) vanguard; **essere all'avanguardia** to be in the vanguard **b** (*Arte*) avant-garde; **d'avanguardia** avant-garde *attr*.

avanguardismo [avangwar'dizmo] SM avant-garde trend.

avanguardista, i, e [avangwar'dista] SM/F avant-garde artist.

avanscoperta [avansko'pɛrta] SF (*Mil*) reconnaissance; **andare in avanscoperta** to reconnoitre.

avanspettacolo [avanspet'takolo] SM (*Teatro*) curtain raiser.

avanti [a'vanti] **1** AVV **a** (*moto: andare, venire*) forward; **fare un passo avanti** to take a step forward; **farsi avanti** to come forward; **piegarsi in avanti** to bend forward; **avanti e indietro** backwards and forwards, to and fro; **essere avanti negli studi** (*a scuola*) to be well ahead in one's studies; **essere avanti di 5 punti** (*Sport ecc*) to be ahead *o* be leading by 5 points; **tirare avanti** (*fig*) to get by, survive
b (*tempo: prima*) before; **l'anno avanti** the year before
c (*tempo: posteriore a*): **d'ora in avanti** from now on; **essere avanti con gli *o* negli anni** to be well on in years; **il mio orologio è *o* va avanti** my watch is fast; **mettere avanti l'orologio** to put the clock forward; **guardare avanti** to look ahead
d : **andare avanti** to go forward; (*continuare*) to go on, carry on; (*fig: fare progressi*) to get on; (*: sopravvivere*) to get by; **non aspettatemi, andate avanti!** don't wait for me, go on (ahead)!; **non possiamo andare avanti così** we can't carry *o* go on like this; **la mia tesi sta andando avanti** my thesis is coming on
e : **mandare avanti la famiglia** to provide for one's family; **mandare avanti un'azienda** to run a business
f : **avanti!** (*entra*) come in!; (*non fare così*) come on!; **avanti! si accomodi!** come (*o* go) in and sit down!; **avanti il prossimo!** next please!; **avanti, march!** forward, march!; **avanti tutta!** (*Naut*) full speed ahead!.

2 PREP: **avanti a** (*luogo*) before, in front of; (*tempo*) before; **avanti Cristo** before Christ.
3 SM INV (*Sport*) forward.

avantielenco [avantie'lɛnko] SM *general information section of the phone book.*

avantreno [avan'trɛno] SM (*Aut*) front chassis.

avanzamento [avantsa'mento] SM (*gen*) advance; (*progresso*) progress; (*promozione di grado*) promotion.

avanzare[1] [avan'tsare] **1** VT (*proposta ecc*) to put forward; (*spostare in avanti: oggetto*) to move forward; **avanzare qn di grado** to promote sb.
2 VI (*aus essere o avere*) (*procedere*) to advance, move forward; (*stagioni*) approach; (*fig: nello studio ecc*) to make progress; **avanzare negli anni** to grow older, get on; **con l'avanzare degli anni** with the passing of time; **avanzare di grado** to be promoted.

avanzare[2] [avan'tsare] **1** VI (*aus essere*) **a** (*essere d'avanzo*) to be left over, remain; **è avanzato del pane da ieri** there is some bread left over from yesterday; **non m'avanza molto tempo** I haven't (got) much time left; **basta e avanza** that's more than enough
b (*Mat*): **sette diviso tre fa due e avanza uno** seven divided by three is two remainder one.
2 VT: **avanzare qc (da qn)** (*essere creditore*) to be owed sth by sb; **avanzo diecimila lire da te** you owe me ten thousand lire.

avanzata [avan'tsata] SF (*Mil*) advance.

avanzato, a [avan'tsato] AGG (*teoria, tecnica*) advanced; **essere in età avanzata** to be of an advanced age; **a primavera avanzata** late on in *o* in late spring; **a un'ora avanzata della notte** late at night.

avanzo [a'vantso] SM **a** (*gen, Mat*) remainder; (*di stoffa*) remnant; (*di carta*) scrap; **avanzo di galera** (*fig*) jailbird; **avanzi** SMPL (*di cibo*) leftovers **b** (*sovrappiù*): **averne d'avanzo (di qc)** to have more than enough (of sth); **ce n'è d'avanzo** there is more than enough **c** (*Comm*) surplus; (*eccedenza di bilancio*) profit carried forward.

avaramente [avara'mente] AVV meanly, stingily.

avaria [ava'ria] SF (*guasto meccanico*) breakdown, failure; (*danneggiamento*) damage; **motore in avaria** engine out of action; **subire un'avaria all'elica** to suffer *o* have a damaged propeller.

avariare [ava'rjare] **1** VT to damage.
2 **avariarsi** VIP (*cibo*) to go off, go bad.

avariato, a [ava'rjato] AGG (*cibo*) off; (*merce*) damaged.

avarizia [ava'rittsja] SF (*peccato*) avarice; (*tirchieria*) meanness, stinginess; **crepi l'avarizia!** to hang with the expense!

avaro, a [a'varo] **1** AGG **a** (*tirchio*) mean, stingy, tight-fisted **b** : **avaro di** (*complimenti, parole*) sparing (with).
2 SM/F miser.

avemaria [avema'ria] SF INV (*preghiera*) Hail Mary, Ave Maria; (*suono delle campane*) Angelus.

avena [a'vena] SF oats *pl*.

---

avere [a'vere] VB IRREG
1 VT
a (*gen*) to have; (*ricevere, ottenere*) to get; (*indossare*) to wear, have on;
▷**avere da *bere*** to have something to drink
▷**avere da *mangiare*** to have something to eat
▷**non ha soldi** he has no money, he doesn't have any money, he hasn't got any money

▷**ho le mani sporche** my hands are dirty

▷**aveva le mani che gli tremavano** his hands were shaking

b (*età, forma, colore*) to be;

▷**quanti** *anni* **hai?** how old are you?

▷**ho vent'***anni* I am twenty (years old)

▷**ha 2** *anni* **più di me** he's two years older than me

▷**aveva la mia stessa** *età* he was the same age as me

▷**avere** *fame* to be hungry

▷**avere** *paura* to be afraid

c (*tempo*)

▷**ne hai ancora** *per* **molto?** have you got much longer to go?

▷**ne avremo ancora** *per* **due giorni prima di arrivare a Londra** we've got another two days to go before we get to London

▷**quanti ne abbiamo oggi?** what's the date today?

d (*fraseologia*)

▷**averne fin sopra i** *capelli* (*fam*) to be fed up to the teeth

▷**ce l'hai** *con* **me?** are you angry with me?

▷**cos'hai?** what's wrong *o* what's the matter (with you)?

▷**avere qc** *da* fare to have sth to do;

▷**ho ancora due lettere** *da* **scrivere** I have to *o* must write another two letters, I've still got two letters to write

▷**non hai che** *da* **dirglielo** you only have to tell him

▷**non hai** *da* **preoccuparti per me** you don't have to *o* needn't worry about me.

▷**ma cos'hai** *da* **lamentarti?** what have you got to complain about?

▷**questo non ha niente a che** *vedere o fare* **con me** that's got nothing to do with me.

2 VB AUS

(*con participio passato*): **lo hai/avevi sentito?** have/had you heard from him?;

▷**l'ho incontrata ieri** I met her yesterday

▷**quando l'avrò visto, ti dirò** when I've seen him, I'll let you know

3 VB IMPERS

▷*si* **è avuto un risultato imprevisto** there was a surprising result

▷**ieri** *si* **è avuto un abbassamento di temperatura** there was a drop in temperature yesterday.

4 SM

a : **il** *dare* **e l'avere** (*Fin*) debits and credits *pl*

b (*ricchezze*): **gli averi** SMPL wealth *sg*, fortune *sg*.

averla [a'vɛrla] SF (*Zool*) red-backed shrike.

aviatore, trice [avja'tore] SM/F pilot, aviator.

aviatorio, ria, ri, rie [avja'tɔrjo] AGG air *attr*, aviation *attr*.

aviazione [avjat'tsjone] SF aviation ▶**aviazione civile** civil aviation ▶**aviazione militare** air force.

avicoltura [avikol'tura] SF (*di pollame*) poultry farming; (*di uccelli*) bird breeding.

avidamente [avida'mente] AVV (*gen*) greedily; (*leggere*) avidly.

avidità [avidi'ta] SF: **avidità (di)** (*denaro ecc*) greed (for); (*gloria*) thirst (for).

avido, a ['avido] AGG: **avido (di)** (*pegg*) greedy (for); (*fig: di conoscenza*) eager (for).

aviere [a'vjɛre] SM (*Mil*) airman.

aviogetto [avjo'dʒɛtto] SM jet.

aviorimessa [avjori'messa] SF hangar.

aviotrasportato, a [avjotraspor'tato] AGG (*truppe*) airborne.

avitaminosi [avitami'nɔzi] SF vitamin deficiency.

avo ['avo] SM (*antenato*) ancestor; (*letter: nonno*) grandfather; **i miei avi** my forebears; **i nostri avi** our ancestors.

avocado [avo'kado] SM INV (*albero*) avocado; (*frutto*) avocado (pear).

avorio, ri [a'vɔrjo] SM ivory; **torre d'avorio** (*fig*) ivory tower.

avulso, a [a'vulso] AGG: **parole avulse dal contesto** words taken out of context; **avulso dalla società** (*fig*) cut off from society.

avuto [a'vuto] PP di **avere**.

avv. ABBR = *avvocato*.

avvalersi [avva'lersi] VIP: **avvalersi di** to avail o.s. of.

avvallamento [avvalla'mento] SM (*Geol*) depression, sinking *no pl*; (*di strada ecc*) subsidence.

avvalorare [avvalo'rare] VT (*comprovare*) to confirm; **avvalorare una tesi** to confirm a theory.

avvampare [avvam'pare] VI (*aus essere*) (*fuoco*) to flare up; (*fig: cielo, nuvole*) to become red; (: *arrossire*) to blush; **avvampare per la collera** to flare up with anger.

avvantaggiare [avvantad'dʒare] **1** VT (*favorire*) to favour (*Brit*), favor (*Am*).
2 **avvantaggiarsi** VR **a** (*acquistare vantaggio*) to gain an advantage *o* get ahead; **avvantaggiarsi nella carriera/nello studio** to get ahead in one's career/in one's studies; **avvantaggiarsi di qualche metro/minuto** to gain a few metres/minutes; **avvantaggiarsi su qn** to get ahead of sb
b (*avvalersi*): **avvantaggiarsi di** to take advantage of.

avvedersi [avve'dersi] VIP IRREG: **avvedersi di qn/qc** to notice sb/sth.

avvedutamente [avveduta'mente] AVV (*vedi agg*) prudently; astutely.

avvedutezza [avvedu'tettsa] SF (*vedi agg*) prudence; astuteness.

avveduto, a [avve'duto] AGG (*accorto*) prudent; (*scaltro*) astute.

avvelenamento [avvelena'mento] SM poisoning.

avvelenare [avvele'nare] **1** VT to poison; **avvelenare l'esistenza a qn** to make sb's life a misery; **è inutile avvelenarsi il sangue per così poco** there's no point in making yourself miserable over nothing.
2 **avvelenarsi** VR to poison o.s.

avvelenatore, trice [avvelena'tore] SM/F poisoner.

avvenente [avve'nɛnte] AGG attractive.

avvenenza [avve'nɛntsa] SF attractiveness.

avvengo *ecc* [av'vɛngo] VB vedi **avvenire**.

avvenimento [avveni'mento] SM event.

avvenire [avve'nire] **1** VI IRREG (*aus essere*) to happen, occur.
2 AGG INV future *attr*.
3 SM (*gen*) future; (*carriera*) future, prospects *pl*; **in avvenire** in the future.

avveniristico, a, ci, che [avveni'ristiko] AGG futuristic.

avvenni *ecc* [av'venni] VB vedi **avvenire**.

avventare [avven'tare] **1** VT (*scagliare*): **gli avventò contro il cane** he set the dog on him.
2 **avventarsi** VR (*scagliarsi*): **avventarsi su** *o* **contro qn/qc** to hurl o.s. at sb/sth.

avventatamente [avventata'mente] AVV rashly.

avventatezza [avventa'tettsa] SF rashness.

avventato, a [avven'tato] AGG (giudizio) rash.

avventiziato [avventit'tsjato] SM (di impiegato) temporary employment; (di operaio) casual labour o work.

avventizio, zia, zi, zie [avven'tittsjo] [1] AGG (impiegato) temporary; (guadagno) casual.
[2] SM temporary clerk.

avvento [av'vɛnto] SM **a** (venuta) coming, advent; **avvento al trono** accession to the throne **b** (Rel): **l'Avvento** Advent.

avventore [avven'tore] SM customer.

avventura [avven'tura] SF (gen) adventure; (vicenda amorosa) (love) affair; **avere spirito d'avventura** to be adventurous.

avventurarsi [avventu'rarsi] VR: **avventurarsi (in qc)** to venture (into sth).

avventuriero, a [avventu'rjɛro] SM/F adventurer/tress.

avventurosamente [avventurosa'mente] AVV adventurously; **vivere avventurosamente** to lead an adventurous life.

avventuroso, a [avventu'roso] AGG adventurous.

avvenuto, a [avve'nuto] PP di **avvenire**.

avverarsi [avve'rarsi] VIP to come true.

avverbiale [avver'bjale] AGG adverbial.

avverbialmente [avverbjal'mente] AVV adverbially.

avverbio, bi [av'vɛrbjo] SM adverb.

avverrà ecc [avver'ra] VB vedi **avvenire**.

avversare [avver'sare] VT to oppose.

avversario, ria, ri, rie [avver'sarjo] [1] AGG opposing.
[2] SM/F (Sport) opponent; (Pol) adversary, opponent.

avversione [avver'sjone] SF: **avversione (per)** loathing (for), aversion (to); **nutrire un'avversione per** to harbour a dislike for.

avversità [avversi'ta] SF INV adversity; **le avversità della vita** life's tribulations.

avverso, a [av'vɛrso] AGG (forze, sorte) adverse, hostile; (tempo) unfavourable (Brit), unfavorable (Am), adverse; (persona: contrario): **avverso a** against.

avvertenza [avver'tɛntsa] SF **a** (avviso) warning; **avvertenza ai lettori** (prefazione) foreword **b** (cautela) care no pl **c** (per l'uso): **avvertenze** SFPL instructions.

avvertibile [avver'tibile] AGG (suono, movimento) perceptible.

avvertimento [avverti'mento] SM warning.

avvertire [avver'tire] VT **a** (informare): **avvertire (di)** to inform (of), let know (of); **avvertimi prima di partire** let me know when you're leaving **b** (ammonire) to warn **c** (percepire: suono) to perceive, hear; (sentire: dolore) to feel.

avvezzo, a [av'vettso] AGG: **avvezzo a** accustomed to, used to.

avviamento [avvia'mento] SM **a** (gen, atto) starting; (: effetto) start
b (insegnamento preparatorio: ad una carriera) training; (: ad uno studio) introduction
c (Meccanica: messa in moto) starting; **avviamento a freddo** cold start; **motorino d'avviamento** starter (motor)
d (Comm) goodwill.

avviare [avvi'are] [1] VT **a** (indirizzare: a studi, mestiere) to lead, direct
b (mettere in moto) to start (up); **avviare con la manovella** (Aut) to crank, give a crank start to

c (iniziare: attività, impresa) to start up, set up; (: trattative) to set in motion; (: discussione) to get going; (: lavoro a maglia) to cast on.
[2] **avviarsi** VIP (incamminarsi): **avviarsi (a o verso qc)** to set out o off (for sth); (fig: essere sul punto di): **avviarsi a fare qc** to be about to do sth, be on the point of doing sth; **avviati, poi ti raggiungo** you go on ahead and I'll catch you up; **l'estate si avvia alla fine** summer is drawing to an end.

avviato, a [avvi'ato] [1] AGG (attività, negozio) thriving; **"vendesi attività ben avviata"** "profitable business for sale".
[2] SM/F person who has found his (o her) first job.

avvicendamento [avvitʃenda'mento] SM (gen) alternation; (Agr: delle colture) rotation; **c'è molto avvicendamento di personale** there is a high turnover of staff.

avvicendare [avvitʃen'dare] [1] VT to alternate.
[2] **avvicendarsi** VR (uso reciproco) to alternate; **si avvicendano in cucina** they take it in turns in the kitchen.

avvicinabile [avvitʃi'nabile] AGG (fig: persona) approachable.

avvicinamento [avvitʃina'mento] SM (Mil, Aer) approach; **ha ottenuto un avvicinamento** (soldato) he has been posted nearer home; (in un lavoro) he has been given a transfer nearer home; **l'avvicinamento dei due paesi** the rapprochement between the two countries.

avvicinare [avvitʃi'nare] [1] VT **a** (mettere vicino): **avvicinare (a)** to bring near (to); **avvicina la sedia al tavolo** bring the chair nearer to the table, draw the chair up to the table; **il dolore li ha avvicinati** (fig) their sorrow has brought them closer together
b (farsi vicino a: persona) to approach; **lo avvicinò per strada e si presentò** she came up to him in the street and introduced herself.
[2] **avvicinarsi** VIP (andare vicino): **avvicinarsi (a)** to approach, go (o come) up to; **il treno si avvicinava alla stazione** the train was approaching the station; **avvicinati!** come here!, come closer!; **mi si avvicinò un mendicante** a beggar came up to me
b (essere imminente: stagione, periodo) to draw near
c (somigliare): **avvicinarsi (a)** to be similar (to), be close (to).

avvilente [avvi'lɛnte] AGG (umiliante) humiliating; (scoraggiante) discouraging, disheartening.

avvilimento [avvili'mento] SM (vedi vb) humiliation; discouragement.

avvilire [avvi'lire] [1] VT (mortificare) to humiliate; (scoraggiare) to dishearten, discourage; (degradare) to degrade.
[2] **avvilirsi** VIP to lose heart, become discouraged.

avvilito, a [avvi'lito] AGG (scoraggiato) disheartened, discouraged; (depresso) depressed.

avviluppare [avvilup'pare] [1] VT **a** (avvolgere): **avviluppare (in)** to wrap up (in); (sogg: nebbia) to envelop
b (ingarbugliare) to entangle.
[2] **avvilupparsi** VR (avvolgersi): **avvilupparsi in qc** to wrap o.s. up in sth.
[3] **avvilupparsi** VIP (aggrovigliarsi) to get entangled o tangled up.

avvinazzato, a [avvinat'tsato] [1] AGG drunken.
[2] SM/F drunkard.

avvincente [avvin'tʃɛnte] AGG (spettacolo, lettura) enthralling.

avvincere [av'vintʃere] VT IRREG (*sogg: spettacolo, lettura*) to enthral, fascinate.

avvinghiare [avvin'gjare] [1] VT to clutch, clasp.

[2] **avvinghiarsi** VR: **avvinghiarsi a** to cling to; **gli si avvinghiò al collo** she threw her arms round his neck.

avvinsi *ecc* [av'vinsi] VB vedi **avvincere**.

avvinto, a [av'vinto] PP di **avvincere**.

avvio, vii [av'vio] SM start, beginning; **dare l'avvio a qc** to start sth off; **prendere l'avvio** to get going, get under way.

avvisaglia [avvi'zaʎʎa] SF: **le prime avvisaglie** (*sintomo: di temporale ecc*) the first signs; (: *di malattia*) the first signs, the first symptoms.

avvisare [avvi'zare] VT **a** (*informare*) to inform, notify **b** (*mettere in guardia*) to warn; **uomo avvisato, mezzo salvato** (*Proverbio*) forewarned is forearmed.

avvisatore [avviza'tore] SM (*apparecchio d'allarme*) alarm ▶**avvisatore acustico** horn ▶**avvisatore d'incendio** fire alarm.

avviso [av'vizo] SM **a** (*comunicazione: al pubblico*) notice; **dare l'avviso a qn di qc** to give sb notice of sth; **fino a nuovo avviso** until further notice

b (*documento di notificazione*) notice ▶**avviso di garanzia** notification (*of impending investigation and of the right to name a defence lawyer*) ▶**avviso di sfratto** eviction order

c (*Comm*): **avviso di consegna** consignment note ▶**avviso di pagamento** payment advice ▶**avviso di spedizione** delivery note

d (*consiglio, avvertimento*) warning; **dare un avviso a qn** to warn sb; **mettere qn sull'avviso** to put sb on their guard

e (*opinione*) opinion; **a mio avviso** in my opinion

f (*inserzione pubblicitaria*) advertisement, ad.

avvistamento [avvista'mento] SM sighting.

avvistare [avvis'tare] VT to sight.

avvitare [avvi'tare] [1] VT (*vite*) to screw in (*o* down); (*fissare con viti*) to screw; (*lampadina*) to screw in.

[2] **avvitarsi** VR (*vite, lampadina*) to screw in; (*Aer*) to spin, go into a spin.

avvizzimento [avvittsi'mento] SM withering.

avvizzire [avvit'tsire] VI (*aus* essere), **avvizzirsi** VIP to wither, shrivel.

avvizzito, a [avvit'tsito] AGG withered, shrivelled.

avvocatessa [avvoka'tessa] SF (*fam*) (female) lawyer.

avvocato [avvo'kato] SM **a** (*gen*) lawyer; (*in corti inferiori*) solicitor; (*in corti superiori*) barrister (*Brit*), attorney(-at-law) (*Am*); **consultare il proprio avvocato** to consult one's lawyer; **avvocato di parte civile/difensore** counsel for the plaintiff/the defence

b (*fig*) advocate, defender ▶**avvocato delle cause perse** defender of lost causes ▶**avvocato del diavolo** devil's advocate; **fare l'avvocato del diavolo** to play devil's advocate.

avvocatura [avvoka'tura] SF **a** (*professione*) legal profession; **esercitare l'avvocatura** to practise law **b** (*insieme degli avvocati*): **l'avvocatura** the Bar.

avvolgere [av'vɔldʒere] VB IRREG [1] VT **a** (*bambino, oggetto*) to wrap (up); (*arrotolare: tappeto*) to roll up; (: *bobina*) to wind up; **avvolto dalla nebbia** enveloped in fog; **avvolto dal mistero/silenzio** shrouded in mystery/silence

b : **avvolgere qc intorno a qc** to wind sth round sth.

[2] **avvolgersi** VR: **si avvolse nel mantello** he wrapped himself (up) in his cloak.

avvolgibile [avvol'dʒibile] [1] AGG roll-up *attr*, roller *attr*.

[2] SM (roller) blind (*Brit*), window shade (*Am*).

avvolgimento [avvoldʒi'mento] SM (*Elettr*) winding.

avvolsi *ecc* [av'vɔlsi] VB vedi **avvolgere**.

avvolto, a [av'vɔlto] PP di **avvolgere**.

avvoltoio, oi [avvol'tojo] SM (*gen, fig*) vulture.

avvoltolare [avvolto'lare] [1] VT to roll up.

[2] **avvoltolarsi** VR (*rotolarsi: nel fango*) to roll (around).

azalea [addza'lɛa] SF azalea.

Azerbaigian [addzɛrbai'dʒan] SM Azerbaijan.

azerbaigiano, a [addzerbai'dzano] [1] AGG Azerbaijani.

[2] SM/F Azerbaijani.

[3] SM (*lingua*) Azerbaijani.

azero [ad'dʒɛro] AGG, SM/F Azeri.

azienda [ad'dzjɛnda] SF (*gen*) company, business, firm, concern ▶**azienda agricola** commercial farm ▶**azienda (autonoma) di soggiorno e turismo** tourist board ▶**azienda avicola** poultry farm ▶**azienda a partecipazione statale** *company in which the state has a controlling interest* ▶**azienda pubblica** state (run) company.

aziendale [addzjen'dale] AGG company *attr*; **mensa aziendale** company canteen; **organizzazione aziendale** business administration.

azimut ['addzimut] SM INV (*Astron*) azimuth.

azionabile [attsjo'nabile] AGG (*macchina ecc*) that can be operated; **questa macchina è azionabile tramite l'uso di questa leva** this machine is operated by this lever.

azionare [attsjo'nare] VT to activate.

azionario, ria, ri, rie [attsjo'narjo] AGG share *attr*; **mercato azionario** stock market; **capitale azionario** share capital.

azione[1] [at'tsjone] SF **a** (*l'agire*) action; **entrare in azione** (*piano*) to come into operation; **passare all'azione** to take action; (*Mil*) to go into action

b (*atto*) action, act; **buona/cattiva azione** good/bad deed

c (*effetto*) action; **l'azione dei gas tossici** the action of toxic gases

d (*Teatro, Sport*) action; (*trama*) plot; **film d'azione** action movie

e (*Dir: processo*) (law)suit, action.

azione[2] [at'tsjone] SF (*Fin: titolo*) share (*Brit*), stock (*Am*) ▶**azioni ordinarie** ordinary shares ▶**azioni preferenziali** preference shares (*Brit*), preferred stock *sg* (*Am*).

azionista, i, e [attsjo'nista] SM/F shareholder.

azoto [ad'dzɔto] SM nitrogen.

azteco, a, chi, che [as'tɛko] AGG, SM/F Aztec.

azzannare [attsan'nare] VT to maul, bite.

azzardare [addzar'dare] [1] VT (*domanda, ipotesi*) to hazard, venture; (*uso assoluto*) to take a risk.

[2] **azzardarsi** VIP: **azzardarsi a fare qc** to dare (to) do sth.

azzardato, a [addzar'dato] AGG (*ipotesi, risposta*) rash; (*impresa*) risky; **non voglio dare un parere azzardato, ma... I don't want to be hasty** *o* rash, but ... .

azzardo [ad'dzardo] SM risk; **gioco d'azzardo** game of chance; **gli piace giocare d'azzardo** (*anche fig*) he likes gambling.

azzeccare [attsek'kare] VT (*bersaglio*) to hit, strike; (*indovinare: risposta, pronostico*) to guess; **ha azzeccato il pronostico al totocalcio** he had a win on the pools; **non ne azzecca mai una** he never gets anything right.

azzeramento [addzera'mento] SM (*Inform*) reset.

azzerare [addze'rare] VT **a** (*Mat, Fis*) to make equal to zero, reduce to zero **b** (*Tecn: strumento*) to (re)set to zero; (*Inform*) to reset.

azzimato, a [addzi'mato] AGG dressed up, spruced up.

azzimo, a ['addzimo] ① AGG (*non lievitato: pane*) unleavened.
② SM unleavened bread.

azzittire [attsit'tire] ① VT: **azzittire qn** to silence sb, shut sb up.
② VI (*aus* **essere**) to fall *o* become silent.

azzoppare [attsop'pare] ① VT to lame, make lame.

② **azzopparsi** VIP to become lame.

Azzorre [ad'dzɔrre] SFPL: **le Azzorre** the Azores.

azzuffarsi [attsuf'farsi] VIP (*gen*) to come to blows; (*bambini*) to squabble.

azzurrino, a [addzur'rino] AGG light blue, pale blue.

azzurro, a [ad'dzurro] ① AGG **a** (*colore*) blue, azure; **il principe azzurro** Prince Charming **b** (*Sport: della nazionale italiana*) of the Italian team.
② SM **a** (*colore*) blue, azure **b** (*Sport: atleta*) member of the Italian team; **gli azzurri** SMPL the Italian team.

azzurrognolo, a [addzur'roɲɲolo] AGG bluish.

B

B, b [bi] SF O M INV (*lettera*) B, b; **B come Bologna** ≈ B for Benjamin (*Brit*), ≈ B for Baker (*Am*).

BA SIGLA = *Bari*.

babà [ba'ba] SM INV: **babà (al rum)** rum baba.

babau [ba'bau] SM INV ogre, bogey man.

babbeo [bab'bɛo] SM fool, idiot.

babbo ['babbo] SM (*fam*) dad, daddy ▶**Babbo Natale** Father Christmas, Santa Claus.

babbuccia, ce [bab'buttʃa] SF (Turkish) slipper; (*per neonati*) bootee.

babbuino [babbu'ino] SM baboon.

Babele [ba'bɛle] SF **a** (*confusione*) chaos, confuṣion **b** (*Bibbia*) Babel; **la torre di Babele** the tower of Babel.

babilonese [babilo'nese] AGG, SM/F Babylonian.

Babilonia [babi'lɔnja] SF Babylon.

babordo [ba'bordo] SM (*Naut*) port side; **a babordo** to port.

baby ['beibi] SM/F INV (*neonato*) (newborn) baby, infant; (*fam: piccola dose di whisky*) tot, shot.

baby-doll ['beibi dɔl] SM INV baby-dolls *pl*.

babysitter ['beɪbɪsitə'] SM/F INV baby-sitter.

bacato, a [ba'kato] AGG (*frutto*) worm-eaten, maggoty; (*fig: mente*) diseased; (: *persona*) corrupt.

bacca, che ['bakka] SF berry.

baccalà [bakka'la] SM INV (*pesce*) dried salted cod; (*fig: persona sciocca*) dummy; **secco come un baccalà** (*magro*) as thin as a rake.

baccano [bak'kano] SM row, din; **fare baccano** to make a row o din.

baccello [bat'tʃɛllo] SM pod.

bacchetta [bak'ketta] SF (*bastoncino*) rod, stick; (*di tamburo*) drumstick; (*di direttore d'orchestra*) baton; **comandare a bacchetta** to rule with a rod of iron ▶**bacchetta magica** magic wand.

bacchettata [bakket'tata] SF: **dare una bacchettata a qn** to hit sb with a stick.

bacchiare [bak'kjare] VT to knock down (*fruit, nuts*).

Bacco ['bakko] SM Bacchus.

bacheca, che [ba'kɛka] SF **a** (*per affissione*) notice board

(*Brit*), bulletin board (*Am*) **b** (*mobile*) showcase, display case.

bachelite [bake'lite] SF bakelite ®.

bachicoltura [bakikol'tura] SF breeding of silkworms.

baciamano [batʃa'mano] SM: **fare il baciamano a qn** to kiss sb's hand.

baciare [ba'tʃare] **1** VT to kiss; **lo baciò sulla guancia** she kissed him on the cheek, she kissed his cheek; **le sponde baciate dal sole** (*fig*) the sun-kissed shores. **2 baciarsi** VR (*uso reciproco*) to kiss (each other o one another).

bacillare [batʃil'lare] AGG bacterial.

bacillo [ba'tʃillo] SM bacillus, germ.

bacinella [batʃi'nɛlla] SF (*gen: recipiente*) bowl; (*per lavarsi*) basin.

bacino [ba'tʃino] SM **a** (*Anat*) pelvis **b** (*Geog*) basin **c** (*Geol*) field, bed ▶**bacino carbonifero** coalfield ▶**bacino petrolifero** oilfield **d** (*Naut*) dock ▶**bacino di carenaggio** dry dock ▶**bacino galleggiante** floating dock.

bacio, ci ['batʃo] SM kiss; **dare un bacio a qn** to give sb a kiss; **coprire qn di baci** to smother sb with kisses; **dare il bacio della buonanotte a qn** to kiss sb goodnight; **tanti baci** (*fine di lettera*) love and kisses.

baco, chi ['bako] SM (*gen: verme*) worm, maggot; (*larva*) grub ▶**baco da seta** silkworm.

bacucco, a, chi, che [ba'kukko] AGG senile; **è un vecchio bacucco** he's an old fool.

bada ['bada] SF: **tenere qn a bada** (*tener d'occhio*) to keep an eye on sb; (*tenere a distanza*) to hold sb at bay.

badare [ba'dare] VI (*aus avere*): **badare a a** (*occuparsi di: negozio, casa*) to look after, mind; (: *bambino, malato*) to take care of, look after; (: *cliente*) to attend to; **bada agli affari tuoi!** OR **bada ai fatti tuoi!** mind your own business!
b (*fare attenzione*) to pay attention to, mind; **nessuno gli ha badato** nobody paid any attention to him; **bada (a te)!** watch out!; **bada a non cadere** mind o be careful you don't fall

c (*preoccuparsi*) to care about; **non bada a ciò che dice la gente** he doesn't care what people say; **è un tipo che non bada a spese** he doesn't mind how much he spends.

badessa [ba'dessa] SF (*Rel*) abbess.

badia [ba'dia] SF abbey.

badile [ba'dile] SM shovel.

baffo ['baffo] SM **a** : **baffi** SMPL (*di persona*) moustache *sg*; (*di animale*) whiskers; **un pranzo da leccarsi i baffi** a mouth-watering meal; **ridere sotto i baffi** to laugh up one's sleeve; **di quello che mi ha detto me ne faccio un baffo** (*fam*) I don't give *o* care a damn about what he said **b** (*sgorbio, sbavatura*) smear, smudge.

baffuto, a [baf'futo] AGG (*persona*) with a moustache.

bagagliaio, ai [bagaʎ'ʎajo] SM **a** (*di auto*) boot (*Brit*), trunk (*Am*); (*di treno*) luggage van (*Brit*), baggage car (*Am*); (*di aereo*) hold **b** (*deposito bagagli*) left-luggage office.

bagaglio, gli [ba'gaʎʎo] SM luggage *no pl*, baggage *no pl*; **fare/disfare i bagagli** to pack/unpack; **ho preso armi e bagagli e me ne sono andato** I packed up and left; **un bagaglio culturale** a store of knowledge ▶ **bagaglio appresso** accompanied luggage ▶ **bagaglio consentito** free luggage allowance ▶ **bagaglio in eccesso** excess luggage ▶ **bagaglio a mano** hand luggage.

bagarino [baga'rino] SM ticket tout.

bagarre [ba'gar] SF INV **a** (*Ciclismo*): **fare bagarre** to jostle **b** (*baruffa*) row.

bagascia, sce [ba'gaʃʃa] SF (*fam!*) whore.

bagattella [bagat'tɛlla] SF **a** (*inezia*) trifle, trifling matter **b** (*Mus*) bagatelle.

baggianata [baddʒa'nata] SF foolish action; **dire baggianate** to talk nonsense.

Baghdad [bag'dad] SF Baghdad.

bagliore [baʎ'ʎore] SM (*di fuoco*) glow; (*di fari*) glare; (*di lampi*) flash; **un bagliore di speranza** a gleam *o* ray of hope.

bagnante [baɲ'ɲante] SM/F bather.

bagnare [baɲ'ɲare] **1** VT **a** (*gen*) to wet; (*inzuppare*) to soak; (*labbra*) to moisten; (*annaffiare*) to water; **bagna la camicia prima di stirarla** damp the shirt before you iron it; **bagnarsi le labbra** to moisten one's lips; **le lacrime bagnavano il suo viso** her face was bathed in tears **b** (*sogg: fiume*) to flow through; (: *mare*) to wash, bathe; **il Mediterraneo bagna Genova** Genoa stands on the Mediterranean coast **c** (*fam: festeggiare bevendo*) to drink to, toast; **abbiamo bagnato la sua promozione** we celebrated his promotion. **2 bagnarsi** VR (*fare il bagno*) to bathe; **il bambino si è bagnato** the baby has wet himself. **3 bagnarsi** VIP (*prendere acqua*) to get wet; (*inzupparsi*) to get soaked, get drenched.

bagnasciuga [baɲɲaʃ'ʃuga] SM INV (*battigia*) water's edge.

bagnata [baɲ'ɲata] SF: **dare una bagnata a** (*pianta*) to water; (*stoffa*) to sprinkle with water.

bagnato, a [baɲ'ɲato] **1** AGG wet; **bagnato di lacrime** bathed in tears; **bagnato di sudore** (*viso, fronte*) bathed in sweat; (*camicia*) soaked with sweat; **bagnato fino alle ossa** soaked to the skin; **bagnato fradicio** wet through, drenched; **essere bagnato come un pulcino** to be like a drowned rat, be sopping wet; **sembrare un pulcino bagnato** to look a pathetic sight. **2** SM wet surface; **piove sempre sul bagnato** (*fig*) it

never rains but it pours.

bagnino, a [baɲ'ɲino] SM/F lifeguard; (*in piscina*) swimming pool attendant.

bagno ['baɲɲo] **1** SM **a** (*gen, Chim, Fot*) bath; (*in piscina*) swim; (*al mare*) swim, bathe; **fare il bagno** (*nella vasca*) to have a bath; (*in piscina*) to go swimming; (*al mare*) to go swimming *o* bathing; **fare il bagno a qn** to give sb a bath; **mettere qc a bagno** to leave sth to soak; **vasca da bagno** bath, bathtub **b** (*locale: anche:* **stanza da bagno**) bathroom; **scusi, dov'è il bagno?** where's the toilet *o* loo, please? (*Brit*), where's the bathroom, please? (*Am*) **c** (*stabilimento balneare*) private beach. **2** ▶ **bagni di mare** sea bathing *sg* ▶ **bagni pubblici** public baths ▶ **bagno di fango** mud bath ▶ **bagno di folla** (*fig*) adulation of the crowd ▶ **bagno di sabbia** sand bath ▶ **bagno di sangue** (*fig*) blood bath ▶ **bagno turco** Turkish bath.

bagnomaria [baɲɲoma'ria] SM INV: **cuocere a bagnomaria** to cook in a double saucepan (*Brit*), to cook in a double boiler (*Am*).

bagnoschiuma [baɲɲo'skjuma] SM INV bubble bath.

Bahama [ba'hama] SFPL: **le Bahama** the Bahamas.

Bahrein [ba'rein] SM: **il Bahrein** Bahrain *o* Bahrein.

baia ['baja] SF (*Geog*) bay.

baiadera [baja'dera] AGG INV (*tessuto*) bayadere.

baio, aia, ai, aie ['bajo] AGG (*cavallo*) bay.

baionetta [bajo'netta] SF bayonet; **innesto a baionetta** bayonet fitting.

baionettata [bajonet'tata] SF (*colpo*) bayonet thrust; (*ferita*) bayonet wound.

baita ['baita] SF mountain hut.

balalaica, che [bala'laika] SF balalaika.

balaustra [bala'ustra], **balaustrata** [balaus'trata] SF balustrade.

balbettare [balbet'tare] **1** VT (*gen*) to stammer (out); (*sogg: bambino*) to babble; **balbettare delle scuse** to mumble an excuse. **2** VI (*aus avere*) (*vedi vt*) to stammer; to babble.

balbettio, ii [balbet'tio] SM (*vedi vb*) stammering; babbling.

balbuzie [bal'buttsje] SF INV stammer; **essere affetto da balbuzie** to have a stammer.

balbuziente [balbut'tsjɛnte] **1** AGG stammering; **essere balbuziente** to stammer. **2** SM/F stammerer.

Balcani [bal'kani] SMPL: **i Balcani** the Balkans.

balcanico, a, ci, che [bal'kaniko] AGG Balkan.

balconata [balko'nata] SF (*Archit*) balcony; (*galleria*) gallery.

balcone [bal'kone] SM balcony.

baldacchino [baldak'kino] SM canopy; **letto a baldacchino** four-poster (bed).

baldanza [bal'dantsa] SF (*sicurezza*) self-confidence; (*spavalderia*) audacity, boldness.

baldanzosamente [baldantsosa'mente] AVV (*vedi sf*) self-confidently; boldly.

baldanzoso, a [baldan'tsoso] AGG (*vedi sf*) self-confident; audacious, bold.

baldo, a ['baldo] AGG bold.

baldoria [bal'dorja] SF merrymaking, revelry; **fare baldoria** to have a good time.

baldracca, che [bal'drakka] SF (*fam!*) whore.

Baleari [bale'ari] SFPL: **le (isole) Baleari** the Balearic

Islands.

balena [ba'lena] SF (*Zool*) whale; (*fig pegg*) barrel of lard; **caccia alla balena** whaling; **olio di balena** whale oil.

balenare [bale'nare] VI (*aus essere*) (*gen*) to flash; **mi è balenata un'idea** an idea flashed into o through my mind; **l'ira balenò nel suo sguardo** his eyes flashed with rage.

baleniera [bale'njɛra] SF (*per la caccia*) whaler, whaling ship.

baleno [ba'leno] SM flash of lightning; **in un baleno** in a flash.

balera [ba'lɛra] SF (*locale*) dance hall; (*pista*) dance floor.

balestra [ba'lɛstra] SF **a** (*arma*) crossbow **b** (*Tecn*) leaf spring.

balestruccio, ci [bales'truttʃo] SM house martin.

balia[1] ['balja] SF (*anche fig*) wet-nurse ►**balia asciutta** nanny.

balia[2] [ba'lia] SF (*potere assoluto*): **essere in balia di** to be at the mercy of; **la nave era in balia delle onde** the ship was at the mercy of the waves; **essere lasciato in balia di se stesso** to be left to one's own devices.

balilla [ba'lilla] SM INV (*Storia*) *member of Fascist youth group*.

balistica [ba'listika] SF ballistics *sg*.

balistico, a, ci, che [ba'listiko] AGG ballistic; **perito balistico** ballistics expert.

balla ['balla] SF **a** (*quantità*) bale **b** (*fam: fandonia*) rubbish *no pl*; **raccontare una balla a qn** to tell sb a lie; **un sacco di balle** a pack of lies, a load of rubbish.

ballabile [bal'labile] SM (*Mus*) dance number, dance tune.

ballare [bal'lare] [1] VI (*aus avere*) **a** to dance; **andare a ballare** to go dancing; **ballare come un orso** to dance like an elephant
b (*traballare: mobile*) to wobble; **le onde facevano ballare la nave** the waves tossed the ship about; **abbiamo ballato in volo** we had a bumpy flight; **quella giacca gli balla addosso** he's lost in that jacket.
[2] VT to dance; **ballare il valzer** to (dance the) waltz.

ballata [bal'lata] SF ballad.

ballatoio, oi [balla'tojo] SM (*balcone*) gallery, walkway.

ballerina [balle'rina] SF **a** (*female*) dancer; **prima ballerina** prima ballerina ►**ballerina classica** ballerina, ballet dancer ►**ballerina di rivista** chorus girl **b** (*scarpa*) pump **c** (*uccello*) wagtail ►**ballerina gialla** grey wagtail.

ballerino [balle'rino] SM (*male*) dancer; (*classico*) ballet dancer.

balletto [bal'letto] SM **a** (*spettacolo*) ballet; (*Mus*) ballet music **b** (*corpo di ballo*) dance troupe; (: *classico*) corps de ballet.

ballo ['ballo] SM (*danza, festa*) dance, ball; (*giro di danza*) dance; **fare un ballo** to have a dance; **essere in ballo** (*fig*) to be at stake; **tirare in ballo qn** (*fig*) to involve sb; **tirare in ballo qc** to bring sth up, raise sth; **entrare in ballo** (*fig: persona*) to become o get involved; (: *cosa*) to come into the picture, become a factor ►**ballo in maschera** o **mascherato** fancy-dress ball.

ballottaggio, gi [ballot'taddʒo] SM (*Pol*) second ballot.

balneare [balne'are] AGG bathing *attr*; **località balneare** seaside town; **governo balneare** (*Pol*) caretaker government.

baloccare [balok'kare] [1] VT (*trastullare*) to keep amused.
[2] **baloccarsi** VR (*perder tempo*) to fritter (one's) time

away.

balocco, chi [ba'lɔkko] SM toy, plaything.

balordaggine [balor'daddʒine] SF (*vedi agg*) stupidity, foolishness; unreliability; peculiarity; **non dire balordaggini!** don't talk nonsense!

balordamente [balorda'mente] AVV (*vedi agg*) stupidly, foolishly; unreliably; oddly, peculiarly.

balordo, a [ba'lordo] [1] AGG (*sciocco*) stupid, silly, foolish; (*di poco affidamento*) unreliable; (*strampalato*) odd, peculiar.
[2] SM/F (*sciocco*) fool, stupid person; (*tipo strampalato*) odd sort.

balsamico, a, ci, che [bal'samiko] AGG (*aria, brezza*) balmy; **pomata balsamica** balsam.

balsamo ['balsamo] SM (*lenimento*) balsam, balm; (*fig*) balm ►**balsamo (per capelli)** (hair) conditioner.

baltico, a, ci, che [ba'baltiko] [1] AGG Baltic.
[2] SM: **il (mar) Baltico** the Baltic (Sea).

baluardo [balu'ardo] SM (*bastione*) bulwark, rampart; (*fig*) bulwark.

baluginare [baludʒi'nare] VI (*aus essere*) to flicker; **gli baluginò il sospetto che...** (*fig*) suddenly the suspicion came into his mind that ... .

balza ['baltsa] SF **a** (*di stoffa*) frill **b** (*rupe*) crag **c** (*di cavallo*) white sock.

balzana [bal'tsana] SF (*di cavallo*) sock.

balzano, a [bal'tsano] AGG (*persona, idea*) queer, odd; **è un cervello balzano** he's a queer fish.

balzare [bal'tsare] VI (*aus essere*) to leap, to jump; **balzare in piedi** to leap o jump to one's feet; **balzare giù dal letto/dalla sedia** to leap o jump out of bed/up from one's chair; **balzare in macchina/a cavallo** to jump into a car/onto a horse; **il cuore le balzò in gola per la gioia/paura** her heart leapt with joy/fear; **la verità balza agli occhi** the truth is obvious; **gli balzò in mente che...** it came to him that ... .

balzo[1] ['baltso] SM (*salto*) leap, jump; (*di palla*) bounce; **fare un balzo** to jump; **un balzo in avanti** (*fig*) a great leap forward; **prendere la palla al balzo** (*fig*) to seize one's opportunity.

balzo[2] ['baltso] SM (*di rupe*) crag, cliff.

bambagia, gie [bam'badʒa] SF (*ovatta*) cottonwool (*Brit*), absorbent cotton (*Am*); (*cascame*) cotton waste; **tenere qn nella bambagia** (*fig*) to mollycoddle sb.

bambinaia [bambi'naja] SF nursemaid.

bambino, a [bam'bino] [1] SM/F (*gen*) child, (little) boy/girl; (*neonato*) baby; **quando ero bambino** when I was a child; **fare il bambino** to behave childishly; **è un bambino!** he's really childish!.
[2] AGG: **una scienza ancora bambina** a science still in its infancy.

bamboccio, ci [bam'bɔttʃo] SM (*bambino*) bouncing child; (*pupazzo*) rag doll; (*fig*) big baby.

bambola ['bambola] SF (*giocattolo*) doll, dolly; (*fig: donna*) doll.

bambolotto [bambo'lɔtto] SM male doll.

bambù [bam'bu] SM INV bamboo; **di bambù** bamboo.

banale [ba'nale] AGG (*gen*) banal, commonplace; (*idea, scusa*) trite; (*incidente*) trivial; (*persona*) ordinary; (*vita*) humdrum, dull; **è solo un banale raffreddore** it's just a common o garden cold, it's just an ordinary cold.

banalità [banali'ta] SF INV **a** (*vedi agg*) banality; triteness; triviality; ordinariness; dullness **b** (*parole*) truism, trite remark; **dire una banalità** to make a trite remark.

banalmente [banal'mente] AVV in a banal way, without originality.

banana [ba'nana] SF banana.

banano [ba'nano] SM banana tree.

banca, che ['banka] SF (istituto, edificio) bank; **in banca** in the bank; **andare in banca** to go to the bank; **avere un conto in banca** to have a bank account ▶**banca dati** (Inform) data bank ▶**banca del sangue** blood bank.

bancarella [banka'rɛlla] SF stall.

bancario, ria, ri, rie [ban'karjo] 1 AGG bank attr, banking; **assegno bancario** (bank) cheque. 2 SM/F bank employee.

bancarotta [banka'rotta] SF (Fin) bankruptcy; (fig) failure; **andare in bancarotta** OR **fare bancarotta** to go bankrupt.

bancarottiere, a [bankarot'tjɛre] SM/F bankrupt.

banchettare [banket'tare] VI (aus avere) to banquet, feast.

banchetto [ban'ketto] SM banquet; **fare un banchetto (a base di qc)** to feast (on sth).

banchiere [ban'kjɛre] SM (Fin, nei giochi) banker.

banchina [ban'kina] 1 SF a (di porto) quay, wharf b (di stazione) platform c (per pedoni) footway; (per ciclisti) cycle path ▶**banchina cedevole** (Aut) soft verge (Brit) o shoulder (Am) ▶**banchina spartitraffico** (Aut) central reservation (Brit), median (strip) (Am).

banchisa [ban'kiza] SF pack ice.

banco, chi ['banko] SM a (sedile) seat, bench; (: in Parlamento) bench ▶**banco di chiesa** pew ▶**banco degli imputati** (Dir) dock ▶**banco di scuola** desk ▶**banco dei testimoni** witness box (Brit) o stand (Am) b (di negozio) counter; (di mercato) stall; **medicinali da banco** over-the-counter medicines; **sotto banco** (fig) under the counter ▶**banco del Lotto** lottery-ticket office
c (di officina) (work)bench ▶**banco di prova** test bed; (fig) testing ground
d (Fin) bank; **tenere il banco** (nei giochi) to be (the) banker; **tener banco** (fig) to monopolize the conversation
e (Meteor) bank, patch ▶**banco di nebbia** fog bank
f (Geol: strato) layer; (: di coralli) reef ▶**banco di ghiaccio** ice floe ▶**banco di sabbia** sandbank
g (di pesci) shoal.

bancogiro [banko'dʒiro] SM credit transfer.

Bancomat® ['bankomat] SM INV automated banking; (tessera) cash card.

banconota [banko'nɔta] SF banknote.

banda¹ ['banda] SF (di suonatori) band; (di ladri, guerriglieri) band, gang; (di amici) gang, group.

banda² ['banda] SF a (di stoffa) band, strip; (di metallo) band, strip; (di carta) strip; (di calcolatore) tape ▶**banda perforata** (Inform) punch tape b (Fis, Radio) band.

banderuola [bande'rwɔla] SF (Meteor) weathercock, weathervane; **essere una banderuola** (fig) to be fickle.

bandiera [ban'djɛra] SF flag; **alzare bandiera bianca** to show the white flag; **battere bandiera italiana** (nave) to fly the Italian flag; **cambiare bandiera** (fig) to change sides ▶**bandiera ombra** o **di comodo** flag of convenience.

bandierina [bandje'rina] SF (Naut) pennant; (Calcio): **tiro dalla bandierina** corner.

bandire [ban'dire] VT a (annunciare) to announce, proclaim; **bandire un concorso** to announce a competition (for posts in large organizations)
b (porre al bando: prodotto) to ban; (: sentimenti) to banish; (: complimenti, ciance) to dispense with; (: persona) to exile; **l'hanno bandito dall'ordine degli avvocati** he has been struck off.

bandita [ban'dita] SF reserve.

banditismo [bandi'tizmo] SM banditry.

bandito [ban'dito] SM bandit, outlaw; (fig: persona senza scrupoli) rogue.

banditore [bandi'tore] SM a (Storia) town crier b (di aste) auctioneer.

bando ['bando] SM a (annuncio) (public) announcement, (public) notice b (esilio) exile; **mettere al bando qn** to exile sb; (fig) to freeze sb out; **bando alle ciance!** that's enough talk!

bandolo ['bandolo] SM (di matassa) end; **trovare il bandolo della matassa** (fig) to find the key to the problem.

bang [bæŋ] SM INV: **bang sonico** sonic boom.

Bangkok [ban'kɔk] SF Bangkok.

Bangladesh [bangla'dɛʃ] SM Bangladesh.

banjo ['bændʒou] SM INV banjo.

baobab [bao'bab] SM INV baobab, monkey bread tree.

bar [bar] SM INV (locale) bar (serving coffee, alcoholic drinks, snacks ecc); (mobile) cocktail cabinet.

bara ['bara] SF coffin.

baracca, che [ba'rakka] SF hut; (pegg) hovel; (fam pegg: oggetto) piece of junk; **mandare avanti la baracca** to keep things going; **come va la baracca?** how are you managing?; **piantare baracca e burattini** to throw everything up.

baraccato, a [barak'kato] SM/F person living in temporary camp or shanty town.

baracchino [barak'kino] SM a (chiosco) stall b (apparecchio) CB radio.

baraccone [barak'kone] SM booth, stall; **baracconi** SMPL (parco dei divertimenti) funfair sg; **fenomeno da baraccone** circus freak.

baraccopoli [barak'kɔpoli] SF INV shanty town.

baraonda [bara'onda] SF (confusione) chaos; (movimento di gente) hubbub, bustle.

barare [ba'rare] VI (aus avere) to cheat.

baratro ['baratro] SM (anche fig) abyss.

barattare [barat'tare] VT: **barattare qc con qc** (merce) to barter sth for sth; (francobolli, dischi) to swap sth for sth (Brit), to trade sth for sth (Am).

baratto [ba'ratto] SM (Comm) barter; (scambio) exchange; **fare un baratto con qn** to swap with sb (Brit), to trade with sb (Am).

barattolo [ba'rattolo] SM (di vetro) jar; (di latta) tin, can; (di plastica) pot.

barba ['barba] SF a beard; **farsi la barba** to shave; **una barba di 3 giorni** 3 days' growth; **farla in barba a qn** (fig) to fool sb; **servire qn di barba e capelli** (fig) to teach sb a lesson; **che barba!** (persona, libro) what a bore! b (Bot) (fine) root.

barbabietola [barba'bjɛtola] SF beetroot (Brit), beet (Am) ▶**barbabietola da zucchero** sugar beet.

Barbados [bar'bados] SF Barbados sg.

barbagianni [barba'dʒanni] SM INV barn owl.

barbaramente [barbara'mente] AVV (uccidere) savagely; (saccheggiare) barbarously.

barbarico, a, ci, che [bar'bariko] AGG (invasione) barbarian; (usanze, metodi) barbaric.

barbarie [bar'barje] SF INV (*condizione*) barbarism; (*crudeltà*) barbarity.

barbaro, a ['barbaro] [1] AGG (*popolo*) barbarian; (*comportamento, crimine*) barbaric, barbarous; (*stile, gusto*) appalling.
[2] SM barbarian; **i Barbari** SMPL the Barbarians.

barbecue ['ba:bikju:] SM INV barbecue.

barbiere [bar'bjɛre] SM barber.

barbiturico, a, ci, che [barbi'turiko] [1] AGG barbituric.
[2] SM barbiturate.

barboncino [barbon'tʃino] SM poodle.

barbone[1] [bar'bone] SM (*anche:* **cane barbone**) (French) poodle.

barbone[2]**, a** SM/F (*vagabondo*) tramp, vagrant.

barboso, a [bar'boso] AGG boring.

barbuto, a [bar'buto] AGG bearded.

barca[1]**, che** ['barka] SF boat; **andare in barca** (*a vela*) to go sailing; (*a remi*) to go boating; **mandare avanti la barca** (*fig*) to keep things going ▶**barca a motore** motorboat ▶**barca a remi** rowing boat (*Brit*), rowboat (*Am*) ▶**barca a vela** sailing boat (*Brit*), sailboat (*Am*).

barca[2]**, che** ['barka] SF (*fig: quantità*): **una barca di** heaps of, tons of.

barcaiolo [barka'jɔlo] SM boatman.

barcamenarsi [barkame'narsi] VIP (*nel lavoro*) to get by.

Barcellona [bartʃel'lona] SF Barcelona.

barcollamento [barkolla'mento] SM staggering.

barcollare [barkol'lare] VI (*aus* **avere**) to stagger.

barcone [bar'kone] SM (*quadrangolare*) scow; (*per costruzione di ponti*) pontoon.

bardare [bar'dare] [1] VT (*cavallo*) to harness; (*fig: persona*) to dress up.
[2] **bardarsi** VR to dress up.

bardatura [barda'tura] SF (*di cavallo*) harness; (*fig*) finery.

bardo ['bardo] SM bard.

bardotto [bar'dɔtto] SM (*Zool*) hinny.

barella [ba'rɛlla] SF (*per malati*) stretcher.

barelliere [barel'ljɛre] SM stretcher bearer.

Barents ['barents] SM: **il mare di Barents** the Barents Sea.

barese [ba'rese] [1] AGG of *o* from Bari.
[2] SM/F inhabitant *o* native of Bari.

bargiglio, gli [bar'dʒiʎʎo] SM wattle.

baricentro [bari'tʃentro] SM centre (*Brit*) *o* center (*Am*) of gravity.

barile [ba'rile] SM (*gen*) barrel; (*di vino*) cask, barrel.

bario ['barjo] SM barium.

barista, i, e [ba'rista] SM/F (*cameriere*) barman/barmaid; (*proprietario*) bar owner.

baritonale [barito'nale] AGG baritone *attr*.

baritono [ba'ritono] SM baritone.

barlume [bar'lume] SM (*faint*) light; (*fig: di speranza, idea*) glimmer.

baro ['baro] SM (*Carte*) cardsharp.

barocco, a, chi, che [ba'rɔkko] AGG, SM baroque.

barometro [ba'rɔmetro] SM barometer.

baronale [baro'nale] AGG baronial.

barone [ba'rone] SM baron; **i baroni della medicina** (*fig pegg*) the big shots in the medical profession.

baronessa [baro'nessa] SF baroness.

baronetto [baro'netto] SM baronet.

barra ['barra] SF **a** (*gen*) bar; (*di legno, metallo*) rod, bar ▶**barra di rimorchio** (*Aut*) tow bar ▶**barra spaziatrice** space-bar ▶**barra stabilizzatrice** (*Aut*) anti-roll bar ▶**barre laterali** (*Aut*) side impact bars **b** (*Naut*) helm; (*: piccola*) tiller **c** (*segno grafico*) stroke.

barracano [barra'kano] SM barracan.

barracuda [barra'kuda] SM INV barracuda.

barrage [ba'raʒ] SM (*Equitazione*) jump-off.

barrare [bar'rare] VT to bar.

barricare [barri'kare] [1] VT to barricade.
[2] **barricarsi** VR: **barricarsi in/dietro** to barricade o.s. in/behind; **barricarsi in camera** to shut o.s. up in one's room.

barricata [barri'kata] SF barricade; **essere dall'altra parte della barricata** (*fig*) to be on the other side of the fence.

barriera [bar'rjɛra] SF (*gen, fig, Fis*) barrier; (*corallina*) reef; (*Calcio*) wall; (*Equitazione: ostacolo*) pole; **la Grande Barriera Corallina** the Great Barrier Reef ▶**barriera doganale** trade *o* tariff barrier ▶**la barriera del suono** the sound barrier ▶**le barriere architettoniche** physical obstacles (*preventing access to buildings by the disabled*).

barrire [bar'rire] VI (*aus* **avere**) to trumpet.

barrito [bar'rito] SM trumpeting.

barroccio, ci [bar'rɔttʃo] SM cart.

baruffa [ba'ruffa] SF quarrel, row; **fare baruffa** to quarrel, have a row.

barzelletta [bardzel'letta] SF joke, funny story; **raccontare una barzelletta** to tell a joke.

basalto [ba'zalto] SM basalt.

basamento [baza'mento] SM (*parte inferiore, piedistallo*) base; (*Tecn*) bed, base plate.

basare [ba'zare] [1] VT: **basare (su)** (*argomento*) to base (on), found (on); (*edificio*) to build on.
[2] **basarsi** VR: **basarsi su** (*sogg: argomento, fatti, prove*) to be based on, be founded on; (*: persona*) to base o.s. on, base one's arguments on; (*: edificio*) to be built on.

basco, a, schi, sche ['basko] [1] AGG Basque.
[2] SM/F Basque.
[3] SM **a** (*lingua*) Basque **b** (*berretto*) beret.

bascula ['baskula]**, basculla** [bas'kulla] SF weighing machine, weighbridge.

basculante [basku'lante] AGG (*bussola, tavolo*) self-stabilizing.

base ['baze] [1] SF **a** (*gen, Mil, Chim, Mat*) base; **la base del partito** (*Pol*) the rank and file of the party
b (*fig: fondamento*) basis; (*: di problema, idea*) origin, root; **base di partenza** starting point
c : **basi** SFPL (*fondamento*) basis *sg*, foundation *sg*; **gettare le basi per qc** to lay the basis *o* foundations for sth; **avere buone basi** (*Scol*) to have a sound educational background
d (*fraseologia*): **prodotto a base di carne** meat-based product; **essere alla base di qc** to be at the root of sth; **servire da** *o* **come base a** (*punto di partenza*) to act as the basis for; **in base a** (*notizie, informazioni*) according to; **in base a ciò...** on that basis ...; **sulla base di** on the basis of; **regole di base** basic rules.
[2] AGG INV (*prezzo, problema, stipendio*) basic.

baseball ['beisbɔ:l] SM INV baseball.

basetta [ba'zetta] SF side whisker, sideburn.

BASIC ['beisik] SIGLA M (*Inform*) BASIC.

basico, a, ci, che ['baziko] AGG (*Chim*) basic.

basilare [bazi'lare] AGG basic, fundamental.

Basilea [basi'lɛa] SF Basle.

basilica, che [ba'zilika] SF basilica.

basilico [ba'ziliko] SM (*Bot*) (sweet) basil.

basket ['ba:skit] SM INV (*sport*) basketball.

bassa ['bassa] SF lowlands *pl*.

bassamente [bassa'mente] AVV (*in modo vile*) meanly.

bassezza [bas'settsa] SF (*d'animo, di sentimenti*) baseness; (*azione*) base action.

basso, a ['basso] **1** AGG **a** (*gen*) low; (*persona*) short; (*suono*) soft, low; (: *profondo*) deep; **i rami bassi** the lower *o* bottom branches; **a occhi bassi** with lowered eyes; **l'ho avuto a basso prezzo** I got it cheap; **c'è bassa marea** it's low tide, the tide is out **b** (*inferiore: qualità*) poor, inferior; (*abietto: azione, istinto*) base, mean **c** (*Geog*): **il basso Po** the lower Po; **i Paesi Bassi** the Netherlands **d** (*Storia: tardo*) late; **il basso Medioevo** the late Middle Ages; **basso latino** low Latin. **2** AVV (*volare, mirare*) low; (*parlare*) softly, in a low voice. **3** SM **a** (*parte inferiore*) bottom, lower part; (: *di pagina*) foot, bottom; **in basso** at the bottom; **devo spostare quel bottone più in basso** I'll have to move that button lower down; **scendere da basso** to go downstairs; **cadere in basso** (*fig*) to come down in the world **b** (*Mus*) bass.

bassofondo [basso'fondo] SM (*pl* **bassifondi**) shallows *pl*; **i bassifondi (della città)** (*quartieri emarginati*) the seediest parts of the town.

bassopiano [basso'pjano] SM (*pl* **bassopiani** *o* **bassipiani**) low-lying plain.

bassorilievo [bassori'ljevo] SM (*pl* **bassorilievi**) bas-relief.

bassotto, a [bas'sotto] **1** AGG squat. **2** SM (*cane*) dachshund.

bastante [bas'tante] AGG sufficient.

bastardaggine [bastar'daddʒine] SF (*pegg*) meanness, rottenness.

bastardo, a [bas'tardo] **1** AGG bastard *attr*; (*animale*) crossbred; (*pianta*) hybrid; **cane bastardo** mongrel. **2** SM/F (*figlio, anche insulto*) bastard; **bastardo!** (*fam*) (you) bastard!. **3** SM (*cane*) mongrel.

bastare [bas'tare] **1** VI (*aus essere*) **a** to be enough, be sufficient; **bastare a qn** to be enough for sb; **mi bastano 15.000 lire per oggi** 15.000 lire will do me *o* will be sufficient (for me) for today; **150.000 lire ti bastano per 2 giorni** 150.000 lire will last you 2 days; **fatti bastare questi soldi!** mind you make this money last!; **bastare a se stesso** to be self-sufficient **b** (*fraseologia*): **basta!** that's enough!, stop it!, that will do!; **punto e basta!** and that's that!; **basta con queste scuse** enough of these excuses; **dimmi basta** (*versando da bere*) say when!; **basta così?** (*al bar ecc*) will that be all?; **basta così, grazie** that's enough, thank you; (*nei negozi*) that's all, thank you; **basta e avanza** that's more than enough. **2** VB IMPERS: **basta chiedere** *o* **che chieda a un vigile** you have only to *o* need only ask a policeman; **basta rivolgersi all'ufficio competente** you just have to contact the relevant department; **non basta volerlo, bisogna sapere come fare** it's not enough to want to, you have to know how to; **e come se non bastasse...** and as if that wasn't enough ...; **basti dire che...** suffice it to say that ...; **basta un niente per farla arrabbiare** the slightest thing will get her annoyed, it only takes the slightest thing to annoy her; **quanto basta** as much as is necessary; **basta che** (*purché*) provided (that); **basta che tu lo chieda** you only have to ask.

bastian [bas'tjan] SM: **bastian contrario** awkward customer.

bastimento [basti'mento] SM ship, vessel.

bastione [bas'tjone] SM bastion.

basto ['basto] SM pack saddle.

bastonare [basto'nare] VT to beat, thrash; **avere l'aria di un cane bastonato** to look crestfallen.

bastonata [basto'nata] SF blow (*with a stick*); **prendere qn a bastonate** to give sb a beating; **l'hanno ucciso a bastonate** they beat him to death.

bastoncello [baston'tʃello] SM (*Anat*) retinal rod.

bastoncino [baston'tʃino] SM (*piccolo bastone*) small stick; (*Tecn*) rod; (*Sci*) ski pole ▶ **bastoncini di pesce** (*Culin*) fish fingers (*Brit*), fish sticks (*Am*).

bastone [bas'tone] SM **a** (*gen*) stick; (*Rel*) staff; **mettere i bastoni fra le ruote a qn** (*fig*) to put a spoke in sb's wheel ▶ **bastone da passeggio** walking stick **b** : **bastoni** SMPL (*Carte*) *suit in Neapolitan pack of cards*.

batacchio, chi [ba'takkjo] SM (*di campana*) clapper; (*di porta*) (door-)knocker.

batiscafo [batis'kafo] SM bathyscaph.

batista [ba'tista] SF (*tessuto*) batiste.

batosta [ba'tɔsta] SF (*colpo, smacco*) blow; (*Sport: sconfitta*) beating.

battage [ba'taʒ] SM INV: **battage promozionale** *o* **pubblicitario** hype.

battaglia [bat'taʎʎa] SF (*Mil*) battle; (*fig*) fight.

battagliero, a [battaʎ'ʎɛro] AGG (*esercito, popolo*) warlike; (*fig: spirito, persona*) aggressive.

battaglio, gli [bat'taʎʎo] SM (*di campana*) clapper; (*di porta*) (door-)knocker.

battaglione [battaʎ'ʎone] SM battalion.

battelliere [battel'ljɛre] SM boatman.

battello [bat'tɛllo] SM (*gen*) boat; (*canotto*) dinghy ▶ **battello pneumatico** rubber dinghy ▶ **battello di salvataggio** lifeboat.

battente [bat'tɛnte] SM **a** (*di finestra*) shutter; (*di porta*) *one side of a double door*; **porta a due battenti** double door; **chiudere i battenti** (*fig*) to shut up shop **b** (*per bussare*) (door-)knocker **c** (*di orologio*) hammer.

battere ['battere] **1** VT **a** (*percuotere: persona*) to beat, strike, hit; (: *panni, tappeti*) to beat; (: *ferro*) to hammer; (: *grano*) to thresh; **battere il ferro finché è caldo** (*fig*) to strike while the iron is hot; **battè un pugno sul tavolo** he beat his fist on the table; **battersi il petto** to beat one's breast; (*fig*) to repent; **battere (a macchina)** to type; **battere il tempo** OR **battere il ritmo** (*Mus*) to beat time **b** (*avversario*) to beat, defeat; (*concorrenza, record*) to beat; **in matematica nessuno lo batte** there's no one to beat him at maths **c** (*urtare: parte del corpo*) to hit; **ha battuto il mento sul gradino** he hit his chin on the step; **batteva i denti per il freddo** his teeth were chattering with the cold; **battere i piedi** to stamp one's feet; **battere i tacchi** to click one's heels; **battere le mani** to clap one's hands **d** (*sbattere: ali*) to beat; **senza battere ciglio** without batting an eyelid; **in un batter d'occhio** in the twinkling of an eye **e** (*rintoccare: le ore*) to strike; **il pendolo batteva le 8** the grandfather clock was striking 8 o'clock **f** (*Culin*) to beat **g** (*Sport: palla*) to hit; **battere un rigore** (*Calcio*) to take a penalty **h** (*percorrere: campagna, paese*) to scour, comb;

(*Caccia*) to beat; **battere (il marciapiede)** (*esercitare la prostituzione*) to be on the game
i : **battersela** to run off
j (*Fin*): **battere moneta** to mint coin.
[2] VI (*aus avere*) **a** (*cuore, polso*) to beat; (*pioggia, sole*): **battere (su)** to beat down (on); **la pioggia batteva sui vetri** the rain beat *o* lashed against the window panes; **battere in testa** (*Aut*) to knock
b (*insistere*): **battere su** to insist on; **battere su un argomento** to harp on a topic
c (*bussare*): **battere (a)** to knock (at)
d : **battere in ritirata** to beat a retreat, fall back.
[3] **battersi** VIP (*lottare*) to fight; (: *fig*) to fight, battle; **battersi all'ultimo sangue** to fight to the last.
batteria [batte'ria] SF **a** (*Elettr, Mil, Agr*) battery ►**batteria da cucina** pots and pans *pl* **b** (*Sport*) heat **c** (*Mus*): **la batteria** the drums *pl*.
battericida, i [batteri'tʃida] SM germicide.
batterico, a, ci, che [bat'tɛriko] AGG bacterial.
batterio, ri [bat'tɛrjo] SM bacterium; **batteri patogeni** bacteria which cause disease.
batteriologia [batterjolo'dʒia] SF bacteriology.
batteriologico, a, ci, che [batterjo'lɔdʒiko] AGG bacteriological; **guerra batteriologica** germ warfare.
batteriologo, gi [batte'rjɔlogo] SM bacteriologist.
batterista, i [batte'rista] SM/F drummer.
battesimale [battezi'male] AGG baptismal.
battesimo [bat'tezimo] SM **a** (*sacramento*) baptism; (*rito*) christening, baptism; **tenere qn a battesimo** to be godfather (*o* godmother) to sb **b** (*cerimonia inaugurativa*: *di nave*) christening ►**battesimo dell'aria** first flight ►**battesimo del fuoco** baptism of fire.
battezzare [batted'dzare] VT **a** (*Rel*) to baptize, christen; (*nave*) to christen **b** (*chiamare*) to call, name, christen; (*fig: dare un soprannome*) to nickname.
battibaleno [battiba'leno] SM: **in un battibaleno** in a flash.
battibecco, chi [batti'bekko] SM squabble.
batticarne [batti'karne] SM INV steak hammer.
batticuore [batti'kwɔre] SM palpitations *pl*; **avevo il batticuore** (*fig*) my heart was thumping.
battigia, gie [bat'tidʒa] SF water's edge.
battimano [batti'mano] SM applause *no pl*, clapping *no pl*.
battipanni [batti'panni] SM INV carpet beater.
battiscopa [battis'kopa] SM INV skirting (board).
battista, i, e [bat'tista] AGG, SM/F Baptist; **San Giovanni Battista** Saint John the Baptist.
battistero [battis'tɛro] SM baptist(e)ry.
battistrada [battis'trada] SM INV **a** (*di pneumatico*) tread **b** (*Sport*) pacemaker; **fare da battistrada** (*in una gara*) to set the pace, make the running; **fare da battistrada a qn** (*fig*) to prepare the way for sb.
battitappeto [battitap'peto] SM INV upright vacuum cleaner; **passare il battitappeto** to vacuum, hoover.
battito ['battito] SM (*pulsazione*) beat, throb; **battito della pioggia/dell'orologio** drumming of the rain/ticking of the clock ►**battito cardiaco** heartbeat.
battitore [batti'tore] SM **a** (*Cricket*) batsman; (*Baseball*) batter **b** (*Caccia*) beater.
battitura [batti'tura] SF **a** (*anche:* **battitura a macchina**) typing **b** (*del grano*) threshing.
battuta [bat'tuta] SF **a** (*Teatro*) cue; (*osservazione*) remark; (*spiritosaggine*) witty remark; **fare una battuta** to crack a joke, make a witty remark; **aver la battuta pronta** (*fig*) to have a ready answer; **non ho perso una**

battuta della loro conversazione I didn't miss a word of what they were saying; **è ancora alle prime battute** (*progetto, commedia*) it's just started
b (*di caccia*) beat, beating; (*di polizia*): **fare una battuta in una zona** to scour *o* comb an area
c (*Tennis*) service; **alla battuta Sampras** Sampras is now serving
d (*Mus*) bar ►**battuta d'arresto** *o* **d'aspetto** bar rest; **gli affari hanno subito una battuta d'arresto** it's a slack period for business
e (*di macchina da scrivere*) key stroke.
battuto [bat'tuto] SM (*Culin*) mirepoix.
batuffolo [ba'tuffolo] SM wad.
bau bau ['bau 'bau] ESCL woof woof!, bow wow!
baud [bod] SM INV (*Telec*) baud.
baule [ba'ule] SM (*valigia*) trunk; (*Aut*) boot (*Brit*), trunk (*Am*).
bauxite [bauk'site] SF bauxite.
bava ['bava] SF (*di persona, bambino*) dribble; (*di animale*) slaver, slobber; (*di cane idrofobo*) foam; (*di lumaca*) slime; (*di baco da seta*) silk filament; **aver la bava alla bocca** (*anche fig*) to be foaming at the mouth; **non c'era nemmeno una bava di vento** there wasn't a breath of wind.
bavaglino [bavaʎ'ʎino] SM bib.
bavaglio, gli [ba'vaʎʎo] SM gag; **mettere il bavaglio a qn/qc** (*anche fig*) to gag sb/sth.
bavarese [bava'rese] [1] AGG, SM/F Bavarian.
[2] SF (*Culin*) bavarois.
bavero ['bavero] SM collar.
Baviera [ba'vjɛra] SF Bavaria.
bavoso, a [ba'voso] AGG dribbling.
bazar [bad'dzar] SM INV bazaar.
bazooka [bə'zu:kə] SM INV bazooka.
bazzecola [bad'dzɛkola] SF (*mere*) trifle.
bazzicare [battsi'kare] [1] VT (*persona*) to hang about with; (*posto*) to hang about *o* around.
[2] VI (*aus avere*): **bazzicare con qn** to hang about with sb; **bazzicare in un posto** to hang about *o* around a place.
bearsi [be'arsi] VIP: **bearsi di qc/a fare qc** to delight in sth/in doing sth; **bearsi alla vista di** to feast one's eyes on.
beatamente [beata'mente] AVV blissfully; **vivere beatamente** to lead a life of bliss.
beatificare [beatifi'kare] VT (*Rel*) to beatify.
beatitudine [beati'tudine] SF (*Rel*) beatitude; (*felicità*) bliss.
beato, a [be'ato] AGG (*Rel*) blessed; (*felice*) blissfully happy; **una vita beata** a life of bliss; **beata ignoranza** blissful ignorance; **beato lui!** lucky him!, how lucky he is!; **beato chi ti vede!** (*fam*) long time no see!
beauty-case ['bju:ti'keis] SM INV beauty case.
bebè [be'bɛ] SM INV baby.
beccaccia, ce [bek'kattʃa] SF woodcock ►**beccaccia di mare** oystercatcher.
beccaccino [bekkat'tʃino] SM snipe.
beccare [bek'kare] [1] VT **a** (*sogg: uccello*) to peck (at) **b** (*fam: cogliere sul fatto*) to nab; **non mi becchi più un'altra volta!** you won't catch me out like that again! **c** (*fam: anche:* **beccarsi**) to get; **beccarsi un raffreddore** to catch a cold.
[2] **beccarsi** VR (*uso reciproco: uccelli*) to peck (at) one another; (: *fig: litigare*) to squabble.

beccata [bek'kata] SF peck.

beccheggiare [bekked'dʒare] VI (*aus* avere) (*Aer, Naut*) to pitch.

beccheggio, gi [bek'keddʒo] SM (*Aer, Naut*) pitching.

beccherò *ecc* [bekke'rɔ] VB vedi **beccare**.

becchime [bek'kime] SM birdseed.

becchino [bek'kino] SM gravedigger.

becco¹, chi ['bekko] SM **a** (*di uccello*) beak, bill; **non ho il becco di un quattrino** (*fam*) I'm broke **b** (*fam: bocca*) mouth; **chiudi il becco!** shut your mouth!, shut your trap!; **mettere il becco in qc** to poke one's nose into sth; **tu non mettere becco!** you keep out of this! **c** (*bruciatore*) burner ▶ **becco Bunsen** Bunsen burner **d** (*di caffettiera*) spout.

becco², chi ['bekko] SM (*Zool*) billy-goat; (*fig fam*) cuckold.

beccofrusone [bekkofru'zone] SM waxwing.

beccuccio, ci [bek'kuttʃo] SM (*di ampolla, bricco*) lip; (*di teiera*) spout.

beduino, a [bedu'ino] AGG, SM/F Bedouin.

Befana [be'fana] SF **a** (*festività*) *national holiday (Jan 6, feast of the Epiphany)* **b** (*personaggio*) *kind old woman who, according to legend, comes down the chimney during the night, bringing gifts for good children and coal for naughty ones* **c** (*donna brutta*) old hag, old witch.

beffa ['beffa] SF: **farsi beffa** *o* **beffe di qn** to make a fool of sb; **farsi beffa** *o* **beffe di qc** to make fun of sth; **ma questa è una beffa!** this is some kind of sick joke!

beffardamente [beffarda'mente] AVV mockingly.

beffardo, a [bef'fardo] AGG mocking.

beffare [bef'fare] **1** VT to make a fool of, mock. **2 beffarsi** VIP: **beffarsi di** to scoff at.

beffeggiare [beffed'dʒare] VT to laugh at, mock.

bega, ghe ['bega] SF (*litigio*) quarrel, dispute; (*problema*): **non voglio beghe** I don't want any trouble.

begli ['beʎʎi] AGG vedi **bello**.

begonia [be'gɔnja] SF begonia.

beh [bɛ] ESCL well!

bei ['bɛi] AGG vedi **bello**.

beige [bɛʒ] AGG INV beige.

Beirut [bei'rut] SF Beirut.

bel¹ [bɛl] AGG vedi **bello**.

bel² [bɛl] SM INV (*Fis*) bel.

belare [be'lare] VI (*aus* avere) (*Zool, fig*) to bleat.

belato [be'lato] SM bleating.

belga, gi, ghe ['bɛlga] AGG, SM/F Belgian.

Belgio ['bɛldʒo] SM: **il Belgio** Belgium.

Belgrado [bel'grado] SF Belgrade.

bella ['bɛlla] SF **a** beauty, belle; (*innamorata*) sweetheart; **la Bella addormentata nel bosco** Sleeping Beauty **b** (*anche:* bella copia) fair copy **c** (*Sport, Carte*) deciding match.

belladonna [bella'dɔnna] SF (*Bot*) deadly nightshade.

bellamente [bella'mente] AVV (*gentilmente*) nicely; (*comodamente*) comfortably, at one's ease.

belletto [bel'letto] SM (*ant*) rouge.

bellezza [bel'lettsa] SF **a** (*qualità*) beauty; (: *di donna*) beauty, loveliness; (: *di uomo*) handsomeness; **una donna di eccezionale bellezza** an exceptionally beautiful woman; **chiudere** *o* **finire qc in bellezza** to finish sth with a flourish; **e per finire in bellezza...** (*iro*) and to round it all off perfectly ...; **che bellezza!** fantastic! **b** (*persona, cosa*) beauty; **ciao bellezza!** hello

gorgeous!; **le bellezze di Roma** the beauties *o* sights of Rome; **questo vestito è una bellezza** this dress is really lovely **c** (*quantità*): **ho pagato la bellezza di 160.000 lire** I paid 160,000 lire, no less; **ha impiegato la bellezza di 2 anni a finirlo** he took a good 2 years to finish it.

bellico, a, ci, che ['bɛlliko] AGG war *attr.*

bellicosamente [bellikosa'mente] AVV belligerently.

bellicosità [bellikosi'ta] SF belligerence.

bellicoso, a [belli'koso] AGG (*popolo, nazione*) warlike; (*fig: persona*) quarrelsome.

belligerante [bellidʒe'rante] AGG belligerent.

belligeranza [bellidʒe'rantsa] SF belligerence.

bellimbusto [bellim'busto] SM dandy.

bello , a ['bɛllo]

1 AGG

> davanti sm **bel** + consonante, **bell'** + vocale, **bello** + s impura, gn, pn, ps, x, y, z, pl **bei** + consonante, **begli** + s impura ecc o vocale

a (*oggetto, donna, paesaggio*) beautiful, lovely; (*uomo*) handsome, good-looking;
▷ **le Belle *Arti*** fine arts
▷ *che* **bello!** how lovely!
▷ **è una *gran* bella donna** she's a very good-looking woman
▷ **belle *maniere*** elegant manners
▷ **il bel *mondo*** high society
▷ **una bella *pettinatura*** a nice hairstyle
b (*tempo*) fine, beautiful, lovely;
▷ **fa bello** the weather's lovely *o* beautiful
▷ **è una bella *giornata*** it's a lovely *o* beautiful day
▷ **fa bel *tempo*** it's lovely weather
c (*quantità*) considerable;
▷ **una bella *cifra*** a considerable sum of money
▷ **ha avuto un bel *coraggio*** he was very brave; (*iro*) he had a nerve
▷ **ce n'è rimasto un bel *pezzo*** there's still a good bit left
d (*buono*) good, fine;
▷ **una bella *azione*** a good deed
▷ **fare una bella *dormita*** to have a nice long sleep
▷ **una bella *idea*** a good *o* nice idea
▷ **un bel *lavoro*** a good job
▷ **un bel *pensiero*** a kind thought
▷ **una bella *tazza* di tè** a nice cup of tea
e (*rafforzativo*)
▷ **è una truffa bella e *buona*!** it's a real con!
▷ **è bell'e *fatto*** it's done now
▷ **sei un bel *matto*** you're absolutely crazy
▷ **nel bel *mezzo* di** right in the middle of
▷ **non mi ha dato un bel *niente*** he gave me absolutely nothing
f (*fraseologia*)
▷ **dirne delle belle** to tell some whoppers
▷ **farne delle belle** to get up to mischief
▷ **farsi (più) bello** to get better looking
▷ **è andata a farsi bella** she's gone to make herself beautiful
▷ **farsi bello di qc** (*vantarsi*) to show off about sth
▷ **alla bell'e *meglio*** somehow or other
▷ **oh bella!** OR **questa è bella!** (*iro*) that's nice!

▷**fare la bella** *vita* to lead an easy life.

2 SM

a : *il* **bello** the beautiful, beauty

▷**amare** *il* **bello** to love beauty *o* beautiful things

▷*il* **bello è che**... the best bit about it is that ...

▷**adesso viene** *il* **bello** (*iro*) now comes the best bit

▷**che fai** *di* **bello stasera?** what are you doing this evening?

▷**proprio** *sul* **più bello** at that very moment

b (*tempo*): **si sta mettendo al bello** the weather is clearing up.

3 SMF (*fidanzato*) sweetheart

bellunese [bellu'nese] **1** AGG of *o* from Belluno. **2** SM/F inhabitant *o* native of Belluno.
belva ['belva] SF wild beast *o* animal; **essere una belva** (*fig*) to be an animal.
belvedere [belve'dere] SM INV panoramic viewpoint.
bemolle [be'mɔlle] SM INV (*Mus*) flat.
benché [ben'ke] CONG although, though.
benda ['benda] SF (*Med*) bandage; (*per gli occhi*) blindfold; **avere gli occhi coperti da una benda** to be blindfolded; **avere la benda agli occhi** (*fig*) to be blind.
bendaggio, gi [ben'daddʒo] SM (*atto*) bandaging; (*effetto*) bandage.
bendare [ben'dare] VT (*ferita*) to bandage; (*occhi*) to blindfold.
bendisposto, a [bendis'posto] AGG: **essere bendisposto verso qn/qc** to be well-disposed towards sb/sth.

bene ['bɛne]

1 AVV

a (*gen*) well; (*funzionare*) properly, well;

▷*faresti* **bene a studiare** you'd do well *o* you'd be well advised to study

▷**hai** *fatto* **bene** you did the right thing

▷**ben** *fatto*! well done!

▷*guida* **bene** he drives well, he's a good driver

▷*parla* **bene l'italiano** he speaks Italian well, he speaks good Italian

▷*parlare* **bene di qn** to speak well of sb

▷**gente** *per* **bene** respectable people

▷**sto** *poco* **bene** I'm not very well

▷**ha** *preso* **bene la notizia** he took the news well

▷**se ben** *ricordo* OR **se** *ricordo* **bene** if I remember correctly

▷ **sto bene** I'm fine

▷*va* **bene** all right, okay

b (*con attenzione, completamente*)

▷*ascoltami* **bene** listen to me carefully

▷*ben* **bene** thoroughly

▷**ho legato il pacco** *ben* **bene** I've tied the parcel securely

▷**hai** *capito* **bene?** do you understand?

▷*chiudi* **bene la porta** close the door properly

▷*per* **bene** thoroughly

▷**ho sistemato le cose** *per* **bene** I've sorted things out properly

c (*molto*: + *aggettivo*) very; (: + *comparativo, avverbio*) very much;

▷**ben** *contento* very pleased

▷**è ben** *difficile* it's very difficult

▷**ben** *più* **caro** much more expensive

▷**ben** *più* **lungo** much longer

d (*rafforzativo*: *appunto*)

▷**lo** *credo* **bene** I'm not surprised

▷**te l'avevo ben** *detto* **io che...** I DID tell you that ..., I certainly did tell you that ...

▷*sai* **bene che non dovresti uscire** you know perfectly well you shouldn't go out

▷**come tu ben** *sai* as you well know

▷**lo** *so* **ben io** OR **lo** *so* **fin troppo bene** I know only too well

▷**lo** *spero* **bene** I certainly hope so

e (*addirittura, non meno di*) at least;

▷**hai fatto ben 7 errori** you've made at least 7 mistakes

▷**sono ben 3 giorni che non la vedo** I haven't seen her for at least 3 days

f (*in esclamazioni*)

▷**ho finito — bene!** I've finished — good!

▷**bene, allora possiamo partire** right then, we can go

▷**bene, puoi continuare da solo** all right, you can continue on your own

▷**bene bene!** good (good)!

g (*fraseologia*)

▷**né bene né** *male* so-so

▷**di bene in** *meglio* better and better

▷*tutto* **è bene quel che finisce bene** all's well that ends well.

2 AGG INV

▷**la** *gente* **bene** (*ricca, snob*) well-to-do people

▷**la** *Roma* **bene** the Roman bourgeois.

3 SM

a good

▷*far* **del bene** to do good

▷*fare* **del bene a qn** to do sb a good turn

▷*fare* **bene a** (*salute*) to be good for

▷**quella vacanza ti ha** *fatto* **bene** that holiday has done you good

▷**a** *fin* **di bene** for a good reason

▷**sul tavolo c'era** *ogni* **ben di Dio** there were all sorts of good things on the table

▷**l'ho fatto** *per* **il suo bene** I did it for his own good

▷**è** *stato* **un bene** it was a good thing

▷*volere* **un bene dell'anima a qn** to love sb very much

▷*vuole* **molto bene a suo padre** he loves his father very much, he's very fond of his father

b : **beni** SMPL (*proprietà, anche Dir*) possessions, property *sg*; (*Econ*) goods ▶**beni ambientali** the environment *sg* ▶**beni di consumo** consumer goods ▶**beni culturali** cultural heritage *sg* ▶**beni (di) rifugio** safe assets bought during periods of inflation ▶**beni immobili** real estate *sg* ▶**beni mobili** personal *o* movable property *sg* ▶**beni patrimoniali** fixed assets ▶**beni privati** private property *sg* ▶**beni pubblici** public property *sg*.

benedettino, a [benedet'tino] AGG, SM/F Benedictine.
benedetto, a [bene'detto] **1** PP di **benedire**.
2 AGG blessed; (*santo*) holy; **acqua benedetta** holy water; **Dio benedetto!** Good Lord!
benedire [bene'dire] VT IRREG (*persona*) to bless; (*chiesa*) to consecrate; **che Dio ti benedica!** God bless you!; **l'ho mandato a farsi benedire** (*fig*) I told him to go to hell.

benedizione [benedit'tsjone] SF (*atto*) blessing; (*funzione*) benediction.

beneducato, a [benedu'kato] AGG well-mannered, polite.

benefattore, trice [benefat'tore] SM/F benefactor/benefactress.

beneficenza [benefi'tʃɛntsa] SF charity; **fare opere di beneficenza** to do charity work; **istituto di beneficenza** charitable organization; **festa di beneficenza** charity event.

beneficiare [benefi'tʃare] VI (*aus* avere): **beneficiare di** to benefit by, benefit from; **beneficiare di una borsa di studio** to be awarded a scholarship.

beneficiario, ria, ri, rie [benefi'tʃarjo] AGG, SM/F (*Dir*) beneficiary.

beneficio, ci [bene'fitʃo] SM benefit; **trarre beneficio da** to benefit from *o* by; **il beneficio del dubbio** the benefit of the doubt; **con beneficio d'inventario** (*fig*) with reservations.

benefico, a, ci, che [be'nefiko] AGG (*gen*) beneficial; (*persona*) charitable.

Benelux ['bɛneluks] SM: **il Benelux** the Benelux countries, Benelux.

benemerenza [beneme'rɛntsa] SF merit; **attestato di benemerenza** certificate of merit.

benemerito, a [bene'mɛrito] AGG meritorious.

beneplacito [bene'platʃito] SM (*approvazione*) approval; (*permesso*) permission.

benessere [be'nɛssere] SM, SOLO SG (*salute*) well-being; (*agiatezza*) comfort.

benestante [benes'tante] [1] AGG well-to-do.
  [2] SM/F: **essere un benestante** to be well-off; **i benestanti** SMPL the well-off.

benestare [benes'tare] SM INV approval.

benevolente [benevo'lɛnte] AGG (*letter*) benevolent.

benevolenza [benevo'lɛntsa] SF benevolence; **trattare qn con benevolenza** to treat sb kindly.

benevolmente [benevol'mente] AVV kindly, benevolently.

benevolo, a [be'nɛvolo] AGG benevolent.

benfatto, a [ben'fatto] AGG (*lavoro*) good; (*mobile*) well made; (*pietanza*) well cooked; **una ragazza benfatta** a girl with a good figure.

Bengala [ben'gala] SM Bengal.

bengala [ben'gala] SM INV Bengal light.

bengalese [benga'lese] [1] AGG, SM/F Bengali.
  [2] SM (*lingua*) Bengali.

bengodi [ben'gɔdi] SM land of plenty.

beniamino, a [benja'mino] SM/F favourite (*Brit*), favorite (*Am*); **è il beniamino della maestra** he's the teacher's pet.

benignamente [beniɲɲa'mente] AVV kindly.

benignità [beniɲɲi'ta] SF (*cortesia*) kindness; **trattare con benignità** to treat kindly.

benigno, a [be'niɲɲo] AGG (*gen, Med*) benign; (*sguardo, sorriso*) kindly, kind; (*critica*) favourable (*Brit*), favorable (*Am*).

benintenzionato, a [benintentsjo'nato] AGG well-meaning; **in fondo era benintenzionato** after all he meant well.

beninteso [benin'teso] [1] AVV (*certamente*) of course, certainly.
  [2]: **beninteso che** CONG provided that.

benpensante [benpen'sante] SM/F conformist.

benservito [benser'vito] SM reference; **dare il benservito a qn** (*sul lavoro*) to give sb the sack, fire sb; (*fig*) to send sb packing.

bensì [ben'si] CONG (*ma*) but (rather); (*anzi*) on the contrary.

benvenuto, a [benve'nuto] [1] AGG welcome.
  [2] SM/F: **essere il(la) benvenuto(a)** to be welcome.
  [3] SM welcome; **dare il benvenuto a qn** to welcome sb.

benvisto, a [ben'visto] AGG: **essere benvisto (da)** to be well thought of (by).

benvolere [benvo'lere] VT DIF: **farsi benvolere da tutti** to win everybody's affection; **prendere a benvolere qn/qc** to take a liking to sb/sth.

benvoluto, a [benvo'luto] AGG loved, well liked.

benzina [ben'dzina] SF petrol (*Brit*), gas(oline) (*Am*); **rimanere senza benzina** to run out of petrol *o* gas; **fare benzina** to get petrol *o* gas ►**benzina normale** 3-star petrol (*Brit*), normal grade gasoline (*Am*) ►**benzina super** 4-star petrol (*Brit*), premium gasoline (*Am*) ►**benzina verde** *o* **senza piombo** unleaded petrol *o* gas, lead-free petrol *o* gas.

benzinaio, aia, ai, aie [bendzi'najo] [1] SM/F (*persona*) petrol (*Brit*) *o* gas (*Am*) pump attendant.
  [2] SM (*posto*) petrol station.

beone, a [be'one] SM heavy drinker.

bequadro [be'kwadro] SM INV(*Mus*) natural.

bere ['bere] [1] VT IRREG (*gen*) to drink; (*fig: assorbire*) to soak up; **bere un bicchiere di vino/un caffè** to have a glass of wine/a (cup of) coffee; **ti offro** *o* **ti pago da bere** I'll buy you a drink; **bere qc tutto d'un fiato** to down sth in one gulp; **bevi un po' d'acqua** have a drink of water; **sono le preoccupazioni a farlo bere** his problems have made him turn to drink; **bere come una spugna** to drink like a fish; **bere per dimenticare** to drown one's sorrows (in drink); **bere alla salute di qn** to drink to sb's health; **il motore beve la benzina** the engine is heavy on petrol; **bere le parole di qn** to drink in sb's words; **questa volta non me la dai a bere!** I won't be taken in this time!.
  [2] SM drink; **si è dato al bere** he has turned to drink.

bergamasco, a, schi, sche [berga'masko] [1] AGG of *o* from Bergamo.
  [2] SM/F inhabitant *o* native of Bergamo.

bergamotto [berga'mɔtto] SM bergamot.

berillio [be'rilljo] SM (*Chim*) beryllium.

Bering ['berɛŋ] SM: **il mar di Bering** the Bering Sea.

berlina¹ [ber'lina] SF: **mettere alla berlina** (*fig*) to hold up to ridicule.

berlina² [ber'lina] SF (*Aut*) saloon (car) (*Brit*), sedan (*Am*).

berlinese [berli'nese] [1] AGG Berlin *attr*, of *o* from Berlin.
  [2] SM/F Berliner.

Berlino [ber'lino] SF Berlin.

Bermuda [ber'muda] SFPL: **le Bermuda** Bermuda *sg*.

bermuda [ber'muda] SMPL (*calzoni*) Bermuda shorts.

Berna ['bɛrna] SF Bern.

bernoccolo [ber'nɔkkolo] SM bump; **avere il bernoccolo di qc** (*fig: disposizione*) to have a bent *o* flair for sth.

berretta [ber'retta] SF cap ►**berretta da prete** biretta.

berretto [ber'retto] SM cap ►**berretto con visiera** peaked cap.

berrò *ecc* [ber'rɔ] VB vedi **bere**.

bersagliare [bersaʎ'ʎare] VT (*colpire ripetutamente*) to bombard; **bersagliare di pugni** to rain blows on; **bersagliare di domande** to bombard with questions; **è bersagliato dalla sfortuna** he's dogged by ill fortune.

bersagliere [bersaʎ'ʎere] SM *member of rifle regiment in*

bersaglio, gli [ber'saʎʎo] SM (*anche fig*) target; **colpire il bersaglio** to hit the target; (*fig*) to reach one's target; **era il bersaglio di tutti i loro scherzi** he was the butt of all their jokes.

bertuccia, ce [ber'tuttʃa] SF Barbary ape.

besciamella [beʃʃa'mɛlla] SF béchamel sauce.

bestemmia [bes'temmja] SF (*gen*) curse; (*Rel*) blasphemy; **dire una bestemmia** to swear; (*Rel*) to blaspheme.

bestemmiare [bestem'mjare] VT (*gen*) to curse, swear; (*Rel*) to blaspheme; **bestemmiare come un turco** to swear like a trooper.

bestemmiatore, trice [bestemmja'tore] SM/F (*gen*) swearer; (*Rel*) blasphemer.

bestia ['bestja] SF (*anche fig*) beast, animal; **andare in bestia** (*fig*) to fly into a rage; **lavorare come una bestia** to work like a dog; **mi guardavano come se fossi una bestia rara** they looked at me as if I came from another planet; **bestia!** (*sciocco*) you stupid fool! ►**bestia feroce** wild beast *o* animal ►**bestia da macello** animal for slaughter ►**bestia da soma** beast of burden ►**bestia da tiro** draught animal.

bestiale [bes'tjale] AGG (*gen*) brutal; (*passione, istinto*) animal *attr*; (*fam: terribile*) beastly, terrible; **ha fatto un freddo bestiale** it's been beastly cold; **ho una fame bestiale** I could eat a horse; **fa un caldo bestiale** it's terribly hot.

bestialità [bestjali'ta] SF INV **a** (*qualità*) brutality; (*perversione sessuale*) bestiality **b** : **dire/fare una bestialità dopo l'altra** to say/do one idiotic thing after another.

bestialmente [bestjal'mente] AVV brutishly, like an animal.

bestiame [bes'tjame] SM livestock; (*bovino*) cattle *pl*.

bestiola [bes'tjɔla] SF (small) animal.

Betlemme [bet'lɛmme] SF Bethlehem.

betoniera [beto'njɛra] SF cement mixer.

bettola ['bettola] SF tavern; (*pegg*) dive; **contegno da bettola** coarse behaviour.

betulla [be'tulla] SF birch ►**betulla argentata** *o* **bianca** silver birch.

bevanda [be'vanda] SF drink, beverage (*frm*); **bevanda alcolica/non alcolica** alcoholic/soft drink.

beveraggio, gi [beve'raddʒo] SM (*per animali*) bran mash; (*pozione*) potion; **beveraggi** SMPL (*bevande*) drinks.

beverone [beve'rone] SM (*per animali*) bran mash.

bevibile [be'vibile] AGG drinkable.

bevitore, trice [bevi'tore] SM/F drinker; **un gran bevitore** a heavy drinker.

bevo *ecc* ['bevo] VB *vedi* **bere**.

bevuta [be'vuta] SF drink; **fare una (bella) bevuta** to have a booze-up (*fam*).

bevuto, a [be'vuto] PP di **bere**.

bevvi *ecc* ['bevvi] VB *vedi* **bere**.

BG SIGLA = *Bergamo*.

BI [bi] ☐1 SIGLA F = *Banca d'Italia*. ☐2 SIGLA = *Biella*.

biacca, che ['bjakka] SF (*anche:* **biacca di piombo**) white lead.

biada ['bjada] SF fodder.

Biancaneve [bjanka'neve] SF Snow White.

biancheggiare [bjanked'dʒare] VI (*aus* **avere**) to look white.

biancheria [bjanke'ria] SF (*per casa*) linen ►**biancheria da donna** ladies' underwear, lingerie ►**biancheria intima** underwear.

bianchetto [bjan'ketto] SM **a** (*per scarpe*) whitener; **dare il bianchetto alle scarpe** to whiten one's shoes **b** (*correttore*) whiteout, Tippex ®.

bianchezza [bjan'kettsa] SF whiteness.

bianchiccio, cia, ci, ce [bjan'kittʃo] AGG whitish, off-white; (*persona*) pale.

bianco, a, chi, che ['bjanko] ☐1 AGG **a** (*gen*) white; **essere bianco come un cencio** to be as white as a sheet; **avere i capelli bianchi** to have white hair, be white-haired; **far venire i capelli bianchi a qn** (*fig*) to make sb's hair turn white; **notte bianca** *o* **in bianco** sleepless night

b (*pagina*) blank; **votare scheda bianca** to return a blank voting slip

c (*Mus*): **voce bianca** treble (voice).

☐2 SM **a** (*colore*) white; (*intonaco*) whitewash; (*vino*) white wine; **vestire di bianco** to dress in white; **in bianco e nero** (*TV, Fot*) black and white; **passare una notte in bianco** to have a sleepless night; **andare in bianco** (*non riuscire*) to fail; (*fam: in amore*) to fail to score

b (*non scritto*): **un assegno in bianco** a blank cheque; **lasciare in bianco** to leave blank

c (*Culin*): **bianco d'uovo** egg-white; **pesce/carne in bianco** boiled fish/meat; **mangiare in bianco** to be on a light *o* bland diet.

☐3 SM/F (*persona*) white man/white woman.

biancosegno [bjanko'seɲɲo] SM (*Dir*) signature to a blank document.

biancospino [bjankos'pino] SM hawthorn.

biascicare [bjaʃʃi'kare] VT to mumble.

biasimare [bjazi'mare] VT (*persona*) to blame; (*condotta, azione*) to disapprove of, censure.

biasimevole [bjazi'mevole] AGG blameworthy.

biasimo ['bjazimo] SM (*vedi vt*) blame; disapproval, censure; **degno di biasimo** blameworthy.

Bibbia ['bibbja] SF Bible.

biberon [bibe'rɔn] SM INV (baby's) bottle, feeding bottle.

bibita ['bibita] SF drink ►**bibita analcolica** non-alcoholic drink.

biblico, a, ci, che ['bibliko] AGG biblical.

bibliografia [bibljogra'fia] SF bibliography.

bibliografico, a, ci, che [bibljo'grafiko] AGG bibliographical.

bibliografo, a [bibli'ografo] SM/F bibliographer.

biblioteca, che [bibljo'tɛka] SF (*edificio*) library; (*mobile*) bookcase.

bibliotecario, ria, ri, rie [bibljote'karjo] SM/F librarian.

biblioteconomia [bibljotekono'mia] SF librarianship.

bicamerale [bikame'rale] AGG (*Pol*) two-chamber *attr*.

bicarbonato [bikarbo'nato] SM: **bicarbonato (di sodio)** bicarbonate (of soda).

bicchierata [bikkje'rata] SF (*bevuta*) drink.

bicchiere [bik'kjɛre] SM glass; **bicchiere di vino** glass of wine; **bere un bicchiere** to have a drink; **è (facile) come bere un bicchier d'acqua** it's as easy as pie ►**bicchiere a calice** goblet ►**bicchiere di carta** paper cup ►**bicchiere graduato** measuring jug ►**bicchiere da vino** wine glass.

bicefalo, a [bi'tʃɛfalo] AGG two-headed.

bici ['bitʃi] SF INV (*fam*) bike.

bicicletta [bitʃi'kletta] SF bicycle, bike; **andare in bicicletta** to cycle; **sai andare in bicicletta?** can you ride a bike? ►**bicicletta da corsa** racing cycle.

bicilindrico, a, ci, che [bitʃi'lindriko] AGG (*Tecn*) two-

cylinder *attr.*

bicipite [bi'tʃipite] ① AGG **a** (*Anat*): **(muscolo) bicipite** biceps *sg o pl* **b** (*che ha due teste*) two-headed. ② SM biceps *sg o pl*.

bicocca, che [bi'kɔkka] SF hovel.

bicolore [biko'lore] AGG two-tone; **governo bicolore** (*Pol*) two-party government.

bicromato [bikro'mato] SM dichromate.

bicromia [bikro'mia] SF (*procedimento*) two-colour printing; (*illustrazione*) two-colour print.

bidè, bidet [bi'dɛ] SM INV bidet.

bidello, a [bi'dɛllo] SM/F (*di scuola*) janitor; (*di università*) porter.

bidimensionale [bidimensjo'nale] AGG two-dimensional.

bidirezionale [bidirettsjo'nale] AGG bidirectional.

bidonare [bido'nare] VT (*fam: imbrogliare*) to cheat, swindle;'(: *piantare in asso*) to let down.

bidonata [bido'nata] SF (*fam: imbroglio*) swindle; (: *delusione*) let-down; **fare o tirare una bidonata a qn** (*imbrogliare*) to cheat o do sb; (*deludere*) to let sb down.

bidone [bi'done] SM **a** (*recipiente*) drum; (*più piccolo*) can ▶ **bidone da latte** churn ▶ **bidone per la spazzatura** o **dei rifiuti** dustbin **b** vedi **bidonata**.

bidonville [bidɔ]'vil] SF INV shanty town.

biecamente [bjeka'mente] AVV sinisterly, in a sinister way.

bieco, a, chi, che ['bjɛko] AGG sinister.

biella ['bjɛlla] SF (*Tecn*) connecting rod.

Bielorussia [bjelo'russja] SF Belarus, Belorussia.

bielorusso, a AGG, SM/F Belarussian, Belorussian.

biennale [bien'nale] ① AGG (*che dura 2 anni*) two-year *attr*; (*che avviene ogni 2 anni*) two-yearly, biennial; **la mostra è biennale** the exhibition is held every two years. ② SF: **la Biennale di Venezia** *the Venice Arts Festival: an international event which includes national pavilions, an exhibition on a particular theme and a section for young artists.*

biennalmente [biennal'mente] AVV (*vedi agg*) every two years; biennially.

biennio, ni [bi'ɛnnjo] SM **a** period of two years; **nel prossimo biennio** over the next two years **b** (*Univ*) two-year foundation course.

bierre [bi'ɛrre] SM/F *member of the Red Brigades.*

bietola ['bjɛtola] SF (*Bot*) chard; (*fam: barbabietola*) beet.

bifase [bi'faze] AGG (*Elettr*) two-phase *attr*.

bifocale [bifo'kale] AGG bifocal.

bifolco, a, chi, che [bi'folko] SM/F (*pegg*) bumpkin, yokel.

bifora ['bifora] SF (*Archit*) mullioned window.

biforcarsi [bifor'karsi] VIP (*fiume, strada*) to divide, fork; (*Ferr*) to branch.

biforcazione [biforkat'tsjone] SF (*di fiume, strada*) fork; (*Ferr*) junction.

biforcuto, a [bifor'kuto] AGG (*anche fig*) forked; **lingua biforcuta** forked tongue.

bifronte [bi'fronte] AGG (*anche fig*) two-faced.

big [big] SM INV (*dello spettacolo*) star; (*dell'industria*) big noise, big shot.

bigamia [biga'mia] SF bigamy.

bigamo, a ['bigamo] ① AGG bigamous. ② SM/F bigamist.

bighellonare [bigello'nare] VI (*aus avere*) to loaf about.

bighellone, a [bigel'lone] SM/F loafer.

bigio, gia, gi, ge o gie ['bidʒo] AGG dull grey.

bigiotteria [bidʒotte'ria] SF (*gioielli*) costume jewellery

(*Brit*) o jewelry (*Am*); (*negozio*) shop selling costume jewel(le)ry.

biglia ['biʎʎa] SF = **bilia**.

bigliardo [biʎ'ʎardo] SM = **biliardo**.

bigliettaio, aia, ai, aie [biʎʎet'tajo] SM/F (*in treno*) ticket inspector; (*in autobus*) conductor/conductress; (*in cinema, teatro*) box-office attendant.

bigliettazione [biʎʎettat'tsjone] SF: **bigliettazione automatica** (*su autobus*) automatic ticketing system.

biglietteria [biʎʎette'ria] SF (*gen*) ticket office; (*di teatro*) box office; (*per prenotazioni*) booking office.

biglietto [biʎ'ʎetto] ① SM **a** (*per viaggio, entrata*) ticket; **fare/comprare il biglietto** to get/buy one's ticket ▶ **biglietto di andata e ritorno** return (ticket) (*Brit*), round-trip ticket (*Am*) ▶ **biglietto aperto** (*Aer*) open ticket ▶ **biglietto chiuso** (*Aer*) closed ticket ▶ **biglietto omaggio** complimentary ticket ▶ **biglietto di (sola) andata** single (ticket) (*Brit*), one-way ticket (*Am*) **b** (*banconota*): **biglietto (di banca)** banknote, note, bill (*Am*); **un biglietto da 10.000 (lire)** a 10.000 lire note **c** (*nota*) note; (*cartoncino*) card ▶ **biglietto d'auguri** greetings card ▶ **biglietto da visita** visiting card.

bignè [biɲ'ɲɛ] SM INV cream puff.

bigodino [bigo'dino] SM roller.

bigoncia, ce [bi'gontʃa] SF wooden tub.

bigotteria [bigotte'ria] SF pharisaism.

bigotto, a [bi'gotto] ① AGG pharisaic. ② SM/F pharisee.

bijou [bi'ʒu] SM INV (*gioiello*) piece of costume jewellery; (*fig*) jewel, gem.

bikini [bi'kini] SM INV bikini.

bilancia, ce [bi'lantʃa] SF **a** (*gen*) scales *pl*; (*a due piatti*) pair of scales; (*di precisione*) balance; (*bascula*) weighing machine; **mettere qc sulla bilancia** to weigh sth; (*fig*) to weigh sth up **b** (*Astrol: anche:* **Bilancia**) Libra; **essere della Bilancia** to be Libra **c** (*Econ*): **bilancia commerciale/dei pagamenti** balance of trade/payments **d** (*Pesca*) drop-net.

bilanciare [bilan'tʃare] ① VT **a** (*tenere in equilibrio*) to balance; **bilanciare il carico** to spread the load evenly **b** (*Comm*) to balance; **bilanciare le uscite e le entrate** to balance expenditure and revenue; **le uscite bilanciano le entrate** expenditure and revenue balance out **c** (*fig: valutare*) to weigh up. ② **bilanciarsi** VR **a** (*uso reciproco: equipararsi*) to be equal **b** (*stare in equilibrio*) to balance (o.s.).

bilanciato, a [bilan'tʃato] AGG balanced.

bilanciere [bilan'tʃere] SM (*di orologio*) balance wheel; (*di motore*) compensator; (*per sollevamento pesi*) bar.

bilancino [bilan'tʃino] SM (*bilancia*) balance; (*sci nautico*) ski rope handle; **dobbiamo pesare la questione col bilancino** (*fig*) we must weigh up the problem very carefully.

bilancio, ci [bi'lantʃo] SM (*Comm: cifre*) balance; (: *documento*) balance sheet; **fare il bilancio** OR **chiudere il bilancio** to draw up the balance sheet; **far quadrare il bilancio** to balance the books; **chiudere il bilancio in attivo/passivo** to make a profit/loss; **fare il bilancio della situazione** (*fig*) to assess the situation ▶ **bilancio consolidato** consolidated balance ▶ **bilancio consuntivo** final balance ▶ **bilancio preventivo** budget

▶**bilancio settimanale/mensile** weekly/monthly balance ▶**bilancio dello stato** budget ▶**bilancio di verifica** trial balance.

bilaterale [bilate'rale] AGG bilateral.

bilateralmente [bilateral'mente] AVV bilaterally.

bile ['bile] SF (*Med*) bile; (*fig: rabbia*) anger, rage; **era verde dalla bile** he was white with rage.

bilia ['bilja] SF **a** (*di vetro*) marble; **giocare a bilie** to play marbles **b** (*da biliardo: pallina*) billiard ball; (: *buca*) (billiard) pocket.

biliardino [biljar'dino] SM (small) billiard table; (*elettrico*) pinball.

biliardo [bi'ljardo] SM billiards *sg*; (*tavolo*) billiard table; **giocare a biliardo** to play billiards; **sala da biliardo** poolroom.

biliare [bi'ljare] AGG (*Med*) biliary; **calcolo biliare** gallstone.

bilico ['biliko] SM: **essere** *o* **stare in bilico** to be balanced; (*fig*) to be undecided; **essere in bilico tra la vita e la morte** to be suspended between life and death; **tenere qn in bilico** to keep sb in suspense.

bilingue [bi'lingwe] AGG bilingual.

bilinguismo [bilin'gwizmo] SM bilingualism.

bilione [bi'ljone] SM (*mille milioni*) thousand million, billion (*Am*); (*milione di milioni*) billion (*Brit*), trillion (*Am*).

bilioso, a [bi'ljoso] AGG (*fig*) bad-tempered.

bimbo, a ['bimbo] SM/F (*bambino*) child, little boy/girl; (*bebè*) baby.

bimensile [bimen'sile] AGG twice-monthly, fortnightly (*Brit*).

bimestrale [bimes'trale] AGG (*che dura 2 mesi*) two-month *attr*; (*che avviene ogni 2 mesi*) two-monthly, bimonthly; **pagamento bimestrale** payment every 2 months; **rivista bimestrale** bimonthly magazine.

bimestralmente [bimestral'mente] AVV every two months.

bimestre [bi'mɛstre] SM two-month period; **ogni bimestre** every two months.

bimetallico, a, ci, che [bime'talliko] AGG bimetallic.

bimotore [bimo'tore] [1] AGG twin-engined.

[2] SM (*aereo*) twin-engined plane.

binario¹, ria, ri, rie [bi'narjo] AGG (*Astron, Chim, Mat, Mus*) binary.

binario², ri [bi'narjo] SM (*rotaie*) (railway) track *o* line; (*piattaforma*) platform; **uscire dai binari** to come off the rails; (*fig*) to go off the rails ▶**binario morto** dead-end track; **siamo su un binario morto** (*fig*) we're not going to get anywhere ▶**binario unico/doppio** single/double track.

binocolo [bi'nɔkolo] SM (*gen*) binoculars *pl*; (*da teatro*) opera glasses *pl* ▶**binocolo prismatico** prism binoculars.

binoculare [binoku'lare] AGG binocular.

binomio, mia, mi, mie [bi'nɔmjo] [1] AGG binomial.

[2] SM **a** (*Mat*) binomial **b** (*fig: due persone*): **il binomio Laurel e Hardy** the Laurel and Hardy duo.

bio... ['bio] PREF bio... .

biochimica [bio'kimika] SF biochemistry.

biochimico, a, ci, che [bio'kimiko] [1] AGG biochemical.

[2] SM/F biochemist.

biodegradabile [biodegra'dabile] AGG biodegradable.

biodegradabilità [biodegradabili'ta] SF biodegradability.

biodiversità [biodiversi'ta] SF INV biodiversity.

bioetica [bio'ɛtika] SF bioethics *sg*.

bioetico, a, ci, che [bio'ɛtiko] AGG bioethical.

biofabbrica [bio'fabbrika] SF factory producing biological control agents.

biofisica [bio'fizika] SF biophysics *sg*.

biofisico, a, ci, che [bio'fiziko] [1] AGG biophysical.

[2] SM/F biophysicist.

biografia [biogra'fia] SF biography.

biografico, a, ci, che [bio'grafiko] AGG biographical.

biografo, a [bi'ɔgrafo] SM/F biographer.

biologia [biolo'dʒia] SF biology.

biologico, a, ci, che [bio'lɔdʒiko] AGG biological.

biologo, a, gi, ghe [bi'ɔlogo] SM/F biologist.

biondeggiare [bjonded'dʒare] VI (*aus avere*) (*letter: messi*) to be golden.

biondiccio, cia, ci, ce [bjon'dittʃo] AGG fairish, blondish.

biondo, a ['bjondo] [1] AGG (*capelli*) fair, blond; (*persona*) fair, fair-haired; **biondo cenere/platino** ash/platinum blond.

[2] SM (*colore*) blond; (*uomo*) fair-haired man.

[3] SF (*donna*) blonde.

bionica [bi'ɔnika] SF bionics *sg*.

bionico, a, ci, che [bi'ɔniko] AGG bionic.

biopsia [bio'psia] SF biopsy.

bioritmo [bio'ritmo] SM biorhythm.

biosfera [bios'fɛra] SF biosphere.

bipartitico, a, ci, che [bipar'titiko] AGG (*Pol*) two-party *attr*.

bipartitismo [biparti'tizmo] SM (*Pol*) two-party system.

bipartito, a [bipar'tito] (*Pol*) [1] AGG two-party *attr*.

[2] SM two-party alliance.

bipede ['bipede] AGG, SM biped.

biplano [bi'plano] SM biplane.

bipolare [bipo'lare] AGG bipolar.

biposto [bi'posto] AGG INV two-seater *attr*.

birba ['birba] SF rascal, rogue.

birbante [bir'bante] SM rascal, rogue.

birbanteria [birbante'ria] SF (*qualità*) mischievousness; (*azione*) mischievous trick.

birbonata [birbo'nata] SF naughty trick.

birbone, a [bir'bone] [1] AGG (*bambino*) naughty; **fare un tiro birbone a qn** to play a naughty trick on sb.

[2] SM/F (*bambino*) little rascal.

bireattore [bireat'tore] SM twin-engined jet.

birichinata [biriki'nata] SF prank, practical joke.

birichino, a [biri'kino] [1] AGG (*bambino*) mischievous, impish; (*adulto*) sly; **sguardo birichino** sly look.

[2] SM/F (*bambino*) little rascal, scamp.

birillo [bi'rillo] SM skittle (*Brit*), pin (*Am*); **birilli** SMPL (*gioco*) skittles *sg*.

Birmania [bir'manja] SF: **la Birmania** Burma.

birmano, a [bir'mano] AGG, SM/F, SM Burmese.

biro® ['biro] SF INV biro®.

birra ['birra] SF (*gen*) beer, ale; **fabbrica di birra** brewery; **a tutta birra** (*fig: veloce*) at top speed, flat out ▶**birra in bottiglia** bottled beer ▶**birra chiara** lager ▶**birra scura** stout ▶**birra alla spina** draught beer.

birraio, ai [bir'rajo] SM (*fabbricante*) brewer.

birreria [birre'ria] SF (*locale*) ≈ bierkeller; (*fabbrica*) brewery.

bis [bis] [1] ESCL encore!.

[2] SM INV encore; **chiedere il bis** (*Teatro*) to call for an encore; (*fig: a tavola*) to ask for a second helping.

[3] AGG INV (*treno, autobus*) relief *attr* (*Brit*), additional;

(*numero*): **12 bis** 12a.

bisaccia, ce [bi'zattʃa] SF knapsack.

Bisanzio [bi'zantsjo] SF Byzantium.

bisavolo, a [bi'zavolo], **bisavo, a** [bi'zavo] SM/F great-grandfather *m*, great-grandmother *f*; **bisavoli** SMPL (*antenati*) forefathers.

bisbeticamente [bizbetika'mente] AVV ill-temperedly, crabbily.

bisbetico, a, ci, che [biz'bɛtiko] AGG ill-tempered, crabby.

bisbigliare [bizbiʎ'ʎare] VT, VI (*aus* **avere**) (*anche fig*) to whisper.

bisbiglio[1]**, glii** [bizbiʎ'ʎio] SM (*anche fig*) whisper.

bisbiglio[2]**, gli** [biz'biʎʎo] SM (*anche fig*) whispering.

bisboccia, ce [biz'bottʃa] SF binge, spree; **fare bisboccia** to go on a binge.

bisca, sche ['biska] SF gambling den.

Biscaglia [bis'kaʎʎa] SF: **il golfo di Biscaglia** the Bay of Biscay.

biscazziere [biskat'tsjɛre] SM *manager* (*o owner*) *of a gambling den*.

bischero ['biskero] SM **a** (*fam: toscano*) fool, idiot **b** (*Mus*) peg.

biscia, sce ['biʃʃa] SF grass snake ▶ **biscia d'acqua** water snake.

biscottato, a [biskot'tato] AGG crisp; **fette biscottate** rusks.

biscottiera [biskot'tjɛra] SF biscuit barrel; (*di latta*) biscuit tin.

biscottificio, ci [biskotti'fitʃo] SM biscuit factory.

biscotto [bis'kɔtto] SM biscuit.

biscuit [bis'kɥt] SM INV (*anche:* **porcellana di biscuit**) biscuit.

bisdrucciolo, a [biz'druttʃolo] AGG (*Gramm*) *with the stress on the fourth-last syllable*.

bisecare [bise'kare] VT (*Mat*) to bisect.

bisessuale [bisessu'ale] AGG, SM/F bisexual.

bisessualità [bisessuali'ta] SF INV bisexuality.

bisestile [bizes'tile] AGG: **anno bisestile** leap year.

bisettimanale [bisettima'nale] AGG twice-weekly.

bisettore, trice [biset'tore] [1] AGG bisecting. [2] SF bisector.

bisex [bi'sɛks] AGG INV, SM/F INV (*fam*) bi (*fam*), bisexual.

bisezione [biset'tsjone] SF (*Geom*) bisection.

bisillabo, a [bi'sillabo] [1] AGG disyllabic. [2] SM disyllable.

bislacco, a, chi, che [biz'lakko] AGG odd, weird; **è una testa bislacca** he's an odd fellow.

bislungo, a, ghi, ghe [biz'lungo] AGG oblong.

bismuto [biz'muto] SM (*Chim*) bismuth.

bisnipote [bizni'pote] SM/F (*di nonni*) great-grandchild, great-grandson/granddaughter; (*di zii*) great-nephew/niece.

bisnonno, a [biz'nɔnno] SM/F great-grandfather/grandmother.

bisognare [bizoɲ'ɲare] [1] VB IMPERS: **bisogna partire** we must leave, we've got to leave, we'll have to leave; **bisogna parlargli** we'll (*o* I'll) have to talk to him; **bisogna che arriviate in tempo** you must *o* you'll have to arrive on time; **bisognerebbe che si decidesse** he should make up his mind; **non bisogna lamentarsi sempre** one *o* you shouldn't complain all the time; **bisogna vedere!** (*dipende*) I'll (*o* you'll *ecc*) have to see how things go!; **bisogna proprio dire che...** it has to be

said that ....

[2] VI (*aus* **essere**) (*aver bisogno*) to need, want; **cosa le bisogna?** (*ant: in negozio*) can I help you?

bisognevole [bizoɲ'ɲevole] AGG (*letter*): **bisognevole di** in need of.

bisogno [bi'zoɲɲo] SM **a** (*necessità*) need, necessity; **aver bisogno di** to need, be in need of; **aver bisogno di fare qc** to need to do sth; **sentire il bisogno di qc/di fare qc** to feel the need for sth/to do sth; **c'è bisogno di te qui** we need you here; **non c'è bisogno che venga anche tu** there's no need for you to come too; **in caso di bisogno** if need be, if necessary; **non c'è bisogno di gridare** there's no need to shout; **nel momento del bisogno** in one's hour of need

b (*povertà*) poverty, need; **trovarsi nel bisogno** to be in want

c (*euf: necessità corporali*): **fare i bisogni** (*persona*) to go to the toilet; (*animale*) to do its business.

bisognoso, a [bizoɲ'ɲoso] AGG **a** (*che ha bisogno*): **bisognoso di** in need of, needing **b** (*povero*) poor, needy.

bisonte [bi'zonte] SM (*Zool*) bison.

bisso ['bisso] SM (*tessuto*) fine linen.

bistecca, che [bis'tekka] SF steak; **bistecca al sangue/ai ferri** rare/grilled steak.

bistecchiera [bistek'kjɛra] SF gridiron.

bisticciare [bistit'tʃare] VI (*aus* **avere**), **bisticciarsi** VR (*uso reciproco*) to bicker, squabble.

bisticcio, ci [bis'tittʃo] SM **a** (*litigio*) quarrel, squabble **b** (*gioco di parole*) pun, play on words.

bistrattare [bistrat'tare] VT to maltreat.

bistro ['bistro] SM bistre.

bistrò [bis'trɔ'] **bistrot** [bis'tro] SM INV (*locale*) bistro.

bisturi ['bisturi] SM INV (*Med*) scalpel.

bisunto, a [bi'zunto] AGG (*unto*) very greasy; **un cappotto unto e bisunto** a filthy, greasy coat.

bit [bit] SM INV (*Inform*) bit.

bitorzolo [bi'tortsolo] SM (*sulla testa*) bump; (*sul corpo*) lump.

bitorzoluto, a [bitortso'luto] AGG (*albero*) gnarled, knotted; (*faccia*) warty.

bitta ['bitta] SF (*Naut: sulla banchina*) bollard; (: *sulla nave*) bitt.

bitter ['bitter] SM INV bitters *pl*.

bitumare [bitu'mare] VT to bituminize.

bitume [bi'tume] SM bitumen.

bituminoso, a [bitumi'noso] AGG bituminous.

bivaccare [bivak'kare] VI (*aus* **avere**) (*Mil*) to bivouac; (*fig*) to bed down.

bivacco, chi [bi'vakko] SM bivouac.

bivio, vi ['bivjo] SM (*di una strada*) fork, junction; **trovarsi davanti a un bivio** (*fig*) to be at a crossroads.

bizantino, a [biddzan'tino] AGG Byzantine; (*fig: pedante*) pedantic; **questioni bizantine** convoluted questions.

bizza ['biddza] SF tantrum; **fare le bizze** to throw a tantrum; **la macchina fa le bizze oggi** the car is playing up today.

bizzarramente [biddzarra'mente] AVV oddly, strangely.

bizzarria [biddzar'ria] SF **a** (*qualità*) eccentricity, weirdness **b** (*azione*) whim, caprice; (*cosa*) oddity.

bizzarro, a [bid'dzarro] AGG **a** (*strano, eccentrico*) odd, queer, eccentric **b** (*focoso: cavallo*) frisky.

bizzeffe [bid'dzɛffe] AVV: **a bizzeffe** in abundance, in plenty, galore; **avere soldi a bizzeffe** to be rolling in money.

bizzosamente [biddzosa'mente] AVV (*vedi agg*) irritably; capriciously.

bizzoso, a [bid'dzoso] AGG **a** (*irascibile*) irritable, quick-tempered; (*capriccioso*) capricious, self-willed **b** (*ombroso: cavallo*) frisky.

BL SIGLA = *Belluno*.

blandamente [blanda'mente] AVV mildly.

blandire [blan'dire] VT (*alleviare*) to soothe; (*lusingare*) to flatter.

blando, a ['blando] AGG (*medicina, rimedio*) mild, gentle; (*liquore*) weak; (*sapore, cibo*) bland; (*punizione*) light, mild.

blasfemo, a [blas'fɛmo] **1** AGG blasphemous. **2** SM/F blasphemer.

blasone [bla'zone] SM coat of arms, escutcheon.

blaterare [blate'rare] **1** VI (*aus* **avere**) to blether. **2** VT to blether about; **ma cosa vai blaterando?** what are you blethering about?

blatta ['blatta] SF cockroach.

blazer ['bleizə] SM INV blazer.

blindare [blin'dare] VT (*veicolo*) to armour; (*porta*) to reinforce.

blindata [blin'data] SF (*macchina*) armoured car o limousine.

blindato, a [blin'dato] AGG armoured (*Brit*), armored (*Am*); **camera blindata** strongroom; **mezzo blindato** armoured vehicle; **porta blindata** reinforced door; **vetro blindato** bulletproof glass; **condurre una vita blindata** (*fig*) to live surrounded by maximum security.

blister ['blista] SM INV blister pack.

blitz [blits] SM INV (*Mil*) blitz; (*di polizia*) swoop, raid.

bloccare [blok'kare] **1** VT **a** (*ostruire: strada*) to block (up); (*fermare: assegno, pallone, persona*) to stop; (: *comandi, meccanismo*) to jam; (: *merci*) to stop, hold up; (: *negoziati*) to block, hold up; (: *prezzi, affitti*) to freeze; **la strada è bloccata da una frana** the road is blocked by a landslide; **la neve ha bloccato molti paesi** the snow has cut off many villages, many villages are snow-bound; **la polizia ha bloccato le vie d'accesso alla città** the police have blocked off the roads leading to the city; **sono rimasto bloccato in un ingorgo/nell'ascensore** I was stuck in a traffic jam/in the lift; **ha bloccato la macchina** he braked suddenly, he slammed on the brakes; **blocca la sicura** put on the safety catch
b (*Mil*) to blockade
c (*Inform*) to block.
2 **bloccarsi** VIP (*motore*) to stall; (*freni, porta*) to jam, stick; (*ascensore*) to get stuck, stop; **si è bloccato nel bel mezzo del discorso** he suddenly stopped in the middle of what he was saying.

bloccasterzo [blokkas'tɛrtso] SM (*Aut*) steering lock.

bloccherò ecc [blokke'rɔ] VB *vedi* **bloccare**.

blocchetto [blok'ketto] SM notebook ►**blocchetto delle ricevute** receipt book.

blocchista, i [blok'kista] SM (*Comm*) wholesale dealer.

blocco¹, chi ['blɔkko] SM **a** (*gen*) block; **in blocco** (*Comm*) in bulk; **considerare/condannare qc in blocco** (*fig*) to take/condemn sth as a whole ►**blocchi di partenza** (*Sport*) starting blocks
b (*per appunti*) notebook; (*di carta da lettere*) (writing) pad
c (*Pol*) bloc, coalition; **l'ex blocco orientale** the former Eastern bloc
d (*Aut*): **blocco cilindri** cylinder block ►**blocco motore** engine block.

blocco², chi ['blɔkko] SM **a** (*Mil*) blockade; **posto di blocco** (*sul confine*) frontier post; (*di polizia: anche:* **blocco stradale**) road block **b** (*Comm*) freeze ►**blocco degli affitti** rent freeze ►**blocco dei salari** wage freeze **c** (*Med*): **blocco cardiaco** cardiac arrest ►**blocco renale** kidney failure.

bloc-notes [blɔk'nɔt] SM INV notebook, notepad.

blu [blu] AGG INV, SM INV dark blue; **blu scuro** navy (blue).

bluastro, a [blu'astro] AGG bluish.

blue jeans [bludʒi:nz] SMPL (blue) jeans.

blues [blu:z] SM INV (*Mus*) blues *pl*.

bluette [bly'ɛt] AGG INV, SM INV bright blue.

bluff [blɛf] SM INV (*anche fig*) bluff; **un bluff pubblicitario** a publicity stunt.

bluffare [bluf'fare] VI (*aus* **avere**) (*anche fig*) to bluff.

bluffatore, trice [bluffa'tore] SM/F bluffer.

blusa ['bluza] SF (*camicetta*) blouse; (*per pittore*) smock; (*per operaio*) overall.

blusante [blu'zante] AGG loose-fitting.

blusotto [blu'zɔtto] SM jerkin.

BN SIGLA = *Benevento*.

BO SIGLA = *Bologna*.

boa¹ ['bɔa] SM INV **a** (*serpente*) boa (constrictor) **b** (*sciarpa*) feather boa.

boa² ['bɔa] SF (*Naut*) buoy.

boato [bo'ato] SM (*di esplosione*) noise; (*di folla*) roar; (*di tuono*) rumble; **boato sonico** sonic boom.

bob [bɔb] SM INV bobsleigh.

bobbista, i, e [bob'bista] SM/F (*Sport*) bobsledder, bobsleigh rider.

bobina [bo'bina] SF **a** (*Elettr*) coil ►**bobina d'accensione** (*Aut*) ignition coil **b** (*di film*) reel; (*di pellicola*) spool **c** (*di cotone*) reel, bobbin, spool.

bocca, che ['bokka] SF **a** (*gen*) mouth; **per bocca** orally; **rimanere a bocca asciutta** to have nothing to eat; (*fig*) to be disappointed; **rimanere a bocca aperta** (*fig*) to be taken aback; **non ha aperto bocca** (*parlare*) he didn't open his mouth; **vuoi chiudere la bocca?** (*star zitto*) will you shut up?; **essere sulla bocca di tutti** (*persona, notizia*) to be the talk of the town; **essere di bocca buona** to eat anything; (*fig*) to be easily satisfied; **fare la bocca a qc** to acquire a taste for sth; **non voglio metter bocca in questa storia** I don't want to interfere; **mi hai tolto la parola di bocca** you took the words out of my mouth; **in bocca al lupo!** good luck!; **respirazione bocca a bocca** mouth-to-mouth resuscitation, kiss of life (*fam*)
b (*di fiume, recipiente*) mouth ►**bocca d'acqua** hydrant **c** (*Bot*): **bocca di leone** snapdragon.

boccaccia, ce [bok'kattʃa] SF **a** (*smorfia*): **fare le boccacce** to pull faces **b** (*persona maldicente*) foul-mouthed person.

boccaglio, gli [bok'kaʎʎo] SM (*Tecn*) nozzle; (*di respiratore*) mouthpiece.

boccale¹ [bok'kale] AGG (*Anat*) oral.

boccale² [bok'kale] SM (*recipiente*) jug; (*per bere*) mug ►**boccale da birra** beer mug, tankard.

boccaporto [bokka'porto] SM (*Naut*) hatch.

boccascena [bokkaʃ'ʃɛna] SM INV proscenium.

boccata [bok'kata] SF mouthful; (*di fumo*) puff; **prendere una boccata d'aria** to go out for a breath of (fresh) air.

boccetta [bot'tʃetta] SF phial, small bottle.

boccheggiante [bokked'dʒante] AGG **a** (*che boccheggia*) gasping (for breath) **b** (*morente*) at one's last gasp.

boccheggiare [bokked'dʒare] VI (*aus* **avere**) to gasp.

bocchetta [bok'ketta] SF **a** (*di strumento musicale*) mouth-piece; (*di tasca da pasticciere*) nozzle **b** (*di serratura*) plate **c** : **bocchetta stradale** drain cover.

bocchettone [bokket'tone] SM (*Tecn*) (pipe) union.

bocchino [bok'kino] SM (*di pipa, strumento musicale*) mouthpiece; (*per sigarette*) cigarette holder.

boccia, ce ['bɔttʃa] SF **a** (*palla di legno, metallo*) bowl; **il gioco delle bocce** bowls *sg*; **giocare a bocce** to play bowls **b** (*bottiglia*) bottle; (: *da vino*) carafe.

bocciare [bot'tʃare] VT **a** (*respingere*) to reject; (: *agli esami*) to fail **b** (*alle bocce*) to hit.

bocciatura [bottʃa'tura] SF (*agli esami*) failure.

boccino [bot'tʃino] SM (*Bocce*) jack.

boccio, ci ['bɔttʃo] SM bud; **in boccio** (*albero, pianta*) in bud.

bocciodromo [bot'tʃɔdromo] SM bowling ground.

bocciolo [bot'tʃɔlo] SM bud ▶ **bocciolo di rosa** rosebud.

boccola ['bɔkkola] SF (*fibbia*) buckle.

boccolo ['bɔkkolo] SM curl.

bocconcino [bokkon'tʃino] SM (*pietanza deliziosa*) delicacy.

boccone [bok'kone] SM (*quantità di cibo*) mouthful; **mangiare un boccone** to have a bite to eat; **inghiottire un boccone amaro** (*fig*) to swallow a bitter pill; **finire tutto in un boccone** to down everything at one gulp ▶ **boccone del prete** (*Culin*) parson's nose.

bocconi [bok'koni] AVV face downwards; **cadere bocconi** to fall flat on one's face.

body ['bɔdi] SM INV (*intimo*) body stocking; (*per danza, ginnastica*) leotard.

Boemia [bo'ɛmja] SF Bohemia.

boemo, a [bo'ɛmo] AGG, SM/F Bohemian.

boero, a [bo'ɛro] AGG, SM/F Boer.

bofonchiare [bofon'kjare] VI (*aus* **avere**) to grumble.

Bogotà [bogo'ta] SF Bogotá.

bohemien [boe'mjɛ̃] AGG INV, SM/F INV bohemian.

boia ['bɔja] **1** SM INV **a** (*carnefice*) executioner; (: *in impiccagione*) hangman; (*fig: mascalzone*) rogue, scoundrel **b** (*in escl: fam*): **boia d'una miseria!, boia d'un mondo ladro!** damn!, blast!.
2 AGG INV (*fam*): **fa un freddo boia** it's cold as hell.

boiata [bo'jata] SF (*fam: robaccia*) rubbish; **quel film era una boiata** that film was (a load of) rubbish; **non dire boiate!** (*sciocchezze*) don't talk rubbish!

boicottaggio, gi [boikot'taddʒo] SM boycott; (*fig*) sabotage.

boicottare [boikot'tare] VT (*Econ, fig: persona*) to boycott; (: *piani*) to sabotage.

boiler ['bɔilə] SM INV water heater.

bolentino [bolen'tino] SM (*Pesca*) fishing line.

bolero [bo'lɛro] SM bolero.

bolgia, ge ['bɔldʒa] SF (*fig*): **c'era una tale bolgia al cinema** the cinema was absolutely mobbed.

bolide ['bɔlide] SM **a** (*Astron*) meteor; **come un bolide** like a flash, at top speed; **entrare/uscire come un bolide** to charge in/out **b** (*auto da corsa*) racing car (*Brit*), race car (*Am*).

bolina [bo'lina] SF (*Naut*): **di bolina** close-hauled, on the wind.

Bolivia [bo'livja] SF: **la Bolivia** Bolivia.

boliviano, a [boli'vjano] AGG, SM/F Bolivian.

bolla¹ ['bolla] SF bubble; (*Med*) blister; **fare le bolle di sapone** to blow bubbles; **finire in una bolla di sapone**

(*fig*) to come to nothing.

bolla² ['bolla] SF **a** (*Comm*) bill, receipt ▶ **bolla di accompagnamento** waybill ▶ **bolla di consegna** delivery note **b** (*Rel*): **bolla papale** papal bull.

bollare [bol'lare] VT (*timbrare*) to stamp; (*sigillare*) to seal; (*fig*) to brand; **bollato a vita** (*fig*) branded for life; **carta bollata** official stamped paper.

bollatrice [bolla'tritʃe] SF stamping machine.

bollente [bol'lɛnte] AGG (*che bolle*) boiling; (*caldissimo*) boiling (hot); **calmare i bollenti spiriti** to calm down.

bolletta [bol'letta] SF **a** (*conto: del gas, telefono*) bill ▶ **bolletta della luce** electricity bill **b** (*ricevuta*) receipt ▶ **bolletta di carico** bill of lading ▶ **bolletta di consegna** delivery note ▶ **bolletta doganale** clearance certificate ▶ **bolletta di trasporto aereo** air waybill **c** (*fam: senza soldi*): **essere in bolletta** to be broke, be hard up.

bollettario, ri [bollet'tarjo] SM duplicate receipt pad.

bollettino [bollet'tino] SM **a** (*comunicato, periodico*) bulletin ▶ **bollettino meteorologico** weather report **b** (*Comm: dei prezzi, cambi*) list; (: *modulo*) form ▶ **bollettino di ordinazione** order form ▶ **bollettino di spedizione** consignment note.

bollilatte [bolli'latte] SM INV milk pan.

bollino [bol'lino] SM coupon.

bollire [bol'lire] **1** VT to boil; **fare bollire** (*acqua*) to boil, bring to the boil; (*biberon*) to sterilize; (*panni*) to boil.
2 VI (*aus* **avere**) to boil, be boiling; **qui dentro si bolle** (*dal caldo*) it's boiling (hot) in here; **qualcosa bolle in pentola** (*fig*) there's something brewing.

bollito, a [bol'lito] **1** AGG boiled.
2 SM (*Culin*) ≈ boiled beef.

bollitore [bolli'tore] SM **a** (*per acqua*) kettle; (*per latte*) milk pan **b** (*Tecn*) boiler.

bollitura [bolli'tura] SF **a** (*azione*) boiling **b** (*acqua*) cooking liquid.

bollo ['bollo] SM (*timbro*) stamp; (*sigillo*) seal; (*su bestiame*) brand; **carta da bollo** official stamped paper; **marca da bollo** revenue stamp; **tassa di bollo** stamp duty ▶ **bollo di circolazione** (*Aut*) road tax ▶ **bollo per patente** driving licence tax ▶ **bollo postale** postmark.

bollore [bol'lore] SM: **dare un bollore a qc** to bring sth to the boil (*Brit*) *o* a boil (*Am*); **i bollori della gioventù** (*fig*) youthful enthusiasm *sg*; **ti sono passati i bollori?** have you calmed down?

bolo ['bolo] SM (*alimentare*) bolus; (*di ruminante*) cud.

Bologna [bo'loɲɲa] SF Bologna.

bolognese [boloɲ'ɲese] **1** AGG Bolognese, of *o* from Bologna; **spaghetti alla bolognese** spaghetti bolognese.
2 SM/F inhabitant *o* native of Bologna.

bolsaggine [bol'saddʒine] SF (*di cavallo*) heaves *sg*, broken wind.

bolscevico, a, chi, che [bolʃe'viko] AGG, SM/F Bolshevik.

Bolscevismo [bolʃe'vizmo] SM Bolshevism.

bolso, a ['bolso] AGG (*cavallo*) broken-winded.

boma ['bɔma] SM INV (*Naut*) boom.

bomba ['bomba] SF bomb; **la notizia fu una bomba** the news came as a bombshell; **sei stato una bomba!** you were tremendous!; **guarda che bomba!** (*donna, macchina*) what a beauty!; **tornare a bomba** (*al punto*) to get back to the point ▶ **bomba atomica** atom bomb ▶ **bomba a mano** hand grenade ▶ **bomba N** Neutron bomb ▶ **bomba ad orologeria** time bomb.

bombarda [bomˈbarda] SF **a** (*arma: antica*) bombard; (: *moderna*) mortar **b** (*Mus*) bombardon.

bombardamento [bombardaˈmento] SM (*vedi vb*) bombardment; bombing; shelling; **un bombardamento aereo** an air raid; **morto sotto un bombardamento** killed during a bomb attack ▶**bombardamento a tappeto** saturation bombing.

bombardare [bombarˈdare] VT (*gen, Fis*) to bombard; (*con bombe*) to bomb; (*con cannone*) to shell; **bombardare di domande/lettere** to bombard with questions/letters.

bombardiere [bombarˈdjɛre] SM (*aereo*) bomber; (*persona*) bombardier.

bombarolo, a [bombaˈrɔlo] SM/F terrorist bomber.

bombato, a [bomˈbato] AGG (*cappello, scatola*) rounded.

bombé [bõˈbe] AGG INV rounded.

bombetta [bomˈbetta] SF bowler (hat) (*Brit*), derby (*Am*).

bombola [ˈbombola] SF cylinder ▶**bombola del gas** gas cylinder ▶**bombola d'insetticida** fly spray ▶**bombola di ossigeno** oxygen cylinder.

bomboniera [bomboˈnjɛra] SF box of sweets (*as souvenir at weddings, first communions*).

bonaccia [boˈnattʃa] SF (*Naut*) dead calm; (*fig*) lull; **il mare è in bonaccia** the sea is dead calm.

bonaccione, a [bonatˈtʃone] **1** AGG good-natured, easy-going.
2 SM/F good-natured sort.

bonariamente [bonarjaˈmente] AVV (*vedi agg*) good-naturedly; kindly.

bonarietà [bonarjeˈta] SF (*vedi agg*) good nature, affability; kindliness.

bonario, ria, ri, rie [boˈnarjo] AGG (*persona*) good-natured, affable; (*modi, aspetto*) kindly.

bonifica, che [boˈnifika], **bonificazione** [bonifikatˈtsjone] SF (*operazione*) reclamation; (*terreno*) reclaimed land; **opere di bonifica** land reclamation works.

bonificabile [bonifiˈkabile] AGG reclaimable.

bonificare [bonifiˈkare] VT **a** (*terreno*) to reclaim; (*Mil*) to clear of mines **b** (*Comm*) to give a discount to.

bonifico, ci [boˈnifiko] SM (*Comm: riduzione, abbuono*) discount; (*Banca*) credit transfer.

Bonn [bɔn] SF Bonn.

bonsai [ˈbonsai] SM INV (*tecnica, pianta*) bonsai.

bontà [bonˈta] SF (*gen*) goodness, kindness; (*di prodotti*) quality; **bontà d'animo** *o* **di cuore** goodness of heart; **bontà sua!** (*iro*) how kind of him!; **abbia la bontà di ascoltarmi!** will you please listen to me?

bonus malus [ˈbɔnusˈmalus] SM INV (*Assicurazioni*) no-claims bonus.

bonzo [ˈbondzo] SM Buddhist monk, bonze.

borace [boˈratʃe] SM borax.

borbonico, a, ci, che [borˈbɔniko] **1** AGG Bourbon; (*pegg*) backward, out of date.
2 SM/F Bourbon.

borbottamento [borbottaˈmento] SM (*vedi vb*) muttering; moaning, grumbling; rumbling.

borbottare [borbotˈtare] **1** VT (*pronunciare confusamente*) to mutter.
2 VI (*aus* avere) to mutter; (*lamentarsi*) to moan, grumble; (*tuono, stomaco*) to rumble.

borbottio, tii [borbotˈtio] SM (*vedi vb*) muttering; moaning, grumbling; rumbling.

borchia [ˈbɔrkja] SF (*di abiti, cinture, borse*) stud; (*Tecn*) boss; (*da tappezziere*) upholsterer's nail.

bordare [borˈdare] VT **a** (*fare il bordo a*) to hem, edge; **un**

vestito bordato di rosso a dress with a red border **b** (*Naut: vele*) to spread.

bordata [borˈdata] SF **a** (*di cannoni, anche fig*) broadside **b** (*Naut*) tack.

bordatura [bordaˈtura] SF (*di abiti, tende*) border, edge.

bordeaux [borˈdo] SM INV (*colore*) burgundy, maroon; (*vino*) Bordeaux.

bordello [borˈdɛllo] SM brothel; **fare bordello** (*fam!*) to kick up a hell of a row; **questa stanza è un bordello** (*fam!*) this room's a shambles.

bordo [ˈbordo] SM **a** (*orlo*) edge; (*guarnizione*) border; (*di cratere, ruota*) rim; **il bordo del tavolo/letto** the edge of the table/bed; **sul bordo della strada** at the roadside
b (*Naut: fiancata di nave*) ship's side; **virare di bordo** (*anche fig*) to change course; **fuori bordo** overboard; **a bordo di** (*nave, aereo*) aboard, on board; **era a bordo di una macchina rossa** he was in a red car; **salire a bordo (di qc)** (*aereo, nave*) to go on board (sth), board (sth); (*macchina*) to get in(to sth); **persona d'alto bordo** (*fig*) VIP; **prostituta d'alto bordo** high-class prostitute.

bordura [borˈdura] SF (*di abiti, aiuole*) border; (*di pietanze*) garnish.

boreale [boreˈale] AGG northern; **aurora boreale** northern lights *pl*, aurora borealis.

borgata [borˈgata] SF (*in campagna*) hamlet; (*a Roma*) working-class suburb.

borghese [borˈgese] **1** AGG **a** (*gen*) middle-class; (*pegg*) bourgeois **b** : **essere in (abito) borghese** to be in civilian clothes *o* in civvies; **poliziotto in borghese** plainclothes policeman.
2 SM/F (*vedi agg*) middle-class person; bourgeois; **piccolo borghese** (*pegg*) petty bourgeois.

borghesemente [borgeseˈmente] AVV in a middle class fashion; (*pegg*) in a bourgeois way.

borghesia [borgeˈzia] SF bourgeoisie, middle classes *pl*; **alta/piccola borghesia** upper/lower middle classes *pl*.

borgo, ghi [ˈborgo] SM (*paese*) village; (*quartiere cittadino*) district; (*sobborgo*) suburb.

Borgogna [borˈgoɲɲa] SF Burgundy.

borgomastro [borgoˈmastro] SM burgomaster.

boria [ˈbɔrja] SF conceit, arrogance.

boriosamente [borjosaˈmente] AVV conceitedly, arrogantly.

borioso, a [boˈrjoso] AGG conceited, arrogant.

borlotto [borˈlɔtto] SM kidney bean.

Borneo [ˈbɔrneo] SM: **il Borneo** Borneo.

boro [ˈbɔro] SM (*Chim*) boron.

borotalco® [boroˈtalko] SM talcum powder.

borraccia, ce [borˈrattʃa] SF (*per soldati, cowboy*) water-bottle, flask.

borraccina [borratˈtʃina] SF (*Bot*) moss.

borragine [borˈradʒine] SF borage.

Borsa [ˈborsa] SF (*Fin*): **la Borsa (valori)** the Stock Exchange; **giocare in Borsa** to speculate on the Stock Exchange ▶**Borsa merci** commodity exchange.

borsa [ˈborsa] **1** SF (*gen*) bag; (*borsetta*) handbag (*Brit*), purse (*Am*); (*Ciclismo*) pannier; **o la borsa o la vita!** your money or your life!; **aver le borse sotto gli occhi** to have bags under one's eyes.
2 ▶**borsa dell'acqua calda** hot water bottle ▶**borsa del ghiaccio** ice bag ▶**borsa portalavoro** knitting bag ▶**borsa del postino** mailbag ▶**borsa della spesa** shopping bag ▶**borsa di studio** (student's) grant ▶**borsa del tabacco** tobacco pouch ▶**borsa degli**

utensili toolbag ▶ **borsa da viaggio** travelling bag.

borsaiolo, a [borsa'jɔlo] SM/F pickpocket.

borsanera [borsa'nera] SF black market.

borseggiare [borsed'dʒare] VT: **mi hanno borseggiato!** I've been robbed!, I've had my pocket picked!; **mi hanno borseggiato del portafoglio** my wallet has been stolen.

borseggiatore, trice [borseddʒa'tore] SM/F pickpocket.

borseggio, gi [bor'seddʒo] SM pickpocketing.

borsellino [borsel'lino] SM purse.

borsello [bor'sɛllo], **borsetto** [bor'setto] SM handbag (for man).

borsetta [bor'setta] SF handbag ▶ **borsetta da sera** evening bag.

borsista, i, e [bor'sista] SM/F **a** (di borsa di studio) grant holder **b** (Borsa) speculator.

borsistico, a, ci, che [bor'sistiko] AGG Stock-Exchange attr, on the Stock Exchange.

boscaglia [bos'kaʎʎa] SF brush.

boscaiolo [boska'jɔlo], **boscaiuolo** [boska'jwɔlo] SM (legnaiuolo) woodcutter, lumberjack (Am); (guardiano) forester.

boschereccio, cia, ci, ce [boske'rettʃo] AGG woodland attr.

boschetto [bos'ketto] SM copse, grove.

boschivo, a [bos'kivo] AGG (terreno) wooded, woody; (flora, vegetazione) woodland attr.

bosco, schi ['bɔsko] SM wood.

boscosità [boskosi'ta] SF density of woodland.

boscoso, a [bos'koso] AGG wooded.

bosniaco, a, ci, che [boz'niako] AGG, SM/F Bosnian.

Bosnia-Erzegovina ['bɔznja erdze'govina] SF: **la Bosnia-Erzegovina** Bosnia-Herzegovina.

boss [bɔs] SM INV boss.

bosso ['bɔsso] SM (pianta) box; (legno) boxwood.

bossolo ['bɔssolo] SM cartridge case.

Bot, bot [bɔt] SIGLA M = **buono ordinario del Tesoro**.

botanica [bo'tanika] SF botany.

botanico, a, ci, che [bo'taniko] ☐1 AGG botanic(al); **orto** o **giardino botanico** botanical gardens pl. ☐2 SM/F botanist.

botola ['bɔtola] SF trap door.

Botswana [bots'wana] SM: **il Botswana** Botswana.

botta ['bɔtta] SF **a** (percossa) blow; (fig: colpo, danno) blow, shock; **gli menò una botta in testa** he struck him a blow on the head; **dare (un sacco di) botte a qn** to give sb a good thrashing **b** (Scherma) thrust; **botta e risposta** (fig) cut and thrust.

bottaio, ai [bot'tajo] SM cooper.

botte ['bɔtte] SF barrel, cask; **volta a botte** (Archit) barrel vault; **volere la botte piena e la moglie ubriaca** (Proverbio) to want to have one's cake and eat it; **essere in una botte di ferro** (fig) to be (as) safe as houses.

bottega, ghe [bot'tega] SF (negozio) shop; (laboratorio) workshop; **aprire/mettere su bottega** to open/set up shop; **chiudere bottega** to shut up shop; (fig) to give up; **stare a bottega (da qn)** to serve one's apprenticeship (with sb); **avere la bottega aperta** (fam) to have one's flies undone ▶ **le Botteghe Oscure** (Pol) headquarters of P.D.S.

bottegaio, aia, ai, aie [botte'gajo] SM/F shopkeeper.

botteghino [botte'gino] SM (Teatro, Cine) box office; (del lotto) lottery office.

bottiglia [bot'tiʎʎa] ☐1 SF bottle; **bottiglia di vino** bottle of wine; **una bottiglia da 1 litro** a litre bottle; **birra in bottiglia** bottled beer ▶ **bottiglia Molotov** Molotov cocktail ▶ **bottiglia da vino** wine bottle. ☐2 AGG INV: **verde bottiglia** bottle green.

bottiglieria [bottiʎʎe'ria] SF (negozio) wine shop; (deposito) wine cellar.

bottiglione [bottiʎ'ʎone] SM large bottle.

bottino[1] [bot'tino] SM (di guerra) booty; (di rapina, furto) loot; **fare bottino di qc** to make off with sth.

bottino[2] [bot'tino] SM (pozzonero) cesspool, cesspit.

botto ['bɔtto] SM (di mortaretti) thud; (spari) rattle; **di botto** (fam) suddenly; **in un botto** (fam) in a flash.

bottone [bot'tone] SM **a** (di giacca, radio) button; **premere** o **spingere un bottone** to press a button; **stanza dei bottoni** control room; (fig) nerve centre; **attaccare un bottone** (alla camicia) to sew on a button; **attaccare un bottone a qn** (fig: trattenere) to buttonhole sb; **attaccare bottone con qn** (fig: conversare) to strike up a conversation with sb ▶ **bottone automatico** press stud **b** (Bot) bud ▶ **botton d'oro** buttercup.

bottoniera [botto'njɛra] SF (Tecn) control panel.

bottonificio, ci [bottoni'fitʃo] SM button factory.

botulino [botu'lino] AGG: **bacillo botulino** botulinus.

botulismo [botu'lizmo] SM botulism.

bouclé [bu'kle] AGG INV bouclé.

boule [bul] SF INV hot water bottle.

bouquet [bu'kɛ] SM INV (di fiori, del vino) bouquet.

boutique [bu'tik] SF INV boutique.

bovaro [bo'varo] SM herdsman.

bove ['bove] SM = **bue**.

bovino, a [bo'vino] ☐1 AGG bovine; (allevamento) cattle attr; **occhi bovini** (fig) protruding eyes. ☐2: **bovini** SMPL cattle.

bowling ['bouliŋ] SM INV (gioco) (tenpin) bowling; (luogo) bowling alley.

box [bɔks] SM INV (per cavalli) horsebox; (per macchina) lock-up, garage; (per macchina da corsa) pit; (per bambini) playpen ▶ **box doccia** shower cubicle.

boxare [bok'sare] VI (aus avere) to box.

boxe [bɔks] SF INV boxing.

boxer ['bɔkser] ☐1 SM INV (cane) boxer. ☐2 SMPL (mutande): **un paio di boxer** a pair of boxer shorts.

boxeur [bok'sœr] SM INV (pugile) boxer.

boy ['bɔi] SM INV (ballerino di rivista) dancer; (in albergo) bellboy.

bozza[1] ['bottsa] SF (fam: bernoccolo) bump.

bozza[2] ['bottsa] SF (di lettera, contratto, romanzo) draft; (Tip: di stampa) proof; **rivedere** o **correggere le bozze** to proofread; **prima/seconda/terza bozza** first/revised proof ▶ **bozza in colonna** galley proof ▶ **bozza impaginata** page proof.

bozzettista, i, e [bottset'tista] SM/F (di pubblicità) commercial artist; (scrittore) sketch writer.

bozzetto [bot'tsetto] SM (disegno) sketch; (modello) scale model.

bozzo ['bottso] SM bump.

bozzolo ['bottsolo] SM cocoon; **uscire dal bozzolo** (fig) to come out of one's shell; **chiudersi nel proprio bozzolo** (fig) to withdraw into one's shell.

BR [bi'ɛrre] ☐1 SIGLA FPL = **Brigate Rosse**. ☐2 SIGLA = Brindisi.

braca, che ['braka] SF **a**: **brache** SFPL (fam: pantaloni) trousers, pants (Am); (: mutandoni) drawers; **calare** o

calarsi le brache (*fig fam*) to chicken out **b** (*allacciatura*: *per operai*) (safety) harness.

braccare [brak'kare] VT (*anche fig*) to hunt.

braccetto [brat'tʃetto] AVV: **a braccetto** arm in arm; **prendere qn a braccetto** to take sb by the arm; **tenersi a braccetto** to be arm in arm.

braccherò *ecc* [brakke'rɔ] VB *vedi* **braccare**.

bracciale [brat'tʃale] SM (*ornamento*) bracelet; (*distintivo*) armband.

braccialetto [brattʃa'letto] SM bracelet, bangle.

bracciante [brat'tʃante] SM/F (day) labourer.

bracciata [brat'tʃata] SF **a** (*quantità*) armful; **a bracciate** by the armful **b** (*nel nuoto*) stroke.

braccio ['brattʃo] SM **a** (*pl f* **braccia**) (*Anat*) arm; **tenere/ prendere in braccio** to hold/take in one's arms; **dare** *o* **offrire il braccio a qn** to give sb one's arm; **camminare sotto braccio** to walk arm in arm; **è il suo braccio destro** (*fig*) he's his right-hand man; **braccio di ferro** (*anche fig*) trial of strength; **alzare le braccia al cielo** to throw up one's arms; **a braccia** (*sollevare, portare*) with one's own hands; **a braccia aperte** with open arms; **incrociare le braccia** to fold one's arms; (*fig*) to down tools; **gettare le braccia al collo a qn** to throw one's arms round sb's neck; **mi sono cascate le braccia** (*fig*) I could have wept; **avere buone braccia** to be big and strong

b (*pl f* **braccia**) (*Naut: unità di misura*) fathom

c (*pl m* **bracci**) (*di croce, gru, fiume, grammofono*) arm; (*di edificio*) wing ▶ **braccio di mare** sound ▶ **braccio della morte** death row.

bracciolo [brat'tʃɔlo] SM arm.

bracco, chi ['brakko] SM hound.

bracconiere [brakko'njɛre] SM poacher.

brace ['bratʃe] SF embers *pl*.

braciere [bra'tʃɛre] SM brazier.

braciola [bra'tʃɔla] SF (*con osso*) chop; (*senza osso*) steak.

bradipo ['bradipo] SM (*Zool*) sloth.

brado, a ['brado] AGG (*animale*) wild; **allo stato brado** in the wild *o* natural state.

braille [braj] AGG INV, SM INV braille.

brama ['brama] SF: **brama (di/di fare)** longing (for/to do), yearning (for/to do).

bramare [bra'mare] VT: **bramare (qc/di fare qc)** to long (for sth/to do sth), yearn (for sth/to do sth).

bramire [bra'mire] VI (*aus* **avere**) (*cervo*) to bell; (*orso*) to roar.

bramito [bra'mito] SM (*di cervo*) bell; (*di orso*) roar.

bramosamente [bramosa'mente] AVV (*guardare*) longingly, yearningly.

bramosia [bramo'sia] SF: **bramosia (di)** longing (for), yearning (for).

bramoso, a [bra'moso] AGG (*sguardo*) longing; **essere bramoso di qc** to long *o* yearn for sth.

branca, che ['branka] SF **a** (*settore, ramo*) branch; **una branca dello scibile** a branch of knowledge **b** (*fig: artigli*): **branche** SFPL (*di vizio*) grip; (*di usuraio*) clutches.

branchia ['brankja] SF (*Zool*) gill.

branchiale [bran'kjale] AGG branchial.

branco, chi ['branko] SM (*di uccelli, pecore*) flock; (*di cani, lupi*) pack; (*di balene, delfini*) school; (*fig pegg: di persone*) gang, pack; **entrare nel branco** (*fig*) to go with the crowd.

brancolare [branko'lare] VI (*aus* **avere**) to grope, feel one's way; **brancolare nel buio** (*fig*) to grope in the dark.

branda ['branda] SF (*da campo, per militari*) camp bed,

folding bed; (*per marinai*) hammock; **giù dalle brande!** everybody up!

brandello [bran'dɛllo] SM scrap, shred; **a brandelli** in tatters, in rags; **fare a brandelli** to tear to shreds.

brandina [bran'dina] SF camp bed (*Brit*), cot (*Am*).

brandire [bran'dire] VT to brandish.

brano ['brano] SM (*gen*) piece; (*di libro*) passage; **fare a brani** (*fig*) to tear to pieces.

branzino [bran'tsino] SM sea-bass.

brasare [bra'zare] VT **a** (*Culin*) to braise **b** (*Tecn*) to braze.

brasato, a [bra'zato] ① AGG (*Culin*) braised. ② SM braised beef.

Brasile [bra'zile] SM: **il Brasile** Brazil.

Brasilia [bra'zilja] SF Brasilia.

brasiliano, a [brazi'ljano] AGG, SM/F Brazilian.

bravata [bra'vata] SF (*azione spavalda*) act of bravado; (*millanterie*): **bravate** SFPL bravado *sg*.

bravo, a ['bravo] AGG **a** (*abile*) good, clever, skilful, capable; **essere bravo in qc/a fare qc** to be good at sth/at doing sth; **un bravo insegnante/medico** a good teacher/doctor; **essere bravo a scuola** to do well at school; **bravo!** well done!; **bravi!** (*in chiusura di spettacolo*) bravo!

b (*buono*) good; (*onesto*) honest; **è un brav'uomo** he's a decent chap; **sono brave persone** they're good people; **fai il bravo** be good; **su da bravo!** (*fam*) there's a good boy!

c (*coraggioso*) brave

d (*rafforzativo*): **mi sono fatto le mie brave 8 ore di lavoro** I put in a full 8 hours' work; **si beve il suo bravo mezzo litro ogni giorno** he drinks his pint every day.

bravura [bra'vura] SF cleverness, skill; **pezzo di bravura** (*Mus*) bravura piece.

breccia[1], ce ['brettʃa] SF breach; (*Geol*) breccia; **essere sulla breccia** (*fig*) to be going strong; **fare breccia nell'animo** *o* **nel cuore di qn** to find the way to sb's heart.

breccia[2], ce ['brettʃa] SF, **brecciame** [bret'tʃame] SM road metal.

brefotrofio, fi [brefo'trɔfjo] SM orphanage (*for abandoned children*).

Brema ['brɛma] SF Bremen.

bresaola [bre'zaola] SF (*Culin*) *kind of dried salted beef*.

bresciano, a [breʃ'ʃano] ① AGG *o* from Brescia. ② SM/F inhabitant *o* native of Brescia.

Bretagna [bre'taɲɲa] SF: **la Bretagna** Brittany; **Gran Bretagna** Great Britain.

bretella [bre'tɛlla] SF **a** (*di sottoveste, reggiseno*) strap; **bretelle** (*di calzoni*) braces **b** (*raccordo stradale*) motorway link road; (*Aer*) exit runway.

bretone ['brɛtone] AGG, SM/F Breton.

breve ['brɛve] ① AGG (*gen*) brief, short; (*vita, strada*) short; **tra breve** shortly; **a breve distanza** near, not far; **sarò breve** I'll be brief; **per farla breve** to cut a long story short; **in breve** in short; **a breve** (*Comm*) short-term. ② SF **a** (*Mus*) breve **b** (*vocale*) short vowel; (*sillaba*) short syllable.

brevemente [breve'mente] AVV briefly.

brevettabile [brevet'tabile] AGG patentable.

brevettare [brevet'tare] VT to patent.

brevettato, a [brevet'tato] AGG patented; (*scherz*) tried and tested.

brevetto [bre'vetto] SM **a** (*d'invenzione*) patent; **Ufficio Brevetti** Patent Office **b** (*patente*): **brevetto di pilota** pilot's licence (*Brit*) *o* license (*Am*).

breviario, ri [bre'vjarjo] SM (*Rel*) breviary; (*compendio*) compendium.

brevi manu ['brɛvi 'manu] AVV: **consegnare qc brevi manu a qn** to hand sth directly to sb.

brevità [brevi'ta] SF brevity.

brezza ['breddza] SF breeze; **brezza di terra/mare** land/sea breeze.

bric-à-brac ['brika'brak] SM INV bric-à-brac.

bricco, chi ['brikko] SM jug ▶**bricco del caffè** coffeepot ▶**bricco del latte** milk jug.

bricconata [brikko'nata] SF mischievous trick.

briccone [brik'kone] SM/F rascal, rogue.

briciola ['britʃola] SF (*di pane*) crumb; (*frammento*) scrap; **non ha lasciato che le briciole** (*anche fig*) he only left the scraps; **ridurre in briciole** (*biscotto*) to crumble up; (*fig: persona*) to take to pieces.

briciolo ['britʃolo] SM bit; (*fig: di buon senso, verità*) grain.

bricolage [briko'laʒ] SM INV do-it-yourself; **negozio/rivista di bricolage** do-it-yourself shop/magazine.

bridge [bridʒ] SM INV bridge.

briga, ghe ['briga] SF **a** (*cura, fastidio*) bother, trouble; **darsi** o **prendersi la briga di fare qc** to take the trouble to do sth **b** (*lite*): **attaccar briga** to start a quarrel.

brigadiere [briga'djɛre] SM (*dei Carabinieri, Finanza*) ≈ sergeant.

brigantaggio, gi [brigan'taddʒo] SM brigandage; (*organizzazione*) brigands *pl*.

brigante [bri'gante] SM brigand, bandit; (*fig: bambino*) rascal.

brigantino [brigan'tino] SM (*Naut*) brig, brigantine.

brigata [bri'gata] SF **a** (*gruppo*) group; (*comitiva*) party; **un'allegra brigata di amici** a lively bunch of friends **b** (*Mil*) brigade; **generale di brigata** brigadier (*Brit*), brigadier general (*Am*) ▶**le Brigate Rosse** (*Pol*) the Red Brigades.

brigatismo [briga'tizmo] SM *phenomenon of the Red Brigades.*

brigatista, i, e [briga'tista] SM/F (*Pol*) *member of the Red Brigades.*

briglia ['briʎʎa] SF (*di cavallo*) rein, bridle; (*per bambino*) rein; **a briglia sciolta** at full gallop; (*fig*) at full speed; **allentare/tirare la briglia** (*anche fig*) to slacken/tighten the reins.

brillante [bril'lante] ① AGG **a** (*luce, raggi, colori*) bright; (: *più intenso*) brilliant; (*che luccica*) shining; (: *occhi*) sparkling

b (*successo, carriera, studioso*) brilliant; (*conversazione*) brilliant, sparkling; **è una persona brillante** he has a sparkling wit.

② SM (*diamante*) diamond; (*anello*) diamond ring.

brillantemente [brillante'mente] AVV (*superare un esame, conversare*) brilliantly.

brillantina [brillan'tina] SF brilliantine.

brillare[1] [bril'lare] VT (*riso*) to husk.

brillare[2] [bril'lare] ① VI (*aus avere*) **a** (*sole*) to shine; (*stelle*) to shine, twinkle; (*occhi*) to shine, sparkle; (*diamante*) to sparkle; **gli occhi le brillavano di gioia** her eyes sparkled o shone with joy; **brilla per la sua bellezza/intelligenza** she is outstandingly beautiful/intelligent; **brillare per la propria assenza** to be conspicuous by one's absence

b (*mina*) to go off, explode.

② VT (*mina*) to set off.

brillo, a ['brillo] AGG (*fam*) tipsy, merry.

brina ['brina] SF (hoar)frost.

brinare [bri'nare] VB IMPERS (*aus essere*): **stanotte è brinato** there was a frost last night.

brinata [bri'nata] SF (hoar)frost.

brindare [brin'dare] VI (*aus avere*) to make a toast; **brindare a qn/qc** to drink to o toast sb/sth; **brindare alla salute di qn** to drink to sb's health.

brindello [brin'dɛllo] SM = **brandello**.

brindisi ['brindizi] SM INV toast; **fare un brindisi (a qn/qc)** to drink a toast (to sb/sth).

brio ['brio] SM, SOLO SG liveliness; **essere pieno di brio** to be very lively o full of life.

brioche [bri'ɔʃ] SF INV brioche.

briosamente [briosa'mente] AVV with spirit, in a lively manner.

brioso, a [bri'oso] AGG lively.

briscola ['briskola] SF (*gioco di carte*) type of card game; (*seme vincente*) trump(s); (*carta*) trump card.

britannico, a, ci, che [bri'tanniko] ① AGG British.

② SM/F British person, Briton; **i britannici** the British.

brivido ['brivido] SM (*di freddo*) shiver; (*di ribrezzo*) shudder; (*di piacere*) thrill; **avere i brividi** (*anche fig*) to have the shivers; **far venire i brividi a qn** (*fig*) to give sb the shivers; **racconti del brivido** suspense stories.

brizzolato, a [brittso'lato] AGG (*barba, capelli*) grizzled; (*persona*) grey-haired, greying.

brocca, che ['brɔkka] SF jug.

broccato [brok'kato] SM brocade.

broccolo ['brɔkkolo] SM (*Bot, Culin*) broccoli *no pl*.

broda ['brɔda] SF (*pegg*) dishwater.

brodaglia [bro'daʎʎa] SF (*pegg*) dishwater.

brodetto [bro'detto] SM (*brodo leggero*) light broth ▶**brodetto alla marinara** *sort of bouillabaisse.*

brodo ['brɔdo] SM broth; (*per cucinare*) stock; **riso/pasta in brodo** rice/noodle soup; **tutto fa brodo** (*fig*) every little helps; **lasciare (cuocere) qn nel suo brodo** (*fig*) to let sb stew (in his own juice) ▶**brodo di manzo** beef tea ▶**brodo ristretto** consommé.

brogliaccio, ci [broʎ'ʎattʃo] SM (*Amm*) daybook.

broglio, gli ['brɔʎʎo] SM: **broglio elettorale** gerrymandering.

bromo ['brɔmo] SM (*Chim*) bromine.

bromuro [bro'muro] SM bromide.

bronchiale [bron'kjale] AGG bronchial.

bronchiolo [bron'kiolo] SM bronchiole.

bronchite [bron'kite] SF bronchitis.

broncio, ci ['brontʃo] SM sulky expression; (*malumore*) sulkiness; **avere** o **tenere il broncio** to sulk; **gli tiene il broncio** he's not speaking to him.

bronco, chi ['bronko] SM bronchial tube.

broncopolmonite [bronkopolmo'nite] SF bronchial pneumonia.

brontolare [bronto'lare] ① VT to mutter, mumble.

② VI (*aus avere*) (*mormorare*) to mutter, mumble; (*protestare*) to grumble; **mi brontola lo stomaco** my stomach is rumbling.

brontolio, lii [bronto'lio] SM (*vedi vb*) muttering, mumbling; grumbling; rumbling.

brontolone, a [bronto'lone] ① AGG grumbling.

② SM/F grumbler.

brontosauro [bronto'sauro] SM brontosaurus.

bronzare [bron'dzare] VT (*rivestire*) to bronze; (*brunire*) to burnish.

bronzatura [brondza'tura] SF (*vedi vb*) bronzing; bur

nishing.

bronzeo, a ['brondzeo] AGG (*di bronzo*) bronze; (*color bronzo*) bronze(-coloured).

bronzetto [bron'dzetto] SM bronze statuette.

bronzina [bron'dzina] SF (*Tecn*) bush.

bronzo ['brondzo] SM (*metallo, oggetto*) bronze; **che faccia di bronzo!** what (brazen) cheek!

bross. ABBR = **in brossura**; vedi **brossura**.

brossura [bros'sura] SF: **in brossura** (*libro*) paperback.

brucare [bru'kare] VT to browse on, nibble at.

brucherà ecc [bruke'ra] VB vedi **brucare**.

bruciacchiare [brutʃak'kjare] ① VT to singe, scorch.

② **bruciacchiarsi** VIP to get singed o scorched.

bruciapelo [brutʃa'pelo] AVV: **a bruciapelo** point-blank; **sparare a bruciapelo** to fire at point-blank range.

bruciare [bru'tʃare] ① VT **a** (*gen*) to burn; (*edificio*) to burn down; (*stoffa: stirando*) to scorch; (*Med: verruca*) to cauterize; **bruciato dal sole** (*terreno*) sun-scorched; (*volto*) sunburnt; (: *ustionato*) burnt by the sun

b (*fraseologia*): **bruciare gli avversari** (*Sport, fig*) to leave the rest of the field behind; **bruciare le cervella a qn** to blow sb's brains out; **bruciare le tappe** o **i tempi** (*Sport, fig*) to shoot ahead; **bruciarsi le ali** (*fig*) to burn one's fingers; **bruciarsi la carriera** to ruin one's career.

② VI (*aus* **essere**) **a** (*gen*) to burn; (*edificio, bosco*) to be on fire

b (*essere molto caldo*) to be burning (hot); (: *sole*) to be scorching, be burning; **bruciare di febbre** to run a high temperature

c (*produrre bruciore*): **gli occhi mi bruciano** my eyes are smarting o stinging; **il viso mi brucia** my face is burning; **mi brucia molto questa offesa** that insult really rankles.

③ **bruciarsi** VR, VIP (*persona*) to burn o.s.; **si è bruciato l'arrosto** the joint is burnt; **si è bruciata una lampadina** a bulb has blown.

bruciato, a [bru'tʃato] ① AGG burnt; **gioventù bruciata** Beat Generation.

② SM: **odore di bruciato** (smell of) burning; **questa zuppa sa di bruciato** this soup tastes burnt.

bruciatore [brutʃa'tore] SM (*Tecn*) burner.

bruciatura [brutʃa'tura] SF **a** (*atto*) burning *no pl* **b** (*parte bruciata*) burn; (*scottatura*) scald.

bruciore [bru'tʃore] SM burning o smarting sensation; **provocare bruciore** to sting.

bruco, chi ['bruko] SM (*Zool*) grub; (: *di farfalla*) caterpillar.

brufolo ['brufolo] SM pimple, spot.

brufoloso, a [brufo'loso] AGG pimply, spotty.

brughiera [bru'gjɛra] SF moor, heath.

brugo, ghi ['brugo] SM (*Bot*) heather.

brûlé [bry'le] AGG INV: **vin brûlé** mulled wine.

brulicante [bruli'kante] AGG: **brulicante di** (*anche fig*) swarming with, teeming with.

brulicare [bruli'kare] VI (*aus* **avere**) to swarm; **il mercato brulicava di gente** the market was heaving with people.

brulichio, chii [bruli'kio] SM swarming.

brullo, a ['brullo] AGG bare.

bruma ['bruma] SF mist, haze.

brunire [bru'nire] VT (*metallo: levigare*) to burnish, polish.

brunitura [bruni'tura] SF burnishing, polishing.

bruno, a ['bruno] ① AGG (*capelli*) brown, dark; (*carnagione*) dark; (*persona*) dark(-haired).

② SM/F dark-haired person.

brusca, sche ['bruska] SF scrubbing brush; (*per cavalli*) horse brush.

bruscamente [bruska'mente] AVV (*frenare, fermarsi*) suddenly; (*rispondere, reagire*) sharply.

bruschetta [brus'ketta] SF *slice of toasted bread seasoned with oil and garlic.*

bruschezza [brus'kettsa] SF brusqueness, abruptness.

brusco, a, schi, sche ['brusko] AGG (*movimento*) abrupt, sudden; (*modi, persona*) abrupt, brusque.

bruscolo ['bruskolo] SM speck.

brusio, sii [bru'zio] SM hubbub, buzz; **il brusio degli insetti** the buzzing of the insects.

brutale [bru'tale] AGG rough, brutal; **per dirla in modo brutale** to put it bluntly.

brutalità [brutali'ta] SF INV brutality.

brutalizzare [brutalid'dzare] VT to brutalize.

brutalmente [brutal'mente] AVV brutally.

Bruto ['bruto] SM Brutus.

bruto, a ['bruto] ① AGG brute; **forza bruta** brute force o strength.

② SM (*uomo violento*) brute.

brutta ['brutta] SF rough copy, first draft.

bruttezza [brut'tettsa] SF ugliness.

brutto, a ['brutto] ① AGG **a** (*persona, vestito, casa*) ugly; **brutto come la fame** as ugly as sin

b (*cattivo: gen*) bad; (: *ferita, malattia, strada, affare*) nasty; (: *carattere*) unpleasant, nasty; **brutto cattivo!** you naughty boy!; **brutto stupido!** you stupid clown!; **ha fatto brutto (tempo) ieri** yesterday the weather was bad; **avere un brutto male** (*euf*) to have cancer; **passare un brutto momento** to go through a difficult period; **passare un brutto quarto d'ora** to have a nasty time of it; **vedersela brutta** (*per un attimo*) to have a nasty moment; (*per un periodo*) to have a bad time of it.

② SM **a**: **il brutto** the ugly; **è il brutto della famiglia** he's the ugly member of the family; **il brutto è che...** the problem o unfortunate thing is that ...; **stiamo andando verso il brutto** (*Meteor*) the weather is taking a turn for the worse.

③ AVV: **guardare qn di brutto** to give sb a nasty look; **picchiare qn di brutto** to give sb a bad o nasty beating; **sta lavorando di brutto** he's working furiously.

bruttura [brut'tura] SF (*oggetto*) ugly thing.

Bruxelles [bry'sɛl] SF Brussels.

BS SIGLA = *Brescia*.

BT [bi'ti] ① ABBR (= *bassa tensione*) LT.

② SIGLA M = **buono del Tesoro**.

btg. ABBR = **battaglione**.

Btp [biti'pi] SIGLA M = **buono del tesoro poliennale**.

bubbone [bub'bone] SM swelling.

bubbonico, a, ci, che [bub'bɔniko] AGG: **peste bubbonica** bubonic plague.

buca, che ['buka] SF (*gen, Golf*) hole; (*più profondo*) pit; (*di biliardo*) pocket; (*avvallamento*) hollow ▶**buca delle lettere** letterbox ▶**buca del suggeritore** (*Teatro*) prompter's box.

bucaneve [buka'neve] SM INV snowdrop.

bucaniere [buka'njɛre] SM buccaneer.

bucare [bu'kare] ① VT (*forare*) to make a hole (o holes) in; (: *biglietto*) to punch; (: *gomma*) to puncture; (*pungere*) to pierce; **ho bucato (una gomma)** I've got a puncture; **avere le mani bucate** (*fig*) to be a spendthrift.

② **bucarsi** VR (*pungersi*) to prick o.s..

③ **bucarsi** VIP (*forarsi: gomma, palla*) to puncture; (*fam: drogarsi*) to mainline; **si è bucata una gomma** I've got a puncture.

Bucarest ['bukarest] SF Bucharest.

bucato [bu'kato] SM washing; **fare il bucato** to do the washing; **stirare il bucato** to do the ironing; **lenzuola di bucato** freshly-laundered sheets.

buccia, ce ['buttʃa] SF **a** (*di verdura, frutta: gen*) skin; (: *di agrumi, patate*) skin, peel; (: *di piselli*) pod **b** (*di salumi*) skin; (*di formaggio*) rind **c** (*corteccia*) bark.

bucherellare [bukerel'lare] VT to riddle with holes.

bucherellato, a [bukerel'lato] AGG riddled (with holes).

bucherò ecc [buke'rɔ] VB vedi **bucare**.

buco, chi ['buko] SM (*gen*) hole; (*omissione*) gap; (*orifizio, apertura*) aperture; **il buco della serratura** keyhole; **fare un buco nell'acqua** to fail, draw a blank; **farsi un buco** (*fam: drogarsi*) to have a fix ▶**buco nero** (*anche fig*) black hole.

bucolicamente [bukolika'mente] AVV bucolically, pastorally.

bucolico, a, ci, che [bu'kɔliko] AGG bucolic, pastoral.

Budapest ['budapest] SF Budapest.

Budda ['budda] SM INV Buddha.

buddismo [bud'dizmo] SM Buddhism.

buddista, i, e [bud'dista] AGG, SM/F Buddhist.

buddistico, a, ci, che [bud'distiko] AGG Buddhist.

budello [bu'dɛllo] SM **a** (*pl f* **budella**) (*intestino*) bowel, intestine, gut **b** (*materiale*) gut **c** (*vicolo*) alley.

budget ['bʌdʒit] SM INV budget ▶**budget pubblicitario** advertising budget.

budgetario, ria, ri, rie [buddʒe'tarjo] AGG budgetary.

budino [bu'dino] SM pudding.

bue ['bue] SM (*pl* **buoi**) **a** (*Zool*) ox ▶**bue marino** dugong ▶**bue muschiato** musk ox ▶**bue selvatico** bison **b** (*Culin*) beef.

Buenos Aires [bwenos 'aires] SF Buenos Aires.

bufala ['bufala] SF (*fam*) **a** (*errore*) howler; (*notizia non vera*) unfounded story **b** : **quel film è una bufala** that film is utter rubbish.

bufalo, a ['bufalo] SM buffalo ▶**bufalo indiano** water buffalo.

bufera [bu'fɛra] SF (*anche fig*) storm.

buffamente [buffa'mente] AVV in a funny way.

buffet [by'fɛ] SM INV **a** (*mobile*) sideboard **b** (*bar*) buffet, refreshment bar.

buffetteria [buffette'ria] SF buffet service.

buffetto [buf'fetto] SM flick.

buffo, a ['buffo] AGG (*ridicolo*) funny, comical; (*divertente*) funny, amusing; (*strano*) funny, odd; (*Teatro*) comic.

buffonata [buffo'nata] SF (*azione*) prank, jest; (*parola*) jest; **fare buffonate** (*anche fig*) to clown about; **dire buffonate** to joke; (*fig*) to talk rubbish.

buffone [buf'fone] SM (*anche fig*) clown, buffoon; (*pegg*) joker; **fare il buffone** (*fig*) to play the fool, clown about ▶**buffone di corte** court jester.

buffoneria [buffone'ria] SF buffoonery.

buffonesco, a, schi, sche [buffo'nesko] AGG clownish, comical.

buggerare [buddʒe'rare] VT (*fam*) to swindle, cheat.

bugia¹, gie [bu'dʒia] SF (*menzogna*) lie; **dire** o **raccontare bugie** to tell lies; **bugia pietosa** white lie; **le bugie hanno le gambe corte** (*Proverbio*) truth will out.

bugia², gie [bu'dʒia] SF (*candeliere*) candleholder.

bugiardo, a [bu'dʒardo] **1** AGG lying, deceitful. **2** SM/F liar.

bugigattolo [budʒi'gattolo] SM (*ripostiglio*) boxroom; (*pegg*) poky little room.

bugliolo [buʎ'ʎɔlo] SM (*Naut*) (ship's) bucket.

bugna ['buɲɲa] SF (*Archit*) boss; (*Naut*) clew cringle.

buio, a, i o **ii, e** ['bujo] **1** AGG (*oscuro*) dark; (*tetro, triste*) gloomy, dismal. **2** SM dark, darkness; **al buio** in the dark; **si sta facendo buio** (*imbrunisce*) it is growing o getting dark; **buio pesto** pitch-dark, pitch-black.

bulbo ['bulbo] SM **a** (*gen, Bot*) bulb **b** : **bulbo oculare** eyeball **c** (*Naut*) ballast.

Bulgaria [bulga'ria] SF: **la Bulgaria** Bulgaria.

bulgaro, a ['bulgaro] AGG, SM/F, SM Bulgarian.

bulimia [buli'mia] SF bulimia.

bulimico, a, ci, che [bu'limiko] AGG, SM/F bulimic.

bulino [bu'lino] SM (*Tecn*) burin, graver; **lavorare a bulino** to engrave.

bulldozer ['buldouzə] SM INV bulldozer.

bulletta [bul'letta] SF tack, stud.

bullo ['bullo] SM (*persona*) tough; **fare il bullo** to act tough.

bullonare [bullo'nare] VT (*Tecn*) to bolt.

bullone [bul'lone] SM bolt.

bum [bum] **1** ESCL (*scoppio*) boom!, bang!. **2** SM INV bang; **fare bum** to bang.

bungalow ['bʌngəlou] SM INV (*casa*) bungalow; (*per vacanze*) holiday chalet.

bunker ['bunker] SM INV (*Mil*) bunker.

buoi ['bwɔji] SMPL di **bue**.

buonafede [bwona'fede] SF good faith; **in buonafede** in good faith.

buonanima [bwo'nanima] SF: **mio nonno buonanima...** [OR] **la buonanima di mio nonno** my grandfather, God rest his soul ... .

buonanotte [bwona'nɔtte] **1** ESCL good night!. **2** SF: **dare la buonanotte a qn** to say good night to sb.

buonasera [bwona'sera] **1** ESCL (*anche:* **buona sera**) good evening!. **2** SF: **dare la buonasera a qn** to wish sb good evening; **signorina buonasera** (*TV*) female TV announcer.

buoncostume [bwonkos'tume] **1** SM public morality. **2** SF: **la (squadra del) buoncostume** (*Polizia*) the vice squad.

buondì [bwon'di] ESCL hello!

buongiorno [bwon'dʒorno] **1** ESCL good morning (o afternoon)!. **2** SM: **dare il buongiorno a qn** to wish sb good morning.

buongrado [bwon'grado] AVV: **di buongrado** willingly.

buongustaio, aia, ai, aie [bwongus'tajo] SM/F gourmet.

buongusto [bwɔn'gusto] SM (good) taste; **abbi il buongusto di non farti più vedere** I hope you'll have the decency not to show your face again.

---

buono¹, a ['bwɔno]

1 AGG (*comp* **migliore**, *superl* **ottimo**)

davanti sm: **buon** + consonante, vocale, **buono** + s impura, gn, pn, ps, x, z; davanti sf: **buona** + consonante, **buon'** + vocale

a (*gen*) good; (*prodotto*) good (quality); (*odore, ambiente, atmosfera*) good, nice, pleasant; (*posizione, ditta, impresa*) sound;

▷**essere in buona *compagnia*** to be in good company

▷**essere di buona *famiglia*** to come from a good family

▷**avere un buon *odore*** to smell good o nice

▷*più* buono better

▷avere un buon *sapore* to taste good *o* nice

▷buon *senso* = buonsenso

▷buona *società* polite society

▷*stai* buono! behave!

▷*tenere* buono qn (*bambino*) to keep sb quiet; (*fig:* *persona influente*) to keep sb sweet

b (*generoso: persona, azione*) good, kind, kindly;

▷una persona di buon *cuore* a good-hearted person

▷essere buono come il *pane* to have a heart of gold

▷è una buona *ragazza* she's a good-hearted girl

c (*abile, idoneo*)

▷essere buono *a* nulla to be no good *o* use at anything; vedi anche **sm/f**

▷quest'acqua non è buona *da* bersi this water isn't safe to drink

▷buono *da* buttar via fit for the dustbin

▷mi sembra buono *per* questo lavoro he seems suitable for the job

d (*utile, vantaggioso*)

▷a buon *mercato* cheap

▷buono a *sapersi* that's good to know

▷è stata una buona *scelta* it was a good choice

e (*giusto, valido*) correct, right; (: *motivo*) valid;

▷ad ogni buon *conto* in any case

▷a buon *diritto* rightfully

▷al *momento* buono at the right moment

f (*utilizzabile*) usable; (: *biglietto, passaporto*) valid;

▷è ancora buona questa vernice? is this paint still okay *o* usable?

▷non è più buono (*latte*) it's off; (*pane*) it's stale

g (*con valore intensivo*) good;

▷peserà dieci *chili* buoni it must weigh a good ten kilos

▷di buon *mattino* early in the morning

▷ci vuole un *mesetto* buono it takes a good month *o* a month at least

▷un buon *numero* a good *o* large number

▷decìditi una buona *volta*! make up your mind once and for all!

h (*auguri*)

▷buon *appetito*! enjoy your meal!

▷buon *compleanno*! happy birthday!

▷tante buone *cose*! all the best!

▷buon *divertimento*! have a nice time!

▷buona *fortuna*! good luck!

▷buon *giorno*! (*in mattinata*) good morning!; (*di pomeriggio*) good afternoon!

▷buon *Natale*! happy Christmas!

▷buona *notte*! good night!

▷buona *permanenza*! enjoy your stay!

▷buon *riposo*! sleep well!

▷buona *sera*! good evening!

▷buon *viaggio*! have a good trip!

i (*fraseologia*)

▷fare qc *alla* buona to do sth simply *o* in a simple way

▷stasera mi vesto *alla* buona I'm not getting dressed up this evening

▷è un tipo *alla* buona he's an easy-going sort

▷accetterà *con* le buone o con le cattive he'll have to agree whether he wants to or not

▷l'ho fatto di buon *grado* I did it willingly

▷che Dio ce la *mandi* buona! here's hoping!

▷essere in buone *mani* to be in good hands

▷con le buone *maniere* in a kind *o* friendly way

▷mettere una buona *parola* per qn to put in a good word for sb

▷essere a buon *punto* to be well advanced

▷siamo a buon *punto* con il pranzo dinner's nearly ready

▷*questa* sì che è buona! that's a good one!

▷mi dica, buon *uomo* tell me, my good man

▷fare buon *viso* a cattivo gioco to put a brave face on things.

2 SM/F (*persona*) good *o* upright person;

▷i buoni e i *cattivi* (*in* film) the goodies and the baddies

▷un buono a *nulla* a good-for-nothing

3 SM, SOLO SG (*bontà*) goodness, good;

▷*di* buono c'è che... the good thing about it is that ...

▷essere un *poco* di buono to be a nasty piece of work

▷è una *poco* di buono she's a slut.

buono² ['bwɔno] SM **a** (*Comm*) coupon, voucher **b** (*Fin*) bill, bond ▶**buono d'acquisto** credit note, credit slip ▶ **buono benzina** petrol coupon ▶**buono di cassa** cash voucher ▶**buono di consegna** delivery note ▶**buono fruttifero** interest-bearing bond ▶ **buono d'imbarco** shipping note ▶**buono d'imposta** *special credit instrument for tax-relief purposes* ▶ **buono mensa** canteen voucher ▶ **buono (ordinario) del Tesoro** short-term treasury bond, treasury bill ▶ **buono postale fruttifero** interest-bearing bond (*issued by Italian Post Office*) ▶**buono del Tesoro poliennale** (*Econ*) long-term treasury bond.

buonora [bwo'nora] SF (*anche:* **buon'ora**): **di buonora** early; **alla buonora** finally, at last.

buonsenso [bwon'sɛnso] SM, SOLO SG common sense.

buontempone, a [bwontem'pone] SM/F jovial person.

buonumore [bwonu'more] SM (*anche:* **buon umore**): **essere di buonumore** to be in a good mood.

buonuomo [bwo'nwɔmo] SM = **buon uomo**.

buonuscita [bwonuʃ'ʃita] SF **a** (*Industria*) golden handshake **b** (*di affitti*) *sum paid for the relinquishing of tenancy rights.*

burattinaio, ai [buratti'najo] SM puppeteer, puppet master.

burattino [burat'tino] SM (*anche fig*) puppet.

burberamente [burbera'mente] AVV grumpily, gruffly.

burbero, a ['burbero] **1** AGG surly, gruff.
2 SM/F surly person, gruff person; **un burbero benefico** a rough diamond.

bureau [by'ro] SM INV (*mobile*) writing desk, bureau.

buretta [bu'retta] SF (*Chim*) burette.

burino, a [bu'rino] SM/F (*romanesco*) country bumpkin.

burla ['burla] SF prank, trick; **per burla** for fun, for a joke.

burlare [bur'lare] **1** VT to make fun of.
2 **burlarsi** VIP: **burlarsi di** = **vt.**

burlescamente [burleska'mente] AVV (*per burla*) in jest; (*in chiave burlesca*) as a burlesque.

burlesco, a, schi, sche [bur'lesko] AGG (*tono, voce*) jesting; (*stile*) burlesque.

burlone, a [bur'lone] SM/F joker.

burocrate [bu'rɔkrate] SM (*anche pegg*) bureaucrat.

burocraticamente [burokratika'mente] AVV bureaucratically.

burocratico, a, ci, che [buro'kratiko] AGG bureaucratic; **lungaggini burocratiche** red tape.

burocratismo [burokra'tizmo] SM bureaucratic attitude.

burocratizzare [burokratid'dzare] VT to bureaucratize.

burocrazia [burokrat'tsia] SF bureaucracy.

burrasca, sche [bur'raska] SF (*anche fig*) storm; **c'è** *o* **tira aria di burrasca** (*anche fig*) there's a storm brewing *o* in the air; **mare in burrasca** stormy sea; **c'è burrasca in famiglia** there's trouble at home.

burrascosamente [burraskosa'mente] AVV stormily.

burrascoso, a [burras'koso] AGG (*anche fig*) stormy.

burrificio, ci [burri'fitʃo] SM creamery.

burro ['burro] SM butter; **pasta/riso al burro** buttered pasta/rice; **uovo al burro** egg fried in butter; **questa bistecca è un burro** (*tenero*) this steak melts in your mouth; **avere le mani di burro** (*fig*) to be butter-fingered ▶ **burro di cacao** cocoa butter; (*per labbra*) lip salve.

burrone [bur'rone] SM ravine, gorge.

burroso, a [bur'roso] AGG buttery.

buscare [bus'kare] VT (*anche:* **buscarsi:** *raffreddore, schiaffo*) to get; **buscarle** to catch it, get a good hiding; (*essere battuto*) to get a drubbing.

buscherò *ecc* [buske'rɔ] VB *vedi* **buscare.**

busillis [bu'zillis] SM INV: **qui sta il busillis** there's the rub.

bussare [bus'sare] VI (*aus avere*) **a** to knock; **bussare alla porta** to knock at the door; **stanno bussando** there's somebody at the door **b** (*Carte*) *to knock on the table to induce partner to play his highest card.*

bussola ['bussola] SF **a** (*strumento nautico*) compass; **bussola giroscopica/magnetica** gyro/magnetic compass; **perdere la bussola** (*fig*) to lose one's head, lose one's bearings **b** (*porta*) revolving door **c** (*cassetta sigillata*) collection box.

bussolotto [busso'lotto] SM (*per dadi*) dice-shaker.

busta ['busta] SF **a** (*da lettera*) envelope; **in busta aperta/chiusa** in an unsealed/sealed envelope ▶ **busta a finestra** window envelope ▶ **busta paga** pay packet; (*listino*) pay slip **b** (*astuccio: di occhiali*) case ▶ **busta portatrucco** make-up bag.

bustarella [busta'rella] SF bribe, backhander; **dare una bustarella a qn** to slip sb a backhander.

bustina [bus'tina] SF **a** (*piccola busta*) envelope **b** (*di cibi, farmaci*) sachet ▶ **bustina di tè** tea bag **c** (*Mil*) forage cap.

bustino [bus'tino] SM corselet(te).

busto ['busto] SM **a** (*Anat, Scultura*) bust; **a mezzo busto** (*fotografia, ritratto*) half-length; **stare a busto eretto** to stand up straight **b** (*indumento*) corset.

butano [bu'tano] SM butane.

buttafuori [butta'fwɔri] SM INV bouncer.

buttare [but'tare] 1 VT **a** (*gettare*) to throw; **buttare fuori qn** to throw sb out; **buttare qc addosso a qn** to throw sth at sb; **buttare qc a qn** to throw sth to sb; **buttare qc per terra** to throw sth on the ground; **buttare (giù) la pasta/il riso** (*Culin*) to put pasta/rice into boiling water; **buttarsi il cappotto sulle spalle** to throw one's coat round one's shoulders; **buttarsi qc dietro le spalle** to throw sth over one's shoulder; (*fig: passato*) to put sth behind one

b (*anche:* **buttare via:** *nella spazzatura*) to throw away, discard; (*sprecare: soldi, tempo*) to waste; **non è un tipo da buttar via** he's not bad looking

c: **buttare giù** (*scritto*) to jot down, scribble down; (*cibo, boccone*) to gulp down; (*edificio*) to pull down, knock down; (*governo*) to bring down; **buttare giù due righe** to scribble a couple of lines; **buttare giù qn** (*deprimere*) to get sb down

d (*fraseologia*): **buttare la colpa addosso a qn** to lay the blame on sb; **buttare a mare** (*fig: soldi, occasione*) to throw away; **buttare i soldi dalla finestra** to throw money down the drain; **ho buttato là una frase** I mentioned it in passing; **gli ha buttato in faccia tutto il suo disprezzo** she told him to his face how much she despised him; **mi ha buttato in faccia tutta la verità** he flung the truth at me.

2 VI (*aus avere*) (*fam: apparire*): **la faccenda butta male** things are looking bad.

3 **buttarsi** VR (*saltare*) to jump; **buttiamoci!** (*saltiamo*) let's jump!; (*rischiamo*) let's have a go!; **buttarsi in acqua** to jump into the water; **buttarsi dalla finestra** to jump out of the window; **buttarsi su** *o* **addosso a qn** to launch o.s. at sb; **buttarsi nelle braccia di qn** to throw o.s. into sb's arms; **buttarsi in ginocchio** to throw o.s. down on one's knees; **buttarsi (anima e corpo) in qc** to throw o.s. (wholeheartedly) into sth; **buttarsi giù** (*stendersi*) to lie down; (*stimarsi poco*) to have a low opinion of o.s.; (*scoraggiarsi*) to get depressed *o* miserable; **buttarsi nella mischia** (*anche fig*) to throw o.s. into the fray; **buttarsi sulla preda** (*anche fig*) to pounce on one's prey.

buttata [but'tata] SF (*Bot*) sprouting.

butterare [butte'rare] VT to pock-mark.

butterato, a [butte'rato] AGG pock-marked, pitted.

buzzo ['buddzo] SM: **di buzzo buono** (*con impegno*) with a will.

buzzurro, a [bud'dzurro] SM/F (*pegg*) boor.

C

C, c [tʃi] SF O M INV (*lettera*) C, c; **C come Como** ≈ C for Charlie.

C [tʃi] ABBR **a** (*Geog*) = **capo b** (= *Celsius, centigrado*) C **c** (= *conto*) a/c.

CA SIGLA = *Cagliari*.

c.a. ABBR **a** (*Elettr*: = *corrente alternata*) AC **b** (*Comm*)= *corrente anno*.

cab. ABBR = **cablogramma.**

cabala ['kabala] SF (*intrigo*) cabal.

cabaret [kaba'rɛ] SM INV cabaret.

cabina [ka'bina] ① SF (*di nave*) cabin; (*di ascensore*) cage; (*di funivia*) car; (*in spiaggia*) beach hut; (*in piscina*) cubicle.

② ▶**cabina di blocco** *o* **di manovra** (*Ferr*) signal box ▶**cabina elettorale** polling booth ▶**cabina elettrica** substation ▶**cabina di guida** driver's cab ▶**cabina passeggeri** (*Aer*) passenger cabin *o* compartment ▶**cabina di pilotaggio** (*Aer: gen*) cockpit; (: *in aereo di linea*) flight deck ▶**cabina di proiezione** (*Cine*) projection booth ▶**cabina di prova** changing room (*in shop*) ▶**cabina di regia** control room (*Radio, TV*) ▶**cabina telefonica** telephone booth *o* box, callbox.

cabinato, a [kabi'nato] ① AGG (*Naut*) with a cabin. ② SM cabin cruiser.

cabinovia [kabino'via] SF two-seater cablecar.

cablaggio, gi [ka'bladdʒo] SM wiring.

cablare [ka'blare] VT to cable.

cablografia [kablogra'fia] SF cable telegraphy.

cablogramma, i [kablo'gramma] SM cable(gram).

cabotaggio, gi [kabo'taddʒo] SM **a** (*Naut*) coastal navigation; **nave da cabotaggio** tramp, coaster **b** : **di piccolo cabotaggio** (*fig: di poco conto: attività*) small-scale.

cabotare [kabo'tare] VI (*aus avere*) to ply along the coast.

cabrare [ka'brare] VI (*aus avere*) (*Aer*) to nose up.

cabrata [ka'brata] SF (*Aer*) nose-up.

cabriolet [kabriɔ'lɛ] SM INV (*auto*) convertible.

cacao [ka'kao] SM INV (*albero*) cacao; (*polvere*) cocoa.

cacare [ka'kare] (*fam!*) VI (*aus avere*) VT to shit (*fam!*); **cacarsi sotto** *o* **addosso** (*fig: avere paura*) to shit o.s.

(*fam!*); **va' a cacare!** piss off! (*fam!*)

cacarella [kaka'rɛlla] SF (*fam: dissenteria*) runs *pl*; **far venire la cacarella a qn** (*fig fam*) to scare the shit out of sb (*fam!*)

cacata [ka'kata] SF (*fig fam!: cosa brutta, mal fatta*) shit (*fam!*)

cacatoa [kaka'tɔa], **cacatua** [kaka'tua] SM INV cockatoo.

cacca ['kakka] SF (*fam: anche fig*) shit (*fam!*); **dover fare la cacca** (*linguaggio infantile*) to have to do a jobbie.

caccia[1] ['kattʃa] ① SF **a** hunting; (*con fucile*) shooting, hunting; **andare a caccia** to go hunting; **andare a caccia di leoni** to go lion-hunting; **battuta di caccia** hunting party

b (*anche: stagione di caccia*) hunting (*o* shooting) season

c (*cacciagione*) game

d (*fig: inseguimento, ricerca*) chase; **dare la caccia a qn** to give chase to sb; **essere a caccia di notizie/libri** to be on the lookout for news/books; **essere a caccia di un impiego/una casa** to be job-hunting *o* house-hunting; **essere a caccia di uomini/soldi** to be after men/money; **andare a caccia di guai** to go looking for trouble.

② ▶**caccia al cervo** deer hunting, deerstalking ▶**caccia grossa** big game hunting ▶**caccia alle streghe** witch-hunt ▶**caccia subacquea** harpoon fishing ▶**caccia al tesoro** treasure hunt ▶**caccia all'uomo** manhunt.

caccia[2] ['kattʃa] SM INV (*aereo*) fighter; (*nave*) destroyer.

cacciabombardiere [kattʃabombar'djɛre] SM fighter-bomber.

cacciagione [kattʃa'dʒone] SF game.

cacciare [kat'tʃare] ① VT **a** (*Sport*) to hunt; (*con fucile*) to shoot, hunt

b (*mandar via: persona*): **cacciare qn di casa/dal paese/dalla scuola** to throw sb out of the house/the country/school; (: *nemico*) to drive away; (: *tristezza, malinconia, dubbio*) to chase away

c (*fam: mettere*): **cacciare qn in prigione** to throw sb into prison; **cacciarsi qc in testa** (*cappello*) to pull sth on;

(*idea*) to get sth into one's head; **dove hai cacciato quel libro?** where have you put that book?

d (*fam: emettere*): **cacciare un grido** to let out a cry *o* yell

e (*fam: estrarre*): **cacciare fuori** to pull out; **cacciare fuori un coltello** to pull out a knife; **cacciare fuori la lingua** to stick out one's tongue; **caccia fuori i soldi!** pay up!, cough up!.

2 **cacciarsi** VR **a** (*fam: nascondersi*) to hide o.s.; **ma dove si sarà cacciato?** where can he (*o* it) have got to? **b** (*fam: mettersi*): **cacciarsi nei guai** *o* **in un bel pasticcio** to get into a lot of trouble.

cacciata [kat'tʃata] SF: **la cacciata dell'invasore** the driving out of the invader.

cacciatora [kattʃa'tora] SF **a** (*giacca*) hunting jacket **b** (*Culin*): **pollo** *ecc* **alla cacciatora** chicken *ecc* chasseur.

cacciatore [kattʃa'tore] SM hunter ►**cacciatore di dote** fortune-hunter ►**cacciatore di frodo** poacher ►**cacciatore di teste** (*anche fig*) headhunter.

cacciatorpediniere [kattʃatorpedi'njɛre] SM destroyer.

cacciavite [kattʃa'vite] SM INV screwdriver ►**cacciavite cercafase** mains tester ►**cacciavite a croce** *o* **a stella** Philips screwdriver ®.

cacciucco [kat'tʃukko] SM *spiced fish soup*.

cachemire [kaʃ'mir] SM INV cashmere.

cachet [ka'ʃɛ] SM INV **a** (*Med: compressa*) tablet; (: *capsula*) capsule **b** (*compenso*) fee **c** (*colorante per capelli*) rinse.

cachi¹ ['kaki] SM INV (*albero, frutto*) persimmon.

cachi² ['kaki] AGG INV, SM khaki.

cacio, ci ['katʃo] SM cheese; **venire** *o* **cadere come il cacio sui maccheroni** (*fig*) to turn up at the right moment.

cacofonia [kakofo'nia] SF cacophony.

cacofonico, a, ci, che [kako'fɔniko] AGG cacophonous.

cactus ['kaktus] SM INV cactus.

cadauno, a [kada'uno] AGG, PRON INDEF each.

cadavere [ka'davere] SM corpse, (dead) body; **sembrare un cadavere ambulante** to look like death warmed up.

cadaverico, a, ci, che [kada'vɛriko] AGG (*fig*) deathly pale; **rigidità cadaverica** rigor mortis.

caddi *ecc* ['kaddi] VB vedi **cadere**.

cadente [ka'dɛnte] AGG falling; (*fig: edificio*) tumbledown; (: *persona*) decrepit; **stella cadente** falling *o* shooting star.

cadenza [ka'dɛntsa] SF (*gen*) cadence; (*ritmo*) rhythm; (*inflessione*) intonation; (*Mus*) cadenza.

cadenzare [kaden'tsare] VT to mark the rhythm of; **marciare con passo cadenzato** to march in time.

cadere [ka'dere] VI IRREG (*aus essere*) **a** (*persona, oggetto*) to fall; (*tetto*) to fall in; (*aereo*) to crash; **cadere dalla bicicletta/da un albero/dalle scale** to fall off one's bicycle/from a tree/down the stairs; **cadere bocconi** to fall flat on one's face; **cadere in ginocchio** to fall on(to) one's knees; **cadere lungo disteso** to fall flat on one's back; **cadere in piedi** (*anche fig*) to land on one's feet; **cadere ai piedi di qn** to fall at sb's feet; **cadere dal sonno** to be falling asleep on one's feet; **cadere a terra** to fall down, fall to the ground; **far cadere** to knock over *o* down; **cadere dalle nuvole** (*fig*) to be taken aback; **la conversazione cadde su Garibaldi** the conversation came round to Garibaldi; **mi è caduto lo sguardo su una vecchia foto** my eye fell upon an old photo; **questi pantaloni cadono bene** these trousers hang well

b (*staccarsi: denti, capelli*) to fall out; (: *foglie*) to fall **c** (*scendere: pioggia, neve*) to fall, come down; (: *notte, stella*) to fall

d (*cessare: vento*) to drop; **è caduta la linea** I (*o* you *ecc*) have been cut off

e (*data*) to fall; **quest'anno il mio compleanno cade di martedì** my birthday falls on a Tuesday this year

f (*venire a trovarsi*): **cadere ammalato** to fall ill; **cadere in disgrazia** to fall into disgrace; **cadere in errore** to make a mistake; **cadere in trappola** fall into a trap; **cadere in miseria/oblio** to sink into poverty/oblivion

g (*soldato, fortezza, governo*) to fall; **far cadere il governo** to bring down the government

h : **lasciar cadere** (*oggetto, fig: discorso, proposta*) to drop; (*frase, parola*) to slip in; **si lasciò cadere sulla poltrona** he dropped *o* fell into the armchair.

cadetto, a [ka'detto] **1** AGG **a** younger; **ramo cadetto** cadet branch **b** (*Sport*) junior *attr*. **2** SM (*gen, Mil*) cadet; (*Sport*) junior.

cadmio ['kadmjo] SM cadmium.

cadrò *ecc* [ka'drɔ] VB vedi **cadere**.

caducità [kadutʃi'ta] SF transience.

caduco, a, chi, che [ka'duko] AGG **a** (*fig letter*) short-lived, fleeting **b** (*Bot*) deciduous.

caduta [ka'duta] SF **1** (*gen, Rel*) fall; **ha fatto una brutta caduta** he had a nasty fall; **la caduta dei capelli** hair loss. **2** ►**caduta libera** (*Fis*) free fall ►**caduta massi** falling rocks ►**caduta del sistema** (*Inform*) system failure ►**caduta di tensione** (*Elettr*) voltage drop.

caduto, a [ka'duto] **1** PP di **cadere**. **2** AGG (*morto*) dead. **3** SM dead soldier; **monumento ai caduti** war memorial.

caffè [kaf'fɛ] SM INV (*bevanda*) coffee; (*bar*) cafè ►**caffè corretto** coffee with a shot of spirits ►**caffè decaffeinato** decaffeinated coffee ►**caffè espresso** espresso coffee ►**caffè in grani** coffee beans ►**caffè lungo** weak black coffee ►**caffè macchiato** coffee with a dash of milk ►**caffè macinato** ground coffee ►**caffè d'orzo** barley coffee ►**caffè ristretto** strong black coffee ►**caffè solubile** instant coffee.

caffeario, ria, ri, rie [kaffe'arjo] AGG coffee *attr*.

caffeina [kaffe'ina] SF caffeine.

caffellatte [kaffel'latte] SM INV white coffee.

caffettano [kaffet'tano] SM kaftan.

caffetteria [kaffette'ria] SF coffee shop, coffee bar.

caffettiera [kaffet'tjɛra] SF (*per fare il caffè*) coffee-maker; (*per servire il caffè*) coffeepot.

cafonaggine [kafo'naddʒine] SF boorishness.

cafone, a [ka'fone] **1** SM/F (*persona*) boor, ill-mannered person; **comportarsi da cafone** to be ill-mannered. **2** AGG (*persona, comportamento, risposta*) boorish, ill-mannered.

cagionare [kadʒo'nare] VT to cause, be the cause of.

cagione [ka'dʒone] SF cause.

cagionevole [kadʒo'nevole] AGG (*salute*) delicate, weak.

cagliare [kaʎ'ʎare] VI (*aus essere*) VT to curdle.

cagliaritano, a [kaʎʎari'tano] **1** AGG of *o* from Cagliari. **2** SM/F inhabitant *o* native of Cagliari.

cagliata [kaʎ'ʎata] SF curd.

cagliatura [kaʎʎa'tura] SF curdling.

caglio, gli ['kaʎʎo] SM rennet.

cagna ['kaɲɲa] SF (*Zool*) bitch.

cagnara [kaɲ'ɲara] SF uproar; **far cagnara** to make a din.

cagnesco [kaɲ'ɲesko] AGG: **guardare qn in cagnesco** to scowl at sb.

C.A.I. ['kai] SIGLA M = *Club Alpino Italiano*.

caimano [kai'mano] SM cayman.

Caino [ka'ino] SM Cain.

Cairo ['kairo] SF: **il Cairo** Cairo.

cala ['kala] SF **a** (*baia*) bay **b** (*Naut*) hold.

calabrese [kala'brese] AGG, SM/F Calabrian.

calabrone [kala'brone] SM hornet.

calafatare [kalafa'tare] VT (*Naut*) to caulk.

calamaio, ai [kala'majo] SM inkpot, inkwell.

calamaro [kala'maro] SM squid.

calamita [kala'mita] SF (*anche fig*) magnet.

calamità [kalami'ta] SF INV disaster, calamity; **è una calamità naturale** (*fig*) he's a walking disaster ▶**calamità naturale** natural disaster.

calamitare [kalami'tare] VT (*anche fig*) to magnetize.

calamitato, a [kalami'tato] AGG (*ago della bussola*) magnetic.

calamo ['kalamo] SM (*Zool, penna*) quill.

calandra [ka'landra] SF (*machine*) calender; (*Aut*) radiator grill.

calante [ka'lante] AGG falling; **sole calante** setting sun; **luna calante** waning moon.

calare [ka'lare] **1** VT (*gen*) to lower; (*Maglia*) to decrease; (*ancora*) to drop, lower; (*perpendicolare*) to drop. **2** VI (*aus* **essere**) **a** (*gen*) to come down, fall; (*sole*) to set, go down; (*notte, silenzio*) to fall **b** (*diminuire: vento, febbre*) to drop; (: *temperatura, prezzo*) to drop, fall; (: *suono*) to die away; **calare di peso** to lose weight; **sono calato (di) 3 chili** I've lost 3 kilos; **cala!** (*non esagerare*) come off it! **c** (*invadere*): **calare (su)** to descend (on). **3 calarsi** VR **a** (*discendere*) to lower o.s.; **calarsi da una finestra/in un crepaccio** to lower o.s. from a window/into a crevasse **b**: **calarsi nella parte** (*Teatro*): **si è calato bene nella parte** he has really got into the part; **si è calato un po' troppo nella parte del giovane dirigente** (*fig*) he goes a bit too far in playing the young executive. **4** SM: **al calar del sole** at sunset; **al calar della luna** when the moon goes down.

calata [ka'lata] SF (*invasione*) invasion.

calca ['kalka] SF throng, press.

calcagno [kal'kaɲɲo] SM (*pl* **calcagna** (negli usi figurati)) (*Anat, di scarpa*) heel; **aveva la polizia alle calcagna** the police were hot on his heels; **il mio capo mi sta sempre alle calcagna** my boss is never off my back.

calcare[1] [kal'kare] VT **a** (*premere*) to press down; (: *coi piedi*) to tread, press down; **calcarsi il cappello sugli occhi** to pull one's hat down over one's eyes; **le scene** (*fig*) to be on the stage; **calcare le orme di qn** (*fig*) to follow in sb's footsteps; **calcare la mano** (*fig*) to overdo it, exaggerate **b** (*mettere in rilievo*) to stress; **calcare le parole** to accentuate each syllable.

calcare[2] [kal'kare] SM limestone.

calcareo, a [kal'kareo] AGG limestone *attr*.

calce[1] ['kaltʃe] SF lime ▶**calce spenta** slaked lime ▶**calce viva** quicklime.

calce[2] ['kaltʃe] SM (*Amm*): **in calce a** at the foot of; **"firma in calce"** "please sign below".

calcedonio [kaltʃe'dɔnjo] SM chalcedony.

calcestruzzo [kaltʃes'truttso] SM concrete.

calcetto [kal'tʃetto] SM (*calcio-balilla*) table football; (*calcio a cinque*) five-a-side (football).

calcherò *ecc* [kalke'rɔ] VB *vedi* **calcare**.

calciare [kal'tʃare] VI (*aus* **avere**) VT to kick.

calciatore [kaltʃa'tore] SM (*Calcio*) (football) player, footballer; (*Rugby*) kicker.

calcificarsi [kaltʃifi'karsi] VIP to calcify.

calcificazione [kaltʃifikat'tsjone] SF calcification.

calcina [kal'tʃina] SF (*lime*) mortar.

calcinaccio, ci [kaltʃi'nattʃo] SM flake of plaster; **un mucchio di calcinacci** a pile of rubble.

calcio[1]**, ci** ['kaltʃo] **1** SM **a** (*pedata: anche Sport*) kick; **dare un calcio a qn** to give sb a kick, kick sb **b** (*sport*) football, soccer; **squadra di calcio** football team **c** (*di pistola, fucile*) butt. **2** ▶**calcio d'angolo** corner (kick) ▶**calcio di punizione** free kick ▶**calcio di rigore** penalty kick ▶**calcio di rinvio** (*Rugby*) drop-out.

calcio[2] ['kaltʃo] SM (*Chim*) calcium.

calcio-balilla ['kaltʃo ba'lilla] SM INV table football.

calcio-mercato ['kaltʃo mer'kato] SM football market.

calcisticamente [kaltʃistika'mente] AVV from a footballing point of view, as regards football.

calcistico, a, ci, che [kal'tʃistiko] AGG football *attr*.

calco, chi ['kalko] SM (*Scultura*) cast, mould (*Brit*), mold (*Am*), casting, moulding (*Brit*), molding (*Am*); (*di disegno*) tracing; (*Ling*) calque, loan translation.

calcografia [kalkogra'fia] SF (*incisione, arte*) copper engraving.

calcolare [kalko'lare] VI (*fare il conto di*) to calculate, work out; (*considerare*) to reckon on, take into account; (*ponderare*) to weigh (up); **calcolo che sarò di ritorno fra 5 giorni** I reckon I'll be back in 5 days' time; **calcolare i pro e i contro** to weigh up the pros and cons.

calcolatore, trice [kalkola'tore] **1** AGG (*fig*) calculating. **2** SM computer. **3** SF (*anche:* **macchina calcolatrice**) calculator. **4** SM/F (*persona*) calculating person.

calcolo ['kalkolo] **1** SM **a** (*anche Mat*) calculation; **fare il calcolo di qc** to work sth out; **fare i propri calcoli** (*fig*) to weigh up the pros and cons; **per calcolo** out of self-interest; **a un calcolo approssimativo** at a rough estimate ▶**calcolo differenziale** differential calculus ▶**calcolo infinitesimale** infinitesimal calculus ▶**calcolo integrale** integral calculus **b** (*Med*) stone, calculus (*termine tecn*) ▶**calcolo renale** (*Med*) stone in the kidneys.

caldaia [kal'daja] SF boiler.

caldamente [kalda'mente] AVV (*fig: con cordialità*) warmly; (: *con fervore*) fervently.

caldarrosta [kaldar'rɔsta] SF roast chestnut.

caldeggiare [kalded'dʒare] VT to support.

calderone [kalde'rone] SM cauldron; (*fig*) hotchpotch; **mettere tutto nello stesso calderone** (*fig*) to treat everything in the same way.

caldo, a ['kaldo] **1** AGG (*gen, fig*) warm; (*molto caldo*) hot; (*appassionato*) keen; (*cordiale: persona, accoglienza*) warm, friendly, cordial; **batti il ferro finché è caldo** strike while the iron is hot; **piangere a calde lacrime** to weep bitterly; **essere una testa calda** to be hot-headed. **2** SM heat; **fa caldo** it's warm; (*molto caldo*) it's hot; **col caldo che fa...** in this heat ...; **ho caldo** I'm warm; (*molto caldo*) I'm hot; **ti tengo in caldo la minestra** I'm keeping your soup hot for you; **non mi fa né caldo né freddo** I couldn't care less; **quel ragazzo non mi fa né caldo né freddo** I'm indifferent to that boy; **a caldo** (*fig*) in the heat of the moment.

caleidoscopico, a, ci, che [kaleidos'kɔpiko] AGG kaleidoscopic.

caleidoscopio, pi [kaleidos'kɔpjo] SM kaleidoscope.

calendario, ri [kalen'darjo] SM calendar; **calendario degli incontri** (*Calcio*) fixtures list.

calende [ka'lɛnde] SFPL calends; **rimandare qc alle calende greche** to put sth off indefinitely.

calesse [ka'lɛsse] SM (*carrozza*) gig.

calibrare [kali'brare] VT (*Tecn*) to calibrate; (*fig: misurare attentamente*) to gauge.

calibrato, a [kali'brato] AGG (*Tecn*) calibrated; (*fig: discorso, giudizio*) balanced; **abiti a taglie calibrate** (*Sartoria*) outsize clothes.

calibratura [kalibra'tura] SF calibration.

calibro ['kalibro] SM (*di arma*) calibre, bore; (*strumento*) callipers *pl*; (*fig*) calibre; **di grosso calibro** (*fig*) prominent.

calice¹ ['kalitʃe] SM (*Bot*) calyx.

calice² ['kalitʃe] SM (*coppa*) goblet; (*bicchiere*) stem glass; (*Rel*) chalice.

califfo [ka'liffo] SM (*Storia*) caliph.

California [kali'fɔrnja] SF: **la California** California.

californiano, a [kalifor'njano] AGG, SM/F Californian.

caligine [ka'lidʒine] SF (*nebbia*) fog; (*: mista a fumo*) smog.

caliginoso, a [kalidʒi'noso] AGG (*nebbioso*) foggy.

Caligola [ka'ligola] SM Caligula.

calle ['kalle] SF narrow street (*in Venice*).

callifugo, ghi [kal'lifugo] SM (*pomata*) anti-corn cream; (*cerotto*) corn plaster.

calligrafia [kalligra'fia] SF (*scrittura*) handwriting; (*arte*) calligraphy.

calligrafico, a, ci, che [kalli'grafiko] AGG (*vedi sf*) handwriting *attr*; calligraphic.

Calliope [kal'liope] SF Calliope.

callista, i, e [kal'lista] SM/F chiropodist.

callo ['kallo] SM callus; (*sui piedi*) corn; **pestare i calli a qn** (*fig*) to tread on sb's toes; **fare il callo a qc** to get used to sth ▶ **callo osseo** callus.

calloso, a [kal'loso] AGG (*mano*) callous.

calma ['kalma] SF (*vedi agg*) quietness, peacefulness; stillness; calm; (*tranquillità*) peace (and quiet), quietness; **con calma** (*senza fretta*) slowly; **fai con calma** take your time; **mare in calma** calm sea; **è un giorno di calma nel negozio** it's a quiet day in the shop; **calma e sangue freddo!** keep cool *o* calm!

calmante [kal'mante] ① AGG relaxing.

② SM (*Med: analgesico*) painkiller; (*: sedativo*) tranquillizer, sedative.

calmare [kal'mare] ① VT (*gen*) to calm; (*persona*) to calm (down); (*dolore*) to soothe.

② **calmarsi** VIP (*mare, persona*) to calm down, grow calm; (*dolore*) to ease; (*febbre, rabbia*) to subside; (*vento*) to abate.

calmierare [kalmje'rare] VT (*Comm: prezzi*) to control.

calmiere [kal'mjɛre] SM (*Comm*): **calmiere dei prezzi** price control(s).

calmo, a ['kalmo] AGG (*atmosfera*) quiet, peaceful; (*aria, cielo*) still; (*persona, mare*) calm.

calo ['kalo] SM: **calo (di)** (*gen*) fall (in), drop (in); (*di prezzi*) fall (in); (*di peso*) loss (of); (*di volume*) shrinkage; **la sua popolarità ha subito un grosso calo** his popularity has fallen sharply.

calore [ka'lore] SM (*gen*) warmth; (*intenso, Fis*) heat; (*fig: entusiasmo*) fervour; **accogliere qn con calore** to welcome sb warmly; **essere in calore** (*animale*) to be on heat.

caloria [kalo'ria] SF calorie.

calorico, a, ci, che [ka'lɔriko] AGG calorific.

calorifero [kalo'rifero] SM radiator.

calorifico, a, ci, che [kalo'rifiko] AGG calorific, heat producing.

calorosamente [kalorosa'mente] AVV (*con cordialità*) warmly; (*con entusiasmo*) fervently.

calorosità [kalorosi'ta] SF (*vedi agg*) warmth; heartiness.

caloroso, a [kalo'roso] AGG (*persona, accoglienza*) warm; (*applauso*) hearty, enthusiastic.

caloscia, sce [ka'lɔʃʃa] SF galosh.

calotta [ka'lɔtta] SF ① (*di cappello*) crown.

② ▶ **calotta cranica** (*Anat*) skullcap ▶ **calotta glaciale** (*Geog*) icecap ▶ **calotta polare** (*Geog*) polar icecap ▶ **calotta sferica** (*Mat*) segment of a sphere ▶ **calotta dello spinterogeno** (*Aut*) distributor cap.

calpestare [kalpes'tare] VT to tread on, trample on; **"vietato calpestare le aiuole"** "keep off the grass"; **calpestare i diritti di qn** to encroach on sb's rights; **non farti calpestare** (*fig*) don't let people walk all over you.

calpestio, tii [kalpes'tio] SM (*di piedi*) tread, treading; (*: rumore*) stamping.

calumet [kaly'mɛ] SM INV (*anche:* **calumet della pace**) peace pipe.

calunnia [ka'lunnja] SF slander; **spargere calunnie sul conto di qn** to spread slander about sb.

calunniare [kalun'njare] VT to slander.

calunniatore, trice [kalunnja'tore] ① AGG slanderous.

② SM/F slanderer.

calunniosamente [kalunnjosa'mente] AVV slanderously.

calunnioso, a [kalun'njoso] AGG slanderous.

Calvario [kal'varjo] SM (*Rel*) Calvary; (*fig*) ordeal, trial; **da allora la sua vita è stata un calvario** her life since then has been one of suffering.

calvinismo [kalvi'nizmo] SM Calvinism.

calvinista, i, e [kalvi'nista] AGG, SM/F Calvinist.

calvizie [kal'vittsje] SF baldness.

calvo, a ['kalvo] ① AGG bald.

② SM bald man.

calza ['kaltsa] SF (*da uomo*) sock; (*da donna*) stocking; **fare la calza** to knit ▶ **calze elastiche** support stockings ▶ **calze di nailon** nylons, (nylon) stockings.

calzamaglia [kaltsa'maʎʎa] SF tights *pl*; (*per danza, ginnastica*) leotard.

calzante [kal'tsante] ① AGG (*fig*) appropriate, fitting.

② SM shoehorn.

calzare [kal'tsare] ① VT (*scarpe, guanti: portare*) to wear; (*: mettere*) to put on.

② VI (*aus* avere*, nel senso fig* essere*) to fit; **calzare a pennello** to fit like a glove; **questa descrizione gli calza a pennello** that describes him to a T.

calzascarpe [kaltsas'karpe] SM INV shoehorn.

calzatura [kaltsa'tura] SF footwear; **negozio di calzature** shoeshop.

calzaturiero, a [kaltsatu'rjero] AGG shoe *attr*.

calzaturificio, ci [kaltsaturi'fitʃo] SM shoe factory.

calzetta [kal'tsetta] SF ankle sock; **una mezza calzetta** (*fig*) a nobody.

calzettone [kaltset'tone] SM knee-length sock.

calzificio, ci [kaltsi'fitʃo] SM hosiery factory.

calzino [kal'tsino] SM (*short*) sock.

calzolaio, ai [kaltso'lajo] SM (*che ripara*) cobbler; (*che fabbrica*) shoemaker.

calzoleria [kaltsole'ria] SF (*negozio*) shoe shop; (*arte*)

shoemaking.

calzoncini [kaltson'tʃini] SMPL shorts ▶**calzoncini da bagno** (swimming) trunks.

calzone [kal'tsone] SM **a** : **calzone destro/sinistro** right/left trouser leg **b** : **calzoni** SMPL trousers (Brit), pants (Am); **portare i calzoni** (anche fig) to wear the trousers ▶**calzoni alla cavallerizza** jodhpurs ▶**calzoni corti** shorts ▶**calzoni alla zuava** knickerbockers **c** (Culin) calzone (savoury turnover made with pizza dough).

camaleonte [kamale'onte] SM (Zool, fig) chameleon.

camaleontismo [kamaleon'tizmo] SM (Pol) opportunism.

cambiadischi [kambja'diski] SM INV (anche: **cambiadischi automatico**) record changer.

cambiale [kam'bjale] SF (Comm) bill (of exchange); (: pagherò cambiario) promissory note; **firmare cambiali per qc** to pay sth up in instalments ▶**cambiale di comodo** o **favore** accommodation bill.

cambiamento [kambja'mento] SM change.

cambiare [kam'bjare] ① VT **a** (gen) to change; (modificare) to alter; **cambiare (l')aria in una stanza** to air a room; **vado in montagna per cambiare aria** I'm going to the mountains for a change of air; **è ora di cambiare aria** (andarsene) it's time to move on; **cambiare casa** to move (house); **cambiare indirizzo** to change address; **cambiare treno** to change trains; **cambiare marcia** (Aut) to change gear; **cambiare idea** to change one's mind; **cambiare le carte in tavola** (fig) to change one's tune **b** (barattare): **cambiare (qc con qn/qc per qc)** to exchange (sth with sb/sth for sth); **ho cambiato la mia macchina con quella del mio amico** I exchanged cars with my friend **c** (valuta) to change; **mi puoi cambiare centomila lire?** can you change a hundred thousand lire for me?.

② VI (aus essere) (variare) to change, alter.

③ **cambiarsi** VIP (modificarsi) to change.

④ **cambiarsi** VR **cambiarsi (d'abito)** to get changed, change (one's clothes).

cambiario, ria, ri, rie [kam'bjarjo] AGG (Fin) exchange attr.

cambiavalute [kambjava'lute] SM INV exchange office.

cambio, bi ['kambjo] SM **a** (gen) change; (modifica) alteration, change; **dare il cambio a qn** to take over from sb, relieve sb; **fare il** o **un cambio** to change (over); **facciamo a cambio** let's change over o swap; **effettuare il cambio di campo** (Sport) to change ends; **in cambio di** in exchange for **b** (Fin) exchange; (anche: **tasso di cambio**) rate of exchange ▶**cambio a termine** forward exchange **c** (Aut, Ciclismo) gears pl; **cambio di marcia** gear change; **macchina con il cambio automatico** automatic (car).

cambista, i [kam'bista] SM (foreign-)exchange agent.

Cambital ['kambital] SIGLA M = Ufficio Italiano dei Cambi.

Cambogia [kam'bodʒa] SF Cambodia.

cambogiano, a [kambo'dʒano] AGG, SM/F Cambodian.

cambusa [kam'buza] SF pantry (on ship).

camelia [ka'mɛlja] SF camellia.

camera ['kamera] ① SF **a** (gen) room; (anche: **camera da letto**) bedroom; (mobili) bedroom suite **b** (Pol) Chamber, House; **le Camere** ≈ (the Houses of) Parliament (Brit), Congress (Am). ② ▶**camera ardente** chapel of rest ▶**camera d'aria** (di pneumatico) inner tube; (di pallone) bladder ▶**camera blindata** strongroom ▶**camera a bolle** (Fis) bubble chamber ▶**camera di combustione** combus-

tion chamber ▶**Camera di commercio** Chamber of Commerce ▶**camera di decompressione** decompression chamber ▶**Camera dei Deputati** Chamber of Deputies, ≈ House of Commons (Brit), ≈ House of Representatives (Am), in this lower chamber of the Italian Parliament there are 630 deputati, elected by a combination of a first-past-the-post system and proportional representation: they elect the Presidente della Camera ▶**camera a due letti** twin-bedded room ▶**camera a gas** gas chamber ▶**camera del lavoro** trades union centre (Brit), labor union centre (Am) ▶**camera matrimoniale** double room ▶**camera a nube** (Fis) cloud chamber ▶**camera oscura** (Fot) darkroom ▶**camera da pranzo** dining room ▶**camera singola** single room.

cameraman ['kæmərəmən] SM INV (TV) cameraman.

camerata[1] [kame'rata] SF (dormitorio) dormitory.

camerata[2] [kame'rata] SM/F comrade (of right-wing group).

cameratesco, a, schi, sche [kamera'tesko] AGG: **spirito cameratesco** sense of comradeship.

cameratismo [kamera'tizmo] SM comradeship.

cameretta [kame'retta] SF (piccola camera) small bedroom; (su piano stradale) manhole.

cameriera [kame'rjɛra] SF (domestica) maid; (che serve a tavola) waitress; (che fa le camere) chambermaid.

cameriere [kame'rjɛre] SM (domestico) (man)servant; (di ristorante) waiter.

camerino [kame'rino] SM (Teatro) dressing room.

cameristico, a, ci, che [kame'ristiko] AGG chamber-music attr.

Camerun ['kamerun] SM: **il Camerun** Cameroon.

camice ['kamitʃe] SM (di medico, tecnico) white coat; (di chirurgo) gown; (di sacerdote) alb.

camiceria [kamitʃe'ria] SF (fabbrica) shirt factory; (negozio) shirt shop (Brit), shirt store (Am).

camicetta [kami'tʃetta] SF blouse.

camicia, cie [ka'mitʃa] ① SF **a** (da uomo) shirt; (da donna) blouse; **nascere con la camicia** (fig) to be born lucky; **sudare sette camicie** (fig) to have a hell of a time **b** (Tecn: involucro) jacket. ② ▶**camicia di forza** straitjacket ▶**camicia nera** (fascista) Blackshirt ▶**camicia da notte** (da donna) nightdress; (da uomo) nightshirt.

camiciaio, aia, ai, aie [kami'tʃajo] SM/F (sarto) shirtmaker; (che vende camicie) shirtseller.

camiciola [kami'tʃɔla] SF vest.

camiciotto [kami'tʃɔtto] SM (camicia sportiva) casual shirt; (per operai) smock.

caminetto [kami'netto] SM hearth, fireplace.

camino [ka'mino] SM **a** (focolare) fireplace, hearth; **accendere il camino** to light the fire **b** (comignolo, ciminiera, di vulcano) chimney.

camion ['kamjon] SM INV lorry (Brit), truck (Am).

camionabile [kamjo'nabile] ① AGG for heavy vehicles. ② SF road for heavy vehicles.

camioncino [kamjon'tʃino] SM van.

camionetta [kamjo'netta] SF jeep.

camionista, i [kamjo'nista] SM/F lorry driver (Brit), truck driver (Am).

camma ['kamma] SF cam; **albero a camme** camshaft.

cammello [kam'mello] SM (Zool, colore) camel; (stoffa) camel hair.

cammeo [kam'mɛo] SM cameo.

camminare [kammi'nare] VI (aus avere) **a** (gen) to walk;

camminare a carponi *o* a quattro zampe to go on all fours, crawl; camminare a grandi passi to stride (along); camminare a testa alta (*fig*) to walk with one's head held high; con questo traffico non si cammina you can't move with all this traffic; cammina cammina, siamo arrivati after a long walk, we arrived; cammina! (*spicciati*) come on!; (*levati di torno*) go away!
 b (*funzionare*) to work, go; il mio orologio non cammina più my watch has stopped.

camminata [kammi'nata] SF walk; fare una camminata to go for a walk.

camminatore, trice [kammina'tore] SM/F walker.

cammino [kam'mino] SM (*viaggio*) walk; (*sentiero*) path; (*itinerario, direzione, tragitto*) way; un'ora di cammino an hour's walk; mettersi in cammino to set *o* start off; riprendere il cammino to continue on one's way; cammin facendo on the way; il cammino della virtù (*fig*) the path of virtue.

camomilla [kamo'milla] SF (*Bot*) camomile; (*infuso*) camomile tea.

camorra [ka'mɔrra] SF Camorra; (*fig*) racket.

camorrista, i, e [kamor'rista] SM/F member of the Camorra; (*fig*) racketeer.

camorristico, a, ci, che [kamor'ristiko] AGG Camorra *attr*, of the Camorra.

camoscio, sci [ka'mɔʃʃo] SM (*Zool, pelle*) chamois; scarpe di camoscio suede shoes.

campagna [kam'paɲɲa] SF a (*gen*) country, countryside; (*paesaggio*) countryside; vivere in campagna to live in the country; andare in campagna to go to the country b (*terra coltivata*) land c (*Pol, Comm, Mil*) campaign; fare una campagna to campaign ▶ campagna promozionale vendite sales campaign.

campagnolo, a [kampaɲ'ɲɔlo] 1 AGG country *attr*. 2 SM/F countryman/woman. 3 SF (*Aut*) cross-country vehicle.

campale [kam'pale] AGG (*Mil*) field *attr*; una giornata campale (*fig*) a hectic *o* hard day.

campana [kam'pana] SF a bell; suonare le campane a martello/a morte to sound the alarm bell/death knell; sordo come una campana as deaf as a doorpost; sentire l'altra campana (*fig*) to hear the other side of the story ▶ campana pneumatica diving bell ▶ campana di vetro bell jar; tenere qn sotto una campana di vetro (*fig*) to wrap sb up in cotton wool.

campanaccio, ci [kampa'nattʃo] SM (*di mucca*) cowbell; (*di capra*) goatbell.

campanaro [kampa'naro] SM bell-ringer.

campanella [kampa'nɛlla] SF a (*a scuola*) (school) bell b (*di tenda*) curtain ring c (*Bot*) campanula ▶ campanella scozzese harebell.

campanello [kampa'nɛllo] SM (*di porta, bicicletta, da tavola*) bell ▶ campanello d'allarme (*anche fig*) alarm bell.

campanile [kampa'nile] SM bell tower, belfry.

campanilismo [kampani'lizmo] SM parochialism.

campanilista, i, e [kampani'lista] 1 AGG parochial. 2 SM/F parochial (-minded) person.

campanilisticamente [kampanilistika'mente] AVV parochially.

campanilistico, a, ci, che [kampani'listiko] AGG parochial.

campano, a [kam'pano] AGG of *o* from Campania.

campanula [kam'panula] SF (*Bot*) bellflower; (: *genere*) campanula.

campare [kam'pare] VI (*aus essere*) (*vivere*) to live; (*tirare avanti*) to get by, manage; campare d'aria (*fig*) to live on air; campare alla giornata, tirare a campare to live from day to day.

campata [kam'pata] SF (*Archit, Elettr*) span.

campato, a [kam'pato] AGG: campato in aria (*ragionamento ecc*) unsound, unfounded.

campeggiamento [kampeddʒa'mento] SM (*Mil*) encampment.

campeggiare [kamped'dʒare] VI (*aus avere*) a (*gen, Mil*) to camp b (*risaltare*) to stand out.

campeggiatore, trice [kampeddʒa'tore] SM/F camper.

campeggio, gi [kam'peddʒo] SM (*luogo*) camp site; (*attività*) camping; nel campeggio on the camp site; andare in campeggio to go camping; "vietato il campeggio" "no camping".

camper ['kæmpəʳ] SM INV motor caravan (*Brit*), motor home (*Am*).

campestre [kam'pɛstre] AGG country *attr*, rural; corsa campestre cross-country race.

campetto [kam'petto] SM (*Sport*) small playing field; (*Sci*) nursery slope.

Campidoglio [kampi'dɔʎʎo] SM: il Campidoglio the Capitol (*one of the seven hills of Rome*).

camping ['kæmpiŋ] SM INV camp site.

campionamento [kampjona'mento] SM sampling.

campionare [kampjo'nare] VT (*Statistica, Mus*) to sample.

campionario, ria, ri, rie [kampjo'narjo] 1 SM (*Comm*) collection of samples. 2 AGG: fiera campionaria trade fair.

campionato [kampjo'nato] SM championship; il campionato di calcio the league championship (*Brit Ftbl*).

campionatura [kampjona'tura] SF (*Statistica*: *azione*) sampling; (: *campioni*) range of samples, collection of samples; (*Mus*) sampling.

campione¹, essa [kam'pjone] SM/F (*Sport*) champion; campione di tennis/del mondo tennis/world champion; sei un campione in matematica (*fig*) you're brilliant at mathematics.

campione² [kam'pjone] 1 AGG INV a (*Sport*: *squadra, pugile*) champion *attr* b (*Statistica*: *test, analisi, indagine*) sample *attr*. 2 SM (*Comm, Statistica*) sample; vendita su campione sale on sample. 3 ▶ campione casuale (*Statistica*) random sample ▶ campione gratuito free sample ▶ campione di misura (*Fis*) standard measure ▶ campione senza valore sample only.

campo ['kampo] 1 SM a (*gen, Agr, Fis*) field; campo di grano cornfield; la vita dei campi life in the country, country life; fiori di campo wild flowers b (*di calcio*) field, pitch; (*da golf*) course; (*da tennis*) court; (*da cricket*) pitch; campo ostacoli (*Equitazione*) jumping arena; campo in terra battuta (*Tennis*) clay court c (*Mil*) field, battlefield; (: *accampamento*) camp; abbandonare il campo (*anche fig*) to leave the field; scendere in campo (*anche fig*) to enter the field, join the fray d (*pittura*) background; (*Araldica*) field. 2 ▶ campo da aviazione airfield ▶ campo base (*Alpinismo*) base camp ▶ campo carbonifero coalfield ▶ campo di concentramento concentration camp

►campo di forze (*Fis*) force field ►campo giochi play area ►campo lungo (*Cine, TV, Fot*) long shot ►campo petrolifero oilfield ►campo profughi refugee camp ►campo sportivo sports ground ►campo di visibilità range of visibility ►campo visivo field of vision.

campobassano, a [kampobas'sano] [1] AGG of *o* from Campobasso.

[2] SM/F inhabitant *o* native of Campobasso.

camposanto [kampo'santo] SM (*pl* campisanti) cemetery.

camuffamento [kamuffa'mento] SM disguise.

camuffare [kamuf'fare] [1] VT: **camuffare (da)** to disguise (as).

[2] **camuffarsi** VR: **camuffarsi (da)** to disguise o.s. (as).

camuso, a [ka'muzo] AGG (*naso*) snub; (*persona*) snub-nosed.

Can. ABBR = canale.

Cana ['kana] SF Cana.

Canada [kana'da] SM: **il Canada** Canada.

canadese [kana'dese] [1] AGG, SM/F Canadian.

[2] SF (*anche:* tenda canadese) ridge tent.

canaglia [ka'naʎʎa] SF (*persona*) scoundrel, rogue.

canale [ka'nale] SM (*gen, Elettr, TV, fig*) channel; (*artificiale*) canal; (*condotto*) conduit; (*Anat*) duct, canal; (*Alpinismo*) gully; **canale di bonifica** *o* **di drenaggio** drainage canal; **il canale di Panama** the Panama Canal; **il Canal Grande** the Grand Canal; **il canale della Manica** the English Channel.

canalizzare [kanalid'dzare] VT to canalize, channel.

canalizzato, a [kanalid'dzato] AGG: **traffico canalizzato** directed traffic.

canalizzazione [kanaliddzat'tsjone] SF canalization.

canalone [kana'lone] SM (*Geol*) gorge.

canapa ['kanapa] SF (*Bot, tessuto*) hemp ►canapa indiana (*Bot*) Indian hemp; (*droga*) cannabis.

canapè [kana'pɛ] SM INV (*divano*) settee, couch; (*Culin*) canapé.

canapo ['kanapo] SM (*Naut*) hawser.

Canarie [ka'narje] SFPL: **le (isole) Canarie** the Canary Islands, the Canaries.

canarino [kana'rino] SM canary.

canasta [ka'nasta] SF canasta.

Canberra [kan'bɛrra] SF Canberra.

cancan [kan'kan] SM INV (*ballo*) cancan; (*fig: confusione*) din, row; (: *scandalo*) fuss.

cancellabile [kantʃel'labile] AGG erasable.

cancellare [kantʃel'lare] [1] VT **a** (*con gomma*) to erase, rub out; (*con penna*) to cross out, score out **b** (*fig: ricordo*) erase; (*volo, treno, appuntamento*) to cancel; **cancellare la lavagna** to clean the blackboard; **cancellare qn dalla faccia della terra** to wipe sb off the face of the earth.

[2] **cancellarsi** VIP (*ricordo*) to fade.

cancellata [kantʃel'lata] SF railing(s *pl*).

cancellatura [kantʃella'tura] SF (*con gomma*) erasure; (*con penna*) crossing out.

cancellazione [kantʃellat'tsjone] SF (*Dir, Comm*) cancellation.

cancelleria [kantʃelle'ria] SF **a** (*materiale per scrivere*) stationery **b** (*Dir, Amm*) chancery.

cancellierato [kantʃellje'rato] SM (*Amm*) chancellery.

cancelliere [kantʃel'ljɛre] SM **a** (*di tribunale*) clerk of the court **b** (*Pol*) chancellor; **Cancelliere dello Scacchiere** Chancellor of the Exchequer (*Brit*).

cancello [kan'tʃɛllo] SM gate.

cancerizzarsi [kantʃerid'dzarsi] VIP to become cancerous.

cancerizzazione [kantʃeriddzat'tsjone] SF cancerization.

cancerogeno, a [kantʃe'rɔdʒeno] [1] AGG carcinogenic.

[2] SM carcinogen.

canceroso, a [kantʃe'roso] [1] AGG (*Med*) cancerous.

[2] SM/F cancer patient.

cancrena [kan'krɛna] SF (*Med*) gangrene; (*fig: corruzione*) corruption; **andare in cancrena** to become gangrenous.

cancro ['kankro] SM **a** (*Med, fig*) cancer; (*Bot*) canker **b** (*Astron, Astrol*): **Cancro** Cancer; **essere del Cancro** to be Cancer.

candeggiante [kanded'dʒante] [1] SM bleach.

[2] AGG bleaching *attr*.

candeggiare [kanded'dʒare] VT to bleach.

candeggina [kanded'dʒina] SF bleach.

candeggio, gi [kan'deddʒo] SM bleaching; **fare il candeggio (di qc)** to bleach (sth).

candela [kan'dela] SF **a** candle; **a lume di candela** by candlelight; **tenere la candela** (*fig*) to play gooseberry (*Brit*), be a third wheel (*Am*) **b** (*Aut*) spark(ing) plug **3** (*Elettr*): **una lampadina da 100 candele** a 100 watt bulb.

candelabro [kande'labro] SM candelabra *inv*.

candeletta [kande'letta] SF (*Med*) pessary.

candeliere [kande'ljɛre] SM **a** candlestick **b** (*Naut*) stanchion.

Candelora [kande'lɔra] SF: **la Candelora** Candlemas.

candelotto [kande'lɔtto] SM candle ►candelotto di dinamite stick of dynamite ►candelotto fumogeno smoke-bomb ►candelotto lacrimogeno tear gas grenade.

candidamente [kandida'mente] AVV (*vedi agg b*) ingenuously, naïvely; candidly, frankly; innocently.

candidare [kandi'dare] [1] VT to present as candidate.

[2] **candidarsi** VR: **candidarsi (per *o* a)** (*Pol*) to stand (*Brit*) *o* run (*Am*) as candidate (for).

candidato, a [kandi'dato] SM/F: **candidato (a)** (*a una carica*) candidate (for); (*a un lavoro*) applicant (for).

candidatura [kandida'tura] SF (*a una carica*) candidature; (*a un lavoro*) application; **presentare la propria candidatura alle elezioni** to stand (*Brit*) *o* run (*Am*) for election.

candido, a ['kandido] AGG **a** (*bianco*) (pure) white; **candido come la neve** (as) white as snow **b** (*fig: ingenuo*) ingenuous, naïve; (: *sincero*) candid, frank; (: *innocente*) pure, innocent.

candito, a [kan'dito] [1] AGG candied.

[2]: **canditi** SMPL candied fruit *sg*.

candore [kan'dore] SM (*vedi agg*) brilliant white; ingenuousness, naïvety; candour (*Brit*), candor (*Am*), frankness; purity, innocence.

cane ['kane] [1] SM (*Zool*) dog; (*di pistola*) cock, hammer; **qui si mangia da cani** the food is rotten here; **che vita da cani!** it's a dog's life!; **questo lavoro è fatto da cani** this job is a real botch; **quell'attore è un cane** he's a rotten actor; **fa un freddo cane** it's bitterly cold; **non c'era un cane** there wasn't a soul; **essere solo come un cane** to be all on one's own; **essere come cane e gatto** to fight like cat and dog.

[2] ►cane barbone (French) poodle ►cane da caccia hunting dog ►cane per ciechi guide dog (*Brit*), seeing eye dog (*Am*) ►cane da guardia watchdog, guard dog ►cane lupo alsatian (dog) (*Brit*), German shepherd (dog) (*Am*) ►cane delle praterie prairie dog ►cane da punta pointer ►cane di razza pedigree dog ►cane da salotto lap dog ►cane da slitta husky.

canestro [ka'nɛstro] SM (*gen, Sport*) basket; **centrare il canestro** *o* **fare (un) canestro** (*Sport*) to shoot a basket.

canfora ['kanfora] SF camphor.

canforato, a [kanfo'rato] AGG camphorated.

cangiante [kan'dʒante] AGG iridescent; **seta cangiante** shot silk.

canguro [kan'guro] SM kangaroo.

canicola [ka'nikola] SF scorching heat.

canile [ka'nile] SM kennel; (*di allevamento*) kennels *pl*
► **canile municipale** dog pound.

canino, a [ka'nino] ①AGG **a** (*razza*) canine; (*mostra*) dog *attr*; **tosse canina** whooping cough; **rosa canina** dog rose **b** (*dente*) canine.
②SM (*dente*) canine, eyetooth.

canizie [ka'nittsje] SF (*letter: chioma bianca*) white hair.

canna ['kanna] SF **a** (*Bot*) reed ► **canna da zucchero** sugar cane **b** (*bastone*) stick, cane ► **canna da pesca** (fishing) rod **c** (*di fucile*) barrel; (*di organo*) pipe; (*di bicicletta*) crossbar ► **canna fumaria** chimney flue **d** (*Droga: gergo*) joint.

cannaiola [kanna'jɔla] SF (*uccello*) reed warbler.

cannella¹ [kan'nɛlla] SF (*di conduttura, botte*) tap.

cannella² [kan'nɛlla] SF (*Bot, Culin*) cinnamon.

cannello [kan'nɛllo] SM (*forato*) tube; (*Chim*) pipette; (*non forato*) stick; (*Tecn*) blowpipe.

cannelloni [kannel'loni] SMPL (*Culin*) cannelloni *sg*.

canneto [kan'neto] SM bed of reeds.

cannetta [kan'netta] SF (*da passeggio*) walking stick.

cannibale [kan'nibale] SM/F cannibal.

cannibalesco, a, schi, sche [kanniba'lesko] AGG cannibalistic.

cannibalismo [kanniba'lizmo] SM cannibalism.

cannocchiale [kannok'kjale] SM telescope.

cannolo [kan'nɔlo] SM (*Culin*) cream horn; **cannolo alla siciliana** *pastry horn filled with cream cheese, candied fruit and chocolate.*

cannonata [kanno'nata] SF cannon shot; **cannonata a salve** gun salute; **è una vera cannonata!** (*fig*) it's (*o* he's *ecc*) fantastic.

cannoncino [kannon'tʃino] SM **a** (*Mil*) light gun **b** (*di abito*) box pleat **c** (*Culin*) cream horn.

cannone [kan'none] SM **a** (*arma*) gun; (*Storia*) cannon; (*fig: chi eccelle*) ace; **donna cannone** (*in circo*) fat lady **b** (*tubo*) pipe, tube **c** (*di abito*) box pleat **d** (*Sci*): **cannone per innevamento artificiale** snow cannon.

cannoneggiare [kannoned'dʒare] VT to shell.

cannoniera [kanno'njɛra] SF (*Naut*) gunboat; (*di fortificazione*) embrasure.

cannoniere [kanno'njɛre] SM **a** (*Naut*) gunner **b** (*Calcio*) goal scorer.

cannuccia, ce [kan'nuttʃa] SF (drinking) straw.

canoa [ka'nɔa] SF canoe; **andare in canoa** to go canoeing.

canoismo [kano'izmo] SM canoeing.

canoista, i, e [kano'ista] SM/F canoeist.

cañon [ka'ɲon] SM INV canyon.

canone ['kanone] SM **a** : **canoni** SMPL (*criteri*) canons, rules; (*di comportamento*) norm **b** (*pagamento periodico*) rent, fee; **legge dell'equo canone** fair rent act ► **canone d'abbonamento alla TV** TV licence fee (*Brit*) ► **canone d'affitto** rent ► **canone agricolo** land rent **c** (*Rel, Mus*) canon.

canonica [ka'nɔnika] SF presbytery.

canonico, a, ci, che [ka'nɔniko] (*Rel*) ①AGG canonical; **diritto canonico** canon law.
②SM canon.

canonizzare [kanonid'dzare] VT to canonize.

canonizzazione [kanoniddzat'tsjone] SF canonization.

canorità [kanori'ta] SF INV melodiousness.

canoro, a [ka'nɔro] AGG: **uccello canoro** songbird.

canotta [ka'nɔtta] SF vest (*Brit*), undershirt (*Am*).

canottaggio, gi [kanot'taddʒo] SM rowing; **circolo di canottaggio** rowing club; **gara di canottaggio** boat race.

canottiera [kanot'tjɛra], SF vest (*Brit*), undershirt (*Am*).

canotto [ka'nɔtto] SM dinghy ► **canotto pneumatico** rubber dinghy ► **canotto di salvataggio** lifeboat.

canovaccio, ci [kano'vattʃo] SM **a** (*tela*) canvas; (*per lavare i piatti*) dishcloth; (*per asciugare i piatti*) tea towel (*Brit*), dish towel (*Am*); (*per pulire*) duster **b** (*Teatro: trama*) plot.

cantante [kan'tante] SM/F singer; **fare il cantante** to be a singer; **cantante lirico** *o* **d'opera** opera singer.

cantare [kan'tare] ①VI (*aus avere*) (*gen, uccelli*) to sing; (*gallo*) to crow; **cantare da tenore/da soprano** to be a tenor/soprano; **fare cantare qn** (*fig*) to make sb talk; **i complici hanno cantato** (*fam*) his accomplices talked.
②VT (*Mus*) to sing; (*Poesia: anche: cantare in versi*) to sing of; **cantare messa** to sing mass; **cantare vittoria** to crow.

cantastorie [kantas'tɔrje] SM/F INV story-teller.

cantata [kan'tata] SF singsong; (*Mus*) cantata.

cantautore, trice [kantau'tore] SM/F singer-songwriter.

canterellare [kanterel'lare] VT, VI (*aus avere*) to sing to o.s.; (*a bocca chiusa*) to hum.

canticchiare [kantik'kjare] VT, VI (*aus avere*) sing to o.s.; (*a bocca chiusa*) to hum.

cantico, ci ['kantiko] SM canticle.

cantiere [kan'tjere] SM **a** (*anche: cantiere navale*) shipyard **b** (*anche: cantiere edile*) building site.

cantieristico, a, ci, che [kantje'ristiko] AGG: **industria cantieristica** shipbuilding industry.

cantilena [kanti'lɛna] SF (*filastrocca*) lullaby; (*intonazione*) singsong; (*fig: lamentela*) whining.

cantilenare [kantile'nare] VT to speak in a singsong voice.

cantina [kan'tina] SF (*locale*) cellar ► **cantina sociale** cooperative winegrowers' association.

canto¹ ['kanto] SM (*il cantare, arte*) singing; (*canzone*) song; (*Poesia*) lyric poem; (: *capitolo*) canto; **lezioni di canto** singing lessons; **il canto dell'usignolo** (*il cantare*) the singing of the nightingale; (*melodia*) the song of the nightingale; **al canto del gallo** at cockcrow; **il canto del cigno** (*fig*) swan song ► **canto gregoriano** Gregorian chant ► **canto di Natale** (Christmas) carol.

canto² ['kanto] SM: **da un canto... d'altro canto** on the one hand ...on the other hand; **da un canto ti capisco** in a way I understand you; **dal canto mio** (*per ciò che mi riguarda*) for my part, as for me, as far as I'm concerned.

cantonata [kanto'nata] SF (*di edificio*) corner; **prendere una cantonata** (*fig*) to blunder.

cantone¹ [kan'tone] SM (*angolo*) corner; **in un cantone** (*fig: in disparte*) in a corner.

cantone² [kan'tone] SM (*Pol, Amm*) canton.

cantoniera [kanto'njera] AGG: **(casa) cantoniera** road inspector's house.

cantore, a [kan'tore] SM/F (*Rel*) singer; (*poeta*) poet.

cantoria [kanto'ria] SF (*luogo, persone*) choir.

cantuccio, ci [kan'tuttʃo] SM corner, nook.

canuto, a [ka'nuto] AGG (*persona*) white-haired; (*barba,*

capelli) white.

canzonare [kantso'nare] VT to tease, make fun of.

canzonatore, trice [kantsona'tore] [1] AGG teasing. [2] SM/F teaser, tease.

canzonatorio, ria, ri, rie [kantsona'tɔrjo] AGG teasing.

canzonatura [kantsona'tura] SF teasing; (*beffa*) joke.

canzone [kan'tsone] SF (*Mus*) song; (*poesia*) canzone; **è sempre la stessa canzone** (*fig*) it's always the same old story ▶ **canzone di gesta** (*poema epico*) chanson de geste.

canzonetta [kantso'netta] SF popular song.

canzonettista, i, e [kantsonet'tista] SM/F (*cabaret*) singer.

canzoniere [kantso'njɛre] SM (*Mus*) song book; (*Letterat*) collection of poems.

caolino [kao'lino] SM kaolin.

caos ['kaos] SM INV (*anche fig*) chaos.

caoticamente [kaotika'mente] AVV chaotically.

caotico, a, ci, che [ka'ɔtiko] AGG chaotic.

C.A.P. [kap] SIGLA M = **codice di avviamento postale**.

cap. ABBR (= *capitolo*) ch.

capace [ka'patʃe] AGG **a** (*capiente*) large, capacious; **questa borsa è poco capace** this bag doesn't hold much **b** (*in grado, dotato*) able, capable; **capace di fare qc** able to do sth, capable of doing sth; **sei capace di farlo da solo?** can you *o* are you able to do it on your own?; **è capace di tutto** he's capable of anything; **capace d'intendere e di volere** (*Dir*) in full possession of one's faculties; **è capace di venire nonostante tutto** he's quite likely to come in spite of everything.

capacità [kapatʃi'ta] SF INV **a** (*capienza*) capacity; **misure di capacità** measures of capacity **b** (*abilità*) ability, capability; **è un compito superiore alle sue capacità** it's a task beyond his capabilities **c** (*Dir, Fis*) capacity ▶ **capacità giuridica** legal capacity **d** : **capacità produttiva** (*di impresa*) production capacity.

capacitarsi [kapatʃi'tarsi] VIP: **capacitarsi (di qc)** to comprehend.

capanna [ka'panna] SF hut.

capannello [kapan'nello] SM knot (of people).

capanno [ka'panno] SM (*di cacciatori*) hide; (*da spiaggia*) bathing hut; (*degli attrezzi*) tool shed.

capannone [kapan'none] SM (*gen*) shed; (*Agr*) barn; (*Aer*) hangar.

caparbiamente [kaparbja'mente] AVV stubbornly, obstinately.

caparbietà [kaparbje'ta] SF stubbornness, obstinacy.

caparbio, bia, bi, bie [ka'parbjo] AGG stubborn, obstinate.

caparra [ka'parra] SF deposit, down payment.

capatina [kapa'tina] SF: **fare una capatina da qn/in centro** to pop in on sb/into town.

capeggiare [kaped'dʒare] VT (*rivolta*) to head, lead.

capello [ka'pello] SM (*uno*) hair; (*capigliatura*): **capelli** SMPL hair *sg*; **dai capelli scuri** dark-haired; **avere i capelli bianchi** to have white hair; **capelli d'angelo** (*Culin*) *long thin pasta*; **avere un diavolo per capello** to be in a foul temper; **averne fin sopra i capelli di qc/qn** to be fed up to the (back) teeth with sth/sb; **mettersi le mani nei capelli** (*fig*) to be in despair; **prendersi per i capelli** (*fig*) to come to blows; **strapparsi i capelli** (*fig*) to tear one's hair out; **mi ci hanno tirato per i capelli** (*fig*) they dragged me into it; **tirato per i capelli** (*spiegazione*) far-fetched.

capellone, a [kapel'lone] SM/F hippie.

capelluto, a [kapel'luto] AGG: **il cuoio capelluto** the scalp.

capelvenere [kapel'vɛnere] SM (*Bot*) maidenhair.

capestro [ka'pɛstro] SM (*di forca*) noose; (*per animali*) halter.

capezzale [kapet'tsale] SM bolster; (*fig*) bedside; **accorrere al capezzale di qn** to rush to sb's bedside.

capezzolo [ka'pettsolo] SM nipple.

capidoglio, gli [kapi'dɔʎʎo] SM = **capodoglio**.

capiente [ka'pjɛnte] AGG capacious.

capienza [ka'pjɛntsa] SF capacity.

capigliatura [kapiʎʎa'tura] SF hair, head of hair.

capillare [kapil'lare] [1] AGG (*Anat, Fis*) capillary; (*fig*: *analisi, ricerca*) detailed. [2] SM (*Anat*: *anche*: **vaso capillare**) capillary.

capillarità [kapillari'ta] SF (*Fis*) capillarity; (*fig*) comprehensiveness.

capinera [kapi'nera] SF (*uccello*) blackcap.

capire [ka'pire] [1] VT to understand; **si capisce che...** it is clear that ...; **si capisce!** (*certamente!*) of course!, certainly!; **capisco** I see, I understand; **fammi capire...** let's get this straight ...; **capisci, è un problema di soldi** you see, it's a problem of money; **bisogna capirla, poverina** you've got to try and understand her, poor thing; **capire al volo** to catch on straight away; **farsi capire** to make o.s. understood; **capirai!** (*sai che sforzo!*) big deal!. [2] **capirsi** VR (*uso reciproco*) to understand each other *o* one another.

capitale [kapi'tale] [1] AGG **a** (*mortale*): **pena capitale** capital punishment; **sentenza capitale** death sentence; **i sette peccati capitali** the seven deadly sins **b** (*fondamentale*) main *attr*, chief *attr*; **d'importanza capitale** of capital *o* the utmost importance. [2] SF (*Amm*) capital (city); (*fig*: *centro*) centre. [3] SM (*Fin, Econ*) capital; **ho speso un capitale per quella macchina** (*fig*) I've spent a fortune on that car ▶ **capitale azionario** equity capital, share capital ▶ **capitale d'esercizio** working capital ▶ **capitale fisso** capital assets *pl*, fixed capital ▶ **capitale immobile** real estate ▶ **capitale liquido** cash assets *pl* ▶ **capitale mobile** movables *pl* ▶ **capitale nominale** authorized capital ▶ **capitale di rischio** risk capital ▶ **capitale sociale** (*di società*) authorized capital; (*di club*) funds *pl* ▶ **capitale di ventura** venture capital, risk capital.

capitalismo [kapita'lizmo] SM capitalism.

capitalista, i, e [kapita'lista] AGG, SM/F capitalist.

capitalisticamente [kapitalistika'mente] AVV in a capitalist way.

capitalistico, a, ci, che [kapita'listiko] AGG capitalist.

capitalizzare [kapitalid'dzare] VT to capitalize.

capitalizzazione [kapitaliddzat'tsjone] SF capitalization.

capitanare [kapita'nare] VT to lead; (*Calcio*) to captain.

capitaneria [kapitane'ria] SF: **capitaneria (di porto)** port authorities *pl*.

capitano [kapi'tano] SM (*Mil, Naut, Sport*) captain; (*Aer*: *di squadriglia*) flight lieutenant (*Brit*), captain (*Am*) ▶ **capitano di industria** captain of industry ▶ **capitano di lungo corso** master mariner ▶ **capitano di ventura** (*Storia*) mercenary leader.

capitare [kapi'tare] [1] VI (*aus essere*) **a** (*giungere casualmente*) to arrive, find o.s.; (*presentarsi*: *cosa*) to turn up, present itself; **capitare a proposito/bene/male** to turn up at the right moment/at a good time/at a bad time

b (*accadere*) to happen; **se ti capita di vederlo** if you happen to see him; **mi è capitato un guaio** I had a spot of trouble; **sono cose che capitano** these things happen. ② VB IMPERS (*aus* **essere**) to happen; **capita spesso di incontrarci** *o* **che ci incontriamo** we often bump into one another.

capitello [kapi'tɛllo] SM (*Archit*) capital.

capitolare [kapito'lare] VI (*aus* **avere**) (*Mil*) to capitulate, surrender; (*fig*) to give in.

capitolato [kapito'lato] SM (*Dir*) terms *pl*, specifications *pl*.

capitolazione [kapitolat'tsjone] SF (*Mil*, *fig*) capitulation.

capitolino, a [kapito'lino] AGG Capitoline.

capitolo [ka'pitolo] SM **a** (*di testo*, *Rel*) chapter; **non ho voce in capitolo** (*fig*) I have no say in the matter **b** (*di bilancio*) item.

capitombolare [kapitombo'lare] VI (*aus* **essere**) to tumble, fall headlong.

capitombolo [kapi'tombolo] SM tumble, headlong fall; **fare un capitombolo** to take a tumble.

capitone [kapi'tone] SM (*Zool*) large (female) eel.

capo ['kapo] ① SM **a** (*Anat*) head; **a capo chino/alto** with one's head bowed/held high; **da capo a piedi** from head to foot; **mal di capo** headache; **rompersi il capo** (*fig*) to rack one's brains; **fra capo e collo** (*all'improvviso*) out of the blue
b (*di fabbrica*, *ufficio*) head, boss; (*di tribù*) chief; (*di partito*, *movimento*) leader; **essere a capo di qc** to head sth, be at the head of sth ▶ **capo del personale** personnel manager ▶ **capo di stato** head of state
c (*oggetto*) item, article; **un capo di biancheria (intima)/vestiario** an item of underwear/clothing ▶ **capo di bestiame** head *inv* of cattle
d (*estremità*: *di tavolo*, *scale*) head, top; (: *di filo*) end; **da un capo all'altro** from one end to the other; **in capo a** (*tempo*) within; (*luogo*) at the top of; **andare in capo al mondo per qn** (*fig*) to go to the ends of the earth for sb; **ricominciare da capo** to start all over again; **andare a capo** to start a new paragraph; **"punto a capo"** "full stop - new paragraph"; **un discorso senza né capo né coda** a senseless *o* meaningless speech
e (*di corda*, *lana*) ply; **lana a 3 capi** 3-ply wool
f (*Geog*) cape ▶ **Capo di Buona Speranza** Cape of Good Hope
g (*Dir*): **capo d'accusa** charge.
② AGG INV (*giardiniere*, *sorvegliante*) head *attr*; **redattore capo** chief editor.

capobanda [kapo'banda] SM (*pl* **capibanda**) (*Mus*) bandmaster; (*di malviventi*, *fig*) gang leader.

capobarca [kapo'barka] SM (*pl* **capibarca**) skipper.

capocannoniere [kapokanno'njɛre] SM (*pl* **capicannonieri**) (*Calcio*) leading goal scorer; (*Naut*) head gunner.

capocchia [ka'pɔkkja] SF head; **capocchia di spillo** pin head.

capoccia [ka'pɔttʃa] SM INV (*di lavoranti*) overseer; (*pegg*: *capobanda*) boss.

capoccione [kapot'tʃone] SM (*persona intelligente*) brainbox; (*fig pegg*: *persona importante*) bigwig.

capocellula [kapo'tʃɛllula] SM/F (*pl m* **capicellula**, *pl f* **capocellula**) (*Pol*) leader of a cell.

capoclasse [kapo'klasse] SM/F (*pl m* **capiclasse**, *pl f* **capoclasse**) (*Scol*) ≈ form captain (*Brit*), ≈ class president (*Am*).

capocomico, a, ci, che [kapo'kɔmiko] SM/F leader of a theatre company.

capocordata [kapokor'data] SM/F (*pl m* **capicordata**, *pl f* **capocordata**) (*Alpinismo*) leader (of a roped party).

capocronista [kapokro'nista] SM/F (*pl m* **capicronisti**, *pl f* **capocroniste**) news editor.

capocuoco, a [kapo'kwɔko] SM/F (*pl m* **capocuochi** *o* **capicuochi**, *pl f* **capocuoche**) head cook *o* chef.

Capodanno [kapo'danno] SM New Year.

capodivisione [kapodivi'zjone] SM/F (*pl m* **capidivisione**, *pl f* **capodivisione**) (*Amm*) head of department.

capodoglio, gli [kapo'dɔʎʎo] SM sperm whale.

capofabbrica [kapo'fabbrika] SM/F (*pl m* **capifabbrica**, *pl f* **capofabbrica**) (factory) supervisor.

capofamiglia [kapofa'miʎʎa] SM/F (*pl m* **capifamiglia**, *pl f* **capofamiglia**) head of the family.

capofila [kapo'fila] SM/F (*pl m* **capifila**, *pl f* **capofila**) leader; **a capofila** at the head of the queue (*Brit*) *o* line (*Am*).

capofitto [kapo'fitto]: **a capofitto** AVV headlong, headfirst; **gettarsi a capofitto in qc** (*fig*) to rush headlong into sth.

capogabinetto [kapogabi'netto] SM/F (*pl m* **capigabinetto**, *pl f* **capogabinetto**) ≈ parliamentary private secretary (*Brit*).

capogiro [kapo'dʒiro] SM dizziness *no pl*; **aver un capogiro** to have a dizzy spell; **far venire il capogiro a qn** to make sb dizzy; **da capogiro** (*fig*) astonishing, staggering.

capogruppo [kapo'gruppo] SM/F (*pl m* **capigruppo**, *pl f* **capogruppo**) group leader.

capolavoro [kapola'voro] SM (*anche fig*) masterpiece.

capolinea [kapo'linea] SM (*pl* **capilinea**) terminus; (*fig*) the end of the line.

capolino [kapo'lino] SM: **far capolino** to peep out (*o* in ecc).

capolista [kapo'lista] SM/F (*pl m* **capilista**, *pl f* **capolista**) (*Pol*) top candidate on electoral list.

capoluogo [kapo'lwɔgo] (*pl* **capoluoghi** *o* **capiluoghi**) SM: **capoluogo (di provincia)** ≈ county town (*Brit*), county seat (*Am*), administrative centre (*Brit*) *o* center (*Am*).

capomastro [kapo'mastro] SM (*pl* **capomastri** *o* **capimastri**) master builder.

capopartito [kapopar'tito] SM/F (*pl m* **capipartito**, *pl f* **capopartito**) party leader.

capopattuglia [kapopat'tuʎʎa] SM (*pl* **capipattuglia**) patrol leader.

caporale [kapo'rale] SM (*Mil*) lance corporal (*Brit*), private first class (*Am*).

caporalesco, a, schi, sche [kapora'lesko] AGG (*pegg*) bossy.

caporalmaggiore [kaporalmad'dʒore] SM (*Mil*) corporal.

caporedattore, trice [kaporedat'tore] SM/F (*pl m* **capiredattore**, *pl f* **caporedattrici**) editor in chief.

capoparto ~ **caporeparto** [kapore'parto] SM/F (*pl m* **capireparto**, *pl f* **caporeparto**) (*di operai*) foreman; (*di ufficio*) head of department; (*di negozio*) floor-manager.

caporione [kapo'rjone] SM gang leader; (*istigatore*) ringleader.

caposala [kapo'sala] SM/F (*pl m* **capisala**, *pl f* **caposala**) (*in ospedale*) head nurse; (: *donna*) ward sister.

caposaldo [kapo'saldo] SM (*pl* **capisaldi**) (*Mil*) stronghold; (*Topografia*) datum point; (*fig*: *fondamento*) cornerstone, basis.

caposcalo [kapos'kalo] SM/F (*pl m* **capiscalo**, *pl f* **caposcalo**) (*di linea aerea*) airline manager.

caposcuola [kapos'kwɔla] SM/F (*pl m* **capiscuola**, *pl f* **caposcuola**) (*Arte*, *Mus*, *Letterat*) founder.

caposervizio [kaposer'vittsjo] SM/F (*pl m* **capiservizio**, *pl f*

caposervizio) departmental *o* section head; **caposervizio della redazione sportiva** Sports editor.

caposezione [kaposet'tsjone] SM/F (*pl m* **capisezione**, *pl f* **caposezione**) section *o* departmental head.

caposquadra [kapos'kwadra] SM/F (*pl m* **capisquadra**, *pl f* **caposquadra**) (*di operai*) foreman, ganger; (*Mil*) squad leader; (*Sport*) team captain.

caposquadriglia [kaposkwa'driʎʎa] SM (*pl* **capisquadriglia**) (*Aer, Naut*) squadron leader (*Brit*), major (*Am*).

capostazione [kapostat'tsjone] SM/F (*pl m* **capistazione**, *pl f* **capostazione**) (*Ferr*) station master.

capostipite [kapos'tipite] SM/F (*pl* **capostipiti**) progenitor; (*fig*) earliest example.

capotasto [kapo'tasto] SM (*Mus*) capo.

capotavola [kapo'tavola] SM/F (*pl m* **capitavola**, *pl f* **capotavola**) (*persona*) head of the table; **sedere a capotavola** to sit at the head of the table.

capote [ka'pɔt] SF INV (*Aut*) hood (*Brit*), top.

capotreno [kapo'treno] SM/F (*pl m* **capitreno** *o* **capotreni**, *pl f* **capotreno**) (*Ferr*) guard (*Brit*), conductor (*Am*).

capotribù [kapotri'bu] SM/F (*pl m* **capitribù**, *pl f* **capotribù**) chief.

capottare [kapot'tare] VI = **cappottare**.

capoturno [kapo'turno] SM/F (*pl m* **capiturno**, *pl f* **capoturno**) shift supervisor.

capoufficio [kapouf'fitʃo] SM/F (*pl m* **capiufficio**, *pl f* **capoufficio**) head clerk.

Capo Verde ['kapo 'verde] SM: **il Capo Verde** Cape Verde.

capoverso [kapo'vɛrso] SM **a** (*di verso, periodo*) first line; (*Tip*) indent; (*paragrafo*) paragraph **b** (*Dir*: *comma*) section.

capovolgere [kapo'vɔldʒere] VB IRREG ①VT (*gen*) to turn upside down; (*barca*) to capsize, overturn; (*macchina*) to overturn; (*fig*: *situazione, posizione*) to reverse, change completely.
②**capovolgersi** VIP (*gen*) to overturn; (*barca*) to capsize; (*fig*) to be reversed.

capovolgimento [kapovoldʒi'mento] SM (*fig*) reversal, complete change.

capovolto, a [kapo'vɔlto] ①PP di **capovolgere**.
②AGG upside down; (*barca*) capsized.

cappa¹ ['kappa] SF **a** (*mantello*) cloak, cape; **film/romanzo di cappa e spada** swashbuckler; **sentirsi sotto una cappa di piombo** to feel oppressed **b** (*del camino*) hood; (*Industria*) chimney ▶**cappa aspirante** (*per cucina*) extractor hood **c** (*Naut*): **mettersi in cappa** to heave to.

cappa² ['kappa] SM O F INV (*lettera*) K, k.

cappella [kap'pɛlla] SF (*Rel*) chapel; (: *cantori*) choir.

cappellaio, aia, ai, aie [kappel'lajo] SM/F hatter.

cappellano [kappel'lano] SM chaplain; **cappellano militare** army chaplain.

cappelleria [kappelle'ria] SF hat shop.

cappelletti [kappel'letti] SMPL *type of ring-shaped ravioli filled with meat.*

cappelliera [kappel'ljɛra] SF hat box.

cappello [kap'pɛllo] SM hat; (*di fungo*) cap; **cappello di paglia** straw hat; **levarsi/togliersi il cappello** to raise/take off one's hat; **ti faccio tanto di cappello!** (*fig*) I take my hat off to you! ▶**cappello a bombetta** bowler (hat) (*Brit*), derby (*Am*) ▶**cappello a cilindro** top hat.

cappero ['kappero] SM (*Bot, Culin*) caper; **capperi!** (*fam*) gosh!

cappio, pi ['kappjo] SM (*nodo*) slip-knot; (*capestro*) noose.

cappone [kap'pone] SM capon.

cappottare [kappot'tare] VI (*aus* **avere**) (*Aut*) to overturn.

cappotto¹ [kap'pɔtto] SM (over)coat.

cappotto² [kap'pɔtto] SM: **dare** *o* **fare cappotto** (*nei giochi*) to win the grand slam.

cappuccino¹ [kapput'tʃino] AGG, SM (*Rel*) Capuchin.

cappuccino² [kapput'tʃino] SM (*caffè*) cappuccino.

cappuccio, ci [kap'puttʃo] SM **a** (*copricapo*) hood; (*di frate*) cowl; (*di biro*) cap **b** (*fam*) = **cappuccino²**.

capra ['kapra] SF **a** (*Zool*) (she-)goat, nanny-goat (*fam*) **b** (*Tecn*) trestle.

capraio, aia, ai, aie [ka'prajo] SM/F goatherd.

caprese [ka'prese] ①AGG from *o* of Capri.
②SM/F inhabitant *o* native of Capri.

capretto [ka'pretto] SM kid.

Capri ['kapri] SF Capri.

capriata [kapri'ata] SF (*Edil*) truss.

capriccio, ci [ka'prittʃo] SM **a** (*gen*) whim, caprice; (*di bambino*) tantrum; **levarsi** *o* **togliersi il capriccio** to indulge one's whim; **fare i capricci** to be awkward, be naughty; **fare un capriccio** to throw a tantrum; **capricci della moda** whims of fashion; **capriccio della natura** freak of nature; **capriccio della sorte** quirk of fate **b** (*Mus*) capriccio.

capricciosamente [kaprittʃosa'mente] AVV (*vedi agg*) capriciously, naughtily.

capriccioso, a [kaprit'tʃoso] AGG (*donna*) capricious; (*bambino*) naughty; (*tempo*) changeable; **insalata capricciosa** (*Culin*) *mixed salad with mayonnaise.*

Capricorno [kapri'kɔrno] SM Capricorn; **essere del Capricorno** (*Astrol*) to be Capricorn.

caprifoglio, gli [kapri'fɔʎʎo] SM honeysuckle.

caprimulgo, gi [kapri'mulgo] SM (*uccello*) nightjar.

caprino, a [ka'prino] ①AGG goat *attr*.
②SM (*formaggio*) goat's (milk) cheese.

capriola [kapri'ɔla] SF (*salto*) somersault; (*Danza*) cabriole; (*Equitazione*) capriole; **fare una capriola** to turn a somersault; **fare le capriole per la gioia** to be jumping for joy.

capriolo [kapri'ɔlo] SM roe deer; (*maschio*) roebuck.

capro ['kapro] SM (he-)goat, billy-goat (*fam*); **capro espiatorio** (*fig*) scapegoat.

caprone [ka'prone] SM (he-)goat, billy-goat (*fam*).

capsula ['kapsula] SF (*di medicinali, spaziale, Anat*) capsule; (*di dente*) crown; (*di arma, bottiglia*) cap.

captare [kap'tare] VT (*segnale radio*) to pick up; (*pensiero*) to read; **captare lo sguardo di qn** to catch sb's eye.

capziosamente [kaptsjosa'mente] AVV speciously.

capziosità [kaptsjosi'ta] SF speciousness.

capzioso, a [kap'tsjoso] AGG specious.

C.A.R. [kar] SIGLA M = *Centro Addestramento Reclute*.

carabattole [kara'battole] SFPL odds and ends.

carabina [kara'bina] SF rifle.

carabiniere [karabi'njɛre] SM carabiniere (*member of the Carabinieri: police with military and civil duties - the force includes paratroop units and mounted divisions*).

Caracas [ka'rakas] SF Caracas.

caracollare [karakol'lare] VI (*aus* **avere**) (*Equitazione*) to caracole.

caraffa [ka'raffa] SF carafe.

Caraibi [ka'raibi] SMPL: **il mar dei Caraibi** the Caribbean (Sea).

caraibico, a, ci, che [kara'ibiko] AGG Caribbean.

carambola [ka'rambola] SF (*Biliardo*) cannon.

caramella [kara'mɛlla] SF (*dolciume*) sweet; (*monocolo*)

monocle.

caramellare [karamel'lare] VT (*zucchero*) to caramelize; (*stampo, arance*) to coat with caramel.

caramellato, a [karamel'lato] AGG caramelized; **mela caramellata** toffee apple.

caramello [kara'mɛllo] SM caramel.

caramente [kara'mente] AVV affectionately.

carato [ka'rato] SM **a** (*di oro, diamante*) carat **b** (*Naut*) *twenty-fourth part of the ownership of a ship.*

carattere [ka'rattere] SM **a** (*gen*) character, nature; **avere un buon/brutto carattere** to be good-/ill-natured, be good-/bad-tempered; **aver carattere** to have character; **mancare di carattere** to lack character, have no backbone; **informazione di carattere tecnico/confidenziale** information of a technical/confidential nature; **essere in carattere con qc** (*intonarsi*) to be in harmony with sth
b SPESSO PL (*caratteristica*) characteristic, feature, trait; **caratteri sessuali** sexual characteristics
c (*Tip*) character, letter; **in carattere corsivo/neretto** *o* **grassetto** in italic/bold type.

caratteriale [karatte'rjale] AGG (*studio, indagine*) character *attr*; (*disturbi*) emotional.

caratterino [karatte'rino] SM difficult nature *o* character.

caratterista, i, e [karatte'rista] SM/F character actor/actress.

caratteristica, che [karatte'ristika] SF characteristic, feature.

caratteristicamente [karatteristika'mente] AVV characteristically, typically.

caratteristico, a, ci, che [karatte'ristiko] AGG (*tipico*) typical, characteristic; (*distintivo*) distinctive; **segni caratteristici** (*su passaporto*) distinguishing marks.

caratterizzare [karatterid'dzare] VT (*essere tipico*) to characterize, be typical *o* characteristic of; (*descrivere*) distinguish.

caratterizzazione [karatteriddzat'tsjone] SF characterization.

caravanserraglio, gli [karavanser'raʎʎo] SM caravanserai.

caravella [kara'vɛlla] SF (*nave*) caravel.

carboidrato [karboi'drato] SM carbohydrate.

carbonaia [karbo'naja] SF (*catasta di legna*) charcoal pit; (*locale*) coal cellar.

carbonaio, ai [karbo'najo] SM (*chi fa carbone*) charcoal-burner; (*commerciante*) coalman, coal merchant.

carbonaro [karbo'naro] SM (*Storia*) member of the Carbonari society.

carbonato [karbo'nato] SM carbonate; **carbonato acido** hydrogen carbonate.

carbonchio, chi [kar'bonkjo] SM (*Med, Veterinaria*) anthrax; (*Bot*) smut.

carboncino [karbon'tʃino] SM (*bastoncino*) charcoal crayon; (*disegno*) charcoal drawing.

carbone [kar'bone] SM coal; (*anche:* **carbone dolce** *o* **di legna**) charcoal; (*di lampada ad arco*) carbon; **essere** *o* **stare sui carboni ardenti** to be like a cat on hot bricks (*Brit*) *o* on a hot tin roof (*Am*) ▶**carbone bianco** hydroelectric power ▶**carbone fossile** (pit) coal.

carbonella [karbo'nɛlla] SF charcoal slack.

carboneria [karbone'ria] SF (*Storia*) secret society of the Carbonari.

carbonico, a, ci, che [kar'boniko] AGG carbonic.

carbonifero, a [karbo'nifero] AGG carboniferous, coal *attr*.

carbonio [kar'bɔnjo] SM (*Chim*) carbon.

carbonizzare [karbonid'dzare] VT (*legna*) to carbonize; (: *parzialmente*) to char; **morire carbonizzato** to be burned to death; **hanno trovato i resti carbonizzati della vittima** they found the charred remains of the victim.

carburante [karbu'rante] ① AGG combustible.
② SM (motor) fuel.

carburare [karbu'rare] VI (*aus* **avere**): **carburare bene/male** (*Aut*) to be well/badly tuned; **oggi non carburo** (*fig: persona*) I'm half asleep today, my brain's not working today.

carburatore [karbura'tore] SM carburettor (*Brit*), carburetor (*Am*).

carburazione [karburat'tsjone] SF carburation.

carburo [kar'buro] SM carbide.

carcassa [kar'kassa] SF **a** (*di animale*) carcass; (*fig pegg: macchina*) (old) wreck **b** (*struttura portante*) framework, frame; (: *di nave*) hulk **c** (*Aut: pneumatico*) carcass; **pneumatico a carcassa radiale/diagonale** radial/cross-ply tyre (*Brit*) *o* tire (*Am*).

carcerario, ria, ri, rie [kartʃe'rarjo] AGG prison *attr*.

carcerato, a [kartʃe'rato] SM/F prisoner.

carcerazione [kartʃerat'tsjone] SF imprisonment.

carcere ['kartʃere] SM (*pl f* **carceri**) (*edificio*) prison, jail; (*pena*) imprisonment; **condannato a due anni di carcere** sentenced to two years' imprisonment; **essere/mettere in carcere** to be in/send to prison *o* jail ▶**carcere di massima sicurezza** top-security prison.

carceriere, a [kartʃe'rjɛre] SM/F (*anche fig*) jailer.

carcinoma [kartʃi'nɔma] SM carcinoma.

carciofo [kar'tʃɔfo] SM artichoke.

cardamomo [karda'mɔmo] SM cardamom.

cardanico, a, ci, che [kar'daniko] AGG: **giunto cardanico** universal joint.

cardano [kar'dano] SM: **trasmissione a cardano** shaft drive.

cardare [kar'dare] VT to card.

cardellino [kardel'lino] SM goldfinch.

cardiaco, a, ci, che [kar'diako] AGG cardiac, heart *attr*; **attacco cardiaco** heart attack.

cardigan ['kardigan] SM INV cardigan.

cardinalato [kardina'lato] SM cardinalship, cardinalate.

cardinale [kardi'nale] ① AGG cardinal.
② SM (*Rel*) cardinal.

cardinalizio, zia, zi, zie [kardina'littsjo] AGG (*titolo, cappello*) of a cardinal.

cardine ['kardine] SM (*di porta, finestra*) hinge; (*fig: fondamento*) cornerstone, foundation.

cardiochirurgia [kardjokirur'dʒia] SF heart surgery.

cardiochirurgo, ghi *o* **gi** [kardjoki'rurgo] SM heart surgeon.

cardiologia [kardjolo'dʒia] SF cardiology.

cardiologo, a, gi [kar'djɔlogo] SM/F heart specialist, cardiologist.

cardiopalmo [kardjo'palmo] SM palpitation.

cardiopatico, a, ci, che [kardjo'patiko] ① AGG suffering from a heart complaint.
② SM/F person suffering from a heart complaint.

cardo ['kardo] SM (*Bot*) thistle; (*commestibile*) cardoon.

carena [ka'rɛna] SF (*Naut*) keel.

carenare [kare'nare] VT (*Naut*) to careen; (*veicolo*) to streamline.

carente [ka'rɛnte] AGG: **carente di** lacking in.

carenza [ka'rɛntsa] SF shortage, lack, scarcity; (*Med*)

deficiency; **carenza vitaminica** vitamin deficiency.

carestia [kares'tia] SF famine; (*fig: penuria*) scarcity, lack, dearth.

carezza [ka'rettsa] SF caress; **dare** *o* **fare una carezza a** (*persona*) to caress; (*animale*) to stroke, pat.

carezzare [karet'tsare] VT = **accarezzare**.

carezzevole [karet'tsevole] AGG sweet, endearing.

carezzevolmente [karettsevol'mente] AVV endearingly.

cargo, ghi ['kargo] SM (*nave*) cargo boat, freighter; (*aereo*) freighter.

cariare [ka'rjare] ① VT to decay; **lo zucchero caria i denti** sugar decays teeth.
 ② **cariarsi** VIP (*denti*) to decay.

cariatide [ka'rjatide] SF caryatid.

cariato, a [ka'rjato] AGG (*dente*) decayed, bad.

carica, che ['karika] SF **a** (*ufficio, funzione*) position, office; **ricoprire** *o* **rivestire una carica** to hold a position; **entrare/essere in carica** to come into/be in office; **uscire di carica** to leave office ▶ **carica onorifica** honorary appointment
 b (*di orologio*) winding; **è finita la carica** it's wound down; **dare la carica all'orologio** to wind up the clock
 c (*di arma, missile*) charge
 d (*attacco: Mil, di animali*) charge; **tornare alla carica** (*fig*) to insist, persist; **entrare a passo di carica** to charge in
 e (*fig: energia*) drive; **dare la carica a qn** to give sb strength, encourage sb; **ha una forte carica di simpatia** he's very likeable.

caricabatteria [karikabatte'ria] SM INV (*Aut*) battery charger.

caricare [kari'kare] ① VT **a** (*gen*) to load; (*fig: esagerare*) to exaggerate; (*tinta*) to deepen
 b : **caricare su/in** (*merci ecc*) to load on/into; **caricare in macchina** (*passeggero*) to give a lift to; (*valigie*) to put into the car
 c (*sovraccaricare*): **caricare di** (*merci ecc*) to overload with; (*fig: di lavoro, responsabilità*) to overload with, to overburden with
 d (*orologio*) to wind up; (*batteria, accumulatore*) to charge; (*fucile, macchina fotografica*) to load; (*pipa, stufa*) to fill; (*caldaia, altoforno*) to stoke; **caricare un programma** (*Inform*) to load a program
 e (*attaccare: Mil*) to charge; (: *Sport*) to tackle.
 ② **caricarsi** VR **a** : **caricarsi di** to overburden *o* overload o.s. with; (*fig: di responsabilità, impegni*) to overburden o.s. with
 b (*concentrarsi*): **caricarsi per una gara** to gear o.s. up for a race.

caricato, a [kari'kato] AGG (*affettato*) affected.

caricatore [karika'tore] ① SM **a** (*di armi*) magazine; (*Fot*) cartridge **b** (*operaio*) loader.
 ② AGG: **piano caricatore** loading platform.

caricatura [karika'tura] SF caricature; **fare la caricatura di qn** to do a caricature of sb.

caricaturale [karikatu'rale] AGG ridiculous, grotesque.

caricaturista, i, e [karikatu'rista] SM/F caricaturist.

carico, a, chi, che ['kariko] ① AGG **a** (*veicolo*): **carico (di)** loaded *o* laden (with), full (of); (*persona*): **carico di** laden with; **carico di debiti** up to one's ears in debt; **carico di lavoro** weighed down with work
 b (*forte: colore*) strong, deep; (: *caffè, tè*) strong
 c (*caricato: orologio*) wound up; (: *fucile, macchina fotografica*) loaded; (: *pipa*) full; (: *batteria*) charged;

(*bomba*) live.
 ② SM **a** (*il caricare*) loading; **fare il carico** to load
 b (*materiale caricato*) load; (: *su nave*) freight, cargo; (*Comm*) shipment; **a pieno carico** with a full load; **capacità di carico** cargo capacity ▶ **carico utile** pay load
 c (*Elettr*) charge
 d (*Econ*): **essere a carico di qn** (*onere, spese ecc*) to be charged to sb, be payable by sb; (*persona*) to be dependent on sb, be supported by sb; **a carico del cliente** at the customer's expense; **ha dei familiari a carico?** do you have any dependants?
 e (*Dir*) charge; **ha carichi pendenti?** do you have any charges pending?; **essere a carico di qn** (*accusa, prova*) to be against sb; **testimone a carico** witness for the prosecution
 f (*fig: peso*) burden, weight; **farsi carico di** (*problema, responsabilità*) to take on ▶ **carico di lavoro** (*di ditta, reparto*) workload.

Cariddi [ka'riddi] SF Charybdis.

carie ['karje] SF (*Med*) decay; (*Bot*) rot.

carillon [kari'jɔ̃] SM INV musical box.

carino, a [ka'rino] AGG (*gen*) nice; (*ragazza, bambino*) pretty, lovely; (*ragazzo*) good-looking; **è stato molto carino da parte tua** that was really nice *o* kind of you.

carisma [ka'rizma] SM charisma.

carismatico, a, ci, che [kariz'matiko] AGG charismatic.

carissimo, a [ka'rissimo] AGG (*molto caro*) very dear; (*molto costoso*) very expensive; **Carissimo Paolo** (*nelle lettere*) Dearest Paul.

carità [kari'ta] SF INV (*gen, Rel*) charity; **chiedere la carità (a qn)** to beg for charity (from sb); (*fig*) to come begging (to sb); **fare la carità a** to give (something) to; **per carità!** (*figurarsi*) you've got to be joking!; (*per favore*) please!; (*non ti disturbare!*) please don't bother!; (*non è un disturbo*) not at all!, it's no trouble at all!; (*neanche per sogno*) good heavens, no!; **fammi la carità di star zitto** please be so kind as to keep quiet.

caritatevole [karita'tevole] AGG charitable.

caritatevolmente [karitatevol'mente] AVV charitably.

carlinga, ghe [kar'linga] SF fuselage.

Carlo Magno ['karlo 'maɲɲo] SM Charlemagne.

carlona [kar'lona] SF: **alla carlona** carelessly, roughly.

carme ['karme] SM solemn poem.

carmelitano, a [karmeli'tano] AGG, SM/F Carmelite.

carminio [kar'minjo] ① SM (*colorante*) carmine.
 ② AGG INV carmine, crimson.

carnagione [karna'dʒone] SF complexion.

carnaio, ai [kar'najo] SM (*ammasso di cadaveri*) charnel house; (*fig: luogo affollato*): **è un carnaio** it's swarming with people.

carnale [kar'nale] AGG **a** (*sessuale: desiderio, conoscenza*) carnal; **violenza carnale** rape **b** (*consanguineo: fratello, sorella*) full *attr*, blood *attr*.

carnalità [karnali'ta] SF carnality.

carnalmente [karnal'mente] AVV (*gen*) carnally; **unirsi carnalmente** to have (sexual) intercourse.

carne ['karne] SF **a** (*gen, fig*) flesh; **in carne e ossa** in the flesh, in person; **carne da macello** (*fig*) cannon fodder; **color carne** flesh coloured; **carne viva** raw flesh; **essere (bene) in carne** to be well padded, be plump; **è carne della mia carne** he's my own flesh and blood
 b (*Culin*) meat; **non essere né carne né pesce** (*fig*) to be neither fish nor fowl; **mettere troppa carne al fuoco** (*fig*)

to have too many irons in the fire; **carne arrosto/ai ferri** roast/grilled meat ►**carne bianca** (*di pollo, agnello, coniglio*) white meat ►**carne bovina** *o* **di manzo** beef ►**carne di cavallo** *o* **equina** horseflesh, horse meat ►**carne suina** *o* **di maiale** pork ►**carne ovina** *o* **di pecora** mutton ►**carne rossa** (*di manzo o maiale*) red meat ►**carne in scatola** tinned (*Brit*) *o* canned (*Am*) meat ►**carne tritata** mince (*Brit*), hamburger meat (*Am*), minced (*Brit*) *o* ground (*Am*) meat ►**carne di vitello** veal.

carnefice [kar'nefitʃe] SM (*boia*) executioner; (*nell'impiccagione*) hangman; (*fig*) torturer.

carneficina [karnefi'tʃina] SF carnage; (*fig*) disaster; **fare una carneficina** to carry out a massacre.

carnevale [karne'vale] SM *carnival period between Epiphany (Jan 6) and the beginning of Lent: it culminates in the festivities of Martedì Grasso (Shrove Tuesday).*

carnevalesco, a, schi, sche [karneva'lesko] AGG carnival *attr*.

carniere [kar'njɛre] SM game bag.

carnivoro, a [kar'nivoro] ① AGG carnivorous. ② SM carnivore.

carnosità [karnosi'ta] SF fleshiness; (*di labbra*) fullness.

carnoso, a [kar'noso] AGG (*gen*) fleshy; (*pianta, frutto, radice*) pulpy; (*labbra*) full.

caro, a ['karo] ① AGG **a** (*amato*): **caro (a)** dear (to); (: *ricordo*) fond; **mi è tanto caro** it (*o* he) is very dear to me; **Caro Paolo** (*nelle lettere*) Dear Paul; **tanti cari saluti** best wishes; **cara signora!** my dear lady!; **se ti è cara la vita** if you value your life; **tener caro il ricordo di qn/qc** to cherish the memory of sb/sth
b (*costoso*) dear, expensive; **a caro prezzo** at a high price; **vendere cara la pelle** (*fig*) to sell one's life dear. ② SM/F: **mio caro, mia cara** my dear; **i miei cari** my dear ones. ③ AVV (*costare, pagare*) a lot, a great deal; **questo insulto ti costerà caro** you'll pay dearly for that insult.

carogna [ka'roɲɲa] SF carrion *inv*; (*fam: persona vile*) swine *inv*.

carognata [karoɲ'ɲata] SF (*fam*) rotten trick; **fare una carognata a qn** to play a rotten trick on sb.

Caronte [ka'ronte] SM Charon.

carosello [karo'zɛllo] SM (*giostra*) merry-go-round, carousel (*Am*); (*movimento vorticoso: di automobili, idee*) whirl; **all'uscita dello stadio si sono formati dei caroselli** outside the stadium there was a whirl of cars.

carota [ka'rɔta] SF **a** carrot **b** (*Mineralogia*) core.

carotide [ka'rɔtide] SF carotid.

carovana [karo'vana] SF (*gen*) caravan; (*convoglio*) convoy.

carovaniero, a [karova'njɛro] AGG caravan *attr*; **strada carovaniera** caravan route.

carovita [karo'vita] SM INV high cost of living; (*indennità*) cost of living allowance.

carpa ['karpa] SF (*pesce*) carp.

Carpazi [kar'pattsi] SMPL: **i Carpazi** the Carpathian Mountains, the Carpathians.

carpello [kar'pɛllo] SM (*Bot*) carpel.

carpenteria [karpente'ria] SF carpentry.

carpentiere [karpen'tjɛre] SM carpenter.

carpino ['karpino] SM (*albero*) hornbeam.

carpione [kar'pjone] SM (*Culin*): **pesce in carpione** soused fish.

carpire [kar'pire] VT: **carpire qc a qn** (*denaro*) to get sth out of sb; **carpire un segreto/un'informazione a qn** to worm a secret/information out of sb.

carpo ['karpo] SM (*Anat*) wrist joint, carpus (*termine tecn*).

carponi [kar'poni] AVV on all fours, on one's hands and knees; **mettersi/stare a carponi** to get down/be on all fours.

carrabile [kar'rabile] AGG suitable for vehicles; **"passo carrabile"** "keep clear".

carraio, aia, ai, aie [kar'rajo] AGG carriage *attr*; **passo carraio** driveway.

carré [kar're] ① SM INV **a** (*Culin: lombata*) loin **b** (*taglio di capelli*) bob. ② AGG INV: **pan carré** toasting loaf.

carreggiabile [karred'dʒabile] SF (*anche:* **strada carreggiabile**) road open to light traffic.

carreggiata [karred'dʒata] SF (*Aut*) carriageway (*Brit*), roadway; **strada a due carreggiate** dual carriageway (*Brit*), divided highway (*Am*); **tenersi in carreggiata** (*fig*) to keep to the right path; **rimettersi in carreggiata** (*fig: recuperare*) to catch up.

carrellare [karrel'lare] VI (*aus* **avere**) (*Cine, TV*) to track.

carrellata [karrel'lata] SF (*Cine, TV: tecnica*) tracking; (: *scena*) tracking shot; **carrellata di successi** medley of hits; **una carrellata su...** a brief look at ... .

carrellista, i [karrel'lista] SM/F (*Cine, TV*) dolly operator.

carrello [kar'rɛllo] SM (*gen, Ferr*) trolley; (*di teleferica*) car; (*Aer*) undercarriage; (*di macchina da scrivere*) carriage; (*Cine, TV*) dolly ►**carrello elevatore** fork-lift truck ►**carrello portaverdure** vegetable rack ►**carrello portavivande** (food) trolley.

carretta [kar'retta] SF (*piccolo carro*) cart; (*pegg: veicolo*) old wreck; **tirare la carretta** (*fig*) to plod along.

carrettata [karret'tata] SF cartload.

carrettiere [karret'tjɛre] SM carter; **usa un linguaggio da carrettiere** he talks like a navvy.

carretto [kar'retto] SM handcart; **carretto a mano** wheelbarrow.

carriera [kar'rjɛra] SF career; **fare carriera** to get on (in one's job), to have a successful career; **una brillante carriera universitaria** a brilliant university career; **prospettive di carriera** career prospects; **ufficiale di carriera** (*Mil*) regular officer; **di** *o* **a gran carriera** (*fig*) at full speed.

carrierista, i, e [karrje'rista] SM/F careerist.

carrieristico, a, ci, che [karrje'ristiko] AGG career *attr*.

carriola [karri'ɔla] SF wheelbarrow.

carrista, i [kar'rista] SM (*Mil: guidatore*) tank driver; (: *soldato*) tank soldier.

carro ['karro] ① SM **a** cart, wagon; (*per carnevale*) float; **mettere il carro davanti ai buoi** (*fig*) to put the cart before the horse
b (*Astron*): **il Gran/Piccolo Carro** the Great/Little Bear. ② ►**carro armato** (*Mil*) tank ►**carro attrezzi** (*Aut*) breakdown van (*Brit*), tow truck (*Am*) ►**carro bestiame** (*Ferr*) animal wagon ►**carro funebre** hearse ►**carro merci** (*Ferr*) goods wagon (*Brit*), freight car (*Am*).

carroccio [kar'rottʃo] SM (*Pol*): **il Carroccio** *symbol of Lega Nord.*

carrozza [kar'rɔttsa] SF (*gen, Ferr*) carriage, coach; **(signori) in carrozza!** all aboard! ►**carrozza belvedere** observation car ►**carrozza letto** sleeper (*Brit*), Pullman ® (*Am*) ►**carrozza ristorante** dining *o* restaurant car.

carrozzabile [karrot'tsabile] AGG: **(strada) carrozzabile** road open to vehicles.

carrozzato, a [karrot'tsato] AGG **a** (Aut): **macchina carrozzata da Bertone** car designed by Bertone **b** (fam: donna) well-stacked.

carrozzella [karrot'tsɛlla] SF (per bambini) pram (Brit), baby carriage (Am); (per invalidi) wheelchair.

carrozzeria [karrottse'ria] SF **a** (Aut: rivestimento) bodywork, body, coachwork (Brit); **carrozzeria portante** chassis **b** (Aut: officina) body shop.

carrozziere [karrot'tsjɛre] SM (Aut: progettista) car designer; (: meccanico) panel beater (Brit), auto bodyworker (Am).

carrozzina [karrot'tsina] SF pram (Brit), baby carriage (Am).

carrozzino [karrot'tsino] SM (di motocicletta) side-car.

carrozzone [karrot'tsone] SM (di circo, zingari) caravan (Brit), wagon (Am).

carruba [kar'ruba] SF (frutta) carob.

carrubo [kar'rubo] SM (albero) carob (tree).

carrucola [kar'rukola] SF pulley.

carta ['karta] **1** SF **a** (gen) paper; (statuto) charter; **sulla carta** (in teoria) on paper
b (da gioco) card; **dare le carte** to deal the cards; **giocare una carta** to play a card; **giocare l'ultima carta** (anche fig) to play one's last card; **a carte scoperte** (anche fig) cards on the table; **mettere le carte in tavola** to lay one's cards on the table; **cambiare le carte in tavola** (fig) to shift one's ground; **fare le carte a qn** (Cartomanzia) to tell sb's fortune using cards
c (documenti): SFPL papers, documents; **devo fare tutte le carte per il passaporto** I've got to sort out all the documents and forms for the passport application; **fare carte false** (fig) to go to great lengths; **avrebbe fatto carte false pur di ottenere quel posto** he would have gone to any lengths to get that job
d (al ristorante) menu; **alla carta** à la carte ▶ **carta dei vini** wine list.
2 ▶ **carta di alluminio** aluminium (Brit) o aluminum (Am) foil ▶ **carta assegni** bank card ▶ **carta assorbente** blotting paper ▶ **carta automobilistica** road map ▶ **carta bianca:dare carta bianca a qn** to give sb carte blanche ▶ **carta da bollo** o **bollata** o **legale** (Amm) official stamped paper ▶ **carta di credito** credit card ▶ **carta da cucina** kitchen roll o paper o towel (Brit), paper towel (Am) ▶ **carta da disegno** drawing paper ▶ **carta geografica** map ▶ **carta di giornale** newsprint ▶ **carta d'identità** identity card ▶ **carta igienica** toilet paper ▶ **carta d'imbarco** boarding card ▶ **carta da lettere** writing paper ▶ **carta libera** o **semplice** (Amm) unstamped paper ▶ **carta lucida** tracing paper ▶ **carta millimetrata** graph paper ▶ **carta moschicida** fly-paper ▶ **carta oleata** waxed o wax paper (spec Am) ▶ **carta da pacchi** o **da imballaggio** wrapping paper, brown paper ▶ **carta paraffinata** o **vegetale** (Culin) greaseproof paper (Brit) ▶ **carta da parati** wallpaper ▶ **carta per prelievi automatici** cash card ▶ **carta da regalo** (gift) wrapping paper ▶ **carta stagnola** tinfoil (Brit) ▶ **carta velina** tissue paper ▶ **carta verde** (Aut) green card (Brit) ▶ **carta vetrata** glasspaper, sandpaper ▶ **carta da visita** visiting card ▶ **(color) carta da zucchero** mid blue.

cartacarbone [kartakar'bone] SF carbon paper.

cartaccia, ce [kar'tattʃa] SF waste paper.

cartaceo, a, cei, cee [kar'tatʃeo] AGG paper attr.

Cartagine [kar'tadʒine] SF Carthage.

cartaginese [kartadʒi'nese] AGG, SM/F Carthaginian.

cartamodello [kartamo'dɛllo] SM (Cucito) paper pattern.

cartamoneta [kartamo'neta] SF paper money.

cartapecora [karta'pɛkora] SF parchment, vellum.

cartapesta [karta'pesta] SF papier-mâché; **di cartapesta** papier-mâché attr; (fig) weak; **eroe di cartapesta** tin god.

cartario, ria, ri, rie [kar'tarjo] AGG paper attr.

cartastraccia, ce [kartas'trattʃa] SF waste paper.

cartavetrare [kartave'trare] VT (legno, metallo) to sand (down).

carteggio, gi [kar'teddʒo] SM correspondence.

cartella [kar'tɛlla] SF **a** (custodia: di cartoncino) folder; (borsa: di professionista) briefcase; (: di scolaro) schoolbag, satchel; (pratica, incartamento) file, dossier ▶ **cartella trasparente** transparent folder
b (Tip) page
c (Lotteria) lottery ticket; (Tombola) tombola card
d ▶ **cartella clinica** (Med) case sheet.

cartellino [kartel'lino] SM (del prezzo) price label, price tag; (scheda) card; **timbrare il cartellino** (all'entrata) to clock in o on; (all'uscita) to clock out o off ▶ **cartellino orario** o **di presenza** clock card, timecard.

cartellista, i [kartel'lista] SM (Econ, Pol) member of a cartel.

cartello¹ [kar'tɛllo] SM (avviso) notice, sign; (stradale) sign, signpost; (di dimostranti, pubblicitario) placard, poster; (di negozio) sign.

cartello² [kar'tɛllo] SM (Econ, Pol) cartel.

cartellone [kartel'lone] SM (pubblicitario) placard, (advertising) poster; (Teatro) bill, playbill; (Cine) poster; (di tombola) scoring frame, board; **tenere il cartellone** (Teatro) to have a long run.

cartellonista, i, e [kartello'nista] SM/F poster designer.

cartellonistica [kartello'nistika] SF poster designing.

carter ['karter] SM INV (di bicicletta, moto) chain guard; (Aut) oil sump.

cartesiano, a [karte'zjano] AGG Cartesian.

cartiera [kar'tjɛra] SF paper mill.

cartiglio, gli [kar'tiʎʎo] SM scroll.

cartilagine [karti'ladʒine] SF cartilage.

cartina [kar'tina] SF **a** (Geog) map **b** (di sigarette) cigarette paper; (piccolo involto) packet.

cartoccio, ci [kar'tɔttʃo] SM **a** (involucro) cornet; **cuocere al cartoccio** (Culin) to bake in tinfoil o aluminium (Brit) o aluminum (Am); **patate al cartoccio** ≈ jacket potatoes (Brit) **b** (Mil) powder charge.

cartografia [kartogra'fia] SF cartography.

cartografo, a [kar'tɔgrafo] SM/F cartographer.

cartolaio, aia, ai, aie [karto'lajo] SM/F stationer.

cartoleria [kartole'ria] SF stationer's (shop).

cartolina [karto'lina] SF postcard ▶ **cartolina di auguri** greetings card ▶ **cartolina illustrata** picture postcard ▶ **cartolina postale** stamped postcard ▶ **cartolina precetto** o **rosa** (Mil) call-up papers pl (Brit), draft card (Am).

cartomante [karto'mante] SM/F fortune-teller (using cards).

cartomanzia [kartoman'tsia] SF fortune-telling (using cards).

cartonato, a [karto'nato] AGG (carta, busta) stiffened; **copertina cartonata** hard cover.

cartoncino [karton'tʃino] SM (*materiale*) thin cardboard; (*biglietto*) card.

cartone [kar'tone] SM **a** (*materiale*) cardboard **b** (*Arte*) cartoon ▶ **cartone animato** (*Cine*) cartoon **c** (*imballaggio*) large cardboard box; (*scatola*: *del latte*, *dell'aranciata*) carton.

cartonificio, ci [kartoni'fitʃo] SM cardboard mill.

cartonista, i, e [karto'nista] SM/F (*Cine*) cartoonist.

cartuccia, ce [kar'tuttʃa] SF (*di arma*) cartridge; (*di penna*) refill, cartridge; **mezza cartuccia** (*fig*: *persona da poco*) good-for-nothing ▶ **cartuccia a salve** blank (cartridge).

cartucciera [kartut'tʃɛra] SF cartridge belt.

casa ['kasa] **1** SF **a** (*edificio*) house; **casa a quattro piani** four-storey(ed) (*Brit*) o four-storied (*Am*) house; **casa di campagna** (*grande*) house in the country; (*piccola*) country cottage; **casa di mattoni** brick house; **case a schiera** terraced (*Brit*) o row (*Am*) houses; **la Casa Bianca** (*Pol*) the White House

b (*abitazione*) home; **essere/stare a** o **in casa** to be/stay at home; **tornare a casa** to come/go back home; **vado a casa mia/tua** I'm going home/to your house; **c'è nessuno in casa?** is anybody in?; **vieni a casa nostra?** are you coming to our house o place?; **uscire di casa** to leave home; **dove sta di casa?** where does he live?; **non sa dove stia di casa la cortesia** he doesn't know the meaning of courtesy; **essere di casa** to be like one of the family; **è una ragazza tutta casa e chiesa** she is a home-loving, church-going girl; **fatto in casa** home-made; **fai come se fossi a casa tua** make yourself at home; **abitare a casa del diavolo** to live in the back of beyond

c (*casato, stirpe*) house, family; **casa d'Asburgo** House of Hapsburg

d (*ditta*) firm, company.

2 ▶ **casa di correzione** ≈ community home (*Brit*), ≈ reform school (*Am*), reformatory (*Am*) ▶ **casa di cura** nursing home ▶ **casa discografica** record company ▶ **casa editrice** publishing house ▶ **casa madre** head office ▶ **casa di moda** fashion house ▶ **casa popolare** ≈ council house o flat (*Brit*), ≈ public housing unit (*Am*) ▶ **casa dello studente** hall of residence (*Brit*), dormitory (*Am*) ▶ **casa di tolleranza** o **d'appuntamenti** brothel.

Casablanca [kasa'blanka] SF Casablanca.

casacca, che [ka'zakka] SF (*Mil*) coat; (*giacca*) jacket; (*di fantino*) blouse.

casaccio [ka'zattʃo] SM: **a casaccio** (*per caso*) at random; (*senza cura*) any old how; (*senza riflettere*) off the top of one's head.

casale [ka'sale] SM (*gruppo di case*) hamlet; (*casolare*) farmhouse.

casalinga, ghe [kasa'linga] SF housewife.

casalingo, a, ghi, ghe [kasa'lingo] **1** AGG **a** (*occupazione, lavoro*) domestic, household *attr*

b (*fatto in casa*) home-made; (*semplice*) homely; (*amante della casa*) home-loving; **cucina casalinga** (plain) home cooking.

2 (*oggetti*): **casalinghi** SMPL household articles.

casamento [kasa'mento] SM block (of flats) (*Brit*), apartment building o house (*Am*).

casata [ka'sata] SF family, (family) lineage.

casato [ka'sato] SM family name; **è di nobile casato** he's of noble birth.

casba ['kazba] SF kasbah.

Casc. ABBR = **cascata**.

cascame [kas'kame] SM (*Tessile*) waste.

cascamorto [kaska'mɔrto] SM love-sick Romeo; **fare il cascamorto** to play the love-sick Romeo; **non fare il cascamorto con me** there's no point in chasing after me.

cascante [kas'kante] AGG drooping, droopy; **avere le guance/le spalle cascanti** to be heavy-jowled/round-shouldered.

cascare [kas'kare] VI (*aus* **essere**) to fall; **far cascare qc** to drop sth; **cascare per terra** to fall to the ground, fall down; **cascare dalla fame** to be faint with hunger; **cascare dal sonno** to be falling asleep on one's feet; **cascare dalle nuvole** (*fig*) to be taken aback; **cascare bene/male** (*fig*) to land lucky/unlucky; **gli ho detto che tu eri partito e lui c'è cascato** I told him you had left and he fell for it; **caschi il mondo** no matter what; **non cascherà il mondo se...** it won't be the end of the world if ... .

cascata [kas'kata] SF (*di acqua*) waterfall, cascade; (*fig*: *di capelli*) cascade; **cascata di ghiaccio** icefall; **le cascate Vittoria** the Victoria Falls.

cascatore, trice [kaska'tore] SM/F (*Cine*) stuntman/stuntwoman.

cascherò *ecc* [kaske'rɔ] VB *vedi* **cascare**.

caschetto [kas'ketto] SM (*pettinatura*) pageboy.

cascina [kaʃ'ʃina] SF farmstead.

cascinale [kaʃʃi'nale] SM (*casolare*) farmhouse; (*cascina*) farmstead.

casco, schi ['kasko] SM **a** (*Mil, Sport*) helmet; (*da motociclista*) crash helmet; (*da parrucchiere*) (hair-)dryer; **i caschi blu** the UN troops **b** (*di banane*) bunch.

caseario, ria, ri, rie [kaze'arjo] AGG dairy *attr*.

caseggiato [kased'dʒato] SM (*edificio*) large block of flats (*Brit*), large apartment building (*Am*) o house; (*gruppo di case*) group of houses.

caseificio, ci [kazei'fitʃo] SM creamery.

caseina [kaze'ina] SF casein.

casella [ka'sɛlla] SF (*quadretto*) box; (*di scacchiera*) square; (*di mobile, schedario*) pigeonhole ▶ **casella postale** post office box ▶ **casella di ricezione** (*Inform*) stacker.

casellante [kasel'lante] SM (*Ferr*) signalman; (*: al passaggio livello*) level-crossing keeper; (*su autostrada*) toll collector.

casellario, ri [kasel'larjo] SM (*mobile*) filing cabinet; (*raccolta di pratiche*) files *pl* ▶ **casellario giudiziale** o **giudiziario** court records *pl* ▶ **casellario penale** police files *pl*.

casello [ka'sɛllo] SM (*Ferr*) signal box (*Brit*), signal tower (*Am*); (*di autostrada*) tollgate.

casereccio, cia, ci, ce [kase'rettʃo] AGG home-made.

caserma [ka'sɛrma] SF barracks *pl*.

casermone [kaser'mone] SM (*pegg*) barracks *pl*.

casertano, a [kaser'tano] **1** AGG of o from Caserta. **2** SM/F inhabitant o native of Caserta.

casetta [ka'setta] SF (*piccola casa*) small house; (*tenda*) family tent.

casinista, i, e [kasi'nista] SM/F muddler.

casino [ka'sino] SM **a** (*fam*: *bordello*) brothel

b (*fig fam*: *rumore*) row, racket; (*: disordine*) mess; (*: guaio*) trouble; **ha fatto un casino** he made an awful row; he messed everything up; **mettere qn nei casini** put sb in a hell of a mess

c (*fam*: *grande quantità*) loads; **mi piace un casino** I really like it; **c'era un casino di macchine** there was a hell of a lot of traffic

b : **casino di caccia** hunting lodge.

casinò [kazi'nɔ] SM INV casino.

casistica [ka'zistika] SF record of cases; **secondo la casistica degli incidenti stradali** according to road accident data.

caso ['kazo] SM **a** (*fatalità, destino*) chance; **è un puro caso** it's sheer chance; **il caso ha voluto che...** by chance ...; **non è un caso** it's no coincidence; **si dà il caso che...** it so happens that ...; **guarda caso** strangely enough; **a caso** at random

b (*fatto, Gramm, Med, Dir*) case; **per lui è un caso di coscienza** he is in a moral dilemma; **questi sono i casi della vita!** that's life!; **caso limite** borderline case

c (*bisogno*): **fare al caso di qn** to be just what sb needs; **non è il caso che tu te la prenda** there's no need for you to be upset; **non mi sembra il caso di insistere** I wouldn't insist on that; **è il caso che ce ne andiamo** we'd better go

d (*possibilità, evenienza*) possibility, event; **i casi sono due** there are two possibilities; **in ogni caso** in any case; **in caso contrario** otherwise; **in tal caso** OR **in quel caso** in that case; **in caso di necessità** *o* **bisogno** in case of need; **al caso** if need be, should the opportunity arise; **per caso** by chance, by accident; **nel caso che...** in case ...; **caso mai** if by chance; **caso mai non possiate venire...** if (by chance) you can't come ...; **dovrei essere lì alle 5, caso mai aspetta** I should be there for 5; if (by any chance) I'm not, wait; **fare** *o* **porre** *o* **mettere il caso che...** to suppose that ...; **a seconda dei casi** depending on the circumstances

e (*attenzione*): **far caso a qn/qc** to pay attention to sb/sth; **hai fatto caso al suo cappello?** did you notice his hat?; **non farci caso** don't pay any attention.

casolare [kaso'lare] SM cottage.

casomai [kazo'mai] CONG = **caso mai**.

casotto [ka'sɔtto] SM **a** (*di sentinella*) sentry box; (*di guardiano*) shelter; (*in spiaggia*) bathing hut, bathing cabin **b** (*fam*) = **casino a, b**.

Caspio ['kaspjo] SM: **il mar Caspio** the Caspian Sea.

caspita ['kaspita] ESCL (*di sorpresa*) good heavens!; (*di impazienza*) for goodness' sake!

cassa ['kassa] ① SF **a** (*gen, Tip, di orologio*) case; (*gabbia*) crate; (*mobile*) chest; (*scatola*) box

b (*Comm*: *macchina*) cash register; (: *sportello*) cash desk; (: *in supermercato*) checkout (counter); **"si prega di pagare alla cassa"** "please pay at the desk"; **"cassa"** "pay here"; **piccola cassa** petty cash; **battere cassa** (*fig*) to come looking for money

c (*ente finanziario*) fund

d (*istituto bancario*) bank.

② ▶**cassa acustica** (*Mus*) speaker ▶**cassa d'aria** (*Naut*) airlock ▶**cassa armonica** (*Mus*) soundbox ▶**cassa automatica prelievi** cashpoint (*Am*), cash dispenser (*Brit*), automatic telling machine (*Brit*) ▶**cassa continua** night safe (*Brit*), night depository (*Am*) ▶**cassa del fucile** rifle stock ▶**cassa integrazione:mettere in cassa integrazione** ≈ to lay off ▶**Cassa del Mezzogiorno** *development fund for the South of Italy, now abolished* ▶**cassa da morto** coffin ▶**cassa mutua** *o* **malattia** health insurance scheme ▶**cassa di risonanza** (*Fis*) resonance chamber; (*fig*) platform ▶**cassa di risparmio** savings bank ▶**cassa rurale e**

artigiana credit institution (*for farmers and craftsmen*) ▶**cassa toracica** (*Anat*) chest.

cassaforte [kassa'fɔrte] SF (*pl* **casseforti**) safe.

Cassandra [kas'sandra] SF (*Mitol, fig*) Cassandra.

cassapanca, che [kassa'panka] SF settle.

cassare [kas'sare] VT (*Dir: annullare*) to annul, repeal.

cassata [kas'sata] SF (*gelato*) tutti-frutti.

cassazione [kassat'tsjone] SF (*Dir*) cassation.

casseruola [kasse'rwɔla] SF saucepan; **pollo in casseruola** chicken casserole.

cassetta [kas'setta] SF **a** (*gen*) box; (*musicassetta*) cassette; **pane a** *o* **in cassetta** toasting loaf ▶**cassetta degli arnesi** toolbox ▶**cassetta delle lettere** letterbox ▶**cassetta di sicurezza** strongbox

b (*Cine, Teatro*: *incasso*) box-office takings *pl*; **far cassetta** to be a box-office success; **film di cassetta** (*commerciale*) box-office draw.

cassettiera [kasset'tjɛra] SF chest of drawers.

cassetto [kas'setto] SM drawer.

cassettone [kasset'tone] SM (*mobile*) chest of drawers; **soffitto a cassettoni** (*Archit*) panelled ceiling.

cassia ['kassja] SF cassia.

cassiere, a [kas'sjɛre] SM/F cashier; (*in supermercato*) check-out assistant (*Brit*), check-out clerk (*Am*); **cassiere di banca** bank teller.

cassintegrato, a [kassinte'grato] SM/F person who has been laid off.

Cassio ['kassjo] SM Cassius.

cassone [kas'sone] SM (*cassa*) large case, large chest.

cassonetto [kasso'netto] SM (*per rifiuti*) wheelie-bin.

cast [ka:st] SM INV (*Cine*) cast.

Cast. ABBR = **castello**.

casta ['kasta] SF caste.

castagna [kas'taɲɲa] SF chestnut; **prendere qn in castagna** (*fig*) to catch sb in the act ▶**castagna d'acqua** water chestnut.

castagnaccio, ci [kastaɲ'nattʃo] SM chestnut cake.

castagno [kas'taɲɲo] SM (*albero*) chestnut (tree); (*legno*) chestnut ▶**castagno comune** *o* **dolce** sweet chestnut.

castagnola [kastaɲ'nɔla] SF (*petardo*) firecrack.

castamente [kasta'mente] AVV chastely.

castano, a [kas'tano] AGG (*capelli*) chestnut (brown); (*occhi*) brown; (*persona*) brown-haired.

castellano, a [kastel'lano] SM/F lord/lady of the manor.

castello [kas'tɛllo] SM **a** castle; **castello di carte** house of cards; **fare castelli in aria** to build castles in the air; **letti a castello** bunk-beds **b** (*Naut*): **castello di poppa** quarter-deck ▶**castello di prua** fo'c'sle **c** (*Tecn*) scaffolding.

castigare [kasti'gare] VT to punish, chastise.

castigatamente [kastigata'mente] AVV (*vestirsi*) demurely.

castigatezza [kastiga'tettsa] SF (*irreprensibilità*) faultlessness.

castigato, a [kasti'gato] AGG (*casto, modesto*) pure, chaste; (*abbigliamento*) demure; (*emendato*: *prosa, versione*) expurgated, amended.

Castiglia [kas'tiʎʎa] SF Castille.

castigliano, a [kastiʎ'ʎano] AGG, SM/F Castilian.

castigo, ghi [kas'tigo] SM punishment; **mettere/essere in castigo** to punish/be punished; **castigo di Dio** (*fig*) scourge.

castità [kasti'ta] SF chastity.

casto, a ['kasto] AGG chaste, pure.

Castore ['kastore] SM (*Mitol, Astron*) Castor.

castorino [kasto'rino] SM coypu; **pelliccia di castorino** nutria fur.

castoro [kas'tɔro] SM beaver.

castrante [kas'trante] AGG frustrating.

castrare [kas'trare] VT (*gen*) to castrate; (*cavallo*) to geld; (*gatto*) to neuter, doctor (*Brit*), fix (*Am*); (*fig: iniziativa*) to frustrate.

castrato, a [kas'trato] [1] AGG (*vedi vb*) castrated; gelded; neutered.

[2] SM (*agnello*) wether; (*Culin*) mutton.

castrazione [kastrat'tsjone] SF castration.

castronaggine [kastro'naddʒine] SF (*fam*) stupidity.

castrone [kas'trone] SM gelding.

castroneria [kastrone'ria] SF (*fam*): **dire castronerie** to talk rubbish.

casual ['kæʒual] [1] AGG INV (*abito, moda*) casual.

[2] SM INV (*abbigliamento*) casual wear.

casuale [kazu'ale] AGG chance *attr*, fortuitous.

casualità [kazuali'ta] SF chance nature.

casupola [ka'supola] SF simple little cottage.

casus belli ['kazus'bɛlli] SM INV (*Pol, fig*) casus belli.

catabolismo [katabo'lizmo] SM catabolism.

cataclisma, i [kata'klizma] SM cataclysm; (*fig*) catastrophe; **sembra che ci sia stato un cataclisma qui** this place looks as though a bomb has hit it.

catacomba [kata'komba] SF catacomb.

catafalco, chi [kata'falko] SM catafalque.

catafascio [kata'faʃʃo] SM: **mandare a catafascio** to wreck; **andare a catafascio** to go to rack and ruin.

catalessi [kata'lɛssi] SF INV (*Med*) catalepsy; **entrare** o **cadere in catalessi** to have a cataleptic fit; (*fig*) to go into a trance.

catalisi [ka'talizi] SF INV catalysis.

catalitico, a, ci, che [kata'litiko] AGG: **marmitta catalitica** catalytic converter.

catalizzare [katalid'dzare] VT (*anche fig*) to act as a catalyst (up)on.

catalizzato, a [katalid'dzato] AGG (*Aut*) fitted with a catalytic converter.

catalizzatore [kataliddza'tore] SM (*Aut*) catalytic converter; (*Chim, fig*) catalyst.

catalogare [katalo'gare] VT to catalogue, list.

Catalogna [kata'loɲɲa] SF: **la Catalonia** Catalonia.

catalogo [ka'talogo] SM catalogue.

catamarano [katama'rano] SM catamaran.

catanese [kata'nese] [1] AGG of o from Catania.

[2] SM/F inhabitant o native of Catania.

catanzarese [katandza'rese] [1] AGG of o from Catanzaro.

[2] SM/F inhabitant o native of Catanzaro.

catapecchia [kata'pekkja] SF hovel.

cataplasma, i [kata'plazma] SM (*Med*) poultice.

catapulta [kata'pulta] SF catapult.

catapultare [katapul'tare] [1] VT to catapult.

[2] **catapultarsi** VR to catapult.

cataratta [kata'ratta] SF = **cateratta**.

catarifrangente [katarifran'dʒɛnte] [1] AGG reflecting.

[2] SM reflector.

catarro [ka'tarro] SM catarrh.

catarsi [ka'tarsi] SF INV catharsis.

catasta [ka'tasta] SF pile, stack.

catastale [katas'tale] AGG (*Amm*): **ufficio catastale** land registry (office); **rilievo catastale** cadastral survey.

catasto [ka'tasto] SM (*Amm: inventario*) land register,

cadaster; (*anche:* **ufficio del catasto**) land registry (office).

catastrofe [ka'tastrofe] SF catastrophe, disaster.

catastroficamente [katastrofika'mente] AVV catastrophically.

catastrofico, a, ci, che [katas'trɔfiko] AGG (*evento*) catastrophic, disastrous; (*persona, previsione*) pessimistic.

catechesi [kate'kɛzi] SF INV catechesis.

catechismo [kate'kizmo] SM catechism.

catechista, i, e [kate'kista] SM/F catechist.

catechistico, a, ci, che [kate'kistiko] AGG catechistic.

catechizzare [katekid'dzare] VT (*Rel*) to catechize; (*fig*) to indoctrinate.

catecumeno [kate'kumeno] SM catechumen.

categoria [katego'ria] SF (*gen*) category; (*di albergo*) class; **di terza categoria** (*albergo, locale, anche pegg*) third-class.

categoricamente [kategorika'mente] AVV categorically.

categorico, a, ci, che [kate'gɔriko] AGG (*gen*) categorical; (*rifiuto*) categorical, flat.

catena [ka'tena] SF (*gen, di negozi*) chain; (*di montagne*) range, chain; (*fig: legame*) bond, chain; **reazione a catena** (*anche fig*) chain reaction; **susseguirsi a catena** to happen in quick succession; **tenere un cane alla catena** to keep a dog on a chain ▸ **catena alimentare** food chain ▸ **catena di montaggio** (*Tecn*) assembly line ▸ **catene da neve** (*Aut*) snow chains.

catenaccio, ci [kate'nattʃo] SM bolt; **chiudere con il catenaccio** to bolt; **fare catenaccio** (*Calcio*) to play defensively.

catenella [kate'nɛlla] SF (*ornamento*) chain; (*di orologio*) watch chain; (*di porta*) door chain; **punto catenella** (*in ricamo, maglia*) chain stitch.

cateratta [kate'ratta] SF **a** (*Med, Geog*) cataract **b** (*saracinesca*) sluice(gate).

caterva [ka'tɛrva] SF (*di cose*) loads *pl*, heaps *pl*; (*di persone*) horde.

catetere [kate'tɛre] SM (*Med*) catheter.

cateto [ka'tɛto] SM (*Geom*) cathetus; **in un triangolo rettangolo l'ipotenusa è uguale alla somma dei cateti** in a right-angled triangle the length of the hypotenuse equals the sum of the other two sides.

Catilina [kati'lina] SM Catiline.

catinella [kati'nɛlla] SF basin; **piovere a catinelle** to rain cats and dogs.

catino [ka'tino] SM basin.

catione [ka'tjone] SM cation.

catodico, a, ci, che [ka'tɔdiko] AGG cathode *attr*; **tubo a raggi catodici** cathode-ray tube.

catodo ['katodo] SM cathode.

Catone [ka'tone] SM Cato.

catorcio, ci [ka'tɔrtʃo] SM (*pegg*) old wreck.

catramare [katra'mare] VT to tar.

catrame [ka'trame] SM tar.

cattedra ['kattedra] SF **a** (*mobile*) (teacher's) desk; **cattedra episcopale** bishop's throne; **salire** o **montare in cattedra** (*fig*) to pontificate **b** (*incarico: Scol*) teaching post; (*: Univ*) chair, professorship.

cattedrale [katte'drale] SF cathedral.

cattedraticamente [kattedratika'mente] AVV (*pegg*) pedantically.

cattedratico, a, ci, che [katte'dratiko] [1] AGG (*insegnamento*) university *attr*; (*pegg*) pedantic.

[2] SM/F professor.

cattivello, a [katti'vɛllo] AGG naughty.

cattiveria [katti'vɛrja] SF **a** (qualità) wickedness, nastiness; (: di bambino) naughtiness; **lo ha fatto per pura cattiveria** he did it out of sheer spite **b** (azione) nasty o wicked action; **fare una cattiveria** to do something nasty o wicked; (bambino) to be naughty.

cattività [kattivi'ta] SF (di animali) captivity.

cattivo, a [kat'tivo] **1** AGG **a** (persona, azione) bad, wicked; (bambino: birichino) naughty, bad; **brutto cattivo!** you naughty boy!; **quel ragazzo è un cattivo soggetto** that boy's a bit of a rascal; **farsi cattivo sangue** to worry, get in a state; **farsi un cattivo nome** to earn a bad reputation for o.s., earn o.s. a bad reputation **b** (di qualità, gen) bad; (odore, sapore) bad, nasty; (cibo guasto) off; (insegnante, salute) bad, poor; (mare) rough; **con le buone o con le cattive (maniere)** by hook or by crook.

2 SM/F bad o wicked person; (nei film) villain; **fare il cattivo** (bambino) to be naughty; **i cattivi** (nei film) the baddies (Brit), the bad guys (Am).

cattocomunista, i, e **1** AGG combining Catholic and Communist ideas.

2 SM/F Catholic-communist.

cattolicamente [kattolika'mente] AVV according to the Catholic faith.

cattolicesimo [kattoli'tʃezimo] SM Catholicism.

cattolico, a, ci, che [kat'tɔliko] AGG, SM/F (Roman) Catholic.

cattura [kat'tura] SF capture; **ordine di cattura** (Dir) warrant of o for arrest.

catturare [kattu'rare] VT (gen, fig: attenzione) to capture, catch.

Catullo [ka'tullo] SM Catullus.

caucasico, a, ci, che [kau'kaziko] AGG, SM/F Caucasian.

Caucaso [ˈkaukazo] SM: **il Caucaso** the Caucasus.

caucciù [kaut'tʃu] SM INV India rubber.

causa [ˈkauza] SF **a** (motivo, ragione) cause, reason; (ideale) cause; **essere causa di qc** to be the cause of sth, be the reason for sth; **a causa di** because of; **per causa sua** because of him; **causa persa** (anche fig) lost cause; **far causa comune** to make common cause; **giusta causa** true and just cause **b** (Dir) case, lawsuit, action; **intentare o fare o muovere causa a qn** to take legal action against sb; **perorare una causa** to plead a case; **parte in causa** litigant; **tu non sei parte in causa in tutto ciò** all this doesn't concern you; **rimettere qc in causa** (fig) to bring sth up again **c** (Gramm): **complemento di causa** complement of cause.

causale [kauˈzale] **1** AGG (rapporto, nesso, Gramm) causal. **2** SF cause, reason ▶ **causale di versamento** (Amm) description of payment.

causalità [kauzaliˈta] SF causality.

causare [kauˈzare] VT to cause.

causticamente [kaustikaˈmente] AVV caustically.

caustico, a, ci, che [ˈkaustiko] AGG (Chim, fig) caustic.

cautamente [kautaˈmente] AVV cautiously, carefully.

cautela [kauˈtɛla] SF **a** (prudenza) caution, prudence; **"maneggiare con cautela"** "handle with care" **b** (precauzione) precaution.

cautelare¹ [kauteˈlare] AGG precautionary.

cautelare² [kauteˈlare] **1** VT to protect. **2** **cautelarsi** VR: **cautelarsi (da o contro)** to take precautions (against).

cauterizzare [kauteridˈdzare] VT (Med) to cauterize.

cauto, a [ˈkauto] AGG prudent, cautious; **andare cauto** (fig) to tread carefully.

cauzionare [kauttsjoˈnare] VT to guarantee.

cauzione [kautˈtsjone] SF **a** (Dir: deposito) security, guarantee; (: per libertà provvisoria) bail; **rilasciare dietro cauzione** to release on bail **b** (somma) caution money.

cav. ABBR = **cavaliere**.

cava [ˈkava] SF quarry (Geol).

cavalcare [kavalˈkare] **1** VT (sogg: persona: cavallo) to ride; (: muro) to sit astride; (sogg: ponte) to span. **2** VI (aus avere) (andare a cavallo) to ride.

cavalcata [kavalˈkata] SF ride; **fare una cavalcata** to go for a ride.

cavalcatura [kavalkaˈtura] SF mount.

cavalcavia [kavalkaˈvia] SM INV flyover (Brit), overpass (Am); (sopra ferrovia) railway bridge.

cavalcioni [kavalˈtʃoni]: **a cavalcioni (di)** AVV astride.

cavaliere [kavaˈljɛre] SM **a** rider, horseman; (Mil) cavalryman, trooper **b** (accompagnatore) escort; (nel ballo) partner; (gentiluomo) gentleman **c** (titolo, Storia) knight; **l'hanno fatto cavaliere del lavoro** he has been knighted for services to industry.

cavalla [kaˈvalla] SF mare.

cavalleggero [kavalledˈdʒero] SM light cavalryman.

cavallerescamente [kavallereskaˈmente] AVV chivalrously.

cavalleresco, a, schi, sche [kavalleˈresko] AGG knightly; (fig: comportamento) chivalrous, noble; **poema cavalleresco** poem of chivalry.

cavalleria [kavalleˈria] SF **a** (Mil) cavalry **b** (Storia, fig: lealtà, cortesia) chivalry.

cavallerizza [kavalleˈrittsa] SF (maneggio) riding school; **alla cavallerizza** (abbigliamento, stivali) riding attr.

cavallerizzo, a [kavalleˈrittso] SM/F (nel circo) circus rider; (maestro di equitazione) riding instructor.

cavalletta [kavalˈletta] SF (Zool) grasshopper; (: dannosa) locust.

cavalletto [kavalˈletto] SM (supporto) trestle; (da pittore) easel; (Fot) tripod.

cavallina [kavalˈlina] SF **a** (Zool) filly **b** (gioco) leapfrog **c** (attrezzo ginnico) (vaulting) horse; **correre la cavallina** (fig) to sow one's wild oats.

cavallino, a [kavalˈlino] AGG (fig: volto, risata) horsy.

cavallo [kaˈvallo] **1** SM **a** horse; **a cavallo** on horseback; **a cavallo di** (sedia, moto, bici) astride, straddling; **andare a cavallo** to go on horseback, ride; **essere a cavallo** to ride; **siamo a cavallo** (fig) we've made it; **montare a/scendere da cavallo** to mount/dismount; **denti da cavallo** horsy teeth; **da cavallo** (fig: dose) drastic; (: febbre) raging; **vivere a cavallo tra due periodi** to straddle two periods; **a caval donato non si guarda in bocca** (Proverbio) don't look a gift horse in the mouth **b** (dei pantaloni) crotch; (Scacchi) knight; (attrezzo ginnico) (vaulting) horse; **c** (anche: cavallo vapore) horsepower. **2** ▶ **cavallo di battaglia** (Teatro) tour de force; (fig) hobby-horse ▶ **cavallo da corsa** racehorse ▶ **cavallo a dondolo** rocking horse ▶ **cavallo di Frisia** (Mil) cheval-de-frise ▶ **cavallo purosangue** o **di razza** thoroughbred ▶ **cavallo da sella** saddle horse ▶ **cavallo da soma** packhorse.

cavallona SF (donna) tall ungainly girl.

cavallone [kaval'lone] SM (*onda*) breaker.

cavalluccio, ci [kaval'luttʃo] SM: **cavalluccio marino** sea horse.

cavapietre [kava'pjɛtre] SM INV quarryman.

cavare [ka'vare] VT **a** (*gen*) to take out, draw out; (*marmo*) to extract; (*dente*) to pull, extract; (*informazioni, soldi*) to obtain, get; **cavare gli occhi a qn** (*anche fig*) to scratch sb's eyes out; **me l'hai cavato di bocca** you took the words out of my mouth; **non gli ho cavato una parola (di bocca)** I couldn't get a word out of him
b : **cavarsi** (*capriccio, voglia*) to satisfy; (*fame*) to satisfy, appease; (*sete*) to quench, slake; (*giacca, scarpe*) to take off; **cavarsi il pane di bocca** (*fig*) to make sacrifices
c : **cavarsela** (*farcela*) to manage, get on all right; (*da impiccio*) to find a way out; **come te la cavi?** how are things?; **cavarsela (a buon mercato)** to come off lightly, get away with it; **se l'è cavata bene** (*in un processo*) he got off lightly; (*in un esame*) he did quite well; **se l'è cavata con qualche graffio** she came out of it with only a few scratches.

cavastivali [kavasti'vali] SM INV bootjack.

cavatappi [kava'tappi], **cavaturaccioli** [kavatu'rattʃoli] SM INV corkscrew.

cavatorsoli [kava'torsoli] SM INV apple corer.

caveau [ka'vo] SM INV vault.

cavedano [ka'vedano] SM (*pesce*) chub.

caverna [ka'vɛrna] SF cave, cavern; **uomo delle caverne** caveman.

cavernicolo, a [kaver'nikolo] SM/F cave-dweller.

cavernoso, a [kaver'noso] AGG (*voce*) deep.

cavetto [ka'vetto] SM (*Elettr*) lead.

cavezza [ka'vettsa] SF halter.

cavia ['kavja] SF (*anche fig*) guinea pig; **fare da cavia** (*fig*) to act as a guinea pig.

caviale [ka'vjale] SM caviar.

cavicchio, chi [ka'vikkjo] SM (*Tecn*) wooden pin; (*Agr*) dibble.

caviglia [ka'viʎʎa] SF (*Anat*) ankle; (*cavicchio*) pin, peg.

cavigliera [kaviʎ'ʎɛra] SF (*fascia elastica*) ankle bandage.

cavillare [kavil'lare] VI (*aus avere*) to quibble, split hairs.

cavillo [ka'villo] SM quibble.

cavillosamente [kavillosa'mente] AVV: **discutere cavillosamente su qc** to quibble over sth.

cavilloso, a [kavil'loso] AGG quibbling, hairsplitting.

cavità [kavi'ta] SF INV hollow; (*Anat*) cavity; **cavità sotterranea** underground cave.

cavo[1], a ['kavo] [1] AGG hollow.
[2] SM (*Anat*) cavity.

cavo[2] ['kavo] SM (*gen, Tecn, Telec*) cable; (*Naut*) rope
► **cavo di traino** (*Aut*) tow rope.

cavolata [kavo'lata] SF (*fam*) stupid thing, foolish thing; **dire cavolate** to talk rubbish o nonsense; **fare cavolate** to do stupid things.

cavolfiore [kavol'fjore] SM cauliflower.

cavolino [kavo'lino] SM: **cavolino di Bruxelles** Brussels sprout.

cavolo ['kavolo] SM **a** (*Bot*) cabbage; **cavolo cappuccio** spring cabbage; **cavolo da foraggio** kale; **questo c'entra come il cavolo a merenda** that's completely beside the point
b (*fam: euf per cazzo*): **non fa un cavolo dalla mattina alla sera** he doesn't do a damn thing from morning till night; **non m'importa un cavolo** I don't give a damn; **che cavolo vuoi?** what the heck do you want?; **cavolo!**

(*imprecazione*) damn!; (*di ammirazione*) wow!; **ci presterà la macchina? — sì, col cavolo!** will she lend us the car? — fat chance!

cazzata [kat'tsata] SF (*fam!: stupidaggine*) stupid thing, something stupid; **dire cazzate** to talk crap (*fam!*); **ha fatto un'altra delle sue cazzate!** he's boobed again!, he's ballsed things up again; **quel film è una vera cazzata** that film is a load of crap (*fam!*).

cazzo ['kattso] SM **a** (*fam!: pene*) prick (*fam!*)
b (*fig fam!*): **non gliene importa un cazzo** he doesn't give a shit (*fam!*) o fuck (*fam!*) about it; **che cazzo vuoi?** what the fuck (*fam!*) do you want?; **non ha fatto un cazzo oggi** he's been pissing about (*fam!*) all day today; **fatti i cazzi tuoi** mind your own fucking (*fam!*) business; **cazzo!** fuck! (*fam!*); **testa di cazzo** dickhead (*fam!*), prick (*fam!*); **che film del cazzo!** what a crap (*fam!*) film!; **grazie al cazzo!** thanks for nothing!; **stare sul cazzo a qn** to get up sb's nose.

cazzotto [kat'tsotto] SM punch; **tirare un cazzotto** to throw a punch; **fare a cazzotti** to have a punch-up (*Brit*).

cazzuola [kat'tswola], **cazzola** [kat'tsola] SF trowel.

CB SIGLA = *Campobasso*.

CC ABBR = *Carabinieri*.

cc ABBR (= *centimetro cubico*) cc.

C.C. ABBR = **codice civile.**

C.C. ABBR **a** (= *conto corrente*) c/a, a/c **b** (*Elettr. = corrente continua*) DC.

c/c ABBR (= *conto corrente*) c/a, a/c.

C.C.D. [tʃitʃi'di] SIGLA M (*Pol: = Centro Cristiano Democratico*) *party originating from Democrazia Cristiana.*

C.C.I. SIGLA F (= *Camera di Commercio Internazionale*) ICC (= *International Chamber of Commerce*).

C.C.I.A.A. ABBR = *Camera di Commercio, Industria, Agricoltura e Artigianato.*

C.C.T. [tʃitʃi'ti] SIGLA M = **certificato di credito del Tesoro.**

CD [tʃi'di] SM INV (= *compact disc*) CD.

C.D. ABBR (= *Corpo Diplomatico*) CD.

c.d. ABBR = **cosiddetto.**

c.d.d. ABBR (= *come dovevasi dimostrare*) QED (= *quod erat demonstrandum*).

CD-ROM [tʃidi'rɔm] SM INV (= *Compact Disc Read Only Memory*) CD-Rom.

CE SIGLA = *Caserta*.

ce [tʃe] PRON, AVV vedi **ci**.

C.E. [tʃi'e] SIGLA F **a** = **Consiglio d'Europa b** = **Comunità Europea.**

C.E.C.A. [tʃe'ka] SIGLA F (= *Comunità Europea del Carbone e dell'Acciaio*) ECSC (= *European Coal and Steel Community*).

cecchino [tʃek'kino] SM sniper; (*Pol*) *member of parliament who votes against his own party.*

cece ['tʃetʃe] SM chickpea, garbanzo (*Am*).

cecità [tʃetʃi'ta] SF blindness; **cecità da neve** snow blindness.

ceco, a, chi, che ['tʃɛko] [1] AGG, SM/F Czech; **la Repubblica ceca** the Czech Republic.
[2] SM (*lingua*) Czech.

Cecoslovacchia [tʃekozlo'vakkja] SF: **la Cecoslovacchia** Czechoslovakia.

cecoslovacco, a, chi, che [tʃekozlo'vakko] AGG, SM/F Czechoslovakian.

C.E.D. [tʃed] SIGLA M = **centro elaborazione dati.**

cedenze [tʃe'dɛntse] SFPL (*Fin: di azioni, titoli*) drop *sg* in value.

cedere ['tʃɛdere] ① VT **a** (*concedere*): **cedere qc (a qn)** to give sth up (to sb); (*eredità, diritto*) to transfer sth (to sb), make sth over (to sb); **cedere il posto a qn** (*in autobus*) to give sb one's seat; **cedere il passo (a qn)** to let (sb) pass in front; **cedere il passo a qc** (*fig*) to give way to sth; **cedere la parola (a qn)** to hand over (to sb)
b (*Comm: vendere*) to sell; **"cedo"** OR **"cedesi"** "for sale".
② VI (*aus* **avere**) **a** (*crollare: persona*) to give in; (: *terreno*) to give way, subside; (: *muro*) to collapse, fall down; **il suo cuore ha ceduto** his heart couldn't take the strain
b (*soccombere*): **cedere a** to give way to, to surrender to, yield to, give in to
c (*deformarsi: tessuto, scarpe*) to give.

cedevole [tʃe'devole] AGG (*materiale*) supple, pliable, yielding; (*terreno*) soft.

cedibilità [tʃedibili'ta] SF (*Comm*) transferability.

cediglia [tʃe'diʎʎa] SF cedilla.

cedimento [tʃedi'mento] SM (*di terreno*) sinking, subsiding; **ha avuto un cedimento** (*terreno*) it has subsided; (*fig: persona*) he broke down.

cedola ['tʃedola] SF (*Comm, Fin*) coupon, voucher; (*di assegno*) counterfoil.

cedrata [tʃe'drata] SF citron juice.

cedro[1] ['tʃedro] SM (*frutto, albero*) citron.

cedro[2] ['tʃedro] SM (*legno, albero*) cedar; **cedro bianco** Lawson's cypress; **cedro del Libano** cedar of Lebanon.

cedrone [tʃe'drone] AGG INV: **gallo cedrone** capercaillie.

ceduo, a ['tʃeduo] AGG: **bosco ceduo** copse, coppice.

C.E.E. ['tʃɛɛ] SIGLA F (= *Comunità Economica Europea*) EEC (= *European Economic Community*).

cefalea [tʃefa'lɛa] SF (*Med*) headache.

cefalo ['tʃɛfalo] SM grey mullet (*Brit*), mullet (*Am*).

ceffo ['tʃɛffo] SM (*pegg*) ugly mug.

ceffone [tʃef'fone] SM slap, smack; **dare un ceffone a qn** to slap sb.

ceko, a ['tʃɛko] AGG, SM/F, SM = **ceco**.

celare [tʃe'lare] ① VT to conceal; **celare qc alla vista di qn** to conceal sth from sb.
② **celarsi** VR (*nascondersi*) to hide, conceal o.s.; (*stare nascosto*) to be hidden, be concealed.

celeberrimo, a [tʃele'bɛrrimo] AGG (*superl di* **celebre**).

celebrante [tʃele'brante] SM (*Rel*) celebrant.

celebrare [tʃele'brare] VT (*messa, matrimonio, festa*) to celebrate; (*cerimonia*) to hold; **celebrare le lodi di qn/qc** to sing the praises of sb/sth.

celebrato, a [tʃele'brato] AGG famous, well-known, celebrated.

celebrazione [tʃelebrat'tsjone] SF celebration.

celebre ['tʃɛlebre] AGG famous, celebrated.

celebrità [tʃelebri'ta] SF INV (*fama, notorietà*) fame; (*persona*) celebrity; **arrivare alla celebrità** to become famous; **raggiungere la celebrità** to rise to fame.

celere ['tʃɛlere] ① AGG quick, fast, swift; (*Scol, Univ: corso*) crash *attr*.
② SF (*Polizia*) riot police.

celerità [tʃeleri'ta] SF quickness, speed.

celeste [tʃe'lɛste] ① AGG **a** (*colore*) pale blue, sky-blue **b** (*di cielo*) celestial; (*divino*) heavenly, celestial; **la volta celeste** the vault o canopy of heaven.
② SM (*colore*) pale blue, sky blue.

celestiale [tʃeles'tjale] AGG heavenly, celestial.

celestialmente [tʃelestjal'mente] AVV (*fig*) divinely.

celia ['tʃɛlja] SF joke; **per celia** as a joke, in jest.

celibato [tʃeli'bato] SM celibacy; **addio al celibato** stag night.

celibe ['tʃɛlibe] ① AGG single, unmarried; (*prete*) celibate.
② SM single o unmarried man, bachelor.

celidonia [tʃeli'dɔnja] SF (*pianta*) celandine.

cella ['tʃɛlla] SF cell ▸**cella a combustione** (*Fis*) fuel cell ▸**cella frigorifera** cold store ▸**cella di isolamento:essere in cella di isolamento** to be in solitary confinement ▸**cella di rigore** punishment cell ▸**cella a secco** (*Chim*) dry cell.

cellophane® [sɛlɔ'fan] SM cellophane ®.

cellula ['tʃɛllula] SF (*in ogni senso*) cell ▸**cellula nervosa** neuron, nerve cell ▸**cellula uovo** ovum.

cellulare [tʃellu'lare] ① AGG cellular; **differenziazione/divisione cellulare** (*Bio*) cell differentiation/division; **segregazione cellulare** (*Dir*) solitary confinement.
② SM (*furgone*) police van; (*telefono*) cellphone.

cellulite [tʃellu'lite] SF cellulitis.

celluloide [tʃellu'lɔide] SF celluloid.

cellulosa [tʃellu'losa] SF cellulose.

celta ['tʃɛlta] SM/F Celt.

celtico, a, ci, che ['tʃɛltiko] AGG, SM Celtic.

cembalo ['tʃembalo] SM (*Mus*) harpsichord.

cementare [tʃemen'tare] VT (*anche fig*) to cement.

cemento [tʃe'mento] SM cement ▸**cemento armato** reinforced concrete.

cena ['tʃena] SF dinner; (*leggera*) supper; **invitare qn a cena** to invite sb to dinner; **andare fuori a cena** to go out for dinner; **l'Ultima Cena** (*Rel*) the Last Supper.

cenacolo [tʃe'nakolo] SM (*circolo*) coterie, circle; (*Rel, dipinto*) (the) Last Supper.

cenare [tʃe'nare] VI (*aus* **avere**) to have dinner, dine.

cenciaiolo, a [tʃentʃa'jɔlo] SM/F rag-merchant.

cencio, ci ['tʃentʃo] SM (*straccio*) rag; (: *per pulire*) cloth; (: *per spolverare*) duster; **vestito di cenci** dressed in rags; **essere ridotto a un cencio** to feel washed out; **essere bianco come un cencio** to be as white as a sheet.

cencioso, a [tʃen'tʃoso] AGG (*persona*) (dressed) in rags; (*indumento*) tattered.

cenere ['tʃenere] SF ash, ashes *pl*; (*di carbone, legno*) cinders *pl*; (*di defunto*): **ceneri** SFPL ashes; **biondo cenere** ash blonde.

Cenerentola [tʃene'rɛntola] SF (*anche fig*) Cinderella.

cenno ['tʃenno] SM **a** (*segno*) sign, signal; (: *con la testa*) nod; (: *con gli occhi*) wink; (: *con la mano*) gesture; (: *di saluto*) wave; **capirsi/parlare a cenni** to understand each other/speak with gestures; **cenno d'intesa** sign of agreement; **fare cenno di sì/no** to nod (one's head)/shake one's head; **mi fece un cenno di saluto con la mano/con la testa** he waved/nodded to me; **mi ha fatto cenno di avvicinarmi** he beckoned to me to come forward
b (*breve esposizione*) mention, short account; (*allusione*) hint; **fare cenno a qn/qc** to mention sb/sth; **cenni di storia dell'arte** an outline of the history of art
c (*indizio*) sign; **al primo cenno di pioggia** at the first sign of rain.

cenone [tʃe'none] SM: **cenone di Capodanno** New Year's Eve dinner.

cenotafio, fi [tʃeno'tafjo] SM cenotaph.

censimento [tʃensi'mento] SM census; **fare il censimento** to take a census.

censire [tʃen'sire] VT: **censire qc** to take a census of sth.

CENSIS ['tʃɛnsis] SIGLA M (= *Centro Studi Investimenti Sociali*) *independent institute carrying out research on social conditions in Italy.*

censo ['tʃɛnso] SM (*Storia*) census; (*ricchezza*) wealth.

censore [tʃen'sore] SM (*anche Storia*) censor; (*fig: critico*) critic.

censura [tʃen'sura] SF (*Psic, Cine, Stampa*: *controllo*) censors; (*ufficio*) board of censors, censor's office; (*fig, Pol, Rel*) censure.

censurare [tʃensu'rare] VT (*Psic, Cine, Stampa*) to censor; (*fig, Pol, Rel*) to censure.

cent. ABBR = **centesimo.**

centauro [tʃen'tauro] SM (*Mitol*) centaur; (*fig*) motorcycle rider.

centellinare [tʃentelli'nare] VT to sip; (*fig*) to savour (*Brit*), savor (*Am*).

centenario, ria, ri, rie [tʃente'narjo] **1** AGG **a** (*che ha cento anni*) hundred-year-old; **un edificio centenario** a (one) hundred-year-old building **b** (*che ricorre ogni cento anni*) centennial *attr*, centenary *attr*.
2 SM/F (*persona*) centenarian.
3 SM (*anniversario*) centenary, centennial (*Am*).

centennale [tʃenten'nale] AGG centennial *attr*; **tradizione centennale** age-old tradition.

centerbe [tʃen'tɛrbe] SM INV *liqueur from the Abruzzi made with herbs.*

centesimale [tʃentezi'male] AGG hundredth.

centesimo, a [tʃen'tɛzimo] **1** AGG hundredth.
2 SM (*centesima parte*) hundredth; (*moneta*: *di dollaro*) cent; (: *di franco*) centime; **non vale un centesimo** it's not worth a penny (*Brit*) *o* a red cent (*Am*); **essere senza un centesimo** to be penniless.

centigrado, a [tʃen'tigrado] AGG centigrade; **20 gradi centigradi** 20 degrees centigrade.

centilitro [tʃen'tilitro] SM centilitre (*Brit*), centiliter (*Am*).

centimetro [tʃen'timetro] SM **a** (*misura*) centimetre (*Brit*), centimeter (*Am*) **b** (*nastro*) measuring tape (*in centimetres*).

centinaio [tʃenti'najo] SM (*pl(f)* **centinaia**) hundred; **un centinaio di persone** about a hundred people, a hundred or so people; **a centinaia** (*merce*: *vendere*) by the hundred; (*persone*: *venire*) in (their) hundreds.

centinodia [tʃenti'nɔdja] SF (*pianta*) knotgrass.

cento ['tʃɛnto] **1** AGG INV a hundred, one hundred; **centouno** one *o* a hundred and one; **seicento** six hundred; **cento di questi giorni!** many happy returns (of the day)!.
2 SM INV a hundred, one hundred; **per cento** per cent; **al cento per cento** a hundred per cent *per fraseologia vedi* **cinque.**

centodieci [tʃento'djɛtʃi] AGG, SM INV one hundred and ten; **laurearsi con centodieci e lode** (*Univ*) ≈ to graduate with first-class honours (*Brit*), ≈ to graduate summa cum laude (*Am*).

centometrista, i, e [tʃentome'trista] SM/F one hundred metres runner *o* swimmer.

centomila [tʃento'mila] AGG INV a *o* one hundred thousand; **te l'ho detto centomila volte** (*fig*) I've told you a thousand times.

centone [tʃen'tone] SM **a** (*fam*: *centomila lire*) *one hundred thousand lire note* **b** (*Letteratura*) cento.

centrafricano, a [tʃentrafri'kano] AGG of the Central African Republic; **la Repubblica Centrafricana** the Central African Republic.

centrale [tʃen'trale] **1** AGG (*gen*) central; (*stazione, ufficio*) main; **sede centrale** head office.
2 SF (*sede principale*) head office ►**centrale elettrica** power station *o* plant (*Am*) ►**centrale del latte** dairy ►**centrale nucleare** nuclear power station *o* plant (*Am*) ►**centrale di polizia** police headquarters *pl* ►**centrale telefonica** (telephone) exchange ►**centrale termoelettrica** thermal power station *o* plant (*Am*).

centralina [tʃentra'lina] SF (*elettrica, telefonica*) junction box.

centralinista, i, e [tʃentrali'nista] SM/F (*Telec*) operator; (*in ditta, albergo*) switchboard operator.

centralino [tʃentra'lino] SM (*Telec*) (telephone) exchange; (*di ditta, albergo*) switchboard.

centralismo SM centralism.

centralità [tʃentrali'ta] SF (*gen*) centrality; (*Pol*) centre.

centralizzare [tʃentralid'dzare] VT to centralize.

centralizzazione [tʃentraliddzat'tsjone] SF centralization.

centrare [tʃen'trare] VT (*gen*) to hit the centre (*Brit*) *o* center (*Am*) of; (*Sport, Tecn*) to centre; (*bersaglio*) to hit in the centre; **centrare (in pieno)** (*freccette*) to score a bull's eye; **centrare una risposta** to get the right answer; **hai centrato il problema** you've hit the nail on the head.

centrato, a [tʃen'trato] AGG (*colpo, pugno*): **ben centrato** well-aimed.

centrattacco, chi [tʃentrat'takko] SM, **centravanti** [tʃentra'vanti] SM INV centre forward.

centrifuga, ghe [tʃen'trifuga] SF (*Tecn*) centrifuge; (*di lavatrice*) spin-dryer; **centrifuga lunga/corta** long/short spin ►**centrifuga elettrica** juice extractor ►**centrifuga scolaverdure** (*Culin*) salad spinner.

centrifugare [tʃentrifu'gare] VT (*Tecn*) to centrifuge; (*biancheria*) to spin-dry; (*Culin*: *verdura, frutta*) to extract the juice from.

centrifugo, a, ghi, ghe [tʃen'trifugo] AGG: **forza centrifuga** centrifugal force.

centrino [tʃen'trino] SM doily.

centripeto, a [tʃen'tripeto] AGG: **forza centripeta** centripetal force.

centrista, i, e [tʃen'trista] AGG (*Pol*) centrist, centre *attr*.

centro ['tʃɛntro] **1** SM (*gen*) centre (*Brit*), center (*Am*); (*di città*) (town *o* city) centre; (*di bersaglio*) bull's eye; **fare centro** to hit the bull's eye; (*Calcio*) to score; (*fig*) to hit the nail on the head.
2 ►**centri vitali** (*anche fig*) vital organs. ►**centro balneare** seaside resort ►**centro commerciale** shopping centre *o* mall (*Am*); (*città*) commercial centre ►**centro di costo** cost centre ►**centro elaborazione dati** data-processing unit ►**centro nervoso** (*Anat*) nerve centre ►**centro ospedaliero** hospital complex ►**centro di ricerche** research centre ►**centro sociale** community centre ►**centro sportivo** sports centre.

centrocampo [tʃentro'kampo] SM (*Sport*) midfield.

centrodestra [tʃentro'dɛstra] SM (*Pol*) centre right.

centrodestro [tʃentro'dɛstro] SM (*Calcio*) inside right.

centromediano [tʃentrome'djano] SM (*Calcio*) centre half.

centrosinistra [tʃentrosi'nistra] SM (*Pol*) centre left.

centrosinistro [tʃentrosi'nistro] SM (*Calcio*) inside left.

centrotavola [tʃentro'tavola] SM (*pl* **centritavola**) centrepiece.

centroterzino [tʃentroter'tsino] SM (*Calcio*) central defender.

centuplicare [tʃɛntupli'kare] vт to increase a hundred times, increase a hundredfold.

centuplo, a ['tʃɛntuplo] 1 AGG a hundred times as much. 2 SM: **il centuplo di 2** a hundred times 2.

centurione [tʃɛntu'rjone] SM centurion.

ceppo ['tʃeppo] SM a (*di albero*) (tree) stump; (*fig: genealogico*) stock b (*ciocco*) log; (*per decapitazione*) (chopping) block c (*di aratro, ancora*) stock; (*Tecn*) brake shoe d : **ceppi** SMPL (*di prigioniero*) shackles, fetters.

cera ['tʃera] SF a (*sostanza*) wax; **cera per pavimenti** floor polish; **dare la cera (a qc)** to polish (sth); **museo delle cere** waxworks *sg* ► **cera d'api** beeswax b (*fig: aspetto*): **avere una bella/brutta cera** to look well/ill.

ceralacca [tʃera'lakka] SF sealing wax.

ceramica [tʃe'ramika] SF a (*materiale*) baked clay, ceramic; (*Arte*) ceramics *sg* b : **ceramiche** SFPL pottery.

ceramista, i, e [tʃera'mista] SM/F ceramist, ceramic artist.

cerato, a [tʃe'rato] 1 AGG waxed, wax *attr*; **tela cerata** oilskin.
2 SM oilcloth.
3 SF (*indumento*) oilskins *pl*.

Cerbero ['tʃɛrbero] SM Cerberus.

cerbiatto [tʃer'bjatto] SM (*animale*) fawn.

cerbottana [tʃerbot'tana] SF (*arma*) blowpipe; (*giocattolo*) peashooter.

cerca ['tʃerka] SF: **andare/essere in cerca di** to go/be looking for, go/be in search of.

cercafase [tʃerka'faze] SM INV mains tester.

cercafughe [tʃerka'fuge] SM INV leak detector.

cercapersone [tʃerkaper'sone] SM INV pager, bleeper (*Brit*), beeper (*Am*).

cercare [tʃer'kare] 1 vт (*gen*) to look for, search for; (*fama, gloria*) to seek; **l'hai cercato sul dizionario?** have you looked it up in the dictionary?; **cercare lavoro/casa** to look for work/a house; **cercare moglie/marito** to be looking for a wife/husband; **cercare qn con gli occhi** to look round for sb; **cercare le parole** to search for words; **cercare guai** to be looking for trouble; **cercare fortuna** to seek one's fortune.
2 vı (*aus avere*): **cercare di fare qc** to try to do sth; **cerca di non far tardi** try not to be late.

cercatore, trice [tʃerka'tore] SM/F searcher, seeker ► **cercatore d'oro** gold digger.

cercherò *ecc* [tʃerke'rɔ] VB vedi **cercare**.

cerchia ['tʃerkja] SF (*anche fig*) circle; **cerchia di mura** city walls.

cerchiare [tʃer'kjare] vт (*botte*) to hoop.

cerchiato, a [tʃer'kjato] AGG: **occhiali cerchiati d'osso** horn-rimmed spectacles; **hai gli occhi cerchiati** you've got dark rings under your eyes.

cerchietto [tʃer'kjetto] SM a (*per capelli*) hairband; **cerchietto d'oro** (*anello*) gold band b (*gioco*): **cerchietti** SMPL *game between 2 players in which each tries to throw a hoop over the other's stick.*

cerchio, chi ['tʃerkjo] SM (*gen, Geom, di persone*) circle; (*di ruota*) rim; (*giocattolo, di botte*) hoop; **mettersi in cerchio** to stand in a circle; **dare un colpo al cerchio e uno alla botte** (*fig*) to keep two things going at the same time; **avere un cerchio alla testa** (*fig: mal di testa*) to have a headache ► **cerchi in lega leggera** (*Aut*) light-alloy wheels.

cerchione [tʃer'kjone] SM (wheel)rim.

cereale [tʃere'ale] AGG, SM cereal.

cerebrale [tʃere'brale] AGG cerebral.

cerebralmente [tʃerebral'mente] AVV in a cerebral way.

cerebroleso, a [tʃerebro'lezo] SM/F person suffering from brain damage.

cereo, a ['tʃɛreo] AGG (*volto*) wan, waxen.

Cerere ['tʃɛrere] SF Ceres.

ceretta [tʃe'retta] SF (*per depilazione*) depilatory wax ► **ceretta a caldo/freddo** hot/cold (depilatory) wax.

cerfoglio, gli [tʃer'fɔʎʎo] SM chervil; **cerfoglio selvatico** cow parsley.

cerimonia [tʃeri'mɔnja] SF a ceremony; (*Rel*) service b : **cerimonie** SFPL ceremony *sg*; **fare cerimonie** to stand on ceremony; **senza tante cerimonie** (*senza formalità*) informally; (*bruscamente*) unceremoniously, without so much as a by-your-leave.

cerimoniale [tʃerimo'njale] SM (*regole*) ritual, custom, etiquette; (*libro*) book of etiquette, ceremonial; **cerimoniale di corte** court etiquette.

cerimoniere [tʃerimo'njɛre] SM master of ceremonies.

cerimoniosamente [tʃerimonjosa'mente] AVV ceremoniously.

cerimonioso, a [tʃerimo'njoso] AGG ceremonious, formal.

cerino [tʃe'rino] SM (*fiammifero*) wax match; (*stoppino*) taper.

C.E.R.N. [tʃɛrn] SIGLA M (= *Comitato Europeo di Ricerche Nucleari*) CERN.

cernia ['tʃɛrnja] SF (*anche:* **cernia gigante**) groper; (*anche:* **cernia di fondo**) stone bass.

cerniera [tʃer'njɛra] SF (*di porte, finestre*) hinge; (*di abito: anche:* **cerniera lampo**) žip (fastener) (*Brit*), zipper (*Am*); (*di bracciale*) clasp.

cernita ['tʃɛrnita] SF selection; **fare una cernita di** to select.

cero ['tʃero] SM (church) candle.

cerone [tʃe'rone] SM (*trucco*) greasepaint.

cerotto [tʃe'rɔtto] SM (*Med*) (sticking) plaster (*Brit*), Bandaid ® (*Am*).

cerro ['tʃɛrro] SM (*albero*) Turkey oak.

certamente [tʃerta'mente] AVV certainly, surely.

certezza [tʃer'tettsa] SF certainty; **avere la certezza che...** to be certain *o* sure that ...; **sapere con certezza che...** to know for sure that ... .

certificare [tʃertifi'kare] vт to certify.

certificato [tʃertifi'kato] SM certificate ► **certificato azionario** share certificate ► **certificato di credito del Tesoro** government bond, treasury bill (*Am*) ► **certificato di matrimonio** marriage certificate ► **certificato medico** doctor's certificate, medical certificate ► **certificato di nascita** birth certificate.

certificazione [tʃertifikat'tsjone] SF a (*di documento*) certification b : **certificazione di bilancio** (*Econ*) external audit.

certo, a ['tʃɛrto] 1 AGG a (*dopo sostantivo: indubbio: gen*) certain; (: *prova*) positive, definite; **è cosa certa** it's quite certain, there's no doubt about it; **è un sintomo certo di malattia** it's a sure sign of illness
b (*sicuro*) certain, sure; **essere certo di qc/di fare qc** to be sure *o* certain of sth/of doing sth; **sono certo che verrà** I'm sure she'll come.
2 AGG INDEF (*prima del sostantivo*) a certain; **devo sbrigare una certa faccenda** there is a certain matter I must attend to; **un certo signor Bonanno** a (certain) Mr Bonanno; **c'è un certo Stefano che ti cerca** someone called Stefano is looking for you; **in un certo senso** in a

way, in a certain sense; **in certi casi** in some *o* certain cases; **un certo non so che** an indefinable something **b** (*con valore intensivo*) some; **avere una certa età** to be getting on; **di una certa età** past one's prime, not so young; **un fatto di una certa importanza** a fact of some importance; **in quel locale c'erano certe facce!** there were some really unpleasant faces in that place!; **ho visto certe borse oggi - le avrei comprate tutte** I saw some terrific handbags today - I could have bought the lot.

3 PRON INDEF PL: **certi/e** (*persone*) some (people); (*cose*) some.

4 AVV certainly; (*senz'altro*) of course; **certo che sì/no** certainly/certainly not; **certo che puoi!** of course you can!; **sì certo** yes indeed; **no certo** certainly not.

5 SM: **di certo** certainly.

certosino [tʃerto'zino] SM Carthusian monk; (*liquore*) chartreuse; **è un lavoro da certosino** it's a pernickety job.

certuni [tʃer'tuni] PRON PL INDEF some (people).

cerume [tʃe'rume] SM (ear) wax.

cerva ['tʃɛrva] SF female (deer), doe.

cervella [tʃer'vɛlla] SF PL (*Culin*) brains *pl*.

cervelletto [tʃervel'letto] SM cerebellum.

cervello [tʃer'vɛllo] SM **a** (*Anat*) (*pl f* **cervella**) brain, brains: **far saltare le cervella a qn** to blow sb's brains out

b (*fig: intelligenza*): **avere molto cervello** to be very clever; **ha poco cervello** he's not very bright; **avere il cervello fino** to be sharp-witted; **avere il cervello di una gallina** to be brainless *o* peabrained; **dovevi avere abbastanza cervello da evitarlo** you should have had enough sense to avoid it; **gli ha dato di volta il cervello** he's gone off his head ▶ **cervello elettronico** computer **c** (*persona*) mind; **è lui il cervello della banda?** is he the brains behind the operation?; **fuga dei cervelli** brain drain.

cervelloticamente [tʃervellotika'mente] AVV bizarrely, oddly.

cervellotico, a, ci, che [tʃervel'lɔtiko] AGG bizarre, odd.

cervicale [tʃervi'kale] AGG cervical.

cervice [tʃer'vitʃe] SF cervix.

Cervino [tʃer'vino] SM Matterhorn.

cervo ['tʃɛrvo] SM **a** (*mammifero*) deer; (: *maschio*) stag; (: *femmina*) doe; **carne di cervo** venison **b** (*insetto*): **cervo volante** stag beetle.

Cesare ['tʃezare] SM Caesar.

cesareo, a [tʃe'zareo] AGG (*anche Med*) Caesarean (*Brit*), Cesarean (*Am*); **parto cesareo** Caesarean (section).

cesellare [tʃezel'lare] VT to chisel; (*incidere*) to engrave.

cesellatore, trice [tʃezella'tore] SM/F engraver.

cesellatura [tʃezella'tura] SF (*lavoro*) chiselling; (*Arte*) engraving.

cesello [tʃe'zɛllo] SM (*strumento*) chisel; (*Arte*) engraving.

C.E.S.I.S. [tʃezis] SIGLA M (= *Comitato Esecutivo per i Servizi di Informazione e di Sicurezza*) *committee on intelligence and security matters, reporting to the Prime Minister.*

cesoie [tʃe'zoje] SFPL shears.

cespite ['tʃɛspite] SM (source of) income.

cespo ['tʃɛspo] SM tuft.

cespuglio, gli [tʃes'puʎʎo] SM bush.

cespuglioso, a [tʃespuʎ'ʎoso] AGG (*anche fig*) bushy.

cessare [tʃes'sare] **1** VI **a** (*aus* **essere**) (*aver termine*: *pioggia, vento, rumore*) to stop **b** (*aus* **avere**) (*smettere*):

cessare di fare qc to stop doing sth.

2 VT to stop, put an end to; (*produzione*) to discontinue; **cessare il fuoco** (*Mil*) to cease fire; **"cessato allarme"** "all clear".

cessate il fuoco [tʃes'sate il 'fwɔko] SM INV ceasefire.

cessazione [tʃessat'tsjone] SF cessation; (*interruzione*) suspension.

cessione [tʃes'sjone] SF transfer.

cesso ['tʃɛsso] SM (*fam: gabinetto*) bog (*Brit*), john (*Am*); (: *pegg: luogo*) dive; **quel film era proprio un cesso** that film was a load of shit (*fam!*).

cesta ['tʃesta] SF (large) basket.

cestello [tʃes'tɛllo] SM (*per bottiglie*) crate; (*di lavatrice*) drum.

cestinare [tʃesti'nare] VT to throw away; (*fig: proposta*) to turn down; (: *romanzo*) to reject.

cestino [tʃes'tino] SM basket; (*per la carta straccia*) wastepaper basket ▶ **cestino da lavoro** (*Cucito*) work basket, sewing basket ▶ **cestino dei rifiuti** litter bin (*Brit*), trashcan (*Am*) ▶ **cestino da viaggio** packed lunch *o* dinner (*for train travellers*).

cesto ['tʃesto] SM (*gen, Sport*) basket.

cesura [tʃe'zura] SF caesura.

cetaceo [tʃe'tatʃeo] SM sea mammal.

ceto ['tʃɛto] SM (social) class.

cetra ['tʃetra] SF zither.

cetriolino [tʃetrio'lino] SM gherkin.

cetriolo [tʃetri'ɔlo] SM cucumber.

cf., cfr. ABBR (= *confronta*) cf.

CFC [tʃieffe'tʃi] SIGLA MPL (= *clorofluorocarburi*) CFC.

C.F.S. [tʃieffe'ɛsse] SIGLA M (= *Corpo Forestale dello Stato*) *body responsible for the planting and management of forests.*

cg ABBR (= *centigrammo*) cg.

C.G.I.L. [tʃidʒi'ɛlle] SIGLA F (= *Confederazione Generale Italiana del Lavoro*) *trades union organization.*

CH SIGLA = *Chieti.*

chalet [ʃa'lɛ] SM INV chalet.

champagne [ʃã'paɲ] SM INV champagne.

chance [ʃãs] SF INV chance.

charlotte [ʃar'lɔt] SF INV (*Culin*) charlotte.

charme [ʃarm] SM charm.

charter ['tʃa:tə] **1** AGG INV (*volo*) charter *attr*; (*aereo*) chartered.

2 SM INV (*aereo*) chartered plane.

chassis [ʃa'si] SM INV chassis.

---

che [ke]

1 PRON

a (*relativo: persona: soggetto*) who; (: *oggetto*) whom, that; (: *cosa, animale*) which, that (*spesso omesso*);

▷ **l'uomo che sta parlando** the man who is speaking

▷ **la ragazza che hai visto** the girl whom you saw

▷ **i bambini che vedi nel cortile** the children whom *o* that you see in the yard

▷ **il giorno che...** the day (that) ...

▷ **la sera che ti ho visto** the evening I saw you

▷ **il libro che è sul tavolo** the book which *o* that is on the table

b (*la qual cosa*) which;

▷ **dovrei ottenere il massimo dei voti, il che è improbabile** I would have to get top marks, which is unlikely

c (*indefinito*)

▷**quell'uomo ha *un* che di losco** there's something suspicious about that man
▷***un certo* non so che** an indefinable something
▷**quel film non era *un gran* che** that film was nothing special
▷**quella ragazza ha *un non so* che di affascinante** there's something fascinating about that girl
d (*interrogativo*) what;
▷**che (cosa) fai?** what are you doing?
▷**di che (cosa) hai bisogno?** what do you need?
▷**non so che dire** I don't know what to say
▷**ma che dite!** what are you saying!
2 AGG
a (*interrogativo*) what; (: *di numero limitato*) which;
▷**che giorno è oggi?** what day is it today?
▷**che vestito ti vuoi mettere?** what (*o* which) dress do you want to put on?
▷**di che attore stai parlando?** which actor are you talking about?
b ESCL what;
▷**che *bel* vestito!** what a lovely dress!
▷**che *buono*!** how delicious!
▷**guarda in che *stato* sei ridotto!** look at the mess you're in!
3 CONG
a (*con proposizioni subordinate*) that (*talvolta omesso*);
▷**ero *così* felice che corsi a dirlo a tutti** I was so happy (that) I ran off to tell everyone
▷**nasconditi qui che *non* ti veda nessuno** hide here, so nobody can see you
▷**so che tu c'eri** I know (that) you were there
▷***voglio* che tu venga** I want you to come
b (*temporale*)
▷**mi sono svegliato che era ancora buio** it was still dark when I woke up
▷**sono anni che non lo vedo** I haven't seen him for *o* in years, it's years since I saw him
▷**era *appena* uscita di casa che suonò il telefono** she had no sooner gone out than *o* she had hardly gone out when the telephone rang
▷**arrivai che eri *già* partito** you had already left when I arrived
c (*in frasi imperative, in concessive*)
▷**che venga pure!** let him come by all means!
▷**che sia benedetto!** may God bless him!
d
▷***non* che sia stupido** not that he's stupid
▷***non* è che non mi interessi la commedia, è che sono stanco e vorrei andare a letto** it's not that the play doesn't interest me, it's just that I'm tired and I'd like to go to bed
▷**che tu venga *o* no, noi partiamo lo stesso** we're leaving whether you come or not
e (*comparativo: con più, meno*) than;
▷**è *più* furbo che intelligente** he's more cunning than intelligent; vedi anche **non, più, meno, così** ecc.

chef [ʃɛf] SM INV chef.
chela ['kɛla] SF nipper.
chemin de fer [ʃəˈmɛ̃dˈfɛr] SM INV (*Carte*) chemin de fer.
chemioterapia [kemjoteraˈpia] SF chemotherapy.
chemiotropismo [kemjotroˈpizmo] SM chemotropism.
chemisier [ʃəmiˈzje] SM INV shirtwaister (*Brit*), shirtwaist (*Am*).

chepì [keˈpi] SM INV kepi.
chèque [ʃɛk] SM INV cheque (*Brit*), check (*Am*).
cheratina [keraˈtina] SF keratin.
cherosene [keroˈzɛne] SM paraffin (*Brit*), kerosene (*Am*).
cherubino [keruˈbino] SM (*anche fig*) cherub.
chetare [keˈtare] **1** VT to hush, silence.
  2 chetarsi VIP to quieten down, fall silent.
chetichella [ketiˈkɛlla] AVV: **alla chetichella** unobtrusively, stealthily; **andarsene alla chetichella** to slip away.
cheto, a ['keto] AGG quiet, silent.
chetone [keˈtone] SM (*Chim*) ketone.

chi [ki] PRON
a (*interrogativo: soggetto*) who; (: *oggetto*) who, whom;
▷**non sapevo a chi rivolgermi** I didn't know who to ask
▷**con chi desidera parlare?** who do you wish to speak to (*Brit*) *o* with (*Am*)?
▷**con chi parli?** who are you talking to?, to whom are you talking?
▷**di chi è questo libro?** whose book is this?, whose is this book?
▷**di chi stai parlando?** who are you talking about?
▷**dimmi chi ti piace *di più* tra loro** tell me which of them you like best
▷**ha telefonato *non so* chi per te** somebody or other phoned up for you
▷**chi l'ha visto?** who saw him?
▷**chi viene di voi?** which of you is coming?
▷**chi hai visto?** who *o* whom did you see?
b (*relativo*) whoever, anyone who;
▷**lo racconterò *a* chi so io** I know who I'll tell about it
▷**lo riferirò *a* chi di dovere** I'll pass it on to the relevant person
▷**esco *con* chi mi pare** I'll go out with whoever I like
▷**so io *di* chi parlo** I'm naming no names
▷**invita chi *vuoi*** invite whoever *o* anyone you like
▷**chi arriva prima vince** whoever gets there first wins
c (*indefinito*): **chi... chi...** some ...some ..., some ...others ...;
▷**i bambini hanno avuto i regali: chi dolci, chi giocattoli e così via** the children have had their presents: some got sweets, others toys and so on
▷**chi dice una cosa, chi un'altra** some say one thing, some another
d (*fraseologia*)
▷***ride* bene chi ride ultimo** (*Proverbio*) he who laughs last laughs longest (*Brit*) *o* best (*Am*)
▷**si *salvi* chi può** every man for himself
▷**chi si *somiglia* si piglia** (*Proverbio*) birds of a feather flock together
▷**chi *va piano* va sano e va lontano** (*Proverbio*) more haste less speed.

chiacchiera ['kjakkjera] SF **a** : **chiacchiere** SFPL (*conversazione*) chatter *sg*; (*pettegolezzi*) gossip *sg*, talk *sg*; **fare due o quattro chiacchiere** to have a chat; **perdersi in chiacchiere** to waste time talking **c** (*loquacità*) talkativeness; **con la sua chiacchiera convincerebbe chiunque** with his gift of the gab he could persuade anyone.
chiacchierare [kjakkjeˈrare] VI (*aus avere*) to chat; (*discorrere futilmente*) to chatter; (*spettegolare*) to gossip; **una**

relazione molto chiacchierata a much talked about relationship.

chiacchierata [kjakkje'rata] SF chat; **farsi una chiacchierata** to have a chat.

chiacchierio, rii [kjakkje'rio] SM chattering.

chiacchierone, a [kjakkje'rone] 1 SM/F chatterbox; (*pegg*) gossip.
2 AGG talkative, chatty; (*pegg*) gossipy.

chiamare [kja'mare] 1 VT **a** (*persona*) to call; (*nome*) to call out; (*per telefono*) to call, phone; **chiamare qn per nome** to call *o* address sb by his (*o* her) name; **chiamare qn a gran voce** to call out loudly to sb; **chiamare qn da parte** to take sb aside; **chiamare (qn in) aiuto** to call (sb) for help; **mandare a chiamare qn** to send for sb, call sb in; **mi sono fatto chiamare presto stamattina** (*svegliare*) I asked to be called early this morning
b (*dare un nome*) to call, name; (*soprannominare*) to (nick)name, call; **e chiamala sfortuna!** and you call that bad luck!
c (*Mil*): **chiamare alle armi** to call up
d (*Dir*): **chiamare qn in giudizio** *o* **in causa** to summons sb; **non mi chiamare in causa!** (*fig*) don't bring me into it!.
2 **chiamarsi** VIP: **come ti chiami? — mi chiamo Michela** what's your name? *o* what are you called? — my name is Michela *o* I'm called Michela; **questo è quello che si chiama un buon affare** that's what you call a bargain.

chiamata [kja'mata] SF (*gen*) call; (*Dir*) summons; **fare una chiamata** (*Telec*) to make a (phone) call ▶**chiamata alle armi** (*Mil*) call-up (*Brit*), draft (*Am*) ▶**chiamata alle urne** (*Pol*) election.

chiappa ['kjappa] SF (*fam*: *natica*) cheek; **chiappe** SFPL backside *sg*; **alza le chiappe!** get up off your backside!

chiara ['kjara] SF (*fam*) egg white.

chiaramente [kjara'mente] AVV (*in modo chiaro*) clearly; (*francamente*) frankly; **chiaramente, potremmo farlo così** obviously, we could do it this way.

chiarezza [kja'rettsa] SF (*anche fig*) clearness, clarity.

chiarificare [kjarifi'kare] VT (*anche fig*) to clarify, make clear.

chiarificatore, trice [kjarifika'tore] AGG clarifying, explanatory; **avere un incontro chiarificatore** to have a meeting to clarify matters.

chiarificazione [kjarifikat'tsjone] SF clarification *no pl*, explanation.

chiarimento [kjari'mento] SM clarification *no pl*, explanation.

chiarire [kja'rire] VT (*gen*) to clarify, make clear, explain; (*mistero, dubbio*) to clear up; **chiarire le idee a qn** to clarify things for sb; **ti chiarisco io le idee!** I'll sort you out!

chiaro, a ['kjaro] 1 AGG **a** (*di colore: mobili, vestiti*) light-coloured; (*colore*) light; (*capelli, carnagione*) fair; **pantaloni verde chiaro** light green trousers
b (*limpido: anche fig*) clear; (*luminoso*) bright; **si sta facendo chiaro** it's getting light, the day is dawning; **un no chiaro e tondo** a very definite no; **sarò chiaro** I'll come to the point; **sia chiara una cosa** let's get one thing straight
c (*evidente, ovvio*) obvious, clear; **è chiaro!** it's blatantly obvious.
2 SM **a** (*colore*): **vestirsi di chiaro** to wear light colours *o* light-coloured clothes
b (*luce, luminosità*) day, daylight; **fa chiaro alle 7** it gets

light at 7 o'clock; **chiaro di luna** moonlight; **mettere in chiaro qc** (*fig*) to clear sth up; **trasmissione in chiaro** (*TV*) uncoded broadcast.
3 AVV (*parlare, vedere*) clearly; **parliamoci chiaro** let's be frank.

chiarore [kja'rore] SM (diffuse) light; **col chiarore della luna** in the moonlight.

chiaroscuro [kjaros'kuro] SM (*Pittura*) chiaroscuro.

chiaroveggente [kjaroved'dʒɛnte] AGG, SM/F clairvoyant.

chiaroveggenza [kjaroved'dʒɛntsa] SF clairvoyance.

chiasso ['kjasso] SM din, uproar; **far chiasso** to make a din; (*fig*) to make a fuss; (*scalpore*) to cause a stir.

chiassosamente [kjassosa'mente] AVV (*vedi agg*) noisily; gaudily.

chiassoso, a [kjas'soso] AGG (*rumoroso*) noisy, rowdy; (*vistoso: colori*) showy, gaudy.

chiatta ['kjatta] SF barge.

chiavare [kja'vare] VT, VI (*aus avere*) (*fam!*) to screw (*fam!*)

chiavata [kja'vata] SF (*fam!*) screw (*fam!*)

chiave ['kjave] 1 SF **a** (*gen, fig*) key; **chiudere a chiave** to lock; **tenere sotto chiave** (*anche fig*) to keep under lock and key; **prezzo chiavi in mano** (*di macchina*) on-the-road price (*Brit*), sticker price (*Am*); (*di casa*) price with immediate entry *o* possession; **in chiave politica** in political terms; **rifare qc in chiave moderna** to produce a modern version of sth; **la chiave di lettura di questo brano...** the key to an understanding of this passage ...; **chiave di basso/di violino** (*Mus*) bass/treble clef ▶**chiave d'accensione** (*Aut*) ignition key
b (*Tecn*) spanner (*Brit*), wrench (*Am*) ▶**chiave a brugola** Allen key ▶**chiave a bussola** socket wrench ▶**chiave a croce** spider ▶**chiave fissa** spanner (*Brit*), wrench (*Am*) ▶**chiave a forcella** fork spanner (*Brit*) *o* wrench (*Am*) ▶**chiave inglese** monkey wrench ▶**chiave a rullino** adjustable spanner (*Brit*) *o* wrench (*Am*) ▶**chiave torsiometrica** *o* **tarata** torque wrench
c (*Archit*): **chiave di volta** (*anche fig*) keystone.
2 AGG INV key *attr*.

chiavetta [kja'vetta] SF (*Tecn*) key; (*di orologio*) winder.

chiavistello [kjavis'tɛllo] SM bolt.

chiazza ['kjattsa] SF stain, splash; **chiazza di petrolio** oil slick.

chiazzare [kjat'tsare] VT to stain, splash.

chic [ʃik] AGG INV chic, elegant.

chicane [ʃi'kan] SF INV (*Aut*) chicane.

chicchessia [kikkes'sia] PRON INDEF anyone, anybody.

chicchirichì [kikkiri'ki] ESCL, SM INV cock-a-doodle-doo.

chicco, chi ['kikko] SM (*di cereale, riso*) grain; (*di caffè*) bean; (*d'uva*) grape; (*di rosario*) bead; (*di grandine*) hailstone.

chiedere ['kjɛdere] VB IRREG 1 VT **a** (*per sapere*) to ask; (*per avere*) to ask for; (: *intervista*) to ask for, request; (: *intervento, volontari*) to call for; **chiedere qc a qn** to ask sb for sth; **chiedere scusa a qn** to apologize to sb; **chiedersi (se)** to wonder (whether); **chiedo scusa!** I'm sorry!; **chiedere a qn di fare qc** *o* **che faccia qc** to ask sb to do sth; **chiedere il permesso di fare qc** to ask permission to do sth; **chiedere notizie di qn** to inquire *o* ask after sb; **mi ha chiesto del mio viaggio** he asked me about my trip; **ci chiede di partire** he wants us *o* is asking us to go
b (*fraseologia*): **chiedere il divorzio** to ask for a divorce; **chiedere l'elemosina** to beg; **chiedere giustizia** to demand justice; **chiedere l'impossibile** to ask (for) the impossible; **chiedere la mano di qn** to ask for sb's hand

in marriage; **chiedere la pace** to sue for peace; **non chiedo altro** that's all I want; **non chiedo altro che partire con te** all I want is to leave with you.

  [2] VI (*aus* avere): **chiedere di qn** (*salute*) to ask about *o* after sb; (*al telefono*) to ask for sb, want sb; (*per vederlo*) to ask for sb; **il padrone chiede di te** the boss wants to see you.

chierica ['kjɛrika] SF (*Rel*) tonsure; (*fig*) bald patch.

chierichetto [kjeri'ketto] SM altar boy.

chierico, ci ['kjɛriko] SM (*Rel*) cleric; (: *seminarista*) seminarist.

chiesa ['kjɛza] SF church; **Chiesa anglicana** Church of England; **Chiesa cattolica** (Roman) Catholic Church; **essere di chiesa** to be a churchgoer.

chiesi ecc ['kjɛzi] VB vedi **chiedere**.

chiesto, a ['kjɛsto] PP di **chiedere**.

chiffon [ʃi'fɔ̃] SM INV chiffon.

Chigi ['kidʒi] SM: **palazzo Chigi** (*Pol*) *offices of the Italian Prime Minister.*

chiglia ['kiʎʎa] SF keel.

chignon [ʃi'ɲɔ̃] SM INV chignon.

chihuahua SM INV chihuahua.

chilo ['kilo] [1] SM kilo.

  [2] PREF: **chilo-** kilo ... .

chilogrammo [kilo'grammo] SM kilogram(me).

chilohertz SM INV kilohertz.

chilometraggio, gi [kilome'traddʒo] SM (*Aut*) ≈ mileage.

chilometrico, a, ci, che [kilo'mɛtriko] AGG kilometric; (*fig*) endless.

chilometro [ki'lɔmetro] SM kilometre (*Brit*), kilometer (*Am*).

chilowatt ['kilovat] SM INV kilowatt.

chilowattora [kilovat'tora] SM INV kilowatt hour.

chimera [ki'mɛra] SF chimera.

chimica ['kimika] SF chemistry.

chimicamente [kimika'mente] AVV chemically.

chimico, a, ci, che ['kimiko] [1] AGG chemical; **sostanza chimica** chemical.

  [2] SM/F chemist.

chimono [ki'mɔno] SM INV kimono.

china[1] ['kina] SF (*pendio*) slope, descent; (*salita*) incline; **risalire la china** (*fig*) to be on the road to recovery.

china[2] ['kina] SF (*albero*) cinchona; (*liquore*) *drink made with alcohol and cinchona bark.*

china[3] ['kina] SF (*inchiostro*) Indian ink.

chinare [ki'nare] [1] VT to lower, bend; **chinare il capo** (*anche fig*) to bow one's head.

  [2] **chinarsi** VR to stoop, bend (over).

chincaglieria [kinkaʎʎe'ria] SF **a** (*negozio*) fancy-goods shop **b**: **chincaglierie** SFPL (*cianfrusaglie*) fancy goods, knick-knacks.

chinino [ki'nino] SM quinine.

chino, a ['kino] AGG: **a capo chino, a testa china** head bent *o* bowed.

chinotto [ki'nɔtto] SM (*bevanda*) *type of bitter orange drink.*

chintz [tʃints] SM INV chintz.

chioccia, ce ['kjɔttʃa] SF broody hen.

chioccio, cia, ci, ce ['kjɔttʃo] AGG (*voce*) clucking.

chiocciola ['kjɔttʃola] SF (*Zool*) snail; **scala a chiocciola** spiral staircase.

chiodato, a [kjo'dato] AGG (*scarpe, bastone*) spiked; **pneumatici chiodati** snow tyres (*Brit*) *o* tires (*Am*).

chiodino [kjo'dino] SM **a** (*piccolo chiodo*) tack, small nail

b (*fungo*) honey fungus.

chiodo ['kjɔdo] SM **a** (*Tecn*) nail; (: *per lamiere*) rivet; (*da scarpone*) hobnail; (*Alpinismo*) piton; (*di scarpe da calcio*) stud; (*di scarpe da atleta, pneumatico*) spike; **per lui è diventato un chiodo fisso** it's become a fixation with him; **roba da chiodi!** it's unbelievable!; **chiodo scaccia chiodo** (*Proverbio*) one problem drives away another ▶ **chiodo a espansione** expansion bolt ▶ **chiodo da ghiaccio** (*Alpinismo*) ice piton

  b (*Culin*): **chiodo di garofano** clove.

chioma ['kjɔma] SF (*capelli*) head of hair; (*di cavallo*) mane; (*di albero*) foliage; (*di cometa*) tail.

chiomato, a [kjo'mato] AGG (*letter*: *frondoso: albero*) leafy; (: *con pennacchio: elmo*) plumed.

chiosa ['kjoza] SF gloss, note.

chiosare [kjo'zare] VT to gloss, annotate.

chiosco, schi ['kjɔsko] SM kiosk, stall.

chiostro ['kjɔstro] SM cloister.

chiromante [kiro'mante] SM/F palmist; (*indovino*) fortune-teller.

chiromanzia [kiroman'tsia] SF (*vedi sm/f*) palmistry; fortune-telling.

chiropratico, a, ci, che [kiro'pratiko] SM/F chiropractor.

chiroterapia [kirotera'pia] SF chiropractic.

chirurgia [kirur'dʒia] SF surgery; **chirurgia plastica** plastic surgery; **specialista in chirurgia plastica** plastic surgeon.

chirurgicamente [kirurdʒika'mente] AVV surgically; **intervenire chirurgicamente** to operate.

chirurgico, a, ci, che [ki'rurdʒiko] AGG (*Med, anche fig*) surgical.

chirurgo, ghi *o* **gi** [ki'rurgo] SM surgeon.

chissà [kis'sa] AVV: **chissà!** who knows!, I wonder!; **chissà chi/come** goodness knows who/how; **chissà che non riesca** you never know, he might succeed.

chitarra [ki'tarra] SF guitar.

chitarrista, i, e [kitar'rista] SM/F guitarist, guitar player.

chiudere ['kjudere] VB IRREG [1] VT **a** to close, shut; (*pugno, lista, caso*) to close; (*busta, lettera*) to seal; (*giacca, camicia*) to do up, fasten; (*gas, rubinetto*) to switch off, turn off; **chiudere a chiave** to lock; **chiudere col catenaccio** to bolt; **sta sempre chiusa in casa** she never goes out; **chiudere la porta in faccia a qn** (*anche fig*) to slam the door in sb's face; **chiudere un occhio su** (*fig*) to turn a blind eye to; **chiudere gli occhi davanti a** (*fig*) to close one's eyes to; **chiudersi le dita nella porta** to catch one's fingers in the door; **non ho chiuso occhio tutta la notte** I didn't sleep a wink all night; **chiudi la bocca!** *o* **il becco!** (*fam*) shut up!

  b (*strada*) to block off; (*frontiera*) to close; (*aeroporto, negozio, scuola*) to close (down), shut (down); (*definitivamente: fabbrica*) to close down, shut down

  c (*recingere*) to enclose

  d (*terminare*) to end.

  [2] VI (*aus* avere) (*scuola, negozio*) to close, shut; (: *definitivamente*) to close down, shut down.

  [3] **chiudersi** VIP (*porta, ombrello*) to close, shut; (*fiore, ferita*) to close up; (*periodo lungo, vacanze*) to finish.

  [4] **chiudersi** VR: **chiudersi in casa** to shut o.s. up in the house; **chiudersi in se stesso** to withdraw into o.s.

chiunque [ki'unkwe] [1] PRON REL whoever, anyone who; **chiunque sia** whoever it is; **chiunque chiami, di' che non ci sono** if anyone phones, tell them I'm not in; **chiunque sia, fallo entrare** whoever that is, let them in; **di**

chiunque sia la colpa, nessuno la passerà liscia I don't care who is to blame, nobody's going to get away with it; **chiunque lo abbia fatto...** whoever did it ....

2 PRON INDEF anyone, anybody; **chiunque ti direbbe che hai torto** ask anybody and they'd tell you you're wrong; **potrebbe farlo chiunque** anyone could do it; **puoi chiederlo a chiunque** you can ask anybody; **chiunque altro** anyone else, anybody else; **posso farlo meglio di chiunque altro** I can do it better than anyone else.

chiurlo ['kjurlo] SM (*uccello*) curlew.

chiusa ['kjusa] SF **a** (*terreno circondato*) enclosure **b** (*sbarramento fluviale*) sluice; (: *per navigazione*) lock **c** (*di discorso*) conclusion, ending.

chiusi *ecc* ['kjusi] VB *vedi* **chiudere**.

chiuso, a ['kjuso] 1 PP *di* **chiudere**.

2 AGG **a** (*porta*) shut, closed; (: *a chiave*) locked; (*senza uscita: strada, corridoio*) blocked off; (*rubinetto*) off; **"chiuso"** (*negozio ecc*) "closed"; **"chiuso al pubblico"** "no admittance to the public"

b (*persona*) uncommunicative; (*mente*) narrow; (*ambiente, club*) exclusive

c (*concluso: discussione, seduta*) finished; (: *iscrizione, lista*) closed.

3 SM: **stare al chiuso** (*fig*) to be shut up; **odore di chiuso** musty smell.

chiusura [kju'sura] SF **a** (*fine*) end; (*Comm: definitiva*) closing down; **chiusura anticipata** early closing; **orario di chiusura** closing time; **termine di chiusura** closing date; **discorso di chiusura** closing speech

b (*di porta, cassaforte*) lock; (*di vestito*) fastening, fastener ►**chiusura centralizzata (delle porte)** (*Aut*) central locking (device) ►**chiusura ermetica** hermetic seal ►**chiusura lampo** zip (fastener) (*Brit*), zipper (*Am*) ►**chiusura di sicurezza** safety lock ►**chiusura sicurezza bambini** (*Aut*) child-proof lock

c (*Pol*): **chiusura verso la destra/sinistra** refusal to collaborate with the right/left.

ci [tʃi] (dav lo la, li, le, ne diventa **ce**) 1 PRON PERS **a** (*ogg diretto*) us; **ci hanno visto** they saw us; **ascoltaci** listen to us

b (*complemento di termine*) (to) us; **ci dai da mangiare?** will you give us something to eat?; **ce l'hanno dato** they gave it to us; **ci dissero di tornare più tardi** they told us to come back later

c (*con verbi riflessivi, pronominali, reciproci*): **ci siamo divertiti** we enjoyed ourselves; **ci siamo annoiati** we got bored; **ci vediamo più tardi!** see you later!; **ci amiamo** we love each other.

2 PRON DIMOSTR (*di ciò, su ciò, in ciò ecc*) about (*o* on *o* of) it; **non so che farci** I don't know what to do about it; **che c'entro io?** what have I got to do with it?; **ci puoi giurare, ci puoi scommettere** you can bet on it; **ci puoi contare** you can depend on it; **ci penserò** I'll think about it.

3 AVV **a** (*qui*) here; (*lì*) there; **qui non ci ritorno più** I'm not coming back here again; **son qui e ci resto** here I am and here I stay; **ci andiamo?** shall we go there?; **ci sei mai stato?** have you ever been there?; **ci sei?** (*sei pronto*) are you ready?; (*hai capito*) do you follow?; **non ci si sta tutti, non ci stiamo tutti** we won't all fit in

b : **c'è** there is; **ci sono** there are; **non c'era nessuno** there was nobody there; **c'è nessuno in casa?** is (there) anybody in?; **c'era una volta...** once upon a time ...

c (*con verbi di moto*): **ci passa sopra un ponte** a bridge passes over it; **non ci passa più nessuno per di qua**

nobody comes this way anymore; vedi **mancare**; **stare**; **volere** *ecc*.

C.I.A. ['tʃia] SIGLA F (= *Central Intelligence Agency*) CIA.

C.ia ABBR (= *compagnia*) Co.

ciabatta [tʃa'batta] SF slipper; **trattare qn come una ciabatta** to treat sb like dirt.

ciabattare [tʃabat'tare] VI (*aus* **avere**) to shuffle about (in one's slippers).

ciabattino [tʃabat'tino] SM cobbler.

ciac [tʃak] 1 ESCL (*camminando sul fango ecc*) squelch!; **ciac, si gira!** action!.

2 SM (*Cine*) clapper board.

Ciad [tʃad] SM: **il Ciad** Chad.

cialda ['tʃalda] SF wafer.

cialtrone, a [tʃal'trone] SM/F rascal, scoundrel.

ciambella [tʃam'bɛlla] SF **a** (*Culin*) *ring-shaped cake*; **non tutte le ciambelle riescono col buco** (*Proverbio*) things can't be expected to turn out right every time **b** (*oggetto: gen*) ring; (: *cuscino*) round cushion; (: *salvagente*) rubber ring; **a ciambella** ring-shaped.

ciambellano [tʃambel'lano] SM chamberlain.

ciancia, ce ['tʃantʃa] SF gossip *no pl*, tittle-tattle *no pl*.

cianciare [tʃan'tʃare] VI (*aus* **avere**) to gossip, tittle-tattle.

ciancicare [tʃantʃi'kare] VT (*parole*) to mumble; (*cibo*) to chew slowly; (*vestito*) to crush.

cianfrusaglia [tʃanfru'zaʎʎa] SF knick-knack; **cianfrusaglie** SFPL bits and pieces.

cianotico, a, ci, che [tʃa'nɔtiko] AGG cyanotic.

cianuro [tʃa'nuro] SM cyanide.

ciao ['tʃao] ESCL (*all'arrivo*) hello!, hi!; (*alla partenza*) bye(-bye)!

ciarlare [tʃar'lare] VI (*aus* **avere**) to chatter; (*pegg*) to gossip.

ciarlatano [tʃarla'tano] SM (*pegg: gen*) charlatan; (: *medico*) quack.

ciarliero, a [tʃar'ljɛro] AGG chatty, talkative.

ciarpame [tʃar'pame] SM rubbish, junk.

ciascuno, a [tʃas'kuno] 1 AGG (dav sm: **ciascun** + consonante, vocale, **ciascuno** + s impura, gn, pn, ps, x, z; dav sf: **ciascuna** + consonante, **ciascun'** + vocale) (*con valore distributivo*) every, each; (*ogni*) every; **ciascun ragazzo** every *o* each boy; **ciascun uomo nasce libero** every man is born free.

2 PRON INDEF (*con valore distributivo*) each (one); **ciascuno di** each (one) *o* every one of; **ciascuno di noi avrà la sua parte** each of us will have his share; **ci ha dato 10.000 lire (per) ciascuno** he gave each of us 10,000 lire; **costano 50.000 lire ciascuno** they cost 50,000 lire each.

cibare [tʃi'bare] 1 VT to feed.

2 **cibarsi** VR: **cibarsi di** (*anche fig*) to live on.

cibarie [tʃi'barje] SFPL foodstuffs, provisions.

cibernetica [tʃiber'nɛtika] SF cybernetics *sg*.

cibo ['tʃibo] SM food; **cibi precotti** ready-cooked food; **son 2 giorni che non tocca cibo** he hasn't eaten for 2 days.

ciborio, ri [tʃi'bɔrjo] SM (*Rel*) ciborium.

cicala [tʃi'kala] SF (*Zool*) cicada ►**cicala di mare** squilla.

cicalare [tʃika'lare] VI (*aus* **avere**) to chatter (away), jabber (away).

cicaleccio, ci [tʃika'lettʃo] SM (*di persone*) chatter, chattering; (*di uccelli*) chirping.

cicalino [tʃika'lino] SM (*cercapersone*) pager (*Brit*), bleeper (*Am*).

cicalio, lii [tʃika'lio] SM chatter, chattering.

cicatrice [tʃika'tritʃe] SF (*anche fig*) scar.

cicatrizzante [tʃikatridˈdzante] ①︎ AGG healing. ②︎ SM healing substance.

cicatrizzare [tʃikatridˈdzare] ①︎ VT, VI (aus avere) to heal ②︎ **cicatrizzarsi** VIP to form a scar, heal (up).

cicca, che [ˈtʃikka] SF **a** (mozzicone: di sigaretta) cigarette end, stub; (: di sigaro) cigar butt; **non vale una cicca** (fig) it's not worth tuppence (Brit) o a red cent (Am), it's worthless **b** (fam: sigaretta) fag.

cicchetto [tʃikˈketto] SM **a** (bicchierino) drop, nip; **andiamo a farci un cicchetto** let's go for a drink **b** (rimprovero) telling-off, ticking-off (Brit).

ciccia [ˈtʃittʃa] SF (fam: grasso umano) fat, flab; (: carne) meat; **avere troppa ciccia** to be on the plump side.

ciccione, a [tʃitˈtʃone] SM/F (fam) fatty.

Cicerone [tʃitʃeˈrone] SM (Storia) Cicero.

cicerone [tʃitʃeˈrone] SM (guida turistica) guide; **fare da cicerone a qn** to show sb around.

cicisbeo [tʃitʃizˈbɛo] SM (Storia) gallant; (damerino) dandy.

ciclabile [tʃiˈklabile] AGG suitable for cycling, cycle attr.

ciclamino [tʃiklaˈmino] SM cyclamen.

ciclicamente [tʃiklikaˈmente] AVV cyclically.

ciclicità [tʃiklitʃiˈta] SF cyclic nature.

ciclico, a, ci, che [ˈtʃikliko] AGG cyclical.

ciclismo [tʃiˈklizmo] SM cycling.

ciclista, i, e [tʃiˈklista] SM/F cyclist.

ciclistico, a, ci, che [tʃiˈklistiko] AGG cycle attr.

ciclo [ˈtʃiklo] SM (gen, Chim, Fis) cycle; (di lezioni, conferenze) series, course; **la malattia deve fare il suo ciclo** the illness must run its course ▶ **ciclo dell'azoto** nitrogen cycle ▶ **ciclo biologico** life history ▶ **ciclo del carbonio** carbon cycle.

ciclocross [tʃikloˈkrɔs] SM INV cyclocross.

cicloescursionismo [tʃikloeskursjoˈnizmo] SM cycling trips pl.

ciclomotore [tʃiklomoˈtore] SM moped.

ciclone [tʃiˈklone] SM cyclone; (fig) whirlwind.

ciclonico, a, ci, che [tʃiˈklɔniko] AGG cyclonic.

Ciclope [tʃiˈklɔpe] SM (Mitol) Cyclops sg.

ciclopico, a, ci, che [tʃiˈklɔpiko] AGG (fig) gigantic, huge.

ciclopista [tʃikloˈpista] SF cycle path, cycle track.

ciclostilare [tʃiklostiˈlare] VT to cyclostyle (Brit), mimeograph (Am), duplicate.

ciclostilato [tʃiklostiˈlato] SM duplicate (copy).

ciclostile [tʃiklosˈtile] SM **a** (macchina) cyclostyle (Brit), Mimeograph ® (Am), duplicator **b** (foglio) duplicate copy.

ciclotrone [tʃikloˈtrone] SM cyclotron.

cicloturismo [tʃiklotuˈrizmo] SM cycling holidays pl.

cicogna [tʃiˈkoɲɲa] SF **a** (uccello) stork **b** (autotreno) trailer lorry o truck.

cicoria [tʃiˈkɔrja] SF chicory.

cicuta [tʃiˈkuta] SF hemlock.

C.I.D.A. [ˈtʃida] SIGLA F = Confederazione Italiana Dirigenti d'Azienda.

ciecamente [tʃɛkaˈmente] AVV (anche fig) blindly.

cieco[1], a, chi, che [ˈtʃɛko] ①︎ AGG (anche fig) blind; **essere cieco da un occhio** to be blind in one eye; **alla cieca** (anche fig) blindly; **andare alla cieca** to grope along; **cieco come una talpa** as blind as a bat; **essere cieco d'amore** to be blinded by love; **vicolo cieco** (anche fig) blind alley. ②︎ SM/F blind man/woman; **i ciechi** the blind.

cieco[2] [ˈtʃɛko] SM (Anat) caecum (Brit), cecum (Am).

ciellino, a [tʃielˈlino] SM/F (Pol) member of CL movement.

cielo [ˈtʃɛlo] SM **a** sky; (letter) heavens pl; **miniera a cielo aperto** opencast mine; **toccare il cielo con un dito** (fig) to walk on air; **essere al settimo cielo** to be in seventh heaven; **volare nel cielo italiano** (Aer) to fly in Italian airspace **b** (Rel) heaven; **il regno dei cieli** the kingdom of heaven; **santo cielo!** good heavens!; **per amor del cielo!** for heaven's sake!; **voglia il cielo che torni presto** I hope to heaven (that) he comes back soon.

cifra [ˈtʃifra] SF **a** (numero) figure, numeral; **un numero di 5 cifre** a five-figure number; **scrivere un numero in cifre** to write a number in figures; **fare cifra tonda** to make a round figure **b** (somma di denaro) figure, sum; **è una cifra astronomica** it's an astronomical figure; **mi è costato una cifra** (fam) it cost me a fortune **c** : **cifre** SFPL (monogram) initials, monogram sg **d** (codice) code, cipher.

cifrare [tʃiˈfrare] VT **a** (messaggio) to (put into) code, encode, cipher **b** (lenzuola, camicie) to embroider initials o a monogram on.

cifrario, ri [tʃiˈfrarjo] SM code book.

cifrato, a [tʃiˈfrato] AGG **a** (codice) coded, ciphered **b** (lenzuola, camicie) monogrammed.

ciglio, gli [ˈtʃiʎʎo] SM **a** (pl f ciglia) (eye)lash: **ciglia finte** false eyelashes; **non ha battuto ciglio** (fig) he didn't bat an eyelid **b** (di strada, fossato) edge, side.

cigno [ˈtʃiɲɲo] SM swan.

cigolante [tʃigoˈlante] AGG (vedi vb) squeaking, creaking.

cigolare [tʃigoˈlare] VI (aus avere) (porta) to squeak, creak; (ruota) to squeak; (parquet) to creak.

cigolio, lii [tʃigoˈlio] SM (vedi vb) squeaking; creaking.

C.I.I.S. [ˈtʃiis] SIGLA M (= Comitato Interparlamentare per l'Informazione e la Sicurezza) all-party committee on intelligence and security.

Cile [ˈtʃile] SM: **il Cile** Chile.

cilecca [tʃiˈlekka] SF: **far cilecca** (fucile) to misfire; (fig) to fail; **le ginocchia mi hanno fatto cilecca** my knees gave way.

cileno, a [tʃiˈlɛno] AGG, SM/F Chilean.

ciliare [tʃiˈljare] AGG (Anat) ciliary.

cilicio, ci [tʃiˈlitʃo] SM hair shirt.

ciliegia, gie o **ge** [tʃiˈljɛdʒa] SF cherry.

ciliegina [tʃiljeˈdʒina] SF glacé cherry; **la ciliegina sulla torta** (fig) the icing o cherry on the cake.

ciliegio, gi [tʃiˈljɛdʒo] SM (albero) cherry (tree); (legno) cherry (wood); **ciliegio dolce** wild cherry.

cilindrata [tʃilinˈdrata] SF (Aut) (cubic) capacity; **macchina di grossa/piccola cilindrata** a big-engined/small-engined car.

cilindrico, a, ci, che [tʃiˈlindriko] AGG cylindrical.

cilindro [tʃiˈlindro] SM (gen, Tecn, Geom) cylinder; (di macchina da scrivere) roller; (cappello) top hat.

C.I.M. [ˈtʃim] SIGLA M (= centro d'igiene mentale) mental health centre.

cima [ˈtʃima] SF **a** (gen) top; (estremità) end; (di montagna) top, summit, peak; **conquistare una cima** (Alpinismo) to conquer a peak; **in cima a** (lista, classifica) at the top of; (montagna) at the top of, on the summit of; **da cima a fondo** from top to bottom; **leggere qc da cima a fondo** to read sth from beginning to end **b** (persona) genius; **è una cima in matematica** he's a genius at maths; **c** (Naut) rope, cable

d (*Bot*) top, head.

cimare [tʃi'mare] VT (*albero*) to pollard; (*tessuto*) to trim.

cimasa [tʃi'maza] SF moulding.

cimelio, li [tʃi'mɛljo] SM relic.

cimentare [tʃimen'tare] ① VT (*pazienza, persona*) to try, to put to the test.
② **cimentarsi** VR: **cimentarsi in qc** to undertake (the challenge of) sth; (*atleta, concorrente*) to try one's hand at sth; **cimentarsi con qn** to compete with sb.

cimento [tʃi'mento] SM (*prova rischiosa*) trial.

cimice ['tʃimitʃe] SF **a** (*Zool*) (bed)bug **b** (*radiotrasmittente*) bug.

cimiero [tʃi'mjɛro] SM crest; (*fig: elmo*) helmet.

ciminiera [tʃimi'njɛra] SF (*di fabbrica*) chimney (stack); (*di nave*) funnel.

cimitero [tʃimi'tɛro] SM cemetery, graveyard; **cimitero di automobili** scrapyard; **questo posto è un cimitero!** (*fig*) this place is like a morgue!

cimosa [tʃi'mosa] SF (*Tessitura*) selvage.

cimurro [tʃi'murro] SM distemper.

Cina ['tʃina] SF: **la Cina** China.

cinabro [tʃi'nabro] SM cinnabar.

cincia, ce ['tʃintʃa] SF (*uccello*) tit; **cincia mora** coal tit.

cinciallegra [tʃintʃal'legra] SF (*uccello*) great tit.

cinciarella [tʃintʃa'rɛlla] SF (*uccello*) bluetit.

cincillà [tʃintʃil'la] SM INV chinchilla.

cincin, cin cin [tʃin'tʃin] ESCL cheers!

Cincinnato [tʃintʃin'nato] SM (*Storia*) Cincinnatus.

cincischiare [tʃintʃis'kjare] VI (*aus avere*) (*perder tempo*) to mess about, fiddle about.

cine ['tʃine] SM INV (*fam*) cinema; **andare al cine** to go to the cinema.

cineamatore [tʃineama'tore] SM amateur film-maker (*Brit*) o moviemaker (*Am*).

cineasta, i, e [tʃine'asta] SM/F **a** person in the film (*Brit*) o movie (*Am*) industry; **è un cineasta** he's in films **b** film-maker (*Brit*), moviemaker (*Am*).

cinecamera [tʃine'kamera] SF cine camera.

cineclub [tʃine'klub] SM INV film club.

cineforum [tʃine'fɔrum] SM INV cinema discussion.

cinegiornale [tʃinedʒor'nale] SM newsreel.

cinema ['tʃinema] SM INV cinema; **andare al cinema** to go to the cinema *o* movies (*Am*); **cosa danno al cinema stasera?** what's on at the cinema tonight?; **fare del cinema** to be in the film business; **industria/divo del cinema** film industry/star ► **cinema muto** silent films.

cinema d'essai [sine'ma dɛ'sɛ] SM INV avant-garde cinema, experimental cinema.

cinemascope ['sinmǝskoup] SM INV Cinemascope ®.

cinematica [tʃine'matika] SF (*Fis*) kinematics *sg*.

cinematico, a, ci, che [tʃine'matiko] AGG kinematic.

cinematografare [tʃinematogra'fare] VT to film.

cinematografia [tʃinematogra'fia] SF (*arte, tecnica*) cinematography; (*industria*) film-making (*Brit*) *o* moviemaking (*Am*) industry, cinema.

cinematograficamente [tʃinematografika'mente] AVV cinematographically; **realizzare cinematograficamente** to make into a film (*Brit*) *o* movie (*Am*).

cinematografico, a, ci, che [tʃinemato'grafiko] AGG **a** (*attore, critica, festival*) film (*Brit*) *attr*, movie (*Am*) *attr*; **casa cinematografica** film studio, film company; **regista cinematografico** film director; **sala cinematografica** cinema; **successo cinematografico** box-office success **b** (*fig: stile*) cinematographic.

cinematografo [tʃinema'tɔgrafo] SM (*locale*) cinema (*Brit*), movie theatre (*Am*); (*arte*) cinema, films *pl* (*Brit*), movies *pl* (*Am*).

cinepresa [tʃine'presa] SF cine camera.

cinerario, ria, ri, rie [tʃine'rarjo] AGG: **urna cineraria** funeral urn.

cinereo, a [tʃi'nɛreo] AGG (*colore*) ash-grey; (*pallido*) pale, ashen.

cinescopio, pi [tʃines'kɔpjo] SM (*TV*) cathode-ray tube.

cinese [tʃi'nese] ① AGG Chinese.
② SM/F Chinese man/woman; **i Cinesi** the Chinese.
③ SM (*lingua*) Chinese.

cineseria [tʃinese'ria] SF chinoiserie.

cineteca, che [tʃine'tɛka] SF (*collezione*) film collection, film library; (*locale*) film library.

cinetica [tʃi'nɛtika] SF kinetics *sg*.

cinetico, a, ci, che [tʃi'nɛtiko] AGG kinetic.

cingere ['tʃindʒere] VT IRREG **a** (*circondare*) to surround, encircle; **cingere una città di mura** to surround a city with walls; **cingere d'assedio** to besiege, lay siege to **b** (*avvolgere*): **le cinse la vita con le braccia** he put his arms round her waist; **cingersi la vita con una corda** to tie a rope round one's waist; **cingersi la testa con fiori** to wreath one's head with flowers.

cinghia ['tʃingja] SF (*cintura*) belt, strap; (*di portabagagli, zaino*) strap; (*Tecn*) belt; (*Equitazione*) girth; **tirare la cinghia** (*fig*) to tighten one's belt ► **cinghia di trasmissione** drive belt ► **cinghia del ventilatore** fan belt.

cinghiale [tʃin'gjale] SM (*animale*) wild boar; (*pelle*) pigskin.

cinghiata [tʃin'gjata] SF: **prendere qn a cinghiate** to give sb a leathering.

cingolato, a [tʃingo'lato] AGG (*veicolo*) caterpillar *attr*.

cingolo ['tʃingolo] SM (*di veicoli*) caterpillar.

cinguettare [tʃingwet'tare] VI (*aus avere*) (*uccelli*) to twitter; (*bambini*) to chatter.

cinguettio, tii [tʃingwet'tio] SM (*vedi vb*) twittering; chattering.

cinicamente [tʃinika'mente] AVV cynically.

cinico, a, ci, che ['tʃiniko] ① AGG cynical.
② SM/F cynic.

ciniglia [tʃi'niʎʎa] SF chenille.

cinismo [tʃi'nizmo] SM cynicism.

cinofilo, a [tʃi'nɔfilo] SM/F dog lover.

cinquanta [tʃin'kwanta] AGG INV, SM INV fifty; **gli anni cinquanta** the Fifties, the 50s; **cinquantuno** fifty-one.

cinquantenario, ri [tʃinkwante'narjo] SM fiftieth anniversary.

cinquantenne [tʃinkwan'tɛnne] ① AGG fifty-year-old; **un signore cinquantenne** a man of fifty, a fifty-year-old man.
② SM/F fifty-year-old man/woman; (*sulla cinquantina*) man/woman in his/her fifties.

cinquantennio, ni [tʃinkwan'tɛnnjo] SM (period of) fifty years.

cinquantesimo, a [tʃinkwan'tɛzimo] AGG, SM/F, SM fiftieth.

cinquantina [tʃinkwan'tina] SF **a**: **una cinquantina (di)** about fifty, fifty or so; **eravamo una cinquantina** there were about fifty of us **b** (*età*): **avere una cinquantina d'anni** OR **essere sulla cinquantina** (*persona*) to be about fifty, be in one's fifties; **avere una cinquantina d'anni** (*mobile, casa*) to be about fifty years old.

cinque ['tʃinkwe] ① AGG INV five; **paragrafo/pagina/capitolo cinque** paragraph/page/chapter five; **i cinque**

settimi della cifra five-sevenths of the amount; **abito in Via Cavour, numero cinque** I live at number five Via Cavour; **un bambino di cinque anni** a child of five; **ha cinque anni** he is five; **un biglietto da cinque sterline** a five-pound note; **siamo in cinque** there are five of us; **sono le due meno cinque** it's five to two; **sono arrivati alle cinque** they arrived at five o'clock; **le cinque di sera** five o'clock in the evening; **cinque volte su dieci** five times out of ten; **mettersi in fila per cinque** to form rows of five.

[2] SM INV five; **due più tre fa cinque** two plus three make five; **il cinque nel dieci ci sta due volte** five goes into ten twice; **uno sconto del cinque per cento** a five percent discount; **abito in Via Cavour cinque** I live at 5 Via Cavour; **il cinque dicembre 1988** the fifth of December 1988; **arrivare il cinque ottobre** to arrive on October 5th; **prendere un cinque** (Scol) to get five out of ten; **il cinque di fiori** (Carte) the five of clubs.

cinquecentesco, a, schi, sche [tʃinkwetʃen'tesko] AGG sixteenth-century.

cinquecento [tʃinkwe'tʃɛnto] [1] AGG INV five hundred.

[2] SM INV five hundred; **il Cinquecento** (secolo) the sixteenth century.

[3] SF INV (Aut) Fiat 500.

cinquemila [tʃinkwe'mila] AGG INV, SM INV five thousand.

cinquina [tʃin'kwina] SF (Lotto, Tombola) set of five winning numbers.

cinsi ecc ['tʃinsi] VB vedi **cingere.**

cinta ['tʃinta] SF (anche: **cinta muraria**) city walls pl; **muro di cinta** (di giardino) surrounding wall.

cintare [tʃin'tare] VT to enclose.

cinto, a ['tʃinto] [1] PP di **cingere.**

[2] SM: **cinto erniario** truss.

cintola ['tʃintola] SF (cintura) belt; (vita) waist.

cintura [tʃin'tura] SF **a** belt ▶**cintura dei pesi** (di subacqueo) weight belt ▶**cintura di salvataggio** life-belt (Brit), life preserver (Am) ▶**cintura di sicurezza** (Aut, Aer) safety o seat belt; **allacciare la cintura (di sicurezza)** to fasten one's safety o seat belt

b (vita) waist

c (Urbanistica): ▶**cintura industriale** industrial belt ▶**cintura verde** green belt.

cinturare [tʃintu'rare] VT (Calcio) to grab around the waist; (Lotta) to hold in a waist lock.

cinturato, a [tʃintu'rato] [1] AGG (pneumatico) radial(-ply).

[2] SM radial tyre (Brit) o tire (Am).

cinturino [tʃintu'rino] SM strap ▶**cinturino dell'orologio** watch strap.

cinturone [tʃintu'rone] SM gun belt.

ciò [tʃɔ] PRON DIMOSTR **a** (questa cosa) this; (quella cosa) that; **ciò è vero** this (o that) is true; **di ciò parleremo più tardi** we'll talk about this (o that) later; **con tutto ciò** for all that, in spite of everything; **e con ciò me ne vado!** and now I'm off!; **e con ciò ha concluso il suo discorso** and with that he finished his speech; **e con ciò?** so what?; **oltre a ciò** besides that, furthermore; **nonostante ciò** [OR] **ciò nonostante** nevertheless, in spite of that; **detto ciò...** having said that ...

b : **ciò che** what; **ciò che voglio dirti è importante** what I want to tell you is important; **gli sarò sempre grato per ciò che ha fatto** I'll always be grateful to him for what he's done; **è questo tutto ciò che hai fatto?** is this all (that) you've done?

C.I.O. ['tʃio] SIGLA M (= Comitato Internazionale Olimpico)

IOC (= International Olympic Committee).

ciocca, che ['tʃɔkka] SF (di capelli) lock; **perde i capelli a ciocche** her hair is coming out in handfuls.

ciocco, chi ['tʃɔkko] SM log.

cioccolata [tʃokko'lata] SF chocolate; **una tavoletta di cioccolata** a bar of chocolate; **una (tazza di) cioccolata calda** a (cup of) hot chocolate.

cioccolatino [tʃokkola'tino] SM chocolate; **una scatola di cioccolatini** a box of chocolates.

cioccolato [tʃokko'lato] SM chocolate; **cioccolato al latte/fondente** milk/plain chocolate.

cioè [tʃo'ɛ] AVV that is (to say); **vengo tra poco — cioè?** I'll come soon — what do you mean by soon?; **questo è il mio, cioè no, il tuo!** this is mine, or rather, I mean yours!

ciondolare [tʃondo'lare] [1] VI (aus avere) to dangle; (fig: bighellonare) to hang around, loaf (about); **l'ubriaco camminava ciondolando** the drunk swayed from side to side as he walked.

[2] VT (far dondolare) to dangle, swing.

ciondolo ['tʃondolo] SM pendant ▶**ciondolo portafortuna** good-luck charm.

ciondoloni [tʃondo'loni] AVV: **con le braccia/gambe ciondoloni** with arms/legs dangling.

ciononostante [tʃononos'tante] AVV nonetheless, nevertheless.

ciotola ['tʃɔtola] SF bowl.

ciottolo ['tʃɔttolo] SM (di fiume) pebble; (di strada) cobble (stone).

C.I.P. [tʃip] SIGLA M = **Comitato Interministeriale dei Prezzi.**

cip [tʃip] SM INV (Poker) stake.

C.I.P.E. ['tʃipe] SIGLA M = **Comitato Interministeriale per la Programmazione Economica.**

C.I.P.I. ['tʃipi] SIGLA M = **Comitato Interministeriale di Coordinamento per la Politica Industriale.**

cipiglio [tʃi'piʎʎo] SM frown.

cipolla [tʃi'polla] SF **a** onion; (di tulipano) bulb; **mangiare pane e cipolla** (fig) to live on bread and dripping **b** (Med) bunion **c** (scherz: orologio) timepiece.

cippo ['tʃippo] SM (celebrativo) memorial stone; (di confine) boundary stone.

cipresso [tʃi'presso] SM cypress.

cipria ['tʃiprja] SF (face) powder; **cipria compatta/in polvere** solid/loose powder.

cipriota, i, e [tʃipri'ɔta] [1] AGG Cypriot; **la questione cipriota** the Cyprus question.

[2] SM/F Cypriot.

Cipro ['tʃipro] SM Cyprus.

circa ['tʃirka] [1] PREP: **circa (a)** regarding, concerning, about; **circa gli accordi presi in precedenza** with reference to previous agreements.

[2] AVV (quasi) about, approximately, roughly; **erano circa le 3 quando è partita** [OR] **è partita alle 3 circa** she left at about 3; **mancano 20 minuti circa all'arrivo del treno** the train is due in about 20 minutes; **a mezzogiorno circa** (at) about midday.

Circe ['tʃirtʃe] SF (Mitol) Circe.

circo, chi ['tʃirko] SM **a** (Storia romana) circus; **circo (equestre)** (spettacolo) circus **b** (Geog) cirque, corrie.

circolante [tʃirko'lante] AGG circulating.

circolare[1] [tʃirko'lare] VI (aus avere e essere) (gen, Anat, Econ) to circulate; (persone) to go about; (notizie, idee) to circulate, go about; **circolare!** move along!; **circolare in città diventa sempre più difficile** (Aut) driving in town is getting more and more difficult; **i camion non possono**

circolare di domenica lorries are not allowed on the roads on Sundays; **circola voce che...** there is a rumour going about that ...; **far circolare qc** to pass sth round.

circolare[2] [tʃirkoˈlare] [1] AGG circular; **assegno circolare** banker's draft.

[2] SF a (*Amm*) circular (letter) b (*linea di autobus*) circle line.

circolatorio, ria, ri, rie [tʃirkolaˈtɔrjo] AGG circulatory.

circolazione [tʃirkolatˈtsjone] SF (*di sangue, aria, moneta*) circulation; (*di merci, veicoli*) movement; **mettere in circolazione** (*moneta*) to put into circulation; (*fig: voce, notizie*) to spread, put about; **togliere dalla circolazione** (*moneta*) to withdraw from circulation; (*fig: persona*) to remove; **tassa di circolazione** (*Aut*) road tax; **libretto di circolazione** (*Aut*) registration document (*Brit*), registration (*Am*) ▶ **circolazione monetaria** money in circulation ▶ **circolazione stradale** (*Aut*) traffic.

circolo ['tʃirkolo] SM a (*gen, Geog, Mat*) circle; **entrare in circolo** (*Med*) to enter the bloodstream; **circolo vizioso** vicious circle b (*club*) club ▶ **circolo giovanile** youth club ▶ **circolo letterario** literary circle *o* society ▶ **circolo ufficiali** officers' club.

circoncidere [tʃirkonˈtʃidere] VT IRREG to circumcize.

circoncisione [tʃirkontʃiˈzjone] SF circumcision.

circonciso, a [tʃirkonˈtʃizo] PP di **circoncidere**.

circondare [tʃirkonˈdare] [1] VT (*gen*) to surround; (*racchiudere*) to encircle; (: *con uno steccato*) to enclose; **circondare qn di cure** to give sb the best of attention; **circondare qn di attenzioni** to be very attentive towards sb; **è sempre stato circondato d'affetto** he has always been surrounded by affection.

[2] **circondarsi** VR: **circondarsi di** to surround o.s. with.

circondariale [tʃirkondaˈrjale] AGG: **casa circondariale di pena** district prison.

circondario, ri [tʃirkonˈdarjo] SM a (*Dir*) administrative district b (*zona circostante*) neighbourhood (*Brit*), neighborhood (*Am*).

circonferenza [tʃirkonfeˈrentsa] SF circumference; **circonferenza fianchi/vita** hip/waist measurement.

circonflessione [tʃirkonflesˈsjone] SF curving, bending.

circonflesso, a [tʃirkonˈflesso] [1] PP di **circonflettere**.

[2] AGG: **accento circonflesso** circumflex accent.

circonflettere [tʃirkonˈflettere] VT IRREG to curve, bend.

circonlocuzione [tʃirkonlokutˈtsjone] SF circumlocution.

circonvallazione [tʃirkonvallatˈtsjone] SF ring road (*Brit*), beltway (*Am*); (*per evitare una città*) by-pass.

circoscritto, a [tʃirkosˈkritto] [1] PP di **circoscrivere**.

[2] AGG (*zona*) limited; (*fenomeno, contagio*) localized.

circoscrivere [tʃirkosˈkrivere] VT IRREG (*Geom*) to circumscribe; (*zona*) to mark out; (*incendio, contagio*) to contain, confine; (*fig: problema, concetto*) to define, describe.

circoscrizionale [tʃirkoskrittsjoˈnale] AGG area *attr*, district *attr*.

circoscrizione [tʃirkoskritˈtsjone] SF (*Amm*) district, area ▶ **circoscrizione elettorale** constituency.

circospetto, a [tʃirkosˈpetto] AGG circumspect, cautious; **con fare circospetto** with a suspicious air.

circospezione [tʃirkospetˈtsjone] SF circumspection, prudence, caution.

circostante [tʃirkosˈtante] AGG (*territorio*) surrounding, neighbouring (*Brit*), neighboring (*Am*); (*persone*) in the vicinity.

circostanza [tʃirkosˈtantsa] SF (*occasione*) occasion; (*situazione*): **circostanze** SFPL circumstances; **in questa circostanza** on this occasion; **date le circostanze** in view of *o* under the circumstances; **circostanze aggravanti/attenuanti** (*Dir*) aggravating/mitigating circumstances; **parole di circostanza** words suited to the occasion.

circostanziare [tʃirkostanˈtsjare] VT (*evento, fatto*) to give a detailed account of.

circostanziatamente [tʃirkostantsjataˈmente] AVV in detail.

circostanziato, a [tʃirkoskanˈtsjato] AGG detailed.

circuire [tʃirkuˈire] VT (*fig*) to fool, take in.

circuito [tʃirˈkuito] SM a (*Elettr*) circuit; **andare in** *o* **fare corto circuito** to short-circuit; **circuito chiuso/integrato** closed/integrated circuit

b (*Aut*) track, circuit ▶ **circuito di attesa** (*Aer*) holding pattern ▶ **circuito di gara** racing track ▶ **circuito di prova** test circuit

c (*sale cinematografiche*) circuit.

circumnavigare [tʃirkumnaviˈgare] VT to circumnavigate.

circumnavigazione [tʃirkumnavigatˈtsjone] SF circumnavigation.

cireneo [tʃireˈnɛo] SM: **il Cireneo** Simon of Cyrene.

cirillico, a, ci, che [tʃiˈrilliko] AGG Cyrillic.

Ciro ['tʃiro] SM (*Storia*) Cyrus.

cirro ['tʃirro] SM (*Meteor*) cirrus.

cirrocumulo [tʃirroˈkumulo] SM cirrocumulus.

cirrosi [tʃirˈrɔzi] SF (*Med*) cirrhosis ▶ **cirrosi epatica** cirrhosis (of the liver).

C.I.S.A.L. ['tʃizal] SIGLA F (= *Confederazione Italiana Sindacati Autonomi dei Lavoratori*) *trades union organization*.

cisalpino, a [tʃizalˈpino] AGG cisalpine.

C.I.S.L. [tʃizl] SIGLA F (= *Confederazione Italiana Sindacati Lavoratori*) *trades union organization*.

C.I.S.N.A.L. ['tʃiznal] SIGLA F (= *Confederazione Italiana Sindacati Nazionali dei Lavoratori*) *trades union organization*.

cisposo, a [tʃisˈpozo] AGG: **avere gli occhi cisposi** to be bleary-eyed.

ciste ['tʃiste] SF = **cisti**.

cistercense [tʃisterˈtʃense] AGG, SM Cistercian.

cisterna [tʃisˈterna] [1] SF tank, cistern.

[2] AGG INV: **nave cisterna** (*per petrolio*) tanker; (*per acqua*) water-supply ship; **camion cisterna** tanker (lorry).

cisti ['tʃisti] SF INV cyst.

cistifellea [tʃistiˈfɛllea] SF (*Anat*) gall bladder.

cistite [tʃisˈtite] SF cystitis.

C.I.T. [tʃit] SIGLA F = *Compagnia Italiana Turismo*.

cit. ABBR (= *citato, citata*) cit.

citare [tʃiˈtare] VT a (*Dir*) to summon; (: *testimone*) to subpoena; **citare qn per danni** to sue sb for damages b (*passo, testo, autore*) to cite; **citare qn/qc a modello** *o* **ad esempio** to cite sb/sth as an example.

citazione [tʃitatˈtsjone] SF a (*Dir*:) summons *sg*; subpoena b (*di testo*) quotation, citation c (*menzione*) citation; **citazione all'ordine del giorno** (*Mil*) mention in dispatches.

citofonare [tʃitofoˈnare] VI (*aus avere*) to call on the entry phone.

citofono [tʃiˈtɔfono] SM (*di appartamento*) entry phone; (*in uffici*) intercom.

citologia [tʃitoloˈdʒia] SF cytology.

citologico, a, ci, che [tʃitoˈlɔdʒiko] AGG: **esame citologico** *test for detection of cancerous cells.*

citologo, gi [tʃi'tɔlogo] SM cytologist.

citoplasma, i [tʃito'plazma] SM cytoplasm.

citrato [tʃi'trato] SM citrate; (*anche:* **citrato di magnesia effervescente**) ≈ milk of magnesia.

citrico, a, ci, che ['tʃitriko] AGG citric.

citrullo, a [tʃi'trullo] SM/F (*fam*) half-wit.

città [tʃit'ta] SF INV **a** (*gen*) town; (*grande*) city; **abitare in città** to live in town *o* in the city; **andare in città** to go to *o* into town; **vita di città** town *o* city life; **la città vecchia/nuova** the old/new (part of) town; **Città del Capo** Cape Town; **città di mare/di provincia** seaside/provincial town; **la Città Santa** (*Gerusalemme*) the Holy City ► **città dormitorio** dormitory town ► **città giardino** garden city ► **città mercato** shopping centre *o* mall (*Am*) ► **città satellite** satellite town ► **città degli studi** *o* **universitaria** university campus.

cittadella [tʃitta'dɛlla] SF citadel, stronghold.

cittadinanza [tʃittadi'nantsa] SF **a** (*città, popolazione*) town, citizens *pl*, inhabitants *pl* of a town *o* city; **tutta la città** the whole town **b** (*Dir*) citizenship; **avere/prendere la cittadinanza britannica** to have/take British citizenship.

cittadino, a [tʃitta'dino] 1 AGG (*vie, popolazione, vita*) town *attr*, city *attr*.
2 SM/F (*abitante di città*) city *o* town dweller; (*di uno Stato*) citizen; **privato cittadino** private citizen; **cittadino britannico** British subject *o* citizen.

ciuccio, ci ['tʃuttʃo] SM (*fam*) comforter, dummy (*Brit*), pacifier (*Am*).

ciuco, a, chi, che ['tʃuko] SM/F ass; (*fig: persona*) ass, fool.

ciuffo ['tʃuffo] SM (*gen*) tuft; (*di prezzemolo*) bunch; (*di capelli*): **porta il ciuffo di lato** she wears her fringe to the side.

ciuffolotto [tʃuffo'lɔtto] SM bullfinch.

ciurma ['tʃurma] SF (*di nave*) crew.

ciurmaglia [tʃur'maʎʎa] SF mob, rabble.

civetta [tʃi'vetta] 1 SF **a** owl; **civetta notturna** little owl **b** (*fig: donna*) flirt, coquette; **fare la civetta con qn** to flirt with sb.
2 AGG INV: **auto/nave civetta** decoy car/ship.

civettare [tʃivet'tare] VI (*aus avere*): **civettare (con qn)** to flirt (with sb).

civetteria [tʃivette'ria] SF flirtatiousness, coquetry.

civettuolo, a [tʃivet'twɔlo] AGG flirtatious, coquettish; **un cappellino civettuolo** a pert little hat.

civicamente [tʃivika'mente] AVV (*con civismo*) public-spiritedly.

civico, a, ci, che ['tʃiviko] AGG **a** (*museo*) town *attr*, municipal; **centro civico** civic centre; **guardia civica** (town) policeman **b** (*dovere*) civic; **senso civico** public spirit; **educazione civica** civics *sg*.

civile [tʃi'vile] 1 AGG **a** civil; **Diritto Civile** Civil Law; **diritti civili** civil rights; **convivenza civile** life in society; **società civile** civil society; **stato civile** marital status **b** (*non militare*) civilian; **abiti civili** civilian clothes **c** (*civilizzato*) civilized; (*educato*) polite, civil.
2 SM private citizen, civilian.

civilista, i, e [tʃivi'lista] SM/F (*avvocato*) civil lawyer; (*studioso*) expert in civil law.

civilizzare [tʃivilid'dzare] 1 VT (*paese, popolo*) to civilize.
2 **civilizzarsi** VR (*fig*) to become civilized, become more refined.

civilizzato, a [tʃivilid'dzato] AGG civilized.

civilizzatore, trice [tʃiviliddza'tore] 1 AGG civilizing.
2 SM/F civilizer.

civilizzazione [tʃiviliddzat'tsjone] SF civilization.

civilmente [tʃivil'mente] AVV (*vedi agg c*) in a civilized way; politely, civilly.

civiltà [tʃivil'ta] SF INV **a** (*civilizzazione*) civilization; **una società con un alto grado di civiltà** a highly civilized society **b** (*gentilezza, educazione*) courtesy, civility; **con civiltà** in a civilized manner.

civismo [tʃi'vizmo] SM civic-mindedness, public spirit.

CL [tʃi'ɛlle] 1 SIGLA F (*Pol:* = *Comunione e Liberazione*) Catholic youth movement.
2 SIGLA = *Caltanissetta*.

cl ABBR (= *centilitro*) cl.

clacson ['klakson] SM INV (*Aut*) horn, hooter (*Brit*); **suonare il clacson** to sound the horn.

clamore [kla'more] SM (*frastuono*) din, uproar, clamour (*Brit*), clamor (*Am*); (*fig: scalpore*) outcry; **suscitare** *o* **destare clamore** to cause a sensation.

clamorosamente [klamorosa'mente] AVV (*gen*) sensationally; **essere clamorosamente sconfitto** to be resoundingly defeated.

clamoroso, a [klamo'roso] AGG (*sconfitta*) resounding; (*applausi*) noisy; (*fig: notizia, processo*) sensational.

clan [klan] SM INV clan; (*fig: gruppo*) team; (: *mafioso*) gang, clan.

clandestinamente [klandestina'mente] AVV (*riunirsi, sposarsi*) secretly; **viaggiare clandestinamente** (*in aereo, nave*) to stow away; **importare clandestinamente** (*gen*) to import illegally; (*di contrabbando*) to smuggle.

clandestinità [klandestini'ta] SF INV (*di attività*) secret nature; **vivere nella clandestinità** to live in hiding; (*ricercato politico*) to live underground.

clandestino, a [klandes'tino] 1 AGG (*illecito*) illicit; (*segreto: matrimonio, incontro*) clandestine, secret; (: *movimento, radio*) underground *attr*.
2 SM/F (*anche:* **passeggero clandestino**) stowaway.

claque [klak] SF INV claque.

clarinetto [klari'netto] SM clarinet.

clarinista, i, e [klari'nista] SM/F clarinet player, clarinettist.

clarino [kla'rino] SM clarinet.

clarissa [kla'rissa] SF (*Rel*) Poor Clare.

classe ['klasse] SF **a** (*gen, fig*) class; **lotta di classe** class struggle; **classe di leva 1958** (*Mil*) class of 1958; **viaggiare in prima/seconda classe** to travel first/second class; **un albergo di prima classe** a first-class hotel; **classe turistica** (*Aer*) economy class; **una donna di (gran) classe** a woman with class **b** (*Scol*) class; (: *aula*) classroom; **compagno di classe** schoolmate; **che classe fai quest'anno?** what class are you in this year?

classicamente [klassika'mente] AVV classically.

classicheggiante [klassiked'dʒante] AGG in the classical style.

classicismo [klassi'tʃizmo] SM classicism.

classicista, i, e [klassi'tʃista] SM/F classicist.

classicità [klassitʃi'ta] SF **a** (*di opera artistica, letteraria*) classical nature **b** (*mondo greco, latino*) classical antiquity.

classico, a, ci, che ['klassiko] 1 AGG **a** (*arte, letteratura, civiltà*) classical; **studi classici** classical studies; **danza classica** ballet dancing; **musica classica** classical music **b** (*moda, esempio*) classic; **un film classico** a classic film; **classico!** that's typical!.

[2] SM a (*autore antico*) classical author; (*opera famosa*) classic
b (*anche:* liceo classico) *secondary school with emphasis on the humanities.*

classifica, che [klas'sifika] SF (*di gara sportiva*) placings *pl*; (*di concorso, esame*) list; (*di dischi*) charts *pl*; essere primo in classifica to be placed first, come first; (*disco*) to be number one (in the charts); classifica finale final results *pl*; classifica generale overall placings *pl*; classifica del campionato (*Calcio*) league table.

classificare [klassifi'kare] [1] VT (*catalogare*) to classify; (*candidato, compito*) to grade.
[2] classificarsi VIP (*Sport*) to be placed; classificarsi primo/secondo to be placed first/second.

classificatore [klassifika'tore] SM (*cartella*) loose-leaf file; (*mobile*) filing cabinet.

classificazione [klassifikat'tsjone] SF (*vedi vt*) classification; grading.

classismo [klas'sizmo] SM class consciousness.

classista, i, e [klas'sista] [1] AGG class-conscious.
[2] SM/F class-conscious person.

classistico, a, ci, che [klas'sistiko] AGG (*politica*) class *attr.*

claudicante [klaudi'kante] AGG (*zoppo*) lame; (*fig: prosa*) halting.

claunesco, a, schi, sche [klau'nesko] AGG (*aspetto, espressione*) clownish.

clausola ['klauzola] SF clause.

claustrofobia [klaustrofo'bia] SF claustrophobia.

claustrofobico, a, ci, che [klaustrofo'biko] AGG claustrophobic.

clausura [klau'zura] SF (*Rel*): monaca di clausura nun belonging to an enclosed order; fare una vita di clausura (*fig*) to lead a cloistered life.

clava ['klava] SF (*arma primitiva*) club; (*attrezzo da ginnastica*) Indian club.

clavicembalista, i, e [klavitʃemba'lista] SM/F harpsichord player, harpsichordist.

clavicembalo [klavi'tʃembalo] SM harpsichord.

clavicola [kla'vikola] SF collarbone, clavicle (*termine tecn*).

clavicordo [klavi'kordo] SM clavichord.

clemente [kle'mɛnte] AGG (*persona*) merciful; (*tempo, stagione*) mild.

clementina [klemen'tina] SF clementine.

clemenza [kle'mɛntsa] SF (*di persona*) mercy, clemency; (*di tempo, stagione*) mildness.

Cleopatra [kleo'patra] SF Cleopatra.

cleptomane [klep'tomane] SM/F kleptomaniac.

cleptomania [kleptoma'nia] SF kleptomania.

clergyman ['klə:dʒimən] SM INV clergyman's suit.

clericale [kleri'kale] [1] AGG clerical; potere clericale power of the clergy.
[2] SM/F clericalist, supporter of the power of the clergy.

clero ['klɛro] SM clergy.

clessidra [kles'sidra] SF (*a sabbia*) hourglass; (*ad acqua*) water clock.

cliché [kli'ʃe] SM INV (*Tip*) plate; (*fig*) cliché.

cliente [kli'ɛnte] SM/F (*gen*) customer; (*di albergo*) guest; (*di professionista*) client; cliente abituale/occasionale regular/occasional customer; sono un cliente fisso di quel bar I'm a regular at that bar.

clientela [klien'tɛla] SF (*di negozio*) customers *pl*; (*di professionista*) clients *pl*; (*di sartoria*) clientele.

clientelare [kliente'lare] AGG = clientelistico.

clientelismo [kliente'lizmo] SM: clientelismo politico po-

litical nepotism.

clientelistico, a, ci, che [kliente'listiko] AGG: favoritismo clientelistico political nepotism.

clima, i ['klima] SM (*anche fig*) climate; c'è un clima piuttosto teso there's a rather tense atmosphere.

climaterio [klima'tɛrjo] SM climacteric.

climatico, a, ci, che [kli'matiko] AGG climatic; stazione climatica health resort.

climatizzazione [klimatiddzat'tsjone] SF air conditioning.

clinica, che ['klinika] SF a (*Med: disciplina*): clinica medica/chirurgica clinical medicine/surgery b (*settore d'ospedale*) clinic; (*casa di cura*) clinic, nursing home.

clinicamente [klinika'mente] AVV clinically.

clinico, a, ci, che ['kliniko] [1] AGG (*medico, esame*) clinical; quadro clinico case history; avere l'occhio clinico (*fig*) to have an expert eye. [2] SM (*medico*) clinician; (*docente*) professor of clinical medicine.

Clio ['klio] SF Clio.

clip [klip] SF INV (*per foglio*) paper clip; (*di orecchino, abito*) clip; orecchini a clip clip-on earrings.

clistere [klis'tɛre] SM (*Med*) enema; (: *apparecchio*) enema (syringe).

clitoride [kli'toride] SM O F (*Anat*) clitoris.

cloaca, che [klo'aka] SF a (*fogna*) sewer; (*pozzo nero*) cesspool, cesspit b (*Anat*) cloaca.

cloche [klɔʃ] SF INV (*Aer*) control stick, joystick; cambio a cloche (*Aut*) (floor-mounted) gear lever (*Brit*) o stick (*Brit*) o shaft (*Am*); cappello a cloche cloche hat.

clone ['klone] SM clone.

cloridrico, a, ci, che [klo'ridriko] AGG hydrochloric.

cloro ['klɔro] SM chlorine.

clorofilla [kloro'filla] SF chlorophyll (*Brit*), chlorophyl (*Am*).

clorofilliano, a [klorofil'ljano] AGG (*Bot*): fotosintesi clorofilliana photosynthesis.

cloroformio [kloro'formjo] SM chloroform.

cloroformizzare [kloroformid'dzare] VT to chloroform.

clorosi [klo'rɔzi] SF INV (*Med, Bot*) chlorosis.

cloruro [klo'ruro] SM chloride ▶ cloruro di sodio sodium chloride.

clou [klu] SM INV: il clou della serata the highlight of the evening.

club [klub] SM INV club.

cm ABBR (= *centimetro*) cm.

c.m. ABBR (= *corrente mese*) inst.

CN SIGLA = *Cuneo.*

c/n ABBR = *conto nuovo.*

C.N.E.N. [knen] SIGLA M (= *Comitato Nazionale per l'Energia Nucleare*) ≈ AEA (*Brit*), ≈ AEC (*Am*).

C.N.I.O.P. [kn'iop] SIGLA M = *Centro Nazionale per l'Istruzione e l'Orientamento Professionale.*

C.N.R. [tʃi'ɛnne'ɛrre] SIGLA M (= *Consiglio Nazionale delle Ricerche*) *science research council.*

C.N.R.N. SIGLA M = *Comitato Nazionale Ricerche Nucleari.*

CO SIGLA = *Como.*

Co. ABBR (= *compagnia*) Co.

c/o ABBR (= *care of*) c/o.

coabitare [koabi'tare] VI (*aus avere*) to live in the same flat (*Brit*) o apartment (*Am*) o house.

coabitazione [koabitat'tsjone] SF living in the same flat (*Brit*) o apartment (*Am*) o house.

coadiutore, trice [koadju'tore] SM/F assistant.

coadiuvante [koadju'vante] AGG (*farmaco*) adjuvant.

coadiuvare [koadju'vare] VT: coadiuvare qn in qc to

cooperate with sb on sth.

coagulante [koagu'lante] [1] AGG coagulative.
[2] SM coagulant.

coagulare [koagu'lare] VT, **coagularsi** VIP (*sangue*) to coagulate, clot; (*latte*) to curdle.

coagulazione [koagulat'tsjone] SF (*vedi vb*) coagulation, clotting; curdling.

coagulo [ko'agulo] SM (*di sangue*) clot; (*di latte*) curd.

coalizione [koalit'tsjone] SF coalition; **governo di coalizione** coalition government.

coalizzare [koalid'dzare] [1] VT to unite in a coalition.
[2] **coalizzarsi** VR (*uso reciproco*) to form a coalition.

coartare [koar'tare] VT (*letter*): **coartare qn a fare qc** to coerce sb into doing sth.

coatto, a [ko'atto] AGG (*Dir*) compulsory, forced; **condannare al domicilio coatto** to place under house arrest.

coautore, trice [koau'tore] SM/F co-author.

cobalto [ko'balto] SM cobalt.

cobaltoterapia [kobaltotera'pia] SF (*Med*) cobalt treatment, cobalt therapy.

COBAS ['kɔbas] SIGLA MPL (= *Comitati di base*) *independent trades unions*.

COBOL ['kɔbol] ABBR (*Inform*) COBOL.

cobra ['kɔbra] SM INV cobra.

coca[1] ['kɔka] SF (*Bot*) coca.

coca[2] ['kɔka] SF **a** (*bevanda*) Coke ® **b** (*fam: cocaina*) coke.

Coca cola® ['kɔka'kɔla] SF Coca Cola ®.

cocaina [koka'ina] SF cocaine.

cocainismo [kokai'nizmo] SM cocaine addiction.

cocainomane [kokai'nɔmane] SM/F cocaine addict.

cocca, che ['kɔkka] SF (*di freccia*) (arrow) notch.

coccarda [kok'karda] SF cockade.

cocchiere [kok'kjɛre] SM coachman.

cocchio, chi ['kɔkkjo] SM (*carrozza*) coach; (*biga*) chariot.

coccige [kot'tʃidʒe] SM (*Anat*) coccyx.

coccinella [kottʃi'nɛlla] SF ladybird (*Brit*), ladybug (*Am*).

cocciniglia [kottʃi'niʎʎa] SF (*Zool*) cochineal; **rosso di cocciniglia** cochineal.

coccio, ci ['kɔttʃo] SM **a** earthenware; **un vaso di coccio** an earthenware pot **b** (*frammento*) fragment (of pottery), potsherd; **chi rompe paga e i cocci sono suoi** (*Proverbio*) any damage must be paid for.

cocciutaggine [kottʃu'taddʒine] SF stubbornness, pigheadedness.

cocciuto, a [kot'tʃuto] AGG stubborn, pig-headed.

cocco[1], **chi** ['kɔkko] SM coconut palm; **noce di cocco** coconut; **latte di cocco** coconut milk.

cocco[2], **chi** ['kɔkko] SM (*batterio*) coccus.

cocco[3], **a, chi, che** ['kɔkko] SM/F (*fam*) love, darling; **è il cocco della mamma** he's mummy's darling.

coccodrillo [kokko'drillo] SM crocodile; **lacrime di coccodrillo** (*fig*) crocodile tears.

coccolare [kokko'lare] [1] VT to cuddle.
[2] **coccolarsi** VR (*uso reciproco*) to cuddle.

cocente [ko'tʃɛnte] AGG (*sole*) burning, scorching; (*fig: dolore*) burning; (: *rimorso*) bitter.

cocker ['kɔkə] SM INV cocker (spaniel).

cocktail ['kɔkteil] SM INV (*bevanda*) cocktail; (*festa*) cocktail party.

coclea ['kɔklea] SF (*Anat*) cochlea.

cocomero [ko'komero] SM watermelon.

cocotte [kɔ'kɔt] SF INV (*Culin*) cast-iron casserole.

cocuzzolo [ko'kuttsolo] SM (*di montagna*) summit, top;

(*della testa*) crown, top (of the head).

cod. ABBR = **codice**.

coda ['koda] SF **a** tail; (*di abiti*) train; **coda di cavallo** (*acconciatura*) ponytail; **vettura/fanale di coda** rear coach/light; **in coda a** (*veicolo, treno*) at the rear of; (*processione*) at the tail end of; **con la coda fra le gambe** (*fig*) with one's tail between one's legs; **avere la coda di paglia** (*fig*) to have a guilty conscience; **guardare con la coda dell'occhio** to look out of the corner of one's eye; **incastro a coda di rondine** dovetail joint
b (*fila*) queue (*Brit*), line (*Am*); **fare la coda, mettersi in coda** to join the queue, queue (up) (*Brit*), line up (*Am*)
c (*Culin*): **coda di rospo** frogfish tail.

codardamente [kodarda'mente] AVV like a coward, in a cowardly way.

codardia [kodar'dia] SF cowardice.

codardo, a [ko'dardo] [1] AGG cowardly.
[2] SM/F coward.

codazzo [ko'dattso] SM throng.

codesto, a [ko'desto] AGG, PRON DIMOSTR (*letter, toscano*) this, that.

codibugnolo [kodi'buɲɲolo] SM (*uccello*) long-tailed tit.

codice ['kɔditʃe] [1] SM **a** code; **messaggio in codice** message in code, coded message
b (*manoscritto antico*) codex.
[2] ▶ **codice di avviamento postale** postcode (*Brit*), zip code (*Am*) ▶ **codice a barre** bar code ▶ **codice di carattere** (*Inform*) character code ▶ **codice civile** civil code ▶ **codice fiscale** tax code ▶ **codice genetico** genetic code ▶ **codice macchina** (*Inform*) machine code ▶ **codice penale** penal code ▶ **codice professionale** code of practice ▶ **codice segreto** (*di tessera magnetica*) PIN (number) ▶ **codice della strada** highway code (*Brit*).

codicillo [kodi'tʃillo] SM codicil.

codifica [ko'difika] SF codification; (*Inform: di programma*) coding.

codificare [kodifi'kare] VT (*Dir*) to codify; (*informazioni, segreti, dati*) to encode.

codificazione [kodifikat'tsjone] SF (*vedi vb*) codification; encoding.

codino[1] [ko'dino] SM (*di capelli*) pigtail.

codino[2], **a** [ko'dino] [1] AGG reactionary.
[2] SM/F (*fig: persona*) reactionary.

coeditore [koedi'tore] SM co-publisher.

coedizione [koedit'tsjone] SF co-edition.

coefficiente [koeffi'tʃɛnte] SM coefficient; **coefficiente di resistenza** drag coefficient *o* factor.

coercibile [koer'tʃibile] AGG coercible; (*Fis*) compressible.

coercibilità [koertʃibili'ta] SF (*vedi agg*) coercibility; compressibility.

coercitivo, a [koertʃi'tivo] AGG coercive.

coercizione [koertʃit'tsjone] SF coercion.

coerente [koe'rɛnte] AGG (*Geol*) coherent; (*fig: pensiero, azione*) consistent, coherent.

coerentemente [koerente'mente] AVV (*fig*) consistently.

coerenza [koe'rɛntsa] SF (*vedi agg*) coherence; consistency.

coesione [koe'zjone] SF cohesion.

coesistente [koezis'tɛnte] AGG coexistent.

coesistenza [koezis'tɛntsa] SF coexistence.

coesistere [koe'zistere] VI IRREG (*aus essere*) to coexist.

coesistito, a [koezis'tito] PP di **coesistere**.

coesivo, a [koe'sivo] AGG cohesive.

coetaneo, a [koe'taneo] [1] AGG (of) the same age; **essere coetaneo di qn** to be the same age as sb.

[2] SM/F contemporary; **preferisco la compagnia dei miei coetanei** I prefer the company of people my own age.

coevo, a [ko'ɛvo] AGG contemporary.

cofanetto [kofa'netto] SM casket; **cofanetto dei gioielli** jewel case; **cofanetto da lavoro** workbox; **cofanetto regalo** gift box.

cofano ['kofano] SM **a** coffer **b** (Aut) bonnet (Brit), hood (Am).

coffa ['kɔffa] SF (Naut) top.

cogitabondo, a [kodʒita'bondo] AGG (letter) thoughtful, deep in thought.

cogli ['koʎʎi] PREP + ART vedi **con**.

cogliere ['kɔʎʎere] VT IRREG **a** (fiori, frutta) to pick, gather **b** (fig: afferrare) to grasp, seize, take; **cogliere il significato di qc** to grasp the meaning of sth; **cogliere l'occasione (per fare)** to take the opportunity (to do); **ha colto l'occasione buona** he chose the right moment; **cogliere nel segno** (fig) to hit the nail on the head **c** (sorprendere) to catch, surprise; **cogliere sul fatto** o **in flagrante/alla sprovvista** to catch red-handed/unprepared; **cogliere qn in fallo** to catch sb out.

coglionaggine [koʎʎo'naddʒine] SF (fam!) (bloody) stupidity.

coglionata [koʎʎo'nata], **coglioneria** ['koʎʎone'ria] SF (fam!): **dire una coglionata** to talk a load of balls (fam!)

coglione, a [koʎ'ʎone] [1] SM (fam!: testicolo): **coglioni** SMPL balls (fam!); **rompere i coglioni a qn** to get on sb's tits (Brit fam!).

[2] SM/F (fam!: persona sciocca) dickhead (fam!).

cognac [kɔ'ɲak] SM INV cognac.

cognato, a [koɲ'ɲato] SM/F brother-/sister-in-law.

cognitivismo [koɲɲiti'vizmo] SM cognitivism.

cognitivo, a [koɲɲi'tivo] AGG cognitive.

cognizione [koɲɲit'tsjone] SF (conoscenza) knowledge; (Dir) cognizance; (Filosofia) cognition; **con cognizione di causa** with full knowledge of the facts.

cognome [koɲ'ɲome] SM surname.

coi ['koi] PREP + ART vedi **con**.

coibente [koi'bɛnte] AGG insulating.

coincidenza [kointʃi'dɛntsa] SF **a** coincidence **b** (Ferr, Aer, di autobus) connection.

coincidere [koin'tʃidere] VI IRREG (aus **avere**) to coincide.

coinciso, a [koin'tʃizo] PP di **coincidere**.

coinquilino [koinkwi'lino] SM (in condominio) fellow tenant; (in appartamento) flatmate (Brit), roommate (Am).

cointeressato, a [kointeres'sato] SM/F (Comm) associate.

cointeressenza [kointeres'sɛntsa] SF (Comm): **avere una cointeressenza in qc** to own shares in sth; **cointeressenza dei lavoratori** profit-sharing.

coinvolgere [koin'vɔldʒere] VT IRREG to involve, implicate; **coinvolgere qn in qc** to involve sb in sth.

coinvolgimento [koinvoldzi'mento] SM involvement.

coinvolsi ecc VB vedi **coinvolgere**.

coinvolto, a [koin'vɔlto] PP di **coinvolgere**.

coito ['kɔito] SM coitus; **coito interrotto** coitus interruptus.

coke ['kouk] SM INV: (carbone) coke coke.

col [kol] PREP + ART vedi **con**.

Col. ABBR (= colonnello) Col.

colà [ko'la] AVV there.

colabrodo [kola'brɔdo] SM INV colander, strainer.

colapasta [kola'pasta] SM INV colander.

colare [ko'lare] [1] VT **a** (liquido) to strain; (pasta) drain **b** (metalli) to cast; (oro fuso) to pour.

[2] VI (aus **essere**) **a** (cadere a gocce) to drip; (cera, formaggio) to run; **il sudore gli colava dalla fronte** sweat dripped from his brow; **mi cola il naso** my nose is running; **mi cola il sangue dal naso** my nose is bleeding **b** (perdere: botte) to leak **c** (nave): **colare a picco** to sink straight to the bottom.

colata [ko'lata] SF (di metallo fuso) casting; (di lava) flow.

colazione [kolat'tsjone] SF (anche: **prima colazione**) breakfast; (anche: **seconda colazione**) lunch; **fare colazione** to have breakfast o lunch; **colazione all'inglese** English o full breakfast ▶ **colazione di lavoro** working lunch.

colbacco, chi [kol'bakko] SM (Mil) busby; (da donna, uomo) fur hat.

Coldiretti [koldi'retti] SIGLA F (= Confederazione nazionale coltivatori diretti) federation of Italian farmers.

colecisti [kole'tʃisti] SF INV (Anat) gall bladder.

colei [ko'lɛi] PRON DIMOSTR (sogg) she; (complemento) her; **colei che** the woman who, the one who.

coleotteri [kole'ɔtteri] SMPL coleoptera pl.

colera [ko'lɛra] SM INV cholera.

colesterolo [koleste'rɔlo] SM cholesterol.

colf [kɔlf] SF INV home help.

colgo ecc ['kɔlgo] VB vedi **cogliere**.

colibrì [koli'bri] SM INV hummingbird.

colica ['kɔlika] SF (Med) colic.

colino [ko'lino] SM strainer; **colino per il tè** tea strainer.

colite [ko'lite] SF (Med) colitis.

colla¹ ['kɔlla] SF glue ▶ **colla di farina** paste ▶ **colla di pesce** fish glue, isinglass.

colla² ['kolla] PREP + ART vedi **con**.

collaborare [kollabo'rare] VI (aus **avere**) (lavorare insieme) to cooperate; (Pol) to collaborate; **collaborare a** (progetto) to contribute to, collaborate on; **collaborare ad un giornale** to contribute to a newspaper; **collaborare con la polizia** to help the police with their enquiries.

collaboratore, trice [kollabora'tore] SM/F (vedi vb) contributor; collaborator; **collaboratore di un giornale** contributor to a newspaper ▶ **collaboratore esterno** freelance, freelancer ▶ **collaboratore di giustizia** = pentito ▶ **collaboratrice familiare** home help.

collaborazione [kollabora't'tsjone] SF (vedi vb) cooperation; collaboration; contribution; **in collaborazione con** in collaboration with.

collaborazionismo [kollaborattsjo'nizmo] SM (Pol) collaboration.

collaborazionista, i, e [kollaborattsjo'nista] SM/F collaborationist.

collage [kɔ'laʒ] SM INV collage.

collagene [kolla'dʒɛne] SM collagen.

collana [kol'lana] SF **a** necklace; **collana di fiori** garland of flowers **b** (raccolta di libri, scritti) collection, series sg.

collant [kɔ'lã] SM INV tights pl.

collare [kol'lare] SM collar.

collarino [kolla'rino] SM (Rel) clerical collar.

collasso [kol'lasso] SM (Med) collapse; **un collasso cardiaco** heart failure.

collaterale [kollate'rale] AGG collateral; **effetti collaterali** side effects.

collaudare [kollau'dare] VT to test, try out.

collaudatore, trice [kollauda'tore] SM/F tester; **collauda-**

tore di aeroplani/automobili test pilot/driver.
collaudo [kol'laudo] SM (*azione*) testing *no pl*; (*prova*) test; **fare il collaudo di qc** to test sth; **volo/giro di collaudo** test flight/run.
collazionare [kollattsjo'nare] VT to collate.
collazione [kollat'tsjone] SF collation.
colle¹ ['kɔlle] SM (*collina*) hill; (*valico*) pass.
colle² ['kolle] PREP + ART vedi **con**.
collega, ghi, ghe [kol'lɛga] SM/F colleague.
collegamento [kollega'mento] SM **a** (*gen, fig: legame*) connection **b** (*Mil*) liaison; **ufficiale di collegamento** liaison officer **c** (*Radio*) link(-up); **siamo ora in collegamento con...** we are now linked to ... .
collegare [kolle'gare] ① VT to connect, join, link; (*città, zone*) to join, link; (*Elettr*) to connect (up).
 ② **collegarsi** VIP to join, meet; (*Radio, TV*) to link up; **collegarsi con** (*Telec*) to get through to.
collegiale [kolle'dʒale] ① AGG (*riunione, decisione*) collective; (*Scol*) boarding school *attr*.
 ② SM/F boarder; (*fig: persona timida e inesperta*) schoolboy/schoolgirl.
collegialità [kolledʒali'ta] SF **a** collegial nature; (*di decisione*) joint nature **b** (*Rel*) collegiality.
collegialmente [kolledʒal'mente] AVV (*decidere*) as a body.
collegio, gi [kol'lɛdʒo] SM **a** (*ordine di professionisti, Rel*) college **b** (*convitto*) boarding school; **collegio militare** military college **c** (*Amm*): **collegio elettorale** constituency.
collera ['kɔllera] SF anger; **andare in collera** to get angry; **essere in collera con qn** to be angry with sb.
collerico, a, ci, che [kol'lɛriko] AGG (*persona*) quick-tempered, irascible; (*parole*) angry; (*temperamento*) choleric.
colletta [kol'lɛtta] SF collection.
collettivamente [kollettiva'mente] AVV collectively.
collettivismo [kolletti'vizmo] SM collectivism.
collettività [kollettivi'ta] SF community.
collettivizzare [kollettivid'dzare] VT to collectivize.
collettivo, a [kollet'tivo] ① AGG (*benessere, bisogno, interesse*) common, general; (*responsabilità*) collective; (*impresa*) group *attr*; **fenomeno collettivo** popular phenomenon; **nome collettivo** (*Gramm*) collective noun; **società in nome collettivo** (*Comm*) partnership.
 ② SM (*Pol*) collective.
colletto [kol'letto] SM (*di vestito, Bot: di albero*) collar; (*di dente*) neck ▶**colletti bianchi** (*fig*) white-collar workers.
collettore [kollet'tore] SM (*Aut*) manifold ▶**collettore di aspirazione** inlet manifold ▶**collettore di scarico** exhaust manifold.
collezionare [kollettsjo'nare] VT to collect.
collezione [kollet'tsjone] SF (*gen*) collection; **fare collezione di** (*francobolli*) to collect.
collezionismo [kollettsjo'nizmo] SM collecting.
collezionista, i, e [kollettsjo'nista] SM/F collector.
collier [kɔ'lje] SM INV necklace.
collimare [kolli'mare] VI (*aus* avere): **collimare (con)** (*idee*) to coincide (with), agree (with).
collimatore [kollima'tore] SM (*gen*) telescopic sight; (*Ottica*) collimator.
collimazione [kollimat'tsjone] SF (*Ottica*) collimation; (*fig: di idee*) coincidence.
collina [kol'lina] SF hill; (*zona*) hills; **una città di collina** a town in the hills, a hill town.

collinare [kolli'nare] AGG hill *attr*.
collinoso, a [kolli'noso] AGG hilly.
collirio, ri [kol'lirjo] SM eyedrops *pl*.
collisione [kolli'zjone] SF (*di veicoli*) collision; (*fig*) clash, conflict; **entrare in collisione con qc** to collide with sth.
collo¹ ['kɔllo] SM neck; (*di abito*) neck, collar; **a collo alto** (*maglione*) high-necked; **portare qc al collo** to wear sth round one's neck; **buttare le braccia al collo di qn** to throw one's arms round sb; **fino al collo** (*anche fig*) up to one's neck; **è nei guai fino al collo** he's up to his neck in it ▶**collo del piede** instep.
collo² ['kɔllo] SM (*pacco*) parcel, package; (*bagaglio*) piece of luggage.
collo³ ['kollo] PREP + ART vedi **con**.
collocamento [kolloka'mento] SM (*impiego*) employment; (*disposizione*) placing, arrangement; **agenzia di collocamento** employment agency; **ufficio di collocamento** ≈ Jobcentre (*Brit*), state *o* federal employment agency (*Am*) ▶**collocamento a riposo** retirement.
collocare [kollo'kare] VT **a** (*porre: libri, mobili*) to place, position; (: *cavi*) to lay; **questo libro va collocato fra le sue opere migliori** this book ranks among his best works **b** (*trovare un impiego a qn*) to place, find a job for; **collocare qn a riposo** to pension sb off, retire sb **c** (*Comm: merce*) to place, find a market for.
collocazione [kollokat'tsjone] SF **a** (*gen*) placing, positioning; **l'opera va considerata nella sua collocazione storica** the work has to be considered within its historical setting **b** (*in biblioteca*) classification.
colloidale [kolloi'dale] AGG colloidal.
colloquiale [kollo'kwjale] AGG (*gen*) colloquial; (*tono*) informal.
colloquialmente [kollokwjal'mente] AVV colloquially.
colloquiare [kollo'kwjare] VI (*aus* avere) to talk, converse.
colloquio, qui [kol'lɔkwjo] SM **a** (*conversazione*) talk, conversation; (*ufficiale, per un lavoro*) interview; **concedere un colloquio a qn** to grant sb an interview; **avviare un colloquio con qn** (*Pol*) to start talks with sb **b** (*Univ*) preliminary oral exam.
colloso, a [kol'loso] AGG sticky.
collottola [kol'lɔttola] SF nape of the neck; **afferrare qn per la collottola** to grab sb by the scruff of the neck.
collusione [kollu'zjone] SF (*Dir*) collusion.
collutorio, ri [kollu'tɔrjo] SM mouthwash.
colluttazione [kolluttat'tsjone] SF scuffle.
colma ['kolma] SF (*di fiume*) high-water level.
colmare [kol'mare] VT: **colmare (di)** (*riempire*) to fill (to the brim) (with); (*fig*) to fill (with); **colmare una lacuna** (*fig*) to fill a gap; **colmare un divario** (*fig*) to bridge a gap; **colmare qn di gentilezze** to overwhelm sb with kindness.
colmo¹, a ['kolmo] AGG: **colmo (di)** full (of).
colmo² ['kolmo] SM (*punto più alto*) summit, top; (*fig*): **il colmo della maleducazione** the height of bad manners; **essere al colmo della disperazione** to be in the depths of despair; **essere al colmo dell'ira** to be in a towering rage; **e per colmo di sfortuna...** and to cap it all ...; **è il colmo!** that beats everything!
colomba [ko'lomba] SF dove; **colomba dal collare** collared dove ▶**colomba pasquale** (*Culin*) *dove-shaped Easter cake*.
colombaccio, ci [kolom'battʃo] SM wood pigeon, ring-dove.
colombaia [kolom'baja] SF dovecote; (*piccionaia*) pigeon

coop.

Colombia [ko'lombja] SF: **la Colombia** Colombia.

colombiano, a [kolom'bjano] AGG, SM/F Colombian.

Colombo [ko'lombo] SM: **Cristoforo Colombo** Christopher Columbus.

colombo [ko'lombo] SM (*Zool*) pigeon; (*fig fam*): **colombi** SMPL lovebirds.

colon ['kɔlon] SM INV (*Anat*) colon.

Colonia [ko'lɔnja] SF Cologne.

colonia¹ [ko'lɔnja] SF (*gen*) colony; (*per bambini*) holiday camp; **colonia marina** seaside holiday camp.

colonia² [ko'lɔnja] SF (*anche*: **acqua di colonia**) (eau de) cologne.

coloniale [kolo'njale] ① AGG colonial.

② SM/F colonist, settler.

colonialismo [kolonja'lizmo] SM colonialism.

colonialista, i, e [kolonja'lista] AGG, SM/F colonialist.

colonialistico, a, ci, che [kolonja'listiko] AGG colonialist.

colonico, a, ci, che [ko'lɔniko] AGG: **casa colonica** farmhouse.

colonizzare [kolonid'dzare] VT to colonize.

colonizzatore, trice [kolonidzza'tore] ① AGG colonizing.

② SM/F colonizer.

colonizzazione [koloniddzat'tsjone] SF colonization.

colonna [ko'lonna] SF (*gen*) column; **le colonne di Ercole** (*Geog*) the Pillars of Hercules; **in colonna** in a column; **stare in colonna** (*Aut*) to be caught in a tailback (*Brit*) o backup (*Am*); **una colonna di 10 chilometri** (*Aut*) a 10-kilometre tailback ▸**colonna sonora** (*Cine*) sound track ▸**colonna vertebrale** spine, spinal column.

colonnato [kolon'nato] SM colonnade.

colonnello [kolon'nɛllo] SM colonel.

colono [ko'lɔno] SM **a** (*contadino*) (tenant) farmer **b** (*abitante di una colonia*) colonist, settler.

colorante [kolo'rante] ① AGG colouring (*Brit*), coloring (*Am*).

② SM colorant; (*alimentare*) colo(u)ring.

colorare [kolo'rare] ① VT to colour (*Brit*), color (*Am*); (*disegno*) to colo(u)r in.

② **colorarsi** VIP: **il cielo si colorava di rosso** the sky was turning red.

colorato, a [kolo'rato] AGG coloured (*Brit*), colored (*Am*).

colorazione [kolorat'tsjone] SF (*atto*) colouring (*Brit*), coloring (*Am*); (*colore*) colour (*Brit*), color (*Am*), colo(u)ring; **colorazione politica** political sympathies *pl*.

colore [ko'lore] SM **a** (*gen, fig*) colour (*Brit*), color (*Am*); (*pittura*) paint; (*Carte*) suit; **di che colore è?** what colo(u)r is it?; **di (un) colore chiaro/scuro** light-/dark-colo(u)red; **color fragola** strawberry-colo(u)red; **senza** o **privo di colore** (*fig*) colo(u)rless; **gente di colore** colo(u)red people; **cambiare colore** (*anche fig*) to change colo(u)r; **a colori** (*film, TV, foto*) colo(u)r *attr*, in colo(u)r; **colori a olio/a tempera** oil/tempera paints **b** (*fraseologia*): **riprendere colore** (*fig*) to get one's colo(u)r back; **diventare di tutti i colori** to turn scarlet; **dirne di tutti i colori a qn** to hurl insults at sb; **farne di tutti i colori** to get up to all sorts of tricks o mischief; **passarne di tutti i colori** to go through all sorts of problems.

colorificio, ci [kolori'fitʃo] SM dye factory.

colorire [kolo'rire] VT (*colorare*) to colour (*Brit*), color (*Am*); (*fig*) to enliven, embellish.

colorito, a [kolo'rito] ① AGG (*guance, viso*) rosy, pink; (*racconto, linguaggio*) colourful (*Brit*), colorful (*Am*); **sei**

più colorito oggi you've got more colo(u)r in your cheeks today.

② SM (*carnagione*) complexion.

coloro [ko'loro] PRON DIMOSTR PL (*sogg*) they; (*complemento*) them; **coloro che** those who; vedi anche **colui**.

colossale [kolos'sale] AGG colossal, huge, enormous.

colosso [ko'lɔsso] SM (*statua*) colossus; (*fig*) giant, colossus; **è un colosso!** (*fisicamente*) he's enormous!

colpa ['kolpa] SF (*responsabilità*) fault; (*colpevolezza*) guilt; (*biasimo*) blame; (*morale*) sin; **di chi è la colpa?** whose fault is it?; **è colpa mia** it's my fault; **per colpa di** because of, thanks to; **per colpa sua** because of him, thanks to him; **essere in colpa** to be at fault; **sentirsi in colpa** to feel guilty; **senso di colpa** sense of guilt; **confessare le proprie colpe** to admit one's faults; **dare la colpa di qc a qn** to blame sb for sth; **addossarsi la colpa di qc** to take the blame for sth.

colpevole [kol'pevole] ① AGG guilty; **dichiarare qn colpevole (di qc)** to find sb guilty (of sth); **dichiararsi colpevole** to plead guilty.

② SM/F culprit.

colpevolezza [kolpevo'lettsa] SF guilt.

colpevolizzare [kolpevolid'dzare] VT: **colpevolizzare qn** to make sb feel guilty.

colpevolmente [kolpevol'mente] AVV guiltily.

colpire [kol'pire] VT (*anche fig*) to hit, strike; (*toccare*) to affect; **è stata colpita alla testa** she was hit o struck on the head; **lo ha colpito con un pugno** he punched him; **colpire qn a morte** to strike sb dead; **il nuovo provvedimento colpirà gli spacciatori** the new measure will hit drug pushers; **colpire nel segno** (*fig*) to hit the nail on the head, be spot on (*Brit*); **rimanere colpito da qc** to be amazed o struck by sth; **la sua bellezza mi ha colpito** I was struck by her beauty; **colpire l'immaginazione** to catch the imagination; **un'epidemia che colpisce le persone anziane** an epidemic which affects old people; **colpito dalla paralisi/dalla sfortuna** stricken with paralysis/by misfortune; **è stato colpito da ordine di cattura** there is a warrant out for his arrest.

colpo ['kolpo] ① SM **a** (*aggressivo*) blow; (*urto*) knock; (*fig: affettivo*) blow, shock; **colpo mortale** mortal blow; **colpo di spada** sword blow; **colpo di remo** oar stroke; **dare un colpo in testa a qn** to hit sb over the head; **prendere un colpo in** o **alla testa** to bump one's head; **prendere qn a colpi di bastone** to set about sb with a stick; **darsi un colpo di pettine** to run a comb through one's hair; **è stato un brutto colpo per lui** (*fig*) it came as a hard blow to him; **un colpo di coda** (*di cavallo*) a flick of the tail; **con un colpo d'ala l'uccello si è librato in volo** with a flap of its wings the bird took flight

b (*di arma da fuoco*) shot; **hanno sparato 10 colpi di cannone** they fired 10 cannon shots; **mi restano solo 2 colpi** I've only got 2 rounds left

c (*Med*) stroke; **colpo (apoplettico)** (apopleptic) fit; **ti venisse un colpo!** (*fam*) drop dead!; **mi hai fatto venire un colpo!** what a fright you gave me! ▸**colpo d'aria** chill ▸**colpo di calore** heat stroke ▸**colpo di frusta** o **della strega** whiplash ▸**colpo di sole** sunstroke ▸**colpo di tosse** fit of coughing

d (*Pugilato*) punch; (*Scherma*) hit ▸**colpo basso** (*Pugilato, fig*) blow o punch below the belt

e (*furto*) raid; **fare un colpo** to carry out a raid; **hanno preso gli autori di quel colpo in banca** they caught those responsible for the bank job o raid; **tentare il colpo** (*fig*)

to have a go; **ho fatto un buon colpo** I pulled it off
f (*fraseologia*): **al primo colpo** at the first attempt; **di
colpo** OR **tutto d'un colpo** suddenly; **far colpo** to cause a
sensation; **è morto sul colpo** he died instantly; **sono
andato in quel negozio a colpo sicuro** I went into that
shop knowing I would find what I wanted; **il motore
perde colpi** (*Aut*) the engine is misfiring.

2 ►**colpi di sole** (*nei capelli*) highlights ►**colpo
d'approccio** (*Tennis*) approach shot ► **colpo di fortuna**
stroke of (good) luck ►**colpo di fulmine** love at first
sight ►**colpo giornalistico** newspaper coup ►**colpo
gobbo** smart move; (*al gioco*) lucky strike ►**colpo di
grazia** (*fig*) coup de grâce ►**colpo di mano** (*Mil*)
surprise attack; (*fig*) surprise action ► **colpo d'occhio:a
colpo d'occhio** at a glance; **avere colpo d'occhio** to have
a good eye ►**colpo di rimbalzo** (*Tennis*) ground stroke
►**colpo di scena** (*Teatro*) coup de théâtre; (*fig*) dramatic turn of events ►**colpo di Stato** coup (d'état)
►**colpo di telefono** phone call; **dare un colpo di
telefono a qn** to give sb a ring ►**colpo di testa** (*Calcio*)
header (*Brit*); (*fig*) (sudden) impulse *o* whim ►**colpo di
vento** gust (of wind).

colposo, a [kol'poso] AGG: **omicidio colposo** manslaughter.

colsi *ecc* ['kɔlsi] VB vedi **cogliere**.

coltellata [koltel'lata] SF (*colpo*) stab; (*ferita*) knife *o* stab
wound.

coltelleria [koltelle'ria] SF (*assortimento*) set of knives;
(*fabbrica*) cutlery works *sg*; (*negozio*) cutler's (shop).

coltelliera [koltel'ljɛra] SF knife box.

coltello [kol'tɛllo] SM knife; **avere il coltello dalla parte del
manico** (*fig*) to have the whip hand; **c'era una nebbia
che si tagliava con il coltello** the fog was so thick you
could have cut it with a knife ►**coltello da cucina**
kitchen knife ►**coltello a serramanico** flick knife,
clasp knife.

coltivabile [kolti'vabile] AGG (*pianta, varietà*) fit for cultivation; (*terreno*) cultivable, cultivatable.

coltivabilità [koltivabili'ta] SF cultivability.

coltivare [kolti'vare] VT (*terreno, fig: amicizia*) to cultivate;
(*piante*) to grow, cultivate; **coltivare un campo a grano** to
plant a field with corn; **coltivare la mente** to cultivate
one's mind.

coltivatore, trice [koltiva'tore] SM grower, farmer
►**coltivatore diretto** small independent farmer.

coltivazione [koltivat'tsjone] SF growing, cultivation
►**coltivazione intensiva** intensive farming.

coltivo, a [kol'tivo] AGG (*terreno*) cultivated, under cultivation.

colto¹, a ['kolto] AGG (*istruito*) cultured, well-educated.

colto², a ['kɔlto] PP di **cogliere**.

coltre ['koltre] SF (*anche fig*) blanket.

coltura [kol'tura] SF **a** cultivation ►**coltura alternata**
crop rotation **b** (*Bio*) culture; **coltura batterica** bacterial culture.

colui [ko'lui] PRON DIMOSTR (*sogg*) he; (*complemento*) him;
colui che the man who, the one who; **colui che parla** the
one *o* the man *o* the person who is speaking.

colza ['kɔltsa] SF (*Bot*) rape.

com. ABBR = **comunale; commissione**.

coma ['kɔma] SM INV coma; **essere in coma** to be in a coma;
(*fig*) to be dead tired.

comandamento [komanda'mento] SM commandment.

comandante [koman'dante] SM (*Mil*) commander,

commandant; (*di reggimento*) commanding officer;
(*Aer, Naut*) captain ►**comandante del porto** harbour
master ►**comandante in seconda** second-in-
command.

comandare [koman'dare] **1** VT **a** (*ordinare*) to order,
command; (*essere al comando di*) to command, be in
charge of; **comandare a qn di fare qc** to order sb to do
sth; **comandare a bacchetta** (*fig*) to rule with a rod of
iron
b (*azionare*) to operate, control; **comandare a distanza**
to operate by remote control.
2 VI (*aus avere*) to be in charge, be in command; **qui
comando io!** I'm in charge here!

comando [ko'mando] SM **a** (*ordine*) command, order;
(: *Inform*) command; **ubbidire a un comando** to obey an
order
b (*autorità, sede*) command; **essere al comando (di)** to
be in command *o* in charge (of); (*Sport: di classifica*) to
be at the top (of); (: *di gara*) to be in the lead (in);
assumere il comando di to assume command of; (*Sport*)
to take the lead in ►**comando generale** general
headquarters *pl*
c (*Tecn*) control; **doppi comandi** dual controls; **comandi
manuali** hand controls ►**comando a distanza** remote
control.

comare [ko'mare] SF (*madrina*) godmother; (*donna pettegola*) gossip; **le allegre comari di Windsor** the Merry
Wives of Windsor.

comasco, a, schi, sche [ko'masko] **1** AGG of *o* from
Como.
2 SM/F inhabitant *o* native of Como.

comatoso, a [koma'toso] AGG comatose.

combaciare [komba'tʃare] VI (*aus avere*) to fit together;
(*fig: coincidere*) to agree, coincide, correspond.

combattente [kombat'tɛnte] **1** AGG fighting, combatant.
2 SM fighter, combatant; **ex-combattente** ex-serviceman.

combattere [kom'battere] **1** VT to fight; (*fig: teoria,
malattia*) to combat, fight (against).
2 VI (*aus avere*) to fight.

combattimento [kombatti'mento] SM (*Mil*) battle, fight,
fighting *no pl*; (*Pugilato*) match; **mettere fuori combattimento** to knock out; **combattimento (a) corpo a corpo**
hand-to-hand combat; **combattimento di galli** cock-
fighting.

combattività [kombattivi'ta] SF fighting spirit.

combattivo, a [kombat'tivo] AGG pugnacious.

combattuto, a [kombat'tuto] AGG **a** (*incerto: persona*)
uncertain, undecided; **combattuto tra due possibilità**
torn between two possibilities **b** (*gara, partita*) hard-
fought.

combinare [kombi'nare] **1** VT **a** (*mettere insieme*) to
combine
b (*organizzare: incontro*) to arrange; (*concludere: affare*)
to conclude; **che cosa stai combinando?** what are you
up to?; **ci hai combinato un bel guaio!** you've got us into
a nice mess!.
2 VI (*aus avere*) (*corrispondere*): **combinare (con)** to
correspond (with).
3 combinarsi VR (*fam: conciarsi*): **ma come ti sei combinato?** what on earth have you got on?, what on earth
have you done to yourself?.
4 combinarsi VIP (*Chim*) to combine.

combinata [kombi'nata] SF (*Sci*) combination.

combinazione [kombinat'tsjone] SF **a** (*accostamento, unione*) combination **b** (*caso fortuito*) chance, coincidence; **per combinazione** by chance; **(guarda) che combinazione!** what a coincidence! **c** (*di cassaforte*) combination.

combriccola [kom'brikkola] SF (*gruppo di amici*) party; (*banda*) gang.

comburente [kombu'rɛnte] SM (*Chim*) combustive agent.

combustibile [kombus'tibile] ①AGG combustible. ②SM fuel.

combustibilità [kombustibili'ta] SF combustibility.

combustione [kombus'tjone] SF combustion; **a lenta combustione** slow-burning.

combutta [kom'butta] SF: **essere in combutta** to be in league o in cahoots; **fare combutta con qn** to be in league o in cahoots with sb.

---

come ['kome]
①AVV
a (*alla maniera di, nel modo che*) as, like (*davanti a sostantivo, pronome*);
▷**com'è *vero* Dio** as God is my witness
▷**bianco come la neve** (as) white as snow
▷**veste come suo padre** he dresses like his father
▷**a scuola come a casa** both at school and at home, at school as well as at home
▷**ci vuole uno come lui** we need somebody like him
▷**è come parlare al muro** it's like talking to the wall
▷**non hanno accettato il progetto: come *dire* che siamo fregati** they didn't accept the plan: which means we've had it
b (*in quale modo: interrogativo, esclamativo*) how;
▷**come *mai*?** how come?
▷**come *mai* non sei partito?** whyever didn't you leave?
▷**non hanno accettato il mio assegno — come *mai*?** they didn't accept my cheque — whyever not?
▷**vieni? — come *no*!** are you coming? — of course!
▷**come *stai*?** how are you?
▷**come glielo dico?** how will I tell him?
▷**non so come dirglielo** I don't know how to tell him
▷**come?** OR **come *dici*?** pardon? (*Brit*), sorry?, excuse me? (*Am*), what did you say?
▷**com'è il tuo amico?** what's your friend like?
▷**com'è *che* non hai telefonato?** how come you didn't phone?
c (*il modo in cui*): **mi piace come scrive** I like the way he writes, I like his style of writing;
▷**ecco come è successo** this is how it happened
▷**attento a come parli!** mind your tongue!
d (*in qualità di*) as;
▷**ti parlo come *amico*** I'm speaking to you as a friend
▷**come *presidente*, dirò che...** speaking as your president I must say that ...
▷**lo hanno scelto come *rappresentante*** they've chosen him as their representative
e (*quanto*)
▷**come è brutto!** how ugly he (o it) is!
▷**come mi dispiace!** I'm terribly sorry!
f
▷**A come *Ancona*** ≈ A for Andrew
▷**come non *detto*** let's forget it
▷**oggi come *oggi*** at the present time

▷**ora come *ora*** right now; vedi anche **così, tanto.**
②CONG
a (*in quale modo*)
▷**mi scrisse come si era rotto un braccio** he wrote to tell me about how he had broken an arm
▷**mi ha spiegato come l'ha conosciuto** he told me how he met him
▷**dovevi vedere come lo picchiava** you should have seen the way he was hitting him
b (*quanto*) how;
▷**sai come sia sensibile** you know how sensitive he is
c (*correlativo*) as; (*con comparativi di maggioranza*) than;
▷**si comporta come ha sempre fatto** he behaves as he has always done
▷**è meglio/peggio di come mi aspettavo** it is better/worse than I expected
d (*appena che, quando*)
▷**come arrivò si mise a lavorare** as soon as he arrived he set to work, no sooner had he arrived than he set to work
▷**come se n'è andato, tutti sono scoppiati a ridere** as soon as he left, everyone burst out laughing
e : **come *(se)*** as if, as though;
▷**la trattano come *(se)* fosse la loro schiava** they treat her like a slave o as if she were their slave
f (*in proposizioni incidentali*) as;
▷**come *puoi* constatare** as you can see
▷**come *sai*** as you know.
③SM INV
▷**il come e il *perché*** the whys and the wherefores
▷**non so dirti il come e il *quando* di tutta questa faccenda** I couldn't tell you how and when all this happened.

COMECON ['komekon] SIGLA M (= *Consiglio di Mutua Assistenza Economica*) COMECON.

comedone [kome'done] SM blackhead.

cometa [ko'meta] SF comet.

comica, che ['komika] SF *short slapstick silent film*.

comicamente [komika'mente] AVV comically, funnily.

comicità [komitʃi'ta] SF (*di libro, film, attore*) comic quality; (*di situazione*) funny side.

comico, a, ci, che ['kɔmiko] ①AGG (*gen, buffo*) comic(al); (*Teatro*) comic. ②SM **a** (*comicità*) comic spirit, comedy; **il comico è che...** the funny thing is that ... **b** (*attore*) comedian, comic actor.

comignolo [ko'miɲɲolo] SM chimney (top).

cominciare [komin'tʃare] ①VT to start, begin; **cominciare a fare/col fare** to begin to do/by doing. ②VI (*aus* essere) to start, begin; **una parola che comincia per J** a word beginning with J; **tanto per cominciare** to start with; **a cominciare da domani** starting (from) tomorrow; **cominciamo bene!** (*iro*) we're off to a fine start!

comitato [komi'tato] SM committee, board; **far parte di un comitato** to be on a committee ▶**comitato direttivo** steering committee ▶**comitato di gestione** works council ▶**Comitato Interministeriale per la Programmazione Economica** interdepartmental committee for economic planning ▶**Comitato Inter-**

ministeriale di coordinamento per la Politica Industriale interdepartmental committee for industrial development ▶**Comitato Interministeriale dei Prezzi** interdepartmental committee on prices.

comitiva [komi'tiva] SF group, party; **viaggiare in comitiva** to travel in *o* as a group.

comizio, zi [ko'mittsjo] SM rally ▶**comizio elettorale** election rally.

comma, i ['kɔmma] SM (*Dir*) subsection.

commando [kom'mando] SM INV commando unit.

commedia [kom'mɛdja] SF **a** (*Teatro*) play; (: *comica*) comedy; **commedia musicale** musical; **la Divina Commedia** the Divine Comedy **b** (*finzione*) sham, play-acting *no pl*; **è tutta una commedia** it's just play-acting; **fare la commedia** to play-act.

commediante [komme'djante] SM/F comedian/comedienne; (*pegg*) third-rate actor/actress; (*fig: ipocrita*) sham.

commediografo, a [komme'djɔgrafo] SM/F (*autore*) comedy writer.

commemorabile [kommemo'rabile] AGG commemorable.

commemorare [kommemo'rare] VT to commemorate.

commemorativo, a [kommemora'tivo] AGG commemorative, memorial.

commemorazione [kommemorat'tsjone] SF commemoration.

commendatore [kommenda'tore] SM *official title awarded for services to one's country.*

commensale [kommen'sale] SM/F table companion.

commensurabile [kommensu'rabile] AGG (*Mat*) commensurable.

commensurabilità [kommensurabili'ta] SF (*Mat*) commensurability.

commentare [kommen'tare] VT (*dare un giudizio su: fatto, avvenimento*) to comment on; (*Radio, TV*) to give a commentary on; (*annotare*) to annotate.

commentatore, trice [kommenta'tore] SM/F (*Radio, TV*) commentator; (*di testo*) annotator.

commento [kom'mento] SM (*osservazione*) comment; (*letterario, Radio, TV*) commentary; **fare un commento su qn/qc** to comment on sb/sth; **fare il commento di una partita** to give the commentary on a match; **senza fare commenti** without passing comment; **è meglio che io non faccia commenti** it is better if I don't say anything ▶**commento musicale** (*Cine*) background music.

commerciabile [kommer'tʃabile] AGG marketable, saleable.

commerciabilità [kommertʃabili'ta] SF marketability, saleability.

commerciale [kommer'tʃale] AGG (*gen*) commercial; (*corrispondenza*) business *attr*, commercial; (*fiera, bilancio*) trade *attr*; (*pegg: film*) commercial; **interrompere i rapporti commerciali con** to interrupt trade with.

commercialista, i, e [kommertʃa'lista] SM/F (*laureato*) graduate in economics and commerce; (*consulente*) business consultant; (: *fiscale, per contabilità*) accountant.

commercializzabile [kommertʃalid'dzabile] AGG marketable.

commercializzare [kommertʃalid'dzare] VT (*prodotto*) to market; (*pegg: arte*) to commercialize.

commercializzazione [kommertʃaliddzat'tsjone] SF marketing.

commercialmente [kommertʃal'mente] AVV commercially.

commerciante [kommer'tʃante] SM/F trader, dealer; (*negoziante*) shopkeeper, tradesman; **commerciante di legname** timber merchant ▶**commerciante all'ingrosso** wholesaler ▶**commerciante in proprio** sole trader.

commerciare [kommer'tʃare] **1** VI (*aus avere*): **commerciare in** to deal *o* trade in; **commerciare con qn** to do business with sb. **2** VT to deal *o* trade in.

commercio, ci [kom'mɛrtʃo] SM (*vendita, affari*) trade, commerce; **il commercio della lana** the wool trade; **essere in commercio** (*prodotto*) to be in the shops, be on the market *o* on sale; **mettere in commercio** to put on the market; **essere nel commercio** (*persona*) to be in business ▶**commercio all'ingrosso** wholesale trade ▶**commercio al minuto** retail trade.

commessa [kom'messa] SF (*ordinazione*) order.

commesso, a [kom'messo] **1** PP di **commettere**. **2** SM/F (*addetto alla vendita*) shop assistant (*Brit*), sales clerk (*Am*); ▶**commesso viaggiatore** travelling salesman. **3** SM (*impiegato*) clerk; **commesso di banca** bank clerk.

commestibile [kommes'tibile] **1** AGG edible. **2**: **commestibili** SMPL foodstuffs.

commestibilità [kommestibili'ta] SF edibility.

commettere [kom'mettere] VT IRREG **a** (*errore*) to make; (*delitto, peccato*) to commit **b** (*ordinare*) to commission, order.

commiato [kom'mjato] SM leave-taking; **prendere commiato da qn** to take one's leave of sb.

commilitone [kommili'tone] SM fellow soldier, comrade-in-arms.

comminare [kommi'nare] VT (*Dir*) to make provision for.

commiserare [kommize'rare] VT to commiserate with, sympathize with.

commiserazione [kommizerat'tsjone] SF commiseration; **sorriso di commiserazione** (*anche pegg*) pitying smile.

commisi *ecc* [kom'mizi] VB *vedi* **commettere**.

commissariamento [kommissarja'mento] SM temporary receivership.

commissariare [kommissa'rjare] VT to put under temporary receivership.

commissariato [kommissa'rjato] SM **a** (*di polizia*) police station **b** (*carica*) commissionership; (*sede*) commissioner's office.

commissario, ri [kommis'sarjo] SM **a** (*funzionario*): **commissario (di Pubblica Sicurezza)** ≈ (police) superintendent (*Brit*), (police) captain (*Am*); **alto commissario** high commissioner ▶**commissario di bordo** (*Naut*) purser; (*Aer*) chief steward, purser ▶**commissario d'esame** member of an examining board **b** (*Sport*) steward ▶**commissario di gara** race official ▶**commissario tecnico (della Nazionale)** national team manager.

commissionare [kommissjo'nare] VT to order, place an order for.

commissionario, ri [kommissjo'narjo] SM (*Comm, Fin*) agent, broker.

commissione [kommis'sjone] SF **a** (*incarico*) errand; **fare una commissione** to go on an errand; **devo fare delle commissioni** I have some shopping to do **b** (*Comm: ordinazione*) order; (: *percentuale*) commis-

sion; **fatto su commissione** made to order; **vendere su commissione** to sell on commission ▶**commissioni bancarie** bank charges **c** (*comitato*) committee, board ▶**commissione d'esame** examining board ▶**commissione d'inchiesta** committee of enquiry ▶**commissione parlamentare** parliamentary (*Brit*) *o* Congressional (*Am*) commission ▶**commissione permanente** standing committee.

commisurare [kommizu'rare] VT: **commisurare (a)** to adapt (to); **bisogna commisurare la retribuzione alle ore di lavoro** payment must be in proportion to the number of hours worked.

commisurato, a [kommizu'rato] AGG: **commisurato a** in proportion to.

committente [kommit'tɛnte] SM/F (*Comm*) purchaser, customer.

commosso, a [kom'mɔsso] [1] PP di **commuovere**. [2] AGG moved, touched; **essere commosso fino alle lacrime** to be moved to tears.

commovente [kommo'vɛnte] AGG moving, touching.

commozione [kommot'tsjone] SF **a** (*emozione*) emotion, deep feeling **b** (*Med*): **commozione cerebrale** concussion.

commuovere [kom'mwɔvere] VB IRREG [1] VT to move, touch, affect. [2] **commuoversi** VIP to be moved.

commutare [kommu'tare] VT **a** (*Dir*: *pena*) to commute **b** (*Elettr*) to switch *o* change over, commutate (*termine tecn*).

commutatore [kommuta'tore] SM (*Elettr*) commutator.

commutazione [kommutat'tsjone] SF (*Dir*, *Elettr*) commutation ▶**commutazione di pacchetto** (*Inform*) packet switching.

comò [ko'mɔ] SM INV chest of drawers, bureau (*Am*).

comodamente [komoda'mente] AVV (*in modo comodo*) comfortably; (*senza sforzo*) easily.

comodino [komo'dino] SM bedside table.

comodità [komodi'ta] SF INV **a** (*vedi agg*) convenience; handiness; comfort **b** : **le comodità della vita moderna** modern conveniences.

comodo, a ['kɔmodo] [1] AGG (*conveniente*) convenient; (*pratico*) handy; (*utile*) useful; (*confortevole*) comfortable; (*facile*) easy; **gli piace la vita comoda** he likes an easy life; **stia comodo!** don't bother to get up!. [2] SM: **con comodo** at one's convenience *o* leisure; **fai con comodo** take your time; **fare il proprio comodo** to please o.s., do as one pleases; **amare il proprio comodo** to like one's comforts; **quei soldi mi hanno fatto comodo** that money came in handy; **una macchina mi farebbe comodo** a car would do me nicely, a car would be very handy; **una soluzione di comodo** a convenient arrangement.

compact disc ['kɔmpakt 'disk] SM INV compact disc.

compaesano, a [kompae'zano] SM/F (*dello stesso paese*) fellow countryman/woman; (*della stessa città*) person from the same town; **è un mio compaesano** he comes from the same town *o* country as I do.

compagine [kom'padʒine] SF **a** (*Pol*): **la compagine del partito** the party en bloc; **la compagine dello Stato** the government as a whole **b** (*squadra*) team.

compagnia [kompaɲ'ɲia] SF **a** company; **fare compagnia a qn** to keep sb company; **essere di compagnia** to be sociable; **dama di compagnia** lady-in-waiting **b** (*gruppo di persone*) group, party; (*Mil, Comm, Teatro*) company; **compagnia aerea** airline; **compagnia di bandiera** (*aerea*) national airline; **frequentare cattive compagnie** to keep bad company; **... e compagnia bella** (*e gli altri*) ...and co.; (*eccetera, eccetera*) ...and so on.

compagno, a [kom'paɲɲo] SM/F (*gen*) companion; (*nel gioco*) partner; (*della vita*) life companion; (*Pol*) comrade ▶**compagno di giochi** playmate ▶**compagno di lavoro** workmate ▶**compagno di scuola** schoolfriend ▶**compagno di squadra** teammate ▶**compagno di sventura** companion in misfortune ▶**compagno di viaggio** fellow traveller.

compaio ecc [kom'pajo] VB vedi **comparire**.

companatico [kompa'natiko] SM: **pane e companatico** ≈ bread and dripping.

comparare [kompa'rare] VT to compare.

comparativamente [komparativa'mente] AVV comparatively.

comparativo, a [kompara'tivo] AGG, SM comparative.

comparato, a [kompa'rato] AGG comparative.

comparazione [komparat'tsjone] SF comparison.

compare [kom'pare] SM (*padrino*) godfather; (*complice*) accomplice; (*fam*: *amico*) old pal, old mate.

comparire [kompa'rire] VI IRREG (*aus* **essere**) (*presentarsi*) to appear; (*uscire*: *libro, giornale*) to come out; **comparire in giudizio** (*Dir*) to appear before the court.

comparizione [komparit'tsjone] SF (*Dir*) appearance; **mandato di comparizione** summons *sg*.

comparsa [kom'parsa] SF **a** (*apparizione*) appearance; **fare la propria comparsa** to put in an appearance; **nessuno si aspettava la sua comparsa** no one expected him to turn up **b** (*persona*: *Cine*) extra; (: *Teatro*) walk-on.

comparso, a [kom'parso] PP di **comparire**.

compartecipare [kompartetʃi'pare] VI (*aus* **avere**) (*Comm*): **compartecipare a** to have a share in; **compartecipare agli utili** to share in the profits.

compartecipazione [kompartetʃipat'tsjone] SF (*divisione con altri*) sharing; (*quota*) share; **compartecipazione agli utili** profit-sharing; **in compartecipazione** jointly.

compartecipe [kompar'tetʃipe] AGG: **essere compartecipe agli utili** to share in the profits.

compartimentale [kompartimen'tale] AGG district *attr*.

compartimentazione [kompartimentat'tsjone] SF compartmentation, division into compartments.

compartimento [komparti'mento] SM **a** (*Amm*: *circoscrizione*) district **b** (*Naut*): **compartimento stagno** watertight compartment.

comparvi ecc [kom'parvi] VB vedi **comparire**.

compassatamente [kompassata'mente] AVV imperturbably.

compassato, a [kompas'sato] AGG (*persona*) composed; **freddo e compassato** cool and collected.

compassione [kompas'sjone] SF compassion, pity; **provare** *o* **sentire compassione per qn** [OR] **avere compassione di qn** to pity sb, feel sorry for sb; **fare compassione** to arouse pity; **mi ha fatto compassione vederli ridotti così** I was sorry to see them in such a state.

compassionevole [kompassjo'nevole] AGG (*che sente compassione*) compassionate; (*che suscita compassione*) pitiful, pathetic.

compassionevolmente [kompassjonevol'mente] AVV (*vedi agg*) compassionately; pitifully, pathetically.

compasso [kom'passo] SM (pair of) compasses *pl*;

compasso per spessori callipers *pl.*

compatibile [kompa'tibile] AGG **a** (*conciliabile, Inform*) compatible **b** (*scusabile*) understandable, excusable.

compatibilità [kompatibili'ta] SF (*gen, Inform*) compatibility.

compatibilmente [kompatibil'mente] AVV: **compatibilmente con i miei impegni** depending on my commitments.

compatimento [kompati'mento] SM: **con aria di compatimento** with a condescending air.

compatire [kompa'tire] VT (*aver compassione di*) to feel sorry for, sympathize with; (*scusare*) to make allowances for; **bisogna compatirlo, poveretto** (*iro*) you've got to make allowances for him, poor thing.

compatriota, i, e [kompatri'ɔta] SM/F fellow countryman/woman, compatriot.

compattezza [kompat'tettsa] SF (*solidità*) compactness; (*fig: unità*) solidarity.

compatto, a [kom'patto] AGG (*roccia*) solid; (*folla*) dense; (*partito*) united; (*gruppo*) close-knit.

compendio, di [kom'pɛndjo] SM compendium, outline.

compensare [kompen'sare] **1** VT **a** (*lavoro*) to pay for; (*danno*) to give compensation for; **è stato compensato per il danno ricevuto** he has received compensation for the damage

b (*bilanciare*) to compensate for, make up for; **le perdite dell'anno scorso saranno compensate dagli utili di quest'anno** this year's profits will compensate for last year's losses.

2 **compensarsi** VR (*uso reciproco*) to balance each other out.

compensato [kompen'sato] SM (*anche:* **legno compensato**) plywood.

compensazione [kompensat'tsjone] SF compensation.

compenso [kom'pɛnso] SM (*retribuzione*) remuneration, payment; (*onorario*) fee; (*ricompensa*) reward, compensation; **in compenso** (*d'altra parte*) on the other hand.

compera ['kompera] SF: **fare le compere** to do the shopping.

comperare [kompe'rare] VT = comprare.

competente [kompe'tɛnte] AGG (*gen, Dir*) competent; (*capace*) qualified; **è lui il competente in materia** he's the expert; **rivolgersi all'ufficio competente** to apply to the office concerned.

competentemente [kompetente'mente] AVV competently.

competenza [kompe'tɛntsa] SF **a** (*capacità*) competence, expertise; (*Dir: autorità*) jurisdiction; **non ho competenza in materia** I'm not an expert on that; **è di competenza del tribunale di Milano** it comes under the jurisdiction of the Milan courts; **l'argomento non è di mia competenza** I am not qualified to speak on that subject; **questo lavoro non è di mia competenza** that's not my job; **definire le competenze** to establish responsibilities

b (*onorario*): **competenze** SFPL fees.

competere [kom'pɛtere] VI DIF **a** (*gareggiare*) to compete, vie **b** (*Dir*): **competere a** to lie with, come under the jurisdiction of, lie within the competence of; (*spettare: compito*) to lie with; (*: denaro*) to be due to; **avrai ciò che ti compete** you'll have what is due to you.

competitivamente [kompetitiva'mente] AVV competitively.

competitività [kompetitivi'ta] SF competitiveness.

competitivo, a [kompeti'tivo] AGG competitive.

competitore, trice [kompeti'tore] SM/F competitor.

competizione [kompetit'tsjone] SF competition, contest; **spirito di competizione** competitive spirit; **auto da competizione** racing car.

compiacente [kompja'tʃɛnte] AGG obliging, courteous; (*pegg*) accommodating.

compiacenza [kompja'tʃɛntsa] SF courtesy; **abbiate la compiacenza di aspettarmi** please be so good as to wait for me.

compiacere [kompja'tʃere] VB IRREG **1** VI (*aus* avere): **compiacere a** to gratify, please.

2 VT to please, make happy.

3 **compiacersi** VIP (*provare soddisfazione*): **compiacersi di** o **per qc** to be delighted at sth, be pleased with sth; (*rallegrarsi*): **compiacersi con qn per qc** to congratulate sb for o on sth.

compiacimento [kompjatʃi'mento] SM satisfaction.

compiaciuto, a [kompja'tʃuto] PP di compiacere.

compiacqui *ecc* VB vedi compiacere.

compiangere [kom'pjandʒere] VT IRREG to feel sorry for, sympathize with.

compiansi *ecc* VB vedi compiangere.

compianto, a [kom'pjanto] **1** PP di compiangere.

2 AGG: **il compianto presidente** the late lamented president.

3 SM mourning, grief.

compiere ['kompjere] **1** VT (*adempiere*) to carry out, fulfil (*Brit*), fulfill (*Am*); (*finire*) complete; **compiere gli anni** to have one's birthday; **quando compi gli anni?** when is your birthday?; **quanti anni compi?** how old will you be?; **ha compiuto 18 anni il mese scorso** he turned 18 last month; **compiere il proprio dovere** to carry out one's duty; **compiere una buona azione** to do a good deed.

2 **compiersi** VIP **a** (*giungere a termine*) to end **b** (*avverarsi: speranze*) to be fulfilled; (*: profezie*) to come true.

compieta [kom'pjɛta] SF (*Rel*) compline.

compilare [kompi'lare] VT (*gen*) to compile; (*modulo*) to complete, fill in, fill out (*Am*).

compilatore, trice [kompila'tore] SM/F compiler.

compilazione [kompilat'tsjone] SF (*vedi vb*) compilation; completion.

compimento [kompi'mento] SM (*termine, conclusione*) completion, fulfilment (*Brit*), fulfillment (*Am*); **portare a compimento qc** to conclude sth, bring sth to a conclusion.

compire *ecc* VB = compiere.

compitare [kompi'tare] VT to spell out.

compitezza [kompi'tettsa] SF politeness, courtesy.

compito¹, a [kom'pito] AGG well-mannered, polite.

compito² ['kompito] SM **a** (*incarico*) job, task, duty; (*dovere*) duty **b** (*Scol: a casa*) piece of homework; (*: in classe*) class test; **fare i compiti** to do one's homework.

compiutamente [kompjuta'mente] AVV completely.

compiutezza [kompju'tettsa] SF (*completezza*) completeness; (*perfezione*) perfection.

compiuto, a [kom'pjuto] AGG: **a 20 anni compiuti** at 20 years of age, at age 20; **un fatto compiuto** a fait accompli.

compleanno [komple'anno] SM birthday.

complementare [komplemen'tare] AGG (*gen, Geom*) complementary; (*materia di studio, esame*) subsidiary.

complementarità [komplementari'ta] SF complementarity.

complemento [komple'mento] SM **a** (*Gramm*) complement; **complemento oggetto** *o* **diretto/indiretto** direct/indirect object **b** (*Mil*) reserve (troops *pl*); **di complemento** reserve *attr*.

complessato, **a** [komples'sato] AGG, SM/F: **essere (un) complessato** to be full of complexes.

complessità [komplessi'ta] SF complexity.

complessivamente [komplessiva'mente] AVV (*nell'insieme*) on the whole, in all; (*in tutto*) altogether.

complessivo, **a** [komples'sivo] AGG (*ammontare, prezzo, spesa*) total; (*voti*) overall; **visione complessiva** overview.

complesso, **a** [kom'plesso] ① AGG complex, complicated; **numeri complessi** complex numbers; **proposizione complessa** compound sentence.

② SM **a** (*insieme*) whole; (*di leggi*) body; (*organizzazione, posto*) complex; **nel** *o* **in complesso** by and large, generally speaking, on the whole; **è stato un complesso di cose a farmi cambiare idea** it was a combination of things that made me change my mind; **il complesso delle manifestazioni culturali avverrà in luglio** the vast majority of cultural events will take place in July
► **complesso industriale** industrial complex
b (*Psic*) complex ► **complesso d'inferiorità** inferiority complex
c (*Mus*) band, ensemble; (: *di musica leggera*) group.

completamente [kompleta'mente] AVV completely.

completamento [kompleta'mento] SM completion.

completare [komple'tare] VT to complete, finish.

completezza [komple'tettsa] SF completeness.

completo, **a** [kom'plɛto] ① AGG (*gen*) complete; (*resoconto, elenco*) full, complete; (*fiasco, fallimento*) complete, utter; **computer completo di stampante** computer complete with printer.

② SM (*abito*) suit; (*di lenzuola*) set; **completo di lenzuola singolo/matrimoniali** set of sheets for a single/double bed; **completo da sci** ski suit; **essere al completo** (*albergo*) to be full; (*teatro*) to be sold out.

complicare [kompli'kare] ① VT to complicate; **non per complicarti la vita, ma...** not that I want to make life difficult for you, but ....

② **complicarsi** VIP to become complicated.

complicazione [komplikat'tsjone] SF complication; **salvo complicazioni** unless any difficulties arise; (*Med*) unless there are any complications.

complice ['kɔmplitʃe] SM/F accomplice.

complicità [komplitʃi'ta] SF INV complicity; **un sorriso/uno sguardo di complicità** a knowing smile/look.

complimentarsi [komplimen'tarsi] VIP: **complimentarsi con qn per qc** to congratulate sb on sth.

complimento [kompli'mento] SM **a** (*lode*) compliment; **fare un complimento a qn** to compliment sb, pay sb a compliment
b : **complimenti** SMPL (*congratulazioni*) congratulations; **le faccio i miei complimenti per...** may I congratulate you on ...; **complimenti!** congratulations!
c : **complimenti** SMPL (*cerimonie*) ceremony *sg*; **fa sempre tanti complimenti** he always stands on ceremony; **senza complimenti!** (*offrendo qualcosa*) help yourself!; **non fare complimenti** *o* **senza complimenti, se ti fa piacere resta con noi** feel free to stay with us if you'd like to; **senza tanti complimenti ha preso la mia**

macchina e se n'è andato without so much as a by your leave he took my car and off he went.

complimentoso, **a** [komplimen'toso] AGG ceremonious.

complottare [komplot'tare] VI (*aus avere*) to plot, conspire.

complotto [kom'plɔtto] SM plot, conspiracy.

compone *ecc* [kom'pone] VB *vedi* **comporre**.

componente [kompo'nɛnte] ① AGG component.
② SM/F (*persona*) member.
③ SM (*Elettr*) component, part; (*Chim*) component.
④ SF (*fig: elemento*) element; **c'era in lui una componente di sadismo** there was an element of sadism in his character.

compongo *ecc* [kom'pongo] VB *vedi* **comporre**.

componibile [kompo'nibile] AGG (*mobili, cucina*) fitted.

componimento [komponi'mento] SM **a** (*gen, Mus*) composition; (*Letteratura*) work, writing **b** (*Dir*) settlement.

comporre [kom'porre] VB IRREG ① VT **a** (*creare: musica, poesia*) to compose; **essere composto di** to be composed of, consist of **b** (*mettere in ordine*) to arrange **c** (*Telec*) to dial **d** (*Tip*) to set **e** (*Dir: vertenza*) to settle.
② **comporsi** VIP: **comporsi di** to consist of, be composed of.

comportamentale [komportamen'tale] AGG behavioural (*Brit*), behavioral (*Am*).

comportamentismo [komportamen'tizmo] SM (*Psic*) behaviourism (*Brit*), behaviorism (*Am*).

comportamentista, **i**, **e** [komportamen'tista] SM/F behaviourist (*Brit*), behaviorist (*Am*).

comportamento [komporta'mento] SM (*umano, animale*) behaviour (*Brit*), behavior (*Am*); (*di prodotto*) performance.

comportare [kompor'tare] ① VT (*richiedere*) to call for, require; (*implicare*) to imply, involve, entail; **ciò comporta una spesa ingente** it involves a huge financial outlay.
② **comportarsi** VIP to behave; **comportati bene!** behave!; **non ci si comporta così** that's no way to behave; **comportarsi da vigliacco** to behave like a coward.

composi *ecc* [kom'pozi] VB *vedi* **comporre**.

composito, **a** [kom'pozito] AGG composite.

compositore, **trice** [kompozi'tore] ① SM/F (*Mus*) composer.
② SM (*Tip*) compositor, typesetter.
③ SF (*Tip*) typesetting machine.

composizione [kompozit'tsjone] SF **a** (*gen, Chim, Mus*) composition **b** (*Tip*) typesetting, composition **c** (*Dir*) settlement.

compossesso [kompos'sɛsso] SM (*Dir*) joint possession.

composta [kom'posta] SF (*Culin*) stewed fruit, compote.

compostamente [komposta'mente] AVV composedly; **stai seduto compostamente!** sit properly!

compostezza [kompos'tettsa] SF (*vedi agg*) composure; decorum.

composto, **a** [kom'posto] ① PP *di* **comporre**.
② AGG **a** (*Gramm*) compound *attr*; (*Mat*) composite; (*formato da più elementi*) compound *attr* **b** (*atteggiamento*) composed; (*persona: decoroso*) dignified; **stai seduto composto** sit properly.
③ SM (*Chim*) compound; (*Culin*) mixture; (*Agr*) compost.

comprare [kom'prare] VT **a** to buy; **comprare qc a qn** to

buy sth for sb, buy sb sth; **comprare qc a occhi chiusi** *o* **a scatola chiusa** to buy sth with complete confidence **b** (*corrompere*: *giudice, testimone*) to bribe; (*voti*) to buy; **comprare il silenzio di qn** to bribe sb to keep quiet, buy sb's silence.

compratore, trice [kompra'tore] SM/F buyer, purchaser.

compravendita [kompra'vendita] SF (*Comm*) (contract of) sale; **un atto di compravendita** a deed of sale.

comprendere [kom'prɛndere] VT IRREG **a** (*includere*) to include; (*contenere*) to comprise, consist of **b** (*capire*) to understand.

comprendonio [kompren'dɔnjo] SM: **essere duro di comprendonio** to be slow on the uptake.

comprensibile [kompren'sibile] AGG understandable.

comprensibilmente [komprensibil'mente] AVV (*in modo giustificabile*) understandably; (*con chiarezza*) clearly, comprehensibly.

comprensione [kompren'sjone] SF understanding.

comprensivamente [komprensiva'mente] AVV **a** (*così da includere*) inclusively **b** (*con tolleranza*) understandingly.

comprensivo, a [kompren'sivo] AGG **a** (*Comm*): **comprensivo (di)** (*prezzo*) inclusive (of) **b** (*tollerante*) understanding.

comprensorio, ri [kompren'sɔrjo] SM (*Amm*: *territorio*) district.

compreso, a [kom'preso] [1] PP di **comprendere**.
[2] AGG (*incluso*) inclusive, included; **tutto compreso** all inclusive, all-in (*Brit*); **dall'8 al 22 compreso** from the 8th to the 22nd inclusive; **aperto tutta la settimana domenica compresa** open all week including Sunday.

compressa [kom'prɛssa] SF (*Med*: *pastiglia*) tablet; (: *garza*) compress.

compressione [kompres'sjone] SF compression.

compresso, a [kom'prɛsso] [1] PP di **comprimere**.
[2] AGG compressed, pressed.

compressore [kompres'sore] SM **a** compressor **b** (*anche*: **rullo compressore**) steamroller.

comprimario, ria, ri, rie [kompri'marjo] SM/F (*Teatro*) supporting actor/actress.

comprimere [kom'primere] VT IRREG to compress, press.

compromesso, a [kompro'messo] [1] PP di **compromettere**.
[2] SM (*accordo*) compromise; (*Dir*) arbitration agreement; **arrivare a un compromesso** to reach a compromise; **soluzione di compromesso** compromise solution; **vive di compromessi** his life is a series of compromises.

compromettente [kompromet'tɛnte] AGG compromising.

compromettere [kompro'mettere] VB IRREG [1] VT (*reputazione*) to compromise, jeopardize; (*libertà, avvenire, risultato*) to jeopardize; **compromettersi la reputazione** to compromise *o* jeopardize one's reputation.
[2] **compromettersi** VR to compromise o.s.

comproprietà [komproprje'ta] SF (*Dir*) joint ownership.

comproprietario, ria, ri, rie [komproprje'tarjo] SM/F (*Dir*) joint owner.

comprova [kom'prɔva] SF: **a comprova di** as proof of.

comprovabile [kompro'vabile] AGG provable, demonstrable.

comprovare [kompro'vare] VT to prove, confirm.

compuntamente [kompunta'mente] AVV contritely.

compunto, a [kom'punto] AGG (*contrito*) contrite; **con fare**

compunto (*iro*) with a solemn air.

compunzione [kompun'tsjone] SF (*vedi agg*) contrition; solemnity.

computabile [kompu'tabile] AGG calculable.

computare [kompu'tare] VT to calculate, estimate.

computer [kəm'pju:tər] SM INV computer.

computerizzare [kompjuterid'dzare] VT to computerize.

computerizzato, a [kompjuterid'dzato] AGG computerized.

computerizzazione [kompjuteriddzat'tsjone] SF computerization.

computisteria [komputiste'ria] SF (*Comm*) book-keeping, accounting.

computo ['kɔmputo] SM (*calcolo*) counting, calculation; **fare il computo di** to count.

comunale [komu'nale] AGG (*del comune*) town *attr*, municipal; **è un impiegato comunale** he works for the local council; **consiglio/palazzo comunale** town council/hall.

comunanza [komu'nantsa] SF: **comunanza di interessi** community of interests.

comune¹ [ko'mune] [1] AGG **a** (*gen, Gramm*) common; (*diffuso*) common, widespread; (*consueto*) everyday; **è un problema molto comune** it's a very common *o* widespread problem; **di intelligenza non comune** of exceptional intelligence; **un nostro comune amico** a mutual friend of ours; **il bene comune** the common good; **di comune accordo** by common consent; **di uso comune** in common use; **un luogo comune** a commonplace; **cassa comune** kitty; **fare cassa comune** to pool one's money; **mal comune, mezzo gaudio** a trouble shared is a trouble halved **b** (*ordinario*) ordinary; (*di livello medio*) average; **la gente comune** ordinary folk.
[2] SM **a** (*di più persone*): **avere qc in comune** to have sth in common, share sth; **avere il bagno in comune** to share a bathroom, have a communal bathroom; **mettere le provviste in comune** to pool *o* share one's provisions **b** : **fuori del comune** out of the ordinary.

comune² [ko'mune] SM (*Amm*: *sede*) town hall; (: *autorità*) town council (*the smallest autonomous political and administrative unit: it keeps records of births, marriages and deaths, approves plans for public works and can impose taxes*); **l'età dei Comuni** (*Storia*) the age of the city states; **la Camera dei Comuni** OR **i Comuni** (*Brit Pol*) the House of Commons, the Commons.

comune³ [ko'mune] SF (*comunità, anche Storia*) commune.

comunella [komu'nella] SF: **fare comunella** to band together.

comunemente [komune'mente] AVV (*gen*) commonly; (*normalmente*) normally.

comunicabile [komuni'kabile] AGG communicable.

comunicabilità [komunikabili'ta] SF communicability.

comunicando, a [komuni'kando] SM/F (*Rel*) communicant.

comunicante [komuni'kante] AGG communicating.

comunicare [komuni'kare] [1] VT **a** (*trasmettere*) to communicate; **comunicare una notizia a qn** to give sb a piece of news; **comunicare qc a qn** to inform sb of sth **b** (*Rel*) to administer communion to.
[2] VI (*aus avere*) (*stanze, persone*) to communicate; **questa porta comunica con l'esterno** this door leads outside.
[3] **comunicarsi** VIP **a** (*propagarsi*) to spread

b (*Rel*) to receive communion.

comunicativa [komunika'tiva] SF communicativeness; **ha molta comunicativa** she is very communicative.

comunicativo, a [komunika'tivo] AGG communicative.

comunicato [komuni'kato] SM communiqué ►**comunicato stampa** press release.

comunicazione [komunikat'tsjone] SF **a** (*collegamento*) communication; **porta di comunicazione** communicating door; **essere in comunicazione (con)** (*Anat, Tecn*) to be connected (with); **mettersi in comunicazione con qn** to contact sb; **vie di comunicazione** means of communication; **le comunicazioni ferroviarie/stradali/telefoniche sono interrotte** rail/road/telephone communications have broken down

b (*Telec*) call; **le passo la comunicazione** I'll put the call through to you; **non riesco ad avere la comunicazione** I can't get through; **si è interrotta la comunicazione** we've been cut off

c (*messaggio*) message, communication; (*annuncio*) announcement; **ho una comunicazione urgente per lei** I have an urgent message for you; **salvo comunicazioni contrarie da parte Vostra** unless we hear from you to the contrary.

comunione [komu'njone] SF (*Rel, fig*) communion; **fare la comunione** to receive communion; **fare la prima comunione** to make one's first communion ►**comunione dei beni** (*Dir*: *tra coniugi*) joint ownership of property.

comunismo [komu'nizmo] SM communism.

comunista, i, e [komu'nista] AGG, SM/F communist.

comunità [komuni'ta] SF INV community ►**Comunità Economica Europea** European Economic Community ►**comunità terapeutica** therapeutic community (*rehabilitation centre run by voluntary organization for people with drug, alcohol etc dependency*).

comunitario, ria, ri, rie [komuni'tarjo] AGG community *attr*.

comunque [ko'munkwe] **1** AVV (*in ogni modo*) anyhow, anyway, in any case; **devi farlo comunque** you'll have to do it anyway; **accetterà comunque** he'll accept in any case; **e comunque al biglietto ci penso io** and as for the ticket I'll see to that.

2 CONG **a** (*in qualunque modo*) however, no matter how; **comunque vada** whatever happens; **comunque sia** however that may be

b (*tuttavia*) however, nevertheless; **comunque potevi avvertirmi** however *o* nevertheless you could have let me know, you could have let me know though.

con [kon] PREP (può fondersi con l'articolo determinativo: con + il = col, con + lo = collo, con + l' = coll', con + la = colla, con + i = coi, con + gli = cogli, con + le = colle) **a** (*gen*) with; **ci andrò con lei** I'll go with her; **con chi sei stato?** who were you with?; **con chi era il film?** who was in the film?; **riso col burro** rice with butter; **un ragazzo con gli occhi azzurri** a boy with blue eyes, a blue-eyed boy; **è a letto con la febbre** he's in bed with a temperature

b (*complemento di relazione*) with; (*nei confronti di*) with, towards; **sono in contatto con loro** I am in touch with them; **è sposata con uno scozzese** she's married to a Scot; **si è sposata con uno scozzese** she married a Scot, she got married to a Scot; **hai parlato con lui?** have you spoken to him?; **essere gentile con qn** to be kind to sb; **è brava con i bambini** she's good with children; **confrontare qc con qc** to compare sth with *o* to sth; **sono tutti**

con lui (*dalla sua parte*) they are all on his side, they are all behind him

c (*per mezzo di*) with; (: *aereo, macchina*) by; **scrivere con la penna** to write with a pen; **prendilo con le mani** pick it up with your hands; **condisci l'insalata con l'olio** dress the salad with oil; **arrivare col treno/l'aereo/con la macchina** to arrive by train/by plane/by car; **lo hanno fatto venire con una scusa** they used a pretext to get him to come, they got him to come by means of a pretext

d (*complemento di modo o maniera*) with; **con pazienza** with patience, patiently; **con la forza** by force; **con molta attenzione** with great attention, very attentively; **con mia grande sorpresa/stupore** to my great surprise/astonishment; **lo accolse con un sorriso** she greeted him with a smile

e (*complemento di causa*): **con questo freddo non potremo partire** we can't leave in this cold weather; **con tutti i debiti che ha…** with all his debts …, given all his debts …; **con il 1 di ottobre** as of October 1st; **con l'autunno cadono le foglie** with the coming of autumn the leaves fall from the trees

f (*nonostante*): **con tutti i suoi difetti…** in spite of all his faults …; **con tutto ciò** in spite of that, for all that; **con tutto che era arrabbiato** even though he was angry, in spite of the fact that he was angry

g (*con l'infinito*): **se vuoi dimagrire, comincia col mangiare meno** if you want to lose weight, start by eating less; **finì col dirgli che aveva ragione lei** he ended up saying she was right; **con l'insistere tanto l'hai fatto arrabbiare** you've annoyed him with your pestering; **col passar del tempo** with the passing of time, in the course of time; **col sorgere del sole** with the dawn

h : **e con ciò se n'è andato** and with that he left; **e con questo?** so what?; **come va con la tua gamba?** how's your leg?; **come va con Alberto?** how are you getting on with Alberto?

conato [ko'nato] SM: **conato di vomito** retching; **avere un conato di vomito** to retch.

conca, che ['konka] SF (*Geog*) valley, basin.

concatenare [konkate'nare] **1** VT to link up, connect.

2 concatenarsi VR (*uso reciproco*) to be connected.

concatenato, a [konkate'nato] AGG (*eventi*) connected; (*Geol*) interlocking.

concatenazione [konkatenat'tsjone] SF connection, link.

concavo, a ['konkavo] AGG concave.

concedente [kontʃe'dɛnte] SM/F (*Dir*) conveyor.

concedere [kon'tʃedere] VB IRREG **1** VT **a** (*permettere*): **concedere a qn di fare qc** to allow sb to do sth; (*dare*): **concedere qc a qn** to grant sb sth; **gli concesse di uscire** he gave him permission to go out; **concedere un prestito** to grant a loan; **mi concedi un minuto d'attenzione** may I have your attention?

b (*ammettere*): **concedere (che)** to concede (that)

c : **concedersi qc/di fare qc** (*permettersi*) to allow o.s. sth/to do sth; **concedersi il lusso di andare in vacanza** to allow o.s. the luxury of a holiday.

2 concedersi VR: **concedersi a qc** (*donna*: *sessualmente*) to give o.s. to sb.

concentramento [kontʃentra'mento] SM concentration.

concentrare [kontʃen'trare] **1** VT to concentrate; **concentrare l'attenzione su qc** to focus one's attention on sth.

2 concentrarsi VR: **concentrarsi (in)** (*raccogliere l'attenzione*) to concentrate (on); (*adunarsi*) to assemble (in).

concentrato, a [kontʃen'trato] SM concentrate ▶ **concentrato di pomodoro** tomato purée.

concentrazione [kontʃentrat'tsjone] SF (*gen*) concentration; **concentrazione orizzontale/verticale** (*Econ*) horizontal/vertical integration.

concentricità [kontʃentritʃi'ta] SF (*Geom*) concentricity.

concentrico, a, ci, che [kon'tʃɛntriko] AGG (*Geom*) concentric.

concepibile [kontʃe'pibile] AGG conceivable.

concepimento [kontʃepi'mento] SM conception.

concepire [kontʃe'pire] VT **a** (*bambino*) to conceive **b** (*idea*) to conceive; (*progetto*) to devise, conceive; (*metodo, piano*) to devise; **un elettrodomestico concepito per vari usi** an electrical appliance devised for various purposes **c** (*immaginare*) to imagine, understand, conceive (of); **non riesco a concepire una cosa simile** I just can't imagine such a thing.

conceria [kontʃe'ria] SF tannery.

concernere [kon'tʃɛrnere] VT DIF to concern, regard; **per quanto mi concerne** as far as I'm concerned.

concertare [kontʃer'tare] VT (*ordire: piano*) to devise, plan; (*Mus: spartito*) to harmonize; (*: sinfonia*) to rehearse.

concertino [kontʃer'tino] SM concertino.

concertista, i, e [kontʃer'tista] SM/F concert performer.

concertistico, a, ci, che [kontʃer'tistiko] AGG concert *attr*.

concerto [kon'tʃɛrto] SM (*Mus*) concert; (*: componimento*) concerto; **sala per concerti** concert hall.

concessi [kon'tʃɛssi] VB vedi **concedere**.

concessionaria [kontʃessjo'narja] SF (*Comm: ditta*) authorized dealer *o* agency.

concessionario, ria, ri, rie [kontʃessjo'narjo] **1** AGG concessionary. **2** SM (*Comm*) agent, dealer ▶ **concessionario esclusivo (di)** sole agent (for).

concessione [kontʃes'sjone] SF concession.

concessiva [kontʃes'siva] SF (*Gramm*) concessive clause.

concessivo, a [kontʃes'sivo] AGG concessive.

concesso, a [kon'tʃɛsso] PP di **concedere**.

concettismo [kontʃet'tizmo] SM (*Arte*) conceptism; (*fig: di scrittore*) use of conceits; ≈ euphuism.

concettistico, a, ci, che [kontʃet'tistiko] AGG (*fig: stile*) marked by the use of conceits; ≈ euphuistic.

concetto [kon'tʃɛtto] SM (*nozione*) concept; (*opinione*) opinion; **farsi un concetto di** to form an opinion of; **è un impiegato di concetto** ≈ he's a white-collar worker; **lascialo in pace, sta facendo un lavoro di concetto** (*iro*) leave him alone, he's concentrating.

concettoso, a [kontʃet'toso] AGG full of conceits.

concettuale [kontʃettu'ale] AGG conceptual.

concezione [kontʃet'tsjone] SF **a** (*idea*) view, idea; **che concezione hai della vita?** how do you see life?, what is your view of life? **b** (*ideazione*) conception.

conchiglia [kon'kiʎʎa] SF (*Zool*) shell; (*Culin*) pasta shell.

concia ['kontʃa] SF (*vedi vt a*) tanning; curing.

conciare [kon'tʃare] **1** VT **a** (*pelli*) to tan; (*tabacco*) to cure **b** (*maltrattare: scarpe, libri*) to treat badly; (*: persona*) to ill-treat; **guarda come hai conciato quei libri** look at the mess you've made of those books; **ti hanno conciato male** *o* **per le feste!** they've really beaten you up! **2 conciarsi** VR (*ridursi male*) to get into a mess; (*vestirsi male*): **ma guarda come si è conciata!** look at the state she's in!

conciatore [kontʃa'tore] SM (*vedi vt a*) tanner; curer.

conciatura [kontʃa'tura] SF (*vedi vt a*) tanning; curing.

conciliabile [kontʃi'ljabile] AGG compatible.

conciliabilità [kontʃiljabili'ta] SF compatibility.

conciliabolo [kontʃi'ljabolo] SM secret meeting.

conciliante [kontʃi'ljante] AGG conciliatory.

conciliare[1] [kontʃi'ljare] **1** VT **a** (*mettere d'accordo*) to reconcile; **conciliare una contravvenzione** to settle a fine on the spot **b** (*favorire: sonno*) to be conducive to, induce **c**: **conciliarsi qc** (*stima, simpatia*) to gain *o* win sth (for o.s.). **2 conciliarsi** VIP: **lo studio non si concilia con il mio lavoro** I can't combine studying with my job.

conciliare[2] [kontʃi'ljare] AGG council *attr*.

conciliazione [kontʃiljat'tsjone] SF (*accordo*) reconciliation; (*Dir*) settlement; **la Conciliazione** (*Storia*) the Lateran Pact.

concilio, lii [kon'tʃiljo] SM **a** (*Rel*) council **b** (*riunione*) conference, meeting.

concimare [kontʃi'mare] VT to fertilize; (*con letame*) to manure.

concime [kon'tʃime] SM (*chimico*) fertilizer; (*letame*) manure.

concione [kon'tʃone] SF: **tenere una concione** (*iro*) to speechify.

concisione [kontʃi'zjone] SF concision, conciseness.

conciso, a [kon'tʃizo] AGG concise, succinct.

concistoro [kontʃis'tɔro] SM (*Rel*) consistory.

concitatamente [kontʃitata'mente] AVV excitedly.

concitato, a [kontʃi'tato] AGG excited, agitated.

concitazione [kontʃitat'tsjone] SF excitement, agitation.

concittadino, a [kontʃitta'dino] SM/F fellow citizen.

conclave [kon'klave] SM (*Rel*) conclave.

concludente [konklu'dɛnte] AGG (*argomentazione*) conclusive, convincing; (*persona*): **poco concludente** inefficient.

concludere [kon'kludere] VB IRREG **1** VT **a** (*affare, trattato*) to conclude; (*discorso*) to finish, end, conclude, bring to an end; (*operare positivamente*) to achieve; **non ho concluso nulla oggi** I haven't achieved anything today; **per concludere...** and to conclude ...; **cerchiamo di concludere** let's try to come to a conclusion **b** (*dedurre*): **concludere che** to conclude that, come to the conclusion that. **2 concludersi** VIP (*finire*) to end, conclude, come to an end.

conclusionale [konkluzjo'nale] AGG (*Dir*): **comparsa conclusionale** summing up, summation.

conclusione [konklu'zjone] SF (*gen*) conclusion; (*di discorso*) close, end; (*risultato*) result; **in conclusione** in conclusion.

conclusivo, a [konklu'zivo] AGG (*finale*) final, closing, conclusive.

concluso, a [kon'kluzo] PP di **concludere**.

concomitante [konkomi'tante] AGG concomitant.

concomitanza [konkomi'tantsa] SF (*di circostanze, fatti*) combination.

concordabile [konkor'dabile] AGG (*prezzo*) negotiable.

concordante [konkor'dante] AGG (*testimonianze, Gramm*): **essere concordanti** to agree.

concordanza [konkor'dantsa] SF (*anche Gramm*) agreement; (*elenco*): **concordanze** SFPL concordances.

concordare [konkor'dare] **1** VT (*fissare: prezzo*) to agree

on; (*Gramm*) to make agree; **concordare una tregua** to agree to a truce.
[2] VI (*aus* **avere**) (*essere d'accordo*) to agree, coincide; (: *testimonianze*) to agree, tally.

concordato [konkor'dato] SM (*patto*) agreement; (*Rel*) concordat.

concorde [kon'korde] AGG (*d'accordo*) in agreement; (*simultaneo*) simultaneous; **concordi nel condannarlo** unanimous in their condemnation of him.

concordemente [konkorde'mente] AVV by mutual consent.

concordia [kon'kordja] SF concord, harmony.

concorrente [konkor'rɛnte] [1] AGG **a** (*Geom*) concurrent **b** (*Comm*) competing *attr.*
[2] SM/F (*Comm, Sport*) competitor; (*a un concorso di bellezza*) contestant.

concorrenza [konkor'rɛntsa] SF competition; **le due ditte si fanno una concorrenza spietata** the two firms are in fierce competition with each other, there is fierce competition between the two firms; **non temono la concorrenza** they are unbeatable; **a prezzi di concorrenza** at competitive prices ►**concorrenza sleale** unfair competition.

concorrenziale [konkorren'tsjale] AGG competitive.

concorrere [kon'korrere] VI IRREG (*aus* **avere**) **a** : **concorrere (a)** (*contribuire: a guarigione, spesa*) to contribute (to); (*partecipare: a un'impresa*) to take part (in) **b** (*competere*): **concorrere (a)** to compete (for); (*a una cattedra*) to apply (for) **c** : **concorrere (in)** (*Mat*) to converge *o* meet (in).

concorso, a [kon'korso] [1] PP di **concorrere**.
[2] SM **a** (*gen*) competition; (*esame*) competitive examination; **partecipanti fuori concorso** non-competitors ►**concorso di bellezza** beauty contest ►**concorso ippico** showjumping event ►**concorso per titoli** competitive examination for qualified candidates **b** (*partecipazione*): **concorso (a)** contribution (to) ►**concorso di colpa** (*Dir*) contributory negligence ►**concorso in reato** (*Dir*) complicity in a crime **c** (*affluenza*) gathering ►**concorso di circostanze** combination of circumstances.

concretamente [konkreta'mente] AVV concretely.

concretare [konkre'tare] [1] VT (*attuare*) to put into practice.
[2] **concretarsi** VIP (*attuarsi*) to materialize, be realized.

concretezza [konkre'tettsa] SF concreteness.

concretizzare [konkretid'dzare] VT = **concretare**.

concreto, a [kon'krɛto] [1] AGG (*gen*) concrete; (*vantaggi*) positive.
[2] SM: **in concreto** in reality; **fare qualcosa di concreto** to get something concrete done.

concubina [konku'bina] SF concubine.

concubinato [konkubi'nato] SM concubinage.

concubino, a [konku'bino] SM/F: **sono concubini** (*scherz*) they are living together.

concupire [konku'pire] VT to lust after.

concupiscente [konkupiʃ'ʃɛnte] AGG (*letter*) concupiscent.

concupiscenza [konkupiʃ'ʃɛntsa] SF lust, concupiscence.

concussione [konkus'sjone] SF (*Dir*) extortion.

condanna [kon'danna] SF **a** (*Dir: sentenza*) sentence; **scontare una condanna** to serve a sentence; **ha già avuto due condanne per furto** he has two previous convictions for theft ►**condanna a morte** death

sentence **b** (*disapprovazione*) condemnation.

condannabile [kondan'nabile] AGG (*biasimevole*) open to censure.

condannare [kondan'nare] VT **a** (*Dir*): **condannare (a)** to sentence (to); **condannare qn a 5 anni di prigione** to sentence sb to 5 years' imprisonment; **condannare qn per rapina a mano armata** to convict sb *o* find sb guilty of armed robbery; **è condannato al letto** he is confined to bed **b** (*disapprovare*) to condemn, censure.

condannato, a [kondan'nato] SM/F prisoner, convict.

condensa [kon'dɛnsa] SF condensation.

condensare [konden'sare] VT, **condensarsi** VIP to condense.

condensato, a [konden'sato] [1] AGG (*denso*) condensed; (*riassunto*) summarized; **latte condensato** condensed milk.
[2] SM (*di bugie, errori*) heap.

condensatore [kondensa'tore] SM condenser, capacitor.

condensazione [kondensat'tsjone] SF condensation.

condimento [kondi'mento] SM (*di insalata*) dressing; (*di carne*) seasoning; (*salsa*) sauce.

condire [kon'dire] VT (*cibo*) to season, flavour; (*insalata*) to dress; (*fig*) to spice, season; **hai condito la pasta?** have you mixed the sauce with the pasta?

condirettore, trice [kondiret'tore] SM/F (*gen*) joint manager/manageress; (*di giornale*) co-editor.

condiscendente [kondiʃʃen'dɛnte] AGG (*indulgente*) obliging; (*arrendevole*) compliant.

condiscendenza [kondiʃʃen'dɛntsa] SF (*disponibilità*) obligingness; (*arrendevolezza*) compliance.

condiscendere [kondiʃ'ʃendere] VI IRREG (*aus* **avere**): **condiscendere a** to agree to.

condiscepolo, a [kondiʃ'ʃepolo] SM/F fellow disciple.

condisceso, a [kondiʃ'ʃeso] PP di **condiscendere**.

condividere [kondi'videre] VT IRREG to share.

condiviso, a [kondi'vizo] PP di **condividere**.

condizionale [kondittsjo'nale] [1] AGG (*Gramm*) conditional.
[2] SM (*Gramm*) conditional (mood).
[3] SF **a** (*Gramm*) conditional clause **b** (*Dir*) suspended sentence.

condizionamento [kondittsjona'mento] SM conditioning ►**condizionamento d'aria** air conditioning.

condizionare [kondittsjo'nare] VT (*gen, Psic*) to condition.

condizionatamente [kondittsjonata'mente] AVV conditionally.

condizionato, a [kondittsjo'nato] AGG conditioned; **ad aria condizionata** air-conditioned.

condizionatore [kondittsjona'tore] SM: **condizionatore (d'aria)** air conditioner.

condizione [kondit'tsjone] SF **a** (*stato*) condition; **in buone condizioni** in good condition; **in condizioni pessime** in a very bad state, in poor condition; **condizioni di salute** state of health; **migliorare le proprie condizioni finanziarie** to improve one's financial position ►**condizioni di lavoro** working conditions **b** (*situazione*) situation; **essere** *o* **trovarsi in condizione di fare qc** to be in a position to do sth; **mettere qn in condizione di fare qc** to make it possible for sb to do sth; **mi trovo in una condizione assurda** I'm in an absurd situation **c** (*di patto*) condition; (*di contratto*) condition, term; (*di pagamento*) term, condition; **porre una condizione** to lay down *o* make a condition; **ad un'unica condizione** on

one condition; **non lo farò a nessuna condizione** on no account will I do it; **a condizione che** on condition that, provided that; **condizioni a convenirsi** terms to be arranged ▶ **condizioni di vendita** sales terms.

condoglianze [kondoʎˈʎantse] SFPL condolences; **fare le proprie condoglianze a qn** to offer one's sympathy o condolences to sb.

condominiale [kondomiˈnjale] AGG: **riunione condominiale** residents' meeting; **spese condominiali** common charges.

condominio, nii [kondoˈminjo] SM (*Dir*) condominium, joint ownership; (*edificio*) jointly-owned block of flats (*Brit*), condominium (*Am*).

condomino [konˈdomino] SM joint owner.

condonare [kondoˈnare] VT (*Dir*) to remit.

condono [konˈdono] SM (*Dir*) remission ▶ **condono edilizio** *conditional amnesty for work done without planning permission* ▶ **condono fiscale** *conditional amnesty for people evading tax.*

condor [ˈkɔndor] SM INV condor.

condotta [konˈdotta] SF **a** (*comportamento*) conduct, behaviour (*Brit*), behavior (*Am*); (*di un affare ecc*) handling; **tenere una buona/cattiva condotta** to behave well/badly **b** (*Amm: di medico*) *country medical practice controlled by a local authority* **c** (*Tecn: tubature*) piping.

condottiero [kondotˈtjɛro] SM (mercenary) leader; (*Storia*) condottiere.

condotto, a 1 PP di **condurre**.

2 AGG: **medico condotto** local authority doctor (*in a country district*).

3 SM **a** (*Anat*) duct ▶ **condotto uditivo** auditory canal **b** (*Tecn: di liquido*) pipe, conduit; (: *di aria*) duct.

conducente [konduˈtʃɛnte] SM/F driver.

conducibilità [kondutʃibiliˈta] SF = **conduttività**.

conduco *ecc* [konˈduko] VB vedi **condurre**.

condurre [konˈdurre] VB IRREG 1 VT **a** (*persona: accompagnare*) to take; (: *guidare*) to lead; **condurre qn a casa** (*a piedi*) to walk sb home; (*in macchina*) to drive o take sb home; **condurre qn per mano** to take sb by the hand; **condurre alla vittoria** to lead to victory; **condurre in salvo qn** to lead sb to safety; **condurre qn alla follia** to drive sb mad; **questo ci conduce a pensare che...** this leads us to think that ...

b (*azienda, affari*) to run, manage; (*trattative*) to hold, conduct; (*orchestra*) to conduct; **condurre (la gara)** (*Sport*) to lead, be in the lead; **condurre a termine** to conclude

c (*automobile*) to drive; (*aereo*) to pilot; (*barca*) to steer **d** (*trasportare: acqua, gas*) to convey

e (*Fis*) to conduct.

2 **condursi** VR to behave, conduct o.s.

condussi *ecc* [konˈdussi] VB vedi **condurre**.

conduttività [konduttiviˈta] SF (*Fis*) conductivity.

conduttivo, a [kondutˈtivo] AGG conductive.

conduttore, trice [kondutˈtore] 1 AGG: **filo conduttore** (*fig*) thread; **motivo conduttore** leitmotiv.

2 SM **a** (*Fis*) conductor **b** (*di mezzi pubblici*) driver.

conduttura [kondutˈtura] SF (*gen*) pipe; (*di acqua, gas*) main.

conduzione [kondutˈtsjone] SF **a** (*di affari, ditta*) management **b** (*Dir: locazione*) lease **c** (*Fis*) conduction.

confabulare [konfabuˈlare] VI (*aus avere*) to confab.

confabulazione [konfabulatˈtsjone] SF confab.

confacente [konfaˈtʃɛnte] AGG: **confacente a qn/qc** suitable for sb/sth; **clima confacente alla salute** healthy climate.

Confagricoltura [konfagrikolˈtura] SIGLA F (= *Confederazione generale dell'Agricoltura Italiana*) *confederation of Italian farmers.*

CONFAPI [konˈfabi] SIGLA F = *Confederazione Nazionale della Piccola Industria.*

confarsi [konˈfarsi] VIP (*essere adatto*): **confarsi a qn/qc** to be suitable for sb/sth, suit sb/sth; **questo modo di parlare non ti si confà** it doesn't become you to speak like that; **questo clima non mi si confà** this climate isn't good for me; **il lavoro non gli si confà** (*scherz*) work doesn't agree with him!

Confartigianato [konfartidʒaˈnato] SIGLA F = *Confederazione Generale dell'Artigianato Italiano.*

Confcommercio [konfkomˈmɛrtʃjo] SIGLA F = *Confederazione Generale del Commercio.*

confederale [konfedeˈrale] AGG confederal.

confederarsi [konfedeˈrarsi] VR to form a confederation.

confederativo, a [konfederaˈtivo] AGG confederal, confederative.

confederato, a [konfedeˈrato] AGG, SM/F confederate.

confederazione [konfederatˈtsjone] SF confederacy, confederation ▶ **confederazione imprenditoriale** employers' association.

conferenza [konfeˈrɛntsa] SF **a** (*discorso*) lecture; **fare o tenere una conferenza su qc** to give a lecture on sth, lecture on sth; **sala conferenze** lecture theatre **b** (*Pol, Amm: riunione*) conference ▶ **conferenza stampa** press conference ▶ **conferenza al vertice** summit conference.

conferenziere, a [konferenˈtsjere] SM/F lecturer, speaker.

conferimento [konferiˈmento] SM conferring, awarding.

conferire [konfeˈrire] 1 VT: **conferire (a)** (*premio, titolo, incarico*) to confer (on); (*tono, aria*) to give (to).

2 VI (*aus avere*) **a** (*avere un colloquio*) to confer **b** (*contribuire, giovare*): **conferire a qn/qc** to be good for sb/sth.

conferma [konˈferma] SF confirmation; **dare conferma** to confirm; **a conferma di** in confirmation of.

confermare [konferˈmare] VT to confirm; **l'eccezione conferma la regola** the exception proves the rule; **si è confermato campione** he has confirmed his position as champion.

confessabile [konfesˈsabile] AGG which can be disclosed.

confessare [konfesˈsare] 1 VT (*gen*) to confess, admit; (*Rel*) to confess; **confesso di essere stupito** I must admit I'm amazed; **l'omicida ha confessato** the murderer confessed.

2 **confessarsi** VR **a** (*Rel*): **(andare a) confessarsi** to go to confession **b** : **confessarsi colpevole** to admit one's guilt.

confessionale [konfessjoˈnale] 1 AGG confessional.

2 SM (*Rel*) confessional (box).

confessione [konfesˈsjone] SF **a** (*gen, Rel*) confession **b** (*fede*) denomination.

confesso, a [konˈfɛsso] AGG: **essere reo confesso** to have pleaded guilty.

confessore [konfesˈsore] SM (*Rel*) confessor.

confettiera [konfetˈtjɛra] SF sweet (*Brit*) o candy (*Am*) box, bonbonnière.

confetto [konˈfetto] SM: **a** (*dolciume*) sugared almond; **a quando i confetti?** when are we going to be hearing wedding bells? **b** (*pillola*) pill.

confettura [konfet'tura] SF (*gen*) jam; (*di arance*) marmalade.

confezionare [konfettsjo'nare] VT **a** (*pacco, merce: involgere*) to wrap up; (: *per vendita*) to package **b** (*articoli di abbigliamento*) to make (up).

confezionato, a [konfettsjo'nato] AGG (*gelato, pollo*) prepacked; (*abiti*) ready-made; **confezionato a mano** hand-made; **confezionato su misura** made to measure.

confezione [konfet'tsjone] SF **a** (*gen*) making, preparation; (*di abiti da uomo*) tailoring; (*di abiti da donna*) dressmaking

b (*imballaggio*) packaging; **confezione natalizia** Christmas pack; **mi può fare una confezione regalo?** could you giftwrap it for me? ► **confezione regalo** gift pack ► **confezione risparmio** economy size ► **confezione da viaggio** travel pack ► **confezioni per signora** ladies' wear *no pl* ► **confezioni da uomo** menswear *no pl*.

conficcare [konfik'kare] **1** VT: **conficcare in** (*chiodo, punta*) to hammer into, drive into, stick into; (*unghie*) to stick into, dig into. **2 conficcarsi** VIP to stick.

confidare [konfi'dare] **1** VT: **confidare qc a qn** to confide sth to sb.

2 VI (*aus avere*): **confidare in** (*persona, capacità ecc*) to have confidence in; **confido nella tua discrezione** I am relying on your discretion; **confido in una buona riuscita** I am confident of a successful outcome.

3 confidarsi VR: **confidarsi con qn** to confide in sb.

confidente [konfi'dεnte] **1** AGG confiding, trusting.

2 SM/F (*persona amica*) confidant/confidante; (*informatore*) informer; **è un confidente della polizia** he is a police informer.

confidenza [konfi'dεntsa] SF **a** (*familiarità*) intimacy, familiarity; **essere in confidenza** *o* **avere confidenza con qn** to be on friendly terms with sb; **prendersi (troppe) confidenze** to take liberties

b (*rivelazione*) confidence; **fare una confidenza a qn** to confide something to sb; **dire qc in confidenza a qn** to tell sb sth in confidence

c (*dimestichezza*): **prendere confidenza col proprio lavoro** to become more confident about one's work.

confidenziale [konfiden'tsjale] AGG (*lettera, informazione*) confidential; (*maniere, parole*) familiar; **in via confidenziale** confidentially.

configurare [konfigu'rare] **1** VT (*Inform*) to set. **2 configurarsi** VIP (*fig*) to take shape.

configurazione [konfigurat'tsjone] SF (*gen*) shape, configuration; (*Astron, Geog*) configuration; (*Inform*) setting.

confinante [konfi'nante] AGG neighbouring (*Brit*), neighboring (*Am*).

confinare [konfi'nare] **1** VI (*aus avere*): **confinare con** (*anche fig*) to border on. **2** VT **a** (*relegare*): **confinare qn in** to confine sb to; **la malattia l'ha confinata in casa** her illness confined her to the house **b** (*Pol*) to intern. **3 confinarsi** VR (*isolarsi*): **confinarsi in** to shut o.s. up in.

confinato, a [konfi'nato] **1** AGG interned. **2** SM/F internee.

Confindustria [konfin'dustrja] SIGLA F (= *Confederazione Generale dell'Industria*) ≈ CBI (*Brit*).

confine [kon'fine] SM (*di territorio, nazione*) border, frontier; (*di proprietà*) boundary; **territorio di confine** border zone; **senza confine** (*fig*) boundless; **i confini della scienza** the frontiers of science.

confino [kon'fino] SM (*Pol*) internment; **mandare al confino qn** to send sb into internal exile.

confisca [kon'fiska] SF confiscation.

confiscare [konfis'kare] VT to confiscate.

confiteor [kon'fiteor] SM INV Confiteor.

conflagrazione [konflagrat'tsjone] SF (*incendio*) conflagration; (*fig: guerra*) sudden outbreak of hostilities.

conflitto [kon'flitto] SM (*gen, Mil*) conflict; (*fig: contrasto*) clash, conflict; **essere in conflitto con qc** to clash with sth; **essere in conflitto con qn** to be at loggerheads with sb.

conflittuale [konflittu'ale] AGG: **rapporto conflittuale** relationship based on conflict.

conflittualità [konflittuali'ta] SF INV conflicts *pl*.

confluenza [konflu'εntsa] SF (*di fiumi, fig*) confluence; (*di strade*) junction.

confluire [konflu'ire] VI (*aus essere e avere*) (*fiumi*) to meet, flow into each other; (*strade*) to meet; (*fig: idee, persone*) to meet, come together.

confondere [kon'fondere] VB IRREG **1** VT **a** (*mischiare*) to mix up, confuse; **confondere le idee a qn** to mix sb up, confuse sb; **confondere le carte in tavola** (*fig*) to confuse the issue

b (*scambiare*): **confondere qc con qc** to confuse sth with sth; **confondo sempre i due fratelli** I always get the two brothers mixed up

c (*turbare*) to confuse; (*imbarazzare*) to embarrass; (*disorientare: nemico, avversario*) to trick.

2 confondersi VIP **a** (*colori, sagoma*) to merge; (*ricordi*) to become confused; (*persona*): **confondersi tra la folla** to mingle with the crowd

b (*sbagliarsi*) to be mistaken, get mixed up

c (*turbarsi*) to become confused.

conformare [konfor'mare] **1** VT: **conformare (a)** (*adeguare*) to adapt (to). **2 conformarsi** VR: **conformarsi (a)** to conform (to).

conformazione [konformat'tsjone] SF conformation.

conforme [kon'forme] AGG: **conforme a** (*simile*) similar to; (*corrispondente*) in keeping with.

conformemente [konforme'mente] AVV accordingly; **conformemente a** in accordance with, according to.

conformismo [konfor'mizmo] SM conformity.

conformista [konfor'mista] SM/F (*gen*) conformist.

conformità [konformi'ta] SF conformity; **in conformità a** in conformity with.

confortante [konfor'tante] AGG comforting.

confortare [konfor'tare] VT **a** (*consolare*) to comfort, console **b** (*tesi, accusa*) to strengthen, support.

confortevole [konfor'tevole] AGG (*comodo*) comfortable; (*confortante*) comforting.

conforto [kon'forto] SM **a** (*consolazione, sollievo*) comfort, consolation; **i conforti (religiosi)** the last sacraments **b** (*conferma*) support; **a conforto di qc** in support of sth.

confratello [konfra'tεllo] SM (*Rel*) brother.

confraternita [konfra'tεrnita] SF brotherhood.

confrontabile [konfron'tabile] AGG comparable.

confrontare [konfron'tare] **1** VT (*paragonare*) to compare. **2 confrontarsi** VR (*scontrarsi*) to have a confrontation.

confronto [kon'fronto] SM **a** (*paragone*) comparison; (*Dir, Mil, Pol*) confrontation; **a confronto di** *o* **in confronto a** compared with *o* to, in comparison with *o* to; **mettere a confronto** to compare; (*Dir*) to confront; **senza confronti** beyond comparison; **reggere al**

confronto con to stand comparison with ► **confronto all'americana** (*Dir*) identity parade **b** (*di testi*) collation **c** : **nei miei** (*o* **tuoi** *ecc*) **confronti** towards me (*o* you *ecc*).

confusamente [konfuza'mente] AVV (*distinguere, vedere*) vaguely; (*capire*) in a confused way, vaguely; (*parlare*) confusedly; (: *timidamente*) in an embarrassed way.

confusi *ecc* [kon'fuzi] VB *vedi* **confondere**.

confusionale [konfuzjo'nale] AGG: **stato confusionale** (*Med*) confused state.

confusionario, ria, ri, rie [konfuzjo'narjo] ☐ AGG muddle-headed. ☐ SM/F muddle-headed person.

confusione [konfu'zjone] SF (*disordine, errore*) confusion; (*chiasso*) racket, noise; (*imbarazzo*) embarrassment; **c'è stata confusione tra i due nomi** there's been a mix-up over the two names, the two names have been confused; **far confusione** (*disordine*) to make a mess; (*chiasso*) to make a racket; (*confondere*) to confuse things; **essere in uno stato di confusione mentale** to be confused in one's mind.

confuso, a [kon'fuzo] ☐ PP *di* **confondere**. ☐ AGG (*gen*) confused; (*discorso, stile*) muddled; (*persona: turbato*) embarrassed; (*immagine, ricordo*) hazy.

confutare [konfu'tare] VT to confute, refute.

confutazione [konfutat'tsjone] SF confutation, refutation.

congedando [kondʒe'dando] SM (*Mil*) serviceman about to be discharged.

congedare [kondʒe'dare] ☐ VT (*gen*) to dismiss; (*Mil: soldati*) to demobilize; (*licenziare*) to sack; **congedare per invalidità** to invalid out. ☐ **congedarsi** VR: **congedarsi (da)** to take one's leave (of); (*soldato*) to be demobilized (from).

congedo [kon'dʒɛdo] SM **a** (*permesso, Mil*) leave; **andare in congedo** to go on leave; **chiedere un congedo per motivi di salute** to apply for sick leave ► **congedo assoluto** (*Mil*) discharge **b** (*commiato*): **prendere congedo da qn** to take one's leave of sb **c** (*Teatro: finale*) finale; (*Poesia: coda*) envoy.

congegnare [kondʒeɲ'ɲare] VT (*motore*) to construct, put together; (*fig: trama, scherzo*) to devise.

congegno [kon'dʒeɲɲo] SM (*dispositivo*) device; (*meccanismo*) mechanism.

congelamento [kondʒela'mento] SM (*gen*) freezing; (*Med*) frostbite ► **congelamento dei prezzi** (*Econ*) price freeze ► **congelamento salariale** wage freeze.

congelare [kondʒe'lare] ☐ VT (*gen, Econ*) to freeze. ☐ **congelarsi** VIP to freeze.

congelato, a [kondʒe'lato] AGG (*gen, Econ*) frozen.

congelatore [kondʒela'tore] ☐ AGG freezer *attr.* ☐ SM (*macchina*) deepfreeze, freezer.

congelazione [kondʒelat'tsjone] SF = **congelamento**.

congeniale [kondʒe'njale] AGG congenial.

congenialità [kondʒenjali'ta] SF congeniality.

congenito, a [kon'dʒɛnito] AGG congenital.

congerie [kon'dʒɛrje] SF INV (*di oggetti*) heap; (*di idee*) muddle, jumble.

congestionare [kondʒestjo'nare] VT (*Med, strada*) to congest; **essere congestionato** (*persona, viso*) to be flushed; (*zona: per traffico*) to be congested.

congestione [kondʒes'tjone] SF congestion.

congettura [kondʒet'tura] SF conjecture, supposition; **fare mille congetture** to let one's imagination run riot.

congetturare [kondʒettu'rare] VT to conjecture.

congiungere [kon'dʒundʒere] VB IRREG ☐ VT (*gen*) to join (together); (*punti*) to join, connect; (*luoghi*) to link, connect. ☐ **congiungersi** VIP (*gen*) to join (together); (*Mil*) to join forces; **congiungersi in matrimonio** to be joined in matrimony.

congiungimento [kondʒundʒi'mento] SM (*di punti*) joining, connecting, linking; (*di luoghi*) connecting; **mettere in atto un congiungimento** (*Mil*) to join forces.

congiuntivite [kondʒunti'vite] SF (*Med*) conjunctivitis.

congiuntivo, a [kondʒun'tivo] AGG, SM (*Gramm*) subjunctive.

congiunto, a [kon'dʒunto] ☐ PP *di* **congiungere**. ☐ AGG (*mani*) clasped, joined; (*azione, sforzo*) joint. ☐ SM/F (*parente*) relative.

congiuntura [kondʒun'tura] SF **a** (*punto di contatto*) join, junction; (*Anat*) joint **b** (*circostanza*) juncture, circumstance; (*opportunità*) occasion; **in questa congiuntura** at this juncture **c** (*Econ*) economic situation; **superare la (bassa) congiuntura** to overcome the economic crisis.

congiunturale [kondʒuntu'rale] AGG of the economic situation; **crisi congiunturale** economic crisis.

congiunzione [kondʒun'tsjone] SF (*gen*) join; (*Anat*) joint; (*di due linee ferroviarie*) junction; (*Astron, Gramm*) conjunction.

congiura [kon'dʒura] SF (*anche fig*) conspiracy, plot.

congiurare [kondʒu'rare] VI (*aus avere*): **congiurare (ai danni di** *o* **contro qn)** to conspire (against sb), plot (against sb); **tutto sembra congiurare contro di me** everything seems to be conspiring against me.

congiurato, a [kondʒu'rato] SM/F conspirator.

conglobare [konglo'bare] VT to merge.

conglomerare [konglome'rare] VT (*gen*) to amass.

conglomerato [konglome'rato] SM (*gen*) conglomeration; (*Geol*) conglomerate; (*Edil*) concrete.

Congo ['kongo] SM (*paese, fiume*): **il Congo** the Congo.

congolese [kongo'lese] AGG, SM/F Congolese *inv.*

congratularsi [kongratu'larsi] VIP: **congratularsi con qn (per qc)** to congratulate sb (on sth).

congratulazioni [kongratulat'tsjoni] SFPL congratulations; **fare le (proprie) congratulazioni a qn per qc** to congratulate sb on sth.

congrega, ghe [kon'grega] SF gang, band, bunch.

congregazionalismo [kongregattsjona'lizmo] SM Congregationalism.

congregazione [kongregat'tsjone] SF congregation.

congressista, i, e [kongres'sista] SM/F participant at a congress.

congresso [kon'grɛsso] SM congress; **sala (dei) congressi** conference hall.

congressuale [kongressu'ale] AGG congressional.

congruamente [kongrua'mente] AVV (*pagare, rimunerare*) fairly, suitably.

congruente [kongru'ɛnte] AGG congruent.

congruenza [kongru'ɛntsa] SF coherence.

congruo, a ['kongruo] AGG (*prezzo, compenso*) adequate, fair; (*ragionamento*) coherent, consistent.

conguagliare [kongwaʎ'ʎare] VT (*Comm*) to balance; (*stipendio*) to adjust.

conguaglio, gli [kon'gwaʎʎo] SM **a** (*vedi vb*) balancing; adjusting **b** (*somma di denaro*) balance.

coniare [ko'njare] VT (*monete*) to mint; (*medaglie*) to strike; (*fig: parole nuove*) to coin.

coniazione [konjat'tsjone] SF (*vedi vb*) minting; striking; coining.

conico, a, ci, che ['kɔniko] AGG conic(al), cone-shaped.

conifera [ko'nifera] SF conifer.

coniglia [ko'niʎʎa] SF (doe) rabbit.

conigliera [koniʎ'ʎɛra] SF (*gabbia*) rabbit hutch; (*più grande*) rabbit run.

coniglietta [koniʎ'ʎetta] SF (*fam*) bunny girl.

coniglietto [koniʎ'ʎetto] SM bunny.

coniglio, gli [ko'niʎʎo] SM (*Zool*) rabbit; (*maschio*) buck; **pelliccia di coniglio** rabbit fur; **sei un coniglio!** (*fig*) you're chicken!

conio, nii ['kɔnjo] SM a (*punzone*) minting die b (*impronta*) stamp; **moneta di nuovo conio** newly-minted coin c (*invenzione*) coining; **parole di nuovo conio** newly-coined words.

coniugale [konju'gale] AGG (*amore, diritti*) conjugal; (*vita*) married, conjugal.

coniugare [konju'gare] VT a (*Gramm*) to conjugate b (*far coesistere*) to combine; **coniugare lo sviluppo industriale con il rispetto dell'ambiente** to combine industrial development with respect for the environment.

coniugato, a [konju'gato] AGG (*Amm*) married.

coniugazione [konjugat'tsjone] SF (*Gramm*) conjugation.

coniuge ['kɔnjudʒe] SM/F spouse; **i coniugi** the couple, the husband and wife; **i coniugi Bianchi** Mr and Mrs Bianchi.

connaturale [konnatu'rale] AGG: **connaturale a qn/qc** natural to sb/sth.

connaturarsi [konnatu'rarsi] VIP (*abitudine, vizio*): **connaturarsi in qn** to become second nature to sb.

connaturato, a [konnatu'rato] AGG inborn.

connazionale [konnattsjo'nale] 1 AGG of the same country.
2 SM/F compatriot, fellow-countryman/woman.

connessione [konnes'sjone] SF connection; **connessione di idee** association of ideas.

connesso, a [kon'nɛsso] 1 PP di **connettere**.
2 AGG connected.

connettere [kon'nɛttere] VT IRREG a (*uso assoluto: ragionare*) to think straight b : **connettere (a)** (*gen, fig*) to connect (with), link (to); (*Elettr*) to connect (with).

connettivo, a [konnet'tivo] AGG: **tessuto connettivo** connective tissue.

connettore [konnet'tore] SM (*Elettr*) connector.

connivente [konni'vɛnte] AGG: **essere connivente (in qc con qn)** to connive (at sth with sb).

connivenza [konni'vɛntsa] SF (*Dir*) connivance.

connotare [konno'tare] VT to connote.

connotati [konno'tati] SMPL distinguishing marks; **dare i connotati di qn** to give a description of sb; **rispondere ai connotati** to fit the description; **cambiare i connotati a qn** (*fam*) to beat sb up.

connotativo, a [konnota'tivo] AGG connotative.

connotazione [konnotat'tsjone] SF connotation.

connubio, bi [kon'nubjo] SM (*matrimonio*) marriage; (*fig*) union.

cono ['kɔno] SM (*in tutti i sensi*) cone ▶**cono gelato** ice-cream cone.

conobbi ecc [ko'nobbi] VB vedi **conoscere**.

conoide [ko'nɔide] SM (*Geom*) conoid.

conoscente [konoʃ'ʃɛnte] SM/F acquaintance.

conoscenza [konoʃ'ʃɛntsa] SF a (*sapere, nozione*) knowledge *no pl*; (*Filosofia*) cognition; **essere a conoscenza di qc** to know sth; **venire a conoscenza di qc** to get to know sth, learn of sth; **portare qn a conoscenza di qc** to inform sb of sth; **la polizia è venuta a conoscenza (del fatto) che...** it has come to the knowledge of the police that ...; **le mie conoscenze in questo campo** my knowledge in this field; **per vostra conoscenza** for your information; **prendere conoscenza di qc** (*Dir, Amm*) to take cognizance of sth ▶**conoscenza tecnica** know-how

b (*amicizia, persona*) acquaintance; **fare la conoscenza di qn** to make sb's acquaintance; **lieto di fare la sua conoscenza** pleased to meet you; **ha ottenuto il lavoro grazie alle sue conoscenze** she got the job because of her contacts

c (*sensi, coscienza*) consciousness; **perdere/riprendere conoscenza** to lose/regain consciousness.

conoscere [ko'noʃʃere] VB IRREG 1 VT a (*gen*) to know; (*persona, avvenimento*) to be acquainted with, know; (*testo, abitudine*) to be familiar with, know; (*posto, ristorante*) to know of; **conoscere qn di vista** to know sb by sight; **l'ha conosciuto all'università** she met him at university; **conosci i motori?** do you know anything about engines?; **conosco la canzone** (*fig*) I've heard it all before; **conosce il fatto suo** he knows what he's talking about; **non conosce il mondo** he isn't very worldly-wise

b (*successo*) to enjoy, have; (*privazioni*) to know, experience; **conoscere tempi difficili** to go through hard times

c : **far conoscere qn/qc** to make sb/sth known; **ti farò conoscere mio marito** I'll introduce you to my husband; **mi ha fatto conoscere la musica classica** he introduced me to classical music; **farsi conoscere** (*fig*) to make a name for o.s.

d (*riconoscere*): **conoscere qn dalla voce** to recognize sb by his voice.

2 **conoscersi** VR a (*se stessi*) to know o.s.

b (*uso reciproco*) to know each other; (: *incontrarsi*) to meet; **si sono conosciuti un anno fa** they (first) met a year ago; **da quanto vi conoscete?** how long have you known one another?

conoscitivo, a [konoʃʃi'tivo] AGG cognitive.

conoscitore, trice [konoʃʃi'tore] SM/F connoisseur.

conosciuto, a [konoʃ'ʃuto] 1 PP di **conoscere**.
2 AGG (*universo*) known; (*attore, autore, artista*) well-known; **conosciuto in tutto il mondo** well-known throughout the world, world-famous.

conquista [kon'kwista] SF (*anche fig*) conquest; **partire alla conquista di qc** to set out to conquer sth; **le conquiste della scienza** the achievements of science.

conquistare [konkwis'tare] VT (*territorio, fortezza*) to conquer; (*felicità, successo, ricchezza*) to gain; (*simpatia, fiducia*) to win, gain; (*cuore*) to win over; **si è conquistato la simpatia di tutti** he's made himself popular with everybody.

conquistatore, trice [konkwista'tore] 1 AGG (*esercito, truppe*) conquering.
2 SM (*in guerra*) conqueror; (*seduttore*) lady-killer.

cons. ABBR = **consiglio**.

consacrare [konsa'krare] 1 VT a (*Rel*) to consecrate; (: *sacerdote*) to ordain; (: *re*) to anoint; (*abitudine, tradizione, uso*) to establish b (*vita, tempo, sforzi*):

consacrare (a) to dedicate (to), devote (to).

2 **consacrarsi** VR (*dedicarsi*): **consacrarsi a qn/qc** to dedicate o.s. to sb/sth.

consacrazione [konsakrat'tsjone] SF (*Rel*: *vedi vb*) consecration; ordination; anointing.

consanguineità [konsangwinei'ta] SF consanguinity, blood relationship.

consanguineo, a [konsan'gwineo] 1 AGG related by blood.

2 SM/F blood relation.

consapevole [konsa'pevole] AGG: **consapevole di qc** aware *o* conscious of sth; **rendere qn consapevole di qc** to make sb aware of sth.

consapevolezza [konsapevo'lettsa] SF awareness, consciousness; **acquistare consapevolezza di qc** to become aware *o* conscious of sth.

consapevolmente [konsapevol'mente] AVV consciously; **l'ha fatto consapevolmente** he was fully aware of what he was doing.

consciamente [konʃa'mente] AVV consciously; **non l'ha fatto consciamente** he didn't know what he was doing.

conscienzioso, a [kon'ʃentsjoso] AGG conscientious.

conscio, a, sci, sce ['konʃo] 1 AGG: **conscio (di)** aware (of), conscious (of); **è conscio dei suoi limiti** he is aware of *o* knows his limitations.

2 SM (*Psic*): **il conscio** the conscious.

consecutiva [konseku'tiva] SF (*Gramm*) consecutive clause.

consecutivo, a [konseku'tivo] AGG (*Gramm, senza interruzione*) consecutive; (*successivo*: *giorno*) following, next; **consecutivo a** following upon.

consegna [kon'seɲɲa] SF **a** (*Comm*: *il consegnare*) delivery; (: *merce consegnata*) consignment; **pagamento alla consegna** cash on delivery ▸ **consegna in contrassegno** cash on delivery ▸ **consegna a domicilio** home delivery ▸ **consegna sollecita** prompt delivery

b (*custodia*) care; **prendere in consegna qn** (*bambino*) to take sb into one's care; (*prigioniero*) to take custody of sb; **prendere qc in consegna** to take sth into safekeeping; **dare qc in consegna a qn** to give sth to sb for safekeeping, entrust sth to sb

c (*Mil: ordine*) orders *pl*; (: *punizione*) confinement to barracks; **un soldato fedele alla consegna** a soldier who obeys orders; **passare le consegne a qn** to hand over to sb.

consegnare [konseɲ'ɲare] VT **a** : **consegnare qc (a qn)** (*lettera, pacco, merce*) to deliver sth (to sb); (*lavoro finito*) to hand sth in (to sb), submit sth (to sb); **il meccanico non mi ha ancora consegnato la macchina** I haven't had the car back from the mechanic yet; **consegnare qn alla polizia** to hand sb over to the police

b (*Mil: soldato*) to confine to barracks.

consegnatario, ria, ri, rie [konseɲɲa'tarjo] SM/F consignee.

consegnato [konseɲ'ɲato] SM (*Mil*) soldier confined to barracks.

conseguente [konse'gwɛnte] AGG consequent.

conseguentemente [konsegwɛnte'mente] AVV (*come conseguenza*) consequently; (*comportarsi*) consistently.

conseguenza [konse'gwɛntsa] SF consequence; **di** *o* **per conseguenza** consequently; **senza lasciare conseguenze** without having any effect; **pagare le conseguenze** to pay the consequences.

conseguibile [konse'gwibile] AGG achievable, attainable.

conseguimento [konsegwi'mento] SM (*di scopo, risultato*) achievement, attainment; **al conseguimento della laurea** on graduation.

conseguire [konse'gwire] 1 VT (*scopo*) to achieve, attain; (*vittoria*) to gain; **conseguire la laurea** to graduate, obtain one's degree.

2 VI (*aus essere*) (*derivare*): **ne consegue che…** it follows that … .

consenso [kon'sɛnso] SM (*permesso*) consent; (*approvazione*) approval; **dare/negare il proprio consenso a qc** to give/refuse one's consent to sth; **per consenso unanime** unanimously.

consensuale [konsensu'ale] AGG (*Dir*) by mutual consent.

consensualmente [konsenswal'mente] AVV: **separarsi consensualmente** to separate by mutual consent.

consentire [konsen'tire] 1 VI (*aus avere*): **consentire a qc/a fare qc** to agree *o* consent to sth/to do sth.

2 VT: **consentire a qn qc/di fare qc** to allow *o* permit sb sth/to do sth; **è un lavoro che non consente distrazioni** you can't afford to be distracted in this kind of job; **mi si consenta di ringraziare…** I would like to thank … .

consenziente [konsen'tsjɛnte] AGG (*gen, Dir*) consenting.

consequenziale [konsekwen'tsjale] AGG consequential.

conserto, a [kon'sɛrto] AGG: **a braccia conserte** with one's arms folded.

conserva [kon'sɛrva] SF: **mettere cibi in conserva** to preserve food ▸ **conserva di frutta** jam, preserve ▸ **conserva di pomodoro** tomato purée ▸ **conserve alimentari** tinned (*Brit*) *o* canned (*Am*) *o* bottled foods.

conservare [konser'vare] 1 VT **a** (*gen*) to keep; (*andatura, velocità*) to maintain; **conservare la calma** to keep calm; **conservare il proprio sangue freddo** (*fig*) to keep one's head; **conservo sempre un buon ricordo di lui** I still have fond memories of him

b (*monumenti*) to preserve

c (*Culin*) to preserve; (: *in frigo*) to keep; **conservare le cipolline sott'aceto** to pickle onions; **conservare i pomodori in bottiglia** to bottle tomatoes.

2 **conservarsi** VIP (*cibo*) to keep; **conservarsi in buona salute** to keep healthy; **si conserva bene** (*persona*) he (*o* she) is well-preserved.

conservatore, trice [konserva'tore] 1 AGG (*gen, Pol*) conservative; **il partito Conservatore** the Conservative Party.

2 SM/F **a** (*di museo*) curator; (*di biblioteca*) librarian; (*di archivio*) keeper **b** (*Pol*) Conservative.

conservatorio, ri [konserva'tɔrjo] SM (*di musica*) conservatory.

conservatorismo [konservato'rizmo] SM (*Pol*) conservatism.

conservazione [konservat'tsjone] SF **a** (*di cibi, monumenti*) preservation; **in buono stato di conservazione** well-preserved; **istinto di conservazione** instinct of self-preservation; **a lunga conservazione** (*latte, panna*) long-life *attr* **b** (*di energia, dell'ambiente naturale*) conservation.

conserviero, a [konser'vjɛro] AGG: **industria conserviera** canning industry.

consesso [kon'sɛsso] SM (*assemblea*) assembly; (*riunione*) meeting.

considerabile [konside'rabile] AGG worthy of consideration.

considerare [konside'rare] 1 VT **a** (*gen*) to consider, regard; **considerato che…** considering that …; **tutto**

considerato all things considered; **ti considero un amico** I think of you as o consider you a friend; **considerare un onore fare qc** to consider it an honour to do sth
b (stimare): **considerare molto qn** to think highly of sb
c (Dir: contemplare): **la legge non considera questo caso** the law does not provide for this case.
2 considerarsi VR: **considerarsi un genio** to consider o.s. a genius; **si considerano amici** they consider themselves friends.

consideratamente [konsiderata'mente] AVV cautiously, carefully.

considerato, a [konside'rato] AGG **a** (stimato) highly thought of, esteemed **b** (prudente) cautious, careful.

considerazione [konsiderat'tsjone] SF **a** (esame, riflessione) consideration; **agire senza considerazione** to act rashly; **voglio che tu agisca con considerazione** I'd like you to think carefully about what you're doing; **meritare considerazione** to be worthy of consideration; **prendere qn/qc in considerzione** to take sb/sth into consideration
b (stima) esteem, regard; **godere di molta considerazione** to be very highly thought of; **avere (una grande) considerazione per qn** to think highly of sb
c (pensiero, osservazione) observation.

considerevole [konside'revole] AGG considerable.

considerevolmente [konsiderevol'mente] AVV considerably.

consigliabile [konsiʎ'ʎabile] AGG advisable.

consigliare [konsiʎ'ʎare] **1** VT **a** (raccomandare: ristorante, film, prudenza): **consigliare (a qn)** to recommend (to sb); **che cosa mi consigli?** what do you recommend?
b (suggerire): **consigliare a qn di fare qc** to advise sb to do sth; **si consiglia ai passeggeri di...** passengers are advised to ....
2 consigliarsi VIP: **consigliarsi con qn** to ask sb's advice, ask sb for advice; **consigliarsi col proprio avvocato** to consult one's lawyer.

consigliere, a [konsiʎ'ʎɛre] SM/F (gen) adviser; (Pol, Amm) councillor, council member ▶**consigliere d'amministrazione** (Comm) board member ▶**consigliere comunale** town councillor ▶**consigliere delegato** (Comm) managing director.

consiglio, gli [kon'siʎʎo] SM **a** advice no pl; **un consiglio** some advice, a piece of advice; **un consiglio da amico** a friendly piece of advice; **seguire il consiglio o i consigli di qn** to take sb's advice
b (assemblea) council; **hanno fatto un consiglio di famiglia** they held a family conference ▶**consiglio d'amministrazione** board of directors, board ▶**consiglio comunale** town council (headed by the sindaco (mayor): it elects the giunta comunale, which is responsible for running a comune) ▶**Consiglio d'Europa** Council of Europe ▶**consiglio di fabbrica** works council ▶**Consiglio dei Ministri: il Consiglio dei Ministri** the Italian Cabinet, headed by the prime minister, the Presidente del Consiglio ▶**Consiglio di stato** advisory body to the Italian government on administrative matters and their legal implications ▶**Consiglio superiore della magistratura** magistrates' governing body responsible for appointments and maintaining professional independence and discipline: it consists of 30 magistrates and is chaired by the Presidente della Repubblica.

consiliare [konsi'ljare] AGG (decisione, assemblea) council attr; (: direzionale) board attr.

consimile [kon'simile] AGG similar.

consistente [konsis'tɛnte] AGG (tessuto) solid; (fig: prova, testimonianza) sound; (somma) sizeable.

consistenza [konsis'tɛntsa] SF **a** (di impasto) consistency; (di stoffa) texture **b** (di sospetti, voci, ragionamenti): **senza consistenza** ill-founded, groundless; **acquistare consistenza** to gain substance **c** (Comm): **consistenza di cassa** cash in hand ▶**consistenza di magazzino** stock in hand ▶**consistenza patrimoniale** financial solidity.

consistere [kon'sistere] VI IRREG (aus essere) (essere composto di): **consistere di qc** to consist of sth, be made up of sth; (fondarsi, risiedere in): **consistere in qc/nel fare qc** to consist in sth/in doing sth; **in che consiste il tuo lavoro?** what does your job entail?

consistito, a [konsis'tito] PP di **consistere**.

CONSOB ['kɔnsob] SIGLA F (= Commissione nazionale per le società e la borsa) regulatory body for the Italian Stock Exchange.

consociarsi [konso'tʃarsi] VR to go into partnership.

consociativismo [konsotʃati'vismo] SM (Pol) pact-building.

consociativo, a [konsotʃa'tivo] AGG (Pol: democrazia) based on pacts.

consociato, a [konso'tʃato] **1** AGG associated.
2 SM/F associate.
3 SF associated company.

consociazione [konsotʃat'tsjone] SF (lega) association.

consocio, cia, ci, cie [kon'sɔtʃo] SM/F associate, partner.

consolante [konso'lante] AGG consoling, comforting.

consolare¹ [konso'lare] **1** VT (confortare) to console, comfort; (rallegrare) to cheer up; **se ti può consolare...** if it is of any consolation o comfort to you ....
2 consolarsi VIP (trovare conforto) to console o.s., be comforted; (rallegrarsi) to cheer up; **la vedova si è consolata presto** the widow got over her loss quickly; **il bambino si è consolato vedendo le caramelle** the child cheered up when he saw the sweets.

consolare² [konso'lare] AGG consular.

consolato [konso'lato] SM (officio) consulate; (carica) consulship.

consolatore, trice [konsola'tore] AGG consoling, comforting.

consolazione [konsolat'tsjone] SF **a** comfort, consolation; **sei la mia unica consolazione** you're my one consolation; **premio di consolazione** consolation prize
b (piacere): **è una consolazione vederlo di nuovo in salute** it's a pleasure o joy to see him well again.

console ['kɔnsole] SM consul.

consolidamento [konsolida'mento] SM consolidation, strengthening.

consolidare [konsoli'dare] **1** VT (anche fig) to consolidate, strengthen, reinforce; **consolidare le proprie posizioni** (Mil) to consolidate one's position.
2 consolidarsi VIP (Geol) to consolidate; (fig: patrimonio, posizione) to become more stable; **la società si è consolidata** the company has consolidated its position.

consolidato, a [konsoli'dato] AGG consolidated; **è un'amicizia ormai consolidata** it's a firm friendship; **debito consolidato** (Econ) funded debt.

consolidazione [konsolidat'tsjone] SF consolidation, strengthening.

consolle [kon'sɔlle] SF INV console ▶**consolle di comando**

control panel.

consommé [kɔ̃sɔ'me] SM INV consommé.

consonante [konso'nante] SF consonant.

consonantico, a, ci, che [konso'nantiko] AGG consonantal.

consonanza [konso'nantsa] SF consonance.

consono, a ['kɔnsono] AGG: **consono a** consistent with, consonant with.

consorella [konso'rɛlla] AGG F sister *attr*.

consorte [kon'sɔrte] 1 SM/F (*coniuge*) consort.
2 AGG: **principe consorte** prince consort.

consorteria [konsorte'ria] SF clique.

consorziale [konsor'tsjale] AGG consortium *attr*.

consorziarsi [konsor'tsjarsi] VR to form a consortium.

consorzio, zi [kon'sɔrtsjo] SM consortium ▶**consorzio agrario** farmers' cooperative ▶**consorzio di garanzia** (*Comm*) underwriting syndicate.

constare [kon'stare] 1 VI (*aus* **essere**) (*essere composto*): **constare di** to consist of, be composed of, be made up of.
2 VB IMPERS (*essere noto*): **mi consta che...** I know that ...; **a quanto mi consta** as far as I know.

constatare [konsta'tare] VT DIF a (*notare*) to notice, note, observe; **come può constatare** as you can see; **non faccio che constatare** I'm merely making an observation b (*verificare*) to establish, verify; (*decesso*) to certify.

constatazione [konstatat'tsjone] SF observation; **fare una constatazione** to make an observation ▶**constatazione amichevole** (*in incidenti stradali*) *jointly-agreed statement for insurance purposes*.

consuetamente [konsueta'mente] AVV usually, normally.

consueto, a [konsu'ɛto] 1 AGG usual, habitual.
2 SM: **come di consueto** as usual; **più/meno del consueto** more/less than usual.

consuetudinario, ria, ri, rie [konsuetudi'narjo] 1 AGG (*abituale*) usual, habitual; **diritto consuetudinario** (*Dir*) common law.
2 SM/F (*persona: abitudinario*) creature of habit, lover of routine.

consuetudine [konsue'tudine] SF a (*abitudine*) habit; (*tradizione*) custom; **è sua consuetudine alzarsi prestissimo** he usually gets up very early, he is in the habit of getting up very early; **secondo la consuetudine** according to custom b (*Dir*) common law.

consulente [konsu'lɛnte] 1 AGG consulting.
2 SM/F (*tecnico, amministrativo*) consultant ▶**consulente aziendale** management consultant ▶**consulente legale** legal adviser.

consulenza [konsu'lɛntsa] SF (*prestazione professionale*) consultancy; (*consigli*) advice; **chiedere una consulenza** to ask for professional advice; **contratto di consulenza** consultancy agreement; **ufficio di consulenza fiscale** tax consultancy office ▶**consulenza legale** legal advice ▶**consulenza medica** medical advice ▶**consulenza tecnica** technical consultancy *o* advice.

consulta [kon'sulta] SF (*riunione*) meeting.

consultare [konsul'tare] 1 VT (*medico, esperto*) to consult, seek the advice of; (*dizionario*) to look up, consult.
2 **consultarsi** VR (*scambiarsi pareri: uso reciproco*) to confer, consult each other.
3 **consultarsi** VIP (*chiedere consiglio*): **consultarsi con qn** to consult (with) sb, seek the advice of sb.

consultazione [konsultat'tsjone] SF consultation; (*Pol*) **consultazioni** SFPL talks, consultations; **dopo lunga consultazione** after much consultation; **libro di consultazione** reference book ▶**consultazione popolare** referendum.

consultivo, a [konsul'tivo] AGG consultative.

consulto [kon'sulto] SM (*Med*) consultation.

consultorio, ri [konsul'tɔrjo] SM: **consultorio familiare** family planning clinic ▶**consultorio pediatrico** children's clinic.

consumare [konsu'mare] 1 VT a (*logorare: scarpe, vestiti*) to wear out
b (*cibo*) to consume; (*sogg: malattia, passione*) to consume, devour; **desidera consumare i pasti in camera?** (*in albergo*) would you like to have your meals brought up to your room?
c (*usare: acqua, luce, benzina*) to use; (*finire*) to use up; **quanto consuma questa macchina?** what sort of mileage does this car do?; **la mia moto consuma molto** my motorbike uses a lot of petrol (*Brit*) *o* gas (*Am*)
d (*Dir: matrimonio*) to consummate.
2 **consumarsi** VIP (*vestiario*) to wear (out); (*candela*) to burn down; (*penna, pennarello*) to run dry; (*persona: per malattia*) to waste away; **consumarsi (di)** to be consumed (with).

consumato, a [konsu'mato] AGG a (*vestiti, scarpe, tappeto*) worn b (*persona: esperto*) accomplished.

consumatore, trice [konsuma'tore] SM/F (*Comm*) consumer.

consumazione [konsumat'tsjone] SF a (*al bar: bibita*) drink; (: *spuntino*) snack b (*Dir: del matrimonio*) consummation.

consumismo [konsu'mizmo] SM consumerism.

consumista, i, e [konsu'mista] SM/F consumerist.

consumistico, a, ci, che [konsu'mistiko] AGG consumer *attr*.

consumo [kon'sumo] SM a (*gen*) consumption, use; **consumo di benzina** petrol (*Brit*) *o* gas (*Am*) consumption; **fare largo consumo di qc** to use sth heavily; **per mio uso e consumo** for my personal use
b (*Econ*): **generi** *o* **beni di consumo** consumer goods; **beni di largo consumo** basic commodities; **imposta di consumo** tax on consumer goods; **la società dei consumi** the consumer society.

consuntivo, a [konsun'tivo] 1 AGG (*Econ: bilancio*) final.
2 SM (*Econ*) final balance; **fare un consuntivo (della situazione)** (*fig*) to take stock (of the situation).

consunto, a [kon'sunto] AGG (*abiti*) worn out, shabby; (*volto*) wasted.

consunzione [konsun'tsjone] SF (*Med*) consumption.

consuocero, a [kon'swɔtʃero] SM/F son-in-law's *o* daughter-in-law's father/mother.

conta ['konta] SF (*nei giochi*): **fare la conta** to see who is going to be 'it'.

contabile [kon'tabile] 1 AGG (*Comm*) book-keeping *attr*, accounts *attr*, accounting *attr*.
2 SM/F book-keeper, accountant.

contabilità [kontabili'ta] SF INV (*attività, tecnica*) accounting, accountancy; (*insieme dei libri*) books *pl*, accounts *pl*; **tenere la contabilità** to keep the accounts; (*ufficio*) **contabilità** accounts department ▶**contabilità finanziaria** financial accounting ▶**contabilità di gestione** management accounting.

contachilometri [kontaki'lɔmetri] SM INV ≈ mileometer

(*Brit*), odometer (*Am*).

contadinesco, a, schi, sche [kontadi'nesko] AGG (*campagnolo*) country *attr*; (*pegg*) coarse, oafish.

contadino, a [konta'dino] ① AGG (*di campagna*) country *attr*; (*rurale*) peasant *attr*; **la rivolta contadina** the peasant revolt.

  ② SM/F **a** countryman/woman; (*bracciante*) farm worker **b** (*Storia, pegg*) peasant.

  ③ SM (*fattore*) tenant farmer.

contagiare [konta'dʒare] VT (*anche fig*) to infect.

contagio, gi [kon'tadʒo] SM **a** infection; (*per contatto diretto*) contagion; **il vaiolo si prende per contagio** smallpox is contracted by touch **b** (*malattia*) disease; (*epidemia*) epidemic.

contagiosamente [kontadʒosa'mente] AVV (*vedi agg*) infectiously; contagiously.

contagioso, a [konta'dʒoso] AGG (*gen*) infectious; (*per contatto*) contagious; (*fig: riso, allegria*) infectious, contagious.

contagiri [konta'dʒiri] SM INV (*Aut*) rev counter.

contagocce [konta'gottʃe] SM INV dropper; **mi dà i soldi con il contagocce** he counts every penny he gives me.

container [kən'teinə] SM INV container.

contaminare [kontami'nare] VT (*gen*) to contaminate; (*buon nome*) to tarnish; (*testo*) to corrupt.

contaminazione [kontaminat'tsjone] SF contamination.

contaminuti [kontami'nuti] SM INV timer.

contante [kon'tante] ① AGG: **denaro contante** cash.

  ②: **contanti** SMPL cash *sg*; **pagare in contanti** to pay cash.

contare [kon'tare] ① VT **a** (*calcolare, enumerare*) to count; **le telefonate non si contavano più** I (*o you ecc*) couldn't keep count of the telephone calls; **ha sempre i minuti contati** he never has a spare moment; **ha i giorni contati** [OR] **ha le ore contate** his days are numbered; **ho i soldi contati** I haven't a penny to spare; **amici così si contano sulla punta delle dita** you can count the number of friends like that on the fingers of one hand

  b (*considerare*) to include, count (in), consider; **senza contare** (*senza includere*) not counting; (*senza parlare di*) not to mention; **contare di fare qc** to intend to do sth

  c (*fam: raccontare*) to tell; **contarle grosse** to tell tall stories.

  ② VI (*aus avere*) **a** (*calcolare*) to count; **contare fino a 100** to count to 100

  b (*fare assegnamento*): **contare su qn/qc** to count on sb/sth, rely on sb/sth; **puoi contarci** you can count on it **c** (*avere importanza*) to count, matter, be of importance; **la gente che conta** the people who matter; **alla sua festa c'era tutta la Milano che conta** everybody who is anybody in Milan was at her party.

contascatti [kontas'katti] SM INV telephone meter.

contatore [konta'tore] SM counter; (*della luce*) meter ▶**contatore del gas** gas meter.

contattare [kontat'tare] VT to contact.

contatto [kon'tatto] SM **a** (*gen*) contact; **essere/venire a contatto con qc** to be in/come into contact with sth; **a contatto con l'aria** in contact with (the) air; **non sopporto la lana a contatto con la pelle** I can't wear wool next to my skin; **mettere qc a contatto con qc** to put sth against sth; **essere in contatto con qn** to be in touch with sb; **prendere contatto con qn** to get in touch *o* contact with sb; **mantenere i contatti (con qn)** to maintain contact (with sb), keep in touch (with sb)

  b (*Elettr, Radio*) contact; **aprire/chiudere il contatto**

(*Elettr*) to make/break contact; **fare contatto** (*Elettr: fili*) to touch; **stabilire il contatto** (*Radio*) to make contact.

conte ['konte] SM (*in Europa*) count; (*in Gran Bretagna*) earl.

contea [kon'tɛa] SF **a** (*Storia: in Europa*) count; (: *in Gran Bretagna*) earldom **b** (*Amm: nei paesi anglosassoni*) county.

conteggiare [konted'dʒare] VT (*fare il conto di*) to work out; (*addebitare*) to charge (for), put on the bill.

conteggio, gi [kon'teddʒo] SM **a** (*gen*) reckoning, calculation; **fare il conteggio di** to calculate **b** : **conteggio alla rovescia** countdown **c** (*Pugilato*) count.

contegno [kon'teɲɲo] SM (*comportamento*) behaviour (*Brit*), behavior (*Am*); (*atteggiamento*) attitude; **avere *o* tenere un contegno esemplare** to behave perfectly; **ha assunto un contegno poco simpatico nei nostri confronti** he assumed a rather unpleasant attitude towards us; **darsi un contegno** (*ostentare disinvoltura*) to act nonchalant; (*ricomporsi*) to pull o.s. together.

contegnosamente [konteɲɲosa'mente] AVV in a dignified way.

contegnoso, a [konteɲ'ɲoso] AGG (*dignitoso*) dignified; (*riservato*) reserved.

contemplare [kontem'plare] VT (*paesaggio*) to gaze at; (*possibilità*) to contemplate; (*Dir: considerare*) to provide for, make provision for.

contemplativamente [kontemplativa'mente] AVV: **vivere contemplativamente** to lead a contemplative life.

contemplativo, a [kontempla'tivo] AGG contemplative.

contemplazione [kontemplat'tsjone] SF contemplation.

contempo [kon'tɛmpo] SM: **nel contempo** meanwhile, in the meantime.

contemporaneamente [kontemporanea'mente] AVV at the same time, simultaneously, contemporaneously; **contemporaneamente a** at the same time as.

contemporaneo, a [kontempo'raneo] ① AGG: **contemporaneo (di *o* a)** contemporary (with); **la sua partenza fu contemporanea al mio arrivo** his departure coincided with my arrival; **l'arte contemporanea** contemporary *o* modern art.

  ② SM/F contemporary.

contendente [konten'dɛnte] ① AGG contending.

  ② SM/F (*avversario*) opponent, adversary; (*per un titolo*) contestant.

contendere [kon'tɛndere] VB IRREG ① VT (*contestare*): **contendere qc a qn** to contend with *o* be in competition with sb for sth; **si contendono il titolo** they are competing for the title; **si contendevano l'affetto della madre** they were vying with each other for their mother's affection.

  ② VI (*aus avere*) (*disputare, litigare*) to quarrel; (*competere*) to compete; **contendere per qc** to quarrel over *o* about sth.

contenere [konte'nere] VB IRREG ① VT **a** (*racchiudere*) to contain; (: *sogg: recipienti, locali pubblici*) to hold; (: *cinema, veicoli*) to hold, seat **b** (*frenare: entusiasmo, sentimenti, epidemia*) to contain; (: *truppe, avanzata nemica*) to hold in check.

  ② **contenersi** VR to contain o.s.

contenimento [konteni'mento] SM (*di fluidi*) containing, holding; (*di prezzi, spesa pubblica*) control.

contenitore [konteni'tore] SM container.

contentabile [konten'tabile] AGG: **essere difficilmente contentabile** to be hard *o* difficult to please.

contentare [konten'tare] ① VT to please; (*soddisfare*) to

satisfy.

[2] **contentarsi** VIP: **contentarsi (di)** to content o.s. (with); **si contenta di poco** he is easily satisfied; **chi si contenta gode** (*Proverbio*) a contented mind is a perpetual feast.

contentezza [konten'tettsa] SF (*felicità*) happiness; (*soddisfazione*) contentment.

contentino [konten'tino] SM sop.

contento, a [kon'tɛnto] AGG (*lieto*) happy, glad; (*soddisfatto*) satisfied, pleased; **contento di** (*auto, persona*) pleased with; (*promozione, cambiamento*) happy *o* pleased about; **sono contento di averti ritrovato** I'm happy to have met up with you again; **e non contento di ciò...** and not content with that ...; **sono contento così** (*mi basta*) I've got enough.

contenuto, a [konte'nuto] [1] AGG (*ira, entusiasmo*) restrained, suppressed; (*forza*) contained.
[2] SM (*di cassa, valigia*) contents *pl*; (*di libro, film, discorso*) content.

contenzioso, a [konten'tsjoso] [1] AGG (*Dir*) contentious.
[2] SM (*Amm: ufficio*) legal department.

conterraneo, a [konter'raneo] SM/F fellow countryman/woman.

contesa [kon'tesa] SF (*litigio, contrasto*) quarrel, argument; (*Dir*) dispute.

conteso, a [kon'teso] [1] PP di **contendere**.
[2] AGG (*premio, carica*) sought after.

contessa [kon'tessa] SF countess.

contessina [kontes'sina] SF (*in Europa*) daughter of a count; (*in Gran Bretagna*) daughter of an earl.

contestabile [kontes'tabile] AGG questionable, disputable.

contestare [kontes'tare] VT **a** (*criticare*) to question, protest against; **contestare il sistema** to protest against the system
b (*disputare*) to dispute, contest; **contestare a qn il diritto di fare qc** to contest sb's right to do sth
c (*Dir: notificare*) to notify; **contestare un reato a qn** to charge sb with a crime; **contestare una contravvenzione a qn** to issue sb with a fine.

contestatario, ria, ri, rie [kontesta'tarjo] AGG, SM/F = **contestatore**.

contestatore, trice [kontesta'tore] [1] AGG anti-establishment.
[2] SM/F protester.

contestazione [kontestat'tsjone] SF **a** (*Pol*) anti-establishment activity; **la contestazione studentesca del '68** the student protests of '68 **b** (*Dir: disputa*) dispute; **in caso di contestazione** if there are any objections **c** (*Dir: notifica*) notification; **si proceda alla contestazione delle accuse** please read out the charges.

contesto [kon'tɛsto] SM context; **visto nel contesto** seen in context.

contestuale [kontestu'ale] AGG (*gen*) contextual; (*Dir*) contemporary.

contestualmente [kontestual'mente] AVV (*contemporaneamente*) at the same time.

contiguità [kontigui'ta] SF proximity.

contiguo, a [kon'tiguo] AGG (*camere, case*) adjoining, adjacent; **essere contiguo a** to be adjacent *o* next to.

continentale [kontinen'tale] AGG continental; **l'Europa continentale** (*Geog*) continental Europe; (*per gli inglesi*) the Continent.

continentalità [kontinentali'ta] SF (*di clima*) continental nature, continentality.

continente[1] [konti'nɛnte] SM (*gen*) continent; (*terraferma*) mainland.

continente[2] [konti'nɛnte] AGG moderate; **essere continente nel bere/mangiare** to drink/eat in moderation.

continenza [konti'nɛntsa] SF continence.

contingentare [kontindʒen'tare] VT (*Econ*) to place a quota on, fix a quota on.

contingente [kontin'dʒɛnte] [1] AGG contingent.
[2] SM **a** (*gen, Mil, Filosofia*) contingent ▶ **contingente di leva** draft (*Am*), *group of soldiers called up for military service* **b** (*Comm*) quota.

contingenza [kontin'dʒɛntsa] SF **a** (*gen*) contingency; (*circostanza*) circumstance **b** (*anche: indennità di contingenza*) cost-of-living allowance.

continuamente [kontinua'mente] AVV (*senza interruzione*) continuously, nonstop; (*ripetutamente*) continually; **perché vieni continuamente a disturbarmi?** why do you keep coming and bothering me?

continuare [kontinu'are] [1] VT (*studi, progetto*) to continue (with), carry on with, go on with; (*viaggio*) to continue; (*tradizione*) to continue, carry on; **continuò la lettura** he went on reading.
[2] VI (*riferito a persona: aus* **avere**; *riferito a cosa: aus* **avere** *o* **essere**) to continue, go on; **continuare a fare qc** to go on *o* keep on *o* continue doing sth; **continuò per la sua strada** he continued on his way; **la strada continua fino al bosco** the road carries on *o* continues as far as the wood; **se continua così...** if it (*o* he *o* she) goes on like this ...; **se i dolori continuano...** if the pain persists ...; **"continua"** (*di romanzi a puntate*) "to be continued"; **"continua a pagina 9"** "continued on page 9".
[3] (*aus* **essere** *e* **avere**) VB IMPERS: **continua a nevicare/a fare freddo** it's still snowing/cold.

continuativamente [kontinuativa'mente] AVV uninterruptedly.

continuativo, a [kontinua'tivo] AGG (*occupazione*) permanent; (*periodo*) consecutive.

continuatore, trice [kontinua'tore] SM/F: **essere continuatore di** (*tradizione*) to continue, carry on.

continuazione [kontinuat'tsjone] SF continuation; **la continuazione di un romanzo** the sequel to a novel; **in continuazione** continuously.

continuità [kontinui'ta] SF continuity.

continuo, a [kon'tinuo] AGG (*ininterrotto*) continuous; (*che si ripete*) continual; (*Elettr: corrente*) direct; **di continuo** continually.

contitolare [kontito'lare] SM/F co-owner.

conto ['konto] [1] SM **a** (*calcolo*) calculation; **fare di conto** to count
b (*Banca, Comm*) account; (*fattura: di ristorante, albergo*) bill; (*: di prestazione*) account, bill; **pagare** *o* **saldare il conto** to pay the bill; **fare i conti** to do the accounts; **dobbiamo fare il conto delle spese** we must work out the expenses; **far bene/male i propri conti** (*anche fig*) to get one's sums right/wrong; **non aveva fatto i conti con possibili imprevisti** he hadn't allowed for anything unexpected happening; **fare i conti senza l'oste** to forget the most important thing; **fare i conti con qn** to settle one's account with sb; **farò i conti con te più tardi!** (*fig*) I'll sort you out later!; **avere un conto in sospeso (con qn)** to have an outstanding account (with sb); (*fig*) to have a score to settle (with sb); **fare i conti in tasca a**

qn (*fig*) to pry into sb's financial affairs

c (*stima, considerazione*): **di poco/nessun conto** of little/no importance; **tener conto di qn/qc** to take sb/sth into consideration *o* account; **tenere qc da conto** to take great care of sth

d (*fraseologia*): **a conti fatti, in fin dei conti** all things considered, when all is said and done; **ad ogni buon conto** in any case; **per conto mio** (*a mio avviso*) in my opinion, as far as I'm concerned; (*a nome mio*) on my behalf; **voglio starmene per conto mio** I want to be on my own; **mi hanno detto strane cose sul suo conto** I've heard some strange things about him; **fare conto che...** (*supporre*) to suppose that ...; **fare conto su qn/qc** to rely *o* depend *o* count on sb/sth; **chiedere conto di qc a qn** to ask sb to give an account *o* explanation of sth; **rendere conto a qn di qc** to be accountable to sb for sth; **rendersi conto di qc/che...** to realize sth/that; **essere alla resa dei conti ...** to come to the day of reckoning.

2 ▶ **conto in banca** *o* **bancario** bank account ▶ **conto capitale** capital account ▶ **conto cassa** cash account ▶ **conto cifrato** numbered account ▶ **conto corrente** current account (*Brit*), checking account (*Am*) ▶ **conto corrente postale** ≈ National Girobank payment, post office account ▶ **conto in partecipazione** joint account ▶ **conto passivo** account payable ▶ **conto profitti e perdite** profit and loss account ▶ **conto alla rovescia** countdown ▶ **conto scoperto** overdrawn account; **avere il conto scoperto** to be overdrawn ▶ **conto valutario** foreign currency account.

contorcere [kon'tɔrtʃere] VB IRREG [1] VT to twist; (*viso*) to contort.

2 **contorcersi** VR: **contorcersi dal dolore** to writhe with pain; **contorcersi dalle risa** to double up with laughter.

contorcimento [kontortʃi'mento] SM = **contorsione**.

contornare [kontor'nare] [1] VT (*gen, fig*) to surround; (*ornare*) to decorate, trim.

2 **contornarsi** VR: **contornarsi di** to surround o.s. with.

contorno [kon'torno] SM **a** (*linea esterna*) outline, contour; (*ornamento*) border; **fare da contorno a** to surround **b** (*Culin*) vegetables *pl*; **arrosto con contorno di piselli** roast meat served with peas.

contorsione [kontor'sjone] SF contortion.

contorsionismo [kontorsjo'nizmo] SM contortionism.

contorsionista, i, e [kontorsjo'nista] SM/F contortionist.

contortamente [kontorta'mente] AVV (*fig: ragionare*) tortuously.

contorto, a [kon'tɔrto] [1] PP di **contorcere**.

2 AGG twisted; (*fig: ragionamento, stile*) tortuous.

contrabbandare [kontrabban'dare] VT to smuggle.

contrabbandiere, a [kontrabban'djere] SM/F smuggler.

contrabbando [kontrab'bando] SM smuggling, contraband; **fare il contrabbando** to smuggle; **di contrabbando** contraband, smuggled; **merce di contrabbando** contraband *no pl*, smuggled goods *pl*.

contrabbasso [kontrab'basso] SM (*Mus*) (double) bass.

contraccambiare [kontrakkam'bjare] VT (*favore, auguri*) to return; (*gentilezza*) to repay; **vorrei contraccambiare** I'd like to show my appreciation.

contraccettivo, a [kontrattʃet'tivo] AGG, SM contraceptive.

contraccolpo [kontrak'kolpo] SM (*gen*) rebound; (*di arma da fuoco*) recoil; (*fig*) repercussion.

contraccusa [kontrak'kuza] SF (*Dir*) countercharge.

contrada [kon'trada] SF (*letter: paese*) land; (*quartiere*) quarter, district; (*via*) street.

contraddetto, a [kontrad'detto] PP di **contraddire**.

contraddire [kontrad'dire] VB IRREG [1] VT to contradict.

2 **contraddirsi** VR to contradict o.s.; (*uso reciproco: persone*) to contradict each other; (: *testimonianze*) to be contradictory.

contraddistinguere [kontraddis'tingwere] VB IRREG [1] VT (*merce*) to mark; (*fig: atteggiamento, persona*) to distinguish.

2 **contraddistinguersi** VIP: **l'opera si contraddistingue per rigore scientifico** the work stands out because of its scientific accuracy.

contraddistinto, a [kontraddis'tinto] PP di **contraddistinguere**.

contraddittorietà [kontraddittorje'ta] SF contradictory nature.

contraddittorio, ria, ri, rie [kontraddit'tɔrjo] [1] AGG (*affermazione, testimonianza, personaggio*) contradictory; (*comportamento*) inconsistent; (*sentimenti*) conflicting.

2 SM (*Dir: di testimoni*) cross-examination; (*Pol: dibattito*) debate.

contraddizione [kontraddit'tsjone] SF contradiction; **cadere in contraddizione** to contradict o.s.; **essere in contraddizione** (*tesi, affermazioni*) to contradict one another; **essere in contraddizione con** to contradict; **spirito di contraddizione** argumentativeness.

contrae *ecc* [kon'trae] VB vedi **contrarre**.

contraente [kontra'ɛnte] [1] AGG (*Dir: parte*) contracting.

2 SM/F contracting party, contractor.

contraerea [kontra'ɛrea] SF (*Mil*) anti-aircraft artillery.

contraereo, a [kontra'ɛreo] AGG (*Mil*) anti-aircraft *attr*.

contraffare [kontraf'fare] VT IRREG (*firma*) to forge; (*banconota*) to forge, counterfeit; (*voce*) to disguise; (*cibo, vino*) to adulterate.

contraffatto, a [kontraf'fatto] [1] PP di **contraffare**.

2 AGG (*firma*) forged; (*banconota*) forged, counterfeit; (*voce*) disguised; (*cibo, vino*) adulterated.

contraffattore, trice [kontraffat'tore] SM/F (*di firme*) forger; (*di monete*) forger, counterfeiter.

contraffazione [kontraffat'tsjone] SF **a** (*vedi vb*) forging *no pl*, forgery; counterfeiting; disguising *no pl*; adulteration **b** (*esemplare contraffatto*) forgery.

contrafforte [kontraf'fɔrte] SM **a** (*Archit*) buttress **b** (*Geog*) spur.

contraggo *ecc* [kon'traggo] VB vedi **contrarre**.

contralto [kon'tralto] SM (*Mus*) contralto; (: *voce maschile*) alto.

contrammiraglio, gli [kontrammi'raʎʎo] SM rear admiral.

contrappello [kontrap'pɛllo] SM (*Mil*) second roll call.

contrappesare [kontrappe'sare] [1] VT to counterbalance; (*fig: decisione*) to weigh up.

2 **contrappesarsi** VR (*uso reciproco*) to counterbalance each other.

contrappeso [kontrap'peso] SM counterbalance, counterweight.

contrapporre [kontrap'porre] VB IRREG [1] VT **a** (*opporre*): **contrapporre qc a qc** to counter sth with sth; **contrapporre un rifiuto ad una richiesta** to counter a request with a refusal; **contrapporre un ostacolo a qc** to set an obstacle in the way of sth

b (*paragonare*): **contrapporre qc (a qc)** to compare sth (with sth).

2 **contrapporsi** VR: **contrapporsi a qc** to contrast with sth, be opposed to sth; **i loro punti di vista si contrap-**

pongono they hold opposing points of view.

contrapposizione [kontrappozit'tsjone] SF (*opposizione*) juxtaposition; (*confronto*) comparison; (*contrasto*) contrast; **due interpretazioni in contrapposizione** two conflicting interpretations.

contrapposto, a [kontrap'posto] ⬛1 PP di **contrapporre**. ⬛2 AGG (*argomenti, concetti*) contrasting; (*posizioni*) opposing.

contrappunto [kontrap'punto] SM counterpoint.

contrariamente [kontrarja'mente] AVV: **contrariamente a** contrary to; **contrariamente al solito** just for once; **contrariamente al solito non ha ottenuto un buon risultato** unusually for him he wasn't successful.

contrariare [kontra'rjare] VT (*ostacolare: persona*) to oppose; (: *piani*) to thwart; (*irritare*) to annoy.

contrariato, a [kontra'rjato] AGG annoyed.

contrarietà [kontrarje'ta] SF INV (*avversità*) adversity, misfortune; (*fastidio*) trouble; (*avversione*) aversion.

contrario, ria, ri, rie [kon'trarjo] ⬛1 AGG (*gen*) opposite; (*sfavorevole*) unfavourable (*Brit*), unfavorable (*Am*); (*avverso: sorte*) adverse; (: *venti*) contrary; **essere contrario a qc** (*persona*) to be against sth; **sono contrario a questo tuo modo di comportarti** I disapprove of the way you're behaving; **è contrario ai miei principi** it's against my principles; **in caso contrario** otherwise; **in direzione contraria** in the opposite direction.

⬛2 SM opposite; **al contrario** on the contrary; **avere qualcosa in contrario** to have some objection; **non ho niente in contrario** I've no objection; **è esattamente il contrario** it's quite the opposite *o* reverse.

contrarre [kon'trarre] VB IRREG ⬛1 VT **a** (*muscoli, volto*) to tense **b** (*malattia, debito, prestito*) to contract; (*abitudine, vizio*) to pick up; (*accordo, patto*) to enter into; **contrarre matrimonio** to marry. ⬛2 **contrarsi** VIP (*gen, Gramm*) to contract.

contrassegnare [kontrasseɲ'ɲare] VT to mark.

contrassegnato, a [kontrasseɲ'ɲato] AGG marked; **contrassegnato da un'etichetta** labelled.

contrassegno [kontras'seɲɲo] ⬛1 SM (distinguishing) mark. ⬛2 AVV (*Comm*): **spedire in contrassegno** to send COD.

contrassi *ecc* [kon'trassi] VB vedi **contrarre**.

contrastante [kontras'tante] AGG contrasting.

contrastare [kontras'tare] ⬛1 VT (*avanzata, piano*) to hinder; (*desiderio, diritto*) to dispute, contest; **una vittoria contrastata** a hard-fought victory. ⬛2 VI (*aus* avere) (*discordare*): **contrastare (con)** to clash (with), contrast (with); **questi colori contrastano fra di loro** these colours clash.

contrastivo, a [kontras'tivo] AGG (*Ling*) contrastive.

contrasto [kon'trasto] SM **a** (*gen, TV, Fot*) contrast; **per contrasto** in contrast **b** (*conflitto*) conflict; (*disputa, litigio*) quarrel, dispute; **un contrasto di opinioni** a difference of opinion; **essere in/venire a contrasto con qn** to be in/get into a disagreement with sb.

contrattabile [kontrat'tabile] AGG negotiable.

contrattaccare [kontrattak'kare] VT to counterattack.

contrattacco [kontrat'takko] SM counterattack; **passare al contrattacco** (*fig*) to fight back.

contrattare [kontrat'tare] VT (*uso assoluto: trattare*) to negotiate; (: *mercanteggiare*) to bargain; (*terreno, merce*) to bargain over, negotiate the price of; **contrattare il prezzo** to negotiate the price.

contrattazione [kontrattat'tsjone] SF (*trattativa*) negotia-tion; **dopo lunghe contrattazioni ho spuntato un buon prezzo** after much bargaining I managed to get a good price.

contrattempo [kontrat'tempo] SM hitch; **per una serie di contrattempi** because of a series of difficulties.

contrattile [kon'trattile] AGG contractile.

contratto, a [kon'tratto] ⬛1 PP di **contrarre**. ⬛2 AGG (*volto, mani*) tense; (*muscoli*) tense, contracted; (*Gramm*) contracted. ⬛3 SM contract ▶**contratto di acquisto** purchase agreement ▶**contratto di affitto** lease ▶**contratto collettivo di lavoro** collective agreement ▶**contratto di lavoro** contract of employment ▶**contratto di locazione** lease ▶**contratto a termine** forward contract.

contrattuale [kontrattu'ale] AGG contractual; **forza contrattuale** (*di sindacato*) bargaining power.

contrattualmente [kontrattual'mente] AVV contractually; **è stato deciso contrattualmente che...** it has been decided in the contract that... .

contravvenire [kontravve'nire] VI IRREG (*aus* avere): **contravvenire a** (*legge, regolamento*) to contravene; (*obbligo*) to fail to meet.

contravventore, trice [kontravven'tore] SM/F offender.

contravvenuto, a [kontravve'nuto] PP di **contravvenire**.

contravvenzione [kontravven'tsjone] SF **a** (*Aut: multa*) fine; **elevare una contravvenzione a qn** to fine sb **b** (*trasgressione*): **contravvenzione (a)** contravention (of).

contrazione [kontrat'tsjone] SF (*gen, Med, Gramm*) contraction; **contrazione (di)** (*di prezzi, vendite*) decrease (in), fall (in).

contribuente [kontribu'ɛnte] SM/F (*Fisco*) taxpayer.

contribuire [kontribu'ire] VI (*aus* avere): **contribuire a qc** to contribute to sth; **contribuire a fare qc** to help do sth; **tutto ciò ha contribuito a peggiorare la situazione** all this has made things worse.

contributivo, a [kontribu'tivo] AGG contributory.

contributo [kontri'buto] SM **a** (*gen*) contribution; **dare il proprio contributo a qc** to make one's contribution to sth **b** : **contributi** SMPL (*tasse*) charges, tax; (*sovvenzioni*) subsidy, contribution ▶**contributi previdenziali** ≈ national insurance (*Brit*) *o* welfare (*Am*) contributions ▶**contributi sindacali** trade (*Brit*) *o* labor (*Am*) union dues.

contribuzione [kontribut'tsjone] SF contribution.

contrito, a [kon'trito] AGG contrite, penitent; **con aria contrita** penitently.

contrizione [kontrit'tsjone] SF contrition.

contro ['kontro] ⬛1 PREP **a** (*gen*) against; **sono tutti contro di me** they are all against me; **lottare contro qn/qc** to fight against sb/sth; **è contro il divorzio** he's against *o* opposed to divorce; **il Milan contro la Juventus** Milan versus *o* against Juventus; **pastiglie contro la tosse** throat lozenges; **un ottimo rimedio contro l'influenza** an excellent treatment for flu

b (*contatto, direzione*) against; **si appoggiò contro la porta** he leaned against the door; **ho sbattuto contro la porta** I bumped into the door; **puntò la pistola contro di me** he pointed his gun at me; **spararono contro la polizia** they shot at the police

c (*Comm: in cambio di*): **contro pagamento/ricevuta** on payment/receipt

d (*contrariamente a*): **contro ogni mia aspettativa**

contrary to my expectations
e : **contro corrente, contro luce, contro voglia** *ecc*; vedi **controcorrente, controluce, controvoglia** *ecc*.
2 AVV against; **votare contro** to vote against; **dar contro a qn** to contradict sb; **per contro** on the other hand.
3 SM INV con; **il pro e il contro** the pros and cons.
4 PREF counter... .
controbattere [kontro'battere] VT (*ribattere*) to answer back; (*confutare*) to refute.
controbilanciare [kontrobilan'tʃare] VT (*gen*, *fig*) to counterbalance.
controcampo [kontro'kampo] SM (*Cine*) reverse shot.
controcorrente [kontrokor'rɛnte] AVV: **nuotare controcorrente** (*in un fiume*) to swim upstream; (*nel mare*) to swim against the tide; **andare controcorrente** (*fig*) to swim against the tide.
controcultura [kontrokul'tura] SF counterculture.
controcurva [kontro'kurva] SF (*Sci*) counter-turn.
controdado [kontro'dado] SM locknut.
controfagotto [kontrofa'gotto] SM (*Mus*) double bassoon.
controfax [kontro'faks] SM INV reply to a fax.
controffensiva [kontroffen'siva] SF (*Mil*, *fig*) counteroffensive.
controfigura [kontrofi'gura] SF (*Cine*) stuntman/woman, double; **essere la controfigura di qn** to play sb's double.
controfiletto [kontrofi'letto] SM sirloin.
controfinestra [kontrofi'nɛstra] SF: **mettere le controfinestre** to have double glazing installed.
controfirma [kontro'firma] SF countersignature.
controfirmare [kontrofir'mare] VT to countersign.
controindicazione [kontroindikat'tsjone] SF contra-indication.
controinterrogatorio, ri [kontrointerroga'tɔrjo] SM cross-examination.
controllare [kontrol'lare] **1** VT **a** (*verificare*: *gen*) to check; (: *biglietto*) to inspect, check **b** (*sorvegliare*) to watch, keep a close watch on; (: *ufficio*, *impiegato*) to supervise **c** (*tenere a freno*, *dominare*: *anche Mil*, *Calcio*) to control.
2 controllarsi VR to control o.s.
controllata [kontrol'lata] SF (*Comm*: *società*) associated company.
controllato, a [kontrol'lato] AGG (*persona*: *non impulsivo*) self-controlled, self-possessed; (*reazioni*) controlled.
controllo [kon'trollo] SM **1** **a** (*verifica*: *gen*) check; (: *di biglietti*) inspection; **fare un controllo di** to check sth, to inspect sth; **visita di controllo** (*Med*) checkup **b** (*sorveglianza*) supervision; **telefono sotto controllo** tapped telephone; **base di controllo** (*Aer*) ground control
c (*padronanza*, *regolamentazione*) control; **esercitare il controllo su qc** to have control over sth; **perdere il controllo (di qc)** (*di macchina*, *situazione*) to lose control (of sth); **ha perso il controllo (di sé)** he lost control (of himself), he lost his self-control.
2 ▸**controllo bagagli** baggage *o* luggage check ▸**controllo dei costi** cost control ▸**controllo doganale** customs inspection ▸**controllo di gestione** management control ▸**controllo delle nascite** birth control ▸**controllo passaporti** passport control ▸**controllo dei prezzi** price control ▸**controllo qualità** quality control ▸**controllo di sicurezza** (*in aeroporto*) security check ▸**controllo del traffico aereo** air-traffic control.

controllore [kontrol'lore] SM (*di autobus*, *treno*) (ticket) inspector; (*doganale*) customs officer ▸**controllore di volo** air-traffic controller.
controluce [kontro'lutʃe] **1** SF INV (*Fot*) backlit shot.
2 AVV: **(in) controluce** against the light; (*fotografare*) into the light.
contromano [kontro'mano] AVV: **guidare contromano** to drive on the wrong side of the road; (*in un senso unico*) to drive the wrong way up a one-way street.
contromarca, che [kontro'marka] SF pass-out (ticket).
contromarcia [kontro'martʃa] SF (*Mil*) countermarch.
controparte [kontro'parte] SF (*Dir*) opposing party.
contropartita [kontropar'tita] SF (*fig*: *compenso*): **come contropartita** in return.
contropelo [kontro'pelo] **1** AVV (*di stoffa*) against the nap; **radersi contropelo** to shave against the growth; **accarezzare un gatto contropelo** to stroke a cat the wrong way.
2 SM: **fare il contropelo** to shave against the growth.
contropiede [kontro'pjɛde] SM (*Sport*): **azione di contropiede** sudden counter-attack; **prendere qn in contropiede** to wrong-foot sb; (*fig*) to catch sb off his (*o* her) guard.
controproducente [kontroprodu'tʃɛnte] AGG counterproductive.
controproposta [kontropro'posta] SF counterproposal.
controprova [kontro'prɔva] SF (*di esperimento*, *conti*) countercheck.
contrordine [kon'trordine] SM counter-order; **salvo contrordine** unless I (*o* you *ecc*) hear to the contrary.
controriforma [kontrori'forma] SF (*Storia*) Counter-Reformation.
controrivoluzionario, a [kontrorivoluttsjo'narjo] AGG, SM/F counter-revolutionary.
controrivoluzione [kontrorivolut'tsjone] SF counter-revolution.
controsenso [kontro'sɛnso] SM (*contraddizione*) contradiction in terms; (*assurdità*) nonsense.
controsoffitto [kontrosof'fitto] SM false ceiling.
controspionaggio, gi [kontrospio'naddʒo] SM counter-espionage.
controsterzare [kontroster'tsare] VI (*aus* **avere**) (*Aut*) to steer the other way.
controvalore [kontrova'lore] SM equivalent (value).
controvento [kontro'vɛnto] AVV against the wind; **navigare controvento** to sail to windward.
controversia [kontro'vɛrsja] SF (*gen*) controversy; (*Dir*) dispute; **ha suscitato molte controversie** it provoked a great deal of controversy ▸**controversia sindacale** industrial dispute.
controverso, a [kontro'vɛrso] AGG controversial.
controvoglia [kontro'vɔʎʎa] AVV: **(di) controvoglia** reluctantly, unwillingly.
contumace [kontu'matʃe] **1** AGG (*Dir*): **rendersi contumace** to default, fail to appear in court.
2 SM/F (*Dir*) defaulter.
contumacia [kontu'matʃa] SF (*Dir*) default; **processare qn in contumacia** to try sb in his (*o* her) absence; **giudizio in contumacia** judgment by default.
contumaciale [kontuma'tʃale] AGG (*Dir*: *processo*) by default; (*Med*: *ospedale*) quarantine *attr*.
contundente [kontun'dɛnte] AGG: **corpo contundente** blunt instrument.
conturbante [kontur'bante] AGG (*sguardo*, *bellezza*) per-

turbing, thrilling.

conturbare [kontur'bare] VT to perturb, thrill.

contusione [kontu'zjone] SF (*Med*) bruise.

contuso, a [kon'tuzo] [1] AGG bruised.

[2] SM/F (*in incidente*) person suffering from cuts and bruises; **numerosi i contusi negli scontri con la polizia** the number of people slightly hurt in the clashes with the police was high.

conurbazione [konurbat'tsjone] SF conurbation.

convalescente [konvaleʃ'ʃɛnte] AGG, SM/F convalescent.

convalescenza [konvaleʃ'ʃɛntsa] SF convalescence; **essere in convalescenza** to be convalescing; **ha fatto una convalescenza di 3 mesi** he spent 3 months convalescing.

convalida [kon'valida] SF (*vedi vb*) validation; stamping; confirmation.

convalidare [konvali'dare] VT (*Amm*) to validate; (*biglietto*) to stamp; (*Dir, fig: dubbi, sospetti*) to confirm.

convegno [kon'veɲɲo] SM (*incontro*) meeting; (*riunione ufficiale*) convention, conference, congress; **darsi convegno** (*appuntamento*) to arrange to meet.

convenevoli [konve'nevoli] SMPL courtesies, civilities; **scambiarsi i convenevoli** to exchange the usual courtesies.

conveniente [konve'njɛnte] AGG **a** (*adatto, opportuno*): **conveniente (a)** suitable (for), fitting (for) **b** (*vantaggioso: prezzo*) cheap; (: *affare*) profitable.

convenientemente [konvenjɛnte'mente] AVV (*opportunamente*) suitably; (*vantaggiosamente*) profitably.

convenienza [konve'njɛntsa] SF **a** (*l'essere vantaggioso di: prezzo*) cheapness; (: *affare*) advantage, profit; **non vedo la convenienza di trovarci a Milano** I don't think Milan is the most convenient place to meet; **fare qc per convenienza** to do sth out of self-interest; **non c'è convenienza a vendere adesso** there's no advantage in selling at the moment; **la convenienza di abitare in centro** the advantage of living in the centre; **matrimonio di convenienza** marriage of convenience **b** (*decoro*) propriety; **andare oltre i limiti della convenienza** to go beyond the pale **c** (*norme sociali*): **le convenienze** SFPL the proprieties, social conventions.

convenire [konve'nire] VB IRREG [1] VT to agree upon; **come convenuto** as agreed; **resta convenuto che... ** it is agreed that ...; **in data da convenire** on a date to be agreed.

[2] VI (*aus essere*) **a** (*aus avere*) (*essere d'accordo*): **convenire (su qc/che...)** to agree (upon sth/that ...); **devi convenire che hai torto** you must admit you are in the wrong; **ne convengo** I agree **b** (*riunirsi*) to gather, assemble **c** : **convenire a qn** (*essere vantaggioso*) to be worthwhile for sb; (*essere consigliabile*) to be advisable for sb; **questo affare non mi conviene** this transaction isn't worth my while; **ti conviene accettare** you would be well advised to accept; **non gli conviene fare il furbo** he'd better not try to get clever.

[3] VB IMPERS (*aus essere*): **conviene fare così** it is advisable to do this; **conviene andarsene** we'd better go, we should go.

[4] **convenirsi** VIP: **convenirsi a** to suit, befit; **come si conviene ad una signorina** as befits a young lady.

conventicola [konven'tikola] SF (*cricca*) clique.

convento [kon'vɛnto] SM (*di suore*) convent; (*di frati*) monastery; **entrare in convento** (*suora*) to enter a convent; **accontentiamoci di quel che passa il convento** let's make the best of things.

conventuale [konventu'ale] AGG of a convent.

convenuto, a [konve'nuto] [1] PP di **convenire**.

[2] AGG (*ora, luogo, prezzo*) agreed.

[3] SM **a** (*cosa pattuita*) agreement; **secondo il convenuto** as agreed **b** (*Dir*) defendant **c** (*i presenti*): **i convenuti** SMPL those present.

convenzionale [konventsjo'nale] AGG (*gen*) conventional.

convenzionalmente [konventsjonal'mente] AVV conventionally, in a conventional way.

convenzionato, a [konventsjo'nato] AGG (*ospedale, clinica*) providing free health care, ≈ National Health Service *attr* (*Brit*).

convenzione [konven'tsjone] SF **a** (*Dir, Pol*) agreement **b** (*assunto generale, tradizione*) convention; (*tacito accordo*) understanding; **le convenzioni (sociali)** social conventions **c** (*Pol, Dir: convegno*) convention.

convergente [konver'dʒɛnte] AGG convergent.

convergenza [konver'dʒɛntsa] SF convergence; (*Aut*) toe-in.

convergere [kon'vɛrdʒere] VI IRREG E DIF (*aus essere*): **convergere (su)** (*gen, Mat*) to converge (on); (*interesse*) to centre (on).

conversa [kon'vɛrsa] SF (*Rel*) lay sister.

conversare [konver'sare] VI (*aus avere*) to talk, to have a conversation.

conversazione [konversat'tsjone] SF conversation; **fare conversazione** (*chiacchierare*) to chat, have a chat.

conversione [konver'sjone] SF (*gen*): **conversione (a/in)** conversion (to/into) ▸**conversione a U** (*Aut*) U-turn.

converso, a [kon'vɛrso] [1] PP di **convergere**.

[2]: **per converso** AVV conversely.

convertibile [konver'tibile] [1] AGG: **convertibile (in)** convertible (into).

[2] SF (*Aut*) convertible.

convertibilità [konvertibili'ta] SF convertibility.

convertire [konver'tire] [1] VT (*gen, Inform*) to convert; (*persuadere*): **convertire qn (a qc)** to convert sb (to sth); **convertire qc in qc** to convert sth into sth.

[2] **convertirsi** VR: **convertirsi (a qc)** to be converted (to sth).

[3] **convertirsi** VIP: **l'amore si convertì in odio** love turned to hate.

convertito, a [konver'tito] [1] AGG converted.

[2] SM/F convert.

convertitore [konverti'tore] SM (*Elettr*) converter ▸**convertitore di coppia** (*Aut*) torque converter.

convessità [konvessi'ta] SF INV convexity.

convesso, a [kon'vɛsso] AGG convex.

convettore [konvet'tore] SM convector.

convezione [konvet'tsjone] SF convection.

convincente [konvin'tʃɛnte] AGG convincing.

convincere [kon'vintʃere] VB IRREG [1] VT to convince; **convincere qn di qc** to convince sb of sth; **convincere qn a fare qc** to persuade sb to do sth, talk sb into doing sth.

[2] **convincersi** VR: **convincersi di qc/che... ** to convince o.s. of sth/that ... .

convincimento [konvintʃi'mento] SM conviction, belief.

convinto, a [kon'vinto] [1] PP di **convincere**.

[2] AGG convinced; **in tono convinto** with conviction.

convinzione [konvin'tsjone] SF conviction, firm belief; **fare opera di convinzione su qn** to try to convince sb.

convissuto [konvis'suto] PP di **convivere**.

convitato, a [konvi'tato] SM/F guest.

convitto [kon'vitto] SM boarding school.

convivenza [konvi'vɛntsa] SF living together; (*Dir*) cohabitation; **la convivenza con quell'uomo non dev'esser facile** it can't be easy living with that man.

convivere [kon'vivere] VI IRREG (*aus avere*) to live together; (*Dir*) to cohabit; **convivere con qn** to live with sb.

conviviale [konvi'vjale] AGG convivial.

convocare [konvo'kare] VT (*riunione*) to convene, call; (*parlamento*) to convene; (*persona subordinata*) to summon, send for; **tutti i genitori sono stati convocati** all parents have been asked to attend; **il giocatore è stato convocato in nazionale** the player has been chosen to play for the national team.

convocazione [konvokat'tsjone] SF **a** (*atto: vedi vb*) convening; summoning; **lettera di convocazione** (letter of) notification to appear *o* attend **b** (*riunione*) meeting, summons *sg*.

convogliare [konvoʎ'ʎare] VT **a** (*dirigere*) to direct, send; (: *acque*) to channel; (: *fig: energie*): **convogliare su** to channel into **b** (*trasportare*) to carry, transport, convey.

convoglio, gli [kon'vɔʎʎo] SM **a** (*Naut, Mil*) convoy; **convoglio (ferroviario)** train **b** (*corteo funebre*) funeral procession.

convolare [konvo'lare] VI (*aus essere*): **convolare a (giuste) nozze** (*scherz*) to tie the knot.

convolvolo [kon'vɔlvolo] SM bindweed.

convulsamente [konvulsa'mente] AVV convulsively.

convulsione [konvul'sjone] SF (*Med*) convulsion; (*di riso*) fit.

convulsivo, a [konvul'sivo] AGG convulsive.

convulso, a [kon'vulso] AGG (*gen*) convulsive; (*pianto*) uncontrollable, violent; (*fig: stile, parlare*) jerky; (: *attività, ritmo*) feverish.

COOP. [ko'op] ABBR F = **cooperativa**.

cooperare [koope'rare] VI (*aus avere*): **cooperare (a qc/a fare qc)** to cooperate (in sth/to do sth).

cooperativa [koopera'tiva] SF cooperative ▶**cooperativa edilizia** building cooperative (*selling houses to its members*).

cooperativo, a [koopera'tivo] AGG cooperative.

cooperatore, trice [koopera'tore] SM/F (*collaboratore*) collaborator; (*socio di cooperativa*) cooperative member.

cooperazione [kooperat'tsjone] SF cooperation.

coordinamento [koordina'mento] SM coordination.

coordinare [koordi'nare] VT to coordinate.

coordinata [koordi'nata] SF (*Ling, Mat, Geog*) coordinate; **coordinate chilometriche est/nord** (*Cartografia*) eastings/northings.

coordinato, a [koordi'nato] ① AGG (*Mat, Ling*) coordinate; (*movimenti*) coordinated.
② (*abbigliamento, arredamento*): **coordinati** SMPL coordinates.

coordinatore, trice [koordina'tore] SM/F coordinator.

coordinazione [koordinat'tsjone] SF coordination.

coorte [ko'ɔrte] SF (*Storia*) cohort.

Copenaghen [kope'nagen] SF Copenhagen.

coperchio, chi [ko'pɛrkjo] SM cover; (*di pentola*) lid.

Copernico [ko'pɛrniko] SM Copernicus.

coperta [ko'pɛrta] SF **a** (*di lana*) blanket; (*da viaggio*) rug ▶**coperta elettrica** electric blanket **b** (*Naut*) deck; **tutti in coperta!** all hands on deck!

copertamente [koperta'mente] AVV covertly, secretly.

copertina [koper'tina] SF (*di libro, rivista*) cover; (: *sovraccoperta*) jacket; **in copertina** on the cover; **ragazza copertina** cover girl.

coperto, a [ko'pɛrto] ① PP di **coprire**.
② AGG (*gen, Assicurazione*) covered; (*luogo: riparato*) sheltered; (*piscina, campo da tennis*) indoor *attr*; (*cielo*) overcast; **coperto di** covered with; **tieni il bambino ben coperto** keep the child well wrapped up.
③ SM **a**: **al coperto** under cover; **mettersi al coperto** to take shelter; **essere al coperto** (*fig*) to be safe
b (*posto a tavola*) place; **ho messo 12 coperti** I've set the table for 12; **(prezzo del) coperto** (*al ristorante*) cover charge.

copertone [koper'tone] SM **a** (*Aut*) tyre (*Brit*), tire (*Am*) **b** (*telone impermeabile*) tarpaulin.

copertura [koper'tura] SF **a** (*gen: atto*) covering; (*Edil*) roofing; **attività di copertura** cover-up; **materiali da copertura** roofing (materials) **b** (*Econ, Comm, Assicurazione*) cover **c** (*Sport*): **fare un gioco di copertura** to play a defensive game **d** (*Mil*) cover.

copia ['kɔpja] SF (*gen*) copy; (*Fot*) print; **brutta/bella copia** rough/final copy; **essere l'esatta copia di qn/qc** to be the spitting image of sb/sth ▶**copia carbone** carbon copy ▶**copia conforme** (*Dir*) certified copy ▶**copia omaggio** presentation copy.

copiacommissione [kopjakommis'sjone] SM INV order book.

copiare [ko'pjare] VT to copy; (*Inform*) to back up, copy; **copiare (qc da qn)** (*in compito a scuola*) to copy (sth from sb).

copiativo, a [kopja'tivo] AGG: **carta copiativa** carbon paper; **inchiostro copiativo** indelible ink; **matita copiativa** indelible pencil.

copiatrice [kopja'tritʃe] SF copier, copying machine.

copiatura [kopja'tura] SF copying.

copiglia [ko'piʎʎa] SF (*Tecn*) cotter (pin).

copilota, i [kopi'lɔta] SM/F copilot.

copione [ko'pjone] SM (*Cine, Teatro*) script; **come da *o* secondo copione** according to plan, as planned.

copiosamente [kopjosa'mente] AVV copiously.

copioso, a [kopjoso] AGG copious.

copisteria [kopiste'ria] SF copy bureau.

coppa¹ ['kɔppa] SF **a** (*gen*) cup; (*Sport*) trophy, cup; (*per gelato, frutta*) bowl; (*per spumante*) champagne glass; (*Rel*) chalice; **coppa di gelato** (*in confezione*) tub of ice cream ▶**coppa dell'olio** (*Aut*) oil sump (*Brit*) *o* pan (*Am*) ▶**coppa della ruota** (*Aut*) hubcap **b** (*Carte*): **coppe** SFPL *suit in Neapolitan pack of cards*.

coppa² ['kɔppa] SF (*Culin*) large pork sausage.

coppia ['kɔppja] SF (*di persone*) couple; (*di animali, Sport*) pair; **una coppia di sposi** a married couple; **a coppie** OR **in coppia** in pairs; **fare una bella coppia** to make a nice couple; **gara a coppie** competition for pairs ▶**coppia di forze** (*Fis*) torque.

coppola ['kɔppola] SF peaked cap.

copra ['kɔpra] SF copra.

coprente [ko'prɛnte] AGG (*colore, cosmetico*) covering; (*calze*) opaque.

copricapo [kopri'kapo] SM headgear *no pl*; (*cappello*) hat.

copricostume [koprikos'tume] SM beach robe.

coprifuoco, chi [kopri'fwɔko] SM curfew.

copriletto [kopri'lɛtto] SM INV bedspread.

coprimaterasso [koprimate'rasso] SM mattress cover.

coprimozzo [kopri'mɔddzo] SM hubcap.

coprire [ko'prire] VB IRREG [1] VT (gen) to cover; (occupare: carica, posto) to hold; (persona: proteggere: anche fig) to cover, shield; (fig: suono) to drown; (: segreto, sentimenti) to conceal; **copri bene il bambino** wrap the child up well; **coprire di** o **con** (gen) to cover with; **era coperto di lividi** he was bruised all over o covered in bruises; **coprire qn di insulti/di doni** to shower insults/gifts on sb; **coprire qn di ridicolo** to cover sb with ridicule; **coprire qn di baci** to smother sb with kisses; **coprire (le spalle a) qn** (in una sparatoria) to cover sb; **coprire un rischio** (Econ, Assicurazione) to cover a risk; **coprire le spese** to break even; **coprire un percorso in un'ora** to cover a distance in one hour.

[2] **coprirsi** VR (persona) to wrap (o.s.) up; (: Assicurazione): **coprirsi contro** to insure o.s. against; **coprirsi di gloria/di ridicolo** to cover o.s. with glory/with ridicule.

[3] **coprirsi** VIP (cielo) to cloud over; (rivestirsi): **coprirsi di** (muffa, macchie) to be covered in.

coprisedile [koprise'dile] SM (per auto) seat cover.

coproduzione [koprodut'tsjone] SF (Cine) co-production.

copula ['kɔpula] SF (Gramm) copula; (congiunzione) conjunction.

copulativo, a [kopula'tivo] AGG copulative.

copulazione [kopulat'tsjone] SF copulation.

copyright ['kɔpirait] SM INV copyright.

coque [kɔk] SF INV: **uovo alla coque** (soft-)boiled egg.

coraggio [ko'raddʒo] SM [a] courage, bravery; **aver coraggio** to be courageous, be brave; **dimostrare coraggio in battaglia** to show courage o bravery in battle; **aver un coraggio da leone** to be as brave as a lion; **non ho avuto il coraggio di chiederglielo** I hadn't the nerve to ask him; **avere il coraggio delle proprie azioni** to have the courage of one's convictions; **farsi coraggio** to pluck up courage; **fare coraggio a qn** to cheer sb up; **coraggio!** (forza!) come on!; (animo!) cheer up!

[b] (sfacciataggine) nerve; **hai un bel coraggio!** you've got a nerve!

coraggiosamente [koraddʒosa'mente] AVV bravely, courageously.

coraggioso, a [korad'dʒoso] AGG brave, courageous.

corale [ko'rale] AGG (Mus) choral; (adesione, consenso) unanimous.

corallino, a [koral'lino] AGG coral attr.

corallo [ko'rallo] SM coral; **il mar dei Coralli** the Coral Sea.

coralmente [koral'mente] AVV (rispondere, approvare) unanimously.

Corano [ko'rano] SM: **il Corano** the Koran.

corazza [ko'rattsa] SF (Storia) cuirass; (Mil) armo(u)r(-plate); (Sport) protective clothing; (di animali) carapace, shell; **corazza di indifferenza** hard shell of indifference.

corazzare [korat'tsare] [1] VT to armour.

[2] **corazzarsi** VR (proteggersi): **corazzarsi contro qc** to protect o.s. from sth.

corazzata [korat'tsata] SF battleship.

corazzato, a [korat'tsato] AGG (Mil) armo(u)red; **essere corazzato contro le avversità** to be hardened o proof against adversities.

corazziere [korat'tsjɛre] SM (Storia) cuirassier; (guardia presidenziale) carabiniere of the President's guard.

corbelleria [korbelle'ria] SF (parola) stupid remark; (azione) foolish action; **non dire corbellerie!** don't talk nonsense!, don't be so silly!

corda ['kɔrda] SF [a] (fune) rope; (Pugilato): **le corde** the ropes; **di corda** (suole) rope attr; **scarpe di corda** espadrilles; **saltare la corda** to skip (Brit), jump rope (Am)

[b] (di violino, arco, racchetta) string; **strumenti a corda** stringed instruments

[c] (Anat): **corde vocali** vocal cords ▸ **corda dorsale** (Zool) spinal chord

[d] (Geom) chord

[e] (fraseologia): **dare corda a qn** to let sb have his (o her) way; **dare la corda a un orologio** to wind a clock; **mettersi la corda al collo** (fig) to put one's head in the noose; **tenere sulla corda qn** to keep sb on tenterhooks; **essere giù di corda** to feel down; **tagliare la corda** to sneak off, slip away; **tendere** o **tirare troppo la corda** (fig) to push one's luck.

cordame [kor'dame] SM ropes pl; (Naut) rigging.

cordata [kor'data] SF (Alpinismo) roped party; (fig: Pol) network, alliance system in financial and business world; **in cordata** roped together.

cordiale [kor'djale] [1] AGG (accoglienza) warm, cordial; (persona) warm; **cordiali saluti** (in lettere) best regards; **c'è una cordiale antipatia tra noi** we cordially dislike one another.

[2] SM (bevanda) cordial.

cordialità [kordjali'ta] SF [a] warmth, cordiality [b] (saluti): **cordialità** SFPL best wishes.

cordialmente [kordjal'mente] AVV warmly, cordially.

cordigliera [kordiʎ'ʎɛra] SF cordillera.

cordiglio, gli [kor'diʎʎo] SM (di frate, monaca) (knotted) cord; (di sacerdote) priest's girdle.

cordoglio [kor'dɔʎʎo] SM grief, sorrow; (lutto) mourning; **esprimere il proprio cordoglio a qn** to offer sb one's sympathy o condolences.

cordone [kor'done] SM (gen) cord; (di telefono) cord, flex; (di borsa) string; (linea: di poliziotti, soldati) cordon ▸ **cordone litoraneo** (Geog) offshore bar ▸ **cordone ombelicale** (Anat) umbilical cord ▸ **cordone sanitario** quarantine line, cordon sanitaire.

Corea [ko'rɛa] SF: **la Corea** Korea; **la Corea del Nord/Sud** North/South Korea.

corea [ko'rɛa] SF (Med) chorea.

coreano, a [kore'ano] AGG, SM/F Korean.

coreografia [koreogra'fia] SF choreography.

coreograficamente [koreografika'mente] AVV choreographically.

coreografico, a, ci, che [koreo'grafiko] AGG choreographic.

coreografo, a [kore'ɔgrafo] SM/F choreographer.

coriaceo, a [ko'rjatʃeo] AGG (Bot, Zool) coriaceous; (fig) tough.

coriandolo [ko'rjandolo] SM [a] (per carnevale): **coriandoli** SMPL confetti sg [b] (Bot) coriander.

coricare [kori'kare] [1] VT (persona: a letto) to put to bed; (: a terra, su divano) to put down, lay down; (bottiglia) to rest, lay.

[2] **coricarsi** VR (andare a letto) to go to bed; (riposarsi) to lie down.

coricherò ecc VB vedi **coricare**.

Corinto [ko'rinto] SF Corinth.

corinzio, zia, zi, zie [ko'rintsjo] AGG (Arte) Corinthian; **ordine/capitello corinzio** Corinthian order/capital.

corista, i, e [ko'rista] [1] SM/F (Rel) choir member, chorister; (Teatro) member of the chorus; **i coristi** (Teatro) the chorus.

[2] SM tuning fork.

cormorano [kormo'rano] SM cormorant.

corna ['korna] SFPL vedi **corno**.

cornacchia [kor'nakkja] SF crow ▶**cornacchia grigia** hooded crow ▶**cornacchia nera** carrion crow.

cornalina [korna'lina] SF carnelian, cornelian.

cornamusa [korna'muza] SF bagpipes *pl*.

cornata [kor'nata] SF butt; **dare una cornata a qn** to butt sb; (*infilzare*) to gore sb.

cornea ['kornea] SF (*Anat*) cornea.

corneo, a ['korneo] AGG horny.

corner ['korner] SM INV (*Calcio*) corner (kick); **salvarsi in corner** (*fig*: *in gara, esame*) to get through by the skin of one's teeth; **mi son salvato in corner** (*in situazione imbarazzante*) I just managed to wriggle out of it.

cornetta [kor'netta] SF (*Mus*) cornet; (*di telefono*) receiver; **riattaccare la cornetta** to hang up.

cornetto [kor'netto] SM **a** (*Culin*: *brioche*) croissant; (: *gelato*) cone, cornet (*Brit*); (: *fagiolino*) runner bean (*Brit*), string bean (*Am*) **b** (*amuleto*) horn-shaped talisman **c** : **cornetto acustico** ear trumpet.

cornice [kor'nitʃe] SF (*gen*) frame; (*Archit, Sci*) cornice; (*Geog*) ledge; (*fig*) background, setting; **fare da cornice a** (*fig*) to frame.

corniciaio, ai [korni'tʃajo] SM picture framer.

corniciatura [kornitʃa'tura] SF framing.

cornicione [korni'tʃone] SM (*di edificio*) ledge; (: *Archit*) cornice.

cornificare [kornifi'kare] VT (*fam*: *marito, moglie*) to cheat on.

corno ['korno] 1 SM (*pl m* **corni**) (*Mus*) horn ▶**corno da caccia** hunting horn ▶**corno inglese** (*Mus*) English horn, cor anglais.

2 SM, NO PL **a** (*materiale*) horn; **di corno** (*bottone, manico*) horn *attr*

b (*fam*): **un corno!** not on your life!; **felice? — un corno!** happy? — anything but!; **non me ne importa un corno!** I don't give a damn!; **non è vero un corno!** that's rubbish!

c (*Geog*): **il Corno d'Africa** Horn of Africa; **i paesi del Corno d'Africa** Somaliland.

3 SM (*pl f* **corna**) **a** (*Zool*: *di toro, lumaca*) horn; (: *di cervo*) antler

b (*fam*): **fare le corna** (*per scaramanzia*) to keep one's fingers crossed; **fare le corna a qn** (*a marito, moglie*) to cheat on sb; **dire peste e corna di qn** to call sb every name under the sun; **rompersi le corna** to burn one's fingers.

Cornovaglia [korno'vaʎʎa] SF: **la Cornovaglia** Cornwall.

cornuto, a [kor'nuto] 1 AGG **a** (*con corna*) horned **b** (*fam*: *tradito*) cheated on; **arbitro cornuto!** bloody ref!.

2 SM/F (*fam*) cheated-on husband/wife; **cornuto!** (*fam!*) bastard! (*fam!*)

coro ['koro] SM (*gen, fig*) chorus; (*Rel*: *cantori, luogo*) choir; **in coro** in chorus.

coroide [ko'rɔide] SF (*Anat*) choroid.

corolla [ko'rɔlla] SF (*Bot*) corolla.

corollario, ri [korol'larjo] SM corollary.

corona [ko'rona] SF **a** (*di re*) crown; (*di nobile*) coronet; **cingere la corona** to assume the crown; **fare corona intorno a qn** (*fig*) to form a circle round sb

b (*di fiori*) wreath ▶**corona d'alloro** laurel wreath ▶**corona funebre** *o* **mortuaria** funeral wreath ▶**corona del rosario** rosary, rosary beads *pl* ▶**corona di spine** crown of thorns

c (*di dente*) crown

d (*Geom*): **corona circolare** outer circle.

coronamento [korona'mento] SM **a** (*di impresa*) completion; (*di carriera*) crowning achievement; **il coronamento dei propri sogni** the fulfilment of one's dreams **b** (*Edil*) crown; (*Naut*) taffrail.

coronare [koro'nare] VT **a** (*cingere*): **coronare (di)** (*anche fig*) to crown (with) **b** (*realizzare*: *impresa*) to bring to a successful conclusion; **coronare i propri sogni** to fulfil one's dreams; **uno sforzo coronato dal successo** an effort crowned with success.

coronaria [koro'narja] SF coronary artery.

coronario, ria, ri, rie [koro'narjo] AGG coronary.

corpetto [kor'petto] SM (*da donna*) bodice; (*da uomo*) waistcoat.

corpo ['kɔrpo] 1 SM (*gen, Chim, fig*) body; (*cadavere*) corpse, (dead) body; (*di opere*) corpus; **corpo liquido/ gassoso** liquid/gaseous substance; **non ho niente in corpo da stamattina** I haven't eaten anything since this morning; **darsi anima e corpo a** to give o.s. heart and soul to; (a) **corpo a corpo** *agg* hand-to-hand; **andare di corpo** to empty one's bowels; **dare corpo a qc** to give substance to sth; **prendere corpo** (*idea, progetto*) to take shape; **a corpo morto** (*fig*) like a dead weight, heavily; **lo colpì con tutta la forza che aveva in corpo** she hit him with all her strength; **l'incendio ha divorato l'intero corpo dell'edificio** the fire destroyed the entire building; **l'intero corpo delle opere di Leopardi** the entire works of Leopardi.

2 ▶**corpo d'armata** army corps *sg* ▶**corpo di ballo** corps de ballet ▶**corpo dei carabinieri** ≈ police force ▶**corpo celeste** heavenly body ▶**corpo a corpo** (*lotta*) hand-to-hand fight ▶**corpo diplomatico** diplomatic corps *sg* ▶**corpo elettorale** electorate ▶**corpo estraneo** foreign body ▶**corpo di guardia** (*soldati*) guard; (*locale*) guardroom ▶**corpo insegnante** teachers *pl*, teaching staff ▶**corpo dei pompieri** fire brigade ▶**corpo del reato** material evidence ▶**corpo di spedizione** (*Mil*) task force.

corporale [korpo'rale] 1 AGG (*bisogni*) bodily; (*punizione*) corporal.

2 SM (*Rel*) corporal.

corporativismo [korporati'vizmo] SM corporatism.

corporativistico, a, ci, che [korporati'vistiko] AGG corporatist.

corporativo, a [korpora'tivo] AGG corporate.

corporatura [korpora'tura] SF build, physique.

corporazione [korporat'tsjone] SF professional body, corporation; (*Storia*) guild.

corporeo, a [kor'pɔreo] AGG bodily, physical.

corposo, a [kor'poso] AGG (*vino*) full-bodied.

corpulento, a [korpu'lɛnto] AGG stout, corpulent.

corpulenza [korpu'lɛntsa] SF stoutness, corpulence.

corpuscolo [kor'puskolo] SM corpuscle.

Corpus Domini ['kɔrpus'domini] SM (*Rel*: *festa*) Corpus Christi.

corredare ['kɔpus'domini] 1 VT: **corredare di** (*apparecchio, laboratorio*) to provide *o* furnish *o* equip with; **un elettrodomestico corredato di vari accessori** an electrical appliance complete with various accessories; **domanda corredata dai seguenti documenti** application accompanied by the following documents.

2 **corredarsi** VR: **corredarsi di** to equip o.s. with.

corredo [kor'rɛdo] SM (*di attrezzi*) kit; (*da sposa*) trousseau.

correggere [kor'rɛddʒere] VB IRREG [1] VT (*gen*) to correct; (*compiti*) to correct, mark (*Brit*), grade (*Am*); (*Tip*) to proofread; (*fig*: *abuso*) to remedy; **correggere il caffè con la grappa** to lace one's coffee with grappa.

[2] **correggersi** VR to correct o.s.

corregionale [korredʒo'nale] [1] AGG: **sono corregionali** they come from the same area.

[2] SM/F: **è un mio corregionale** he comes from the same area as me.

correlativo, a [korrela'tivo] AGG correlative.

correlatore, trice [korrela'tore] SM/F (*Univ*: *di tesi*) assistant supervisor.

correlazione [korrelat'tsjone] SF (*gen*) correlation; **correlazione dei tempi** (*Gramm*) sequence of tenses.

corrente [kor'rɛnte] [1] AGG **a** (*acqua del rubinetto*) running
b (*uso, anno*) current; (*moneta*) valid; **è opinione corrente che...** it is commonly believed that ...; **la vostra lettera del 5 corrente mese** (*in lettere commerciali*) in your letter of the 5th of this month, in your letter of the 5th inst. (*Brit frm*)
c (*ordinario*: *merce*) ordinary; **articoli di qualità corrente** average-quality products
d (*quotidiano*: *spese, affari*) everyday.

[2] SM: **essere al corrente di** (*notizia*) to know about; (*scoperte scientifiche*) to be well-informed about; **tenere qn al corrente** to keep sb informed; **mettere qn al corrente (di)** to inform sb (of).

[3] SF (*Elettr, di acque*) current; (*di aria*) airstream, current of air; (*spiffero*) draught (*Brit*), draft (*Am*); (*di opinioni*) trend; **c'è corrente qui dentro** there's a draught in here; **tagliare la corrente** (*Elettr*) to cut off the power; **una corrente di simpatia** a wave of sympathy; **andare contro corrente** (*anche fig*) to swim against the stream; **seguire la corrente** (*fig*) to follow the trend ► **corrente alternata** alternating current ► **corrente continua** direct current ► **la Corrente del Golfo** the Gulf Stream ► **corrente di risacca** (*Geog*) undertow.

correntemente [korrente'mente] AVV (*comunemente*) commonly; **parlare una lingua correntemente** to speak a language fluently.

correntista, i, e [korren'tista] SM/F (*Fin*) (current (*Brit*) o checking (*Am*)) account holder.

correo, a ['kɔrreo] SM/F (*Dir*) accomplice.

correre ['korrere] VB IRREG [1] VI (*quando si esprime o sottindende una meta*: *aus* **essere**) (*senza una meta e nel senso Sport*: *aus* **avere**) (*gen*) to run; (*affrettarsi*) to hurry; (*precipitarsi*) to rush; (*Sport*) to race, run; (*diffondersi*: *notizie*) to go round; **non correre!** (*anche fig*) not so fast!; **correre dietro a qn** (*anche fig*) to run after sb; **ci corre!** (*c'è una differenza*) there's a big difference!; **correva l'anno 1265** it was the year 1265; **corre voce che...** it is rumoured that ...; **il tempo corre** time is getting on.

[2] VT (*gen*) to run; (*pericolo*) to face; (*Sport*) to run; (: *gara*) to compete in; **correre i 100 metri** to run in the 100 metres; **correre i 100 metri a tempo di record** to run the 100 metres in record time; **correre un rischio** to run a risk.

corresponsabile [korrespon'sabile] [1] AGG jointly responsible; (*Dir*) jointly liable.

[2] SM/F person jointly responsible; (*Dir*: *civile*) person jointly liable; (: *penale*) accomplice.

corresponsabilità [korresponsabili'ta] SF (*vedi agg*) joint responsibility; joint liability.

corresponsione [korrespon'sjone] SF payment.

corressi *ecc* [kor'rɛssi] VB *vedi* **correggere**.

correttamente [korretta'mente] AVV (*gen*) correctly; (*comportarsi*) properly; (: *nello sport*) fairly.

correttezza [korret'tettsa] SF (*di comportamento*) correctness; (*Sport*) fair play; **è questione di correttezza** it's a question of propriety o good manners.

correttivo, a [korret'tivo] AGG corrective.

corretto, a [kor'rɛtto] [1] PP di **correggere**.

[2] AGG (*gen*) correct; (*comportamento*) proper, correct; **caffè corretto al cognac** coffee with a shot of cognac.

correttore, trice [korret'tore] [1] SM/F: **correttore di bozze** proofreader.

[2] SM **a** : (**liquido**) **correttore** correction o correcting fluid, Tipp-Ex® (*Brit*), White Out® (*Am*) **b** (*cosmetico*) blemish cover.

correzione [korret'tsjone] SF **a** (*gen*) correction; (*di compiti*) marking (*Brit*), grading (*Am*); (*miglioramento*) improvement ► **correzione di bozze** proofreading **b** (*castigo*): **casa di correzione** ≈ community home (*Brit*), ≈ reform school (*Am*), reformatory (*Am*).

corrida [kor'rida] SF bullfight.

corridoio, oi [korri'dojo] SM (*gen*) corridor, passage; (*laterale*: *di aereo, treno*) corridor; (*centrale*: *di aereo, pullman*) aisle; (*Tennis*) alley; **manovre di corridoio** (*Pol*) lobbying *sg* ► **corridoio aereo** air corridor.

corridore [korri'dore] SM (*Sport*) runner; (: *su veicolo*) racer.

corriera [kor'rjɛra] SF bus, coach (*Brit*).

corriere [kor'rjɛre] SM **a** (*gen*) messenger; (*Mil, diplomatico*) courier; (*spedizioniere*) carrier **b** (*Zool*): **corriere grosso** ringed plover.

corrimano [korri'mano] SM handrail.

corrispettivo [korrispet'tivo] SM amount due; **versare a qn il corrispettivo di una prestazione** to pay sb the amount due for his (o her) services.

corrispondente [korrispon'dɛnte] [1] AGG corresponding.

[2] SM/F (*gen, Stampa, TV*) correspondent.

corrispondenza [korrispon'dɛntsa] SF **a** (*conformità*) correspondence; (*fig*:) connection, relation; **non c'è corrispondenza tra le due versioni** the two versions do not correspond
b (*posta*: *atto di scrivere*) correspondence; (*insieme di lettere*) mail; **evadere la corrispondenza** to deal with one's correspondence; **corrispondenza in arrivo/partenza** incoming/outgoing mail; **corso per corrispondenza** correspondence course; **vendita per corrispondenza** mail-order shopping
c (*Mat*) relation.

corrispondere [korris'pondere] VB IRREG [1] VT **a** (*pagare*) to pay **b** (*ricambiare*: *amore*) to return.

[2] VI (*aus* **avere**) **a** (*equivalere*): **corrispondere (a)** to correspond (to); **quello che ha detto non corrisponde a verità** what he said doesn't fit the facts **b** (*per lettera*): **corrispondere con** to correspond with.

corrisposto, a [korris'posto] [1] PP di **corrispondere**.

[2] AGG (*affetto, sentimento*) reciprocated.

corroborante [korrobo'rante] [1] AGG fortifying, stimulating; **clima corroborante** bracing climate.

[2] SM (*liquore*) pick-me-up.

corroborare [korrobo'rare] VT (*rinvigorire*) to invigorate, strengthen, fortify; (*fig*: *ipotesi*) to corroborate, bear out.

corrodere [kor'rodere] VB IRREG ⓵ VT (*metalli*, *fig*) to corrode; (*legno*) to eat into; **la carie corrode i denti** teeth are eaten away by decay.

⓶ **corrodersi** VIP to corrode; (*roccia*) to erode, wear away.

corrompere [kor'rompere] VB IRREG ⓵ VT (*gen*, *fig*) to corrupt; (*testimone, giudice*) to bribe, corrupt; (*linguaggio*) to debase.

⓶ **corrompersi** VIP (*costumi*) to become corrupt.

corrosione [korro'zjone] SF corrosion.

corrosivamente [korroziva'mente] AVV corrosively.

corrosività [korrozivi'ta] SF corrosiveness.

corrosivo, a [korro'sivo] AGG, SM corrosive.

corroso, a [kor'roso] PP di **corrodere**.

corrottamente [korrotta'mente] AVV corruptly.

corrotto, a [kor'rotto] ⓵ PP di **corrompere**.

⓶ AGG corrupt.

corrucciarsi [korrut'tʃarsi] VIP to become upset; **si corruc- ciò in viso** his face took on a worried expression.

corrucciato, a [korrut'tʃato] AGG (*volto, sguardo*) worried.

corrugare [korru'gare] VT: **corrugare la fronte** o **le soprac- ciglia** to frown, knit one's brows.

corruppi *ecc* [kor'ruppi] VB vedi **corrompere**.

corruttela [korrut'tɛla] SF (*letter*) corruption, depravity.

corruttibile [korrut'tibile] AGG corruptible.

corruttibilità [korruttibili'ta] SF corruptibility.

corruttore, trice [korrut'tore] SM/F corrupter; (*con denaro*) briber.

corruzione [korrut'tsjone] SF corruption; (*con denaro*) bribery ▶**corruzione di minorenne** (*Dir*) corruption of a minor.

corsa ['korsa] SF **a** (*azione*) running *no pl*; **andare** o **essere di corsa** to be in a hurry; **andarsene/arrivare di corsa** to rush off/in; **ho dovuto fare una corsa** I had to dash; **"vietato scendere dal treno in corsa"** "do not alight from the train while it is in motion"; **abbiamo preso i cappotti e via di corsa** we grabbed our coats and off we went; **faccio una corsa e torno!** I'll be straight back!; **è una corsa contro il tempo** it's a race against time; **corsa all'oro** gold rush

b (*Sport: gara*) race; (: *disciplina*) racing *no pl*; (: *atletica*) running *no pl*; **da corsa** (*auto, moto*) racing; **cavallo da corsa** racehorse; **fare una corsa** to run a race; **va spesso alle corse** he often goes to the races; **corsa automobili- stica/ciclistica** motor/cycle racing; **corsa con i sacchi** sack race ▶**corsa campestre** cross-country race ▶**corsa ad ostacoli** (*Ippica*) steeplechase; (*Atletica*) hurdles *sg* ▶**corsa piana** o **in piano** (*Ippica*) flat race ▶**corsa a siepi** (*Ippica*) hurdle race

c (*di autobus, taxi*) trip, journey; **a che ora c'è l'ultima corsa?** when is the last bus?; **quanto costa la corsa?** what's the fare?

d (*Fis: di pendolo*) movement; (: *di pistone*) stroke

e (*Naut, Mil*): **guerra di corsa** privateering.

corsaro, a [kor'saro] ⓵ AGG: **nave corsara** privateer.

⓶ SM privateer, corsair.

corsetteria [korsette'ria] SF corsetry.

corsetto [kor'setto] SM corset.

corsi *ecc* ['korsi] VB vedi **correre**.

corsia [kor'sia] SF **a** (*gen*) gangway, passage; (*Aut, Sport*) lane; **autostrada a 4 corsie** 4-lane motorway (*Brit*) o freeway (*Am*) ▶**corsia di accelerazione** (*Aut*) accelera- tion lane ▶**corsia di decelerazione** (*Aut*) deceleration lane ▶**corsia di emergenza** (*Aut*) hard shoulder (*Brit*),

shoulder (*Am*) ▶**corsia preferenziale** ≈ bus lane; (*fig*) fast track ▶**corsia di sorpasso** (*Aut*) overtaking lane, fast lane

b (*in ospedale*) ward; **è ricoverato in corsia** he's a patient in the ward.

Corsica ['korsika] SF: **la Corsica** Corsica.

corsivo, a [kor'sivo] ⓵ AGG (*scrittura*) cursive; (*Tip*) italic.

⓶ SM **a** cursive (writing); (*Tip*) italics *pl* **b** (*Stampa*) brief article of comment (*in italics*).

corso¹, a ['korso] PP di **correre**.

corso², a ['korso] AGG, SM/F Corsican.

corso³ ['korso] SM **a** (*fluire: di acqua, tempo*) course; **corso d'acqua** (*naturale*) river, stream; (*artificiale*) waterway; **discendere il corso del Nilo** to go down the Nile; **dare corso a** to start; **dar libero corso a** to give free expres- sion to; **in corso** (*lavori*) in progress, under way; (*anno, mese*) current; **in corso di riparazione** in the process of being repaired; **nel corso di** during; **nel corso del tempo** in the course of time; **il nuovo corso del partito laburista** the new direction of the Labour Party

b (*Scol, Univ*) course; **seguire un corso serale** to go to an evening class; **tenere un corso su** to give a course on; **primo anno di corso** first year; **studente fuori corso** *undergraduate who has not completed course in due time*

c (*strada cittadina*) main street; (*nei nomi di strada*) avenue

d (*Fin: di moneta*) circulation; (: *di titoli, valori*) rate, price; **aver corso legale** to be legal tender; **una banco- nota fuori corso** a banknote no longer legal tender.

corte ['korte] SF **a** (*seguito del re*) court

b (*attenzioni, gentilezze*): **fare la corte a qn** (*per amore*) to court sb; (*per interesse*) to butter sb up

c (*Dir*) court ▶**corte d'appello** court of appeal ▶**Corte di Cassazione** Court of Cassation, *the highest judicial authority, responsible for ensuring that the law is correctly applied: it assesses the legitimacy of judicial decisions and can authorize re-trials* ▶**Corte dei Conti** *audit court overseeing the management of the state budget and the finances of nationalized industries: it reports directly to Parliament* ▶**Corte Costituzionale** *politically independent body responsible for ensuring that laws comply with the principles of the constitution: it has the power to impeach the Presidente della Repubblica* ▶**corte marziale** court-martial

d (*cortile*) (court)yard.

corteccia, ce [kor'tettʃa] SF (*di albero*) bark; (*Anat*) cortex.

corteggiamento [kortedd3a'mento] SM courtship.

corteggiare [korted'd3are] VT to court, woo.

corteggiatore [kortedd3a'tore] SM suitor.

corteo [kor'tɛo] SM procession; **i dimostranti hanno sfilato in corteo** the demonstrators marched past ▶**corteo funebre** funeral cortège.

cortese [kor'teze] AGG courteous; (*Letteratura*) courtly.

cortesemente [korteze'mente] AVV courteously; **la preghiamo cortesemente di...** (*in lettera*) we should be most grateful if you would ... .

cortesia [korte'zia] SF (*qualità*) courtesy; (*atto*) favour; **fare una cortesia a qn** to do sb a favour; **fammi una cortesia, spegni quella radio** would you please turn off that radio; **per cortesia, dov'è...?** excuse me, please, where is ...?

cortigiano, a [korti'd3ano] ⓵ SM/F courtier.

⓶ SF (*euf: prostituta*) courtesan.

cortile [kor'tile] SM (*di edificio*: *all'interno*) (court)yard; (: *davanti*) forecourt; (: *all'esterno*, *dietro*) yard; (*di cascina*) farmyard.

cortina [kor'tina] SF curtain, drape (*Am*); (*anche fig*) screen; **una cortina di fumo/nebbia** a wall of smoke/mist; **la cortina di ferro** the Iron Curtain; **una cortina di silenzio** a wall of silence.

cortisone [korti'zone] SM cortisone.

corto, a ['kɔrto] ① AGG (*tutti i sensi*) short; **la settimana corta** the 5-day week; **la strada più corta** (*anche fig*) the quickest way; **avere la vista corta** (*anche fig*) to be short-sighted; **essere** o **rimanere a corto di qc** to be short of sth; **essere a corto di parole** to be at a loss for words.

② AVV: **tagliare corto** to come straight to the point.

cortocircuito [kortotʃir'kuito] SM short-circuit.

cortometraggio, gi [kortome'traddʒo] SM (*Cine*) short (feature film).

corvé [kor've] SF INV (*Mil*) fatigue duty; **sabato siamo di corvé** (*scherz*) we are on chores on Saturday.

corvetta [kor'vetta] SF corvette.

corvino, a [kor'vino] AGG: **capelli corvini** jet-black hair.

corvo ['kɔrvo] SM (*anche*: **corvo imperiale**) raven ▶**corvo comune** o **nero** rook.

cosa ['kɔsa] ① SF **a** (*gen*) thing; **ogni cosa** OR **tutte le cose** everything; **qualche cosa** something; **nessuna cosa** nothing; **è una cosa da poco** it's nothing; **devo dirti una cosa** I've got something to tell you; **come prima cosa** first of all; **facciamo le cose per bene** let's do things properly; **tante belle cose!** all the best!

b (*situazione, fatto*) it, things *pl*; **la cosa non è chiara** it isn't clear, things aren't clear; **ti voglio spiegare la cosa** let me explain things to you; **è successa una cosa strana** something strange has happened; **sono cose da ragazzi** that's kids for you; **ormai è cosa fatta!** (*positivo*) it's in the bag!; (*negativo*) it's done now!; **a cose fatte** when all is said and done, when it's all over; **le cose stanno così** this is how things stand

c (*preoccupazione, problema*) matter, affair, business *no pl*; **brutta cosa!** it's a nasty business o matter!; **la cosa non mi riguarda** the matter doesn't concern me; **è tutt'altra cosa** that's quite another matter.

② PRON INTERROG: **(che) cosa?** what?; **(che) cos'è?** what is it?; **a cosa pensi?** what are you thinking about?; vedi anche **che**.

cosacco, chi [ko'zakko] SM Cossack.

Cosa Nostra [koza 'nɔstra] SF Cosa Nostra.

cosare [ko'sare] VT (*fam*): **hai cosato la macchina?** have you thingummy'd the car?

cosca, sche ['kɔska] SF (*di mafiosi*) clan.

coscia, sce ['kɔʃʃa] SF (*Anat*) thigh; (*Culin*: *di pollo*) leg.

cosciente [koʃ'ʃɛnte] AGG (*gen, Med*) conscious; (*consapevole*): **cosciente di** conscious o aware of.

coscientemente [koʃʃente'mente] AVV consciously.

coscienza [koʃ'ʃɛntsa] SF **a** (*morale*) conscience; **aver qc sulla coscienza** to have sth on one's conscience; **avere la coscienza a posto/sporca** to have a good o clear/bad o guilty conscience; **in (tutta) coscienza** in all conscience o honesty

b (*sensi*) consciousness; **perdere/riacquistare coscienza** to lose/regain consciousness

c (*psicologica*) awareness; **avere coscienza di/che...** to be aware o conscious of/that ...; **prendere coscienza di qc** to become aware of sth, realize sth ▶**coscienza politica** political awareness

d (*serietà*) conscientiousness; **coscienza professionale** conscientiousness; **persona di coscienza** honest o conscientious person.

coscienziosamente [koʃʃentsjosa'mente] AVV conscientiously.

coscienziosità [koʃʃentsjosi'ta] SF conscientiousness.

coscienzioso, a [koʃʃen'tsjoso] AGG conscientious.

cosciotto [koʃ'ʃɔtto] SM (*Culin*) leg.

coscritto [kos'kritto] SM (*Mil*) conscript.

coscrizione [koskrit'tsjone] SF (*Mil*) conscription.

cosecante [kose'kante] SF (*Mat*) cosecant.

coseno [ko'seno] SM (*Mat*) cosine.

così [ko'si] ① AVV **a** (*in tal modo*) so; (*in questo modo*) (in) this way, like this, like that; **ho detto così** that's what I said; **ha detto così: "sei bugiardo"** this is what he said: "you're a liar"; **non ho detto così** I didn't say that; **se fosse così** if this were the case; **le cose stanno così** this is how things stand; **vorrei una scatola larga così e lunga così** (*accompagnato da gesti*) I'd like a box this o so wide and this o so long; **non scriverlo così, ma così!** don't write it like that, write it like this!; **e così feci anch'io** and I did likewise

b (*talmente*) so; **fa così bello oggi** it's such a lovely day, the weather's so lovely today; **una persona così gentile** such a kind person; **è così lontano** it's so far away; **non sono così stupido!** I'm not that stupid!

c : **così... come** as ...as; **non è così onesto come credi** he's not as o so honest as you think; **se si comporta così come ha sempre fatto...** if he goes on behaving like this ...; **me lo dia così com'è** give it to me as it is

d : **per così dire** so to speak, so to say; **e così via** and so on; **è così o non è così?** isn't that so?; **così così** so so; **e così?** well?.

② AGG INV (*tale*): **non ho mai visto un film così** I've never seen such a film; **non ho mai conosciuto una persona così** I've never met such a person, I've never met a person like that.

③ CONG (*perciò*) so, therefore; **pioveva, così sono rimasto a casa** it was raining so I stayed at home.

cosicché [kosik'ke] CONG so (that).

cosiddetto, a [kosid'detto] AGG so-called.

cosmesi [koz'mɛzi] SF INV (*scienza*) cosmetics *sg*; (*prodotti*) cosmetics *pl*; (*trattamento*) beauty treatment.

cosmetico, a, ci, che [koz'metiko] AGG, SM cosmetic.

cosmico, a, ci, che ['kɔzmiko] AGG cosmic.

cosmo ['kɔzmo] SM (*universo*) cosmos; (*spazio*) outer space.

cosmologia [kozmolo'dʒia] SF cosmology.

cosmonauta, i, e [kozmo'nauta] SM/F cosmonaut.

cosmonave [kozmo'nave] SF spaceship.

cosmopolita, i, e [kozmopo'lita] AGG, SM/F (*anche fig*) cosmopolitan.

cosmopolitico, a, ci, che [kozmopo'litiko] AGG cosmopolitan.

cosmopolitismo [kozmopoli'tizmo] SM cosmopolitanism.

coso ['kɔso] SM (*fam*: *oggetto*) thing, thingummy; (: *aggeggio*) contraption; (: *persona*) what's his name, thingummy.

cospargere [kos'pardʒere] VT IRREG: **cospargere di** to sprinkle with.

cosparso, a [kos'parzo] PP di **cospargere**.

cospetto [kos'petto] SM (*presenza*): **in** o **al cospetto di** in

the presence of, in front of; **giurare al cospetto di Dio** to swear before God.

cospicuamente [kospikua'mente] AVV: **remunerato cospicuamente** generously paid.

cospicuità [kospikui'ta] SF vast quantity; **la cospicuità delle sue risorse** his considerable resources.

cospicuo, a [kos'pikuo] AGG considerable, large.

cospirare [kospi'rare] VI (*aus* avere) (*gen*) to conspire, plot; (*fig*: *circostanze*) to conspire.

cospiratore, trice [kospira'tore] SM/F plotter, conspirator; **con fare da cospiratore** with a conspiratorial air.

cospirazione [kospirat'tsjone] SF (*anche fig*) plot, conspiracy.

cossi *ecc* ['kɔssi] VB *vedi* **cuocere**.

Cost. ABBR = **costituzione**.

costa ['kɔsta] SF **a** (*litorale*) coast; (*spiaggia*) shore; (*tra terra e mare*) coastline; **navigare sotto costa** to hug the coast ▶**la Costa d'Avorio** the Ivory Coast ▶**la Costa Azzurra** the French Riviera
b (*di montagna*) slope; **a mezza costa** halfway up (*o* down) the slope
c (*nervatura*: *di nave, Bot*) rib; (: *di tessuto*) ribbing *no pl*; (*dorso*: *di libro*) spine; **punto a coste** (*Maglia*) rib (stitch); **velluto a coste** corduroy.

costà [kos'ta] AVV (*letter*) there.

costante [kos'tante] 1 AGG (*gen, Mat*) constant; (*persona*) steadfast.
2 SF (*Mat*) constant; **è una costante della letteratura del '900** it is a standard feature of 20th century literature.

costantemente [kostante'mente] AVV constantly.

costanza [kos'tantsa] SF (*gen*) constancy; (*fig*: *fermezza*) constancy, steadfastness; **il Lago di Costanza** Lake Constance.

costare [kos'tare] VI (*aus* essere) (*anche fig*) to cost; **costare caro** to be expensive, cost a lot; **costare poco** to be cheap; **cosa vuoi che ti costi** I am not asking much of you; **costare un occhio della testa** to cost a fortune; **costi quel che costi** no matter what; **gli è costato la vita** it cost him his life.

Costa Rica ['kɔsta 'rika] SF: **la Costa Rica** Costa Rica.

costaricano, a [kostari'kano] AGG, SM/F Costa Rican.

costata [kos'tata] SF (*Culin*: *di manzo*) large chop.

costato [kos'tato] SM (*Anat*) ribs *pl*.

costeggiare [kosted'dʒare] VT (*Naut*) to hug, skirt; (*sogg*: *persona*) to walk (*o* drive *ecc*) alongside; (: *strada*) to run alongside.

costei [kos'tɛi] PRON DIMOSTR (*sogg*) she; (*complemento*) her; (*pegg*) this woman.

costellare [kostel'lare] VT: **costellare (di)** to stud (with); **il prato era costellato di margherite** the field was studded with daisies.

costellazione [kostellat'tsjone] SF constellation.

costernare [koster'nare] VT to dismay, fill with consternation.

costernato, a [koster'nato] AGG dismayed.

costernazione [kosternat'tsjone] SF dismay, consternation.

costì [kos'ti] AVV (*letter*) here.

costiera [kos'tjɛra] SF (stretch of) coast; (*strada*) coast road.

costiero, a [kos'tjɛro] AGG coastal, coast *attr*; **nave costiera** coaster.

costina [kos'tina] SF: **costine di maiale** spareribs.

costipato, a [kosti'pato] AGG (*stitico*) constipated; (*raffreddato*): **essere costipato** to have a bad cold.

costipazione [kostipat'tsjone] SF (*vedi agg*) constipation; bad cold.

costituente [kostitu'ɛnte] 1 AGG (*gen, Chim, Pol*) constituent *attr*.
2 SM (*Chim*) constituent.
3 SF: **la Costituente** OR **l'Assemblea costituente** the Constituent Assembly.

costituire [kostitu'ire] 1 VT **a** (*fondare*: *società, comitato, governo*) to set up, form; (*accumulare*: *patrimonio, raccolta*) to build up, put together
b (*formare*: *sogg*: *elementi, parti*) to constitute, make up
c (*essere, rappresentare*) to be, constitute; **costituisce un vero problema!** it's a real problem!; **il fatto non costituisce reato** (*Dir*) this is not a crime
d (*Dir*: *nominare*) to appoint; **costituire qn presidente/erede** to appoint sb chairman/one's heir.
2 **costituirsi** VR **a** (*organizzarsi*): **costituirsi in società** to form a company; **costituirsi in regione autonoma** to become an independent region
b (*ricercato*): **costituirsi (alla polizia)** to give o.s. up (to the police)
c (*Dir*): **costituirsi parte civile** *to associate in an action with the public prosecutor for damages.*

costitutivo, a [kostitu'tivo] AGG constituent, component; **atto costitutivo** (*Dir*: *di società*) memorandum of association.

costituzionale [kostituttsjo'nale] AGG constitutional.

costituzionalismo [kostituttsjona'lizmo] SM constitutionalism.

costituzionalità [kostituttsjonali'ta] SF constitutionality.

costituzionalmente [kostituttsjonal'mente] AVV constitutionally.

costituzione [kostitut'tsjone] SF **a** (*formazione*) setting-up, establishment; (*struttura*) composition, make-up; (*Med*) constitution; **certificato di sana e robusta costituzione** certificate of good health **b** (*Dir*) constitution.

costo ['kɔsto] 1 SM (*anche fig*) cost; **determinazione dei costi** costing; **sotto costo** for less than cost price; **a ogni** *o* **qualunque costo** OR **a tutti i costi** at all costs; **non vuol cedere a nessun costo** there's no way he'll give in, he won't give in no matter what.
2 ▶**costi di esercizio** running costs ▶**costi fissi** fixed costs ▶**costi di gestione** operating costs ▶**costi d'impianto** set-up costs ▶**costi indiretti** indirect costs ▶**costi di produzione** production costs ▶**costo, assicurazione e freight** cost, insurance and freight ▶**costo e nolo** cost and freight ▶**costo della vita** cost of living.

costola ['kɔstola] SF (*Anat, Bot, Archit*) rib; **è magrissimo, gli si contano le costole** he's so thin you can see his ribs; **se lo prendo gli rompo le costole!** if I catch him I'll break every bone in his body!; **ha la polizia alle costole** the police are hard on his heels.

costoletta [kosto'letta] SF (*Culin*) cutlet.

costolone [kosto'lone] SM (*Archit*) rib.

costoro [kos'toro] PRON DIMOSTR PL (*sogg*) they; (*complemento*) them; (*pegg*) these people.

costosamente [kostosa'mente] AVV expensively.

costoso, a [kos'toso] AGG costly, expensive.

costretto, a [kos'tretto] PP *di* **costringere**.

costringere [kos'trindʒere] VT IRREG: **costringere qn (a fare qc)** to force *o* compel sb (to do sth); **mi ci hanno**

costretto con la forza they forced me to do it; la paralisi lo costringe a una sedia a rotelle the paralysis confines him to a wheelchair; vedersi costretto a fare qc to find o.s. forced o compelled to do sth.

costrittivo, a [kostrit'tivo] AGG coercive.

costrittore [kostrit'tore] AGG: muscolo costrittore constrictor.

costrizione [kostrit'tsjone] SF **a** (obbligo) compulsion; è legato da costrizione morale he is morally obliged **b** (violenza) coercion, duress.

costruire [kostru'ire] VT IRREG (gen) to build, construct; (fig: teoria, frasi, fortuna) to construct, build up; in questa città non si costruisce più da anni there's been no building work done in this town for years; questo verbo si costruisce con il congiuntivo this verb takes the subjunctive; costruire sulla sabbia (fig) to build on sand.

costruttivo, a [kostrut'tivo] AGG (Edil) building attr; (fig) constructive; schema costruttivo (Tecn) design, plan; tecnica costruttiva (Edil) building techniques pl; (Ingegneria) assembly techniques pl.

costrutto [kos'trutto] SM (Gramm) construction.

costruttore, trice [kostrut'tore] [1] AGG building attr. [2] SM (fabbricante) manufacturer; (Edil) builder.

costruzione [kostrut'tsjone] SF **a** (fabbricazione) building, construction; (struttura: anche Tecn, Gramm) construction; di recente costruzione of recent construction, recently built; in (via di) costruzione under construction; materiali/legno da costruzione building materials/timber; scienza delle costruzioni construction theory; le costruzioni (gioco) building blocks **b** (edificio) building.

costui [kos'tui] PRON DIMOSTR (sogg) he; (complemento) him; (pegg) this fellow, this man; si può sapere chi è costui? (pegg) just who is that fellow?

costume [kos'tume] SM **a** (gen) custom; (abitudine) habit; usi e costumi di una popolazione habits and customs of a people; di facili costumi of loose morals, of easy virtue; il buon costume public morality **b** (indumento) costume; costume nazionale national costume o dress ▶costume da bagno (da donna) bathing o swimming costume (Brit), swimsuit; (da uomo) bathing o swimming trunks pl.

costumista, i, e [kostu'mista] SM/F (Cine, Teatro, TV) costume maker, costume designer.

cotangente [kotan'dʒɛnte] SF (Mat) cotangent.

cote ['kote] SF whetstone.

cotechino [kote'kino] SM (Culin) pork sausage.

cotenna [ko'tenna] SF bacon rind.

cotiledone [koti'lɛdone] SM cotyledon.

cotillon [koti'jõ] SM INV (piccolo omaggio) favour.

cotogna [ko'toɲɲa] SF (anche: mela cotogna) quince.

cotognata [kotoɲ'ɲata] SF quince jelly.

cotogno [ko'toɲɲo] SM quince (tree).

cotoletta [koto'letta] SF (di maiale, montone) chop; (di vitello, agnello) cutlet.

cotonare [koto'nare] VT (capelli) to backcomb.

cotonato [koto'nato] [1] SM (tessuto: di cotone) cotton fabric; (: misto) cotton mix. [2] AGG (capelli) backcombed.

cotonatura [kotona'tura] SF (di capelli) backcombing.

cotone [ko'tone] SM **a** (gen) cotton; di cotone cotton attr ▶cotone mercerizzato mercerised cotton ▶cotone pettinato brushed cotton ▶cotone da rammendo

darning thread **b** (anche: cotone idrofilo) cotton wool (Brit), cotton (Am); batuffolo di cotone wad of cotton wool (Brit) o cotton (Am).

cotoniero, a [koto'njɛro] AGG cotton attr.

cotonificio, ci [kotoni'fitʃo] SM cotton mill.

cotta¹ ['kɔtta] SF (fam): prendersi una cotta (per qn) to get a crush (on sb).

cotta² ['kɔtta] SF **a** (Rel) surplice **b** (Storia): cotta d'arme surcoat ▶cotta di maglia chain mail.

cottimista, i, e [kotti'mista] SM/F pieceworker.

cottimo ['kottimo] SM (anche: lavoro a cottimo) piecework; lavorare a cottimo to do piecework.

cotto, a ['kɔtto] [1] PP di cuocere. [2] AGG (Culin) cooked; ben cotto well cooked; (carne) well done; poco cotto underdone; troppo cotto overdone; cotto a puntino cooked to perfection; essere cotto (di qn) (fig fam) to have a crush (on sb); è proprio cotto! he's smitten!, he's head-over-heels in love; essere cotto (di sonno/stanchezza) (fam) to be done in; dirne di cotte e di crude a qn to call sb every name under the sun; farne di cotte e di crude to get up to all kinds of mischief. [3] SM brickwork; mattone di cotto fired brick; pavimento in cotto tile floor.

cotton fioc® ['kɔtton'fiɔk] SM INV cotton bud.

cottura [kot'tura] SF (Culin, gen) cooking; (: in forno) baking; (: di arrosto) roasting; (: in umido) stewing; cottura a fuoco lento simmering.

coupé [ku'pe] SM INV (Aut) coupé.

couperose [kupəroz] SF INV blotches pl (on the face).

coupon [ku'põ] SM INV coupon.

court-bouillon ['kuət'bu:jAn] SM INV court-bouillon.

cova ['kova] SF (di uccello: atto, periodo) brooding; fare la cova to brood, sit.

covalente [kova'lɛnte] AGG covalent; legame covalente covalent bond.

covare [ko'vare] [1] VI (aus avere) (fuoco, fig: odio, rancore) to smoulder (Brit), smolder (Am); qui gatta ci cova there's something fishy about this. [2] VT **a** (sogg: uccello: uova) to sit on; (uso assoluto) to sit on its eggs **b** (fig: malattia) to be sickening for; (: odio, rancore) to nurse; sta covando un raffreddore he is sickening for a cold; covare odio verso qn to nurse hatred for sb.

covata [ko'vata] SF (anche fig) brood.

covo ['kovo] SM den, lair; un covo di terroristi a terrorist base; quel bar è un covo di spacciatori that bar is a haunt for drug pushers.

covone [ko'vone] SM sheaf.

coyote [ko'jote] SM INV coyote.

cozza ['kɔttsa] SF mussel.

cozzare [kot'tsare] [1] VI (aus avere) (animali: con le corna) to butt; (veicoli) to collide; (fig: caratteri, idee) to clash; cozzare contro un muro to crash into a wall. [2] VT (fig): cozzare il capo contro il muro to bang one's head against a brick wall.

cozzo ['kɔttso] SM (di corna) butt; (di veicoli) crash, collision; (fig: di idee) clash.

C.P. ABBR **a** (= cartolina postale) pc **b** (= casella postale) P.O. box **c** (Naut) = capitaneria (di porto) **d** (Dir) = codice penale.

crac [krak] SM INV **a** (rumore) crack **b** (rovina: economica) crash.

crack [krak] SM INV (droga) crack.

cracking ['krækɪŋ] SM (*Chim*) cracking.
Cracovia [kra'kɔvja] SF Cracow.
crampo ['krampo] SM cramp; **avere un crampo alla gamba** to have cramp in one's leg; **avere i crampi allo stomaco** to have stomach cramps; **ho i crampi allo stomaco dalla fame** I've got hunger pangs.
cranico, a, ci, che ['kraniko] AGG cranial.
cranio, ni ['kranjo] SM **a** skull; (*Anat*) cranium; **avere il cranio duro** (*fig*) to be pig-headed; **fa trentamila lire a cranio** (*fam*) it's thirty thousand lire a head **b** (*genio*): **essere un cranio (in qc)** to be a genius (at sth).
crasi ['krazi] SF INV (*Gramm*) syneresis, crasis.
cratere [kra'tɛre] SM crater.
crauti ['krauti] SMPL sauerkraut *sg*.
cravatta [kra'vatta] SF tie; **fare il nodo alla cravatta** to tie one's tie ▶ **cravatta a farfalla** bow tie.
cravattino [kravat'tino] SM bow tie.
crawl [krɔ:l] SM INV crawl; **nuotare a crawl** to do the crawl.
creanza [kre'antsa] SF (good) manners *pl*; **per buona creanza** out of politeness.
creare [kre'are] VT (*gen*) to create; (*eleggere*) to make, appoint; (*fondare*) to set up; **creare un precedente** to create a precedent; **creare un problema a qn** to create a problem for sb; **crearsi una clientela** to build up a clientele.
creatina [krea'tina] SF creatin(e).
creativamente [kreativa'mente] AVV creatively.
creatività [kreativi'ta] SF INV creativity.
creativo, a [krea'tivo] AGG creative.
creato [kre'ato] SM: **il creato** the Creation.
creatore, trice [krea'tore] [1] AGG creative.
  [2] SM/F creator; (*fondatore*) founder; **un creatore di alta moda** fashion designer; **il Creatore** (*Dio*) the Creator; **andare al Creatore** to go to meet one's maker.
creatura [krea'tura] SF creature; (*bimbo*) baby, infant; **povera creatura!** poor thing!; **le mie creature** my babies.
creazione [kreat'tsjone] SF (*gen*) creation; (*fondazione*) foundation, establishment.
crebbi *ecc* VB *vedi* **crescere**.
credente [kre'dɛnte] SM/F (*Rel*) believer.
credenza¹ [kre'dɛntsa] SF (*fede, opinione*) belief.
credenza² [kre'dɛntsa] SF (*armadio*) sideboard.
credenziale [kreden'tsjale] [1] AGG: **lettere credenziali** credentials.
  [2]: **credenziali** SFPL (*anche fig*) credentials.
credere ['kredere] [1] VT **a** to believe; **lo *o* ci credo** I believe it; **come puoi credere una cosa simile?** how can you believe such a thing?; **lo credo bene!** I should think so too!
  b (*pensare*) to believe, think; **lo credo onesto** I believe him to be honest; **ti credevo morto** I thought you were dead; **credo che sia stato lui (a farlo)** I think it was him, I think he did it; **credeva di aver perso le chiavi** she thought she had lost her keys; **credo di sì/no** I think/don't think so; **voleva farmi credere che...** he wanted me to think that ...; **voleva darmi a credere che non la conosceva** he tried to convince me that he didn't know her
  c (*ritenere opportuno*): **fai quello che credi *o* come credi** do as you please; **ha creduto bene di mollare tutto** he thought it best to let everything go.
  [2] VI (*aus* avere) to believe; **credere a qn/qc** to believe sb/sth; **credere in qn/qc** to believe in sb/sth; **credere in**

Dio to believe in God; **ti credo sulla parola** I'll take your word for it; **gli credo poco** I have little faith in him; **non credeva ai suoi occhi/alle sue orecchie** he could not believe his eyes/ears; **credevo a uno scherzo** I thought it was a joke; **si è creduto ad una truffa** it looked like a swindle.
  [3] **credersi** VR: **si crede furbo** he thinks he's smart; **chi ti credi di essere!** who do you think you are!
credibile [kre'dibile] AGG credible, believable.
credibilità [kredibili'ta] SF credibility.
credibilmente [kredibil'mente] AVV credibly.
creditizio, zia, zi, zie [kredi'tittsjo] AGG credit *attr*.
credito ['kredito] SM **a** (*Fin*) credit; **comprare/vendere a credito** to buy/sell on credit *o* easy terms; **"non facciamo credito"** "no credit", "cash terms only"; **essere in credito** to be owed money; (*Banca*) to be in credit ▶ **credito agevolato** easy credit terms ▶ **credito d'imposta** tax credit
  b (*credibilità*) credit; **acquistare credito** (*teoria, partito*) to gain acceptance; **dare credito a qc** to give credit to sth; **non puoi dar credito alla sua parola** you can't trust him; **trovare credito presso qn** to win sb's trust.
creditore, trice [kredi'tore] AGG, SM/F creditor.
credo ['krɛdo] SM INV (*Rel, fig*) creed; **credo politico** political credo.
credulità [kreduli'ta] SF credulity, gullibility.
credulo, a [kre'dulo] AGG credulous.
credulone, a [kredu'lone] SM/F gullible person.
crema ['krɛma] [1] SF (*Culin*) cream; (: *con uova, zucchero ecc*) custard; (*cosmetico, fig*) cream; **un gelato alla crema** a vanilla ice.
  [2] ▶ **crema da barba** shaving cream ▶ **crema di bellezza** beauty cream ▶ **crema di cacao** (*liquore*) crème de cacao ▶ **crema al cioccolato** chocolate custard ▶ **crema idratante** moisturizing cream ▶ **crema pasticciera** confectioner's custard ▶ **crema di riso** rice custard ▶ **crema solare** sun cream.
cremagliera [kremaʎ'ʎɛra] SF rack; **ferrovia a cremagliera** rack railway.
cremare [kre'mare] VT to cremate.
crematorio, ria, ri, rie [krema'tɔrjo] [1] AGG crematory.
  [2] SM crematorium.
cremazione [kremat'tsjone] SF cremation.
cremisi ['krɛmizi] AGG INV, SM INV crimson.
Cremlino [krem'lino] SM: **il Cremlino** the Kremlin.
cremlinologia [kremlinolo'dʒia] SF Kremlinology.
cremlinologo, gi [kremli'nɔlogo] SM Kremlinologist.
cremonese [kremo'nese] [1] AGG *o* from Cremona.
  [2] SM/F inhabitant *o* native of Cremona.
cremortartaro [kremor'tartaro] SM cream of tartar.
cremoso, a [kre'moso] AGG creamy.
cren [krɛn] SM (*Bot*) horseradish; (*salsa*) horseradish sauce.
crepa ['krɛpa] SF crack.
crepaccio, ci [kre'pattʃo] SM (*nella roccia*) large crack, fissure; (*nel ghiaccio*) crevasse.
crepacuore [krepa'kwɔre] SM: **morire di crepacuore** to die of a broken heart.
crepapelle [krepa'pɛlle] AVV: **ridere a crepapelle** to split one's sides laughing; **mangiare a crepapelle** to eat till one bursts.
crepare [kre'pare] [1] VI (*aus* essere) (*fam: morire*) to kick the bucket, snuff it (*Brit*); **crepare dal ridere *o* dalle risa** to kill o.s. laughing, split one's sides laughing; **crepare**

dall'invidia to be green with envy.
[2] **creparsi** VIP (*spaccarsi*) to crack.
crêpe [krɛp] SF INV (*Culin*) pancake.
crepitare [krepi'tare] VI (*aus* avere) (*fuoco*) to crackle; (*pioggia*) to patter; (*foglie*) to rustle.
crepitio, tii [krepi'tio] SM (*vedi vb*) crackling; pattering; rustling.
crepuscolare [krepusko'lare] AGG twilight *attr*; **luce crepuscolare** twilight.
crepuscolo [kre'puskolo] SM (*anche fig*) twilight, dusk; **al crepuscolo** at twilight.
crescendo [kreʃ'ʃɛndo] SM (*Mus, anche fig*) crescendo; **suonare in crescendo** to play a crescendo; **la sua carriera è stata un crescendo di successi** his career has gone from strength to strength.
crescente [kreʃ'ʃɛnte] AGG (*gen*) growing, increasing; (*luna*) waxing.
crescere ['kreʃʃere] VB IRREG [1] VI (*aus* essere) **a** (*gen*) to grow; (*persona: diventare adulto*) to grow up; (: *diventare più alto*) to grow taller; **il bambino/l'albero è cresciuto** the child/tree has grown; **i suoi capelli non crescono molto** her hair doesn't grow very fast; **sono cresciuto in Sardegna** I grew up in Sardinia; **farsi crescere la barba/i capelli** to grow a beard/one's hair
  b (*aumentare: rumore, prezzo, numero*) to increase; (: *città, quartiere*) to expand; (: *luna*) to wax; **la popolazione mondiale cresce velocemente** the world's population is increasing rapidly; **i prezzi crescono ogni giorno** prices are going up daily; **la città è cresciuta a vista d'occhio** the city has grown before our very eyes.
  [2] VT (*fam: coltivare*) to grow; (: *allevare: figli*) to raise.
crescione [kreʃ'ʃone] SM watercress ▶ **crescione inglese** o **degli orti** garden cress.
crescita ['kreʃʃita] SF: **crescita (di)** growth (in); **crescita zero** zero growth.
cresciuto, a [kreʃ'ʃuto] PP di **crescere**.
cresima ['krɛzima] SF (*Rel*) confirmation.
cresimare [krezi'mare] (*Rel*) [1] VT to confirm.
  [2] **cresimarsi** VIP to be confirmed.
Creso ['krɛzo] SM Croesus.
crespella [kres'pɛlla] SF (stuffed) pancake.
crespo, a ['krespo] [1] AGG (*capelli*) frizzy; (*tessuto*) puckered.
  [2] SM (*tessuto*) crêpe.
cresta ['kresta] SF (*gen*) crest; (*di uccello*) crest; (*di pollo*) comb; (*di montagna*) ridge; **alzare la cresta** (*fig*) to become cocky; **abbassare la cresta** (*fig*) to climb down; **far abbassare la cresta a qn** to take sb down a peg or two; **far la cresta sulla spesa** to keep some of the shopping money for o.s.; **essere sulla cresta dell'onda** to be riding high ▶ **cresta di gallo** (*Bot*) cockscomb; (*Med fam*) condyloma.
Creta ['krɛta] SF Crete.
creta ['krɛta] SF (*argilla*) clay.
cretese [kre'tese] AGG, SM/F Cretan.
cretinata [kreti'nata] SF (*fam*): **dire/fare una cretinata** to say/do something stupid; **non dire cretinate!** don't talk rubbish!
cretineria [kretine'ria] SF stupidity.
cretinismo [kreti'nizmo] SM (*Med*) cretinism.
cretino, a [kre'tino] [1] AGG (*Med*) cretinous; (*pegg*) cretinous, moronic.
  [2] SM/F (*vedi agg*) cretin; cretin, moron.
C.R.I. [kri] SIGLA F = *Croce Rossa Italiana*.

cric¹ [krik] SM INV (*rumore*) creak.
cric² [krik] SM INV (*martinetto*) jack.
cricca, che ['krikka] SF clique.
criceto [kri'tʃɛto] SM hamster.
criminale [krimi'nale] [1] AGG criminal.
  [2] SM/F criminal ▶ **criminale di guerra** war criminal.
criminalità [kriminali'ta] SF **a** criminal nature **b** (*delinquenza*) crime ▶ **la criminalità organizzata** organized crime.
criminalizzare [kriminalid'dzare] VT to criminalize.
Criminalpol [kriminal'pɔl] SIGLA F = *polizia criminale*.
crimine ['krimine] SM (*anche fig*) crime ▶ **crimini di guerra** war crimes.
criminologia [kriminolo'dʒia] SF criminology.
criminosamente [kriminosa'mente] AVV criminally.
criminosità [kriminosi'ta] SF criminality.
criminoso, a [krimi'noso] AGG criminal.
crinale [kri'nale] SM ridge, crest.
crine ['krine] SM horsehair; **di crine** horsehair *attr* ▶ **crine vegetale** vegetable fibre.
criniera [kri'njɛra] SF (*di animale*) mane.
crinolina [krino'lina] SF crinoline.
criochirurgia [kriokirur'dʒia] SF cryosurgery.
criolite [krio'lite] SF cryolite.
cripta ['kripta] SF crypt.
criptare [krip'tare] VT (*TV*) to encrypt.
criptato, a [krip'tato] AGG (*programma, messaggio*) encrypted.
criptico, a, ci, che ['kriptiko] AGG cryptic.
crisalide [kri'zalide] SF chrysalis.
crisantemo [krizan'tɛmo] SM chrysanthemum.
crisi ['krizi] SF INV **a** (*gen, Pol, Econ*) crisis; **il paese sta uscendo dalla crisi (economica)** the country is emerging from the (economic) crisis; **essere in crisi** (*partito, impresa*) to be in a state of crisis; (*persona*) to be upset; **mettere qn in crisi** to put sb in a difficult position; **la crisi degli alloggi** the housing crisis ▶ **crisi energetica** energy crisis
  b (*Med*) attack; (*di epilessia*) fit ▶ **crisi da astinenza** withdrawal symptoms *pl* ▶ **crisi di nervi** fit of hysterics, attack of nerves ▶ **crisi di pianto** fit of tears.
crisma ['krizma] SF (*Rel*) chrism; **un matrimonio con tutti i crismi** a proper wedding.
cristalleria [kristalle'ria] SF (*fabbrica*) crystal glassworks *sg*; (*oggetti*) crystalware.
cristallino, a [kristal'lino] [1] AGG (*Mineralogia*) crystalline; (*fig: suono, acque*) crystal clear.
  [2] SM (*Anat*) crystalline lens.
cristallizzare [kristallid'dzare] [1] VI (*aus* essere), **cristallizzarsi** VIP to crystallize; (*fig*) to become fossilized.
  [2] VT (*gen*) to crystallize, turn into crystals; **zucchero cristallizzato** granulated sugar.
cristallizzazione [kristalliddzat'tsjone] SF crystallization.
cristallo [kris'tallo] SM crystal; (*di finestra*) pane (of glass) ▶ **cristallo liquido** liquid crystal ▶ **cristallo di rocca** rock crystal.
cristianamente [kristjana'mente] AVV like a Christian, in a Christian way.
cristianesimo [kristja'nezimo] SM Christianity.
cristiania [kris'tjanja] SM INV (*Sci*) Christy, Christie.
cristianità [kristjani'ta] SF (*condizione*) Christianity; (*popoli, territorio*) Christendom.
cristianizzare [kristjanid'dzare] VT to convert to Christianity.

cristiano, a [kris'tjano] [1] AGG Christian. [2] SM/F (*anche fig*) Christian; **un povero cristiano** (*fig*) a poor soul *o* beggar; **non c'era un cristiano per le strade** there wasn't a soul on the streets; **comportarsi da cristiano** (*fig*) to behave in a civilized manner.

cristo ['kristo] SM [a] : **Cristo** Christ; **nell'anno 54 avanti/dopo Cristo** in 54 B.C./A.D; **(un) povero cristo** (a) poor beggar [b] (*immagine, oggetto*) figure of Christ.

criterio, ri [kri'tɛrjo] SM [a] (*norma*) criterion, rule; **con criterio approssimativo** approximately [b] (*buon senso*) (common) sense; **dovresti avere più criterio** you should have more sense; **è una persona di poco criterio** he doesn't have much common sense.

critica ['kritika] SF [a] (*biasimo*) criticism [b] : **la critica** (*attività*) criticism; (*i critici*) critics *pl*; (*opera, studio*) appreciation, critique; (*recensione*) review; **fare la critica di** (*libro, film*) to review.

criticabile [kriti'kabile] AGG open to criticism.

criticamente [kritika'mente] AVV critically.

criticare [kriti'kare] VT (*biasimare*) to criticize, find fault with; (*giudicare: opera*) to give a critique of.

critico, a, ci, che ['kritiko] [1] AGG critical; **aver spirito critico** to have a critical mind; **al momento critico** at the critical moment; **età critica** (*gen*) difficult age; (*menopausa*) change of life. [2] SM (*gen*) critic; (*recensore*) reviewer ▶ **critico cinematografico** film critic ▶ **critico letterario** literary critic.

criticone, a [kriti'kone] SM/F faultfinder; **sei il solito criticone!** you're always finding fault!

crittogramma [kritto'gramma] SM (*testo in cifre*) cryptograph; (*Enigmistica*) cryptogram.

crivellare [krivel'lare] VT: **crivellare (di)** to riddle (with).

crivello [kri'vɛllo] SM riddle.

croato, a [kro'ato] AGG, SM/F Croatian, Croat.

Croazia [kro'attsja] SF: **la Croazia** Croatia.

croccante [krok'kante] [1] AGG crisp, crunchy. [2] SM (*Culin*) almond crunch.

crocchetta [krok'ketta] SF (*Culin*) croquette.

crocchia ['krɔkkja] SF chignon, bun.

crocchio ['krɔkkjo] SM (*di persone*) small group, cluster.

croce ['krotʃe] SF (*gen*) cross; **farsi il segno della croce** to make the sign of the cross, cross o.s.; **Cristo in croce** *o* **sulla croce** Christ on the cross; **in croce** (*di traverso*) crosswise; (*fig*) on tenterhooks; **mettere in croce** (*anche fig: criticare*) to crucify; (*tormentare*) to nag to death; **facciamoci una croce sopra** let's forget about it; **quella malattia è la sua croce** that illness is her cross in life; **ognuno ha la sua croce da portare** we each have our cross to bear; **punto croce** (*Maglia*) cross stitch ▶ **croce greca** Greek cross ▶ **croce latina** Latin cross ▶ **Croce di Malta** Maltese cross ▶ **croce uncinata** swastika ▶ **la Croce Rossa** the Red Cross; **chiama la Croce Rossa!** (*uso improprio*) call an ambulance!

crocefiggere *ecc* = **crocifiggere** *ecc*.

crocerossina [krotʃeros'sina] SF Red Cross nurse.

crocetta [kro'tʃetta] SF (*Naut*) crosstree.

crocevia [krotʃe'via] SM INV crossroads *sg*.

crochet [krɔ'ʃɛ] SM INV [a] (*arnese*) crochet hook [b] (*lavoro*) crochet.

crociata [kro'tʃata] SF (*anche fig*) crusade.

crociato, a [kro'tʃato] [1] AGG cross-shaped; **parole crociate** crossword puzzle *sg*. [2] SM (*anche fig*) crusader.

crocicchio, chi [kro'tʃikkjo] SM crossroads *sg*.

crociera [kro'tʃera] SF [a] (*viaggio*) cruise; **velocità di crociera** (*Aut, Aer, Naut*) cruising speed; **altezza di crociera** (*Aer*) cruising height; **andare in crociera** [OR] **fare una crociera** to go on a cruise [b] (*Archit*) transept; **volta a crociera** cross vault.

crociere [kro'tʃere] SM (*Zool*) crossbill.

crocifiggere [krotʃi'fiddʒere] VT IRREG (*anche fig*) to crucify.

crocifissione [krotʃifis'sjone] SF (*anche fig*) crucifixion.

crocifisso, a [krotʃi'fisso] [1] PP di **crocifiggere**. [2] SM crucifix.

croco, chi ['krɔko] SM crocus.

crogiolarsi [krodʒo'larsi] VIP [a] (*scaldarsi*): **crogiolarsi al sole** to bask in the sun [b] (*bearsi*): **crogiolarsi nelle illusioni** to harbour (*Brit*) *o* harbor (*Am*) illusions.

crogiolo [kro'dʒɔlo], **crogiuolo** [kro'dʒwɔlo] SM (*Chim, Metallurgia*) crucible; (*Vetreria*) pot; (*fig: di popoli*) melting pot.

crollare [krol'lare] VI (*aus essere*) (*gen, fig*) to collapse; (*tetto*) to cave in; (*prezzi, titoli*) to slump; **si lasciò crollare sul letto** he collapsed onto the bed; **dopo 2 giorni di interrogatorio è crollato** he broke down after 2 days of interrogation.

crollo ['krɔllo] SM (*anche fig*) collapse; (*Fin*) slump, sudden fall; **avere un crollo** (*fisico*) to collapse; (*psichico*) to have a breakdown; **crollo in Borsa** slump in prices on the Stock Exchange; **il crollo del '29** the Wall Street Crash.

croma ['krɔma] SF (*Mus*) quaver (*Brit*), eighth note (*Am*).

cromare [kro'mare] VT to chromium-plate.

cromatico, a, ci, che [kro'matiko] AGG chromatic; **sfumature cromatiche** shades of colour.

cromatismo [kroma'tizmo] SM (*Ottica*) chromatism; (*Mus*) chromaticism.

cromato, a [kro'mato] AGG chromium-plated.

cromatografia [kromatogra'fia] SF chromatography.

cromatura [kroma'tura] SF chromium plating.

cromo ['krɔmo] [1] SM (*Chim*) chromium. [2] AGG INV: **giallo cromo** chrome yellow.

cromosoma, i [kromo'sɔma] SM chromosome.

cronaca, che ['krɔnaka] SF [a] (*Storia*) chronicle [b] (*di giornale*) news *sg*; (*resoconto: sportivo*) commentary; (: *di viaggio*) coverage; **fatto** *o* **episodio di cronaca** news item ▶ **cronaca mondana** *o* **rosa** gossip column ▶ **cronaca nera** crime news *sg*; (*rubrica*) crime column.

cronicizzarsi [kronitʃid'dzarsi] VIP to become chronic.

cronico, a, ci, che ['krɔniko] [1] AGG (*anche fig*) chronic. [2] SM (*Med*) chronic invalid.

cronista, i, e [kro'nista] SM/F (*Stampa*) columnist; (*Radio, TV*) commentator; (*storico*) chronicler.

cronistoria [kronis'tɔrja] SF chronicle; (*fig*) blow-by-blow account.

Crono ['krɔno] SM Cronus.

cronografo [kro'nɔgrafo] SM chronograph.

cronologia [kronolo'dʒia] SF chronology.

cronologicamente [kronolodʒika'mente] AVV chronologically.

cronologico, a, ci, che [krono'lɔdʒiko] AGG chronological.

cronometraggio, gi [kronome'traddʒo] SM (precision) timing.

cronometrare [kronome'trare] VT to time.

cronometrico, a, ci, che [krono'mɛtriko] AGG chronometric(al); (*fig: puntualità*) perfect.

cronometrista, i, e [kronome'trista] SM/F timekeeper.

cronometro [kro'nɔmetro] SM chronometer; (a scatto) stopwatch.

cross [krɔs] SM INV (Sport: motocross) motocross; (in Pugilato, Calcio) cross; **moto da cross** rally bike.

crosta ['krɔsta] SF (di formaggio, pane) crust; (Med) scab; (Zool) shell; (di ghiaccio) layer; (fig pegg: quadro) daub ▶**crosta lattea** (Anat) cradle cap ▶**crosta terrestre** earth's crust.

crostaceo [kros'tatʃeo] SM (Zool) shellfish no pl.

crostata [kros'tata] SF (Culin) tart.

crostino [kros'tino] SM (da brodo) croûton; (da antipasto) canapé.

crotalo ['krɔtalo] SM (Zool) rattlesnake.

croton ['krɔton] SM INV (Bot) croton.

croupier [kru'pje] SM INV croupier.

crucciare [krut'tʃare] [1] VT to torment, worry. [2] **crucciarsi** VIP: **crucciarsi per** to torment o.s. over.

crucciato, a [krut'tʃato] AGG worried.

cruccio, ci ['kruttʃo] SM torment, worry.

cruciale [kru'tʃale] AGG crucial.

cruciverba [krutʃi'vɛrba] SM INV crossword (puzzle).

crudamente [kruda'mente] AVV (descrivere, esprimersi) bluntly.

crudele [kru'dɛle] AGG (anche fig) cruel.

crudelmente [krudel'mente] AVV cruelly.

crudeltà [krudel'ta] SF INV (anche fig) cruelty.

crudezza [kru'dettsa] SF (di linguaggio) bluntness.

crudo, a ['krudo] AGG **a** (Culin, Tecn) raw; **la bistecca è un po' cruda** the steak is underdone **b** (fig: descrizione, linguaggio) blunt; **cruda realtà** harsh reality.

cruento, a [kru'ɛnto] AGG bloody.

cruiser ['kru:zə] SM INV cruiser.

crumiro, a [kru'miro] SM/F (pegg) scab, blackleg (Brit).

cruna ['kruna] SF eye (of a needle).

crusca ['kruska] SF bran.

cruscotto [krus'kɔtto] SM (Aut) dashboard.

CS SIGLA = Cosenza.

C.S. ABBR **a** (Mil) = comando supremo **b** (Aut) = codice della strada.

c.s. ABBR = come sopra; vedi sopra.

Csce [tʃi'ɛssetʃi'e] SIGLA F (= Conferenza sulla sicurezza e la cooperazione in Europa) CSCE.

C.S.I. [tʃi'ɛsse'tʃi] SIGLA F (= Comunità di stati indipendenti) CIS.

C.S.M., Csm [tʃi'ɛsse'ɛmme] SIGLA M (= Consiglio Superiore della Magistratura) magistrates' internal board of supervisors.

CT SIGLA = Catania.

c.t. ABBR = commissario tecnico.

Cuba ['kuba] SF Cuba.

cubano, a [ku'bano] AGG, SM/F Cuban.

cubatura [kuba'tura] SF cubic capacity.

cubetto [ku'betto] SM (small) cube ▶**cubetto di ghiaccio** ice cube.

cubico, a, ci, che ['kubiko] AGG (gen) cubic; **radice cubica** cube root.

cubismo [ku'bizmo] SM cubism.

cubito ['kubito] SM (Anat) ulna.

cubo ['kubo] [1] AGG cubic. [2] SM (gen) cube; **elevare al cubo** (Mat) to cube.

cuccagna [kuk'kaɲɲa] SF abundance, plenty; **paese della cuccagna** land of plenty; **è finita la cuccagna!** the party's over!; **albero della cuccagna** greasy pole (fig).

cuccare [kuk'kare] VT (fam) **a** (beccare) to catch; **l'ho cuccato che frugava nella mia borsa** I caught him going through my bag **b** (rubare) to pinch; **mi hanno cuccato il portafoglio** my wallet has been pinched **c** (sopportare): **ho dovuto cuccarmela tutta la sera** I had to put up with her all evening.

cuccetta [kut'tʃetta] SF (di treno) couchette; (di nave) berth.

cucchiaiata [kukkja'jata] SF spoonful, tablespoonful.

cucchiaino [kukkja'ino] SM coffee spoon, ≈ teaspoon; (contenuto) ≈ teaspoonful; (Pesca) spinner.

cucchiaio, ai [kuk'kjajo] SM (gen) spoon; (da tavola) tablespoon; (cucchiaiata) spoonful; tablespoonful ▶**cucchiaio da portata** serving spoon.

cucchiaione [kukkja'jone] SM (Culin) basting spoon.

cuccia, ce ['kuttʃa] SF (di cane: letto) dog's basket; (: canile) kennel; **a cuccia!** [OR] **fai la cuccia!** down (boy)!

cucciolata [kuttʃo'lata] SF litter.

cucciolo ['kuttʃolo] SM (gen) cub; (di cane) pup, puppy; (fig: persona): **vieni qua, cucciolo!** come here, pet!

cucina [ku'tʃina] SF (locale) kitchen; (arte culinaria) cooking, cookery; (cibo) cooking, food; (elettrodomestico) cooker; **mi piace la cucina greca** I like Greek cooking; **è molto brava in cucina** she's very good at cooking; **da cucina** (utensile) kitchen attr; **di cucina** (libro, lezione) cookery attr ▶**cucina da campo** primus stove ▶**cucina componibile** fitted kitchen ▶**cucina economica** kitchen range.

cucinare [kutʃi'nare] VT to cook; **chi ha cucinato?** who did the cooking?

cuciniere, a [kutʃi'njɛre] SM/F cook.

cucinino [kutʃi'nino] SM kitchenette.

cucire [ku'tʃire] VT (gen) to sew; (vestito, Med: ferita) to sew up; (libro, cuoio) to stitch; **cucire a macchina** to machine-sew; **macchina da cucire** sewing machine; **cucire la bocca a qn** (fig) to shut sb up.

cucito, a [ku'tʃito] [1] AGG (vedi vb) sewn; stitched; **cucito a mano** hand-sewn; **stare cucito addosso a qn** (fig: persona) to cling to sb. [2] SM sewing.

cucitrice [kutʃi'tritʃe] SF (per fogli) stapler; (Tip: per libri) stitching machine.

cucitura [kutʃi'tura] SF (di stoffa, cuoio, libro) stitching; (costura) seam.

cucù [ku'ku] SM INV **a** (Zool: anche: **cuculo**) cuckoo **b** (verso del cuculo): **far cucù** to go boo; **cucù, eccomi qua!** peek-a-boo!; **orologio a cucù** cuckoo clock.

cuculo [ku'kulo] SM cuckoo.

cuffia ['kuffja] SF bonnet, cap; (da infermiera) cap; (per ascoltare) headphones pl, headset; (Tecn) casing; (Bot) root cap ▶**cuffia da bagno** (da piscina) bathing cap; (da doccia) shower cap.

cugino, a [ku'dʒino] SM/F cousin.

cui ['kui] PRON REL **a** (nei complementi indiretti: riferito a persona) whom; (: riferito a oggetto, animale) which; **la persona (a) cui si riferiva** the person he referred to o to whom he referred; **le ragazze di cui ti ho parlato** the girls I spoke to you about o about whom I spoke to you; **il libro di cui parlavo** the book I was talking about o about which I was talking; **il motivo per cui non insisto** the reason I'm not insisting; **il quartiere in cui abito** the area o district where I live; **l'anno in cui prese la laurea** the year he took his degree, the year when o in which he took his degree **b** (come genitivo possessivo: riferito a persona) whose;

(: *riferito a oggetto, animale*) of which, whose; **il signore la cui figlia ho incontrato ieri** the gentleman whose daughter I met yesterday; **la persona di cui ti ho dato il numero di telefono ieri** the person whose telephone number I gave you yesterday
c : **per cui** (*perciò*) therefore, so.

culaccio, ci [ku'lattʃo] SM (*Culin*) rump.

culbianco, chi [kul'bjanko] SM (*Zool*) wheatear.

culinaria [kuli'narja] SF cuisine, cookery.

culinario, ria, ri, rie [kuli'narjo] AGG culinary.

culla ['kulla] SF (*anche fig*) cradle; **fin dalla culla** from the cradle, since I was (*o* you were *ecc*) a baby.

cullare [kul'lare] ① VT (*bambino*) to rock; (*fig*: *idea, speranza*) to cherish.

② **cullarsi** VR (*gen*) to sway; **cullarsi in vane speranze** to cherish fond hopes; **cullarsi nel dolce far niente** to sit back and relax.

culminante [kulmi'nante] AGG: **posizione culminante** (*Astron*) highest point; **punto** *o* **momento culminante** (*fig*) climax.

culminare [kulmi'nare] VI (*aus* **essere**): **culminare (in)** (*Astron*) to reach its highest point (at); **culminare in** *o* **con** (*fig*) to culminate in.

culminazione [kulminat'tsjone] SF (*Astron*) culmination.

culmine ['kulmine] SM (*di torre, monte*) summit, top; (*fig*): **ero al culmine della felicità** my happiness knew no bounds; **era al culmine del successo** he was at the peak of his success.

culo ['kulo] SM (*fam!*) **a** (*sedere*) arse (*Brit fam!*), ass (*Am fam!*); **alza il culo!** get off your arse!; **prendere qn per il culo** to take the piss out of sb (*Brit fam!*); **essere culo e camicia con qc** to be really close to sb **b** (*fortuna*): **aver culo** to be lucky; **che culo!** lucky bastard! (*fam!*)

culottes [ky'lɔt] SFPL French knickers.

culto ['kulto] SM (*religione*) religion; (*adorazione*) worship, adoration; (*venerazione*: *anche fig*) cult; **culto della personalità** personality cult; **culto degli eroi** hero worship; **avere il culto della propria persona** to be vain about one's personal appearance.

cultore, trice [kul'tore] SM/F: **essere un cultore di** to have a keen interest in.

cultura [kul'tura] SF (*gen*) culture; (*conoscenza*) learning, knowledge, education; **di cultura** (*persona*) cultured; (*istituto*) cultural, of culture ▶ **cultura generale** general knowledge ▶ **cultura di massa** mass culture.

culturale [kultu'rale] AGG cultural.

culturalmente [kultural'mente] AVV culturally.

culturismo [kultu'rizmo] SM body-building.

culturista, i, e [kultu'rista] SM/F body-builder.

cumino [ku'mino] SM cumin.

cumulare [kumu'lare] VT (*gen*) to accumulate, amass; (*Amm*: *impieghi*) to hold concurrently.

cumulativamente [kumulativa'mente] AVV (*pagare*) in one go.

cumulativo, a [kumula'tivo] AGG (*gen*) cumulative; (*prezzo*) (all-)inclusive; (*biglietto*) group *attr*.

cumulo ['kumulo] SM **a** (*mucchio*) heap, pile ▶ **cumulo delle pene** (*Dir*) consecutive sentences ▶ **cumulo dei redditi** (*Fisco*) combined incomes **b** (*Meteor*) cumulus.

cumulonembo [kumulo'nembo] SM cumulonimbus.

cuneese [kune'ese] ① AGG of *o* from Cuneo.

② SM/F inhabitant *o* native of Cuneo.

cuneiforme [kunei'forme] AGG, SM cuneiform.

cuneo ['kuneo] SM wedge.

cunetta [ku'netta] SF **a** (*di strada*) bump; (*Sci*) mogul, bump; **pieno di cunette** bumpy **b** (*scolo*: *nelle strade di città*) gutter; (: *di campagna*) ditch.

cunicolo [ku'nikolo] SM (*galleria*) tunnel; (*di miniera*) pit, shaft; (*di talpa*) hole.

cuocere ['kwɔtʃere] VB IRREG ① VT **a** (*gen*): **(far) cuocere** to cook; **cuocere al forno** (*pane*) to bake; (*arrosto*) to roast; **cuocere in umido/a vapore/in padella** to stew/steam/fry; **da cuocere** (*frutta*) cooking *attr* **b** (*mattoni*) to fire.

② VI (*aus* **essere**) to cook.

③ **cuocersi** VIP (*cibo*) to cook.

cuoco, a, chi, che ['kwɔko] SM/F cook; (*di ristorante*) chef.

cuoiame [kwo'jame] SM leather goods *pl*.

cuoio, oi ['kwɔjo] SM **a** (*pelle di animale*) leather; (*prima della concia*) hide; **in** *o* **di cuoio** leather *attr* **b** (*Anat*): **il cuoio capelluto** the scalp **c** : **cuoia** SFPL: **tirare le cuoia** (*fam*) to kick the bucket.

cuore ['kwɔre] SM **a** (*Anat, fig*: *cosa centrale*) heart; **a cuore** heart-shaped; **nel cuore della città/della notte/della mischia** in the heart of the city/middle of the night/midst of the fight; **intervento a cuore aperto** open-heart operation

b (*fig*: *animo*): **aver buon cuore** to be kind-hearted; **una persona di buon cuore** a kind-hearted soul; **parlare col cuore in mano** to speak frankly; **col cuore in gola** with one's heart in one's mouth; **senza cuore** heartless; **aprire il proprio cuore a qn** to open one's heart to sb; **non ho il cuore di dirglielo** I haven't the heart to tell him; **il cuore mi dice che...** I feel in my heart that ...; **avere un cuore da leone** to be brave-hearted; **mettiti il cuore in pace, non tornerà mai più** you'll have to accept that he'll never come back; **avere la morte nel cuore** to be sick at heart; **nel profondo del cuore** in one's heart of hearts; **ringraziare di cuore** to thank sincerely; **un grazie di cuore** heartfelt thanks; **ho a cuore il successo del progetto** the success of the project matters to me; **mi sta molto a cuore** it's very important to me; **mi si stringeva il cuore** [OR] **mi piangeva il cuore** my heart ached; **mi piange il cuore a vedere questo spreco** I hate to see such waste; **toccare il cuore a qn** to move sb; **club dei cuori solitari** lonely hearts club

c (*Carte*): **cuori** SMPL hearts.

cupamente [kupa'mente] AVV (*pensierosamente*) gloomily, morosely; (*fig*: *descrivere*) gloomily, bleakly.

cupidamente [kupida'mente] AVV (*vedi agg*) greedily; lustfully.

cupidigia [kupi'didʒa] SF greed, covetousness.

Cupido [ku'pido] SM Cupid; **cupido** (*Arte*) cupid.

cupido, a ['kupido] AGG (*bramoso*) greedy; (*lascivo*) lustful.

cupo, a ['kupo] AGG (*caverna, notte*) pitch-black; (*voce, abisso*) deep; (*colore, cielo*) dark; (*suono*) dull; (*fig*: *carattere*) sullen, morose.

cupola ['kupola] SF (*di chiesa, osservatorio*) dome; (*più piccola*) cupola; (*fig*: *della Mafia*) Mafia high command; **a cupola** dome-shaped.

cura ['kura] SF **a** care; **avere** *o* **prendersi cura di qn/qc** to look after sb/sth; **abbi cura di fare come ti ho detto** be sure to do exactly as I've told you, take care to do exactly as I've told you; **abbi cura di te** take care of yourself, look after yourself; **si dedica completamente alla cura dell'azienda** he devotes all his time to running the company; **questa pianta ha bisogno di molte cure** this plant needs a lot of attention; **a cura di** (*Stampa*)

edited by; **trasmissione a cura di** (*TV, Radio*) programme produced by

b (*accuratezza*) care, accuracy; **con cura** carefully; **senza cura** carelessly; **se lo facessi con un po' più di cura...** if you took a bit more care over it ...

c (*Med: trattamento*) (course of) treatment; **fare una cura** to follow a course of treatment; **è in cura presso il dott. Bianchi** she's one of Dr Bianchi's patients; **è stato in cura presso i migliori medici** he has received treatment from the best doctors; **le hanno dato una cura a base di ormoni** they prescribed a course of hormone treatment for her ▶**cura dimagrante** diet ▶**cura del sonno** sleep therapy.

curabile [ku'rabile] AGG curable.

curante [ku'rante] AGG: **medico curante** doctor (in charge of a patient).

curapipe [kura'pipe] SM INV pipe cleaner.

curare [ku'rare] [1] VT **a** (*Med*) to treat; (: *guarire*) to cure; **gli curarono la pertosse** they treated him for whooping cough; **farsi curare da qn per qc** to be treated by sb for sth; **devi curare o curarti questo raffreddore** you must see about that cold

b (*occuparsi di*) to look after; (: *azienda*) to run, look after; (: *libro*) to edit; **curare l'edizione di un'antologia** to be the editor of an anthology.

[2] **curarsi** VR **a** (*gen*) to take care of o.s., look after o.s.; (*Med*) to follow a course of treatment; **si sta curando con delle vitamine** he's taking vitamins

b (*esteticamente*) to take trouble over one's appearance.

[3] **curarsi di** VIP (*occuparsi di*) to look after; (*preoccuparsi di*) to bother about.

curaro [ku'raro] SM curare.

curatela [kura'tɛla] SF (*Dir*) guardianship.

curativo, a [kura'tivo] AGG curative.

curato [ku'rato] SM (*Rel*) parish priest; (: *protestante*) vicar, minister.

curatore, trice [kura'tore] SM/F **a** (*Dir*:) guardian; (: *di testamento*) administrator ▶**curatore fallimentare** (official) receiver **b** (*di antologia*) editor.

curdo, a ['kurdo] [1] AGG, SM (*lingua*) Kurdish.

[2] SM/F Kurd.

curia ['kurja] SF **a** (*Rel*): **la Curia (Romana)** the (Roman) Curia ▶**curia vescovile** diocesan administration **b** (*Dir*) local lawyers' association ▶**curia notarile** notaries' association o guild.

curiosaggine [kurjo'saddʒine] SF nosiness.

curiosamente [kurjosa'mente] AVV (*con curiosità*) curiously; (*insolitamente*) strangely, oddly.

curiosare [kurjo'sare] VI (*aus avere*) (*aggirarsi*) to look round, wander round; **curiosare nei negozi** to look round o wander around the shops; **curiosare tra vecchi giornali** to browse through old newspapers; **curiosare nelle faccende altrui** to poke one's nose into other people's affairs.

curiosità [kurjosi'ta] SF INV **a** (*gen*) curiosity; (*pegg*) curiosity, inquisitiveness; **provare curiosità per** to be curious about **b** (*cosa rara*) curio, curiosity.

curioso, a [ku'rjoso] [1] AGG (*gen*) curious; (*che vuol sapere*) inquiring; (*pegg*) curious, inquisitive; (*strano*) odd, strange, curious; **un fatto/tipo curioso** an odd thing/person; **essere curioso di qc/di sapere qc** to be curious about sth/to know sth.

[2] SM/F busybody, nosy parker (*Brit fam*); **una folla di curiosi** a crowd of onlookers.

[3] SM: **il curioso è che...** the funny o curious thing is that ... .

curriculum [kur'rikulum] SM INV: **curriculum (vitae)** curriculum vitae.

curry ['kʌri] SM INV curry; **riso al curry** curried rice; **pollo al curry** chicken curry, curried chicken.

cursore [kur'sore] SM (*su strumento di misura, videoterminale*) cursor; (*su radio*) slider.

curva ['kurva] SF **a** (*gen, Mat, Tecn*) curve; (*traiettoria*) trajectory; **una bionda tutta curve** (*fam*) a curvaceous blonde

b (*di strada, fiume*) bend; **prendere una curva** (*Aut*) to take a bend; **sorpassare in curva** to overtake on a bend ▶**curva a gomito** hairpin bend ▶**curva stretta** sharp bend

c (*Geog*) contour ▶**curva di livello** contour line

d (*Sci*) turn ▶**curva a sci uniti** parallel turn ▶**curva a spazzaneve** snow-plough turn, basic turn.

curvare [kur'vare] [1] VT to bend.

[2] VI (*aus avere*) **a** (*strada*) to bend; **curvare a sinistra/destra** to bend to the left/right

b (*veicolo*) to take a bend; **curvare a sinistra/destra** to follow the road to the left/right.

[3] **curvarsi** VR (*chinarsi*) to bend down.

[4] **curvarsi** VIP (*legno*) to warp; (*persona*): **curvarsi con la vecchiaia** to become bent with age.

curvatura [kurva'tura] SF (*gen, Mat*) curvature; (*di strada*) camber; **curvatura alla spina dorsale** (*Med*) curvature of the spine.

curvilineo, a [kurvi'lineo] [1] AGG (*gen, Mat*) curvilinear.

[2] SM (*strumento*) drawing stencil.

curvo, a ['kurvo] AGG (*gen*) curved; (*piegato*) bent; **camminare curvo** to walk with a stoop.

C.U.S. [kus] SIGLA M = *Centro Universitario Sportivo*.

cuscinetto [kuʃʃi'netto] [1] SM **a** (*per timbri*) pad; (*puntaspilli*) pincushion; (*Tecn*) bearing ▶**cuscinetto a sfere** ball bearing **b** (*fam: deposito adiposo*) spare tyre (*Brit*) o tire (*Am*).

[2] AGG INV: **stato cuscinetto** (*fig*) buffer state.

cuscino [kuʃ'ʃino] SM (*gen*) cushion; (*guanciale*) pillow ▶**cuscino di fiori** wreath.

cuscus [kus'kus] SM INV couscous.

cuspide ['kuspide] SF (*Mat, Astron, Astrol*) cusp; (*Archit*) spire.

custode [kus'tɔde] SM/F (*di museo*) keeper, custodian; (*di parco*) warden; (*di casa*) concierge; (*di fabbrica, carcere*) guard.

custodia [kus'tɔdja] SF **a** care; **avere qc in custodia** to look after sth; **dare qc in custodia a qn** to entrust sth to sb's care **b** (*Dir*) custody; **affidare a qn la custodia di** to give sb custody of; **agente di custodia** prison warder ▶**custodia delle carceri** prison security ▶**custodia cautelare** remand (*Brit*) **c** (*astuccio*) case, holder.

custodire [kusto'dire] VT (*conservare*) to keep; (*fare la guardia*: *casa, carcere*) to guard; **i gioielli sono custoditi in cassaforte** the jewels are kept in a safe.

cutaneo, a [ku'taneo] AGG skin *attr*.

cute ['kute] SF (*Anat*) skin.

cuticola [ku'tikola] SF cuticle.

cutrettola [ku'trettola] SF (*uccello*) wagtail.

C.V. ABBR (= *cavallo vapore*) h.p.

c.v.d. ABBR (= *come volevasi dimostrare*) QED (= *quod erat demonstrandum*).

C.VO ABBR = *corsivo*.

cyclette® [si'klɛt] SF INV exercise bike.

D

D, d [di] SF O M INV (*lettera*) D, d; **D come Domodossola** ≈ D for David (*Brit*), ≈ D for Dog (*Am*).

D [di] ABBR **a** (= *destra*) R **b** (*Ferr*) = diretto.

---

da [da] PREP

> da + il= **dal**, da + lo= **dallo**, da + l'= **dall'**, da + la= **dalla**, da + i= **dai**, da + gli= **dagli**, da + le= **dalle**

a (*agente, mezzo*) by;
▷**fare qc da *sé*** to do sth (for) o.s.
▷**dipinto da un grande artista** painted by a great artist
▷**riconoscere qn dal passo** to recognize sb by his (*o* her) step
b (*causa*)
▷**tremare dal *freddo*** to shiver with cold
▷**morire dallo *spavento*** to die of fright
c (*provenienza, distanza, separazione*) from; (: *fuori di*) out of; (: *giù da*) off;
▷**a 3 km da Roma** 3 km(s)from Rome
▷**arrivare da Milano** to arrive from Milan
▷**da *dove* vieni?** where do you come from?
▷**l'aereo *parte* da Gatwick** the plane departs from Gatwick
▷**scendere dal treno** to get off the train
▷**staccarsi da qn** to leave *o* part from sb
▷**toglitelo dalla testa** get it out of your head
▷**uscire dalla scuola** to come out of school
d (*stato in luogo*) at; (: *presso*) at, with;
▷**abita da quelle parti** he lives somewhere round there, he lives in that area
▷**ti aspetto dal macellaio** I'll wait for you at the butcher's
▷**sono da Pietro** I'm at Pietro's (house)
▷**vive da un amico** he's living at a friend's *o* with a friend
e (*moto a luogo*) to; (*moto per luogo*) through;
▷**questo treno *passa* da Genova** this train goes through Genoa
▷**è *uscito* dalla finestra** he went out through *o* by (way of) the window
▷**vado da Pietro/dal giornalaio** I'm going to Pietro's (house)/to the newsagent's
f (*tempo: durata*) for; (: *a partire da: nel passato*) since; (: *nel futuro*) from;
▷**da *allora*** since then
▷**vivo qui da un *anno*** I've been living here for a year
▷**è a Londra da *martedì*** he has been in London since Tuesday
▷**da *oggi* in poi** from today onwards
▷**d'*ora* in poi *o* in avanti** from now on
▷**da *quando* sei qui** since you have been here
▷**sono qui dalle *sei*** I've been here since 6 o'clock
g (*qualità, caratteristica*)
▷**una ragazza dai *capelli* biondi** a fair-haired girl, a girl with fair hair
▷**un vestito da 300.000 *lire*** a 300,000 lire dress
▷**un ragazzo dagli *occhi* azzurri** a blue-eyed boy, a boy with blue eyes
▷**sordo da un *orecchio*** deaf in one ear
▷**è una cosa da *poco*** it's nothing special
h (*modo*) like;
▷**trattare qn da *amico*** to treat sb like *o* as a friend
▷**non è da *lui*** it's not like him
▷**comportarsi da *uomo*** to behave like a man
▷**è da *vigliacchi* fare così** that's a spineless way to behave
i (*predicativo*) as;
▷**da *bambino* piangevo molto** I cried a lot as a child *o* when I was a child
▷**da *giovane*** as a young man (*o* woman)
▷**fare da *guida*** to act as a guide
▷**fare da *maestro*** to act as a teacher
▷**fare da *padre* a** to be a father to
▷**da *studente*** as a student
j (*fine, scopo*)
▷**cavallo da *corsa*** racehorse

▷macchina da *corsa* racing car
▷vino da *pasto* table wine
▷abito da *sera* evening dress
k (*seguito da infinito: consecutivo*) that (*spesso omesso*); (*: finale*) to;
▷casa da *affittare* house to let
▷qualcosa da *bere* something to drink
▷qualcosa da *mangiare* something to eat
▷ero così stanco da *non* stare più in piedi I was so tired (that) I couldn't stand
▷casa da *vendere* house for sale
l: da... *a*... from ...to ...;
▷contare da 1 *a* 10 to count from 1 to 10
▷dalle 3 *alle* 5 from 3 to *o* till 5 (o'clock)
▷c'erano dalle 30 *alle* 40 persone there were between 30 and 40 people there
▷è cambiato dall'oggi *al* domani he changed overnight.

dà [da] VB vedi **dare**.
dabbasso [dab'basso] AVV = **da basso**; vedi **basso**.
dabbenaggine [dabbe'naddʒine] SF (*pegg*) simple-mindedness, credulity.
dabbene [dab'bɛne] AGG INV honest, decent.
Dacca ['dakka] SF Dacca.
daccapo [dak'kapo] AVV = **da capo**; vedi **capo**.
dacché [dak'ke] CONG (*letter*) since.
dacia, cie ['datʃa] SF dacha.
dado ['dado] SM (*nel gioco*) dice *pl inv*; (*Culin*) stock cube (*Brit*), bouillon cube (*Am*); (*Tecn*) (screw) nut; (*Archit*) dado; **giocare a dadi** to play dice; **tagliare a dadi** (*Culin*) to dice; **il dado è tratto** (*fig*) the die is cast.
daffare [daf'fare] SM INV work; **avere un gran daffare** to be very busy; **darsi daffare perché si faccia qc** to work hard to get sth done.
dagherrotipo [dager'rɔtipo] SM daguerreotype.
dagli ['daʎʎi], **dai** [dai] PREP + ART vedi **da**.
daino ['daino] SM (*maschio*) (fallow) deer *pl inv*; (*femmina*) female fallow deer *pl inv*, doe; **pelle di daino** buckskin.
Dakar [da'kar] SF Dakar.
dal¹ [dal] PREP + ART vedi **da**.
dal² ABBR (= *decalitro*) dal.
dalia ['dalja] SF dahlia.
dall' [dall], **dalla** ['dalla], **dalle** ['dalle], **dallo** ['dallo] PREP + ART vedi **da**.
dalmata, i ['dalmata] SM (*cane*) Dalmatian.
dalmatica, che [dal'matika] SF (*Rel*) dalmatic.
daltonico, a, ci, che [dal'tɔniko] 1 AGG colour-blind (*Brit*), colorblind (*Am*). 2 SM/F colo(u)r-blind person.
daltonismo [dalto'nizmo] SM colo(u)r blindness.
dam ABBR (= *decametro*) dam.
dama ['dama] SF a lady; (*nei balli*) partner ▷**dama di compagnia** lady's companion ▷**dama di corte** lady-in-waiting b (*gioco*) draughts *sg* (*Brit*), checkers *sg* (*Am*); **far dama** to crown a draughtsman.
damascare [damas'kare] VT to damask.
damaschino [damas'kino] SM (*tessuto*) damask cloth.
Damasco [da'masko] SF Damascus.
damasco, schi [da'masko] SM damask.
damigella [dami'dʒɛlla] SF (*Storia*) damsel ▷**damigella d'onore** (*di sposa*) bridesmaid.
damigiana [dami'dʒana] SF demijohn.
dammeno [dam'meno] AGG INV: **per non essere dammeno**

di qn so as not to be outdone by sb; **è un grande imbroglione e sua moglie non è dammeno** he's an out-and-out crook and so is his wife.
DAMS [dams] SIGLA M (= *Disciplina delle Arti, della Musica, dello Spettacolo*) *faculty of the performing arts*.
danaro [da'naro] SM = **denaro**.
danaroso, a [dana'roso] AGG wealthy.
dancing ['da:nsiŋ] SM INV dance hall.
danese [da'nese] 1 AGG Danish. 2 SM/F Dane. 3 SM a (*lingua*) Danish b (*cane*) Great Dane.
Daniele [dan'jɛle] SM Daniel.
Danimarca [dani'marka] SF: **la Danimarca** Denmark.
dannare [dan'nare] 1 VT (*Rel*) to damn; **far dannare qn** (*fig*) to drive sb mad; **dannarsi l'anima per qc** (*affannarsi*) to work o.s. to death for sth. 2 **dannarsi** VR (*affannarsi*): **dannarsi per fare qc** to wear o.s. out doing sth.
dannato, a [dan'nato] 1 AGG damned; **quella dannata macchina!** (*fam*) that damned car!. 2: **i dannati** SMPL the damned.
dannazione [dannat'tsjone] 1 SF damnation. 2 ESCL: **dannazione!** damn!
danneggiare [danned'dʒare] VT (*gen*) to damage; (*rovinare*) to spoil; (*fig: persona*) to harm; **la parte danneggiata** (*Dir*) the injured party.
danno¹ ['danno] SM (*gen*) damage; (*a persona*) harm, injury; **arrecare danno a qc** to damage sth; **arrecare danno a qn** to harm sb, do sb harm; **il maltempo ha provocato ingenti danni** the bad weather caused serious damage; **a danno di qn** to sb's detriment; **non c'è stato nessun danno alle persone** nobody was hurt; **in caso di perdita o danno** in case of loss or damage; **chiedere/risarcire i danni** to sue for/pay damages.
danno² ['danno] VB vedi **dare**.
dannosamente [dannosa'mente] AVV harmfully.
dannosità [dannosi'ta] SF harmfulness.
dannoso, a [dan'noso] AGG: **dannoso (a *o* per)** harmful (to), bad (for); **il fumo è dannoso alla salute** smoking damages your health.
dantesco, a, schi, sche [dan'tesko] AGG Dantesque; **l'opera dantesca** Dante's work.
dantista, i, e [dan'tista] SM/F Dante scholar.
Danubio [da'nubjo] SM: **il Danubio** the Danube.
danza ['dantsa] SF: **la danza** dancing; **una danza** a dance; **fare danza** to study dancing; **scuola/maestro di danza** dancing school/master ▷**danza classica** ballet dancing ▷**danza di guerra** war dance.
danzante [dan'tsante] AGG dancing; **serata danzante** dance.
danzare [dan'tsare] VT, VI (*aus* avere) to dance.
danzatore, trice [dantsa'tore] SM/F dancer.
dappertutto [dapper'tutto] AVV everywhere.
dappocaggine [dappo'kaddʒine] SF ineptitude.
dappoco [dap'pɔko] AGG INV (*anche:* **da poco**: *inetto*) inept; (*insignificante*) insignificant, negligible.
dapprima [dap'prima] AVV at first.
Dardanelli [darda'nɛlli] SMPL: **i Dardanelli** the Dardanelles.
dardo ['dardo] SM dart, arrow.
dare ['dare] VB IRREG 1 VT a (*gen*) to give; (*premio, borsa di studio*) to give, award; **dare qc a qn** to give sb sth, give sth to sb; **dare qc da fare a qn** to give sb sth to do; **dare da mangiare/bere a qn** to give sb sth to eat/drink; **dare**

uno schiaffo/un calcio a qn to give sb a slap/kick, slap/kick sb; **mi dai la macchina?** can I have the car?; **dare a qn il permesso di fare qc** to give sb permission to do sth; **gli hanno dato ordine di sparare** they gave him the order to fire; **questo trucco ti dà un'aria volgare** that make-up makes you look common; **ha dato 16 milioni per la macchina** he paid 16 million (lire) for the car; **gli hanno dato 5 anni** (*di prigione*) they gave him 5 years; **quanti anni mi dai?** how old do you think I am?; **queste scene mi danno il voltastomaco** these scenes make me feel sick; **dare del cretino a qn** to call sb a fool; **dare la vita per qc** to give (up) one's life for sth; **dare tutto se stesso a qn/qc** to give one's all to sb/sth; **darsi una pettinata** to give one's hair a comb

b (*organizzare: festa, banchetto*) to hold, give; (: *spettacolo*) to perform, put on; (: *film*) to show; **danno ancora quel film?** is that film still showing?

c (*produrre: frutti, soldi*) to yield, produce; (: *calore*) to give off; (: *suono*) to make; **gli investimenti hanno dato il 10% di interesse** the investments yielded 10% interest; **gli ha dato un figlio** she bore him a son

d : **dare qc per certo** to be sure of sth; **dare qn per disperso** to report sb missing; **dare qn per morto** to give sb up for dead; **dare qc/qn per perso** to give sth/sb up for lost; **dare qc per scontato** to take sth for granted; **dare ad intendere a qn che...** to lead sb to believe that ...; **ciò mi dà da pensare** (*insospettire*) that gives me food for thought; (*preoccupare*) that worries me; **non è dato a tutti di essere intelligenti** not everyone is blessed with intelligence; **dar via** to give away.

2 VI (*aus avere*) **a** (*finestra, casa: guardare*): **dare su** to overlook, give onto, look (out) onto; **il giardino dà sulla strada** the garden faces onto the road

b (*colore: tendere*): **dare su** to tend towards; **un colore che dà sul verde** a greenish colour.

3 **darsi** VR: **darsi a** (*musica, politica*) to devote o.s. to; **darsi al bere/al gioco** to take to drink/to gambling; **darsi alla bella vita** to have a good time; **darsi ammalato** to report sick; **darsi prigioniero** to surrender; **darsi per vinto** to give in; **darsi da fare per fare qc** to go to a lot of bother to do sth; **coraggio, diamoci da fare!** come on, let's get on with it!.

4 **darsi** VIP **a** : **può darsi** maybe, perhaps; **può darsi che venga** he may come, perhaps he will come; **si dà il caso che...** it so happens that ...

b : **darsela a gambe** to take to one's heels.

5 SM (*Fin*): **il dare e l'avere** debits and credits *pl*.

Dar-es-Salaam [daresa'lam] SF Dar-es-Salaam.

darsena ['darsena] SF (*Naut*) dock.

data ['data] SF date; **che data è oggi?** what's today's date?; **in data da destinarsi** on a date still to be announced; **lettera in data 4 febbraio** letter dated the 4th February; **in data odierna** as of today; **senza data** undated; **amicizia di lunga** o **vecchia data** long-standing friendship ▶**data di emissione** date of issue ▶**data di nascita** date of birth ▶**data di scadenza** expiry date.

datare [da'tare] **1** VT to date; **non datato** undated.

2 VI: **datare da** to date back to, date from; **a datare da oggi** dating from today.

datario, ri [da'tarjo] SM (*timbro*) date stamp; (*di orologio*) (universal) calendar.

datato, a [da'tato] AGG (*film, romanzo*) dated.

datazione [datat'tsjone] SF (*Archeol, Geol*) dating.

dativo [da'tivo] SM (*Gramm*) dative.

dato, a ['dato] **1** AGG **a** (*certo*): **in quel dato giorno** on that particular day; **in dati casi** in certain cases

b (*stabilito*): **entro quel dato giorno** by that particular day

c (*considerato*): **data la situazione** given o considering o in view of the situation; **dato che...** given that ....

2 SM (*Mat, Scienza*) datum; **dati** SMPL data *pl inv*; **è un dato di fatto** it's a fact.

datore, trice [da'tore] SM/F: **datore di lavoro** employer.

dattero ['dattero] SM **a** (*Bot: albero*) date palm; (: *frutto*) date **b** (*Zool*): **dattero di mare** date mussel.

dattilografare [dattilogra'fare] VT to type.

dattilografia [dattilogra'fia] SF typing.

dattilografo, a [datti'lografo] SM/F typist.

dattiloscritto, a [dattilos'kritto] **1** AGG typewritten.

2 SM typescript.

dattorno [dat'torno] AVV = **di torno**; vedi **torno**.

davanti [da'vanti] **1** AVV in front; (*all'inizio di: gruppo*) at the front; (*dirimpetto*) opposite; **posso andare davanti?** (*in macchina*) can I go o sit in front?; **davanti c'era un bel giardino** at the front there was a nice garden.

2 : **davanti a** PREP **a** (*posizione: gen*) in front of; (: *dirimpetto a*) opposite; (*distanza*) ahead of; **ogni mattina passo davanti a casa tua** every morning I go past your house; **camminava davanti a me** he was walking ahead of o in front of me; **era seduto davanti a me** (*più in là*) he was sitting in front of me; (*faccia a faccia*) he was sitting opposite o facing me; **la mia casa è davanti al municipio** my house is opposite o faces the town hall

b (*al cospetto di*) before, in front of; **comparire davanti al giudice** to appear before the judge; **davanti a Dio** before God; **davanti al pericolo** in the face of danger.

3 AGG INV front *attr*; **le file davanti sono occupate** the front rows are taken; **le zampe davanti** the front o fore paws.

4 SM INV front.

davanzale [davan'tsale] SM (window)sill.

davanzo [da'vantso] AVV = **d'avanzo**; vedi **avanzo**.

Davide ['davide] SM David.

davvero [dav'vero] AVV really; **è successo davvero** it really happened; **dico davvero** I mean it.

dazebao [daddze'bao] SM INV political poster.

daziario, ria, ri, rie [dat'tsjarjo] AGG excise *attr*.

dazio, zi ['dattsjo] SM (*somma*) duty, tax; (*luogo*) customs *pl* ▶**dazio doganale** customs duty ▶**dazio d'importazione** import duty.

dB ABBR (= *decibel*) dB, db.

D.C. [di't∫i] SIGLA F = **Democrazia Cristiana** *former political party.*

d.C. ABBR (= *dopo Cristo*) A.D.

DD ABBR (*Ferr*) = **direttissimo**.

D.D.T. [didi'ti] SIGLA M (= *dicloro-difenil-tricloroetano*) D.D.T.

dea ['dɛa] SF (*anche fig*) goddess.

debbo *ecc* ['dɛbbo] VB vedi **dovere**.

debellare [debel'lare] VT to overcome.

debilitante [debili'tante] AGG debilitating.

debilitare [debili'tare] **1** VT to debilitate.

2 **debilitarsi** VIP to become debilitated.

debilitazione [debilitat'tsjone] SF debilitation.

debitamente [debita'mente] AVV (*vedi agg*) duly; properly.

debito¹, a ['debito] AGG (*dovuto*) due; (*appropriato*) proper; **a tempo debito** at the right o appropriate time; **ogni cosa a tempo debito** I'll (o we'll) think about it

when the time comes, everything in due time.

debito² ['debito] SM **a** (*anche fig*) debt; **far debiti** to get into debt; **essere/sentirsi in debito verso qn** to be/feel indebted to sb **b** (*Comm*) debit ▶**debito consolidato** consolidated debt ▶**debito d'imposta** tax liability ▶**debito pubblico** national debt.

debitore, trice [debi'tore] SM/F debtor; **ti sono debitore** (*anche fig*) I'm in your debt; **ti sono debitore di un favore** I owe you a favour.

debole ['debole] ☐ AGG (*gen*) weak, feeble; (*luce*) dim, faint; (*speranza, lamento, suono*) faint; (*polso*) faint, weak; (*argomentazioni*) weak, poor; **essere debole di vista** to have weak o poor eyesight; **essere debole di stomaco** to have a delicate stomach; **essere debole in matematica** to be bad at mathematics; **è troppo debole con lei** he's too soft with her.
☐ SM/F (*persona*) weakling; **i deboli** the weak.
☐ SM weakness; **ha un debole per la cioccolata** he's got a weakness for chocolate.

debolezza [debo'lettsa] SF (*anche fig*) weakness.

debolmente [debol'mente] AVV (*vedi agg*) weakly; dimly; faintly.

debosciato, a [deboʃ'ʃato] ☐ AGG debauched.
☐ SM/F debauchee.

debuttante [debut'tante] SM/F (*gen*) beginner, novice; (*Teatro*) actor o actress at the beginning of his (o her) career; **ballo delle debuttanti** debutantes' ball.

debuttare [debut'tare] VI (*aus avere*) to make one's debut.

debutto [de'butto] SM (*anche fig*) debut; **fare il proprio debutto** (*anche fig*) to make one's debut.

decade ['dɛkade] SF period of ten days.

decadente [deka'dɛnte] AGG, SM/F (*gen, Arte*) decadent.

decadentismo [dekaden'tizmo] SM (*Arte*) Decadence.

decadentista, i, e [dekaden'tista] SM/F (*Arte*) Decadent.

decadenza [deka'dɛntsa] SF **a** (*processo*) decline; (*stato*) decadence; **una civiltà in decadenza** a civilisation in decline **b** (*Dir*) loss, forfeiture.

decadere [deka'dere] VI IRREG (*aus essere*) **a** (*costumi*) to fall into decline **b** (*scadere*) to lapse.

decadimento [dekadi'mento] SM (*Fis*) decay.

decaduto, a [deka'duto] AGG (*nobile*) impoverished; (*norma*) no longer in force.

decaedro [deka'ɛdro] SM (*Mat*) decahedron.

decaffeinato, a [dekaffei'nato] ☐ AGG decaffeinated.
☐ SM decaffeinated coffee, decaff (*fam*).

decalcificare [dekaltʃifi'kare] VT (*Med*) to decalcify.

decalcificazione [dekaltʃifikat'tsjone] SF (*Med, Geol*) decalcification.

decalcomania [dekalkoma'nia] SF (*figura*) transfer (*of design, drawing*).

decalitro [de'kalitro] SM decalitre (*Brit*), decaliter (*Am*), ten litres.

decalogo, ghi [de'kalogo] SM (*Rel*) Decalogue; (*fig*) rule-book.

decametro [de'kametro] SM decametre (*Brit*), decameter (*Am*), ten metres.

decano [de'kano] SM (*Rel*) dean; (*fig*) doyen.

decantare¹ [dekan'tare] VT (*virtù, bravura*) to hymn; (*persona*) to sing the praises of.

decantare² [dekan'tare] (*Chim*) ☐ VT to leave to settle.
☐ VI to settle.

decantazione [dekantat'tsjone] SF (*Chim*) settling.

decapitare [dekapi'tare] VT (*gen*) to decapitate; (*per pena*

capitale) to behead.

decapitazione [dekapitat'tsjone] SF (*vedi vb*) decapitation; beheading.

decappottabile [dekappot'tabile] AGG, SF (*Aut*) convertible.

decathlon, decatlon ['dɛkatlon] SM INV (*Sport*) decathlon.

decedere [de'tʃedere] VI (*aus essere*) (*frm*) to die.

deceduto, a [detʃe'duto] AGG deceased.

decelerare [detʃele'rare] VT, VI (*aus avere*) to decelerate, slow down.

decelerazione [detʃelerat'tsjone] SF deceleration.

decennale [detʃen'nale] ☐ AGG (*che dura 10 anni*) ten-year *attr*; (*che ricorre ogni 10 anni*) ten-yearly, every ten years.
☐ SM (*ricorrenza*) tenth anniversary.

decenne [de'tʃɛnne] AGG: **un bambino decenne** a ten-year-old child, a child of ten.

decennio, ni [de'tʃɛnnjo] SM decade.

decente [de'tʃɛnte] AGG (*decoroso: abiti*) decent, respectable; (*contegno*) proper; (*accettabile*) satisfactory, decent.

decentemente [detʃente'mente] AVV decently; **cerca di fare questo lavoro decentemente** try and do this job properly, try and make a decent job of this.

decentramento [detʃentra'mento] SM, **decentralizzazione** [detʃentraliddzat'tsjone] SF decentralization.

decentrare [detʃen'trare], **decentralizzare** [detʃentralid'dzare] VT to decentralize.

decentrato, a [detʃen'trato] AGG (*amministrazione*) decentralized; **ufficio decentrato** (*del comune*) local office.

decenza [de'tʃɛntsa] SF decency, propriety.

decesso [de'tʃɛsso] SM (*frm*) death; **atto di decesso** death certificate.

decibel [detʃi'bɛl] SM INV decibel.

decidere [de'tʃidere] VB IRREG ☐ VT **a** (*stabilire*): **decidere qc** to decide on sth; **decidere una data/un'ora** to agree on a date/time, fix a date/time; **decidere che** to decide that; **decidere di fare qc/di non fare qc** to decide to do sth/against doing sth; **sta a lui decidere** it's up to him to decide; **ha deciso il nostro futuro** it determined our future **b** (*risolvere: disputa*) to settle, resolve; **decidere una lite** (*Dir*) to settle a dispute.
☐ VI (*aus avere*) (*persona*) to decide, make up one's mind; **è venuto il momento di decidere** it's time to decide o make a decision; **non so decidere tra questi modelli** I can't decide which of these models to choose; **fu quel fatto a decidere del mio futuro** that was what decided o determined my future.
☐ **decidersi** VIP (*persona*) to come to o make a decision; **decidersi a fare** to make up one's mind to do; **finalmente si è deciso a parlare** he finally made up his mind to talk.

deciduo, a [de'tʃiduo] AGG deciduous.

deciframento [detʃifra'mento] SM (*di calligrafia*) deciphering.

decifrare [detʃi'frare] VT (*codice*) to decode, decipher; (*calligrafia*) to decipher, make out; (*enigma*) to find the key to; (*fig: intenzioni, atteggiamento*) to work out.

decilitro [de'tʃilitro] SM decilitre (*Brit*), deciliter (*Am*).

decimale [detʃi'male] AGG, SM decimal.

decimare [detʃi'mare] VT (*anche fig*) to decimate.

decimazione [detʃimat'tsjone] SF (*anche fig*) decimation.

decimetro [de'tʃimetro] SM decimetre (*Brit*), decimeter (*Am*).

decimo, a ['dɛtʃimo] [1] AGG tenth

[2] SM **a** (*Mat*) tenth **b** (*Med*): **avere dieci decimi di vista** to have twenty-twenty vision.

[3] SM/F (*in ordine, graduatoria*): **il decimo da sinistra** the tenth from the left *per fraseologia vedi* **quinto**.

decina [de'tʃina] SF **a** (*Mat*): **la colonna delle decine** the tens column **b** (*circa 10*) ten or so, about ten; **decine di lettere** ≈ dozens of letters, ≈ letters by the dozen; *vedi anche* **cinquantina**.

decisamente [detʃiza'mente] AVV definitely, decidedly.

decisi *ecc* [de'tʃizi] VB *vedi* **decidere**.

decisionale [detʃizjo'nale] AGG decision-making *attr*.

decisione [detʃi'zjone] SF **a** (*scelta, Dir*) decision; **prendere una decisione** to take *o* make a decision **b** (*risolutezza*) decisiveness; **con decisione** decisively, resolutely.

decisivamente [detʃiziva'mente] AVV decisively.

decisivo, a [detʃi'zivo] AGG (*gen*) decisive; (*fattore*) deciding.

deciso, a [de'tʃizo] [1] PP *di* **decidere**.

[2] AGG **a** (*persona, carattere*) determined; (*tono*) firm, resolute; **essere deciso a fare qc** to be determined to do sth; **essere deciso a tutto** to be ready to do anything; **sei proprio deciso?** are you quite sure?; **entrò con passo deciso** he marched in resolutely **b** (*netto: colpo*) clean **c** (*definitivo*): **non c'è ancora niente di deciso** nothing has been decided yet.

declamare [dekla'mare] VT, VI (*aus* avere) to declaim.

declamatorio, ria, ri, rie [deklama'tɔrjo] AGG declamatory.

declassare [deklas'sare] VT to downgrade; **1ª declassata** (*Ferr*) *first-class carriage which may be used by second-class passengers.*

declinabile [dekli'nabile] AGG (*Gramm*) declinable.

declinare [dekli'nare] [1] VI (*aus* avere) (*pendio*) to slope down; (*fig: popolarità*) to decline.

[2] VT **a** (*Gramm*) to decline **b** (*rifiutare: invito, offerta*) to decline, turn down; **declinare ogni responsabilità** to disclaim all responsibility **c**: **declinare le proprie generalità** (*frm*) to give one's particulars.

declinazione [deklinat'tsjone] SF **a** (*Gramm*) declension **b** (*Fis, Astron*) declination.

declino [de'klino] SM decline; **in declino** declining, on the decline.

declivio, vi [de'klivjo] SM (downward) slope.

decodificare [dekodifi'kare] VT to decode.

decodificatore [dekodifika'tore] SM decoder.

decodificazione [dekodifikat'tsjone] SF decoding.

decollare [dekol'lare] VI (*aus* avere) (*anche fig*) to take off.

décolleté [dekolə'te] [1] AGG INV (*abito*) low-necked, low-cut; **scarpa décolleté** court shoe.

[2] SM INV (*di abito*) low neckline; (*di donna*) cleavage.

decollo [de'kɔllo] SM (*Aer, fig*) take-off; **al decollo** on take-off; **in fase di decollo** during take-off ▶ **decollo verticale** vertical take-off.

decolorante [dekolo'rante] [1] AGG (*Chim*) decolorizing *o* decolouring; (*per capelli*) bleaching.

[2] SM (*vedi agg*) decolorizing *o* decolouring agent; bleach.

decolorare [dekolo'rare] VT (*vedi agg*) to decolorize *o* decolour; to bleach.

decolorazione [dekolorat'tsjone] SF (*vedi agg*) decolorizing *o* decolouring; bleaching.

decomporre [dekom'porre] (VB IRREG) VT, **decomporsi** VIP to decompose.

decomposizione [dekompozit'tsjone] SF decomposition; **un cadavere in decomposizione** a decomposing corpse.

decomposto, a [dekom'posto] PP *di* **decomporre**.

decompressimetro [dekompres'simetro] SM (*nuoto subacqueo*) decompression gauge.

decompressione [dekompres'sjone] SF decompression; **fare la decompressione** to decompress.

decongelare [dekondʒe'lare] VT to defrost.

decongestionamento [dekondʒestjona'mento] SM relieving of congestion.

decongestionante [dekondʒestjo'nante] SM decongestant.

decongestionare [dekondʒestjo'nare] VT (*Med, traffico*) to relieve congestion in.

decorare [deko'rare] VT (*ornare, anche Mil*) to decorate; **decorare qn al valor militare** to decorate sb for bravery.

decorativo, a [dekora'tivo] AGG decorative.

decoratore, trice [dekora'tore] SM/F **a** (interior) decorator **b** (*Teatro*) set designer.

decorazione [dekorat'tsjone] SF (*ornamento, medaglia*) decoration.

decoro [de'kɔro] SM (*decenza*) decorum; (*dignità*) dignity; **vestirsi con decoro** to be properly dressed.

decoroso, a [deko'roso] AGG (*contegno, abito*) dignified, decorous; (*fig: stipendio*) decent.

decorrenza [dekor'rɛntsa] SF: **con decorrenza da** (as) from.

decorrere [de'korrere] VI IRREG (*aus* essere) **a**: **decorrere da** to have effect from, run from; **a decorrere da** (as) from, starting from **b** (*trascorrere*) to pass, elapse (*frm*); **è decorso un anno dalla sua morte** a year has passed *o* elapsed since he died.

decorso, a [de'korso] [1] PP *di* **decorrere**.

[2] SM (*di malattia*) course.

decotto [de'kɔtto] SM (*Farmacologia*) decoction.

decrebbi *ecc* [de'krebbi] VB *vedi* **decrescere**.

decrepito, a [de'krɛpito] AGG (*vecchio*) decrepit; (*fig*) obsolete.

decrescere [de'kreʃʃere] VI IRREG (*aus* essere) (*gen*) to decrease, diminish; (*prezzi, febbre*) to go down; (*piena*) to subside; (*luna*) to wane; (*marea*) to ebb.

decresciuto, a [dekreʃ'ʃuto] PP *di* **decrescere**.

decretare [dekre'tare] VT (*Dir*) to decree; (*stabilire*) to order; **decretare lo stato d'emergenza** to declare a state of emergency; **decretare la nomina di qn** to nominate sb for appointment.

decreto [de'kreto] SM decree ▶ **decreto legge** ≈ decree with the force of law ▶ **decreto di sfratto** eviction order.

decubito [de'kubito] SM (*Med*): **piaghe da decubito** bedsores.

decuplicare [dekupli'kare] VT to increase tenfold.

decuplo, a ['dɛkuplo] [1] AGG tenfold.

[2] SM: **guadagno il decuplo di prima** I earn ten times more than I used to.

decurtare [dekur'tare] VT (*debito, somma*) to reduce.

decurtazione [dekurtat'tsjone] SF reduction.

Dedalo ['dɛdalo] SM Daedalus.

dedalo ['dɛdalo] SM maze, labyrinth.

dedica, che ['dɛdika] SF dedication.

dedicare [dedi'kare] [1] VT (*gen, Rel*) to dedicate; (*energie, sforzi*) to devote.

2 dedicarsi VR: **dedicarsi a** (*votarsi*) to devote o.s. to; **dedicarsi alla casa** (*occuparsene*) to look after the house; **dedicarsi anima e corpo a** to give o.s. up body and soul to.

dedicatorio, ria, ri, rie [dedika'tɔrjo] AGG dedicatory.

dedicherò *ecc* [dedike'rɔ] VB vedi **dedicare**.

dedito, a ['dɛdito] AGG: **dedito a** (*studio*) dedicated *o* devoted to; (*vizio*) addicted to; **essere dedito al bere** to be a heavy drinker.

dedizione [dedit'tsjone] SF dedication, devotion.

dedotto, a [de'dotto] PP di **dedurre**.

deducibile [dedu'tʃibile] AGG **a** (*per deduzione*) which can be deduced, deducible **b** (*detraibile*) deductible; **spese deducibili (dalle tasse)** (tax-)deductible expenses.

deduco *ecc* [de'duco] VB vedi **dedurre**.

dedurre [de'durre] VT IRREG **a** (*capire, concludere*) to deduce, infer; **dal suo comportamento ho dedotto che era stanco** I realized from the way he was behaving that he was tired **b** (*togliere*): **dedurre (da)** to deduct (from).

dedussi *ecc* [de'dussi] VB vedi **dedurre**.

deduttivamente [deduttiva'mente] AVV by deduction, deductively.

deduttivo, a [dedut'tivo] AGG deductive.

deduzione [dedut'tsjone] SF (*in tutti i sensi*) deduction.

défaillance [defa'jãs] SF INV (*Sport: crisi*) collapse; **avere un attimo di défaillance** (*debolezza*) to have a moment of weakness.

defalcare [defal'kare] VT to deduct.

defecare [defe'kare] **1** VI (*aus* **avere**) to defecate. **2** VT (*Chim*) to refine.

defenestrare [defenes'trare] VT (*fig*) to remove from office; (*in senso proprio*) to throw out of the window.

defenestrazione [defenestrat'tsjone] SF (*fig*: *azione*) removal from office, dismissal.

deferente [defe'rɛnte] AGG **a** (*persona*) deferential **b** (*Anat*: *dotto, canale*) deferent.

deferenza [defe'rɛntsa] SF deference.

deferire [defe'rire] VT: **deferire qc a** (*Dir*) to refer sth to.

defezionare [defettsjo'nare] VI (*aus* **avere**) to defect; (*Mil*) to desert.

defezione [defet'tsjone] SF (*vedi vb*) defection; desertion.

deficiente [defi'tʃɛnte] **1** AGG **a** (*fam pegg*: *sciocco*) half-witted, half-wit **b** (*mancante*): **deficiente di** deficient in. **2** SM/F mentally handicapped person; (*fam pegg*: *sciocco*) idiot.

deficienza [defi'tʃɛntsa] SF (*gen*) deficiency; (*carenza*) shortage; (*fig*: *lacuna*) weakness.

deficit ['dɛfitʃit] SM INV deficit.

deficitario, ria, ri, rie [defitʃi'tarjo] AGG (*Fin*) in deficit; **bilancio deficitario** deficit; **a causa della gestione deficitaria dello scorso anno...** due to last year's deficit ... .

defilarsi [defi'larsi] VR (*svignarsela*) to slip away, slip off.

défilé [defi'le] SM INV fashion show.

definire [defi'nire] VT **a** (*descrivere*) to define; **il suo comportamento si può definire irresponsabile** his behaviour can be described as irresponsible **b** (*risolvere*: *vertenza*) to settle **c** (*determinare*) to define.

definitamente [definita'mente] AVV clearly.

definitiva [defini'tiva] SF: **in definitiva** (*dopotutto*) in the end.

definitivamente [definitiva'mente] AVV (*decidere*) once and for all, definitively; (*stabilirsi*) for good, permanently; (*lasciarsi*) for good; (*assumere*) on a permanent basis, permanently.

definitivo, a [defini'tivo] AGG (*gen*) final, definitive; (*chiusura, vittoria, edizione*) definitive.

definito, a [defi'nito] AGG (*gen*) definite; **ben definito** clear, clear cut.

definizione [definit'tsjone] SF (*gen*) definition; (*di disputa, vertenza*) settlement; (*di tempi, obiettivi*) establishment; **ad alta definizione** (*Fot, TV*) high definition.

deflagrare [defla'grare] VI (*aus* **avere**) (*anche fig*) to explode.

deflagrazione [deflagrat'tsjone] SF explosion.

deflazionare [deflattsjo'nare] VT (*Econ*) to deflate.

deflazione [deflat'tsjone] SF (*Econ*) deflation.

deflettore [deflet'tore] SM (*Aut*) quarterlight (*Brit*), deflector (*Am*).

deflorare VT deflower.

deflorazione [deflorat'tsjone] SF deflowering, defloration.

defluire [deflu'ire] VI (*aus* **essere**): **defluire da** (*liquido*) to flow away from; (*folla*) to stream.

deflusso [de'flusso] SM (*anche fig*) flow; (*di marea*) ebb.

defogliante [defoʎ'ʎante] SM defoliant.

deformabile [defor'mabile] AGG (*gen, Fis*) deformable.

deformante [defor'mante] AGG (*Med*) deforming; (*specchio*) distorting.

deformare [defor'mare] **1** VT (*oggetto*) to put out of shape; (*legno*) to warp; (*corpo*) to deform; (*fig*: *immagine, visione, verità, fatto*) to distort. **2** **deformarsi** VIP (*vedi vt*) to lose its shape; to warp; to become deformed; (*fig*: *immagine*) to become distorted.

deformazione [deformat'tsjone] SF (*Med*) deformation; **questa è deformazione professionale!** that's how you get when you do this job!

deforme [de'forme] AGG (*mani, piedi, corpo*) misshapen; (*volto*) disfigured; (*fig*: *brutto, sgradevole*) hideous.

deformità [deformi'ta] SF INV (*Med*) deformity.

defraudare [defrau'dare] VT: **defraudare qn di qc** to cheat *o* swindle sb out of sth, defraud sb of sth.

defunto, a [de'funto] **1** AGG dead, late *attr*; **il defunto presidente** the late president. **2** SM/F deceased person; **il defunto** the deceased; **commemorazione dei defunti** (*ricorrenza*) All Souls' Day.

degenerare [dedʒene'rare] VI (*aus* **avere**): **degenerare (in)** to degenerate (into).

degenerativo, a AGG degenerative.

degenerato, a [dedʒene'rato] AGG, SM/F degenerate.

degenerazione [dedʒenerat'tsjone] SF degeneration, degeneracy.

degenere [de'dʒenere] AGG degenerate.

degente [de'dʒɛnte] SM/F (*di ospedale*) in-patient.

degenza [de'dʒɛntsa] SF confinement in *o* to bed; **degenza ospedaliera** period in hospital.

degli ['deʎʎi] PREP + ART vedi **di**.

deglutire [deglu'tire] VT to swallow.

deglutizione [deglutit'tsjone] SF swallowing.

degnamente [deɲɲa'mente] AVV worthily.

degnare [deɲ'ɲare] **1** VT: **non mi ha degnato di uno sguardo** he didn't so much as look at me; **non mi ha degnato di una risposta** he didn't deign to answer me. **2** **degnarsi** VIP: **degnarsi di fare qc** to deign *o* condescend to do sth; **vedo che ti sei degnato!** (*iro*) how gracious of you!

degno, a ['deɲɲo] AGG (*gen*) worthy; (*dignitoso*) dignified; **degno di** worthy of; **degno di fiducia** trustworthy; **degno**

di fede (*persona, testimonianza*) reliable; **degno di lode** praiseworthy; **non è degno di te** (*persona*) he is not worthy of you; **fare una cosa del genere non è degno di te** it's unworthy of you to do a thing like that; **non è degno di essere chiamato padre** he is not fit to be called a father; **il suo degno figlio** (*anche iro*) his good *o* worthy son.

degradante [degra'dante] AGG degrading.

degradare [degra'dare] ① VT (*Mil*) to demote; (*fig: persona*) to degrade.

  ② **degradarsi** VR to degrade o.s., demean o.s.

degradazione [degradat'tsjone] SF (*vedi vt*) demotion; degradation.

degrado [de'grado] SM: **degrado urbano** urban decline.

degustare [degus'tare] VT to sample, taste.

degustazione [degustat'tsjone] SF a (*azione*) tasting, sampling b (*negozio*): **degustazione di vini** specialist wine bar; **degustazione di caffè** specialist coffee shop.

dei ['dei] PREP + ART vedi **di**.

deificare [deifi'kare] VT to deify.

deiscente [deiʃ'ʃɛnte] AGG (*Bot*) dehiscent.

del [del] PREP + ART vedi **di**.

delatore, trice [dela'tore] SM/F (*police*) informer.

delazione [delat'tsjone] SF informing.

delega, ghe ['dɛlega] SF a (*di autorità, poteri*) delegation b (*procura*) proxy; **per delega** by proxy; **per delega notarile** ≈ through a solicitor (*Brit*) *o* lawyer.

delegare [dele'gare] VT to delegate; **delegare qn a fare qc** to delegate sb to do sth; (*Dir*) to empower *o* authorise sb to do sth.

delegato, a [dele'gato] ① AGG: **amministratore delegato, consigliere delegato** managing director.

  ② SM/F delegate.

delegazione [delegat'tsjone] SF delegation.

delegherò ecc [delege'rɔ] VB vedi **delegare**.

deleterio, ria, ri, rie [dele'tɛrjo] AGG (*effetto*) deleterious; (*sostanza*) noxious.

delfino[1] [del'fino] SM (*Zool*) dolphin; **nuotare a delfino** (*Sport*) ≈ to do the butterfly (stroke).

delfino[2] [del'fino] SM (*Storia*) dauphin; (*fig: successore*) probable successor.

Delhi ['deli] SF Delhi.

delibera [de'libera] SF decision; (*del Parlamento*) resolution.

deliberare [delibe'rare] ① VT: **deliberare qc** to come to a decision on sth; **deliberare di fare qc** to decide to do sth.

  ② VI (*aus avere*) (*Dir*): **deliberare su qc** to rule on sth.

deliberatamente [deliberata'mente] AVV deliberately, on purpose.

deliberato, a [delibe'rato] AGG (*intenzionale*) deliberate.

deliberazione [deliberat'tsjone] SF = **delibera**.

delicatamente [delikata'mente] AVV (*toccare*) delicately; (*accarezzare, appoggiare*) gently.

delicatezza [delika'tettsa] SF (*vedi agg*) delicacy; softness, paleness; lightness; gentleness; frailty; fragility; thoughtfulness, considerateness, tactfulness.

delicato, a [deli'kato] AGG a (*gen*) delicate, fine; (*tessuto*) delicate, fine; (*colore*) delicate, soft, pale; (*profumo*) delicate, light; (*carezza*) gentle, soft; (*salute*) delicate, frail; (*meccanismo*) delicate, fragile; **è delicato di stomaco** he has a delicate stomach b (*che richiede tatto*) delicate; (*che dimostra tatto*) thoughtful, considerate, tactful.

delimitare [delimi'tare] VT (*anche fig*) to delimit (*frm*).

delimitazione [delimitat'tsjone] SF delimitation (*frm*).

delineare [deline'are] ① VT (*anche fig*) to outline.

  ② **delinearsi** VIP to be outlined; (*fig: situazione*) to take shape; **si sta delineando un periodo difficile** there are hard times ahead.

delinquente [delin'kwɛnte] SM/F delinquent, criminal; (*fig: mascalzone*) scoundrel, wretch ►**delinquente abituale** (*Dir*) persistent offender.

delinquenza [delin'kwɛntsa] SF delinquency, criminality ►**delinquenza minorile** juvenile delinquency ►**delinquenza organizzata** organized crime.

deliquio, qui [de'likwjo] SM (*frm*) swoon; **cadere in deliquio** to swoon.

delirante [deli'rante] AGG (*Med*) delirious; (*fig: folla*) frenzied; (: *discorso, mente*) insane.

delirare [deli'rare] VI (*aus avere*) (*Med*) to be delirious; (*fig*) to rave.

delirio, ri [de'lirjo] SM (*Med*) delirium; **in delirio** (*Med*) delirious; **andare in delirio per qc** to go wild about sth; **mandare in delirio** to send into a frenzy; **la folla in delirio** the frenzied crowd.

delirium tremens [de'lirjum'trɛmens] SM INV (*Med*) delirium tremens.

delitto [de'litto] SM (*misfatto, anche fig*) crime; (*Dir*) crime, offence.

delittuoso, a [delittu'oso] AGG criminal.

delizia [de'littsja] SF delight; **con mia grande delizia** to my great delight; **che delizia!** how delightful!

deliziare [delit'tsjare] ① VT to delight.

  ② **deliziarsi** VIP: **deliziarsi di qc/a fare qc** to take delight in sth/in doing sth.

deliziosamente [delittsjosa'mente] AVV (*vedi agg*) delightfully; deliciously.

delizioso, a [delit'tsjoso] AGG (*gen*) delightful; (*sapore, odore, cibo*) delicious.

della ['della], **delle** ['delle], **dello** ['dello] PREP + ART vedi **di**.

delta ['dɛlta] ① SM INV (*Geog*) delta.

  ② SM O F INV a (*in alfabeto greco*) delta b (*Aer*): **ala a delta** delta wing.

deltaplanista, i, e [deltapla'nista] SM/F hang-glider (*person*).

deltaplano [delta'plano] SM hang-glider; **volo col deltaplano** hang-gliding.

delucidazione [delutʃidat'tsjone] SF clarification *no pl*; **vorrei delle delucidazioni in merito** I would like some more details on that.

deludente [de'lɛnte] AGG disappointing.

deludere [de'ludere] VT IRREG to disappoint.

delusi ecc [de'luzi] VB vedi **deludere**.

delusione [delu'zjone] SF disappointment; **dare una delusione a qn** to disappoint sb.

deluso, a [de'luzo] ① PP di **deludere**.

  ② AGG disappointed.

demagogia [demago'dʒia] SF demagogy.

demagogico, a, ci, che [dema'gɔdʒiko] AGG (*politica, iniziativa*) popularity-seeking.

demagogo, ghi [dema'gogo] SM demagogue.

demandare [deman'dare] VT (*Amm*) to transfer.

demaniale [dema'njale] AGG state *attr*.

demanio, ni [de'manjo] SM (*Amm*) state property; (: *ufficio*) state property office.

demarcare [demar'kare] VT to demarcate.

demarcazione [demarkat'tsjone] SF demarcation; **linea di**

demarcazione demarcation line.

demente [de'mɛnte] ① SM/F (anche fig) lunatic.
② AGG (Med) demented, mentally deranged; (fam) crazy, mad.

demenza [de'mɛntsa] SF (anche fig) madness, insanity ►demenza senile (Med) senile dementia.

demenziale [demen'tsjale] AGG insane; (comicità) surreal, off-the-wall.

demerito [de'mɛrito] SM demerit; ciò torna a tuo demerito that reflects badly on you.

demistificare [demistifi'kare] VT (mito) to demystify, to debunk (fam).

demi-volée [demivo'le] SF INV (Tennis) half volley.

demmo ['demmo] VB vedi **dare**.

democraticamente [demokratika'mente] AVV democratically.

democraticità [demokratitʃi'ta] SF INV democratic nature.

democratico, a, ci, che [demo'kratiko] ① AGG democratic.
② SM/F democrat.

democratizzare [demokratid'dzare] VT to democratize.

democrazia [demokrat'tsia] SF democracy; le democrazie occidentali the western democracies ►la Democrazia Cristiana the Christian Democrat Party.

democristiano, a [demokris'tjano] AGG, SM/F Christian Democrat.

Democrito [de'mɔkrito] SM Democritus.

démodé [demɔ'de] AGG INV old-fashioned, out-of-date.

demografia [demogra'fia] SF demography.

demograficamente [demografika'mente] AVV demographically.

demografico, a, ci, che [demo'grafiko] AGG demographic; incremento demografico increase in population.

demolire [demo'lire] VT (casa, oggetto, teoria) to demolish; (persona: criticare) to tear to pieces.

demolitore, trice [demoli'tore] ① AGG (anche fig) destructive.
② SM (operaio) demolition worker.

demolizione [demolit'tsjone] SF (anche fig) demolition.

demone ['dɛmone] SM demon.

demoniaco, a, ci, che [demo'niako] AGG demoniac(al); (fig: diabolico) fiendish, diabolic.

demonico, a, ci, che [de'mɔniko] AGG, SM (letter) demonic.

demonio, ni [de'mɔnjo] SM demon, devil; (fig: genio) genius; il Demonio the Devil; quel ragazzino è un demonio that child is a little devil.

demonizzare [demonid'dzare] VT to make a monster of.

demonizzazione [demoniddzat'tsjone] SF demonizing, demonization.

demoralizzare [demoralid'dzare] ① VT to demoralize.
② demoralizzarsi VIP to become demoralized; non demoralizzarti don't let it get you down.

demoralizzato, a [demoralid'dzato] AGG demoralized.

demoralizzazione [demoraliddzat'tsjone] SF demoralization.

demordere [de'mɔrdere] VI IRREG (aus avere) to give up; non demordere (da) to refuse to give up.

demoscopia [demosko'pia] SF analysis of public opinion.

demoscopico, a, ci, che [demos'kɔpiko] AGG: indagine demoscopica opinion poll.

Demostene [de'mɔstene] SM Demosthenes.

demotivare [demoti'vare] VT: demotivare qn to take away sb's motivation.

demotivato, a [demoti'vato] AGG demotivated, lacking motivation.

denaro [de'naro] SM **a** money ►denaro contante o liquido cash **b** (misura di fibre tessili) denier **c** : denari SMPL (Carte) suit in Neapolitan pack of cards.

denaturato, a [denatu'rato] AGG: alcol denaturato methylated spirits, denatured alcohol (Am).

denaturazione [denaturat'tsjone] SF denaturation.

denazionalizzare [denattsjonalid'dzare] VT (industria) to denationalize.

denazionalizzazione [denattsjonaliddzat'tsjone] SF denationalization.

dendrite [den'drite] SF (Anat) dendrite.

denigrare [deni'grare] VT to denigrate, run down.

denigratorio, ria, ri, rie [denigra'tɔrjo] AGG disparaging, denigrating.

denigrazione [denigrat'tsjone] SF denigration.

denitrificazione [denitrifikat'tsjone] SF (Chim) denitrification.

denominare [denomi'nare] VT to name.

denominatore [denomina'tore] SM (Mat) denominator ►denominatore comune (anche fig) common denominator.

denominazione [denominat'tsjone] SF (gen) name, designation (frm); (classificazione) denomination ►denominazione di origine controllata mark guaranteeing the quality and origin of a wine.

denotare [deno'tare] VT to indicate, denote.

densamente [densa'mente] AVV densely.

densità [densi'ta] SF (gen, Fis) density; (di nebbia) thickness, denseness; (di vernice) thickness; (di folla) denseness; ad alta/bassa densità di popolazione densely/sparsely populated; a doppia/alta densità (Inform) double-/high-density.

denso, a ['dɛnso] AGG (gen) dense, thick; (vernice, fumo, minestra) thick; una frase densa di significato a phrase charged with meaning.

dentale [den'tale] AGG dental.

dentario, ria, ri, rie [den'tarjo] AGG dental.

dentaruolo [denta'rwɔlo] SM teething ring.

dentata [den'tata] SF (morso) bite; (segno) toothmark.

dentato, a [den'tato] AGG (Tecn) toothed; (Bot) dentate.

dentatura [denta'tura] SF **a** set of teeth, teeth pl **b** (Tecn: di ruota) serration.

dente ['dɛnte] SM **a** (Anat) tooth; denti sporgenti buck teeth; mettere i denti to teethe; mal di denti toothache; lavarsi i denti to clean o brush one's teeth ►dente del giudizio wisdom tooth ►dente da latte milk tooth
b (di sega, pettine) tooth; (di ingranaggio) cog; (di forchetta, tridente) prong
c (Geog) jagged peak
d (Bot): dente di leone dandelion
e (fraseologia): al dente (Culin) al dente; avere il dente avvelenato contro o con qn to bear sb a grudge; via il dente, via il dolore once it's over I'll (o you'll ecc) feel better; mettere qc sotto i denti to have a bite to eat; mostrare i denti to show one's teeth; parlare a denti stretti to speak unwillingly; stringere i denti to grit one's teeth.

dentellare [dentel'lare] VT (gen) to indent, notch; (lama) to serrate; (stoffa) to pink.

dentellato, a [dentel'lato] AGG (gen) indented, notched; (francobollo) perforated; (foglia) serrated; (Geog: cresta)

jagged; (*pizzo*) scalloped.

dentellatura [dentella'tura] SF (*gen*) indentation; (*di francobollo*) perforation; (*di cresta*) jagged outline; (*di pizzo*) scalloping.

dentice ['dɛntitʃe] SM (*Zool*) sea bream.

dentiera [den'tjɛra] SF **a** (*Med*) dentures *pl*, (set of) false teeth *pl* (*fam*) **b** (*Tecn*) rack.

dentifricio, cia, ci, cie [denti'fritʃo] [1] SM toothpaste. [2] AGG: **pasta dentifricia** toothpaste.

dentista, i, e [den'tista] SM/F dentist.

dentistico, a, ci, che [den'tistiko] AGG (*gabinetto, studio*) dentist's; **studi dentistici** dentistry *sg*.

dentizione [dentit'tsjone] SF dentition.

dentro ['dentro] [1] AVV **a** (*all'interno*) inside; (*in casa*) indoors; **qui/là dentro** in here/there; **andare dentro** to go inside (*o* indoors); **non va dentro** it won't go in (here); **vieni dentro** come inside *o* in; **col freddo che c'era, dentro si stava bene** with the cold weather we were better off indoors; **hai visto dentro?** have you seen inside?; **cioccolatini con dentro le nocciole** chocolates with hazelnut centres; **piegato in dentro** folded over; **o dentro o fuori!** either come in or go out!; **darci dentro** (*fig fam*) to slog away, work hard

b (*fam: in carcere*) inside; **l'hanno messo dentro** they've put him away *o* inside; **è dentro da un anno** he's been inside for a year

c (*fig: nell'intimo*) inwardly; **sentire qc dentro** to feel sth deep down inside o.s.; **tenere tutto dentro** to keep everything bottled up (inside o.s.).

[2] PREP: **dentro (a)** in; **dentro l'armadio** in the cupboard; **dentro le mura/i confini** within the walls/frontiers; **è dentro a quel cassetto** it's in that drawer; **è dentro alla politica/agli affari** he's involved in politics/business; **dentro di me pensai...** I thought to myself ...; **ci sono dentro fino al collo** (*fig*) I'm in it up to my neck.

[3] SM inside.

denuclearizzare VT to denuclearize.

denuclearizzato, a [denuklearid'dzato] AGG (*comune, zona*) denuclearized, nuclear-free.

denudare [denu'dare] [1] VT (*persona*) to strip; (*parte del corpo*) to bare.

[2] **denudarsi** VR to strip.

denudazione [denudat'tsjone] SF (*Geol*) denudation.

denuncia, ce *o* **cie** [de'nuntʃa], **denunzia** [de'nuntsja] SF **a** (*Dir*): **sporgere denuncia contro qn** to report sb to the police **b** (*dichiarazione*) notification ▶**denuncia delle nascite** registration of births ▶**denuncia dei redditi** income tax return.

denunciare [denun'tʃare], **denunziare** [denun'tsjare] VT **a** (*Dir*): **denunciare qn/qc (alla polizia)** to report sb/sth (to the police) **b** (*dichiarare: nascite, redditi*) to declare; (*accusare pubblicamente*) to denounce; (*rivelare*) to expose.

denutrito, a [denu'trito] AGG undernourished.

denutrizione [denutrit'tsjone] SF malnutrition.

deodorante [deodo'rante] AGG, SM deodorant.

deodorare [deodo'rare] VT to deodorize.

deontologia [deontolo'dʒia] SF: **deontologia professionale** professional code of conduct.

depauperare [depaupe'rare] VT (*frm*) to impoverish.

depenalizzazione [depenaliddzat'tsjone] SF decriminalization.

dépendance [depã'dãs] SF INV outbuilding.

deperibile [depe'ribile] AGG perishable; **merce deperibile**

perishables *pl*, perishable goods *pl*.

deperibilità [deperibili'ta] SF INV perishability.

deperimento [deperi'mento] SM (*di persona*) wasting away; (*di merci*) deterioration; **il loro deperimento è dovuto a denutrizione** they are in a serious state because of malnutrition.

deperire [depe'rire] VI (*aus* essere) (*persona*) to waste away; (*pianta*) to wilt; **ti trovo un po' deperito** you look rather run-down to me.

depilare [depi'lare] VT to depilate; **depilarsi le sopracciglia** to pluck one's eyebrows; **depilarsi le gambe** to shave one's legs.

depilatorio, ria, ri, rie [depila'tɔrjo] [1] AGG hair-removing *attr*, depilatory.

[2] SM (*sostanza*) hair-remover, depilatory.

depilazione [depilat'tsjone] SF depilation, hair-removal.

depistaggio, gi [depis'taddʒo] SM: **un tentativo di depistaggio delle indagini** an attempt to throw the inquiry off the track.

depistare [depis'tare] VT (*polizia, autorità*) to set on the wrong track.

dépliant [depli'ã] SM INV leaflet; (*opuscolo*) brochure.

deplorare [deplo'rare] VT (*biasimare*) to deplore; (*perdita*) to lament.

deplorazione [deplorat'tsjone] SF censure, disapproval.

deplorevole [deplo'revole], **deplorabile** [deplo'rabile] AGG deplorable.

deplorevolmente [deplorevol'mente], **deplorabilmente** [deplorabil'mente] AVV deplorably.

depone *ecc* [de'pone] VB vedi **deporre**.

deponente [depo'nɛnte] SM (*Gramm*) deponent.

depongo *ecc* [de'pongo] VB vedi **deporre**.

deporre [de'porre] VB IRREG [1] VT **a** (*gen: valigia*) to put down; (*fig: abbandonare: orgoglio, vecchio rancore*) to put aside, forget; **deporre le armi** (*Mil*) to lay down arms

b (*rimuovere: persona*) to remove; (: *re*) to depose; **lo deposero dalla carica** they removed him from office

c (*sogg: uccello*): **deporre le uova** to lay eggs

d (*Dir*): **deporre il vero** to tell the truth; **deporre il falso** to give false evidence.

[2] VI (*aus* avere) (*Dir*) to testify.

deportare [depor'tare] VT to deport.

deportato, a [depor'tato] [1] AGG deported. [2] SM/F deportee.

deportazione [deportat'tsjone] SF deportation.

deposi *ecc* [de'posi] VB vedi **deporre**.

depositante [depozi'tante] SM/F (*Comm*) depositor.

depositare [depozi'tare] [1] VT **a** (*gen: oggetto*) to put down, lay down; (*merci*) to store; **depositare qc per terra** to put sth down; **ha depositato qui tutti i libri e se n'è andato** he dumped all his books here and left

b (*Banca*) to deposit; **depositare una somma in banca** to pay a sum of money into the bank

c (*sogg: fiume, vino*) to deposit.

[2] VI (*aus* avere) (*liquido*) to leave some sediment.

[3] **depositarsi** VIP (*sabbia, polvere*) to settle.

depositario, ria, ri, rie [depozi'tarjo] SM/F (*gen*) depository; (*fig: confidente*) repository; (: *custode: di verità, tradizioni*) custodian.

deposito [de'pɔzito] SM **a** (*atto*): **il deposito della merce ci è costato molto** storing the goods cost us a lot; **il deposito dei bagagli è gratuito** there is no charge for left luggage

b (*di liquidi*) sediment, deposit; (*di acqua calcarea*) fur,

(lime) scale ▶**deposito alluvionale** drift

c (*Fin*) deposit; **fare** *o* **eseguire un deposito** to put down *o* pay a deposit; **denaro in deposito** money on deposit **d** (*magazzino*) warehouse; (*Mil*, *di autobus*) depot; **lasciare in deposito** (*merce*) to store ▶**deposito bagagli** left-luggage office ▶**deposito di munizioni** ammunition dump.

deposizione [depozit'tsjone] SF **a** (*gen*, *Dir*) deposition; (*da una carica*) removal; **fare una falsa deposizione** to perjure o.s. **b** (*Arte*, *Rel*): **la Deposizione** the Deposition.

deposto, a [de'posto] PP di **deporre**.

depravare [depra'vare] VT to corrupt, pervert.

depravato, a [depra'vato] ①AGG depraved.

②SM/F degenerate.

depravazione [depravat'tsjone] SF depravity.

deprecabile [depre'kabile] AGG deplorable.

deprecare [depre'kare] VT to deplore, deprecate.

depredare [depre'dare] VT to plunder, loot; **depredare qn di qc** to rob sb of sth.

depressione [depres'sjone] SF (*in tutti i sensi*) depression; **area** *o* **zona di depressione** (*Meteor*) area of low pressure; **essere in uno stato di depressione** (*Med*) to be depressed, be in a state of depression.

depressivo, a [depres'sivo] AGG depressive; **in uno stato depressivo** in a depressed state, in a state of depression.

depresso, a [de'prɛsso] ①PP di **deprimere**.

②AGG depressed; **zona depressa** (*Econ*) depressed area.

deprezzamento [deprettsa'mento] SM: **deprezzamento (di)** depreciation (of).

deprezzare [depret'tsare] ①VT to bring down the value of.

②**deprezzarsi** VIP to depreciate.

deprimente [depri'mɛnte] AGG depressing.

deprimere [de'primere] VB IRREG ①VT to depress.

②**deprimersi** VIP to become depressed.

depurare [depu'rare] ①VT (*liquido*) to purify; (*sangue*) to cleanse.

②**depurarsi** VIP (*liquido*) to be purified; (*corpo*) to be cleansed.

depurativo, a [depura'tivo] AGG, SM depurative.

depuratore, trice [depura'tore] ①AGG purifying.

②SM: **depuratore d'acqua** water purifier ▶**depuratore di gas** scrubber.

depurazione [depurat'tsjone] SF purification; **impianto di depurazione** purification plant.

deputare [depu'tare] VT (*incaricare*): **deputare qn a fare qc** to delegate sb to do sth.

deputato, a [depu'tato] SM/F **a** (*Pol*) deputy, ≈ member of Parliament (*Brit*), ≈ representative (*Am*), ≈ Congressman/Congresswoman (*Am*) **b** (*Amm*) delegate, representative.

deputazione [deputat'tsjone] SF (*gruppo*) deputation, delegation.

deragliamento [deraʎʎa'mento] SM derailment.

deragliare [deraʎ'ʎare] VI (*aus* **avere**) to be derailed, go off the rails; **far deragliare un treno** to derail a train.

dérapage [dera'paʒ] SM INV (*di veicolo*, *Aer*) skid; (*Sci*) sideslipping.

derapare [dera'pare] VI (*aus* **avere**) (*veicolo*, *Aer*) to skid; (*Sci*) to sideslip.

derapata [dera'pata] SF (*vedi vb*) skid; sideslip; **fare una derapata** (*di veicolo*) to skid, go into a skid; (*sugli sci*) to

sideslip.

derattizzazione [derattiddzat'tsjone] SF rodent control.

derby ['dɛrbi] SM INV (*Calcio*) local derby (*Brit*).

deregolamentare [deregolamen'tare] VT to deregulate.

deregolamentazione [deregolamentat'tsjone] SF deregulation.

derelitto, a [dere'litto] ①AGG abandoned; (*casa*) derelict, abandoned.

②SM/F destitute person; **i derelitti** the destitute.

deretano [dere'tano] SM (*fam*) backside.

deridere [de'ridere] VT IRREG to mock, deride.

derisi *ecc* [de'risi] VB vedi **deridere**.

derisione [deri'zjone] SF mockery, derision.

deriso, a [de'rizo] PP di **deridere**.

derisorio, ria, ri, rie [deri'zɔrjo] AGG (*gesto*, *tono*) mocking.

deriva [de'riva] SF **a** (*Aer*, *Naut*) drift; **andare alla deriva** (*anche fig*) to drift; **la deriva dei continenti** (*Geol*) continental drift **b** (*dispositivo*: *Aer*) fin; (: *Naut*) centreboard (*Brit*), centerboard (*Am*) **c** (*Naut*: *barca*) dinghy.

derivare [deri'vare] ①VI (*aus* **essere**): **derivare da** to derive from; (*corso d'acqua*) to spring from; **da quella decisione non sono derivati altro che guai** nothing but trouble has come out of that decision.

②VT **a** (*Chim*, *Gramm*, *Mat*) to derive; **da ciò ha derivato che...** hence he concluded that ... **b** (*corso d'acqua*) to divert.

derivata [deri'vata] SF (*Mat*) derivative.

derivato, a [deri'vato] ①AGG derived.

②SM (*Chim*, *Gramm*) derivative; (*prodotto*) by-product.

derivazione [derivat'tsjone] SF (*gen*) derivation; (*di acque*) diversion; (*Elettr*) shunt; (*Telec*) extension (*in house*).

dermatite [derma'tite] SF dermatitis.

dermatologia [dermatolo'dʒia] SF dermatology.

dermatologico, a, ci, che [dermato'lɔdʒiko] AGG dermatological.

dermatologo, a, gi, ghe [derma'tɔlogo] SM/F dermatologist.

dermatosi [derma'tɔzi] SF INV dermatosis.

dermoprotettivo, a [dermoprotet'tivo] AGG (*crema*, *azione*) protecting the skin.

deroga, ghe ['dɛroga] SF (special) dispensation; **in deroga a** as a (special) dispensation to; **è una norma che non ammette deroghe** there can be no exceptions to this rule.

derogare [dero'gare] VI (*aus* **avere**) (*Dir*): **derogare a** to repeal in part.

derrate [der'rate] SFPL: **derrate alimentari** foodstuffs.

derubare [deru'bare] VT: **derubare qn di qc** to rob sb of sth.

derubato, a [deru'bato] SM/F victim of a theft.

deruralizzazione [deruraliddzat'tsjone] SF rural depopulation.

desalatore [desala'tore] SM = **dissalatore**.

desalinizzare [desalinid'dzare] VT = **dissalare**.

desalinizzazione [desaliniddzat'tsjone] SF = **dissalazione**.

descrittivo, a [deskrit'tivo] AGG descriptive.

descritto, a [des'kritto] PP di **descrivere**.

descrivere [des'krivere] VT IRREG (*in tutti i sensi*) to describe.

descrivibile [deskri'vibile] AGG: **facilmente descrivibile** easy to describe; **non è descrivibile** it's indescribable.

descrizione [deskrit'tsjone] SF description.

desensibilizzare [desensibilid'dzare] VT (*Med*, *fig*) to

desensitize.

desertico, a, ci, che [de'zɛrtiko] AGG desert *attr*.

desertificazione [dezertifikat'tsjone] SF desertification.

deserto, a [de'zɛrto] 1 AGG deserted; **isola deserta** desert island.

2 SM desert.

déshabillé [dezabi'je] SM INV: **essere in déshabillé** to be half-dressed; **sono ancora in déshabillé** I'm not dressed yet.

desiderabile [deside'rabile] AGG desirable.

desiderare [deside'rare] VT **a** (*volere*) to want, wish for; **desiderare (di) fare qc** to want *o* wish to do sth; **desidererei andarmene** I would like to leave; **desidero che lei venga domani** I'd like you to come tomorrow; **desidera?** (*in bar*) what would you like?; (*in negozio, ufficio*) can I help you?; **sei desiderato al telefono** you're wanted on the phone; **farsi desiderare** (*fare il prezioso*) to play hard to get; (*farsi aspettare*) to take one's time; **lascia molto a desiderare** it leaves a lot to be desired; **la casa lascia un po' a desiderare** the house is not ideal **b** (*sessualmente*) to desire.

desiderio, ri [desi'dɛrjo] SM (*gen*) wish; (*più intenso, carnale*) desire; **sentì il desiderio di andarsene** he felt a desire to leave; **esprimi un desiderio!** make a wish!

desideroso, a [deside'roso] AGG: **desideroso di** longing *o* eager for.

designare [desiɲ'ɲare] VT (*persona*) to designate, appoint; (*data, ora*) to fix; **la vittima designata** the intended victim.

designazione [desiɲɲat'tsjone] SF designation, appointment.

desinare [dezi'nare] (*toscano*) 1 VI (*aus* **avere**) to dine, have dinner.

2 SM dinner.

desinenza [dezi'nɛntsa] SF (*Gramm*) ending, inflexion.

desistere [de'sistere] VI IRREG (*aus* **avere**): **desistere (da qc/dal fare qc)** to give up (sth/doing sth), desist from (doing sth) (*frm*).

desistito, a [desis'tito] PP di **desistere**.

desolante [dezo'lante] AGG distressing.

desolatamente [dezolata'mente] AVV desolately.

desolato, a [dezo'lato] AGG (*paesaggio*) desolate; (*persona: sconsolato*) distressed; **essere desolato (per qc)** (*spiacente*) to be terribly sorry (about sth).

desolazione [dezolat'tsjone] SF desolation.

despota, i ['dɛspota] SM despot.

dessert [de'sɛr] SM INV dessert; **da dessert** dessert *attr*.

dessi *ecc* ['dessi] VB vedi **dare**.

destabilizzante [destabilid'dzante] AGG destabilizing.

destabilizzare [destabilid'dzare] VT to destabilize.

destare [des'tare] 1 VT (*svegliare*) to wake (up); (*fig: dubbio, sospetti, pietà*) to arouse; (: *curiosità, invidia*) to arouse, to awaken; **destare la preoccupazione/la sorpresa di qn** to cause sb concern/surprise; **non destare il can che dorme** (*Proverbio*) let sleeping dogs lie.

2 **destarsi** VIP to wake up.

deste *ecc* ['deste] VB vedi **dare**.

destinare [desti'nare] VT **a** (*designare*): **destinare qc a qn** to intend *o* mean sth for sb; **era destinato a morir giovane** he was destined *o* fated to die young; **la sorte che gli è stata destinata** the fate that was in store for him; **libri destinati ai bambini** books (written) for children

b (*devolvere*): **destinare una somma all'acquisto di qc** to intend to use *o* earmark a sum to buy sth; **i fondi saranno destinati alla ricerca** the money will be used for research

c (*assegnare*) to appoint, assign; **è destinato alla nuova filiale** he's been appointed to the new branch

d (*indirizzare*) to address; **sai dov'è destinata la lettera?** do you know where the letter is going?

e (*decidere*): **destinare un giorno a qc/a fare qc** to set aside a day for sth/to do sth; **in data da destinarsi** at some future date, at a date to be decided.

destinatario, ria, ri, rie [destina'tarjo] SM/F (*di lettera*) addressee; (*di merce*) consignee; (*di mandato*) payee.

destinazione [destinat'tsjone] SF destination; (*scopo*) purpose; **giungere a destinazione** to reach one's destination.

destino [des'tino] SM (*sorte*) fate, destiny; (*futuro*) destiny; **era destino che accadesse** it was fated *o* destined to happen.

destituire [destitu'ire] VT (*funzionario*) to dismiss, remove.

destituzione [destitut'tsjone] SF dismissal, removal.

desto, a ['desto] AGG (wide) awake; **tener desto l'interesse del pubblico** to hold the public's attention; **sogno o son desto?** am I dreaming?

destra ['dɛstra] SF **a** (*mano*) right hand **b** (*parte*) right, right-hand side; **a destra** (*stato in luogo*) on the right; (*moto a luogo*) to the right; **a destra di** to the right of; **corsia di destra** right-hand lane; **guida a destra** right-hand drive; **tenere la destra** to keep to the right **c** (*Pol*): **la destra** the right; **di destra** right-wing.

destreggiarsi [destred'dʒarsi] VIP to manoeuvre (*Brit*), maneuver (*Am*).

destrezza [des'trettsa] SF skill, dexterity.

destriero [des'trjɛro] SM steed; (*da battaglia*) warhorse, charger.

destrismo [des'trizmo] SM **a** (*Med*) right-handedness **b** (*Pol*) right-wing tendencies.

destro, a ['dɛstro] 1 AGG **a** (*mano, braccio*) right; (*lato*) right-hand **b** (*persona: abile*) adroit, skilful (*Brit*), skillful (*Am*).

2 SM (*Boxe*) right.

destrorso, a [des'trorso] 1 AGG (*moto*) clockwise; (*Pol: scherz*) rightist.

2 SM/F (*Pol: scherz*) rightist.

destrosio [des'trɔzjo] SM dextrose.

desueto, a [desu'ɛto] AGG (*letter: parola, uso*) obsolete.

desumere [de'sumere] VT IRREG (*dedurre*) to infer, deduce; (*trarre: informazioni*) to obtain; **desumo da ciò che te ne vuoi andare** I gather from this that you want to leave.

desunto, a [de'sunto] PP di **desumere**.

detassare [detas'sare] VT to remove the duty (*o* tax) from.

detective [di'tektiv] SM INV (*anche:* **detective privato**) private detective.

detenere [dete'nere] VT IRREG (*incarico, primato*) to hold; (*proprietà*) to have, possess; (*prigioniero*) to detain, hold.

detengo *ecc* [de'tɛngo] VB vedi **detenere**.

detenni *ecc* [de'tenni] VB vedi **detenere**.

detentivo, a [deten'tivo] AGG: **pena detentiva** prison sentence.

detentore, trice [deten'tore] SM/F (*di titolo, primato*) holder.

detenuto, a [dete'nuto] SM/F prisoner.

detenzione [deten'tsjone] SF **a** (*di titolo, primato*) holding; (*di armi, stupefacenti*) possession **b** (*Dir*) detention.

detergente [deter'dʒɛnte] [1] AGG (*gen*) detergent; (*crema, latte*) cleansing *attr*.
[2] SM (*detersivo*) detergent; (*cosmetico*) cleanser.

detergere [de'tɛrdʒere] VT IRREG (*gen*) to clean; (*pelle, viso*) to cleanse; (*sudore*) to wipe (away).

deteriorabile [deterjo'rabile] AGG (*gen*) liable to deteriorate; (*cibi*) perishable.

deterioramento [deterjora'mento] SM: **deterioramento (di)** deterioration (in).

deteriorare [deterjo'rare] [1] VT (*macchinari, merce*) to damage, cause to deteriorate; (*alimenti*) to spoil, cause to go bad.
[2] **deteriorarsi** VIP (*vedi vt*) to deteriorate; to go bad.

deteriore [dete'rjore] AGG (*merce*) second-rate; (*significato*) pejorative.

determinante [determi'nante] AGG decisive, determining.

determinare [determi'nare] VT (*gen*) to determine; (*causare*) to bring about, cause.

determinativo, a [determina'tivo] AGG determining; **articolo determinativo** (*Gramm*) definite article.

determinato, a [determi'nato] AGG **a** (*gen*) certain; (*particolare*) specific **b** (*risoluto*) determined, resolute.

determinazione [determinat'tsjone] SF (*atto*) determining; (*decisione*) decision; (*risolutezza*) determination. ▶**determinazione dei costi** (*Econ*) costing.

determinismo [determi'nizmo] SM determinism.

determinista, i, e [determi'nista] SM/F determinist.

deterrente [deter'rɛnte] AGG, SM deterrent.

deterrò *ecc* [deter'rɔ] VB *vedi* **detenere**.

detersivo [deter'sivo] SM (*gen*) detergent; (*per bucato*) washing powder (*Brit*), soap powder ▶**detersivo per bucato a mano** hand-washing powder/liquid ▶**detersivo per lavatrice** detergent for use in washing machines ▶**detersivo per i pavimenti** floor cleaner ▶**detersivo per i piatti** washing-up liquid.

deterso, a [de'tɛrso] PP di **detergere**.

detestabile [detes'tabile] AGG (*carattere, abitudine*) detestable, odious; (*tempo, cibo*) dreadful, appalling.

detestabilmente [detestabil'mente] AVV detestably.

detestare [detes'tare] VT to detest, hate, loathe.

detiene *ecc* [de'tjɛne] VB *vedi* **detenere**.

detonante [deto'nante] [1] AGG detonating, explosive.
[2] SM explosive.

detonare [deto'nare] VI (*aus* avere) to detonate, explode.

detonatore [detona'tore] SM detonator.

detonazione [detonat'tsjone] SF (*di esplosivo*) detonation, explosion; (*di arma*) bang; (*di motore*) knocking, pinking (*Brit*).

detrae *ecc* [de'trae] VB *vedi* **detrarre**.

detraggo *ecc* [de'traggo] VB *vedi* **detrarre**.

detrarre [de'trarre] VT IRREG: **detrarre (da)** to deduct (from), take away (from).

detrassi *ecc* [de'trassi] VB *vedi* **detrarre**.

detratto, a [de'tratto] PP di **detrarre**.

detrazione [detrat'tsjone] SF deduction ▶**detrazione d'imposta** tax allowance.

detrimento [detri'mento] SM: **a detrimento di** to the detriment of.

detrito [de'trito] SM (*Geol*) detritus; (: *fluviale*) silt, alluvium.

detronizzare [detronid'dzare] VT (*anche fig*) to dethrone.

detta ['detta] SF: **a detta di** according to; **a detta sua** according to him (*o* her).

dettagliante [dettaʎ'ʎante] SM/F (*Comm*) retailer, retail

dealer.

dettagliare [dettaʎ'ʎare] VT (*racconto, descrizione*) to detail, give full details of.

dettagliatamente [dettaʎʎata'mente] AVV in detail.

dettaglio, gli [det'taʎʎo] SM **a** detail; **entrare** *o* **scendere nei dettagli** to go into details *o* particulars **b** (*Comm*): **al dettaglio** (*prezzo, vendita*) retail; **vendere al dettaglio** to (sell) retail.

dettame [det'tame] SM dictate.

dettare [det'tare] VT (*lettera, condizioni*) to dictate; **dettare legge** (*fig*) to lay down the law; **fa' come ti detta il cuore** follow your heart.

dettato [det'tato] SM dictation.

dettatura [detta'tura] SF dictation; **scrivere qc sotto dettatura** to take sth down from dictation; **l'ha scritto sotto dettatura** it was dictated to him.

detto, a ['detto] [1] PP di **dire**.
[2] AGG **a** (*Amm, Comm: suddetto*) above-mentioned, aforementioned; **detti prodotti vi saranno consegnati in settimana** the above-mentioned products will be delivered to you by the end of the week; **nel detto giorno** on that day
b (*soprannominato*) called, known as
c (*fraseologia*): **detto fatto** no sooner said than done; **è presto detto!** it's easier said than done!; **come non detto** let's forget it.
[3] SM (*motto*) saying.

deturpare [detur'pare] VT (*anche fig*) to disfigure; (*moralmente*) to sully.

deturpazione [deturpat'tsjone] SF disfigurement.

deuterio, ri [deu'tɛrjo] SM (*Chim*) deuterium.

Deuteronomio [deutero'nɔmjo] SM (*Bibbia*) Deuteronomy.

devastante [devas'tante] AGG (*anche fig*) devastating.

devastare [devas'tare] VT to devastate; (*fig: sogg: malattia*) to ravage.

devastatore, trice [devasta'tore] AGG destructive.

devastazione [devastat'tsjone] SF devastation, destruction.

deviante [devi'ante] AGG deviant.

deviare [devi'are] [1] VI (*aus* avere) (*veicolo*): **deviare (da)** to turn off (from); (*pallone*) to deflect; **il viale devia dal corso principale** the avenue leads off the main road; **deviare dalla retta via** to go astray.
[2] VT (*traffico, fiume, conversazione*) to divert; (*proiettile, colpo, pallone*) to deflect; **deviare qn dalla retta via** to lead sb astray.

deviato, a [devi'ato] AGG (*fig: organizzazione*) corrupt, bent (*fam*).

deviatore [devia'tore] SM (*Ferr: persona*) signalman.

deviazione [deviat'tsjone] SF (*gen*) deviation; (*Aut*) diversion; **fare una deviazione** to make a detour; **deviazione della colonna vertebrale** curvature of the spine.

devitalizzare [devitalid'dzare] VT (*dente, nervo*) to devitalize, kill.

devitalizzazione [devitaliddzat'tsjone] SF devitalization.

devo *ecc* ['devo] VB *vedi* **dovere**.

devoluto, a [devo'luto] PP di **devolvere**.

devoluzione [devolut'tsjone] SF transfer.

devolvere [de'volvere] VT IRREG (*somma*) to transfer; **devolvere qc in beneficenza** to give sth to charity.

devotamente [devota'mente] AVV devoutly.

devoto, a [de'vɔto] [1] AGG (*Rel*) devout, pious; (*affezionato*) devoted.

2 SM/F devout person; **i devoti** (*i fedeli*) the faithful.

devozione [devot'tsjone] SF (*Rel*) devoutness; (*affetto, dedizione*) devotion; **avere una devozione per qn** to worship sb; **dire/fare le devozioni** (*Rel: preghiere*) to say/make one's devotions.

dg ABBR (= *decigrammo*) dg.

---

dì [di]

di + il = del, di + lo = dello, di + l' = dell', di + la = della, di + i = dei, di + gli = degli, di + le = delle

1 PREP

a (*possesso*) of; (*composto da, scritto da*) by;

▷ **la macchina del mio amico/dei miei amici** my friend's/friends' car

▷ **la figlia dell'amica di mia madre** the daughter of my mother's friend, my mother's friend's daughter

▷ **una commedia di Goldoni** a play by Goldoni

▷ **l'ultimo libro di Umberto Eco** Umberto Eco's latest book, the latest book by Umberto Eco

b (*specificazione, denominazione*) of;

▷ **il sindaco di Milano** the mayor of Milan

▷ **il mese di marzo** the month of March

▷ **la vita di campagna** country life

▷ **tavolo di cucina** kitchen table

▷ **sala di lettura** reading-room

▷ **il direttore dell'azienda** the manager of the company

▷ **il professore d'inglese** the English teacher, the teacher of English

▷ **il nome di Maria** the name Mary

c (*materiale*)

▷ **fatto di legno** made of wood

▷ **una casa di mattoni** a brick house, a house made of brick(s)

▷ **un'orologio d'oro** a gold watch

▷ **un sacchetto di plastica** a plastic bag

d (*provenienza*) from, out of; (*posizione*) in, on;

▷ **uscire di casa** to come out of *o* leave the house

▷ **i negozi di Milano** the Milan shops, the shops in Milan

▷ **i vicini del piano di sopra** the upstairs neighbours, the people who live on the floor above us

▷ **sono di Roma** I am *o* come from Rome

e (*tempo*)

▷ **di domenica** on Sundays

▷ **d'estate** in (the) summer

▷ **di giorno** by day, during the day

▷ **di mattina** in the morning

▷ **di notte** by night; at night; in the night

▷ **di sera** in the evening

f (*misura*)

▷ **un bimbo di 2 anni** a 2-year-old child, a child of two

▷ **un viaggio di 100 chilometri** a 100-kilometre journey

▷ **un chilo di farina** a kilo of flour

▷ **un viaggio di 2 giorni** a 2-day journey

▷ **un milione di lire** a million lire

▷ **una stanza di 2 metri per 3** a room measuring 2 metres by 3

▷ **un gioiello di valore** a valuable piece of jewellery

▷ **un bicchiere di vino** a glass of wine

g (*mezzo, modo, causa*)

▷ **vestirsi di bianco** to dress in white

▷ **fermarsi di botto** to stop dead *o* suddenly

▷ **rispondere di brutto** to answer brusquely

▷ **è debole di cuore** he has a weak heart

▷ **urlare di dolore** to scream with pain

▷ **ridere di gusto** to laugh heartily

▷ **morire di cancro** to die of cancer

▷ **spalmare di burro** to spread with butter

▷ **sporcare qc di sugo** to get sauce on sth

h (*argomento*) about, of;

▷ **discutere del tempo** to talk about the weather

▷ **trattato di medicina** medical treatise

▷ **parlare di qc** to talk about sth

▷ **libro di storia** history book

i (*abbondanza, privazione*)

▷ **pieno di** full of

▷ **povero di carbone** poor in coal

▷ **privo di** lacking in

▷ **ricco di risorse naturali** rich in natural resources

j (*paragone nei comparativi*) than; (*paragone nei superlativi*) of;

▷ **il migliore della classe** the best in the class

▷ **è meglio di me** he's better than me

▷ **è il migliore di tutti** he is the best of all

▷ **il migliore dei suoi libri** his best book, the best of his books

▷ **il migliore della città** the best in the city

k (*seguito da infinito*)

▷ **sa di aver sbagliato** he knows (that) he did the wrong thing

▷ **credo di capire** I think (that) I understand

▷ **ti chiedo di dirmi la verità** I beg you to tell me the truth

▷ **è degno di esser ricordato** it's worth remembering

▷ **tentò di scappare** he tried to escape.

2 ART PARTITIVO (*affermativo*) some; (*negativo*) any; (*interrogativo*) any, some;

▷ **vuoi dei biscotti?** would you like some biscuits?, do you want any biscuits?

▷ **non ho dei libri** I haven't any books, I have no books

▷ **non vedo niente di meglio** I can't see anything better

▷ **c'erano delle persone che non conoscevo** there were some people I didn't know

▷ **ho dei soldi** I've got some money

▷ **non c'è nulla di strano** there's nothing odd about it

▷ **c'è del vero in quello che dici** there's some truth in what you say

▷ **vuoi del vino?** would you like some wine?, do you want any wine?

---

dì [di] SM (*letter*) day; **buon dì!** good day (to you)!; **a dì =** addì.

DIA ['dia] SIGLA F = *Direzione Investigativa Antimafia*.

diabete [dia'bɛte] SM diabetes *sg*.

diabetico, a, ci, che [dia'bɛtiko] AGG, SM/F diabetic.

diabolicamente [djabolika'mente] AVV diabolically.

diabolico, a, ci, che [dja'bɔliko] AGG (*anche fig*) diabolical.

diaconato [diako'nato] SM diaconate.

diacono [di'akono] SM (*Rel*) deacon.

diadema, i [dia'dɛma] SM (*di sovrano*) diadem; (*di donna*)

tiara.

diafano, a [di'afano] AGG diaphanous; (*fig: mani, volto*) transparent.

diaframma, i [dia'framma] SM (*Anat, Fot*) diaphragm; (*contraccettivo*) diaphragm, Dutch cap; (*schermo*) screen.

diagnosi [di'aɲɲozi] SF INV (*anche fig*) diagnosis *sg*.

diagnostica [diaɲ'nɔstika] SF diagnostics *sg*.

diagnosticamente [diaɲɲostika'mente] AVV diagnostically.

diagnosticare [diaɲɲosti'kare] VT (*anche fig*) to diagnose.

diagnostico, a, ci, che [diaɲ'nɔstiko] ① AGG diagnostic; **aiuti diagnostici** (*Inform*) debugging aids.
② SM diagnostician.

diagonale [diago'nale] ① AGG (*motivo, disegno*) diagonal; **in linea diagonale** diagonally; **tessuto diagonale** twill; **tiro diagonale** (*Calcio*) cross.
② SF diagonal; **in diagonale** diagonally.
③ SM **a** (*tessuto*) twill **b** (*Calcio*) cross; (*Tennis*) crosscourt shot; **diagonale incrociato** (*Tennis*) return crosscourt shot.

diagonalmente [diagonal'mente] AVV diagonally.

diagramma, i [dia'gramma] SM (*gen, Mat*) diagram; (*grafico*) chart, graph ▶ **diagramma a barre** bar chart ▶ **diagramma di flusso** flow chart ▶ **diagramma a torta** pie chart.

dialettale [dialet'tale] AGG dialectal; **poesia dialettale** poetry in dialect.

dialettalmente [dialettal'mente] AVV in dialect.

dialettica [dia'lɛttika] SF dialectic; **ha una dialettica travolgente** he's highly articulate.

dialetticamente [dialettika'mente] AVV dialectically.

dialettico, a, ci, che [dia'lɛttiko] AGG dialectic.

dialetto [dia'lɛtto] SM dialect.

dialisi [di'alizi] SF INV (*Chim, Med*) dialysis *sg*.

dialogante [dialo'gante] AGG: **unità dialogante** (*Inform*) interactive terminal.

dialogare [dialo'gare] ① VI (*aus* avere): **dialogare (con)** to have a dialogue (*Brit*) *o* dialog (*Am*) (with); (*conversare*) to converse (with).
② VT (*scena*) to write the dialogue (*Brit*) *o* dialog (*Am*) for.

dialogico, a, ci, che [dia'lɔdʒiko] AGG dialogue (*Brit*) *attr*, dialog (*Am*) *attr*.

dialogo, ghi [di'alogo] SM dialogue (*Brit*), dialog (*Am*); **tra noi non c'è più dialogo** we don't talk anymore.

diamante [dia'mante] SM **a** (*gen*) diamond; (*di diamante*) diamond *attr*; **nozze di diamante** diamond wedding anniversary **b** (*Naut: di ancora*) crown.

diametralmente [diametral'mente] AVV diametrically.

diametro [di'ametro] SM diameter.

diamine ['djamine] ESCL: **che diamine?** what on earth?

Diana ['djana] SF Diana.

diapason [di'apazon] SM INV (*Mus: strumento*) tuning fork; (: *tono*) diapason.

diapositiva [diapozi'tiva] SF slide, transparency.

diaria [di'arja] SF daily (expense) allowance.

diario, ri [di'arjo] SM (*gen*) diary, journal ▶ **diario di bordo** (*Naut*) log(book) ▶ **diario di classe** (*Scol*) class register ▶ **diario degli esami** (*Scol*) exam timetable ▶ **diario scolastico** homework diary.

diarrea [diar'rɛa] SF diarrhoea (*Brit*), diarrhea (*Am*).

diaspora [di'aspora] SF (*Storia*) Diaspora.

diastole [di'astole] SF (*Anat*) diastole.

diatriba [di'atriba] SF diatribe.

diavoleria [djavole'ria] SF **a** (*azione*) act *o* piece of mischief
b (*aggeggio*) weird contraption.

diavoletto¹, a [djavo'letto] SM/F (*fig: bambino*) little devil, imp.

diavoletto² SM (*bigodino*) hair-curler.

diavolo ['djavolo] SM **a** devil; **povero diavolo!** poor devil!; **è un buon diavolo** he's a good sort; **avere un diavolo per capello** to be in a foul temper; **avere il diavolo in corpo** (*bambino*) to have the devil in one; (*adulto*) to be fidgety; **avere una fame/un freddo del diavolo** to be ravenously hungry/frozen stiff; **mandare qn al diavolo** (*fam*) to tell sb to go to hell; **va al diavolo!** (*fam*) go to hell!; **fare il diavolo a quattro** to kick up a fuss
b : **diavolo!** for goodness' sake!; **che diavolo vuoi?** what the hell do you want?; **dove diavolo è finito?** where the hell has it (*o* he) got to?
c (*Zool*): **diavolo orsino** Tasmanian devil.

dibattere [di'battere] ① VT (*argomento*) to debate, discuss.
② **dibattersi** VR (*anche fig*) to struggle, wrestle; **dibattersi tra mille difficoltà** to have to contend with a host of difficulties; **dibattersi nel dubbio** to be racked by indecision.

dibattimento [dibatti'mento] SM (*dibattito*) debate, discussion; (*Dir*) hearing.

dibattito [di'battito] SM (*gen*) debate, discussion; (*in parlamento*) debate.

diboscare [dibos'kare] VT (*zona, montagna*) to deforest.

dicastero [dikas'tɛro] SM ministry.

dice *ecc* VB *vedi* **dire**.

dicembre [di'tʃembre] SM December *per fraseologia vedi* **luglio**.

dicembrino, a [ditʃem'brino] AGG December *attr*.

diceria [ditʃe'ria] SF rumour (*Brit*), rumor (*Am*), piece of gossip; **sono solo dicerie** it's just gossip.

dichiarare [dikja'rare] ① VT (*gen*) to declare; (*annunciare*) to announce; **dichiarare guerra (a)** to declare war (on); **dichiarare qn colpevole** to declare sb guilty; **si dichiara che...** it is hereby declared that ...; **il portavoce ha dichiarato che...** the spokesman said that ...; **vi dichiaro marito e moglie** I pronounce you man and wife; **articoli da dichiarare** (*Dogana*) goods to declare; **nulla da dichiarare** (*Dogana*) nothing to declare.
② **dichiararsi** VR **a** to declare o.s.; **dichiararsi soddisfatto** to declare o.s. satisfied; **dichiararsi a favore di/contro** to declare o.s. *o* come out in favour of/against; **dichiararsi vinto** to acknowledge defeat
b (*innamorato*) to declare one's love.

dichiaratamente [dikjarata'mente] AVV openly.

dichiarato, a [dikja'rato] AGG (*nemico, ateo*) avowed; (*cocainomane, anarchico*) self-confessed.

dichiarazione [dikjarat'tsjone] SF (*proclamazione*) declaration; (*discorso, commento*) statement ▶ **dichiarazione (d'amore)** declaration of love ▶ **dichiarazione doganale** customs declaration ▶ **dichiarazione di guerra** declaration of war ▶ **dichiarazione dei redditi** statement of income; (*modulo*) tax return.

diciannove [ditʃan'nɔve] AGG INV, SM INV nineteen *per fraseologia vedi* **cinque**.

diciannovenne [ditʃanno'vɛnne] AGG, SM/F nineteen-year-old *per fraseologia vedi* **cinquantenne**.

diciannovesimo, a [ditʃanno'vɛzimo] AGG, SM/F nine-

teenth *per fraseologia vedi* **quinto**.

diciassette [ditʃas'sɛtte] AGG INV, SM INV seventeen *per fraseologia vedi* **cinque**.

diciassettenne [ditʃasset'tɛnne] AGG, SM/F seventeen-year-old *per fraseologia vedi* **cinquantenne**.

diciassettesimo, a [ditʃasset'tɛzimo] AGG, SM/F seventeenth *per fraseologia vedi* **quinto**.

diciottenne [ditʃot'tɛnne] AGG, SM/F eighteen-year-old *per fraseologia vedi* **cinquantenne**.

diciottesimo, a [ditʃot'tɛzimo] AGG, SM/F eighteenth *per fraseologia vedi* **quinto**.

diciotto [di'tʃotto] **1** AGG INV eighteen.
2 SM INV eighteen; (*Univ*) *minimum (pass) mark awarded in Italian universities for any individual exam per fraseologia vedi* **cinque**.

dicitore, trice [ditʃi'tore] SM/F (*frm*) speaker.

dicitura [ditʃi'tura] SF wording, words *pl*.

dico *ecc* ['diko] VB *vedi* **dire**.

dicotiledone [dikoti'lɛdone] AGG (*Bot*) dicotyledon.

dicotomia [dikoto'mia] SF dichotomy.

didascalia [didaska'lia] SF (*di illustrazione*) caption; (*Teatro*) stage directions *pl*; (*Cine*) subtitle; (: *in film muto*) title.

didascalico, a, ci, che [didas'kaliko] AGG didactic.

didattica [di'dattika] SF (*scienza*) didactics *sg*; (*metodologia*) teaching methodology.

didatticamente [didattika'mente] AVV didactically.

didattico, a, ci, che [di'dattiko] AGG (*gen*) didactic; (*programma, metodo*) teaching; (*centro, libro*) educational.

didentro [di'dentro] SM INV (*gen*) inside; (*di casa, auto*) interior; **dal didentro** from inside.

didietro [di'djɛtro] SM INV (*di casa*) rear, back; (*euf*) bottom; **dal didietro** from behind.

Didone [di'done] SF Dido.

dieci ['djɛtʃi] **1** AGG INV ten.
2 SM INV ten; **dare un dieci a qn** (*voto*) to give sb ten out of ten *per fraseologia vedi* **cinque**.

diecimila [djetʃi'mila] AGG INV, SM INV ten thousand.

diecina [dje'tʃina] SF = **decina**.

diedi *ecc* ['djɛdi] VB *vedi* **dare**.

diedro [di'ɛdro] SM (*Geom: anche:* (**angolo**) **diedro**) dihedral (angle), dihedron.

dielettrico, ci [die'lɛttriko] SM, AGG (*Fis*) dielectric.

dieresi [di'ɛrezi] SF INV dieresis *sg*.

diesel ['di:zəl] AGG INV, SM INV (*motore, automobile*) diesel.

dieta ['djɛta] SF **a** diet; **essere** *o* **stare a dieta** to be on a diet; **mettersi a dieta** to diet, go on a diet; **rompere la dieta** to break one's diet **b** (*Storia*) diet, Diet.

dietetica [die'tɛtika] SF dietetics *sg*.

dieteticamente [dietetika'mente] AVV dietetically.

dietetico, a, ci, che [die'tɛtiko] AGG diet *attr*.

dietologo, a, gi, ghe [dje'tɔlogo] SM/F dietician.

dietro ['djɛtro] **1** AVV behind; (*in fondo: di gruppo, stanza*) at the back; **qua/là dietro** behind here/there; **2 file dietro** 2 rows (further) back; **vestito che si abbottona dietro** dress which buttons at the back; **non guardar dietro** don't look back; **guarda se arriva qualcuno (da) dietro** look and see if anyone is coming up behind us; **ti metti tu dietro?** (*in macchina*) are you going to go in the back?; **la firma è dietro** the signature is on the back; **attacca il foglio dietro** attach the sheet to the back; **passa dietro!** go round the back!; **di dietro** (*entrare, stare*) at the back; **la porta di dietro** the back door;

zampe di dietro hind legs; **da dietro** (*assalire*) from behind, from the rear; **da dietro non ti ho riconosciuto** I didn't recognize you from the back.
2 PREP **a** (*anche:* **dietro a**: *posizione*) behind; **dietro la casa/il banco** behind the house/the counter; **dietro l'angolo** round the corner; **dietro di** *o* **a lui/lei** behind him/her; **guarda cosa c'è scritto dietro il foglio** look what is written on the other side of the page; **camminare uno dietro l'altro** to walk one behind the other *o* in single file; **andare dietro a** (*anche fig*) to follow; **stare dietro a qn** (*sorvegliare*) to keep an eye on sb; (*corteggiare*) to hang around sb; **portarsi dietro qn/qc** to bring sb/sth with one, bring sb/sth along; **gli hanno riso/parlato dietro** they laughed at/talked about him behind his back
b (*anche:* **dietro a**: *dopo*) after; **sono arrivati uno dietro l'altro** they arrived one after the other
c (*Amm, Comm*): **dietro pagamento/consegna** on payment/delivery; **dietro ricevuta di pagamento** on receipt of payment; **dietro richiesta** (*orale*) on demand, upon request; (*scritta*) on application.
3 SM INV (*di foglio, quadro, giacca*) back; (*di casa*) back, rear; (*di pantaloni*) seat.
4 AGG INV (*vedi sm*): **la parte dietro** the back; the rear; the seat.

dietro front ['djɛtro 'front] **1** ESCL about turn! (*Brit*), about face! (*Am*).
2 SM INV (*Mil*) about-turn, about-face; (*fig*) volte-face, about-turn, about-face; **fare dietro front** (*Mil, fig*) to about-turn, about-face; (*tornare indietro*) to turn (a)round; **dietro front da fermo** (*Sci*) kick turn.

difatti [di'fatti] CONG in fact, as a matter of fact.

difendere [di'fɛndere] VB IRREG **1** VT (*gen, Dir: proteggere*) to defend; (: *opinioni*) to defend, stand up for, uphold; (: *dal freddo*) to protect; **difendere gli interessi di qn** to look after sb's interests; **sapersi difendere** to know how to look after o.s.
2 difendersi VR **a** (*proteggersi*): **difendersi (da/contro)** to defend o.s. (from/against); **difendersi dal freddo** to protect o.s. from the cold
b (*cavarsela*) to get by; **in matematica mi difendo** I get by at maths.

difensiva [difen'siva] SF: **sulla difensiva** (*anche fig*) on the defensive.

difensivo, a [difen'sivo] AGG defensive.

difensore [difen'sore] **1** SM/F (*gen*) defender; (*di moralità*) upholder; (*Dir*) counsel for the defence.
2 AGG: **avvocato difensore** defence counsel, defense lawyer (*Am*), counsel for the defence (*Brit*) *o* defense (*Am*).

difesa [di'fesa] SF (*gen, Mil, Dir, Sport*) defence (*Brit*), defense (*Am*); **senza difese** defenceless; **prendere le difese di qn** to defend sb, take sb's part; **la parola alla difesa** (*Dir*) the defence may speak; **giocare in difesa** (*Sport*) to play in defence; **Ministro/Ministero della Difesa** Minister/Ministry of Defence; **la difesa dell'ambiente** protection of the environment.

difesi *ecc* [di'fesi] VB *vedi* **difendere**.

difeso, a [di'feso] PP *di* **difendere**.

difettare [difet'tare] VI (*aus avere*) **a** (*essere difettoso*) to be defective **b** (*mancare*): **difettare di** to be lacking in, lack.

difettivo, a [difet'tivo] AGG (*Gramm*) defective.

difetto [di'fɛtto] SM **a** (*imperfezione: di fabbricazione*) fault,

flaw, defect; (: *morale*) fault, failing, defect; (: *fisico*) defect; **è senza difetti** (*persona*) he has no faults; **l'arroganza è il suo difetto** pride is his failing; **difetto di pronuncia** speech defect

b (*mancanza*): **difetto di** lack of; **se la memoria non mi fa difetto** if my memory serves me well.

difettosamente [difettosa'mente] AVV defectively.

difettosità [difettosi'ta] SF faultiness, defective nature.

difettoso, a [difet'toso] AGG defective, faulty, imperfect.

diffamare [diffa'mare] VT (*a parole*) to slander; (*per iscritto*) to libel.

diffamatore, trice [diffama'tore] SM/F (*vedi vb*) slanderer; libeller, libelist.

diffamatorio, ria, ri, rie [diffama'torjo] AGG (*vedi vb*) slanderous; libellous (*Brit*), libelous (*Am*).

diffamazione [diffamat'tsjone] SF (*vedi vb*) slander; libel.

differente [diffe'rɛnte] AGG: **differente (da)** different (from).

differentemente [differente'mente] AVV differently, in a different way.

differenza [diffe'rɛntsa] SF **a** (*diversità*): **differenza (di)** difference (in); **differenza di età** age difference, difference in age; **non fare differenza (tra)** to make no distinction (between); **a differenza di** unlike; **con la differenza che...** with the difference that ...; **non fa differenza che venga o meno** it makes no difference whether he comes or not

b (*Mat*) difference ▶ **differenza di potenziale** (*Mat, Fis*) potential difference.

differenziale [differen'tsjale] ① AGG differential. ② SM (*Aut, Mat*) differential.

differenziare [differen'tsjare] ① VT to differentiate. ② **differenziarsi** VIP (*essere differente*) to be different, differ; (*diventare differente*) to become different.

differenziazione [differentsjat'tsjone] SF differentiation.

differimento [differi'mento] SM deferment, postponement.

differire [diffe'rire] ① VT to defer, postpone, put off; **differire qc di un mese** to postpone o defer sth for a month. ② VI (*aus essere*) (*essere differente*): **differire (da/in)** to differ (from/in), be different (from/in); **differire per grandezza** to differ o be different in size.

differita [diffe'rita] SF: **in differita** (*trasmettere*) prerecorded.

difficile [dif'fitʃile] ① AGG **a** (*problema, lavoro, periodo*) difficult; (*situazione*) difficult, awkward; **difficile da fare** difficult o hard to do; **sta attraversando momenti difficili** he's going through a difficult period; **non farla tanto difficile** don't make it more difficult than it is **b** (*persona: intrattabile*) difficult, awkward; (: *nei gusti*) fussy; **suo marito ha un carattere difficile** her husband is hard to get on with, her husband is an awkward character; **difficile da accontentare** hard to please; **essere difficile nel mangiare** to be fussy about one's food **c** (*improbabile*) unlikely; **è difficile che venga** he's unlikely to come. ② SM/F: **fare il (la) difficile** to be difficult, be awkward. ③ SM difficulty, difficult part; **il difficile è finire in tempo** the difficulty lies in finishing in time, the problem is getting finished in time; **ora che il difficile è fatto...** now that the difficult part has been done ... .

difficilmente [diffitʃil'mente] AVV **a** (*con difficoltà*) with difficulty **b** (*con scarsa probabilità*): **difficilmente verrà** he's unlikely to come; **verrai? — difficilmente** will you come? — probably not.

difficoltà [diffikol'ta] SF INV difficulty; **difficoltà finanziarie** financial difficulties; **trovare difficoltà a fare qc** to find it difficult to do sth; **fare delle difficoltà** to make difficulties, raise objections.

difficoltoso, a [diffikol'toso] AGG (*compito*) difficult, hard; (*persona*) difficult, hard to please; **digestione difficoltosa** poor digestion.

diffida [dif'fida] SF (*Dir*) notice, warning.

diffidare [diffi'dare] ① VI (*aus avere*) (*sospettare*): **diffidare di** to distrust, be suspicious o distrustful of. ② VT (*Dir*): **diffidare qn dal fare qc** to warn sb not to do sth, caution sb against doing sth.

diffidente [diffi'dɛnte] AGG: **diffidente (nei confronti di)** distrustful (of), suspicious (of).

diffidenza [diffi'dɛntsa] SF distrust, suspicion.

diffondere [dif'fondere] VB IRREG ① VT (*luce, calore*) to give out, spread, diffuse (*frm*); (*malattia, idea, notizie, scritto*) to spread, circulate; **la notizia è stata diffusa per radio** the news was broadcast o given out on the radio. ② **diffondersi** VIP (*anche fig*) to spread.

diffrazione [diffrat'tsjone] SF (*Fis*) diffraction.

diffusamente [diffuza'mente] AVV (*trattare*) at length.

diffusi ecc [dif'fuzi] VB vedi **diffondere**.

diffusione [diffu'zjone] SF (*gen*) diffusion; (*di giornale*) circulation; (*di cultura, religione, malattia*) spread; (*Fis*) scattering.

diffuso, a [dif'fuzo] ① PP di **diffondere**. ② AGG **a** (*notizia, malattia*) widespread; **è opinione diffusa che...** it's widely held that ... **b** (*Fis*) diffuse; **luce diffusa** diffused light.

diffusore [diffu'zore] SM (*Tecn*) diffuser.

difilato [difi'lato] AVV (*subito*) straightaway, straight away; (*direttamente*) straight, directly; **ho lavorato per 8 ore difilato** I worked 8 hours without a break.

difterite [difte'rite] SF (*Med*) diphtheria.

diga, ghe ['diga] SF (*sbarramento*) dam, dyke (*against flooding*); (: *portuale*) breakwater.

digerente [didʒe'rɛnte] AGG digestive.

digeribile [didʒe'ribile] AGG digestible.

digeribilità [didʒeribili'ta] SF INV digestibility.

digerire [didʒe'rire] VT (*cibo, fig: nozioni*) to digest; (: *insulto*) to stomach, put up with.

digestione [didʒes'tjone] SF digestion.

digestivo, a [didʒes'tivo] ① AGG digestive. ② SM (after-dinner) liqueur.

Digione [di'dʒone] SF Dijon.

digitale [didʒi'tale] ① AGG (*Anat, Tecn*) digital; **impronta digitale** fingerprint. ② SF (*Bot*) foxglove.

digitare [didʒi'tare] VT (*dati*) to key (in).

digiunare [didʒu'nare] VI (*aus avere*) (*gen, Rel*) to fast; **digiunare per protesta** to go on hunger strike.

digiuno, a [di'dʒuno] ① SM fast, fasting; **a digiuno** on an empty stomach; **sono a digiuno** I haven't eaten; **stare a digiuno** to fast; **è una medicina da prendersi a digiuno** this medicine should be taken before meals. ② AGG: **digiuno di** (*fig: cognizioni*) ignorant of; **sono completamente digiuno di informatica** I haven't a clue about computers, I don't know anything about computers.

dignità [diɲɲi'ta] SF dignity.

dignitario, ri [diɲɲi'tarjo] SM dignitary.
dignitosamente [diɲɲitosa'mente] AVV in a dignified way, with dignity.
dignitoso, a [diɲɲi'toso] AGG (*contegno, abito*) dignified; (*fig: stipendio*) decent.
Digos ['digos] SIGLA F (= *Divisione investigazioni generali e operazioni speciali*) *police department dealing with political security*, ≈ Special Branch.
digradare [digra'dare] VI (*pendio*) to slope, decline.
digressione [digres'sjone] SF digression.
digrignare [digriɲ'ɲare] VT: **digrignare i denti** (*animale*) to bare its teeth; (*persona*) to grind one's teeth.
digrossare [digros'sare] VT (*tronco*) to trim; (*pietra, marmo*) to rough-hew.
dilagare [dila'gare] VI (*aus* **essere**) to overflow, flood; (*fig: corruzione*) to spread, be rampant; (: *malattia*) to spread.
dilaniare [dila'njare] VT to tear to pieces; **era dilaniato dal rimorso** (*fig*) he was overwhelmed by remorse.
dilapidare [dilapi'dare] VT to squander.
dilapidatore, trice [dilapida'tore] SM/F squanderer.
dilatare [dila'tare] ① VT (*pupille*) to dilate; (*stomaco*) to dilate, cause to expand; (*gas, metallo*) to cause to expand; (*tubo, buco*) to enlarge; (*passaggio, cavità*) to open (up).
  ② **dilatarsi** VIP (*vedi vt*) to dilate; to expand; to become enlarged; to open up.
dilatazione [dilatat'tsjone] SF (*Anat*) dilation; (*di gas, metallo*) expansion.
dilazionabile [dilattsjo'nabile] AGG deferrable.
dilazionare [dilattsjo'nare] VT to defer, delay.
dilazione [dilat'tsjone] SF deferment.
dileggiare [diled'dʒare] VT to mock, scoff at, deride.
dileggio, gi [di'leddʒo] SM mockery, scoffing, derision; **per dileggio** in derision *o* mockery.
dileguare [dile'gware] ① VT to dispel, disperse; **il vento ha dileguato le nubi** the wind has dispersed the clouds.
  ② **dileguarsi** VIP (*nebbia*) to disperse; (*fig: dubbio, persona*) to vanish, disappear.
dilemma, i [di'lɛmma] SM dilemma.
dilettante [dilet'tante] ① AGG amateur *attr*; (*pegg*) amateur *attr*, dilettante *attr*.
  ② SM/F (*vedi agg*) amateur; dilettante.
dilettantismo [dilettan'tizmo] SM (*pegg*) amateurishness; (*Sport*) amateurism.
dilettantistico, a, ci, che [dilettan'tistiko] AGG (*pegg*) amateurish; (*Sport*) amateur *attr*.
dilettare [dilet'tare] ① VT **a** (*dar piacere*) to delight, please, give pleasure to; **mi dilettava l'idea di partire** the thought of going away was a delight
  b (*intrattenere*) to amuse, entertain.
  ② **dilettarsi** VIP: **dilettarsi a fare qc** to delight *o* take pleasure in doing sth, enjoy doing sth; **dilettarsi di qc** to have sth as a hobby; **si diletta di pittura** painting is a hobby of his.
dilettevole [dilet'tevole] AGG delightful.
diletto¹, a [di'lɛtto] ① AGG beloved.
  ② SM/F beloved, loved one.
diletto² [di'lɛtto] SM delight, pleasure; **trarre diletto da** to take pleasure *o* delight in; **per diletto** for pleasure.
diligente [dili'dʒente] AGG (*scrupoloso*) diligent, hard-working, assiduous; (*accurato*) careful, accurate.
diligentemente [dilidʒente'mente] AVV (*vedi agg*) diligently, assiduously; carefully.
diligenza¹ [dili'dʒɛntsa] SF (*qualità*) diligence.

diligenza² [dili'dʒɛntsa] SF (*carrozza*) stagecoach.
diliscare [dilis'kare] VT (*pesce*) to bone.
diluire [dilu'ire] VT (*gen: liquidi*) to dilute; (*vernice*) to thin (down); (*polverina, medicina*) to dissolve.
diluizione [diluit'tsjone] SF (*vedi vb*) dilution; thinning; dissolving.
dilungarsi [dilun'garsi] VIP to talk at length; **dilungarsi in una descrizione** to go into a detailed description.
diluviare [dilu'vjare] VB IMPERS (*aus* **essere** *o* **avere**) to pour (down), rain hard.
diluvio, vi [di'luvjo] SM (*pioggia*) downpour, deluge; (*fig: di insulti*) torrent; **il diluvio universale** the Flood.
dimagrante [dima'grante] AGG slimming *attr*; **fare una cura dimagrante** to go on a (slimming) diet.
dimagrimento [dimagri'mento] SM loss of weight.
dimagrire [dima'grire] VI (*aus* **essere**) to become thin, lose weight, get thinner; **è dimagrito di 5 kg** he has lost 5 kg.
dimenare [dime'nare] ① VT (*braccia*) to wave (about); (*coda*) to wag; (*corpo, testa*) to shake; (*sedere*) to wiggle.
  ② **dimenarsi** VR (*agitarsi: nel letto*) to toss (about), toss and turn; (: *per liberarsi, ballando*) to fling o.s. about; (*gesticolare*) to gesticulate wildly.
dimensionale [dimensjo'nale] AGG dimensional.
dimensione [dimen'sjone] SF **a** (*Mat, Filosofia, Fis*) dimension, size; **a 3 dimensioni** 3-dimensional
  b (*misura*): **dimensioni** SFPL dimensions, measurements, size *sg*; **di quali dimensioni è la stanza?** what are the dimensions *o* measurements of the room?, what size is the room?, what does the room measure?
  c (*fig*): **ricondurre qc alle giuste dimensioni** to get sth back in perspective; **considerare un discorso nella sua dimensione politica** to look at a speech in terms of its political significance; **di dimensioni allarmanti** of alarming proportions.
dimenticanza [dimenti'kantsa] SF (*svista*) oversight.
dimenticare [dimenti'kare] ① VT (*gen*) to forget; (*preoccupazioni*) to forget (about); (*omettere*) to leave out; **dimenticare di fare qc** to forget to do sth; **dimenticare o dimenticarsi qc** to forget sth; **ho dimenticato l'ombrello in ufficio** I left my umbrella at the office.
  ② **dimenticarsi** VIP: **dimenticarsi di qc/di fare qc** to forget (about) sth/to do sth; **non me ne dimenticherò** I won't forget.
dimenticatoio [dimentika'tojo] SM (*scherz*): **cadere/ mettere nel dimenticatoio** to sink into/consign to oblivion.
dimentico, a, chi, che [di'mentiko] AGG: **dimentico di** (*che non ricorda*) forgetful of; (*incurante*) oblivious of, unmindful of.
dimero ['dimero] SM (*Chim*) dimer.
dimessamente [dimessa'mente] AVV (*vestire, vivere*) modestly, simply.
dimesso, a [di'messo] ① PP di **dimettere**.
  ② AGG modest, unassuming, humble; **in abiti dimessi** simply dressed; **con voce dimessa** humbly.
dimestichezza [dimesti'kettsa] SF (*familiarità*) familiarity; **avere dimestichezza con qc** to be familiar with sth.
dimettere [di'mettere] VB IRREG ① VT (*da ospedale*) to discharge; (*da carcere*) to release; (*da carica*) to dismiss; **far dimettere qn** to have sb dismissed.
  ② **dimettersi** VR: **dimettersi (da)** to resign, hand *o* give in one's notice.
dimezzare [dimed'dzare] VT to cut in half, halve.

diminuendo [diminu'ɛndo] SM (*Mus*) diminuendo.

diminuire [diminu'ire] ① VT (*gen*) to reduce, decrease, diminish; (*prezzi*) to bring down, reduce.

② VI (*aus* **essere**) (*gen*) to diminish, to decrease; (*vento, rumore*) to die down, die away; (*prezzo, valore, pressione*) to go down, fall, decrease; **diminuire d'intensità** to decrease in intensity, subside; **diminuire di volume** (*massa*) to be reduced in volume; **diminuire di peso** (*persona*) to lose weight; (*Fis*) to be reduced in weight.

diminutivo, a [diminu'tivo] AGG, SM diminutive.

diminuzione [diminut'tsjone] SF reduction; (*calo*) decrease; (: *di temperatura, pressione*) fall; **in diminuzione** on the decrease; **temperature in diminuzione** drop in temperatures; **diminuzione della produttività** fall in productivity; **diminuzione di peso** loss of weight.

dimisi *ecc* [di'mizi] VB *vedi* **dimettere**.

dimissionare [dimissjo'nare] VT (*Amm*) to dismiss.

dimissionario, ria, ri, rie [dimissjo'narjo] AGG outgoing.

dimissioni [dimis'sjoni] SFPL resignation *sg*; **dare** *o* **rassegnare le dimissioni** to give/hand in *o* tender one's resignation, resign.

dimora [di'mɔra] SF (*abitazione*) residence; **senza fissa dimora** of no fixed address *o* abode; **estrema dimora** (*euf*) last resting place.

dimorare [dimo'rare] VI (*aus* **avere**) (*anche fig: sentimenti*) to dwell.

dimostrabile [dimos'trabile] AGG demonstrable.

dimostrante [dimos'trante] SM/F (*Pol*) demonstrator.

dimostrare [dimos'trare] ① VT **a** (*verità, funzionamento*) to demonstrate, show; (*colpevolezza, teorema, tesi*) to prove, demonstrate; **ciò dimostra che hai ragione** this proves *o* shows you are right
b (*simpatia, affetto, interesse*) to show, display; **non dimostra la sua età** he doesn't look his age
c (*Pol*) to demonstrate.

② **dimostrarsi** VR **a** (*rivelarsi*) to prove to be; **si è dimostrato coraggioso** he showed courage
b (*apparire*): **dimostrarsi entusiasta/interessato** to show one's enthusiasm/interest.

dimostrativo, a [dimostra'tivo] AGG (*gen, Gramm*) demonstrative; **azione dimostrativa** (*Mil*) demonstration.

dimostratore, trice [dimostra'tore] SM/F (*Comm*) demonstrator.

dimostrazione [dimostrat'tsjone] SF **a** demonstration, proof; **una dimostrazione d'affetto** a show of affection; **una chiara dimostrazione di inefficienza** (*prova*) clear proof of inefficiency **b** (*manifestazione, Mat*) demonstration.

dina ['dina] SF (*Fis*) dyne.

dinamica [di'namika] SF (*gen, Fis*) dynamics *sg*.

dinamicamente [dinamika'mente] AVV dynamically.

dinamicità [dinamitʃi'ta] SF dynamism.

dinamico, a, ci, che [di'namiko] AGG (*fig: persona, vita*) dynamic, dynamical; (*Fis, Mus*) dynamic.

dinamismo [dina'mizmo] SM dynamism.

dinamitardo, a [dinami'tardo] ① AGG: **attentato dinamitardo** dynamite attack.
② SM/F dynamiter.

dinamite [dina'mite] SF dynamite.

dinamo ['dinamo] SF INV dynamo.

dinamometro [dina'mɔmetro] SM dynamometer.

dinanzi [di'nantsi] ① AVV ahead.
② : **dinanzi a** PREP (*di fronte*) in front of; (*al cospetto*) in the presence of, before; **si presentò dinanzi a me** he appeared before me; **dinanzi ad una tale situazione...** faced with such a situation ....

dinastia [dinas'tia] SF dynasty.

dinastico, a, ci, che [di'nastiko] AGG dynastic(al).

dingo, ghi ['dingo] SM dingo.

diniego, ghi [di'njɛgo] SM (*rifiuto*) refusal; (*negazione*) denial; **ha opposto un netto diniego** he refused point-blank; **scuotere la testa in segno di diniego** to shake one's head.

dinoccolato, a [dinokko'lato] AGG lanky; **andatura dinoccolata** slouching walk.

dinosauro [dino'sauro] SM dinosaur.

dintorni [din'torni] SMPL outskirts; **nei dintorni di** in the vicinity *o* neighbourhood of; **Palermo e dintorni** Palermo and the surrounding area.

dintorno [din'torno] AVV (a)round, (round)about.

dio, dei ['dio] SM **a** (*Mitol, fig*) god; **gli dei** the gods; **si crede un dio** he thinks he's wonderful; **canta come un dio** he sings divinely
b (*Rel*): **Dio** God; **Dio padre** God the Father; **un senza Dio** a godless person; **il buon Dio** the good Lord
c (*fraseologia*): **Dio mio!** my goodness!, my God!; **Dio buono** *o* **santo!** for God's sake!; **per Dio!** by God!; **grazie a Dio!** *o* **Dio sia lodato** *o* **ringraziato!** thank God!; **com'è vero Dio** as God is my witness; **Dio sa quando finirà** God knows when it's going to come to an end; **viene giù che Dio la manda** it's raining cats and dogs, it's pouring with rain; **come Dio volle arrivammo** somehow or other we got there; **se Dio vuole...** God willing ...; **(che) Dio ce la mandi buona** let's hope for the best; **Dio ce ne scampi e liberi** God forbid.

diocesi [di'ɔtʃezi] SF INV diocese.

Diocleziano [dioklet'tsjano] SM Diocletian.

diodo ['diodo] SM diode.

Diogene [di'ɔdʒene] SM Diogenes.

dionea [dio'nɛa] SF (*Bot*) Venus's-flytrap, Venus flytrap.

Dioniso [di'ɔniso] SM Dionysus.

diossina [dios'sina] SF dioxin.

diottria [diot'tria] SF (*Fis*) dioptre (*Brit*), diopter (*Am*).

dipanare [dipa'nare] VT (*matassa*) to wind (up *o* into, a ball); (*fig: questione*) to sort out, disentangle.

dipartimentale [dipartimen'tale] AGG (*Amm*) departmental.

dipartimento [diparti'mento] SM (*gen, Univ*) department.

dipartita [dipar'tita] SF (*euf: decesso*) passing (away).

dipendente [dipen'dɛnte] ① AGG **a** : **personale dipendente** employees *pl*
b (*gen*): **dipendente da** (*alcol, droga*) addicted to; **è completamente dipendente da sua madre** he's completely dependent on his mother.
② SM/F employee; **dipendenti** SM/F PL employees, staff *sg o pl*, personnel *pl*.
③ SF (*Gramm: anche:* **(proposizione) dipendente**) subordinate *o* dependent clause.

dipendenza [dipen'dɛntsa] SF **a** dependency; (*economica*) dependence; (*da droga*) addiction; **un farmaco che provoca dipendenza** an addictive drug **b** : **alle dipendenze di** employed by; **ha 10 persone alle sue dipendenze** (*datore di lavoro*) he employs 10 people; (*caporeparto*) he has 10 people under him.

dipendere [di'pɛndere] VI IRREG (*aus* **essere**): **dipendere da a** (*gen*) to depend on; **dipende!** it depends!; **dipende solo da te** it depends entirely on you, it's entirely up to you; **la sua risposta è dipesa dal fatto che era nervosa**

she answered that way because she was irritated
b (*impiegato, filiale*) to be answerable to; **la ditta dipendeva da una compagnia americana** the firm was controlled by an American company
c (*essere mantenuto, soggetto*) to depend (up)on, be dependent on
d (*Gramm*) to be subordinate (to).

dipesi *ecc* [di'pesi] VB vedi **dipendere**.

dipeso, a [di'peso] PP di **dipendere**.

dipingere [di'pindʒere] VB IRREG ☐ VT (*gen, Arte*) to paint; (*fig*) to describe, depict.
☐ **dipingersi** VIP (*tingersi*): **il cielo si dipinse di rosso** the sky turned red; **gli si dipinse sul viso la delusione** (*fig*) his face expressed *o* clearly showed his disappointment.

dipinsi *ecc* [di'pinsi] VB vedi **dipingere**.

dipinto, a [di'pinto] ☐ PP di **dipingere**.
☐ SM (*quadro*) painting.

diploma, i [di'plɔma] SM diploma, certificate ▸ **diploma di laurea** degree (certificate) ▸ **diploma di maturità** school-leaving certificate.

diplomare [diplo'mare] ☐ VT to award a diploma to, graduate (*Am*).
☐ **diplomarsi** VIP to obtain a diploma, graduate (*Am*).

diplomaticamente [diplomatika'mente] AVV diplomatically.

diplomatico, a, ci, che [diplo'matiko] ☐ AGG diplomatic; **rompere le relazioni diplomatiche** to break off diplomatic relations.
☐ SM (*anche fig*) diplomat.

diplomato, a [diplo'mato] ☐ AGG qualified.
☐ SM/F qualified person, holder of a diploma, graduate (*Am*).

diplomazia [diplomat'tsia] SF (*anche fig*) diplomacy; (*corpo diplomatico*) diplomatic corps *sg*; **entrare in diplomazia** to enter *o* join the diplomatic service.

dipolo [di'pɔlo] SM (*Fis*) dipole; **antenna a dipolo** (*Radiotecnica*) dipole aerial.

diportista, i, e [dipor'tista] SM/F pleasure-boat owner.

diporto [di'pɔrto] SM: **imbarcazione da diporto** pleasure craft *inv*.

diradare [dira'dare] ☐ VT (*vegetazione*) to thin (out); (*nebbia, gas*) to clear, dissipate; **diradare le visite** to call less frequently.
☐ VI (*aus* **essere**), **diradarsi** VIP (*vegetazione*) to thin out; (*folla*) to disperse; (*nebbia*) to clear (up); (*visite*) to become less frequent.

diramare [dira'mare] ☐ VT (*comunicato, ordine*) to issue; (*notizia*) to circulate; **diramare gli inviti** (*spedire*) to send out invitations.
☐ **diramarsi** VIP **a** (*sentiero, strada*) to branch off; (*vene*) to spread; (*fusti*) to branch **b** (*diffondersi*): **la notizia si è diramata** the news spread.

diramazione [diramat'tsjone] SF **a** (*diffusione*: *di ordine*) issuing; (: *di notizia*) circulation **b** (*biforcazione*) fork **c** (*ramificazione*) branch.

---

dire ['dire]
☐ VT IRREG
a (*gen*) to say;
▷ **dire qc** *a* **qn** to say sth to sb, tell sb sth
▷ **disse** *che* **accettava** he said he would accept
▷ **dicono** *o* **si dice** *che*... (*impersonale*) they say that ..., it is said that ...

▷ **dicono** *o* **si dice** *che* **siano ricchissimi** they are said to be very rich, people say they are very rich
▷ *come* **dicono gli inglesi** as the English say
▷ *come* **si dice in inglese?** how do you say it in English?
▷ *come* **si dice 'penna' in inglese?** what is the English for 'penna'?
▷ *lascialo* **dire** (*esprimersi*) let him have his say; (*ignoralo*) just ignore him, don't take any notice of him
▷ **non disse una** *parola* he didn't say *o* utter a word
▷ **dice sempre quello che** *pensa* he always says what he thinks
▷ **di' liberamente ciò che** *pensi* feel free to say what you think
▷ **dicano** *pure* **quello che vogliono!** let them say what they like!
▷ *sa* **quello che dice** he knows what he's talking about
▷ **Roberta...** — *sì*, **dimmi** Roberta ... — yes, what is it?
▷ **dire di** *sì/no* to say yes/no
▷ **"non ci vado" - disse** "I'm not going" - he said
▷ **dica?** (*in negozio*) what can I do for you?
b (*raccontare, riferire, indicare*) to tell;
▷ **dire** *a* **qn qc** to tell sb sth
▷ **dire a qn di** *fare* **qc** to tell sb to do sth
▷ *mi* **si dice che...** I am told that ...
▷ *può* **dirmi da che parte devo andare?** can you tell me which way to go?
▷ **mi ha detto** *tutto* he told me everything
c (*significare*) to mean;
▷ **ti dice** *niente* **questo nome?** does this name mean anything to you?, does this name ring a bell?
▷ **quel libro non mi ha detto** *niente* that book didn't appeal to me
▷ **come** *sarebbe* **a dire?** what do you mean?
d (*recitare*) to say, recite;
▷ **dire a** *memoria* to recite by heart
▷ **dire (la)** *Messa* to say Mass
▷ **dire le** *preghiere* to say one's prayers
e (*pensare*) to think;
▷ *chi* **l'avrebbe mai detto!** who would have thought it!
▷ **cosa** *o* **che** *ne* **dici di questa musica?** what do you think of this music?
▷ **che** *ne* **diresti di andarcene?** let's make a move, shall we?
▷ *si* **direbbe che non menta** (*impersonale*) you would think he was telling the truth
f (*ammettere*) to say, admit;
▷ *devi* **dire che ha ragione** you must admit that he's right
g: *far* **dire qc a qn** to make sb say sth;
▷ **non me lo** *farò* **dire due volte** I won't need to be asked twice
▷ **gliel'ho** *fatto* **dire dalla segretaria** I had his secretary tell him about it, I got his secretary to tell him about it
▷ *mandare* **a dire qc a qn** (*riferire*) to let sb know sth
h: **dirsi** to say to o.s.; (*definirsi*) to call o.s., claim to be; (*uso reciproco*) to say to each other
▷ **"coraggio" - si disse** "come on" - he said to himself
▷ *si* **dicono esperti** they claim to be experts
▷ *si* **dissero addio** they said goodbye (to each other)

▷*si son detti qualcosa all'orecchio* they whispered something to one another
⚀ (*fraseologia*):
▷*per così* dire so to speak
▷*sono stanco — e a me lo dici!* I'm tired — you're telling ME YOU'RE tired!
▷*non c'è che* dire there's no doubt about it
▷*avere a che* dire con qn to have words with sb
▷*e chi mi dice che è vero?* and who's to say that's true?
▷*dimmi con chi vai e ti dirò chi sei* (*Proverbio*) you can tell what somebody is like by the company they keep
▷*trovare da dire su qc/qn* to find fault with sth/sb
▷*l'idea mi stuzzica, non dico di no* the idea is tempting, I don't deny it
▷*non ti dico la scena!* you can't imagine the scene!
▷*lo conosco per sentito* dire I've heard about him
▷*a dir poco* to say the least
▷*dico sul serio* I'm serious
▷*il che è tutto dire* need I say more?
▷*a dire il vero...* to tell the truth ... .
⚁ SM
▷*tra il dire e il fare c'è di mezzo il mare* (*Proverbio*) it's easier said than done
▷*è un bel dire il suo* what he says is all very well.

diressi *ecc* [di'rɛssi] VB *vedi* **dirigere.**
diretta [di'rɛtta] SF: **in diretta** (*trasmettere*) live.
direttamente [diretta'mente] AVV (*immediatamente*) directly, straight; (*personalmente*) directly; (*senza intermediari*) direct, straight; **andiamo direttamente a casa** let's go straight home; **non mi riguarda direttamente** it doesn't directly concern me; **parla direttamente col preside** speak to the headmaster direct.
direttissima [diret'tissima] SF (*Dir*): **processo per direttissima** summary trial.
direttissimo [diret'tissimo] SM (*Ferr*) fast (through) train.
direttiva [diret'tiva] SF directive, instruction; **seguire le direttive del partito** to stick to the party line.
direttivo, a [diret'tivo] ⚀ AGG (*Pol, Amm*) executive; (*Comm*) managerial, executive.
⚁ SM leadership, leaders *pl.*
diretto, a [di'rɛtto] ⚀ PP di **dirigere.**
⚁ AGG (*gen, Gramm*) direct; **è il suo diretto superiore** he's his immediate superior; **c'è una diretta dipendenza tra i due fatti** the two events are directly connected.
⚂ SM a (*Ferr: anche:* **treno diretto**) through train b (*Boxe*) jab.
direttore [diret'tore] SM (*gen*) director; (*responsabile: di banca, fabbrica*) manager ▶**direttore artistico** (*Teatro, Mus*) artistic director ▶**direttore di carcere** prison governor (*Brit*) o warden (*Am*) ▶**direttore didattico** (primary school) headmaster (*Brit*), (elementary school) principal (*Am*) ▶**direttore di macchina** (*Naut*) chief engineer ▶**direttore d'orchestra** conductor ▶**direttore del personale** personnel manager ▶**direttore di produzione** (*Cine*) producer; (*Industria*) production manager ▶**direttore responsabile** (*Stampa*) editor (in chief) ▶**direttore sportivo** team manager ▶**direttore tecnico** (*Sport*) trainer, coach.
direttrice¹ [diret'tritʃe] SF (*vedi sm*); director; manager

▶**direttrice didattica** (primary school) headmistress (*Brit*), (elementary school) principal (*Am*).
direttrice² [diret'tritʃe] SF a (*Geom*) directrix b (*fig: di partito*) policy, line.
direzionale [direttsjo'nale] AGG directional.
direzione [diret'tsjone] SF a (*senso: anche fig*) direction; **in direzione di** towards, in the direction of; **in che direzione vai?** which way are you going?; **prendere la direzione giusta/sbagliata** to go the right/wrong way; **sbagliare direzione** to go the wrong way
b (*conduzione: gen*) running; (: *di società*) management; (: *di giornale*) editorship; (: *di partito*) leadership; **assumere la direzione delle operazioni** to take charge of operations
c : **la direzione** (*direttori*) the management; (*ufficio*) director's (o manager's o editor's o headmaster's *ecc*) office.
dirigente [diri'dʒɛnte] ⚀ AGG managerial; **classe dirigente** ruling class. ⚁ SM/F executive.
dirigenza [diri'dʒɛntsa] SF (*di ditta*) management; (*di partito*) leadership.
dirigenziale [diridʒen'tsjale] AGG managerial.
dirigere [di'ridʒere] VB IRREG ⚀ VT a (*condurre*) to run; (*ditta*) to manage; (*giornale*) to edit; (*partito, inchiesta*) to lead; (*operazioni, traffico*) to direct; (*orchestra*) to conduct
b (*arma*): **dirigere verso** o **contro** to point at; **dirigere contro** (*critiche*) to direct at, aim at; **dirigere l'attenzione su qc/qn** to turn one's attention to sth/sb; **dirigere i propri passi verso** to make one's way towards; **dirigere lo sguardo verso** to look towards; **a chi era diretta quell'osservazione?** who was that remark intended for?; **era diretto verso casa** he was heading home; **dove sei diretto?** where are you heading?; **il treno era diretto a Pavia** the train was en route for Pavia; **eravamo diretti a nord** we were heading north; **mi hanno diretto qui** they sent me here
c (*pacco, lettera*) to address.
⚁ **dirigersi** VR (*prendere una direzione*): **dirigersi a** o **verso** (*luogo*) to make one's way towards, make o head for; **dirigersi verso** (*persona*) to come/go towards; **l'aereo si dirigeva a nord** the plane was on its way o flying north; **si diresse a** o **verso casa** he headed home, he set off home; **dove si è diretto?** which way did he go?
dirigibile [diri'dʒibile] SM airship.
dirimpetto [dirim'pɛtto] ⚀ AVV opposite.
⚁ : **dirimpetto a** PREP opposite; **era seduto dirimpetto a me** he was sitting opposite me.
⚂ AGG INV opposite; **la casa dirimpetto** the house opposite.
diritto¹, a [di'ritto] ⚀ AGG a (*strada, palo, linea*) straight; (*persona: eretto*) erect, upright; (*fig: onesto*) upright, honest, straight; **stare su diritto** to stand up straight; **è andata diritta dal direttore** she went straight to the manager
b (*Maglia*): **punto diritto** plain (stitch).
⚁ AVV straight, directly; **verrò diritto al punto** I'll come straight to the point; **vai sempre diritto fino al semaforo** keep straight on till you get to the traffic lights.
⚂ SM a (*di vestito*) right side
b (*Tennis*) forehand
c (*Maglia*) plain stitch, knit stitch.
diritto² [di'ritto] SM a (*prerogativa*) right; **ti spetta di diritto** it is yours by right; **a buon diritto** quite rightly;

avere il **diritto di fare** qc to have the right to do sth; **aver diritto a** qc to be entitled to sth; **ho il diritto di sapere** I have a right to know ▶**diritto d'asilo** right of asylum ▶**diritto di voto** (*elettore*) right to vote; (*azionista*) voting right

b (*Dir*): **il diritto** (the) law

c: **diritti** SMPL (*tasse*) fees, dues ▶**diritti d'autore** royalties ▶**diritti di magazzinaggio** demurrage *sg* ▶**diritti di segreteria** administrative charges.

dirittura [dirit'tura] SF **a** (*Sport*): **dirittura (d'arrivo)** (home *o* final) straight **b** (*fig*: *rettitudine*) rectitude.

diroccato, a [dirok'kato] AGG (*semidistrutto*) in ruins; (*cadente*) dilapidated, tumbledown.

dirompente [dirom'pɛnte] AGG (*anche fig*) explosive; **bomba dirompente** fragmentation bomb.

dirottamente [dirotta'mente] AVV: **piangere dirottamente** to cry one's heart out; **pioveva dirottamente** it was raining very heavily, it was pouring (with rain).

dirottamento [dirotta'mento] SM: **dirottamento (aereo)** hijacking, hijack.

dirottare [dirot'tare] **1** VT (*aereo*: *sotto minaccia*) to hijack; (*traffico*) to divert; (*nave, aereo*) to change the course of.

2 VI (*aus* avere) (*Naut*) to change course.

dirottatore, trice [dirotta'tore] SM/F hijacker.

dirotto, a [di'rotto] AGG: **scoppiare in un pianto dirotto** to burst into tears; **piove a dirotto** it's pouring (with rain), it's raining cats and dogs.

dirozzare [dirod'dzare] VT (*pietra, marmo*) to rough-hew; (*fig*: *stile, maniere*) to polish, refine; (: *persona*) to smooth the rough edges off.

dirupo [di'rupo] SM precipice, crag.

diruttore [dirut'tore] SM (*Aer*) spoiler.

disabitato, a [dizabi'tato] AGG uninhabited.

disabituare [dizabitu'are] **1** VT: **disabituare qn a qc/a fare qc** to break sb of a habit/the habit of doing sth.

2 **disabituarsi** VIP: **disabituarsi a qc/a fare qc** to get out of the habit of sth/of doing sth.

disaccordo [dizak'kɔrdo] SM **a** disagreement; **essere in disaccordo** to disagree **b** (*Mus*) discord.

disadattamento [dizadatta'mento] SM maladjustment.

disadattato, a [dizadat'tato] **1** AGG maladjusted.

2 SM/F maladjusted person, misfit.

disadorno, a [diza'dorno] AGG plain, unadorned.

disaffezione [dizaffet'tsjone] SF disaffection.

disagevole [diza'dʒevole] AGG (*scomodo*) uncomfortable; (*difficile*) difficult.

disagevolmente [dizadʒevol'mente] AVV uncomfortably.

disagiatamente [dizadʒata'mente] AVV (*vivere*) in hardship, in poverty.

disagiato, a [diza'dʒato] AGG (*povero*) poor, needy; **vivere in condizioni disagiate** to live in poverty.

disagio, gi [di'zadʒo] SM **a** (*scomodità*) discomfort; (*difficoltà*) difficulty **b** (*imbarazzo*) awkwardness; **essere** *o* **trovarsi a disagio** to be ill-at-ease *o* uncomfortable; **mettere qn a disagio** to make sb feel ill-at-ease *o* uncomfortable.

disalberare [dizalbe'rare] VT (*Naut*) to dismast.

disamina [di'zamina] SF close examination; **sottoporre a disamina** to put under close scrutiny.

disamorarsi [dizamo'rarsi] VIP: **disamorarsi di** (*persona*) to fall out of love with, cease to love; (*studio, lavoro*) to lose interest in.

disappannare [dizappan'nare] VT to demist.

disappetenza [dizappe'tɛntsa] SF lack of appetite.

disapprovare [dizappro'vare] VT: **disapprovare (qc)** to disapprove (of sth).

disapprovazione [dizapprovat'tsjone] SF disapproval; **un'occhiata di disapprovazione** a disapproving glance; **con aria di disapprovazione** disapprovingly.

disappunto [dizap'punto] SM (*delusione*) disappointment; (*fastidio*) annoyance; **con mio disappunto** to my disappointment (*o* annoyance).

disarcionare [dizartʃo'nare] VT to unseat.

disarmante [dizar'mante] AGG (*sorriso*) disarming; (*calma*) soothing.

disarmare [dizar'mare] **1** VT (*Mil, fig*) to disarm; (*Naut*) to lay up.

2 VI (*aus* avere) (*Mil*) to disarm; (*fig*) to surrender, give in.

disarmo [di'zarmo] SM (*Mil*) disarmament; (*di nave*) laying up.

disarmonia [dizarmo'nia] SF disharmony.

disarticolare [dizartiko'lare] VT to dislocate.

disarticolato, a [dizartiko'lato] AGG (*suoni, discorso*) disjointed.

disastrato, a [dizas'trato] **1** AGG devastated; **zona disastrata** disaster area.

2 SM/F (*di alluvione, terremoto*) victim.

disastro [di'zastro] SM (*anche fig*) disaster; **i disastri dovuti alla grandine** the damage caused by the hailstorm.

disastrosamente [dizastrosa'mente] AVV disastrously.

disastroso, a [dizas'troso] AGG (*gen*) disastrous; **in condizioni disastrose** in a terrible *o* appalling state.

disattento, a [dizat'tɛnto] AGG careless, inattentive.

disattenzione [dizatten'tsjone] SF carelessness, lack of attention.

disattivare [dizatti'vare] VT (*bomba*) to de-activate, defuse.

disavanzo [diza'vantso] SM (*Econ*) deficit.

disavventura [dizavven'tura] SF misadventure, mishap.

disbrigo, ghi [diz'brigo] SM: **disbrigo (di)** (*corrispondenza, pratiche*) dealing (with).

discapito [dis'kapito] SM: **a discapito di** to the detriment of; **lo fai a tuo discapito** if you do this it will be to your disadvantage.

discarica, che [dis'karika] SF (*di rifiuti*) rubbish tip *o* dump.

discendente [diʃʃen'dɛnte] **1** AGG descending.

2 SM/F descendant.

discendenza [diʃʃen'dɛntsa] SF **a** (*origine*) descent, lineage; **di nobile/umile discendenza** of noble/humble descent **b** (*discendenti*) descendants *pl*.

discendere [diʃ'ʃendere] VB IRREG **1** VI (*aus* essere) **a** (*scendere*) to come (*o* go) down, descend; **discendere da** (*treno*) to get off; (*macchina*) to get out of; (*tetto*) to get down from; **discendere da cavallo** to dismount, get off one's horse; **le tenebre discesero sulla città** darkness descended on the town

b (*provenire*): **discendere da** to be descended from, come from.

2 VT (*scale*) to come (*o* go) down, descend.

discepolo, a [diʃ'ʃepolo] SM/F (*Rel*) disciple; (*seguace*) follower, disciple; (*scolaro*) pupil.

discernere [diʃ'ʃɛrnere] VT DIF (*distinguere*: *anche fig*) to discern; **discernere il bene dal male** to distinguish good

from evil.

discernimento [diʃʃerni'mento] SM discernment.

discesa [diʃ'ʃesa] SF a (*atto*) descent; **la discesa dei barbari** the barbarian invasion; **fare una discesa in corda doppia** (*Alpinismo*) to abseil ▶ **discesa libera** (*Sci*) downhill (race) b (*pendio*) slope, downhill stretch; **in discesa** downhill *attr*.

discesista, i, e [diʃʃe'sista] SM/F (*Sci*) downhill skier.

disceso, a [diʃ'ʃeso] PP di **discendere.**

dischetto [dis'ketto] SM a (*Inform*) diskette, floppy disk b (*Calcio*) penalty spot.

dischiudere [dis'kjudere] VT IRREG (*aprire*) to open; (*fig: rivelare*) to disclose, reveal.

dischiusi *ecc* [dis'kjusi] VB vedi **dischiudere.**

dischiuso, a [dis'kjuso] PP di **dischiudere.**

discinto, a [diʃ'ʃinto] AGG half-undressed.

disciogliere [diʃ'ʃɔʎʎere] VB IRREG 1 VT a (*sciogliere: medicina*) to dissolve; (*liquefare*) to melt.
2 **disciogliersi** VIP (*vedi vt*) to dissolve; to melt.

disciolto, a [diʃ'ʃɔlto] PP di **disciogliere.**

disciplina [diʃʃi'plina] SF (*regola*) discipline; (*materia*) discipline, subject.

disciplinare[1] [diʃʃipli'nare] VT to discipline.

disciplinare[2] [diʃʃipli'nare] AGG (*provvedimento*) disciplinary.

disciplinatamente [diʃʃiplinata'mente] AVV in a disciplined way.

disciplinato, a [diʃʃipli'nato] AGG disciplined.

disc-jockey ['disk 'dʒɔki] SM/F INV disc jockey.

disco, schi ['disko] SM a (*gen, Anat*) disc (*Brit*), disk (*Am*); (*Inform*) disk; (*Sport*) discus b (*Mus*) record, disc; **cambia disco!** (*fam*) change the subject! ▶ **disco magnetico** (*Inform*) magnetic disk ▶ **disco orario** (*Aut*) parking disc ▶ **disco rigido** o **fisso** (*Inform*) hard o fixed disk ▶ **disco volante** flying saucer.

discofilo, a [dis'kɔfilo] SM/F record collector.

discografia [diskogra'fia] SF a (*tecnica*) recording, record-making b (*industria*) record industry c (*elenco*) discography.

discografico, a, ci, che [disko'grafiko] 1 AGG record *attr*, recording *attr*; **casa discografica** record(ing) company.
2 SM record producer.

discoide [dis'kɔide] AGG disc-shaped.

discolo, a ['diskolo] 1 AGG (*bambino*) undisciplined, unruly.
2 SM/F rascal.

discolpa [dis'kolpa] SF defence, excuse; **a discolpa di qn** in sb's defence.

discolpare [diskol'pare] 1 VT: **discolpare qn** to prove sb's innocence, clear sb (of blame).
2 **discolparsi** VR to clear o.s., prove one's innocence; (*giustificarsi*) to excuse o.s.

disconoscere [disko'noʃʃere] VT IRREG (*meriti*) to ignore, disregard; **disconoscere la paternità di un figlio** (*Dir*) to deny paternity.

disconosciuto, a [diskonoʃ'ʃuto] PP di **disconoscere.**

discontinuamente [diskontinua'mente] AVV sporadically.

discontinuità [diskontinui'ta] SF INV (*vedi agg*) discontinuity; irregularity.

discontinuo, a [diskon'tinuo] AGG (*linea*) discontinuous, broken; (*rendimento, stile*) irregular, erratic; (*interesse*): **essere discontinuo nel lavoro** to lack application.

discordante [diskor'dante] AGG (*gen, suoni*) discordant; (*testimonianze, opinioni*) conflicting; (*colori*) clashing.

discordanza [diskor'dantsa] SF (*gen*) discordance, dissonance; (*Mus*) discord; **discordanza di opinioni** difference of opinion; **ci sono discordanze tra le due versioni** the two versions conflict.

discordare [diskor'dare] VI (*aus* avere) a : **discordare (da)** (*opinioni*) to conflict (with) b (*stonare: suono, colore*) to clash (with).

discorde [dis'kɔrde] AGG conflicting; **essere di parere discorde** to be of a different opinion.

discordia [dis'kɔrdja] SF discord, dissension; **essere in discordia con** to be at variance with.

discorrere [dis'korrere] VI IRREG (*aus* avere): **discorrere (di)** to talk (about), chat (about).

discorsività [diskorsivi'ta] SF (*di stile*) conversational nature.

discorsivo, a [diskor'sivo] AGG (*stile*) conversational, colloquial.

discorso [dis'korso] 1 PP di **discorrere.**
2 SM a (*gen*) speech; **fare un discorso** (*in pubblico*) to make a speech; **gli ho fatto un bel discorso ieri** (*iro*) I gave him a piece of my mind yesterday; **cambiare discorso** to change the subject; **è un altro discorso** that's another matter; **non son discorsi da fare!** what sort of attitude is that?
b (*Ling*): **analisi del discorso** discourse analysis; **discorso diretto/indiretto** direct/indirect o reported speech.

discostare [diskos'tare] 1 VT (*letter*) to move away.
2 **discostarsi** VR, VIP (*anche fig*): **discostarsi da** to move away from.

discosto, a [dis'kɔsto] 1 AGG (*letter*): **discosto da** remote from; **tenersi discosto da** to stay away from.
2 AVV at a distance, at some distance, far away.

discoteca, che [disko'tɛka] SF a (*sala da ballo*) disco b (*raccolta*) record library c (*negozio*) record shop.

discredito [dis'kredito] SM discredit, disrepute; **gettare il discredito su** to bring discredit on; **cadere in discredito** to fall into disrepute; **tornare a discredito di qn** to redound to sb's discredit (*frm*).

discrepanza [diskre'pantsa] SF discrepancy.

discretamente [diskreta'mente] AVV (*con discrezione*) discreetly, tactfully; (*sufficientemente*) fairly.

discreto, a [dis'kreto] AGG a (*abbastanza buono*) reasonable, fair b (*non forte: tinta, trucco*) subtle c (*persona: riservato*) discreet; **fu discreto da parte sua andarsene** it was tactful of him to leave.

discrezionale [diskrettsjo'nale] AGG discretionary.

discrezione [diskret'tsjone] SF a (*riservatezza*) discretion; **ti prego la massima discrezione** I'm relying on your absolute discretion b (*arbitrio*): **a propria discrezione** at one's own discretion c (*discernimento*): **l'età della discrezione** the age of discretion.

discriminante [diskrimi'nante] 1 AGG (*fattore, elemento*) decisive.
2 SF (*Dir*) extenuating circumstance.
3 SM (*Mat*) discriminant.

discriminare [diskrimi'nare] VT to discriminate.

discriminazione [diskriminat'tsjone] SF discrimination.

discussi *ecc* [dis'kussi] VB vedi **discutere.**

discussione [diskus'sjone] SF (*gen*) discussion; (*lite*) argument; **fare una discussione** to have a discussion; **avere una discussione** to have an argument; **ho avuto una discussione col capo** (*lite*) I had words with my boss; **mettere in discussione** to bring into question; **questo è**

fuori discussione this is out of the question; la sua onestà è fuori discussione his honesty is beyond question; fila a letto, senza discussioni! go to bed and don't argue!

discusso, a [dis'kusso] ① PP di **discutere.**
② AGG controversial.

discutere [dis'kutere] VB IRREG ① VT (*dibattere*) to discuss, debate; (*contestare*) to question, dispute; è da discutere (*se ne parlerà ancora*) it remains to be discussed; (*è in dubbio*) it's questionable; **discutere una proposta di legge** to debate a (parliamentary) bill; **discutere la tesi (di laurea)** to present *o* submit one's (degree) thesis.
② VI (*aus* avere) a (*conversare*): **discutere (di)** to talk (about), to discuss
b (*litigare*) to argue.

discutibile [disku'tibile] AGG questionable.
discutibilità [diskutibili'ta] SF questionable nature.
discutibilmente [diskutibil'mente] AVV questionably.
disdegnare [dizdeɲ'ɲare] VT to disdain, to scorn.
disdegno [diz'deɲɲo] SM disdain, contempt, scorn.
disdegnosamente [dizdeɲɲosa'mente] AVV disdainfully, scornfully, contemptuously.
disdegnoso, a [dizdeɲ'ɲoso] AGG (*letter*) disdainful, scornful, contemptuous.
disdetta [diz'detta] SF a : **dare la disdetta di** (*contratto*) to cancel; **dare la disdetta di un contratto d'affitto** (*locatario*) to give notice; (*locatore*) to give notice (to quit) b (*sfortuna*): **per disdetta** unfortunately; **che disdetta!** hard luck!
disdetto, a [dis'detto] PP di **disdire.**
disdicevole [dizdi'tʃevole] AGG improper, unseemly.
disdicevolmente [dizditʃevol'mente] AVV in an unseemly fashion.
disdire [diz'dire] VT IRREG (*prenotazione, appuntamento*) to cancel; **disdire un contratto d'affitto** (*locatario*) to give notice; (*locatore*) to give notice (to quit).
diseducare [dizedu'kare] VT to have a negative influence on.
disegnare [diseɲ'ɲare] VT a (*gen*) to draw; (*a contorno*) to outline; (*fig: descrivere*) to describe, portray b (*progettare: mobile, casa*) to design.
disegnatore, trice [diseɲɲa'tore] SM/F (*tecnico*) draughtsman/draughtwoman; (*progettista*) designer.
disegno [di'seɲɲo] SM a drawing; (*schizzo*) sketch; **disegno a matita** pencil drawing; **disegno dal vero** from life drawing b (*su carta, stoffa*) design, pattern c (*fig: schema*) outline, plan; (: *progetto*) plan, project ▸ **disegno di legge** (*Dir*) bill.
disequazione [dizekwat'tsjone] SF (*Mat*) inequality.
diserbante [dizer'bante] ① AGG herbicidal.
② SM herbicide, weed-killer.
diserbare [dizer'bare] VT to weed.
diserbo [di'zɛrbo] SM weeding.
diseredare [dizere'dare] VT to disinherit.
diseredato, a [dizere'dato] ① AGG disinherited; (*fig*) deprived.
② SM/F disinherited person; (*fig*) deprived person.
disertare [dizer'tare] ① VT to desert, abandon, leave; **ieri ho disertato la riunione** yesterday I gave the meeting a miss.
② VI (*aus* avere) (*Mil, fig*): **disertare (da qc)** to desert (sth).
disertore [dizer'tore] SM (*Mil, fig*) deserter.
diserzione [dizer'tsjone] SF (*Mil, fig*) desertion.

disfacimento [disfatʃi'mento] SM (*di cadavere*) decay; (*fig: di istituzione, impero, società*) decline, decay; **in disfacimento** in decay.
disfare [dis'fare] VB IRREG ① VT a (*gen*) to undo; (*nodo*) to untie, undo; (*sciogliere*) to melt; (*meccanismo*) to take to pieces; **disfare il letto** to strip the bed; **disfare le valigie** to unpack (one's cases)
b (*distruggere*) to destroy.
② **disfarsi** VR: **disfarsi di** (*liberarsi*) to get rid of.
③ **disfarsi** VIP a (*nodo, pacco*) to come undone; (*neve*) to melt
b (*andare a pezzi*) to fall to pieces.
disfatta [dis'fatta] SF (*anche fig*) (utter) defeat.
disfattismo [disfat'tizmo] SM defeatism.
disfattista, i, e [disfat'tista] SM/F defeatist.
disfatto, a [dis'fatto] ① PP di **disfare.**
② AGG (*gen*) undone, untied; (*letto*) unmade.
disfida [dis'fida] SF (*letter, sfida*) challenge; (*duello*) duel.
disfunzione [disfun'tsjone] SF (*Med*) dysfunction ▸ **disfunzione cardiaca** heart trouble.
disgelare [dizdʒe'lare] VT, VI (*aus* essere), VB IMPERS, **disgelarsi** VIP to thaw.
disgelo [diz'dʒɛlo] SM thaw.
disgiungere [diz'dʒundʒere] VT IRREG to separate.
disgiuntivo, a [dizdʒun'tivo] AGG (*Gramm*) disjunctive.
disgiunto, a [dis'dʒunto] PP di **disgiungere.**
disgrazia [diz'grattsja] SF a (*sventura*) bad luck, misfortune; **per disgrazia** unfortunately b (*incidente*) accident; (*calamità*) disaster c (*sfavore*) disgrace; **cadere in disgrazia** to fall into disgrace.
disgraziatamente [dizgrattsjata'mente] AVV unfortunately.
disgraziato, a [dizgrat'tsjato] ① AGG (*persona: povero*) poor, wretched; (: *sfortunato*) unfortunate, unlucky; (: *pegg: sciagurato*) good-for-nothing; (*periodo, attività, impresa*) ill-fated.
② SM/F (*povero*) poor wretch; (*sciagurato*) rascal, rogue, scoundrel.
disgregamento [dizgrega'mento] SM disintegration; (*fig*) break-up.
disgregare [dizgre'gare] ① VT to cause to disintegrate, break up; (*fig: partito, famiglia*) to break up.
② **disgregarsi** VIP to disintegrate, break up; (*fig*) to break up.
disgregazione [dizgregat'tsjone] SF disintegration; (*fig*) break-up.
disguido [diz'gwido] SM hitch ▸ **disguido postale** error in postal delivery.
disgustare [dizgus'tare] ① VT to disgust, sicken, make sick.
② **disgustarsi** VIP: **disgustarsi di** to be disgusted by, be sickened by.
disgusto [diz'gusto] SM (*anche fig*) disgust.
disgustosamente [dizgustosa'mente] AVV disgustingly.
disgustoso, a [dizgus'toso] AGG disgusting.
disidratante [dizidra'tante] ① AGG dehydrating.
② SM (*Chim*) dehydrating agent.
disidratare [dizidra'tare] VT to dehydrate.
disidratato, a [dizidra'tato] AGG dehydrated.
disidratazione [dizidratat'tsjone] SF dehydration.
disilludere [dizil'ludere] VB IRREG ① VT to disillusion, disenchant.
② **disilludersi** VIP to be disillusioned, be disenchanted.
disillusione [dizillu'zjone] SF disillusion, disenchant-

ment.

disilluso, a [dizil'luzo] ① PP di **disilludere**.
② AGG disillusioned, disenchanted.
③ SM/F disillusioned *o* disenchanted person.

disimballare [dizimbal'lare] VT (*merci*) to unpack.

disimparare [dizimpa'rare] VT to forget; **ho disimparato il francese** I've forgotten my French.

disimpegnare [dizimpeɲ'ɲare] ① VT **a** (*persona*: *da obblighi*): **disimpegnare da** to release (from); (*àncora*) to clear **b** (*oggetto in pegno*) to redeem, get out of pawn.
② **disimpegnarsi** VR: **disimpegnarsi da** (*obblighi*) to release o.s. from, free o.s. from.

disincagliare [dizinkaʎ'ʎare] ① VT (*barca*) to refloat.
② **disincagliarsi** VIP to get afloat again.

disincantare [dizinkan'tare] VT to disenchant.

disincantato, a [dizinkan'tato] AGG disenchanted, disillusioned.

disincentivare [dizintʃenti'vare] VT to discourage.

disincrostare [dizinkros'tare] VT to descale.

disinfestante [dizinfes'tante] ① AGG disinfesting.
② SM pesticide.

disinfestare [dizinfes'tare] VT to disinfest.

disinfestazione [dizinfestat'tsjone] SF disinfestation.

disinfettante [dizinfet'tante] AGG, SM disinfectant.

disinfettare [dizinfet'tare] VT to disinfect.

disinfezione [dizinfet'tsjone] SF disinfection.

disinformazione [dizinformat'tsjone] SF misinformation.

disingannare [dizingan'nare] VT to disillusion.

disinganno [dizin'ganno] SM disillusion.

disinibito, a [dizini'bito] AGG uninhibited.

disinnescare [dizinnes'kare] VT to defuse.

disinnestare [dizinnes'tare] VT (*marcia*) to disengage.

disinquinare [dizinkwi'nare] VT to free from pollution.

disinserire [dizinse'rire] VT (*Elettr*) to disconnect.

disintasare [dizinta'sare] VT (*tubo*) to unblock, clear.

disintegrare [dizinte'grare] ① VT (*gen*) to cause to disintegrate; (*edificio*) to shatter; (*fig: opposizione, avversari*) to annihilate.
② **disintegrarsi** VIP (*anche fig*) to disintegrate.

disintegrazione [dizintegrat'tsjone] SF disintegration.

disinteressare [dizinteres'sare] ① VT: **disinteressare qn a qc** to cause sb to lose interest in sth. ② **disinteressarsi** VIP: **disinteressarsi di** to take no interest in.

disinteressatamente [dizinteressata'mente] AVV disinterestedly.

disinteressato, a [dizinteres'sato] AGG disinterested.

disinteresse [dizinte'rɛsse] SM **a** (*indifferenza*) disinterest, indifference **b** (*generosità*) disinterestedness, unselfishness.

disintossicante [dizintossi'kante] AGG detoxifying.

disintossicare [dizintossi'kare] ① VT to detoxify; (*alcolizzato, drogato*) to treat for alcoholism (*o* drug addiction); **disintossicare l'organismo** to clear out one's system.
② **disintossicarsi** VR to clear out one's system; (*alcolizzato, drogato*) to be treated for alcoholism (*o* drug addiction).

disintossicazione [dizintossikat'tsjone] SF (*vedi vb*) detoxification; treatment for alcoholism (*o* drug addiction).

disinvoltamente [dizinvolta'mente] AVV (*vedi agg*) confidently; casually.

disinvolto, a [dizin'vɔlto] AGG (*sicuro*) confident; (*spigliato*) casual, nonchalant, free and easy; **con fare disinvolto** nonchalantly.

disinvoltura [dizinvol'tura] SF (*vedi agg*) confidence; casualness, nonchalance, ease; **con disinvoltura** with ease, easily.

dislessia [dizles'sia] SF dyslexia.

dislessico, a, ci, che [dis'lɛssiko] AGG, SM/F dyslexic.

dislivello [dizli'vɛllo] SM difference in height; (*fig*) gap.

dislocamento [dizloka'mento] SM (*Naut*) displacement.

dislocare [dizlo'kare] VT **a** (*Mil, Amm*) to post **b** (*Naut*) to displace.

dislocazione [dizlokat'tsjone] SF **a** (*di truppe*) stationing **b** (*Med*) dislocation.

dismisura [dizmi'sura] SF: **a dismisura** excessively.

disobbedire ecc [dizobbe'dire] = **disubbidire** ecc.

disobbligare [dizobbli'gare] ① VT: **disobbligare (da)** to free *o* release from an obligation.
② **disobbligarsi** VR (*sdebitarsi*): **disobbligarsi con qn per qc** to repay sb for sth.

disoccupato, a [dizokku'pato] ① AGG unemployed, out of work.
② SM/F unemployed person; **i disoccupati** the unemployed, people out of work.

disoccupazione [dizokkupat'tsjone] SF unemployment.

disonestà [dizones'ta] SF INV dishonesty; **è una disonestà** it's dishonest.

disonestamente [dizonesta'mente] AVV dishonestly.

disonesto, a [dizo'nɛsto] ① AGG dishonest.
② SM/F dishonest person.

disonorare [dizono'rare] ① VT (*nome, famiglia*) to disgrace, bring disgrace upon, to dishonour (*Brit*), dishonor (*Am*).
② **disonorarsi** VR to bring disgrace on o.s., bring dishono(u)r on o.s.

disonorato, a [dizono'rato] AGG (*famiglia*) dishono(u)red, disgraced.

disonore [dizo'nore] SM disgrace, dishonour (*Brit*), dishonor (*Am*); **essere il disonore della propria famiglia** to be a disgrace to one's family.

disonorevole [dizono'revole] AGG dishono(u)rable.

disonorevolmente [dizonorevol'mente] AVV dishono(u)rably.

disopra [di'sopra] ① AVV = **di sopra**; vedi **sopra**.
② SM INV top, upper part.

disordinare [dizordi'nare] VT to mess up, disarrange; (*Mil*) to throw into disorder.

disordinatamente [dizordinata'mente] AVV (*alla rinfusa*) untidily; (*senza chiarezza*) incoherently; (*sregolatamente*) uncontrollably, immoderately.

disordinato, a [dizordi'nato] AGG (*persona*) untidy, disorderly; (*compito*) untidy; (*fuga, vita*) disorderly; **disordinato nel lavoro** disorganized in one's work.

disordine [di'zordine] SM **a** (*confusione*) untidiness, disorder; **essere/mettere in disordine** to be/make untidy; **ho i capelli in disordine** my hair is in a mess; **disordine mentale** mental confusion; **che disordine!** what a mess!
b: **disordini** SMPL (*Pol*) disorder *sg*; (*tumulti*) riots.

disorganicamente [dizorganika'mente] AVV piecemeal.

disorganico, a, ci, che [dizor'ganiko] AGG incoherent, disorganized.

disorganizzare [dizorganid'dzare] VT to disorganize.

disorganizzato, a [dizorganid'dzato] AGG disorganized.

disorganizzazione [dizorganiddzat'tsjone] SF disorganization.

disorientamento [dizorjenta'mento] SM (*fig*) disorienta-

tion.

disorientare [dizorjen'tare] ☐ VT (*anche fig*) to disorientate, disorient.
☐ **disorientarsi** VIP (*anche fig*) to lose one's bearings, become disorientated.

disorientato, a [dizorjen'tato] AGG disorientated, disoriented.

disossare [dizos'sare] VT (*Culin*) to bone.

disotto [di'sotto] ☐ AVV = **di sotto**; vedi **sotto**.
☐ SM INV bottom, underside.

dispaccio, ci [dis'pattʃo] SM dispatch, despatch.

disparato, a [dispa'rato] AGG disparate; **le cose più disparate** the most oddly assorted things.

dispari ['dispari] AGG INV (*numero*) odd, uneven; (*Mil: forze*) unequal.

disparità [dispari'ta] SF INV: **disparità (di)** (*disuguaglianza*) disparity (in); (*divergenza*) difference (in).

disparte [dis'parte]: **in disparte** AVV (*da lato*) aside, apart; **mettere qc in disparte** to put *o* set sth aside; **stare** *o* **tenersi in disparte** to stand apart; (*fig*) to keep to o.s., hold *o* keep o.s. aloof.

dispendio, di [dis'pɛndjo] SM (*di denaro, energie*) expenditure; (: *spreco*) waste.

dispendiosamente [dispendjosa'mente] AVV extravagantly.

dispendioso, a [dispen'djoso] AGG (*tenore di vita*) extravagant; (*impresa, viaggio*) expensive.

dispensa [dis'pɛnsa] SF **a** (*fascicolo*) instalment; (*Univ*) duplicated lecture notes *pl*, handout **b** (*esenzione*): **dispensa (da)** exemption (from); (*Rel*) dispensation (from) **c** (*locale*) larder, pantry; (*mobile*) sideboard.

dispensare [dispen'sare] ☐ VT **a** (*esonerare*): **dispensare qn da/dal fare qc** to exempt sb from/from doing sth **b** (*elemosine, favori*) to distribute, hand out.
☐ **dispensarsi** VR: **dispensarsi dal fare qc** to get out of *o* avoid doing sth.

disperare [dispe'rare] ☐ VI (*aus* avere): **disperare (di)** to despair (of); **disperare di fare qc** to despair of doing sth.
☐ **disperarsi** VIP to despair; **non disperarti in quel modo!** don't get so upset!; **far disperare qn** to drive sb mad.

disperata [dispe'rata]: **alla disperata** AVV recklessly.

disperatamente [disperata'mente] AVV desperately.

disperato, a [dispe'rato] ☐ AGG (*persona*) in despair; (*caso*) hopeless; (*tentativo, gesto*) desperate; **grido disperato** cry of despair.
☐ SM/F **a** (*fam: spiantato*): **è un povero disperato** he's a no-hoper **b**: **lavorare come un disperato** to work furiously *o* like mad.

disperazione [disperat'tsjone] SF despair; **in preda alla disperazione** overcome by despair; **quel bambino è la mia disperazione** that child drives me mad.

disperdere [dis'pɛrdere] VB IRREG ☐ VT (*folla*) to disperse; (*nemico*) to scatter; (*fig: energia, sostanze*) to waste, squander; **"non disperdere nell'ambiente"** (*vetro, lattine*) ≈ "please recycle"; (*pile, batterie*) ≈ "please dispose of carefully".
☐ **disperdersi** VIP (*folla*) to disperse; (*nemico*) to scatter; (*energia, sostanze*) to be wasted; (*calore*) to be lost.

dispersione [disper'sjone] SF (*vedi vb*) scattering, dispersal; waste; (*Chim, Fis*) dispersion; **dispersione di calore** heat loss.

dispersivamente [dispersiva'mente] AVV in a disorganized way.

dispersività [dispersivi'ta] SF lack of organization.

dispersivo, a [disper'sivo] AGG (*lavoro*) disorganized.

disperso, a [dis'pɛrso] ☐ PP di **disperdere**.
☐ AGG (*sparpagliato*) scattered, dispersed; (*smarrito*: *persona*) missing.
☐ SM/F missing person; (*Mil*) missing soldier.

dispetto [dis'pɛtto] SM **a** (*molestia*) piece of spite; **fare un dispetto a qn** to play a nasty *o* spiteful trick on sb; **a dispetto di** in spite of, despite; **per dispetto** out of spite **b** (*stizza*) vexation; **con suo grande dispetto** much to his annoyance.

dispettosamente [dispettosa'mente] AVV spitefully.

dispettoso, a [dispet'toso] AGG spiteful.

dispiacere [dispja'tʃere] ☐ SM **a** (*rammarico*) regret, sorrow; (*dolore*) grief; **con mio grande dispiacere** much to my regret; **con grande dispiacere vi annuncio...** I regret to announce ...; **impazzire dal dispiacere** to go mad with grief
b (*disappunto*) disappointment; **non puoi dare questo dispiacere a tua madre** you can't upset your mother in this way
c: **dispiaceri** SMPL (*preoccupazioni*) worries, troubles; **il figlio le ha dato molti dispiaceri** her son has given her a lot of trouble.
☐ VI IRREG (*aus* essere): **dispiacere a** **a** (*causare dolore*) to upset; (*causare disagio, noia*) to displease; **ciò che hai fatto è dispiaciuto ai tuoi** your parents are upset (*o* displeased) at your behaviour, you have upset your parents by what you have done; **non posso venire, mi dispiace** I'm sorry I can't come
b (*risultare sgradito*): **ti dispiace se fumo?** do you mind if I smoke?; **se non le dispiace...** if you don't mind ...; **ti dispiace prestarmelo?** would you mind lending it to me?.
☐ **dispiacersi** VIP: **dispiacersi (per** *o* **di qc)** to regret (sth).

dispiaciuto, a [dispja'tʃuto] ☐ PP di **dispiacere**.
☐ AGG sorry.

displuvio, vi [dis'pluvjo] SM **a** (*Geog*) watershed **b** (*di tetto*) ridge.

dispone ecc [dis'pone] VB vedi **disporre**.

dispongo ecc [dis'pongo] VB vedi **disporre**.

disponibile [dispo'nibile] AGG (*posto, merce*) available; (*persona*: *solerte, gentile*) helpful; **sei disponibile stasera?** are you free this evening?; **è sempre molto disponibile** he's always willing to help.

disponibilità [disponibili'ta] SF INV **a** (*gen*) availability; (*solerzia, gentilezza*) helpfulness **b** (*Fin*): **disponibilità** SFPL available funds, resources.

disporre [dis'porre] VB IRREG ☐ VT **a** (*mettere*) to place, put; (*sistemare*) to arrange; (*preparare*) to prepare, make ready
b (*ordinare*) to order; **la legge dispone che...** the law lays down that ...; **ha disposto che nessuno se ne andasse** he gave orders that no-one should leave.
☐ VI (*aus* avere) **a** (*decidere*) to decide; **abbiamo disposto diversamente** we have decided otherwise, we have made other arrangements
b: **disporre di** to have, have at one's disposal; **lo stadio dispone di 50.000 posti** the stadium holds 50,000 people.
☐ **disporsi** VR **a** (*posizione*) to put o.s., place o.s., arrange o.s.; **disporsi in fila** to line up; **disporsi in cerchio** to form a circle

b (*prepararsi*): **disporsi a fare qc** to prepare o.s. *o* get ready to do sth; **disporsi all'attacco** to prepare for an attack.

disposi *ecc* [dis'posi] VB *vedi* **disporre**.

dispositivo [dispozi'tivo] SM a (*meccanismo*) device ▶**dispositivo di controllo** *o* **di comando** control device ▶**dispositivo di sicurezza** (*gen*) safety device; (*di arma da fuoco*) safety catch b (*Mil*: *posizione*) order; **dispositivo di marcia** marching order c (*Dir*) pronouncement.

disposizione [disposit'tsjone] SF a (*sistemazione*: *di mobili*) arrangement; (: *di locali*) layout; (*Sport*: *di squadra*) positioning

b (*ordine*) order; (: *Dir*) provision; **disposizioni** (*preparativi, misure*) measures; **dare disposizione** *o* **disposizioni a qn affinché faccia qc** to give orders to sb to do sth; **per disposizione di legge** by law; **le sue ultime disposizioni furono...** his last instructions were ... ▶**disposizione testamentaria** provisions of a will ▶**disposizioni di sicurezza** safety measures

c : **a disposizione** at one's disposal; **avere a disposizione** to have available *o* at one's disposal; **sono a tua disposizione** I am at your disposal; **resti a disposizione della polizia** be prepared to assist the police with their enquiries

d : **disposizione d'animo** mood, frame of mind

e (*tendenza*) bent.

disposto, a [dis'posto] 1 PP di **disporre**.

2 AGG (*incline*): **disposto a fare** disposed *o* prepared to do; **essere ben/mal disposto verso qn** to be well-/ill-disposed towards sb.

3 SM (*Dir*) provision.

dispoticamente [dispotika'mente] AVV (*vedi agg*) despotically; tyrannically.

dispotico, a, ci, che [dis'pɔtiko] AGG despotic; (*fig*) tyrannical, overbearing.

dispotismo [dispo'tizmo] SM despotism; (*fig*) tyranny.

dispregiativo, a [dispredʒa'tivo] AGG disparaging; (*Ling*) pejorative.

dispregio, gi [dis'prɛdʒo] SM disparagement.

disprezzabile [dispret'tsabile] AGG contemptible, despicable; **una somma non disprezzabile** a not inconsiderable sum of money.

disprezzare [dispret'tsare] VT (*gen*) to scorn, to despise; (*persona*) to look down on.

disprezzo [dis'prɛttso] SM scorn, contempt; **ha agito con disprezzo del pericolo** he acted with a total disregard for the danger involved.

disputa ['disputa] SF a (*dibattito*) discussion b (*lite*) argument, dispute.

disputare [dispu'tare] 1 VI (*aus avere*): **disputare di** (*dibattere*) to discuss.

2 VT a (*gara*) to take part in; (*partita*) to play; **quando si disputerà la gara?** when will the competition take place?

b (*contrastare*) to contest, dispute; **gli hanno disputato il diritto di farlo** they disputed his right to do it

c : **disputarsi qc** to compete for sth, fight for sth; **disputarsi il pallone** to fight for the ball.

disquisire [diskwi'zire] VI to discourse on.

disquisizione [diskwizit'tsjone] SF detailed analysis; **è inutile stare a fare disquisizioni sul perché** there's no point discussing all the ins and outs of it.

dissacrante [dissa'krante] AGG debunking.

dissacrare [dissa'krare] VT to debunk.

dissalare [dissa'lare] VT (*acqua di mare*) to desalinate.

dissalatore [dissala'tore] SM desalination plant.

dissalazione [dissalat'tsjone] SF desalination.

dissanguamento [dissangwa'mento] SM (*Med*) loss of blood.

dissanguare [dissan'gware] 1 VT (*fig*: *persona*) to bleed white *o* dry; **morire dissanguato** to bleed to death.

2 **dissanguarsi** VIP (*Med*) to lose blood; (*fig*) to ruin o.s.

dissapore [dissa'pore] SM slight disagreement.

disse *ecc* VB *vedi* **dire**.

dissecare [disse'kare] VT to dissect.

disseccare [dissek'kare] VT, **disseccarsi** VIP to dry up.

dissellare [dissel'lare] VT to unsaddle.

disseminare [dissemi'nare] VT to scatter, spread; (*fig*: *malcontento*) to breed.

disseminazione [disseminat'tsjone] SF (*Bot*) dispersal.

dissennatezza [dissenna'tettsa] SF foolishness.

dissennato, a [dissen'nato] AGG (*persona*) foolish; (*idea*) senseless.

dissenso [dis'sɛnso] SM (*protesta*) dissent; (*disapprovazione*) disapproval; **scrittori del dissenso** dissident writers.

dissenteria [dissente'ria] SF dysentery.

dissentire [dissen'tire] VI (*aus avere*) to dissent; **dissentire da qn su qc** to disagree with sb on sth.

dissenziente [dissen'tsjɛnte] 1 AGG dissenting.

2 SM/F dissenter.

disseppellire [disseppel'lire] VT (*esumare*: *cadavere*) to disinter, exhume; (*dissotterrare*: *anche fig*) to dig up, unearth.

dissertare [disser'tare] VI (*aus avere*): **dissertare di** *o* **su** (*parlare*) to speak on; (*scrivere*) to write on.

dissertazione [dissertat'tsjone] SF dissertation.

disservizio, zi [disser'vittsjo] SM inefficiency.

dissestare [disses'tare] VT (*anche fig*) to upset, disturb; **dissestare il bilancio** to unbalance the budget.

dissestato, a [disses'tato] AGG (*fondo stradale*) uneven; (*economia, finanze*) shaky; **"strada dissestata"** (*per lavori in corso*) "road up" (*Brit*), "road out" (*Am*).

dissesto [dis'sɛsto] SM (*Fin, Econ*) disorder; **dissesto finanziario** serious financial difficulties; **in dissesto** in disorder.

dissetante [disse'tante] AGG refreshing, thirst-quenching.

dissetare [disse'tare] 1 VT (*persona*) to quench the thirst of; (*animale*) to water, give water to.

2 **dissetarsi** VR to quench one's thirst.

dissezione [disset'tsjone] SF dissection.

dissi *ecc* VB *vedi* **dire**.

dissidente [dissi'dɛnte] AGG, SM/F dissident.

dissidenza [dissi'dɛntsa] SF dissidence.

dissidio, di [dis'sidjo] SM disagreement; **dissidio di opinioni** difference of opinion.

dissimile [dis'simile] AGG: **dissimile (da)** different (from), dissimilar (to).

dissimulare [dissimu'lare] VT (*nascondere*) to hide, conceal; (*mentire*) to dissemble (*frm*); **non sa dissimulare** he's not good at pretending.

dissimulatore, trice [dissimula'tore] SM/F dissembler.

dissimulazione [dissimulat'tsjone] SF (*vedi vb*) concealment; dissembling.

dissipare [dissi'pare] 1 VT a (*disperdere*: *nubi, nebbia*) to disperse; (*fig*: *dubbi, timori*) to dispel b (*sprecare*) to

squander.

2 dissiparsi VIP (*nubi*) to disperse; (*nebbia*) to clear, lift; (*dubbi, timori*) to vanish, disappear.

dissipatamente [dissipata'mente] AVV dissolutely.

dissipatezza [dissipa'tettsa] SF dissipation.

dissipato, a [dissi'pato] AGG dissolute, dissipated.

dissipatore, trice [dissipa'tore] SM/F squanderer.

dissipazione [dissipat'tsjone] SF **a** (*sperpero*) squandering, waste **b** (*dissipatezza*) dissipation.

dissociare [disso'tʃare] **1** VT to dissociate.

2 dissociarsi VR: **dissociarsi da** to dissociate o.s. from.

dissociativo, a [dissotʃa'tivo] AGG dissociative.

dissociato, a [disso'tʃato] AGG (*terrorista*) who disowns his (*or* her) criminal past.

dissociazione [dissotʃat'tsjone] SF dissociation.

dissodamento [dissoda'mento] SM (*Agr*) tillage.

dissodare [disso'dare] VT (*Agr*) to till, turn over.

dissolto, a [dis'sɔlto] PP di **dissolvere**.

dissolutamente [dissoluta'mente] AVV dissolutely.

dissolutezza [dissolu'tettsa] SF dissoluteness; **vivere nella dissolutezza** to lead a dissolute life.

dissolutivo, a [dissolu'tivo] AGG (*forza*) divisive; **processo dissolutivo** (*anche fig*) process of dissolution.

dissoluto, a [disso'luto] **1** AGG dissolute, licentious.

2 SM/F dissolute person.

dissoluzione [dissolut'tsjone] SF dissolution.

dissolvenza [dissol'ventsa] SF (*Cine*) fade-out.

dissolvere [dis'sɔlvere] VB IRREG **1** VT (*sostanza*) to dissolve; (*nebbia*) to disperse, dispel, clear (away); (*neve*) to melt; (*fig: dubbio*) to dispel.

2 dissolversi VIP (*vedi vt*) to dissolve; to disperse, dispel, clear (away); to melt; to be dispelled.

dissonante [disso'nante] AGG (*suono*) dissonant, discordant.

dissonanza [disso'nantsa] SF (*di suoni*) dissonance, discord; (*fig: di opinioni*) clash.

dissotterrare [dissotter'rare] VT (*cadavere*) to disinter, exhume; (*tesori, rovine*) to dig up, unearth; (*fig: sentimenti, odio*) to bring up again, resurrect.

dissuadere [dissua'dere] VT IRREG to dissuade; **dissuadere qn da qc/da fare qc** to dissuade sb from sth/from doing sth.

dissuasione [dissua'zjone] SF dissuasion.

dissuasivo, a [dissua'zivo] AGG dissuasive.

dissuaso, a [dissu'azo] PP di **dissuadere**.

distaccamento [distakka'mento] SM (*Mil*) detachment.

distaccare [distak'kare] **1** VT **a**: **distaccare (da)** (*persona*) to separate (from), take away (from); (*etichetta, francobollo*) to remove, take off; (*vagone, ricevuta*) to detach (from); **distaccare lo sguardo da qn** to look away from sb

b (*Amm: dipendente*) to transfer; (*Mil: reparto*) to detach **c** (*Sport*) to outdistance, leave behind; **li distaccò di 20 metri** he outdistanced them by 20 metres.

2 distaccarsi VIP **a** (*bottone, etichetta*): **distaccarsi (da qc)** to come off (sth)

b: **distaccarsi (da)** (*persona, famiglia: gradualmente*) to grow away (from); (*: nettamente*) to leave; (*mondo*) to become detached (from)

c (*distinguersi*) to stand out (from).

distaccato, a [distak'kato] AGG detached.

distacco, chi [dis'takko] SM **a** (*separazione*) detachment; (*: fig*) parting; **il distacco fu molto doloroso** it was very painful to part **b** (*indifferenza*) coldness **c** (*Sport*):

vincere con un distacco di 100m to win by a 100m.

distante [dis'tante] **1** AGG **a** (*luogo*): **essere distante (da)** to be a long way (from); **la casa è molto distante dal centro** the house is a long way (away) from the (town) centre; **è distante da qui?** is it far from here?, is it a long way from here?; **non è distante** it's not far

b (*tempo*): **essere distante nel tempo** to be in the distant past; **sono distanti gli anni in cui...** it's a long time since ...

c (*fig: persona, atteggiamento*) distant.

2 AVV far away, a long way away; **non si vede da così distante** you can't see it from this distance *o* from so far away; **non abitano distante** they don't live far away.

distanza [dis'tantsa] SF **a** (*gen*) distance; **abito ad una certa distanza dal centro** I live a fair distance *o* quite a distance from the (town) centre; **qual è la distanza tra Glasgow ed Edimburgo?** how far is it from Glasgow to Edinburgh?, how far is Glasgow from Edinburgh?; **le 2 barche erano a 3 metri di distanza** the 2 boats were 3 metres apart; **comando a distanza** remote control ▶ **distanza focale** focal length ▶ **distanza di sicurezza** (*Aut*) braking distance ▶ **distanza di tiro** (*Mil*) range ▶ **distanza di visibilità** (*Aer, Naut*) visibility

b (*tempo*): **a distanza di 2 giorni** 2 days later; **sono nati a qualche anno di distanza** they were born within a few years of one another

c (*Sport*) distance; **gara su media/lunga distanza** middle-/long-distance race

d (*fraseologia*): **prendere le distanze da qc/qn** to dissociate o.s. from sth/sb; **tenere** *o* **mantenere le distanze** to keep one's distance; **tenere qn a distanza** to keep sb at arm's length.

distanziare [distan'tsjare] VT **a** (*oggetti*) to place at intervals; (*piante*) to space out **b**: **distanziare qn** (*Sport*) to leave sb behind, outdistance sb; (*superare*) to outstrip, surpass.

distare [dis'tare] VI DIF: **distare (da)** to be a long way (from); **dista molto da qui?** is it far (away) from here?; **non dista molto** it's not far (away); **quanto dista?** how far is it?; **distiamo pochi chilometri da Roma** we are only a few kilometres (away) from Rome.

distendere [dis'tɛndere] VB IRREG **1** VT (*braccia, gambe*) to stretch (out); (*muscoli*) to relax; (*tovaglia*) to spread; (*bucato*) to hang out; **fecero distendere il ferito sul letto** they laid the injured man on the bed; **è ottimo per distendere i nervi** it's just the thing to help you relax.

2 distendersi VR (*persona*) to lie down, stretch out; (*fig: rilassarsi*) to relax.

3 distendersi VIP (*estendersi*): **i prati si distendevano a perdita d'occhio** the fields stretched out as far as the eye could see.

distensione [disten'sjone] SF (*Pol*) détente; (*rilassamento*) relaxation; (*estensione*) stretching.

distensivo, a [disten'sivo] AGG (*gen*) relaxing, restful; (*Pol*) conciliatory.

distesa [dis'tesa] SF **a** expanse, stretch; **la distesa del mare** the expanse of the sea **b**: **le campane suonavano a distesa** the bells pealed out.

distesamente [distesa'mente] AVV in detail.

disteso, a [dis'teso] **1** PP di **distendere**.

2 AGG (*allungato: persona, gamba*) stretched out; (*rilassato: persona, atmosfera*) relaxed; **cadere lungo disteso** to fall flat on one's face; **se ne stava disteso sul letto** he was stretched out on the bed; **avere un volto disteso** to

look relaxed.

distillare [distil'lare] VT to distil; **acqua distillata** distilled water.

distillato [distil'lato] SM distillate.

distillazione [distillat'tsjone] SF distillation.

distilleria [distille'ria] SF distillery.

distinguere [dis'tingwere] VB IRREG [1] VT a (differenziare) to distinguish, single out; **distinguere il vero dal falso** to tell truth from falsehood; **la sua energia lo distingue dagli altri** his energy distinguishes him o sets him apart from the others
b (percepire) to distinguish, discern; **era troppo buio per distinguere la sua faccia** it was too dark to see o make out his (o her) face
c (contrassegnare: con etichetta) to mark, indicate
d (frm: dividere) to divide, separate.
[2] **distinguersi** VIP a (essere riconoscibile) to be distinguished
b (emergere) to stand out, be conspicuous, distinguish o.s.; **un whisky che si distingue per il suo aroma** a whisky with a distinctive bouquet; **si è sempre distinta per la sua eleganza** her elegance always makes her stand out from the crowd.

distinguo [dis'tingwo] SM INV distinction.

distinta [dis'tinta] SF (Comm) note; (elenco) list ▶**distinta di pagamento** receipt ▶**distinta di versamento** paying-in slip.

distintamente [distinta'mente] AVV (con chiarezza) distinctly, clearly; (separatamente) individually.

distintivo, a [distin'tivo] [1] SM badge.
[2] AGG distinguishing.

distinto, a [dis'tinto] [1] PP di **distinguere**.
[2] AGG a (differente) different, distinct b (chiaro) distinct, clear c (elegante, dignitoso: signore) distinguished; (: modi) refined; **distinti saluti** (in lettera) yours faithfully o truly.

distinzione [distin'tsjone] SF a (gen) distinction; **non faccio distinzioni** (tra persone) I don't discriminate; (tra cose) it's all one o the same to me; **senza distinzione di razza/religione**... without distinction of race/religion ...
b (signorilità) distinction, refinement
c (onore) honour, distinction.

distogliere [dis'tɔʎʎere] VT IRREG a (allontanare) to remove, take away; **distogliere lo sguardo** to look away
b (fig: dissuadere) to dissuade, deter; **distogliere qn da qc** to dissuade sb from sth.

distolto, a [dis'tɔlto] PP di **distogliere**.

distorcere [dis'tɔrtʃere] VB IRREG [1] VT a (contorcere) to twist; (fig: verità, versione dei fatti) to twist, distort; **distorcersi una caviglia** to sprain one's ankle b (Fis, Ottica) to distort.
[2] **distorcersi** VR (contorcersi) to twist.

distorsione [distor'sjone] SF a (Med) sprain b (Fis, Ottica) distortion.

distorto, a [dis'tɔrto] [1] PP di **distorcere**.
[2] AGG (Fis, Ottica, fig) distorted.

distrarre [dis'trarre] VB IRREG [1] VT (distogliere) to distract, divert; (divertire) to amuse, entertain; **distrarre lo sguardo** to look away.
[2] **distrarsi** VR (non fare attenzione) to let one's mind wander; (svagarsi) to take one's mind off things; **non distrarti!** pay attention!

distrattamente [distratta'mente] AVV absent-mindedly, without thinking.

distratto, a [dis'tratto] [1] PP di **distrarre**.
[2] AGG (persona) absent-minded; (pegg) inattentive.

distrazione [distrat'tsjone] SF a (caratteristica) absent-mindedness; (disattenzione) carelessness; **errori di distrazione** slips of the pen b (divertimento) distraction, amusement, entertainment.

distretto [dis'tretto] SM (circoscrizione) district ▶**distretto militare** recruiting office.

distrettuale [distrettu'ale] AGG district attr.

distribuire [distribu'ire] VT a (dare: gen) to distribute; (posta) to deliver; (lavoro, mansioni: assegnare) to allocate, assign; (: ripartire) to share out; (carte) to deal (out) b (disporre) to arrange; (Mil) to deploy.

distributivo, a [distribu'tivo] AGG distributive.

distributore, trice [distribu'tore] [1] SM (apparecchio) dispenser; (Aut, Elettr) distributor ▶**distributore automatico** slot machine, vending machine ▶**distributore di biglietti** ticket machine ▶**distributore (di benzina)** (pompa) petrol (Brit) o gas (Am) pump; (stazione) petrol (Brit) o gas (Am) station.
[2] SM/F distributor.

distribuzione [distribut'tsjone] SF a (vedi vb) distribution; delivery; allocation, assignment; sharing out, dealing; arrangement; deployment b (Comm, Tecn) distribution; **regolare la distribuzione** (Aut) to set the timing.

districare [distri'kare] [1] VT (sbrogliare) to unravel, to disentangle; (fig: chiarire) to unravel, sort out.
[2] **districarsi** VR a (tirarsi fuori): **districarsi da** to extricate o.s. from b (fig: cavarsela) to manage, get by.

distrofia [distro'fia] SF (Med) dystrophy ▶**distrofia muscolare** muscular dystrophy.

distruggere [dis'truddʒere] VT IRREG (gen) to destroy; (popolazione) to wipe out; (fig: speranze) to ruin, destroy; (: persona) to shatter.

distruttibile [distrut'tibile] AGG destructible.

distruttivo, a [distrut'tivo] AGG destructive.

distrutto, a [dis'trutto] [1] PP di **distruggere**.
[2] AGG (fig): **sono distrutto!** I'm exhausted o knackered (fam)!.

distruttore, trice [distrut'tore] [1] AGG destructive.
[2] SM/F destroyer.
[3] SM: **distruttore di documenti** shredder.

distruzione [distrut'tsjone] SF destruction.

disturbare [distur'bare] [1] VT (importunare) to disturb, trouble, bother; (portar scompiglio) to disturb, interrupt; **disturbo?** am I disturbing you?; **non vorrei disturbare** I don't want to be a nuisance; **"non disturbare"** "do not disturb"; **la disturba se fumo?** — **non mi disturba affatto** do you mind if I smoke? — no, I don't mind at all.
[2] **disturbarsi** VR to bother, to put o.s. out; **stia comodo, non si disturbi** please don't get up; **non doveva disturbarsi!** you shouldn't have gone to all that trouble!

disturbo [dis'turbo] SM a (incomodo) trouble, bother, inconvenience; **non è affatto un disturbo** it's no trouble at all; **prendersi il disturbo di fare qc** to take the trouble to do sth ▶**disturbo della quiete pubblica** (Dir) breach of the peace
b (Med) (slight) problem, ailment; **disturbi di stomaco** stomach trouble sg
c (Radio, TV): **disturbi** SMPL noise sg, interference sg, static sg.

disubbidiente [dizubbi'djɛnte] AGG disobedient.

disubbidienza [dizubbi'djɛntsa] SF disobedience

▶**disubbidienza civile** civil disobedience.

disubbidire [dizubbi'dire] VI (*aus* avere): disubbidire (a qn) to disobey (sb); **disubbidire alla legge** to break the law.

disuguaglianza [dizugwaʎ'ʎantsa] SF inequality.

disuguale [dizu'gwale] AGG **a** (*gen: differente*) different; (*grandezze, altezze*) unequal **b** (*non uniforme: superficie*) uneven, irregular.

disumanamente [dizumana'mente] AVV (*senza umanità*) inhumanly, cruelly; (*atrocemente*) terribly.

disumanità [dizumani'ta] SF INV inhumanity.

disumano, a [dizu'mano] AGG inhuman; **un grido disumano** a terrible cry.

disunione [dizu'njone] SF (*separazione*) disunity.

disunire [dizu'nire] **1** VT (*separare*) to take apart, separate; (*fig: disgregare*) to divide, disunite. **2** **disunirsi** VIP (*oggetti*) to come apart; (*elementi*) separate.

disunito, a [dizu'nito] AGG disunited, divided.

disuso [di'zuzo] SM disuse; **cadere in disuso** to fall into disuse.

disvalore [dizva'lore] SM (*Econ*) non-value.

dita ['dita] SFPL di **dito**.

ditale [di'tale] SM (*per cucire*) thimble; (*per ferita*) finger-stall.

ditata [di'tata] SF (*colpo*) jab (with one's finger), poke; (*segno*) fingermark.

dito ['dito] SM (*pl(f)* dita) **a** (*di mano, guanto*) finger; **dito del piede** toe; **mettersi le dita nel naso** to pick one's nose **b** (*misura*): **per me solo un dito di vino** just a drop of wine for me; **accorciare una gonna di un dito** to shorten a skirt by an inch **c** (*fraseologia*): **avere sulla punta delle dita** (*materia*) to have at one's fingertips; **si possono contare sulle dita di una mano** you can count them on the fingers of one hand; **un pranzetto da leccarsi le dita** a scrumptious meal; **mettere il dito sulla piaga** (*fig*) to touch a sore spot; **non ha mosso un dito (per aiutarmi)** he didn't lift a finger (to help me); **ormai è segnato a dito** everyone knows about him now.

ditta ['ditta] SF firm, business; **Spett. Ditta F.lli Gobi** (*su busta*) Messrs Gobi; (*su lettera*) Dear Sirs; **usa la macchina della ditta** he has the use of a company car; **son due giorni che non viene in ditta** he hasn't been into the office for the past two days.

dittafono® [dit'tafono] SM Dictaphone®.

dittatore [ditta'tore] SM dictator; **fare il dittatore** to be bossy.

dittatoriale [dittato'rjale] AGG dictatorial.

dittatorio, ria, ri, rie [ditta'torjo] AGG dictatorial.

dittatura [ditta'tura] SF dictatorship.

dittongo, ghi [dit'tongo] SM diphthong.

diuresi [diu'rɛzi] SF INV (*Med*) diuresis.

diuretico, a, ci, che [diu'rɛtiko] AGG, SM (*Med*) diuretic.

diurnista, i, e [diur'nista] SM/F *temporary employee paid by the day*.

diurno, a [di'urno] AGG day *attr*, daytime *attr*; **ore diurne** daytime *sg*; **spettacolo diurno** matinée; **albergo diurno** *public toilets with washing and shaving facilities*.

diva ['diva] SF vedi **divo**.

divagare [diva'gare] VI (*aus* avere) to digress; **divagare dal tema** to stray *o* wander from the point.

divagazione [divagat'tsjone] SF digression.

divampare [divam'pare] VI (*aus* essere) (*incendio*) to flare up, break out, blaze up; (*fig: rivolta*) to break out; (: *passione*) to blaze.

divano [di'vano] SM sofa, settee; (*senza schienale*) divan ▶**divano letto** bed settee, sofa bed.

divaricare [divari'kare] VT to open (wide); **a gambe divaricate** with his (*o* her) legs wide apart.

divario, ri [di'varjo] SM (*differenza*) difference ▶**divario tecnologico** technological gap.

divengo *ecc* [di'vɛngo] VB vedi **divenire**.

divenire [dive'nire] **1** VI IRREG (*aus* essere) to become. **2** SM (*Filosofia*) becoming.

divenni *ecc* [di'venni] VB vedi **divenire**.

diventare [diven'tare] VI (*aus* essere) (*gen*) to become; **diventare famoso/medico** to become famous/a doctor; **diventare vecchio** to grow old; **le foglie sono diventate gialle** the leaves have turned yellow; **è diventato rosso in faccia** he turned *o* grew red in the face; **come sei diventato grande!** how tall you've got!; **ora che sei diventato grande** now that you're grown up; **mangia la minestra, non farla diventare fredda** eat your soup, don't let it go *o* get cold; **c'è da diventare matti** it's enough to drive you mad.

divenuto, a [dive'nuto] PP di **divenire**.

diverbio, bi [di'vɛrbjo] SM dispute, quarrel, altercation (*frm*).

divergente [diver'dʒɛnte] AGG divergent.

divergenza [diver'dʒɛntsa] SF divergence; **divergenza d'opinioni** difference of opinion.

divergere [di'vɛrdʒere] VI DIF (*Mat*) to diverge, be divergent; (*fig: opinioni*) to differ, diverge.

diverrò *ecc* [diver'rɔ] VB vedi **divenire**.

diversamente [diversa'mente] AVV **a** (*in modo differente*) differently; **diversamente da quanto stabilito** contrary to what had been decided **b** (*altrimenti*) otherwise.

diversificare [diversifi'kare] **1** VT (*gen*) to vary; (*Comm: prodotti*) to diversify. **2** **diversificarsi** VIP: **diversificarsi (per)** to differ (in).

diversificazione [diversifikat'tsjone] SF **a** (*il diversificare*) diversification **b** (*diversità*) difference.

diversione [diver'sjone] SF (*anche Mil*) diversion.

diversità [diversi'ta] SF INV (*differenza*) difference; (*varietà*) variety, diversity.

diversivo, a [diver'sivo] **1** AGG diversionary; **fare un'azione diversiva** to create a diversion. **2** SM (*divertimento*) diversion, distraction.

diverso, a [di'vɛrso] **1** AGG (*differente*): **diverso (da)** different (from); **secondo me è diverso** I don't see it like that. **2** AGG INDEF: **diversi(e)** PL (*alcuni, parecchi*) several; **diversi mesi fa** some *o* several months ago; **gliel'ho detto diverse volte** I told him several times; **c'era diversa gente** there were quite a few people; **diverse persone me l'hanno detto** several *o* various people told me that. **3** PRON INDEF: **diversi(e)** PL several; (*persone*) several (people); **diversi dicono che...** various people say that ...; **ne ho presi diversi** (*libri, bicchieri*) I took several (of them). **4** SM/F (*euf: handicappato*) handicapped person; (: *omosessuale*) homosexual.

divertente [diver'tɛnte] AGG (*piacevole*) amusing, entertaining; (*comico*) funny, amusing; **era molto divertente** it was great *o* good fun.

divertimento [diverti'mento] SM **a** (*passatempo*)

pastime; (*piacere*) amusement, pleasure, entertainment; **fare qc per divertimento** to do sth for fun; **buon divertimento!** enjoy yourself!, have a good time!; **bel divertimento!** (*iro*) that sounds like fun! **b** (*Mus*) divertimento, divertissement.

divertire [diver'tire] **1** VT to amuse, entertain; **far divertire qn** to amuse sb.

2 divertirsi VR to enjoy o.s., amuse o.s., have fun; **divertiti!** have a good time!; **divertirsi a fare qc** to enjoy doing sth; **divertirsi alle spalle di qn** to have a laugh at sb's expense.

divertito, a [diver'tito] AGG amused.

divetta [di'vetta] SF starlet.

divezzare [divet'tsare] VT (*anche fig*): **divezzare (da)** to wean (from).

dividendo [divi'dɛndo] SM (*Fin, Mat*) dividend.

dividere [di'videre] VB IRREG **1** VT **a** (*gen, Mat*) to divide; (*compito, risorse*) to share out; (*dolce*) to divide (up); **dividere in 5 parti/per 5** to divide o split into 5 parts/in 5; **dividere 100 per 2** to divide 100 by 2; **su questo argomento gli studiosi sono divisi** scholars are divided on this matter; **si stavano picchiando e hanno dovuto dividerli** they were fighting and had to be separated; **niente potrà dividerci** nothing can come between us; **è diviso dalla moglie** he's separated from his wife; **si sono divisi il bottino** they split o divided the loot between them

b (*condividere*) to share; **non ho niente da dividere con te** I have nothing in common with you.

2 dividersi VR **a**: **si divide tra casa e lavoro** he divides his time between home and work

b (*uso reciproco: persone*) to separate, part; (: *coppia*) to separate.

3 dividersi VIP (*scindersi*): **dividersi (in)** to divide (into), split up (into); (*ramificarsi*) to fork; **il libro si divide in 5 capitoli** the book is divided into 5 chapters; **a questo punto le nostre strade si dividono** we must now go our separate ways.

divieto [di'vjɛto] SM prohibition ►"**divieto di accesso**" "no entry" ►"**divieto di caccia**" "no hunting" ►"**divieto di parcheggio**" "no parking" ►"**divieto di sosta**" "no waiting" ►"**divieto di transito**" "no thoroughfare".

divinamente [divina'mente] AVV (*gen*) divinely (*ant*), beautifully; (*come rafforzativo*) extremely.

divinatorio, ria, ri, rie [divina'tɔrjo] AGG: **arte divinatoria** divination.

divinazione [divinat'tsjone] SF divination.

divincolarsi [divinko'larsi] VR to wriggle (free), struggle (free); **cercava di divincolarsi** he was struggling to free himself.

divinità [divini'ta] SF INV divinity.

divinizzare [divinid'dzare] VT to deify.

divino, a [di'vino] AGG (*gen*) divine; (*fig fam*) divine, heavenly.

divisa[1] [di'viza] SF (*uniforme*) uniform.

divisa[2] [di'viza] SF (*Fin*) (foreign) currency.

divisi *ecc* [di'vizi] VB *vedi* **dividere**.

divisibile [divi'zibile] AGG divisible.

divisionale [divizjo'nale] AGG (*Mil: comandante*) divisional; (: *raggruppamento*) in divisions.

divisione [divi'zjone] SF (*gen*) division; **divisione del lavoro** division of labour; **divisione in sillabe** syllable division; (*a fine riga*) hyphenation.

divismo [di'vizmo] SM (*esibizionismo*) prima donna behaviour; (*fanatismo di massa*) hero worship.

diviso, a [di'vizo] PP di **dividere**.

divisore [divi'zore] SM (*Mat*) divisor; **massimo comun divisore** highest common denominator.

divisorio, ria, ri, rie [divi'zɔrjo] **1** AGG (*siepe, muro esterno*) dividing; (*muro interno*) dividing, partition *attr.*

2 SM (*in una stanza*) partition.

divo, a ['divo] SM/F star; **come una diva** like a prima donna.

divorare [divo'rare] **1** VT (*fig: cibo, libro*) to devour; (: *patrimonio*) to squander; (*sogg: passione, malattia, fuoco*) to consume, devour; **divorare qn con gli occhi** to devour sb with one's eyes; **divorare qc con gli occhi** to eye sth greedily; **questa macchina divora i chilometri** ≈ this car eats up the miles.

2 divorarsi VIP: **divorarsi da** (*rabbia, odio*) to be consumed o eaten up with.

divoratore, trice [divora'tore] **1** AGG (*passione*) consuming; (*febbre*) burning.

2 SM/F: **è un divoratore di carne** he's a great meat eater; **una divoratrice di uomini** (*fig*) a man-eater; **un divoratore di libri** (*fig*) an avid reader, a bookworm.

divorziare [divor'tsjare] VI (*aus* avere) to get divorced; **divorziare dalla moglie/dal marito** to divorce one's wife/husband.

divorziato, a [divor'tsjato] **1** AGG divorced.

2 SM/F divorcé(e).

divorzio, zi [di'vortsjo] SM divorce.

divorzista, i, e [divor'tsista] SM/F **a** supporter of divorce **b** (*avvocato*) divorce lawyer.

divulgare [divul'gare] **1** VT **a** (*segreto*) to divulge, disclose **b** (*rendere accessibile: teoria, scienza*) to popularize.

2 divulgarsi VIP (*notizia, dottrina*) to spread.

divulgativo, a [divulga'tivo] AGG popular.

divulgatore, trice [divulga'tore] SM/F popularizer.

divulgazione [divulgat'tsjone] SF (*vedi vb*) disclosure; popularization; spread.

dizionario, ri [dittsjo'narjo] SM dictionary.

dizione [dit'tsjone] SF **a** (*modo di parlare*) diction, delivery; (*recitazione*) recitation; (*pronuncia*) pronunciation; **corso di dizione** elocution classes *pl* **b** (*locuzione*) idiom, expression.

Djakarta [dʒa'karta] SF Djakarta.

dl ABBR (= *decilitro*) dl.

dm ABBR (= *decimetro*) dm.

DNA [di'ɛnne'a] **1** SIGLA M (= *acido deossiribonucleico*) DNA.

2 SIGLA F = *Direzione Nazionale Antimafia*.

do [dɔ] SM INV (*Mus*) C; (: *solfeggiando la scala*) do(h).

dobbiamo [dob'bjamo] VB *vedi* **dovere**.

doberman ['do:bərman] SM INV Doberman (pinscher).

D.O.C., doc [dɔk] **1** ABBR = **denominazione di origine controllata.**

2 AGG INV: **vini doc** quality wines; **un fiorentino doc** a Florentine born and bred.

doc. ABBR = *documento*.

doccia, ce ['dottʃa] SF **a** (*impianto*) shower; **fare la doccia** to have a shower ►**doccia fredda** (*fig*) slap in the face **b** (*grondaia*) gutter.

docciaschiuma [dottʃas'kjuma] SF INV shower gel.

docente [do'tʃɛnte] **1** AGG teaching; **personale non docente** non-teaching staff.

2 SM/F (*di università*) lecturer (*Brit*), professor (*Am*).

docenza [do'tʃɛntsa] SF (*Univ*): **ottenere la libera docenza** to become a lecturer.

D.O.C.G. [dɔtʃi'dʒi] ABBR (= *denominazione di origine controllata e garantita*) *label guaranteeing the quality and origin of a wine.*

docile ['dɔtʃile] AGG (*persona*) docile, meek; (*cavallo*) docile, well-behaved; **capelli docili al pettine** manageable hair.

docilità [dotʃili'ta] SF (*vedi agg*) docility; meekness.

docilmente [dotʃil'mente] AVV (*vedi agg*) docilely; meekly.

documentabile [dokumen'tabile] AGG which can be documented.

documentare [dokumen'tare] ☐1 VT to document.
☐2 **documentarsi** VR: **documentarsi (su)** to gather information *o* material (about).

documentario, ria, ri, rie [dokumen'tarjo] ☐1 AGG documentary.
☐2 SM documentary (film).

documentazione [dokumentat'tsjone] SF documentation.

documento [doku'mento] SM **a** (*gen*) document; **ha un documento (d'identità)?** do you have any identification?; **documenti prego!** may I see your papers, please? **b** (*storico*) historical document; **i dolmen sono un importante documento della preistoria** dolmen provide important evidence on the prehistoric period.

Dodecanneso [dodekan'nɛzo] SM: **le isole del Dodecanneso** the Dodecanese Islands.

dodicenne [dodi'tʃɛnne] AGG, SM/F twelve-year-old *per fraseologia vedi* **cinquantenne**.

dodicesimo, a [dodi'tʃɛzimo] AGG, SM/F twelfth *per fraseologia vedi* **quinto**.

dodici ['doditʃi] AGG INV, SM INV twelve *per fraseologia vedi* **cinque**.

doga, ghe ['doga] SF stave.

dogana [do'gana] SF customs *pl*; (*tassa*) (customs) duty; **passare la dogana** to go through customs; **pagare la dogana su qc** to pay duty on sth.

doganale [doga'nale] AGG customs *attr.*

doganiere [doga'njɛre] SM customs officer.

doge ['dɔdʒe] SM doge.

doglie ['dɔʎʎe] SFPL (*Med*) labour *sg* (*Brit*), labor *sg* (*Am*); **avere le doglie** to be in labour.

dogma, i ['dɔgma] SM dogma.

dogmaticamente [dogmatika'mente] AVV dogmatically.

dogmatico, a, ci, che [dog'matiko] ☐1 AGG dogmatic.
☐2 SM/F dogmatic person.

dolce ['doltʃe] ☐1 AGG **a** (*zuccherato, piacevole*) sweet; (*formaggio, clima*) mild; (*modi, carattere*) gentle, mild; (*suono, voce, colore*) soft; (*ricordo*) pleasant; (*pendio*) gentle; (*decollo*) smooth; (*legno, carbone*) soft; **cerca di essere più dolce con tua madre** try to be nicer to your mother; **il caffè mi piace dolce** I like my coffee sweet; **nutriva la dolce speranza di rivederlo** she cherished the hope of seeing him again; **il dolce far niente** sweet idleness; **la dolce vita** the good life **b** (*Fonetica*) soft.
☐2 SM **a**: **preferire il dolce al salato** to prefer sweet things to savoury foods **b** (*Culin: portata*) sweet, dessert; (: *torta*) cake; **mi piacciono i dolci** I like sweet things.

dolceamaro, a, ri, re [doltʃea'maro] AGG bittersweet.

dolcemente [doltʃe'mente] AVV (*sorridere, cantare*) sweetly; (*parlare*) softly; (*baciare, trattare*) gently; **il pendio**

digradava dolcemente verso il mare the land sloped gently down towards the sea.

dolcevita [doltʃe'vita] SF (*anche*: **maglione (a) dolcevita**) rollneck (sweater).

dolcezza [dol'tʃettsa] SF (*vedi agg a*) sweetness; mildness; gentleness; softness; pleasantness; smoothness; **parlare con dolcezza** to speak gently.

dolciario, ria, ri, rie [dol'tʃarjo] AGG confectionery *attr.*

dolciastro, a [dol'tʃastro] AGG (*sapore*) sweetish; (: *stucchevole*) sickly sweet; (*fig: tono*) ingratiating.

dolcificante [doltʃifi'kante] ☐1 AGG sweetening.
☐2 SM sweetener.

dolcificare [doltʃifi'kare] VT to sweeten.

dolciumi [dol'tʃumi] SMPL sweets, confectionery *sg.*

dolente [do'lɛnte] AGG **a** (*addolorato: espressione*) sorrowful, doleful, sad; **essere dolente per qc** to be very sorry about sth, regret sth profoundly **b** (*dolorante: braccio, gamba*) sore, painful; (: *dente, testa*) aching.

dolere [do'lere] VB IRREG ☐1 VI (*aus essere*) (*dente*) to ache; (*gamba, schiena*) to hurt, ache; **mi duole la testa** my head is aching, I've got a headache.
☐2 **dolersi** VIP **a**: **dolersi di** (*errore, cattiva azione*) to regret; (*peccato*) to repent of **b** (*protestare*) to complain.

dolgo *ecc* ['dɔlgo] VB vedi **dolere**.

dollaro ['dɔllaro] SM dollar.

dolmen ['dɔlmen] SM INV dolmen.

dolo ['dɔlo] SM **a** (*Dir*) malice **b** (*letter: frode*) fraud, deceit.

Dolomiti [dolo'miti] SFPL: **le Dolomiti** the Dolomites.

dolomitico, a, ci, che [dolo'mitiko] AGG (*Geol*) dolomite, dolomitic; (*delle Dolomiti*) of (*o* from) the Dolomites.

dolorante [dolo'rante] AGG aching, sore; **sono ancora dolorante** I'm still aching.

dolore [do'lore] SM (*fisico*) pain; (*morale*) distress, sorrow, grief; **avere un dolore a** (*braccio, dito*) to have a pain in; **ha dei dolori di testa** he gets headaches; **se lo scoprono sono dolori!** if they find out there'll be trouble!

dolorosamente [dolorosa'mente] AVV (*con dolore*) painfully; (*con angoscia*) with anguish.

doloroso, a [dolo'roso] AGG (*operazione*) painful; (*situazione*) distressing; (*notizia*) sad.

dolosamente [dolosa'mente] AVV (*Dir*) maliciously.

doloso, a [do'loso] AGG (*Dir*) malicious; **incendio doloso** arson.

dolsi *ecc* ['dɔlsi] VB vedi **dolere**.

domanda [do'manda] SF **a** (*interrogazione*) question; **fare una domanda a qn** to ask sb a question **b**: **domanda (di)** (*richiesta*) request (for); (: *d'impiego, iscrizione*) application (for); **fare domanda d'impiego** to apply for a job; **presentare una domanda** to send in an application; **fare domanda all'autorità giudiziaria** to apply to the courts; **far regolare domanda (di qc)** to apply through the proper channels (for sth) **c** (*Econ*): **la domanda** demand.

domandare [doman'dare] ☐1 VT **a** (*per sapere: ora, nome, indirizzo*) to ask; **domandare qc a qn** to ask sb sth **b** (*per ottenere: informazione, consiglio, aiuto*) to ask for; **domandare qc a qn** to ask sb for sth; **domandare il permesso di** *o* **per fare qc** to ask permission to do sth; **domandare scusa a qn** to beg sb's pardon, say sorry to sb; **domandare un favore a qn** to ask sb a favour, ask a favour of sb; **domandare la parola** to ask leave *o* permission to speak

c : **domandarsi** to wonder, ask o.s.; **mi domando e dico perché devo rimanere qua?** why on earth have I got to stay here?.

[2] VI (*aus* **avere**): **domandare di qn** (*chiedere come sta*) to ask after sb; (*voler vedere o parlare a*) to ask for sb; **c'è un signore che domanda di te** (*al telefono*) there's a gentleman asking to speak to you; (*voler vedere*) there's a gentleman asking to speak to *o* see you.

domani [do'mani] [1] AVV tomorrow; **domani mattina** tomorrow morning; **domani l'altro** the day after tomorrow; **domani a mezzogiorno** at midday tomorrow; **domani (a) otto** tomorrow week, a week tomorrow; **a domani!** see you tomorrow!; **credi che ci presterà la macchina? — sì, domani!** (*fam iro*) do you think he'll lend us the car? — fat chance!.

[2] SM INV **a** (*il giorno dopo*) next day, the next *o* following day

b : **il domani** (*il futuro*) the future; **un domani** some day; **chi sa cosa ci riserva il domani** who knows what the future holds.

domare [do'mare] VT (*belva*) to tame; (*cavallo*) to break in; (*fig: popolo, rivolta*) to subdue; (: *incendio*) to bring under control; (: *passione*) to master, control.

domatore, trice [doma'tore] SM/F (*gen*) tamer ▶**domatore di cavalli** horsebreaker ▶**domatore di leoni** lion tamer.

domattina [domat'tina] AVV tomorrow morning.

domenica, che [do'menika] SF Sunday; **ha messo il vestito della domenica** he is dressed in his Sunday best ▶**domenica delle Palme** Palm Sunday ▶**domenica di Pasqua** Easter Sunday *per fraseologia vedi* **martedì**.

domenicale [domeni'kale] AGG Sunday *attr*.

domenicano, a [domeni'kano] AGG, SM/F (*Rel*) Dominican.

domestico, a, ci, che [do'mɛstiko] [1] AGG (*lavori*) domestic, household *attr*; (*vita*) domestic, family *attr*; (*animale*: *addomesticato*) domestic, domesticated; **animale domestico** (*di compagnia*) pet; **le pareti domestiche** one's own four walls.

[2] SM/F (domestic) servant ▶**domestica a ore** cleaning woman.

domiciliare [domitʃi'ljare] [1] AGG domiciliary; **essere agli arresti domiciliari** to be under house arrest; **fare una perquisizione domiciliare** to carry out a house search; **visita domiciliare** (*di medico*) home visit.

[2] **domiciliarsi** VR to take up residence.

domiciliato, a [domitʃi'ljato] AGG: **domiciliato (a)** resident (in), domiciled (in).

domicilio, li [domi'tʃiljo] SM (*gen*) residence; (*Dir*) domicile; (*indirizzo*) address, place of residence (*frm*); **cambiare domicilio** to change one's address; **visita a domicilio** (*di medico*) house call; **"recapito a domicilio"** "deliveries"; **violazione di domicilio** (*Dir*) breaking and entering.

dominante [domi'nante] [1] AGG (*colore, nota, anche Bio*) dominant; (*opinione*) prevailing; (*idea*) main *attr*, chief *attr*; (*posizione*) dominating *attr*; (*classe, partito*) ruling *attr*.

[2] SF (*Mus*) dominant.

dominare [domi'nare] [1] VT (*gen*) to dominate; (*governare*) to rule; (*situazione*) to control; (*passioni, sentimenti*) to master; **la fortezza domina la pianura** the fortress has a commanding position overlooking the plain; **dominare i mari** to rule the seas *o* waves; **è dominato dal padre** he is dominated by his father; **da lassù si domina**

uno stupendo panorama there is a wonderful view from up there.

[2] VI (*aus* **avere**) **a** (*regnare*): **dominare (su)** to reign (over)

b (*primeggiare*): **dominare su tutti per intelligenza** to excel everyone in intelligence.

[3] **dominarsi** VR (*controllarsi*) to control o.s.

dominatore, trice [domina'tore] [1] AGG ruling *attr*.

[2] SM/F ruler.

dominazione [dominat'tsjone] SF domination.

dominicano, a [domini'kano] AGG, SM/F Dominican; **la Repubblica Dominicana** the Dominican Republic.

dominio, ni [do'minjo] SM **a** (*Pol: supremazia*) dominion; (: *potere*) power; **esercitare il dominio su** to exercise power over; **domini coloniali** colonies; **il dominio indiscusso di un artista** an artist's undisputed pre-eminence; **essere di dominio pubblico** (*notizia*) to be common knowledge

b (*controllo*: *gen*) control; (: *delle passioni, di una materia*) mastery; **dominio di sé** self-control.

domino ['dɔmino] SM INV (*gioco*) dominoes *sg*.

don [dɔn] SM (*sacerdote*) Father; (*titolo spagnolo o meridionale*) Don.

donare [do'nare] [1] VT (*gen*) to give; (*organo*) to donate; **donare il sangue** to give blood; **donare qc a qn** to give sb sth; **donare tutto se stesso a qn** to devote o.s. entirely to sb; **donare la vita per** to give one's life for.

[2] VI (*aus* **avere**) (*abito, colore*): **donare a** to suit, become.

donatore, trice [dona'tore] SM/F (*gen*) giver; (*Med*) donor ▶**donatore di organi** organ donor ▶**donatore di sangue** blood donor.

donazione [donat'tsjone] SF donation; **atto di donazione** (*Dir*) deed of gift.

donde ['donde] AVV (*letter*) whence.

dondolare [dondo'lare] [1] VT (*sedia*) to rock; (*ciondolare*: *corda, gambe*) to dangle.

[2] VI (*aus* **avere**) (*barca*) to rock, sway; (*altalena*) to sway; (*corda, lampadario*) to swing (to and fro).

[3] **dondolarsi** VR (*su sedia*) to rock (backwards and forwards); (*su altalena*) to swing (backwards and forwards).

dondolio, lii [dondo'lio] SM (*gentle*) rocking.

dondolo ['dondolo] SM: **cavallo/sedia a dondolo** rocking horse/chair.

dongiovanni [dondʒo'vanni] SM INV Don Juan, lady-killer.

donna ['dɔnna] SF **a** woman; **da donna** (*abito*) woman's, lady's; **figlio di buona donna!** (*fam*) son of a bitch! ▶**donna di casa** housewife ▶**donna a ore** daily (help) ▶**donna delle pulizie** cleaning lady, cleaner ▶**donna di servizio** maid ▶**donna di strada** prostitute, streetwalker **b** (*titolo*) Donna **c** (*Carte*) queen.

donnaiolo [donna'jolo] SM womanizer.

donnola ['dɔnnola] SF weasel.

dono ['dono] SM **a** (*regalo*) gift, present; (*donazione*) donation; **fare un dono a qn** to give sb a present; **portare qc in dono a qn** to bring sth as a gift *o* present for sb **b** (*dote*) gift, talent; **un dono di natura** a natural gift *o* talent; **il dono della parola** the gift of speech.

dopo ['dopo] [1] AVV **a** (*in seguito*) afterwards, after; (*poi*) then; (*più tardi*) later; **il giorno dopo** the next *o* following day; **un anno dopo** a year later; **parecchio/poco** (*tempo*) **dopo** long/not long after(wards); **prima studia, dopo usciremo** get your (school) work done first then we'll go out; **prima pensa e dopo parla** think before you speak; **è**

accaduto **2 mesi dopo** it happened 2 months later; **ci vediamo dopo** see you later; **ho rimandato tutto a dopo** I've postponed everything till later

b (*oltre*) after, next; **ecco la chiesa - la mia casa è subito dopo** there's the church - my house is just past it; **non questa strada, quella dopo** not this street but the next one.

2 PREP (*gen*) after; **dopo un anno** after a year, a year later; **dopo le vacanze** after the holidays; **rimandare qc a dopo Natale** to postpone sth till after Christmas; **è arrivato dopo cena/di me** he arrived after supper/me; **non l'ho più sentito dopo la sua partenza** I haven't heard from him since he left; **uno dopo l'altro** one after the other; **è subito dopo la chiesa** it's just past the church; **la Cina del dopo Mao** post-Mao China; **dopo tutto = dopotutto**.

3 CONG (*temporale*): **dopo mangiato va a dormire** after eating *o* after a meal he has a sleep; **dopo aver mangiato è uscito** after having something to eat *o* after eating he went out; **dopo che è partito** after he left; **dopo tutto ciò che gli ho detto** after all I said to him; **dopo che = dopoché**.

dopobarba [dopo'barba] SM INV after-shave.

dopoché [dopo'ke] CONG after, when.

dopodiché [dopodi'ke] AVV after which.

dopodomani [dopodo'mani] AVV, SM the day after tomorrow.

dopoguerra [dopo'gwɛrra] SM INV post-war period, post-war years *pl*.

dopolavoro [dopola'voro] SM recreational club.

dopopranzo [dopo'prandzo] **1** SM INV afternoon.

2 AVV: **studierò dopopranzo** I'm going to study after lunch *o* this afternoon.

doposci [dopoʃ'ʃi] SM INV: **i doposci** (*stivali*) après-ski boots.

doposcuola [dopos'kwɔla] SM INV *supervised study and recreation after school hours*.

dopotutto [dopo'tutto] AVV after all.

doppiaggio, gi [dop'pjaddʒo] SM (*Cine*) dubbing.

doppiamente [doppja'mente] AVV **a** doubly **b** (*con falsità*): **ha agito doppiamente** he acted deceitfully.

doppiare[1] [dop'pjare] VT (*Cine*) to dub.

doppiare[2] [dop'pjare] VT **a** (*Naut*) to round **b** (*Sport*) to lap.

doppiatore, trice [doppja'tore] SM/F dubber.

doppietta [dop'pjetta] SF **a** (*fucile*) double-barrelled (*Brit*) *o* double-barreled (*Am*) shotgun; (*sparo*) shot from both barrels **b** (*Calcio*) double; (*Boxe*) one-two **c** (*Aut*) double-declutch (*Brit*), double-clutch (*Am*).

doppiezza [dop'pjettsa] SF (*fig: di persona*) duplicity.

doppio, pia, pi, pie ['doppjo] **1** AGG (*gen*) double; (*vantaggio*) double, twofold; (*fig: persona*) deceitful; **battere una lettera in doppia copia** to type a letter with a carbon copy; **chiudere a doppia mandata** to double-lock; **un utensile a doppio uso** a dual-purpose utensil; **fare il doppio gioco** (*fig*) to play a double game; **doppio senso** double entendre; **frase a doppio senso** sentence with a double meaning.

2 SM **a**: **pagare il doppio** to pay twice as much *o* double the amount; **10 è il doppio di 5** 10 is twice *o* two times 5

b (*Tennis*) doubles (match); **facciamo un doppio** let's have a game of doubles ▶ **doppio misto** mixed doubles **c** (*attore*) understudy.

3 AVV double; **vedere** *o* **vederci doppio** to see double.

doppiofondo [doppjo'fondo] SM (*di valigia*) false bottom; (*Naut*) double hull.

doppione [dop'pjone] SM duplicate (copy).

doppiopetto [doppjo'pɛtto] SM INV double-breasted jacket.

doppista, i, e [dop'pista] SM/F (*Tennis*) doubles player.

dorare [do'rare] VT (*oggetto*) to gild; (*metallo*) to gold-plate; (*Culin: arrosto*) to brown; **dorare la pillola** (*fig*) to sugar the pill.

dorato, a [do'rato] AGG (*oggetto*) gilt, gilded; (*abbronzatura, giallo*) golden.

doratura [dora'tura] SF **a** (*vedi vb*) gilding; gold-plating; browning **b** (*ornamento*) gilt, decoration.

dorifora [do'rifora] SF (*Zool*) Colorado beetle.

dormicchiare [dormik'kjare] VI (*aus* avere) to doze.

dormiente [dor'mjɛnte] **1** AGG sleeping.

2 SM/F sleeper.

dormiglione, a [dormiʎ'ʎone] SM/F sleepyhead.

dormire [dor'mire] **1** VI (*aus* avere) **a** to sleep; (*essere addormentato*) to be asleep, be sleeping; **vado a dormire** I'm going to bed; **il caffè non mi fa dormire** coffee keeps me awake; **sono pensieri che non mi fanno dormire** I'm losing sleep thinking about all this; **i campi dormono sotto la neve** (*fig*) the fields slumber under the snow

b (*fraseologia*): **dormire come un ghiro** to sleep like a log; **dormire della grossa** to sleep soundly, be dead to the world; **dormire con gli occhi aperti** to sleep with one eye open; **dormire in piedi** (*essere stanco*) to be asleep on one's feet; (*essere imbambolato*) to be half asleep; **dormire tranquillo** *o* **tra due guanciali** (*senza preoccupazioni*) to rest easy; **è meglio dormirci sopra** you'd (*o* we'd *ecc*) better sleep on it.

2 VT: **dormire sonni tranquilli/agitati** to have a good/bad night's sleep, sleep well/badly; **dormire il sonno del giusto** to sleep the sleep of the just; **dormire il sonno eterno** to sleep the sleep of the dead.

dormita [dor'mita] SF sleep; **fare una bella dormita** to have a good sleep.

dormitorio, ri [dormi'tɔrjo] **1** SM (*gen*) dormitory ▶ **dormitorio pubblico** night shelter (*run by local authority*).

2 AGG INV: **città dormitorio** dormitory town, commuter town.

dormiveglia [dormi've ʎʎa] SM INV: **essere nel dormiveglia** to be half-asleep, be drowsy; **nel dormiveglia ha sentito un rumore** he was half-asleep when he heard a noise.

dorrò *ecc* [dor'rɔ] VB vedi **dolere**.

dorsale [dor'sale] **1** AGG **a** (*Anat*) dorsal, back *attr*; **spina dorsale** backbone, spine **b** (*Sport*): **nuoto dorsale** backstroke; **salto dorsale** Fosbury flop.

2 SF (*catena montuosa*) ridge.

3 SM (*di sedia*) back.

dorsalmente [dorsal'mente] AVV dorsally.

dorsista, i, e [dor'sista] SM/F (*Nuoto*) backstroke swimmer.

dorso ['dɔrso] SM **a** (*gen*) back; (*di libro*) spine; (*di monte*) ridge, crest; **a dorso di cavallo** on horseback **b** (*Nuoto*) backstroke.

dosaggio, gi [do'zaddʒo] SM (*atto*) measuring out; (*dose*) dosage (*frm*); **sbagliare il dosaggio** to get the amount wrong.

dosare [do'zare] VT (*ingredienti*) to measure out; (*Med*) to dose; (*fig: forze, risorse*) to husband; **saper dosare le**

proprie forze to know how much effort to make.

dosatore [doza'tore] SM (*apparecchio*) dispenser; (*su bottiglia*) optic ® (*Brit*); (*recipiente*) measuring cap.

dose ['doze] SF (*Med*) dose; (*di farina, zucchero*) amount, quantity; (*di whisky, vodka*) measure; **ha avuto la sua dose di preoccupazioni** he's had his fair share of worries; **ci vuole una buona dose di coraggio** it takes a lot of courage.

dossale [dos'sale] SM (*di altare*) reredos.

dossier [do'sje] SM INV dossier, file.

dosso ['dɔsso] SM **a** (*rilievo*) rise; (: *di strada*) bump **b** : **levarsi i vestiti di dosso** to take one's clothes off; **levarsi un peso di dosso** (*fig*) to take a weight off one's mind.

dotare [do'tare] VT: **dotare di** (*attrezzature*) to equip with, provide *o* supply with; (*fig: qualità*) to endow with.

dotato, a [do'tato] AGG: **dotato di** (*attrezzature*) equipped with; (*bellezza, intelligenza*) endowed with; **un bambino molto dotato** a highly gifted *o* talented child.

dotazione [dotat'tsjone] SF **a** (*gen, Mil, Naut*) equipment; **dare qc in dotazione a qn** to issue sb with sth, issue sth to sb; **avere in dotazione una somma** to have a sum at one's disposal; **i macchinari in dotazione alla fabbrica** the machinery in use in the factory **b** (*rendita*) endowment.

dote ['dɔte] SF (*di sposa*) dowry; (*Fin*) endowment; (*fig*) gift, talent; **portare qc in dote** to bring a dowry of sth; **avere doti naturali per** to have a natural talent for.

Dott. ABBR (= *dottore*) Dr.

dotto[1], a ['dɔtto] **1** AGG (*persona*) erudite, learned; (*citazione*) learned; **lingue dotte** classical languages. **2** SM/F scholar.

dotto[2] ['dɔtto] SM (*Anat*) duct.

dottorale [dotto'rale] AGG doctoral; (*iro: tono*) pedantic.

dottorato [dotto'rato] SM degree ▶ **dottorato di ricerca** doctorate, doctor's degree.

dottore, essa [dot'tore] SM/F **a** (*medico*) doctor; **andare dal dottore** to go to the doctor **b** (*laureato*) graduate ▶ **dottore in lettere** ≈ Bachelor of Arts **c** (*studioso*) scholar.

dottrina [dot'trina] SF (*Filosofia, Rel*) doctrine; (*cultura*) learning, erudition.

dottrinale [dottri'nale] AGG doctrinal.

dottrinario, ria, ri, rie [dottri'narjo] **1** AGG doctrinaire. **2** SM/F doctrinarian.

Dott.ssa ABBR (= *dottoressa*) Dr.

double face [dubl'fas] AGG INV reversible.

dove ['dove] **1** AVV (*gen*) where; (*in cui*) where, in which; (*dovunque*) wherever; **dove vivi?** where do you live?; **di dove sei?** where are you from?, where do you come from?; **non so da dove iniziare** I don't know where to begin; **da dove è entrato?** where did he get in?; **la città dove abito** the city where *o* in which I live; **da dove abito vedo...** from where I live I can see ...; **per** *o* **da dove sei passato?** which way did you go?; **siediti dove vuoi** sit wherever you like; **ti do una mano fin dove posso** I'll help you as much as I can; **(fin) dove è arrivato con il programma?** (*insegnante*) how far has he got with the syllabus?. **2** CONG (*letter: allorquando*): **e dove non vi piacesse fate come volete** and if you are not happy about it do what you like. **3** SM where; **gente arrivava da ogni dove** people were arriving from all over; **per ogni dove** everywhere.

dovere [do'vere] **1** VT IRREG (*soldi, riconoscenza*) to owe; ▷ **gli devo il mio** *successo* I owe my success to him, I have him to thank for my success ▷ **devo** *tutto* **ai miei genitori** I owe everything to my parents ▷ **crede che** *tutto* **gli sia dovuto** he thinks he has a god-given right to everything. **2** VB AUS (*nei tempi composti prende l'ausiliare del verbo che accompagna*) **a** (*obbligo*) to have to; ▷ **come si deve** (*bene*) properly; (*meritatamente*) properly, as he (*o* she *ecc*) deserves ▷ **è una persona** *come* **si deve** he is a very decent person ▷ **non avrebbe dovuto** *esserne informata* **che il giorno dopo** she was not supposed to hear about it until the following day ▷ **non devi** *fare* **rumore** you mustn't *o* you're not to make a noise ▷ **avrebbe dovuto** *farlo* he should have *o* ought to have done it ▷ **lui deve** *farlo* he has (got) to do it, he must do it ▷ **devo** *farlo* **subito?** do I have to *o* have I got to do it immediately? ▷ **ha dovuto** *pagare* he had to pay ▷ **è dovuto** *partire* he had to leave ▷ **devo** *partire* **domani** I'm leaving tomorrow; (*purtroppo*) I've got to leave tomorrow ▷ **non devi** *zuccherarlo* (*non è necessario*) there's no need to add sugar **b** (*fatalità*) ▷ **doveva** *accadere* it was bound to happen ▷ **lo farò, dovessi** *morire* I'll do it if it kills me ▷ **tutti dobbiamo** *morire* we all have to die **c** (*previsione*) ▷ **deve arrivare alle 10** he should *o* is due to arrive at 10 ▷ **sembra che le cose si debbano sistemare** things seem to be sorting themselves out **d** (*probabilità*) ▷ **deve essere difficile farlo** it must be difficult to do ▷ **non deve essere uno stupido** he can't be stupid ▷ **dev'essere tardi** it must be late ▷ **devono essere le 4** it must be 4 o'clock ▷ **devo averlo fatto** I must have done it. **3** SM (*obbligo*) duty; ▷ **a dovere** (*bene*) properly; (*debitamente*) as he (*o* she *ecc*) deserves ▷ **rivolgersi a chi di dovere** to apply to the appropriate authority *o* person ▷ **fare il proprio dovere di elettore** to do one's duty as a voter ▷ **farsi un dovere di qc** to make sth one's duty ▷ **avere il** *senso* **del dovere** to have a sense of duty.

doverosamente [doverosa'mente] AVV duly.

doveroso, a [dove'roso] AGG (*ubbidienza*) dutiful; (*rispetto*) (right and) proper, due; **è doveroso avvertirlo** we (*o* you *ecc*) ought to warn him.

dovizia [do'vittsja] SF abundance; **descrivere qc con dovizia di particolari** to give a very detailed description of sth.

dovrò *ecc* [do'vrɔ] VB vedi **dovere**.

dovunque [do'vunkwe] AVV **a** (*in qualsiasi luogo*) wherever; **dovunque vada** wherever I go; **dovunque tu sia** wherever you are **b** (*dappertutto*) everywhere; **si trovano dovunque** they can be found everywhere; **c'erano libri un po' dovunque** there were books all over the place.

dovutamente [dovuta'mente] AVV (*debitamente: redigere, compilare*) correctly; (: *rimproverare*) as he (*o* she *ecc*) deserves.

dovuto, a [do'vuto] [1] AGG (*denaro*) owing, owed; (*rispetto*) due; **è dovuto al temporale** it's due to the storm, it's because of the storm; **nel modo dovuto** in the proper way, properly. [2] SM due; **mi hanno pagato più del dovuto** they paid me more than what I was owed; **ho lavorato più del dovuto** I worked more than I actually had to.

dozzina [dod'dzina] SF dozen; **c'erano persone/libri a dozzine** there were dozens of people/books; **una dozzina di uova** a dozen eggs; **di** *o* **da dozzina** (*scrittore, spettacolo*) second-rate.

dozzinale [doddzi'nale] AGG (*prodotto*) cheap, shoddy; (*persona*) second-rate.

draga, ghe ['draga] SF dredger.

dragaggio, gi [dra'gaddʒo] SM dredging ▶ **dragaggio di mine** minesweeping.

dragare [dra'gare] VT to dredge; **dragare il mare** (*per mine*) to sweep the sea (*for mines*).

dragherò *ecc* [drage'rɔ] VB vedi **dragare**.

drago, ghi ['drago] SM dragon; **in inglese è un drago** (*fig fam*) he's a genius at English.

dragoncello [dragon'tʃɛllo] SM tarragon.

dramma, i ['dramma] SM **a** (*Teatro*) drama **b** (*fig: vicenda tragica*) drama, tragedy; **fare un dramma di qc** to make a drama out of sth.

drammaticamente [drammatika'mente] AVV dramatically.

drammaticità [drammatitʃi'ta] SF **a** (*Teatro*) dramatic force **b** (*fig: di situazione*) drama.

drammatico, a, ci, che [dram'matiko] AGG **a** (*Teatro*): **arte drammatica** dramatics *sg*; **scuola d'arte drammatica** drama school; **autore drammatico** dramatist **b** (*situazione*) terrible **c** (*emotivo*) dramatic.

drammatizzare [drammatid'dzare] VT to dramatize.

drammaturgia [drammatur'dʒia] SF drama.

drammaturgo, a, ghi, ghe [dramma'turgo] SM/F dramatist, playwright.

drappeggiare [drapped'dʒare] [1] VT to drape. [2] **drappeggiarsi** VR to drape o.s.

drappeggio, gi [drap'peddʒo] SM (*tessuto*) drapery; (*di abito*) folds.

drappello [drap'pɛllo] SM (*Mil*) squad, platoon; (*gruppo*) group.

drappo ['drappo] SM cloth.

drasticamente [drastika'mente] AVV drastically.

drastico, a, ci, che ['drastiko] AGG drastic.

drenaggio, gi [dre'naddʒo] SM drainage.

drenare [dre'nare] VT to drain.

Dresda ['drɛsda] SF Dresden.

dressage [drɛ'saʒ] SM INV (*Equitazione*) dressage.

dribblare [drib'blare] (*Calcio*) [1] VI (*aus* **avere**) to dribble (the ball). [2] VT (*avversario*) to avoid, dodge.

dribbling ['driblin] SM INV (*Calcio*) dribbling.

dritta ['dritta] SF (*destra*) right, right hand (side); (*Naut*)

starboard; **a dritta e a manca** (*fig*) on all sides, right, left and centre; **dare una dritta a qn** (*fam: informazione*) to give sb a few (useful) tips.

dritto, a ['dritto] [1] AGG **a** = **diritto¹** **b** (*fam: scaltro*) sharp, crafty. [2] SM = **diritto¹**. [3] SM/F (*fam: furbo*): **è un dritto** he's a crafty *o* sly one. [4] AVV = **diritto¹**.

drittofilo [dritto'filo] SM INV (*di tessuto*) grain; **tagliare in drittofilo** to cut on the grain.

drizzare [drit'tsare] [1] VT (*palo, quadro*) to straighten; (*innalzare: antenna, muro*) to erect; (*volgere: sguardo, occhi*) to turn, direct; **drizzare le orecchie** to prick up one's ears. [2] **drizzarsi** VR: **drizzarsi in piedi** to rise to one's feet, stand up; **drizzarsi a sedere** to sit up.

droga, ghe ['drɔga] SF **a** (*stupefacente*) drug; **la droga** drugs *pl*; **spacciare droga** to peddle drugs; **fare uso di droga** to take *o* be on drugs ▶ **droghe leggere** soft drugs ▶ **droghe pesanti** hard drugs **b** (*spezia*) spice.

drogare [dro'gare] [1] VT **a** (*persona, animale*) to drug, dope; **questa bevanda è drogata** this drink has been doped **b** (*Culin*) to season, spice. [2] **drogarsi** VR to take drugs, be on drugs.

drogato, a [dro'gato] SM/F drug addict.

drogheria [droge'ria] SF ≈ grocer's (shop) (*Brit*), ≈ grocery (store) (*Am*).

drogherò *ecc* [droge'rɔ] VB vedi **drogare**.

droghiere, a [dro'gjɛre] SM/F ≈ grocer.

dromedario, ri [drome'darjo] SM dromedary.

D.T. ABBR = **direttore tecnico**.

duale [du'ale] AGG, SM (*Gramm*) dual.

dualismo [dua'lizmo] SM (*Filosofia*) dualism; (*fig: contrasto*) conflict.

dualista, i, e [dua'lista] SM/F dualist.

dubbio, bia, bi, bie ['dubbjo] [1] SM (*incertezza*) doubt; **mettere in dubbio** (*affermazione, buona fede*) to doubt, question; (*esito, successo*) to put in doubt; **avere il dubbio che** to suspect (that), be afraid that; **essere in dubbio** (*risultato*) to be doubtful *o* uncertain; **sono in dubbio se partire o no** I don't know whether to go or not; **essere in dubbio fra** to hesitate between; **nutrire seri dubbi su qc** to have grave doubts about sth; **senza dubbio** doubtless, no doubt; **senza alcun dubbio** without a doubt; **esprimere un dubbio su** to express (one's) doubts about. [2] AGG **a** (*incerto: gen*) doubtful; (: *avvenire*) uncertain **b** (*equivoco, discutibile: qualità, gusto*) dubious, questionable; **uno scherzo di dubbio gusto** a joke in poor taste.

dubbiosamente [dubbjosa'mente] AVV (*vedi agg*) hesitantly, uncertainly; in a puzzled way.

dubbioso, a [dub'bjoso] AGG **a** (*esitante*) hesitant, uncertain; (*perplesso: persona*) uncertain; (: *sguardo, aria*) puzzled; **essere dubbioso su qc** to be uncertain about sth, question the truth of sth **b** (*incerto: esito*) uncertain, doubtful.

dubitare [dubi'tare] VI (*aus* **avere**) **a** : **dubitare di** (*onestà*) to doubt, have (one's) doubts as to; (*autenticità*) to question; (*riuscita*) to be doubtful of **b** (*ritenere improbabile*): **dubito che venga** I doubt if *o* whether he'll come; **non dubito che verrà** I have no doubt that he'll come, I'm sure he'll come **c** (*diffidare*): **dubitare di sé** to be unsure of o.s.;

dubitare di qn to mistrust sb.
Dublino [du'blino] SF Dublin.
duca, chi ['duka] SM duke.
ducale [du'kale] AGG ducal.
ducato[1] [du'kato] SM (*titolo*) dukedom; (*territorio*) duchy, dukedom.
ducato[2] [du'kato] SM (*moneta*) ducat.
duce ['dutʃe] SM (*Storia*) (Roman) commander; (: *del fascismo*) Duce.
duchessa [du'kessa] SF duchess.
due ['due] [1] AGG INV a two; **due volte** twice; **a due a due** two at a time, two by two b (*fig: pochi*) a couple, a few; **dire due parole** to say a few words; **starò via due o tre giorni** I'll be away for two or three days; **ci metto due minuti** it'll only take me a couple of minutes.
  [2] SM INV two *per fraseologia vedi* **cinque.**
due alberi ['due'alberi] SM INV (*Naut*) two-master.
duecentesco, a, schi, sche [duetʃen'tesko] AGG thirteenth-century.
duecento [due'tʃɛnto] [1] AGG INV two hundred.
  [2] SM INV two hundred; **il Duecento** (*secolo*) the thirteenth century.
duellante [duel'lante] SM duellist.
duellare [duel'lare] VI (*aus* **avere**) to fight a duel.
duello [du'ɛllo] SM duel; **sfidare a duello** to challenge to a duel.
duemila [due'mila] [1] AGG INV two thousand.
  [2] SM INV two thousand; **il duemila** the year two thousand.
duepezzi, due pezzi [due'pɛttsi] SM INV (*da bagno*) bikini, two-piece swimsuit; (*abito*) two-piece (suit).
duetto [du'etto] SM (*Mus*) duet.
dulcis in fundo ['dultʃis in'fundo] AVV to cap it all.
duna ['duna] SF dune.
dune buggy ['dju:n'bʌgi] SM INV beach buggy.
dunque ['dunkwe] [1] CONG (*perciò*) therefore, so; (*allora*) well (now), well (then); **fallo dunque!** do it then!.
  [2] SM INV: **venire al dunque** to come to the point.
duo ['duo] SM INV (*Mus*) duet; (*Teatro, Cine, fig*) duo; **formano un duo ben assortito** they're a well-matched pair *o* couple.
duodeno [duo'dɛno] SM (*Anat*) duodenum.
duole *ecc* ['dwɔle] VB *vedi* **dolere.**
duomo[1] ['dwɔmo] SM cathedral.
duomo[2] ['dwɔmo] SM (*Tecn*) dome.
duplex ['dupleks] SM INV (*Telec*) party line.
duplicare [dupli'kare] VT to duplicate.
duplicato [dupli'kato] SM duplicate.
duplicatore [duplika'tore] SM duplicator.
duplicazione [duplikat'tsjone] SF duplication.
duplice ['duplitʃe] AGG (*gen*) double, twofold; (*incarico,*

scopo) dual; **in duplice copia** in duplicate; **il problema ha un duplice aspetto** the problem is twofold.
duplicità [duplitʃi'ta] SF (*fig*) duplicity.
duralluminio [durallu'minjo] SM Duralumin ®.
duramente [dura'mente] AVV harshly, severely.
durante [du'rante] PREP (*nel corso di*) during, in the course of; (*per tutta la durata di*) throughout, for; **durante la notte** during the night; **durante l'intera giornata** throughout the day, for the entire day; **vita natural durante** for life.
durare [du'rare] [1] VI (*aus* **essere** *o* **avere**) (*gen*) to last; **la festa durò tutta la notte** the party went on all night; **lo stipendio ti deve durare tutto il mese** your salary will have to last you the month; **così non può durare!** this can't go on any longer!; **questa storia dura da un pezzo** this business has been going on for some time; **durare in carica** to remain in office.
  [2] VT: **durare fatica a fare qc** to have a hard job doing sth, have difficulty in doing sth.
durata [du'rata] SF (*gen*) duration, length; (*di prodotto, pianta*) life; **per tutta la durata di** throughout; **di breve durata** (*vacanza*) short; (*felicità*) short-lived; **di lunga durata** long-lasting; **durata della vita** life span ▶ **durata media della vita** (*Statistica*) life expectancy.
duraturo, a [dura'turo] AGG (*ricordo, fama*) enduring; (*pace*) lasting.
durevole [du'revole] AGG (*materiale*) durable; **beni durevoli** (*Econ*) durable goods.
durezza [du'rettsa] SF (*gen, di acque*) hardness; (*di metallo*) strength; (*di spazzola*) stiffness; (*di voce*) harshness; (*fig: severità*) severity; (: *rigidità*) rigidity, severity; (: *ostinazione*) stubbornness.
duro, a ['duro] [1] AGG a (*resistente: gen*) hard; (: *serratura*) stiff; (: *carne*) tough; **duro d'orecchi** (*sordo*) hard of hearing; **duro di comprendonio** *o* **di testa** slow-witted; **avere la pelle dura** (*fig: persona*) to be tough; **pane duro** stale bread
  b (*fig: severo: persona*) harsh, hard; (: *disciplina*) harsh, strict; (: *atteggiamento*) harsh, unbending; (: *inverno*) hard; **duro di cuore** hard-hearted
  c (*ostinato*) stubborn, obstinate.
  [2] SM a (*durezza*) hardness; (*parte dura*) hard part; **dormire sul duro** to sleep on a hard bed
  b (*fig: difficoltà*) hard part; **il duro deve ancora venire** the hard part is still to come.
  [3] SM/F (*persona*) tough one; **fare il duro** to act tough.
  [4] AVV: **tener duro** (*resistere*) to stand firm, hold out.
durone [du'rone] SM (*callo*) hard skin.
duttile ['duttile] AGG (*sostanza*) malleable; (*fig: carattere*) flexible; (: *stile*) adaptable.
duvet [dyve] SM INV down jacket.

E

E, e [e] SF O M INV (*lettera*) E, e; **E come Empoli** ≈ E for Edward (*Brit*), ≈ E for Easy (*Am*).

E ABBR (= *est*) E.

e [e] CONG (spesso **ed** dav a vocale) **a** and; **io e te** me and you; **Davide ed un suo amico** David and a friend of his; **un metro e novanta** one metre ninety; **ho speso settemila e duecento lire** I spent seven thousand two hundred lire; **tutt'e tre** all three of them; **tutt'e due** both (of them); **è bell'e fatto** it's well and truly finished; **mi piace molto, e a te?** I like it a lot, what about you?
b (*avversativo*) but; (*eppure*) and yet; **lo credevo onesto e non lo è** I thought he was honest but he isn't; **sapeva di sbagliare e l'ha fatto ugualmente** he knew it was a mistake but he did it all the same
c (*ebbene*) well, well then; **e deciditi dunque!** well make up your mind then!; **e smettila!** stop it!

è [ɛ] VB vedi **essere**.

E.A. ABBR = **ente autonomo**; vedi **ente**.

E.A.D. ABBR (= *elaborazione automatica dei dati*) A.D.P.

ebanista, i [eba'nista] SM cabinet-maker.

ebanisteria [ebaniste'ria] SF cabinet-making.

ebano ['ɛbano] SM ebony.

ebbene [eb'bɛne] CONG well (then).

ebbi ecc ['ɛbbi] VB vedi **avere**.

ebbrezza [eb'brettsa] SF intoxication, inebriation; **in stato di ebbrezza** inebriated; (*ubriaco*) intoxicated; (*autista*) under the influence of drink; **l'ebbrezza del successo** the exhilaration of success.

ebbro, a ['ɛbbro] AGG intoxicated, inebriated; **ebbro di gioia** drunk with joy.

ebdomadario, ria, ri, rie [ebdoma'darjo] AGG, SM weekly.

Ebe ['ebe] SF Hebe.

ebetaggine [ebe'taddʒine] SF (*letter*) obtuseness.

ebete ['ebete] **1** AGG slow-witted, moronic (*fam*).
2 SM/F half-wit, moron (*fam*).

ebetismo [ebe'tizmo] SM feeble mindedness.

ebollizione [ebollit'tsjone] SF boiling; **in ebollizione** boiling; **portare ad ebollizione** to bring to the boil; **punto di ebollizione** boiling point.

ebraico, a, ci, che [e'braiko] **1** AGG Jewish; (*scritture*) Hebrew; (*tradizione*) Hebraic.
2 SM (*lingua*) Hebrew.

ebraismo [ebra'izmo] SM (*Rel, Storia*) Judaism; (*language*) Hebraism.

ebraista, i, e [ebra'ista] SM/F Hebraist.

ebreo, a [e'brɛo] **1** AGG Jewish.
2 SM/F Jewish man/woman; (*Storia*) Jew/Jewess; **l'Ebreo errante** the Wandering Jew.

Ebridi ['ɛbridi] SFPL: **le (isole) Ebridi** the Hebrides.

eburneo, a [e'burneo] AGG (*letter: di avorio, anche fig*) ivory *attr*.

E/C ABBR = **estratto conto**.

ecatombe [eka'tombe] SF (*fig: strage*) slaughter, massacre.

ecc. ABBR (= *eccetera*) etc.

eccedente [ettʃe'dɛnte] SM excess.

eccedenza [ettʃe'dɛntsa] SF excess; **un'eccedenza di peso** some excess weight; **bagaglio in eccedenza** excess baggage.

eccedere [et'tʃɛdere] **1** VT (*competenza, aspettative*) to exceed; (*limiti*) to overstep.
2 VI (*aus avere*) to go too far; **eccedere nel mangiare** to eat too much; **eccedere nel bere** to drink to excess.

eccellente [ettʃel'lɛnte] AGG excellent; (*cadavere, arresto*) of a prominent person.

eccellentemente [ettʃellente'mente] AVV excellently.

eccellentissimo, a [ettʃellen'tissimo] AGG (*titolo onorifico*) most excellent.

eccellenza [ettʃel'lɛntsa] SF **a** excellence; **per eccellenza** par excellence **b** (*titolo*): **Sua Eccellenza** His Excellency.

eccellere [et'tʃɛllere] VI IRREG (*aus avere o essere*): **eccellere (in)** to excel (at); **eccellere in tutto** to excel at everything; **eccellere su tutti** to surpass everyone.

eccelsamente [ettʃelsa'mente] AVV sublimely.

eccelso, a [et'tʃɛlso] **1** PP di **eccellere**.
2 AGG (*cima*) lofty; (*fig*) towering, lofty.
3 SM: **l'Eccelso** (*Rel*) the Almighty.

eccentricamente [ettʃentrika'mente] AVV eccentrically.

eccentricità [ettʃentritʃi'ta] SF INV eccentricity.

eccentrico, a, ci, che [et'tʃɛntriko] ① AGG (*persona, Mat*) eccentric.

② SM (*Tecn*) cam.

eccepibile [ettʃe'pibile] AGG (*argomento, decisione*) questionable.

eccepire [ettʃe'pire] VT: **eccepire che** to object that; **non avere niente da eccepire** to have no objections.

eccessivamente [ettʃessiva'mente] AVV excessively.

eccessivo, a [ettʃes'sivo] AGG excessive.

eccesso [et'tʃɛsso] SM excess; **gentile fino all'eccesso** kind to a fault; **arrotondare una cifra per eccesso** to round up a figure; **dare in eccessi** to fly off the handle, fly into a rage ►**eccesso di velocità** (*Aut*) speeding ►**eccesso di zelo** excess of zeal; **peccare per eccesso di zelo** to be overzealous.

eccetera [et'tʃɛtera] AVV et cetera, and so on.

eccetto [et'tʃɛtto] ① PREP except; **tutti eccetto lui** everybody except him.

② CONG: **eccetto che** (*tranne che*) except; **eccetto che (non) piova...** unless it rains ... .

eccettuare [ettʃettu'are] VT: **se si eccettua...** apart from ..., other than ...; **eccettuati i presenti** present company excepted.

eccezionale [ettʃettsjo'nale] AGG exceptional; **in via del tutto eccezionale** in this one instance, exceptionally.

eccezionalità [ettʃettsjonali'ta] SF INV exceptional nature.

eccezionalmente [ettʃettsjonal'mente] AVV exceptionally.

eccezione [ettʃet'tsjone] SF **a** exception; **d'eccezione** (*provvedimento*) exceptional, special; (*ospite*) special; **a eccezione o con l'eccezione di** with the exception of; **l'eccezione che conferma la regola** the exception which proves the rule; **fare un'eccezione alla regola** to make an exception to the rule **b** (*Dir: obiezione*) objection.

ecchimosi [ek'kimozi] SF INV bruise.

eccidio, di [et'tʃidjo] SM massacre.

eccipiente [ettʃi'pjɛnte] SM (*Med*) excipient.

eccitabile [ettʃi'tabile] AGG excitable.

eccitabiltà [ettʃitabili'ta] SF INV excitability.

eccitamento [ettʃita'mento] SM (*gen*) stimulation; (*incitamento*) incitement.

eccitante [ettʃi'tante] ① AGG (*gen*) exciting; (*sostanza*) stimulating.

② SM stimulant.

eccitare [ettʃi'tare] ① VT **a** (*persona: sessualmente*) to arouse; (*curiosità, interesse*) to arouse, excite; (*sensi, fantasia*) to stir; (*folla*) to incite **b** (*agitare*) to excite; **il caffè eccita** coffee acts as a stimulant.

② **eccitarsi** VIP (*sessualmente*) to become aroused; (*entusiasmarsi*) to get excited; (*innervosirsi*) to get worked up.

eccitato, a [ettʃi'tato] AGG (*sessualmente*) aroused; (*emozionato*) excited; (*innervosito*) worked up.

eccitazione [ettʃitat'tsjone] SF (*gen*) excitement; (*del sistema nervoso*) stimulation; (*Elettr*) excitation.

ecclesiale [ekkle'zjale] AGG church *attr*.

ecclesiastico, a, ci, che [ekkle'zjastiko] ① AGG (*ufficio*) ecclesiastical; (*gerarchia, beni*) ecclesiastical, church *attr*; (*abito*) clerical.

② SM ecclesiastic.

ecco ['ɛkko] AVV: **ecco qui/là** here/there it is; **ecco i nostri amici** here are our friends; **ecco il treno** here comes *o* here's the train; **ecco! (prendi)** here you are!; **eccomi** here I am; **eccone due** here are two (of them); **ecco**

perché that's why; **ed ecco che sul più bello...** and just at that moment ...; **ecco fatto** there, that's that done, there we are.

eccome [ek'kome] AVV rather; **ti piace? — eccome!** do you like it? — I certainly do!; **lo so eccome!** don't I know it!

ECG [etʃi'dʒi] SIGLA M (= *elettrocardiogramma*) ECG.

echeggiare [eked'dʒare] VI (*aus* **essere** *o* **avere**) to echo; **echeggiare di** to echo *o* resound with.

echinococco, chi [ekino'kɔkko] SM (*Zool*) echinococcus.

echinodermi [ekino'dɛrmi] SMPL (*Zool*) echinoderms.

eclatante [ekla'tante] AGG (*notizia*) extraordinary; (*esempio*) striking.

eclettico, a, ci, che [e'klɛttiko] AGG, SM/F eclectic.

eclettismo [eklet'tizmo] SM eclecticism.

eclissare [eklis'sare] ① VT (*anche fig*) to eclipse.

② **eclissarsi** VIP (*persona: scherz*) to disappear.

eclissi [e'klissi] SF INV eclipse.

eco ['ɛko] SM O F (*pl m* **echi**) echo; **fare eco a qc/qn** to echo sth/sb; **suscitò** *o* **ebbe una vasta eco** it caused a considerable stir.

ecografia [ekogra'fia] SF (*Med*) ultrasound, echography.

ecografico, a, ci, che [eko'grafiko] AGG (*Med*) ultrasound *attr*.

ecologia [ekolo'dʒia] SF ecology; **i problemi dell'ecologia** environmental issues.

ecologicamente [ekolodʒika'mente] AVV ecologically; (*sicuro, dannoso*) environmentally.

ecologico, a, ci, che [eko'lɔdʒiko] AGG ecological; (*detersivo, vernice ecc*) environmentally friendly, eco-friendly; **pelliccia ecologica** fake fur.

ecologista, i, e [ekolo'dʒista] ① SM/F ecologist; (*ambientalista*) environmentalist.

② AGG (*movimento*) ecology *attr*; (*gruppo, attivista*) environmental.

ecologo, a, gi, ghe [e'kɔlogo] SM/F ecologist.

economato [ekono'mato] SM (*Scol, Univ*) bursar's office.

econometria [ekonome'tria] SF econometrics *sg*.

econometro [eko'nɔmetro] SM (*Aut*) trip computer.

economia [ekono'mia] SF **a** (*scienza*) economics *sg*; (*di paese, nazione*) economy ►**economia aziendale** business management ►**economia domestica** home economics *sg* ►**economia di mercato** market economy ►**economia pianificata** planned economy ►**economia politica** (*Univ*) political economy ►**economia di scala** economy of scale ►**economia sommersa** black (*Brit*) *o* underground (*Am*) economy **b** (*impiego razionale*) economy; (*risparmio*) saving; **dobbiamo fare economia** we must economize *o* make economies; **vivere in economia** to live frugally; **lavori in economia** (*nei cantieri edili*) building work involving direct labour.

economicamente [ekonomika'mente] AVV economically.

economico, a, ci, che [eko'nɔmiko] AGG (*Econ*) economic; (*che costa poco*) inexpensive; (*che fa risparmiare*) economical; **edizione economica** low price edition.

economista, i, e [ekono'mista] SM/F economist.

economizzare [ekonomid'dzare] ① VT (*soldi, forze*) to save.

② VI (*aus* **avere**): **economizzare (su)** to economize (on), cut down (on).

economizzatore [ekonomiddza'tore] SM (*Tecn*) fuel-saving device.

economo, a [e'kɔnomo] ① AGG thrifty.

② SM/F (*Amm*) bursar.

ecoscandaglio, gli [ekoskan'daʎʎo] SM echo sounder.
ecosistema, i [ekosis'tɛma] SM ecosystem.
ecoterrorismo [ekoterro'rizmo] SM ecoterrorism.
ecoterrorista, i, e [ekoterro'rista] SM/F ecoterrorist.
écru [e'kry] AGG INV (*tessuto*) raw; (*colore*) ecru, natural-coloured; **lino écru** unbleached linen; **seta écru** raw silk.
ectoplasma, i [ekto'plazma] SM ectoplasm.
ECU, ecu ['ɛku] SIGLA M O F INV ECU, ecu (= *European Currency Unit*).
Ecuador [ekwa'dɔr] SM: **l'Ecuador** Ecuador.
ecumenico, a, ci, che [eku'mɛniko] AGG ecumenical.
ecumenismo [ekume'nizmo] SM ecumenicalism.
eczema, i [ek'dzɛma] SM eczema.
ed [ed] CONG vedi **e**.
Ed. ABBR = **editore**.
ed. ABBR = **edizione**.
Eden ['ɛden] SM: **l'Eden** Eden.
edera ['edera] SF ivy.
edicola [e'dikola] SF newspaper kiosk o stand, newsstand (*Am*).
edicolante [ediko'lante] SM/F newspaper-seller.
edificante [edifi'kante] AGG edifying; **è uno spettacolo poco edificante** it isn't a very edifying spectacle.
edificare [edifi'kare] VT a (*casa*) to build; (*teoria*) to construct; (*azienda*) to set up b (*indurre al bene*) to edify.
edificazione [edifikat'tsjone] SF a building b (*morale*) edification.
edificio, ci [edi'fitʃo] SM (*costruzione*) building; (*struttura: sociale*) structure; (: *filosofico, critico*) framework.
edile [e'dile] 1 AGG building *attr*, construction *attr*.
  2 SM construction worker.
edilizia [edi'littsja] SF building (trade).
edilizio, zia, zi, zie [edi'littsjo] AGG building *attr*.
Edimburgo [edim'burgo] SF Edinburgh.
Edipo [e'dipo] SM Oedipus; **complesso di Edipo** Oedipus complex.
editare [edi'tare] VT (*Inform*) to edit.
edito, a ['ɛdito] AGG published.
editore, trice [edi'tore] 1 AGG publishing *attr*.
  2 SM/F (*imprenditore*) publisher; (*chi cura la pubblicazione*) editor.
editoria [edito'ria] SF publishing.
editoriale [edito'rjale] 1 AGG publishing *attr*.
  2 SM (*articolo di fondo*) leader, editorial.
editorialista, i, e [editorja'lista] SM/F leader writer.
editto [e'ditto] SM edict.
edizione [edit'tsjone] SF a (*di libro, giornale*) edition; **edizione a tiratura limitata** limited edition b : **la quarantesima edizione della Fiera di Milano** the fortieth Milan Trade Fair.
edonismo [edo'nizmo] SM hedonism.
edonista, i, e [edo'nista] SM/F hedonist.
edonistico, a, ci, che [edo'nistiko] AGG hedonistic.
edotto, a [e'dɔtto] AGG informed; **rendere qn edotto su qc** to inform sb about sth.
edredone [edre'done] SM (*Zool*) eider (duck).
educanda [edu'kanda] SF boarder (*girl*).
educare [edu'kare] VT (*gen, fig: gusto*) to educate; (*allevare*) to bring up; **educare qn a rispettare qc** to bring sb up to respect sth.
educatamente [edukata'mente] AVV politely.
educativo, a [eduka'tivo] AGG educational.

educato, a [edu'kato] AGG (*gen*) polite; (*bambino*) well-behaved, well-mannered; **non è educato fare così** it's not good manners o polite o nice to do that.
educatore, trice [eduka'tore] SM/F educator; (*pedagogista*) educationalist.
educazione [edukat'tsjone] SF a (*comportamento*) (good) manners *pl*; **per educazione** out of politeness; **buona/cattiva educazione** good/bad manners; **questa è pura mancanza d'educazione!** this is sheer bad manners!
  b (*formazione*) education; (*familiare*) upbringing ►**educazione fisica** physical education o training.
educherò *ecc* [eduke'rɔ] VB vedi **educare**.
E.E.D. [ee'di] SIGLA F (= *elaborazione elettronica dei dati*) EDP.
EEG [ee'dʒi] SIGLA M (= *elettroencefalogramma*) EEG.
efebo [e'fɛbo] SM (*Storia*) ephebe; (*fig*) youth.
efelide [e'fɛlide] SF freckle.
efemera [e'fɛmera] SF (*Zool*) mayfly.
effemeride [effe'mɛride] SF (*Astron*) ephemeris.
effeminatezza [effemina'tettsa] SF effeminacy.
effeminato, a [effemi'nato] AGG effeminate.
efferatezza [effera'tettsa] SF brutality.
efferato, a [effe'rato] AGG brutal, savage.
effervescente [efferveʃ'ʃente] AGG (*gen*) effervescent; (*fig: persona, personalità*) bubbly; **bibita effervescente** fizzy drink; **digestivo effervescente** liver salts.
effervescenza [efferveʃ'ʃentsa] SF effervescence.
effettivamente [effettiva'mente] AVV (*in effetti*) in fact; (*a dire il vero*) really, actually.
effettivo, a [effet'tivo] 1 AGG a (*vero e proprio*) real b (*impiegato, professore*) permanent; (*Mil*) regular.
  2 SM a (*Amm*): **effettivi** SMPL permanent staff; (*Mil*) strength b (*di patrimonio*) sum total.
effetto[1] [ef'fɛtto] SM a (*risultato*) effect; **avere** o **produrre un effetto (su)** to have o produce an effect (on); **l'effetto voluto** the desired effect; **far effetto** (*medicina*) to take effect, (start to) work; **sotto l'effetto dell'alcool** under the influence of alcohol; **in effetti** in fact; **a questo** o **tale effetto** to this end; **la legge ha effetto retroattivo** the law is retroactive
  b (*fig: impressione*) effect, impression; **ebbe l'effetto di una bomba** it had a shattering effect; **fare effetto su qn** to make an impression on sb; **il sangue mi fa effetto** I can't take the sight of blood; **mi fa un effetto strano pensare che...** it gives me a strange feeling to think that ...; **cercare l'effetto** to try to impress ►**effetti speciali** (*Cine*) special effects ►**effetto cocktail** (*Med*) cocktail effect ►**effetto neve** (*TV*) snow ►**effetto serra** (*Meteor*) greenhouse effect
  c (*Sport: di palla*) spin; **colpire d'effetto una palla** to put a spin on a ball
  d (*Comm: cambiale*) bill.
effetto[2] [ef'fɛtto] SM, SPEC PL: **effetti personali** personal effects, personal belongings.
effettore [effet'tore] SM (*Anat*) effector.
effettuare [effettu'are] 1 VT (*gen*) to make; (*controllo, volontà altrui*) to carry out.
  2 **effettuarsi** VIP to take place.
efficace [effi'katʃe] AGG (*provvedimento, rimedio*) effective.
efficacemente [effikatʃe'mente] AVV effectively.
efficacia [effi'katʃa] SF effectiveness.
efficiente [effi'tʃente] AGG (*persona, macchina*) efficient; (*misura*) effective.
efficientemente [effitʃente'mente] AVV efficiently.

efficientismo [effitʃen'tizmo] SM (show of) hyper-efficiency.

efficienza [effi'tʃɛntsa] SF efficiency.

effigiare [effi'dʒare] VT to represent, portray.

effigie, gi [ef'fidʒe] SF effigy; (*ritratto*) portrait.

effimero, a [ef'fimero] AGG (*gen*) ephemeral, fleeting; (*speranza, gloria*) short-lived.

efflorescenza [effloreʃ'ʃɛntsa] SF (*Chim, Geol*) efflorescence.

effluvio, vi [ef'fluvjo] SM (*anche iro*) scent, perfume.

effusione [effu'zjone] SF **a** (*gen*) effusion ► **effusione lavica** (*Geol*) lava flow **b** : **con effusione** (*salutare, abbracciare*) warmly.

e.g. ABBR (= *exempli gratia*) e.g.

egemone [e'dʒɛmone] AGG (*stato*) hegemonic.

egemonia [edʒemo'nia] SF hegemony.

Egeo [e'dʒɛo] SM: **l'Egeo, il mar Egeo** the Aegean (Sea).

egida ['ɛdʒida] SF: **sotto l'egida di** under the aegis of.

Egitto [e'dʒitto] SM: **l'Egitto** Egypt.

egiziano, a [edʒit'tsjano] 1 AGG Egyptian.
2 SM/F Egyptian.
3 SM (*lingua*) Ancient Egyptian.

egizio, zia, zi, zie [e'dʒittsjo] AGG, SM/F Ancient Egyptian.

egli ['eʎʎi] PRON PERS (*little used*) he; **egli stesso** he himself.

ego ['ɛgo] SM INV (*Psic*) ego.

egocentrico, a, ci, che [ego'tʃɛntriko] 1 AGG egocentric, self-centred (*Brit*), self-centered (*Am*).
2 SM/F self-centred (*Brit*) o self-centered (*Am*) person.

egocentrismo [egotʃen'trizmo] SM egocentricity.

egoismo [ego'izmo] SM selfishness; (*Psic*) egoism.

egoista, i, e [ego'ista] 1 AGG selfish; (*Psic*) egoistic.
2 SM/F selfish person; (*Psic*) egoist.

egoisticamente [egoistika'mente] AVV selfishly; (*Psic*) egoistically.

egoistico, a, ci, che [ego'istiko] AGG selfish; (*Psic*) egoistic.

egotismo [ego'tizmo] SM egotism.

egotista, i, e [ego'tista] 1 AGG egotistic.
2 SM/F egotist.

Egr., egr. ABBR = **Egregio**.

egregio, gia, gi, gie [e'grɛdʒo] AGG distinguished; **Egregio Signore** (*nelle lettere*) Dear Sir.

eguaglianza *ecc* [egwaʎ'ʎantsa] = **uguaglianza** *ecc*.

egualitario, ria, ri, rie [egwali'tarjo] AGG, SM/F egalitarian.

egualitarismo [egwalita'rizmo] SM egalitarianism.

E.I. ABBR = *Esercito Italiano*.

eiaculazione [ejakulat'tsjone] SF (*Fisiologia*) ejaculation ► **eiaculazione precoce** premature ejaculation.

eiettabile [ejet'tabile] AGG: **seggiolino eiettabile** ejector seat.

elaborare [elabo'rare] VT (*proposta*) to elaborate, develop; (*concetto, idea*) to work out; (*dati*) to process.

elaborato, a [elabo'rato] AGG elaborate; **motore elaborato** (*Aut*) souped-up engine.

elaboratore [elabora'tore] SM (*Inform*): **elaboratore elettronico** computer.

elaborazione [elaborat'tsjone] 1 SF (*gen*) elaboration; (*di concetto, idea*) working out.
2 (*Inform*) ► **elaborazione (automatica) dei dati** (automatic) data processing ► **elaborazione a blocchi** batch processing ► **elaborazione conversazionale** interactive computing ► **elaborazione elettronica dei dati** electronic data processing ► **elaborazione testi** word processing.

elargire [elar'dʒire] VT to give (generously).

elargizione [elardʒit'tsjone] SF donation.

elasticamente [elastika'mente] AVV elastically.

elasticità [elastitʃi'ta] SF (*vedi agg*) elasticity; spring; flexibility; laxness.

elasticizzato, a [elastitʃid'dzato] AGG (*tessuto*) stretch *attr*.

elastico, a, ci, che [e'lastiko] 1 AGG (*materiale*) elastic; (*fig: andatura*) springy; (: *mente, vedute, misure*) flexible; (: *principi morali*) lax.
2 SM (*per cucito: nastro*) elastic *no pl*; (*di gomma*) elastic band, rubber band.

elefante [ele'fante] SM elephant.

elefantesco, a, schi, sche [elefan'tesko] AGG elephantine.

elegante [ele'gante] AGG elegant, smart.

elegantemente [elegante'mente] AVV elegantly; (*vestirsi*) elegantly, smartly.

eleganza [ele'gantsa] SF elegance; (*nel vestirsi*) elegance, smartness.

eleggere [e'lɛddʒere] VT IRREG: **eleggere (a)** to elect (to).

elegia, gie [ele'dʒia] SF elegy.

elementare [elemen'tare] 1 AGG (*gen*) elementary; (*rozzo, rudimentale*) rudimentary; (*principi, nozioni*) basic; (*Chim*) elemental; **scuola elementare** primary (*Brit*) o grade (*Am*) school; **la prima elementare** the first year of primary (*Brit*) o grade (*Am*) school.
2 SFPL: **le elementari** primary (*Brit*) o grade (*Am*) school *sg*.

elemento [ele'mento] SM (*gen, Chim*) element; (*di meccanismo*) part, component; (*di pila*) cell; (*di cucina componibile*) unit; **elementi di algebra** basic algebra; **la furia degli elementi** the fury of the elements; **non è stato scoperto nessun nuovo elemento** no new facts have come to light; **è il migliore elemento della squadra** he's the best player in the team; **essere nel proprio elemento** to be in one's element ► **elementi in parallelo/in serie** (*Fis*) parallel/series elements.

elemosina [ele'mɔzina] SF charity, alms *pl* (*ant*); **chiedere l'elemosina** to beg; **dare qc in elemosina** to give sth to charity; **cassetta delle elemosine** (*in chiesa*) alms box; **non ho bisogno della tua elemosina** (*fig*) I don't need your charity.

elemosinare [elemozi'nare] 1 VT to beg for.
2 VI (*aus* **avere**) to beg.

Elena ['ɛlena] SF Helen.

elencare [elen'kare] VT to list.

elencherò *ecc* [elenke'rɔ] VB *vedi* **elencare**.

elenco, chi [e'lɛnko] SM list; **fare un elenco di** (*scritto*) to make a list of, list; (*orale*) to list ► **elenco telefonico** telephone directory.

elessi *ecc* [e'lɛssi] VB *vedi* **eleggere**.

elettivo, a [elet'tivo] AGG (*carica*) elective.

eletto, a [e'lɛtto] 1 PP di **eleggere**.
2 AGG (*Pol*) elected; (*pubblico*) select; **il popolo eletto** the chosen people.
3 SM **a** (*Pol*) elected member **b** (*Rel*): **gli eletti** SMPL the elect, the chosen.

elettorale [eletto'rale] AGG electoral, election *attr*.

elettorato [eletto'rato] SM: **elettorato (attivo)** electorate.

elettore, trice [elet'tore] SM/F voter.

Elettra [e'lɛttra] SF Electra.

elettrauto [elet'trauto] SM INV (*Aut: officina*) workshop for electrical repairs; (: *tecnico*) electrician.

elettricamente [elettrika'mente] AVV electrically.
elettricista, i [elettri'tʃista] SM electrician.
elettricità [elettritʃi'ta] SF electricity; **c'è elettricità nell'aria** (fig) the atmosphere is electric.
elettrico, a, ci, che [e'lɛttriko] ① AGG (gen) electric; (impianto, corrente) electric(al); **tariffe elettriche** electricity charges; **blu elettrico** electric blue.
② SM (operaio) electricity worker, power worker.
elettrificare [elettrifi'kare] VT (linea ferroviaria) to electrify.
elettrificazione [elettrifikat'tsjone] SF electrification.
elettrizzante [elettrid'dzante] AGG (fig) electrifying.
elettrizzare [elettrid'dzare] ① VT to charge (with electricity); (fig: pubblico, atmosfera) to electrify.
② **elettrizzarsi** VIP to become charged with electricity; (fig: persona) to be electrified, be thrilled.
elettrizzato, a [elettrid'dzato] AGG charged with electricity; (fig) electrified, thrilled.
elettrizzazione [elettriddzat'tsjone] SF electrification; (Fis) charging.
elettro... [e'lɛttro] PREF electro... .
elettrocalamita [elettrokala'mita] SF electromagnet.
elettrocardiogramma, i [elettrokardjo'gramma] SM electrocardiogram.
elettrochimica [elettro'kimika] SF electrochemistry.
elettrochimico, a, ci, che [elettro'kimiko] AGG electrochemical.
elettrodinamica [elettrodi'namika] SF electrodynamics sg.
elettrodo [e'lɛttrodo] SM electrode.
elettrodomestico, a, ci, che [elettrodo'mɛstiko] AGG: (apparecchio) **elettrodomestico** domestic (electrical) appliance.
elettroencefalogramma, i [elettroentʃefalo'gramma] SM electroencephalogram, EEG.
elettroesecuzione [elettroezekut'tsjone] SF electrocution.
elettrogeno, a [elet'trɔdʒeno] AGG: **gruppo elettrogeno** generator.
elettrolisi [elet'trɔlizi] SF electrolysis.
elettrolita, i [elet'trɔlita] SM electrolyte.
elettromagnete [elettromaɲ'ɲɛte] SM electromagnet.
elettromagnetico, a, ci, che [elettromaɲ'ɲɛtiko] AGG electromagnetic.
elettromagnetismo [elettromaɲɲe'tizmo] SM electromagnetism.
elettromeccanico, a, ci, che [elettromek'kaniko] AGG electromechanical.
elettromotore, trice [elettromo'tore] AGG: **forza elettromotrice** electromotive force.
elettromotrice [elettromo'tritʃe] SF electric train.
elettrone [elet'trone] SM electron.
elettronegatività [elettronegativi'ta] SF INV electronegativity.
elettronica [elet'trɔnika] SF electronics sg.
elettronicamente [elettronika'mente] AVV electronically; **elaborato elettronicamente** computerized.
elettronico, a, ci, che [elet'trɔniko] AGG (gen) electronic; (carica, microscopio) electron attr; **ingegneria elettronica** electronic engineering.
elettroscopio, pi [elettros'kɔpjo] SM electroscope.
elettroshock [elettroʃ'ʃɔk] SM INV electroconvulsive therapy, (electro)shock treatment.
elettrostatica [elettros'tatika] SF electrostatics sg.

elettrostatico, a, ci, che [elettros'tatiko] AGG electrostatic.
elettrotecnica [elettro'tɛknika] SF electrotechnology.
elettrotecnico, a, ci, che [elettro'tɛkniko] ① AGG electrotechnical.
② SM electrical engineer.
elettrovalente [elettrova'lɛnte] AGG (Chim, Fis) electrovalent.
elevare [ele'vare] ① VT ⓐ (alzare: muro) to put up; (sguardo, occhi) to raise, lift; (tenore di vita) to raise; **elevare un edificio di un piano** to add a floor to a building; **elevare qn al rango di** to raise o elevate sb to the rank of; **elevare al trono** to raise to the throne
ⓑ (Mat) to raise; **elevare un numero al quadrato** to square a number
ⓒ (Amm): **elevare una contravvenzione a qn** to fine sb.
② **elevarsi** VIP, VR (gen) to rise; **elevarsi (con lo spirito)** (fig) to be uplifted.
elevatezza [eleva'tettsa] SF (altezza) elevation; (di animo, pensiero) loftiness.
elevato, a [ele'vato] AGG (gen) high; (cime) high, lofty; (fig: stile, sentimenti) lofty; **poco elevato** not very high.
elevatore [eleva'tore] SM elevator.
elevazione [elevat'tsjone] SF (gen, Mat) raising; (di terreno) elevation; (Sport) lift; **l'Elevazione** (Rel) the Elevation.
elezione [elet'tsjone] SF ⓐ (Pol, Amm) election; **indire le elezioni** to hold an election; **giorno delle elezioni** election day ▸ **elezioni amministrative** ≈ local council election ▸ **elezioni anticipate** early election (held before end of fixed term of legislature) ▸ **elezioni politiche** general election
ⓑ (scelta) choice; **patria d'elezione** adopted country.
elfo ['ɛlfo] SM elf.
elica, che ['ɛlika] SF (Aer, Naut) propeller, screw; (Mat) helix.
elicoidale [elikoi'dale] AGG helicoidal.
elicottero [eli'kɔttero] SM helicopter.
elidere [e'lidere] VB IRREG ① VT (Fonetica) to elide.
② **elidersi** VR (uso reciproco) to cancel each other out, neutralize each other.
eliminare [elimi'nare] VT (anche fig) to eliminate.
eliminatorio, ria, ri, rie [elimina'tɔrjo] ① AGG (prova, gara) eliminatory.
② SF (Sport) heat, eliminating round.
eliminazione [eliminat'tsjone] SF elimination; **per eliminazione** by a process of elimination.
Elio ['ɛljo] SM (Mitol) Helios.
elio ['ɛljo] SM (Chim) helium.
eliocentrico, a, ci, che [eljo'tʃɛntriko] AGG heliocentric.
eliporto [eli'pɔrto] SM heliport.
elisabettiano, a [elizabet'tjano] AGG Elizabethan.
elisione [eli'zjone] SF (Fonetica) elision.
elisir [eli'zir] SM INV elixir ▸ **elisir di lunga vita** elixir of life.
eliso, a [e'lizo] PP di **elidere**.
elitario, ria, ri, rie [eli'tarjo] AGG elitist.
élite [e'lit] SF INV élite.
ella ['ella] PRON PERS (letter) she; **ella stessa** she herself.
Ellade ['ɛllade] SF Hellas.
ellenico, a, ci, che [el'lɛniko] AGG Hellenic.
ellisse [el'lisse] SF (Geom) ellipse.
ellissi [el'lissi] SF INV (Gramm) ellipsis; (Geom) = **ellisse**.
ellittico, a, ci, che [el'littiko] AGG (Geom, Gramm) elliptic(al).
elmetto [el'metto] SM helmet.

elmo ['elmo] SM helmet.

elogiare [elo'dʒare] VT to praise, laud (frm).

elogiativo, a [elodʒa'tivo] AGG laudatory.

elogio, gi [e'lɔdʒo] SM **a** praise; **fare l'elogio di qn/qc** to praise sb/sth, speak highly of sb/sth **b** (ufficiale) eulogy; **elogio funebre** funeral oration.

eloquente [elo'kwɛnte] AGG eloquent; **questi dati sono eloquenti** these facts speak for themselves.

eloquentemente [elokwente'mente] AVV eloquently.

eloquenza [elo'kwɛntsa] SF eloquence.

eloquio, qui [e'lɔkwjo] SM (letter) discourse.

elsa ['elsa] SF hilt.

El Salvador ['el salva'dɔr] SM El Salvador.

elucubrare [eluku'brare] VT (anche iro) to ponder (on o over); **che cosa stai elucubrando?** what are you dreaming up now?

elucubrazioni [elukubrat'tsjoni] SFPL (anche iro) cogitations, ponderings.

eludere [e'ludere] VT IRREG (gen) to evade, elude; (sorveglianza, nemico) to evade, dodge.

elusi ecc [e'luzi] VB vedi **eludere**.

elusione [elu'zjone] SF: **elusione fiscale** tax avoidance.

elusivamente [eluziva'mente] AVV (rispondere) evasively.

elusivo, a [elu'zivo] AGG (risposta, parole) evasive.

eluso, a [e'luzo] PP di **eludere**.

elvetico, a, ci, che [el'vetiko] AGG Swiss.

emaciato, a [ema'tʃato] AGG emaciated.

emanare [ema'nare] **1** VT **a** (odore, calore) to give off o out; (raggi) to emit; (fascino) to radiate **b** (emettere: legge) to promulgate; (: ordine, circolare) to issue.
2 VI (aus essere): **emanare da** to emanate from.

emanazione [emanat'tsjone] SF **a** (di raggi, calore) emission; (di odori) exhalation **b** (di legge) promulgation; (di ordine, circolare) issuing.

emancipare [emantʃi'pare] **1** VT to emancipate.
2 emanciparsi VR to become liberated o emancipated.

emancipato, a [emantʃi'pato] AGG emancipated.

emancipazione [emantʃipat'tsjone] SF emancipation.

emarginare [emardʒi'nare] VT (socialmente) to marginalize.

emarginato, a [emardʒi'nato] SM/F marginalized person, disadvantaged person.

emarginazione [emardʒinat'tsjone] SF marginalization.

ematologia [ematolo'dʒia] SF (Med) haematology (Brit), hematology (Am).

ematoma, i [ema'tɔma] SM bruise; (termine tecn) haematoma (Brit), hematoma (Am).

embargo, ghi [em'bargo] SM embargo.

emblema, i [em'blɛma] SM emblem.

emblematicamente [emblematika'mente] AVV (vedi agg) emblematically; symbolically.

emblematico, a, ci, che [emble'matiko] AGG emblematic; (atteggiamento, parole) symbolic.

embolia [embo'lia] SF embolism.

embrionale [embrio'nale] AGG embryonic, embryo attr; **sacco embrionale** embryo sac; **allo stadio embrionale** (progetto, piano) at the embryo stage.

embrione [embri'one] SM embryo.

emendamento [emenda'mento] SM (Dir) amendment; (di scritto) emendation.

emendare [emen'dare] VT (legge) to amend; (testo) to emend.

emergente [emer'dʒɛnte] AGG emerging; **paesi emergenti** developing countries.

emergenza [emer'dʒɛntsa] SF emergency; **in caso di emergenza** in case of an emergency; **stato di emergenza** state of emergency.

emergere [e'mɛrdʒere] VI IRREG (aus essere) (sommergibile) to surface; (fig: verità, fatti) to emerge; (: persona: distinguersi) to stand out.

emerito, a [e'mɛrito] AGG (insigne) distinguished; **professore emerito** professor emeritus; **è un emerito cretino!** he's a complete idiot!

emersi ecc [e'mɛrsi] VB vedi **emergere**.

emersione [emer'sjone] SF (sottomarino): **navigare in emersione** to sail on the surface; **pronto all'emersione** ready to surface.

emerso, a [e'mɛrso] **1** PP di **emergere**.
2 AGG (Geog): **le terre emerse** the world's land surface.

emesso, a [e'messo] PP di **emettere**.

emetico, a, ci, che [e'mɛtiko] AGG, SM emetic.

emettere [e'mettere] VT IRREG **a** (Fis) to emit; (luce) to give out; (calore, odore) to give off; (suono, fischio) to give, let out; (Radio) to transmit; (Inform) to output; **emettere un grido di dolore** to give a cry of pain; **emettere un gemito** to groan, utter a groan
b (Fin: titoli, assegno) to issue; (: moneta) to put into circulation, issue
c (pronunciare: giudizio) to express, voice; (Dir: ordine, mandato di cattura) to issue; **emettere una sentenza** to pass sentence.

emiciclo [emi'tʃiklo] SM semicircle, hemicycle; (della Camera dei deputati) floor.

emicrania [emi'kranja] SF migraine.

emigrante [emi'grante] AGG, SM/F emigrant.

emigrare [emi'grare] VI (aus essere): **emigrare (in)** (persona) to emigrate (to); (animale: migrare) to migrate (to).

emigrato, a [emi'grato] **1** AGG emigrant.
2 SM/F emigrant; (Storia) émigré.

emigrazione [emigrat'tsjone] SF (vedi vb) emigration; migration; **emigrazione di capitali** flight of capital.

emiliano, a [emi'ljano] **1** AGG of o from Emilia.
2 SM/F inhabitant o native of Emilia.

eminente [emi'nɛnte] AGG (posizione) high, lofty; (scienziato ecc) eminent, distinguished.

eminentemente [eminente'mente] AVV (principalmente) mainly, principally.

eminentissimo [eminen'tissimo] SM (in lettere) His Eminence; (nel rivolgersi personalmente) Your Eminence.

eminenza [emi'nɛntsa] SF **a** (titolo: di cardinale): **Eminenza** Eminence ▶ **eminenza grigia** (fig) éminence grise **b** (qualità) distinction, eminence.

emirato [emi'rato] SM emirate; **gli Emirati Arabi Uniti** the United Arab Emirates.

emiro [e'miro] SM emir.

emisfero [emis'fɛro] SM (gen) hemisphere; **emisfero australe/boreale** southern/northern hemisphere.

emisi ecc [e'mizi] VB vedi **emettere**.

emissario, ri [emis'sarjo] SM **a** (Geog) outflowing river **b** (inviato) emissary.

emissione [emis'sjone] SF (di suoni, onde, calore, radiazioni) emission; (di energia) output; (di francobolli, titoli, assegni) issue.

emittente [emit'tɛnte] **1** AGG (Radio, TV) transmitting, broadcasting; (banca) issuing.
2 SF (stazione) transmitting station, broadcasting

station; **emittente privata** independent station.

emofilia [emofiˈlia] SF haemophilia (*Brit*), hemophilia (*Am*).

emofiliaco, a, ci, che [emofiˈliako] AGG, SM/F haemophiliac (*Brit*), hemophiliac (*Am*).

emoglobina [emogloˈbina] SF haemoglobin (*Brit*), hemoglobin (*Am*).

emolisi [emoˈlizi] SF (*Bio*) haemolysis.

emolliente [emolˈljɛnte] AGG, SM (*crema, preparato*) soothing.

emorragia, gie [emorraˈdʒia] SF haemorrhage (*Brit*), hemorrhage (*Am*) ▶**emorragia interna** internal bleeding.

emorroidi [emorˈrɔidi] SFPL haemorrhoids (*Brit*), hemorrhoids (*Am*), piles.

emostatico, a, ci, che [emosˈtatiko] AGG haemostatic (*Brit*), hemostatic (*Am*); **laccio emostatico** tourniquet; **matita emostatica** styptic pencil.

emotivamente [emotivaˈmente] AVV emotionally.

emotività [emotiviˈta] SF INV emotional nature.

emotivo, a [emoˈtivo] AGG emotional.

emozionale [emottsjoˈnale] AGG emotional.

emozionante [emottsjoˈnante] AGG (*che appassiona*) thrilling, exciting; (*che commuove*) moving.

emozionare [emottsjoˈnare] ① VT (*appassionare*) to thrill, excite; (*commuovere*) to move.

② **emozionarsi** VIP (*vedi vt*) to get excited; to be moved; **emozionarsi facilmente** to be excitable; to be easily moved.

emozionato, a [emotsjoˈnato] AGG (*commosso*) moved; (*agitato*) nervous; **scusami sono un po' emozionato** sorry, I feel a bit overwhelmed.

emozione [emotˈtsjone] SF emotion; **a caccia di emozioni** in search of excitement.

empatia [empaˈtia] SF empathy.

Empedocle [emˈpɛdokle] SM Empedocles.

empiamente [empjaˈmente] AVV (*Rel*) impiously, blasphemously; (*crudelmente*) cruelly.

empietà [empjeˈta] SF INV (*Rel*) impiety; (*crudeltà*) cruelty; (*azione crudele*) cruel deed.

empio, pia, pi, pie [ˈempjo] AGG (*Rel*) impious; (*crudele*) cruel.

empiricamente [empirikaˈmente] AVV empirically.

empirico, a, ci, che [emˈpiriko] AGG empirical.

empirismo [empiˈrizmo] SM empiricism.

emporio, ri [emˈpɔrjo] SM emporium, general store.

emù [eˈmu] SM INV emu.

emulare [emuˈlare] VT to emulate.

emulazione [emulatˈtsjone] SF emulation.

emulo, a [ˈɛmulo] SM/F imitator.

emulsionare [emulsjoˈnare] VT to emulsify.

emulsione [emulˈsjone] SF emulsion.

EN SIGLA = *Enna*.

enciclica, che [enˈtʃiklika] SF (*Rel*) encyclical.

enciclopedia [entʃiklopeˈdia] SF encyclopaedia (*Brit*), encyclopedia (*Am*).

enciclopedico, a, ci, che [entʃikloˈpɛdiko] AGG encyclopaedic (*Brit*), encyclopedic (*Am*).

enclave [ãˈklav] SF INV enclave.

enclitico, a, ci, che [enˈklitiko] AGG (*Gramm*) enclitic; **particella enclitica** enclitic particle.

encomiabile [enkoˈmjabile] AGG commendable, praiseworthy.

encomiabilmente [enkomjabilˈmente] AVV admirably, in a praiseworthy manner.

encomiare [enkoˈmjare] VT to commend, praise.

encomio, mi [enˈkɔmjo] SM commendation; **encomio solenne** (*Mil*) mention in dispatches.

endemico, a, ci, che [enˈdɛmiko] AGG endemic.

endocrino, a [enˈdɔkrino] AGG endocrine.

endogeno, a [enˈdɔdʒeno] AGG a (*gen, Bio, Med*) endogenous b (*Geol*): **fenomeni endogeni** internal processes; **rocce endogene** endogenous rocks.

endoscheletro [endosˈkɛletro] SM (*Anat*) endoskeleton.

endotermico, a, ci, che [endoˈtɛrmiko] AGG endothermic.

endovena [endoˈvena] ① SF (*Med*) intravenous injection.

② AVV: **iniettare qc endovena** to inject sth intravenously.

endovenoso, a [endoveˈnoso] ① AGG (*Med*) intravenous; **per via endovenosa** intravenously.

② SF intravenous injection.

Enea [eˈnɛa] SM (*Storia*) Aeneas.

E.N.E.A. [eˈnɛa] SIGLA M (= *Comitato nazionale per la ricerca e lo sviluppo dell'Energia Nucleare e delle Energie Alternative*) national committee for research into nuclear and alternative energy sources.

E.N.E.L. [ˈenel] SIGLA M (= *Ente Nazionale per l'Energia Elettrica*) national electricity board.

energetico, a, ci, che [enerˈdʒɛtiko] AGG (*risorse, crisi*) energy *attr*; (*sostanza, alimento*) energy-giving.

energia, gie [enerˈdʒia] SF a (*vigore*) energy, strength, vigour (*Brit*), vigor (*Am*); **avere molta energia** to be very energetic; **avere poca energia** to lack energy, have little energy; **dedicare tutte le proprie energie a qc** to devote all one's energies to sth

b (*Fis*) energy; (*Tecn*) power; **liberare energia** to release energy; **consumo di energia** power consumption ▶**energia alternativa: fonti di energia alternativa** sources of alternative energy ▶**energia nucleare** nuclear energy ▶**energia termica** heat energy.

energicamente [enerdʒikaˈmente] AVV energetically, vigorously.

energico, a, ci, che [eˈnɛrdʒiko] AGG (*persona*) energetic, vigorous; (*resistenza, rifiuto*) forceful, vigorous; (*cura*) potent, powerful; (*provvedimenti*) drastic.

energumeno [enerˈgumeno] SM (*scherz*) brute.

enfasi [ˈɛnfazi] SF INV emphasis; (*pegg*) pomposity; **con enfasi** emphatically; (*pegg*) pompously; **porre l'enfasi su** to stress, place the emphasis on, emphasize.

enfaticamente [enfatikaˈmente] AVV emphatically; **sottolineare enfaticamente il fatto che...** to lay great stress on the fact that ... .

enfatico, a, ci, che [enˈfatiko] AGG (*tono, discorso*) emphatic; (: *pegg*) pompous.

enfatizzare [enfatidˈdzare] VT to emphasize, stress.

enfisema, i [enfiˈzɛma] SM (*Med*) emphysema ▶**enfisema polmonare** pulmonary emphysema.

E.N.I. [ˈɛni] SIGLA M = *Ente Nazionale Idrocarburi*.

enigma, i [eˈnigma] SM (*mistero*) enigma, riddle; (*gioco*) puzzle, riddle; **quell'uomo è un enigma** that man is an enigma; **il suo comportamento rimane un enigma** his behaviour is inexplicable.

enigmaticamente [enigmatikaˈmente] AVV enigmatically.

enigmatico, a, ci, che [enigˈmatiko] AGG enigmatic.

enigmistica [enigˈmistika] SF: **essere un appassionato di enigmistica** to be very keen on doing puzzles; **rivista di enigmistica** puzzles magazine.

E.N.I.T. ['enit] SIGLA M (= *Ente Nazionale Italiano per il Turismo*) *Italian tourist board*.

ennesimo, a [en'nɛzimo] AGG (*Mat, fam*) nth; **all'ennesima potenza** to the nth power *o* degree; **per l'ennesima volta** for the umpteenth time.

enologia [enolo'dʒia] SF oenology (*Brit*), enology (*Am*).

enologico, a, ci, che [eno'lɔdziko] AGG oenological (*Brit*), enological (*Am*); **l'industria enologica** the wine industry.

enologo, a, gi [e'nɔlogo] SM/F oenologist (*Brit*), enologist (*Am*), wine expert.

enorme [e'norme] AGG (*gen*) enormous, huge; (*distesa, riserva*) vast, enormous; (*pazienza, forza*) tremendous, enormous.

enormemente [enorme'mente] AVV enormously, tremendously; **ci siamo divertiti enormemente** we enjoyed ourselves tremendously *o* hugely; **ciò mi ha deluso enormemente** I was greatly *o* tremendously disappointed by it.

enormità [enormi'ta] SF INV **a** (*di peso, somma*) hugeness; (*di distesa*) vastness; (*di richiesta*) enormity; (*di prezzo*) unreasonableness **b** (*stupidaggine*) blunder, howler; **non dire enormità!** don't talk nonsense!; **l'ho pagato un'enormità** I paid a fortune for it.

enoteca, che [eno'tɛka] SF (*per vendita*) wine shop, ≈ off-licence; (*per degustazione*) wine bar.

E.N.P.A. ['ɛnpa] SIGLA M (= *Ente Nazionale Protezione Animali*) ≈ RSPCA (*Brit*), ≈ SPCA (*Am*).

E.N.P.A.S. ['ɛnpas] SIGLA M (= *Ente Nazionale di Previdenza e Assistenza per i Dipendenti Statali*) *welfare organization for State employees*.

ensemble [ã'sãbl] SM INV (*Mus*) ensemble.

entalpia [ental'pia] SF (*Fis*) enthalpy.

ente ['ɛnte] SM **a** (*Amm*) body, corporation, board ▸ **ente autonomo** ≈ local board ▸ **ente locale** ≈ local authority (*Brit*), local government (*Am*) ▸ **ente pubblico** public body ▸ **ente di ricerca** research organization **b** (*Filosofia*) being.

enterite [ente'rite] SF (*Med*) enteritis.

entità [enti'ta] SF INV **a** (*di perdita, danni, investimenti*) extent; (*di popolazione*) size; **di scarsa/una certa entità** (*avvenimento, incidente*) of slight/some importance **b** (*Filosofia*) entity.

entomologia [entomolo'dʒia] SF (*Zool*) entomology.

entourage [ãtu'raʒ] SM INV entourage.

entraîneuse [ãtrɛ'nø:z] SF INV night-club hostess.

entrambi, e [en'trambi] AGG, PRON both; **entrambi i ragazzi** both boys, both of the boys; **entrambe le sorelle** both sisters, both of the sisters; **vennero entrambi** they both came, both of them came; **mi piacciono entrambi** I like them both, I like both of them.

entrante [en'trante] AGG (*prossimo: mese, anno*) next, coming.

entrare [en'trare] VI (*aus* **essere**)
a to go (*o* come) in, enter; (*con la macchina*) to drive in;
▷ **entri pure!** do come in!
▷ **"si prega di bussare prima di entrare"** "knock before entering"
▷ **entrare dalla finestra** to get in by the window
▷ **entrare in automobile** to get into the car
▷ **non entrare in acqua subito dopo aver mangiato!** don't go into the water when you've just eaten!
▷ **mi è entrato qualcosa nell'occhio** I've got something in my eye
b (*soldi, prodotti*) to enter, come in; (*contenuto*) to go in; (: *adattarsi*) to fit in;
▷ **il regalo non entra nella scatola** the present won't go *o* fit into the box
▷ **queste scarpe non mi entrano** I can't get into these shoes
▷ **entra acqua dal tetto** there's water coming in through the roof
▷ **la matematica non mi entra proprio in testa** I just can't get the hang of maths, I just can't get maths to sink in
c: **far entrare** (*visitatore, cliente*) to show in; (*animale*) to let in; (*oggetto*) to fit in; (*merce: d'importazione*) to bring in; (: *di contrabbando*) to smuggle in
▷ **far entrare qn in banca** (*come impiegato*) to get sb a job in a bank
▷ **far entrare qn in un club** (*ammettere*) to let sb into a club
▷ **non riesco a fargli entrare in testa che ce la può fare** I can't get him to understand that he can do it
▷ **gli hanno fatto entrare in testa la trigonometria** they've managed to teach him trigonometry
d: **entrare in** (*club, partito*) to join, become a member of; (*professione*) to go into
▷ **entrare in affari** to go into business
▷ **entrare nei vent'anni di età** to turn twenty
▷ **entrare in argomento** to get onto the subject
▷ **entrare in ballo** to come into play
▷ **entrare in carica** to take up office
▷ **entrare in commercio con qn** to go into business with sb
▷ **entrare in convalescenza** to begin one's convalescence
▷ **entrare in convento** to enter a convent
▷ **entrare in discussione con qn** to enter into discussions with sb
▷ **entrare in gioco** to come into play
▷ **entrare in guerra** (*all'inizio*) to go to war; (*a conflitto iniziato*) to come into the war
▷ **entrare nella professione legale** to go into the law
▷ **entrare al servizio di qn** to enter sb's service
▷ **entrare in società con qn** to go into partnership with sb
▷ **entrare nella storia** to go down in history
▷ **entrare in vigore** (*legge*) to come into force *o* effect
e: **entrarci** to have to do with
▷ **quello che dici non c'entra (niente)** what you say has nothing to do with it
▷ **tu non c'entri in questa faccenda** this is none of your business
▷ **io non c'entro** it's got nothing to do with me.

entrata [en'trata] SF **a** (*ingresso: di persona*) entry, entrance; (: *di merci, veicoli*) entry; **alla sua entrata** as he entered; **alla sua entrata in scena** (*Teatro*) on his entrance; (*fig*) when he came on to the scene; **all'entrata in guerra degli Stati Uniti** when the United States came into the war; **dopo la sua entrata in carica** after he took office; **con l'entrata in vigore dei nuovi provvedimenti...** once the new measures come into effect ...

b (*accesso*) admission; **"entrata libera"** "admission free"; **biglietto di entrata** (entrance) ticket

c (*porta*) entrance; (*vestibolo*) entrance (hall) ▶ **entrata degli artisti** (*Teatro*) stage door ▶ **entrata di servizio** service *o* tradesmen's entrance

d : **entrate** SFPL (*Econ*) income *sg*; (*Comm*) takings, receipts; **entrate e uscite** income and expenditure ▶ **entrate tributarie** tax revenue *sg*.

entrecôte [ātrə'kot] SF INV (*Culin*) entrecôte, rib steak.

entro ['entro] PREP within; **entro un mese** within a month; **entro domani** by tomorrow; **entro febbraio** by the end of February; **entro e non oltre il 25 aprile** no later than 25th April.

entrobordo [entro'bordo] (*Naut*) ①︎ AGG INV inboard.
②︎ SM INV (*motore*) inboard motor; (*motoscafo*) boat with an inboard engine.

entropia [entro'pia] SF (*Fis*) entropy.

entroterra [entro'tɛrra] SM INV hinterland; **l'entroterra australiano** the (Australian) outback.

entusiasmante [entuzjaz'mante] AGG exciting.

entusiasmare [entuzjaz'mare] ①︎ VT to fill with enthusiasm, excite.
②︎ **entusiasmarsi** VIP: **entusiasmarsi per qc** to be enthusiastic about *o* over sth.

entusiasmo [entu'zjazmo] SM enthusiasm.

entusiasta, i, e [entu'zjasta] ①︎ AGG: **entusiasta (di)** enthusiastic (about *o* over); **non sono entusiasta dei risultati** I'm not too happy about the results.
②︎ SM/F enthusiast.

entusiasticamente [entuzjastika'mente] AVV enthusiastically.

entusiastico, a, ci, che [entu'zjastiko] AGG enthusiastic.

enucleare [enukle'are] VT (*frm: problema*) to clarify.

enumerare [enume'rare] VT to enumerate, list.

enumerazione [enumerat'tsjone] SF enumeration.

enunciare [enun'tʃare] VT (*pensiero*) to express; (*fatti*) to state; (*teorema, teoria*) to set out.

enzima, i [en'dzima] SM enzyme.

eolico, a, ci, che [e'ɔliko] AGG (*Geog*) aeolian.

epatico, a, ci, che [e'patiko] AGG hepatic; **cirrosi epatica** cirrhosis of the liver.

epatite [epa'tite] SF hepatitis ▶ **epatite virale** viral hepatitis.

epatta [e'patta] SF (*Astron*) epact.

epica ['ɛpika] SF epic (poetry).

epicentro [epi'tʃentro] SM epicentre.

epico, a, ci, che ['ɛpiko] AGG (*anche fig*) epic.

epicureo, a [epiku'rɛo] AGG, SM/F epicurean.

Epicuro [epi'kuro] SM Epicurus.

epidemia [epide'mia] SF epidemic.

epidemicamente [epidemika'mente] AVV: **diffondersi epidemicamente** (*anche fig*) to spread like wildfire.

epidemico, a, ci, che [epi'dɛmiko] AGG epidemic.

epidermico, a, ci, che [epi'dɛrmiko] AGG (*Anat*) skin *attr*; (*fig: interesse, impressione*) superficial.

epidermide [epi'dɛrmide] SF (*Anat*) skin, epidermis.

Epifania [epifa'nia] SF Epiphany.

epiglottide [epi'glɔttide] SF (*Med*) epiglottis.

epigono [e'pigono] SM imitator.

epigrafe [e'pigrafe] SF epigraph; (*su libro*) dedication.

epigrafico, a, ci, che [epi'grafiko] AGG epigraphic; (*fig: stile*) concise.

epigramma, i [epi'gramma] SM epigram.

epigrammatica [epigram'matika] SF epigrammatic poetry.

epigrammatico, a, ci, che [epigram'matiko] AGG epigrammatic.

epilessia [epiles'sia] SF epilepsy.

epilettico, a, ci, che [epi'lɛttiko] AGG, SM/F epileptic.

epilobio, bi [epi'lɔbjo] SM (*Bot*) willowherb.

epilogo, ghi [e'pilogo] SM epilogue; (*fig*) conclusion.

episcopale [episko'pale] AGG episcopal.

episcopato [episko'pato] SM episcopacy.

episodicamente [epizodika'mente] AVV occasionally.

episodico, a, ci, che [epi'zɔdiko] AGG (*romanzo, narrazione*) episodic; (*fig: occasionale*) occasional.

episodio, di [epi'zɔdjo] SM episode; **sceneggiato a episodi** serial.

epistola [e'pistola] SF epistle.

epistolare [episto'lare] AGG epistolary; **essere in rapporto ˙o relazione epistolare con qn** to correspond *o* be in correspondence with sb.

epistolario, ri [episto'larjo] SM letters *pl*.

epitaffio, fi [epi'taffjo] SM epitaph.

epitelio, li [epi'tɛljo] SM (*Anat*) epithelium.

epiteto [e'piteto] SM (*Gramm*) attribute; (*fig*) epithet; **un epiteto irripetibile** an unrepeatable insult.

epoca, che ['ɛpoka] SF (*gen*) time; (*periodo storico*) age, era, epoch; (*Geol*) age; **all'epoca di** at the time of; **viviamo in un'epoca difficile** we live in difficult times *o* in a difficult age; **mobili d'epoca** period furniture; **fare epoca** (*scandalo*) to cause a stir; (*cantante, moda*) to mark a new era; **lo sbarco sulla luna ha fatto epoca** the moon landing was an epoch-making event.

epopea [epo'pɛa] SF (*anche fig*) epic.

eppure [ep'pure] CONG and yet, nevertheless.

E.P.T. [epi'ti] SIGLA M (= *Ente Provinciale per il Turismo*) *local tourist bureau*.

epurare [epu'rare] VT (*Pol*) to purge.

epurazione [epurat'tsjone] SF purge ▶ **epurazione etnica** ethnic cleansing.

equalizzatore [ekwaliddza'tore] SM (*Elettr*) equalizer.

equamente [ekwa'mente] AVV equitably, fairly.

equanime [e'kwanime] AGG (*imparziale*) impartial.

equanimità [ekwanimi'ta] SF INV (*imparzialità*) impartiality.

equatore [ekwa'tore] SM equator.

equatoriale [ekwato'rjale] AGG equatorial.

equazione [ekwat'tsjone] SF equation.

equestre [e'kwɛstre] AGG equestrian; **circo equestre** circus.

equidistante [ekwidis'tante] AGG equidistant.

equilatero [ekwi'latero] AGG equilateral.

equilibrare [ekwili'brare] ①︎ VT (*gen*) to balance; (*controbilanciare*) to counterbalance; **equilibrare qc con qc** to balance sth against sth (else).
②︎ **equilibrarsi** VR (*uso reciproco: forze ecc*) to counterbalance each other.

equilibratamente [ekwilibrata'mente] AVV (*giudicare, decidere*) sensibly, judiciously.

equilibrato, a [ekwili'brato] AGG (*carico, giudizio, dieta, alimentazione*) balanced; (*persona*) well-balanced.

equilibratura [ekwilibra'tura] SF (*Aut*) balancing.

equilibrio, ri [ekwi'librjo] SM (*gen*) balance, equilibrium; (*armonia*) harmony; **perdere l'equilibrio** to lose one's balance; **stare in equilibrio su** (*persona*) to balance on; (*oggetto*) to be balanced on; **equilibrio mentale** (mental) equilibrium *o* stability; **equilibrio economico**

economic stability; **equilibrio politico** balance of power; **è una persona priva di equilibrio** he is not a well-balanced person, he is rather unstable.

equilibrismo [ekwili'brizmo] SM tightrope walking; (*fig*) juggling; (*Pol*) balancing act.

equilibrista, i, e [ekwili'brista] SM/F tightrope walker.

equino, a [e'kwino] AGG horse *attr*, equine; **carne equina** horsemeat; **una razza equina** a breed of horses.

equinozio, zi [ekwi'nɔttsjo] SM equinox.

equipaggiamento [ekwipaddʒa'mento] SM **a** (*operazione: di nave*) equipping, fitting out; (: *di spedizione, esercito*) equipping, kitting out (*fam*) **b** (*attrezzatura*) equipment, gear; **equipaggiamento da sci/da sub** skiing/diving equipment.

equipaggiare [ekwipad'dʒare] **1** VT (*nave, esercito, spedizione*) to equip; (*per uno sport*) to kit out.
2 equipaggiarsi VR to equip o.s.

equipaggio, gi [ekwi'paddʒo] SM (*gen, Naut*) crew; (*Aer*) (air)crew.

equiparabile [ekwipa'rabile] AGG comparable.

equiparare [ekwipa'rare] VT (*Amm: stipendi, gradi*) to make equal, level.

equiparazione [ekwiparat'tsjone] SF levelling.

équipe [e'kip] SF INV (*gen, Sport*) team; **lavorare in équipe** to work as a team; **lavoro d'équipe** teamwork.

equipollente [ekwipol'lɛnte] AGG equivalent.

equità [ekwi'ta] SF INV equity, fairness.

equitazione [ekwitat'tsjone] SF (horse-)riding.

equivalente [ekwiva'lɛnte] **1** AGG: **equivalente (a)** equivalent (to).
2 SM equivalent.

equivalenza [ekwiva'lɛntsa] SF equivalence.

equivalere [ekwiva'lere] VB IRREG **1** VI (*aus* **essere** *o* **avere**): **equivalere a** (*valore*) to be equivalent to; (*affermazione*) to be tantamount to; **equivale a dire che...** that is the same as saying that ....
2 equivalersi VR (*uso reciproco: forze*) to counterbalance each other; (: *soluzioni*) to amount to the same thing.

equivalso, a [ekwi'valso] PP di **equivalere**.

equivocare [ekwivo'kare] VI (*aus* **avere**) (*capire male*): **equivocare (su qc)** to misunderstand (sth).

equivoco, a, ci, che [e'kwivoko] **1** AGG (*risposta, discorso*) equivocal, ambiguous; (*persona*) shady; (*locale*) disreputable.
2 SM (*malinteso*) misunderstanding; **dar luogo a un equivoco** to cause a misunderstanding; **cadere in un equivoco** to misunderstand; **ci dev'essere stato un equivoco** there must have been some misunderstanding; **a scanso di equivoci** (so as) to avoid any misunderstanding, so that it will be perfectly clear.

equo, a ['ɛkwo] AGG (*gen*) equitable, fair; **un equo compenso** a fair *o* adequate reward.

Era ['ɛra] SF (*Mitol*) Hera.

era ['ɛra] SF (*gen*) era; (*Geol*) period; **l'era cristiana** the Christian era; **l'era glaciale** the ice age; **l'era spaziale** the space age.

era *ecc* ['ɛra] VB vedi **essere**.

erariale [era'rjale] AGG: **ufficio erariale** ≈ tax office; **spese erariali** public expenditure *sg*; **imposte erariali** revenue taxes.

erario, ri [e'rarjo] SM: **l'erario** ≈ the Treasury.

erba ['ɛrba] **1** SF grass; (*Culin, Med*) herb; (*fam: marijuana*) grass, pot; **in erba** (*fig: pittore, scultore*) budding; **fare di ogni erba un fascio** (*fig*) to lump everything (*o* everybody) together ▶**erba cipollina** chives *pl* ▶**erba medica** lucerne ▶**erbe aromatiche** herbs.

erbaccia, ce [er'battʃa] SF weed.

erbaceo, a [er'batʃeo] AGG herbaceous.

erbario, ri [er'barjo] SM (*raccolta*) herbarium; (*libro*) herbal.

erbette [er'bette] SFPL beet tops.

erbicida, i, e [erbi'tʃida] **1** AGG herbicidal.
2 SM weed-killer.

erbivendolo, a [erbi'vendolo] SM/F greengrocer.

erbivoro, a [er'bivoro] **1** AGG herbivorous.
2 SM/F herbivore.

erborista, i, e [erbo'rista] SM/F herbalist.

erboristeria [erboriste'ria] SF (*scienza*) herbalism; (*negozio*) herbalist's (shop).

erboso, a [er'boso] AGG grassy; **tappeto erboso** lawn.

Ercole ['ɛrkole] SM (*Mit*) Hercules.

erculeo, a [er'kuleo] AGG (*anche fig*) Herculean.

erede [e'rɛde] SM/F heir/heiress; **erede di qc** heir to sth; **erede al trono** heir to the throne; **erede legittimo** heir-at-law; **nominare qn proprio erede** to make sb one's heir.

eredità [eredi'ta] SF INV **a** (*Dir*) inheritance; (*fig*) heritage; **lasciare qc in eredità a qn** to leave *o* bequeath sth to sb; **ricevere qc in eredità** to inherit sth **b** (*Bio*) heredity.

ereditare [eredi'tare] VT to inherit; **ereditare qc da qn** to inherit sth from sb.

ereditarietà [ereditarje'ta] SF INV heredity.

ereditario, ria, ri, rie [eredi'tarjo] AGG hereditary.

ereditiera [eredi'tjɛra] SF heiress.

eremita, i [ere'mita] SM hermit.

eremitaggio, gi [eremi'taddʒo] SM hermitage.

eremo ['ɛremo] SM hermitage; (*fig*) retreat.

eresia [ere'zia] SF (*Rel, fig*) heresy; **dire eresie** (*fig*) to talk nonsense.

eressi *ecc* [e'rɛssi] VB vedi **erigere**.

ereticamente [eretika'mente] AVV heretically.

eretico, a, ci, che [e'rɛtiko] **1** AGG heretical.
2 SM/F heretic.

eretto, a [e'rɛtto] **1** PP di **erigere**.
2 AGG (*capo, busto*) erect, upright.

erezione [eret'tsjone] SF **a** (*Fisiol*) erection **b** (*costruzione: di monumento*) raising; (: *di palazzo, chiesa*) building.

ergastolano, a [ergasto'lano] SM/F prisoner serving a life sentence, lifer (*fam*).

ergastolo [er'gastolo] SM (*pena*) life imprisonment; (*luogo di pena*) prison (*for those serving life sentence*); **condannato all'ergastolo** given a life sentence; **gli hanno dato tre ergastoli** he was given three life sentences.

ergonomia [ergono'mia] SF ergonomics *sg*, biotechnology (*Am*).

ergonomico, a, ci, che [ergo'nɔmiko] AGG ergonomic(al).

ergoterapia [ergotera'pia] SF occupational therapy.

erica, che ['ɛrika] SF heather.

erigere [e'ridʒere] **1** VT (*monumento*) to erect, raise; (*fig: fondare*) to found.
2 erigersi VR (*fig: costituirsi*): **erigersi a giudice/difensore (di)** to set o.s. up as a judge/a defender (of).

eritema, i [eri'tɛma] SM (*Med*) inflammation, erythema (*termine tecn*) ▶**eritema solare** sunburn.

Eritrea [eri'trɛa] SF Eritrea.

eritrocita, i [eritro'tʃita] SM (*Anat*) erythrocyte.

ermafrodito, a [ermafro'dito] AGG, SM hermaphrodite.

ermellino [ermel'lino] SM (*animale*: *d'inverno*) ermine; (: *d'estate*) stoat; (*pelliccia*) ermine.

ermeticamente [ermetika'mente] AVV hermetically; (*fig*) impenetrably.

ermetico, a, ci, che [er'mɛtiko] AGG **a** (*contenitore*) airtight; (*fig*: *sguardo, volto*) inscrutable, impenetrable; **a chiusura ermetica** hermetically sealed **b** (*Letteratura*) hermetic.

ermetismo [erme'tizmo] SM (*Letteratura*) Hermeticism.

ernia ['ɛrnja] SF (*Med*) hernia ▶**ernia del disco** slipped disc.

ero *ecc* ['ɛro] VB *vedi* **essere**.

Erode [e'rɔde] SM Herod.

erodere [e'rodere] VT to erode.

Erodoto [e'rɔdoto] SM Herodotus.

eroe [e'rɔe] SM hero.

erogare [ero'gare] VT (*gas, luce*) to supply; (*somma*) to distribute.

erogatore [eroga'tore] SM supply valve.

erogazione [erogat'tsjone] SF (*vedi vb*) supply; distribution.

erogeno, a [e'rɔdʒeno] AGG erogenous; **zona erogena** erogenous zone.

eroicamente [eroika'mente] AVV heroically.

eroico, a, ci, che [e'rɔiko] AGG heroic.

eroicomico, a, ci, che [eroi'kɔmiko] AGG mock-heroic.

eroina[1] [ero'ina] SF (*donna*) heroine.

eroina[2] [ero'ina] SF (*droga*) heroin.

eroinomane [eroi'nɔmane] SM/F heroin addict.

eroinomania [eroinoma'nia] SF heroin addiction.

eroismo [ero'izmo] SM heroism.

erompere [e'rompere] VI IRREG: **erompere (da)** (*lava, folla*) to erupt (from); **erompere in un pianto dirotto** to burst into tears.

eros ['ɛros] SM INV Eros.

erosione [ero'zjone] SF erosion.

erosivo, a [ero'zivo] AGG erosive.

eroso, a [e'roso] PP di **erodere**.

eroticamente [erotika'mente] AVV erotically.

erotico, a, ci, che [e'rɔtiko] AGG erotic.

erotismo [ero'tizmo] SM eroticism.

erotomane [ero'tɔmane] SM erotomaniac; (*scherz*) sex maniac.

erotto [e'rotto] PP di **erompere**.

erpete ['ɛrpete] SM (*Med*) herpes *sg*.

erpice ['ɛrpitʃe] SM (*Agr*) harrow.

errabondo, a [erra'bondo] AGG (*letter*) wandering.

errante [er'rante] AGG (*letter*) wandering; **cavaliere errante** knight errant.

errare [er'rare] VI (*aus avere*) **a** (*letter*: *vagare*): **errare (per)** to wander (about), roam (about); **errare con la fantasia** (*fig*) to let one's imagination wander **b** (*frm*: *sbagliare*) to be mistaken, make a mistake; **se non erro...** if I'm not mistaken ... .

errata corrige [er'rata 'kɔrridʒe] SM INV erratum, corrigendum.

erratamente [errata'mente] AVV (*vedi agg*) wrongly; mistakenly.

errato, a [er'rato] AGG (*calcolo*) wrong, incorrect; (*idea, interpretazione*) mistaken, erroneous; **se non vado errato** if I am not mistaken.

erroneamente [erronea'mente] AVV erroneously, mistakenly.

erroneo, a [er'rɔneo] AGG erroneous, mistaken.

errore [er'rore] SM mistake, error; **fare un errore** to make a mistake; **per errore** by mistake; **salvo errori** (*scritto*) errors excepted; (*nel parlare*) if I am not mistaken; **salvo errori ed omissioni** errors and omissions excepted; **è stato un errore di gioventù** it was a youthful error ▶**errore di calcolo** (*anche fig*) miscalculation ▶**errore giudiziario** miscarriage of justice ▶**errore di giudizio** *o* **di valutazione** error of judgment ▶**errore di ortografia** spelling mistake ▶**errore di stampa** printing error, misprint.

erta ['erta] SF **a** (*salita*) steep slope **b**: **stare all'erta** (*vigilare*) to be on the alert.

erto, a ['erto] AGG (*letter*) (very) steep.

erudire [eru'dire] VT (*frm, scherz*) to teach, educate.

eruditamente [erudita'mente] AVV eruditely.

erudito, a [eru'dito] [1] AGG (*persona*) learned, erudite; (*opera*) scholarly, learned.

[2] SM/F scholar.

erudizione [erudit'tsjone] SF erudition.

eruttare [erut'tare] VT (*lava*) to spew (out).

eruttivo, a [erut'tivo] AGG eruptive; **roccia eruttiva** igneous rock.

eruzione [erut'tsjone] SF (*Geol*) eruption; (*Med*) rash.

E.S. ABBR (= *elettroshock*) ECT.

es. ABBR (= *esempio*) e.g.

E.S.A. SIGLA M (= *European Space Agency*) ESA.

esacerbare [ezatʃer'bare] VT to exacerbate.

esacerbato, a [ezatʃer'bato] AGG embittered.

esagerare [ezadʒe'rare] [1] VI (*aus avere*) (*gen*) to exaggerate; (*eccedere*) to go too far; **esagerare con le pretese** to demand too much, expect too much; **esagerare con la prudenza** to be overcautious; **senza esagerare** without exaggeration; **non ti sembra di esagerare un po'?** don't you think that's a bit of an exaggeration?; **esagerare nel bere/nel mangiare** to drink/eat too much.

[2] VT to exaggerate.

esageratamente [ezadʒerata'mente] AVV excessively.

esagerato, a [ezadʒe'rato] [1] AGG (*notizia, proporzioni*) exaggerated; (*curiosità, pignoleria*) excessive; (*prezzo*) exorbitant; **sarebbe esagerato dire che...** it would be an exaggeration to say that ....

[2] SM/F: **sei il solito esagerato** you're exaggerating as usual.

esagerazione [ezadʒerat'tsjone] SF exaggeration; **costare un'esagerazione** to cost the earth; **che esagerazione!** what nonsense!

esagitato, a [ezadʒi'tato] AGG (*persona, animo*) agitated.

esagonale [ezago'nale] AGG hexagonal.

esagono [e'zagono] SM hexagon.

esalare [eza'lare] [1] VT (*odori*) to give off; **esalare l'ultimo respiro** to breathe one's last.

[2] VI (*aus essere*) **esalare (da)** to emanate (from).

esalazione [ezalat'tsjone] SF (*emissione*) exhalation; (*odore*) fumes *pl*.

esaltante [ezal'tante] AGG exciting.

esaltare [ezal'tare] [1] VT **a** (*lodare: pregi, virtù*) to extol **b** (*eccitare: immaginazione*) to fire; (: *folla*) to excite, stir.

[2] **esaltarsi** VR: **esaltarsi (per qc)** to grow excited (about sth).

esaltato, a [ezal'tato] [1] AGG (*giovane, mente*) overexcited.

[2] SM/F fanatic.

esaltazione [ezalat'tsjone] SF **a** (*elogio*) extolling **b** (*mistica*) exaltation.

esame [e'zame] SM **a** (*gen*) examination, exam; **essere all'esame** to be under examination; **prendere in esame** to examine, consider; **fare un esame di coscienza** to examine one's conscience; **dopo un attento esame della situazione** after careful study *o* consideration of the situation

b (*Scol*) exam, examination; **dare** *o* **sostenere un esame** to sit (*Brit*) *o* take an exam ►**esame di guida** driving test

c (*Med*) examination, test; **farsi fare degli esami** to have some tests done *o* carried out ►**esame del sangue** blood test ► **esame della vista** eye test.

esaminando, a [ezami'nando] SM/F examinee.

esaminare [ezami'nare] VT **a** (*gen*) to examine; (*proposta, elementi*) to consider, examine **b** (*oggetto*) to examine, study **c** (*candidati*) to interview; (*Scol*) to examine.

esaminatore, trice [ezamina'tore] 1 AGG examining *attr.* 2 SM/F examiner.

esangue [e'zangwe] AGG (*pallido*) pale, wan; (*privo di vigore*) lifeless.

esanime [e'zanime] AGG lifeless.

esasperare [ezaspe'rare] 1 VT (*persona*) to exasperate; (*situazione*) to exacerbate.

2 **esasperarsi** VIP to become exasperated.

esasperato, a [ezaspe'rato] AGG exasperated.

esasperazione [ezasperat'tsjone] SF exasperation.

esattamente [ezatta'mente] AVV exactly.

esattezza [ezat'tettsa] SF **a** (*correttezza: di calcolo, affermazione*) accuracy; **per l'esattezza** to be precise; **con esattezza** exactly; **rispondere con esattezza** (*in modo corretto*) to answer correctly, give a *o* the correct answer; (*in modo preciso*) to give a detailed answer **b** (*accuratezza: di persona*) precision.

esatto, a [e'zatto] 1 PP di **esigere**.

2 AGG **a** (*corretto: calcolo, risposta*) correct, right; (*ora*) exact, right; (*dimensioni, quantità*) exact, precise; (*prezzo, peso*) exact; **sono le tre esatte** it's exactly three o'clock; **è l'esatto contrario** it's the exact opposite *o* it's just the opposite; **allora, hai deciso di partire? — esatto!** so, you've decided to leave? — that's right!

b (*accurato: resoconto, descrizione*) accurate; (: *impiegato*) careful; **le scienze esatte** the exact sciences.

esattore, trice [ezat'tore] SM/F: **esattore delle tasse** tax collector; **esattore del gas/della luce** gas/electricity man.

esattoria [ezatto'ria] SF: **esattoria comunale** council tax office (*Brit*), assessor's office (*Am*).

esaudibile [ezau'dibile] AGG (*desiderio, richiesta*) which can be granted.

esaudire [ezau'dire] VT (*desiderio, richiesta*) to grant, fulfil (*Brit*), fulfill (*Am*); (*preghiera*) to answer, grant.

esauribile [ezau'ribile] AGG exhaustible.

esauriente [ezau'rjɛnte] AGG (*gen*) exhaustive; (*risposta*) complete.

esaurientemente [ezaurjɛnte'mente] AVV exhaustively.

esaurimento [ezauri'mento] SM (*gen*) exhaustion; **svendita (fino) ad esaurimento della merce** clearance sale ►**esaurimento nervoso** nervous breakdown.

esaurire [ezau'rire] 1 VT IRREG **a** (*consumare: scorte, risorse*) to exhaust, use up; (: *pozzo, miniera*) to exhaust; (: *carburante*) to use up; (: *forze, energie*) to expend, use up **b** (*portare a termine: indagine*) to conclude; (: *argomento*) to exhaust **c** (*persona*) to exhaust, wear out.

2 **esaurirsi** VR (*persona*) to exhaust o.s., wear o.s. out.

3 **esaurirsi** VIP (*provviste*) to run out; (*fondi*) to run out, dry up; (*ispirazione*) to dry up.

esaurito, a [ezau'rito] AGG (*gen*) exhausted; (*esausto: persona*) run-down *attr.*; (*merci*) sold out; (*libro: non più stampato*) out of print; **tutto esaurito** sold out; **registrare il tutto esaurito** (*teatro*) to have a full house; **essere esaurito** (*persona*) to be worn out.

esausto, a [e'zausto] AGG (*spossato*) exhausted, worn out.

esautorare [ezauto'rare] VT (*dirigente, funzionario*) to deprive of authority; (*parlamento, istituzione*) to reduce the authority of.

esazione [ezat'tsjone] SF collection (of taxes).

esborso [ez'borso] SM (*Amm*) disbursement.

esca ['eska] SF (*anche fig*) bait; **mettere l'esca all'amo** to bait the hook.

escalation [eska'leiʃən] SF INV (*Mil*) escalation; **un'escalation di violenza** a rising spiral of violence.

escamotage [eskamɔ'taʒ] SM INV subterfuge.

escandescenza [eskandeʃ'ʃɛntsa] SF: **dare in escandescenze** to fly into a rage.

escatologia [eskatolo'dʒia] SF (*Rel*) eschatology.

escavatore, trice [eskava'tore] 1 AGG excavating. 2 SM/F (*macchina*) excavator.

escavazione [eskavat'tsjone] SF excavation.

esce *ecc* ['ɛʃʃe] VB vedi **uscire**.

Eschilo ['ɛskilo] SM Aeschylus.

eschimese [eski'mese] AGG, SM/F, SM Eskimo.

esci *ecc* ['ɛʃʃi] VB vedi **uscire**.

escl. ABBR (= *escluso*) excl.

esclamare [eskla'mare] VI (*aus* avere) to exclaim, cry out.

esclamativo, a [esklama'tivo] AGG: **punto esclamativo** exclamation mark.

esclamazione [esklamat'tsjone] SF exclamation.

escludere [es'kludere] VT IRREG **a** (*estromettere*): **escludere qn (da)** to exclude sb (from); **fu escluso dall'elenco** his name was left off the list

b (*ritenere o rendere impossibile*) to rule out, exclude; **escludo che si tratti di omicidio** I think we can rule out murder; **la polizia ha escluso la tesi del suicidio** the police ruled out *o* excluded the possibility of suicide; **una teoria esclude l'altra** one theory excludes another; **vieni domani? — lo escludo!** *o* **è escluso!** are you coming tomorrow? — it's out of the question!

esclusi *ecc* [es'kluzi] VB vedi **escludere**.

esclusione [esklu'zjone] SF exclusion; **a esclusione di** *o* **fatta esclusione per** except (for), apart from; **senza esclusione (alcuna)** without exception; **senza esclusione di colpi** (*fig*) with no holds barred; **procedere per esclusione** to follow a process of elimination.

esclusiva [esklu'ziva] SF **a** (*Comm*): **avere l'esclusiva di qc** to be the sole agent for sth; **avere l'esclusiva di vendita** to have the exclusive *o* sole selling rights **b** (*Stampa*) exclusive; **intervista in esclusiva** exclusive interview.

esclusivamente [eskluziva'mente] AVV exclusively, solely.

esclusivismo [eskluzi'vizmo] SM intransigence; (*Pol, Econ*) preferential treatment.

esclusivista, i, e [eskluzi'vista] SM/F **a** intransigent person **b** (*Comm*) sole agent.

esclusivo, a [esklu'zivo] AGG exclusive.

escluso, a [es'kluzo] 1 PP di **escludere**.

2 AGG: **nessuno escluso** without exception; **è escluso che venga** there is no question of his coming; **non è escluso che lo si faccia** the possibility can't be ruled out,

we (o they) might do it; IVA **esclusa** excluding VAT, exclusive of VAT.

esco ecc ['ɛsko] VB vedi **uscire.**

escogitare [eskodʒi'tare] VT to devise, think up.

escono ['ɛskono] VB vedi **uscire.**

escoriare [esko'rjare] [1] VT to graze.

[2] **escoriarsi** VR to graze o.s.

escoriazione [eskorjat'tsjone] SF abrasion, graze.

escrementi [eskre'menti] SMPL excrement sg, faeces pl.

escrescenza [eskreʃ'ʃɛntsa] SF (Bio) excrescence.

escrezione [eskret'tsjone] SF excretion.

escudo [es'kudo] SM (pl **escudos**) escudo.

escursione [eskur'sjone] SF **a** (gita) excursion, trip; (: a piedi) hike, walk **b** (Meteor): **escursione termica** temperature range.

escursionista, i, e [eskursjo'nista] SM/F (gitante) (day) tripper; (: a piedi) hiker, walker.

esecrabile [ese'krabile] AGG execrable, abominable.

esecrabilmente [esekrabil'mente] AVV abominably.

esecrando, a [ese'krando] AGG (letter) abhorrent, abominable.

esecrare [ese'krare] VT to abhor, loathe; (persona) to loathe.

esecutivo, a [eseku'tivo] [1] AGG executive; **(potere) esecutivo** executive power.

[2] SM (comitato) executive committee.

esecutore, trice [eseku'tore] SM/F **a** (Dir): **esecutore (testamentario)** executor/executrix; **l'esecutore del progetto** the person who realized the project **b** (Mus) performer.

esecuzione [esekut'tsjone] SF **a** (di lavoro, ordini, piano) execution, carrying out; (Mus) performance; **mettere in esecuzione** o **dare esecuzione a** (progetto, ordine) to carry out **b** (Dir) execution ▶**esecuzione capitale** execution.

esegesi [ese'dʒɛzi] SF exegesis.

esegeta, i, e [ese'dʒɛta] SM/F commentator.

eseguire [ese'gwire] VT (lavoro, ordini, piano) to carry out, execute; (Mus: sinfonia, pezzo) to perform, execute; **ha fatto eseguire dei lavori** he had some work done; **eseguire un pagamento** to make a payment; **eseguire un programma** (Inform) to run a program.

esempio, pi [e'zɛmpjo] SM example; **ad** o **per esempio** for example o instance; **citare come** o **ad esempio** to quote as an example; **dare il buon/cattivo esempio** to set a good/bad example; **essere un esempio di virtù** to be a paragon of virtue; **fare un esempio** to give an example; **prendere (l')esempio da qn** to follow sb's example; **che ti serva d'esempio!** let that be a lesson to you!

esemplare[1] [ezem'plare] AGG (vita, punizione) exemplary; (allievo) model attr; **dare una punizione esemplare a qn** to make an example of sb.

esemplare[2] [ezem'plare] SM (Bot, Zool, Geol) specimen; (di francobollo, moneta) example; (di libro) copy.

esemplarmente [ezemplar'mente] AVV in an exemplary way.

esemplificare [ezemplifi'kare] VT to illustrate.

esemplificativo, a [ezemplifika'tivo] AGG illustrative.

esemplificazione [ezemplifikat'tsjone] SF (atto) exemplification; (esempio) example.

esentare [ezen'tare] VT: **esentare qn/qc (da qc)** to exempt sb/sth (from sth).

esentasse [ezen'tasse] AGG INV tax-free.

esente [e'zɛnte] AGG: **esente da** (dispensato da) exempt from; **esente da dazio** duty-free; **esente da tasse** o **imposte** untaxed; **anche lui non è esente da difetti** even he has his failings.

esenzione [ezen'tsjone] SF: **esenzione (da)** exemption (from) ▶**esenzione fiscale** tax exemption.

esequie [e'zɛkwje] SFPL funeral rites, obsequies.

esercente [ezer'tʃɛnte] SM/F (gestore) trader, owner of a business.

esercitare [ezertʃi'tare] [1] VT **a** (professione) to practise (Brit), practice (Am); (diritto) to exercise; **esercitare (su)** (controllo, influenza) to exert (over); (pressione) to exert (on); (autorità, potere) to exercise (over); **quel medico non esercita più** that doctor is no longer in practice **b** (corpo, mente, voce) to train, exercise.

[2] **esercitarsi** VR (sportivo) to train; (musicista) to practise; **esercitarsi nella guida** to practise one's driving; **esecitarsi a fare qc** to practise doing sth; **esercitarsi in palestra** to train in the gym.

esercitazione [ezertʃitat'tsjone] SF **a** (Univ: di materie scientifiche) practical (class); (: di lingue) language class ▪**b** (Mil): **esercitazione navale/militare** naval/military exercise; **esercitazioni di tiro** target practice sg.

esercito [e'zɛrtʃito] SM (Mil) army; (fig: di persone) host.

esercizio, zi [ezer'tʃittsjo] SM **a** (compito, movimento) exercise; **essere fuori esercizio** to be out of practice; **fare (molto) esercizio** (pratica) to practise (Brit) o practice (Am) a lot; (movimento) to take a lot of exercise **b** (di professione, culto) practice; (di diritto) exercising; (di funzioni) exercise; **nell'esercizio delle proprie funzioni** in the execution of one's duties **c** (Comm, Amm: gestione) running, management; (: azienda gestita) business, concern; **costi d'esercizio** overheads; **quella ditta è in esercizio da pochi mesi** that firm has only been in business for a few months; **aprire un esercizio** to set up a business, open a shop (o bar o restaurant ecc); **pubblico esercizio** commercial concern; **licenza d'esercizio** licence to trade **d** (Fin: anche: **esercizio finanziario**) financial year; **il bilancio dell'esercizio 1994** the budget for the 1994 financial year.

esfoliante [esfo'ljante] SM exfoliator.

esfoliazione [esfoljat'tsjone] SF (Med) exfoliation.

esibire [ezi'bire] [1] VT (bravura, capacità) to exhibit, display; (documenti) to produce, present.

[2] **esibirsi** VR (attore, artista) to perform; (fig) to show off.

esibizione [ezibit'tsjone] SF **a** (spettacolo) performance, show **b** (sfoggio) exhibition, showing off **c** (di documento) presentation.

esibizionismo [ezibittsjo'nizmo] SM **a** (mettersi in mostra) exhibitionism **b** (Psic) exhibitionism; (Dir) indecent exposure.

esibizionista, i, e [ezibittsjo'nista] SM/F exhibitionist; (Psic) exhibitionist, flasher (Brit fam).

esigente [ezi'dʒɛnte] AGG demanding; **un cliente molto esigente** a very demanding customer; **è esigente nel mangiare** he's particular about his food.

esigenza [ezi'dʒɛntsa] SF requirement, need; **avere troppe esigenze** to be too demanding; **andare incontro alle esigenze del mercato** o **dei consumatori** to meet the demands of the market o of consumers; **sentire l'esigenza di qc/di fare qc** to feel the need for sth/to do sth.

esigere [e'zidʒere] VT IRREG **a** (pretendere) to demand; (comportare, richiedere) to require, call for; **esigere qc da**

qn to demand sth from o of sb; **esigere che qn faccia qc** to expect sb to do sth; **esige il rispetto di tutti** he demands everybody's respect; **esigere troppo da se stessi** to expect too much of oneself **b** (*riscuotere*: *debito*) to collect.

esigibile [ezi'dʒibile] AGG (*assegno, somma*) payable.

esiguità [ezigui'ta] SF INV (*di patrimonio, compenso*) meagreness; (*di risorse*) scarcity.

esiguo, a [e'ziguo] AGG (*numero, quantità*) small, tiny; (*patrimonio, compenso*) meagre; (*risorse*) scanty.

esilarante [ezila'rante] AGG hilarious; **gas esilarante** laughing gas.

esile ['ezile] AGG (*persona*) slender, slim; (*stelo*) thin; (*voce*) faint; **un esile filo di speranza** a faint ray of hope, a glimmer of hope.

esiliare [ezi'ljare] ① VT (*Pol*) to exile; (*fig*) to banish. ② **esiliarsi** VR (*Pol*) to go into exile.

esiliato, a [ezi'ljato] ① AGG exiled. ② SM/F exile.

esilio, li [e'ziljo] SM exile.

esilità [ezili'ta] SF INV (*vedi agg*) slenderness, slimness; thinness; faintness.

esilmente [ezil'mente] AVV (*debolmente*) faintly, feebly.

esimere [e'zimere] ① VT: **esimere qn da qc** to exempt sb from sth. ② **esimersi** VR: **esimersi da qc/dal fare qc** to get out of sth/doing sth.

esimio, mia, mi, mie [e'zimjo] AGG distinguished, eminent; **un esimio cretino** (*iro*) a prize idiot.

Esiodo [e'ziodo] SM Hesiod.

esistente [ezis'tɛnte] AGG (*gen*) existing; **tuttora esistente** (*persona*) still alive o living; (*casa*) which still stands.

esistenza [ezis'tɛntsa] SF (*gen*) existence; (*vita*) life, existence.

esistenziale [ezisten'tsjale] AGG existential.

esistenzialismo [ezistentsja'lizmo] SM existentialism.

esistenzialista, i, e [ezistentsja'lista] AGG, SM/F existentialist.

esistenzialistico, a, ci, che [ezistentsja'listiko] AGG existentialist.

esistere [e'zistere] VI IRREG (*aus* essere) (*gen*) to exist; **esistono ancora dubbi in merito** there are still some doubts about it; **questo modello esiste in due colori** this model comes o is available in two colours; **non esiste!** (*fam*) no way!

esistito, a [ezis'tito] PP di **esistere**.

esitante [ezi'tante] AGG hesitant, faltering.

esitare [ezi'tare] VI (*aus* avere) to hesitate; **esitava a prendere una decisione** he was reluctant to take a decision; **esitava tra il sì e il no** he wasn't sure whether to say yes or no; **esitò a rispondere** he hesitated before answering; **senza esitare** without (any) hesitation.

esitazione [ezitat'tsjone] SF hesitation; **dopo molte esitazioni** after much hesitation; **senza esitazioni** unhesitatingly, without (any) hesitation.

esito ['ezito] SM result, outcome; **avere buon esito** to be successful; **le analisi hanno avuto esito negativo** the results of the tests were negative.

esiziale [ezit'tsjale] AGG (*frm*) fatal, disastrous.

eskimo ['ɛskimo] SM (*giaccone*) parka.

esodo ['ɛzodo] SM exodus; **l'esodo di Ferragosto** ≈ the August bank holiday exodus; **l'esodo dei capitali all'estero** the outflow of funds into overseas investments; **l'Esodo** (*Bibbia*) the Exodus.

esofago, gi [e'zɔfago] SM oesophagus (*Brit*), esophagus (*Am*).

esogeno, a [e'zɔdʒeno] AGG (*Med, Geog, Geol*) external; **fenomeni esogeni** external processes.

esonerare [ezone'rare] VT: **esonerare da** (*servizio militare*) to exempt from; (*lezioni*) to excuse from.

esonero [e'zɔnero] SM exemption.

Esopo [e'zɔpo] SM Aesop.

esorbitante [ezorbi'tante] AGG exorbitant, excessive.

esorbitare [ezorbi'tare] VI (*aus* avere): **esorbitare da** to go beyond.

esorcismo [ezor'tʃizmo] SM exorcism.

esorcista, i [ezor'tʃista] SM exorcist.

esorcizzare [ezortʃid'dzare] VT (*anche fig*) to exorcize.

esordiente [ezor'djɛnte] ① AGG: **un attore/calciatore esordiente** an actor/footballer making his professional debut. ② SM/F (*attore, giocatore*) newcomer.

esordio, di [e'zɔrdjo] SM debut, first appearance; **un'attrice al suo esordio come regista** an actress making her directorial debut; **la sua carriera è ancora agli esordi** his career is just beginning.

esordire [ezor'dire] VI IRREG (*aus* avere) (*Cine, Teatro, Mus, Sport*) to make one's debut; (*fig*) to start out, begin (one's career); **esordì giovanissima** she made her debut when she was very young; **esordì dicendo che...** he began by saying (that) ... .

esortare [ezor'tare] VT to exhort, urge; **lo esortai a partire al più presto** I urged him to leave as soon as possible.

esortativo, a [ezorta'tivo] AGG exhortatory.

esortazione [ezortat'tsjone] SF exhortation.

esosità [ezozi'ta] SF INV (*vedi agg*) exorbitance; greed.

esoso, a [e'zozo] AGG **a** (*prezzo*) exorbitant **b** (*persona*: *avido*) grasping.

esoterico, a, ci, che [ezo'tɛriko] AGG esoteric.

esotermico, a, ci, che [ezo'tɛrmiko] AGG (*Chim*) exothermic.

esoticamente [ezotika'mente] AVV exotically.

esotico, a, ci, che [e'zɔtiko] AGG exotic.

esotismo [ezo'tizmo] SM exoticism.

espadrilles [ɛspa'drij] SFPL espadrilles.

espandere [es'pandere] ① VT IRREG (*gen*) to expand; (*confini*) to extend; (*influenza*) to extend, widen. ② **espandersi** VIP to expand; (*influenza*) to spread.

espansione [espan'sjone] SF (*estensione*) expansion; **in espansione** (*economia*) booming; (*universo*) expanding; **a espansione** (*Tecn*: *motori*) expansion *attr*.

espansionismo [espansjo'nizmo] SM expansionism.

espansionistico, a, ci, che [espansjo'nistiko] AGG expansionist.

espansività [espansivi'ta] SF INV expansiveness.

espansivo, a [espan'sivo] AGG (*persona*) expansive, communicative; **poco espansivo** reserved, not very forthcoming.

espanso, a [es'panso] PP di **espandere**.

espatriare [espa'trjare] VI (*aus* essere) to leave the country.

espatrio, ri [es'patrjo] SM expatriation; **permesso di espatrio** authorization to leave the country.

espediente [espe'djɛnte] SM expedient; **cercare un espediente per trarsi d'impaccio** to try and find a way out of a difficult situation; **vivere di espedienti** to live by o on one's wits.

espellere [es'pɛllere] VT IRREG **a**: **espellere (da)** (*da partito,*

associazione, scuola) to expel (from); (da paese) to deport (from); **espellere (dal campo)** (*Sport*) to send off (the field) **b** (*gas*) to discharge; (*cartucce usate*) to eject.

esperanto [espe'ranto] SM Esperanto.

Esperidi [es'pɛridi] SFPL Hesperides.

esperienza [espe'rjɛntsa] SF **a** experience; **senza esperienza** inexperienced; **avere molta esperienza di/in** to have a lot of experience of/in; **parlare/sapere per esperienza** to speak/know from experience; **fare** *o* **acquisire esperienza** to gain experience; **ha dieci anni di esperienza nell'insegnamento** he has ten years' teaching experience; **esperienze di lavoro** work experience
b (*scientifico*) experiment.

esperimento [esperi'mento] SM experiment; **a titolo di esperimento** by way of experiment; **sottoporre qc ad esperimento** to carry out an experiment on sth; **fare un esperimento** to carry out *o* do an experiment; **esperimenti nucleari** nuclear tests.

espertamente [esperta'mente] AVV expertly.

esperto, a [es'pɛrto] [1] AGG **a** (*competente*) expert; (*operaio*) skilled **b** (*che ha esperienza*) experienced; **è abbastanza esperto nella guida** he is a fairly experienced driver.
[2] SM/F expert; **è un esperto di botanica** he is an expert on botany.

espettorare [espetto'rare] VT (*Med*) to expectorate.

espianto [es'pjanto] SM (*Med*) removal.

espiare [espi'are] VT to expiate, atone for.

espiatorio, ria, ri, rie [espia'tɔrjo] AGG expiatory.

espiazione [espiat'tsjone] SF: **espiazione (di)** expiation (of), atonement (for).

espirare [espi'rare] VT, VI (*aus* avere) to breathe out, exhale.

espirazione [espirat'tsjone] SF breathing out, exhalation.

espletamento [espleta'mento] SM (*Amm*) carrying out; **l'espletamento delle pratiche richiede due mesi** the completion of all formalities will require two months.

espletare [esple'tare] VT (*Amm*) to carry out.

esplicare [espli'kare] VT (*incarico, attività*) to carry out, perform.

esplicativo, a [esplika'tivo] AGG explanatory.

esplicazione [esplikat'tsjone] SF (*di incarico, attività*) carrying out, performance.

esplicitamente [esplitʃita'mente] AVV explicitly.

esplicito, a [es'plitʃito] AGG explicit; **proposizione esplicita** (*Gramm*) sentence (*containing finite verb*).

esplodere [es'plɔdere] [1] VI IRREG (*aus* essere) (*anche fig*) to explode; (*bomba*) to explode, blow up; **far esplodere una bomba** to explode a bomb; **esplodere per la rabbia** to explode with anger; **esplodere in una risata** to burst out laughing; **è esplosa l'estate** summer has arrived with a bang.
[2] VT: **esplodere un colpo contro qn** to fire a shot at sb.

esplorare [esplo'rare] VT **a** (*gen, fig*) to explore **b** (*Mil*) to reconnoitre.

esplorativo, a [esplora'tivo] AGG exploratory.

esploratore, trice [esplora'tore] [1] SM/F explorer; **giovani esploratori** (boy) scouts.
[2] SM (*militare*) scout; (: *nave*) scout (ship).

esplorazione [esplorat'tsjone] SF exploration; (*Mil*) reconnaissance; **mandare qn in esplorazione** to send sb to scout ahead.

esplosione [esplo'zjone] SF (*gen, fig: di moda, crisi*) explosion; (: *di rabbia, gioia*) outburst; **esplosione demografica** population explosion.

esplosivo, a [esplo'zivo] AGG, SM explosive; **una notizia esplosiva** a bombshell.

esploso, a [es'plɔzo] [1] PP di **esplodere**.
[2] AGG (*disegno*) exploded.
[3] SM exploded view.

esponente [espo'nɛnte] [1] SM/F (*rappresentante*) exponent, representative.
[2] SM (*Mat*) exponent.

esponenziale [esponen'tsjale] AGG (*Mat*) exponential.

espongo [es'pongo], **esponi** [es'poni] *ecc* VB vedi **esporre**.

esporre [es'porre] VB IRREG [1] VT **a** (*esibire: merce*) to put on display, display; (: *quadri*) to exhibit, show; (: *avviso*) to put up; (: *bandiera*) to put out, raise; **esposto al pubblico** on display to the public
b (*spiegare*) to explain; (*argomento, teoria*) to put forward, expound; (*fatti, ragionamenti*) to set out; (*dubbi, riserve*) to express; **esporre a voce/per iscritto** to explain verbally/in writing
c (*mettere in pericolo*): **esporre qn al pericolo** to expose sb to danger; **esporre il fianco a critiche** to lay o.s. open to criticism
d (*alla luce, all'aria, anche Fot*) to expose.
[2]: **esporsi** VR: **esporsi a** (*sole, pericolo*) to expose o.s. to; (*critiche*) to lay o.s. open to; **stai attento a non esporti troppo** (*compromettersi*) be careful about sticking your neck out.

esportare [espor'tare] VT to export.

esportatore, trice [esporta'tore] [1] AGG exporting *attr*.
[2] SM/F exporter.

esportazione [esportat'tsjone] SF (*azione*) exportation, export; (*di prodotti*) exports *pl*; **di esportazione** (*agenzia, permesso*) export *attr*.

espose *ecc* [es'pose] VB vedi **esporre**.

esposimetro [espo'zimetro] SM (*Fot*) exposure meter, light meter.

espositore, trice [espozi'tore] [1] AGG exhibiting.
[2] SM/F exhibitor.

esposizione [espozit'tsjone] SF **a** (*di merce*) display; (*di fatti, ragioni: narrazione*) exposition; (: *spiegazione*) explanation
b (*fiera, mostra*) exhibition, show
c (*posizione di casa*) aspect; **casa con esposizione a nord** house facing north, north-facing house
d (*Fot, al sole*) exposure.

esposto, a [es'posto] [1] PP di **esporre**.
[2] AGG **a** (*edificio*): **esposto a nord** facing north, north-facing **b** (*Med: frattura*) compound *attr* **c** (*Alpinismo: passaggio, via*) exposed.
[3] SM (*Amm*) statement, account; (: *petizione*) petition; **fare un esposto a qn** to submit a report to sb, give sb a report.

espressamente [espressa'mente] AVV (*esplicitamente*) expressly, explicitly; (*appositamente*) especially.

espressione [espres'sjone] SF (*gen, Mat*) expression.

espressionismo [espressjo'nizmo] SM expressionism.

espressionista, i, e [espressjo'nista] AGG, SM/F expressionist.

espressività [espressivi'ta] SF INV expressiveness.

espressivo, a [espres'sivo] AGG expressive; **silenzio espressivo** eloquent silence.

espresso[1], a [es'prɛsso] PP di **esprimere**.

espresso[2], a [es'prɛsso] [1] AGG (*desiderio, treno*) express;

(*caffè*) espresso.

2 SM (*lettera*) express letter; (*treno*) express; (*caffè*) espresso (coffee).

esprimere [es'primere] VB IRREG **1** VT to express; (*opinione*) to voice, express.

2 esprimersi VIP to express o.s.; **esprimersi a gesti** to use sign language.

esprimibile [espri'mibile] AGG expressible.

espropriare [espro'prjare] VT (*terreni, edifici*) to place a compulsory purchase order on; **l'hanno espropriato dei suoi beni** they dispossessed him of his property, they expropriated his property.

espropriazione [esproprjat'tsjone] SF, **esproprio, pri** [es'prɔprjo] SM expropriation; **espropriazione per pubblica utilità** compulsory purchase.

espugnare [espuɲ'ɲare] VT to take by force, storm.

espulsi ecc [es'pulsi] VB vedi **espellere**.

espulsione [espul'sjone] SF (*da partito, scuola ecc*) expulsion; (*da paese*) deportation; (*dal campo di gioco*) sending off.

espulso, a [es'pulso] PP di **espellere**.

essa ['essa] PRON F (*fpl* **esse**) vedi **esso**.

essenza [es'sɛntsa] SF **a** (*di argomento*) gist, essence; (*Filosofia*) essence **b** (*estratto: di piante*) (essential) oil, essence; (: *alimentare*) essence.

essenziale [essen'tsjale] **1** AGG: **essenziale (a)** essential (to o for); (*stile, linguaggio*) simple; **olio essenziale** essential oil; **requisiti essenziali** prerequisites.

2 SM: **l'essenziale** (*l'importante*) the main o most important thing; (*oggetti necessari*) the (basic) essentials *pl*; (*punti principali*) the essentials *pl*; **riduciamo il discorso all'essenziale** let's restrict our discussion to the basic o essential points; **l'essenziale è che venga** the main o important thing is that he should come.

essenzialmente [essentsjal'mente] AVV essentially, basically.

essere ['ɛssere] (*aus* **essere**)

1 VB COPULATIVO

a (*gen*) to be;

▷ *chi* è quel tipo? — è Giovanni who is that (guy)? — it's Giovanni

▷ è *giovane/malato* he is young/ill

▷ siamo *in dieci* a volerci andare there are ten of us wanting to go o who want to go

▷ è (un) *professore* he is a teacher

▷ non è *vero* that's not true

b (*data*)

▷ è il 12 giugno it is June 12th;

▷ era il 1962 it was 1962

▷ erano gli anni Sessanta it was the Sixties

c (*ora*)

▷ che *ora* è? o che *ore* sono? — sono le due what's the time? o what time is it? — it's two o'clock

▷ saranno state le cinque it must have been five o'clock

d (*appartenenza*)

▷ *di chi* è questo libro? — è mio whose book is this? — it's mine

▷ non potrò essere *dei vostri* quest'estate I won't be able to join you this summer.

2 VB AUS

a (*tempi composti: attivo*)

▷ è arrivato? has he arrived?

▷ è arrivato ieri? did he arrive yesterday?

▷ è andato in Inghilterra he has gone to England

▷ è stato in Inghilterra he has been to England

▷ sono cresciuto in Italia I grew up in Italy

b (*tempi composti: passivo*)

▷ è stato fabbricato in India it was made in India

▷ è stato investito da un'auto he was run over by a car

c (*tempi composti: riflessivo*): *si* sono **vestiti** they dressed, they got dressed; (: *reciproco*): *si* sono **baciati** they kissed;

▷ non *si* sono visti they didn't see each other

3 VI (*aus* **essere**)

a (*esistere*) to be;

▷ essere o non essere to be or not to be

▷ sia la luce - e la luce fu let there be light - and there was light

▷ è il miglior meccanico che ci sia he is the best mechanic there is

b (*trovarsi*) to be; (*vivere*) to live;

▷ essere in *piedi* to be standing

▷ sono *qui* da tre ore I've been here for three hours

▷ è a *Roma* dal 1990 he's been (living) in Rome since 1990

▷ è a *tavola* he is eating

c (*diventare*) to be;

▷ quando sarai *calmo* when you calm down

▷ quando sarai *grande* when you grow up o are grown up

▷ quando sarai *medico* when you are a doctor

d (*provenire*)

▷ è *di* Genova he is o comes from Genoa.

e (+ *da* + *infinito*)

▷ è *da* fare subito it should be done o needs to be done o is to be done immediately

▷ è *da* spedire stasera it has (got) to be sent tonight.

4 VB IMPERS

a

▷ è *che* non mi piace the fact is I don't like it

▷ *che* ne sarà della macchina? what will happen to the car?

▷ sarà *come* dici tu you may be right

▷ *come* sarebbe a dire? what do you mean?

▷ *come* se niente fosse as if nothing had happened

▷ è *da* tre ore che ti aspetto I've been waiting for you for three hours

▷ non è *da* te it's not like you

▷ sia *detto* fra noi between you and me

▷ è *Pasqua* it's Easter

▷ è *possibile* che venga he may come

▷ *può* essere perhaps

▷ sarà *quel* che sarà what will be will be

▷ *sia* quel che sia, io me ne vado whatever happens I'm off

▷ è *tardi* it's late

b (*costare*)

▷ sono 20.000 *lire* that's 20,000 lire, that comes to 20,000 lire

▷ *quant'*è? how much is it?

▷ *quant'*è in tutto? how much does that come to?

c: esserci: *c'è* there is;

▷ *ci* sono there are

▷ non c'è *altro* da dire there's nothing else to be said o there's nothing more one can say

▷*che* (cosa) c'è? what's wrong *o* the matter?
▷*che* c'è di nuovo? what's new?
▷ci sono 60 *chilometri* it's 60 kilometres
▷*cosa* c'è what's wrong *o* the matter?
▷c'è *da* strapparsi i capelli it's enough to drive you up the wall
▷ce n'è *per* tutti there's enough for everybody
▷*quanti* invitati ci saranno? how many guests will there be?
▷*quanto* c'è da qui a Edimburgo? how far is it from here to Edinburgh?
▷c'era una *volta*... once upon a time there was ...; vedi anche ci.
[5] SM being;
▷essere *umano* human being
▷gli esseri *viventi* the living *pl.*

essi ['essi] PRON MPL vedi esso.
essiccare [essik'kare] [1] VT (*gen*) to dry; (*legname*) to season; (*bacino, palude*) to drain. [2] **essiccarsi** VIP (*fiume, pozzo*) to dry up; (*vernice*) to dry (out).
essiccatoio, oi [essikka'tojo] SM (*Industria tessile*) dryer; (*per grano, mais*) drying warehouse; (*per pelli*) drying room.
essiccatore [essikka'tore] SM (*Chim*) desiccator.
essiccazione [essikkat'tsjone] SF drying (process); (*Chim*) desiccation.
esso, a ['esso] PRON PERS (NEUTRO) it; (*riferito a persona*: *sogg*) he/she; (: *complemento*) him/her; **essi** *o* **esse** (*sogg*) they; (*complemento*) them; ... **o chi per esso** ...or his delegate *o* representative.
est [ɛst] [1] SM **a** east; **a est (di)** east (of); **verso est** eastward(s); **il vento dell'est** the east wind **b** (*Pol*): **l'Est** the East; **i paesi dell'Est** the Eastern bloc *sg.* [2] AGG INV (*gen*) east; (*regione*) eastern; **è partito in direzione est** he set off eastwards *o* in an eastward direction.
estasi ['ɛstazi] SF INV (*Rel, fig*) ecstasy; **andare in estasi (per)** (*fig*) to go into ecstasies *o* raptures (over); **mandare in estasi** to send into ecstasies *o* raptures.
estasiare [esta'zjare] [1] VT to send into raptures. [2] **estasiarsi** VIP: **estasiarsi (a, davanti a)** to go into ecstasies *o* raptures (over).
estate [es'tate] SF summer; **d'estate** *o* **in estate** in (the) summer; **un giorno d'estate** one summer's day, one day in summer.
estaticamente [estatika'mente] AVV ecstatically.
estatico, a, ci, che [es'tatiko] AGG ecstatic.
estemporaneamente [estemporanea'mente] AVV in an improvised way, in an impromptu manner.
estemporaneo, a [estempo'raneo] AGG (*discorso*) extempore, impromptu; (*brano musicale*) impromptu.
estendere [es'tɛndere] VB IRREG [1] VT (*gen*) to extend. [2] **estendersi** VIP **a** (*diffondersi: epidemia, rivolta*) to spread; (*allargarsi: città*) to spread, expand; (: *attività commerciale*) to increase, expand **b** (*foresta*) to stretch, extend; **la pianura si estendeva a perdita d'occhio** the plain stretched (away) as far as the eye could see.
estensibile [esten'sibile] AGG **a** (*materiale*) stretch *attr* **b** : **una norma estensibile a tutti i cittadini** a law which applies to all citizens.
estensione [esten'sjone] SF **a** (*ampliamento: di diritto,*

significato, contratto) extension; (: *di commercio, dominio*) expansion; **per estensione** by extension, in a wider sense; **in tutta l'estensione del termine** in the widest sense of the word **b** (*ampiezza: di fenomeno, territorio*) extent; (*superficie*) expanse **c** (*Mus*) range, compass.
estensivamente [estensiva'mente] AVV extensively.
estensivo, a [esten'sivo] AGG extensive; **agricoltura estensiva** extensive agriculture.
estensore [esten'sore] SM **a** (*Anat: anche:* muscolo estensore) extensor (muscle) **b** (*compilatore*) writer, compiler **b** (*attrezzo*) chest expander.
estenuante [estenu'ante] AGG wearing, tiring.
estenuare [estenu'are] VT (*stancare*) to wear out, tire out.
estenuato, a [estenu'ato] AGG worn out, exhausted.
estere ['ɛstere] SM (*Chim*) ester.
esteriore [este'rjore] AGG (*esterno: aspetto, segni, manifestazioni*) outward *attr*; **il mondo esteriore** the external world.
esteriorità [esterjori'ta] SF INV outward appearance.
esteriorizzare [esterjorid'dzare] VT (*gioia, sentimenti*) to show.
esteriormente [esterjor'mente] AVV outwardly.
esternamente [esterna'mente] AVV (*fuori*) on the outside.
esternare [ester'nare] VT to express; **esternare un sospetto** to voice a suspicion.
esternazione [esternat'tsjone] SF expression of one's own opinion.
esterno, a [es'tɛrno] [1] AGG **a** (*muro, superficie*) outer, exterior; (*scala, gabinetto*) outside *attr*; (*rivestimento*) exterior; **aspetto esterno** (*di persona*) outward appearance; **l'aspetto esterno della casa** the outside of the house; **per uso esterno** (*Med*) for external use only **b** (*fig: influenze, mondo*) external, outside *attr*; (: *interessi*) outside *attr*; (: *realtà*) external **c** (*Geom*): **angolo esterno** exterior angle **d** (*allievo*) day *attr*; (*candidato*) external; **commissione esterna** external examiners *pl.* [2] SM (*di edificio*) outside, exterior; (*di scatola*) outside; **all'esterno** on the outside; **dall'esterno** from outside; **gli esterni sono stati girati a Glasgow** (*Cine*) the location shots were taken in Glasgow. [3] SM/F (*allievo*) day pupil; (*candidato*) external candidate.
estero, a ['ɛstero] [1] AGG foreign. [2] SM: **andare all'estero** *o* **partire per l'estero** to go abroad; **vivere all'estero** to live abroad *o* in a foreign country; **commercio con l'estero** foreign trade; **ministero degli Esteri** *o* **gli Esteri** Ministry for Foreign Affairs, ≈ Foreign Office (*Brit*), ≈ State Department (*Am*).
esterofilia [esterofi'lia] SF passion for foreign things.
esterrefatto, a [esterre'fatto] AGG (*costernato*) horrified; (*sbalordito*) astounded.
estesamente [estesa'mente] AVV extensively.
estesi *ecc* [e'stesi] VB vedi estendere.
esteso, a [es'teso] [1] PP di estendere. [2] AGG (*gen*) extensive, large; (*territorio*) vast; (*cultura, ricerca*) wide-ranging; (*scrivere*) **per esteso** (to write) in full.
esteta, i, e [es'tɛta] SM/F aesthete.
estetica [es'tɛtika] SF (*disciplina*) aesthetics *sg*; (*bellezza*) attractiveness; **tiene molto all'estetica** he's very concerned about his appearance; **gli manca completamente il senso dell'estetica** he has absolutely no taste.
esteticamente [estetika'mente] AVV aesthetically; **esteticamente non è il massimo, però funziona bene** it isn't

estetico, a, ci, che [es'tɛtiko] AGG aesthetic; **chirurgia estetica** plastic surgery, cosmetic surgery; **cura estetica** beauty treatment.

estetista, i, e [este'tista] SM/F beautician.

estimo ['ɛstimo] SM (*stima*) valuation; (*disciplina*) surveying.

estinguere [es'tingwere] VB IRREG ☐1 VT **a** (*spegnere*) to put out, extinguish **b** (*Comm: debito*) to pay off; (: *conto in banca*) to close.

☐2 **estinguersi** VIP (*fuoco*) to go out, die out; (*fama*) to fade away; (*stirpe*) to die out; (*specie*) to become extinct.

estinsi *ecc* [es'tinsi] VB vedi **estinguere.**

estinto, a [es'tinto] ☐1 PP di **estinguere.**

☐2 AGG **a** (*specie, stirpe*) extinct **b** (*Comm: debito*) paid off; (: *conto*) closed.

☐3 SM/F: **il caro estinto** the dear departed.

estintore [estin'tore] SM (fire) extinguisher.

estinzione [estin'tsjone] SF (*gen, di specie*) extinction; (*di debito*) payment; (*di conto*) closing; (*di incendio*) putting out.

estirpare [estir'pare] VT (*pianta*) to uproot, pull up; (*dente*) to extract; (*tumore*) to remove; (*fig: vizio*) to eradicate.

estivo, a [es'tivo] AGG summer *attr*; **nei mesi estivi** in the summer months.

estone ['ɛstone] ☐1 AGG, SM/F Estonian ☐2 SM (*lingua*) Estonian.

Estonia [es'tɔnja] SF: **l'Estonia** Estonia.

estorcere [es'tortʃere] VT IRREG: **estorcere qc (a qn)** to extort sth (from sb).

estorsione [estor'sjone] SF extortion; **il denaro frutto delle estorsioni** money acquired by extortion.

estorto, a [es'tɔrto] PP di **estorcere.**

estradare [estra'dare] VT (*Dir*) to extradite.

estradizione [estradit'tsjone] SF (*Dir*) extradition.

estraggo [es'traggo], **estrai** [es'trai] *ecc* VB vedi **estrarre.**

estraibile [estra'ibile] AGG (*autoradio*) removable.

estraneità [estranei'ta] SF INV (*non implicazione*): **ha tentato di dimostrare la propria estraneità alla faccenda** he tried to prove that he had nothing to do with it, he tried to prove that he was not involved in the matter.

estraneo, a [es'traneo] ☐1 AGG (*gen*) extraneous; **corpo estraneo** foreign body; **estraneo a** (*tema, argomento*) unrelated to; **sentirsi estraneo a** (*famiglia, società*) to feel alienated from; **mantenersi** *o* **rimanere estraneo a** (*litigio, complotto*) to take no part in.

☐2 SM/F stranger; **ingresso vietato agli estranei** no admittance to unauthorized personnel.

estraniarsi [estra'njarsi] VR: **estraniarsi (da)** to cut o.s. off (from).

estrapolare [estrapo'lare] VT to extrapolate.

estrapolazione [estrapolat'tsjone] SF extrapolation.

estrarre [es'trarre] VT IRREG **a** (*gen, Med, Mat*) to extract; (*carbone*) to mine; (*marmo*) to quarry **b** (*sorteggiare*) to draw; **estrarre a sorte** to draw lots.

estrassi *ecc* [es'trassi] VB vedi **estrarre.**

estratto, a [es'tratto] ☐1 PP di **estrarre.**

☐2 SM **a** (*alimentare*) extract; (*per profumeria*) essence ▶**estratto di carne** meat extract

b (*sommario: di discorso, documento*) resumé; (*brano: di libro*) extract, excerpt ▶**estratto conto** (*Banca*) (bank) statement ▶**estratto di nascita** (*Amm*) birth certificate.

estrazione [estrat'tsjone] SF **a** (*vedi vb*) extraction; mining; quarrying; drawing **b** (*sorteggio*) draw **c** (*fig: origine*): **essere di estrazione borghese** to come from a middle-class family.

estremamente [estrema'mente] AVV extremely.

estremismo [estre'mizmo] SM extremism.

estremista, i, e [estre'mista] SM/F extremist.

estremistico, a, ci, che [estre'mistiko] AGG extremist.

estremità [estremi'ta] SF INV **a** (*gen*) end, extremity; (*di ago, matita*) point; (*di villaggio, lago, isola*) far end; **da un'estremità all'altra** from one end to the other **b** (*Anat*): **estremità** SFPL extremities.

estremizzare [estremid'dzare] VT: **estremizzare qc** to take sth to extremes.

estremo, a [es'trɛmo] ☐1 AGG (*gen*) extreme; (*ultimo: ora, tentativo*) final, last; (*misure*) drastic, extreme; **estrema destra/sinistra** (*Pol*) extreme right/left; **l'Estrema Unzione** (*Rel*) Extreme Unction; **l'Estremo Oriente** the Far East.

☐2 SM **a** (*gen*) extreme; (*limite: di pazienza, forze*) limit, end; **all'estremo della disperazione** in the depths of despair; **passare da un estremo all'altro** to go from one extreme to the other; **è pignolo (fino) all'estremo** he is extremely *o* exceedingly fussy; **spingere le cose agli estremi** to go too far

b : **estremi** SMPL (*Amm: dati essenziali*) details, particulars; (*Dir*) essential elements.

estrinsecare [estrinse'kare] ☐1 VT to express, show.

☐2 **estrinsecarsi** VIP to express o.s.

estrinseco, a, ci, che [es'trinseko] AGG extrinsic.

estro ['ɛstro] SM (*ispirazione*) inspiration; (*talento*) gift, bent; (*capriccio*) whim, fancy; **gli è venuto l'estro di scrivere** he has taken it into his head to become a writer.

estrogeno, a [es'trɔdʒeno] AGG, SM oestrogen.

estromesso, a [estro'messo] PP di **estromettere.**

estromettere [estro'mettere] VT IRREG: **estromettere (da)** (*partito, club*) to expel (from); (*discussione*) to exclude (from).

estromissione [estromis'sjone] SF (*vedi vb*) expulsion; exclusion.

estrosamente [estrosa'mente] AVV (*con estro*) imaginatively; (*in modo imprevedibile*) unpredictably.

estroso, a [es'troso] AGG (*capriccioso*) fanciful; (*creativo*) talented, creative.

estroverso, a [estro'vɛrso] ☐1 AGG extrovert(ed).

☐2 SM/F extrovert.

estuario, ri [estu'arjo] SM estuary.

esuberante [ezube'rante] AGG exuberant.

esuberanza [ezube'rantsa] SF (*vitalità*) exuberance; **esuberanza di personale** (*eccedenza*) surplus staff.

esubero [e'zubero] SM: **esubero di personale** surplus staff; **in esubero** (*personale*) due to be laid off.

esulare [ezu'lare] VI (*aus avere*): **esulare da** (*competenza*) to be beyond; (*compiti*) not to be part of; **esula dalle mie possibilità aiutarti** it is not within my power to help you.

esule ['ɛzule] SM/F exile.

esultante [ezul'tante] AGG exultant.

esultanza [ezul'tantsa] SF exultation.

esultare [ezul'tare] VI (*aus avere*): **esultare di gioia** to be full of joy; **esultare per la vittoria** to rejoice at one's victory.

esumare [ezu'mare] VT (*salma*) to exhume, disinter; (*fig*)

to unearth.

esumazione [ezumat'tsjone] SF exhumation, disinterment.

età [e'ta] SF INV (gen) age; **all'età di 8 anni** at the age of 8, at 8 years of age, at (age) 8; **avere l'età per fare qc** to be old enough to do sth; **non ho più l'età per fare queste cose** I'm too old to do this sort of thing; **di mezza età** middle-aged; **con l'età è migliorato** he has improved with age; **in età avanzata** of advanced years; **gente della nostra età** people our age; **raggiungere la maggior età** to come of age; **essere in età minore** to be under age; **è giunto ad una bella età** he has reached a good age; **limite di età** age limit; **l'età della ragione** the age of reason; **l'età della pietra** the Stone Age; **lei ha la mia età** she is the same age as me o as I am.

etano [e'tano] SM (Chim) ethane.

etanolo [eta'nɔlo] SM ethanol.

etc. ABBR etc.

etere ['ɛtere] SM (Chim, letter) ether; **via etere** on the airwaves.

etereo, a [e'tɛreo] AGG ethereal.

eternamente [eterna'mente] AVV (gen) eternally; **è eternamente al verde** he's always broke.

eternare [eter'nare] VT to immortalize.

eternità [eterni'ta] SF INV (anche fig) eternity; **impiegare o mettere un'eternità a fare qc** to take ages to do sth; **ti aspetto da un'eternità** I've been waiting for you for ages.

eterno, a [e'tɛrno] **1** AGG (Rel, Filosofia) eternal; (senza fine) eternal, everlasting; (duraturo) perpetual; (interminabile: lamenti, attesa) never-ending; **in eterno** for ever, eternally.

2 SM eternity; **l'Eterno** (Dio) the Eternal (being).

eterodossia [eterodos'sia] SF heterodoxy.

eterodosso, a [etero'dɔsso] **1** AGG heterodox.

2 SM/F heterodox person.

eterogeneità [eterodʒenei'ta] SF INV heterogeneity, heterogeneousness.

eterogeneo, a [etero'dʒɛneo] AGG heterogeneous, mixed, varied.

eterosessuale [eterosessu'ale] AGG, SM/F heterosexual.

eterozigote [eteroddzi'gɔte] SM heterozygote.

etica ['ɛtika] SF ethics sg; **etica professionale** professional ethics.

eticamente [etika'mente] AVV ethically.

etichetta [eti'ketta] SF label; **l'etichetta** (cerimoniale) etiquette.

etichettare [etiket'tare] VT to label.

etichettatrice [etiketta'tritʃe] SF (macchina) labelling machine, labeller.

etico, a, ci, che ['ɛtiko] AGG ethical.

etilene [eti'lɛne] SM (Chim) ethene, ethylene.

etilico, a, ci, che [e'tiliko] AGG: **alcol etilico** ethyl alcohol.

etilismo [eti'lizmo] SM (Med) alcoholism.

etilista, i, e [eti'lista] SM/F (Med) alcoholic.

etilometro [eti'lɔmetro] SM Breathalyzer ® (Brit), drunkometer (Am).

etimologia [etimolo'dʒia] SF etymology.

etimologicamente [etimolodʒika'mente] AVV etymologically.

etimologico, a, ci, che [etimo'lɔdʒiko] AGG etymological.

etiope [e'tiope] AGG, SM/F Ethiopian.

Etiopia [eti'ɔpja] SF: **l'Etiopia** Ethiopia.

etiopico, a, ci, che [eti'ɔpiko] **1** AGG Ethiopian.

2 SM (lingua) Amharic.

Etna ['ɛtna] SM: **l'Etna** Etna.

etnicamente [etnika'mente] AVV ethnically.

etnico, a, ci, che ['ɛtniko] AGG ethnic.

etnografia [etnogra'fia] SF ethnography.

etnologia [etnolo'dʒia] SF ethnology.

etnologico, a, ci, che [etno'lɔdʒiko] AGG ethnological.

etrusco, a, schi, sche [e'trusko] AGG, SM/F Etruscan.

ettaro ['ɛttaro] SM hectare (= 10,000 m²).

etto ['ɛtto] **1** PREF: **etto...** hecto....

2 ABBR SM di **ettogrammo**.

ettogrammo [etto'grammo] SM hectogram(me) (= 100 grams).

ettolitro [et'tɔlitro] SM hectolitre (Brit), hectoliter (Am).

ettometro [et'tɔmetro] SM hectometre.

Ettore ['ɛttore] SM Hector.

EU ABBR (= Europa) E.

eucalipto [euka'lipto] SM eucalyptus.

eucaristia [eukaris'tia] SF: **l'eucaristia** the Eucharist.

Euclide [eu'klide] SM Euclid.

eufemismo [eufe'mizmo] SM euphemism.

eufemisticamente [eufemistika'mente] AVV euphemistically.

eufemistico, a, ci, che [eufe'mistiko] AGG euphemistic.

euforia [eufo'ria] SF euphoria.

euforicamente [euforika'mente] AVV euphorically.

euforico, a, ci, che [eu'fɔriko] AGG euphoric.

eunuco, chi [eu'nuko] SM eunuch.

Eurasia [eu'razja] SF: **l'Eurasia** Eurasia.

eurasiatico, a, ci, che [eura'zjatiko] AGG, SM/F Eurasian.

Euratom ['euratom] SIGLA F (= Comunità Europea dell'Energia Atomica) Euratom.

Euridice [euri'ditʃe] SF Eurydice.

Euripide [eu'ripide] SM Euripides.

eurocorpo [euro'kɔrpo] SM European force.

eurodeputato, a [eurodepu'tato] SM/F Euro MP.

eurodivisa [eurodi'viza] SF Eurocurrency.

eurodollaro [euro'dollaro] SM Eurodollar.

euromercato [euromer'kato] SM Euromarket.

euromissile [euro'missile] SM Euro-missile.

Europa [eu'rɔpa] SF: **l'Europa** Europe.

europeismo [europe'izmo] SM (Pol) Europeanism.

europeizzare [europeid'dzare] VT to europeanize.

europeo, a [euro'pɛo] AGG, SM/F European.

euroscettico, a, ci, che [euroʃ'ʃettiko] SM/F Euro-sceptic.

eurovisione [eurovi'zjone] SF eurovision.

eutanasia [eutana'zia] SF euthanasia.

E.V. ABBR = Eccellenza Vostra.

Eva ['ɛva] SF Eve.

evacuamento [evakua'mento] SM evacuation.

evacuare [evaku'are] VT, VI (aus avere) (gen, Med) to evacuate.

evacuazione [evakuat'tsjone] SF evacuation.

evadere [e'vadere] VB IRREG **1** VT **a** (tasse, imposte) to evade; **evadere il fisco** to evade (income) tax

b (Amm: pratica) to deal with, dispatch; (: corrispondenza) to deal with, clear; (: ordine) to deal with.

2 VI (aus essere): **evadere (da)** (prigione) to escape (from); **far evadere qn** to help sb to escape; **evadere dalla realtà quotidiana** to get away from the realities of daily life.

evanescente [evaneʃ'ʃɛnte] AGG evanescent.

evanescenza [evaneʃ'ʃɛntsa] SF evanescence.

evangelico, a, ci, che [evan'dʒɛliko] AGG, SM/F evangelical.

evangelista, i [evandʒe'lista] SM Evangelist.

evangelizzare [evandʒelid'dzare] VT to evangelize.

evaporare [evapo'rare] VT, VI (aus **essere** nel senso di 'trasformarsi in vapore'; **avere** nel senso di 'ridursi per evaporazione') to evaporate.

evaporazione [evaporat'tsjone] SF evaporation.

evasi ecc [e'vazi] VB vedi **evadere**.

evasione [eva'zjone] SF **a** (da prigione, anche fig) escape; **letteratura d'evasione** escapist literature **b** (Amm: disbrigo: di ordine) carrying out, fulfilment; **occuparsi dell'evasione della corrispondenza** to deal with the correspondence **c** (Fisco) evasion ▸**evasione fiscale** tax evasion.

evasivamente [evaziva'mente] AVV evasively.

evasivo, a [eva'zivo] AGG evasive.

evaso, a [e'vazo] [1] PP di **evadere**. [2] SM/F escaped prisoner.

evasore [eva'zore] SM: **evasore (fiscale)** tax evader.

evenienza [eve'njɛntsa] SF: **nell'evenienza che ciò succeda** should that happen; **essere pronto ad ogni evenienza** to be ready for any eventuality; **in ogni evenienza puoi metterti in contatto con me** you can get in touch with me should the need arise.

evento [e'vɛnto] SM event.

eventuale [eventu'ale] [1] AGG: **contro eventuali danni** against any possible damage; **per scongiurare il pericolo di eventuali complicazioni** to avoid the risk of possible complications; **gli eventuali guadagni saranno devoluti in beneficenza** any profit will be given to charity; **per eventuali reclami rivolgersi a...** (any) claims should be addressed to .... [2] SFPL: **varie ed eventuali** any other business.

eventualità [eventuali'ta] SF INV eventuality, possibility; **tenersi pronto a ogni eventualità** o **a tutte le eventualità** to be prepared for any eventuality o for all eventualities; **nell'eventualità di** in the event of; **nell'eventualità che non dovesse tornare...** should he not return ... .

eventualmente [eventual'mente] AVV if need be, if necessary; **eventualmente ci fossero difficoltà...** should there be any problems ... .

Everest ['ɛverest] SM: **l'Everest, il monte Everest** (Mount) Everest.

eversione [ever'sjone] SF subversion.

eversivo, a [ever'sivo] AGG subversive.

evidente [evi'dɛnte] AGG obvious, evident; **è una prova evidente di...** it's clear proof of ...; **è evidente che** it is obvious o evident that; **è evidente!** obviously!

evidentemente [evidente'mente] AVV (palesemente) obviously, clearly, evidently.

evidenza [evi'dɛntsa] SF: **l'evidenza dei fatti è schiacciante** the facts are incontrovertible; **arrendersi (di fronte) all'evidenza** to yield to the evidence; **negare l'evidenza** to deny the facts o the obvious; **mettere in evidenza** (problemi) to highlight, bring to the fore.

evidenziare [eviden'tsjare] VT (sottolineare) to emphasize, highlight; (con evidenziatore) to highlight.

evidenziatore [evidentsja'tore] SM (penna) highlighter.

evirare [evi'rare] VT to castrate.

evirazione [evirat'tsjone] SF castration.

evitabile [evi'tabile] AGG avoidable.

evitare [evi'tare] VT (gen) to avoid; (colpo) to dodge; (sguardo) to evade; **evitare di fare qc** to avoid doing sth; **evitare che qc accada** to prevent sth (from) happening; **evitare qc a qn** to spare sb sth; **ciò gli ha evitato il fastidio di tornare indietro** that saved him the bother of going back; **evita di fare rumore** try not to make any noise.

evo ['ɛvo] SM: **l'evo moderno/antico** modern/ancient times.

evocare [evo'kare] VT IRREG (gen) to evoke; (ricordo) to recall, evoke.

evocativo, a [evoka'tivo] AGG evocative.

evocazione [evokat'tsjone] SF evocation.

evocherò ecc [evoke'rɔ] VB vedi **evocare**.

evolutivo, a [evolu'tivo] AGG (gen, Bio) evolutionary; (Med) progressive.

evoluto, a [evo'luto] [1] PP di **evolversi**. [2] AGG (popolo, civiltà) (highly) developed, advanced; (persona: emancipato) independent; (: senza pregiudizi) broad-minded.

evoluzione [evolut'tsjone] SF **a** (gen) evolution; (progresso) progress, development; **teoria dell'evoluzione** theory of evolution **b** (movimento) movement; (Mil) manoeuvre.

evoluzionismo [evoluttsjo'nizmo] SM evolutionism.

evoluzionista, i, e [evoluttsjo'nista] SM/F evolutionist.

evoluzionistico, a, ci, che [evoluttsjo'nistiko] AGG evolutionist.

evolversi [e'vɔlversi] [1] VIP IRREG to develop, evolve. [2] SM: **con l'evolversi della situazione** as the situation developed o develops.

evviva [ev'viva] [1] ESCL hurrah!; **evviva il re!** long live the King!. [2] SM INV applause no pl.

ex [ɛks] [1] PREF ex, ex-, former. [2] SM/F INV: **il mio ex** my ex.

ex aequo [ɛg'z ɛkwo] AVV: **classificarsi primo ex aequo** to come joint first, come first equal.

excursus [eks'kursus] SM INV digression.

ex novo [ɛks 'nɔvo] AVV (daccapo) from the beginning.

expertise [ɛksper'tiz] SF INV (di opera d'arte) authentication.

exploit [ɛks'plwa] SM INV feat, achievement.

extra ['ɛkstra] AGG INV, SM INV extra.

extracomunitario, ria, ri, rie [ɛkstracomuni'tarjo] [1] AGG non-EEC. [2] SM/F non-EEC national (often referring to non-European immigrant).

extraconiugale [ɛkstrakonju'gale] AGG extramarital.

extraeuropeo, a [ɛkstraeuro'pɛo] AGG non-European.

extraparlamentare [ɛkstraparlamen'tare] AGG, SM/F extraparliamentary.

extrasensoriale [ɛkstrasenso'rjale] AGG extrasensory; **percezione extrasensoriale** extrasensory perception.

extrasistole [ɛkstra'sistole] SF (Med) extrasystole.

extraterrestre [ɛkstrater'rɛstre] AGG, SM/F extraterrestrial.

extraterritoriale [ɛkstraterrito'rjale] AGG extraterritorial.

extraurbano, a [ɛkstraur'bano] AGG suburban.

ex voto [eks'vɔto] SM INV ex voto.

Ezechiele [edze'kjɛle] SM Ezekiel.

F

F, f ['effe] SF O M INV (*lettera*) F, f; **F come Firenze** ≈ F for Frederick (*Brit*), ≈ F for Fox (*Am*).

F ABBR **a** (= *Fahrenheit*) F **b** (= *fiume*) R.

fa¹ [fa] ⌐1⌐ 3A PERS SG DEL PRESENTE di **fare.**
⌐2⌐ AVV: **10 anni fa** 10 years ago; **quanto tempo fa?** how long ago?

fa² [fa] SM INV (*Mus*) F; (: *solfeggiando*) fa.

fabbisogno [fabbi'zoɲɲo] SM needs *pl*, requirements *pl*; **il fabbisogno nazionale di petrolio** the country's oil requirements; **il fabbisogno del settore pubblico** public sector borrowing requirement (*Brit*), government debt borrowing (*Am*).

fabbrica, che ['fabbrika] SF factory; **fabbrica di mattoni** brickyard.

fabbricabile [fabbri'kabile] AGG **a** (*terreno, area*) that can be built on **b** (*prodotto industriale*) manufacturable.

fabbricante [fabbri'kante] SM/F manufacturer, maker.

fabbricare [fabbri'kare] VT (*produrre: gen*) to make, manufacture; (: *a livello industriale*) to manufacture; (*costruire: edificio*) to build, put up; (*fig: inventare: alibi, accuse*) to fabricate.

fabbricato [fabbri'kato] SM building.

fabbricazione [fabbrikat'tsjone] SF (*vedi vb*) making; manufacture, manufacturing; building; fabrication; **di fabbricazione italiana** made in Italy, Italian made; **difetto di fabbricazione** manufacturing defect.

fabbro ['fabbro] SM smith ▶ **fabbro ferraio** (black) smith.

faccenda [fat'tʃɛnda] SF (*affare*) business, affair, matter; **una brutta faccenda** a nasty business; **devo sbrigare alcune faccende** I've got a few things to see to; **le faccende domestiche** the housework *sg*.

faccendiere [fattʃen'djɛre] SM wheeler-dealer, (shady) operator.

faccetta [fat'tʃetta] SF (*di pietra preziosa*) facet.

faccettatura [fattʃetta'tura] SF (*operazione*) facetting.

facchinaggio, gi [fakki'naddʒo] SM porterage.

facchino [fak'kino] SM (*gen*) porter; **lavoro da facchino** (*fig*) hard graft.

faccia, ce ['fattʃa] SF **a** (*viso, espressione*) face; **una faccia amica** a friendly face; **avere la faccia stanca** to look tired; **fare la faccia imbronciata** to sulk; **dovevi vedere la sua faccia quando...** you should have seen his face when ...; **avere il sole in faccia** to have the sun in one's eyes; **gliel'ho detto in faccia** I told him to his face; **ridere in faccia a qn** to laugh in sb's face; **leggere qc in faccia a qn** to see sth written all over sb's face; **perdere/salvare la faccia** to lose/save (one's) face; **avere la faccia (tosta) di dire/fare qc** to have the cheek *o* nerve to say/do sth **b** (*lato: gen*) side; (: *Geom*) face, side; (: *della terra*) face; (: *fig: di problema, questione*) side, aspect; **vorrei cancellarlo dalla faccia della terra** I'd like to wipe him off the face of the earth
c (*fraseologia*): **(a) faccia a faccia** face to face; **a faccia in su/giù** face up(wards)/down(wards); **fare qc alla faccia di qn** to do sth to spite sb; **di faccia a** opposite, facing; **visto di faccia** seen from the front.

facciale [fat'tʃale] AGG facial.

facciata [fat'tʃata] SF **a** (*Archit*) façade; (*fig: apparenza esterna*) appearances *pl*; **non giudicare dalla facciata** don't judge by appearances **b** (*di pagina*) side; **una lettera di 4 facciate** a 4-page letter.

faccio ecc ['fattʃo] VB vedi **fare.**

facente [fa'tʃɛnte]: **facente funzione** SM/F (*Amm*) deputy.

facessi ecc [fa'tʃessi] VB vedi **fare.**

faceto, a [fa'tʃɛto] AGG humorous.

facevo ecc [fa'tʃevo] VB vedi **fare.**

facezia [fa'tʃettsja] SF witticism, witty remark.

fachiro [fa'kiro] SM fakir.

facile ['fatʃile] AGG **a** (*gen*) easy; **è più facile a dirsi che a farsi** it's easier said than done; **è meno facile di quanto sembri** it's harder than it looks, it's not as easy as it looks; **far tutto facile** to make light *o* little of everything; **avere la pistola facile** to be trigger-happy; **avere la lacrima facile** to be easily moved to tears; **è facile all'ira/alla malinconia** he's apt to lose his temper/to get depressed; **avere un carattere facile** to be an easy-going person; **donna di facili costumi** woman of easy

virtue, loose woman
b (*probabile*): **è facile che piova** it's probably going to rain; **è facile che venga** he may well come, he'll probably come.

facilità [fatʃili'ta] SF INV **a** (*di lavoro, compito*) easiness; (*di vittoria*) ease; **studia con facilità** he has no problem studying; **arrabbiarsi con facilità** to be apt to lose one's temper **b** (*disposizione, dono*) ability, aptitude; **ha facilità a fare amicizia** he makes friends easily.

facilitare [fatʃili'tare] VT to facilitate (*frm*), make easier; **non faciliterà la situazione** it's not going to make matters any easier.

facilitazione [fatʃilitat'tsjone] SF: **facilitazioni di paga-mento** easy terms, credit facilities.

facilmente [fatʃil'mente] AVV (*gen*) easily; (*probabilmente*) probably.

facilone, a [fatʃi'lone] SM/F (*pegg*) laid-back type.

faciloneria [fatʃilone'ria] SF slapdash attitude.

facinoroso, a [fatʃino'roso] [1] AGG violent. [2] SM/F thug.

facocero [fako'tʃero] SM (*Zool*) warthog.

facoltà [fakol'ta] SF INV **a** (*capacità mentale*) faculty; (*Chim*) property; **nel pieno possesso delle proprie facoltà mentali** in full possession of one's faculties **b** (*autorità*) power; **dare facoltà a qn di fare qc** to give sb the power *o* authority to do sth; **esula dalle mie facoltà** it's not within my power **c** (*Univ*) department, faculty; **è iscritta alla facoltà di legge** she's a student in the law department.

facoltativo, a [fakolta'tivo] AGG optional; **fermata facoltativa** request stop.

facoltoso, a [fakol'toso] AGG wealthy.

façon [fa'sɔ̃] SF INV: **una pelliccia façon visone** an imitation mink (coat).

facsimile [fak'simile] SM INV facsimile; (*fig: cosa simile*) copy.

factotum [fak'tɔtum] SM/F INV: **è il factotum della ditta** he's the one who does most of the work in the firm; **sarebbe una semplice segretaria ma in pratica è la factotum** she's supposed to be a secretary but in reality she does a bit of everything.

faggio, gi ['faddʒo] SM (*albero, legno*) beech; **mobili di** *o* **in faggio** beech(wood) furniture.

fagiano [fa'dʒano] SM pheasant ▶**fagiano di monte** black grouse.

fagiolino [fadʒo'lino] SM French (*Brit*) *o* string bean.

fagiolo [fa'dʒɔlo] SM bean; **capitare a fagiolo** to come at the right time.

faglia ['faʎʎa] SF (*Geol*) fault.

fagliatura [faʎʎa'tura] SF (*Geol*): **fagliatura a blocchi** block faulting.

fagocitare [fagotʃi'tare] VT (*Bio*) to perform phagocytosis on; (*fig: industria*) to absorb, swallow up.

fagocitosi [fagotʃi'tɔzi] SF (*Bio*) phagocytosis.

fagotto¹ [fa'gɔtto] SM bundle; **fare fagotto** to pack up and go.

fagotto² [fa'gɔtto] SM (*Mus*) bassoon.

Fahrenheit ['faːrənhait] SM INV Fahrenheit.

fai ['fai] VB vedi **fare**.

faida ['faida] SF feud.

fai da te [faida'te] SM INV DIY, do-it-yourself.

faina [fa'ina] SF (*Zool*) stone marten.

falange [fa'landʒe] SF (*Anat, Mil*) phalanx.

falcata [fal'kata] SF stride.

falce ['faltʃe] SF scythe; **una falce di luna** a crescent moon; **falce e martello** (*Pol*) hammer and sickle.

falcetto [fal'tʃetto] SM sickle.

falchetta [fal'ketta] SF (*Naut*) gunwale.

falciare [fal'tʃare] VT **a** (*grano*) to reap; (*erba*) to mow, cut; (*con la falce*) to scythe **b** (*fig: uccidere*): **furono falciati da una raffica di mitra** they were mown down by a hail of machine-gun fire; **migliaia di vite falciate dall'epidemia** thousands of lives wiped out by the epidemic **c** (*Calcio*) to bring down.

falciatrice [faltʃa'tritʃe] SF (*per grano*) reaping machine; (*per erba*) mowing machine.

falciatura [faltʃa'tura] SF (*vedi vb*) reaping; mowing.

falcidia [fal'tʃidja] SF (*fig: strage*) extermination; **all'e-same di anatomia hanno fatto una falcidia** they were failing students en masse at the Anatomy exam.

falco, chi ['falko] SM (*Zool, fig Pol*) hawk; **occhio di falco!** you're sharp-eyed!; ▶**falco migratore** *o* **pellegrino** peregrine falcon ▶**falco di palude** marsh harrier ▶**falco pescatore** osprey.

falcone [fal'kone] SM falcon.

falconeria [falkone'ria] SF falconry.

falda ['falda] SF (*Geol*) layer, stratum; (*di cappello*) brim; (*di cappotto*) tails *pl*; (*di monte*) lower slope; (*di tetto*) pitch; (*di neve*) flake.

falegname [falen'name] SM carpenter, joiner (*Brit*).

falegnameria [falennname'ria] SF **a** (*mestiere*) carpentry **b** (*locale*) carpenter's shop.

falena [fa'lɛna] SF (*Zool*) moth.

falesia [fa'lɛzja] SF cliff.

Falkland ['fɔːlklənd] SFPL: **le (isole) Falkland** the Falkland Islands.

falla ['falla] SF leak.

fallace [fal'latʃe] AGG deceptive.

fallacia, cie [fal'latʃa] SF fallacy.

fallico, a, ci, che ['falliko] AGG phallic.

fallimentare [fallimen'tare] AGG (*Comm*) bankruptcy *attr*; **bilancio fallimentare** negative balance, deficit; **diritto fallimentare** bankruptcy law; **"tutto a prezzi fallimen-tari"** "everything at drastically reduced prices"; **il bilancio della sua vita era fallimentare** his life was a total failure; **fu un'esperienza fallimentare** it was a failure.

fallimento [falli'mento] SM **a** (*fiasco*) failure, flop **b** (*Comm, Dir*) bankruptcy; **essere/andare in fallimento** to be/go bankrupt.

fallire [fal'lire] [1] VT (*colpo, bersaglio*) to miss. [2] VI (*aus essere*) **a**: **fallire (in)** (*non riuscire*) to fail (in), be unsuccessful (in) **b** (*Comm, Dir*) to go bankrupt.

fallito, a [fal'lito] [1] AGG (*commerciante*) bankrupt; (*tenta-tivo*) unsuccessful. [2] SM/F (*Comm*) bankrupt; (*fig*) failure.

fallo¹ ['fallo] SM **a** (*errore*) fault; **essere in fallo** to be at fault *o* in error; **mettere il piede in fallo** to slip; **cogliere qn in fallo** to catch sb out; **senza fallo** without fail **b** (*difetto*) fault, defect, flaw **c** (*Sport*) fault, foul; (*Tennis*) fault; **fallo di piede** (*Tennis*) foot fault; **fare un fallo di mano** (*Calcio*) to handle the ball.

fallo² ['fallo] SM (*Anat*) phallus.

fallocrate [fal'lɔkrate] SM (*pegg*) male chauvinist.

fallosamente [fallosa'mente] AVV (*Sport*): **giocare fallosa-mente** to commit fouls, play a dirty game.

falloso, a [fal'loso] AGG (*Sport*): **gioco falloso** foul play, unfair play.

falò [fa'lɔ] SM INV bonfire.

falsamente [falsa'mente] AVV (gen) falsely; (rispondere, dichiarare) untruthfully.

falsare [fal'sare] VT (notizia, realtà) to distort.

falsariga, ghe [falsa'riga] SF lined page, ruled page; **sulla falsariga di...** (fig) along the lines of ... .

falsario, ri [fal'sarjo] SM (di documenti, quadri) forger; (di monete) counterfeiter.

falsetto [fal'setto] SM (Mus) falsetto; **cantare in falsetto** to sing falsetto.

falsificare [falsifi'kare] VT (firma, documento) to forge; (conti) to falsify; (monete) to forge, counterfeit.

falsificazione [falsifikat'tsjone] SF forging; **di difficile falsificazione** difficult to forge.

falsità [falsi'ta] SF INV (di persona, notizia) falseness; (bugia) lie.

falso, a ['falso] ① AGG (denaro, documenti) forged, fake, counterfeit; (oro, gioielli) imitation attr; (pudore, promessa) false; **fare un passo falso** to stumble; (fig) to slip up; **sotto falsa luce** in a false light; **essere un falso magro** to be heavier than one looks ►**falsa partenza** (anche fig) false start ►**falso allarme** false alarm.
② SM a falsehood; **dire il falso** to lie, not to tell the truth; **giurare il falso** (Dir) to commit perjury
b (Dir) forgery; **falso in atto pubblico** forgery (of a legal document)
c (opera d'arte) fake.

falsopiano [falso'pjano] SM (pl falsipiani) slight slope.

fama ['fama] SF a (celebrità) fame, renown; **raggiungere la fama** to become famous; **di fama mondiale** world famous **b** (reputazione) reputation, name; **conoscere qn di o per fama** to know sb by reputation; **ha (la) fama di essere un dongiovanni** he has a reputation as a Don Juan.

fame ['fame] SF hunger; **aver fame** to be hungry; **ho una fame da lupo** I'm famished o starving, I could eat a horse; **aver fame di** (fig: giustizia) to hunger o long for; **fare la fame** (fig) to starve, scrape a living.

famelico, a, ci, che [fa'mɛliko] AGG ravenous.

famigerato, a [famidʒe'rato] AGG notorious.

famiglia [fa'miʎʎa] SF (gen, Zool, Bot) family; **essere di buona famiglia** to come from a good family; **metter su famiglia** to start a family; **amico/festa di famiglia** family friend/celebration; **in famiglia** (matrimonio) quiet; (funerale) private; **passare il Natale in famiglia** to spend Christmas with one's family; **è uno della famiglia** (fig) he's (quite) one of the family; **la Sacra Famiglia** the Holy Family.

familiare [fami'ljare] ① AGG a (di famiglia) family attr; **vita familiare** family life; **una FIAT familiare** a FIAT estate (Brit) o station wagon (Am)
b (noto) familiar; **questo nome mi è familiare** I've heard this name before, I know the name
c (intimo: rapporti, atmosfera) friendly; (: tono) informal; (lessico: colloquiale) informal, colloquial.
② SM/F relative, relation; **i miei familiari** my relations o family sg.

familiarità [familjari'ta] SF (dimestichezza) familiarity; (confidenza) informality; **trattare qn con familiarità** to treat sb in a friendly way; **aver familiarità con qc** to be familiar with sth.

familiarizzare [familjarid'dzare] VI (aus avere): **familiarizzare con qn** to get to know sb; **abbiamo familiarizzato subito** we got on well together from the start; **familiarizzare o familiarizzarsi con l'ambiente** to familiarize o.s. with one's surroundings.

famoso, a [fa'moso] AGG famous, well-known.

fanale [fa'nale] SM (Aut) light; (luce stradale) lamp; (Naut) light; (di faro) beacon ►**fanale di poppa** (Naut) stern light.

fanalino [fana'lino] SM light ►**fanalino di coda** (Aut, Aer) rear o tail light; (fig) tail end ►**fanalino di posizione** (Aut) sidelight.

fanaticamente [fanatika'mente] AVV fanatically.

fanatico, a, ci, che [fa'natiko] ① AGG fanatical; **fanatico di o per** (teatro, calcio) wild o mad o crazy about.
② SM/F fanatic; (tifoso) fan; **è un fanatico del golf/di Fellini** he is a golf/Fellini fanatic.

fanatismo [fana'tizmo] SM fanaticism.

fanatizzare [fanatid'dzare] VT to rouse to fanaticism.

fanciullesco, a, schi, sche [fantʃul'lesko] AGG childlike; (pegg) childish.

fanciullezza [fantʃul'lettsa] SF childhood.

fanciullo, a [fan'tʃullo] SM/F child.

fandonia [fan'dɔnja] SF (tall) story, whopper; **fandonie!** nonsense! sg, rubbish! sg.

fanello [fa'nɛllo] SM linnet.

fanfara [fan'fara] SF (banda) brass band; (musica) fanfare.

fanfarone [fanfa'rone] SM braggart.

fanghiglia [fan'giʎʎa] SF mire, mud.

fango, ghi ['fango] SM mud; **gettare fango addosso a qn** (fig) to sling mud at sb; **fare i fanghi** (Med) to take a course of mud baths.

fangosità [fangosi'ta] SF INV muddiness.

fangoso, a [fan'goso] AGG muddy.

fanno ['fanno] VB vedi fare.

fannullone, a [fannul'lone] SM/F layabout.

fantapolitica [fantapo'litika] SF political fiction.

fantascientifico, a, ci, che [fantaʃʃen'tifiko] AGG science fiction attr.

fantascienza [fantaʃ'ʃɛntsa] SF science fiction.

fantasia [fanta'zia] SF a (facoltà) imagination, fancy; **avere fantasia** to have imagination; **non ha fantasia** he hasn't got any imagination; **lavori troppo di fantasia** your imagination is running away with you; **sono fantasie le tue!** it's just your imagination!; **nel mondo della fantasia** in the realm(s) of fantasy o fancy
b (capriccio) whim, caprice; **fantasia passeggera** passing fancy
c (decorazione) pattern; **lo vuole tinta unita o fantasia?** would you like it plain or patterned?
d (Mus) fantasia.

fantasiosamente [fantazjosa'mente] AVV imaginatively.

fantasioso, a [fanta'zjoso] AGG (dotato di fantasia) imaginative; (bizzarro) fanciful, strange.

fantasista, i, e [fanta'zista] SM/F variety artist.

fantasma, i [fan'tazma] ① SM (spettro) ghost, spectre (letter), phantom (letter).
② AGG: **governo fantasma** shadow cabinet; **città/scrittore fantasma** ghost town/writer.

fantasmagoria [fantazmago'ria] SF phantasmagoria.

fantasmagorico, a, ci, che [fantazma'gɔriko] AGG phantasmagoric(al).

fantasticamente [fantastika'mente] AVV (in modo meraviglioso) fantastically; (con fantasia) imaginatively.

fantasticare [fantasti'kare] VI (aus avere) to daydream.

fantasticheria [fantastike'ria] SF daydream.

fantastico, a, ci, che [fan'tastiko] AGG (gen) fantastic;

(*potenza, ingegno*) imaginative; **un mondo fantastico** a world of fantasy, a fantasy world; **fantastico!** fantastic!, terrific!

fante ['fante] SM **a** (*Mil*) infantryman **b** (*Carte*) jack.

fanteria [fante'ria] SF (*Mil*) infantry.

fantino [fan'tino] SM jockey.

fantoccio, ci [fan'tɔttʃo] **1** SM (*manichino*) dummy; (*bambola*) doll; (*fig: persona*) puppet; **fantoccio di pezza** rag doll.
2 AGG INV: **governo fantoccio** puppet government.

fantomatico, a, ci, che [fanto'matiko] AGG (*personaggio*) mythical.

F.A.O. ['fao] SIGLA F (= *Food and Agriculture Organization*) FAO.

farabutto [fara'butto] SM crook.

faraglione [faraʎ'ʎone] SM (*Geog*) stack.

faraona [fara'ona] SF (*anche*: **gallina faraona**) guinea fowl.

faraone [fara'one] SM **a** (*Storia*) Pharaoh **b** (*Carte*) faro.

faraonico, a, ci, che [fara'ɔniko] AGG of the Pharaohs; (*fig*) enormous, huge.

farcire [far'tʃire] VT (*carni, peperoni, pomodori*) to stuff; (*torte*) to fill; **farcito di errori** (*fig*) riddled with mistakes.

fard [far] SM INV blusher.

fardello [far'dello] SM bundle; (*fig*) burden.

---

fare ['fare] VB IRREG
1 VT
a (*fabbricare: gen*) to make; (: *casa*) to build; (*quadro*) to paint; (*disegno*) to draw; (*pasto*) to cook; (*pane, dolci*) to bake; (*assegno*) to make out;
▷**fanno la stessa classe** they are in the same year
▷**fare un corso** (*tenere*) to give a series of lessons, teach a course; (*seguire*) to do a course
▷**che cosa ne hai fatto di quei pantaloni?** what have you done with those trousers?
▷**fare un errore** to make a mistake
▷**ha fatto la mia felicità** he made me so happy
▷**fare una festa** to have o hold a party
▷**ha fatto un figlio** she's had a baby
▷**quest'albero non fa frutti** this tree doesn't bear fruit
▷**hai fatto il letto?** have you made the bed?
▷**lo hanno fatto presidente** they made him president
▷**fare una promessa** to make a promise
▷**hai fatto la stanza?** have you cleaned the room?
b (*attività: gen*) to do; (*vacanza, sogno*) to have;
▷**a scuola facciamo chimica** at school we do chemistry
▷**fare i compiti** to do one's homework
▷**cosa fai?** (*adesso*) what are you doing?; (*nella vita*) what do you do?, what is your job?
▷**non posso farci nulla** I can't do anything about it
▷**fare la spesa** to do the shopping
▷**fare del tennis** to play tennis
c (*funzione*) to be; (*Teatro*) to play, be, act;
▷**fare l'avvocato** to be a lawyer
▷**fare finta di essere stanco** to pretend to be tired
▷**fare l'innocente** to act the innocent
▷**fare il malato** to pretend to be ill
▷**fare il medico** to be a doctor
▷**fare il morto** (*in acqua*) to float
▷**nel film fa il padre** in the film he plays the father
d (*percorrere*) to do;
▷**fare i 100 metri** (*competere*) to go in for o run in the 100 metres
▷**fa i 100 metri in 10,5** he does the 100 metres in 10.5
▷**abbiamo fatto 5 chilometri** we've done 5 kilometres
▷**fare una passeggiata** to go for o take a walk
▷**fare un viaggio** to go on a trip, make a journey
e (*suscitare: sentimenti*) to arouse;
▷**fa niente** it doesn't matter
▷**mi fa orrore** it horrifies me
▷**fare paura a** to frighten
▷**mi fa rabbia** it makes me angry
f (*considerare*)
▷**ti facevo più intelligente** I thought you had more sense
▷**ti facevo al mare** I thought you were at the seaside
▷**io facevo più vecchio** I thought he was older
g (*ammontare*)
▷**due più due fa quattro** two plus two make(s) o equal(s) 4
▷**la città non fa più di 2 milioni di abitanti** the city hasn't more than 2 million inhabitants
▷**che differenza fa?** what difference does it make?
▷**fa 5.000 lire, signora** that'll be 5,000 lire, madam
▷**glielo faccio 100.000 lire** I'll give it to you o I'll let you have it for 100,000 lire
▷**che ora fa il tuo orologio?** what time is it by your watch?
h (+ *infinito*)
▷**le faremo avere la merce** we'll get the goods to you
▷**l'hanno fatto entrare in macchina** (*costringere*) they forced him into the car, they made him get into the car; (*lasciare*) they let him get into the car
▷**lo farò fare a lei** I'll get her to do it, I'll have her do it
▷**farsi fregare** to be taken for a ride
▷**far piangere qn** to make sb cry
▷**far riparare la macchina** to have one's car repaired
▷**far scongelare** to defrost, thaw out
▷**far soffrire qn** to make sb suffer
▷**mi son fatto tagliare i capelli** I've had my hair cut
▷**fammi vedere** let me see
▷**fare venire qn** to send for sb
i: *farsi*
▷**farsi la barba** to have a shave
▷**farsi la barca** to get a boat
▷**farsi una gonna** to make o.s. a skirt
▷**farsi la macchina** to get a car
▷**si fa da mangiare da solo** he does his own cooking
▷**si è fatto mia moglie** (*fam*) he's had it off with my wife
▷**farsi un nome** to make a name for o.s.
j (*fraseologia*)
▷**farla a qn** to get the better of sb
▷**me l'hanno fatta!** (*imbrogliare*) I've been done!; (*derubare*) I've been robbed!; (*lasciare nei guai*) I've been lumbered!
▷**farcela** to succeed, manage
▷**ne ha fatta una delle sue** he's done it again
▷**non ce la faccio più** (*a camminare*) I can't go on; (*a sopportare*) I can't take any more
▷**ce la facciamo?** do you think we'll make it?
▷**farla finita con qc** to have done with sth
▷**fare del proprio meglio** to do one's best
▷**non c'è niente da fare** it's no use

▷ormai è stato deciso e non c'è *niente* da fare it's been decided and there's nothing we can do about it

▷ha fatto di *sì* con la testa he nodded.

2 VI (*aus* avere)

a (*agire*) to do;

▷fare *presto* to be quick

▷faccia *pure*! go ahead!

▷*saperci* fare con (*situazioni, persone*) to know how to deal with

▷ci sa fare coi bambini/con le macchine he's good with children/cars

▷ci sa fare con le donne he's a smooth operator with women

▷ci sa fare he's quite good

▷fate come *volete* do as you please

b (*dire*): "davvero?" fece "really?" he said

c questo non *si* fa it's not done, you (just) can't do that;

▷*si* fa così! you do it like this, this is the way it's done

▷non *si* fa così! (*rimprovero*) that's no way to behave!

▷questa festa non *si* farà! this party won't take place!

d (*fraseologia*)

▷fa proprio al *caso* nostro it's just what we need

▷avere a *che* fare con qn to have sth to do with sb

▷non so *che* farmene di lui I don't know what to do with him

▷fare *da* (*funzioni*) to act as

▷fare *da* padre a qn to be like a father to sb

▷la cucina fa anche *da* sala da pranzo the kitchen also serves as *o* is also used as a dining room

▷fai in *modo* che non ti vedano make sure they don't see you

▷fare *per* (*essere adatto*) to be suitable for; (*essere sul punto di*) to be about to

▷fece *per* uscire e poi si fermò he made as if to go out and then stopped

▷non fa *per* me it isn't (suitable) for me

▷fare a *pugni* to come to blows; (*fig*) to clash

▷fare in *tempo* a... to be in time to ...

▷il grigio fa *vecchio* grey makes you *o* one look older.

3 VB IMPERS

▷fa *caldo* it's hot

▷fa *freddo* it's cold

▷fa *notte* it's getting dark.

4 farsi VR

a (*rendersi*)

▷farsi *amico* di qn to make friends with sb

▷è andata a farsi *bella* she's gone to make herself beautiful

▷farsi *notare* to get o.s. noticed

▷farsi *prete* to become a priest

b (*spostarsi*): farsi *avanti* to move forward; (*fig*) to come forward;

▷fatti *più in là*! move along a bit!

c (*gergo: drogarsi*) to do drugs.

5 farsi VIP (*divenire*) to become

▷farsi *bello* to grow beautiful

▷farsi *grande* to grow tall

▷si fa *notte* it's getting dark

▷farsi *vecchio* to grow old.

6 SM: con fare *distratto* absent-mindedly

▷ha un fare *simpatico* he has a pleasant manner

▷sul far del giorno/della notte at daybreak/nightfall.

faretra [fa'rɛtra] SF (*per frecce*) quiver.

faretto [fa'retto] SM spot lamp.

farfalla [far'falla] SF **a** (*Zool*) butterfly **b** (*cravatta*) bow tie **c** (*Nuoto*) butterfly (stroke); nuotare a farfalla to do the butterfly (stroke) **d** (*pasta*) bow **e** (*Aut*): valvola a farfalla butterfly valve **f** (*Naut*): navigare a farfalla to goosewing.

farfallino [farfal'lino] SM (*cravattino*) bow tie.

farfallone [farfal'lone] SM (*fig*) philanderer.

farfara ['farfara] SF (*Bot*) coltsfoot.

farfugliare [farfuʎ'ʎare] VT, VI (*aus* avere) to mumble, mutter.

farina [fa'rina] SF flour; questa non è farina del tuo sacco (*fig*) this isn't your own idea (*o* work) ►farina di castagne chestnut flour ►farina di grano saraceno buckwheat ►farina di granoturco *o* di mais *o* gialla maize (*Brit*) *o* corn (*Am*) flour ►farina integrale wholemeal (*Brit*) *o* whole-wheat (*Am*) flour ►farina di riso ground rice ►farina di soia soya flour.

farinaceo, a [fari'natʃeo] **1** AGG farinaceous. **2**: farinacei SMPL starches, starchy foods.

faringe [fa'rindʒe] SF (*Anat*) pharynx.

faringeo, a [farin'dʒɛo] AGG (*Anat*) pharyngeal.

faringite [farin'dʒite] SF (*Med*) pharyngitis.

farinoso, a [fari'noso] AGG (*patate*) floury; (*mela*) woolly; (*neve*) powdery.

farisaico, a, ci, che [fari'zaiko] AGG (*Storia*) Pharisaic; (*fig*) pharisaic.

fariseo [fari'zɛo] SM (*Storia*) Pharisee; (*fig*) pharisee.

farmaceutica [farma'tʃɛutika] SF pharmaceutics *sg*.

farmaceutico, a, ci, che [farma'tʃɛutiko] AGG pharmaceutical.

farmacia, cie [farma'tʃia] SF **a** (*negozio*) chemist's (shop) *o* chemist (*Brit*), pharmacy **b** (*professione*) pharmacy.

farmacista, i, e [farma'tʃista] SM/F (dispensing) chemist (*Brit*), pharmacist.

farmaco, ci ['farmako] SM drug, medicine.

farmacologia [farmakolo'dʒia] SF pharmacology.

farmacologicamente [farmakolodʒika'mente] AVV pharmacologically.

farmacologico, a, ci, che [farmako'lɔdʒiko] AGG pharmacological.

farmacopea [farmako'pɛa] SF (*catalogo*) pharmacopoeia.

farneticare [farneti'kare] VI (*aus* avere) (*anche fig*) to be delirious; stai farneticando! you're talking nonsense!

farnia ['farnja] SF (*Bot*) English oak.

faro ['faro] SM **a** (*Naut*) lighthouse; (*Aer*) beacon; faro d'atterraggio landing light **b** (*Aut*) headlight, headlamp (*Brit*) ►fari abbaglianti headlights on full beam ►fari anabbaglianti dipped headlights ►fari antinebbia fog lights *o* lamps.

Faroar [fa'roar] SFPL (*anche:* le isole Faroar) the Faroes, the Faroe Islands.

farragine [far'radʒine] SF (*di libri*) jumble; (*di opinioni, citazioni*) mishmash.

farraginoso, a [farradʒi'noso] AGG (*stile*) muddled, confused.

farsa ['farsa] SF (*anche fig*) farce.

farsesco, a, schi, sche [far'sesko] AGG farcical.

fasc. ABBR = fascicolo.

fascetta [faʃ'ʃetta] SF (*gen*) narrow band, narrow strip; (*di medaglia*) ribbon; (*Med*) bandage; (*di giornale*) wrapper.

fascia, sce ['faʃʃa] SF a (di tessuto, carta, anche fig) strip, band; (Med) bandage; (di sindaco, ufficiale) sash; **fascia del cappello** hatband; **essere in fasce** (anche fig) to be in one's infancy; **ti conosco da quando eri ancora in fasce** I've known you since you were a baby; **fascia di contribuenti** tax group o band ►**fascia oraria** (Radio, TV) slot; (Telec) time band

b (Geog) strip, belt; **fascia equatoriale** equatorial belt c (Tecn)► **fascia elastica** piston ring.

fasciame [faʃ'ʃame] SM (Naut: di legno) planking; (: di metallo) plating.

fasciante [faʃ'ʃante] AGG (aderente) tight(-fitting).

fasciare [faʃ'ʃare] VT (gen) to bind; (Med) to bandage; **fasciare un bambino** to put on a baby's nappy (Brit) o diaper (Am); **fasciati il piede** bandage your foot; **quel vestito le fasciava i fianchi** the dress clung to her hips.

fasciato, a [faʃ'ʃato] AGG bandaged.

fasciatura [faʃʃa'tura] SF (azione) bandaging; (fascia) bandage.

fascicolo [faʃ'ʃikolo] SM (opuscolo) booklet, pamphlet; (Amm) file, dossier; (di pubblicazione) instalment; (di rivista) issue, number.

fascina [faʃ'ʃina] SF faggot.

fascino ['faʃʃino] SM charm, fascination; **avere fascino** (persona) to be fascinating; **subire il fascino di qn** to succumb to sb's charm.

fascio, sci ['faʃʃo] SM a (di legna) bundle; (di fieno, frecce) sheaf; (di fiori) bunch; (di luce) beam b (Storia) fasces pl c (Pol): **il Fascio** the Fascist Party.

fascismo [faʃ'ʃizmo] SM fascism.

fascista, i, e [faʃ'ʃista] AGG, SM/F fascist.

fase ['faze] SF a (gen, Chim, Astron) phase; **in fase avanzata** at an advanced stage; **essere in fase di miglioramento** to be getting better, be improving; **in fase preliminare** in the preliminary stages; **in fase di espansione** in a period of expansion

b (Tecn) stroke; **essere fuori fase** (motore) to be rough (Brit), run roughly; (fig) to feel rough (Brit) o rotten; **mettere il motore in fase** to tune the engine.

fastello [fas'tɛllo] SM bundle.

fastidio, di [fas'tidjo] SM (disturbo) trouble, bother; **che fastidio!** what a nuisance!; **dare fastidio a qn** to bother o annoy sb; **sento un po' di fastidio** it hurts a bit; **il rumore mi dava fastidio** the noise was annoying me; **mi dà fastidio il suo modo di fare** his whole attitude gets on my nerves; **le dà fastidio se fumo?** do you mind if I smoke?; **ha avuto dei fastidi con la polizia** he has had some trouble o bother with the police.

fastidiosamente [fastidjosa'mente] AVV (vedi agg) annoyingly; irritably.

fastidioso, a [fasti'djoso] AGG a (gen) annoying; (persona) tiresome, annoying; **un dolore fastidioso** a nagging pain b (irritabile) irritable.

fasto ['fasto] SM pomp, splendor (Brit), splendor (Am); **i fasti dell'antica Roma** the splendour(s) of ancient Rome.

fastosità [fastosi'ta] SF INV pomp, splendour.

fastoso, a [fas'toso] AGG sumptuous, lavish.

fasullo, a [fa'zullo] AGG a (gen) fake; (dichiarazione, persona) false; (pretesto) bogus.

fata ['fata] SF fairy ►**fata morgana** (miraggio) Fata Morgana.

fatale [fa'tale] AGG a (inevitabile) inevitable; **era fatale che succedesse** it was bound to happen b (mortale: inci-

dente, malattia) fatal; (: colpo) fatal, mortal; **errore fatale** fatal error; **essere fatale a qn** to be o prove fatal to sb c (irresistibile: sguardo) irresistible; **donna fatale** femme fatale.

fatalismo [fata'lizmo] SM fatalism.

fatalista, i, e [fata'lista] SM/F fatalist.

fatalisticamente [fatalistika'mente] AVV fatalistically.

fatalistico, a, ci, che [fata'listiko] AGG fatalistic.

fatalità [fatali'ta] SF INV (fato) fate, destiny; (inevitabilità) inevitability; (disgrazia) misfortune.

fatalmente [fatal'mente] AVV a (inevitabilmente) inevitably; **doveva fatalmente accadere** it was bound to happen b (con gravi conseguenze) with fatal consequences.

fatato, a [fa'tato] AGG (spada, chiave) magic; (castello) enchanted.

fatica, che [fa'tika] SF a (sforzo fisico) hard work, toil; **animale da fatica** beast of burden; **divisa di fatica** (Mil) fatigues pl; **uomo di fatica** odd-job man; **fare fatica a fare qc** to have a job doing sth, find it difficult to do sth; **faccio fatica a crederlo** I find that hard to believe; **il paziente deve evitare ogni fatica** the patient must avoid any kind of physical exertion; **accusare o sentire fatica** to feel tired; **non si è preso nemmeno la fatica di dirmelo** he didn't even take the trouble to tell me; **risparmiarsi la fatica di fare qc** to save o.s. the bother o effort of doing sth; **le fatiche di Ercole** the labours of Hercules

b (difficoltà): **a fatica** with difficulty; **respirare a fatica** to have difficulty (in) breathing; **riusciva a fatica a tenere la testa dritta** he could hardly keep his head up; **l'ho convinto a fatica** I had a hard job convincing him c (di metalli) fatigue.

faticaccia, ce [fati'kattʃa] SF (fam): **fu una faticaccia** it was a hell of a job.

faticare [fati'kare] VI (aus **avere**) to work hard, toil; **faticare per fare qc** to struggle to do sth; **faticare a fare qc** to have difficulty in doing sth, have difficulty doing sth.

faticata [fati'kata] SF hard work.

fatichi ecc [fa'tiki] VB vedi **faticare**.

faticosamente [fatikosa'mente] AVV with effort, laboriously.

faticoso, a [fati'koso] AGG (viaggio, camminata) tiring, exhausting; (lavoro) laborious.

fatidicamente [fatidika'mente] AVV as fate would have it.

fatidico, a, ci, che [fa'tidiko] AGG fateful.

fato ['fato] SM fate, destiny.

fatt. ABBR (= fattura) inv.

fatta ['fatta] SF (genere, tipo) kind.

fattaccio, ci [fat'tattʃo] SM foul deed.

fatterello [fatte'rɛllo] SM insignificant event.

fattezze [fat'tettse] SFPL (del viso) features.

fattibile [fat'tibile] AGG feasible, possible.

fattispecie [fattis'pɛtʃe] SF: **nella o in fattispecie** in this case o instance.

fatto¹, a ['fatto] 1 PP di **fare**.

2 AGG a (prodotto) made; **fatto a macchina/a mano** machine/hand made; **fatto in casa** home-made; **abiti fatti** ready-made o off-the-peg clothes

b (fraseologia): **sono fatto così** that's how I am, I'm like that; **è ben fatta** she has a nice figure; **essere fatto per qc** to be made o meant for sth; **è fatto per l'archeologia** he's got what it takes to be an archeologist; **è un uomo fatto** he's a grown man; **a giorno fatto** in broad

daylight; **è fatta!** that's it!, I've (*o* you've *ecc*) done it!; **è completamente fatto** (*fam*: *drogato, ubriaco*) he's (completely) stoned.

fatto² ['fatto] SM **a** (*accaduto*) fact; **i fatti parlano chiaro** the facts speak for themselves; **questo è un altro fatto** that's another matter; **di fatto** in fact; **il fatto sta** *o* **è che** the fact remains *o* is that; **in fatto di macchine è un genio** when it comes to cars he's a genius

b (*azione*) deed, act; **cogliere qn sul fatto** to catch sb red-handed *o* in the act; **porre qn di fronte al fatto compiuto** to present sb with a fait accompli; **c'è stato un nuovo fatto di sangue** there has been further bloodshed; **fatto d'arme** (*frm*) feat of arms; **è uno che sa il fatto suo** he knows what he's about; **gli ho detto il fatto suo** I told him what I thought of him; **fare i fatti propri** to mind one's own business; **immischiarsi nei fatti altrui** to stick one's nose into other people's business **c** (*avvenimento*) event, occurrence; (*di romanzo, film*) action, story; **fatto di cronaca** news item; **fatto nuovo** new development.

fattore [fat'tore] SM **a** (*elemento, Mat*) factor **b** (*Agr*) farm manager.

fattoria [fatto'ria] SF (*gen*) farm; (*casa*) farmhouse.

fattorino [fatto'rino] SM (*gen*) errand boy; (*di ufficio*) office junior, office boy; (*d'albergo*) porter.

fattrice [fat'tritʃe] SF (*cavalla*) brood mare; (*mucca*) brood cow.

fattucchiera [fattuk'kjɛra] SF witch.

fattura [fat'tura] SF **a** (*Comm*) invoice **b** (*confezione*: *di abito*) tailoring **c** (*stregoneria*) spell; **fare una fattura a qn** to cast a spell on sb.

fatturare [fattu'rare] VT **a** (*Comm*) to invoice **b** (*adulterare*) to adulterate.

fatturato [fattu'rato] SM (*Comm*) turnover.

fatturatrice [fattura'tritʃe] SF invoicing machine.

fatturazione [fatturat'tsjone] SF invoicing, billing.

fatturista, i, e [fattu'rista] SM/F invoice clerk.

fatuamente [fatua'mente] AVV fatuously.

fatuità [fatui'ta] SF INV fatuousness.

fatuo, a ['fatuo] AGG fatuous, vain; **fuoco fatuo** (*anche fig*) will-o'-the-wisp.

fauci ['fautʃi] SFPL (*di leone*) jaws; (*di vulcano*) mouth *sg*; **cadere nelle fauci di qn** (*fig*) to fall prey to sb.

fauna ['fauna] SF (*Zool*) fauna.

fauno ['fauno] SM (*Mitol*) faun.

fausto, a ['fausto] AGG (*frm*) happy, propitious; **un fausto evento** a happy event; **un fausto presagio** a good omen.

fautore, trice [fau'tore] SM/F advocate, supporter.

fava ['fava] SF broad bean.

favella [fa'vɛlla] SF speech; **perdere il dono della favella** to be struck dumb.

favilla [fa'villa] SF spark; (*fig*: *di speranza*) glimmer; **fare faville** (*fig*: *cantante*) to give a sparkling performance.

favo ['favo] SM (*di api*) honeycomb.

favola ['favola] SF (*fiaba*) fairy tale; (*d'intento morale*) fable; (*fig*: *fandonia*) tall tale, yarn; **essere la favola del paese** (*oggetto di chiacchiere*) to be the talk of the town; (*zimbello*) to be a laughing stock in the town; **la casa è una favola** the house is a dream.

favoleggiare [favoled'dʒare] VI (*aus* avere) to tell stories.

favolistica [favo'listika] SF folk tales *pl*.

favolosamente [favolosa'mente] AVV fabulously; **è stato favolosamente bravo** he was exceptionally good.

favoloso, a [favo'loso] AGG (*gen*) fabulous; (*incredibile*) incredible; **prezzi favolosi** incredible prices.

favore [fa'vore] SM favour (*Brit*), favor (*Am*); **chiedere/fare un favore a qn** to ask/do sb a favour; **per favore** please; **godere del favore del pubblico** to enjoy public favour; **prezzo/trattamento di favore** preferential price/treatment; **condizioni di favore** (*Comm*) favourable terms; **biglietto di favore** complimentary ticket; **a favore di** (*votare*) in favour of; (*testimoniare, raccogliere aiuti*) on behalf of; **col favore delle tenebre** under cover of darkness.

favoreggiamento [favoreddʒa'mento] SM (*Dir*) aiding and abetting ▶**favoreggiamento bellico** collaboration (with the enemy).

favoreggiare [favored'dʒare] VT **a** to favour (*Brit*), favor (*Am*) **b** (*Dir*) to aid and abet.

favorevole [favo'revole] AGG: **favorevole (a)** (*situazione, vento*) favourable (*Brit*) *o* favorable (*Am*) (to); (*persona*) in favour (of), favourable (to); **hanno avuto 70 voti favorevoli** they got 70 votes in favour; **aspettare il momento favorevole** to wait for the right moment.

favorevolmente [favorevol'mente] AVV favourably (*Brit*), favorably (*Am*); **la proposta è stata accolta favorevolmente** the proposal was greeted favourably.

favorire [favo'rire] VT **a** (*gen*) to favour (*Brit*), favor (*Am*); (*commercio, industria, arti*) to promote, encourage; (*partito, opinione*) to support

b (*in espressioni di cortesia*): **favorisca da questa parte** please come this way; **vuole favorire?** won't you help yourself?; **mi favorisca i documenti** please may I see your papers?; **favorisca alla cassa** please pay at the cash-desk.

favoritismo [favori'tizmo] SM favouritism (*Brit*), favoritism (*Am*).

favorito, a [favo'rito] AGG, SM/F favourite (*Brit*), favorite (*Am*).

fax [faks] SM INV (*anche*: **telefax**) fax; **mandare qc via fax** to fax sth.

faxare [fak'sare] VT to fax.

fazione [fat'tsjone] SF faction.

faziosamente [fattsjosa'mente] AVV in a partisan manner.

faziosità [fattsjosi'ta] SF INV bias.

fazioso, a [fat'tsjoso] AGG partisan.

fazzoletto [fattso'letto] SM (*da naso*) handkerchief; (: *di carta*) (paper) tissue (*Brit*), Kleenex® (*Am*); (*da collo*) neckerchief; **un fazzoletto di terra** a patch of land.

F.B.I. [efbi'ai] SIGLA F FBI (= *Federal Bureau of Investigation*).

FC ABBR vedi **fuoricorso**.

f.co ABBR = **franco¹ b.**

FE SIGLA = *Ferrara*.

febbraio [feb'brajo] SM February *per fraseologia vedi* **luglio**.

febbre ['fɛbbre] SF **a** fever; **avere la febbre** to have a (high) temperature; **misurarsi la febbre** to take one's temperature ▶**febbre da fieno** hay fever ▶**febbre gialla** yellow fever ▶**febbre reumatica** rheumatic fever **b** (*herpes*) cold sore **c** (*fig*): **la febbre dell'oro** gold fever.

febbricitante [febbritʃi'tante] AGG feverish.

febbrile [feb'brile] AGG (*anche fig*) feverish.

febbrilmente [febbril'mente] AVV feverishly.

febbrone [feb'brone] SM high temperature.

Febo ['fɛbo] SM Phoebus.

fecale [fe'kale] AGG faecal (*Brit*), fecal (*Am*).

feccia, ce ['fɛttʃa] SF (*anche fig*) dregs *pl.*

feci ['fɛtʃi] SFPL faeces (*Brit*), feces (*Am*), excrement *sg.*

feci *ecc* ['fetʃi] VB vedi **fare**.

fecola ['fɛkola] SF starch ▶ **fecola di patate** ≈ cornflour.

fecondamente [fekonda'mente] AVV fruitfully.

fecondare [fekon'dare] VT to fertilize.

fecondativo, a [fekonda'tivo] AGG: **un farmaco fecondativo** a fertility drug.

fecondazione [fekondat'tsjone] SF fertilization ▶ **fecondazione artificiale** artificial insemination.

fecondità [fekondi'ta] SF INV (*Bio, di terreno, fig*: *ingegno*) fertility, productiveness; (*di scrittore*) prolificness.

fecondo, a [fe'kondo] AGG (*terreno, donna, fig*: *ingegno*) fertile; (*albero, fig*: *pensiero, lavoro*) fruitful; (: *scrittore*) prolific.

Fedcom [fed'kɔm] SIGLA M (= *Fondo Europeo di Cooperazione Monetaria*) EMCF.

fede ['fede] SF **a** (*credenza*) faith, belief; (*Rel*) faith **b** (*fiducia*) faith, trust; (*fedeltà*) loyalty; **aver fede in** to have faith in; **degno di fede** trustworthy, reliable; **tener fede a** (*ideale*) to remain loyal to; (*giuramento, promessa*) to keep; **essere in buona/cattiva fede** to act in good/bad faith; **in fede mia!** on my word! **c** (*anello nuziale*) wedding ring **d** (*attestato*) certificate; **in fede di** in proof of *o* as evidence of; **far fede di** to be proof *o* evidence of; **"in fede"** (*Dir*) "in witness whereof".

fedele [fe'dele] **1** AGG **a** (*leale*): **fedele (a)** faithful (to); **essere fedele alla parola data** to keep one's word; **suddito fedele** loyal subject **b** (*veritiero*) true, accurate. **2** SM/F (*Rel*) believer; (*seguace*) follower; **i fedeli** (*Rel*) the faithful *pl.*

fedelmente [fedel'mente] AVV (*servire, amare*) faithfully.

fedeltà [fedel'ta] SF INV **a** (*devozione*) loyalty, faithfulness; (*coniugale*) fidelity; **fedeltà verso** *o* **a qn** loyalty to sb **b** (*esattezza: di copia, traduzione*) accuracy **c** (*Radio ecc*): **alta fedeltà** high fidelity.

federa ['fɛdera] SF pillowslip, pillowcase.

federale [fede'rale] AGG federal.

federalismo [federa'lizmo] SM federalism.

federalista, i, e [federa'lista] AGG, SM/F federalist.

federarsi [fede'rarsi] VIP to form a federation.

federativo, a [federa'tivo] AGG federative.

federazione [federat'tsjone] SF federation.

Federcaccia [feder'kattʃa] ABBR F (= *Federazione Italiana della Caccia*) *Italian hunting federation.*

Federcalcio [feder'kaltʃo] ABBR M (= *Federazione Italiana Gioco Calcio*) *Italian football association.*

Federconsorzi [federkon'sɔrtsi] ABBR F (= *Federazione Italiana dei Consorzi Agrari*) *Italian federation of farmers' cooperatives.*

fedifrago, a, ghi, ghe [fe'difrago] AGG faithless, perfidious.

fedina [fe'dina] SF (*Dir*: *anche*: **fedina penale**) record; **avere la fedina (penale) pulita** to have a clean record; **avere la fedina (penale) sporca** to have a police record.

Fedra ['fɛdra] SF Phaedra.

fegatino [fega'tino] SM (*di pollame*) liver; **fegatino di pollo** chicken liver.

fegato ['fegato] SM **a** (*Anat, Culin*) liver; **fegato di vitello** calf's liver; **mangiarsi** *o* **rodersi il fegato** to be consumed with rage; **fegato ingrossato** (*Med*) enlarged liver **b** (*fig: coraggio*) guts *pl*, nerve.

felce ['feltʃe] SF fern.

feldmaresciallo [feldmareʃ'ʃallo] SM (*Mil*) field marshal.

felice [fe'litʃe] AGG **a** (*contento*) happy; **sono felice di fare la sua conoscenza** pleased to meet you; **felice come una pasqua** as happy as a sandboy **b** (*fortunato*) lucky; (: *scelta*) fortunate, happy; (: *vento*) favourable; **avere la mano felice** to have nimble fingers; **non ho scelto il momento più felice per venire** I don't seem to have chosen the best moment to come.

felicemente [felitʃe'mente] AVV (*in modo felice*) happily; (*bene*) successfully, happily; **l'esperimento si è concluso felicemente** the experiment was successful.

felicità [felitʃi'ta] SF INV happiness.

felicitarsi [felitʃi'tarsi] VIP: **felicitarsi con qn (per qc)** (*congratularsi*) to congratulate sb (on sth).

felicitazioni [felitʃitat'tsjoni] SFPL congratulations.

felino, a [fe'lino] **1** AGG (*Zool*) feline; (*fig*) feline, catlike. **2** SM feline.

felpa ['felpa] SF (*maglia*) sweatshirt.

felpato, a [fel'pato] **1** AGG (*tessuto*) brushed; (*passo*) stealthy; **con passo felpato** stealthily. **2** SM brushed cotton (*o* nylon *ecc*).

feltro ['feltro] SM felt; **cappello di feltro** felt hat.

feluca, che [fe'luka] SF **a** (*Naut*) felucca **b** (*cappello*) cocked hat.

femmina ['femmina] SF (*Zool, Tecn*) female; **ho due figli, un maschio e una femmina** I've got two children, a boy and a girl; **una femmina di panda** OR **un panda femmina** a female panda.

femmineo, a [fem'mineo] AGG (*effeminato*) effeminate.

femminile [femmi'nile] AGG (*gen, Gramm*) feminine; (*sesso*) female; **moda femminile** women's fashion.

femminilità [femminili'ta] SF INV femininity; **un tocco di femminilità** a feminine touch.

femminismo [femmi'nizmo] SM feminism.

femminista, i, e [femmi'nista] SM/F, AGG feminist.

femminuccia, ce [femmi'nuttʃa] SF (*bambina*) baby girl; (*pegg*) sissy.

femore ['femore] SM (*Anat*) thighbone, femur.

fendente [fen'dɛnte] SM (*con sciabola*) cut; (*Calcio*) powerful shot; **con un fendente mandò il pallone in rete** he slammed the ball into the back of the net.

fendere ['fɛndere] VT IRREG (*fig: aria, flutti, onde*) to cut through, slice (through); **i fari fendevano la nebbia** the headlights pierced the fog; **fendere la folla** to push through the crowd.

fendinebbia [fendi'nebbja] SM INV (*Aut*) fog lamp.

fenditura [fendi'tura] SF (*gen*) crack; (*di roccia*) cleft, crack.

fenice [fe'nitʃe] SF (*anche:* **araba fenice**) phoenix.

fenicottero [feni'kɔttero] SM flamingo.

fenolftaleina [fenolftale'ina] SF (*Chim*) phenolphthalein.

fenolo [fe'nɔlo] SM (*Chim*) phenol.

fenomenale [fenome'nale] AGG phenomenal.

fenomenico, a, ci, che [feno'mɛniko] AGG phenomenal; **mondo fenomenico** external world.

fenomeno [fe'nɔmeno] SM (*gen*) phenomenon; (*persona: eccezionale*) character; (: *anormale*) freak.

fenotipo [feno'tipo] SM (*Bio*) phenotype.

feretro ['fɛretro] SM coffin; **il feretro si avviava verso il cimitero** the funeral procession wound its way to the cemetery.

feriale [fe'rjale] AGG: **giorno feriale** working day, weekday.

ferie ['fɛrje] SFPL holidays (*Brit*), vacation *sg* (*Am*); **ferie**

retribuite paid holiday, holiday with pay; **andare in ferie** to go on holiday *o* vacation; **ho fatto le ferie al mare** I spent my holidays at the seaside; **ho 2 settimane di ferie** I have 2 weeks' holidays.

ferimento [feri'mento] SM wounding; **nella sparatoria si è avuto il ferimento di 3 persone** 3 people were hurt *o* wounded in the shooting.

ferire [fe'rire] ☐ VT **a** (*gen*) to injure; (*Mil*) to wound; **fu ferito a morte** he was fatally wounded; **nell'incidente sono state ferite 4 persone** 4 people were injured in the accident
b (*fig*) to hurt, wound; **ferire qn nell'orgoglio** to hurt *o* wound *o* injure sb's pride; **le sue parole la ferirono** she was wounded *o* hurt by what he said.
☐ **ferirsi** VR to hurt o.s., injure o.s.; **ferirsi con un coltello** to cut o.s. with a knife; **mi sono ferito ad una mano** I've injured my hand.

ferita [fe'rita] SF (*vedi vb*) injury; wound; **riportò gravi ferite** he was seriously wounded.

ferito, a [fe'rito] SM/F wounded *o* injured man/woman; **un ferito grave** a seriously injured person.

feritoia [feri'toja] SF slit.

ferma ['ferma] SF **a** (*Mil*) (period of) service **b** (*Caccia*): **cane da ferma** pointer.

fermacapelli [fermaka'pelli] SM INV hair slide.

fermacarte [ferma'karte] SM INV paperweight.

fermacravatta [fermakra'vatta] SM INV tiepin (*Brit*), tie tack (*Am*).

fermaglio, gli [fer'maʎʎo] SM (*gen*) clasp; (*per documenti*) clip.

fermamente [ferma'mente] AVV firmly.

fermare [fer'mare] ☐ VT **a** (*gen*) to stop, halt; **lo fermò con un gesto della mano** (*far cenno*) he gestured to him to stop; (*bloccare*) he put his hand out to stop him
b (*fissare: bottone*) to make secure; (*: porta*) to stop
c (*prenotare: stanza, albergo*) to book
d (*Polizia*) to detain, hold.
☐ VI (*aus* **avere**) to stop; **il treno ferma a...** the train calls at ....
☐ **fermarsi** VIP (*gen*) to stop, halt; **fermarsi a guardare/fare** to stop to look/do; **non posso fermarmi di più** I can't stop *o* stay any longer; **far segno di fermarsi a qn** to signal to sb to stop; (*ad automobilista*) to wave sb down; **la sua attenzione si fermò sul dipinto** his attention focused on the painting.

fermata [fer'mata] SF stop; **scendo tra 2 fermate** I get off 2 stops from here; **la corriera fa una fermata a Montelupo** the coach stops *o* makes a stop at Montelupo ►**fermata dell'autobus** bus stop ►**fermata facoltativa** *o* **a richiesta** request stop.

fermentare [fermen'tare] ☐ VI (*aus* **avere**) to ferment.
☐ VT to ferment; (*fig*) to be in ferment.

fermentazione [fermentat'tsjone] SF fermentation.

fermento [fer'mento] SM **a** (*anche fig*) ferment; **in fermento** in a ferment **b** (*Culin: lievito*) yeast.

fermezza [fer'mettsa] SF firmness, steadfastness; **fermezza di mente/d'animo** strength of mind/of character; **fermezza di propositi** steadiness of purpose; **rispondere con fermezza** to answer firmly, give a firm answer.

fermo, a ['fermo] ☐ AGG **a** (*immobile: persona*) still, motionless; (*: veicolo, traffico*) at a standstill, stationary; (*non in funzione*) not working; **era fermo in piedi** he was standing still; **stai fermo!** keep still!; **stai fermo con le**

mani! keep your hands still!; (*non toccarmi*) keep your hands to yourself!; **fermo!** don't move!, stay where you are!; **c'era una macchina ferma al bordo della strada** there was a car stopped at the side of the road; **il treno era fermo in stazione** the train was standing in the station; **gli affari sono fermi** business is at a standstill; **l'orologio è fermo** the clock has stopped
b (*costante, risoluto*) firm; (*non tremante: voce, mano*) steady; **restare fermo sulle proprie posizioni** to stick to one's position; **resta fermo che...** it is settled that ...; **fermo restando che...** it being understood that ....
☐ SM **a** (*Dir*): **fermo di polizia** police custody (*before formal accusation of a crime*)
b (*di porta: gancio*) catch.

fermo posta ['fermo 'pɔsta] AVV, SM, AGG poste restante (*Brit*), general delivery (*Am*).

feroce [fe'rotʃe] AGG (*animale*) ferocious, fierce; (*persona*) fierce, cruel; (*critica*) savage; (*fame, dolore*) raging; **le bestie feroci** wild animals.

ferocemente [ferotʃe'mente] AVV (*aggredire*) ferociously, fiercely; (*criticare*) savagely.

ferocia [fe'rɔtʃa] SF ferocity.

ferodo® [fe'rɔdo] SM brake lining.

Ferr. ABBR = **ferrovia**.

ferraglia [fer'raʎʎa] SF scrap iron; **rumore di ferraglia** clanking noise.

ferragosto [ferra'gosto] SM *national holiday (August 15th: feast of the Assumption)*; (*periodo*) *period around the 15th when most people take a holiday and when much of industry and commerce is at a standstill*.

ferraio, aia, ai, aie [fer'rajo] AGG: **fabbro ferraio** blacksmith.

ferramenta [ferra'menta] ☐ SFPL ironmongery *sg* (*Brit*), hardware *sg*.
☐ SF (*anche: negozio di ferramenta*) ironmonger's (*Brit*), hardware shop *o* store (*Am*).

ferrare [fer'rare] VT (*cavallo*) to shoe; (*botte*) to hoop.

ferrato, a [fer'rato] AGG **a** (*Ferr*): **strada ferrata** railway line (*Brit*), railroad line (*Am*) **b** (*fig*): **essere ferrato in** (*materia*) to be well up in.

ferratura [ferra'tura] SF (*di cavallo*) shoeing.

ferravecchio, chi [ferra'vɛkkjo] SM = **ferrovecchio**.

ferreo, a ['fɛrreo] AGG (*anche fig*) iron *attr*; **volontà ferrea** iron will; **salute ferrea** iron constitution.

ferriera [fer'rjɛra] SF ironworks *sg o pl*.

ferrigno, a [fer'riɲɲo] AGG (*che contiene ferro*) ferrous; **grigio ferrigno** iron-grey.

ferro ['fɛrro] SM **a** (*metallo*) iron; **ferro battuto** wrought iron; **l'età del ferro** the Iron Age; **minerali di ferro** iron ore; **ha una memoria di ferro** he has an excellent memory; **ha una salute di ferro** he has an iron constitution; **avere uno stomaco di ferro** to have a cast-iron stomach; **avere un alibi di ferro** to have a cast-iron alibi; **tocca ferro!** touch wood!; **battere il ferro finché è caldo** to strike while the iron is hot
b (*strumento: gen*) tool; **i ferri del mestiere** the tools of the trade; **a ferro di cavallo** in the shape of a horseshoe; **i ferri del chirurgo** surgical instruments; **essere sotto i ferri** (*di chirurgo*) to be under the knife; **carne ai ferri** grilled meat; **cucinare** *o* **fare qc ai ferri** to grill sth ►**ferri da calza** knitting needles ►**ferro di cavallo** horseshoe ►**ferro da stiro** iron
c (*arma*) sword; **ferri** SMPL (*ceppi*) irons, chains; **incrociare i ferri** to cross swords; **mettere a ferro e fuoco** to

put to the sword; **essere ai ferri corti** (*fig*) to be at daggers drawn.

ferroso, a [fer'roso] AGG ferrous.

ferrotranviario, ria, ri, rie [ferrotran'vjarjo] AGG public transport *attr*.

ferrotranviere [ferrotran'vjɛre] SM public transport employee.

Ferrotranvieri [ferrotran'vjɛri] ABBR F (= *Federazione Nazionale Lavoratori Autoferrotranvieri e Internavigatori*) *transport workers' union.*

ferrovecchio, chi [ferro'vɛkkjo] SM (*commerciante: di oggetti di scarso valore*) junk dealer; (: *di ferro vecchio*) scrap merchant.

ferrovia [ferro'via] SF railway (*Brit*), railroad (*Am*).

ferroviario, ria, rie, ri [ferro'vjarjo] AGG railway *attr* (*Brit*), railroad *attr* (*Am*).

ferroviere [ferro'vjɛre] SM railwayman (*Brit*), railroad man (*Am*).

ferry-boat ['fɛri 'bout] SM INV ferry.

fertile ['fɛrtile] AGG (*anche fig*) fertile.

fertilità [fertili'ta] SF INV fertility.

fertilizzante [fertilid'dzante] ① AGG fertilizing. ② SM fertilizer.

fertilizzare [fertilid'dzare] VT to fertilize.

fertilizzazione [fertiliddzat'tsjone] SF fertilization.

fervente [fer'vɛnte] AGG fervent, ardent.

ferventemente [fervente'mente] AVV fervently, ardently.

fervere ['fɛrvere] VI DIF: **fervono i preparativi per l'arrivo del presidente** preparations for the president's arrival are in full swing.

fervidamente [fervida'mente] AVV fervently, fervidly.

fervido, a ['fɛrvido] AGG fervent, fervid, ardent; **fervide preghiere** impassioned pleas; **i miei più fervidi auguri** my very best wishes.

fervore [fer'vore] SM fervour (*Brit*), fervor (*Am*), ardour (*Brit*), ardor (*Am*); **nel fervore di** (*discussione, lotta*) in the heat of.

fesa ['feza] SF (*Culin*) rump of veal.

fesseria [fesse'ria] SF stupidity; **quel film è una fesseria** that film is rubbish; **dire fesserie** to talk nonsense; **fare una fesseria** to do something stupid.

fesso, a ['fesso] ① PP di **fendere**. ② SM/F idiot, fool; **fare il fesso** to play the fool; **dare del fesso a qn** to call sb a fool. ③ AGG **a** (*fam*) stupid, daft **b** (*spaccato*) cracked; **con voce fessa** in a cracked voice.

fessura [fes'sura] SF (*gen*) crack, split; (*per gettone, moneta*) slot; (*Alpinismo*) crack.

festa ['fɛsta] ① SF **a** (*religiosa*) feast (day); (*civile*) holiday; **giorno di festa** holiday; **il Natale è la festa dei bambini** Christmas is a time for children
b (*vacanza*) holidays *pl*, vacation (*Am*); **cosa fai per le feste?** what are you doing over the holidays?; **la settimana scorsa ho avuto 3 giorni di festa** last week I was on holiday for 3 days, I had 3 days off (work) last week
c (*ricorrenza: compleanno*) birthday; (: *onomastico*) name day; **quand'è la tua festa?** when is your birthday?; **la festa di San Giovanni** St John's Day, the feast of St John
d (*sagra*) fair; **la festa del paese** the town festival; **festa della birra** beer festival
e (*ricevimento*) party, celebration; **dare** *o* **fare una festa** to give *o* have a party

f (*fraseologia*): **un'aria di festa** a festive air; **fare festa** (*non lavorare*) to have a holiday; (*far baldoria*) to live it up; **fare le feste a qn** to give sb a warm welcome; **tutta la città era in festa** the whole town was celebrating; **le campane suonavano a festa** the bells were pealing; **essere vestito a festa** to be dressed up to the nines.
② ▶**festa comandata** (*Rel*) holiday *o* holy day of obligation ▶**la festa della donna** International Women's Day ▶**la festa della mamma/del papà** Mother's/Father's Day ▶**festa nazionale** national *o* public holiday ▶**la festa della repubblica** *national holiday (June 2) which celebrates the founding of the republic after the fall of the monarchy in 1946: it is marked by military parades and political speeches.*

festaiolo, a [festa'jɔlo] AGG (*atmosfera*) festive; **è un tipo festaiolo** he's a great one for parties.

festeggiamenti [festeddʒa'menti] SMPL celebrations.

festeggiare [fested'dʒare] VT (*anniversario*) to celebrate; (*persona*) to have a celebration for, fête.

festeggiato, a [fested'dʒato] SM/F guest of honour; **sei tu il festeggiato!** it's your party!

festino [fes'tino] SM (*festa*) party; (*con balli*) ball.

festival ['fɛstival] SM INV festival.

festività [festivi'ta] SF INV festivity; **festività civile** public holiday.

festivo, a [fes'tivo] AGG (*atmosfera*) festive; **giorno festivo** holiday.

festone [fes'tone] SM festoon.

festosamente [festosa'mente] AVV joyfully; **accogliere festosamente qn** to give sb a warm welcome, greet sb warmly.

festoso, a [fes'toso] AGG merry, joyful; **un'accoglienza festosa** a warm welcome.

fetale [fe'tale] AGG foetal (*Brit*), fetal (*Am*).

fetente [fe'tɛnte] ① AGG (*puzzolente*) fetid; (*comportamento*) disgusting. ② SM/F (*fam*) stinker, rotter (*Brit*).

feticcio, ci [fe'tittʃo] SM fetish.

feticismo [feti'tʃizmo] SM fetishism.

feticista, i, e [feti'tʃista] AGG, SM/F fetishist.

fetido, a ['fɛtido] AGG fetid, stinking.

feto ['fɛto] SM foetus (*Brit*), fetus (*Am*).

fetore [fe'tore] SM stench, stink.

fetta ['fetta] SF (*gen*) slice; (*di terra*) strip; (*fig: porzione*) share; **fare a fette** (*pane, prosciutto*) to slice; (*fig: persona*) to make mincemeat of; **una fetta di pane** a slice of bread; **una fetta del bottino** a share of the loot; **si vedeva solo una fetta di luna/cielo** you could just glimpse the moon/sky.

fettuccia, ce [fet'tuttʃa] SF tape, ribbon.

fettuccine [fettut'tʃine] SFPL (*Culin*) fettu(c)cine (*ribbon-shaped pasta*).

feudale [feu'dale] AGG feudal.

feudalesimo [feuda'lezimo] SM feudalism.

feudatario, ri [feuda'tarjo] SM feudal lord.

feudo ['fɛudo] SM (*Storia*) fief; **un feudo democristiano** (*fig*) a Christian Democrat stronghold.

ff ABBR **a** (*Amm*) = **facente funzione b** (= *fogli*) pp.

FF.AA ABBR = **forze armate.**

FF.SS. ABBR (= *Ferrovie dello Stato*) *Italian railways.*

FG SIGLA = *Foggia.*

FI SIGLA = *Firenze.*

fiaba ['fjaba] SF fairy tale; **paesaggio di fiaba** fairy-tale landscape.

fiabesco, a, schi, sche [fja'besko] AGG fairy-tale *attr.*

fiacca ['fjakka] SF (*stanchezza*) weariness; (*svogliatezza*) listlessness; **avere la fiacca** to be listless; **battere la fiacca** to shirk.

fiaccamente [fjakka'mente] AVV weakly.

fiaccare [fjak'kare] VT to weaken; **l'artiglieria ha fiaccato le difese nemiche** the artillery wore down the enemy's defences (*Brit*) *o* defenses (*Am*).

fiaccherò *ecc* [fjakke'rɔ] VB vedi **fiaccare**.

fiacchezza [fjak'kettsa] SF weariness.

fiacco, a, chi, che ['fjakko] AGG (*stanco*) tired, weary; (*svogliato*) listless; (*debole*) weak; (: *discorso*) weak, dull; (*fermo: mercato*) stagnant.

fiaccola ['fjakkola] SF torch (*with flame*).

fiaccolata [fjakko'lata] SF torchlight procession; (*Sci*) torchlit descent.

fiala ['fjala] SF phial.

fiamma ['fjamma] SF **a** flame; **andare in fiamme** to go up in flames; **dare alle fiamme** to set on fire, burn; **le fiamme dell'inferno** hellfire *sg*, **cucinare alla fiamma** (*Culin*) to flambé **b** (*fig: persona amata*) love, flame; **una vecchia fiamma** an old flame **c** (*Mil, Naut*) pennant.

fiammante [fjam'mante] AGG (*colore*) flaming; **rosso fiammante** flame red, bright red; **nuovo fiammante** brand new.

fiammata [fjam'mata] SF blaze.

fiammato [fjam'mato] SM (*anche: tessuto fiammato*) iridescent fabric.

fiammeggiante [fjammed'dʒante] AGG flaming, blazing; (*fig: occhi*) flashing.

fiammeggiare [fjammed'dʒare] 1 VI (*aus avere*) (*anche fig: cielo*) to blaze; (: *occhi*) to flash; (: *spada*) to gleam. 2 VT (*Culin: pollo*) to singe.

fiammifero [fjam'mifero] SM match.

fiammingo, a, ghi, ghe [fjam'mingo] 1 AGG Flemish. 2 SM/F Fleming; **i fiamminghi** the Flemish. 3 SM (*lingua*) Flemish.

fiancata [fjan'kata] SF (*di nave, auto*) side.

fiancheggiare [fjanked'dʒare] VT (*gen*) to border; (*Mil*) to flank; (*fig: sostenere*) to support, back (up).

fiancheggiatore, trice [fjankeddʒa'tore] SM/F supporter.

fianco, chi ['fjanko] SM (*gen*) side; (*di persona*) hip; (*di animale, esercito*) flank; (*di montagna*) slope; **di fianco** from the side, sideways; **di fianco a** *o* **a fianco di qn/qc** beside *o* next to sb/sth; **avere un dolore al fianco** to have a pain in one's side; **stare al fianco di qn** (*anche fig*) to stand by sb, stay by sb's side; **ho sempre avuto qualcuno al mio fianco** I have always had somebody by my side; **fianco a fianco** side by side; **stare con le mani sui fianchi** to stand with one's hands on one's hips; **avere fianchi larghi/stretti** (*persona*) to have broad/narrow hips, be broad-/narrow-hipped; **una spina nel fianco** (*fig*) a thorn in one's side; **mostrare il fianco al nemico** (*fig*) to reveal one's weak spot *o* Achilles' heel to one's enemy; **offrire** *o* **prestare il fianco a critiche** to leave o.s. open to criticism; **fianco destr/sinistr!** (*Mil*) right/left turn!

fiandra ['fjandra] SF damask linen.

Fiandre ['fjandre] SFPL: **le Fiandre** Flanders *sg*.

fiasca, sche ['fjaska] SF (hip) flask.

fiaschetteria [fjaskette'ria] SF wine shop.

fiasco, schi ['fjasko] SM bottle (*in straw holder*); (*fig: fallimento*) fiasco; **fare fiasco** (*persona*) to come a cropper; (*spettacolo*) to be a flop, be a fiasco.

fiatare [fja'tare] VI (*aus avere*) (*fig: parlare*): **senza fiatare** without saying a word; **non osarono fiatare** they didn't dare breathe.

fiato ['fjato] SM **a** breath; **fiato cattivo** bad breath; **avere il fiato grosso** to pant, be out of breath; **riprendere fiato** (*anche fig*) to get one's breath back, catch one's breath; **tirare il fiato** to draw breath; (*fig*) to have a breather; **essere senza fiato** to be out of breath; **restare senza fiato** to be breathless; **sono rimasto senza fiato** (*fig*) it took my breath away; **bere tutto d'un fiato** to drink all in one go *o* gulp; **me l'ha raccontato tutto d'un fiato** he told me the whole story without drawing breath; **è fiato sprecato** (*fig*) it's a waste of breath; **quella scena mi ha mozzato il fiato** that scene took my breath away **b** (*capacità di resistenza*) stamina, staying power **c** (*Mus*): **i fiati** wind instruments, the winds; **strumento a fiato** wind instrument.

fiatone [fja'tone] SM: **avere il fiatone** to be out of breath.

fibbia ['fibbja] SF buckle.

fibra ['fibra] 1 SF **a** (*gen*) fibre (*Brit*), fiber (*Am*) **b** (*costituzione*) constitution; **persona di fibra forte** person with a strong constitution. 2 ▸**fibra di vetro** fibreglass (*Brit*), fiberglass (*Am*) ▸**fibre grezze** roughage *sg*, (dietary) fibre *sg* ▸**fibre ottiche** optic fibres ▸**fibre tessili** textile fibres.

fibrillazione [fibrillat'tsjone] SF (*Med*) fibrillation.

fibrina [fi'brina] SF (*Bio*) fibrin.

fibrinogeno [fibri'nɔdʒeno] SM (*Bio*) fibrinogen.

fibroma, i [fi'brɔma] SM (*Med*) fibroma.

fibrosità [fibrosi'ta] SF INV (*vedi agg*) fibrousness; stringiness.

fibroso, a [fi'broso] AGG fibrous; (*carne*) stringy.

fibula ['fibula] SF (*Anat, Archeol*) fibula.

ficcanaso [fikka'naso] SM/F (*pl m* **ficcanasi**, *pl f* **ficcanaso**) busybody, nos(e)y parker.

ficcare [fik'kare] 1 VT **a** (*infilare: in borsa, cassetto*) to put; (: *con forza*) to thrust, push; (*palo, chiodo*) to drive; **mi ha ficcato un dito nell'occhio** he poked his finger in my eye; **ficcalo da qualche parte** (*fam*) stick it somewhere; **ficcare il naso negli affari altrui** (*fig*) to poke *o* stick one's nose into other people's business; **lo hanno ficcato dentro** (*fam: in prigione*) they put him away *o* inside **b**: **ficcarsi: ficcarsi le dita nel naso** to pick one's nose; **ficcarsi il cappello in testa** to put *o* thrust one's hat on one's head; **ficcarsi in testa qc** (*fig*) to get sth into one's head; **ficcarsi in testa di fare qc** (*fig*) to take it into one's head to do sth. 2 **ficcarsi** VR (*andare a finire*) to get to; **dove si sarà ficcato?** where can he (*o* it *ecc*) have got to?; **ficcarsi nei pasticci** *o* **nei guai** to get into hot water *o* a fix; **perché ti devi sempre ficcare in mezzo?** why do you always have to stick your oar in?

ficcherò *ecc* [fikke'rɔ] VB vedi **ficcare**.

fiche [fiʃ] SF INV (*nei giochi d'azzardo*) chip.

fico[1], chi ['fiko] SM (*Bot*) fig ▸**fico d'India** prickly pear ▸**fico secco** dried fig; **non vale un fico secco** (*fig*) it's not worth a fig *o* a straw; **non ci capisco un fico secco** I don't understand a thing.

fico[2], a, chi, che ['fiko], **figo, a, ghi, ghe** ['figo] (*fam*) 1 AGG great. 2 SM/F great guy/girl.

ficus ['fikus] SM INV (*Bot*) ficus.

fidanzamento [fidantsa'mento] SM engagement; **anello/festa di fidanzamento** engagement ring/party.

fidanzare [fidan'tsare] 1 VT: **fidanzare a** to betroth to.

2 **fidanzarsi** VR (*uso reciproco*) to get engaged.
fidanzato, a [fidan'tsato] 1 AGG engaged.
2 SM/F fiancé/fiancée; **i fidanzati** the engaged couple.
fidarsi [fi'darsi] VIP: **fidarsi di** to trust; (*fare affidamento*) to rely on; **non mi fido di uscire con questo tempo** I daren't go out in this weather; **fidarsi è bene non fidarsi è meglio** (*Proverbio*) better safe than sorry.
fidatezza [fida'tettsa] SF trustworthiness, reliability.
fidato, a [fi'dato] AGG (*degno di fiducia*) trustworthy, reliable; (*leale*) loyal, faithful.
fideismo [fide'izmo] SM unquestioning belief.
fideistico, a, ci, che [fide'istiko] AGG (*atteggiamento, posizione*) totally uncritical.
fideiussione [fidejus'sjone] SF (*Dir*) guarantee.
fideiussore [fidejus'sore] SM (*Dir*) guarantor.
Fidia ['fidja] SM Phidias.
fido¹, a ['fido] AGG faithful, loyal.
fido² ['fido] SM (*Comm*) credit ►**fido bancario** banker's credit.
fiducia [fi'dutʃa] SF a trust, confidence; **avere fiducia in qn** to have faith in sb, trust sb; **abbi fiducia in Dio** have faith in the Lord; **riporre la propria fiducia in qn/qc** to place one's trust in sb/sth; **devi avere più fiducia in te stesso** you should have more confidence in yourself; **una persona di fiducia** a trustworthy *o* reliable person; **un prodotto di fiducia** a reliable product; **è il mio uomo di fiducia** he is my right-hand man; **ha un incarico di fiducia** he holds a responsible position
b (*Pol*): **voto di fiducia** vote of confidence; **fiducia del Parlamento al Governo** parliamentary vote of confidence; **porre la questione di fiducia** to ask for a vote of confidence.
fiduciario, ria, ri, rie [fidu'tʃarjo] AGG, SM (*Dir, Comm*) fiduciary.
fiduciosamente [fidutʃosa'mente] AVV trustingly; **guardare fiduciosamente all'avvenire** to look to the future with confidence.
fiducioso, a [fidu'tʃoso] AGG trusting.
fiele ['fjɛle] SM (*amarezza*) bitterness, bile (*letter*); **parole piene di fiele** (*fig*) bitter words.
fienagione [fjena'dʒone] SF (*operazione*) haymaking; (*stagione*) haymaking season.
fienile [fje'nile] SM hayloft.
fieno ['fjɛno] SM hay.
fiera¹ ['fjɛra] SF (*letter: animale*) wild beast.
fiera² ['fjɛra] SF fair ►**fiera di beneficenza** charity bazaar, (garden) fête *o* fete ►**fiera del bianco** linen sale ►**fiera campionaria** trade fair.
fieramente [fjera'mente] AVV (*vedi agg*) proudly; boldly.
fierezza [fje'rettsa] SF pride.
fiero, a ['fjɛro] AGG a (*orgoglioso*) proud; **essere** *o* **andare fiero di qn/qc** to be proud of sb/sth b (*valente*) bold, intrepid.
fievole ['fjevole] AGG (*luce*) dim; (*suono*) faint.
fievolmente [fjevol'mente] AVV (*risuonare*) faintly; (*illuminare*) dimly; (*sussurrare*) softly.
fifa ['fifa] SF (*fam*): **che fifa!** what a fright!; **avere fifa** to have the jitters.
F.I.F.A. ['fifa] SIGLA F (= *Fédération Internationale de Football Association*) FIFA.
fifo ['fifo] SM INV (*Comm*: = *first in first out*) FIFO.
fifone, a [fi'fone] SM/F (*fam scherz*) chicken, scaredy cat (*used by children*).
fig. ABBR (= *figura*) fig.

F.I.G.C. [fidʒi'tʃi] SIGLA F (= *Federazione Italiana Gioco Calcio*) *Italian football association.*
Figi ['fidʒi] SFPL: **le (isole) Figi** Fiji *sg*, the Fiji Islands.
figlia ['fiʎʎa] SF a daughter; **è figlia unica** she's an only child ►**figlia di papà** daddy's girl b (*Comm*) counterfoil (*Brit*), stub.
figliare [fiʎ'ʎare] VI (*aus* avere) (*animali*) to give birth.
figliastro, a [fiʎ'ʎastro] SM/F stepchild, stepson/stepdaughter.
figlio, gli ['fiʎʎo] SM son; (*senza distinzione di sesso*) child; **hanno 2 figli** they have 2 children; **aspetta un figlio** she's expecting a baby; **suo figlio è all'estero** his son is abroad; **essere figlio d'arte** to come from a theatrical (*o* artistic *ecc*) family; **il Figlio di Dio/dell'uomo** (*Rel*) the Son of God/of Man ►**figlio di papà** daddy's boy, spoilt and wealthy young man ►**figlio di puttana** (*fam!*) son of a bitch (*fam!*) ►**figlio unico** only child.
figlioccio, cia, ci, ce [fiʎ'ʎottʃo] SM/F godchild, godson/goddaughter.
figliola [fiʎ'ʎɔla] SF daughter; **una bella figliola** (*ragazza*) a fine figure of a girl.
figliolo [fiʎ'ʎɔlo] SM son; **un figliolo ubbidiente** (*ragazzo*) an obedient young boy *o* man.
figura [fi'gura] SF (*gen, Mat*) figure; (*illustrazione*) illustration, picture; (*Carte*) face card; **ritratto a mezza figura** half-length portrait; **fare bella/brutta figura** to create *o* make a good/bad impression; **far fare una brutta figura a qn** to show sb up, make sb look a fool; **fare la figura dello scemo** to look a fool; **che figura!** how embarrassing!; **fare figura** to look good *o* smart ►**figura retorica** figure of speech.
figuraccia, ce [figu'rattʃa] SF: **fare una figuraccia** to create a bad impression.
figurante [figu'rante] SM (*Teatro, Cine*) extra.
figurare [figu'rare] 1 VT: **non riesco a figurarmelo** I can't picture it; **ti disturbo? — ma no, figurati!** am I disturbing you? — no, not at all!; **figurati che... ** would you believe that ...?; **figurarsi se non accettava!** wouldn't you just know it — he accepted it!.
2 VI (*aus* avere) to appear, figure.
figuratamente [figurata'mente] AVV figuratively.
figurativo, a [figura'tivo] AGG figurative.
figurato, a [figu'rato] AGG a (*allegorico*) figurative; **linguaggio figurato** figurative language b (*illustrato*) illustrated.
figurazione [figurat'tsjone] SF (*rappresentazione*) representation, depiction.
figurina [figu'rina] SF a (*statuetta*) figurine b (*da collezione*) picture card.
figurinista, i, e [figuri'nista] SM/F dress designer.
figurino [figu'rino] SM fashion sketch; **sembra un figurino** she looks like a fashion plate.
figuro [fi'guro] SM: **un losco figuro** a suspicious character.
figurona [figu'rona] SF, **figurone** [figu'rone] SM (*fam*): **fare una figurona** *o* **un figurone** (*persona, oggetto*) to look terrific; (*persona: con un discorso*) to make an excellent impression.
fila ['fila] SF a (*gen*) line, row; (*coda*) queue; (*Mil*) rank; (*Teatro*) row; **in fila** in a row *o* line; **in fila indiana** in single file; **mettetevi in fila per due** line up in twos; **fare la fila** to queue; **serrare/rompere le file** (*Mil*) to close/break ranks
b (*successione*): **di fila** in succession, one after the other; **è piovuto per due mesi di fila** it rained for two

months on the trot o non-stop; **una fila di avvenimenti** a series of events; **fuoco di fila** (*di armi da fuoco, anche fig*: *di domande ecc*) volley.

filamento [fila'mento] SM filament.

filamentoso, a [filamen'toso] AGG (*verdura, carne*) stringy.

filanca° [fi'lanka] SF *stretch material*.

filanda [fi'landa] SF spinning mill.

filante [fi'lante] AGG: **stella filante** (*stella cadente*) shooting star; (*striscia di carta*) streamer.

filantropia [filantro'pia] SF philanthropy.

filantropicamente [filantropika'mente] AVV philan-thropically.

filantropico, a, ci, che [filan'trɔpiko] AGG philanthropic (al).

filantropo [fi'lantropo] SM philanthropist.

filare¹ [fi'lare] ① VT **a** (*lana*) to spin; (*metallo*) to draw; **quando Berta filava** in the good old days **b** (*Naut*: *gomena*) to pay out; (: *remi*) to trail. ② VI (*aus essere nel significato* **a**, *avere negli altri signifi-cati*) **a** (*persona*) to dash off, run; **filare via** OR **filarsela** to run away, make off, make o.s. scarce; **fila (via)!** clear off!; **fila a letto subito** off to bed with you; **far filare qn** (*fig*) to make sb behave; **filare dritto** to behave, toe the line; **la macchina fila che è una bellezza** the car goes like a bomb **b** (*discorso, ragionamento*) to be coherent, hang to-gether **c** (*amoreggiare*): **filare (con)** to go out (with), go steady (with) (*ant*) **d** (*liquido*) to trickle; (*candela*) to smoke; (*formaggio*) to go stringy.

filare² [fi'lare] SM (*di alberi*) row, line.

filarmonica, che [filar'mɔnika] SF music society.

filarmonico, a, ci, che [filar'mɔniko] AGG philharmonic.

filastrocca, che [filas'trɔkka] SF nursery rhyme.

filatelia [filate'lia] SF philately (*frm*), stamp collecting.

filatelica [fila'tɛlika] SF philately (*frm*), stamp collecting.

filatelico, a, ci, che [fila'tɛliko] ① AGG philatelic. ② SM/F philatelist (*frm*), stamp collector.

filato¹, a [fi'lato] ① AGG **a** : **zucchero filato** candy floss **b** (*di seguito*) without a break, straight off; **ha parlato per 4 ore filate** he spoke for 4 hours without stopping. ② AVV: **vai dritto filato a casa** go straight home.

filato² [fi'lato] SM (*di lana*) yarn; (*di altri tessuti*) thread.

filatoio, oi [fila'tojo] SM (*macchina*) spinning wheel.

filatore, trice [fila'tore] SM/F spinner.

filatura [fila'tura] SF **a** (*operazione*) spinning **b** (*fabbrica*) spinning mill.

fileggiare [filed'dʒare] VI (*aus avere*) (*Naut*: *vela*) to luff.

filettare [filet'tare] VT (*Tecn*: *vite*) to thread.

filettatura [filetta'tura] SF (*di viti*) thread.

filetto¹ [fi'letto] SM **a** (*ornamento*) braid, trimming **b** (*Tecn*) thread **c** (*Equitazione*) snaffle (bit).

filetto² [fi'letto] SM (*di carne, pesce*) fillet.

filiale¹ [fi'ljale] AGG filial.

filiale² [fi'ljale] SF (*Comm*) branch; (*impresa dipendente*) subsidiary (company).

filibustiere [filibus'tjɛre] SM pirate; (*fig*) adventurer.

filiforme [fili'forme] AGG threadlike; (*fig*: *magrissimo*) spindly.

filigrana [fili'grana] SF (*di oro*) filigree; (*di banconota, francobollo*) watermark.

filigranato, a [filigra'nato] AGG (*carta*) water-marked.

filippica [fi'lippika] SF invective.

Filippine [filip'pine] SFPL: **le Filippine** the Philippines.

filippino, a [filip'pino] AGG, SM/F Filipino.

filisteismo [filiste'izmo] SM stuffy bourgeois attitudes.

filisteo, a [filis'tɛo] AGG, SM/F stuffy bourgeois.

film [film] SM INV (*Fot*) film; (*Cine*) film, movie (*Am*).

filmare [fil'mare] VT (*persona*) to film; (*scena*) to film, shoot.

filmato [fil'mato] SM short film.

filmina [fil'mina] SF film strip.

filo ['filo] SM **a** (*di cotone*) thread; (*di lana*) yarn; (*di perle, burattini*) string; (*di telefono, lampada*) wire, flex; **maglietta di filo di Scozia** fine cotton T-shirt; **calzettoni di filo di Scozia** lisle socks; **i fili della luce/del telefono** the electricity/telephone wires; **il filo del traguardo** the finishing tape; **in fil di ruota** (*Naut*) on a dead run; **un filo d'erba** a blade of grass; **filo a piombo** plumb line; **un filo d'acqua** a trickle of water; **un filo d'aria** (*fig*) a breath of air; **un filo di luce** (*fig*) a ray of light; **un filo di speranza** (*fig*) a ray o glimmer of hope; **con un filo di voce** in a weak o feeble voice, in a whisper ►**filo elettrico** electric wire ►**filo di ferro/spinato** wire/barbed wire ►**filo interdentale** dental floss **b** (*di lama, rasoio*) edge; **essere** o **camminare** o **trovarsi sul filo del rasoio** (*fig*) to be on the razor's edge **c** (*di legno*) grain **d** (*fraseologia*): **perdere il filo** (*di un discorso*) to lose the thread; **ripetere qc per filo e per segno** to repeat sth word for word; **dare del filo da torcere a qn** to create difficulties for sb, make life difficult for sb; **è appeso a un filo** it's hanging by a thread; **fare il filo a qn** (*corteggiare*) to be after sb, chase sb **e** : **fila** SFPL: **le fila di un complotto** the threads of a plot.

filoamericano, a [filoameri'kano] AGG pro-American.

filobus ['filobus] SM INV trolley bus.

filocinese [filotʃi'nese] AGG pro-Chinese.

filodendro [filo'dɛndro] SM philodendron.

filodiffusione [filodiffu'zjone] SF rediffusion.

filodrammatico, a, ci, che [filodram'matiko] ① AGG: (**compagnia) filodrammatica** amateur dramatic society. ② SM/F amateur actor/amateur actress.

filologia [filolo'dʒia] SF philology.

filologicamente [filolodʒika'mente] AVV philologically.

filologico, a, ci, che [filo'lɔdʒiko] AGG philological.

filologo, gi [fi'lɔlogo] SM philologist.

filoncino [filon'tʃino] SM ≈ French stick.

filone [fi'lone] SM **a** (*di minerale*) seam, vein; (*fig*: *culturale*) tradition; **un film che appartiene al filone western** a film in the Western genre **b** (*di pane*) ≈ Vienna loaf.

filosofale [filozo'fale] AGG: **pietra filosofale** philosopher's stone.

filosofare [filozo'fare] VI (*aus avere*) to philosophize.

filosofeggiare [filozofed'dʒare] VI (*aus avere*) (*pegg*) to philosophize.

filosofia [filozo'fia] SF philosophy; **con filosofia** (*fig*) philosophically.

filosoficamente [filozofika'mente] AVV philosophically.

filosofico, a, ci, che [filo'zɔfiko] AGG philosophical.

filosofo, a [fi'lɔzofo] SM/F philosopher.

filosovietico, a, ci, che [filoso'vjɛtiko] AGG pro-Soviet.

filovia [filo'via] SF (*linea*) trolley line; (*bus*) trolley bus.

filtraggio, gi [fil'traddʒo] SM (*gen*) filtering.

filtrare [fil'trare] ① VT to filter; (*fig*: *selezionare*) to screen. ② VI (*aus essere*) to filter; **la luce filtrava dalla finestra** the light filtered in through the window.

filtrazione [filtrat'tsjone] SF (*vedi vb*) filtration; screening.

filtro[1] ['filtro] SM (*gen*, *Fot*) filter; **sigaretta con filtro** filter-tipped cigarette, filter tip ▶**filtro dell'aria** (*Aut*) air filter ▶**filtro dell'olio** (*Aut*) oil filter.

filtro[2] ['filtro] SM (*pozione*) potion.

filza ['filtsa] SF (*gen*, *anche fig*) string; **mi ha raccontato una filza di bugie** he told me a string of lies.

F.I.N. [fin] SIGLA F (= *Federazione Italiana Nuoto*) *Italian Swimming Federation.*

finale [fi'nale] [1] AGG final; **il giudizio finale** (*Rel*) the Last Judgment; **proposizione finale** (*Gramm*) purpose clause.

  [2] SM (*di libro*, *film*) ending, end; (*Mus*, *di spettacolo*) finale; **finale a sorpresa** surprise ending.

  [3] SF **a** (*Sport*) final; **entrare in finale** to reach the final(s)

  b (*Gramm*) last syllable (*o* letter).

finalismo [fina'lizmo] SM (*Filosofia*) finalism.

finalissima [fina'lissima] SF (*Sport*) final(s); (*di concorso di bellezza*) grand final.

finalista, i, e [fina'lista] SM/F finalist.

finalità [finali'ta] SF INV **a** (*scopo*) aim, purpose; **gioco a finalità educativa** educational game **b** (*Filosofia*) finality.

finalizzare [finalid'dzare] VT: **finalizzare a** (*ricerca, iniziativa*) to direct towards, aim at; **l'iniziativa è finalizzata alla salvaguardia dell'ambiente** the aim of this project is to protect the environment.

finalmente [final'mente] AVV at (long) last, finally; **finalmente!** at (long) last!

finanza [fi'nantsa] SF **a** finance; **alta finanza** high finance **b** : **finanze** SFPL finances; **Ministro delle finanze** Minister of Finance, ≈ Chancellor of the Exchequer (*Brit*), ≈ Secretary of the Treasury (*Am*)

  c (*Amm*): **(Guardia di) finanza** (*di frontiera*) ≈ Customs and Excise (*Brit*), ≈ Customs Service (*Am*); **Intendenza di finanza** ≈ Inland Revenue (*Brit*), ≈ Internal Revenue Service (*Am*).

finanziamento [finantsja'mento] SM (*azione*) financing; (*denaro fornito*) funds *pl*; **la banca ha concesso un finanziamento alla ditta** the bank has agreed to finance *o* fund the company.

finanziare [finan'tsjare] VT to finance, fund.

finanziaria [finan'tsjarja] SF (*anche:* **legge finanziaria**) finance act, ≈ budget (*Brit*); (*anche:* **società finanziaria**) investment company.

finanziariamente [finantsjarja'mente] AVV financially.

finanziario, ria, ri, rie [finan'tsjarjo] AGG financial.

finanziatore, trice [finantsja'tore] [1] AGG: **ente finanziatore** financing body.

  [2] SM/F backer.

finanziere [finan'tsjɛre] SM **a** (*esperto di finanze*) financier **b** (*guardia*) ≈ customs officer.

finché [fin'ke] CONG (*fino a quando*) until; (*per tutto il tempo che*) as long as; **ti amerò finché vivrò** I'll love you as long as I live; **non uscirai finché non avrai finito il lavoro** you won't leave until you have finished your work; **finché vorrai** as long as you like; **aspetta finché non sia uscito** wait until he goes (*o* comes) out.

fine[1] ['fine] AGG **a** (*sottile: lamina, fetta*) thin; (: *capelli, lineamenti, pioggia*) fine; (: *voce*) thin, frail; **penna a punta fine** fine-point pen

  b (*acuto: vista, udito*) sharp, keen; (: *odorato*) fine; (*fig: ingegno*) shrewd; (: *osservazione, ironia*) subtle

  c (*raffinato: persona*) refined, distinguished; **non è fine mangiare con le mani** it's not polite to eat with your fingers.

fine[2] ['fine] SM **a** (*scopo*) aim, end, purpose; (*Filosofia*) end; **avere un secondo fine** to have an ulterior motive; **a fin di bene** with the best of intentions; **il fine giustifica i mezzi** the end justifies the means; **al fine di fare qc** (in order) to do sth **b** (*conclusione*) end; **condurre qc a buon fine** to bring sth to a successful conclusion.

fine[3] ['fine] SF (*gen*) end; (*di libro, film*) ending; **alla fine** in the end, finally; **senza fine** endlessly (*avv*), endless (*agg*); **porre fine a** to put an end to; **a fine anno/mese** at the end of the year/month; **alla fine della giornata** at the end of the day; **verso la fine di giugno** in late June; **alla fin fine** at the end of the day, in the end; **in fin dei conti** when all is said and done; (*tutto sommato*) after all; **volgere alla fine** to draw to an end; **fare una brutta fine** to come to a bad end; **che fine ha fatto?** what became of him?; **essere in fin di vita** to be at death's door; **è la fine del mondo!** (*fig: stupendo*) it's out of this world!; (*pegg*) what's the world coming to?; **buona fine e buon principio!** (*augurio*) happy New Year!; **un quadro fine Ottocento** a late nineteenth-century painting; **articoli di fine serie** oddments; **svendita di fine stagione** end-of-season sale.

finemente [fine'mente] AVV (*tagliare*) thinly; (*fig: osservare*) shrewdly; **un ricamo finemente lavorato** a finely worked embroidery.

fine settimana [fine setti'mana] SM INV weekend.

finestra [fi'nɛstra] SF (*gen*, *Inform*) window; **affacciarsi alla finestra** to appear at the window; **buttare il denaro dalla finestra** (*fig*) to throw money down the drain ▶**finestra a battenti** casement window ▶**finestra a ghigliottina** sash window.

finestrino [fines'trino] SM (*di treno, auto*) window.

finezza [fi'nettsa] SF (*vedi* **fine**[1]) thinness; fineness; sharpness; keenness; shrewdness; subtleness, subtlety; refinement.

fingere ['findʒere] VB IRREG [1] VT to feign (*letter*); **fingere di fare qc** to pretend to do sth; **fingere un grande dolore** to pretend to be very upset.

  [2] VI (*aus* avere) to dissemble (*letter*); **sa fingere molto bene** he's very good at hiding his feelings.

  [3] **fingersi** VR to pretend to be; **fingersi medico** to pretend to be a doctor.

finimenti [fini'menti] SMPL (*di cavallo*) harness *sg*.

finimondo [fini'mondo] SM pandemonium; **successe un finimondo** all hell broke loose.

finire [fi'nire] [1] VI (*aus* essere) **a** (*gen*) to finish, end; (*pioggia, neve*) to stop, cease; **un altro giorno è finito** another day is over *o* has come to an end; **tra noi è tutto finito** it's all over between us; **è finito di piovere/nevicare** it has stopped raining/snowing; **finire bene/male** (*film, libro*) to have a happy/an unhappy ending; **finire male** (*persona*) to come to a bad end; **per fortuna tutto è finito bene** luckily everything turned out well in the end; **finire per** *o* **col fare qc** to end up (by) doing sth; **finì col fare il lavoro lui** he ended up doing the job himself; **com'è andata a finire?** what happened in the end?; **dov'è andato a finire quel libro?** [OR] **dov'è finito quel libro?** where has that book got to?; **dove vuoi andare a finire con questo discorso?** what are you driving *o* getting at?; **è finita!** (*non c'è rimedio*) it's all over!; **finire in galera** to end up *o* finish up in prison

b (*esaurirsi*) to be finished; **l'olio è finito** we have run out of oil, there's no oil left.
2 vt **a** (*gen*) to finish; (*lavoro, corso*) to finish, complete; (*discorso*) to end; **ha finito i propri giorni in prigione** he ended his days in prison; **finisci la minestra** finish *o* eat up your soup
b (*smettere*) to stop; **finire di fare qc** to stop doing sth; **non finire più di fare qc** to keep on doing sth; **non finisco di meravigliarmi della sua pazienza** her patience never ceases to amaze me
c (*dare il colpo di grazia*) to finish off
d (*rifinire*) to finish off, put the finishing touches to
e (*fam*): **finirla** to pack in; **è ora di finirla con queste storie!** it's time you stopped this nonsense!; **finiscila!** stop it!; **farla finita con qc** to have done with sth; **devi farla finita con questi capricci** you'll have to stop these tantrums; **l'ho fatta finita con la droga** I'm off drugs now; **ho deciso di farla finita con Maria** I've decided to finish with Maria; **farla finita (con la vita)** to put an end to one's life.
3 sm (*fine*) end; **sul finire della festa** towards the end of the party.

finissaggio, gi [finis'saddʒo] sm (*Tecn: operazione*) finishing; (: *risultato*) finish.
finito, a [fi'nito] AGG **a** (*Gramm, Mat, Filosofia*) finite **b** (*terminato, rifinito*) finished; **è un uomo finito** (*fig: rovinato*) he's finished **c** (*esperto: cuoco*) expert; (: *operaio, artigiano*) skilled.
finitrice [fini'tritʃe] sf (*Tecn*) finishing machine.
finitura [fini'tura] sf finish; **le ultime finiture** the finishing touches.
finlandese [finlan'dese] **1** AGG Finnish.
2 sm/f Finn.
3 sm (*lingua*) Finnish.
Finlandia [fin'landja] sf: **la Finlandia** Finland.
fino¹, a ['fino] AGG **a** = **fine¹** **b** (*oro, argento*) pure; **cervello fino** quick brain; vedi **fine¹**.
fino² ['fino] (*spesso troncato, davanti a consonante, in* fin) **1** AVV (*pure, anche*) even; **hai detto fin troppo** you have said too much *o* more than enough.
2 PREP **a**: **fino a** (*tempo*) until, up to, till; (*luogo*) as far as; (+ *infin*) so that; **resto fino a venerdì/al 15 gennaio** I'm staying until Friday/until the 15th of January; **vengo con te fino al cinema** I'll come as far as the cinema with you; **ha lavorato fino ad ammalarsi** he worked so hard that he made himself ill; **fino a quando?** [OR] **fin quando?** until when?; **fino all'ultimo** until the end, to the end, till the end; **fino all'ultimo ha negato poi ha ceduto** he denied it up till the last minute, then gave way; **averne fin sopra i capelli** (*fig*) to be fed up to the back teeth; **andare fino in fondo a qc** to get to the bottom of sth
b: **fin da** since, from; **fin dalla nascita/dall'infanzia** from *o* since birth/infancy; **fin da quando sei arrivato** since you arrived, from the time you arrived; **fin d'ora** as of *o* from now; **fin dall'alba** since daybreak; **fin da domani** from tomorrow onwards; **fin da ieri** since yesterday.
finocchio, chi [fi'nɔkkjo] sm **a** (*Bot*) fennel **b** (*offensivo: omosessuale*) queer, poof (*Brit*).
finora [fi'nora] AVV up till now, so far; **finora Marco non si è visto** Marco hasn't turned up yet.
finsi ecc ['finsi] vB vedi **fingere**.
finta ['finta] sf **a** (*finzione*): **fare finta di fare qc** to pretend

to do sth; **fa finta di niente** he pretends not to notice; (*comportarsi normalmente*) he's behaving as if nothing had happened; **l'ho detto per finta** I was only pretending; (*per scherzo*) I was only kidding
b (*Pugilato*) feint; (*Calcio ecc*) dummy; **fare una finta** to feint
c (*Cucito*) flap.
fintantoché [fintanto'ke] AVV (*per tutto il tempo che*) as long as; (*fino al momento in cui*) until.
finto, a ['finto] **1** PP di **fingere**.
2 AGG (*capelli, denti*) false; (*fiori*) artificial; (*cuoio, pelle*) imitation *attr*; (*fig: simulato: pazzia*) feigned, pretended.
finzione [fin'tsjone] sf (*simulazione*) pretence (*Brit*), pretense (*Am*), sham; **la finzione scenica** the stage illusion.
fio, fii ['fio] sm (*frm*): **pagare il fio (di)** to pay the penalty (for).
fiocamente [fjoka'mente] AVV (*vedi agg*) dimly; faintly.
fioccare [fjok'kare] **1** vi (*aus essere*) (*neve*) to fall; (*fig: insulti*) to come thick and fast.
2 vB IMPERS to snow.
fiocchetto [fjok'ketto] sm (*cravattino*) bow.
fiocco¹, chi ['fjɔkko] sm **a** (*di neve, cereali*) flake **b** (*di lana*) flock **c** (*nastro*) bow; **coi fiocchi** (*fig*) first-rate; **un pranzo coi fiocchi** a slap-up meal.
fiocco², chi ['fjɔkko] sm (*Naut*) jib.
fiocina ['fjotʃina] sf (*Naut*) harpoon.
fioco, a, chi, che ['fjɔko] AGG (*luce*) dim, weak; (*suono, voce*) faint, weak.
fionda ['fjonda] sf (*arma*) sling; (*giocattolo*) catapult.
fiondarsi [fjon'darsi] vR (*fam: andare precipitosamente*) to make a dash; **si è fiondato al telefono** he rushed to the phone, he made a dash for the phone.
fioraio, aia, ai, aie [fjo'rajo] sm/f (*in negozio*) florist; (*ambulante*) flower seller.
fiorato, a [fjo'rato] AGG floral.
fiordaliso [fjorda'lizo] sm (*Bot*) cornflower; (*Araldica*) fleur-de-lis *o* -lys.
fiordo ['fjɔrdo] sm fjord.
fiore ['fjore] sm **a** (*gen, anche fig*) flower; (*di albero*) blossom; **essere in fiore** (*pianta, giardino*) to be in bloom; (*albero*) to be in blossom; (*fig*) to be in full bloom; **fiori d'arancio** orange blossom *sg*, **disegno a fiori** floral design; **nel fiore degli anni** in one's prime; **oggi sei un fiore** you're looking lovely today; "**non fiori ma opere di bene**" (*negli annunci mortuari*) "no flowers please, but donations to charity"
b (*Carte*): **fiori** smpl clubs
c : **a fior di**: **a fior d'acqua** on (the surface of) the water; **a fior di labbra** in a whisper; **ho i nervi a fior di pelle** my nerves are all on edge
d (*fraseologia*): **un fior di ragazza** a really lovely girl; **è costato fior di quattrini** it cost a pretty penny; **aver fior di quattrini** to be rolling in money; **il fior fiore della società** the cream of society ▶**fiore all'occhiello** feather in the cap
e : **fior di latte** cream.
fiorente [fjo'rɛnte] AGG (*industria, paese*) flourishing; (*salute*) blooming; (*petto*) ample; **fiorente di** (*boschi, vigneti*) rich in.
fiorentina [fjoren'tina] sf (*Culin*) T-bone steak.
fiorentino, a [fjoren'tino] **1** AGG of *o* from Florence, Florentine.
2 sm/f inhabitant *o* native of Florence.

fioretto[1] [fjo'retto] SM (*piccola rinuncia*) small sacrifice; (*buona azione*) good deed.

fioretto[2] [fjo'retto] SM **a** (*Scherma*) foil **b** (*Tecn*) drilling bit.

fioriera [fjo'rjɛra] SF (*per piante*) flowerpot; (*per fiori recisi*) vase.

fiorino [fjo'rino] SM florin.

fiorire [fjo'rire] VI (*aus essere*) (*fiore*) to flower, bloom; (*albero*) to blossom, flower; (*fig: sentimento*) to blossom; (*: commercio, arte*) to flourish.

fiorista, i, e [fjo'rista] SM/F florist.

fiorito, a [fjo'rito] AGG (*giardino*) in flower, in bloom; (*pianta*) in bloom; (*ramo*) covered with blossom; (*tessuto*) floral, flowered; (*stile*) flowery; **fiorito di errori** full of errors.

fioritura [fjori'tura] SF **a** (*di pianta*) flowering, blooming; (*di albero*) blossoming; (*fig: di commercio, arte*) flourishing **b** (*insieme dei fiori*) flowers pl; **il ciliegio ha avuto una fioritura abbondante quest'anno** the cherry tree produced a lot of flowers *o* blossom this year **c** (*Mus*) fioritura.

fiotto ['fjotto] SM (*di lacrime*) flood; (*di sangue*) gush, spurt; **scorrere a fiotti** to gush out *o* forth.

F.I.P.E. ['fipe] SIGLA F (= *Federazione Italiana Pubblici Esercizi*) Italian Federation of Commercial Concerns.

Firenze [fi'rɛntse] SF Florence.

firma ['firma] SF signature; (*fig*) name; **apporre la propria firma a** to put one's signature to; **le grandi firme della moda** the big names in fashion.

firmamento [firma'mento] SM firmament.

firmare [fir'mare] VT to sign; **un maglione firmato da Missoni** a Missoni sweater, a sweater by Missoni.

firmatario, ria, ri, rie [firma'tarjo] SM/F signatory.

fisarmonica, che [fizar'mɔnika] SF accordion.

fiscale [fis'kale] AGG **a** fiscal, tax *attr*; **anno fiscale** tax year; **scontrino fiscale** (shop) receipt; **ricevuta fiscale** official receipt (*for tax purposes*); **medico fiscale** *doctor employed by Social Security to examine people on sick leave* **b** (*fig pegg: meticoloso*) nitpicking.

fiscalista, i, e [fiska'lista] SM/F tax consultant.

fiscalità [fiskali'ta] SF INV (*vedi agg*) tax system; punctiliousness.

fiscalmente [fiskal'mente] AVV (*vedi agg*) from the tax point of view; over-punctiliously.

fischiare [fis'kjare] **1** VT **a** (*canzone, motivo*) to whistle; **l'arbitro ha fischiato un rigore** the referee blew his whistle for a penalty **b** (*in segno di disapprovazione*) to hiss, boo. **2** VI (*aus avere*) (*gen, fig*) to whistle; (*serpente*) to hiss; (*uccello*) to sing; **mi fischiano le orecchie** I've got a ringing in my ears; (*fig fam*) my ears are burning; **fischiare al cane** to whistle for one's dog.

fischiata [fis'kjata] SF (*azione*) whistling; (*fischio*) whistle; **le fischiate del pubblico** the booing *o* boos of the audience.

fischiettare [fiskjet'tare] VI (*aus avere*), VT to whistle.

fischietto [fis'kjetto] SM (*strumento*) whistle.

fischio, chi ['fiskjo] SM (*suono*) whistle; **fare un fischio** to whistle, give a whistle; **prendere fischi per fiaschi** to get hold of the wrong end of the stick.

fischione [fis'kjone] SM (*Zool*) wigeon.

fisco ['fisko] SM tax authorities pl; (*Amm*) ≈ Inland Revenue (*Brit*), ≈ Internal Revenue (Service) (*Am*); (*fam*): **il fisco** the taxman.

fisica ['fizika] SF physics *sg*.

fisicamente [fizika'mente] AVV physically; **sono fisicamente impossibilitato a venire** it's physically impossible for me to come.

fisico, a, ci, che ['fiziko] **1** AGG (*gen*) physical. **2** SM (*corpo*) physique; **avere un bel fisico** (*donna*) to have a good figure; (*uomo*) to have a good physique; **hai il fisico dell'atleta** you have an athletic physique *o* the physique of an athlete. **3** SM/F (*studioso*) physicist.

fisima ['fizima] SF fixation.

fisiologia [fizjolo'dʒia] SF physiology.

fisiologicamente [fizjolodʒika'mente] AVV physiologically.

fisiologico, a, ci, che [fizjo'lɔdʒiko] AGG physiological.

fisiologo, a, gi, ghe [fi'zjɔlogo] SM/F physiologist.

fisionomia [fizjono'mia] SF physiognomy; **non ricordo bene la sua fisionomia** I don't remember his face very well.

fisionomista, i, e [fizjono'mista] SM/F: **sei un buon fisionomista** you have a good memory for faces.

fisioterapia [fizjotera'pia] SF physiotherapy.

fisioterapico, a, ci, che [fizjote'rapiko] AGG physiotherapy *attr*.

fisioterapista, i, e [fizjotera'pista] SM/F physiotherapist.

fissaggio, gi [fis'saddʒo] SM (*Fot*) fixing; **bisogna aspettare 2 ore per il fissaggio di questa vernice** you must wait 2 hours for this paint to dry.

fissamente [fissa'mente] AVV: **guardare qn/qc fissamente** to stare at sb/sth.

fissante [fis'sante] AGG (*spray, lozione*) holding.

fissare [fis'sare] **1** VT **a** (*attaccare*): **fissare (a *o* su)** to fix (to), fasten (to); **fissare (su)** (*sguardo*) to fix (on), fasten (on); **fissare qn/qc** (*guardare*) to stare at sb/sth; **fissare qc in mente** to fix sth firmly in one's mind **b** (*prezzo, data, condizioni*) to fix, set; (*regola*) to lay down; (*appuntamento*) to arrange, fix; **all'ora fissata** at the agreed time; **è tutto fissato** it's all fixed *o* arranged **c** (*prenotare*) to book, reserve **d** (*Fot, Chim*) to fix. **2** **fissarsi** VIP **a**: **fissarsi di fare qc** (*mettersi in testa di*) to set one's heart on doing sth; (*ostinarsi*) to insist on doing sth; **si è fissato di partire con noi** he has set his heart on coming with us; **si è fissato che vuole vederlo subito** he insists on seeing him at once **b** (*concentrarsi*): **l'attenzione del pubblico si fissò su di lui** everybody was staring at him **c** (*uso reciproco*) to stare at each other.

fissativo, a [fissa'tivo] AGG, SM fixative.

fissato, a [fis'sato] **1** AGG (*gen*) fixed; (*ora*) set, agreed; (*prezzo*) agreed; **essere fissato con qc** to have a thing about sth. **2** SM/F person with an obsession; **ma quello è un fissato!** he is obsessed!

fissatore [fissa'tore] SM (*Chim*) fixative; (*Fot*) fixer; (*per capelli*) setting lotion.

fissazione [fissat'tsjone] SF (*Psic*) obsession, fixation.

fissione [fis'sjone] SF fission.

fissità [fissi'ta] SF INV (*di sguardo*) steadiness; (*di principi*) firmness.

fisso, a ['fisso] **1** AGG (*gen*) fixed; (*lavoro, lavoratore*) permanent; (*stipendio*) regular; (*presenza*) constant; (*immagine, elemento*) recurring; **avere un ragazzo fisso** to have a steady boyfriend; **senza fissa dimora** of no

fixed abode.
2 SM (*compenso*) fixed sum.
3 AVV: **guardar fisso** (qn/qc) to stare (at sb/sth).
fistola ['fistola] SF (*Med*) fistula.
fitotermalismo [fitoterma'lizmo] SM herbal hydro-
therapy.
fitta ['fitta] SF sharp pain; **una fitta di dolore** a sharp
twinge of pain; **una fitta al cuore** (*fig*) a pang of grief.
fittamente [fitta'mente] AVV (*intrecciato, tessuto*) thickly;
(*in modo denso*) densely; **parlare fittamente** to be deep
in conversation.
fittavolo [fit'tavolo] SM tenant.
fittiziamente [fittittsja'mente] AVV fictitiously.
fittizio, zia, zi, zie [fit'tittsjo] AGG (*nome, personaggio*)
fictitious, imaginary.
fitto[1], a ['fitto] **1** AGG **a** (*bosco, pelo*) thick; (*nebbia*) thick,
dense; (*tessuto*) closely-woven; (*pettine*) fine; (*mistero*)
impenetrable; **è buio fitto** it's pitch dark
b (*intenso: fuoco d'artiglieria, pioggia*) heavy; **una giornata fitta di eventi** an eventful day.
2 AVV (*nevicare, piovere*) hard; **parlare fitto fitto** to be
deep in conversation; **scritto fitto fitto** closely written.
3 SM: **nel fitto del bosco** in the heart *o* depths of the
wood.
fitto[2] ['fitto] SM (*affitto*) rent; **blocco dei fitti** rents freeze.
fiumana [fju'mana] SF (*fiume in piena*) torrent; (*fig: di gente*)
flood, stream.
fiumara [fju'mara] SF torrent.
fiume ['fjume] **1** SM river; (*fig: di gente, parole*) stream;
scorrere a fiumi (*vino, sangue*) to flow in torrents;
sgorgare a fiumi (da) (*acqua, sangue*) to pour out (from);
versare fiumi di inchiostro su qc to write reams about
sth.
2 AGG INV: **romanzo fiume** roman-fleuve; **processo fiume**
long-drawn-out *o* long-running trial.
fiutare [fju'tare] VT **a** (*annusare*) to smell, sniff; (*sogg:
cane da caccia*) to scent; **fiutare tabacco** to take snuff;
fiutare cocaina to snort cocaine **b** (*intuire*): **fiutare un
pericolo** to smell danger; **fiutare un buon affare** to sniff
out a bargain; **fiutare qc di losco** to smell a rat.
fiuto ['fjuto] SM (*odorato*) sense of smell; (*fig: intuito*) nose;
avere fiuto nel fare qc to have a flair for doing sth.
flaccido, a ['flattʃido] AGG flabby.
flacone [fla'kone] SM (*di profumo ecc*) bottle.
flagellare [fladʒel'lare] **1** VT to flog, scourge; (*sogg: onde*)
to beat against.
2 flagellarsi VR to whip o.s.
flagellazione [fladʒellat'tsjone] SF flogging, scourging.
flagello [fla'dʒɛllo] SM **a** (*frusta, fig*) scourge **b** (*Bio*)
flagellum.
flagrante [fla'grante] AGG: **cogliere qn in flagrante** to catch
sb red-handed *o* in the act; **essere in flagrante contraddizione** (*evidente*) to be in blatant contradiction.
flamenco [fla'menko] SM flamenco.
flan [flɑ̃] SM INV (*Culin*) mould (*Brit*), mold (*Am*).
flanella [fla'nɛlla] SF flannel.
flangia, ge ['flandʒa] SF (*Tecn*) flange.
flash [flæʃ] SM INV **a** (*Fot, Elettr*) flash **b** (*Radio, TV*)
newsflash.
flashback ['flæʃbæk] SM INV (*Cine*): **flashback (su *o* di)**
flashback (to).
flatting ['flætiŋ] SM INV clear varnish.
flautista, i, e [flau'tista] SM/F flautist.
flauto ['flauto] SM: **flauto (traverso)** flute ▶**flauto dolce**

recorder.
flebile ['flɛbile] AGG feeble, faint.
flebilmente [flebil'mente] AVV faintly.
flebite [fle'bite] SF phlebitis.
flebo ['flɛbo] ABBR F INV = **fleboclisi**.
fleboclisi [flebo'klizi] SF INV (*Med*) drip.
flemma ['flɛmma] SF (*calma*) composure, coolness;
rispose con molta flemma he answered very coolly.
flemmaticamente [flemmatika'mente] AVV phlegmati-
cally.
flemmatico, a, ci, che [flem'matiko] AGG cool.
flessibile [fles'sibile] **1** AGG (*materiale*) flexible, pliable;
(*fig: carattere*) flexible, adaptable; **orario flessibile** flexitime.
2 SM flex.
flessibilità [flessibili'ta] SF INV flexibility.
flessione [fles'sjone] SF **a** (*gen*) bending; (*Ginnastica: a
terra*) sit-up; (: *in piedi*) forward bend; (: *sulle gambe*)
knee-bend; (: *sulle braccia*) press-up; **fare una flessione**
to bend **b** (*diminuzione*) slight drop *o* fall, blip; **una
flessione economica** a downward trend in the economy
c (*Ling*) inflection.
flesso, a ['flɛsso] PP di **flettere**.
flessuosamente [flessuosa'mente] AVV gracefully.
flessuosità [flessuosi'ta] SF INV (*vedi agg*) suppleness;
grace(fulness).
flessuoso, a [flessu'oso] AGG (*elastico*) supple, lithe;
(*armonico: corpo femminile*) graceful; (: *movimenti*)
flowing, graceful.
flettere ['flɛttere] VB IRREG **1** VT **a** (*gen*) to bend; **flettere il
busto in avanti** to bend forward from the waist **b** (*Ling*)
to inflect.
2 flettersi VR to bend.
flipper ['flipper] SM INV pinball machine.
flirt [fləːt] SM INV brief romance, flirtation.
flirtare [flir'tare] VI (*aus avere*) to flirt.
F.lli ABBR (= *fratelli*) Bros.
floema, i [flo'ɛma] SM (*Bot*) phloem.
flora ['flora] SF flora.
floreale [flore'ale] AGG floral; **una lampada in stile floreale**
an Art Nouveau lamp.
floricoltore, trice [florikol'tore] SM/F flower grower.
floricoltura [florikol'tura] SF flower-growing, floricul-
ture.
floridamente [florida'mente] AVV flourishingly; (*svilupparsi*) greatly.
floridezza [flori'dettsa] SF (*di economia, industria*) flourishing state, prosperity; (*di persona*) glowing health.
florido, a ['florido] AGG (*industria*) flourishing, thriving,
prosperous; (*aspetto*) healthy, glowing with health;
(*salute*) excellent.
flosciamente [floʃʃa'mente] AVV (*vedi agg*) floppily; flab-
bily.
floscio, scia, sci, sce ['floʃʃo] AGG (*cappello, tessuto*) soft,
floppy; (*muscoli, carni*) flabby.
flotta ['flotta] SF fleet; **flotta aerea** fleet of aircraft.
flottante [flot'tante] SM (*Borsa*): **titoli a largo flottante**
blue chips.
flou [flu] AGG INV **a** (*Fot, Cine: sfumato*) blurred **b** (*abito*)
flowing, loose(-fitting).
fluente [flu'ɛnte] AGG (*fig: chioma, barba*) flowing; (:
discorso) fluent.
fluidificante [fluidifi'kante] AGG **a**: **sostanza fluidificante**
fluidizer **b** (*Calcio*): **terzino fluidificante** attacking full-

back.

fluidificare [fluidifi'kare] vt to fluidify, fluidize; **fluidificare il traffico** (*fig*) to improve the flow of traffic.

fluidità [fluidi'ta] sf inv (*gen*) fluidity; (*fig: di stile*) fluency.

fluido, a ['fluido] 1 agg (*gen*) fluid.
2 sm fluid; (*forza magica*) mysterious power.

fluire [flu'ire] vi (*aus essere*) to flow.

fluorescente [fluoreʃ'ɛnte] agg fluorescent.

fluorescenza [fluoreʃ'ʃɛntsa] sf fluorescence.

fluoro [flu'ɔro] sm fluorine.

fluoruro [fluo'ruro] sm fluoride.

flusso ['flusso] sm (*gen, fig*) flow; (*Fis, Elettr*) flux; **flusso e riflusso** ebb and flow ► **flusso di cassa** (*Comm*) cash flow.

flutto ['flutto] sm (*letter: onda*) billow; **tra i flutti** among the waves.

fluttuante [fluttu'ante] agg (*Econ: moneta, prezzi*) fluctuating; **debito fluttuante** floating debt.

fluttuare [fluttu'are] vi (*aus avere*) a (*ondeggiare: mare*) to rise and fall; (: *barca*) to toss, rock; (: *bandiera*) to flutter b (*Econ: moneta*) to fluctuate.

fluttuazione [fluttuat'tsjone] sf (*Econ, Fis, fig*) fluctuation.

fluviale [flu'vjale] agg river *attr*; **pesca fluviale** freshwater fishing; **navigazione fluviale** river o inland navigation.

FM abbr (= *modulazione di frequenza*) FM (= *frequency modulation*).

F.M.E. ['effe'ɛmme'e] sigla m (= *Fondo Monetario Europeo*) EMF (= *European Monetary Fund*).

F.M.I. ['effe'ɛmme'i] sigla m (= *Fondo Monetario Internazionale*) IMF (= *International Monetary Fund*).

FO sigla = *Forlì*.

fobia [fo'bia] sf (*Med*) phobia; **ha la fobia dei ragni** he has a phobia about spiders.

foca, che ['fɔka] sf (*Zool*) seal.

focaccia, ce [fo'kattʃa] sf (*Culin*) *kind of pizza*; (: *dolce*) bun; **rendere pan per focaccia** to get one's own back, give tit for tat.

focaia [fo'kaja] agg f: **pietra focaia** flint.

focale [fo'kale] agg focal.

focalizzare [fokalid'dzare] vt (*Fot: immagine*) to get into focus; **focalizzare la situazione** to get the situation into perspective; **focalizzare l'attenzione su** to focus one's attention on.

foce ['fotʃe] sf (*Geog*) mouth.

focena [fo'tʃɛna] sf porpoise.

focolaio, ai [foko'lajo] sm (*Med*) centre (*Brit*) o center (*Am*) of infection, focus; (*fig*) hotbed, breeding ground; **il focolaio della rivolta** the breeding ground of the rebellion.

focolare [foko'lare] sm hearth, fireside; (*Tecn*) furnace; **ritornare al focolare domestico** to return to hearth and home.

focomelico, a, ci, che [foko'mɛliko] agg, sm/f (*Med*) phocomelic.

focosamente [fokosa'mente] avv passionately.

focoso, a [fo'koso] agg fiery; (*cavallo*) mettlesome, fiery.

fodera ['fɔdera] sf (*interna: di vestito*) lining; (*di libro*) dust jacket; (*di divano, poltrona*) cover.

foderare [fode'rare] vt (*vestito*) to line; (*Culin*) to line (with pastry; (*libro*) to cover.

fodero ['fɔdero] sm (*di spada*) scabbard; (*di pugnale*) sheath; (*di pistola*) holster.

foga ['fɔga] sf enthusiasm, ardour (*Brit*), ardor (*Am*); **nella foga della passione/discussione** in the heat of passion/

the discussion; **lavora con foga** he throws himself into his work (with great enthusiasm); **si precipitò con foga ad aprire** he rushed excitedly to the door.

foggia, ge ['fɔddʒa] sf (*forma*) shape, form; (*moda*) style, fashion; **un abito di foggia strana** an odd looking suit/dress; **alla foggia degli anni venti** twenties style.

foggiare [fod'dʒare] vt to fashion; (*carattere*) to form.

foglia ['fɔʎʎa] sf (*Bot, di metallo*) leaf; **gli alberi stanno mettendo le foglie** the trees are coming into leaf; **ha mangiato la foglia** (*fig*) he's caught on; **tremare come una foglia** (*fig*) to shake like a leaf; **foglia d'argento/oro** silver/gold leaf; **foglia di fico** fig leaf.

fogliame [foʎ'ʎame] sm foliage, leaves *pl*.

foglietto [foʎ'ʎetto] sm a (*piccolo foglio*) slip o piece of paper; (*manifestino*) leaflet, handout b (*Anat*): **foglietto pleurico** pleural layer.

foglio, gli ['fɔʎʎo] sm a (*gen, di metallo*) sheet; (*di libro*) page, leaf; **foglio rigato** o **a righe** sheet of lined o ruled paper; **foglio a quadretti** sheet of squared paper; **foglio protocollo** foolscap; **foglio volante** leaflet
b ► **foglio rosa** (*Aut: documento*) ≈ provisional driving licence ► **foglio di via** (*Dir*) expulsion order
c (*banconota*) (bank)note
d (*Tip*): **in foglio** folio *attr*.

fogliolina [foʎʎo'lina] sf leaflet.

foglioso, a [foʎ'ʎoso] agg leafy.

fogna ['fɔɲɲa] sf sewer; (*fig: luogo sporco*) pigsty; **topo di fogna** sewer rat; **sei una fogna!** (*fig fam: ghiottone*) you're a greedy pig!

fognatura [foɲɲa'tura] sf sewerage.

föhn [føːn] sm inv hair-dryer.

folaga, ghe ['fɔlaga] sf coot.

folata [fo'lata] sf gust; **il tuo arrivo ha portato una folata di novità** your arrival was like a breath of fresh air.

folclore [fol'klore] sm folklore.

folcloristico, a, ci, che [folklo'ristiko] agg (*spettacolo, canzone*) folk *attr*; (*scherz: bizzarro*) wierd, freakish; **costume folcloristico** traditional dress.

folgorante [folgo'rante] agg (*luce*) dazzling; (*fig: sguardo*) withering; (: *passione*) violent; (: *dolore, male*) sudden.

folgorare [folgo'rare] 1 vt (*sogg: fulmine*) to strike (down); (: *alta tensione*) to electrocute; **mi folgorò con uno sguardo** (*fig*) he gave me a withering look.
2 vi (*aus avere*) (*rilucere*) to flash.

folgorazione [folgorat'tsjone] sf electrocution; **ebbe una folgorazione** (*fig: idea*) he had a brainwave.

folgore ['folgore] sf thunderbolt.

folk ['fouk] 1 agg (*cantante*) folk *attr*; (*abito*) peasant *attr*.
2 sm (*Mus*) folk; (*moda*) peasant look.

folla ['folla] sf (*di persone*) crowd, throng; (: *pegg*) mob; **una folla di idee** a multitude o host of ideas.

folle ['folle] 1 agg a (*anche fig: idee, trovata*) mad, insane; **a ritmo** o **velocità folle** at breakneck speed b (*Tecn: ingranaggio*) idle.
2 sm/f madman/madwoman.
3 sf (*Aut*): **in folle** in neutral.

folleggiare [folled'dʒare] vi (*aus avere*) (*divertirsi*) to paint the town red.

follemente [folle'mente] avv madly.

folletto [fol'letto] sm elf.

follia [fol'lia] sf (*pazzia*) madness; (*atto*) act of madness o folly; **fare una follia** (*fig*) to do sth mad o crazy; **è stata una follia fare ciò che ha fatto** it was madness o folly to do what he did; **costare una follia** to cost the earth;

amare qn alla follia to love sb to distraction; che follia! what folly!, what madness!

follicolo [fol'likolo] SM follicle.

folto, a ['folto] [1] AGG (capelli, pelo, bosco) thick; (schiera) dense.
[2] SM: **nel folto della mischia** in the thick of the fray.

fomentare [fomen'tare] VT to stir up, foment (frm).

fomentatore, trice [fomenta'tore] SM/F agitator.

fomento [fo'mento] SM **a** (letter: stimolo): **dare fomento a** to stir up, foment **b** (Med) poultice.

fon [fɔn] SM INV = föhn.

fonda ['fonda] SF (Naut): **alla fonda** at anchor.

fondale [fon'dale] SM **a** (del mare) bottom; **il fondale marino** the sea bed **b** (Teatro) backdrop.

fondamentale [fondamen'tale] AGG fundamental, basic; **è fondamentale che...** it's of prime importance that ... .

fondamentalismo [fondamenta'lizmo] SM (Rel) fundamentalism.

fondamentalista, i, e [fondamenta'lista] AGG, SM/F (Rel) fundamentalist.

fondamentalmente [fondamental'mente] AVV fundamentally, basically.

fondamento [fonda'mento] SM **a** foundation, basis; **i fondamenti della matematica** the principles of mathematics **b** : **fondamenta** SFPL (Edil) foundations; **gettare le fondamenta** (anche fig) to lay the foundations.

fondant [fɔ'dã] SM fondant.

fondare [fon'dare] [1] VT (istituzione, città) to found; (fig: teoria, sospetti) to base.
[2] **fondarsi** VIP: **fondarsi (su)** (teorie) to be based (on).

fondatamente [fondata'mente] AVV with good reason.

fondatezza [fonda'tettsa] SF (di ragioni) soundness; (di dubbio, sospetto) basis in fact.

fondato, a [fon'dato] AGG (sospetto) well-founded, valid; (ragione) valid, sound.

fondatore, trice [fonda'tore] SM/F founder.

fondazione [fondat'tsjone] SF foundation.

fondello [fon'dɛllo] SM (fig fam): **prendere qn per i fondelli** to pull sb's leg.

fondente [fon'dɛnte] SM (Metallurgia) flux.

fondere ['fondere] VB IRREG [1] VT **a** (gen) to melt; (metallo) to fuse, melt; (fig: colori) to blend, merge; (: enti, classi, Inform) to merge **b** (statua, campana) to cast.
[2] VI (aus avere) to melt; **mi fonde il cervello** (fig) I can't think straight any more, my brain has seized up.
[3] **fondersi** VR (uso reciproco: unirsi: correnti, enti) to merge, unite.
[4] **fondersi** VIP (sciogliersi) to melt.

fonderia [fonde'ria] SF foundry.

fondiario, ria, ri, rie [fon'djarjo] AGG land attr; **possidente fondiario** landowner.

fondina [fon'dina] SF **a** (portapistola) holster **b** (piatto fondo) soup plate.

fondista, i, e [fon'dista] SM/F (long-)distance runner; (sciatore) cross-country skier, langlauf skier.

fondo[1], a ['fondo] [1] AGG deep; **piatto fondo** soup plate; **a notte fonda** at dead of night; **una buca fonda 3 metri** a hole 3 metres deep.
[2] SM **a** (di recipiente, vallata, pozzo) bottom; (dei pantaloni) seat; (di mare, fiume) bottom, bed; **fondo marino** sea floor; **fondo stradale** road surface; **doppio fondo** false bottom; **andare o colare a fondo** (nave) to go to the bottom, sink; **dar fondo (all'ancora)** (Naut) to drop

anchor; **in fondo alla pagina** at the bottom of the page; **in fondo al vicolo** at the end of the alley; **laggiù in fondo** (lontano) over there; (in profondità) down there; **nel fondo del bosco** in the depths o heart of the wood; **nel fondo del suo cuore** deep down, in his (o her) heart of hearts

b : **fondi** SMPL (di vino, aceto) dregs; (di vino, birra) lees; (di caffè) grounds; (di tè) leaves ▶**fondi di magazzino** old o unsold stock sg

c (sfondo) background; (Araldica) ground

d (Sport): **di fondo** long-distance; **sci di fondo** cross-country o langlauf skiing; **linea di fondo** (Tennis) baseline; (Calcio) bye-line; **prova di fondo** (Equitazione) speed and endurance (test)

e (Giornalismo): **articolo di fondo** editorial

f (fraseologia): **conoscere a fondo** (persona) to know through and through; (argomento, materia) to have a thorough knowledge of, know inside out; **studiare a fondo qc** to study sth thoroughly o in depth; **andare in fondo a/fino in fondo** (fig) to examine thoroughly; **dar fondo a qc** (risorse) to use up, consume; **senza fondo** (risorse) infinite, inexhaustible; (pozzo) bottomless; **in fondo** after all, all things considered; **in fondo in fondo** actually; **in fondo in fondo avevi ragione** in fact you were right; **toccare il fondo** (fig) to plumb the depths.

fondo[2] ['fondo] SM **a** (riserva) fund; **a fondo perduto** unsecured, without security ▶**fondo (comune) d'investimento** investment trust ▶**fondo (di) cassa** cash in hand; (per piccole spese) petty cash ▶**Fondo Monetario Europeo** European Monetary Fund ▶**Fondo Monetario Internazionale** International Monetary Fund ▶**fondo di previdenza** social insurance fund ▶**fondo di riserva** reserve fund

b : **fondi** SMPL funds; (capitale): **fondi pubblici/segreti** public/secret funds ▶**fondi d'esercizio** working capital sg ▶**fondi neri** slush fund sg

c (bene immobile) land, property, estate; **fondo rustico** country estate; **fondo urbano** town property.

fondotinta [fondo'tinta] SM INV (cosmetico) foundation.

fondovalle [fondo'valle] SM (pl fondivalle) valley bottom.

fonduta [fon'duta] SF (Culin) fondue.

fonema [fo'nɛma] SM phoneme.

fonetica [fo'nɛtika] SF phonetics sg.

foneticamente [fonetika'mente] AVV phonetically.

fonetico, a, ci, che [fo'nɛtiko] AGG phonetic.

fonico, a, ci, che ['fɔniko] [1] AGG phonic; **accento fonico** stress.
[2] SM (tecnico del suono) sound technician.

fonoassorbente [fonoassor'bɛnte] AGG sound-absorbent.

fonografo [fo'nɔgrafo] SM gramophone, phonograph (Am).

fonologia [fonolo'dʒia] SF phonology.

fonologico, a, ci, che [fono'lɔdʒiko] AGG phonological.

fontana [fon'tana] SF fountain; **piangere come una fontana** to weep (great) buckets of tears; **fare la fontana** (Culin) to make a well.

fontanella [fonta'nɛlla] SF **a** (fontana) drinking fountain **b** (Anat) fontanelle.

fonte ['fonte] [1] SF (sorgente) spring; (fig: di calore, informazioni) source; **risalire alle fonti** to go back to the origins o roots.
[2] SM: **fonte battesimale** (Rel) font.

fontina [fon'tina] SF *full fat, hard, sweet cheese from Valle d'Aosta.*

footing ['futiŋ] SM jogging; **fare footing** to jog.

foraggiare [forad'dʒare] VT (*cavalli*) to fodder; (*fig fam*: *sovvenzionare*) to bankroll; (: *illegalmente*) to bribe.

foraggio, gi [fo'raddʒo] SM fodder, forage.

foraneo, a [fo'raneo] AGG: **diga foranea** breakwater.

forapaglie [fora'paʎʎe] SM INV (*Zool*) sedge warbler.

forare [fo'rare] ①① VT (*gen*) to make a hole in, pierce; (*biglietto*) to punch; (*pneumatico*) to puncture; (*pallone*) to burst; **forare una gomma** to burst a tyre (*Brit*) o tire (*Am*).
②② VI (*aus avere*) (*Aut*) to have a puncture.
③③ **forarsi** VIP (*gen*) to develop a hole; (*Aut*, *pallone*, *timpano*) to burst.

foratura [fora'tura] SF (*vedi vb*) piercing; punching; puncturing, puncture; bursting.

forbice ['fɔrbitʃe] SF, SPEC PL scissors *pl*; **un paio di forbici** a pair of scissors; **dare un colpo di forbici a qc** to snip sth; **forbici da giardiniere** (gardening) shears; **forbici per potare** secateurs.

forbicina [forbi'tʃina] SF (*Zool*) earwig.

forbitamente [forbita'mente] AVV (*parlare*) in a refined way.

forbito, a [for'bito] AGG (*stile, modi*) polished; **parla una lingua forbita** he has an elegant turn of phrase.

forca, che ['forka] SF ⓐ (*Agr*) (pitch)fork ⓑ (*per impiccagione*) gallows *sg o pl*.

forcella [for'tʃɛlla] SF (*gen, Tecn*) fork; (*per capelli*) hairpin; (*di volatile*) wishbone; (*di monte*) pass.

forchetta [for'ketta] SF fork; **essere una buona forchetta** to enjoy one's food, be a big eater.

forchettata [forket'tata] AVV (*gen*) forkful; **ne prendo solo una forchettata** I'll just have a little.

forchettone [forket'tone] SM (*Culin*) carving fork.

forcina [for'tʃina] SF hairpin.

forcipe ['fɔrtʃipe] SM forceps *pl*.

forcone [for'kone] SM pitchfork.

forcuto, a [for'kuto] AGG forked.

forense [fo'rɛnse] AGG (*linguaggio*) legal; **avvocato forense** barrister (*Brit*), lawyer.

foresta [fo'rɛsta] SF (*anche fig*) forest; **foresta pluviale** rain forest.

forestale [fores'tale] AGG forest *attr*; **guardia forestale** forester, (forest) ranger.

foresteria [foreste'ria] SF (*di convento, palazzo*) guest rooms *pl*, guest quarters *pl*.

forestiero, a [fores'tjɛro] ①① SM/F stranger; (*dall'estero*) foreigner.
②② AGG foreign.

forfait [for'fɛ] SM INV ⓐ : (*prezzo a*) **forfait** fixed o set price; **le diamo un forfait per il suo lavoro** we'll give you a lump sum for your work; **a forfait** on a lump-sum basis ⓑ : **dichiarare forfait** (*Sport*) to withdraw; (*fig*) to give up.

forfetario, ria, ri, rie [forfe'tarjo], **forfettario, ria, ri, rie** [forfet'tarjo] AGG: **prezzo forfetario** fixed o set price; **somma forfetaria** lump sum.

forfora ['forfora] SF dandruff.

forgiare [for'dʒare] VT to forge; (*fig: carattere*) to mould, form.

foriero, a [fo'rjɛro] AGG (*poet*): **essere foriero di** to herald.

forma ['forma] SF ⓐ (*gen, Gramm, Filosofia*) form; (*contorno*) form, shape; **di forma quadrata** square; a

forma di cuore heart-shaped; **senza forma** (*oggetto*) shapeless; (*pensiero*) unformed; **prendere forma** (*delinearsi*) to take shape; **prendere una medicina in** o **sotto forma di compresse** to take a medicine in tablet form; **in forma ufficiale/privata** officially/privately; **forma mentale** o **mentis** way of thinking; **non c'è alcuna forma di vita sulla luna** there is no form of life on the moon
ⓑ (*stampo*) mould (*Brit*), mold (*Am*); (*per scarpe*) last; **una forma di formaggio** a (whole) cheese
ⓒ (*modo di esprimersi*) form; **errori di forma** stylistic errors
ⓓ (*anche*: **forma fisica**) form; **essere/non essere in forma** (*atleta, squadra*) to be on/off form; (*persona*) to be in/out of shape; **tenersi in forma** to keep fit o in shape
ⓔ (*apparenze*) appearances *pl*; **tenere alla forma** to care about appearances
ⓕ : **forme** SFPL (*del corpo*) figure, shape.

formaggiera [formad'dʒɛra] SF cheese bowl (*for grated Parmesan*).

formaggino [formad'dʒino] SM processed cheese; **un formaggino** a portion of processed cheese.

formaggio, gi [for'maddʒo] SM cheese.

formaldeide [formal'dɛide] SF (*Chim*) formaldehyde.

formale [for'male] AGG formal.

formalina [forma'lina] SF (*Chim*) formalin.

formalismo [forma'lizmo] SM (*Arte, Filosofia*) formalism.

formalista, i, e [forma'lista] AGG, SM/F formalist.

formalistico, a, ci, che [forma'listiko] AGG formalistic.

formalità [formali'ta] SF INV formality; **senza tante formalità** (*pasto*) informal.

formalizzare [formalid'dzare] ①① VT to formalize.
②② **formalizzarsi** VIP (*farsi scrupoli sulla forma*) to stand on ceremony; (*scandalizzarsi*) to be easily shocked.

formalizzazione [formaliddzat'tsjone] SF formalization.

formalmente [formal'mente] AVV formally.

formare [for'mare] ①① VT ⓐ (*gen*) to form, shape, make; (*numero telefonico*) to dial; **questi pezzi formano una croce** these pieces make o form a cross; **l'appartamento è formato da 3 stanze** the flat comprises 3 rooms; **formare una famiglia** to (get married and) start a family
ⓑ (*educare: soldati, attori*) to train; (*carattere*) to form, mould (*Brit*), mold (*Am*).
②② **formarsi** VIP ⓐ to form, take shape; **il treno si forma a Milano** the train starts from Milan
ⓑ (*educarsi*) to be educated; **Leopardi si formò sui classici greci** Leopardi had a classical Greek background.

formativo, a [forma'tivo] AGG formative.

formato, a [for'mato] ①① AGG (*maturo*) fully-developed, fully-grown.
②② SM (*dimensioni*) size, format; (*Inform*) format; **foto formato tessera** passport-size photo; **formato famiglia** family size.

formattare [format'tare] VT (*Inform*) to format.

formattazione [formattat'tsjone] SF (*Inform*) formatting.

formazione [format'tsjone] SF ⓐ (*gen, Mil, Sport*) formation; (*educazione*) education; (*addestramento*) training ▸**formazione professionale** vocational training.

formella [for'mɛlla] SF tile.

formica[1], che [for'mika] SF (*Zool*) ant.

formica[2]* ['formika] SF Formica ®.

formicaio, ai [formi'kajo] SM (*sporgente*) anthill; (*sotterra-*

neo) ants' nest; **quella spiaggia è un formicaio** (*fig*) that beach is always swarming with people.

formichiere [formi'kjɛre] SM anteater.

formicolare [formiko'lare] VI (*aus* **avere** *nel significato* **a**, **essere** *nel significato* **b**) **a** (*anche fig*: *brulicare*): **formicolare di** to swarm with, be crawling *o* swarming with **b** : **mi formicola un braccio** I've got pins and needles in my arm.

formicolio, lii [formiko'lio] SM (*brulichio*) swarming; (*prurito*) tingling; **sento un formicolio al braccio** I've got pins and needles in my arm.

formidabile [formi'dabile] AGG (*temibile*) formidable; (*meraviglioso*) amazing, tremendous, fantastic; (*straordinario*) remarkable; **ho una fame formidabile** I'm incredibly hungry.

formidabilmente [formidabil'mente] AVV terribly, incredibly.

formoso, a [for'moso] AGG shapely.

formula ['fɔrmula] SF (*gen*, *Chim*, *Mat*) formula; **formula di struttura** (*Chim*) structural formula; **formula di cortesia** (*nelle lettere*) set phrase; **formula pubblicitaria** advertising slogan ▶**formula 1** (*Sport*) formula 1.

formulare [formu'lare] VT (*giudizio*, *pensiero*) to formulate.

formulario, ri [formu'larjo] SM (*modulo*) form.

formulazione [formulat'tsjone] SF formulation; **è un pensiero di difficile formulazione verbale** it's a difficult concept to put into words.

fornace [for'natʃe] SF (*Tecn*) kiln.

fornaio, ai [for'najo] SM baker; **dal fornaio** at the baker's.

fornello [for'nɛllo] SM **a** (*cuocivivande*: *a spirito*, *petrolio*) stove; (: *elettrico*) hotplate; (: *a gas*) ring **b** (*di pipa*) bowl.

fornicare [forni'kare] VI (*aus* **avere**) to fornicate.

fornicazione [fornikat'tsjone] SF fornication.

fornire [for'nire] ▶①VT **a** (*Comm*): **fornire qc a qn** to supply sth to sb, supply sb with sth

b (*procurare*: *abiti*, *viveri*): **fornire qc a qn, fornire qn di qc** to supply *o* provide sb with sth; **fornire qn di informazioni** to supply *o* provide sb with information, supply *o* provide information to sb.

② **fornirsi** VR: **fornirsi di** (*procurarsi*) to provide o.s. with; **mi fornisco di pane da quel fornaio** I get my bread from that baker; **dobbiamo fornirci di legna per l'inverno** we'll have to stock up with wood for the winter.

fornito, a [for'nito] AGG: **ben fornito** (*negozio*) well-stocked.

fornitore, trice [forni'tore] ① AGG: **ditta fornitrice di...** company supplying ....

② SM/F supplier.

fornitura [forni'tura] SF supply; **forniture per ufficio** office supplies; **negozio** *o* **società di forniture navali** ship's chandler.

forno ['forno] SM (*gen*) oven; (*panetteria*) bakery; (*Industria*) furnace; (*per ceramica*) kiln; **cuocere al forno** (*dolci*, *patate*) to bake; (*carne*, *patate*) to roast; **pasta al forno** oven-baked pasta; **pollo al forno** roast chicken; **fare i forni** (*Med*) to have heat treatment; **questa stanza è un forno!** this room's like an oven! ▶**forno crematorio** cremator, cinerator (*Am*) ▶**forno a microonde** microwave (oven).

foro¹ ['foro] SM (*buco*) hole.

foro² ['foro] SM **a** (*Storia*) forum **b** (*Dir*: *tribunale*) (law) court; (: *autorità competente*): **del caso si occuperà il foro**

di Milano the case will be dealt with by the Milan judiciary; **gli avvocati del foro** ≈ the Bar.

forse ['forse] ① AVV **a** perhaps, maybe; **forse verrà più tardi** he may *o* might come later

b (*circa*) about; **ti devo forse 10.000 lire** I must owe you about 10,000 lire; **mancheranno forse 500.000 lire** we're about 500,000 lire short; **sei forse tu il mio padrone?** so you think you own me, do you?.

② SM: **essere in forse** (*persona*) to be undecided; (*evento*) to be in doubt; **mettere in forse la propria vita** to put one's life in danger.

forsennatamente [forsennata'mente] AVV (*gridare*) like a madman.

forsennato, a [forsen'nato] ① SM/F madman/madwoman, lunatic.

② AGG mad, crazy, insane.

forte¹ ['fɔrte] ① AGG **a** (*gen*, *fig*) strong; (*luce*, *tinta*) strong, bright; (*nevicata*, *pioggia*) heavy; (*voce*, *musica*) loud; (*ceffone*, *colpo*) hard; (*somma*, *aumento*) large, big; (*spesa*) considerable; **ho un forte mal di testa/raffreddore** I have a bad headache/heavy cold; **questo curry è un po' forte** this curry is rather hot; **taglie forti** (*Abbigliamento*) outsize; **usare le maniere forti** to use strong-arm methods *o* tactics; **piatto forte** (*Culin*) main dish; **pezzo forte** pièce de résistance; **dare man forte a qn** to back sb up, support sb; **è forte in matematica** he is good at maths; **essere forte di qc** to be confident of sth; **farsi forte di qc** to make use of sth, avail o.s. of sth; **non voglio piangere ma è più forte di me** I don't want to cry but I can't help it

b (*fam*: *bello*, *bravo*) amazing, great; **che forte!** (*fam*) amazing!, fantastic!.

② AVV (*velocemente*) fast; (*a volume alto*) loud(ly); (*violentemente*) hard; **tenersi forte** to hold tight; **giocare forte** to play for high stakes; **andare forte** (*fam*: *essere bravo*) to be amazing, be fantastic; (: *aver successo*) to be all the rage.

③ SM (*persona*): **il forte e il debole** the strong and the weak; (*punto forte*) strong point, forte.

forte² ['fɔrte] SM (*fortezza*) fort.

fortemente [forte'mente] AVV (*insistere*, *consigliare*) strongly; (*stringere*) hard, tight(ly); **fortemente attratto** strongly attracted; **temo fortemente di essere ammalato** I'm very much afraid I'm ill.

fortezza [for'tettsa] SF (*luogo fortificato*) fortress; (*morale*) strength.

fortificare [fortifi'kare] VT to strengthen, fortify.

fortificazione [fortifikat'tsjone] SF fortification.

fortino [for'tino] SM fort.

Fortran ['fɔ:træn] SIGLA M (*Inform*) Fortran.

fortuitamente [fortuita'mente] AVV by chance, fortuitously.

fortuito, a [for'tuito] AGG chance, fortuitous, chance *attr*; **per un caso fortuito** by pure chance.

fortuna [for'tuna] SF **a** (*destino*) fortune, destiny; (: *favorevole*) luck; **predire la fortuna a qn** to tell sb's future; **la ruota della fortuna** the wheel of fortune; **è girata la fortuna** my (*o* your *ecc*) luck's changed; **tentare la fortuna** to try one's luck; **portare fortuna** to bring luck; **colpo di fortuna** stroke of luck; **per fortuna** luckily, fortunately; **(per) fortuna che sei passato** OR **è una fortuna che tu sia passato** it's lucky that you were passing; **aver fortuna** to be lucky; **avere la fortuna di fare qc** to be lucky enough to do sth; **è tutta fortuna la**

sua he's just lucky; **che fortuna!** what luck!; **buona fortuna!** good luck!

b (*successo, ricchezza*) fortune; **costa una fortuna** it costs a fortune; **fare fortuna** (*persona*) to make one's fortune; (*libro, film ecc*) to be successful; **cercare fortuna** to seek one's fortune

c : **di fortuna** (*riparazione*) makeshift, emergency *attr*; **atterraggio di fortuna** emergency landing; **albero/ timone di fortuna** (*Naut*) jury mast.

fortunale [fortu'nale] SM storm.

fortunatamente [fortunata'mente] AVV luckily, fortunately.

fortunato, a [fortu'nato] AGG lucky, fortunate; (*felice*) happy; (*coronato da successo*) successful; **numero fortunato** lucky number.

fortunoso, a [fortu'noso] AGG (*vita*) eventful; (*avvenimenti, vicende*) unlucky.

foruncolo [fo'runkolo] SM boil.

forviare [forvi'are] **1** VI (*aus* avere) to go astray.
2 VT (*inseguitori, polizia*) to mislead; (*sospetti*) to allay; (*giovani: traviare*) to lead astray.

forza ['fortsa] SF **a** (*vigore*) strength; **perdere/riacquistare le forze** to lose/regain one's strength; **avere forza nelle braccia** to be strong in the arm; **senza forza** o **forze** weak; **bella forza!** (*iro*) how clever of you (*o* him *ecc*)!; **farsi forza** (*coraggio*) to pluck up one's courage; **fatti forza!** chin up!, come on!; **forza!** come on!; **con la forza della disperazione** with the strength born of desperation; **l'unione fa la forza** unity is strength ▸ **forza d'animo** strength of mind ▸ **forza di volontà** willpower

b (*di vento, tempesta*) force; **vento forza 4** force 4 gale
c (*violenza*) force; **ricorrere alla/adoperare la forza** to resort to/use violence; **a viva forza** by force; **forza bruta** brute force

d (*Mil*): **le forze armate** the armed forces; **la forza pubblica** the police *pl*

e (*Dir*): **in forza** in force; **avere forza di legge** to have force of law

f (*Fis, Tecn*) force ▸ **forza di gravità** force of gravity ▸ **forza motrice** motive power

g : **a forza, con la forza** by force; **a forza di rimproveri/di lavorare** by dint of scolding/working; **con forza** (*violentemente*) violently; (*fermamente*) firmly; **per forza** (*ovviamente*) of course; (*contro la sua volontà*) against one's will; **lo devi fare per forza?** have you got to do it?; **l'ha fatto per forza** he had no choice but to do it, he was forced to do it; **per causa di forza maggiore** (*Dir*) by reason of force majeure; (*per estensione*) due to circumstances beyond one's control; **per forza di cose** through force of circumstances

h : **forza lavoro** (*Econ*) workforce
i ▸ **Forza Italia** (*Pol*) moderate right-wing party.

forzare [for'tsare] VT **a** (*costringere*): **forzare qn (a fare qc)** to force sb (to do sth), compel sb (to do sth); **hanno forzato la mia volontà** they forced me to do it

b (*cassaforte, porta*) to force (open); (*serratura*) to force
c (*sforzare: voce*) to strain; **forzare l'andatura** to force the pace; **forzare il significato** (*di parola, testo*) to stretch the meaning; **non voglio forzare la situazione** I don't want to push things.

forzatamente [fortsata'mente] AVV (*con sforzo*): **sorridere/ ridere forzatamente** to force a smile/a laugh.

forzato, a [for'tsato] **1** AGG forced; (*situazione*) artificial;

la mia è stata un'assenza forzata my absence was due to circumstances beyond my control; **fare un sorriso forzato** to force a smile.
2 SM prisoner sentenced to hard labour (*Brit*) o labor (*Am*).

forzatura [fortsa'tura] SF **a** (*di cassaforte*) forcing (open)
b (*di voce*) straining; (*di significato*) stretching; **è una forzatura usare questo termine in quel modo** you're stretching its meaning if you use the word like that.

forziere [for'tsjɛre] SM strongbox; (*di pirati*) treasure chest.

forzista, i, e [for'tsista] (*Pol*) **1** AGG of Forza Italia.
2 SM/F member (*o* supporter) of Forza Italia.

forzuto, a [for'tsuto] AGG (*scherz*) big and strong.

foschia [fos'kia] SF haze, mist; **oggi c'è molta foschia** it's very hazy o misty today.

fosco, a, schi, sche ['fosko] AGG (*colore*) dark; (*cielo*) dull, overcast; (*fig: futuro, pensiero*) dark, gloomy; **dipingere qc a tinte fosche** (*fig*) to paint a gloomy picture of sth.

fosfato [fos'fato] SM (*Chim*) phosphate; **fosfato di sodio** sodium phosphate.

fosforescente [fosfore∫'∫ɛnte] AGG phosphorescent; (*insegna, lancetta dell'orologio*) luminous.

fosforescenza [fosfore∫'∫ɛntsa] SF phosphorescence.

fosforico, a, ci, che [fos'fɔriko] AGG (*Chim*) phosphoric.

fosforo ['fɔsforo] SM (*Chim*) phosphorus.

fossa ['fɔssa] SF **a** pit, hole; (*Oceanografia, Mil*) trench ▸ **fossa biologica** cesspool, cesspit ▸ **fossa tettonica** (*Geol*) rift valley **b** (*tomba*) grave; **essere con un piede nella fossa** to have one foot in the grave ▸ **fossa comune** mass grave **c** (*Anat*) fossa.

fossato [fos'sato] SM ditch; (*di castello*) moat.

fossetta [fos'setta] SF dimple.

fossi *ecc* ['fɔssi] VB vedi **essere**.

fossile ['fɔssile] AGG, SM (*anche fig*) fossil *attr*.

fossilizzare [fossilid'dzare] VT, **fossilizzarsi** VR, VIP (*anche fig*) to fossilize.

fossilizzazione [fossiliddzat'tsjone] SF (*anche fig*) fossilization.

fosso ['fosso] SM ditch; (*di castello*) moat; **saltare il fosso** (*fig*) to take the plunge.

foste ['foste] VB vedi **essere**.

foto ['foto] SF INV, ABBR di **fotografia**; photo, snap; **fare una foto** to take a photo o a snap ▸ **foto ricordo** souvenir photo ▸ **foto tessera** passport (-type) photo.

foto... ['foto] PREF photo... .

fotocellula [foto'tʃɛllula] SF photocell, electric eye, photoelectric cell.

fotochimica [foto'kimika] SF photochemistry.

fotochimico, a, ci, che [foto'kimiko] AGG photochemical.

fotocomporre [fotokom'porre] VT to filmset, photocompose (*Am*).

fotocompositore [fotokompozi'tore] SM filmsetter, photocomposer (*Am*).

fotocomposizione [fotokomposit'tsjone] SF filmsetting, (photo)typesetting, photocomposition (*Am*).

fotocopia [foto'kɔpja] SF photocopy.

fotocopiare [fotoko'pjare] VT to photocopy.

fotocopiatrice [fotokopja'tritʃe] SF photocopier, photocopying machine.

fotocopiatura [fotokopja'tura] SF photocopying.

fotocromatico, a, ci, che [fotokro'matiko] AGG (*lente*) light-sensitive.

fotoelettricità [fotoelettritʃi'ta] SF INV photoelectricity.

fotoelettrico, a, ci, che [fotoe'lɛttriko] AGG photoelectric.

fotogenico, a, ci, che [foto'dʒɛniko] AGG photogenic.

fotografare [fotogra'fare] VT to photograph.

fotografia [fotogra'fia] SF (*arte, procedimento*) photography; (*immagine*) photograph; **fotografia a colori/in bianco e nero** colour/black and white photograph; **fare una fotografia** to take a photograph; **farsi fare una fotografia** to have one's photograph taken.

fotograficamente [fotografika'mente] AVV photographically.

fotografico, a, ci, che [foto'grafiko] AGG photographic; **macchina fotografica** camera; **servizio** *o* **reportage fotografico** photo feature; **studio fotografico** photographer's studio.

fotografo, a [fo'tɔgrafo] SM/F photographer.

fotogramma, i [foto'gramma] SM (*Cine*) frame.

fotoincisione [fotointʃi'zjone] SF photogravure, photoengraving.

fotomodello, a [fotomo'dɛllo] SM/F fashion *o* photographic model.

fotomontaggio, gi [fotomon'taddʒo] SM photomontage.

fotoreporter [fotore'pɔrter] SM/F INV newspaper (*o* magazine) photographer.

fotoromanzo [fotoro'mandzo] SM photo love story.

fotosensibile [fotosen'sibile] AGG photosensitive.

fotosintesi [foto'sintezi] SF (*Bot*) photosynthesis.

fototropismo [fototro'pizmo] SM (*Bot*) phototropism.

fottere ['fottere] VT (*fam!*) a (*avere rapporti sessuali*) to fuck (*fam!*), screw (*fam!*); **vai a farti fottere!** fuck off! (*fam!*) b (*rubare*) to pinch, swipe c (*fregare*): **mi hanno fottuto** they did the dirty on me, they played a dirty trick on me, I've been screwed (*fam*).

fottuto, a [fot'tuto] AGG (*fam!*) bloody, fucking *attr* (*fam!*)

foulard [fu'lar] SM INV (head)scarf.

foyer [fwa'je] SM INV foyer.

FR SIGLA = *Frosinone.*

fr. ABBR (*moneta : = franco*) fr.

fra¹ [fra] PREP = **tra.**

fra² [fra] SM (*dav a nomi propri*) = **frate.**

frac [frak] SM INV (*abito maschile*) tails *pl.*

fracassare [frakas'sare] ☐1☐ VT to smash, shatter.
☐2☐ **fracassarsi** VIP to smash, break, shatter; (*veicolo*) to crash; (*fare a piccoli pezzi*) to smash to smithereens, shatter.

fracasso [fra'kasso] SM (*baccano, confusione*) din; (*di piatti*) crash; **fare fracasso** to make a din.

fradicio, cia, ci, ce ['fraditʃo] AGG soaked, soaking (wet), drenched; **bagnato fradicio** soaking wet; **ubriaco fradicio** blind drunk.

fragile ['fradʒile] AGG (*gen, fig*) fragile; (*salute, nervi*) delicate; (*vetro*) brittle; **"fragile"** (*sui pacchi*) "fragile, (handle) with care".

fragilità [fradʒili'ta] SF INV (*vedi agg*) fragility; delicacy; brittleness.

fragola ['fragola] SF strawberry.

fragore [fra'gore] SM (*di cascate, carro armato*) roar; (*di tuono*) rumble.

fragorosamente [fragorosa'mente] AVV (*ridere*) uproariously; (*scoppiare*) deafeningly.

fragoroso, a [frago'roso] AGG deafening, ear-splitting; **un fragoroso ceffone** a resounding slap; **una risata fragorosa** an uproarious burst of laughter; **scoppiare in una**

risata fragorosa to roar with laughter.

fragrante [fra'grante] AGG fragrant.

fragranza [fra'grantsa] SF fragrance.

fraintendere [frain'tɛndere] VT IRREG to misunderstand.

fraintendimento [fraintendi'mento] SM misunderstanding.

frainteso, a [frain'teso] PP di **fraintendere.**

frammentariamente [frammentarja'mente] AVV in a fragmented fashion.

frammentarietà [frammentarje'ta] SF INV fragmentary nature.

frammentario, ria, ri, rie [frammen'tarjo] AGG sketchy, fragmentary; **le notizie giungono frammentarie** as yet we don't have a complete picture of events.

frammento [fram'mento] SM (*di roccia*) fragment, bit; (*di testo*) passage, extract.

frammesso, a [fram'messo] PP di **frammettere.**

frammettere [fram'mettere] VB IRREG ☐1☐ VT to interpose.
☐2☐ **frammettersi** VR to intervene, interfere.

frammezzo [fram'meddzo] ☐1☐ AVV in between.
☐2☐: **frammezzo a** PREP among.

frammischiare [frammis'kjare] VT: **frammischiare (a)** to mix up (with).

frammisto, a [fram'misto] AGG: **frammisto a** interspersed with, mixed with.

frana ['frana] SF landslip, landslide; (*fig: persona*): **essere una frana** to be useless *o* hopeless, be a walking disaster area.

franamento [frana'mento] SM landslide.

franare [fra'nare] VI (*aus essere*) (*Geol*) to slip, slide down; (: *roccia*) to fall; (*fig: resistenza*) to collapse.

francamente [franka'mente] AVV frankly.

francescano, a [frantʃes'kano] AGG, SM Franciscan.

francese [fran'tʃeze] ☐1☐ AGG French.
☐2☐ SM/F Frenchman/Frenchwoman; **i francesi** the French.
☐3☐ SM (*lingua*) French.

francesismo [frantʃe'zizmo] SM Gallicism.

franchezza [fran'kettsa] SF frankness, openness.

franchigia, gie [fran'kidʒa] SF a (*Amm*) exemption; **franchigia doganale** exemption from customs duty; **bagaglio in franchigia** (*Aer*) free baggage allowance b: **franchigia assicurativa** insurance excess franchise c (*Naut*) shore leave.

Francia ['frantʃa] SF: **la Francia** France.

franco¹, a, chi, che ['franko] ☐1☐ AGG a (*persona, sguardo*: *sincero*) frank, candid, open, sincere; **rispondere in modo franco** to answer frankly
b (*Comm*): **porto franco** free port ▶**franco bordo** free on board ▶**franco di dazio** *o* **dogana** duty-free ▶**franco fabbrica** ex factory, ex works; **prezzo franco fabbrica** ex-works price ▶**franco magazzino** ex warehouse ▶**franco di porto** carriage free ▶**franco vagone** free on rail
c: **franco tiratore** (*Mil*) irregular (soldier); (*cecchino*) sniper; (*Pol*) *member of parliament who votes against his own party*
d: **farla franca** to get away with it, get off scot-free.
☐2☐ AVV (*francamente*) frankly.

franco², a, chi, che ['franko] (*Storia*) ☐1☐ AGG Frankish.
☐2☐ SM Frank.
☐3☐ PREF: **franco... Franco... .**

franco³, chi ['franko] SM (*moneta*) franc.

francobollo [franko'bollo] SM (postage) stamp.

franco-canadese [frankokana'dese] AGG, SM/F French Canadian.

francofilo, a [fran'kɔfilo] AGG, SM/F Francophile.

Francoforte [franko'fɔrte] SF Frankfurt.

frangente [fran'dʒɛnte] SM **a** (onda) breaker **b** (scoglio affiorante) reef **c** (circostanza) situation, circumstance.

frangia, ge ['frandʒa] SF (gen) fringe; **frangia costiera** coastal strip; **le frange estremiste del partito** (fig) the extremist fringe of the party.

frangiflutti [frandʒi'flutti] SM INV breakwater.

frangivento [frandʒi'vento] SM windbreak.

franoso, a [fra'noso] AGG (terreno) unstable, subject to landslides.

frantoio, oi [fran'tojo] SM (Agr) olive-press; (Tecn) crusher.

frantumare [frantu'mare] ①VT to break (up), break into pieces, shatter. ②**frantumarsi** VIP to break, shatter, break into pieces.

frantumazione [frantumat'tsjone] SF breaking, shattering.

frantume [fran'tume] SM: **andare in frantumi, mandare in frantumi** to shatter, smash to pieces o smithereens.

frappé [frap'pe] SM INV (Culin) milk shake.

frapporre [frap'porre] VB IRREG ①VT: **frapporre ostacoli (a qn)** to place obstacles in the way (of sb); **senza frapporre indugi** without hesitating. ②**frapporsi** VR: **frapporsi tra** (intromettersi) to come between.

frapposizione [frapposit'tsjone] SF interference.

frapposto, a [frap'posto] PP di **frapporre**.

frasario, ri [fra'zarjo] SM (gergo) language.

frasca, sche ['fraska] SF bough, (leafy) branch; **saltare di palo in frasca** to jump from one subject to another.

frase ['fraze] SF **a** (proposizione) sentence; **la frase che ha detto non mi è piaciuta** I didn't like what he said ▶**frase fatta** stock o set phrase **b** (Mus) phrase.

fraseggio, gi [fra'zeddʒo] SM (Mus) phrasing.

fraseologia [frazeolo'dʒia] SF phraseology.

fraseologico, a, ci, che [frazeo'lɔdʒiko] AGG phraseological.

frassino ['frassino] SM ash (tree).

frastagliare [frastaʎ'ʎare] VT to indent.

frastagliato, a [frastaʎ'ʎato] AGG (costa) indented, jagged.

frastornare [frastor'nare] VT (intontire) to daze; (confondere) to befuddle, bewilder.

frastornato, a [frastor'nato] AGG deafened; (vedi vt) dazed; bewildered.

frastuono [fras'twɔno] SM noise, din.

frate ['frate] SM (Rel) brother, friar, monk; **farsi frate** to become a monk.

fratellanza [fratel'lantsa] SF (sentimento) brotherliness; (associazione) brotherhood, fraternity.

fratellastro [fratel'lastro] SM stepbrother.

fratello [fra'tɛllo] SM **a** (gen) brother; **siamo fratelli, disse la donna** we are brother and sister, said the woman ▶**fratello d'armi** brother in arms ▶**fratello gemello** twin (brother) ▶**fratello siamese** Siamese twin **b** (Rel) brother; **i fratelli cristiani** the Christian brethren.

fraternamente [fraterna'mente] AVV fraternally, in a brotherly way.

fraternità [fraterni'ta] SF INV fraternity.

fraternizzare [fraternid'dzare] VI (aus **avere**) to fraternize.

fraterno, a [fra'tɛrno] AGG fraternal, brotherly.

fratricida, i, e [fratri'tʃida] ①AGG fratricidal; **guerra fratricida** civil war. ②SM/F fratricide (person).

fratta ['fratta] SF thicket.

frattaglie [frat'taʎʎe] SFPL (Culin: gen) offal sg; (: di pollo) giblets.

frattanto [frat'tanto] AVV meanwhile, in the meantime.

frattempo [frat'tempo]: **nel frattempo** AVV in the meantime, meanwhile.

fratto, a ['fratto] AGG (Mat: numero, equazione) fractional; (: diviso): **due fratto cinque** 2 divided by 5.

frattura [frat'tura] SF (Med, Geol) fracture; (fig: dissenso) split, break.

fratturare [frattu'rare] ①VT (Med) to fracture, break; **fratturarsi un braccio/una gamba** to break one's arm/one's leg. ②**fratturarsi** VIP (Med) to fracture, break; (partito, gruppo) to split.

fraudolento, a [fraudo'lɛnto] AGG fraudulent.

fraudolenza [fraudo'lɛntsa] SF fraudulence.

frazionamento [frattsjona'mento] SM division, splitting up.

frazionare [frattsjo'nare] VT to divide, split up.

frazione [frat'tsjone] SF **a** (gen, Mat) fraction; **una frazione di secondo** a fraction of a second **b** (borgata) ≈ hamlet.

freatico, a, ci, che [fre'atiko] AGG (Geol): **acqua freatica** groundwater; **falda freatica** phreatic layer.

freccetta [fret'tʃetta] SF (Sport) dart; **freccette** SFPL: **giocare a freccette** to play darts.

freccia, ce ['frettʃa] SF **a** (di arco) arrow; **entrare/uscire come una freccia** to dash o shoot in/out **b** (Aut) indicator; **mettere la freccia (a destra/sinistra)** to indicate that one is turning (right/left) **c** (segnale stradale) signpost.

frecciata [fret'tʃata] SF: **lanciare una frecciata** to make a cutting remark.

freddamente [fredda'mente] AVV coldly, coolly.

freddare [fred'dare] ①VT (minestra) to cool; (fig: entusiasmo) to put a damper on; (uccidere) to kill, shoot dead; **fai freddare la minestra** let the soup cool; **freddare qn con lo sguardo** to silence sb with an icy stare. ②**freddarsi** VIP to cool, become cold.

freddezza [fred'dettsa] SF **a** (indifferenza) coldness, coolness; **accogliere qn/qc con freddezza** to greet sb/sth coolly **b** (autocontrollo) sang-froid; **la sua freddezza ha evitato il peggio** her cool-headedness prevented anything worse happening.

freddo, a ['freddo] ①AGG (gen) cold; (accoglienza) cool, cold; **a mente fredda capì di avere torto** when he had cooled down he realized that he was wrong; **la macchina è ancora fredda** the engine is still cold. ②SM **a** (gen) cold; **aver freddo** to be cold; **prendere freddo** to catch cold; **soffrire il freddo** to feel the cold; **sudare freddo** to be in a cold sweat; **fa freddo** it's cold; **c'è stata un'ondata di freddo** there's been a cold spell **b**: **a freddo** (lavare) in cold water; (fig) deliberately; **a freddo ha poi negato di averlo detto** when he had cooled down, he denied having said it.

freddoloso, a [freddo'loso] AGG: **essere freddoloso** to feel o be sensitive to the cold.

freddura [fred'dura] SF dry comment, pun.

freezer ['fri:zə] SM INV fridge-freezer.

fregare [fre'gare] VT **a** (sfregare) to rub; (per pulire) to

polish; **fregarsi le mani/gli occhi** to rub one's hands/one's eyes

b (*fig fam*): **fregare qn** (*imbrogliare*) to cheat sb, rip sb off, take sb in; **mi frega sempre a carte** (*vincere*) he always beats me at cards

c (*rubare*): **fregare qc a qn** to pinch *o* swipe sth from sb; **mi ha fregato il ragazzo** she pinched my boyfriend

d (*fig fam*): **fregarsene (di qc/qn)** (*infischiarsene*) not to give a damn (about sth/sb); **non gliene frega niente** he doesn't give a damn; **me ne frego** I don't give a damn; **che ti frega?** none of your business!

fregata[1] [fre'gata] SF **a** (*vedi vb a*) rub; polish; **dare una fregata a qc** to rub sth, polish sth **b** (*fam*) = **fregatura**.

fregata[2] [fre'gata] SF (*Naut*) frigate.

fregatura [frega'tura] SF (*fam: imbroglio*) rip-off, con; **mi hanno tirato una fregatura** they ripped me off; **è stata una fregatura** (*delusione*) it's been a let-down.

fregherò *ecc* [frege'rɔ] VB *vedi* **fregare**.

fregiare [fre'dʒare] **1** VT (*Archit*) to adorn, embellish.

2 fregiarsi VR: **fregiarsi di** (*titolo, onore*) to be the proud holder of.

fregio, gi ['fredʒo] SM (*gen*) decoration, ornament; (*Archit*) frieze.

frego, ghi ['frego] SM line, mark.

fregola ['fregola] SF **a** (*Zool: calore*) heat **b** (*fig: smania*): **avere la fregola di fare qc** to have an itch to do sth.

fremente [fre'mɛnte] AGG: **essere fremente di** (*gen*) to be trembling with.

fremere ['fremere] VI (*aus* **avere**) to shake, tremble; **fremere di** to tremble *o* quiver with; **fremere d'impazienza** to be champing at the bit.

fremito ['fremito] SM shudder, shiver; (*di passione*) wave; **ebbe un fremito d'ira** he shook with anger.

frenaggio, gi [fre'naddʒo] SM (*Sport, Aut: azione*) braking; (: *meccanismi*) braking system.

frenare [fre'nare] **1** VT (*sogg: veicolo*) to pull up, slow down; (*progresso, avanzata*) to hold up; (*gioia, evoluzione*) to check; (*cavallo*) to rein in; **frenare la lingua** to hold one's tongue; **frenare le lacrime** to hold back one's tears.

2 VI (*aus* **avere**) (*Aut*) to brake; (*Sci*) to slow down.

3 frenarsi VR to restrain o.s., stop o.s., control o.s.

frenata [fre'nata] SF braking; **fare una brusca frenata** to brake suddenly, hit the brakes.

frenesia [frene'zia] SF frenzy; **con frenesia** frenziedly.

freneticamente [frenetika'mente] AVV frantically.

frenetico, a, ci, che [fre'nɛtiko] AGG frenetic.

freno ['freno] SM **a** (*Aut*) brake; (*di cavallo*) bit; (*fig*) restraint; **bloccare i freni** [OR] **azionare i freni** to apply the brakes ▶**freno a disco** disc brake ▶**freno a mano** handbrake, parking brake (*Am*)

b (*fraseologia*): **mettere** *o* **porre un freno a** (*inflazione, tendenza*) to put a brake on, keep in check; **tenere a freno** (*passioni*) to restrain; **tenere a freno la lingua** to hold one's tongue; **agire da freno** to act as a restraint.

frenologia [frenolo'dʒia] SF phrenology.

frenulo ['frenulo] SM (*Anat*) fraenum.

freon® ['frɛon] SM INV (*Chim*) Freon ®.

frequentare [frekwen'tare] **1** VT (*scuola, corso*) to attend; (*persona*) to see (regularly *o* often); (*locale, casa, bar*) to go to, frequent; **frequentare cattive compagnie** to keep bad company; **è un locale mal frequentato** you get some shady types at that place *o* in that bar.

2 frequentarsi VR (*uso reciproco*) to see each other

(regularly); **si frequentano da anni** they have been seeing each other for years.

frequentato, a [frekwen'tato] AGG (*locale*) busy.

frequentatore, trice [frekwenta'tore] SM/F: **frequentatore (di)** frequent visitor (to).

frequente [fre'kwɛnte] AGG frequent; **di frequente** frequently.

frequentemente [frekwente'mente] AVV frequently, often.

frequenza [fre'kwɛntsa] SF (*gen, Fis, Radio, Elettr*) frequency; (*Scol*) attendance; **frequenza respiratoria** breathing rate.

fresa ['freza] SF (*Tecn*) milling cutter.

fresare [fre'zare] VT (*Tecn*) to mill.

fresatrice [freza'tritʃe] SF (*Tecn*) milling machine.

freschezza [fres'kettsa] SF (*gen*) freshness; (*di serata*) coolness.

fresco, a, schi, sche ['fresko] **1** AGG (*gen*) fresh; (*temperatura, clima*) fresh, cool; (*vernice*) wet; (*traccia, notizia, ferita*) recent, new; **fresco e riposato** (completely) refreshed; **fresca come una rosa** as fresh as a daisy; **bere qc di fresco** to have a cold drink; **fresco di bucato** freshly laundered, newly washed; **fresco di studi** (*fam*) fresh out of university *o* school; **se continui così stai fresco** (*fig*) if you go on like this you'll be in trouble.

2 SM (*temperatura*) cool; **è** *o* **fa fresco** it is cool; **mettere/tenere al fresco** (*oggetto*) to put/keep in a cool place; (*fig: persona: in prigione*) to put/keep inside *o* in the cooler; **fatto di fresco** newly done; **godersi il fresco** to enjoy the cool air.

frescura [fres'kura] SF cool; **la frescura della sera** the cool of the evening.

fresia ['frɛzja] SF freesia.

fretta ['fretta] SF hurry, haste; **in fretta** in a hurry; **in tutta fretta** hurriedly, quickly; **in fretta e furia** in a great *o* tearing hurry, in a mad rush; **avere fretta (di fare qc)** to be in a hurry (to do sth); **fare qc in fretta** (*velocemente*) to do sth quickly, hurry up with sth; (*troppo velocemente*) to do sth in a hurry; **l'ho fatto un po' troppo in fretta** I did it in too much of a hurry; **far fretta a qn** to hurry sb; **fai in fretta!** hurry up!; **che fretta c'è?** what's the hurry?

frettolosamente [frettolosa'mente] AVV hurriedly, in a rush; **salutò frettolosamente e se ne andò** he said a hurried goodbye and left.

frettoloso, a [fretto'loso] AGG (*persona*) in a hurry; (*lavoro*) hurried, rushed; **diede una scorsa frettolosa al libro** he flicked through the book; **è un po' troppo frettoloso in quello che fa** he tends to rush things.

friabile [fri'abile] AGG (*roccia, terreno*) friable; (*biscotto*) crumbly.

friabilità [friabili'ta] SF INV (*vedi agg*) friability; crumbliness.

fricassea [frikas'sɛa] SF (*Culin*) fricassee; **pollo in fricassea** chicken fricassee.

fricativo, a [frika'tivo] AGG, SF fricative.

fricchettone, a [frikket'tone] SM (*fam*) freak.

friggere ['friddʒere] VB IRREG **1** VT to fry; **vai a farti friggere!** (*fam*) get lost!.

2 VI (*aus* **avere**) (*grasso, olio*) to sizzle; (*fig*): **friggere dalla rabbia** to seethe with rage; **friggere d'impazienza** to fume with impatience.

friggitoria [friddʒito'ria] SF ≈ fish and chip shop.

friggitrice [friddʒi'tritʃe] SF deep fryer.

frigidaire [friʒi'dɛr] SM INV refrigerator.
frigidità [fridʒidi'ta] SF INV frigidity.
frigido, a ['fridʒido] AGG frigid.
frignare [friɲ'ɲare] VI (aus avere) to whine, snivel.
frignone, a [friɲ'ɲone] SM/F whiner, sniveller.
frigo, ghi ['frigo] SM fridge.
frigobar [frigo'bar] SM INV minibar.
frigorifero, a [frigo'rifero] 1 AGG refrigerated; **cella frigorifera** cold store.
  2 SM refrigerator.
fringuello [frin'gwɛllo] SM chaffinch.
frinire [fri'nire] VI (aus avere) to chirp.
frisbee® ['frisbi:] SM INV Frisbee ®.
frissi ecc ['frissi] VB vedi **friggere**.
frittata [frit'tata] SF (Culin) omelette, omelet (Am); **la frittata è fatta!** (fig) that's torn it!, the damage is done.
frittella [frit'tɛlla] SF (Culin) fritter.
fritto, a ['fritto] 1 PP di **friggere**.
  2 AGG (patatine, pesce) fried; **ormai siamo fritti!** (fig fam) now we've had it!; **è un argomento fritto e rifritto** that's old hat.
  3 SM fried food; **odore di fritto** smell of frying ► **fritto misto** mixed fried fish.
frittura [frit'tura] SF (cibo) fried food; **frittura di pesce** mixed fried fish.
friulano, a [friu'lano] 1 AGG of o from Friuli, Friulian.
  2 inhabitant o native of Friuli.
frivolamente [frivola'mente] AVV frivolously.
frivolezza [frivo'lettsa] SF frivolity.
frivolo, a ['frivolo] AGG frivolous.
frizionare [frittsjo'nare] VT to rub, massage; **frizionarsi il braccio** to rub one's arm.
frizione [frit'tsjone] SF **a** (massaggio) rubbing, massage; **fare delle frizioni con una pomata** to rub in an ointment **b** (lozione) lotion **c** (tensione) friction **d** (Aut) clutch **e** (Fis) friction.
frizzante [frid'dzante] AGG (gen) fizzy, sparkling; (vino) sparkling; (persona) effervescent, bubbly (fam).
frizzare [frid'dzare] VI (aus avere) to sparkle, be fizzy.
frizzo ['friddzo] SM witticism.
frodare [fro'dare] VT to defraud, cheat; **frodare il fisco** to evade tax.
frode ['frɔde] SF (Dir) fraud ► **frode fiscale** tax evasion.
frodo ['frɔdo] SM: **di frodo** illegal, contraband; **pescatore/cacciatore di frodo** poacher; **pescare/cacciare di frodo** to poach.
frogia, gie o **ge** ['frɔdʒa] SF (di cavallo) nostril.
frollare [frol'lare] VI (aus essere) (carne) to become high.
frollino [frol'lino] SM (Culin) pastry (with candied fruit).
frollo, a ['frɔllo] AGG (Culin: carne) high; **pasta frolla** short(crust) pastry; (fig: persona) soft.
fronda¹ ['fronda] SF (Bot) leafy branch; (spec al pl) foliage sg.
fronda² ['fronda] SF (fig Pol) rebellion, internal opposition.
frondista, i, e [fron'dista] SM/F (fig Pol) rebel.
frondoso, a [fron'doso] AGG (albero) leafy; (fig: stile) ornate.
frontale [fron'tale] AGG (Anat, Mil) frontal; **scontro frontale** (Aut) head-on collision.
frontalmente [frontal'mente] AVV frontally.
fronte ['fronte] 1 SF **a** (Anat) brow, forehead; **a fronte alta** (anche fig) with one's head held high; **col sudore della fronte** by the sweat of one's brow

  b : **di fronte** (dirimpetto) opposite; **di fronte a** opposite, facing, in front of; (a paragone di) compared with; **testo a fronte** parallel text; **vista di fronte la casa è più bella** seen from the front the house looks much more attractive.
  2 SM (Mil, Pol, Meteor) front; **far fronte a** (nemico, problema) to confront; (responsabilità) to face up to; (spese) to meet.
fronteggiare [fronted'dʒare] VT (affrontare: nemico, problema, avversità) to face, confront, stand up to; (sostenere: spese) to meet.
frontespizio, zi [frontes'pittsjo] SM (di libro) title page.
frontiera [fron'tjɛra] SF frontier, border; (fig) frontier; **zona di frontiera** frontier o border area; **guardia di frontiera** border guard; **polizia di frontiera** border police.
frontone [fron'tone] SM pediment.
fronzolo ['frondzolo] SM frill; **senza fronzoli** (fig) without (any) frills, plainly.
fronzuto, a [fron'dzuto] AGG leafy.
frotta ['frotta] SF crowd; **in frotta** OR **a frotte** in their hundreds, in droves.
frottola ['frottola] SF (fam: bugia) lie, fib; **raccontare un sacco di frottole** to tell a pack of lies.
fru fru [fruf'fru] AGG INV frilly.
frugale [fru'gale] AGG frugal.
frugalità [frugali'ta] SF INV frugality.
frugalmente [frugal'mente] AVV frugally.
frugare [fru'gare] 1 VT to search; **frugarsi le tasche** to search through one's pockets.
  2 VI (aus avere): **frugare in** to search, rummage around in.
frugherò ecc [fruge'rɔ] VB vedi **frugare**.
frugoletto [frugo'letto] SM cutie-pie (fam).
fruibile [fru'ibile] AGG usable; **è fruibile da tutti** it's available to everybody.
fruire [fru'ire] VI (aus avere): **fruire di qc** to enjoy the use of sth.
fruitore, trice [frui'tore] SM user.
fruizione [fruit'tsjone] SF use.
frullare [frul'lare] 1 VT (gen) to blend; (frutta) to blend, liquidize; (uova) to whisk.
  2 VI (aus avere) (uccelli) to flutter, whirr; **cosa ti frulla in mente?** (fig) what is going on in that mind of yours?
frullato [frul'lato] SM (Culin) milk shake (made with fresh fruit, cocoa etc).
frullatore [frulla'tore] SM blender, liquidizer ► **frullatore a immersione** hand-held liquidizer.
frullino [frul'lino] SM whisk.
frullio, lii [frul'lio] SM (di ali) flutter.
frumentario, ria, ri, rie [frumen'tarjo] AGG grain attr, wheat attr.
frumento [fru'mento] SM grain, wheat.
frusciare [fruʃ'ʃare] VI (aus avere) to rustle.
fruscio, scii [fruʃ'ʃio] SM rustling, rustle.
frusta ['frusta] SF **a** (per cavalli) whip; **colpo di frusta** whiplash **b** (Culin) whisk.
frustare [frus'tare] VT to whip.
frustata [frus'tata] SF lash.
frustino [frus'tino] SM riding crop.
frusto, a ['frusto] AGG (logoro: abito) threadbare; (: argomento) trite, hackneyed.
frustrare [frus'trare] VT to frustrate.
frustrato, a [frus'trato] 1 AGG frustrated.

[2] SM/F frustrated person.

frustrazione [frustrat'tsjone] SF frustration.

frutta ['frutta] SF fruit; (*portata*) dessert; **torta alla frutta** fruit gateau; **gelato alla frutta** fruit-flavoured ice cream ►**frutta candita** candied fruit ►**frutta sciroppata** fruit in heavy syrup ►**frutta secca** (*fichi ecc*) dried fruit; (*noci, mandorle ecc*) nuts.

fruttare [frut'tare] [1] VT: **il mio deposito in banca (mi) frutta il 5%** I get 5% interest on my bank deposits; **quella gara gli fruttò la medaglia d'oro** he won the gold medal in that competition.

[2] VI (*aus* **avere**) (*investimenti, deposito*) to bear dividends, give a return; **questo investimento ha fruttato poco** this investment did not give much of a return *o* gave a poor yield.

fruttato, a [frut'tato] AGG (*vino*) fruity.

frutteto [frut'teto] SM orchard.

frutticolo, a [frut'tikolo] AGG fruit *attr*.

frutticoltore, trice [fruttikol'tore] SM/F fruit grower.

frutticoltura [fruttikol'tura] SF fruit growing.

fruttiera [frut'tjɛra] SF fruit dish.

fruttifero, a [frut'tifero] AGG **a** (*albero*) fruit-bearing **b** (*fig: che frutta*) fruitful, profitable; **deposito fruttifero** interest-bearing deposit.

fruttificare [fruttifi'kare] VI (*aus* **avere**) to bear fruit.

fruttivendolo, a [frutti'vendolo] SM/F fruiterer, greengrocer (*Brit*), produce dealer (*Am*); **dal fruttivendolo** at the fruit shop *o* greengrocer's *o* fruiterer's.

frutto ['frutto] SM (*anche fig*) fruit; **dare frutti** (*anche fig*) to bear fruit; **raccogliere i frutti di qc** (*fig*) to reap the rewards of sth; **essere frutto di** (*fig*) to be the fruit of; **è frutto della tua immaginazione** it's a figment of your imagination; **il frutto del mio lavoro** (*fig*) the fruits of my labour; **senza alcun frutto** (*fig*) fruitlessly, in vain ►**frutti di bosco** berries ►**frutti di mare** shellfish *sg o pl*, seafood *sg*.

fruttosio [frut'tozjo] SM fructose.

fruttuosamente [fruttuosa'mente] AVV profitably.

fruttuoso, a [fruttu'oso] AGG fruitful, profitable.

F.S. ['effe'ɛsse] SIGLA F (= *Ferrovie dello Stato*) *Italian railways.*

f.t. ABBR = **fuori testo**.

f.to ABBR (= *firmato*) signed.

fu [fu] [1] *3a pers sg del passato remoto di* **essere.**

[2] AGG INV (*defunto*): **il fu Mario Rossi** the late Mario Rossi.

fucilare [futʃi'lare] VT to shoot *o* execute (by firing squad).

fucilata [futʃi'lata] SF (*rifle*) shot; **fu ucciso da una fucilata alla schiena** it was a bullet in the back which killed him.

fucilazione [futʃilat'tsjone] SF execution (by firing squad).

fucile [fu'tʃile] SM rifle, gun ►**fucile da caccia** shotgun ►**fucile a canne mozze** sawn-off shotgun ►**fucile subacqueo** (*underwater*) spear gun.

fucina [fu'tʃina] SF (*Tecn*) forge; (*fig: di ingegni*) breeding ground.

fuco, chi ['fuko] SM (*ape*) drone.

fucsia ['fuksja] [1] SF (*Bot*) fuchsia.

[2] SM, AGG (*colore*) fuchsia.

fuga, ghe ['fuga] SF **a** escape; (*letter*) flight; **mettere qn in fuga** to put sb to flight **b** (*perdita: di gas, notizie*) leak ►**fuga di capitali** flight of capital ►**fuga di cervelli** brain drain **c** (*Mus*) fugue **d** (*Sport*) breakaway.

fugace [fu'gatʃe] AGG fleeting, transient.

fugacemente [fugatʃe'mente] AVV fleetingly.

fugare [fu'gare] VT (*dubbi, incertezze*) to dispel, drive out.

fuggevole [fud'dʒevole] AGG fleeting.

fuggevolmente [fuddʒevol'mente] AVV fleetingly.

fuggiasco, a, schi, sche [fud'dʒasko] [1] AGG runaway *attr*.

[2] SM/F fugitive; (*Mil*) deserter.

fuggifuggi [fuddʒi'fuddʒi] SM INV stampede.

fuggire [fud'dʒire] [1] VT (*anche fig*) to avoid, shun.

[2] VI (*aus* **essere**) (*ladro*) to run away, flee (*frm*); (*prigioniero*) to escape; (*fig: vita*) to fly *o* slip by; **il tempo fugge** time flies.

fuggitivo, a [fuddʒi'tivo] [1] AGG **a** (*in fuga*) fleeing, escaping **b** (*fugace*) fleeting.

[2] SM/F fugitive; (*Mil*) deserter.

fui *ecc* ['fui] VB vedi **essere.**

fulcro ['fulkro] SM (*Tecn*) fulcrum; (*fig: di discussione, teoria*) central *o* key point.

fulgidamente [fuldʒida'mente] AVV brilliantly.

fulgido, a ['fuldʒido] AGG bright, shining; (*fig: esempio*) shining.

fulgore [ful'gore] SM brilliance; (*fig*) splendour (*Brit*), splendor (*Am*).

fuliggine [fu'liddʒine] SF soot.

fuligginoso, a [fuliddʒi'noso] AGG sooty.

fulminante [fulmi'nante] AGG (*sguardo*) blazing; **è morto per un polmonite fulminante** he died after suddenly contracting pneumonia.

fulminare [fulmi'nare] [1] VB IMPERS: **fulmina** there is lightning.

[2] VT **a** : **essere fulminato** (*da fulmine*) to be struck (by lightning); (*da elettricità*) to be electrocuted **b** (*fig: uccidere*) to shoot dead; **mi fulminò con uno sguardo** he looked daggers at me.

[3] **fulminarsi** VIP (*lampadina*) to go, blow.

fulminato [fulmi'nato] SM (*Chim*) fulminate.

fulmine ['fulmine] SM bolt of lightning; **fulmini** lightning *sg*; **come un fulmine** like lightning; **fulmine a ciel sereno** bolt from the blue; **un colpo di fulmine** (*fig*) love at first sight.

fulmineamente [fulminea'mente] AVV like lightning, quick as a flash.

fulmineo, a [ful'mineo] AGG (*fig: scatto*) rapid; (*minaccioso: sguardo*) threatening; **una morte fulminea** a sudden death.

fulvo, a ['fulvo] AGG tawny.

fumaiolo [fuma'jɔlo] SM (*gen*) chimney; (*Naut, Ferr*) funnel.

fumante [fu'mante] AGG (*piatto*) steaming.

fumare [fu'mare] [1] VT (*sigaretta, pipa*) to smoke.

[2] VI (*aus* **avere**) (*esalare: fumo*) to smoke; (: *vapore*) to steam; **smettere di fumare** to give up smoking; **fumare come un turco** to smoke like a chimney; **"vietato fumare"** "no smoking".

fumario, ria, ri, rie [fu'marjo] AGG: **canna fumaria** flue.

fumarola [fuma'rɔla] SF fumarole.

fumata [fu'mata] SF **a** (*il fumare*): **farsi una fumata** to have a smoke **b** (*emissione di fumo*) cloud of smoke ►**fumata bianca/nera** (*in Vaticano*) *signal that a new pope has/has not been elected.*

fumatore, trice [fuma'tore] SM/F smoker.

fumé [fy'me] AGG INV smoky grey.

fumeria [fume'ria] SF: **una fumeria d'oppio** opium den.

fumettista, i, e [fumet'tista] SM/F cartoonist.

fumettistico, a, ci, che [fumet'tistiko] AGG comic *attr*; **un**

personaggio fumettistico (*pegg*) a stereotype.

fumetto [fu'metto] SM a (*nuvoletta con parole*) bubble b (*storia a vignette*) cartoon, comic strip; **giornale a fumetti** comic (*Brit*), comic book (*Am*).

fummo *ecc* ['fummo] VB vedi **essere**.

fumo ['fumo] 1 SM a (*di fuoco, sigaretta*) smoke; (*vapore*) steam; **fare fumo** (*camino ecc*) to smoke; **i fumi industriali** industrial fumes; **essere in preda ai fumi dell'alcol** (*fig*) to be under the influence of alcohol b (*il fumare*) smoking; **il fumo fa male** smoking is bad for you ▶ **fumo passivo** passive smoking c (*fam: hascisc*) dope d (*fraseologia*): **andare in fumo** to go up in smoke; **è solo fumo** it's worthless; **è tutto fumo e niente arrosto** there's no substance to it; **gettare fumo negli occhi a qn** to pull the wool over sb's eyes; **lo vedo come il fumo negli occhi** I can't stand him; **vendere fumo** to deceive, cheat. 2 AGG INV: **grigio fumo** smoky grey.

fumogeno, a [fu'mɔdʒeno] 1 AGG (*candelotto*) smoke *attr*; **cortina fumogena** smoke screen. 2 SM smoke bomb.

fumosamente [fumosa'mente] AVV (*fig*) vaguely.

fumoso, a [fu'moso] AGG a (*ambiente, stanza*) smoky b (*fig: idee*) woolly, (: *progetto*) muddled.

funambolo, a [fu'nambolo] SM/F tightrope walker.

fune ['fune] SF rope, cord; (*più grossa*) cable.

funebre ['funebre] AGG (*gen, corteo, cerimonia*) funeral *attr*; (*atmosfera*) gloomy, funereal; (*voce, sguardo*) funereal, mournful.

funerale [fune'rale] SM funeral; **una faccia da funerale** a long face.

funerario, ria, ri, rie [fune'rarjo] AGG (*urna*) funeral *attr*; (*iscrizione*) tombstone *attr*.

funereo, a [fu'nɛreo] AGG (*frm*) funeral *attr*; (*sguardo, aspetto*) funereal, mournful.

funesto, a [fu'nɛsto] AGG (*incidente*) fatal; (*errore, decisione*) fatal, disastrous; (*atmosfera*) gloomy, dismal.

fungaia [fun'gaja] SF mushroom bed.

fungere ['fundʒere] VI IRREG (*aus* avere): **fungere da** to act as.

fungo, ghi ['fungo] SM a (*commestibile*) mushroom; **fungo velenoso** toadstool; **funghi secchi** dried mushrooms; **andare a** o **per funghi** to go mushrooming; **crescere come i funghi** (*fig*) to spring up overnight ▶ **fungo atomico** mushroom cloud b (*Med*) fungus c (*di annaffiatoio*) rose.

funicolare [funiko'lare] SF funicular railway.

funivia [funi'via] SF cablecar.

funsi *ecc* ['funsi] VB vedi **fungere**.

funto, a ['funto] PP di **fungere**.

funzionale [funtsjo'nale] AGG functional.

funzionalità [funtsjonali'ta] SF INV functionality.

funzionamento [funtsjona'mento] SM (*vedi vb a*) working; functioning.

funzionante [funtsjo'nante] AGG working.

funzionare [funtsjo'nare] VI (*aus* avere) a (*gen*) to work, function; (*sistema*) to function; **funziona a benzina** it runs on petrol; **far funzionare** to operate; **il telefono non funziona** the telephone is out of order b: **funzionare da** to act as.

funzionario, ria, ri, rie [funtsjo'narjo] SM/F (*Amm: dirigente*) official; (: *impiegato*) employee; **funzionario dell'amministrazione comunale** local authority

employee ▶ **funzionario statale** civil servant.

funzione [fun'tsjone] SF a (*gen, Gramm, Mat*) function; **in funzione** (*macchina*) in operation; **vive in funzione dei figli/della carriera** he lives for his children/his job; **participio usato in funzione di aggettivo** participle used as an adjective b (*carica*) post, office, position; **cessare dalle funzioni** to leave office; **far funzione di sindaco** to act as mayor; **non il presidente ma il facente funzione** not the president but his deputy; **nell'esercizio delle sue funzioni** in the performance of his duties c (*Rel*) service, religious ceremony.

fuochista, i [fwo'kista] SM stoker; (*Ferr*) stoker, fireman.

fuoco, chi ['fwɔko] 1 SM a fire; **prendere fuoco** to catch fire; **dare fuoco a qc** to set fire to sth; **al fuoco!** fire!; **scherzare col fuoco** (*fig*) to play with fire; **soffiare sul fuoco** (*fig*) to add fuel to the flames b (*Culin: fornello*) ring; **mettere qc sul fuoco** to put sth on the stove; **cuocere a fuoco lento/vivo** to cook over a low/high heat c (*Mil: sparo*) fire; **far fuoco** to fire; **cessare/aprire il fuoco** to cease/open fire ▶ **fuoco incrociato** crossfire d (*ardore, vivacità*) fire; **parole di fuoco** heated words e (*Mat, Ottica*) focus; **mettere a fuoco** to focus; (*fig: problema*) to clarify f (*fraseologia*): **fare fuoco e fiamme (per fare)** to do one's utmost (to do); **mettere la mano sul fuoco per qc** to stake one's life on sth; **mettere a ferro e fuoco** to put to fire and the sword. 2 AGG INV: **rosso fuoco** flame red. 3 ▶ **fuoco d'artificio** firework ▶ **fuoco fatuo** will-o'-the-wisp ▶ **fuoco di paglia** flash in the pan ▶ **fuoco sacro** o **di Sant'Antonio** (*Med fam*) shingles *pl*.

fuorché [fwor'ke] CONG, PREP except, apart from.

FUORI ['fwɔri] SIGLA M (= *Fronte Unitario Omosessuale Rivoluzionario Italiano*) *Italian gay liberation movement*.

fuori ['fwɔri] 1 AVV a (*gen*) outside; (*all'aperto*) outdoors, outside; (*fuori casa*) out; (*all'estero*) abroad; **era lì fuori ad aspettarmi** he was outside waiting for me; **ceniamo fuori?** (*all'aperto*) shall we eat outside?; (*al ristorante*) shall we go out for a meal?, shall we eat out?; **mandali a giocare fuori** send them out to play; **mio marito è fuori** my husband is out o is not at home; **ho vissuto in Italia e fuori** I've lived in Italy and abroad; **tiralo fuori dalla scatola** take it out of the box b (*fraseologia*): **fuori di qui!** get out (of here)!; **fuori i soldi!** hand over your money!; **essere di fuori** to be a stranger; **essere in fuori** (*sporgere*) to stick out; (*denti, occhi*) to be prominent; **finalmente ne sono fuori** (*da un vizio*) I've managed to break the habit; **far fuori** (*fam: soldi*) to spend; (: *cioccolatini*) to eat up; (: *rubare*) to nick; **far fuori qn** (*fam*) to do sb in; **lasciare/mettere fuori** to leave/put out; **essere tagliato fuori** (*da un gruppo, ambiente*) to be excluded; **mi sento tagliato fuori qui** I feel cut off here; **uscire fuori** to come out; **andare/venire fuori** to go/come out; **giocare fuori** (*Sport*) to play away. 2 PREP a: **fuori (di)** out of, outside; **è fuori città** he's out of town; **abita fuori Roma** he lives outside Rome b (*fraseologia*): **è fuori di sé (dalla gioia/rabbia)** he's beside himself (with joy/anger); **è fuori commercio** it's not for sale; **fuori fase** (*motore*) out of phase; **fuori mano** (*casa, paese*) out of the way, remote; **abitare fuori mano** to live in an out-of-the-way place; **fuori luogo** (*osservazione*) out of place, uncalled for; **fuori orario** outside

working hours; **fuori pasto** between meals; **fuori pericolo** out of danger; **fuori dai piedi!** get out of the way!; **fuori programma** unscheduled; **è fuori questione** o **discussione** it's out of the question; **fuori servizio** out of order; **fuori stagione** out of season; **la macchina è andata fuori strada** the car left the road; **essere fuori tempo** (*Mus*) to be out of time; **è arrivato fuori tempo massimo** he arrived outside the time limit; **illustrazione fuori testo** plate; **fuori uso** out of use.

<u>3</u> SM outside; **dal di fuori** from the outside.

fuoribordo [fwori'bordo] SM INV (*Naut*: *imbarcazione*) outboard, speedboat (with outboard motor); (: *motore*) outboard motor.

fuoribusta [fwori'busta] SM INV unofficial payment.

fuoricampo [fwori'kampo] AGG INV (*Cine*) out of the picture.

fuoriclasse [fwori'klasse] <u>1</u> AGG INV unrivalled, unequalled.

<u>2</u> SM/F INV undisputed champion.

fuoricorso [fwori'korso] AGG INV **a** (*moneta*) no longer in circulation **b** (*Univ*): **(studente) fuoricorso** *student who takes longer than normal to complete his* o *her university course*.

fuorigioco [fwori'dʒɔko] SM INV (*Sport*): **in fuorigioco** offside; **fischiare un fuorigioco** to blow the whistle for offside.

fuorilegge [fwori'leddʒe] SM/F INV outlaw.

fuoripista [fwori'pista] SM INV, AVV (*Sci*) off-piste.

fuoriprogramma [fworipro'gramma] SM INV (*TV*, *Radio*) unscheduled programme; (*fig*) change of plan o programme.

fuoriserie [fwori'sɛrje] <u>1</u> AGG INV (*macchina*) specially built; (*fig*: *eccezionale*) outstanding.

<u>2</u> SF INV custom-built car.

fuoristrada [fwori'strada] SM INV (*Aut*) Land Rover ®, jeep; **fare del fuoristrada** to drive cross-country.

fuoriuscita [fworiuʃ'ʃita], **fuoruscita** [fworuʃ'ʃita] SF (*di gas*) leakage, escape; (*di sangue, linfa*) seepage.

fuoriuscito, a [fworiuʃ'ʃito], **fuoruscito, a** [fworuʃ'ʃito] SM/F exile, refugee.

fuorviare [fworvi'are] VI = **forviare**.

furbacchione, a [furbak'kjone] SM/F cunning o crafty old devil.

furbamente [furba'mente] AVV (*vedi agg*) cleverly; cunningly.

furberia [furbe'ria] SF (*qualità*) cunning, slyness; (*azione*) sly trick.

furbescamente [furbeska'mente] AVV cunningly, slyly, craftily.

furbesco, a, schi, sche [fur'besko] AGG cunning, sly, crafty; **lingua furbesca** thieves' cant.

furbizia [fur'bittsja] SF (*vedi agg*) cleverness; cunning; **una furbizia** a cunning trick.

furbo, a ['furbo] <u>1</u> AGG clever, smart; (*pegg*) cunning, sly.

<u>2</u> SM/F clever person, cunning person; **fare il furbo** to (try to) be clever o smart; **fatti furbo!** show a bit of sense!

furente [fu'rɛnte] AGG: **furente (contro)** furious (with).

fureria [fure'ria] SF (*Mil*) orderly room.

furetto [fu'retto] SM ferret.

furfante [fur'fante] SM/F rascal, scoundrel.

furfanteria [furfante'ria] SF roguery.

furgoncino [furgon'tʃino] SM small van.

furgone [fur'gone] SM van.

furia ['furja] SF **a** (*ira, furore*) fury, rage; (*velocità*) hurry, haste; **andare** o **montare su tutte le furie** to get into a towering rage, fly into a rage o frenzy; **la furia del vento** the violence of the wind; **a furia di fare qc** by constantly doing sth, by dint of sth/doing sth (*old*); **si è fatto largo nella folla a furia di spinte** he shoved his way through the crowd

b (*Mitol*): **le Furie** the Furies.

furibondo, a [furi'bondo] AGG furious.

furiere [fu'rjɛre] SM quartermaster.

furiosamente [furjosa'mente] AVV furiously.

furioso, a [fu'rjoso] AGG (*gen*) furious; (*vento, assalto*) violent, raging; **è un pazzo furioso** he is a raving lunatic.

furono ['furono] VB vedi **essere**.

furore [fu'rore] SM fury; **nel furore della battaglia** in the heat of the battle; **a furor di popolo** by popular acclaim; **far furore** to be all the rage.

furoreggiare [furored'dʒare] VI (*aus* **avere**) to be all the rage.

furtivamente [furtiva'mente] AVV (*vedi agg*) furtively; stealthily.

furtivo, a [fur'tivo] AGG (*sguardo*) furtive; (*passo*) stealthy.

furto ['furto] SM theft; **commettere un furto** to commit a robbery ▶ **furto con scasso** (*Dir*) burglary.

fusa ['fusa] SFPL: **fare le fusa** to purr.

fuscello [fuʃ'ʃɛllo] SM twig; **magro come un fuscello** thin as a lath.

fusciacca, che [fuʃ'ʃakka] SF sash.

fuseaux [fy'zo] SMPL leggings.

fusi *ecc* ['fuzi] VB vedi **fondere**.

fusibile [fu'zibile] SM (*Elettr*) fuse.

fusillo [fu'sillo] SM (*Culin*) *pasta spiral*.

fusione [fu'zjone] SF **a** (*gen, Fis*) fusion; (*di metalli*) melting; (*fig*: *di idee*) merging, blending **b** (*Comm*) merger, amalgamation.

fuso¹, a ['fuzo] PP di **fondere**.

fuso² ['fuzo] SM **a** (*Tessile*) spindle; **diritto come un fuso** as straight as a ramrod **b**: **fuso orario** time zone.

fusoliera [fuzo'ljɛra] SF (*Aer*) fusillage.

fustagno [fus'taɲɲo] SM fustian, corduroy.

fustella [fus'tɛlla] SF (*su scatola di medicinali*) tear-off tab.

fustigare [fusti'gare] VT (*frustare*) to flog; (*fig*: *costumi*) to censure, denounce.

fustigatore, trice [fustiga'tore] SM/F (*fig*) critic.

fustigazione [fustigat'tsjone] SF flogging, beating.

fustino [fus'tino] SM (*di detersivo*) tub.

fusto ['fusto] SM **a** (*Anat, Bot*: *di albero*) trunk; (: *di pianta*) stem; (*colonna*) shaft **b** (*recipiente*: *di metallo*) drum **c** (*fam*) he-man.

futile ['futile] AGG futile, vain.

futilità [futili'ta] SF INV futility.

futilmente [futil'mente] AVV futilely.

futurismo [futu'rizmo] SM futurism.

futurista, i, e [futu'rista] SM/F futurist.

futuristico, a, ci, che [futu'ristiko] AGG futuristic.

futuro, a [fu'turo] <u>1</u> AGG future.

<u>2</u> SM future; **futuro anteriore** future perfect.

G

G, g [dʒi] SF O M INV (*lettera*) G, g; **G come Genova** ≈ G for George.

g. ABBR (= *grammo, grammi*) g.

gabardine [gabar'din] SM (*tessuto*) gabardine; (*soprabito*) gabardine raincoat.

gabbare [gab'bare] VT to deceive, trick, dupe.

gabbia ['gabbja] SF **a** (*gen*) cage; (*da imballaggio*) crate ▶ **la gabbia degli accusati** (*Dir*) the dock ▶ **gabbia di matti** (*fig*) madhouse ▶ **gabbia toracica** (*Anat*) rib cage **b** (*Equitazione: ostacolo*) double.

gabbiano [gab'bjano] SM (sea)gull ▶ **gabbiano comune** black-headed gull ▶ **gabbiano reale** herring gull.

gabella [ga'bɛlla] SF (*Storia: tassa*) duty.

gabinetto [gabi'netto] SM **a** (*WC*) lavatory, toilet **b** (*di medico*) surgery, consulting room **c** (*Pol: ministero*) ≈ ministry; (: *di ministro*) advisers PL.

Gabon [ga'bon] SM: **il Gabon** Gabon.

gaelico, a, ci, che [ga'ɛliko] AGG, SM Gaelic.

gaffe [gaf] SF INV blunder, boob (*fam*); **fare una gaffe** to put one's foot in it (*fam*).

gag [gæg] SF INV (*Cine, Teatro*) gag.

gagà [ga'ga] SM INV fop, dandy.

gaggia, gie [gad'dʒia] SF (*Bot*) locust tree, false acacia.

gagliardamente [gaʎʎarda'mente] AVV (*in modo valoroso*) courageously, bravely; (*efficacemente*) vigorously, strongly.

gagliardetto [gaʎʎar'detto] SM pennant.

gagliardo, a [gaʎ'ʎardo] AGG strong, robust.

Gaia ['gaja] SF Gaea.

gaiamente [gaja'mente] AVV cheerfully, happily.

gaiezza [ga'jettsa] SF (*di persona*) gaiety, cheerfulness; (*di colori*) brightness.

gaio, aia, ai, aie ['gajo] AGG (*persona*) cheerful, happy; (*colore*) bright, gay.

gala ['gala] **1** SF **a** (*ornamento*) bow **b** : **serata di gala** gala evening; **uniforme di gran gala** full-dress uniform; **pranzo di gala** banquet. **2** SM gala, festivity.

galante [ga'lante] **1** AGG **a** (*cortese*) gallant, chivalrous **b** (*amoroso*) romantic; **avventura galante** love affair. **2** SM gallant.

galantemente [galante'mente] AVV gallantly.

galanteria [galante'ria] SF gallantry.

galantuomo [galan'twɔmo] SM (*pl* **-uomini**) gentleman.

Galapagos [gala'pagos] SFPL (*anche:* **le isole Galapagos**) the Galápagos Islands.

galassia [ga'lassja] SF galaxy.

galateo [gala'tɛo] SM etiquette.

galattico, a, ci, che [ga'lattiko] AGG galactic.

galea [ga'lɛa] SF (*Storia: nave*) galley.

galeone [gale'one] SM galleon.

galeotto [gale'ɔtto] SM (*Storia*) galley slave; (*carcerato*) convict.

galera [ga'lɛra] SF **a** (*fam*) prison, gaol; **avanzo di galera** criminal type; **vita da galera** (*fig*) dog's life **b** (*Naut*) galley.

galla¹ ['galla]: **a galla** AVV afloat; **stare a galla** to float; (*fig*) to keep one's head above water; **venire a galla** to surface, come to the surface; (*fig: verità*) to come out, come to light.

galla² ['galla] SF (*Bot*) gall.

galleggiabilità [galleddʒabili'ta] SF buoyancy.

galleggiamento [galleddʒa'mento] SM floating; **linea di galleggiamento** (*di nave*) waterline.

galleggiante [galled'dʒante] **1** AGG floating. **2** SM (*Tecn, Aer, Pesca*) float; (*natante*) barge; (*boa*) buoy.

galleggiare [galled'dʒare] VI (*aus* **avere**) to float.

galleria [galle'ria] SF **a** (*traforo*) tunnel ▶ **galleria del vento** o **aerodinamica** (*Aer*) wind tunnel **b** (*Archit, d'arte*) gallery; (*strada coperta con negozi*) arcade; (*Cine*) balcony; (*Teatro*) circle.

Galles ['galles] SM: **il Galles** Wales.

gallese [gal'lese] **1** AGG Welsh. **2** SM/F Welshman/Welshwoman; **i gallesi** the Welsh. **3** SM (*lingua*) Welsh.

galletta [gal'letta] SF cracker.

galletto [gal'letto] SM young cock, cockerel; (*fig*) cocky

young man; **fare il galletto** to show off (*in front of girls*).
Gallia [gal'lja] SF: **la Gallia** Gaul.
gallicismo [galli'tʃizmo] SM gallicism.
gallico, a, ci, che ['gallico] AGG Gallic.
gallina [gal'lina] SF hen; **gallina lessa** boiled chicken; **andare a letto con le galline** to go to bed early; **la gallina dalla uova d'oro** the goose that lays the golden eggs; **gallina vecchia fa buon brodo** (*Proverbio*) an old hen makes good broth.
gallinacei [galli'natʃei] SMPL gallinaceans.
gallinella [galli'nɛlla] SF: **gallinella d'acqua** moorhen.
gallismo [gal'lizmo] SM machismo.
gallo[1] ['gallo] [1] SM cock; **al canto del gallo** at daybreak, at cockcrow; **fare il gallo** to show off (*in front of girls*) ▶**gallo cedrone** capercaillie ▶**gallo da combattimento** fighting cock.
[2] AGG INV (*Pugilato*): **peso gallo** bantamweight.
gallo[2], **a** ['gallo] SM/F (*Storia*) Gaul.
galloccia, ce [gal'lɔttʃa] SF (*Naut*) cleat.
gallone[1] [gal'lone] SM **a** (*Mil*) stripe; **guadagnarsi i galloni** to be promoted; **perdere i galloni** to lose one's stripes **b** (*ornamento*) braid, piece of braid.
gallone[2] [gal'lone] SM (*unità di misura*) gallon.
galoppante [galop'pante] AGG (*inflazione, tisi*) galloping.
galoppare [galop'pare] VI (*aus* **avere**) (*cavallo*) to gallop; (*fig: correre affannosamente*) to rush about; (: *fantasia, immaginazione*) to run wild, run riot; **sua madre lo fa galoppare!** his mother runs him off his feet!
galoppata [galop'pata] SF (*di cavallo*) gallop; **ho fatto una galoppata per arrivare in tempo** (*fig*) I had to dash to get here in time.
galoppino [galop'pino] SM **a** errand boy **b** (*Pol*) canvasser.
galoppo [ga'lɔppo] SM gallop; **piccolo galoppo** canter; **al galoppo** (*anche fig*) at a gallop; **andare al galoppo** to gallop; **partire al galoppo** to set off at a gallop; (*fig*) to rush off *o* away.
galoscia, sce [ga'lɔʃʃa] SF = **caloscia**.
galvanizzare [galvanid'dzare] VT (*Med, Tecn, anche fig*) to galvanize.
galvanizzazione [galvaniddzat'tsjone] SF (*Med, Tecn*) galvanization.
gamba ['gamba] SF (*Anat, di mobile*) leg; (*di lettera, nota musicale*) tail; **le gambe del tavolo** the table legs; **con le proprie gambe** on one's own two feet; **essere di buona gamba** *o* **di gamba lesta** to be a good walker; **scappare a gambe levate** *o* **in spalla** to take to one's heels; **darsela a gambe** to take to one's heels; **gambe!** scatter!; **andare a gambe all'aria** to fall headlong; (*fig: progetto*) to fall through; **prendere qc sotto gamba** to treat sth too lightly; **prendere qn sotto gamba** not to take sb seriously; **in gamba** (*in buona salute*) well; (*capace, sveglio*) bright, smart.
gambale [gam'bale] SM legging.
gambaletto [gamba'letto] SM knee-high sock.
gamberetto [gambe'retto] SM shrimp.
gambero ['gambero] SM (*di mare*) prawn; (*di fiume*) crayfish; **fare come i gamberi** to go backwards; **rosso come un gambero** as red as a beetroot (*o* lobster).
gamberone [gambe'rone] SM Dublin Bay prawn.
gambetto [gam'betto] SM (*Scacchi*) gambit.
Gambia ['gambja] SM: **il Gambia** the Gambia.
gambizzare [gambid'dzare] VT to kneecap.
gambizzazione [gambiddzat'tsjone] SF kneecapping.

gambo ['gambo] SM (*di fiore, bicchiere*) stem; (*di frutta, fungo*) stalk ▶**gambo della punteria** (*Aut*) push rod.
gamella [ga'mɛlla] SF mess tin.
gamete [ga'mɛte] SM (*Bio*) gamete.
gamma[1] ['gamma] AGG INV: **raggi gamma** gamma rays.
gamma[2] ['gamma] SF (*Mus*) scale; (*fig*) range ▶**gamma d'onda** (*Radio*) waveband ▶**gamma di prodotti** product range.
ganascia, sce [ga'naʃʃa] SF (*Zool, Tecn*) jaw; (*Aut: del freno*) brake shoes; **mangiare a quattro ganasce** to eat like a horse.
gancio, ci ['gantʃo] SM (*gen, Pugilato*) hook.
gang [gæŋ] SF INV gang.
Gange ['gandʒe] SM: **il Gange** the Ganges.
ganghero ['gangero] SM (*di porta*) hinge; **uscire dai gangheri** (*fig*) to lose one's temper, go off at the deep end, fly into a rage; **essere fuori dai gangheri** (*fig*) to be beside o.s. with rage.
ganglio, gli ['gangljo] SM (*Anat, Med*) ganglion.
gangrena [gan'grɛna] SF = **cancrena**.
gangster ['gæŋstə] SM INV gangster; (*fig*) shark, crook.
Ganimede [gani'mɛde] SM (*Mitol*) Ganymede.
gara ['gara] SF **a** (*concorso*) competition, contest; (*di velocità*) race; **gara di canto/nuoto/tiro** singing/swimming/shooting competition; **gare automobilistiche/ciclistiche** car/cycle races; **entrare in gara** to enter a competition (*o* race); **essere in gara** to be competing; **hanno fatto a gara a chi riusciva meglio** they competed *o* vied with each other to see who could do it best **b** (*Comm, Econ*): **gara d'appalto** call for bids.
garage [ga'raʒ] SM INV (*autorimessa*) garage.
garagista, i, e [gara'dʒista] SM/F (*proprietario*) garage owner; (*gestore*) garage manager.
garante [ga'rante] [1] AGG: **farsi garante di** *o* **per qc** to vouch for sth, guarantee sth; **farsi garante di** *o* **per qn** to stand surety for sb.
[2] SM/F guarantor.
garantire [garan'tire] [1] VT (*gen*) to guarantee; (*dare per certo*) to assure; **ti garantisco che sarà pronto domani** I guarantee that it will be ready tomorrow; **garantire un debito** to stand surety for a debt.
[2] **garantirsi** VIP: **garantirsi da** *o* **contro** to insure o.s. against.
garantismo [garan'tizmo] SM protection of civil liberties.
garantista, i, e [garan'tista] [1] AGG protecting civil liberties.
[2] SM/F civil libertarian.
garantito, a [garan'tito] AGG guaranteed; **il successo sembra ormai garantito** success now seems certain; **è garantito che pioverà** it's bound to rain; **se glielo chiedi dirà di no, garantito!** if you ask him he'll be bound to say no!
garanzia [garan'tsia] SF (*gen, Comm*) guarantee; (*pegno*) security, surety; **in garanzia** under guarantee; **questa persona non dà alcuna garanzia** this person is not to be trusted, this person is unreliable.
garbare [gar'bare] VI (*aus* **essere**): **non mi garba** I don't like it (*o* him *ecc*).
garbatamente [garbata'mente] AVV (*vedi agg*) courteously, politely; kindly.
garbato, a [gar'bato] AGG (*cortese*) courteous, polite; (*gentile*) kind.
garbo ['garbo] SM **a** (*grazia*) grace; **muoversi con garbo**/

senza garbo to move gracefully/awkwardly; **non ha garbo nel vestire** she doesn't dress well **b** (*gentilezza*) politeness, courtesy; **una persona di garbo** a well-mannered person.

garbuglio, gli [gar'buʎʎo] SM tangle; (*fig*) muddle, mess.

garçonnière [garso'njɛr] SF INV bachelor pad.

gardenia [gar'dɛnja] SF gardenia.

gareggiare [gared'dʒare] VI (*aus* avere): **gareggiare in qc** to compete in sth; **gareggiare con qn** to compete *o* vie with sb.

garganella [garga'nɛlla] SF: **a garganella** from the bottle.

gargarismo [garga'rizmo] SM gargle; **fare un gargarismo** *o* **dei gargarismi** to gargle.

garibaldino, a [garibal'dino] ① AGG (*Storia*) of (*o* relating to) Garibaldi; **alla garibaldina** impetuously. ② SM soldier in Garibaldi's army.

garitta [ga'ritta] SF (*di caserma*) sentry box.

garofano [ga'rɔfano] SM carnation.

garrese [gar'rese] SM withers *pl*.

garretto [gar'retto] SM hock.

garrire [gar'rire] VI (*aus* avere) (*uccelli*) to chirp.

garrotta [gar'rɔtta] SF garrotte.

garrottare [garrot'tare] VT to garrotte.

garrulo, a ['garrulo] AGG **a** (*uccello*) chirping **b** (*loquace*) garrulous, talkative.

garza ['gardza] SF (*tessuto*, *Med*) gauze; **una garza** (*Med*) a gauze bandage.

garzone [gar'dzone] SM (*di negozio*) boy; **il garzone del macellaio** the butcher's boy.

gas [gas] ① SM INV **a** gas; **l'uomo del gas** the gasman; **scaldabagno/stufa a gas** gas waterheater/stove **b** (*Aut*): **dare gas** to step on the gas, accelerate; **a tutto gas** (*anche fig*) at full speed; **è partito a tutto gas** he roared off. ② ▶**gas asfissiante** poison gas ▶**gas esilarante** laughing gas ▶ **gas illuminante** town gas ▶ **gas inerti** *o* **nobili** inert gases ▶**gas lacrimogeno** tear gas ▶**gas liquido** liquid gas ▶**gas naturale** natural gas.

gasare [ga'zare] ① VT = **gassare**. ② **gasarsi** VR (*fam*) to get excited; (*montarsi*) to become too full of o.s.

gasato, a [ga'zato] ① AGG **a** (*bibita*) = **gassato b** (*fam*: *persona*) excited; (: *montato*) big-headed. ② SM/F (*fam*: *persona*) big-head.

gasdotto [gaz'dotto] SM gas pipeline.

gasista, i [ga'zista] SM = **gassista**.

gasolina [gazo'lina] SF gasoline.

gasolio [ga'zɔljo] SM diesel (oil).

gasometro [ga'zɔmetro] SM gasometer.

gassa ['gassa] SF (*Naut*): **gassa d'amante** bowline knot.

gassare [gas'sare] VT **a** (*liquido*) to aerate, make fizzy **b** (*uccidere col gas*) to gas.

gassato, a [gas'sato] AGG (*bibita*) fizzy.

gassificare [gassifi'kare] VT to gasify.

gassista, i [gas'sista] SM gasman.

gassometro [gas'sɔmetro] SM = **gasometro**.

gassosa [gas'sosa] SF = **gazzosa**.

gassoso, a [gas'soso] AGG gaseous.

gastrico, a, ci, che ['gastriko] AGG gastric.

gastrite [gas'trite] SF gastritis.

gastroenterite [gastroente'rite] SF gastroenteritis.

gastronomia [gastrono'mia] SF gastronomy.

gastronomico, a, ci, che [gastro'nɔmiko] AGG gastronomic.

gastronomo, a [gas'trɔnomo] SM/F gourmet, gastronome.

G.A.T.T. [gat] SIGLA M (= *General Agreement on Tariffs and Trade*) GATT.

gatta ['gatta] SF (female) cat, she-cat; **una gatta da pelare** (*fam*) a thankless task; **qui gatta ci cova!** I smell a rat!, there's something fishy going on here!

gattabuia [gatta'buja] SF (*fam scherz*: *prigione*) clink.

gattino, a [gat'tino] SM/F kitten.

gatto ['gatto] ① SM (*gen*) cat; (*maschio*) tomcat; **siamo rimasti in quattro gatti** there were only a few of us left; **quando il gatto non c'è i topi ballano** (*Proverbio*) when the cat's away the mice will play. ② ▶**gatto delle nevi** (*Sci*) snowcat ▶**gatto a nove code** cat-o'-nine-tails ▶**gatto selvatico** wildcat.

gattoni [gat'toni] AVV on all fours.

gattopardo [gatto'pardo] SM: **gattopardo africano** serval ▶**gattopardo americano** ocelot.

gattuccio, ci [gat'tuttʃo] SM dogfish.

gaudente [gau'dɛnte] SM/F pleasure-seeker; **fare la vita del gaudente** to live like a lord.

gaudio, di ['gaudjo] SM joy, happiness.

gavetta [ga'vetta] SF (*Mil*) mess tin; **venire dalla gavetta** (*fig*) to rise from the ranks.

gavina [ga'vina] SF (*Zool*) common gull.

gavitello [gavi'tɛllo] SM (*Naut*) mooring buoy.

gavone [ga'vone] SM (*Naut*) locker.

gazebo [gə'zi:bou] SM INV summerhouse, gazebo.

gazolina [gaddzo'lina] SF = **gasolina**.

gazza ['gaddza] SF magpie.

gazzarra [gad'dzarra] SF racket, din; **fare gazzarra** to make a din.

gazzella [gad'dzɛlla] SF **a** (*Zool*) gazelle **b** (*auto dei Carabinieri*) (high-speed) police car.

gazzetta [gad'dzetta] SF gazette ▶**Gazzetta Ufficiale** *official publication containing the text of new laws.*

gazzettino [gaddzet'tino] SM **a** (*di giornale*: *titolo*) gazette; (: *sezione*) page; **gazzettino teatrale** theatre page; **gazzettino regionale** (*alla radio*) regional news *sg* **b** (*fig*: *persona pettegola*) gossip.

gazzosa [gad'dzosa] SF fizzy drink, ≈ lemonade.

Gazz. Uff. ABBR = **Gazzetta Ufficiale**.

GB SIGLA (= *Gran Bretagna*) GB.

G.C. ABBR = **genio civile**.

G.d.F. ABBR = **guardia di finanza**.

GE SIGLA = *Genova*.

geco, chi ['dʒɛko] SM (*Zool*) gecko.

gel [dʒɛl] SM INV gel.

gelare [dʒe'lare] ① VT to freeze; **mi ha gelato il sangue** (*fig*) it made my blood run cold. ② VI (*aus* essere) to freeze; **il lago è gelato** the lake has frozen over; **chiudi la porta, si gela!** close the door, it's freezing!. ③ VB IMPERS to freeze; **gela** it's freezing.

gelata [dʒe'lata] SF frost.

gelataio, aia, ai, aie [dʒela'tajo] SM/F (*venditore*) ice-cream seller; (*produttore*) ice-cream maker.

gelateria [dʒelate'ria] SF ice-cream shop, ice-cream parlour (*Am*).

gelatiera [dʒela'tjɛra] SF ice-cream machine.

gelatina [dʒela'tina] SF (*gen*, *Culin*) gelatine ▶**gelatina esplosiva** gelignite ▶**gelatina di frutta** fruit jelly.

gelatinoso, a [dʒelati'noso] AGG gelatinous.

gelato, a [dʒe'lato] ① AGG frozen; **ho le mani gelate** my hands are frozen (stiff).

[2] SM ice cream; **gelato di fragola/di crema** strawberry/dairy ice.

gelidamente [dʒelida'mente] AVV (fig) icily.

gelido, a ['dʒɛlido] AGG (aria, vento) icy, freezing; (mani, acqua) freezing, ice-cold; (fig: accoglienza, espressione, sguardo) icy, frosty.

gelo ['dʒɛlo] SM (temperatura) intense cold; (brina) frost; (fig: inverno) cold weather; **il gelo invernale** the cold winter weather; **sentirsi il gelo nelle ossa** to feel a chill of fear; **il gelo della morte** the chill hand of death.

gelone [dʒe'lone] SM chilblain.

gelosamente [dʒelosa'mente] AVV jealously.

gelosia[1] [dʒelo'sia] SF (sentimento) jealousy; **conservare qc con gran gelosia** to guard sth jealously.

gelosia[2] [dʒelo'sia] SF (persiana) shutter.

geloso, a [dʒe'loso] AGG jealous.

gelso ['dʒɛlso] SM mulberry (tree) ▶ **gelso nero** black mulberry.

gelsomino [dʒelso'mino] SM jasmine.

gemellaggio, gi [dʒemel'laddʒo] SM twinning.

gemellare [dʒemel'lare] **[1]** AGG twin attr.
[2] VT (città) to twin.

gemello, a [dʒe'mɛllo] **[1]** AGG (fratelli, letti) twin attr.
[2] SM/F (persona, oggetto) twin.
[3]: **gemelli** SMPL **a** (di camicia) cufflinks **b** (Astrol): **Gemelli** Gemini sg; **essere dei Gemelli** to be Gemini.

gemere ['dʒemere] VI (aus avere) (ferito): **gemere (di)** to groan (with), moan (with); (cane) to whine; (piccione, tortora: tubare) to coo; (fig: cigolare) to creak.

gemito ['dʒemito] SM groan, moan.

gemma ['dʒemma] SF **a** (Bot) bud **b** (gioiello) gem, jewel.

gemmazione [dʒemmat'tsjone] SF (Bot) budding; (Bio) gemmation.

gemmologia [dʒemmolo'dʒia] SF gemology.

Gen. ABBR (Mil: = generale) Gen.

gen. ABBR (= generale, generalmente) gen.

gendarme [dʒen'darme] SM **a** policeman; **essere un gendarme** (fig) to be a martinet **b** (Alpinismo) gendarme.

gene ['dʒɛne] SM gene.

genealogia, gie [dʒenealo'dʒia] SF genealogy.

genealogico, a, ci, che [dʒenea'lɔdʒiko] AGG genealogical; **albero genealogico** family tree.

generale[1] [dʒene'rale] AGG general; **nell'interesse generale** in the interest of everyone, for the common good; **un quadro generale della situazione** a general o overall view of the situation; **l'opinione generale** public opinion; **direttore generale** managing director; **console generale** consul general; **in generale** generally, in general; (parlare) in general terms; **in generale sto bene** on the whole I am quite well; **mantenersi o stare sulle generali** to stick to generalities.

generale[2] [dʒene'rale] SM general; **generale di brigata** brigadier.

generalesco, a, schi, sche [dʒenera'lesko] AGG (scherz) as of a general.

generalità [dʒenerali'ta] SF INV **a** (qualità) generality **b** (maggioranza) majority; **nella generalità dei casi** in most cases **c** (dati anagrafici): **generalità** SFPL particulars; **dare le generalità** give one's name and address.

generalizzare [dʒeneralid'dzare] VT, VI (aus avere) to generalize.

generalizzazione [dʒeneraliddzat'tsjone] SF generalization.

generalmente [dʒeneral'mente] AVV generally, usually.

generare [dʒene'rare] VT **a** (dar vita, anche fig) to give birth to **b** (produrre: Tecn) to generate, produce; (: Geom) to generate, form **c** (causare: sospetti) to arouse; (: confusione) to create.

generativo, a [dʒenera'tivo] AGG generative.

generatore [dʒenera'tore] SM (Elettr) generator.

generazionale [dʒenerattsjo'nale] AGG generation attr.

generazione [dʒenerat'tsjone] SF generation; **la nuova generazione** the new o younger generation.

genere ['dʒɛnere] SM **a** kind, type, sort; **oggetti di ogni genere** all kinds of things; **cose del o di questo genere** such things; **non farmi più uno scherzo del genere!** don't ever play such a trick on me again!; **è bravo nel suo genere** in his own way he is quite good; **questo vaso è bello, nel suo genere** this is a nice vase of its kind; **in genere** generally, usually, as a rule; **i documentari non sono il mio genere** documentaries aren't my cup of tea **b** (prodotti): **generi** SMPL article, product ▶ **generi alimentari** foodstuffs ▶ **generi di consumo** consumer goods ▶ **generi di prima necessità** basic essentials **c** (Bio, Zool, Bot) genus ▶ **il genere umano** mankind, the human race **d** (Gramm) gender **e** (Letteratura, Arte) genre.

genericamente [dʒenerika'mente] AVV generically.

genericità [dʒenerritʃi'ta] SF vagueness, generality.

generico, a, ci, che [dʒe'nɛriko] **[1]** AGG **a** generic; (vago: descrizione, accuse) vague, imprecise **b** (non specializzato): **medico generico** general practitioner.
[2] SM generality; **i suoi discorsi non escono dal generico** his speeches never get beyond generalities.

genero ['dʒɛnero] SM son-in-law.

generosamente [dʒenerosa'mente] AVV generously.

generosità [dʒenerosi'ta] SF INV generosity; **è un uomo di grande generosità** he's a very generous man.

generoso, a [dʒene'roso] AGG generous; **non è generoso da parte tua** that's not very nice of you; **un vino generoso** a full-bodied wine.

genesi ['dʒɛnezi] SF genesis; (Bibbia): **la Genesi** Genesis.

genetica [dʒe'nɛtika] SF genetics sg.

geneticamente [dʒenetika'mente] AVV genetically.

genetico, a, ci, che [dʒe'nɛtiko] AGG genetic.

gengiva [dʒen'dʒiva] SF gum.

gengivale [dʒendʒi'vale] AGG gum attr.

genia [dʒe'nia] SF (pegg) mob, gang.

geniale [dʒe'njale] AGG (persona, artista) of genius; (idea, soluzione) brilliant, inspired.

genialità [dʒenjali'ta] SF (vedi agg) genius; brilliance.

genialmente [dʒenjal'mente] AVV brilliantly.

genialoide [dʒenja'lɔide] SM/F eccentric genius.

geniere [dʒe'njɛre] SM (Mil) sapper.

genio[1], ni ['dʒɛnjo] SM **a** (persona) genius; **essere un genio in matematica** he is a mathematical genius o wizard; **essere un genio incompreso** to be a misunderstood genius; **avere un colpo di genio** to have a brainwave **b** (talento): **avere il genio degli affari** to have a genius o flair for business **c** (gusto): **andare a genio a qn** to be to sb's liking; **non mi va a genio** I am not very keen on it (o him ecc) **b** (Mitol: gen) spirit; (: arabo) genie.

genio[2] ['dʒɛnjo] SM **a** (Mil): **il genio (militare)** the Engineers **b**: **genio civile** civil engineers pl.

genitale [dʒeni'tale] ① AGG genital.
  ② : **genitali** SMPL genitals.
genitivo, a [dʒeni'tivo] AGG, SM genitive.
genitore, trice [dʒeni'tore] SM/F parent, father (*o* mother); **genitori** SMPL parents.
gennaio [dʒen'najo] SM January *per fraseologia vedi* **luglio.**
genoa ['dʒɛnoa] SM INV (*Naut*) genoa (jib).
genocidio, di [dʒeno'tʃidjo] SM genocide.
genoma [dʒe'nɔma] SM (*Bio*) genom(e).
genotipo [dʒeno'tipo] SM (*Bio*) genotype.
Genova ['dʒɛnova] SF Genoa.
genovese [dʒeno'vese] AGG, SM/F Genoese *pl inv.*
gentaglia [dʒen'taʎʎa] SF (*pegg*) rabble, scum.
gente ['dʒɛnte] SF people *pl*; **c'era tanta gente** there were lots of people there; **gente di campagna** country people; **gente di città** townspeople; **gente di mare** seafaring folk; **è brava gente** they are nice people; **aspetto gente** I'm waiting for somebody; **ho gente a cena** I've got people to dinner; **le genti anglosassoni** (*letter: papolazioni*) the Anglo-Saxon peoples; **diritto delle genti** law of nations.
gentildonna [dʒentil'dɔnna] SF gentlewoman, lady.
gentile[1] [dʒen'tile] AGG **a** (*buono*) kind; (*garbato*) courteous, polite; **è molto gentile da parte sua** it's very kind *o* nice of you; **vuoi essere tanto gentile da...?** would you be so kind as to ...?; **i commessi sono sempre così gentili** the shop assistants are always so helpful
  b (*delicato: lineamenti*) fine; (: *profumo*) delicate; **il gentil sesso** the fair sex
  c (*nelle lettere*): **Gentile Signore** Dear Sir; (*sulla busta*): **Gentile Signor Fernando Villa** Mr Fernando Villa.
gentile[2] [dʒen'tile] SM (*Rel*) Gentile.
gentilezza [dʒenti'lettsa] SF **a** (*bontà*) kindness; (*garbatezza*) courtesy; **gentilezze** SFPL acts of kindness; **fare una gentilezza a qn** to do sb a favour; **fammi la gentilezza di chiudere la porta** be so kind as to close the door; **per gentilezza** (*per favore*) please **b** (*grazia: di lineamenti*) delicacy; (: *di movimento*) grace.
gentilmente [dʒentil'mente] AVV (*vedi agg a*) kindly; courteously, politely.
gentiluomo [dʒenti'lwɔmo] SM (*pl* -**uomini**) gentleman.
genuflessione [dʒenufles'sjone] SF genuflection, genuflexion (*Brit*).
genuflesso, a [dʒenu'flɛsso] PP di **genuflettersi.**
genuflettersi [dʒenu'flɛttersi] VR IRREG to genuflect, kneel.
genuinamente [dʒenuina'mente] AVV genuinely.
genuinità [dʒenuini'ta] SF (*di prodotti*) naturalness; (*di sentimento*) sincerity, genuineness.
genuino, a [dʒenu'ino] AGG (*prodotto*) natural; (*persona, sentimento*) genuine, sincere; (*risata*) natural, unaffected; **ha una genuina vocazione** he has a true *o* real vocation.
genziana [dʒen'tsjana] SF gentian.
genzianella [dʒentsja'nɛlla] SF gentianella.
geodesia [dʒeode'sia] SF geodesy.
geofisica [dʒeo'fizika] SF geophysics *sg.*
geografia [dʒeogra'fia] SF geography.
geograficamente [dʒeografika'mente] AVV geographically.
geografico, a, ci, che [dʒeo'grafiko] AGG geographical; **atlante geografico** atlas; **carta geografica** map.
geografo, a [dʒe'ɔgrafo] SM/F geographer.
geologia [dʒeolo'dʒia] SF geology.
geologicamente [dʒeolodʒika'mente] AVV geologically.

geologico, a, ci, che [dʒeo'lɔdʒiko] AGG geological.
geometra, i, e [dʒe'ɔmetra] SM/F surveyor.
geometria [dʒeome'tria] SF geometry.
geometricamente [dʒeometrika'mente] AVV geometrically.
geometrico, a, ci, che [dʒeo'mɛtriko] AGG geometric(al).
geopolitica [dʒeopo'litika] SF geopolitics *sg.*
geopolitico, a, ci, che [dʒeopo'litiko] AGG geopolitical.
geotermico, a, ci, che [dʒeo'tɛrmiko] AGG geothermal.
geotropismo [dʒeotro'pizmo] SM geotropism.
geranio, ni [dʒe'ranjo] SM geranium.
gerarca, chi [dʒe'rarka] SM (*Storia: nel fascismo*) party official.
gerarchia [dʒerar'kia] SF hierarchy; **le più alte gerarchie** the upper echelons.
gerarchicamente [dʒerarkika'mente] AVV hierarchically.
gerarchico, a, ci, che [dʒe'rarkiko] AGG hierarchical.
Geremia [dʒere'mia] SM Jeremiah.
gerente [dʒe'rɛnte] SM/F manager/manageress.
gerenza [dʒe'rɛntsa] SF management.
gergale [dʒer'gale] AGG (*vedi sm*) slang *attr*; jargon *attr.*
gergo ['dʒergo] SM (*gen*) slang; (*professionale*) jargon; **gergo della malavita** criminals' slang.
geriatria [dʒerja'tria] SF geriatrics *sg.*
geriatrico, a, ci, che [dʒe'rjatriko] AGG geriatric.
Gerico ['dʒeriko] SM Jericho.
gerla ['dʒɛrla] SF *conical wicker basket.*
Germania [dʒer'manja] SF: **la Germania** Germany.
germanico, a, ci, che [dʒer'maniko] AGG Germanic.
germanismo [dʒerma'nizmo] SM Germanism.
germano [dʒer'mano] SM (*Zool*): **germano reale** mallard.
germe ['dʒerme] SM (*gen*) germ; (*fig*) seed; **germi dell'influenza** flu germs; **i germi della ribellione** the seeds of rebellion.
germinale [dʒermi'nale] AGG germinal.
germinare [dʒermi'nare] VI (*aus* **essere** *o* **avere**) to germinate.
germinazione [dʒerminat'tsjone] SF germination.
germogliare [dʒermoʎ'ʎare] VI (*aus* **essere** *o* **avere**) (*germinare*) to germinate; (*emettere germogli*) to sprout.
germoglio, gli [dʒer'moʎʎo] SM (*gen*) shoot; (*gemma*) bud.
geroglifico, ci [dʒero'glifiko] SM hieroglyphic.
gerontologia [dʒerontolo'dʒia] SF gerontology.
gerontologo, a, gi, ghe [dʒeron'tologo] SM/F specialist in geriatrics.
gerundio, di [dʒe'rundjo] SM gerund.
Gerusalemme [dʒeruza'lɛmme] SF Jerusalem.
gessato, a [dʒes'sato] AGG: **abito gessato** pinstripe suit.
gessetto [dʒes'setto] SM piece of chalk.
gesso ['dʒɛsso] SM (*gen*) chalk; (*minerale*) gypsum; (*Scultura, Med, Edil*) plaster; (*statuetta*) plaster figure; **mi hanno tolto il gesso** (*Med*) they've taken off my plaster (cast).
gesta ['dʒɛsta] SFPL (*letter*) deeds, feats.
gestante [dʒes'tante] SF expectant mother.
gestazione [dʒestat'tsjone] SF gestation; **il progetto è ancora in gestazione** (*fig*) the project is still at the planning stage.
gesticolare [dʒestiko'lare] VI (*aus* **avere**) to gesticulate.
gestionale [dʒestjo'nale] AGG management *attr.*
gestione [dʒes'tjone] SF management; **gestione finanziaria** financial management.
gestire [dʒes'tire] VT to manage, run.
gesto ['dʒɛsto] SM gesture; **ha fatto un gesto di rabbia** he

made an angry gesture; **non ha fatto un gesto per aiutarmi** he didn't lift a finger to help me.

gestore [dʒes'tore] SM manager.

gestuale [dʒestu'ale] AGG: **linguaggio gestuale** sign language.

gestualità [dʒestuali'ta] SF (*Arte*) gestural art; (*insieme di gesti*) gestures *pl*.

Gesù [dʒe'zu] SM Jesus; **Gesù Bambino** the Christ Child, baby Jesus (*fam*).

gesuita, i [dʒezu'ita] SM Jesuit.

Getsemani [dʒet'sɛmani] SM (*Bibbia*) Gethsemane.

gettare [dʒet'tare] ⓵ VT **a** (*lanciare*) to throw; (: *con forza*) to fling, hurl; (: *in aria*) to toss; **gettare (via)** (*liberarsi di*) to throw away; **gettare qc a qn** to throw sth to sb; **gettare qc addosso a qn** (*sasso*) to throw sth at sb; (*acqua, sabbia*) to throw sth over sb; **si gettò un mantello sulle spalle** he threw a coat round his shoulders; **gettare a terra qn** to throw sb to the ground; **gettare le braccia al collo di qn** to throw *o* fling one's arms round sb's neck; **gettare la colpa addosso a qn** to cast the blame on sb; **gettare qc in faccia a qn** (*anche fig*) to throw sth in sb's face; **gettò un rapido sguardo intorno** he had a quick look round; **gettare l'ancora** (*Naut*) to drop anchor; **gettare le reti** to cast the nets; **gettare a mare** (*fig: persona*) to abandon; **quella notizia l'ha gettato nella disperazione** he was plunged into despair at the news

b (*metalli, cera*) to cast; (*fondamenta*) to lay; **gettare un ponte su un fiume** to throw a bridge over a river

c (*emettere: acqua*) to spout; (: *grido*) to utter, give

d (*fraseologia*): **gettare le armi** (*anche fig*) to throw down one's weapons; **gettare la spugna** to throw in the sponge; **gettare la polvere negli occhi a qn** (*fig*) to throw dust in sb's eyes; **gettare luce su qc** to shed light on sth.

⓶ VI (*aus* **avere**) (*pianta*) to sprout.

⓷ VR **a** : **gettarsi in un'impresa** to throw o.s. into an enterprise; **gettarsi nella mischia** to hurl o.s. into the fray; **gettarsi contro** *o* **addosso a qn** to hurl o.s. at sb; **gettarsi sulla preda** to pounce on one's prey; **gettarsi ai piedi di qn** to throw o.s. at sb's feet

b (*fiume*): **gettarsi in** to flow into.

gettata [dʒet'tata] SF **a** (*di cemento, bronzo, reti*) cast **b** (*in balistica*) range **c** (*diga*) jetty.

gettito ['dʒettito] SM (*Econ: rendita, introito*) yield, revenue.

getto¹ ['dʒetto] SM **a** (*azione*) throwing; (*risultato*) throw, cast

b (*di acqua*) jet; **di getto** (*scrivere*) in one go, straight off; **a getto continuo** in a continuous stream, uninterruptedly; **scrive novelle a getto continuo** he writes one short story after another, he produces a constant stream of short stories; **a getto d'inchiostro** (*stampante*) ink-jet

c (*Bot*) shoot

d (*Metallurgia, Edil*) casting.

getto² ['dʒetto] SM (*Meteor*): **corrente a getto** jet stream.

gettonare [dʒetto'nare] VT (*fam: canzone in juke-box*) to play; **una canzone molto gettonata** a very popular song.

gettone [dʒet'tone] SM (*gen*) token; (*per giochi*) counter; (: *roulette*) chip ▶ **gettone di presenza** attendance fee ▶ **gettone del telefono** telephone token.

gettoniera [dʒetto'njɛra] SF telephone-token vending machine.

geyser ['gaizə] SM INV geyser.

Ghana ['gana] SM: **il Ghana** Ghana.

ghenga, ghe ['gɛnga] SF (*fam*) gang, crowd.

ghepardo [ge'pardo] SM cheetah.

gheppio, pi ['geppjo] SM (*Zool*) kestrel.

gheriglio, gli [ge'riʎʎo] SM kernel.

ghermire [ger'mire] VT to grasp, clasp, clutch.

ghetta ['getta] SF (*gambale*) gaiter.

ghettizzare [gettid'dzare] VT to confine to a ghetto; (*fig: isolare*) to ghettoize.

ghettizzazione [gettiddzat'tsjone] SF ghettoization.

ghetto ['getto] SM ghetto.

ghiacciaia [gjat'tʃaja] SF (*anche fig*) icebox.

ghiacciaio, ai [gjat'tʃajo] SM glacier ▶ **ghiacciaio continentale** ice sheet.

ghiacciare [gjat'tʃare] ⓵ VI (*aus* **essere**) to freeze; (*lago, fiume*) to ice over, freeze (over); **mi si è ghiacciato il sangue** my blood ran cold; **questa notte è ghiacciato** there was a frost last night.

⓶ VT to freeze.

⓷ VB IMPERS to freeze.

ghiacciato, a [gjat'tʃato] AGG (*gen*) frozen; (*bevanda*) ice-cold; **avevo le mani ghiacciate** my hands were frozen.

ghiaccio ['gjattʃo] SM ice; **hai le mani di ghiaccio** your hands are like ice; **restare di ghiaccio** to be dumbfounded; **rompere il ghiaccio** (*fig*) to break the ice; **quella donna è un pezzo di ghiaccio** that woman is as cold as ice ▶ **ghiaccio secco** dry ice.

ghiacciolo [gjat'tʃolo] SM **a** (*formazione di ghiaccio*) icicle **b** (*gelato*) ice lolly (*Brit*), popsicle (*Am*).

ghiaia ['gjaja] SF gravel.

ghiaioso, a [gja'joso] AGG gravelly.

ghianda ['gjanda] SF (*Bot*) acorn.

ghiandaia [gjan'daja] SF (*Zool*) jay.

ghiandola ['gjandola] SF (*Anat*) gland ▶ **ghiandole endocrine** *o* **a secrezione interna** endocrine *o* ductless glands ▶ **ghiandole esocrine** *o* **a secrezione esterna** exocrine glands.

ghiandolare [gjando'lare] AGG glandular.

ghiera ['gjɛra] SF (*Tecn*) ring nut.

ghigliottina [giʎʎot'tina] SF guillotine.

ghigliottinare [giʎʎotti'nare] VT to guillotine.

ghignare [giɲ'ɲare] VI (*aus* **avere**) to sneer, laugh derisively.

ghignata [giɲ'ɲata] SF (*fam*) laugh; **fare una ghignata** to have a good laugh.

ghigno ['giɲɲo] SM (*espressione*) sneer; (*risata*) mocking laugh.

ghingheri ['gingeri] SMPL: **in ghingheri** all dolled up; **mettersi in ghingheri** to dress up to the nines.

ghiottamente [gjotta'mente] AVV greedily.

ghiotto, a ['gjotto] AGG (*persona*): **ghiotto (di)** greedy (for); (*cibi*) appetizing, delicious; (*fig: notizia*) juicy.

ghiottone, a [gjot'tone] SM/F **a** (*persona*) glutton **b** (*Zool*) wolverine.

ghiottoneria [gjottone'ria] SF (*di persona*) greed, gluttony; (*cibo*) delicacy.

ghiribizzo [giri'biddzo] SM whim; **gli è venuto il ghiribizzo della pittura** he's taken it into his head to paint.

ghirigoro [giri'gɔro] SM (*scarabocchio*) doodle, scribble; (*arabesco*) flourish.

ghirlanda [gir'landa] SF garland, wreath.

ghiro ['giro] SM dormouse; **dormire come un ghiro** to sleep like a log *o* top.

ghisa ['giza] SF cast iron.

GI ABBR = **giudice istruttore**.

già [dʒa] AVV **a** (*gen*) already; **te l'ho già detto** I have already told you; **ho finito — di già?** I've finished — already?; **già che ci sei...** while you are at it ...; **è successo già da molto tempo** it happened a long time ago; **fra qualche anno sarà già un pianista famoso** in just a few years he will be a famous pianist; **già da bambino amava la musica** even as a child he loved music; **già sua madre lo faceva** his mother used to do it too

b (*ex*) formerly; **lo Zimbabwe, già Rodesia** Zimbabwe, formerly Rhodesia

c (*naturalmente*) of course, naturally; **già, avrei dovuto saperlo!** of course, I should have known!

giacca, che ['dʒakka] SF jacket ▶**giacca a vento** windcheater (*Brit*), windbreaker (*Am*), anorak.

giacché [dʒak'ke] CONG since, as.

giacchetta [dʒak'ketta] SF (light) jacket.

giaccio *ecc* ['dʒattʃo] VB vedi **giacere**.

giaccone [dʒak'kone] SM heavy jacket.

giacente [dʒa'tʃɛnte] AGG (*merce*) unsold; (*posta*) undelivered; (: *non ritirata*) unclaimed; (*Fin: capitale*) idle, uninvested.

giacenza [dʒa'tʃɛntsa] SF **a** (*Comm*): **merce in giacenza** (*non reclamata*) unclaimed goods; (*non recapitata*) undelivered goods; **giacenze di cassa** cash on *o* in hand; **giacenze di magazzino** unsold stock **b** (*Fin*): **capitale in giacenza** uninvested *o* idle capital.

giacere [dʒa'tʃere] VI IRREG (*aus essere*) (*gen*) to lie; (*Fin: capitale*) to lie idle; **il paese giace ai piedi della montagna** the village lies *o* is situated at the foot of the mountain; **giacere nell'ozio** to live in idleness; **la mia domanda giace ancora negli uffici del consolato** my application is still buried somewhere in the consulate.

giaciglio, gli [dʒa'tʃiʎʎo] SM bed, pallet.

giacimento [dʒatʃi'mento] SM (*Mineralogia*) deposit; **giacimento petrolifero** oil field.

giacinto [dʒa'tʃinto] SM hyacinth.

giaciuto, a [dʒa'tʃuto] PP di **giacere**.

giacqui *ecc* ['dʒakkwi] VB vedi **giacere**.

giaculatoria [dʒakula'tɔrja] SF short prayer; (*scherz: discorso noioso*) boring words *pl*.

giada ['dʒada] SF jade.

giaggiolo [dʒad'dʒɔlo] SM iris.

giaguaro [dʒa'gwaro] SM jaguar.

giallastro, a [dʒal'lastro] AGG yellowish; (*carnagione*) sallow.

giallistica [dʒal'listika] SF detective stories *pl*.

giallo, a ['dʒallo] ① AGG **a** (*colore*) yellow; (*carnagione*) sallow **b** : **film/libro giallo** detective film/novel.

② SM **a** (*colore*) yellow; (*di semaforo*) amber; **il giallo dell'uovo** (egg) yolk **b** (*romanzo*) detective story; (*film*) thriller.

giallognolo, a [dʒal'loɲɲolo] AGG yellowish, dirty yellow.

Giamaica [dʒa'maika] SF: **la Giamaica** Jamaica.

giamaicano, a [dʒamai'kano] AGG, SM/F Jamaican.

giammai [dʒam'mai] AVV never.

Giano ['dʒano] SM Janus.

Giappone [dʒap'pone] SM: **il Giappone** Japan.

giapponese [dʒappo'nese] ① AGG, SM/F Japanese *inv*. ② SM (*lingua*) Japanese.

giara ['dʒara] SF earthenware vessel.

giardinaggio [dʒardi'naddʒo] SM gardening.

giardinetta [dʒardi'netta] SF estate car (*Brit*), station wagon (*Am*).

giardiniera [dʒardi'njɛra] SF (*Culin*) mixed pickles *pl*.

giardiniere, a [dʒardi'njɛre] SM/F gardener.

giardino [dʒar'dino] SM garden ▶**giardino d'infanzia** nursery school, kindergarten ▶**giardino pensile** roof garden ▶**giardino pubblico** public gardens *pl*, (public) park ▶**giardino zoologico** zoo.

giarrettiera [dʒarret'tjɛra] SF garter; **Ordine della Giarrettiera** Order of the Garter.

Giasone [dʒa'zone] SM Jason.

Giava ['dʒava] SF Java.

giavellotto [dʒavel'lɔtto] SM javelin.

gibbone [dʒib'bone] SM (*Zool*) gibbon.

gibbosità [dʒibbosi'ta] SF INV: **le gibbosità del terreno** the bumps in the ground.

gibboso, a [dʒib'boso] AGG (*superficie*) bumpy; (*naso*) crooked.

giberna [dʒi'bɛrna] SF (*Mil*) cartridge case.

Gibilterra [dʒibil'tɛrra] SF Gibraltar.

gigante [dʒi'gante] ① AGG gigantic, giant; **confezione/formato gigante** (*Comm*) giant-size.

② SM giant; **gigante della letteratura** literary giant; **compiere passi da gigante** (*scienza*) to make huge strides.

giganteggiare [dʒiganted'dʒare] VI (*aus avere*): **giganteggiare su** to tower over.

gigantesco, a, schi, sche [dʒigan'tesko] AGG gigantic, huge.

gigantismo [dʒigan'tizmo] SM (*Med*) gigantism.

gigantografia [dʒigantogra'fia] SF (*Fot*) blow-up.

giglio, gli ['dʒiʎʎo] SM lily.

gigolo [ʒigɔ'lo] SM INV gigolo.

gilè [dʒi'lɛ] SM INV (*panciotto*) waistcoat; (*fatto a maglia*) sleeveless cardigan.

gin [dʒin] SM INV gin.

gincana [dʒin'kana] SF gymkhana.

gineceo [dʒine'tʃɛo] SM (*Archeol*) gynaeceum (*Brit*), gyneceum (*Am*); (*Bot*) gynoecium.

ginecologia [dʒinekolo'dʒia] SF gynaecology (*Brit*), gynecology (*Am*).

ginecologicamente [dʒinekolodʒika'mente] AVV gynaecologically (*Brit*), gynecologically (*Am*).

ginecologico, a, ci, che [dʒineko'lɔdʒiko] AGG gynaecological (*Brit*), gynecological (*Am*).

ginecologo, a, gi, ghe [dʒine'kɔlogo] SM/F gynaecologist (*Brit*), gynecologist (*Am*).

ginepraio [dʒine'prajo] SM (*fig*): **cacciarsi in un ginepraio** to get o.s. into a fine mess.

ginepro [dʒi'nepro] SM juniper.

ginestra [dʒi'nɛstra] SF (*Bot*) broom.

ginestrone [dʒines'trone] SM (*Bot*) whin.

Ginevra [dʒi'nevra] SF Geneva; **il lago di Ginevra** Lake Geneva.

ginevrino, a [dʒine'vrino] AGG, SM/F Genevan.

gingillarsi [dʒindʒil'larsi] VIP **a** (*perdere tempo*) to fritter away one's time **b** (*trastullarsi*): **gingillarsi con** to fiddle with.

gingillo [dʒin'dʒillo] SM (*ninnolo*) knick-knack, trinket; (*balocco*) plaything.

ginnasio, si [dʒin'nazjo] SM *the 4th and 5th year of secondary school*.

ginnasta, i, e [dʒin'nasta] SM/F gymnast.

ginnastica [dʒin'nastika] SF (*disciplina*) gymnastics *sg*; (*educazione fisica*) physical education; **fare ginnastica** (*Scol*) to do gym; **dovresti fare un po' di ginnastica** you

should take some exercise.

ginnico, a, ci, che [ˈdʒinniko] AGG gymnastic.

ginocchiata [dʒinokˈkjata] SF: **mi ha dato una ginocchiata nello stomaco** he kneed me in the stomach; **ho preso** *o* **battuto una ginocchiata contro il letto** I bumped my knee on the bed.

ginocchiera [dʒinokˈkjɛra] SF (*Sport*) kneepad; (*Med*) elasticated knee bandage.

ginocchio [dʒiˈnɔkkjo] (*pl f* **ginocchia**) SM knee; **al ginocchio** (*lunghezza*) knee-length; **in ginocchio** on one's knees, kneeling; **mettersi in ginocchio** to kneel (down); **mettere qn in ginocchio** (*vincere*) to bring sb to his knees; **sedersi sulle ginocchia di qn** to sit on sb's lap.

ginocchioni [dʒinokˈkjoni] AVV on one's knees; **cadere ginocchioni** to fall to one's knees.

Giobbe [ˈdʒɔbbe] SM Job.

giocare [dʒoˈkare] **1** VI (*aus* **avere**) **a** (*gen, Sport*) to play; **giocare a scacchi/ai soldatini/al pallone** to play (at) chess/soldiers/football; **giocava con l'accendino** (*trastullarsi*) he was toying *o* playing with the lighter; **giocare in Nazionale** (*Calcio*) to play for Italy; **il Milan gioca in casa** Milan is playing at home; **giocare i minuti di recupero** (*Calcio*) to play injury time

b (*scommettere, anche:* **giocare d'azzardo**) to gamble; **giocare in Borsa** to speculate *o* gamble on the Stock Exchange; **giocare alla roulette** to play roulette; **giocare ai cavalli** to bet on the horses

c (*intervenire: fattore*) to matter, count, come into play; **ciò ha giocato a suo favore** that worked in his favour; **qui gioca l'elemento sorpresa** this is where the surprise element counts

d (*muoversi liberamente: meccanismo*) to play freely

e (*fraseologia*): **a che gioco giochiamo?** what are you playing at?; **giocare a carte scoperte** to act openly; **giocare sul sicuro** to play safe; **giocare d'astuzia** to be crafty.

2 VT **a** (*partita, carta*) to play; **giocare l'atout** to play trumps; **giocare l'ultima carta** (*fig*) to play one's last card

b (*scommettere*): **giocare (su)** (*Casinò*) to stake (on), wager (on); (*Corse*) to bet (on); **giocare forte** to gamble heavily; **giocarsi una cena** to play for a meal; **si è giocato anche la camicia** he has gambled away his last penny; **ci giocherei l'anima** I'd stake my life on it; **giocarsi tutto** to risk everything; **si sta giocando la carriera** he's putting his career at risk; **ormai è troppo tardi, ti sei giocato la carriera** it's too late now, your career is ruined

c (*imbrogliare*) to deceive, trick, take in; **ci hanno giocato un brutto tiro** they played a dirty trick on us.

giocata [dʒoˈkata] SF **a** (*partita*) game **b** (*scommessa*) wager, bet.

giocatore, trice [dʒokaˈtore] SM/F **a** (*gen, Sport*) player **b** (*d'azzardo*) gambler.

giocattolaio, aia, ai, aie [dʒokattoˈlajo] SM/F (*costruttore*) toy-maker; (*venditore*) toy-seller.

giocattolo [dʒoˈkattolo] SM toy.

giocherellare [dʒokerelˈlare] VI (*aus* **avere**): **giocherellare con** (*giocattolo*) to play with; (*distrattamente*) to fiddle with.

giocherellone [dʒokerelˈlone] SM joker.

giocherò *ecc* [dʒokeˈrɔ] VB *vedi* **giocare**.

giochetto [dʒoˈketto] SM **a** (*gioco*) game; **è un giochetto** (*cosa molto facile*) it's child's play, it's a piece of cake **b** (*tranello*) trick.

gioco, chi [ˈdʒɔko] SM **a** (*gen*) game; **il gioco degli scacchi/delle bocce** (the game of) chess/bowls *sg* ▶**gioco d'abilità** game of skill ▶**gioco d'azzardo** game of chance ▶**gioco di pazienza** puzzle ▶**gioco di società** parlour game

b (*Sport: partita, modo di giocare*) game; **gioco di squadra** team game; **due giochi a uno** (*Tennis*) two games to one; **i giochi olimpici** the Olympic Games

c (*Carte: mano*) hand; **non avere gioco** to have a poor hand

d : **il gioco** (*Casinò*) gambling; (*Corse*) betting; **avere il vizio del gioco** to be a gambler; **casa/tavolo da gioco** gaming house/table; **fortunato al gioco, sfortunato in amore** lucky at cards, unlucky in love

e (*Tecn*) play; **lo sterzo ha troppo gioco** there is too much play in the steering wheel

f : **giochi di luce** play of light and shade ▶**giochi d'acqua** play of water

g (*fraseologia*): **gioco di parole** play on words, pun; **è un gioco da ragazzi** it's child's play; **entrano in gioco diversi fattori** various factors come into play; **è in gioco la mia reputazione** my reputation is at stake; **ho deciso di fare il suo gioco** I've decided to play his game; **stare al gioco di qn** to play along with sb; **scoprire il proprio gioco** to show one's hand; **prendersi gioco di qn** to pull sb's leg; **per gioco** in *o* for fun; **far buon viso a cattivo gioco** to make the best of a bad job; **fare il doppio gioco con qn** to double-cross sb

h (*Proverbi*): **un bel gioco dura poco** never take a joke too far; **gioco di mano, gioco di villano** never use your fists; **il gioco non vale la candela** the game's not worth the candle.

giocoforza [dʒokoˈfɔrtsa] SM: **essere giocoforza** to be inevitable.

giocoliere [dʒokoˈljɛre] SM juggler.

giocondità [dʒokondiˈta] SF cheerfulness.

giocondo, a [dʒoˈkondo] AGG cheerful, smiling.

giocosamente [dʒokosaˈmente] AVV playfully.

giocosità [dʒokosiˈta] SF playfulness.

giocoso, a [dʒoˈkoso] AGG playful, jocular.

giogaia [dʒoˈgaja] SF (*Geog*) range of mountains.

giogo, ghi [ˈdʒogo] SM (*Agr, fig*) yoke; (*di montagna*) range; (*di bilancia*) beam; **sotto il giogo di** under the yoke of.

gioia[1] [ˈdʒɔja] SF **a** (*felicità*) joy, delight; **essere pazzo di gioia** to be beside o.s. with joy, be overjoyed; **darsi alla pazza gioia** to live it up; **le gioie della vita** the joys of life

b (*fig*): **gioia mia!** darling!; **è la nostra gioia** he's the light of our life.

gioia[2] [ˈdʒɔja] SF (*pietra preziosa*) jewel, precious stone.

gioielleria [dʒojelleˈria] SF **a** (*negozio*) jeweller's (*Brit*) *o* jeweler's (*Am*) (shop) **b** (*arte*) jeweller's (*Brit*) *o* jeweler's (*Am*) craft.

gioielliere [dʒojelˈljɛre] SM/F jeweller (*Brit*), jeweler (*Am*).

gioiello [dʒoˈjɛllo] SM jewel, piece of jewellery (*Brit*) *o* jewelry (*Am*); (*fig*) jewel, treasure.

gioiosamente [dʒojosaˈmente] AVV joyfully, cheerfully.

gioioso, a [dʒoˈjoso] AGG joyful, cheerful.

gioire [dʒoˈire] VT: **gioire di qc** to rejoice in sth, be delighted by sth.

Giona [ˈdʒona] SM Jonah.

Giordania [dʒorˈdanja] SF: **la Giordania** Jordan.

Giordano [dʒorˈdano] SM: **il Giordano** the Jordan.

giordano, a [dʒorˈdano] AGG, SM/F Jordanian.

giornalaio, aia, ai, aie [dʒornaˈlajo] SM/F newsagent

(*Brit*), newsdealer (*Am*).

giornale [dʒor'nale] SM **a** (news)paper; (*periodico*) journal; **lo dicono i giornali** OR **è sui giornali** it's in the papers ▶**giornale a fumetti** comic ▶**giornale murale** wall poster ▶**il giornale radio** the (radio) news **b** (*diario*) diary, journal ▶**giornale di bordo** (*Naut*) logbook, ship's log.

giornaletto [dʒorna'letto] SM (*fam*) (children's) comic.

giornaliero, a [dʒorna'ljɛro] **1** AGG daily.
2 SM **a** (*operaio*) day labourer (*Brit*) o laborer (*Am*) **b** (*abbonamento*) day pass, day ticket.

giornalino [dʒorna'lino] SM (*fam*) children's comic.

giornalismo [dʒorna'lizmo] SM journalism.

giornalista, i, e [dʒorna'lista] SM/F journalist.

giornalistico, a, ci, che [dʒorna'listiko] AGG (*stile*) journalistic.

giornalmente [dʒornal'mente] AVV daily.

giornata [dʒor'nata] SF **a** day; **durante la giornata** during the day; **durante la giornata di ieri** yesterday; **in giornata** by the end of the day; **fresco di giornata** (*uovo*) new-laid; **è a una giornata di cammino/macchina** it's a day's walk/drive away; **come stai? — mah, va a giornate** how are you? — well, a bit up and down; **vivere alla giornata** to live one day to the next; **è proprio la mia giornata!** (*iro*) it's not my day today!; **giornata lavorativa** working day
b (*paga*) day's wages, day's pay; **lavorare/pagare a giornata** to work/pay by the day.

giorno ['dʒorno] SM **a** (*periodo di luce*) day(light), day(time); **giorno e notte** day and night; **si fa giorno** it's getting light; **è già giorno** it's daylight; **di giorno** by day, during the daytime; **in pieno giorno** in full daylight; **ci corre come dal giorno alla notte** there's absolutely no comparison
b (*periodo di tempo*) day; **giorno feriale** weekday; **giorno festivo** holiday; **giorno di paga** payday; **tutti i santi giorni** every blessed day; **tutto il santo giorno** all day long; **fra 2 giorni** in 2 days' time; **uno di questi giorni** one of these days; **il giorno prima** the day before, the previous day; **il giorno dopo** the day after, the next day, the following day; **un giorno sì e uno no** on alternate days; **due giorni fa** two days ago; **fra quindici giorni** in a fortnight, in two weeks' time; **al giorno** a o per day, per day; **giorno per giorno** day by day; **a giorni** o **da un giorno all'altro** any day now
c (*periodo indeterminato*): **al giorno d'oggi** nowadays; **ha i giorni contati** his days are numbered; **mettere fine ai propri giorni** to put an end to one's life; **passare i propri giorni a fare qc** to spend one's time doing sth ▶**il giorno dei Morti** All Souls' Day (*Nov 2nd: relatives visit the graves of loved ones to lay flowers*).

giostra ['dʒostra] SF **a** (*nei luna-park*) merry-go-round **b** (*Storia*) joust.

giostrare [dʒos'trare] **1** VI (*aus* avere) (*Storia*) to joust, tilt.
2 giostrarsi VIP to manage; **giostrarsi fra i creditori** to manage one's creditors.

Giosuè [dʒo'zwɛ] SM Joshua.

giovamento [dʒova'mento] SM benefit, help; **trarre giovamento da qc** to benefit from sth; **non ho avuto nessun giovamento dalla cura** the treatment hasn't done me any good.

giovane ['dʒovane] **1** AGG (*gen*) young; (*aspetto*) youthful; **non è più tanto giovane** he is not as young as he was; **è più giovane di me** he is younger than me; **vestirsi giovane** to wear young styles; **è morto in giovane età** he died young; **giovane di spirito** young at heart; **è giovane del mestiere** he's new to the job.
2 SM youth, young man; **i giovani** the young, young people; **giovane di bottega** apprentice; **da giovane** when I was young.
3 SF girl, young woman.

giovanetto, a [dʒova'netto] SM/F young man/woman.

giovanile [dʒova'nile] AGG (*aspetto*) youthful; (*scritti*) early; (*errore*) of youth.

giovanotto [dʒova'nɔtto] SM young man.

giovare [dʒo'vare] **1** VI (*aus* avere o essere): **giovare a** (*essere utile*) to be useful to; (*far bene*) to be good for; **nascondere la verità non ti gioverà di sicuro** it certainly won't do you any good to conceal the truth; **lavorare fino a tardi non ti giova** working late isn't good for you.
2 VB IMPERS (*essere bene, utile*) to be useful; **a che giova prendersela?** what's the point of getting upset?; **giova sapere che...** it's useful to know that ....
3 giovarsi VIP: **giovarsi di qn/qc** to make use of sb/sth.

Giove ['dʒove] SM (*Mitol*) Jove; (*Astron*) Jupiter.

giovedì [dʒove'di] SM INV Thursday *per fraseologia vedi* **martedì**.

giovenca, che [dʒo'venka] SF heifer.

giovenco, chi [dʒo'venko] SM young ox.

gioventù [dʒoven'tu] SF **a** (*gen*) youth; **errori di gioventù** errors of youth; **in gioventù** in one's youth, in one's younger days **b** (*persone*) young (people); **la gioventù del giorno d'oggi** young people today; **libri per la gioventù** books for the young.

gioviale [dʒo'vjale] AGG jolly, jovial.

giovialità [dʒovjali'ta] SF jollity, joviality.

giovialmente [dʒovjal'mente] AVV jovially.

giovialone, a [dʒovja'lone] SM/F jovial person.

giovinastro [dʒovi'nastro] SM young thug.

giovincello [dʒovin'tʃɛllo] SM young lad.

giovinezza [dʒovi'nettsa] SF (*gen*) youth; (*di spirito*) youthfulness; **godersi la giovinezza** to enjoy one's youth.

GIP, gip [dʒip] ABBR M (*Dir*) = **giudice per le indagini preliminari**.

girabile [dʒi'rabile] AGG (*cambiale, assegno*) endorsable.

giradischi [dʒira'diski] SM INV record player.

giraffa [dʒi'raffa] SF (*Zool*) giraffe; (*TV, Cine, Radio*) boom.

giramento [dʒira'mento] SM: **giramento di testa** fit of dizziness; **mi è venuto un giramento di testa** I feel dizzy.

giramondo [dʒira'mondo] SM/F INV globetrotter.

girandola [dʒi'randola] SF (*fuochi artificiali*) Catherine wheel; (*giocattolo*) toy windmill; (*banderuola*) weathervane, weathercock.

girante [dʒi'rante] SM/F (*chi gira un assegno*) endorser.

girare [dʒi'rare] **1** VT **a** (*ruota, chiave, sguardo*) to turn; (*pagina*) to turn (over); **ha girato la testa dall'altra parte** he looked the other way; **girare l'angolo** to turn the corner; **ha girato la domanda al presidente** he referred the question to the president; **non girare il discorso** don't change the subject; **girala come ti pare** (*fig*) look at it whichever way you like
b (*museo, città, negozio*) to go round; **ha girato il mondo** he has travelled the world; **ho girato tutta Londra per trovarlo** I searched all over London for it
c (*cambiale, assegno*) to endorse
d (*Cine, TV: scena*) to shoot, film; (: *film: fare le riprese*) to shoot; (: *esserne il regista*) to make.

2 VI (*aus* **avere** *o* **essere**) **a** (*gen*) to turn; (*trottola*) to spin; (*ruota*) to revolve; (*tassametro*) to tick away; **girare su se stesso** (*persona*) to turn right round; (: *rapidamente*) to spin round; **la terra gira intorno al proprio asse** the earth turns on its axis; **continuavano a girare intorno allo stesso argomento** they kept on discussing the same topic; **gli gira intorno da mesi** she's been hanging round him for months; **la strada gira intorno al lago** the road goes round the lake

b (*errare*) to go round, wander round; **girare per i negozi** to go *o* wander round the shops

c (*voltare*) to turn; **giri subito a destra** take the first turning on the right

d (*denaro, notizie*) to circulate; **girano troppi drogati** there are too many drug addicts about

e (*fraseologia*): **mi gira la testa** I feel dizzy, my head's spinning; **quella ragazza fa girare la testa a tutti** that girl is a real show stopper; **gira al largo!** keep your distance!; **gira e rigira...** after a lot of driving (*o* walking) about ...; (*fig*) whichever way you look at it ...; **cosa ti gira?** (*fam*) what's got into you?; **mi ha fatto girare le scatole** (*fam*) he drove me crazy *o* round the bend.

3 girarsi VR (*voltarsi*) to turn (round); (: *nel letto*) to turn over; **si girava e rigirava nel letto** he tossed and turned in bed; **non so più da che parte girarmi** (*fig*) I don't know which way to turn.

girarrosto [dʒirar'rɔsto] SM (*Culin*) spit.

girasole [dʒira'sole] SM sunflower.

girata [dʒi'rata] SF (*di cambiale, assegno*) endorsement.

giratario, ria, ri, rie [dʒira'tarjo] SM/F endorsee.

giratubi [dʒira'tubi] SM INV pipe wrench.

giravolta [dʒira'vɔlta] SF turn, twirl; (*di strada*) sharp bend; (*fig*) about-face, about-turn.

girella [dʒi'rɛlla] SF (*carrucola*) pulley; (*giocattolo*) spinning top.

girellare [dʒirel'lare] VI (*aus* **avere**) to wander about, stroll about.

girello [dʒi'rɛllo] SM **a** (*di bambino*) Babywalker ® (*Brit*), go-cart (*Am*) **b** (*taglio di carne*) topside (*Brit*), top round (*Am*).

giretto [dʒi'retto] SM (*passeggiata*) walk, stroll; (: *in macchina*) drive, spin; (: *in bicicletta*) ride.

girevole [dʒi'revole] AGG (*sedia*) swivel *attr*; (*porta, piattaforma*) revolving.

girino [dʒi'rino] SM tadpole.

giro ['dʒiro] SM **a** (*circuito, cerchio*) circle; (*di manovella, chiave*) turn; (*Tecn*) revolution; **3000 giri al minuto** 3000 revolutions *o* revs per minute; **compiere un intero giro** to go full circle; **un giro di vite** a turn of the screw; **dare un giro di vite** (*fig*) to put the screws on, put pressure on; **essere nel giro** to belong to a circle (of friends); **un giro di parole** (*fig*) a circumlocution; **essere giù di giri** (*fig*) to be depressed; **essere su di giri** (*fig*) to be on top of the world; ▸**giro d'affari** (*Comm*) turnover

b (*passeggiata*) walk, stroll; (: *in macchina*) drive; (: *in bicicletta, a cavallo*) ride; (*viaggio*) tour, trip; (*percorso intorno a*): **fare il giro di** (*parco, città*) to go round; **abbiamo dovuto fare un giro intorno all'isolato** we had to go round the block; **abbiamo dovuto fare un lungo giro** we had to take the long way round; **abbiamo fatto un giro in campagna** we went for a walk (*o* a drive *o* a ride) in the country; **giro turistico della città** sightseeing tour of the city; **fare il giro del mondo** to go round the world; **giro d'ispezione** tour of inspection; **il medico sta**

facendo il giro dei malati the doctor is doing his rounds **c** (*Sport: di pista*) lap; (*Carte*) hand; **sono al primo giro** they are on the first lap ▸**giro di Francia** Tour de France ▸**giro d'onore** lap of honour ▸**giro di prova** (*Aut*) test lap

d (*di parte del corpo*) measurement ▸**giro manica** armhole ▸ **giro vita** waist measurement

e (*di tempo*): **nel giro di** in the course of; **nel giro di un mese** in a month's time; **a (stretto) giro di posta** by return of post

f (*cerchia, ambiente*): **non ti preoccupare, è del nostro giro** don't worry, he's one of us; **essere nel** *o* **del giro** to be one of a circle; **entrare in un giro** to become one of a group; **essere fuori dal giro** to be no longer part of a group

g : **in giro: guardarsi in giro** to look around; **andare in giro** to wander about, go about, walk around; **sono stato in giro tutto il giorno** I've been on the go all day; **non trovo la penna, ma dev'essere in giro** I can't find my pen, but it must be around somewhere; **prendere in giro qn** (*stuzzicare*) to pull sb's leg; (*imbrogliare*) take sb for a ride; **lascia sempre tutto in giro** he always leaves everything lying about; **mettere in giro** (*voci, denaro*) to circulate; **c'è parecchio denaro falso in giro** there is a lot of counterfeit money in circulation; **c'è molta droga in giro** there are a lot of drugs around.

girocollo [dʒiro'kɔllo] SM: **a girocollo** crewneck *attr*.

giroconto [dʒiro'konto] SM (*Fin*) giro credit transfer.

girone [dʒi'rone] SM **a** (*dantesco*) circle **b** (*Sport*) series of games; **girone di andata/ritorno** first/second half of the season.

gironzolare [dʒirondzo'lare] VI (*aus* **avere**) to wander *o* stroll about; **gironzolare intorno a qn** (*pegg: importunare*) to hang around sb.

giroscopio, pi [dʒiros'kɔpjo] SM gyroscope.

girotondo [dʒiro'tondo] SM ring-a-ring-o'roses (*Brit*), ring-around-the-rosey (*Am*).

girovagare [dʒirova'gare] VI (*aus* **avere**) to wander about.

girovago, a, ghi, ghe [dʒi'rɔvago] **1** AGG wandering, strolling; **vita girovaga** itinerant life.

2 SM/F (*vagabondo*) tramp; (*venditore*) peddler.

gita ['dʒita] SF trip, outing; **andare in gita** OR **fare una gita** to go for a trip, go on an outing; **gita in barca** boat trip.

gitano, a [dʒi'tano] AGG, SM/F gipsy.

gitante [dʒi'tante] SM/F member of a tour.

gittata [dʒit'tata] SF (*di arma*) range.

giù [dʒu] AVV **a** (*gen*) down; (*dabbasso*) downstairs; **è sceso giù in giardino** he's gone down to the garden; **scese giù per le scale** he came down the stairs; **è giù in cantina** he's down in the cellar; **scendi giù dal tavolo!** get down off the table!; **mi tiri giù quella scatola?** can you get that box down for me?; **vieni giù un minuto** come down a minute; **è venuto giù il tetto** the roof came down; **veniva giù un'acqua!** it was pouring with rain!; **fagli mettere giù quel libro** make him put that book down; **due isolati più in giù** two blocks further down; **la mia casa è un po' più in giù** my house is a bit further on; **cadere a testa in giù** to fall head first; **vai giù di là** go down that way

b (*al di sotto di*) below; **bambini dai 6 anni in giù** children aged 6 and under; **ce n'erano 30** *o* **giù di lì** there were about 30, there were 30 or thereabouts

c (*nelle esclamazioni*): **giù!** down!; **giù le mani!** hands off!; **giù di lì!** get down from there!; **e giù botte!** and the fists

flew!

d (*fraseologia*): **essere giù** (*persona: di morale*) to be depressed; (: *di salute*) to be run down; **quel tipo non mi va giù** I can't stand that bloke (*Brit*) *o* guy; **non riesco a mandarla giù** (*fig*) it really sticks in my throat; **buttare giù** vedi **buttare** c.

giubba ['dʒubba] SF jacket.

giubbetto [dʒub'betto] SM short jacket; **giubbetto equilibratore** (*Sub*) adjustable buoyancy life jacket, stabilizing jacket.

giubbone [dʒub'bone] SM heavy jacket.

giubbotto [dʒub'bɔtto] SM jerkin ▶**giubbotto antiproiettile** bulletproof vest ▶**giubbotto salvagente** life jacket.

giubilare [dʒubi'lare] **1** AGG jubilee *attr*.
2 VI (*aus* **avere**) to rejoice.

giubileo [dʒubi'lɛo] SM jubilee.

giubilo ['dʒubilo] SM rejoicing; **grida di giubilo** shouts of joy.

Giuda ['dʒuda] SM INV Judas; (*fig*) Judas, traitor.

giudaico, a, ci, che [dʒu'daiko] AGG Jewish.

giudaismo [dʒuda'izmo] SM Judaism.

Giudea [dʒu'dɛa] SF Judea.

giudeo, a [dʒu'dɛo] **1** AGG Jewish.
2 SM/F Jew.

giudicabile [dʒudi'kabile] AGG that can be judged.

giudicare [dʒudi'kare] **1** VT **a** (*Dir: causa*) to judge; (: *lite*) to arbitrate in; (: *accusato*): **giudicare (per)** to try (for); **l'hanno giudicato e l'hanno trovato colpevole** they tried him and found him guilty; **l'hanno giudicato colpevole** they found him guilty; **il caso verrà giudicato il prossimo anno** the case will be heard next year
b (*valutare*) to judge; **non giudicarla con tanta severità** don't judge her so harshly; **giudicare qn abile alla leva/idoneo ad un lavoro** to judge sb fit for military service/suitable for a job
c (*stimare*): **giudicare qn capace di fare qc** to consider sb capable of doing sth; **anche se mi giudicherai pazzo** even though you think I'm mad; **giudicare qn bene/male** to think well/badly of sb; **giudicare opportuno fare** to consider it advisable to do.
2 VI (*aus* **avere**) (*dare un giudizio*): **giudicare di** to judge; **se devo giudicare in base alla mia esperienza** judging by my experience; **a giudicare da ciò che dice** judging by what he says; **giudicare dalle apparenze** to judge *o* go by appearances; **sta a voi giudicare** it's up to you to decide *o* judge .

giudicato [dʒudi'kato] SM (*Dir*): **passare in giudicato** to pass final judgment.

giudicatore, trice [dʒudika'tore] AGG judging; **commissione giudicatrice** examining board.

giudice ['dʒuditʃe] SM (*gen*) judge; **farsi giudice** *o* **erigersi a giudice di qc** to set o.s. up as a judge of sth ▶**giudice collegiale** member of the court ▶**giudice conciliatore** magistrate, justice of the peace ▶**giudice di gara** (*Sport*) umpire ▶**giudice per le indagini preliminari** magistrate in charge of preliminary investigations ▶**giudice istruttore** examining (*Brit*) *o* committing (*Am*) magistrate ▶**giudice di linea** (*Tennis*) linesman ▶**giudice popolare** member of a jury.

giudiziale [dʒudit'tsjale] AGG judicial.

giudiziario, ria, ri, rie [dʒudit'tsjarjo] AGG legal, judicial.

giudizio, zi [dʒu'dittsjo] SM **a** (*opinione*) judgment, opinion; **dare** *o* **esprimere un giudizio su qn/qc** to express an opinion on sb/sth; **non vorrei esprimere un giudizio troppo affrettato** I wouldn't like to pass judgment *o* to judge too hastily; **a giudizio di qn** in sb's opinion; **chiedere il giudizio di qn** to ask sb's opinion
b (*discernimento*) judgment; **essere privo di giudizio** to lack judgment; **l'età del giudizio** the age of reason; **denti del giudizio** wisdom teeth; **fai giudizio!** be good!
c (*Dir: processo*) trial; (: *verdetto*) judgment, verdict; (: *in processi civili*) decision; **essere in attesa di giudizio** to be awaiting trial; **l'imputato è stato rinviato a giudizio** the accused has been committed for trial; **citare in giudizio** to summons
d (*Rel*) judgment ▶**il giudizio universale** the Last Judgment.

giudiziosamente [dʒudittsjosa'mente] AVV judiciously.

giudizioso, a [dʒudit'tsjoso] AGG judicious.

giuggiola ['dʒuddʒola] SF: **andare in brodo di giuggiole** (*fam*) to be over the moon.

giuggiolone [dʒuddʒo'lone] SM (*fig: fam*) silly-billy.

giugno ['dʒuɲɲo] SM June *per fraseologia vedi* **luglio**.

giugulare [dʒugu'lare] AGG (*Anat*) jugular.

giulivamente [dʒuliva'mente] AVV (*letter*) merrily.

giulivo, a [dʒu'livo] AGG (*letter*) merry.

giullare [dʒul'lare] SM (*Storia*) jester.

giumenta [dʒu'menta] SF mare.

giunca, che ['dʒunka] SF junk (*boat*).

giunchiglia [dʒun'kiʎʎa] SF (*Bot*) jonquil.

giunco, chi ['dʒunko] SM (*Bot*) rush.

giungere ['dʒundʒere] VB IRREG **1** VI (*aus* **essere**): **giungere a** to arrive at, reach; **giungere all'orecchio di qn** to come to sb's attention *o* notice; **giungere nuovo a qn** to come as news to sb; **giungere alla meta** to achieve one's aim; **giungere in porto** to reach harbour; (*fig*) to have a successful outcome.
2 VT (*unire*) to join.

giungla ['dʒungla] SF jungle.

Giunone [dʒu'none] SF (*Mitol, Astron*) Juno.

giunonico, a, ci, che [dʒu'nɔniko] AGG Junoesque.

giunsi ecc ['dʒunsi] VB vedi **giungere**.

giunta[1] ['dʒunta] SF (*aggiunta*) addition; (*punto in cui due cose si uniscono*) join; (*Cine*) splice; **questa gonna è troppo corta, dovrò fare una giunta** this skirt is too short, I'll have to add a piece of material; **per giunta** (*inoltre*) what's more.

giunta[2] ['dʒunta] SF (*Amm*) council, board; (*Mil*) junta.

giuntare [dʒun'tare] VT to join; (*Cine*) to splice.

giuntatrice [dʒunta'tritʃe] SF (*Cine*) splicer.

giunto, a ['dʒunto] **1** PP di **giungere**.
2 SM (*Tecn*) coupling, joint ▶**giunto cardanico** universal joint ▶**giunto elastico** flexible joint.

giuntura [dʒun'tura] SF **a** (*Cucitura*) seam **b** (*Anat*) joint.

giunzione [dʒun'tsjone] SF (*Tecn*) joint; (*Elettr*) junction.

giuocare ecc [dʒwo'kare] VT, VI = **giocare** ecc.

giuramento [dʒura'mento] SM oath; **fare** *o* **prestare un giuramento** to take an oath; **venir meno a un giuramento** to break an oath.

giurare [dʒu'rare] **1** VT to swear; **giurare di fare qc** to swear to do sth; **giurare fedeltà a qn** to swear *o* pledge loyalty to sb; **giurare il falso** to commit perjury; **ti giuro che non ne posso più** I swear I've had more than I can take; **giurerei di averlo visto prima** I'd swear I have seen him somewhere before; **io non ci giurerei** I wouldn't swear to it; **gliel'ho giurata** I swore I would get even with him.

2 VI (*aus* avere) to swear, take an oath; **giurare su qc** to swear on sth; **giurare su qn** to swear by sb.

giurato, a [dʒuˈrato] **1** AGG sworn; **nemico giurato** sworn enemy.

2 SM/F juror, juryman/jurywoman.

giureconsulto [dʒurekonˈsulto] SM jurist.

giurì [dʒuˈri] SM INV (*letter*) jury.

giuria [dʒuˈria] SF (*Dir*) jury; (*di gara, concorso*) (panel of) judges.

giuridicamente [dʒuridikaˈmente] AVV juridically.

giuridico, a, ci, che [dʒuˈridiko] AGG legal.

giurisdizione [dʒurizditˈtsjone] SF jurisdiction.

giurisprudenza [dʒurispruˈdɛntsa] SF jurisprudence.

giurista, i, e [dʒuˈrista] SM/F jurist.

giustamente [dʒustaˈmente] AVV (*gen*) fairly, justly; (*offendersi, seccarsi*) with good reason.

giustapporre [dʒustapˈporre] VT IRREG to juxtapose.

giustapposizione [dʒustappozitˈtsjone] SF juxtaposition.

giustapposto, a [dʒustapˈposto] PP di **giustapporre**.

giustezza [dʒusˈtettsa] SF **a** (*di calcoli*) accuracy; (*di ragionamento*) soundness; (*di osservazione*) aptness **b** (*Tip*) justification.

giustificabile [dʒustifiˈkabile] AGG justifiable.

giustificare [dʒustifiˈkare] **1** VT (*gen*) to justify; (*Amm: spese*) to account for; **il fine giustifica i mezzi** the end justifies the means; **posso giustificarlo** I can understand why he did it; **giustificare il proprio ritardo** to give a reason for one's lateness.

2 giustificarsi VR: **giustificarsi per il ritardo** to excuse one's lateness.

giustificativo, a [dʒustifikaˈtivo] AGG (*Amm*): **nota** *o* **pezza giustificativa** receipt.

giustificazione [dʒustifikatˈtsjone] SF **a** (*spiegazione*) justification, explanation; (*prova*) proof; (*Scol*) excuse note, (note of) excuse **b** (*Tip*) justification.

giustizia [dʒusˈtittsja] SF **a** (*gen*) justice; **render giustizia a qn** to do sb justice; **farsi giustizia (da sé)** (*vendicarsi*) to take the law into one's own hands; **con giustizia** justly, with justice **b** (*autorità*) law; **ricorrere alla giustizia** to have recourse to the law; **affidarsi alla giustizia** to give o.s. up.

giustiziare [dʒustitˈtsjare] VT to execute, put to death.

giustiziere [dʒustitˈtsjɛre] SM executioner.

giusto, a [ˈdʒusto] **1** AGG **a** (*persona, sentenza*) just, fair; **per essere giusto verso di lui** *o* **nei suoi confronti** in fairness to him, to be fair to him; **non mi sembra giusto** it doesn't seem fair to me; **il giusto prezzo** the right price; **il giusto mezzo** the happy medium **b** (*calcolo, risposta*) right, correct; (*ragionamento*) sound; (*osservazione*) apt; (*misura, peso, ora*) correct, exact; **tre ore giuste** exactly three hours; **queste scarpe mi sono un po' troppo giuste** these shoes are a bit tight on me; **giusto di sale** with enough *o* the right amount of salt; **giusto di cottura** well-cooked.

2 SM **a** righteous person; **i giusti** SMPL the just; (*Rel*) the righteous

b (*il dovuto*): **chiedere/dare il giusto** ask for/give what's right.

3 AVV **a** (*proprio*) just, exactly; **arrivare giusto in tempo** to arrive just in time; **volevo giusto te** you're just *o* exactly the person I wanted; **saranno state giusto le quattro quando mi sono svegliato** it must have been exactly four o'clock when I woke up; **ho finito giusto**

adesso I've only just finished; **è andato via giusto adesso** he's just left; **giusto!** right!, of course!; (*a proposito*) that reminds me!; **giusto a me dovevi dare questo lavoro!** why did you have to give this job to me? **b** (*rispondere, capire*) correctly; (*indovinare*) rightly; **mirare giusto** to aim straight.

glabro, a [ˈglabro] AGG hairless.

glaciale [glaˈtʃale] AGG icy, freezing; (*fig*) icy, frosty; **periodo glaciale** (*Geol*) glacial period, Ice Age.

glacialmente [glatʃalˈmente] AVV (*fig*) icily, frostily.

glaciazione [glatʃatˈtsjone] SF glaciation.

gladiatore [gladjaˈtore] SM gladiator.

gladiolo [glaˈdiolo] SM gladiolus.

glande [ˈglande] SM (*Anat*) glans.

glandola [ˈglandola] SF = **ghiandola**.

glassa [ˈglassa] SF (*Culin*) icing; **glassa alla vaniglia** vanilla icing.

glassare [glasˈsare] VT (*Culin*) to ice.

glaucoma [glauˈkɔma] SM glaucoma.

gli¹ [ʎi] ART DET MPL vedi **il**.

gli² [ʎi] PRON PERS **a** (*a lui*) (to) him; (*a esso: riferito ad animale*) (to) it, (to) him; **dagli qualcosa da mangiare** (*persona*) give him something to eat; (*animale*) give it something to eat

b (*in coppia con lo, la, li, le, ne: a lui, a lei, a loro, a esso ecc*): **dagliela** give it to him (*o* her *o* them); **glieli hai promessi** you promised them to him (*o* her *o* them); **glielo ha detto** he told him (*o* her *o* them); **gliele ha spedite** he sent them to him (*o* her *o* them); **gliene ho parlato** I spoke to him (*o* her *o* them) about it.

glicemia [glitʃeˈmia] SF (*Med*) glycaemia.

glicerina [glitʃeˈrina] SF glycerine.

glicine [ˈglitʃine] SM wistaria.

glicogeno [gliˈkɔdʒeno] SM (*Bio*) glycogen.

glicol [ˈglikol] SM (*Chim*) glycol.

gliela ecc; vedi **gli²**.

glissare [glisˈsare] VI (*aus* avere): **glissare su** (*argomento*) to skate over.

globale [gloˈbale] AGG (*gen*) overall, inclusive; (*spesa, reddito*) total; (*visione*) global.

globalmente [globalˈmente] AVV globally; **preso globalmente** taken as a whole.

globo [ˈglɔbo] SM globe ▶ **globo oculare** eyeball ▶ **il globo terrestre** the globe.

globulare [globuˈlare] AGG (*sferico*) globular; (*Anat*) corpuscular.

globulina [globuˈlina] SF (*Bio*) globulin.

globulo [ˈglɔbulo] SM globule; (*Anat*) ▶ **globulo bianco/rosso** white/red corpuscle, white/red blood cell.

glomerulo [gloˈmɛrulo] SM (*Anat*) glomerulus; (*Bot*) glomerule.

gloria¹ [ˈglɔrja] SF **a** (*fama*) glory, fame; **coprirsi di gloria** to cover o.s. in glory; **lavorare per la gloria** (*iro*) to work for peanuts **b** (*vanto*) pride; **farsi gloria di qc** to pride o.s. on sth, take pride in sth.

gloria² [ˈglɔrja] SM (*Rel*) Gloria.

gloriarsi [gloˈrjarsi] VIP: **gloriarsi di qc** to glory in sth.

glorificare [glorifiˈkare] VT to glorify.

glorificazione [glorifikatˈtsjone] SF glorification.

gloriosamente [glorjosaˈmente] AVV gloriously.

glorioso, a [gloˈrjoso] AGG glorious.

glossa [ˈglɔssa] SF gloss.

glossario, ri [glosˈsarjo] SM glossary.

glottide [ˈglɔttide] SF (*Anat*) glottis.

glottologia [glottolo'dʒia] SF linguistics *sg*.

glottologico, a, ci, che [glotto'lɔdʒiko] AGG linguistic.

glottologo, a, gi, ghe [glot'tɔlogo] SM/F linguist.

glucosio [glu'kɔzjo] SM glucose.

glutammato [glutam'mato] SM: **glutammato monosodico** monosodium glutamate.

gluteo ['gluteo] SM gluteus (*Anat*); **glutei** SMPL buttocks.

GM ABBR = **genio militare**.

G.N. ABBR = **gas naturale**.

gnocco, chi ['ɲɔkko] SM a (*Culin*) *small dumpling made of potato or semolina* b (*fig fam*) dolt, idiot.

gnomico, a, ci, che ['ɲɔmiko] AGG gnomic.

gnomo ['ɲɔmo] SM gnome.

gnorri ['ɲɔrri] SM/F INV: **non fare lo gnorri!** stop acting as if you didn't know anything about it!

gnu [nu] SM INV (*Zool*) gnu.

GO SIGLA = *Gorizia*.

goal ['goul] SM INV (*Sport*) goal.

gobba ['gobba] SF (*Anat, Zool*) hump; (*di terreno, naso*) bump.

gobbo, a ['gobbo] 1 AGG (*che ha una gobba*) hunchbacked; (*ricurvo*) bent.
2 SM/F hunchback.

Gobi ['gobi] SM: **il Deserto dei Gobi** the Gobi Desert.

goccia, ce ['gottʃa] SF (*gen*) drop; (*di sudore*) bead; **goccia a goccia** drop by drop; **goccia di rugiada** dewdrop; **le prime gocce di pioggia** the first drops *o* spots of rain; **gocce per il naso/gli occhi** nose/eyedrops; **vuoi ancora una goccia di caffè?** would you like another drop *o* spot of coffee?; **orecchini a goccia** drop earrings; **somigliarsi come due gocce d'acqua** to be as like as two peas in a pod; **avere la goccia al naso** to have a runny nose; **è la goccia che fa traboccare il vaso!** it's the last straw!

goccio, ci ['gottʃo] SM drop, spot; **vuoi un goccio di vino?** would you like some wine?

gocciola ['gottʃola] SF (*di lampadario, gioiello*) drop.

gocciolare [gottʃo'lare] 1 VI (*aus* **avere** *o* **essere**) to drip; **mi gocciola il naso** I have got a runny nose; **l'acqua gocciola dal rubinetto** OR **il rubinetto gocciola** the tap's dripping; **l'acqua gocciola dal soffitto** there's water coming in through the ceiling.
2 VB IMPERS to drizzle.

gocciolatoio, oi [gottʃola'tojo] SM (*Archit*) dripstone.

gocciolio, lii [gottʃo'lio] SM dripping.

godere [go'dere] 1 a VT (*gustare: pace, fresco*) to enjoy; (: *bene, rendita*) to enjoy, benefit from
b : **godersi il sole** to soak up the sun; **godersi la vita** to enjoy life; **godersela** to enjoy o.s., have a good time; **si è goduta sua suocera per due mesi** (*iro*) she had the pleasure of her mother-in-law's company for two months.
2 VI (*aus* **avere**) a (*essere felice*): **godere di** to enjoy, rejoice at *o* in, be delighted (at); **godere nel fare qc** to enjoy *o* delight in doing sth; **godere delle disgrazie altrui** to take pleasure in other people's misfortunes; **godere della compagnia di qn** to enjoy sb's company; **godere all'idea che...** to rejoice at the thought of ...
b (*possedere*): **godere di** (*buona salute, reputazione*) to enjoy; **godere di riduzioni speciali** to benefit from special reductions.

godereccio, cia, ci, ce [gode'rettʃo] AGG (*persona*) pleasure-loving.

godimento [godi'mento] SM a (*piacere*) pleasure, enjoyment b (*Dir*) enjoyment, possession.

godrò *ecc* [go'drɔ] VB *vedi* **godere**.

goduria [go'durja] SF (*scherz*) pleasure; **che goduria starsene sdraiati al sole** what bliss to lie in the sun.

goffaggine [gof'faddʒine] SF clumsiness.

goffamente [goffa'mente] AVV clumsily, awkwardly.

goffo, a ['gɔffo] AGG (*persona, gesto*) clumsy, awkward; (*vestito*) inelegant.

goffrare [gof'frare] VT (*carta*) to emboss.

gogna ['gɔɲɲa] SF pillory; **mettere qn alla gogna** (*anche fig*) to pillory sb.

go-kart ['gou ka:t] SM INV go-kart.

gol [gɔl] SM INV = **goal**.

gola ['gola] SF a (*Anat*) throat; **avere mal di gola** to have a sore throat; **tagliare la gola a qn** to cut sb's throat; **ricacciare il pianto** *o* **le lacrime in gola** to swallow one's tears b (*golosità*) gluttony, greed; **fare gola a qn** to tempt sb c (*di montagna*) gorge d (*di camino*) flue.

goleador [golea'dor] SM INV (*Calcio*) goal scorer.

goletta [go'letta] SF (*Naut*) schooner.

golf[1] [gɔlf] SM (*sport*) golf; **campo da golf** golf course; **giocatore di golf** golfer.

golf[2] [gɔlf] SM INV jumper; (*con bottoni*) cardigan.

golfo ['golfo] SM gulf.

Golgota ['gɔlgota] SM Golgotha.

Golia [go'lia] SM Goliath.

goliardico, a, ci, che [go'ljardiko] AGG (*canto, vita*) student *attr*.

gollismo [gol'lizmo] SM Gaullism.

gollista, i, e [gol'lista] AGG, SM/F Gaullist.

golosamente [golosa'mente] AVV greedily.

golosità [golosi'ta] SF INV greed; (*peccato*) gluttony; (*leccornia*) delicacy.

goloso, a [go'loso] AGG greedy; **è golosa di dolci** she has a sweet tooth.

golpe ['golpe] SM INV (*Pol*) coup.

golpista, i, e [gol'pista] SM/F (*Pol*) leader of a coup.

gomena ['gomena] SF (*Naut*) hawser.

gomitata [gomi'tata] SF: **dare una gomitata a qn** to elbow sb; (*per zittire ecc*) to nudge sb; **farsi avanti a (forza** *o* **furia di) gomitate** to elbow one's way through; **fare a gomitate per qc** to fight to get sth.

gomito ['gomito] SM (*Anat*) elbow; (*di tubatura*) bend; **a gomito** (*tubo, giunto*) L-shaped; **curva a gomito** hairpin bend; **gomito a gomito** shoulder to shoulder; **alzare il gomito** (*fig*) to drink too much.

gomitolo [go'mitolo] SM (*di lana, filo*) ball.

gomma ['gomma] SF a (*caucciù*) rubber; (*per cancellare*) rubber (*Brit*), eraser ▶ **gomma arabica** gum arabic ▶ **gomma da masticare** chewing gum b (*pneumatico*) tyre (*Brit*), tire (*Am*); **avere una gomma a terra** to have a flat tyre; **trasporto su gomma** road transport ▶ **gomma rigenerata** (*Aut*) remould.

gommapiuma® [gomma'pjuma] SF foam rubber.

gommare [gom'mare] VT to rubberize.

gommato, a [gom'mato] AGG (*tela*) rubberized; (*carta*) gummed; **nastro gommato** adhesive tape.

gommino [gom'mino] SM (*gen*) rubber tip; (*rondella*) rubber washer.

gommista, i, e [gom'mista] SM/F tyre (*Brit*) *o* tire (*Am*) specialist; (*rivenditore*) tyre *o* tire merchant.

gommone [gom'mone] SM rubber dinghy.

gommosità [gommosi'ta] SF rubberiness.

gommoso, a [gom'moso] AGG rubbery.

gonade ['gonade] SF (*Anat*) gonad.

gondola ['gondola] SF a gondola b (*Aer*): **gondola del**

motore engine pod.

gondoliere [gondo'ljɛre] SM gondolier.

gonfalone [gonfa'lone] SM (*Storia*) banner.

gonfiagomme [gonfia'gomme] AGG INV: **bomboletta gonfiagomme** instant puncture sealant.

gonfiare [gon'fjare] ① VT **a** (*palloncino*) to blow up, inflate; (: *con pompa*) to inflate, pump up; (*le guance*) to puff out, blow out **b** (*fiume, vele*) to swell; **la birra mi gonfia lo stomaco** beer makes me feel bloated **c** (*fig*: *notizia, fatto*) to exaggerate.

② **gonfiarsi** VIP (*gen*) to swell (up); (*fiume*) to rise.

gonfio, fia, fi, fie ['gonfjo] AGG **a** (*occhi, piedi*) swollen; (*fiume*) swollen; (*vela*) full; (*stile*) bombastic, wordy; **gonfio di orgoglio** (*persona*) puffed up (with pride); **aveva il cuore gonfio (di dolore)** her heart was heavy; **occhi gonfi di pianto** eyes swollen with tears; **mi sento gonfio** I feel bloated; **avere il portafoglio gonfio** to have a bulging wallet

b (*palloncino, gomme*) inflated, blown up; (*con pompa*) inflated, pumped up.

gonfiore [gon'fjore] SM swelling.

gong [gɔŋg] SM INV gong.

gongolare [gongo'lare] VI (*aus* avere): **gongolare (per)** to look pleased with o.s. (about); **gongolare di gioia** to be overjoyed.

goniometro [go'njɔmetro] SM protractor.

gonna ['gonna] SF skirt; **stare attaccato alle gonne della madre** to cling to one's mother's apron strings ▶ **gonna pantalone** culottes *pl.*

gonzo ['gondzo] SM simpleton, dolt, fool.

gorgheggiare [gorged'dʒare] VI (*aus* avere) (*cantante*) to trill; (*uccello*) to warble.

gorgheggio, gi [gor'geddʒo] SM (*Mus*) trill; (*di uccello*) warbling.

gorgo, ghi ['gorgo] SM whirlpool; **essere preso nel gorgo della passione** to be in the grip of passion.

gorgogliare [gorgoʎ'ʎare] VI (*aus* avere) to gurgle.

gorgoglio¹ [gor'goʎʎo] SM gurgle.

gorgoglio², glii [gorgoʎ'ʎio] SM gurgling.

Gorgone [gor'gone] SF Gorgon.

gorgonzola [gorgon'dzɔla] SM INV gorgonzola.

gorilla [go'rilla] SM INV **a** (*Zool*) gorilla **b** (*fig*: *guardia del corpo*) bodyguard.

gotha ['go:ta] SM (*di cinema, letteratura, industria*) leading figures *pl.*

gotico, a, ci, che ['gɔtiko] AGG, SM (*scrittura, architettura*) Gothic.

Goto ['gɔto] SM (*Storia*) Goth.

gotta ['gotta] SF gout.

gottoso, a [got'toso] AGG (*attacco*) of gout, gout *attr*; (*persona*) gouty.

governante¹ [gover'nante] SM ruler.

governante² [gover'nante] SF (*donna di servizio*) housekeeper; (*di bambini*) governess.

governare [gover'nare] VT **a** (*stato, nazione*) to govern, rule **b** (*barca, nave*) to steer; (*bestiame*) to look after, tend.

governativo, a [governa'tivo] AGG (*politica, decreto*) government *attr*, governmental; (*stampa*) pro-government.

governatore, trice [governa'tore] SM/F governor.

governo [go'vɛrno] SM **a** (*regime*) government; (*gabinetto*) Cabinet, Government; **crisi di governo** Government crisis; **governo ponte** caretaker govern-

ment; **i partiti al governo** the parties in power *o* in office **b** (*di cavallo*) grooming.

gozzo ['gottso] SM (*di uccello*) crop; (*Med*) goitre; (*fig fam*) throat; **restare sul gozzo** (*fig*) to stick in one's throat; **se hai qualcosa sul gozzo sarà meglio che parli** if something is bothering you, you'd better spit it out.

gozzovigliare [gottsoviʎ'ʎare] VI (*aus* avere) to make merry, carouse.

gpm ABBR (= *giri per minuto*) rpm.

GR [dʒi'ɛrre] ① SIGLA = Grosseto.

② SIGLA M = **giornale radio.**

gracchiare [grak'kjare] VI (*aus* avere) (*cornacchia*) to caw, croak; (*telefono, radio*) to crackle; (*persona*) to croak.

gracchio, chi ['grakkjo] SM (*il gracchiare*) caw, croak.

gracidare [gratʃi'dare] VI (*aus* avere) (*rana*) to croak.

gracidio, dii [gratʃi'dio] SM croaking.

gracile ['gratʃile] AGG (*persona, costituzione*) delicate, frail; (*braccia, gambe*) slender.

gracilità [gratʃili'ta] SF delicateness, frailness.

gradasso [gra'dasso] SM braggart, boaster; **che gradasso!** what a loudmouth!

gradatamente [gradata'mente] AVV gradually, by degrees.

gradazione [gradat'tsjone] SF (*sfumatura*) gradation; **gradazione alcolica** alcoholic content *o* strength.

gradevole [gra'devole] AGG agreeable, pleasant.

gradevolmente [gradevol'mente] AVV agreeably, pleasantly.

gradiente [gra'djɛnte] SM gradient.

gradimento [gradi'mento] SM pleasure, satisfaction; **non è di mio gradimento** it's not to my taste *o* liking.

gradinata [gradi'nata] SF (*scalinata*) (flight of) steps *pl*; (*di stadio*) terraces (*Brit*) *pl*, terracing (*Brit*); (*in anfiteatro*) tiers *pl.*

gradino [gra'dino] SM (*gen*) step; (*Alpinismo*) foothold; **"attenti al gradino"** "mind the step"; **è salito di un gradino nella carriera** he has taken a step forward in his career; **è l'ultimo gradino della scala sociale** it's the bottom rung of the social ladder.

gradire [gra'dire] VT **a** (*accogliere, ricevere con piacere*) to accept (with pleasure); **gradire un dono/un invito** to accept a gift/an invitation with pleasure; ... **tanto per gradire** I shouldn't, but ...; **gradisca i miei omaggi** please accept my best wishes; **ho gradito la sua visita** I enjoyed your visit

b (*frm*: *desiderare*) to like, want, wish; **gradisce un caffè?** would you like a coffee?; **gradirei avere un po' di pace** I should like some peace and quiet.

gradito, a [gra'dito] AGG welcome.

grado¹ ['grado] SM: **di buon grado** willingly.

grado² ['grado] SM **a** (*gen*) degree; (*livello*) degree, level; (*Alpinismo*) grade; **per gradi** by degrees; **un cugino di primo/secondo grado** a first/second cousin; **essere in grado di fare qc** to be able to do sth; **subire il terzo grado** (*anche fig*) to be given the third degree

b (*Mil, sociale*) rank; **salire di grado** to be promoted; **perdere i gradi** to lose one's stripes.

graduale [gradu'ale] AGG gradual.

gradualità [graduali'ta] SF INV gradualness.

gradualmente [gradual'mente] AVV gradually.

graduare [gradu'are] VT (*scala, termometro*) to graduate; (*difficoltà*) to increase by degrees.

graduato, a [gradu'ato] ① AGG (*scala, termometro*) graduated; (*esercizi*) graded.

2 SM (*Mil*) non-commissioned officer.

graduatoria [gradua'tɔrja] SF (*di concorso*) list; (*per promozione*) order of seniority.

graduazione [graduat'tsjone] SF graduation.

graffa ['graffa] SF (*Tip: parentesi*) brace; (*punto metallico*) staple.

graffetta [graf'fetta] SF (*fermaglio*) paper clip; (*punto metallico*) staple.

graffiante [graf'fjante] AGG (*critica, commento*) caustic, biting.

graffiare [graf'fjare] VT to scratch.

graffiatura [graffja'tura] SF scratch.

graffio, fi ['graffjo] SM scratch.

graffiti [graf'fiti] SMPL graffiti *sg*.

grafia [gra'fia] SF (*di parola*) spelling; (*scrittura*) handwriting.

grafica ['grafika] SF graphic arts *pl*.

graficamente [grafika'mente] AVV graphically; **parole graficamente differenti** words which are spelt differently.

grafico, a, ci, che ['grafiko] **1** AGG graphic.
2 SM **a** (*diagramma*) graph **b** (*disegnatore*) commercial artist, graphic designer; ▶**grafico industriale** draughtsman (*Brit*), draftsman (*Am*).

grafite [gra'fite] SF (*minerale*) graphite.

grafomane [gra'fɔmane] SM/F compulsive scribbler.

grafomania [grafoma'nia] SF mania for writing.

gramaglie [gra'maʎʎe] SFPL: **in gramaglie** in mourning.

gramigna [gra'miɲɲa] SF (*Bot*) couch grass; (*erbaccia*) weed.

graminacee [grami'natʃee] SFPL (*Bot*) grasses.

grammatica, che [gram'matika] SF grammar; **un errore di grammatica** a grammatical error; **libro di grammatica** grammar book.

grammaticale [grammati'kale] AGG grammatical.

grammaticamente [grammatika'mente] AVV grammatically.

grammatico, ci [gram'matiko] SM (*studioso*) grammarian.

grammo ['grammo] SM gram, gramme (*Brit*).

grammofono [gram'mɔfono] SM gramophone.

gramo, a ['gramo] AGG (*vita*) wretched.

gran [gran] AGG vedi **grande**.

grana¹ ['grana] SF grain; **di grana grossa** coarse-grained.

grana² ['grana] SF (*fam: seccatura*) trouble; **avere delle grane** to have problems; **piantare grane** to stir up trouble.

grana³ ['grana] SM INV *cheese similar to Parmesan*.

grana⁴ ['grana] SF INV (*fam*) cash; **essere pieno di grana** to be rolling in it, be stinking rich.

granaglie [gra'naʎʎe] SFPL corn seed *sg*, corn *sg*.

granaio, ai [gra'najo] SM barn, granary.

granata¹ [gra'nata] SF (*Mil*) grenade.

granata² [gra'nata] **1** SF (*Bot*) pomegranate.
2 AGG (*colore*) garnet(-coloured).

granatiere [grana'tjɛre] SM (*Mil*) grenadier; (*fig*) fine figure of a man.

granato [gra'nato] SM (*pietra preziosa*) garnet.

Gran Bretagna [granbre'taɲɲa] SF: **la Gran Bretagna** Great Britain.

grancassa [gran'kassa] SF (*Mus*) bass drum.

grancevola [gran'tʃɛvola] SF spider crab.

granché [gran'ke] PRON = **gran che**; vedi **grande**.

granchio, chi ['grankjo] SM (*Zool*) crab; (*fig: errore*) blunder; **prendere un granchio** (*fig*) to blunder.

grandangolo [gran'dangolo], **grandangolare** [grandango'lare] SM (*Fot*) wide-angle lens *sg*.

grande ['grande]
1 AGG

a volte **gran** + consonante, **grand'** + vocale

a (*gen*) big; (*quantità*) large; (*alto*) tall; (: *montagna*) high; (*largo*) wide, broad; (*lungo*) long; (*forte: rumore*) loud; (: *vento*) strong, high; (: *pioggia*) heavy; (: *caldo*) intense; (: *affetto, bisogno*) great; (: *sospiro*) deep;
▷**è grande per la sua *età*** he's big for his age
▷**un ragazzo grande e *grosso*** a big strong boy
▷**un grande *invalido*** a seriously disabled person
▷**la gran *maggioranza* degli italiani** the great *o* vast majority of Italians
▷**ha una grande *opinione* di sé** he has a high opinion of himself
▷**il gran *pubblico*** the general public
▷**una *taglia* più grande** a larger *o* bigger size
b (*di età*)
▷**sei *abbastanza* grande per capire** you're big *o* old enough to understand
▷**farsi grande** to grow up
▷**hanno due *figli* grandi** they have two grown-up children
▷**mio fratello *più* grande** my big *o* older brother
▷**è più grande di me** he's older than me
c (*importante, rilevante*) great; (*illustre, nobile*) noble, great;
▷**è arrivato il gran *giorno*** the great day dawned
▷**un grande *musicista*** a great musician
▷**un grande *poeta*** a great poet
▷**le grandi *potenze*** (*Pol*) the major powers
▷**è un gran *signore*** he's a real gentleman
▷**ha fatto grandi *spese*** he's been spending his money
d (*rafforzativo*: *lavoratore*) hard; (: *bevitore*) heavy; (: *amico, bugiardo*) great;
▷**è una gran *bella* donna** she's a very beautiful woman
▷**una gran *bella* vita** a great life
▷**oggi fa un gran *caldo*** it's extremely hot today
▷**di gran *classe*** (*prodotto*) high-class
▷**una donna di gran *classe*** a woman with class
▷**la famiglia al gran *completo*** the entire family
▷**è un gran *cretino*** he's an utter fool
▷**per sua gran *fortuna* non c'era la polizia** he was really lucky that the police weren't around
▷**oggi fa un gran *freddo*** it's extremely cold today
▷**in gran *parte*** to a large extent, mainly
▷**ha fatto una gran *risata*** he laughed loudly
▷**con mia gran *sorpresa*** to my great surprise
e (*fraseologia*)
▷**ti farà un gran *bene*** it'll do you good
▷**non ci ho fatto gran *caso*** I didn't really notice
▷**non ne so (un) gran *che*** I don't know very much about it
▷**non è *o* non vale (un) gran *che*** it (*o* he *ecc*) is nothing special, it (*o* he *ecc*) is not up to much
▷**quel quadro non è poi (una) gran *cosa*** that painting's nothing special.
2 SM/F

a (*persona adulta*) adult, grown-up;
▷**cosa farai *da* grande?** what will you be *o* do when you grow up?
b (*persona importante*) great man/woman;
▷**fare il grande** (*strafare*) to act big
▷**Pietro il Grande** Peter the Great.
3 SM: **fare le cose *in* grande** to do things on a grand scale, do things in style.

grandeggiare [granded'dʒare] VI (*aus* avere) **a** : **grandeggiare (su)** to tower (over) **b** (*darsi arie*) to put on airs, give o.s. airs.

grandemente [grande'mente] AVV greatly, very much.

grandezza [gran'dettsa] SF **a** (*dimensione*) size; (*Astron*) magnitude; (*Mat, Fis*) quantity; **di media grandezza** of average size; **a** *o* **in grandezza naturale** life-size(d) **b** (*fig: qualità*) greatness; **grandezza d'animo** nobility of soul **c** (*fasto*) grandeur; **manie di grandezza** delusions of grandeur.

grandinare [grandi'nare] **1** VB IMPERS to hail.
2 VI (*aus* essere) (*fig: bombe, proiettili*) to hail down.

grandine ['grandine] SF hail; **un chicco di grandine** a hailstone.

grandiosamente [grandjosa'mente] AVV magnificently.

grandiosità [grandjosi'ta] SF grandeur, magnificence.

grandioso, a [gran'djoso] AGG grandiose, magnificent; **dalle idee grandiose** with grandiose ideas; **avere un'idea grandiosa** to have a great idea.

granduca, chi [gran'duka] SM grand duke.

granducato [grandu'kato] SM grand duchy.

granduchessa [grandu'kessa] SF grand duchess.

granello [gra'nɛllo] SM (*di sabbia, sale*) grain; (*di polvere*) speck; **un granello di pepe** a peppercorn.

granita [gra'nita] SF *kind of water ice*.

granitico, a, ci, che [gra'nitiko] AGG (*roccia*) granite *attr*; (*fig: fede*) rock-like.

granito [gra'nito] SM (*Geol*) granite.

grano ['grano] SM **a** (*Bot*) grain, wheat **b** (*chicco: gen*) grain; (: *di rosario*) bead; **un grano di pepe** a peppercorn; **pepe in grani** peppercorns.

granturco [gran'turko] SM (*Bot*) maize (*Brit*), (Indian) corn (*Am*); **pannocchia di granturco** corncob.

granulare [granu'lare] AGG granular.

granulo ['granulo] SM granule; (*Med*) pellet.

granuloma, i [granu'lɔma] SM (*Med*) granuloma.

granuloso, a [granu'loso] AGG granular.

grappa ['grappa] SF grappa.

grappolo ['grappolo] SM bunch, cluster; **un grappolo d'uva** a bunch of grapes.

grassaggio, gi [gras'saddʒo] SM greasing.

grassetto [gras'setto] SM (*Tip*) bold (type) (*Brit*), bold face.

grassezza [gras'settsa] SF fatness, stoutness.

grasso, a ['grasso] **1** AGG **a** (*gen*) fat; (*cibo*) fatty; (*pelle, capelli*) greasy; (*terreno*) rich, fertile; **cucina grassa** oily cooking; **formaggio grasso** full-fat cheese; **un'annata grassa** (*Agr*) a good year; **pianta grassa** succulent plant **b** (*volgare*) lewd, coarse; **una grassa risata** a coarse laugh.
2 SM (*adipe, Culin*) fat; (*unto*) grease; **senza grassi** fat free; **grasso per cucinare** cooking fat; **grasso (per lubrificare)** (lubricating) grease ▶**grasso di balena** blubber.

grassoccio, cia, ci, ce [gras'sɔttʃo] AGG plump, podgy.

grassone, a [gras'sone] SM/F (*fam: persona*) dumpling.

grata ['grata] SF grating.

graticcio, ci [gra'tittʃo] SM (*di vimini ecc*) trellis; (*stuoia*) mat.

graticola [gra'tikola] SF (*Culin*) grill.

gratifica, che [gra'tifika] SF bonus.

gratificare [gratifi'kare] VT (*soddisfare*): **questo lavoro non mi gratifica** OR **non mi sento gratificato in questo lavoro** I don't find this job rewarding.

gratificazione [gratifikat'tsjone] SF (*soddisfazione*) satisfaction, reward.

gratin [gra'tɛ̃] SM INV (*Culin*): **al gratin** au gratin.

gratinare [grati'nare] VT (*Culin*) to cook au gratin.

gratinato, a [grati'nato] AGG (*Culin*) au gratin.

gratis ['gratis] AVV (*viaggiare*) free; (*lavorare*) for nothing; **biglietto gratis** free ticket; **ingresso gratis** admission free.

gratitudine [grati'tudine] SF gratitude.

grato, a ['grato] AGG (*riconoscente*) grateful; **ti sono molto grato** I am very grateful to you.

grattacapo [gratta'kapo] SM worry, headache (*fig*).

grattacielo [gratta'tʃɛlo] SM skyscraper.

grattare [grat'tare] **1** VT **a** to scratch; **grattar via** (*vernice*) to scrape off; **grattarsi la testa** to scratch one's head; **grattarsi la pancia** (*fig*) to twiddle one's thumbs; **grattare il violino** (*fam*) to scrape on the violin **b** (*grattugiare*) to grate **c** (*fam: rubare*) to pinch, nick (*Brit*).
2 VI (*aus* avere) (*stridere*) to grate; (*Aut: marcia*) to grind.
3 **grattarsi** VR to scratch (o.s.).

grattata [grat'tata] SF **a** (*alla testa*) scratch; **darsi una grattata alla testa** to scratch one's head **b** (*Aut fam*): **fare una grattata** to grind the gears.

grattugia, gie [grat'tudʒa] SF grater.

grattugiare [grattu'dʒare] VT to grate; **pane grattugiato** breadcrumbs *pl*.

gratuità [gratui'ta] SF (*anche fig*) gratuitousness.

gratuitamente [gratuita'mente] AVV (*senza compenso*) free (of charge), without payment; (*fig: senza prove, scopo*) gratuitously.

gratuito, a [gra'tuito] AGG **a** (*gratis*) free **b** (*fig: critiche, commenti*) gratuitous, uncalled-for.

gravame [gra'vame] SM: **gravame fiscale** tax.

gravare [gra'vare] **1** VT: **gravare di** (*responsabilità, imposte*) to burden with.
2 VI (*aus* essere): **gravare su** to weigh on, lie heavy on.

grave ['grave] **1** AGG **a** (*pericolo, errore*) grave, serious; (*responsabilità*) heavy, grave; (*contegno*) grave, solemn; **un malato grave** a seriously ill patient, a person who is seriously ill; **non è grave** it's not serious **b** (*suono, voce*) deep, low-pitched **c** (*Gramm*): **accento grave** grave accent.
2 SM (*Fis*) (heavy) body.

gravemente [grave'mente] AVV (*in modo solenne*) gravely, solemnly; (*seriamente*) seriously, gravely.

gravidanza [gravi'dantsa] SF pregnancy.

gravido, a ['gravido] AGG pregnant; **gravido di minaccia** fraught with *o* full of menace.

gravità [gravi'ta] SF INV **a** (*di errore, situazione, malattia*) seriousness, gravity; (*di comportamento, occasione*) solemnity, gravity; (*di punizione*) severity **b** (*Fis*) gravity.

gravitare [gravi'tare] VI (*aus* avere) (*Fis, fig*): **gravitare intorno a** to gravitate round; **gravitare verso** to gravitate towards.

gravitazionale [gravitattsjo'nale] AGG (*Fis*) gravitational.

gravitazione [gravitat'tsjone] SF (*Fis*) gravitation.

gravosamente [gravosa'mente] AVV heavily.

gravoso, a [gra'voso] AGG (*tasso, imposta*) heavy, onerous; **un compito gravoso** a hard *o* onerous task.

grazia ['grattsja] SF **a** (*di persona*) grace; **piena di grazia** graceful; **muoversi con grazia** to move gracefully; **di buona/mala grazia** with good/bad grace

b (*favore, benevolenza*) favour (*Brit*), favor (*Am*); **entrare nelle grazie di qn** to win sb's favo(u)r; **essere nelle grazie di qn** to be in sb's good graces *o* books; **di grazia** (*iro*) if you please; **troppa grazia!** (*iro*) you're too generous!

c (*misericordia*) mercy; (*Dir*) pardon; **concedere la grazia a qn** to pardon sb; **ottenere la grazia** to be pardoned; **Ministero di Grazia e Giustizia** Ministry of Justice, ≈ Lord Chancellor's Office (*Brit*), ≈ Department of Justice (*Am*)

d (*Rel*) grace; **quanta grazia di Dio!** what abundance!

e (*Mitol*): **le tre Grazie** the three Graces

f (*titolo*): **Sua Grazia** Your Grace.

graziare [grat'tsjare] VT (*Dir*) to pardon.

grazie ['grattsje] [1] ESCL thank you, thanks; **vuole un caffè? — (sì) grazie/no grazie** would you like some coffee? — yes, please/no, thank you; **hai trovato i libri? — sì grazie** did you find the books? — yes, thanks; **mille *o* tante grazie!** many thanks!; **Marco non è mai stanco — grazie al cavolo *o* grazie tante, lui non fa mai niente!** Marco is never tired — and neither he should be, since he never does a thing!.

[2] : **grazie a** PREP thanks to.

[3] SM INV thank you; **non ho avuto neanche un grazie** I did not get a word of thanks; **dille un grazie da parte mia** thank her for me.

graziosamente [grattsjosa'mente] AVV (*con grazia*) gracefully; (*cortesemente*) graciously.

grazioso, a [grat'tsjoso] AGG (*piacevole*) delightful, charming; (*gentile*) kind, gracious.

greca ['grɛka] SF (Greek) fret.

Grecia ['grɛtʃa] SF: **la Grecia** Greece.

greco, a, ci, che ['grɛko] [1] AGG, SM/F Greek.

[2] SM (*lingua*) Greek; **greco antico/moderno** Ancient/ Modern Greek.

gregario, ria, ri, rie [gre'garjo] [1] AGG (*Bot, Zool*) gregarious.

[2] SM (*Ciclismo*) supporting rider; (*Pol*) follower, supporter.

gregge ['greddʒe] (*pl f* **greggi**) SM (*gen, fig*) flock.

greggio, gia, gi, ge ['greddʒo] [1] AGG (*materia*) raw, unrefined; (*petrolio*) crude; (*diamante*) rough, uncut; (*cuoio*) untanned, untreated; (*tessuto*) unbleached.

[2] SM crude oil.

gregoriano, a [grego'rjano] AGG Gregorian.

grembiule [grem'bjule] SM apron; (*sopravveste*) overall (*Brit*), work coat (*Am*).

grembo ['grembo] SM **a** (*ginocchia*) lap; **tenere qn in grembo** to have sb on one's knee *o* in one's arms **b** (*ventre materno*) womb; **in grembo alla famiglia** in the bosom of one's family.

gremire [gre'mire] VT (*affollare*) to crowd, pack.

gremito, a [gre'mito] AGG: **gremito di** packed *o* crowded *o* crammed with.

Grenada [gre'nada] SF Grenada.

greppia ['greppja] SF manger.

greto ['greto] SM (exposed) gravel bed of a river.

grettamente [gretta'mente] AVV (*vedi agg*) pettily, narrow-mindedly; meanly, stingily.

grettezza [gret'tettsa] SF (*vedi agg*) pettiness; meanness, stinginess; **grettezza d'animo** narrow-mindedness.

gretto, a ['gretto] AGG **a** (*meschino*) petty, narrow-minded **b** (*avaro*) mean, stingy.

greve ['grɛve] AGG heavy.

grezzo, a ['greddzo] AGG **a** = **greggio b** (*poco raffinato*) coarse, rough.

gridare [gri'dare] [1] VI (*aus* **avere**) (*gen*) to shout, cry (out); (*strillare*) to scream, yell; (*animale*) to call; **smettila di gridare!** stop shouting!; **gridare a squarciagola** to yell at the top of one's voice; **gridare di dolore** to cry out *o* scream out in pain.

[2] VT to shout (out), yell (out); **gridare aiuto** to cry *o* shout for help; **gridare qc ai quattro venti** to shout *o* cry sth from the rooftops; **gridare vendetta** to cry out for vengeance.

grido ['grido] SM **a** (*pl f* **grida**) (*gen*) shout, cry; (*strillo*) scream, yell

b (*pl m* **gridi**) (*di animale*) cry; **un grido di dolore** a cry of pain; **un grido di aiuto** a cry for help; **lanciare grida di gioia** to shout for joy; **un cantante di grido** a famous singer; **è l'ultimo grido (della moda)** it's the latest fashion; **vestito all'ultimo grido** dressed in the latest style.

grifone [gri'fone] SM (*cane*) griffon; (*Mitol*) griffin.

grigiastro, a [gri'dʒastro] AGG greyish (*Brit*), grayish (*Am*).

grigio, gia, gi, gie ['gridʒo] [1] AGG grey (*Brit*), gray (*Am*); (*fig*) dull, boring; **materia grigia** (*Anat*) grey matter.

[2] SM grey (*Brit*), gray (*Am*); **grigio argento** silver grey.

grigioverde [gridʒo'verde] AGG grey-green (*Brit*), gray-green (*Am*).

griglia ['griʎʎa] SF **a** (*Culin*) grill (*Brit*), broiler (*Am*); **alla griglia** grilled (*Brit*), broiled (*Am*) **b** (*di stufa, focolare*) grate; (*di apertura*) grating **c** (*Aut*) grille **d** (*Elettr*) grid.

grigliante [griʎ'ʎante] AGG: **piatto grigliante** grill (*Brit*) *o* broiler (*Am*) tray.

grigliata [griʎ'ʎata] SF (*Culin*) grill; **fare una grigliata sulla spiaggia** to have a beach barbecue; **grigliata mista** mixed grill.

grilletto [gril'letto] SM trigger; **premere il grilletto** to pull the trigger.

grillo ['grillo] SM **a** (*Zool*) cricket **b** (*fig*) whim; **gli è saltato il grillo di...** he's taken it into his head to ...; **ha dei grilli per la testa** his head is full of nonsense **c** (*Naut*) shackle.

grimaldello [grimal'dɛllo] SM picklock.

grinfia ['grinfja] SF: **cadere nelle grinfie di qn** to fall into sb's clutches.

grinta ['grinta] SF (*di persona*) determination; (*nello Sport*) pluck; **avere molta grinta** to be very determined; **una macchina che ha grinta** a car with aggressive acceleration.

grintosamente [grintosa'mente] AVV determinedly.

grintoso, a [grin'toso] AGG (*persona*) forceful; (: *nello Sport*) plucky, combative.

grinza ['grintsa] SF (*di pelle*) wrinkle; (*di stoffa*) wrinkle, crease; **il tuo ragionamento non fa una grinza** your argument is faultless.

grinzoso, a [grin'tsoso] AGG (*vedi sf*) wrinkled; creased.

grippare [grip'pare] VI (*aus* **avere**), **gripparsi** VIP (*Tecn*) to seize (up), jam.

grisou [gri'zu] SM firedamp.

grissino [gris'sino] SM bread-stick.

groenlandese [groenlan'dese] ① SM/F Greenlander.
② AGG Greenland attr.

Groenlandia [groen'landja] SF: **la Groenlandia** Greenland.

gronda ['gronda] SF eaves pl.

grondaia [gron'daja] SF gutter.

grondante [gron'dante] AGG dripping; **un impermeabile grondante di pioggia** a soaking wet o dripping raincoat; **grondante di sudore** in o dripping with sweat.

grondare [gron'dare] ① VI (aus essere) to pour; **il sudore gli grondava dalla fronte** the sweat was pouring down his face.
② VT to drip with.

grongo, ghi ['grongo] SM (Zool) conger (eel).

groppa ['grɔppa] SF (di quadrupede) back, rump; (fam: di persona) back, shoulders pl; **salire in groppa a un cavallo** to mount a horse; **ha un bel po' di anni sulla groppa** she's getting on a bit.

groppo ['grɔppo] SM (groviglio) tangle; **avere un groppo alla gola** (fig) to have a lump in one's throat.

groppone [grop'pone] SM (scherz: di persona) back, shoulders pl.

gros-grain [gro'grɛ̃] SM (nastro) petersham.

grossa ['grɔssa] SF (unità di misura) gross.

grossezza [gros'settsa] SF (dimensione) size; (spessore) thickness.

grossista, i, e [gros'sista] SM/F (Comm) wholesaler.

grosso, a ['grɔsso] ① AGG ⓐ (gen) big, large; (spesso) thick; (pesante) heavy
ⓑ (fig: errore, rischio) serious, great; (: patrimonio) large; (: tempo, mare) rough; **un pezzo grosso** (fig) a big shot; **un grosso industriale** a business magnate
ⓒ (non raffinato: sale, anche fig) coarse
ⓓ (fraseologia): **avere il fiato grosso** to be short of breath; **fare la voce grossa** to raise one's voice; **farla grossa** to do something very stupid; **questa volta l'hai fatta grossa!** now you've done it!; **dirla** o **spararla grossa** to shoot a line, to tell tall stories (Brit) o tales (Am); **sbagliarsi di grosso** to be completely wrong o mistaken; **questa è grossa!** that's a good one!; **dormire della grossa** to sleep like a log; **grosso modo = grossomodo**.
② SM: **il grosso del lavoro è fatto** the bulk o the main part of the work is over; **il grosso dell'esercito** the main body of the army.

grossolanamente [grossolana'mente] AVV (gen) coarsely; **un lavoro fatto grossolanamente** a rough piece of work.

grossolanità [grossolani'ta] SF INV coarseness.

grossolano, a [grosso'lano] AGG (gen) coarse; (lavoro) roughly done; (linguaggio) coarse, crude; (errore) stupid, gross.

grossomodo [grosso'mɔdo] AVV roughly.

grotta ['grɔtta] SF cave.

grottescamente [grotteska'mente] AVV grotesquely.

grottesco, a, schi, sche [grot'tesko] ① AGG grotesque.
② SM: **il suo atteggiamento ha del grottesco** his attitude is somewhat ridiculous.

groviera [gro'vjɛra] SF O M INV gruyère (cheese).

groviglio, gli [gro'viʎʎo] SM (di fili, lana) tangle; (fig: di idee) muddle.

gru [gru] SF INV (Zool, Tecn) crane.

gruccia, ce ['gruttʃa] SF ⓐ (stampella) crutch ⓑ (per abiti) coat hanger.

grufolare [grufo'lare] VI (aus avere) to root about.

grugnire [grun'ɲire] ① VI (aus avere) (maiale) to grunt; (fig: persona) to grumble, growl.
② VT to mutter, growl out.

grugnito [grun'ɲito] SM grunt.

grugno ['grunɲo] SM (di maiale) snout; (fam: faccia) mug; **rompere il grugno a qn** to smash sb's face in.

grullaggine [grul'laddʒine] SF stupidity.

grullo, a ['grullo] ① AGG stupid, silly.
② SM/F fool, idiot.

grumo ['grumo] SM (di sangue, latte) clot; (di farina) lump.

grumoso, a [gru'moso] AGG lumpy.

gruppetto [grup'petto] SM small group.

gruppo ['gruppo] SM ⓐ group; **suddividere in gruppi di 10** to divide into groups of 10; **arrivare a gruppi di 3** to arrive in groups of 3 o in threes; **un gruppo di turisti** a group o party of tourists; **un gruppo letterario** a literary circle o group ▶ **gruppo elettrogeno** generating set ▶ **gruppo sanguigno** blood group ⓑ (Ciclismo) pack.

gruppuscolo [grup'puskolo] SM (pegg) small group.

gruviera [gru'vjɛra] SF O M INV = **groviera**.

gruzzolo ['gruttsolo] SM (di denaro) hoard; **ha messo da parte un bel gruzzolo** he has saved a fair bit.

GT ABBR (Aut: = gran turismo) GT.

G.U. ABBR = **Gazzetta Ufficiale**.

guadagnare [gwadan'ɲare] VT ⓐ (stipendio, percentuale, anche fig) to earn; **guadagnarsi la vita/il pane** to earn one's living/one's bread and butter
ⓑ (conquistare) to win; **guadagnare la fiducia/l'affetto di qn** to win sb's confidence/affection
ⓒ (ottenere) to gain; **guadagnare tempo** (temporeggiare) to gain time; (risparmiare) to save time; **guadagnare terreno** (Mil, fig) to gain ground; **che cosa ci guadagni a fare così?** what will you gain by doing that?; **in tutti i casi ci guadagni** you can't loose; **tanto di guadagnato!** so much the better!
ⓓ (raggiungere: riva, porto) to reach.

guadagno [gwa'danɲo] SM ⓐ (gen) earnings pl; (Comm) profit; **guadagno lordo/netto** gross/net earnings pl; **fare grossi guadagni** to earn a packet; (Comm) to make a large profit ⓑ (fig: vantaggio) advantage, gain.

guadare [gwa'dare] VT (fiume) to ford.

guado ['gwado] SM ford; **passare a guado** to ford.

guai ['gwai] ESCL: **guai a te** (o **lui** ecc)! woe betide you (o him ecc)!; **se non lo fai subito guai!** there will be trouble if you don't do it straight away!

guaina [gwa'ina] SF ⓐ (fodero) sheath ⓑ (busto) girdle.

guaio, ai ['gwajo] SM trouble, difficulty; (inconveniente) trouble, snag; **essere nei guai** to be in trouble o in a mess; **mettersi** o **ficcarsi nei guai** (fam) to get into trouble, get into a spot of bother; **andare a caccia di guai** (fam) to go looking for trouble; **il guaio è che...** the trouble o snag is that ... .

guaire [gwa'ire] VI (aus avere) (cane) to yelp, to whine; (persona) to whine.

guaito [gwa'ito] SM (di cane) yelp, whine; (il guaire) yelping, whining.

gualdrappa [gwal'drappa] SF (di cavallo) caparison.

guancia, ce ['gwantʃa] SF cheek; **porgere l'altra guancia** to turn the other cheek.

guanciale [gwan'tʃale] SM pillow; **dormire fra due guanciali** (fig) to sleep easy, have no worries.

guano ['gwano] SM guano.

guanto ['gwanto] SM glove; **un paio di guanti** a pair of gloves; **trattare qn con i guanti** (fig) to handle sb with kid gloves; **gettare/raccogliere il guanto** (fig) to throw down/take up the gauntlet ▶**guanto da forno** oven glove ▶**guanto di spugna** (per lavarsi) wash glove.

guantone [gwan'tone] SM boxing glove.

guardaboschi [gwarda'bɔski] SM INV forester.

guardacaccia [gwarda'kattʃa] SM INV gamekeeper.

guardacoste [gwarda'kɔste] SM INV (persona) coastguard; (nave) coastguard patrol vessel.

guardalinee [gwarda'linee] SM INV (Sport) linesman.

guardamacchine [gwarda'makkine] SM/F INV car-park (Brit) o parking lot (Am) attendant.

guardapesca [gwarda'peska] SM INV gamekeeper (for fish).

guardare [gwar'dare] ① VT a (oggetto, paesaggio) to look at; (persona, cosa in movimento) to watch; **guardare la televisione** to watch television; **guarda chi c'è** o **chi si vede!** look who's here!; **e guarda caso...** as if by coincidence ...
b (rapidamente) to glance at; (a lungo) to gaze at; **guardare di sfuggita** to steal a glance at; **guardare con diffidenza** to look warily at; **guardare di traverso** to scowl o frown at; **guardare fisso** to stare at; **guardare qc di buon/mal occhio** to look on o view sth favourably (Brit) o favorably (Am)/unfavourably (Brit) o unfavorably (Am); **guardare qn dall'alto in basso** to look down on sb; **guardare qn in faccia** to look sb in the face; **non guardare in faccia a nessuno** (fig) to have no regard for anybody
c (esaminare) to (have a) look at, check; **guardare una parola sul dizionario** to look sth up o check a word in the dictionary
d (custodire) to look after, take care of; (proteggere) to guard; **guardare a vista qn** (prigioniero) to keep a close watch on sb; **chi guarda i bambini?** who is looking after the children?; **i soldati guardano il ponte** the soldiers are guarding the bridge; **Dio me ne guardi!** God forbid!.
② VI (aus avere) a : **guardare di** to try to; **guarda di non arrivare in ritardo** try not to be late
b (badare): **guardare a** to mind, be careful about, pay attention to; **comprare qc senza guardare a spese** to buy sth without worrying about the expense; **per il matrimonio di sua figlia non ha guardato a spese** he spared no expense when his daughter got married
c (essere rivolto): **guardare a** to face; **guardare su** to give o look onto
d (fraseologia): **guardare dalla finestra** to look out of the window; **guarda un po' lì** (cerca) take a look over there; **ma guarda un po'!** good heavens!.
③ **guardarsi** VR a (uso reciproco) to look at each other
b (in vetrina, specchio) to look at o.s.; **guardarsi allo specchio** to look at o.s. in the mirror
c : **guardarsi da** (astenersi) to refrain from; (stare in guardia) to be wary of, beware of; **guardarsi dal fare qc** to take care o be careful not to do sth.

guardaroba [gwarda'rɔba] SM INV a (armadio) wardrobe b (locale) cloakroom, checkroom (Am).

guardarobiere, a [gwardaro'bjɛre] SM/F a (in albergo, grande casa) housekeeper b (in locale pubblico) cloakroom o checkroom (Am) attendant.

guardasigilli [gwardasi'dʒilli] SM INV a (Storia) keeper of the seals b (ministro) ≈ Lord Chancellor (Brit), ≈ Attorney General (Am).

guardia ['gwardja] ① SF a (individuo, corpo) guard; il cambio della guardia the changing of the guard; **essere della vecchia guardia** to be one of the old guard; **giocare a guardie e ladri** to play cops and robbers
b (sorveglianza: gen, Naut) watch; (Mil: servizio) guard duty, sentry duty; **lasciare qn a guardia di qc** to leave sb to look after sth, leave sb to keep an eye on sth, leave sth in sb's care; **fare la guardia a qn/qc** to guard sb/sth; **essere di guardia** to be on duty; **il medico di guardia** the doctor on call; **il fiume ha raggiunto il livello di guardia** the river has reached the high-water mark; **cane da guardia** guard dog
c (Pugilato, Scherma) guard; (di spada) hilt; **in guardia!** on guard!; **stare in guardia** (fig) to be on one's guard; **mettersi in guardia** to take one's guard; **mettere qn in guardia contro** (fig) to put sb on his guard against.
② ▶**guardia carceraria** (prison) warder (Brit) o guard (Am) ▶**guardia del corpo** bodyguard ▶**guardia di finanza** (corpo) a military body responsible for enforcing the law on income tax and monopolies; (persona) customs officer ▶**guardia forestale** forest ranger ▶**guardia giurata** security guard ▶**guardia medica** emergency doctor service ▶**guardia municipale** town policeman ▶**guardia notturna** night security guard ▶**guardia di pubblica sicurezza** policeman.

guardiacaccia [gwardja'kattʃa] SM INV = **guardacaccia**.

guardiano [gwar'djano] SM (di carcere) warder (Brit), guard (Am); (di stabilmento, villa) caretaker; (di faro, zoo) keeper; (di museo) attendant; (Rel, anche: **padre guardiano**) Father Guardian; **guardiano dei porci** swineherd; **un guardiano notturno** a night watchman.

guardina [gwar'dina] SF cell.

guardingo, a, ghi, ghe [gwar'dingo] AGG wary, cautious.

guardiola [gwar'djɔla] SF porter's lodge.

guardone [gwar'done] SM (fam pegg) voyeur, peeping Tom.

guardrail ['ga:dreil] SM INV guardrail.

guaribile [gwa'ribile] AGG curable.

guarigione [gwari'dʒone] SF recovery; **essere in via di guarigione** to be on the way o road to recovery.

guarire [gwa'rire] ① VT (anche fig) to cure; (ferita) to heal; **guarire qn da qc** to cure sb of sth.
② VI (aus essere) (persona) to recover; (ferita) to heal (up); **far guarire qn** to cure sb; **è guarito dal vizio del fumo** he is cured of smoking.

guaritore, trice [gwari'tore] SM/F healer.

guarnigione [gwarni'dʒone] SF (Mil) garrison.

guarnire [gwar'nire] VT (ornare: abiti) to trim; (: Culin) to garnish.

guarnizione [gwarnit'tsjone] SF a (vedi vb) trimming; garnish b (di rubinetto) washer; (Aut) gasket; **guarnizione della testata** cylinder head gasket; **guarnizioni dei freni** brake linings; **cambiare le guarnizioni dei freni** to reline the brakes.

Guascogna [gwas'koɲɲa] SF: **la Guascogna** Gascony.

guastafeste [gwasta'fɛste] SM/F INV spoilsport.

guastare [gwas'tare] ① VT (danneggiare: gen) to spoil, ruin; (: meccanismo) to break; (: cibo) to spoil.
② **guastarsi** VIP (meccanismo) to break down; (cibo) to go bad, go off; (tempo, persona) to change for the worse.

guasto, a ['gwasto] ① AGG a (non funzionante: gen) broken; (: telefono, distributore) out of order b (andato a male) bad, rotten; (: dente) decayed, bad; (fig: corrotto) depraved.
② SM (rottura completa) breakdown; (avaria) failure;

guasto al motore engine failure.

Guatemala [gwate'mala] SM: **il Guatemala** Guatemala.

guatemalteco, a, chi, che [gwatemal'tɛko] AGG, SM/F Guatemalan.

guazza ['gwattsa] SF heavy dew.

guazzabuglio, gli [gwattsa'buʎʎo] SM muddle, confusion.

guazzare [gwat'tsare] VI = **sguazzare**.

guazzo ['gwattso] SM (*Pittura*) gouache.

guercio, cia, ci, ce ['gwertʃo] ①AGG cross-eyed.
② SM/F cross-eyed person.

guereza [gwe'rɛddza] SF (*scimmia*) black colobus.

guerra ['gwɛrra] SF (*conflitto*) war; (*tecnica bellica*) warfare; **corrispondente di guerra** war correspondent; **in guerra con** at war with *o* against; **fare la guerra (a)** to wage war (against); **essere sul piede di guerra** to be on a war footing; **ha fatto la prima guerra mondiale** he fought in World War I; **sembra che abbia fatto la guerra** (*fig*) it looks as if it has been in the wars; **tra di loro ormai è guerra aperta** there is open war between them now ▶**guerra batteriologica** germ warfare ▶**guerra chimica** chemical warfare ▶**guerra fredda** cold war ▶**guerra mondiale** world war.

guerrafondaio, ai [gwerrafon'dajo] SM warmonger.

guerreggiare [gwerred'dʒare] VI (*aus* avere): **guerreggiare (contro)** to wage war (on, against).

guerresco, a, schi, sche [gwer'resko] AGG (*di guerra*) war *attr*; (*bellicoso*) warlike.

guerriero, a [gwer'rjɛro] ①AGG warlike.
② SM warrior.

guerriglia [gwer'riʎʎa] SF guerrilla warfare.

guerrigliero, a [gwerriʎ'ʎɛro] SM/F guerrilla.

gufo ['gufo] SM owl ▶**gufo comune** long-eared owl ▶**gufo reale** eagle-owl.

guglia ['guʎʎa] SF (*Archit*) spire; (*di roccia*) needle.

gugliata [guʎ'ʎata] SF length of thread.

Guiana [gu'jana] SF: **la Guiana francese** French Guiana.

guida ['gwida] SF ⓐ (*manuale*) guide, manual ▶**guida telefonica** telephone directory
ⓑ (*capo*) guide; (*direzione*) guidance, direction; **sotto la guida di qn** with sb's guidance; **essere alla guida di** (*governo*) to head; (*spedizione, paese*) to lead; **far da guida a qn** (*mostrare la strada*) to show sb the way; (*in una città*) to show sb (a)round ▶**guida alpina** mountain guide ▶**guida turistica** (*persona*) guide; (*libro*) guide(book)
ⓒ (*Aut*) driving; **avere guida a destra/sinistra** to be a right-/left-hand drive; **lezioni di guida** driving lessons; **patente di guida** driving licence (*Brit*), driver's license (*Am*); **posto di guida** driving seat
ⓓ (*tappeto, cassetto*) runner; (*Tecn*) runner, guide
ⓔ (*scout*) (girl) guide (*Brit*), girl scout.

guidare [gwi'dare] VT ⓐ (*gen*) to guide; (*capeggiare*) to lead; **lasciarsi guidare dal proprio istinto** to let o.s. be guided by one's instincts; **guidare qn sulla retta via** (*fig*) to steer sb in the right direction; **guidare una spedizione** to lead an expedition; **guidare la classifica** (*Sport*) to head the table
ⓑ (*auto*) to drive; **guidare bene/male** to drive well/badly; **sa guidare?** can you drive?

guidatore, trice [gwida'tore] SM/F (*conducente*) driver.

Guinea [gwi'nɛa] SF: **la Guinea Equatoriale** Equatorial Guinea; **la (Repubblica di) Guinea** (Republic of) Guinea.

guinzaglio, gli [gwin'tsaʎʎo] SM lead (*Brit*), leash (*Am frm*); **tenere qn al guinzaglio** (*fig*) to keep sb on a tight rein.

guisa ['gwisa] SF manner, way; **a guisa di** like, in the manner of; **in tal guisa** in such a way.

guizzante [gwit'tsante] AGG (*luce, fiamma*) flickering; (*pesce*) darting, flashing.

guizzare [gwit'tsare] VI (*aus* essere) ⓐ (*pesce, serpente*) to dart; (*fiamma*) to flicker ⓑ (*balzare*) to leap, slip; **mi guizzò via dalle mani** it leapt *o* slipped out of my hands; **il ladro riuscì a guizzare via** the thief managed to slip away.

guizzo ['gwittso] SM (*di animale*) dart; (*di fulmine*) flash; (*di persona*) spring, leap.

guru ['guru] SM INV (*Rel, anche fig*) guru.

guscio, sci ['guʃʃo] SM shell; **uscire dal proprio guscio** (*fig*) to come out of one's shell; **chiudersi nel proprio guscio** (*fig*) to retreat into one's shell; **guscio di noce** nutshell; (*fig: barca*) cockleshell.

gustare [gus'tare] ① VT ⓐ (*assaggiare*) to taste ⓑ to enjoy, savour (*Brit*), savor (*Am*); (*fig: apprezzare*) to relish, enjoy, appreciate.
② VI (*aus* avere): **gustare (a qn)** to please (sb); **non mi gusta affatto** I don't like it at all.

gustativo, a [gusta'tivo] AGG (*Anat*): **papille gustative** taste buds.

gusto ['gusto] SM ⓐ (*senso*) taste; (*sapore*) taste, flavour (*Brit*), flavor (*Am*); **ha un gusto amaro/di lampone** it tastes bitter/of raspberries, it has a bitter/a raspberry taste; **al gusto di fragola** strawberry-flavo(u)red; **privo di gusto** tasteless, flavo(u)rless
ⓑ (*senso estetico*) taste; **con gusto** tastefully; **veste con buon gusto** she has very good dress sense; **di buon/cattivo gusto** in good/bad taste; **abbiamo gli stessi gusti** we like the same things, we have the same tastes; **non è di mio gusto** it is not my taste
ⓒ (*piacere*): **fare qc di** *o* **con gusto** to do sth with pleasure; **mangiare/ridere di gusto** to eat/laugh heartily; **prendere gusto a qc/a fare qc** to get a taste for sth/for doing sth, get to like sth/doing sth; **ci ha preso gusto** he's acquired a taste for it, he's got to like it; **non c'è gusto a...** there's no pleasure in ...; **tutti i gusti sono gusti** there is no accounting for taste
ⓓ (*stile*) style; **di gusto barocco** in the baroque style.

gustosamente [gustosa'mente] AVV (*saporito, cucinato*) deliciously.

gustoso, a [gus'toso] AGG (*piatto*) tasty; (*romanzo, commedia*) enjoyable, agreeable.

gutturale [guttu'rale] AGG guttural.

Guyana [gu'jana] SF = **Guiana**.

H

H, h ['akka] [1] SF O M INV (*lettera*) H, h; **H come hotel** ≈ H for Harry (*Brit*), ≈ H for How (*Am*).
[2] ABBR **a** = ora **b** = altezza.

ha¹ ABBR (= *ettaro*) ha.

ha² *ecc* [a] VB vedi **avere**.

habitat ['abitat] SM INV (*Bot, Zool*) habitat.

habitué [abi'tɥe] SM/F INV (*di locale, ristorante*) regular customer.

hai *ecc* ['ai] VB vedi **avere**.

Haiti [a'iti] SF Haiti.

haitiano, a [ai'tjano] AGG, SM/F Haitian.

hall [hɔːl] SF INV (*di albergo*) hall, foyer.

hamburger [am'burger] SM INV hamburger.

handicap ['hændikap] SM INV (*Sport, fig*) handicap.

handicappato, a [andikap'pato] [1] AGG handicapped.
[2] SM/F handicapped person, disabled person; **gli handicappati** the handicapped.

hangar [ã'gar] SM INV (*Aer*) hangar.

hanno *ecc* ['anno] VB vedi **avere**.

happening ['hæpəniŋ] SM INV happening.

hardware ['haːdwɛə] SM INV hardware.

harem [a'rɛm] SM INV harem.

hascisc [aʃ'ʃiʃ] SM INV hashish.

haute-couture ['otku'tyr] SF haute couture.

hawaiano, a [ava'jano] AGG, SM/F Hawaiian.

Hawaii [ə'waːiː] SFPL: **le Hawaii** Hawaii *sg*.

Helsinki ['ɛlsinki] SF Helsinki.

henna ['ɛnna] SF henna.

herpes ['ɛrpes] SM (*Med*) herpes *sg* ▶**herpes zoster** shingles *sg*.

hg ABBR (= *ettogrammo*) hg.

hi-fi ['haifai] SM INV, AGG INV hi-fi.

Himalaia [ima'laja] SM: **l'Himalaia** the Himalayas *pl*.

hinterland ['hintərlant] SM INV hinterland.

hippy ['hipi] AGG INV, SM/F INV hippy.

hitleriano, a [itle'rjano] [1] AGG ATTR Hitler *attr*.
[2] SM Hitlerite.

hit-parade ['hit pə'reid] SF INV hit parade; **è in testa alla hit-parade** it's top of the pops.

hl ABBR (= *ettolitro*) hl.

ho *ecc* [ɔ] VB vedi **avere**.

hobby ['hɔbi] SM INV hobby.

hockey ['hɔki] SM hockey ▶**hockey su ghiaccio** ice hockey ▶**hockey su prato** field hockey, hockey (*Brit*).

holding ['houldiŋ] SF INV holding company.

hollywoodiano, a [ollivu'djano] AGG Hollywood *attr*; (*fig*) spectacular.

Honduras [on'duras] SM: **l'Honduras** Honduras.

Hong Kong [ong'kɔng] SF Hong Kong.

Honolulu [ono'lulu] SF Honolulu.

honoris causa [o'nɔris 'kauza] AVV honoris causa.

hostess ['houstis] SF INV (*assistente di volo*) air hostess (*Brit*), (air) stewardess, flight attendant; (*accompagnatrice*) escort.

hot dog ['hɔtdɔg] SM INV **a** (*panino*) hot dog **b** (*Sport: sci acrobatico*) hot-dogging.

hotel [o'tɛl] SM INV hotel.

hovercraft ['hɔvəkraːft] SM INV hovercraft.

humour ['hjuːmə] SM (sense of) humour.

humus ['umus] SM humus.

Hz ABBR (= *hertz*) Hz.

I

I, i [i] SF O M INV (*lettera*) I, i; **I come Imola** ≈ I for Isaac (*Brit*), ≈ I for Item (*Am*).

i [i] ART DET MPL vedi **il**.

I.A.C.P. [iatʃi'pi] SIGLA M (= *Istituto Autonomo per le Case Popolari*) *public housing association*.

iato [i'ato] SM hiatus.

iberico, a, ci, che [i'bɛriko] AGG Iberian; **la penisola iberica** the Iberian Peninsula.

ibernare [iber'nare] 1 VI (*aus* **avere**) to hibernate. 2 VT (*Med*) to induce hypothermia in.

ibernazione [ibernat'tsjone] SF hibernation.

ibid. ABBR (= *ibidem*) ib(id).

ibidem [i'bidem] AVV ibid.

ibisco, schi [i'bisko] SM hibiscus.

ibrido, a [i'brido] AGG, SM hybrid.

I.C.E. [i'tʃe] SIGLA M (= *Istituto nazionale per il Commercio Estero*) *overseas trade board*.

iceberg ['aisbəːg] SM INV iceberg; **la punta dell'iceberg** (*anche fig*) the tip of the iceberg.

icona [i'kɔna] SF icon.

iconoclasta, i, e [ikono'klasta] AGG, SM/F iconoclast.

iconografia [ikonogra'fia] SF iconography.

iconografico, a, ci, che [ikono'grafiko] AGG iconographic(al).

ictus ['iktus] SM INV (*Med, Metrica*) ictus.

id. ABBR (= *idem*) do.

Iddio [id'dio] SM God.

idea [i'dɛa] SF **a** (*gen*) idea; **non ne ho la minima idea** I haven't the faintest *o* foggiest idea; **farsi un'idea di qc** to get an idea of sth; **non hai idea di quanto sia difficile** you have no idea how difficult it is; **un'idea geniale** a brilliant *o* clever idea; **chissà che idea gli è saltata in mente adesso?** who knows what idea he may have got into his head now?; **tremo solo all'idea che possa venire** just the thought that he might come is enough to terrify me; **ho idea che...** I have an idea *o* a feeling that ...; **nemmeno** *o* **neanche** *o* **neppure per idea!** not on your life!, certainly not!, no way!; **dare l'idea di** to seem, look like; **idea fissa** obsession

b (*opinione*) opinion, view; **avere le idee chiare** to know one's mind; **cambiare idea** to change one's mind; **essere dell'idea (che)** to be of the opinion (that), think (that)

c (*intenzione*): **avere una mezza idea di fare qc** to have half a mind to do sth; **la mia idea era di andare al cinema** I had thought of going to the pictures

d (*ideale*) ideal; **l'idea del bello/della pace** the ideal of beauty/of peace.

ideale [ide'ale] 1 AGG ideal. 2 SM ideal; **l'ideale sarebbe andarsene** the best thing would be to leave; **il mio ideale di casa** my ideal home.

idealismo [idea'lizmo] SM idealism.

idealista, i, e [idea'lista] SM/F idealist.

idealistico, a, ci, che [idea'listiko] AGG idealistic.

idealizzare [idealid'dzare] VT to idealize.

idealizzazione [idealiddzat'tsjone] SF idealization.

idealmente [ideal'mente] AVV ideally.

ideare [ide'are] VT (*escogitare: scherzo*) to think of; (: *piano*) to think out, conceive; (*progettare: congegno*) to invent.

ideatore, trice [idea'tore] SM/F (*di piano*) originator; (*di metodo*) inventor.

ideazione [ideat'tsjone] SF conception.

idem ['idem] AVV idem.

identico, a, ci, che [i'dɛntiko] AGG: **identico (a)** identical (to); **è la stessa identica cosa** it's exactly the same thing.

identificabile [identifi'kabile] AGG identifiable.

identificare [identifi'kare] 1 VT to identify. 2 **identificarsi** VR: **identificarsi con** to identify o.s. with.

identificazione [identifikat'tsjone] SF identification.

identikit [identi'kit] SM INV identikit ®; **fare l'identikit di** to produce an identikit picture of.

identità [identi'ta] SF INV identity; **carta d'identità** identity card.

ideogramma, i [ideo'gramma] SM ideogram.

ideologia, gie [ideolo'dʒia] SF ideology.

ideologico, a, ci, che [ideo'lɔdʒiko] AGG ideological.

idilliaco, a, ci, che [idil'liako], **idillico, a, ci, che** [i'dilliko] AGG idyllic.

idillicamente [idillika'mente] AVV idyllically.

idillio, li [i'dilljo] SM idyll; **tra di loro è nato un idillio** they have fallen in love.

idioma, i [i'djɔma] SM language.

idiomatico, a, ci, che [idjo'matiko] AGG idiomatic; **frase idiomatica** idiom.

idiosincrasia [idjosinkra'zia] SF **a** (*avversione*) dislike; **avere un'idiosincrasia per qc** to dislike sth **b** (*Med*) idiosyncrasy.

idiosincratico, a, ci, che [idjosin'kratiko] AGG (*Med*) idiosyncratic.

idiota, i, e [i'djɔta] **1** AGG (*Med*) idiotic; (*fig*) idiotic, stupid.
2 SM/F idiot.

idiotismo [idjo'tizmo] SM (*Med*) idiocy.

idiozia [idjɔt'tsia] SF (*Med*) idiocy; (*fig*) idiocy, stupidity; (: *atto, discorso*) idiotic thing to do (*o* say).

idolatra, i, e [ido'latra] **1** AGG idolatrous.
2 SM/F idolater/idolatress.

idolatrare [idola'trare] VT (*divinità*) to worship; (*fig*: *persona*) to idolize.

idolatria [idola'tria] SF idolatry.

idolo ['idolo] SM (*Rel, fig*) idol.

idoneità [idonei'ta] SF suitability, fitness; **esame di idoneità** qualifying examination.

idoneo, a [i'dɔneo] AGG: **idoneo (a)** suitable (for), fit (for); **idoneo all'insegnamento** qualified to teach; **fare qn idoneo (al servizio militare)** to pass sb as fit (for military service).

idrante [i'drante] SM hydrant.

idratante [idra'tante] **1** AGG (*crema*) moisturizing.
2 SM moisturizer.

idratare [idra'tare] VT (*pelle*) to moisturize.

idratazione [idratat'tsjone] SF (*della pelle*) moisturizing.

idraulica [i'draulika] SF hydraulics *sg.*

idraulico, a, ci, che [i'drauliko] **1** AGG hydraulic.
2 SM plumber.

idrico, a, ci, che ['idriko] AGG water *attr.*

idrocarburo [idrokar'buro] SM hydrocarbon.

idroelettricità [idroelettritʃi'ta] SF hydroelectricity.

idroelettrico, a, ci, che [idroe'lɛttriko] AGG hydroelectric.

idrofilo, a [i'drɔfilo] AGG hydrophilic; **cotone idrofilo** cotton wool (*Brit*), absorbent cotton (*Am*).

idrofobia [idrofo'bia] SF (*Med*) rabies *sg.*

idrofobo, a [i'drɔfobo] AGG rabid; (*fig*) furious.

idrofugo, a, ghi, ghe [i'drɔfugo] AGG (*Chim*) hydrophobic.

idrogenazione [idrodʒenat'tsjone] SF hydrogenation.

idrogeno [i'drɔdʒeno] SM hydrogen.

idrografia [idrogra'fia] SF hydrography.

idrografico, a, ci, che [idro'grafiko] AGG hydrographic.

idrolipidico, a, ci, che [idroli'pidiko] AGG hydrolipid.

idrolisi [i'drɔlizi] SF hydrolysis.

idrologico, a, ci, che [idro'lɔdʒiko] AGG hydrological.

idromassaggio, gi [idromas'saddʒo] SM water massage; **vasca per idromassaggio** Jacuzzi ®.

idromele [idro'mɛle] SM mead.

idrometro [i'drometro] SM hydrometer.

idropisia [idropi'zia] SF (*Med*) dropsy.

idrorepellente [idrorepel'lɛnte] **1** AGG water-repellent.
2 SM water-repellent substance.

idroscalo [idros'kalo] SM (*Aer*) seaplane base.

idrosolubile [idroso'lubile] AGG water-soluble.

idrovolante [idrovo'lante] SM seaplane.

idrovora [i'drɔvora] SF water pump.

idruro [i'druro] SM hydride.

iella ['jɛlla] SF bad luck; **essere perseguitato dalla iella** to be plagued by bad luck.

iellato, a [jel'lato] AGG plagued by bad luck.

iena ['jɛna] SF hyena; (*fig*: *persona crudele*) nasty piece of work.

ieratico, a, ci, che [je'ratiko] AGG (*Rel*: *scrittura*) hieratic; (*fig*: *atteggiamento*) solemn.

ieri ['jɛri] **1** AVV yesterday; **ieri l'altro** OR **l'altro ieri** the day before yesterday; **ieri sera** yesterday evening, last night; **non sono nato ieri** I wasn't born yesterday.
2 SM yesterday; **il giornale di ieri** yesterday's paper.

iettatore, trice [jetta'tore] SM/F jinx; **smettila di fare lo iettatore!** stop trying to put a jinx on things!

iettatura [jetta'tura] SF evil eye; **ho la iettatura addosso!** there must be a jinx on me!

Ifigenia [ifidʒe'nia] SF Iphigenia.

igiene [i'dʒɛne] SF hygiene; **igiene del corpo** personal hygiene; **norme d'igiene** sanitary regulations; **ufficio d'igiene** ≈ Environmental Health Service (*Brit*) ► **igiene mentale** mental health ► **igiene pubblica** public health.

igienicamente [idʒenika'mente] AVV hygienically.

igienico, a, ci, che [i'dʒɛniko] AGG (*gen*) hygienic; (*salubre*: *clima*) healthy; **carta igienica** toilet paper; **impianto igienico** sanitary fittings.

igienista, i, e [idʒe'nista] SM/F hygienist.

igloo ['iglu] SM INV igloo.

I.G.M. [idʒi'emme] SIGLA M (= *Ispettorato Generale della Motorizzazione*) *road traffic inspectorate.*

ignaro, a [iɲ'ɲaro] AGG: **ignaro (di)** unaware (of), ignorant (of).

ignifugo, a [iɲ'ɲifugo] AGG flame-resistant, fireproof.

ignobile [iɲ'ɲɔbile] AGG vile, despicable.

ignobilmente [iɲɲobil'mente] AVV vilely, despicably.

ignominia [iɲɲo'minja] SF ignominy; **questo monumento è un'ignominia!** (*scherz*) this monument is a disgrace!

ignominioso, a [iɲɲomi'njoso] AGG ignominious.

ignorante [iɲɲo'rante] **1** AGG ignorant.
2 SM/F ignoramus; (*villano*) boor.

ignoranza [iɲɲo'rantsa] SF ignorance; **è di un'ignoranza spaventosa** he is appallingly ignorant.

ignorare [iɲɲo'rare] VT **a** (*non conoscere*) to be ignorant *o* unaware of, not to know; **ignoravo che...** I was unaware that..., I was ignorant of the fact that...; **ignoravo che tu fossi qui** I was unaware *o* I didn't know that you were here **b** (*fingere di non conoscere*) to ignore; **ha ignorato la mia domanda** he ignored my question.

ignoto, a [iɲ'ɲɔto] **1** AGG unknown; **il Milite Ignoto** the Unknown Soldier.
2 SM/F stranger, unknown person.
3 SM: **l'ignoto** the unknown.

igrometro [i'grometro] SM hygrometer.

igroscopico, a, ci, che [igros'kɔpiko] AGG hygroscopic.

iguana [i'gwana] SF iguana.

il [il] ART DET M (pl(m) **i**; diventa **lo** (pl **gli**) dav s impura, gn, pn, ps, x, z; f **la** (pl **le**)) **a** (*determinazione*) the; **il bambino ha la febbre** the baby has a temperature; **le ragazze non sono arrivate** the girls aren't here yet; **i figli dell'architetto** the architect's children; **lo zio di Roberta** Roberta's uncle; **gli studenti del primo anno** first-year students; **l'ora di cena** dinner time

b (*generalizzazione, astrazione*) *gen non tradotto*; **l'uomo è un animale sociale** man is a social animal; **i cavalli dormono in piedi** horses sleep on their feet; **l'oro è un metallo prezioso** gold is a precious metal; **la leucemia** leukemia; **lo zucchero caria i denti** sugar causes tooth decay; **mi piace la musica classica** I like classical music; **non sopporto il rumore** I can't stand noise; **il bello** the beautiful; **i poveri** the poor

c (*tempo*) the (*spesso omesso*); **siamo arrivati il lunedì di Pasqua** we arrived on Easter Monday; **la settimana prossima** next week; **l'inverno scorso** last winter; **il venerdì** ecc (*abitualmente*) on Fridays *ecc*; (*quel giorno*) on (the) Friday *ecc*; **riceve il venerdì** he sees people on Fridays *o* on a Friday; **la sera** in the evening; **verso le 6** at about 6 o'clock; **è partito il 20 luglio** he left on the 20th of July *o* on July the 20th (*lingua parlata*), he left on July 20th (*lingua scritta*)

d (*distributivo*) a, an; **costano 20.000 lire il chilo** they cost 20,000 lire a *o* per kilo; **li vendono a 5.000 lire il paio** they are sold at 5,000 lire a *o* per pair; **120 km l'ora** 120 km an *o* per hour; **ne abbiamo fatto la metà** we have done half of it

e (*partitivo*) some, any; **hai messo lo zucchero?** have you put sugar in it?; **hai comprato il pane?** did you buy (some *o* any) bread?

f (*possesso*): **ha aperto gli occhi** he opened his eyes; **mi fa male la gamba** my leg is hurting; **mettiti le scarpe** her mother smiled at her; **prendo il caffè senza zucchero** I take my coffee without sugar; **avere i capelli neri/il naso rosso** to have dark hair/a red nose

g (*con nomi propri*): **Plinio il giovane** Pliny the Younger; **il Petrarca** Petrarch; **il Presidente Mitterrand** President Mitterrand; **sono arrivati i Martinoni** the Martinonis have arrived; **le sorelle Clari** the Clari sisters; **dov'è la Giovanna?** where's Giovanna?; **ma dov'è finito il Cozzi?** whatever happened to the Cozzi boy?

h (*con nomi geografici*): **il Tevere** the Tiber; **i Pirenei** the Pyrenees; **l'Everest** Everest; **l'Italia** Italy; **il Regno Unito** the United Kingdom.

ilare ['ilare] AGG cheerful.

ilarità [ilari'ta] SF hilarity, mirth.

ileo ['ileo] SM (*Anat: intestino*) ileum; (: *osso*) hipbone, ilium.

ill. ABBR (= *illustrazione, illustrato*) ill.

illanguidimento [illangwidi'mento] SM languidness, languor.

illanguidire [illangwi'dire] **1** VT to weaken.
2 VI (*aus* essere) to grow weak *o* feeble.

illazione [illat'tsjone] SF inference, deduction.

illecitamente [illetʃita'mente] AVV illicitly.

illecito, a [il'letʃito] AGG illicit.

illegale [ille'gale] AGG illegal, unlawful.

illegalità [illegali'ta] SF illegality, unlawfulness.

illegalmente [illegal'mente] AVV illegally, unlawfully.

illeggibile [illed'dʒibile] AGG (*scrittura*) illegible; (*romanzo*) unreadable.

illegittimamente [illedʒittima'mente] AVV illegitimately.

illegittimità [illedʒittimi'ta] SF illegitimacy.

illegittimo, a [ille'dʒittimo] AGG illegitimate.

illeso, a [il'lezo] AGG unharmed, unhurt.

illetterato, a [illette'rato] AGG, SM/F illiterate.

illibatezza [illiba'tettsa] SF (*verginità*) virginity; (*purezza*) purity.

illibato, a [illi'bato] AGG (*vergine*) virgin; (*puro*) pure.

illimitatamente [illimitata'mente] AVV (*protrarsi*) indefinitely; (*estendersi*) without limits.

illimitato, a [illimi'tato] AGG (*gen*) unlimited, boundless; (*fiducia*) absolute; (*congedo, visto*) indefinite.

illividire [illivi'dire] VI (*aus* essere) (*volto, mani*) to go blue; (*cielo*) to grow leaden.

ill.mo ABBR = **illustrissimo**.

illogicamente [illodʒika'mente] AVV illogically.

illogicità [illodʒitʃi'ta] SF INV illogicality.

illogico, a, ci, che [il'lodʒiko] AGG illogical.

illudere [il'ludere] VB IRREG **1** VT to deceive, fool, delude.
2 **illudersi** VR to deceive o.s., delude o.s.; **illudersi sul conto di qn** to be mistaken about sb; **si illuse di poter cambiare tutto** he flattered himself that he could change everything.

illuminante [illumi'nante] AGG illuminating, enlightening.

illuminare [illumi'nare] **1** VT **a** (*strada, stanza*) to light; (*volto*) to illuminate; **illuminare a giorno** (*con riflettori*) to floodlight **b** (*fig: informare*) to enlighten.
2 **illuminarsi** VIP (*stanza*) to grow lighter; (*volto*) to light up.

illuminato, a [illumi'nato] AGG (*fig: sovrano, spirito*) enlightened.

illuminazione [illuminat'tsjone] SF **a** (*vedi vb*) lighting, illumination; floodlighting; enlightenment **b** (*lampo di genio*) flash of inspiration.

illuminismo [illumi'nizmo] SM (*Storia*): **l'Illuminismo** the Enlightenment.

illusi ecc [il'luzi] VB vedi **illudere**.

illusione [illu'zjone] SF illusion; **illusione ottica** optical illusion; **farsi illusioni** to deceive *o* delude o.s.; **non farti illusioni** don't delude yourself, don't kid yourself (*fam*); **ha perso ogni illusione** he has become thoroughly disillusioned.

illusionismo [illuzjo'nizmo] SM conjuring.

illusionista, i, e [illuzjo'nista] SM/F conjurer.

illuso, a [il'luzo] **1** PP di **illudere**.
2 AGG deluded.
3 SM/F: **sei un illuso** you are suffering from delusions.

illusoriamente [illuzorja'mente] AVV illusorily, deceptively.

illusorio, ria, ri, rie [illu'zorjo] AGG illusory.

illustrare [illus'trare] VT to illustrate.

illustrativo, a [illustra'tivo] AGG illustrative; **un catalogo illustrativo** a descriptive catalogue.

illustrazione [illustrat'tsjone] SF illustration.

illustre [il'lustre] AGG eminent, renowned, illustrious.

ILOR ['ilor] SIGLA F = **imposta locale sui redditi**.

IM SIGLA = *Imperia*.

imbacuccare [imbakuk'kare] **1** VT to wrap up.
2 **imbacuccarsi** VR to wrap (o.s.) up.

imbacuccato, a [imbakuk'kato] AGG muffled up, wrapped up.

imbaldanzire [imbaldan'tsire] **1** VT to give confidence to.
2 **imbaldanzirsi** VIP to grow bold, get cocky (*fam*).

imballaggio, gi [imbal'laddʒo] SM **a** (*gen*) packing *no pl*; **cassa da imballaggio** packing case; **carta da imballaggio** brown paper **b** (*costo*) cost of packing.

imballare[1] [imbal'lare] VT to pack.

imballare[2] [imbal'lare] **1** VT (*Aut: motore*) to race, rev up (*fam*).
2 **imballarsi** VIP (*Aut*) to race.

imballatore, trice [imballa'tore] SM/F packer.

imballo [im'ballo] SM packing.

imbalsamare [imbalsa'mare] VT to embalm; (*animale*) to stuff.

imbalsamato, a [imbalsa'mato] AGG embalmed.

imbalsamatore, trice [imbalsama'tore] SM/F embalmer; (*tassidermista*) taxidermist.

imbalsamazione [imbalsamat'tsjone] SF embalming; (*tassidermia*) taxidermy.

imbambolato, a [imbambo'lato] AGG (*sguardo, espressione*) vacant, blank.

imbandierare [imbandje'rare] VT to deck with flags.

imbandire [imban'dire] VT: **imbandire un banchetto** to prepare a lavish feast.

imbandito, a [imban'dito] AGG: **tavola imbandita** lavishly o sumptuously decked table.

imbarazzante [imbarat'tsante] AGG embarrassing, awkward.

imbarazzare [imbarat'tsare] ⬜1 VT a (*mettere a disagio*) to embarrass b (*ostacolare: movimenti*) to hamper; (*ingombrare: stanza*) to clutter up; (*appesantire: stomaco*) to lie heavily on.

⬜2 **imbarazzarsi** VIP to become embarrassed.

imbarazzato, a [imbarat'tsato] AGG (*persona*) embarrassed; **avere lo stomaco imbarazzato** to have an upset stomach.

imbarazzo [imba'rattso] SM a (*disagio*) embarrassment; **essere o trovarsi in imbarazzo** to be in an awkward situation o predicament; **mettere in imbarazzo** to embarrass b (*perplessità*) bewilderment, puzzlement; **non hai che l'imbarazzo della scelta** you are spoilt for choice c (*pesantezza*): **imbarazzo di stomaco** indigestion.

imbarbarimento [imbarbari'mento] SM (*di civiltà, costumi*) barbarization.

imbarbarire [imbarba'rire] ⬜1 VT (*costumi*) to make less civilized; (*lingua*) to barbarize.

⬜2 **imbarbarirsi** VIP (*costumi*) to become less civilized; (*lingua*) to become barbarized.

imbarcadero [imbarka'dɛro] SM landing stage.

imbarcare [imbar'kare] ⬜1 VT (*passeggeri*) to embark; (*merci*) to load; **imbarcare acqua** (*Naut*) to ship water.

⬜2 **imbarcarsi** VR a: **imbarcarsi su** (*nave*) to board, embark on; (*altro veicolo*) to board; **imbarcarsi per l'America** to sail for America b (*fig*): **imbarcarsi in** (*affare ecc*) to embark on.

imbarcazione [imbarkat'tsjone] SF (small) boat, (small) craft *pl inv*; **imbarcazione da pesca** fishing boat.

imbarco [im'barko] SM a (*di persone*) embarkation, boarding; (*di merci*) loading; **carta d'imbarco** boarding card b (*banchina*) embarkation point, departure point.

imbastardire [imbastar'dire] ⬜1 VT to bastardize, debase.

⬜2 **imbastardirsi** VIP to degenerate, become debased.

imbastire [imbas'tire] VT (*Cucito*) to baste, to tack; (*fig: piano*) to sketch out, outline.

imbastitura [imbasti'tura] SF (*Cucito*) tacking.

imbattersi [im'battersi] VIP: **imbattersi in** to bump o run into.

imbattibile [imbat'tibile] AGG unbeatable, invincible.

imbattuto, a [imbat'tuto] AGG unbeaten.

imbavagliare [imbavaʎ'ʎare] VT (*anche fig*) to gag.

imbeccare [imbek'kare] VT (*uccelli*) to feed; (*fig*) to prompt, put words into sb's mouth.

imbeccata [imbek'kata] SF (*di uccelli*) beakful of food;

(*Teatro*) prompt; **dare l'imbeccata a qn** (*Teatro*) to prompt sb; (*fig*) to give sb their cue.

imbecillaggine [imbetʃil'laddʒine] SF stupidity, foolishness; **questa è una vera imbecillaggine** this is a really idiotic thing to do (*o say*).

imbecille [imbe'tʃille] ⬜1 AGG (*Psic*) imbecilic; (*fig*) idiotic, stupid.

⬜2 SM/F (*Psic*) idiot, imbecile; **fare l'imbecille** to play the fool.

imbecillità [imbetʃilli'ta] SF INV (*Med, fig*) imbecility, idiocy; **dire imbecillità** to talk nonsense.

imbellettare [imbellet'tare] ⬜1 VT (*viso*) to make up, put make-up on.

⬜2 **imbellettarsi** VR to make o.s. up, put on one's make-up.

imbellettatura [imbelletta'tura] SF (*pegg*) frill.

imbellire [imbel'lire] ⬜1 VT to adorn, embellish.

⬜2 VI (*aus essere*), **imbellirsi** VIP to grow more beautiful.

imberbe [im'bɛrbe] AGG beardless; **un giovanotto imberbe** a callow youth.

imbestialire [imbestja'lire] ⬜1 VT to infuriate.

⬜2 **imbestialirsi** VIP to become infuriated, fly into a rage.

imbestialito, a [imbestja'lito] AGG furious, enraged.

imbevere [im'bevere] ⬜1 VT: **imbevere qc di** to soak sth in.

⬜2 **imbeversi** VIP (*anche fig*): **imbeversi di** to soak up, absorb.

imbevuto, a [imbe'vuto] AGG (*spugna*) **imbevuto (di)** soaked (in); (*fig: nozioni*): **imbevuto di** imbued with.

imbiancare [imbjan'kare] ⬜1 VT (*gen*) to whiten; (*muro: con il bianco di calce*) to whitewash; (: *con qualsiasi pittura*) to paint; **sepolcro imbiancato** (*fig*) whited sepulchre.

⬜2 VI (*aus essere*), **imbiancarsi** VIP to turn white, go white.

imbiancatura [imbjanka'tura] SF (*di muro: con bianco di calce*) whitewashing; (: *con altre pitture*) painting.

imbianchino [imbjan'kino] SM (house) painter, painter and decorator.

imbiondire [imbjon'dire] ⬜1 VT (*capelli*) to lighten; (*Culin: cipolla*) to brown.

⬜2 VI (*aus essere*), **imbiondirsi** VIP (*capelli*) to lighten, bleach; (*messi*) to turn golden, ripen.

imbizzarrire [imbiddzar'rire] VI (*aus essere*), **imbizzarrirsi** VIP (*cavallo*) to become frisky, get excited.

imbizzarrito, a [imbiddzar'rito] AGG (*cavallo*) skittish.

imboccare [imbok'kare] VT a (*bambino*) to feed b (*tromba*) to put to one's mouth c (*entrare in: strada*) to turn into, enter.

imboccatura [imbokka'tura] SF a (*di grotta, galleria, fiume*) mouth; (*di strada, porto*) entrance b (*Mus*) mouthpiece; (*per cavallo*) bit.

imbocco, chi [im'bokko] SM (*di autostrada, galleria*) entrance; (*di valle*) mouth.

imbonimento [imboni'mento] SM spiel, patter.

imbonitore [imboni'tore] SM (*di spettacolo, circo*) barker.

imborghesimento [imborgezi'mento] SM embourgeoisement.

imborghesire [imborge'zire] VI (*aus essere*), **imborghesirsi** VIP to become bourgeois.

imboscare [imbos'kare] ⬜1 VT (*nascondere*) to hide.

⬜2 **imboscarsi** VR (*Mil*) to evade military service, dodge the draft (*Am*); **quei due si sono imboscati di nuovo** (*fig*) those two have disappeared again.

imboscata [imbos'kata] SF ambush; **tendere un'imbo-**

scata to lay an ambush.

imboscato [imbos'kato] SM draft dodger (*Am*).

imboschimento [imboski'mento] SM afforestation.

imboschire [imbos'kire] 1 VT to afforest.

2 **imboschirsi** VIP to become wooded.

imbottigliamento [imbottiʎʎa'mento] SM (*di vino*) bottling; (*di traffico*) congestion.

imbottigliare [imbottiʎ'ʎare] 1 VT **a** (*vino*) to bottle **b** (*Mil: nemico*) to hem in, bottle up; (: *porto*) to blockade; **siamo rimasti imbottigliati** we got stuck in a traffic jam.

2 **imbottigliarsi** VIP to get *o* be stuck in a traffic jam.

imbottigliato, a [imbottiʎ'ʎato] AGG (*vino*) bottled; (*nave, esercito*) hemmed in, bottled up; (*auto*) stuck in a traffic jam.

imbottigliatrice [imbottiʎʎa'tritʃe] SF bottling machine.

imbottire [imbot'tire] 1 VT (*sedia, cuscino*) to stuff; (*giacca*) to pad; (*panino*) to fill; **gli hanno imbottito la testa di idee strane** they filled his head with silly notions.

2 **imbottirsi** VR (*coprirsi*) to wrap o.s. up; (*rimpinzarsi*): **imbottirsi di** to stuff o.s. with.

imbottito, a [imbot'tito] AGG (*sedia*) upholstered; (*giacca*) padded; **panino imbottito** filled roll.

imbottitura [imbotti'tura] SF (*vedi vb*) stuffing; padding; filling.

imbracare [imbra'kare] VT (*carico, container*) to secure for hoisting; (*cavallo, ferito*) to put into a harness.

imbracciare [imbrat'tʃare] VT (*fucile*) to shoulder; (*scudo*) to grasp.

imbranato, a [imbra'nato] (*fam*) 1 AGG clumsy, awkward.

2 SM/F clumsy person.

imbrattacarte [imbratta'karte] SM/F (*pegg*) scribbler.

imbrattare [imbrat'tare] 1 VT: **imbrattare (di)** to dirty (with), smear (with), daub (with).

2 **imbrattarsi** VR: **imbrattarsi (di)** to dirty o.s. (with).

imbrattatele [imbratta'tele] SM/F (*pegg*) dauber.

imbrigliare [imbriʎ'ʎare] VT (*cavallo*) to bridle; (*acque*) to dam; (*passioni*) to curb.

imbroccare [imbrok'kare] VT (*bersaglio*) to hit; (*fig: risposta*) to guess correctly; **non riesco mai ad imbroccarne una!** I never manage to get anything right!

imbrogliare [imbroʎ'ʎare] 1 VT **a** (*ingannare*) to trick, deceive

b (*confondere: documenti*) to muddle up; (: *idee*) to confuse, muddle, mix up; (: *fili*) to tangle up; **e per imbrogliare la faccenda...** and to complicate matters ...; **imbrogliare le carte** to confuse the issue

c (*Naut: vele*) to clew up.

2 **imbrogliarsi** VIP (*vedi vt b*) to become muddled up; to become confused, become muddled, get mixed up; to get tangled up; **s'imbrogliò nel parlare** his speech became confused.

imbroglio, gli [im'brɔʎʎo] SM **a** (*truffa*) swindle, con (*fam*); **niente imbrogli!** no cheating! **b** (*groviglio*) tangle; (*fig: situazione confusa*) mess; **cacciarsi in un imbroglio** to get into a mess.

imbroglione, a [imbroʎ'ʎone] SM/F cheat, swindler.

imbronciarsi [imbron'tʃarsi] VIP (*persona*) to sulk; (*cielo*) to cloud over.

imbronciato, a [imbron'tʃato] AGG (*persona*) sulky; (*cielo*) cloudy, threatening.

imbrunire [imbru'nire] 1 (*aus essere*) VI, VB IMPERS to grow dark.

2 SM: **all'imbrunire** at dusk.

imbruttire [imbrut'tire] 1 VT to make ugly.

2 VI (*aus essere*), **imbruttirsi** VIP to grow ugly.

imbucare [imbu'kare] 1 VT to post, mail (*Am*).

2 **imbucarsi** VR (*fam*) to gate-crash.

imbufalirsi [imbufa'lirsi] VIP (*fam*) to go up the wall.

imbullonare [imbullo'nare] VT to bolt.

imburrare [imbur'rare] VT to butter; (*stampo, teglia*) to grease.

imbutiforme [imbuti'forme] AGG funnel-shaped.

imbuto [im'buto] SM funnel.

imene [i'mɛne] SM hymen.

imitare [imi'tare] VT (*gen*) to imitate; (*Teatro*) to impersonate, do an impression of; (*gesti*) to mimic; (*firma*) to forge; **un materiale che imita il cuoio** a material which looks like leather.

imitativo, a [imita'tivo] AGG imitative.

imitatore, trice [imita'tore] SM/F (*gen*) imitator; (*Teatro*) impersonator, impressionist.

imitazione [imitat'tsjone] SF (*vedi vb*) imitation; impersonation, impression; mimicry; forgery.

immacolato, a [immako'lato] AGG immaculate, spotless; **l'Immacolata Concezione** (*Rel*) the Immaculate Conception.

immagazzinaggio, gi [immagaddzi'naddʒo] SM (*di merce, energia*) storing.

immagazzinamento [immagaddzina'mento] SM (*di merce, energia*) storing; (*di nozioni, idee*) accumulation.

immagazzinare [immagaddzi'nare] VT (*merce, energia*) to store; (*nozioni, idee*) to accumulate.

immaginabile [immadʒi'nabile] AGG conceivable, imaginable.

immaginare [immadʒi'nare] VT **a** (*credere, supporre*) to imagine, suppose; **immaginare che** to imagine *o* think that; **me lo immaginavo più giovane** I'd thought he was younger; **me lo immaginavo** I thought as much; **dovevo immaginarmelo** I should have expected it **b** (*in espressioni di cortesia*): **s'immagini!** don't mention it!, not at all!

immaginariamente [immadʒinarja'mente] AVV in an imaginary way.

immaginario, ria, ri, rie [immadʒi'narjo] 1 AGG imaginary; (*mondo*) make-believe; **un malato immaginario** a hypochondriac.

2 SM: **l'immaginario collettivo** the collective imagination.

immaginativa [immadʒina'tiva] SF imagination; **mancare d'immaginativa** to lack imagination.

immaginativo, a [immadʒina'tivo] AGG imaginative.

immaginazione [immadʒinat'tsjone] SF imagination; **è frutto della tua immaginazione** it's a figment of your imagination.

immagine [im'madʒine] SF (*gen, Fis*) image; (*rappresentazione, fotografia*) picture; **è l'immagine della salute** he's the picture of health; **è l'immagine di suo padre** he's the image of his father; **avere nella mente l'immagine di qn/qc** to have a mental picture of sb/sth; **diritto all'immagine** (*Dir*) right to privacy (*prohibiting unauthorised publication of photographs of a person*); **salvaguardare la propria immagine pubblica** to safeguard one's public image; **immagine dell'azienda** (*Comm*) corporate image *o* identity.

immaginoso, a [immadʒi'noso] AGG (*linguaggio, stile*) full of imagery.

immalinconire [immalinko'nire] 1 VT to sadden, depress.

2 **immalinconirsi** VIP to become depressed, become melancholy.

immancabile [imman'kabile] AGG unfailing; **ecco l'immancabile Giovanna** here comes Giovanna as usual.

immancabilmente [immankabil'mente] AVV without fail, unfailingly.

immane [im'mane] AGG (*smisurato*) huge; (*spaventoso, inumano*) terrible.

immanente [imma'nɛnte] AGG (*Filosofia*) inherent, immanent.

immanentismo [immanen'tizmo] SM (*Filosofia*) immanentism.

immanenza [imma'nɛntsa] SF (*Filosofia*) immanence.

immangiabile [imman'dʒabile] AGG (*non commestibile*) inedible; (*ripugnante*) uneatable, unpalatable; **è immangiabile** I can't stomach it.

immateriale [immate'rjale] AGG incorporeal, immaterial.

immatricolare [immatriko'lare] 1 VT (*veicolo*) to register.

2 **immatricolarsi** VR (*Univ*) to matriculate, enrol.

immatricolazione [immatrikolat'tsjone] SF (*vedi vb*) registration; matriculation, enrolment.

immaturamente [immatura'mente] AVV prematurely.

immaturità [immaturi'ta] SF immaturity.

immaturo, a [imma'turo] AGG (*frutto*) unripe; (*persona*) immature; (*neonato*) premature.

immedesimarsi [immedezi'marsi] VR: **immedesimarsi in** to identify with; **immedesimarsi nella parte** (*Cine, Teatro*) to get into a part, live a part.

immedesimazione [immedezimat'tsjone] SF: **immedesimazione (in)** identification (with).

immediatamente [immedjata'mente] AVV (*subito*) immediately, at once; (*direttamente*) immediately.

immediatezza [immedja'tettsa] SF immediacy.

immediato, a [imme'djato] AGG (*gen*) immediate; (*intervento*) prompt.

immemorabile [immemo'rabile] AGG immemorial; **da tempo immemorabile** from time immemorial.

immemore [im'mɛmore] AGG (*letter*): **immemore di** forgetful of.

immensamente [immensa'mente] AVV immensely, infinitely.

immensità [immensi'ta] SF immensity.

immenso, a [im'mɛnso] AGG (*gen*) immense, huge; (*spazio*) boundless; (*folla*) huge, enormous; (*fig: dolore, tristezza*) immense; **odio immenso** deep hatred.

immergere [im'mɛrdʒere] VB IRREG 1 VT (*gen*) to immerse, plunge; **immergere in acqua** (*mani*) to put in water; (*stoffa*) to soak in water; **immerso nello studio** immersed o absorbed in one's studies.

2 **immergersi** VR to plunge; (*sommergibile*) to dive, submerge; **immergersi in** (*fig*) to immerse o.s. in, become absorbed in.

immeritatamente [immeritata'mente] AVV (*senza merito*) undeservedly; (*senza colpa*) unjustly.

immeritato, a [immeri'tato] AGG (*non meritato*) undeserved, unmerited; (*ingiusto*) unjust.

immeritevole [immeri'tevole] AGG undeserving, unworthy.

immersione [immer'sjone] SF **a** (*gen*) immersion; (*di sommergibile*) submersion, dive; (*di palombaro*) dive; **navigare in immersione** to sail underwater; **linea di immersione** (*Naut*) water line **b** (*Geol*) hade.

immerso, a [im'mɛrso] PP di **immergere**.

immesso, a [im'messo] PP di **immettere**.

immettere [im'mettere] VT IRREG: **immettere (in)** (*gen*) to introduce (into); **immettere aria nei polmoni** to take air into the lungs; **immettere dati in un computer** to feed information into a computer, enter data on a computer.

immigrante [immi'grante] AGG, SM/F immigrant.

immigrare [immi'grare] VI (*aus essere*) to immigrate.

immigrato, a [immi'grato] AGG, SM/F immigrant.

immigrazione [immigrat'tsjone] SF immigration.

imminente [immi'nɛnte] AGG imminent.

imminenza [immi'nɛntsa] SF imminence.

immischiare [immis'kjare] 1 VT to involve; **immischiare qn in** to involve sb in; **trovarsi immischiato in uno scandalo** to find o.s. mixed up o involved in a scandal.

2 **immischiarsi** VIP: **immischiarsi in** to interfere o meddle in.

immiscibile [immiʃ'ʃibile] AGG (*Chim*) immiscible.

immiserimento [immizeri'mento] SM impoverishment.

immiserire [immize'rire] VT to impoverish.

immissario, ri [immis'sarjo] SM (*Geog*) affluent, tributary.

immissione [immis'sjone] SF (*gen*) introduction; (*Tecn, Med*) intake ▶ **immissione di dati** (*Inform*) data entry.

immobile [im'mɔbile] 1 AGG motionless, stationary, still.

2 SM item of real estate; (**beni) immobili** real estate *sg.*

immobiliare [immobi'ljare] 1 AGG property *attr*; **patrimonio immobiliare** real estate; **agenzia immobiliare** estate agent's (*Brit*), realtor (*Am*); **società immobiliare** property company. 2 SF = **società immobiliare**.

immobilismo [immobi'lizmo] SM (*Pol*) opposition to progress.

immobilità [immobili'ta] SF immobility; **immobilità politica** political inertia.

immobilizzare [immobilid'dzare] VT (*gen*) to immobilize; (*Econ: capitali*) to lock up.

immobilizzato, a [immobilid'dzato] AGG (*gen*) immobilized; **essere immobilizzato a letto** to be confined to bed.

immobilizzazione [immobiliddzat'tsjone] SF (*vedi vb*) immobilization; locking up ▶ **immobilizzazioni tecniche** (*Econ*) fixed assets.

immobilizzo [immobi'liddzo] SM: **spese d'immobilizzo** capital expenditure.

immodestia [immo'dɛstja] SF immodesty.

immodesto, a [immo'dɛsto] AGG immodest, conceited.

immolare [immo'lare] 1 VT: **immolare (a)** to sacrifice (to).

2 **immolarsi** VR: **immolarsi per** to sacrifice o.s. for.

immolazione [immolat'tsjone] SF sacrifice.

immondezzaio, ai [immondet'tsajo] SM rubbish dump.

immondizia [immon'dittsja] SF (*spazzatura*) rubbish *no pl*, refuse *no pl*, trash *no pl* (*Am*).

immondo, a [im'mondo] AGG (*luogo*) filthy, foul; (*azione*) base, vile.

immorale [immo'rale] AGG immoral.

immoralità [immorali'ta] SF immorality.

immoralmente [immoral'mente] AVV immorally.

immortalare [immorta'lare] 1 VT to immortalize.

2 **immortalarsi** VIP to win immortality for o.s.

immortale [immor'tale] AGG immortal.

immortalità [immortali'ta] SF immortality.

immotivato, a [immoti'vato] AGG (*azione*) unmotivated; (*critica*) groundless.

immune [im'mune] AGG: **immune da** (*esente*) exempt from; (*Med*) immune to; (*Dir*) immune from.

immunità [immuni'ta] SF (*Med, Dir*) immunity

▶ **immunità diplomatica** diplomatic immunity
▶ **immunità parlamentare** ≈ parliamentary privilege.

immunizzare [immunid'dzare] ☐ vт: **immunizzare contro** to immunize against.
☐ **immunizzarsi** vʀ (*fig*): **immunizzarsi contro** to become immune to.

immunizzazione [immuniddzat'tsjone] sf immunization.

immunodeficienza [immunodefi'tʃɛntsa] sf: **sindrome da immunodeficienza acquista** acquired immunodeficiency syndrome.

immunologia [immunolo'dʒia] sf immunology.

immunologico, a, ci, che [immuno'lɔdʒiko] AGG immunological.

immunoterapia [immunotera'pia] sf immunotherapy.

immusonirsi [immuzo'nirsi] vɪᴘ (*fam*) to sulk.

immusonito, a [immuzo'nito] AGG sulky.

immutabile [immu'tabile] AGG (*gen*) unchanging; (*decreto, decisione*) immutable.

immutato, a [immu'tato] AGG unchanged.

impaccare [impak'kare] vт to pack.

impaccatura [impakka'tura] sf packaging.

impacchettare [impakket'tare] vт to wrap up, parcel up.

impacciare [impat'tʃare] vт to hamper, hinder; **impacciare qn nei movimenti** to hamper sb's movements.

impacciatamente [impattʃata'mente] AVV (*muoversi*) clumsily; (*rispondere*) awkwardly, with embarrassment.

impacciato, a [impat'tʃato] AGG **a** (*imbarazzato*) embarrassed **b** (*goffo*) awkward, clumsy.

impaccio, ci [im'pattʃo] sm **a** (*imbarazzo*) embarrassment; (*situazione imbarazzante*) awkward situation; **trarsi d'impaccio** to get out of an awkward situation **b** (*ostacolo*) obstacle; **essere d'impaccio a qn** to be in sb's way.

impacco, chi [im'pakko] sm (*Med*) compress.

impadronirsi [impadro'nirsi] vɪᴘ: **impadronirsi di** (*città, ricchezze*) to seize, take possession of; (*fig: lingua*) to master.

impagabile [impa'gabile] AGG priceless.

impaginare [impadʒi'nare] vт (*Tip*) to make up.

impaginazione [impadʒinat'tsjone] sf (*Tip*) make-up.

impagliare [impaʎ'ʎare] vт **a** (*animale: imbalsamare*) to stuff (with straw) **b**: **impagliare una sedia** to cane a chair.

impagliatore, trice [impaʎʎa'tore] sм/ꜰ (*di animali*) taxidermist; (*di sedie*) chair-mender.

impala [im'pala] sм ɪɴᴠ (*Zool*) impala.

impalare [impa'lare] ☐ vт **a** (*persona*) to impale **b** (*viti, piante*) to stake, prop up.
☐ **impalarsi** vɪᴘ (*fig: bloccarsi*) to stand stock-still.

impalato, a [impa'lato] AGG (*fig*) stock-still; **non startene lì impalato, fai qualcosa!** don't just stand there, do something!

impalcatura [impalka'tura] sf scaffolding; (*fig*) framework, structure.

impallidire [impalli'dire] vɪ (*aus essere*) to turn pale; (*colore, ricordo*) to fade.

impallinare [impalli'nare] vт to riddle with shot.

impalpabile [impal'pabile] AGG impalpable.

impalpabilmente [impalpabil'mente] AVV impalpably.

impanare [impa'nare] vт **a** (*Culin*) to roll (*o coat*) in breadcrumbs, bread (*Am*) **b** (*Tecn: vite*) to thread.

impanatura [impana'tura] sf **a** (*vedi vb*) coating in breadcrumbs; threading **b** (*Culin*) breadcrumbs *pl*.

impantanarsi [impanta'narsi] vɪᴘ to sink into mud; (*fig*) to get bogged down.

impaperarsi [impape'rarsi] vɪᴘ to stumble over a word.

impappinarsi [impappi'narsi] vɪᴘ to falter, stammer.

imparabile [impa'rabile] AGG (*Sport: tiro, pallone*) unstoppable.

imparare [impa'rare] vт to learn; **imparare a fare qc** to learn to do sth; **imparare qc a memoria** to learn sth (off) by heart; **imparare qc a proprie spese** to learn sth to one's cost; **così impari!** that'll teach you!; **sbagliando s'impara** (*Proverbio*) practice makes perfect.

imparaticcio, ci [impara'tittʃo] sm half-baked notions *pl*.

impareggiabile [impared'dʒabile] AGG incomparable.

impareggiabilmente [impareddʒabil'mente] AVV incomparably.

imparentare [imparen'tare] ☐ vт (*famiglie*) to ally by marriage. ☐ **imparentarsi** vɪᴘ: **imparentarsi con** to marry into, become related by marriage to.

imparentato, a [imparen'tato] AGG: **essere imparentato con** to be related by marriage to.

impari ['impari] AGG ɪɴᴠ (*disuguale*) unequal.

impartire [impar'tire] vт (*ordine*) to give; (*benedizione*) to bestow.

imparziale [impar'tsjale] AGG impartial, unbiased.

imparzialità [impartsjali'ta] sf impartiality.

impasse [ɛ̃'pas] sf ɪɴᴠ (*fig*) impasse.

impassibile [impas'sibile] AGG impassive.

impastare [impas'tare] vт (*pane*) to knead; (*cemento, malta*) to mix.

impastato, a [impas'tato] AGG: **impastato di fango** covered in mud; **avere la lingua impastata** to have a furry tongue; **avere gli occhi impastati di sonno** to be half asleep.

impasticcarsi [impastik'karsi] vʀ (*fam*) to pop pills.

impasticcato, a [impastik'kato] AGG (*fam*) pill-popping.

impasto [im'pasto] sm **a** (*l'impastare: di pane*) kneading; (: *cemento*) mixing **b** (*pasta*) dough; (*miscuglio, anche fig*) mixture, blend.

impatto [im'patto] sm (*urto, effetto*) impact ▶ **impatto ambientale** impact on the environment.

impaurire [impau'rire] ☐ vт to frighten, scare.
☐ **impaurirsi** vɪᴘ to get *o* grow scared *o* frightened.

impavidamente [impavida'mente] AVV fearlessly.

impavido, a [im'pavido] AGG intrepid, fearless.

impaziente [impat'tsjɛnte] AGG impatient; **impaziente di fare qc** eager to do sth.

impazientemente [impattsjɛnte'mente] AVV impatiently.

impazienza [impat'tsjɛntsa] sf (*vedi agg*) impatience; eagerness.

impazzata [impat'tsata]: **all'impazzata** AVV (*correre*) at breakneck speed; (*colpire*) wildly.

impazzire [impat'tsire] vɪ (*aus essere*) **a** to go mad; **impazzire per qn/qc** to be mad *o* crazy about sb/sth; **impazzire per lo sport/il gelato** to be mad about sport/ice cream; **impazzire per il dolore** to go mad with grief; **impazzisco d'amore per te** I'm mad *o* crazy about you; **questo compito mi fa impazzire** this homework's driving me mad; **sono impazzito a cercare un taxi** I nearly went crazy trying to find a taxi; **ho un mal di testa da impazzire** I've got a splitting headache **b** (*Culin: salsa, maionese*) to curdle.

impeccabile [impek'kabile] AGG impeccable.

impeccabilmente [impekkabil'mente] AVV impeccably.

impedenza [impe'dɛntsa] sf (*Fis*) impedance.

impedimento [impedi'mento] SM **a** (*ostacolo*) obstacle, hindrance; **essere un impedimento** *o* **d'impedimento a qc/qn** to stand in the way of sth/sb **b** (*Dir*) impediment.

impedire [impe'dire] VT **a** (*proibire*): **impedire a qn di fare qc** to prevent *o* stop sb (from) doing sth **b** (*ostruire*) to obstruct **c** (*impacciare*) to hamper, hinder; **era impedita dal vestito lungo** she was hampered by her long dress.

impegnare [impeɲ'ɲare] 1 VT **a** (*dare in pegno*) to pawn **b** (*vincolare*) to bind **c** (*sogg*: *lavoro*) to keep busy; **quel compito di matematica ha impegnato tutta la classe** the maths exercise kept the whole class busy **d** (*Mil*) to engage; (*Sport*) to put under pressure. 2 **impegnarsi** VR (*vincolarsi*): **impegnarsi a fare qc** to undertake to do sth; **impegnarsi con un contratto** to enter into a contract; **impegnarsi con qn** (*accordarsi*) to come to an agreement with sb; **impegnarsi in qc** (*dedicarsi*) to devote o.s. to sth.

impegnativa [impeɲɲa'tiva] SF (*Amm*) ≈ referral (*Health Service authorization for hospital or specialist treatment*).

impegnativo, a [impeɲɲa'tivo] AGG (*lavoro*) demanding; (*promessa*) binding.

impegnato, a [impeɲ'ɲato] AGG **a** (*persona*: *occupata*) busy; **sono già impegnato** I have a prior engagement; **essere impegnato con** (*lavoro*) to be busy with; (*ditta*) to be involved with **b** (*gioielli*) pawned **c** (*fig*: *romanzo, autore, film*) serious, engagé.

impegno [im'peɲɲo] SM **a** (*obbligo*) obligation; (*promessa*) promise, pledge; (*compito, di scrittore*) commitment; **assumere un impegno** to take on a commitment; **penso di venire, ma senza impegno** I'll probably come but I can't promise **b** (*affare, incombenza*) engagement, appointment; **un impegno precedente** a previous engagement **c** (*zelo*) enthusiasm, diligence; **studiare con impegno** to study hard.

impegolarsi [impego'larsi], **impelagarsi** [impela'garsi] VR: **impegolarsi in** to get heavily involved in.

impellente [impel'lɛnte] AGG pressing, urgent.

impellicciato, a [impellit'tʃato] AGG dressed in furs.

impenetrabile [impene'trabile] AGG (*volto*) inscrutable; (*mistero*) complete; (*segreto*) closely-guarded; (*bosco*) impenetrable.

impenitente [impeni'tɛnte] AGG impenitent, unrepentant; **scapolo impenitente** confirmed bachelor.

impennacchiarsi [impennak'kjarsi] VR (*scherz*) to get all dolled up.

impennare [impen'nare] 1 VT (*Aer*): **far impennare l'aereo** to go into a climb. 2 **impennarsi** VIP **a** (*aereo*) to go into a climb; (*cavallo*) to rear (up) **b** (*fig*: *arrabbiarsi*) to flare up.

impennata [impen'nata] SF **a** (*di cavallo*) rearing (up); (*di aereo*) climb, nose-up; (*di motociclo*) wheelie **b** (*fig*: *scatto d'ira*) burst of anger **c** (*rialzo*: *di prezzi, valuta*) sharp rise.

impensabile [impen'sabile] AGG (*inaccettabile*) unthinkable; (*difficile da concepire*) inconceivable.

impensato, a [impen'sato] AGG unexpected, unforeseen.

impensierire [impensje'rire] 1 VT to worry. 2 **impensierirsi** VIP: **impensierirsi (per)** to worry (about).

imperante [impe'rante] AGG (*tendenza, moda*) prevailing.

imperare [impe'rare] VI (*aus avere*) (*anche fig*) to rule,

reign.

imperativo, a [impera'tivo] 1 AGG (*tono, discorso*) commanding; (*Gramm*) imperative. 2 SM (*Gramm*): **l'imperativo** the imperative.

imperatore, trice [impera'tore] SM/F emperor/empress.

impercettibile [impertʃet'tibile] AGG imperceptible.

impercettibilmente [impertʃettibil'mente] AVV imperceptibly.

imperdonabile [imperdo'nabile] AGG unforgivable, unpardonable.

imperdonabilmente [imperdonabil'mente] AVV unforgivably, unpardonably.

imperfettamente [imperfetta'mente] AVV imperfectly.

imperfetto, a [imper'fɛtto] 1 AGG (*gen, Gramm*) imperfect; (*difettoso*) faulty, defective; (*incompleto*) unfinished. 2 SM (*Gramm*): **l'imperfetto** the imperfect (tense).

imperfezione [imperfet'tsjone] SF (*gen*) imperfection; (*di gioiello*) flaw; (*della pelle*) blemish, imperfection.

imperiale [impe'rjale] AGG imperial.

imperialismo [imperja'lizmo] SM imperialism.

imperialista, i, e [imperja'lista] AGG, SM/F imperialist.

imperialistico, a, ci, che [imperja'listiko] AGG imperialist(ic).

imperiosamente [imperjosa'mente] AVV imperiously.

imperioso, a [impe'rjoso] AGG (*autoritario*: *persona, tono*) imperious; (*motivo, esigenza*) urgent, pressing.

imperituro, a [imperi'turo] AGG (*letter*) everlasting.

imperizia [impe'rittsja] SF inexperience, lack of experience.

imperlare [imper'lare] 1 VT: **il sudore gli imperlava la fronte** his brow was beaded with perspiration, beads of sweat formed on his forehead. 2 **imperlarsi** VIP: **imperlarsi di sudore** to be (*o* become) beaded with perspiration.

impermalire [imperma'lire] 1 VT: **far impermalire qn** to offend sb. 2 **impermalirsi** VIP: **impermalirsi (per)** to take offence *o* umbrage (at).

impermeabile [imperme'abile] 1 AGG (*terreno, roccia*) impermeable; (*tessuto*) waterproof; (*orologio*) water-resistant; **essere impermeabile alle offese** to be thick-skinned, have a thick skin. 2 SM (*indumento*) raincoat, mac (*Brit*).

impermeabilizzare [impermeabilid'dzare] VT to waterproof.

impermeabilizzazione [impermeabiliddzat'tsjone] SF waterproofing.

imperniare [imper'njare] 1 VT: **imperniare qc su** to hinge sth on; (*fig*: *discorso, relazione*) to base sth on; **il mio discorso è imperniato su un unico concetto** my talk hinges on one basic concept. 2 **imperniarsi** VIP (*fig*): **imperniarsi su** to be based on.

impero [im'pɛro] 1 SM empire; **l'impero della ragione** (*fig*) the rule of reason. 2 AGG INV Empire *attr*.

imperscrutabile [imperskru'tabile] AGG inscrutable.

imperscrutabilità [imperskrutabili'ta] SF inscrutability.

impersonale [imperso'nale] AGG impersonal.

impersonalità [impersonali'ta] SF impersonality.

impersonare [imperso'nare] 1 VT **a** (*qualità, concetto astratto*) to personify **b** (*Teatro*) to play (the part of), act (the part of). 2 **impersonarsi** VIP (*incarnarsi*): **in lei s'impersona la cupidigia** she is the personification of greed.

imperterrito, a [imper'tɛrrito] AGG unperturbed; **continuare imperterrito (a fare qc)** to carry on (doing sth) regardless *o* unperturbed.

impertinente [imperti'nɛnte] AGG impertinent.

impertinenza [imperti'nɛntsa] SF impertinence.

imperturbabile [impertur'babile] AGG imperturbable.

imperturbabilità [imperturbabili'ta] SF imperturbability.

imperturbato, a [impertur'bato] AGG unperturbed.

imperversare [imperver'sare] VI (*aus* avere) (*persona, tempesta, malattia*) to rage; (*scherz: moda, costumi*) to be all the rage.

impervio, via, vi, vie [im'pɛrvjo] AGG (*luogo*) inaccessible; (*strada*) impassable.

impetigine [impe'tidʒine] SF (*Med*) impetigo.

impeto ['impeto] SM (*moto, forza*) force, impetus; (*assalto*) onslaught; (*fig: d'odio, amore*) surge; **lo uccise in un impeto d'ira** he killed him in a fit of rage; **agire d'impeto** to act on impulse; **con impeto** (*parlare*) forcefully, energetically.

impetrare [impe'trare] VT (*letter*) to beg for, beseech.

impettinabile [impetti'nabile] AGG (*capelli*) unruly.

impettito, a [impet'tito] AGG: **essere tutto impettito** to be as stiff as a ramrod; **camminare impettito** to strut.

impetuosamente [impetuosa'mente] AVV (*reagire*) impetuously; (*soffiare: vento*) violently, furiously.

impetuosità [impetuosi'ta] SF impetuosity.

impetuoso, a [impetu'oso] AGG (*gen*) impetuous; (*vento, corrente*) raging, strong.

impiallacciare [impjallat'tʃare] VT (*mobile*) to veneer.

impiallacciatura [impjallattʃa'tura] SF (*tecnica*) veneering; (*materiale*) veneer.

impiantare [impjan'tare] VT (*installare*) to install; (*avviare: azienda*) to set up, establish.

impiantistica [impjan'tistika] SF plant design and installation.

impiantito [impjan'tito] SM flooring, floor.

impianto [im'pjanto] SM **a** (*installazione*) installation; **spese d'impianto** installation costs **b** (*Anat: di embrione*) implantation **c** (*apparecchiature*) plant; (*sistema*) system ▶ **impianti di risalita** (*Sci*) ski lifts ▶ **impianto elettrico** wiring ▶ **impianto industriale** plant ▶ **impianto di raffreddamento** cooling system ▶ **impianto di riscaldamento** heating system ▶ **impianto sportivo** sports complex ▶ **impianto stereo** stereo system.

impiastrare [impjas'trare], **impiastricciare** [impjastrit'tʃare] VT: **impiastrare di** (*fango ecc*) to dirty with; (*pittura, trucco*) to smear with.

impiastro [im'pjastro] SM **a** (*Med*) poultice **b** (*fig fam: persona*) nuisance.

impiccagione [impikka'dʒone] SF hanging.

impiccare [impik'kare] ① VT to hang; **questo colletto m'impicca** (*fig*) this collar's choking me; **non lo farò nemmeno se m'impicchi!** there's no way I'll do that!

② **impiccarsi** VR to hang o.s.; **impiccati!** (*fam*) go to hell!

impiccato, a [impik'kato] SM/F hanged man/woman.

impicciare [impit'tʃare] ① VT (*sogg: persona, tavolo*) to be in the way of, get in the way of; (*: abiti*) to hinder, hamper.

② **impicciarsi** VIP to meddle, interfere; **impicciarsi di** *o* **in qc** to interfere *o* meddle in sth; **impicciati degli affari tuoi!** mind your own business!

impiccio, ci [im'pittʃo] SM **a** (*ostacolo*) hindrance; (*seccatura*) trouble, bother; **essere d'impiccio** to be in the way **b** (*affare imbrogliato*) mess *no pl*; **cavare** *o* **togliere qn dagli impicci** to get sb out of trouble.

impiccione, a [impit'tʃone] SM/F busybody.

impiccolimento [impikkoli'mento] SM (*di immagine*) reduction.

impiccolire [impikko'lire] ① VT to make smaller, reduce.

② VI (*aus* essere), **impiccolirsi** VIP to get smaller.

impiegabile [impje'gabile] AVV usable.

impiegare [impje'gare] ① VT **a** (*utilizzare*) to use, employ; (*: tempo*) to spend; (*metterci: tempo*) to take; (*investire: denaro*) to invest; **impiega il tempo libero a dipingere** he spends his free time painting; **impiego un quarto d'ora per andare a casa** it takes me *o* I take a quarter of an hour to get home **b** (*lavoratore*) to employ.

② **impiegarsi** VR to get a job, obtain employment.

impiegatizio, zia, zi, zie [impjega'tittsjo] AGG clerical, white-collar *attr*; **il ceto impiegatizio** clerical *o* white-collar workers *pl*.

impiegato, a [impje'gato] SM/F employee ▶ **impiegato di banca** bank clerk ▶ **impiegato statale** state employee.

impiego, ghi [im'pjɛgo] SM **a** (*gen*) use; (*Econ*) investment **b** (*occupazione*) employment; (*posto di lavoro*) post, (regular) job; **un impiego fisso** a permanent job; **pubblico impiego** public sector.

impietosire [impjeto'sire] ① VT to move (to pity).

② **impietosirsi** VIP to be moved (to pity).

impietoso, a [impje'toso] AGG pitiless, cruel.

impietrire [impje'trire] VT (*anche fig*) to petrify.

impigliare [impiʎ'ʎare] ① VT to catch, entangle.

② **impigliarsi** VIP: **impigliarsi (in qc)** to get caught *o* entangled (in sth).

impigrire [impi'grire] ① VT to make lazy.

② VI (*aus* essere), **impigrirsi** VIP to get *o* grow lazy.

impilare [impi'lare] VT to stack, pile (up).

impinguare [impin'gware] VT (*fig: tasche, casse dello Stato*) to fill; (*maiale*) to fatten.

impiombare [impjom'bare] VT **a** (*saldare: tubo ecc*) to seal (with lead); (*sigillare: baule, cassa*) to seal **b** (*dente*) to fill.

implacabile [impla'kabile] AGG implacable.

implacabilità [implakabili'ta] SF implacability.

implacabilmente [implakabil'mente] AVV implacably.

implantologia [implantolo'dʒia] SF (*tecnica di trapianto: di capelli*) hair-replacement; (*: di denti*) implantology.

implementare [implemen'tare] VT (*Inform*) to implement.

implicare [impli'kare] ① VT **a** (*sottintendere*) to imply; (*comportare*) to entail **b** (*coinvolgere*): **implicare qn (in)** to involve sb (in), implicate sb (in).

② **implicarsi** VR: **implicarsi (in)** to get *o* become involved (in).

implicazione [implikat'tsjone] SF implication.

implicitamente [implitʃita'mente] AVV implicitly.

implicito, a [im'plitʃito] AGG implicit.

implorante [implo'rante] AGG imploring, beseeching.

implorare [implo'rare] VT to implore, beseech.

implorazione [implorat'tsjone] SF plea, entreaty.

impluvio, vi [im'pluvjo] SM (*Geol*): **linea di impluvio** watershed.

impollinare [impolli'nare] VT to pollinate.

impollinazione [impollinat'tsjone] SF pollination.

impoltronirsi [impoltro'nirsi] VIP to become lazy.

impolverare [impolve'rare] ① VT to cover with dust.

② **impolverarsi** VIP to get dusty.

impomatare [impoma'tare] ① VT (*capelli*) to pomade; (*baffi*) to wax; (*pelle*) to put ointment on.
② **impomatarsi** VR (*fam*) to get spruced up.

imponderabile [imponde'rabile] AGG, SM imponderable.

impone *ecc* [im'pone] VB vedi **imporre**.

imponente [impo'nɛnte] AGG (*persona, monumento*) imposing, impressive.

impongo *ecc* [im'pongo] VB vedi **imporre**.

imponibile [impo'nibile] ① AGG taxable.
② SM taxable income.

impopolare [impopo'lare] AGG unpopular.

impopolarità [impopolari'ta] SF unpopularity.

imporporare [imporpo'rare] ① VT (*sogg: tramonto*) to redden.
② **imporporarsi** VIP (*cielo*) to redden; (*persona*) to blush, go red.

imporre [im'porre] VB IRREG ① VT (*gen*) to impose; (*compito*) to set, impose; (*condizioni*) to impose, lay down; **imporre qc a qn** to impose sth on sb; **imporre a qn di fare qc** to oblige *o* force sb to do sth, make sb do sth; **imporre la propria autorità** to assert one's authority, make one's authority felt; **imporre la propria volontà** to have one's way; **imporsi qc** to impose sth on o.s.; **imporsi di fare qc** to make o.s. do sth, force o.s. to do sth.
② **imporsi** VR **a** (*farsi valere*) to assert o.s., make o.s. respected; **si è imposto sugli altri per la sua competenza** he commanded the others' respect because of his ability **b** (*aver successo: musicista, attore, sportivo*) to come to the fore, become popular; **imporsi al pubblico** to come into the public eye.
③: **imporsi** VIP **a** (*diventare necessario*) to become necessary; **s'impone una scelta** a choice is called for **b** (*avere successo: moda*) to become established, become popular.

importante [impor'tante] ① AGG (*gen*) important; (*fatti*) important, significant; (*somma*) sizeable; **poco importante** of little importance *o* significance; **è importante che ci sia anche lui** it is important that he should be there too.
② SM: **l'importante è...** the important thing is ..., what is important is ... .

importanza [impor'tantsa] SF (*vedi agg*) importance; significance; size; **di una certa importanza** of considerable importance; **della massima importanza** of the utmost importance; **avere importanza** to be important; **assumere importanza** to become more important; **dare importanza a qc** to attach importance to sth; **dare troppa importanza a qc** to make too much of sth, attach too much importance to sth; **darsi importanza** (*darsi arie*) to give o.s. airs.

importare¹ [impor'tare] VT (*introdurre dall'estero*) to import.

importare² [impor'tare] VI, VB IMPERS (*aus* essere) (*essere importante*) to matter, be important; **le tue ragioni non mi importano** your reasons aren't important to me, I don't care about your reasons; **ciò che importa di più è...** the most important thing is ...; **non importa!** it doesn't matter!, never mind!; **non m'importa niente** I couldn't care less, I don't care; **che importa?** what does that matter?; **non importa cosa/quando/dove** it doesn't matter what/when/where.

importatore, trice [importa'tore] ① AGG importing; la

ditta **importatrice di questo prodotto** the firm which imports this product.
② SM/F importer.

importazione [importat'tsjone] SF (*operazione*) importation; (*merci importate*) imports *pl*; **merci/prodotti d'importazione** imported goods/products.

importo [im'porto] SM (*total*) amount.

importunare [importu'nare] VT **a** (*disturbare*) to bother, disturb; **non vorrei importunarti con le mie richieste** I don't want to bother you with my requests **b** (*molestare*) to pester, annoy; (: *sessualmente*) to harass.

importunità [importuni'ta] SF (*di visita*) inopportuneness; (*di persona*) irksomeness, tiresomeness.

importuno, a [impor'tuno] ① AGG (*visita*) inopportune, ill-timed; (*persona*) irksome, annoying.
② SM/F troublesome individual.

imposi [im'posi] *ecc* VB vedi **imporre**.

imposizione [impozit'tsjone] SF **a** (*atto*) imposition **b** (*ordine*) order, command; **non accetto imposizioni da nessuno** I don't take orders from anyone **c** (*onere, imposta*) tax.

impossessarsi [imposses'sarsi] VIP: **impossessarsi di** (*terreno, beni*) to seize, take possession of; (*segreto*) to get hold of; **si è impossessato della mia stanza** (*fig*) he has taken over my room.

impossibile [impos'sibile] ① AGG impossible; **mi è impossibile farlo** it's impossible for me to do it, I can't (possibly) do it.
② SM: **fare l'impossibile** to do one's utmost, do all one can.

impossibilità [impossibili'ta] SF impossibility; **essere** *o* **trovarsi nell'impossibilità di fare qc** to be unable *o* find it impossible to do sth.

impossibilitare [impossibili'tare] VT: **impossibilitare qc a qn** to make sth impossible for sb; **impossibilitare qn a fare qc** to prevent sb from doing sth, make it impossible for sb to do sth.

impossibilitato, a [impossibili'tato] AGG: **essere impossibilitato a fare qc** to be unable to do sth.

imposta¹ [im'posta] SF (*di finestra*) shutter.

imposta² [im'posta] SF (*tassa*) tax; **imposte dirette/indirette** direct/indirect taxation *sg*; **ufficio imposte** tax office ►**imposta indiretta sui consumi** excise duty *o* tax ►**imposta locale sui redditi** tax on unearned income ►**imposta patrimoniale** property tax ►**imposta sul reddito** income tax ►**imposta sul reddito delle persone fisiche** personal income tax ►**imposta di successione** capital transfer tax (*Brit*), inheritance tax (*Am*) ►**imposta sugli utili** tax on profits ►**imposta sul valore aggiunto** value added tax (*Brit*), sales tax (*Am*).

impostare¹ [impos'tare] VT **a** (*servizio, organizzazione*) to set up; (*lavoro*) to organize, plan; (*resoconto, rapporto*) to plan; (*questione, problema*) to formulate, set out; (*Tip: pagina*) to lay out, make up **b** (*Mus*): **impostare la voce** to pitch one's voice.

impostare² [impos'tare] VT (*lettera*) to post (*Brit*), mail (*Am*).

impostazione¹ [impostat'tsjone] SF (*di problema, questione*) formulation, statement; (*di lavoro*) organization, planning; (*di attività*) setting up; (*Mus: di voce*) pitch.

impostazione² [impostat'tsjone] SF (*di lettera*) posting (*Brit*), mailing (*Am*).

imposto, a [im'posto] PP di **imporre**.

impostore, a [impos'tore] SM/F impostor.

impostura [impos'tura] SF imposture.

impotente [impo'tɛnte] ☐ AGG **a** (*persona, governo*) impotent, powerless; **essere impotente di fronte a qc** to be powerless in the face of sth; **sentirsi impotente** to feel helpless **b** (*Med: incapace sessualmente*) impotent. ☐ SM (*Med*) impotent man.

impotenza [impo'tɛntsa] SF (*debolezza*) impotence, powerlessness; (*Med*) impotence.

impoverimento [impoveri'mento] SM impoverishment.

impoverire [impove'rire] ☐ VT to impoverish. ☐ VI (*aus essere*), **impoverirsi** VIP to become poor(er).

impraticabile [imprati'kabile] AGG (*strada*) impassable; (*Sport: campo*) unfit for play, unplayable.

impraticabilità [impratikabili'ta] SF: **l'impraticabilità delle strade** the fact that the roads are impassable; **partita sospesa per impraticabilità del campo** (*Sport*) match abandoned due to the pitch being unplayable.

impratichirsi [imprati'kirsi] VIP (*fare pratica*) to get practice, gain experience; **impratichirsi in qc** to gain experience in (doing) sth.

imprecare [impre'kare] VI (*aus avere*) to curse, swear; **imprecare contro** to hurl abuse at.

imprecazione [imprekat'tsjone] SF abuse, curse; **lanciare un'imprecazione** to curse.

imprecisabile [impretʃi'zabile] AGG indeterminable.

imprecisato, a [impretʃi'zato] AGG **a** (*non preciso*: *quantità, numero*) indeterminate **b** (*non chiaro*: *dettagli, particolari*) unclear; **per motivi imprecisati** for reasons which are not clear; **ad un'ora imprecisata** at an unspecified time.

imprecisione [impretʃi'zjone] SF (*vedi agg*) imprecision; inaccuracy.

impreciso, a [impre'tʃizo] AGG (*definizione, descrizione*) imprecise, vague; (*calcolo*) inaccurate; **è impreciso nel suo lavoro** he's a careless worker.

impregnare [impreɲ'ɲare] ☐ VT: **impregnare (di)** (*imbevere*) to soak o impregnate (with); (*riempire: anche fig*) to fill (with). ☐ **impregnarsi** VIP: **impregnarsi di** (*vedi vt*) to become impregnated with; to become filled with.

imprenditore [imprendi'tore] SM (*industriale*) entrepreneur; (*appaltatore*) contractor; **piccolo imprenditore** small businessman ▶ **imprenditore edile** building contractor.

imprenditoria [imprendito'ria] SF enterprise; (*imprenditori*) entrepreneurs pl.

imprenditoriale [imprendito'rjale] AGG (*ceto, classe*) entrepreneurial.

impreparato, a [imprepa'rato] AGG: **impreparato (a)** (*gen*) unprepared (for); (*lavoratore*) untrained (for); **quel professore di matematica è impreparato** that maths teacher has a poor knowledge of his subject; **cogliere qn impreparato** to catch sb unawares.

impreparazione [impreparat'tsjone] SF lack of preparation.

impresa [im'presa] SF **a** (*iniziativa*) enterprise, undertaking; **abbandonare un'impresa** to abandon an enterprise o an undertaking; **è un'impresa!** that's quite an undertaking!

b (*azione gloriosa*) feat, exploit

c (*ditta, azienda*) firm, concern; **mettere su un'impresa** to set up a business ▶ **impresa familiare** family firm

▶ **impresa pubblica** state-owned enterprise.

impresario, ria, ri, rie [impre'sarjo] SM/F (*Teatro*) theatre manager; (: *di teatri maggiori, o più teatri*) impresario ▶ **impresario di pompe funebri** funeral director.

imprescindibile [impreʃʃin'dibile] AGG (*necessità*) inescapable, unavoidable; (*condizione*) essential; (*obbligo*) binding.

impressi ecc [im'prɛssi] VB vedi **imprimere**.

impressionabile [impressjo'nabile] AGG (*persona*) impressionable.

impressionabilità [impressjonabili'ta] SF (*di persona*) impressionability.

impressionante [impressjo'nante] AGG **a** (*che suscita turbamento*) disturbing, upsetting **b** (*che suscita sensazione*) impressive.

impressionare [impressjo'nare] ☐ VT **a** (*turbare*) to upset; (*colpire*) to impress **b** (*Fot*) to expose. ☐ **impressionarsi** VIP (*spaventarsi*) to get o be upset; **non impressionarti!** don't get upset!

impressione [impres'sjone] SF **a** (*sensazione*) impression, sensation, feeling; **ho l'impressione che mi nasconda qualcosa** I have the feeling that he's hiding something from me; **far impressione a qn** (*colpire*) to impress sb; (*turbare*) to upset sb, frighten sb; **fare una buona/cattiva o brutta impressione a qn** to make a good/bad impression on sb; **che impressione ti ha fatto?** what was your impression of it (o him ecc)?, what did you make of it (o him ecc)?; **che impressione!** how awful!, how ghastly!

b (*Tip: stampa*) printing; (: *ristampa*) impression.

impressionismo [impressjo'nizmo] SM impressionism.

impresso, a [im'prɛsso] PP di **imprimere**.

imprestare [impres'tare] VT (*fam*): **imprestare qc a qn** to lend sth to sb.

imprevedibile [impreve'dibile] AGG (*destino, futuro*) unforeseeable; (*cambiamento*) unexpected; (*persona, risultato*) unpredictable.

imprevidente [imprevi'dɛnte] AGG lacking in foresight, improvident.

imprevidenza [imprevi'dɛntsa] SF lack of foresight, improvidence.

imprevidibilmente [imprevedibil'mente] AVV unexpectedly.

imprevisto, a [impre'visto] ☐ AGG (*arrivo, cambiamento*) unexpected; (*circostanza*) unforeseen, unexpected. ☐ SM unexpected o unforeseen event; **salvo imprevisti** unless anything unexpected happens.

impreziosire [imprettsjo'sire] VT: **impreziosire con** to embellish with.

imprigionamento [impridʒona'mento] SM imprisonment.

imprigionare [impridʒo'nare] VT (*chiudere in prigione*) to imprison; (*rinchiudere: in casa ecc*) to shut up, confine; (*fig: intrappolare*) to trap; **la nave era imprigionata nel ghiaccio** the ship was icebound.

imprimatur [impri'matur] SM INV imprimatur.

imprimé [ɛ̃pri'me] AGG INV (*tessuto*) printed.

imprimere [im'primere] VB IRREG ☐ VT **a** (*marchio*) to impress, stamp; **imprimersi qc nella mente** to fix sth firmly in one's mind; **mi è rimasto impresso ciò che hai detto** I have never forgotten what you said

b (*trasmettere*): **imprimere (un) movimento a** to impart o transmit movement to. ☐ **imprimersi** VIP (*fig: ricordo*) to stamp itself, imprint itself.

improbabile [impro'babile] AGG improbable, unlikely; **è improbabile che venga** he's unlikely to come.

improbabilità [improbabili'ta] SF improbability, unlikelihood.

improbo, a ['improbo] AGG (letter: fatica, lavoro) gruelling (Brit) o grueling (Am), laborious.

improduttività [improduttivi'ta] SF unproductiveness.

improduttivo, a [improdut'tivo] AGG (investimento) unprofitable; (terreno) unfruitful; (fig: sforzo) fruitless, futile.

impronta [im'pronta] SF **a** (di piede, mano) print; (fig: di genio, maestro) mark, stamp; **lasciare la propria impronta in qc** (fig) to leave one's mark on sth; **impronta del piede** footprint; **rilevamento delle impronte genetiche** genetic fingerprinting ▶**impronte digitali** fingerprints **b** (di moneta) impression.

improntare [impron'tare] VT (dare una certa espressione a): **improntò il suo discorso alla massima semplicità** his speech was couched in terms of the utmost simplicity; **improntò il suo viso al dolore** his face assumed a sad expression.

impronunciabile [impronun'tʃabile], **impronunziabile** [impronun'tsjabile] AGG unpronounceable.

improperio, ri [impro'pɛrjo] SM (insulto) insult; **lanciare un improperio** to swear; **coprire qn d'improperi** to hurl abuse at sb.

improponibile [impropo'nibile] AGG (idea, patto, accordo) which cannot be proposed o suggested.

improprietà [improprje'ta] SF INV impropriety; **improprietà (di linguaggio)** incorrect usage.

improprio, ria, ri, rie [im'prɔprjo] AGG (non corretto: uso) incorrect, improper; (sconveniente: tono, abbigliamento) improper, inappropriate; **arma impropria** something used as a weapon.

improrogabile [improro'gabile] AGG (termine) that cannot be extended.

improrogabilità [improrogabili'ta] SF (di termine) unalterable nature.

improvvisamente [improvviza'mente] AVV suddenly, unexpectedly.

improvvisare [improvvi'zare] **1** VT (gen) to improvise; (cena, piatto) to knock up, throw together, improvise; **improvvisare una festa** to hold an impromptu party. **2 improvvisarsi** VR to act as; **si è improvvisato cuoco per l'occasione** he took on the role of chef on that occasion.

improvvisata [improvvi'zata] SF (pleasant) surprise; **fare un'improvvisata a qn** to give sb a surprise.

improvvisatore, trice [improvviza'tore] SM/F improviser; **è un abile improvvisatore** he's good at improvising.

improvvisazione [improvvizat'tsjone] SF improvisation; **spirito d'improvvisazione** spirit of invention; **capacità d'improvvisazione** ability to improvise.

improvviso [improv'vizo] AGG (inaspettato: arrivo ecc) unexpected; (subitaneo: simpatia, cambiamento d'umore) sudden; **all'improvviso** OR **d'improvviso** (inaspettatamente) unexpectedly; (tutto d'un tratto) suddenly.

imprudente [impru'dɛnte] **1** AGG (gen) careless, foolish, imprudent; (osservazione) unwise. **2** SM/F imprudent person.

imprudentemente [imprudente'mente] AVV imprudently.

imprudenza [impru'dɛntsa] SF (qualità) carelessness, foolishness, imprudence; (azione): **è stata un'impru-**

denza that was a rash o an imprudent thing to do.

impudente [impu'dɛnte] **1** AGG impudent, cheeky. **2** SM/F impudent person.

impudentemente [impudente'mente] AVV impudently, cheekily.

impudenza [impu'dɛntsa] SF impudence, cheek; **avere l'impudenza di fare qc** to have the cheek to do sth.

impudicizia [impudi'tʃittsja] SF immodesty.

impudico, a, chi, che [impu'diko] AGG immodest.

impugnabile [impuɲ'ɲabile] AGG (Dir) subject to appeal.

impugnare [impuɲ'ɲare] VT **a** (arma) to grasp, seize **b** (Dir: sentenza) to contest.

impugnatura [impuɲɲa'tura] SF (di coltello, frusta) handle; (di spada) hilt; (di remo, racchetta) grip; **impugnatura a due mani** (Tennis) two-handed grip o grasp.

impulsivamente [impulsiva'mente] AVV impulsively.

impulsività [impulsivi'ta] SF impulsiveness; **fare qc per impulsività** to do sth impulsively.

impulsivo, a [impul'sivo] **1** AGG impulsive. **2** SM/F impulsive person.

impulso [im'pulso] SM **a** (Fis, moto istintivo) impulse; **agire d'impulso** to act on impulse; **sentì l'impulso di picchiarlo** he was seized with an urge to hit him **b** (fig: spinta) boost; **dare un impulso alle vendite** to boost sales.

impunemente [impune'mente] AVV with impunity; **fare qc impunemente** to get away with sth.

impunità [impuni'ta] SF impunity.

impunito, a [impu'nito] AGG unpunished; **restare impunito** to go unpunished.

impuntarsi [impun'tarsi] VIP (cavallo, asino) to jib, refuse to budge; (fig: ostinarsi) to dig one's heels in, be obstinate.

impuntura [impun'tura] SF stitching.

impurità [impuri'ta] SF INV impurity.

impuro, a [im'puro] AGG impure; **esse impura** (Fonetica) "s" impure ("s" + consonant).

imputabile [impu'tabile] AGG **a** (Dir) chargeable **b** (attribuibile): **imputabile a** attributable to.

imputare [impu'tare] VT (Dir): **imputare qn di** to charge sb with, accuse sb of **b**: **imputare qc a** (attribuire) to attribute o ascribe sth to; (Contabilità) to charge sth to.

imputato, a [impu'tato] SM/F (Dir) defendant, accused.

imputazione [imputat'tsjone] SF (Dir) charge; **capo d'imputazione** charge, count (of indictment); **imputazione delle spese generali** (Contabilità) allocation of overheads.

imputridimento [imputridi'mento] SM putrefaction.

imputridire [imputri'dire] **1** VT to rot. **2** VI (aus essere) to putrefy, rot.

imputridito, a [imputri'dito] AGG putrefied.

impuzzolentire [imputtsolen'tire] VT to stink out.

---

in [in]

1 PREP

in + il = **nel**, in + lo = **nello**, in + l' = **nell'**, in + la = **nella**, in + i = **nei**, in + gli = **negli**, in + le = **nelle**

a (stato in luogo) in; (: all'interno) inside;
▷**sono rimasto in** casa I stayed at home, I stayed indoors
▷**è nell'**editoria/**nell'**esercito he is in publishing/in the army

▷è in *fondo* all'armadio it is at the back of the wardrobe
▷è bravo in *latino* he's good at Latin
▷dottore in *legge* doctor of law
▷in *lei* ho trovato una sorella I found a sister in her
▷in *lui* non c'era più speranza there was no hope left in him
▷nell'*opera* di Shakespeare in Shakespeare's works
▷vivo in *Scozia* I live in Scotland
▷aveva le mani in *tasca* he had his hands in his pockets
▷il pranzo è in *tavola* lunch is on the table
▷se fossi in *te* if I were you
▷un giornale diffuso in *tutta* Italia a newspaper read all over o throughout Italy
b (*moto a luogo*) to; (: *dentro*) into;
▷*andare* in campagna/in montagna to go into the country/to the mountains
▷*andrò* in Francia I'm going to France
▷*entrare* in casa to go into the house
▷*entrare* in macchina to get into the car
▷*gettare* qc in acqua to throw sth into the water
▷*inciampò* in una radice he tripped over a root
▷l'ho *messo* là in alto/basso I put it up/down there
▷*spostarsi* di città in città to move from town to town
c (*moto per luogo*)
▷il corteo è passato in piazza the procession passed through the square
▷sta facendo un viaggio in Egitto he's travelling in o around Egypt
d (*tempo*) in;
▷negli *anni* ottanta in the eighties
▷nel 1960 in 1960
▷è cambiata molto in un *anno* she has changed a lot in a year
▷in *autunno* in autumn
▷di giorno in *giorno* from day to day
▷in *gioventù* in one's youth
▷in questo *istante* at the moment
▷in *luglio*, nel *mese* di luglio in July
▷lo farò in *settimana* I'll do it within the week
e (*mezzo*) by;
▷mi piace viaggiare in *aereo* I like travelling by plane, I like flying
▷pagare in *contanti*/in *dollari* to pay cash/in dollars
▷ci andremo in *macchina* we'll go there by car, we'll drive there
▷siamo andati in *treno* we went by train
f (*modo, maniera*) in;
▷in *abito* da sera in evening dress
▷tagliare in *due* to cut in two
▷in *fiamme* on fire, in flames
▷in *gruppo* in a group
▷in *guerra* at war
▷tradurre in *italiano* to translate into Italian
▷parlare in *italiano* to speak Italian
▷nell'*oscurità* in the darkness
▷in *piedi* standing, on one's feet
▷in *prosa* in prose
▷in *silenzio* in silence
▷scrivere in *stampatello* to write in block letters
▷in *versi* in verse
▷Maria Bianchi in Rossi Maria Rossi née Bianchi

g (*materia*) made of;
▷in *marmo* made of marble, marble *attr*
▷braccialetto in *oro* gold bracelet
▷lo stesso modello in *seta* the same model in silk
h (*fine, scopo*)
▷spende tutto in *divertimenti* he spends all his money on entertainment
▷me lo hanno dato in *dono* they gave it to me as a gift
▷in *favore* di in favour of
▷in *onore* di in honour of
i (*misura*) in;
▷in *altezza* in height
▷arrivarono in *gran numero* they arrived in large numbers
▷in *lunghezza* in length
▷siamo in *quattro* there are four of us
▷in *tutto* in all
j (*con infinito*)
▷ha sbagliato nel *rispondere* male he was wrong to be rude
▷si è fatto male nel *salire* sull'autobus he hurt himself as he was getting onto the bus
▷nell'*udire* la notizia on hearing the news.
2 AVV: *essere* in (*di moda, attuale*) to be in.
3 AGG INV: la *gente* in the in-crowd.

inabbordabile [inabbor'dabile] AGG unapproachable.
inabile [i'nabile] AGG (*fisicamente, Mil*): **inabile (a)** unfit (for); (*per infortunio*) disabled; **inabile al servizio militare** unfit for military service.
inabilità [inabili'ta] SF (*fisica, Mil*): **inabilità (a)** unfitness (for); (*per infortunio*) disablement.
inabissare [inabis'sare] **1** VT (*nave*) to sink.
2 **inabissarsi** VIP to sink, go down.
inabitabile [inabi'tabile] AGG uninhabitable.
inabitato, a [inabi'tato] AGG uninhabited.
inaccessibile [inattʃes'sibile] AGG (*luogo*) inaccessible; (*spesa*) prohibitive; (*persona*) unapproachable; (*mistero*) unfathomable; (*teoria*) incomprehensible.
inaccessibilità [inattʃessibili'ta] SF (*di luogo*) inaccessibility; (*di persona*) unapproachableness; (*di teoria ecc*) incomprehensibility; **l'inaccessibilità del prezzo mi ha impedito di comprarlo** the price was so prohibitive that I couldn't buy it.
inaccettabile [inattʃet'tabile] AGG unacceptable.
inaccettabilità [inattʃettabili'ta] SF unacceptableness.
inaccostabile [inakkos'tabile] AGG (*persona*) unapproachable.
inacerbire [inatʃer'bire] **1** VT to exacerbate.
2 **inacerbirsi** VIP (*persona*) to become embittered.
inacidire [inatʃi'dire] **1** VT (*persona, carattere*) to embitter.
2 VI (*aus essere*), **inacidirsi** VIP (*latte*) to go sour; (*fig: persona, carattere*) to become sour, become embittered.
inadatto, a [ina'datto] AGG: **inadatto (a)** (*persona*) unsuited (to), unfit (for); (*luogo, costruzione, lavoro*) unsuitable (for); (*parole, azione*) inappropriate (to).
inadeguatamente [inadegwata'mente] AVV (*vedi agg*) inadequately; unsuitably.
inadeguatezza [inadegwa'tettsa] SF (*vedi agg*) inadequacy; unsuitability.
inadeguato, a [inade'gwato] AGG: **inadeguato (a)** (*non*

sufficiente) inadequate (for); (*inadatto*) not suitable (for).

inadempiente [inadem'pjɛnte] [1] AGG defaulting.
[2] SM/F defaulter.

inadempienza [inadem'pjɛntsa] SF: **inadempienza a un contratto** non-fulfilment of a contract; **dovuto alle inadempienze dei funzionari** due to negligence on the part of the officials.

inadempimento [inadempi'mento] SM non-fulfilment.

inadempiuto, a [inadem'pjuto] AGG unfulfilled, broken.

inafferrabile [inaffer'rabile] AGG (*ladro, criminale*) elusive; (*fig: concetto, significato*) incomprehensible, difficult to grasp.

I.N.A.I.L. ['inail] SIGLA M (= *Istituto Nazionale per l'Assicurazione contro gli Infortuni sul Lavoro*) *state body providing sickness benefit to people injured at work.*

inalare [ina'lare] VT to inhale.

inalatore [inala'tore] SM inhaler.

inalazione [inalat'tsjone] SF inhalation.

inalberare [inalbe'rare] [1] VT (*bandiera, insegna*) to hoist, run up, raise.
[2] **inalberarsi** VIP (*fig: arrabbiarsi*) to flare up, fly off the handle.

inalienabile [inalje'nabile] AGG inalienable.

inalterabile [inalte'rabile] AGG (*colore*) permanent, fast; (*prezzo, qualità*) stable; (*amicizia*) steadfast; (*affetto*) unchanging, constant; **i termini del contratto sono inalterabili** the terms of the contract cannot be changed.

inalterato, a [inalte'rato] AGG (*prezzi*) stable; (*affetto, amicizia, termini di contratto*) unaltered, unchanged.

inamidare [inami'dare] VT to starch.

inamidato, a [inami'dato] AGG (*colletto, camicia*) starched.

inammissibile [inammis'sibile] AGG (*comportamento, reazione*) intolerable; (*Dir: prova*) inadmissible.

inamovibile [inamo'vibile] AGG (*Amm: magistrato*) irremovable.

inanellato, a [inanel'lato] AGG (*dita, mano*) bejewelled.

inanimato, a [inani'mato] AGG (*gen*) inanimate; (*svenuto*) unconscious; (*morto*) lifeless.

inappagabile [inappa'gabile] AGG (*desiderio*) insatiable.

inappagato, a [inappa'gato] AGG unfulfilled.

inappellabile [inappel'labile] AGG (*decisione*) final, irrevocable; (*Dir*) not open to appeal, final.

inappellabilità [inappellabili'ta] SF (*di decisione*) finality; **vista l'inappellabilità della sentenza...** (*Dir*) given that no appeal can be made against the sentence ... .

inappetenza [inappe'tɛntsa] SF lack of appetite; **soffrire di inappetenza** to have no appetite.

inappuntabile [inappun'tabile] AGG (*persona*) irreproachable; (*contegno*) faultless, irreproachable; (*eleganza*) faultless, impeccable.

inarcamento [inarka'mento] SM (*vedi vb*) arching; raising; warping.

inarcare [inar'kare] [1] VT (*schiena*) to arch; (*sopracciglia*) to raise.
[2] **inarcarsi** VIP (*legno*) to warp.

inaridimento [inaridi'mento] SM (*anche fig*) drying up.

inaridire [inari'dire] [1] VT (*terreno*) to parch, dry up; (*fig: vena poetica*) to dry up; (*: persona*) to sour.
[2] VI (*aus essere*), **inaridirsi** VIP (*anche fig*) to dry up, become arid; (*persona*) to become soured.

inarrestabile [inarres'tabile] AGG **a** (*processo*) irreversible; (*emorragia*) that cannot be staunched **b** (*corsa del tempo*) relentless.

inarticolato, a [inartiko'lato] AGG (*suono*) inarticulate.

inascoltato, a [inaskol'tato] AGG unheeded, unheard; **rimanere inascoltato** to go unheeded *o* unheard.

inaspettatamente [inaspettata'mente] AVV unexpectedly.

inaspettato, a [inaspet'tato] AGG unexpected.

inasprimento [inaspri'mento] SM (*vedi vt*) tightening up; embitterment; worsening.

inasprire [inas'prire] [1] VT (*disciplina*) to tighten up, make harsher; (*persona, carattere*) to embitter, sour; (*rapporti*) to make worse.
[2] **inasprirsi** VIP (*vedi vt*) to become harsher; to become bitter; to become worse; **si sono inasprite le ostilità** hostilities have intensified.

inattaccabile [inattak'kabile] AGG (*fortezza, castello*) unassailable, impregnable; (*fig: alibi*) cast-iron; (*: posizione*) unassailable; **inattaccabile dagli acidi** proof against acids.

inattendibile [inatten'dibile] AGG (*versione dei fatti*) unreliable; (*testimone*) unreliable, untrustworthy.

inatteso, a [inat'teso] AGG unexpected.

inattivo, a [inat'tivo] AGG (*persona*) idle, inactive; (*vulcano*) inactive, dormant; (*Chim*) inactive.

inattuabile [inattu'abile] AGG impracticable.

inattuabilità [inattuabili'ta] SF impracticability.

inaudito, a [inau'dito] AGG (*crudeltà, ferocia*) unheard-of, unprecedented; (*somma, prezzo*) outrageous; **è inaudito!** it's outrageous!

inaugurale [inaugu'rale] AGG inaugural; **la fase inaugurale** the opening stages.

inaugurare [inaugu'rare] VT (*scuola, linea ferroviaria*) to open, inaugurate; (*mostra*) to open; (*monumento*) to unveil; (*era, periodo*) to usher in, inaugurate; (*sistema*) to inaugurate; (*scherz: scarpe, vestito*) to christen.

inaugurazione [inaugurat'tsjone] SF (*vedi vt*) opening, inauguration; unveiling; **fare l'inaugurazione di** to inaugurate, open.

inavveduto, a [inavve'duto] AGG (*gesto*) inadvertent, unintentional, careless.

inavvertenza [inavver'tɛntsa] SF carelessness, inadvertence.

inavvertitamente [inavvertita'mente] AVV inadvertently, unintentionally.

inavvicinabile [inavvitʃi'nabile] AGG unapproachable.

Inca ['inka] AGG, SM/F INV Inca.

incagliarsi [inkaʎ'ʎarsi] VIP (*nave, barca*) to run aground; (*fig: trattative*) to become bogged down, grind to a halt.

incaico, a, ci, che [in'kaiko] AGG Inca, Incan.

incalcolabile [inkalko'labile] AGG incalculable.

incallito, a [inkal'lito] AGG **a** (*mani*) calloused **b** (*fig: ladro*) hardened; (*: bugiardo*) inveterate; (*: fumatore, bevitore*) heavy; **è un incallito rubacuori** he's a real heartbreaker.

incalzante [inkal'tsante] AGG (*richiesta*) urgent, insistent; (*crisi*) imminent.

incalzare [inkal'tsare] [1] VT (*inseguire*) to pursue, follow closely; (*fig*) to press.
[2] VI (*aus essere*) (*urgere: tempo*) to be pressing; (*essere imminente: pericolo*) to be imminent.

incamerare [inkame'rare] VT (*Dir*) to expropriate, confiscate.

incamminarsi [inkammi'narsi] VIP to set forth, set out; **incamminarsi verso** to set out for, head for; (*fig*) to head for.

incanalamento [inkanala'mento] SM (*di acque*) canalization.

incanalare [inkana'lare] [1] VT (*acque*) to canalize; (*traffico, folla*) to direct, channel. [2] **incanalarsi** VIP: **incanalarsi verso** (*folla*) to converge on.

incancrenire [inkankre'nire] VI (*aus* **essere**), **incancrenirsi** VIP to become gangrenous.

incandescente [inkandeʃ'ʃɛnte] AGG incandescent, white-hot.

incandescenza [inkandeʃ'ʃɛntsa] SF incandescence.

incantare [inkan'tare] [1] VT (*per magia, anche fig: persona*) to enchant, bewitch; (*serpente*) to charm; **non m'incanti con le tue chiacchiere!** you don't fool me with your fine words!. [2] **incantarsi** VIP (*bloccarsi: meccanismo*) to stick, jam; (: *persona*) to be spellbound, be in a daze; **incantarsi nel parlare** to hesitate in one's speech; **incantarsi a guardare qn/qc** to stop and stare at sb/sth.

incantato, a [inkan'tato] AGG (*anello, castello*) enchanted; (*fig: affascinato*) spellbound, entranced; **rimanere incantato davanti a qc** to stand entranced *o* spellbound before sth.

incantatore, trice [inkanta'tore] [1] AGG enchanting, bewitching. [2] SM/F enchanter/enchantress; **incantatore di serpenti** snake charmer.

incantesimo [inkan'tezimo] SM spell, charm; **rompere l'incantesimo** (*anche fig*) to break the spell.

incantevole [inkan'tevole] AGG enchanting, delightful, charming.

incanto¹ [in'kanto] SM (*incantesimo*) spell, charm, enchantment; **quella ragazza/quel paese è un incanto** that girl/village is enchanting; **sei un incanto stasera** you look enchanting this evening; **l'incanto della montagna** the magic of the mountains; **come per incanto** as if by magic; **ti sta d'incanto!** (*vestito ecc*) it really suits you!

incanto² [in'kanto] SM (*asta*) auction; **vendita all'incanto** sale by auction; **mettere all'incanto** to put up for auction.

incanutire [inkanu'tire] VI (*aus* **essere**) to go white.

incapace [inka'patʃe] [1] AGG incapable; **essere incapace (di fare qc)** to be incapable (of doing sth). [2] SM/F: **essere un incapace** to be useless, be a dead loss; (*fam*) **solo un incapace poteva... only an idiot could ... .**

incapacità [inkapatʃi'ta] SF **a** (*inabilità*) incapability, inability; **incapacità a fare qc** inability to do sth **b** (*Dir*) incapacity ▶**incapacità d'intendere e di volere** diminished responsibility.

incaponirsi [inkapo'nirsi] VIP (*ostinarsi*) to be set on; **incaponirsi a fare qc** to insist on doing sth.

incappare [inkap'pare] VI (*aus* **essere**): **incappare in** (*problema, guaio*) to run into, get into; (*persona*) to run into.

incappucciare [inkapput'tʃare] [1] VT to put a hood on; **la neve incappuccia le cime dei monti** snow covers the mountain tops. [2] **incappucciarsi** VR (*persona*) to put on a hood.

incaprettamento [inkapretta'mento] SM *method of strangulation used by the Mafia whereby a rope is passed around the victim's wrists, ankles and throat.*

incapricciarsi [inkaprit'tʃarsi] VIP: **incapricciarsi di** to take a fancy to.

incapsulare [inkapsu'lare] VT (*Med: dente*) to crown.

incarcerare [inkartʃe'rare] VT to imprison, jail.

incaricare [inkari'kare] [1] VT: **incaricare qn di fare qc** to give sb the responsibility of doing sth, ask sb to do sth. [2] **incaricarsi** VIP: **incaricarsi di fare qc** to take it upon o.s. to do sth; **me ne incarico io** I'll see to it.

incaricato, a [inkari'kato] [1] AGG: **incaricato (di)** in charge (of), responsible (for); **docente incaricato** (*Univ*) lecturer without tenure. [2] SM/F representative, delegate ▶**incaricato d'affari** (*Pol*) chargé d'affaires.

incarico, chi [in'kariko] SM **a** (*gen, compito*) task, job; **dare un incarico a qn** to give sb a task *o* job to do; **ricevere un incarico** to be given a task *or* job to do; **avere l'incarico di fare qc** to have the job of doing sth; **per incarico di qn** on sb's behalf **b** (*Scol, Univ*) temporary post.

incarnare [inkar'nare] [1] VT (*rappresentare*) to embody. [2] **incarnarsi** VIP (*Rel*) to become incarnate; (*concretarsi*) to be embodied.

incarnato¹, a [inkar'nato] AGG (*Rel*) incarnate; **è l'avarizia incarnata** he's avarice personified.

incarnato² [inkar'nato] SM (*carnagione*) rosy.

incarnazione [inkarnat'tsjone] SF (*Rel*) incarnation; (*fig*) embodiment; **è l'incarnazione della virtù** he (*o* she) is the embodiment of virtue; **sembra l'incarnazione di suo nonno** he (*o* she) is the image of his (*o* her) grandfather.

incarnire [inkar'nire] VI (*aus* **essere**), **incarnirsi** VIP (*unghia*) to become ingrown.

incarnito, a [inkar'nito] AGG (*unghia*) ingrown.

incartamento [inkarta'mento] SM dossier, file.

incartapecorire [inkartapeko'rire] VI (*aus* **essere**), **incartapecorirsi** VIP to shrivel (up).

incartapecorito, a [inkartapeko'rito] AGG (*pelle*) wizened, shrivelled (*Brit*), shriveled (*Am*).

incartare [inkar'tare] VT to wrap (in paper).

incasellare [inkasel'lare] VT (*posta*) to sort; (*fig: nozioni*) to pigeonhole.

incasinare [inkasi'nare] VT (*fam: creare disordine in*) to mess up; (: *creare problemi a*) to screw up.

incasinato, a [inkasi'nato] AGG (*fam: gen*) in a mess; (: *mentalmente*) screwed up.

incassare [inkas'sare] VT **a** (*Comm: denaro*) to take, receive; (: *assegno, cambiale*) to cash **b** (*Pugilato: colpi*) to take, stand up to; (*fig: offese*) to take **c** (*montare: pietra preziosa*) to set; (: *mobile*) to build in **d** (*imballare: merce*) to pack (in cases).

incassatore, trice [inkassa'tore] SM/F: **è un buon incassatore** (*pugile*) he can take a lot of punishment; (*fig*) he can take it.

incasso [in'kasso] SM **a** (*somma incassata*) takings *pl*; (: *per un incontro sportivo*) take; **incasso giornaliero/mensile** daily/monthly takings; **fare un buon incasso** to take a lot of cash *o* money **b** (*cavità*): **frigorifero da incasso** fitted refrigerator.

incastonare [inkasto'nare] VT to set.

incastonatura [inkastona'tura] SF setting.

incastrare [inkas'trare] [1] VT **a** (*gen: far combaciare*) to fit in, insert **b** (*intrappolare*) to catch; (: *con false accuse*) to frame. [2] **incastrarsi** VIP **a** (*combaciare, pezzi meccanici*) to fit together; **questo pezzo s'incastra qui** this part fits here **b** (*rimanere bloccato*) to get stuck; **la chiave si è incastrata nella serratura** the key got stuck in the lock.

incastro [in'kastro] SM (*punto di unione*) joint; (*scanalatura*) slot, groove; **gioco a incastro** interlocking puzzle; **sistema a incastro** interlocking system ▶**incastro a coda di rondine** dovetail joint.

incatenare [inkate'nare] ☐ VT: **incatenare qc/qn a qc** to chain sth/sb to sth.

☐ **incatenarsi** VR: **incatenarsi a qc** to chain o.s. to sth.

incatramare [inkatra'mare] VT to tar.

incattivire [inkatti'vire] ☐ VT to make wicked.

☐ (*aus essere*), **incattivirsi** VIP to turn nasty.

incautamente [inkauta'mente] AVV imprudently, rashly.

incauto, a [in'kauto] AGG imprudent, rash.

incavare [inka'vare] VT to hollow out.

incavato, a [inka'vato] AGG (*gen*) hollow; (*occhi*) sunken.

incavo [in'kavo] SM hollow; (*solco*) groove.

incavolarsi [inkavo'larsi] VIP (*fam*) to lose one's temper, fly off the handle; **incavolarsi per** *o* **a causa di qc** to get annoyed about sth, lose one's temper over sth; **incavolarsi con qn** to get annoyed *o* lose one's temper with sb.

incazzarsi [inkat'tsarsi] VIP (*fam!*) to get pissed off (*fam!*).

incazzato, a [inkat'tsato] AGG (*fam!*) pissed off (*fam!*); **sono incazzato nero!** I'm really pissed off!

incedere [in'tʃedere] ☐ VI (*aus* **avere**) to advance solemnly. ☐ SM solemn gait.

incendiare [intʃen'djare] ☐ VT (*gen*) to set fire to; (*fig*: *animi*) to fire.

☐ **incendiarsi** VIP to catch fire, burst into flames.

incendiario, ria, ri, rie [intʃen'djarjo] ☐ AGG incendiary.

☐ SM/F arsonist.

incendio, di [in'tʃendjo] SM fire; **provocare l'incendio di** to set fire to ▶**incendio doloso** arson.

incenerimento [intʃeneri'mento] SM incineration.

incenerire [intʃene'rire] ☐ VT (*gen*) to incinerate; (*casa, albero*) to burn (down), burn to ashes; **incenerire qn con uno sguardo** to give sb a withering look.

☐ **incenerirsi** VIP to be burnt to ashes.

inceneritore [intʃeneri'tore] SM incinerator.

incensiere [intʃen'sjɛre] SM censer, thurible.

incenso [in'tʃenso] SM incense.

incensurabile [intʃensu'rabile] AGG irreproachable.

incensurato, a [intʃensu'rato] AGG (*Dir*): **essere incensurato** to have a clean record.

incentivare [intʃenti'vare] VT (*produzione, vendite*) to boost; (*dipendente*) to motivate.

incentivazione [intʃentivat'tsjone] SF (*di produzione*) boosting ▶**incentivazione vendite** sales promotion.

incentivo [intʃen'tivo] SM incentive.

incentrarsi [intʃen'trarsi] VIP: **incentrarsi su** (*fig*) to centre (*Brit*) *o* center (*Am*) on.

inceppare [intʃep'pare] ☐ VT (*fig: operazione*) to obstruct, hamper. ☐ **incepparsi** VIP (*fucile ecc*) to jam.

incerare [intʃe'rare] VT to wax.

incerata [intʃe'rata] SF (*impermeabile*) oilskins *pl*; (*tela*) oilcloth, tarpaulin; (: *da letto*) waterproof sheet.

incernierato, a [intʃernje'rato] AGG hinged.

incerottato, a [intʃerot'tato] AGG: **avere un dito incerottato** to have a plaster (*Brit*) *o* Bandaid ®(*Am*) on one's finger.

incertamente [intʃerta'mente] AVV (*rispondere*) uncertainly, doubtfully.

incertezza [intʃer'tettsa] SF **a** (*di notizie, fonti*) uncertainty, doubtful nature

b (*esitazione*) uncertainty, hesitation; **un momento d'incertezza** a moment's uncertainty *o* hesitation;

rispondere con incertezza to answer hesitantly

c (*insicurezza, instabilità*) uncertainty, doubt; **essere nell'incertezza** to be in a state of uncertainty; **tenere qn nell'incertezza** to keep sb in suspense; **vivere nell'incertezza** to live in a state of uncertainty.

incerto, a [in'tʃerto] ☐ AGG (*esito, risultato*) uncertain, doubtful; (*tempo*) uncertain; (*persona*) undecided, hesitating; **essere incerto su qc** to be uncertain *o* unsure about sth; **essere incerto sul da farsi** not to know what to do, be uncertain what to do; **camminare con passo incerto** to walk unsteadily.

☐ SM uncertainty; **lasciare il certo per l'incerto** to step out into the unknown, leave certainty behind one; **gli incerti del mestiere** the risks of the job.

incespicare [intʃespi'kare] VI (*aus* **avere**): **incespicare (in qc)** to trip (over sth); **incespicare nel parlare** to stumble over one's words.

incessante [intʃes'sante] AGG (*gen*) unceasing, incessant; (*serie*) never-ending.

incessantemente [intʃessante'mente] AVV incessantly.

incesto [in'tʃesto] SM incest.

incestuoso, a [intʃestu'oso] AGG incestuous.

incetta [in'tʃetta] SF buying up, hoarding; **fare incetta di** (*prodotti, merce*) to stockpile, buy up; **cercare di fare incetta di voti** to try to get as many votes as possible.

inchiesta [in'kjɛsta] SF (*gen, Dir*) inquiry, investigation; (*giornalistica*) report; **fare un'inchiesta su qc** to investigate sth, carry out an investigation *o* inquiry into sth; to report on sth ▶**inchiesta parlamentare** ≈ parliamentary inquiry (*Brit*), ≈ congressional investigation (*Am*).

inchinare [inki'nare] ☐ VT (*schiena*) to bend; (*testa, fronte*) to bow.

☐ **inchinarsi** VR to bend down; (*per riverenza*) to bow; (: *donna*) to curts(e)y; **inchinarsi davanti a qn** to bow (*o* curts(e)y) to sb; **m'inchino davanti alla tua bravura** I take off my hat to you.

inchino [in'kino] SM (*gen*) bow; (*di donna*) curts(e)y; **fare un inchino** to bow; to curts(e)y.

inchiodare [inkjo'dare] ☐ VT to nail (down); **inchiodare qc a qc** to nail sth to sth; **il lavoro lo inchioda al tavolino** his work keeps him chained to his desk; **sta tutto il giorno inchiodato davanti alla TV** he spends all day glued to the TV; **con queste prove lo hanno inchiodato** they nailed him with this evidence; **inchiodare la macchina** to jam on the brakes.

☐ **inchiodarsi** VIP (*fermarsi di colpo*) to stop dead.

inchiodatura [inkjoda'tura] SF (*operazione*) nailing down; (*chiodi*) nails *pl*.

inchiostro [in'kjostro] SM ink; **una macchia d'inchiostro** an ink blot ▶**inchiostro di china** Indian ink ▶**inchiostro simpatico** invisible ink.

inciampare [intʃam'pare] VI (*aus* **essere** *o* **avere**) to trip, stumble; **inciampare in** (*gradino, pietra*) to trip over; (*fig: persona*) to run into; **far inciampare qn** to trip sb (up).

inciampo [in'tʃampo] SM obstacle; **proseguire senza inciampi** to proceed smoothly.

incidentale [intʃiden'tale] AGG **a** (*casuale*) accidental **b** (*secondario*) incidental; **questione incidentale** (*Dir*) interlocutory matter; **proposizione incidentale** (*Gramm*) parenthetical clause.

incidentalmente [intʃidental'mente] AVV (*per caso*) by chance; (*per inciso*) incidentally, by the way.

incidente [intʃi'dɛnte] SM **a** (*disgrazia*) accident

▶**incidente aereo** plane crash ▶**incidente d'auto** car crash *o* accident ▶**incidente mortale** fatal accident ▶**incidente stradale** road accident **b** (*episodio*) incident; **e con questo l'incidente è chiuso** and that is the end of the matter ▶**incidente diplomatico** diplomatic incident.

incidenza [intʃi'dɛntsa] SF **a** (*fig*: *effetto*): **avere una forte incidenza su qc** to affect sth greatly, have a considerable effect on sth **b** (*Mat*): **angolo di incidenza** angle of incidence.

incidere[1] [in'tʃidere] VT IRREG **a** (*tagliare*: *corteccia, legno*) to cut into, carve; (*scolpire*: *pietra*) to engrave; **incidere un'iscrizione su** to engrave an inscription on; **incidere ad acquaforte** to etch; **incidere una ferita** (*Med*) to lance a wound **b** (*canzone*) to record; **incidere un disco** to make a record.

incidere[2] [in'tʃidere] VI IRREG (*aus* **avere**) (*influire*): **incidere su** to influence, affect, have a bearing upon; **le spese di riscaldamento incidono molto sull'economia domestica** heating costs are an important item of household expenditure.

incinta [in'tʃinta] AGG F pregnant; **restare incinta** to become *o* get pregnant; **incinta di 5 mesi** 5 months pregnant.

incipiente [intʃi'pjɛnte] AGG incipient.

incipriare [intʃi'prjare] **1** VT to powder; **andare ad incipriarsi il naso** (*euf*) to go and powder one's nose. **2 incipriarsi** VR to powder one's face.

incirca [in'tʃirka] AVV: **all'incirca** approximately, more or less, very nearly.

incisi *ecc* [in'tʃizi] VB *vedi* **incidere**.

incisione [intʃi'zjone] SF **a** (*taglio*) cut; (*Med*) incision **b** (*Arte*) engraving ▶**incisione ad acquaforte** etching ▶**incisione su legno** woodcut ▶**incisione su rame** copperplate engraving **c** (*registrazione*) recording; **sala d'incisione** recording studio ▶**incisione su nastro** tape recording.

incisivamente [intʃiziva'mente] AVV (*criticare, scrivere*) incisively.

incisività [intʃizivi'ta] SF incisiveness.

incisivo, a [intʃi'zivo] AGG **a** (*Anat*): **(dente) incisivo** incisor **b** (*fig*: *parole, stile*) incisive.

inciso, a [in'tʃizo] **1** PP di **incidere**. **2** SM (*Gramm*) parenthesis; **per inciso** incidentally, by the way.

incisore [intʃi'zore] SM (*Arte*) engraver.

incitamento [intʃita'mento] SM incitement; **essere d'incitamento per** *o* **a** to be an incitement to.

incitare [intʃi'tare] VT: **incitare qn a (fare) qc** to incite sb to (do) sth.

incivile [intʃi'vile] **1** AGG (*popolazione, costumi*) uncivilized; (*fig*: *persona, comportamento*) rude, impolite. **2** SM/F boor.

incivilimento [intʃivili'mento] SM civilization.

incivilire [intʃivi'lire] **1** VT to civilize. **2 incivilirsi** VIP to become civilized.

incivilmente [intʃivil'mente] AVV (*villanamente*) uncivilly, rudely; (*barbaramente*) in an uncivilized manner.

inciviltà [intʃivil'ta] SF **a** (*di popolazione*) barbarism **b** (*fig*: *di trattamento*) barbarity; (: *maleducazione*) incivility, rudeness.

incl. ABBR (= *incluso*) encl.

inclassificabile [inklassifi'kabile] AGG **a** unclassifiable **b** (*fig*: *pessimo*: *compito*) unmarkable; (: *azione, comporta-*

mento) abominable.

inclemente [inkle'mɛnte] AGG (*fig*: *clima*) harsh; (: *tempo*) inclement; (*giudice, critica*) severe, harsh.

inclemenza [inkle'mɛntsa] SF (*vedi agg*) harshness; inclemency; severity.

inclinabile [inkli'nabile] AGG (*schienale*) reclinable.

inclinare [inkli'nare] **1** VT (*recipiente*) to tilt, tip; (*schienale*) to tilt (back), recline; **inclinare il busto in avanti** to bend forward, lean forward. **2** VI (*aus* **avere**): **inclinare a qc/a fare** to incline towards sth/doing, tend towards sth/to do. **3 inclinarsi** VIP (*barca*) to list, heel; (*aereo*) to bank; (*ago magnetico*) to dip.

inclinato, a [inkli'nato] AGG (*recipiente*) tilted; (*strada*) sloping; **piano inclinato** (*Mat*) inclined plane.

inclinazione [inklinat'tsjone] SF **a** (*pendenza*: *di strada*) gradient; (: *di superficie*) slope; (: *di tetto*) slope, pitch; (: *di retta, piano*) inclination **b** (*fig*: *tendenza*) inclination, bent, tendency; **seguire le proprie inclinazioni** to follow one's inclinations.

incline [in'kline] AGG: **essere incline a pensare che...** to be inclined to think that ...; **essere incline alla collera** to be prone to anger, be irascible.

includere [in'kludere] VT IRREG: **includere (in)** (*accludere*) to enclose (in); (*comprendere*) to include (in).

inclusione [inklu'zjone] SF inclusion.

inclusivo, a [inklu'zivo] AGG: **inclusivo di** inclusive of.

incluso, a [in'kluzo] **1** PP di **includere**. **2** AGG **a** (*accluso*) attached, enclosed **b** (*compreso*) inclusive, included; **fino a giovedì incluso** up to and including Thursday; **incluso mio cugino** including my cousin, my cousin included; **spese incluse** inclusive of expenses.

incoerente [inkoe'rɛnte] AGG **a** (*terreno, materiali*) loose **b** (*fig*: *confuso*) incoherent; (: *illogico*) inconsistent.

incoerentemente [inkoerente'mente] AVV (*vedi agg* **b**) incoherently; inconsistently.

incoerenza [inkoe'rɛntsa] SF (*vedi agg*) looseness; incoherence; inconsistency.

incognita [in'kɔɲɲita] SF (*Mat, fig*: *persona*) unknown quantity; (: *fatto, evento*) matter of uncertainty.

incognito, a [in'kɔɲɲito] **1** AGG unknown. **2** SM: **mantenere l'incognito** to remain incognito; **viaggiare in incognito** to travel incognito.

incollare [inkol'lare] **1** VT (*gen*) to stick, gum; (*legno, porcellana*) to glue, stick; **incollare un francobollo ad una lettera** to put *o* stick a stamp on a letter; **incollare insieme dei cartoncini** to stick *o* glue pieces of card together; **incollare gli occhi addosso a qn** to fix one's eyes on sb. **2 incollarsi** VIP (*gen*): **incollarsi (a)** to stick (to); **incollarsi a qn** (*fig*) to stick close to sb; **le pagine si sono incollate** the pages have stuck together; **la camicia bagnata gli si incollò addosso** his wet shirt stuck to him.

incollato, a [inkol'lato] AGG (*gen*) stuck; **passa il pomeriggio incollato alla TV** he spends his afternoons glued to the TV.

incollatura [inkolla'tura] SF (*Ippica*): **vincere/perdere di un'incollatura** to win/lose by a head.

incollerire [inkolle'rire] VI (*aus* **essere**), **incollerirsi** VIP to lose one's temper.

incolmabile [inkol'mabile] AGG (*vuoto*) unfillable; (*lacuna*) overwhelming; (*Sport*: *distacco*) irretrievable.

incolonnamento [inkolonna'mento] SM (*di cifre*) putting into columns; (*di persone, soldati*) formation (in

columns); (*Tip*) printing in columns.

incolonnare [inkolon'nare] **1** VT (*cifre*) to put in columns; (*Mil: truppe*) to draw up in columns; (*Tip*) to set up in columns; (*con macchina da scrivere*) to tabulate.

2 incolonnarsi VIP (*truppe*) to draw up in columns.

incolore [inko'lore] AGG (*senza colore*) colourless (*Brit*), colorless (*Am*); (*monotono*) dull.

incolpare [inkol'pare] VT (*gen*): **incolpare (di)** to blame (for); **incolpare qn di aver fatto qc** to accuse sb of having done sth; **incolpare l'inesperienza** to blame one's inexperience.

incolto, a [in'kolto] AGG **a** (*terreno*) uncultivated **b** (*trascurato: barba*) neglected; (*ignorante: persona*) uneducated.

incolume [in'kolume] AGG unhurt, safe and sound.

incolumità [inkolumi'ta] SF safety; **attentato all'incolumità di qn** attempt on sb's life.

incombente [inkom'bɛnte] AGG (*pericolo*) imminent, impending.

incombenza [inkom'bɛntsa] SF duty, task.

incombere [in'kombere] VI DIF: **incombere su** (*sovrastare minacciando*) to hang over, threaten.

incombustibile [inkombus'tibile] AGG incombustible.

incominciare [inkomin'tʃare] **1** VT to begin, start; **incominciare a fare qc** to begin *o* start doing sth.

2 VI (*aus essere*) to begin, start.

incommensurabile [inkommensu'rabile] AGG (*Mat*) incommensurable; (*fig: pregi*) incalculable; (*: distanza*) immeasurable.

incommensurabilmente [inkommensurabil'mente] AVV (*vedi agg*) incommensurably; incalculably; immeasurably.

incomodare [inkomo'dare] **1** VT to trouble, inconvenience.

2 incomodarsi VR to put o.s. out.

incomodo [in'komodo] **1** AGG: **fare il terzo incomodo** to play gooseberry.

2 SM trouble, inconvenience, bother; **prendersi l'incomodo di fare qc** to take the trouble to do sth; **essere d'incomodo a qn** to be in sb's way; **togliere l'incomodo** (*andarsene*) to take o.s. off.

incomparabile [inkompa'rabile] AGG incomparable.

incomparabilmente [inkomparabil'mente] AVV incomparably.

incompatibile [inkompa'tibile] AGG (*inconciliabile*) incompatible.

incompatibilità [inkompatibili'ta] SF incompatibility ▶ **incompatibilità di carattere** (mutual) incompatibility.

incompetente [inkompe'tɛnte] **1** AGG (*gen, Dir*) incompetent; **essere incompetente in qc** to be incompetent *o* useless (*fam*) at sth.

2 SM/F incompetent person; **è un incompetente** he is incompetent.

incompetenza [inkompe'tɛntsa] SF incompetence.

incompiuto, a [inkom'pjuto] AGG unfinished, incomplete; **rimanere incompiuto** to be left unfinished.

incompleto, a [inkom'plɛto] AGG incomplete.

incomprensibile [inkompren'sibile] AGG (*gen*) incomprehensible.

incomprensibilmente [inkomprensibil'mente] AVV incomprehensibly.

incomprensione [inkompren'sjone] SF **a** (*mancanza di comprensione*) lack of understanding, incomprehen-

sion **b** (*malinteso*) misunderstanding.

incompreso, a [inkom'preso] **1** AGG misunderstood, not understood; **sono un genio incompreso** (*scherz*) I'm a misunderstood genius.

2 SM/F: **è un incompreso** people don't understand him.

incomunicabile [inkomuni'kabile] AGG (*sentimento, sensazione*) incommunicable.

inconcepibile [inkontʃe'pibile] AGG (*impensabile*) inconceivable, unthinkable; (*assurdo*) incredible.

inconciliabile [inkontʃi'ljabile] AGG irreconcilable.

inconcludente [inkonklu'dɛnte] AGG (*persona*) ineffectual; (*sforzi*) unavailing; (*discorso: sconclusionato*) disconnected.

incondizionatamente [inkondittsjonata'mente] AVV unconditionally.

incondizionato, a [inkondittsjo'nato] AGG (*approvazione ecc*) unconditional; (*fiducia*) unquestioning, complete; **resa incondizionata** (*anche fig*) unconditional surrender.

inconfessabile [inkonfes'sabile] AGG (*pensiero, peccato*) unmentionable.

inconfessato, a [inkonfes'sato] AGG (*desiderio, voglia*) unconfessed, secret.

inconfondibile [inkonfon'dibile] AGG unmistakable.

inconfondibilmente [inkonfondibil'mente] AVV unmistakably.

inconfutabile [inkonfu'tabile] AGG irrefutable.

incongruente [inkongru'ɛnte] AGG inconsistent.

incongruenza [inkongru'ɛntsa] SF inconsistency.

incongruo, a [in'kongruo] AGG insufficient, inadequate.

inconoscibile [inkonoʃ'ʃibile] SM: **l'inconoscibile** (*Filosofia*) the unknowable.

inconsapevole [inkonsa'pevole] AGG: **inconsapevole di** unaware of, ignorant of.

inconsapevolezza [inkonsapevo'lettsa] SF ignorance, lack of awareness.

inconsapevolmente [inkonsapevol'mente] AVV unwittingly.

inconsciamente [inkonʃa'mente] AVV unconsciously.

inconscio, scia, sci, sce [in'konʃo] **1** AGG (*desiderio, impulso*) unconscious.

2 SM: **l'inconscio** (*Psic*) the unconscious.

inconsistente [inkonsis'tɛnte] AGG (*dubbio*) unfounded; (*ragionamento, prove*) tenuous, flimsy.

inconsistenza [inkonsis'tɛntsa] SF (*di dubbio*) lack of foundation; (*di ragionamento, prove*) flimsiness.

inconsolabile [inkonso'labile] AGG inconsolable.

inconsueto, a [inkonsu'ɛto] AGG unusual.

inconsulto, a [inkon'sulto] AGG (*gesto, azione*) rash, impetuous.

incontaminato, a [inkontami'nato] AGG uncontaminated.

incontenibile [inkonte'nibile] AGG (*rabbia*) uncontrollable; (*entusiasmo*) irrepressible.

incontentabile [inkonten'tabile] AGG (*desiderio, avidità*) insatiable; (*persona: capriccioso*) hard to please, very demanding.

incontestabile [inkontes'tabile] AGG incontrovertible, indisputable.

incontestato, a [inkontes'tato] AGG undisputed.

incontinenza [inkonti'nɛntsa] SF (*Med*) incontinence.

incontrare [inkon'trare] **1** VT **a** (*gen*) to meet; (*in riunione*) to have a meeting with; (*difficoltà, pericolo*) to meet with, run into, come up against; **incontrare qn per caso** to run *o* bump into sb; **incontrare il favore del**

pubblico (*attore, prodotto ecc*) to find favour with *o* be popular with the public; **questo prodotto non incontra** (*uso assoluto*) this product hasn't caught on **b** (*Sport: squadra*) to meet, play (against); (: *pugile*) to meet, fight.

[2] **incontrarsi** VR (*uso reciproco*) **a** (*trovarsi: su appuntamento*) to meet (each other); (: *in riunione*) to have a meeting **b** (*Sport*) to meet.

incontrario [inkon'trarjo]: **all'incontrario** AVV (*sottosopra*) upside down; (*alla rovescia*) back to front; (*all'indietro*) backwards; (*nel senso contrario*) the other way round.

incontrastabile [inkontras'tabile] AGG incontrovertible, indisputable.

incontrastato, a [inkontras'tato] AGG (*successo, vittoria, verità*) undisputed.

incontro¹ [in'kontro] SM **a** (*gen*) meeting; (*fortuito*) encounter; **un incontro al vertice** a summit (meeting); **a tarda notte si possono fare brutti incontri** you can have some unpleasant encounters late at night **b** (*Sport*) match ▶ **incontro di calcio** football match (*Brit*), soccer game (*Am*) ▶ **incontro di pugilato** boxing match.

incontro² [in'kontro]: **incontro a** PREP (*verso*) towards; **andare incontro a qn** to go to meet sb; (*fig: aiutare*) to meet sb halfway; **andare incontro a** (*brutte sorprese*) to come up against, meet; (*spese*) to incur; **andare incontro alla morte** to go to one's death; **stiamo ormai andando incontro alla primavera** we're moving towards spring now, it'll soon be spring; **venire incontro a** (*richieste, esigenze*) to comply with.

incontrollabile [inkontrol'labile] AGG uncontrollable.

inconveniente [inkonve'njɛnte] SM **a** (*difficoltà*) setback, mishap; **ho avuto degli inconvenienti con la macchina** I had some problems with the car **b** (*svantaggio*) drawback, disadvantage, snag.

incoraggiamento [inkoraddʒa'mento] SM encouragement; **premio d'incoraggiamento** consolation prize.

incoraggiare [inkorad'dʒare] VT (*esortare*) to encourage; **incoraggiare qn a fare qc** to encourage sb to do sth; **incoraggiare qn allo studio** to encourage sb to study.

incornare [inkor'nare] VT to gore.

incorniciare [inkorni'tʃare] VT (*quadro, ritratto*) to frame; (*fig*): **i lunghi capelli le incorniciavano il volto** her long hair framed her face.

incoronare [inkoro'nare] VT (*anche fig*) to crown.

Incoronata [inkoro'nata] SF (*Rel*) feast of the Coronation of the Virgin Mary.

incoronazione [inkoronat'tsjone] SF coronation.

incorporare [inkorpo'rare] VT: **incorporare (in)** (*gen, Comm*) to incorporate (into); (*sostanza*) to mix (in); **"incorporare gli albumi nell'impasto"** (*Culin*) "fold the egg whites into the mixture".

incorporato, a [inkorpo'rato] AGG (*parte di impianto*) built-in.

incorporeo, a [inkor'pɔreo] AGG incorporeal; **esseri incorporei** spirits.

incorreggibile [inkorred'dʒibile] AGG (*gen*) incorrigible; (*giocatore*) inveterate.

incorreggibilmente [inkorreddʒibil'mente] AVV (*gen*) incorrigibly.

incorrere [in'korrere] VI IRREG (*aus essere*): **incorrere in** (*pericolo, guaio*) to run into, come up against, meet with.

incorruttibile [inkorrut'tibile] AGG (*funzionario*) incorruptible; (*fig: fede*) unshakeable; (: *bellezza*) unfading.

incorso, a [in'korso] PP di **incorrere.**

incosciente [inkoʃ'ʃɛnte] [1] AGG **a** (*irresponsabile*) reckless, thoughtless **b** (*privo di sensi*) unconscious. [2] SM/F reckless person, thoughtless person.

incoscientemente [inkoʃʃente'mente] AVV recklessly, thoughtlessly.

incoscienza [inkoʃ'ʃɛntsa] SF (*vedi agg*) recklessness, thoughtlessness; unconsciousness.

incostante [inkos'tante] AGG (*studente, impiegato*) inconsistent; (*carattere*) fickle, inconstant; (*rendimento*) sporadic.

incostanza [inkos'tantsa] SF inconstancy, fickleness.

incostituzionale [inkostituttsjo'nale] AGG unconstitutional.

incostituzionalità [inkostituttsjonali'ta] SF unconstitutionality.

incredibile [inkre'dibile] AGG incredible, unbelievable.

incredibilmente [inkredibil'mente] AVV incredibly, unbelievably.

incredulità [inkreduli'ta] SF incredulity.

incredulo, a [in'krɛdulo] AGG incredulous, disbelieving.

incrementare [inkremen'tare] VT (*aumentare: vendite, produzione*) to increase; (*dar sviluppo a: commercio*) to promote.

incremento [inkre'mento] SM: **incremento (di)** (*aumento numerico*) increase (in), growth (in); (*sviluppo*) development ▶ **incremento demografico** population rise *o* growth.

increscioso, a [inkreʃ'ʃoso] AGG (*spiacevole*) unpleasant; **incidente increscioso** regrettable incident.

increspare [inkres'pare] [1] VT (*capelli*) to curl; (*stoffa*) to gather; (*superficie: del mare*) to ripple. [2] **incresparsi** VIP (*superficie: di mare, lago*) to ripple.

incriminabile [inkrimi'nabile] AGG (*Dir*) chargeable.

incriminare [inkrimi'nare] VT (*Dir*): **incriminare qn per qc** to charge sb with sth.

incriminato, a [inkrimi'nato] AGG (*Dir*) indicted; **questa è la frase incriminata** (*scherz*) this was the fateful expression.

incriminazione [inkriminat'tsjone] SF (*atto d'accusa*) indictment, charge; **non c'erano prove sufficienti per la sua incriminazione** there wasn't sufficient evidence to charge him.

incrinare [inkri'nare] [1] VT (*vetro, specchio, vaso*) to crack; (*fig: rapporti, amicizia*) to spoil, create a rift in. [2] **incrinarsi** VIP (*vetro, ghiaccio, roccia*) to crack; (*rapporti, amicizia*) to deteriorate.

incrinatura [inkrina'tura] SF (*crepa*) crack; (*fig: di rapporti*) rift.

incrociare [inkro'tʃare] [1] VT **a** (*gen*) to cross; (*strada, linea*) to cut across; **incrociare le gambe** to cross one's legs; **incrociare le braccia** to fold one's arms; (*fig*) to down tools, refuse to work **b** (*autoveicolo, persona*) to meet; **l'ho incrociato per strada** I met him in the street **c** (*animali, piante*) to cross. [2] VI (*aus avere*) (*Naut, Aer*) to cruise. [3] **incrociarsi** VR (*uso reciproco: strade, rette*) to cross, intersect; (: *persone, veicoli*) to pass each other; (*fig: sguardi*) to meet; (: *battute*) to fly thick and fast.

incrociato, a [inkro'tʃato] AGG: **fuoco incrociato** (*Mil*) crossfire.

incrociatore [inkrotʃa'tore] SM (*Naut*) cruiser.

incrocio, ci [in'krotʃo] SM **a** (*di strade*) crossroads, junc-

tion; (*Ferr*) crossing **b** : **l'incrocio dei pali** (*Calcio*) the top corner of the goalposts **c** (*Zool, Bot*) cross.

incrollabile [inkrol'labile] AGG (*fede*) unshakeable, firm.

incrostare [inkros'tare] ① VT to encrust. ② **incrostarsi** VIP: **incrostarsi di** to become encrusted with.

incrostato, a [inkros'tato] AGG (*tubi*) furred up; **incrostato (di)** (*fango ecc*) encrusted (with); (*pietre preziose*) studded (with), encrusted (with).

incrostazione [inkrostat'tsjone] SF incrustation, encrustation; (*di calcare*) scale; (*nelle tubature*) scale, fur (*Brit*).

incruento, a [inkru'ɛnto] AGG (*battaglia*) without bloodshed, bloodless.

incubatrice [inkuba'tritʃe] SF incubator.

incubazione [inkubat'tsjone] SF incubation.

incubo ['inkubo] SM (*anche fig*) nightmare; **ho l'incubo degli esami** exams are a nightmare for me.

incudine [in'kudine] SF anvil; **trovarsi** *o* **essere tra l'incudine e il martello** (*fig*) to be between the devil and the deep blue sea.

inculata [inku'lata] SF (*fam!: solenne fregatura*): **ho preso una bella inculata** they really screwed me (*fam!*)

inculcare [inkul'kare] VT: **inculcare qc in qn** to inculcate sth into sb, instil sth into sb.

incuneare [inkune'are] ① VT to wedge. ② **incunearsi** VIP to slot in.

incupire [inku'pire] ① VT (*rendere scuro*) to darken; (*fig: intristire*) to fill with gloom. ② VI (*aus essere*), **incupirsi** VIP (*vedi vt*) to darken; to become gloomy.

incurabile [inku'rabile] AGG, SM/F incurable.

incurabilmente [inkurabil'mente] AVV incurably.

incurante [inku'rante] AGG: **incurante (di)** heedless (of), careless (of).

incuria [in'kurja] SF negligence.

incuriosire [inkurjo'sire] ① VT to arouse the curiosity of, make curious. ② **incuriosirsi** VIP to become curious.

incuriosito, a [inkurjo'sito] AGG curious.

incursione [inkur'sjone] SF (*Mil, Aer*) incursion, foray, raid; (*di ladri ecc*) raid.

incurvare [inkur'vare] ① VT (*piegare*) to curve, bend; **non incurvare la schiena!** sit *o* stand up straight!; **il lavoro a tavolino gli ha incurvato la schiena** *o* **le spalle** deskwork has made him round-shouldered *o* has given him a stoop. ② **incurvarsi** VIP (*gen*) to bend; (*legno*) to warp; (*persona*) to develop a stoop, become bent.

incurvato, a [inkur'vato] AGG bent.

incusso, a [in'kusso] PP di **incutere**.

incustodito, a [inkusto'dito] AGG (*bagaglio*) unattended, unguarded; **passaggio a livello incustodito** unmanned level crossing.

incutere [in'kutere] VT IRREG: **incutere rispetto a qn** to command sb's respect; **incutere paura a qn** to strike fear into sb; **incutere soggezione a qn** to cow sb.

indaco, chi ['indako] AGG INV, SM indigo.

indaffarato, a [indaffa'rato] AGG: **indaffarato (a fare qc)** busy (doing sth).

indagare [inda'gare] ① VI (*aus avere*): **indagare su** to investigate; **indagare sul conto di qn** to investigate sb, make enquiries about sb; **è meglio non indagare** it's better not to enquire too closely. ② VT to investigate, look into.

indagatore, trice [indaga'tore] AGG (*sguardo, domanda*) searching; (*mente*) inquiring; **rivolgere a qn uno sguardo indagatore** to give sb a searching look.

indagine [in'dadʒine] SF **a** (*inchiesta*) investigation, inquiry, enquiry; **fare** *o* **svolgere un'indagine (su)** to carry out an investigation *o* inquiry (into) **b** (*ricerca*) research, study; **fare** *o* **svolgere un'indagine su** to carry out *o* do research into, make a study of ▶**indagine su campione** sample survey ▶**indagine demoscopica** public opinion poll ▶**indagine di mercato** market survey.

indebitamente [indebita'mente] AVV (*immeritatamente*) undeservedly; (*erroneamente*) wrongfully.

indebitamento [indebita'mento] SM debt.

indebitare [indebi'tare] ① VT: **indebitare qn** to get sb into debt. ② **indebitarsi** VR: **si è indebitato fino al collo** he is up to his eyes in debt; **indebitarsi con qn/con la banca** to owe money to sb/to the bank.

indebito, a [in'debito] AGG (*onori, accuse*) undeserved; **appropriazione indebita** embezzlement.

indebolimento [indeboli'mento] SM **a** weakening **b** (*debolezza*) weakness.

indebolire [indebo'lire] ① VT to weaken. ② VI (*aus essere*), **indebolirsi** VIP (*persona*) to grow weak; (*vista*) to deteriorate.

indecente [inde'tʃɛnte] AGG indecent; **in quel ristorante il servizio è indecente** (*inaccettabile*) the service is disgraceful at that restaurant.

indecentemente [indetʃente'mente] AVV (*gen*) indecently; **esprimersi indecentemente** (*oscenamente*) to use obscene language.

indecenza [inde'tʃɛntsa] SF indecency; **è un'indecenza!** (*vergogna*) it's scandalous!, it's a disgrace!

indecifrabile [indetʃi'frabile] AGG (*scrittura*) illegible, indecipherable; (*messaggio, testo*) incomprehensible.

indecisione [indetʃi'zjone] SF indecision, indecisiveness.

indeciso, a [inde'tʃizo] AGG (*persona: titubante*) indecisive; (: *che non ha ancora deciso, questione, risultato*) undecided; (*tempo*) unsettled; (*colore, forma*) indistinct.

indeclinabile [indekli'nabile] AGG (*Gramm*) indeclinable.

indecorosamente [indekorosa'mente] AVV indecorously.

indecoroso, a [indeko'roso] AGG (*comportamento*) indecorous, unseemly.

indefessamente [indefessa'mente] AVV indefatigably, tirelessly.

indefesso, a [inde'fɛsso] AGG indefatigable, untiring.

indefinibile [indefi'nibile] AGG indefinable.

indefinito, a [indefi'nito] AGG (*indeterminato: anche Gramm*) indefinite; (*impreciso*) undefined; (*irrisolto: questione, controversia*) unresolved.

indeformabile [indefor'mabile] AGG crushproof.

indegnamente [indeɲɲa'mente] AVV (*comportarsi*) shamefully.

indegno, a [in'deɲɲo] AGG (*atto*) shameful; (*persona*) unworthy; **è indegno di tanta ammirazione** he doesn't deserve so much admiration.

indeiscente [indeiʃ'ʃɛnte] AGG (*Bot*) indehiscent.

indelebile [inde'lɛbile] AGG indelible, permanent.

indelebilmente [indelebil'mente] AVV indelibly.

indelicatamente [indelikata'mente] AVV indiscreetly, tactlessly.

indelicatezza [indelika'tettsa] SF tactlessness; **è stata un'indelicatezza da parte sua** it was tactless of him.

indelicato, a [indeli'kato] AGG (*domanda*) indiscreet, tactless.

indemagliabile [indemaʎˈʎabile] AGG (*calze, tessuto*) runresist.

indemoniato, a [indemoˈnjato] [1] AGG possessed (by the devil); **quel ragazzino è indemoniato** (*fig*) that boy is a little demon.

[2] SM/F person possessed by the devil; **gridare come un indemoniato** to shout like one possessed.

indenne [inˈdɛnne] AGG (*illeso*) unscathed, unharmed, unhurt.

indennità [indenniˈta] SF INV (*rimborso: di spese*) reimbursement; (: *di perdita*) indemnity, compensation ▶**indennità di contingenza** cost-of-living allowance ▶**indennità di fine rapporto** severance payment ▶**indennità parlamentare** member of parliament's salary ▶**indennità di trasferta** travel allowance, travel expenses *pl*.

indennizzare [indennidˈdzare] VT to indemnify, compensate.

indennizzo [indenˈniddzo] SM (*somma*) indemnity, compensation.

inderogabile [inderoˈgabile] AGG binding.

indescrivibile [indeskriˈvibile] AGG indescribable.

indescrivibilmente [indeskrivibilˈmente] AVV indescribably.

indesiderabile [indesideˈrabile] AGG undesirable; **persona indesiderabile** persona non grata.

indesiderato, a [indesideˈrato] AGG unwanted.

indeterminatezza [indeterminaˈtettsa] SF vagueness.

indeterminativo, a [indeterminaˈtivo] AGG (*Gramm*) indefinite.

indeterminato, a [indetermiˈnato] AGG (*tempo*) unspecified, indefinite; (*quantità, spazio*) indeterminate; **rimandare qc a tempo indeterminato** to postpone sth indefinitely.

indetto, a [inˈdetto] PP di **indire**.

India [ˈindja] SF: **l'India** India ▶**le Indie occidentali** the West Indies.

indiano, a [inˈdjano] [1] AGG Indian; **l'oceano Indiano** the Indian Ocean.

[2] SM/F (*dell'India*) Indian; (*dell'America*) (American) Indian; **fare l'indiano** (*fig*) to feign ignorance.

indiavolato, a [indjavoˈlato] AGG (*persona: arrabbiato*) furious; (: *vivace, violento*) wild; (*bambino*) high-spirited; (*chiasso*) terrible, awful; (*danza, ritmo*) frenzied.

indicare [indiˈkare] VT a (*mostrare*) to show, indicate; (: *col dito*) to point to, point out; **indicare qc a qn** to show sb sth; **indicare la strada a qn** to show sb the way; **indicare qn col dito** to point to *o* at sb; **m'indicò l'uscita** he showed me where the exit was; **la lancetta grande indica i minuti** the big hand shows the minutes; **cosa indica questo segnale?** what does this signal mean?; **le varie tappe erano indicate sulla carta** the various stops were indicated *o* shown *o* marked on the map; **i risultati indicano che...** the results indicate *o* show that ...

b (*consigliare*) to suggest, recommend; **mi indicò un medico** he recommended a doctor to me.

indicativamente [indikativaˈmente] AVV as an indication; **qual è il prezzo, indicativamente?** can you give me an idea of the price?

indicativo, a [indikaˈtivo] [1] AGG (*gen, Gramm*) indicative; (*prezzo*) approximate; **a titolo puramente indicativo** just as an indication.

[2] SM (*Gramm*) indicative (mood).

indicato, a [indiˈkato] AGG (*consigliato*) advisable; (*adatto*):

indicato per suitable for, appropriate for; **questa cura non è indicata in caso di gravidanza** this treatment is not advisable during pregnancy.

indicatore, trice [indikaˈtore] [1] AGG indicating; **cartello indicatore** sign.

[2] SM (*Tecn*) gauge, indicator; (*Chim*) indicator ▶**indicatore della benzina** fuel gauge, petrol (*Brit*) *o* gas (*Am*) gauge ▶**indicatore ecologico** indicator species ▶**indicatore di radiazioni** radiation detector ▶**indicatore di velocità** (*Aut*) speedometer; (*Aer*) airspeed indicator ▶**indicatori di direzione** (*Aut*) indicator lights.

indicazione [indikatˈtsjone] SF (*gen*) indication; (*istruzione*) instruction, direction; (*informazione*) piece of information; **indicazioni** SFPL (*Med*) directions; **non è stato in grado di fornirmi indicazioni utili** he was unable to give me any useful information; **mi ha dato le indicazioni sbagliate per arrivare lì** he didn't tell me the right way to get there.

indice [ˈinditʃe] [1] SM a (*Anat*) index finger, forefinger

b (*indicatore*) needle, pointer; (*fig: indizio*) sign; **tale comportamento è indice d'ignoranza/di pigrizia** such behaviour is a sign of ignorance/laziness

c (*di libro*) (table of) contents *pl* ▶**indice analitico** index

d (*Rel*): **l'Indice (dei libri proibiti)** the Index; **mettere all'indice** (*fig*) to blacklist

e (*Mat, Statistica: rapporto*) index ▶**indice azionario** (*Borsa*) share index ▶**indice di gradimento** (*Radio, TV*) popularity rating ▶**indice dei prezzi al consumo** ≈ retail price index (*Brit*), ≈ consumer price index (*Am*) ▶**indice di produzione** production index ▶**indice di rifrazione costante** (*Fis*) refractive constant.

[2] AGG: **dito indice** index finger, forefinger.

indicherò *ecc* [indikeˈrɔ] VB vedi **indicare**.

indicibile [indiˈtʃibile] AGG inexpressible, unspeakable.

indicizzare [inditʃidˈdzare] VT (*salari*) to index-link (*Brit*), index (*Am*).

indicizzato, a [inditʃidˈdzato] AGG (*polizza, salario ecc*) index-linked (*Brit*), indexed (*Am*).

indicizzazione [inditʃiddzatˈtsjone] SF indexing.

indietreggiare [indjetredˈdzare] VI (*aus avere o essere*) (*anche fig*) to draw back, retreat; (*Mil*) to retreat.

indietro [inˈdjɛtro] AVV a (*stato, tempo*) behind; **essere indietro negli studi** to be behind in one's studies; **rimanere indietro** (*persona: di proposito*) to stay back *o* behind; (: *proprio malgrado*) to drop *o* lag behind, be left behind; **mentre dettava sono rimasto indietro** while he was dictating I got behind, I couldn't keep up with his dictation; **mettere indietro l'orologio** to put one's watch back; **essere indietro** (*orologio*) to be slow; (*persona: col lavoro*) to be behind; **essere indietro con i pagamenti** to be behind *o* in arrears with one's payments

b (*moto*) back, backwards; **tornare indietro** to go back; **mandare *o* rimandare qc indietro** to send sth back; **andare avanti e indietro** to walk up and down; **non vado né avanti né indietro** (*fig*) I'm not getting anywhere, I'm getting nowhere; **voltarsi indietro** to look back, look round; **farsi indietro** to move back; **fare un passo indietro** to take a step back *o* backwards; **facciamo un passo indietro negli anni venti** let's go back *o* cast our minds back to the twenties; (*state*) **indietro!** get back!

c: **dare qc indietro a qn** (*restituire*) to give sth back to sb

d : **all'indietro** backwards; **camminare all'indietro** to walk backwards; **cadere all'indietro** to fall over backwards.

indifeso, a [indiˈfeso] AGG (*città, confine*) undefended; (*persona*) helpless, defenceless (*Brit*), defenseless (*Am*).

indifferente [indiffeˈrɛnte] ① AGG **a** : **indifferente (a)** indifferent (to); **mi è indifferente** I don't mind, it's all the same to me; **quell'uomo mi è indifferente** that man means nothing to me, I feel quite indifferent towards that man; **a piedi o in auto è indifferente** on foot or by car, it's all the same to me

b : **non indifferente** (*notevole: somma, spesa*) sizeable, not inconsiderable.

② SM: **fare l'indifferente** to pretend to be indifferent, be *o* act casual; (*fingere di non vedere o sentire*) to pretend not to notice.

indifferentemente [indifferenteˈmente] AVV without distinction; **bevo indifferentemente tè o caffè** I drink tea or coffee; **prenderei indifferentemente questo o quello** I'd be quite happy with either one, either would do nicely.

indifferenza [indiffeˈrɛntsa] SF indifference.

indifferibile [indiffeˈribile] AGG not deferable.

indigeno, a [inˈdidʒeno] ① AGG indigenous, native.

② SM/F native.

indigente [indiˈdʒɛnte] ① AGG destitute, poverty-stricken.

② SM/F pauper; **gli indigenti** the poor *o* needy.

indigenza [indiˈdʒɛntsa] SF extreme poverty, destitution; **vivere nell'indigenza** to live in extreme poverty.

indigestione [indidʒesˈtjone] SF indigestion; **fare indigestione di qc** to eat too much of sth; (*fig: di romanzi, film*) to have a surfeit of sth, be sick of.

indigesto, a [indiˈdʒɛsto] AGG indigestible; (*fig: persona, libro*) unbearable; **il latte mi è indigesto** I find milk indigestible.

indignare [indiɲˈɲare] ① VT: **indignare qn** to make sb indignant, fill sb with indignation.

② **indignarsi** VIP: **indignarsi per** to be (*o* get) indignant about *o* at.

indignato, a [indiɲˈɲato] AGG: **indignato (per)** indignant (about *o* at).

indignazione [indiɲɲatˈtsjone] SF indignation; **con sua grande indignazione** much to his indignation.

indimenticabile [indimentiˈkabile] AGG unforgettable.

indio, dia, di, die [ˈindjo] AGG, SM/F (South American) Indian.

indipendente [indipenˈdɛnte] ① AGG (*gen, Pol, Gramm*): **indipendente (da)** independent (of); **è indipendente dalla mia volontà** it is beyond my control; **"affittasi camera con ingresso indipendente"** "room to let with independent access".

② SM/F (*Pol*) independent.

indipendentemente [indipendenteˈmente] AVV **a** (*in modo libero*) independently

b (*a prescindere da*): **verrò indipendentemente dal fatto che lui venga o meno** I'll come anyway, whether he comes or not; **indipendentemente dal fatto che gli piaccia o meno, verrà!** whether he likes it or not, he's coming!, he's coming, whether he likes it or not!

indipendenza [indipenˈdɛntsa] SF independence.

indire [inˈdire] VT IRREG (*concorso*) to announce; (*elezioni*) to call.

indirettamente [indirettaˈmente] AVV indirectly.

indiretto, a [indiˈrɛtto] AGG (*gen*) indirect; **per vie indirette** indirectly.

indirizzare [indiritˈtsare] ① VT (*lettera, osservazione, richiesta*) to address; **indirizzare la parola a qn** to address sb; **mi hanno indirizzato qui** they sent me here; **un libro indirizzato ai ragazzi** a book intended *o* written for young people; **indirizzare i propri sforzi verso** to direct one's efforts towards; **l'hanno indirizzato alla segreteria del personale** he was referred to the personnel officer.

② **indirizzarsi** VR (*rivolgersi*): **indirizzarsi a qn** to speak to sb.

indirizzario, ri [indiritˈtsarjo] SM mailing list.

indirizzo [indiˈrittso] SM **a** (*di domicilio*) address; **sbagliare indirizzo** to have the wrong address; **se vieni da me in cerca di aiuto, hai sbagliato indirizzo** if you're looking for help from me, you've come to the wrong person

b (*fig: direzione*) direction, course; (: *tendenza*) trend; **mutare indirizzo** to change course *o* direction; **stanno seguendo l'indirizzo giusto** they're on the right lines, they're going in the right direction; **l'attuale indirizzo politico** the present political trend

c (*Inform*): **indirizzo assoluto** absolute address
▶ **indirizzo relativo** relative address.

indisciplina [indiʃʃiˈplina] SF indiscipline, lack of discipline.

indisciplinato, a [indiʃʃipliˈnato] AGG undisciplined, unruly.

indiscretamente [indiskretaˈmente] AVV indiscreetly.

indiscreto, a [indisˈkreto] AGG indiscreet.

indiscrezione [indiskretˈtsjone] SF **a** (*qualità*) indiscretion **b** (*azione*) indiscretion; (*fuga di notizie*) unconfirmed report.

indiscriminatamente [indiskriminataˈmente] AVV indiscriminately.

indiscriminato, a [indiskrimiˈnato] AGG indiscriminate.

indiscusso, a [indisˈkusso] AGG (*autorità, campione*) undisputed.

indiscutibile [indiskuˈtibile] AGG indisputable, unquestionable.

indiscutibilmente [indiskutibilˈmente] AVV indisputably, unquestionably.

indispensabile [indispenˈsabile] ① AGG (*essenziale*) essential, indispensable; (*necessario*) necessary; **rendersi indispensabile** to make o.s. indispensable.

② SM: **porterò con me solo l'indispensabile** I'll take the absolute minimum with me; **ho l'indispensabile per il picnic** I've got everything I need for the picnic.

indispettire [indispetˈtire] ① VT to irritate, annoy.

② VI (*aus essere*), **indispettirsi** VIP to get *o* grow irritated *o* annoyed.

indisponente [indispoˈnɛnte] AGG irritating, annoying.

indisporre [indisˈporre] VT IRREG to antagonize; **il suo modo di fare mi indispone** I find his manner irritating.

indisposizione [indispozitˈtsjone] SF (slight) indisposition.

indisposto, a [indisˈposto] ① PP di **indisporre**.

② AGG indisposed (*frm*), unwell.

indissolubile [indissoˈlubile] AGG indissoluble.

indissolubilmente [indissolubilˈmente] AVV indissolubly.

indistintamente [indistintaˈmente] AVV **a** (*senza distinzioni*) indiscriminately, without exception **b** (*in modo indefinito: vedere, sentire*) vaguely, faintly.

indistinto, a [indisˈtinto] AGG (*gen*) indistinct; (*colori*)

vague.

indistruttibile [indistrut'tibile] AGG indestructible.

indisturbato, a [indistur'bato] AGG undisturbed.

indivia [in'divja] SF endive.

individuale [individu'ale] AGG (*gen*) individual; (*libertà*) personal; (*qualità*) distinctive; **lezioni individuali** individual tuition.

individualismo [individua'lizmo] SM individualism.

individualista, i, e [individua'lista] SM/F individualist.

individualistico, a, ci, che [individua'listiko] AGG individualistic.

individualità [individuali'ta] SF (*unicità*) individuality; (*personalità*) personality.

individualizzare [individualid'dzare] VT to individualize.

individualizzazione [individualiddzat'tsjone] SF individualization.

individualmente [individual'mente] AVV individually.

individuare [individu'are] ☐ VT **a** (*determinare*) to identify; (: *posizione*) to locate **b** (*riconoscere*) to pick out, single out; **sono riuscito ad individuarlo tra la folla** I managed to pick him out in the crowd.

☐: **individuarsi** VIP (*assumere forma distinta*) to be characterized.

individuazione [individuat'tsjone] SF (*gen*) identification; (*di posizione, relitto ecc*) location.

individuo [indi'viduo] SM (*gen*) individual; (*pegg: uomo*) character, fellow; **un losco individuo** a shady character.

indivisibile [indivi'zibile] AGG (*Mat*) indivisible; **quei due sono indivisibili** those two are inseparable.

indivisibilità [indivizibili'ta] SF (*Mat*) indivisibility.

indiviso, a [indi'vizo] AGG undivided.

indiziare [indit'tsjare] VT: **indiziare qn** to cast suspicion on sb; **essere indiziato di qc** to be suspected of sth.

indiziato, a [indit'tsjato] ☐ AGG suspected.

☐ SM/F suspect.

indizio, zi [in'dittsjo] SM (*segno*) indication, sign; (*traccia*) clue; (*Dir*) piece of evidence.

Indocina [indo'tʃina] SF: **l'Indocina** Indochina.

indoeuropeo, a [indoeuro'pɛo] AGG, SM/F Indo-European.

indole ['indole] SF nature, character; **di indole buona** good-natured.

indolente [indo'lɛnte] AGG indolent, lazy.

indolentemente [indolente'mente] AVV indolently, lazily.

indolenza [indo'lɛntsa] SF indolence, laziness.

indolenzimento [indolentsi'mento] SM (*vedi vb*) stiffness, ache; numbness.

indolenzire [indolen'tsire] ☐ VT (*gambe, braccia ecc*) to make stiff, cause to ache; (: *intorpidire*) to numb.

☐ VI (*aus essere*), **indolenzirsi** VIP (*vedi vt*) to become stiff; to go numb.

indolenzito, a [indolen'tsito] AGG stiff, aching; (*intorpidito*) numb.

indolore [indo'lore] AGG (*anche fig*) painless.

indomabile [indo'mabile] AGG (*fig: volontà*) indomitable; (: *incendio*) uncontrollable; (*animale*) untameable.

indomani [indo'mani] SM: **l'indomani** the next day, the following day.

indomito, a [in'dɔmito] AGG (*coraggio*) indomitable.

Indonesia [indo'nɛzja] SF: **l'Indonesia** Indonesia.

indonesiano, a [indone'zjano] AGG, SM/F, SM Indonesian.

indorare [indo'rare] VT (*rivestire in oro*) to gild; (*Culin*) to dip in egg yolk; **indorare la pillola** (*fig*) to sugar the pill.

indossare [indos'sare] VT (*mettere indosso*) to put on; (*avere indosso*) to wear, have on.

indossatore, trice [indossa'tore] SM/F model; **fare l'indossatore** to be a model; **indossatrice volante** freelance model.

indotto, a [in'dotto] PP di **indurre**.

indottrinamento [indottrina'mento] SM indoctrination.

indottrinare [indottri'nare] VT to indoctrinate.

indovinare [indovi'nare] VT **a** (*gen*) to guess; (*il futuro*) to predict, foretell; **tirare a indovinare** to hazard a guess; **indovina chi viene a cena!** guess who's coming to dinner! **b** (*azzeccare: risposta*) to get right; **non ne indovini una** you never get anything right.

indovinato, a [indovi'nato] AGG successful; (*scelta*) inspired; **una festa indovinata** a successful party.

indovinello [indovi'nɛllo] SM riddle.

indovino, a [indo'vino] SM/F fortune-teller, soothsayer.

indù [in'du] AGG, SM/F Hindu.

indubbiamente [indubbja'mente] AVV undoubtedly; **sarai a Parigi per la fine del mese? — indubbiamente** will you be in Paris by the end of the month? — definitely.

indubbio, bia, bi, bie [in'dubbjo] AGG undoubted, undeniable; **è indubbio che...** there is no doubt that ... .

indubitabile [indubi'tabile] AGG indubitable.

induco *ecc* [in'duko] VB vedi **indurre**.

indugiare [indu'dʒare] VI (*aus avere*) (*attardarsi*) to take one's time, delay; **non ha indugiato ad accettare l'invito** he wasted no time in accepting the invitation.

indugio, gi [in'dudʒo] SM (*ritardo*) delay; **senza indugio** without delay, straight away.

induismo [indu'izmo] SM Hinduism.

indulgente [indul'dʒɛnte] AGG (*gen*) indulgent; (*giudice*) lenient.

indulgenza [indul'dʒɛntsa] SF **a** (*vedi agg*) indulgence; leniency **b** (*Rel*) indulgence ▶ **indulgenza plenaria** plenary indulgence.

indulgere [in'duldʒere] VI IRREG (*aus avere*): **indulgere a qc** (*abbandonarsi*) to indulge in sth; (*accondiscendere*) to comply with sth.

indulto [in'dulto] ☐ PP di **indulgere**.

☐ SM (*Dir*) pardon.

indumento [indu'mento] SM garment, article of clothing; **un negozio di indumenti usati** a secondhand clothes shop ▶ **indumenti intimi** underwear *sg*, underclothing *sg*, underclothes *pl*.

indurimento [induri'mento] SM hardening.

indurire [indu'rire] VB IRREG ☐ VT (*anche fig: cuore*) to harden.

☐ VI (*aus essere*), **indurirsi** VIP to harden, become hard.

indurre [in'durre] VT IRREC: **indurre qn a fare qc** to induce *o* persuade sb to do sth; **indurre con lusinghe qn a fare qc** to cajole sb into doing sth; **indurre in errore** to mislead, lead astray; **indurre in tentazione** to lead into temptation.

indussi *ecc* [in'dussi] VB vedi **indurre**.

industria [in'dustrja] SF **a** (*attività*) industry; **industria pesante/leggera** heavy/light industry; **la piccola/grande industria** small/big business **b** (*impresa*) factory, industrial concern ▶ **industria di assemblaggio** assembly industry ▶ **industria automobilistica** motor industry ▶ **industria tessile** textile industry.

industriale [indus'trjale] ☐ AGG industrial.

☐ SM/F industrialist.

industrialismo [industrja'lizmo] SM industrialism.

industrializzare [industrjalid'dzare] VT to industrialize.

industrializzato, a [industrjalid'dzato] AGG industrialized.

industrializzazione [industrjaliddzat'tsjone] SF industrialization.

industrialmente [industrjal'mente] AVV industrially.

industriarsi [indus'trjarsi] VIP to do one's best, try hard.

industriosamente [industrjosa'mente] AVV industriously.

industrioso, a [indus'trjoso] AGG industrious, hard-working.

induttivo, a [indut'tivo] AGG inductive.

induttore, trice [indut'tore] ① AGG (Elettr) inductive.

② SM (Elettr) inductor.

induzione [indut'tsjone] SF induction.

inebetire [inebe'tire] ① VT to stupefy, daze.

② VI (aus essere), **inebetirsi** VIP to become stupid.

inebetito, a [inebe'tito] AGG dazed, stunned.

inebriante [inebri'ante] AGG (alcolico) intoxicating; (fig: eccitante) heady, exciting, exhilarating.

inebriare [inebri'are] ① VT (anche fig) to intoxicate.

② **inebriarsi** VIP to become intoxicated; **inebriarsi alla vista di qc** to go into raptures at the sight of sth.

inebriato, a [inebri'ato] AGG (anche fig) intoxicated, inebriated.

ineccepibile [inettʃe'pibile] AGG (comportamento) exemplary, unexceptionable.

inedia [i'nɛdja] SF starvation; **morire d'inedia** to starve to death.

inedito, a [i'nɛdito] ① AGG (non pubblicato) unpublished; **notizia inedita** fresh piece of news.

② SM unpublished work.

ineffabile [inef'fabile] AGG ineffable.

inefficace [ineffi'katʃe] AGG ineffective.

inefficacia [ineffi'katʃa] SF inefficacy, ineffectiveness.

inefficiente [ineffi'tʃɛnte] AGG inefficient.

inefficienza [ineffi'tʃɛntsa] SF inefficiency.

ineguagliabile [inegwaʎ'ʎabile] AGG incomparable, matchless.

ineguaglianza [inegwaʎ'ʎantsa] SF (sociale) inequality; (di trattamento) disparity; (di superficie, livello) unevenness.

ineguale [ine'gwale] AGG (non uguale) unequal; (irregolare) uneven.

inelegante [inele'gante] AGG (persona, abito) inelegant.

ineluttabile [inelut'tabile] AGG inescapable.

ineluttabilità [ineluttabili'ta] SF inescapability.

inenarrabile [inenar'rabile] AGG unutterable.

inequivocabile [inekwivo'kabile] AGG unequivocal.

inequivocabilmente [inekwivokabil'mente] AVV unequivocally.

inerente [ine'rɛnte] AGG: **inerente a** concerning, regarding.

inerme [i'nɛrme] AGG unarmed, defenceless (Brit), defenseless (Am).

inerpicarsi [inerpi'karsi] VIP: **inerpicarsi (su o per)** (persona) to clamber (up); **la strada si inerpicava fino in cima al colle** the road wound steeply up to the top of the hill.

inerte [i'nɛrte] AGG **a** (corpo) lifeless; (persona) inactive; **peso inerte** (anche fig) dead weight **b** (Chim) inert.

inerzia [i'nɛrtsja] SF (gen, Fis) inertia; (inoperosità) inactivity; **per forza d'inerzia** (anche fig) through inertia.

inesattezza [inezat'tettsa] SF inaccuracy.

inesatto[1], a [ine'zatto] AGG (impreciso) inaccurate, inexact; (erroneo) incorrect.

inesatto[2], a [ine'zatto] AGG (Amm: non riscosso) uncol-

lected.

inesauribile [inezau'ribile] AGG inexhaustible.

inesistente [inezis'tɛnte] AGG non-existent.

inesistenza [inezis'tɛntsa] SF non-existence.

inesorabile [inezo'rabile] AGG (destino, nemico, ostilità) inexorable, relentless; (giudice) inflexible.

inesorabilità [inezorabili'ta] SF (vedi agg) inexorability, relentlessness; inflexibility.

inesorabilmente [inezorabil'mente] AVV inexorably, relentlessly.

inesperienza [inespe'rjɛntsa] SF inexperience.

inesperto, a [ines'pɛrto] AGG inexperienced.

inesplicabile [inespli'kabile] AGG inexplicable.

inesplicabilità [inesplikabili'ta] SF inexplicableness.

inesplicabilmente [inesplikabil'mente] AVV inexplicably.

inesplorato, a [inesplo'rato] AGG unexplored.

inesploso, a [ines'plɔzo] AGG unexploded.

inespressivo, a [inespres'sivo] AGG (viso) expressionless, inexpressive.

inespresso, a [ines'prɛsso] AGG unexpressed.

inesprimibile [inespri'mibile] AGG inexpressible.

inespugnabile [inespuɲ'ɲabile] AGG (fortezza, torre) impregnable.

inespugnato, a [inespuɲ'ɲato] AGG (fortezza) unconquered.

inestetismo [ineste'tizmo] SM beauty problem, (slight) blemish.

inestimabile [inesti'mabile] AGG (bene, qualità) inestimable; (valore) incalculable; **un quadro di valore inestimabile** a priceless painting.

inestinguibile [inestin'gwibile] AGG inextinguishable.

inestirpabile [inestir'pabile] AGG ineradicable.

inestricabile [inestri'kabile] AGG (anche fig) impenetrable.

inestricabilmente [inestrikabil'mente] AVV (anche fig) inextricably.

inettitudine [inetti'tudine] SF ineptitude.

inetto, a [i'nɛtto] ① AGG (incapace) incompetent; (sciocco) inept.

② SM/F incompetent.

inevaso, a [ine'vazo] AGG (pratica) pending; (corrispondenza) unanswered.

inevitabile [inevi'tabile] ① AGG (ostacolo) unavoidable; (risultato) inevitable; **era inevitabile!** it was inevitable!, it was bound to happen!; **era inevitabile che lo scoprisse** he was bound to discover it.

② SM: **l'inevitabile** the inevitable.

inevitabilmente [inevitabil'mente] AVV inevitably.

in extremis [in eks'trɛmis] AVV in the nick of time.

inezia [i'nɛttsja] SF trifle, bagatelle, thing of no importance.

infagottare [infagot'tare] ① VT to bundle up, wrap up; **essere infagottato** to be well wrapped up.

② **infagottarsi** VR to wrap (o.s.) up.

infallibile [infal'libile] AGG infallible.

infallibilità [infallibili'ta] SF infallibility.

infamante [infa'mante] AGG (accusa) defamatory, slanderous.

infamare [infa'mare] VT to defame.

infame [in'fame] AGG (persona) wicked; (calunnia) vile; (fig: pessimo) awful, dreadful.

infamia [in'famja] SF **a** (disonore) infamy **b** (azione) infamous deed, vile deed.

infangare [infan'gare] ① VT to cover with mud; (fig: reputazione, nome) to sully.

2 **infangarsi** VIP to get covered in mud; (*fig*) to be sullied.

infanticida, i, e [infanti'tʃida] SM/F infanticide (*person*).

infanticidio, di [infanti'tʃidjo] SM infanticide.

infantile [infan'tile] AGG **a** (*per bambini*) child *attr*; (*malattia*) childhood *attr*; (*di bambino: grazia, ingenuità*) childlike; **asilo infantile** nursery school; **letteratura infantile** children's books *pl* **b** (*immaturo: adulto, azione*) childish, infantile.

infantilismo [infanti'lizmo] SM infantilism.

infanzia [in'fantsja] SF **a** (*periodo*) childhood; **prima infanzia** infancy, babyhood **b** (*bambini*) children *pl*; **l'infanzia abbandonata** abandoned children.

infarcire [infar'tʃire] VT: **infarcire (di)** to fill (with), stuff (with).

infarinare [infari'nare] VT to cover with (*o* sprinkle with *o* dip in) flour; **infarinare di zucchero** to sprinkle with sugar.

infarinatura [infarina'tura] SF (*fig: conoscenza superficiale*) smattering.

infarto [in'farto] SM (*Med*): **infarto (cardiaco)** heart attack.

infartuato, a [infartu'ato] 1 AGG who has suffered a heart attack. 2 SM/F person who has suffered a heart attack, cardiac patient; **reparto infartuati** cardiology (ward), ward for patients treated for heart attack.

infastidire [infasti'dire] 1 VT to annoy, irritate. 2 **infastidirsi** VIP to get annoyed *o* irritated.

infastidito, a [infasti'dito] AGG annoyed, irritated.

infaticabile [infati'kabile] AGG indefatigable, tireless, untiring.

infaticabilmente [infatikabil'mente] AVV indefatigably, tirelessly.

infatti [in'fatti] CONG as a matter of fact, in fact, actually.

infatuarsi [infatu'arsi] VIP: **infatuarsi di** to become infatuated with.

infatuazione [infatuat'tsjone] SF infatuation; **avere un'infatuazione per qn** to be infatuated with sb.

infausto, a [in'fausto] AGG (*infelice*) unhappy, unpropitious, unfavourable (*Brit*), unfavorable (*Am*); **presagio infausto** ill omen; **prognosi infausta** (*Med*) fatal prognosis.

infecondità [infekondi'ta] SF infertility.

infecondo, a [infe'kondo] AGG (*anche fig*) infertile.

infedele [infe'dele] 1 AGG unfaithful; **essere infedele a qn** to be unfaithful to sb. 2 SM/F (*Storia*) infidel.

infedeltà [infedel'ta] SF INV infidelity.

infelice [infe'litʃe] 1 AGG **a** (*persona, sguardo, vita*) unhappy; (*incontro, osservazione, posizione*) unfortunate; **una frase infelice** an unfortunate choice of words **b** (*mal riuscito: traduzione, lavoro*) bad, poor; **esito infelice** unsuccessful outcome. 2 SM/F poor wretch.

infelicità [infelitʃi'ta] SF (*gen*) unhappiness; (*inopportunità*) inopportuneness.

infeltrire [infel'trire] VI (*aus* essere), **infeltrirsi** VIP (*lana*) to become matted.

inferenza [infe'rɛntsa] SF inference.

inferiore [infe'rjore] 1 AGG (*parte, rango, velocità*) lower; (*quantità, numero*) smaller; (*qualità, intelligenza*) inferior; **inferiore alla media** below average; **il piano inferiore** the next floor down, the floor below; **inferiore a** (*numero, quantità*) less *o* smaller than; below; (*meno buono*) inferior to. 2 SM/F inferior.

inferiorità [inferjori'ta] SF inferiority; **complesso di inferiorità** inferiority complex.

inferire[1] [infe'rire] (*pass rem* **inferii**, *pp* **inferto**) VT IRREG: **inferire un colpo a** to strike.

inferire[2] [infe'rire] (*pass rem* **inferii**, *pp* **inferito**) VT IRREG (*dedurre*) to infer, deduce.

inferito, a [infe'rito] PP di **inferire[2]**.

infermeria [inferme'ria] SF (*gen*) infirmary; (*di scuola, nave*) sick bay.

infermiera [infer'mjɛra] SF nurse.

infermiere [infer'mjɛre] SM male nurse.

infermità [infermi'ta] SF INV (*stato*) infirmity; (*malattia*) illness ▶**infermità mentale** mental illness; (*Dir*) insanity.

infermo, a [in'fermo] 1 AGG (*fisicamente debole*) infirm; (*malato*) ill ▶**infermo di mente** mentally ill; (*Dir*) insane. 2 SM/F invalid.

infernale [infer'nale] AGG (*gen*) infernal; (*complotto, proposito*) diabolical; **fa un caldo infernale** (*fam*) it's roasting; **un tempo infernale** (*fam*) hellish weather.

inferno [in'fɛrno] SM hell; **la mia vita è un inferno** my life is hell; **mandare qn all'inferno** to tell sb to go to hell; **soffrire le pene dell'inferno** to go through hell.

inferocire [infero'tʃire] 1 VT to make fierce. 2 VI (*aus* essere), **inferocirsi** VIP to become fierce.

inferriata [infer'rjata] SF grating.

inferto, a [in'ferto] PP di **inferire[1]**.

infervorare [infervo'rare] 1 VT to arouse enthusiasm in. 2 **infervorarsi** VIP: **infervorarsi (per qc)** to get excited (about sth), get carried away (by sth); **infervorarsi in una discussione** to get carried away in a discussion.

infestare [infes'tare] VT to infest; **infestato dai topi** infested with *o* overrun by mice; **le erbacce infestavano il giardino** the garden was full of *o* overgrown with weeds.

infettare [infet'tare] 1 VT (*gen*) to infect; (*acqua, aria*) to pollute, contaminate. 2 **infettarsi** VIP to become infected.

infettivo, a [infet'tivo] AGG infectious; **malattia infettiva** infectious disease.

infetto, a [in'fetto] AGG (*ferita*) infected; (*acque, aria*) polluted, contaminated.

infezione [infet'tsjone] SF infection.

infiacchire [infjak'kire] 1 VT (*anche fig*) to weaken, exhaust. 2 VI (*aus* essere), **infiacchirsi** VIP to grow weak.

infiammabile [infjam'mabile] AGG, SM inflammable.

infiammabilità [infjammabili'ta] SF flammability.

infiammare [infjam'mare] 1 VT (*gen*) to set fire to, set alight; (*Med: ferita, organo*) to inflame; **il suo discorso infiammò gli animi dei rivoltosi** his speech inflamed the rebels. 2 **infiammarsi** VIP (*gen*) to catch fire; (*Med*) to become inflamed; **infiammarsi d'amore** to be fired with love.

infiammatorio, ria, ri, rie [infjamma'tɔrjo] AGG inflammatory.

infiammazione [infjammat'tsjone] SF inflammation.

infiascare [infjas'kare] VT (*vino, olio*) to bottle.

inficiare [infi'tʃare] VT (*Dir: testimonianza, dichiarazione*) to invalidate.

infido, a [in'fido] AGG unreliable, treacherous.

infierire [infje'rire] VI (*aus* avere) **a** (*comportarsi con ferocia*): **infierire su** (*fisicamente*) to attack furiously; (*verbalmente*) to rage at **b** (*imperversare: epidemia,*

peste) to rage *o* sweep through.

infiggere [in'fiddʒere] VT IRREG: **infiggere qc in** to thrust *o* drive sth into.

infilare [infi'lare] **1** VT **a** (*introdurre: moneta, chiave*) to insert; **infilò le mani in tasca** he put *o* slipped his hands into his pockets; **le infilò un anello al dito** he put *o* slipped a ring on her finger; **infilò la mano nel cassetto** he slid his hand into the drawer; **puoi infilare anche questo nella busta?** can you put this in the same envelope?; **riesci ad infilarci ancora qualcosa?** (*in borsa, valigia*) can you squeeze anything else in?

b (*ago, perle*) to thread

c (*indossare: vestito*) to slip *o* put on; **infilarsi la giacca** to put on one's jacket

d (*imboccare: strada*) to turn into, take; **infilò la porta e se ne andò** he slipped through the door and off he went

e (*far seguire in successione*): **infilare uno sbaglio dopo l'altro** to make one mistake after the other; **infilare sette vittorie consecutive** to win seven matches *o* times on the trot; **abbiamo infilato cinque semafori verdi** we met five green lights in succession.

2 **infilarsi** VR (*introdursi*): **infilarsi in** to slip into; **infilarsi tra la folla** to merge into the crowd; **il gatto si è infilato lì sotto e non riesco a prenderlo** the cat slipped under there and I can't get at it; **infilarsi a letto** to slip into bed; **infilarsi in un taxi** to jump into a taxi.

infiltrarsi [infil'trarsi] VIP (*persona*): **infiltrarsi in** to infiltrate; (*fumo, gas, luce*) to penetrate into, filter into; (*umidità, liquido*) to penetrate, seep (into).

infiltrato, a [infil'trato] SM/F infiltrator.

infiltrazione [infiltrat'tsjone] SF (*vedi vb*) infiltration; penetration; seepage.

infilzare [infil'tsare] VT (*trafiggere*) to run through, pierce; (*sullo spiedo*) to skewer; (*infilare*) to string together; **infilzare un pollo sullo spiedo** to spit a chicken.

infimo, a ['infimo] AGG (*qualità*) very poor, lowest; **un albergo di infimo ordine** a third-rate hotel.

infine [in'fine] AVV (*alla fine*) finally; (*per concludere*) in short.

infingardo, a [infin'gardo] **1** AGG slothful.

2 SM/F sluggard.

infinità [infini'ta] SF infinity; **un'infinità di** an infinite number of; **ho un'infinità di cose da fare** I have masses of things to do.

infinitamente [infinita'mente] AVV (*anche fig*) infinitely; **mi dispiace infinitamente** I'm extremely sorry.

infinitesimale [infinitezi'male] AGG infinitesimal.

infinitesimo, a [infini'tezimo] AGG, SM infinitesimal.

infinito, a [infi'nito] **1** AGG (*gen*) infinite; **con infinito rammarico** with deep regret; **con infinita gioia** with great pleasure.

2 SM **a** (*Filosofia*): **l'infinito** the infinite; (*Mat, Fot*) infinity; **all'infinito** (*senza fine*) endlessly; (*Mat*) to infinity; **te l'ho ripetuto all'infinito!** I've told you a thousand times!

b (*Gramm*) infinitive; **all'infinito** in the infinitive.

infinocchiare [infinok'kjare] VT (*fam*) to hoodwink, bamboozle.

infiocchettare [infjokket'tare] VT (*pacchetto*) to tie up with ribbons.

infiorare [infjo'rare] VT to deck with flowers; **infiorare un discorso di citazioni** to embellish a speech with quotations.

infiorescenza [infjoreʃ'ʃɛntsa] SF inflorescence.

infirmare [infir'mare] VT (*Dir*) to invalidate.

infischiarsi [infis'kjarsi] VIP: **infischiarsi di** not to care about; **me ne infischio!** I couldn't care less!

infisso, a [in'fisso] **1** PP di **infiggere**.

2 SM (*di porta, finestra*) frame.

infittire [infit'tire] **1** VT to thicken.

2 VI (*aus* **essere**), **infittirsi** VIP to become thicker, thicken.

inflazionare [inflattsjo'nare] VT (*Econ*) to inflate; **inflazionare un'espressione** to overwork an expression; **un titolo di studio inflazionato** an overrated qualification.

inflazione [inflat'tsjone] SF **a** (*Econ*) inflation
▶ **inflazione galoppante** galloping inflation
▶ **inflazione strisciante** creeping inflation

b (*pegg: quantità esagerata*) proliferation; **un'inflazione di telefonini** a proliferation of mobile phones; **un'inflazione di laureati in medicina** an over-abundance of people graduating in medicine.

inflazionistico, a, ci, che [inflattsjo'nistiko] AGG (*Econ*) inflationary.

inflessibile [infles'sibile] AGG (*gen*) inflexible; (*carattere*) unyielding; (*volontà*) iron *attr*.

inflessibilità [inflessibili'ta] SF inflexibility.

inflessione [infles'sjone] SF inflexion.

infliggere [in'fliddʒere] VT IRREG (*pena, castigo*) to inflict; (*multa*) to impose.

inflissi *ecc* [in'flissi] VB vedi **infliggere**.

inflitto, a [in'flitto] PP di **infliggere**.

influente [influ'ɛnte] AGG influential.

influenza [influ'ɛntsa] SF **a** (*ascendente, peso*) influence; **è una persona che ha influenza** he's an influential person; **avere influenza su qn/qc** to have an influence on sb/sth; **subire l'influenza di qn/qc** to be influenced by sb/sth; **zona o sfera d'influenza** (*Pol*) sphere of influence

b (*Med*) influenza, flu; **prendere l'influenza** to catch *o* get (the) flu.

influenzabile [influen'tsabile] AGG easily influenced.

influenzale [influen'tsale] AGG (*Med*) influenza *attr*.

influenzare [influen'tsare] VT to influence, have an influence on; **lasciarsi o farsi influenzare** to be (easily) influenced.

influenzato, a [influen'tsato] AGG (*ammalato*): **essere influenzato** to have (the) flu; **è a letto influenzato** he's in bed with flu.

influire [influ'ire] VI (*aus* **avere**): **influire su** to influence, affect.

influsso [in'flusso] SM influence.

I.N.F.N. [i'ɛnne'ɛffe'ɛnne] SIGLA M = *Istituto Nazionale di Fisica Nucleare*.

infocare [info'kare] = **infuocare**.

infocato, a [info'kato] AGG = **infuocato**.

infognarsi [infoɲ'ɲarsi] VIP (*fam*) to get into a mess; **infognarsi in un mare di debiti** to be up to one's *o* eyes in debt.

in folio [in 'fɔljo] AGG INV: **edizione in folio** folio edition.

infoltire [infol'tire] **1** VT to thicken, make thicker.

2 VI (*aus* **essere**), **infoltirsi** VIP to become thicker, thicken.

infondatezza [infonda'tettsa] SF groundlessness.

infondato, a [infon'dato] AGG unfounded, groundless.

infondere [in'fondere] VT IRREG: **infondere qc in qn** to instil (*Brit*) *o* instill (*Am*) sth in sb; **infondere fiducia in qn** to inspire sb with confidence.

inforcare [infor'kare] VT **a** (*prendere con la forca*) to fork

(up) **b** (*bicicletta, cavallo*) to mount, get on; (*occhiali*) to put on.

informale [infor'male] AGG informal.

informare [infor'mare] ☐ VT to inform, tell; **informare qn di qc** to inform sb of *o* about sth, tell sb of *o* about sth. ☐ **informarsi** VIP to make inquiries; **informarsi di** *o* **su** to inquire about, ask about, find out about; **un'altra volta informati!** next time make sure you're better informed!

informatica [infor'matika] SF (*scienza*) computer science, computing; (*tecnica*) data processing.

informatico, a, ci, che [infor'matiko] AGG (*settore*) computer *attr*.

informativa [informa'tiva] SF (*Amm*) office circular.

informativo, a [informa'tivo] AGG informative; **a titolo informativo** for information only.

informatizzare [informatid'dzare] VT to computerize.

informato, a [infor'mato] AGG informed; **tenersi informato** to keep o.s. (well-)informed.

informatore, trice [informa'tore] ☐ AGG informative. ☐ SM/F (*della polizia*) informer ▶ **informatore medico scientifico** representative (*of pharmaceutical company*).

informazione [informat'tsjone] SF **a** (*ragguaglio*) piece of information; **può darmi un'informazione?** can you give me some information?; **chiedere un'informazione** to ask for (some) information; **chiedere/prendere informazioni sul conto di qn** to ask for/get information about sb, to make inquiries about sb; **a titolo d'informazione** for information; **ufficio informazioni** information *o* inquiry office
b (*Inform*) information; **teoria dell'informazione** information theory
c (*Dir*) ▶ **informazione di garanzia** = **avviso di garanzia** ▶ **informazione genetica** (*Bio*) genetic code.

informe [in'forme] AGG formless, shapeless.

informicolarsi [informiko'larsi], **informicolirsi** [informiko'lirsi] VIP: **mi si è informicolata una gamba** I've got pins and needles in my leg.

infornare [infor'nare] VT to put in the oven.

infornata [infor'nata] SF (*anche fig*) batch.

infortunarsi [infortu'narsi] VIP to injure o.s., have an accident.

infortunato, a [infortu'nato] ☐ AGG injured, hurt. ☐ SM/F injured person.

infortunio, ni [infor'tunjo] SM accident ▶ **infortunio sul lavoro** industrial accident, accident at work.

infortunistica [infortu'nistika] SF study of (industrial) accidents.

infossamento [infossa'mento] SM (*nel terreno*) hollow, depression.

infossarsi [infos'sarsi] VIP (*terreno*) to sink; (*guance*) to become hollow.

infossato, a [infos'sato] AGG (*guance*) hollow; (*occhi*) deep-set; (: *per malattia*) sunken.

infradiciare [infradi'tʃare] ☐ VT (*inzuppare*) to soak, drench; (*marcire*) to rot. ☐ **infradiciarsi** VIP (*vedi vt*) to get soaked, get drenched; to rot.

infradiciato, a [infradi'tʃato] AGG soaked, drenched.

infrangere [in'frandʒere] VB IRREG ☐ VT (*legge, patto*) to violate, break; (*vetro, vaso*) to smash. ☐ **infrangersi** VIP (*onde*) to break, smash; **le onde s'infrangevano sugli scogli** the waves were breaking on the rocks.

infrangibile [infran'dʒibile] AGG unbreakable.

infranto, a [in'franto] ☐ PP di **infrangere**. ☐ AGG (*anche fig*: *cuore*) broken.

infrarosso, a [infra'rosso] AGG, SM infrared.

infrasettimanale [infrasettima'nale] AGG midweek *attr*.

infrastruttura [infrastrut'tura] SF infrastructure.

infrasuono [infra'swɔno] SM infrasound.

infrazione [infrat'tsjone] SF infringement; **infrazione al codice della strada** traffic offence.

infreddatura [infredda'tura] SF slight cold.

infreddolire [infreddo'lire] VI (*aus* **essere**), **infreddolirsi** VIP to get cold.

infreddolito, a [infreddo'lito] AGG cold, chilled; **sono tutto infreddolito** I'm chilled to the bone.

infrequente [infre'kwɛnte] AGG infrequent, rare.

infrequentemente [infrekwente'mente] AVV infrequently, rarely.

infrollire [infrol'lire] VI (*aus* **essere**), **infrollirsi** VIP (*selvaggina*) to become high.

infruttuoso, a [infruttu'oso] AGG (*anche fig*) unfruitful, fruitless.

infuocare [infwo'kare] ☐ VT to make red-hot. ☐ **infuocarsi** VIP (*metallo*) to become red-hot; (*fig*: *persona*) to become excited.

infuocato, a [infwo'kato] AGG (*metallo*) red-hot; (*sabbia*) burning; (*discorso*) heated, passionate.

infuori [in'fwɔri] AVV **a** : **infuori** [OR] **all'infuori** (*sporgere*) out, outwards; **avere i denti/gli occhi infuori** to have prominent *o* protuberant teeth/eyes **b** : **all'infuori di** (*eccetto*) except, apart from, with the exception of; **non so altro all'infuori di questo** that's all I know.

infuriare [infu'rjare] ☐ VT to enrage, make furious. ☐ VI (*aus* **avere**) (*tempesta, vento*) to rage. ☐ **infuriarsi** VIP to fly into a rage.

infuriato, a [infu'rjato] AGG furious.

infusione [infu'zjone] SF (*operazione*) infusion; (*infuso*) infusion, herb tea; **lasciare in infusione** to leave to infuse.

infuso, a [in'fuzo] ☐ PP di **infondere**. ☐ AGG: **scienza infusa** (*anche iro*) innate knowledge. ☐ SM infusion, herb tea ▶ **infuso di camomilla** camomile tea.

Ing. ABBR = **ingegnere**.

ingabbiare [ingab'bjare] VT (*animali*) to (put in a) cage; (*fig*: *persona*) to cage in.

ingaggiare [ingad'dʒare] VT (*assumere*: *operai*) to take on, hire; (: *Sport*: *giocatore*) to sign; **ingaggiare battaglia** (*Mil*) to engage the enemy.

ingaggio, gi [in'gaddʒo] SM (*di operaio*) taking on, hiring; (*Sport*) signing; (: *somma*) signing-on fee.

ingagliardire [ingaʎʎar'dire] ☐ VT to strengthen, to invigorate. ☐ VI (*aus* **essere**), **ingagliardirsi** VIP to grow stronger.

ingannare [ingan'nare] ☐ VT (*imbrogliare*) to deceive; (*tradire*: *moglie, marito*) to cheat on, be unfaithful to; **le apparenze spesso ingannano** appearances are often deceptive; **ingannare il tempo** to while away the time; **abbiamo giocato a carte per ingannare l'attesa** while we waited we played cards to kill time. ☐ **ingannarsi** VIP to be mistaken, be wrong; **ingannarsi sul conto di qn** to be mistaken *o* wrong about sb.

ingannatore, trice [inganna'tore] AGG (*gen*) deceptive; (*persona, sguardo*) deceitful.

ingannevole [ingan'nevole] AGG (*gen*) deceptive; (*consi-*

glio) misleading.

inganno [in'ganno] SM (*imbroglio*) deceit, deception; (*menzogna, frode*) con, swindle; (*insidia*) trick; (*illusione*) illusion; **trarre in inganno** to deceive, mislead; **con l'inganno** by a trick; **inganno dei sensi** sensory illusion.

ingarbugliare [ingarbuʎ'ʎare] [1] VT (*fili, corde*) to tangle; (*fig: situazione*) to muddle, confuse.

[2] **ingarbugliarsi** VIP (*fili, corde, capelli*) to get tangled; (*fig: situazione*) to become confused o muddled.

ingarbugliato, a [ingarbuʎ'ʎato] AGG (*vedi vb*) tangled; muddled, confused.

ingegnarsi [indʒeɲ'ɲarsi] VIP to use one's ingenuity; **non avevamo l'occorrente ma ci siamo ingegnati** we didn't have what we needed but we made do; **ingegnarsi per vivere** to live by one's wits; **basta ingegnarsi un po'** you just need a bit of ingenuity.

ingegnere [indʒeɲ'ɲere] SM engineer ▶ **ingegnere civile** civil engineer ▶ **ingegnere navale** naval engineer.

ingegneria [indʒeɲɲe'ria] SF engineering.

ingegno [in'dʒeɲɲo] SM **a** (*intelligenza*) intelligence, brains *pl*; (*attitudine, talento*) talent; (*ingegnosità*) ingenuity; **avere dell'ingegno** to have a creative mind; **aguzzare l'ingegno** to sharpen one's wits; **un'alzata d'ingegno** (*anche iro*) a bright idea

b (*persona*) mind; **è un bell'ingegno** he has a good brain; **i più grandi ingegni del secolo** the greatest minds of the century.

ingegnosamente [indʒeɲɲosa'mente] AVV ingeniously.

ingegnosità [indʒeɲɲosi'ta] SF ingenuity.

ingegnoso, a [indʒeɲ'ɲoso] AGG ingenious, clever.

ingelosire [indʒelo'sire] [1] VT to make jealous.

[2] VI (*aus* **essere**), **ingelosirsi** VIP to become jealous.

ingente [in'dʒɛnte] AGG huge, enormous.

ingentilire [indʒenti'lire] [1] VT to refine, civilize.

[2] **ingentilirsi** VIP to become more refined o civilized.

ingenuamente [indʒenua'mente] AVV naïvely, ingenuously.

ingenuità [indʒenui'ta] SF naïvety, ingenuousness.

ingenuo, a [in'dʒɛnuo] [1] AGG naïve, ingenuous.

[2] SM/F: **è un ingenuo** he is naïve; **fare l'ingenuo** to act the innocent.

ingerenza [indʒe'rɛntsa] SF interference.

ingerire [indʒe'rire] VT to ingest.

ingessare [indʒes'sare] VT to put in plaster.

ingessatura [indʒessa'tura] SF plaster (cast).

ingestione [indʒes'tjone] SF ingestion.

Inghilterra [ingil'tɛrra] SF: **l'Inghilterra** England.

inghiottire [ingjot'tire] VT (*anche fig*) to swallow; **la barca fu inghiottita dai flutti** the boat was swallowed up o engulfed by the waves; **essere inghiottito dal buio** to be swallowed up by the darkness; **ne ha inghiottite tante nella vita** (*fig: dispiaceri*) he's had so much to put up with in life.

inghippo [in'gippo] SM trick.

ingiallire [indʒal'lire] [1] VT to turn yellow.

[2] VI (*aus* **essere**), **ingiallirsi** VIP to (turn o go) yellow.

ingiallito, a [indʒal'lito] AGG yellowed.

ingigantire [indʒigan'tire] [1] VT (*immagine*) to enlarge, magnify; (*fig: problema*) to exaggerate.

[2] VI (*aus* **essere**), **ingigantirsi** VIP to become gigantic o enormous.

inginocchiarsi [indʒinok'kjarsi] VIP to kneel (down); **essere inginocchiato** to be kneeling down, be on one's knees.

inginocchiatoio, oi [indʒinokkja'tojo] SM prie-dieu.

ingioiellare [indʒojel'lare] [1] VT to bejewel, adorn with jewels.

[2] **ingioiellarsi** VR to put on one's jewels.

ingiù [in'dʒu] AVV down, downwards; **con la testa all'ingiù** head downwards; (*capovolto*) upside down.

ingiungere [in'dʒundʒere] VT IRREG: **ingiungere a qn di fare qc** to enjoin o order sb to do sth.

ingiuntivo, a [indʒun'tivo] AGG (*Dir*): **decreto ingiuntivo** order to pay.

ingiunto, a [in'dʒunto] PP di **ingiungere**.

ingiunzione [indʒun'tsjone] SF injunction, command ▶ **ingiunzione di pagamento** final demand.

ingiuria [in'dʒurja] SF (*insulto*) insult; **coprire qn di ingiurie** to heap abuse on sb; **le ingiurie del tempo** the ravages of time.

ingiuriare [indʒu'rjare] VT to insult, abuse.

ingiurioso, a [indʒu'rjoso] AGG insulting, abusive.

ingiustamente [indʒusta'mente] AVV unjustly.

ingiustificabile [indʒustifi'kabile] AGG unjustifiable.

ingiustificato, a [indʒustifi'kato] AGG unjustified; **assenza ingiustificata** unexplained absence; (*Scol*) absence without permission; (*Mil*) absence without leave.

ingiustizia [indʒus'tittsja] SF injustice; **ha commesso un'ingiustizia** he was unjust, he acted unjustly; **è un'ingiustizia!** that's not fair!

ingiusto, a [in'dʒusto] AGG unjust, unfair; **essere ingiusto con qn** to be unfair o unjust to sb.

inglese [in'glese] [1] AGG English; **andarsene** o **filarsela all'inglese** to take French leave.

[2] SM/F Englishman/Englishwoman; **gli Inglesi** the English, English people.

[3] SM (*lingua*) English; **parlare (l')inglese** to speak English.

inglorioso, a [inglo'rjoso] AGG (*privo di gloria*) inglorious; (*ignominioso*) ignominious.

ingobbire [ingob'bire] VI (*aus* **essere**), **ingobbirsi** VIP to become stooped.

ingoiare [ingo'jare] VT (*inghiottire*) to swallow; (: *in fretta*) to gulp (down); (*fig*) to swallow (up); **se l'ingoiò in un boccone** he swallowed it in one go; **furono ingoiati dai flutti** they were swallowed up o engulfed by the waves; **è stato un boccone amaro da ingoiare** (*fig*) it was a bitter pill to swallow; **ha dovuto ingoiare tante amarezze** he has had to endure so many disappointments; **ha dovuto ingoiare il rospo** he had to accept the situation, whether he liked it or not.

ingolfare [ingol'fare] [1] VT (*Aut*) to flood.

[2] **ingolfarsi** VIP (*Aut*) to flood; **ingolfarsi nei debiti** to get up to one's o the ears in debt.

ingollare [ingol'lare] VT (*cibo*) to gulp down.

ingolosire [ingolo'sire] [1] VT: **ingolosire qn** to make sb's mouth water; (*fig*) to attract sb.

[2] VI (*aus* **essere**), **ingolosirsi** VIP to become greedy.

ingombrante [ingom'brante] AGG cumbersome.

ingombrare [ingom'brare] VT (*strada*) to block, obstruct; (*stanza, tavolo*) to clutter up.

ingombro[1], a [in'gombro] AGG: **ingombro di** (*strada*) blocked by; (*stanza*) cluttered up with.

ingombro[2] [in'gombro] SM **a** obstacle; **essere d'ingombro** to be in the way; **per ragioni di ingombro** for reasons of space **b** (*di auto*) overall dimensions *pl*.

ingordamente [ingorda'mente] AVV greedily.

ingordigia [ingor'didʒa] SF: **ingordigia (di)** (*vedi agg*) greed

(for); avidity (for).

ingordo, a [in'gordo] [1] AGG: **ingordo (di)** (*cibo*) greedy (for); (*fig: denaro*) greedy *o* avid (for).
[2] SM/F glutton.

ingorgare [ingor'gare] [1] VT to block.
[2] **ingorgarsi** VIP to get blocked.

ingorgo, ghi [in'gorgo] SM **a** (*di tubo*) blockage, obstruction **b** (*anche:* **ingorgo stradale**) (traffic) jam.

ingozzare [ingot'tsare] [1] VT (*animali*) to fatten; **ingozzare (di cibo)** (*persona*) to stuff (with food).
[2] **ingozzarsi** VR: **ingozzarsi (di qc)** to stuff o.s. (with sth).

ingranaggio, gi [ingra'naddʒo] SM (*Tecn*) gear; (: *di orologio*) mechanism; **gli ingranaggi della burocrazia** the bureaucratic machinery; **essere preso nell'ingranaggio** (*fig*) to be caught in the system.

ingranare [ingra'nare] [1] VI (*aus avere*) (*Tecn*) to engage, mesh; **non riesco ad ingranare nel nuovo lavoro** I can't seem to get into my stride in the new job; **gli affari cominciano ad ingranare** business is beginning to move.
[2] VT: **ingranare la marcia** (*Aut*) to engage gear, get into gear.

ingrandimento [ingrandi'mento] SM (*di città, azienda*) development, growth, expansion; (*di casa*) extension; (*di strada*) widening; (*Ottica, Fis*) magnification; (*Fot*) enlargement; **lente d'ingrandimento** magnifying glass.

ingrandire [ingran'dire] [1] VT (*azienda, città*) to develop, expand; (*locale*) to extend; (*strada*) to widen; (*Ottica*) to magnify; (*Fot*) to enlarge; (*fig: storia: esagerare*) to embroider.
[2] VI (*aus essere*), **ingrandirsi** VIP (*gen*) to get larger *o* bigger; (*azienda, città*) to grow, expand; (*strada*) to get wider; (*potere*) to grow, increase; (*problema*) to become more serious *o* worse.

ingranditore [ingrandi'tore] SM (*Fot*) enlarger.

ingrassaggio, gi [ingras'saddʒo] SM greasing.

ingrassare [ingras'sare] [1] VT **a** (*animali*) to fatten (up); (*persone*) to make fat; **questo vestito ti ingrassa** this dress makes you look fat; **i dolci ingrassano** sweets are fattening
b (*lubrificare*) to grease
c (*concimare: terreno*) to manure.
[2] VI (*aus essere*), **ingrassarsi** VIP to get fat, put on weight; **sei molto ingrassato** you've put on a lot of weight; **ingrassarsi alle spalle altrui** (*fig*) to thrive at the expense of others.

ingrassatore [ingrassa'tore] SM (*dispositivo*) lubricator.

ingrasso [in'grasso] SM: **mettere all'ingrasso** to forcefeed; **essere all'ingrasso** to be forcefed.

ingratitudine [ingrati'tudine] SF ingratitude, ungratefulness.

ingrato, a [in'grato] [1] AGG (*persona*) ungrateful; (*lavoro*) thankless, unrewarding.
[2] SM/F ungrateful person; **sei un ingrato!** you're an ungrateful wretch!

ingraziarsi [ingrat'tsjarsi] VT: **ingraziarsi qn** to ingratiate o.s. with sb.

ingrediente [ingre'djɛnte] SM ingredient.

ingresso [in'grɛsso] SM **a** (*porta*) entrance, entry; (*atrio*) hall ▶**ingresso principale** main entrance ▶**ingresso di servizio** tradesmen's entrance
b (*accesso*) admission; **fare il proprio ingresso** to make one's entrance; **vietato l'ingresso** no admittance;

ingresso libero admission free; **biglietto d'ingresso** admission ticket, entrance ticket; **prezzo d'ingresso** cost of admission.

ingrossamento [ingrossa'mento] SM swelling.

ingrossare [ingros'sare] [1] VT (*spessore, patrimonio*) to increase; (*fiume, folla*) to swell; (*muscoli*) to develop; **ingrossare le file** (*Mil, fig*) to swell the ranks; **quest'abito ti ingrossa** this dress makes you look fat.
[2] VI (*aus essere*), **ingrossarsi** VIP (*vedi vt*) to increase; to swell; to develop; (*persona*) to put on weight.

ingrosso [in'grɔsso] [1] AVV: **all'ingrosso** (*Comm*) wholesale; (*all'incirca*) roughly, about; **prezzo all'ingrosso** wholesale price; **vendere all'ingrosso** [OR] **effettuare vendite all'ingrosso** to sell wholesale.
[2] SM: **un ingrosso di calzature** a shoe wholesaler.

ingrugnato, a [ingruɲ'ɲato] AGG grumpy.

inguaiare [ingwa'jare] (*fam*) [1] VT to get (sb) into trouble.
[2] **inguaiarsi** VR to get into trouble.

inguainare [ingwai'nare] VT to sheathe.

ingualcibile [ingwal'tʃibile] AGG crease-resistant.

inguaribile [ingwa'ribile] AGG (*anche fig*) incurable.

inguaribilmente [ingwaribil'mente] AVV incurably.

inguine ['ingwine] SM (*Anat*) groin.

ingurgitare [ingurdʒi'tare] VT to gulp down.

inibire [ini'bire] VT to inhibit.

inibito, a [ini'bito] [1] AGG inhibited.
[2] SM/F inhibited person.

inibitorio, ria, ri, rie [inibi'tɔrjo] AGG (*Psic*) inhibitory, inhibitive; (*Dir: provvedimento, misure*) restrictive.

inibizione [inibit'tsjone] SF inhibition.

iniettare [injet'tare] [1] VT to inject; **iniettare qc a qn** to inject sb with sth; **iniettarsi una sostanza stupefacente** to inject o.s. with a drug; **con gli occhi iniettati di sangue** with bloodshot eyes.
[2] **iniettarsi** VIP: **iniettarsi di sangue** (*occhi*) to become bloodshot.

iniettore [injet'tore] SM (*Tecn*) injector.

iniezione [injet'tsjone] SF **a** (*Med*) injection; **fare** *o* **farsi fare un'iniezione** to get an injection; **fare un'iniezione (a qn)** to give (sb) an injection; **dare un'iniezione di fiducia a qn** to boost sb's morale *o* confidence **b** (*Aut*): **motore a iniezione** injection engine.

inimicare [inimi'kare] [1] VT to alienate, make hostile; **si è inimicato gli amici di un tempo** he has alienated his old friends.
[2] **inimicarsi** VIP: **inimicarsi con qn** to fall out with sb.

inimicizia [inimi'tʃittsja] SF enmity, animosity.

inimitabile [inimi'tabile] AGG inimitable.

inimitabilmente [inimitabil'mente] AVV inimitably.

inimmaginabile [inimmadʒi'nabile] AGG unimaginable.

ininfiammabile [ininfjam'mabile] AGG non-flammable.

inintelligibile [inintelli'dʒibile] AGG unintelligible.

ininterrottamente [ininterrotta'mente] AVV non-stop, continuously; **è piovuto ininterrottamente per 2 settimane** it rained non-stop *o* continuously for 2 weeks.

ininterrotto, a [ininter'rotto] AGG (*fila*) continuous, unbroken; (*viavai, rumore*) constant.

iniquamente [inikwa'mente] AVV iniquitously.

iniquità [inikwi'ta] SF INV (*qualità*) iniquity; (*atto*) wicked action.

iniquo, a [i'nikwo] AGG iniquitous.

iniziale [init'tsjale] [1] AGG initial; **stipendio iniziale** starting salary.
[2] SF initial; **firmare con le iniziali** to initial.

inizializzare [inittsjalid'dzare] VT (*Inform*) to boot.

inizialmente [inittsjal'mente] AVV initially, at first.

iniziare [init'tsjare] ①VT **a** (*cominciare*) to begin, start; (*dibattito, ostilità*) to open; **iniziare a fare qc** to start doing sth **b** (*person: a un culto*) to initiate into; (: *a un'attività*) to introduce to.

②VI (*aus essere*) to begin, start.

iniziativa [inittsja'tiva] SF (*gen*) initiative; **di propria iniziativa** on one's own initiative; **spirito d'iniziativa** spirit of initiative, drive ►**iniziativa privata** (*Comm*) private enterprise.

iniziato, a [init'tsjato] ①AGG (*a un culto*) initiated.

②SM/F initiate; **gli iniziati** the initiated.

iniziatore, trice [inittsja'tore] SM/F initiator.

iniziazione [inittsjat'tsjone] SF initiation.

inizio, zi [i'nittsjo] SM beginning, start; **fin dall'inizio** from the beginning; **all'inizio** at the beginning, at the start; **essere agli inizi** (*progetto, lavoro ecc*) to be in the initial stages; **dare inizio a qc** to start sth, get sth going.

in loco [in 'loko] AVV (*sul posto*) on the spot.

innaffiare ecc [innaf'fjare] = **annaffiare** ecc.

innalzamento [innaltsa'mento] SM (*gen*) raising.

innalzare [innal'tsare] ①VT (*gen: sollevare*) to raise; (*costruire: monumento*) to erect; **innalzare gli occhi al cielo** to raise one's eyes to heaven; **innalzare al trono** to raise to the throne.

②**innalzarsi** VIP to rise.

innamoramento [innamora'mento] SM falling in love.

innamorare [innamo'rare] ①VT to enchant, charm; **un viso che innamora** an enchanting *o* a delightful face.

②**innamorarsi** VR (*uso reciproco*) to fall in love (with each other).

③VIP: **innamorarsi (di)** to fall in love (with).

innamorato, a [innamo'rato] ①AGG: **innamorato (di)** (*anche fig: di lavoro ecc*) in love (with), very fond (of); **è innamorato del suo bambino** he dotes on his child.

②SM/F boyfriend/girlfriend; (*anche scherz*) sweetheart.

innanzi [in'nantsi] ①AVV **a** (*stato in luogo*) in front, ahead; (*moto a luogo*) forward, on; **stare** *o* **essere innanzi** to be in front *o* ahead; **farsi innanzi** to step forward **b** (*tempo*) before, earlier; **il giorno innanzi** the day before; **d'ora innanzi** from now on.

②PREP **a** (*davanti*): **innanzi a** in front of, before; **lo giuro innanzi a Dio** I swear before God **b** (*prima*) before; **innanzi tempo** ahead of time; **morire innanzi tempo** to die before one's time.

innanzitutto [innantsi'tutto] AVV (*soprattutto*) above all; (*per prima cosa*) first of all.

innato, a [in'nato] AGG innate, inborn.

innaturale [innatu'rale] AGG unnatural.

innegabile [inne'gabile] AGG undeniable.

innegabilmente [innegabil'mente] AVV undeniably.

inneggiare [inned'dʒare] VI (*aus avere*): **inneggiare a** to sing hymns to; (*fig*) to sing the praises of.

innervosire [innervo'sire] ①VT: **innervosire qn** (*rendere nervoso*) to make sb nervous; (*irritare*) to get on sb's nerves, annoy sb.

②**innervosirsi** VIP (*vedi vt*) to become nervous; to get irritated *o* upset.

innescare [innes'kare] VT **a** (*ordigno esplosivo*) to prime; (*fig: serie di eventi ecc*) to trigger off **b** (*amo*) to bait.

innesco, schi [in'nesko] SM primer, fuse.

innestare [innes'tare] VT (*Agr, Med*) to graft; (*Tecn*) to engage; (*Elettr: presa*) to put in.

innesto [in'nesto] SM (*Agr, Med*) graft; (: *azione*) grafting *no pl*; (*Tecn*) clutch; (*Elettr*) connection.

innevamento [inneva'mento] SM snowfall ►**innevamento artificiale** production of artificial snow.

innevato, a [inne'vato] AGG covered in snow; **le discese sono ben innevate quest'anno** the slopes have a good covering of snow this year.

inno ['inno] SM (*anche fig*) hymn ►**inno nazionale** national anthem.

innocente [inno'tʃɛnte] ①AGG **a** (*gen*) innocent; (*scherzo*) harmless **b** (*Dir*) not guilty.

②SM/F innocent person; (*bambino*) innocent.

innocentemente [innotʃɛnte'mente] AVV innocently; **l'ha detto innocentemente** he said it in all innocence.

innocenza [inno'tʃɛntsa] SF innocence.

innocuo, a [in'nɔkuo] AGG innocuous, harmless.

innominabile [innomi'nabile] AGG unmentionable.

innominato, a [innomi'nato] AGG unnamed.

innovare [inno'vare] VT to make changes to.

innovativo, a [innova'tivo] AGG innovative.

innovatore, trice [innova'tore] ①AGG innovatory.

②SM/F innovator.

innovazione [innovat'tsjone] SF innovation.

in nuce [in 'nutʃe] AVV (*in embrione*) in embryo; (*in breve*) in a nutshell.

innumerevole [innume'revole] AGG innumerable, countless.

inoculare [inoku'lare] VT (*Med*) to inoculate.

inodore [ino'dore], **inodoro, a** [ino'doro] AGG (*gen*) odourless (*Brit*), odorless (*Am*); (*fiore*) scentless.

inoffensivo, a [inoffen'sivo] AGG harmless.

inoltrare [inol'trare] ①VT (*Amm: pratica*) to pass on, forward; (*lettera*) to send on, forward.

②**inoltrarsi** VIP: **inoltrarsi (in)** to advance (into), go forward (into).

inoltrato, a [inol'trato] AGG: **a notte inoltrata** late at night; **a primavera inoltrata** late in the spring.

inoltre [i'noltre] AVV besides, moreover.

inoltro [i'noltro] SM (*Amm*) forwarding.

inondare [inon'dare] VT (*anche fig*) to flood; (*mercato*): **inondare (di)** to flood (with); **la folla inondava la piazza** the crowd flooded into the square; **il sole inondava la stanza** the sun flooded into the room; **le lacrime le inondavano il viso** her face was bathed in tears.

inondazione [inondat'tsjone] SF flood, flooding *no pl*.

inoperante [inope'rante] AGG (*provvedimento, piano*) inoperative.

inoperosità [inoperosi'ta] SF idleness, inactivity.

inoperoso, a [inope'roso] AGG idle, inactive.

inopinabile [inopi'nabile] AGG (*letter: impensabile*) unimaginable.

inopinato, a [inopi'nato] AGG (*letter*) unexpected.

inopportunamente [inopportuna'mente] AVV (*arrivare*) inopportunely; **commentare inopportunamente** to make an ill-timed remark.

inopportunità [inopportuni'ta] SF (*vedi agg*) inappropriateness; untimeliness.

inopportuno, a [inoppor'tuno] AGG (*poco adatto*) inappropriate; (*intempestivo*) untimely, ill-timed; **è arrivato in un momento inopportuno** he arrived at an awkward *o* inopportune moment.

inoppugnabile [inoppuɲ'ɲabile] AGG incontrovertible.

inorganicità [inorganitʃi'ta] SF (*di sostanza*) inorganic

nature; (*di libro, discorso*) lack of structure.

inorganico, a, ci, che [inor'ganiko] AGG inorganic.

inorgoglire [inorgoʎ'ʎire] 1 VT to make proud. 2 VI (*aus* **essere**), **inorgoglirsi** VIP to become proud; **inorgoglirsi per qc** to pride o.s. on sth.

inorgoglito, a [inorgoʎ'ʎito] AGG proud.

inorridire [inorri'dire] 1 VT to horrify. 2 VI (*aus* **essere**) to be horrified.

inospitale [inospi'tale] AGG inhospitable.

inosservante [inosser'vante] AGG: **essere inosservante di** to fail to comply with.

inosservanza [inosser'vantsa] SF non-observance.

inosservato, a [inosser'vato] AGG (*non notato*) unobserved; (*non rispettato*) not observed, not kept; **passare inosservato** to go unobserved, escape notice.

inossidabile [inossi'dabile] AGG (*acciaio*) stainless.

inox ['inoks] AGG INV (*acciaio*) stainless; (*pentole, posate, lavello*) stainless steel.

in primis [in 'primis] AVV first of all, firstly.

I.N.P.S. [inps] SIGLA M (= *Istituto Nazionale Previdenza Sociale*) social security service.

input ['input] SM INV (*Inform*) input; (*fig*: *avvio*): **dare l'input ad un'iniziativa** to set a project in motion; **un comportamento condizionato da input esterni** behaviour conditioned by external factors.

inquadramento [inkwadra'mento] SM (*Amm*) placement ▶ **inquadramento unico** integrated salary scheme.

inquadrare [inkwa'drare] 1 VT **a** (*foto, immagine*) to frame; **inquadrare un autore nel suo periodo** to place an author in his historical context; **l'ho inquadrato appena l'ho visto** I recognized his sort as soon as I saw him **b** (*Mil*) to regiment; (*personale*) to organize. 2 **inquadrarsi** VIP (*collocarsi*): **inquadrarsi in** to fit in.

inquadratura [inkwadra'tura] SF (*Cine, Fot*: *atto*) framing; (*: immagine*) shot; (*: sequenza*) sequence.

inqualificabile [inkwalifi'kabile] AGG unspeakable.

inquietante [inkwje'tante] AGG disturbing, worrying.

inquietare [inkwje'tare] 1 VT (*preoccupare*) to disturb, worry; (*irritare*) to upset. 2 **inquietarsi** VIP (*vedi vt*) to worry, become anxious; to get upset.

inquieto, a [in'kwjɛto] AGG (*agitato*) restless; (*preoccupato*) worried, anxious; (*arrabbiato*) upset.

inquietudine [inkwje'tudine] SF anxiety, worry.

inquilino, a [inkwi'lino] SM/F tenant.

inquinamento [inkwina'mento] SM pollution ▶ **inquinamento acustico** noise pollution ▶ **inquinamento delle prove** (*Dir*) tampering with the evidence.

inquinare [inkwi'nare] VT to pollute.

inquinato, a [inkwi'nato] AGG polluted.

inquirente [inkwi'rɛnte] AGG (*Dir*): **magistrato inquirente** examining (*Brit*) *o* committing (*Am*) magistrate; **commissione inquirente** commission of inquiry.

inquisire [inkwi'zire] VT, VI (*aus* **avere**) to investigate.

inquisito, a [inkwi'zito] 1 AGG (*persona*) under investigation. 2 SM person under investigation.

inquisitore, trice [inkwizi'tore] 1 AGG (*sguardo*) inquiring. 2 SM inquisitor.

inquisizione [inkwizit'tsjone] SF inquisition.

insabbiamento [insabbja'mento] SM (*fig*: *di pratica*) shelving.

insabbiare [insab'bjare] 1 VT (*fig*: *pratica*) to shelve.

2 **insabbiarsi** VIP (*barca*) to run aground; (*fig*: *pratica*) to be shelved.

insaccare [insak'kare] VT (*grano, farina ecc*) to bag, put into sacks; (*carne*) to put into sausage skins.

insaccati [insak'kati] SMPL sausages.

insalata [insa'lata] SF (*pianta*) lettuce (*or other green-leaf vegetable*); (*piatto*) salad ▶ **insalata mista** mixed salad ▶ **insalata russa** Russian salad.

insalatiera [insala'tjɛra] SF salad bowl.

insalubre [insa'lubre] AGG insalubrious (*frm*), unhealthy.

insalubrità [insalubri'ta] SF insalubrity (*frm*), unhealthiness.

insanabile [insa'nabile] AGG (*piaga*) which cannot be healed; (*fig*: *situazione*) irremediable; **fra di loro si è creata una rottura insanabile** a rift has developed between them which cannot be healed.

insanguinare [insangwi'nare] 1 VT to stain with blood; **arrivò tutto insanguinato** he arrived all covered in blood; **una feroce rivolta insanguinò la Francia** France was plunged into a bloody revolution. 2 **insanguinarsi** VR to get covered in blood.

insania [in'sanja] SF (*letter*) insanity.

insano, a [in'sano] AGG (*letter*: *gesto, proposito*) insane.

insaponare [insapo'nare] VT to soap; (*con sapone da barba*) to lather; **insaponarsi le mani** to soap one's hands.

insaponata [insapo'nata] SF: **dare un'insaponata a ˙qc** to give sth a (quick) soaping.

insaponatura [insapona'tura] SF soaping.

insapore [insa'pore], **insaporo, a** [insa'poro] AGG tasteless, insipid.

insaporire [insapo'rire] 1 VT to flavour (*Brit*) *o* flavor (*Am*); (*con spezie*) to season. 2 **insaporirsi** VIP to gain flavo(u)r.

insaputa [insa'puta] SF: **all'insaputa di qn** without sb's knowledge, unbeknown to sb, without sb knowing.

insaturo, a [in'saturo] AGG (*Chim*) unsaturated.

insaziabile [insat'tsjabile] AGG insatiable.

insaziabilmente [insattsjabil'mente] AVV insatiably.

inscatolare [inskato'lare] VT (*frutta, carne*) to can.

inscatolatrice [inskatola'tritʃe] SF canning machine.

inscenare [inʃe'nare] VT (*Teatro*) to stage, put on; (*fig*: *protesta, sciopero*) to stage; **inscenare una commedia** (*fig*) to put on an act.

inscindibile [inʃin'dibile] AGG (*fattori*) inseparable; (*legame*) indissoluble.

inscritto, a [in'skritto] PP di **inscrivere**.

inscrivere [in'skrivere] VT IRREG (*Geom*) to inscribe.

insecchire [insek'kire] 1 VT (*seccare*) to dry up; (*: piante*) to wither. 2 VI (*aus* **essere**), **insecchirsi** VIP (*vedi vt*) to dry up, become dry; to wither.

insediamento [insedja'mento] SM **a** (*Amm*: *in carica, ufficio*) installation **b** (*villaggio, colonia*) settlement.

insediare [inse'djare] 1 VT (*Amm*) to install. 2 **insediarsi** VIP **a** (*Amm*) to take up office **b** (*colonia, profughi ecc*) to settle; (*Mil*) to take up positions.

insegna [in'seɲɲa] SF **a** (*stradale, di negozio*) sign ▶ **insegna al neon** neon sign **b** (*bandiera*) flag, banner; (*emblema*) emblem, sign; **insegne** SFPL (*decorazioni*) insignia *pl*; **un'estate all'insegna del maltempo** a summer marked by bad weather.

insegnamento [inseɲɲa'mento] SM teaching; **che ti serva da insegnamento** let this be a lesson to you; **trarre insegnamento da un'esperienza** to learn from an ex-

perience.

insegnante [inseɲˈɲante] [1] AGG teaching *attr.*
[2] SM/F teacher; **fare l'insegnante** to be a teacher; **insegnante di storia** history teacher ▶**insegnante di sostegno** support teacher.

insegnare [inseɲˈɲare] VT to teach; **insegnare alle elementari** to be primary school teacher; **insegnare a qn qc/a fare qc** to teach sb sth/(how) to do sth; **vi insegno io a comportarvi bene!** I'll teach you how to behave!; **come lei ben m'insegna...** (*iro*) as you will doubtless be aware ... .

inseguimento [insegwiˈmento] SM pursuit, chase; **darsi all'inseguimento di qn** to give chase to sb; **(gara di) inseguimento** (*Ciclismo*) pursuit (race).

inseguire [inseˈgwire] VT (*anche fig*) to pursue, chase.

inseguitore, trice [insegwiˈtore] SM/F pursuer; (*Ciclismo*) track rider.

insellare [inselˈlare] [1] VT (*curvare*) to curve.
[2] **insellarsi** VIP (*curvarsi*) to sag.

inselvatichire [inselvatiˈkire] [1] VT (*persona*) to make unsociable.
[2] VI (*aus* essere), **inselvatichirsi** VIP (*giardino, animale domestico*) to grow wild; (*persona*) to become unsociable.

inseminazione [inseminatˈtsjone] SF insemination ▶**inseminazione artificiale** artificial insemination.

insenatura [insenaˈtura] SF inlet, creek.

insensatamente [insensataˈmente] AVV foolishly, stupidly.

insensatezza [insensaˈtettsa] SF foolishness, stupidity.

insensato, a [insenˈsato] AGG senseless, stupid.

insensibile [insenˈsibile] AGG (*anche fig*) insensitive; **è insensibile al freddo** he doesn't feel the cold; **insensibile ai complimenti** indifferent to compliments.

insensibilità [insensibiliˈta] SF insensitivity, insensibility.

insensibilmente [insensibilˈmente] AVV insensitively.

inseparabile [insepaˈrabile] AGG inseparable.

insepolto, a [inseˈpolto] AGG unburied.

inserimento [inseriˈmento] SM (*gen*) insertion; **ha avuto problemi di inserimento nella nuova scuola** he has had problems settling in at his new school.

inserire [inseˈrire] [1] VT (*introdurre*) to insert; (*Elettr: spina*) to insert, put in; (*allegare*) to enclose; **inserire un annuncio sul giornale** to put *o* place an advertisement in the newspaper; **inserire un apparecchio in un circuito elettrico** to connect a machine to an electrical circuit.
[2] **inserirsi** VR: **inserirsi in** (*ambiente*) to fit into, become part of.
[3] **inserirsi** VIP: **inserirsi in** (*contesto*) to be a part of, be included in.

inserto [inˈsɛrto] SM (*pubblicazione*) insert, supplement ▶**inserto filmato** (film) clip.

inservibile [inserˈvibile] AGG useless.

inserviente [inserˈvjɛnte] SM/F attendant.

inserzione [inserˈtsjone] SF (*aggiunta*) insertion; (*avviso*) advertisement; **mettere un'inserzione sul giornale** to put *o* place an advertisement in the newspaper.

inserzionista, i, e [insertsjoˈnista] SM/F advertiser.

inserzionistico, a, ci, che [insertsjoˈnistiko] AGG: **spazio inserzionistico** advertising space.

insetticida, i, e [insettiˈtʃida] AGG, SM insecticide.

insettivoro, a [insettiˈvoro] [1] AGG insectivorous.
[2] SM insectivore.

insetto [inˈsɛtto] SM insect; **è un insetto** (*pegg: persona*)

he's a louse.

insicurezza [insicuˈrettsa] SF insecurity.

insicuro, a [insiˈkuro] AGG insecure.

insidia [inˈsidja] SF (*pericolo*) hidden danger; (*inganno*) trap, snare; **tendere un'insidia a qn** to lay *o* set a trap for sb.

insidiare [insiˈdjare] VT **a** (*Mil*) to harass **b** : **insidiare la vita di qn** to make an attempt on sb's life; **insidiare la virtù di una donna** to make an attempt on a woman's virtue.

insidiosamente [insidjosaˈmente] AVV insidiously.

insidioso, a [insiˈdjoso] AGG insidious.

insieme [inˈsjɛme] [1] AVV **a** together; **tutti insieme** all together; **stanno bene insieme** (*persone*) they get on well together; (*colori*) they go well together; **quei due stanno proprio bene insieme** (*coppia*) those two make a nice couple; **stanno insieme da due anni** they have been (going out) together for two years; **questo libro non sta più insieme** this book is falling apart
b (*contemporaneamente*) at the same time; **vuol fare troppe cose insieme** she wants to do too many things at the same time; **abbiamo finito insieme** we finished together *o* at the same time; **l'ha bevuto tutto insieme** (*in una volta*) he drank it at one go *o* in one draught.
[2] : **insieme a** PREP together with; **bevilo insieme al succo di frutta** take it with a drink of fruit juice; **mettilo insieme al mio** put it along with mine.
[3] SM **a** (*totalità*) whole; **l'insieme degli elettori** the whole electorate; **l'insieme dei cittadini/degli edifici** all the citizens/buildings; **nell'insieme** on the whole; **bisogna considerare la cosa nell'insieme** *o* **nel suo insieme** we will have to take an overall view of the matter; **d'insieme** (*sguardo, veduta*) overall, general
b (*Mat, assortimento*) set; (*Moda*) outfit, ensemble; **nella stanza c'era uno strano insieme di persone/ oggetti** there was a strange collection of people/ objects in the room.

insiemistica [insjeˈmistika] SF (*Mat*) set theory.

insigne [inˈsiɲɲe] AGG (*persona*) distinguished, eminent; (*città, monumento*) notable.

insignificante [insiɲɲifiˈkante] AGG (*gen*) insignificant; (*somma*) trifling, insignificant.

insignire [insiɲˈɲire] VT: **insignire qn di** to honour (*Brit*) *o* honor (*Am*) sb with, decorate sb with; **insignire qn del titolo di cavaliere** to knight sb.

insilare [insiˈlare] VT (*Agr: mangimi*) to ensile.

insincero, a [insinˈtʃɛro] AGG insincere.

insindacabile [insindaˈkabile] AGG unquestionable, unchallengeable; **la decisione è insindacabile** (*di giuria*) the decision is final.

insinuante [insinuˈante] AGG (*osservazione, sguardo*) insinuating; (*maniere*) ingratiating.

insinuare [insinuˈare] [1] VT **a** (*introdurre*): **insinuare qc in** to slip *o* slide sth into
b (*alludere*) to insinuate, imply; **fu lei ad insinuargli il sospetto che...** she was the one who created the suspicion in his mind *o* made him suspect that ...; **cosa vorresti insinuare?** what are you trying to insinuate?.
[2] **insinuarsi** VIP (*umidità, acqua*): **insinuarsi (in qc)** to seep in(to sth), penetrate (sth); (*dubbio*): **insinuarsi in** to creep into.
[3] **insinuarsi** VR (*persona*): **insinuarsi in** to worm one's way into, insinuate o.s. into.

insinuazione [insinuatˈtsjone] SF insinuation, innuendo;

fare insinuazioni su qn to make insinuations about sb.

insipido, a [in'sipido] AGG (anche fig) insipid.

insistente [insis'tɛnte] AGG (che insiste) insistent; (: pioggia, dolore) persistent.

insistentemente [insistente'mente] AVV repeatedly, persistently.

insistenza [insis'tɛntsa] SF (vedi agg) insistence; persistence; **chiedere con insistenza** to ask insistently.

insistere [in'sistere] VI IRREG (aus avere): **insistere (su qc/a fare qc)** to insist (on sth/on doing sth); **insistere (in qc/a fare qc)** (perseverare) to persist in sth/in doing sth.

insistito, a [insis'tito] PP di **insistere**.

insito, a ['insito] AGG: **insito (in)** inherent (in).

insoddisfacente [insoddisfa't∫ɛnte] AGG unsatisfactory.

insoddisfatto, a [insoddis'fatto] AGG (persona) dissatisfied; (desiderio) unfulfilled, unsatisfied.

insoddisfazione [insoddisfat'tsjone] SF dissatisfaction.

insofferente [insoffe'rɛnte] AGG (impaziente) impatient; (irrequieto) edgy.

insofferenza [insoffe'rɛntsa] SF impatience.

insolazione [insolat'tsjone] SF (Med) sunstroke; **prendere un'insolazione** to get sunstroke.

insolente [inso'lɛnte] **1** AGG insolent. **2** SM/F insolent person.

insolentemente [insolente'mente] AVV insolently.

insolentire [insolen'tire] **1** VI (aus essere) to grow insolent. **2** VT to insult, be rude to.

insolenza [inso'lɛntsa] SF (arroganza) insolence; (osservazione) insolent remark; **è stata un'insolenza da parte sua** (azione) that was a piece of insolence on his part.

insolito, a [in'sɔlito] AGG unusual, out of the ordinary, strange.

insolubile [inso'lubile] AGG **a** (problema) insoluble, insolvable **b** (sostanza) insoluble.

insoluto, a [inso'luto] AGG (problema) unsolved; (debito) unpaid, outstanding.

insolvente [insol'vɛnte] AGG (Dir) insolvent.

insolvenza [insol'vɛntsa] SF (Dir) insolvency.

insolvibile [insol'vibile] AGG (Dir) insolvent.

insomma [in'somma] **1** AVV (in breve, in conclusione) in short, all in all; (dunque) well. **2** ESCL: **insomma!** for heaven's sake!; **come stai? — insomma...!** how are you? — not too bad.

insondabile [inson'dabile] AGG unfathomable.

insonne [in'sɔnne] AGG (notte) sleepless.

insonnia [in'sɔnnja] SF insomnia, sleeplessness; **soffrire d'insonnia** to suffer from insomnia.

insonnolito, a [insonno'lito] AGG sleepy, drowsy.

insonorizzato, a [insonorid'dzato] AGG (stanza) soundproofed.

insonorizzazione [insonoriddzat'tsjone] SF soundproofing.

insopportabile [insoppor'tabile] AGG unbearable.

insopportabilmente [insopportabil'mente] AVV unbearably.

insopprimibile [insoppri'mibile] AGG unsuppressible, insuppressible.

insorgente [insor'dʒɛnte] AGG: **viste le insorgenti difficoltà...** given the problems which are arising o cropping up ... .

insorgenza [insor'dʒɛntsa] SF (di malattia) onset.

insorgere [in'sordʒere] VI IRREG (aus essere) **a** (ribellarsi): **insorgere (contro)** to rise up (against), rebel (against)

b (manifestarsi improvvisamente) to arise, come o crop up.

insormontabile [insormon'tabile] AGG (ostacolo) unsurmountable, insurmountable, insuperable.

insorsi ecc [in'sorsi] VB vedi **insorgere**.

insorto, a [in'sorto] **1** PP di **insorgere**. **2** AGG: **il popolo insorto** the rebels, the insurgents. **3** SM/F rebel, insurgent.

insospettabile [insospet'tabile] AGG **a** (al di sopra di ogni sospetto) above suspicion **b** (inatteso) unsuspected.

insospettato, a [insospet'tato] AGG unsuspected.

insospettire [insospet'tire] **1** VT to make suspicious, arouse suspicions in. **2** VI (aus essere), **insospettirsi** VIP: **insospettirsi (per/di qc)** to become suspicious (because of/about sth).

insostenibile [insoste'nibile] AGG **a** (posizione, teoria) untenable **b** (dolore, situazione) intolerable, unbearable; **le spese di manutenzione sono insostenibili** the maintenance costs are prohibitive.

insostituibile [insostitu'ibile] AGG (persona) irreplaceable; (aiuto, presenza) invaluable.

insozzare [insot'tsare] **1** VT **a** (pavimento) to (make) dirty **b** (fig: reputazione, memoria di qn) to tarnish, sully. **2** **insozzarsi** VR, VIP to get dirty.

insperabile [inspe'rabile] AGG: **la guarigione/salvezza era insperabile** there was no hope of a cure/of rescue; **abbiamo ottenuto risultati insperabili** the results we achieved were beyond our expectations.

insperato, a [inspe'rato] AGG unhoped-for.

inspiegabile [inspje'gabile] AGG inexplicable.

inspiegabilmente [inspjegabil'mente] AVV inexplicably.

inspirare [inspi'rare] VT to inhale, breathe in.

inspirazione [inspirat'tsjone] SF inhaling, breathing in.

instabile [in'stabile] AGG (carico, carattere, situazione) unstable; (tempo) unsettled, changeable; (umore) uncertain, changeable; (equilibrio) unsteady.

instabilità [instabili'ta] SF (gen) instability; (del tempo) changeability; (di umore) inconstancy.

installare [instal'lare] **1** VT (impianto, telefono) to install, put in. **2** **installarsi** VR: **installarsi in** (sistemarsi) to set up house, settle in; **si è installata in casa mia** (scherz) she has taken up residence at my house.

installazione [installat'tsjone] SF **a** (di telefono ecc) installation **b** (impianto) system ▶**installazioni di bordo** (Aer, Naut) on-board equipment.

instancabile [instan'kabile] AGG tireless, untiring.

instancabilmente [instankabil'mente] AVV tirelessly.

instaurare [instau'rare] **1** VT (regola, sistema) to establish, institute; (moda ecc) to introduce. **2** **instaurarsi** VIP to be o become established.

instaurazione [instaurat'tsjone] SF (vedi vt) establishment, institution; introduction.

instillare [instil'lare] VT to instil.

instillazione [instillat'tsjone] SF instillation, instillment (Brit), instilment (Am).

instradare [instra'dare] VT = **istradare**.

insù [in'su] AVV up, upwards; **guardare all'insù** to look up o upwards; **nasino all'insù** turned-up nose.

insubordinato, a [insubordi'nato] AGG insubordinate.

insubordinazione [insubordinat'tsjone] SF insubordination.

insuccesso [insut't∫ɛsso] SM failure, flop.

insudiciare [insudi't∫are] **1** VT to dirty, soil; (fig: reputa-

zione, nome) to sully, tarnish; **insudiciarsi i vestiti** to get one's clothes dirty, dirty one's clothes.

2 **insudiciarsi** VR, VIP to get dirty.

insufficiente [insuffi'tʃɛnte] AGG **a** : **insufficiente a** *o* **per** (*quantità*) insufficient (for); (*qualità*) inadequate (for); **200 sterline al mese sono insufficienti per vivere** £200 a month is not enough *o* sufficient to live on **b** (*Scol*: *voto*) unsatisfactory; (: *compito*) below standard.

insufficientemente [insuffitʃente'mente] AVV (*vedi agg a*) insufficiently; inadequately.

insufficienza [insuffi'tʃɛntsa] SF **a** (*di denaro, viveri*) shortage; (*di tempo, spazio*) lack; (*di preparazione*) inadequacy; (*Med*) insufficiency ▶ **insufficienza di prove** (*Dir*) lack of evidence
b (*Scol*) fail; **ho preso un'insufficienza in chimica** I got a fail in chemistry.

insulare [insu'lare] AGG island *attr*.

insulina [insu'lina] SF (*Chim*) insulin.

insulsaggine [insul'saddʒine] SF (*vedi agg*) dullness, insipidity; inanity; silliness.

insulso, a [in'sulso] AGG (*persona*) dull, insipid; (*osserva-zione*) inane, silly; (*film, romanzo*) crass, silly.

insultare [insul'tare] VT to insult.

insulto [in'sulto] SM insult, affront; **coprire qn di insulti** to hurl abuse at sb, heap abuse on sb.

insuperabile [insupe'rabile] AGG **a** (*ostacolo, difficoltà*) insuperable, unsurmountable, insurmountable **b** (*eccellente: qualità, prodotto*) unbeatable; (: *persona, interpretazione*) unequalled.

insuperato, a [insupe'rato] AGG unsurpassed, unequalled.

insuperbire [insuper'bire] 1 VT to make proud, make arrogant; **il successo lo ha insuperbito** success has gone to his head.
2 VI (*aus essere*), **insuperbirsi** VIP to become arrogant.

insurrezionale [insurrettsjo'nale] AGG insurrectionary.

insurrezione [insurret'tsjone] SF insurrection, revolt.

insussistente [insussis'tɛnte] AGG (*accusa, paura*) unfounded, groundless; (*pericolo*) non-existent.

insussistenza [insussis'tɛntsa] SF (*vedi agg*) groundlessness; non-existence.

intabarrato, a [intabar'rato] AGG well wrapped up, muffled up.

intaccabile [intak'kabile] AGG (*metallo*) subject to corrosion; (*fig: teoria*) open to criticism.

intaccare [intak'kare] VT **a** (*sogg: ruggine*) to corrode; (: *acido*) to eat into; **non vorrei intaccare i miei risparmi** I wouldn't want to break into my savings **b** (*fare tacche in*) to cut into, nick **c** (*infettare, fig: reputazione*) to affect, damage.

intacco, chi [in'takko] SM notch, nick.

intagliare [intaʎ'ʎare] VT (*pietre*) to engrave, carve; (*legno*) to carve.

intagliatore, trice [intaʎʎa'tore] SM/F engraver.

intaglio, gli [in'taʎʎo] SM intaglio.

intangibile [intan'dʒibile] AGG **a** (*eredità, patrimonio*) tied-up **b** (*fig: diritto*) inviolable; (: *differenza*) intangible.

intanto [in'tanto] AVV (*nel frattempo*) meanwhile, in the meantime; (*per cominciare*) just to begin with; **intanto che** while; **intanto che aspetti leggiti questo** you can read this while you're waiting; **puoi scusarti quanto vuoi, intanto il male è già stato fatto** it's all very well saying you're sorry, but (the fact remains that) the

damage has been done; **intanto prendi questo, poi ti darò il resto** take this for now *o* the time being and I'll give you the rest later.

intarsiare [intar'sjare] VT to inlay.

intarsio, si [in'tarsjo] SM (*arte, tecnica*) inlaying *no pl*, marquetry *no pl*; (*parte lavorata*) marquetry, inlay; **mobili lavorati a intarsio** inlaid furniture.

intasamento [intasa'mento] SM (*ostruzione*) blockage, obstruction; (*Aut: ingorgo*) traffic jam.

intasare [inta'sare] 1 VT (*tubo*) to block (up); (*traffico*) to hold up; **ho il naso intasato** I've got a blocked *o* stuffed-up nose.
2 **intasarsi** VIP to become choked *o* blocked.

intasato, a [inta'sato] AGG (*lavandino, naso, strada*) blocked.

intascare [intas'kare] VT (*denaro, premio*) to pocket.

intatto, a [in'tatto] AGG (*gen*) intact; (*puro*) unsullied; **la neve era intatta** there were no footprints in the snow.

intavolare [intavo'lare] VT (*discussione, trattative*) to open, start, enter into.

integerrimo, a [inte'dʒerrimo] AGG honest, upright; **è un uomo integerrimo** he's a man of the utmost integrity.

integrale [inte'grale] 1 AGG **a** (*gen*) complete; (*rimborso*) full; (*pane, farina*) wholemeal (*Brit*), wholewheat (*Am*); **edizione integrale** unabridged edition; **film in versione integrale** uncut version of a film **b** (*Mat*) integral.
2 SM (*Mat*) integral.

integralismo [integra'lizmo] SM integralism.

integralista, i, e [integra'lista] AGG, SM/F integralist.

integralmente [integral'mente] AVV in full, fully.

integrante [inte'grante] AGG: **essere parte integrante di** to be an integral part of.

integrare [inte'grare] 1 VT **a** (*completare*) to complete; (: *personale*) to bring up to strength; (: *stipendio, dieta ecc*) to supplement; **integra il proprio stipendio dando lezioni private** he supplements his income by giving private lessons **b** (*Sociol, Mat*) to integrate.
2 **integrarsi** VIP (*Sociol*) to become integrated.

integrativo, a [integra'tivo] AGG (*assegno*) supplementary; (*Scol*): **esame integrativo** *assessment test sat when changing schools.*

integrato, a [inte'grato] AGG (*Elettr*) integrated.

integratore [integra'tore] SM: **integratori alimentari** nutritional supplements.

integrazione [integrat'tsjone] SF integration.

integrità [integri'ta] SF **a** (*interezza: di patrimonio*) intact state; **tutelare l'integrità fisica dei prigionieri** to guarantee the physical well-being of (the) prisoners **b** (*onestà*) integrity, honesty, uprightness.

integro, a ['integro] AGG **a** (*intero*) intact, complete, whole **b** (*onesto*) honest, upright.

intelaiatura [intelaja'tura] SF (*Edil*) skeleton, framework, frame; (*fig: economica, sociale*) framework, structure.

intellegibile [intelle'dʒibile] AGG = **intelligibile**.

intellettivo, a [intellet'tivo] AGG (*facoltà*) intellectual.

intelletto [intel'letto] SM intellect; **perdere il ben dell'intelletto** (*impazzire*) to go out of one's mind.

intellettuale [intellettu'ale] 1 AGG intellectual; **sforzo intellettuale** mental effort.
2 SM/F intellectual.

intellettualizzare [intellettualid'dzare] VT to intellectualize.

intellettualmente [intellettual'mente] AVV intellectually.

intellettualoide [intellettua'lɔide] (*pegg*) 1 AGG (*atteggia-*

mento) highbrow, pseudo-intellectual.

2 SM/F pseudo-intellectual, would-be intellectual.

intelligente [intelli'dʒɛnte] AGG (*gen*) intelligent; (*brillante*) clever, bright; (*capace*) clever, able.

intelligentemente [intellidʒente'mente] AVV intelligently.

intelligenza [intelli'dʒɛntsa] SF intelligence; **ha un'intelligenza viva** he's got a quick *o* sharp mind; **è una bella intelligenza** he has a fine mind *o* a good brain; **un lavoro fatto con intelligenza** a clever piece of work; **giocato con intelligenza** cleverly played ▶ **intelligenza artificiale** artificial intelligence.

intellighenzia [intelli'gɛntsia] SF intelligentsia.

intelligibile [intelli'dʒibile] AGG intelligible; **ripetilo in modo chiaro e intelligibile** repeat it loudly and clearly; **un messaggio poco intelligibile** an unclear message; **ha una scrittura chiara e intelligibile** he has clear, legible handwriting.

intelligibilità [intellidʒibili'ta] SF intelligibility.

intelligibilmente [intellidʒibil'mente] AVV intelligibly.

intemerato, a [inteme'rato] (*letter*) AGG (*persona, vita*) blameless, irreproachable; (*coscienza*) clear; (*fama*) unblemished.

intemperante [intempe'rante] AGG intemperate, immoderate.

intemperanza [intempe'rantsa] SF (*qualità*) intemperance; **intemperanze** SFPL (*eccessi*) excesses.

intemperie [intem'pɛrje] SFPL bad weather *sg*; **esposto alle intemperie** exposed to the elements; **resistente alle intemperie** weatherproof.

intempestivo, a [intempes'tivo] AGG (*intervento*) untimely, ill-timed.

intendente [inten'dɛnte] SM: **intendente di Finanza** inland (*Brit*) *o* internal (*Am*) revenue officer.

intendenza [inten'dɛntsa] SF: **intendenza di Finanza** inland (*Brit*) *o* internal (*Am*) revenue office.

intendere [in'tɛndere] VB IRREG **1** VT **a** (*avere intenzione*): **intendere fare qc** to intend *o* mean to do sth, have the intention of doing sth; **non intendo farlo** I have no intention of doing it, I don't intend to do it

b (*significare*) to mean; **cosa intendevi (dire)?** what did you mean?

c (*capire*) to understand; **mi ha dato a intendere che...** he led me to believe that ...; **ha lasciato intendere che...** he gave (me *o* us) to understand that ...; **ma io non la intendo così** I don't see things that way; **puoi intenderla come vuoi** you can take it how you like; **non riesce a farsi intendere** he cannot make himself understood; **s'intende!** naturally!, of course!; **s'intende che verrai anche tu!** you'll be coming too, of course!

d (*udire*) to hear; **ho inteso dire che...** I've heard (it said) that ...; **non vuole intendere ragione** he won't listen to reason.

2 **intendersi** VR (*uso reciproco: capirsi*) to understand each other, get on (well); **intendersi con qn su qc** (*accordarsi*) to come to an agreement with sb about sth; **intendiamoci** let's get it quite clear; **ci siamo intesi?** is that clear?, is that understood?.

3 **intendersi** VIP **a** (*conoscere bene*): **intendersi di qc** to know a lot about sth; (: *cibi, vini*) to be a connoisseur of sth; **me ne intendo poco** I know very little about it

b (*avere una relazione amorosa*): **intendersela (con qn)** to have an affair with sb.

intendimento [intendi'mento] SM (*proposito*) intention.

intenditore, trice [intendi'tore] SM/F expert; (*di vini, cibi*)

connoisseur; **a buon intenditor poche parole** (*Proverbio*) a word to the wise ... .

intenerire [intene'rire] **1** VT (*commuovere*) to touch, move (to pity).

2 **intenerirsi** VIP to be touched, be moved.

intensamente [intensa'mente] AVV intensely.

intensificare [intensifi'kare] VT, **intensificarsi** VIP to intensify, increase.

intensificazione [intensifikat'tsjone] SF intensification.

intensità [intensi'ta] SF INV (*gen, Fis*) intensity; (*del vento*) force, strength.

intensivamente [intensiva'mente] AVV intensively.

intensivo, a [inten'sivo] AGG intensive.

intenso, a [in'tɛnso] AGG (*gen*) intense; (*luce, profumo*) strong; (*colore*) intense, deep.

intentare [inten'tare] VT (*Dir*): **intentare causa a** *o* **contro qn** to start *o* institute proceedings against sb.

intentato, a [inten'tato] AGG: **non lasciare nulla d'intentato** to leave no stone unturned, try everything.

intento[1], a [in'tɛnto] AGG intent; **essere intento a qc/a fare qc** to be intent on sth/absorbed in doing sth.

intento[2] [in'tɛnto] SM intention, aim, purpose; **fare qc con l'intento di** to do sth with the intention of; **riuscire nell'intento** to achieve one's aim.

intenzionale [intentsjo'nale] AGG (*gen*) intentional, deliberate; (*Dir: omicidio*) premeditated; **fallo intenzionale** (*Sport*) deliberate foul.

intenzionalmente [intentsjonal'mente] AVV intentionally.

intenzionato, a [intentsjo'nato] AGG: **essere intenzionato a fare qc** to intend to do sth, have the intention of doing sth; **ben intenzionato** well-meaning, well-intentioned; **mal intenzionato** ill-intentioned.

intenzione [inten'tsjone] SF intention; **avere (l')intenzione di fare qc** to intend to do sth, have the intention of doing sth; **è mia intenzione farlo** I intend to do it; **non era mia intenzione offenderti** I didn't mean to offend you; **è l'intenzione che conta** it's the thought that counts; **con intenzione** intentionally, deliberately; **senza intenzione** unintentionally; **secondo l'intenzione** *o* **le intenzioni di qn** in accordance with sb's wishes; **animato dalle migliori intenzioni** with the best of intentions.

intepidire [intepi'dire] VT = **intiepidire**.

interagire [intera'dʒire] VI (*aus avere*) to interact.

interamente [intera'mente] AVV entirely, completely.

interattivo, a [interat'tivo] AGG interactive.

interazione [interat'tsjone] SF interaction.

intercalare [interka'lare] **1** VT: **intercalare a, intercalare in** (*testo, discorso ecc*) to insert into.

2 SM pet phrase, stock phrase; **il suo intercalare preferito è "cioè"** one of his favourite expressions is "cioè".

intercambiabile [interkam'bjabile] AGG interchangeable.

intercambiabilità [interkambjabili'ta] SF interchangeability.

intercapedine [interka'pɛdine] SF gap, cavity.

intercedere [inter'tʃɛdere] VI (*aus avere*): **intercedere (presso/in favore di)** to intercede (with/on behalf of).

intercessione [intertʃes'sjone] SF intercession.

intercettare [intertʃet'tare] VT (*gen, Sport, Telec*) to intercept.

intercettazione [intertʃettat'tsjone], **intercettamento** [intertʃetta'mento] SF interception ▶ **intercettazione telefonica** telephone tapping.

intercettore [intert∫et'tore] SM (*Mil*) interceptor.

intercity [inter'siti] SM INV (*Ferr*) ≈ intercity (train).

intercomunicante [interkomuni'kante] AGG (inter)communicating.

interconfessionale [interkonfessjo'nale] AGG (*Rel*) interdenominational.

interconnettere [interkon'nεttere] VT IRREG to interconnect.

intercontinentale [interkontinen'tale] AGG intercontinental.

intercorrere [inter'korrere] VI IRREG (*aus* essere) **a** (*passare, tempo*) to elapse **b** (*esserci*) to exist; **fra loro intercorrono ottimi rapporti** they are on the very best of terms.

intercorso, a [inter'korso] PP di **intercorrere**.

intercostale [interkos'tale] AGG (*Anat*) intercostal.

interdentale [interden'tale] AGG (*Anat*) interdental; **filo interdentale** dental floss.

interdetto, a [inter'detto] [1] PP di **interdire**.

[2] AGG (*sconcertato*) dumbfounded; **rimanere interdetto** to be taken aback; **lasciare qn interdetto** to take sb aback, dumbfound.

[3] SM (*Rel, Dir*) interdict; **gli interdetti per infermità mentale** those who are debarred on the grounds of mental incapacity.

interdipendente [interdipen'dεnte] AGG interdependent.

interdipendenza [interdipen'dεntsa] SF interdependence.

interdire [inter'dire] VT IRREG (*gen: vietare*) to forbid, ban, prohibit; (*Rel*) to interdict; (*Dir*) to deprive of civil rights; **interdire qn dai pubblici uffici** to ban *o* debar sb from public office.

interdisciplinare [interdi∫∫ipli'nare] AGG interdisciplinary.

interdizione [interdit'tsjone] SF (*divieto*) prohibition, ban; (*Rel*) interdict; (*Dir*) debarment ▶**interdizione giudiziale** debarment (*resulting from certification of insanity*) ▶**interdizione legale** deprivation of civil rights.

interessamento [interessa'mento] SM (*interesse*) interest; (*intervento*) intervention, good offices *pl*; **grazie al suo interessamento sono riuscito ad avere il lavoro** it was thanks to his good offices that I managed to get the job.

interessante [interes'sante] AGG (*gen*) interesting; **essere in stato interessante** (*fam*) to be expecting (a baby).

interessare [interes'sare] [1] VI (*aus* essere): **interessare (a qn)** to interest (sb); **forse ti interesserà sapere che...** perhaps you might be interested to know that ...; **se ti interessa ti posso dare il suo indirizzo** if you are interested I can give you his address; **non m'interessa!** I'm not interested!; **a lui non interessano che i suoi libri** he's only interested in his books; **ci interessa che tutto vada bene** what matters to us is that everything should go *o* goes well.

[2] VT **a** (*suscitare interesse in*) to interest; **interessare qn a qc** to interest sb in sth

b (*riguardare*) to affect, concern; **la notizia interesserà gli appassionati di cinema** the news will interest cinema fans; **precipitazioni che interessano le regioni settentrionali** rainfall affecting the north; **un provvedimento che interessa gli automobilisti** a regulation affecting *o* concerning motorists

c (*Comm*): **interessare qn in** (*utili*) to give sb a share *o* an interest in.

[3] **interessarsi** VIP **a** (*mostrare curiosità*): **interessarsi** (a) to show interest (in); **si è interessato molto a quel progetto** he showed a lot of interest in the project

b (*occuparsi*): **interessarsi di** *o* **a** (*politica, pittura ecc*) to be interested in, take an interest in; **si sono interessati al suo caso** they took up his case; **si è interessato alla mia promozione** he helped me get promotion; **si è interessato di farmi avere quei biglietti** he took the trouble to get me those tickets; **interessati degli affari tuoi!** mind your own business!

interessatamente [interessata'mente] AVV selfinterestedly.

interessato, a [interes'sato] [1] AGG **a** (*coinvolto*) interested, involved; **le parti interessate** the interested parties; **le regioni interessate dal maltempo** the regions affected by the bad weather

b (*pegg*): **essere interessato** to act out of self-interest.

[2] SM/F (*coinvolto*) person concerned; **a tutti gli interessati** to all those concerned, to all interested parties.

interesse [inte'rεsse] SM **a** (*gen*) interest; **ho sempre avuto un certo interesse per...** I've always had a certain interest in ..., I've always been rather interested in ...

b (*affare, attività*): **badare ai propri interessi** to look after one's own interests *o* affairs; **ha degli interessi in quell'azienda** he has a financial interest in that company; **curare gli interessi del proprio cliente** (*avvocato*) to act in the interests of one's client ▶**interesse privato in atti di ufficio** (*Amm*) abuse of public office

c (*tornaconto*): **fare qc per interesse** to do sth out of self-interest; **non pensa che a fare il proprio interesse** he only thinks of his own interests; **nell'interesse dell'umanità** in the interests of mankind; **agire nell'interesse comune** to act for the common good *o* in the common interest; **non ho alcun interesse a farlo** [OR] **non è nel mio interesse farlo** it is not in my interest to do it; **l'ha sposata per interesse** he married her for her money; **quando c'è di mezzo l'interesse...** when personal interests are involved ...

d (*Fin, Comm*) interest; **un interesse del 5%** 5% interest ▶**interesse composto** compound interest ▶**interesse maturato** accrued interest ▶**interesse semplice** simple interest.

interessenza [interes'sεntsa] SF (*Econ*) profit-sharing.

interfaccia [inter'fatt∫a] SF INV (*Inform*) interface ▶**interfaccia utente** user interface.

interfacciare [interfat't∫are] VT (*Inform*) to interface.

interferenza [interfe'rεntsa] SF (*gen, Tecn*) interference; **ci sono delle interferenze nella linea** (*Telec*) there is interference on the line.

interferire [interfe'rire] VI (*aus* avere): **interferire (in)** to interfere (in).

interfono [inter'fono] SM intercom (*fam*); (*in una casa*) house phone, internal phone.

intergalattico, a, ci, che [interga'lattiko] AGG intergalactic.

interiezione [interjet'tsjone] SF (*Gramm*) interjection, exclamation.

interim ['interim] SM INV **a** (*periodo*) interim, interval; **ministro ad interim** acting *o* interim minister **b** (*incarico*) temporary appointment.

interiora [inte'rjora] SFPL entrails *pl*.

interiore [inte'rjore] AGG **a** (*interno*) inner *attr*; **parte interiore** inside **b** (*fig: vita, mondo*) inner *attr*.

interiorità [interjori'ta] SF inner being.

interiorizzare [interjorid'dzare] VT to internalize.

interiorizzazione [interjoriddzat'tsjone] SF internalization.

interiormente [interjor'mente] AVV (gen) internally; (soffrire) inwardly, inside.

interlinea [inter'linea] SF **a** (Dattilografia) line spacing; **interlinea doppia** double spacing **b** (Tip) lead, leading.

interlineare [interline'are] [1] AGG interlinear.

[2] VT **a** (spaziare le righe) to space (out) **b** (Tip) to lead (out).

interlocutore, trice [interloku'tore] SM/F speaker; **il suo interlocutore** the person he was speaking to.

interlocutorio, ria, ri, rie [interloku'tɔrjo] AGG interlocutory.

interludio, di [inter'ludjo] SM (Mus, fig) interlude.

intermediario, ria, ri, rie [interme'djarjo] [1] AGG intermediary.

[2] SM/F intermediary, go-between; (Comm, Econ) middleman.

intermediazione [intermedjat'tsjone] SF mediation.

intermedio, dia, di, die [inter'mɛdjo] AGG intermediate attr.

intermezzo [inter'mɛddzo] SM (intervallo) interval; (breve spettacolo) interlude.

interminabile [intermi'nabile] AGG interminable, endless, never-ending.

interministeriale [interministe'rjale] AGG interministerial.

intermittente [intermit'tɛnte] AGG intermittent.

intermittentemente [intermittente'mente] AVV intermittently.

intermittenza [intermit'tɛntsa] SF: **ad intermittenza** intermittent.

internamente [interna'mente] AVV internally.

internamento [interna'mento] SM (vedi vb) internment; confinement (to a mental hospital).

internare [inter'nare] VT (Pol) to intern; (Med) to confine to a mental hospital.

internato¹, a [inter'nato] (vedi vb) [1] AGG interned; confined (to a mental hospital).

[2] SM/F internee; inmate (of a mental hospital).

internato² [inter'nato] SM **a** (collegio) boarding school **b** (di medico) period as a houseman (Brit) o an intern (Am).

internazionale [internattsjo'nale] [1] AGG international.

[2] SF: **l'Internazionale** (Pol: associazione) the International; (: inno) the Internationale.

internazionalmente [internattsjonal'mente] AVV internationally.

internista, i, e [inter'nista] SM/F internist.

interno, a [in'tɛrno] [1] AGG (gen, Med) internal; (tasca) inside attr; (regione, navigazione, mare) inland attr; (politica, commercio) domestic; **alunno interno** boarder; **commissione interna** (Scol) internal examination board.

[2] SM **a** (di edificio) inside, interior; (di scatola) inside; (di cappotto: fodera) lining; **dall'interno** from the inside; **all'interno (della casa)** inside (the house)

b (Cine): **interni** SMPL interior shots; **girare gli interni** to film the indoor shots

c (di paese) interior; **regioni dell'interno** inland areas, areas of the interior; **notizie dall'interno** (Stampa) home news; **Ministero degli Interni** Ministry of the Interior, ≈ Home Office (Brit), ≈ Department of the Interior (Am)

d (di telefono) extension; (di appartamento) flat (Brit) o apartment (Am) (number); **abita in Via Mangili 6, 2**

piano, interno 5 he lives at number 6 Via Mangili, 2nd floor, flat 5.

[3] SM/F (Scol) boarder.

intero, a [in'tero] [1] AGG **a** (gen) whole, entire; (quantità) whole, full; (Mat: numero) whole; **latte intero** full-cream milk; **ti ho aspettato per un'ora intera** I waited for you for a whole o full hour; **pagare il prezzo intero** to pay the full price; **ha ingoiato una prugna tutta intera** he swallowed a plum whole; **ho trascorso l'intera settimana a studiare** I spent the whole o entire week studying; **ha girato il mondo intero** he's travelled all over the world, he's been all round the world

b (intatto) intact; **ho 50.000 lire intere, me le cambi?** I have a 50,000 lire note, can you give me change for it?.

[2] SM (anche Mat) whole; **scrivere per intero qc** to write sth in full.

interparlamentare [interparlamen'tare] AGG interparliamentary.

interpellanza [interpel'lantsa] SF (Pol: anche: **interpellanza parlamentare**) (parliamentary) question; **presentare un'interpellanza** to ask a (parliamentary) question.

interpellare [interpel'lare] VT (consultare) to consult, ask; (Pol) to question.

interpellato, a [interpel'lato] SM/F person being questioned.

interpersonale [interperso'nale] AGG: **rapporti interpersonali** interpersonal relations.

interplanetario, ria, ri, rie [interplane'tarjo] AGG interplanetary.

Interpol [inter'pol] SF Interpol.

interpolare [interpo'lare] VT to interpolate.

interpolazione [interpolat'tsjone] SF interpolation.

interporre [inter'porre] VB IRREG [1] VT **a** (ostacoli, difficoltà): **interporre qc a qc** to put sth in the way of sth; (influenza) to use; **ha interposto i suoi buoni uffici per aiutarlo** he used his good offices to help him **b** : **interporre appello** (Dir) to appeal.

[2] **interporsi** VIP (intervenire) to intervene; **interporsi fra** (mettersi in mezzo) to come between.

interposto, a [inter'posto] [1] PP di **interporre**.

[2] AGG: **per interposta persona** through a third party.

interpretare [interpre'tare] VT **a** (gen: spiegare, tradurre, capire) to interpret; **interpretare male** to misinterpret **b** (Mus, Teatro) to perform; (personaggio, sonata) to play; (canzone) to sing.

interpretariato [interpreta'rjato] SM interpreting.

interpretazione [interpretat'tsjone] SF interpretation.

interprete [in'tɛrprete] SM/F **a** (traduttore) interpreter; (portavoce): **farsi interprete di** to act as a spokesman for **b** (Teatro, Cine) performer, actor/actress; (Mus) performer.

interpunzione [interpun'tsjone] SF punctuation; **segni di interpunzione** punctuation marks.

interrare [inter'rare] VT **a** (seme, pianta) to plant; (tubature, cavi) to lay underground; (Mil: pezzo d'artiglieria) to dig in **b** (riempire di terra: canale) to fill in.

interrato [inter'rato] SM (anche: **piano interrato**) basement.

interregionale [interredʒo'nale] SM long distance train (stopping frequently).

interregno [inter'reɲɲo] SM interregnum.

interrogare [interro'gare] VT (gen) to question; (Dir) to examine; (Scol) to examine, test; **lo interrogarono in**

merito agli ultimi avvenimenti they questioned him regarding recent events; **mi ha interrogato in matematica** he examined me in maths; **interrogare gli astri** (*Astrol*) to consult the stars.

interrogativamente [interrogativa'mente] AVV (*vedi agg*) questioningly, inquiringly; interrogatively.

interrogativo, a [interroga'tivo] ① AGG (*sguardo, espressione*) questioning, inquiring; (*Gramm*) interrogative; **punto interrogativo** (*anche fig*) question mark.

② SM question; (*fig: persona, futuro*) mystery; **porsi un interrogativo** to ask o.s. a question.

interrogato, a [interro'gato] SM/F person examined (*o* questioned).

interrogatorio, ri [interroga'torjo] SM questioning *no pl*; (*più severo*) interrogation; **subire un interrogatorio** to be questioned; (*anche fig*) to be interrogated.

interrogazione [interrogat'tsjone] SF **a** (*Scol*): **interrogazione (di)** (oral) examination (in), oral test (in) ▶ **interrogazione ciclica** (*Inform*) polling

b (*Pol*): **interrogazione (parlamentare)** (parliamentary) question.

interrompere [inter'rompere] VB IRREG ① VT (*viaggio, studi, trattative*) to interrupt, break off; (*conversazione*) to interrupt; (*gravidanza*) to terminate; (*Elettr: circuito*) to break; **interrompere l'erogazione del gas/dell'acqua** to cut off the gas/water supply; **le comunicazioni con il nord sono interrotte** the north is cut off; **non interrompere!** don't interrupt!.

② **interrompersi** VIP (*gen*) to break off, stop; (*corrente, linea telefonica*) to be cut off; (*circuito elettrico*) to be broken; (*trasmissione*) to be interrupted.

interrotto, a [inter'rotto] PP *di* **interrompere**.

interruttore [interrut'tore] SM switch.

interruzione [interrut'tsjone] SF (*azione*) interruption; (*stato*) break, interruption; **senza interruzione** (*lavorare*) without a break; (*dormire, parlare*) non-stop ▶ **interruzione di gravidanza** termination of pregnancy.

interscambio, bi [inter'skambjo] SM import-export trade.

intersecare [interse'kare] VT, **intersecarsi** VR (*uso reciproco*) to intersect.

intersezione [interset'tsjone] SF intersection.

interstizio, zi [inter'stittsjo] SM interstice.

interurbano, a [interur'bano] ① AGG intercity *attr*; (*Telec*: *telefonata*) long-distance *attr*.

② SF (*Telec*) long-distance call.

intervallare [interval'lare] VT to space out.

intervallo [inter'vallo] SM **a** (*di tempo*: *Teatro, Cine, Mus*) interval; (*a scuola*) break; (*in ufficio*) (tea *o* coffee) break; (*Sport*: *fra due tempi*) half-time; **fare un intervallo di 10 minuti** to have a 10-minute break; **a intervalli regolari** at regular intervals **b** (*di spazio*) space, gap; **a intervalli di 10 cm** at intervals of 10 cm, every 10 cm.

intervenire [interve'nire] VI IRREG (*aus essere*) **a** : **intervenire (in)** (*discussione*) to intervene (in); **intervenire a** (*riunione, cerimonia, manifestazione*) to take part in; **hanno dovuto far intervenire l'esercito** the army had to be brought in; **i vigili del fuoco sono intervenuti immediatamente** the firemen took immediate action

b (*insorgere*: *nuovi elementi*) to arise

c (*Med*: *operare*) to operate; **intervenire d'urgenza su un paziente** to perform emergency surgery on a patient.

interventismo [interven'tizmo] SM (*Pol, Econ*) interven-

tionism.

interventista, i, e [interven'tista] AGG, SM/F interventionist.

intervento [inter'vento] SM **a** (*gen, Pol, Mil*) intervention; **politica del non intervento** policy of non-intervention; **hanno chiesto l'intervento della polizia** they asked for police assistance, they asked the police to intervene; **un intervento falloso** (*Sport*) a foul

b (*breve discorso*) speech; (*partecipazione*) participation; **fare un intervento nel corso di** (*dibattito, programma*) to take part in

c (*Med*) operation; **subire un intervento** to be operated on, undergo an operation.

intervenuto, a [interve'nuto] ① PP *di* **intervenire**.

② : **gli intervenuti** those present.

intervista [inter'vista] SF interview; **fare un'intervista a qn** to interview sb.

intervistare [intervis'tare] VT to interview.

intervistato, a [intervis'tato] SM/F person interviewed.

intervistatore, trice [intervista'tore] SM/F interviewer.

intesa [in'tesa] SF (*amicizia*) understanding; (*accordo*) agreement; **raggiungere un'intesa** (*comprendersi*) to come to understand each other; (*accordarsi*) to reach an agreement; **uno sguardo d'intesa** a knowing look.

inteso, a [in'teso] ① PP *di* **intendere**.

② AGG **a** (*pattuito*) agreed; (*capito*) understood; **resta inteso che...** it is understood that ...; **non darsi per inteso di qc** to take no notice of sth; **siamo intesi?** ok? **b** (*destinato*): **inteso a fare qc** intended to do sth.

intessere [in'tessere] VT to weave together; (*fig: trama, storia*) to weave; **intessere lodi a qn** to sing sb's praises.

intestardirsi [intestar'dirsi] VIP: **intestardirsi (su qc/a fare qc)** to insist (on sth/on doing sth).

intestare [intes'tare] VT **a** (*lettera, busta*) to address **b** : **intestare a** (*casa, proprietà*) to register in the name of; **a chi è intestata la macchina?** whose name is the car registered in ?; **intestare un assegno a qn** to make out a cheque to sb.

intestatario, ria, ri, rie [intesta'tarjo] SM/F holder.

intestato, a [intes'tato] AGG (*proprietà, casa, conto*) in the name of; (*assegno*) made out to; **carta intestata** headed paper.

intestazione [intestat'tsjone] SF (*gen*) heading; (*su carta da lettere*) letterhead; **qual è l'intestazione dell'assegno?** who is the cheque made out to?

intestinale [intesti'nale] AGG intestinal.

intestino, a [intes'tino] ① AGG internal; **guerra intestina** civil war.

② SM (*Anat*) intestine; **intestino tenue/crasso** small/large intestine.

intiepidire [intjepi'dire] ① VT (*riscaldare*) to warm (up); (*raffreddare*) to cool (down); (*fig: amicizia ecc*) to cool.

② **intiepidirsi** VIP (*vedi vt*) to warm (up); to cool (down); to cool.

Intifada [inti'fada] SF Intifada.

intimamente [intima'mente] AVV intimately; **sono intimamente convinto che...** I'm firmly *o* deeply convinced that ...; **i fatti sono intimamente connessi** the two events are closely connected.

intimare [inti'mare] VT (*ordinare*) to order, command; (*notificare*) to give notice of; **intimare a qn di fare qc** to order sb to do sth; **intimare la resa a qn** (*Mil*) to call upon sb to surrender; **intimare l'alt** to order sb to stop *o* halt; **intimare lo sfratto a qn** (*Dir*) to serve an eviction

notice *o* order on sb.

intimazione [intimat'tsjone] SF order, command
▶**intimazione di sfratto** (*Dir*) eviction notice *o* order.

intimidatorio, ria, ri, rie [intimida'tɔrjo] AGG threatening; **sparare (in aria) a scopo intimidatorio** to fire warning shots.

intimidazione [intimidat'tsjone] SF intimidation; **vittima di intimidazioni** victim of intimidation *o* threats.

intimidire [intimi'dire] ☐1☐ VT to intimidate.
☐2☐ VI (*aus* **essere**), **intimidirsi** VIP to become *o* grow shy.

intimità [intimi'ta] SF (*vita privata*) privacy; (*familiarità*) familiarity; (*di rapporto*) intimacy; **nell'intimità della propria casa** in the privacy of one's own home.

intimo, a ['intimo] ☐1☐ AGG (*amico*) close, intimate; (*affetti, vita*) private; (*gioia, dolore*) deep; (*cerimonia*) quiet; (*atmosfera*) cosy, intimate; (*igiene*) personal; **biancheria intima** underwear; **parti intime** (*genitali*) private parts; **rapporti intimi** (*sessuali*) intimate relations.
☐2☐ SM a (*persona*) close friend
b : **nell'intimo della sua coscienza** deep down in his conscience; **nell'intimo del suo cuore** in his heart of hearts
c (*biancheria intima*) underwear; (: *per donna*) lingerie; **saldi del 30% sull'intimo uomo** 30% reductions on men's underwear.

intimorire [intimo'rire] ☐1☐ VT to frighten, make afraid.
☐2☐ **intimorirsi** VIP to become frightened.

intimorito, a [intimo'rito] AGG frightened.

intingere [in'tindʒere] VT IRREG (*biscotto, pane*) to dunk; (*penna, pennello*) to dip.

intingolo [in'tingolo] SM (*sugo*) sauce; (*pietanza*) tasty dish.

intinto, a [in'tinto] PP di **intingere**.

intirizzire [intirid'dzire] ☐1☐ VT to numb.
☐2☐ VI (*aus* **essere**), **intirizzirsi** VIP to grow numb (with cold).

intirizzito, a [intirid'dzito] AGG numb (with cold).

intitolare [intito'lare] ☐1☐ VT a (*dare un titolo a*) to entitle, give a title to; **come ha intitolato il suo ultimo romanzo?** what title has he given to his latest book? b (*dedicare: chiesa, monumento*) to dedicate.
☐2☐ **intitolarsi** VIP (*libro, film*) to be called.

intoccabile [intok'kabile] AGG, SM/F untouchable.

intollerabile [intolle'rabile] AGG intolerable, unbearable.

intollerante [intolle'rante] ☐1☐ AGG: **intollerante (di)** intolerant (of).
☐2☐ SM/F intolerant person.

intolleranza [intolle'rantsa] SF intolerance.

intonacare [intona'kare] VT to plaster.

intonaco, ci [in'tɔnako] SM plaster.

intonare [into'nare] ☐1☐ VT (*Mus: canzone*) to sing the opening phrases of; (*fig: armonizzare*) to match; **intonare a** *o* **con** to tone in with, match with; **intonare due colori tra di loro** to match two colours.
☐2☐ **intonarsi** VIP (*colori*) to go together; **intonarsi a** *o* **con** (*circostanza, carnagione*) to suit; (*abito*) to match, go with.

intonato, a [into'nato] AGG (*strumento, voce*) tuneful; (*persona*) able to sing in tune; (*colori*) matching; **una borsa intonata alle scarpe** a bag which matched her shoes.

intonazione [intonat'tsjone] SF (*nel cantare*) pitch; (*nel parlare*) intonation.

intonso, a [in'tonso] AGG untouched.

intontire [inton'tire] ☐1☐ VT (*sogg: botta*) to stun, daze; (: *gas, alcolici*) to make dizzy, make woozy (*fam*).
☐2☐ VI (*aus* **essere**), **intontirsi** VIP to be stunned *o* dazed.

intontito, a [inton'tito] AGG (*persona: da botta*) stunned, dazed; (: *da gas, alcolici*) dizzy, woozy (*fam*); (*sguardo*) glazed; **intontito dal sonno** befuddled with sleep.

intoppare [intop'pare] VI (*aus* **essere**), **intopparsi** VIP (*congegno*) to stick; **intoppare in** (*parola difficile, difficoltà*) to stumble over.

intoppo [in'tɔppo] SM (*ostacolo*) hitch, stumbling block, obstacle; (*difficoltà*) difficulty.

intorbidare [intorbi'dare], **intorbidire** [intorbi'dire] ☐1☐ VT (*liquido*) to make turbid; (*mente*) to cloud; **intorbidare le acque** (*fig*) to muddy the waters.
☐2☐ VI (*aus* **essere**), **intorbidarsi** VIP (*vedi vt*) to become turbid; to cloud, become confused.

intorno [in'torno] ☐1☐ AVV around, round; **qui/lì intorno** round here/there; **c'è un castello e tutt'intorno un giardino** there is a castle with a garden surrounding it.
☐2☐: **intorno a** PREP a (*attorno a, circa*) (a)round about; **smettila di girarmi intorno** stop hanging around me; **successe intorno al 1910** it happened (a)round about 1910
b (*riguardo*) about.

intorpidimento [intorpidi'mento] SM (*delle membra*) numbness; (*della mente*) torpor, sluggishness.

intorpidire [intorpi'dire] ☐1☐ VT (*membra*) to numb; (*mente*) to slow down, make sluggish.
☐2☐ VI (*aus* **essere**), **intorpidirsi** VIP (*membra*) to grow numb; (*mente, persona*) to become sluggish.

intossicare [intossi'kare] ☐1☐ VT to poison.
☐2☐ **intossicarsi** VR: **intossicarsi (con)** to poison o.s. (with).

intossicazione [intossikat'tsjone] SF poisoning
▶**intossicazione alimentare** food poisoning.

intra... ['intra] PREF intra...

intraducibile [intradu'tʃibile] AGG untranslatable.

intraducibilità [intradutʃibili'ta] SF untranslatability.

intralciare [intral'tʃare] VT to hamper, hinder, hold up.

intralcio, ci [in'traltʃo] SM hitch.

intrallazzare [intrallat'tsare] VI (*aus* **avere**) to intrigue, scheme.

intrallazzatore, trice [intrallattsa'tore] SM/F wheeler dealer.

intrallazzo [intral'lattso] SM (*Pol*) intrigue, manoeuvre (*Brit*), maneuver (*Am*); (*traffico losco*) racket.

intramontabile [intramon'tabile] AGG timeless.

intramuscolare [intramusko'lare] AGG intramuscular.

intransigente [intransi'dʒɛnte] AGG uncompromising, intransigent; **è piuttosto intransigente in fatto di amicizie** he's rather choosy about who he makes friends with.

intransigenza [intransi'dʒɛntsa] SF intransigence.

intransitivo, a [intransi'tivo] AGG, SM (*Gramm*) intransitive.

intrappolare [intrappo'lare] VT to trap; **rimanere intrappolato** to be trapped; **farsi intrappolare** to get caught.

intraprendente [intrapren'dɛnte] AGG (*che si dà da fare*) enterprising, go-ahead; (*audace*) forward, bold.

intraprendenza [intrapren'dɛntsa] SF (*spirito d'iniziativa*) initiative; (*audacità*) audacity, boldness.

intraprendere [intra'prɛndere] VT IRREG (*riforme*) to undertake; (*carriera*) to embark (up)on; **intraprendere una spedizione** to set out on an expedition.

intrapreso, a [intra'preso] PP di **intraprendere**.
intrattabile [intrat'tabile] AGG intractable; **il capo oggi è intrattabile** the boss is impossible today.
intrattenere [intratte'nere] ① VT **a** (divertire) to entertain; (chiacchierando) to engage in conversation **b** (rapporti) to have, maintain.
② **intrattenersi** VIP (fermarsi: con ospiti) to linger; **intrattenersi su** (argomento, questione) to dwell on.
intrattenimento [intratteni'mento] SM entertainment.
intrattenitore, trice [intratteni'tore] SM/F entertainer.
intravedere [intrave'dere] VT IRREG **a** (vedere appena) to make out, catch a glimpse of **b** (presagire: difficoltà, pericoli) to foresee; (: verità) to have an inkling of.
intravisto, a [intra'visto] PP di **intravedere**.
intrecciare [intret't∫are] ① VT (gen) to plait, braid; (intessere) to weave, interweave, intertwine; **intrecciare una relazione amorosa** to begin an affair.
② **intrecciarsi** VIP (rami, corde) to become interwoven, intertwine.
intreccio, ci [in'trett∫o] SM **a** (di tessuto) weave; (di paglia) plaiting **b** (fig: trama) plot, story.
intrepido, a [in'trεpido] AGG intrepid, dauntless, fearless.
intricare [intri'kare] ① VT (fili) to tangle; (fig: faccenda) to complicate.
② **intricarsi** VIP (vedi vt) to become tangled; to become complicated.
intricato, a [intri'kato] AGG (fili ecc) tangled; (fig: faccenda) complicated.
intrico, chi [in'triko] SM (anche fig) tangle.
intrigante [intri'gante] ① AGG (persona: imbroglione) scheming; (misterioso: sorriso, sguardo) enigmatic; (: romanzo) intriguing.
② SM/F schemer, intriguer.
intrigare [intri'gare] ① VT (affascinare) to intrigue.
② VI (aus avere) to scheme, intrigue, manoeuvre (Brit), maneuver (Am).
intrigo, ghi [in'trigo] SM (complotto) intrigue, scheme, plot; (situazione complicata) tricky situation.
intrinsecamente [intrinseka'mente] AVV intrinsically.
intrinseco, a, ci, che [in'trinseko] AGG intrinsic.
intrippato, a [intrip'pato] AGG (fam) **a** (sotto effetto di droghe) on a trip **b** : **essere intrippato con** (fissato) to be mad o crazy about.
intriso, a [in'trizo] AGG: **intriso di** (inzuppato) soaked with; **un film intriso di sentimentalismo** a film dripping with sentimentality.
intristire [intris'tire] VI (aus essere) (persona: diventare triste) to grow sad; (pianta) to wilt.
introdotto, a [intro'dotto] ① PP di **introdurre**.
② AGG: **essere bene introdotto** to know all the right people.
introdurre [intro'durre] VB IRREG ① VT (gen) to introduce; (moneta, chiave) to insert, put in; (descrizione, elemento) to introduce, bring in; (persona) to show in; **gli ospiti venivano introdotti in sala** the guests were shown o ushered into the room; **introdurre prodotti di contrabbando** to smuggle in goods.
② **introdursi** VIP (penetrare): **introdursi in** to enter, get into; (: furtivamente) to sneak in, slip in; (moda, tecniche) to be introduced.
introduttivo, a [introdut'tivo] AGG introductory.
introduzione [introdut'tsjone] SF introduction.
introito [in'trɔito] SM (Comm: entrata) revenue, income.
intromesso, a [intro'messo] PP di **intromettersi**.

intromettersi [intro'mettersi] VR IRREG (immischiarsi) to interfere, meddle; (in conversazione) to intervene.
intromissione [intromis'sjone] SF (vedi vb) interference, meddling; intervention.
introspettivo, a [introspet'tivo] AGG introspective.
introspezione [introspet'tsjone] SF introspection.
introvabile [intro'vabile] AGG (persona, oggetto) who (o which) cannot be found; (libro) unobtainable.
introversione [introver'sjone] SF introversion.
introverso, a [intro'vεrso] ① AGG introverted.
② SM/F introvert.
intrufolarsi [intrufo'larsi] VR: **intrufolarsi (in)** (stanza, casa) to sneak in(to), slip in(to).
intruglio, gli [in'truʎʎo] SM concoction.
intrupparsi [intrup'parsi] VR (fam) to band together; **spero che tu non vada ad intruparti con quei mascalzoni** I hope you aren't going to get involved with that bunch of thugs.
intrusione [intru'zjone] SF intrusion, interference.
intrusivo, a [intru'zivo] AGG intrusive.
intruso, a [in'truzo] SM/F (estraneo) intruder; (: ad un ricevimento) gatecrasher; **mi trattano come un intruso** they treat me as if I had no right to be there.
intuibile [intu'ibile] AGG deducible; **è facilmente intuibile che...** one soon realizes that ... .
intuire [intu'ire] VT (presentire, accorgersi) to realize; (capire) to know intuitively; (indovinare) to guess.
intuitivamente [intuitiva'mente] AVV intuitively.
intuitivo, a [intui'tivo] AGG intuitive.
intuito [in'tuito] SM (intuizione) intuition; (perspicacia) perspicacity; **capire per intuito** to know intuitively.
intuizione [intuit'tsjone] SF intuition.
inturgidire [inturdʒi'dire] VI (aus essere), **inturgidirsi** VIP to swell.
inumanamente [inumana'mente] AVV inhumanely.
inumanità [inumani'ta] SF inhumanity.
inumano, a [inu'mano] AGG inhuman.
inumare [inu'mare] VT (seppellire) to bury, inter.
inumazione [inumat'tsjone] SF burial, interment.
inumidire [inumi'dire] ① VT (labbra) to moisten; (biancheria) to dampen; **inumidirsi le labbra** to moisten one's lips.
② **inumidirsi** VIP to get damp o wet.
inurbamento [inurba'mento] SM urbanization.
inusitato, a [inuzi'tato] AGG unusual.
inutile [i'nutile] AGG (che non serve) useless; (superfluo) needless, unnecessary; **è inutile insistere** o **che tu insista** it's no use o no good insisting, there's no point in insisting; **è stato tutto inutile!** it was all in vain!
inutilità [inutili'ta] SF (vedi agg) uselessness; needlessness.
inutilizzabile [inutilid'dzabile] AGG unusable.
inutilizzato, a [inutilid'dzato] AGG unused.
inutilmente [inutil'mente] AVV (senza risultato) fruitlessly; (senza utilità, scopo) unnecessarily, needlessly; **l'ho cercato inutilmente** I looked for him in vain; **ti preoccupi inutilmente** you're worrying unnecessarily, there's no need for you to worry.
invadente [inva'dεnte] ① AGG interfering; **non vorrei essere invadente** I don't want to interfere.
② SM/F interfering person, busy-body.
invadenza [inva'dεntsa] SF intrusiveness.
invadere [in'vadere] VT IRREG (gen) to invade; (affollare) to overrun, swarm into; (sogg: acque) to flood; **i tifosi**

hanno invaso il campo the fans invaded the pitch; **le auto giapponesi hanno invaso il mercato** Japanese cars have flooded the market; **invadere la privacy di qn** to invade sb's privacy.

invaghirsi [inva'girsi] VIP: **invaghirsi di** to take a fancy to.

invalicabile [invali'kabile] AGG (*montagna*) impassable; (*fig*: *difficoltà*) insurmountable; **limite invalicabile** (*zona militare*) no unauthorised access.

invalidare [invali'dare] VT to invalidate.

invalidità [invalidi'ta] SF INV (*vedi agg*) disablement, disability; infirmity; invalidity.

invalido, a [in'valido] 1 AGG **a** (*inabile*) disabled; (*malato*) infirm **b** (*Dir*: *nullo*) invalid.
2 SM/F (*inabile*) disabled person; (*malato*) invalid ▶**invalido di guerra** disabled ex-serviceman ▶**invalido del lavoro** industrially disabled person.

invalso, a [in'valso] AGG (*diffuso*) established.

invano [in'vano] AVV in vain.

invariabile [inva'rjabile] AGG invariable.

invariabilmente [invarjabil'mente] AVV invariably.

invariato, a [inva'rjato] AGG unchanged.

invasare [inva'zare] VT (*pianta*) to pot.

invasato, a [inva'zato] 1 AGG possessed (by the devil).
2 SM/F person possessed by the devil; **urlare come un invasato** to shout like one possessed.

invasatura [invaza'tura] SF (*Naut*) slipway, slips *pl*.

invasione [inva'zjone] SF invasion.

invaso, a [in'vazo] PP di **invadere**.

invasore [inva'zore] 1 AGG invading.
2 SM invader.

invecchiamento [invekkja'mento] SM (*di persona*) ageing; **questo whisky ha un invecchiamento di 12 anni** this whisky has been matured for 12 years.

invecchiare [invek'kjare] 1 VI (*aus* **essere**) (*diventare vecchio*) to grow old; (*sembrare più vecchio*) to age; (*vino*) to age; **lo trovo invecchiato** I think he has aged.
2 VT (*persona*) to make look older, age, put years on; (*vino*) to age.

invece [in'vetʃe] AVV (*gen*) instead; (*ma*) but; **credevo di aver ragione e invece no** I thought I was right but I wasn't; **io preferisco i romanzi; Peter invece i gialli** I like novels but Peter prefers detective stories; **invece di qc/di** *o* **che fare qc** instead of sth/of doing sth; **potresti aiutarmi invece di** *o* **che stare lì a guardare la** TV you could help me instead of sitting there watching TV; **preferisco lavorare in Italia invece che all'estero** I prefer to work in Italy rather than abroad.

inveire [inve'ire] VI (*aus* **avere**): **inveire contro** to rail against.

invelenire [invele'nire] 1 VT to embitter.
2 VI (*aus* **essere**), **invelenirsi** VIP to become bitter.

invendibile [inven'dibile] AGG unsaleable.

invenduto, a [inven'duto] 1 AGG unsold.
2 SM (*Comm*): **rendere l'invenduto** to return unsold goods.

inventare [inven'tare] VT (*gen*) to invent; (*metodo*) to invent, devise; (*gioco, scusa*) to invent, make up, think up; **lui ne inventa di tutti i colori!** what will he think up next!; **se l'è inventata di sana pianta** he made the whole thing up.

inventariare [inventa'rjare] VT to make an inventory of, inventory.

inventario, ri [inven'tarjo] SM (*gen*) inventory; (*Comm*: *registro*) stock list; (: *operazione*) stocktaking *no pl*;

inventario fisico physical stocktaking; **fare l'inventario di** to make an inventory of; **mi ha fatto l'inventario delle sue malattie** (*fig*) he regaled me with his medical history.

inventiva [inven'tiva] SF inventiveness.

inventivo, a [inven'tivo] AGG inventive.

inventore, trice [inven'tore] 1 AGG inventive.
2 SM/F inventor.

invenzione [inven'tsjone] SF (*gen*) invention; **è tutta un'invenzione** it's pure invention; **una ricetta di mia invenzione** a recipe I made up myself.

inverecondia [invere'kondja] SF shamelessness, immodesty.

inverecondo, a [invere'kondo] AGG shameless, immodest.

invernale [inver'nale] AGG (*gen*) winter *attr*; (*simile all'inverno*) wintry.

inverno [in'vɛrno] SM winter; **d'inverno** in (the) winter; **essere in pieno inverno** to be in the depths of winter.

inverosimiglianza [inverosimiʎ'ʎantsa] SF improbability, unlikelihood.

inverosimile [invero'simile] 1 AGG (*racconto*) unlikely, improbable; (*scusa*) far-fetched.
2 SM: **l'inverosimile** the improbable; **ha dell'inverosimile** it's hard to believe, it's incredible.

inverosimilmente [inverosimil'mente] AVV unbelievably.

inversamente [inversa'mente] AVV inversely; **inversamente proporzionale** in inverse proportion.

inversione [inver'sjone] SF inversion; **inversione di tendenza** (*fig*) radical change of direction; (*pegg*: *spec Pol*) U-turn; **"divieto d'inversione"** (*Aut*) "no U-turns" ▶**inversione di fondo** (*Inform*) reverse video.

inverso, a [in'vɛrso] 1 AGG **a** (*direzione*) opposite; **in ordine inverso** in reverse order; **si è scontrato con una macchina che veniva in senso inverso** he collided with a car coming in the opposite direction **b** (*Mat*) inverse; **in ragione inversa** (*Mat*) in inverse ratio.
2 SM: **l'inverso** the opposite, the reverse, the contrary; **capisce tutto all'inverso** he always gets hold of the wrong end of the stick; **fa tutto all'inverso** he does everything the wrong way round.

invertebrato, a [inverte'brato] AGG, SM invertebrate.

invertire [inver'tire] VT (*gen*) to invert; (*disposizione, posti*) to change; (*ruoli*) to exchange; **invertire la marcia** (*Aut*) to do a U-turn; **invertire la rotta** (*Naut*) to go about; (*fig*) to do a U-turn.

invertito, a [inver'tito] 1 AGG (*Chim*): **zucchero invertito** invert sugar.
2 SM (*omosessuale*) homosexual.

investigare [investi'gare] 1 VT (*indagare*) to investigate; (*analizzare*) to examine.
2 VI (*aus* **avere**): **investigare su** to investigate.

investigativo, a [investiga'tivo] AGG: **squadra investigativa** detective squad; **agente investigativo** detective.

investigatore, trice [investiga'tore] SM/F investigator, detective ▶**investigatore privato** private detective, private investigator.

investigazione [investigat'tsjone] SF investigation, inquiry.

investimento [investi'mento] SM **a** (*Econ*) investment **b** (*di pedone*) running down, knocking down; (*di veicolo*) collision, crash.

investire [inves'tire] 1 VT **a** (*Econ*) to invest

b (*sogg: veicolo: pedone*) to run over, knock down; (: *altro veicolo*) to crash into, hit

c (*apostrofare*) to assail; **investire qn di** *o* **con qc** (*domande*) to besiege sb with sth; (*ingiurie, insulti*) to heap sth on sb

d (*Dir, Amm: incaricare*): **investire qn di** (*poteri*) to invest sb with; (*incarico*) to appoint sb to.

2 **investirsi** VR (*fig*): **investirsi di una parte** to enter thoroughly into a role.

investitore, trice [investi'tore] SM/F driver responsible for an accident; (*Econ*) investor.

investitura [investi'tura] SF (*Amm, Pol*) appointment, nomination; (*Rel*) investiture.

inveterato, a [invete'rato] AGG (*abitudine, vizio*) ingrained; (*giocatore, bugiardo*) inveterate.

invetriata [inve'trjata] SF (*vetrata*) picture window.

invettiva [invet'tiva] SF invective; **lanciare invettive contro qn/qc** to hurl abuse at sb/sth.

inviare [invi'are] VT (*gen*) to send; (*merce*) to dispatch.

inviato, a [invi'ato] SM/F (*Pol*) envoy; (*Stampa*) correspondent.

invidia [in'vidja] SF envy; **fare invidia a qn** to make sb envious; **farebbe invidia ai migliori ristoranti** it would be the envy of the best restaurants; **avere** *o* **provare invidia per qn/qc** to be envious of sb/sth; **per invidia** out of envy; **morire d'invidia** to be green with envy; **degno d'invidia** enviable; **che invidia!** how I envy you!

invidiabile [invi'djabile] AGG enviable.

invidiabilmente [invidjabil'mente] AVV enviably.

invidiare [invi'djare] VT: **invidiare qc a qn** to envy sb sth; **invidiare qn per qc** to envy sb for sth; **non aver nulla da invidiare a nessuno** to be as good as the next one.

invidioso, a [invi'djoso] AGG envious.

invincibile [invin'tʃibile] AGG (*esercito, nemico*) invincible; (*fig: antipatia, timidezza*) insurmountable.

invio, vii [in'vio] SM **a** (*vedi vb*) sending; dispatching; **chiedere l'invio di qc** to ask for sth to be sent (*o* dispatched) **b** (*insieme di merci*) consignment.

inviolabile [invio'labile] AGG inviolable.

inviolato, a [invio'lato] AGG **a** (*diritto, segreto*) inviolate **b** (*foresta*) virgin *attr*; (*montagna, vetta*) unscaled.

inviperire [invipe'rire] VI (*aus essere*), **inviperirsi** VIP to become furious, fly into a temper; **mi ha fatto inviperire** he made me furious.

inviperito, a [invipe'rito] AGG furious.

invischiare [invis'kjare] 1 VT (*fig*): **invischiare qn in qc** to involve sb in sth, mix sb up in sth.

2 **invischiarsi** VIP: **invischiarsi con qn/in qc** to get mixed up *o* involved with sb/in sth.

invisibile [invi'zibile] AGG (*gen, Econ*) invisible; **rendersi invisibile** (*scherz*) to make o.s. scarce.

invisibilità [invizibili'ta] SF invisibility.

inviso, a [in'vizo] AGG: **inviso a** unpopular with.

invitante [invi'tante] AGG (*proposta, odorino*) inviting; (*sorriso*) appealing, attractive.

invitare [invi'tare] 1 VT (*gen*) to invite; **invitare qn a fare qc** to invite sb to do sth; **invitare a cena gli amici** to invite *o* ask friends to dinner; **furono invitati a entrare** they were invited *o* asked in; **è stato invitato a dimettersi** he was asked to resign; **è una giornata che invita a uscire** it's the sort of day that tempts one to go out.

2 **invitarsi** VR: **si invita sempre da solo** he always invites himself along.

invitato, a [invi'tato] SM/F guest.

invito [in'vito] SM invitation; **fare un invito a qn** to extend an invitation to sb; **su** *o* **dietro invito di qn** at sb's invitation.

in vitro [in 'vitro] AVV, AGG INV in vitro.

invocare [invo'kare] VT (*aiuto, pietà*) to beg for, cry out for; (*Dio*) to invoke, call upon, appeal to; (*articolo*) to cite, quote.

invocazione [invokat'tsjone] SF invocation.

invogliare [invoʎ'ʎare] VT (*stimolare*) to encourage; (*invitare*) to tempt, entice; **invogliare qn a fare qc** to tempt sb to do sth, induce sb to do sth; **bisognerebbe invogliarlo a studiare** we should encourage him to study; **la giornata di sole invogliava ad uscire** the sunny weather tempted one out of doors.

involgarire [involga'rire] 1 VT (*sogg: abito, trucco*) to make (sb) look vulgar.

2 VI (*aus essere*), **involgarirsi** VIP to become vulgar.

involontariamente [involontarja'mente] AVV (*sorridere*) involuntarily; (*spingere*) unintentionally; **l'incidente di cui fu involontariamente responsabile** the accident of which he was the involuntary cause; **scusami, l'ho fatto involontariamente** I'm sorry, I didn't mean to do it.

involontario, ria, ri, rie [involon'tarjo] AGG (*movimento, muscolo*) involuntary; (*offesa, errore*) unintentional.

involtino [invol'tino] SM (*Culin*) roulade.

involto [in'volto] SM (*fagotto*) bundle; (*pacco*) parcel.

involucro [in'volukro] SM (*rivestimento*) covering, cover; (*confezione*) wrapping.

involutivo, a [involu'tivo] AGG: **subire un processo involutivo** to regress.

involuto, a [invo'luto] AGG (*stile*) convoluted.

involuzione [involut'tsjone] SF **a** (*di stile*) convolutedness **b** (*regresso*): **subire un'involuzione** to regress.

invulnerabile [invulne'rabile] AGG invulnerable.

invulnerabilità [invulnerabili'ta] SF invulnerability.

inzaccherare [intsakke'rare] 1 VT to spatter with mud.

2 **inzaccherarsi** VR, VIP to get muddy.

inzaccherato, a [intsakke'rato] AGG muddy.

inzuppare [intsup'pare] 1 VT (*gen*): **inzuppare qc (di)** to soak sth (in); **inzuppò i biscotti nel latte** he dipped the biscuits in the milk; **abiti inzuppati di pioggia** rain-soaked clothes.

2 **inzupparsi** VIP to get soaked, get drenched.

io ['io] 1 PRON PERS I; **sono io** it's me; (*più formale*) it is I; **io e te** you and I, you and me (*fam*); **il mio amico ed io ci andremo** my friend and I will go; **lo farò io** [OR] **io lo farò** I'LL do it; **io stesso(a)** I myself.

2 SM INV: **l'io** the self, the ego.

iodato, a [jo'dato] AGG iodized.

iodio ['jodjo] SM iodine.

ioduro [jo'duro] SM iodide.

ione ['jone] SM ion ▶ **ione idrogeno** hydrogen ion ▶ **ioni complessi** complex ions.

ionico¹, a, ci, che ['joniko] AGG **a** (*stile, periodo*) Ionic **b** (*Geog*) Ionian.

ionico², a, ci, che ['joniko] AGG (*Chim: legame*) ionic.

Ionio ['jonjo] SM: **lo Ionio, il mar Ionio** the Ionian (Sea).

ionizzare [jonid'dzare] VT to ionize.

ionizzatore [joniddza'tore] SM ionizer.

ionizzazione [joniddzat'tsjone] SF ionization.

ionosfera [jonos'fɛra] SF ionosphere.

iosa ['jɔsa]: **a iosa** AVV in abundance, in great quantity; **ce ne sono a iosa** there are thousands of them; **avere matite a iosa** to have pencils galore.

IPAB ['ipab] SIGLA FPL (= *Istituzioni pubbliche di Assistenza e Beneficenza*) *charitable institutions*.

iperbole [i'pɛrbole] SF (*Letteratura*) hyberbole; (*Mat*) hyperbola.

iperbolico, a, ci, che [iper'bɔliko] AGG (*Letteratura, Mat*) hyperbolic(al); (*fig: esagerato*) exaggerated.

ipercritico, a, ci, che [iper'kritiko] AGG hypercritical.

ipermercato [ipermer'kato] SM hypermarket.

ipermetrope [iper'mɛtrope] AGG (*Med*) long-sighted, hyperopic (*termine tecn*).

ipermetropia [ipermetro'pia] SF (*Med*) long-sightedness, hyperopia (*termine tecn*).

ipersensibile [ipersen'sibile] AGG (*persona*) hypersensitive; (*Fot: lastra, pellicola*) hypersensitized.

ipersensibilità [ipersensibili'ta] SF hypersensitivity.

ipertecnologico, a, ci, che [ipertekno'lodʒiko] AGG hi-tech.

ipertensione [iperten'sjone] SF (*Med*) high blood pressure, hypertension (*termine tecn*).

iperteso, a [iper'teso] AGG, SM/F (*Med*) suffering from high blood pressure.

ipertesto [iper'tɛsto] SM (*Inform*) hypertext.

iperventilazione [iperventilat'tsjone] SF (*Med, di subacqueo*) hyperventilation.

ipnosi [ip'nɔzi] SF INV hypnosis.

ipnotico, a, ci, che [ip'nɔtiko] AGG, SM hypnotic.

ipnotismo [ipno'tizmo] SM hypnotism.

ipnotizzare [ipnotid'dzare] VT to hypnotize.

ipoallergenico, a, ci, che [ipoaller'dʒɛniko], **ipoallergico, a, ci, che** [ipoal'lɛrdʒiko] AGG (*crema, sapone, rossetto*) hypoallergenic.

ipocalorico, a, ci, che [ipoka'lɔriko] AGG low-calorie *attr*.

ipocentro [ipo'tʃɛntro] SM (*Geol*) focus.

ipocondria [ipokon'dria] SF hypochondria.

ipocondriaco, a, ci, che [ipokon'driako] AGG, SM/F hypochondriac.

ipocrisia [ipokri'zia] SF hypocrisy; **è stata un'ipocrisia da parte sua** that was sheer hypocrisy on his part.

ipocrita, i, e [i'pɔkrita] 1 AGG hypocritical.
2 SM/F hypocrite.

ipocritamente [ipokrita'mente] AVV hypocritically.

ipofisi [i'pɔfizi] SF INV hypophysis (*termine tecn*), pituitary gland.

iposodico, a, ci, che [ipo'sɔdiko] AGG (*sale*) low sodium *attr*.

ipoteca, che [ipo'tɛka] SF mortgage; **fare** *o* **mettere un'ipoteca su qc** to mortgage sth, raise a mortgage on sth; **la squadra ha messo una seria ipoteca sullo scudetto** the team has practically put its name on the cup.

ipotecabile [ipote'kabile] AGG mortgageable.

ipotecare [ipote'kare] VT (*Dir, fig*) to mortgage.

ipotecario, ria, ri, rie [ipote'karjo] AGG mortgage *attr*.

ipotensione [ipoten'sjone] SF (*Med*): **ipotensione arteriosa** low blood pressure, hypotension (*termine tecn*).

ipotenusa [ipote'nuza] SF hypotenuse.

ipotesi [i'pɔtezi] SF INV hypothesis; **facciamo l'ipotesi che...** OR ammettiamo per ipotesi che... let's suppose *o* assume that ...; **nella peggiore/migliore delle ipotesi** at worst/best; **nell'ipotesi che venga** should he come, if he comes; **se per ipotesi io partissi...** just supposing I were to leave ... .

ipoteticamente [ipotetika'mente] AVV hypothetically.

ipotetico, a, ci, che [ipo'tɛtiko] AGG (*gen*) hypothetical;

(*guadagni, profitti*) theoretical, hypothetical; (*mondo*) imaginary; **nel caso ipotetico che tu non arrivi in tempo** should you not arrive in time; **periodo ipotetico** (*Gramm*) conditional clause.

ipotizzare [ipotid'dzare] VT: **ipotizzare che** to form the hypothesis that, hypothesize.

ippica ['ippika] SF horseracing.

ippico, a, ci, che ['ippiko] AGG horse *attr*.

ippocastano [ippokas'tano] SM horse chestnut (tree).

Ippocrate [ip'pɔkrate] SM Hippocrates.

ippodromo [ip'pɔdromo] SM racecourse, racetrack.

Ippolito [ip'pɔlito] SM Hippolytus.

ippopotamo [ippo'pɔtamo] SM hippopotamus.

ipsilon ['ipsilon] SF O M INV (*lettera*) Y, y; (: *dell'alfabeto greco*) upsilon.

I.P.S.O.A. [ip'soa] SIGLA M (= *Istituto Post-Universitario per lo Studio dell'Organizzazione Aziendale*) *postgraduate institute of business administration*.

IRA ['ira] SIGLA F (= *Irish Republican Army*) IRA.

ira ['ira] SF anger, fury, wrath; **l'ira di Dio** the wrath of God; **ha fatto un'ira di Dio** she made a terrible scene; **costa un'ira di Dio** it costs a king's ransom; **con uno scatto d'ira** in a fit of anger; **farsi prendere dall'ira** to lose one's temper.

iracheno, a [ira'kɛno] AGG, SM/F Iraqi.

iracondo, a [ira'kondo] AGG irascible, quick-tempered.

Irak [i'rak] SM: **l'Irak** Iraq.

Iran ['iran] SM: **l'Iran** Iran.

iraniano, a [ira'njano] AGG, SM/F Iranian.

irascibile [iraʃ'ʃibile] AGG irascible, quick-tempered.

irascibilità [iraʃʃibili'ta] SF irascibilty.

irato, a [i'rato] AGG (*persona, sguardo*) irate, furious.

I.R.C.E. ['irtʃe] SIGLA M (= *Istituto per le relazioni culturali con l'Estero*) ≈ British Council.

I.R.I. ['iri] SIGLA M (= *Istituto per la Ricostruzione Industriale*) *state-controlled industrial investment office*.

iride ['iride] SF a (*Anat*) iris b (*arcobaleno*) rainbow.

iridescente [irideʃ'ʃente] AGG iridescent.

iridescenza [irideʃ'ʃentsa] SF iridescence.

Irlanda [ir'landa] SF: **l'Irlanda** Ireland; **il mar d'Irlanda** the Irish Sea; **la Repubblica d'Irlanda** Eire, the Republic of Ireland ▶ **l'Irlanda del Nord** Northern Ireland, Ulster.

irlandese [irlan'dese] 1 AGG Irish.
2 SM/F Irishman/Irishwoman; **gli Irlandesi** the Irish.

ironia [iro'nia] SF irony; **fare dell'ironia su qc** to be sarcastic about sth; **l'ironia della sorte** the irony of fate.

ironicamente [ironika'mente] AVV ironically.

ironico, a, ci, che [i'rɔniko] AGG ironic(al).

ironizzare [ironid'dzare] VT, VI (*aus* **avere**): **ironizzare su** to be ironical about.

iroso, a [i'roso] AGG (*sguardo, tono*) angry, wrathful; (*persona*) irascible.

IRPEF ['irpef] SIGLA F = **imposta sul reddito delle persone fisiche**.

irpino, a [ir'pino] 1 AGG of *o* from Irpinia.
2 SM/F inhabitant *o* native of Irpinia.

irradiare [irra'djare] 1 VT a (*illuminare, anche fig*) to light up b (*diffondere: calore, energia*) to radiate.
2 VI (*aus* **essere**) to radiate.
3 **irradiarsi** VIP: **irradiarsi (da)** (*strade, rette*) to radiate (from).

irradiazione [irradjat'tsjone] SF (*di calore, energia*) radiation.

irraggiamento [irraddʒa'mento] SM (*Fis*) radiation.

irraggiungibile [irraddʒun'dʒibile] AGG unreachable; (fig: meta) unattainable.

irragionevole [irradʒo'nevole] AGG (privo di ragione) irrational; (fig: persona, pretese, prezzo) unreasonable.

irrancidire [irrantʃi'dire] VI (aus essere) to go rancid.

irrazionale [irrattsjo'nale] AGG (gen, Mat) irrational.

irrazionalità [irrattsjonali'ta] SF irrationality.

irrazionalmente [irrattsjonal'mente] AVV irrationally.

irreale [irre'ale] AGG unreal.

irrealizzabile [irrealid'dzabile] AGG (sogno, desiderio) unattainable, unrealizable; (progetto) unworkable, impracticable.

irrealtà [irreal'ta] SF unreality.

irrecuperabile [irrekupe'rabile] AGG (gen) irretrievable; (fig: persona) irredeemable.

irrecusabile [irreku'zabile] AGG **a** (prova) indisputable, irrefutable **b** (offerta) which cannot be refused, not to be refused.

irredentismo [irreden'tizmo] SM (Storia) irredentism.

irredentista, i, e [irreden'tista] AGG, SM/F (Storia) Irredentist.

irredimibile [irredi'mibile] AGG irredeemable.

irrefrenabile [irrefre'nabile] AGG uncontrollable.

irrefutabile [irrefu'tabile] AGG irrefutable.

irregolare [irrego'lare] ① AGG (gen) irregular; (terreno) uneven; (sonno) fitful; (risultati, sviluppo) erratic.
② SM (Mil) irregular.

irregolarità [irregolari'ta] SF INV **a** (vedi agg) irregularity; unevenness no pl; fitfulness; erratic nature **b** (azione irregolare) irregularity; (Sport) foul.

irregolarmente [irregolar'mente] AVV (vedi agg) irregularly; unevenly; fitfully; erratically.

irreligioso, a [irreli'dʒoso] AGG irreligious.

irremovibile [irremo'vibile] AGG (fig) unshakable, unyielding; **essere irremovibile in qc** to be adamant about sth.

irreparabile [irrepa'rabile] AGG irreparable.

irreperibile [irrepe'ribile] AGG who (o which) cannot be found, nowhere to be found.

irreperibilità [irreperibili'ta] SF: **causa l'irreperibilità dell'imputato...** given that the accused cannot be found ... .

irreprensibile [irrepren'sibile] AGG irreproachable.

irrequietezza [irrekwje'tettsa] SF restlessness.

irrequieto, a [irre'kwjeto] AGG (agitato) restless; (vivace) lively.

irresistibile [irresis'tibile] AGG irresistible.

irresistibilmente [irresistibil'mente] AVV irresistibly.

irresolubile [irreso'lubile] AGG (mistero) insoluble.

irresolutezza [irresolu'tettsa] SF irresoluteness, indecisiveness.

irresoluto, a [irreso'luto] AGG irresolute, indecisive.

irresoluzione [irresolut'tsjone] SF irresolution, indecision.

irrespirabile [irrespi'rabile] AGG (aria) unbreathable; (: malsano) unhealthy; (fig: opprimente) stifling, oppressive.

irresponsabile [irrespon'sabile] ① AGG irresponsible.
② SM/F irresponsible person.

irresponsabilità [irresponsabili'ta] SF irresponsibility.

irresponsabilmente [irresponsabil'mente] AVV irresponsibly.

irrestringibile [irrestrin'dʒibile] AGG unshrinkable, non-shrink (Brit).

irretire [irre'tire] VT to seduce.

irreversibile [irrever'sibile] AGG irreversible.

irrevocabile [irrevo'kabile] AGG irrevocable.

irrevocabilmente [irrevokabil'mente] AVV irrevocably.

irriconoscibile [irrikonoʃ'ʃibile] AGG unrecognizable.

irriducibile [irridu'tʃibile] AGG (frazione, cifra) irreducible; (fig: avversario) indomitable, unshakable; (: ostinazione) unyielding.

irriflessivo, a [irrifles'sivo] AGG thoughtless.

irrigare [irri'gare] VT (Agr, Med) to irrigate.

irrigazione [irrigat'tsjone] SF (Agr, Med) irrigation.

irrigidimento [irridʒidi'mento] SM (di muscoli) stiffening; (fig: di disciplina) tightening; (: di posizione, atteggiamento) hardening.

irrigidire [irridʒi'dire] ① VT (gen) to stiffen; (fig: disciplina) to tighten.
② **irrigidirsi** VIP to stiffen; **irrigidirsi sulle proprie posizioni** to become entrenched in one's position.

irriguardoso, a [irrigwar'doso] AGG disrespectful.

irriguo, a [ir'riguo] AGG (terreno) irrigated; (acque) irrigation attr.

irrilevante [irrile'vante] AGG (trascurabile) insignificant.

irrimediabile [irrime'djabile] AGG: **un errore irrimediabile** a mistake which cannot be rectified; **danneggiato in modo irrimediabile** irreparably o irremediably damaged; **non è irrimediabile!** we can do something about it!

irrimediabilmente [irrimedjabil'mente] AVV irremediably, irreparably.

irrinunciabile [irrinun'tʃabile] AGG (bene, diritto) that cannot be renounced, which cannot be abandoned.

irripetibile [irripe'tibile] AGG unrepeatable.

irrisolto, a [irri'sɔlto] AGG (problema) unresolved.

irrisorio, ria, ri, rie [irri'zɔrjo] AGG ridiculous.

irrispettoso, a [irrispet'toso] AGG disrespectful.

irritabile [irri'tabile] AGG irritable.

irritabilità [irritabili'ta] SF irritability.

irritante [irri'tante] AGG (atteggiamento) irritating, annoying; (Med) irritant.

irritare [irri'tare] ① VT **a** (infastidire) to irritate, annoy **b** (pelle, occhi) to irritate.
② **irritarsi** VIP **a**: **irritarsi per qc/con qn** (infastidirsi) to get irritated o annoyed at sth/with sb **b** (infiammarsi: pelle, occhi) to become irritated.

irritato, a [irri'tato] AGG irritated; **aver la gola irritata** to have a sore throat.

irritazione [irritat'tsjone] SF (fastidio) irritation, annoyance; (Med) irritation.

irriverente [irrive'rɛnte] AGG irreverent.

irriverenza [irrive'rɛntsa] SF (qualità) irreverence; (azione) irreverent action.

irrobustire [irrobus'tire] ① VT (persona) to make stronger, make more robust; (muscoli) to strengthen.
② **irrobustirsi** VIP to become stronger.

irrompere [ir'rompere] VI DIF: **irrompere in** to burst into.

irrorare [irro'rare] VT (bagnare) to bathe; (Agr) to spray.

irroratrice [irrora'tritʃe] SF (Agr) spraying machine.

irrorazione [irrorat'tsjone] SF: **irrorazione sanguigna** blood supply.

irruente [irru'ɛnte] AGG (impetuoso) impetuous; (chiassoso) boisterous.

irruenza [irru'ɛntsa] SF impetuousness; **con irruenza** impetuously.

irruppi ecc [ir'ruppi] VB vedi **irrompere**.

irruvidire [irruvi'dire] ① VT to roughen.
② VI (aus essere), **irruvidirsi** VIP to become rough.

irruzione [irrut'tsjone] SF: **fare irruzione in** (*sogg*: *polizia*) to raid, burst into; **i tifosi hanno fatto irruzione nel campo** the fans invaded the pitch.

irsuto, a [ir'suto] AGG (*petto*) hairy; (*barba*) bristly.

irto, a ['irto] AGG (*barba*) bristly; **irto di** (*anche fig*) bristling with.

Is. ABBR (= *isola*) I.

Isacco [i'zakko] SM Isaac.

Isaia [iza'ia] SM Isaiah.

ISBN ABBR (= *International Standard Book Number*) ISBN.

iscrissi *ecc* [is'krissi] VB vedi **iscrivere**.

iscritto¹, a [is'kritto] ① PP di **iscrivere**.
② SM/F registered member (*o* student *o* candidate); **gli iscritti alla gara** the competitors.

iscritto² [is'kritto]: **per iscritto** AVV in writing.

iscrivere [is'krivere] VB IRREG ① VT ⓐ (*Scol*): **iscrivere (a)** to register (in), enrol (in); (*all'anagrafe*) to register; **iscrivere qn a un club** to enrol sb as a member of a club
ⓑ (*Comm*) to enter; **iscrivere una spesa nel bilancio** to enter an item on the balance sheet.
② **iscriversi** VR: **iscriversi a** (*partito, club*) to join; (*gara*) to enter; (*concorso*) to register *o* enter for; (*corso*) to enrol for; (*università*) to register *o* enrol at.

iscrizione [iskrit'tsjone] SF ⓐ (*epigrafe*) inscription
ⓑ (*a scuola, università*) enrolment; (*all'anagrafe*) registration; **chiedere/fare l'iscrizione a un club** to apply for membership of/join a club; **tassa di iscrizione** (*a una gara*) entry fee; (*a un circolo*) membership fee
ⓒ (*Comm*) entering.

I.S.E.F. ['izef] SIGLA M = *Istituto Superiore di Educazione Fisica*.

Islam [iz'lam] SM: **l'Islam** Islam.

islamico, a, ci, che [iz'lamiko] AGG Islamic.

islamismo [izla'mizmo] SM Islamism.

Islanda [iz'landa] SF: **l'Islanda** Iceland.

islandese [izlan'dese] ① AGG Icelandic.
② SM/F Icelander.
③ SM (*lingua*) Icelandic.

isobara [i'zɔbara] SF isobar.

isobaro, a [i'zɔbaro] AGG isobaric.

isola ['izola] SF island; **le Isole britanniche** the British Isles ►**isola pedonale** (*Aut*) pedestrian precinct ►**isola spartitraffico** *o* **salvagente** traffic island.

isolamento [izola'mento] SM ⓐ (*gen*) isolation; (*solitudine*) loneliness, solitude; **reparto d'isolamento** (*in ospedale*) isolation ward; **mettere qn in cella di isolamento** to put sb in solitary confinement ⓑ (*Tecn, Elettr*) insulation ►**isolamento acustico** soundproofing ►**isolamento termico** thermal insulation.

isolano, a [izo'lano] ① AGG island *attr*.
② SM/F islander.

isolante [izo'lante] ① AGG insulating.
② SM insulator.

isolare [izo'lare] ① VT ⓐ (*gen*) to isolate; **la neve ha isolato il paese dal resto del mondo** snow has cut the village off from the rest of the world ⓑ (*Tecn, Elettr*) to insulate; (: *acusticamente*) to soundproof ⓒ (*Bio*: *virus*) to isolate.
② **isolarsi** VR to isolate o.s.

isolato¹, a [izo'lato] AGG (*gen*) isolated; (*luogo*) lonely, remote.

isolato² [izo'lato] SM (*gruppo di palazzi*) block; **fare il giro dell'isolato** to walk round the block.

isolatore [izola'tore] SM insulator.

isolazionismo [izolattsjo'nizmo] SM isolationism.

isolazionista, i, e [izolattsjo'nista] SM/F isolationist.

isolotto [izo'lɔtto] SM islet.

isomero [i'zɔmero] SM isomer.

isometrico, a, ci, che [izo'mɛtriko] AGG isometric.

isoscele [i'zɔʃʃele] AGG (*Geom*) isosceles *attr*.

isoterma [izo'tɛrma] SF isotherm.

isotopo, a [i'zɔtopo] ① AGG isotopic.
② SM isotope.

ispanico, a, ci, che [is'paniko] AGG Hispanic.

ispessimento [ispessi'mento] SM thickening.

ispessire [ispes'sire] ① VT to thicken.
② **ispessirsi** VIP to get thicker, thicken.

ispettorato [ispetto'rato] SM inspectorate.

ispettore, trice [ispet'tore] SM/F (*Amm*) inspector ►**ispettore di polizia** police inspector ►**ispettore di reparto** shop walker (*Brit*), floor walker (*Am*) ►**ispettore alle vendite** (*Comm*) supervisor ►**ispettore di zona** (*Comm*) area supervisor *o* manager.

ispezionare [ispettsjo'nare] VT to inspect.

ispezione [ispet'tsjone] SF inspection.

ispido, a ['ispido] AGG (*barba*) bristly, shaggy; (*fig*: *carattere*) prickly, touchy.

ispirare [ispi'rare] ① VT (*gen*) to inspire; **ispirare fiducia a qn** to inspire sb with confidence; **è un tipo/un'idea che non mi ispira** *o* **che mi ispira poco** I'm not all that keen on him/the idea; **l'idea m'ispira** the idea appeals to me.
② **ispirarsi** VIP ⓐ: **ispirarsi a** (*prendere ispirazione*) to be inspired by, draw one's inspiration from
ⓑ (*conformarsi*): **ispirarsi a qc** to be based on sth.

ispirato, a [ispi'rato] AGG inspired.

ispiratore, trice [ispira'tore] ① AGG inspiring.
② SM/F inspirer.

ispirazione [ispirat'tsjone] SF inspiration; **secondo l'ispirazione del momento** according to the mood of the moment; **mi è venuta l'ispirazione di telefonargli** I suddenly thought of phoning him.

Israele [izra'ɛle] SM Israel.

israeliano, a [izrae'ljano] AGG, SM/F Israeli.

israelita, i, e [izrae'lita] SM/F Jew/Jewess; (*Storia*) Israelite.

israelitico, a, ci, che [izrae'litiko] AGG Jewish.

issare [is'sare] VT (*bandiera, vela*) to hoist; (*oggetto*) to hoist, haul up; **issare l'ancora** to weigh anchor; **issare qn in spalla** to lift sb onto one's shoulders.

Istanbul [istan'bul] SF Istanbul.

istantanea [istan'tanea] SF (*Fot*) snapshot.

istantaneamente [istantanea'mente] AVV instantaneously.

istantaneità [istantanei'ta] SF instantaneousness, immediacy.

istantaneo, a [istan'taneo] AGG (*gen*) instantaneous; (*che dura un istante*) momentary.

istante [is'tante] SM moment, instant; **all'istante** OR **sull'istante** at once, immediately, instantly; **in un istante** in a flash; **fra un istante** OR **tra qualche istante** in a moment *o* minute; **abbiamo saputo proprio in questo istante che...** we have just (this moment) heard that ...; **l'aereo dovrebbe essere atterrato proprio in questo istante** the plane should be landing at this very moment; **in quell'istante** at that very *o* precise moment.

istanza [is'tantsa] SF (*richiesta*: *Amm, Dir*) request, petition; **fare** *o* **presentare un'istanza a qn** to present a petition to sb; **su istanza di qn** at sb's request; **giudice di prima istanza** (*Dir*) judge of the court of first instance; **giudizio**

di seconda istanza judg(e)ment on appeal; in ultima istanza (*fig*) finally ►istanza di divorzio petition for divorce.

ISTAT ['istat] SIGLA M = *Istituto Centrale di Statistica*.

ISTEL ['istel] SIGLA F = *Indagine sull'ascolto delle televisioni in Italia*.

isterectomia [isterekto'mia] SF hysterectomy.

isteria [iste'ria] SF hysteria.

isterico, a, ci, che [is'tɛriko] 1 AGG hysterical.

2 SM/F (*Med*) hysteric; (*pegg*) hysterical type.

isterilire [isteri'lire] 1 VT (*terreno*) to render infertile; (*fig*: *fantasia*) to dry up.

2: isterilirsi VIP (*vedi vt*) to become infertile; to dry up.

isterismo [iste'rizmo] SM hysteria.

istigare [isti'gare] VT: istigare qn a (fare) qc to incite sb to (do) sth; istigare alla prostituzione (*Dir*) to force into prostitution.

istigatore, trice [istiga'tore] SM/F instigator.

istigazione [istigat'tsjone] SF incitement, instigation; su istigazione di qn (up)on sb's instigation ►istigazione a delinquere (*Dir*) incitement to crime.

istintivamente [istintiva'mente] AVV instinctively.

istintivo, a [istin'tivo] 1 AGG instinctive.

2 SM/F: essere un istintivo to be guided by one's instincts.

istinto [is'tinto] SM instinct; istinto di conservazione instinct of self-preservation; per o d'istinto instinctively.

istituire [istitu'ire] VT (*gen*) to institute; (*borsa di studio*) to found, endow; (*commissione d'inchiesta*) to set up; (*stabilire*: *parallelo*) to establish.

istituto [isti'tuto] 1 SM a (*gen*) institute; (*Univ*) department; (*Scol*) college, school, institute; istituto di francese/storia (*Univ*) French/history department; capo d'istituto headteacher

b (*istituzione*) institution.

2 ►istituto di bellezza beauty salon ►istituto di credito bank, banking institution ►istituto tecnico commerciale *school specializing in commercial subjects* ►istituto tecnico industriale statale ≈ technical college.

istitutore, trice [istitu'tore] SM/F a (*fondatore*) founder b (*precettore*) tutor/governess.

istituzionale [istituttsjo'nale] AGG institutional.

istituzionalizzare [istituttsjonalid'dzare] VT to institutionalize.

istituzionalizzato, a [istituttsjonalid'dzato] AGG institutionalized.

istituzione [istitut'tsjone] SF a (*atto*) institution, founding b (*ente, tradizione*) institution; essere un'istituzione (*fig*) to be an institution c (*stato*): istituzioni SFPL state institutions.

istmo ['istmo] SM isthmus.

istogramma, i [isto'gramma] SM (*Statistica*) histogram.

istologia [istolo'dʒia] SF (*Med*) histology.

istradare [istra'dare] VT (*fig*: *persona*): istradare (in o verso) to guide sb's steps (in o towards); istradare qn nella via del bene to set sb on the right path.

istriano, a [istri'ano] AGG, SM/F Istrian.

istrice ['istritʃe] SM (*Zool*) porcupine; (*fig*: *persona*): essere un istrice to be prickly.

istrione [istri'one] SM (*Teatro, fig*) ham (actor); fare l'istrione to ham.

istrionico, a, ci, che [istri'ɔniko] AGG histrionic.

istruire [istru'ire] VB IRREG 1 VT a (*dare un'istruzione a*) to educate; (*Mil*) to drill b (*dare istruzioni a*): istruire qn sul da farsi to instruct o tell sb what to do c (*Dir*): istruire una causa o un processo to prepare a case. 2 istruirsi VR (*informarsi*): istruirsi su qc to find out about sth.

istruito, a [istru'ito] AGG educated.

istruttivo, a [istrut'tivo] AGG (*esempio*) instructive; (*libro, film, discussione*) informative.

istruttore, trice [istrut'tore] 1 AGG: giudice istruttore (*Dir*) examining (*Brit*) o committing (*Am*) magistrate.

2 SM/F instructor ►istruttore di nuoto swimming instructor ►istruttore di scuola guida driving instructor ►istruttore di volo flying instructor.

istruttoria [istrut'tɔrja] SF (*Dir*) (preliminary) investigation and hearing; formalizzare un'istruttoria to proceed to a formal hearing.

istruttorio, ria, ri, rie [istrut'tɔrjo] AGG (*Dir*) preliminary; segreto istruttorio *obligation to maintain secrecy of disclosures in legal hearings*.

istruzione [istrut'tsjone] SF a (*gen*) training, instruction; (*Mil*) training; (*Scol*) education; Ministero della pubblica istruzione Ministry of Education

b: istruzioni SFPL (*direttive, avvertenze*) instructions, directions ►istruzioni per l'uso instructions (for use) c (*Dir*) investigation.

istupidimento [istupidi'mento] SM dazed state.

istupidire [istupi'dire] 1 VT (*sogg*: *colpo*) to stun, daze; (: *droga, stanchezza*) to stupefy.

2 VI (*aus essere*), istupidirsi VIP to become stupid.

I.S.V.E. ['izve] SIGLA M (= *Istituto di Studi per lo Sviluppo Economico*) *institute for research into economic development*.

Italia [i'talja] SF: l'Italia Italy; in Italia in Italy.

italianità [italjani'ta] SF Italian character.

italianizzare [italjanid'dzare] 1 VT to make Italian, italianize.

2 italianizzarsi VIP to become Italian, be italianized.

italiano, a [ita'ljano] 1 AGG Italian; all'italiana in the Italian style.

2 SM/F (*abitante*) Italian; gli Italiani the Italians.

3 SM (*lingua*) Italian; parlare (l')italiano to speak Italian.

italico, a, ci, che [i'taliko] AGG (*Storia*) Italic.

I.T.C. ['i'ti'tʃi] SIGLA M = istituto tecnico commerciale.

iter ['iter] SM passage, course ►iter burocratico bureaucratic process ►iter parlamentare parliamentary procedure.

iterativo, a [itera'tivo] AGG iterative, repetitive.

iterazione [iterat'tsjone] SF (*Inform*) loop.

itinerante [itine'rante] AGG wandering, itinerant; spettacolo itinerante touring show, travelling (*Brit*) o traveling (*Am*) show; mostra itinerante touring exhibition.

itinerario, ria, ri, rie [itine'rarjo] SM (*percorso*) route, itinerary; (*Alpinismo*) route; itinerario turistico tourist route.

I.T.I.S. ['itis] SIGLA M = istituto tecnico industriale statale.

itterizia [itte'rittsja] SF (*Med*) jaundice.

ittico, a, ci, che ['ittiko] AGG fish *attr*.

IUD [jud] SIGLA M INV (= *intra-uterine device*) IUD.

Iugoslavia [jugoz'lavja] SF = Jugoslavia.

iugoslavo, a [jugoz'lavo] = jugoslavo.

iuta ['juta] SF jute.

I.V.A. ['iva] SIGLA F (= *imposta sul valore aggiunto*) V.A.T. (*Brit*).

ivi ['ivi] AVV (*letter*) therein; (*nelle citazioni*) ibid.

J

J, j [i'lunga] SM O F INV (*lettera*) J, j; **J come Jersey** ≈ J for Jack (*Brit*), ≈ J for Jig (*Am*).

jabot [ʒa'bo] SM INV (*abbigliamento*) jabot.

jack [ʒæk] SM INV (*Carte*) jack, knave (*Brit*); (*Elettr*) jack (plug).

jacquard [ʒa'kar] AGG INV (*tessuto, disegno, maglione*) jacquard *attr*.

jais [ʒɛ] SM (*Min*) jet.

jazz [dʒaz] **1** SM INV jazz.
2 AGG INV jazz *attr*.

jazzista, i, e [dʒad'dzista] SM/F jazz player.

jeans [dʒinz] SMPL jeans.

jeanseria [dʒinse'ria] SF jeans shop.

jeep [dʒip] SF INV jeep.

jersey ['dʒɛrzi] SM INV jersey (cloth); **jersey di lana/cotone** jersey wool/cotton.

jet lag [dʒɛt lag] SM INV jet lag.

jet set [dʒɛt sɛt] SM INV jet set.

jingle ['dʒiŋɡəl] SM INV jingle.

jockey ['dʒɔki] SM INV (*fantino*) jockey.

jodel ['jodel] SM INV yodel.

jogging ['dʒɔɡiŋ] SM INV jogging; **fare jogging** to go jogging.

joint-venture [dʒɔint 'ventʃə] SF INV (*Fin*) joint venture.

jolly ['dʒɔli] SM INV joker.

jr. ABBR (= *junior*) Jr., jr.

judo [dʒu'dɔ] SM judo.

Jugoslavia [jugoz'lavja] SF: **la Jugoslavia** Yugoslavia.

jugoslavo, a [jugoz'lavo] AGG, SM/F Yugoslav(ian).

jujitsu ['zu:zitsu] SM jujitsu.

jukebox ['dʒuk'bɔks] SM INV jukebox.

julienne [ʒy'ljɛn] SF INV (*zuppa*) julienne; **tagliare le carote alla julienne** to cut carrots into julienne strips.

jumbo jet ['dʒumbo'dʒɛt], **jumbo** ['dʒumbo] SM INV jumbo (jet).

junghiano, a [jun'ɡjano] AGG, SM/F Jungian.

junior ['junjor] **1** AGG INV junior.
2 SM (*pl* **juniores**) (*Sport*) under-21; **la Nazionale juniores** the national under-21 team.

juta ['juta] SF = **iuta**.

K

K, k ['kappa] SF O M INV (*lettera*) K, k; **K come Kursaal** ≈ K for King.

k ABBR (= *kilo-*) k; (*Inform*) K.

Kabul [ka'bul] SF Kabul.

kafkiano, a [kaf'kjano] AGG Kafkaesque.

Kaiser ['kaizer] SM INV Kaiser.

kajal [ka'dʒal] SM INV kohl.

kaki ['kaki] AGG INV, SM INV = **cachi**.

Kalahari [kala'ari] SM: **il (deserto del) Kalahari** the Kalahari (Desert).

kalashnikov [kalaʃni'kof] SM INV kalashnikov.

kamasutra [kama'sutra] SM INV: **il kamasutra** the kamasutra.

kamikaze [kami'kaddze] [1] SM INV kamikaze; **una politica economica da kamikaze** (*fig*) a suicidal economic policy.
[2] AGG INV (*terrorista, commando, missione*) kamikaze *attr.*

Kampala [kam'pala] SF Kampala.

kantiano, a [kan'tjano] AGG Kantian.

kapoc [ka'pɔk] SM INV kapok.

kaputt [ka'put] AGG INV (*fam*) kaput.

karakiri [kara'kiri] SM INV hara-kiri; **fare karakiri** to commit hara-kiri.

karatè [kara'tɛ] SM INV karate.

karma ['karma] SM INV karma.

kasher [ka'ʃer] AGG INV kosher.

Kashmir [kaʃ'mir] SM: **il Kashmir** Kashmir.

kayak [ka'jak] SM INV kayak.

Kelvin ['kɛlvin] SM: **la scala Kelvin** the Kelvin scale.

keniota, i, e [ke'njɔta], **keniano, a** [ke'njano] AGG, SM/F Kenyan.

Kenya ['kɛnja] SM: **il Kenya** Kenya.

képi [ke'pi] SM INV kepi.

kermesse [ker'mɛs] SF INV (*nei Paesi Bassi*) kermis; (*fig*) carnival.

kerosene [kero'zɛne] SM INV = **cherosene**.

ketchup ['ketʃup] SM INV (tomato) ketchup.

kg ABBR (= *chilogrammo*) kg.

KGB ['kappa'dʒi'bi] SIGLA M: **il KGB** the KGB.

Khmer ['kmɛr] [1] AGG INV Khmer.
[2] SM/F INV Khmer; **i Khmer rossi** the Khmer Rouge *pl.*

kibbutz [kib'buts] SM INV kibbutz.

Kilimangiaro [kiliman'dʒaro] SM: **il Kilimangiaro** Kilimanjaro.

killer ['killer] [1] SM INV killer, hit man/woman (*fam*).
[2] AGG (*squalo, cellule*) killer *attr.*

kilo *ecc* ['kilo] = **chilo** *ecc.*

kilt [kilt] SM INV kilt.

kimono [ki'mɔno] SM INV = **chimono**.

kinesiterapia [kinezitera'pia] SF = **cinesiterapia**.

kit [kit] SM INV (*gen*) kit; (*Med, Bio*) (testing) kit.

kitsch [kitʃ] SM INV, AGG INV kitsch; **un arredamento kitsch** (*pegg*) tacky furniture.

kiwi ['kiwi] SM INV **a** (*frutto*) kiwi (fruit) **b** (*uccello*) kiwi.

kleenex® ['kli:neks] SM INV tissue, Kleenex ®.

km ABBR (= *chilometro*) km.

km/h ABBR (= *chilometri all'ora*) kmh, kph.

kmq ABBR (= *chilometro quadrato*) km².

knock out [nɔk'aut] [1] AGG knocked out.
[2] AVV: **mettere qn knock out** to knock sb out.
[3] SM INV (*colpo*) knockout punch ▶**knock out tecnico** technical knockout.

know-how ['nou hau] SM INV know-how.

K.O. [kappa'o], **k.o.**= *knock out* [1] AVV: **mettere qn k.o.** to knock sb out.
[2] SM INV KO, k.o.; **ha vinto per k.o. tecnico** he won on a technical knockout.

koala [ko'ala] SM INV koala (bear).

KR SIGLA = *Crotone.*

krapfen ['krapfən] SM INV ≈ doughnut.

krypton ['kripton] SM INV (*gas*) krypton.

Kuala Lumpur ['kwala 'lumpur] SF Kuala Lumpur.

Ku Klux Klan [kukluks'klan] SM Ku Klux Klan.

Kuwait [ku'vait] SM: **il Kuwait** Kuwait.

kuwaitiano, a [kuwai'tjano] AGG, SM/F Kuwaiti.

kW ABBR (= *kilowatt*) kW.

K-way® [kei'wei] SM INV cagoule.

kWh ABBR (= *kilowattora*) kW/h.

L

L, l ['ɛlle] SF O M INV (*lettera*) L, l; **L come Livorno** ≈ L for Lucy (*Brit*), ≈ L for Love (*Am*).

L, l ABBR (= *lira*) L, l.

l ABBR (= *litro*) L, l.

l' vedi **il**, **la²**; vedi **lo²**.

là [la] AVV **a** there; **mettilo là** put it there; **eccolo là!** there he (*o* it) is; **resta là dove sei** stay where you are; **là dentro/fuori/sopra/sotto** *ecc* in/out/up (*o* on)/under there *ecc*; **più in là** (*spazio*) further on; (*tempo*) later on; **chi va là?** who goes there?; **alto là!** halt!
b : **di là**: **di là dal fiume** beyond the river, on the other side of the river; **vieni via di là** come away from there; **mia madre è di là** my mother's in the other room; **per di là** (*andare, passare*) that way; **se vai per di là allunghi** if you go that way it'll take you longer; **essere più di là che di qua** to be more dead than alive; **cerca di guardare al di là del fatto in sé** try to look beyond the event itself
c (*fraseologia*): **là per là** (*sul momento*) there and then; **va' là!** come off it!; **stavolta è andato troppo in là** this time he's gone too far; **essere in là con gli anni** to be getting on (in years).

la¹ [la] ART DET F vedi **il**.

la² [la] PRON (dav vocale **l'**) **a** (*oggetto: riferito a persona*) her; (: *riferito a cosa*) it *per fraseologia vedi* **lo b** (*oggetto: forma di cortesia, anche:* **La**) you; **in attesa di risentirla** I (*o* we) look forward to hearing from you; **molto lieto di conoscerla** pleased to meet you.

la³ [la] SM INV (*Mus*) A; (: *solfeggiando la scala*) lah.

labbo ['labbo] SM (*uccello*) arctic skua.

labbro ['labbro] SM **a** (*Anat*) (*pl f* **labbra**) lip; **leccarsi le labbra** to lick one's lips; **mordersi le labbra** (*fig*) to bite one's tongue; **parlare a fior di labbra** to murmur; **sorridere a fior di labbra** to smile faintly; **pendere dalle labbra di qn** to hang on sb's every word **b** (*pl m* **labbri**) (*di ferita, vaso*) lip.

labiale [la'bjale] AGG, SF labial.

labile ['labile] AGG fleeting, ephemeral; **avere una memoria labile** to have a poor memory.

labirinto [labi'rinto] SM (*Mitol*) labyrinth; (*di stradine*) maze.

laboratorio, ri [labora'tɔrjo] SM **a** (*di ricerca*) laboratory; **esperimento di** *o* **da laboratorio** laboratory experiment ▶**laboratorio linguistico** language laboratory **b** (*per lavori manuali*) workshop; (*stanza*) workroom; **laboratorio fotografico** darkroom.

laboriosamente [laborjosa'mente] AVV (*vedi agg*) industriously; laboriously, with difficulty.

laboriosità [laborjosi'ta] SF (*industriosità*) industriousness.

laborioso, a [labo'rjoso] AGG (*operoso*) industrious, hard-working; (*faticoso*) laborious, difficult.

laburismo [labu'rizmo] SM (*Pol*) Labour movement.

laburista, i, e [labu'rista] [1] AGG Labour *attr* (*Brit*).
[2] SM/F Labour Party member (*Brit*).

lacca, che ['lakka] SF (*per mobili*) varnish, lacquer; (*per capelli*) (hair) lacquer, hair spray; (*per unghie*) nail polish, nail varnish (*Brit*).

laccare [lak'kare] VT (*mobili*) to varnish, lacquer.

laccatura [lakka'tura] SF lacquering, varnishing.

lacchè [lak'kɛ] SM INV lackey.

laccio, ci ['lattʃo] SM lace, string; **lacci delle scarpe** shoelaces ▶**laccio emostatico** (*Med*) tourniquet.

laccolite [lakko'lite] SM O F (*Geol*) laccolith.

lacerante [latʃe'rante] AGG (*suono*) piercing, shrill.

lacerare [latʃe'rare] [1] VT (*vestiti, stoffa*) to rip, tear; (: *fare a pezzi*) to tear *o* rip to shreds; (*Med, fig*) to lacerate; **un grido lacerò il silenzio** a piercing cry broke the silence; **lacerato dai dubbi/dal rimorso/dal dolore** racked by doubt/remorse/pain.
[2] **lacerarsi** VIP to tear, rip.

lacerazione [latʃerat'tsjone] SF (*anche Med*) tear.

lacero, a ['latʃero] AGG **a** (*abiti*) ripped, torn, tattered; (*persona*) ragged, in rags **b** (*Med*) lacerated; **ferita lacero-contusa** injury with lacerations and bruising.

laconicamente [lakonika'mente] AVV laconically.

laconico, a, ci, che [la'kɔniko] AGG laconic.

lacrima ['lakrima] SF **a** tear; **con le lacrime agli occhi** with tears in one's eyes; **essere/scoppiare in lacrime** to be

in/burst into tears ►**lacrime di coccodrillo** crocodile tears **b** (*goccia*) drop.

lacrimale [lakri'male] AGG (*Anat*) tear *attr*; (*ghiandola*) lachrymal (*Med*).

lacrimare [lakri'mare] VI (*aus* **avere**) (*occhi*) to water; (*persona*) to cry, weep.

lacrimevole [lakri'mevole] AGG heart-rending, pitiful.

lacrimogeno, a [lakri'mɔdʒeno] ①AGG: **gas lacrimogeno** tear gas.

②SM tear-gas grenade; **hanno lanciato dei lacrimogeni** they fired tear gas.

lacrimoso, a [lakri'moso] AGG (*viso, occhi*) tearful; (*commuovente: storia, film*) moving.

lacuna [la'kuna] SF (*vuoto*) gap; (: *in un testo*) blank (space); (: *di memoria*) lapse; **colmare una lacuna** to fill a gap.

lacunoso, a [laku'noso] AGG full of blanks *o* gaps.

lacustre [la'kustre] AGG lake *attr*.

laddove [lad'dove] CONG whereas.

ladro, a ['ladro] ① AGG thieving; **governo ladro!** (*fam*) damned government!.

② SM/F thief; (*di case*) burglar; **al ladro!** stop thief!; **l'occasione fa l'uomo ladro** (*Proverbio*) opportunity makes the thief.

ladrocinio, ni [ladro'tʃinjo] SM theft, robbery.

ladroneria [ladrone'ria] SF robbery.

ladruncolo, a [la'druŋkolo] SM/F petty thief.

lager ['la:gər] SM INV lager.

laggiù [lad'dʒu] AVV (*in basso*) down there; (*di là*) down *o* over there.

lagna ['laɲɲa] SF (*fam: persona, cosa*) drag, bore; **lagne** SFPL whining *sg*, moaning *sg*; **fare la lagna** to whine, moan.

lagnanza [laɲ'ɲantsa] SF complaint.

lagnarsi [laɲ'ɲarsi] VIP: **lagnarsi (di** *o* **per)** to complain (about), grumble (about).

lagnoso, a [laɲ'ɲoso] AGG (*noioso: film*) boring; **un tipo lagnoso** a moaner.

lago, ghi ['lago] SM lake; **il lago di Garda** Lake Garda; **un lago di sangue** a pool of blood ►**lago vulcanico** (*Geol*) crater lake.

Lagos ['lagos] SF: **il Lagos** Lagos.

lagrima *ecc* ['lagrima] = **lacrima** *ecc*.

laguna [la'guna] SF lagoon.

lagunare [lagu'nare] ①AGG lagoon *attr*.

②SM: **i lagunari** SMPL ≈ the marines.

laicismo [lai'tʃizmo] SM laicism.

laicizzare [laitʃid'dzare] VT to secularize.

laico, a, ci, che ['laiko] ①AGG (*Rel*) lay *attr*; (*stato, potere*) secular; (*scuola*) non-denominational.

②SM/F layman/laywoman.

③SM (*frate converso*) lay brother.

laido, a ['laido] AGG filthy, foul; (*osceno*) obscene, filthy.

lama¹ ['lama] SF (*di rasoio, spada*) blade; (*spada*) sword; **rasoio a doppia lama** double-edged razor.

lama² ['lama] SM INV (*Rel*) lama.

lama³ ['lama] SM INV (*animale*) llama.

lamantino [laman'tino] SM (*animale*) manatee.

lambiccare [lambik'kare] VT to distil; **lambiccarsi il cervello** to rack one's brains.

lambire [lam'bire] VT (*fig: acqua*) to lap; (: *fiamme*) to lick.

lambretta° [lam'bretta] SF (motor)scooter.

lamé [la'me] SM INV lamé; **di lamé** lamé *attr*.

lamella [la'mɛlla] SF **a** (*di metallo*) thin sheet **b** (*Bio*) lamella; (*di fungo*) gill, lamella (*termine tecn*).

lamentare [lamen'tare] ①VT to lament; **si lamentano**

gravi perdite heavy losses are reported.

② **lamentarsi** VIP **a** (*gemere*) to moan, groan **b** (*lagnarsi*): **lamentarsi (di)** to complain (about); **non mi lamento!** I can't complain!

lamentela [lamen'tɛla] SF complaint; **lamentele** SFPL complaining *sg*, grumbling *sg*; **smettila con queste lamentele!** stop grumbling!

lamentevole [lamen'tevole] AGG (*voce*) plaintive, mournful, complaining; (*stato*) lamentable, pitiful.

lamento [la'mento] SM (*gemito*) groan, moan; (: *per la morte di qn*) lament.

lamentoso, a [lamen'toso] AGG plaintive, mournful.

lametta [la'metta] SF (*da rasoio*) razor blade.

lamiera [la'mjɛra] SF (*Tecn*) sheet (metal); **lamiera di ferro/d'acciaio** sheet iron/steel; **lamiera ondulata** corrugated iron.

lamina ['lamina] SF (*di metallo*) thin layer *o* sheet *o* plate; (*di sci*) edge; (*Bot, Anat*) lamina; **lamina d'oro** gold leaf *o* foil.

laminare¹ [lami'nare] AGG laminar.

laminare² [lami'nare] VT to laminate.

laminato [lami'nato] ① SM (*metallico*) rolled section ►**laminato plastico** laminated plastic.

②AGG laminated.

lampada ['lampada] SF light, lamp ►**lampada abbronzante** sun lamp ►**lampada alogena** halogen lamp ►**lampada a gas** gas lamp ►**lampada al neon** neon light ►**lampada a petrolio** oil lamp ►**lampada da scrivania** reading lamp ►**lampada di sicurezza** safety lamp ►**lampada a spirito** blowlamp (*Brit*), blowtorch ►**lampada a stelo** standard lamp (*Brit*), floor lamp (*Am*) ►**lampada da tavolo** table lamp.

lampadario, ri [lampa'darjo] SM chandelier.

lampadina [lampa'dina] SF (*Elettr*) (light) bulb; **una lampadina da 100 watt** a 100 watt bulb; **lampadina tascabile** torch (*Brit*), flashlight (*Am*).

lampante [lam'pante] AGG **a** (*fig: evidente*) blindingly obvious, crystal clear; **prova lampante** clear proof **b** : **olio lampante** lamp oil.

lampara [lam'para] SF (*lampada*) fishing lamp; (*barca*) *boat for fishing by lamplight in Mediterranean*.

lampeggiamento [lampeddʒa'mento] SM flashing.

lampeggiare [lamped'dʒare] ①VI (*aus* **avere**) (*luce, occhi*) to flash; (*Aut*) to flash one's lights.

②VB IMPERS: **lampeggia** it is lightning.

lampeggiatore [lampeddʒa'tore] SM (*Aut*) indicator; (*Fot*) flash(gun).

lampione [lam'pjone] SM street light *o* lamp (*Brit*); (*palo*) lamppost.

lampo ['lampo] ① SM (*gen*) flash; (*Meteor*) flash of lightning; **lampi** SMPL (*Meteor*) lightning *sg*; **in un lampo** in a flash; **passare come un lampo** to flash past *o* by; **lampo di speranza** glimmer of hope ►**lampo di genio** flash of genius, sudden inspiration ►**lampo al magnesio** (*Fot*) magnesium flash.

② AGG INV (*cerimonia, Mil: operazione*) lightning *attr*; **la (cerniera) lampo** zip (fastener) (*Brit*), zipper (*Am*); **guerra lampo** blitzkrieg; **visita lampo** flying visit.

lampone [lam'pone] SM (*Bot*) raspberry.

lana ['lana] SF wool; **di lana** wool, woollen (*Brit*), woolen (*Am*); **pura lana vergine** pure new wool; **essere una buona lana** (*fig*) to be a scoundrel *o* rogue ►**lana d'acciaio** steel wool ►**lana di cammello** camel hair ►**lana di vetro** fibreglass (*Brit*), fiberglass (*Am*), glass wool.

lancetta [lan'tʃetta] SF (*di orologio*) hand; (*di barometro*) needle, pointer.

lancia[1], **ce** ['lantʃa] SF (*arma*) lance, spear; (*Pesca*) harpoon; (*di pompa antincendio*) nozzle; **spezzare una lancia in favore di qn** to come to sb's defence; **partire lancia in resta** (*fig*) to set off ready for battle.

lancia[2], **ce** ['lantʃa] SF (*Naut*) launch ▶ **lancia di salvataggio** lifeboat.

lanciabombe [lantʃa'bombe] SM INV (*Mil*) mortar.

lanciafiamme [lantʃa'fjamme] SM INV (*Mil*) flame-thrower.

lanciamissili [lantʃa'missili] [1] AGG INV missile-launching. [2] SM INV missile launcher.

lanciapalle [lantʃa'palle] AGG INV: **macchina lanciapalle** (*Tennis*) ball machine.

lanciarazzi [lantʃa'raddzi] [1] AGG INV rocket-launching. [2] SM INV rocket launcher.

lanciare [lan'tʃare] [1] VT **a** (*gen*) to throw; (*con forza*) to hurl, fling; (*bombe*) to drop; (*missili, siluri*) to launch; **lanciare qc a qn** to throw sth to sb; (*per colpirlo*) to throw sth at sb; **lanciare qc in aria** to throw sth into the air; **lanciare una moneta in aria** to toss a coin; **lanciare il peso** (*Sport*) to put the shot; **lanciare il disco** (*Sport*) to throw the discus

b (*emettere: grido*) to give out; (*: invettiva*) to hurl; (*: S.O.S.*) to send out; **mi ha lanciato un'occhiataccia** he flashed me a nasty look; **ha lanciato un urlo** he let out a yell

c (*introdurre: idea, nave, prodotto, moda*) to launch; **fu quel regista a lanciarla** it was that director who started her on her career

d (*far andare veloce: macchina*) to get up to top speed; **lanciare un cavallo** to set a horse off (at a gallop).

[2] **lanciarsi** VR **a** (*gen*): **lanciarsi in qc** (*anche fig*) to throw o.s. into sth; **lanciarsi contro qn** to hurl *o* fling o.s. at sb; **lanciarsi nella mischia** to throw o.s. into the fray; **lanciarsi all'inseguimento di qn** to set off in pursuit of sb; **lanciarsi col paracadute** to parachute

b (*fig: fare il primo passo*): **lanciarsi in** to launch into, embark upon *o* on; **che aspetti? — lanciati!** what are you waiting for? — off you go!

lanciasiluri [lantʃasi'luri] SM INV torpedo tube.

lanciato, a [lan'tʃato] AGG **a** (*affermato: attore, prodotto*) well-known, famous **b** (*veicolo*) speeding *o* racing along; **lanciato a tutta velocità** racing along at top speed; **chilometro lanciato** (*Sport*) flying start kilometre.

lanciere [lan'tʃɛre] SM (*Mil*) lancer.

lancinante [lantʃi'nante] AGG (*dolore*) stabbing, shooting; (*grido*) piercing.

lancio, ci ['lantʃo] SM **a** (*vedi vb 1a, c*) throwing *no pl*; hurling *no pl*, flinging *no pl*; dropping *no pl*; launching *no pl* **b** (*Sport*) throw ▶ **lancio di corda** (*Alpinismo*) lassoing ▶ **lancio del disco** throwing the discus ▶ **lancio del giavellotto** throwing the javelin ▶ **lancio del peso** putting the shot.

landa ['landa] SF (*terreno*) moor.

languidamente [langwida'mente] AVV languidly.

languido, a ['langwido] AGG (*voce*) languid; (*sguardo, atteggiamento*) languishing.

languire [lan'gwire] VI (*aus avere*) **a** (*struggersi*) to pine, languish; **languire d'amore** to be languishing with love **b** (*perdere forza: persona*) to languish; (*: conversazione*) to flag; (*: affari, commercio*) to be slack; **languire in carcere** to languish in prison.

languore [lan'gwore] SM **a** (*debolezza*) weakness, faint-

ness; **sento un languore allo stomaco** I'm feeling a bit peckish **b** (*comportamento*) languor; **mi guardava con languore** he gave me a languishing look.

laniero, a [la'njɛro] AGG (*industria, commercio*) wool *attr*, woollen (*Brit*), woolen (*Am*).

lanificio, ci [lani'fitʃo] SM wool mill, woollen (*Brit*) *o* woolen (*Am*) mill.

lanolina [lano'lina] SF (*Chim*) lanolin(e).

lanoso, a [la'noso] AGG woolly (*Brit*), wooly (*Am*).

lanterna [lan'tɛrna] SF (*lume, Archit*) lantern; (*faro*) lighthouse ▶ **lanterna magica** (*Cine*) magic lantern.

lanternino [lanter'nino] SM: **cercarsele col lanternino** (*fig*) to be asking for trouble.

lanugine [la'nudʒine] SF down.

lanuginoso, a [lanudʒi'noso] AGG downy.

Laocoonte [laoko'onte] SM Laocoon.

Laos ['laos] SM: **il Laos** Laos.

laotiano, a [lao'tjano] AGG, SM/F Laotian.

lapalissiano, a [lapalis'sjano] AGG self-evident.

laparoscopia [laparosko'pia] SF (*Med*) laparoscopy.

La Paz [la'pats] SF La Paz.

lapidare [lapi'dare] VT to stone (to death); (*fig*) to tear to pieces.

lapidario, ria, ri, rie [lapi'darjo] AGG (*arte*) lapidary; (*fig: stile*) succinct, terse.

lapide ['lapide] SF (*di sepolcro*) tombstone; (*lastra commemorativa*) memorial stone, plaque.

lapin [la'pɛ̃] SM INV rabbit fur, cony.

lapis ['lapis] SM INV pencil.

lapislazzuli [lapiz'laddzuli] SM INV lapis lazuli.

lappone ['lappone] [1] AGG Lappish, Lapp. [2] SM/F Laplander, Lapp. [3] SM (*lingua*) Lapp, Lappish.

Lapponia [lap'ponja] SF: **la Lapponia** Lapland.

lapsus ['lapsus] SM INV (*parlando*) slip (of the tongue); (*scrivendo*) slip (of the pen); **lapsus freudiano** Freudian slip.

laptop ['læptɔp] SM INV laptop (computer).

lardellare [lardel'lare] VT (*Culin*) to lard.

lardo ['lardo] SM (*per cucinare*) lard; (*da affettare*) pork fat (*salted or smoked*).

larga ['larga] SF vedi **largo 3**.

largamente [larga'mente] AVV (*ampiamente*) widely; (*generosamente*) generously.

largheggiare [larged'dʒare] VI (*aus avere*) to spend freely.

larghezza [lar'gettsa] SF **a** (*Mat, misura*) width, breadth; (*di barca*) beam; **una stanza della larghezza di 3 metri** a room 3 metres wide **b** (*generosità*) generosity; **larghezza di vedute** (*fig*) broad-mindedness.

largire [lar'dʒire] VT (*letter*) to give generously.

largo, a, ghi, ghe ['largo] [1] AGG **a** (*dimensione, misura*) wide, broad; **un cappello a larghe falde** a wide-brimmed hat; **un uomo largo di spalle** *o* **di spalle larghe** a broad-shouldered man; **a gambe larghe** with legs wide apart; **un corridoio largo 2 metri** a corridor 2 metres wide

b (*abiti*) loose; (*: maniche*) wide; **questa gonna mi sta larga** this skirt is loose on me; **questa giacca mi sta larga di spalle** this jacket is too big around the shoulders for me

c (*ampio: parte, percentuale*) large, big; **in larga misura** to a great *o* large extent; **su larga scala** on a large scale; **di larghe vedute** (*fig: liberale*) broad-minded; **di manica larga** (*fig*) generous, open-handed.

2 SM **a** : **fate largo!** make room o way!; **farsi largo tra la folla** to make o push one's way through the crowd; **farsi largo a gomitate** to elbow one's way
b (*piazzetta*) (small) square
c (*Naut*) open sea; **andare al largo** to sail on the open sea; **non andare al largo** (*nuotando*) don't go too far out; **prendere il largo** to put out to sea; (*fig*) to make off, escape; **al largo di Genova** off (the coast of) Genoa
d (*Mus*) largo.
3 SF: **stare** o **tenersi alla larga (da qn/qc)** to keep one's distance (from sb/sth), keep away (from sb/sth).
larice ['laritʃe] SM (*albero*) larch.
laringe [la'rindʒe] SF larynx.
laringite [larin'dʒite] SF laryngitis.
laringoiatra, i, e [laringo'jatra] SM/F (*medico*) throat specialist.
larva ['larva] SF (*Zool, Bio*) larva; (*fig pegg: apatico*) zombie; **essere (ridotto a) una larva** (*fig*) to be (all) skin and bone(s).
larvale [lar'vale] AGG (*Zool*) larval; **allo stato larvale** (*fig*) in embryo.
larvato, a [lar'vato] AGG (*fig: minacce*) veiled.
lasagne [la'zaɲɲe] SFPL lasagna *sg*; **lasagne al forno** baked lasagna *sg*.
lascare [las'kare] VT (*Naut*) to slack.
lasciapassare [laʃʃapas'sare] SM INV pass, permit.
lasciare [laʃ'ʃare] **1** VT **a** (*gen*) to leave; **lasciare qc a qn** to leave sb sth o sth to sb; **ha lasciato Roma nel '76** he left Rome in '76; **ho lasciato i soldi a casa** I've left my money at home; **devo lasciare l'università** I have to leave university, I have to give up university; **ha lasciato la scuola a 16 anni** he left school at 16; **lasciare la porta aperta** to leave the door open; **lasciare qn solo (a casa)** to leave sb (at home) alone; **ha lasciato la moglie** he's left his wife; **lascia la moglie e due bambini** he leaves a wife and two children; **lasciare qn erede** to make sb one's heir; **lasciare qn perplesso/confuso** to leave sb perplexed/confused
b (*permettere*): **lasciare qn fare qc** o **che qn faccia qc** to let sb do sth, allow sb to do sth; **lascia fare a me** let me do it; **lascia stare** o **correre** o **perdere** let it drop, forget it
c (*deporre: cose*) to leave, deposit; (: *persone*) to leave, drop (off); **ti lascio all'angolo** I'll drop you off at the corner
d (*dare, concedere*) to give, let have; **mi puoi lasciare la macchina oggi?** can you let me have the car today?; **lasciami il tempo di farlo** give me time to do it
e (*omettere*) to leave out, forget; **non lasciare tutti i particolari interessanti** don't leave out all the interesting bits
f (*serbare*) to leave, keep; **lasciami un po' di vino** leave some wine for me
g : **lasciare stare qn** to let sb be, leave sb alone; **lasciare stare qc** to leave sth alone; **lascia stare quel povero gatto!** leave that poor cat alone!; **lascia stare, ci penso io** leave it, I'll see to it; **lascialo stare, non vale la pena di arrabbiarsi** just ignore him, it's not worth getting annoyed; **lascia stare, offro io** it's all right, I'm paying o it's on me; **è meglio lasciar stare certi argomenti** it's better not to bring up certain subjects; **volevo insistere ma poi ho lasciato stare** I was going to insist but then I decided to let it go
h : **lasciarsi sfruttare** to let o.s. be exploited; **lasciarsi andare** to let o.s. go

I (*fraseologia*): **lasciare in bianco** to leave blank; **lasciare (molto) a desiderare** to leave much o a lot to be desired; **lasciare detto** o **scritto (a qn)** to leave word (for sb); **lasciare qn indifferente** to leave sb unmoved; **non lascia mai niente al caso** he never leaves anything to chance; **lasciami in pace** leave me alone o in peace; **lasciare la presa** to lose one's grip; **lasciare il segno (su qc)** to mark (sth); (*fig*) to leave one's o a mark (on sth); **ci ha lasciato la vita** it cost him his life.
2 **lasciarsi** VR (*uso reciproco*) to part (from each other); (*coniugi*) to leave each other, split up; **si sono lasciati all'aeroporto** they left each other at the airport, they said goodbye at the airport.
lascito ['laʃʃito] SM (*Dir*) legacy, bequest.
lascivia [laʃ'ʃivja] SF lust, lasciviousness.
lascivo, a [laʃ'ʃivo] AGG lascivious, wanton.
lasco ['lasko] SM (*Naut*): **al lasco** on a close reach; **al gran lasco** on a broad reach.
laser ['lazer] SM INV, AGG INV: **(raggio) laser** laser (beam).
lassativo, a [lassa'tivo] AGG, SM laxative.
lassismo [las'sizmo] SM laxity.
lasso ['lasso] SM: **lasso di tempo** interval, lapse of time.
lassù [las'su] AVV (*in alto*) up there; (*in paradiso*) in heaven above.
lastra ['lastra] SF **a** (*di marmo, pietra*) slab; (*di vetro, ghiaccio*) sheet; (*di finestra*) pane; (*di metallo*) plate **b** (*Fot*) plate; (*Med*) X-ray; **fare le lastre a qn** (*fam*) to X-ray sb.
lastricare [lastri'kare] VT to pave.
lastricato [lastri'kato] SM paving(stone).
lastrico, ci o **chi** ['lastriko] SM paving; **essere sul lastrico** to be penniless; **gettare qn sul lastrico** to leave sb destitute.
lastrone [las'trone] SM (*di pietra*) slab; (*Alpinismo*) sheer rock face.
latente [la'tɛnte] AGG latent.
laterale [late'rale] **1** AGG (*gen*) side *attr*, lateral; (*uscita, ingresso, linea*) side *attr*; **rimessa laterale** throw-in.
2 SM (*Calcio, anche:* **mediano laterale**) halfback.
lateralmente [lateral'mente] AVV sideways.
laterite [late'rite] SF (*Geol*) laterite.
laterizio, zi [late'rittsjo] SM (perforated) brick.
latice ['latitʃe] SM = **lattice**.
latifondista, i, e [latifon'dista] SM/F large (agricultural) landowner.
latifondo [lati'fondo] SM large (agricultural) estate.
latinismo [lati'nizmo] SM Latinism.
latinista, i, e [lati'nista] SM/F Latin scholar, Latinist.
latino, a [la'tino] **1** AGG Latin.
2 SM (*lingua*) Latin.
latino-americano, a [la'tino ameri'kano] AGG, SM/F Latin-American.
latitante [lati'tante] **1** AGG: **essere latitante** (*persona*) to be in hiding o on the run; (*fig*) to be an absent force; (*potere, governo*) to be inactive.
2 SM/F fugitive (from justice).
latitanza [lati'tantsa] SF (*fig: assenza*) absence; **darsi alla latitanza** (*nascondersi*) to go into hiding.
latitudine [lati'tudine] SF latitude.
lato[1] ['lato] SM (*gen*) side, part; (*Mat, Geom*) side; (*fig: di problema*) aspect; **da ogni lato** OR **da tutti i lati** from all sides; **dal lato opposto (di)** from the other o opposite side (of); **d'altro lato** (*d'altra parte*) on the other hand; **da un lato... dall'altro lato...** on the one hand ...on the

other hand ...; **l'altro lato della medaglia** (*fig*) the other side of the coin.

lato² ['lato] AGG: **in senso lato** broadly speaking.

latore, trice [la'tore] SM/F (*Comm*) bearer.

latrare [la'trare] VI (*aus* **avere**) to bark.

latrato [la'trato] SM howling.

latrina [la'trina] SF (public) lavatory (*Brit*), rest room (*Am*).

latrocinio, ni [latrot'ʃinjo] SM = **ladrocinio**.

latta ['latta] SF (*sostanza*) tin (plate); (*recipiente*) tin (*Brit*), can.

lattaio, aia, ai, aie [lat'tajo] SM/F (*commerciante*) dairyman/dairywoman; (*distributore*) milkman/milkwoman; **vado dal lattaio** I'm going to the dairy.

lattante [lat'tante] ① AGG unweaned.

② SM/F unweaned baby.

latte ['latte] ① SM milk; **al latte** milk *attr*; **dare il latte (a un bambino)** (*al seno*) to (breast)feed (a baby); (*con il biberon*) to (bottle-)feed (a baby); **avere ancora il latte alla bocca** (*fig*) to be still wet behind the ears; **tutto latte e miele** (*fig*) all smiles.

② ▶**latte di bellezza** beauty lotion ▶**latte di cocco** coconut milk ▶**latte condensato** condensed milk ▶**latte detergente** cleansing milk *o* lotion ▶**latte di gallina** eggnog ▶**latte intero** full-cream milk ▶**latte a lunga conservazione** long-life milk, UHT milk ▶**latte magro** *o* **scremato** skimmed milk ▶**latte materno** mother's milk, breast milk ▶**latte in polvere** dried *o* powdered milk.

latteo, a ['latteo] AGG (*di latte*) milk *attr*; (*colore*) milky (-white); **la Via Lattea** the Milky Way.

latteria [latte'ria] SF dairy.

lattice ['lattitʃe] SM latex.

latticino [latti'tʃino] SM dairy product.

lattico, a, ci, che ['lattiko] AGG lactic.

lattiera [lat'tjɛra] SF milk jug.

lattiero, a [lat'tjɛro] AGG (*prodotti*) dairy *attr*; **industria lattiero-casearia** dairying.

lattiginoso, a [lattidʒi'noso] AGG milky.

lattina [lat'tina] SF can.

lattosio [lat'tɔzjo] SM (*Chim*) lactose.

lattuga, ghe [lat'tuga] SF lettuce.

laudano ['laudano] SM laudanum.

laurea ['laurea] SF degree (*gained after 4-6 years' study and the presentation of a dissertation*); **prendere** *o* **conseguire la laurea** to take *o* obtain one's degree, graduate; **ha preso la laurea in legge** he graduated *o* got a degree in law ▶**laurea breve** *diploma awarded at the end of a more vocational university course lasting 2-3 years.*

laureando, a [laure'ando] ① AGG final year *attr* (*Brit*), senior (*Am*).

② SM/F final-year student (*Brit*), senior (*Am*).

laureare [laure'are] ① VT to confer a degree on.

② **laurearsi** VIP to graduate; **si è laureato in legge** he graduated in law.

laureato, a [laure'ato] ① AGG graduate *attr*.

② SM/F graduate.

lauro ['lauro] SM (*Bot*) laurel; **il lauro della vittoria** the laurels of victory.

lauto, a ['lauto] AGG (*pranzo, mancia*) lavish; **lauti guadagni** handsome profits.

lava ['lava] SF lava.

lavabicchieri [lavabik'kjɛri] SM INV glass-washer (*machine*).

lavabo [la'vabo] SM washbasin (*Brit*), washbowl (*Am*).

lavabottiglie [lavabot'tiʎʎe] SM INV bottle-washer (*machine*).

lavacristallo [lavakris'tallo] SM (*Aut*) windscreen (*Brit*) *o* windshield (*Am*) washer.

lavaggio, gi [la'vaddʒo] SM (*gen*) washing *no pl* ▶**lavaggio auto** car wash ▶**lavaggio del cervello** brainwashing ▶**lavaggio a secco** dry cleaning.

lavagna [la'vaɲɲa] SF ⓐ (*nelle scuole*) blackboard, chalkboard (*Am*); **scrivere alla lavagna** to write on the blackboard *o* chalkboard; **lavagna luminosa** overhead projector

ⓑ (*minerale*) slate.

lavamano [lava'mano] SM INV washstand.

lavanda¹ [la'vanda] SF (*gen*) washing; (*Med*) lavage; **fare una lavanda gastrica a qn** to pump sb's stomach.

lavanda² [la'vanda] SF (*Bot*) lavender.

lavandaia [lavan'daja] SF washerwoman; (*fig pegg*) fishwife.

lavanderia [lavande'ria] SF (*di ospedale, caserma*) laundry; (*negozio*) laund(e)rette (*Brit*), laundromat ® (*Am*); (: *lavanderia a secco*) dry-cleaner's.

lavandino [lavan'dino] SM (*del bagno*) washbasin (*Brit*), washbowl (*Am*); (*della cucina*) sink.

lavapiatti [lava'pjatti] ① SM/F INV (*persona*) dishwasher.

② SF INV (*macchina*) dishwasher, dishwashing machine.

lavare [la'vare] ① VT ⓐ (*gen*) to wash; **lavare a mano** to wash by hand, handwash; **lavare a secco** to dry-clean; **lavare i piatti** to wash the dishes, do the washing up; **lavare la testa a qn** to wash sb's hair

ⓑ (*fig: purificare*) to cleanse, purify

ⓒ : **lavarsi le mani/i capelli** to wash one's hands/hair; **lavarsi i denti** to clean *o* brush one's teeth; **me ne lavo le mani** (*fig*) I wash my hands of it.

② **lavarsi** VR to wash o.s., have a wash.

lavascale [lavas'kale] SM/F INV (*persona*) stair cleaner (*in block of flats*).

lavasecco [lava'sekko] ① SM INV (*negozio*) dry-cleaner's.

② SF INV dry-cleaning machine.

lavastoviglie [lavasto'viʎʎe] SF INV dishwasher.

lavata [la'vata] SF wash; **dare una lavata a qc** to give sth a wash; **dare una lavata di capo a qn** (*fig*) to give sb a good telling-off.

lavativo [lava'tivo] SM (*buono a nulla*) good-for-nothing, idler.

lavatoio, oi [lava'tojo] SM (public) washhouse.

lavatrice [lava'tritʃe] SF washing machine.

lavatura [lava'tura] SF ⓐ (*atto*) washing *no pl* ⓑ (*liquido*) dirty water; **lavatura di piatti** dishwater; **questa minestra è lavatura di piatti** this soup is like dishwater.

lavavetri [lava'vetri] SM INV (*apparecchio*) window cleaner.

lavello [la'vɛllo] SM (kitchen) sink.

lavico, a, ci, che ['laviko] AGG lava *attr*.

lavina [la'vina] SF snowslide.

lavorante [lavo'rante] SM/F worker.

lavorare [lavo'rare] ① VI (*aus* **avere**) ⓐ (*persona*) to work; **andare a lavorare** to go to work; **va a lavorare!** go and get on with your work!; **lavorare duro** *o* **sodo** to work hard; **lavorare in proprio** to work for o.s., be self-employed; **lavorare a maglia/ad ago** to knit/do needlework; **lavorare a qc** to work on sth; **lavorare di fantasia** (*suggestionarsi*) to imagine things; (*fantasticare*) to let one's imagination run free

ⓑ (*funzionare: macchinari*) to work, run, operate; (*negozi, uffici: far affari*) to do well, do good business; **quel bar**

non lavora molto that bar isn't doing very well; **far lavorare il cervello** to use one's brains.

[2] VT (*creta, ferro*) to work; (*legno*) to carve; (*Culin: pane, pasta*) to work, knead; (: *burro*) to beat; (*Agr: terra*) to work, cultivate; **lavorarsi qn** (*fig: convincere*) to work on sb.

lavorativo, a [lavora'tivo] AGG (*giorno, capacità*) working *attr*; **attività lavorativa** occupation.

lavorato, a [lavo'rato] AGG (*cuoio*) tooled; (*legno, pietra*) carved; (*metallo*) wrought; (: *oro*) worked; (*prodotto*) finished; (*terreno*) cultivated; **lavorato a mano** hand-made.

lavoratore, trice [lavora'tore] [1] AGG working *attr*; **la classe lavoratrice** the working class.

[2] SM/F worker; **è un gran lavoratore** he's a hard worker.

lavorazione [lavorat'tsjone] SF a (*gen*) working; (*di legno, pietra*) carving; (*di film*) making; (*del terreno*) cultivation; (*di pane, pasta*) working, kneading; (*di prodotto*) manufacture; **lavorazione della carta** paper making; **"lavorazione a mano"** "handmade" ▶**lavorazione a macchina** machine production ▶**lavorazione in serie** mass production

b (*modo di esecuzione*) workmanship.

lavorio, rii [lavo'rio] SM intense activity.

lavoro [la'voro] SM a (*attività*): **il lavoro** work; **lavoro manuale/dei campi** manual/farm work; **avere molto/poco lavoro** to have a lot of/little work to do; **essere al lavoro (su qc)** to be at work (on sth); **mettersi al lavoro** to set to *o* get down to work

b (*compito*) job, task, work *no pl*; **è un lavoro da specialisti** it's a skilled job, it's a job for a professional; **sta svolgendo un lavoro di ricerca** he is carrying out *o* doing research work; **è un lavoro da niente!** it's no job at all!; **eseguire** *o* **fare (bene/male) un lavoro** to do a job (well/badly)

c (*posto, impiego*): **il lavoro** work; **un lavoro** a job, an occupation; **avere un buon lavoro** to have a good job; **essere senza lavoro** to be out of work *o* unemployed; **i senza lavoro** the jobless, the unemployed; **incidente sul lavoro** industrial accident, accident at work; **Ministero del Lavoro e della Previdenza Sociale** ≈ Department of Employment (*Brit*), ≈ Department of Labor (*Am*) ▶**lavoro d'équipe** teamwork ▶**lavoro nero** moonlighting (*Brit*), double-dipping (*Am*) ▶**lavoro straordinario** overtime

d : **lavori** SMPL work *sg*; **lavori scientifici/di ricerca** scientific/research work; **lavori pesanti/leggeri** heavy/light work *o* jobs; **(fare) i lavori di casa** (to do) the housework; **far fare dei lavori in casa** to have some work done in the house; **aprire/chiudere i lavori del parlamento** to open/close the parliamentary session; **il convegno conclude domani i suoi lavori** the conference comes to an end tomorrow; **lavori di scavo** (*Archeol*) excavation works; **Ministero dei Lavori Pubblici** Ministry of Public Works; **"lavori in corso"** "work in progress"; (*segnale stradale*) "road works ahead"; **questi lavori non si fanno!** you just don't do these things! ▶**lavori forzati** hard labour *sg*

e (*opera*) piece of work; (: *artistica*) work

f (*Econ*) labour (*Brit*), labor (*Am*)

g (*Fis*) work.

laziale [lat'tsjale] [1] AGG of *o* from Lazio.

[2] SM/F inhabitant *o* native of Lazio.

lazzaretto [laddza'retto] SM leper hospital.

Lazzaro ['laddzaro] SM Lazarus.

lazzarone [laddza'rone] SM scoundrel.

lazzo ['laddzo] SM jest.

LC SIGLA = Lecco.

LE SIGLA = Lecce.

le¹ [le] ART DET FPL vedi **il**.

le² [le] PRON PERS a (*complemento oggetto*) them; vedi anche **lo²**

b (*complemento di termine: a lei*) (to) her; **le ho detto tutto** I told her everything; **le appartiene** it belongs to her

c (*forma di cortesia, anche:* **Le**: *complemento di termine*) (to) you; **le posso dire una cosa?** may I tell you something?; **le dispiace attendere?** would you mind waiting?; **le chiedo scusa** I beg your pardon.

leader ['li:də] SM/F INV leader.

leale [le'ale] AGG (*fedele*) loyal, faithful; (*onesto*) fair, honest.

lealista, i, e [lea'lista] SM/F loyalist.

lealmente [leal'mente] AVV (*vedi agg*) loyally, faithfully; fairly, honestly.

lealtà [leal'ta] SF a (*fedeltà*) loyalty, faithfulness b (*onestà*) fairness, honesty; **comportarsi con lealtà** to behave fairly.

leasing ['li:zin] SM INV (*Comm*) leasing.

lebbra ['lebbra] SF leprosy.

lebbroso, a [leb'broso] [1] AGG leprous.

[2] SM/F leper.

leccaculo [lekka'kulo] SM/F INV (*pegg*) arselicker (*Brit fam!*), arsekisser (*Am fam!*)

lecca lecca ['lekka 'lekka] SM INV lollipop, lolly.

leccapiedi [lekka'pjedi] SM/F INV (*pegg*) bootlicker.

leccarda [lek'karda] SF (*Culin*) dripping pan.

leccare [lek'kare] [1] VT to lick; **leccarsi le labbra** *o* **i baffi/le dita** to lick one's lips/fingers; **leccarsi le ferite** (*anche fig*) to lick one's wounds; **leccare (i piedi a) qn** (*fig*) to suck up to sb.

[2] **leccarsi** VR (*fig*) to preen o.s.

leccata [lek'kata] SF lick.

leccato, a [lek'kato] AGG affected.

leccherò *ecc* [lekke'rɔ] VB vedi **leccare**.

leccio, ci ['lettʃo] SM (*albero*) holm oak, ilex.

leccornia [lekkor'nia] SF delicacy, titbit.

lecitamente [letʃita'mente] AVV rightly, correctly.

lecito, a ['letʃito] [1] AGG (*domanda, comportamento*) permissible; (*Dir*) lawful, legal; **ti par** *o* **sembra lecito che...?** does it seem right to you that ...?; **crede che tutto gli sia lecito** he thinks he can do whatever he likes; **mi sia lecito far presente che...?** may I point out that ...?; **se mi è lecito** if I may.

[2] SM (what is) right.

lectio brevis ['lɛktsjo 'brɛvis] SF INV (*Scol*) *shorter school day*.

ledere ['lɛdere] VT IRREG to damage; **ledere gli interessi di qn** to prejudice sb's interests.

lega¹, ghe ['lega] SF a (*Pol, Calcio*) league; **lega doganale** customs union; **far lega (con qn) contro qn/qc** to be in league (with sb) against sb/sth ▶**la Lega delle Nazioni** the League of Nations ▶**Lega Nord** (*Pol*) *Italian federalist party*

b (*Chim*) alloy; **metallo di bassa lega** base metal; **gente di bassa lega** (*fig*) common *o* vulgar people.

lega², ghe ['lega] SF (*misura*) league.

legaccio, ci [le'gattʃo] SM lace, string.

legale [le'gale] [1] AGG (*gen*) legal; **medicina legale** forensic

medicine; **studio legale** lawyer's office; **numero legale** quorum; **corso legale delle monete** official exchange rate.
[2] SM/F lawyer.

legalità [legali'ta] SF lawfulness, legality.

legalizzare [legalid'dzare] VT **a** (*rendere legale*) to legalize **b** (*autenticare*) to authenticate.

legalizzazione [legalid'dzattsjone] SF (*vedi vb*) legalization; authentication.

legalmente [legal'mente] AVV legally.

legame [le'game] SM **a** (*gen, fig*) tie, bond; **legame di sangue/di parentela** blood/family tie; **legame di amicizia** bond of friendship; **rompere i legami con qn/qc** to break one's ties with sb/sth **b** (*rapporto logico*) link, connection **c** (*Chim*) bond.

legamento [lega'mento] SM (*Anat*) ligament.

legare [le'gare] [1] VT **a** (*gen*) to bind, tie (up); (*Tip: libro*) to bind; **legare le mani a qn** (*anche fig*) to tie sb's hands; **è pazzo da legare** (*fam*) he should be locked up **b** (*persone: unire*) to bind (together), unite; (*vincolare*) to bind; **sono legati da amicizia** they are friends; **siamo legati da questioni di interesse** we have financial interests in common; **questo posto è legato ai ricordi della mia infanzia** this place is bound up with memories of my childhood; **è legata al ricordo di suo marito** she is very attached to her husband's memory; **legarsela al dito** (*fig*) to bear a grudge **c** (*connettere*) to connect, link up; **questi due fatti sono strettamente legati** these two facts are closely linked *o* connected **d** (*Culin: ingredienti, salsa*) to bind; (: *arrosto, pollo*) to truss.
[2] VI (*aus avere*) **a** (*persone*) to get on; **non hanno mai legato** they've never got on **b** (*metalli*) to alloy **c** (*Culin*) to bind.
[3] **legarsi** VR **a** (*fig*): **legarsi (a qn)** to become attached (to sb) **b** (*Alpinismo*): **legarsi in cordata** to rope up.

legatario, ria, ri, rie [lega'tarjo] SM/F (*Dir*) legatee.

legato¹, a [le'gato] [1] AGG **a** (*inibito*) awkward; **essere legato nei movimenti** to be stiff in one's movements; **ho le mani legate** (*fig*) my hands are tied **b** (*Mus*): **note legate** notes played legato.
[2] SM (*Mus*) legato.

legato² [le'gato] SM: **legato pontificio** papal legate.

legato³ [le'gato] SM (*Dir*) legacy, bequest.

legatore, trice [lega'tore] SM/F bookbinder.

legatoria [legato'ria] SF (*attività*) bookbinding; (*negozio*) bookbinder's.

legatura [lega'tura] SF (*di libri*) binding; (*Tip, Mus*) ligature.

legazione [legat'tsjone] SF legation.

legenda [le'dʒɛnda] SF vedi **leggenda b**.

legge ['leddʒe] SF (*gen*) law; (*Parlamento*) act; **a norma** *o* **termini di legge** according to the law; **per legge** by law; **la legge è uguale per tutti** everybody is equal before the law; **la legge del più forte** the law of survival of the fittest; **ogni suo desiderio è legge** your wish is my command; **la sua parola è legge** his word is law; **le leggi della società** the rules *o* laws of society ►**legge marziale** martial law.

leggenda [led'dʒɛnda] SF **a** (*mito*) legend; (*diceria*) old wives' tale **b** (*iscrizione: di moneta*) legend **c** (*chiave di lettura*) key.

leggendario, ria, ri, rie [leddʒen'darjo] AGG legendary.

leggere ['leddʒere] VT IRREG (*gen, Mus*) to read; (*discorso, comunicato*) to read (out); **leggere ad alta voce** to read aloud; **l'ho letto sul giornale** I read (about) it in the newspaper; **leggere nel futuro** (*chiromante*) to read the future; **leggere la mano a qn** to read sb's palm; **leggere qc negli occhi di qn** to see sth in sb's eyes; **leggere nel pensiero a qn** to read sb's mind *o* thoughts; **leggere fra le righe** (*fig*) to read between the lines; **letto e approvato** read and approved.

leggerezza [leddʒe'rettsa] SF **a** (*gen*) lightness; (*di ballerina*) lightness, nimbleness **b** (*sconsideratezza*) thoughtlessness; (*volubilità*) fickleness; **con leggerezza** (*agire*) thoughtlessly.

leggermente [leddʒer'mente] AVV (*con leggerezza*) lightly; (*con agilità*) lightly, nimbly; (*un po'*) slightly; **è leggermente cambiato** he has changed a little; **la macchina ha urtato leggermente il muro** the car just grazed the wall.

leggero, a [led'dʒero] AGG (*gen*) light; (*agile*) light, nimble, agile; (*rumore, dolore*) slight; (*malattia, punizione*) mild, slight; (*cibo, vino*) light; (*caffè, tè*) weak; **leggero come una piuma** light as a feather; **avere il sonno leggero** to be a light sleeper; **a passi leggeri** with a light step; **avere un leggero accento straniero** to have a slight foreign accent; **ha avuto la malattia in forma leggera** she had a mild form of the illness; **fanteria/cavalleria leggera** light infantry/cavalry; **una ragazza leggera** (*fig*) a flirtatious *o* flighty girl; **prendere le cose alla leggera** to take things lightly; **a cuor leggero** light-heartedly.

leggiadria [leddʒa'dria] SF loveliness, prettiness; **leggiadria di stile** elegance of style.

leggiadro, a [led'dʒadro] AGG (*gen*) lovely, pretty; (*stile, movimenti*) elegant, graceful.

leggibile [led'dʒibile] AGG (*calligrafia*) legible; (*libro*) readable.

leggio, gii [led'dʒio] SM (*per libri*) bookrest; (*Mus*) music stand; (*in chiesa, Univ*) lectern.

legherò *ecc* [lege'rɔ] VB vedi **legare**.

leghismo [le'gizmo] SM (*Pol*) *in Italy, political movement with federalist tendencies*.

leghista, i, e [le'gista] (*Pol*) [1] AGG *of a "lega", especially Lega Nord*.
[2] SM/F *member o supporter of a "lega", especially Lega Nord*.

legiferare [ledʒife'rare] VI (*aus avere*) to legislate.

legionario, ri [ledʒo'narjo] SM (*volontario*) legionnaire; (*Storia*) legionary.

legione [le'dʒone] SF (*Mil*) legion; (*fig*) host, multitude ►**la Legione straniera** the Foreign Legion.

legislativo, a [ledʒizla'tivo] AGG legislative.

legislatore [ledʒizla'tore] SM legislator.

legislatura [ledʒizla'tura] SF legislature.

legislazione [ledʒizlat'tsjone] SF legislation.

legittima [le'dʒittima] SF (*Dir*) *portion of estate of which a testator cannot dispose freely*.

legittimamente [ledʒittima'mente] AVV (*possedere*) legitimately.

legittimare [ledʒitti'mare] VT (*figlio*) to legitimize; (*giustificare: comportamento*) to justify.

legittimità [ledʒittimi'ta] SF legitimacy.

legittimo, a [le'dʒittimo] AGG (*figlio*) legitimate; (*orgoglio*) justifiable; (*dubbio, desiderio*) reasonable; (*fondato: paura, sospetto*) justified; **per legittima difesa** in self-defence (*Brit*), in self-defense (*Am*).

legna ['leɲɲa] SF (fire)wood; **legna da ardere** firewood; **stufa a legna** wood stove; **far legna** to gather firewood; **mettere legna al fuoco** (*fig*) to add fuel to the fire.

legnaia [leɲ'ɲaja] SF woodshed.

legnaiolo [leɲɲa'jɔlo] SM woodcutter.

legname [leɲ'ɲame] SM timber, wood.

legnata [leɲ'ɲata] SF blow with a stick; **dare a qn un sacco di legnate** to give sb a good hiding.

legno ['leɲɲo] SM **a** (*gen*) wood; **di legno** wood *attr*, wooden; **legno stagionato** seasoned wood; **legno dolce/duro** soft/hardwood; **testa di legno** (*fig*) blockhead **b** (*pezzo di legno*) piece of wood **c** (*fig*: *nave*) sailing ship **d** (*Mus*): **i legni** SMPL the woodwind *sg o pl.*

legnoso, a [leɲ'ɲoso] AGG (*di legno*) woody; (*come legno*: *movimenti*) stiff, wooden.

legume [le'gume] SM pulse; **legumi** SMPL pulses.

leguminosa [legumi'nosa] SF leguminous plant.

lei[1] ['lɛi] **1** PRON PERS F **a** (*complemento: dopo prep, con valore enfatico*) her; **sono venuto con lei** I came with her; **senza di lei** without her; **se non fosse per lei** if it were not for her; **hanno accusato lei, non me** they accused her, not me; **chiedilo a lei** ask her; **lei qui non la voglio** I don't want her here **b** (*sogg*: *al posto di 'ella', con valore enfatico*) she; **lei è meglio di te** she is better than you; **prendetela, è lei** catch her, she's the one; **è stata lei a dirmelo** she told me herself, it was she who told me; **ha ragione lei, non tu** she's right, not you; **neanche lei ha tutti i torti** even she isn't completely in the wrong **c** (*nelle comparazioni*: *sogg*) she, her; (: *complemento*) her; **ne so quanto lei** I know as much as she does, I know as much as her. **2** SF INV (*scherz*): **la mia lei** my beloved.

lei[2] ['lɛi] **1** PRON PERS (*forma di cortesia, anche*: **Lei**) **a** you; **lei per cortesia venga con noi** be so good as to come with us; **senza di lei** without you; **riconosco lei senz'altro** I certainly recognize you **b** (*nelle comparazioni*) you; **farò come lei** I'll do the same as you (do). **2** SM: **dare del lei a qn** to address sb as 'lei'.

leitmotiv ['laitmoti:f] SM INV (*Mus, fig*) leitmotiv.

lembo ['lembo] SM (*orlo*) hem; (*striscia: di stoffa, fig: di terra*) strip.

lemma, i ['lɛmma] SM **a** (*di dizionario*) headword; (*di enciclopedia*) (main) entry **b** (*Mat, Filosofia*) lemma.

lemmario, ri [lem'marjo] SM word list.

lemme lemme ['lɛmme 'lɛmme] AVV (*fam*) (very) very slowly.

lemuridi [le'muridi] SMPL (*Zool*) lemurs.

lena ['lena] SF: **di buona lena** (*lavorare, camminare*) at a good pace.

leninismo [leni'nizmo] SM Leninism.

leninista, i, e [leni'nista] AGG, SM/F Leninist.

lenire [le'nire] VT to soothe, relieve.

lente ['lɛnte] SF (*Ottica, Fot*) lens ▶ **lente d'ingrandimento** magnifying glass ▶ **lenti (a contatto) morbide** soft lenses ▶ **lenti (a contatto) rigide** hard lenses ▶ **lenti a contatto** contact lenses; **portare le lenti (a contatto)** to wear contacts *o* contact lenses.

lentezza [len'tettsa] SF slowness; (*di mente*) slowwittedness; **con lentezza** slowly.

lenticchia [len'tikkja] SF (*Bot*) lentil; **per un piatto di lenticchie** (*fig*) for nothing, for peanuts.

lenticella [lenti't∫ella] SF (*Bot*) lenticel.

lentiggine [len'tiddʒine] SF freckle.

lentigginoso, a [lentidd ʒi'noso] AGG freckled.

lento, a ['lɛnto] **1** AGG **a** (*gen*) slow; **lento a** *o* **nel fare qc** slow in doing sth; **a passi lenti** slowly, with a slow step; **il bambino è un po' lento** (*fig*) the child is a bit slow; **cuocere a fuoco lento** to cook over a low heat **b** (*allentato*) loose; (: *fune*) slack. **2** SM (*ballo*) slow dance.

lenza ['lɛntsa] SF (fishing) line.

lenzuolo [len'tswɔlo] (*pl m* **lenzuoli**, *pl f* **lenzuola**) SM sheet; **lenzuolo (di) sopra/sotto** top/bottom sheet ▶ **lenzuolo funebre** shroud.

leoncino [leon't∫ino] SM lion cub.

leone [le'one] SM **a** (*Zool*) lion; **fare la parte del leone** (*fig*) to take the lion's share ▶ **leone marino** sea-lion **b** (*Astrol*): **Leone** Leo; **essere del Leone** to be Leo.

leonessa [leo'nessa] SF lioness.

leonino, a [leo'nino] AGG lion's, leonine.

leopardo [leo'pardo] SM leopard.

leporino, a [lepo'rino] AGG (*Med*): **labbro leporino** harelip.

lepre ['lɛpre] SF hare ▶ **lepre delle nevi** mountain *o* blue hare.

leprotto [le'prɔtto] SM leveret.

leptospirosi [leptospi'rɔzi] SF (*Med*) leptospirosis.

lercio, cia, ci, ce ['lɛrt∫o] AGG filthy, foul.

lerciume [ler't∫ume] SM filth.

lesbica, che ['lɛzbika] SF lesbian.

lesbico, a, ci, che ['lɛzbiko] AGG lesbian.

lesbismo [lez'bizmo] SM lesbianism.

lesinare [lezi'nare] **1** VI (*aus* **avere**): **lesinare (su)** to skimp (on), be stingy (with). **2** VT: **lesinare la lira** to count the pennies.

lesione [le'zjone] SF **a** (*danno*) damage ▶ **lesione personale** (*Dir*) personal injury **b** (*Med*) lesion ▶ **lesioni interne** internal injuries **c** (*Edil*) crack.

lesivo, a [le'zivo] AGG: **lesivo (di)** detrimental (to), damaging (to).

leso, a ['lezo] **1** PP *di* **ledere**. **2** AGG (*Dir*): **parte lesa** injured party ▶ **lesa maestà** lese-majesty.

Lesotho [le'sɔto] SM: **il Lesotho** Lesotho.

lessare [les'sare] VT (*Culin*) to boil.

lessatura [lessa'tura] SF boiling.

lessi *ecc* ['lɛssi] VB *vedi* **leggere**.

lessicale [lessi'kale] AGG lexical.

lessicalmente [lessikal'mente] AVV lexically.

lessico, ci ['lɛssiko] SM (*Ling*) lexis, vocabulary; (*dizionario*) lexicon.

lessicografia [lessikogra'fia] SF lexicography.

lessicografo, a [lessi'kɔgrafo] SM/F lexicographer.

lessicologia [lessikolo'dʒia] SF lexicology.

lessicologo, a, gi, ghe [lessi'kɔlogo] SM/F lexicologist.

lesso, a ['lesso] (*Culin*) **1** AGG boiled. **2** SM (*gen*) boiled meat; (*manzo*) boiled beef.

lestamente [lesta'mente] AVV quickly.

lesto, a ['lesto] AGG quick, fast; **lesto di mano** (*fig*: *per rubare*) light-fingered; (: *per picchiare*) free with one's fists.

lestofante [lesto'fante] SM swindler, con man.

letale [le'tale] AGG lethal, deadly.

letamaio, ai [leta'majo] SM dung *o* manure heap; (*fig*) pigsty.

letame [le'tame] SM manure, dung; (*fig*) filth, muck.

letargo [le'targo] SM **a** (*di animale*) hibernation; **essere/andare** *o* **cadere in letargo** to be in/go into hibernation

b (*di persona: Med, anche fig*) lethargy.

letizia [le'tittsja] SF joy, happiness.

lettera ['lɛttera] **1** SF **a** (*dell'alfabeto*) letter; **scrivere qc con lettere maiuscole/minuscole** to write sth in capitals *o* capital letters/in small letters; **scrivere un numero in lettere** to write out a number in full; **prendere qc alla lettera** to take sth literally; **eseguire qc alla lettera** (*legge, ordine*) to carry out sth to the letter; **restar lettera morta** (*consiglio, invito*) to go unheeded; **diventar lettera morta** (*legge*) to become a dead letter ▶ **lettere maiuscole** capitals *o* capital letters ▶ **lettere minuscole** small letters

b (*missiva*) letter; **lettera d'affari/d'amore** business/love letter

c : **lettere** SFPL (*letteratura*) literature *sg*; **fa lettere all'università** he is doing an arts degree at university; **lettere antiche** classics *sg*; **un uomo di lettere** a man of letters.

2 ▶ **lettera di accompagnamento** accompanying letter ▶ **lettera assicurata** registered letter ▶ **lettera di cambio** (*Comm*) bill of exchange ▶ **lettera di credito** (*Comm*) letter of credit ▶ **lettera di intenti** (*Comm*) letter of intent ▶ **lettera di presentazione** letter of presentation ▶ **lettera raccomandata** recorded delivery (*Brit*) *o* certified (*Am*) letter.

letterale [lette'rale] AGG literal.

letteralmente [letteral'mente] AVV literally.

letterario, ria, ri, rie [lette'rarjo] AGG literary.

letterato, a [lette'rato] **1** AGG cultured.

2 SM/F scholar.

letteratura [lettera'tura] SF literature.

lettiera [let'tjɛra] SF (*per bestiame*) bedding, litter.

lettiga, ghe [let'tiga] SF **a** (*barella*) stretcher **b** (*portantina*) litter.

lettino [let'tino] SM (*anche: lettino solare*) sunbed; (*per bambini*) cot (*Brit*), crib (*Am*).

letto¹, a ['lɛtto] PP di **leggere**.

letto² ['lɛtto] SM (*gen, di fiume, lago*) bed; **(ri)fare il letto** to make the bed; **essere a letto** to be in bed; **andare a letto** OR **mettersi a letto** to go to bed; **andare a letto con qn** to go to bed with sb, sleep with sb; **a letto, bambini!** bedtime, children!; **figlio di primo/secondo letto** child by one's first/second marriage; **sul letto di morte** on one's deathbed ▶ **letti a castello** bunk beds ▶ **letti gemelli** twin beds ▶ **letto matrimoniale** *o* **a due piazze** double bed ▶ **letto a una piazza** single bed.

lettone ['lɛttone] **1** AGG, SM/F Latvian.

2 SM (*lingua*) Latvian, Lettish.

Lettonia [let'tɔnja] SF: **la Lettonia** Latvia.

lettorato [letto'rato] SM **a** (*Univ*) lectorship, assistantship **b** (*Rel*) lectorate, lectorship.

lettore, trice [let'tore] **1** SM/F **a** (*gen*) reader; **il pubblico dei lettori** the reading public **b** (*Univ*) lector, assistant.

2 SM **a** (*Rel*) lector **b** ▶ **lettore CD** CD player ▶ **lettore ottico** (*Inform*) optical character reader.

lettura [let'tura] SF (*gen*) reading; **un libro di piacevole lettura** a very readable book; **un libro di facile lettura** an easy book to read; **libro di lettura** (*Scol*) reading book; **letture obbligatorie** (*Scol*) set books.

leucemia [leutʃe'mia] SF leukaemia (*Brit*), leukemia (*Am*).

leucocita, i [leuko'tʃita] SM (*Bio*) leucocyte.

leva¹ ['lɛva] SF (*anche fig*) lever; **far leva su qc** to lever sth up; (*fig*) to take advantage of sth; **far leva su qn** to work on sb; **leva del freno a mano** handbrake (lever); **avere in**

mano le leve del comando (*fig*) to hold the reins ▶ **leva del cambio** gear lever *o* stick (*Brit*), gear shift (*Am*) ▶ **leva di comando** control lever.

leva² ['lɛva] SF (*Mil*) conscription, call-up (*Brit*), draft (*Am*); **essere di leva** to be due for call-up *o* draft; (*in servizio*) to be a conscript; **le nuove leve** (*fig*) the younger generation.

levante [le'vante] SM (*Geog*) east; (*vento*) east wind; (: *nel Mediterraneo*) levanter; **il Levante** the Levant.

levapunti [leva'punti] SM INV staple remover.

levare [le'vare] **1** VT **a** (*gen: togliere*) to remove, take away; (: *coperchio*) to take off; (: *tassa*) to abolish; (: *dente*) to take out; (*Mat*) to subtract, take away; **levare la sete** to quench one's thirst; **levare qn/qc di mezzo** *o* **di torno** to get rid of sb/sth; **levare l'assedio** (*Mil*) to raise the siege; **levare un divieto** to lift a ban; **levare le tende** (*fig*) to pack up and leave

b (*sollevare: occhi, testa*) to lift (up), raise; **levare l'ancora** (*Naut*) to lift *o* weigh anchor; **levare un grido** to let out a cry

c : **levarsi qc** (*vestito*) to take sth off, remove sth; **si è levato le scarpe** he took off his shoes; **levarsi il pensiero** to put one's mind at rest.

2 **levarsi** VR (*persona: alzarsi*) to get up; **levati di mezzo** *o* **di lì** *o* **di torno!** get out of my way!; **puoi levarti dalla luce?** can you get out of my light?.

3 **levarsi** VIP (*vento, burrasca, sole*) to rise.

levata [le'vata] SF **a** (*della posta*) collection; **una levata di scudi** concerted opposition **b** (*Mil*) reveille.

levataccia, ce [leva'tattʃa] SF: **fare una levataccia** to get up at an ungodly hour.

levatoio, oi [leva'tojo] AGG: **ponte levatoio** drawbridge.

levatrice [leva'tritʃe] SF midwife.

levatura [leva'tura] SF intellect, intellectual capacity.

levigare [levi'gare] VT (*gen*) to smooth; (*marmo*) to polish; (*con carta vetrata*) to sand; (*fig: discorso*) polish.

levigato, a [levi'gato] AGG (*superficie*) smooth; (*fig: stile*) polished; (: *pelle*) flawless.

levigatrice [leviga'tritʃe] SF (*Tecn*) polisher.

levità [levi'ta] SF (*letter*) lightness.

levitare [levi'tare] VI (*aus avere o essere*) to levitate.

levitazione [levitat'tsjone] SF levitation.

Levitico, a, ci, che [le'vitiko] (*Rel*) **1** SM Leviticus.

2 AGG Levitical, Levitic.

levriere [le'vrjɛre] SM greyhound.

lezione [let'tsjone] SF (*Scol*) lesson; (*Univ*) lecture; **ora di lezione** (*Scol*) period; **far lezione (a qn)** to teach (sb), give lessons (to sb); (*Univ*) to give a lecture (to sb); **una lezione di generosità** a lesson in generosity; **servire di lezione a qn** to be a lesson to sb ▶ **lezione privata** private lesson.

leziosità [lettsjosi'ta] SF affectation.

lezioso, a [let'tsjoso] AGG (*stile*) affected; (*sorriso*) simpering.

lezzo ['leddzo] SM stink, stench.

lg ABBR (= *lira sterlina*) £.

LI SIGLA = Livorno.

li [li] PRON PERS PL them; vedi anche **lo²**.

lì [li] AVV **a** there; **mettilo lì** put it there; **eccolo lì!** there he (*o* it) is!; **è rimasto lì dov'era** he stayed where he was; **lì dentro/fuori/sopra/sotto** *ecc* in/out/on (*o* up)/under there *ecc*; **di** *o* **da lì** from there; **da lì non si entra** you can't come in that way; **per di lì** that way; **di lì a pochi giorni** a few days later; **la discussione è finita lì** the discussion

ended there; **fin ll tutto sembrava normale** up until then everything seemed normal; vedi anche **quello**

b (*fraseologia*): **ll per ll** (*sul momento*) there and then, then and there; (*dapprima*) at first; **è arrabbiato, tutto ll** he's angry, that's all; **essere ll (lì) per fare qc** to be on the point of doing sth, be about to do sth; **se non l'ha offeso apertamente siamo ll** he may not have insulted him openly but that's what it amounts to.

liana [li'ana] SF liana, liane.

libagione [liba'dʒone] SF libation.

libanese [liba'nese] AGG, SM/F Lebanese *inv.*

Libano ['libano] SM: **il Libano** the Lebanon.

libbra ['libbra] SF pound.

libeccio, ci [li'bettʃo] SM libeccio, libecchio, *south-west wind.*

libellista, i, e [libel'lista] SM/F libeller.

libello [li'bɛllo] SM libel.

libellula [li'bɛllula] SF dragonfly.

liberale [libe'rale] **1** AGG (*gen, Pol*) liberal.

2 SM/F (*Pol*) Liberal.

liberalismo [libera'lizmo] SM liberalism.

liberalità [liberali'ta] SF generosity; **con liberalità** generously.

liberalizzare [liberalid'dzare] VT to liberalize.

liberalizzazione [liberalid'dzattsjone] SF liberalization.

liberalmente [liberal'mente] AVV liberally.

liberare [libe'rare] **1** VT **a** (*rendere libero: prigioniero*) to release; (: *popolo*) to liberate, free; **liberaci dal male** (*Rel*) deliver us from evil

b (*sgombrare: passaggio*) to clear; (: *stanza*) to vacate

c (*produrre: energia*) to release.

2 liberarsi VR: **liberarsi di qn/qc** to get rid of sb/sth; **liberarsi dagli impegni** to free o.s. from one's commitments; **se riesco a liberarmi per le 5...** if I can manage to be free by 5 o'clock ....

3 liberarsi VIP (*stanza*) to become vacant; (*telefono, posto*) to become free.

liberatore, trice [libera'tore] **1** AGG liberating; **guerra liberatrice** war of liberation.

2 SM/F liberator.

liberatorio, ria, ri, rie [libera'tɔrjo] AGG **a** (*Psic*) liberating **b** (*Fin*): **pagamento liberatorio** payment in full.

liberazione [liberat'tsjone] SF **a** (*di prigioniero*) release; (*di popolo*) liberation; **è stata una liberazione per lui** (*sollievo*) it was a release for him; **che liberazione!** what a relief! ▸ **la liberazione della donna** women's liberation **b** : **la Liberazione** *holiday (April 25th) commemorating the liberation of Italy in 1945.*

libercolo [li'bɛrkolo] SM (*pegg*) worthless book.

Liberia [li'bɛrja] SF: **la Liberia** Liberia.

liberiano, a [libe'rjano] AGG, SM/F Liberian.

liberismo [libe'rizmo] SM (*Econ*) laissez-faire.

liberistico, a, ci, che [libe'ristiko] AGG laissez-faire *attr.*

libero, a ['libero] **1** AGG **a** (*senza costrizioni*) free; (*persona: non sposata*) unattached; **libero da** (*legami, preoccupazioni*) free of *o* from; **essere libero di fare qc** to be free to do sth; **sei libero di rifiutare** you're free *o* at liberty to refuse; **dar libero corso a** to give free rein to; **dar libero sfogo a** to give vent to; **libera discussione** free *o* open discussion; **"ingresso libero"** (*gratuito*) "entrance free"

b (*non occupato: gen*) free; (: *passaggio*) clear; (: *posto*) vacant, free; (: *linea telefonica*) free; **non ha mai un momento libero** he never has a free moment; **cosa fai nel tuo tempo libero?** what do you do in your free *o*

spare time?; **via libera!** all clear!; **avere via libera** to have a free hand; **dare via libera a qn** to give sb the go-ahead.

2 SM (*Calcio, anche: battitore libero*) sweeper.

3 ▸ **libera professione** self-employment ▸ **libera uscita** (*Mil*) leave; (*in Marina*) liberty ▸ **libero arbitrio** free will ▸ **libero professionista** self-employed (professional) person; (*che lavora per varie aziende*) freelance, freelancer ▸ **libero scambio** free trade.

liberoscambismo [liberoskam'bizmo] SM (*Econ*) free trade.

libertà [liber'ta] SF INV **a** (*gen*) freedom, liberty; **combattere per la libertà** to fight for freedom; **il ladro è ancora in libertà** the thief is still at large; **nei momenti di libertà** (*tempo libero*) in one's free time ▸ **libertà di espressione** freedom of expression ▸ **libertà di pensiero** freedom of thought ▸ **libertà di stampa** freedom of the press

b (*Dir*) freedom, liberty; **concedere la libertà a qn** to release sb; **rimettere qn in libertà** to set sb free, release sb; **essere in libertà provvisoria** to be released on (*o* without) bail; **essere in libertà vigilata** to be on probation

c (*licenza*) liberty; **prendersi la libertà di** to take the liberty of; **prendersi delle libertà** to take liberties.

libertario, ria, ri, rie [liber'tarjo] AGG libertarian.

liberticida, i, e [liberti'tʃida] **1** AGG liberticidal.

2 SM/F liberticide.

libertino, a [liber'tino] AGG, SM/F libertine.

liberty ['liberti] AGG INV, SM INV art nouveau.

Libia ['libja] SF: **la Libia** Libya.

libico, a, ci, che ['libiko] AGG, SM/F Libyan.

libidine [li'bidine] SF lust, lechery.

libidinoso, a [libidi'noso] AGG lustful, lecherous, libidinous.

libido [li'bido] SF INV (*Psic*) libido.

libraio, ai [li'brajo] SM bookseller.

librario, ria, ri, rie [li'brarjo] AGG book *attr.*

librarsi [li'brarsi] VR to hover; **librarsi in volo** to soar.

libreria [libre'ria] SF **a** (*negozio*) bookshop **b** (*mobile*) bookcase.

libresco, a, schi, sche [li'bresko] AGG (*pegg: cultura*) bookish.

librettista, i, e [libret'tista] SM/F librettist.

libretto [li'bretto] **1** SM booklet; (*Mus*) libretto.

2 ▸ **libretto degli assegni** chequebook (*Brit*), checkbook (*Am*) ▸ **libretto di banca** bank book ▸ **libretto di circolazione** (*Aut*) registration document (*Brit*), logbook (*Brit*), registration (*Am*) ▸ **libretto d'istruzioni** user's manual ▸ **libretto di lavoro** employment card ▸ **libretto di risparmio** bankbook (*Brit*), passbook (*Am*) ▸ **libretto universitario** university student's academic record card.

libro ['libro] SM **a** (*gen*) book; **essere sul libro nero di qn** to be in sb's bad books; **essere un libro aperto** (*fig: persona*) to be an open book; **a libro** (*scala*) folding ▸ **libro bianco** (*Pol*) white paper (*Brit*) ▸ **libro di consultazione** reference book ▸ **libro di cucina** cookery book ▸ **libro giallo** detective story, thriller ▸ **libro tascabile** paperback ▸ **libro di testo** textbook ▸ **libro usato** second-hand book

b (*registro*) book, register; **tenere i libri** to keep the books ▸ **libri contabili** (account) books ▸ **libri sociali** company records ▸ **libro di cassa** cash book ▸ **libro mastro** ledger ▸ **libro paga** payroll.

licantropo [li'kantropo] SM werewolf.

liceale [litʃe'ale] ① AGG secondary school *attr* (*Brit*), high school *attr* (*Am*).
② SM/F secondary school (*Brit*) *o* high school (*Am*) pupil.

licenza [li'tʃɛntsa] SF **a** (*gen, permesso*) permission, leave; **chiedere/dare licenza di fare qc** to ask/give permission to do sth; **prendersi la licenza di fare qc** to take the liberty of doing sth
b (*autorizzazione*) licence (*Brit*), license (*Am*), permit; **licenza di caccia/di pesca/ matrimoniale** hunting/ fishing/marriage licence; **licenza di esportazione/ importazione** export/import licence; **licenza di fabbricazione** manufacturer's licence; **su licenza di...** (*Comm*) under licence from ...
c (*Scol*) school-leaving certificate
d (*Mil*: *documento*) pass; **essere/andare in licenza** to be/go on leave
c (*sfrenatezza*) licence (*Brit*), license (*Am*), licentiousness ▶ **licenza poetica** poetic licence.

licenziamento [litʃentsja'mento] SM dismissal; (*per eccesso di personale*) redundancy; **licenziamento ingiustificato** unfair dismissal; **licenziamento in massa** mass dismissals *pl o* redundancies *pl*.

licenziare [litʃen'tsjare] ① VT **a** to dismiss; (*per eccesso di personale*) to make redundant
b (*Scol*) to award a school-leaving certificate to.
② **licenziarsi** VR **a** (*andare via*) to take one's leave; (*dal lavoro*) to resign, hand in one's notice
b (*Scol*) to obtain one's school-leaving certificate.

licenziosamente [litʃentsjosa'mente] AVV licentiously.

licenziosità [litʃentsjosi'ta] SF licentiousness.

licenzioso, a [litʃen'tsjoso] AGG licentious.

liceo [li'tʃɛo] SM ≈ secondary school (*Brit*), ≈ high school (*Am*); **liceo classico/scientifico** secondary *or* high school *specializing in classics/scientific subjects*.

lichene [li'kɛne] SM (*Bot*) lichen.

licitazione [litʃitat'tsjone] SF (*vendita all'asta*) auction; (*offerta di prezzo*) bid; **mettere in licitazione** to put up for auction.

licnide ['liknide] SF (*pianta*) campion.

lido ['lido] SM (*spiaggia*) beach; (*letter: paese*) shore; **il lido di Venezia** the Venice Lido.

Liechtenstein ['liktenʃtain] SM: **il Liechtenstein** Liechtenstein.

lietamente [ljeta'mente] AVV joyfully, gladly.

lieto, a ['ljɛto] AGG glad, happy; **a lieto fine** with a happy ending; **lieto evento** happy event; **molto lieto (di fare la sua conoscenza)** pleased to meet you.

lieve ['ljeve] AGG (*tocco, brezza*) soft, light, faint; (*ferita*) slight.

lievemente [ljeve'mente] AVV (*vedi agg*) softly, lightly, faintly; slightly.

lievità [ljevi'ta] SF = **levità**.

lievitare [ljevi'tare] ① VI (*aus* **essere**) (*pane, pasta, anche fig*) to rise.
② VT to leaven.

lievitazione [ljevitat'tsjone] SF rising.

lievito ['ljevito] SM yeast ▶ **lievito di birra** brewer's yeast ▶ **lievito in polvere** baking powder.

lifo ['lifo] SM (*Comm, Fin*) LIFO (= *last in first out*).

lifting ['liftiŋ] SM INV face-lift; **farsi fare il lifting** to have a face-lift.

ligio, a, gi, gie *o* **ge** ['lidʒo] AGG: **ligio (a)** faithful (to), loyal (to); **ligio al dovere** devoted to duty.

lignaggio, gi [liɲ'naddʒo] SM descent, lineage.

ligneo, a ['liɲɲeo] AGG wooden.

lignite [liɲ'ɲite] SF lignite.

ligure ['ligure] AGG, SM/F Ligurian; **la Riviera Ligure** the Italian Riviera.

Liguria [li'gurja] SF Liguria.

ligustro [li'gustro] SM (*arbusto*) privet.

Likud ['likud] SM Likud.

lilla ['lilla] AGG INV, SM INV (*colore*) lilac.

lillà [lil'la] SM INV (*arbusto*) lilac.

lillipuziano, a [lilliput'tsjano] AGG, SM/F Lilliputian.

Lima ['lima] SF Lima.

lima ['lima] SF file; **lima per le unghie** nailfile.

limaccioso, a [limat'tʃoso] AGG muddy.

limanda [li'manda] SF (*pesce*) dab.

limare [li'mare] VT (*superficie, unghie*) to file; (*fig: scritti*) to polish, perfect.

limatura [lima'tura] SF (*azione*) filing (down); (*residuo*) filings *pl*.

limbo ['limbo] SM (*Rel, fig*) limbo.

limetta [li'metta] SF **a** (*per le unghie*) nailfile **b** (*Bot*) lime (*fruit*).

limitare [limi'tare] ① VT **a** (*circoscrivere*) to bound, mark the bounds of, surround **b** (*contenere*): **limitare (a)** to limit (to), restrict (to).
② **limitarsi** VR: **limitarsi a qc/a fare qc** to limit *o* confine o.s. to sth/to doing sth; **limitarsi nel fumare** to limit one's smoking; **mi limiterò a dire che...** all I'm prepared to say *o* all I'll say is that ... .

limitatamente [limitata'mente] AVV to a limited extent; **limitatamente alle mie possibilità** in so far as I am able.

limitatezza [limita'tettsa] SF: **limitatezza di idee** narrow-mindedness.

limitativo, a [limita'tivo] AGG limiting, restrictive, restricting.

limitato, a [limi'tato] AGG (*ristretto*) limited, restricted; (*scarso*) scarce, limited; **persona di idee limitate** narrow-minded person.

limitazione [limitat'tsjone] SF (*gen*) limitation, restriction; **limitazione degli armamenti** arms limitation *o* control.

limite ['limite] ① SM (*gen, fig*) limit; (*confine*) boundary, limit, border; **c'è un limite a tutto!** OR **tutto ha un limite!** there are limits!; **senza limite** *o* **limiti** boundless, limitless; **conoscere i propri limiti** to know one's limitations; **nei limiti del possibile** as far as possible; **passare il** *o* **ogni limite** to go too far; **entro certi limiti** within certain limits; **al limite** if the worst comes to the worst (*Brit*), if worst comes to worst (*Am*) ▶ **limite d'età** age limit ▶ **limite delle nevi perenni** snow line ▶ **limite di rottura** breaking point ▶ **limite di tempo** time limit ▶ **limite della vegetazione arborea** tree line ▶ **limite di velocità** speed limit.
② AGG INV: **caso limite** extreme case.

limitrofo, a [li'mitrofo] AGG neighbouring (*Brit*), neighboring (*Am*).

limo ['limo] SM (*fango*) mud, slime; (*Geog*) silt.

limonata [limo'nata] SF lemonade (*Brit*), (lemon) soda (*Am*); (*spremuta*) lemon squash (*Brit*), lemonade (*Am*).

limone [li'mone] SM (*frutto*) lemon; (*albero*) lemon (tree); **l'hanno spremuto come un limone e poi l'hanno licenziato** they worked him to death and then sacked him.

limpidamente [limpida'mente] AVV (*esporre*) clearly, lucidly.

limpidezza [limpi'dettsa] SF (*di acqua, cielo*) clearness; (*di*

discorso) clarity.

limpido, a ['limpido] AGG (*acqua*) limpid, clear; (*cielo*) clear; (*fig: discorso*) clear, lucid.

lince ['lintʃe] SF lynx; **avere un occhio di lince** to be eagle-eyed.

linciaggio, gi [lin'tʃaddʒo] SM lynching.

linciare [lin'tʃare] VT to lynch.

lindo, a ['lindo] AGG (*casa, stanza*) neat and tidy, spick and span; (*biancheria, abiti*) clean.

linea ['linea] SF **a** (*gen, Mat*) line; **a grandi linee** in outline; **in linea di massima** on the whole; **in linea d'aria** as the crow flies; **avere qualche linea di febbre** to have a slight temperature ►**linea di confine** boundary line ►**linea continua** solid line ►**linea punteggiata** dotted line ►**linea tratteggiata** broken line
b (*fig: direzione*) line; **linea d'azione/di condotta** line of action/of conduct; **rimanere in linea col proprio partito** to toe the party line
c (*figura: di persona*) figure; (: *Moda, Aut*) line; **mantenere la linea** to keep one's figure; **la linea Dior** (*collezione*) the Dior collection; **una giacca con una linea classica** a classically styled jacket
d (*Ferr, Aer*) line; **linea d'autobus** (*percorso*) bus route; (*servizio*) bus service; **aereo di linea** airliner; **volo di linea** scheduled flight; **linea aerea** airline; **nave di linea** (ocean) liner
e (*Elettr*) line; **linee di alta tensione** high tension cables
f (*Telec*) line; **la linea è occupata** the line is engaged (*Brit*) o busy (*Am*); **è caduta la linea** I (*o you ecc*) have been cut off
g (*Mil*) line; **essere in prima linea** to be in the front line; **linea di mira/tiro** line of sight/fire
h (*Sport*) line ►**linea d'arrivo** finishing line ►**linea laterale** sideline ►**linea di massima pendenza** (*Sci*) fall line ►**linea mediana** (*Calcio*) half-way line ►**linea di pallone morto** (*Rugby*) dead-ball line ►**linea di partenza** starting line.

lineamenti [linea'menti] SMPL (*di volto*) features; (*fig: elementi essenziali*): **lineamenti di fisica** introduction *sg* to physics.

lineare [line'are] AGG (*Mat, disegno*) linear; (*fig*) consistent, coherent, logical.

lineetta [line'etta] SF (*trattino*) dash; (*in composti, a fine riga*) hyphen.

linfa ['linfa] SF (*Bot*) sap; (*Anat*) lymph ►**linfa vitale** (*fig*) lifeblood.

linfatico, a, ci, che [lin'fatiko] AGG (*Anat*) lymphatic.

linfonodo [linfo'nɔdo] SM (*Anat*) lymph node.

lingottiera [lingot'tjɛra] SF ingot mould.

lingotto [lin'gɔtto] SM ingot, bar.

lingua ['lingwa] SF **a** (*Anat, Culin, fig*) tongue; **mostrare la lingua a qn** to stick *o* put out one's tongue at sb; **avere qc sulla punta della lingua** (*fig*) to have sth on the tip of one's tongue; **avere la lingua sciolta** to have the gift of the gab; **avere una lingua velenosa** (*fig*) to have a nasty tongue; **tenere a freno la lingua** to hold one's tongue; **avere la lingua lunga** (*fig*) to talk too much; **la lingua batte dove il dente duole** (*Proverbio*) it is human nature to dwell on one's misfortunes ►**lingua di bue** (*Culin*) ox tongue ►**lingue di gatto** (*biscotti*) langues de chat
b (*linguaggio*) language, tongue; **lingua viva/morta** living/dead language; **la lingua italiana** the Italian language; **paesi di lingua inglese** English-speaking countries; **non parliamo la stessa lingua** (*anche fig*) we

don't talk the same language; **studiare lingue** to study languages ►**lingua franca** lingua franca ►**lingua madre** mother tongue
c ►**lingua di fuoco** tongue of flame ►**lingua di terra** spit of land.

linguaccia [lin'gwattʃa] SF (*pegg: persona*) spiteful gossip.

linguacciuto, a [lingwat'tʃuto] ¹ AGG gossipy.
² SM/F gossip.

linguaggio, gi [lin'gwaddʒo] SM language; **linguaggio infantile** baby talk.

linguetta [lin'gwetta] SF (*di scarpe*) tongue; (*di busta*) flap; (*di strumento*) reed.

linguista, i, e [lin'gwista] SM/F linguist.

linguistica [lin'gwistika] SF linguistics *sg*.

linguistico, a, ci, che [lin'gwistiko] ¹ AGG linguistic.
² SM (*anche: liceo linguistico*) *secondary or high school specializing in modern languages*.

linimento [lini'mento] SM liniment.

lino ['lino] SM (*pianta*) flax; (*tessuto*) linen; **seme di lino** linseed.

linoleum [li'nɔleum] SM INV linoleum, lino (*Brit*).

liofilizzare [liofilid'dzare] VT to freeze-dry.

liofilizzato, a [liofilid'dzato] ¹ AGG freeze-dried.
² SM freeze-dried food.

Lione [li'one] SF Lyons.

lipasi [li'pazi] SF INV (*Bio*) lipase.

lipide [li'pide] SM (*Chim*) lipid.

liposuzione [liposut'tsjone] SF liposuction.

LIPU ['lipu] SIGLA F (= *Lega Italiana Protezione Uccelli*) ≈ RSPB (*Royal Society for the Protection of Birds*).

liquame [li'kwame] SM liquid sewage.

liquefare [likwe'fare] VB IRREG ¹ VT (*render liquido*) to liquefy; (*fondere*) to melt.
² **liquefarsi** VIP to liquefy; (*burro, ghiaccio*) to melt.

liquefatto, a [likwe'fatto] PP di **liquefare**.

liquefazione [likwefat'tsjone] SF liquefaction.

liquefeci *ecc* VB vedi **liquefare**.

liquidare [likwi'dare] VT **a** (*debiti*) to settle, pay off; (*società*) to wind up, liquidate; (*merci*) to sell off, clear; (*pensione*) to pay **b** (*fig: sbarazzarsi di: persona*) to get rid of; (: *uccidere*) to kill, liquidate; **liquidare una questione** to settle a matter once and for all.

liquidatore, trice [likwida'tore] SM/F (*Dir, Comm*) liquidator; (*Assicurazioni*) claims adjuster.

liquidazione [likwidat'tsjone] SF **a** (*pagamento*) settlement, payment; (*di società*) liquidation; (*di merci*) clearance; **vendita/prezzi di liquidazione** clearance sale/prices **b** (*Amm*) severance pay.

liquidità [likwidi'ta] SF INV liquidity.

liquido, a ['likwido] ¹ AGG (*gen, Comm, Fonetica*) liquid; (*Culin*) runny; **denaro liquido** cash, ready money.
² SM **a** (*corpo liquido*) liquid, fluid **b** (*Econ: denaro contante*) ready money *o* cash.

liquigas® [likwi'gas] SM INV Calor gas ® (*Brit*), butane.

liquirizia [likwi'rittsja] SF liquorice.

liquore [li'kwore] SM liqueur; **liquori** SMPL (*bevande alcoliche*) spirits.

liquoroso, a [likwo'roso] AGG: **vino liquoroso** dessert wine.

lira¹ ['lira] SF (*unità monetaria*) lira; **1000 lire** 1000 lire; **non vale una lira** it's worthless; **non avere una lira** to be penniless ►**lira sterlina** pound sterling.

lira² ['lira] SF **a** (*Mus*) lyre **b** (*anche: uccello lira*) lyrebird.

lirica, che ['lirika] SF **a** (*genere di poesia*) lyric poetry; (*poema*) lyric poem **b** (*Mus: anche: opera lirica*) opera.

liricamente [lirika'mente] AVV lyrically.
liricità [lirit∫i'ta] SF = **lirismo.**
lirico, a, ci, che ['liriko] [1] AGG [a] (*poesia*) lyric; (*impeto, descrizione*) lyrical [b] (*Mus*) opera *attr*; **la stagione lirica** the opera season.
[2] SM lyric poet.
lirismo [li'rizmo] SM lyricism.
Lisbona [lis'bona] SF Lisbon.
lisca, sche ['liska] SF (fish)bone.
lisciare [li∫'∫are] [1] VT (*gen*) to smooth; (*fig: adulare*) to flatter; **lisciarsi i capelli** to smooth (down) one's hair.
[2] **lisciarsi** VR (*fig*) to preen o.s.
lisciatura [li∫∫a'tura] SF (*Tecn*) polishing.
liscio, scia, sci, sce ['li∫∫o] AGG (*pelo, capelli*) sleek; (*affare, faccenda*) simple, straightforward; (*liquore*) neat, straight; **avere i capelli lisci** to have straight hair; **è andato tutto liscio** it all went off smoothly o without a hitch; **non la passerà liscia** he won't get away with it; **com'è andata? — liscia come l'olio** how did it go? — it went like a dream.
liscivia [li∫'∫ivja], **lisciva** [li∫'∫iva] SF lye.
liseuse [li'zøz] SF INV bed jacket.
liso, a ['lizo] AGG worn(-out), threadbare.
lisoformio [lizo'formjo] SM Lysol ®.
lista ['lista] SF [a] (*gen: elenco*) list; (*menù*) menu; **lista della spesa/degli invitati** shopping/guest list; **fare la lista di qc** to make a list of sth; **mettersi in lista per** to put one's name down for o on the list for ► **lista elettorale** electoral roll o register ► **lista nera** (*fig*) blacklist ► **lista di nozze** wedding list [b] (*striscia*) strip.
listare [lis'tare] VT [a]: **listare (di)** to border (with), edge (with) [b] (*Inform*) to list.
listato [lis'tato] SM (*Inform*) list, listing.
listello [lis'tɛllo] SM (*Archit*) listel, fillet.
listino [lis'tino] SM list; **prezzo di listino** list price ► **listino di borsa** (*Fin*) Stock Exchange listing ► **listino dei cambi** (*Fin*) (foreign) exchange rate ► **listino dei prezzi** price list.
litania [lita'nia] SF (*Rel*) litany; (*fig: di nomi, titoli*) string.
lite ['lite] SF [a] (*gen*) quarrel, argument; **attaccar lite (con qn)** to pick a fight (with sb) [b] (*Dir*) lawsuit.
litigante [liti'gante] SM/F (*gen*) quarreller; (*Dir*) litigant.
litigare [liti'gare] VI (*aus* **avere**) (*gen*) to quarrel, argue; (*Dir*) to litigate.
litigio, gi [li'tidʒo] SM quarrel, dispute.
litigioso, a [liti'dʒoso] AGG (*gen*) quarrelsome; (*Dir*) litigious, contentious.
litio ['litjo] SM (*Chim*) lithium.
litografia [litogra'fia] SF (*metodo*) lithography; (*stampa*) lithograph; (*stabilimento*) lithographic printing works *sg*.
litografico, a, ci, che [lito'grafiko] AGG lithographic.
litografo, a [li'tografo] SM/F lithographer.
litorale [lito'rale] [1] SM coast.
[2] AGG coastal, coast *attr*.
litoraneo, a [lito'raneo] AGG coastal.
litorina [lito'rina] SF (*mollusco*) periwinkle.
litro ['litro] SM litre (*Brit*), liter (*Am*).
littorina [litto'rina] SF (*Ferr*) diesel engine.
littorio, ria, ri, rie [lit'tɔrjo] AGG (*Storia romana*) lictorial; **fascio littorio** (*anche Fascismo*) fasces *pl*.
Lituania [litu'anja] SF: **la Lituania** Lithuania.
lituano [litu'ano] AGG, SM/F, SM Lithuanian.
liturgia, gie [litur'dʒia] SF liturgy.
liturgico, a, ci, che [li'turdʒiko] AGG liturgical.

liuto [li'uto] SM lute.
livella [li'vɛlla] SF (*Tecn*) level ► **livella a bolla (d'aria)** spirit level.
livellamento [livella'mento] SM levelling.
livellare [livel'lare] [1] VT (*anche fig*) to level.
[2] **livellarsi** VIP to become level; (*fig*) to level out, balance out.
livellatore, trice [livella'tore] AGG levelling.
livellatrice [livella'tritʃe] SF steamroller.
livello [li'vɛllo] [1] SM [a] (*di olio, acqua*) level; **allo stesso livello** at the same level; **a livello della strada** at street o ground level; **livello di guardia** (*anche fig*) danger level; **sotto il/sul livello del mare** (*Geog*) below/above sea level [b] (*grado*) standard; (: *intellettuale, sociale*) level; **un alto livello di vita** a high standard of living; **una conferenza ad alto livello** high-level o top-level talks; **contatti ad alto livello** high-level contacts; **non è al tuo livello** he is not on the same level as you; **a livello economico/politico** at an economic/a political level; **a livello mondiale** world-wide.
[2] ► **livello impiegatizio** employment grading ► **livello di magazzino** stock level ► **livello occupazionale** level of employment ► **livello retributivo** salary grade.
livido, a ['livido] [1] AGG (*bluastro*) livid; (*per percosse*) bruised, black and blue; (*plumbeo: cielo*) leaden; **labbra livide dal freddo** lips blue with cold; **livido di collera** o **rabbia** livid with rage; **livido di invidia** green with envy.
[2] SM bruise.
livore [li'vore] SM venom.
Livorno [li'vorno] SF Livorno, Leghorn.
livrea [li'vrɛa] SF (*uniforme*) livery; (*di animale*) coat; (*di uccello*) plumage.
lizza ['littsa] SF: **entrare** o **scendere in lizza** (*anche fig*) to enter the lists; **essere in lizza per** (*fig*) to be competing for; **rimanere in lizza** (*fig*) to be left in the running.
LO SIGLA = *Lodi.*
lo¹ [lo] ART DET M vedi **il.**
lo² [lo] PRON (dav vocale **l'**) [a] (*riferito a persona*) him; (*riferito ad animale*) it; (: *affettuosamente*) him; (*riferito a cosa*) it; **lo vuoi conoscere?** [OR] **vuoi conoscerlo?** would you like to meet him?; **Paolo lo conosco bene, ma Giovanna no** I know Paolo well, but not Giovanna; **guardalo!** look at him (o it)!
[b] (*con valore neutro: spesso non tradotto*): **vieni? — non lo so** are you coming? — I don't know; **te lo dicevo io!** I told you so!; **non lo vedi che stai sbagliando?** can't you see you're wrong?; **può sembrare innocuo ma non lo è** he may look harmless but he's not.
lobbia ['lɔbbja] SF (*cappello*) homburg.
lobbista, i, e [lob'bista] SM/F lobbyist.
lobby ['lɔbi] SF INV lobby.
lobelia [lo'bɛlja] SF (*pianta*) lobelia.
lobo ['lɔbo] SM (*Anat, Bot*) lobe ► **lobo dell'orecchio** ear lobe.
lobotomia [loboto'mia] SF lobotomy.
locale [lo'kale] [1] AGG local; (*treno*) stopping (*Brit*), local (*Am*).
[2] SM [a] (*stanza*) room; (*luogo pubblico*) place, premises *pl*; **non si servono alcolici in questo locale** no alcohol is served on the premises; **locale caldaie** boiler room ► **locale (notturno)** nightclub [b] (*anche:* **treno locale**) stopping train (*Brit*), local train (*Am*).
località [lokali'ta] SF INV locality; **località balneare/di villeggiatura** seaside/holiday resort.

localizzare [lokalid'dzare] ① VT (*individuare*) to locate, place; (*circoscrivere*: *epidemia, incendio*) to confine, localize.
② **localizzarsi** VIP: **localizzarsi in** to become localized in.

localizzazione [lokaliddzat'tsjone] SF (*vedi vb*) location; confinement.

localmente [lokal'mente] AVV locally.

locanda [lo'kanda] SF inn.

locandiere, a [lokan'djɛre] SM/F landlord/landlady.

locandina [lokan'dina] SF poster.

locare [lo'kare] VT (*Dir*) to rent out, let.

locatario, ria, ri, rie [loka'tarjo] SM/F (*di casa, appartamento*) tenant; (*di camera*) lodger.

locativo, a [loka'tivo] AGG (*Dir*): **valore locativo** rental value.

locatore, trice [loka'tore] SM/F landlord/landlady.

locazione [lokat'tsjone] SF a (*da parte del locatario*) renting; (*da parte del locatore*) renting out, letting; **dare in locazione** to rent out, let b (*anche:* **contratto di locazione**) lease; **canone di locazione** rent.

locomotiva [lokomo'tiva] SF locomotive, engine.

locomotore [lokomo'tore] SM, **locomotrice** [lokomo'd tritʃe] SF (*electric*) locomotive, engine.

locomozione [lokomot'tsjone] SF locomotion; **mezzi di locomozione** means of transport.

loculo ['lɔkulo] SM burial recess.

locusta [lo'kusta] SF locust.

locuzione [lokut'tsjone] SF phrase, locution, expression.

lodare [lo'dare] VT to praise; **lodare qn per qc/per aver fatto qc** to praise sb for sth/for having done sth; **sia lodato Dio!** God be praised!

lode ['lɔde] SF praise; **degno di lode** praiseworthy; **tessere le lodi di qn** to sing sb's praises; **in lode di** in praise of; **torna a sua lode** it's to his credit; **laurearsi con 110 e lode** (*Univ*) ≈ to graduate with first-class honours *o* a first-class honours degree (*Brit*), ≈ to graduate summa cum laude (*Am*).

loden ['lɔdən] SM INV (*stoffa*) loden; (*cappotto*) loden overcoat.

lodevole [lo'devole] AGG praiseworthy.

logaritmo [loga'ritmo] SM (*Mat*) logarithm.

loggia, ge ['lɔddʒa] SF (*Archit*) loggia; (*circolo massonico*) lodge.

loggione [lod'dʒone] SM (*Teatro*): **il loggione** the gods *sg*.

logica ['lɔdʒika] SF logic; **è nella logica delle cose** it is in the nature of things; **a rigor di logica** logically; **privo di logica** illogical.

logicamente [lɔdʒika'mente] AVV naturally, obviously.

logicità [lɔdʒitʃi'ta] SF logicality.

logico, a, ci, che ['lɔdʒiko] ① AGG logical.
② SM logician.

logistica [lo'dʒistika] SF logistics *sg*.

logistico, a, ci, che [lo'dʒistiko] AGG logistic.

loglio ['lɔʎʎo] SM (*Bot*): **loglio perenne** rye-grass.

logo ['lɔgo] SM INV logo.

logopedista, i, e [logope'dista] SM/F speech therapist.

logorabile [logo'rabile] AGG: **essere logorabile** (*vista, salute*) to be easily ruined.

logoramento [logora'mento] SM (*di vestiti*) wear.

logorante [logo'rante] AGG exhausting; (*attesa, giornata*) wearing.

logorare [logo'rare] ① VT (*abiti, scarpe*) to wear out; (*scalini, pietra*) to wear away; (*occhi, salute*) to ruin; (*nervi, resistenza*) to wear down; (*persona*) to wear out, exhaust;

(*volto*) to line, mark; **logorarsi l'anima** *o* **la vita su qc** to wear o.s. out over sth; **logorarsi la vista** to ruin one's eyesight.
② **logorarsi** VIP (*abiti, scarpe*) to wear out; (*occhi*) to become ruined; (*nervi*) to go.
③ **logorarsi** VR (*persona*) to wear o.s. out.

logorio, rii [logo'rio] SM wear and tear, strain; **il logorio della vita moderna** the stresses and strains *pl* of life today.

logoro, a ['logoro] AGG (*scarpe*) worn (out); (*abiti, tappeto*) worn out, threadbare; (*fig*: *occhi, vista*) ruined; (: *aspetto*) worn out, exhausted.

logorroico, a, ci, che [logor'rɔiko] AGG (*che parla troppo*) loquacious.

Loira ['lɔira] SF: **la Loira** the Loire.

lombaggine [lom'baddʒine] SF (*Med*) lumbago.

Lombardia [lombar'dia] SF: **la Lombardia** Lombardy.

lombardo, a [lom'bardo] AGG, SM/F Lombard.

lombare [lom'bare] AGG (*Anat, Med*) lumbar.

lombata [lom'bata] SF (*Culin*) loin.

lombo ['lombo] SM (*Anat, Culin*) loin.

lombrico, chi [lom'briko] SM earthworm.

londinese [londi'nese] ① AGG London *attr*.
② SM/F Londoner.

Londra ['londra] SF London.

longanime [lon'ganime] AGG forbearing.

longanimità [longanimi'ta] SF forbearance.

longevità [londʒevi'ta] SF longevity.

longevo, a [lon'dʒevo] AGG long-lived.

longherone [longe'rone] SM (*Tecn*) metal strut; (*Aer*) longeron.

longilineo, a [londʒi'lineo] AGG long-limbed.

longitudinale [londʒitudi'nale] AGG longitudinal.

longitudinalmente [londʒitudinal'mente] AVV longways, lengthways.

longitudine [londʒi'tudine] SF longitude.

longobardo, a [longo'bardo] ① AGG Longobardic.
② SM/F Longobard.

long playing ['lɔŋ pleiiŋ] SM INV long-playing record, L.P.

lontanamente [lontana'mente] AVV remotely; **non ci pensavo neppure lontanamente** it didn't even occur to me.

lontananza [lonta'nantsa] SF (*distanza*) distance; (*assenza*) absence; **in lontananza** in the distance; **la lontananza da casa lo faceva soffrire** being far away from home upset him.

lontano, a [lon'tano] ① AGG a (*nello spazio, nel tempo*) distant, faraway, far-off; (*di parentela*) distant; **lontano da** far from, a long way from; **essere ben lontano dal pensare che...** to be far from thinking that ...; **tenere qn lontano** to keep sb at a distance; **tenersi lontano da** to keep one's distance from; **lontano dagli occhi lontano dal cuore** (*Proverbio*) out of sight out of mind; **il giorno della sua partenza non era lontano** the day when he was due to leave was not far off *o* away; **amici lontani** absent friends; **siamo parenti alla lontana** we are distantly related; **i nostri ricordi più lontani** our earliest memories; **i tempi lontani dell'università** those far-off days at university; **terre lontane** faraway places
b (*vago*) vague, slight.
② AVV far; **più lontano** farther, further; **è meno lontano di quello che pensi** it's not as far as you think; **abita lontano** he lives a long way off *o* away; **è lontano 10 chilometri** it's 10 kilometres away; **da lontano** from a distance;

vengo da lontano I've come quite a distance; **lontano nel passato** far back in the past; **lontano nel futuro** in the distant future; **andar lontano** (*anche fig*) to go far; **mirare lontano** (*fig*) to aim high; **vedere lontano** (*fig*) to see far ahead.

lontra ['lontra] SF otter.

lonza ['lontsa] SF (*Culin*) loin of pork.

loquace [lo'kwatʃe] AGG talkative, loquacious; (*fig*: *occhiata, gesto*) expressive, eloquent.

loquacemente [lokwatʃe'mente] AVV (*vedi agg*) loquaciously; eloquently.

loquacità [lokwatʃi'ta] SF talkativeness, loquacity.

lordo, a ['lordo] **1** AGG **a** (*Comm*: *peso, stipendio*) gross **b** (*sporco*) dirty, filthy; **lordo di sangue** bloody.
  2 SM: **al lordo d'imposta** before tax.

Lorena [lo'rɛna] SF: **la Lorena** Lorraine.

loro¹ ['loro] PRON PERS PL **a** (*complemento*) them; **chiedi (a) loro** ask them; **disse loro che non sarebbe venuto** he told them he wouldn't be coming; **sono venuto con loro** I came with them; **senza di loro** without them; **loro qui non li voglio** I don't want them here
  b (*sogg*: *al posto di "essi", "esse", con valore enfatico*) they; **loro sono meglio di te** they are better than you; **prendeteli, sono loro** catch them, they're the ones; **sono stati loro a dirmelo** they told me themselves, it was they (*frm*) *o* them who told me; **hanno ragione loro, non tu** they are right, not you; **neanche loro hanno tutti i torti** even they aren't completely in the wrong
  c (*nelle comparazioni*: *sogg*) they, them; (: *complemento*) them; **ne so quanto loro** I know as much as they do, I know as much as them.

loro² ['loro] PRON PERS PL (*forma di cortesia*: *anche*: **Loro**) **a** you; **loro capiscono quanto ciò sia penoso** you are aware of how distressing that is; **chiedo lor signori di seguirmi** be so good as to follow me, (if you would) gentlemen **b** (*nelle comparazioni*) you.

loro³ ['loro] **1** AGG POSS INV: **il(la) loro** OR **i(le) loro a** their; **i loro amici** their friends; **un loro amico** a friend of theirs
  b (*forma di cortesia*: *anche*: **Loro**) your.
  2 PRON POSS INV: **il(la) loro** OR **i(le) loro a** theirs; **questi libri sono i loro** those books are theirs
  b (*forma di cortesia*: *anche*: **Loro**) yours
  c : **vivono del loro** they live on what they have; **i loro** (*famiglia*) their family; (*amici*) their own people; **siamo dei loro** OR **stiamo dalla loro** (*parte*) we're on their side, we're with them; **vogliono sempre dire la loro** they've always got something to say; **ne hanno fatto un'altra delle loro** they've (gone and) done it again.

losanga, ghe [lo'zanga] SF lozenge.

Losanna [lo'zanna] SF Lausanne.

loscamente [loska'mente] AVV suspiciously.

losco, a, schi, sche ['losko] **1** AGG **a** (*occhiata, aspetto*) sullen, surly **b** (*fig*: *equivoco*: *persona, affare*) shady, suspicious.
  2 SM: **qui c'è del losco** I smell a rat.

loto ['loto] SM lotus.

lotta ['lotta] **1** SF (*combattimento*) fight, struggle; (*conflitto*) conflict; (*Sport*) wrestling; **essere in lotta (con)** to be in conflict (with); **fare la lotta (con)** to wrestle (with); **lotta all'ultimo sangue** (*anche fig*) fight to the death; **lotta mortale** mortal combat.
  2 ▶**lotta armata** armed struggle ▶**lotta di classe** (*Pol*) class struggle ▶ **lotta contro la droga** war against drugs ▶**lotta corpo a corpo** hand-to-hand combat

▶**lotta libera** (*Sport*) all-in wrestling, freestyle ▶**lotta per la sopravvivenza** struggle *o* fight for survival.

lottare [lot'tare] VI (*aus* avere): **lottare (con** *o* **contro)** to fight (with *o* against), struggle (with *o* against); (*Sport*) to wrestle; **lottare contro il sonno** to struggle to keep awake; **lottare con la morte** to battle against death.

lottatore, trice [lotta'tore] SM/F fighter; (*Sport*) wrestler.

lotteria [lotte'ria] SF lottery; (*di gara ippica*) sweepstake.

lottizzare [lottid'dzare] VT (*terreno*) to divide into plots; (*fig*) to share out.

lottizzazione [lottiddzat'tsjone] SF (*di terreno*) division into plots; (*fig*) share-out.

lotto¹ ['lotto] SM (*gen*) lot; (*di terreno*) plot; **lotto fabbricabile** *o* **edificabile** building lot.

lotto² ['lotto] SM (*gioco*) (state) lottery; **vincere un terno al lotto** (*anche fig*) to hit the jackpot.

love story [lʌv'stɔːri] SF INV affair.

lozione [lot'tsjone] SF lotion.

L.st. ABBR (= *lire sterline*) £.

LT SIGLA = *Latina*.

LU SIGLA = *Lucca*.

lubrificante [lubrifi'kante] **1** AGG lubricating.
  2 SM lubricant.

lubrificare [lubrifi'kare] VT to lubricate.

lubrificazione [lubrifikat'tsjone] SF lubrication.

lucano, a [lu'kano] **1** AGG of *o* from Lucania.
  2 SM/F inhabitant *o* native of Lucania.

lucchetto [luk'ketto] SM padlock.

luccicante [luttʃi'kante] AGG (*vedi vb*) sparkling; twinkling; glittering; glistening.

luccicare [luttʃi'kare] VI (*aus* avere) (*gen*) to sparkle; (*stella*) to twinkle; (*oro*) to glitter; (*occhi*) to glisten; **non è tutt'oro quel che luccica** (*Proverbio*) all that glitters is not gold.

luccichio, chii [luttʃi'kio] SM (*vedi vb*) sparkling; twinkling; glittering; glistening.

luccicone [luttʃi'kone] SM: **avere i lucciconi agli occhi** to have tears in one's eyes.

luccio, ci ['luttʃo] SM (*pesce*) pike.

lucciola ['luttʃola] SF **a** (*Zool*) firefly, glow-worm; **prendere lucciole per lanterne** (*fig*) to get hold of the wrong end of the stick **b** (*euf*: *prostituta*) working girl.

luce ['lutʃe] SF **a** (*gen*) light; **alla luce del giorno** in daylight; **luce del sole/della luna** sun/moonlight; **accendere/spegnere la luce** to turn *o* switch the light on/off; **fare luce su qc** (*fig*) to shed *o* throw light on sth; **mettere in luce** (*fig*) to spotlight, highlight; **mettere qn in buona/cattiva luce** (*fig*) to put sb in a good/bad light; **fare qc alla luce del sole** (*fig*) to do sth in the open; **dare alla luce** (*bambino*) to give birth to; **venire alla luce** (*fatto*) to come to light; (*bambino*) to come into the world; **alla luce di questi fatti** in the light of this ▶**luci della ribalta** (*Teatro*) footlights
  b (*Aut*): **luci di arresto** brake lights ▶**luci di emergenza** hazard warning lights ▶**luci di posizione** sidelights (*Brit*), parking lights (*Am*) ▶**luci di retromarcia** reversing lights
  c (*Archit*: *di ponte, arco*) span; (*finestra*) window; **negozio a una luce** shop with one window.

lucente [lu'tʃente] AGG shining.

lucentezza [lutʃen'tettsa] SF shine.

lucerna [lu'tʃɛrna] SF oil lamp.

lucernario, ri [lutʃer'narjo] SM skylight.

lucertola [lu'tʃɛrtola] SF (*animale*) lizard; (*pellame*) lizard-

skin.

lucertolone [lutʃerto'lone] SM (*iguana*) iguana; (*ramarro*) green lizard.

lucherino [luke'rino] SM (*uccello*) siskin.

lucidalabbra [lutʃida'labbra] SM INV lip gloss.

lucidare [lutʃi'dare] VT **a** (*mobili, scarpe, pavimenti*) to polish **b** (*ricalcare: disegno*) to trace.

lucidatrice [lutʃida'tritʃe] SF floor polisher.

lucidatura [lutʃida'tura] SF polishing.

lucidità [lutʃidi'ta] SF lucidity.

lucido, a ['lutʃido] [1] AGG **a** shining, bright; **occhi lucidi di pianto/per la febbre** eyes bright with tears/with fever **b** (*pavimento, argento, scarpe*) polished; **è lucido come uno specchio** you can see your face in it **c** (*mente, discorso*) lucid, clear; (*malato*) lucid. [2] SM **a** (*lucentezza*) shine, lustre (*Brit*), luster (*Am*); **perdere il lucido** to lose its shine **b** (*sostanza*) polish; **lucido da scarpe** shoe polish **c** (*disegno, ricalco*) tracing; **carta da lucido** tracing paper.

lucignolo [lu'tʃiɲɲolo] SM wick.

lucrare [lu'krare] VT to make money (out of).

lucrativo, a [lukra'tivo] AGG lucrative.

lucro ['lukro] SM profit, gain; **a scopo di lucro** for gain; **associazione a scopo di lucro** profit-making organization.

lucroso, a [lu'kroso] AGG lucrative, profitable.

luculliano, a [lukul'ljano] AGG (*pasto*) sumptuous.

ludibrio [lu'dibrjo] SM **a** (*scherno*) mockery, scorn **b** (*zimbello*) laughing stock.

lue ['lue] SF (*Med*) syphilis.

luglio ['luʎʎo] SM July; **nel mese di luglio** in July *o* in the month of July; **il primo luglio** the first of July; **arrivare il 2 luglio** to arrive on the 2nd of July; **all'inizio/alla fine di luglio** at the beginning/at the end of July; **durante il mese di luglio** during July; **a luglio del prossimo anno** in July (of) next year; **ogni anno a luglio** every July; **che fai a luglio?** what are you doing in July?; **è piovuto molto a luglio quest'anno** July was very wet this year.

lugubre ['lugubre] AGG gloomy, dismal.

lugubremente [lugubre'mente] AVV gloomily, dismally.

lui ['lui] [1] PRON PERS M **a** (*complemento: dopo prep, con valore enfatico*) him; **sono venuto con lui** I came with him; **senza di lui** without him; **se non fosse per lui** if it were not for him; **hanno accusato lui, non me** they accused him, not me; **chiedilo a lui** ask him; **lui qui non lo voglio** I don't want him here **b** (*sogg: al posto di 'egli', con valore enfatico*) he; **lui è meglio di te** he is better than you; **prendetelo, è lui** catch him, he's the one; **è stato lui a dirmelo** he told me himself, it was he who told me; **ha ragione lui, non tu** he's right, not you; **neanche lui ha tutti i torti** even he isn't completely in the wrong **c** (*nelle comparazioni: sogg*) he, him; **ne so quanto lui** I know as much as he does, I know as much as him. [2] SM INV (*scherz*): **il mio lui** my beloved.

luì [lu'i] SM (*uccello*) willow warbler.

lumaca, che [lu'maka] SF (*Zool*) slug; (*fam: chiocciola*) snail; (*fig*) slowcoach (*Brit*), slowpoke (*Am*); **a passo di lumaca** at a snail's pace.

lumacone [luma'kone] SM (*Zool*) (large) slug; (*fig*) slowcoach (*Brit*), slowpoke (*Am*).

lume ['lume] SM **a** (*gen*) light; **a lume di candela** by candlelight; **a lume di naso** by rule of thumb; **chiedere lumi a qn** (*fig*) to ask sb for advice; **perdere il lume della ragione** to be blinded by rage **b** (*lampada*) lamp ▶ **lume a olio** oil lamp.

lumicino [lumi'tʃino] SM small *o* faint light; **essere (ridotto) al lumicino** (*fig*) to be at death's door.

luminaria [lumi'narja] SF (*per feste*) illuminations *pl*.

luminescente [luminef'ʃente] AGG luminescent.

luminescenza [luminef'ʃentsa] SF luminescence.

lumino [lu'mino] SM small light; **lumino da notte** nightlight; **lumino per i morti** candle for the dead.

luminosamente [luminosa'mente] AVV brightly.

luminosità [luminosi'ta] SF brightness; (*fig: di sorriso, volto*) radiance; **c'è una luminosità diffusa sopra la città** there's a hazy glow over the city.

luminoso, a [lumi'noso] AGG **a** (*gen*) luminous; (*sorgente*) of light, light *attr*; (*fig: sorriso, volto*) radiant; **insegna luminosa** neon sign **b** (*cielo, occhi, avvenire, idea*) bright; (*sorriso, viso*) bright, radiant.

luna ['luna] SF moon; **una notte di luna** a moonlit night; **avere la luna** to be in a bad mood; **svegliarsi con la luna** (*fig*) to get out of bed on the wrong side; **chiedere la luna** to ask for the moon ▶ **luna di miele** honeymoon ▶ **luna nuova** new moon ▶ **luna piena** full moon.

luna park ['luna 'park] SM INV amusement park, funfair.

lunare [lu'nare] AGG lunar, moon *attr*; **paesaggio lunare** (*fig*) lunar landscape.

lunaria [lu'narja] SF (*pietra*) moonstone.

lunario, ri [lu'narjo] SM almanac; **sbarcare il lunario** (*fig*) to make ends meet.

lunatico, a, ci, che [lu'natiko] [1] AGG quirky, temperamental. [2] SM/F temperamental person.

lunedì [lune'di] SM INV Monday; **lunedì dell'Angelo** Easter Monday *per fraseologia vedi* **martedì**.

lunetta [lu'netta] SF (*Archit*) lunette.

lunga ['lunga] SF vedi **lungo 3**.

lungaggine [lun'gaddʒine] SF slowness; **le lungaggini della burocrazia** red tape *sg*.

lungamente [lunga'mente] AVV (*a lungo*) for a long time; (*diffusamente*) at length; **un figlio lungamente atteso** a long-awaited child; **dopo aver lungamente sofferto** after long suffering.

lungarno [lun'garno] SM *embankment along the Arno*.

lunghezza [lun'gettsa] [1] SF length; **il lungomare si estende per una lunghezza di 5 km** the promenade stretches for 5 km; **nel senso della lunghezza** lengthways, along its length; **vincere per una lunghezza** (*cavallo*) to win by a length ▶ **lunghezza d'onda** wavelength.

lungi ['lundʒi]: **lungi da** PREP far from; **lungi da me l'idea di offenderti!** far be it from me to offend you!; **lungi dall'essere** far from being.

lungimirante [lundʒimi'rante] AGG far-sighted.

lungimiranza [lundʒimi'rantsa] SF far-sightedness.

lungo, a, ghi, ghe ['lungo] [1] AGG **a** (*gen*) long; (*persona*) tall; (*viaggio*) lengthy; **una fila di macchine lunga 2 km** a tailback of cars 2 km long; **amici da lunga data** long-standing *o* old friends; **lo conosco da lungo tempo** I've known him for a long time; **un discorso lungo 2 ore** a 2-hour speech **b** (*lento: persona*) slow; **essere lungo a *o* nel fare qc** to be slow at doing sth, take a long time to do sth; **essere lungo come la fame** to be a slowcoach (*Brit*) *o* slowpoke (*Am*)

c (*diluito*: *caffè*) weak, watery; (*brodo*) thin
d (*fraseologia*): **avere la barba lunga** to be unshaven; **avere le mani lunghe** to be light-fingered; **fare il passo più lungo della gamba** to bite off more than one can chew; **cadere lungo disteso** to measure one's length on the ground; **fare la faccia lunga** *o* **il muso lungo** *o* **il viso lungo** to pull a long face; **a lunga gittata** (*Mil*) long-range; **saperla lunga** (*fam*) to know a thing or two, know what's what; **a lunga scadenza** long term; **a lungo andare** in the long run.

2 SM length; **per il lungo** along its length, lengthways; **in lungo e in largo** (*girare, cercare*) far and wide; **a lungo** (*aspettare*) for a long time; (*spiegare*) in great detail.

3 SF: **di gran lunga** far and away; **è di gran lunga il migliore** he's far and away the best, he's the best by far; **andare per le lunghe** to drag on; **alla lunga** in the long run.

4 PREP (*spazio*) along, beside; (*tempo*) during; **camminare lungo il fiume** to walk along *o* beside the river; **lungo il corso dei secoli** throughout the centuries, in the course of the centuries; **lungo il viaggio** during the journey.

lungofiume [lungo'fjume] SM embankment.

lungolago [lungo'lago] SM *road round a lake.*

lungolinea [lungo'linea] SM INV (*Tennis*) down-the-line shot.

lungomare [lungo'mare] SM promenade.

lungometraggio, gi [lungome'traddʒo] SM (*Cine*) feature film.

lungotevere [lungo'tevere] SM *embankment along the Tiber.*

lunotto [lu'nɔtto] SM (*Aut*) rear *o* back window ▸**lunotto termico** heated rear window.

luogo, ghi ['lwɔgo] 1 SM **a** (*gen*) place; **in ogni luogo** everywhere; **in qualsiasi luogo** anywhere; **in qualsiasi luogo vada** wherever you go; **in nessun luogo** nowhere; **sul luogo** on the spot; **fuori luogo** (*fig*) out of place, inopportune; **uno del luogo** a native, a local
b (*fraseologia*): **aver luogo** to take place; **far luogo a** to give way to, make room for; **dar luogo a** (*critiche, dubbi*) to give rise to; **in luogo di** in place of, instead of; **in primo/secondo luogo** in the first/ second place.
2 ▸**luogo comune** commonplace, cliché ▸**luogo del delitto** scene of the crime ▸**luogo geometrico** locus ▸**luogo di nascita** (*gen*) birthplace; (*Amm*) place of birth ▸**luogo di origine** *o* **di provenienza** place of origin ▸**luogo di pena** penitentiary (*Am*), prison ▸**luogo pubblico** public place.

luogotenente [lwogote'nɛnte] SM (*Mil, fig*) lieutenant.

lupa ['lupa] SF she-wolf.

lupacchiotto [lupak'kjɔtto] SM (*Zool*) (wolf) cub.

lupara [lu'para] SF (*fucile*) sawn-off shotgun.

luparia [lu'parja] SF (*pianta*) globeflower.

lupetto [lu'petto] SM (*Zool*) (wolf) cub; (*negli scouts*) cub (scout).

lupinella [lupi'nɛlla] SF (*pianta*) sainfoin.

lupino [lu'pino] SM (*pianta*) lupin.

lupo ['lupo] 1 SM wolf; **cane lupo** alsatian (*Brit*), German

shepherd (*Am*); **avere una fame da lupi** to be ravenous *o* famished; **gridare al lupo** to cry wolf; **tempo da lupi** filthy weather; **in bocca al lupo!** good luck!; **il lupo perde il pelo ma non il vizio** (*Proverbio*) the leopard cannot change its spots ▸**lupo mannaro** (*licantropo*) werewolf ▸**lupo di mare** (*fig*) old salt.

luppolo ['luppolo] SM (*pianta*) hop.

lurido, a ['lurido] AGG (*anche fig*) filthy, foul.

luridume [luri'dume] SM filth.

lusco ['lusko] SM: **tra il lusco e il brusco** at dusk.

lusinga, ghe [lu'zinga] SF flattery; **con la lusinga di un lauto stipendio** with the promise of a high salary; **non mi convincerai con le lusinghe** flattery will get you nowhere.

lusingare [luzin'gare] VT (*adulare*) to flatter; **si è fatto lusingare dalle promesse di una brillante carriera** he let himself be swayed by promises of a brilliant career; **lusingatissimo!** (*onorato*) I'm honoured!

lusinghiero, a [luzin'gjɛro] AGG flattering.

lussare [lus'sare] VT (*Med*) to dislocate.

lussazione [lussat'tsjone] SF (*Med*) dislocation.

lussemburghese [lussembur'gese] 1 AGG of *o* from Luxembourg.
2 SM/F native *o* inhabitant of Luxembourg.

Lussemburgo [lussem'burgo] 1 SM (*stato*): **il Lussemburgo** Luxembourg.
2 SF (*città*) Luxembourg.

lusso ['lusso] SM luxury; **di lusso** (*macchina, appartamento*) luxury *attr*, (*prodotto*) de luxe *attr*; **vivere nel lusso più sfacciato** to live in unashamed luxury; **non posso permettermi il lusso di una vacanza** I can't afford the luxury of a holiday.

lussuosamente [lussuosa'mente] AVV luxuriously.

lussuoso, a [lussu'oso] AGG luxurious.

lussureggiante [lussured'dʒante] AGG (*vegetazione, pianta*) luxuriant; (*fig: stile*) profuse, rich.

lussureggiare [lussured'dʒare] VI (*aus* **avere**) to be luxuriant.

lussuria [lus'surja] SF lust.

lussuriosamente [lussurjosa'mente] AVV lasciviously.

lussurioso, a [lussu'rjoso] AGG lascivious, lustful.

lustrare [lus'trare] VT (*mobili, pavimenti*) to polish; (*scarpe*) to polish, shine.

lustrascarpe [lustras'karpe] SM/F INV shoeshine.

lustrino [lus'trino] SM sequin.

lustro, a ['lustro] 1 AGG (*superficie*) shiny; (*capelli, pelo*) glossy; (*occhi*) moist.
2 SM **a** shine, gloss **b** (*fig: gloria*) prestige, glory **c** (*quinquennio*) five-year period.

luteranesimo [lutera'nezimo] SM Lutheranism.

luterano, a [lute'rano] AGG, SM/F Lutheran.

Lutero [lu'tɛro] SM Luther.

lutreola [lu'trɛola] SF (*Zool*) European mink.

lutto ['lutto] SM (*gen*) mourning; (*perdita*) loss, bereavement; **essere in/portare il lutto** to be in/wear mourning; **un lutto nazionale** an occasion for national mourning; **è stato un lutto per il paese** it was a great loss to the country.

luttuoso, a [luttu'oso] AGG sad, mournful.

M

M, m ['emme] SF O M INV (*lettera*) M, m; **M come Milano** ≈ M for Mary (*Brit*), ≈ M for Mike (*Am*).

m ['emme] ABBR = **metro**.

m. ABBR = **mese, miglia, monte**.

ma [ma] **1** CONG but; (*tuttavia*) yet, still, but; (*comunque*) however; **mi piacerebbe venire ma non posso** I would love to come but I can't; **non solo non beve più ma ha anche smesso di fumare** he's not just given up drinking - he's stopped smoking too; **hanno fatto quel che potevano ma non sono riusciti a salvarlo** they did what they could, but they couldn't save him; **non se lo merita ma dovremmo cercare di capirlo** even though he doesn't deserve it, we should try to understand him; **ma non se lo merita** he doesn't deserve it though; **incredibile ma vero** incredible but true; **ma si può sapere che cosa vuoi?** just what do you want?; **ma smettila!** give over!, stop it!; **ma va'?** (*dubitativo*) really?; (*esclamazione*) surely not!; **ma davvero?** really?; **ma sì!** (*certo*) yes, of course!; **ma no!** of course not!; **ma insomma!** for goodness sake!.
2 SM INV but; **ci sono ancora dei ma** there are still some uncertainties; **non c'è ma che tenga** I'm not going to take no for an answer.

ma' [ma] SF (*fam*) mum, mom (*Am*).

macabro, a ['makabro] **1** AGG macabre, gruesome.
2 SM: **il gusto del macabro** a taste for the macabre.

macaco, chi [ma'kako] SM (*Zool*) macaque; (*fig fam*) clod.

macadam [maka'dam] SM macadam.

macadamizzare [makadamid'dzare] VT to macadamize.

macché [mak'ke] ESCL (*fam*) certainly not!, you must be joking!; **avete finito il lavoro? — macché!, abbiamo appena incominciato!** have you finished the work? — you must be joking, we've hardly started!

maccheroni [makke'roni] SMPL macaroni *sg*.

maccheronico, a, ci, che [makke'rɔniko] AGG (*latino, greco*) macaronic; (*pegg*) abysmal.

macchia¹ ['makkja] SF **a** (*chiazza*) mark, spot; (*sulla pelle*) blotch, mark; (*sul pelo*) patch; (*di sporco*) stain, mark; **macchie di colore** splashes of colour; **coprirsi di macchie** (*pelle*) to come out in a rash; **estendersi a macchia d'olio** (*fig: rivolta, epidemia*) to spread rapidly; (*: città*) to grow rapidly ▶ **macchia di grasso** greasy mark, grease stain ▶ **macchia d'inchiostro** ink stain; (*su foglio*) (ink) blot ▶ **macchia di sangue** bloodstain ▶ **macchia di vino** wine stain ▶ **macchie solari** (*Astron*) sunspots
b (*fig: su reputazione*) blot, stain.

macchia² ['makkja] SF (*boscaglia*) scrub; **darsi/vivere alla macchia** (*fig*) to go into/live in hiding.

macchiare [mak'kjare] **1** VT **a** (*sporcare: tovaglia, camicia*) to stain; (*con inchiostro: quaderno*) to blot; (*fig: reputazione*) to sully, tarnish; **hai macchiato la tovaglia di caffè** you've got coffee on the tablecloth; **la birra non macchia** beer doesn't stain *o* leave a mark; **mi sono macchiata il vestito** I've got a stain on my dress
b: **macchiare il caffè (col latte)** to add a drop of milk to (one's) coffee.
2 **macchiarsi** VIP (*persona*) to get stains *o* marks on one's clothes, get o.s. dirty; (*tessuto*) to get stained *o* marked; **ti sei macchiato tutto!** you've got yourself all dirty!; **macchiarsi di un delitto** to be guilty of a crime.

macchiato, a [mak'kjato] AGG **a** (*gen*): **macchiato (di)** stained (with); **caffè macchiato** coffee with a dash of milk **b** (*pelo*) spotted.

macchietta [mak'kjetta] SF **a** (*piccola macchia*) spot **b** (*vignetta, Teatro*) caricature; (*fig: persona*) character.

macchiettista, i, e [makkjet'tista] SM/F caricaturist.

macchina ['makkina] **1** SF **a** (*automobile*) car; **salire in macchina** to get into the car; **andare/venire in macchina** to go/come by car
b (*gen, fig*) machine; (*motore, locomotiva*) engine; **sala macchine** (*Naut*) engine room; **la macchina burocratica** the bureaucratic machinery; **andare in macchina** (*Stampa*) to go to press.
2 ▶ **macchina per caffè** espresso (machine) ▶ **macchina da cucire** sewing machine ▶ **macchina fotografica** camera ▶ **macchina da presa** cine *o* movie camera ▶ **macchina da scrivere** typewriter ▶ **macchina utensile** machine tool ▶ **macchina a**

vapore steam engine.

macchinalmente [makkinal'mente] AVV mechanically.

macchinare [makki'nare] VT to plot.

macchinario, ri [makki'narjo] SM machinery.

macchinata [makki'nata] SF (*fam: carico di lavatrice o lavastoviglie*) load.

macchinazione [makkinat'tsjone] SF plot, machination.

macchinetta [makki'netta] SF (*fam: caffettiera*) espresso coffee maker; (: *accendino*) lighter; (: *per il taglio dei capelli*) hair clippers; (: *per i denti*) brace; **parlare come una macchinetta** (*fig*) to talk nineteen to the dozen.

macchinista, i [makki'nista] SM (*di treno*) engine-driver; (*di nave*) engineer; (*Teatro, Cine, TV*) stagehand.

macchinoso, a [makki'noso] AGG complex, complicated.

Macedonia [matʃe'dɔnja] SF: **la Macedonia** Macedonia.

macedonia [matʃe'dɔnja] SF (*Culin*) fruit salad.

macellaio, ai [matʃel'lajo] SM (*anche fig*) butcher.

macellare [matʃel'lare] VT (*anche fig*) to slaughter, butcher.

macellazione [matʃellat'tsjone] SF slaughtering, butchering.

macelleria [matʃelle'ria] SF butcher's (shop).

macello [ma'tʃɛllo] SM **a** (*mattatoio*) slaughterhouse, abattoir (*Brit*) **b** (*azione, anche fig*) slaughter, massacre; **mandare al macello** (*soldati*) to send to their deaths **c** (*fig fam: disordine*) mess, shambles *sg*; (: *disastro*) disaster.

macerare [matʃe'rare] **1** VT (*canapa, carta*) to macerate; (*Culin*) to marinate.
2 macerarsi VR (*consumarsi*): **macerarsi nel rimorso** to be consumed with remorse.

macerazione [matʃerat'tsjone] SF maceration.

macerie [ma'tʃɛrje] SFPL rubble *sg*, debris *sg*.

macero ['matʃero] SM (*operazione*) pulping; (*stabilimento*) pulping mill; **carta da macero** paper for pulping.

mach [makh] SM INV Mach (number).

machete [ma'tʃete] SM INV machete.

machiavellicamente [makjavellika'mente] AVV craftily.

machiavellico, a, ci, che [makja'vɛlliko] AGG (*anche fig*) Machiavellian.

macho ['matʃo] **1** AGG INV macho.
2 SM INV macho type.

macigno [ma'tʃiɲɲo] SM (*masso*) rock, boulder; **duro come un macigno** as hard as rock.

macilento, a [matʃi'lɛnto] AGG emaciated.

macina ['matʃina] SF (*pietra*) millstone; (*macchina*) grinder.

macinacaffè [matʃinakaf'fɛ] SM INV coffee grinder, coffee mill.

macinapepe [matʃina'pepe] SM INV pepper mill.

macinare [matʃi'nare] VT (*grano, caffè*) to grind; (*carne*) to mince (*Brit*), grind (*Am*); **macinare i chilometri** (*fig*) to eat up the miles.

macinato [matʃi'nato] SM **a** (*cereali, farina*) meal **b** (*carne*) mince, minced (*Brit*) *o* ground (*Am*) meat.

macinatura [matʃina'tura], **macinazione** [matʃinat'tsjone] SF grinding.

macinino [matʃi'nino] SM **a** (*per caffè*) mill, coffee grinder; (*per pepe*) mill, pepper mill **b** (*scherz: macchina*) old banger (*Brit*), clunker (*Am*).

maciste [ma'tʃiste] SM (*scherz*) colossus.

maciullare [matʃul'lare] VT (*canapa, lino*) to brake; (*fig: braccio ecc*) to crush.

macramè [makra'mɛ] SM macramé.

macro... ['makro] PREF macro... .

macrobiotica [makrobi'ɔtika] SF macrobiotics *sg*.

macrobiotico, a, ci, che [makrobi'ɔtiko] AGG (*dieta, alimenti*) macrobiotic.

macroclima, i [makro'klima] SM macroclimate.

macrocosmo [makro'kɔzmo] SM macrocosm.

macroeconomia [makroekono'mia] SF macroeconomics *sg*.

macrofotografia [makrofotogra'fia] SF (*Fot: tecnica*) macrography; (: *singola immagine*) macrograph.

macromolecola [makromo'lɛkola] SF macromolecule.

macropo ['makropo] SM (*Zool*) red-necked wallaby.

macroscopicamente [makroskopika'mente] AVV (*rafforzativo*) glaringly.

macroscopico, a, ci, che [makros'kɔpiko] AGG (*dimensione*) macroscopic; (*errore*) glaring.

maculato, a [maku'lato] AGG (*pelo*) spotted.

madama [ma'dama] SF **a** (*scherz*) madam **b** (*gergo: polizia*) cops *pl*.

madamigella [madami'dʒɛlla] SF (*scherz*) young lady.

Maddalena [madda'lena] SF (*Rel*) Mary Magdalen(e).

made in Italy SM: **il made in Italy** Italian exports *pl* (*especially fashion goods*).

Madera [ma'dɛra] **1** SF (*Geog*) Madeira.
2 SM INV (*vino*) Madeira.

madia ['madja] SF *chest for the making and storage of bread*.

madido, a ['madido] AGG (*letter*): **madido (di)** wet *o* moist (with); **madido di sudore** bathed in sweat.

madonna [ma'dɔnna] SF (*Rel*): **Madonna** Our Lady; (*Arte*) madonna; (*letter, Storia*) my lady, madam; **madonna!** (*fam*) good God!

madonnina [madon'nina] SF (*Arte*) madonna; **con quell'aria da madonnina infilzata** (*iro*) with that look of a demure little madonna.

madornale [mador'nale] AGG enormous, huge.

madras [ma'dras] SM INV madras cotton.

madre ['madre] **1** SF **a** mother; **senza madre** motherless ▶**madre adottiva** adoptive mother ▶**madre coraggio** Mother Courage (*mother who defies the mafia, state etc to defend her child*) ▶**madre di famiglia** mother ▶**madre natura** Mother Nature ▶**madre superiora** (*Rel*) mother superior
b : **madre dell'aceto** mother of vinegar
c (*matrice di bolletta*) counterfoil.
2 AGG INV mother *attr*; **casa madre** (*Rel*) mother house; **ragazza madre** unmarried mother; **regina madre** queen mother; **scena madre** (*Teatro*) principal scene; **ha fatto una scena madre** (*fig*) she made a terrible scene.

madrelingua [madre'lingwa] SF mother tongue, native language.

madrepatria [madre'patrja] SF mother country, native land.

madreperla [madre'pɛrla] SF mother-of-pearl.

madreperlaceo, a [madreper'latʃeo] AGG pearly.

madrepora [ma'drɛpora] SF madrepore.

Madrid [ma'drid] SF Madrid.

madrigale [madri'gale] SM madrigal.

madrileno, a [madri'lɛno] **1** AGG of *o* from Madrid.
2 SM/F native *o* inhabitant of Madrid.

madrina [ma'drina] SF (*di bambino*) godmother; (*di nave*) christener.

maestà [maes'ta] SF INV (*gen*) majesty; **Sua Maestà il Re**

His Majesty the King; **Sua Maestà la Regina** Her Majesty the Queen.

maestosamente [maestosa'mente] AVV majestically.

maestosità [maestosi'ta] SF majesty.

maestoso, a [maes'toso] AGG majestic.

maestra [ma'ɛstra] SF vedi **maestro**.

maestrale [maes'trale] [1] SM northwest wind, north-westerly.

[2] AGG northwest *attr*, northwesterly.

maestranze [maes'trantse] SFPL workforce *sg*, workers.

maestria [maes'tria] SF mastery, skill.

maestro, a [ma'ɛstro] [1] SM/F **a** (*anche:* **maestro di scuola** *o* **elementare**) primary (*Brit*) *o* grade school (*Am*) teacher

b (*fig: esperto*) expert; **è maestra nella cucina** she's an expert cook; **è stato un colpo da maestro** (*fig*) that was a masterstroke.

[2] SM **a** (*artigiano*) master; **i Maestri del Rinascimento** the Masters of the Renaissance

b (*Mus*) maestro

c (*vento*) northwest wind.

[3] AGG (*di grande abilità*) masterly, skilful (*Brit*), skillful (*Am*); **albero maestro** (*Naut*) main mast; **muro maestro** main wall; **strada maestra** main road.

[4] ►**maestra d'asilo** nursery teacher ►**maestro di ballo** dancing master ►**maestro di cerimonie** master of ceremonies ►**maestro d'orchestra** conductor, director (*Am*) ►**maestro di piano** piano teacher ►**maestro di scherma** fencing master ►**maestro di sci** ski *o* skiing instructor.

mafia ['mafja] SF Mafia.

mafioso, a [ma'fjoso] [1] AGG mafia *attr*.

[2] SM/F member of the Mafia.

maga, ghe ['maga] SF sorceress.

magagna [ma'gaɲɲa] SF **a** (*anche fig*) defect, flaw, blemish **b** (*noia, guaio*) problem.

magari [ma'gari] [1] ESCL (*esprime desiderio*): **magari fosse vero!** if only it were true!; **ti piacerebbe andare in Italia? — magari!** would you like to go to Italy? — I certainly would! *o* you bet!; **hai avuto l'aumento? — sì, magari!** did you get the increase? — I should have been so lucky!.

[2] AVV (*anche*) even; (*forse*) perhaps; **saremo in 5, magari in 6** there will be 5, or perhaps 6, of us; **a uscire tutto sudato magari ti prendi un raffreddore** if you go out all sweaty you're likely to *o* you may catch a cold.

magazzinaggio, gi [magaddzi'naddʒo] SM storage; **(spese di) magazzinaggio** storage charges *pl*, warehousing charges *pl*.

magazziniere [magaddzi'njɛre] SM warehouseman.

magazzino [magad'dzino] SM **a** (*deposito*) warehouse; **avere merci in magazzino** to have goods in stock; **fondi di magazzino** unsold stock ►**magazzino doganale** bonded warehouse **b**: **grande magazzino** department store.

maggese [mad'dʒese] SM (*Agr*) fallow field; **lasciare a maggese** to leave fallow.

maggio ['maddʒo] SM May *per fraseologia vedi* **luglio**.

maggiolino [maddʒo'lino] SM **a** (*Zool*) cockchafer, May bug **b** (*automobile*) beetle.

maggiorana [maddʒo'rana] SF (*Bot*) (sweet) marjoram.

maggioranza [maddʒo'rantsa] SF (*gen*) majority; **partito di maggioranza** majority party; **eletto con una maggioranza di** elected by a majority of; **essere in maggioranza**

to be in the majority; **nella maggioranza dei casi** in most cases; **la maggioranza degli italiani** most Italians, the majority of Italians; **la maggioranza silenziosa** the silent majority.

maggiorare [maddʒo'rare] VT (*Comm: prezzo, conto*): **maggiorare (di)** to increase (by).

maggiorazione [maddʒorat'tsjone] SF (*Comm*) rise, increase.

maggiordomo [maddʒor'dɔmo] SM butler.

maggiore [mad'dʒore] [1] AGG (*comp di* **grande**) **a** (*più grande*) bigger, larger; (: *di quantità*) greater; **le spese sono state maggiori del previsto** expenses were higher than expected; **ha dimostrato maggior entusiasmo di te** he showed greater enthusiasm than you; **a maggior ragione dovresti parlargli tu** all the more reason for you to speak to him yourself

b (*più importante*) more important; (*di notevole rilevanza*) major; **opere maggiori** major works

c (*più anziano: sorella, fratello*) elder, older

d (*di grado*): **sergente maggiore** sergeant major; **Stato Maggiore** (*Mil*) general staff

e (*Mus*) major; **do maggiore** C major.

[2] AGG (*superl di* **grande**) (*vedi 1a, b, c*) biggest, largest; greatest; most important; eldest, oldest; **la maggior parte della gente** most people, the majority (of people); **andare per la maggiore** (*cantante, attore ecc*) to be very popular, be "in"; **raggiungere la maggior età** to reach the age of majority.

[3] SM/F **a** (*grado: Mil*) major; (: *Aer*) squadron leader

b (*d'età: tra due*) older, elder; (: *tra più di due*) oldest, eldest.

maggiorenne [maddʒo'rɛnne] [1] AGG of age.

[2] SM/F person who has come of age; **diventare maggiorenne** to come of age, reach one's majority.

maggiorità [maddʒori'ta] SF (*Mil: di battaglione*) orderly room; (: *di reggimento*) regimental office.

maggioritario, ria, ri, rie [maddʒori'tarjo] [1] AGG majority *attr*.

[2] SM (*Pol: anche:* **sistema maggioritario**) first-past-the-post system.

maggiormente [maddʒor'mente] AVV more; **impegnandoti maggiormente supereresti l'esame** if you were to work harder you'd pass the exam; **l'artista che lo ha maggiormente influenzato è Rembrandt** the artist who most influenced him was Rembrandt.

magia [ma'dʒia] SF magic; **come per magia** as if by magic, like magic.

magicamente [madʒika'mente] AVV magically.

magico, a, ci, che ['madʒiko] AGG magic; (*fig: serata, incontro*) magical; (: *sorriso*) charming; **pronunciare la formula magica** to say the magic words.

magio, gi ['madʒo] SM (*Rel*): **i re Magi** the Magi, the Three Wise Men.

magistero [madʒis'tɛro] SM: **Facoltà di Magistero** ≈ teacher(s') training college.

magistrale [madʒis'trale] [1] AGG **a** (*Scol*) primary (*Brit*) *o* grade school (*Am*) teachers', primary *o* grade school teaching *attr*; **abilitazione magistrale** *teaching diploma for primary teachers*; **istituto magistrale** *secondary school for the training of primary teachers: attended by students aged 14 - 18*

b (*abile: colpo, intervento*) masterly, skilful (*Brit*), skillful (*Am*).

[2]: **magistrali** SFPL = **istituto magistrale**.

magistralmente [madʒistral'mente] AVV in a masterly manner, skilfully (*Brit*), skillfully (*Am*).

magistrato [madʒis'trato] SM magistrate.

magistratura [madʒistra'tura] SF: **la magistratura** the magistracy, the magistrature.

maglia ['maʎʎa] SF **a** (*punto*) stitch; **avviare/calare le maglie** to cast on/off ▶**maglia dritta** plain ▶**maglia rovescia** purl; **lavora una maglia dritta, una rovescia** knit one, purl one

  b (*lavoro ai ferri*) knitting *no pl*; **lavorare a maglia** OR **fare la maglia** to knit

  c (*indumento intimo*) vest; (*Sport, maglione, tessuto*) jersey; (*Storia: di armatura*) coat of mail; **indossa la maglia iridata** (*Ciclismo*) he's the world cycling champion

  d (*di catena*) link; (*di armatura*) coat of mail; (*di rete, Tecn*) mesh; **una rete a maglie fitte/grosse** a fine-/wide-mesh net; **passare per le maglie della rete** (*anche fig*) to slip through the net.

magliaia [maʎ'ʎaja] SF knitter.

maglieria [maʎʎe'ria] SF **a** (*indumenti*) knitwear; **macchina per maglieria** knitting machine **b** (*negozio*) knitwear shop.

maglietta [maʎ'ʎetta] SF (*con maniche*) T-shirt; (*canottiera*) vest.

maglificio, ci [maʎʎi'fitʃo] SM knitwear factory.

maglina [maʎ'ʎina] SF (*tessuto*) jersey.

maglio, gli ['maʎʎo] SM (*martello*) mallet; (*Tecn: macchina*) power hammer.

maglione [maʎ'ʎone] SM jersey, sweater.

magma, i ['magma] SM (*Geol*) magma; **allo stato di magma** (*fig*) inchoate.

magnaccia [maɲ'ɲattʃa] SM INV (*pegg*) pimp.

Magna Grecia [maɲɲa'gretʃa] SF: **la Magna Grecia** Magna Graecia.

magnanimamente [maɲɲanima'mente] AVV magnanimously.

magnanimità [maɲɲanimi'ta] SF magnanimity.

magnanimo, a [maɲ'ɲanimo] AGG magnanimous.

magnate [maɲ'ɲate] SM tycoon, magnate.

magnesia [maɲ'ɲezja] SF magnesia.

magnesio [maɲ'ɲezjo] SM magnesium; **al magnesio** (*lampada, flash*) magnesium *attr*.

magnete [maɲ'ɲete] SM (*calamita*) magnet; (*Elettr, Aut*) magneto.

magneticamente [maɲɲetika'mente] AVV magnetically.

magnetico, a, ci, che [maɲ'ɲetiko] AGG (*anche fig*) magnetic.

magnetismo [maɲɲe'tizmo] SM (*anche fig*) magnetism; **il magnetismo terrestre** the earth's magnetism.

magnetizzare [maɲɲetid'dzare] VT (*Fis*) to magnetize; (*fig*) to mesmerize.

magnetizzazione [maɲɲetiddzat'tsjone] SF (*Fis*) magnetization.

magnetofono° [maɲɲe'tɔfono] SM tape recorder.

magnificamente [maɲɲifika'mente] AVV magnificently, extremely well.

magnificare [maɲɲifi'kare] VT (*celebrare*) to extol, praise; **magnificare i pregi di qn/qc** to sing the praises of sb/sth.

Magnificat [maɲ'ɲifikat] SM INV Magnificat.

magnificenza [maɲɲifi'tʃɛntsa] SF magnificence, splendour (*Brit*), splendor (*Am*).

magnifico, a, ci, che [maɲ'ɲifiko] AGG (*gen*) magnificent, splendid; (*serata*) marvellous, wonderful; (*tempo*) gorgeous, superb; **domani si parte — magnifico!** we're setting off tomorrow — terrific!

magnitudine [maɲɲi'tudine] SF (*Astron, Geol*) magnitude.

magno, a ['maɲɲo] AGG: **aula magna** main hall.

magnolia [maɲ'ɲɔlja] SF magnolia.

magnum ['maɲɲum] ① SM INV (*bottiglia*) magnum.

  ② SF INV (*pistola*) magnum.

mago, ghi ['mago] SM (*stregone*) magician, wizard; (*illusionista*) magician; (*fam: persona abilissima*) wizard.

magone [ma'gone] SM (*fam*): **avere il magone** to have a lump in one's throat.

magra ['magra] SF **a** (*di fiume*) low water; **essere in magra** to be very low; **periodo di magra** (*fig*) lean times **b** (*fam: brutta figura*): **fare una magra** to boob (*Brit*), make a boob (*Brit*).

magramente [magra'mente] AVV (*ricompensato*) poorly.

magrezza [ma'grettsa] SF (*di persona, corpo*) thinness; (*di risorse*) scarcity.

magro, a ['magro] ① AGG **a** (*persona, corpo*) thin, skinny (*pegg*); (*viso*) thin

  b (*latte*) skimmed; (*carne*) lean; (*formaggio*) low-fat

  c (*stipendio, guadagno*) poor, meagre (*Brit*), meager (*Am*); (*profitti*) small, slim; (*annata, raccolto*) poor; (*scusa*) poor, lame; (*soddisfazione, consolazione*) scant; (*cena, pasto*) skimpy.

  ② SM **a** (*carne*) lean meat

  b (*Rel*): **giorno di magro** day of abstinence; **mangiare di magro** not to eat meat.

  ③ SM/F (*persona magra*) slim person; **questi vestiti stanno bene solo alle magre** these clothes only look good on slim women.

mah [ma] ESCL (*fam*) well!

mai ['mai] AVV **a** (*negativo*) never, not ...ever; **non esce mai** she never goes out; **non sono mai stato in Russia** I've never *o* I haven't ever been to Russia; **non me ne dimenticherò mai** I'll never *o* won't ever forget it; **non avrei mai detto che...** I would never have said that ...; **non le ha mai più telefonato** he never phoned her again, he has never phoned her since; **non si sa mai** you never can tell; **mai e poi mai!** no way!; **mai più** never again; (*assolutamente no*) no way; **quasi mai** hardly ever, practically never; **ora o mai più** it's now or never

  b (*con tempi indefiniti*) ever; **l'hai mai visto prima?** have you ever seen him before?; **sei mai in ufficio il sabato?** are you ever in the office on a Saturday?; **se mai ne trovassi uno te lo farei sapere** if I ever found one I would let you know; **i prezzi delle case sono più alti che mai** house prices are higher than ever; **caso mai si mettesse a piovere** in case it starts raining, should it start to rain; **se mai direi che ha sbagliato lui** if anything, I would say that he was in the wrong; **caso mai ti telefono domenica** I might phone you on Sunday; **come mai?** why (*o* how) on earth?; **come mai non ci hai avvisato?** why (on earth) didn't you let us know?; **che dici mai?** what (on earth) are you saying?; **chi/dove/quando mai?** whoever/wherever/whenever?; **quando mai ho detto una cosa simile?** when did I ever say any such thing?

maiale [ma'jale] SM **a** (*Zool, fig pegg*) pig; **mangiare come un maiale** to eat like a pig **b** (*Culin*) pork.

mailing ['meiliŋ] SM direct mail.

maiolica [ma'jɔlika] SF majolica.

maionese [majo'nese] SF mayonnaise.

Maiorca [ma'jɔrka] SF Majorca.

mais ['mais] SM (*coltura*) maize (*Brit*), corn (*Am*); (*in scatola*) sweetcorn.

maître [mɛtr] SM INV head waiter, maître d'hôtel.

maiuscola [ma'juskola] SF (*anche:* **lettera maiuscola**) capital (letter).

maiuscoletto [majusko'letto] SM (*Tip*) small capitals *pl*.

maiuscolo, a [ma'juskolo] ① AGG capital.

② SM capital letters *pl*; (*Tip*) upper case; **scrivere tutto in maiuscolo** to write everything in capitals *o* in capital letters.

maizena [maid'dzɛna] SF cornflour.

makò [ma'kɔ] SM (*cotone*) *high quality Egyptian cotton.*

mal ['mal] AVV, SM vedi **male**.

mala ['mala] SF (*gergo*) underworld.

malaccorto, a [malak'kɔrto] AGG rash, careless.

malachite [mala'kite] SF malachite.

malacreanza [malakre'antsa] SF bad manners *pl*.

malafede [mala'fede] SF bad faith.

malaffare [malaf'fare]: **di malaffare** AGG (*gente*) shady, dishonest; **donna di malaffare** prostitute.

malagevole [mala'dʒevole] AGG difficult, hard.

malagrazia [mala'grattsja] SF: **con malagrazia** with bad grace, impolitely.

malalingua [mala'lingwa] SF (*pl* **malelingue**) gossip (*person*).

malamente [mala'mente] AVV (*gen*) badly; (*sgarbatamente*) rudely; **finire malamente** (*persona*) to come to a bad end.

malandato, a [malan'dato] AGG (*persona: di salute*) in poor health, in a bad way; (: *di condizioni finanziarie*) badly off; (*trascurato: persona*) shabby; (: *cosa*) dilapidated.

malandrino, a [malan'drino] ① AGG (*scherz: occhi, sguardo*) mischievous, roguish.

② SM/F rogue, rascal.

malanimo [ma'lanimo] SM ill will, malevolence; **di malanimo** unwillingly, grudgingly.

malanno [ma'lanno] SM **a** (*disgrazia*) misfortune **b** (*malattia*) ailment; **mi devo essere preso un malanno** I must have caught something.

malaparata [malapa'rata] SF (*fam*) approaching danger; **vista la malaparata...** as things were looking ominous ... .

malapena [mala'pena]: **a malapena** AVV hardly, scarcely; **ti sento a malapena** I can hardly hear you.

malaria [ma'larja] SF malaria.

malarico, a, ci, che [ma'lariko] AGG malarial.

malasanità [malasani'ta] SF INV health service malfunction.

malasorte [mala'sɔrte] SF bad luck, ill luck.

malaticcio, cia, ci, ce [mala'tittʃo] AGG sickly.

malato, a [ma'lato] ① AGG (*persona*) ill, sick, unwell; (*organo, pianta*) diseased; **ho una gamba malata** I've got a bad leg; **essere malato di cuore** to have heart trouble *o* a bad heart; **malato di mente** mentally ill; **tu sei malato al cervello!** (*fig*) you're off your head!; **una mente/fantasia malata** a sick mind/morbid imagination; **darsi malato** (*sul lavoro ecc*) to go sick; **essere malato d'amore** (*fig*) to be lovesick.

② SM/F (*infermo*) sick person; (*paziente*) patient; **i malati** the sick; **un malato grave** a person who is seriously ill.

malattia [malat'tia] SF **a** (*Med*) illness, disease; (*di pianta*) disease; (*cattiva salute*) illness, sickness; **malattie nervose** nervous diseases; **malattie del lavoro** industrial diseases; **mettersi in malattia** to go on sick

leave; **fare una malattia di qc** (*fig: disperarsi*) to get in a state about sth

b (*fissazione*) mania; **ha la malattia del gioco** he's addicted to gambling, he's hooked on gambling.

malauguratamente [malauguratamente] AVV unluckily, unfortunately.

malaugurato, a [malaugu'rato] AGG ill-fated, unlucky.

malaugurio, ri [malau'gurjo] SM bad *o* ill omen; **uccello del malaugurio** bird of ill omen; (*fig*) jinx, Jonah.

malavita [mala'vita] SF underworld; **darsi alla malavita** to turn to crime.

malavitoso, a [malavi'toso] SM/F gangster.

malavoglia [mala'vɔʎʎa]: **di malavoglia** AVV reluctantly, unwillingly.

Malawi [ma'lawi] SM: **il Malawi** Malawi.

Malaysia [ma'laizja] SF: **la Malaysia** Malaysia.

malaysiano, a [malai'zjano] AGG, SM/F Malaysian.

malcapitato, a [malkapi'tato] ① AGG unlucky, unfortunate.

② SM/F unfortunate person.

malcelato [maltʃe'lato] AGG (*evidente*) ill-concealed, unconcealed; **lo guardò con malcelato disprezzo** she looked at him with ill-concealed contempt; **... disse con malcelato orgoglio** ...he said with obvious pride.

malconcio, cia, ci, ce [mal'kontʃo] AGG (*abiti, persona*) in a sorry state; **uscire malconcio da qc** (*fig*) to come out of sth badly.

malcontento, a [malkon'tɛnto] ① AGG: **malcontento (di)** dissatisfied (with).

② SM (*sentimento*) discontent.

malcostume [malkos'tume] SM corruption.

maldestramente [maldestra'mente] AVV clumsily.

maldestro, a [mal'dɛstro] AGG (*goffo*) clumsy, awkward; (*persona: inesperto*) inexperienced, inexpert.

maldicente [maldi'tʃɛnte] SM/F gossip.

maldicenza [maldi'tʃɛntsa] SF malicious gossip; **è solo una maldicenza** OR **sono solo maldicenze** it's just gossip.

maldisposto, a [maldis'posto] AGG: **maldisposto (verso)** ill-disposed (towards).

Maldive [mal'dive] SFPL: **le Maldive** the Maldives, the Maldive Islands.

male ['male] ① AVV **a** (*in modo insoddisfacente*) badly; (*in modo errato*) badly, wrongly; **male! non avresti dovuto farlo** that was wrong of you - you shouldn't have done it; **questa porta chiude male** this door doesn't shut properly; **scrivere/comportarsi male** to write/behave badly; **pronunciare male una parola** to pronounce a word wrongly; **rispondere male** (*in modo errato*) to answer wrongly *o* incorrectly; (*in modo sgarbato*) to answer back; **riuscire male** to turn out badly; **qui si mangia molto male** the food is very bad *o* poor here; **pensi che abbia fatto male ad andare?** do you think it was wrong of me to go?; **parlar male di qn** to speak ill of sb; **trattar male qn** to ill-treat sb

b: **sentirsi/star male** (*di salute*) to feel/be ill

c (*fraseologia*): **gli è andata male di nuovo** he failed again; **per male che vada** however badly things go; **capire male** to misunderstand; **le cose si stanno mettendo male** things are taking a turn for the worse; **ha preso molto male la cosa** he took it very badly; **restare** *o* **rimanere male** (*deluso*) to be disappointed; (*dispiaciuto*) to be sorry; (*offeso*) to be hurt *o* offended; **sta male comportarsi così** that's no way to behave; **quell'abito le sta proprio male** that dress just doesn't

suit her, that dress looks terrible on her; **il giallo sta male con il rosa** yellow looks awful with pink; **la vedo male** things look bad (to me), it doesn't look good to me; **bene o male ce la farò** one way or the other I'll manage; **niente male quel ragazzo** that boy's not bad, that boy's a bit of alright (*fam*); **di male in peggio** from bad to worse; **non faresti male a dirglielo** it wouldn't be a bad idea to tell him.

2 SM **a** (*ciò che è ingiusto, disonesto*) evil; **il male** evil; **un male necessario** a necessary evil; **le forze del male** the forces of evil; **il minore dei due mali** the lesser of two evils; **mali sociali** social evils

 b (*danno*) harm; **fare del male a qn** to harm *o* hurt sb; **le sigarette fanno male** cigarettes are bad for you; **che c'è di male se esco con lui?** what harm is there in my going out with him?; **non ho fatto niente di male** I haven't done anything wrong; **non sarebbe (un) male se gliene parlassi** it wouldn't do any harm to talk to him about it; **non farebbe (del) male a una mosca** he wouldn't hurt a fly; **non gli voglio male** I don't bear him ill-will

 c (*dolore*) pain, ache; (*malattia*) illness, disease; **farsi male** to hurt o.s.; **fare (del) male a qn** to hurt *o* harm sb; **far male alla salute** to be bad for one's health; **mi fa male la gamba** OR **ho male ad una gamba** my leg hurts, I've got a pain in my leg; **mi fa male** it hurts; **avere mal di testa/di stomaco** to have a headache/stomach ache; **aver mal di denti/d'orecchi/di gola** to have toothache/earache/a sore throat; **avere mal di cuore/di fegato** to have a heart/liver complaint; **avere un brutto male** (*euf: cancro*) to have cancer; **i mali della vecchiaia** the infirmities of old age ► **mal d'aria** air sickness ► **mal d'auto** car sickness ► **mal di mare** seasickness; **avere il mal di mare** to be seasick

 d (*fraseologia*): **andare a male** (*carne*) to go off *o* bad; (*latte*) to go off; **non avertene a male** OR **non prendertela a male** don't take it to heart; **come va? — non c'è male** how are you? — not bad *o* O.K. (*fam*); **mal comune mezzo gaudio** (*Proverbio*) a trouble shared is a trouble halved; **a mali estremi, estremi rimedi** (*Proverbio*) desperate circumstances call for desperate remedies; **non tutto il male vien per nuocere** (*Proverbio*) it's an ill wind that blows nobody any good.

maledetto, a [male'detto] **1** PP di **maledire**.

 2 AGG **a** (*dannato*) accursed; (*nelle imprecazioni*) cursed, damned

 b (*fig fam*) damned, blasted, confounded; **avere una fame maledetta** to be damned hungry; **spegni quella maledetta radio!** turn that blasted radio off!; **ho una paura maledetta dei ragni** I'm scared stiff of spiders; **è stato un giorno maledetto** it's been a bloody awful day; **non vedo l'ora di finire questo maledetto lavoro** I can't wait to finish this damn work.

maledire [male'dire] VT IRREG to curse.

maledizione [maledit'tsjone] SF (*condanna, imprecazione*) curse; **maledizione!** damn!; **devo avere la maledizione addosso!** I must be fated!

maleducatamente [maledukata'mente] AVV rudely.

maleducato, a [maledu'kato] **1** AGG (*persona*) rude, ill-mannered.

 2 SM/F ill-mannered person; **fare il maleducato** to be rude.

maleducazione [maledukat'tsjone] SF rudeness; **è maleducazione fare così** it's bad manners to do that.

malefatta [male'fatta] SF misdeed.

maleficio, ci [male'fitʃo] SM evil spell, witchcraft.

malefico, a, ci, che [ma'lɛfiko] AGG (*influsso*) evil; (*clima*) harmful, bad.

maleodorante [maleodo'rante] AGG foul-smelling, malodorous.

malese [ma'lese] **1** AGG, SM/F Malaysian.

 2 SM (*lingua*) Malay.

Malesia [ma'lesja] SF: **la Malesia** Malaysia.

malessere [ma'lɛssere] SM **a** (*indisposizione*) indisposition, slight illness; **ha avuto un leggero malessere** he didn't feel quite right **b** (*fig: disagio*) disquiet, uneasiness.

malevolenza [malevo'lɛntsa] SF malevolence.

malevolo, a [ma'lɛvolo] AGG malevolent.

malfamato, a [malfa'mato] AGG of ill repute, notorious.

malfatto, a [mal'fatto] AGG (*lavoro*) badly done; (*oggetto*) badly made; (*persona, corpo*) deformed.

malfattore, trice [malfat'tore] SM/F wrongdoer; **è una banda di malfattori!** they're a bunch of crooks!

malfermo, a [mal'fermo] AGG (*voce, mano*) shaky; (*passo*) unsteady; (*salute*) poor, delicate; **essere malfermo sulle gambe** to be unsteady on one's legs.

malfidato, a [malfi'dato], **malfidente** [malfi'dɛnte] AGG distrustful, suspicious.

malformato, a [malfor'mato] AGG (*Med*) malformed.

malformazione [malformat'tsjone] SF (*Med*) malformation.

malga, ghe ['malga] SF Alpine hut.

malgoverno [malgo'vɛrno] SM (*Pol*) mismanagement, misrule.

malgrado [mal'grado] **1** PREP in spite of, despite; **malgrado tutto le sono ancora amico** we are still friends in spite of *o* despite everything; **mio** (*o* **tuo** *ecc*) **malgrado** against my (*o* your *ecc*) will; **suo malgrado ha dovuto fare il lavoro** he had to do the work much against his will.

 2 CONG even though, although; **malgrado fossi in ritardo sono riuscito a prendere il treno** even though I was late I managed to get the train.

malia [ma'lia] SF (*incantesimo*) spell; (*fig: fascino*) charm.

maliarda [mali'arda] SF enchantress.

maliardo, a [mali'ardo] AGG (*occhi, sorriso*) bewitching.

malignamente [maliɲɲa'mente] AVV maliciously.

malignare [maliɲ'ɲare] VI (*aus* avere): **malignare su** to malign, speak ill of.

malignità [maliɲɲi'ta] SF INV **a** (*qualità*) malice, spite; **con malignità** spitefully, maliciously **b** (*osservazione*) spiteful remark.

maligno, a [ma'liɲɲo] **1** AGG **a** (*persona, parole*) malicious; **spirito maligno** evil spirit **b** (*Med*) malignant.

 2 SM/F malicious person.

malinconia [malinko'nia] SF melancholy, gloom.

malinconicamente [malinkonika'mente] AVV melancholically, with a melancholy air.

malinconico, a, ci, che [malin'kɔniko] AGG melancholy.

malincuore [malin'kwɔre]: **a malincuore** AVV reluctantly, unwillingly.

malinformato, a [malinfor'mato] AGG misinformed.

malintenzionato, a [malintentsjo'nato] **1** AGG ill-intentioned.

 2 SM/F ill-intentioned person; **è stato aggredito da un malintenzionato** he was attacked by a mugger.

malinteso [malin'teso] **1** AGG (*riguardo, senso del dovere*) mistaken, misguided.

2 SM misunderstanding.

malizia [ma'littsja] SF (*cattiveria*) malice, spite; (*furbizia*) mischievousness; (*astuzia*) clever trick; **con malizia** maliciously, spitefully; mischievously; cleverly.

maliziosamente [malittsjosa'mente] AVV (*vedi agg*) maliciously, spitefully; mischievously; cleverly.

malizioso, a [malit'tsjoso] AGG (*cattivo*) malicious, spiteful; (*vivace, birichino*) mischievous; (*astuto*) clever.

malleabile [malle'abile] AGG malleable.

malleolo [mal'lɛolo] SM (*Anat*) malleolus.

mallevadore [malleva'dore] SM guarantor.

malleveria [malleve'ria] SF guarantee, surety.

mallo ['mallo] SM (*Bot*) husk.

malloppo [mal'lɔppo] SM (*fam: refurtiva*) loot.

malmenare [malme'nare] VT to beat up.

malmesso, a [mal'mɛsso] AGG (*persona*) in a difficult situation; (: *vestito male*) poorly dressed, shabby; (: *economicamente*) badly off; (*casa, macchina*) in a poor state of repair.

malnutrito, a [malnu'trito] AGG undernourished.

malnutrizione [malnutrit'tsjone] SF malnutrition.

malo, a ['malo] AGG: **in malo modo** badly; (*sgarbatamente*) rudely; **essere a mal partito** to be in an awkward situation; **mala lingua = malalingua; mala sorte = malasorte; mala voglia = malavoglia**.

malocchio [ma'lɔkkjo] SM evil eye; **guardare di malocchio** to look at with disfavour.

malora [ma'lora] SF (*fam*): **andare in malora** to go to the dogs; **alla malora!** hell!; **va in malora!** go to hell!; **è un tirchio della malora!** he's a bloody miser!

malore [ma'lore] SM sudden illness; **venire** *o* **essere colto da malore** to be taken ill suddenly.

malpreparato, a [malprepa'rato] AGG ill-prepared.

malridotto, a [malri'dotto] AGG (*abiti, scarpe, persona*) in a sorry state; (*casa*) dilapidated; (*macchina*) in a poor state of repair.

malsano, a [mal'sano] AGG unhealthy.

malsicuro, a [malsi'kuro] AGG (*scala, edificio*) unsafe.

Malta ['malta] SF Malta.

malta ['malta] SF (*Edil*) mortar.

maltagliati [maltaʎ'ʎati] SMPL (*Culin*) *irregularly cut pasta squares.*

maltempo [mal'tɛmpo] SM bad weather.

maltenuto, a [malte'nuto] AGG badly looked after, badly kept.

maltese [mal'tese] AGG, SM/F, SM Maltese *inv.*

malto ['malto] SM malt.

maltolto [mal'tɔlto] SM: **resituire il maltolto** to give back one's ill-gotten gains.

maltosio [mal'tɔzjo] SM maltose.

maltrattamento [maltratta'mento] SM ill-treatment; **subire maltrattamenti** to be ill-treated; **maltrattamento di animali** cruelty to animals.

maltrattare [maltrat'tare] VT to ill-treat, abuse.

maluccio [ma'luttʃo] AVV: **stare maluccio** to be poorly; **com'è andato l'esame? — maluccio** how did the exam go? — pretty badly.

malumore [malu'more] SM (*irritabilità*) bad temper, ill humour; (*discordia*) ill feeling; **di malumore** in a bad mood.

malva ['malva] **1** SF (*Bot*) mallow.
2 SM INV (*colore*) mauve.
3 AGG INV mauve.

malvagiamente [malvadʒa'mente] AVV wickedly.

malvagio, gia, gi, gie [mal'vadʒo] **1** AGG (*uomo, azione*) evil, wicked; **non è malvagio** (*fig: vino, cibo*) it's not unpleasant *o* bad; (: *spettacolo, film*) it's not bad.
2 SM/F wicked person.

malvagità [malvadʒi'ta] SF INV (*qualità*) wickedness; (*azione*) wicked deed.

malvasia [malva'zia] SF *Italian dessert wine.*

malversazione [malversat'tsjone] SF (*Dir*) embezzlement.

malvestito, a [malves'tito] AGG badly dressed, ill-clad.

Malvine [mal'vine] SFPL: **le (isole) Malvine** the Falkland Islands, the Falklands.

malvisto, a [mal'visto] AGG (*persona, idea, proposta*): **malvisto (da)** unpopular (with).

malvivente [malvi'vɛnte] SM/F criminal.

malvolentieri [malvolen'tjɛri] AVV unwillingly, reluctantly.

malvolere [malvo'lere] VT DIF: **farsi malvolere (da)** to make o.s. unpopular (with); **essere malvoluto da qn** to be disliked by sb; **prendere qn a malvolere** to take a dislike to sb.

mamma ['mamma] SF (*fam*) mum(my) (*Brit*), mom (*Am*); **come l'ha fatto mamma** in one's birthday suit; **mamma mia!** good heavens!, my goodness!

mammalucco, chi [mamma'lukko] SM dolt, idiot.

mammario, ria, ri, rie [mam'marjo] AGG (*Anat*) mammary.

mammasantissima [mammasan'tissima] SM INV (*nel crimine organizzato*) boss of bosses.

mammella [mam'mɛlla] SF (*di donna*) breast; (*di animale*) udder.

mammifero, a [mam'mifero] **1** AGG (*Zool*) mammalian.
2 SM (*Zool*) mammal.

mammismo [mam'mizmo] SM *excessive attachment to one's mother.*

mammografia [mammogra'fia] SF (*Med*) mammography.

mammola ['mammola] SF (*Bot*) violet; **è una mammoletta** (*fig scherz*) he's a shrinking violet.

mammone, a [mam'mone] SM/F (*fam*) mummy's boy/girl.

mammut [mam'mut] SM INV (*Zool*) mammoth.

manager ['mænidʒə] SM/F INV manager.

manageriale [manadʒe'rjale] AGG managerial.

manata [ma'nata] SF (*colpo*) slap; (*quantità*) handful; **a manate** by the handful.

manca ['manka] SF left (hand); **a destra e a manca** left, right and centre, on all sides.

mancamento [manka'mento] SM (*di forze*) (feeling of) faintness, weakness.

mancante [man'kante] AGG (*pagina, tassello, parte ecc*) missing.

mancanza [man'kantsa] SF **a** : **mancanza di** (*assenza*) lack of; (*carenza*) shortage of, scarcity of; **mancanza di rispetto** lack of respect; **mancanza di soldi** lack (*o* shortage) of money; **in mancanza di vino berremo acqua** as there is no wine we'll drink water; **in mancanza d'altro/di meglio** for want *o* lack of anything else/better; **per mancanza di tempo** through lack of time; **sentire la mancanza di qc/qn** to miss sth/sb; **sento la tua mancanza** I miss you
b (*fallo*) fault; (*difetto*) failing, shortcoming; **commettere una mancanza** to commit an error.

mancare [man'kare] **1** VI (*aus essere; nei sensi (d), (e) ed (f) avere*) **a** (*far difetto*) to be lacking; **mancano i fondi per la ricerca** there aren't the funds to do research; **manca sempre il tempo** there's never enough time; **mi mancano le parole per esprimerti la mia gratitudine** I

can't find words to express my gratitude to you; **ci manca il pane** we've run out of bread, we don't have *o* haven't got any bread; **fammi sapere se ti manca qualcosa** let me know if you need anything; **i suoi non gli fanno mancar niente** his family doesn't let him want for anything; **gli sono venuti a mancare i soldi** his money ran out, he ran out of money; **quanto manca all'arrivo del treno?** how long before the train arrives?; **manca un quarto alle 6** it's a quarter to (*Brit*) *o* of (*Am*) 6
b (*non esserci*) to be missing, not to be there; (*persona: essere assente*) to be absent; **mancano ancora 10 ster-line** we're still £10 short; **quanti pezzi mancano?** how many pieces are missing?; **mancavi solo tu** you were the only one missing, you were the only one who wasn't there; **mi manchi** I miss you; **mancano prove** there's not enough evidence; **mancare da casa** to be away from home; **mancare all'appello** (*persona*) to be absent from roll call; (*cose*) to be missing
c (*venir meno: coraggio, forze*) to fail; (*morire*) to die; **gli è mancato il coraggio** his courage failed him; **gli sono mancate le parole** words failed him; **sentirsi mancare** to feel faint; **gli sono venuti a mancare i genitori** he lost his parents; **è mancata la luce** the electricity went off
d (*essere in errore*) to be wrong, make a mistake; **mi dispiace se ho mancato** I'm sorry if I was wrong
e : **mancare di** (*coraggio, giudizio*) to lack, be lacking in; (*risorse, soldi*) to be short of, lack; **mancare di rispetto a qn** to be lacking in respect towards sb, be disrespectful towards sb; **mancare di parola** not to keep one's word, go back on one's word; **non mancherò di salutarlo da parte tua** of course I'll give him your regards; **non mancherò** I won't forget, I'll make sure I do
f : **mancare a** (*doveri*) to neglect; (*promessa*) to fail to keep; (*appuntamento*) to miss; **mancare alla parola data** to break one's promise
g (*fraseologia*): **ci mancherebbe altro!** of course I (*o* you *ecc*) will!; **ci mancava solo questa!** that's all we need!; **c'è mancato poco** it was a near thing; **c'è mancato poco** *o* **poco è mancato che si facesse male** he very nearly hurt himself; **gli manca una rotella** (*fig*) he's got a screw loose; **a questo cane manca solo la parola** that dog is almost human.
2 VT (*bersaglio*) to miss; **ha mancato la presa ed è caduto** he lost his grip and fell.

mancato, a [man'kato] AGG (*tentativo*) abortive, unsuccessful; (*appuntamento*) missed; (*occasione*) lost, wasted; (*artista*) failed; **è un dottore mancato** (*fallito*) he's a failure as a doctor; (*non realizzato*) he should have been a doctor; **mancato pagamento** non-payment; **mancato arrivo** failure to arrive.

manche [mãʃ] SF INV (*Sport*) heat.

mancherò *ecc* [manke'rɔ] VB vedi **mancare**.

manchevole [man'kevole] AGG (*insufficiente*) inadequate, insufficient.

manchevolezza [mankevo'lettsa] SF (*scorrettezza*) fault, shortcoming; **è stata una manchevolezza non invitarlo** it was remiss of us not to invite him.

mancia, ce ['mantʃa] SF tip; **dare una mancia a qn** to tip sb, give sb a tip ▶ **mancia competente** reward.

manciata [man'tʃata] SF handful; **a manciate** by the handful.

mancina [man'tʃina] SF (*mano*) left hand; (*parte*) left, left-hand side.

mancinismo [mantʃi'nizmo] SM left-handedness.

mancino, a [man'tʃino] **1** AGG (*persona*) left-handed; (*calciatore*) left-footed; (*pugile*) southpaw *attr*; (*fig*): **tiro mancino** dirty trick.
2 SM/F left-handed person, left-hander.

manco ['manko] AVV (*fam: nemmeno*) not even; **manco per sogno!** [OR] **manco per idea!** not on your life!, (I) wouldn't dream of it!

mandante [man'dante] SM/F (*Dir*) principal; (*istigatore*) instigator.

mandarancio, ci [manda'rantʃo] SM clementine.

mandare [man'dare] VT **a** (*gen*) to send; **mandare qc per posta/per via aerea** to send sth through the *o* by post/by air; **mandare a chiamare qn** to send for sb; **mandare a dire (a qn)** to send word (to sb); **mandare due righe a qn** to drop sb a line; **mandare qn in prigione** to send sb to prison; **mandare un bacio a qn** to blow sb a kiss; **mandare in pezzi** (*vaso, vetro*) to shatter; **mandare in rovina** to ruin; **che Dio ce la mandi buona!** God help us!
b : **mandare avanti** (*persona*) to send ahead; (*fig: famiglia*) to provide for; (: *ditta*) to keep going, run; (: *pratica*) to attend to; **mandare giù** (*persona*) to send down; (*cibo, fig*) to swallow; **mandare via** (*persona*) to send away; (: *licenziare*) to sack, fire
c (*emettere: segnali*) to send out; (: *grido*) to give, utter, let out; **mandare in onda** (*Radio, TV*) to broadcast.

mandarino¹ [manda'rino] SM (*Bot*) mandarin (orange).

mandarino² [manda'rino] SM (*in Cina*) mandarin.

mandata [man'data] SF **a** (*di chiave*) turn; **chiudere a doppia mandata** to double-lock **b** (*quantità*) consignment, lot, batch.

mandatario, ri [manda'tarjo] SM (*Dir*) representative, agent.

mandato [man'dato] SM **a** (*incarico: di deputato*) mandate; (*durata dell'incarico*) term of office; **su mandato di** by order of
b (*Dir: penale*) warrant ▶ **mandato d'arresto** *o* **di cattura** warrant for arrest ▶ **mandato di comparizione** summons *sg* ▶ **mandato di perquisizione** search warrant
c (*Dir: civile*) mandate
d : **mandato di pagamento** postal *o* money order.

mandibola [man'dibola] SF (*Anat*) jaw, mandible.

mandolino [mando'lino] SM (*Mus*) mandolin(e).

mandorla ['mandorla] SF (*frutto*) almond; **occhi a mandorla** almond(-shaped) eyes.

mandorlato [mandor'lato] SM nut brittle.

mandorlo ['mandorlo] SM almond tree.

mandragola [man'dragola] SF (*Bot*) mandrake.

mandria ['mandrja] SF herd.

mandriano [mandri'ano] SM cowherd, herdsman.

mandrillo [man'drillo] SM (*Zool*) mandrill; (*fig scherz*) lecher.

mandrino [man'drino] SM (*Tecn*) mandrel.

maneggevole [maned'dʒevole] AGG easy to handle; **poco maneggevole** difficult to handle.

maneggiare [maned'dʒare] VT (*utensili, arnesi*) to handle, use; (*cera, creta*) to work; (*fig: persone, denaro*) to handle, deal with.

maneggio, gi [ma'neddʒo] SM **a** (*Equitazione: scuola*) riding school; (: *pista*) ring; **maneggio coperto/all'aperto** indoor/outdoor school
b (*di denaro, affari*) management, handling
c (*fig: manovra, intrigo*) scheme, ploy.

manesco, a, schi, sche [ma'nesko] AGG ready with one's fists; **una mamma manesca** a mother who smacks a lot.

manetta [ma'netta] SF (di gas, aria) lever; **andare a manetta** (Aut fam) to drive flat out.

manette [ma'nette] SFPL handcuffs; **mettere le manette a qn** to handcuff sb.

manforte [man'fɔrte] SF INV: **dare manforte a qn** to support sb.

manganellare [manganel'lare] VT to club.

manganellata [manganel'lata] SF blow with a club o cudgel.

manganello [manga'nɛllo] SM club, cudgel; (della polizia) truncheon, night stick (Am).

manganese [manga'nese] SM manganese.

mangano ['mangano] SM mangle.

mangereccio, cia, ci, ce [mandʒe'rettʃo] AGG edible.

mangeria [mandʒe'ria] SF (fam) embezzlement of public money.

mangiabile [man'dʒabile] AGG edible, eatable.

mangiadischi° [mandʒa'diski] SM INV portable record player.

mangia-e-bevi ['mandʒa e b'bevi] SM INV (gelato) ice-cream sundae.

mangiafumo [mandʒa'fumo] AGG INV: **candela mangia-fumo** candle which acts as an air purifier.

mangianastri° [mandʒa'nastri] SM INV cassette-recorder.

mangiapane [mandʒa'pane] SM/F: **mangiapane a tradimento** scrounger.

mangiapreti [mandʒa'preti] SM/F INV hater of priests.

mangiare [man'dʒare] **1** VT **a** (gen) to eat; **mangiare di tutto** to eat anything o everything; **qui si mangia bene/male** the food is good/bad here; **non avere da mangiare** not to have enough to eat; **dare da mangiare a qn** to give sb something to eat; **fare da mangiare** to do the cooking; **farsi qc da mangiare** to make o.s. sth to eat; **mangiare fuori** to eat out, have a meal out; **resta a mangiare un boccone con noi** stay and have a bite with us; **allora, si mangia?** is it ready then?; **si mangiano questi funghi?** are these mushrooms edible?; **mangiare per due/quattro** (fig) to eat enough for two/like a horse; **mangiare come un uccellino** (fig) to eat like a bird; **mangiare alle spalle di qn** (fig) to live off sb; **sembrava volesse mangiarmi** (fig) I thought he was going to kill me; **mangiarsi qn con gli occhi** to devour sb with one's eyes; **mangiarsi qn di baci** to smother sb with kisses; **mangiarsi il patrimonio** to squander one's inheritance; **mangiarsi il fegato** (fig) to be consumed with rage; **mi sarei mangiato le mani** I could have kicked myself; **mangiarsi le parole** to mumble; **mangiarsi le unghie** to bite one's nails; **questo mobile è mangiato dai tarli** this piece of furniture has woodworm; **esser mangiato vivo dalle zanzare** to be eaten alive by mosquitoes
b (Carte, Scacchi) to take.
2 SM (cibo) food; **essere difficile nel mangiare** to be a fussy eater; **il mangiare è pronto** lunch/breakfast/dinner is ready.

mangiasoldi [mandʒa'sɔldi] AGG INV (fam): **macchinetta mangiasoldi** one-armed bandit.

mangiata [man'dʒata] SF: **che mangiata!** what a huge meal!; **una mangiata coi fiocchi** a slap-up meal.

mangiatoia [mandʒa'toja] SF (feeding-)trough.

mangiatore, trice [mandʒa'tore] SM/F eater ▶**mangiatore di fuoco** fire-eater ▶**mangiatore di spade** sword swallower ▶**mangiatrice di uomini**

(scherz) man-eater.

mangiaufo [mandʒa'ufo] SM/F INV (scroccone) scrounger; (poltrone) idler.

mangime [man'dʒime] SM (foraggio) fodder; (becchime) birdseed.

mangione, a [man'dʒone] SM/F (fam) glutton.

mangiucchiare [mandʒuk'kjare] VT to nibble.

mango, ghi ['mango] SM (frutto) mango; (albero) mango tree.

mangrovia [man'grɔvja] SF mangrove.

mangusta [man'gusta] SF mongoose.

mania [ma'nia] SF (Psic) mania; (fissazione) obsession; (abitudine) odd o strange habit; **gli è presa la mania dei francobolli** his latest craze is stamp collecting; **una delle sue manie** one of his funny habits; **ha la mania della puntualità/della pulizia** he's obsessively punctual/clean; **avere la mania di fare qc** to have a habit of doing sth ▶**mania di grandezza** delusions pl of grandeur ▶**mania di persecuzione** persecution complex o mania.

maniacale [mania'kale] AGG (Psic) maniacal; (fanatico) fanatical; **è un igienista maniacale** (fig) he's fanatical about hygiene.

maniaco, a, ci, che [ma'niako] **1** AGG (Med: stato) maniac; (: persona) suffering from a mania; **essere maniaco dell'ordine** (fig) to be obsessively tidy.
2 SM/F (Med) maniac; (fanatico) fanatic; **un maniaco sessuale** (anche scherz) sex maniac; **è un maniaco del calcio** he's football mad o crazy.

maniaco-depressivo, a [ma'niakodepres'sivo] AGG, SM/F manic-depressive.

manica, che ['manika] SF **a** sleeve; **manica (a) kimono** bat sleeve; **a maniche lunghe** long-sleeved; **senza maniche** sleeveless; **essere in maniche di camicia** to be in (one's) shirt sleeves; **essere di manica larga** (prodigo) to be free with one's money; (indulgente) to be easy-going; **essere di manica stretta** (tirchio) to be stingy, be tight (fam); (rigoroso) to be strict
b (fig: banda) gang; **una manica di delinquenti** a bunch of criminals; **una manica di ladri** a pack of thieves
c (Geog): **la Manica** OR **il Canale della Manica** the (English) Channel
d: **manica a vento** (Aer) wind sock; (Naut) ventilator.

manicaretto [manika'retto] SM delicious dish.

manicheismo [manike'izmo] SM **a** (Rel) Manich(a)eism
b: **non mi piace il suo manicheismo** I don't like the way he sees everything as black or white.

manichetta [mani'ketta] SF (Tecn) hose.

manichino [mani'kino] SM (di sarto, vetrina) dummy.

manico, ci o chi ['maniko] SM (gen) handle; (di strumento musicale) neck ▶**manico di scopa** broomstick.

manicomio, mi [mani'kɔmjo] SM lunatic asylum, mental hospital; (fig) madhouse; **è roba da manicomio!** this is complete lunacy!

manicotto [mani'kɔtto] SM (di pelliccia) muff; (Tecn) sleeve, coupling; (Aut) hose.

manicure [mani'kure] **1** SM o F INV manicure; **farsi il o la manicure** to do one's nails, give o.s. a manicure.
2 SF INV (persona) manicurist.

maniera [ma'njɛra] SF **a** (modo) way, manner; **maniera di vivere/di parlare** way of life/of speaking; **fare qc alla propria maniera** to do sth one's own way; **in una maniera o nell'altra** one way or another; **in qualche maniera** somehow or other; **in maniera che** so that; **in**

maniera da so as to; **fa' in maniera che sia tutto pronto per domani** see to it that everything's ready for tomorrow; **dobbiamo fare in maniera da non ripetere gli stessi errori** we must see that we don't make the same mistakes again; **in tutte le maniere** (*a tutti i costi*) at all costs; **usare le maniere forti** to take tough action; **in nessuna maniera** in no way

b (*Arte: stile*) style, manner; **alla maniera di** in *o* after the style of; **è un Picasso prima maniera** it's an early Picasso

c (*comportamento*): **maniere** SFPL manners; **usare buone maniere con qn** to be polite to sb; **non mi piacciono le sue maniere** I don't like the way he behaves.

manierato, a [manje'rato] AGG (*affettato*) affected; (*Arte*) mannered.

manierismo [manje'rizmo] SM (*Arte*) mannerism.

manieristico, a, ci, che [manje'ristiko] AGG (*Arte*) manneristic.

maniero [ma'njɛro] SM manor.

manifattura [manifat'tura] SF (*stabilimento*) factory; (*lavorazione*) manufacture.

manifatturiero, a [manifattu'rjɛro] AGG manufacturing *attr.*

manifestamente [manifesta'mente] AVV manifestly.

manifestante [manifes'tante] SM/F demonstrator.

manifestare [manifes'tare] **1** VT (*gen*) to show, display; (*opinioni, intenzioni*) to reveal, disclose; **manifestare il desiderio di fare qc** to express a desire to do sth, indicate one's wish to do sth.

2 VI (*aus* avere): **manifestare contro/a favore di** to demonstrate against/in favour of.

3 manifestarsi VR: **si è manifestato per quello che è** he has shown his true colours; **manifestarsi contrario a un progetto** to reveal one's opposition to a plan; **manifestarsi amico/nemico** to prove to be a friend/an enemy.

4 manifestarsi VIP (*sintomi, malattia*) to appear.

manifestazione [manifestat'tsjone] SF **a** (*di opinione, sentimento*) expression; (*di affetto*) demonstration; (*di malattia: comparsa*) manifestation; (: *sintomo*) sign, symptom

b (*spettacolo*) event, show, display; (*Pol*) demonstration; **manifestazione sportiva** sporting event.

manifestino [manifes'tino] SM leaflet.

manifesto, a [mani'fɛsto] **1** AGG (*errore, verità*) obvious, manifest; (*fatto*) well-known; **i giornali hanno reso manifesto il suo rapporto con la mafia** the newspapers have uncovered his links with the Mafia.

2 SM **a** (*Letteratura, Arte, Pol*) manifesto **b** (*cartellone*) poster, bill; **manifesto pubblicitario** advertising poster.

maniglia [ma'niʎʎa] SF (*di porta, cassetta*) handle; (*sostegno: in autobus*) strap; (*fig fam: appoggio influente*) help from a highly-placed friend; (*Naut*) shackle.

manigoldo [mani'goldo] SM (*anche scherz*) rogue.

Manila [ma'nila] SF Manila.

manipolare [manipo'lare] VT **a** (*gen*) to manipulate, handle; (*creta, cera*) to work, fashion **b** (*alterare: elezione*) to rig; (: *conti*) to falsify, doctor, fiddle (*fam*); (: *notizia, informazioni*) to manipulate; (: *vino*) to adulterate.

manipolatore, trice [manipola'tore] **1** SM/F (*di elezioni, imbrogli*) fixer.

2 SM (*Tecn*) key.

manipolazione [manipolat'tsjone] SF (*gen, Med*) manipulation; (*di conti*) falsification, fiddling (*fam*).

manipolo [ma'nipolo] SM **a** (*drappello*) handful **b** (*Storia, Rel*) maniple.

maniscalco, chi [manis'kalko] SM blacksmith, farrier (*Brit*).

manna ['manna] SF (*Rel*) manna; **è una manna dal cielo!** (*fig*) it is a godsend!

mannaia [man'naja] SF (*del boia*) (executioner's) axe *o* ax (*Am*); (*per carni*) cleaver.

mannaro [man'naro] AGG: **lupo mannaro** werewolf.

mannequin [manə'kɛ̃] SF INV model.

mano, i ['mano] SF **a** hand; **dare la mano a qn** to give sb one's hand; (*per salutare*) to shake hands with sb; **darsi** *o* **stringersi la mano** to hold hands; (*per salutarsi*) to shake hands; **tenersi per mano** to hold hands; **mano nella mano** hand in hand; **battere le mani** to clap (one's hands); **mani in alto!** hands up!; **cadere nelle mani di qn** (*fig*) to fall into sb's hands; ►**mani pulite** *the judicial operation which brought to trial politicians and industrialists implicated in corruption scandals.*

b (*locuzioni*): **di seconda mano** second-hand; **di prima mano** (*notizia*) first-hand; **a portata di mano** within reach; **sotto mano** (*vicino*) to hand; (*furtivamente*) secretly; **ce l'hai sotto mano?** have you got it to hand?; **fuori mano** out of the way; **in mani fidate** in safe hands; **in buone mani** in good hands; **a mani vuote** empty-handed; **rapina a mano armata** armed robbery; **recapitato a mano** (*lettera, pacco*) (delivered) by hand; **fatto a mano** handmade; **cucito a mano** hand-sewn; **bagaglio a mano** hand luggage; **alla mano** (*persona*) easy-going; **con i soldi alla mano** cash in hand; **con i fatti alla mano** with his (*o* her *ecc*) facts at the ready; **a mano a mano che** OR **man mano che** (*mentre*) as; **man mano** (*gradualmente*) little by little, gradually

c (*locuzioni verbali*): **andare contro mano** (*Aut*) to go against the (flow of) traffic; **ho le mani legate** (*fig*) my hands are tied; **restare a mani vuote** to be left empty-handed; **avere le mani bucate** to spend money like water; **avere mani di fata** to have a light touch; **aver le mani in pasta** to have a finger in the pie; **avere qc per le mani** (*progetto, lavoro*) to have sth in hand; **alzare le mani su qn** to raise one's hand to sb; **dare una mano a qn** to lend sb a hand; **gli dai una mano e si prende il braccio** give him an inch and he'll take a mile; **fare man bassa di qc** to run off with sth; **forzare la mano** to go too far; **sai com'è, una mano lava l'altra...** you know how it is - you scratch my back and I'll scratch yours ...; **mettere la mano sul fuoco per qc** (*fig*) to stake one's life on sth; **mettere le mani su qc** to lay one's hands on sth; **mettere mano a qc** to have a hand in sth; **mettere le mani avanti** to safeguard o.s.; **mettere le mani addosso a qn** to lay hands on sb; (*molestare*) to touch sb up; **mettersi una mano sulla coscienza** to examine one's conscience; **ci ho preso la mano** I've got the hang of it; **starsene con le mani in mano** to twiddle one's thumbs; **venire alle mani** to come to blows

d (*strato*) coat; **dare una mano di vernice a qc** to give sth a coat of paint

e (*Carte*) hand; **facciamo ancora una mano** let's play one more hand.

manodopera [mano'dɔpera] SF manpower, labour (*Brit*), labor (*Am*).

manomesso, a [mano'messo] PP di **manomettere**.

manometro [ma'nɔmetro] SM manometer.

manomettere [mano'mettere] VT IRREG (*alterare: docu-*

mento, prove) to tamper with; (*aprire indebitamente*: *lettera*) to open (without permission); (: *serratura*) to force; (: *cassaforte*) to break open; **la serratura sembrava manomessa** the lock looked as though it had been tampered with.

manomissione [manomis'sjone] SF (*di prove*) tampering; (*di lettera*) (unauthorized) opening.

manomorta [mano'mɔrta] SF (*Dir*) mortmain.

manopola [ma'nɔpola] SF **a** (*di televisore, radio*) knob; (*impugnatura*) hand-grip; (*sostegno: su autobus, vetture*) strap **b** (*di armatura*) gauntlet; (*guanto*) mitten, mitt; (: *di spugna*) wash mitt.

manoscritto, a [manos'kritto] **1** AGG handwritten. **2** SM manuscript.

manovalanza [manova'lantsa] SF (*lavoratori*) unskilled workers *pl*; **la manovalanza mafiosa** (*criminali*) mafia henchmen *pl*, *small-time Mafiosi who do the dirty work*.

manovale [mano'vale] SM unskilled worker, labourer (*Brit*), laborer (*Am*).

manovella [mano'vɛlla] SF (*gen*) handle; (*Tecn*) crank; **manovella alzacristalli** (window) winder; **manovella d'avviamento** starting handle; **dare il primo giro di manovella** (*Cine*) to begin filming.

manovra [ma'nɔvra] SF **a** (*Mil, fig*) manoeuvre (*Brit*), maneuver (*Am*); (*Pol, Econ*) measures *pl*; **la nuova manovra fiscale** the new tax(ation) measures; **manovra di accerchiamento** encircling movement; **grandi manovre** army manoeuvres *o* exercises ▶**manovre di corridoio** lobbying
b (*Ferr*) shunting; **fare manovra** (*Aut*) to manoeuvre; **fare manovra di parcheggio** to park
c: **manovre** SFPL (*Naut*) rigging *sg*; **manovre fisse/correnti** standing/running rigging.

manovrabile [mano'vrabile] AGG (*anche fig*) easy to manipulate.

manovrare [mano'vrare] **1** VT (*veicolo*) to manoeuvre (*Brit*), maneuver (*Am*); (*macchinario*) to operate, work; (*fig: persona*) to manipulate.
2 VI (*aus avere*): **manovrare per parcheggiare l'auto** to pull/back into a parking space.

manovrato, a [mano'vrato] AGG (*Calcio*): **fare un gioco manovrato** to play a well-organized attacking game.

manovratore, trice [manovra'tore] SM/F (*di tram*) driver; (*di treno*) shunter.

manrovescio, sci [manro'veʃʃo] SM slap, back hander.

mansalva [man'salva]: **a mansalva** AVV freely.

mansarda [man'sarda] SF attic.

mansione [man'sjone] SF duty, job, task; **non rientra nelle mie mansioni** it's not part of my job; **svolgere** *o* **esplicare le proprie mansioni** to carry out one's duties.

mansuetamente [mansueta'mente] AVV (*vedi agg*) tamely; docilely.

mansueto, a [mansu'ɛto] AGG (*animale*) tame; (*persona*) gentle, docile.

mansuetudine [mansue'tudine] SF (*vedi agg*) tameness; gentleness, docility.

manta [ˈmanta] SF (*Zool*) manta (ray).

mantecare [mante'kare] VT (*Culin*) to cook until creamy.

mantecato, a [mante'kato] (*Culin*) **1** AGG (*risotto*) creamy. **2** SM soft ice cream.

mantella [man'tɛlla] SF cloak.

mantellina [mantel'lina] SF cape.

mantello [man'tɛllo] SM **a** (*cappotto*) cloak; (*Zool*) coat; (*fig*: *di neve*) blanket, mantle **b** (*Tecn*: *rivestimento*) casing, shell **c** (*Geol*) mantle.

mantenere [mante'nere] **1** VT **a** (*gen*) to keep; (*decisione*) to stand by, abide by; (*promessa*) to keep, maintain; (*tradizione*) to maintain, uphold; (*edificio*) to maintain; **mantenere l'equilibrio/la linea** to keep one's balance/one's figure; **mantenere qn in vita** to keep sb alive; **mantenere i prezzi bassi** to hold prices down; **mantenere i contatti con qn** to keep in touch with sb; **mantenere l'ordine** (*Polizia*) to maintain law and order; (*in assemblea ecc*) to keep order
b (*famiglia*) to maintain, support.
2 **mantenersi** VR **a** (*conservarsi*): **mantenersi calmo/giovane** to stay *o* keep *o* remain calm/young; **mantenersi bene** to look good for one's age
b (*sostentarsi*) to keep o.s.; **si mantiene da anni** he has supported himself financially for years; **lavora per mantenersi** he works for a living; **si mantiene facendo la cameriera** (*studentessa*) she supports herself by waitressing.
3 **mantenersi** VIP (*cibi*) to keep; **il tempo si mantiene bello** the weather is holding.

mantenimento [manteni'mento] SM (*gen*) maintenance; **provvedere al mantenimento della famiglia** to provide for one's family; **dieta/ginnastica di mantenimento** maintenance diet/gymnastics.

mantenuta [mante'nuta] SF (*pegg*) kept woman.

mantenuto [mante'nuto] SM (*pegg*) gigolo.

mantice [man'titʃe] SM bellows *pl*; **sbuffare** *o* **soffiare come un mantice** to puff like a grampus.

mantide [ˈmantide] SF: **mantide religiosa** praying mantis.

mantiglia [man'tiʎʎa] SF mantilla.

manto [ˈmanto] SM (*cappotto*) cloak; (*Zool*) coat; (*fig: di neve*) blanket, mantle ▶**manto stradale** road surface.

Mantova [ˈmantova] SF Mantua.

mantovana [manto'vana] SF (*di tenda*) pelmet.

mantovano, a [manto'vano] **1** AGG of *o* from Mantua. **2** SM/F native *o* inhabitant of Mantua.

manuale [manu'ale] **1** AGG (*lavoro*) manual. **2** SM (*libro*) manual, handbook; **manuale di fotografia** Teach Yourself Photography; **un caso da manuale** (*fig*) a textbook example.

manualistico, a, ci, che [manua'listiko] AGG: **cultura manualistica** (*pegg*) superficial knowledge.

manualmente [manual'mente] AVV manually, by hand.

manubrio, ri [ma'nubrjo] SM (*gen*) handle; (*di bicicletta*) handlebars *pl*; (*attrezzo da ginnastica*) dumbbell.

manufatto [manu'fatto] SM manufactured article; **manufatti** SMPL manufactured goods.

manutenzione [manuten'tsjone] SF (*gen*) maintenance; (*di edifici, locali*) upkeep; (*d'impianti*) maintenance, servicing.

manzo [ˈmandzo] SM (*animale*) steer, bullock; (*carne*) beef.

maoista, i, e [mao'ista] AGG, SM/F Maoist.

Maometto [mao'metto] SM Mohammed.

maori [ma'ɔri] AGG, SM/F, SM Maori.

mappa [ˈmappa] SF map.

mappamondo [mappa'mondo] SM (*globo*) globe; (*carta*) map of the world.

maquillage [maki'jaʒ] SM INV make-up; **fare il maquillage** (*al centro storico*) to smarten up.

marabù [mara'bu] SM INV (*Zool*) marabou.

marachella [mara'kɛlla] SF mischievous trick.

maragià [mara'dʒa] SM INV maharaja(h).

marameo [mara'mɛo] SM: **fare marameo a** to thumb one's nose at.

marasca [ma'raska] SF marasca cherry.

maraschino [maras'kino] SM maraschino.

marasco [ma'rasko] SM marasca.

marasma, i [ma'razma] SM (fig) decline, decay; **un marasma generale** (fig: disordine) chaos.

maratona [mara'tona] SF (Sport, fig) marathon.

maratoneta, i, e [marato'nɛta] SM/F (Sport) marathon runner.

marca, che ['marka] SF **a** (Comm: di sigarette, caffè) brand; (: di scarpe, vestito) make; (: marchio di fabbrica) trademark; **prodotti di (gran) marca** high-class products **b** (bollo) stamp ▶ **marca da bollo** official stamp **c** (contrassegno, scontrino) ticket, check.

marcamento [marka'mento] SM (Sport) marking.

marcare [mar'kare] VT **a** (segnare) to mark; (a fuoco: animale) to brand; (biancheria) to mark; **marcare visita** (Mil) to report sick **b** (accentuare) to stress **c** (Sport: gol) to score; (: avversario) to mark.

marcatamente [markata'mente] AVV markedly.

marcato, a [mar'kato] AGG (lineamenti, accento) pronounced.

marcatore [marka'tore] SM **a** (Calcio: chi segna i gol) scorer; (: chi marca l'avversario) marker **b** (penna) marker (pen).

Marche ['marke] SFPL: **le Marche** the Marches (region of central Italy).

marcherò ecc [marke'rɔ] VB vedi **marcare**.

marchesa [mar'keza] SF marchioness.

marchese [mar'keze] SM marquis, marquess.

marchetta [mar'ketta] SF **a** (Amm) ≈ National Insurance Stamp **b**: **fare marchette** (prostituirsi) to be on the game.

marchiano, a [mar'kjano] AGG (errore) glaring, gross.

marchiare [mar'kjare] VT (bestiame) to mark; **marchiare a fuoco** to brand; **marchiare a vita** (fig) to brand for life.

marchigiano, a [marki'dʒano] **1** AGG of o from the Marches. **2** SM/F inhabitant o native of the Marches.

marchingegno [markin'dʒeɲɲo] SM contraption.

marchio, chi ['markjo] SM **a** (Comm) mark ▶ **marchio depositato** registered trademark ▶ **marchio di fabbrica** trademark **b** (per bestiame: segno) brand; (: strumento) branding iron; **ha il marchio di bugiardo** he has been branded a liar.

marcia, ce ['martʃa] SF **a** (gen, Mil, Mus) march ▶ **marcia forzata** forced march ▶ **marcia funebre** funeral march
b : **mettersi in marcia** to get moving; **mettere in marcia** (veicolo) to start (up); (apparecchio) to set going, start; **essere in marcia verso** to be marching towards
c (Aut) gear; **cambiare marcia** to change gear; **fare marcia indietro** to reverse; (fig) to back-pedal, backtrack
d (Sport) walking.

marcialonga, ghe [martʃa'longa] SF (sci di fondo) crosscountry skiing race; (a piedi) long-distance race.

marciapiede [martʃa'pjɛde] SM (di strada) pavement (Brit), sidewalk (Am); (Ferr) platform.

marciare [mar'tʃare] VI (aus avere) **a** (Mil) to march; (Sport) to walk; **far marciare dritto qn** (fig) to make sb toe the line **b** (veicolo) to go, travel; (fig: funzionare) to run, work; **il treno marcia a 70 km/h** the train goes o travels at 70 km/h; **la ditta marcia bene** the firm is running smoothly.

marciatore, trice [martʃa'tore] SM/F (Sport) walker.

marcio, cia, ci ce ['martʃo] **1** AGG (uovo, legno) rotten; (foglie) rotting; (frutta) rotten, bad; (ferita, piaga) festering; (fig: corrotto) corrupt, rotten; **avere torto marcio** to be utterly wrong.
2 SM (di frutto ecc) rotten o bad part; **c'è del marcio in questa storia** (fig) there's something fishy about this business.

marcire [mar'tʃire] **1** VI (aus essere) (cibi, frutta) to go rotten o bad; (cadaveri, legno, foglie) to rot; (ferita) to fester; **marcire in prigione** (fig) to rot in prison.
2 VT to rot.

marcita [mar'tʃita] SF water meadow.

marciume [mar'tʃume] SM **a** (parte guasta: di cibi) rotten part, bad part **b** (di radice, pianta) rot; (fig: corruzione) rottenness, corruption.

marco, chi ['marko] SM (moneta) mark.

marconista, i [marko'nista] SM radiotelegraphist.

marconiterapia [markonitera'pia] SF (Med) diathermy.

mare ['mare] **1** SM **a** (gen) sea; **mare interno** inland sea; **mare calmo/mosso/grosso** calm/rough/heavy sea; **per mare** by sea; **sul mare** (barca) on the sea; (villaggio, località) by o beside the sea; **in mare** at sea; **una vacanza al mare** a holiday beside o by the sea, a seaside holiday; **andare al mare** (in vacanza) to go to the seaside; **mettersi in mare** to put out to sea; **c'è un po' di mare oggi** there's a bit of a swell today; **uomo in mare!** man overboard!; **di mare** (brezza, acqua, uccelli, pesce) sea attr; **essere in alto mare** (fig) to have a long way to go; **è una goccia nel mare** (fig) it's a drop in the ocean
b (gran quantità di: lettere, lamentele) flood; (: gente, problemi, difficoltà) host; (: lavoro) pile; **ho un mare di cose da fare** I've got stacks of things to do; **essere in un mare di guai** to be surrounded by problems; **essere in un mare di lacrime** to be in floods of tears; **promettere mari e monti a qn** to promise sb the earth.
2 ▶ **il mar Caspio** the Caspian Sea ▶ **il mare del Nord** the North Sea ▶ **il mar Morto** the Dead Sea ▶ **il mar Nero** the Black Sea ▶ **il mar Rosso** the Red Sea ▶ **il mar dei Sargassi** the Sargasso Sea ▶ **i mari del Sud** the South Seas ▶ **il mare della Tranquillità** (sulla luna) the Sea of Tranquillity ▶ **il mar Mediterraneo** the Mediterranean Sea.

marea [ma'rɛa] SF **a** tide; **alta/bassa marea** high/low tide; **marea calante/montante** ebb/flood o rising tide **b** (fig) flood; **una marea di gente affollava la piazza** there were hordes of people in the square.

mareggiata [mared'dʒata] SF rough seas (inshore).

maremma [ma'remma] SF (Geog) maremma, swampy coastal area.

maremmano, a [marem'mano] **1** AGG **a** (zona, macchia) swampy **b** (della Maremma) of o from the Maremma. **2** SM/F inhabitant o native of the Maremma.

maremoto [mare'mɔto] SM seaquake.

maresciallo [mareʃ'ʃallo] SM (Mil) marshal; (: sottufficiale) warrant officer.

maretta [ma'retta] SF **a** (movimento di mare) choppiness **b** (tensione, disaccordo) tension.

marezzato, a [mared'dzato] AGG (seta) watered, moiré; (legno) veined; (carta) marbled.

margarina [marga'rina] SF margarine.

margherita [marge'rita] SF **a** (Bot) oxeye daisy, margue-

rite **b** (*di stampante*) daisy wheel.

margheritina [margeri'tina] SF (*Bot*) daisy.

marginale [mardʒi'nale] AGG marginal.

marginalità [mardʒinali'ta] SF INV (*di problema, questione*) marginality.

marginalmente [mardʒinal'mente] AVV marginally; **l'argomento è stato trattato marginalmente** this point was not the main focus of the discussion.

marginare [mardʒi'nare] VT (*foglio, pagina*) to set the margins for.

marginatore [mardʒina'tore] SM (*di macchina da scrivere*) margin stop.

marginazione [mardʒinat'tsjone] SF margin setting.

margine ['mardʒine] ① SM (*gen*) margin; (*di bosco, via*) edge; **al margine di** on the edge of; **ai margini della società** on the fringes of society; **note in** *o* **a margine** notes in the margin; **avere un buon margine di tempo/denaro** to have plenty of time/money (to spare). ② ▶**margine di errore** margin of error ▶**margine di guadagno** *o* **di utile** profit margin ▶**margine operativo** operating margin ▶**margine sul prezzo** mark-up ▶**margine di sicurezza** safety margin.

margotta [mar'gɔtta] SF layer.

mariano, a [mari'ano] AGG (*Rel*) Marian; **mese mariano** month of Mary.

marijuana [mæri'waːnə] SF marijuana.

marina [ma'rina] SF **a** (*costa*) coast; (*quadro*) seascape **b** (*Mil*) navy ▶**marina mercantile** merchant navy (*Brit*) *o* marine (*Am*) ▶**marina militare** ≈ Royal Navy (*Brit*), ≈ United States Navy (*Am*).

marinaio, ai [mari'najo] SM sailor; **marinaio di acqua dolce** (*pegg*) landlubber.

marinare [mari'nare] VT **a** (*Culin*) to marinate; **aringhe marinate** soused *o* pickled herring **b** (*disertare*): **marinare la scuola** to play truant, play hooky (*spec Am*).

marinaresco, a, schi, sche [marina'resko] AGG sailor's *attr*.

marinaro, a [mari'naro] AGG (*tradizione, popolo*) seafaring; **borgo marinaro** fishing village/town; **alla marinara** (*vestito, cappello*) sailor *attr*, (*Culin*) with seafood.

marinata [mari'nata] SF (*Culin*) marinade.

marinato, a [mari'nato] AGG (*Culin*) marinated.

marinatura [marina'tura] SF marinading.

marine [mə'riːn] SM INV (*Mil*) marine.

marino, a [ma'rino] AGG (*aria, fondali*) sea *attr*; (*fauna*) marine; (*città, colonia*) seaside *attr*.

mariolo [mari'ɔlo] SM (*scherz*) rascal.

marionetta [marjo'netta] SF puppet, marionette; (*fig: persona debole*) puppet; **teatrino/spettacolo di marionette** puppet theatre/show.

maritare [mari'tare] ① VT to marry, give in marriage. ② **maritarsi** VR: **maritarsi (a** *o* **con qn)** to get married (to sb), marry (sb).

maritato, a [mari'tato] AGG married.

marito [ma'rito] SM husband; **prendere marito** to get married.

maritozzo [mari'tɔttso] SM *type of currant bun*.

marittimo, a [ma'rittimo] ① AGG (*gen*) maritime, sea *attr*; (*città*) coastal; **linee marittime** shipping lines. ② SM seaman.

marmaglia [mar'maʎʎa] SF (*gente ignobile*) riff-raff, mob; (*ragazzacci*) gang of kids.

marmellata [marmel'lata] SF jam; (*di agrumi*) marmalade.

marmista, i [mar'mista] SM (*operaio*) marble-cutter; (*arti-*

giano) marble worker.

marmitta [mar'mitta] SF **a** (*Aut*) silencer ▶**marmitta catalitica** catalytic converter **b** (*recipiente*) cauldron **c** (*Geol*) pothole.

marmittone [marmit'tone] SM (*scherz: recluta*) raw recruit, rookie (*Am*).

marmo ['marmo] SM marble; **di marmo** marble *attr*, made of marble; **avere un cuore duro come il marmo** to have a heart of stone.

marmocchio, chi [mar'mɔkkjo] SM (*fam*) (tiny) tot, (little) kid.

marmoreo, a [mar'mɔreo] AGG (*di marmo*) marble *attr*.

marmorizzato, a [marmorid'dzato] AGG marbled.

marmotta [mar'mɔtta] SF (*Zool*) marmot; (*fig: persona lenta*) slowcoach.

marna ['marna] SF (*Geol*) marl.

marocchino, a [marok'kino] ① AGG, SM/F Moroccan. ② SM (*cuoio*) morocco (leather).

Marocco [ma'rɔkko] SM: **il Marocco** Morocco.

maroso [ma'roso] SM breaker.

marpione, a [mar'pjone] SM/F (*fam*) cunning old devil.

marra ['marra] SF (*Agr*) hoe; (*Naut*) fluke.

Marrakesh [marra'keʃ] SF Marrakesh.

marrano [mar'rano] SM (*scherz*) boor.

marrone [mar'rone] ① AGG INV brown. ② SM **a** (*colore*) brown **b** (*Bot*) chestnut.

marron glacé [ma'rɔɡla'se] SM INV marron glacé.

marsala [mar'sala] SM INV (*vino*) Marsala.

marsc' [marʃ] ESCL: **(avanti) marsc'!** quick march!

Marsiglia [mar'siʎʎa] SF Marseilles.

marsigliese [marsiʎ'ʎese] ① AGG of *o* from Marseilles. ② SM/F inhabitant *o* native of Marseilles.

marsina [mar'sina] SF tails *pl*, tail coat.

marsupiale [marsu'pjale] SM marsupial.

marsupio, pi [mar'supjo] SM **a** (*Zool*) pouch, marsupium (*termine tecn*) **b** (*per neonati*) sling; (*per denaro*) bumbag.

Marte ['marte] SM (*Astron, Mitol*) Mars.

martedì [marte'di] SM INV Tuesday; **oggi è martedì 3 aprile** (the date) today is Tuesday 3rd April; **martedì stavo male** I wasn't well on Tuesday; **ogni martedì** [OR] **tutti i martedì** every Tuesday, on Tuesdays; **di** *o* **il martedì** on Tuesdays; **un martedì sì un martedì no** every other Tuesday; **martedì scorso/prossimo** last/next Tuesday; **il martedì successivo** [OR] **il martedì dopo** the following Tuesday; **2 settimane fa, di martedì** a fortnight ago on Tuesday; **martedì fra una settimana/quindici giorni** a week/fortnight on Tuesday, Tuesday week/fortnight; **martedì mattina/pomeriggio/sera** Tuesday morning/afternoon/evening; **il film del martedì** the Tuesday film; **il giornale di martedì** Tuesday's newspaper ▶**martedì grasso** Shrove Tuesday.

martellamento [martella'mento] SM hammering, pounding; **mi fu difficile far fronte al martellamento delle sue domande** I found it hard to stand up to his constant questioning.

martellante [martel'lante] AGG (*fig: dolore*) throbbing; **una martellante campagna elettorale** a high-pressure electoral campaign.

martellare [martel'lare] ① VT (*gen*) to hammer; **martellare qn di domande** to fire questions at sb. ② VI (*aus* avere) (*pulsare: tempie*) to throb; (: *cuore*) to thump.

martellata [martel'lata] SF hammer blow; **dare una**

martellata a qn/qc to hit sb/sth with a hammer.

martelletto [martel'letto] SM (di pianoforte) hammer; (di macchina da scrivere) typebar; (di giudice, nelle vendite all'asta) gavel; (Med) percussion hammer.

martellio, lii [martel'lio] SM hammering.

martello [mar'tɛllo] ① SM (gen, Sport, Anat) hammer; **battere col martello** to hit with a hammer, hammer; **piantare un chiodo col martello** to hammer in a nail; **lancio del martello** (Sport) hammer throw; **suonare a martello** (fig: campane) to sound the tocsin ►**martello pneumatico** pneumatic drill.

martinetto [marti'netto] SM (Tecn) jack.

martingala [martin'gala] SF (di giacca) half-belt; (di cavallo) martingale.

martin pescatore [mar'tin peska'tore] SM kingfisher.

martire ['martire] SM/F (anche fig) martyr; **fare il o atteggiarsi a martire** to play the martyr.

martirio, ri [mar'tirjo] SM martyrdom; (fig) agony, torture; **vivere con quell'uomo è un martirio** living with that man is hell.

martirizzare [martirid'dzare] VT (Rel) to martyr; (persona, animali) to torture.

martora ['martora] SF marten.

martoriare [marto'rjare] VT to torment, torture.

marxismo [mark'sizmo] SM Marxism.

marxista, i, e [mark'sista] AGG, SM/F Marxist.

marzapane [martsa'pane] SM marzipan.

marziale [mar'tsjale] AGG martial.

marziano, a [mar'tsjano] ① AGG Martian. ② SM/F (di Marte) Martian; (extraterrestre) Martian, little green man; **mi guardavano come se fossi un marziano** (fam) they looked at me as if I had two heads.

marzo ['martso] SM March per fraseologia vedi **luglio**.

marzolino, a [martso'lino] AGG March attr.

mas [mas] SM INV motor torpedo boat.

mascalzonata [maskaltso'nata] SF dirty trick.

mascalzone [maskal'tsone] SM (anche scherz) rascal, scoundrel.

mascara [mas'kara] SM INV mascara.

mascarpone [maskar'pone] SM soft cream cheese often used in desserts.

mascella [maʃ'ʃɛlla] SF (Anat) jaw.

mascellare [maʃʃel'lare] AGG jaw attr.

maschera ['maskera] ① SF a (gen) mask; (costume) fancy dress; **in maschera** (mascherato) masked; **mettersi o vestirsi in maschera** to put on a fancy-dress; **ballo in maschera** fancy-dress ball; **gettare la maschera** (fig) to reveal o.s.; **giù la maschera!** (fig) stop acting!
b (Cine) usher/usherette
c (Teatro) stock character.
② ►**maschera antigas** gas mask ►**maschera di bellezza** face pack ►**maschera ad ossigeno** oxygen mask ►**maschera subacquea** diving mask.

mascherare [maske'rare] ① VT (viso) to mask; (entrata, fig: sentimenti, intenzioni) to hide, conceal; (Mil) to camouflage; **mascherare i bambini per una festa** to get the children into fancy dress for a party.
② **mascherarsi** VR: **mascherarsi (da)** (travestirsi) to disguise o.s. (as); (per un ballo) to dress up (as).

mascherata [maske'rata] SF (anche fig) masquerade.

mascherato, a [maske'rato] AGG (ladro) masked; (bambino) dressed up; (ballo) masked; (fig: nascosto) concealed.

mascherina [maske'rina] SF a (bambino in maschera)

child in fancy dress; (piccola maschera) mask; (di animale) patch; (di scarpe) toe-cap b (Aut) radiator grille.

mascherone [maske'rone] SM (grotesque) mask.

maschiaccio, ci [mas'kjattʃo] SM (scherz: ragazza) tomboy.

maschietto [mas'kjetto] SM little boy.

maschile [mas'kile] ① AGG (gen, Gramm) masculine; (sesso, popolazione) male attr; (abiti) men's; (per ragazzi: scuola) boys'.
② SM (Gramm): **il maschile** the masculine.

maschilismo [maski'lizmo] SM (male) chauvinism, sexism.

maschilista, i, e [maski'lista] AGG, SM/F (uomo) (male) chauvinist, sexist; (donna) sexist.

maschio, chia, chi, chie ['maskjo] ① AGG (figlio) male; (comportamento, atteggiamento) male, masculine; (volto, voce) masculine.
② AGG INV (animale) male; **una tigre maschio** a male tiger.
③ SM (gen, Tecn, Bio, Zool) male; (uomo) man; (ragazzo) boy; (figlio) son; **hanno un maschio e una femmina** they've got a boy and a girl; **il maschio della tigre** the male tiger; **maschio della vite** screw tap.

mascolinità [maskolini'ta] SF masculinity.

mascolino, a [masko'lino] AGG masculine.

mascotte [mas'kɔt] SF INV mascot.

masnada [maz'nada] SF (pegg: gruppo) gang, band.

masnadiere [mazna'djɛre] SM (furfante) ruffian, scoundrel.

masochismo [mazo'kizmo] SM masochism.

masochista, i, e [mazo'kista] ① AGG masochistic.
② SM/F masochist.

massa ['massa] SF a (volume, Fis) mass ►**massa d'acqua** body of water ►**massa atomica** atomic mass ►**massa cerebrale** brain, cerebral mass
b (Sociol): **la massa** OR **le masse** the masses pl; **la massa dei cittadini** the majority of the townspeople; **manifestazione/cultura di massa** mass demonstration/culture
c: **una massa di** (oggetti) heaps of, loads of; (errori) masses of; (persone) crowds of, masses of; **siete una massa di idioti!** (fam) you're a bunch of idiots!
d: **produzione in massa** mass production; **produrre in massa** to mass-produce; **vendere in massa** (Comm) to sell in bulk; **esecuzioni in massa** mass executions; **arrivare in massa** to arrive en masse
e (Elettr) earth; **collegare o mettere a massa** to earth.

massacrante [massa'krante] AGG exhausting, gruelling.

massacrare [massa'krare] VT (uccidere) to massacre, slaughter; (: animali) to slaughter; (fig: avversario) to make mincemeat of; (: brano musicale) to murder.

massacro [mas'sakro] SM massacre, slaughter; (fig) disaster, mess; **fare un massacro** to carry out a massacre; **all'esame i professori hanno fatto un massacro** the lecturers were failing exam candidates left, right and centre.

massaggiare [massad'dʒare] VT to massage; **farsi massaggiare** to have a massage.

massaggiatore, trice [massadʒa'tore] ① SM/F masseur/ masseuse.
② SM (apparecchio) massager.

massaggio, gi [mas'saddʒo] SM massage ►**massaggio cardiaco** heart massage.

massaia [mas'saja] SF housewife.

massaio, ai [mas'sajo] SM (di podere) estate manager.

massello [mas'sɛllo] SM **a** (*di oro ecc*) ingot **b** : **mobili in massello di noce** furniture *sg* made of solid walnut.

masseria [masse'ria] SF large farm.

masserizie [masse'rittsje] SFPL (household) furnishings.

massicciamente [massittʃa'mente] AVV (*intervenire*) on a massive scale; **hanno dovuto intervenire massicciamente sul testo** the text had to be heavily edited.

massicciata [massit'tʃata] SF (*di strada, ferrovia*) ballast.

massiccio, cia, ci, ce [mas'sittʃo] **1** AGG **a** (*mobile, edificio*) massive, solid; (*corporatura*) stout **b** : **oro/legno massiccio** solid gold/wood **c** (*fig: attacco*) massive; (: *dose*) heavy, massive. **2** SM (*Geog*) massif.

massificare [massifi'kare] VT (*individui*) to depersonalize.

massificazione [massifikat'tsjone] SF: **la massificazione della cultura** the homogenization of culture.

massima ['massima] SF **a** (*motto*) maxim **b** (*Meteor*) maximum temperature **c** : **in linea di massima** generally speaking.

massimale [massi'male] SM (*Assicurazione*) maximum sum payable by insurers.

massimalismo [massima'lizmo] SM (*Pol*) maximalism; (*fig*) radical ideology.

massimo, a ['massimo] **1** AGG (*superl di* **grande**) (*gen*) greatest; (*temperatura, livello, prezzo*) maximum, highest; (*importanza, cura*) utmost, greatest; **è della massima importanza che tu ci sia** it is of the utmost importance *o* it is vital that you be *o* are there; **è il massimo poeta del secolo** he is the greatest poet of the century; **erano presenti le massime autorità** all the most important dignitaries were there; **al massimo grado** to the highest degree; **stupido al massimo grado** stupid beyond belief; **ha la mia massima stima/il mio massimo rispetto** I have the highest regard/greatest respect for him; **ottenere il massimo effetto con la minima spesa** to get the best results at the least cost; **in massima parte** for the most part, mainly; **arrivare entro il tempo massimo** to arrive within the time limit; **il tempo massimo concesso** the maximum time allowed; **la velocità massima che questa macchina può raggiungere è...** the top *o* maximum speed of this car is ...; **la velocità massima permessa nei centri abitati** the speed limit in built-up areas. **2** SM (*gen*) maximum; **è il massimo che io possa fare** it's the most I can do; **è il massimo della stupidità** (*persona*) you can't get much more stupid than him; (*gesto*) it's the height of stupidity; **è il massimo!** (*colmo*) that's the limit *o* end!; **costerà al massimo 5 sterline** it'll cost 5 pounds at (the) most; **lavorare al massimo** to work flat out; **sfruttare qc al massimo** to make full use of sth; **al massimo finiamo lunedì** we'll finish on Monday at the outside; **arriverò al massimo alle 5** I'll arrive at 5 at the latest; **ottenere il massimo dei voti** (*Scol*) to get full marks; (*in votazione*) to be accepted unanimously; **il massimo della pena** (*Dir*) the maximum penalty.

massivo, a [mas'sivo] AGG (*intervento*) en masse; (*emigrazione*) mass; (*emorragia*) massive.

masso ['masso] SM rock, boulder; **caduta (di) massi** (*cartello*) (beware!) falling rocks; **dormire come un masso** to sleep like a log ▶**masso erratico** (*Geol*) erratic.

massone [mas'sone] SM freemason.

massoneria [massone'ria] SF freemasonry.

massonico, a, ci, che [mas'sɔniko] AGG masonic.

massoterapia [massotera'pia] SF (*Med*) deep massage.

mastectomia [mastekto'mia] SF (*Med*) mastectomy.

mastello [mas'tɛllo] SM tub.

masticabile [masti'kabile] AGG which can be chewed, chewable.

masticare [masti'kare] VT to chew, masticate (*frm*); (*tabacco, gomma*) to chew; **mastico un po' di inglese** I have a smattering of English.

mastice ['mastitʃe] SM (*resina*) mastic; (*per vetri*) putty.

mastino [mas'tino] SM mastiff.

mastodonte [masto'donte] SM mastodon; **è un mastodonte** (*fig*) he's a hulking great brute.

mastodontico, a, ci, che [masto'dontiko] AGG (*fig*) gigantic, colossal.

mastoide [mas'tɔide] SF mastoid.

mastoideo, a [mastoi'dɛo] AGG mastoid *attr*.

mastro ['mastro] SM **a** (*persona*): **mastro falegname** master carpenter **b** (*Comm*): (**libro**) **mastro** ledger.

masturbare [mastur'bare] VT, **masturbarsi** VR to masturbate.

masturbazione [masturbat'tsjone] SF masturbation; **masturbazione intellettuale** *o* **mentale** (*fig*) intellectual masturbation.

matassa [ma'tassa] SF (*gen*) skein, hank; **venire a capo della matassa** (*fig*) to unravel the problem; **ingarbugliare** *o* **imbrogliare la matassa** (*fig*) to confuse the issue.

matematica [mate'matika] SF mathematics *sg*.

matematicamente [matematika'mente] AVV mathematically; **sono matematicamente sicuro di quello che dico** I am absolutely sure of what I'm saying.

matematico, a, ci, che [mate'matiko] **1** AGG mathematical; **avere la certezza matematica che** to be absolutely certain that. **2** SM/F mathematician.

materassino [materas'sino] SM mat ▶**materassino gonfiabile** air bed.

materasso [mate'rasso] SM mattress ▶**materasso ad acqua** water bed ▶**materasso di gommapiuma** foam mattress ▶**materasso a molle** spring *o* interior-sprung mattress.

materia [ma'tɛrja] **1** SF (*gen, Filosofia, Fis*) matter; (*Scol: argomento*) subject matter, material; (*disciplina*) subject; (*sostanza: Tecn, Comm*) material, substance; **prima di entrare in materia...** before discussing the matter in hand ...; **un esperto in materia (di musica** *ecc*) an expert on the subject (of music *ecc*); **sono ignorante in materia** I know nothing about it. **2** ▶**materia cerebrale** cerebral matter ▶**materia grassa** fat ▶**materia grigia** (*anche fig*) grey matter ▶**materie plastiche** plastics ▶**materie prime** raw materials.

materiale [mate'rjale] **1** AGG (*interessi, necessità, danni*) material; (*persona: materialista*) materialistic; **non ho avuto il tempo materiale di farlo** I simply haven't had the time to do it; **non ha avuto la possibilità materiale di evitarlo** he just couldn't avoid it. **2** SM (*gen*) material; (*insieme di strumenti*) equipment *no pl*; **di che materiale è fatto?** what is it made of?; **hai il materiale per scrivere?** have you got pen and paper?. **3** ▶**materiale bellico** war materiel *o* matériel ▶**materiale da costruzione** building materials *pl* ▶**materiale rotabile** rolling stock ▶**materiale di scarto** waste material.

materialismo [materja'lizmo] SM materialism.

materialista, i, e [materja'lista] [1] AGG materialistic. [2] SM/F materialist.

materialistico, a, ci, che [materja'listiko] AGG materialistic.

materializzarsi [materjalid'dzarsi] VIP to materialize.

materialmente [materjal'mente] AVV: **è materialmente impossibile farlo** it's a physical impossibility.

maternamente [materna'mente] AVV maternally, like a mother.

maternità [materni'ta] SF INV **a** (condizione) motherhood; **in (congedo di) maternità** on maternity leave **b** (clinica) maternity hospital; **reparto maternità** maternity ward.

materno, a [ma'tɛrno] AGG (gen) maternal; (amore, cura) motherly, maternal; (nonno) maternal; (lingua, terra) mother attr; **scuola materna** nursery school (attended by children aged 3).

matinée [mati'ne] SF INV (Cine, Teatro) matinée, afternoon performance.

matita [ma'tita] [1] SF pencil; **scrivere a matita** to write in pencil; **disegno a matita** pencil drawing. [2] ▶**matita emostatica** styptic pencil ▶**matita per (gli) occhi** eyeliner (pencil) ▶**matita per (le) labbra** lip liner ▶**matite colorate** coloured pencils.

matriarca [matri'arka] SF matriarch.

matriarcale [matriar'kale] AGG matriarchal.

matriarcato [matriar'kato] SM matriarchy.

matrice [ma'tritʃe] SF **a** (Bio, Mat, Tip, Tecn) matrix; (per duplicatore) stencil **b** (Comm) counterfoil; (di assegno) (cheque) stub **c** (fig: origine) background; **l'attentato è di chiara matrice fascista** the fascists are undoubtedly behind this bombing.

matricida, i, e [matri'tʃida] [1] AGG matricidal. [2] SM/F matricide (person).

matricidio, di [matri'tʃidjo] SM matricide (act).

matricola [ma'trikola] SF **a** (registro) register **b** (anche: numero di matricola) registration number; (: Mil) regimental number; (: Tecn) part number **c** (studente: nell'università) freshman, fresher (Brit fam).

matricolato, a [matriko'lato] AGG (ladro, bugiardo) downright attr, out-and-out attr.

matrigna [ma'trinna] SF stepmother.

matrimoniale [matrimo'njale] AGG (gen) matrimonial, marriage attr; (rapporto) marital; (vita) married; (anello) wedding attr; **camera/letto matrimoniale** double room/bed.

matrimonio, ni [matri'monjo] SM (unione) marriage; (cerimonia) wedding; (durata) marriage, married life; **dopo 5 anni di matrimonio** after 5 years of marriage; **pubblicazioni di matrimonio** (marriage) banns; **matrimonio religioso/civile** religious/civil wedding; **matrimonio d'amore** love match; **matrimonio di convenienza** marriage of convenience.

matrona [ma'trona] SF (fig) matronly woman.

matronale [matro'nale] AGG matronly.

matta ['matta] SF (Carte) joker.

mattacchione, a [mattak'kjone] SM/F joker.

mattanza [mat'tantsa] SF (pesca dei tonni) tuna fishing; (fig: serie di uccisioni) killings pl.

mattatoio, oi [matta'tojo] SM slaughterhouse, abattoir (Brit).

mattatore [matta'tore] SM (di spettacolo) star performer.

matterello [matte'rello] SM rolling pin.

mattina [mat'tina] SF morning; **la o alla o di mattina** in the morning; **di prima mattina** OR **la mattina presto** early in the morning; **la mattina prima/dopo** the previous/following morning; **la mattina prima di...** the morning before ...; **dalla mattina alla sera** (continuamente) from morning to night; (improvvisamente: cambiare) overnight; **alle due di mattina** at 2 a.m.

mattinata [matti'nata] SF **a** morning; **in mattinata** in the course of the morning; **sarà pronto in mattinata** it will be ready before noon; **nella mattinata** in the morning; **nella tarda mattinata** at the end of the morning; **nella tarda mattinata di sabato** late on Saturday morning **b** (spettacolo) matinée, afternoon performance.

mattiniero, a [matti'njero] AGG: **essere mattiniero** to be an early riser.

mattino [mat'tino] SM morning; **di buon mattino** early in the morning; **sul far del mattino** at daybreak; **il mattino ha l'oro in bocca** (Proverbio) the early bird catches the worm.

matto, a ['matto] [1] AGG **a** (gen, fig) mad, crazy; (Med) insane; **diventare matto** to go mad; **far diventare matto qn** to drive sb mad o crazy; **andare matto per qc** to be crazy about sth; **quella testa matta ne ha combinato un'altra** that lunatic has done it again; **matto da legare** as mad as a hatter; **fossi matto!** (neanche per sogno) not on your life!; **avere una voglia matta di** (cibo, cioccolato) to have a craving for; **ho una voglia matta di incontrarlo** I'm dying to meet him, I can't wait to meet him **b** (falso): **oro matto** imitation gold **c** (opaco) matt. [2] SM/F madman/madwoman, lunatic; **ridere come un matto** to laugh hysterically; **fare il matto** to act the fool; **mi piace da matti la tua giacca** I just love your jacket; **roba da matti!** it's unbelievable!; **una gabbia di matti** (fig) a madhouse.

mattoide [mat'tɔide] (fam) [1] AGG nutty, screwy. [2] SM/F nutcase, screwball (spec Am).

mattone [mat'tone] SM **a** brick; **casa di mattoni** brick house; **color mattone** OR **rosso mattone** brick red **b** (fig): **questo libro/film è un mattone** this book/film is really heavy going; **ho un mattone sullo stomaco** I feel as though I've got a lead weight in my stomach.

mattonella [matto'nɛlla] SF **a** (piastrella) tile; **a mattonelle** tiled **b** (di carbone) briquette **c** (del biliardo) cushion.

mattutino, a [mattu'tino] AGG morning attr.

maturando, a [matu'rando] SM/F ≈ G.C.E. A-level candidate (Brit), graduating high-school senior (Am).

maturare [matu'rare] [1] VT (frutta) to ripen; (fig: persona) to (make) mature; **maturare una decisione** to come to a decision. [2] VI (aus essere), **maturarsi** VIP (frutta, grano) to ripen; (ascesso) to come to a head; (fig: persona, idea, Econ: interessi) to mature.

maturazione [matural'tsjone] SF (di frutta) ripening; (di formaggio) maturing; (di interessi) maturity.

maturità [maturi'ta] SF **a** maturity; **se avessi un minimo di maturità** if you were a responsible adult **b** (Scol: anche: esame di maturità) school-leaving examination, ≈ G.C.E. A levels (Brit), ≈ (high-school) graduation (Am).

maturo, a [ma'turo] AGG **a** (frutto) ripe, mature; **troppo maturo** overripe **b** (persona) mature; **è un uomo maturo** he's middle-aged; **i tempi sono maturi per agire** the time is ripe for action **c** (Scol: studente) student who has gained A levels (Brit),

≈ high-school graduate (*Am*).

matusa [ma'tuza] SM/F INV (*scherz*) old fogey.

Mauritania [mauri'tanja] SF: **la Mauritania** Mauritania.

Maurizio [mau'rittsjo] SF: **(l'isola di) Maurizio** Mauritius.

mausoleo [mauzo'lɛo] SM mausoleum.

max. ABBR (= *massimo*) max.

maxi... ['maksi] PREF maxi... .

maxiprocesso [maksipro'tʃɛsso] SM *trial involving a large number of accused: usually members of terrorist or criminal organizations.*

mazurca [mad'dzurka] SF mazurka.

mazza ['mattsa] SF (*bastone*) club; (*Mil*) baton; (*nelle cerimonie*) mace; (*martello*) sledgehammer; (*Sport*: *da golf*) (golf) club; (: *da baseball, cricket*) bat.

mazzata [mat'tsata] SF (*anche fig*) heavy blow.

mazzetta [mat'tsetta] SF (*di banconote*) bundle; (*fig*) rake-off; (: *tangente*) bribe.

mazziere [mat'tsjɛre] SM **a** (*in processioni*) macebearer **b** (*Carte*) dealer.

mazzo ['mattso] SM **a** (*di fiori, chiavi*) bunch **b** (*di carte da gioco*) pack; **tenere il mazzo** to be dealer; **fare il mazzo** (*mescolare*) to shuffle the cards **c** (*fam!*: *culo*): **farsi un** o **il mazzo** (*faticare molto*) to work bloody hard, work one's guts out.

MC SIGLA = *Macerata*.

m.c.d. ABBR (= *minimo comune denominatore*) lcd.

m.c.m. ABBR (= *minimo comune multiplo*) lcm.

ME SIGLA = *Messina*.

me [me] PRON PERS **a** (*forma tonica*) me; **parlavate di me?** were you talking about me?; **vieni con me?** are you coming with me?; **dietro di me** behind me; **lo ha dato a me, non a te** he gave it to me o ME, not to you o YOU; **vieni da me?** are you coming to my place?; **l'ho fatto da me** I did it (all) by myself; **pensavo tra me e me che...** I was thinking to myself that ...; **se fossi in me cosa faresti?** what would you do if you were me? o if you were in my position?

b (*nelle comparazioni*) I, me; (*in espressioni esclamative*) me; **è alta come me** she's as tall as I am o as me; **fai come me** do the same as me, do as I do; **sei bravo quanto me** you are as clever as I (am) o as me; **è più giovane di me** he's younger than I (am) o than me; **povero me!** poor me!

c vedi **mi**.

mea culpa ['mɛa'kulpa] SM INV mea culpa; **recitare il mea culpa** (*fig*) to admit one is to blame.

meandro [me'andro] SM (*di fiume*) meander; **si è perso nei meandri del palazzo** he lost his way in the building's maze of corridors; **i meandri del pensiero** the mind's meanderings.

M.E.C. [mɛk] SIGLA M = **Mercato Comune Europeo.**

mecca ['mɛkka] SF (*Geog*): **la Mecca** Mecca; **la mecca del cinema** (*fig*) the mecca of the film world.

meccanica [mek'kanika] SF **a** (*scienza*) mechanics *sg*; (*attività tecnologica*) mechanical engineering; **meccanica agraria** agricultural technology

b (*meccanismo: di orologio, congegno*) mechanism; **c'è qualcosa che non va nella meccanica di questa macchina** there's something mechanically wrong with this car; **spiegami la meccanica dei fatti** o **dell'accaduto** tell me how it happened; **ricostruire la meccanica di un delitto/ incidente** to reconstruct all the factors involved in a crime/accident.

meccanicamente [mekkanika'mente] AVV mechanically.

meccanicistico, a, ci, che [mekkani'tʃistiko] AGG mechanistic.

meccanico, a, ci, che [mek'kaniko] **1** AGG (*anche fig*) mechanical; **officina meccanica** garage.

2 SM mechanic.

meccanismo [mekka'nizmo] SM mechanism.

meccanizzare [mekkanid'dzare] VT to mechanize.

meccanizzazione [mekkaniddzat'tsjone] SF mechanization.

meccanografia [mekkanogra'fia] SF (mechanical) data processing.

meccanografico, a, ci, che [mekkano'grafiko] AGG: **centro meccanografico** data processing department.

mecenate [metʃe'nate] SM/F patron.

mecenatismo [metʃena'tizmo] SM patronage (of the arts).

mèche [mɛʃ] SF INV streak; **farsi le mèche** to have one's hair streaked.

medaglia [me'daʎʎa] SF (*gen*) medal; (*distintivo*) badge; **il rovescio della medaglia** (*fig*) the other side of the coin ▸ **medaglia d'oro** (*oggetto*) gold medal; (*atleta*) gold medallist (*Brit*) o medalist (*Am*).

medagliere [medaʎ'ʎɛre] SM **a** (*raccolta*) medal collection; **il medagliere dell'Italia alle Olimpiadi** (*Sport*) the (total number of) Olympic medals won by Italy **b** (*mobile*) medal cabinet.

medaglietta [medaʎ'ʎetta] SF (small) medal; (*per cani*) name tag.

medaglione [medaʎ'ʎone] SM **a** (*Arte*) medallion; (*Culin*) médaillon **b** (*gioiello*) locket.

Medea [me'dɛa] SF Medea.

medesimo, a [me'dezimo] **1** AGG **a** (*identico, uguale*) same; **mi ha detto le medesime cose** he said the same things to me; **sono della medesima taglia** they are the same size

b (*enfatizzato*) very; **arrivò il medesimo giorno in cui io dovevo partire** he arrived the very day I was due to leave; **è la stessa medesima cosa** it's the very same thing; **le regole medesime del gioco impongono ciò** the very rules of the game require this

c (*in persona*): **io medesimo/tu medesimo** I myself/you yourself; **il presidente medesimo** the president himself.

2 PRON: **il (la) medesimo(a)** the same one.

media ['mɛdja] SF **a** (*valore intermedio*) average; **al di sopra/sotto della media** above/below average; **in media** on average; **questa macchina fa in media i 120 km/h** this car has an average speed of 120 km/h; **viaggiare ad una media di...** to travel at an average speed of ...; **riceve in media 700.000 lire al mese** he earns 700,000 lire per month on average, he has an average income of 700,000 lire per month

b (*Scol: voto*) end-of-term average; **fu promosso con la media del 7** he passed with an average of 7 out of 10; **ha avuto una media molto bassa** his average marks were very low, he had a very low average mark

c: **medie** SFPL = **scuola media**; vedi **medio**

d (*Mat*) mean; **media aritmetica/geometrica** arithmetic/geometric mean.

mediamente [medja'mente] AVV on average.

medianico, a, ci, che [me'djaniko] AGG (*poteri*) extrasensory.

mediano, a [me'djano] **1** AGG (*Geom*) median.

2 SM (*Calcio*) half-back; **mediano sinistro/destro** left/ right half; **mediano di mischia** (*Rugby*) scrum half.

3 SF (*Geom*) median.

mediante [me'djante] PREP (*per mezzo di*) by (means of).

mediare [me'djare] VT (*fare da mediatore*) to act as mediator in, mediate.

mediato, a [me'djato] AGG indirect.

mediatore, trice [medja'tore] SM/F (*gen, Pol*) mediator; (*Comm*) middleman, agent; **fare da mediatore tra** to mediate between ▶**mediatore d'affari** business agent.

mediazione [medjat'tsjone] SF (*gen, Pol*) mediation; (*Industria*) arbitration; (*Comm: azione, compenso*) brokerage.

medicamento [medika'mento] SM medicament.

medicamentoso, a [medikamen'toso] AGG medicinal.

medicare [medi'kare] VT (*paziente*) to treat; (*ferita*) to dress; **medicarsi un piede ferito** to dress one's injured foot.

medicato, a [medi'kato] AGG (*garza, shampoo*) medicated.

medicazione [medikat'tsjone] SF (*di ferita*) dressing; **fare una medicazione a qn** to dress sb's wounds; **togliere/cambiare la medicazione** to remove/change the dressings.

medicina [medi'tʃina] SF **a** (*scienza, preparato medicinale*) medicine; **il tempo è la miglior medicina** (*fig*) time is a great healer ▶**medicina legale** forensic medicine **b** (*Univ: anche: facoltà di medicina*) medical faculty/school; **studente in medicina** medical student; **laurea in medicina** degree in medicine.

medicinale [meditʃi'nale] [1] AGG medicinal. [2] SM medicine, drug.

medico, a, ci, che ['mɛdiko] [1] AGG (*gen*) medical; (*sostanza, erba*) medicinal; **ricetta medica** prescription; **visita medica** medical (examination). [2] SM (*gen*) doctor; **chi è il tuo medico curante?** who's your doctor o GP?; (*in ospedale*) which doctor is in charge of your case? ▶**medico di bordo** ship's doctor ▶**medico chirurgo** surgeon ▶**medico di famiglia** family doctor ▶**medico fiscale** *doctor who checks that the sick leave given to patients by GPs is reasonable* ▶**medico generico** o **di base** general practitioner ▶**medico legale** forensic scientist.

medievale [medje'vale] AGG (*anche fig*) medi(a)eval.

medievalistica [medjeva'listika] SF medieval studies *pl*.

medio, dia, di, die ['mɛdjo] [1] AGG (*gen*) average; (*misura, corporatura*) average, medium; (*peso, ceto*) middle; **persona di statura media** person of average o medium height; (*dito*) **medio** middle finger; **scuola media** *school for pupils aged 11 - 14: education beyond this level is not compulsory*; **licenza media** *leaving certificate at the end of 3 years of secondary education* ▶**il Medio Oriente** the Middle East. [2] SM (*dito*) middle finger.

mediocre [me'djɔkre] AGG (*gen*) mediocre; (*qualità, stipendio*) poor; (*persona, impiego*) mediocre, second-rate.

mediocremente [medjokre'mente] AVV (*suonare, cantare*) indifferently; **quell'impiegato/quella fabbrica rende mediocremente** that employee/factory isn't very efficient; **lo pagano mediocremente** he's poorly paid.

mediocrità [medjokri'ta] SF (*vedi agg*) mediocrity; poorness.

Medioevo [medjo'ɛvo] SM: **il Medioevo** the Middle Ages *pl*.

medioleggero [medjoled'dʒero] SM welterweight.

mediomassimo [medjo'massimo] SM light heavyweight.

meditabondo, a [medita'bondo] AGG meditative, thoughtful.

meditare [medi'tare] [1] VT to ponder over, meditate on; (*progettare*) to plan, think out; **meditare di fare qc** to contemplate doing sth. [2] VI (*aus avere*): **meditare (su)** to meditate (on/upon).

meditativo, a [medita'tivo] AGG meditative, thoughtful.

meditato, a [medi'tato] AGG (*gen*) meditated; (*parole*) carefully-weighed; (*vendetta*) premeditated; **ben meditato** (*piano*) well worked-out, neat.

meditazione [meditat'tsjone] SF meditation; **dopo lunga meditazione si risolse a partire** after much thought he decided to leave.

mediterraneo, a [mediter'raneo] [1] AGG Mediterranean. [2] SM: **il (mare) Mediterraneo** the Mediterranean (Sea).

medium ['mɛdjum] SM/F INV medium.

Medusa [me'duza] SF (*Mitol*) Medusa.

medusa [me'duza] SF (*Zool*) jellyfish.

mefitico, a, ci, che [me'fitiko] AGG putrid, foul-smelling.

mega... ['mɛga] PREF mega... .

megaciclo [mega'tʃiklo] SM (*Radio*) megacycle.

megafono [me'gafono] SM megaphone.

megagalattico, a, ci, che [megaga'lattiko] AGG (*scherz: grandissimo*) gigantic, mega-; (: *importantissimo*) mega-important.

megahertz [mega'ɛrts] SM INV megahertz.

megalite [mega'lite] SM megalith.

megalomane [mega'lɔmane] AGG, SM/F megalomaniac.

megalomania [megaloma'nia] SF megalomania.

megalopoli [mega'lɔpoli] SF INV megalopolis.

megaton ['mɛgaton] SM INV (*Fis*) megaton.

megera [me'dʒɛra] SF (*pegg: donna*) shrew.

meglio ['mɛʎʎo] (*comp, superl di bene*) [1] AVV **a** better; **sto meglio** I feel better; **gioca meglio di lui** she plays better than he does; **è cambiato in meglio** he has changed for the better, he has improved; **meglio non passare per quella strada** it's better not to take that road **b** (*con senso superlativo*) best; **i meglio allenati** the best trained; **sono le ragazze meglio vestite della scuola** they are the best dressed girls in the school **c** : **meglio che mai** better than ever; **meglio tardi che mai** better late than never; **meglio poco che niente** half a loaf is better than no bread; **faresti meglio ad andartene** you had better leave; **andare di bene in meglio** [OR] **andare sempre meglio** to get better and better. [2] AGG INV **a** better; **questa casa è meglio dell'altra** this house is better than the other one; **è meglio che tu te ne vada** you'd better leave, it would be better for you to go; **è meglio non raccontargli niente** it would be better not to tell him anything o if you didn't tell him anything; **ha trovato di meglio da fare** he's found something better to do **b** : **alla meglio** as best one can; **alla bell'e meglio** somehow or other. [3] SM best; **al meglio delle proprie possibilità** as best one can, to the best of one's ability; **è il meglio che io possa fare** it's the best I can do; **fare del proprio meglio** to do one's best; **le cose si sono messe per il meglio** things turned out for the best; **essere al meglio della forma** to be in top form. [4] SF: **avere la meglio** to come off best; **aver la meglio su qn** to get the better of sb.

mela ['mela] SF apple; **torta di mele** apple tart; **mele cotte** stewed apples ▶**mela cotogna** quince ▶**mela selvatica** crab apple.

melagrana [mela'grana] SF pomegranate.

melammina [melam'mina] SF (*Chim*) melamine.

melanconia [melanko'nia] *ecc* = **malinconia** *ecc.*

mélange [me'lɑ̃ʒ] SM INV mixture.

melanina [mela'nina] SF melanin.

melanzana [melan'dzana] SF aubergine (*Brit*), eggplant (*Am*).

melassa [me'lassa] SF (*Culin*) treacle, molasses *sg* (*Am*).

melenso, a [me'lɛnso] AGG dull, stupid.

melissa [me'lissa] SF (lemon) balm.

mellifluamente [melliflua'mente] AVV (*pegg: rispondere, sorridere*) with sugary sweetness.

mellifluo, a [mel'lifluo] AGG (*pegg*) sugary, honeyed.

melma ['melma] SF slime.

melmosità [melmosi'ta] SF sliminess.

melmoso, a [mel'moso] AGG slimy.

melo ['melo] SM apple tree.

melodia [melo'dia] SF (*Mus*) melody; (*aria*) melody, tune; **cantare una melodia** to hum a tune.

melodico, a, ci, che [me'lɔdiko] AGG melodic.

melodiosamente [melodjosa'mente] AVV melodiously, tunefully.

melodioso, a [melo'djoso] AGG melodious, tuneful.

melodramma, i [melo'dramma] SM (*Teatro, pegg*) melodrama.

melodrammaticamente [melodrammatika'mente] AVV melodramatically.

melodrammatico, a, ci, che [melodram'matiko] AGG (*Teatro, pegg*) melodramatic.

melograno [melo'grano] SM pomegranate tree.

melone [me'lone] SM (musk) melon.

membrana [mem'brana] SF membrane.

membro ['mɛmbro] SM **a** (*pl m* **membri**) (*persona, Mat, Gramm*) member; **diventare membro di** to become a member of **b** (*pl f* **membra**) (*Anat*) limb; **riposare le stanche membra** to rest one's weary limbs **c** (*pl m* **membri**): **membro (virile)** male sexual organ.

memorabile [memo'rabile] AGG memorable.

memorandum [memo'randum] SM INV memorandum.

memore ['mɛmore] AGG (*letter*): **memore di** (*ricordando*) mindful of; (*riconoscente*) grateful for.

memoria [me'mɔrja] **1** SF **a** (*gen, Inform*) memory; **avere molta memoria** to have a good memory; **non avere memoria** to have a bad memory; **avere una memoria fotografica** to have a photographic memory; **imparare/sapere qc a memoria** to learn/know sth by heart; **frugare nella memoria** to search one's memory; **mi è rimasto impresso nella memoria** it was imprinted in my memory; **se la memoria non m'inganna** if I remember correctly **b** (*ricordo*) recollection, memory; **non resta memoria di quel fatto** no one remembers that event; **fatto degno di memoria** memorable deed; **a memoria d'uomo** within living memory; (*da tempo immemorabile*) from time immemorial; **in** *o* **alla memoria di** in (loving) memory of; **medaglia alla memoria** commemorative medal **c**: **memorie** SFPL (*opera autobiografica*) memoirs. **2** (*Inform*) ▸ **memoria permanente** nonvolatile memory ▸**memoria di sola lettura** read-only memory ▸**memoria tampone** buffer ▸**memoria volatile** volatile memory.

memoriale [memo'rjale] SM (*raccolta di memorie*) memoirs *pl.*

memorizzare [memorid'dzare] VT (*gen*) to memorize;

(*Inform*) to store.

memorizzazione [memoriddzat'tsjone] SF (*vedi vb*) memorization; storage ▸**memorizzazione transitoria** (*Inform*) buffering.

menadito [mena'dito]: **a menadito** AVV perfectly, thoroughly; **sapere** *o* **conoscere qc a menadito** to know sth inside out.

ménage [me'naʒ] SM INV: **un ménage tranquillo** a happy relationship; **ménage a tre** ménage à trois.

menagramo [mena'gramo] SM/F INV jinx, Jonah.

menare [me'nare] **1** VT **a** (*letter: condurre*) to take, lead; **qual buon vento ti mena?** what brings you here?; **menare qn per il naso** (*fig*) to lead sb by the nose; **menare il can per l'aia** (*fig*) to beat about (*Brit*) *o* around (*Am*) the bush; **menare qc per le lunghe** to drag sth out; **menar vanto di qc** to boast about sth **b** (*picchiare*): **menare qn** to hit *o* beat sb; **menare le mani** (*essere manesco*) to be free with one's fists; (*picchiarsi*) to come to blows; **menare calci** to kick; **menare colpi** to deal blows **c**: **menarla a qc** (*fam: infastidire*) to bore sb, drone on to sb. **2 menarsi** VR (*uso reciproco*) to come to blows.

menata [me'nata] SF **a** (*bastonata*) beating, hiding **b** (*fam: lamentela*) moaning; (*: cosa noiosa*) bore.

mendace [men'datʃe] AGG (*letter*) lying, mendacious.

mendicante [mendi'kante] SM/F beggar.

mendicare [mendi'kare] **1** VT (*anche fig*) to beg for; **mendicare qc da qn** to beg sb for sth, beg sth from sb. **2** VI (*anche fig*) to beg.

menefreghismo [menefre'gizmo] SM (*fam*) couldn't-care-less attitude; **il suo è menefreghismo bello e buono!** he simply doesn't give a damn!

menefreghista, i, e [menefre'gista] **1** AGG couldn't-care-less *attr.* **2** SM/F person who couldn't care less; **quella donna è una menefreghista** that woman couldn't care less about anything *o* doesn't give a damn about anything.

Menelao [mene'lao] SM Menelaus.

menestrello [menes'trɛllo] SM minstrel.

menhir [me'nir] SM INV menhir.

meninge [me'nindʒe] SF (*Anat*) meninx; **spremersi le meningi** to rack one's brains.

meningite [menin'dʒite] SF (*Med*) meningitis.

menisco [me'nisko] SM (*Anat, Mat, Fis*) meniscus.

meno ['meno]
1 AVV
a less;
▸**meno** *caro* less expensive, cheaper
▸**è meno alto** *di* **suo fratello/***di* **quel che pensavo** he is not as tall as his brother/as I thought, he is less tall than his brother/than I thought
▸**ha due anni meno** *di* **me** he's two years younger than me
▸**dovresti** *mangiare* **meno** you should eat less, you shouldn't eat so much
▸**meno ne discutiamo,** *meglio* **è** the less we talk about it, the better
▸**deve avere** *non* **meno di trent'anni** he must be at least thirty
▸**meno fumo** *più* **mangio** the less I smoke the more I eat

▷andare all'università diventa *sempre* meno facile it's getting less and less easy to go to university

▷ho *speso* (di) meno I spent less

▷arrivo *tra* meno di un'ora I'll be there in less than *o* in under an hour

[b] (*con senso superlativo*) least;

▷è il meno dotato dei miei studenti he's the least gifted of my pupils

▷è quello che leggo meno spesso it's the one I read least often

[c] (*sottrazione: Mat*) minus, less;

▷5 meno 2 5 minus 2, 5 take away 2

▷sono le otto meno un quarto it's a quarter to eight (*Brit*) *o* of eight (*Am*)

▷mi hai dato due carte *di* meno you gave me two cards too few

▷eh, se avessi dieci anni *di* meno! oh, if only I were ten years younger!

▷ho una sterlina *in* meno I am one pound short

▷ci sono meno 25 it's minus 25, it is 25 below (zero)

▷ha preso sette meno ≈ he got (a) B minus

[d] (*fraseologia*)

▷non è *da* meno di lui she is (every bit) as good as he is

▷non voglio essere *da* meno di lui I don't want to be outdone by him

▷*fare a* meno di to do *o* manage without

▷se non c'è zucchero ne *faremo a* meno if there isn't any sugar we'll do without

▷potresti *fare a* meno di fumare in macchina? would you mind not smoking in the car?

▷non ho potuto *fare a* meno di ridere I couldn't help laughing

▷*in* men che non si dica in less than no time, quick as a flash

▷meno *male*! good!, thank goodness!, just as well!

▷meno *male* che sei arrivato it's a good job that you have come

▷*men che* meno gli inglesi least of all the English

▷fammi sapere se verrai *o* meno let me know if you are coming or not

▷*quanto* meno poteva avvertire he could at least have let us know

▷non mi piace come scrive e *tanto* meno come parla I don't like the way he writes let alone the way he talks

[2] AGG INV (*acqua, lavoro, soldi*) less; (*persone, libri, errori*) fewer;

▷meno bambini ci sono, *meglio* è the fewer children there are the better

▷meno *storie*! stop messing around!

▷meno *tempo* less time

▷meno *turisti* fewer tourists.

[3] SM INV

[a] (*la minor cosa*)

▷*il* meno the least

▷era *il* meno che ti potesse capitare (*rimprovero*) you were asking for it

▷parlare del *più* e del meno to talk about this and that

▷per lo meno = perlomeno

▷*i* meno (*la minoranza*) the minority

[b] (*Mat*) minus (sign).

[4] PREP (*fuorché, eccetto che*) except (for);

▷a meno *che* non faccia caldo unless it is hot

▷a meno *di* prendere un giorno di ferie unless I (*o* you *ecc*) take a day off

▷ci siamo *tutti* meno lui we are all here except (for) him

▷*tutti* meno uno all but one.

menomare [meno'mare] VT to maim, disable.

menomato, a [meno'mato] [1] AGG (*persona*) disabled. [2] SM/F disabled person.

menomazione [menomat'tsjone] SF disablement.

menopausa [meno'pauza] SF menopause; **essere in menopausa** to be menopausal.

menorah [meno'ra] SF INV menorah.

mensa ['mɛnsa] SF **a** (*locale*) canteen; (: *Mil*) mess; (: *nelle università*) refectory **b** (*fig*) table; **i piaceri della mensa** the pleasures of the table.

mensile [men'sile] [1] AGG monthly. [2] SM (*periodico*) monthly (magazine); (*stipendio*) monthly salary.

mensilità [mensili'ta] SF INV (*stipendio*) monthly salary; **riscuotere due mensilità arretrate** to get two months' back pay; **13ª/14ª/15ª mensilità** ≈ once-/twice-/thrice-yearly bonus.

mensilmente [mensil'mente] AVV (*ogni mese*) every month; (*una volta al mese*) monthly.

mensola ['mɛnsola] SF (*supporto*) bracket; (*ripiano*) shelf; (*Archit*) corbel; **mensola del camino** mantelpiece; **mensola portaspezie** spice rack.

menta ['menta] SF (*Bot*) mint; (*caramella*) mint, peppermint; (*bibita*) peppermint cordial; **alla menta** [OR] **di menta** mint *attr* ▶**menta da giardino** *o* **comune** *o* **verde** spearmint ▶**menta piperita** peppermint.

mentale [men'tale] AGG mental.

mentalità [mentali'ta] SF INV mentality; **mentalità aperta/ristretta** open/narrow mind.

mentalmente [mental'mente] AVV mentally.

mente ['mente] SF **a** (*gen, fig*) mind; **mente aperta/lucida** open/clear mind; **mente agile/acuta** quick/sharp mind; **mente malata** sick mind; **malato di mente** mentally ill; **avevo la mente altrove** my mind was elsewhere, I was miles away

b (*fraseologia*): **a mente fredda** objectively; **rivedere qc a mente fresca** to take another look at sth when one's mind is fresh; **avere in mente serena** calmly; **avere in mente qc/qn** to have sth/sb in mind; **lo ha sempre in mente** she's always thinking of him; **avere in mente di fare qc** to intend to do sth; **lasciami fare mente locale** let me think; **fare venire in mente qc a qn** to remind sb of sth; **mettersi in mente di fare qc** to make up one's mind to do sth; **mi è scappato di mente ciò che ti volevo dire** I've forgotten what I was going to say to you; **volevo farlo ma mi è scappato di mente** I meant to do it, but it went out of my head *o* slipped my mind; **ma cosa ti salta in mente?** what are you thinking of?; **tenere a mente qc** to bear sth in mind; **toglitelo dalla mente** forget about it, put it out of your mind; **mi è tornato in mente quell'indirizzo** that address has come back to me, I've remembered that address; **mi è venuto in mente che...** it occurred to me that ...; **non mi passa neppure per la mente** I wouldn't even consider it.

mentecatto, a [mente'katto] [1] AGG half-witted. [2] SM/F half-wit, imbecile.

mentina [men'tina] SF peppermint.

mentire [men'tire] VI (*aus* avere): **mentire (a qn su qc)** to lie (to sb about sth); **non saper mentire** to be a poor liar; **mentire spudoratamente** to lie through *o* in one's teeth.

mentito, a [men'tito] AGG: **sotto mentite spoglie** under false pretences (*Brit*) *o* pretenses (*Am*).

mentitore, trice [menti'tore] SM/F liar.

mento ['mento] SM chin; **doppio mento** double chin.

mentolo [men'tɔlo] SM menthol.

mentre ['mentre] ① CONG **a** (*temporale*) while, as; **è successo mentre ero fuori** it happened while I was out; **l'ho incontrato mentre entravo nel negozio** I met him as I was going into the shop **b** (*avversativo*) whereas, while; **lui è biondo mentre sua sorella è mora** he's blond while his sister is dark. ② SM: **in quel mentre** at that very moment.

menu [me'nu] SM INV **a** (*Culin*) (set) menu; **menu turistico** tourists' menu **b** (*Inform*) menu.

menzionare [mentsjo'nare] VT to mention.

menzione [men'tsjone] SF mention; **fare menzione di** to mention; **degno di menzione** worthy of note.

menzogna [men'tsoɲɲa] SF lie, falsehood.

menzognero, a [mentsoɲ'ɲero] AGG (*scuse*) false, untrue; (*persona*) lying.

meramente [mera'mente] AVV simply, purely.

meraviglia [mera'viʎʎa] SF **a** (*stupore*) amazement, wonder; **non ti nascondo la mia meraviglia** you can imagine my surprise; **con mia (grande) meraviglia** to my amazement; **suscitare gran meraviglia** to cause quite a stir; **mi fa meraviglia che...** I'm amazed that ...; **quest'abito ti sta a meraviglia** you look wonderful in that dress; **tutto va a meraviglia** everything is going perfectly **b** (*persona, cosa*) marvel, wonder; **hai un bimbo che è una meraviglia** isn't your baby gorgeous!; **le sette meraviglie del mondo** the seven Wonders of the World.

meravigliare [meraviʎ'ʎare] ① VT to amaze, surprise, astonish; **sono rimasto meravigliato** I was amazed *o* astonished; **mi meraviglierebbe se...** I'd be surprised if ..., it would surprise me if .... ② **meravigliarsi** VIP: **meravigliarsi (di *o* per)** (*stupirsi*) to be amazed (at), be astonished (at); **mi meraviglio di te!** I'm surprised at you!; **non c'è da meravigliarsi** it's not surprising.

meravigliosamente [meraviʎʎosa'mente] AVV marvellously, wonderfully.

meraviglioso, a [meraviʎ'ʎoso] AGG wonderful, marvellous (*Brit*), marvelous (*Am*).

merc. ABBR (= *mercoledì*) Wed.

mercante [mer'kante] SM dealer, trader; (*ant*) merchant ▶**mercante d'arte** art dealer ▶**mercante di cavalli** horse dealer ▶**mercante di schiavi** slave trader.

mercanteggiare [merkanted'dʒare] ① VI (*aus* avere) to bargain, haggle; **mercanteggiare sul prezzo** to haggle over the price. ② VT (*pegg: onore, voto*) to sell.

mercantile [merkan'tile] ① AGG (*gen*) mercantile, commercial; (*marina, nave*) merchant *attr*. ② SM (*nave*) merchantman.

mercantilismo [merkanti'lizmo] SM mercantilism.

mercanzia [merkan'tsia] SF (*pegg*) stuff.

mercatino [merka'tino] SM **a** (*rionale*) local street market **b** (*Econ*) unlisted securities market.

mercato [mer'kato] ① SM **a** (*luogo*) market; **giorno di mercato** market day; **mercato ortofrutticolo/del pesce**

fruit/fish market; **mercati generali** wholesale market *sg*; **mercato delle pulci** flea market **b** (*Econ, Fin*) market; **mettere *o* lanciare qc sul mercato** to put sth on the market; **a buon mercato** (*agg*) cheap; (*avv*) cheaply; **di mercato** (*economia, prezzo, ricerche*) market *attr*. ② ▶**il Mercato Comune (Europeo)** the (European) Common Market ▶**mercato dei cambi** exchange market ▶**mercato dei capitali** capital market ▶**mercato interno *o* nazionale** domestic market ▶**mercato del lavoro** labour market, job market ▶**mercato libero** free market ▶**mercato nero** black market ▶**mercato al rialzo** (*Borsa*) bull market ▶**mercato al ribasso** (*Borsa*) bear market ▶**mercato a termine** forward *o* futures market ▶**mercato dei valori** stock market.

merce ['mertʃe] SF goods *pl*, merchandise *no pl* ▶**merce in conto vendita** sale or return goods ▶**merce deperibile** perishable goods *pl*.

mercé [mer'tʃe] SF mercy; **essere alla mercé di qn** to be at sb's mercy.

mercenario, ria, ri, rie [mertʃe'narjo] AGG, SM/F mercenary.

merceologia [mertʃeolo'dʒia] SF study *o* knowledge of commodities.

merceria [mertʃe'ria] SF (*articoli*) haberdashery (*Brit*), notions *pl* (*Am*); (*bottega*) haberdasher's shop (*Brit*), notions store (*Am*).

mercerizzare [mertʃerid'dzare] VT (*cotone*) to mercerize.

merciaio, aia, ai, aie [mer'tʃajo] SM/F haberdasher.

mercificare [mertʃifi'kare] VT to commercialize.

mercificazione [mertʃifikat'tsjone] SF commercialization.

mercoledì [merkole'di] SM INV Wednesday ▶**mercoledì delle Ceneri** Ash Wednesday (*a fast day: churchgoers are marked on the forehead with ash*) *per fraseologia vedi* **martedì**.

Mercurio [mer'kurjo] SM (*Astron, Mitol*) Mercury.

mercurio [mer'kurjo] SM mercury.

merda ['mɛrda] SF (*fam!*) shit (*fam!*); **che giornata di merda!** what a lousy/shitty day!; **ho fatto una figura di merda** I looked a right git; **a quelle parole sono rimasto di merda** I felt bloody awful when I heard that; **essere nella merda (fino al collo)** (*nei guai*) to be (right) in the shit.

merdoso, a [mer'doso] AGG (*fam!*) shitty.

merenda [me'rɛnda] SF afternoon snack; **far merenda** to have an afternoon snack.

merendina [meren'dina] SF *prepacked cakes ecc sold as snacks for children*.

meretrice [mere'tritʃe] SF (*letter*) harlot.

meridiana [meri'djana] SF sundial.

meridiano, a [meri'djano] ① AGG (*di mezzogiorno*) midday *attr*, noonday *attr*. ② SM (*Geog: anche:* **meridiano terrestre**) meridian.

meridionale [meridjo'nale] ① AGG (*gen*) southern; (*dell'Italia*) Southern Italian. ② SM/F (*gen*) southerner; (*dell'Italia*) Southern Italian.

meridione [meri'djone] SM: **il meridione** the South; (*dell'Italia*) the South of Italy, Southern Italy.

meringa, ghe [me'ringa] SF meringue.

meringata [merin'gata] SF *meringue and ice-cream based dessert*.

merino [me'rino] AGG INV, SM merino.

meritare [meri'tare] ☐1 VT **a** (*premio, stima*) to deserve; **(si) merita un premio/un ceffone** he deserves a prize/a smack; **si è meritato la stima di tutti** he earned everybody's respect; **è una persona che merita** he deserves our respect (*o affection ecc*); **se l'è proprio meritato!** it serves him right

b (*richiedere*): **meritare attenzione/considerazione** to require *o* need attention/consideration

c (*valere*) to be worth; **questo pranzo non merita il prezzo** this meal's not worth the money.

☐2 VB IMPERS (*valere la pena*): **merita andare** it's worth going; **non merita neanche parlarne** it's not worth talking about; **per quel che merita** for what it's worth.

meritatamente [meritata'mente] AVV deservedly.

meritato, a [meri'tato] AGG (*vacanza, premio, riposo*) well-deserved.

meritevole [meri'tevole] AGG: **meritevole (di)** (*di lode, biasimo*) worthy (of).

merito ['mɛrito] SM **a** (*gen*) merit; (*valore*) worth; **dare (il) merito a qn di qc/di aver fatto qc** to give sb credit for sth/for doing sth; **è merito mio se hai avuto quel lavoro** it's thanks to me that you got that job; **Dio ve ne renda merito!** may God reward you!; **finire a pari merito** to finish joint first (*o* second *ecc*); **le due squadre hanno finito a pari merito** the two teams tied; **medaglia al merito** (*Mil*) medal for bravery

b (*argomento*): **entrare nel merito di una questione** to go into a matter; **non so niente in merito** I don't know anything about it; **in merito a** as regards, with regard to; **in merito a ciò di cui si è parlato** with reference to what was discussed.

meritocratico, a, ci, che [merito'kratiko] AGG meritocratic, based on merit.

meritocrazia [meritokrat'tsia] SF meritocracy.

meritorio, ria, ri, rie [meri'tɔrjo] AGG praiseworthy.

merlato, a [mer'lato] AGG (*Archit*) crenellated.

merlatura [merla'tura] SF (*Archit*) battlements *pl*.

merlettaia [merlet'taja] SF lacemaker.

merletto [mer'letto] SM lace.

merlo¹ ['mɛrlo] SM **a** (*Zool*) blackbird ▶ **merlo acquaiolo** dipper ▶ **merlo dal petto bianco** ring ouzel **b** (*sciocco*) fool, idiot.

merlo² ['mɛrlo] SM (*Archit*) battlement.

merluzzo [mer'luttso] SM cod.

mero, a ['mɛro] AGG mere, sheer; **per mero caso** by mere *o* sheer chance.

mescalina [meska'lina] SF mescaline.

mescere ['meʃʃere] VT to pour (out).

meschinamente [meskina'mente] AVV (*grettamente*) meanly, pettily.

meschinità [meskini'ta] SF INV (*grettezza*) meanness, pettiness, narrow-mindedness; (*spilorceria*) stinginess; **è stata una meschinità** it was a mean *o* petty trick.

meschino, a [mes'kino] ☐1 AGG (*avaro*) mean; (*gretto*) narrow-minded, mean, petty; (*scarso: guadagno*) meagre (*Brit*), meager (*Am*); **fare una figura meschina** to cut a poor figure.

☐2 SM/F: **non fare il meschino** (*gretto*) don't be so petty.

mescita ['meʃʃita] SF wine bar.

mesciuto, a [meʃ'ʃuto] PP di **mescere**.

mescolanza [mesko'lantsa] SF (*gen*) mixture; (*di ingredienti*) blend, mixture; **una mescolanza di gente/di idee** a mix of people/ideas.

mescolare [mesko'lare] ☐1 VT (*gen, Culin*) to mix; (*col cucchiaio*) to stir; (*vini, colori*) to blend; (*mettere in disordine: fogli, schede*) to mix up, muddle up; (*carte*) to shuffle.

☐2 **mescolarsi** VR: **mescolarsi alla folla** to mingle with the crowd.

☐3 **mescolarsi** VIP (*Culin*) to mix; (*vini, colori*) to blend; (*fogli, schede*) to get mixed up.

mescolata [mesko'lata] SF: **dare una mescolata a** (*Culin*) to stir; (*Carte*) to shuffle.

mese ['mese] SM month; **fra un mese** in a month('s time); **un mese di vacanza** a month's holiday; **un mese di sciopero** a month-long strike; **il mese scorso** last month; **il corrente mese** this month; **guadagna un milione al mese** she earns a million lira a *o* per month; **tre mesi d'affitto** three months' rent; **un bambino di sei mesi** a six-month-old baby; **è al settimo mese (di gravidanza)** she's six months pregnant.

mesetto [me'setto] SM: **un mesetto** about a month.

messa¹ ['messa] SF (*Rel*) mass; **andare a** *o* **alla messa** to go to mass; **dire la messa** (*celebrarla*) to say mass ▶ **messa nera** black *o* Satanic mass.

messa² ['messa] SF (*il mettere*): **messa a fuoco** focusing ▶ **messa in moto** starting-up ▶ **messa in opera** installation ▶ **messa in orbita** launching ▶ **messa in piega** set ▶ **messa in posizione** installation ▶ **messa a punto** (*termine tecn*) adjustment; (*Aut*) tuning; (*di progetto*) finalization ▶ **messa in scena** (*Teatro*) production ▶ **messa a terra** earthing.

messaggerie [messaddʒe'rie] SFPL (*ditta: di distribuzione*) distributors; (*: di trasporto*) freight company *sg*.

messaggero, a [messad'dʒero] SM/F messenger.

messaggio, gi [mes'saddʒo] SM message; **il messaggio augurale del capo dello stato** ≈ the Queen's Christmas message ▶ **messaggio di errore** (*Inform*) error message.

messale [mes'sale] SM (*Rel*) missal.

messe ['messe] SF (*letter*) harvest; **fare messe di** (*fig: lodi, consensi*) to win.

messia [mes'sia] SM INV messiah; **il Messia** the Messiah.

messianico, a, ci, che [messi'aniko] AGG Messianic.

messicano, a [messi'kano] AGG, SM/F Mexican.

Messico ['mɛssiko] SM: **il Messico** Mexico; **Città del Messico** Mexico City.

Messina [mes'sina] SF Messina; **lo stretto di Messina** the Strait of Messina.

messinscena [messin'ʃena] SF INV (*Teatro*) production; (*fig*) performance; **è tutta una messinscena** it's all an act.

messo¹ ['messo] SM messenger.

messo², a ['messo] ☐1 PP di **mettere**.

☐2 AGG: **essere ben/mal messo** (*economicamente*) to be well-/badly-off; (*di salute*) to be in good/bad health.

mestamente [mesta'mente] AVV sadly.

mestierante [mestje'rante] SM/F (*pegg*) money-grubber; (*: scrittore*) hack.

mestiere [mes'tjɛre] SM (*gen: lavoro*) job; (*: manuale*) trade; (*: artigianale*) craft; (*fig: abilità nel lavoro*) skill, technique; (*di mestiere* by trade; **fa il mestiere di calzolaio** he is a shoemaker; **imparare un mestiere** to learn a trade; **essere del mestiere** to be in the trade; (*fig*) to be an expert; **conoscere i trucchi del mestiere** to know the tricks of the trade; **essere padrone del mestiere** to know one's job.

mestizia [mes'tittsja] SF sadness, melancholy.

mesto, a ['mɛsto] AGG sad, melancholy.

mestola ['mestola] SF (*Culin*) ladle; (*Edil*) trowel.

mestolo ['mestolo] SM ladle.

mestolone [mesto'lone] SM (*Zool*) shoveler.

mestruale [mestru'ale] AGG menstrual.

mestruato, a [mestru'ato] AGG menstruating.

mestruazione [mestruat'tsjone] SF menstruation; **avere le mestruazioni** to have one's period.

mestruo ['mɛstruo] SM menstrual fluid.

meta ['mɛta] SF **a** (*destinazione*) destination; (*fig: scopo*) aim, goal; **vagare senza meta** to wander aimlessly **b** (*Rugby*) try; **segnare una meta** to score a try.

metà [me'ta] SF INV **a** half; **dividere qc a metà** to divide sth in half *o* into two halves, halve sth; **fare a metà di qc con qn** to go halves with sb in sth; **facciamo a metà** let's go halves; **dammene la metà** give me half (of it); **ho impiegato la metà del tempo** it only took me half the time; **siamo arrivati a metà del concerto** we arrived halfway through the concert; **dire le cose a metà** to leave some things unsaid; **fare le cose a metà** to leave things half-done; **la mia dolce metà** (*fam scherz*) my better half; **a metà prezzo** at half price, half-price; **a metà strada** halfway

b (*punto di mezzo*) middle; **tagliare una pagina per metà** to cut a page down the middle; **a metà settimana** mid-week; **verso la metà del mese** halfway through the month, towards the middle of the month.

metabolico, a, ci, che [meta'bɔliko] AGG metabolic.

metabolismo [metabo'lizmo] SM metabolism; **metabolismo basale** basal metabolism.

metacarpo [meta'karpo] SM metacarpus.

metadone [meta'done] SM methadone.

metafisica [meta'fizika] SF metaphysics *sg*.

metafisicamente [metafizika'mente] AVV metaphysically.

metafisico, a, ci, che [meta'fiziko] AGG metaphysical.

metafora [me'tafora] SF metaphor; **parlare per metafore** to speak metaphorically; **fuor di metafora** without beating about the bush.

metaforicamente [metaforika'mente] AVV metaphorically.

metaforico, a, ci, che [meta'fɔriko] AGG metaphorical.

metallaro, a [metal'laro] SM/F (*fam*) head-banger.

metallico, a, ci, che [me'talliko] AGG (*simile al metallo*) metallic; (*di metallo*) metal *attr*.

metallizzato, a [metallid'dzato] AGG (*vernice*) metallic.

metallo [me'tallo] SM metal; **di metallo** metal *attr*.

metalloide [metal'lɔide] SM metalloid.

metallurgia [metallur'dʒia] SF metallurgy.

metallurgico, a, ci, che [metal'lurdʒiko] **1** AGG metallurgical; **l'industria metallurgica** the iron and steel industry.

2 SM/F metal-worker.

metalmeccanico, a, ci, che [metalmek'kaniko] **1** AGG engineering *attr*.

2 SM/F engineering worker.

metamorfico, a, ci, che [meta'mɔrfiko] AGG metamorphic.

metamorfosi [meta'mɔrfozi] SF INV metamorphosis.

metano [me'tano] SM methane.

metanodotto [metano'dotto] SM methane pipeline.

metanolo [meta'nɔlo] SM methanol.

metastasi [me'tastazi] SF INV (*Med*) metastasis.

metatarso [meta'tarso] SM metatarsus.

metempsicosi [metempsi'kɔzi] SF INV metempsychosis.

meteo ['mɛteo] SM INV weather forecast.

meteora [me'tɛora] SF meteor; **quell'attore è passato come una meteora** that actor's success was a flash in the pan.

meteorico, a, ci, che [mete'ɔriko] AGG meteoric.

meteorismo [meteo'rizmo] SM (*Med*) meteorism.

meteorite [meteo'rite] SM meteorite.

meteorologia [meteorolo'dʒia] SF meteorology.

meteorologico, a, ci, che [meteoro'lɔdʒiko] AGG (*fenomeno*) meteorological; (*previsione, stazione, carta*) weather *attr*; **bollettino meteorologico** weather report; **ufficio meteorologico dell'Aeronautica** Airforce Meteorological Office.

meteorologo, a, gi, ghe [meteo'rɔlogo] SM/F meteorologist.

meticcio, cia, ci, ce [me'tittʃo] **1** AGG (*persona*) half-cast; (*animale*) crossbreed.

2 SM/F half-caste, half-breed.

meticolosamente [metikolosa'mente] AVV meticulously.

meticolosità [metikolosi'ta] SF INV meticulousness.

meticoloso, a [metiko'loso] AGG meticulous.

metile [me'tile] SM methyl.

metilico, a, ci, che [me'tiliko] AGG methyl *attr*; **alcol metilico** methyl alcohol.

metodicità [metoditʃi'ta] SF methodicalness.

metodico, a, ci, che [me'tɔdiko] AGG methodical.

metodismo [meto'dismo] SM (*Rel*) Methodism.

metodista, i, e [meto'dista] AGG, SM/F (*Rel*) Methodist.

metodo ['mɛtodo] SM (*procedimento*) method; (*manuale*) tutor (*Brit*), manual; **far qc con/senza metodo** to do sth methodically/unmethodically; **aver il proprio metodo per fare qc** to have one's own way *o* method of doing sth.

metodologia [metodolo'dʒia] SF methodology.

metraggio, gi [me'traddʒo] SM **a** (*Sartoria*) length; **vendere a metraggio** to sell by the metre **b** (*Cine*) footage; (**film a) lungo metraggio** feature film; (**film a) corto metraggio** short (film).

metratura [metra'tura] SF length.

metrica ['mɛtrika] SF (*Poesia*) metrics *sg*, prosody.

metrico, a, ci, che ['mɛtriko] AGG metric; (*Poesia*) metrical; **il sistema metrico decimale** the metric system.

metro ['mɛtro] SM (*gen*) metre (*Brit*), meter (*Am*); (*strumento: a nastro*) tape measure; (: *ad asta*) (metre) rule; (*fig: criterio*) yardstick; **metro cubo/quadrato** cubic/square metre; **i cento metri** (*Sport*) the hundred metres (race).

metrò [me'tro] SM INV underground (*Brit*), subway (*Am*).

metronomo [me'trɔnomo] SM INV metronome.

metronotte [metro'nɔtte] SM INV night security guard.

metropoli [me'trɔpoli] SF INV metropolis.

metropolitana [metropoli'tana] SF (*anche:* **ferrovia metropolitana**) underground (*Brit*), subway (*Am*) ▶ **metropolitana leggera** metro (*mainly on the surface*).

metropolitano, a [metropoli'tano] AGG metropolitan; **leggende metropolitane** urban myths.

mettere ['mettere] VB IRREG **1** VT **a** (*porre*) to put; **dove hai messo la mia penna?** where did you put my pen?; **guarda dove metti i piedi** be careful where you step; **gli ha messo una mano sulla spalla** he put *o* laid a hand on his shoulder; **mettere qc diritto** to put *o* set sth straight; **mettere un bambino a letto** to put a child to bed; **mettere un annuncio sul giornale** to put an advert in the paper; **mettere il lavoro al di sopra di tutto** to put work

before all else; **quando si mette una cosa in testa...** when he gets an idea into his head ...; **mettere qn sulla strada giusta** (*fig*) to set sb right

b (*infondere*): **mettere fame/allegria/malinconia a qn** to make sb (feel) hungry/happy/sad

c (*anche:* **mettersi**: *abito: indossare*) to put on; (: *portare*) to wear; **non metto più quelle scarpe** I've stopped wearing those shoes; **mettersi il cappello** to put on one's hat; **non so cosa mettermi** I don't know what to wear; **ma che cosa ti sei messo?** what on earth have you got on?

d (*installare: telefono, gas, finestre*) to put in; (*acqua*) to lay on

e (*sveglia, allarme*) to set; **hai messo la sicura?** (*Aut*) have you locked the door?

f (*supporre*): **mettiamo che...** let's suppose *o* say that ...

g : **metterci**: **metterci molta cura/molto tempo** to take a lot of care/a lot of time; **ci ho messo 3 ore per venire** it's taken me 3 hours to get here; **mettercela tutta** to do one's utmost

h (*fraseologia*): **mettere a confronto** to compare; **mettere in conto** (*somma ecc*) to put on account; **mettere qn contro qn** (*fig*) to turn sb against sb; **mettere qn al corrente di qc** to put sb in the picture about sth; **mettere dentro qn** (*fam: imprigionare*) to put sb inside; **mettere in giro** (*pettegolezzi, voci*) to spread; **mettere insieme** (*gen*) to put together; (*organizzare: spettacolo, gruppo*) to organize, get together; (*soldi*) to save; **mettere in luce** (*problemi, errori*) to show up, highlight; **mettere qn a sedere** to sit sb down; **mettere sotto** (*sopraffare*) to get the better of; **mettere su il caffè** (*fam*) to put the coffee on; **mettere su casa** to set up house; **mettere su un negozio** to start a shop; **mettere su pancia** to develop a paunch; **mettere su peso** to put on weight; **mettere a tacere qn/qc** to keep sb/sth quiet; **mettere via** to put away.

2 **mettersi** VR **a** to put o.s.; **non metterti là** (*seduto*) don't sit there; (*in piedi*) don't stand there; **mettersi a sedere** to sit down; **mettersi a letto** to go to bed; (*malato*) to take to one's bed

b (*vestirsi*): **mettersi in costume** to put on one's swimming things; **ti dispiace se mi metto in maniche di camicia?** do you mind if I take off my jacket?

c (*in gruppo*): **mettersi in società** to set up in business; **si sono messi insieme** (*coppia*) they've started going out together (*Brit*) *o* dating (*Am*)

3 **mettersi** VIP **a** (*incominciare*): **mettersi a piangere/ridere** to start crying/laughing, start *o* begin to cry/laugh; **mettersi a bere** to take to drink; **mettersi al lavoro** to set to work

b (*prendere un andamento*): **si mette al bello** (*tempo*) the weather's turning fine; **mettersi bene/male** (*faccenda*) to turn out well/badly; **vediamo come si mettono le cose** let's see how things go.

mezza ['mɛddza] SF (*mezzogiorno e mezzo*): **è la mezza** it's half-past twelve (in the afternoon).

mezzadria [meddza'dria] SF (*Agr*) sharecropping.

mezzadro [med'dzadro] SM (*Agr*) sharecropper.

mezzala [med'dzala] SF (*Calcio*) inside forward; **mezzala destra/sinistra** inside right/left.

mezzaluna [meddza'luna] SF (*pl* **mezzelune**) half-moon; (*dell'islamismo*) crescent; (*coltello*) (semicircular) chopping knife.

mezzamanica [meddza'manika] SF (*pl* **mezzemaniche**)

sleeve guard; (*fig: impiegato*) penpusher.

mezzanino [meddza'nino] SM mezzanine (floor).

mezzano, a [med'dzano] **1** AGG (*medio*) average, medium; (*figlio*) middle *attr*; (*vela*) mizzen *attr*.
2 SM/F (*intermediario*) go-between; (*ruffiano*) procurer.
3 SF (*Naut*): **albero di mezzana** mizzen mast.

mezzanotte [meddza'nɔtte] SF midnight.

mezz'asta [mɛd'dzasta]: **a mezz'asta** AVV at half-mast; **bandiera a mezz'asta** flag (flying) at half-mast.

mezzeria [meddze'ria] SF (*di strada*) centre line.

mezzo¹ ['mɛddzo] SM **a** (*strumento*) means *sg*; (*metodo*) means, way; **mezzi di produzione** means of production; **per mezzo di** by means of, through; **a mezzo corriere** by carrier; **cercherò di ottenere il posto con qualsiasi mezzo** I'll try to get the job by whatever means; **non c'è mezzo di fermarlo** there's no way of stopping him; **ci siamo arrangiati con mezzi di fortuna** we managed as best we could ▶ **mezzi di comunicazione di massa** mass media *pl*

b (*veicolo*) vehicle ▶ **mezzi pubblici** public transport *sg* ▶ **mezzi di trasporto** means of transport

c : **mezzi** SMPL (*possibilità economiche*) means; **è una persona che ha molti mezzi** he has a large income, he's very well off; **farcela con i propri mezzi** to manage on one's own; **fare una vita al di sopra dei propri mezzi** to live beyond one's means

d (*Fis*) medium.

mezzo², a ['mɛddzo] **1** AGG **a** half; **mezza bottiglia di vino** half a bottle of wine; **una mezza bottiglia di vino** a half-bottle of wine; **una mezza dozzina di uova** half a dozen eggs; **ha lasciato mezzo panino** he left half of his sandwich; **c'era mezza città al concerto** half the town was at the concert; **mi ha fatto una mezza promessa** he half-promised me; **aver una mezza idea di fare qc** to have half a mind to do sth; **è venuto mezzo mondo** just about everybody was there; **è stato un mezzo scandalo** it almost caused a scandal; **me l'ha detto a mezza voce** he said it to me in an undertone; **non mi piacciono le mezze misure** I don't like half measures; **mezz'ora = mezzora**

b (*medio*): **di mezza età** middle-aged; **un soprabito di mezza stagione** a spring (*o* autumn) coat.

2 AVV half-; **mezzo pieno/vuoto** *ecc* half-full/empty *ecc*; **mezzo morto** half-dead.

3 SM **a** (*metà*) half; **un chilo e mezzo** a kilo and a half, one and a half kilos; **è l'una e mezzo** it's half past one; **una volta e mezzo più grande** one and a half times bigger

b (*parte centrale*) middle; **nel mezzo della piazza** in the middle of the square; **la porta di mezzo** the middle door; **in mezzo a** in the middle of; (*folla*) in the midst of; **nel bel mezzo (di)** right in the middle (of)

c (*fraseologia*): **esserci di mezzo** (*ostacolo*) to be in the way; **quando ci sono di mezzo i numeri non ci capisco più niente** when numbers are involved I get completely lost; **non voglio andarci di mezzo** I don't want to suffer for it; **mettersi di mezzo** to interfere; **non mettermi in mezzo!** don't drag me into it!; **è meglio non porre tempo in mezzo** it'd be better not to delay; **togliere di mezzo** (*persona, cosa*) to get rid of; (*fam: uccidere*) to bump off; **levarsi** *o* **togliersi di mezzo** to get out of the way; **il giusto mezzo** the happy medium; **non c'è una via di mezzo** there's no middle course.

mezzobusto [meddzo'busto] SM (*pl* **mezzibusti**) **a** (*statua*)

bust; **a mezzobusto** (*ritratto, fotografia*) half-length **b**
(*scherz: giornalista televisivo*) talking-head.

mezzodì [meddzo'di] SM INV midday, noon.

mezzofondista, i, e [meddzofon'dista] SM/F middle-
distance runner.

mezzofondo [meddzo'fondo] SM middle-distance
running.

mezzogiorno [meddzo'dʒorno] SM **a** (*ora*) midday, noon;
a mezzogiorno at 12 (o'clock) *o* midday *o* noon; **a
mezzogiorno e mezzo** at half past twelve **b** (*Geog*)
south; **il mezzogiorno d'Italia** the South of Italy,
Southern Italy.

mezzoguanto [meddzo'gwanto] SM (*pl* **mezziguanti**)
fingerless glove.

mezzomarinaro [meddzomari'naro] SM (*pl* **mezzimari-
nari**) (*Naut*) boathook.

mezzora, mezz'ora [med'dzora] SF half an hour, half-
hour; **ti aspetterò una mezzora** I'll wait for you for half
an hour; **la prima mezzora** the first half-hour.

mezzosangue [meddzo'sangwe] SM/F INV (*cavallo*) crossbreed.

mezzoservizio [meddzoser'vittsjo] SM INV: **lavorare a
mezzoservizio** to do part-time cleaning *o* domestic
work.

mezzosoprano [meddzoso'prano] SM (*pl* **mezzisoprani**)
mezzo-soprano.

mezzuccio, ci [med'dzuttʃo] SM mean trick.

MI SIGLA = *Milano*.

mi[1] [mi] PRON PERS (dav lo, la, li, le, ne diventa **me**) **a** (*ogg
diretto*) me; **mi aiuti?** will you help me?
b (*complemento di termine*) (to) me; **mi dai il libro?** will
you give me the book?; **mi compri il libro?** will you buy
me the book?, will you buy the book for me?; **me ne ha
parlato** he spoke to me about it, he told me about it
c (*riflessivo*) myself; **mi servo da solo** I'll help myself; **mi
sono pettinato** I combed my hair.

mi[2] [mi] SM INV (*Mus*) E; (: *solfeggiando la scala*) mi.

mia ['mia] vedi **mio**.

miagolare [mjago'lare] VI (*aus* **avere**) to miaow, mew.

miagolio, lii [mjago'lio] SM miaowing, mewing.

miao ['mjao] ESCL, SM INV miaow.

miasma, i [mi'azma] SM miasma.

Mib [mib] SIGLA M, AGG (= *Milano indice Borsa*) Milan Stock
Exchange; **l'indice Mib** the Milan (Stock Exchange)
index.

Mibtel [mibtel] SIGLA M: **indice telematico borsa Milano**
Milan Stock Exchange Index.

mica[1] ['mika] AVV: **non... mica** (*fam*) not ...at all; **non ci
credo mica!** I don't believe that for a minute!; **non sarà
mica partito?** he wouldn't have left, would he?; **non
sono mica stanco** I'm not at all tired; **mica male!** not bad
(at all)!

mica[2] ['mika] SF (*minerale*) mica.

miccia, ce ['mittʃa] SF fuse.

micidiale [mitʃi'djale] AGG (*letale*) fatal, deadly; (*fig:
musica*) excruciating; (: *liquore*) deadly; **fa un caldo
micidiale oggi** the heat's killing today.

micio, cia, ci, cie ['mitʃo] SM/F (*fam*) pussy (cat).

micologo, a, gi, ghe [mi'kɔlogo] SM/F: **esperto micologo**
mycologist (*employed to check wild mushrooms before
they are sold*).

micosi [mi'kɔzi] SF INV mycosis.

micro... ['mikro] PREF micro ... .

microbiologia [mikrobiolo'dʒia] SF microbiology.

microbo ['mikrobo] SM microbe.

microcircuito [mikrotʃir'kuito] SM microcircuit.

microclima, i [mikro'klima] SM microclimate.

microcosmo [mikro'kɔzmo] SM microcosm.

microcriminalità [mikrokriminali'ta] SF INV petty crime.

microelettronica [mikroelet'trɔnika] SF microelectronics
sg.

microfiche [mikro'fiʃ] SF INV microfiche.

microfilm [mikro'film] SM INV microfilm.

microfono [mi'krɔfono] SM microphone.

microfotografia [mikrofotogra'fia] SF (*Fot: tecnica*)
micrography; (: *singola immagine*) micrograph.

microinformatica [mikroinfor'matika] SF microcom-
puting.

micrometrico, a, ci, che [mikro'mɛtriko] AGG micro-
metric; **vite micrometrica** micrometer screw.

micrometro [mi'krɔmetro] SM micrometer.

micron ['mikron] SM INV micron.

microonda [mikro'onda] SF microwave; **forno a
microonde** microwave (oven).

microorganismo [mikroorga'nizmo] SM microorganism.

microprocessore [mikroprotʃes'sore] SM microproces-
sor.

microscopico, a, ci, che [mikros'kɔpiko] AGG micro-
scopic; **un microscopico bikini** (*scherz*) a micro-
scopic bikini.

microscopio, pi [mikros'kɔpjo] SM microscope
▶ **microscopio elettronico** electron microscope
▶ **microscopio ottico** light microscope.

microsecondo [mikrose'kondo] SM microsecond.

microsolco, chi [mikro'solko] SM (*solco*) microgroove;
(*disco a 33 giri*) long-playing record, LP.

microspia [mikros'pia] SF hidden microphone, bug (*fam*).

Mida ['mida] SM Midas; **il tocco di Mida** the Midas touch.

midollo [mi'dollo] SM (*pl f* **midolla**) (*Anat*) marrow; (*Bot*)
pith; **bagnarsi fino alle midolla** *o* **al midollo** (*fig*) to get
soaking wet *o* drenched ▶ **midollo allungato** medulla
oblungata ▶ **midollo osseo** bone marrow ▶ **midollo
spinale** spinal cord.

mie ['mie] vedi **mio**.

miei ['mjɛi] vedi **mio**.

miele ['mjɛle] SM honey; **color miele** honey-coloured.

mietere ['mjɛtere] VT (*Agr, fig*) to reap, harvest; **l'epidemia
ha mietuto molte vittime** the epidemic has claimed
many victims.

mietitrebbiatrice [mjetitrebbja'tritʃe] SF combine harvester.

mietitrice [mjeti'tritʃe] SF (*macchina*) harvester.

mietitura [mjeti'tura] SF (*raccolto*) harvest; (*lavoro*) harvesting; (*tempo*) harvest time.

migliaio [miʎ'ʎajo] SM (*pl f* **migliaia**) thousand; **un migliaio
(di)** about a thousand, a thousand or so; **a migliaia** by
the thousand, in thousands; **poche migliaia di persone**
a few thousand people; **centinaia di migliaia di persone**
hundreds of thousands of people.

migliarino [miʎʎa'rino] SM (*Zool*): **migliarino di palude**
reed bunting.

miglio[1] ['miʎʎo] SM (*pl f* **miglia**) mile; **si vede lontano un
miglio che è falso** you can see a mile off that it's a fake
▶ **miglio inglese** *o* **terrestre** (= *1609,33 metri*) mile
▶ **miglio marino** *o* **nautico** (= *1852,28 metri*) nautical
mile.

miglio[2] ['miʎʎo] SM (*Bot*) millet.

miglioramento [miʎʎora'mento] SM improvement.

migliorare [miʎʎo'rare] [1] VT, VI (*aus* **essere**; *riferito a persone, anche* **avere**) to improve.
[2] **migliorarsi** VR to improve o.s.

migliore [miʎ'ʎore] (*comp, superl di* **buono**) [1] AGG (*comparativo*) better; (*superlativo*) best; **migliore (di)** better (than); **molto migliore** much better; **rendere migliore** to make better, improve; **i migliori auguri** best wishes; **la cosa migliore sarebbe partire subito** the best thing would be to leave immediately.
[2] SM/F: **il/la migliore** (*comparativo*) the better (one); (*superlativo*) the best (one); **il migliore dei due** the better of the two; **il migliore della classe** the best in the class; **nella migliore delle ipotesi** at best; **vinca il migliore** let the best man/woman win.

miglioria [miʎʎo'ria] SF improvement; **fare** *o* **apportare delle migliorie** to make *o* carry out improvements.

migliorista, i, e [miʎʎo'rista] (*Pol*) [1] AGG (*corrente, candidato, posizione*) *connected with the gradualist wing of the PDS (former communist party).*
[2] SM/F PDS gradualist.

mignatta [miɲ'ɲatta] SF (*Zool*) leech.

mignolo ['miɲɲolo] SM (*di mano*) little finger, pinkie (*fam*); (*di piede*) little toe.

mignon [mi'ɲõ] AGG INV: **bottiglia mignon** miniature (bottle); **pasticceria mignon** petit fours *pl.*

migrare [mi'grare] VI (*aus* **essere**) to migrate.

migratore, trice [migra'tore] [1] AGG migratory.
[2] SM/F migrant.

migratorio, ria, ri, rie [migra'tɔrjo] AGG migratory; **movimento migratorio** migration.

migrazione [migrat'tsjone] SF migration.

mila ['mila] (in combinazione con **due, tre** ecc); *vedi* **mille**.

milanese [mila'nese] [1] AGG Milanese; **cotoletta alla milanese** Wiener schnitzel; **risotto alla milanese** *risotto with saffron.*
[2] SM/F inhabitant *o* native of Milan; **i milanesi** the Milanese.

Milano [mi'lano] SF Milan.

miliardario, ria, ri, rie [miljar'darjo] AGG, SM/F ≈ millionaire, ≈ billionaire (*Am*).

miliardo [mi'ljardo] SM thousand million (*Brit*), billion (*Am*); **un miliardo di lire** a thousand million lire.

miliare [mi'ljare] AGG: **pietra miliare** (*anche fig*) milestone.

milieu [mi'ljø] SM INV milieu.

milionario, ria, ri, rie [miljo'narjo] AGG, SM/F millionaire.

milione [mi'ljone] SM million; **un milione di lire** a million lire.

milionesimo, a [miljo'nɛzimo] AGG, SM/F, SM millionth.

militante [mili'tante] AGG, SM/F militant.

militanza [mili'tantsa] SF militancy.

militare[1] [mili'tare] VI (*aus* **avere**): **militare in** (*partito, gruppo*) to be active in; (*marina, aeronautica*) to serve in; **militare in una squadra** (*Sport*) to play for/in a team; **una squadra che milita in serie A** ≈ a team (which plays) in the Premier division.

militare[2] [mili'tare] [1] AGG army *attr*, military; **governo militare** military government.
[2] SM serviceman; **fare il militare** to do one's military service ► **militare di carriera** regular (soldier).

militaresco, a, schi, sche [milita'resko] AGG (*portamento*) military *attr*, soldierly.

militarismo [milita'rizmo] SM militarism.

militarista [milita'rista] [1] AGG militaristic.

[2] SM/F militarist.

militarizzare [militarid'dzare] VT to militarize.

militarmente [militar'mente] AVV (*invadere*) by force of arms; (*educare*) in a military fashion.

militassolto, a [militas'sɔlto] (*in annunci economici*) [1] AGG having done National Service.
[2] SM person who has done National Service.

milite ['milite] SM (*soldato*) soldier; **il Milite ignoto** the Unknown Soldier *o* Warrior.

militesente [milite'zɛnte] [1] AGG exempt from National Service.
[2] SM person who is exempt from National Service.

milizia [mi'littsja] SF militia.

miliziano [milit'tsjano] SM militiaman.

millantare [millan'tare] VT to boast (of), brag (about).

millantato [millan'tato] AGG: **millantato credito** (*Dir*) *fraudulent claim to influence with public officials, made so as to obtain a bribe.*

millantatore, trice [millanta'tore] SM/F boaster.

millanteria [millante'ria] SF (*qualità*) boastfulness; **queste sono millanterie** that's just boasting.

mille ['mille] [1] AGG INV a *o* one thousand; **duemila** two thousand; **tremila** three thousand; **milleuno** a *o* one thousand and one; **mille grazie** thanks a lot; **a mille (a mille)** in their thousands.
[2] SM INV a *o* one thousand; **nel mille d.C.** in one thousand A.D.

millefoglie [mille'fɔʎʎe] SM INV (*Culin*) millefeuille.

millenario, ria, ri, rie [mille'narjo] [1] AGG millennial; (*fig: molto vecchio*) ancient; (: *dominazione*) age-old.
[2] SM (*anniversario*) thousandth anniversary, millennium.

millennio, ni [mil'lɛnnjo] SM millennium.

millepiedi [mille'pjɛdi] SM INV millipede.

millerighe [mille'rige] AGG INV needlecord.

millesimo, a [mil'lɛzimo] AGG, SM thousandth.

milleusi [mille'uzi] AGG INV all-purpose.

milli... ['milli] PREF milli... .

millibar [milli'bar] SM INV millibar.

milligrammo [milli'grammo] SM milligram(me).

millilitro [mil'lilitro] SM millilitre (*Brit*), milliliter (*Am*).

millimetro [mil'limetro] SM millimetre (*Brit*), millimeter (*Am*).

milza ['miltsa] SF (*Anat*) spleen.

mimare [mi'mare] VT (*Teatro*) to mime; (*fig: imitare*) to mimic, take off.

mimetico, a, ci, che [mi'mɛtiko] AGG (*arte*) mimetic; **tuta mimetica** (*Mil*) camouflage.

mimetismo [mime'tizmo] SM (*Bio, Mil*) camouflage.

mimetizzare [mimetid'dzare] [1] VT to camouflage.
[2] **mimetizzarsi** VR to camouflage o.s.

mimica ['mimika] SF **a** (*arte*) mime **b** (*insieme di gesti*) gestures *pl*; **mimica facciale** facial expressions.

mimico, a, ci, che ['mimiko] AGG mime *attr*; (*linguaggio*) sign *attr*; **arte mimica** mime.

mimo ['mimo] SM **a** (*attore, spettacolo*) mime **b** (*Zool*) mocking bird.

mimosa [mi'mosa] SF mimosa.

min. ABBR (= *minuto, minimo*) min.

mina ['mina] SF **a** (*ordigno*) mine ► **mina terrestre** landmine ► **mina vagante** time bomb **b** (*di matita*) lead.

minaccia, ce [mi'nattʃa] SF threat; **è una grave minaccia per la nazione** it is a serious threat to the nation; **in**

segno di minaccia as a threat; sotto la minaccia di under threat of; avere una minaccia di aborto to have a threatened miscarriage.

minacciare [minat'tʃare] VT to threaten; minacciare qn di morte to threaten sb with death, threaten to kill sb; minacciare qn con una pistola to threaten sb with a gun; lo sciopero minaccia di durare the strike looks set to continue; ha minacciato di andarsene he threatened to leave; minaccia di piovere it looks like rain; minaccia tempesta there's a storm brewing.

minacciosamente [minattʃosa'mente] AVV threateningly, menacingly.

minaccioso, a [minat'tʃoso] AGG threatening, menacing.

minare [mi'nare] VT (ponte) to mine; (fig: salute, reputazione) to undermine; questo campo è minato this field has been mined; ha la salute minata dall'alcol his health has been ruined by drink.

minareto [mina'reto] SM minaret.

minatore [mina'tore] SM miner.

minatorio, ria, ri, rie [mina'tɔrjo] AGG threatening.

minchione, a [min'kjone] (fam) [1] AGG idiotic.
[2] SM/F idiot.

minchioneria [minkjone'ria] SF (fam: qualità) stupidity; (: azione) foolish thing.

minerale [mine'rale] [1] AGG mineral.
[2] SM mineral; minerale di ferro iron ore.
[3] SF (anche: acqua minerale) mineral water.

mineralogia [mineralo'dʒia] SF mineralogy.

mineralogico, a, ci, che [minera'lɔdʒiko] AGG mineralogical.

mineralogista, i, e [mineralo'dʒista] SM/F mineralogist.

minerario, ria, ri, rie [mine'rarjo] AGG (delle miniere) mining attr; (dei minerali) ore attr.

Minerva [mi'nɛrva] SF Minerva.

minerva° [mi'nɛrva] SMPL safety matches.

minestra [mi'nɛstra] SF soup; "minestre" (sul menu) "first courses"; è sempre la solita minestra (fig) it's always the same old story; o mangi questa minestra o salti dalla finestra (Proverbio) take it or leave it ▶ minestra in brodo noodle soup ▶ minestra di verdura vegetable soup.

minestrina [mines'trina] SF broth.

minestrone [mines'trone] SM (Culin) minestrone (thick vegetable and pasta soup); (fig) mix-up, confusion.

mingherlino, a [minger'lino] AGG skinny.

mini ['mini] [1] AGG INV mini.
[2] SF INV (Moda) miniskirt, mini.

mini... ['mini] PREF mini... .

miniabito [mini'abito] SM mini-dress.

miniappartamento [miniapparta'mento] SM studio flat.

miniare [mi'njare] VT to paint in miniature.

miniatura [minja'tura] SF (dipinto) miniature; (arte, genere) miniature painting; in miniatura in miniature; una città/un giardino in miniatura a model town/garden.

miniaturista, i, e [minjatu'rista] SM/F (pittore) miniaturist.

miniaturizzare [minjaturid'dzare] VT to miniaturize.

miniaturizzato, a [minjaturid'dzato] AGG (Elettr) miniaturized; (molto piccolo) minuscule.

miniaturizzazione [minjaturiddzat'tsjone] SF miniaturization.

minibus ['minibus] SM INV minibus.

minidisco, chi [mini'disko] SM (Inform) diskette.

minielaboratore [minielabora'tore] SM minicomputer.

miniera [mi'njɛra] SF mine; una miniera di informazioni (fig) a mine of information ▶ miniera di carbone (gen) coalmine; (impresa) colliery (Brit), coalmine ▶ miniera a cielo aperto open-cast mine ▶ miniera sotterranea pit, mine.

minigolf [mini'gɔlf] SM INV (gioco) minigolf; (campo da gioco) minigolf course.

minigonna [mini'gonna] SF miniskirt.

minima ['minima] SF (Meteor) minimum temperature; (Med) minimum blood-pressure level.

minimalismo [minima'lizmo] SM (Arte, Letterat) minimalism.

minimalista, i, e [minima'lista] AGG, SM/F (Arte, Letteratura) minimalist.

minimizzare [minimid'dzare] VT to minimize.

minimo, a ['minimo] [1] AGG (il più piccolo) least, slightest; (piccolissimo) very small, slight; (il più basso) lowest, minimum; non c'è la minima differenza there isn't the slightest difference; la differenza è minima the difference is minimal o very small o slight; il prezzo minimo è 10.000 lire the lowest o minimum price is 10,000 lire; gli effetti collaterali della medicina sono minimi the drug's side effects are minimal; non ne ho la minima idea I haven't the slightest idea; ridurre una frazione ai minimi termini (Mat) to reduce a fraction to its lowest terms; queste scarpe sono ridotte ai minimi termini (fig: molto consumate) these shoes are completely worn out. [2] SM a minimum; è il minimo che tu possa fare it's the least you can do; non ha un minimo di comprensione he is totally lacking in understanding; gli hanno dato il minimo della pena they gave him the minimum sentence; come minimo avrebbe potuto dirmelo he could at least have told me; il minimo indispensabile the bare minimum
b (Aut): girare al minimo to idle; questo motore ha il minimo basso this engine has a low idling speed.

minio ['minjo] SM red lead.

ministeriale [ministe'rjale] AGG (del ministero) ministerial; (del governo) government attr.

ministero [minis'tɛro] SM a (Pol) ministry, department (spec Am) ▶ ministero delle Finanze Ministry of Finance, ≈ Treasury ▶ ministero degli Interni Ministry of the Interior, ≈ Home Office (Brit), ≈ Department of the Interior (Am) ▶ ministero della Pubblica Istruzione ≈ Department of Education and Science (Brit)
b (Dir): pubblico ministero State Prosecutor
c (Rel) ministry.

ministro [mi'nistro] SM a (Pol) minister, secretary (spec Am) ▶ ministro delle Finanze Minister of Finance, ≈ Chancellor of the Exchequer (Brit) ▶ ministro degli Interni Minister of the Interior, ≈ Home Secretary (Brit), ≈ Secretary of the Interior (Am) b (Rel) minister.

minoranza [mino'rantsa] SF (gen) minority; (gruppo) minority (group); essere in minoranza to be in the minority.

minorato, a [mino'rato] [1] AGG handicapped.
[2] SM/F physically (o mentally) handicapped person.

minorazione [minorat'tsjone] SF handicap.

Minorca [mi'nɔrka] SF Minorca.

minore [mi'nore] [1] AGG (comp di piccolo) a less; (più piccolo) smaller; (più breve) shorter; (meno grave) lesser; (numero) lower; le vendite sono state minori del previsto sales were less o lower than expected; questo è il male minore this is the lesser evil; vocabolario in edizione

minore shorter *o* concise edition of a dictionary; **in misura minore** to a lesser extent

b (*meno importante*) less important; (*inferiore*) lower, inferior; (*di poco rilievo*) minor; **opere minori** minor works; **di minor pregio** of inferior quality

c (*più giovane*) younger; **il fratello minore** the younger brother

d (*Mus*) minor; **do minore** C minor.

2 AGG (*superl di* **piccolo**) (*vedi 1a, b, c*) least; smallest; shortest; lowest; least important; youngest.

3 SM/F **a** (*d'età: tra due*) younger; (: *tra più di due*) youngest

b (*minorenne*) minor, person under age; **minore non accompagnato** unaccompanied minor; **spettacolo vietato ai minori** no admittance to persons under the age of 18 (*to film, show ecc*).

minorenne [mino'rɛnne] **1** AGG under age.

2 SM/F minor, person under age; **tribunale dei minorenni** (*Dir*) juvenile court.

minorile [mino'rile] AGG juvenile; **carcere minorile** young offenders' institution; **delinquenza minorile** juvenile delinquency.

minoritario, ria, ri, rie [minori'tarjo] AGG minority *attr.*

Minosse [mi'nɔsse] SM Minos.

Minotauro [mino'tauro] SM Minotaur.

minuetto [minu'etto] SM (*Mus*) minuet.

minuscola [mi'nuskola] SF (*anche:* **lettera minuscola**) small letter.

minuscolo, a [mi'nuskolo] **1** AGG **a** (*piccolissimo*) tiny, minuscule, minute **b** (*lettera*) small.

2 SM small letters *pl*; (*Tip*) lower case; **scrivere tutto (in) minuscolo** to write everything in small letters.

minuta [mi'nuta] SF rough copy, draft.

minutamente [minuta'mente] AVV (*tritato*) finely; (*intarsiato, decorato*) delicately, finely; (*analizzato, discusso*) in minute detail.

minuto¹, a [mi'nuto] AGG tiny, minute; (*pioggia*) fine; (*corporatura*) delicate, fine; (*lavoro, descrizione*) detailed; **spese minute** minor expenses; **al minuto** (*Comm*) retail; **comprare al minuto** to buy at retail prices, buy retail.

minuto² [mi'nuto] SM (*gen*) minute; (*momento*) moment, minute; **all'ultimo minuto** at the (very) last minute *o* moment; **a minuti** OR **da un minuto all'altro** any second *o* minute now; **in un minuto** in one minute; (*fig: rapidamente*) in a flash; **tra pochi minuti** in a few minutes, in a few minutes' time; **avere i minuti contati** to have very little time; **spaccare il minuto** (*fig: persona*) to be (always) on the dot; (: *orologio*) to be accurate to a split second.

minuzia [mi'nuttsja] SF (*cura*) meticulousness; (*particolare*) detail; **perdersi in minuzie** to waste one's time with trifling details.

minuziosamente [minuttsjosa'mente] AVV (*vedi agg*) meticulously; in minute detail.

minuziosità [minuttsjosi'ta] SF meticulousness.

minuzioso, a [minut'tsjoso] AGG (*persona*) meticulous; (*descrizione*) detailed; (*esame*) minute.

mio, a ['mio] (*pl* **miei, mie**) **1** AGG POSS: **il mio** OR **la mia** *ecc* my; **il mio cane** my dog; **mia madre** my mother; **un mio amico** a friend of mine; **è colpa mia** it's my fault; **è casa mia** OR **è la mia casa** it's my house; **per amor mio** for my sake.

2 PRON POSS: **il mio** OR **la mia** *ecc* mine, my own; **la sua**

barca è più lunga della mia his boat is longer than mine; **è questo il mio?** is this mine?; **il mio è stato solo un errore** it was simply an error on my part.

3 PRON POSS M **a** : **ho speso del mio** I spent my own money; **vivo del mio** I live on my own income

b : **i miei** (*genitori, famiglia*) my family; (*amici*) my side; **lui è dei miei** he is on my side.

4 PRON POSS F: **la mia** (*opinione*) my view; **è dalla mia** she is on my side; **sono riuscita a dire la mia** I managed to say my piece; **anch'io ho avuto le mie** (*disavventure*) I've had my problems too; **ne ho fatta una della mie!** (*sciocchezze*) I've done it again!; **cerco di stare sulle mie** I try to keep myself to myself.

miope ['miope] **1** AGG short-sighted, myopic (*frm*); (*fig*) short-sighted.

2 SM/F myopic *o* short-sighted person.

miopia [mio'pia] SF short-sightedness, myopia (*frm*); (*fig*) short-sightedness.

mira ['mira] SF (*anche fig*) aim; **prendere la mira** to take aim; **prendere di mira qn** (*fig*) to pick on sb; **avere una buona/cattiva mira** to be a good/bad shot.

mirabile [mi'rabile] AGG admirable, wonderful.

mirabilmente [mirabil'mente] AVV admirably, wonderfully.

mirabolante [mirabo'lante] AGG astonishing, amazing.

miracolare [mirako'lare] VT to cure *o* heal miraculously.

miracolato, a [mirako'lato] SM/F miraculously-cured person.

miracolo [mi'rakolo] SM (*anche fig*) miracle; (*persona*) wonder, prodigy; **miracolo economico** economic miracle; **fare miracoli** to perform *o* do miracles; (*fig*) to work wonders; **sapere vita, morte e miracoli di qn** to know everything there is to know about sb; **per miracolo** by a miracle.

miracolosamente [mirakolosa'mente] AVV miraculously.

miracoloso, a [mirako'loso] **1** AGG miraculous, prodigious; **non c'è niente di miracoloso** here's nothing extraordinary about it.

2 SM, SOLO SG: **la sua guarigione ha del miracoloso** his recovery is well nigh miraculous.

miraggio, gi [mi'raddʒo] SM (*anche fig*) mirage.

mirare [mi'rare] **1** VI (*aus* **avere**): **mirare (a)** (*anche fig*) to aim (at); **ha sempre mirato a diventare presidente** it has always been his aim to become president; **mirare al potere** to aspire to power.

2 **mirarsi** VR: **mirarsi allo specchio** to look at o.s. in the mirror.

miriade [mi'riade] SF myriad, host.

mirino [mi'rino] SM (*di arma da fuoco, strumento ottico*) sight; (*Fot*) viewfinder, viewer; **essere nel mirino della Mafia** (*fig*) to be a target of the Mafia.

mirra ['mirra] SF myrrh.

mirtillo [mir'tillo] SM bilberry (*Brit*), blueberry (*Am*).

mirto ['mirto] SM myrtle.

misantropia [mizantro'pia] SF misanthropy.

misantropico, a, ci, che [mizan'tropiko] AGG misanthropic.

misantropo, a [mi'zantropo] **1** AGG misanthropic.

2 SM/F misanthrope, misanthropist.

miscela [miʃ'ʃɛla] SF (*gen*) mixture; (*di caffè, tè, tabacco*) blend; (*per motorino*) petrol and oil mixture; **miscela pronta** (*per dolci*) cake mix ▶**miscela carburante** mixture.

miscelare [miʃʃe'lare] VT (*gen*) to mix; (*caffè, tè, tabacco*)

to blend.

miscelatore, trice [miʃʃela'tore] (*vedi vt*) 1 AGG mixing; blending.

2 SM (*macchinario, operaio*) mixer; blender; (*dell'acqua*) mixer tap.

miscellanea [miʃʃel'lanea] SF miscellany.

miscellaneo, a [miʃʃel'laneo] AGG miscellaneous.

mischia ['miskja] SF (*rissa, zuffa*) scuffle, brawl; (*Rugby*) scrum, scrummage; **stare al di fuori della mischia** (*fig*) to stay out of the fray; **mischia aperta/chiusa** (*Rugby*) loose/set scrum.

mischiare [mis'kjare] 1 VT (*gen*) to mix; (*caffè, tè*) to blend; (*carte*) to shuffle.

2 **mischiarsi** VIP (*liquidi ecc*) to mix, blend.

misconoscere [misko'noʃʃere] VT IRREG (*qualità, coraggio ecc*) to fail to appreciate; **non puoi misconoscere l'arte moderna solo perché non ti piace Picasso** you can't ignore modern art just because you don't like Picasso.

misconosciuto, a [miskonoʃ'ʃuto] 1 PP di **misconoscere**.

2 AGG disregarded, ignored.

miscredente [miskre'dɛnte] 1 SM/F (*Rel*) heretic; (: *indifferente*) unbeliever.

2 AGG (*vedi sm/f*) heretical; unbelieving.

miscuglio, gli [mis'kuʎʎo] SM (*gen*) mixture; (*accozzaglia*) jumble, hotchpotch.

mise *ecc* VB vedi **mettere**.

miserabile [mize'rabile] 1 AGG **a** (*pietoso: vita, condizioni*) miserable, wretched, pitiful; (: *persona*) pitiful, wretched

b (*povero*) poor, destitute, poverty-stricken; **vivere in condizioni miserabili** to live in abject poverty; **una somma miserabile** a miserable *o* paltry sum of money **c** (*spregevole: azione, persona*) mean, wretched.

2 SM/F (*persona spregevole*) wretch.

miseramente [mizera'mente] AVV (*vivere*) in wretched poverty; (*fallire*) miserably; **essere ridotto miseramente** (*persona, oggetto*) to be in a wretched *o* pitiful state; **è pagato miseramente** he earns a pittance; **una casa miseramente arredata** a poorly furnished house.

miserando, a [mize'rando] AGG (*letter*) pitiful.

miserevole [mize'revole] AGG pitiful, wretched, miserable.

miseria [mi'zɛrja] SF **a** (*povertà*) (extreme) poverty, destitution; **cadere in miseria** to become destitute; **ridursi in miseria** to be reduced to poverty; **vivere nella miseria più nera** to live in dire poverty; **piangere miseria** to plead poverty; **porca miseria!** (*fam*) (bloody) hell!

b (*somma*): **comprare qc per una miseria** to buy sth for next to nothing *o* for a song; **costare una miseria** to cost next to nothing; **lo pagano una miseria** they pay him a pittance

c: **miserie** SFPL (*brutture*) misfortunes, troubles; **le miserie del mondo** the wretchedness of this world **d** (*Bot*) wandering Jew.

misericordia [mizeri'kɔrdja] SF mercy, pity; **avere misericordia di qn** to have pity on sb; **misericordia divina** Divine mercy; **invocare la misericordia di qn** to beg sb for mercy; **misericordia!** my goodness!

misericordiosamente [mizerikordjosa'mente] AVV mercifully.

misericordioso, a [mizerikor'djoso] AGG merciful.

misero, a ['mizero] AGG **a** (*pietoso: vita, condizioni*) miserable, wretched, pitiful; (: *persona*) pitiful, wretched; **fare una misera figura** to cut a poor figure

b (*povero*) poor, poverty-stricken; **una misera somma** a miserable *o* paltry sum

c (*spregevole, meschino*) mean, wretched; **ho preso un misero 22 all'esame** ≈ I didn't get a very good pass in the exam; **è un misero impiegatuccio** he's a miserable pen-pusher; **una misera scusa** a lame excuse.

misfatto [mis'fatto] SM (*cattiva azione*) misdeed; (*delitto*) crime.

misi *ecc* VB vedi **mettere**.

misoginia [mizodʒi'nia] SF misogyny.

misogino, a [mi'zɔdʒino] 1 AGG misogynous.

2 SM misogynist.

miss [mis] SF INV (*in concorso di bellezza*) beauty queen; **Miss Mondo** Miss World.

missaggio, gi [mis'saddʒo] SM (*Cine, TV, Mus*) mixing.

missile ['missile] SM missile ▶**missile cruise** *o* **da crociera** cruise missile ▶**missile teleguidato** guided missile ▶**missile terra-aria** surface-to-air missile.

missilistica [missi'listika] SF rocketry.

missilistico, a, ci, che [missi'listiko] AGG missile *attr*.

missino, a [mis'sino] (*Pol*) 1 AGG of/belonging to the Movimento Sociale Italiano (*Italian extreme right-wing party*).

2 SM/F member (*o* supporter) of Movimento Sociale Italiano.

missionario, ria, ri, rie [missjo'narjo] AGG, SM/F missionary.

missione [mis'sjone] SF mission; **essere/partire in missione** to be/leave on a mission; **missione compiuta** mission accomplished.

Mississippi [missis'sippi] SM: **il Mississippi** the Mississippi.

missiva [mis'siva] SF (*spec scherz*) missive.

mister ['mistə] SM INV **a** (*Calcio*) trainer **b** (*in concorso di bellezza*): **Mister Universo** Mr Universe; **mister muscolo** Mr Muscle.

misteriosamente [misterjosa'mente] AVV mysteriously.

misterioso, a [miste'rjoso] 1 AGG mysterious.

2 SM/F: **fare il misterioso** to act mysterious.

mistero [mis'tɛro] SM mystery; **fare mistero di qc** to make a mystery out of sth; **non se ne fa un mistero** there's no mystery about it; **quanti misteri!** why all the mystery?

mistica ['mistika] SF mysticism.

misticismo [misti'tʃizmo] SM mysticism.

mistico, a, ci, che ['mistiko] 1 AGG mystic(al).

2 SM mystic.

mistificare [mistifi'kare] VT **a** (*dato, fatti*) to falsify **b** (*ingannare*) to fool, take in.

mistificatore, trice [mistifika'tore] SM/F: **è un mistificatore** he is distorting the facts.

mistificatorio, ria, ri, rie [mistifika'tɔrjo] AGG (*intervento, comportamento*) intentionally misleading.

mistificazione [mistifikat'tsjone] SF (*di fatti*) falsification.

misto, a ['misto] 1 AGG (*tutti i sensi*) mixed; (*classe*) mixed, coeducational; **misto a qc** mixed with sth; **un tessuto in misto lino** a linen mix; **cane di razza mista** a mixed breed of dog, crossbreed dog.

2 SM mixture.

mistral [mis'tral] SM mistral.

mistura [mis'tura] SF (*miscuglio*) mixture.

misura [mi'zura] SF **a** (*Mat*) measure; **unità di misura** unit of measurement ▶**misura di capacità** unit of capacity

▶**misura di lunghezza** unit of length
b (*dimensione*) measurement; (*taglia*) size; **prendere le misure a qn** to take sb's measurements, measure sb; **prendere le misure di qc** to measure sth; **di misura grande/piccola** (*scarpe, abito*) in a large/small size; **(fatto) su misura** made to measure; **a misura d'uomo** on a human scale; **l'episodio dà la misura del livello di corruzione raggiunto** the affair gives an indication of the prevailing level of corruption
c (*proporzione*): **in misura di** in accordance with, according to; **i prezzi aumenteranno in misura del 5%** prices will increase by 5%
d (*provvedimento*) measure, step; **ho preso le mie misure** I've taken the necessary steps; **mezze misure** (*fig*) half measures ▶**misure di prevenzione** precautionary measures ▶**misure di sicurezza** safety measures
e (*Mus*) time; (: *gruppo di note*) bar
f (*Poesia*) measure, metre
g (*fraseologia*): **in ugual misura** equally, in the same way; **non ha il senso della misura** he doesn't know when to stop; **passare la misura** to overstep the mark, go too far; **bere senza misura** to drink to excess; **oltre misura** beyond measure, excessively; **vincere di stretta misura** to win by a narrow margin.

misurare [mizu'rare] ⓵ VT **a** (*gen*) to measure; (*vista, udito*) to test; (*valore*) to estimate; (*capacità*) to judge; (*terreno*) to survey; **misurare a occhio** to measure roughly, give a rough estimate; **misurare a passi una stanza** to pace out a room
b (*fig: limitare: spese*) to limit; **misurare le parole** to weigh one's words
c (*provare*): **misurare o misurarsi qc** (*abito, scarpe, cappotto*) to try sth on.
⓶ VI (*aus* avere) to measure; **quanto misura questa stanza?** how big is this room?, what are the measurements of this room?.
⓷ **misurarsi** VR **a** (*contenersi, regolarsi*): **misurarsi nel bere** to control one's drinking
b (*provare le proprie forze*): **misurarsi con qn** to compete with sb, pit o.s. against sb.

misuratezza [mizura'tettsa] SF moderation.
misurato, a [mizu'rato] AGG (*ponderato*) measured; (*prudente*) cautious; (*moderato*) moderate.
misuratore [mizura'tore] SM **a** (*strumento*) gauge **b** (*persona: di terreno*) surveyor.
misurazione [mizurat'tsjone] SF measuring, measurement; (*di terreno*) surveying.
misurino [mizu'rino] SM (*recipiente*) measuring cup.
mite ['mite] AGG (*tempo, persona*) mild; (*condanna*) lenient; (*animale*) meek.
mitezza [mi'tettsa] SF (*vedi agg*) mildness; leniency; meekness.
mitico, a, ci, che ['mitiko] AGG mythical; (*leggendario*) legendary.
mitigare [miti'gare] ⓵ VT (*gen*) to mitigate, lessen; (*dolore*) to soothe, relieve; (*sapore*) to sweeten.
⓶ **mitigarsi** VIP (*dolore*) to lessen; (*odio*) to subside; (*clima*) to become milder.
mitilo [mi'tilo] SM mussel.
mitizzare [mitid'dzare] VT: **mitizzare qn/qc** to mythicize sb/sth, turn sb/sth into a myth.
mitizzazione [mitiddzat'tsjone] SF mythicization.
mito ['mito] SM myth; **far crollare un mito** to explode a

myth.
mitologia, gie [mitolo'dʒia] SF mythology.
mitologico, a, ci, che [mito'lɔdʒiko] AGG mythological.
mitomane [mi'tɔmane] SM/F mythomaniac.
mitomania [mitoma'nia] SF mythomania.
mitosi [mi'tɔzi] SF INV (*Bio*) mitosis.
mitra[1] ['mitra] SM INV (*arma*) sub-machine gun.
mitra[2] ['mitra] SF (*Rel*) mitre (*Brit*), miter (*Am*).
mitraglia [mi'traʎʎa] SF **a** (*tipo di munizione*) grapeshot **b** (*arma*) machine gun.
mitragliare [mitraʎ'ʎare] VT to machine-gun; **mitragliare qn di domande** (*fig*) to fire questions at sb, bombard sb with questions.
mitragliatore, trice [mitraʎʎa'tore] AGG: **fucile mitragliatore** sub-machine gun.
mitragliatrice [mitraʎʎa'tritʃe] SF machine gun.
mitragliere [mitraʎ'ʎɛre] SM machine-gunner.
mitrale [mi'trale] AGG (*Anat*): **valvola mitrale** mitral valve.
mitralico, a, ci, che [mi'traliko] AGG (*Anat*) mitral.
mitteleuropeo, a [mitteleuro'pɛo] AGG Central European.
mittente [mit'tɛnte] SM/F sender.
mixer ['miksə] SM INV (*per cocktail, Cine, TV*) mixer; (*frullatore*) blender.
ml ABBR (= *millilitro*) ml.
M.L.D. SIGLA M = **Movimento per la Liberazione della Donna**.
mm ABBR (= *millimetro*) mm.
M.M. ABBR (= *marina militare*) ≈ RN (*Brit*) (= *Royal Navy*).
MN SIGLA = *Mantova*.
M/N, m/n ABBR (= *motonave*) MV (= *motor vessel*).
mnemonico, a, ci, che [mne'mɔniko] AGG (*gen*) mnemonic; (*pegg: studio, apprendimento*) mechanical.
MO SIGLA = *Modena*.
mo' [mɔ]: **a mo' di** PREP as; **a mo' di esempio** by way of example.
M.O. ABBR = **Medio Oriente**.
mobile ['mɔbile] ⓵ AGG **a** (*gen*) mobile; (*parte di meccanismo*) moving; (*Rel: festa*) movable; **beni mobili** (*Fin*) movable property
b (*occhi*) darting.
⓶ SM **a** (*per arredamento*) piece of furniture; **mobili** furniture *sg*; **mobile componibile** unit
b (*Fin*): **mobili** SMPL movable property, movables.
⓷ SF: **la (squadra) mobile** the flying squad.
mobilia [mo'bilja] SF furniture.
mobiliare [mobi'ljare] AGG (*credito*) personal; (*beni*) movable.
mobiliere [mobi'ljɛre] SM (*fabbricante*) furniture-maker; (*commerciante*) furniture-seller.
mobilificio, ci [mobili'fitʃo] SM furniture factory.
mobilio [mo'biljo] SM furniture.
mobilità [mobili'ta] SF (*gen*) mobility; **mobilità del lavoro** o **della manodopera** labour mobility; **lista di mobilità** redeployment list.
mobilitare [mobili'tare] ⓵ VT (*Mil, fig*) to mobilize; **mobilitare l'opinione pubblica** to mobilize public opinion.
⓶ **mobilitarsi** VR: **mobilitarsi per fare qc** to go into action to do sth.
mobilitazione [mobilitat'tsjone] SF mobilization.
moca ['mɔka] ⓵ SM INV (*tipo di caffè*) mocha coffee.
⓶ SF INV (*macchina*) mocha coffee pot.
mocassino [mokas'sino] SM moccasin.
moccio, ci ['mottʃo] SM (*fam: muco*) snot.

moccioso, a [mot'tʃoso] SM/F (*bambino piccolo*) little kid; (*pegg*) snotty-nosed kid.

moccolo ['mɔkkolo] SM **a** (*di candela*) candle end; **reggere il moccolo** (*fig*) to play gooseberry (*Brit*) **b** (*fam: bestemmia*): **tirare o mandare un moccolo** to curse, swear **c** (*fam: moccio*) snot.

moda ['mɔda] SF (*gen*) fashion; (*pegg*) craze; **l'alta moda** haute couture; **la moda pronta** ready-to-wear (clothes); **essere alla moda** (*persona*) to be fashionable; **seguire la moda** to follow fashion; **essere di moda** [OR] **andare di moda** (*abbigliamento, acconciatura ecc*) to be fashionable, be in fashion; **veste sempre all'ultima moda** she's always dressed in the latest fashion; **è tornata di moda la mini** the mini is back in fashion; **non è più di moda** [OR] **è fuori moda** it's gone out of fashion, it's no longer fashionable; **è diventato una moda** it has become the fashion; **rivista di moda** fashion magazine.

modale [mo'dale] AGG (*Gramm, Mus*) modal.

modalità [modali'ta] SF INV (*procedura*) formality; **secondo le modalità previste dalla legge** in accordance with what is laid down by the law; **seguire attentamente le modalità d'uso** to follow the instructions carefully ▶ **modalità di pagamento** method of payment.

modanare [moda'nare] VT (*Archit, mobili*) to decorate with mouldings.

modanatura [modana'tura] SF (*Archit, di mobili*) moulding; (*Aut*) trim.

modella [mo'dɛlla] SF model.

modellamento [modella'mento] SM modelling, moulding.

modellare [model'lare] **1** VT (*creta, statua*) to model, mould; **modellare qc su qc** (*fig: opera, stile ecc*) to model sth on sth; **un vestito che modella la figura** a figure-hugging dress.
2 modellarsi VR: **modellarsi su qn/qc** to model o.s. on sb/sth, take sb/sth as a model.

modellino [model'lino] SM model.

modellismo [model'lizmo] SM model-making.

modellista, i, e [model'lista] SM/F (*di cappelli, abiti*) designer.

modello [mo'dɛllo] **1** SM **a** (*gen, fig*) model; (*stampo*) mould (*Brit*), mold (*Am*); **un modello in cera** a wax model; **ha comprato l'ultimo modello della FIAT** he's bought the latest Fiat; **prendere a modello** (*fig*) to take as one's model; **modello di serie/in scala** production/scale model
b (*Sartoria*) model, style; (: *forma*) style; **gli ultimi modelli di Armani** the latest Armani models o styles **c** (*Amm*) form.
2 AGG INV (*madre, marito, ospedale ecc*) model *attr*.

modem ['mɔdem] SM INV modem.

modenese [mode'nese] **1** AGG of o from Modena.
2 SM/F inhabitant o native of Modena.

moderare [mode'rare] **1** VT (*gen*) to moderate, curb; **moderare la velocità** to reduce speed; **moderare i termini** to weigh one's words.
2 moderarsi VR to restrain o.s.; **moderarsi nel mangiare/nelle spese** to control one's eating/one's spending.

moderatamente [modera'mente] AVV in moderation.

moderatezza [modera'tettsa] SF moderation.

moderato, a [mode'rato] **1** AGG **a** (*gen, Pol*) moderate **b** (*Mus*) moderato.
2 SM (*Pol*) moderate.

moderatore, trice [modera'tore] SM/F **a** (*in una discussione*) moderator; **fare da moderatore** to act as moderator **b** (*Fis*) moderator.

moderazione [moderat'tsjone] SF (*vedi vb*) moderation; restraint; **bere con moderazione** to drink in moderation; **usare moderazione** (*nel bere, nello spendere*) to be moderate.

modernamente [moderna'mente] AVV (*in modo moderno*) in a modern style; (*nei tempi moderni*) nowadays.

modernariato [moderna'rjato] SM *collecting of 20th century products and objets d'art.*

modernità [moderni'ta] SF INV modernity.

modernizzare [modernid'dzare] **1** VT to bring up to date, modernize.
2 modernizzarsi VR to get up to date.

modernizzazione [moderniddzat'tsjone] SF modernization.

moderno, a [mo'dɛrno] **1** AGG (*gen*) modern; **una mamma moderna** an up-to-date young mother, a modern mum.
2 SM **a** (*stile*) modern style **b** : **gli antichi e i moderni** (the) ancient and (the) modern.

modestamente [modesta'mente] AVV modestly; **modestamente, io lo faccio meglio** in all modesty, I'm better at it.

modestia [mo'dɛstja] SF modesty; **modestia a parte...** in all modesty..., though I say it myself...; **certo non pecca di modestia** modesty isn't one of his faults.

modesto, a [mo'dɛsto] AGG modest; **di modeste origini** from humble origins; **una casa modesta** a modest house o home.

modico, a, ci, che ['mɔdiko] AGG (*gen*) modest, moderate; **prezzi modici** low prices.

modifica, che [mo'difika] SF (*a motore*) adjustment; (*ad abito*) alteration; (*a piano*) modification; **fare una modifica** to make an adjustment (o alteration o modification); **subire delle modifiche** (*cambiamenti*) to undergo some modifications; (*miglioramenti*) to be revamped.

modificabile [modifi'kabile] AGG modifiable.

modificare [modifi'kare] **1** VT to modify, alter.
2 modificarsi VIP to alter, change.

modificazione [modifikat'tsjone] SF (*vedi modifica*) adjustment; alteration; modification.

modista [mo'dista] SF milliner.

modisteria [modiste'ria] SF (*laboratorio*) milliner's (shop).

modo ['mɔdo] SM **a** (*maniera*) way, manner; **allo stesso modo** in the same way; **in modo strano** strangely, in a strange way; **a o in questo/quel modo** (in) this/that way; **va fatto in questo modo** it should be done this way o like this; **in nessun modo** in no way; **fare a modo proprio** to do as one likes; **lo farò a modo mio** I'll do it my own way; **non è il modo di comportarsi** this is no way to behave; **a suo modo o a modo suo le vuole bene** he loves her in his own way; **ha un modo tutto suo di giocare a tennis** he has a highly idiosyncratic way of playing tennis; **un modo di dire** a turn of phrase, an expression; **per modo di dire** so to speak, as it were; **l'ha perdonata per modo di dire** he's forgiven her in a manner of speaking; **non mi piace il suo modo di fare** I don't like the way he goes about things; **non c'è modo di convincerlo** there's no way of persuading him; **c'è modo e modo di farlo** there's a right way and a wrong way of doing it; **aver modo di fare qc** to have the opportunity o chance of doing sth;

trovare il modo di fare qc to find a way *o* the means of doing sth; **ad** *o* **in ogni modo** anyway; **in qualche modo** somehow or other; **in un certo qual modo** in a way, in some ways; **in tutti i modi** at all costs; (*comunque sia*) anyway; (*in ogni caso*) in any case; **di** *o* **in modo che** so that; **lo sgriderò in modo che capisca che deve studiare** I'll give him a good telling-off, that way he'll understand he's got to study; **dovrò fare in modo che non mi vedano** I'll have to make sure they don't see me; **in modo da** so as to, in such a way as to; **in modo da non disturbarlo** so as not to disturb him; **fate in modo di tornare per le 5** try and be back for 5 o'clock

b (*misura, regola*): **oltre modo** extremely; **fare le cose a modo** to do things properly; **una persona a modo** a well-mannered person

c : **modi** SMPL (*maniere*) manners; **ha dei modi molto brutti** he has dreadful manners

d (*Gramm*) mood; **modo congiuntivo/indicativo** subjunctive/indicative mood

e (*Mus, Inform*) mode; **modo conversazionale** (*Inform*) conversation mode.

modulare[1] [modu'lare] VT (*voce, Fis*) to modulate.

modulare[2] [modu'lare] AGG modular.

modulatore [modula'tore] SM (*Fis*) modulator; **modulatore di frequenza/di luce** frequency/light modulator.

modulazione [modulat'tsjone] SF modulation ▶ **modulazione di frequenza** frequency modulation.

modulo ['mɔdulo] SM **a** (*modello*) form; **riempire un modulo** to fill in a form ▶ **modulo continuo** continuous stationery ▶ **modulo di domanda** application form ▶ **modulo d'iscrizione** enrolment form ▶ **modulo di versamento** deposit slip

b (*Archit, Aer*) module; **modulo di comando/lunare** command/lunar module

c (*Mat*) modulus.

modus vivendi ['mɔdus vi'vɛndi] SM INV modus vivendi.

moffetta [mof'fetta] SF skunk.

Mogadiscio [moga'diʃʃo] SF Mogadishu.

mogano ['mɔgano] SM mahogany.

mogio, a, gi, ge *o* **gie** ['mɔdʒo] AGG down in the dumps, dejected; **se n'è andato mogio mogio** he went off with his tail between his legs.

moglie ['moʎʎe] SF wife; **prendere moglie** to get married, take a wife; **tra moglie e marito non mettere il dito** (*Proverbio*) never interfere between husband and wife.

mohair [mɔ'ɛr] SM mohair.

moicano, a [moi'kano] AGG, SM/F (*indiano*) Mohican; (*acconciatura*) mohican.

moine [mo'ine] SFPL (*carezze*) endearments; (*lusinghe*) flattery *sg*, cajolery *sg*; (*smancerie*) affectation *sg*; **fare le moine a qn** to cajole sb; **è una ragazza tutta moine** she's a very affected girl; **non mi convincerai con le tue moine** you're not going to sweet-talk me into it.

moka ['mɔka] = **moca.**

mola ['mɔla] SF (*di mulino*) millstone; (*per utensili ecc*) grindstone.

molare[1] [mo'lare] AGG, SM (*dente*) molar.

molare[2] [mo'lare] VT to grind, polish.

molare[3] [mo'lare] AGG (*Chim, Fis*) molar.

molarità [molari'ta] SF INV (*Chim, Fis*) molarity.

molato, a [mo'lato] AGG: **vetro molato** cut glass.

molatrice [mola'tritʃe] SF grinder.

mole ['mɔle] SF (*gen*) massive shape; (*dimensioni*) size; (*Chim*) mole; **una mole di lavoro** masses (*Brit fam*) *o* loads

of work; **una mole di lavoro arretrato**, a massive backlog of work; **è comparso sulla porta in tutta la sua mole** his massive shape appeared at the door.

molecola [mo'lɛkola] SF molecule.

molecolare [moleko'lare] AGG molecular.

molestare [moles'tare] VT (*infastidire*) to annoy, bother; (*sessualmente*) to harass.

molestatore, trice [molesta'tore] SM/F (*di bambini*) molester.

molestia [mo'lɛstja] SF (*noia, fastidio*) annoyance, bother; (*azione molesta*): **molestie** SFPL trouble *sg*, bother *sg*; **molestie sessuali** sexual harassment *sg*.

molesto, a [mo'lɛsto] AGG annoying.

molisano, a [moli'zano] **[1]** AGG of *o* from Molise.

[2] SM/F inhabitant *o* native of Molise.

molla ['mɔlla] SF **a** (*Tecn*) spring; (*fig: incentivo*) motivating force; **molla elicoidale** helical spring, coil spring; **molla di orologio** watch spring; **materasso a molle** spring mattress; **a molla** (*giocattolo*) clockwork; **i soldi sono la molla che lo spinge ad agire** money is the driving force as far as he's concerned

b (*per camino*): **molle** SFPL tongs; **prendere qn con le molle** to treat sb with kid gloves.

mollare [mol'lare] **[1]** VT (*gen*) to let go; (*far cadere*) to drop; **mollare la presa** to let go; **mollare gli ormeggi** (*Naut*) to cast off; **mollare un pugno a qn** (*fig fam*) to punch sb; **mollare uno schiaffo a qn** (*fig fam*) to slap sb; **ha mollato il suo ragazzo** she's ditched her boyfriend; **ha mollato il pacco qua e se n'è andato** he dumped the parcel here and left; **mi ha mollato il soldi per il cine** he let me have the money to go to the cinema.

[2] VI (*aus avere*) (*cedere, arrendersi*) to give in; (*fig fam: smettere*) stop.

molle ['mɔlle] AGG **a** (*gen*) soft; (*muscoli*) flabby **b** (*fig: debole*) weak, feeble.

molleggiare [molled'dʒare] **[1]** VT to spring.

[2] VI (*aus avere*) (*letto*) to be springy.

[3] **molleggiarsi** VR: **molleggiarsi sulle gambe** (*Ginnastica*) to do knee-bends; (*camminando*) to have a spring in one's step.

molleggiato, a [molled'dʒato] AGG (*letto*) sprung; (*auto*) with good suspension; (*passo, camminata*) springy.

molleggio, gi [mol'leddʒo] SM **a** (*per veicoli*) suspension; (*per letti*) springs *pl* **b** (*elasticità*) springiness **c** (*Ginnastica*) knee-bends *pl*.

mollemente [molle'mente] AVV (*sdraiarsi, muoversi*) languidly.

molletta [mol'letta] SF (*per capelli*) hairgrip; (*per panni*) clothes peg (*Brit*) *o* pin (*Am*); **mollette** SFPL (*per zucchero, ghiaccio*) tongs.

mollettone [mollet'tone] SM (*per tavolo*) padded table cover; (*per asse da stiro*) ironing-board cover.

mollezza [mol'lettsa] SF **a** (*fig: di carattere*) weakness, feebleness **b** : **mollezze** SFPL (*agi, comodità*) luxury *sg*; **vivere nelle mollezze** to live in the lap of luxury.

mollica, che [mol'lika] SF soft part of loaf; **molliche** SFPL (*briciole*) crumbs.

molliccio, cia, ci, ce [mol'littʃo] AGG **a** (*terreno, impasto*) soggy; (*frutta*) soft **b** (*floscio: mano*) limp; (*: muscolo*) flabby.

mollusco, schi [mol'lusko] SM (*Zool*) mollusc.

molo ['mɔlo] SM jetty, pier; **attraccare al molo** to dock.

molotov ['mɔlotov] SF INV (*anche:* **bottiglia molotov**) Molotov cocktail.

molteplice [mol'teplitʃe] AGG (*formato di più elementi*) complex; **molteplici** P (*svariati: interessi, attività ecc*) numerous, various.

molteplicità [molteplitʃi'ta] SF multiplicity; **una molteplicità di interessi** a wide range of interests.

moltiplica, che [mol'tiplika] SF (*di bicicletta*) gear ratio.

moltiplicare [moltipli'kare] **1** VT (*anche fig*) to multiply; **moltiplicare 5 per 3** to multiply 5 by 3.

2 moltiplicarsi VIP (*gen*) to multiply; (*spese, richieste*) to increase.

moltiplicatore, trice [moltiplika'tore] SM (*Tecn, Fis, Mat*) multiplier.

moltiplicazione [moltiplikat'tsjone] SF multiplication.

moltitudine [molti'tudine] SF **a**: **una moltitudine di** a vast number *o* a multitude of **b** (*letter: folla*) multitude.

---

molto , a ['molto]

1 AVV

a a lot, (very) much, a great deal;

▷ **non legge molto** he doesn't read much *o* a great deal

▷ **ha viaggiato molto** he has travelled a lot *o* a great deal

▷ **ti è piaciuto? — sì, molto** did you like it? — yes, very much

▷ **questo libro è molto meglio dell'altro** this book is a lot *o* much better than the other one

▷ **ci vorranno a dir molto 3 giorni** it will take 3 days at the most

b (*con aggettivi, avverbi*) very; (*con participio passato*) (very) much;

▷ **l'ha fatto molto** *bene* he did it very well

▷ **molto** *lodato* highly *o* (very) much praised

▷ **sono molto** *stanco* I'm very tired

c (*distanza, tempo*)

▷ **c'è ancora molta da camminare** there's still a long way to go

▷ **ci vuole molto?** (*tempo*) will it take long?

▷ **non la vedo da molto** I haven't seen her for quite a while *o* for a long time

▷ **ne hai ancora per molto?** will you be much longer?

▷ **arriverà fra non molto** he'll arrive soon.

2 AGG (*quantità*) a great deal of, a lot of, lots of, much (*in domande e con negazioni*); (*numero*) a lot of, lots of, many (*in domande e con negazioni*);

▷ **molta** *gente* a lot of people, many people

▷ **molti** *libri* a lot of books, many books

▷ **c'è molta** *neve* there's a great deal of *o* a lot of snow

▷ **non c'è molto** *pane* there isn't a lot of bread, there isn't (very) much bread

▷ **non ho molto** *tempo* I don't have *o* haven't got much time

▷ **non c'erano molti** *turisti* there weren't many tourists.

3 PRON much, a lot;

▷ **molti** OR ▷ **molte** many, a lot

▷ **c'è pane? — sì, molto** is there any bread? — yes plenty *o* lots (*fam*)

▷ **molti pensano che sia giusto** many (people) think it's right

▷ **molti di noi** many of *o* a lot of us.

---

molva ['molva] SF ling (*fish*).

momentaneamente [momentanea'mente] AVV at the moment, at present.

momentaneo, a [momen'taneo] AGG (*gioia, dolore*) momentary; (*assenza, scarsità*) temporary.

momento [mo'mento] SM **a** (*gen*) moment; **in questo momento** at the moment, at present; **in questo momento è al telefono** he's on the phone at the moment; **la situazione non è rosea in questo momento** *o* **al momento** things don't look too rosy at the moment *o* at present; **da un momento all'altro** any moment now, at any moment; (*all'improvviso*) suddenly; **il tempo è cambiato da un momento all'altro** the weather changed suddenly; **per il momento** for the time being; **sul momento** there and then; **fino a questo momento** up till now, until now; **in qualunque momento** at any time; **un momento prego!** just a moment, please!; **proprio in quel momento** at that very moment, just at that moment; **non sta fermo un momento** he can't keep still; **posso parlarti un momento?** could I have a word with you?; **dal momento che** given that, since

b (*contingenza*) time; (*occasione*) opportunity; **sono momenti difficili** OR **è un momento difficile** it's a difficult time; **aspettare il momento favorevole** to wait for the right moment; **è successo al momento sbagliato** it came at the wrong time; **momento culminante** climax; **abbiamo passato momenti bellissimi insieme** we had some great times together; **verremo in un altro momento** we'll come another time; **è l'uomo del momento** he's the man of the moment; **non è il momento di scherzare** this is no time to joke; **al momento di pagare...** when it came to paying ...; **al momento di partire mi sono accorto che...** just as I was leaving, I realised ...

c: **a momenti** (*da un momento all'altro*) any time *o* moment now; (*quasi*) nearly; **arriverà a momenti** he should arrive any time now; **a momenti cadevo** I nearly fell

d (*Fis*) moment.

monaca, che ['monaka] SF (*Rel*) nun; **farsi monaca** to become a nun.

monacale [mona'kale] AGG monastic.

monachesimo [mona'kezimo] SM monasticism.

Monaco ['monako] SF: **(Principato di) Monaco** Monaco ▶ **Monaco (di Baviera)** Munich.

monaco, ci ['monako] SM monk.

monade ['monade] SF (*Filosofia*) monad.

monarca, chi [mo'narka] SM monarch.

monarchia [monar'kia] SF monarchy.

monarchico, a, ci, che [mo'narkiko] **1** AGG (*stato, autorità*) monarchic; (*partito, fede*) monarchist attr.

2 SM/F monarchist.

monastero [monas'tero] SM (*di monaci*) monastery; (*di monache*) convent.

monastico, a, ci, che [mo'nastiko] AGG monastic.

moncherino [monke'rino] SM stump.

monco, a, chi, che ['monco] **1** AGG maimed, mutilated; (*fig*) incomplete; **monco di un braccio** one-armed.

2 SM/F maimed *o* mutilated person.

moncone [mon'kone] SM stump.

mondana [mon'dana] SF (*euf*) prostitute.

mondanamente [mondana'mente] AVV: **vivere mondanamente** to move in fashionable circles.

mondanità [mondani'ta] SF INV **a** (*frivolezza*) worldliness

b : **le mondanità** SFPL (*piaceri*) worldy pleasures.
mondano, a [mon'dano] AGG (*Rel*: *terrestre*) worldly, earthly; (*riunione, cronaca, vita*) society *attr*; (*obblighi*) social.
mondare [mon'dare] VT (*piselli*) to shell; (*frutta, patate*) to peel; (*grano*) to winnow; (*fig*: *anima*) to cleanse.
mondezza [mon'dettsa] SF (*fam*) rubbish *no pl*, refuse *no pl*, trash *no pl* (*Am*).
mondezzaio, ai [mondet'tsajo] SM rubbish (*Brit*) o garbage (*Am*) dump; (*fig*) tip (*Brit*).
mondiale [mon'djale] AGG (*gen*) world *attr*; (*crisi, successo*) world-wide; **di fama mondiale** world famous; **la prima guerra mondiale** the First World War; **su scala mondiale** on a world-wide scale.
mondina [mon'dina] SF worker in the paddy fields.
mondo[1] ['mondo] SM **a** (*gen, fig*) world; **in tutto il mondo** all over the world, throughout the world; **il migliore del mondo** the best in the world; **nessuno al mondo** no-one in the world; **essere solo al mondo** to have no family; **il mondo dell'aldilà** the next life, the after life; **il gran** o **bel mondo** high society; **il mondo del teatro** the world of the theatre
b (*fraseologia*): **ti faccio un mondo di auguri** [OR] **ti auguro un mondo di bene** all the best!; **ti voglio un mondo di bene** I really love you!; **gli voglio tutto il bene di questo mondo ma...** I'm very fond of him but ...; **per niente al mondo** [OR] **per nessuna cosa al mondo** not for all the world; **da che mondo è mondo** since time o the world began; **(sono) cose dell'altro mondo!** it's incredible!; **non è poi la fine del mondo se non vengo** it won't be the end of the world if I can't make it; **una moto che è la fine del mondo** one hell of a motorbike; **mettere/venire al mondo** to bring/come into the world; **com'è piccolo il mondo!** it's a small world!; **è un uomo di mondo** he's a man of the world; **così va il mondo** that's life; **vivere fuori dal mondo** to be out of touch with the real world; **ma in che mondo vivi?** what planet are you living on?; **vive in un mondo tutto suo** he lives in a world of his own; **mandare qn all'altro mondo** to kill sb; **il mondo è bello perché è vario** (*Proverbio*) variety is the spice of life; **mondo cane!** bloody hell!
mondo[2], **a** ['mondo] AGG (*verdura*) cleaned; (*frutta, patate*) peeled.
mondovisione [mondovi'zjone] SF: **trasmettere in mondovisione** to show on TV worldwide.
monegasco, a, schi, sche [mone'gasko] [1] AGG Monegasque.
[2] SM/F native o inhabitant of Monaco.
monelleria [monelle'ria] SF prank, naughty trick; **fare una monelleria** to play a trick o prank.
monello, a [mo'nɛllo] SM/F (*ragazzo di strada*) (street) urchin; (*ragazzo vivace*) rascal, scamp.
moneta [mo'neta] SF **a** (*pezzo*) coin; **una moneta da 100 lire** a 100 lire coin o piece; **ripagare qn della stessa moneta** (*fig*) to pay sb back in his own coin
b (*denaro*) money; (*spiccioli*) (small) change; **non ho moneta** I have no change; **moneta cartacea** paper money
c (*valuta*) currency; **il marco è moneta forte** the mark is a strong currency ►**moneta corrente** currency ►**moneta estera** foreign currency ►**moneta legale** legal tender.
monetario, ria, ri, rie [mone'tarjo] AGG monetary.
monetarismo [moneta'rizmo] SM monetarism.

mongolfiera [mongol'fjɛra] SF hot-air balloon.
Mongolia [mon'gɔlja] SF: **la Mongolia** Mongolia.
mongolico, a, ci, che [mon'gɔliko] AGG Mongolian.
mongolo, a ['mongolo] AGG, SM/F, SM Mongolian, Mongol.
monile [mo'nile] SM (*collana*) necklace; (*gioiello*) jewel.
monito ['mɔnito] SM warning; **che ti serva di monito!** let this be a lesson to you!
monitor ['mɔnitə] SM INV monitor.
monitoraggio, gi [monito'raddʒo] SM monitoring.
monitorare [monito'rare] VT to monitor.
monoalbero [mono'albero] AGG INV single-camshaft *attr*.
monoblocco, chi [mono'blɔkko] SM (*Aut*) cylinder block.
monocamera [mono'kamera] SF one-room flat.
monocamerale [monokame'rale] AGG (*Pol*: *sistema*) single chamber *attr*.
monocilindrico, a, ci, che [monotʃi'lindriko] AGG single-cylinder *attr*.
monocolo [mo'nɔkolo] SM monocle, eyeglass.
monocolore [monoko'lore] SM (*Pol*: *anche*: **governo monocolore**) one-party government.
monocorde [mono'kɔrde] AGG (*monotono*) monotonous.
monocotiledone [monokoti'lɛdone] AGG monocotyledon.
monocromatico, a, ci, che [monokro'matiko] AGG (*pittura*) monochrome; (*Fis*) monochromatic.
monocromatismo [monokroma'tizmo] SM (*Med*) monochromatism.
monocromo, a [mo'nɔkromo] AGG monochrome.
monodose [mono'dɔze] AGG INV single dose.
monoelica [mono'ɛlika] AGG INV (*aereo*) single-propellor *attr*.
monofase [mono'faze] AGG (*Elettr*) single-phase.
monogamia [monoga'mia] SF monogamy.
monogamo, a [mo'nɔgamo] [1] AGG monogamous.
[2] SM/F monogamist.
monogenitore [monodʒeni'tore] AGG INV: **famiglia monogenitore** one-parent family.
monografia [monogra'fia] SF monograph.
monografico, a, ci, che [mono'grafiko] AGG monographic; **corso monografico** (*Univ*) *course on a single author or topic*.
monogramma, i [mono'gramma] SM monogram.
monokini [mono'kini] SM INV monokini.
monolingue [mono'lingwe] [1] AGG monolingual.
[2] SM (*dizionario*) monolingual dictionary.
monolito [mo'nɔlito] SM monolith.
monolocale [monolo'kale] SM studio flat.
monologo, ghi [mo'nɔlogo] SM monologue; **il monologo di Amleto** Hamlet's soliloquy ►**monologo interiore** (*Letterat*) interior monolgue.
monomio, mi [mo'nɔmjo] SM (*Mat*) monomial.
monomotore [monomo'tore] AGG (*aereo*) single-engined.
mononucleosi [mononukle'ozi] SF INV glandular fever, mononucleosis (*termine tecn*).
monopartitismo [monoparti'tizmo] SM single-party system.
monopattino [mono'pattino] SM scooter.
monopetto [mono'pɛtto] AGG INV (*giacca*) single-breasted.
monopezzo [mono'pɛttso] [1] AGG INV one-piece *attr*.
[2] SM INV one-piece.
monopoli° [mo'nɔpoli] SM (*gioco*) Monopoly ®.
monopolio, li [mono'pɔljo] SM (*Econ, fig*) monopoly ►**monopolio di stato** state monopoly.
monopolizzare [monopolid'dzare] VT (*Comm, fig*) to

monopolize.

monopolizzatore, trice [monopoliddza'tore] 1 AGG monopolizing *attr.*
2 SM/F monopolizer.

monopolizzazione [monopoliddzat'tsjone] SF monopolization.

monoposto [mono'posto] AGG INV, SM single-seater.

monoreddito [mono'rɛddito] AGG INV: **famiglia monoreddito** single-income family.

monoscì [mono'ʃi] SM INV (*sci d'acqua*) water-ski; (*sci alpino*) monoski.

monosillabico, a, ci, che [monosil'labiko] AGG monosyllabic.

monosillabo, a [mono'sillabo] 1 AGG monosyllabic.
2 SM monosyllable; **rispondere a monosillabi** (*fig*) to answer in monosyllables.

monossido [mo'nɔssido] SM monoxide ▶**monossido di carbonio** carbon monoxide.

monostadio [monos'tadjo] AGG INV (*missile*) single-stage.

monoteismo [monote'izmo] SM monotheism.

monoteistico, a, ci, che [monote'istiko] AGG monotheistic.

monotonamente [monotona'mente] AVV monotonously.

monotonia [monoto'nia] SF monotony, dullness.

monotono, a [mo'nɔtono] AGG (*gen*) monotonous; (*vita*) humdrum; (*lavoro*) dull, monotonous.

monouso [mono'uzo] AGG INV (*siringa*) disposable.

monovalente [monova'lɛnte] AGG (*Chim*) monovalent.

Mons. ABBR (= *Monsignore*) Mgr.

monsignore [monsiɲ'ɲore] SM **a** (*titolo ecclesiastico*) monsignor **b** (*titolo: parlando a arcivescovo, vescovo*) Your Grace; (: *parlando di terzi*) His Grace.

monsone [mon'sone] SM monsoon.

monta ['monta] SF (*accoppiamento*) covering; **stazione di monta** stud farm.

montacarichi [monta'kariki] SM INV goods lift, service elevator (*Am*).

montaggio, gi [mon'taddʒo] SM **a** (*di macchina, telaio, mobile*) assembly; **scatola/catena di montaggio** assembly kit/line **b** (*Cine*) editing.

montagna [mon'taɲɲa] SF **a** (*monte*) mountain; **una montagna di** (*fig: gran quantità*) a mountain *o* pile *o* heap of ▶**montagne russe** (*giostra*) roller coaster *sg*, big dipper *sg* (*Brit*)
b (*zona, regione*): **la montagna** the mountains *pl*; **andare in montagna** to go to the mountains; **casa di montagna** house in the mountains; **aria/strada di montagna** mountain air/road.

montagnoso, a [montaɲ'ɲoso] AGG mountainous.

montanaro, a [monta'naro] 1 AGG mountain *attr.*
2 SM/F (*persona*) mountain dweller.

montano, a [mon'tano] AGG mountain *attr.*

montante [mon'tante] SM **a** (*di porta*) jamb; (*di finestra*) upright; (*Calcio: palo*) post **b** (*Pugilato*) upper cut **c** (*Comm*) total amount.

montare [mon'tare] 1 VI (*aus essere*) **a** (*salire*) to go (*o* come) up; **montare in bicicletta/macchina/in treno** to get on a bicycle/into a car/on a train; **montare su una scala** to climb a ladder; **montare in cima a** to climb to the top of; **montare su tutte le furie** (*fig*) to lose one's temper
b (*cavalcare*): **montare bene/male** to ride well/badly; **montare a cavallo** to mount *o* get on a horse

c (*aumentare*: *vento, marea*) to rise.
2 VT **a** (*salire*) to go (*o* come) up; **montare le scale** to go upstairs, climb the stairs
b (*cavallo*) to ride
c (*Zool*) to cover
d : **montare la guardia** (*Mil*) to mount guard
e (*costruire: macchina, mobile ecc*) to assemble; (*tenda*) to pitch; (*film*) to edit; (*gioielli*) to set; (*fotografia*) to mount; (*Aut: gomma*) to put on
f (*fig: esagerare: notizia*) to blow up, exaggerate
g (*fig*): **montare la testa a qn** to turn sb's head; **montarsi la testa** to become big-headed
h (*Culin: panna*) to whip; (: *albume*) to whisk; **montare a neve** to whisk until stiff.
3 **montarsi** VIP (*insuperbirsi*) to become big-headed.

montatura [monta'tura] SF (*di gioiello*) setting; (*di occhiali*) frames *pl*; (*fig: esagerazione*) exaggeration; **una montatura pubblicitaria** (*fig*) a publicity stunt.

montavivande [montavi'vande] SM INV dumbwaiter.

monte ['monte] SM **a** mountain; **a monte (di)** (*fiume*) upstream (from); (*vallata*) at the head (of); **un monte di** (*gran quantità*) a mountain *o* pile *o* heap of; **il problema è a monte** (*fig*) the problem goes back to the early stages; **andare a monte** (*fig*) to come to nothing; **mandare a monte** (*fig: piano, progetto*) to put paid to; **fu quel fatto a mandare a monte il matrimonio** that's what caused the wedding to be called off ▶**il Monte Bianco** Mont Blanc ▶**il Monte Everest** Mount Everest ▶**il Monte degli Ulivi** the Mount of Olives
b : **monte di pietà** pawnbroker's, pawnshop; **portare qc al monte di pietà** (*impegnare*) to pawn sth.

montepremi [monte'prɛmi] SM INV jackpot.

montgomery [mɛnt'ɡʌməri] SM INV duffle *o* duffel coat.

montone [mon'tone] SM **a** (*Zool*) ram; **carne di montone** mutton **b** (*anche: giacca di montone*) sheepskin (jacket).

montuosità [montuosi'ta] SF mountainous nature.

montuoso, a [montu'oso] AGG mountainous.

monumentale [monumen'tale] AGG monumental.

monumentalità [monumentali'ta] SF monumental nature.

monumento [monu'mento] SM monument; **visitare i monumenti** to go sightseeing; **ti farei un monumento!** (*fig*) you deserve a medal!

moplen® [mo'plɛn] SM moulded plastic.

moquette [mɔ'kɛt] SF INV fitted carpet.

mora[1] ['mɔra] SF (*Bot: di gelso*) mulberry; (: *di rovo*) blackberry.

mora[2] ['mɔra] SF (*Dir*) **a** delay **b** (*somma dovuta*) arrears *pl*.

morale [mo'rale] 1 AGG (*gen*) moral.
2 SF **a** (*norme, consuetudini*) morals *pl*, morality; (*Filosofia*) moral philosophy, ethics *sg*; **la morale corrente** current moral standards *pl*
b (*insegnamento*) moral; **la morale della favola** the moral of the story; **così, morale della favola, siamo rimasti a casa** and the result was that we stayed at home.
3 SM (*stato d'animo*) morale; **essere giù di morale** to be feeling down; **su col morale!** cheer up!; **aver il morale alto/a terra** to be in good/low spirits; **bisogna tener alto il morale delle truppe** we must keep the troops' morale high.

moraleggiare [moraled'dʒare] VI (*aus avere*) to moralize,

sermonize.

moralista, i, e [mora'lista] ☐1 AGG moralistic.
☐2 SM/F moralist.

moralisticamente [moralistika'mente] AVV (*analizzare*) from a moral point of view; (*parlare, comportarsi*) in a moralizing way.

moralistico, a, ci, che [mora'listiko] AGG moralistic.

moralità [morali'ta] SF **a** (*norme di vita, morale*) morality, morals *pl*, moral standards *pl*; **una persona di alta moralità** a person of high moral standards **b** (*di comportamento*) morality.

moralizzare [moralid'dzare] ☐1 VT (*costumi, vita pubblica*) to set moral standards for.
☐2 VI (*aus* avere): **moralizzare (su)** to moralize (on, about).

moralizzatore, trice [moraliddza'tore] ☐1 AGG moralizing.
☐2 SM/F moralizer.

moralizzazione [moraliddzat'tsjone] SF setting of moral standards.

moralmente [moral'mente] AVV morally.

moratoria [mora'tɔrja] SF (*Dir*) moratorium.

morbidamente [morbida'mente] AVV softly.

morbidezza [morbi'dettsa] SF (*vedi agg*) softness; tenderness; smoothness.

morbido, a ['mɔrbido] AGG (*gen*) soft; (*carne*) tender; (*pelle*) soft, smooth.

morbillo [mor'billo] SM measles *sg*.

morbo ['mɔrbo] SM (*Med*) disease; (: *epidemia*) epidemic.

morbosamente [morbosa'mente] AVV morbidly.

morbosità [morbosi'ta] SF morbidity.

morboso, a [mor'boso] AGG (*Med, fig*) morbid; **una gelosia morbosa** pathological jealousy.

morchia ['mɔrkja] SF sludge, oily deposit.

mordace [mor'datʃe] AGG (*fig: satira*) biting; (: *persona, parole*) cutting.

mordente [mor'dɛnte] SM **a** (*Chim*) mordant **b** (*fig: di satira, critica, stile*) bite; (: *di persona*) drive.

mordere ['mɔrdere] VT IRREG (*sogg: persona, cane, insetto*) to bite; (*addentare: mela, panino*) to bite into; **mordere la gamba a qn** to bite sb's leg, bite sb in the leg; **mordersi le labbra/la lingua** (*anche fig*) to bite one's lips/one's tongue; **mordere il freno** (*anche fig*) to champ at the bit; **mordere l'asfalto** (*Aut*) to grip the road; **mi sarei morso le mani** I could have kicked myself; **can che abbaia non morde** (*Proverbio*) his (*o* her *ecc*) bark is worse than his (*o* her *ecc*) bite.

mordicchiare [mordik'kjare] VT (*gen*) to chew at; **mordicchiarsi le labbra** to bite one's lips.

morello, a [mo'rɛllo] AGG, SM/F: **(cavallo) morello** black horse.

morena [mo'rɛna] SF (*Geol*) moraine.

morente [mo'rɛnte] ☐1 AGG dying.
☐2 SM/F (*persona*) dying man/woman; **i morenti** the dying.

moresco, a, schi, sche [mo'resko] AGG Moorish.

more uxorio ['mɔre uk'sɔrjo] AVV as man and wife.

morfina [mor'fina] SF morphine.

morfinomane [morfi'nɔmane] SM/F morphine addict.

morfologia [morfolo'dʒia] SF morphology.

morfologicamente [morfolodʒika'mente] AVV morphologically.

morfologico, a, ci, che [morfo'lɔdʒiko] AGG morphological.

moria [mo'ria] SF (*di bestiame*) disease; (*Bot*) blight.

moribondo, a [mori'bondo] ☐1 AGG (*persona*) dying.
☐2 SM/F dying man/woman.

morigerato, a [moridʒe'rato] AGG (*persona, vita*) moderate, sober.

morire [mo'rire] VI IRREG (*aus* essere) **a** (*gen*) to die; **morire di malattia** to die after an illness; **morire di morte violenta/naturale** to die a violent/natural death; **morire di stenti** to die from hardship; **morire in guerra** to die in battle; **morire assassinato** to be murdered; **morire di dolore** to die of a broken heart; **morire di fame** to starve to death, die of hunger; (*fig*) to be starving, be famished; **morire di freddo** to freeze to death; (*fig*) to be frozen (stiff); **morire di sete** (*anche fig*) to die of thirst **b** (*fig*): **morire d'invidia** to be green with envy; **morire di noia** to be bored to death *o* to tears; **morire di paura** to be scared to death; **morire dalle risate** *o* **dal ridere** to kill o.s. laughing, die laughing; **morire di sonno** to be dog tired; **morire dalla voglia di fare qc** to be dying to do sth; **fa un caldo da morire** it's terribly hot; **ho un caldo da morire** I'm terribly hot; **mi fa male da morire questo braccio** my arm is killing me; **bella da morire** stunning; **le muore dietro e lei neanche lo vede** he worships the ground she treads on, and she doesn't even notice he's there; **chi non muore si rivede!** (*scherz*) fancy meeting you! (after all this time) **c** (*luce, giorno*) to fade, die; (*fiamma*) to die down; (*fuoco, tradizione, civiltà*) to die out; **il blu sul nero muore un po'** blue doesn't show up well on a black background.

mormone [mor'mone] SM (*Rel*) Mormon.

mormorare [mormo'rare] ☐1 VI (*aus* avere) **a** (*gen*) to murmur; (*sussurrare: persona, vento*) to murmur, whisper; (*brontolare*) to grumble, mutter; **si mormora che...** it's rumoured (*Brit*) *o* rumored (*Am*) that ... **b** (*parlare male*): **mormorare sul conto di qn** to speak ill of sb; **la gente mormora** people are talking.
☐2 VT (*parole d'amore ecc*) to whisper, murmur.

mormorio, rii [mormo'rio] SM (*di persone, vento, acque*) murmur, murmuring; (*di foglie, fronde*) rustling.

moro[1], a ['mɔro] ☐1 AGG **a** (*Storia*) Moorish **b** (*persona: dai capelli scuri*) dark, dark-haired; (: *di carnagione scura*) dark, dark-skinned.
☐2 SM/F (*vedi agg*) Moor; dark-haired person; dark-skinned person; **i Mori** SMPL (*Storia*) the Moors.

moro[2] ['mɔro] SM mulberry tree.

moroso, a [mo'roso] ☐1 AGG (*Dir*) defaulting, in arrears.
☐2 SM/F (*fam: innamorato*) sweetheart.

morra ['mɔrra] SF *betting game: each of two players shows a number of fingers, simultaneously shouting out a guess at the joint total.*

morsa ['mɔrsa] SF (*Tecn*) vice (*Brit*), vise (*Am*); (*fig: stretta*) grip; **stretto in una morsa d'acciaio** (*fig*) held in an iron grip.

morse [mɔːs] AGG INV: **alfabeto morse** Morse (code).

morsetto [mor'setto] SM (*Tecn*) clamp; (*Elettr*) terminal; **morsetto della batteria** (*Aut*) battery lead connection.

morsicare [morsi'kare] VT to bite.

morso, a ['mɔrso] ☐1 PP di mordere.
☐2 SM **a** (*gen*) bite; (*di insetto*) sting; **dare un morso a qc/qn** to bite sth/sb; **mi dai un morso di panino?** can I have a bite of your sandwich?; **i morsi della fame** hunger pangs **b** (*parte della briglia*) bit.

mortadella [morta'dɛlla] SF (*Culin*) mortadella (*type of*

salted pork meat).

mortaio, ai [mor'tajo] SM mortar.

mortale [mor'tale] [1] AGG **a** (*vita, uomo*) mortal **b** (*veleno*) deadly; (*ferita, incidente*) fatal; **un colpo mortale** a deadly *o* fatal blow; **peccato mortale** (*Rel*) mortal sin. [2] SM/F mortal.

mortalità [mortali'ta] SF **a** (*l'essere mortale*) mortality **b** (*Statistica*) mortality, death rate; **mortalità infantile** infant mortality.

mortalmente [mortal'mente] AVV (*gen, fig: offendersi*) mortally; **mi sono mortalmente annoiato** I was bored to death.

mortaretto [morta'retto] SM firecracker.

morte ['morte] SF **a** (*gen*) death; (*fig: fine, rovina*) death, end; **morte clinica** brain death; **alla morte di sua madre** on the death of his mother; **in punto di morte** at death's door; **in punto di morte ha confessato** he confessed on his deathbed; **essere tra la vita e la morte** to be fighting for one's life; **ferito a morte** (*soldato*) mortally wounded; (*in incidente*) fatally injured; **condannare qn a morte** to sentence sb to death; **pena di/condanna a morte** death penalty/sentence **b** (*fraseologia*): **è questione di vita o di morte** it's a matter of life or death; **essere annoiato a morte** to be bored to death *o* to tears; **avercela a morte con qn** to hate sb like poison; **si odiano a morte** they can't stand the sight of each other; **avere la morte nel cuore** to have a heavy heart; **così facendo ha firmato la sua condanna a morte** by doing that he signed his own death warrant.

mortificante [mortifi'kante] AVV mortifying.

mortificare [mortifi'kare] [1] VT to mortify. [2] **mortificarsi** VR (*Rel*) to mortify o.s.. [3] **mortificarsi** VIP (*vergognarsi, spiacersi*) to feel mortified.

mortificato, a [mortifi'kato] AGG: **essere mortificato (per qc)** to be mortified (about sth).

mortificazione [mortifikat'tsjone] SF mortification.

morto, a ['morto] [1] PP di **morire**. [2] AGG (*gen, fig*) dead; **sono morto di freddo** I'm frozen stiff; **sono stanco morto** I'm dead tired; **l'inverno è una stagione morta per noi** winter is our slack season; **morto e sepolto** (*fig*) dead and buried. [3] SM/F **a** dead man/woman; **i morti** the dead; **fare il morto** (*in acqua*) to float on one's back; **un morto di fame** (*fig pegg*) a down-and-out; **sembri un morto che cammina** you look like death warmed up; **le campane suonavano a morto** the funeral bells were tolling; **giorno dei morti** All Souls' Day; **il regno dei morti** the world beyond the grave **b** (*Carte*) dummy.

mortorio, ri [mor'torjo] SM (*fig: cerimonia, festa*): **quella festa è stata un mortorio** that party was more like a funeral *o* wake.

mosaico, ci [mo'zaiko] SM **a** (*Arte*) mosaic; **pavimento a mosaico** mosaic floor; **l'ultimo tassello del mosaico** (*fig*) the final piece of the puzzle **b** (*fig: di lingue, popoli*) mixture.

Mosca ['moska] SF Moscow.

mosca ['moska] [1] SF (*pl* **mosche**) **a** (*Zool, Pesca*) fly ►**mosca della carne** bluebottle, blowfly ►**mosca cavallina** horsefly ►**mosca tse-tse** tsetse fly **b** (*fraseologia*): **non farebbe male a una mosca** he wouldn't hurt a fly; **morire come mosche** to die like flies; **non si sentiva volare una mosca** you could have heard a

pin drop; **gli è saltata la mosca al naso** he lost his temper; **giocare a mosca cieca** to play blind-man's buff; **essere una mosca bianca** to be like hen's teeth; **rimanere** *o* **restare con un pugno di mosche** (*fig*) to be left empty-handed **c** (*barba*) goatee. [2] AGG INV (*Pugilato*): **peso mosca** flyweight.

moscato, a [mos'kato] [1] AGG (*uva*) muscat. [2] SM (*uva*) muscat grape; (*vino*) muscatel, muscat.

moscerino [moʃʃe'rino] SM midge, gnat.

moschea [mos'kɛa] SF mosque.

moschettiere [mosket'tjɛre] SM musketeer.

moschetto [mos'ketto] SM musket.

moschettone [mosket'tone] SM (*gancio*) spring clip; (*Alpinismo*) karabiner, snaplink; (*Naut*) snapshackle.

moschicida, i, e [moski'tʃida] [1] SM flykiller. [2] AGG: **carta moschicida** flypaper.

moscio, scia, sci, sce ['moʃʃo] AGG **a** (*cappello*) soft; (*fig: persona*) lifeless, dull **b** : **ha la "r" moscia** he can't roll his "r"s.

moscone [mos'kone] SM **a** (*insetto*) bluebottle **b** (*pattino*) pedalo; (: *a remi*) pedalo with oars **c** (*corteggiatore*) suitor.

moscovita, i, e [mosko'vita] AGG, SM/F Muscovite.

Mosè [mo'zɛ] SM Moses.

mossa ['mossa] SF **a** (*gen: movimento*) movement; **prendere le mosse da qc** to come about as the result of sth; **datti una mossa!** (*fig*) get a move on! **b** (*Scacchi, Dama, fig*) move; **fare una mossa sbagliata** (*anche fig*) to make a wrong move.

mossi *ecc* ['mossi] VB vedi **muovere**.

mosso, a ['mosso] [1] PP di **muovere**. [2] AGG **a** (*mare*) rough; (*capelli*) wavy; (*fotografia*) blurred **b** (*Mus*) mosso.

mostarda [mos'tarda] SF (*Culin*) mustard ►**mostarda di Cremona** *pickled fruit with mustard.*

mosto ['mosto] SM must.

mostra ['mostra] SF **a** (*di oggetti*) exhibition; (*di animali, fiori*) show; **fare una mostra** to put on an exhibition *o* a show; **il negozio ha messo in mostra gli ultimi arrivi** the shop has put its latest stock on display; **essere in mostra** to be on show ►**mostra d'arte** art exhibition ►**mostra canina** dog show **b** (*locale*) exhibition hall **c** (*fraseologia*): **far mostra di sé** to show off; **fare mostra di fare qc** (*fingere*) to pretend to do sth; **mettersi in mostra** to draw attention to o.s.; **mettere qc in bella mostra** to show sth off.

mostrare [mos'trare] [1] VT: **mostrare (qc a qn)** to show (sb sth), show (sth to sb); **mi mostri come si fa?** will you show me how to do it?; **ha mostrato un notevole coraggio** he displayed great courage; **mostrare i denti** (*anche fig*) to bare one's teeth; **mostrare la lingua** to stick out one's tongue; **mostrare i pugni a qn** to shake one's fist at sb; **ha mostrato di non conoscermi** he pretended not to know me. [2] **mostrarsi** VR **a** (*dimostrarsi*) to appear; **si è mostrato felice** he appeared *o* looked happy **b** (*comparire*) to appear, show o.s.; **mostrarsi in pubblico** to appear in public.

mostrina [mos'trina] SF (*Mil*) flash.

mostro ['mostro] SM (*anche fig*) monster; **sei un mostro di bravura!** you're a genius!; **i mostri sacri del cinema italiano** the giants of the Italian cinema.

mostruosamente [mostruosa'mente] AVV monstrously.

mostruosità [mostruosi'ta] SF monstrosity.

mostruoso, a [mostru'oso] AGG (*anche fig*) monstrous; (*fam: enorme: intelligenza, cultura*) mega, vast.

mota ['mɔta] SF (*letter*) mire.

motel [mo'tɛl] SM INV motel.

motilità [motili'ta] SF motility.

motivare [moti'vare] VT **a** (*giustificare*) to give reasons for **b** (*causare*) to cause **c** (*stimolare*) to motivate.

motivato, a [moti'vato] AGG (*azione*) justified, reasoned; (*persona*) motivated.

motivazione [motivat'tsjone] SF (*ragione*) justification; (*stimolo*) motivation.

motivo [mo'tivo] SM **a** (*causa, ragione*) reason, grounds *pl*, cause; **senza motivo** for no reason; **qual è il motivo del tuo ritardo?** what is the reason for your lateness?; **avere un motivo valido per fare qc** to have a valid reason for doing sth; **per motivi di salute** for health reasons, on health grounds; **per quale motivo?** why?, for what reason?; **per questo motivo** for this reason, therefore; **motivi personali** personal reasons; **mia madre sta male, motivo per cui non potrò venire** my mother is ill so I won't be able to come **b** (*Mus*) motif; (*di opera letteraria*) (central) theme; (*disegno*) design, pattern.

moto¹ ['mɔto] SM **a** (*di mare, macchina, pianeti*) movement; (*Fis, Tecn*) motion; **quantità di moto** (*Fis*) momentum; **moto armonico semplice** (*Fis*) simple harmonic motion; **verbi di moto** verbs of motion; **mettere in moto qc** (*anche fig*) to set sth in motion; (*motore, macchina*) to start sth (up); **mettersi in moto** (*macchina*) to start; (*persona*) to set off **b** (*esercizio fisico*) exercise; **fare del moto** to take some exercise **c** (*gesto*) movement; **un moto d'impazienza** an impatient gesture **d** (*rivolta*) rising, revolt.

moto² ['mɔto] SF INV (*fam*) bike.

motobarca, che [moto'barka] SF motorboat.

motocarro [moto'karro] SM three-wheeler van.

motocicletta [mototʃi'kletta] SF motorcycle.

motociclismo [mototʃi'klizmo] SM motorcycling, motorcycle racing.

motociclista, i, e [mototʃi'klista] SM/F motorcyclist.

motociclistico, a, ci, che [mototʃi'klistiko] AGG motorcycle *attr*.

motociclo [moto'tʃiklo] SM motorcycle, motorbike (*fam*).

motocross [moto'krɔs] SM motocross.

motofurgone [motofur'gone] SM three-wheel van.

motonautica [moto'nautika] SF speedboat racing.

motonautico, a, ci, che [moto'nautiko] AGG motorboat *attr*, speedboat *attr*.

motonave [moto'nave] SF motor vessel.

motopeschereccio, ci [motopeske'rettʃo] SM trawler.

motopompa [moto'pompa] SF (motor) pump.

motore, trice [mo'tore] **1** AGG **a** (*Anat: organo*) motor *attr* **b** (*Tecn*) driving; **albero motore** drive shaft; **forza motrice** driving force. **2** SM **a** (*Tecn*) engine, motor; (*di macchina, treno, nave*) engine; **a motore** power-driven, motor *attr* ►**motore a 2/4 tempi** 2-/4-stroke engine ►**motore diesel** diesel engine ►**motore a iniezione** fuel-injection engine ►**motore a reazione** jet engine ►**motore a scoppio** internal combustion engine ►**motore turbo** turbo(-charged) engine **b** (*Filosofia*) mover; **il primo motore** the Prime Mover.

motoretta [moto'retta] SF motor scooter.

motorino [moto'rino] SM **a** (*Aut*): **motorino d'avviamento** starter(-motor) **b** (*fam: ciclomotore*) moped.

motorio, ria, ri, rie [mo'tɔrjo] AGG (*Anat*) motor *attr*.

motoristica [moto'ristika] SF engine design (*of racing cars*).

motorizzare [motorid'dzare] **1** VT (*polizia, soldati*) to motorize. **2 motorizzarsi** VR (*fam*) to get a car (o motorbike).

motorizzato, a [motorid'dzato] AGG: **reparto motorizzato** (*Mil*) motorized division; **sei motorizzato?** have you got transport?

motorizzazione [motoriddzat'tsjone] SF (*ufficio tecnico e organizzativo*): **(ufficio della) motorizzazione** road traffic office.

motorscooter ['moutəskuːtə] SM INV motor scooter.

motoscafo [motos'kafo] SM motorboat.

motosega, ghe [moto'sega] SF electric saw.

motoslitta [motoz'litta] SF motorized sledge.

motovedetta [motove'detta] SF (motor) patrol vessel.

motrice [mo'tritʃe] SF (*Tecn*) engine, motor.

motteggiare [motted'dʒare] VT (*letter*) to jest, banter.

motteggio, gi [mot'teddʒo] SM (*letter*) banter.

mottetto [mot'tetto] SM (*Poesia*) witty poem.

motto ['mɔtto] SM (*detto arguto*) witty remark; (*massima*) motto, maxim.

mountain bike ['mauntin 'baik] SF INV mountain bike.

mousse [mus] SF INV (*Culin*) mousse.

movente [mo'vɛnte] SM (*Dir*) motive.

movenza [mo'vɛntsa] SF movement; **sciolto nelle movenze** graceful in one's movements.

movimentare [movimen'tare] VT to liven up.

movimentato, a [movimen'tato] AGG (*festa, partita*) lively; (*riunione*) animated; (*strada, vita*) busy; (*soggiorno*) eventful.

movimento [movi'mento] **1** SM (*gen, Pol, Letterat*) movement; (*Mus: grado di velocità*) tempo; (*: parte*) movement; (*fig: animazione*) activity, hustle and bustle; **un movimento di rotazione/rivoluzione** a rotation/revolution; **essere sempre in movimento** to be always on the go; **è vietato salire sul treno in movimento** do not get on the train while it is in motion; **fare un movimento falso** to make an awkward movement; **fece un movimento all'indietro** he stepped back; **fare un po' di movimento** (*esercizio fisico*) to take some exercise; **c'è molto movimento in città** the town is very busy. **2** ►**movimento di capitali** movement of capital ►**movimento di conto** (*Banca*) (bank) account transaction ►**movimento passeggeri e merci** passenger and freight traffic ►**Movimento per la Liberazione della Donna** women's liberation movement ►**movimento di truppe** troop movement.

moviola [mo'vjɔla] SF moviola; **rivedere qc alla moviola** to see an action (*Brit*) or instant (*Am*) replay of sth.

Mozambico [mottsam'biko] SM: **il Mozambico** Mozambique.

mozione [mot'tsjone] SF (*Pol*) motion ►**mozione d'ordine** point of order.

mozzafiato [mottsa'fjato] AGG INV breathtaking.

mozzare [mot'tsare] VT (*testa*) to cut off; (*coda*) to dock; **mozzare il fiato o il respiro a qn** (*fig*) to take sb's breath away.

mozzarella [mottsa'rɛlla] SF mozzarella.

mozzatura [mottsa'tura] SF a (azione: di coda) docking b (parte mozzata) end.

mozzicone [mottsi'kone] SM (di sigaretta) stub, end, butt; (di candela) end; (di matita) stub.

mozzo¹, a ['mottso] AGG (testa) cut off; (coda) docked.

mozzo² ['mottso] SM a (Naut) ship's boy b : mozzo di stalla stable boy.

mozzo³ ['mɔttso] SM (Tecn) hub.

mq ABBR (= metro quadro) sq.m.

MS SIGLA = Massa Carrara.

ms. ABBR (= manoscritto) ms.

M.S.I. ['ɛmme'ɛsse'i] SIGLA M (= Movimento Sociale Italiano) former right-wing political party.

Mti ABBR = monti.

mucca, che ['mukka] SF cow.

mucchio, chi ['mukkjo] SM (gen) heap, pile; a mucchi in piles; un mucchio di (molto) heaps pl of, lots pl of, piles pl of; ha detto un mucchio di sciocchezze he came out with a load of rubbish.

mucillagine [mutʃil'ladʒine] SF (Bot) mucilage (termine tecn), green slime produced by plants growing in water.

muco ['muko] SM (Med) mucus.

mucosa [mu'kosa] SF (Anat) mucous membrane.

muffa ['muffa] SF (biancastra) mildew; (verdognola) mould (Brit), mold (Am); fare la muffa to go mouldy (Brit) o moldy (Am); non ho intenzione di restare a casa a fare la muffa (fig) I'm not going to moulder (Brit) o molder (Am) away at home; avere odore di muffa to smell mouldy.

muffola ['muffola] SF mitten.

muflone [mu'flone] SM mouflon.

mugghiare [mug'gjare] VI (aus avere) (letter fig: mare, tuono) to roar; (: vento) to howl.

muggire [mud'dʒire] VI (aus avere) (bovini) to low; (vacca) to moo, low; (toro) to bellow; (fig) to roar.

muggito [mud'dʒito] SM (vedi vb) lowing; mooing; bellow; roar; i muggiti del bestiame the lowing of the cattle.

mughetto [mu'getto] SM a (Bot) lily of the valley b (Med) thrush.

mugnaio, aia, ai, aie [muɲ'najo] SM/F miller.

mugolare [mugo'lare] 1 VI (cane) to whimper, whine; mugolare (di) (fig: persona) to moan (in o with).
2 VT (borbottare) to mutter.

mugolio, lii [mugo'lio] SM (vedi vb) whimpering, whining; moaning; muttering.

mugugnare [muguɲ'ɲare] VI (aus avere) (fam) to mutter, mumble.

mulattiera [mulat'tjɛra] SF mule track.

mulattiere [mulat'tjɛre] SM mule-driver.

mulatto, a [mu'latto] AGG, SM/F mulatto.

muleta [mu'leta] SF INV muleta.

muliebre [mu'ljɛbre] AGG (letter) feminine, womanly.

mulinare [muli'nare] VI (aus avere) to whirl, spin (round and round).

mulinello [muli'nɛllo] SM a (di vento, acqua) eddy b (di canna da pesca) reel c (Naut) windlass.

mulino [mu'lino] SM mill; lottare o combattere contro i mulini a vento (fig) to tilt at windmills ▶mulino ad acqua water mill ▶mulino a vento windmill.

mulo ['mulo] SM mule; testardo o ostinato o cocciuto come un mulo as stubborn as a mule.

multa ['multa] SF fine; fare o dare una multa a qn to fine sb; ho preso una multa di 50.000 lire I was fined 50,000 lire, I got a 50,000 lire fine.

multare [mul'tare] VT to fine.

multicolore [multiko'lore] AGG multicoloured (Brit), multicolored (Am).

multiforme [multi'forme] AGG (interessi) varied; (ingegno) versatile.

multilaterale [multilate'rale] AGG multilateral.

multilingue [multi'lingwe] AGG multilingual.

multimediale [multime'djale] AGG multimedia attr.

multimiliardario, ria, ri, rie [multimiljar'darjo] AGG, SM/F ≈ billionaire.

multimilionario, ria, ri, rie [multimiljo'narjo] AGG, SM/F multimillionaire.

multinazionale [multinattsjo'nale] AGG, SF multinational; forza multinazionale di pace multinational peacekeeping force.

multiplo, a ['multiplo] 1 AGG multiple.
2 SM (Mat): multiplo (di) multiple (of); minimo comune multiplo lowest common multiple.

multiproprietà [multiproprje'ta] SF INV time-sharing.

multisala [multi'sala] AGG INV (cinema) multi-screen attr.

multiscafo [multis'kafo] SM INV (Naut) multihull.

multiuso [multi'uzo] AGG INV multipurpose.

multiutenza [multiu'tɛntsa] SF (Inform) time sharing.

mummia ['mummja] SF mummy; (fig: persona) old fogey.

mummificare [mummifi'kare] 1 VT to mummify.
2 mummificarsi VIP to become mummified.

mummificazione [mummifikat'tsjone] SF mummification.

mungere ['mundʒere] VT IRREG (anche fig) to milk.

mungitrice [mundʒi'tritʃe] SF (macchina) milking machine.

mungitura [mundʒi'tura] SF milking.

municipale [munitʃi'pale] AGG (gen) municipal; palazzo municipale town hall; autorità municipali local authority sg (Brit), local government sg.

municipalità [munitʃipali'ta] SF INV town council.

municipio, pi [muni'tʃipjo] SM (comune) town council; (palazzo) town hall; sposarsi in municipio ≈ to get married in a registry office (Brit).

munificamente [munifika'mente] AVV munificently, generously.

munificenza [munifi'tʃɛntsa] SF munificence, generosity.

munifico, a, ci, che [mu'nifiko] AGG munificent, generous.

munire [mu'nire] 1 VT: munire di (fortificare: città) to fortify with; (equipaggiare: persona, stanza ecc) to equip with; munire una nave di uomini to man a ship; munire di firma (documento) to sign.
2 munirsi VR: munirsi di (gen: denaro, documenti) to provide o.s. with; (armi) to arm o.s. with; munirsi di coraggio/pazienza to arm o.s. with courage/ patience; "si pregano i clienti di munirsi di scontrino" (in bar) "customers must pay at the desk and obtain a receipt before being served"; si è munito di ombrello ed è uscito arming himself with an umbrella he sallied out.

munizioni [munit'tsjoni] SFPL ammunition sg.

munsi ecc ['munsi] VB vedi mungere.

munto, a ['munto] PP di mungere.

muoio ecc ['mwɔjo] VB vedi morire.

muovere ['mwɔvere] VB IRREG 1 VT a (gen) to move; (macchina, ruota) to drive; il cane muoveva festosamente la coda the dog was joyfully wagging its tail; muovere i primi passi to take one's first steps; (fig) to be

starting out; **mosse un passo verso di me** he took a step towards me; **non muove un passo senza interpellare la moglie** (*fig*) he never does anything without asking his wife; **non ha mosso un dito per aiutarmi** he didn't lift a finger to help me; **muovere mari e monti** to move heaven and earth

b (*fig*: *sollevare*): **muovere un'accusa a** *o* **contro qn** to make an accusation against sb; **muovere causa a qn** (*Dir*) to take legal action against sb; **muovere guerra a** *o* **contro qn** to wage war against sb; **muovere un'obiezione** to raise an objection

c (*commuovere*): **muovere a compassione** to move to pity; **muovere al pianto** to move to tears

d (*Scacchi*) to move; **tocca a te muovere** it's your move.

2 VI (*aus* **essere** *o* **avere**) **a** (*gen*) to move; **muovere verso** OR **muovere in direzione di** to move towards

b (*derivare*): **muovere da** to derive from; **le sue osservazioni muovono da una premessa errata** his comments are based on a mistaken *o* wrong assumption.

3 **muoversi** VR **a** to move; **muoversi in aiuto di qn** to go to sb's aid; **non si muove dalle sue posizioni** (*fig*) he won't budge

b (*sbrigarsi*) to hurry up, get a move on; **muoviti, cammina!** hurry up and get moving!.

4 **muoversi** VIP **c** (*commuoversi*): **muoversi a compassione** *o* **pietà** to be moved to pity

b (*essere in movimento*) to move; **finalmente qualcosa si è mosso** (*fig*) at last things are moving.

mura ['mura] SFPL di **muro b.**

muraglia [mu'raʎʎa] SF (high) wall; **la grande muraglia cinese** the Great Wall of China.

muraglione [muraʎ'ʎone] SM massive wall.

murale [mu'rale] **1** AGG wall *attr*; (*Arte*) mural *attr*; **carta murale** wall map; **pittura murale** mural.

2 SM (*Arte*) mural.

murare [mu'rare] **1** VT (*porta, finestra*) to wall up; (*mensola*) to embed into a wall; **murare qn vivo** to wall sb up.

2 **murarsi** VR: **murarsi in casa** (*fig*: *rinchiudersi*) to shut o.s. away at home.

murario, ria, ri, rie [mu'rarjo] AGG (*tecnica*) building *attr*; **arte muraria** masonry; **opera muraria** piece of masonry work.

muratore [mura'tore] SM (*che costruisce con pietre*) mason; (*che costruisce con mattoni*) bricklayer.

muratura [mura'tura] SF **a** (*atto del murare*) walling (up)

b (*lavoro murario*: *con pietra*) masonry; (: *con mattoni*) bricklaying; **casa in muratura** (*di pietra*) stonebuilt house; (*di mattoni*) brick house.

murena [mu'rɛna] SF moray eel.

muro ['muro] **1** SM **a** (*anche fig*) wall; **armadio a muro** built-in cupboard; **il muro di Berlino** the Berlin Wall; **alzare un muro** to build a wall; **attaccare qc al muro** to hang sth on the wall; **chiudere qc con un muro** (*campo, giardino*) to build a wall around sth; **mettere al muro** (*fucilare*) to shoot *o* execute (by firing squad); **è come parlare al muro** it's like talking to a brick wall; **tra noi c'è un muro** (*fig*) there's a barrier between us; **un muro d'incomprensione** a total lack of understanding

b: **mura** SFPL (*di città, castello*) walls; **chiudersi fra quattro mura** (*fig*) to shut o.s. up at home.

2 ▶**muro di cinta** surrounding wall ▶**muro divisorio** dividing wall ▶**muro di gomma** (*fig*: *indifferenza*) the wall of indifference ▶**muro maestro** main wall

▶**muro di mattoni** brick wall ▶**muro a secco** drystone wall ▶**muro del suono** (*Fis*) sound barrier.

musa ['muza] SF (*Mitol*) Muse; (*fig*) muse, inspiration.

muschiato, a [mus'kjato] AGG **a** (*che odora di muschio*) musky **b** (*Zool*): **bue muschiato** musk ox; **topo muschiato** muskrat.

muschio¹, chi ['muskjo] SM (*profumo*) musk.

muschio², chi ['muskjo] SM (*Bot*) moss.

muscolare [musko'lare] AGG (*Anat, tessuto, fascio*) muscular, muscle *attr*; **strappo muscolare** torn muscle.

muscolatura [muskola'tura] SF musculature; **muscolatura atletica** athletic build.

muscolo ['muskolo] SM **a** (*Anat*) muscle; **scaldare i muscoli** to warm up; **è tutto muscoli e niente cervello** (*fig*) he's all brawn and no brains ▶**muscolo involontario** involuntary muscle ▶**muscolo volontario** voluntary muscle **b** (*Culin*) lean meat **c** (*Zool*) mussel.

muscoloso, a [musko'loso] AGG muscular.

muscoso, a [mus'koso] AGG mossy.

museo [mu'zɛo] SM museum; **un pezzo da museo** (*fig*) a museum piece.

museruola [muze'rwɔla] SF (*per cani*) muzzle; **mettere la museruola a un cane** to muzzle a dog; **mettere la museruola a qn** (*fig*) to muzzle sb, shut sb up.

musica ['muzika] SF (*gen, fig*) music; **musica di sottofondo** background music; **un pezzo** *o* **brano di musica** a piece of music; **mettere in musica** to set to music; **è sempre la stessa musica** (*fig*) it's always the same old story; **è ora di cambiare musica** (*fig*) it's time you changed your tune ▶**musica da ballo** dance music ▶**musica da camera** chamber music.

musical ['mju:zikəl] SM INV musical.

musicale [muzi'kale] AGG musical; **avere orecchio musicale** to have an ear for music.

musicalmente [musikal'mente] AVV musically.

musicare [muzi'kare] VT to set to music.

musicassetta [muzikas'setta] SF (pre-recorded) cassette.

musicista, i, e [muzi'tʃista] SM/F musician.

musicomane [muzi'kɔmane] SM/F music lover.

musivo, a [mu'zivo] AGG mosaic *attr*.

muso ['muzo] SM (*di animale*) muzzle; (*fig*: *di persona*) face; (: *pegg*) mug; (: *di aereo*) nose; (: *di auto, moto*) front (end); **rompere il muso a qn** to smash sb's face in; **mettere** *o* **fare il muso** to pull a long face; **tenere il muso** to sulk; **tenere il muso a qn** to be in a huff with sb; **ha storto il muso quando gliene ho parlato** he didn't look at all pleased when I mentioned it; **gliel'ho detto sul muso** I told him so to his face.

musone, a [mu'zone] SM/F sulky person.

mussola ['mussola] SF muslin.

mussoliniano, a [mussoli'njano] AGG (*vita, politica*) of Mussolini; (*stile*) Mussolini-like.

mustacchi [mus'takki] SMPL (*scherz*) mustachio *sg*.

musulmano, a [musul'mano], **mussulmano, a** [mussul'mano] AGG, SM/F Muslim, Moslem.

muta¹ ['muta] SF **a** (*di animali*: *gen*) moulting (*Brit*), molting (*Am*); (: *di serpenti*) shedding of skin; **andare in muta** to moult; shed (one's) skin **b** (*di subacqueo*) wet suit.

muta² ['muta] SF (*gruppo di cani*) pack.

mutabile [mu'tabile] AGG changeable.

mutabilità [mutabili'ta] SF changeability.

mutamento [muta'mento] SM change.

mutande [mu'tande] SFPL (*da uomo*) (under)pants; (*da*

donna) pants, knickers.

mutandine [mutan'dine] SFPL (*da bambino*) pants; (*da donna*) panties, knickers ►**mutandine di plastica** plastic pants.

mutandoni [mutan'doni] SMPL long johns (*fam*).

mutante [mu'tante] SM/F (*Bio, in fantascienza*) mutant.

mutare [mu'tare] ⊡ VT **a** (*gen*) to change; (*opinione, carattere*) to change, alter; **mutare qc in** to change sth into

b (*Zool: sogg: rettili*) to slough; (: *animali*): **mutare il pelo** to moult.

⊡ VI (*aus essere*) to change; **mutare di colore** to change colour; **qualcosa è mutato in lui** there's something different about him; **mutare in meglio/in peggio** to change for the better/for the worse.

⊡ **mutarsi** VIP: **mutarsi in** to change into, turn into; **il ghiaccio si mutò in acqua** the ice turned to water; **mutarsi d'abito** to change one's clothes.

mutazione [mutat'tsjone] SF change, alteration; (*Bio*) mutation.

mutevole [mu'tevole] AGG changeable; **umore mutevole** moodiness.

mutevolmente [mutevol'mente] AVV (*comportarsi*) unpredictably.

mutilare [muti'lare] VT (*gen, fig*) to mutilate; (*persona*) to maim; (*statua*) to deface; **la fresatrice gli ha mutilato la mano** the milling machine chopped off his hand.

mutilato, a [muti'lato] ⊡ AGG (*vedi vb*) mutilated; maimed; defaced.

⊡ SM/F cripple, disabled person (*through loss of limbs*) ►**mutilato di guerra** disabled ex-serviceman (*Brit*) o war veteran (*Am*) ►**mutilato del lavoro** person disabled at work.

mutilazione [mutilat'tsjone] SF (*vedi vb*) mutilation; maiming; defaçement.

mutismo [mu'tizmo] SM **a** (*Med*) muteness, mutism **b** (*atteggiamento*) (stubborn) silence; **chiudersi in un mutismo ostinato** to maintain a stubborn silence.

muto, a ['muto] ⊡ AGG (*Med*) dumb; (*Ling*) silent, mute; (*Geog: cartina, atlante*) blank; **il cinema muto** the silent cinema; **muto per lo stupore** *ecc* speechless with amazement *ecc*; **ha fatto scena muta** he didn't utter a word; **giuro che sarò muto come un pesce** I swear I won't open my mouth; **un muto rimprovero** a silent reproach.

⊡ SM/F (*Med*) dumb person, mute.

mutua ['mutua] SF: **medico della mutua** ≈ National Health Service doctor (*Brit*).

mutuabile [mutu'abile] AGG (*farmaco*) *prescribable on the NHS*.

mutuare [mutu'are] VT (*fig*) to borrow.

mutuato, a [mutu'ato] SM/F ≈ NHS patient.

mutuo[1], a ['mutuo] AGG (*reciproco*) mutual; **società di mutuo soccorso** friendly society (*Brit*), benefit society (*Am*).

mutuo[2] ['mutuo] SM (long-term) loan ►**mutuo ipotecario** mortgage.

N

N, n [ˈɛnne] SF O M INV (*lettera*) N, n; **N come Napoli** ≈ N for
Nellie (*Brit*), ≈ N for Nan (*Am*).

n ABBR (= *numero*) no.

N. ABBR (= *Nord*) N.

NA SIGLA = *Napoli*.

nababbo [naˈbabbo] SM (*anche fig*) nabob.

nacchere [ˈnakkere] SFPL castanets.

N.A.D. [nad] SIGLA M = **nucleo antidroga**.

nadir [naˈdir] SM (*Astron*) nadir.

nafta [ˈnafta] SF (*Chim*) naphtha; (*carburante*) diesel oil;
motore a nafta diesel engine.

naftalina [naftaˈlina] SF (*Chim*) naphthalene; (*tarmicida*)
mothballs *pl*.

naia [ˈnaja] SF (*Mil fam*) national service (*Brit*), draft (*Am*).

naiade [ˈnajade] SF (*Bot, Mitol*) naiad.

naif [naˈif] AGG INV naïve.

nailon [ˈnailon] SM = **nylon**.

Nairobi [naiˈrɔbi] SF Nairobi.

nanismo [naˈnizmo] SM (*Med*) dwarfism.

nanna [ˈnanna] SF (*fam*) bye-byes (*Brit*), beddy-bye (*Am*);
andare a nanna to go bye-byes o beddy-bye; **fare la
nanna** to sleep.

nano, a [ˈnano] ① SM/F dwarf.
② AGG dwarf *attr*.

nanometro [nanoˈmetro] SM nanometre.

napalm° [ˈnapalm] SM napalm.

Napoleone [napoleˈone] SM Napoleon.

napoleonico, a, ci, che [napoleˈɔniko] AGG Napoleonic.

napoletana [napoleˈtana] SF (*macchinetta da caffè*) Neapolitan coffeepot.

napoletano, a [napoleˈtano] AGG, SM/F Neapolitan.

Napoli [ˈnapoli] SF Naples.

nappa [ˈnappa] SF ⓐ (*ornamento per tende*) tassel ⓑ (*pelle*)
nappa, soft leather.

narcisismo [nartʃiˈzizmo] SM narcissism.

narcisista, i, e [nartʃiˈzista] SM/F narcissist; **essere narcisista** to have a Narcissus complex.

Narciso [narˈtʃizo] SM (*Mitol*) Narcissus.

narciso [narˈtʃizo] SM (*Bot*) narcissus.

narcodollari [narcoˈdollari] SMPL drug money *sg*.

narcos [ˈnarkos] SM INV (*colombiano*) Colombian drug
trafficker.

narcosi [narˈkɔzi] SF INV (*Med*) general anaesthesia (*Brit*) o
anesthesia (*Am*), narcosis; **essere sotto narcosi** to be
under general anaesthetic (*Brit*) o anesthetic (*Am*).

narcotico, a, ci, che [narˈkɔtiko] AGG, SM narcotic.

narcotizzare [narkotidˈdzare] VT to narcotize.

narcotrafficante [narkotraffiˈkante] SM/F drug trafficker.

narcotraffico [narkoˈtraffiko] SM drug trade.

narghilè [nargiˈlɛ] SM INV hookah, narghile.

narice [naˈritʃe] SF nostril.

narrare [narˈrare] ① VT to tell, narrate, recount.
② VI (*aus avere*): **narrare di** to tell the story of.

narrativa [narraˈtiva] SF (*branca letteraria*) fiction.

narrativo, a [narraˈtivo] AGG narrative.

narratore, trice [narraˈtore] SM/F narrator.

narrazione [narratˈtsjone] SF ⓐ (*di fatto, avvenimento*)
narration, account ⓑ (*storia, racconto*) story, tale.

narvalo [narˈvalo] SM (*pesce*) narwhal.

N.A.S. [nas] SIGLA M (= *Nucleo Antisofisticazioni*) *department of the carabinieri responsible for controls of
foodstuff, drinks, medicine etc.*

N.A.S.A. [ˈnaza] SIGLA F (= *National Aeronautics and Space
Administration*) NASA.

nasale [naˈsale] ① AGG (*Anat, Fonetica*) nasal.
② SF nasal consonant.

nascente [naʃˈʃɛnte] AGG (*sole, luna*) rising.

nascere [ˈnaʃʃere] VI IRREG (*aus essere*) ⓐ (*bambino,
animale*) to be born; (*pianta*) to come o spring up; **è nata
nel 1952** she was born in 1952; **sono nato il 4 febbraio** I
was born on the 4th of February; **l'uomo nasce libero**
man is born free; **nascono più femmine che maschi** there
are more girls being born than boys; **è appena nato** he's
a newborn baby; **nascere da genitori ricchi/poveri** to be
born of rich/poor parents; **essere nato per qc/per fare
qc** (*fig*) to be destined for sth/to do sth; **non sono nato
ieri** I wasn't born yesterday
ⓑ (*fiume*) to rise, have its source; (*sole*) to rise; (*giorno*)

to break; (*dente*) to come through; (*idea, speranza*) to be born; (*difficoltà, dubbio*) to arise; (*industria, movimento*) to start up; **il sole nasce ad oriente** the sun rises in the east; **far nascere** (*industria*) to create; (*sospetto, desiderio*) to arouse; **nascere da** (*fig: derivare, conseguire*) to arise from, be born out of; **l'odio che nasce da tali conflitti** the hatred which springs from such conflicts; **nasce spontanea la domanda...** the question which springs to mind is ...; **da cosa nasce cosa** one thing leads to another; **la rivolta è stata stroncata sul nascere** the revolt was nipped in the bud.

nascita ['naʃʃita] SF birth; **di nascita** by birth; **nobile di nascita** of noble birth; **dalla nascita** from birth; **è cieco dalla nascita** he has been blind from birth, he was born blind.

nascituro, a [naʃʃi'turo] SM/F future child; **come si chiamerà il nascituro?** what's the baby going to be called?

nascondere [nas'kondere] VB IRREG [1] VT (*gen*) to hide, conceal; **nascondere il viso tra le mani** to bury one's face in one's hands; **nascondere qc alla vista di qn** to hide sth from sb; **nascondere la verità a qn** to hide *o* keep the truth from sb; **non nascondo che mi farebbe molto piacere** I make no secret of the fact that I would like it.

[2] **nascondersi** VR to hide; **nascondersi alla vista di qn** to hide from sb, keep out of sb's sight; **dove si è nascosto?** where is he hiding?, where has he got to?; **dovresti nasconderti** you had better hide; (*fig*) you should be ashamed of yourself.

nascondiglio, gli [naskon'diʎʎo] SM hiding place.

nascondino [naskon'dino] SM: **giocare a nascondino** to play hide-and-seek *o* hide-and-go-seek (*Am*).

nascosi *ecc* [nas'kosi] VB *vedi* **nascondere**.

nascostamente [naskosta'mente] AVV furtively, secretly.

nascosto, a [nas'kosto] [1] PP di **nascondere**.

[2] AGG hidden; **tenere nascosto qc** to keep sth hidden; **gli hanno tenuto nascosta la notizia** they concealed *o* kept the news from him; **fare qc di nascosto** to do sth secretly; **andarsene di nascosto** to slip away.

nasello [na'sɛllo] SM (*pesce*) hake.

naso ['naso] SM nose; **parlare col naso** to talk through one's nose; **torcere** *o* **arricciare il naso (di fronte a qc)** to turn up one's nose (at sth); **avere naso per gli affari** to have a flair for business; **mettere il naso negli affari altrui** to poke one's nose into other people's business; **son 2 settimane che non metto il naso fuori di casa** it's 2 weeks since I last stuck my nose out of the door; **guarda, ce l'hai sotto il naso** look, it's right under your nose.

nassa ['nassa] SF (*per pesci*) fish trap; (*per aragoste*) lobster pot.

Nassau [nas'sau] SF Nassau.

nastrino [nas'trino] SM ribbon.

nastro ['nastro] SM (*gen, di macchina da scrivere*) ribbon; (*Tecn, Sport*) tape ▶**nastro adesivo** adhesive tape ▶**nastro isolante** insulating tape ▶**nastro magnetico** magnetic tape ▶**nastro trasportatore** conveyor belt.

nastroteca, che [nastro'tɛka] SF tape library.

nasturzio, zi [nas'turtsjo] SM cress ▶**nasturzio indiano** nasturtium.

Natale [na'tale] SM Christmas; **cosa fai a Natale?** what are you doing at Christmas? *o* at Christmastime?; **Buon Natale!** Merry Christmas!; **albero di Natale** Christmas tree; **Babbo Natale** Santa Claus, Father Christmas (*Brit*).

natale [na'tale] [1] AGG (*paese, città*) native, of one's birth.

[2]: **natali** SMPL: **di illustri/umili natali** of noble/humble birth.

natalità [natali'ta] SF birth rate.

natalizio, zia, zi, zie [nata'littsjo] AGG (*del Natale*) Christmas *attr*.

natante [na'tante] SM craft *inv*, boat.

natatorio, ria, ri, rie [nata'tɔrjo] AGG (*Zool*): **vescica natatoria** swim bladder.

natica, che ['natika] SF (*Anat*) buttock.

natio, tia, tii, tie [na'tio] AGG native.

Natività [nativi'ta] SF INV (*Rel*) Nativity.

nativo, a [na'tivo] AGG, SM/F (*gen*) native.

nato, a ['nato] [1] PP di **nascere**.

[2] AGG **a** (*artista ecc*) born; **un attore nato** a born actor **b** (*di donna, prima di sposarsi*): **la sig.ra Rossi, nata Bianchi** Mrs Rossi, née Bianchi.

[3] SM: **un nuovo nato** a newborn child; **i nati del** *o* **nel 1960** those born in 1960.

N.A.T.O. ['nato] SIGLA F NATO (= *North Atlantic Treaty Organization*).

natura [na'tura] SF **a** (*mondo naturale*): **la natura** nature; **il mondo della natura** the world of nature; **vivere a contatto con la natura** to live close to nature; **questa sostanza non esiste in natura** this substance does not exist naturally; **contro natura** unnatural

b (*carattere*) nature; **la natura umana** human nature; **è nella natura delle cose** it's in the nature of things; **è allegro di natura** he's naturally cheerful; **non è nella sua natura fare così** he's not the sort of person who would do that; **i nostri rapporti sono di natura professionale** our relationship is of a professional nature

c (*tipo*) nature, kind; **scritti di varia natura** writings of various kinds; **pagare in natura** to pay in kind

d (*Pittura*): **natura morta** still life.

naturale [natu'rale] [1] AGG (*gen*) natural; **è naturale che sia così** it's natural that it should be so; **gli viene naturale comportarsi così** it comes naturally to him to behave like that; **(ma) è naturale!** (*in risposte*) of course!; **a grandezza naturale** life-size; **figlio naturale** natural child; **acqua naturale** spring water; **i suoi capelli sono biondi naturali** her hair is naturally blonde.

[2] SM: **al naturale** (*alimenti*) served plain; (*ritratto*) life-size; **tonno al naturale** tuna in brine; **pesche/fragole al naturale** peaches/strawberries in fruit juice; **è più bella al naturale** (*senza trucco*) she's prettier without make-up.

naturalezza [natura'lettsa] SF naturalness; **con naturalezza** naturally.

naturalista, i, e [natura'lista] SM/F naturalist.

naturalistico, a, ci, che [natura'listiko] AGG naturalistic.

naturalizzare [naturalid'dzare] [1] VT to naturalize.

[2] **naturalizzarsi** VIP to become naturalized; **si è naturalizzato italiano** he's become a naturalized Italian.

naturalizzazione [naturaliddzat'tsjone] SF naturalization.

naturalmente [natural'mente] AVV naturally; **vieni? — naturalmente** are you coming? — of course *o* naturally.

naturismo [natu'rizmo] SM naturism, nudism.

naturista, i, e [natu'rista] AGG, SM/F naturist, nudist.

naufragare [naufra'gare] VI (*aus* essere *o* avere) (*nave*) to be wrecked; (*persona*) to be shipwrecked; (*fig: progetto, disegno*) to fall through; **tutte le nostre speranze naufragarono** all our hopes were dashed.

naufragio, gi [nau'fradʒo] SM shipwreck; (*fig*) ruin, failure; **fare naufragio** to be shipwrecked; (*fig*) to fail, fall through.

naufrago, a, ghi, ghe ['naufrago] SM/F shipwrecked person, shipwreck victim; (*su un'isola*) castaway.

nausea ['nauzea] SF (*Med*) nausea; **avere la nausea** to feel sick (*Brit*) *o* sick to one's stomach (*Am*); **mi dai la nausea!** (*fig*) you make me sick!; **fino alla nausea** ad nauseam; **ho bevuto fino alla nausea** I drank till I felt sick (to my stomach).

nauseabondo, a [nauzea'bondo], **nauseante** [nauze-'ante] AGG nauseating, sickening.

nauseare [nauze'are] VT to nauseate, make (feel) sick (*Brit*) *o* sick to one's stomach (*Am*); **ho mangiato tanti funghi che ora ne sono nauseato** I've eaten so many mushrooms that now I'm sick of them; **il suo comportamento mi ha nauseato** his behaviour sickened me.

nautica ['nautika] SF navigation, nautical science; **nautica da diporto** yachting.

nautico, a, ci, che ['nautiko] AGG (*gen*) nautical; **salone nautico** (*mostra*) boat show; **sci nautico** water-skiing.

navale [na'vale] AGG (*gen*) naval; **battaglia navale** naval battle; (*gioco*) battleships *sg*; **cantiere navale** shipyard.

navata [na'vata] SF: **navata centrale** nave ►**navata laterale** aisle.

nave ['nave] SF ship, vessel ►**nave ammiraglia** flagship ►**nave da carico** cargo ship, freighter ►**nave cisterna** tanker ►**nave da guerra** warship ►**nave di linea** liner ►**nave mercantile** merchant ship ►**nave passeggeri** passenger ship ►**nave portaerei** aircraft carrier ►**nave scuola** training ship ►**nave spaziale** spaceship ►**nave da trasporto** cargo ship ►**nave a vapore** steamship ►**nave a vela** sailing ship.

navetta [na'vetta] SF **a** (*di telaio*) shuttle **b** (*servizio di collegamento*) shuttle (service).

navicella [navi'tʃɛlla] SF **a** (*di pallone, dirigibile*) gondola ►**navicella spaziale** spaceship **b** (*per l'incenso*) incense boat.

navigabile [navi'gabile] AGG (*canale, fiume*) navigable.

navigante [navi'gante] SM sailor, seaman.

navigare [navi'gare] VI (*aus avere*) to sail; **suo marito naviga** her husband is a sailor; **navigare in cattive acque** (*fig: finanziariamente*) to be hard up.

navigato, a [navi'gato] AGG (*fig: esperto*) experienced.

navigatore, trice [naviga'tore] SM/F (*gen*) navigator ►**navigatore solitario** single-handed sailor.

navigazione [navigat'tsjone] SF (*Naut, Aer*) navigation; **navigazione aerea/interna/fluviale** air/inland/river navigation; **compagnia di navigazione** shipping company; **durante la navigazione** during the (sea *o* river) voyage; **dopo una settimana di navigazione** after a week at sea.

naviglio, gli [na'viʎʎo] SM **a** (*letter: imbarcazione*) ship; (*flotta*) fleet, ships *pl* ►**naviglio da pesca** fishing fleet **b** (*canale artificiale*) canal; (*canale navigabile*) (navigable) canal.

Nazareno [naddza'rɛno] SM: **Gesù Nazareno** Jesus of Nazareth; **il Nazareno** the Nazarene.

Nazaret, Nazareth ['nadzaret] SF Nazareth.

nazionale [nattsjo'nale] **1** AGG (*gen*) national; (*arrivi, passeggeri, economia*) domestic. **2** SF (*Sport*) national team.

nazionalismo [nattsjona'lizmo] SM nationalism.

nazionalista, i, e [nattsjona'lista] AGG, SM/F nationalist.

nazionalistico, a, ci, che [nattsjona'listiko] AGG nationalist.

nazionalità [nattsjonali'ta] SF INV nationality.

nazionalizzare [nattsjonalid'dzare] VT to nationalize.

nazionalizzato, a [nattsjonalid'dzato] AGG nationalized; **industria nazionalizzata** nationalized industry.

nazionalizzazione [nattsjonaliddzat'tsjone] SF nationalization.

nazionalsocialismo [nattsjonalsotʃa'lizmo] SM National Socialism, Nazism.

nazione [nat'tsjone] SF nation.

naziskin ['na:tsi skin] SM/F INV skinhead (*belonging to extreme right-wing group*).

nazismo [nat'tsizmo] SM Nazism.

nazista, i, e [nat'tsista] AGG, SM/F Nazi (*inv*).

nazistico, a, ci, che [nat'tsistiko] AGG Nazi *attr*.

N.B., n.b. ABBR (= *nota bene*) N.B.

N.d.A. ABBR (= *nota dell'autore*) author's note.

N.d.D. ABBR (= *nota della direzione*) editor's note.

N.d.E. ABBR (= *nota dell'editore*) publisher's note.

N.d.R. ABBR (= *nota della redazione*) editor's note.

'ndrangheta ['ndrangeta] SF *Mafia-like criminal organization in Calabria*.

N.d.T. ABBR (= *nota del traduttore*) translator's note.

NE ABBR (= *nordest*) NE.

ne [ne] **1** PRON **a** (*di lui, lei, loro*) of him (*o* her *o* them); about him (*o* her *o* them); **ne riconosco la voce** I recognize his (*o* her) voice; **non lo vedo da anni, parlamene** I haven't seen him for years, tell me about him

b (*con valore partitivo*) of it; of them (*spesso omesso*); **ne voglio ancora** I want some more (of it *o* them); **dammene un po'** give me some; **hai dei libri? — sì, ne ho** have you got any books? — yes I have; **hai del pane? — no, non ne ho** have you got any bread? — no I haven't any; **quanti anni hai? — ne ho 17** how old are you? — I'm 17

c (*riguardo*) about it; about them; **non me ne importa niente** I couldn't care less about it; **cosa ne pensi?** what do you think (about it)?; **cosa ne faremo?** what will we do with it (o them)?; **non parliamone più!** let's not talk about it any more!

d (*da ciò*): **ne deduco che l'avete trovato** I gather you've found it; **ne consegue che...** it follows therefore that ....

2 AVV (*moto da luogo: da lì*) from there; (: *da qui*) from here; **ne vengo ora** I've just come from there; **me ne vado immediatamente** I'm leaving (here) right away; **siamo arrivati alle 7 e ne siamo venuti via alle 10** we got to the theatre at 7 and left at 10.

né [ne] CONG: **né... né...** neither ...nor ...; **né mio padre né mia madre parlano l'italiano** neither my father nor my mother speaks Italian; **non parla né l'italiano né il tedesco** he speaks neither Italian nor German, he doesn't speak either Italian or German; **non voglio discutere né con lui né con mio fratello** I don't want to speak to him or to my brother; **non l'ho più vista né sentita** I haven't seen or heard from her again; **non voglio né posso accettare** I neither wish to nor can accept; **non piove né nevica** it isn't raining or snowing; **né da una parte né dall'altra** on neither side; **né più né meno** no more no less; **né l'uno né l'altro** neither of them, neither the one nor the other; **né l'uno né l'altro lo vuole** neither of them wants it; **non mi fa né caldo né freddo** it makes no odds to me.

neanche [ne'anke] **1** AVV not even; **non mi ha neanche pagato** he didn't even pay me; **non ci vado — neanch'io** I'm not going — neither *o* nor am I; **non l'ho visto — neanch'io** I didn't see him — neither did I *o* I didn't either; **neanche lui lo farebbe** not even he would do it, even he wouldn't do it; **non ho neanche un soldo** I haven't got a single penny; **non ci penso neanche!** I wouldn't dream of it!; **neanche per idea** *o* **per sogno!** not on your life!; **se ne è partito senza neanche salutare** he went off without even saying goodbye; **non parlo spagnolo — e lui? — neanche** I don't speak Spanish — what about him? — he doesn't either *o* neither does he; **lui non è inglese e neanche sua moglie** he isn't English and neither is his wife.

2 CONG not even; **non lo sposerei neanche se fosse un re** I wouldn't marry him even if he were a king; **neanche se volesse potrebbe venire** he couldn't come even if he wanted to; **neanche a pagarlo lo farebbe** he wouldn't do it even if you paid him.

nebbia ['nebbja] SF (*densa*) fog; (*foschia*) mist.

nebbiolina [nebbjo'lina] SF mist.

nebbione [neb'bjone] SM thick fog.

nebbiosità [nebbjosi'ta] SF fogginess.

nebbioso, a [neb'bjoso] AGG (*vedi sf*) foggy; misty.

nebulizzatore [nebuliddza'tore] SM atomizer.

nebulosa [nebu'losa] SF nebula.

nebulosità [nebulosi'ta] SF haziness.

nebuloso, a [nebu'loso] AGG (*atmosfera, cielo*) hazy; (*fig*) hazy, vague.

nécessaire [nesɛ'sɛr] SM INV: **nécessaire da cucito** sewing kit ►**nécessaire da toilette** make-up bag *o* case ►**nécessaire da viaggio** overnight case *o* bag.

necessariamente [netʃessarja'mente] AVV necessarily.

necessario, ria, ri, rie [netʃes'sarjo] **1** AGG (*gen*) necessary; (*persona*) indispensable; **è necessario che tu vada** you will have to go, you must go, it is necessary for you to go; **non è necessario che ti fermi** you don't need to stay; **non ho avuto il tempo necessario** I didn't have enough *o* sufficient time; **se necessario** if need be, if necessary; **rendersi necessario** (*persona*) to make o.s. indispensable; **si rende necessario partire** it has become necessary for me (*o* you *ecc*) to leave; **portami i documenti necessari** bring me the necessary documents.

2 SM: **fare il necessario** to do what is necessary; **lo stretto necessario** the bare essentials *pl*; **hanno appena il necessario per vivere** they have barely enough to live on; **non ho con me il necessario** I haven't got what I need with me; **hai tutto il necessario per scrivere?** have you got all your writing materials?; **lavorare/preoccuparsi più del necessario** to work/worry more than is necessary *o* more than one has to.

necessità [netʃessi'ta] SF INV (*bisogno*) necessity, need; (*povertà*) poverty; **per necessità** out of need *o* necessity; **di necessità** (*necessariamente*) of necessity; **in caso di necessità** in case of need, if need be; **non vedo la necessità di andare tutti quanti** I don't see any necessity for us all to go; **trovarsi nella necessità di fare qc** to be forced *o* obliged to do sth, have to do sth; **fare di necessità virtù** to make a virtue of necessity.

necessitare [netʃessi'tare] **1** VI (*aus essere*) (*aiuto, intervento*) to be necessary, be needed, be required; **necessita il vostro aiuto** your help is needed *o* necessary *o* required; **necessitare di** (*aver bisogno*) to need; **necessita di un'attenzione maggiore** it requires greater attention *o* care; **prima di essere pronto necessita di molte altre cose** a lot of other things are needed before it will be ready.

2 VT to need, require.

necrofilia [nekrofi'lia] SF necrophilia.

necrofilo, a [ne'krɔfilo] SM/F necrophiliac.

necrologio, gi [nekro'lɔdʒo] SM (*annuncio*) obituary notice; (*registro*) register of deaths.

necropoli [ne'krɔpoli] SF INV necropolis.

necroscopia [nekrosko'pia] SF necroscopy, necropsy.

necrosi [ne'krɔzi] SF INV necrosis.

nefando, a [ne'fando] AGG vile.

nefasto, a [ne'fasto] AGG (*giorno*) fateful, fatal; (*segno, presagio*) inauspicious, ill-omened; (*fam: persona*) full of gloom and doom.

nefrite [ne'frite] SF (*Med*) nephritis.

nefritico, a, ci, che [ne'fritiko] **1** AGG nephritic. **2** SM/F person suffering from nephritis.

negabile [ne'gabile] AGG deniable; **non è negabile** it's undeniable.

negare [ne'gare] VT (*gen*) to deny; (*rifiutare*) to deny, refuse; **negare qc/di aver fatto qc** to deny sth/having done sth; **negare a qn il permesso (di fare qc)** to refuse sb permission (to do sth); **negare a qn la possibilità di fare qc** to deny sb the possibility of doing sth; **mi hanno negato un aumento** they turned down my request for a rise (*Brit*) *o* raise; **negare obbedienza a qn** to refuse to obey sb.

negativa [nega'tiva] SF (*Gramm, Fot*) negative.

negativamente [negativa'mente] AVV negatively; **rispondere negativamente** to give a negative response, reply in the negative.

negatività [negativi'ta] SF (*di atteggiamento*) negativeness, negativity; (*Fis*) negativity.

negativizzarsi [negativid'dzarsi] VIP (*Med*) to become HIV negative.

negativo, a [nega'tivo] **1** AGG negative. **2** SM (*Fot*) negative.

negato, a [ne'gato] AGG (*persona*): **essere negato per** *o* **in qc** to be hopeless at sth, be no good at sth.

negazione [negat'tsjone] SF negation.

negherò ecc [nege'rɔ] VB vedi **negare**.

negletto, a [ne'gletto] AGG (*trascurato*) neglected.

negli ['neʎʎi] PREP + ART vedi **in**.

négligé [negli'ʒe] SM INV negligee.

negligente [negli'dʒɛnte] AGG (*gen*) negligent; (*non diligente*) careless.

negligenza [negli'dʒɛntsa] SF (*vedi agg*) negligence; carelessness.

negoziabile [negot'tsjabile] AGG negotiable.

negoziante [negot'tsjante] SM/F shopkeeper (*Brit*), storekeeper (*Am*).

negoziare [negot'tsjare] **1** VT to negotiate. **2** VI (*aus avere*): **negoziare in** to trade *o* deal in.

negoziato [negot'tsjato] SM negotiation ►**negoziati per la pace** peace talks *o* negotiations.

negoziatore, trice [negottsja'tore] SM/F negotiator.

negoziazione [negottsjat'tsjone] SF negotiation.

negozio, zi [ne'gɔttsjo] SM **a** (*bottega*) shop (*Brit*), store (*Am*) ►**negozio di scarpe** shoe shop *o* store **b** (*Dir*): **negozio giuridico** legal transaction.

negriere, a [ne'grjɛre], **negriero, a** [ne'grjɛro] **1** SM (*Storia*) slaver, slave-trader.

2 SM/F (*fig pegg*) slave-driver.

negro, a ['negro] 1 AGG (*razza, popolo*) black, Negro (*frm*).

2 SM/F Negro/Negress; **lavorare come un negro** (*fig*) to work like a slave.

negroide [ne'grɔide] AGG, SM/F negroid.

negromante [negro'mante] SM/F necromancer.

negromanzia [negroman'tsia] SF necromancy.

Negus ['negus] SM INV Negus.

nei ['nei] PREP + ART vedi **in**.

nembo ['nembo] SM (*Meteor*) nimbus.

Nemesi ['nɛmezi] SF (*Mitol, fig*) Nemesis.

nemico, a, ci, che [ne'miko] 1 SM/F enemy.

2 AGG (*Mil*) enemy *attr*; (*ostile*) hostile; **farsi nemico qn** to make an enemy of sb; **essere nemico di qc** to be strongly averse *o* opposed to sth; **il gelo è nemico delle piante** frost is harmful to plants.

nemmeno [nem'meno] AVV, CONG = **neanche**.

nenia ['nɛnja] SF (*canto*) dirge; (*motivo monotono*) monotonous tune; (*fig: discorso*) tale of woe.

neo ['nɛo] SM (*gen*) mole; (*sul viso*) beauty spot; (*fig: imperfezione*) (slight) flaw; (: *di persona*) slight defect.

neo... ['nɛo] PREF neo... .

neoclassico, a, ci, che [neo'klassiko] 1 AGG (*stile, epoca, artista*) neoclassical.

2 SM (*stile*) neoclassical; (*artista*) neoclassicist.

neocolonialismo [neokolonja'lizmo] SM neocolonialism.

neofascismo [neofaʃ'ʃizmo] SM neofascism.

neofascista, i, e [neofaʃ'ʃista] AGG, SM/F neofascist.

neofita, i, e [ne'ɔfita] SM/F (*Rel*) neophyte; (*fig*) novice.

neoformazione [neoformat'tsjone] SF (*Med*) neoplasm.

neolatino, a [neola'tino] AGG Romance *attr*.

neolaureato, a [neolaure'ato] 1 AGG recently graduated.

2 SM/F recent graduate.

neologismo [neolo'dʒizmo] SM neologism.

neon ['nɛon] SM INV (*Chim*) neon; (*lampadario*) neon lamp; **luce al neon** neon light.

neonato, a [neo'nato] 1 AGG newborn.

2 SM/F newborn baby.

neonazismo [neonat'tsizmo] SM neonazism.

neonazista, i, e [neonat'tsista] AGG, SM/F neonazi.

neoprene® [neo'prɛne] SM neoprene.

neorealismo [neorea'lizmo] SM neorealism.

neozelandese [neoddzelan'dese] 1 AGG New Zealand *attr*.

2 SM/F New Zealander.

Nepal ['nepal] SM: **il Nepal** Nepal.

nepotismo [nepo'tizmo] SM nepotism.

neppure [nep'pure] AVV, CONG = **neanche**.

nerastro, a [ne'rastro] AGG (*gen*) blackish; (*labbra*) purple.

nerbata [ner'bata] SF (*colpo*) blow; (*sferzata*) whiplash.

nerbo ['nɛrbo] SM whip, lash; (*fig: di esercito*) backbone.

nerboruto, a [nerbo'ruto] AGG brawny, muscular; (*robusto*) robust.

nereide [ne'rɛide] SF (*Mitol*) Nereid.

neretto [ne'retto] SM a (*Tip*) bold (type) (*Brit*), bold face b (*articolo di giornale*) article in bold type *o* face.

nero, a ['nero] 1 AGG a (*colore*) black; (*scuro*) dark; (*pelle: abbronzata*) tanned; **mettere qc nero su bianco** to put sth down in black and white; **nero come il carbone/la pece** as black as coal/pitch; **quel colletto è nero** (*sporco*) that collar is black *o* filthy

b (*negro: razza*) black; **l'Africa nera** black Africa

c (*fig: disperazione, futuro*) black; (: *giornata*) awful; **essere (di umore) nero** to be in a filthy mood; **sono in un periodo nero** I'm going through a bad time; **vedere**

tutto nero to look on the black side (of things); **vivono nella miseria più nera** they live in utter *o* abject poverty d (*illegale*): **lavoro nero** moonlighting (*Brit*), double-dipping (*Am*); **mercato nero** black market; **fondi neri** slush fund *sg*.

2 SM (*colore*) black; **vestirsi di *o* in nero** to dress in black; **essere pagato in nero** to be paid in cash (*to evade payment of taxes*); **lavorare in nero** to moonlight (*Brit*) *o* double-dip (*Am*) (*without statutory deductions of payment of taxes*).

3 SM/F (*persona*) black, black man/woman.

nerofumo [nero'fumo] SM lampblack.

Nerone [ne'rone] SM Nero.

nervatura [nerva'tura] SF (*Anat*) nerves *pl*, nervous system; (*Bot*) veining; (*Archit, Tecn*) rib.

nervino, a [ner'vino] AGG (*Chim*): **gas nervino** nerve gas.

nervo ['nɛrvo] SM a (*Anat*) nerve; (*Bot*) vein ▶**nervo ottico** optic nerve b : **avere i nervi** to be very irritable; **avere i nervi a fior di pelle** to be on edge, be nervy (*Brit*); **ho i nervi scossi** my nerves are shattered; **far venire i nervi a qn** OR **dare sui nervi a qn** to get on sb's nerves; **avere i nervi saldi** to be calm; **che nervi!** damn (it)!

nervosamente [nervosa'mente] AVV nervously.

nervosismo [nervo'sizmo] SM (*Psic*) nervousness; (*irritazione*) irritability; **farsi prendere dal nervosismo** to let one's nerves get the better of one.

nervoso, a [ner'voso] 1 AGG a (*tensione, sistema*) nervous; (*centro*) nerve *attr*; **esaurimento nervoso** nervous breakdown

b (*agitato*) nervous, tense; (*irritabile*) irritable, touchy

c (*gambe, corpo*) sinewy.

2 SM: **far venire il nervoso a qn** (*fam*) to get on sb's nerves; **farsi prendere dal nervoso** to let o.s. get irritated.

nespola ['nɛspola] SF (*frutto*) medlar; (*fig*) blow, punch.

nespolo ['nɛspolo] SM medlar (tree).

nesso ['nɛsso] SM connection, link.

nessuno, a [nes'suno] 1 AGG (dav sm: **nessun** + consonante, vocale, **nessuno** + s impura, gn, pn, ps, x, z,; dav sf: **nessuna** + consonante, **nessun'** + vocale) a (*non uno*) no, not any; (*espressione negativa*) + any; **nessun uomo è immortale** no man is immortal; **nessun altro** no-one else, nobody else; **nessun altro ti crederà** no one else will believe you; **non ho nessun dubbio** I have no doubts; **non c'è nessun bisogno** there's no need, there isn't any need; **in nessun caso** under no circumstances; **in nessun luogo** nowhere; **nessun'altra cosa** nothing else; **per nessuna cosa nel mondo** not for anything in the world

b (*qualche*) any; **nessuna obiezione?** any objections?.

2 PRON a (*non uno*) no-one, nobody, *espressione negativa* + anyone; (: *cosa*) none, *espressione negativa* + any; **nessuno di** (*riferito a persone, cose*) none of; **nessuno mi crede** no-one believes me; **nessuno si muova!** nobody move!; **non c'era nessuno** there was no-one there, there wasn't anyone there; **non è venuto nessuno** nobody came; **nessuno di loro/dei presenti** none of them/of those present; **ha molti libri ma non me ne piace nessuno** he has lots of books but I don't like any of them; **non ne ho letto nessuno** I haven't read any of them, I have read none of them

b (*qualcuno*) anyone, anybody; **ha telefonato nessuno?** did anyone phone?.

3 SM (*pegg: nullità*) nobody, nonentity; **e io chi sono,**

nessuno? and who am I then, nobody?; **con tutte quelle arie resta comunque un nessuno** despite his airs and graces, he's still a nobody.

nettamente [netta'mente] AVV (*chiaramente*) clearly; (*decisamente*) decidedly.

nettapiedi [netta'pjɛdi] SM INV (*zerbino*) (door)mat.

nettapipe [netta'pipe] SM INV pipe cleaner.

nettare¹ [net'tare] VT to clean.

nettare² ['nɛttare] SM nectar.

nettezza [net'tettsa] SF **a** (*pulizia*) cleanness, cleanliness ▶ **nettezza urbana** cleansing department (*Brit*), department of sanitation (*Am*) **b** (*chiarezza*) clarity.

netto, a ['nɛtto] ① AGG **a** (*pulito*) clean **b** (*chiaro: contorni, immagine*) clear, sharp, clear-cut; (*deciso: rifiuto, vittoria*) clear, definite; **tagliare qc di netto** to cut sth clean off; **taglio netto** clean cut; **un taglio netto col passato** a clean break with the past **c** (*stipendio, peso*) net. ② SM: **al netto delle tasse** after tax, net of tax. ③ AVV: **chiaro e netto** plainly.

Nettuno [net'tuno] SM (*Mitol, Astron*) Neptune.

netturbino [nettur'bino] SM dustman (*Brit*), dustbin man (*Brit*), garbage collector (*Am*) o man, trash man (*Am*).

neurite [neu'rite] SF = **nevrite**.

neuro ['neuro] SIGLA F = **clinica neurologica**; vedi **neurologico**.

neuro... ['neuro] PREF neuro... .

neurochirurgia [neurokirur'dʒia] SF neurosurgery.

neurochirurgo, ghi o **-gi** [neuroki'rurgo] SM neurosurgeon.

neurologia [neurolo'dʒia] SF neurology.

neurologico, a, ci, che [neuro'lɔdʒiko] AGG neurological; **clinica neurologica** neurological clinic.

neurologo, a, gi, ghe [neu'rɔlogo] SM/F neurologist.

neurone [neu'rone] SM neuron, nerve cell.

neuropatia [neuropa'tia] SF neuropathy.

neuropatico, a, ci, che [neuro'patiko] ① AGG neuropathic. ② SM/F neuropath.

neuropsichiatra, i, e [neuropsi'kjatra] SM/F neuropsychiatrist.

neuropsichiatria [neuropsikja'tria] SF neuropsychiatry.

neurosi [neu'rɔzi] SF INV = **nevrosi**.

neurovegetativo, a [neurovedʒeta'tivo] AGG (*Med*): **sistema neurovegetativo** autonomic nervous system.

neutrale [neu'trale] AGG, SM neutral.

neutralità [neutrali'ta] SF neutrality.

neutralizzare [neutralid'dzare] VT (*gen, Chim*) to neutralize.

neutralizzazione [neutraliddzat'tsjone] SF neutralization.

neutrino [neu'trino] SM neutrino.

neutro, a ['nɛutro] ① AGG (*gen*) neutral; (*Gramm, Zool*) neuter. ② SM (*Gramm*) neuter.

neutrone [neu'trone] SM neutron.

nevaio, ai [ne'vajo] SM snowfield.

nevato [ne'vato] SM (*Geog*) nevé.

neve ['neve] SF snow; **c'era un tempo da neve** it was snowy; **montare a neve** (*Culin*) to whip up ▶ **neve carbonica** dry ice.

nevicare [nevi'kare] VB IMPERS to snow, be snowing.

nevicata [nevi'kata] SF snowfall.

nevischio, chi [ne'viskjo] SM sleet.

nevoso, a [ne'voso] AGG (*montagna*) snow-covered;

(*tempo, inverno*) snowy.

nevralgia [nevral'dʒia] SF neuralgia.

nevralgico, a, ci, che [ne'vraldʒiko] AGG: **punto nevralgico** (*Med*) nerve centre (*Brit*) o center (*Am*); (*fig*) crucial point; **è un punto nevralgico del traffico** it is one of the main areas of traffic congestion.

nevrastenia [nevraste'nia] SF neurasthenia.

nevrastenico, a, ci, che [nevras'tɛniko] ① AGG (*Med*) neurasthenic; (*fig*) hot-tempered. ② SM/F (*vedi agg*) neurasthenic; hot-tempered person.

nevrite [ne'vrite] SF neuritis.

nevrosi [ne'vrɔzi] SF INV neurosis.

nevrotico, a, ci, che [ne'vrɔtiko] AGG, SM/F (*anche fig*) neurotic.

newyorchese [njujor'kese] ① AGG of o from New York. ② SM/F New Yorker.

Niagara [nja'gara] SM: **le cascate del Niagara** the Niagara Falls.

nibbio, bi ['nibbjo] SM (*uccello*) kite.

Nicaragua [nika'ragwa] SM: **il Nicaragua** Nicaragua.

nicaraguense [nikara'gwɛnse], **nicaraguese** [nikara'gwese] AGG, SM/F Nicaraguan.

nicchia ['nikkja] SF (*gen, fig*) niche; (*naturale*) cavity, hollow ▶ **nicchia ecologica** niche ▶ **nicchia di mercato** (*Comm*) niche market.

nicchiare [nik'kjare] VI (*aus avere*) to shilly-shally, hesitate.

nichel ['nikel] SM nickel.

nichelare [nike'lare] VT to nickel-plate.

nichelato, a [nike'lato] AGG nickel-plated.

nichelatura [nikela'tura] SF nickel-plating.

nichelio [ni'kɛljo] SM = **nichel**.

nichilismo [niki'lizmo] SM nihilism.

nichilista, i, e [niki'lista] ① AGG nihilistic. ② SM/F nihilist.

Nicosia [niko'zia] SF Nicosia.

nicotina [niko'tina] SF nicotine.

nidiata [ni'djata] SF (*di uccelli, fig: di bambini*) brood; (*di altri animali*) litter.

nidificare [nidifi'kare] VI (*aus avere*) to nest.

nido ['nido] ① SM (*Zool*) nest; (*fig: casa*) nest, home; **a nido d'ape** (*tessuto, ricamo*) honeycomb *attr*. ② AGG INV: **asilo nido** crèche (*Brit*), day-care center (*Am*).

niente ['njɛnte] ① PRON (*nessuna cosa*) nothing; (*qualcosa*) anything; **non... niente** nothing, *espressione negativa* + anything; **niente lo fermerà** nothing will stop him; **non ho visto niente** I saw nothing, I didn't see anything; **ti serve niente?** do you need anything?; **niente di grave/nuovo** nothing serious/new; **non gli va bene niente** he's never satisfied; **un uomo da niente** a nobody, a nonentity; **una cosa da niente** a trivial thing; **non fa niente!** it doesn't matter!; **fa niente se non vengo?** does it matter if I don't come?; **non mi sono fatto niente** I haven't hurt myself at all; **la cura non gli ha fatto niente** the treatment hasn't done anything for him; **non ho niente a che fare con lui** I have nothing to do with him; **ha niente in contrario se...?** would you object if ...?; **come se niente fosse** as if nothing had happened; **niente al mondo** nothing on earth o in the world; **niente di niente** absolutely nothing; **nessuno fa niente per niente** no one does anything for nothing; **ho parlato per niente** I spoke to no purpose, I wasted my breath; **sono venuto per niente** there was no point in my coming; **si arrabbia per niente** he gets annoyed at the slightest thing;

nient'altro nothing else; **nient'altro?** (*in negozio*) is that all?, is there anything else?; **nient'altro che** nothing but; (*solamente*) just, only; **so poco o niente di lui** I know next to nothing about him; **non so niente di niente** I know nothing at all; **quel brodo non sa di niente** that soup is tasteless; **niente meno = nientemeno**.

2 AGG: **non ho niente voglia di farlo** I'm not at all keen to do it; **niente paura!** never fear!; **e niente scuse!** don't try to make excuses!; **niente male!** not bad at all!.

3 SM nothing; **si è fatto dal niente** he's a self-made man; **il mondo è stato creato dal niente** the world was created out of nothing; **un bel niente** absolutely nothing; **basta un niente per farlo piangere** the slightest thing is enough to make him cry; **si è ridotto al niente** he has lost everything; **si è ridotto a un niente** he's just skin and bone.

4 AVV (*in nessuna misura*): **non... niente** not ...at all; **non è niente buono** it's not good at all; **non... per niente** (*affatto*) not ...at all; **non si è visto per niente** he hasn't been seen at all; **non è per niente vero** it's not true at all; **niente affatto** not at all, not in the least; **poco o niente** next to nothing.

nientedimeno [njentedi'meno], **nientemeno** [njente'-meno] 1 AVV (*addirittura*) actually, even; **è diventata nientedimeno che amministratore delegato** she has become managing director, no less.

2 ESCL really!, you don't say!

nietzschiano, a [nit'tʃano] AGG Nietzschean.

Niger ['nidʒer] SM: **il Niger** (*stato*) Niger; (*fiume*) the Niger.

Nigeria [ni'dʒɛrja] SF: **la Nigeria** Nigeria.

nigeriano, a [nidʒe'rjano] AGG, SM/F Nigerian.

night [nait], **night-club** ['naitklʌb] SM INV nightclub.

Nilo ['nilo] SM: **il Nilo** the Nile.

nimbo ['nimbo] SM halo.

ninfa ['ninfa] SF nymph.

ninfea [nin'fɛa] SF water lily.

ninfetta [nin'fetta] SF nymphet.

ninfomane [nin'fomane] SF nymphomaniac.

ninfomania [ninfoma'nia] SF nymphomania.

ninnananna [ninna'nanna] SF lullaby.

ninnolo ['ninnolo] SM (*gingillo*) knick-knack; (*balocco*) plaything.

nipote [ni'pote] SM/F (*di nonni*) grandchild, grandson/granddaughter; (*di zii*) nephew/niece.

nipponico, a, ci, che [nip'poniko] AGG Japanese, Nipponese.

nirvana [nir'vana] SM nirvana.

nitidamente [nitida'mente] AVV clearly.

nitidezza [niti'dettsa] SF (*gen*) clearness; (*di stile*) clarity; (*Fot, TV: di immagine*) sharpness.

nitido, a ['nitido] AGG (*gen*) clear; (*immagine*) sharp, well-defined.

nitrato [ni'trato] SM nitrate.

nitrico, a, ci, che ['nitriko] AGG nitric.

nitrificazione [nitrifikat'tsjone] SF nitrification.

nitrire [ni'trire] VI (*aus avere*) to neigh.

nitrito[1] [ni'trito] SM (*di cavallo*) neigh; **nitriti** SMPL neighing *no pl.*

nitrito[2] [ni'trito] SM (*Chim*) nitrite.

nitroglicerina [nitroglitʃe'rina] SF nitroglycerine.

nitroso, a [ni'troso] AGG nitrous.

niveo, a ['niveo] AGG snow-white, snowy.

Nizza ['nittsa] SF Nice.

nizzardo, a [nit'tsardo] 1 AGG of *o* from Nice.

2 SM/F inhabitant *o* native of Nice.

nn ABBR (= *numeri*) nos.

NO 1 SIGLA = *Novara*.

2 ABBR (= *nordovest*) NW.

no [nɔ] 1 AVV **a** no; **vieni? — no** are you coming? — no (I'm not); **la conosce? — no** does he know her? — no (he doesn't); **lo conosciamo? — tu no ma io sì** do we know him? — you don't but I do; **verrai, no?** you'll come, won't you?

b (*con avverbio, congiunzione*) not; **perché no?** why not?; **no di certo!** certainly not!; **vieni? — come no!** are you coming? — of course! *o* certainly!; **come no?** what do you mean, no?; **vieni o no?** are you coming or not?; **simpatico o no lo devo sopportare** (whether he's) nice or not, I'll have to put up with him

c: **credo di no** I think not, I don't think so; **spero di no** I hope not; **sembra di no** apparently not; **direi di no** I don't think so; **ha detto di no** he said no.

2 SM no; **da lui un no non me l'aspettavo** I didn't expect him to say no; **ci sono stati molti no** (*voti, pareri contrari*) there were a lot of votes against, there were a lot of noes.

nobildonna [nobil'donna] SF noblewoman.

nobile ['nobile] 1 AGG noble; **di animo nobile** noble-hearted.

2 SM/F noble, nobleman/noblewoman; **i nobili** the nobility.

nobiliare [nobi'ljare] AGG noble.

nobilitare [nobili'tare] 1 VT (*anche fig*) to ennoble.

2 **nobilitarsi** VR (*rendersi insigne*) to distinguish o.s.

nobilmente [nobil'mente] AVV nobly.

nobiltà [nobil'ta] SF INV (*condizione, classe sociale*) nobility; (*fig: di azione, animo*) nobleness.

nobiluomo [nobi'lwomo] SM (*pl* **nobiluomini**) nobleman.

nocca, che ['nɔkka] SF (*Anat*) knuckle; (*di cavallo*) fetlock.

nocchiere [nok'kjɛre] SM (*letter*) helmsman.

noccio *ecc* ['nɔttʃo] VB vedi **nuocere**.

nocciola [not'tʃola] 1 SF hazelnut.

2 AGG INV (*anche*: **color nocciola**) hazel, light brown.

nocciolina [nottʃo'lina] SF (*anche*: **nocciolina americana**) peanut.

nocciolo[1] ['nɔttʃolo] SM (*di frutto*) stone; (*fig*) heart, core; **veniamo al nocciolo!** let's get to the point!

nocciolo[2] [not'tʃolo] SM (*albero*) hazel.

noce ['notʃe] 1 SM (*albero*) walnut (tree); (*legno*) walnut.

2 SF (*frutto*) walnut ►**noce di cocco** coconut ►**noce moscata** nutmeg **b**: **una noce di burro** (*Culin*) a knob of butter (*Brit*), a dab of butter (*Am*); **noce di manzo/vitello** beef/veal fillet.

nocepesca, sche [notʃe'peska] SF nectarine.

nocevo *ecc* [no'tʃevo] VB vedi **nuocere**.

nociuto [no'tʃuto] PP di **nuocere**.

nocivo, a [no'tʃivo] AGG (*gen*) harmful; (*fumi*) noxious; **insetti nocivi** pests.

nocqui *ecc* VB vedi **nuocere**.

nodo ['nodo] SM **a** (*gen: di cravatta, fune*) knot; (*fig: legame*) bond, tie; (: *punto centrale*) heart, crux; (*Med, Astron, Bot*) node; **fare/sciogliere un nodo** to tie/untie a knot; **avere i capelli pieni di nodi** to have tangles in one's hair; **avere un nodo alla gola** to have a lump in one's throat; **fare un nodo al fazzoletto** (*fig*) to tie a knot in one's handkerchief; **tutti i nodi vengono al pettine** (*Proverbio*) your sins will find you out ►**nodo d'amore** love knot ►**nodo scorsoio** slipknot

b (*Aut, Ferr: incrocio*) junction
c (*Naut: velocità*) knot.

nodosità [nodosi'ta] SF **a** (*di corteccia*) knottiness **b**
(*Med*) lump.

nodoso, a [no'doso] AGG (*tronco, mani*) gnarled.

nodulo ['nɔdulo] SM (*Anat, Bot*) nodule.

Noè [no'ɛ] SM Noah; **l'arca di Noè** Noah's ark.

noi ['noi] PRON PERS **a** (*soggetto*) we; **noi andiamo** we're
going; **noi stessi(e)** we ourselves; **tutti noi pensiamo che
sia giusto** we all think it's right, all of us think it's right;
noi italiani we Italians; **siamo stati noi a dirglielo** it was
us who told him, we were the ones to tell him; **noi
accettare? non sia mai detto!** us accept that? never!
b (*oggetto: per dare rilievo, con preposizione*) us; **noi
stessi(e)** ourselves; **vuol vedere proprio noi** it's us he
wants to see; **dice a noi?** is he talking to us?; **tocca a noi?**
is it our turn?; **da noi** (*nel nostro paese*) in our country,
where we come from; (*a casa nostra*) at our house
c (*comparazioni*) we, us; **vanno veloce come noi** they are
going as fast as we are, they are going as fast as us; **fate
come noi** do as we do, do the same as us; **sono più
giovani di noi** they are younger than we are *o* than us.

noia ['nɔja] SF (*tedio*) boredom; (*disturbo, impaccio*) bother
no pl, trouble *no pl*; (*fastidio*) nuisance; **morire di noia** to
die of boredom; **mi è venuto a noia** I'm tired of it; **dare
noia a qn** to bother *o* annoy sb; **avere qn/qc a noia** not to
like sb/sth; **avere (delle) noie con la polizia** to have
trouble with the police; **che noia!** what a bore!; (*fastidio*)
what a nuisance!

noialtri, e [no'jaltri] PRON PERS we.

noiosità [nojosi'ta] SF (*di libro, discorso*) dullness.

noioso, a [no'joso] AGG (*tedioso*) boring; (*fastidioso*) tiresome, annoying.

noleggiare [noled'dʒare] VT (*auto, bicicletta: prendere a
noleggio*) to hire (*Brit*), rent; (*: dare a noleggio*) to hire out
(*Brit*), rent out; (*aereo, nave*) to charter.

noleggiatore, trice [noleddʒa'tore] SM/F (*vedi vb*) hirer
(*Brit*), renter; charterer.

noleggio, gi [no'leddʒo] SM (*di auto, bicicletta*) hire (*Brit*),
rental; (*di nave, barca*) charter; **prendere/dare a noleggio** to hire/hire (out) *o* rent/rent out; **contratto di
noleggio** (*Naut*) charter party (contract); **c'è un noleggio
di biciclette?** is there a place where you can hire *o* rent
bikes?

nolente [no'lɛnte] AGG: **volente o nolente** whether one
likes it *o* not, willy-nilly.

nolo ['nɔlo] SM (*di auto*) hire (charge) (*Brit*), rental
(charge); (*di nave*) charter (fee); (*per trasporto merci*)
freight (charge); **prendere/dare a nolo qc** to hire/hire
out *o* rent/rent out.

nomade ['nɔmade] **1** AGG nomadic.
2 SM/F nomad.

nomadismo [noma'dizmo] SM nomadism.

nome ['nome] **1** SM (*gen*) name; **a nome di** on behalf of;
un uomo di nome Giovanni a man by the name of John, a
man called John; **solo di nome** in name only; **in nome
della legge** in the name of the law; **in nome del cielo!** in
heaven's name!; **sotto il nome di** under the name of;
sotto falso nome under an assumed name *o* an alias;
chiamare qn per nome to call sb by name; **posso
chiamarla per nome?** can I call you by your first name?;
li conosce tutti per nome she knows them all by name;
lo conosco solo di nome I know him only by name; **fare
il nome di qn** to name sb; **faccia pure il mio nome** feel

free to mention my name; **farsi un buon/cattivo nome**
to get a good/bad name; **ormai si è fatto un nome** he
has made a name for himself now; **porta** *o* **gli hanno
dato il nome di suo nonno** he is named after his
grandfather; **senza nome** nameless.
2 ▶**nome d'arte** stage name ▶**nome astratto**
(*Gramm*) abstract noun ▶**nome di battaglia** nom de
guerre ▶**nome di battesimo** Christian name ▶**nome
comune** (*Gramm*) common noun ▶**nome depositato**
trade name ▶**nome di famiglia** surname ▶**nome
proprio** (*Gramm*) proper noun ▶**nome da ragazza**
maiden name ▶**nome da sposata** married name.

nomea [no'mɛa] SF notoriety.

nomenclatura [nomenkla'tura] SF nomenclature.

nomenklatura [nomenkla'tura] SF (*di partito, di stato*)
nomenklatura.

nomignolo [no'miɲɲolo] SM nickname.

nomina ['nɔmina] SF appointment; **conferire una nomina
a qn** to appoint sb; **ottenere la nomina a presidente** to
be appointed president.

nominale [nomi'nale] AGG (*gen*) nominal; (*Gramm*) noun
attr; **valore nominale** face *o* nominal value.

nominalmente [nominal'mente] AVV nominally, in name
only.

nominare [nomi'nare] VT (*citare*) to mention; (*: per nome*)
to name; (*eleggere*) to appoint; **non l'ho mai sentito
nominare** I've never heard of it (*o* him); **l'hanno
nominato segretario generale** he has been appointed
secretary-general.

nominativo, a [nomina'tivo] **1** AGG (*Gramm*) nominative;
(*Comm*) registered; **elenco nominativo** list of names.
2 SM **a** (*Gramm: anche:* **caso nominativo**) nominative
(case) **b** (*Comm, Amm: nome*) name.

non [non] **1** AVV **a** not; **non sono inglesi** they are not *o*
aren't English; **non ne ho** I haven't (got) any; **non devi
farlo** you must not *o* mustn't do it; **non puoi venire** you
cannot *o* can't come; **non vieni?** aren't you coming?;
non parli francese? don't you speak French?; **non è
venuto nessuno** nobody came; **non l'ho mai visto** I have
never seen it; **non lo capisco affatto** I do not *o* don't
understand him at all; **non più di 5 minuti** no more than
5 minutes; **non oltre il 15 luglio** no later than (the) 15th
(of) July; **grazie — non c'è di che** thank you — don't
mention it
b (*con sostantivo, aggettivo, pronome, avverbio*) not; **un
guadagno non indifferente** a not inconsiderable gain;
non pochi sono d'accordo not a few are in agreement,
many are in agreement; **non uno dei presenti si è alzato**
not one of those present stood up
c (*con valore rafforzativo*): **non puoi non vederlo** you
can't not see him, you'll have to see him; **finché non
torno** until I get back; **per poco non cadevo in acqua** I
almost fell into the water
2 PREF non-, un-...; **politica di non intervento** policy of
non-intervention; **i non credenti** the unbelievers; **i non
abbienti** the have-nots; **i paesi non allineati** the non-
aligned countries.

nona ['nɔna] SF (*Mus: intervallo*) ninth.

nonché [non'ke] CONG **a** (*tanto più, tanto meno*) let alone **b**
(*e inoltre*) as well as; **lo ricorderò a lui, nonché a suo
fratello** I'll remind him as well as his brother.

nonconformista, i, e [nonkonfor'mista] AGG, SM/F
nonconformist.

noncurante [nonku'rante] AGG: **noncurante (di)** indif-

ferent (to), careless (of); **con fare noncurante** with a nonchalant air.

noncuranza [nonku'rantsa] SF carelessness, indifference; **assumere un'aria di noncuranza** to take on a nonchalant air.

nondimeno [nondi'meno] CONG (*tuttavia*) however; (*nonostante*) nevertheless.

nonno, a ['nɔnno] SM/F grandfather/grandmother; (*in senso più familiare*) grandpa/grandma; **nonni** SMPL grandparents.

nonnulla [non'nulla] SM INV: **un nonnulla** nothing, a trifle; **se la prende per un nonnulla** he gets annoyed over the slightest thing.

nono, a ['nɔno] AGG, SM/F, SM ninth *per fraseologia vedi* **quinto**.

nonostante [nonos'tante] ☐ PREP in spite of, notwithstanding.

☐ CONG even though, although, in spite of the fact that; **nonostante fosse notte fonda** in spite of the fact that it was late at night; **nonostante piovesse** even though *o* in spite of the fact that it was raining.

non plus ultra ['non plus 'ultra] SM INV: **il non plus ultra (di)** the last word (in).

nonsenso [non'sɛnso] SM absurdity.

nontiscordardimé [nontiskordardi'me] SM INV (*Bot*) forget-me-not.

nord [nɔrd] ☐ SM north; **a nord (di)** north (of); **esposto a nord** north-facing; **verso nord** northward(s), north; **il mare del Nord** the North Sea; **l'America del Nord** North America.

☐ AGG INV (*gen*) north; (*regione*) northern; **è partito in direzione nord** he set off northwards *o* in a northward direction.

nord-est [nor'dɛst] SM northeast; **vento di nord-est** northeasterly wind.

nordico, a, ci, che ['nɔrdiko] ☐ AGG Nordic; (*sci*) nordic.

☐ SM/F Northern European.

nordista, i, e [nor'dista] AGG, SM/F Yankee.

nord-ovest [nor'dɔvest] SM northwest; **vento di nord-ovest** northwesterly wind.

Norimberga [norim'bɛrga] SF Nuremberg.

norma ['nɔrma] SF (*principio*) norm; (*regola*) regulation, rule; (*consuetudine*) custom, rule; **scostarsi dalla norma** to diverge from the norm; **al di sopra della norma** above average, above the norm; **di norma** normally; **a norma di legge** in accordance with the law, according to the law, as laid down by law; **per tua norma e regola** for your information; **proporsi una norma di vita** to set o.s. rules to live by ▶ **norme per l'uso** instructions for use ▶ **norme di sicurezza** safety regulations.

normale [nor'male] ☐ AGG normal; (*solito*) usual, normal; **ma tu non sei normale!** there must be something wrong with you!; **è normale che sia così** it is quite normal for it to be like that.

☐ SM: **più alto del normale** taller than average; **ha un'intelligenza al di sopra del normale** he is of above average intelligence.

☐ SF (*Mat*) normal.

normalità [normali'ta] SF normality.

normalizzare [normalid'dzare] ☐ VT to bring back to normal, normalize; (*Pol, Mat*) normalize.

☐ **normalizzarsi** VIP to return to normal.

normalizzazione [normaliddzat'tsjone] SF (*Pol, Mat*) normalization; **si è avuta una normalizzazione dei**

rapporti tra Italia e Cina relations between Italy and China have returned to normal.

normalmente [normal'mente] AVV (*in modo normale*) normally; (*abitualmente*) normally, usually, ordinarily.

Normandia [norman'dia] SF: **la Normandia** Normandy.

normanno, a [nor'manno] AGG, SM/F Norman.

normativa [norma'tiva] SF regulations *pl.*

normativo, a [norma'tivo] AGG normative.

normografo [nor'mɔgrafo] SM (*Disegno*) stencil.

norvegese [norve'dʒese] AGG, SM/F, SM Norwegian.

Norvegia [nor'vɛdʒa] SF: **la Norvegia** Norway.

nosocomio, mi [nozo'kɔmjo] SM hospital.

nostalgia [nostal'dʒia] SF (*di casa, paese*) homesickness; (*del passato*) nostalgia; **soffrire di nostalgia** to be homesick; **aver nostalgia di casa** to be homesick.

nostalgicamente [nostaldʒika'mente] AVV nostalgically.

nostalgico, a, ci, che [nos'taldʒiko] ☐ AGG (*vedi sf*) homesick; nostalgic.

☐ SM/F (*Pol*) person *who hopes for the return of Fascism*.

nostrano, a [nos'trano] AGG (*gen*) local; (*pianta, frutta*) home-grown.

nostro, a ['nɔstro] ☐ AGG POSS: **il(la) nostro(a)** ecc our; **il nostro giardino** our garden; **nostra madre** our mother; **un nostro amico** a friend of ours; **è colpa nostra** it's our fault; **a casa nostra** at our house, at home.

☐ PRON POSS: **il(la) nostro(a)**ecc ours, our own; **la vostra barca è più lunga della nostra** your boat is longer than ours; **il nostro è stato solo un errore** it was simply an error on our part.

☐ PRON POSS M **a** : **abbiamo speso del nostro** we spent our own money; **viviamo del nostro** we live on our own income

b : **i nostri** (*famiglia*) our family; (*amici*) our own people, our side; **è dei nostri** he's one of us.

☐ PRON POSS F: **la nostra** (*opinione*) our view; **è dalla nostra** (*parte*) he's on our side; **anche noi abbiamo avuto le nostre** (*disavventure*) we've had our problems too; **alla nostra!** (*brindisi*) to us!

nostromo [nos'trɔmo] SM boatswain.

nota ['nɔta] SF **a** (*gen, Mus*) note; **prendere nota di qc** to note sth, make a note of sth, write sth down; (*fig*: *fare attenzione*) to note sth, take note of sth; **degno di nota** noteworthy, worthy of note; **una nota di tristezza/allegria** a note of sadness/happiness ▶ **nota fondamentale** (*Mus*) tonic ▶ **note caratteristiche** (*di carattere, stile*) distinguishing marks *o* features ▶ **note a piè di pagina** footnotes

b (*fattura*) bill; (*elenco*) list ▶ **nota di addebito** debit note ▶ **nota della spesa** shopping list ▶ **nota spese** list of expenses.

notabile [no'tabile] ☐ AGG (*letter*: *mutamento, avvenimento*) notable; (*persona*) important.

☐ SM notable.

notaio, ai [no'tajo] SM notary (public).

notare [no'tare] VT (*rilevare, osservare*) to notice, note; (*segnare*: *errori*) to mark; (*registrare*) to note (down), write down; **hai notato com'era strano?** did you notice how strange he was?; **vi faccio notare che...** I would have you note *o* I wish to point out that ...; **notare qc a margine** to write sth in the margin; **farsi notare** to get o.s. noticed.

notarile [nota'rile] AGG: **studio notarile** notary's office; **atto notarile** legal document (*authorized by a notary*).

notazione [notat'tsjone] SF (*Mus*) notation.

notes ['nɔtes] SM INV notepad.

notevole [no'tevole] AGG (*talento*) notable, remarkable; (*peso*) considerable.

notevolmente [notevol'mente] AVV considerably.

notifica, che [no'tifika] SF notification.

notificare [notifi'kare] VT (*Dir*): **notificare qc a qn** to notify sb of sth, give sb notice of sth.

notificazione [notifikat'tskjone] SF notification.

notizia [no'tittsja] SF (piece of) news *sg*; (*informazione*) piece of information; **notizie** SFPL news *sg*, information *sg*; **aver una bella/brutta notizia** to have some good/bad news; **aver notizie di qn** to hear from sb; **fammi avere tue notizie!** keep in touch!; **è un avvenimento che fa notizia** it's a sensational event.

notiziario, ri [notit'tsjarjo] SM (*Radio, TV, Stampa*) news *sg*.

noto, a ['nɔto] [1] AGG (well-)known; **noto a tutti** (well) known to everybody; **rendere noto qc** to make sth known.
[2] SM: **il noto e l'ignoto** the known and the unknown.

notoriamente [notorja'mente] AVV: **è notoriamente risaputo che...** it's generally recognized that ..., it's well known that ...; **è notoriamente disonesto** he's notoriously dishonest.

notorietà [notorje'ta] SF fame; (*pegg*) notoriety.

notorio, ria, ri, rie [no'tɔrjo] AGG **a** well-known; (*pegg*) notorious **b** (*Dir*): **atto notorio = atto notarile**; vedi **notarile**.

nottambulo, a [not'tambulo] SM/F night owl (*fig*), nighthawk (*Am fig*).

nottata [not'tata] SF night; **ho passato la nottata in piedi** I was up all night.

notte ['nɔtte] SF night; (*oscurità*) darkness, night; (*periodo*) night, night-time; **di notte** at night; (*durante la notte*) in the night, during the night; **è meglio non uscire di notte** it's better not to go out at night; **è successo di notte** it happened during the night; **la notte è meglio dormire** it's better to sleep at night; **la notte di sabato** OR **sabato notte** (on) Saturday night; **questa notte** (*passata*) last night; (*che viene*) tonight; **rientrare prima di notte** to come back home before dark; **col favore della notte** under cover of darkness; **nella notte dei tempi** in the mists of time; **come va? — peggio che andare di notte** how are things? — worse than ever; **camicia da notte** nightgown; **portiere di notte** night porter ▶**notte bianca** *o* **in bianco** sleepless night.

nottetempo [notte'tɛmpo] AVV at night, during the night.

nottola ['nɔttola] SF (*pipistrello*) noctule.

notturno, a [not'turno] [1] AGG (*locale, servizio, guardiano*) night *attr*; (*Zool, fig*) nocturnal.
[2] SM (*Mus*) nocturne.
[3] SF (*Sport*) evening match *o* fixture (*Brit*); **in notturna** (*partita*) under floodlights.

noumeno [no'umeno] SM (*Filosofia*) noumenon.

nova ['nɔva] SF (*Astron*) nova.

novanta [no'vanta] AGG INV, SM INV ninety *per fraseologia vedi* **cinquanta**.

novantenne [novan'tɛnne] AGG, SM/F ninety-year-old *per fraseologia vedi* **cinquantenne**.

novantesimo, a [novan'tɛzimo] AGG, SM/F, SM ninetieth *per fraseologia vedi* **quinto**.

novantina [novan'tina] SF: **una novantina (di)** about ninety *per fraseologia vedi* **cinquantina**.

nove ['nɔve] AGG INV, SM INV nine *per fraseologia vedi* **cinque**.

novecentesco, a, schi, sche [novetʃen'tesko] AGG twentieth-century.

novecento [nove'tʃɛnto] [1] AGG INV nine hundred.
[2] SM INV nine hundred; (*secolo*): **il Novecento** the twentieth century.

novella [no'vɛlla] SF (*Letterat*) short story.

novelliere [novel'ljɛre] SM short-story writer.

novellino, a [novel'lino] [1] SM/F beginner, greenhorn.
[2] AGG (*pivello*) green, inexperienced.

novellista, i, e [novel'lista] SM/F short-story writer.

novellistica [novel'listika] SF (*arte*) short-story writing; (*insieme di racconti*) short stories *pl*.

novello, a [no'vɛllo] AGG (*piante, patate*) new; (*insalata, verdura*) early; (*sposo*) newly-married; **pollo novello** spring chicken.

novembre [no'vɛmbre] SM November *per fraseologia vedi* **luglio**.

novembrino, a [novem'brino] AGG November *attr*.

novemila [nove'mila] AGG INV, SM INV nine thousand.

novena [no'vena] SF (*Rel*) novena.

novennale [noven'nale] AGG (*che dura 9 anni*) nine-year *attr*; (*ogni 9 anni*) nine-yearly.

novero ['nɔvero] SM (*di fortunati, vincitori*) group; **non è nel novero dei miei amici** I don't number him amongst my friends.

novilunio, ni [novi'lunjo] SM (*Astron*) new moon.

novità [novi'ta] SF INV **a** (*originalità*) novelty; (*innovazione*) innovation; (*cosa originale, insolita*) something new; (*libro*) new publication; **questa è una novità!** that's new!; **le novità della moda francese** the latest French fashions **b** (*notizia*) (piece of) news *sg*; **che novità ci sono?** what's the news?

noviziato [novit'tsjato] SM (*Rel*) novitiate; (*tirocinio*) apprenticeship.

novizio, zia, zi, zie [no'vittsjo] SM/F (*Rel*) novice; (*tirocinante*) beginner, apprentice.

nozione [not'tsjone] SF notion, idea; **nozioni** SFPL (*rudimenti*) basic knowledge *sg*, rudiments; **ho perso la nozione del tempo** I've lost all notion of time; **le prime nozioni di matematica** the first elements of mathematics; **non ha che alcune nozioni di filosofia** he only has a vague notion of philosophy.

nozionismo [nottsjo'nizmo] SM superficial knowledge.

nozionistico, a, ci, che [nottsjo'nistiko] AGG superficial.

nozze ['nɔttse] SFPL wedding *sg*, marriage *sg*; **regalo di nozze** wedding present; **viaggio di nozze** honeymoon; **offrendomi quel lavoro mi hanno invitato a nozze** (*fig*) when they offered me that job it was just what I wanted ▶**nozze d'argento** silver wedding *sg* ▶**nozze d'oro** golden wedding *sg*.

N.P.A. ABBR = **nave portaerei**.

ns. ABBR (*Comm*) = **nostro**.

NU SIGLA = *Nuoro*.

N.U. ABBR (= *Nazioni Unite*) UN.

nube ['nube] SF (*anche fig*) cloud.

nubifragio, gi [nubi'fradʒo] SM cloudburst.

nubilato [nubi'lato] SM single status.

nubile ['nubile] [1] AGG (*donna*) unmarried, single.
[2] SF single *o* unmarried woman.

nuca, che ['nuka] SF nape (of the neck).

nucleare [nukle'are] [1] AGG nuclear.
[2] SM: **il nucleare** nuclear energy.

nucleico, a, ci, che [nu'klɛiko] AGG nucleic.

nucleo ['nukleo] SM (*Bio, Fis*) nucleus; (*Geog*) core; (*fig: parte centrale*) core, nucleus; (*gruppo*) unit, group,

team; (*Mil, Polizia*) unit, squad ►**il nucleo familiare** the family unit ►**nucleo antidroga** anti-drugs squad.

nucleone [nukle'one] SM nucleon.

nudismo [nu'dizmo] SM nudism.

nudista, i, e [nu'dista] SM/F nudist.

nudità [nudi'ta] SF INV (*di persona*) nudity, nakedness *sg*; (*parti nude del corpo*) nakedness; (*di paesaggio*) bareness *sg*; **le proprie nudità** one's nakedness.

nudo, a ['nudo] [1] AGG (*persona, membra*) bare, naked, nude; (*albero, parete, montagna*) bare; (*verità*) plain, naked; **mezzo/tutto nudo** half-/stark-naked; **a piedi nudi** barefoot; **a occhio nudo** to the naked eye; **gli ha detto nudo e crudo che...** he said to him bluntly that ...; **questa è la verità nuda e cruda** this is the plain, unvarnished truth; **mettere a nudo** (*cuore, verità*) to lay bare.

[2] SM (*Arte*) nude.

nugolo ['nugolo] SM: **un nugolo di** a whole host of.

nulla ['nulla] [1] PRON, AVV = **niente**.

[2] SM [a]: **il nulla** nothing, nothingness; **Dio creò il mondo dal nulla** God created the world out of nothing; **svanire nel nulla** to vanish into thin air

[b] (*minima quantità*): **basta un nulla per farlo arrabbiare** he gets annoyed over the slightest thing; **te lo cedo per (un) nulla** I am giving it to you for a song *o* for next to nothing.

nullaosta [nulla'ɔsta] SM INV authorization, permission.

nullatenente [nullate'nɛnte] [1] AGG: **essere nullatenente** to own nothing.

[2] SM/F person with no property.

nullità [nulli'ta] SF INV [a] (*Dir*) nullity; (*di idea, ragionamento*) invalidity [b] (*persona*) nonentity.

nullo, a ['nullo] AGG (*tentativo, sforzo*) vain, pointless; (*Dir*) null (and void); **scheda nulla** (*Pol*) spoiled vote; **incontro nullo** (*Sport*) draw; **colpo nullo** (*Tennis*) let.

nume ['nume] SM numen; **santi numi!** good heavens!

numerale [nume'rale] AGG, SM numeral.

numerare [nume'rare] VT to number.

numeratore [numera'tore] SM [a] (*Mat*) numerator [b] (*macchina*) numbering device.

numerazione [numerat'tsjone] SF numbering ►**numerazione araba** arabic numerals *pl* ►**numerazione romana** roman numerals *pl*.

numericamente [numerika'mente] AVV numerically.

numerico, a, ci, che [nu'mɛriko] AGG numerical.

numero ['numero] SM [a] (*gen*) number; (*arabo, romano*) numeral; **i Numeri** (*Bibbia*) the Book of Numbers; **dodici di numero** twelve in number; **abito al numero 6** I live at number 6; **ha tutti i numeri per riuscire** he's got what it takes to succeed; **dare i numeri** (*farneticare*) to be not all there; **tanto per fare numero invitiamo anche lui** why don't we invite him to make up the numbers?; **che numero tuo fratello!** your brother is a real character! ►**numero chiuso** (*Univ*) selective entry system ►**numero civico** house number ►**numero legale** quorum ►**numero di scarpe** shoe size; **che numero di scarpe porti?** what size (of) shoe do you take?

[b] (*Telec, anche:* **numero di telefono**) (tele)phone number ►**numero verde** (*Telec*) ≈ Freephone *o* Freefone number (*Brit*), ≈ toll-free number (*Am*); **fare un numero** to dial a number

[c] (*di giornale, rivista*) issue, number ►**numero arretrato** back number ►**numero doppio** issue with supplement

[d] (*di spettacolo*) act, turn

[e] (*Chim, Fis*) number ►**numero di massa** mass number.

numeroso, a [nume'roso] AGG [a] numerous, many; **le personalità sono intervenute numerose** celebrities were present in large numbers [b] (*folla, famiglia*) large.

numismatica [numiz'matika] SF numismatics *sg*, coin collecting.

nunzio, zi ['nuntsjo] SM (*Rel*) nuncio.

nuoccio *ecc* ['nwɔttʃo] VB *vedi* **nuocere**.

nuocere ['nwɔtʃere] VI IRREG (*aus* **avere**): **nuocere a** to harm, damage; **tentar non nuoce** (*Proverbio*) there's no harm in trying.

nuociuto, a [nwo'tʃuto] PP di **nuocere**.

nuora ['nwora] SF daughter-in-law.

nuotare [nwo'tare] [1] VI (*aus* **avere**) to swim; (*galleggiare*: *oggetti*) to float; **nuotare a rana/sul dorso** to do the breaststroke/backstroke; **nuotare nell'oro** to be rolling in money. [2] VT to swim.

nuotata [nwo'tata] SF swim.

nuotatore, trice [nwota'tore] SM/F swimmer.

nuoto ['nwoto] SM swimming; **attraversare la Manica a nuoto** to swim (across) the Channel ►**nuoto pinnato** fin swimming.

nuova ['nwɔva] SF news *sg*; **che nuove ci sono?** is there any news?; **nessuna nuova buona nuova** (*Proverbio*) no news is good news.

Nuova Guinea ['nwɔva gwi'nɛa] SF: **la Nuova Guinea** New Guinea.

Nuova Inghilterra ['nwɔva ingil'tɛrra] SF: **la Nuova Inghilterra** New England.

nuovamente [nwɔva'mente] AVV again.

Nuova Scozia ['nwɔva'skɔttsja] SF: **la Nuova Scozia** Nova Scotia.

nuovayorchese [nwovajor'kese] AGG, SM/F = **newyorchese**.

Nuova York ['nwɔva 'jork] SF New York.

Nuova Zelanda ['nwɔva dze'landa] SF: **la Nuova Zelanda** New Zealand.

nuovo, a ['nwɔvo] [1] AGG [a] (*gen*) new; (*originale: idea*) novel, new; (: *metodo*) new, up-to-date; **nuovo fiammante** OR **nuovo di zecca** brand-new; **il nuovo presidente** the new *o* newly-elected president; **sono nuovo del mestiere** I am new to this job; **sono nuova di questo posto/di Glasgow** I am new here/to Glasgow; **il suo volto non mi è nuovo** I know his face; **come nuovo** as good as new; **sembra nuovo** it looks like new

[b] (*altro, secondo*) new, fresh; (*diverso*) new, different; **usa un foglio nuovo** take a fresh sheet of paper; **hai letto il suo nuovo libro?** have you read his new *o* latest book?; **fino a nuovo ordine** until further notice; **c'è stata una nuova serie di scosse** there has been a new *o* further series of tremors; **fare un nuovo tentativo** to make another attempt; **anno nuovo, vita nuova!** it's time to turn over a new leaf!

[c]: **di nuovo** again; **di nuovo tu?** (is that) you again?.

[2] SM: **che c'è di nuovo?** what's the news?, what's new?; **non c'è niente di nuovo** there's no news *o* nothing new; **rimettere a nuovo** (*cosa, macchina*) to do up like new; **questa cura mi ha rimesso a nuovo** this treatment has given me a new lease of life.

nutria ['nutrja] SF (*animale*) coypu; (*pelliccia*) nutria.

nutrice [nu'tritʃe] SF wet nurse.

nutriente [nutri'ɛnte] AGG nutritious, nourishing;

(*balsamo*) nourishing; **crema nutriente** (*Cosmetica*) nourishing cream.

nutrimento [nutri'mento] SM nourishment, food.

nutrire [nu'trire] [1] VT to feed; (*fig: sentimenti*) to harbour (*Brit*), harbor (*Am*); (: *risentimento, rancore*) to nurse, feel; **nutrivo profonda stima per lui** I felt great respect for him.

[2] VI (*aus* **avere**) (*cibo*) to be nourishing.

[3] **nutrirsi** VR: **nutrirsi di** to feed on, eat.

nutritivo, a [nutri'tivo] AGG (*proprietà*) nutritional; (*sostanza*) nutritious.

nutrito, a [nu'trito] AGG a : **ben/mal nutrito** well/poorly fed b (*numeroso*) large; (*fitto*) heavy.

nutrizione [nutrit'tsjone] SF (*atto*) feeding, nutrition; (*dieta*) nutrition; **una scarsa nutrizione** a poor diet.

nuvola ['nuvola] SF cloud; **avere la testa fra le nuvole** to have one's head in the clouds; **cascare dalle nuvole** to be astounded, be taken aback.

nuvolo, a ['nuvolo] AGG cloudy.

nuvolosità [nuvolosi'ta] SF INV cloudiness; **nuvolosità persistente** persistent cloud cover.

nuvoloso, a [nuvo'loso] AGG (*tempo*) cloudy; (*cielo*) cloudy, overcast.

nuziale [nut'tsjale] AGG wedding *attr*, nuptial.

nylon° ['nailən] SM nylon.

O

O, o [ɔ] SF O M INV (*lettera*) O, o; **O come Otranto** ≈ O for Oliver (*Brit*), ≈ O for Oboe (*Am*).

O ABBR (= *ovest*) W.

o¹ [o] (dav vocale talvolta **od**) CONG **a** (*gen*) or; **o... o...** either ...or ...; **o meglio** or rather; **due o tre volte** two or three times; **oggi o domani** (either) today or tomorrow; **lo farò o oggi o domani** I'll do it either today or tomorrow; **(o) l'uno o l'altro** either (of them); **sono decisa: o lui o nessuno** I've made up my mind: it's him or nobody **b** (*altrimenti*) (or) else; **sbrigati o faremo tardi** hurry up or (else) we'll be late.

o², oh [o] ESCL **a** oh! **b** (*fam: per chiamare*) hey!

oasi ['ɔazi] SF INV (*anche fig*) oasis; **oasi di pace** haven of peace.

obbediente *ecc* [obbe'djɛnte]; vedi **ubbidiente** *ecc*.

obbiettare *ecc*; vedi **obiettare** *ecc*.

obbligare [obbli'gare] [1] VT: **obbligare qn a fare qc** (*sogg: circostanze, persona*) to force o oblige sb to do sth; (*legalmente*) to require sb to do sth; (*Dir*) to bind sb to do sth; **sono obbligato (a farlo)** I have to (do it); **e chi ti obbliga?** who's forcing you (to do it)?; **la mia coscienza mi obbligò a tacere** I was bound by conscience to remain silent; **l'influenza lo obbliga a letto** he's confined to bed with flu.

[2] **obbligarsi** VR **a** (*Dir*): **obbligarsi per qn** to stand surety for sb, act as guarantor for sb **b** (*impegnarsi*): **obbligarsi a fare qc** to undertake to do sth.

obbligatissimo, a [obbliga'tissimo] AGG: **obbligatissimo!** (*ringraziamento*) much obliged!

obbligato, a [obbli'gato] AGG **a** (*riconoscente*): **obbligato verso qn** obliged o indebted to sb; **le sono molto obbligato!** I'm much obliged! **b** (*imposto: percorso, tappa*) set, fixed; **passaggio obbligato** (*fig*) essential requirement; **è stata una scelta obbligata** I (*o you ecc*) had no choice.

obbligatoriamente [obbligatorja'mente] AVV: **dovete seguire obbligatoriamente le lezioni** the classes are compulsory; **non devi obbligatoriamente farlo** you are not obliged to do it.

obbligatorio, ria, ri, rie [obbliga'tɔrjo] AGG (*assicurazione, esame*) compulsory; (*clausola*) (legally) binding.

obbligazione [obbligat'tsjone] SF **a** (*gen, Dir*) obligation **b** (*Fin*) bond, debenture ►**obbligazione al portatore** bearer bond ►**obbligazione dello Stato** government bond ►**obbligazioni convertibili** convertible loan stock *sg*, convertible debentures.

obbligazionista, i, e [obbligattsjo'nista] SM/F bondholder.

obbligo, ghi ['ɔbbligo] SM obligation; (*dovere*) obligation, duty; **avere degli obblighi con o verso qn** to be under an obligation to sb; (*essere riconoscente*) to be indebted to sb; **sentire/avere l'obbligo di fare qc** to feel/be obliged to do sth, feel/be under an obligation to do sth; **mi sono sentito in obbligo (di farlo)** I felt obliged to (do it); **i libri vengono dati in prestito con l'obbligo di restituirli entro 15 giorni** books are lent on condition that they are returned within a fortnight; **essere d'obbligo** (*discorso, applauso*) to be called for; **fare una visita d'obbligo** to make a duty call; **le formalità d'obbligo** the necessary formalities; **frasi d'obbligo** civilities; **"è d'obbligo l'abito scuro"** "black tie"; **scuola dell'obbligo** compulsory education ►**obblighi militari** compulsory military service *sg*.

obb.mo ABBR = **obbligatissimo**.

obbrobrio, bri [ob'brɔbrjo] SM **a** (*infamia*) disgrace, shame **b** (*fig: cosa brutta*) mess, eyesore; **quel palazzo è un obbrobrio** that building's an eyesore.

obbrobriosamente [obbrobrjosa'mente] AVV (*in modo infame*) disgracefully, shamefully; (*in modo orribile*) atrociously.

obbrobrioso, a [obbrobrj'oso] AGG (*infame*) disgraceful, shameful; (*fig*) ghastly.

obelisco, schi [obe'lisko] SM obelisk.

oberare [obe'rare] VT: **oberare qn di** (*lavoro, responsabilità, impegni*) to overload sb with.

oberato, a [obe'rato] AGG: **oberato di** (*lavoro*) overloaded

o overburdened with; **oberato di** *o* **da debiti** crippled with debts.

obesità [obesi'ta] SF obesity.

obeso, a [o'beso] AGG obese.

obice ['ɔbitʃe] SM (*Mil*) howitzer.

obiettare [objet'tare] VT: **obiettare che...** to object that ...; **non ho nulla da obiettare** I have no objection (to make); **ha obiettato che non aveva tempo** he pleaded lack of time; **obiettare su qc** to object to sth, raise objections concerning sth.

obiettivamente [objettiva'mente] AVV objectively.

obiettività [objettivi'ta] SF objectivity.

obiettivo, a [objet'tivo] [1] AGG objective.
[2] SM **a** (*Mil, fig*) objective **b** (*Ottica, Fot*) lens *sg*, objective ▶**obiettivo a fuoco fisso** fixed-focus lens ▶**obiettivo grandangolare** wide-angle lens.

obiettore [objet'tore] SM objector ▶**obiettore di coscienza** conscientious objector.

obiezione [objet'tsjone] SF objection; **fare** *o* **muovere** *o* **sollevare un'obiezione** to make *o* raise an objection, object; **obiezione accolta/respinta** (*Dir*) objection sustained/overruled.

obitorio, ri [obi'tɔrjo] SM mortuary, morgue.

oblato, a [o'blato] SM/F oblate.

oblazione [oblat'tsjone] SF oblation.

oblio, oblii [o'blio] SM oblivion; **cadere nell'oblio** to sink into oblivion.

obliquamente [oblikwa'mente] AVV (*in modo inclinato*) on the slant, slantwise.

obliquità [oblikwi'ta] SF obliqueness.

obliquo, a [o'blikwo] AGG (*gen, Mat*) oblique; (*calligrafia, raggi*) slanting; (*fig*) devious, underhand.

obliterare [oblite'rare] VT (*francobollo*) to cancel; (*biglietto: con timbro*) to stamp; (: *con foratura*) to punch.

obliteratrice [oblitera'tritʃe] SF (*anche:* **macchina obliteratrice**) (*vedi vb*) cancelling machine; stamping machine; punch.

oblò [o'blɔ] SM INV (*Naut*) porthole.

oblungo, a, ghi, ghe [o'blungo] AGG oblong.

obnubilato, a [obnubi'lato] AGG (*letter fig: mente*) clouded.

oboe ['ɔboe] SM oboe.

oboista, i, e [obo'ista] SM/F oboist.

obolo ['ɔbolo] SM (*elemosina*) (small) offering, mite.

obsolescente [obsoleʃ'ʃente] AGG obsolescent.

obsolescenza [obsoleʃ'ʃentsa] SF (*Econ*) obsolescence.

obsoleto, a [obso'lɛto] AGG obsolete.

OC ABBR (= *onde corte*) SW (= *short wave*).

oca ['ɔka] SF (*pl* **oche**) (*Zool*) goose; (*fig pegg: anche:* **un'oca giuliva**) silly goose; **gioco dell'oca** ≈ snakes and ladders ▶**oca maschio** gander.

ocaggine [o'kaddʒine] SF silliness, stupidity.

ocarina [oka'rina] SF (*Mus*) ocarina.

occasionale [okkazjo'nale] AGG (*incontro*) chance *attr*; (*cliente, guadagni*) casual, occasional.

occasionalmente [okkazjonal'mente] AVV occasionally, from time to time.

occasionare [okkazjo'nare] VT to cause, bring about.

occasione [okka'zjone] SF **a** (*opportunità*) opportunity; (*caso favorevole*) chance; **sarebbe l'occasione buona per fare...** it would be an ideal opportunity to do ...; **avere occasione di fare qc** to have the chance *o* opportunity of doing sth; **alla prima occasione** at the first opportunity; **all'occasione** should the need arise
b (*circostanza*) occasion; **in occasione di** on the occa-

sion of; **a seconda delle** *o* **secondo le occasioni** depending on circumstances *o* on the situation
c (*motivo, pretesto*) occasion, cause; **dare occasione a** to cause, give rise to
d (*buon affare*) bargain; **d'occasione** (*a buon prezzo*) bargain *attr*, (*di seconda mano*) secondhand.

occhiacci [ok'kjattʃi] SMPL: **fare gli occhiacci a qn** to scowl at sb.

occhiaia [ok'kjaja] SF **a** (*orbita*) eye socket **b**: **occhiaie** SFPL: **avere le occhiaie** to have bags under one's eyes.

occhiali [ok'kjali] SMPL (*da vista*) glasses, spectacles; (*di protezione*) goggles ▶**occhiali da sole** sunglasses.

occhialuto, a [okkja'luto] AGG (*scherz*): **un signore occhialuto** a bespectacled man.

occhiata [ok'kjata] SF look, glance; **dare un'occhiata a** (*guardare*) to have a look at, glance at; (*badare*) to keep an eye on; **un'occhiata d'intesa** a knowing look *o* glance.

occhieggiare [okkjed'dʒare] VI (*aus* avere) (*apparire qua e là*) to appear here and there, peep out.

occhiello [ok'kjɛllo] SM **a** (*asola*) buttonhole; (*di scarpe*) eyelet **b** (*Tip*) half-title.

occhio, chi ['ɔkkjo] SM **a** (*Anat*) eye; **avere gli occhi blu** to have blue eyes; **dagli occhi castani** brown-eyed; **avere occhi buoni** to have good eyesight; **logorarsi gli occhi** to strain one's eyes; **fare un occhio nero a qn** to give sb a black eye; **a occhio nudo** with the naked eye
b (*sguardo, espressione*) look; **alzò gli occhi dal libro** he looked up from *o* raised his eyes from his book; **cercare qn con gli occhi** to look *o* glance around for sb; **ha l'occhio smorto oggi** he's looking rather bleary-eyed today
c (*accortezza, capacità di giudicare*): **avere occhio** to have a good eye; **ci vuole occhio per fare questo lavoro** this job requires a good eye; **vedere di buon/mal occhio qn/qc** to view sb/sth favourably/unfavourably, look favourably/unfavourably on sb/sth
d (*attenzione*): **occhio!** look out!, watch out!, careful!; **occhio alla borsa!** watch your bag!, keep an eye on your bag!; **essere tutt'occhi** to be all eyes
e (*cosa a forma d'occhio: di ciclone, patata*) eye ▶**occhio magico** (*su porta*) peephole
f (*fraseologia*): **a occhio (e croce)** roughly, approximately; **tieni gli occhi aperti per...** keep an eye out for ...; **non riuscivo a tener gli occhi aperti** I couldn't keep my eyes open; **non ho chiuso occhio stanotte** I didn't sleep a wink last night; **aprire gli occhi a qn su qc** to open sb's eyes to sth; **chiudere un occhio (su)** (*fig*) to turn a blind eye (to), shut one's eyes (to); **sognare a occhi aperti** to daydream; **a occhi chiusi** (*anche fig*) with one's eyes shut; **costare un occhio della testa** to cost a fortune; **darei un occhio per sapere** I'd give my eyeteeth to know; **dare nell'occhio** to attract attention; (*spiccare*) to stand out a mile; (*vestito, colore*) to be loud *o* gaudy; **dare all'occhio** *o* **nell'occhio a qn** to catch sb's eye; **tenere d'occhio qn/qc** to keep an eye on sb/sth; **fare l'occhio a qc** to get used to sth; **fare gli occhi dolci a qn** to make sheep's eyes at sb; **guardare con tanto d'occhi** to gaze wide-eyed at; **lasciare gli occhi su qc** to set one's heart on sth; **mettere gli occhi addosso a qn/su qc** to have got one's eyes on sb/sth; **a quattr'occhi** privately, in private; **vedendo tutti quei bei vestiti mi sono rifatta gli occhi** it was a real pleasure to see so many lovely clothes; **ce l'hai sotto gli occhi** it's right there in front of

you; **mi è capitato sott'occhio un articolo interessante** I happened to see an interesting article; **occhio non vede cuore non duole** (*Proverbio*) what the eye doesn't see the heart doesn't grieve over; **occhio per occhio, dente per dente** (*Proverbio*) an eye for an eye, a tooth for a tooth; **lontano dagli occhi lontano dal cuore** (*Proverbio*) out of sight, out of mind.

occhiolino [okkjo'lino] SM: **fare l'occhiolino a qn** to wink at sb.

occidentale [ottʃiden'tale] 1 AGG (*Geog*) western, west; (: *vento*) westerly; (*cultura, paesi*) Western.

2 SM/F Westerner.

occidentalizzare [ottʃidentalid'dzare] 1 VT to westernize.

2 **occidentalizzarsi** VIP to become westernized.

occidentalizzazione [ottʃidentaliddzat'tsjone] SF westernization.

occidente [ottʃi'dɛnte] SM west; **a occidente** in the west; **a occidente di** (to the) west of; **il sole tramonta a occidente** the sun sets in the west; **l'Occidente** (*Pol*) the West.

occipitale [ottʃipi'tale] AGG: **osso occipitale** occipital bone.

occipite [ot'tʃipite] SM back of the head, occiput (*Anat*).

occludere [ok'kludere] VT IRREG to block, occlude (*Med*).

occlusione [okklu'zjone] SF blockage, obstruction, occlusion (*Med*).

occlusivo, a [okklu'zivo] (*Ling*) 1 AGG occlusive.

2 SF occlusive.

occluso, a [ok'kluzo] PP di **occludere**.

occorrente [okkor'rɛnte] 1 AGG necessary.

2 SM all that is necessary; **porta con te tutto l'occorrente** bring everything you need; **l'occorrente per scrivere/disegnare** writing/drawing materials *pl*.

occorrenza [okkor'rɛntsa] SF a (*evenienza*) eventuality b (*bisogno*) necessity, need; **all'occorrenza** if need be, if necessary, in case of need.

occorrere [ok'korrere] 1 VI IRREG (*aus essere*) (*essere necessario*) to be needed, be required; **mi occorrono 2 milioni di lire** I need 2 million lire; **mi occorre un'ora per arrivarci** it takes me *o* I need an hour to get there.

2 VB IMPERS: **occorre farlo** it must be done; **occorre far presto** we'll (*o* you'll *ecc*) have to hurry; **non occorre che gli scriva subito** there's no need to write to him at once.

occorso, a [ok'korso] PP di **occorrere**.

occultamento [okkulta'mento] SM concealment.

occultare [okkul'tare] 1 VT to hide, conceal.

2 **occultarsi** VR: **occultarsi (a)** to hide (from), conceal o.s. (from).

occultismo [okkul'tizmo] SM occultism.

occulto, a [ok'kulto] 1 AGG (*segreto*) hidden, secret, concealed; (*arcano*) occult; **le scienze occulte** the occult *sg*, the occult sciences.

2 SM: **l'occulto** the occult.

occupante [okku'pante] 1 AGG (*Mil*) occupying.

2 SM/F (*di casa*) occupier, occupant ▶**occupante abusivo** squatter.

occupare [okku'pare] 1 VT (*gen, Mil*) to occupy; (*spazio, tempo*) to occupy, take up; (*casa*) to live in; (*carica*) to hold; (*manodopera*) to employ; **l'esercito ha occupato il paese** the army has occupied *o* taken over the country; **l'insegnamento occupa tutte le mie mattinate** teaching takes up all my mornings; **la casa è stata occupata (abusivamente)** the house has been taken over by squatters.

2 **occuparsi** VIP a : **occuparsi di** (*interessarsi*) to be interested in, take an interest in; (*prendersi cura*) to take care of, look after; (*impicciarsi*) to interfere in, meddle in; **si occupa di assicurazione** he's in insurance; **occupati dei fatti tuoi!** mind your own business!

b : **occuparsi in** (*impiegarsi*) to get a job in.

occupato, a [okku'pato] AGG 1 (*telefono, gabinetto*) engaged; (*posto, sedia*) taken, occupied; (*zona, fabbrica, scuola*) occupied; (*persona: affaccendato*) busy; **essere occupato a fare qc** to be busy doing sth.

2 SM: **gli occupati e i disoccupati** the employed and the unemployed.

occupazionale [okkupattsjo'nale] AGG employment *attr*, of employment.

occupazione [okkupat'tsjone] SF a (*Mil, di fabbrica, scuola*) occupation; (*di casa*) occupancy, occupation; (*interesse, attività*) occupation ▶**occupazione abusiva** squatting b (*gen*) employment; (*impiego, lavoro*) job, occupation; **la piena occupazione** full employment.

Oceania [otʃe'anja] SF: **l'Oceania** Oceania.

oceanico, a, ci, che [otʃe'aniko] AGG oceanic, ocean *attr*; (*fig: immenso*) vast, huge.

oceano [o'tʃɛano] SM ocean.

oceanografia [otʃeanogra'fia] SF oceanography.

oceanografico, a, ci, che [otʃeano'grafiko] AGG oceanographic(al).

oceanografo, a [otʃea'nografo] SM/F oceanographer.

ocelot [otʃe'lɔt] SM INV = **ozelot**.

ocra [ˈɔkra] SF ochre.

OCSE [ˈɔkse] SIGLA F (= *Organizzazione per la Cooperazione e lo Sviluppo Economico*) OECD (= *Organization for Economic Cooperation and Development*).

oculare [oku'lare] AGG (*bulbo, lenti*) ocular, eye *attr*; **testimone oculare** eyewitness.

oculatezza [okula'tettsa] SF (*vedi agg*) caution; shrewdness.

oculato, a [oku'lato] AGG (*attento*) cautious, prudent; (*accorto*) shrewd.

oculista, i, e [oku'lista] SM/F eye specialist, ophtalmologist.

oculistica [oku'listika] SF ophthalmology.

oculistico, a, ci, che [oku'listiko] AGG (*gen*) ophthalmic; **studio oculistico** eye clinic; **fare una visita oculistica** to have one's eyes tested.

od [od] CONG vedi **o'**.

ode [ˈɔde] SF ode.

ode *ecc* [ˈɔde] VB vedi **udire**.

odiare [o'djare] 1 VT to hate, detest, loathe.

2 **odiarsi** VR to hate o.s.; (*uso reciproco*) to hate each other.

odiernamente [odjerna'mente] AVV nowadays.

odierno, a [o'djɛrno] AGG (*di oggi*) today's, of today; (*attuale*) present, current; **in data odierna** (*frm*) today.

odio, odi [ˈɔdjo] SM hatred, hate; **avere in odio qn/qc** to hate *o* detest sb/sth; **prendere in odio qn/qch** to take a strong dislike to sb/sth.

odiosamente [odjosa'mente] AVV hatefully, odiously.

odioso, a [o'djoso] AGG (*detestabile*) hateful, odious; (*antipatico*) unpleasant, obnoxious; **rendersi odioso (a)** to make o.s. thoroughly unpopular (with).

odissea [odis'sɛa] SF odyssey.

odo *ecc* [ˈɔdo] VB vedi **udire**.

odontoiatra, i, e [odonto'jatra] SM/F dentist, dental

surgeon.

odontoiatria [odontoja'tria] SF dentistry.

odontoiatrico, a, ci, che·[odonto'jatriko] AGG dental.

odontotecnico, ci [odonto'tɛkniko] SM dental technician.

odorare [odo'rare] **1** VT (*anche fig*) to smell; (*profumare*) to perfume, scent.

2 VI (*aus* **avere**) (*anche fig*): **odorare (di)** to smell (of); **questi fiori non odorano** these flowers don't have any smell *o* perfume; **odorare di pulito/fresco** to smell clean/fresh; **odorare di muffa/d'aglio** to smell mouldy/of garlic.

odorato [odo'rato] SM sense of smell.

odore [o'dore] SM **a** (*gen*) smell, odour (*Brit*), odor (*Am*); (*fragranza*) scent, fragrance; **senza odore** odo(u)rless; **sentire odore di qc** to smell sth; **avere buon/cattivo odore** to smell nice/bad, have a nice *o* good/bad smell; **odore di cucina** smell of cooking; **morire in odore di santità** (*Rel*) to die in the odo(u)r of sanctity

b : **odori** SMPL (*Culin*) (aromatic) herbs.

odoroso, a [odo'roso] AGG sweet-smelling.

off [ɔːf] AGG **a** (*spento*) off **b** (*Cine, Teatro: alternativo, sperimentale*) alternative.

offendere [of'fɛndere] VB IRREG **1** VT **a** (*persona, morale pubblica, senso estetico*) to offend; (*ferire*) to hurt; **offendere qn nell'onore** to offend sb's honour (*Brit*) *o* honor (*Am*); **offendere la vista** (*fig*) to offend the eye

b (*insultare*) to insult, offend

c (*violare: libertà, diritti*) to violate; (: *legge*) to break; **offendere i diritti di qn** to infringe on sb's rights.

2 **offendersi** VR (*uso reciproco*) to insult each other.

3 **offendersi** VIP (*risentirsi*): **offendersi (per)** to take offence (*Brit*) *o* offense (*Am*) (at), be offended (by).

offensiva [offen'siva] SF offensive; **passare all'offensiva** to take the offensive.

offensivamente [offensiva'mente] AVV (*in modo ingiurioso*) offensively, insultingly.

offensivo, a [offen'sivo] AGG (*parole*) offensive, insulting; (*armi*) offensive.

offensore [offen'sore] SM (*Mil*) aggressor.

offerente [offe'rɛnte] **1** PART PRES di **offrire**.

2 SM/F (*ad un'asta*) bidder; **vendere al migliore offerente** to sell to the highest bidder.

offerta [of'fɛrta] SF **a** (*gen*) offer; (*in gara d'appalto*) tender; (*ad un'asta*) bid; (*Econ*) supply; **fare un'offerta** to make an offer; (*per appalto*) to tender; (*ad un'asta*) to bid; **ci sono poche offerte d'impiego** there aren't many jobs advertised; **"offerte d'impiego"** (*Stampa*) "situations vacant" (*Brit*), "help wanted" (*Am*) ►**offerta pubblica d'acquisto** takeover bid ►**offerta pubblica di vendita** public offer for sale ►**offerta reale** tender ►**offerta speciale; (in) offerta speciale** (*Comm*) (on) special offer

b (*donazione, anche Rel*) offering, donation.

offerto, a [of'fɛrto] SF PP di **offrire**.

offertorio, ri [offer'tɔrjo] SM (*Rel*) offertory.

offesa [of'fesa] SF **a** (*insulto*) offence (*Brit*), offense (*Am*), insult, affront; (*Dir*) offence, offense; **fare *o* recare offesa a qn** to give offence *o* offense to sb **b** (*Mil*) attack.

offeso, a [of'feso] **1** PP di **offendere**.

2 AGG **a** (*nei sentimenti*) offended, hurt; (*fisicamente*) hurt, injured; **sei ancora offeso con me?** are you still annoyed with me? **b** (*Dir*): **la parte offesa** the plaintiff.

3 SM/F: **fare l'offeso** to go into a huff.

office ['ɔfis] SM INV pantry.

officiante [offi'tʃante] AGG (*Rel*) officiating.

officiare [offi'tʃare] VI (*aus* **avere**) (*Rel*) to officiate.

officina [offi'tʃina] SF workshop ►**officina meccanica** (*Aut*) garage.

offrire [of'frire] VB IRREG **1** VT **a** (*sigaretta, lavoro, merce, aiuto*) to offer; (*preghiere, messa*) to offer (up); (*ad un'asta*) to bid; **offrire qc a qn** to offer sth to sb, offer sb sth; **mi offri una sigaretta?** can I have a cigarette?; **ti offro da bere** I'll buy you a drink; **offro io (da bere)** the drinks are on me; **lo offre la casa** it's on the house; **ti va una pizza? offro io** do you feel like a pizza? my treat

b (*regalare*): **offrire a** to give to; **offrire qc in dono a qn** to present sb with sth

c (*opportunità, vantaggio*) to offer, present; **offrire il fianco alle critiche** to expose o.s. to criticism; **"offresi posto di segretaria"** "secretarial vacancy", "vacancy for secretary".

2 **offrirsi** VR: **offrirsi volontario** to offer (o.s.), volunteer; **offrirsi di fare qc** to offer *o* volunteer to do sth; **"segretaria offresi"** "secretary seeks post".

3 **offrirsi** VIP (*presentarsi: occasione*) to present itself, arise; **una vista stupenda si offrì ai loro occhi** a wonderful view lay before them.

offset ['ɔːfset] SM (*Tip*) offset; **realizzato in offset** printed in offset; **stampa in offset** offset printing.

offuscare [offus'kare] **1** VT (*cielo*) to darken; (*sole*) to obscure; (*fig: fama*) to obscure, overshadow; (: *mente*) to dim, cloud.

2 **offuscarsi** VIP (*vedi vt*) to darken, grow dark; to become obscured; to grow dim; (*fig: sguardo*) to cloud over.

oftalmia [oftal'mia] SF ophthalmia.

oftalmico, a, ci, che [of'talmiko] AGG ophthalmic.

oftalmoscopio [oftalmos'kɔpjo] SM ophthalmoscope.

oggettivamente [oddʒettiva'mente] AVV objectively.

oggettivare [oddʒetti'vare] **1** VT to objectify.

2 **oggettivarsi** VIP to become concrete.

oggettività [oddʒettivi'ta] SF objectivity.

oggettivo, a [oddʒet'tivo] AGG objective; **proposizione oggettiva** (*Gramm*) object clause.

oggetto [od'dʒetto] SM **a** (*cosa, articolo*) object, thing ►**oggetti preziosi** valuables, articles of value ►**oggetti smarriti** lost property *sg* (*Brit*), lost and found *sg* (*Am*)

b (*di disputa, discorso, studio*) subject; (*di sogni, pensieri*) object; **essere oggetto di** (*critiche, controversia*) to be the subject of; (*odio, pietà*) to be the object of; **essere oggetto di scherno** to be a laughing stock; **essere oggetto di persecuzione** to be subjected to persecution

c (*di attività, contratto*) object, purpose

d (*in lettere commerciali*): **oggetto... re ...**; **in oggetto a quanto detto** as regards the (matter mentioned) above

e (*Gramm, Filosofia*) object.

oggi ['ɔddʒi] **1** AVV today; (*al presente, al giorno d'oggi*) today, nowadays, these days; **oggi stesso** today, this very day; **oggi nel pomeriggio** this afternoon; **oggi (a) otto** a week today, today week; **quanti ne abbiamo oggi?** what's the date today?; **oggi come oggi** at present, as things stand; **oggi qui, domani là** (*fig*) here today, gone tomorrow; **oggi o domani** (*fig*) sooner or later; **oggi a me, domani a te** (*fig*) your day will come; **dagli oggi, dagli domani** in the long run, over time.

2 SM today; **dall'oggi al domani** from one day to the

next; **a tutt'oggi** up till now, till today; **le spese a tutt'oggi sono...** expenses to date are ... .

oggidì [odd͡ʒi'di] AVV nowadays.

oggigiorno [odd͡ʒi'd͡ʒorno] 1 AVV nowadays, these days. 2 SM today.

ogiva [o'd͡ʒiva] SF ogive, pointed arch.

ogni ['oɲɲi] AGG a (ciascuno) every, each; (tutti) all; **ogni passeggero** every o each passenger; **ogni cosa** everything; **ogni sorta di articoli** all sorts pl of goods b (qualsiasi) any, all; **ad ogni costo** at any price, at all costs; **gente d'ogni tipo** people of all sorts c (con valore distributivo) every; **ogni due giorni** every two days, every other day; **l'autobus passa ogni 20 minuti** the bus comes past every 20 minutes; **una persona ogni cento** one person in every hundred d (fraseologia): **in ogni caso** at any rate, in any case; **in ogni luogo** everywhere; **da ogni parte** from everywhere; **in o ad ogni modo** anyway, anyhow; **ogni tanto** every so often, every now and then; **ogni volta che** every time (that), whenever.

ogniqualvolta [oɲɲikwal'vɔlta] CONG whenever.

Ognissanti [oɲɲis'santi] SM All Saints' Day.

ognuno [oɲ'ɲuno] PRON (tutti) everybody, everyone; (ciascuno) each (one); **ognuno di noi sa quello che vuole** each of us knows what he wants, we all know what we want.

oh [ɔ, o] ESCL vedi **o²**.

ohi ['ɔi] ESCL (esprime disappunto, spesso ripetuto) oh!; (esprime dolore) ow!; **ohi là!** hey there!

ohimè [oi'mɛ] ESCL oh dear!

OIL ['ɔil] SIGLA F (= Organizzazione Internazionale del Lavoro) ILO (= International Labour Organisation).

okapi [o'kapi] SM INV (animale) okapi.

okay ['oukei] 1 ESCL O.K.!, okay!. 2 SM INV okay; **ricevere l'okay** to get the okay o the go-ahead; **dare l'okay a qc** to okay sth; **ti hanno messo l'okay sul biglietto?** have they confirmed your ticket?

OL ABBR (= onde lunghe) LW (= long wave).

Olanda [o'landa] SF: **l'Olanda** Holland.

olandese [olan'dese] 1 AGG Dutch. 2 SM/F Dutchman/Dutchwoman; **gli Olandesi** the Dutch. 3 SM a (lingua) Dutch b (formaggio) Dutch cheese.

oleaginoso, a [olead͡ʒi'noso] AGG oleaginous.

oleandro [ole'andro] SM oleander.

oleario, ria, ri, rie [ole'arjo] AGG oil attr.

oleato, a [ole'ato] AGG: **carta oleata** greaseproof paper (Brit), wax paper (Am).

oleificio, ci [olei'fit͡ʃo] SM oil mill.

oleodotto [oleo'dɔtto] SM oil pipeline.

oleografia [oleogra'fia] SF a (tecnica) oleography b (riproduzione) oleograph; (fig pegg) imitative painting.

oleografico, a, ci, che [oleo'grafiko] AGG oleographic; (fig pegg) imitative.

oleoso, a [ole'oso] AGG oily; (che contiene olio) oil attr.

olezzo [o'leddzo] SM fragrance; (scherz: puzzo) aroma.

olfatto [ol'fatto] SM sense of smell.

oliare [o'ljare] VT (meccanismo) to oil, lubricate; (Culin) to grease.

oliatore [olja'tore] SM (recipiente) oilcan; (dispositivo) oiler.

oliera [o'ljɛra] SF oil and vinegar cruet.

oligarchia [oligar'kia] SF oligarchy.

oligarchico, a, ci, che [oli'garkiko] AGG oligarchic(al).

Olimpiadi [olim'piadi] SFPL: **le Olimpiadi** the Olympics, the Olympic games.

olimpico, a, ci, che [o'limpiko] AGG Olympic.

olimpionico, a, ci, che [olim'pjoniko] 1 AGG Olympic. 2 SM/F (concorrente) competitor in the Olympics; (campione) Olympic champion.

Olimpo [o'limpo] SM (Geog, Mitol): **(monte) Olimpo** (Mount) Olympus.

olio, oli ['ɔljo] SM a oil; **sott'olio** (Culin) in oil; **tonno/funghi sott'olio** tuna/mushrooms in oil; **il mare è un olio** the sea is like a millpond; **gettare olio sul fuoco** (fig) to add fuel to the flames ▸**olio di fegato di merluzzo** cod-liver oil ▸**olio dei freni** (Aut) brake fluid ▸**olio di lino** linseed oil ▸**olio lubrificante** lubricating oil ▸**olio d'oliva** olive oil ▸**olio di semi** vegetable oil ▸**olio solare** suntan oil b (Rel): **olio santo** holy oil; **dare l'olio santo a qn** to give sb Extreme Unction c (Pittura): **un (quadro a) olio** an oil painting; **dipingere a olio** to paint in oils.

oliva [o'liva] 1 SF olive. 2 AGG INV (colore) olive(-green).

olivastro, a [oli'vastro] AGG (colore) olive-greenish, olive(-coloured) (Brit), olive(-colored) (Am); (carnagione) olive.

oliveto [oli'veto] SM olive grove.

olivicoltore [olivikol'tore] SM olive grower.

olivicoltura [olivikol'tura] SF olive growing.

olivo [o'livo] SM olive tree.

olmaria [ol'marja] SF (pianta) meadowsweet.

olmo ['ɔlmo] SM elm.

olocausto [olo'kausto] SM (Rel, fig) sacrifice; (genocidio) holocaust.

olofitico, a, ci, che [olo'fitiko] AGG (Bot) holophytic.

olografia [ologra'fia] SF holography.

ologramma, i [olo'gramma] SM hologram.

oloturia [olo'turja] SF (echinoderma) holothurian.

oloturoideo [oloturoi'dɛo] SM sea slug.

OLP [ɔlp] SIGLA F (= Organizzazione per la Liberazione della Palestina) PLO (= Palestine Liberation Organization).

oltraggiare [oltrad'd͡ʒare] VT to offend, insult.

oltraggio, gi [ol'tradd͡ʒo] SM a (insulto) insult, offence (Brit), offense (Am); **fare un oltraggio a** to offend, insult; **subire un oltraggio** to suffer an affront b (Dir): **accusato di oltraggio a pubblico ufficiale** charged with insulting a public official ▸**oltraggio alla corte** contempt of court ▸**oltraggio al pudore** indecent exposure.

oltraggiosamente [oltradd͡ʒosa'mente] AVV insultingly, offensively.

oltraggioso, a [oltrad'd͡ʒoso] AGG (offensivo) insulting, offensive.

oltralpe [ol'tralpe] AVV on the other side of the Alps, beyond the Alps; **un paese d'oltralpe** a country beyond the Alps.

oltranza [ol'trantsa] SF: **a o ad oltranza** to the (bitter) end; **sciopero ad oltranza** all-out strike.

oltranzismo [oltran'tsismo] SM (Pol) extremism.

oltranzista, i, e [oltran'tsista] SM/F (Pol) extremist.

oltre ['oltre] 1 AVV a (di luogo: più in là) farther, further; (: fig) further; **andare troppo oltre** (fig) to go too far b (di tempo: di più): **non... oltre** no more, no longer; **non posso aspettare oltre** I can't wait any longer c (di età) over; **persone di oltre trent'anni** people over thirty (years of age).

2 PREP **a** (*di luogo: di là da*) on the other side of, beyond, over; **sono passati oltre i confini** they crossed the border

b (*di tempo, quantità: più di*) more than, over; **sono oltre 3 mesi che non ti vedo** I haven't seen you in more than *o* in over 3 months; **non oltre il 10 febbraio** not later than 10th February

c (*in aggiunta a*): **oltre a** *o* **che** besides, as well as; **oltre che piovere fa freddo** it's cold as well as wet; **oltre a tutto** on top of all that

d (*all'infuori di, eccetto*): **oltre a** besides, except, apart from.

oltrecortina [oltrekor'tina] AVV behind the Iron Curtain; **paesi d'oltrecortina** Iron Curtain countries.

oltremanica [oltre'manika] AVV across the Channel.

oltremare [oltre'mare] AVV overseas; **paesi d'oltremare** overseas countries.

oltremarino, a [oltrema'rino] AGG (*colore*) ultramarine.

oltremodo [oltre'mɔdo] AVV extremely, greatly.

oltreoceano [oltreo'tʃeano] SM: **paesi d'oltreoceano** overseas countries.

oltrepassare [oltrepas'sare] VT (*varcare*) to cross, go beyond; (*superare*) to exceed, go over; **oltrepassare i limiti** *o* **la misura** (*fig*) to go too far.

oltretomba [oltre'tomba] SM: **l'oltretomba** the hereafter.

OM ABBR **a** (= *onde medie*) MW (= *medium wave*) **b** (*Mil*) = **ospedale militare.**

omaggio, gi [o'maddʒo] **1** SM **a** (*segno di rispetto*) homage, tribute; **rendere omaggio a** to pay homage *o* tribute to

b (*dono*) gift; (*Comm*): **fare omaggio di un libro** to give a presentation copy of a book; **copia in omaggio** presentation *o* complimentary copy; **biglietto in omaggio** complimentary ticket; **è un omaggio della ditta** it's a present from the firm; **"in omaggio"** "free gift"

c : **omaggi** SMPL (*ossequi*) respects, regards; **presentare i propri omaggi a qn** (*frm*) to pay one's respects to sb.

2 AGG INV free.

Oman [o'man] SM: **l'Oman** Oman.

ombelicale [ombeli'kale] AGG umbilical; **cordone ombelicale** umbilical cord.

ombelico, chi [ombe'liko] SM navel.

ombra ['ombra] **1** SF **a** (*sagoma scura*) shadow; (*zona non assolata*) shade; (*oscurità*) darkness; **sedersi all'ombra (di)** to sit in the shade (of); **dare ombra a qn** (*fig*) to put sb in the shade; **essere l'ombra di se stesso** to be a shadow of one's former self; **aver paura della propria ombra** to be afraid of one's own shadow

b (*fantasma*) shade (*letter*), ghost

c (*fig: oscurità*) obscurity; **nell'ombra** (*tramare, agire*) secretly; **restare nell'ombra** (*persona*) to remain in obscurity

d (*parvenza, traccia*): **non c'è ombra di verità in quello che dice** there isn't a grain of truth in what he says; **senza ombra di dubbio** without a shadow of a doubt; **un'ombra di burro** a hint *o* touch of butter.

2 AGG INV: **bandiera ombra** flag of convenience; **governo ombra** (*Pol*) shadow cabinet.

ombratura [ombra'tura] SF dark patch.

ombreggiare [ombred'dʒare] VT to shade.

ombreggiatura [ombreddʒa'tura] SF shading.

ombrellificio, ci [ombrelli'fitʃo] SM umbrella factory.

ombrellino [ombrel'lino] SM (*parasole*) parasol.

ombrello [om'brɛllo] SM (*also fig*) umbrella ► **ombrello**

da sole parasol, sunshade.

ombrellone [ombrel'lone] SM (*da spiaggia*) beach umbrella; (*di caffè, bar*) sunshade.

ombretto [om'bretto] SM eyeshadow.

ombrosità [ombrosi'ta] SF (*vedi agg*) shadiness; skittishness; touchiness.

ombroso, a [om'broso] AGG **a** (*bosco, viale*) shady, shaded **b** (*fig: cavallo*) skittish, nervous; (: *persona*) touchy, easily offended.

omelette [ɔmə'lɛt] SF INV omelette (*Brit*), omelet (*Am*).

omelia [ome'lia] SF (*Rel*) homily, sermon.

omeopata [ome'ɔpata] SM/F homoeopath (*Brit*), homeopath (*Am*).

omeopatia [omeopa'tia] SF homoeopathy (*Brit*), homeopathy (*Am*).

omeopatico, a, ci, che [omeo'patiko] AGG homoeopathic (*Brit*), homeopathic (*Am*).

Omero ['ɔmero] SM Homer.

omero ['ɔmero] SM (*Anat*) humerus.

omertà [omer'ta] SF conspiracy of silence.

omesso, a [o'messo] PP di **omettere.**

omettere [o'mettere] VT IRREG to leave out, omit; **omettere di fare qc** to neglect *o* omit *o* fail to do sth.

ometto [o'metto] SM (*fig: bambino*) good little fellow.

omiciattolo [omi'tʃattolo] SM creep.

omicida, i, e [omi'tʃida] **1** AGG (*maniaco, istinto, furia*) homicidal; (*sguardo, intenzione*) murderous.

2 SM/F murderer/murderess.

omicidio, di [omi'tʃidjo] SM murder, homicide (*Am*). ► **omicidio colposo** (*Dir*) manslaughter, second-degree murder (*Am*) ► **omicidio premeditato** (*Dir*) murder, first-degree murder (*Am*).

ominide [o'minide] SM hominid.

omisi *ecc* [o'mizi] VB *vedi* **omettere.**

omissione [omis'sjone] SF **a** (*non inclusione*) omission; **salvo errori e omissioni** errors and omissions excepted **b** (*Dir*): **reato d'omissione** criminal negligence ► **omissione di atti d'ufficio** negligence (*by a public employee*) ► **omissione di denuncia** failure to report a crime ► **omissione di soccorso** failure to stop and give assistance.

omnibus ['ɔmnibus] SM INV (*Storia*) horse-drawn omnibus.

omogeneamente [omodʒenea'mente] AVV homogeneously.

omogeneità [omodʒenei'ta] SF homogeneity.

omogeneizzare [omodʒeneid'dzare] VT to homogenize.

omogeneizzato, a [omodʒeneid'dzato] **1** AGG homogenized.

2 SM (*per bambini*) baby food.

omogeneo, a [omo'dʒɛneo] AGG (*gen*) homogeneous; (*fig: insieme di colori*) harmonious.

omografo, a [o'mɔgrafo] **1** SM homograph.

2 AGG homographic.

omologare [omolo'gare] VT (*Dir*) to approve, sanction; (*ratificare*) to ratify; **macchina omologata per 5 persone** car authorized to carry 5 people.

omologazione [omologat'tsjone] SF (*vedi vb*) approval, sanction; ratification.

omologo, a, ghi, ghe [o'mɔlogo] **1** AGG homologous, corresponding; (*Chim*) homologous.

2 SM/F opposite number, counterpart.

omonimia [omoni'mia] SF homonymy; **si tratta di un caso di omonimia** it must be somebody else of the same name.

omonimo, a [o'mɔnimo] [1] AGG (*persone, cose*) with the same name; **il film Lolita, tratto dall'omonimo romanzo** the film "Lolita", adapted from the book of the same name.
[2] SM/F (*persona*) namesake.
[3] SM (*Gramm*) homonym.

omosessuale [omosessu'ale] AGG, SM/F homosexual.

omosessualità [omosessuali'ta] SF homosexuality.

omozigote [omoddzi'gɔte] SM homozygote.

O.M.S. [o'ɛmme'ɛsse] SIGLA F (= *Organizzazione Mondiale della Sanità*) WHO (= *World Health Organization*).

omuncolo [o'munkolo] SM = **omiciattolo**.

On. ABBR (*Pol*) = **onorevole**.

onanismo [ona'nizmo] SM onanism.

oncia, ce ['ontʃa] SF (*unità di misura*) ounce.

oncologia [onkolo'dʒia] SF oncology.

oncologico, a, ci, che [onko'lɔdʒiko] AGG oncological.

oncologo, a, gi, ghe [on'kɔlogo] SM/F oncologist.

onda ['onda] SF **a** (*flutto, fig*) wave; **un'onda di commozione** a wave *o* surge of excitement; **capelli a onde** wavy hair ▸**onda lunga** roller ▸**onda verde** (*Aut*) synchronized traffic lights *pl*
b (*Fisica*) wave; **andare in onda** (*Radio, TV*) to go on the air, be broadcast; **mettere** *o* **mandare in onda** (*Radio, TV*) to broadcast ▸**onde corte** short wave *sg* ▸**onde lunghe** long wave *sg* ▸**onde medie** medium wave *sg*.

ondata [on'data] SF (*flutto*) wave; (*fig*) wave, surge; **a ondate** (*muovere, avanzare*) in waves; **un'ondata di turisti** an influx of tourists; **un'ondata di entusiasmo** a wave *o* surge of enthusiasm; **un'ondata di caldo** a heatwave; **un'ondata di freddo** a cold spell *o* snap.

onde ['onde] CONG (*frm: affinché*: con l'infinito*) in order to, so as to; (*: con il congiuntivo*) so that, in order that.

ondeggiare [onded'dʒare] VI (*aus avere*) (*acqua, superficie, grano*) to ripple; (*bandiera*) to flutter; (*muoversi: sulle onde: barca*) to rock, roll; (*fig: folla, alberi, edificio*) to sway; (*: persona: essere incerto*) to waver, hesitate.

ondoso, a [on'doso] AGG (*moto*) of the waves.

ondulare [ondu'lare] VT (*capelli*) to wave.

ondulato, a [ondu'lato] AGG (*capelli*) wavy; (*terreno*) undulating; **cartone ondulato** corrugated paper; **lamiera ondulata** sheet of corrugated iron.

ondulatorio, ria, ri, rie [ondula'tɔrjo] AGG (*movimento*) undulating; (*Fis*) undulatory, wave *attr*.

ondulazione [ondulat'tsjone] SF undulation; (*di capelli*) wave.

onerato, a [one'rato] AGG: **onerato di** burdened with, loaded with.

onere ['ɔnere] SM (*peso*) burden; (*responsabilità*) responsibility ▸**onere finanziario** financial burden ▸**oneri fiscali** taxes.

onerosamente [onerosa'mente] AVV heavily.

oneroso, a [one'roso] AGG (*compito*) onerous; (*tasse, pena*) heavy; (*condizioni di contratto*) hard.

onestà [ones'ta] SF (*vedi agg*) honesty; fairness; virtue; chastity.

onestamente [onesta'mente] AVV (*vedi agg*) honestly; fairly; virtuously; (*in verità*) honestly, frankly.

onesto, a [o'nɛsto] AGG (*probo, retto*) honest; (*giusto: persona, prezzi*) fair; (*virtuoso, pudico*) virtuous; (*casto*) chaste; **con intenzioni poco oneste** with dubious intentions.

onice ['ɔnitʃe] SF onyx.

onirico, a, ci, che [o'niriko] AGG dreamlike, dream *attr*.

onisco, schi [o'nisko] SM woodlouse.

onnipotente [onnipo'tɛnte] [1] AGG omnipotent, all-powerful; **Dio onnipotente** Almighty God.
[2] SM: **l'Onnipotente** (*Rel*) the Almighty.

onnipresente [onnipre'zɛnte] AGG (*of God*) omnipresent; (*fig*) ubiquitous.

onnisciente [onniʃ'ʃɛnte] AGG omniscient.

onniveggente [onnived'dʒɛnte] AGG all-seeing.

onnivoro, a [on'nivoro] [1] AGG omnivorous.
[2] SM omnivore.

onomastico, ci [ono'mastiko] SM name day.

onomatopea [onomato'pɛa] SF onomatopoeia.

onomatopeico, a, ci, che [onomato'pɛiko] AGG onomatopoeic.

onoranze [ono'rantse] SFPL honours (*Brit*), honors (*Am*)
▸**onoranze funebri** funeral hono(u)rs.

onorare [ono'rare] [1] VT (*gen*) to honour (*Brit*), honor (*Am*); (*far onore a*) to be a credit to, do credit to; **onorare qn con** *o* **di qc** to hono(u)r sb with sth; **onorare una cambiale** (*Comm*) to hono(u)r a bill.
[2] **onorarsi** VR: **onorarsi di qc/di fare qc** to feel hono(u)red by sth/to do sth.

onorario, ria, ri, rie [ono'rarjo] [1] AGG honorary.
[2] SM fee.

onoratissimo, a [onora'tissimo] AGG (*in presentazioni*): **onoratissimo!** delighted to meet you!

onorato, a [ono'rato] AGG (*reputazione, famiglia, carriera*) distinguished; **essere onorato di fare qc** to have the honour (*Brit*) *o* honor (*Am*) to do sth *o* of doing sth; **onorato di conoscerla** (it is) a pleasure to meet you.

onore [o'nore] SM **a** (*reputazione, integrità*) honour (*Brit*), honor (*Am*); **giuro sul mio onore che...** I swear on my hono(u)r that ...
b (*omaggio*) hono(u)r; **rendere onore a qn/qc** to hono(u)r sb/sth
c (*privilegio*) hono(u)r, privilege; **aver l'onore di** to have the hono(u)r of; **posto d'onore** place of hono(u)r
d (*merito*) credit; **fare onore ai genitori** to be a credit to one's parents; **si è fatto onore agli esami** he performed very creditably in the exams, he distinguished himself in the exams
e : **onori** SMPL (*onorificenze*) hono(u)rs
f (*Carte*) hono(u)r (card)
g (*fraseologia*): **in onore di** in hono(u)r of; **a onor del vero** to tell the truth; **fare onore alla tavola** to do justice to the dinner; **fare gli onori di casa** to do the hono(u)rs (of the house), to play host (*o* hostess).

onorevole [ono'revole] [1] AGG honourable (*Brit*), honorable (*Am*); (*Pol: titolo*); **l'Onorevole...** the Honourable ....
[2] SM/F (*Pol*): **Onorevole** ≈ Member of Parliament (*Brit*), ≈ Congressman/Congresswoman (*Am*).

onorevolmente [onorevol'mente] AVV honourably (*Brit*), honorably (*Am*).

onorificenza [onorifi'tʃɛntsa] SF honour (*Brit*), honor (*Am*); (*decorazione*) decoration.

onorifico, a, ci, che [ono'rifiko] AGG honorary.

onta ['onta] SF **a** (*vergogna*) shame, disgrace; (*affronto*) insult, affront **b** : **ad onta di** despite, notwithstanding.

ontano [on'tano] SM alder.

ontologia [ontolo'dʒia] SF ontology.

O.N.U. ['ɔnu] SIGLA F (= *Organizzazione delle Nazioni Unite*) UN, UNO (= *United Nations (Organization)*).

OO.PP. ABBR = **opere pubbliche**.

OPA ABBR = **offerta pubblica d'acquisto**.

opacità [opat∫i'ta] SF (*vedi agg*) opaqueness, opacity; matt quality; dullness.

opaco, a, chi, che [o'pako] AGG (*vetro, corpo*) opaque; (*carta*) matt; (*metallo, colore, fig: voce, sguardo, mente*) dull.

opale [o'pale] SM O F opal.

opalescenza [opale∫'∫entsa] SF opalescence.

opalina [opa'lina] SF (*vetro*) opaline.

O.P.E.C. ['opek] SIGLA F OPEC (= *Organization of Petroleum Exporting Countries*).

open ['oupən] 1 AGG INV (*torneo, biglietto*) open.
2 SM INV (*Sport*) open (tournament).

opera ['ɔpera] SF a (*attività, lavoro*) work; (*azione rilevante*) action, deed, work; **mettersi/essere all'opera** to get down to/be at work; **vedere qn all'opera** to see sb in action; **abbiamo ottenuto quell'aumento per opera sua** it was thanks to him that we got the rise; **fare opera di persuasione presso qn** to try to convince sb; **fare opere buone** *o* **di carità** to do good works *o* works of charity
b (*lavoro materiale*) work, piece of work ►**opera di scavo** excavation work *sg* ►**opere pubbliche** (*Amm*) public works ►**opere di restauro** restoration work *sg*
c (*produzione artistica: nell'insieme*) works *pl*; (: *libro, quadro*) work ►**opera d'arte** work of art
d (*ente*) foundation, institution, organization ►**opera pia** religious charity
e (*Mus*) opus; (: *melodramma*) opera; (: *teatro*) opera (house) ►**opera buffa** comic opera ►**opera lirica** (grand) opera
f (*Naut*): **opera morta** topsides *pl* ►**opera viva** bottom.

operaio, aia, ai, aie [ope'rajo] 1 AGG a (*movimento, partito*) workers' *attr*; (*prete*) worker *attr*; **classe operaia** working class
b (*Zool: ape, formica*) worker *attr*.
2 SM worker, workman ►**operaio di fabbrica** factory worker ►**operaio a giornata** day labourer (*Brit*) *o* laborer (*Am*) ►**operaio non specializzato** semi-skilled worker ►**operaio qualificato** *o* **specializzato** skilled worker.
3 SF female worker.

operante [ope'rante] AGG: **divenire operante** (*legge, piano*) to take effect; **essere operante** (*fabbrica*) to be operative.

operare [ope'rare] 1 VT a (*riforma*) to carry out, make; (*effetto*) to produce; **operare miracoli** to work wonders
b (*Med*) to operate on; **il chirurgo ha operato Mario di appendicite/allo stomaco** the surgeon operated on Mario for appendicitis/operated on Mario's stomach; **operare qn d'urgenza** to perform an emergency operation on sb.
2 VI (*aus avere*) a (*agire*) to act, work; (*Mil, Comm*) to operate
b (*Med*) to operate.
3 **operarsi** VIP a (*verificarsi*) to take place, to occur
b (*Med*) to have an operation; **operarsi d'ernia** to have a hernia operation; **operarsi d'appendicite** to have one's appendix out.

operativamente [operativa'mente] AVV (*mettere in atto, entrare in funzione*) effectively.

operativo, a [opera'tivo] AGG operative, operating; **piano operativo** (*Mil*) plan of operations.

operato, a [ope'rato] 1 SM (*comportamento*) actions *pl*.
2 SM/F (*Med*) patient (*who has undergone an operation*).
3 AGG (*tessuto*) diapered; (*carta*) embossed; (*cuoio*)

tooled.

operatore, trice [opera'tore] SM/F a (*TV, Cine*) cameraman/camerawoman; (*Comput*) operator ►**operatore cinematografico** projectionist ►**operatore ecologico** refuse collector ►**operatore del suono** sound recordist
b (*Econ*) agent; **gli operatori economici del settore** those with commercial interests in that sector; **aperto solo agli operatori** (*Comm*) open to the trade only ►**operatore di borsa** dealer on the stock exchange ►**operatore economico** agent, broker ►**operatore turistico** tour operator.

operatorio, ria, ri, rie [opera'tɔrjo] AGG (*Med*) operating.

operazione [operat'tsjone] SF (*gen, Med, Mil, Mat*) operation; (*Econ*) transaction.

opercolo [o'pɛrkolo] SM (*Bot, Zool*) operculum.

operetta [ope'retta] SF (*Mus*) operetta, light opera.

operettistico, a, ci, che [operet'tistiko] AGG operetta *attr*.

operistico, a, ci, che [ope'ristiko] AGG opera *attr*.

operosamente [operosa'mente] AVV industriously.

operosità [operosi'ta] SF industry, industriousness.

operoso, a [ope'roso] AGG (*attivo*) industrious, hard-working.

opificio, ci [opi'fit∫o] SM (*ant*) factory, works *pl*.

opinabile [opi'nabile] AGG (*discutibile*) debatable, questionable; **è opinabile** it is a matter of opinion.

opinione [opi'njone] SF opinion; **secondo la mia opinione** in my opinion; **avere il coraggio delle proprie opinioni** to have the courage of one's convictions ►**l'opinione pubblica** public opinion.

opinionista, i, e [opinjo'nista] SM/F (political) columnist.

op là [op'la] ESCL (*per far saltare*) hup!; (*un bimbo che è caduto*) upsy-daisy!

opossum [o'pɔssum] SM INV opossum.

oppio ['ɔppjo] SM opium.

oppiomane [op'pjɔmane] SM/F opium addict.

opponente [oppo'nente] 1 SM/F opponent.
2 AGG opposing.

oppongo ecc [op'pongo] VB vedi **opporre**.

opporre [op'porre] VB IRREG 1 VT a (*ragioni, argomenti*) to put forward; (*resistenza*) to put up, offer; **opporre un netto rifiuto a** to give a clear-cut refusal to
b (*obiettare*) to object; **non ho nulla da opporre** I have no objection.
2 **opporsi** VR (*fare opposizione*): **opporsi (a)** (*nemico*) to oppose; (*proposta*) to object (to); **mi oppongo alla sua idea** I am opposed to *o* against his idea.

opportunamente [opportuna'mente] AVV (*intervenire*) opportunely, at the right time; (*decidere*) conveniently.

opportunismo [opportu'nizmo] SM opportunism.

opportunista, i, e [opportu'nista] SM/F opportunist.

opportunisticamente [opportunistika'mente] AVV opportunistically.

opportunistico, a, ci, che [opportu'nistiko] AGG opportunist(ic).

opportunità [opportuni'ta] SF INV a (*convenienza*) opportuneness, timeliness; **avere il senso dell'opportunità** to have a sense of timing b (*occasione*) opportunity; **avere l'opportunità di fare qc** to have the opportunity of *o* for doing *o* to do sth; **Commissione per le Pari Opportunità** Equal Opportunities Commission.

opportuno, a [oppor'tuno] AGG (*adatto, conveniente*) opportune, timely; (*giusto*) right, appropriate; **a tempo opportuno** at the right *o* the appropriate time; **ritengo**

opportuno che tu gli scriva I think you should write to him, I think it would be advisable for you to write to him.

opposi *ecc* [op'pɔsi] VB *vedi* **opporre.**

oppositore, trice [oppozi'tore] [1] SM/F opponent, opposer.

[2] AGG opposing.

opposizione [oppozit'tsjone] SF **a** (*resistenza*) opposition; (*Pol*): **l'Opposizione** the Opposition; **fare opposizione a qn/qc** to oppose sb/sth **b** (*contrasto*) opposition; **essere in netta opposizione** (*idee, opinioni*) to clash, be in complete opposition **c** (*Dir*) objection.

opposto, a [op'posto] [1] PP di **opporre.**

[2] AGG **a** (*direzione, lato*) opposite

b (*contrario: idee, vedute*) opposite, conflicting; **le sue idee sono opposte alle mie** his ideas conflict with mine, his ideas are the opposite of mine.

[3] SM: **l'opposto** the opposite, the contrary; **all'opposto** on the contrary; **io, all'opposto di te, non li approvo** unlike you, I don't approve of them.

oppressione [oppres'sjone] SF (*Pol*) oppression; (*fisica, morale*) feeling of oppression.

oppressivo, a [oppres'sivo] AGG oppressive.

oppresso, a [op'prɛsso] [1] PP di **opprimere.**

[2] AGG oppressed.

[3]: **gli oppressi** SMPL the oppressed.

oppressore [oppres'sore] [1] SM oppressor.

[2] AGG oppressive.

opprimente [oppri'mɛnte] AGG (*caldo, noia*) oppressive; (*persona: deprimente*) depressing; (*fidanzato: soffocante*) possessive.

opprimere [op'primere] VT IRREG **a** (*sogg: caldo, afa*) to suffocate, oppress; **cibo che opprime lo stomaco** food that lies heavy on the stomach

b (*sogg: ansia, lavoro*) to weigh down, weigh heavily on; **il lavoro mi opprime** my work is getting me down; **mi opprime con la sua gelosia** his jealousy is suffocating me

c (*tiranneggiare: popolo*) to oppress.

oppugnare [oppuɲ'ɲare] VT (*letter fig: dottrina*) to refute.

oppugnazione [oppuɲɲat'tsjone] SF (*letter fig*) refutation.

oppure [op'pure] CONG (*o invece*) or; (*altrimenti*) otherwise, or (else).

optare [op'tare] VI (*aus* **avere**): **optare per** (*scegliere*) to opt for, decide upon; (*Borsa*) to take (out) an option on.

optimum ['ɔptimum] SM INV optimum.

optional ['ɔpʃənəl] SM INV optional extra.

optometria [optome'tria] SF optometry.

opulento, a [opu'lɛnto] AGG (*ricco: paese, società*) rich, wealthy, affluent; (*: stile letterario*) opulent.

opulenza [opu'lɛntsa] SF (*vedi agg*) richness, wealth, affluence; opulence.

opuscolo [o'puskolo] SM (*letterario, scientifico*) booklet, pamphlet; (*pubblicitario*) brochure, leaflet.

OPV ABBR = **offerta pubblica di vendita.**

opzionale [optsjo'nale] AGG optional.

opzione [op'tsjone] SF (*gen, Comm*) option; **diritto di opzione** (*Borsa*) (right of) option.

OR SIGLA = **Oristano.**

ora ['ora] [1] SF **a** (*unità di tempo, durata*) hour; **durante le ore d'ufficio** during office hours; **è a un'ora di cammino/d'auto dalla stazione** it's an hour's walk/drive from the station; **pagare a ore** to pay by the hour; **mi pagano 50.000 lire all'ora** they pay me 50,000 lire an hour

b (*parte della giornata*): **che ora è?, che ore sono? —sono le 4** what time is it? — it's 4 (o'clock); **che ora fai?** what time do you make it?; **a che ora ci vediamo?** what time o when shall we meet? ▶ **ora legale** summer time (*Brit*), daylight saving time (*Am*) ▶ **ora locale** local time

c (*momento*) time; **domani a quest'ora** this time tomorrow; **l'ora di pranzo** lunchtime; **l'ora dei pasti** mealtimes; **è ora di partire** it's time to go; **era ora!** about time too!; **le notizie dell'ultima ora** the latest news ▶ **ora di punta** (*Aut*) rush hour ▶ **l'ora X** zero hour

d (*fraseologia*): **non vedo l'ora di finire** I'm looking forward to finishing; (*excitement, frustration*) I can't wait to finish; **non vedevo l'ora che arrivasse l'estate** I couldn't wait for summer (to come); **fare le ore piccole** to stay up till the early o small hours (of the morning); **di buon'ora** early; **alla buon'ora!** at last!; **di ora in ora** hourly, hour by hour.

[2] AVV **a** (*adesso*) now; **ora non posso uscire** I can't go out (just) now; **d'ora in avanti** o **poi** from now on; **ora come ora** right now, at present

b (*poco fa*): **è uscito (proprio) ora** he's just gone out; **or ora** just now, a moment ago; **10 anni or sono** 10 years ago

c (*tra poco*) in a moment, presently, in a minute; **ora arrivo** I'm just coming, I'll be right there

d (*correlativo*): **ora... ora...** now ..., now ...; **ora qui ora lì** now here now there; **ora piange ora ride** one minute he's crying, the next he's laughing.

[3] CONG now; **ora che** now (that).

oracolo [o'rakolo] SM oracle.

orafo, a ['ɔrafo] [1] SM goldsmith.

[2] AGG (*arte*) goldsmith's *attr*, of a goldsmith.

orale [o'rale] AGG, SM oral.

oralmente [oral'mente] AVV orally.

oramai [ora'mai] AVV = **ormai.**

orango, ghi [o'rango] SM, **orangutan** [orangu'tan] SM INV orang-utan.

orario, ria, ri, rie [o'rarjo] [1] AGG (*cambiamento, media*) hourly; (*velocità*) per hour; (*fuso, segnale*) time *attr*; **in senso orario** clockwise; **disco orario** parking disc.

[2] SM **a** (*di ufficio, visite*) hours *pl*, time(s *pl*); **fare l'orario ridotto** to be on short time; **in orario** on time ▶ **orario di apertura** opening time ▶ **orario di chiusura** closing time ▶ **orario flessibile** (*Industria*) flexitime ▶ **orario di lavoro** working hours *pl* ▶ **orario di sportello** (*Banca*) bank opening hours *pl* ▶ **orario d'ufficio** office hours *pl*

b (*tabella*) timetable, schedule ▶ **orario ferroviario** railway timetable.

orata [o'rata] SF (*pesce*) sea bream.

oratore, trice [ora'tore] SM/F (public) speaker, orator.

oratoriamente [oratorja'mente] AVV oratorically.

oratorio, ria, ri, rie [ora'tɔrjo] [1] AGG oratorical.

[2] SM **a** (*cappella*) oratory **b** (*Mus*) oratorio.

[3] SF (*arte*) oratory.

Orazio [o'rattsjo] SM Horace.

orazione [orat'tsjone] SF **a** (*preghiera*) prayer **b** (*discorso*) oration, speech ▶ **orazione funebre** funeral oration.

orbene [or'bɛne] CONG (*letter*) well (then), so.

orbita ['ɔrbita] SF **a** (*Anat*) (eye-)socket; **aveva gli occhi fuori dalle orbite** (*fig*) his eyes were popping out of his head **b** (*Astron, Fis*) orbit; **mettere in orbita** to put into orbit **c** (*fig: ambito d'influenza*) sphere of influence.

orbitale [orbi'tale] AGG orbital.

orbitare [orbi'tare] VI (*aus* **essere**) to orbit.

orbo, a ['ɔrbo] AGG (*scherz*) blind; **e giù botte da orbi** and the fists were flying.

orca, che ['ɔrka] SF (*Zool*) killer whale.

Orcadi ['ɔrkadi] SFPL: **le (isole) Orcadi** the Orkney Islands, the Orkneys.

orchestra [or'kɛstra] SF (*complesso di musicisti, strumenti musicali*) orchestra; (: *da ballo, jazz*) band; (*Teatro: spazio*) orchestra pit.

orchestrale [orkes'trale] 1 AGG orchestral.
2 SM/F member of an orchestra, orchestra player.

orchestrare [orkes'trare] VT (*Mus, fig*) to orchestrate.

orchestrazione [orkestrat'tsjone] SF orchestration.

orchidea [orki'dɛa] SF orchid.

orcio, orci ['ɔrtʃo] SM (earthenware) pot.

orco, chi ['ɔrko] SM (*in fiabe*) ogre.

orda ['ɔrda] SF (*Storia, fig*) horde.

ordigno [or'diɲɲo] SM: **ordigno esplosivo** explosive device.

ordinale [ordi'nale] 1 AGG ordinal.
2 SM ordinal (number).

ordinamento [ordina'mento] SM (*organizzazione*) order, arrangement; (*regolamento*) regulations *pl*, rules *pl* ▶ **ordinamento giuridico** legal system ▶ **ordinamento scolastico** education system.

ordinanza [ordi'nantsa] SF **a** (*Dir*) order
b (*Amm, decreto*) decree ▶ **ordinanza municipale** by(e-)law
c (*Mil*) order; (: *prescrizione*) regulation; (: *anche:* **soldato d'ordinanza**) batman, orderly; **d'ordinanza** (*pistola, divisa*) regulation *attr*.

ordinare [ordi'nare] 1 VT **a** (*mettere in ordine*) to organize, put in order, arrange
b (*comandare*) to order; (*prescrivere: cura, medicina*) to prescribe; (*merce, pranzo*) to order; **ordinare che...** to order that ...; **ordinare a qn di fare qc** to order sb to do sth
c (*Rel: sacerdote*) to ordain.
2 **ordinarsi** VR (*disporsi*): **ordinarsi in fila/in colonna** to line up/form a column.

ordinariamente [ordinarja'mente] AVV (*di solito*) ordinarily; (*comunemente*) frequently; (*con mezzi e modi usuali*) as usual, according to the usual practice.

ordinarietà [ordinarje'ta] SF (*l'essere ordinario*) ordinary nature; (*pegg: qualità scadente*) mediocrity.

ordinario, ria, ri, rie [ordi'narjo] 1 AGG **a** (*consueto, normale*) ordinary, usual; (: *tariffa, spedizione, seduta*) ordinary; **di statura ordinaria** of average height; **di ordinaria amministrazione** (*fig*) routine *attr*
b (*rozzo: persona*) common, coarse; (*scadente: materiale, stoffa*) poor-quality
c (*professore: Scol*) permanent; (: *Univ*) full.
2 SM **a** : **l'ordinario** the ordinary; **fuori dall'ordinario** out of the ordinary; **d'ordinario** usually, as a rule
b (*Scol*) permanent teacher; (*Univ*) (full) professor.

ordinata [ordi'nata] SF (*Mat*) ordinate, y-axis.

ordinatamente [ordinata'mente] AVV (*gen*) tidily; (*metodicamente*) methodically.

ordinativo, a [ordina'tivo] 1 AGG governing, regulating.
2 SM (*Comm*) order.

ordinato, a [ordi'nato] AGG (*casa, persona*) tidy, orderly; (*vita*) well-ordered; (*impiegato*) methodical; (*corteo*) orderly.

ordinazione [ordinat'tsjone] SF **a** (*Comm*) order; **fare un'ordinazione di qc** to put in an order for sth, order sth; **eseguire qc su ordinazione** to make sth to order **b** (*Rel*) ordination.

ordine ['ordine] SM **a** (*disposizione, sequenza*) order; **in ordine alfabetico** in alphabetical order; **in ordine di anzianità/importanza** in order of seniority/importance; **in ordine di battaglia** (*Mil*) in battle order; **ritirarsi in buon ordine** (*Mil*) to retreat in good order; (*fig*) to back down gracefully; **ciò è nell'ordine naturale delle cose** it's in the nature of things
b (*di persona, camera*) tidiness, orderliness; **in ordine** (*documenti*) in order; (*casa*) tidy, orderly; **essere/tenere in ordine** to be/keep in order; **mettere in ordine** to tidy (up), put in order; **mettersi in ordine** to tidy (o.s.) up
c (*categoria: Archit, Bio*) order
d (*associazione*) association, order; (: *Rel*) order ▶ **l'ordine degli avvocati** ≈ the Bar ▶ **l'ordine dei medici** ≈ the British *o* American Medical Association
e (*carattere*): **questioni di ordine pratico/generale** questions of a practical/general nature; **un affare dell'ordine di 20 milioni** a deal of the order of 20 million; **di prim'ordine** (*albergo, merce*) first-class; **non rientra nel mio ordine di idee** that's not the way I see things
f (*principio d'organizzazione*) order; **richiamare all'ordine** to call to order; **le forze dell'ordine** the police ▶ **l'ordine pubblico** law and order, public order ▶ **l'ordine costituito** the established order
g : **ordini** SMPL (*Rel*) (Holy) Orders; **ordini minori/maggiori** minor/major orders
h (*comando*) order, command; **dare (l')ordine di fare qc** to give the order to do sth; **essere agli ordini di qn** (*Mil*) to be under sb's command; (*fig*) to be at sb's beck and call; **per ordine del governo** by order of the government; **fino a nuovo ordine** until further orders
i (*Comm, Fin*) order; **pagabile all'ordine di** payable to the order of ▶ **ordine d'acquisto** purchase order ▶ **ordine di pagamento** standing order (*Brit*), automatic payment (*Am*) ▶ **ordine di prova** trial order
j : **l'ordine del giorno** (*in riunioni*) the agenda; (*Mil*) the order of the day; **essere all'ordine del giorno** (*di riunione*) to be on the agenda; **gli scioperi sono ormai all'ordine del giorno** (*fig*) strikes are now the order of the day, strikes are now an everyday affair.

ordire [or'dire] VT (*tessuto*) to warp; (*fig*) to plot, scheme; **ordire una congiura** *o* **una trama** to hatch a plot, to plot.

ordito [or'dito] SM (*di tessuto*) warp.

orditore, trice [ordi'tore] SM/F (*Industria tessile*) warper; **orditore di trame** (*fig*) conspirator, plotter.

orditura [ordi'tura] SF (*di tessuto*) warpage.

orecchia [o'rekkja] SF **a** vedi **orecchio b** : **orecchie** SFPL: **fare le orecchie a un libro** to dog-ear a book.

orecchiabile [orek'kjabile] AGG (*canzone*) catchy.

orecchietta [orek'kjetta] SF (*Anat*) auricle.

orecchino [orek'kino] SM earring.

orecchio, chi [o'rekkjo] SM **a** (*Anat*) (*pl(f)* **orecchie**) ear; **mi fischiano le orecchie** (*lett*) my ears are singing; (*fig*) my ears are burning; **essere tutto orecchi** to be all ears; **venire all'orecchio di qn** to come to sb's attention; **te lo dico in un orecchio** this is for your ears only; **tapparsi** *o* **turarsi le orecchie** to put one's fingers in one's ears; **fare orecchie da mercante (a)** to turn a deaf ear (to); **tirare le orecchie a qn** to tweak sb's ears; (*fig*) to tell sb off, give sb an earful
b (*udito*) hearing; **essere debole d'orecchio** to be hard

of hearing; **avere orecchio** to have a good ear (for music); **cantare/suonare a orecchio** to sing/play by ear.

orecchioni [orek'kjoni] SMPL (*Med*): **gli orecchioni** (the) mumps *sg*.

orefice [o'refitʃe] SM/F (*negoziante*) jeweller (*Brit*), jeweler (*Am*); (*artigiano*) goldsmith.

oreficeria [orefitʃe'ria] SF (*negozio*) jeweller's (shop) (*Brit*), jewelry store (*Am*); (*arte*) goldsmith's (*o* silversmith's) art *o* craft; (*gioielli*) jewellery (*Brit*), jewelry (*Am*).

Oreste [o'rɛste] SM Orestes.

orfano, a ['ɔrfano] ⌐1⌐ AGG orphan(ed).
⌐2⌐ SM/F orphan; **restare orfano** to be left motherless (*o* fatherless), have lost one's mother (*o* father); **essere orfano di madre/padre** to be motherless/fatherless.

orfanotrofio, fi [orfano'trɔfjo] SM orphanage.

Orfeo [or'fɛo] SM Orpheus.

orfico, a, ci, che ['ɔrfiko] AGG Orphic.

orfismo [or'fizmo] SM Orphism.

organetto [orga'netto] SM (*strumento a manovella*) barrel organ, street organ; (*fam*: *armonica a bocca*) mouth organ; (: *fisarmonica*) accordion.

organicamente [organika'mente] AVV organically.

organico, a, ci, che [or'ganiko] ⌐1⌐ AGG (*Chim, Med, Dir*) organic.
⌐2⌐ SM (*personale*) staff, personnel; (: *Mil*) cadre; **essere nell'organico** to be on the permanent staff.

organigramma, i [organi'gramma] SM (*diagramma gerarchico*) organization chart; (*Inform*) computer flow chart.

organismo [orga'nizmo] SM (*vegetale, animale*) organism; (*Anat, Amm*) body, organism.

organista, i, e [orga'nista] SM/F organist.

organizzare [organid'dzare] ⌐1⌐ VT to organize, arrange.
⌐2⌐ **organizzarsi** VR to organize o.s., get (o.s.) organized.

organizzativo, a [organiddza'tivo] AGG organizational.

organizzatore, trice [organiddza'tore] ⌐1⌐ AGG organizing.
⌐2⌐ SM/F organizer.

organizzazione [organiddzat'tsjone] SF ⌐a⌐ (*azione*) organizing, organization, arranging; (*risultato*) organization, arrangement ⌐b⌐ (*associazione*) organization.

organo ['ɔrgano] SM (*Anat, Mus, pubblicazione*) organ; (*di congegno*) part; (*Amm*) organ, body ▶ **organi di comando** (*Tecn*) controls ▶ **organi di trasmissione** (*Tecn*) transmission (unit) *sg*.

organza [or'gandza] SF (*tessuto*) organza.

orgasmo [or'gazmo] SM ⌐a⌐ (*Fisiologia*) orgasm, climax ⌐b⌐ (*fig*: *agitazione, ansia*) anxiety, agitation; **essere/ mettersi in orgasmo** to be/get in a state.

orgia, ge ['ɔrdʒa] SF orgy; **un'orgia di** a profusion *o* riot of; **un'orgia di colori** an orgy of colour (*Brit*) *o* color (*Am*).

orgiastico, a, ci, che [or'dʒastiko] AGG orgiastic.

orgoglio [or'goʎʎo] SM pride.

orgogliosamente [orgoʎʎosa'mente] AVV proudly.

orgoglioso, a [orgoʎ'ʎoso] AGG proud; **sono orgogliosa di te** I'm proud of you.

orientabile [orjen'tabile] AGG adjustable.

orientale [orjen'tale] ⌐1⌐ AGG (*paese, regione*) eastern; (*civiltà, lingua, tappeto*) oriental.
⌐2⌐ SM/F Oriental.

orientaleggiante [orjentaled'dʒante] AGG oriental.

orientalista, i, e [orjenta'lista] SM/F Orientalist.

orientalizzare [orjentalid'dzare] VT to Orientalize.

orientalizzazione [orjentaliddzat'tsjone] SF Orientaliza-

tion.

orientamento [orjenta'mento] SM ⌐a⌐ (*azione*) (*vedi vt*) positioning; orientation; directing
⌐b⌐ (*direzione*) direction; **senso di** *o* **dell'orientamento** sense of direction; **perdere l'orientamento** to lose one's bearings
⌐c⌐ (*tendenza*: *di partito, rivista*) tendencies *pl*, leanings *pl*; (: *di scienze*) trends *pl*; (: *di ricerche*) direction ▶ **orientamento professionale** careers guidance.

orientare [orjen'tare] ⌐1⌐ VT ⌐a⌐ (*disporre*: *antenna, ventilatore*) to position; (*carta, bussola*) to orientate
⌐b⌐ (*fig*: *dirigere*: *ricerche, persona*) to direct; **hanno orientato la conversazione su un tema d'attualità** they steered the conversation round to a topical subject.
⌐2⌐ **orientarsi** VR ⌐a⌐ (*viaggiatore*) to find one's bearings; (*fig*: *raccapezzarsi*) to find one's way; **in questa faccenda non riesco a orientarmi** I can't make head nor tail of this business
⌐b⌐ : **orientarsi per** *o* **verso** (*fig*: *indirizzarsi*) to take up, go in for; (: *propendere*) to lean towards, tend towards; **mi sto orientando verso l'acquisto di una casa** I'm coming round to the idea of buying a house.

orientativamente [orjentativa'mente] AVV: **qual è il prezzo, orientativamente?** can you give me a rough idea of the price?

orientativo, a [orjenta'tivo] AGG indicative, approximate; **a scopo orientativo** for information.

orientazione [orjentat'tsjone] SF (*vedi vt a*) positioning; orientation.

oriente [o'rjɛnte] SM (*levante*) east; **l'Oriente** the East, the Orient; **a oriente** in the east; **il Medio/l'Estremo Oriente** the Middle/Far East.

orificio, ci [ori'fitʃo], **orifizio, zi** [ori'fittsjo] SM (*apertura*) opening; (: *di tubo*) mouth; (*Anat*) orifice.

origano [o'rigano] SM (*Bot*) oregano.

originale [oridʒi'nale] ⌐1⌐ AGG (*gen*) original; (*nuovo*) new, original; (*bizzarro*) eccentric, odd.
⌐2⌐ SM (*opera, documento*) original ▶ **originale radiofonico** radio play ▶ **originale televisivo** television play.
⌐3⌐ SM/F eccentric; **il tuo amico è un bell'originale!** your friend is a real character!

originalità [oridʒinali'ta] SF ⌐a⌐ (*vedi agg*) originality; eccentricity, oddness ⌐b⌐ (*atto da originale*) eccentric behaviour.

originalmente [oridʒinal'mente] AVV (*in origine*) originally; (*in modo originale*) in an original way.

originare [oridʒi'nare] ⌐1⌐ VT to cause, give rise to, bring about, produce.
⌐2⌐ VI (*aus essere*): **originare da** to arise *o* spring from.

originariamente [oridʒinarja'mente] AVV (*in origine*) originally; (*dapprincipio*) at first, originally.

originario, ria, ri, rie [oridʒi'narjo] AGG ⌐a⌐: **essere originario di** (*persona*) to be a native of; (*animale, pianta*) to be indigenous to, be native to; **è originario di Roma** he is a native of Rome, he was born in Rome ⌐b⌐ (*primitivo, originale*) original.

origine [o'ridʒine] SF (*gen*) origin; (*provenienza*: *di persona, famiglia*) origin, extraction; (: *di cosa*) origin, provenance; (*di fiume*) source; (*causa*) origin, cause; **luogo/paese d'origine** place/country of origin; **di origine italiana** of Italian extraction *o* origin; **risalire alle origini** *o* **all'origine di qc** to go back to the origins *o* the beginning of sth; **cominciare dalle origini** to start at the beginning; **dare origine a** to give rise to; **avere**

origine da to originate from; **all'origine** originally.

origliare [oriʎ'ʎare] ① VI (*aus* avere): **stava origliando alla porta** he was listening at the door.
② VT to eavesdrop (on).

orina [o'rina] SF urine.

orinale [ori'nale] SM chamberpot.

orinare [ori'nare] ① VI (*aus* avere) to pass water, urinate.
② VT: **orinare sangue** to pass blood.

orinatoio, oi [orina'tojo] SM (public) urinal.

Orione [ori'one] SM Orion.

oritteropo [orit'tɛropo] SM (*animale*) aardvark.

oriundo, a [o'rjundo] ① AGG: **essere oriundo di Milano** to be of Milanese extraction *o* origin.
② SM/F person of foreign extraction *o* origin; **negli Stati Uniti ci sono molti oriundi italiani** in the United States there are many people of Italian extraction *o* origin.
③ SM (*Sport: in Italia*) foreign player of Italian extraction.

orizzontale [oriddzon'tale] ① AGG horizontal.
② SF (*di cruciverba*) clue (*o* word) across.

orizzontalmente [oriddzontal'mente] AVV horizontally.

orizzontarsi [oriddzon'tarsi] VR (*viaggiatore*) to get one's bearings; (*fig: raccapezzarsi*) to find one's way.

orizzonte [orid'dzonte] SM **a** horizon; **all'orizzonte** (*apparire*) on the horizon; (*sparire*) below the horizon **b** (*fig: prospettiva*) horizon; **l'orizzonte politico** the political scene; **fare un giro d'orizzonte** (*di situazione*) to examine the main aspects.

ORL [ɔrl] SIGLA F (*Med: = otorinolaringoiatria*) ENT (= *ear, nose and throat*).

orlare [or'lare] VT (*gen*) to hem; (*con fettucce, nastri*) to edge, trim.

orlatura [orla'tura] SF (*orlo*) hem; (*azione*) hemming *no pl*.

orlo ['orlo] SM **a** (*di marciapiede*) edge; (*di recipiente*) rim, brim; (*di precipizio*) brink; **pieno fino all'orlo** full to the brim, brimfull; **sull'orlo della pazzia/della rovina** on the brink *o* verge of madness/ruin **b** (*ripiegatura: di vestiti*) hem ▶ **orlo a giorno** hemstitch.

orma ['orma] SF (*di persona*) footprint; (*di animale*) track; (*fig: impronta, traccia*) trace, mark; **seguire** *o* **calcare le orme di qn** to follow in sb's footsteps.

ormai [or'mai] AVV **a** (*riferito al presente*) by now, by this time; (: *a questo punto*) now; **ormai è tardi** it's late now; **ormai dovrebbe essere partito** he must have left by now **b** (*allora*) by then **c** (*riferito al futuro: quasi*) almost, nearly; **ormai siamo arrivati** we're nearly *o* almost there.

ormeggiare [ormed'dʒare] VT, **ormeggiarsi** VR to moor.

ormeggio, gi [or'meddʒo] SM (*atto*) mooring *no pl*; (*luogo*) moorings *pl*; **ormeggi** SMPL (*cavi e catene*) moorings; **le navi erano all'ormeggio** the ships were at their moorings; **posto d'ormeggio** berth.

ormonale [ormo'nale] AGG (*disfunzione*) hormonal, hormone *attr*; (*cura*) hormone *attr*; **terapia ormonale** hormone therapy.

ormone [or'mone] SM hormone.

ornamentale [ornamen'tale] AGG ornamental, decorative.

ornamento [orna'mento] SM (*gen*) ornament, decoration; (*azione*) adornment, decoration; (*Archit, Arte*) embellishment; **privo di ornamenti** (*stile, vestito, stanza*) plain, unadorned.

ornare [or'nare] ① VT **a** (*tavola, vestito*): **ornare (di** *o* **con)** to decorate (with), adorn (with); (*fig: discorso*) to embellish (with) **b** (*sogg: affresco, statua*) to adorn, decorate.
② **ornarsi** VR: **ornarsi (di)** to deck o.s. (out) (with).

ornato, a [or'nato] ① AGG **a** (*adorno*): **ornato di** adorned with, decorated with; **un cappello ornato di piume** a hat trimmed with feathers **b** (*stile*) ornate, florid.
② SM (*Archit*) embellishment.

ornitologia [ornitolo'dʒia] SF ornithology.

ornitologico, a, ci, che [ornito'lɔdʒiko] AGG ornithological.

ornitologo, a, gi *o* **ghi, ghe** [orni'tɔlogo] SM/F ornithologist.

ornitorinco, chi [ornito'rinko] SM (*animale*) (duck-billed) platypus.

oro ['oro] SM **a** gold; **bracciale in oro** *o* **d'oro** gold bracelet ▶ **oro nero** (*petrolio*) black gold ▶ **oro zecchino** pure gold
b : **ori** SMPL (*oggetti d'oro*) gold *sg*; (*gioielli*) jewellery *sg* (*Brit*), jewelry *sg* (*Am*); (*Carte*) *suit in Neapolitan pack of cards*
c : **d'oro** (*oggetto*) gold; (*colore, occasione*) golden; (*persona*) wonderful, marvellous (*Brit*), marvelous (*Am*); **un'occasione d'oro** a golden opportunity; **un affare d'oro** a real bargain; **fare affari d'oro** to do excellent business; **avere un cuore d'oro** to have a heart of gold.
d (*fraseologia*): **nuotare nell'oro** to be rolling in money; **prendere qc per oro colato** to take sth as gospel (truth); **non lo farei per tutto l'oro del mondo** I wouldn't do it for all the money in the world; **quell'uomo vale tanto oro quanto pesa** that man is worth his weight in gold; **non è tutt'oro quel che luccica** all that glitters is not gold.

orogenesi [oro'dʒɛnezi] SF INV (*Geol*) orogeny, orogenis.

orogenetico, a, ci, che [orodʒe'nɛtiko] AGG (*Geol*) orogenic, orogenetic.

orografia [orogra'fia] SF (*Geog*) orography.

orografico, a, ci, che [oro'grafiko] AGG (*Geog*) orographic.

orologeria [orolodʒe'ria] SF (*arte, industria*) watchmaking *no pl*; (*negozio*) watchmaker's (shop); clockmaker's (shop); (*meccanismo*) clockwork; **bomba a orologeria** time bomb.

orologiaio, ai [orolo'dʒajo] SM watchmaker; clockmaker.

orologio, gi [oro'lɔdʒo] SM (*da muro, a pendolo*) clock; (*da tasca, polso*) watch; **il mio orologio va avanti/indietro** my watch is fast/slow; **una mezz'ora di orologio** exactly half an hour; **andare** *o* **funzionare come un orologio** (*meccanismo*) to run like clockwork ▶ **orologio analogico** analogue watch *o* clock ▶ **orologio biologico** biological clock ▶ **orologio digitale** digital watch *o* clock ▶ **orologio al quarzo** quartz watch ▶ **orologio solare** sundial.

oroscopo [o'rɔskopo] SM horoscope.

orrendamente [orrenda'mente] AVV horrifically, horrendously.

orrendo, a [or'rɛndo] AGG (*spaventoso*) horrible, horrendous; (*bruttissimo*) hideous; (*cattivo*) awful, terrible, dreadful; (*ripugnante*) revolting.

orribile [or'ribile] AGG (*brutto*) horrible; (*pessimo*) awful, dreadful; (*ripugnante*) revolting.

orribilmente [orribil'mente] AVV horribly, hideously.

orrido, a ['ɔrrido] AGG horrid, dreadful, fearful.

orripilante [orripi'lante] AGG horrifying, hair-raising.

orrore [or'rore] SM (*gen*) horror; (*ribrezzo*) disgust, loathing; **avere orrore di qc** to loathe *o* detest sth; **avere in orrore qn/qc** to loathe *o* detest sb/sth; **i ragni mi fanno**

orrore I have a horror of spiders, I loathe spiders; **gli orrori della guerra** the horrors of war; **che orrore!** how awful o dreadful!; **quel quadro è un orrore** that painting is hideous; **film dell'orrore** horror film (*Brit*) o movie (*Am*).

orsa ['orsa] SF she-bear; **l'Orsa maggiore/minore** the Great/Little Bear, Ursa Major/Minor (*Astron*).

orsacchiotto [orsak'kjɔtto] SM (*cucciolo*) bear cub; (*giocattolo*) teddy bear.

orso ['orso] SM (*Zool, fig*) bear ▶ **orso bianco** polar bear ▶ **orso bruno** brown bear.

orsolina [orso'lina] SF Ursuline.

orsù [or'su] ESCL (*letter*) come now!

ortaggio, gi [or'taddʒo] SM vegetable.

ortensia [or'tɛnsja] SF hydrangea.

ortica, che [or'tika] SF (stinging) nettle; **falsa ortica** dead-nettle.

orticaria [orti'karja] SF nettle rash.

orticoltura [ortikol'tura] SF horticulture.

orto ['ɔrto] SM vegetable garden, kitchen garden; (*Agr*) market garden (*Brit*), truck farm (*Am*) ▶ **orto botanico** botanical garden(s *pl*).

ortocentro [orto'tʃentro] SM (*Mat*) orthocentre (*Brit*), orthocenter (*Am*).

ortodontia [ortodon'tia] SF orthodontics *sg*, dental orthopaedics (*Brit*) o orthopedics (*Am*) *sg*.

ortodossia [ortodos'sia] SF orthodoxy.

ortodosso, a [orto'dɔsso] AGG, SM/F orthodox.

ortofonia [ortofo'nia] SF (*Ling*) correct pronunciation; (*Med*) speech therapy.

ortofrutticolo, a [ortofrut'tikolo] AGG fruit and vegetable *attr*.

ortofrutticoltore [ortofruttikol'tore], **ortofrutticultore** [ortofruttikul'tore] SM market gardener.

ortofrutticoltura [ortofruttikol'tura], **ortofrutticultura** [ortofruttikul'tura] SF market gardening.

ortogonale [ortogo'nale] AGG perpendicular, orthogonal.

ortografia [ortogra'fia] SF spelling, orthography; **errori di ortografia** spelling mistakes.

ortografico, a, ci, che [orto'grafiko] AGG spelling *attr*, orthographical.

ortolano, a [orto'lano] SM/F (*negoziante*) greengrocer (*Brit*), produce dealer (*Am*).

ortomercato [ortomer'kato] SM fruit market.

ortopedia [ortope'dia] SF orthopaedics *sg* (*Brit*), orthopedics *sg* (*Am*).

ortopedicamente [ortopedika'mente] AVV orthopaedically (*Brit*), orthopedically (*Am*).

ortopedico, a, ci, che [orto'pɛdiko] 1 AGG orthopaedic (*Brit*), orthopedic (*Am*).
2 SM/F orthopaedic specialist (*Brit*), orthopedist (*Am*).

orzaiolo [ordza'jolo], **orzaiuolo** [ordza'jwɔlo] SM (*Med*) sty(e).

orzare [or'tsare] VI (*aus avere*) (*Naut*) to head up.

orzata¹ [or'dzata] SF (*bevanda*) barley water; (*sciroppo*) *almond-based cordial*.

orzata² [or'dzata] SF (*Naut*): **fare un'orzata** to head up.

orzo ['ɔrdzo] SM barley.

OSA ['ɔza] SIGLA F (= *Organizzazione degli Stati Americani*) OAS (= *Organization of American States*).

osanna [o'zanna] SM INV hosanna.

osannare [ozan'nare] VT (*lodare*) to applaud, acclaim.

osare [o'zare] VT **a** : **osare (fare)** to dare (do) o (to do); **non osava domandargli** he didn't dare (to) ask him;

oserei dire che... I dare say that ...; **come osi?** how dare you? **b** (*tentare*) to attempt; (*arrischiare*) to risk.

oscar ['ɔskar] SM INV (*Cine*) Oscar; (*fig: primo premio*): **oscar (di)** prize (for).

oscenamente [oʃʃena'mente] AVV (*in modo indecente*) obscenely; (*in modo pessimo*) appallingly, atrociously.

oscenità [oʃʃeni'ta] SF INV obscenity.

osceno, a [oʃ'ʃɛno] AGG (*indecente*) obscene; (*bruttissimo*) dreadful, awful; (*ripugnante*) ghastly.

oscillante [oʃʃil'lante] AGG **a** (*prezzi, valori*) fluctuating **b** (*Elettr: corrente*) oscillating.

oscillare [oʃʃil'lare] VI (*aus avere*) (*Fis*) to oscillate; (*pendolo*) to swing; (*fiamma*) to flicker; (*dondolare: al vento*) to rock; (*prezzi, temperatura*): **oscillare (fra)** to fluctuate (between); (*persona: essere indeciso*) to waver (between).

oscillatore [oʃʃilla'tore] SM oscillator.

oscillatorio, ria, ri, rie [oʃʃilla'tɔrjo] AGG (*Fis: moto*) swinging, oscillatory (*termine tecn*).

oscillazione [oʃʃillat'tsjone] SF (*Fis*) oscillation; (*di prezzi, temperatura*) fluctuation.

oscilloscopio, pi [oʃʃillos'kɔpjo] SM oscilloscope.

oscuramente [oskura'mente] AVV (*senza chiarezza*) obscurely; **vivere oscuramente** (*senza fama*) to live in obscurity.

oscuramento [oskura'mento] SM **a** (*cielo*) darkening; (*sole*) obscuring; (*vista*) dimming **b** (*in tempo di guerra*) blackout.

oscurantismo [oskuran'tizmo] SM obscurantism.

oscurare [osku'rare] 1 VT **a** (*rendere scuro*) to darken, obscure; (*offuscare: sole, veduta*) to obscure; (*schermare: lampada*) to shade **b** (*fig*) to obscure.
2 **oscurarsi** VIP **a** (*cielo*) to cloud over, darken, get o become darker **b** (*vista, mente*) to dim, grow dim; **si oscurò in volto** his face clouded (over).

oscurità [oskuri'ta] SF (*vedi agg*) darkness; obscurity; gloominess; **sono nell'oscurità più completa per quanto riguarda i loro progetti** I am completely in the dark about their plans.

oscuro, a [os'kuro] 1 AGG (*scuro*) dark; (*fig: incomprensibile, sconosciuto*) obscure; (: *triste: pensiero*) gloomy, sombre; (: *umile: vita, natali*) humble, obscure; **è morto in circostanze oscure** he died in mysterious circumstances.
2 SM darkness; **all'oscuro** in the dark; **tenere qn/essere all'oscuro di qc** to keep sb/be in the dark about sth.

Oslo ['ɔslo] SF Oslo.

osmio ['ɔzmjo] SM osmium.

osmoregolazione [ozmoregolat'tsjone] SF (*Zool*) osmoregulation.

osmosi [oz'mɔzi] SF INV osmosis.

osmotico, a, ci, che [oz'mɔtiko] AGG osmotic.

ospedale [ospe'dale] SM hospital ▶ **ospedale da campo** field hospital ▶ **ospedale militare** military hospital.

ospedaliero, a [ospeda'ljɛro] 1 AGG hospital *attr*; **attrezzatura ospedaliera** hospital facilities *pl*.
2 SM/F hospital worker.

ospedalizzare [ospedalid'dzare] VT to hospitalize.

ospitale [ospi'tale] AGG (*gente*) hospitable; (*casa, paese*) friendly.

ospitalità [ospitali'ta] SF hospitality.

ospitare [ospi'tare] VT **a** (*dare alloggio*) to put up; (: *sogg: albergo*) to accommodate **b** (*accogliere: mostre, gare, avvenimenti*) to hold; (: *Sport*) to play at home to; **il Milan**

ospiterà la Juventus domenica prossima Milan will play at home to Juventus next Sunday.
ospite ['ɔspite] 1 SM/F (*persona ospitata*) guest; (*persona che ospita*) host/hostess.
2 AGG: **squadra ospite** (*Calcio*) visiting team.
ospizio, zi [os'pittsjo] SM (*istituto di ricovero*) home; (*per anziani*) old people's home; (*per viaggiatori, pellegrini*) hospice.
ossa ['ɔssa] SFPL vedi **osso**.
ossalide [os'salide] SF (*pianta*) oxalis.
ossario, ri [os'sarjo] SM war memorial (*with burial place*).
ossatura [ossa'tura] SF (*di corpo*) bone structure, frame, skeletal structure; (*di edificio, ponte, romanzo*) framework; **è di ossatura robusta** he's strongly built.
osseo, a ['ɔsseo] AGG (*Anat, Med*) bone *attr*, bony.
ossequente [osse'kwɛnte], **ossequiente** [osse'kwjɛnte] AGG: **ossequente alle leggi** law-abiding.
ossequio, qui [os'sɛkwjo] SM **a** respect, deference; **in ossequio a** out of respect for
b : **ossequi** SMPL (*saluto*) respects, regards; **ossequi alla signora!** (give my) respects to your wife!; **porgere i propri ossequi a qn** (*frm*) to pay one's respects to sb; **i miei ossequi** (*in una lettera*) sincere regards.
ossequiosamente [ossekwjosa'mente] AVV (*vedi agg*) respectfully; obsequiously.
ossequioso, a [osse'kwjoso] AGG (*rispettoso*) respectful; (*servile*) obsequious.
osservante [osser'vante] AGG (*Rel*) practising.
osservanza [osser'vantsa] SF observance.
osservare [osser'vare] VT **a** (*guardare*) to observe; (: *attentamente: nemico*) to watch; (: *al microscopio*) to examine
b (*notare, rilevare*) to notice, observe; (*far notare*) to point out, remark, observe; **far osservare qc a qn** to point sth out to sb; **ha osservato che...** (*ha detto*) he remarked that ...; (*ha obiettato*) he objected o made the objection that ...; **non ho nulla da osservare** I have no objections
c (*rispettare: legge, regolamento*) to observe, respect; (*mantenere: silenzio*) to keep; **osservare il digiuno** to fast, keep the fast.
osservatore, trice [osserva'tore] 1 AGG observant.
2 SM/F observer.
osservatorio, ri [osserva'tɔrjo] SM (*Astron, Meteor*) observatory; (*Mil*) observation o look-out post.
osservazione [osservat'tsjone] SF **a** observation; **tenere qn in** o **sotto osservazione** (*Med*) to keep sb under observation
b (*considerazione critica*) comment, observation, remark; (*obiezione*) objection; (*rimprovero*) criticism, reproof; **fare un'osservazione** (*considerazione*) to make a remark; (*obiezione*) to raise an objection; **fare un'osservazione a qn** to criticise sb; **fare osservazione a qn** to reprimand sb.
ossessionante [ossessjo'nante] AGG (*vedi vb*) obsessive, haunting; troublesome.
ossessionare [ossessjo'nare] VT (*tormentare: sogg: idea, ricordo*) to obsess, haunt; (: *sogg: persona*) to torment, harass; (*infastidire*) to trouble, bother.
ossessione [osses'sjone] SF **a** (*fissazione*) obsession; **aveva l'ossessione del denaro** he was obsessed with money **b** (*seccatura*) nuisance.
ossessivamente [ossessiva'mente] AVV (*gen*) obsessively; **gli chiedeva ossessivamente la stessa cosa** she kept on

and on asking him the same thing.
ossessivo, a [osses'sivo] AGG obsessive, haunting; (*ricordo, idea, persona*) troublesome; **ma sei proprio ossessivo!** you really are a pest!
ossesso, a [os'sɛsso] 1 AGG (*spiritato*) possessed.
2 SM/F person possessed; (*fig*): **urlare come un ossesso** to shout like a maniac.
ossia [os'sia] CONG (*cioè*) that is, to be precise; (*o meglio*) or rather.
ossiacido [ossi'atʃido] SM acidic oxide.
ossibuchi [ossi'buki] SMPL di **ossobuco**.
ossicino [ossi'tʃino] SM (*Anat*) ossicle.
ossidante [ossi'dante] SM oxidizer.
ossidare [ossi'dare] VT, **ossidarsi** VIP to oxidize.
ossidazione [ossidat'tsjone] SF oxidization, oxidation.
ossidiana [ossi'djana] SF obsidian.
ossido ['ɔssido] SM oxide ▶**ossido di carbonio** carbon monoxide.
ossidoriduzione [ossidoridut'tsjone] SF redox, oxidation-reduction.
ossidrile [ossi'drile] SM hydroxide.
ossificare [ossifi'kare] VT, **ossificarsi** VIP to ossify.
ossificazione [ossifikat'tsjone] SF ossification.
ossigenare [ossidʒe'nare] 1 VT **a** (*Chim*) to oxygenate; (*decolorare: capelli*) to bleach; **ossigenare i polmoni** to get some fresh air (into one's lungs) **b** (*fig*) to inject new life into.
2 **ossigenarsi** VR **a** (*decolorarsi*) to bleach one's hair **b** (*ritemprarsi*) to get some fresh air.
ossigenato, a [ossidʒe'nato] AGG: **acqua ossigenata** hydrogen peroxide; **bionda ossigenata** peroxide blonde.
ossigenazione [ossidʒenat'tsjone] SF (*del sangue*) oxygenation; (*dei capelli*) bleaching.
ossigeno [os'sidʒeno] SM oxygen; **dare l'ossigeno a qn** to give sb oxygen; **dare ossigeno a qn/qc** (*fig*) to give sb/sth a new lease of life.
osso ['ɔsso] SM (pl(f) **ossa** nel senso Anat, o talvolta pl(m) **ossi**) **a** bone; **d'osso** (*bottone, manico*) bone *attr*, of bone; **carne senza ossa** boneless o boned meat ▶**osso di balena** whalebone ▶**osso di seppia** cuttlebone
b (*fam: di pesca*) stone
c (*fraseologia*): **avere le ossa rotte** to be dead o dog tired; **bagnato fino all'osso** soaked to the skin; **rompersi l'osso del collo** to break one's neck; **rimetterci l'osso del collo** (*fig*) to ruin o.s., lose everything; **essere ridotto all'osso** (*fig: magro*) to be just skin and bone; (: *senza soldi*) to be in dire straits; **farsi le ossa** to gain experience; **un osso duro** (*persona*) a hard nut, a tough cookie (*Am*); (*impresa*) a tall order.
ossobuco [osso'buko] SM (*pl* **ossibuchi**) (*Culin*) marrowbone; (: *piatto*) ossobuco, *stew made with knuckle of veal in tomato sauce*.
ossonio, ni [os'sɔnjo] AGG (*Chim*): **ione ossonio** oxonium ion.
ossuto, a [os'suto] AGG (*persona, viso*) angular; (*animale*) scraggy; (*mano*) bony.
ostacolare [ostako'lare] VT (*persona, piano*) to hinder.
ostacolista, i, e [ostako'lista] 1 SM/F (*atleta*) hurdler.
2 SM (*cavallo*) steeplechaser.
ostacolo [os'takolo] SM **a** (*anche fig*) obstacle; **essere di ostacolo a qn/qc** (*fig*) to stand in the way of sb/sth **b** (*Atletica*) hurdle; (*Equitazione*) jump, fence.
ostaggio, gi [os'taddʒo] SM hostage; **prendere/tenere qn**

in ostaggio to take/keep sb hostage.
oste, ostessa ['ɔste] SM/F innkeeper, landlord/landlady.
osteggiare [osted'dʒare] VT to oppose, be opposed to.
ostello [os'tɛllo] SM hostel ►**ostello della gioventù** youth hostel.
ostensorio, ri [osten'sɔrjo] SM (Rel) monstrance.
ostentare [osten'tare] VT (ricchezze, bravura) to show off, flaunt, make a show of; (distacco, indifferenza) to feign.
ostentatamente [ostentata'mente] AVV ostentatiously.
ostentazione [ostentat'tsjone] SF ostentation, show; **con ostentazione** ostentatiously.
osteo... ['ɔsteo] PREF osteo... .
osteoporosi [osteopo'rɔzi] SF osteoporosis.
osteria [oste'ria] SF ≈ pub (Brit), ≈ bar.
ostetricia [oste'tritʃa] SF obstetrics sg.
ostetrico, a, ci, che [os'tɛtriko] [1] AGG obstetric(al); **clinica ostetrica** maternity hospital o home.
[2] SM/F (medico) obstetrician.
[3] SF (levatrice) midwife.
ostia ['ɔstja] SF (Rel) host; (per medicinali) wafer.
ostico, a, ci, che ['ɔstiko] AGG difficult, tough.
ostile [os'tile] AGG: **ostile (a)** hostile (to o towards).
ostilità [ostili'ta] SF INV (stato, atteggiamento) hostility; (atto) act of hostility; (Mil): **le ostilità** hostilities.
ostilmente [ostil'mente] AVV hostilely, in a hostile way.
ostinarsi [osti'narsi] VIP **a** (impuntarsi): **ostinarsi su** o **in qc** to insist on sth, dig one's heels in about sth; **ostinarsi a voler fare qc** to be determined to do sth **b** (persistere): **ostinarsi a fare qc** to persist (obstinately) in doing sth.
ostinatamente [ostinata'mente] AVV obstinately, stubbornly.
ostinato, a [osti'nato] [1] AGG (persona, resistenza) obstinate, stubborn; (tenace) determined; (tosse, pioggia) persistent.
[2] SM/F obstinate o stubborn person.
ostinazione [ostinat'tsjone] SF (di persone) obstinacy, stubbornness; **ostinazione a fare qc** obstinate o stubborn determination to do sth.
ostracismo [ostra'tʃizmo] SM ostracism; **dare l'ostracismo a qn** to ostracize sb.
ostrica, che ['ɔstrika] SF oyster ►**ostrica perlifera** pearl oyster.
ostruire [ostru'ire] [1] VT to obstruct, block.
[2] **ostruirsi** VIP to become obstructed o blocked.
ostruzione [ostrut'tsjone] SF **a** obstruction, blocking **b** (effetto, cosa che ostruisce) obstruction, blockage; (Sport) obstruction; **fare ostruzione** (Calcio) to obstruct.
ostruzionismo [ostruttsjo'nizmo] SM (Pol) obstructionism; (Sport) obstruction; **fare ostruzionismo a** (progetto, legge) to obstruct.
ostruzionista, i, e [ostruttsjo'nista] AGG, SM/F obstructionist.
ostruzionistico, a, ci, che [ostruttsjo'nistiko] AGG obstructionist.
otaria [o'tarja] SF eared seal.
otite [o'tite] SF ear infection.
otorinolaringoiatra, i, e [otorinolaringo'jatra] SM/F, **otorino** [oto'rino] SM ear, nose and throat specialist.
otre ['otre] SM (recipiente) goatskin.
ottagonale [ottago'nale] AGG octagonal, eight-sided.
ottagono [ot'tagono] SM octagon.
ottano [ot'tano] SM octane; **numero di ottani** octane rating o number; **benzina ad alto numero di ottani** high-octane petrol (Brit) o gasoline (Am).

ottanta [ot'tanta] AGG INV, SM INV eighty per fraseologia vedi **cinquanta**.
ottantenne [ottan'tɛnne] [1] AGG eighty-year-old per fraseologia vedi **cinquantenne**.
[2] SM/F octogenarian.
ottantesimo, a [ottan'tɛzimo] AGG, SM/F, SM eightieth per fraseologia vedi **quinto**.
ottantina [ottan'tina] SF: **una ottantina (di)** about eighty per fraseologia vedi **cinquantina**.
ottativo [otta'tivo] SM (Gramm) optative.
ottavino [otta'vino] SM (Mus: flauto) piccolo.
ottavo, a [ot'tavo] [1] AGG, SM/F eighth per fraseologia vedi **quinto**.
[2] SM **a** (frazione) eighth **b** (Tip) octavo; **edizione in ottavo** octavo edition **c** (Sport): **entrare negli ottavi di finale** to get into the last sixteen; **superare gli ottavi di finale** to reach the quarterfinals.
[3] SF (Poesia, Mus, Rel) octave.
ottemperanza [ottempe'rantsa] SF (Amm): **in ottemperanza a** in accordance with, in compliance with.
ottemperare [ottempe'rare] VI (aus avere): **ottemperare a** to comply with, obey.
ottenebrare [ottene'brare] [1] VT (anche fig) to cloud; (sole) to hide, obscure.
[2] **ottenebrarsi** VIP to cloud (over), darken.
ottenere [otte'nere] VT IRREG **a** (risposta, laurea, permesso) to obtain, get; **ottenere una promozione** to get promotion; **ha ottenuto di parlargli lunedì** he managed to arrange a meeting with him for Monday; **ha ottenuto che il ragazzo venisse ricoverato** he managed to get the boy admitted to hospital
b (totale) to reach, arrive at; (risultato) to achieve, obtain; (premio, approvazione, fiducia) to gain, win; **ottenere un buon successo** to have great success; **aggiungendo il giallo al blu si ottiene il verde** green is obtained o you get green by adding yellow to blue.
ottetto [ot'tetto] SM (Mus) octet.
ottica ['ɔttika] SF (Fis: scienza) optics sg; (Fot: lenti, prismi) optics pl; (fig: punto di vista) point of view, viewpoint.
ottico, a, ci, che ['ɔttiko] [1] AGG (nervo) optic; (fenomeno, strumento) optical.
[2] SM optician.
ottimale [otti'male] AGG optimal, optimum.
ottimamente [ottima'mente] AVV very well, excellently.
ottimismo [otti'mizmo] SM optimism.
ottimista, i, e [otti'mista] [1] AGG optimistic.
[2] SM/F optimist.
ottimisticamente [ottimistika'mente] AVV optimistically.
ottimistico, a, ci, che [otti'mistiko] AGG optimistic.
ottimizzare [ottimid'dzare] VT (servizio, produzione) optimize.
ottimizzazione [ottimiddzat'tsjone] SF optimization.
ottimo, a ['ɔttimo] [1] AGG (superl di **buono**) very good, excellent.
[2] SM (condizione ottimale) peak; (Scol) top marks pl.
otto ['ɔtto] [1] AGG INV eight.
[2] SM INV (numero, Canottaggio) eight; (tracciato) figure of eight; **oggi (a) otto** in a week's time, today week ►**otto volante** switchback per fraseologia vedi **cinque**.
ottobre [ot'tobre] SM October per fraseologia vedi **luglio**.
ottobrino, a [otto'brino] AGG October attr.
ottocentesco, a, schi, sche [ottotʃen'tesko] AGG nineteenth-century.
ottocentista, i, e [ottotʃen'tista] SM/F **a** (studioso) nine-

teenth-century scholar *o* specialist; (*artista, scrittore*) nineteenth-century artist (*o* writer) **b** (*Sport*) eight hundred metres runner.

ottocento [otto'tʃɛnto] ☐1 AGG INV eight hundred.

☐2 SM INV eight hundred; (*secolo*): **l'Ottocento** the nineteenth century.

ottomila [otto'mila] AGG INV, SM INV eight thousand.

ottone [ot'tone] SM brass; **di** *o* **in ottone** brass *attr*; **gli ottoni** (*Mus*) the brass *sg*.

ottuagenario, a, ri [ottuadʒe'narjo] AGG, SM/F octogenarian.

ottundere [ot'tundere] VT IRREG (*fig: mente*) to dull.

otturare [ottu'rare] ☐1 VT (*chiudere: falla, apertura*) to stop up, close (up), seal; (*bloccare: lavandino*) to block (up); (*riempire: dente*) to fill.

☐2 **otturarsi** VIP (*bloccarsi*) to become *o* get blocked (up).

otturatore [ottura'tore] SM (*Fot*) shutter; (*nelle armi*) breechblock; (*Tecn*) valve.

otturazione [otturat'tsjone] SF **a** (*vedi vb*) stopping up, closing (up), sealing; blocking; filling **b** (*di dente*) filling; **fare un'otturazione a qn** to give sb a filling.

ottusamente [ottuza'mente] AVV obtusely, slow-wittedly.

ottusità [ottuzi'ta] SF (*vedi agg*) obtuseness; dullness.

ottuso, a [ot'tuzo] ☐1 PP di **ottundere**.

☐2 AGG (*Mat*) obtuse; (*fig*) obtuse, slow-witted; (*suono*) muffled, dull.

ouverture [uver'tyr] SF INV (*Mus*) overture.

ovaia [o'vaja] SF, **ovaio** [o'vajo] SM (*Anat*) ovary.

ovale [o'vale] AGG, SM oval.

ovarico, a, ci, che AGG ovarian.

ovario, ri [o'varjo] SM (*Bot*) ovary.

ovatta [o'vatta] SF (*per medicazione*) cotton wool; (*per imbottiture*) padding, wadding.

ovattare [ovat'tare] VT **a** (*imbottire*) to pad; **ambiente ovattato** (*fig*) cocoon-like environment **b** (*fig: smorzare*) to muffle.

ovazione [ovat'tsjone] SF ovation.

overdose ['ouvədous] SF INV overdose.

overdrive ['ouvədraiv] SM INV (*Aut*) overdrive.

ovest ['ɔvest] ☐1 SM INV west; **a ovest (di)** west (of); **verso ovest** westward(s).

☐2 AGG INV (*gen*) west; (*regione*) western; **è partito in direzione ovest** he set off westwards *o* in a westward direction.

Ovidio [o'vidjo] SM Ovid.

ovidotto [ovi'dotto] SM (*Anat*) oviduct.

ovile [o'vile] SM pen, (sheep)fold; **tornare all'ovile** (*fig*) to return to the fold.

ovino, a [o'vino] AGG (*specie*) ovine (*termine tecn*), sheep *attr*; (*mercato, allevamento*) sheep *attr*.

oviparo, a [o'viparo] AGG oviparous.

ovoviviparo, a [ovovi'viparo] AGG ovoviviparous.

ovulazione [ovulat'tsjone] SF ovulation.

ovulo ['ɔvulo] SM (*Anat*) ovum; (*Bot*) ovule.

ovunque [o'vunkwe] AVV = **dovunque.**

ovvero [ov'vero] CONG (*o meglio*) or (rather); (*ossia*) that is, to be precise; (*oppure*) or (else).

ovviamente [ovvja'mente] AVV obviously.

ovviare [ovvi'are] VI (*aus avere*): **ovviare a** to remedy; **ovviare all'inconveniente (di)** to get round *o* obviate the problem (of).

ovvio, via, vi, vie ['ɔvvjo] AGG obvious; **è ovvio che...** obviously ..., it is obvious *o* clear that ... .

ozelot [oddze'lɔt] SM (*animale*) ocelot.

oziare [ot'tsjare] VI (*aus avere*) to laze around.

ozio, ozi ['ɔttsjo] SM **a** (*peccato*) sloth; (*inattività*) idleness; **stare in ozio** to be idle; **l'ozio è il padre dei vizi** (*Proverbio*) the Devil finds work for idle hands (to do) **b** (*riposo*): **ore d'ozio** leisure *o* spare time *sg*.

oziosamente [ottsjosa'mente] AVV idly.

ozioso, a [ot'tsjoso] ☐1 AGG **a** (*sfaccendato*) idle; (*inattivo: persona, giornata*) lazy; (: *per malattia*) inactive **b** (*fig: discorsi*) idle; (: *domanda*) pointless.

☐2 SM/F layabout, idler.

ozono [od'dzono] SM ozone; **il buco nell'ozono** the hole in the ozone layer; **la fascia** *o* **lo strato d'ozono** the ozone layer.

ozonosfera [oddzonos'fɛra] SF ozonosphere, ozone layer.

P

P, p [pi] SF O M INV (*lettera*) P, p; **P come Padova** ≈ P for Peter.
P ABBR **a** (= *peso*) wt (= *weight*) **b** (= *parcheggio*) P **c** (*Aut*: = *principiante*) L (= *learner*).
p ABBR (= *pagina*) p (= *page*).
P2 [pi'due] SIGLA F: **la (loggia) P2** the P2 masonic lodge.
PA SIGLA = *Palermo*.
pa' [pa] SM (*fam*) dad.
P.A. ABBR = **pubblica amministrazione**.
pacare [pa'kare] **1** VT to calm.
2 pacarsi VIP (*tempesta, disordini*) to subside.
pacatamente [pakata'mente] AVV (*parlare*) placidly.
pacatezza [paka'tettsa] SF (*vedi agg*) placidness; quietness, calmness.
pacato, a [pa'kato] AGG (*carattere*) placid; (*voce, tono*) quiet, calm.
pacca, che ['pakka] SF slap.
pacchetto [pak'ketto] SM (*confezione*) parcel; (: *di sigarette*) packet (*Brit*), pack (*Am*) ▶**pacchetto applicativo** (*Inform*) applications package ▶**pacchetto azionario** (*Fin*) shareholding ▶**pacchetto software** (*Inform*) software package ▶**pacchetto turistico** package holiday (*Brit*) o tour.
pacchia ['pakkja] SF (*fam*): **è stata una pacchia!** (*divertimento*) we had a great time!; (*di esame: molto facile*) it was a piece of cake!; **che pacchia!** what fun!
pacchiano, a [pak'kjano] AGG (*colori*) garish; (*abiti, arredamento*) vulgar, garish; **ha un gusto veramente pacchiano** she has extremely vulgar taste.
pacco, chi ['pakko] SM **a** package; **carta da pacchi** brown paper; (*da regalo*) wrapping paper ▶**pacco postale** parcel **b** (*involto*) bundle.
paccottiglia [pakkot'tiʎʎa] SF trash, junk.
pace ['patʃe] SF (*gen*) peace; **trattato di pace** peace treaty; **firmare la pace** to sign a peace treaty; **fare (la) pace con qn** to make (it) up with sb; **far fare (la) pace a due persone** to make peace between two people; **non si dà pace per quello che è successo** she can't stop thinking about what happened; **non mi dà un momento di pace** he doesn't give me a moment's peace; **mettersi l'animo**

in pace OR **darsi pace** to resign o.s.; **lasciare qn in pace** to leave sb alone; **riposare in pace** to rest in peace; **santa pace!** for heaven's sake!; **pace all'anima sua!** (*anche scherz*) may he rest in peace!; **pace!** (*fa niente*) never mind!
pachiderma, i [paki'dɛrma] SM pachyderm.
pachistano, a [pakis'tano] AGG, SM/F Pakistani.
paciere, a [pa'tʃɛre] SM/F peacemaker.
pacificamente [patʃifika'mente] AVV (*con intenzioni pacifiche*) peaceably; (*con calma*) peacefully.
pacificare [patʃifi'kare] VT (*riconciliare*) to reconcile, make peace between; (*mettere in pace*) to pacify; **riuscì a pacificare gli animi** he managed to pacify o mollify everyone.
pacificazione [patʃifikat'tsjone] SF (*vedi vb*) reconciliation; pacification.
pacifico, a, ci, che [pa'tʃifiko] **1** AGG **a** (*persona, carattere*) peaceable; (*vita, manifestazione*) peaceful **b** (*fig: indiscusso*) indisputable; (: *ovvio*) obvious, clear; **è pacifico che resterà in carica** it is obvious o it goes without saying that he will stay in office.
2 SM: **il Pacifico, l'Oceano Pacifico** the Pacific (Ocean).
pacifismo [patʃi'fizmo] SM pacifism.
pacifista, i, e [patʃi'fista] SM/F pacifist.
padano, a [pa'dano] AGG of the Po; **la pianura padana** the Lombardy plain.
padella [pa'dɛlla] SF **a** (*Culin*) frying pan (*Brit*), skillet (*Am*); **cucinare in padella** to fry; **cadere dalla padella nella brace** (*fig*) to jump out of the frying pan into the fire **b** (*per infermi*) bedpan.
padiglione [padiʎ'ʎone] SM **a** (*di mostra, ospedale*) pavilion ▶**padiglione di caccia** hunting lodge **b** (*Anat*): **padiglione auricolare** auricle, pinna.
Padova ['padova] SF Padua.
padovano, a [pado'vano] **1** AGG of o from Padua.
2 SM/F inhabitant o native of Padova.
padre ['padre] SM **a** father; **Rossi padre** Rossi senior; **di padre in figlio** from father to son; **per parte di padre** on my (o his ecc) father's side ▶**padre di famiglia** father,

family man **b** (*antenati*): **padri** SMPL forefathers, ancestors **c** (*Rel*) father; **Padre mio** Father; **il Santo Padre** (*il Papa*) the Holy Father.

Padrenostro [padre'nɔstro] SM: **il Padrenostro** the Lord's prayer, Our Father.

Padreterno [padre'tɛrno] SM: **il Padreterno** God the Father; **si crede un padreterno** (*fig*) he thinks he is God Almighty.

padrino [pa'drino] SM (*di battesimo*) godfather; (*di cresima*) sponsor; (*di duello*) second.

padronale [padro'nale] AGG (*scala, entrata*) main, principal; **casa padronale** country house.

padronanza [padro'nantsa] SF (*dominio*) command, mastery; **padronanza di sé** self-control; **avere una buona padronanza della lingua inglese** to have a good command of the English language.

padronato [padro'nato] SM: **il padronato** the ruling class.

padrone, a [pa'drone] SM/F **a** (*dominatore: anche fig*) master/mistress; (*proprietario*) owner; **essere padone di sé** to be self-possessed; **non era più padrone di sé** he had lost his self-control; **sono padrone di fare ciò che voglio** I am my own master; **si crede padrone del mondo** he thinks he is God Almighty; **essere padrone di una lingua** to have mastered a language; **essere padrone della situazione** to be master of the situation, have the situation in hand; **farla da padrone** to play the lord and master; **non sono più padrone in casa mia** I am no longer master in my own home ▶**padrona di casa** mistress of the house; (*per gli inquilini*) landlady ▶**padrone di casa** master of the house; (*per gli inquilini*) landlord

b (*datore di lavoro*) employer, boss (*fam*); **essere sotto padrone** to be an employee.

padroneggiare [padroned'dʒare] [1] VT (*fig: istinti, sentimenti*) to control, to master; (: *lingua, materia*) to master, know thoroughly.

[2] **padroneggiarsi** VR to control o.s.

paesaggio, gi [pae'zaddʒo] SM (*panorama, Arte*) landscape; (*aspetto di un luogo*) scenery.

paesaggista, i, e [paezad'dʒista] SM/F (*pittore*) landscape painter.

paesaggistica [paezad'dʒistika] SF (*Pittura*) landscape (painting); (*dipinti*) landscapes *pl*.

paesano, a [pae'zano] [1] AGG country *attr*.

[2] SM/F **a** (*campagnolo*) peasant, rustic; (*abitante di paese*) villager **b** (*concittadino*) fellow countryman/countrywoman.

paese [pa'eze] SM **a** (*nazione*) country, nation; **i paesi in via di sviluppo** the developing countries *o* nations; **l'Iraq è il paese d'origine della mia famiglia** my family comes from Iraq

b (*terra*) country, land; **vorrei visitare paesi lontani** I should like to visit far away places; **la Francia è un paese fertile** France is a fertile country *o* land

c (*villaggio*) village; **gente di paese** village people **d** (*fraseologia*): **paese che vai usanze che trovi** when in Rome do as the Romans do; **tutto il mondo è paese** people are the same the world over; **mandare qn a quel paese** (*fam*) to tell sb to get lost.

Paesi Bassi SMPL: **i Paesi Bassi** the Netherlands.

paffutezza [paffu'tettsa] SF plumpness, chubbiness.

paffuto, a [paf'futo] AGG plump, chubby.

paga, ghe ['paga] SF (*gen*) pay; (*di operaio*) wages *pl*; (*fig: ricompensa*) reward, recompense; **giorno di paga** payday.

pagabile [pa'gabile] AGG payable; **pagabile alla consegna/a vista** payable on delivery/on demand.

pagaia [pa'gaja] SF paddle.

pagamento [paga'mento] SM payment; **non lo faccio nemmeno a pagamento** I won't do it even if they pay me; **la TV a pagamento** pay TV ▶**pagamento anticipato** payment in advance ▶**pagamento alla consegna** payment on delivery ▶**pagamento in contanti** payment in cash ▶**pagamento all'ordine** cash with order.

paganamente [pagana'mente] AVV in a pagan manner.

paganesimo [paga'nezimo] SM paganism.

pagano, a [pa'gano] AGG, SM/F pagan.

pagare [pa'gare] VT **a** (*somma, conto, operaio*) to pay; (*debito*) to pay, settle; **pagare una cambiale** to pay a bill, honour (*Brit*) *o* honor (*Am*) a bill; **pagare in contanti** to pay cash; **pagare con carta di credito** to pay by credit card

b (*merce, lavoro, fig: colpa*) to pay for; **quanto l'hai pagato?** how much did you pay for it?; **pagare una macchina 20 milioni** to pay 20 million lire for a car; **me l'ha fatto pagare duemila lire** he charged me two thousand lire for it; **l'ho pagato caro/poco** I paid a lot/very little for it; **l'ho pagata cara** (*fig*) I paid dearly for it; **pagare qc salato** *o* **un occhio della testa** to pay through the nose for sth; **te la farò pagare!** (*fig*) I'll make you pay for it!, you'll pay for this!; **ha pagato con la vita** it cost him his life; **pagare di persona** (*fig*) to suffer the consequences; **pagare qc di tasca propria** to pay for sth out of one's own pocket; (*fig*) to learn sth to one's cost; **quanto non pagherei per sapere!** what wouldn't I give to know!

c (*offrire*): **ti pago da bere** let me buy you a drink; **pago io** this is on me; **pago io questo giro** this is my round **d** (*contraccambiare*) to repay, pay back.

pagella [pa'dʒella] SF (*Scol*) school report (*Brit*), report card (*Am*).

paggio, gi ['paddʒo] SM page(boy).

pagherò *ecc¹* [page'rɔ] VB vedi **pagare**.

pagherò² [page'rɔ] SM INV IOU ▶**pagherò cambiario** promissory note.

pagina ['padʒina] SF page; **a pagina 5** on page 5; **le più belle pagine del Manzoni** Manzoni's finest passages ▶**le pagine gialle** (*Telec*) the yellow pages.

paginare [padʒi'nare] VT (*Inform*) to page.

paginazione [padʒinat'tsjone] SF (*Inform*) paging.

paglia ['paʎʎa] SF straw; **cappello di paglia** straw hat; **tetto di paglia** thatched roof; **avere la coda di paglia** (*fig*) to have a guilty conscience; **fuoco di paglia** (*fig*) flash in the pan.

pagliaccetto [paʎʎat'tʃetto] SM (*per bambini*) rompers *pl*; (*per signora*) camiknickers (*Brit*) *pl*.

pagliacciata [paʎʎat'tʃata] SF farce.

pagliaccio, ci [paʎ'ʎattʃo] SM clown; **fare il pagliaccio** (*fig*) to play the fool.

pagliaio, ai [paʎ'ʎajo] SM haystack.

pagliericcio, ci [paʎʎe'rittʃo] SM straw mattress.

paglierino, a [paʎʎe'rino] AGG: **giallo paglierino** pale yellow.

paglietta [paʎ'ʎetta] SF **a** (*cappello per uomo*) (straw) boater **b** (*per tegami ecc*) steel wool.

pagliolato [paʎʎo'lato] SM (*Naut*) floor.

pagliuzza [paʎ'ʎuttsa] SF (blade of) straw; (*d'oro ecc*) tiny

particle, speck.

pagnotta [paɲˈɲɔtta] SF round loaf.

pago, a, ghi, ghe [ˈpago] AGG: **essere pago di** to be satisfied with.

pagoda [paˈgɔda] SF pagoda.

paguro [paˈguro] SM hermit crab.

paillette [paˈjɛt] SF INV sequin.

paio ecc[1] [ˈpajo] VB vedi **parere**.

paio[2] [ˈpajo] SM (pl f **paia**) (coppia) pair; **un paio di** (guanti, scarpe) a pair of; (alcuni) a couple of; **un paio di occhiali** a pair of glasses; **fra un paio di settimane** in a couple of weeks; **dare un paio di schiaffi a qn** to box sb's ears; **fanno il paio** they are two of a kind; **è un altro paio di maniche** that's another kettle of fish.

paiolo [paˈjɔlo], **paiuolo** [paˈjwɔlo] SM (copper) pot.

Pakistan [pakisˈtan] SM: **il Pakistan** Pakistan.

pakistano, a [pakisˈtano] AGG, SM/F = **pachistano**.

pal. ABBR = **palude**.

pala [ˈpala] SF **a** shovel; (di remo, ventilatore, elica) blade; (di ruota) paddle **b** (Rel): **pala d'altare** altar piece.

paladino [palaˈdino] SM (Storia) paladin; (fig: difensore) champion.

palafitta [palaˈfitta] SF **a** (abitazione) pile-dwelling **b** (Edil: sostegno) piles pl.

palafitticolo, a [palafitˈtikolo] AGG pile-dwelling attr.

palafreniere [palafreˈnjɛre] SM (Storia) groom.

palamito [paˈlamito] SM (Pesca) trawl line.

palanca, che [paˈlanka] SF lifting beam, lever beam.

palandrana [palanˈdrana] SF (scherz: abito lungo e largo) tent.

palasport [palaˈspɔrt] SM INV indoor sports arena.

palata [paˈlata] SF (contenuto) shovelful; **fa soldi a palate** he is making a mint.

palatale [palaˈtale] AGG, SF (Anat, Ling) palatal.

palatino[1]**, a** [palaˈtino] AGG (Storia, Rel) Palatine.

palatino[2]**, a** [palaˈtino] AGG (Anat: del palato) palatine.

palato [paˈlato] SM (Anat) palate; (gusto) palate, (sense of) taste; **gradevole al palato** palatable; **avere un palato fine** to have a refined palate.

palazzina [palatˈtsina] SF (dimora signorile) villa.

palazzo [paˈlattso] SM (reggia) palace; (edificio) building ▶ **palazzo dei congressi** conference centre ▶ **palazzo di giustizia** law courts pl, courthouse ▶ **palazzo dello sport** sports stadium.

palchetto [palˈketto] SM shelf.

palco, chi [ˈpalko] SM **a** (tavolato) platform, stand; (ripiano) layer **b** (Teatro) box; (tribuna) stand.

palcoscenico [palkoʃˈʃɛniko] SM (Teatro) stage.

paleontologia [paleontoloˈdʒia] SF palaeontology.

palermitano, a [palermiˈtano] [1] AGG of o from Palermo. [2] SM/F inhabitant o native of Palermo.

Palermo [paˈlɛrmo] SF Palermo.

palesare [paleˈzare] [1] VT to reveal, disclose. [2] **palesarsi** VIP (sentimento) to reveal o show itself.

palese [paˈleze] AGG clear, evident; **rendere palesi le proprie intenzioni** to make one's intentions clear.

palesemente [paleze'mente] AVV clearly.

Palestina [palesˈtina] SF: **la Palestina** Palestine.

palestinese [palestiˈnese] AGG, SM/F Palestinian.

palestra [paˈlɛstra] SF (luogo) gymnasium, gym; (esercizio atletico) exercise, training; (fig) training ground, school; **devo fare un po' di palestra** I must take a bit of exercise; **la scuola è palestra di vita** school is a preparation for life.

paletot [palˈto] SM INV = **paltò**.

paletta [paˈletta] SF (giocattolo) spade; (per il focolare) shovel; (del capostazione, vigile) signalling disc; (Culin: da dolce) cake slice.

paletto [paˈletto] SM (picchetto) stake, peg; (spranga) bolt; (Sci) pole (marking run).

palinsesto [palinˈsɛsto] SM (TV, Radio) programme (Brit) o program (Am) schedule; (Storia) palimpsest.

palio, li [ˈpaljo] SM (Storia: drappo) (prize) banner; **il Palio di Siena** horse race in which the different districts of Siena compete; **mettere qc in palio** (fig) to offer sth as a prize.

palissandro [palisˈsandro] SM rosewood.

palizzata [palitˈtsata] SF palisade.

palla[1] [ˈpalla] SF ball; (pallottola) bullet; **giocare a palla** to play (with a) ball; **sei una palla al piede!** you are a drag!; **prendere la palla al balzo** (fig) to seize one's opportunity; **rompere le palle a qn** (fam!) to be a bloody nuisance to sb ▶ **palla da golf** golf ball ▶ **palla di neve** snowball ▶ **palla da tennis** tennis ball.

palla[2] [ˈpalla] SF (Rel) pall.

pallacanestro [pallakaˈnɛstro] SF basketball.

Pallade [ˈpallade] SF (anche: **Pallade Atena**) Pallas (Athena).

palladiano, a [pallaˈdjano] AGG Palladian.

pallamano [pallaˈmano] SF handball.

pallanuoto [pallaˈnwɔto] SF water polo.

pallavolo [pallaˈvolo] SF volleyball.

palleggiare [palledˈdʒare] [1] VI (aus avere) (Calcio) to practise (Brit) o practice (Am) with the ball; (Tennis) to knock up. [2] **palleggiarsi** VR (uso reciproco): **si stanno palleggiando le responsabilità** each is trying to shift the responsibility onto the other.

palleggio, gi [palˈleddʒo] SM (gen) practising (Brit) o practicing (Am) with a ball; (prima di una partita) warm-up; (Tennis) knock-up; (: in partita) rally.

palliativo [palljaˈtivo] SM (Med) palliative; (fig) stopgap measure.

pallidamente [pallidaˈmente] AVV palely.

pallido, a [ˈpallido] AGG (gen) pale; (malaticcio) pallid; (ricordo) faint; (sorriso) faint, wan; **è diventata pallida** she paled, she turned pale; **non ho la più pallida idea** I haven't the faintest o foggiest (idea).

pallina [palˈlina] SF (bilia) marble.

pallino [palˈlino] SM **a** (pois) dot; **bianco a pallini blu** white with blue dots **b** (Biliardo) cue ball; (Bocce) jack **c** (proiettile) pellet **d** (idea fissa) craze, obsession; **avere il pallino di** to be crazy about; **ha il pallino della matematica** he has a passion for mathematics.

pallonata [palloˈnata] SF blow (from a ball).

palloncino [pallonˈtʃino] SM (giocattolo) balloon; (lampioncino) Chinese lantern.

pallone [palˈlone] SM **a** (palla) ball; (Calcio) football; **gioco del pallone** football; **essere un pallone gonfiato** (fig) to be full of o.s. **b** (aerostato) balloon ▶ **pallone sonda** weather balloon **c** (Chim) flask.

pallonetto [palloˈnetto] SM (Calcio, Tennis) lob.

pallore [palˈlore] SM pallor, paleness.

pallottola [palˈlottola] SF **a** (proiettile) bullet; (: di fucile da caccia) pellet **b** (di carta) ball; **c'erano delle pallottole di carta nel cestino** there were some bits of screwed-up paper in the wastepaper basket.

pallottoliere [pallottoˈljɛre] SM abacus.

palma¹ ['palma] SF (*Anat*) palm.

palma² ['palma] SF (*Bot*) palm; **riportare/vincere la palma** (*fig*) to walk off with/win the prize ► **palma da datteri** date palm.

palmato, a [pal'mato] AGG (*Zool*: *piede*) webbed; (*Bot*) palmate.

palmeto [pal'meto] SM palm grove.

palmipede [pal'mipede] AGG web-footed.

palmizio, zi [pal'mittsjo] SM (*palma*) palm tree; (*ramo*) palm.

palmo ['palmo] SM (*misura*) handbreadth; **un palmo di polvere sul tavolo** (*fig*) a layer of dust on the table; **restare con un palmo di naso** (*fig*) to be badly disappointed; **essere alto un palmo** (*fig*) to be tiny.

palombaro [palom'baro] SM (deep-sea) diver.

palombo [pa'lombo] SM (*pesce*) dogfish; (*colombo*) wood pigeon.

palpabile [pal'pabile] AGG (*differenza, errore*) palpable.

palpabilmente [palpabil'mente] AVV palpably.

palpare [pal'pare] VT (*tastare*) to feel, finger; (*Med*) to palpate.

palpebra ['palpebra] SF eyelid.

palpitante [palpi'tante] AGG: **palpitante di** (*paura*) trembling with; (*emozione*) quivering with.

palpitare [palpi'tare] VI (*aus* **avere**) (*cuore*) to beat; (: *più forte*) to pound, throb; (*fremere*) to quiver; **palpitare di paura** to tremble with fear; **palpitare di gioia** to quiver with delight.

palpitazione [palpitat'tsjone] SF (*Med*): **avere le palpitazioni** to have palpitations.

palpito ['palpito] SM (*del cuore*) beat; (*fig*: *d'amore*) throb.

paltò [pal'tɔ] SM INV overcoat.

palude [pa'lude] SF marsh, swamp.

paludoso, a [palu'doso] AGG swampy, marshy.

palustre [pa'lustre] AGG marsh *attr*, swamp *attr*.

pampa ['pampa] SF pampas *sg o pl*.

pampino ['pampino] SM vine leaf.

Pan ['pan] SM Pan.

panacea [pana'tʃɛa] SF panacea.

Panama ['panama] SF Panama; **il canale di Panama** the Panama Canal.

panama ['panama] SM INV (*cappello*) panama (hat).

panamense [pana'mɛnse] AGG, SM/F Panamanian.

panare [pa'nare] VT to dip *o* roll in breadcrumbs.

panca, che ['panka] SF bench.

pancarré [pankar're] SM INV sliced bread.

pancetta [pan'tʃetta] SF (*Culin*) bacon ► **pancetta affumicata** smoked streaky bacon.

panchetto [pan'ketto] SM (*sgabello*) stool.

panchina [pan'kina] SF garden seat; (*di giardino pubblico*) (park) bench; (*Sport*) substitutes' bench.

pancia, ce ['pantʃa] SF belly, stomach; **aver la pancia** to have a potbelly; **aver la pancia piena** to be full; **aver mal di pancia** to have stomach ache *o* a sore stomach; **mettere su pancia** to develop *o* be getting a paunch; **non star lì a grattarti la pancia!** don't sit (*o* stand) there doing nothing!

panciata [pan'tʃata] SF belly flop.

panciera [pan'tʃɛra] SF corset.

panciolle [pan'tʃɔlle] AVV: **stare in panciolle** to lounge

about (*Brit*) *o* around.

pancione, a [pan'tʃone] **1** SM (*pancia*) stomach; **quando la mamma aveva il pancione** when mummy was pregnant. **2** SM/F (*persona grassa*) potbellied man/fat-bellied woman.

panciotto [pan'tʃɔtto] SM waistcoat.

panciuto, a [pan'tʃuto] AGG (*persona*) potbellied; (*vaso, bottiglia*) rounded.

pancreas ['pankreas] SM INV pancreas.

panda ['panda] SM INV panda.

pandemia [pande'mia] SF pandemic.

pandemico, a, ci, che [pan'dɛmiko] AGG pandemic.

pandemonio, ni [pande'mɔnjo] SM pandemonium.

Pandora [pan'dɔra] SF Pandora; **il vaso di Pandora** Pandora's box.

pandoro [pan'dɔro] SM *type of sponge cake eaten at Christmas*.

pane ['pane] **1** SM (*gen*) bread; (*pagnotta*) loaf (of bread); (*di cera*) bar; (*di burro*) block; **il pane quotidiano** one's daily bread; **guadagnarsi il pane** to earn one's living; **mangiare (il) pane a tradimento** to sponge, scrounge; **rendere pan per focaccia** to give tit for tat; **dire pane al pane, vino al vino** to call a spade a spade; **essere buono come il pane** to have a heart of gold; **quella ragazza non è pane per i tuoi denti** that girl's not for you; **per un pezzo di pane** (*comprare, vendere*) for a song. **2** ► **pane a** *o* **in cassetta** sliced bread ► **pane bianco** white bread ► **pane casereccio** homemade bread ► **pane integrale** *o* **nero** wholemeal bread ► **pane al latte** milk bread ► **pane di segale** rye bread ► **pane tostato** toast ► **pan di Spagna** sponge cake ► **pan di zucchero** sugar loaf.

panegirico, ci [pane'dʒiriko] SM panegyric; **fare un panegirico di qn** to sing sb's praises.

panetteria [panette'ria] SF (*forno*) bakery; (*negozio*) baker's (shop), bakery.

panettiere, a [panet'tjɛre] SM/F baker.

panetto [pa'netto] SM (*di burro*) block.

panettone [panet'tone] SM panettone, *a kind of spiced brioche with sultanas, eaten at Christmas*.

panfilo ['panfilo] SM yacht.

panforte [pan'fɔrte] SM *Sienese nougat-type delicacy*.

pangrattato [pangrat'tato] SM breadcrumbs *pl*.

panico, a, ci, che ['paniko] **1** SM panic; **essere in preda al panico** to be panic-stricken; **lasciarsi prendere dal panico** to panic. **2** AGG panic *attr*.

paniere [pa'njɛre] SM basket.

panificare [panifi'kare] VI (*aus* **avere**) to make bread.

panificatore, trice [panifika'tore] SM/F bread-maker, baker.

panificio, ci [pani'fiʃo] SM (*forno*) bakery; (*negozio*) baker's (shop), bakery.

panino [pa'nino] SM roll ► **panino imbottito** filled roll.

paninoteca, che [panino'tɛka] SF ≈ café.

panna¹ ['panna] SF (*Culin*) cream ► **panna acida** sour(ed) cream ► **panna da cucina** long-life cream used for cooking ► **panna montata** whipped cream.

panna² ['panna] SF (*Naut*): **mettersi in panna** to heave to.

panne ['pan] SF INV (*Aut*) breakdown; **la macchina è in panne** the car has broken down; **restare in panne** to break down.

panneggio, gi [pan'neddʒo] SM drapery.

pannello [pan'nɛllo] SM panel ▶**pannello di controllo** control panel ▶**pannello divisorio** partition ▶**pannello fonoisolante** acoustic screen ▶**pannello solare** solar panel.

panno ['panno] SM **a** (*tessuto, straccio*) cloth **b** (*vestiti*): **panni** SMPL clothes; **panni da lavare** laundry, washing; **mettiti nei miei panni** put yourself in my shoes; **non stava più nei panni dalla gioia** he was beside himself with joy.

pannocchia [pan'nɔkkja] SF corncob; (*di mais*) ear.

pannolino [panno'lino] SM (*per bambini*) nappy (*Brit*), diaper (*Am*); (*assorbente*) sanitary towel ▶**pannolino mutandina** disposable nappy *o* diaper.

pannolone [panno'lone] SM (*per adulti*) incontinence pad.

panorama, i [pano'rama] SM panorama.

panoramica, che [pano'ramika] SF **a** (*strada*) scenic route **b** (*Cine*) pan shot; (*Fot*) panorama; **fare una panoramica di qc** (*fig*) to outline sth.

panoramicamente [panoramika'mente] AVV panoramically.

panoramico, a, ci, che [pano'ramiko] AGG (*gen*) panoramic; **strada panoramica** scenic route; **rassegna panoramica** overall view.

panpepato [panpe'pato] SM *type of gingerbread.*

pantacollant [pantakol'lan] SM INV leggings *pl.*

pantagruelico, a, ci, che [pantagru'ɛliko] AGG (*pranzo, appetito*) gigantic.

pantalone [panta'lone] AGG INV: **gonna pantalone** culottes *pl.*

pantaloni [panta'loni] SMPL trousers (*Brit*), pants (*Am*); **una paio di pantaloni** a pair of trousers *o* pants.

pantano [pan'tano] SM marsh, bog.

panteismo [pante'izmo] SM pantheism.

panteistico, a, ci, che [pante'istiko] AGG pantheistic.

pantera [pan'tɛra] SF **a** (*Zool*) panther **b** (*fam: auto della polizia*) (high-speed) police car.

pantheon ['panteon] SM INV pantheon.

pantofola [pan'tɔfola] SF slipper.

pantografo [pan'tɔgrafo] SM pantograph.

pantomima [panto'mima] SF pantomime.

panzana [pan'tsana] SF tall story.

panzarotto [pantsa'rɔtto] SM *large fried piece of ravioli filled with ham, cheese and tomato.*

panzer ['pantsər] SM INV (*Mil*) panzer.

paonazzo, a [pao'nattso] AGG purple.

papa, i ['papa] SM pope; **ad ogni morte di papa** once in a blue moon; **morto un papa se ne fa un altro** nobody's indispensable; **vivere come un papa** to live like a Lord ▶**il papa nero** the Black Pope.

papà [pa'pa] SM INV daddy, dad; **figlio di papà** spoilt young man.

papaia [pa'paja] SF papaya.

papale [pa'pale] AGG papal.

papalina [papa'lina] SF skullcap.

papalino [papa'lino] **1** AGG papal.
2 SM (*soldato*) papal guard; (*Pol*) supporter of the Pope's temporal authority.

paparazzo [papa'rattso] SM paparazzo.

papato [pa'pato] SM papacy.

papaverina [papave'rina] SF papaverine.

papavero [pa'pavero] SM poppy.

papera ['papera] SF (*errore*) slip of the tongue; **ha fatto una papera** that was a slip of the tongue on his (o her) part.

papero, a ['papero] SM/F (*Zool*) gosling.

papilla [pa'pilla] SF (*Anat*): **papilla gustativa** taste bud ▶**papilla ottica** blind spot.

papillon [papi'jɔ̃] SM INV bow tie.

papiro [pa'piro] SM papyrus.

papirologia [papirolo'dʒia] SF papyrology.

pappa ['pappa] SF (*per bambini*) pap; (*pegg: poltiglia*) mush; **hai sempre avuto la pappa pronta** (*fig*) you've never had to stand on your own two feet ▶**pappa reale** royal jelly.

pappagallesco, a, schi, sche [pappagal'lesko] AGG parrot-like.

pappagallo [pappa'gallo] SM (*Zool*) parrot; (*fig pegg: uomo*) wolf; **ripetere tutto a pappagallo** to repeat everything parrot-fashion.

pappagorgia, ge [pappa'gɔrdʒa] SF double chin.

pappardella [pappar'dɛlla] SF (*Culin*) *wide strip of pasta;* (*fig: tiritera*) rigmarole.

pappare [pap'pare] VT (*fam: anche: papparsi: mangiare*) to gobble up; (: *appropriarsi di: soldi*) to walk off with.

paprica ['paprika] SF paprika.

Pap-test ['paptest] SM INV smear test, Pap smear *o* test (*Am*).

par. ABBR (= *paragrafo*) par. (= *paragraph*).

para ['para] SF: **suole di para** crepe soles.

parà [pa'ra] SM INV para.

parabola¹ [pa'rabola] SF (*Mat*) parabola.

parabola² [pa'rabola] SF (*Rel*) parable.

parabolico, a, ci, che [para'bɔliko] AGG parabolic; **antenna parabolica** (satellite) dish.

parabordo [para'bordo] SM (*Naut*) fender.

parabrezza [para'breddza] SM INV (*Aut*) windscreen (*Brit*), windshield (*Am*).

paracadutare [parakadu'tare] VT, **paracadutarsi** VR to parachute.

paracadute [paraka'dute] SM INV parachute.

paracadutismo [parakadu'tizmo] SM parachuting.

paracadutista, i [parakadu'tista] SM parachutist; (*Mil*) paratrooper.

paracarro [para'karro] SM kerbstone (*Brit*), curbstone (*Am*).

paradenti [para'dɛnti] SM INV (*Pugilato*) gumshield.

paradigma, i [para'digma] SM paradigm.

paradigmatico, a, ci, che [paradig'matiko] AGG (*Ling*) paradigmatic; (*fig: esemplificante*) exemplary, paradigmatic.

paradisiaco, a, ci, che [paradi'ziako] AGG heavenly.

paradiso [para'dizo] SM (*anche fig*) paradise, heaven; **sentirsi in paradiso** to be in seventh heaven ▶**paradisi artificiali** drug-induced fantasies ▶**paradiso fiscale** tax haven ▶**il Paradiso terrestre** the Garden of Eden, the Earthly Paradise.

paradossale [parados'sale] AGG paradoxical.

paradossalmente [paradossal'mente] AVV paradoxically.

paradosso [para'dɔsso] SM paradox.

parafango, ghi [para'fango] SM (*di auto*) mudflap (*Brit*) *o* splashguard (*Am*); (*di bicicletta*) mudguard (*Brit*) *o* fender (*Am*).

paraffina [paraf'fina] SF paraffin (wax).

parafrasare [parafra'zare] VT to paraphrase.

parafrasi [pa'rafrazi] SF INV paraphrase.

parafulmine [para'fulmine] SM lightning conductor.

paraggi [pa'raddʒi] SMPL: **nei paraggi (di)** in the vicinity (of), in the neighbourhood (*Brit*) *o* neighborhood (*Am*)

(of); **in questi paraggi** in this neighbo(u)rhood, somewhere around here.

paragonabile [parago'nabile] AGG: **paragonabile (a)** comparable (to).

paragonare [parago'nare] ① VT: **paragonare a/con** to compare to/with.

② **paragonarsi** VR: **paragonarsi a/con** to compare o.s. to/with.

paragone [para'gone] SM comparison; (*esempio analogo*) analogy, parallel; **a paragone di** as compared to, in comparison with; **il paragone non regge** the two just can't be compared; **non regge al paragone** it doesn't stand *o* bear comparison; **senza paragone** incomparable, peerless.

paragrafo [pa'ragrafo] SM (*Gramm, fig*) paragraph.

paraguaiano, a [paragwa'jano] AGG, SM/F Paraguayan.

Paraguay [para'gwai] SM: **il Paraguay** Paraguay.

paralisi [pa'ralizi] SF INV (*Med, fig*) paralysis.

paralitico, a, ci, che [para'litiko] AGG, SM/F paralytic.

paralizzare [paralid'dzare] VT (*Med, fig*) to paralyze.

paralizzato, a [paralid'dzato] AGG paralyzed.

parallasse [paral'lasse] SF parallax.

parallela [paral'lɛla] SF (*Geom*) parallel (line); (*attrezzo ginnico*): **le parallele** SFPL the parallel bars.

parallelamente [parallela'mente] AVV: **parallelamente (a)** (*gen*) parallel (to); (*contemporaneamente*) at the same time (as), in parallel (with).

parallelepipedo [parallele'pipedo] SM parallelepiped.

parallelismo [paralle'lizmo] SM (*Mat*) parallelism; (*fig: corrispondenza*) similarities *pl*.

parallelo, a [paral'lɛlo] ① AGG (*gen, anche Inform*) parallel; **interfaccia parallela** (*Inform*) parallel interface.

② SM (*Geog, fig*) parallel; **fare un parallelo tra** (*comparazione*) to draw a parallel between.

parallelogramma, i [parallelo'gramma] SM parallelogram.

paralume [para'lume] SM lampshade.

paramedico, a, ci, che [para'mɛdiko] ① AGG paramedical; **il personale paramedico** the paramedics *pl*.

② SM paramedic.

paramenti [para'menti] SMPL (*Rel*) vestments.

parametro [pa'rametro] SM parameter.

paramilitare [paramili'tare] AGG paramilitary.

paranco, chi [pa'ranko] SM hoist.

paranoia [para'nɔja] SF (*Psicol*) paranoia; **andare/mandare in paranoia** (*fam*) to freak/be freaked out.

paranoico, a, ci, che [para'nɔiko] AGG, SM/F paranoid; (*fam*) freaked (out).

paranormale [paranor'male] AGG paranormal.

paraocchi [para'ɔkki] SMPL (*anche fig*) blinkers (*Brit*), blinders (*Am*).

paraorecchie [parao'rekkje] SM INV (*di cappello*) earflap.

parapendio, dii [parapen'dio] SM (*paracadute*) paraglider; (*sport*) paragliding.

parapetto [para'petto] SM parapet.

parapiglia [para'piʎʎa] SM INV uproar, commotion.

parapioggia [para'pjɔddʒa] SM INV umbrella.

paraplegia [paraple'dʒia] SF paraplegia.

paraplegico, a, ci, che [para'plɛdʒiko] AGG, SM/F paraplegic.

parapsicologia [parapsikolo'dʒia] SF parapsychology.

parapsicologico, a, ci, che [parapsiko'lodʒiko] AGG parapsychological.

parare [pa'rare] ① VT **a** (*addobbare*) to adorn, deck (out) **b** (*proteggere*: *occhi*) to shield, protect **c** (*scansare*: *colpo*: *anche fig*) to parry; (: *goal, tiro*) to save.

② VI (*aus avere*): **dove vuoi andare a parare?** what are you driving at?.

③ **pararsi** VR (*presentarsi*) to present o.s., to appear.

parascolastico, a, ci, che [parasko'lastiko] AGG (*attività*) extracurricular.

parasole [para'sole] SM INV parasol, sunshade.

parassita, i [paras'sita] (*anche fig*) ① AGG parasitic.

② SM parasite.

parassitario, ria, ri, rie [parassi'tarjo] AGG parasitic.

parassitismo [parassi'tizmo] SM parasitism.

parastatale [parasta'tale] AGG state-controlled.

parastato [paras'tato] SM *employees in the state-controlled sector*.

parastinchi [paras'tinki] SM INV shin guard.

parata¹ [pa'rata] SF (*Sport*) save.

parata² [pa'rata] SF (*Mil*) review, parade.

parati [pa'rati] SMPL hangings; **carta da parati** wallpaper.

paratia [para'tia] SF (*Naut*) bulkhead.

paraurti [para'urti] SM INV (*Aut*) bumper.

paravento [para'vɛnto] SM folding screen; **fare da paravento a qn** (*fig*) to shield sb.

parcella [par'tʃɛlla] SF fee.

Parche ['parke] SFPL: **le Parche** the Fates.

parcheggiare [parked'dʒare] VT to park.

parcheggio, gi [par'keddʒo] SM (*luogo*) car park (*Brit*), parking lot (*Am*); (*azione*) parking *no pl*; (*singolo posto*) parking space; **"divieto di parcheggio"** "no parking".

parchimetro [par'kimetro] SM parking meter.

parco¹, chi ['parko] SM **a** (*giardino*) park ▸**parco di divertimenti** amusement park, funfair ▸**parco giochi** (children's) playground ▸**parco nazionale** national park ▸**parco a tema** theme park **b** (*insieme di veicoli*) fleet ▸**parco macchine** car fleet ▸**parco rotabile** (*Ferr*) rolling stock **c** (*spazio per deposito*) depot.

parco², a, chi, che ['parko] AGG: **parco (in)** (*sobrio*) moderate (in); (*avaro*) sparing (with).

parecchio, a, chi [pa'rekkjo] ① AGG INDEF **a** quite a lot of; **c'è parecchio vino** there is quite a lot of wine; **c'era parecchia gente** there were quite a lot of *o* several people; **ho parecchia fame** I am quite hungry; **parecchio tempo** quite a lot of time, a long time; **non lo vedo da parecchio tempo** I haven't seen him for ages *o* for a long time; **è parecchio tempo che ti aspetto** I have been waiting for you for ages; **parecchio tempo fa** a long time ago, long ago

b: **parecchi(e)** several, quite a lot of; **parecchie persone/volte/cose** several *o* a number of people/times/things; **ho avuto parecchi guai** I have had quite a lot of trouble.

② PRON INDEF quite a lot, quite a bit; **parecchi(e)** several, quite a lot; **c'è del pane? — parecchio** is there any bread? — yes, quite a lot; **quanto tempo hai aspettato? — parecchio** how long did you wait? — quite a long time *o* quite a while; **ci ho pensato parecchio** I gave it quite a lot of thought; **parecchi dicono...** several people *o* a number of people say ...; **eravamo in parecchi** there were several of us; **parecchi di noi** several of us.

③ AVV **a** (*seguito da agg*) quite, rather; **è parecchio intelligente** he is quite intelligent

b (*seguito da vb*) quite a lot, quite a bit; **mangia parecchio** he eats quite a lot; **è dimagrito parecchio** he has lost quite a lot of weight.

pareggiamento [paredd3a'mento] SM (*di conti, bilancio*) balancing.

pareggiare [pared'd3are] **1** VT (*gen*) to make equal; (*terreno*) to level, make level; (*bilancio, conti*) to balance. **2** VI (*aus* avere) (*Sport: durante la partita*) to equalize; (*: risultato*) to draw.

pareggio, gi [pa'redd3o] SM (*Sport*) draw; (*Econ*) balance.

parentado [paren'tado] SM relatives *pl*, relations *pl*; **alla festa c'era tutto il parentado** the whole family was at the party.

parentale [paren'tale] AGG (*autorità*) parental; (*malattia*) hereditary.

parente [pa'rente] SM/F relative, relation.

parentela [paren'tela] SF (*vincolo di sangue, fig*) relationship; (*insieme dei parenti*) relatives *pl*, relations *pl.*

parentesi [pa'rentezi] SF INV (*segno grafico*) bracket, parenthesis; (*digressione*) digression, parenthesis; **tra parentesi** in brackets; (*fig*) incidentally; **fare una parentesi** (*fig*) to digress; **dopo la parentesi estiva** after the summer break ▶**parentesi graffe** curly braces ▶**parentesi quadre** square brackets ▶**parentesi tonde** round brackets.

parentetico, a, ci, che [paren'tetiko] AGG parenthetic(al).

parere[1] [pa'rere] SM (*opinione*) opinion; (*consiglio*) advice; **a mio parere** in my opinion.

parere[2] [pa'rere] VI IRREG (*aus* essere) **a** (*apparire*) to look, seem, appear; **pare onesto** he looks *o* seems *o* appears honest; **pare impossibile ma è così** it doesn't seem possible and yet it's true; **pare di sì/no** it seems/doesn't seem so; **non mi pare vero!** I can scarcely believe it!; **pare che...** it seems *o* appears that ..., they say that ...; **a quanto pare se n'è andato** he seems to have left, he has apparently left

b (*essere dell'opinione*): **mi pare che...** I think (that) ..., it seems to me (that) ...; **mi pare di sì/no** I think/don't think so; **che te ne pare del mio libro?** what do you think of my book?; **che te ne pare di andare al cinema?** how about going to the cinema?, how do you fancy going to the cinema?; **è ora di andare, non ti pare?** don't you think it's time we left?; **disturbo? — ma le pare!** am I disturbing you? — not at all!; **fai come ti pare!** do what *o* as you like!

paresi ['parezi] SF INV paresis.

parete [pa'rete] SF (*muro*) wall; (*di montagna*) face; **fra le pareti domestiche** at home, within one's own four walls ▶**parete cellulare** (*Bio*) cell wall.

pargolo, a ['pargolo] SM/F (*letter o scherz*) child.

pari[1] ['pari] **1** AGG INV **a** (*uguale*) equal, (the) same; **essere pari a qn in qc** to be equal to sb in sth; **essere pari di grado** to have the same rank; **essere pari in bellezza/intelligenza** to be equally beautiful/intelligent; **andare di pari passo (con)** to proceed at the same rate (as)

b (*piano*) level; **una superficie pari** a level *o* an even surface; **saltare qc a piè pari** (*fig: omettere*) to skip sth

c (*Mat: numero*) even

d (*in giochi*) equal, drawn, tied; **la partita è pari** (*Sport*) the match is a draw; **siamo pari, vuoi la rivincita?** it's a draw, do you want a decider?; **siamo pari** (*fig*) we are quits *o* even.

2 SM (*numero*) even number; (*parità*): **mettersi in pari con** to catch up with; **essere intelligente al pari di qn** to be as intelligent as sb; **comportarsi al pari di qn** to behave like sb.

3 SM/F peer, equal.

4 AVV **a**: **copiato pari pari dal libro** copied word for word from the book

b: **alla pari** on the same level; (*Borsa*) at par; **mettersi alla pari con** to place o.s. on the same level as; **ragazza alla pari** au pair (girl).

pari[2] ['pari] SM INV (*Pol: Brit*) peer ▶**pari a vita** life peer.

paria ['parja] SM INV (*anche fig*) pariah.

Paride ['paride] SM (*Mitol*) Paris.

parificare [parifi'kare] VT (*scuola*) to recognize officially.

parificato, a [parifi'kato] AGG: **scuola parificata** *officially recognized private school.*

parificazione [parifikat'tsjone] SF (*di scuola*) official recognition.

Parigi [pa'rid3i] SF Paris.

parigino, a [pari'd3ino] AGG, SM/F Parisian.

pariglia [pa'riʎʎa] SF **a** (*tiro di cavalli*) pair **b** (*fig*): **rendere la pariglia** to give tit for tat.

parimenti [pari'menti] AVV (*letter: ugualmente*) equally.

parità [pari'ta] SF INV parity, equality; **a parità di condizioni** all things being equal; **trattamento di parità** equal treatment; **un risultato di parità** (*Sport*) a draw, a tie.

paritetico, a, ci, che [pari'tetiko] AGG: **rapporto paritetico** equal relationship; **commissione paritetica** joint committee.

parlamentare[1] [parlamen'tare] **1** AGG parliamentary. **2** SM/F ≈ Member of Parliament (*Brit*), ≈ Congressman/Congresswoman (*Am*).

parlamentare[2] [parlamen'tare] VI (*aus* avere) to negotiate, parley.

parlamento [parla'mento] SM parliament.

parlante [par'lante] AGG (*bambola, pappagallo*) talking; **ritratto parlante** (*fig*) lifelike painting.

parlantina [parlan'tina] SF (*fam*) talkativeness; **avere una buona parlantina** to have the gift of the gab.

parlare [par'lare] **1** VI (*aus* avere) **a** (*facoltà*) to talk; (*modo*) to talk, to speak; **il bambino non sa ancora parlare** the baby can't talk yet; **si parlavano a gesti** they were using sign language; **parla piano/più forte** talk *o* speak quietly/louder; **non riusciva a parlare per la gioia** he was speechless with joy; **parla bene!** talk properly!; **parlare tra i denti** to mutter; **parlare come un libro stampato** to talk like a book; **ha occhi che parlano** he has expressive eyes

b (*esprimere il proprio pensiero*) to speak; **parlare chiaro** to speak one's mind; **parlare a caso** *o* a vanvera to ramble on; **parlare male di qn/qc** to speak ill of sb/sth; **fallo** *o* lascialo parlare give him a chance to speak, let him have his say; **con rispetto parlando** with respect; **i dati parlano chiaro** the facts speak for themselves

c (*conversare*) to talk; **parlare a/con qn di qc** to talk *o* speak to/with sb about *o* of sth; **parlare di lavoro** *o* d'affari to talk shop; **non ci parliamo più** we're not on speaking terms; **parlare del più e del meno** to talk of this and that; **è come parlare al vento** *o* a un muro it's like talking to a brick wall; **senti, ne parliamo a quattrocchi** look, we'll discuss it *o* talk about it in private; **non parliamone più** let's just forget about it; **non ne voglio più sentir parlare** let's hear no more about it; **far parlare di sé** to get o.s. talked about; **parlano di matrimonio** they are talking about getting married, they are discussing marriage; **per ora non se ne parla** there's nothing doing for the moment

d (*Telec*): **sta parlando al telefono** he's on the phone;

pronto? chi parla? hello, who's speaking?; parla Bianchi Bianchi here o speaking; posso parlare con il Sig. Rossi? can I speak to Mr Rossi?

e : parlare di (far cenno a) to mention; (trattare di: argomento) to be about, deal with; ne ho sentito parlare I've heard of it (o him o her ecc); ne parlano tutti i giornali it's in all the newspapers; il libro parla del problema della droga the book deals with the drug problem; di cosa parla il suo ultimo romanzo? what is his latest novel about?

f (confessare) to talk; far parlare un prigioniero to make a prisoner talk.

2 VT (una lingua) to speak; sai parlare l'inglese? can you speak English?; per me parla arabo (fig) it's all Greek to me.

3 SM (dialetto) dialect.

parlata [par'lata] SF (dialetto) dialect.

parlato¹, a [par'lato] AGG spoken.

parlato² [par'lato] SM (Naut: nodo) clove hitch.

parlatore, trice [parla'tore] SM/F (oratore) speaker.

parlatorio, ri [parla'tɔrjo] SM (di carcere) visiting room; (di collegio, convento) parlour (Brit), parlor (Am).

parlottare [parlot'tare] VI (aus avere) to mutter.

parlottio, tii [parlot'tio] SM muttering.

parmigiano, a [parmi'dʒano] **1** AGG Parma attr, of o from Parma; alla parmigiana (Culin) with Parmesan cheese. **2** SM/F inhabitant o native of Parma. **3** SM (grana) Parmesan (cheese).

Parnaso [par'nazo] SM (Geog, Mitol) Parnassus.

parodia [paro'dia] SF parody.

parodiare [paro'djare] VT to parody.

parola [pa'rɔla] SF **a** (facoltà) speech; ha perso la parola he's lost the power of speech; a quel cane manca solo la parola that dog is almost human; avere la parola facile to have the gift of the gab

b (vocabolo) word; rimanere senza parole to be speechless; rivolgere la parola a qn to speak to sb; mi hai tolto la parola di bocca you have taken the words right out of my mouth; mettere una buona parola per qn to put in a good word for sb; non è detta l'ultima parola that's not the end of the matter; non farne parola a nessuno! don't breathe a word to anyone!; è una parola! it's easier said than done!; non ho parole per ringraziarti I don't know how to thank you; passare dalle parole ai fatti to get down to business; in parole povere in plain English ▶parola d'ordine password ▶parole incrociate crossword (puzzle) sg

c : parole SFPL (di canzone) words, lyrics; (chiacchiere) talk sg

d (promessa) word; dare la propria parola a qn to give sb one's word; mantenere la parola to keep one's word; è una persona di parola he is a man of his word; rimangiarsi la parola to go back on one's word ▶parola d'onore word of honour

e (in dibattiti): diritto di parola right to speak; chiedere la parola to ask permission to speak; prendere la parola to take the floor; dare la parola a qn to call on sb to speak.

parolaccia, ce [paro'lattʃa] SF bad word, swearword.

parolaio, aia, ai, aie [paro'lajo] SM/F (pegg) windbag.

paroliere [paro'ljɛre] SM lyricist.

parolina [paro'lina] SF: dire una parolina a qn (di rimprovero) to have a few words with sb; (d'amore) to whisper sweet nothings to sb.

parolone [paro'lone] SFPL bombast sg.

parossismo [paros'sizmo] SM (Med) paroxysm; (fig: di amore, odio) height; amare/odiare fino al parossismo to be beside o.s. with love/hate.

parossisticamente [parossistika'mente] AVV (fig) fiercely.

parossistico, a, ci, che [paros'sistiko] AGG (Med) paroxysmal, paroxysmic; (fig) fierce, violent.

parotite [paro'tite] SF (Med) parotitis.

parquet [par'kɛ] SM INV parquet (flooring).

parricida, i, e [parri'tʃida] SM/F parricide (person).

parricidio, di [parri'tʃidjo] SM parricide (action).

parrò ecc [par'rɔ] VB vedi parere.

parrocchia [par'rɔkkja] SF (suddivisione) parish; (chiesa) parish church.

parrocchiale [parrok'kjale] AGG parish attr.

parrocchiano, a [parrok'kjano] SM/F parishioner.

parroco, ci [ˈparroko] SM parish priest.

parrucca, che [par'rukka] SF wig.

parrucchiera [parruk'kjɛra] SF hairdresser.

parrucchiere [parruk'kjɛre] SM (per uomo) barber; (per signora) hairdresser.

parruccone [parruk'kone] SM (pegg) old fogey.

parsimonia [parsi'mɔnja] SF parsimony, frugality, thrift.

parsimoniosamente [parsimonjosa'mente] AVV parsimoniously.

parsimonioso, a [parsimo'njoso] AGG frugal, thrifty.

parso, a [ˈparso] PP di parere.

partaccia, ce [par'tattʃa] SF (figuraccia): fare una partaccia to cut a poor figure; (scenata): fare una partaccia a qn to give sb a telling-off.

parte [ˈparte] SF **a** (gen) part; (quota spettante a ciascuno) share; parte del libro non mi è piaciuta I didn't like some o part of the book; una parte di noi some of us; gran o la maggior parte degli spettatori most of the audience; in parte in part, partly; fare le parti di qc to divide sth up; fare la parte del leone to take the lion's share

b (partecipazione): fare parte di qc to belong to sth; prendere parte a (dibattito, conversazione) to take part in, participate in; (lutto) to share in; mettere qn a parte di qc to inform sb of sth, tell sb about sth

c (lato: anche fig) side; (direzione) direction; la parte destra del corpo the right-hand side of the body; dall'altra parte della strada on the other side of the road; veniva dall'altra parte he was coming from the opposite direction; da parte a parte right through; essere dalla parte della ragione to be in the right; non sapeva da che parte voltarsi (fig) he didn't know which way to turn; stare dalla parte di qn to be on sb's side; prendere le parti di qn to take sb's side; mettere/ prendere da parte to put/take aside

d (luogo, regione): da qualche parte somewhere; da questa parte (in questa direzione) this way; da ogni parte (stato in luogo) everywhere, on all sides; (moto da luogo) from all sides; da nessuna parte nowhere; da queste parti (qui vicino) around here; dalle mie parti where I come from; abita dalle mie parti he lives in the same area as I do; dalle parti di Glasgow Street in the vicinity of Glasgow Street

e (fazione, partito) group, faction; (Dir) party; uomo di parte partisan; la parte lesa (Dir) the injured party; costituirsi parte civile contro qn (Dir) to associate in an action with the public prosecutor against sb; le parti in causa the parties concerned

f (*Teatro*) part, role; **avere una parte secondaria** to have a minor role; **fare la parte dello stupido/della vittima** (*fig*) to act the fool/the martyr

g (*fraseologia*): **a parte** (*con funzione di agg*) separate; (*con funzione di avv*) separately; **fatto a parte** done separately; **inviare a parte** (*campioni*) to send under separate cover; **scherzi a parte** joking aside; **a parte ciò** apart from that; **da un anno a questa parte** for about a year now; **da parte** (*in disparte*) to one side, aside; **da parte mia** as far as I'm concerned, as for me; **da parte di** (*per conto di*) on behalf of; **da parte di madre** on his (*o* her *ecc*) mother's side; **d'altra parte** on the other hand.

partecipante [partetʃi'pante] ☐ AGG: **partecipante a** taking part in, participating in.

☐ SM/F: **partecipante (a)** (*riunione, dibattito*) participant (in); (*gara sportiva*) competitor (in); (*concorso*) entrant (to); **i partecipanti alla cerimonia** those taking part in the ceremony.

partecipare [partetʃi'pare] ☐ VI (*aus avere*): **partecipare a** to take part in, participate in; (*utili*) to share in; (*spese*) to contribute to; (*dolore, successo di qn*) to share (in).

☐ VT: **partecipare le nozze (a)** to announce one's wedding (to).

partecipazione [partetʃipat'tsjone] SF **a** : **partecipazione (a)** (*dibattito, cerimonia*) participation (in); (*spettacolo*) appearance (in); (*complotto*) involvement (in) ▶ **partecipazione a banda armata** (*Dir*) belonging to an armed gang ▶ **partecipazione di nozze** wedding announcement card

b (*Econ*) sharing, interest; **ministro delle Partecipazioni statali** *minister responsible for companies in which the state has a financial interest* ▶ **partecipazione di maggioranza** controlling interest ▶ **partecipazione di minoranza** minority interest ▶ **partecipazione agli utili** profit-sharing.

partecipe [par'tetʃipe] AGG participating; **essere partecipe del dolore/della gioia di qn** to share in sb's sorrow/joy.

parteggiare [parted'dʒare] VI (*aus avere*): **parteggiare per** to side with, be on the side of.

partenza [par'tɛntsa] SF **a** (*gen*) departure; **dopo la mia partenza si deciderà** things will be decided after I leave *o* after my departure; **essere in partenza** (*treno, aereo, nave*) to be about to leave; **prenderò il primo treno in partenza per Milano** I'll catch the first train for Milan; **"il treno per Roma è in partenza dal binario 15"** "the Rome train is leaving from platform 15"; **passeggeri in partenza per** passengers travelling (*Brit*) *o* traveling (*Am*) to; **siamo tornati al punto di partenza** (*fig*) we are back where we started, we are back to square one

b (*Sport*) start; **segnale di partenza** start, starting signal; **linea di partenza** start, starting line; **falsa partenza** (*anche fig*) false start.

particella [parti'tʃɛlla] SF (*Gramm, Fis*) particle ▶ **particelle alfa/beta** (*Fis*) alpha/beta particles.

participio, pi [parti'tʃipjo] SM (*Gramm*) participle ▶ **participio passato** past participle ▶ **participio presente** present participle.

particolare [partiko'lare] ☐ AGG **a** (*specifico*) particular; (*caratteristico*) distinctive; (*speciale*) special, particular; **in questo caso particolare** in this particular case, in this specific instance; **ha un sapore particolare** it has a distinctive flavour; **in particolare** in particular, particularly

b (*strano*) peculiar, odd

c (*insolito*) unusual; **l'ho fatto con cura particolare** I took particular care over it; **amicizie particolari** (*euf*) homosexual relationships

d (*privato*: *udienza, ragioni*) private, personal.

☐ SM detail; **raccontare un fatto in tutti i particolari** to give all the details *o* particulars of an occurrence; **entrare nei particolari** to go into details.

particolareggiato, a [partikolared'dʒato] AGG (extremely) detailed.

particolarità [partikolari'ta] SF INV **a** (*carattere eccezionale*) peculiarity; **data la particolarità del caso** given the peculiarity of the case **b** (*dettaglio*) detail, particularity **c** (*caratteristica specifica*) (distinctive) feature, characteristic.

particolarmente [partikolar'mente] AVV particularly, especially.

partigiano, a [parti'dʒano] ☐ AGG partisan.

☐ SM (*Storia*) partisan; (*fautore*) supporter, champion.

partire [par'tire] VI (*aus essere*) **a** (*gen*) to go, leave; (*lasciare un luogo*) to leave; (*mettersi in cammino*) to set off, set out; (*allontanarsi*) to go away, go off; **partire da/per** to leave from/for; **sono partita da Roma alle 7** I left Rome at 7; **partire in treno/in macchina** to go by train/car; **partire come una freccia** to be off like a shot; **non dargli troppo da bere perché lui parte subito** (*fam*) don't give him too much to drink because it goes straight to his head

b (*cominciare*: *Sport, fig*): **partire (da)** to start (from); **la corsa parte dal nord della città** the race starts *o* leaves from the north of the town; **la loro è una storia partita male** theirs is a relationship which got off to a bad start

c (*motore*) to start; (*aereo*) to take off; (*treno*) to leave; **il volo parte da Linate** the flight leaves from Linate; **partire in quarta** to drive off at top speed; (*fig*) to be very enthusiastic; **far partire la macchina** to start (up) the car

d (*colpo di arma da fuoco, petardo*) to go off; (*tappo*) to pop out, shoot out

e : **a partire da** from; **a partire da oggi** from today onwards; **a partire da ora** from now on; **la seconda a partire da destra** the second from the right; **a partire da 50.000 lire** from 50,000 lire.

partita [par'tita] SF **a** (*Comm*) lot, consignment

b (*Contabilità*) entry, item ▶ **partita doppia** double-entry book-keeping ▶ **partita IVA** VAT registration number (*Brit*) ▶ **partita semplice** single-entry book-keeping

c (*gioco, Carte*) game; (*Sport*) match, game; **facciamo una partita a tennis** let's have a game of tennis; **dare partita vinta a qn** to admit defeat (by sb) ▶ **partita amichevole** friendly (match)

d (*escursione*): **partita di caccia** hunting party.

partitico, a [par'titiko] AGG (*Pol*): **sistema partitico** party system.

partitivo, a [parti'tivo] AGG (*Gramm*) partitive.

partito [par'tito] SM **a** (*Pol*) party

b (*decisione*): **per partito preso** on principle; **non saprei che partito prendere** I wouldn't know what to do; **mettere la testa a partito** to settle down

c (*persona da sposare*) match; **è un buon partito** (*uomo*) he's a very eligible young man, he's a good match

d (*condizione*): **essere ridotto a mal partito** to be in desperate straits.

partitocratico, a, ci, che [partito'kratiko] AGG party-dominated.

partitocrazia [partitokrat'tsia] SF *hijacking of institutions by the party system.*

partitura [parti'tura] SF (*Mus*) score.

partizione [partit'tsjone] SF (*azione*) division; (*parte*) subdivision.

partner ['pa:tnə] SM/F INV partner.

parto ['parto] SM (*Med*) labour (*Brit*), labor (*Am*); **durante il parto** during labo(u)r; **i dolori del parto** labo(u)r pains; **sala parto** labo(u)r room; **al momento del parto il bambino stava bene** at birth the child was in good health; **morire di parto** to die in childbirth ▶ **parto cesareo** Caesarean birth ▶ **parto naturale** natural childbirth ▶ **parto pilotato** induced labo(u)r ▶ **parto plurigemellare** multiple birth ▶ **parto podalico** breech delivery ▶ **parto prematuro** premature birth *o* delivery.

partoriente [parto'rjɛnte] SF woman in labour (*Brit*) *o* labor (*Am*).

partorire [parto'rire] VT to give birth to; (*fig: invenzione*) to produce.

part time ['pa:t 'taim] AVV, AGG INV part-time.

party ['pa:ti] SM INV party.

parure [pa'ryr] SF INV (*di biancheria*) (set of) underwear; (*di gioielli*) (set of) jewellery ▶ **parure da letto** matching sheets and pillow slip(s).

parvenu [parvə'ny] SM INV upstart, nouveau riche.

parvenza [par'vɛntsa] SF semblance.

parvi *ecc* ['parvi] VB *vedi* **parere**.

parziale [par'tsjale] AGG (*limitato*) partial; (*non obiettivo*) biased, partial.

parzialità [partsjali'ta] SF INV **a** : **parzialità (a favore di qn)** partiality (for sb), bias (towards sb); **parzialità (contro qn)** bias (against sb) **b** (*azione*) unfair action.

parzialmente [partsjal'mente] AVV partially; **latte parzialmente scremato** semi-skimmed milk.

pascere ['paʃʃere] VB IRREG **1** VI (*aus* **avere**) to graze.
2 VT (*brucare*) to graze on.
3 **pascersi** VR: **pascersi di** (*erba, fig: illusioni*) to feed on.

pascià [paʃ'ʃa] SM INV pasha; **stare come un pascià** (*fig*) to live like a lord.

pasciuto, a [paʃ'ʃuto] **1** PP *di* **pascere**.
2 AGG: **ben pasciuto** plump.

pascolare [pasko'lare] VT, VI (*aus* **avere**) to graze.

pascolo ['paskolo] SM (*luogo*) pasture; **diritto di pascolo** grazing rights *pl*.

Pasqua ['paskwa] SF **a** Easter; **la domenica di Pasqua** Easter Sunday; **essere contento come una Pasqua** to be as happy as a sandboy **b** : **isola di Pasqua** Easter Island.

pasquale [pas'kwale] AGG Easter *attr*.

pasquetta [pas'kwetta] SF Easter Monday.

passabile [pas'sabile] AGG fairly good, passable.

passabilmente [passabil'mente] AVV fairly *o* reasonably (well).

passaggio, gi [pas'saddʒo] SM **a** (*atto del passare*) passage, passing *no pl*; (*traversata*) crossing *no pl*; **guardare il passaggio degli uccelli** to watch the birds fly past; **sono qui solo di passaggio** I'm just passing through **b** (*trasferimento: di poteri, diritti, calciatore*) transfer; **il passaggio dall'infanzia all'adolescenza** the transition from childhood to adolescence; **il passaggio dal giorno alla notte** the change from day to night ▶ **passaggio di**

proprietà transfer of ownership **c** (*luogo*) passage; (*cammino*) way, passage; (*itinerario*) route; **impedire il passaggio a qn** to block *o* stand in sb's way ▶ **passaggio a livello** level (*Brit*) *o* grade (*Am*) crossing ▶ **passaggio pedonale** pedestrian crossing ▶ **"passaggio di servizio"** "staff only" **d** (*traffico*): **c'è molto passaggio** there's a lot of traffic; **luogo di passaggio** thoroughfare **e** (*Aut*) lift (*Brit*), ride; **dare un passaggio a qn** to give sb a lift **f** (*brano*) passage **g** (*Sport*) pass; **passaggio in avanti/indietro** forward/ back pass.

passamaneria [passamane'ria] SF braid, trimming.

passamano [passa'mano] SM braid.

passamontagna [passamon'taɲɲa] SM INV balaclava.

passante [pas'sante] **1** SM/F passer-by.
2 SM (*di cintura*) loop.

passaparola [passapa'rɔla] SM: **fare il passaparola** (*Mil*) to pass the word; **passaparola!** pass it on!; **giocare a passaparola** to play Chinese whispers (*Brit*), to play telephone (*Am*).

passaporto [passa'porto] SM passport.

passare [pas'sare] **1** VI (*aus* **essere**) **a** (*persona, veicolo*) to go by, pass (by); **l'autobus passa davanti a casa nostra** the bus goes past our house; **siamo passati davanti a casa tua** we went past your house, we walked (*o* drove) past your house; **passare dall'altra parte della strada** to cross (over) to the other side of the street **b** (*fare una breve sosta*) to call in; (: *presso amico*) to call *o* drop in; (*postino*) to come, call; **passare a casa di qn** *o* **da qn** to drop in on sb; **passare a trovare/salutare qn** to drop by to see sb/say "hello" to sb; **passare a prendere qc/qn** to call in and pick sth/sb up; **passare in banca/ ufficio** to call in at the bank/office **c** (*filtrare attraverso: aria, sole, luce*) to pass, get through; (: *acqua*) to seep through **d** (*trasferirsi*): **passare da... a** to pass from ...to; **passare di mano in mano** to be passed *o* handed round; **passare di padre in figlio** to be handed *o* passed down *o* from father to son; **passare da un argomento ad un altro** to go from one subject to another; **passare ad altro** to change the subject; (*in una riunione*) to discuss the next item; **passiamo ad altro!** let's go on!; **passare al nemico** to go over to the enemy; **passare alla storia** to pass into history; (*fig*) to become a legend; **passare di moda** to go out of fashion; **passare a miglior vita** (*euf*) to pass away **e** (*trascorrere: giorni, tempo*) to pass, go by **f** (*allontanarsi: temporale, dolore, voglia*) to pass, go away; **il peggio è passato** the worst is over; **far passare a qn la voglia di qc/di fare qc** to stifle sb's desire for sth/to do sth; **gli passerà!** he'll get over it! **g** (*essere accettato: proposta di legge*) to be passed; (: *candidato*) to pass; **passare a un esame** to go up (to the next class) after an exam; **passare di grado** to be promoted **h** (*Culin*): **passare di cottura** to be overdone **i** (*Carte*) to pass **j** : **30 anni e passa** well over 30 years ago; **c'erano 100 persone e passa** there were well over a 100 people **k** (*esistere*): **ci passa una bella differenza tra i 2 quadri** there's a big difference between the 2 pictures **l** : **passare per uno stupido/un genio** to be taken for a fool/a genius; **passare per buono** to be taken as valid,

be accepted; **passare inosservato** to go unnoticed; **farsi passare per** to pass o.s. off as, pretend to be
m : **passare attraverso, per** (*anche fig*) to go through; **passare sopra** to pass over *o* above; (*fig: lasciar correre*) to pass over, overlook; **passare sotto** to pass below; **cosa ti passa per la testa?** (*a che pensi?*) what is going through your mind?; (*come puoi pensarlo?*) what are you thinking of!; **per dove si passa per arrivare in centro?** which way do I (*o* we) go to get into town?; **lasciar passare qn/qc** to let sb/sth through; **far passare qn per** *o* **da** to let sb in (*o* out) by; **far passare avanti qn** to let sb get past *o* by; **questa volta non ci passo sopra** I'm not prepared to overlook it this time.
2 VT **a** (*attraversare*) to cross
b (*esame*) to pass; (*dogana*) to go through, clear; (*visita medica*) to have
c (*approvare*) to pass, approve
d (*trafiggere*): **passare qn/qc da parte a parte** to pass right through sb/sth
e (*trascorrere*) to spend, pass; **passare le vacanze in montagna** to spend one's holidays in the mountains; **non passerà la notte** he (*o* she) won't survive the night; **non passa giorno che non ne combini una delle sue** hardly a day goes by without him getting up to something
f (*oltrepassare, sorpassare*) to go beyond; (*fig: andare oltre i limiti*) to exceed, go beyond; **ha passato la quarantina** he (*o* she) is over 40
g (*dare: oggetto*) to pass, give, hand; (*Sport: palla*) to pass; **passare qc a qn** to pass sth to sb, give sb sth; (*trasmettere: messaggio*) to pass sth (on) to sb; **passare indietro qc** to pass *o* give *o* hand sth back; **i miei genitori mi passano 500.000 lire al mese** my parents give me 500,000 lire a month; **mi passi Maria?** (*al telefono*) could you put Maria on?; **le passo il signor Rossi** I'm putting you through to Mr Rossi, here's Mr Rossi
h (*brodo, verdura*) to strain
i : **passare lo straccio per terra** to give the floor a wipe; **passare l'aspirapolvere** to hoover (*Brit*), vacuum (*Am*); **passare una mano di vernice su qc** to give sth a coat of paint
l (*fraseologia*): **passarsela bene/male** to get on well/badly; (*economicamente*) to manage well/badly; **come te la passi?** how are you getting on *o* along?; **passarla liscia** to get away with it; **ne ha passate tante** he's been through a lot, he's had some difficult times.
3 SM: **col passare del tempo...** with the passing of time ...; **col passare degli anni** (*riferito al presente*) as time goes by; (*riferito al passato*) as time passed *o* went by.
passata [pas'sata] SF **a** : **dare una passata a qc** (*spolverata*) to dust sth quickly; (*pulita*) to give sth a wipe; (*stirata*) to give sth a quick iron; **dare una passata di vernice a qc** to give sth a coat of paint **b** (*occhiata*) glance, look; **dare una passata al giornale** to skim through *o* have a glance at the paper.
passatempo [passa'tɛmpo] SM pastime, hobby; **per passatempo** as a hobby.
passato, a [pas'sato] **1** AGG **a** (*scorso*) last; **l'anno passato** last year; **nel corso degli anni passati** over the past years
b (*finito: gloria, generazioni*) past; (*usanze*) out of date; (*sfiorito*) faded; **passato di moda** out of fashion; **sono cose ormai passate** that's all over now; **nei tempi passati** in the past; **è acqua passata** it's over and done

with, it's water under the bridge
c (*superato*): **sono le 8 passate** it's past *o* after 8 o'clock; **ha 40 anni passati** he's over 40.
2 SM **a** past; **ha un passato di droga e furti** he has a history of drugs and theft
b (*Gramm*) past (tense) ▶**passato prossimo** present perfect ▶**passato remoto** past historic
c (*Culin*): **passato di verdura** vegetable purée.
passatoia [passa'toja] SF (*di scale*) stair carpet; (*di corridoio*) hall carpet.
passaverdura [passaver'dura] SM INV vegetable mill.
passavivande [passavi'vande] SM INV serving hatch.
passeggero, a [passed'dʒɛro] **1** AGG (*malessere, nuvola, temporale*) passing; (*bellezza, benessere*) transient.
2 SM/F passenger; **passeggero in arrivo/in partenza/in transito** arriving/departing/transit passenger.
passeggiare [passed'dʒare] VI (*aus avere*) to stroll, walk; **passeggiava nervosamente nel corridoio** he was pacing nervously up and down the corridor.
passeggiata [passed'dʒata] SF **a** (*a piedi*) walk; (*in macchina*) drive; **fare una passeggiata** to go for a walk; (*in veicolo*) to go for a drive **b** (*luogo*) promenade.
passeggiatrice [passeddʒa'tritʃe] SF (*euf*) streetwalker.
passeggino [passed'dʒino] SM pushchair (*Brit*), stroller (*Am*).
passeggio [pas'seddʒo] SM walk, stroll; (*luogo*) promenade; **andare a passeggio** to go for a walk *o* a stroll; **guardare il passeggio** to watch people out for a stroll.
passe-partout ['pas par'tu] SM INV **a** (*chiave*) skeleton *o* master key **b** (*per cornici*) passepartout.
passera ['passera] SF (*uccello*) hedge sparrow; (*pesce*) flounder.
passerella [passe'rɛlla] SF (*gen, di aereo*) footbridge; (*di nave*) gangway, gangplank; (*pedana: per sfilate*) catwalk.
passero ['passero] SM sparrow.
passerotto [passe'rɔtto] SM young sparrow.
passibile [pas'sibile] AGG: **passibile di** liable to; **passibile di aumento** liable to go up *o* increase.
passino [pas'sino] SM sieve, strainer.
passionale [passjo'nale] AGG (*temperamento*) passionate; **delitto passionale** crime of passion.
passionalità [passjonali'ta] SF passionate nature.
passionalmente [passjonal'mente] AVV (*amare*) passionately; (*agire*) in a fit of passion.
passione [pas'sjone] SF passion; **aver la passione di** *o* **per** to have a passion for; **domenica di Passione** Passion Sunday.
passivamente [passiva'mente] AVV passively.
passivante [passi'vante] AGG (*Gramm*): **il si passivante** the passive "si".
passività [passivi'ta] SF INV **a** (*qualità*) passivity, passiveness **b** (*Econ*) liability ▶**passività a breve termine** current liabilities *pl*.
passivo, a [pas'sivo] **1** AGG passive; **fumo passivo** passive smoking.
2 SM **a** (*Gramm*) passive **b** (*Econ*) debit; (: *complesso dei debiti*) liabilities *pl*.
passo¹ ['passo] SM **a** (*gen*) step; (*rumore*) (foot)step; (*orma*) footprint; **a due passi da qui** a stone's throw from here; **passo (a) passo** step by step; **seguire qn passo passo** to follow close on sb's heels; **fare i primi passi** (*anche fig*) to take one's first steps; **fare due** *o* **quattro passi** to go for a short walk; **fare un passo avanti/indietro** (*anche fig*) to take a step forward/back;

ha fatto passi da gigante in spagnolo his Spanish has improved by leaps and bounds; fare il gran passo to take the plunge; fare un passo falso to make a wrong move; fare i passi necessari to take the necessary steps; fare il passo più lungo della gamba to bite off more than one can chew; tornare sui propri passi to retrace one's steps; non ho intenzione di tornare sui miei passi (fig) I have no intention of starting all over again

b (andatura) pace; (: Mil, Danza) step; (: Equitazione) walk; fare il passo dell'oca to goose-step; passo di pattinaggio (Sci) skating turn; allungare il passo to quicken one's pace; avere il passo lento to walk slowly, be a slow walker; di buon passo at a good o brisk pace; marciare al passo to march; mettere il cavallo al passo to walk one's horse; a passo d'uomo at walking pace; (Aut) dead slow; le macchine andavano a passo d'uomo the cars were crawling along; andare al passo coi tempi to keep up with the times; di questo passo (fig) at this rate

c (brano) passage

d (Cine) gauge.

passo² ['passo] SM **a** (passaggio): cedere il passo a qn to give way to sb; sbarrare il passo a qn to bar sb's way; uccelli di passo birds of passage, migratory birds ▶"passo carrabile o carraio" "vehicle entrance — keep clear" **b** (valico) pass.

pasta ['pasta] SF **a** (Culin: impasto per pane) dough; (: impasto per dolce) pastry; (: anche: pastasciutta) pasta; (pasticcino) cake, pastry; lavorare la pasta to knead the dough; spianare la pasta to roll pastry ▶pasta in brodo noodle soup ▶pasta fatta in casa home-made pasta ▶pasta frolla shortcrust pastry; hai le mani di pasta frolla! what a butterfingers you are! ▶pasta sfoglia puff pastry ▶pasta all'uovo egg pasta

b (sostanza pastosa) paste ▶pasta di acciughe anchovy paste ▶pasta dentifricia toothpaste ▶pasta di mandorle almond paste

c (fig: indole) nature; sono tutt'e due della stessa pasta they're both cast in the same mould (Brit) o mold (Am).

pastasciutta [pastaʃ'ʃutta] SF pasta.

pasteggiare [pasted'dʒare] VI (aus avere): pasteggiare a vino/champagne to have wine/champagne with one's meal.

pastella [pas'tɛlla] SF batter.

pastello [pas'tɛllo] **1** SM pastel.

2 AGG INV pastel attr.

pastetta [pas'tetta] SF (Culin) = pastella.

pasticca, che [pas'tikka] SF pastille, lozenge.

pasticceria [pastittʃe'ria] SF **a** (negozio) cake shop **b** (pasticcini) pastries pl, cakes pl **c** (arte) confectionery.

pasticciare [pastit'tʃare] VT to mess up, make a mess of.

pasticciere, a [pastit'tʃɛre] SM/F pastry-cook; (gestore di pasticceria) confectioner.

pasticcino [pastit'tʃino] SM petit four.

pasticcio, ci [pas'tittʃo] SM **a** (Culin) pie **b** (lavoro disordinato, imbroglio) mess; cacciarsi nei pasticci to get into trouble.

pasticcione, a [pastit'tʃone] **1** AGG bungling, messy.

2 SM/F bungler, messy person.

pastiera [pas'tjɛra] SF: pastiera (napoletana) puff pastry filled with cream cheese, barley and candied fruit.

pastificio, ci [pasti'fitʃo] SM pasta factory.

pastiglia [pas'tiʎʎa] SF **a** (Med) pastille, lozenge; pastiglie per la gola throat lozenges o pastilles; pastiglie per

la tosse cough drops o pastilles **b** (Aut): pastiglie dei freni brake lining sg.

pastina [pas'tina] SF small pasta shapes used in soup.

pasto ['pasto] SM meal; saltare i pasti to skip meals; da prendersi prima dei pasti to be taken before meals; non mangiare fuori pasto o fuori dei pasti don't eat between meals; vino da pasto table wine; la notizia fu data in pasto al pubblico the news was made common knowledge; lo diedero in pasto ai leoni (anche fig) he was thrown to the lions.

pastoia [pas'toja] SF (fig): pastoia burocratica red tape.

pastone [pas'tone] SM (per animali) mash; (pegg: cibo) overcooked stodge.

pastorale [pasto'rale] **1** AGG (gen) pastoral.

2 SF **a** (Rel: lettera del vescovo) pastoral (letter) **b** (Mus) pastoral(e).

3 SM (Rel: bastone) crook, crosier.

pastore [pas'tore] **a** SM (anche Rel) shepherd; (sacerdote) minister, pastor; il buon Pastore (Rel) the Good Shepherd **b** (anche: cane (da) pastore) sheepdog ▶pastore scozzese collie ▶pastore tedesco Alsatian (Brit), German shepherd.

pastorella [pasto'rɛlla] SF **a** (persona) shepherdess **b** (Poesia) pastoral.

pastorizia [pasto'rittsja] SF sheep-rearing, sheep farming.

pastorizzare [pastorid'dzare] VT to pasteurize; latte pastorizzato pasteurized milk.

pastosità [pastosi'ta] SF (vedi agg) doughiness; pastiness; mellowness, softness; mellowness.

pastoso, a [pas'toso] AGG **a** (miscuglio) doughy; (: più liquido) pasty **b** (fig: colore, voce) mellow, soft; (vino) mellow.

pastrano [pas'trano] SM greatcoat.

pastura [pas'tura] SF (atto) grazing; (luogo) pasture; terreno a pastura grazing land.

patacca, che [pa'takka] SF **a** (distintivo) medal, decoration **b** (fig: macchia) grease spot, grease mark; (: oggetto senza valore) piece of rubbish; li vendono solo patacche they just sell junk there.

patata [pa'tata] SF potato; che spirito di patata! (fam) some joke that! (iro) ▶patata americana o dolce sweet potato, batata, yam (Am) ▶patate fritte chips (Brit), French fries (Am).

patatine [pata'tine] SFPL chips (Brit), French fries (Am); (confezionate) (potato) crisps (Brit) o chips (Am).

patatrac [pata'trak] SM INV (fig: disastro) disaster; (: dissesto economico) crash.

pâté [pa'te] SM INV pâté ▶pâté di fegato d'oca pâté de foie gras.

patella [pa'tɛlla] SF (Zool) limpet.

patema, i [pa'tɛma] SM: patema (d'animo) anxiety, worry.

patentato, a [paten'tato] AGG **a** (munito di patente) licensed, certified **b** (fig scherz: qualificato) utter, thorough; un cretino patentato an utter fool; un ladro patentato an out and out thief.

patente [pa'tɛnte] SF (anche: patente di guida) driving licence (Brit), driver's license (Am).

patentino [paten'tino] SM temporary licence (Brit) o license (Am).

paterazzo [pate'rattso] SM (Naut) backstay.

paternale [pater'nale] SF rebuke, reprimand; fare una paternale a qn to rebuke o reprimand sb.

paternalismo [paterna'lizmo] SM paternalism.

paternalista, i, e [paterna'lista] ① AGG paternalistic. ② SM/F paternalist.

paternalistico, a, ci, che [paterna'listiko] AGG paternalistic.

paternamente [paterna'mente] AVV like a father, in a fatherly fashion.

paternità [paterni'ta] SF INV (gen) fatherhood; (Dir) paternity; **hanno rivendicato la paternità dell'attentato** (fig) they've claimed responsibility for the bombing.

paterno, a [pa'tɛrno] AGG (autorità) paternal; (benevolo: affetto, consigli) fatherly; **lasciare la casa paterna** to leave one's father's house.

Paternostro [pater'nɔstro] SM = Padrenostro.

pateticamente [patetika'mente] AVV pathetically.

patetico, a, ci, che [pa'tɛtiko] ① AGG (gen, Anat, pegg) pathetic; (commovente) moving, touching. ② SM sentimentalism; **cadere nel patetico** to become (over)sentimental.

pathos ['patos] SM INV pathos.

patibolo [pa'tibolo] SM scaffold, gallows sg; **pare che vada al patibolo!** (fig) you'd think his hour had come!

patimento [pati'mento] SM suffering.

patina ['patina] SF (su rame) patina; (su medaglie) coat; (sulla lingua) fur, coating.

patio ['patjo] SM INV patio.

patire [pa'tire] ① VT (ingiurie, offese) to suffer; (fame, sete) to suffer (from); (ingiustizie) to endure. ② VI (aus avere): **patire (di)** to suffer (from); **patire di cuore** to have a weak heart; **ha finito di patire** his sufferings are over.

patito, a [pa'tito] ① AGG (sofferente) run-down; (: volto) wan. ② SM/F: **essere un patito di** (musica, sport) to be a fan o lover of.

patogeno, a [pa'tɔdʒeno] AGG pathogenic; **agente patogeno** pathogen.

patologia [patolo'dʒia] SF (Med) pathology.

patologico, a, ci, che [pato'lɔdʒiko] AGG (Med, fig) pathological.

patologo, a, gi, ghe [pa'tɔlogo] SM/F (Med) pathologist.

patria ['patrja] SF (paese) homeland, fatherland; (fig: città o luogo natale) birthplace; **Vienna, la patria del walzer** Vienna, the home of the waltz; **tornare in patria** to return to one's own country; **amor di patria** patriotism.

patriarca, chi [patri'arka] SM patriarch.

patriarcale [patriar'kale] AGG patriarchal.

patriarcalmente [patriarkal'mente] AVV patriarchally.

patriarcato [patriar'kato] SM (Antropologia) patriarchy; (: sede, territorio, anche Rel) patriarchate.

patrigno [pa'triɲɲo] SM stepfather.

patrimoniale [patrimo'njale] ① AGG patrimonial; **rendita patrimoniale** income from property; **imposta patrimoniale** property tax. ② SF (imposta) property tax.

patrimonio, ni [patri'mɔnjo] SM **a** estate, property; **mi è costato un patrimonio** (fig) it cost me a fortune, I paid a fortune for it ▶ **patrimonio pubblico** public property **b** (fig: eredità) heritage ▶ **patrimonio culturale** cultural heritage ▶ **patrimonio ereditario** hereditary characteristics pl ▶ **patrimonio spirituale** spiritual heritage.

patrio, ria, rii, rie ['patrjo] AGG **a** (di patria) of one's country, native attr; **amor patrio** love of one's country **b** (Dir): **patria potestà** parental authority.

patriota, i, e [patri'ɔta] SM/F patriot.

patriotticamente [patriottika'mente] AVV patriotically.

patriottico, a, ci, che [patri'ɔttiko] AGG patriotic.

patriottismo [patriot'tizmo] SM patriotism.

patrocinare [patrotʃi'nare] VT (Dir) to defend; (fig: candidatura: appoggiare) to support; (: finanziariamente) to sponsor.

patrocinio, nii [patro'tʃinjo] SM (vedi vb) defence (Brit), defense (Am); support; sponsorship, patronage.

patrona [pa'trɔna] SF (Rel) patron saint.

patronato [patro'nato] SM **a** (patrocinio) patronage **b** (istituzione benefica) charitable institution o society.

patronessa [patro'nessa] SF patroness.

patronimico, a, ci, che [patro'nimiko] AGG, SM patronymic.

patrono [pa'trɔno] SM **a** (Rel) patron saint **b** (benefattore) patron **c** (Dir) counsel.

patta¹ ['patta] SF (di tasca) flap; (dei pantaloni) fly.

patta² ['patta] SF (pareggio) draw, tie; **essere pari e patta** (fig) to be even o all square.

patteggiamento [patteddʒa'mento] SM (Dir: anche: **patteggiamento della pena**) plea bargaining.

patteggiare [patted'dʒare] ① VT (negoziare: resa, tregua) to negotiate; (Dir): **patteggiare la pena** to plea-bargain. ② VI (aus avere): **patteggiare con qn** (scendere a patti) to negotiate with sb; (scendere a compromessi) to come to a compromise with sb.

pattinaggio [patti'naddʒo] SM skating; **fare del pattinaggio** to go skating ▶ **pattinaggio artistico** figure skating ▶ **pattinaggio sul ghiaccio** ice skating ▶ **pattinaggio a rotelle** roller skating.

pattinare [patti'nare] VI (aus avere) **a** (Sport) to skate; **pattinare sul ghiaccio/a rotelle** to ice-/roller-skate **b** (Aut: scivolare) to skid.

pattinatore, trice [pattina'tore] SM/F skater.

pattino¹ ['pattino] SM **a** (Sport) skate ▶ **pattini da ghiaccio** ice skates ▶ **pattini a rotelle** roller skates **b** (Tecn) sliding block; (Aer) skid; (di slitta) runner.

pattino² [pat'tino] SM (barca) kind of pedalo with oars.

pattista, i, e [pat'tista] ① AGG (Pol) of Patto per l'Italia. ② SM/F (Pol) member (o supporter) of Patto per l'Italia.

patto ['patto] SM **a** (accordo) pact, agreement; **fare un patto** to make a pact o an agreement; **il Patto di Varsavia** the Warsaw Pact ▶ **patto di non aggressione** non-aggression pact ▶ **il Patto per l'Italia** (Pol) centrist party **b** (condizione) condition, term; **a nessun patto** under no circumstances; **venire o scendere a patti (con)** to come to an agreement (with), come to terms (with); **a patto che** on condition that.

pattuglia [pat'tuʎʎa] SF (Mil) patrol; **essere di pattuglia** to be on patrol.

pattugliare [pattuʎ'ʎare] VT to patrol.

pattuire [pattu'ire] VT to reach an agreement on.

pattume [pat'tume] SM rubbish (Brit), garbage (Am), trash (Am).

pattumiera [pattu'mjɛra] SF (dust)bin (Brit), garbage can (Am), trashcan (Am).

paturnie [pa'turnie] SFPL (fam: malumore): **avere le paturnie** to be in a bad mood.

paura [pa'ura] SF fear; **aver paura di/di fare/che...** to be frightened o afraid of/of doing/that ...; **fare o mettere paura a qn** to frighten sb; **era morto di paura** he was scared to death o frightened out of his wits; **ho paura di sì/no** I am afraid so/not; **ha paura di ingrassare** she's

afraid of *o* worried about putting on weight; **ho paura che non venga** *o* **che non verrà** I'm afraid he won't come; **non aver paura, tutto si risolverà** don't worry, everything will work out in the end; **niente paura, ci penso io** don't worry, I'll see to it; **per paura di/che...** for fear of/that ...; **parlava piano per paura di svegliarlo** she spoke quietly so as not to wake him; **è magro da far paura** he is terribly thin; **ha una faccia da far paura** he looks terrible; **piove da far paura** it's bucketing down.

paurosamente [paurosa'mente] AVV **a** (*in modo pauroso*) frighteningly **b** (*con paura*) timidly, fearfully.

pauroso, a [pau'roso] AGG **a** (*che incute paura*) frightening; (*fig: straordinario*) awful, dreadful **b** (*che ha paura*) timid, fearful, timorous.

pausa ['pauza] SF (*sosta*) break; (*nel parlare, Mus*) pause; **fare una pausa di 10 minuti** to have a 10-minute break; **fece una pausa e poi riprese a parlare** he paused then began speaking again.

pavé [pa've] SM INV cobbles *pl*.

paventato, a [paven'tato] AGG much-feared.

pavese¹ [pa'vese] SM (*Naut*): **gran pavese** bunting.

pavese² [pa'vese] **1** AGG of *o* from Pavia.

2 SM/F inhabitant *o* native of Pavia.

pavido, a ['pavido] AGG (*letter*) fearful.

pavimentare [pavimen'tare] VT (*stanza*) to floor; (*strada*) to pave.

pavimentazione [pavimentat'tsjone] SF (*vedi vb*) flooring; paving.

pavimento [pavi'mento] SM floor.

pavona [pa'vona] SF peahen.

pavoncella [pavon'tʃɛlla] SF lapwing.

pavone [pa'vone] SM peacock.

pavoneggiarsi [pavoned'dʒarsi] VIP to strut about, show off.

pazientare [pattsjen'tare] VI (*aus avere*) to be patient.

paziente [pat'tsjɛnte] **1** AGG patient.

2 SM/F (*Med*) patient.

pazientemente [pattsjɛnte'mente] AVV patiently.

pazienza [pat'tsjɛntsa] SF patience; **aver pazienza** to be patient; **perdere la pazienza** to lose (one's) patience; **pazienza!** never mind!; **santa pazienza!** (God) give me patience!

pazzamente [pattsa'mente] AVV madly; **essere pazzamente innamorato** to be madly in love.

pazzerellone, a [pattserel'lone] SM/F madcap.

pazzescamente [pattseska'mente] AVV (*vedi agg*) crazily; incredibly.

pazzesco, a, schi, sche [pat'tsesko] AGG (*assurdo: persona, comportamento*) crazy, daft, mad; (*incredibile: scena*) incredible; **ad una velocità pazzesca** at breakneck speed; **ha una cultura pazzesca** she's incredibly knowledgeable; **pazzesco!** incredible!

pazzia [pat'tsia] SF (*Med*) madness, lunacy, insanity; (*di azione, decisione*) madness, folly; **dar segni di pazzia** to show signs of madness; **mi sento in vena di far pazzie** I feel like doing something crazy; **è stata una pazzia!** it was sheer madness!

pazzo, a ['pattso] **1** AGG (*Med*) mad, insane, crazy; (*strano: persona, idea*) wild, mad; **essere pazzo da legare** to be raving mad *o* a raving lunatic; **essere pazzo di** (*gioia, dolore*) to be beside o.s. with, to be mad *o* crazy with; **essere pazzo di gelosia** to be insanely jealous; **essere innamorato pazzo** to be madly in love; **è pazzo di lei** he's crazy about her; **pazzo per qn/qc** mad *o* crazy

about sb/sth; **va pazza per il cioccolato** she adores chocolate; **prova un gusto pazzo a prendere in giro la gente** he thoroughly enjoys taking people for a ride; **andava a pazza velocità** he was going at breakneck speed.

2 SM/F lunatic, madman/madwoman; **urlava come un pazzo** he was shouting his head off, he was shouting like a lunatic.

pazzoide [pat'tsɔide] **1** AGG crazy.

2 SM/F (*fam*) nutcase.

PC SIGLA = *Piacenza*.

P.C. ABBR (*Comm*) = **polizza di carico**.

p.c. ABBR **a** = *per condoglianze* **b** = *per conoscenza*.

p.c.c. ABBR (= *per copia conforme*) cc.

P.C.I. [pi'tʃi] SIGLA M (*Pol*: = *Partito Comunista Italiano*) *former political party*.

P.C.U.S. [pkus] SIGLA M (*Pol*: = *Partito Comunista dell'Unione Sovietica*) CPSU.

PD SIGLA = *Padova*.

P.D. ABBR (*Contabilità*) = **partita doppia**.

P.D.S. [pidi'ɛsse] SIGLA M (*Pol*: = *Partito Democratico della Sinistra*) *party originating from P.C.I.*

PE SIGLA = *Pescara*.

pecan [pɛ'kan] SM INV pecan.

pecari ['pɛkari] SM INV (*Zool*) peccary.

pecca, che ['pɛkka] SF defect, flaw, fault.

peccaminoso, a [pekkami'noso] AGG sinful, wicked.

peccare [pek'kare] VI (*aus avere*) **a** (*Rel*) to sin; (*fig*) to err; **peccare di superbia** (*anche fig*) to be guilty of pride; **peccare per troppa bontà** to be too kind **b** (*difettare*): **peccare di** to lack, be lacking in; **peccare di modestia** to be lacking in modesty; **quel romanzo pecca nella struttura** that novel lacks structure.

peccato [pek'kato] SM (*Rel*) sin; **un peccato di gioventù** (*fig*) a youthful error *o* indiscretion; **che peccato!** what a shame *o* pity!; **è un peccato che sia finita così** it's a shame that it had to end like that ▸**peccato di gola** gluttony ▸**peccato mortale** mortal sin ▸**peccato originale** original sin ▸**peccato veniale** venial sin.

peccatore, trice [pekka'tore] SM/F sinner.

peccherò *ecc* [pekke'rɔ] VB *vedi* **peccare**.

pece ['petʃe] SF pitch.

pechinese [peki'nese] **1** AGG, SM/F Pekin(g)ese *inv*.

2 SM (*anche:* **cane pechinese**) Pekin(g)ese *inv*, Peke (*fam*).

Pechino [pe'kino] SF Beijing, Peking (*ant*).

pecora ['pɛkora] SF (*gen, fig*) sheep *inv*; (*femmina*) ewe; **latte di pecora** ewe's milk ▸**pecora nera** (*fig*) black sheep.

pecoraio, ai [peko'rajo] SM shepherd.

pecorella [peko'rɛlla] SF lamb; **la pecorella smarrita** the lost sheep; **cielo a pecorelle** (*fig: nuvole*) mackerel sky.

pecorino [peko'rino] SM (*anche:* **formaggio pecorino**) pecorino, *sheep's* o *ewe's milk cheese*.

pecorone [peko'rone] SM (*fig pegg*) spineless creature.

pectina [pek'tina] SF pectin.

peculato [peku'lato] SM (*Dir*) embezzlement.

peculiare [peku'ljare] AGG: **peculiare di** peculiar to.

peculiarità [pekuljari'ta] SF INV peculiarity.

peculiarmente [pekuljar'mente] AVV peculiarly.

pecuniario, ria, ri, rie [peku'njarjo] AGG financial, monetary, money *attr*.

pedaggio, gi [pe'daddʒo] SM toll.

pedagogia [pedago'dʒia] SF pedagogy, pedagogics *sg*,

educational methods *pl.*

pedagogicamente [pedagodʒika'mente] AVV pedagogically.

pedagogico, a, ci, che [peda'gɔdʒiko] AGG pedagogic(al).

pedagogo, a, ghi, ghe [peda'gɔgo] SM/F pedagogue.

pedalare [peda'lare] VI (*aus* avere) to pedal; (*andare in bicicletta*) to cycle.

pedalata [peda'lata] SF push on the pedals.

pedale [pe'dale] SM (*gen*) pedal; (*di macchina da cucire*) treadle.

pedalò [peda'lɔ] SM INV pedalo.

pedana [pe'dana] SF **a** (*gen*) footboard; **pedana della cattedra** platform, dais **b** (*Sport: nel salto*) springboard; (: *nella scherma*) piste; (: *nel lancio del disco*) throwing circle.

pedante [pe'dante] 1 AGG pedantic. 2 SM/F pedant.

pedantemente [pedante'mente] AVV pedantically.

pedanteria [pedante'ria] SF pedantry.

pedata [pe'data] SF (*colpo*) kick; (*impronta*) footprint; **dare una pedata a qn** to kick sb, give sb a kick; **prendere a pedate qn/qc** to kick sb/sth.

pedemontano, a [pedemon'tano] AGG (*regione, ghiacciaio*) piedmont *attr.*

pederasta, i [pede'rasta] SM pederast.

pederastia [pederas'tia] SF pederasty.

pedestre [pe'dɛstre] AGG pedestrian.

pediatra, i, e [pe'djatra] SM/F paediatrician (*Brit*), pediatrician (*Am*).

pediatria [pedja'tria] SF paediatrics *sg* (*Brit*), pediatrics *sg* (*Am*).

pediatrico, a, ci, che [pe'djatriko] AGG paediatric (*Brit*), pediatric (*Am*), children's *attr.*

pedicello [pedi'tʃɛllo] SM (*Bot*) pedicel.

pedicure [pedi'kure] SM/F INV chiropodist (*Brit*), podiatrist (*Am*).

pedigree ['pedigri:] SM INV pedigree.

pediluvio, vi [pedi'luvjo] SM footbath.

pedina [pe'dina] SF (*Dama*) draughtsman (*Brit*), draftsman (*Am*); (*Scacchi, fig*) pawn.

pedinare [pedi'nare] VT to shadow, tail; **far pedinare qn** to have sb followed, put a tail on sb.

pedissequo, a [pe'dissekwo] AGG (*imitatore*) servile; (*traduzione*) literal.

pedofilia [pedofi'lia] SF paedophilia (*Brit*), pedophilia (*Am*).

pedofilo, a [pe'dɔfilo] AGG, SM/F paedophile (*Brit*), pedophile (*Am*), paedophiliac (*Brit*), pedophiliac (*Am*).

pedologico, a, ci, che [pedo'lɔdʒiko] AGG (*Geol*): **profilo pedologico** soil profile.

pedonale [pedo'nale] AGG (*passaggio, isola, traffico ecc*) pedestrian *attr.*

pedone [pe'done] SM **a** (*persona*) pedestrian **b** (*Scacchi*) pawn.

pedule [pe'dule] SFPL walking boots.

peduncolo [pe'dunkolo] SM peduncle.

peeling ['pi:liŋ] SM INV (*Cosmesi*) facial scrub.

PEEP [piee'pi] SIGLA M (= *Piano per l'Edilizia Economica Popolare*) *council-house building programme.*

Pegaso ['pɛgazo] SM (*Mitol, Astron*) Pegasus.

peggio ['pɛddʒo] (*comp, superl di* **male**) 1 AVV **a** (*con senso comparativo*) worse; **gioca peggio di lui** she plays worse than he does, she's a worse player than he is; **andare peggio** to be worse; **gli affari vanno peggio che mai** business is worse than ever; **cambiare in peggio** to get *o* become worse, change for the worse; **si comporta sempre peggio** his behaviour gets worse and worse; **peggio per te!** so much the worse for you!; **peggio di così si muore** things couldn't be worse; **è peggio che andar di notte!** it's worse than ever!; **non c'è niente di peggio che...** there's nothing worse than ...

b (*con senso superlativo*) worst; **i peggio allenati** the worst trained; **sono le ragazze peggio vestite della scuola** they are the worst dressed girls in the school.

2 AGG INV (*con senso comparativo*) worse; **è peggio di suo fratello** she's worse than her brother.

3 SM worst; **il peggio è che...** the worst thing *o* the worst of it is that ....

4 SF **a** : **avere la peggio** to come off worse, get the worst of it

b : **alla peggio** if the worst comes to the worst, at worst; **tirare avanti alla meno peggio** to get along as best one can.

peggioramento [peddʒora'mento] SM (*gen, di malattia*) worsening; (*di rapporti*) worsening, deterioration; **portare un peggioramento in** [OR] **portare ad un peggioramento di** to worsen, lead to a worsening in; **ci sarà un peggioramento** (*Meteor*) the weather will deteriorate *o* become worse.

peggiorare [peddʒo'rare] 1 VT to worsen, to make worse. 2 VI (*aus* essere) to worsen, become *o* grow worse.

peggiorativamente [peddʒorativa'mente] AVV pejoratively.

peggiorativo, a [peddʒora'tivo] AGG pejorative.

peggiore [ped'dʒore] 1 AGG (*comparativo*) worse; (*superlativo*) worst; **peggiore (di)** worse (than); **molto peggiore** much worse; **nel peggiore dei casi** if the worst comes to the worst; **le cose non potevano concludersi in modo peggiore** things couldn't have come to a worse end; **ho conosciuto tempi peggiori** I've been through worse.

2 SM/F: **il/la peggiore** the worst one, the worst (person); **il peggiore dei due** the worse of the two; **il peggiore della classe** the worst in the class.

pegno ['peɲɲo] SM **a** (*Dir*) pledge, security; **dare in pegno qc** to pawn sth; **banco dei pegni** pawnshop **b** (*fig: segno*) token, pledge; (*nei giochi di società*) forfeit; **un pegno d'amore** a love token; **in pegno d'amicizia** as a token of friendship.

pelame [pe'lame] SM (*di animale*) coat, fur.

pelandrone, a [pelan'drone] SM/F loafer, idler.

pelapatate [pelapa'tate] SM INV potato peeler.

pelare [pe'lare] VT (*spennare*) to pluck; (*spellare*) to skin; (*sbucciare*) to peel; **ti hanno pelato!** (*di capelli*) they've scalped you!; **in quel negozio ti pelano** they make you pay through the nose in that shop.

pelata [pe'lata] SF (*calvizie parziale*) bald patch.

pelato, a [pe'lato] 1 AGG **a** (*sbucciato*) peeled **b** (*calvo*) bald.

2 : **pelati** SMPL (*anche:* **pomodori pelati**) peeled tomatoes.

pellaccia, ce [pel'lattʃa] SF (*fig: persona*): **essere una pellaccia** to be tough.

pellagra [pel'lagra] SF pellagra.

pellame [pel'lame] SM (*di animali*) skins *pl*, hides *pl.*

pelle ['pɛlle] SF **a** (*gen*) skin; **avere la pelle delicata** to have sensitive skin ▶**pelle grassa** greasy skin; (*Cosmesi*) oily skin ▶**pelle mista** combination skin ▶**pelle secca** dry skin

b (*di animale*) skin, hide; (*di rettile*) skin; (*conciata*) leather; **borsa di pelle** leather handbag ▶**pelle di camoscio** suede ▶**pelle di daino** shammy (leather) ▶**pelli di foca** (*Sci*) skins ▶**pelle di montone** sheepskin

c (*buccia*) skin, peel

d (*fraseologia*): **avere la pelle dura** (*fig*) to be tough; **avere la pelle d'oca** to have goose pimples (*Brit*) *o* goose flesh (*Brit*) *o* goose bumps (*Am*); **mi ha fatto venire la pelle d'oca** (*paura, disgusto*) it made my flesh creep; **avere i nervi a fior di pelle** to be edgy; **essere pelle ed ossa** to be skin and bone; **non stare più nella pelle dalla gioia** to be beside o.s. with delight; **lasciarci la pelle** to lose one's life; **salvare la pelle** to save one's skin; **vendere cara la pelle** to put up a fierce struggle; **amici per la pelle** firm *o* close friends.

pellegrinaggio, gi [pellegri'naddʒo] SM pilgrimage; **andare in pellegrinaggio** to go on a pilgrimage.

pellegrino, a [pelle'grino] SM/F pilgrim.

pellerossa [pelle'rossa] SM/F (*pl* **pellirosse**) redskin, Red Indian.

pelletteria [pellette'ria] SF **a** (*negozio*) leather goods shop; **articoli di pelletteria** leather goods **b** (*industria*) leather trade *o* industry.

pellettiere [pellet'tjɛre] SM dealer in leather goods.

pellicano [pelli'kano] SM pelican.

pellicceria [pellittʃe'ria] SF **a** (*negozio*) furrier's (shop) **b** (*pellicce*) furs *pl*.

pelliccia, ce [pel'littʃa] SF **a** (*mantello di animale*) fur, coat **b** (*indumento*) fur (coat) ▶**pelliccia ecologica** fake fur ▶**pelliccia di visone** mink coat.

pellicciaio, ciai [pellit'tʃajo] SM furrier.

pellicola [pel'likola] SF **a** (*membrana*) film, layer ▶**pellicola trasparente** (*Culin*) cling film (*Brit*), plastic wrap (*Am*) **b** (*Fot, Cine*) film.

pellirossa [pelli'rossa] SM/F = **pellerossa**.

pelo ['pelo] SM **a** (*gen*) hair; **ho tanti peli sulle gambe** I've got a lot of hair *o* hairs on my legs; **non aver peli sulla lingua** to speak one's mind; **cercare il pelo nell'uovo** to pick holes, split hairs; **per un pelo non ho perduto il treno** I very nearly missed the train; **l'ha mancato per un pelo** she just missed it; **per un pelo non s'ammazzava** he almost *o* nearly killed himself; **ha perso per un pelo** he lost but only just; **c'è mancato un pelo che affogasse** he narrowly escaped drowning; **è un pelo più grande** (*un po'*) it's a shade bigger

b (*di animale: pelame*) coat, fur; (: *peli*) hair; (: *pelliccia*) fur; **il gatto ha un pelo morbido** the cat has soft fur *o* a soft coat; **impermeabile con l'interno di pelo** fur-lined raincoat; **pelliccia a pelo lungo** long-haired fur coat; **essere di primo pelo** to be wet behind the ears; **fare il pelo e il contropelo a qn** to give sb a good dressing-down; **il lupo perde il pelo ma non il vizio** (*Proverbio*) the leopard cannot change its spots

c (*di tappeto*) pile; (*di tessuto*) pile, nap; **tappeto a pelo lungo** thick pile carpet

d (*superficie: di liquido*) surface; **il pelo dell'acqua** the surface of the water.

peloso, a [pe'loso] AGG hairy.

pelota [pe'lɔta] SF pelota.

peltro ['peltro] SM pewter.

peluche [pə'lyʃ] SM (*tessuto*) plush; **giocattoli di peluche** soft *o* cuddly toys; **un cane di peluche** a fluffy dog.

peluria [pe'lurja] SF down.

pelvi ['pɛlvi] SF INV pelvis.

pelvico, a, ci, che ['pɛlviko] AGG pelvic.

pena ['pena] SF **a** (*dolore*) sorrow, sadness *no pl*; (*angoscia*) worry, anxiety; **essere** *o* **stare in pena (per qn/qc)** to worry *o* be anxious (about sb/sth); **le pene dell'inferno** the torments of hell; **ha passato le pene dell'inferno** (*fig*) she went through hell

b (*pietà*) pity; **far pena** to be pitiful; **mi fa pena** I feel sorry for him; **fa pena vederlo così** it is pitiful to see him like this; **quel cappello fa pena** (*fig*) that hat is a disgrace

c (*Dir*) sentence; (: *punizione*) penalty, punishment; **fu condannato ad una pena di 5 anni** he was sentenced to 5 years' imprisonment; **scontare una pena** to serve a term of imprisonment ▶**pena capitale** capital punishment ▶**pena di morte** death sentence *o* penalty ▶**pena pecuniaria** fine

d (*fatica*) trouble *no pl*, effort; (*difficoltà*) difficulty; **prendersi** *o* **darsi la pena di fare qc** to go to the trouble of doing sth, take the trouble to do sth; **vale la pena farlo** it's worth doing, it's worth it; **non ne vale la pena** it's not worth the effort *o* worth it.

penale [pe'nale] **1** AGG (*Dir*) criminal, penal; **codice penale** penal code; **causa penale** criminal trial; **diritto penale** criminal law.

2 SF (*anche:* **clausola penale**) penalty clause; **pagare la penale** to pay the penalty.

penalista, i, e [pena'lista] SM/F (*avvocato*) criminal lawyer.

penalistico, a, ci, che [pena'listiko] AGG criminal; **fare studi penalistici** to study criminal law.

penalità [penali'ta] SF INV penalty.

penalizzare [penalid'dzare] VT (*Sport*) to penalize.

penalizzazione [penaliddzat'tsjone] SF (*Sport*) penalty.

penare [pe'nare] VI (*aus* **avere**) (*patire*) to suffer; (*faticare*) to struggle; **ha finito di penare** his sufferings are over; **penare a fare qc** to have difficulty in doing sth; **lo fecero senza penare troppo** they did it without too much difficulty.

penati [pe'nati] SMPL household gods.

pencolare [penko'lare] VI (*aus* **avere**) (*dondolare, vacillare*) sway; (*fig: tentennare*) to dither, hesitate.

pendaglio, gli [pen'daʎʎo] SM (*ciondolo*) pendant ▶**pendaglio da forca** (*fig*) gallows bird.

pendente [pen'dɛnte] **1** AGG **a** (*appeso*) hanging; (*inclinato*) leaning **b** (*Dir: causa, lite*) pending.

2 SM (*pendaglio*) pendant; (*orecchino*) drop earring.

pendenza [pen'dɛntsa] SF **a** slope, slant; (*grado d'inclinazione*) gradient; **in pendenza** (*tetto*) sloping; (*strada, terreno*) on a slope; **essere in leggera pendenza** to slope (down) gently; **una strada con una pendenza del 20%** a road with a 1 in 5 gradient **b** (*Dir*) pending suit **c** (*Comm*) outstanding account.

pendere ['pɛndere] VI (*aus* **avere**) **a** (*essere appeso*): **pendere (da)** to hang (from); **pendere dalle labbra di qn** to hang on sb's every word

b (*Dir: causa*) to be pending

c (*essere inclinato: superficie*) to slope, slant; (: *palo, edificio*) to lean; (: *nave*) to list; **pendere da una parte** to slope to one side; **pendere dalla parte di qn** (*fig*) to be inclined to take sb's part; **la bilancia pende in suo favore** things are in his favour

d (*fig: incombere*): **pendere su** to hang over.

pendice [pen'ditʃe] SF (*di monte*) slope.

pendio, dii [pen'dio] SM **a** (*luogo in pendenza*) slope **b**

(*pendenza*) slope, slant.

pendola ['pɛndola] SF pendulum clock.

pendolare [pendo'lare] ① AGG (*moto*) pendular, pendulum *attr.*

② SM/F (*lavoratore*) commuter.

pendolarismo [pendola'rizmo] SM commuting.

pendolo ['pɛndolo] SM (*peso*) pendulum; (*anche:* **orologio a pendolo**) pendulum clock.

pene ['pɛne] SM (*Anat*) penis.

Penelope [pe'nɛlope] SF Penelope.

penetrabile [pene'trabile] AGG penetrable.

penetrante [pene'trante] AGG (*freddo*) biting, piercing; (*odore*) penetrating; (*sguardo*) penetrating, piercing.

penetrare [pene'trare] ① VI (*aus* essere) **a** (*gen*): **penetrare (in qc)** to penetrate (sth), enter (sth); **penetrò in casa di nascosto** he entered the house by stealth, he stole into the house

b (*freddo*) to come *o* get in; (*liquido*) to soak in; **penetrare nella parete** (*chiodo*) to penetrate the wall; (*acqua*) to soak into the wall; **il sole penetrò nella stanza** the sun shone into the room; **il freddo mi penetrava nelle ossa** the cold went right through me; **far penetrare** (*aria, luce*) to let in.

② VT (*gen, fig*) to penetrate; (*sogg: proiettile*) to penetrate; (: *acqua, aria*) to go *o* come into; **penetrare un mistero** to get to the bottom of a mystery.

penetrazione [penetrat'tsjone] SF penetration.

penicillina [penitʃil'lina] SF penicillin.

peninsulare [peninsu'lare] AGG peninsular; **l'Italia peninsulare** mainland Italy.

penisola [pe'nizola] SF peninsula; **la penisola italiana** the Italian mainland.

penitente [peni'tɛnte] SM/F, AGG penitent.

penitenza [peni'tɛntsa] SF **a** (*Rel: pentimento*) repentance, penitence; (: *pena*) penance; **far penitenza** to do penance **b** (*nei giochi*) forfeit.

penitenziario, ri [peniten'tsjarjo] SM prison, penitentiary (*Am*).

penna ['penna] SF **a** (*di uccello*) feather; **mettere le penne** to grow feathers; **lasciarci** *o* **rimetterci le penne** (*fig*) to get one's fingers burnt ▶ **le penne nere** (*Mil*) *the Italian Alpine troops*

b (*per scrivere*) pen ▶ **penna biro** biro ® (*Brit*), ballpoint (*Am*) ▶ **penna luminosa** *o* **ottica** light pen ▶ **penna d'oca** quill ▶ **penna a sfera** ballpoint pen ▶ **penna stilografica** fountain pen

c (*Culin*): **penne** SFPL quills (*type of pasta*)

d (*Mus*) pick.

pennacchio, chi [pen'nakkjo] SM (*ornamento*) plume; **un pennacchio di fumo** (*fig*) a plume *o* spiral of smoke.

pennarello [penna'rɛllo] SM felt(-tip) pen.

pennellare [pennel'lare] VI (*aus* avere) to paint.

pennellata [pennel'lata] SF (*di vernice*) brush stroke; **dare le ultime pennellate a qc** (*anche fig*) to give the finishing touches to sth.

pennellessa [pennel'lessa] SF pasting brush.

pennello¹ [pen'nɛllo] SM (*gen*) brush; (*di pittore, imbianchino*) (paint)brush; **a pennello** (*perfettamente*) to perfection, perfectly; **quest'abito ti sta a pennello** this dress fits you like a glove ▶ **pennello per la barba** shaving brush.

pennello² [pen'nɛllo] SM (*lungo la costa*) breakwater.

Pennini [pen'nini] SMPL: **i Pennini** the Pennines.

pennino [pen'nino] SM (pen) nib.

pennone [pen'none] SM **a** (*Naut*) yard **b** (*bandiera*) banner, standard.

pennuto, a [pen'nuto] ① AGG feathered.

② SM bird.

penombra [pe'nombra] SF half-light, dim light.

penosamente [penosa'mente] AVV (*vedi agg*) painfully; anxiously; with difficulty, laboriously; pathetically.

penoso, a [pe'noso] AGG (*doloroso: esperienza, compito*) painful, distressing; (*angoscioso: attesa*) anxious; (*faticoso: lavoro, viaggio*) difficult, tiring; (*patetico: scena, scusa*) pathetic; **un penoso silenzio** a painful silence.

pensante [pen'sante] ① AGG thinking.

② SM/F: **ben pensante** = benpensante.

pensare [pen'sare] ① VI (*aus* avere) **a** to think; **pensare a** to think of; (*amico, vacanze*) to think of *o* about; (*problema*) to think about; **a chi stai pensando?** who are you thinking about?; **pensava al tempo passato** he was remembering days gone by; **vorrei pensarci su** I would like to think it over *o* give it some thought; **penso di sì** I think so; **penso di no** I don't think so; **a pensarci bene...** on second thoughts (*Brit*) *o* thought (*Am*) ...; **pensare con la propria testa** to think for o.s.; **pensa a come sarebbe bello** think how lovely it would be; **prima di parlare pensa** think before you speak; **se solo ci avessi pensato** if only I had thought about it; **non voglio nemmeno pensarci** I don't even want to think about it; **ciò mi dà da pensare** that gives me something to think about; **pensare bene/male di qn** to think well/badly of sb, have a good/bad opinion of sb; **ma pensa un po'!** just think of that!

b (*provvedere*): **pensare a qc** to see to sth, take care of sth; **ci penso io** I'll see to *o* take care of it; **ha altro a cui pensare ora** he's got other *o* more important things to think about now; **pensa ai fatti tuoi!** mind your own business!.

② VT **a** (*gen*) to think; **che stai pensando?** what are you thinking?; **cosa ne pensi?** what do you think of it?, how do you feel about it?; **penso che sia colpa sua** I think it is his fault *o* that he is to blame; **ciò mi fa pensare che...** that makes me think that ...; **il suo comportamento farebbe pensare che...** his behaviour would lead you to suppose that ..., his behaviour would make you think that ...; **non avrei mai pensato finisse così** I would never have believed it would end like this; **ti pensavo più furbo** I thought you were smarter than that; **chi l'avrebbe mai pensato?** who would have thought it?; **e pensare che...** and to think that ...

b (*prendere in considerazione*) to realize; **devi pensare che ha appena iniziato** you must realize *o* remember that he's only just started; **non pensa che quello che fa può danneggiare gli altri** he doesn't realize that what he does may harm others

c (*avere intenzione*): **pensare di fare qc** to think of doing sth; **pensavo di invitare anche lui** I was thinking of inviting him too; **penso di partire in serata** I'm thinking of leaving in the course of the evening

d (*inventare, escogitare*) to think out; **ne pensa sempre una nuova** he's always got something new up his sleeve; **l'ha pensata bella** he had a bright idea; **una ne fa e cento ne pensa** he's always up to something.

pensata [pen'sata] SF (*trovata*) idea, thought; **ma che bella pensata!** (*anche iro*) what a good idea!

pensatore, trice [pensa'tore] SM/F thinker.

pensée [pã'se] SF INV (*fiore*) pansy.

pensierino [pensje'rino] SM **a** (*pensiero*): **ci farò un pensierino** I'll think about it **b** (*dono*) little gift.

pensiero [pen'sjɛro] SM **a** thought; **riandare col pensiero a** to remember, think back to; **leggere il pensiero di qn** to read sb's thoughts *o* mind; **essere assorto nei propri pensieri** to be deep *o* lost in thought; **un pensiero gentile** (*anche fig*: *dono*) a kind thought; **libertà di pensiero** freedom of thought

b (*preoccupazione*) worry, care, trouble; **ha tanti pensieri** he has so many worries; **stare in pensiero per qn/qc** to be worried about sb/sth; **darsi pensiero per qc** to worry about sth; **è un tipo senza pensieri** he's a carefree chap

c (*modo di pensare, dottrina*) thinking *no pl*; **il pensiero di Hegel** Hegelian thinking.

pensierosamente [pensjerosa'mente] AVV thoughtfully.

pensieroso, a [pensje'roso] AGG pensive, thoughtful.

pensile ['pɛnsile] AGG hanging, suspended; **giardino pensile** hanging garden.

pensilina [pensi'lina] SF projecting roof; (*di stazione*) platform roof.

pensionabile [pensjo'nabile] AGG pensionable.

pensionamento [pensjona'mento] SM retirement ▶ **pensionamento anticipato** early retirement.

pensionante [pensjo'nante] SM/F (*presso una famiglia*) lodger; (*in albergo*) resident, guest.

pensionato¹ [pensjo'nato] SM (*istituto*: *per studenti*) hostel; (: *per anziani*) rest home.

pensionato², a [pensjo'nato] SM/F pensioner.

pensione [pen'sjone] SF **a** (*rendita*) pension; **andare in pensione** to retire ▶ **pensione di anzianità** old-age pension ▶ **pensione di guerra** war pension ▶ **pensione d'invalidità** disability pension

b (*albergo*) boarding house; (*vitto e alloggio*) board and lodging; **essere a pensione da qn** to board with sb; **tenere a pensione qn** to have sb as a lodger; **mezza pensione** half board ▶ **pensione completa** full board.

pensionistico, a, ci, che [pensjo'nistiko] AGG pension *attr*; **fondo pensionistico** pension fund.

pensosamente [pensosa'mente] AVV thoughtfully, pensively.

pensoso, a [pen'soso] AGG thoughtful, pensive.

pentagonale [pentago'nale] AGG pentagonal.

pentagono [pen'tagono] SM **a** (*Geom*) pentagon **b** (*Pol*): **il Pentagono** the Pentagon.

pentagramma, i [penta'gramma] SM (*Mus*) staff, stave.

pentapartito [pentapar'tito] SM (*Pol*) five-party coalition government.

pentathlon ['pɛntatlon] SM INV pentathlon.

Pentecoste [pente'kɔste] SF Pentecost, Whit Sunday (*Brit*).

pentimento [penti'mento] SM repentance, contrition; (*rimpianto*) regret.

pentirsi [pen'tirsi] VIP (*Rel*) to repent; **pentirsi dei propri peccati** to repent of one's sins; **pentirsi di qc/di aver fatto qc** (*rimpiangere*) to regret sth/doing sth; **se segui i miei consigli, non te ne pentirai** if you follow my advice you won't regret it.

pentitismo [penti'tizmo] SM *practice of turning informer*.

pentito, a [pen'tito] **1** AGG (*gen*: *persona, sguardo ecc*) penitent, repentant.

2 SM/F (*terrorista, mafioso*) ≈ supergrass (*Brit*), *terrorist/criminal who turns police informer*.

pentola ['pentola] SF (*recipiente*) pot; (*contenuto*) pot(ful);

qualcosa bolle in pentola (*fig*) there's something brewing ▶ **pentola a pressione** pressure cooker.

pentolino [pento'lino] SM small saucepan ▶ **pentolino del latte** milk pan.

penultimo, a [pe'nultimo] **1** AGG penultimate, last but one (*Brit*), next to last.

2 SM/F: **il(la) penultimo(a)** the last but one (*Brit*).

penuria [pe'nurja] SF shortage.

penzolare [pendzo'lare] VI (*aus* avere) (*pendere*) to hang loosely, dangle.

penzoloni [pendzo'loni] AVV (*anche*: **a penzoloni**) hanging down, dangling; **se ne stava con le braccia penzoloni** he stood there with his arms dangling.

peonia [pe'ɔnja] SF (*Bot*) peony.

pepare [pe'pare] VT to pepper.

pepato, a [pe'pato] AGG **a** (*condito con pepe*) peppery, hot **b** (*fig*: *pungente*) sharp.

pepe ['pepe] SM pepper; **è tutta pepe** (*fig*) she's full of life ▶ **pepe bianco** white pepper ▶ **pepe della Giamaica** allspice ▶ **pepe in grani** whole pepper, peppercorns ▶ **pepe macinato** ground pepper ▶ **pepe nero** black pepper.

peperonata [pepero'nata] SF (*Culin*) *stewed peppers, tomatoes and onions*.

peperoncino [peperon'tʃino] SM chilli pepper.

peperone [pepe'rone] SM capsicum; **rosso come un peperone** as red as a beetroot (*Brit*) *o* beet (*Am*) ▶ **peperone rosso** red pepper, capsicum ▶ **peperone verde** green pepper, capsicum ▶ **peperoni ripieni** stuffed peppers.

pepiera [pe'pjɛra] SF pepper pot.

pepita [pe'pita] SF nugget.

pepsina [pep'sina] SF pepsin.

peptide [pep'tide] SM peptide.

---

per [per] PREP
a (*direzione*) for, to;
▷ l'*autobus* per Milano the Milan bus, the bus for *o* to Milan
▷ quando *parti* per Parigi? when are you leaving for *o* are you off to Paris?
▷ *proseguire* per Londra to go on to London
b (*verso, nei confronti di*) for, towards;
▷ il suo grande *amore* per la sorella his great love for *o* of his sister
▷ ha una *passione* per la musica he is passionately fond of music
c (*moto attraverso luogo*) through;
▷ l'ho *cercata* per tutta la casa I searched the whole house *o* I searched all over the house for it
▷ ti ho *cercato* per mari e per monti I looked everywhere for you
▷ l'ho *incontrato* per le scale I met him on the stairs
▷ sono *passata* per Roma I came through *o* via Rome
▷ il maestro è *passato* per i banchi the teacher went along the rows of desks
▷ i ladri sono *passati* per la finestra the thieves got in (*o* out) through the window
d (*stato in luogo*): **seduto/sdraiato per** *terra* sitting/lying on the ground
e (*tempo*) for;
▷ per *anni* for years
▷ per tutta l'*estate* all summer long, all through the

summer, throughout the summer
▷**per tutta la *giornata*** all day long
▷**per *giorni* e giorni** for days on end
▷**giorno per *giorno*** day by day
▷**dobbiamo finirlo per *lunedì*** we must get it finished by *o* for Monday
▷**ci rivedremo per *Pasqua*** we'll see one another again at Easter
▷**è piovuto per tutta la *settimana*** it has rained all week long
▷**per molto *tempo*** for a long time
▷**sarò di ritorno per le *tre*** I'll be back by three o'clock
f (*mezzo, maniera*) by;
▷**per *ferrovia*** by rail *o* train
▷**l'ha fatto per *gioco*** he did it as a joke
▷**per *lettera*** by letter
▷**l'ha presa per *mano*** he took her by the hand
▷**chiamare qn per *nome*** to call sb by name
▷**l'ha fatto per *scherzo*** he did it as a joke
▷**non mi piace parlare per *telefono*** I don't like using the phone *o* speaking on the phone
▷**per *via aerea*** by air
▷**per *vie legali*** through legal channels
g (*causa*) for, because of, owing to; (*scopo*) for;
▷**per *abitudine*** out of habit, from habit
▷**è morto per *avvelenamento*** he died from poisoning
▷**le tende per la *cucina*** the kitchen curtains, the curtains for the kitchen
▷**per un *errore*** through *o* by error
▷**per il *freddo*** because of the cold
▷**non stare in pena per *lui*** don't worry about him
▷**pastiglie per il *mal di gola*** throat pastilles *o* lozenges
▷**chiuso per *malattia*** closed because of *o* on account of illness
▷**assentarsi per *malattia*** to be off because of *o* through *o* owing to illness
▷**questo lavoro non fa per *me*** this isn't the right job for me
▷**per *motivi* di salute** for health reasons
▷**condannato per *omicidio*** convicted of murder
▷**non l'ha fatto per *pigrizia*** he didn't do it out of laziness
▷**processato per *rapina* a mano armata** tried for armed robbery
h (*prezzo, misura*) for;
▷**assicurato per 10 milioni** insured for 10 million lire
▷**l'ho *comprato* per un milione** I bought it for a million lire
▷**per *miglia* e miglia non si vedeva nulla** you couldn't see anything for miles
▷**il terreno *si estende* per molti chilometri** the land extends for several kilometres
▷**lo *vendo* per poco** I'm selling it for very little, I'm selling it cheap
i (*limitazione*) for;
▷**è troppo difficile per *lui*** it's too hard for him
▷**per *me* è come una madre** she's like a mother to me
▷**per *quel* che mi riguarda** as far as I'm concerned
▷**per questa *volta* ci passerò sopra** I'll forget about it this time
j (*distributivo*)

▷**un interesse del 5 per *cento*** 5 per cent interest
▷***dividere* 12 per 4** to divide 12 by 4
▷**2 per 3 *fa* 6** 2 times 3 equals 6
▷***in fila* per tre!** line up in threes!
▷***moltiplicare* 9 per 3** to multiply 9 by 3
▷**ce n'è una per *parte*** there's one on each side
▷**duemila lire per *persona*** two thousand lire per person *o* a head *o* apiece
▷**vi interrogo uno per *uno*** I'll question you one by one
▷**entrate uno per *volta*** come in one at a time
k (*in qualità di*) as; (*al posto di*) for;
▷**te lo dico per *certo*** I tell you it's gospel
▷**me l'hanno venduto per *lana*** they sold it to me as (if it were) wool
▷**lo hanno dato per *morto*** he was given up for dead
▷**ha avuto suo padre per *professore*** he had his father as one of his teachers, he was taught by his father
▷**prendere qn per uno *sciocco*** to take sb for a fool
▷**ti ho preso per tuo *fratello*** I (mis)took you for your brother
l (*introduce proposizione finale*) to, in order to;
▷**per *fare* qc** (so as) to do sth, in order to do sth
▷**l'ho fatto per *aiutarti*** I did it to help you
▷**dicevo così per *scherzare*** I said it as a joke *o* in fun
m (*introduce proposizione causale*) for;
▷**per *aver fatto* qc** for doing sth
▷**è stato punito per aver picchiato suo fratello** he was punished for hitting his brother
▷**è morta per aver ingerito troppi barbiturici** she died from *o* of an overdose of barbiturates
n (*introduce proposizione concessiva*)
▷**per *poco* che sia** however little it is *o* it may be, little though it is *o* it may be;
▷**per *quanto* si dia da fare...** however hard he tries ...
▷**per *quanto* io sappia** as far as I know.

pera ['pera] SF **a** pear; **pere cotte** stewed pears; **cadere come una pera cotta** (*fig: innamorarsi*) to fall head over heels in love **b** : **pera di gomma** (*Med: per clistere*) rubber syringe; **c** : **farsi una pera** (*fig fam*) to shoot up.

peraltro [pe'raltro] AVV (*per di più*) moreover, what's more; (*comunque*) however.

perbacco [per'bakko] ESCL by Jove!

perbene [per'bɛne] **1** AGG INV (*ammodo*) respectable, decent.
2 AVV (*con cura*) well, properly.

perbenismo [perbe'nizmo] SM (so-called) respectability.

perbenistico, a, ci, che [perbe'nistiko] AGG supposedly respectable.

perborato [perbo'rato] SM perborate.

perca, che ['pɛrka] SF perch (*fish*).

percalle [per'kalle] SM percale.

percento [per'tʃɛnto] **1** SM INV percentage.
2 AVV: **il cinque percento** five percent.

percentuale [pertʃentu'ale] **1** AGG percentage *attr*.
2 SF percentage; (*provvigione*) commission; **percepisce una percentuale del 20% su ciò che vende** he receives a commission of 20% on what he sells.

percepire [pertʃe'pire] VT **a** (*sentire, intuire*) to perceive **b** (*ricevere: somma, compenso*) to receive.

percettibile [pertʃet'tibile] AGG perceptible; **un suono**

appena percettibile a barely audible sound.
percettibilità [pertʃettibili'ta] SF perceptibility.
percezione [pertʃet'tsjone] SF perception.

perché [per'ke] **1** AVV why; **perché no?** why not?; **perché non vuoi andarci?** why don't you want to go?; **spiegami perché l'hai fatto** tell me why you did it; **vorrei sapere perché non te ne vai** I'd like to know why you don't leave.

2 CONG **a** (causale: poiché) because; **non posso uscire perché ho da fare** I can't go out because o as I've a lot to do

b (finale: affinché) so (that), in order that; **te lo do perché tu lo legga** I'm giving it to you so you can read it

c (consecutivo: cosicché): **l'ostacolo era troppo alto perché si potesse scavalcarlo** the obstacle was too high to climb over; **è troppo forte perché si possa vincerlo** he's too strong to be beaten o for anyone to beat him.

3 SM INV (motivo) reason; **non c'è un vero perché** there's no real reason for it; **vorrei sapere il perché di un simile atteggiamento da parte sua** I'd like to know the reason for his attitude; **i perché sono tanti** there are many reasons for it; **voglio sapere il perché e il percome** I want to know the whys and wherefores.

perciò [per'tʃɔ] CONG therefore, so, for this (o that) reason.

percome [per'kome] SM INV: **il perché e il percome** the whys and wherefores.

percorrere [per'korrere] VT IRREG (distanza, circuito, territorio) to cover; (strada) to follow; (luogo) to go all over; (paese) to travel up and down, go all over; **percorrere un paese in lungo e in largo** to travel all over a country.

percorribile [perkor'ribile] AGG (strada) which can be followed.

percorso, a [per'korso] **1** PP di **percorrere**.

2 SM (distanza) distance; (tragitto) journey; (itinerario) route; (Sport) course ▶ **percorso netto** (Ippica) clear round ▶ **percorso obbligato** (Sport) set course.

percossa [per'kɔssa] SF blow.

percosso, a [per'kɔsso] PP di **percuotere**.

percuotere [per'kwɔtere] VT IRREG (gen) to beat, hit, strike; **percuotersi il petto** to beat one's breast.

percussione [perkus'sjone] SF percussion; **strumenti a percussione** (Mus) percussion instruments.

percussore [perkus'sore] SM (in armi) hammer.

perdente [per'dɛnte] **1** AGG losing.

2 SM/F loser.

perdere ['pɛrdere] VB IRREG **1** VT **a** (gen) to lose; (abitudine) to get out of; **perdere di vista qn** (anche fig) to lose sight of sb; **perdere la speranza/l'appetito/la vista** to lose hope/one's appetite/one's sight; **perdere i capelli** to lose one's hair, go bald; **gli albèri perdono le foglie** the trees are losing o shedding their leaves; **perdere al gioco** to lose money gambling; **saper perdere** to be a good loser; **lascia perdere!** (non insistere) forget it!, never mind!; (non ascoltarlo) don't listen to him!; **non ho niente da perdere** I've got nothing to lose

b (lasciar sfuggire: treno, autobus) to miss; **è un'occasione da non perdere** it's a marvellous opportunity; (affare) it's a great bargain

c (sprecare: tempo, danaro) to waste; **ho perso l'intera giornata a cercarlo** I wasted the whole day looking for it; **è fatica persa** it's a waste of effort

d (lasciar uscire: sangue) to lose; **il rubinetto perde** (acqua) the tap is leaking; **la stufa perde gas** the gas fire is leaking

e (rimetterci): **hanno alzato i prezzi per non perderci** they put up their prices so as not to make a loss; **non hai perso niente a non vedere quel film** you haven't missed anything by not seeing that film; **ci perdi a non venire** you are missing out by not coming.

2 VI (aus avere): **perdere di** (diminuire): **perdere di autorità/importanza** to lose authority/importance; **perdere di valore** to go down in value.

3 **perdersi** VIP **a** (smarrirsi) to lose one's way, get lost; **perdersi in un bicchiere d'acqua** to be unable to cope with the slightest problem; **perdersi in chiacchiere** to waste time talking; **perdersi dietro a qn** to waste one's time with o on sb; **non perderti in queste sciocchezze** don't waste your time with this nonsense

b (scomparire: oggetto) to disappear, vanish; (: suono) to fade away; **perdersi alla vista** to disappear from sight

c (uso reciproco): **perdersi di vista** to lose sight of each other; (fig) to lose touch.

perdifiato [perdi'fjato]: **a perdifiato** AVV (correre) at breathtaking speed; (gridare) at the top of one's voice.

perdigiorno [perdi'dʒorno] SM/F INV idler, loafer, waster.

perdimento [perdi'mento] SM (fig) perdition, damnation.

perdinci [per'dintʃi] ESCL (euf: con impazienza) for goodness' sake!; (: con meraviglia) golly!, crikey! (Brit).

perdio [per'dio] ESCL (con impazienza) for God's sake!; (con meraviglia) good God!

perdita ['pɛrdita] SF **a** (gen) loss; (di persona: morte) loss, death; **è una grave perdita** it's a great loss; **a perdita d'occhio** as far as the eye can see

b (Econ) loss, deficit; **siamo in perdita** we are running at a loss

c (spreco) waste; **è una perdita di tempo** it's a waste of time

d (spandimento: di rubinetto) leak; (: di sangue) loss; **le perdite bianche** (Med) the whites.

perditempo [perdi'tɛmpo] SM/F INV waster, idler.

perdizione [perdit'tsjone] SF (Rel) perdition, damnation; **luogo di perdizione** place of ill repute.

perdonabile [perdo'nabile] AGG pardonable, forgivable.

perdonare [perdo'nare] **1** VT **a** to forgive, pardon; **perdonare a qn qc/di aver fatto qc** to forgive sb (for) sth/for doing o having done sth; **mi perdoni?** will you forgive me?; **le ha comprato dei fiori per farsi perdonare** he bought her flowers as a peace offering; **non gliel'ha mai perdonata** he has never forgiven him for that; **non me lo perdonerò mai** I'll never forgive myself

b (scusare) to excuse, pardon; **perdona la domanda** if you don't mind my asking ...; **vogliate perdonare il (mio) ritardo** my apologies for being late; **perdona la mia ignoranza** forgive my ignorance; **bisogna perdonare la sua giovane età** you must make allowances for his youth.

2 VI (aus avere) to forgive; **un male che non perdona** an incurable disease; **un uomo che non perdona** an unforgiving man.

perdono [per'dono] SM (gen) forgiveness; **chiedere perdono a qn (per)** to ask for sb's forgiveness (for); (scusarsi) to apologize to sb (for); **l'ho urtata? chiedo perdono** was that you I hit? I do beg your pardon o I do apologize ▶ **perdono giudiziale** (Dir) pardon.

perdurare [perdu'rare] VI (aus avere; nel senso di perseverare essere) (continuare) to go on, last; (perseverare) to persist; **il cattivo tempo perdura** the bad weather continues; **perdurare nei propositi di vendetta** to

persist in seeking revenge.

perdutamente [perduta'mente] AVV desperately, passionately; **amare perdutamente qn** to be desperately in love with sb.

perduto, a [per'duto] ① PP di **perdere**.
② AGG (*gen*) lost; **sentirsi** *o* **vedersi perduto** (*fig*) to realize the hopelessness of one's position; **una donna perduta** (*fig*) a fallen woman.

peregrinare [peregri'nare] VI (*aus* avere) to wander, roam.

peregrinazione [peregrinat'tsjone] SF (*anche fig*) peregrination.

perenne [pe'rɛnne] AGG (*Bot*) perennial; (*gloria, ricordo*) everlasting; **nevi perenni** perpetual snow *sg*.

perennemente [perenne'mente] AVV perpetually; **un monumento che ricorderà perennemente i caduti** a monument to the eternal memory of those who died in the war.

perentoriamente [perentorja'mente] AVV peremptorily.

perentorio, ria, ri, rie [peren'tɔrjo] AGG (*tono, ordine*) peremptory; (*definitivo*) final.

perequazione [perekwat'tsjone] SF (*Amm*) equal distribution.

perestrojka [peres'trɔika] SF (*Pol*) perestroika.

perfettamente [perfetta'mente] AVV perfectly; **sai perfettamente che...** you know perfectly well that ... .

perfettibile [perfet'tibile] AGG perfectible.

perfetto, a [per'fetto] ① AGG (*gen*) perfect; (*silenzio, accordo*) complete, total; **è un perfetto cretino** he's an utter *o* a perfect idiot.
② SM (*Gramm*) perfect (tense).

perfezionamento [perfettsjona'mento] SM (*vedi vb*): **perfezionamento (di)** perfection (of); improvement (in); **corso di perfezionamento** proficiency course.

perfezionare [perfettsjo'nare] ① VT (*rendere perfetto*) to perfect; (*migliorare*) to improve.
② **perfezionarsi** VIP (*tecnica*) to improve; **perfezionarsi in inglese** to improve one's English.

perfezione [perfet'tsjone] SF perfection; **alla** *o* **a perfezione** to perfection.

perfezionismo [perfettsjo'nizmo] SM perfectionism.

perfezionista, i, e [perfettsjo'nista] SM/F perfectionist.

perfidamente [perfida'mente] AVV perfidiously.

perfidia [per'fidja] SF perfidy.

perfido, a [ˈpɛrfido] AGG perfidious, treacherous.

perfino [per'fino] AVV even; **perfino lui si è commosso** even he was moved; **è un peccato perfino pensarlo** you should be ashamed to even think of such a thing.

perforare [perfo'rare] VT (*gen*) to pierce; (*banda, schede*) to punch; (*trivellare*) to drill; (*Med*) to perforate; **ulcera perforata** (*Med*) perforated ulcer.

perforatore, trice [perfora'tore] ① SM/F (*Inform: persona*) punch-card operator.
② SM (*macchina*) punch ▸**perforatore di schede** (*Inform*) card punch.
③ SF (*Tecn*) boring *o* drilling machine; (*Inform*) card punch.

perforazione [perforat'tsjone] SF a (*di sottosuolo*) boring, drilling; (*Inform: atto*) punching; (: *foro*) punch b (*Med*) perforation.

pergamena [perga'mɛna] SF parchment.

pergola [ˈpɛrgola] SF, **pergolato** [pergo'lato] SM pergola.

pericolante [perikoˈlante] AGG (*muro, edificio*) unsafe; (*fig: economia*) shaky, precarious.

pericolo [pe'rikolo] SM danger; **essere/trovarsi in pericolo** to be/find o.s. in danger; **mettere in pericolo** to endanger, put in danger; **essere fuori pericolo** to be out of danger; (*Med*) to be off the danger list; **"pericolo di morte"** (*su centralina elettrica*) ≈ "danger: high voltage"; **è un pericolo pubblico** (*fig: persona*) he's a public menace; **non c'è pericolo che rifiuti** (*iro*) there's no chance of his refusing, there's no fear that he'll refuse.

pericolosamente [perikolosa'mente] AVV dangerously.

pericolosità [perikolosi'ta] SF (*gen*) danger; **bisogna tener presente la pericolosità di questo criminale** we must bear in mind how dangerous this criminal is.

pericoloso, a [periko'loso] AGG (*gen*) dangerous; (*impresa*) hazardous, risky; **zona pericolosa** danger zone.

periferia [perife'ria] SF (*anche fig*) periphery; (*di città*) outskirts *pl*, suburbs *pl*; **vivere in periferia** to live on the outskirts *o* in the suburbs.

perifericamente [periferika'mente] AVV peripherally.

periferico, a, ci, che [peri'fɛriko] AGG (*Anat, Inform*) peripheral; (*zona*) outlying.

perifrasi [pe'rifrazi] SF INV circumlocution.

perimetrale [perime'trale] AGG (*misura*) perimetral; (*muro*) perimeter *attr*.

perimetro [pe'rimetro] SM (*gen, Mat*) perimeter.

periodicamente [periodika'mente] AVV periodically.

periodico, a, ci, che [peri'ɔdiko] ① AGG periodic(al); (*Mat*) recurring. ② SM (*pubblicazione*) periodical.

periodo [pe'riodo] SM (*gen*) period; **durante il periodo elettorale** at election time; **durante il periodo estivo** during the summer (period) ▸**periodo contabile** accounting period ▸**periodo di prova** trial period.

peripatetica, che [peripa'tɛtika] SF (*euf: prostituta*) streetwalker.

peripezie [peripet'tsie] SFPL vicissitudes, ups and downs.

periplo [ˈperiplo] SM circumnavigation.

perire [pe'rire] VI (*aus* essere) to perish, die.

periscopio, pi [peris'kɔpjo] SM periscope.

peristalsi [peris'talsi] SF INV peristalsis.

perito, a [pe'rito] ① SM (*esperto*) expert; (: *Edil, Agr, Naut*) surveyor; (: *Assicurazioni*) loss adjuster; **è perito chimico/agrario** (*Scol*) he has a qualification *o* diploma in chemistry/agriculture.
② AGG expert, skilled.

peritonite [perito'nite] SF peritonitis.

perizia [pe'rittsja] SF a (*maestria*) skill, ability; **un lavoro fatto con perizia** a skilful piece of work b (*Dir: giudizio tecnico*) expert opinion; (: *scritto*) expert's report; (*stima*) appraisal, valuation ▸**perizia psichiatrica** psychiatrist's report.

perizoma, i [perid'dzɔma] SM loincloth.

perla [ˈpɛrla] ① SF pearl; **una collana di perle** a pearl necklace; **Venezia, la perla dell'Adriatico** Venice, the jewel of the Adriatic; **una perla di marito** a gem of a husband ▸**perla coltivata** cultured pearl.
② AGG INV (*colore*) pearl *attr*; **grigio perla** pearl grey.

perlaceo, a [per'latʃeo] AGG pearly.

perlaquale [perla'kwale] (*fam*) ① AGG INV (*perbene*) respectable; **è un tipo poco perlaquale** he is not to be trusted.
② AVV (*bene*): **oggi non mi sento troppo perlaquale** I don't feel quite right today.

perlifero, a [per'lifero] AGG: **ostrica perlifera** pearl oyster.

perlina [per'lina] SF bead.

perlinato [perli'nato] SM matchboarding.

perlomeno [perlo'meno] AVV (*almeno*) at least.

perlopiù [perlo'pju] AVV (*quasi sempre*) in most cases, usually.

perlustrare [perlus'trare] VT to patrol, reconnoitre.

perlustrazione [perlustrat'tsjone] SF patrol, reconnaissance; **andare in perlustrazione** to go on patrol.

permalosità [permalosi'ta] SF touchiness.

permaloso, a [perma'loso] 1 AGG touchy.
2 SM/F touchy person.

permanente [perma'nɛnte] 1 AGG (*gen*) permanent; (*esercito, commissione*) standing.
2 SF (*acconciatura*) permanent wave, perm.

permanentemente [permanente'mente] AVV permanently.

permanenza [perma'nɛntsa] SF a (*presenza continua*) permanence b (*soggiorno*) stay, sojourn; **buona permanenza!** enjoy your stay!

permanere [perma'nere] VI IRREG (*aus essere*) (*rimanere*) to remain; **il cattivo tempo permane sulla Scozia** the bad weather conditions persist over Scotland.

permanganato [permanga'nato] SM permanganate ▶ **permanganato di potassio** potassium permanganate.

permango *ecc* [per'mango] VB *vedi* **permanere**.

permasi *ecc* [per'masi] VB *vedi* **permanere**.

permeabile [perme'abile] AGG permeable.

permeabilità [permeabili'ta] SF permeability.

permeare [perme'are] VT (*anche fig*): **permeare (di)** to permeate (with).

permesso, a [per'messo] 1 PP di **permettere**.
2 SM a (*autorizzazione*) permission; **chiedere il permesso di fare qc** to ask permission to do sth b (*Amm, Mil*) leave (of absence); **andare in permesso** to go on leave c (*documento*) permit, licence (*Brit*), license (*Am*); (: *Mil*) pass ▶ **permesso di lavoro** work permit ▶ **permesso di soggiorno** residence permit.

permettere [per'mettere] VT IRREG a (*gen, consentire*) to allow, permit; **permettere a qn di fare qc** (*autorizzare*) to allow o permit sb to do sth, let sb do sth; (*dare la possibilità*) to enable sb to do sth; (*dare il diritto*) to entitle sb to do sth; **crede che tutto gli sia permesso** he thinks he can do just as he likes; **i miei impegni non me lo permettono** I'm too busy to be able to do it; **ci andremo, tempo permettendo** we'll go, weather permitting; **non permetto che mi si tratti così** I will not tolerate being treated in this way
b : **permettersi qc/di fare qc** (*concedersi*) to allow o.s. sth/to do sth; (*avere la possibilità*) to afford sth/to do sth; **non possono permettersi una casa più grande** they can't afford a bigger house; **non posso permettermi di perdere neanche un minuto** I can't afford to waste a minute; **sai cosa si è permessa di dire?** do you know what she dared to say?
c (*fraseologia*): **è permesso?** (*posso entrare?*) may I come in?; **scusi, permesso...** (*posso passare?*) excuse me, can I get by o past?; **se permetti avrei un'obiezione** if you don't mind I have an objection to raise; **mi sia permesso di sottolineare che...** may I take the liberty of pointing out that ...; **permettete che mi presenti** let me introduce myself, may I introduce myself?

permisi *ecc* [per'mizi] VB *vedi* **permettere**.

permissivismo [permissi'vizmo] SM (*atteggiamento*) permissiveness.

permissività [permissivi'ta] SF (*qualità*) permissiveness.

permissivo, a [permis'sivo] AGG permissive.

permuta ['pɛrmuta] SF (*Dir*) transfer; **valore di permuta** (*di macchina*) trade-in value; **accettare qc in permuta** to take sth as a trade-in.

permutare [permu'tare] VT to exchange; (*Mat*) to permute.

pernacchia [per'nakkja] SF (*fam*) raspberry; **fare una pernacchia** to blow a raspberry.

pernice [per'nitʃe] SF partridge ▶ **pernice bianca** ptarmigan.

pernicioso, a [perni'tʃoso] AGG pernicious.

perno ['pɛrno] SM (*anche fig*) pivot; **fare perno su qc** to pivot on sth.

pernottamento [pernotta'mento] SM overnight stay.

pernottare [pernot'tare] VI (*aus avere*) to spend the night, stay overnight.

pero ['pero] SM (*Bot*) pear (tree).

però [pe'rɔ] CONG (*ma*) (and) yet, but (nevertheless); (*tuttavia*) nevertheless, however; **però non è giusto che...** and yet o but nevertheless it's not fair that ...; **però avresti potuto dirmelo** you could have told me nevertheless; **sono stanco, non tanto però da non poter finire** I'm tired, but not so tired as not to be able to finish.

perorare [pero'rare] VT (*Dir, fig*): **perorare la causa di qn** to plead sb's case.

perossido [pe'rɔssido] SM peroxide.

perpendicolare [perpendiko'lare] 1 AGG perpendicular.
2 SF (*Mat*) perpendicular (line).

perpendicolarmente [perpendikolar'mente] AVV perpendicularly.

perpendicolo [perpen'dikolo] SM: **a perpendicolo** perpendicularly.

perpetrare [perpe'trare] VT to perpetrate, commit.

perpetua [per'pɛtua] SF priest's housekeeper.

perpetuamente [perpetua'mente] AVV perpetually.

perpetuare [perpetu'are] VT to perpetuate.

perpetuo, a [per'pɛtuo] AGG (*gen*) perpetual; (*rendita*) life *attr*.

perplessamente [perplessa'mente] AVV in o with perplexity, with puzzlement.

perplessità [perplessi'ta] SF INV perplexity.

perplesso, a [per'plɛsso] AGG perplexed, puzzled; **lasciare qn perplesso** to perplex o puzzle sb.

perquisire [perkwi'zire] VT to search.

perquisizione [perkwizit'tsjone] SF search; **mandato di perquisizione** search warrant; **fare una perquisizione (di)** to carry out a search (of).

persecutore, trice [perseku'tore] SM/F persecutor.

persecuzione [persekut'tsjone] SF persecution; **mania di persecuzione** (*Psic*) persecution complex.

Persefone [per'sefone] SF Persephone.

perseguibile [perse'gwibile] AGG (*reato*) prosecutable.

perseguire [perse'gwire] VT a (*scopo, intento*) to pursue b (*Dir*) to prosecute.

perseguitare [persegwi'tare] VT (*anche fig*) to persecute; **essere perseguitato dalla sfortuna** to be dogged by ill luck.

perseguitato, a [persegwi'tato] SM/F victim of persecution.

Perseo [per'sɛo] SM Perseus.

perseverante [perseve'rante] AGG persevering.

perseveranza [perseve'rantsa] SF perseverance.

perseverare [perseve'rare] VI (*aus* avere) to persevere; **perseverare in qc/nel fare qc** to persevere in sth/in doing sth.

persi *ecc* ['pɛrsi] VB vedi **perdere**.

Persia ['pɛrsja] SF: **la Persia** Persia.

persiana [per'sjana] SF shutter ▶**persiana avvolgibile** roller shutter.

persiano, a [per'sjano] ☐1 AGG, SM/F Persian. ☐2 SM **a** (*lingua*) Persian **b** (*Zool*: *gatto*) Persian (cat) **c** (*pelliccia*) Persian lamb.

persico, a, ci, che ['pɛrsiko] AGG: **il golfo Persico** the Persian Gulf; **pesce persico** perch.

persino [per'sino] AVV = **perfino**.

persistente [persis'tɛnte] AGG persistent.

persistentemente [persistente'mente] AVV persistently.

persistenza [persis'tɛntsa] SF persistence.

persistere [per'sistere] VI IRREG (*aus* avere) to persist; **persistere in qc/a fare qc** to persist in sth/in doing sth; **persiste nella sua opinione** he is sticking to his opinion.

persistito, a [persis'tito] PP di **persistere**.

perso, a ['pɛrso] ☐1 PP di **perdere**. ☐2 AGG (*smarrito*: *anche fig*) lost; (*sprecato*) wasted; **questo è tempo perso** this is a waste of time; **fare qc a tempo perso** to do sth in one's spare time; **perso per perso** I've (*o* we've *ecc*) got nothing left *o* more to lose; **dare per perso** to give up for lost.

persona [per'sona] SF **a** (*essere umano*) person; **persone** SFPL people *pl*; **tre persone** three people *o* persons (*Am*); **per persona** (*a testa*) per head *o* person; **per interposta persona** through a third party *o* an intermediary ▶**persona giuridica** (*Dir*) legal person ▶**persona di servizio** domestic servant

b (*corpo*): **aver cura della propria persona** to look after o.s.; **in persona** ☐OR☐ **di persona** in person; **ci andrò di persona** I'll go there personally *o* in person; **è l'onestà in persona** he is honesty personified

c (*Gramm*) person; **alla terza persona singolare** in the third person singular; **vivere qc in prima persona** (*fig*) to experience sth personally

d (*qualcuno*): **una persona** somebody, someone; **c'era una persona che ti cercava** somebody was looking for you.

personaggio, gi [perso'naddʒo] SM **a** (*celebrità*) personage; (*persona ragguardevole*) personality; (*scherz*: *individuo*) character, individual **b** (*di romanzo*) character; (*di quadro*) figure.

personale [perso'nale] ☐1 AGG personal. ☐2 SF (*mostra*) one-man (*o* one-woman) exhibition. ☐3 SM **a** (*complesso di dipendenti*) personnel, staff ▶**personale di terra** (*Aer*) ground personnel **b** (*corpo, figura*) build; **quella ragazza ha un bel personale** that girl's got a lovely figure.

personalità [personali'ta] SF INV (*gen*) personality ▶**personalità giuridica** (*Dir*) legal status ▶**personalità multipla** (*Psic*) multiple personality.

personalizzare [personalid'dzare] VT (*arredamento, stile*) to personalize; (*auto, accessorio*) to customize.

personalizzato, a [personalid'dzato] AGG (*vedi vb*) personalized; customized.

personalmente [personal'mente] AVV personally.

personificare [personifi'kare] VT (*rappresentare*) to personify; (*simboleggiare*) to embody.

personificazione [personifikat'tsjone] SF (*vedi vb*) personification; embodiment; **essere la personificazione**

della gentilezza to be kindness itself.

perspicace [perspi'katʃe] AGG discerning, shrewd.

perspicacemente [perspikatʃe'mente] AVV perspicaciously, shrewdly.

perspicacia [perspi'katʃa] SF perspicacity, shrewdness.

persuadere [persua'dere] VB IRREG ☐1 VT to persuade, convince; **persuadere qn di qc/a fare qc** to persuade *o* convince sb of sth/to do sth; **lasciarsi persuadere** to let o.s. be convinced; **ne sono persuaso** I'm quite sure *o* convinced (of it). ☐2 **persuadersi** VR to convince o.s.

persuasione [persua'zjone] SF (*gen*) persuasion; (*credenza*) conviction, belief.

persuasivamente [persuaziva'mente] AVV persuasively.

persuasivo, a [persua'zivo] AGG persuasive, convincing.

persuaso, a [persu'azo] PP di **persuadere**.

persuasore [persua'zore] SM: **persuasori occulti** hidden persuaders.

pertanto [per'tanto] CONG (*quindi*) therefore, so.

pertica, che ['pɛrtika] SF (*bastone*) pole, rod; (*Sport*) pole; (*fig*: *persona alta e magra*) beanpole.

pertinace [perti'natʃe] AGG pertinacious.

pertinacemente [pertinatʃe'mente] AVV pertinaciously.

pertinacia [perti'natʃa] SF pertinacity.

pertinente [perti'nɛnte] AGG: **pertinente (a)** pertinent (to), relevant (to).

pertinenza [perti'nɛntsa] SF **a** (*attinenza*) pertinence, relevance **b** (*competenza*): **essere di pertinenza di qn** to be sb's business; **è di pertinenza del tribunale di Napoli** it comes under the jurisdiction of the Naples courts.

pertosse [per'tosse] SF (*Med*) whooping cough.

pertugio, gi [per'tudʒo] SM opening, hole.

perturbare [pertur'bare] ☐1 VT (*persona*) to upset, disturb, perturb. ☐2 **perturbarsi** VIP to become *o* get upset.

perturbazione [perturbat'tsjone] SF (*Meteor, Astron*) disturbance.

Perù [pe'ru] SM: **il Perù** Peru.

perugino, a [peru'dʒino] ☐1 AGG of *o* from Perugia. ☐2 SM/F inhabitant *o* native of Perugia.

peruviano, a [peru'vjano] AGG, SM/F Peruvian.

pervadere [per'vadere] VT IRREG to pervade, permeate.

pervaso, a [per'vazo] PP di **pervadere**.

pervenire [perve'nire] VI IRREG (*aus* essere) **a** : **pervenire a** to reach, arrive at, come to; **far pervenire qc a qn** to have sth sent to sb; **ci sono pervenute migliaia di lettere** we have received thousands of letters **b** (*venire in possesso*): **gli pervenne una fortuna** he inherited a fortune.

pervenuto, a [perve'nuto] PP di **pervenire**.

perversamente [perversa'mente] AVV in a perverted fashion.

perversione [perver'sjone] SF perversion.

perversità [perversi'ta] SF INV perversity.

perverso, a [per'vɛrso] AGG perverted.

pervertire [perver'tire] VT to pervert.

pervertito, a [perver'tito] ☐1 AGG perverted. ☐2 SM/F pervert.

pervicace [pervi'katʃe] AGG stubborn, obstinate.

pervicacia [pervi'katʃa] SF stubbornness, obstinacy.

pervinca, che [per'vinka] ☐1 SF (*Bot*) periwinkle. ☐2 SM INV (*colore*) periwinkle (blue).

p.es. ABBR (= *per esempio*) e.g.

pesa ['pesa] SF (*azione*) weighing *no pl*; (*luogo*) weigh-

house; (*apparecchiatura: per merci*) weighing machine; (: *per autoveicoli*) weighbridge; (: *per animali*) cattle-weighing platform.

pesalettere [pesa'lɛttere] SM INV letter scales *pl.*

pesante [pe'sante] AGG (*gen*) heavy; (*cibo*) heavy, rich; (*sonno*) heavy, deep; (*droga*) hard; (*fig: stile*) ponderous; (: *battuta*) crass; (*noioso: conferenza*) dull, boring; (: *persona*) tedious, boring; **questo libro è pesante** (*fig*) this book is heavy going; **il film era un po' pesante** I found the film rather heavy going; **ho gli occhi pesanti** I can't keep my eyes open; **è andata giù pesante** (*ha esagerato*) she was rather heavy-handed; **avere l'alito pesante** to have bad breath; **atletica pesante** weight-lifting and wrestling; **gioco pesante** (*Sport*) physical game; **terreno pesante** (*Sport: per pioggia*) waterlogged pitch.

pesantemente [pesante'mente] AVV heavily; **ripercuotersi pesantemente su** (*situazione*) to have grave consequences for; **ha scherzato pesantemente** he went too far with his jokes.

pesantezza [pesan'tettsa] SF (*anche fig*) heaviness; **avere pesantezza di stomaco** to feel bloated.

pesapersone [pesaper'sone] AGG INV, SF INV: (**bilancia**) **pesapersone** (weighing) scales *pl*; (*automatica*) weighing machine.

pesare [pe'sare] [1] VT to weigh; (*fig: valutare*) to weigh (up); **pesare i pro e i contro** to weigh up the pros and cons; **pesare le parole** to weigh one's words.

[2] VI (*aus* avere) **a** (*avere un peso*) to weigh; (*essere pesante*) to be heavy; (*fig*) to carry weight; **quanto pesi?** how much do you weigh?; **come pesa!** how heavy it is!; **pesare sulla coscienza/sullo stomaco** to lie heavy on one's conscience/on one's stomach; **tutta la responsabilità pesa su di lui** all the responsibility rests on his shoulders; **la responsabilità gli pesa** the responsibility weighs heavy on him; **ha sempre pesato sui genitori** he has always been dependent on his parents; **i figli pesano notevolmente sul bilancio familiare** children weigh heavily on the family budget; **è molto gentile ma lo fa pesare** he is very kind but he makes sure it doesn't go unnoticed; **le ha sempre fatto pesare il fatto che viene da una famiglia povera** he has always made her aware of her humble origins

b (*dispiacere*): **mi pesa partire** I don't want to leave; **mi pesa dirti di no** I regret having to say no to you; **mi pesa sgridarlo** I find it hard to scold him; **è una situazione che mi pesa** it's a difficult situation for me

c (*contare*) to carry weight, count; **il suo parere pesa molto** his opinion counts for a lot *o* carries a lot of weight.

pesatura [pesa'tura] SF weighing.

pesca[1], **sche** [ˈpɛska] SF (*frutto*) peach.

pesca[2] [ˈpeska] SF **a** (*Sport*) fishing; **andare a pesca** to go fishing ▶**pesca con la lenza** angling ▶**pesca subacquea** underwater fishing **b** (*pesce pescato*) catch; **avete fatto una buona pesca?** did you get a good catch? **c** (*lotteria*): **pesca di beneficenza** lucky dip.

pescaggio, gi [pes'kaddʒo] SM (*Naut*) draught (*Brit*), draft (*Am*).

pescare [pes'kare] [1] VT (*essere pescatore di*) to fish for; (*prendere*) to catch; (: *molluschi*) to gather; (*recuperare qc nell'acqua*) to fish out; (*fig: trovare*) to get hold of, find; **pescare nel torbido** (*fig*) to fish in troubled waters; **ma dove le vai a pescare queste idee?** where on earth do you get hold of such ideas?; **dove hai pescato questo cappello?** where on earth did you get that hat?; **l'hanno pescato con le mani nel sacco** they caught him red-handed. [2] VI (*aus* avere) (*Naut*) to draw.

pescatore [peska'tore] SM fisherman; (*con lenza*) angler; **un paesino di pescatori** a fishing village.

pesce [ˈpeʃʃe] [1] SM **a** fish *gen inv*; **c'erano molti pesci** there were a lot of fish *o* fishes; **ti piace il pesce?** do you like fish?

b (*Astrol*): **Pesci** SMPL Pisces; **essere dei Pesci** to be Pisces

c (*Tip*) omission

d (*fraseologia*): **sano come un pesce** as fit as a fiddle; **buttarsi a pesce su un'offerta** to jump at an offer; **sentirsi un pesce fuor d'acqua** to feel like a fish out of water; **prendere qn a pesci in faccia** to treat sb like dirt; **non saper che pesci prendere** not to know which way to turn; **hanno preso solo i pesci piccoli** they only caught the small fry; **chi dorme non piglia pesci** (*Proverbio*) the early bird catches the worm.

[2] ▶**pesce d'aprile** April Fool ▶**pesce azzurro** mackerel, sardines and anchovies ▶**pesce gatto** catfish ▶**pesce martello** hammerhead ▶**pesce ragno** weever ▶**pesce rosso** goldfish ▶**pesce spada** swordfish.

pescecane [peʃʃe'kane] SM (*pl* pescecani *o* pescicani) (*Zool*) shark; (*fig: profittatore*) shark, profiteer.

peschereccio, a, ci, ce [peske'rettʃo] SM fishing boat.

pescheria [peske'ria] SF fishmonger's (shop) (*Brit*), fish shop.

pescherò ecc [peske'rɔ] VB vedi **pescare**.

peschiera [pes'kjɛra] SF fish farm, fishery.

pesciera [peʃ'ʃɛra] SF fish kettle.

pescivendolo, a [peʃʃi'vendolo] SM/F fishmonger (*Brit*), fish merchant (*Am*); (*negozio*) fishmonger's (shop) (*Brit*), fish shop (*Am*).

pesco, schi [ˈpesko] SM (*Bot*) peach (tree).

pescoso, a [pes'koso] AGG teeming with fish.

peseta [pe'zɛta] SF peseta.

pesista, i, e [pe'sista] SM/F (*Sport*) weightlifter.

peso [ˈpeso] [1] SM **a** (*gen*) weight; **comprare a peso** to buy by weight; **rubare sul peso** to give short weight; **eccesso di peso** excess weight; **metter su peso** to put on weight; **piegarsi sotto il peso di** (*sogg: trave*) to bend under the weight of; **lo portarono via di peso** they carried him away bodily; **avere due pesi e due misure** (*fig*) to have double standards ▶**peso lordo** gross weight ▶**peso morto** dead load *o* weight ▶**peso netto** net weight ▶**peso specifico** (*Fis*) specific gravity

b (*fig: onere*) weight; **il peso degli anni** the weight of years; **avere un peso sullo stomaco** to have something lying heavy on one's stomach; **mi sono liberato di un peso** (*preoccupazione*) that's a load off my mind; **togliersi un peso dalla coscienza** to take a load off one's conscience; **essere di peso a qn** to be a burden to sb; **piegarsi sotto il peso di** (*dispiaceri, problemi*) to be weighed down by

c (*fig: importanza*) weight, importance; **una questione di un certo peso** a matter of some weight *o* importance; **dar peso a qc** to attach importance to sth

d (*Sport*) shot; **lancio del peso** putting the shot; **sollevamento pesi** weightlifting ▶**peso gallo** bantamweight ▶**peso massimo** heavyweight ▶**peso medio** middleweight ▶**peso mosca** flyweight ▶**peso piuma**

featherweight.

pessimismo [pessi'mizmo] SM pessimism.

pessimista, i, e [pessi'mista] [1] AGG pessimistic.
[2] SM/F pessimist.

pessimisticamente [pessimistika'mente] AVV pessimistically; **vedere le cose pessimisticamente** to look at things pessimistically.

pessimistico, a, ci, che [pessi'mistiko] AGG pessimistic.

pessimo, a ['pɛssimo] AGG (superl di cattivo) **a** (gen) awful, dreadful, very bad; **abbiamo fatto un pessimo viaggio** we had a dreadful o an awful o an appalling journey; **c'è un pessimo odore in questa stanza** there's an awful o a dreadful smell in this room; **ha fatto un tempo pessimo** the weather has been dreadful; **è un pessimo insegnante** he is a very poor teacher; **di pessima qualità** of very poor quality, very shoddy; **essere di pessimo umore** to be in a foul mood; **hai un pessimo aspetto** o **una pessima cera** you look awful o dreadful; **quello scherzo è di pessimo gusto** that joke is in very bad taste
b (molto riprovevole) very wicked, nasty.

pestaggio, gi [pes'taddʒo] SM (rissa) brawl, punch-up; **è stato vittima di un pestaggio** he was set upon by a gang.

pestare [pes'tare] VT **a** (calpestare) to tread on, trample on; **pestare i piedi** to stamp one's feet; **pestare i piedi a qn** (anche fig) to tread on sb's toes; **pestare qn** (picchiarlo) to beat sb up **b** (frantumare: uva, aglio) to crush; (: pepe) to grind.

pestata [pes'tata] SF **a** : **dare una pestata sul piede a qn** to tread on sb's foot **b** (botte) beating.

peste ['pɛste] SF (Med) plague; (fig: persona) pest, nuisance; **dire peste e corna di qn** to tear sb to bits.

pestello [pes'tɛllo] SM pestle.

pesticida, i [pesti't∫ida] SM pesticide.

pestifero, a [pes'tifero] AGG (anche fig) pestilential, pestiferous; (odore) noxious.

pestilenza [pesti'lɛntsa] SF (peste) plague, pestilence; (fetore) stench.

pestilenziale [pestilen'tsjale] AGG (odore) noxious.

pesto, a ['pesto] [1] AGG : **occhio pesto** black eye; **avere gli occhi pesti** (per la stanchezza) to have bags under one's eyes; **era buio pesto** it was pitch-black.
[2] SM (Culin) pesto, sauce made with basil, garlic, cheese and oil.

petalo ['pɛtalo] SM petal.

petardo [pe'tardo] SM firecracker, banger (Brit); (Ferr) detonator, torpedo (Am).

petizione [petit'tsjone] SF (Dir) petition; **fare una petizione a** to petition.

peto ['peto] SM : **fare un peto** to break wind.

Petrarca [pe'trarka] SM Petrarch.

petrodollaro [petro'dollaro] SM petrodollar.

petrografia [petrogra'fia] SF petrography.

petrolchimica [petrol'kimika] SF petrochemical industry.

petrolchimico, a, ci, che [petrol'kimiko] AGG petrochemical; **prodotto petrolchimico** petrochemical (product).

petroldollaro [petrol'dollaro] SM = petrodollaro.

petroliera [petro'ljɛra] SF (nave) (oil) tanker (ship).

petroliere [petro'ljɛre] SM **a** (industriale) oilman **b** (tecnico) worker in the oil industry.

petroliero, a [petro'ljɛro] AGG oil attr.

petrolifero, a [petro'lifero] AGG (industria, pozzo) oil attr.

petrolio [pe'trɔljo] SM oil, petroleum; (per lampada, fornello) paraffin (Brit), kerosene (Am); **lume a petrolio** oil o paraffin o kerosene lamp ▶ **petrolio grezzo** crude oil.

pettegolare [pettego'lare] VI (aus avere) to gossip.

pettegolezzo [pettego'leddzo] SM gossip no pl, piece of gossip; **non mi piacciono i pettegolezzi** I don't like gossip; **fare pettegolezzi** to gossip.

pettegolo, a [pet'tegolo] [1] AGG gossipy; **è pettegola di carattere** she is given to gossip.
[2] SM/F gossip.

pettinare [petti'nare] [1] VT (capelli) to comb; (tessuto) to comb, tease.
[2] **pettinarsi** VR to comb one's hair, do one's hair.

pettinata [petti'nata] SF comb, combing; **darsi una pettinata** to give one's hair a comb.

pettinato, a [petti'nato] [1] AGG (capelli) combed; (persona) with one's hair combed; (tessuto) carded, combed.
[2] SM worsted.

pettinatura [pettina'tura] SF **a** (acconciatura) hairstyle, hairdo **b** (di tessuto) carding, combing.

pettine ['pettine] SM **a** comb **b** (Zool) scallop.

pettirosso [petti'rosso] SM robin.

petto ['pɛtto] SM **a** (Anat) chest; (: seno) breast, bust; **giacca a doppio petto** double-breasted jacket; **battersi** o **picchiarsi il petto** to beat one's breast; **prendere qn/qc di petto** to face up to sb/sth **b** (Culin: di pollo) breast; **punta di petto** (carne bovina) brisket **c** (Mus): **voce di petto** chest voice.

pettorale [petto'rale] AGG, SM pectoral.

pettorina [petto'rina] SF (di grembiule) bib.

pettoruto, a [petto'ruto] AGG (uomo) broad-chested; (donna) full-breasted.

petulante [petu'lante] AGG insolent.

petulanza [petu'lantsa] SF insolence.

petunia [pe'tunja] SF petunia.

pezza ['pɛttsa] SF **a** (rotolo di tessuto) bolt of cloth **b** (toppa) patch; (cencio) rag, cloth; **bambola di pezza** rag doll; **mettere una pezza su qc** (vestito, camera d'aria) to patch sth; **trattare qn come una pezza da piedi** to treat sb like a doormat **c** (Amm): **pezza d'appoggio** o **giustificativa** voucher.

pezzato, a [pet'tsato] [1] AGG piebald.
[2] SM (anche: cavallo pezzato) piebald (horse).

pezzatura [pettsa'tura] SF (di animale) piebald marking.

pezzente [pet'tsɛnte] SM/F (accattone) beggar, wretch; (fig: tirchio) miser.

pezzo ['pɛttso] SM **a** (gen) piece; (brandello, frammento) piece, bit; **ne vuoi ancora un pezzo?** (di torta, pane) would you like a bit more o another piece?; **ci ha accompagnato per un bel pezzo di strada** he came quite a long way with us; **andare in pezzi** to shatter; **fare a pezzi qc** to pull sth to pieces; **andare a pezzi** to break into pieces; **essere a pezzi** (oggetto) to be in pieces o bits; (fig: persona) to be shattered; **ha i nervi a pezzi** his nerves are shattered
b (oggetto, negli scacchi) piece; (Mil) gun; **da vendersi al pezzo** to be sold separately o individually; **1000 lire al pezzo** 1000 lire each o apiece; **un due pezzi** (costume) a bikini; **un servizio da 24 pezzi** (piatti) a 24-piece dinner service
c (di macchina, arnese) part; **smontare qc pezzo per**

pezzo to dismantle sth piece by piece o bit by bit ▶ **pezzo di ricambio** spare part

d (*brano*: *Mus*) piece; (: *scritto*) piece, passage; (: *Stampa*) article ▶ **pezzo di cronaca** (*Stampa*) report ▶ **pezzo forte** pièce de résistance

e (*tempo*): **è qui da un pezzo** he's been here for quite a while; **resterà per un bel pezzo** he'll stay for quite a long time; **è un pezzo che non lo vedo** I haven't seen him for a while; **aspettare un pezzo** to wait quite a while o some time

f (*fraseologia*): **un pezzo grosso** a big shot, a bigwig; **un (bel) pezzo d'uomo** a fine figure of a man; **essere tutto d'un pezzo** to be a man of integrity; **che pezzo di ragazza!** she's a bit of all right!; **pezzo di cretino** stupid idiot.

PG SIGLA = *Perugia*.

pg [pi'dʒi] SIGLA M = **procuratore generale**.

pH [pi'akka] SIGLA M (*Chim*) pH.

PI SIGLA = *Pisa*.

P.I. ABBR = **Pubblica Istruzione**.

piaccio ecc ['pjattʃo] VB vedi **piacere**.

piacente [pja'tʃɛnte] AGG attractive.

piacentino, a [pjatʃen'tino] **1** AGG o from Piacenza. **2** SM/F inahabitant o native of Piacenza.

piacere¹ [pja'tʃere] SM **a** (*gen*) pleasure; **i piaceri della vita** the pleasures of life; **fare qc per il piacere di farlo** to do sth for the sake of doing it; **ho il piacere di annunciare che...** it gives me great pleasure to tell you that ...; **mi fa piacere per lui** I am pleased for him; **è un piacere averti qui** it's a pleasure to have you here; **che piacere vederti!** how nice to see you!; **piacere!** OR **è un piacere conoscerla** pleased to meet you; **mi farebbe piacere rivederlo** I would like to see him again; **se ti fa piacere** if you like; **con piacere** with pleasure, certainly; **fare qc con piacere** to be happy o glad to do sth; **ho saputo con piacere che ti sposi** I was delighted to hear you're getting married; **un viaggio di piacere** a pleasure trip; **potevi averne a piacere** (*volontà*) you could take as many as you wanted; **tanto piacere!** (*iro*) so what?

b (*favore*) favour (*Brit*), favor (*Am*); **fare un piacere a qn** to do sb a favo(u)r; **mi fai il piacere di smetterla?** would you kindly stop that?; **per piacere** please; **per piacere, potresti...?** could you please ...?; **su mangia la minestra, fammi il piacere** come on, eat your soup like a good boy (o girl); **ma fammi il piacere!** for heaven's sake!

piacere² [pja'tʃere] VI IRREG (*aus essere*) (*persona*): **piacere a qn** to be liked by sb; **mi piace** (*lavoro, film*) I like o enjoy it; (*progetto*) it suits me; (*sport, attività*) I enjoy it; **quei ragazzi non mi piacciono** I don't like those boys; **mi piace molto questo quadro** I like this picture very much; **non credo gli piaccia** I don't think he likes it; **mi piace di più così** I like it better this way; **un gusto che piace** a pleasant o agreeable flavour; **una ragazza che piace** (*piacevole*) a likeable girl; (*attraente*) an attractive girl; **il suo discorso è piaciuto molto** his speech was well received; **che ti piaccia o no** OR **ti piaccia o non ti piaccia** whether you like it or not; **che cosa ti piacerebbe fare?** what would you like to do?, what do you fancy doing?; **gli piacerebbe andare al cinema** he would like to go to the cinema; **mi sarebbe piaciuto andarci** I would have liked to go; **fa' come ti pare e piace** do as you please o like; **a Dio piacendo** God willing.

piacevole [pja'tʃevole] AGG pleasant, nice, agreeable.

piacevolezza [pjatʃevo'lettsa] SF (*di compagnia, persona*) pleasantness.

piacevolmente [pjatʃevol'mente] AVV pleasantly.

piacimento [pjatʃi'mento] SM: **a piacimento** (*a volontà*) as much as one likes, at will; **lo farà a suo piacimento** he'll do it when it suits him.

piaciucchiare [pjatʃuk'kjare] VI (*aus essere*): **lui mi piaciucchia** I quite like him.

piaciuto, a [pja'tʃuto] PP di **piacere²**.

piacqui ecc ['pjakkwi] VB vedi **piacere²**.

piaga, ghe ['pjaga] SF **a** (*Med*) sore; (*ferita*: anche *fig*) wound; (*fig*: *flagello*) scourge, curse; **mettere un dito sulla piaga** to touch a sore point; **rigirare il coltello nella piaga** to twist the knife (in the wound); **le piaghe d'Egitto** the plagues of Egypt ▶ **piaghe da decubito** bedsores

b (*fig pegg*: *persona*) nuisance, pain in the neck, pest.

piagnisteo [pjaɲɲis'tɛo] SM whining, whimpering.

piagnucolare [pjaɲɲuko'lare] VI (*aus avere*) to whine, whimper.

piagnucolio, lii [pjaɲɲuko'lio] SM whimpering, whining.

piagnucolone, a [pjaɲɲuko'lone] SM/F whiner, moaner.

piagnucoloso, a [pjaɲɲuko'loso] AGG whiny, whimpering, moaning.

pialla ['pjalla] SF (*arnese*) plane.

piallare [pjal'lare] VT to plane.

piallatore [pjalla'tore] SM (*operaio*) planer.

piallatrice [pjalla'tritʃe] SF planing machine.

piallatura [pjalla'tura] SF (*lavorazione*) planing.

piamente [pia'mente] AVV (*con devozione*) piously, devoutly; (*con misericordia*) charitably.

piana ['pjana] SF stretch of level ground; (*più estesa*) plain.

pianeggiante [pjaned'dʒante] AGG flat, level.

pianella [pja'nɛlla] SF slipper.

pianerottolo [pjane'rɔttolo] SM landing.

pianeta¹, i [pja'neta] SM (*Astron*) planet.

pianeta² [pja'neta] SF (*Rel*) chasuble.

piangente [pjan'dʒante] AGG (*espressione, viso*) tearful; (*bambino*) weeping, crying; **salice piangente** weeping willow.

piangere ['pjandʒere] VB IRREG **1** VI (*aus avere*) (*gen*) to cry, weep; (*occhi*) to water; **piangere di gioia** to weep for joy; **piangere a calde lacrime** to cry one's heart out; **mi piange il cuore** (*iro*) my heart bleeds; **mi piange il cuore a buttare via tanta roba** I hate having to throw away so much stuff; **è inutile piangere sul latte versato** it's no use crying over spilt milk.

2 VT **a** to cry, weep

b (*lamentare*) to bewail, lament; **piangere la morte di qn** to mourn sb's death; **sta sempre piangendo miseria** he's always claiming he has no money.

pianificare [pjanifi'kare] VT to plan.

pianificatore, trice [pjanifika'tore] SM/F (*Econ*) planner.

pianificazione [pjanifikat'tsjone] SF (*Econ*) planning ▶ **pianificazione aziendale** corporate planning ▶ **pianificazione familiare** family planning.

pianista, i, e [pja'nista] SM/F pianist.

pianistico, a, ci, che [pja'nistiko] AGG (*concerto*) piano attr; (*musica*) for the piano.

piano¹, a ['pjano] **1** AGG **a** (*piatto*) flat, level; (*senza asperità*) smooth; (*Mat*) plane attr; **geometria piana** plane geometry; **corsa piana** (*Sport*) flat race

b (*facile*) straightforward, simple; (*chiaro*) clear, plain.

2 AVV (*lentamente*) slowly; (*con cautela*) carefully, slowly; (*a basso volume o voce*) softly, quietly; **la macchina**

andava piano the car was travelling slowly; vai piano! (*in macchina*) drive slowly!; vacci piano! (*fig*: *non esagerare*: *nel bere*) take it easy with that!; (: *nelle minacce*) calm down!; (: *nel lodarsi*) come off it!; attento, fai piano! (*fa' meno rumore*) don't make so much noise!; (*sta' attento*) watch out!, be careful!; parla più piano (*lentamente*) speak more slowly; (*a bassa voce*) lower your voice; pian piano (*lentamente*) very slowly; (*poco a poco*) little by little; pian pianino *o* pian piano siamo arrivati slowly but surely we got there; pian pianino *o* pian piano ha acquistato una certa esperienza he gradually acquired experience.
[3] SM a (*Geom*) plane; (*superficie*) top, surface; (*fig*: *livello*) level, plane; (*Geog*: *pianura*) plain; mettere tutto sullo stesso piano to lump everything together, give equal importance to everything; quei due alunni sono sullo stesso piano those two pupils are at the same level *o* are on a par ▶ piano inclinato inclined plane ▶ piano di lavoro (*in cucina*) worktop ▶ piano stradale road surface
b (*di edificio*) floor, storey (*Brit*), story (*Am*); (*di autobus*) deck; una casa di 3 piani a 3-storey (*Brit*) *o* 3-storied (*Am*) house; al piano di sopra/di sotto on the floor above/below; all'ultimo piano on the top floor; al piano terra on the ground floor (*Brit*) *o* first floor (*Am*); un autobus a due piani a double-decker (bus)
c (*Fot, Cine, Arte*): primo piano foreground; secondo piano background; in primo/secondo piano in the foreground/background; fare un primo piano to take a close-up; in primissimo piano right in the foreground; di primo piano (*fig*) prominent, high-ranking; uno scrittore di primo piano a major author; mettere qc in secondo piano to consider sth of secondary importance; un fattore di secondo piano a secondary *o* minor factor; passare in secondo piano (*questione*) to become less important.

piano² ['pjano] [1] SM (*progetto*: *anche Mil*) plan; (: *industriale*) design; (*programma*) work plan; facciamo un piano let's draw up a plan; non era nei nostri piani we hadn't intended to do it, we hadn't planned on doing so; tutto secondo i piani all according to plan.
[2] ▶ piano di battaglia (*Mil*) battle plan ▶ piano di guerra (*Mil*) plan of campaign ▶ piano regolatore (*Urbanistica*) town-planning scheme ▶ piano di studi (*Univ*) study programme (*Brit*) *o* program (*Am*), study plan ▶ piano di volo (*Aer*) flight plan.

piano³ ['pjano] SM (*Mus*) piano.
piano-bar [pjano'bar] SM INV piano-bar.
pianoforte [pjano'forte] SM piano, pianoforte.
pianola [pja'nɔla] SF player piano, Pianola ®.
pianoterra [pjano'tɛrra] SM INV ground floor (*Brit*), first floor (*Am*); al pianoterra on the ground *o* first floor.
piansi *ecc* ['pjansi] VB *vedi* **piangere**.
pianta ['pjanta] SF a (*Bot*) plant ▶ pianta d'appartamento house plant ▶ pianta grassa succulent (plant)
b (*Anat*: *anche*: pianta del piede) sole (of the foot)
c (*disegno*) plan; (*cartina topografica*) map, plan ▶ pianta stradale street map *o* plan
d (*fraseologia*): l'ha inventato di sana pianta he made the whole thing up; in pianta stabile on the permanent staff; essere assunto in pianta stabile to be taken on as a permanent employee; ormai è qui da noi in pianta stabile (*fig*) he seems to have taken up residence at our place.

piantagione [pjanta'dʒone] SF plantation.
piantagrane [pjanta'grane] SM/F INV troublemaker.
piantare [pjan'tare] [1] VT a (*pianta*) to plant, put in
b : piantare (in) (*chiodo*) to hammer in(to), knock in(to); (*paletto*) to drive in(to); (*ago*) to stick in(to); piantare una tenda to put up a tent, pitch a tent; piantare grane to cause trouble
c (*fig*: *lasciare*: *moglie, figli*) to leave, abandon, desert; ha piantato il suo ragazzo she has left her boyfriend; piantare qn in asso to leave sb in the lurch; piantala! stop it!, cut it out!.
[2] piantarsi VR (*persona*): mi si piantò davanti OR si piantò davanti a me he planted himself in front of me.
[3] piantarsi VIP (*proiettile*): piantarsi in to enter; mi si è piantata una scheggia nel dito I've got a splinter in my finger.
piantato, a [pjan'tato] AGG: ben piantato (*persona*) well-built.
piantatore [pjanta'tore] SM (*persona*) planter.
pianterreno [pjanter'reno] SM ground floor (*Brit*), first floor (*Am*).
pianto, a ['pjanto] [1] PP di **piangere**.
[2] SM crying, weeping, tears *pl*; scoppiò in un pianto dirotto she burst into tears; è uno che ha il pianto facile he cries easily.
piantonare [pjanto'nare] VT to guard, watch over.
piantone [pjan'tone] SM a (*soldato*) orderly; (*vigilante*) sentry, guard b (*Aut*) steering column.
pianura [pja'nura] SF (*Geog*) plain.
piastra ['pjastra] SF a (*di metallo*) sheet, plate; (*di cemento, pietra*) slab; (*Elettr, Fot, di rivestimento*) plate; (*di cucina*) hotplate ▶ piastra di registrazione tape deck b (*moneta*) piastre.
piastrella [pjas'trɛlla] SF tile.
piastrellare [pjastrel'lare] VT to tile.
piastrina [pjas'trina] SF a (*Anat*) platelet b : piastrina di riconoscimento (*Mil*) name tag, identity disc (*Brit*) *o* tag (*Am*).
piattaforma [pjatta'forma] SF (*pl* piattaforme) (*gen, fig, Pol*) platform; (*per tuffi*) board ▶ piattaforma continentale (*Geog*) continental shelf ▶ piattaforma girevole (*Tecn*) turntable ▶ piattaforma di lancio (*Mil*) launch(ing) pad ▶ piattaforma rivendicativa *document setting out claims of the unions in an industry*.
piattamente [pjatta'mente] AVV (*in modo scialbo*) dully.
piattello [pjat'tɛllo] SM a (*bersaglio*) clay pigeon; tiro al piattello clay-pigeon shooting, skeet shooting, trap-shooting b (*Sci*: *di skilift*) disc.
piattina [pjat'tina] SF (*Elettr*) twin lead.
piattino [pjat'tino] SM (*di tazza*) saucer.
piatto, a ['pjatto] [1] AGG (*gen*) flat; (*fig*: *scialbo*) flat, dreary, dull; piatto come una tavola as flat as a pancake.
[2] SM a (*recipiente*) dish, plate; (*quantità*) plate(ful); un piatto di minestra a plate of soup ▶ piatto fondo soup plate *o* dish ▶ piatto da frutta side plate ▶ piatto piano dinner plate ▶ piatto di portata serving dish
b (*Culin*: *portata*) course; primo/secondo piatto first/second course ▶ piatto forte main course ▶ piatto freddo cold dish (*meat, cheese, pickles ecc*) ▶ piatto del giorno dish of the day, plat du jour ▶ piatti già pronti ready-cooked dishes
c (*Tecn*) plate ▶ piatto della bilancia scale pan ▶ piatto del giradischi turntable
d (*Mus*): piatti SMPL cymbals

e (*parte piana*) flat (part).

piattola ['pjattola] SF (*pidocchio del pube*) crab louse; (*fig*: *persona noiosa*) pain in the neck.

piazza ['pjattsa] SF **a** (*Archit*) square; (*Comm*) market; **piazza del mercato** market place; **scendere in piazza** (*dimostrare*) to take to the streets, demonstrate; **vendere sulla pubblica piazza** to sell in the market place; **fare piazza pulita** to make a clean sweep; **mettere in piazza** (*rendere pubblico*) to make public

b (*Mil*): **piazza d'armi** parade ground

c (*di letto, lenzuolo*): **a una piazza** single *attr*; **a due piazze** double *attr*.

piazzaforte [pjattsa'fɔrte] SF (*pl* **piazzeforti**) (*Mil*) fortified town; (*fig*) stronghold.

piazzale [pjat'tsale] SM (*piazza*) (large) square; (*di auto-strada, stazione*) service area.

piazzamento [pjattsa'mento] SM (*Sport*) place, placing.

piazzare [pjat'tsare] ① VT **a** (*mettere*: *gen*) to place, put; (: *colpo*) to land, place

b (*Comm*: *vendere*) to place, sell, market.

② **piazzarsi** VR **a** (*Sport*) be placed; **piazzarsi bene** to finish with the leaders *o* in a good position; **piazzarsi male** to do badly (in a race)

b (*fig*: *piantarsi*): **si è piazzato di fronte a me** he planted himself in front of me; **si è piazzato a casa mia e non si vuole più muovere** he's moved in at my place and refuses to budge.

piazzista, i, e [pjat'tsista] SM/F (*Comm*) travelling sales-man/saleswoman.

piazzola [pjat'tsɔla] SF **a** (*Aut*) lay-by (*Brit*), (roadside) stopping place **b** (*Mil*) (gun) emplacement.

picaresco, a, schi, sche [pika'resko] AGG picaresque.

picca, che ['pikka] SF (*arma*) pike; (*Carte*): **picche** SFPL spades; **rispondere picche a qn** (*fig*) to give sb a flat refusal.

piccante [pik'kante] AGG (*sapore*) spicy, hot; (*fig*: *sconcio*: *barzelletta*) risqué, racy; (: *dettaglio*) titillating, juicy.

Piccardia [pik'kardja] SF Picardy.

piccarsi [pik'karsi] VIP **a** (*pretendere*): **piccarsi di fare qc** to pride o.s. on one's ability to do sth **b** (*impermalirsi*): **piccarsi per qc** to take offence (*Brit*) *o* offense (*Am*) at sth.

piccata [pik'kata] SF (*Culin*) sautéed veal.

picchettaggio, gi [pikket'taddʒo] SM picketing.

picchettare [pikket'tare] VT **a** (*piantare paletti*) to stake out **b** (*fare picchettaggio*) to picket.

picchettatura [pikketta'tura] SF staking (out).

picchetto [pik'ketto] SM **a** (*paletto*) stake, peg **b** (*Mil*) picket; **essere di picchetto** to be on picket duty; **ufficiale di picchetto** orderly officer **c** (*di scioperanti*) picket.

picchiare [pik'kjare] ① VT **a** (*persona*: *colpire*) to hit, strike; (: *dar botte a*) to beat (up), thrash; **lo picchiarono selvaggiamente** they gave him a savage beating; **picchiare qn a sangue** to beat sb black and blue

b (*battere*) to beat; (*sbattere*) to bang, knock; **picchiare i pugni sul tavolo** to bang *o* beat one's fists on the table; **ho picchiato la testa contro il muro** I banged my head against *o* on the wall.

② VI (*aus* **avere**) **a** (*bussare*) to knock; (: *con forza*) to bang; **picchiare alla porta di qn** to knock at *o* on sb's door

b (*colpire*) to hit, strike; **ha picchiato sodo** he hit out hard; **il sole picchiava forte** the sun was beating down; **picchiare in testa** (*Aut*) to knock; **picchia e ripicchia** by

dint of perseverance.

picchiata [pik'kjata] SF **a** (*bussata*) knock; (: *più forte*) bang; (*percosse*) beating, thrashing **b** (*Aer*) (nose-)dive; **scendere in picchiata** to (nose-)dive.

picchiettare [pikkjet'tare] ① VI (*aus* **avere**) (*gen*) to tap; (*pioggia*) to patter.

② VT (*punteggiare*) to spot, dot, fleck; (*colpire*) to tap.

picchio, chi ['pikkjo] SM (*Zool*) woodpecker ▸**picchio muratore** nuthatch.

piccino, a [pit'tʃino] ① AGG little, tiny, (very) small.

② SM/F (*bambino*) small child, little boy/girl.

picciolo [pit'tʃɔlo] SM (*Bot*) stalk.

piccionaia [pittʃo'naja] SF **a** pigeon loft **b** (*soffitta*) loft **c** (*Teatro*: *loggione*): **la piccionaia** the gods *sg* (*Brit*), the gallery.

piccione [pit'tʃone] SM pigeon; **prendere due piccioni con una fava** to kill two birds with one stone ▸**piccione viaggiatore** carrier pigeon.

picco, chi ['pikko] SM (*cima*) peak, summit; (*valore più alto*: *in diagramma*) peak; **a picco** vertically; **una roccia a picco sul mare** a rock rising straight from the sea; **colare a picco** (*Naut*, *fig*) to sink.

piccolezza [pikko'lettsa] SF **a** (*dimensione*) smallness; (*fig*: *grettezza*) meanness, pettiness **b** (*fig*: *inezia*) trifle; **è inutile che ti arrabbi per delle piccolezze simili** there's no point in getting annoyed over such trifles.

piccolo, a ['pikkolo] ① AGG **a** (*oggetto, misura*) small; (*vezzeggiativo*) little; **è piccolo di statura** he is small, he is of small stature; **è più piccolo di me** he is smaller than me; **com'è piccolo il mondo!** it's a small world!

b (*giovane*) young, small, little; (*vezzeggiativo*) little; **bambini piccoli** young children; **mio fratello più piccolo** my younger *o* little brother

c (*di poco conto*: *difetto*) slight; (: *regalo*) little; (: *dettaglio*) minor

d (*breve*: *viaggio, lettera*) short

e (*modesto*) small; (*fig pegg*: *meschino*) petty, mean; **piccolo possidente** smallholder; **la piccola borghesia** the lower middle-classes *pl*; (*pegg*) the petty bourgeoisie; **farsi piccolo** (*umile*) to make o.s. small, to cower.

② SM/F (*bambino*) (small) child, small boy/girl; (*vezzeggiativo*) little one; **da piccolo** as a child.

③ SM: **in piccolo** in miniature; **mi sembra il Colosseo in piccolo** it's like a miniature version of the Colosseum; **nel mio piccolo** in my own small way **b** (*di animale*): **piccoli** SMPL young *pl*; **la gatta e i suoi piccoli** the cat and her kittens; **la volpe e i suoi piccoli** the vixen and her young *o* cubs.

picconata [pikko'nata] SF blow with a pickaxe (*Brit*) *o* pickax (*Am*).

piccone [pik'kone] SM pick, pickaxe (*Brit*), pickax (*Am*).

piccozza [pik'kɔttsa] SF ice axe (*Brit*), ice ax (*Am*).

pick-up ['pikʌp] SM INV (*di giradischi*) pick-up.

picnic [pik'nik] SM INV picnic; **fare un picnic** to have a picnic.

pidiessino, a [pidiɛs'sino] ① AGG (*Pol*) of *o* belonging to the P.D.S (*successor to Italian communist party*).

② SM/F (*Pol*) member *o* supporter of the P.D.S.

pidocchio, chi [pi'dɔkkjo] SM **a** (*Zool*) louse; **pieno di pidocchi** crawling with lice **b** (*fig*: *persona gretta*) mean person.

pidocchioso, a [pidok'kjoso] AGG **a** (*infestato*) lousy, full of lice **b** (*fig*: *taccagno*) mean, stingy, tight.

piduista, i, e [pidu'ista] ① AGG P2 *attr* (*masonic lodge*).

2 SM *member of the P2 masonic lodge.*

piè [pjɛ] SM INV: **a ogni piè sospinto** (*fig*) at every step; **saltare a piè pari** (*omettere*) to skip; **a piè di pagina** at the foot of the page; **note a piè di pagina** footnotes.

pied-à-terre [pjeta'tɛːr] SM INV pied-à-terre.

pied-de-poule ['pjɛdə'pul] SM INV (*tessuto*) hound's-tooth cloth.

piede ['pjɛde] SM **a** (*gen*) foot; **a piedi nudi** barefoot; **avere i piedi piatti** to have flat feet, be flat-footed; **essere o stare in piedi** to stand, be standing; **alzarsi in piedi** to get to one's feet, stand up; **andare/essere a piedi** to go/be on foot; **rimanere a piedi** to be without transport; **ai piedi della montagna/del letto** at the foot *o* bottom of the mountains/of the bed; **da capo a piedi** from head to foot, from top to toe

b (*di mobile*) leg; (*di lampada*) base

c : **piede di porco** (*Tecn*) crowbar; (*per forzare serrature*) jemmy (*Brit*), jimmy (*Am*); (*Culin*) pig's trotter

d (*Metrica*) foot

e (*fraseologia*): **avere tutti ai propri piedi** to have the world at one's feet; **essere sul piede di guerra** to be ready for action; **fare qc con i piedi** to do sth badly; **ragionare con i piedi** to reason like a fool; **fuori dai piedi!** get out of the way!; **levarsi o togliersi dai piedi** to get out from under sb's feet; **è sempre tra i piedi** he's always in the way; **a piede libero** (*Dir*) on bail; **io non ci ho mai messo piede** I've never set foot in there; **mettere i piedi in testa a qn** to walk all over sb; **mettere qn sotto i piedi** to push sb around; **mettere qc in piedi** (*azienda*) to set sth up; **prendere piede** (*teoria, tendenza*) to gain ground, catch on; **puntare i piedi** to dig one's heels in; **sentirsi mancare la terra sotto i piedi** to feel completely lost; **su due piedi** (*rispondere, accettare*) on the spot, at once; **tenere in piedi** (*persona*) to keep on his (*o* her) feet; (*fig*: *ditta*) to keep going; **non sta in piedi** (*persona*) he can't stand; (*fig*: *scusa*) it doesn't hold water.

piedino [pje'dino] SM: **fare piedino a qn** to play footsie with sb.

piedipiatti [pjedi'pjatti] SM/F INV (*fam*: *poliziotto*) cop.

piedistallo [pjedis'tallo], **piedestallo** [pjedes'tallo] SM (*anche fig*) pedestal.

piega, ghe ['pjɛga] SF **a** (*gen, Geol*) fold; (*Cucito*: *di gonna*) pleat; (: *di pantaloni*) crease; (*grinza*) wrinkle, crease; (*della pelle*) (skin) fold; **è tutto pieno di pieghe** (*spiegazzato*) it's all creased; **prendere una brutta o cattiva piega** (*fig*: *persona*) to get into bad ways; (: *situazione*) to take a turn for the worse; **non fa una piega** (*fig*: *ragionamento*) it's faultless; **non ha fatto una piega** (*fig*: *persona*) he didn't bat an eye(lid) (*Brit*) *o* an eye(lash) (*Am*)

b (*acconciatura*) set; **farsi (fare) la messa in piega** to have one's hair set.

piegaciglia [pjega'tʃiʎʎa] SM INV eyelash curler.

piegamento [pjega'mento] SM **a** (*vedi vt*) folding; bending **b** (*Ginnastica*): **piegamento sulle gambe** knee-bend.

piegare [pje'gare] **1** VT **a** (*ripiegare*: *vestito, tovagliolo, foglio*) to fold (up); (: *sedia, tavola*) to fold up

b (*curvare*: *ramo, schiena, braccia*) to bend; **piegare il capo di fronte a qn** (*fig*) to bow to sb; **piegare qn alla propria volontà** to bend sb to one's will.

2 piegarsi VR (*curvarsi*: *persona*) to bend (over); (*fig*: *cedere*): **piegarsi (a)** to yield (to), submit (to); **piegarsi in due dalle risate/dal dolore** to double up with laughter/with pain.

3 piegarsi VIP (*asse, superficie*) to sag; (*sedia, tavolo*) to fold (up).

piegata [pje'gata] SF: **dare una piegata a qc** to fold sth (up).

piegatura [pjega'tura] SF (*vedi vt*) **a** folding *no pl*; bending *no pl* **b** (*piega*) fold; bend.

piegherò ecc [pjege'rɔ] VB vedi **piegare**.

pieghettare [pjeget'tare] VT to pleat.

pieghettato, a [pjeget'tato] AGG pleated.

pieghettatura [pjegetta'tura] SF (*azione*) pleating; (*pieghe*) pleats *pl*.

pieghevole [pje'gevole] AGG **a** (*ripiegabile*: *porta, sedia*) folding **b** (*flessibile*) pliable, bendable, flexible; (*fig*) pliable, yielding, docile.

Piemonte [pje'monte] SM: **il Piemonte** Piedmont.

piemontese [pjemon'tese] AGG, SM/F Piedmontese.

piena ['pjɛna] SF **a** (*di corso d'acqua*) flood, spate; **essere in piena** to be in flood *o* in spate **b** (*fig*: *calca*) crowd, throng.

pienamente [pjena'mente] AVV completely, wholly.

pienezza [pje'nettsa] SF fullness.

pieno, a ['pjɛno] **1** AGG **a** (*gen*) full; (*giornata, vita*) full, busy; **pieno di** (*gen*) full of; (*idee*) bursting with; (*macchie*) covered in *o* with; **un bicchiere pieno d'acqua** a glass full of water *o* filled with water; **avere la pancia piena** to be full; **il cinema era pieno zeppo (di gente)** the cinema was packed; **luna piena** full moon

b (*completo*: *successo, fiducia*) total, complete; **a tempo pieno** full-time; **avere pieni poteri** to have full powers; **nel pieno possesso delle sue facoltà** in full possession of his faculties

c (*muro, mattone*) solid

d (*fraseologia*): **a piene mani** abundantly; **è una persona che dà a piene mani** he (*o* she) is very generous; **a pieni voti** (*eleggere*) unanimously; **laurearsi a pieni voti** *to graduate with full marks*; **pieno di sé** full of oneself, self-important; **essere pieno di lavoro** to have a lot of work to do; **essere in piena forma** to be in top form; **pieno come un uovo** full to overflowing; **in pieno** (*completamente*: *sbagliare*) completely; (: *colpire, centrare*) bang *o* right in the middle; **in pieno inverno** in the depths of winter; **in piena notte** in the middle of the night; **in pieno giorno** in broad daylight; **in piena stagione** at the height of the season.

2 SM **a** : **fare il pieno (di benzina)** (*Aut*) to fill up (with petrol (*Brit*) *o* gas (*Am*)); **il pieno, per favore** fill her up, please

b (*colmo*) height, peak; **arrivò nel pieno della festa** he arrived when the party was in full swing.

pienone [pje'none] SM: **c'era un tale pienone a teatro!** the theatre was packed!

pienotto, a [pje'nɔtto] AGG plump, chubby.

pietà [pje'ta] SF INV (*gen*) pity, compassion; (*Rel*) piety; **sentire o provare pietà per qn** to pity sb, feel pity for sb; **avere pietà di** (*compassione*) to pity, feel pity for; (*misericordia*) to have pity *o* mercy on; **muovere qn a pietà** to move sb to pity; **senza pietà** (*agire*) ruthlessly; (*persona*) pitiless, ruthless; **far pietà** to arouse pity; (*pegg*) to be terrible; **come pianista fa pietà** he's a useless *o* terrible pianist.

pietanza [pje'tantsa] SF course, dish.

pietismo [pje'tizmo] SM pietism.

pietosamente [pjetosa'mente] AVV (*vedi agg*) compassionately; pitifully.

pietoso, a [pje'toso] AGG **a** (*che prova pietà*) compassionate, pitying **b** (*che fa pietà*) pitiful; **essere ridotto in uno stato pietoso** to be reduced to a pitiful o sorry state; **ho fatto una figura pietosa** I made an awful fool of myself.

pietra ['pjɛtra] ⬚1⬚ SF stone; **di pietra** stone *attr*; **avere un cuore di pietra** to be hard-hearted; **porre la prima pietra** (*fondare*) to set up; **scagliare la prima pietra** to cast the first stone; **mettiamoci una pietra sopra** let bygones be bygones.
⬚2⬚ ▶**pietra dura** semiprecious stone ▶**pietra focaia** flint(stone) ▶**pietra di paragone** (*fig*) touchstone ▶**pietra pomice** pumice stone ▶**pietra preziosa** precious stone, gem ▶**pietra dello scandalo** cause of scandal.

pietraia [pje'traja] SF (*mucchio*) pile of stones; (*terreno*) stony ground; (*cava*) stone quarry.

pietrificare [pjetrifi'kare] ⬚1⬚ VT to petrify; (*fig*) to petrify, transfix, paralyze.
⬚2⬚ **pietrificarsi** VIP (*anche fig*) to be petrified, be turned to stone.

pietrina [pje'trina] SF (*per accendino*) flint.

pietrisco, schi [pje'trisko] SM crushed stone, road metal.

pietroso, a [pje'troso] AGG stony.

pieve ['pjɛve] SF parish church.

piezoelettricità [pjeddzoelettritʃi'ta] SF piezoelectricity.

piezoelettrico, a, ci, che [pjeddzoe'lettriko] AGG piezoelectric.

pifferaio, ai [piffe'rajo] SM piper.

piffero ['piffero] SM (*Mus*) pipe, fife.

pigiama, i [pi'dʒama] SM pyjamas *pl* (*Brit*), pajamas *pl* (*Am*).

pigia pigia ['pidʒa 'pidʒa] SM INV throng, crowd, press.

pigiare [pi'dʒare] VT (*pulsante*) to press; (*uva*) to tread.

pigiatrice [pidʒa'tritʃe] SF (*macchina*) wine press.

pigiatura [pidʒa'tura] SF (*di uva*) pressing, treading.

pigione [pi'dʒone] SF rent.

pigliare [piʎ'ʎare] VT (*fam*) = **prendere**.

piglio¹ ['piʎʎo] SM: **dar di piglio a qc** (*fig*: *incominciare*) to get to grips with sth.

piglio² ['piʎʎo] SM (*aspetto*) look, countenance, expression.

pigmalione [pigma'ljone] SM (*fig*) benefactor.

pigmentazione [pigmentat'tsjone] SF pigmentation.

pigmento [pig'mento] SM pigment.

pigmeo, a [pig'mɛo] AGG, SM/F pigmy.

pigna ['piɲɲa] SF (*Bot*) pine cone.

pignatta [piɲ'ɲatta] SF pot.

pignoleria [piɲɲole'ria] SF fastidiousness, fussiness.

pignolo, a [piɲ'ɲɔlo] ⬚1⬚ AGG pernickety, fussy.
⬚2⬚ SM/F fussy person.

pignone [piɲ'ɲone] SM (*Tecn*) pinion.

pignoramento [piɲɲora'mento] SM (*Dir*) distraint.

pignorare [piɲɲo'rare] VT (*Dir*) to distrain.

pigolare [pigo'lare] VI (*aus avere*) to cheep, chirp.

pigolio, lii [pigo'lio] SM cheeping *no pl*, chirping *no pl*.

pigramente [pigra'mente] AVV lazily.

pigrizia [pi'grittsja] SF laziness.

pigro, a ['pigro] AGG (*persona*) lazy, idle; (*fig*: *mente*) slow, dull; (*andatura*) lazy; (*stomaco*) sluggish; **in un pigro pomeriggio d'agosto** on a lazy August afternoon.

P.I.L. [pil] SIGLA M (= *prodotto interno lordo*) GDP (= *Gross Domestic Product*).

pila ['pila] SF **a** (*mucchio*) pile **b** (*Elettr*) battery; **a pila** ⬚OR⬚ a pile battery-operated ▶**pila atomica** nuclear reactor **c** (*fam*: *torcia*) torch (*Brit*), flashlight (*esp Am*).

pilaf [pi'laf] AGG INV: **riso pilaf** pilaf (rice).

pilastro [pi'lastro] SM (*Archit*) pillar, pilaster; (*Alpinismo*) pillar; (*fig*: *sostegno*) pillar, mainstay.

Pilato [pi'lato] SM: **Ponzio Pilato** Pontius Pilate.

pillola ['pillola] SF pill; **la pillola (anticoncezionale)** the pill; **prendere la pillola** to be on the pill ▶**pillola del giorno dopo** morning-after pill.

pilone [pi'lone] SM **a** (*di linea elettrica*) pylon; (*di ponte*) pier **b** (*Rugby*) prop.

piloro [pi'lɔro] SM (*Anat*) pylorus.

pilota, i, e [pi'lɔta] ⬚1⬚ SM/F (*Naut*, *Aer*) pilot; (*Aut*) driver; **secondo pilota** co-pilot ▶**pilota automatico** automatic pilot. ⬚2⬚ AGG INV pilot *attr*.

pilotaggio [pilo'taddʒo] SM: **cabina di pilotaggio** flight deck.

pilotare [pilo'tare] VT (*Aer*, *Naut*) to pilot; (*Aut*) to drive.

piluccare [piluk'kare] VT to nibble at; **smettila di piluccare** stop nibbling (at) your food.

pimento [pi'mento] SM pimento, allspice.

pimpante [pim'pante] AGG lively, full of beans.

pinacoteca, che [pinako'tɛka] SF art gallery.

pince [pɛ̃s] SF INV (*Sartoria*) dart, tuck.

Pinco ['pinko] SM: **Pinco Pallino** so-and-so.

pindarico, a, ci, che [pin'dariko] AGG Pindaric; **voli pindarici** flights of fancy.

Pindaro ['pindaro] SM Pindar.

pineta [pi'neta] SF pinewood, pine forest.

ping-pong [ping 'pong] SM INV table tennis.

pingue ['pingwe] AGG (*grasso*) fat, corpulent; (*fertile*) rich, fertile; (*fig*: *abbondante*: *guadagno*) huge.

pinguedine [pin'gwɛdine] SF (*adiposità*) fatness, corpulence.

pinguino [pin'gwino] SM **a** (*Zool*) penguin **b** (*gelato*) *chocolate-coated ice cream on a stick*.

pinna ['pinna] SF **a** (*di pesce*) fin; (*di cetacei*) flipper **b** (*per nuotare*) flipper **c** (*Naut*) stabilizer; (*Aer*) fin **d** (*Anat*): **pinna nasale** ala of the nose.

pinnacolo [pin'nakolo] SM pinnacle.

pino ['pino] SM (*albero*) pine (tree); (*legno*) pine(wood) ▶**pino silvestre** o **di Scozia** Scots pine.

pinolo [pi'nɔlo] SM (*seme*) pine kernel.

pinta ['pinta] SF pint.

pinza ['pintsa] SF **a** (*gen*) pliers *pl*; (*tanaglia*) pincers *pl*; (*molle*) tongs *pl* **b** (*Med*) forceps *pl* **c** (*di granchio*) pincer.

pinzatrice [pintsa'tritʃe] SF stapler.

pinzette [pin'tsette] SFPL tweezers.

pio, pia, pii, pie ['pio] AGG (*devoto*) pious, devout; (*misericordioso*: *opere, istituzione*) charitable, charity *attr*.

pioggerella [pjoddʒe'rɛlla] SF drizzle.

pioggia, ge ['pjoddʒa] SF **a** rain; **sorpreso dalla pioggia** caught in the rain; **sotto la pioggia** in the rain; **pioggia fine** drizzle; **pioggia scrosciante** driving rain ▶**pioggia acida** acid rain **b** (*fig*: *di regali, fiori*) shower; (*di insulti*) hail.

piolo [pi'ɔlo] SM peg, stake; (*di scala*) rung; **scala a pioli** ladder.

piombare¹ [pjom'bare] VI (*aus essere*) **a** (*cadere*) to fall heavily; **piombare su** (*sogg: tigre, leone*) to pounce on; (: *rapaci*) to swoop down on; (: *esercito nemico*) to swoop down on, pounce on; **il falco piombò sulla preda** the

hawk swooped (down) on its prey; **gli sono piombati addosso** they swooped down on him, they pounced on him; **piombò nella più cupa disperazione** he plunged *o* sank into blackest despair

b (*arrivare*) to arrive unexpectedly, turn up; **è piombato qui alle 2 di mattina** he turned up here at 2 in the morning.

piombare² [pjom'bare] VT (*pacco*) to seal (with lead); (*dente*) to fill.

piombatura [pjomba'tura] SF **a** (*vedi* **piombare²**) sealing; filling **b** (*sigillo*) seal; (*di dente*) filling.

piombino [pjom'bino] SM (*sigillo*) (lead) seal; (*Pesca*) sinker (weight); (*del filo a piombo*) plummet.

piombo ['pjombo] ⃞1 SM **a** (*metallo*) lead; (*Pesca*) sinker; (*Tip*) type; (*sigillo*) (lead) seal; (*proiettile*) (lead) shot; **di piombo** (*tubo*) lead *attr*; (*fig: cielo*) leaden; **soldatino di piombo** tin soldier; **senza piombo** (*benzina*) unleaded, lead-free; **gli anni di piombo** era of terrorist outrages

b (*fraseologia*): **a piombo** (*muro*) plumb; (*cadere*) straight down; **non essere a piombo** to be out of plumb; **cadere di piombo** to fall suddenly; **andare con i piedi di piombo** to tread carefully; **avere/sentirsi addosso una cappa di piombo** to have/feel a great weight on one's shoulders; **riempire qn di piombo** to fill sb with lead.

⃞2 AGG INV (*colore*) leaden, lead-coloured; **grigio piombo** lead grey.

pioniere, a [pjo'njɛre] SM/F pioneer.

pioppo ['pjɔppo] SM poplar ▶**pioppo bianco** white poplar ▶**pioppo nero** black poplar ▶**pioppo tremolo** aspen, trembling poplar.

piovanello [pjova'nɛllo] SM (*Zool*): **piovanello alpino** dunlin.

piovano, a [pjo'vano] AGG: **acqua piovana** rainwater.

piovere ['pjɔvere] ⃞1 VB IMPERS to rain; **piove** it's raining; **piove a dirotto** *o* **a catinelle** it's pouring; **mi piove in casa** the rain comes in through my roof; **su questo non ci piove** (*fig fam*) there's no doubt about it.

⃞2 VI IRREG (*aus* essere) (*scendere dall'alto*) to rain down; (*fig: lettere, regali*) to pour in; (: *persona: arrivare all'improvviso*) to turn up, arrive unexpectedly.

piovigginare [pjoviddʒi'nare] VB IMPERS to drizzle.

piovigginoso, a [pjoviddʒi'noso] AGG drizzly.

piovosità [pjovosi'ta] SF INV (*Meteor*) rainfall.

piovoso, a [pjo'voso] AGG rainy, wet.

piovra ['pjovra] SF octopus.

piovve *ecc* ['pjɔvve] VB *vedi* **piovere**.

pipa ['pipa] SF pipe; (*quantità di tabacco*) pipe(ful); **fumare la pipa** to smoke a pipe.

pipetta [pi'petta] SF pipette.

pipì [pi'pi] SF INV (*fam*) wee(-wee), pee; **fare (la) pipì** to have a pee, have a wee(-wee).

pipistrello [pipis'trɛllo] SM **a** (*Zool*) bat **b** (*mantello*) cloak.

piqué [pi'ke] SM INV (*tessuto*) piqué.

piramidale [pirami'dale] AGG pyramidal.

piramide [pi'ramide] SF pyramid; **a piramide** pyramid-shaped.

piranha [pi'raɲa] SM INV piranha.

pirata, i [pi'rata] ⃞1 SM pirate; (*fig: ladro*) swindler, shark ▶**pirata dell'aria** hijacker ▶**pirata della strada** hit-and-run driver.

⃞2 AGG INV pirate *attr*.

pirateria [pirate'ria] SF piracy; (*atto*) act of piracy.

pirenaico, a, ci, che [pire'naiko] AGG Pyrenean.

Pirenei [pire'nɛi] SMPL: **i Pirenei** the Pyrenees.

piretro [pi'rɛtro] SM (*Bot*) pyrethrum.

pirex® ['pireks] SM pyrex ®.

pirico, a, ci, che ['piriko] AGG: **polvere pirica** gunpowder.

pirite [pi'rite] SF pyrite.

piro... ['piro] PREF pyro-... .

piroetta [piro'etta] SF pirouette.

piroettare [piroet'tare] VI (*aus* avere) to pirouette.

pirofila [pi'rɔfila] SF (*tegame*) heat-resistant dish.

pirofilo, a [pi'rɔfilo] AGG heat-resistant.

piroga, ghe [pi'rɔga] SF dugout (canoe).

pirolisi [piro'lizi] SF INV pyrolysis.

piromane [pi'romane] SM/F pyromaniac, arsonist.

piromania [piroma'nia] SF pyromania.

piro piro ['piro 'piro] SM INV sandpiper.

piroscafo [pi'rɔskafo] SM steamship, steamer.

pirotecnica [piro'tɛknika] SF pyrotechnics *sg*.

pirotecnico, a, ci, che [piro'tɛkniko] AGG pyrotechnical.

Pisa ['pisa] SF Pisa.

pisano, a [pi'sano] ⃞1 AGG Pisan, of *o* from Pisa.

⃞2 SM/F inhabitant *o* native of Pisa.

piscia ['piʃʃa] SF (*fam*) piss.

pisciare [piʃ'ʃare] VI (*aus* avere) (*fam*) to piss.

pisciata [piʃ'ʃata] SF (*fam*): **fare una pisciata** to take a leak, have a pee.

pisciatoio, toi [piʃʃa'tojo] SM (*fam*) public loo (*Brit*).

piscicoltura [piʃʃikol'tura] SF fish farming.

piscina [piʃ'ʃina] SF (*swimming*) pool; (*pubblica, comunale*) (*swimming*) baths *pl* ▶**piscina coperta** indoor swimming pool ▶**piscina scoperta** open-air *o* outdoor swimming pool.

piscio, sci ['piʃʃo] SM (*fam*) piss.

pisello [pi'sɛllo] SM (*Bot*) pea; (*fam: pene*) willie (*Brit*), peter (*Am*).

pisolino [pizo'lino] SM nap, snooze; **fare un pisolino** to have a nap.

pisside ['pisside] SF (*Rel*) pyx.

pista ['pista] ⃞1 SF **a** (*traccia*) track, trail; **siamo su una buona pista** we are on the right track; **pista!** get out of the way!

b (*Radio*) (sound)track; (*Inform*) track; **registrato a doppia pista** double-tracked

c (*di circo*) ring; (*di stadio*) track; (*Sci*) (ski) run, piste; (*Pattinaggio*) rink; (*Ippica*) course; (*Aer*) runway.

⃞2 ▶**pista artificiale** (*Sci*) dry ski slope ▶**pista (da ballo)** (dance) floor ▶**pista ciclabile** cycle track ▶**pista da fondo** (*Sci*) (cross-country) trail ▶**pista di lancio** launch(ing) pad ▶**pista per principianti** (*Sci*) nursery slope ▶**pista di rullaggio** (*Aer*) taxiway ▶**pista di volo** (*Aer*) runway.

pistacchio, chi [pis'takkjo] SM (*albero*) pistachio (tree); (*seme*) pistachio (nut).

pistard [pis'ta:r] SM INV (*Ciclismo*) track racer, track specialist.

pistillo [pis'tillo] SM (*Bot*) pistil.

pistola [pis'tɔla] SF pistol, gun; **sotto la minaccia della pistola** at gunpoint ▶**pistola ad acqua** water pistol ▶**pistola automatica** automatic (pistol) ▶**pistola a spruzzo** (*per vernice*) spray gun ▶**pistola a tamburo** revolver.

pistolettata [pistolet'tata] SF pistol shot.

pistone [pis'tone] SM (*Tecn*) piston; (*Mus*) valve.

Pitagora [pi'tagora] SM Pythagoras.

pitagorico, a, ci, che [pita'gɔriko] AGG Pythagorean.

pitecantropo [pite'kantropo] SM pithecanthropus.

pitoccare [pitok'kare] VT, VI (aus avere) to beg.

pitocco, a, chi, che [pi'tɔkko] [1] AGG mean, stingy. [2] SM/F miser, skinflint.

pitone [pi'tone] SM python.

pittima ['pittima] SF (fig: persona) bore.

pittore, trice [pit'tore] SM/F a (artista) painter b (imbianchino) (house) painter, decorator.

pittorescamente [pittoreska'mente] AVV (vedi agg) picturesquely; colourfully, vividly.

pittoresco, a, schi, sche [pitto'resko] AGG (veduta, paesaggio) picturesque; (modo di parlare) colourful, vivid.

pittorico, a, ci, che [pit'tɔriko] AGG pictorial, painting attr, of painting.

pittura [pit'tura] SF a (arte) painting; (dipinto) painting, picture ▶**pittura murale** mural b (vernice) paint ▶**pittura fresca** wet paint.

pitturare [pittu'rare] [1] VT to paint; **pitturarsi le labbra** to put on lipstick; **pitturarsi le unghie** to paint one's nails. [2] **pitturarsi** VR (fam: truccarsi) to make o.s. up, put on make-up.

più [pju]

[1] AVV

a (tempo: usato al negativo): **non... più** no longer, no more, not ...any more

▷**non lavora più** he doesn't work any more, he no longer works

▷**non ha più detto una parola** he didn't say another word

▷**non c'è più bisogno che...** there's no longer any need for ...

▷**non riesco più a sopportarla** I can't stand her any more o any longer

▷**non ne posso più!** I can't take any more!

▷**non ritornerò mai più** I'll never come back

▷**non è più così giovane** he is not as young as he was

b (quantità: usato al negativo): **non... più** no more

▷**non abbiamo più vino/soldi** we have no more wine/money, we haven't got any wine/money (left)

▷**non ce n'è più** there isn't any left

▷**non ce n'è quasi più** there's hardly any

▷**non c'è più nessuno** there's no one left

▷**non c'è più niente da fare** there's nothing else to do, there's nothing more to be done

c (uso comparativo) more, aggettivo corto +...er;

▷**più bello** more beautiful

▷**più elegante** smarter, more elegant

▷**parla più forte!** speak up!

▷**e chi più ne ha, più ne metta!** and so on and so forth!

▷**è più furbo che capace** he's cunning rather than able

▷**è più che intelligente** he's clever to say the least

▷**noi lavoriamo più di loro** we work more o harder than they do

▷**mi piace più di ogni altra cosa al mondo** I like it better o more than anything else in the world

▷**non guadagna più di me** he doesn't earn any more than me

▷**è più intelligente di te** he is more intelligent than you (are)

▷**è più povero di te** he is poorer than you (are)

▷**cammina più veloce di me** she walks more quickly than me o than I do

▷**non ce n'erano più di 15** there were no more than 15

▷**ha più di 70 anni** she is over 70

▷**è a più di 10 km da qui** it's more than o over 10 km from here

▷**più di uno gli ha detto che...** several people have told him that ...

▷**si fa sempre più difficile** it is getting more and more difficult

▷**due volte più grande del mio** twice as big as mine

d : **di più, in più,** more

▷**ne voglio di più** I want some more

▷**3 ore/litri di più che** 3 hours/litres more than

▷**una volta di più** once more

▷**ci sono 3 persone in più** there are 3 more o extra people

▷**mi ha dato 3 pacchetti in più** he gave me 3 more o extra packets; (troppi) he gave me 3 packets too many

▷**e in più fa anche...** and in addition to o on top of that he also ...

e (uso superlativo) most, aggettivo corto +...est;

▷**la più bella del mondo** the most beautiful in the world

▷**il più bravo di tutta la classe** the best in the class

▷**il più veloce di tutti** the fastest of all

▷**è ciò che ho di più caro** it's the thing I hold dearest

▷**è quello che mi piace di più** it's the one I like the most o best

▷**ciò che mi ha colpito di più** the thing that struck me most

▷**fare qc il più in fretta possibile** to do sth as quickly as possible

▷**è il programma che guardo più spesso** it's the programme I watch most often

f (Mat) plus;

▷**2 più 2 fa 4** 2 plus 2 equals 4

▷**più due** (gradi) plus two, two degrees above freezing o above zero

g (fraseologia)

▷**a più non posso** as much as possible

▷**urlava a più non posso** she was shouting at the top of her voice

▷**al più presto** as soon as possible

▷**al più tardi** at the latest

▷**più che altro** above all

▷**più che mai** more than ever

▷**chi più chi meno hanno tutti contribuito** everybody made a contribution of some sort

▷**più o meno** more or less

▷**avrà più o meno 30 anni** he must be about 30

▷**sarò lì più o meno alle 4** I'll be there about 4 o'clock

▷**minuto più minuto meno** give or take a minute

▷**né più né meno** no more, no less

▷**né più né meno come sua madre** just like her mother

▷**e per di più** (inoltre) and what's more, moreover

▷**tanto più che non sai neppure parlare l'inglese** all the more so as you can't even speak English.

[2] AGG

a (comparativo) more; (superlativo) the most;

▷**chi ha più voti di tutti?** who has the most votes?

▷**più gente viene meglio è** the more the merrier
▷**ci sono più macchine** there are more cars
▷**ci vuole più sale** it needs more salt
b (*molti, parecchi*) several;
▷**abbiamo discusso per più ore** we argued for several hours.
3 PREP plus;
▷**i genitori, più i figli** parents plus *o* and their children.
4 SM INV
a (*Mat*) plus (sign)
b (*la parte maggiore*): **il più** the most
▷**ottenere il più possibile** to get the best possible
▷**tutt'al più** *o* **al più possiamo andare al cinema** if the worst comes to the worst we can always go to the cinema
▷**il più delle volte** more often than not, generally
▷**il più ormai è fatto** the worst is over, most of it is already done
▷**parlare del più e del meno** to talk about this and that
▷**per lo più = perlopiù**
c: **i più** the majority;
▷**i più pensano così** most people think so
▷**la reazione dei più** the reaction of the majority.

piuccheperfetto [piukkeper'fɛtto] SM past perfect (tense), pluperfect (tense).
piuma ['pjuma] SF (*di uccello*) feather; (*ornamento*) feather, plume; **piume** SFPL down *sg*; (*piumaggio*) plumage, feathers *pl*; **leggero/morbido come una piuma** light/soft as a feather; **guanciale di piume** feather pillow; **cappello con le piume** plumed hat.
piumaggio [pju'maddʒo] SM plumage, feathers *pl*.
piumato, a [pju'mato] AGG plumed.
piumino [pju'mino] SM (*per letto*) eiderdown; (: *tipo danese*) duvet, continental quilt (*Brit*); (*giacca*) quilted jacket (*with goose-feather padding*); (*per cipria*) powder puff; (*per spolverare*) feather duster.
piumoso, a [pju'moso] AGG feathery.
piuttosto [pjut'tɔsto] AVV **a** (*preferibilmente*) rather; **prenderei piuttosto un'aranciata** I'd rather have an orangeade; **piuttosto che** (*anziché*) rather than; **piuttosto che studiare farebbe di tutto** he'd do anything rather than study; **qui piove in primavera piuttosto che in autunno** here it rains in the spring rather than *o* instead of in the autumn; **piuttosto la morte!** I'd rather die!
b (*alquanto*) quite, rather; **fa piuttosto freddo** it's rather *o* fairly cold; **sono piuttosto stanco** I'm quite *o* rather tired; **siamo piuttosto indietro con il lavoro** we're rather *o* somewhat behind with the work.
piva ['piva] SF: **tornarsene con le pive nel sacco** (*fig*) to return empty-handed.
pivello, a [pi'vɛllo] SM/F (*fam*) greenhorn.
piviale [pi'vjale] SM (*Rel*) cope.
piviere [pi'vjɛre] SM (*Zool*) plover.
pizza ['pittsa] SF **a** (*Culin*) pizza; (*fig: persona o cosa noiosa*) bore; **che pizza!** what a bore! **b** (*Cine*) reel.
pizzaiola [pittsa'jɔla] SF (*Culin*): **alla pizzaiola** *with tomato and oregano sauce*.
pizzeria [pittse'ria] SF pizzeria (*place where pizzas are made, sold or eaten*).
pizzicagnolo, a [pittsi'kaɲɲolo] SM/F delicatessen owner.

pizzicare [pittsi'kare] **1** VT **a** (*stringere*) to nip; (: *con pinze*) to pinch; (*pungere: sogg: ape*) to sting; (: *zanzara, pulce*) to bite; (: *sostanza*) to sting; **gli ho pizzicato un braccio** I pinched his arm; **ha un sapore che ti pizzica la gola** the taste makes your mouth tingle; **mi sono pizzicato un dito** I've nipped my finger
b (*fig: acciuffare*) to nab, pinch; (*fig: rubare*) to pinch
c (*Mus*) to pluck.
2 VI (*aus* avere) **a** (*prudere*) to itch, be itchy; **mi pizzica il naso** my nose is itching
b (*essere piccante*) to be spicy, be hot.
pizzicata [pittsi'kata] SF pinch; **dare una pizzicata a qn** to give sb a pinch, pinch sb.
pizzicato [pittsi'kato] SM (*Mus*) pizzicato.
pizzicheria [pittsike'ria] SF (*negozio*) delicatessen.
pizzico, chi ['pittsiko] SM (*pizzicotto*) pinch, nip; (*piccola quantità*) pinch, dash; (*puntura: di ape, vespa*) sting; (: *di zanzara*) bite; **un pizzico di sale** a pinch of salt; **non ha un pizzico di pudore** he hasn't an ounce of common decency.
pizzicore [pittsi'kore] SM (*prurito*) itch.
pizzicotto [pittsi'kɔtto] SM pinch, nip.
pizzo ['pittso] SM **a** (*merletto*) lace **b** (*barbetta*) goatee (beard) **c** (*cima*) peak **d** (*tangente*) protection money.
placare [pla'kare] **1** VT (*persona*) to calm down, pacify; (*desiderio*) to placate, assuage; (*dolore, eccitazione*) to soothe; (*coscienza*) to salve; (*scrupoli*) to allay; **placare la fame** to satisfy one's hunger; **placare la sete** to quench one's thirst; **placare gli animi** to appease the crowd.
2 **placarsi** VIP (*rivolta, tempesta*) to die down; (*persona*) to calm down.
placca, che ['plakka] SF **a** (*gen, Elettr*) plate; (*con iscrizione*) plaque **b** (*Med: anche:* **placca dentaria**) (dental) plaque **c** (*Culin*) **placca da forno** baking sheet.
placcare [plak'kare] VT **a** to plate; **placcato in oro/argento** gold-/silver-plated **b** (*Rugby*) to tackle, bring down.
placenta [pla'tʃɛnta] SF placenta.
placidamente [platʃida'mente] AVV peacefully.
placidità [platʃidi'ta] SF calm, peacefulness.
placido, a ['platʃido] AGG (*persona*) placid, calm; (*acque, vento, sera*) calm.
plafond [pla'fɔ̃] SM INV (*Fin*) ceiling, upper limit.
plafoniera [plafo'njɛra] SF ceiling light.
plagiare [pla'dʒare] VT **a** (*copiare*) to plagiarize **b** (*Dir: influenzare*) to coerce.
plagiario, ria, ri, rie [pla'dʒarjo] SM/F plagiarist.
plagio, gi ['pladʒo] SM **a** (*di opera*) plagiarism **b** (*Dir*) duress.
plaid [plɛd] SM INV (travelling) rug (*Brit*), lap robe (*Am*).
planare¹ [pla'nare] AGG planar.
planare² [pla'nare] VI (*aus* avere) (*Aer*) to glide; (*Naut*) to skim.
plancia, ce ['plantʃa] SF **a** (*Naut*) bridge; (: *passerella*) gangway **b** (*Aut: cruscotto*) dashboard.
plancton ['plankton] SM INV plankton.
planetario, ria, ri, rie [plane'tarjo] **1** AGG planetary.
2 SM **a** (*Astron: locale*) planetarium **b** (*Aut*) crown wheel.
planimetria [planime'tria] SF (*scienza*) planimetry; (*disegno, pianta*) plan.
planisfero [planis'fɛro] SM planisphere.
plantare [plan'tare] SM orthopaedic (*Brit*) *o* orthopedic (*Am*) insole, arch support.

plasma ['plazma] SM plasma.

plasmare [plaz'mare] VT (anche fig) shape, to mould (Brit), mold (Am), shape.

plasmatico, a, ci, che [plaz'matiko] AGG plasma attr.

plasmolisi [plazmo'lizi] SF INV plasmolysis.

plastica, che ['plastika] SF a (materiale) plastic; di plastica plastic attr b (Med: anche: chirurgia plastica) plastic surgery c (Arte) plastic art.

plasticamente [plastika'mente] AVV plastically.

plasticità [plastitʃi'ta] SF (Arte) sculptural quality; (duttilità) plasticity.

plastico, a, ci, che ['plastiko] [1] AGG plastic; in materiale plastico plastic.
[2] SM a (Topografia) plastic model, relief model b (esplosivo) plastic explosive; bomba al plastico plastic bomb.

plastificare [plastifi'kare] VT to coat with plastic.

plastilina® [plasti'lina] SF plasticine ®.

platano ['platano] SM plane tree.

platea [pla'tɛa] SF a (Teatro) stalls pl (Brit), orchestra (Am); (pubblico) audience b (Geol) shelf.

plateale [plate'ale] AGG (gesto, atteggiamento) theatrical.

platealmente [plateal'mente] AVV theatrically.

plateau [pla'to] SM INV (Geog) plateau, tableland.

platino ['platino] SM platinum.

Platone [pla'tone] SM Plato.

platonicamente [platonika'mente] AVV platonically.

platonico, a, ci, che [pla'tɔniko] [1] AGG platonic.
[2] SM Platonist.

plaudire [plau'dire] VI (aus avere) (frm): plaudire a (progetto, iniziativa) to applaud.

plausibile [plau'zibile] AGG plausible.

plausibilità [plauzibili'ta] SF plausibility.

plauso ['plauzo] SM (fig) approbation, approval.

Plauto ['plauto] SM Plautus.

playback ['pleibæk] SM INV: cantare in playback to mime.

playboy ['pleibɔi] SM INV playboy.

playmaker ['pleimeikə] SM/F INV (Sport) playmaker.

play-off ['plei'ɔf] SM INV (Sport) play-off.

plebaglia [ple'baʎʎa] SF (pegg) rabble, riffraff sg o pl.

plebe ['plɛbe] SF common people pl; (pegg) rabble, riffraff sg o pl.

plebeo, a [ple'bɛo] [1] AGG plebeian; (volgare) coarse, common. [2] SM/F plebeian.

plebiscito [plebiʃ'ʃito] SM plebiscite.

plenariamente [plenarja'mente] AVV plenarily.

plenario, ria, ri, rie [ple'narjo] AGG plenary; in sessione plenaria in plenary session.

plenilunio, ni [pleni'lunjo] SM full moon.

plenipotenziario, ria, ri, rie [plenipoten'tsjarjo] AGG, SM plenipotentiary.

plenum ['plɛnum] SM INV plenum.

pleonasmo [pleo'nazmo] SM pleonasm.

pletora ['plɛtora] SF (Med, fig) plethora.

plettro ['plɛttro] SM plectrum.

pleura ['plɛura] SF (Anat) pleura.

pleurico, a, ci, che ['plɛuriko] AGG pleural.

pleurite [pleu'rite] SF pleurisy.

plexiglas® [pleksi'glas] SM perspex ®.

P.L.I. [pi'ɛlle'i] SIGLA M (Pol: = Partito Liberale Italiano) former political party.

plico, chi ['pliko] SM (pacco) parcel; in plico a parte under separate cover.

Plinio ['plinjo] SM: Plinio il Giovane/il Vecchio Pliny the Younger/the Elder.

plissé [pli'se] AGG INV, SM INV = plissettato.

plissettato, a [plisset'tato] [1] AGG: tessuto plissettato plissé attr.
[2] SM plissé.

plotone [plo'tone] SM (Mil) platoon ▶ plotone d'esecuzione firing squad.

plumbeo, a ['plumbeo] AGG (colore, cielo) leaden.

plurale [plu'rale] [1] AGG plural.
[2] SM plural; mettere al plurale to put into the plural, pluralize.

pluralis maiestatis [plu'ralis maies'tatis] SM: il pluralis maiestatis the royal "we".

pluralismo [plura'lizmo] SM pluralism.

pluralista, i, e [plura'lista] SM/F pluralist.

pluralistico, a, ci, che [plura'listiko] AGG pluralistic.

pluralità [plurali'ta] SF plurality; (maggioranza) majority.

pluricellulare [pluritʃellu'lare] AGG multicellular.

pluridecorato, a [plurideko'rato] AGG (Mil) much-decorated.

plurigemellare [pluridʒemel'lare] AGG: parto plurigemellare multiple birth.

plurilaureato, a [plurilaure'ato] SM/F person with several degrees.

plurimiliardario, ria, ri, rie [plurimiljar'darjo] AGG, SM/F multimillionaire.

plurimilionario, ria, ri, rie [plurimiljo'narjo] AGG, SM/F multimillionaire.

plurimo, a ['plurimo] AGG multiple.

plusvalenza [pluzva'lɛntsa] SF capital gain.

plusvalore [plusva'lore] SM (Econ) surplus (value).

Plutarco [plu'tarko] SM Plutarch.

plutocrate [plu'tɔkrate] SM/F plutocrat.

Plutone [plu'tone] SM (Mitol, Astron) Pluto.

plutonico, a, ci, che [plu'tɔniko] AGG (Geol) plutonic.

plutonio [plu'tɔnjo] SM plutonium.

pluviale [plu'vjale] AGG rain attr.

pluviometro [plu'vjɔmetro] SM rain gauge.

pm [pi'ɛmme] [1] SIGLA M (Dir) = Pubblico Ministero.
[2] ABBR = peso molecolare.

P.M. ABBR (= Polizia Militare) MP (= Military Police).

PN SIGLA = Pordenone.

pneumatico, a, ci, che [pneu'matiko] [1] AGG (Tecn) pneumatic; (gonfiabile) inflatable.
[2] SM (Aut) tyre (Brit), tire (Am) ▶ pneumatico chiodato studded tyre o tire ▶ pneumatico da neve snow tyre o tire ▶ pneumatico rigenerato remould.

pneumotorace [pneumoto'ratʃe] SM pneumothorax.

P.N.L. [pi'ɛnne'ɛlle] SIGLA M (= prodotto nazionale lordo) GNP (= Gross National Product).

PO SIGLA = Prato.

Po [pɔ] SM: il Po the Po.

po' [pɔ] AVV, SM vedi poco.

P.O. ABBR = posta ordinaria.

pochette [pɔ'ʃet] SF INV clutch bag.

pochezza [po'kettsa] SF insufficiency, shortage; (fig: meschinità) meanness, smallness.

poco , a, chi, che ['pɔko]
[1] AVV
[a] (piccola quantità) little, negazione + much;
▷ si accontenta di poco he's easily satisfied

▷**c'è poco da ridere** there's nothing to laugh about
▷**guadagna poco** he doesn't earn much, he earns little
▷**dorme troppo poco** she doesn't get enough sleep
b (*con aggettivo, avverbio*) (a) little, *negazione* + very;
▷**sta poco bene** he's not very well
▷**è poco più alta di lui** she's a little *o* slightly taller than him
▷**è poco probabile** it's not very likely
▷**è poco socievole** he's not very sociable
c (*tempo*)
▷**poco dopo** shortly after(wards)
▷**il film dura poco** the film doesn't last long
▷**poco fa** a short while *o* time ago
▷**fra poco** in a little while
▷**manca poco alla fine** it's almost *o* nearly finished, it's more or less finished
▷**poco prima** shortly before
▷**ci vediamo poco** we hardly ever see each other
d: **un po'** a little, a bit
▷**è un po' corto** it's a little *o* a bit short
▷**sono un po' stanco** I'm a bit tired
▷**zoppica un po'** he limps a bit, he has a slight limp
▷**arriverà fra un po'** he'll arrive shortly *o* in a little while
▷**un po' prima del solito** a little earlier than usual
▷**ha dormito un bel po'** he slept for quite a while
▷**fammi un po' vedere** let me have a look
e (*fraseologia*)
▷**(a) poco a poco** bit by bit, little by little
▷**a dir poco** to say the least
▷**eravamo in 30 a dir poco** there were at least 30 of us
▷**è una cosa da poco** it's nothing, it's of no importance
▷**una persona da poco** a worthless individual
▷**ha vinto di poco** he only just won
▷**poco male** never mind, it doesn't matter
▷**per poco non cadevo** I almost *o* nearly fell.
2 AGG INDEF
a (*quantità*) little, *negazione* + (very) much; (*numero*) few, *negazione* + (very) many;
▷**poco denaro** little *o* not much money
▷**poco vino** little *o* not much wine
▷**poche persone** few *o* not many people
▷**poche idee** few *o* not many ideas
▷**c'era poca gente** there were only a few people
▷**è un tipo di poche parole** he's a man of few words
▷**a poco prezzo** at a low price, cheap
▷**con poca spesa** for a small outlay
b (*in espressioni ellittiche*: *tempo*) a short time, a little while; (: *quantità*) (a) little;
▷**ci vediamo fra poco** see you soon *o* shortly
▷**l'ha comprato per poco** he bought it cheap
▷**ne abbiamo ancora per poco** we'll only be a little longer
▷**basta poco per farlo contento** it doesn't take much to make him happy.
3 PRON
a (a) little;
▷**c'è chi ha molto tempo e chi ne ha poco** there are those who have a lot of time and those who have little
b (*persone*): **pochi, poche** few (people);
▷**pochi la pensano come lui** few people think as he

does
▷**pochi di noi** few of us.
4 SM
a little;
▷**il poco che guadagno...** what little I earn ...
▷**vive del poco che ha** she lives on the little she has; (*vedi anche* **buono**)
b: **un po'** a little
▷**un po' di soldi** a little money
▷**un po' di pane** a little bread
▷**un po' di zucchero** a little sugar
▷**un po' di silenzio!** let's have a bit of quiet!
▷**ha un po' di mal di testa** he has a slight headache
▷**ha un po' di influenza** she has a touch of flu
▷**un bel po' di denaro** quite a lot of money, a tidy sum
▷**facciamo un po' per uno** let's do a bit each
c: **po' po'**: **che po' po' di coraggio!** what courage!
▷**niente po' po' di meno che il presidente in persona!** no less than the president himself!

podalico, a, ci, che [po'daliko] AGG: **parto podalico** breech delivery.
podere [po'dere] SM (*Agr*) farm.
poderosamente [poderosa'mente] AVV with great strength.
poderoso, a [pode'roso] AGG powerful.
podestà [podes'ta] SM INV (*nel fascismo*) mayor, podestà.
podio, di ['pɔdjo] SM (*gen*) podium, dais; (*Mus*) platform.
podismo [po'dizmo] SM (*Sport*: *marcia*) walking; (: *corsa*) running.
podista, i, e [po'dista] SM/F (*vedi sm*) walker; runner.
poema, i [po'ɛma] SM poem; **conciato così sei un poema** (*iro*) you look a pretty sight like that; **è tutto un poema!** (*complicato*) it's a real palaver!
poemetto [poe'metto] SM (short) poem.
poesia [poe'zia] SF (*Arte, produzione poetica*) poetry; (*singolo componimento*) poem; (*fig*: *di incontro*) magic; **scrivere poesie** to write poetry.
poeta, i [po'ɛta] SM poet.
poetare [poe'tare] VI (*aus* **avere**) to write poetry, write verse.
poetessa [poe'tessa] SF poet(ess).
poetica [po'ɛtika] SF poetics *sg*.
poeticamente [poetika'mente] AVV poetically.
poeticizzare [poetitʃid'dzare] VT to poeticize.
poetico, a, ci, che [po'ɛtiko] AGG poetic(al); **la produzione poetica di Dante** Dante's poetical works.
poggiare [pod'dʒare] **1** VT to lean, rest; (*posare*) to lay, place; (*mettere*) to put; **non poggiare i gomiti sulla tavola** don't put your elbows on the table. **2** VI (*aus* **avere**) **a** (*anche fig*) to stand, rest **b** (*Naut*) to bear away.
poggiatesta [poddʒa'tɛsta] SM INV (*Aut*) headrest.
poggio, gi ['pɔddʒo] SM hill, hillock, knoll.
poggiolo [pod'dʒɔlo] SM balcony.
pogrom [pa'grɔm] SM INV pogrom.
poi ['pɔi] **1** AVV **a** (*gen*) then; (*più tardi*) later (on); (*alla fine*) finally, at last; **e poi, cos'è successo?** and then, what happened?; **e poi** (*inoltre*) and besides; **non ne ho voglia e poi sono stanco** I don't feel like it and what's more I'm tired; **devi poi sapere che...** you should also know that ...; **prima o poi** sooner or later; **poi te lo dico**

I'll tell you later (on); **a poi** till later; **d'ora in poi** from now on; **da domani in poi** from tomorrow onwards

b (*enfatico*): **lui, poi, non c'entra proprio** he simply doesn't come into it, it's nothing at all to do with him; **questa poi non me l'aspettavo** I just wasn't expecting this at all; **questa poi (è bella)!** (*iro*) that's a good one!.

☐2 SM: **il poi** the future; **pensare al poi** to think of the future.

poiana [po'jana] SF buzzard.

poiché [poi'ke] CONG since, as.

pointer ['pointə] SM INV pointer (*dog*).

pois [pwa] SM INV (polka) dot; **a pois** spotted, dotted; **bianco a pois rossi** white with red dots.

poker ['pɔker] SM INV poker; **un poker d'assi** four aces.

polacchini [polak'kini] SMPL high-laced boots.

polacco, a, chi, che [po'lakko] ☐1 AGG Polish.
☐2 SM/F (*persona*) Pole.
☐3 SM (*lingua*) Polish.

polare [po'lare] AGG polar; **la stella polare** the Pole Star.

polarità [polari'ta] SF INV polarity.

polarizzare [polarid'dzare] ☐1 VT (*Fis*) to polarize; (*fig: attrarre*) to attract; **polarizzare la propria attenzione su** to focus one's attention on.
☐2 **polarizzarsi** VIP (*attenzione, sguardo*): **polarizzarsi su** to focus on.

polarizzazione [polariddzat'tsjone] SF polarization.

polca ['pɔlka] SF = polka.

polemica, che [po'lɛmika] SF controversy, argument, polemic; **fare polemiche** to be contentious.

polemicamente [polemika'mente] AVV contentiously; **perché devi sempre rispondere polemicamente?** why do you always have to argue the point?

polemico, a, ci, che [po'lɛmiko] AGG (*gen*) controversial, polemic(al); (*pegg*) contentious.

polemista, i, e [pole'mista] SM/F polemicist; (*pegg*) contentious person.

polemizzare [polemid'dzare] VI (*aus* avere): **polemizzare (su qc)** to argue (about sth).

polenta [po'lɛnta] SF (*Culin*) polenta, *sort of thick porridge made with maize flour*; (*fig: persona lenta*) slowcoach (*Brit*), slowpoke (*Am*).

polentone, a [polen'tone] SM/F slowcoach (*Brit*), slowpoke (*Am*).

polesano, a [pole'zano] ☐1 AGG of *o* from Polesine (*area between the Po and the Adige*).
☐2 SM/F inhabitant *o* native of Polesine.

Polfer ['polfer] SIGLA F = polizia ferroviaria.

poli... ['pɔli] PREF poly... .

poliambulatorio, ri [poliambula'tɔrjo] SM (*Med*) ≈ health centre (*Brit*).

poliammide [poliam'mide] SF polyamide.

poliammidico, a, ci, che [poliam'midiko] AGG polyamide *attr*.

policlinico, ci [poli'kliniko] SM (*Med*) general hospital.

policromatico, a, ci, che [polikro'matiko] AGG (*Arte, Fis*) polychromatic, polychromous.

policromia [polikro'mia] SF polychromy.

policromo, a [po'likromo] AGG many-coloured, polychrome.

poliedrico, a, ci, che [poli'ɛdriko] AGG (*Mat*) polyhedral; (*fig*) multifaceted.

poliedro [poli'ɛdro] SM (*Mat*) polyhedron.

poliestere [poli'ɛstere] SM polyester.

polietilene [polieti'lɛne] SM polyethylene.

polifase [poli'faze] AGG (*Elettr*) multiphase.

Polifemo [poli'femo] SM Polyphemus.

polifonico, a, ci, che [poli'fɔniko] AGG polyphonic.

poligamia [poliga'mia] SF polygamy.

poligamo, a [po'ligamo] ☐1 AGG polygamous.
☐2 SM/F polygamist.

poliglotta [poli'glɔtta] AGG, SM/F polyglot.

poligonale [poligo'nale] AGG polygonal.

poligono [po'ligono] SM **a** (*Mat*) polygon **b** : **poligono di tiro** rifle range.

polimerizzazione [polimeriddzat'tsjone] SF polymerization.

polimero [po'limero] SM polymer.

Polinesia [poli'nɛzja] SF: **la Polinesia** Polynesia.

polinesiano, a [poline'zjano] ☐1 AGG, SM/F Polynesian.
☐2 SM (*lingua*) Polynesian.

polio ['pɔljo] SF polio.

poliomielite [poljomie'lite] SF polio(myelitis).

polipo ['pɔlipo] SM (*Zool, Med*) polyp.

polipropilene [polipropi'lɛne] SM polypropylene.

polisaccaride [polisak'karide] SM polysaccharide.

polisemico, a, ci, che [poli'sɛmiko] AGG polysemous.

polisillabo, a [poli'sillabo] ☐1 AGG polysyllabic.
☐2 SM polysyllable.

polisportivo, a [polispor'tivo] AGG (*campo, società*) multisports *attr*.

polistirolo [polisti'rɔlo] SM polystyrene.

politecnico, a, ci, che [poli'tɛkniko] ☐1 AGG polytechnic.
☐2 SM *university institution providing courses in science, technology and engineering*.

politeismo [polite'izmo] AGG polytheism.

politeistico, a, ci, che [polite'istiko] AGG polytheistic.

politica, che [po'litika] SF **a** (*scienza, carriera*) politics *sg*; **fare politica** (*militante*) to be a political activist; (*come professione*) to be in politics; **darsi alla politica** to go into politics

b (*linea di condotta*) policy; (*modo di governare*) policies *pl*; **la politica del governo** the government's policies ▶**politica aziendale** company policy ▶**politica estera** foreign policy ▶**politica dei prezzi** prices policy ▶**politica dei redditi** incomes policy.

politicamente [politika'mente] AVV politically.

politicante [politi'kante] SM/F (*pegg*) petty politician.

politichese [politi'kese] SM (*pegg*) political jargon.

politicizzare [polititʃid'dzare] VT to politicize.

politico, a, ci, che [po'litiko] ☐1 AGG political; **uomo politico** politician; **scienze politiche** political sciences; **elezioni politiche** parliamentary (*Brit*) *o* congressional (*Am*) election(s). ☐2 SM politician.

politologo, gi [poli'tɔlogo] SM political analyst.

politonale [polito'nale] AGG (*Mus*) polytonal.

polittico, ci [po'littiko] SM polyptych.

polivalente [poliva'lɛnte] AGG (*Chim*) polyvalent; (*fig*) multi-purpose.

polizia [polit'tsia] SF **a** (*Amm*) police (force); (*poliziotti*) police *pl*; **agente di polizia** policeman ▶**polizia ferroviaria** railway (*Brit*) *o* railroad (*Am*) police ▶**polizia fluviale** river police ▶**polizia giudiziaria** ≈ Criminal Investigation Department (*Brit*), ≈ Federal Bureau of Investigation (*Am*) ▶**polizia sanitaria** health inspectorate ▶**polizia stradale** traffic police (*Brit*), state highway patrol (*Am*) ▶**polizia tributaria** tax inspectorate

b (*commissariato*) police station.

poliziesco, a, schi, sche [polit'tsjesko] AGG (*indagine*) police *attr*; (*film, libro*) detective *attr*; (*pegg: modi*) bullying.

poliziotto [polit'tsjɔtto] ☐1 SM policeman.

☐2 AGG INV: **donna poliziotto** policewoman; **cane poliziotto** police dog.

polizza ['polittsa] SF ⓐ (*Assicurazione*) policy ►**polizza di assicurazione** insurance policy ►**polizza casco** comprehensive insurance policy

ⓑ (*Comm*) bill, voucher ►**polizza di carico** bill of lading ►**polizza di pegno** pawn ticket.

polka ['pɔlka] SF polka.

polla ['polla] SF (*sorgente*) spring.

pollaio, ai [pol'lajo] SM (*edificio*) henhouse; (*recinto*) chicken run.

pollaiolo, a [polla'jɔlo] SM/F poulterer (*Brit*), poultryman/woman.

pollame [pol'lame] SM poultry.

pollastra [pol'lastra] SF pullet; (*fam: ragazza*) chick, bird (*Brit*).

pollastro [pol'lastro] SM (*Zool*) cockerel, young cock; (*fig: persona ingenua*) sucker (*fam*).

polleria [polle'ria] SF poulterer's (shop) (*Brit*).

pollice ['pollitʃe] SM ⓐ (*Anat*) thumb; **avere il pollice verde** to have green fingers (*Brit*) *o* a green thumb (*Am*) ⓑ (*unità di misura*) inch.

polline ['polline] SM pollen.

pollivendolo, a [polli'vendolo] SM/F poulterer (*Brit*), poultryman/woman.

pollo ['pollo] SM ⓐ chicken; (*fig: persona ingenua*) sucker (*fam*) ⓑ (*fraseologia*): **conoscere i propri polli** to know who one is dealing with; **far ridere i polli** (*situazione, persona*) to be utterly ridiculous.

pollone [pol'lone] SM (*Bot*) sucker.

Polluce [pol'lutʃe] SM (*Mitol, Astron*) Pollux.

polluzione [pollut'tsjone] SF (*Med*) pollution.

polmonare [polmo'nare] AGG lung *attr*, pulmonary.

polmone [pol'mone] SM lung; **avere buoni polmoni** to have a good pair of lungs; **gridare a pieni polmoni** to shout at the top of one's voice; **respirare a pieni polmoni** to take deep breaths, breathe deeply ►**polmone d'acciaio** iron lung.

polmonite [polmo'nite] SF (*Med*) pneumonia.

polo¹ ['pɔlo] SM (*Fis, Mat, Geog*) pole; **abitiamo ai poli opposti della città** we live at opposite ends of the city ►**il Polo nord** the North Pole ►**il Polo sud** the South Pole.

polo² ['pɔlo] SM (*Sport*) polo.

polo³ ['pɔlo] SF INV (*maglietta*) polo shirt.

Polonia [po'lɔnja] SF: **la Polonia** Poland.

polpa ['polpa] SF ⓐ (*di frutto*) pulp, flesh ⓑ (*di carne*) lean meat.

polpaccio, ci [pol'pattʃo] SM (*Anat*) calf.

polpastrello [polpas'trɛllo] SM fingertip.

polpetta [pol'petta] SF (*in tegame*) meatball; (*fritta*) rissole; **far polpette di qn** to make mincemeat of sb.

polpettone [polpet'tone] SM (*Culin*) meatloaf; **questo film/libro è un polpettone** this film/book is far too long and involved.

polpo ['polpo] SM octopus.

polposo, a [pol'poso] AGG fleshy.

polsino [pol'sino] SM cuff.

polso ['polso] SM ⓐ (*Anat*) wrist; (*di camicia*) cuff; (*Med: pulsazione*) pulse; **orologio da polso** wristwatch; **con le manette ai polsi** in handcuffs ⓑ (*fig: forza*) drive, vigour (*Brit*), vigor (*Am*); **avere polso** to be strong; **un uomo di polso** a man of nerve.

poltiglia [pol'tiʎʎa] SF (*miscuglio*) paste, mush; (*cibo stracotto*) mush, pulp; (*di fango e neve*) slush; **il riso si era ridotto in poltiglia** the rice had cooked to a mush; **ridurre qn in poltiglia** to make mincemeat of sb.

poltrire [pol'trire] VI (*aus avere*) (*rimanere a letto*) to have a lie(-in); (*oziare*) to loaf about, laze about, idle.

poltrona [pol'trona] ☐1 SF armchair; (*Teatro*) seat in the front stalls (*Brit*) *o* the orchestra (*Am*); **starsene in poltrona** (*fig*) to laze about; **aspirare alla poltrona di direttore generale** to aspire to the managing directorship.

☐2: **poltrona letto** put-you-up.

poltroncina [poltron'tʃina] SF (*Teatro*) seat in the back stalls (*Brit*) *o* the orchestra (*Am*).

poltrone, a [pol'trone] ☐1 SM/F loafer, idler.

☐2 AGG lazy, idle.

poltronissima [poltro'nissima] SF (*Teatro*) front-row seat.

polvere ['polvere] SF (*gen, sostanza ridotta minutissima*) powder, dust; (*pulviscolo*) dust; **caffè in polvere** instant coffee; **latte in polvere** dried *o* powdered milk; **sapone in polvere** soap powder; **fare polvere** to raise clouds of dust; **ridurre in polvere** to pulverize; **buttare** *o* **gettare la polvere negli occhi a qn** (*fig*) to pull the wool over sb's eyes; **far mangiare la polvere a qn** (*fig*) to leave sb far behind ►**polvere di ferro** iron filings *pl* ►**polvere d'oro** gold dust ►**polvere pirica** *o* **da sparo** gunpowder ►**polvere di stelle** stardust.

polveriera [polve'rjɛra] SF (*Mil*) (gun)powder magazine; (*fig: zona calda*) powder keg.

polverificio, ci [polveri'fitʃo] SM explosives factory.

polverina [polve'rina] SF (*gen, Med*) powder; (*gergo: cocaina*) snow.

polverizzare [polverid'dzare] ☐1 VT (*legno, ferro*) to pulverize; (*liquido*) to atomize; (*fig: nemico*) to crush, pulverize; (: *record*) to smash.

☐2 **polverizzarsi** VIP to turn to dust.

polverizzatore [polveriddza'tore] SM (*Tecn*) atomizer.

polverone [polve'rone] SM thick cloud of dust; **sollevare un polverone** (*fig*) to raise a stink.

polveroso, a [polve'roso] AGG dusty, covered with dust.

pomata [po'mata] SF ointment.

pomello [po'mɛllo] SM ⓐ (*impugnatura*) knob ⓑ (*gota*) cheek.

pomeridiano, a [pomeri'djano] AGG afternoon *attr*; **nelle ore pomeridiane** in the afternoon.

pomeriggio, gi [pome'riddʒo] SM afternoon; **il** *o* **di pomeriggio** in the afternoon; **nel primo/tardo pomeriggio** in the early/late afternoon; **alle 2 di** *o* **del pomeriggio** at 2 o'clock in the afternoon, at 2 pm; **tutti i pomeriggi** every afternoon; **tutte le domeniche pomeriggio** every Sunday afternoon; **domani/sabato pomeriggio** tomorrow/Saturday afternoon.

pomice ['pomitʃe] SF: (**pietra**) **pomice** pumice (stone).

pomiciare [pomi'tʃare] VI (*aus avere*) (*fam: sbaciucchiarsi*) to neck.

pomiciata [pomi'tʃata] SF (*fam*): **farsi una pomiciata** to neck.

pomo ['pomo] SM (*frutto*) apple; (*oggetto sferico*) knob; (*di sella*) pommel ►**pomo d'Adamo** (*Anat*) Adam's apple ►**pomo della discordia** (*Mitol*) apple of discord; (*fig*) bone of contention.

pomodoro [pomo'dɔro] SM (*frutto*) tomato; (*pianta*) tomato plant; **spaghetti al pomodoro** spaghetti with tomato sauce.

pompa¹ ['pompa] SF a (*fasto*) pomp (and ceremony); **mettersi in pompa magna** to get all dressed up; **accogliere qn in grande pompa** to roll out the red carpet for sb b : (**impresa di) pompe funebri** undertaker's *sg*, funeral director's *sg* (*Brit*), funeral parlor *o* home (*Am*), mortician's (*Am*).

pompa² ['pompa] SF (*Tecn*) pump ►**pompa antincendio** fire hose ►**pompa di benzina** petrol (*Brit*) *o* gas (*Am*) pump; (*distributore*) filling *o* gas (*Am*) station ►**pompa idraulica** hydraulic pump; (*Aut: dei freni*) master cylinder.

pompare [pom'pare] VT to pump; (*estrarre*) to pump out; (*gonfiare d'aria*) to pump up; (*fig: esagerare*) to exaggerate, blow up.

pompeiano, a [pompe'jano] 1 AGG of *o* from Pompeii. 2 SM/F inhabitant *o* native of Pompeii.

pompelmo [pom'pɛlmo] SM (*frutto*) grapefruit; (*albero*) grapefruit (tree).

Pompeo [pom'pɛo] SM: **Pompeo Magno** Pompey the Great.

pompiere [pom'pjɛre] SM fireman; **chiamare i pompieri** to call the fire brigade (*Brit*) *o* fire department (*Am*).

pompon [pom'pɔn] SM INV pompom, pompon.

pomposamente [pomposa'mente] AVV with great pomp.

pomposo, a [pom'poso] AGG (*cerimonia*) full of pomp (and circumstance); (*fig: discorso, atteggiamento*) pompous.

poncho ['pontʃo] SM INV poncho.

ponderare [ponde'rare] VT to ponder (over), think over, consider carefully; **ponderare i pro ed i contro** to weigh up the pros and cons; **fu una decisione ben ponderata** it was a carefully considered decision.

ponderazione [ponderat'tsjone] SF thought, consideration.

ponderoso, a [ponde'roso] AGG (*anche fig*) weighty.

ponente [po'nɛnte] SM (*direzione*) west; (*vento*) west wind.

pongo ecc ['pongo] VB vedi **porre**.

poni ecc ['poni] VB vedi **porre**.

ponte ['ponte] 1 SM (*Edil, Med, Mil*) bridge; (*Naut*) deck; (: *anche:* **ponte di comando**) bridge; (*Aut*) axle; (*impalcatura*) scaffold; **vivere sotto i ponti** to be a tramp; **tagliare** *o* **rompere i ponti con qn** to break off relations with sb; **fare il ponte** to take the extra day off (*between 2 public holidays*); **abbiamo fatto un ponte di 3 giorni** we had 3 days off ►**ponte aereo** airlift, air bridge (*Brit*) ►**ponte di barche** pontoon bridge ►**ponte di coperta** (*Naut*) upper deck ►**ponte levatoio** drawbridge ►**ponte radio** radio link ►**ponte (sollevatore)** (*Aut*) hydraulic ramp ►**ponte sospeso** suspension bridge. 2 AGG INV: **governo ponte** caretaker *o* interim government; **legge ponte** interim law.

pontefice [pon'tefiʃe] SM (*Rel*) pontiff.

ponticello [ponti'tʃɛllo] SM (*di occhiali, Mus*) bridge.

pontificante [pontifi'kante] AGG (*fig*) pontificating.

pontificare [pontifi'kare] VI (*aus* **avere**) (*anche fig*) to pontificate.

pontificato [pontifi'kato] SM (*Rel*) papacy, pontificate.

pontificio, cia, ci, cie [ponti'fitʃo] AGG pontifical, papal; **Stato pontificio** Papal State.

pontile [pon'tile] SM jetty.

pony ['pɔni] SM INV pony.

pool [pu:l] SM INV (*consorzio*) consortium; (*organismo internazionale*) pool; (*di esperti, ricercatori*) team; (*antimafia, antidroga*) working party.

pop [pɔp] AGG INV pop *attr*.

popcorn ['pɔpkɔ:n] SM INV popcorn.

popeline [pɔpə'lin] SF INV poplin.

popò [po'pɔ] (*linguaggio infantile*) 1 SM INV (*sedere*) botty. 2 SF INV (*cacca*) pooh.

popolano, a [popo'lano] 1 AGG of the people, popular; **saggezza popolana** popular lore. 2 SM/F man/woman of the people.

popolare¹ [popo'lare] 1 VT (*rendere abitato*) to populate. 2 **popolarsi** VIP (*diventare popolato*) to become populated; (*affollarsi*): **popolarsi di** to become crowded with.

popolare² [popo'lare] 1 AGG a (*gen, fig*) popular; (*quartiere, clientela*) working-class; **canzone popolare** folk song; **case popolari** council houses (*Brit*); **manifestazione popolare** mass demonstration; **repubblica popolare** people's republic b (*Pol*) of P.P.I. 2 SM/F (*Pol*) member (*o* supporter) of P.P.I.

popolarità [popolari'ta] SF popularity.

popolarmente [popolar'mente] AVV popularly.

popolato, a [popo'lato] AGG populated.

popolazione [popolat'tsjone] SF population.

popolino [popo'lino] SM (*pegg*): **il popolino** the masses *pl*, the common people.

popolo ['pɔpolo] SM (*gen*) people; (*classe*): **il popolo** the (common) people; **il popolo italiano** the Italian people, the Italians *pl*; **a furor di popolo** by popular acclaim.

popoloso, a [popo'loso] AGG densely populated, populous.

popone [po'pone] SM melon.

poppa¹ ['poppa] SF (*Anat*) breast.

poppa² ['poppa] SF (*Naut*) stern; **a poppa** aft, astern; **andare a poppa** to go aft; **andare col vento in poppa** to sail before the wind.

poppante [pop'pante] SM/F unweaned infant; (*fig: inesperto*) whippersnapper.

poppare [pop'pare] VT to suck.

poppata [pop'pata] SF (*allattamento*) feed; **l'ora della poppata** feeding time.

poppatoio, toi [poppa'tojo] SM (baby's) bottle, feeding bottle (*Brit*), baby bottle (*Am*).

poppiero, a [pop'pjɛro] AGG (*Naut*) after *attr*.

populista, i, e [popu'lista] AGG populist.

porcaio, ai [por'kajo] SM (*anche fig*) pigsty.

porcaro [por'karo] SM swineherd.

porcata [por'kata] SF (*libro, film ecc*) load of rubbish; **fare una porcata a qn** to play a dirty trick on sb.

porcellana [portʃel'lana] SF porcelain, china; (*oggetto*) piece of porcelain.

porcellino [portʃel'lino] SM piglet ►**porcellino d'India** guinea pig.

porcello, a [por'tʃɛllo] 1 SM (*Zool*) piglet. 2 SM/F (*pegg*) pig.

porcellone, a [portʃel'lone] SM/F (*pegg*) pig.

porcheria [porke'ria] SF (*gen*) dirt, muck, filth; (*azione disonesta*) dirty trick; (*oscenità*) obscenity; (*cosa fatta male*) (load of) rubbish *o* trash; **mangia un sacco di porcherie** he eats a lot of rubbish; **non si fanno queste porcherie!** you shouldn't behave like that!

porchetta [por'ketta] SF (*Culin*) roast sucking pig.

porcile [por'tʃile] SM (*anche fig*) pigsty.

porcino, a [por'tʃino] 1 AGG of pigs, pork *attr*; **occhi**

porcini (*fig*) piggy eyes.
② SM (*anche:* **fungo porcino**) cep.
porco, a, ci, che ['pɔrko] ① SM (*Zool*) pig; (*Culin*) pork; **gettare le perle ai porci** (*fig*) to cast pearls before swine.
② SM/F (*pegg*) pig; **un vecchio porco** a dirty old man.
③ AGG (*fam*): **porca miseria!, porco Giuda!** bloody hell! (*Brit*).
porcospino [porkos'pino] SM porcupine; (*fig: persona*): **è chiuso come un porcospino** he doesn't come out of his shell easily.
porfido ['pɔrfido] SM porphyry.
porgere ['pɔrdʒere] VT IRREG to hand, give; (*tendere*) to hold out; **porgere la mano a qn** to hold out one's hand to sb; (*fig*) to give sb a helping hand, lend sb a hand; **porgere l'altra guancia** to turn the other cheek; **porgere orecchio** *o* **ascolto** to pay attention, listen.
porno ['pɔrno] (*fam*) ① AGG INV porno; **film porno** porn film (*Brit*) *o* movie (*Am*).
② SM INV (*pornografia*) porn.
pornodivo, a [porno'divo] SM/F porn star.
pornofilm [porno'film] SM INV porn film (*Brit*) *o* movie (*Am*).
pornografia [pornogra'fia] SF pornography.
pornograficamente [pornografika'mente] AVV pornographically.
pornografico, a, ci, che [porno'grafiko] AGG pornographic.
poro ['pɔro] SM (*Anat*) pore; (*forellino*) hole.
poroso, a [po'roso] AGG porous.
porpora ['pɔrpora] ① AGG, SM (*colore*) crimson.
② SF (*stoffa, simbolo*) purple.
porporino, a [porpo'rino] AGG crimson.
porre ['pɔrre] VB IRREG ① VT **a** (*mettere*) to put; (*collocare*) to place; (*posare*) to lay (down), put (down); **porre le fondamenta di** (*edificio*) to lay the foundations of; **porre le basi di** (*fig*) to lay the foundations of, establish; **abbiamo posto le basi per una futura collaborazione** we have laid the foundations for future cooperation; **fu posto al comando del reggimento** he was placed in command of the regiment; **porre la propria fiducia in qn** to place one's trust in sb; **porre fine** *o* **termine a qc** to put an end *o* a stop to sth
b (*condizioni*) to lay down, set out, state; (*problema*) to pose; (*questione*) to raise; **porre una domanda a qn** to ask sb a question, put a question to sb
c (*supporre*) to suppose; **poniamo (il caso) che...** let's suppose that ...; **posto che...** supposing that ..., on the assumption that ....
② **porsi** VR: **porsi in cammino** to set out *o* forth; **porsi al lavoro** to get down to work; **porsi a sedere** to sit down; **porsi in salvo** to save o.s.
porro ['pɔrro] SM **a** (*Bot*) leek **b** (*Med*) wart.
porsi *ecc* ['pɔrsi] VB *vedi* **porgere.**
porta ['pɔrta] SF (*gen*) door; (*soglia*) doorstep; (*apertura*) doorway; (*di fortezza, Sci*) gate; (*Calcio, Rugby*) goal; (*Inform*) port; (*di città*) **porte** SFPL gates; **abitare porta a porta con qn** to live right next door to sb; **vendere porta a porta** to sell from door to door; **vendita porta a porta** door-to-door selling; **indicare la porta a qn** (*fig*) to show sb the door; **mettere qn alla porta** (*anche fig*) to throw sb out; **prendere la porta ed andarsene** to walk out the door; **sbattere** *o* **chiudere la porta in faccia a qn** (*anche fig*) to slam the door in sb's face; **suonare alla porta** to ring the (door)bell; **suonano alla porta** there's some-

body at the door; **trovare tutte le porte chiuse** (*fig*) to find the way barred; **a porte chiuse** (*processo*) in camera; **cacciamo questo problema dalla porta e rientra dalla finestra** there's no getting rid of this problem; **esce dalla porta e rientra dalla finestra** there's no getting rid of him; **l'inverno è alle porte** winter is upon us; **tirare in porta** (*Sport*) to take a shot at goal ▶ **porta blindata** reinforced door ▶ **porta di servizio** tradesman's entrance ▶ **porta di sicurezza** emergency exit ▶ **porta stagna** watertight door.
portabagagli [portaba'gaʎʎi] SM INV **a** (*facchino*) porter **b** (*Aut*) boot (*Brit*), trunk (*Am*); (: *sul tetto*) roof rack; (*in treno, corriera: anche:* **rete portabagagli**) luggage rack.
portabandiera [portaban'djɛra] SM/F INV (*anche fig*) standard bearer.
portabiancheria [portabjanke'ria] SM INV (*anche:* **cesto portabiancheria**) laundry *o* linen basket, hamper (*Am*).
portabicchiere [portabik'kjɛre] SM (*da bagno*) tooth-mug holder.
portabiciclette [portabitʃi'klette] SM INV bicycle rack (*on car*).
portabiti [por'tabiti] SM INV clothes hanger.
portaborse [porta'borse] SM/F INV (*pegg*) lackey.
portabottiglie [portabot'tiʎʎe] SM INV (*scaffale*) bottle rack; (*per trasporto*) bottle carrier; (*da tavola*) wine cooler.
portacarte [porta'karte] SM INV paper holder, paper rack.
portacenere [porta'tʃenere] SM INV ashtray.
portachiavi [porta'kjavi] SM INV (*anello*) key ring; (*astuccio*) key case.
portacinture [portatʃin'ture] SM INV belt rack.
portacipria [porta'tʃipria] SM INV (powder) compact.
portacravatte [portakra'vatte] SM INV tie rack.
portadocumenti [portadoku'menti] ① SM INV file, folder.
② AGG INV: **valigetta portadocumenti** briefcase.
portaerei [porta'ɛrei] ① SF INV (*anche:* **nave portaerei**) aircraft carrier.
② SM INV (*aereo*) aircraft transporter.
portaferiti [portafe'riti] SM INV (*Mil*) stretcher-bearer.
portafiammiferi [portafjam'miferi] SM INV match holder.
portafinestra [portafi'nɛstra] SF (*pl* **portefinestre**) French window *o* door (*Am*).
portafiori [porta'fjori] SM INV flower stand.
portafoglio, gli [porta'fɔʎʎo] SM **a** (*per soldi*) wallet, billfold (*Am*); (*cartella*) briefcase; **mettere mano al portafoglio** (*fig*) to put one's hand in one's pocket; **gonna a portafoglio** wrapover skirt
b (*Fin, Pol*) portfolio; **ministro senza portafoglio** minister without portfolio ▶ **portafoglio titoli** investment portfolio.
portafortuna [portafor'tuna] ① SM INV (*amuleto*) lucky charm; (*persona, animale*) mascot.
② AGG INV lucky.
portafotografie [portafotogra'fie] SM INV photo(graph) frame.
portaghiaccio [porta'gjattʃo] SM INV (*anche:* **secchiello portaghiaccio**) ice bucket.
portagioie [porta'dʒoje], **portagioielli** [portadʒo'jɛlli] SM INV jewellery (*Brit*) *o* jewelry (*Am*) box.
portalampada [porta'lampada] SM INV bulb socket.
portale [por'tale] SM (*Archit*) portal.
portalettere [porta'lɛttere] SM/F INV postman/postwoman (*Brit*), mailman/mailwoman (*Am*).
portamatite [portama'tite] SM INV (*anche:* **astuccio porta-**

matite) pencil case.

portamento [porta'mento] SM bearing, carriage.

portamonete [portamo'nete] SM INV purse (*Brit*), change purse (*Am*).

portante [por'tante] AGG (*muro*) load-bearing, supporting.

portantina [portan'tina] SF **a** (*sedia*) sedan chair **b** (*barella*) stretcher.

portaoggetti [portaod'dʒetti] AGG INV: **vano portaoggetti** (*Aut*) glove compartment.

portaombrelli [portaom'brelli] SM INV umbrella stand.

portaordini [porta'ordini] SM INV (*Mil*) dispatch rider.

portapacchi [porta'pakki] SM INV (*di moto, automobile*) luggage rack.

portapenne [porta'penne] SM INV pen holder; (*astuccio*) pencil case.

portaposate [portapo'sate] SM INV (*anche*: **vassoio portaposate**) cutlery *o* flatware (*Am*) tray.

portare [por'tare] □ VT **a** (*sostenere, sorreggere: peso, bambino, pacco*) to carry; **portava il pacco sottobraccio** he was carrying the parcel under his arm; **questa macchina porta 4 persone** this car can carry 4 people; **puoi portarmi la valigia?** can you carry my case for me?; **si porta dietro un sacco di roba** he carries masses of stuff round with him; **portare via** to take away; (*rubare*) to take; **schedare questi documenti porta via molto tempo** filing these documents takes (up) a lot of time; **porta bene i suoi anni** he's wearing well, he doesn't look his age; **ognuno ha la propria croce da portare** we all have our cross to bear

b (*consegnare, recare*): **portare qc (a qn)** to take (*o* bring) sth (to sb); **porta il libro in cucina!** (*vicino a chi parla*) bring the book into the kitchen!; (*lontano da chi parla*) take the book into the kitchen!; **portami un bicchiere!** bring me a glass!; **posso portarli a casa?** can I bring (*o* take) them home?; **portare qc alla bocca** to lift *o* put sth to one's lips; **il suo intervento ha portato dei vantaggi** his intervention has brought certain advantages; **portare fortuna/sfortuna a qn** to bring (good) luck/bad luck to sb

c (*condurre*) to take; (*sogg: strada*) to take, lead; (*fig: indurre*): **portare qn a (fare) qc** to lead sb to (do) sth; **dove porta questa strada?** where does this road lead?, where does this road take you?; **portare i bambini a spasso** to take the children for a walk; **il vento ci sta portando al largo** the wind is carrying us out to sea; **dove ti porterà tutto questo?** where will all this lead you?; **portare qn alla disperazione** to drive sb to despair; **stiamo portando avanti il discorso sul disarmo** we are pursuing the topic of disarmament

d (*indossare: scarpe, vestito, occhiali*) to wear, have on; **non porto più queste scarpe** I don't wear these shoes any more; **porta i capelli lunghi** he wears his hair long, he has long hair

e (*avere: nome, titolo, firma*) to have, bear; (*fig: sentimenti*) to bear; **porta il nome di suo nonno** he is called after his grandfather; **il documento porta la tua firma** the document has *o* bears your signature; **Firenze porta ancora i segni dell'alluvione** Florence still bears the signs of the flood; **non gli porto rancore** I don't bear him a grudge.

② **portarsi** VIP (*recarsi*) to go; **la polizia si è portata sul luogo del disastro** the police went to the scene of the disaster.

portaritratti [portari'tratti] SM INV photo(graph) frame.

portariviste [portari'viste] SM INV magazine rack.

portarotolo [porta'rotolo] SM INV (*da bagno*) toilet paper holder; (*da cucina*) kitchen (*Brit*) *o* paper (*Am*) towel holder.

portasapone [portasa'pone] SM INV soap dish.

portascarpe [portas'karpe] SM INV shoe rack.

portascì [porta'ʃʃi] SM INV (*Aut*) ski rack.

portasciugamani [portaʃʃuga'mani] SM INV towel rail.

portascopino [portasko'pino] SM INV lavatory brush holder (*Brit*).

portasigarette [portasiga'rette] SM INV cigarette case.

portaspazzolino [portaspattso'lino] SM INV toothbrush holder.

portaspilli [portas'pilli] SM INV pincushion.

portassegni [portas'seɲɲi] SM INV chequebook (*Brit*) *o* checkbook (*Am*) holder.

portata [por'tata] SF **a** (*Culin*) course; **un pranzo di 7 portate** a 7-course lunch

b (*di veicolo*) carrying (*o* loading) capacity

c (*di arma*) range; (*fig: limite*) scope, capability; **a/fuori portata (di)** within/out of reach (of); **a portata di mano** within (arm's) reach; **alla portata di tutti** (*conoscenza*) within everybody's grasp; (*prezzo*) within everybody's means

d (*fig: importanza*) importance, significance; **di grande portata** of great importance

e (*volume d'acqua*) (rate of) flow.

portatile [por'tatile] AGG portable.

portato, a [por'tato] AGG (*incline*): **portato a** inclined *o* apt to; **essere portato per** (*studio, matematica*) to have a bent for.

portatore, trice [porta'tore] SM/F **a** (*di messaggio, assegno*) bearer; **pagabile al portatore** payable to the bearer **b** (*Med*) carrier ▶ **portatore di handicap** disabled person ▶ **portatore sano** (symptomless) carrier **c** (*Alpinismo*) porter.

portatovagliolo [portatovaʎ'ʎɔlo] SM (*anello*) napkin ring; (*busta*) napkin holder.

portauova [porta'wɔva], **portauovo** [porta'wɔvo] SM INV egg cup; (*scatola*) egg box.

portavoce [porta'votʃe] SM/F INV spokesman/spokeswoman, spokesperson.

porte-enfant ['pɔrtã'fã] SM INV carrycot (*Brit*), portacrib ® (*Am*).

portello [por'tello] SM (*di portone, aereo*) door; (*Naut*) hatch.

portellone [portel'lone] SM (*Aer, Naut*) hold door; (*Aut*) tailgate.

portento [por'tento] SM wonder, marvel.

portentosamente [portentosa'mente] AVV wonderfully.

portentoso, a [porten'toso] AGG wonderful, marvellous (*Brit*), marvelous (*Am*).

portfolio ['pɔːtfouljou] SM INV (*Pubblicità*) portfolio.

porticato [porti'kato] SM portico.

portico ['pɔrtiko] SM (*Archit*) porch, portico; (*riparo*) lean-to.

portiera [por'tjera] SF (*Aut*) door.

portiere, a [por'tjere] SM/F **a** (*portinaio*) concierge, caretaker, janitor (*Am*); (*di hotel*) porter **b** (*Sport*) goalkeeper.

portinaio, a, nai, e [porti'najo] SM/F concierge, caretaker, janitor (*Am*).

portineria [portine'ria] SF caretaker's lodge.

porto[1] ['pɔrto] SM port, harbour (*Brit*), harbor (*Am*); **andare** *o* **giungere in porto** (*fig*) to come to a successful conclusion; **condurre qc in porto** (*fig*) to bring sth to a successful conclusion; **questa casa è un porto di mare** people are always coming and going in this house ▶**porto fluviale** river port ▶**porto franco** free port ▶**porto marittimo** seaport ▶**porto militare** naval base ▶**porto di scalo** port of call.

porto[2] ['pɔrto] SM **a** (*Comm: spesa di trasporto*) carriage; **franco di porto** carriage free **b** : **porto d'armi** gun licence (*Brit*) *o* license (*Am*).

porto[3] ['pɔrto] SM INV (*vino*) port (wine).

porto[4], **a** ['pɔrto] PP di **porgere**.

Portogallo [porto'gallo] SM: **il Portogallo** Portugal.

portoghese [porto'gese] [1] AGG Portuguese.

[2] SM/F **a** (*abitante, nativo*) Portuguese *inv* **b** (*spettatore senza biglietto*) gate-crasher.

[3] SM (*lingua*) Portuguese.

portolano [porto'lano] SM (*Naut*) pilot book.

portone [por'tone] SM main entrance.

portoricano, a [portori'kano] AGG, SM/F Puerto Rican.

Portorico [porto'riko] SM Puerto Rico.

portuale [portu'ale] [1] AGG port *attr*, dock *attr*, harbour *attr* (*Brit*), harbor *attr* (*Am*); **lavoratori portuali** dockers, dock workers, longshoremen (*Am*).

[2] SM docker, dock worker, longshoreman (*Am*).

porzione [por'tsjone] SF (*gen*) portion, share; (*di cibo*) helping, portion.

posa ['pɔsa] SF **a** (*atteggiamento, di modello*) pose; (: *affettato*) posing; **teatro di posa** photographic studio; **mettersi in posa** to pose; **assumere pose da grandonna** to act the lady; **è tutta una posa** it's just an act **b** (*Fot*) exposure **c** (*riposo*): **lavorare senza posa** to work without a break **d** (*collocazione*) laying, placing.

posacavi [posa'kavi] SF INV (*anche*: **nave posacavi**) cable ship.

posacenere [posa'tʃenere] SM INV ashtray.

posamine [posa'mine] SM O F INV minelayer.

posapiano [posa'pjano] SM/F INV (*scherz*) slowcoach (*Brit*), slowpoke (*Am*).

posare [po'sare] [1] VT (*gen*) to put (down); (*piatto, vassoio*) to lay *o* put (down); (*fondamenta, cavo*) to lay; **posare gli occhi su** to gaze at; (*con mire particolari*) to set one'sights on; **posalo contro il muro** stand *o* put it against the wall.

[2] VI (*aus* avere) **a** (*ponte, edificio, teoria*): **posare su** to rest on **b** (*Fot, Arte*) to pose, sit; (*atteggiarsi*) to pose; **posa a grande scrittore** (*fig*) he poses as a great writer.

[3] **posarsi** VIP (*uccello*) to alight; (*ape, mosca*) to land; (*aereo*) to land, touch down; (*sguardo*) to settle, fix.

posata [po'sata] SF piece of cutlery *o* flatware (*Am*); **posate** SFPL cutlery *sg*, flatware *sg*.

posatamente [posata'mente] AVV composedly.

posatezza [posa'tettsa] SF (*di persona*) composure; (*di discorso*) balanced nature.

posato, a [po'sato] AGG (*persona*) steady, level-headed; (*comportamento*) steady, sober; (*discorso*) balanced.

poscia ['pɔʃʃa] AVV (*letter*) thereafter.

poscritto [pos'kritto] SM postscript.

posdomani [pozdo'mani] AVV (*letter*) the day after tomorrow.

Poseidone [pozei'done] SM Poseidon.

posi *ecc* ['pɔsi] VB vedi **porre**.

positiva [pozi'tiva] SF (*Fot*) (positive) print.

positivamente [pozitiva'mente] AVV positively; (*rispondere*) in the affirmative, affirmatively.

positivo, a [pozi'tivo] AGG, SM positive.

posizionare [pozittsjo'nare] VT to position.

posizionatore [pozittsjona'tore] SM (*Tecn*) positioning device.

posizione [pozit'tsjone] SF (*gen, fig*) position; **prendere posizione a favore di/contro** to take up a position in favour (*Brit*) *o* favor (*Am*) of/against; **devi prendere una posizione** you must take a stand; **farsi una posizione** to make one's way in the world; **è arrivato in prima/ seconda posizione** (*Sport*) he arrived first/second; **posizione di attesa** (*Tennis*) ready position; **posizione dei piedi** stance; **luci di posizione** (*Aut*) sidelights (*Brit*), parking lights (*Am*).

posologia [pozolo'dʒia] SF dosage, directions *pl* for use.

posporre [pos'porre] VT IRREG **a** (*rimandare*) to postpone, defer **b** (*subordinare*) to subordinate, place after.

posposto, a [pos'posto] PP di **posporre**.

possedere [posse'dere] VT IRREG (*gen*) to have; (*qualità, virtù, fortuna*) to possess; (*casa, terreno*) to own; (*diploma*) to hold; (*sogg: ira*) to possess; **era posseduto dal demone** he was possessed by the Devil.

possedimento [possedi'mento] SM **a** (*proprietà terriera*) property, estate **b** (*di uno Stato, territorio*) possession.

posseditrice [possedi'tritʃe] SF vedi **possessore**.

possente [pos'sɛnte] AGG strong, powerful.

possentemente [possente'mente] AVV powerfully, mightily.

possessivo, a [posses'sivo] AGG (*gen, Gramm*) possessive.

possesso [pos'sɛsso] SM **a** (*gen, Dir*) possession; **essere in possesso di qc** to be in possession of sth; **prendere possesso di qc** to take possession of sth; **entrare in possesso dell'eredità** to come into one's inheritance **b** (*possedimenti*): **possessi** SMPL property *sg*.

possessore, posseditrice [posses'sore, possedi'tritʃe] SM/F possessor, owner; (*di carica, diploma*) holder.

possibile [pos'sibile] [1] AGG (*gen*) possible; (*fattibile: progetto, piano*) feasible; **non mi sarà possibile farlo** I won't be able to do it; **è possibile che arrivi più tardi** he may *o* might arrive later; **cerca di venir presto, se possibile** try to come early, if possible *o* if you can; **ha trovato tutte le scuse possibili e immaginabili per non venire** he came up with every excuse imaginable for not coming; **vieni prima possibile** come as soon as possible; **fallo meglio possibile** do it as best you can; **porta meno roba possibile** bring as little as possible; **non è possibile!** (*irrealizzabile*) it's not possible!; (*falso*) that can't be true!; **possibile?** (*sorpresa*) well I never!.

[2] SM: **fare il possibile** to do everything possible *o* everything in one's power; **nei limiti del possibile** as far as possible.

possibilista, i, e [possibi'lista] AGG: **essere possibilista** to keep an open mind.

possibilità [possibili'ta] SF INV (*gen*) possibility; **c'è sempre la possibilità che cambi idea** there's always the possibility *o* chance that he'll change his mind; **avere la possibilità di fare qc** (*facoltà*) to be in a position to do sth; (*opportunità*) to have the opportunity to do; **non ha possibilità di salvezza** there's no hope of escape for him; **nella mia posizione non ho avuto la possibilità di aiutarlo** in my position I couldn't assist him *o* I had no means of assisting him **b** (*mezzi*): **possibilità** SFPL

means; **vivere secondo le proprie possibilità** (*finanziarie*) to live according to one's means; **nei limiti delle nostre possibilità** in so far as we can.

possibilmente [possibil'mente] AVV if possible; **ti telefono possibilmente domani** I'll phone you tomorrow if I can.

possidente [possi'dɛnte] SM/F property owner, landowner.

possiedo *ecc* [pos'sjɛdo] VB *vedi* **possedere**.

posso *ecc* ['pɔsso] VB *vedi* **potere**.

post... [pɔst] PREF post... .

posta ['pɔsta] SF **a** (*corrispondenza*) post (*Brit*), mail (*Am*); (*servizio*) postal service, mail service, post; (*ufficio*) post office; **poste** SFPL (*amministrazione*) post office; **c'è posta per me?** are there any letters for me?, is there any post *o* mail for me?; **perché non lo mandi per posta?** why don't you send it by post *o* mail?; **impiegato delle poste** post office clerk; **piccola posta** (*su giornale*) letters to the editor, letters page ►**posta aerea** airmail ►**posta elettronica** electronic mail ►**posta ordinaria** ≈ second-class post *o* mail ► **Poste e Telecomunicazioni** *postal and telecommunications service*; **ministro delle Poste e Telecomunicazioni** Postmaster General
b (*Giochi*: *somma in palio*) stake(s); **la posta in gioco è troppo alta** (*fig*) there's too much at stake
c (*Caccia*) hide (*Brit*), blind (*Am*); **fare la posta a qn** (*fig*) to lie in wait for sb
d (*apposta*): **a bella posta** on purpose.

postacelere [posta'tʃɛlere] SM express postal service (*48-hour delivery*).

postagiro [posta'dʒiro] SM post office cheque (*Brit*) *o* check (*Am*), postal giro (*Brit*).

postale [pos'tale] **1** AGG (*servizio, vaglia*) postal *attr* (*Brit*), mail *attr* (*Am*); (*casella, impiegato*) post office *attr*; (*nave, treno*) mail *attr*; **timbro postale** postmark.
2 SM (*treno*) mail train; (*nave*) mail boat; (*furgone*) mail van.

postazione [postat'tsjone] SF (*Mil*) emplacement.

postbellico, a, ci, che [post'bɛlliko] AGG postwar *attr*.

postdatare [postda'tare] VT to postdate.

posteggiare [posted'dʒare] VT, VI (*aus avere*) to park.

posteggiatore, trice [postedddʒa'tore] SM/F car-park attendant (*Brit*), parking-lot attendant (*Am*).

posteggio, gi [pos'teddʒo] SM **a** car park (*Brit*), parking lot (*Am*) ►**posteggio custodito** attended car park *o* parking lot ►**posteggio di taxi** taxi rank (*Brit*), taxi stand (*Am*) **b** (*di rivenditore*) pitch.

postelegrafonico, a, ci, che [postelegra'fɔniko] AGG postal and telecommunications *attr*.

posteri ['pɔsteri] SMPL posterity *sg*; **i nostri posteri** our descendants.

posteriore [poste'rjore] **1** AGG **a** (*dietro: parte di oggetto*) back *attr*, rear *attr*; (*zampe*) hind *attr* **b** (*tempo*) later; **questi avvenimenti sono posteriori alla mia partenza** these events occurred after my departure.
2 SM (*euf fam: sedere*) behind, bottom.

posteriori [poste'rjori]: **a posteriori** **1** AGG INV after the event (*dopo sostantivo*).
2 AVV looking back.

posteriormente [posterjor'mente] AVV **a** (*nella parte posteriore*) behind, at the back **b** (*in un periodo successivo*) later, subsequently; **posteriormente a** subsequent to.

posterità [posteri'ta] SF posterity.

posticcio, a, ci, ce [pos'tittʃo] **1** AGG (*capelli, barba*) false.
2 SM hairpiece.

posticipare [postitʃi'pare] VT to defer, postpone; **posticipare di 3 giorni** to postpone for 3 days; **la riunione è stata posticipata a sabato** the meeting has been postponed until Saturday.

postilla [pos'tilla] SF marginal note.

postimpressionismo [postimpressjo'nizmo] SM post-impressionism.

post-industriale [postindus'trjale] AGG post-industrial.

post-industrialismo [postindustrja'lizmo] SM post-industrialism.

postino, a [pos'tino] SM/F postman/postwoman (*Brit*), mailman/mailwoman (*Am*).

postmoderno, a [postmo'dɛrno] AGG post-modern.

posto¹, a ['posto] PP *di* **porre**.

posto² ['posto] SM **a** (*luogo*) place; **non è un posto adatto ai bambini** it's no place for children; **sul posto** on the spot; **i pompieri sono accorsi sul posto** the firemen rushed to the spot; **lo faremo sul posto *o* quando saremo sul posto** we'll do it when we get there ►**posto di polizia** police station ►**posto telefonico pubblico** public telephone ►**posto di villeggiatura** holiday (*Brit*) *o* tourist spot, resort
b (*spazio libero*) room, space; (*sedile: al teatro, in treno*) seat; (*di parcheggio*) space; **non c'è più posto in macchina** there's no more room in the car; **fate posto!** make way!; **prender posto** to take a seat; **ci sono 20 posti letto in quell'albergo** they can sleep 20 in that hotel; **vai pure al posto** (*scolaro*) go and sit down; **mi tieni il posto in fila?** will you keep my place in the queue?; **una macchina a 5 posti** a 5-seater car ►**posti in piedi** (*Teatro, in autobus*) standing room ►**posto a sedere** seat
c (*impiego*) job, post; **ha un posto di segretaria** she works as *o* has a job as a secretary, she has a secretarial post ►**posto di lavoro** job
d (*posizione in classifica*): **primo/secondo posto** first/second place; **è arrivato al primo posto** he arrived first
e (*Mil*) post; **tutti ai posti di combattimento!** action stations! ►**posto di blocco** (*di polizia*) roadblock; (*alla frontiera*) frontier post
f (*fraseologia*): **al posto di** in place of; **al posto tuo ci andrei** I'd go if I were in your shoes; **l'hanno assunto al posto tuo** they employed him instead of you; **essere a posto** (*in ordine: stanza*) to be tidy; (: *persona*) to be neat and tidy; (*fig: questione*) to be settled; (: *person*) to be OK; **è gente a posto** they are very respectable (people); **mettere a posto** (*riordinare*) to tidy (up), put in order; (*faccende: sistemare*) to straighten out; **mettere a posto qn** to sort sb out; **sa stare al suo posto** he knows his place; **tenere la lingua a posto** to hold one's tongue; **tieni le mani a posto!** keep your hands to yourself!; **per me non ha la testa tanto a posto!** I don't think he's all there!; **sarebbe ora che mettessi la testa a posto** it's time you got yourself sorted out.

postoperatorio, ria, ri, rie [postopera'tɔrjo] AGG (*Med*) postoperative.

postribolo [pos'tribolo] SM (*letter*) brothel.

postscriptum [post'skriptum] SM INV postscript.

postulare [postu'lare] VT (*Filosofia*) to postulate.

postulato [postu'lato] SM (*Mat, Filosofia*) postulate.

postumo, a ['pɔstumo] **1** AGG posthumous; (*tardivo*) belated.
2 (*conseguenze*): **postumi** SMPL consequences, after-

effects; **soffrire i postumi della sbornia** to have a hangover.

potabile [po'tabile] AGG drinkable; **acqua potabile** drinking water.

potare [po'tare] VT (*albero da frutta*) to prune; (*siepe*) to trim.

potassio [po'tassjo] SM potassium.

potatura [pota'tura] SF pruning.

potente [po'tɛnte] ① AGG (*gen*) powerful; (*nazione*) strong; (*efficace*: *medicina, veleno*) potent, strong; (*argomenti*) potent, forceful; **è potente all'interno dell'azienda** he has a lot of influence in the company.

② SMPL: **i potenti** the mighty, the powerful.

potentemente [potente'mente] AVV with force.

potentino, a [poten'tino] ① AGG of *o* from Potenza.

② SM/F inhabitant *o* native of Potenza.

Potenza [po'tɛntsa] SF Potenza.

potenza [po'tɛntsa] SF ⓐ (*potere, influenza*) power, influence; (*forza: fisica, psicologica*) strength; (*efficacia: di medicina, veleno*) potency; (*di argomenti, onde, pugni, armi*) force; **la potenza della stampa** the power of the press; **le Grandi Potenze** the Great Powers ▶**potenza militare** military might *o* strength

ⓑ (*Fis, Mat*) power; **all'ennesima potenza** to the nth degree; **è un idiota all'ennesima potenza** he's a complete and utter idiot.

potenziale [poten'tsjale] AGG, SM potential.

potenzialmente [potentsjal'mente] AVV potentially; **potenzialmente potrebbe fare molto di più** he has the potential to do far more.

potenziamento [potentsja'mento] SM development.

potenziare [poten'tsjare] VT to develop.

potenziometro [poten'tsjɔmetro] SM potentiometer.

potere[1] [po'tere] SM (*gen*) power; **avere il potere di fare qc** (*capacità*) to have the power *o* ability to do sth; (*autorità*) to have the authority *o* power to do sth; **ha il potere di rovinare sempre tutto** he always manages to ruin everything; **il quarto potere** (*stampa*) the fourth estate; **non ho nessun potere su di lui** I have no power *o* influence over him; **essere al potere** (*Pol*) to be in power *o* in office ▶**potere d'acquisto** purchasing power ▶**potere esecutivo** executive power.

potere[2] [po'tere] ① VB IRREG AUS (*nei tempi composti prende l'ausiliare del verbo che accompagna*) ⓐ (*possibilità, capacità*) can; (*sogg: persona*) can, to be able to; **non posso venire** I can't come; **non è potuto venire** he couldn't come, he was unable to come; **non potrà mai farlo da solo** he'll never be able to do it alone; **non ho potuto farlo** I couldn't *o* wasn't able *o* was unable to do it; **come hai potuto fare una cosa simile?** how could you do a thing like that?; **a più non posso** (*correre*) as fast as one can; (*urlare*) as loud as one can

ⓑ (*permesso*) can, may; **posso entrare?** can *o* may I come in?; **potrei parlarti?** could I have a word with you?; **si può sapere dove sei stato?** where on earth have you been?

ⓒ (*eventualità*): **può anche esser vero** it may *o* might *o* could even be true; **potrebbe avere trent'anni** he must be about thirty; **può accadere di tutto** anything can happen; **si può fare** it can be done; **può darsi** perhaps; **può darsi che non venga** he may not *o* might not come; **può essere che non voglia** he may not *o* might not want to

ⓓ (*augurio*): **potessimo trovare un po' di pace!** if only we could get a little peace!

ⓔ (*rimprovero*): **potresti almeno ringraziare!** you could *o* might at least say thank you!; **avresti potuto dirmelo!** you could *o* might have told me!.

② VT IRREG: **puoi molto per me** you can do a lot for me; **non ha potuto niente** he could do nothing; **non ne posso più!** I can't take any more!

potestà [potes'ta] SF INV (*Dir: potere*) power, authority.

potrò ecc [po'trɔ] VB vedi **potere**.

poveraccio, a, ci, ce [pove'rattʃo] SM/F poor devil.

poveramente [povera'mente] AVV (*vestito*) poorly, shabbily; (*arredato*) poorly; **vivere poveramente** to live in poverty.

povero, a ['pɔvero] ① AGG ⓐ (*gen*) poor; (*stile, scusa*) weak; (*raccolto*) poor, scanty; (*vegetazione*) sparse; (*vestito*) plain; (*stanza*) bare; **povero di** lacking in, having little; **minerale povero di ferro** ore with a low iron content; **aria povera di ossigeno** air low in oxygen; **paese povero di risorse** country short of *o* lacking in resources

ⓑ (*fraseologia*): **essere povero in canna** to be as poor as a church mouse; **povero illuso!** poor fool!; **povera piccola!** poor little thing!; **sei un povero stupido!** you're a stupid fool!; **povera me!** poor me!; **in parole povere** in plain language; **povero di spirito** half-wit; **povero te se lo fai!** just you dare!; **il mio povero marito** my poor (late) husband.

② SM/F poor man/woman; **i poveri** the poor.

povertà [pover'ta] SF (*vedi agg*) poverty; weakness; scantiness; sparseness.

pozione [pot'tsjone] SF potion.

pozza ['pottsa] SF (*pozzanghera*) puddle; **una pozza di sangue** a pool of blood.

pozzanghera [pot'tsangera] SF puddle.

pozzetto [pot'tsetto] SM ⓐ (*di fognatura*) shaft ⓑ (*Naut*) well-deck.

pozzo ['pottso] SM (*di acqua, petrolio*) well; (*di miniera*) shaft; (*cava: di carbone*) pit; **essere un pozzo di scienza** to be a walking encyclopaedia *o* a mine of information; **essere un pozzo senza fondo** (*ghiottone*) to be a bottomless pit ▶**pozzo nero** cesspit ▶**pozzo petrolifero** oil well.

p.p. ABBR (= *per procura*) pp.

pp. ABBR (= *pagine*) pp.

P.P.I. [pipi'i] SIGLA M (*Pol*: = *Partito Popolare Italiano*) *party originating from D.C.*

PP.SS. ABBR = **partecipazioni statali**.

PP.TT. ABBR = **Poste e Telecomunicazioni**.

PR SIGLA = *Parma*.

P.R. [pi'ɛrre] ① SIGLA M (*Pol*)= *Partito Radicale*.

② ABBR ⓐ = **piano regolatore** ⓑ = **procuratore della Repubblica**.

Praga ['praga] SF Prague.

pragmatico, a, ci, che [prag'matiko] AGG pragmatic.

pralina [pra'lina] SF praline.

prammatica [pram'matika] SF custom; **essere di prammatica** to be customary.

prammatico, a, ci, che [pram'matiko] AGG pragmatic.

pranzare [pran'dzare] VI (*aus avere*) to (have) lunch; **siamo andati a pranzare fuori** we went out for lunch.

pranzetto [pran'dzetto] SM: **un bel pranzetto** a lovely little meal.

pranzo ['prandzo] SM (*a mezzogiorno*) lunch ▶**pranzo di nozze** wedding breakfast.

prassi ['prassi] SF normal procedure.

prataiolo [prata'jɔlo] SM field mushroom.

prateria [prate'ria] SF prairie.

pratica, che ['pratika] SF **a** (*attività*) practice; **in pratica** (*praticamente*) in practice; **mettere in pratica qc** to put sth into practice; **ho messo in pratica i tuoi consigli** I have acted on your advice **b** (*esperienza*) (practical) experience; (*conoscenza*) knowledge, familiarity; (*tirocinio*) training; **far pratica presso un avvocato** to be articled to a solicitor (*Brit*) o lawyer (*Am*); **acquistare pratica** to gain experience; **ha fatto pratica presso un altro falegname** he was trained by another carpenter; **non ho pratica di queste cose** I have no experience of this **c** (*Amm*: *incartamento*) file, dossier; (: *affare*) matter, case; **fare le pratiche per** to do the paperwork for **d** (*usanza*) practice ▶**pratica restrittiva** restrictive practice ▶**pratiche illecite** (*abortive*) dishonest practices ▶**pratiche religiose** religious practices.

praticabile [prati'kabile] AGG (*progetto*) practicable, feasible; (*luogo*) passable, practicable.

praticamente [pratika'mente] AVV **a** (*quasi*) practically, almost **b** (*in modo pratico*) in a practical way, practically.

praticante [prati'kante] **1** AGG practising (*Brit*), practicing (*Am*). **2** SM/F apprentice, trainee; (*Rel*) (regular) churchgoer.

praticare [prati'kare] VT **a** (*esercitare*: *arte, medicina*) to practise (*Brit*), practice (*Am*); (*Sport*: *calcio, tennis*) to play; (: *nuoto, scherma*) to go in for, do **b** (*frequentare*: *persona*) to associate with, mix with; (: *luogo*) to frequent **c** (*eseguire*: *apertura, incisione*) to make; **praticare uno sconto** to give a discount.

praticità [pratitʃi'ta] SF practicality, practicalness; **per praticità** for practicality's sake.

pratico, a, ci, che ['pratiko] AGG **a** (*non teorico, realista*) practical; **avere senso pratico** to be practical; **all'atto pratico** in practice **b** (*comodo*: *gen*) practical; (: *strumento*) handy; **mi è più pratico venire di pomeriggio** it's more convenient for me to come in the afternoon; **è pratico avere i negozi così vicino** it's handy o convenient to have the shops so near **c** : **pratico di** (*esperto*) experienced o skilled in; (*familiare*) familiar with; **è pratico di motori** he's good with engines; **è pratico del mestiere** he knows his trade; **è pratica del luogo** she knows the place well.

prato ['prato] SM meadow; (*di giardino*) lawn.

preallarme [preal'larme] SM warning (signal).

Prealpi [pre'alpi] SFPL: **le Prealpi** (the) Pre-Alps.

prealpino, a [preal'pino] AGG of the Pre-Alps.

preambolo [pre'ambolo] SM preamble; **senza tanti preamboli** without beating about (*Brit*) o around (*Am*) the bush.

preannunciare [preannun'tʃare], **preannunziare** [preannun'tsjare] VT to give advance notice of; **le nubi preannunziavano la tempesta** the clouds heralded the storm.

preannuncio [prean'nuntʃo], **preannunzio** [prean'nuntsjo] SM advance warning.

preavvisare [preavvi'zare] VT to give advance notice of.

preavviso [preav'vizo] SM (advance) notice; (*Dir*) notice; **senza preavviso** without notice; **3 giorni di preavviso** 3 days' notice; **telefonata con preavviso** personal o person-to-person call.

prebellico, a, ci, che [pre'bɛlliko] AGG prewar *attr*.

precariamente [prekarja'mente] AVV precariously.

precariato [preka'rjato] SM temporary employment.

precarietà [prekarje'ta] SF precariousness.

precario, ria, ri, rie [pre'karjo] **1** AGG **a** precarious; **in precarie condizioni economiche** in a precarious financial state **b** (*Scol*) temporary, without tenure. **2** SM/F (*Scol*) temporary member of staff.

precauzionale [prekauttsjo'nale] AGG precautionary.

precauzione [prekaut'tsjone] SF **a** (*cautela*) caution, care **b** (*misura*) precaution; **prendere precauzioni** to take precautions.

precedente [pretʃe'dɛnte] **1** AGG previous; **il giorno precedente** the previous day, the day before; **il discorso/film precedente** the previous o preceding speech/film. **2** SM precedent; **senza precedenti** unprecedented ▶**precedenti penali** (*Dir*) criminal record *sg*.

precedentemente [pretʃedente'mente] AVV previously, before.

precedenza [pretʃe'dɛntsa] SF **a** (*priorità*) priority, precedence; **dare precedenza assoluta a qc** to give sth top priority **b** (*Aut*): **avere la precedenza** to have right of way; **dare la precedenza** to give way **c** : **in precedenza** (*precedentemente*) previously, before.

precedere [pre'tʃɛdere] VT to precede, go (o come) before.

precessione [pretʃes'sjone] SF (*Astron*) precession.

precettare [pretʃet'tare] VT (*Mil*) to call up (*Brit*), draft (*Am*); (*scioperanti*) to order back to work (*via an injunction*).

precettazione [pretʃettat'tsjone] SF (*di scioperanti*) labour (*Brit*) o labor (*Am*) injunction (*calling off industrial action*).

precetto [pre'tʃetto] SM (*gen*) precept; (*Mil*) call-up papers *pl* (*Brit*), draft notice (*Am*).

precettore [pretʃet'tore] SM (private) tutor.

precipitare [pretʃipi'tare] **1** VT (*gettare dall'alto in basso*) to hurl down, fling down; (*fig*: *affrettare*) to hurry, rush; **precipitare una decisione** to make a hasty decision; **non precipitiamo le cose** let's not rush o precipitate things. **2** VI (*aus essere*) **a** (*cadere*) fall (headlong); (: *aereo*) to crash; **precipitare da una rupe/in un burrone** to fall off a cliff/down a ravine; **la situazione sta precipitando** the situation is getting out of control **b** (*Chim*) to precipitate. **3** **precipitarsi** VIP (*affrettarsi*) to rush. **4** **precipitarsi** VR (*gettarsi*): **precipitarsi da, in** to hurl o fling o.s. from, into.

precipitato, a [pretʃipi'tato] **1** AGG hasty. **2** SM (*Chim*) precipitate.

precipitazione [pretʃipitat'tsjone] SF (*Meteor*) precipitation; (*fig*) haste; **con precipitazione** hastily.

precipitevolmente [pretʃipitevol'mente], **precipitosamente** [pretʃipitosa'mente] AVV hastily.

precipitoso, a [pretʃipi'toso] AGG (*fig*: *affrettato*) hasty, rushed; (: *avventato*) rash, reckless; (*caduta, fuga*) headlong.

precipizio, zi [pretʃi'pittsjo] SM precipice; **cadere da un precipizio** to fall over a precipice; **scogli a precipizio sul mare** cliffs rising sheer from the sea; **essere sull'orlo del precipizio** (*fig*) to be on the edge of a precipice; **correre a precipizio** (*fig*) to run headlong.

precipuo, a [pre'tʃipuo] AGG main, principal.

precisamente [pretʃiza'mente] AVV (*gen*) precisely; (*con esattezza*) exactly.

precisare [pretʃi'zare] VT to clarify; (*spiegare*) to explain (in detail); **vi preciseremo la data in seguito** we'll let you know the exact date later; **tengo a precisare che... I** must point out that ... .

precisazione [pretʃizat'tsjone] SF clarification.

precisione [pretʃi'zjone] SF (*esattezza*) precision; (*accuratezza*) accuracy; **strumenti di precisione** precision instruments.

preciso, a [pre'tʃizo] AGG **a** (*esatto*) precise; (*accurato*) accurate, precise; (*ben determinato: ordine, idee, piano*) precise, definite; **in quel preciso istante** at that very moment; **queste sono le sue precise parole** these were his very words; **sono le 4 precise** it's exactly 4 o'clock **b** (*uguale*): **2 vestiti precisi** 2 dresses exactly the same; **il tuo cappello è preciso al mio** your hat is exactly the same as *o* identical to mine.

precludere [pre'kludere] VT IRREG to preclude.

precluso, a [pre'kluzo] PP di **precludere**.

precoce [pre'kotʃe] AGG (*stagione*) early; (*bambino*) precocious; (*vecchiaia*) premature; (*morte*) untimely; (*decisione*) hasty, premature.

precocemente [prekotʃe'mente] AVV (*maturare: bambino*) precociously; (*: frutta*) too early.

precocità [prekotʃi'ta] SF (*di morte*) untimeliness; (*di bambino*) precociousness, precocity.

precompresso, a [prekom'prɛsso] AGG (*Edil*) prestressed.

preconcetto [prekon'tʃɛtto] 1 AGG preconceived. 2 SM preconceived idea, prejudice.

preconfezionare [prekonfettsjo'nare] VT to prepack(age).

preconfezionato, a [prekonfettsjo'nato] AGG prepacked, prepackaged.

precorrere [pre'korrere] VT IRREG to anticipate; **precorrere i tempi** to be ahead of one's time.

precorritore, trice [prekorri'tore] SM/F precursor, forerunner.

precorso, a [pre'korso] PP di **precorrere**.

precotto, a [pre'kotto] AGG precooked.

precursore [prekur'sore] SM precursor, forerunner.

preda ['prɛda] SF (*animale, fig*) prey; (*bottino*) booty; **uccello da preda** bird of prey; **essere preda di** to fall prey to; **essere in preda a** (*paura, terrore*) to be prey to; **era in preda all'ira** he was beside himself with rage; **era in preda al panico** he was in a panic.

predare [pre'dare] VT to plunder.

predatore, trice [preda'tore] 1 AGG predatory. 2 SM/F (*Zool*) predator; (*predone*) plunderer.

predecessore, a [predetʃes'sore] SM/F predecessor.

predella [pre'dɛlla] SF (*di cattedra*) platform, dais; (*di altare*) predella, altar-step.

predellino [predel'lino] SM (*di vettura*) step, footboard.

predestinare [predesti'nare] VT to predestine.

predestinazione [predestinat'tsjone] SF predestination.

predetto, a [pre'detto] 1 PP di **predire**. 2 AGG aforesaid, aforementioned.

predica, che ['prɛdika] SF (*Rel*) sermon; (*fig*) lecture, talking-to; **fare una predica** to preach a sermon; **fare una predica a qn** (*fig*) to give sb a lecture *o* a talking-to.

predicare [predi'kare] 1 VT to preach. 2 VI (*aus avere*) (*anche fig*) to preach; **predica bene e razzola male** he doesn't practise what he preaches.

predicativo, a [predika'tivo] AGG predicative.

predicato [predi'kato] SM (*Gramm*) predicate; **in funzione di predicato** predicatively.

predicatore [predika'tore] SM preacher.

predicazione [predikat'tsjone] SF preaching.

predicozzo [predi'kottso] SM (*fam*) lecture, talking-to; **fare un predicozzo a qn** to lecture sb.

prediletto, a [predi'lɛtto] 1 PP di **prediligere**. 2 AGG (*figlio, allievo*) favourite (*Brit*), favorite (*Am*); (*amico*) best, closest. 3 SM/F favourite (*Brit*), favorite (*Am*); **il prediletto della mamma** mummy's pet.

predilezione [predilet'tsjone] SF partiality, predilection, fondness; **avere una predilezione per qc/qn** to be partial to sth/fond of sb.

prediligere [predi'lidʒere] VT IRREG to prefer, have a preference *o* a predilection for.

predire [pre'dire] VT IRREG to predict, foretell; **predire il futuro** to tell *o* predict the future.

predisporre [predis'porre] VB IRREG 1 VT to get ready, prepare; **predisporre qn a qc** to prepare sb for sth. 2 **predisporsi** VR: **predisporsi a qc** to prepare o.s. for sth.

predisposizione [predisposit'tsjone] SF (*Med*) predisposition; (*attitudine*) bent, aptitude; **avere predisposizione alla musica** to have a bent for music.

predisposto, a [predis'posto] 1 PP di **predisporre**. 2 AGG (*gen*) prepared; **le misure predisposte per prevenire gli incidenti stradali...** the measures which have been drawn up to prevent road accidents ...; **predisposto alle malattie** (*persona*) prone to illness.

predizione [predit'tsjone] SF prediction.

predominante [predomi'nante] AGG predominant.

predominare [predomi'nare] VI (*aus avere*) (*prevalere*) to predominate; (*eccellere*) to excel.

predominio [predo'minjo] SM (*il prevalere*) predominance; (*supremazia*) supremacy; (*dominio*) domination; (*:fig*) sway; **avere il predominio** (*prevalere*) to be predominant.

predone [pre'done] SM marauder, plunderer.

preesistente [preezis'tɛnte] AGG pre-existent.

preesistenza [preezis'tɛntsa] SF pre-existence.

preesistere [pree'zistere] VI IRREG (*aus essere*) to pre-exist.

preesistito, a [preezis'tito] PP di **preesistere**.

prefabbricato, a [prefabbri'kato] 1 AGG (*Edil*) prefabricated. 2 SM prefab, prefabricated house.

prefazione [prefat'tsjone] SF preface, foreword.

preferenza [prefe'rɛntsa] SF preference; **di preferenza** preferably, by preference; **a preferenza di** rather than; **dare la preferenza a qn/qc** to prefer sb/sth; **non ho preferenze** I have no preferences either way, I don't mind; **qui non si fanno preferenze** there is no favouritism here.

preferenziale [preferen'tsjale] AGG preferential; **corsia preferenziale** (*Aut*) bus and taxi lane; (*fig*) fast track.

preferibile [prefe'ribile] AGG: **preferibile (a)** preferable (to), better (than); **sarebbe preferibile andarsene** it would be better to go.

preferibilmente [preferibil'mente] AVV preferably.

preferire [prefe'rire] VT to prefer, like better; **preferisco la città alla campagna** I prefer the town to the countryside; **preferirei non farlo** I'd rather not do it, I'd prefer not to do it; **preferirei morire piuttosto che...** I'd rather die than ...; **cosa preferisci, tè o caffè?** what would you like, tea or coffee?; **preferire il caffè al tè** to prefer coffee

to tea, like coffee better than tea.

preferito, a [prefe'rito] AGG, SM/F favourite.

prefettizio, a, zi, e [prefet'tittsjo] AGG prefectorial.

prefetto [pre'fɛtto] SM prefect.

prefettura [prefet'tura] SF prefecture.

prefiggere [pre'fiddʒere] VT IRREG: **prefiggersi qc** (*scopo, meta*) to set o.s. sth.

prefigurare [prefigu'rare] VT (*simboleggiare*) to foreshadow; (*prevedere*) to foresee.

prefigurazione [prefigurat'tsjone] SF prefiguration.

prefissare [prefis'sare] VT to establish in advance.

prefisso, a [pre'fisso] 1 PP di **prefiggere**.
2 SM (*Telec*) dialling (*Brit*) o dial (*Am*) code; (*Gramm*) prefix.

Preg. ABBR = **pregiatissimo**.

pregare [pre'gare] VT (*Rel*) to pray to; (*supplicare*) to beg; (*chiedere*): **pregare qn di fare qc** to ask sb to do sth; **l'ho pregata di venire** I asked her to come; **i passeggeri sono pregati di...** passengers are requested to ...; **farsi pregare** to need coaxing o persuading; **si fa pregare un po' troppo** she plays hard to get; **non si fa pregare due volte** he doesn't wait to be asked twice; **ti prego, lasciami in pace** please leave me alone; **la prego, stia comodo** please don't get up.

pregevole [pre'dʒevole] AGG (*persona, azione*) praiseworthy; (*oggetto, opera*) valuable.

pregherò ecc [prege'rɔ] VB vedi **pregare**.

preghiera [pre'gjɛra] SF (*Rel*) prayer; (*richiesta*) request; (*supplica*) plea, entreaty.

pregiarsi [pre'dʒarsi] VR (*frm*): **pregiarsi di fare qc** to be honoured to do sth; **mi pregio di farle sapere che...** I am pleased o honoured to inform you that ... .

pregiatamente [predʒata'mente] AVV (*lavorato, intarsiato*) finely.

pregiatissimo, a [predʒa'tissimo] AGG (*in lettere*): **pregiatissimo Signor G. Agelli** G. Agelli, Esq(uire).

pregiato, a [pre'dʒato] AGG (*opera*) valuable; (*tessuto*) fine; (*valuta*) strong; **vino pregiato** vintage wine.

pregio, gi ['prɛdʒo] SM (*valore*) worth, value; (*qualità*) (good) quality, merit; (*frm: stima*) esteem, regard; **avere molti pregi** (*persona*) to have a lot of good qualities; **i pregi artistici di un'opera** the artistic merit of a work; **il pregio di questo sistema è...** the merit of this system is ...; **oggetto di pregio** valuable object.

pregiudicare [predʒudi'kare] VT (*compromettere*): **pregiudicare qc** to jeopardize sth, put sth in jeopardy, prejudice sth; **pregiudicare la propria salute** to endanger one's health.

pregiudicato, a [predʒudi'kato] SM/F (*Dir*) person with a criminal record.

pregiudiziale [predʒudit'tsjale] SF precondition.

pregiudizio, zi [predʒu'dittsjo] SM **a** (*opinione errata*) prejudice; (*superstizione*) superstition; **avere dei pregiudizi contro** o **nei confronti di qn** to be prejudiced o biased against sb; **è un pregiudizio largamente diffuso** it's a widely held superstition
b (*danno*) harm *no pl*; **essere di pregiudizio a** to be detrimental to; **con pregiudizio della sua salute** to the detriment of his health.

pregnante [preɲ'ɲante] AGG (*fig: frasi, parole*) pregnant, meaningful.

pregno, a ['preɲɲo] AGG **a** (*gravido: animale*) pregnant **b**: **pregno di** (*odio, passione*) filled with, full of.

prego ['prɛgo] ESCL (*a chi ringrazia*) don't mention it!, you're welcome!, not at all!; (*invitando qn ad accomodarsi*) please sit down!; (*invitando qn ad andare prima*) after you!; **prego, si accomodi** (*entri*) come in please; (*si sieda*) take a seat please; **posso prenderlo? - prego!** can I take it? - please do!; **prego? pardon?, sorry?** (*Brit*).

pregustare [pregus'tare] VT to look forward to; **pregustava il piacere della vendetta** he savoured the idea of vengeance.

pre-industriale [preindus'trjale] AGG pre-industrial.

preistoria [preis'tɔrja] SF prehistory; **fin dalla preistoria** from time immemorial.

preistorico, a, ci, che [preis'tɔriko] AGG prehistoric; (*fig: scherz*) antediluvian.

prelato [pre'lato] SM prelate.

prelavaggio [prela'vaddʒo] SM prewash.

prelazione [prelat'tsjone] SF (*Dir*) pre-emption; **avere il diritto di prelazione su qc** to have the first option on sth.

prelevamento [preleva'mento] SM (*Banca*) withdrawal; (*di merce*) picking up, collection.

prelevare [prele'vare] VT (*Banca*) to withdraw; (*campione di sangue*) to take; (*merce*) to collect, to pick up; (*sogg: polizia*) to arrest.

prelibatamente [prelibata'mente] AVV deliciously.

prelibato, a [preli'bato] AGG delicious.

prelievo [pre'ljɛvo] SM (*Banca*) withdrawal; (*di merce*) collection; (*di tasse*) levying; **fare un prelievo di sangue** to take a blood sample.

preliminare [prelimi'nare] 1 AGG preliminary.
2: **preliminari** SMPL preliminaries; (*in rapporto sessuale*) foreplay *sg*.

preludere [pre'ludere] VI IRREG (*aus avere*): **preludere a a** (*preannunciare: crisi, guerra, temporale*) to herald, be a sign of **b** (*introdurre: dibattito*) to introduce, be a prelude to.

preludio, di [pre'ludjo] SM (*Mus, fig*) prelude; (*introduzione*) introduction.

preluso, a [pre'luzo] PP di **preludere**.

pre-maman [pre ma'mã] 1 AGG INV maternity *attr*.
2 SM INV maternity dress.

prematrimoniale [prematrimo'njale] AGG premarital.

prematuramente [prematura'mente] AVV prematurely; **è morto prematuramente** he died before his time.

prematuro, a [prema'turo] 1 AGG (*gen*) premature; (*morte*) untimely.
2 SM/F premature baby.

premeditare [premedi'tare] VT to premeditate, plan; **omicidio premeditato** premeditated murder.

premeditatamente [premeditata'mente] AVV with premeditation.

premeditazione [premeditat'tsjone] SF (*Dir*) premeditation; **con premeditazione** with intent.

premere ['prɛmere] 1 VT (*gen*) to press; **premere il grilletto** to pull the trigger; **premi forte!** press hard!.
2 VI (*aus avere*) **a**: **premere su** (*gen*) to press on; (*pedale*) to press down on; (*fig*) to put pressure on
b (*fig: stare a cuore*): **è una faccenda che mi preme molto** it's a matter which I am very concerned about; **gli premeva (di) terminare il lavoro** he was anxious to finish the job.

premessa [pre'messa] SF (*introduzione*) introduction; (*Filosofia*) premise; **fare una premessa** to make an introductory statement; **mancano le premesse per una buona riuscita** we lack the basis for a successful outcome.

premesso, a [pre'messo] PP di **premettere**.

premestruale [premestru'ale] AGG premenstrual.

premettere [pre'mettere] VT IRREG **a** (*dire prima*) to start by saying, state first; **vorrei premettere alcune considerazioni di carattere generale** I should like to begin by making a few general points; **premetto che...** I must say first of all that ...; **premesso che...** given that ...; **ciò premesso...** that (having been) said ...

b (*porre prima*) to put before; **premettere una prefazione ad un'opera** to preface a work.

premiare [pre'mjare] VT (*atleta, studente*) to give a prize to, award a prize to; (*libro, film*) to award a prize to; (*fig: merito, onestà*) to reward; **è stata premiata con una medaglia** she was awarded a medal.

premiato, a [pre'mjato] **1** AGG prizewinning.

2 SM/F prizewinner.

premiazione [premjat'tsjone] SF prize-giving.

premier ['prɛmjer] SM INV (*Pol*) premier.

première [prə'mjɛr] SF INV (*Teatro, Cine*) première, first performance.

preminente [premi'nɛnte] AGG prominent, pre-eminent.

preminentemente [preminente'mente] AVV primarily.

preminenza [premi'nɛntsa] SF pre-eminence, superiority.

premio, mi ['prɛmjo] **1** SM **a** (*gen*) prize; (*ricompensa*) reward; **in premio per** as a prize (*o* reward) for ▶**premio di consolazione** consolation prize ▶**premio Nobel** Nobel prize

b (*Fin, Assicurazione*) premium

c (*indennità speciale*) bonus ▶**premio d'ingaggio** (*Sport*) signing-on fee ▶**premio di produzione** productivity bonus.

2 AGG INV: **vincere una vacanza premio** to win a holiday.

premisi ecc [pre'mizi] VB vedi **premettere**.

premonitore, trice [premoni'tore] AGG premonitory.

premonizione [premonit'tsjone] SF premonition.

premunire [premu'nire] **1** VT: **premunire (contro)** (*nemico, influenza*) to protect (against); **premunire qn contro i rischi della droga** to make sb aware of the dangers of drugs.

2 premunirsi VR: **premunirsi (di** *o* **con)** to arm o.s. (with); **premunirsi (contro)** to protect o.s. (from), guard o.s. (against).

premura [pre'mura] SF **a** (*fretta*) haste, hurry; **aver premura** to be in a hurry; **far premura a qn** to hurry sb

b (*riguardo*) attention, care; **usare ogni premura nei riguardi di qn** [OR] **circondare qn di premure** to be very attentive to sb.

premurosamente [premurosa'mente] AVV thoughtfully, kindly.

premuroso, a [premu'roso] AGG attentive, thoughtful, considerate; **un marito e padre premuroso** a devoted husband and father.

prenatale [prena'tale] AGG antenatal, prenatal.

prendere ['prɛndere] VB IRREG **1** VT **a** (*gen*) to take; (*portare: cosa*) to get, fetch; (*: persona*) to pick up, fetch; **ha preso il libro dal tavolo** he picked up *o* took the book from the table; **l'ho preso dal cassetto** I took *o* got it out of the drawer; **l'ha preso per mano** she took his hand *o* took him by the hand; **prendere qc in spalla** to shoulder sth; **prendere qc per il manico** to take sth by the handle; **vieni a prendermi alla stazione** come and pick me up *o* fetch me from the station; **vai a prendermi gli occhiali** go and get my glasses; **abbiamo preso una casa** (*affit-*

tare) we have taken *o* rented a house; (*comprare*) we have bought a house

b (*afferrare*) to seize, grab; (*catturare: ladro, pesce*) to catch; (: *fortezza*) to take; **prendere qn per i capelli** to grab sb by the hair; **è stato preso dalla polizia** he was caught by the police; **l'ho preso mentre tentava di scappare** I caught him trying to escape; **la cintura mi è rimasta presa nella porta** my belt got caught in the door

c (*direzione, scorciatoia, mezzo pubblico*) to take; **non so che strada prendere** I don't know which road to take; **ha preso il treno** he took the train, he went by train; **ha preso il treno delle 10** he took *o* caught the 10 o'clock train; **preferisco prendere l'aereo anziché il treno** I prefer to go by plane rather than by train; **la nave ha preso il largo** the ship put out to sea

d (*registrare*) to take (down); **prendere le misure di qn** to take sb's measurements; **prendere le generalità di qn** to take down sb's particulars; **prendere nota di** to take note of

e (*guadagnare*) to get, earn; (*chiedere: somma, prezzo*) to charge, ask; **prende tre milioni al mese** he makes *o* earns three million lira a month; **quanto prende per un taglio di capelli?** how much do you charge for a haircut?

f (*ricevere: colpi, schiaffi, sgridata*) to get; (*subire: malattia*) to catch; **le ha prese** he got a good hiding; **ho preso uno spavento** I got such a fright; **ho preso freddo** I've caught a chill; **non so come la prenderà** I don't know how he'll take the news

g (*ingoiare: pasto, panino, tè*) to have; (: *medicina*) to take; **non prendo nulla fuori pasto** I don't eat between meals; **prendi qualcosa?** (*da bere, da mangiare*) would you like something to eat (*o* drink)?; **prendo un caffè** I'll have a coffee; **prendi pure** help yourself

h (*assumere: collaboratore, dipendente*) to take on, hire; (: *responsabilità*) to take on, assume; (: *tono, aria*) to put on; (: *colore*) to take on; (*decisione*) to take, make, come to; **prendere un impegno** to take on a commitment; **ha preso uno strano odore** it smells funny; **prendere l'abitudine di** to get into the habit of

i (*pervadere*): **essere preso dai rimorsi** to be full of remorse; **essere preso dal panico** to be panic-stricken; **che cosa ti prende adesso?** now what's got into you!; **quel film mi ha preso** that film caught my imagination

j (*scambiare*): **prendere qn/qc per** to mistake sb/sth for; **ti avevo preso per mio fratello** I mistook you for my brother; **ha preso le mie parole** *o* **come un'offesa** he took offence at my words; **per chi mi prendi?** who do you think I am?, what do you take me for?

k (*trattare: persona*) to handle; **prendere qn per il verso giusto** to handle sb the right way; **prendere qn con le buone/cattive** to handle sb tactfully/rudely

l (*occupare: spazio, tempo*) to take up; **il tavolo prende poco posto** the table doesn't take up much room; **questo lavoro mi sta prendendo troppo tempo** this work is taking up too much of my time

m (*cominciare*): **prendere a fare qc** to begin to do sth, start doing sth

n : **prendersela** (*adirarsi*) to get annoyed; (*preoccuparsi*) to get upset, worry; **prendersela a male** to take offence; **prendersela con qn** to get angry with sb; **perché te la prendi sempre con me?** why do you always pick on me?; **prendersela comoda** to take it easy

o (*fraseologia*): **prendere da qn** (*assomigliare*) to take

after sb; **prendere a calci qn** to kick sb; **prendere qn per fame** to starve sb into submission; **prendere o lasciare** take it or leave it; **prendersi la soddisfazione (di)** to have the satisfaction (of); **prendersi una vacanza** to take a holiday; **prendersi cura di qn/qc** to look after sb/sth; **prendersi gioco di qn** to mock sb; **prendere parte a** to take part in; **prendere fuoco** to catch fire.

2 VI (*aus* **avere**) **a** (*far presa: colla, cemento*) to set; (: *piante*) to take (root); (: *fuoco*) to catch

b (*andare*): **prendere a destra** to go *o* turn right; **prendere per i campi** to go across the fields

c (*fraseologia*): **mi è preso un colpo** I got such a fright; **mi è preso freddo** I started feeling cold; **mi è presa la voglia di andare al mare** I feel like going to the seaside.

3 **prendersi** VR (*uso reciproco: afferrarsi*) to grab each other, seize each other; **prendersi a pugni** to come to blows; **prendersi a calci** to kick each other.

prendisole [prendi'sole] SM INV sundress.

prenotare [preno'tare] 1 VT (*posto, tavolo*) to book, reserve; (*camera*) to book.

2 **prenotarsi** VR: **prenotarsi per qc** to put one's name down for sth.

prenotazione [prenotat'tsjone] SF booking, reservation.

prensile ['prɛnsile] AGG prehensile.

preoccupante [preokku'pante] AGG worrying.

preoccupare [preokku'pare] 1 VT (*impensierire*) to worry; **ciò che mi preoccupa è il viaggio** what's worrying *o* bothering me is the journey; **Giovanna mi preoccupa** OR **sono preoccupato per Giovanna** I am worried about Giovanna; **la sua salute mi preoccupa** I'm concerned *o* anxious about his health.

2 **preoccuparsi** VIP: **preoccuparsi (per qn/qc)** to worry (about sb/sth), be anxious (about sb/sth); **non preoccuparti** don't worry.

preoccupazione [preokkupat'tsjone] SF (*problema*) worry; (*inquietudine*) anxiety, worry; **è pieno di preoccupazioni** he has lots of worries *o* problems; **la sua unica preoccupazione è vestirsi bene** his only concern *o* preoccupation is to dress well.

preordinato, a [preordi'nato] AGG preordained.

prepagato, a [prepa'gato] AGG prepaid.

preparare [prepa'rare] 1 VT **a** (*gen*) to prepare; (*pranzo*) to make, prepare; (*letto*) to make; (*tavola*) to lay; (*valigia*) to get ready, pack; (*esame, concorso*) to prepare for, study for; **preparare da mangiare** to prepare a meal; **preparare il terreno** (*anche fig*) to prepare the ground; **chissà cosa ci prepara il futuro!** who knows what the future has in store for us!

b : **preparare qn a** (*esame*) to prepare *o* coach sb for; (*notizia*) to prepare sb for; **preparare qn per un intervento** to get sb ready for an operation.

2 **prepararsi** VR (*vestirsi*) to get ready; (*atleta: allenarsi*) to train; **prepararsi a qc/a fare qc** to get ready *o* prepare (o.s.) for sth/to do sth; **prepararsi ad un esame** to prepare for *o* study for an exam.

preparativi [prepara'tivi] SMPL: **preparativi (per)** preparations (for).

preparato, a [prepa'rato] 1 AGG (*gen*) prepared; (*pronto*) ready; **un allievo molto preparato** a well-prepared student.

2 SM (*prodotto*) preparation.

preparatorio, ria, ri, rie [prepara'tɔrjo] AGG preparatory.

preparazione [preparat'tsjone] SF (*gen*) preparation; (*Sport*) training; **iniziare la preparazione per gli esami** to begin preparation for the exams; **non ha la necessaria preparazione per svolgere questo lavoro** he doesn't have either the knowledge or the experience necessary for the job.

prepensionamento [prepensjona'mento] SM early retirement.

preponderante [preponde'rante] AGG predominant.

preponderanza [preponde'rantsa] SF (*prevalenza*) preponderance; (*superiorità*) superiority.

preporre [pre'porre] VT IRREG **a** (*porre innanzi*) to place before; (*fig: preferire*) to prefer, put before **b** (*mettere a capo*): **preporre qn a qc** to put sb in charge of sth; **l'ufficiale preposto al comando del reggimento** the officer in command of the regiment.

preposizione [preposit'tsjone] SF (*Gramm*) preposition.

preposto, a [pre'posto] PP di **preporre**.

prepotente [prepo'tɛnte] 1 AGG (*persona*) overbearing, arrogant, domineering; (*fig: desiderio, bisogno*) overwhelming, pressing; **un prepotente desiderio di qc/di fare qc** an overwhelming desire for sth/to do sth; **quel bambino è molto prepotente** that child is a real bully.

2 SM/F bully.

prepotentemente [prepotente'mente] AVV (*vedi agg*) arrogantly; overwhelmingly.

prepotenza [prepo'tɛntsa] SF (*arroganza*) arrogance; (*comportamento*) arrogant behaviour (*Brit*) *o* behavior (*Am*); **agire con prepotenza** to behave arrogantly; **è stata una prepotenza da parte tua** it was very highhanded of you.

prepuzio, zi [pre'puttsjo] SM (*Anat*) foreskin.

prerogativa [preroga'tiva] SF **a** (*privilegio*) prerogative **b** (*peculiarità*) property, quality.

presa ['presa] 1 SF **a** (*gen*) grip; (*appiglio*) hold; (*Lotta*) grip, hold; **allentare la presa (di qc)** to release one's grip *o* hold (on sth); **avere una presa forte** to have a strong grip; **venire alle prese con qc** (*fig*) to come to grips with sth; **essere alle prese con qc** (*fig*) to be struggling with sth; **di forte presa** (*fig*) with wide appeal; **a presa rapida** (*cemento*) quick-setting; **far presa** (*colla*) to set; **ha fatto presa sul pubblico** (*fig*) it caught the public's imagination

b (*conquista: di città*) taking *no pl*, capture; (*Carte*) trick

c (*pizzico: di sale, tabacco*) pinch

d (*Cine*): **macchina da presa** cine camera (*Brit*), movie camera (*Am*).

2 ▸ **presa dell'acqua** water (supply) point ▸ **presa d'aria** air inlet *o* intake ▸ **presa di corrente** (*Elettr*) socket; (: *al muro*) point ▸ **presa diretta** (*Aut*) direct drive ▸ **presa del gas** gas (supply) point ▸ **presa in giro** leg-pull (*Brit*), joke ▸ **presa multipla** (*Elettr*) multiple socket ▸ **presa di posizione** stand ▸ **presa di possesso** taking possession.

presagio, gi [pre'zadʒo] SM omen, sign; (*presentimento*) premonition, presentiment.

presagire [preza'dʒire] VT (*prevedere*) to predict, foresee; (*presentire*) to have a premonition of.

presago, a, ghi, ghe [pre'zago] AGG (*letter*): **essere presago di qc** to have a premonition *o* presentiment of sth.

presalario, ri [presa'larjo] SM (*Univ*) grant.

presbiopia [prezbio'pia] SF long-sightedness.

presbite ['prɛzbite] AGG long-sighted.

presbiterianesimo [prezbiterja'nezimo] SM Presbyteri-

anism.

presbiteriano, a [prezbite'rjano] AGG, SM/F Presbyterian.

presbiterio, ri [prezbi'tɛrjo] SM presbytery.

presbitero [prez'bitero] SM presbyter.

prescegliere [preʃ'ʃeʎʎere] VT IRREG to select, choose.

prescelto, a [preʃ'ʃelto] PP di **prescegliere**.

prescindere [preʃ'ʃindere] VI IRREG (aus avere): **prescindere da** to leave aside, leave out of consideration; **prescindendo da** [OR] **a prescindere da** leaving aside, apart from.

prescisso, a [preʃ'ʃisso] PP di **prescindere**.

prescolastico, a, ci, che [presko'lastiko] AGG preschool attr; **bambini in età prescolastica** children not yet of school age.

prescritto, a [pres'kritto] PP di **prescrivere**.

prescrivere [pres'krivere] VT IRREG (Med, Dir) to prescribe; **prescrivere una medicina a qn** to prescribe medicine for sb.

prescrizione [preskrit'tsjone] SF (Med, Dir) prescription; (norma) rule, regulation; **cadere in prescrizione** (Dir) to become statute-barred.

prese ecc ['prese] VB vedi **prendere**.

preselettore [preselet'tore] SM (Tecn) preselector.

presentare [prezen'tare] [1] VT a (gen) to present; (documento) to present, show, produce; (proposta, conti, bilancio) to present, submit; (domanda, reclamo) to put in
b (nuovo modello) to present; (spettacolo) to present, host; (persona) to introduce; **presentare qn (a)** to introduce sb (to); **presentare qn in società** to introduce sb into society; **presentare qc in un'esposizione** to show o display sth at an exhibition
c (dono) to present, give; (omaggi) to present, pay; **presentare le armi** (Mil) to present arms.
[2] **presentarsi** VR a (recarsi, farsi vedere) to present o.s., appear; **presentarsi davanti al tribunale** to appear before the court; **è così che ti presenti?** is this any way to be seen?; **presentarsi bene/male** to have a good/poor appearance
b (farsi conoscere) to introduce o.s.
c (candidato) to come forward; **presentarsi a** (elezione) to stand for (Brit), run for (Am); (concorso) to enter for; (esame) to sit, take.
[3] **presentarsi** VIP a (capitare: occasione, caso strano) to occur, arise; **se mi si presenterà una simile occasione** should a similar opportunity occur o arise; **presentarsi alla mente** (idea) to come o spring to mind
b (apparire) to look, seem; **la situazione si presenta difficile** things aren't looking too good, things look a bit tricky.

presentatore, trice [prezenta'tore] SM/F (Radio, TV) presenter; **presentatore di quiz** quizmaster.

presentazione [prezentat'tsjone] SF (gen) presentation; (di persona) introduction; **fare le presentazioni** to make the introductions.

presente¹ [pre'zɛnte] [1] AGG (gen) present; (questo): **la presente lettera** this letter; **essere presente a una riunione** to be present at o attend a meeting; **avere presente qn/qc** to remember sb/sth; **tener presente qn/qc** to keep sb/sth in mind.
[2] SM/F person present; **i presenti** those present; **esclusi i presenti** present company excepted.
[3] SM (Gramm) present tense; (tempo attuale): **il presente** the present; **per il presente** for the present; **al presente** at present.
[4] SF (Comm: lettera): **con la presente vi comunico...** this is to inform you that ... .

presente² [pre'zɛnte] SM (regalo) present, gift.

presentemente [prezente'mente] AVV at present.

presentimento [presenti'mento] SM premonition, presentiment; **ho lo strano presentimento che...** I have a strange feeling that ... .

presentire [presen'tire] VT to have a presentiment of; **come presentivo non si è fatto più sentire** as I thought o foresaw he hasn't called since; **presentivo che sarebbe andata a finire così** I thought o had a feeling that it would end like that.

presenza [pre'zɛntsa] SF (gen) presence; (Scol) attendance; **fare atto di presenza** to put in an appearance; **in presenza di** in (the) presence of; **conta 18 presenze in nazionale** (Sport) he's won 18 caps, he's played in the national team 18 times; **di bella presenza** of good appearance ▶ **presenza di spirito** presence of mind.

presenziare [prezen'tsjare] VI (aus avere): **presenziare a** to be present at, attend.

presepio, pi [pre'zɛpjo], **presepe** [pre'zɛpe] SM nativity scene.

preservare [preser'vare] VT to protect; **preservare qn da qc** to protect sb from o against sth; **preservare la salute** to protect one's health.

preservativo [preserva'tivo] SM (profilattico) condom, sheath (Brit).

preservazione [preservat'tsjone] SF preservation, protection.

presi ecc ['presi] VB vedi **prendere**.

preside ['prɛside] SM/F (Scol) headmaster/headmistress (Brit), head (teacher) (Brit), principal (Am) ▶ **preside di facoltà** (Univ) dean of faculty.

presidente, essa [presi'dɛnte] SM (di nazione, club) president; (di assemblea, riunione, società commerciale) chairman/chairwoman; (Dir) presiding judge o magistrate ▶ **Presidente della Camera (dei Deputati)** (Pol) ≈ Speaker ▶ **Presidente della commissione** (Scol) chief examiner ▶ **Presidente del Consiglio (dei Ministri)** (Pol) ≈ Prime Minister ▶ **Presidente della Repubblica** (Pol) President of the Republic.

presidenza [presi'dɛntsa] SF a (vedi presidente) presidency, office of president; chairmanship; **essere alla presidenza** to be president; to be chairman/woman; **assumere la presidenza** to become president; to take the chair; **candidato alla presidenza** presidential candidate; candidate for the chairmanship
b (di preside: carica) headship (Brit), post of principal (Am); (: ufficio) headmaster's/headmistress's office o study (Brit), principal's office (Am).

presidenziale [presiden'tsjale] AGG presidential.

presidiare [presi'djare] VT (Mil) to garrison; (casa, fabbrica) to guard.

presidio, di [pre'sidjo] SM (Mil: guarnigione) garrison; (: comando territoriale) command; (: ufficio) area recruitment office.

presiedere [pre'sjɛdere] VB IRREG [1] VT (assemblea, riunione) to preside over, chair; **presiede la Camera dei Deputati** (Pol) ≈ he (o she) is Speaker of the House of Commons.
[2] VI (aus avere): **presiedere a** (discussione, riunione) to preside over, chair; (realizzazione, svolgimento) direct, be in charge of.

presieduto, a [presje'duto] PP di **presiedere**.

presina [pre'sina] SF (*per le pentole*) pot holder.

preso, a ['preso] PP di **prendere**.

pressa ['pressa] SF (*Tecn*) press.

pressante [pres'sante] AGG (*bisogno*) urgent, pressing; (*richiesta*) urgent.

pressantemente [pressante'mente] AVV urgently.

pressappoco [pressap'pɔko] AVV about, roughly, approximately; **sono pressappoco uguali** they are more or less the same; **pressapoco ha 40 anni** he's about 40.

pressare [pres'sare] VT (*Tecn, fig: schiacciare*) to press; **pressare qn con richieste di aiuti** to press sb for assistance.

pressione [pres'sjone] SF a (*gen, Fis, Med*) pressure; **mettere sotto pressione** (*Tecn*) to pressurize; **la macchina del caffè non è ancora in pressione** there isn't enough steam in the espresso machine yet; **pentola a pressione** pressure cooker; **avere la pressione alta/bassa** (*Med*) to have high/low blood pressure ▶ **pressione atmosferica** atmospheric pressure ▶ **pressione sanguigna** blood pressure
b (*fig: sollecitazione*) pressure; **far pressione su qn** to put pressure on sb; **subire forti pressioni** to be under strong pressure; **essere/mettere qn sotto pressione** to be/put sb under pressure; **gruppo di pressione** pressure group.

presso ['presso] 1 AVV a (*vicino*) nearby, near, close at hand; **abitava lì presso** he lived nearby *o* near there
b : **di** *o* **da presso** (*incalzare*) closely; **da presso** (*esaminare*) closely; **a un di presso** about, approximately.
2 PREP a (*vicino a*) close to, near (to); (*accanto a*) beside, next to; **presso a** near (to), by; **stava presso la finestra** she was standing near the window
b : **presso qn** (*in casa di*) at sb's home; **abita presso i genitori** he lives with his parents; **lavora presso di noi** (*alle dipendenze di*) he works for *o* with us; **'presso'** (*su busta, cartolina*) 'care of', 'c/o'; **ambasciatore presso la Santa Sede** ambassador to the Holy See
c (*nell'ambiente di*) among; **diffuso presso le popolazioni primitive** common among primitive peoples; **ha avuto grande successo presso i giovani** it has been a hit with young people.
3 SMPL: **nei pressi di** near, in the vicinity of; **nei pressi di Londra** near London.

pressoché [presso'ke] AVV nearly, almost.

pressurizzare [pressurid'dzare] VT to pressurize.

pressurizzato, a [pressurid'dzato] AGG pressurized.

pressurizzazione [pressuriddzat'tsjone] SF pressurization.

prestabilire [prestabi'lire] VT to arrange beforehand, arrange in advance; **era già tutto prestabilito** everything had already been arranged.

prestabilito, a [prestabi'lito] AGG prearranged.

prestanome [presta'nome] SM/F INV (*Dir*) nominee; (*pegg*) front man.

prestante [pres'tante] AGG good-looking; **un uomo prestante** a fine figure of a man.

prestanza [pres'tantsa] SF (*robust*) good looks *pl.*

prestare [pres'tare] 1 VT to lend; **prestare qc a qn** to lend sb sth, lend sth to sb; **farsi prestare qc da qn** to borrow sth from sb; **prestare aiuto a qn** to give sb a helping hand, lend sb a hand; **prestare soccorso a** to give assistance to; **prestare ascolto** *o* **orecchio a** to listen to; **prestare attenzione a** to pay attention to; **prestare fede a** to give credence to; **prestare giuramento** to take an oath.
2 **prestarsi** VR (*offrirsi*): **prestarsi (a fare qc)** to offer (to do sth); **si presta sempre volentieri** he's always willing to lend a hand.
3 **prestarsi** VIP (*essere adatto*): **prestarsi per** *o* **a** to lend itself to, be suitable for; **la frase si presta a molteplici interpretazioni** the phrase lends itself to numerous interpretations; **quel vestito non si presta all'occasione** that dress isn't suitable for the occasion.

prestazione [prestat'tsjone] SF a (*Tecn, Sport*) performance b (*opera, servizio*): **prestazioni** SFPL services.

prestigiatore, trice [prestidʒa'tore] SM/F conjurer.

prestigio [pres'tidʒo] SM a (*fama, autorità*) prestige; **di prestigio** prestigious b (*illusione*): **gioco di prestigio** conjuring trick.

prestigiosamente [prestidʒosa'mente] AVV prestigiously.

prestigioso, a [presti'dʒoso] AGG prestigious.

prestito ['prestito] SM loan; **prendere qc in prestito da qn** to borrow sth from sb; **dare qc in prestito a qn** to lend sth to sb, lend sb sth; **mi fai un prestito?** can I borrow some money from you?, will you lend me some money? ▶ **prestito bancario** (*Banca*) bank loan ▶ **prestito linguistico** loan word ▶ **prestito pubblico** (*Fin*) public borrowing.

presto ['presto] AVV a (*fra poco*) soon; **ci rivedremo presto** we'll see one another soon; **presto o tardi** sooner or later; **a presto** see you soon; **arrivederci a presto!** goodbye for now!, see you soon!; **il più presto possibile** as soon as possible; **se non la smette, presto avrà dei guai** if he doesn't stop that he'll be for it
b (*in fretta*) quickly, fast; **fai presto!** hurry up!, be quick (about it)!; **fai presto che è già buio** come on - it's already dark; **più presto che puoi** as quickly *o* fast as you can; **fare presto a fare qc** to hurry up and do sth; (*con facilità*) to have no trouble doing sth; **ha fatto presto a sbrigare quel lavoro** he got through that job quickly; **si fa presto a criticare** it's easy to criticize; **è presto detto** it's easier said than done
c (*di buon'ora*) early; **mi alzo presto** I get up early; **sono arrivato troppo presto all'appuntamento** I arrived too early for the appointment; **è ancora presto per decidere** it's still too early *o* soon to decide.

presumere [pre'zumere] VT IRREG a (*ritenere, credere*): **presumere che...** to presume *o* imagine that ...; **presumo che venga** I presume *o* imagine he'll come
b (*pretendere, avere la presunzione di*) to presume, assume; **e tu presumi di potermi criticare?** you have the nerve to think you can criticize me; **presume di sapere più degli altri** he thinks he knows more *o* better than everybody else.

presumibile [prezu'mibile] AGG (*dati, risultati*) likely.

presumibilmente [prezumibil'mente] AVV presumably.

presunsi ecc [pre'zunsi] VB vedi **presumere**.

presunto, a [pre'zunto] 1 PP di **presumere**.
2 AGG: **il presunto colpevole** the alleged culprit.

presuntuosamente [prezuntuosa'mente] AVV presumptuously.

presuntuoso, a [prezuntu'oso] 1 AGG presumptuous, conceited.
2 SM: **fare il presuntuoso** to be cocksure.

presunzione [prezun'tsjone] SF a (*congettura*) presumption b (*immodestia*) presumptuousness; **peccare di presunzione** to be presumptuous.

presupporre [presup'porre] VT IRREG a (*immaginare, preve-*

dere) to assume, suppose **b** (*implicare*) to presuppose.

presupposto, a [presup'posto] ⃞1 PP di **presupporre**.

⃞2 SM (*premessa*) supposition, premise; **partendo dal presupposto che**... assuming that ...; **mancano i presupposti necessari** the necessary conditions are lacking.

prêt-à-porter ['prɛt a pɔr'te] SM INV ready-to-wear (clothes).

prete ['prɛte] SM priest; **scherzo da prete** (*fig fam*) nasty trick ▶ **prete operaio** worker-priest.

pretendente [preten'dɛnte] SM/F **a** (*aspirante*): **pretendente (a)** pretender (to) **b** (*corteggiatore*) suitor.

pretendere [pre'tɛndere] VT IRREG **a** (*esigere*) to demand, require; (*aspettarsi*) to expect; **pretendo un po' di rispetto** I demand some respect; **pretendo la mia parte** I demand *o* claim my share; **pretende di essere pagato** he expects to be paid; **pretendi troppo da lui** you expect too much of him

b (*sostenere, presumere*): **pretendere (che...)** to claim (that ...); **pretende di aver sempre ragione** he thinks he's always right.

pretensionatore [pretensjona'tore] SM (*Aut*) pre-tensioner.

pretenziosamente [pretentsjosa'mente] AVV pretentiously.

pretenziosità [pretentsjosi'ta] SF pretentiousness.

pretenzioso, a [preten'tsjoso] AGG pretentious.

preterintenzionale [preterintentsjo'nale] AGG (*Dir*): **omicidio preterintenzionale** manslaughter.

preterito [pre'tɛrito] SM (*Gramm*) preterit(e).

pretesa [pre'tesa] SF **a** (*richiesta, esigenza*) claim, demand; **avanzare una pretesa** to put forward a claim *o* demand; **un uomo di poche pretese** a man who is easily pleased *o* who doesn't ask much in life; **è pieno di pretese** he's difficult to please, he expects too much; **senza pretese** (*persona, casa, arredamento*) unpretentious, modest; (*abito*) simple

b (*presunzione*) pretension; **hai la pretesa di criticarmi!** you've got the nerve to criticize me!; **non avrai la pretesa di farmelo credere?** you don't really expect me to believe that; **non ho la pretesa di essere bella** I have no pretensions to beauty, I don't pretend to be beautiful.

preteso, a [pre'teso] PP di **pretendere**.

pretesto [pre'tɛsto] SM excuse, pretext; **con il pretesto di** on the pretext of; **mi ha fornito il pretesto per agire** he has provided me with a pretext for taking action.

pretestuoso, a [pretestu'oso] AGG (*data, motivo*) used as an excuse.

pretore [pre'tore] SM (*Dir*) magistrate.

prettamente [pretta'mente] AVV (*tipicamente*) decidedly.

pretura [pre'tura] SF (*Dir: sede*) magistrate's court (*Brit*), circuit *o* superior court (*Am*); (: *insieme dei pretori*) magistracy.

prevalente [preva'lɛnte] AGG prevalent, prevailing.

prevalentemente [prevalente'mente] AVV predominantly, mainly, for the most part; **in quella zona si parla prevalentemente il tedesco** German is the main *o* predominant language in that area.

prevalenza [preva'lɛntsa] SF predominance; **in prevalenza** predominantly, mainly.

prevalere [preva'lere] VI IRREG (*aus* avere *o* essere) to prevail; **prevalere su tutti per intelligenza** to surpass everyone in intelligence.

prevalso, a [pre'valso] PP di **prevalere**.

prevaricare [prevari'kare] VI (*aus* **avere**) (*abusare del potere*) to abuse one's power.

prevaricazione [prevarikat'tsjone] SF (*abuso di potere*) abuse of power.

prevedere [preve'dere] VT IRREG **a** (*avvenimento, conseguenza*) to foresee, anticipate; (*tempo*) to forecast; **prevedere il futuro** to foretell the future; **era da prevedere** it was to be expected; **non si sarebbe potuto prevedere** that couldn't have been foreseen; **nulla lasciava prevedere che**... there was nothing to suggest *o* to make one think that ...; **non possiamo prevedere tutto** we can't think of everything; **come previsto** as expected; **spese previste** anticipated expenditure; **tempo previsto per domani** weather forecast for tomorrow

b (*programmare*) to plan; **prevedere di fare qc** to plan to do sth; **avevamo previsto di partire oggi** we had planned to leave today; **all'ora prevista** at the appointed *o* scheduled time; **previsto per martedì** scheduled for Tuesday

c (*sogg: contratto, legge*) to make provision for, provide for; **questo caso non è previsto dalla legge** the law makes no provision for such a case.

prevedibile [preve'dibile] AGG predictable; **non era assolutamente prevedibile che**... no one could have foreseen that ... .

prevedibilmente [prevedibil'mente] AVV as one would expect *o* have expected.

preveggenza [preved'dʒɛntsa] SF foresight.

prevendita [pre'vendita] SF (*di biglietti*) advance sale.

prevenire [preve'nire] VT IRREG **a** (*anticipare: domanda*) to anticipate; (: *obiezione*) to forestall

b : **prevenire qn (di)** (*preavvertire*) to inform sb in advance (of); (*mettere sull'avviso*) to warn sb (of); **ti hanno prevenuto contro di me** they have already warned you about me

c (*evitare: malattia, disgrazia*) to prevent; **gli incidenti si possono prevenire** accidents can be prevented.

preventivare [preventi'vare] VT (*Comm: spesa*) to estimate; (: *mettere in bilancio*) to budget for; **non avevamo preventivato un figlio** we hadn't reckoned on having a child.

preventivo [preven'tivo] ⃞1 AGG (*intervento, cura*) preventive; **carcere preventivo** custody (*pending trial*); **bilancio preventivo** (*Comm*) budget.

⃞2 SM (*Comm*) estimate; **fare un preventivo** to give an estimate.

prevenuto, a [preve'nuto] ⃞1 PP di **prevenire**.

⃞2 AGG (*mal disposto*): **prevenuto (contro qn/qc)** prejudiced (against sb/sth).

prevenzione [preven'tsjone] SF **a** prevention; **prevenzione degli infortuni** prevention of accidents **b** (*preconcetto*) prejùdice; **avere prevenzioni contro qn/qc** to be prejudiced against sb/sth.

previamente [prevja'mente] AVV in advance.

previdente [previ'dɛnte] AGG prudent, showing foresight.

previdentemente [previdente'mente] AVV prudently.

previdenza [previ'dɛntsa] SF prudence, foresight; **istituto di previdenza** provident institution ▶ **previdenza sociale** social security (*Brit*), welfare (*Am*).

previdi *ecc* [pre'vidi] VB vedi **prevedere**.

previo, a, vi ['prɛvjo] AGG (*Comm*): **previo avviso** upon (prior) notice; **previo pagamento** upon payment.

previsione [previ'zjone] SF (*gen*) prediction; (*attesa*)

expectation; **tutto è andato secondo le previsioni** everything went according to expectation(s); **in previsione di** in anticipation of ▸**previsioni del tempo** o **metereologiche** weather forecast *sg*.

previsto, a [pre'visto] 1 PP di **prevedere**.
2 SM: **più/meno del previsto** more/less than expected; **prima del previsto** earlier than expected.

prevosto [pre'vɔsto] SM (*parroco*) parish priest.

preziosamente [prettsjosa'mente] AVV (*ornato*) richly; (*fig*: *custodire*) jealously.

prezioso, a [pret'tsjoso] 1 AGG (*gen*) precious; (*documento*) valuable; (*testimonianza, aiuto, consiglio*) invaluable.
2 SM **a** (*gioiello*) jewel; (*oggetto di valore*) valuable; **le hanno rubato tutti i preziosi** they stole all her valuables **b** (*fig: persona*): **fare il prezioso** to play hard to get; **fa il prezioso perché è diventato importante** he puts on airs and graces because he has become important.

prezzare [pret'tsare] VT (*articolo*) to price.

prezzario, ri [pret'tsarjo] SM price list.

prezzemolo [pret'tsemolo] SM (*Bot*) parsley; **essere come il prezzemolo** (*fig*) to turn up everywhere.

prezzo ['prɛttso] 1 SM price; **a buon prezzo** cheaply, at a good price; **a prezzo di costo** at cost, at cost price (*Brit*); **a metà prezzo** at half price; **menu a prezzo fisso** set price menu; **il prezzo pattuito è 1.000.000 di lire** the agreed price is 1,000,000 lire; **tirare sul prezzo** to bargain, haggle; **ti faccio un prezzo d'amico** o **di favore** I'll let you have it at a reduced price; **pagare qc a caro prezzo** (*fig*) to pay dearly for sth; **la libertà non ha prezzo** you can't put a price on freedom; **è una cosa di poco prezzo** it's of little value, it's not worth much.
2 ▸**prezzo d'acquisto** purchase price ▸**prezzo per contanti** cash price ▸**prezzo di fabbrica** factory price ▸**prezzo di listino** list price ▸**prezzo di mercato** market price ▸**prezzo scontato** reduced price ▸**prezzo unitario** unit price ▸**prezzo di vendita** selling price ▸**prezzo di vendita al dettaglio** retail price.

prezzolato, a [prettso'lato] AGG: **soldato prezzolato** mercenary; **giornalista prezzolato** journalist who is in sb's pay; **sicario prezzolato** hired killer.

P.R.I. [pi'ɛrre'i] SIGLA M (*Pol*: = *Partito Repubblicano Italiano*) *former political party*.

Priamo ['priamo] SM Priam.

priapismo [pria'pizmo] SM (*Med*) priapism.

prigione [pri'dʒone] SF (*luogo*) prison, jail; (*pena*) imprisonment; **andare/mettere in prigione** to go/send to prison; **scontare un anno di prigione** to spend a year in prison.

prigionia [pridʒo'nia] SF imprisonment.

prigioniero, a [pridʒo'njɛro] 1 AGG captive; **essere prigioniero** to be a prisoner; **essere prigioniero di un ricordo** to be tormented by a memory.
2 SM/F prisoner; **fare/tenere qn prigioniero** to take/hold sb prisoner.

prima¹ ['prima] 1 AVV **a** (*in precedenza*) before; (*una volta*) once, formerly; **prima non lo sapevo** I didn't know that before; **due giorni prima** two days before o earlier; **ne so quanto prima** I know as much as I did before, I'm none the wiser; **amici come prima!** let's make it up o let's be friends again!; **prima non si faceva così** people used not to do that; **usanze di prima** former customs; **non è più la stessa di prima** she's not the same as she was

b (*in anticipo*) beforehand, in advance; **un'altra volta dimmelo prima** next time let me know in advance o beforehand

c (*più presto*) sooner, earlier; **prima o poi** sooner or later; **credevo di fare prima** I thought I'd be finished sooner o earlier; **prima lo farai prima sarai libero di uscire** the sooner you do it the sooner you can go out; **chi arriva prima compra i biglietti** whoever arrives first gets the tickets

d (*innanzi*) before; (*in primo luogo*) first; **prima la famiglia** family first; **prima il dovere e poi il piacere** duty before pleasure.
2: **prima di** PREP (*tempo, spazio*) before; **prima del suo arrivo** before his arrival; **sono andati via prima di noi** they left before us; **prima d'ora** before now; **c'è un cinema prima del semaforo** there's a cinema before the lights.
3: **prima di, prima che** CONG before; **prima di fare/che tu faccia** before doing/you do; **pensaci prima che sia troppo tardi** give it some thought before it is too late.

prima² ['prima] SF **a** (*gen*) first; (*Teatro*) opening night; (*Cine*) première; (*Ferr*) first class; (*Aut*) first gear; **viaggiare in prima** to travel first class; **ingranare la prima** to engage first gear
b (*Scol: elementare*) ≈ first year (at primary school) (*Brit*), ≈ second grade (*Am*); (: *media*) ≈ first year (at secondary school) (*Brit*), ≈ seventh grade (*Am*); (: *superiore*) ≈ fourth year (at secondary school) (*Brit*), ≈ tenth grade (*Am*).

primadonna [prima'dɔnna] SF leading lady; (*di opera lirica*) prima donna; (*pegg*): **fare la primadonna** to act the prima donna.

primanota [prima'nɔta] SF petty cash book.

primariamente [primarja'mente] AVV primarily.

primario, ria, ri, rie [pri'marjo] 1 AGG **a** (*funzione, motivo, scopo*) main, chief, primary **b** (*Geol*): **roccia primaria** primary rock.
2 SM (*medico*) head o chief physician.

primate [pri'mate] SM (*Rel, Zool*) primate.

primatista, i, e [prima'tista] SM/F (*Sport*) record holder.

primato [pri'mato] SM **a** (*in campo industriale, artistico*) supremacy; **l'Italia ha il primato nel campo della moda** Italy is the leader o holds the lead in the world of fashion **b** (*Sport*) record.

primavera [prima'vɛra] SF spring.

primaverile [primave'rile] AGG spring *attr*.

primeggiare [primed'dʒare] VI (*aus avere*): **primeggiare (in)** to excel (in), be one of the best (in).

primipara [pri'mipara] SF (*Med*) primigravida.

primitivamente [primitiva'mente] AVV primitively, in a primitive manner.

primitivo, a [primi'tivo] 1 AGG (*società, popolazione, usanza*) primitive; (*significato*) original.
2 SM/F (*della preistoria, arcaico*) primitive; (*fig: zotico*) uncivilized person.

primizia [pri'mittsja] SF **a** (*Agr*): **primizie** SFPL early fruit and vegetables, early produce *sg* **b** (*notizia inedita*): **ho una primizia per il tuo giornale** I've got a scoop for your paper.

primo, a ['primo] 1 AGG **a** (*gen*) first; (*impressione*) first, initial; (*infanzia*) early; (*Mat: numero*) prime; **le prime 20 pagine** the first 20 pages; **dalla prima all'ultima pagina** from beginning to end; **in prima pagina** (*Stampa*) on the front page; **i suoi primi quadri** his early paintings;

questo quadro è un Michelangelo prima maniera this is an early Michelangelo; questo film è di Fellini prima maniera this film is in Fellini's early style; di prima mattina early in the morning; le prime ore del mattino the early hours of the morning; posare la prima pietra to lay the foundation stone; ai primi freddi at the first sign of cold weather; ustioni di primo grado first-degree burns

b (in un ordine) first; preferisco il primo pittore al secondo I prefer the former painter to the latter; essere primo in classifica to be placed first, be in first place; essere in prima posizione to be in the lead; sul primo scaffale in alto/in basso on the top/bottom shelf; di prim'ordine o prima qualità first-class, first-rate; è un attore di prim'ordine he is a first-rate actor

c (prossimo) first, next; prendi la prima (strada) a destra take the first o next (street) on the right; scendo alla prima fermata I am getting off at the next stop

d (principale) main, principal; il primo attore the leading man; la causa prima the main reason

e (fraseologia): per prima cosa firstly; in primo luogo in the first place, first of all; in un primo tempo o momento at first; fin dal primo momento from the very first; amore a prima vista love at first sight; fare i primi passi to take one's first steps; fare il primo passo (fig) to make the first move.

[2] SM/F first (one); è stata la prima a farlo she was the first to do it; fu tra i primi ad arrivare he was among the first to arrive; è la prima della classe she is the top of the class; non sposerò il primo venuto I won't marry just anyone.

[3] SM (gen) first; (piano) first floor (Brit), second floor (Am); (Culin) first course; il primo luglio the first of July; il primo d'Aprile April Fools' Day; il primo dell'anno New Year's Day; i primi del Novecento the early twentieth century; ai primi del mese at the beginning of the month.

primogenito, a [primo'dʒɛnito] [1] SM/F first o eldest child, firstborn.

[2] AGG firstborn.

primordi [pri'mɔrdi] SMPL beginnings; ai primordi della storia at the dawn of history.

primordiale [primor'djale] AGG (era, scienza) primordial.

primula ['primula] SF primula, primrose; la primula rossa (fig) the most wanted man.

principale [printʃi'pale] [1] AGG (strada, motivo) main, principal; (opera) major; proposizione principale (Gramm) main clause; sede principale head office.

[2] SM/F (fam) boss.

principalmente [printʃipal'mente] AVV mainly, principally.

principato [printʃi'pato] SM (titolo nobiliare) princedom; (Stato) principality.

principe ['printʃipe] SM (titolo nobiliare) prince; il principe di Galles the Prince of Wales; stare come un principe (fig) to live like a lord ▶principe azzurro (fig) prince charming ▶principe consorte prince consort ▶principe ereditario crown prince.

principescamente [printʃipeska'mente] AVV in a princely fashion.

principesco, a, schi, sche [printʃi'pesko] AGG (anche fig) princely.

principessa [printʃi'pessa] SF princess.

principiante [printʃi'pjante] SM/F beginner; un lavoro da

principianti (pegg) an amateur job.

principiare [printʃi'pjare] (frm) [1] VT (discorso, trattative, lavoro) to start, begin.

[2] VI (aus (persona) avere; (tempo) essere): principiare a fare qc to begin o start doing o to do sth; a principiare da oggi/domani starting from today/tomorrow; a principiare da te/noi starting with you/us.

principio, pi [prin'tʃipjo] SM **a** (inizio) beginning, start; ricominciare dal principio to start from the beginning again, go back to square one; fin dal principio right from the start; al o in principio at first, at the beginning; dal principio alla fine from beginning to end, from start to finish

b (concetto, norma) principle; essere senza principi to have no principles; una persona di sani principi morali a person of sound moral principles; una questione di principio a matter of principle; per principio on principle

c (Mat) principle

d (Chim): principio attivo active ingredient.

priora [pri'ora] SF (Rel) prioress.

priorato [prio'rato] SM (Rel) priorate; (: sede) priory.

priore [pri'ore] SM (Rel, Storia) prior.

priori [pri'ori]: **a priori** [1] AGG INV prior, a priori.

[2] AVV at first glance; (giudicare, valutare) initially; (dedurre, ragionare) a priori.

priorità [priori'ta] SF priority; avere la priorità (su) to have priority (over).

prioritario, ria, ri, rie [priori'tarjo] AGG having priority, of utmost importance.

prisma, i ['prizma] SM prism.

privacy ['praivəsi] SF INV privacy.

privare [pri'vare] [1] VT: privare qn di qc to deprive sb of sth; privare qn della vita to take sb's life; non mi ha privato di niente he didn't deny me anything.

[2] privarsi VR: privarsi di qc to do o go without sth; non privarsi di niente to deny o.s. nothing.

privatista, i, e [priva'tista] SM/F (studente) private student; studiare da o come privatista to study privately; fare un esame da o come privatista to be an external candidate at an exam.

privativa [priva'tiva] SF (Econ) monopoly.

privativo, a [priva'tivo] AGG (Gramm) privative.

privatizzare [privatid'dzare] VT to privatize.

privatizzazione [privatiddzat'tsjone] SF privatization.

privato, a [pri'vato] [1] AGG (gen) private; diritto privato (Dir) civil law; privato cittadino private citizen; ritirarsi a vita privata to withdraw from public life; discutere o parlare in privato to talk in private.

[2] SM **a** (cittadino) private citizen; (persona singola) member of the public; un'azienda gestita da privati a privately owned business; "non vendiamo a privati" "wholesale only"

b (vita privata) private life.

privazione [privat'tsjone] SF **a** (di diritti, genitori) loss **b** (sacrificio: spec pl) hardship, privation.

privilegiare [privile'dʒare] VT to favour (Brit), favor (Am).

privilegiato, a [privile'dʒato] [1] AGG (individuo, classe) privileged; (trattamento) preferential **b** (Comm: credito) preferential; azioni privilegiate preference shares (Brit), preferred stock sg (Am).

[2] SM/F privileged person.

privilegio, gi [privi'lɛdʒo] SM privilege; godere di/concedere un privilegio to enjoy/grant a privilege; avere il

privilegio di fare to have the privilege of doing, be privileged to do.

privo, a ['privo] AGG: **privo di** (senza) without; (carente in) lacking in; **privo di scrupoli** without scruples; **privo di coraggio** lacking in courage; **parole prive di significato** meaningless words.

pro[1] [prɔ] PREP (in favore di) for, in favour (Brit) o favor (Am) of, on o in (Am) behalf of; **pro patria** patriotic; **raccolta pro rifugiati** collection for refugees; **sei pro o contro?** are you for or against?

pro[2] [prɔ] SM, SOLO SG (vantaggio) good; (utilità) advantage, benefit; **a che pro?** what's the use?; **a che pro l'hai fatto?** why did you do it?; **tutta questa fatica, e a che pro?** all this work, and for what?; **buon pro ti faccia!** much good may it do you!; **il pro e il contro** the pros and cons.

probabile [pro'babile] AGG likely, probable; **è probabile che venga** he will probably come, he is likely to come.

probabilità [probabili'ta] SF INV **a** probability, likelihood; (possibilità) chance; **quali o che probabilità ci sono?** what chances are there?; **c'è una probabilità su mille** there's a one in a thousand chance; **con molta probabilità** very probably, in all probability **b** (Mat) probability.

probabilmente [probabil'mente] AVV probably; **probabilmente verrà** he'll probably come.

probante [pro'bante] AGG convincing.

problema, i [pro'blɛma] SM (gen, Mat) problem; (questione) issue.

problematica [proble'matika] SF problems pl.

problematicamente [problematika'mente] AVV problematically; **molti adolescenti vivono problematicamente la loro età** many teenagers find adolescence a difficult time.

problematico, a, ci, che [proble'matiko] AGG (situazione) problematic; (intesa, esito) doubtful.

proboscide [pro'boʃʃide] SF (di elefante) trunk; (di insetto) proboscis.

procacciare [prokat'tʃare] VT to get, obtain; **procacciarsi un lavoro** to get o.s. a job; **procacciarsi il pane** o **da vivere** to earn one's living.

procacciatore [prokattʃa'tore] SM: **procacciatore d'affari** wheeler-dealer (fam).

procace [pro'katʃe] AGG (donna, aspetto) provocative.

procacemente [prokatʃe'mente] AVV provocatively.

pro capite [prɔ'kapite] AVV per capita.

procedere [pro'tʃɛdere] VI (aus avere; nel senso (a) essere) **a** (avanzare) to proceed, advance; (continuare) to proceed, go on; **procedere oltre** to go on ahead; **prima di procedere oltre** before going any further; **procedere con lentezza** (veicolo) to drive along slowly; (trattative) to proceed slowly; **procediamo con ordine** let's do this in an orderly fashion; **gli affari procedono bene** business is going well; **procede nella ricerca scientifica** he is continuing his scientific research

b (passare a): **procedere a** to start, begin; **procediamo alla discussione** let's begin the discussion

c (agire) to proceed; (comportarsi) to behave; **non mi piace il suo modo di procedere** I don't like the way he behaves; **bisogna procedere con cautela** we have to proceed cautiously

d (Dir): **procedere contro qc** to start o take proceedings against sb; **non luogo a procedere** nonsuit.

procedimento [protʃedi'mento] SM **a** (svolgimento) course **b** (metodo) procedure; (: Tecn) process; **il**

procedimento usato per la fabbricazione the manufacturing process **c** (Dir) proceedings pl ▶ **procedimento penale** criminal proceedings pl.

procedura [protʃe'dura] SF (gen, Dir) procedure; **seguire** o **osservare la procedura** to follow procedure.

procedurale [protʃedu'rale] AGG (Dir) procedural.

procellaria [protʃel'larja] SF storm petrel.

processare [protʃes'sare] VT (Dir): **processare qn (per)** to try sb (for).

processione [protʃes'sjone] SF (gen) procession.

processo [pro'tʃɛsso] SM **a** (gen, Chim, Med, Tecn) process ▶ **processo di fabbricazione** manufacturing process ▶ **processo di pace** peace process

b (Dir: civile) (legal) proceedings pl, (court) action, lawsuit; (: penale) trial; **essere sotto processo** to be on trial; **mettere sotto processo** (anche fig) to put on trial; **fare il processo alle intenzioni di qn** to question sb's motives.

processuale [protʃessu'ale] AGG (Dir): **atti processuali** records of a trial; **spese processuali** legal costs.

Proc. Gen. ABBR = **procuratore generale.**

procinto [pro'tʃinto] SM: **in procinto di fare qc** about to do sth, on the point of doing sth; **ero in procinto di partire** I was about to leave o on the point of leaving.

procione [pro'tʃone] SM (Zool) raccoon.

proclama, i [pro'klama] SM (bando, appello) proclamation.

proclamare [prokla'mare] VT (legge) to promulgate; (stato d'assedio, guerra, pace) to declare; **proclamare qn vincitore** to declare sb the winner; **proclamare la propria innocenza** to proclaim one's innocence.

proclamazione [proklamat'tsjone] SF (dichiarazione) declaration; (affermazione) proclamation.

procrastinare [prokrasti'nare] VT (data) to postpone; (pagamento) to defer.

procreare [prokre'are] VT to procreate.

procreazione [prokreat'tsjone] SF procreation.

procura [pro'kura] SF (Dir) **a** proxy, power of attorney; **per procura** by proxy **b** (ufficio): **la procura della Repubblica** the Public Prosecutor's office.

procurare [proku'rare] VT **a** (fornire): **procurare qc a qn** to get o obtain sth for sb, provide sb with sth; **procurare danni** to cause damage; **procurare noie a qn** to cause sb trouble; **hai procurato i biglietti?** did you get the tickets? **b** (fare in modo di): **procurare di fare qc** to try to do sth.

procuratore, trice [prokura'tore] SM/F (Dir) ≈ solicitor (Brit), ≈ lawyer (Am); (chi è munito di procura) holder of power of attorney ▶ **procuratore generale** (in corte d'appello) public prosecutor; (in corte di cassazione) Attorney General ▶ **procuratore legale** ≈ solicitor (Brit), ≈ lawyer ▶ **procuratore della Repubblica** (in corte d'assise, tribunale) public prosecutor.

prode ['prɔde] [1] AGG valiant, brave. [2] SM brave man.

prodezza [pro'dettsa] SF (qualità) valour (Brit), valor (Am), bravery; (fig) feat, exploit.

prodigalità [prodigali'ta] SF INV prodigality.

prodigare [prodi'gare] [1] VT (lodi, affetto) to lavish, be lavish with; **gli prodiga tutte le sue cure** she lavishes all her care on him. [2] **prodigarsi** VR: **prodigarsi per qn** to do all one can for sb.

prodigio, gi [pro'didʒo] [1] SM (miracolo) wonder, marvel;

(*fig: persona*) prodigy; **i prodigi della tecnica/scienza** the wonders of technology/science; **fare prodigi** to work wonders. 2 AGG INV: **bambino prodigio** child prodigy.

prodigiosamente [prodidʒosa'mente] AVV miraculously.

prodigioso, a [prodi'dʒoso] AGG wonderful, marvellous (*Brit*), marvelous (*Am*), prodigious; (*fenomenale*) phenomenal.

prodigo, a, ghi, ghe ['prɔdigo] AGG: **essere prodigo (di)** (*consigli, attenzioni*) to be lavish (with); (*denaro*) to be extravagant (with); **il figliol prodigo** (*Rel, fig*) the prodigal son.

prodotto, a [pro'dotto] 1 PP di **produrre**.

2 SM (*gen, Mat*) product; (*fig: risultato*) result, fruit, product ▶**prodotti agricoli** farm produce *sg* ▶**prodotti alimentari** foodstuffs ▶**prodotti di bellezza** cosmetics ▶**prodotti chimici** chemicals ▶**prodotto di base** primary product ▶**prodotto finale** end product ▶**prodotto interno lordo** (*Econ*) gross domestic product ▶**prodotto nazionale lordo** (*Econ*) gross national product.

prodromo ['prɔdromo] SM (*segno precorritore*) warning sign; (*Med*) prodrome.

produco *ecc* [pro'duko] VB vedi **produrre**.

produrre [pro'durre] VT IRREG a (*gen, Cine*) to produce; (*calore*) to generate; (*fabbricare*) to manufacture, make, produce; **produrre in serie** to mass-produce b (*causare: angoscia, timori*) to cause, give rise to.

produssi *ecc* [pro'dussi] VB vedi **produrre**.

produttività [produttivi'ta] SF productivity.

produttivo, a [produt'tivo] AGG (*lavoro, investimento*) productive; (*metodo, ciclo*) of production, production *attr*.

produttore, trice [produt'tore] 1 SM/F (*gen, Cine, Agr*) producer.

2 AGG (*gen, Agr*) producing *attr*; **paese produttore di petrolio** oil-producing country.

produzione [produt'tsjone] SF a (*gen, Cine, TV*) production; **articolo di produzione italiana** article of Italian manufacture ▶**produzione in serie** mass production b (*quantità prodotta*) production, output; (*Agr*) production, yield.

proemio, mi [pro'ɛmjo] SM introduction, preface.

Prof. ABBR (= *professore*) Prof.

profanare [profa'nare] VT (*Rel*) to profane, to desecrate; (*tomba*) to violate; (*fig: nome, ricordo*) to defile.

profanazione [profanat'tsjone] SF (*vedi vb*) profanation, desecration; violation; defilement.

profano, a [pro'fano] 1 AGG (*non sacro*) secular, profane; (*sacrilego*) profane; (*fig: orecchio, occhio*) untrained.

2 SM/F (*gen*) layman, lay person.

3 SM: **il profano** the profane, the secular.

proferire [profe'rire] VT IRREG (*parola, nome*) to utter; (*giudizio, desiderio*) to express.

proferito, a [profe'rito] PP di **proferire**.

professare [profes'sare] 1 VT (*opinione, dottrina*) to profess; (*medicina, avvocatura*) to practise (*Brit*), practice (*Am*).

2 **professarsi** VR: **professarsi innocente** to declare o.s. innocent.

professionale [professjo'nale] AGG (*gen*) professional; (*malattia*) occupational; **istituto professionale** training college.

professionalità [professjonali'ta] SF professionalism.

professionalmente [professjonal'mente] AVV profes-

sionally.

professione [profes'sjone] SF (*gen*) occupation, profession; (*manuale*) trade; **libera professione** profession; **fare qc di professione** to do sth for a living; **di professione** professional, by profession; **professione di fede** profession of faith.

professionismo [professjo'nizmo] SM professionalism.

professionista, i, e [professjo'nista] SM/F (*gen, Sport*) professional; **libero professionista** (*gen*) self-employed; (*avvocato, medico*) professional man/woman.

professorale [professo'rale] AGG professorial.

professore, essa [profes'sore] SM/F (*Scol*) teacher; (*Univ*) ≈ lecturer; (: *titolare di cattedra*) professor ▶**professore d'orchestra** member of an orchestra.

profeta, i [pro'fɛta] SM prophet.

profetessa [profe'tessa] SF prophetess.

profeticamente [profetika'mente] AVV prophetically.

profetico, a, ci, che [pro'fɛtiko] AGG prophetic.

profetizzare [profetid'dzare] VT to prophesy.

profezia [profet'tsia] SF prophecy.

profferta [prof'fɛrta] SF: **fare profferte amorose a qn** to make (amorous) advances to sb.

profferto, a [prof'fɛrto] PP di **proferire**.

proficuamente [profikua'mente] AVV profitably.

proficuo, a [pro'fikuo] AGG profitable, useful.

profilare [profi'lare] 1 VT a (*descrivere in breve*) to outline b (*ornare: vestito*) to edge c (*Tecn: barra metallica*) to shape.

2 **profilarsi** VIP (*figura*) to stand out, be outlined, be silhouetted; (*soluzione, problemi*) to emerge; (*minaccia, crisi*) to loom up; **profilarsi all'orizzonte** (*anche fig*) to appear on the horizon.

profilassi [profi'lassi] SF INV (*Med*) preventive treatment, prophylaxis.

profilato [profi'lato] SM (*Tecn: trave*) section.

profilattico, a, ci, che [profi'lattiko] (*Med*) 1 AGG prophylactic.

2 SM (*anticoncezionale*) condom, sheat (*Brit*).

profilo [pro'filo] SM (*gen, fig*) profile; (*breve descrizione*) sketch, outline; **di profilo** in profile; **mettersi di profilo** to turn sideways (on); **considerare qc sotto il profilo giuridico** to consider the legal aspects of sth; **una figura di scarso profilo** an insignificant character.

profittare [profit'tare] VI (*aus avere*): **profittare di** (*situazione*) to profit by o from; (*pegg: persona*) to take advantage of.

profitto [pro'fitto] SM (*gen, Econ*) profit; (*fig: progresso*) progress; **ricavare un profitto da** to make a profit from o out of; **vendere con profitto** to sell at a profit; **conto profitti e perdite** profit and loss account; **trarre profitto da** (*lezione, esperienza*) to learn from; (*problemi altrui*) to take advantage of; (*invenzione*) to turn to good account; (*tempo libero*) to make the most of.

profondamente [profonda'mente] AVV (*conficcare, piantare*) deep; (*fig: amare, addolorare, essere radicato*) deeply; (*dormire*) deeply, soundly; **dormiva profondamente** he was sleeping soundly o deeply, he was sound asleep; **sentirsi profondamente legato a qn** to feel very attached to sb; **siamo profondamente addolorati per la perdita del caro Giovanni** we deeply regret dear Giovanni's death.

profondere [pro'fondere] VB IRREG 1 VT (*lodi*) to lavish; (*denaro*) to squander.

2 profondersi VIP: **profondersi in** (*scuse, ringraziamenti*) to be profuse in.

profondimetro [profon'dimetro] SM (*Sub*) depth gauge.

profondità [profondi'ta] SF INV **a** depth; **scavare in profondità** to dig deep; **avere 10 metri di profondità** [OR] **avere una profondità di 10 metri** to be 10 metres deep *o* in depth; **le profondità del mare** the depths of the sea **b** (*di persona, osservazione*) profundity; (*di sentimento, rispetto*) depth **c** (*Cine, Fot*): **profondità di campo** depth of field.

profondo, a [pro'fondo] **1** AGG **a** (*gen*) deep; **poco profondo** shallow; **profondo 5 metri** 5 metres deep **b** (*fig: notte, colore, voce*) deep; (: *sospiro*) deep, heavy; (: *sonno*) deep, sound; (: *silenzio, mistero*) total, profound; (: *interesse, sentimento, meditazione*) profound; (: *inchino*) deep, low; (: *causa, significato*) underlying, deeper; (: *tendenza*) deep-seated, underlying. **2** SM depth, depths *pl*, bottom; **nel profondo del mare** in the depths of the sea, at the bottom of the sea; **dal profondo del cuore** from the bottom of one's heart; **nel profondo del cuore** *o* **dell'animo** in one's heart of hearts.

proforma [pro'forma] **1** AGG routine *attr*. **2** AVV: **fare qc proforma** to do sth as a formality. **3** SM INV formality.

profugo, a, ghi, ghe ['prɔfugo] SM/F refugee.

profumare [profu'mare] **1** VI (*aus* **avere**) to smell good, be fragrant; **profumare di pulito/fresco** to smell clean/fresh. **2** VT **a** (*sogg: fiori*) to perfume, scent; (*fazzoletto*) to put perfume *o* scent on; **l'aroma del caffè profumava l'aria** the smell of coffee filled the air **b** : **profumarsi** (*pelle, capelli*) to put perfume *o* scent on. **3** **profumarsi** VR to put on perfume *o* scent.

profumatamente [profuma'mente] AVV: **pagare qc profumatamente** to pay through the nose for sth; **pagare qn profumatamente** to pay sb handsomely.

profumato, a [profu'mato] AGG (*fiore, aria*) fragrant; (*fazzoletto, saponetta*) scented; (*pelle*) sweet-smelling; (*persona*) with perfume on.

profumeria [profume'ria] SF perfumery.

profumo [pro'fumo] SM (*sostanza*) perfume, scent; (*fragranza*) scent, fragrance; (*di caffè*) aroma; **avere un buon profumo** to smell nice; **senti che profumo!** what a lovely smell!

profusione [profu'zjone] SF profusion; **a profusione** in plenty.

profuso, a [pro'fuzo] PP di **profondere**.

progenie [pro'dʒɛnje] SF INV (*pegg: razza, discendenza*) progeny.

progenitore, trice [prodʒeni'tore] SM/F ancestor.

progesterone [prodʒeste'rone] SM progesterone.

progettare [prodʒet'tare] VT (*ponte, casa*) to plan, design; (*vacanza, fuga, rapina*) to plan; **progettare di fare qc** to plan to do sth.

progettazione [prodʒettat'tsjone] SF planning; **in corso di progettazione** at the planning stage.

progettista, i, e [prodʒet'tista] SM/F designer.

progetto [pro'dʒɛtto] SM **a** (*Archit*) plan; (*idea*) plan, project; **fare il progetto di una casa** to design a house; **fare progetti per il futuro** to make plans for the future; **avere in progetto di fare qc** to be planning to do sth **b** (*Pol*): **progetto di legge** bill.

prognosi ['prɔɲɲozi] SF INV (*Med*) prognosis; **essere in prognosi riservata** to be on the danger list; **sciogliere la prognosi su qn** to take sb off the danger list.

programma, i [pro'gramma] SM **a** (*Pol, Econ, TV, Radio*) programme (*Brit*), program (*Am*); (*Inform*) program ▶**programma applicativo** (*Inform*) application program **b** (*progetto*) plan; **fare programmi** to plan; **avere in programma di fare qc** to be planning to do sth; **hai qualcosa in programma per la serata?** have you anything planned for this evening?; **a causa dello sciopero vi trasmettiamo fuori programma un documentario** because of the strike we are now broadcasting a documentary instead of the scheduled program(me) **c** (*Scol*) syllabus, curriculum; **libri in programma** set texts.

programmare [program'mare] VT (*gen*) to plan; (*Inform*) to program; (*Cine: presentare*) to screen; (*TV, Radio*) to put on; **programmare di fare qc** to plan to do sth.

programmatore, trice [programma'tore] SM/F (*Inform*) (computer) programmer (*Brit*) *o* programer (*Am*).

programmazione [programmat'tsjone] SF (*Econ*) planning; (*Inform*) programming (*Brit*), programing (*Am*); **in programmazione all'Odeon** (*film*) now showing at the Odeon; **linguaggio di programmazione** (*Inform*) progra(m)mming language.

progredire [progre'dire] VI (*aus* (*persona*) **essere**; (*cosa*) **avere**) (*migliorare*) to progress, make progress; **progredire in qc** to make progress in sth.

progredito, a [progre'dito] AGG (*paese, popolo*) advanced.

progressione [progres'sjone] SF progression ▶**progressione aritmetica** (*Mat*) arithmetic progression ▶**progressione geometrica** geometric progression.

progressista, i, e [progres'sista] AGG, SM/F progressive.

progressivamente [progressiva'mente] AVV progressively.

progressivo, a [progres'sivo] AGG progressive.

progresso [pro'grɛsso] SM (*gen*) progress *no pl*; **fare progressi** to make progress.

proibire [proi'bire] VT **a** (*vietare*) to forbid, prohibit; (*per legge, regola*) to prohibit; **proibire a qn di fare qc** to forbid sb to do sth; **gli fu proibito di entrare** he was refused admission **b** (*impedire*): **proibire a qn di fare qc** to prevent sb from doing sth.

proibitivo, a [proibi'tivo] AGG (*prezzo*) prohibitive; (*condizioni del tempo*) adverse.

proibito, a [proi'bito] AGG forbidden; **"è proibito l'accesso"** "no admittance"; **"è proibito fumare"** "no smoking"; **sogni proibiti** impossible dreams; **frutto proibito** (*Rel, fig*) forbidden fruit.

proibizione [proibit'tsjone] SF prohibition.

proibizionismo [proibittsjo'nizmo] SM prohibition.

proiettare [projet'tare] VT **a** (*gen, Geom*) to project; (*Cine: riprodurre su schermo*) to project; (*ombra, luce*) to cast, throw, project **b** (*gettare*) to throw (out); **furono proiettati fuori dalla vettura** they were thrown out of the car **c** (*protendere*): **proiettare le proprie speranze nel futuro** to pin one's hopes on the future.

proiettile [pro'jɛttile] SM (*pallottola*) bullet (*o* shell); (*corpo lanciato in aria*) projectile; **a prova di proiettile** bullet-proof.

proiettore [projet'tore] SM **a** (*Cine, Fot*) projector **b** (*in stadio*) floodlight; (*Aut*) headlight, headlamp; (*Mil*) searchlight.

proiezione [projet'tsjone] SF (*gen*, *Geom*, *Cine*) projection; **cabina di proiezione** (*Cine*) projection room.

prole ['prɔle] SF children *pl*, offspring; **senza prole** childless.

proletariato [proleta'rjato] SM proletariat.

proletario, ria, ri, rie [prole'tarjo] AGG, SM/F proletarian.

proliferare [prolife'rare] VI (*aus* **avere**) (*anche fig*) to proliferate.

prolifico, a, ci, che [pro'lifiko] AGG prolific.

prolissamente [prolissa'mente] AVV verbosely.

prolissità [prolissi'ta] SF verbosity.

prolisso, a [pro'lisso] AGG verbose.

prologo, ghi ['prɔlogo] SM prologue.

prolunga, ghe [pro'lunga] SF (*di cavo elettrico, telefono*) extension.

prolungamento [prolunga'mento] SM (*gen*) extension; (*di strada*) continuation.

prolungare [prolun'gare] ⬚1 VT (*discorso, attesa*) to prolong; (*linea, termine*) to extend; (*strada, muro*) to extend, continue; (*vacanza*) to prolong, extend.

⬚2 **prolungarsi** VIP (*film, discussione*) to go on; (*effetto*) to last; **la vacanza si è prolungata di alcuni giorni** we (*o* they *ecc*) extended our (*o* their *ecc*) holiday (*Brit*) *o* vacation (*Am*) by a few days.

promemoria [prome'mɔrja] SM INV memorandum, memo.

promessa [pro'messa] SF promise; **fare/mantenere una promessa** to make/keep a promise; **gli ha fatto la promessa di tornare** she promised him that she would come back; **è una giovane promessa del teatro** he (*o* she) is a promising young actor (*o* actress); **ogni promessa è debito!** I'll hold you to that!

promesso, a [pro'messo] ⬚1 PP di **promettere**.

⬚2 AGG: **la terra promessa** the promised land; **sposi promessi** betrothed couple *sg*.

⬚3 SM/F (*fidanzato*) betrothed.

Prometeo [pro'mɛteo] SM Prometheus.

promettente [promet'tɛnte] AGG promising.

promettere [pro'mettere] VT IRREG to promise; **te lo prometto** I promise (you); **promettere a qn di fare qc** to promise sb that one will do sth; **ha promesso di venire** *o* **che sarebbe venuto** he promised to come *o* that he would come; **promettere mari e monti a qn** to promise sb the earth; **promettere bene** (*tempo*) to be *o* look promising; (*studente, attore*) to show promise, be very promising; **il tempo promette male** *o* **non promette niente di buono** the weather doesn't look very promising.

prominente [promi'nɛnte] AGG prominent.

prominenza [promi'nɛntsa] SF prominence.

promiscuamente [promiskua'mente] AVV (*pegg*) promiscuously.

promiscuità [promiskui'ta] SF promiscuity, promiscuousness.

promiscuo, a [pro'miskuo] AGG a : **matrimonio promiscuo** mixed marriage b (*Gramm*): **nome promiscuo** common-gender noun.

promisi *ecc* [pro'mizi] VB vedi **promettere**.

promontorio, ri [promon'tɔrjo] SM (*Geog*) promontory, headland.

promosso, a [pro'mɔsso] PP di **promuovere**.

promotore, trice [promo'tore] ⬚1 SM/F (*di iniziativa, campagna*) promoter, organizer.

⬚2 AGG: **comitato promotore** organizing committee.

promozionale [promottsjo'nale] AGG promotional; **"vendita promozionale"** "special offer".

promozione [promot'tsjone] SF (*gen*, *Comm*, *Sport*) promotion; **avere la promozione a** to be promoted to ▶ **promozione delle vendite** sales promotion.

promulgare [promul'gare] VT to promulgate.

promulgazione [promulgat'tsjone] SF promulgation.

promuovere [pro'mwɔvere] VT IRREG (*gen*) to promote; **promuovere qn (a)** to promote sb (to); **lo studente è stato promosso** the student passed (his exams).

pronipote [proni'pote] SM/F (*di nonni*) great-grandchild, great-grandson/granddaughter; (*di zii*) great-nephew/niece; (*discendenti*): **pronipoti** SMPL descendants.

pronome [pro'nome] SM pronoun.

pronominale [pronomi'nale] AGG pronominal.

pronosticare [pronosti'kare] VT to predict, forecast, foretell.

pronostico, ci [pro'nɔstiko] SM forecast.

prontamente [pronta'mente] AVV promptly, quickly.

prontezza [pron'tettsa] SF (*vedi agg*) readiness; quickness, promptness ▶ **prontezza di mente** readiness of mind ▶ **prontezza di riflessi** quick reflexes *pl* ▶ **prontezza di spirito** readiness of wit.

pronto, a ['pronto] ⬚1 AGG a (*gen*) ready; **essere pronto a tutto** to be ready for anything; **essere pronto a fare qc** to be ready to do sth; **tieniti pronto a partire** be ready to leave; **pronto all'ira** quick-tempered

b (*intervento: rapido*) quick, prompt, fast; **ha sempre la risposta pronta** she's always got an answer ▶ **a pronta cassa** (*Comm*) cash (*Brit*) *o* collect (*Am*) on delivery ▶ **pronta consegna** (*Comm*) prompt delivery ▶ **pronto soccorso** first aid.

⬚2 ESCL (*al telefono*) hello; (*in gara, gioco*): **pronti! via!** ready! steady! go!

prontuario, ri [prontu'arjo] SM manual, handbook.

pronuncia [pro'nuntʃa] SF (*articolazione di suono*) pronunciation; (*Dir*) judgment; **difetto di pronuncia** speech defect.

pronunciabile [pronun'tʃabile] AGG pronounceable.

pronunciare [pronun'tʃare] ⬚1 VT (*parola*) to pronounce; (*nome*) to utter; (*discorso*) to deliver; **pronunciare male qc** to mispronounce sth; **pronunciare una sentenza** (*Dir*) to pass sentence.

⬚2 **pronunciarsi** VIP: **pronunciarsi (su qc)** (*dare un'opinione*) to give one's opinion (on sth); **pronunciarsi a favore/contro** to pronounce o.s. in favour (*Brit*) *o* favor (*Am*) of/against; **non mi pronuncio** I don't want to commit myself.

pronunciato, a [pronun'tʃato] AGG a (*accento, tendenza*) pronounced, marked b (*lineamenti*) prominent; (*mento*) protruding.

pronunzia [pro'nuntsja] *ecc* = **pronuncia** *ecc*.

propaganda [propa'ganda] SF propaganda; **fare propaganda per qn/qc** to push sb/sth.

propagandare [propagan'dare] VT (*idea*) to propagandize; (*prodotto, invenzione*) to push.

propagandista, i, e [propagan'dista] SM/F (*politico*) propagandist; (*Comm*) sales promoter.

propagandistico, a, ci, che [propagan'distiko] AGG propaganda *attr*.

propagare [propa'gare] ⬚1 VT (*Fisica, Bio*) to propagate; (*notizia, idea, contagio*) to spread.

⬚2 **propagarsi** VIP (*gen*) to spread; (*Fis: onde*) to be propagated; (*Bio: specie*) to propagate.

propagatore, trice [propaga'tore] SM/F propagator.

propagazione [propagat'tsjone] SF (*vedi vb*) propagation; spreading.

propaggine [pro'paddʒine] SF (*Bot*) layer; (*fig: diramazione*) offshoot.

propano [pro'pano] SM propane.

propedeutica [prope'dɛutika] SF propaedeutics *pl* (*Brit*), propedeutics *pl* (*Am*).

propedeutico, a, ci, che [prope'dɛutiko] AGG (*corso, trattato*) introductory.

propellente [propel'lɛnte] AGG, SM propellent.

propendere [pro'pɛndere] VI IRREG (*aus* avere): **propendere per** to favour (*Brit*), favor (*Am*), lean towards; **propendere a fare qc** to be inclined to do sth; **propendere per il sì** to be in favo(u)r; **propendere per il no** not to be in favo(u)r.

propensione [propen'sjone] SF **a** inclination; **avere propensione a credere che...** to be inclined to think that ... **b** (*disposizione*) bent; **avere propensione per la matematica** to have a bent for mathematics.

propenso, a [pro'pɛnso] ① PP di **propendere**.
② AGG: **essere propenso a qc** to be in favour (*Brit*) *o* favor (*Am*) of sth; **essere propenso a fare qc** to be inclined to do sth.

propinare [propi'nare] VT (*scherz: pietanza*) to serve up; (: *storia, discorso*) to inflict, foist; **propinare veleno a qn** to slip poison to sb; **ci ha propinato tutte le foto di famiglia** he dragged out all the family photographs for us.

propiziare [propit'tsjare] VT: **propiziare qn, propiziarsi qn** to gain sb's favour; **propiziarsi gli dei** to propitiate the gods.

propiziatorio, ria, ri, rie [propittsja'tɔrjo] AGG propitiatory.

propiziazione [propittsjat'tsjone] SF propitiation.

propizio, a, zi, e [pro'pittsjo] AGG: **propizio (per)** (*gen*) favourable (*Brit*) *o* favorable (*Am*) (to); (*momento*) opportune (for).

proponimento [proponi'mento] SM resolution; **fare il proponimento di fare qc** to resolve to do sth; **nonostante i miei proponimenti** in spite of my good intentions.

proporre [pro'porre] VB IRREG ① VT **a** (*suggerire*) to suggest, propose; (*soluzione, candidato*) to put forward; (*legge, brindisi*) to propose; **proporre qc a qn** to suggest *o* propose sth to sb; **proporre di fare qc** to suggest *o* propose doing sth; **gli ho proposto di venire** I suggested that he should come
b (*offrire: aiuto, prezzo*) to offer; **proporre qc a qn** to offer sth to sb, offer sb sth; **proporre di fare qc** to offer to do sth
c : **proporsi qc** (*obiettivo, meta*) to set o.s. sth; **proporsi di fare qc** to propose *o* intend to do sth.
② **proporsi** VR: **proporsi come candidato** to put o.s. forward as a candidate.

proporzionale [proportsjo'nale] AGG proportional; **proporzionale a** proportional to, proportionate to; **sistema proporzionale** (*Pol*) proportional representation system.

proporzionalmente [proportsjonal'mente], **proporzionatamente** [proportsjonata'mente] AVV proportionally, proportionately.

proporzionato, a [proportsjo'nato] AGG: **proporzionato a** proportionate to, proportional to; **ben proporzionato** well-proportioned.

proporzione [propor'tsjone] SF (*gen, Mat*) proportion; **in proporzione (a)** in proportion (to); **in proporzione diretta/inversa** in direct/inverse proportion *o* ratio; **mancare di proporzione** to be out of proportion; **un movimento di grandi proporzioni** (*fig*) an important movement.

proposito [pro'pɔzito] SM **a** (*intenzione*) intention, aim; **avere il proposito di fare qc** to intend to do sth; **fare qc di proposito** to do sth deliberately *o* on purpose; **essere pieno di buoni propositi** to be full of good intentions
b (*argomento*): **a questo proposito** on this subject; **a quale proposito voleva vedermi?** what did he want to see me about?; **a proposito della tua ragazza...** talking of your girlfriend ...; **a proposito di** (*in lettera*) regarding, with regard to; **le scrivo a proposito dell'inserzione** I am writing to you with reference to the advertisement; **a proposito, sai dirmi...** by the way, can you tell me ...; **capitare** *o* **arrivare a proposito** (*cosa, persona*) to turn up at the right time.

proposizione [propozit'tsjone] SF **a** (*Gramm*) clause; (: *periodo*) sentence ▶**proposizione principale** main clause ▶**proposizione secondaria** subordinate clause
b (*Mat*) proposition.

proposta [pro'posta] SF (*gen*) proposal; (*suggerimento*) suggestion; **fare una proposta** to put forward a proposal; to make a suggestion; **proposta di matrimonio** proposal of marriage; **fare una proposta di matrimonio a qn** to propose to sb ▶**proposta di legge** (*Pol*) bill.

proposto, a [pro'posto] PP di **proporre**.

propriamente [proprja'mente] AVV (*correttamente*) properly, correctly; (*in modo specifico*) specifically; **propriamente detto** in the strict sense of the word; **subito dopo l'ingresso propriamente detto** immediately beyond the hall itself.

proprietà [proprje'ta] SF INV **a** (*caratteristica, qualità*) property
b (*possedimento: casa*) property; (: *terreno*) property, land; (: *beni mobili e immobili*) property *gen no pl*, estate; **avere delle proprietà** to own property; **essere di proprietà di qn** to belong to sb ▶**proprietà privata** private property
c (*correttezza: nel parlare, nello scrivere*) correctness; **proprietà di linguaggio** correct use of language.

proprietario, ria, ri, rie [proprje'tarjo] SM/F (*gen*) owner; (*di pensione*) landlord/landlady; (*di albergo*) proprietor/proprietress, owner; **piccolo proprietario** (*Agr*) smallholder ▶**proprietario terriero** landowner.

proprio, a, pri, e ['prɔprjo] ① AGG **a** (*possessivo*) own; (: *impersonale*) one's; **l'ha visto con i (suoi) propri occhi** he saw it with his own eyes; **per motivi miei propri** for my own *o* for personal reasons; **fare qc per conto proprio** to do sth for oneself
b (*tipico, caratteristico*): **proprio di** peculiar to, characteristic of; **è proprio dei mammiferi** it's peculiar to *o* characteristic of mammals; **è un atteggiamento proprio di quel tipo di persona** it's an attitude characteristic *o* typical of that kind of person
c (*esatto*) proper, exact, correct; **senso proprio di un termine** exact *o* proper meaning of a term; **è stata una vera e propria sciocchezza** it was pure foolishness
d (*Gramm*): **nome proprio** proper noun.
② PRON one's own; **ognuno si prenda il proprio** everybody take their own.
③ SM: **mettersi in proprio** (*Comm*) to set up on one's

own; **perderci del proprio** to be out of pocket.

4 AVV a (*precisamente*) exactly, just; **le cose sono andate proprio così** things went just *o* exactly like this b (*veramente*) really; **oggi mi sento proprio bene** I feel really fit today; **ma sei proprio certo?** are you really sure?, are you a hundred per cent certain?

c (*affatto*): **non... proprio** not ... at all; **quel tipo non mi piace proprio** I really can't stand that man; **non voleva proprio farlo** he really didn't want to do it, he didn't want to do it at all.

propugnare [propuɲ'ɲare] VT to support.

propulsione [propul'sjone] SF (*Tecn, Aer, Naut*) propulsion; **a propulsione atomica** atomic-powered.

propulsore [propul'sore] SM (*Tecn*) propeller.

prora ['prɔra] SF (*Naut: prua*) bow, bows *pl*, prow; **vento di prora** headwind.

proroga, ghe ['prɔroga] SF (*vedi vb*) extension; deferment, postponement.

prorogare [proro'gare] VT (*durata*) to extend; (*scadenza, termine*) to defer, postpone.

prorompente [prorom'pɛnte] AGG (*fiume, torrente*) gushing; **il suo entusiasmo era prorompente** he was overflowing with enthusiasm.

prorompere [pro'rompere] VI IRREG (*aus avere*) (*fiume, torrente*): **prorompere dagli argini** to burst its banks; **prorompere in pianto/in una risata** to burst into tears/out laughing.

prorotto, a [pro'rotto] PP di **prorompere**.

proruppi *ecc* [pro'ruppi] VB vedi **prorompere**.

prosa ['prɔza] SF a (*Letteratura*) prose; **scrivere in prosa** to write in prose; **opera in prosa** prose work b (*Teatro*): **la stagione della prosa** the theatre season; **attore di prosa** theatre actor; **compagnia di prosa** theatrical company.

prosaicamente [prozaika'mente] AVV prosaically.

prosaico, a, ci, che [pro'zaiko] AGG prosaic, mundane.

prosatore, trice [proza'tore] SM/F prose writer.

prosciogliere [proʃ'ʃɔʎʎere] VT IRREG: **prosciogliere qn (da)** (*obbligo, giuramento*) to release sb (from); (*Dir: da accusa*) to acquit sb (of).

proscioglimento [proʃʃoʎʎi'mento] SM (*vedi vb*): **proscioglimento (da)** release (from); acquittal (of).

prosciolto, a [proʃ'ʃolto] PP di **prosciogliere**.

prosciugamento [proʃʃuga'mento] SM (*naturale*) drying up; (*artificiale*) draining; (*bonifica*) reclamation.

prosciugare [proʃʃu'gare] 1 VT (*asciugare: naturalmente*) to dry up; (: *artificialmente*) to drain; (*bonificare*) reclaim.

2 **prosciugarsi** VIP to dry up.

prosciutto [proʃ'ʃutto] SM ham ▶ **prosciutto affumicato** smoked ham ▶ **prosciutto cotto** cooked *o* boiled ham ▶ **prosciutto crudo** cured ham.

proscritto, a [pros'kritto] 1 PP di **proscrivere**.

2 SM/F (*fuorilegge*) outlaw; (*esule*) exile.

proscrivere [pros'krivere] VT IRREG (*Storia*) to proscribe; (*esiliare*) to exile, banish; (*fig: abolire*) to ban.

proscrizione [proskrit'tsjone] SF (*vedi vb*) proscription; banishment; banning.

prosecuzione [prosekut'tsjone] SF continuation.

proseguimento [prosegwi'mento] SM (*gen*) continuation; **buon proseguimento!** (*a chi viaggia*) enjoy the rest of your journey!

proseguire [prose'gwire] 1 VT (*studi, viaggio*) to continue, carry on with; (*lavoro*) to continue with; **proseguire il cammino** to continue on one's way; **proseguì dicendo che...** he went on to say that ...;

proseguì la lettura del libro he carried on reading the book.

2 VI (*aus avere*) (*sogg: persona*) to carry on, go on; (: *lavoro, viaggio*) to continue, go on; **proseguire negli studi** to continue *o* pursue one's studies; **come prosegue?** (*lavoro*) how is it coming along?; **la polizia prosegue nelle ricerche** the police are pursuing their inquiries.

proselito, a [pro'zɛlito] SM/F (*Rel, Pol*) convert.

prosodia [prozo'dia] SF prosody.

prosopopea [prozopo'pɛa] SF pomposity.

prosperamente [prospera'mente] AVV (*gen*) prosperously; **vivere prosperamente** to live in affluence.

prosperare [prospe'rare] VI (*aus avere*) (*commercio, salute*) to flourish; (*finanze*) to thrive; (*paese, commerciante*) to prosper.

prosperità [prosperi'ta] SF prosperity.

prospero, a ['prɔspero] AGG (*commercio, salute*) flourishing; (*finanze*) thriving; (*paese, commerciante*) prosperous, affluent.

prosperosamente [prosperosa'mente] AVV prosperously.

prosperoso, a [prospe'roso] AGG (*commercio, salute*) flourishing; (*regione*) prosperous, affluent; **una ragazza prosperosa** (*formosa*) a buxom girl.

prospettare [prospet'tare] 1 VT (*possibilità*) to indicate; (*affare*) to outline; (*ipotesi*) to advance.

2 **prospettarsi** VIP (*possibilità*) to present itself; (*situazione, futuro*) to look, seem; **la vacanza si prospetta bene** it looks like being an enjoyable holiday.

prospettiva [prospet'tiva] SF a (*Disegno*) perspective; (*veduta*) view; **in prospettiva** in perspective b (*fig: previsione, possibilità*) prospect; **che prospettive hai?** what are your prospects?

prospetto [pros'pɛtto] SM a (*Disegno*) elevation; (*veduta*) view, prospect; **guardare qc di prospetto** to get a front view of sth b (*facciata*) front, façade c (*tabella*) table, schedule; (*sommario*) summary ▶ **prospetto delle lezioni** timetable ▶ **prospetto dei verbi** verb table.

prospiciente [prospi'tʃɛnte] AGG: **prospiciente qc** (*casa*) facing sth; (*terrazza*) overlooking sth.

prossimamente [prossima'mente] AVV soon; **"prossimamente su questi schermi"** (*Cine*) "coming shortly to your screens".

prossimità [prossimi'ta] SF proximity, nearness; **in prossimità di** near (to), close to; **in prossimità delle feste natalizie** as Christmas approaches.

prossimo, a ['prɔssimo] 1 AGG a (*successivo: in tempo, spazio*) next; **nei prossimi giorni** in the next few days; **scendo alla prossima fermata** I get off at the next stop; **la prossima volta stai attento!** next time be careful!; **venerdì prossimo** next Friday; **venerdì prossimo venturo** (*frm: Amm*) next Friday

b (*vicino: gen*) near; (: *parente*) close; **in un prossimo futuro** in the near future; **prossimo a** near (to), close to; **essere prossimo alla laurea** *o* **laurearsi** to be about to graduate; **è prossimo alla fine** (*fig: morte*) he is close to death

c (*Gramm*): **passato prossimo** present perfect; **trapassato prossimo** pluperfect.

2 SM a (*Rel*) neighbour (*Brit*), neighbor (*Am*), fellow man

b : **avanti il prossimo!** (*a sportello ecc*) next please!

prostata ['prɔstata] SF (*Anat*) prostate (gland).

prostituire [prostitu'ire] 1 VT to prostitute.

2 **prostituirsi** VR to prostitute o.s.

prostituta [prosti'tuta] SF prostitute.

prostituto [prosti'tuto] SM male prostitute.

prostituzione [prostitut'tsjone] SF prostitution.

prostrare [pros'trare] 1 VT (*sogg: malattia*) to debilitate seriously; (*fig: nel morale*) to exhaust, wear out; **prostrato dal dolore** overcome *o* prostrate with grief.

2 **prostrarsi** VR to prostrate o.s.; (*fig*) to humble o.s.; **prostrarsi ai piedi di qn/davanti a qn** to bow down at sb's feet/before sb.

prostrazione [prostrat'tsjone] SF prostration.

protagonista, i, e [protago'nista] SM/F protagonist.

proteggere [pro'tɛddʒere] VB IRREG 1 VT (*gen*) to protect; (*moralmente*) to guard, shield; (*fig: artista, arte*) to be a patron of.

2 **proteggersi** VR to protect o.s.

proteico, a, ci, che [pro'tɛiko] AGG protein *attr*; **altamente proteico** high in protein.

proteina [prote'ina] SF protein.

protendere [pro'tɛndere] VB IRREG 1 VT to stretch out.

2 **protendersi** VR to stretch forward; **protendersi dalla finestra** to lean out of the window.

protervia [pro'tɛrvja] SF arrogance, haughtiness.

protesi ['prɔtezi] SF INV (*Med*) prosthesis ▶ **protesi dentaria** dentures *pl*.

proteso, a [pro'teso] PP di **protendere**.

protesta [pro'tɛsta] SF protest; **fare una protesta contro** to protest against; **di protesta** (*marcia, sciopero*) protest *attr*.

protestante [protes'tante] AGG, SM/F Protestant.

protestantesimo [protestan'tezimo] SM Protestantism.

protestare [protes'tare] 1 VT to protest; **protestare la propria innocenza** to protest one's innocence.

2 VI (*aus* avere) to protest.

3 **protestarsi** VR: **protestarsi innocente** to protest one's innocence.

protesto [pro'tɛsto] SM (*Dir*) protest; **mandare una cambiale in protesto** to dishonour (*Brit*) *o* dishonor (*Am*) a bill.

protettivo, a [protet'tivo] AGG protective.

protetto, a [pro'tɛtto] 1 PP di **proteggere**.

2 AGG (*porto, baia*) sheltered; **una specie protetta** a protected species.

3 SM/F protégé(e); (*fig: favorito*) favourite (*Brit*), favorite (*Am*).

protettorato [protetto'rato] SM (*Pol*) protectorate.

protettore, trice [protet'tore] 1 SM/F (*difensore*) protector, guardian; (*di artista, arte*) patron.

2 SM (*di prostituta*) pimp.

3 AGG **a** (*Rel*): **santo protettore** patron saint **b** : **società protettrice degli animali** animal protection society.

protezione [protet'tsjone] SF (*difesa*) protection; (*di arte, artista*) patronage; **misure di protezione** protective measures; **prendere qn sotto la propria protezione** to give sb one's patronage ▶ **protezione civile** civil defence (*Brit*) *o* defense (*Am*).

protezionismo [protettsjo'nizmo] SM protectionism.

protezionista, i, e [protettsjo'nista] AGG, SM/F protectionist.

protezionistico, a, ci, che [protettsjo'nistiko] AGG protectionist.

protocollare [protokol'lare] 1 VT (*Amm*) to register.

2 AGG of protocol.

protocollo [proto'kɔllo] 1 SM **a** (*registro*) register of documents; **numero di protocollo** reference number **b** (*accordo internazionale, cerimoniale*) protocol.

2 AGG INV: **foglio protocollo** foolscap.

protone [pro'tone] SM proton.

protoplasma, i [proto'plazma] SM protoplasm.

prototipo [pro'tɔtipo] SM prototype; **il prototipo dell'americano** your typical American.

protozoo [protod'dzɔo] SM protozoan.

protrarre [pro'trarre] VB IRREG 1 VT (*prolungare*) to prolong; **ha deciso di protrarre il suo soggiorno di un mese** he decided to stay on a month longer.

2 **protrarsi** VIP to go on, continue.

protratto, a [pro'tratto] PP di **protrarre**.

protuberanza [protube'rantsa] SF (*gen*) bulge, protuberance; (*Anat*) swelling.

Prov. ABBR (= *provincia*) Prov.

prova ['prɔva] SF **a** (*esperimento*) test, trial; **essere in prova** (*persona: per lavoro*) to be on probation; **assumere in prova** (*per lavoro*) to employ on a trial basis; **mettere alla prova** to put to the test; **sta mettendo a dura prova la mia pazienza** he is trying my patience severely; **sottoporre ad una prova** to test; **a prova di bomba** bombproof; (*fig*) indestructible; **a prova di proiettile** bulletproof; **la prova del fuoco** (*fig*) the acid test; **circuito/volo di prova** test track/flight; **giro di prova** (*Sport*) test *o* trial run ▶ **prova su pista** (*Ciclismo*) track race

b (*dimostrazione, anche Mat*) proof *no pl*; (*Dir*) proof *no pl*, evidence *no pl*; **dare prova di** to give proof of; **hai le prove di ciò che dici?** can you prove what you're saying?; **avevo ragione e tutto ciò ne è la prova** I was right and this all goes to prove it; **fino a prova contraria** until (it's) proved otherwise; **fino a prova contraria questa è casa mia!** until I hear differently this is my house!; **una prova** (*Dir*) a piece of evidence; **assolto per insufficienza di prove** (*Dir*) acquitted because of lack of evidence ▶ **prova a carico** (*Dir*) evidence for the prosecution ▶ **prova a discarico** (*Dir*) evidence for the defence ▶ **prova documentale** (*Dir*) documentary evidence ▶ **prova del nove** (*Mat*) casting out nines; (*fig*) acid test ▶ **prova testimoniale** (*Dir*) testimonial evidence

c (*tentativo*) attempt, try; **fare una prova** to make an attempt, have a try

d (*Scol*) exam, test; **prova orale/scritta** oral/written exam

e (*Teatro, Mus*) rehearsal; **fare le prove** to rehearse ▶ **prova generale** dress rehearsal

f (*di abito*) fitting.

provare [pro'vare] 1 VT **a** (*tentare*) to try, attempt; (*nuova medicina, macchina, freni*) to try out, test; (*scarpe, abito*) to try on; (*assaggiare*) to try, taste; **provare a fare qc** to try *o* attempt to do sth; **prova tu se ci riesci!** you try and see if you can do it!; **provaci e vedrai!** just you try it!; **ci ha provato con tutte in ufficio** (*fam*) he's tried it on with all the women in the office; **provarsi una gonna** to try on a skirt

b (*dimostrare: verità, teoria, Dir*) to prove

c (*mettere alla prova: coraggio ecc*) to put to the test; **è molto provato da quell'esperienza** the experience has left its mark on him

d (*sentimento*) to feel; (*sensazione*) to experience

e (*Teatro, Mus*) to rehearse.

2 **provarsi** VIP: **provarsi a fare qc** to try *o* attempt to do

sth.

provenienza [prove'njɛntsa] SF (*origine*) origin; (*fonte*) source; **luogo di provenienza** place of origin.

provenire [prove'nire] VI IRREG (*aus* **essere**): **provenire da** (*per nascita*) to come from; (*essere causato*) to be due to, be the result of.

proventi [pro'vɛnti] SMPL revenue *sg*, proceeds.

provenuto, a [prove'nuto] PP di **provenire.**

Provenza [pro'vɛntsa] SF: **la Provenza** Provence.

provenzale [proven'tsale] AGG, SM Provençal.

proverbiale [prover'bjale] AGG proverbial.

proverbialmente [proverbjal'mente] AVV proverbially.

proverbio, bi [pro'vɛrbjo] SM proverb; **come dice il proverbio** as the proverb says, as the saying goes.

provetta [pro'vetta] SF (*Chim*) test tube; **bambino in provetta** test-tube baby.

provetto, a [pro'vɛtto] AGG skilled, experienced.

provincia, ce o **cie** [pro'vintʃa] SF province; **gente/vita di provincia** provincial people/life; **venire dalla provincia** to come from the provinces.

provinciale [provin'tʃale] [1] AGG (*anche pegg*) provincial. [2] SM/F (*anche pegg*) provincial. [3] SF (*anche:* **strada provinciale**) main road (*Brit*), highway (*Am*).

provincialismo [provintʃa'lizmo] SM (*pegg*) provincialism.

provino [pro'vino] SM (*Cine*) screen test; (: *anteprima*) trailer; (*campione*) specimen; **fare un provino** (*Cine*) to have a screen test.

provocante [provo'kante] AGG (*attraente*) provocative.

provocare [provo'kare] VT (*incidente, rivolta, risata*) to cause, bring about; (*persona*) to provoke; (*collera, curiosità*) to arouse.

provocatore, trice [provoka'tore] [1] SM/F (*di rivolta*) agitator. [2] AGG: **agente provocatore** agent provocateur.

provocatoriamente [provokatorja'mente] AVV provocatively.

provocatorio, ria, ri, rie [provoka'tɔrjo] AGG provocative.

provocazione [provokat'tsjone] SF provocation.

provvedere [provve'dere] VB IRREG [1] VI (*aus* **avere**) **a**: **provvedere a** (*famiglia*) to provide for **b** (*prendere provvedimenti*) to take steps, act; **hanno provveduto a mandare rinforzi** they arranged for reinforcements to be sent **c**: **provvedere a** (*occuparsi di*) to look after, take charge of; **provvedere alla spesa/a fare la spesa** to do the shopping; **l'azienda che provvede alla raccolta dei rifiuti urbani** the company responsible for refuse collection. [2] VT: **provvedere qn di qc** to provide *o* supply sb with sth. [3] **provvedersi** VR: **provvedersi di** to provide o.s. with.

provvedimento [provvedi'mento] SM measure, step; (*di previdenza*) precaution ▸ **provvedimento disciplinare** disciplinary measure.

provveditorato [provvedito'rato] SM (*Amm*): **provveditorato agli studi** education offices *pl.*

provveditore [provvedi'tore] SM (*Amm*): **provveditore agli studi** director (*Brit*) *o* commissioner (*Am*) of education.

provvidenza [provvi'dɛntsa] SF: **la provvidenza** providence; **un dono della provvidenza** a godsend; **ti ha mandato la provvidenza!** you're a godsend!

provvidenziale [provviden'tsjale] AGG (*arrivo, pioggia*) providential; **il tuo arrivo è stato provvidenziale!** your coming here was a godsend!

provvidenzialmente [provvidentsjal'mente] AVV providentially.

provvido, a ['prɔvvido] AGG (*letter*) prudent.

provvigione [provvi'dʒone] SF (*Comm*) commission; **lavoro/stipendio a provvigione** job/salary on a commission basis.

provvisorietà [provvizorje'ta] SF (*vedi agg*) temporary nature; provisional nature.

provvisorio, ria, ri, rie [provvi'zɔrjo] AGG (*riparo, lavoro*) temporary; (*governo*) temporary, provisional.

provvista [prov'vista] SF supply, stock; **fare provvista di** to stock up with; **fare provviste** to take in supplies ▸ **provviste alimentari** provisions.

provvisto, a [prov'visto] PP di **provvedere.**

prozia [prot'tsia] SF great-aunt.

prozio [prot'tsio] SM great-uncle.

prua ['prua] SF (*Naut*) bow, bows *pl*, prow.

prudente [pru'dɛnte] AGG (*attento*) cautious, prudent; (*assennato*) wise, sensible; **sarebbe prudente che tu lo facessi** you would be well advised to do it; **non è prudente** it's not advisable; **è più prudente** it's wiser *o* safer; **sii prudente!** be careful!, take care!

prudentemente [prudente'mente] AVV (*gen*) prudently; (*guidare*) carefully.

prudenza [pru'dɛntsa] SF (*vedi agg*) caution, prudence; wisdom; **per prudenza** as a precaution, to be on the safe side; **ha avuto la prudenza di non dire niente** he had the good sense *o* he was wise enough to keep quiet.

prudere ['prudere] VI DIF to be itchy, itch; **mi prude un orecchio** my ear is itchy.

prugna ['pruɲɲa] SF (*Bot*) plum ▸ **prugna secca** prune.

pruno ['pruno] SM (*Bot: cespuglio*) blackthorn; (: *spina*) thorn.

pruriginoso, a [pruridʒi'noso] AGG itchy.

prurito [pru'rito] SM (*anche fig*) itch, itchiness *no pl*; **ho prurito alla mano** my hand is itchy.

Prussia ['prussja] SF Prussia.

prussiano, a [prus'sjano] AGG, SM/F Prussian.

PS SIGLA = *Pesaro.*

P.S. [pi'ɛsse] [1] SIGLA F = **Pubblica Sicurezza.** [2] ABBR **a** (= *postscriptum*) P.S. **b** (*Contabilità*) = **partita semplice.**

P.S.D.I. [pi'ɛsse'di'i] SIGLA M (*Pol*: = *Partito Socialista Democratico Italiano*) *former political party.*

pseudo... ['pseudo] PREF pseudo... .

pseudobiografico, a, ci, che [pseudobio'grafiko] AGG pseudobiographic(al).

pseudointellettuale [pseudointellettu'ale] AGG, SM/F pseudo-intellectual.

pseudonimo [pseu'dɔnimo] SM (*gen*) assumed name; (*di scrittore*) pen name, pseudonym; (*di attore*) stage name.

pseudoscientifico, a, ci, che [pseudoʃen'tifiko] AGG pseudoscientific.

pseudoscienza [pseudo'ʃɛntsa] SF pseudoscience.

P.S.I. [pi'ɛsse'i] SIGLA M (*Pol*)= *Partito Socialista Italiano.*

psicanalisi [psika'nalizi] SF INV psychoanalysis.

psicanalista, i, e [psikana'lista] SM/F psychoanalyst.

psicanalitico, a, ci, che [psikana'litiko] AGG psychoanalytic(al).

psicanalizzare [psikanalid'dzare] VT to psychoanalyse (*Brit*) *o* psycoanalyze (*Am*).

psiche ['psike] SF psyche.

psichedelico, a, ci, che [psike'dɛliko] AGG (*Psic, luci*) psychedelic.

psichiatra, i, e [psi'kjatra] SM/F psychiatrist.

psichiatria [psikja'tria] SF psychiatry.

psichiatrico, a, ci, che [psi'kjatriko] AGG (*caso*) psychiatric; (*reparto, ospedale*) psychiatric, mental.

psichico, a, ci, che ['psikiko] AGG psychological.

psicofarmaco, ci [psiko'farmako] SM (*Med*) *drug used in treatment of mental conditions.*

psicofisica [psiko'fisika] SF psychophysics *sg.*

psicofisico, a, ci, che [psiko'fisiko] AGG psychophysical.

psicologia [psikolo'dʒia] SF psychology.

psicologicamente [psikolodʒika'mente] AVV psychologically.

psicologico, a, ci, che [psiko'lɔdʒiko] AGG psychological.

psicologo, a, gi, ghe [psi'kɔlogo] SM/F psychologist.

psicopatico, a, ci, che [psiko'patiko] ☐1 AGG psychopathic.

☐2 SM/F psychopath.

psicosi [psi'kɔzi] SF INV (*Med*) psychosis; (*fig*) obsessive fear.

psicosomatico, a, ci, che [psikoso'matiko] AGG psychosomatic.

psicoterapeuta, i, e [psikotera'pɛuta], **psicoterapista, i, e** [psikotera'pista] SM/F psychotherapist.

psicoterapia [psikotera'pia] SF psychotherapy.

psoriasi [pso'riazi] SF INV psoriasis.

PT SIGLA = Pistoia.

P.T. ABBR **a** (= *posta e telegrafi*) ≈ P.O. (= *post office*) **b** (*Fisco*) = polizia tributaria.

Pta ABBR (*Geog*: = *punta*) Pt.

pterodattilo [ptero'dattilo] SM pterodactyl.

P.T.P. ABBR = posto telefonico pubblico.

pubblicamente [pubblika'mente] AVV publicly.

pubblicare [pubbli'kare] VT to publish.

pubblicazione [pubblikat'tsjone] SF **a** (*gen*) publication ▶ **pubblicazione periodica** periodical **b** (*di matrimonio*): **pubblicazioni** SFPL (marriage) banns; **fare le pubblicazioni** to publish the (marriage) banns.

pubblicista, i, e [pubbli'tʃista] SM/F **a** (*giornalista*) free-lance journalist **b** (*Dir*) expert in public law.

pubblicità [pubblitʃi'ta] SF INV **a** (*Comm: professione*) advertising; **fare pubblicità a qc** to advertise sth; **lavora nella pubblicità** he works in advertising **b** (*annunci in giornali, TV*) advertisements *pl*; **c'è troppa pubblicità su quella rivista** there are too many advertisements in that magazine **c** (*diffusione*) publicity; **fare molta pubblicità a qc** to give sth a lot of publicity.

pubblicitario, ria, ri, rie [pubblitʃi'tarjo] ☐1 AGG (*campagna, agenzia*) advertising *attr*; (*film, trovata*) publicity *attr*; **cartello pubblicitario** advertising poster; **annuncio** *o* **avviso pubblicitario** advertisement.

☐2 SM/F advertising agent.

pubblico, a, ci, che ['pubbliko] ☐1 AGG (*gen*) public; (*statale: scuola*) state *attr*; **funzionario pubblico** civil servant; **la pubblica amministrazione** public administration; **un pubblico esercizio** a catering (*o* hotel *o* entertainment) business; **pubbliche relazioni** public relations; **ministero della Pubblica Istruzione** ≈ Department for Education (*Brit*), ≈ Department of Health, Education and Welfare (*Am*) ▶ **la Pubblica Sicurezza** the police ▶ **Pubblico Ministero** Public Prosecutor's Office.

☐2 SM (*gen*) public; (*spettatori*: *Cine, Teatro*) audience, public; (: *di partita*) spectators *pl*; **il pubblico dei lettori** the reading public; **un libro destinato al grande pubblico** a book written for the general public; **in pubblico** in public.

pube ['pube] SM (*Anat*) pubis.

pubertà [puber'ta] SF puberty.

pudicamente [pudika'mente] AVV modestly.

pudicizia [pudi'tʃittsja] SF modesty.

pudico, a, ci, che [pu'diko] AGG modest.

pudore [pu'dore] SM (sense of) modesty; (*vergogna*) shame; (*riservatezza*) discretion; **falso pudore** false modesty; **oltraggio al pudore** (*Dir*) indecent behaviour.

puericultrice [puerikul'tritʃe] SF paediatric (*Brit*) *o* pediatric (*Am*) nurse.

puericultura [puerikul'tura] SF paedology (*Brit*), pedology (*Am*), infant care.

puerile [pue'rile] AGG (*anche pegg*) childish, puerile.

puerilità [puerili'ta] SF childishness, puerility.

puerilmente [pueril'mente] AVV (*pegg*) childishly, puerilely.

puerpera [pu'ɛrpera] SF *woman who has just given birth.*

pugilato [pudʒi'lato] SM boxing.

pugile ['pudʒile] SM boxer.

pugliese [puʎ'ʎese] ☐1 AGG of *o* from Puglia.

☐2 SM/F inhabitant *o* native of Puglia.

pugnalare [puɲɲa'lare] VT to stab; **pugnalare qn alle spalle** (*anche fig*) to stab sb in the back.

pugnalata [puɲɲa'lata] SF (*ferita*) stab wound; (*fig: colpo*) severe blow; **dare una pugnalata a qn** to stab sb; **una pugnalata alle spalle** (*anche fig*) a stab in the back.

pugnale [puɲ'ɲale] SM dagger; **colpo di pugnale** stab; **uccidere con un pugnale** to stab to death.

pugno ['puɲɲo] SM **a** (*mano*) fist; **a pugni stretti** with clenched fists; **con la pistola in pugno** with one's gun in one's hand; **scrivere qc di proprio pugno** to write sth in one's own hand; **mostrare i pugni a qn** to shake one's fist at sb; **ormai ha la vittoria in pugno** he now has victory within his grasp; **tenere la situazione in pugno** to have control of the situation; **avere qn in pugno** to have sb in the palm of one's hand; **ormai lo abbiamo in pugno** (*con ricatto, minacce*) we've got him in our power now; (*criminale*) we've got him now **b** (*colpo*) punch; **dare un pugno a qn** to punch sb; **gli ha dato un pugno in un occhio** he punched him in the eye; **fare a pugni** to fight; (*fig: colori*) to clash; **essere un pugno in un occhio** (*fig*) to be an eyesore ▶ **pugno di ferro** (*tirapugni*) knuckleduster (*Brit*), brass knuckles *pl* (*Am*) **c** (*manciata*): **un pugno di** a handful of; **un pugno di uomini** a handful of men; **rimanere con un pugno di mosche** to be left empty-handed.

pula ['pula] SF chaff.

pulce ['pultʃe] SF flea; **mercato delle pulci** flea market; **il gioco delle pulci** tiddlywinks *sg*; **mi hai messo una pulce nell'orecchio** (*fig: insospettire*) you've aroused my suspicions ▶ **pulce di mare** sand hopper.

pulcinella [pultʃi'nɛlla] SM: **Pulcinella** (*maschera*) Punch; **il segreto di pulcinella** (*fig*) an open secret.

pulcino [pul'tʃino] SM (*Zool*) chick; (*vezzeggiativo*) pet; **timido come un pulcino** as shy as a mouse; **bagnato come un pulcino** soaked to the skin.

pulcioso, a [pul'tʃoso] AGG flea-bitten.

puledra [pu'ledra] SF filly.

puledro [pu'ledro] SM colt.

puleggia, ge [pu'leddʒa] SF (*Tecn*) pulley.

pulire [pu'lire] ① VT **a** (*gen*) to clean; (*giardino*) to clear; (*cassetto*) to clear out; (*lucidare*) to polish; **pulire a secco** to dry-clean; **far pulire qc** to have sth cleaned; **pulire il piatto** (*fig*) to clear one's plate

  b : **pulirsi** (*mani*) to clean; (*naso, bocca*) to wipe; **pulirsi i denti** to brush o clean one's teeth; **pulisciti i piedi** wipe your feet.

  ② **pulirsi** VR to clean o.s. (up).

pulita [pu'lita] SF quick clean; **dare una pulita a qc** to give sth a quick clean.

pulito, a [pu'lito] AGG (*gen*) clean; (*ordinato*) neat, tidy; (*fig: lavoro, persona*) honest; **una ragazza dalla faccia pulita** (*fig*) an innocent-looking girl; **avere la coscienza pulita** to have a clear conscience.

pulitore, trice [puli'tore] SM/F cleaner.

pulitura [puli'tura] SF cleaning ▸**pulitura a secco** dry cleaning.

pulizia [pulit'tsia] SF (*condizione*) cleanliness, cleanness; (*atto*) cleaning; **fare le pulizie** (*gen*) to do the cleaning, do the housework; **fare le pulizie di primavera** to spring-clean; **far pulizia** (*fig: portarsi via tutto*) to make a clean sweep ▸**pulizia etnica** ethnic cleansing.

pullman ['pulman] SM INV (*per escursioni*) coach (*Brit*), bus (*Am*).

pullover [pul'lover] SM INV pullover, sweater, jumper (*Brit*).

pullulare [pullu'lare] VI (*aus* **avere**) (*pesci*) to teem; (*insetti*) to swarm; **il fiume pullula di pesci** the river is teeming with fish; **la piazza pullulava di turisti** the square was swarming with tourists; **in questa zona i ristoranti cinesi pullulano** there are lots of Chinese restaurants in this area.

pulmino [pul'mino] SM minibus.

pulpito ['pulpito] SM pulpit; **senti da che pulpito viene la predica!** look who's talking!

pulsante [pul'sante] ① AGG pulsating.

  ② SM (push) button.

pulsar ['pulsar] SM/F INV pulsar.

pulsare [pul'sare] VI (*aus* **avere**) (*cuore*) to beat, pulsate; (*vena*) to throb.

pulsazione [pulsat'tsjone] SF (*di cuore*) beat; (*di vena*) throbbing; (*Fis*) pulsation; **(numero di) pulsazioni** (*Med*) pulse rate.

pulsione [pul'sjone] SF (*Psic*) drive.

pulviscolo [pul'viskolo] SM fine dust ▸**pulviscolo atmosferico** specks *pl* of dust.

puma ['puma] SM INV puma.

pungente [pun'dʒɛnte] AGG (*frutto, arbusto, spina*) prickly; (*odore*) pungent; (*fig: freddo, vento*) biting; (: *ironia, critica*) biting, pungent.

pungere ['pundʒere] VB IRREG ① VT **a** (*sogg: spina, ago*) to prick; (: *insetto, ortica*) to sting; (: *freddo*) to bite; **pungere qn sul vivo** to cut sb to the quick; **essere punto dal rimorso** to be stricken with remorse **b** : **pungersi un dito/una mano** to prick one's finger/one's hand.

  ② **pungersi** VR (*con ago, spina*) to prick o.s.

pungiglione [pundʒiʎ'ʎone] SM sting.

pungitopo [pundʒi'tɔpo] SM (*Bot*) butcher's-broom.

pungolare [pungo'lare] VT (*anche fig: spingere*) goad; **pungolare qn a fare qc** to goad sb into doing sth.

pungolo ['pungolo] SM (*per animali*) goad; (*fig: stimolo*)

spur; **il pungolo dell'ambizione** the spur of ambition.

punibile [pu'nibile] AGG punishable.

punire [pu'nire] VT to punish.

punitivo, a [puni'tivo] AGG punitive.

punizione [punit'tsjone] SF punishment; (*Sport*) penalty; **dare una punizione a qn** to punish sb; **dare una punizione esemplare a qn** to make an example of sb; **per punizione** as a punishment.

punk [pʌŋk] ① AGG INV punk *attr*.

  ② SM/F INV punk.

punsi *ecc* ['punsi] VB vedi **pungere**.

punta¹ ['punta] SF **a** (*di matita, ago, coltello*) point; (*di trapano*) drill; (*di perforatrice*) bit; (*di parte del corpo*) tip; (*di capelli, coda*) tip, end; (*di campanile, albero*) top; (*di monte*) top, peak; **fare la punta a una matita** to sharpen a pencil; **le punte degli alberi** the treetops; **punta della freccia** arrowhead; **camminare in punta di piedi** to walk on tiptoe, tiptoe; **ballare sulle punte** (*Danza*) to dance on points; **doppie punte** (*di capelli*) split ends; **avere qc sulla punta delle dita** (*fig*) to have sth at one's fingertips; **avere qc sulla punta della lingua** (*fig*) to have sth on the tip of one's tongue; **prendere qc di punta** (*fig*) to meet sth head on; **uomo di punta** (*Sport, Pol*) front-rank o leading man

  b (*fig: pizzico: di zucchero, farina*) touch; (: *di sale*) pinch; (: *d'invidia, rancore*) touch, hint; (*traccia*) trace; **c'è una punta d'acido nel latte** the milk tastes slightly sour

  c (*Geog*) promontory

  d (*massima frequenza o intensità*) peak; **ore di punta** peak hours; **il traffico delle ore di punta** rush-hour traffic; **punta massima/minima** highest/lowest level.

punta² ['punta] SF: **cane da punta** pointer.

puntale [pun'tale] SM (*di ombrello*) tip; (*Sci: di bastoncino*) point, tip; (: *di attacco*) toe-piece.

puntapiedi [punta'pjɛdi] SM INV (*Ciclismo*) toe-clip.

puntare [pun'tare] ① VT **a** (*arma*) to point, aim; (*cannocchiale, dito*) to point; **puntare un fucile contro qn** to point a gun at sb; **puntare il dito verso qn/qc** to point (one's finger) at sb/sth; **puntare l'attenzione su qn/qc** to turn one's attention to sb/sth; **puntare gli occhi su qn** to fix one's eyes on sb

  b (*piantare: gomiti, piedi*) to plant; **puntare i piedi** (*fig*) to dig one's heels in

  c (*nei giochi*): **puntare su** to bet on

  d (*sogg: cane*) to point to.

  ② VI (*aus* **avere**) **a** : **puntare su, puntare verso** (*aereo, nave*) to make for, head for; **puntare a qc/a fare qc** (*mirare*) to aim for sth/to do sth

  b (*contare*): **puntare su qn/qc** to rely on sb/sth, count on sb/sth.

puntaspilli [puntas'pilli] SM INV = **portaspilli**.

puntata¹ [pun'tata] SF **a** (*in scommessa, gioco*) bet; **fare una puntata** to place a bet **b** (*fig: breve visita*) short trip; **fare una puntata a casa** to pop home; **farò una puntata a Parigi** I'll pay a flying visit to Paris.

puntata² [pun'tata] SF (*di romanzo*) instalment (*Brit*), installment (*Am*); (*di sceneggiato*) episode; **romanzo a puntate** serial; **pubblicare a puntate** to serialize.

punteggiare [punted'dʒare] VT to punctuate.

punteggiatura [punteddʒa'tura] SF punctuation.

punteggio, gi [pun'teddʒo] SM (*in gara*) score; (*in esame*) mark; **sistema di punteggio** scoring system; **totalizzare il punteggio massimo** to score maximum points.

puntellare [puntel'lare] VT (*ponte, muro*) to shore (up);

(*porta, finestra*) to prop up; (*fig: ipotesi*) to back up, support.

puntello [pun'tɛllo] SM prop, support.

punteria [punte'ria] SF (*Aut*) tappet.

punteruolo [punte'rwɔlo] SM (*Tecn*) punch; (: *per stoffa*) bodkin.

puntiglio [pun'tiλλo] SM (*ostinazione*) obstinacy, stubbornness; **fare qc per puntiglio** to do sth out of sheer obstinacy.

puntigliosamente [puntiλλosa'mente] AVV punctiliously.

puntigliosità [puntiλλosi'ta] SF punctiliousness.

puntiglioso, a [puntiλ'λoso] AGG punctilious.

puntina [pun'tina] SF **a** (*da disegno*) drawing pin (*Brit*), thumb tack (*Am*) **b** (*del giradischi*) stylus **c** (*Aut*): **puntine** SFPL points.

puntino [pun'tino] SM (*di punteggiatura*) dot; **mettere i puntini sulle "i"** (*fig*) to dot the i's and cross the "t"s; **fare le cose a puntino** to do things perfectly; **cotto a puntino** cooked to a turn; **arrivare a puntino** to arrive at just the right moment ▶ **puntini di sospensione** suspension points.

punto¹, a ['punto] PP di **pungere**.

punto² ['punto] 1 SM **a** (*gen*) point; (*luogo*) spot, point, place; (*grado*) point, stage; **la casa è in un bel punto** the house is in a nice spot; **a questo punto** OR **al punto in cui siamo** at this stage; **a che punto sei?** (*con lavoro*) where have you got to?; (*nel prepararsi*) how are you getting on?; **ad un certo punto** at a certain point; **ad un certo punto uno si chiede...** there comes a time when one asks oneself ...; **fino ad un certo punto** to a certain extent; **non si può essere ingenui fino a questo** o **tal punto** one cannot be as naïve as that; **era arrabbiato a tal punto che...** he was so angry that ...; **lo odia al punto tale che...** he hates him so much that ...; **passiamo al prossimo punto** (*in discorso*) let's move on to the next item o point; **punto per punto** point by point; **su questo punto siamo d'accordo** we agree on this point; **siamo sempre allo stesso punto** we're still at the same stage; **essere a buon punto** to have reached a satisfactory stage, be getting on well; **aver raggiunto il punto in cui...** to have reached the stage where ...; **venire al punto** to come to the point; **cotto al punto giusto** cooked to a turn; **di punto in bianco** (*improvvisamente*) all of a sudden; (*inaspettatamente*) out of the blue; **sono le 5 in punto** it's exactly 5 o'clock; **alle 6 in punto** at 6 o'clock sharp o on the dot; **vestito di tutto punto** all dressed up; **sul punto di fare qc** (just) about to do sth

b (*Aer, Naut: posizione*) position; **fare il punto** to take a bearing; **fare il punto della situazione** (*analisi*) to take stock of the situation; (*riassunto*) to sum up the situation

c (*in alfabeto, in morse, su 'i'*) dot; (*punteggiatura*) full stop (*Brit*), period (*Am*); **punto e basta!** that's it!, that's enough!; **due punti** colon; **punto e a capo** new paragraph ▶ **punti di sospensione** suspension points ▶ **punto esclamativo** exclamation mark (*Brit*) o point (*Am*) ▶ **punto interrogativo** o **di domanda** question mark ▶ **punto e virgola** semicolon

d (*Cucito, Maglia, Med*) stitch

e (*Tecn*): **mettere a punto** (*gen*) to adjust; (*motore*) to tune; (*cannocchiale*) to focus; (*Inform*) to debug; (*fig: questione*) to define, settle; (: *progetto*) to finalize.

2 ▶ **punto d'appoggio** (*Alpinismo*) point of contact ▶ **punto d'arrivo** arrival point ▶ **punto caldo** (*Mil*)

trouble spot; (*d'attualità*) major issue ▶ **punto cardinale** cardinal point, point of the compass ▶ **punto critico** (*anche fig*) critical point ▶ **punto debole** weak spot, weak point ▶ **punto (di) vendita** retail outlet ▶ **punto di ebollizione** boiling point ▶ **punto d'incontro** meeting place, meeting point ▶ **punto d'intersezione** (*Geom*) point of intersection ▶ **punto morto** standstill ▶ **punto nero** (*comedone*) blackhead ▶ **punto nevralgico** (*anche fig*) nerve centre (*Brit*) o center (*Am*) ▶ **punto d'onore** point of honour (*Brit*) o honor (*Am*) ▶ **punto di partenza** (*anche fig*) starting point ▶ **punto di riferimento** landmark; (*fig*) point of reference ▶ **punto di vista** (*fig*) point of view.

3 AVV: **non... punto** not ... at all.

puntuale [puntu'ale] AGG punctual; **essere puntuale** to be punctual, be on time; **arrivare puntuale** to arrive on time; **essere puntuale nei pagamenti** to pay on time.

puntualità [puntuali'ta] SF punctuality.

puntualizzare [puntualid'dzare] VT to make clear.

puntualizzazione [puntualiddzat'tsjone] SF clarification; **vorrei fare delle puntualizzazioni** I'd like to make some things clear, I'd like to clarify some points.

puntualmente [puntual'mente] AVV (*gen*) on time; (*iro: al solito*) as usual.

puntura [pun'tura] SF **a** (*di insetto*) sting; (*di zanzara, ragno*) bite; (*di spillo*) prick; (*dolore*) sharp pain **b** (*Med: iniezione*) injection; **fare una puntura a qn** to give sb an injection ▶ **puntura lombare** lumbar puncture.

punzecchiare [puntsek'kjare] 1 VT to prick; (*fig: molestare*) to tease.

2 **punzecchiarsi** VR (*uso reciproco*) to tease each other.

punzonare [puntso'nare] VT (*Tecn*) to stamp.

punzone [pun'tsone] SM (*per metalli*) stamp, die.

può [pwɔ] , **puoi** [pwɔi] VB vedi **potere**.

pupa ['pupa] SF **a** (*bambola, fam: ragazza*) doll **b** (*Zool*) pupa.

pupazzo [pu'pattso] SM puppet ▶ **pupazzo di neve** snowman.

pupilla [pu'pilla] SF (*Anat*) pupil.

pupillo, a [pu'pillo] SM/F (*prediletto*) pet, favourite (*Brit*), favorite (*Am*); (*Dir*) ward.

puramente [pura'mente] AVV (*semplicemente*) purely, simply; (*unicamente*) only, solely.

purché [pur'ke] CONG (*a patto che*) as long as, provided that, on condition that; **verrò con te purché non ci sia molto da aspettare** I'll come with you as long as we don't have to wait long; **purché sia vero!** if only it were true!

pure ['pure] 1 AVV **a** (*anche*) too, as well, also; (*in proposizioni negative*) either; **viene suo fratello e pure sua sorella** his brother is coming as is his sister, his brother is coming and his sister is too o as well; **siamo stati a Zurigo e pure a Lucerna** we went to Zurich and to Lucerne as well; **pure lei non lo sa fare** she can't do it either

b (*con valore concessivo*): **faccia pure!** please do!, by all means!, go ahead!; **te l'avevo pur detto di non andarci** I did tell you not to go.

2 CONG **a** (*tuttavia, nondimeno*) but, and yet, nevertheless; **non è facile, pure bisogna riuscirci** it's not easy and yet we have to succeed; **è giovane, pure ha buon senso** he's young but he's sensible

b (*anche se, sebbene*) even though; **pur non volendolo, ho dovuto farlo** I had to do it even though I didn't want

to; **pur essendo fuori mano** even though it is out of the way

c (*con valore finale*): **pur di vederlo contento farebbe di tutto** she would do anything to make him happy.

purè [pu'rɛ] SM INV, **purea** [pu'rɛa] SF (*Culin*) purée ►**purè di patate** mashed potatoes *pl*.

purezza [pu'rettsa] SF (*gen*) purity; (*di colore*) clarity.

purga, ghe ['purga] SF (*Med*) purging *no pl*, purge; (*Pol*) purge.

purgante [pur'gante] 1 SM (*Med*) purge, purgative.

2 AGG (*Med*) purgative.

purgare [pur'gare] 1 VT (*Med: malato*) to purge, give a purgative to; (: *sangue, aria*) to purify; (*fig: testo, discorso*) to expurgate.

2 **purgarsi** VR (*fig*): **purgarsi dei peccati** to purge o.s. of one's sins.

purgativo, a [purga'tivo] AGG (*Med*) purgative.

purgatorio [purga'tɔrjo] SM (*Rel, fig*) purgatory.

purificare [purifi'kare] 1 VT (*gen*) to purify, cleanse; (*metalli*) to refine.

2 **purificarsi** VIP to cleanse o.s.

purificatoio, toi [purifika'tojo] SM (*Rel*) purificator.

purificatore [purifika'tore] SM purifier.

purificatorio, ria, ri, rie [purifika'tɔrjo] AGG purificatory, purifying, cleansing.

purificazione [purifikat'tsjone] SF (*vedi vb*) purification, cleansing; refinement.

puritanesimo [purita'nezimo] SM Puritanism.

puritano, a [puri'tano] 1 AGG (*Rel*) Puritan; (*fig*) puritanical.

2 SM/F (*Rel*) Puritan; (*fig*) puritan.

puro, a ['puro] AGG (*gen*) pure; (*acqua*) clear, limpid; (*vino*) undiluted; (*aria*) pure, clean; (*fig: ragazza*) chaste, pure; **di razza pura** thoroughbred; **è pazzia pura** it's sheer madness; **è la pura verità** that's the simple truth; **per puro caso** by sheer chance, purely by chance.

purosangue [puro'sangwe] 1 AGG INV (*cavallo*) thoroughbred; **un inglese purosangue** a full-blooded Englishman.

2 SM/F INV (*cavallo*) thoroughbred.

purtroppo [pur'trɔppo] AVV unfortunately.

purulento, a [puru'lɛnto] AGG (*Med*) purulent, festering.

pus [pus] SM (*Med*) pus; **fare pus** to ooze pus.

pusillanime [puzil'lanime] 1 AGG cowardly.

2 SM/F coward.

pustola ['pustola] SF (*Med*) pustule; (*foruncolo*) pimple.

putacaso [puta'kazo] AVV just supposing, suppose; **metti, putacaso, che arrivi anche lui** just supposing *o* suppose he comes too.

putativo, a [puta'tivo] AGG putative.

putiferio [puti'fɛrjo] SM row, rumpus; **fare un putiferio** to kick up a row.

putrefare [putre'fare] (VB IRREG) VI (*aus* **essere**), **putrefarsi** VIP to putrefy, rot.

putrefatto, a [putre'fatto] 1 PP di **putrefare**.

2 AGG (*carne, legno*) rotten; (*cadavere*) putrid, decayed.

putrefazione [putrefat'tsjone] SF putrefaction.

putrescente [putreʃ'ʃɛnte] AGG putrefying, decaying.

putrido, a ['putrido] AGG (*acqua*) putrid; (*carne*) rotten.

puttana [put'tana] SF (*fam!*) whore (*fam!*); **figlio di puttana** (*fig*) son of a bitch.

puttanata [putta'nata] SF (*fam: azione, osservazione*) bloody (*Brit*) *o* goddamn (*Am*) stupid thing to do (*o* say); (: *film, libro*) bullshit (*fam*); **dire delle puttanate** to talk bullshit.

puttanella [putta'nɛlla] SF (*fam*) tart.

puttanesco, a, schi, sche [putta'nesko] AGG (*Culin*): **spaghetti alla puttanesca** spaghetti in a sauce made from anchovies, black olives, capers and tomatoes.

putto ['putto] SM cupid.

puzza ['puttsa] SF = **puzzo**.

puzzare [put'tsare] VI (*aus* **avere**): **puzzare (di)** to smell (of), stink (of); **gli puzza l'alito** his breath stinks, he's got very bad breath; **la faccenda puzza (d'imbroglio)** there's something fishy about the matter, the whole business stinks; **mi puzza!** it smells fishy to me!

puzzle [pʌzl] SM INV jigsaw puzzle.

puzzo ['puttso] SM stink, foul smell; **puzzo di bruciato** smell of burning; **puzzo di fritto** stink of fried food; **sento puzzo** there's a horrible smell; **c'è puzzo d'imbroglio** it smells fishy.

puzzola ['puttsola] SF (*Zool*) polecat.

puzzolente [puttso'lɛnte] AGG smelly, stinking.

PV SIGLA = *Pavia*.

p.v. ABBR (*Amm*) = **prossimo venturo**.

P.V.C. [pivi'tʃi] SIGLA M (= *polivinilcloruro*) PVC.

PZ SIGLA = *Potenza*.

p.zza ABBR = *piazza*.

Q

Q, q [ku] SF O M INV (*lettera*) Q, q; **Q come Quarto** ≈ Q for Queen.

q. ABBR (= *quintale*) q.

Qatar ['katar] SM: **il Qatar** Qatar.

q.b. ABBR (*Culin*: = *quanto basta*) as required; **zucchero q.b.** sugar to taste.

Q.G. ABBR = **quartier generale**.

Q.I. ['ku'i] SIGLA M (= *quoziente d'intelligenza*) IQ.

qua [kwa] AVV **a** here; **eccomi qua!** here I am!; **qua dentro/sotto** in/under here; **da o di qua non mi muovo!** I'm not budging from here!; **da o di qua la vista è stupenda** the view is fantastic from here; **(al) di qua del fiume** on this side of the river; **passavo (per) di qua** I was passing this way; **(per) di qua non si passa** you can't get through here o this way; **vieni più in qua** come closer **b** (*temporale*): **da un anno in qua** since last year, for a year now; **da quando in qua?** since when? **c** (*fraseologia*): **ecco qua cosa succede a non fare attenzione!** just look what happens when you don't pay attention!; **prendi qua questi soldi** here, take this money; **(dammi qua, ci penso io!** just give it to me, I'll see to it!; **dammi qua, è mio** give it here, it's mine; **guarda qua che confusione!** just look at this mess!; **qua la mano** let's shake on it; **che diavolo vuole questo qua?** what on earth does he want?

quacchero, a ['kwakkero] SM/F Quaker.

quaderno [kwa'dɛrno] SM (*per scuola*) exercise book ▶ **quaderno a quadretti** arithmetic exercise book ▶ **quaderno a righe** lined exercise book.

quadrangolare [kwadrango'lare] AGG (*Geom*) quadrangular; (*Sport*): **incontro quadrangolare** four-sided tournament.

quadrangolo [kwa'drangolo] SM (*Geom*) quadrangle.

quadrante [kwa'drante] SM **a** (*dell'orologio*) face **b** (*Naut, Geom*) quadrant.

quadrare [kwa'drare] **1** VT **a** (*Geom*) to square **b** (*Contabilità*) to balance, tally; **quadrare il bilancio** to balance the books.

2 VI (*aus* **avere** o **essere**) (*Contabilità*: *conti, bilancio*) to tally, balance; (*fig*: *corrispondere*): **quadrare (con)** to correspond (with); **qui c'è qualcosa che non quadra** something is amiss here o doesn't add up here; **quel tipo non mi quadra** (*fam*) there's something fishy o I don't like about that guy.

quadrato, a [kwa'drato] **1** AGG **a** (*Mat, tavolo, tovaglia*) square; **metro/chilometro quadrato** square metre/kilometre; **radice quadrata** (*Mat*) square root **b** (*equilibrato*) sensible, level-headed.

2 SM **a** (*gen, Mat*) square; **elevare al quadrato** (*Mat*) to square; **6 al quadrato** 6 squared **b** (*Pugilato*) ring **c** (*Naut*) officers' mess.

quadratura [kwadra'tura] SF **a** (*Mat*) squaring; **la quadratura del cerchio** the squaring of the circle **b** (*Contabilità*) balancing.

quadrello [kwa'drɛllo] SM **a** (*mattonella*) square tile **b** (*di guanto*) gusset **c** (*Culin*) loin.

quadrettare [kwadret'tare] VT to divide into squares.

quadrettato, a [kwadret'tato] AGG (*foglio*) squared; (*tessuto*) checked.

quadretto [kwa'dretto] SM **a** (*fig*: *scena, spettacolo*) picture; **siete un bel quadretto!** you make a lovely picture! **b** : **a quadretti** (*stoffa*) checked; (*foglio*) squared.

quadriennale [kwadrien'nale] AGG (*che dura 4 anni*) four-year *attr*; (*che avviene ogni 4 anni*) four-yearly.

quadriennio [kwadri'ɛnnjo] SM quadrennium, four-year period.

quadrifoglio, gli [kwadri'fɔʎʎo] SM **a** (*Bot*) four-leaf clover **b** : **raccordo a quadrifoglio** (*Aut*) cloverleaf.

quadrifonia [kwadrifo'nia] SF quadrophonics *sg*; **in quadrifonia** in quadrophonic sound.

quadrifonico, a, ci, che [kwadri'fɔniko] AGG quadrophonic.

quadrigemino, a [kwadri'dʒɛmino] AGG: **avere un parto quadrigemino** to have quadruplets.

quadrigetto [kwadri'dʒetto] SM (*Aer*) four-engined jet.

quadriglia [kwa'driʎʎa] SF (*danza*) quadrille.

quadrilatero, a [kwadri'latero] AGG, SM quadrilateral.

quadrimestrale [kwadrimes'trale] AGG **a** (*carica, durata*) four-month *attr*, of four months **b** (*rivista, esame*) four-monthly.

quadrimestre [kwadri'mɛstre] SM (*periodo*) four-month period; (*Scol*) term.

quadrimotore [kwadrimo'tore] SM (*Aer*) four-engined plane.

quadrinomio, mi [kwadri'nɔmjo] SM (*Mat*) quadrinomial.

quadripartito, a [kwadripar'tito] ① SM (*Pol*) four-party government.
② AGG (*Pol: governo*) four-party *attr*; (: *alleanza*) four-power *attr*.

quadro¹, a ['kwadro] AGG (*quadrato*) square; **parentesi quadra** square bracket; **essere una testa quadra** (*fig pegg: ostinato*) to be pig-headed; (*tonto*) to be a block-head.

quadro² ['kwadro] SM **a** (*Arte*) picture, painting; **dipingere un quadro** to paint a picture, to do a painting; **quadro a olio** oil painting
b (*quadrato*) square; **a quadri** (*disegno*) checked
c (*fig: descrizione*) outline, description; (*scena*) sight; **fare un quadro della situazione** to outline the situation; **questo ci fornisce un quadro completo della situazione** this gives us a complete picture of the situation
▶ **quadro clinico** (*Med*) case history
d (*Tecn*) panel, board ▶ **quadro di comando** control panel ▶ **quadro di distribuzione** (*Elettr*) switchboard ▶ **quadro degli strumenti** instrument panel
e (*fig: tabella di dati*) table, chart
f (*Teatro*) scene; **quadro!** (*Cine*) focus!
g : **quadri** SMPL (*Mil, di partito, organizzazione*) upper echelons, cadres; (*Comm*) managerial staff *sg o pl*, (senior) management *sg o pl* ▶ **quadri intermedi** (*Comm*) middle management *sg o pl*
h : **quadri** SMPL (*Carte*) diamonds.

quadrumane [kwa'drumane] (*Zool*) ① AGG quadrumanous.
② SM quadrumanous monkey.

quadrupede [kwa'drupede] (*Zool*) ① SM quadruped.
② AGG (*animale*) four-footed.

quadruplicare [kwadrupli'kare] VT, VI (*aus essere*), **quadruplicarsi** VIP to quadruple, increase fourfold.

quadruplice [kwa'druplitʃe] AGG quadruple; **un contratto in quadruplice copia** four copies *pl* of a contract.

quadruplo, a ['kwadruplo] ① AGG quadruple; **il lavoro è quadruplo rispetto a quello iniziale** the workload is four times what it was originally.
② SM (*Mat*) quadruple; **vorrei il quadruplo del denaro che ho ora** I would like four times as much money as I have now.

quaggiù [kwad'dʒu] AVV (*gen*) down here; (*al sud*) here in the south; (*sulla terra*) in this life.

quaglia ['kwaʎʎa] SF quail.

---

qualche ['kwalke] AGG INDEF
a (*alcuni, non molti*) a few;
▷ **per qualche *giorno*** for a few days
▷ **ho comprato qualche *libro*** I've bought some *o* a few books
▷ **fra qualche *mese*** in a few months
▷ **qualche *volta*** sometimes
▷ **l'ho incontrato qualche *volta*** I've met him a few times *o* once or twice
b (*con valore indeterminato*: *in frasi affermative*) some; (: *in frasi negative e domande*) any;
▷ **sai se passa qualche *autobus* da questa parte?** do you know if any buses go this way?
▷ **in qualche *modo*** somehow
▷ **l'ho già visto da qualche *parte*** I've already seen him somewhere
▷ **hai qualche *sigaretta*?** have you any cigarettes?
▷ **hai qualche *soldo* da prestarmi?** can you lend me some money?
c (*un certo*) some;
▷ **c'è qualche fondamento di verità** there's an element of truth in it
▷ **ci vuole qualche tempo per abituarsi** it takes some *o* a little time to get used to it
▷ **un personaggio *di* qualche rilievo** a person of some importance
▷ **non senza qualche esitazione** not without some hesitation
▷ **ci dev'essere *una* qualche spiegazione** there must be some explanation
▷ **qualche cosa = qualcosa.**

---

qualcheduno [kwalke'duno] PRON INDEF **= qualcuno.**

qualcosa [kwal'kɔsa] PRON INDEF (*in frasi affermative*) something; (*in domande*) anything; **ci dev'essere qualcosa che non va** there must be something wrong *o* the matter; **è già qualcosa** that's something; **ho qualcosa da parte** (*soldi*) I've got a little something put aside; **qualcosa mi dice che...** something tells me that ...; **è medico, o qualcosa di simile** *o* **del genere** he's a doctor or something like that; **bevi qualcosa?** would you like something to drink?; **posso fare qualcosa per te?** can I do anything for you?; **c'è qualcos'altro che desideri?** do you want anything else?; **posso chiederti qualcos'altro?** can I ask you something else?; **c'è qualcosa che non va?** is there something *o* anything wrong?; **qualcosa di meglio/di nuovo** something better/new; **la serata fu qualcosa di grande** it was a really great evening.

qualcuno [kwal'kuno] PRON INDEF **a** (*in frasi affermative*) somebody, someone; (*in domande, in proposizioni condizionali e dubitative*) anybody, anyone; **ho visto qualcuno là fuori** I saw somebody out there; **aspetti qualcuno?** are you waiting for somebody?; **c'è qualcuno in casa?** is anybody at home?
b (*con valore partitivo*: *affermazioni*) some; (: *domande*) any; **qualcuno di noi** some of us; **qualcuno di voi vuol venire?** do any of you want to come?; **se ti piacciono, prendine qualcuno in più** if you like them, take some *o* a few more; **qualcun altro** somebody *o* someone else; **ne avresti qualcun altro da prestarmi?** have you got any more you could lend me?; **viene qualcun altro?** is anybody else coming?; **ce n'è rimasto qualcuno?** are there any left?
c (*persona importante, di prestigio*) somebody; **diventerà qualcuno nella vita** he'll become somebody, he'll make something of his life.

---

quale ['kwale]
① AGG
a (*interrogativo*) what;
▷ **a quale *conclusione* è giunta?** what conclusion did

she reach?

▷**per quale** *data* **conti di finire?** when do you hope to finish by?

▷**in quale** *giorno* **vi siete incontrati?** when did you meet?

▷**quali sono i tuoi** *programmi?* what are your plans?

▷**per quale** *ragione?* why?

b *(scegliendo tra due o più cose o persone)* which;

▷**quale stanza preferisci?** which room do you prefer?

c *(esclamazioni)* what;

▷**quale** *onore!* what an honour!

d

▷**è** *tale* **e quale suo padre** he's just *o* exactly like his father

▷**è** *tale* **quale l'avevo lasciato** it's just *o* exactly as I left it

e *(con valore relativo: qualunque)*

▷**quale** *che* whatever

▷**accetterò quali** *che* **siano le condizioni** I'll accept whatever the conditions

f *(fraseologia)*

▷**per la qual** *cosa* for which reason

▷**in un certo qual** *modo* in some way or other, somehow or other.

2 PRON INTERROG *(scegliendo tra due o più cose o persone)* which;

▷**quale** *dei* **due scegli?** which of the two do you want?

3 PRON REL

a *(soggetto: persona)* who; (: *cosa)* which, that;

▷**a tutti coloro** *i* **quali fossero interessati...** to whom it may concern ...

▷**suo padre,** *il* **quale è avvocato,** his father, who is a lawyer

b *(con preposizioni)*

▷**l'albergo** *al* **quale ci siamo fermati** the hotel where we stayed *o* which we stayed at

▷**il signore** *con* **il quale parlavi** the gentleman to whom you were talking

▷**la collina** *della* **quale si vede la cima** the hill whose summit you can see

▷**la ragione** *per* **la quale sono qui** the reason why I am here

c *(in elenchi)* such as, like;

▷**piante quali l'edera e le rose** plants like *o* such as ivy and roses

▷**pittori quali Raffaello e Leonardo** painters like *o* such as Raphael and Leonardo

d: **per la quale** *(fam)*: **non mi sembra una persona troppo** *per la* **quale** he doesn't inspire me with confidence

▷**è stata una cena proprio** *per la* **quale** it was everything a dinner party should be.

4 AVV *(in veste di, in qualità di)* as;

▷**quale legale della signora** as the lady's lawyer

▷**lo hanno assunto quale direttore** they employed him as manager.

qualifica, che [kwa'lifika] SF qualification; **ha la qualifica di insegnante** he has a teaching qualification, he is a qualified teacher; **sono stato assunto con la qualifica di meccanico** I was taken on as a mechanic.

qualificabile [kwalifi'kabile] AGG: **qualificabile (come)**

which can be described (as).

qualificare [kwalifi'kare] **1** VT **a** *(giudicare: persona, lavoro)* to judge

b *(definire)* to define, describe; **qualificare qn/qc come** to describe sb/sth as; **il suo gesto lo qualifica per quello che è** by doing that he shows the kind of person he is.

2 **qualificarsi** VR **a** *(presentarsi)*: **qualificarsi come** to describe o.s. as

b *(ottenere una qualifica)* to qualify; **qualificarsi a un concorso** to pass a exam *(to obtain a post)*; **qualificarsi per le semifinali** *(Sport)* to qualify for the semifinals.

qualificativo, a [kwalifika'tivo] AGG *(Gramm)*: **aggettivo qualificativo** qualifying adjective.

qualificato, a [kwalifi'kato] AGG *(dotato di qualifica)* qualified; *(esperto, abile)* skilled; **operaio qualificato** skilled worker; **è un medico molto qualificato** he is a very distinguished doctor; **non mi ritengo qualificato per questo lavoro** I don't think I'm qualified for this job.

qualificazione [kwalifikat'tsjone] SF **a** *(qualifica)* qualification; **corso di qualificazione professionale** vocational training course **b** *(Sport: anche:* **gara di qualificazione)** qualifying event; **lottare per la qualificazione** to fight to qualify.

qualità [kwali'ta] SF INV **a** *(gen)* quality; *(di suolo, clima)* nature; **di ottima** *o* **prima qualità** top quality; **prodotto di qualità** quality product; **un vino di pessima qualità** a very poor wine; **controllo (di) qualità** quality control; **ci interessa la qualità non la quantità** we are interested in quality not quantity; **la qualità della vita** the quality of life

b *(dote, pregio)* quality; **ha molte qualità** she has many good qualities

c *(genere, tipo)* kind, type; **fiori di varie qualità** flowers of various kinds; **abbiamo sigarette di ogni qualità** we have cigarettes of every kind; **articoli di ogni qualità** all sorts of goods

d *(veste, carica)*: **in qualità di** in one's capacity as; **in qualità di avvocato** in my *(o* your *ecc)* capacity as a lawyer; **in qualità di amica** as a friend.

qualitativamente [kwalitativa'mente] AVV qualitatively.

qualitativo, a [kwalita'tivo] AGG qualitative.

qualora [kwa'lora] CONG in case, if; **qualora cambiassi idea** should you (happen to) change your mind.

qualsiasi [kwal'siasi] AGG INDEF **a** *(tra molti)* any; **in qualsiasi momento** at any time; **qualsiasi cosa** anything; **per lui farei qualsiasi cosa** I'd do anything for him; **a qualsiasi costo** at any cost, whatever the cost

b *(tra due)* either; **prendine uno qualsiasi** take either of them

c *(pegg)* ordinary, indifferent; **non è uno qualsiasi** he's not just anybody; **non voglio un vino qualsiasi** I don't want any old wine; **quale vuoi?** — **uno qualsiasi** which do you want? — any old one *o* whichever

d *(rel)* whatever; **qualsiasi cosa dica** whatever he says; **qualsiasi favore tu mi chieda** whatever you ask of me.

qualsivoglia [kwalsi'voʎʎa] AGG INDEF *(frm)* = **qualsiasi a.**

qualunque [kwa'lunkwe] AGG INDEF **a** *(tra molti)* any; **in qualunque momento** at any time *o* moment; **qualunque persona** anybody, anyone; **qualunque cosa** anything; **per lui farei qualunque cosa** I'd do anything for him; **a qualunque costo** at any cost, whatever the cost

b *(tra due)* either; **prendine uno qualunque** take either

of them

c (*pegg*) ordinary, indifferent; **non è uno qualunque** he's not just anybody; **non voglio un vino qualunque** I don't want any old wine; **quale vuoi? — uno qualunque** which do you want? — any old one *o* whichever; **l'uomo qualunque** the man in the street

d (*rel*) whatever; **qualunque cosa dica** whatever he says; **qualunque cosa accada** whatever happens; **qualunque favore tu mi chieda** whatever you ask of me.

qualunquismo [kwalun'kwizmo] SM (*pegg*) *political apathy.*

qualunquista, i, e [kwalun'kwista] SM/F (*pegg*) *politically apathetic person.*

qualunquistico, a, ci, che [kwalun'kwistiko] AGG (*pegg*) *(politically) apathetic.*

quando ['kwando] **1** AVV when; **quando arriverà?** when is he arriving?, when will he arrive?; **da quando?** since when?; **da quando sei qui?** how long have you been here?; **di quando è quel giornale?** which day's paper is that?; **fino a quando continuerà così?** how long will it go on *o* continue like this?; **quando mai avrei detto una cosa del genere?** whenever did I say anything of the kind?; **di quando in quando** from time to time; **a quando i confetti?** when are we going to be hearing wedding bells?.

2 CONG when; **ti raggiungo quando ho finito** I'll join you when I've finished; **da quando sono arrivato** (ever) since I arrived; **piange sempre quando parto** she always cries when I leave, she cries whenever I leave; **quando fa così non lo sopporto** I can't stand him when he does that; **quand'anche tu volessi parlargli...** even if you wanted to speak to him ...; **si lamenta lui quando ne avrei molto più diritto io** he's the one that's complaining, when in fact I've got much more reason to; **quando te lo dico devi credermi** when I tell you something you should believe me; **ci raccontava di quando era bambino** he told us about when he was a child; **vorrei trovare tutto pronto per quando torno** I'd like to find everything ready for when I come back; **quando si dice la sfortuna...!** talk about bad luck ...!

quantificabile [kwantifi'kabile] AGG quantifiable.

quantificare [kwantifi'kare] VT to quantify.

quantificazione [kwantifikat'tsjone] SF quantification.

quantità [kwanti'ta] SF INV **a** (*entità misurabile*) quantity, amount

b (*gran numero*): **una quantità di** (*denaro, acqua*) a great deal of, a lot of; (*gente, cose*) a great many, a lot of, a great number of; **ho una quantità di cose da fare** I have a lot of things to do; **c'è frutta in quantità** there is plenty of fruit

c (*Mat, di vocale*) quantity.

quantitativamente [kwantitativa'mente] AVV quantitatively.

quantitativo, a [kwantita'tivo] **1** AGG quantitative. **2** SM (*Comm: di merce*) amount, quantity.

---

quanto[1]**, a** ['kwanto]

1 AGG

a (*interrogativo: quantità*) how much; (: *numero*) how many;

▷**quanti** *anni* **hai?** how old are you?

▷**quanti** *metri* **desidera?** how many metres would you like?

▷**quanti** *soldi* **ti hanno chiesto?** how much did they ask you (for it)?

▷**quanta** *stoffa* **ti serve?** how much material do you need?

▷**quanto** *tempo*? how long?, how much time?

▷**quanto** *tempo* **ci metti da qui all'ufficio?** how long does it take you from here to the office?

▷**quante** *volte*? how often?, how many times?

b (*esclamativo*)

▷**quante** *storie*! what a fuss!

▷**quanto** *tempo* **sprecato!** what a waste of time!

c (*relativo: quantità*) as much as; (: *numero*) as many as;

▷**ti darò quanto** *denaro* **ti serve** I'll give you as much money as you need

▷**prendi quanti** *libri* **vuoi** take as many books as you want

▷**fermati quanto** *tempo* **vuoi** stay as long as you want.

2 PRON

a (*interrogativo: quantità*) how much; (: *numero*) how many;

▷**quanto** *costa*? how much does it cost?

▷**quanto credi** *costerà*? how much do you think it will cost?

▷**quanto è** *da* **qui al negozio?** how far is it from here to the shop?

▷**quanti** *di* **loro?** how many of them?

▷**quanto ci hai** *messo* **a farlo?** how long did it take you to do it?

▷**quanti** *ne* **desidera?** how many do you want?

▷**quanti** *ne* **abbiamo oggi?** what's the date today?

▷**quanto stai** *via*? how long will you be away?

▷**so che devo prendere del pane, ma non so quanto** I know I must get some bread, but I don't know how much

▷**quant'è?** how much is it?

b (*esclamativo*)

▷**vedi quanti hanno accettato!** see how many have accepted!

▷**quante me ne ha dette!** (*insulti*) the way he insulted me!; (*bugie*) the number of lies he told me!

c (*relativo: quantità*) as much as; (: *numero*) as many as;

▷**gli darò quanto** *chiede* I'll give him what *o* as much as he asks for

▷**è quanto** *di meglio* **potessi trovare** it's the best you could find

▷**a quanto** *dice* **lui** according to him

▷**in risposta a quanto** *esposto* **nella sua lettera...** in answer to the points raised in your letter ...

▷**saranno scelti quanti** *hanno fatto* **domanda in tempo** all (those) whose applications arrived in time will be selected

▷*per* **quanto ne so** as far as I know

▷**faremo quanto** *potremo* **per aiutarti** we'll do all we can *o* as much as we can to help you

▷**era** *tanto* **felice quanto non lo era mai stato** he was happier than he had ever been

▷**spende** *tanto* **denaro quanto ne guadagna** he spends all that *o* every penny he earns, he spends as much as he earns

▷**fanne venire quanti** *vuoi* get as many as you like to come.

quanto² ['kwanto] AVV

a (*quantità*) how much; (*numero*) how many;
▷**sapessi quanto *abbiamo camminato*!** if you knew how far we have walked!
▷**quanto *fumi* al giorno?** how many (cigarettes) do you smoke a day?
▷**Dio solo sa quanto *mi sono arrabbiato*!** God only knows how angry I was!
▷**quanto *pesi*?** how much do you weigh?
▷**quanto *sono felice*!** how happy I am!

b (*nella misura o quantità che*) as much as;
▷**aggiungere brodo quanto *basta*** add sufficient *o* enough stock, add as much stock as is necessary
▷**dovrai aspettare quanto è *necessario*** you'll have to wait as long as is necessary
▷**strillava quanto *poteva*** she was shouting at the top of her voice *o* as loud as she could

c (*come*)
▷**siamo ricchi quanto *loro*** we are as rich as they are
▷**mi sono riposato quanto *mai* in questi ultimi tempi** I've had more rest than ever recently
▷**è una ragazza quanto *mai* spontanea** she's a very natural girl
▷**è famoso *non tanto* per i romanzi quanto per le poesie** he's famous not so much for his novels as for his poetry
▷**è *tanto* sciocco quanto cafone** he is as stupid as he is rude, he is both stupid and rude
▷**quanto è *vero* Iddio...!** I swear to God ...!

d: **in** quanto (*in qualità di*) as; (*perché, per il fatto che*) as, since
▷**in quanto insegnante** as a teacher
▷**non ho suonato *in* quanto temevo di svegliarti** I didn't ring as *o* since I was afraid I would wake you
▷**in quanto a** (*per ciò che riguarda*) as for
▷**in quanto ai soldi che mi devi...** as for the money you owe me ..., as far as the money you owe me is concerned ...

e: **per** quanto (*nonostante, anche se*) however; (*tuttavia*) although
▷**per quanto si sforzi, non riesce** however hard he tries he can't do it
▷**per quanto sembri complicato** however complicated it may seem
▷**cercherò di fare qualcosa per lui, *per* quanto non se lo meriti** I'll try and do something for him although *o* even though he doesn't deserve it

f
▷**quanto *meno*** the less
▷**quanto *meno* uno insiste tanto più gli viene offerto** the less one demands the more one is offered
▷**quanto *più* mi sforzo di ricordare tanto meno ci riesco** the harder *o* the more I try to remember the less I succeed
▷**quanto *più*** the more
▷**quanto *più* presto potrò** as soon as I can
▷**verrò quanto *prima*** I'll come as soon *o* as early as possible

quanto³ SM (*Fis*) quantum; **teoria dei quanti** quantum

theory.

quantunque [kwan'tunkwe] CONG (*sebbene*) although, even though; **quantunque mi piaccia non ci vivrei mai** even though I like the place I'd never live there; **accetto quantunque non convinto del tutto** I accept although *o* even though I'm not totally convinced.

quaranta [kwa'ranta] AGG INV, SM INV forty *per fraseologia vedi* **cinquanta**.

quarantena [kwaran'tɛna] SF quarantine; **essere in quarantena** to be in quarantine; **mettere in quarantena** to quarantine.

quarantenne [kwaran'tɛnne] AGG, SM/F forty-year-old *per fraseologia vedi* **cinquantenne**.

quarantennio, ni [kwaran'tɛnnjo] SM (period of) forty years.

quarantesimo, a [kwaran'tɛzimo] AGG, SM/F, SM fortieth *per fraseologia vedi* **quinto**.

quarantina [kwaran'tina] SF: **una quarantina (di)** about forty *per fraseologia vedi* **cinquantina**.

quarantotto [kwaran'totto] **1** AGG INV forty-eight.
2 SM INV forty-eight; **fare un quarantotto** (*fam*) to raise hell.

Quaresima [kwa'rezima] SF (*Rel*): **la Quaresima** Lent; **osservare *o* fare la Quaresima** to keep Lent.

Quaresimale [qwarezi'male] AGG (*Rel*) Lenten.

quarta ['kwarta] SF (*gen*) fourth; (*Aut*) fourth gear; (*Scol: elementare*) ≈ third year (at primary school) (*Brit*), ≈ fourth grade (*Am*); (: *superiore*) ≈ lower sixth (*Brit*), ≈ twelfth grade (*Am*); **mettere la quarta** to go into fourth (gear); **partire in quarta** (*fig*) to take off at top speed.

quartettista, i, e [kwartet'tista] SM/F (*Mus*) member of a quartet; (*compositore*) composer of quartets.

quartetto [kwar'tetto] SM (*Mus*) quartet(te); **che bel quartetto!** just look at the four of them!

quartiere [kwar'tjɛre] SM **a** (*di città*) district, area; **la gente del quartiere** the local people; **lo conoscono tutti nel quartiere** everybody in the neighbourhood knows him ▶**quartiere dormitorio** dormitory *o* commuter area ▶**quartiere residenziale** residential area *o* district ▶**i quartieri alti** the smart *o* exclusive areas ▶**i quartieri bassi** the poor areas
b (*Mil*) quarters *pl* ▶**quartier generale** headquarters *pl*
c: **lotta senza quartiere** (*fig*) unrelenting struggle.

quartina [kwar'tina] SF (*Poesia*) quatrain.

quartino [kwar'tino] SM **a** (*di vino*) quarter litre (*Brit*) *o* liter (*Am*) **b** (*Mus*: *strumento*) small clarinet.

quarto, a ['kwarto] **1** AGG, SM/F fourth *per fraseologia vedi* **quinto**.
2 SM **a** (*frazione*) quarter; **un quarto di vino** a quarter-litre (*Brit*) *o* quarter-liter (*Am*) bottle of wine; **un quarto di pollo** a quarter chicken; **primo/ultimo quarto** (*della luna*) first/last quarter; **un chilo e un quarto** a kilo and a quarter
b (*ora*): **un quarto d'ora** a quarter of an hour; **tre quarti d'ora** three quarters of an hour; **tre ore e un quarto** three and a quarter hours; **le sei e un quarto** (a) quarter past six; **le otto e tre quarti** |OR| **le nove meno un quarto** (a) quarter to (*Brit*) *o* of (*Am*) nine; **passare un brutto quarto d'ora** (*fig*) to have a bad *o* nasty time of it
c: **quarti di finale** (*Sport*) quarterfinals
d (*Naut*) watch; **il primo quarto** the first watch
e (*Tip*) quarto.

quartogenito, a [kwarto'dʒenito] SM/F fourth child.

quartultimo, a [kwar'tultimo] AGG, SM/F last but three, fourth from last.

quarzo ['kwartso] SM quartz; **orologio al quarzo** quartz watch ▶ **quarzo rosa** rose quartz.

quasar ['kwazar] SF INV quasar.

quasi ['kwazi] [1] AVV (gen) almost, nearly; (restrittivo) hardly, scarcely; **ha quasi 30 anni** he's almost o nearly 30 (years old); **quasi niente** hardly o scarcely anything; **quasi mai** hardly ever; **quasi cadevo** I almost o nearly fell; **è quasi un fratello per me** he's like a brother to me; **oserei quasi dire che…** I'd almost say that …; **quasi quasi me ne vado** I've half a mind to leave; **quasi quasi è meglio così** it may even be better this way.
[2] CONG (come se) as if; **urla quasi fosse lui il padrone** he shouts as if he were the boss; **non si è fatto vivo, quasi sospettasse qualcosa** he hasn't been in touch, as if he suspected something.

quassù [kwas'su] AVV up here.

quaterna [kwa'tɛrna] SF (Lotto, Tombola) set of four winning numbers; **vincere una quaterna** (Lotto) to draw four winning numbers; **fare quaterna** (Tombola) to cover four numbers in a row.

quaternario, ria, ri, rie [kwater'narjo] (Geol) [1] AGG: **l'era quaternaria** the Quaternary period.
[2] SM: **il quaternario** the Quaternary (period).

quattamente [kwatta'mente] AVV stealthily.

quatto, a ['kwatto] AGG: **stare quatto quatto** to keep as quiet as a mouse; **entrare quatto quatto in una stanza** to creep stealthily into a room; **uscire quatto quatto** to slip away.

quattordicenne [kwattordi'tʃɛnne] AGG, SM/F fourteen-year-old per fraseologia vedi **cinquantenne**.

quattordicesimo, a [kwattordi'tʃɛzimo] AGG, SM/F fourteenth; **la quattordicesima** (di stipendio) annual Christmas bonus equivalent to 1 month's pay per fraseologia vedi **quinto**.

quattordici [kwat'torditʃi] AGG, SM INV fourteen per fraseologia vedi **cinque**.

quattrino [kwat'trino] SM **a**: **non avere un quattrino** o **il becco di un quattrino** (fam) to be penniless o broke **b**: **quattrini** SMPL money sg, cash sg; **fare quattrini** to make money; **essere pieno di quattrini** to be rolling in money; **quattrini a palate** piles of money; **costare fior di quattrini** to cost a fortune.

quattro ['kwattro] [1] AGG INV **a** four; **c'erano quattro persone** there were four people there
b (fig: pochi): **fare quattro passi** to take a stroll; **c'erano quattro gatti allo spettacolo** there was only a handful of people at the show; **fare quattro salti** to go dancing; **fare quattro chiacchiere** to have a chat; **lo pagano quattro soldi** they pay him peanuts o a pittance; **a quattr'occhi** (tra 2 persone) face to face; (privatamente) in private; **a quattro a quattro** four at a time.
[2] SM INV four; **dirne quattro a qn** to give sb a piece of one's mind; **farsi in quattro per qn** to go out of one's way for sb, put o.s. out for sb; **fare il diavolo a quattro** to kick up a rumpus; **in quattro e quattr'otto** in less than no time, in no time at all per fraseologia vedi **cinque**.

quattrocchi [kwat'trɔkki] SM INV (fig fam: persona con occhiali) four-eyes.

quattrocentesco, a, schi, sche [kwattrotʃen'tesko] AGG fifteenth-century attr.

quattrocento [kwattro'tʃɛnto] [1] AGG INV four hundred.
[2] SM INV four hundred; (secolo): **il Quattrocento** the

fifteenth century.

quattromila [kwattro'mila] AGG INV, SM INV four thousand.

Quebec [kwe'bɛk] SM il Quebec.

---

quello , a ['kwello]

davanti a sm **quel** + consonante, **quell'**+ vocale, **quello** + s impura, gn, pn, ps, x, z; pl **quei** + consonante, **quegli** + vocale o s impura, gn, pn, ps, x, z; davanti a sf **quella** + consonante, **quell'** + vocale; pl **quelle**

[1] AGG DIMOSTR
a that, those pl;
▷ **mi passi quel libro?** could you pass me that book?
▷ **voglio quella camicia lì o là** I want that shirt there
▷ **dove hai comprato quei quadri?** where did you buy those paintings?
▷ **dove metto quello scatolone?** where shall I put that box?
▷ **chi sono quegli uomini?** who are those men?
b (seguito da proposizione relativa)
▷ **con quel poco che abbiamo** with what o the little we have
▷ **dov'è quel maglione che mi dicevi?** where's the o that jumper you were telling me about?
c (enfatico)
▷ **ho una di quelle paure!** I'm scared stiff!
▷ **ne ha fatte di quelle!** (sciocchezze) he did some really stupid things!
▷ **una di quelle** (euf: prostituta) a working girl
▷ **in quello stesso istante** at that very moment.
[2] PRON DIMOSTR
a that (one), those (ones) pl;
▷ **quale vuoi? — quello bianco** which do you want? — the white one
▷ **il tuo nome e quello di Roberta** your name and Roberta's
▷ **quello di Giovanna è il voto migliore** Giovanna's is the best mark, Giovanna has the best mark
▷ **prendiamo quello là** we'll take that one there
▷ **chi è quello lì?** who is that (person)?
▷ **e quello cos'è?** and what is that?
▷ **quelle sono le mie scarpe** those are my shoes
▷ **ho incontrato quelli della festa** I met the people from the party
▷ **a che ora viene quello del latte?** when does the milkman come?
b (egli) he; (ella) she; (essi, esse) they;
▷ **sarebbe un'occasione d'oro e quelli non vogliono accettare** it's a golden opportunity but they don't want to accept
c (in proposizione relativa): **quello(a) che** (persona) the one (who); (cosa) the one (which) o (that)
▷ **quelli(e) che** (persone) those who; (cose) those which o that
▷ **quello che hai comprato tu è più bello** the one (which) you bought is nicer
▷ **quello che hai visto è il padre** the person o the one you saw is the father
▷ **quella che hai incontrato è la seconda moglie** the one o woman you met is his second wife
▷ **chiedi a quelli che l'hanno conosciuto** ask those who knew him

d (*ciò*): **quello** *che* what; (*tutto*) all (that), everything
▷**ho detto quello** *che* **sapevo** I've told you all I know
▷**ho fatto quello** *che* **potevo** I did what I could
▷**nega, e quel** *che* **è peggio, ci scherza sopra** he denies it, and what is worse, jokes about it
▷**da quello** *che* **ho sentito** from what I've heard
e (*fraseologia*)
▷*in* **quel** *di* **Milano** in the Milan area *o* region
▷*in* **quel** *mentre* at that very moment.

quercia, ce ['kwɛrtʃa] SF **a** (*albero*) oak (tree); (*legno*) oak ▶**quercia rossa** red oak; **forte come una quercia** as strong as an ox **b** : **la Quercia** (*Pol*) symbol of *P.D.S.*

querela [kwe'rɛla] SF (*Dir*) (legal) action; **sporgere querela contro qn** to bring an action against sb; **querela per diffamazione** libel action.

querelante [kwere'lante] SM/F (*Dir*) plaintiff.

querelare [kwere'lare] VT (*Dir*) to bring an action against.

querelato, a [kwere'lato] SM/F (*Dir*) defendant.

querulo, a ['kwɛrulo] AGG (*letter*) querulous.

quesito [kwe'sito] SM question, query; **porre un quesito (a)** to put a question (to).

questi ['kwesti] PRON DIMOSTR (*letter*) this person.

questionare [kwestjo'nare] VI (*aus* avere) (*litigare*) to quarrel, argue; **questionare di** to discuss.

questionario, ri [kwestjo'narjo] SM questionnaire.

questione [kwes'tjone] SF **a** (*problema, faccenda*) question, matter, problem; (*controversia*) issue; **si tratta di una questione delicata/personale** it's a delicate/personal matter; **è una questione politica** it's a political question *o* matter; **è una questione di vita o di morte** it's a question *o* matter of life and death; **il nocciolo della questione** the heart of the matter; **non conosco i termini della questione** I don't know the details of the matter; **ne ha fatto una questione** he made an issue out of it; **è sorta una questione in merito** they made an issue out of it; **comporre una questione** (*Dir*) to settle an issue; **il caso in questione** the matter at hand; **la persona in questione** the person involved; **non voglio essere chiamato in questione** I don't want to be involved; **è questione di tempo** it's a matter *o* question of time; **non faccio questioni di soldi** it's not a question of money; **litigare per questioni di eredità** OR **essere in questione per l'eredità** to be in dispute over the inheritance; **la questione meridionale** the Southern Question (*the social/political situation in Southern Italy*) **b** (*dubbio*): **mettere qc in questione** to question sth; **è fuori questione** it's out of the question.

questo , a ['kwesto]
1 AGG DIMOSTR
a this, these *pl*;
▷**in questi ultimi** *giorni* these last few days
▷**questo** *libro qui o qua* this book (here)
▷**questo** *lunedì* this Monday
▷**ti piace questo** *maglione*? do you like this jumper?
▷**quest'***oggi* nowadays, today
▷**questa** *sera* this evening
▷**di questi** *tempi* in times like these
b (*enfatico*)
▷**con questo** *caldo* in this heat
▷**non fatemi più prendere queste** *paure* don't give me such a fright again.

2 PRON DIMOSTR
a this (one), these (ones) *pl*;
▷**prendo questo** *qui o qua* I'll take this one
▷**questo è il tuo posto** this is your place
▷**questo cosa significa?** what does this mean?
▷**questo è troppo!** this is too much *o* the limit!
▷**questo mi fa piacere** I am pleased about that
b (*egli*) he; (*ella*) she; (*essi, esse*) they;
▷**e questo mi guarda e ride!** and this guy just looks at me and laughs!
▷**una tale occasione, e questi che fanno? - rifiutano** such a great opportunity, and what do they do? - they refuse
c : **questo... quello...** (*il primo... il secondo...*) the former ...the latter ...; (*l'uno... l'altro...*) the one ...the other ...;
▷**questi... quelli** some ...others
▷**questi gridavano, quelli ridevano** some were shouting, others were laughing
▷**preferisci questo o quello?** do you prefer this one or that one?
d (*fraseologia*)
▷**e con questo?** so what?
▷**e con questo se n'è andato** and with that he left
▷**con tutto questo** in spite of this, despite all this
▷**è per questo che sono venuto** this is why I came
▷**questa poi!** I don't believe it!
▷**questo è quanto** that's all
▷**questo sì che è il colmo!** this is the limit!
▷**questa non me la dovevi fare** you shouldn't have done this to me.

questore [kwes'tore] SM (*Polizia*) *public official in charge of the police in the provincial capital, reporting to the prefetto*, ≈ chief constable (*Brit*), ≈ police commissioner (*Am*).

questua ['kwɛstua] SF collection (of alms).

questura [kwes'tura] SF (*organo*) police force; (*edificio*) police headquarters *pl*.

questurino [kwestu'rino] SM (*fam: poliziotto*) cop.

qui [kwi] AVV **a** here; **eccomi qui!** here I am!; **qui dentro/sopra/vicino** in/up/near here; **da** *o* **di qui** from here; **da** *o* **di qui non mi muovo!** I'm not budging from here!; **da qui la vista è stupenda** the view is fantastic from here; **di qui non si passa** you can't get through here *o* this way **b** (*temporale*): **da qui in avanti** from now on; **di qui a poco/una settimana** in a little while/a week's time **c** (*fraseologia*): **dammi, qui, ci penso io!** just give it to me, I'll see to it!; **fin qui tutto bene** so far so good; **ah, qui ti voglio!** that's the problem!; **non è di qui** he's not from around here; **che diavolo vuole questo qui?** what on earth does he want?

quiescente [kwjeʃ'ʃɛnte] AGG dormant.

quiescenza [kwjeʃ'ʃɛntsa] SF **a** (*di vulcano*) dormancy **b** (*Amm*): **trattamento di quiescenza** retirement package; **porre qn in quiescenza** to retire sb.

quietamente [kwjeta'mente] AVV quietly.

quietanza [kwje'tantsa] SF (*Comm*) receipt.

quietare [kwje'tare] **1** VT to soothe, calm.
2 **quietarsi** VIP (*mare*) to become calm; (*vento*) to die down; (*bambino*) to calm down.

quiete ['kwjɛte] SF **a** (*silenzio*) quiet, stillness, quietness; (*tranquillità*) peace, calmness; **la quiete che precede la**

tempesta the calm before the storm; aver bisogno di quiete (*riposo*) to need peace and quiet; la quiete della campagna the tranquillity *o* peace of the countryside; turbare la quiete pubblica (*Dir*) to disturb the peace **b** (*Fis*): stato di quiete state of rest.

quieto, a ['kwjeto] AGG (*gen*) quiet; (*notte*) quiet, still; (*mare*) calm; l'ho fatto per il quieto vivere I did it for a quiet life.

quindi ['kwindi] ① CONG (*perciò*) therefore, so.
② AVV (*in seguito*) then; devi continuare diritto, quindi girare a destra you should carry straight on, then turn right.

quindicennale [kwindit∫en'nale] ① AGG (*che dura 15 anni*) fifteen-year *attr*; (*che ricorre ogni 15 anni*) every fifteen years, fifteen-yearly.
② SM (*ricorrenza*) fifteenth anniversary.

quindicenne [kwindi't∫εnne] AGG, SM/F fifteen-year-old *per fraseologia vedi* cinquantenne.

quindicennio, ni [kwindi't∫εnnjo] SM (period of) fifteen years.

quindicesimo, a [kwindi't∫εzimo] AGG, SM/F fifteenth *per fraseologia vedi* quinto.

quindici ['kwindit∫i] ① AGG INV fifteen; quindici giorni two weeks, a fortnight (*Brit*); oggi a quindici two weeks *o* a fortnight (*Brit*) today; tra quindici giorni in two weeks *o* a fortnight (*Brit*).
② SM INV fifteen *per fraseologia vedi* cinque.

quindicina [kwindi't∫ina] SF: una quindicina (di) about fifteen; (fra) una quindicina di giorni (in) two weeks *o* a fortnight (*Brit*); la seconda quindicina di marzo the second half of March *per fraseologia vedi* cinquantina.

quindicinale [kwindit∫i'nale] ① AGG fortnightly (*Brit*), semimonthly (*Am*).
② SM (*rivista*) fortnightly magazine (*Brit*), semimonthly (*Am*).

quinquennale [kwinkwen'nale] AGG (*che dura 5 anni*) five-year *attr*; (*che avviene ogni 5 anni*) five-yearly.

quinquennio, ni [kwin'kwεnnjo] SM (period of) five years, quinquennial.

quinta ['kwinta] SF **a** (*gen*) fifth; (*Aut*) fifth gear; (*Scol: elementare*) ≈ fourth year (at primary school) (*Brit*), ≈ fifth grade (*Am*); (: *superiore*) ≈ upper sixth (*Brit*), ≈ freshman year (at college) (*Am*) **b** : le quinte (*Teatro*) the wings; tra *o* dietro le quinte (*fig*) behind the scenes.

quintale [kwin'tale] SM quintal (≈ *100 kg*); pesa un quintale (*fig*) it weighs a ton.

quintessenza [kwintes'sεntsa] SF quintessence.

quintetto [kwin'tetto] SM (*Mus*) quintet(te).

quinto, a ['kwinto] ① AGG fifth; la quinta parte di a fifth of; la quinta volta the fifth time; al quinto piano on the fifth (*Brit*) *o* sixth (*Am*) floor; essere al quinto posto in classifica to be fifth in the championship; in quinta pagina on the fifth page, on page five; quinta colonna (*fig*) fifth column.
② SM/F fifth; sei la quinta a cui faccio la domanda you are the fifth person I have asked; il quinto da destra the fifth from the right; il quinto arrivato vincerà una macchina fotografica whoever comes fifth will win a camera.
③ SM (*frazione*) fifth; un quinto della popolazione a fifth of the population; tre quinti three fifths.

quintultimo, a [kwin'tultimo] AGG, SM/F last but four, fifth from last.

quintuplicare [kwintupli'kare] VT, quintuplicarsi VIP to increase fivefold.

qui pro quo ['kwiprɔ'kwɔ] SM INV misunderstanding.

quisquilia [kwis'kwilja] SF (*inezia, stupidaggine*) trifle.

quiz [kwidz] SM INV **a** (*domanda*) question; risolvere un quiz to answer a question **b** (*anche:* gioco a quiz) quiz game; quiz televisivo television quiz.

quorum ['kwɔrum] SM INV quorum.

quota ['kwɔta] SF **a** (*parte*) quota, share; la sua quota di azioni his quota of shares; le quote del totalizzatore (*Ippica*) the odds ▶quota fissa fixed amount *o* sum ▶quota imponibile (*Fisco*) taxable income ▶quota d'iscrizione (*Univ*) enrolment fee; (*a gara*) entry fee; (*a club*) membership fee ▶quota di mercato market share ▶quota non imponibile (*Fisco*) personal allowance
b (*altitudine*) altitude, height; di alta quota high-altitude *attr*; a quota zero at sea level; a quota 750 metri 750 metres above sea level; prendere/perdere quota (*Aer*) to gain/lose height *o* altitude.

quotare [kwo'tare] VT **a** (*Fin, Borsa*) to quote; il dollaro è quotato a 1700 lire the dollar is quoted at 1700 lire; queste azioni sono quotate in Borsa these shares are quoted on the Stock Exchange
b (*valutare: anche fig*) to value; questo quadro è stato quotato 15 milioni di lire this painting was valued at 15 million lire; è un pittore molto quotato he is rated highly as a painter, he is a highly rated painter.

quotazione [kwotat'tsjone] SF (*Fin*) quotation; (*fig: di artista*) rating.

quotidianamente [kwotidjana'mente] AVV daily, every day.

quotidiano, a [kwoti'djano] ① AGG (*di ogni giorno*) daily; (*normale*) everyday.
② SM (*giornale*) daily (paper).

quoto ['kwɔto] SM (*Mat*) quotient.

quoziente [kwot'tsjεnte] SM **a** (*Mat*) quotient **b** (*tasso*) rate ▶quoziente di crescita zero zero growth rate ▶quoziente d'intelligenza intelligence quotient.

R

R, r ['ɛrre] SF O M INV (*lettera*) R, r; **R come Roma** ≈ R for Robert (*Brit*), R for Roger (*Am*).

R ABBR **a** (*Posta*) = **raccomandata b** (*Ferr*) = **rapido**.

RA SIGLA = *Ravenna*.

rabarbaro [ra'barbaro] SM (*Bot*) rhubarb; (*liquore*) rhubarb liqueur.

Rabat [ra'bat] SF Rabat.

rabberciare [rabber'tʃare] VT (*anche fig*) to patch up.

rabberciatura [rabbertʃa'tura] SF (*anche fig*) patch job.

rabbia ['rabbja] SF **a** (*ira*) anger, rage; (*fig: di onde, vento*) fury; **essere fuori di sé dalla rabbia** to be beside o.s. with rage; **farsi prendere dalla rabbia** to fly into a rage; **fare qc con rabbia** to do sth angrily; **mi fai una rabbia!** you make me so angry!; (*scherz: invidia*) you make me so jealous!; **che rabbia!** what a damned nuisance! **b** (*Med: idrofobia*) rabies *sg*.

rabbico, a, ci, che ['rabbiko] AGG (*Med*): **virus rabbico** rabies virus.

rabbino [rab'bino] SM rabbi.

rabbiosamente [rabbjosa'mente] AVV furiously, angrily.

rabbioso, a [rab'bjoso] AGG **a** (*discorso, tono, sguardo*) furious, angry; (*fig: vento, odio*) raging, furious **b** (*Med*) rabid, mad.

rabboccare [rabbok'kare] VT (*bottiglia*) to top up.

rabbonire [rabbo'nire] VT, **rabbonirsi** VIP to calm down.

rabbrividire [rabbrivi'dire] VI (*aus* **essere**) (*per il freddo*) to shiver, shudder; (*fig: per paura*) to shudder; **rabbrividire al solo pensiero di qc/di fare qc** to shudder at the mere thought of sth/of doing sth.

rabbuffo [rab'buffo] SM reprimand.

rabbuiare [rabbu'jare] VI (*aus* **essere**), **rabbuiarsi** VIP to grow dark, darken; **si rabbuiò in viso** his (*o* her) face darkened.

rabdomante [rabdo'mante] SM water diviner.

rabdomanzia [rabdoman'tsia] SF rhabdomancy, water divining.

racc. ABBR (*Posta*) = **raccomandata**.

raccapezzarsi [rakkapet'tsarsi] VIP: **non raccapezzarsi** to be at a loss; **c'è tanta confusione che non mi raccapezzo più** things are in such a mess that I can't make head nor tail of anything.

raccapricciante [rakkaprit'tʃante] AGG horrifying.

raccapriccio [rakka'prittʃo] SM horror.

raccattapalle [rakkatta'palle] SM INV (*spec Tennis*) ballboy.

raccattare [rakkat'tare] VT (*raccogliere, fig: voti*) to pick up.

racchetta [rak'ketta] SF (*da tennis*) racket; (*da ping-pong*) bat ▶**racchetta da neve** snowshoe ▶**racchetta da sci** ski stick.

racchio, chia, chi, chie ['rakkjo] AGG (*fam*) ugly.

racchiudere [rak'kjudere] VT IRREG to contain.

racchiuso, a [rak'kjuso] PP di **racchiudere**.

raccogliere [rak'koʎʎere] VB IRREG **1** VT **a** (*raccattare*) to pick up; **puoi raccogliere i tuoi giocattoli?** can you pick up your toys?; **l'istituto raccoglie molti bambini abbandonati** the institution takes in many abandoned children; **non ha raccolto il guanto** (*fig*) he didn't take up the gauntlet; **non ha raccolto** (*allusione*) he didn't take the hint; (*frecciata*) he took no notice of it
b (*frutta, fiori*) to pick, pluck; (*Agr*) to harvest; (*fig: onori, successo*) to reap; (*: approvazione, voti*) to win; **raccogliere il grano** to harvest the wheat; **raccogliere l'uva** to pick grapes; **raccogliere i frutti del proprio lavoro** (*fig*) to reap the benefits of one's work
c (*radunare: persone*) to assemble; (*notizie, denaro, firme*) to gather, collect; **ho raccolto le mie cose e me ne sono andata** I took my things and went; **raccogliere le idee** (*fig*) to gather *o* collect one's thoughts
d (*collezionare: francobolli, monete, cartoline*) to collect
e (*ripiegare: ali*) to fold; (*: gambe*) to draw up; (*: vele*) to furl; (*: capelli*) to put up.
2 **raccogliersi** VIP (*radunarsi*) to gather.

raccoglimento [rakkoʎʎi'mento] SM meditation; **un minuto di raccoglimento** a minute's silence.

raccoglitore [rakkoʎʎi'tore] SM (*cartella*) folder, binder; (*: per francobolli*) album ▶**raccoglitore a fogli mobili**

loose-leaf binder.

raccoglitrice [rakkoʎʎi'tritʃe] SF (*Agr*: *macchina*) harvester.

raccolta [rak'kɔlta] SF **a** (*gen*) collection, collecting *no pl*; **fare (la) raccolta di qc** to collect sth; **raccolta dei rifiuti** refuse *o* rubbish (*Brit*) *o* garbage (*Am*) collection **b** (*Agr*) harvesting *no pl*, gathering *no pl*; **fare la raccolta della frutta** to pick fruit **c** (*di persone*) gathering; **chiamare a raccolta** to gather together.

raccolto, a [rak'kɔlto] **1** PP di **raccogliere**.
2 AGG **a** (*persona: assorto*) thoughtful; **raccolto in preghiera** absorbed in prayer **b** (*luogo: appartato*) secluded, quiet **c** (*gambe*) drawn up; **raccolto su se stesso** curled up.
3 SM (*Agr*) crop, harvest; (: *periodo*) harvest time.

raccomandabile [rakkoman'dabile] AGG (highly) commendable; **è un tipo poco raccomandabile** he is not to be trusted.

raccomandare [rakkoman'dare] **1** VT **a** (*consigliare*) to recommend; **te lo raccomando, quello!** (*iro*) watch out for that one!; **raccomandare a qn di fare qc** to recommend that sb does sth; **ti raccomando questo libro/di leggere questo libro** I recommend this book to you/ that you read this book; **raccomandare a qn di non fare qc** (*esortare*) to tell *o* warn sb not to do sth; **ti raccomando di non fare tardi** now remember, don't come in late
b (*affidare*) to entrust; **raccomandare qn a qn/alle cure di qn** to entrust sb to sb/to sb's care
c (*appoggiare*) to recommend; **raccomandare qn per un lavoro** to recommend sb for a job.
2 raccomandarsi VR: **raccomandarsi a qn** to implore sb's help; **raccomandarsi alla pietà di qn** to implore sb's pity; **mi raccomando!** don't forget!; **mi raccomando! non perderlo** please, don't lose it!; **mi raccomando! studia bene** be sure and study hard!

raccomandata [rakkoman'data] SF (*anche:* **lettera raccomandata**) recorded-delivery (*Brit*) *o* certified (*Am*) letter; **raccomandata con ricevuta di ritorno** *recorded-delivery letter with advice of receipt*.

raccomandatizio, zia, zi, zie [rakkomanda'tittsjo] AGG: **lettera raccomandatizia** letter of introduction.

raccomandato, a [rakkoman'dato] **1** AGG **a** (*lettera, pacco*) recorded-delivery (*Brit*), certified (*Am*) **b** (*candidato*) recommended.
2 SM/F: **essere un raccomandato di ferro** to have friends in high places.

raccomandazione [rakkomandat'tsjone] SF **a** (*appoggio*) recommendation; **lettera di raccomandazione** letter of introduction; **qui ci vuole la raccomandazione di qualcuno** we need somebody to pull a few strings here **b** (*esortazione*) piece of advice; **mi ha fatto mille raccomandazioni** he gave me lots of advice.

raccomodare [rakkomo'dare] VT (*riparare*) to repair, mend.

raccontare [rakkon'tare] VT (*storia, bugie*) to tell; (*avventure*) to tell about; **raccontare qc a qn** to tell sb sth; **non raccontarlo a nessuno** don't tell anyone about it; **raccontano che sia fuggito** they say that he escaped; **nel libro racconta delle sue avventure** in the book he speaks of his adventures; **raccontami tutto** tell me the whole story; **a me non la racconti** don't try and kid me; **raccontala a qualcun altro!** try and pull the wool over somebody else's eyes!; **a me lo vieni a raccontare!** don't

tell me!; **se ne raccontano delle belle su di lui** I've heard a few stories about him; **cosa mi racconti di nuovo?** what's new?

racconto [rak'konto] SM **a** (*narrazione*) account, telling *no pl*, relating *no pl*; (*fatto raccontato*) story, tale; **il suo racconto dell'avventura** his account of the adventure **b** (*genere letterario*) short story ▸**racconti per bambini** children's stories.

raccorciare [rakkor'tʃare] **1** VT to shorten.
2 raccorciarsi VIP to become shorter; **le giornate si stanno raccorciando** the days are drawing in.

raccordare [rakkor'dare] VT (*collegare*) to link up, join (up).

raccordo [rak'kɔrdo] SM (*Tecn*: *giunzione*) joint, connection; (*di autostrada*) slip road (*Brit*), entrance (*o* exit) ramp (*Am*); (*Ferr*) siding ▸**raccordo anulare** (*Aut*) ring road (*Brit*), beltway (*Am*).

rachitico, a, ci, che [ra'kitiko] **1** AGG (*Med*) suffering from rickets; (*fig*: *pianta*) spindly; (: *person*) scrawny.
2 SM/F person who suffers from rickets.

rachitismo [raki'tizmo] SM (*Med*) rickets *sg*.

racimolare [ratʃimo'lare] VT (*denaro*) to scrape together; (*fig*: *notizie*) to glean.

racket ['rækit] SM INV racket.

rada ['rada] SF (natural) harbour (*Brit*) *o* harbor (*Am*).

radar ['radar] **1** SM INV radar.
2 AGG INV (*segnale, avvistamento*) radar *attr*; **uomini radar** air traffic controllers.

raddensare [radden'sare] **1** VT (*crema, minestra*) to thicken.
2 raddensarsi VIP (*marmellata*) to set; (*minestra*) to thicken.

raddolcimento [raddoltʃi'mento] SM (*Ling*) palatalization.

raddolcire [raddol'tʃire] **1** VT (*persona, carattere*) to soften.
2 raddolcirsi VIP (*tempo*) to grow milder; (*persona*) to soften, mellow.

raddoppiamento [raddoppja'mento] SM (*gen*) doubling.

raddoppiare [raddop'pjare] **1** VI (*aus* **essere**; *nel signif. sportivo* **avere**) to double; (*Calcio*) to score a second goal.
2 VT to double.

raddoppio, pi [rad'doppjo] SM (*gen*) doubling; (*Biliardo*) double; (*Calcio*) second goal; (*Equitazione*) gallop.

raddrizzabile [raddrit'tsabile] AGG (*gen*) which can be straightened; (*Elettr*) rectifiable.

raddrizzamento [raddrittsa'mento] SM straightening.

raddrizzare [raddrit'tsare] **1** VT **a** (*mettere dritto*) to straighten; (*fig*: *correggere*) to put straight, correct **b** (*Elettr*) to rectify.
2 raddrizzarsi VR (*persona*) to straighten (o.s.) up.

raddrizzatore [raddrittsa'tore] SM (*Elettr*) rectifier.

radente [ra'dɛnte] AGG: **tiro radente** (*Mil*) grazing fire; **attrito radente** (*Fis*) sliding friction.

radere ['radere] VB IRREG **1** VT **a** (*barba*) to shave off; (*mento*) to shave; **radere i capelli a zero** to shave one's hair off **b** (*fig*: *sfiorare*) to graze, skim **c** (*abbattere*): **radere al suolo** to raze to the ground.
2 radersi VR to shave (o.s.).

radiale [ra'djale] AGG, SM (*Anat, Geom, Aut*) radial.

radiante [ra'djante] **1** AGG (*superficie, pannello*) radiant.
2 SM (*Mat*) radian.

radiare [ra'djare] VT (*da scuola, partito*) to expel; (*dall'esercito*) to dismiss; (*da albo professionale*: *medico*) to strike

off; (: *avvocato*) to disbar.

radiatore [radja'tore] SM radiator.

radiazione [radjat'tsjone] SF **a** (*Fis*) radiation; **radiazione nucleare** nuclear radiation **b** (*cancellazione*) striking off; (*espulsione*) expulsion.

radica ['radika] SF (*per pipe*) briar, briarwood; **pipa in radica** briar-pipe ▶ **radica di noce** walnut (wood).

radicale [radi'kale] ① AGG (*gen, Pol*) radical; (*Ling*) root *attr*.
② SM/F (*Pol*) radical.
③ SM (*Mat, Chim*) radical; (*Ling*) root.

radicalismo [radika'lizmo] SM radicalism.

radicalmente [radikal'mente] AVV (*dalla radice*) radically, fundamentally; (*completamente*) thoroughly, completely.

radicando [radi'kando] SM (*Mat*) radicand.

radicare [radi'kare] ① VI (*aus essere*) (*Bot*) to take root.
② **radicarsi** VIP (*fig*) to take root.

radicato, a [radi'kato] AGG (*pregiudizio, credenza*) deep-seated, deeply-rooted.

radicchio [ra'dikkjo] SM radicchio, *variety of chicory*.

radice [ra'ditʃe] SF (*gen, Mat, Anat, Ling, fig*) root; **segno di radice** (*Mat*) radical sign; **colpire alla radice** (*fig*) to strike at the root; **mettere radici** (*idee, odio*) to take root; (*persona*) to put down roots ▶ **radice quadrata** (*Mat*) square root.

radi e getta ['radi e 'dʒetta] AGG INV: **rasoio radi e getta** disposable *o* throwaway razor.

radio[1] ['radjo] ① SF INV **a** (*apparecchio*) radio (set) ▶ **radio portatile** portable radio ▶ **radio ricevente** receiver ▶ **radio a transistor** transistor (radio) ▶ **radio trasmittente** transmitter
b (*radiodiffusione*): **la radio** (the) radio; **trasmettere via radio a qn** (*messaggio*) to radio to sb; **trasmettere per radio** to broadcast.
② AGG INV radio *attr*; **stazione /ponte radio** radio station/ link.

radio[2], **di** ['radjo] SM (*Anat*) radius.

radio[3] ['radjo] SM (*Chim*) radium.

radioabbonato, a [radjoabbo'nato] SM/F radio subscriber.

radioamatore, trice [radjoama'tore] SM/F amateur radio operator.

radioascoltatore, trice [radjoaskolta'tore] SM/F (radio) listener.

radioascolto [radjoas'kolto] SM radio listening.

radioassistito, a [radjoassis'tito] AGG: **navigazione radioassistita** radio navigation.

radioattività [radjoattivi'ta] SF radioactivity.

radioattivo, a [radjoat'tivo] AGG radioactive.

radiobiologia [radjobiolo'dʒia] SF radiobiology.

radiobussola [radjo'bussola] SF (*Naut*) radio compass.

radiocarbonio [radjokar'bɔnjo] SM radiocarbon.

radiocollegamento [radjokollega'mento] SM radio link.

radiocomandare [radjokoman'dare] VT to operate by remote control.

radiocomandato, a [radjokoman'dato] AGG remote-controlled.

radiocomando [radjoko'mando] SM remote control.

radiocomunicazione [radjokomunikat'tsjone] SF radio message.

radiocronaca, che [radjo'krɔnaka] SF radio commentary.

radiocronista, i, e [radjokro'nista] SM/F radio commenta-

tor.

radiodiffusione [radjodiffu'zjone] SF (radio) broadcasting.

radioelettricità [radjoelettritʃi'ta] SF radioelectricity.

radiofaro [radjo'faro] SM radio beacon.

radiofonico, a, ci, che [radjo'fɔniko] AGG radio *attr*.

radiofrequenza [radjofre'kwɛntsa] SF (radio) frequency.

radiogoniometro [radjogo'njɔmetro] SM (*Naut, Aer*) direction finder, radiogoniometer.

radiografare [radjogra'fare] VT to X-ray.

radiografia [radjogra'fia] SF (*procedimento*) radiography; (*foto*) X-ray (photograph).

radiografico, a, ci, che [radjo'grafiko] AGG X-ray *attr*.

radioisotopo [radjoi'zɔtopo] SM radioisotope, radioactive isotope.

radiolina [radjo'lina] SF portable radio, transistor (radio).

radiolocalizzare [radjolokalid'dzare] VT to locate by radar.

radiologia [radjolo'dʒia] SF radiology.

radiologo, a, gi, ghe [ra'djɔlogo] SM/F (*medico*) radiologist; (*tecnico*) radiographer.

radioonda [radjo'onda] SF radio wave.

radioregistratore [radjoredʒistra'tore] SM radio cassette recorder. '

radioricevente [radjoritʃe'vɛnte] SF (*anche:* **apparecchio radioricevente**) receiver.

radioscopia [radjosko'pia] SF (*Med*) radioscopy.

radioscopico, a, ci, che [radjo'skɔpiko] AGG radioscopic.

radiosità [radjosi'ta] SF (*anche fig*) radiance.

radioso, a [ra'djoso] AGG (*anche fig*) radiant.

radiospia [radjos'pia] SF bug.

radiostazione [radjostat'tsjone] SF radio station.

radiosveglia [radjoz'veʎʎa] SF radio alarm.

radiotaxi [radjo'taksi], **radiotassì** [radjotas'si] SM INV radio taxi.

radiotecnica [radjo'tɛknika] SF radio engineering.

radiotecnico, a, ci, che [radjo'tɛkniko] ① AGG radio engineering *attr*.
② SM radio engineer.

radiotelefono [radjote'lɛfono] SM radiotelephone.

radiotelegrafia [radjotelegra'fia] SF radiotelegraphy.

radiotelegrafista, i, e [radjotelegra'fista] SM/F radiotelegrapher.

radiotelescopio, pi [radjoteles'kɔpjo] SM radio telescope.

radioterapia [radjotera'pia] SF radiotherapy.

radiotrasmesso, a [radjotraz'messo] PP di **radiotrasmettere**.

radiotrasmettere [radjotraz'mettere] VT IRREG to broadcast (*by radio*).

radiotrasmettitore [radjotrazmetti'tore] SM radio transmitter.

radiotrasmittente [radjotrazmit'tɛnte] ① AGG (radio) broadcasting *attr*.
② SF (radio) broadcasting station.

rado, a ['rado] AGG (*capelli*) sparse, thin; (*visite*) infrequent; **di rado** rarely; **non di rado** not uncommonly.

radunare [radu'nare] ① VT (*persone*) to gather, assemble; (*Mil: truppe*) to rally; (*cose*) to collect, gather together.
② **radunarsi** VIP to gather, assemble.

radunata [radu'nata] SF (*Mil*) muster; (*Dir*): **radunata sediziosa** seditious assembly (*o* gathering).

raduno [ra'duno] SM gathering, meeting.

radura [ra'dura] SF clearing.

rafano ['rafano] SM (*Bot*) horseradish.

Raffaello [raffa'ɛllo] SM: **Raffaello (Sanzio)** Raphael.

raffazzonare [raffattso'nare] VT (*riparare*) to patch up; (*mettere insieme alla meglio*) to throw together.

raffazzonato, a [raffattsonato] AGG patched up.

raffermo, a [raf'fermo] AGG stale.

raffica, che ['raffika] SF (*Meteor*) gust (of wind); **raffica di mitra** burst of gunfire; **il vento soffiava a raffiche** the wind was very blustery; **raffica di insulti** (*fig*) avalanche of insults; **raffica di domande** (*fig*) barrage of questions.

raffigurare [raffigu'rare] VT (*rappresentare*) to depict, to represent; (*simboleggiare*) to represent, symbolize; **non riesco a raffigurarmelo** I can't picture it.

raffigurazione [raffigurat'tsjone] SF depiction, representation.

raffinare [raffi'nare] ①VT (*zucchero, petrolio, fig*) to refine. ②**raffinarsi** VIP (*fig*) to become refined.

raffinatamente [raffinata'mente] AVV (*vestito, arredato*) elegantly, tastefully.

raffinatezza [raffina'tettsa] SF refinement; **arredato con raffinatezza** tastefully furnished.

raffinato, a [raffi'nato] ① AGG (*zucchero, sale*) refined; (*persona*) cultivated, polished, refined; (*modi*) polished, sophisticated; (*crudeltà, astuzia*) refined, subtle; (*pranzo*) formal; **cibi raffinati** delicacies. ②SM/F refined person.

raffinatore [raffina'tore] SM refiner.

raffinazione [raffinat'tsjone] SF (*di sostanza*) refining ▶**raffinazione del petrolio** oil refining.

raffineria [raffine'ria] SF refinery.

rafforzamento [raffortsa'mento] SM (*di costruzione*) reinforcement; (*di muscoli, carattere*) strengthening.

rafforzare [raffor'tsare] ①VT (*gen, Mil*) to reinforce. ②**rafforzarsi** VIP to strengthen, grow stronger; **i miei dubbi su di lui si sono rafforzati** my doubts about him have grown.

rafforzativo, a [raffortsa'tivo] (*Gramm*) ① AGG intensifying. ②SM intensifier.

raffreddamento [raffredda'mento] SM (*anche fig*) cooling; **c'è stato un raffreddamento nei loro rapporti** (*fig*) their relationship has cooled ▶**raffreddamento ad acqua** (*Aut*) water-cooling ▶**raffreddamento ad aria** (*Aut*) air-cooling.

raffreddare [raffred'dare] ① VT to cool (down); (*fig: entusiasmo*) to have a cooling effect on, dampen; **lascia raffreddare la minestra** leave the soup to cool (down). ②**raffreddarsi** VIP a (*caffè, minestra ecc*) to cool down; (*aria*) to become cooler, become colder; (*fig: entusiasmo, relazione*) to cool (off); **non lasciare che la minestra si raffreddi** don't let the soup get cold; **aspetta che si raffreddi** wait till it cools down b (*prendere un raffreddore*) to catch a cold.

raffreddato, a [raffred'dato] AGG (*Med*): **essere raffreddato** to have a cold.

raffreddore [raffred'dore] SM (*Med*) cold; **prendere/avere il raffreddore** to catch/have a cold ▶**raffreddore da fieno** hay fever.

raffrontare [raffron'tare] VT to compare.

raffronto [raf'fronto] SM comparison.

rafia ['rafja] SF (*fibra*) raffia.

raganella [raga'nɛlla] SF (*Zool*) tree frog.

ragazza [ra'gattsa] SF (*gen*) girl; (*giovane donna*) young woman; (*fidanzata*) girlfriend; **brava ragazza** nice girl,

good sort; **nome da ragazza** maiden name; **da ragazza faceva la commessa** when she was younger she worked as a shop (*Brit*) o sales (*Am*) assistant ▶**ragazza copertina** cover girl ▶**ragazza madre** unmarried mother ▶**ragazza alla pari** au-pair girl ▶**ragazza squillo** call girl.

ragazzata [ragat'tsata] SF childish action; **è stata solo una ragazzata** it was just a boyish prank.

ragazzo [ra'gattso] SM a (*gen*) boy; (*giovanotto*) young man; (*fidanzato*) boyfriend; (*garzone*) boy; **fin da quando era ragazzo** since he was a boy; **da ragazzo faceva il commesso** when he was younger he worked as a shop (*Brit*) o sales (*Am*) assistant ▶**ragazzo padre** unmarried father ▶**ragazzo di strada** street urchin ▶**ragazzo di vita** rent boy (*Brit*), hustler (*Am*) b : **ragazzi** SMPL (*bambini, figli*) children; (*amici*) folks (*fam*), guys (*Am*); **andiamo ragazzi!** let's go children (o folks)!; **film/libro per ragazzi** children's film (*Brit*) o movie (*Am*) /book.

raggelare [raddʒe'lare] ① VI (*aus essere*), **raggelarsi** VIP to freeze; **si sentì raggelare all'idea** his blood froze o ran cold at the idea. ②VT to freeze; **raggelare una conversazione** to stop a conversation dead.

raggiante [rad'dʒante] AGG (*sorriso, espressione*) beaming, radiant; **raggiante di gioia** beaming o radiant with joy.

raggiare [rad'dʒare] VI (*aus avere*) a : **raggiare di gioia** to be radiant with joy b (*Fis*) to radiate.

raggiera [rad'dʒɛra] SF (*di ruota*) spokes pl; **a raggiera** with a sunburst pattern.

raggio, gi ['raddʒo] SM a (*gen, Fis, fig*) ray, beam; **un raggio di sole** (*anche fig*) a ray of sunshine; **raggio di luna** moonbeam; **raggio di speranza** (*fig*) ray o gleam of hope ▶**raggio laser** laser beam ▶ **raggi X** X-rays b (*di ruota*) spoke c (*Mat, fig*) radius; **nel raggio di 20 km** within a radius of 20 km o a 20-km radius; **a largo raggio** (*esplorazione, incursione*) wide-ranging, extensive in scope ▶**raggio d'azione** (*di proiettile*) range; (*fig*) range, scope.

raggirare [raddʒi'rare] VT to deceive, take in, trick; **si è lasciato raggirare dai suoi discorsi** he was taken in by his arguments.

raggiro [rad'dʒiro] SM trick, swindle; **non farti invischiare nei suoi raggiri** don't let yourself get mixed up in his schemes.

raggiungere [rad'dʒundʒere] VT IRREG a (*persona*): **raggiungere qn** to catch sb up, catch up with sb; (: *telefonicamente*) to get in touch with sb, reach sb; **li abbiamo raggiunti per strada/alla stazione** we caught up with them on the way/at the station; **vi raggiungo più tardi** I'll see you later, I'll catch you up later; **nella ricerca nucleare l'Italia non ha ancora raggiunto la Francia** o **il livello della Francia** Italy still hasn't caught up with France in nuclear research b (*luogo, oggetto posto in alto*) to reach; (*obiettivo*) to reach, achieve; **la temperatura ha raggiunto i trenta gradi** the temperature has reached thirty degrees; **la criminalità sta raggiungendo livelli preoccupanti** crime is reaching worrying levels; **raggiungere il proprio scopo** to reach one's goal, achieve one's aim; **raggiungere un accordo** to come to o reach an agreement.

raggiungibile [raddʒun'dʒibile] AGG (*scopo*) attainable, within reach.

raggiungimento [raddʒundʒi'mento] SM (*di scopo*) attain-

ment, achievement.

raggiunto, a [rad'dʒunto] PP di **raggiungere**.

raggomitolare [raggomito'lare] ☐ VT (*avvolgere*) to wind up.

☐ **raggomitolarsi** VR (*fig: rannicchiarsi*) to curl up.

raggranellare [raggranel'lare] VT (*soldi*) to scrape together.

raggrinzire [raggrin'tsire], **raggrinzare** [raggrin'tsare] ☐ VT to crease.

☐ VI (*aus* **essere**), **raggrinzarsi** VIP (*stoffa*) to wrinkle (up); (*viso, pelle*) to become wrinkled.

raggrumare [raggru'mare] VT, **raggrumarsi** VIP (*sangue, latte*) to clot.

raggruppamento [raggruppa'mento] SM **a** (*azione*) grouping **b** (*gruppo*) group; (: *Mil*) unit.

raggruppare [raggrup'pare] ☐ VT (*in un unico gruppo*) to group (together); (*in molti gruppi*) to organize into groups.

☐ **raggrupparsi** VR (*in un unico gruppo*) to group (together); (*in molti gruppi*) to form into groups; **raggrupparsi intorno a qn** to gather around sb.

ragguagliare [raggwaʎ'ʎare] VT **a** (*informare*): **ragguagliare (su)** to inform (about) **b** (*confrontare*): **ragguagliare qc a qc** to compare sth with sth.

ragguaglio, gli [rag'gwaʎʎo] SM **a** (*informazione*) piece of information; **fornire ragguagli su qc** to provide information about sth **b** (*paragone*) comparison.

ragguardevole [raggwar'devole] AGG (*persona*) notable, distinguished; (*somma*) considerable, sizeable; (*successo*) remarkable.

ragia ['radʒa] SF: **acqua ragia = acquaragia**.

ragià [ra'dʒa] SM INV rajah.

ragionamento [radʒona'mento] SM (*facoltà*) reasoning *no pl*; (*argomentazione*) argument, reasoning; **ci sono arrivato con il ragionamento** I got there through reasoning; **è un ragionamento logico** it's a logical argument; **il tuo ragionamento fila** your argument makes sense; **è inutile perdersi in futili ragionamenti** it's pointless getting involved in futile arguments.

ragionare [radʒo'nare] VI (*aus* **avere**) **a** (*pensare*) to reason, think; **ragionaci su!** think about it!, think it over!; **cerca di ragionare** try and be reasonable; **non c'è modo di farla ragionare** you can't make her think clearly (*o* use her head); **quando ho fame non ragiono più** I can't think straight when I'm hungry **b** (*discutere*): **ragionare di** to discuss, talk over.

ragionato, a [radʒo'nato] AGG (*discorso*) reasoned; (*bibliografia*) annotated.

ragione [ra'dʒone] ☐ SF **a** (*facoltà*) reason; **perdere il lume della ragione** to lose one's reason, take leave of one's senses

b (*motivo*) reason, cause, motive; (*argomentazione*) argument; (*diritto*) right; **avrà le sue buone ragioni per agire così** he must have his reasons for behaving that way; **non è una buona ragione!** that's no excuse *o* reason!; **ragione di più per fare così** all the more reason for doing so; ... **ragion per cui sarebbe meglio partire** ...that's why it would be better to leave; **a maggior ragione dovresti fare qualcosa** all the more reason why you should do something; **a** *o* **con ragione** with good reason, rightly, justly; **senza ragione** for no reason; **a torto o a ragione** rightly or wrongly; **per ragioni di famiglia** for family reasons

c (*Mat*) proportion, ratio; **in ragione di 20.000 lire per**

articolo at the rate of 20,000 lire per item; **a ragion veduta** after due consideration; (*intenzionalmente*) deliberately; **far valere le proprie ragioni** to assert one's rights

d (*fraseologia*): **aver ragione (a fare)** to be right (in doing *o* to do); **aver ragione di qn/qc** to get the better of sb/sth; **avere ragione da vendere** to be absolutely right, be dead right (*fam*); **dare ragione a qn** (*sogg: persona*) to side with sb; (: *fatto*) to prove sb right; **farsi una ragione di qc** to accept sth, come to terms with sth; **non sentire ragioni** to refuse to listen to reason; **picchiare qn di santa ragione** to give sb a good hiding.

☐ ►**ragione di scambio** (*Econ*) terms *pl* of trade ►**ragione sociale** (*Comm*) corporate name ►**ragion d'essere** raison d'être ►**ragion di stato** reason of State.

ragioneria [radʒone'ria] SF (*scienza*) accountancy; (*ufficio*) accounts department; (*scuola*) commercial school, institute of commerce.

ragionevole [radʒo'nevole] AGG **a** (*sensato: persona*) reasonable, sensible; (: *consiglio*) sensible, sound **b** (*giusto: prezzo*) reasonable, fair **c** (*fondato: timore, sospetto*) well-founded.

ragionevolezza [radʒonevo'lettsa] SF (*sensatezza*) reasonableness.

ragionevolmente [radʒonevol'mente] AVV (*sensatamente*) sensibly, reasonably; (*giustamente*) reasonably.

ragioniere, a [radʒo'njɛre] SM/F accountant.

raglan [ra'glan] AGG INV (*manica*) raglan.

ragliare [raʎ'ʎare] VI (*aus* **avere**) to bray.

raglio, gli ['raʎʎo] SM bray.

ragnatela [raɲɲa'tela] SF (spider's) web, cobweb; **la casa era piena di ragnatele** the house was full of cobwebs; **una ragnatela d'intrighi** (*fig*) a web of intrigue.

ragno ['raɲɲo] SM spider; **non cavare un ragno dal buco** (*fig*) to draw a blank, get nowhere.

ragù [ra'gu] SM INV (*Culin*) meat sauce (*for pasta*).

RAI-TV ['raiti'vu] SIGLA F (= *Radio televisione italiana*) *Public Italian Broadcasting Company*.

ralenti [ralɑ̃'ti] SM INV: **al ralenti** in slow motion.

rallegramenti [rallegra'menti] SMPL congratulations.

rallegrare [ralle'grare] ☐ VT (*persona*) to cheer up; (*stanza, atmosfera*) to brighten up.

☐ **rallegrarsi** VIP **a** (*diventare allegro*) to cheer up; (*provare allegrezza*) to rejoice; **si rallegrò solo a vederlo** he was glad just to see him **b** (*congratularsi*): **rallegrarsi con qn per qc** to congratulate sb on sth.

rallentamento [rallenta'mento] SM (*di produzione*) slowing down, slackening; (*del traffico*) slowing down; **subire un rallentamento** to slow down, slacken.

rallentando [rallen'tando] SM INV (*Mus*) rallentando.

rallentare [rallen'tare] ☐ VT (*gen*) to slow down; **rallentare il ritmo** to slow down; **rallentare il passo** to slacken one's pace.

☐ VI (*aus* **essere**) to slow down.

rallentatore [rallenta'tore] SM (*Cine*) slow-motion camera; **al rallentatore** (*anche fig*) in slow motion.

rally ['ræli] SM INV (car) rally.

Ramadan [rama'dan] SM INV (*Rel*): **il Ramadan** Ramadan.

ramaiolo [rama'jolo] SM ladle.

ramanzina [raman'dzina] SF lecture, telling-off; **fare una bella ramanzina a qn** to give sb a good lecture.

ramare [ra'mare] VT **a** (*superficie*) to copper, coat with copper **b** (*Agr: vite*) to spray with copper sulphate.

ramarro [ra'marro] SM green lizard.

ramato, a [ra'mato] AGG (*oggetto: rivestito di rame*) copper-coated, coppered; (*capelli, barba*) coppery, copper-coloured (*Brit*), copper-colored (*Am*).

ramatura [rama'tura] SF (*vedi vb*) coppering; spraying with copper sulphate.

ramazza [ra'mattsa] SF (*scopa*) besom.

ramazzare [ramat'tsare] VT to sweep.

rame ['rame] SM copper; **di rame** copper *attr*; **incisione su rame** copperplate.

ramificare [ramifi'kare] [1] VI (*aus* avere) (*Bot*) to put out branches.

  [2] **ramificarsi** VIP (*diramarsi, fig*) to branch out; (*Med: tumore, vene*) to ramify; **ramificarsi in** (*biforcarsi*) to branch into.

ramificato, a [ramifi'kato] AGG (*albero, corna*) branched; (*tumore*) ramified; **il tunnel sotterraneo è ramificato in 4 gallerie** the underground tunnel branches into 4 passages.

ramificazione [ramifikat'tsjone] SF ramification.

ramingo, a, ghi, ghe [ra'mingo] AGG (*letter*): **andare ramingo** to go wandering, wander.

ramino [ra'mino] SM (*Carte*) rummy.

rammagliare [rammaʎ'ʎare] VT (*calze*) to mend a ladder in.

rammaricare [rammari'kare] [1] VT to grieve.

  [2] **rammaricarsi** VIP: **rammaricarsi di** *o* **per qc** (*dispiacersi*) to regret sth, be sorry about sth; (*lamentarsi*) to complain about sth; **è inutile rammaricarsi** there is no point in feeling sorry.

rammarico, chi [ram'mariko] SM regret.

rammendare [rammen'dare] VT to mend, darn.

rammendo [ram'mɛndo] SM (*azione*) darning *no pl*, mending *no pl*; (*risultato*) darn, mend; **fare un rammendo** to darn, mend.

rammentare [rammen'tare] [1] VT to remember, recall; **rammentare qc a qn** to remind sb of sth.

  [2] **rammentarsi** VIP: **rammentarsi (di qc)** to remember (sth).

rammollimento [rammolli'mento] SM softening.

rammollire [rammol'lire] [1] VT to soften.

  [2] VI (*aus* essere), **rammollirsi** VIP to soften, grow *o* go soft.

rammollito, a [rammol'lito] [1] AGG weak.

  [2] SM/F weakling.

ramo ['ramo] SM (*gen, fig*) branch; (*branca: di una scienza*) branch; (: *di commercio*) field; **non è il mio ramo** it's not my field *o* line; **i due rami del parlamento** the two chambers of parliament.

ramoscello [ramoʃ'ʃɛllo] SM twig.

rampa ['rampa] SF **a** (*anche:* **rampa di scale**) flight (of stairs) **b** (*breve salita*) slope ▶**rampa d'accesso** (*in autostrada*) slip road (*Brit*), entrance (*o* exit) ramp (*Am*); (*in marciapiede*) ramp ▶**rampa di lancio** (*Aer*) launching pad.

rampante [ram'pante] [1] AGG (*Araldica*) rampant; (*pegg: arrivista*) aggressively ambitious.

  [2] SM/F (*arrivista*): **un giovane rampante** a yuppie.

rampicante [rampi'kante] (*Bot*) [1] AGG climbing.

  [2] SM creeper, climber.

rampichino [rampi'kino] SM (*Zool*): **rampichino alpestre** tree creeper.

rampino [ram'pino] SM (*gancio*) hook; (*Naut*) grapnel.

rampollo [ram'pollo] SM (*discendente*) descendant;

(*scherz: figlio*): **è tutto orgoglioso del suo rampollo** he's very proud of his son and heir.

rampone [ram'pone] SM (*fiocina*) harpoon; (*Alpinismo*) crampon.

rana ['rana] SF frog; **nuoto a rana** breaststroke; **nuotare a rana** to do the breaststroke; **uomo rana** frogman ▶**rana pescatrice** angler fish.

rancido, a ['rantʃido] [1] AGG rancid.

  [2] SM: **odore di rancido** rank odour; **ha odore di rancido** it smells rancid; **sa di rancido** it tastes rancid.

rancio, ci ['rantʃo] SM (*Mil*) mess; **ora del rancio** mess time.

rancore [ran'kore] SM resentment, rancour (*Brit*), rancor (*Am*); **senza rancore?** no hard feelings?; **serbare rancore a qn** [OR] **nutrire rancore contro** *o* **verso qn** to bear sb a grudge.

randa ['randa] SF (*Naut*) mainsail.

randagio, a, gi, gie *o* **ge** [ran'dadʒo] AGG (*gatto, cane*) stray *attr*.

randellare [randel'lare] VT to cudgel.

randellata [randel'lata] SF blow with a cudgel; **prendere qn a randellate** to set about sb with a cudgel.

randello [ran'dɛllo] SM cudgel, club.

rango, ghi ['rango] SM **a** (*grado*) rank; (*condizione sociale*) station, social standing; **avere il rango di** to hold the rank of; **gli alti ranghi** the upper ranks; **persone di rango inferiore** people of lower standing **b** (*Mil: schiera*) rank; (: *fila*) line; **rientrare nei ranghi** to fall in; (*fig*) to fall into line; **uscire dai ranghi** to fall out; (*fig*) to step out of line.

Rangoon [ran'gun] SF Rangoon.

ranista, i, e [ra'nista] SM/F (*Nuoto*) breast-stroke swimmer.

rannicchiare [rannik'kjare] [1] VT (*gambe*) to tuck up.

  [2] **rannicchiarsi** VR to crouch, huddle; **rannicchiarsi sotto le coperte** to curl up under the blankets.

rannuvolamento [rannuvola'mento] SM clouding over.

rannuvolare [rannuvo'lare] [1] VT to darken.

  [2] **rannuvolarsi** VIP (*cielo*) to cloud over, become overcast; (*fig: viso*) to darken.

ranocchio, chi [ra'nɔkkjo] SM (edible) frog.

rantolare [ranto'lare] VI (*aus* avere) (*respirare affannosamente*) to wheeze; **si sentiva il moribondo rantolare** you could hear the man's death rattle.

rantolio, lii [ranto'lio] SM (*il respirare affannoso*) wheezing; (: *di agonizzante*) death rattle.

rantolo ['rantolo] SM (*respiro affannoso*) wheeze; (: *di agonizzante*) death rattle.

ranuncolo [ra'nunkolo] SM (*Bot*) buttercup.

rapa ['rapa] SF turnip; **cime di rapa** turnip tops; **testa di rapa** (*fig*) fathead, idiot; **è come voler cavar sangue da una rapa** it's like trying to get blood out of a stone.

rapace [ra'patʃe] [1] AGG (*animale*) predatory; (*fig: avido*) rapacious, grasping.

  [2] SM bird of prey.

rapacemente [rapatʃe'mente] AVV rapaciously.

rapacità [rapatʃi'ta] SF (*anche fig*) rapaciousness, rapacity.

rapare [ra'pare] [1] VT (*capelli*) to crop, cut very short; **ti hanno rapato (i capelli) a zero** they have scalped you; **raparsi (i capelli) a zero** to get scalped.

  [2] **raparsi** VR to have one's head shaved (*o* cropped).

rapidamente [rapida'mente] AVV quickly, rapidly, fast.

rapide ['rapide] SFPL (*di fiume*) rapids.

rapidità [rapidi'ta] SF speed, rapidity; **ha colpito con**

rapidità he was quick to strike.

rapido, a ['rapido] [1] AGG (*gen*) fast; (*esame, occhiata*) quick, rapid; **è rapido nell'agire** he is quick to act.
[2] SM (*Ferr*) express (train) (*on which supplement must be paid*).

rapimento [rapi'mento] SM **a** (*di persona*) kidnapping, abduction **b** (*Rel*) ecstasy; (*fig*) rapture; **fu preso da rapimento** he went into ecstasies *o* raptures; **con rapimento** rapturously, ecstatically.

rapina [ra'pina] SF robbery; **rapina in banca** bank robbery ▶**rapina a mano armata** armed robbery.

rapinare [rapi'nare] VT to rob.

rapinatore, trice [rapina'tore] SM/F robber.

rapire [ra'pire] VT **a** (*persona*) to kidnap, abduct **b** (*fig: mandare in estasi*) to enrapture, delight.

rapito, a [ra'pito] [1] AGG **a** (*persona*) kidnapped **b** (*fig: in estasi*): **ascoltare rapito qn** to be captivated by sb's words; **guardava rapito il quadro** he gazed at the painting, entranced.
[2] SM/F kidnapped person.

rapitore, trice [rapi'tore] SM/F kidnapper.

rappacificare [rappatʃifi'kare] [1] VT (*riconciliare*) to reconcile.
[2] **rappacificarsi** VR (*uso reciproco*) to become reconciled, make it up.

rappacificazione [rappatʃifikat'tsjone] SF reconciliation.

rappezzare [rappet'tsare] VT to patch; **rappezzare un discorso** (*fig*) to cobble together a speech.

rapportare [rappor'tare] [1] VT **a**: **rapportare qc a qc** (*confrontare*) to compare sth with sth **b** (*riprodurre disegno*): **rapportare su scala più grande** to reproduce on a larger scale.
[2] **rapportarsi** VIP: **rapportarsi a** to be related to.

rapporto [rap'porto] SM **a** (*legame*) connection, relationship, link; **non avere alcun rapporto con qc** to have nothing to do with sth, be unrelated to sth; **in rapporto a quanto è successo** with regard to *o* in relation to what happened
b (*relazione*) relationship; **abbiamo un ottimo rapporto** we have a very good relationship; **i rapporti tra loro sono piuttosto tesi** relations between them are rather strained; **essere in buoni/cattivi rapporti con qn** to be on good/bad terms with sb ▶**rapporti diplomatici** diplomatic relations ▶**rapporti prematrimoniali** sex *sg* before marriage, premarital sex ▶**rapporto d'affari** business relations *pl* ▶**rapporto coniugale** marital relationship ▶**rapporto intimo** sexual intercourse ▶**rapporto di lavoro** employer-employee relationship; **indennità di fine rapporto (di lavoro)** severance pay ▶**rapporto sessuale** (sexual) intercourse
c (*resoconto*) report; **fare rapporto a qn su qc** to report sth to sb; **chiamare qn a rapporto** (*Mil*) to summon sb; **andare a rapporto da qn** to report to sb
d (*Mat, Tecn*) ratio; (*di bicicletta*) gear; **in rapporto di 1 a 10** in a ratio of 1 to 10 ▶**rapporto di compressione** (*Tecn*) pressure ratio ▶**rapporto di distanza** (*Fis*) distance ratio ▶**rapporto di trasmissione** (*Tecn*) gear.

rapprendersi [rap'prɛndersi] VIP IRREG (*sangue*) to coagulate, clot; (*latte*) to curdle.

rappresaglia [rappre'saʎʎa] SF reprisal, retaliation; **per rappresaglia** in reprisal *o* retaliation.

rappresentante [rapprezen'tante] SM/F (*gen, Pol, Comm*) representative ▶**rappresentante di commercio** sales representative, sales rep (*fam*) ▶**rappresentante sindacale** union delegate *o* representative.

rappresentanza [rapprezen'tantsa] SF **a** (*gen, Pol*) representation; (*gruppo*) delegation, deputation; **in rappresentanza di qn** on behalf of sb; **spese di rappresentanza** entertainment expenses; **macchina di rappresentanza** official car
b (*Comm*) agency; **avere la rappresentanza di** to be the agent for ▶**rappresentanza esclusiva** sole agency; **avere la rappresentanza esclusiva** to be sole agent.

rappresentare [rapprezen'tare] VT **a** (*sogg: pittore, romanziere, quadro*) to depict, portray; (*: fotografia*) to show
b (*simboleggiare, significare*) to represent; **ciò rappresenta un grave pericolo per la nazione** this represents a serious threat to the nation; **quella ragazza non rappresenta più niente per me** that girl means nothing to me any more
c (*Teatro: recitare*) to perform, play; (*: mettere in scena*) to perform, put on; **hanno intenzione di rappresentare la Carmen** they intend to stage *o* put on Carmen
d (*agire per conto di*) to represent; **farsi rappresentare dal proprio legale** to be represented by one's lawyer.

rappresentativa [rapprezenta'tiva] SF (*di partito, sindacale*) representative group; (*Sport*): **la rappresentativa italiana** the Italian team.

rappresentatività [rapprezentativi'ta] SF representativeness.

rappresentativo, a [rapprezenta'tivo] AGG (*gen*) representative; (*tipico*) typical.

rappresentazione [rapprezentat'tsjone] SF **a** (*raffigurazione*) representation; (*: di società, paesaggio*) portrayal
b (*spettacolo*) performance; **prima rappresentazione assoluta** world première; **sacra rappresentazione** religious play.

rappreso, a [rap'preso] [1] PP di **rapprendersi**.
[2] AGG (*sangue*) coagulated, clotted; (*latte*) curdled.

rapsodia [rapso'dia] SF rhapsody.

raptus ['raptus] SM INV: **raptus di follia** fit of madness.

raramente [rara'mente] AVV seldom, rarely.

rarefare [rare'fare] (VB IRREG) VT, **rarefarsi** VIP to rarefy.

rarefatto, a [rare'fatto] AGG rarefied.

rarefazione [rarefat'tsjone] SF rarefaction.

rarità [rari'ta] SF INV **a** (*scarsezza: di oggetto, malattia*) rarity; (*: di visite*) infrequency **b** (*oggetto*) rarity; (*avvenimento*) rare occurrence, unusual occurrence.

raro, a ['raro] AGG **a** (*poco comune*) rare; **è un caso molto raro** it's a very unusual *o* rare case; **è una bestia rara** (*fig*) he's a rare breed
b (*poco numeroso*) few, rare; **le rare persone che passavano** the few people that went by; **c'era qualche rara nuvola** there was the odd cloud; **i clienti sono diventati rari** customers have become scarce *o* few and far between.

ras [ras] SM INV (*titolo etiopico*) ras; (*fig: capetto*) tyrant.

rasare [ra'sare] [1] VT (*barba, capelli*) to shave off; (*siepi, erba*) to trim, cut.
[2] **rasarsi** VR to shave (o.s.).

rasato, a [ra'sato] AGG (*erba*) trimmed, cut; (*tessuto*) smooth; **avere la barba rasata** OR **essere ben rasato** to be clean-shaven.

rasatura [rasa'tura] SF (*atto*) shaving; (*effetto*) shave.

raschiamento [raskja'mento] SM (*Med*) curettage ▶**raschiamento uterino** D and C.

raschiare [ras'kjare] VT to scrape; **raschiare (via) qc** to

scrape sth off; **raschiarsi la gola** to clear one's throat.

raschiata [ras'kjata] SF: **dare una raschiata a qc** to give sth a scrape, scrape sth.

raschietto [ras'kjetto] SM scraper.

raschio, chi ['raskjo] SM (*in gola*) irritation.

rasentare [razen'tare] VT (*muro*) to hug, keep close to; (*terra*) to skim along (*o over*); (*fig: sfiorare*) to border on; **questo rasenta la pazzia!** this is bordering on insanity!; **rasentare la cinquantina** to be getting on for fifty (years of age).

rasente [ra'zɛnte] PREP: **rasente (a)** close to, very near; **camminare rasente il *o* al muro** to hug the wall.

raso, a ['raso] [1] PP di **radere**.
  [2] AGG **a** (*liscio*): **a pelo raso** (*pelliccia*) short-haired; (*tessuto*) smooth **b** (*con misure di capacità*) level *attr*; (*pieno: bicchiere*) full to the brim; **un cucchiaio raso** a level spoonful.
  [3] PREP: **raso terra** close to the ground; **volare raso terra** to hedgehop.
  [4] SM (*tessuto*) satin.

rasoio, oi [ra'sojo] SM razor ▸**rasoio elettrico** electric shaver *o* razor ▸**rasoio a lama** cut-throat *o* straight razor ▸**rasoio radi e getta** disposable *o* throwaway razor.

raspa ['raspa] SF (*lima*) rasp.

raspare [ras'pare] [1] VT **a** (*levigare*) to rasp **b** (*grattare: sogg: gallina, cane*) to scratch; (*: cavallo*) to paw.
  [2] VI (*aus* **avere**) to scrape, scratch.

raspo ['raspo] SM (*di uva*) grape stalk.

rassegna [ras'seɲɲa] SF **a** (*Mil*) inspection, review; **passare in rassegna** (*Mil, fig*) to review **b** (*resoconto*) review, survey; (*rivista*) review; (*mostra*) exhibition, show.

rassegnare [rasseɲ'ɲare] [1] VT: **rassegnare le dimissioni** to resign, hand in one's resignation.
  [2] **rassegnarsi** VIP: **rassegnarsi (a qc)** to resign o.s. (to sth); **bisogna rassegnarsi all'idea** we (*o* you *ecc*) will have to accept *o* get used to the idea; **mai rassegnarsi!** never give up!

rassegnatamente [rasseɲɲata'mente] AVV resignedly.

rassegnato, a [rasseɲ'ɲato] AGG (*aria, sguardo, tono*) resigned; **l'ho visto piuttosto rassegnato** he seemed quite resigned to it when I saw him; **sospirò con fare rassegnato** he sighed resignedly.

rassegnazione [rasseɲɲat'tsjone] SF resignation; **accettare qc con rassegnazione** to resign o.s. to sth.

rasserenamento [rasserena'mento] SM brightening up.

rasserenare [rassere'nare] [1] VT (*Meteor*) to clear up, brighten up.
  [2] VT (*persona*) to cheer up.
  [3] **rasserenarsi** VIP (*Meteor*) to brighten up, clear up; (*persona*) to cheer up.

rassettare [rasset'tare] [1] VT to tidy up, put in order.
  [2] **rassettarsi** VR to tidy o.s. up.

rassicurante [rassiku'rante] AGG reassuring.

rassicurare [rassiku'rare] [1] VT to reassure.
  [2] **rassicurarsi** VIP to take heart, recover one's confidence.

rassicurazione [rassikurat'tsjone] SF reassurance.

rassodamento [rassoda'mento] SM (*di muscoli*) hardening, strengthening; (*di tessuti*) firming.

rassodante [rasso'dante] AGG (*crema, ginnastica*) toning.

rassodare [rasso'dare] [1] VT (*muscoli*) to harden, strengthen; (*tessuti*) to firm (up); (*fig: amicizia*) to

strengthen, consolidate.
  [2] **rassodarsi** VIP (*muscoli*) to harden, strengthen; (*tessuti*) to firm (up).

rassomigliante [rassomiʎ'ʎante] AGG: **questa foto è molto rassomigliante** this photo is a good likeness.

rassomiglianza [rassomiʎ'ʎantsa] SF resemblance.

rassomigliare [rassomiʎ'ʎare] [1] VI (*aus* **essere** *o* **avere**): **rassomigliare a** to resemble, look like.
  [2] **rassomigliarsi** VR (*uso reciproco*) to look alike, resemble each other.

rastrellamento [rastrella'mento] SM (*di erba, fieno*) raking; (*Mil, di polizia*) (thorough) search; **stanno facendo un rastrellamento nella zona** they are combing the area.

rastrellare [rastrel'lare] VT (*erba, fieno*) to rake; (*fig: perlustrare*) to comb.

rastrelliera [rastrel'ljɛra] SF (*per fieno*) hayrack; (*per fucili, biciclette*) rack; (*per piatti*) dish rack.

rastrello [ras'trɛllo] SM rake.

rata ['rata] SF instalment (*Brit*), installment (*Am*); **pagare a rate** to pay by instal(l)ments *o* on hire purchase (*Brit*); **comprare/vendere a rate** to buy/sell on hire purchase (*Brit*) *o* on the installment plan (*Am*).

rateale [rate'ale] AGG: **pagamento rateale** payment by instal(l)ments; **vendita rateale** hire purchase (*Brit*), installment plan (*Am*).

rateare [rate'are] VT to divide into instal(l)ments.

rateazione [rateat'tsjone] SF division into instal(l)ments.

rateizzare [rateid'dzare] VT = **rateare**.

rateo ['rateo] SM (*Econ*) accrual.

ratifica, che [ra'tifika] SF ratification.

ratificare [ratifi'kare] VT (*gen*) to approve, ratify; (*Amm, Dir*) to ratify.

ratificazione [ratifikat'tsjone] SF = **ratifica**.

rat musquè SM INV (*pelliccia*) muskrat, musquash.

ratto[1] ['ratto] SM (*Storia, Dir*) abduction; **il ratto delle Sabine** the rape of the Sabine Women.

ratto[2] ['ratto] SM (*Zool*) rat ▸**ratto comune** black rat.

rattoppare [rattop'pare] VT to patch.

rattoppo [rat'tɔppo] SM (*risultato*) patch; (*azione*) patching *no pl*; **fare un rattoppo a** *o* **su qc** to patch sth.

rattrappire [rattrap'pire] [1] VT (*piedi, mani*) to make stiff.
  [2] **rattrappirsi** VIP to become stiff.

rattristare [rattris'tare] [1] VT (*addolorare*) to sadden.
  [2] **rattristarsi** VIP to grow *o* become sad.

rattristato, a [rattris'tato] AGG saddened.

raucamente [rauka'mente] AVV hoarsely.

raucedine [rau'tʃedine] SF hoarseness; **ho un po' di raucedine** I am a little hoarse.

rauco, a, chi, che ['rauko] AGG hoarse.

ravanello [rava'nɛllo] SM radish.

ravennate [raven'nate] [1] AGG of *o* from Ravenna.
  [2] SM/F inhabitant *o* native of Ravenna.

ravioli [ravi'ɔli] SMPL (*Culin*) ravioli *sg*.

ravvedersi [ravve'dersi] VIP IRREG to mend one's ways.

ravveduto, a [ravve'duto] PP di **ravvedersi**.

ravviare [ravvi'are] VT (*capelli*) to tidy; **ravviarsi i capelli** to tidy one's hair.

ravviata [ravvi'ata] SF tidying up.

ravvicinamento [ravvitʃina'mento] SM (*tra persone*) reconciliation; (*Pol: tra paesi*) rapprochement.

ravvicinare [ravvitʃi'nare] [1] VT (*oggetti*) to bring closer together; (*fig: persone*) to reconcile, bring together again.

2 **ravvicinarsi** VR to be reconciled; **si è ravvicinato alla famiglia** he is now reconciled with his family.

ravvisare [ravvi'zare] VT to recognize.

ravvivare [ravvi'vare] 1 VT (*fuoco, sentimento*) to revive, rekindle; (*fig: rallegrare*) to brighten up.

2 **ravvivarsi** VIP (*fuoco, sentimento*) to be rekindled *o* revived; (*persona, ambiente*) to brighten up.

ravvolgere [rav'voldʒere] VB IRREG 1 VT (*coperta, lenzuolo*) to roll up; **ravvolgere qn in una coperta** to wrap a blanket round sb.

2 **ravvolgersi** VR (*coprirsi*): **ravvolgersi in qc** to wrap o.s. up in sth.

ravvolto, a [rav'vɔlto] PP di **ravvolgere**.

ravvoltolare [ravvolto'lare] 1 VT: **ravvoltolare qn in qc** to wrap sb up in sth.

2 **ravvoltolarsi** VR: **ravvoltolarsi in qc** to wrap o.s. up in sth.

Rawalpindi [rawal'pindi] SF Rawalpindi.

rayon ['rajon] SM rayon.

raziocinio [rattsjo't∫injo] SM (*facoltà di ragionare*) reasoning *no pl*; (*buon senso*) common sense; **essere dotato di raziocinio** to be able to reason, possess the faculty of reason.

razionale [rattsjo'nale] 1 AGG (*gen, Mat*) rational; (*funzionale*) functional; **un razionale sfruttamento dello spazio** an intelligent use of space.

2 SM: **il razionale** the rational.

razionalità [rattsjonali'ta] SF rationality; (*buon senso*) common sense; (*funzionalità*) functionality, practicalness; **con razionalità** rationally, intelligently.

razionalizzare [rattsjonalid'dzare] VT (*metodo, lavoro, programma*) to rationalize; (*problema, situazione*) to approach rationally.

razionalmente [rattsjonal'mente] AVV rationally; (*funzionalmente*) functionally, practically.

razionamento [rattsjona'mento] SM rationing.

razionare [rattsjo'nare] VT to ration.

razione [rat'tsjone] SF (*gen*) ration; (*di soldato*) rations *pl*; (*fig: porzione*) share.

razza ['rattsa] SF a (*etnica*) race; (*Zool*) breed; **di razza** (*gen*) pedigree, purebred; (*cavallo*) thoroughbred; **razza da latte** (*bovini*) dairy breed; **razza da macello** *o* **da carne** (*bovini*) beef breed; **essere di buona razza** to come of good stock

b (*specie, tipo*) sort, kind; **che razza di discorso è?** what sort of argument is that?; **che razza di mascalzone!** what a scoundrel!

razzia [rat'tsia] SF raid, foray; **fare razzia in un pollaio** to raid a henhouse; **ha fatto razzia nel frigorifero** he raided the refrigerator.

razziale [rat'tsjale] AGG racial; **pregiudizi razziali** racial prejudice *sg*.

razziare [rattsi'are] VT (*bestiame*) to raid; (*città: saccheggiare*) to plunder, ravage.

razzismo [rat'tsizmo] SM racism, racialism; (*intolleranza*) prejudice.

razzista, i, e [rat'tsista] AGG, SM/F racist, racialist.

razzistico, a, ci, che [rat'tsistiko] AGG racist, racialist.

razzo ['raddzo] SM rocket; **lanciare un razzo** to send up *o* fire a rocket; **veloce come un razzo** as quick as lightning; **partire come un razzo** to be off like a shot ▶ **razzo di segnalazione** flare ▶ **razzo vettore** vector rocket.

razzolare [rattso'lare] VI (*aus avere*) (*galline*) to scratch about.

RC ['ɛrre't∫i] 1 SIGLA F = *responsabilità civile*; **RC-auto** (*assicurazione*) car insurance (*minimum liability*).

2 SIGLA = *Reggio Calabria*.

RDT ['ɛrre'di'ti] SIGLA F (= *Republica Democratica Tedesca*) GDR.

RE SIGLA = *Reggio Emilia*.

re[1] [re] SM INV (*gen*) king; (*fig: magnate*) tycoon, magnate; **i Re Magi** the Three Wise Men, the Magi; **Cristo re** Christ the King; **fare una vita da re** (*fig*) to live like a king.

re[2] [rɛ] SM INV (*Mus*) D; (: *solfeggiando la scala*) re.

reagente [rea'dʒɛnte] 1 AGG reacting.

2 SM reagent.

reagire [rea'dʒire] VI (*aus avere*) (*gen, Chim*) to react; **reagire (a/contro)** to react (to/against); **il paziente reagisce bene alle cure** the patient is responding well to treatment.

reale[1] [re'ale] 1 AGG (*gen, Mat*) real; (*piacere, miglioramento*) real, genuine; (*Fin: valore, salario*) real, actual; **nella vita reale** in real life.

2 SM: **il reale** reality.

reale[2] [re'ale] 1 AGG (*di, da re*) royal.

2 SMPL: **i Reali** the Royal family *sg o pl*.

realismo [rea'lizmo] SM realism; **con realismo** realistically.

realista[1]**, i, e** [rea'lista] 1 AGG (*gen*) realistic; (*Arte, Letteratura*) realist.

2 SM/F realist.

realista[2]**, i, e** [rea'lista] AGG, SM/F (*Pol*) royalist.

realisticamente [realistika'mente] AVV realistically.

realistico, a, ci, che [rea'listiko] AGG realistic.

realizzabile [realid'dzabile] AGG (*fattibile*) feasible; **questo abito è realizzabile in diversi tessuti** this dress can be made in various materials.

realizzabilità [realiddzabili'ta] SF (*di progetto*) feasibility; (*di ideale*) attainability.

realizzare [realid'dzare] 1 VT a (*opera, progetto*) to carry out, realize; (*scopo*) to achieve; (*sogno, desiderio*) to achieve, fulfil (*Brit*), fulfill (*Am*), realize

b (*fig: capire*) to realize

c (*Fin: capitale*) to realize; **abbiamo realizzato 2.000.000 dalla vendita della macchina** we made 2,000,000 lire from the sale of the car

d (*Sport: goal*) to score.

2 **realizzarsi** VIP (*sogno, speranza*) to come true, be realized.

3 **realizzarsi** VR (*persona*) to fulfil (*Brit*) *o* fulfill (*Am*) o.s.; **non mi sento realizzata nel mio lavoro** I don't feel fulfilled in my job.

realizzazione [realiddzat'tsjone] SF a (*di libro, opera*) realization; (*di sogno*) fulfil(l)ment; (*di persona*) self-fulfil(l)ment b (*opera, creazione*) achievement; (*Cine, Teatro*) production ▶ **realizzazione scenica** stage production c (*Fin*) realization.

realizzo [rea'liddzo] SM a (*conversione in denaro*) conversion into cash b (*vendita forzata*) clearance sale.

realmente [real'mente] AVV (*in realtà*) really; (*effettivamente*) actually.

realtà [real'ta] SF INV reality; **la dura realtà** harsh reality; **il suo sogno è divenuto realtà** his dream has become (a) reality *o* has come true; **in realtà** (*in effetti*) in fact; (*a dire il vero*) really.

reame [re'ame] SM kingdom, realm; (*fig*) realm.

reato [re'ato] SM (*Dir*) crime, offence (*Brit*), offense (*Am*).

reattività [reattivi'ta] SF (*Chim*): **scala di reattività** reac-

tivity series.

reattore [reat'tore] SM (*Aer: aereo*) jet; (: *motore*) jet engine ▶ **reattore nucleare** nuclear reactor.

reazionario, ria, ri, rie [reattsjo'narjo] AGG, SM/F reactionary.

reazione [reat'tsjone] SF **a** (*gen*) reaction; **motore/aereo a reazione** jet engine/plane ▶ **reazione a catena** (*anche fig*) chain reaction ▶ **reazione fisica** physical change ▶ **reazione chimica** chemical reaction **b** (*Pol*) reaction, repression; **forze della reazione** reactionary forces.

rebbio, bi [′rebbjo] SM prong.

rebus [′rɛbus] SM INV (*gioco enigmistico*) rebus; (*fig: persona*) enigma; (: *situazione, comportamento*) puzzle.

recapitare [rekapi'tare] VT to deliver.

recapito [re'kapito] SM **a** (*indirizzo*) address; **ha un recapito telefonico?** do you have a telephone number where you can be reached? **b** (*consegna*) delivery ▶ **recapito a domicilio** home delivery (service).

recare [re'kare] **1** VT **a** (*portare*) to bear, carry; (*contenere*) to bear; **le recò in dono un anello** he brought her a ring as a gift; **il telegramma reca la data di ieri** the telegram bears yesterday's date **b** (*causare, arrecare: gioia, piacere*) to give, bring; (: *danno*) to cause, bring; **non voglio recarvi disturbo** I don't want to cause any inconvenience to you, I don't want to disturb you; **recare danno a qn** to harm sb, cause harm to sb.

2 **recarsi** VIP to go; **recarsi in città/a scuola** to go into town/to school.

recedere [re'tʃɛdere] VI (*aus avere*) (*ritirarsi, Dir*): **recedere (da)** to withdraw (from).

recensione [retʃen'sjone] SF review; **fare la recensione di qc** OR **scrivere una recensione su qc** to review sth.

recensire [retʃen'sire] VT to review.

recensore [retʃen'sore] SM reviewer.

recente [re'tʃɛnte] AGG recent; **più recente** latest, most recent; **di recente** recently.

recentemente [retʃente'mente] AVV recently.

recentissime [retʃen'tissime] SFPL (*TV, Radio*) latest news *sg*; (*Stampa*) stop press *sg.*

recepire [retʃe'pire] VT take in.

recessione [retʃes'sjone] SF recession.

recessivo, a [retʃes'sivo] AGG (*Bio, Econ*) recessive.

recesso [re'tʃɛsso] SM **a** (*Dir*) withdrawal **b** (*luogo*) recess; **i recessi della mente** (*fig*) the recesses of the mind.

recettore [retʃet'tore] SM (*Anat*) receptor.

recherò ecc [reke'rɔ] VB vedi **recare**.

recidere [re'tʃidere] VT IRREG to cut off, chop off.

recidiva [retʃi'diva] SF (*Dir*) recidivism; (*Med*) relapse.

recidività [retʃidivi'ta] SF (*Dir*) recidivism; (*Med*) recurring nature.

recidivo, a [retʃi'divo] SM/F (*Dir*) recidivist, second (*o* habitual) offender.

recintare [retʃin'tare] VT to enclose, fence off.

recinto [re'tʃinto] SM **a** (*gen*) enclosure; (*per animali*) pen; (*per cavalli*) paddock **b** (*staccionata*) fence; (*in muratura*) surrounding wall **c** : **recinto delle grida** (*Borsa*) floor.

recinzione [retʃin'tsjone] SF **a** (*azione*) enclosure, fencing-off **b** (*recinto: di legno*) fence; (: *di mattoni*) wall; (*reticolato*) wire fencing; (*a sbarre*) railings *pl.*

recipiente [retʃi'pjɛnte] SM container.

reciprocamente [retʃiproka'mente] AVV each other, one another, mutually; **aiutarsi reciprocamente** to help

each other *o* one another.

reciprocità [retʃiprotʃi'ta] SF reciprocity.

reciproco, a, ci, che [re'tʃiproko] **1** AGG (*gen*) reciprocal; (*sentimento, interesse*) mutual.

2 SM (*Mat*) reciprocal.

reciso, a [re'tʃizo] **1** PP di **recidere**.

2 AGG (*risposta*) sharp, curt.

recita [′retʃita] SF (*Teatro*) performance; (*di poesie*) recital.

recital [retʃi'tal] SM INV recital.

recitare [retʃi'tare] **1** VI (*Teatro, fig*) to act.

2 VT (*dramma*) to perform; (*poesia, lezione*) to recite; (*ruolo*) to play *o* act (the part of).

recitazione [retʃitat'tsjone] SF (*di poesia*) recitation; (*modo di recitare: di attore*) acting; **scuola di recitazione** drama school.

reclamare [rekla'mare] **1** VI (*aus avere*): **reclamare (contro/presso qn)** to complain (about/to sb).

2 VT (*diritto*) to demand; **reclamare giustizia** to demand justice.

réclame [re'klam] SF INV (*pubblicità*) advertising *no pl*; (*annuncio*) advertisement; **fare la réclame di qc** OR **fare réclame a qc** to advertise sth.

reclamizzare [reklamid'dzare] VT to advertise.

reclamo [re'klamo] SM complaint; **sporgere reclamo presso** to complain to, make a complaint to; **ufficio reclami** complaints department.

reclinabile [rekli'nabile] AGG (*sedile*) reclining.

reclinare [rekli'nare] VT (*capo*) to bow, lower; (*sedile*) to tilt.

reclusione [reklu'zjone] SF (*Dir*) imprisonment.

recluso, a [re'kluzo] **1** AGG (*in prigione*) imprisoned.

2 SM/F (*prigioniero*) prisoner; **fare vita da recluso** (*fig*) to lead the life of a recluse.

recluta [′rɛkluta] SF (*Mil, fig*) recruit.

reclutamento [rekluta'mento] SM recruitment; **ufficio (di) reclutamento** recruiting office.

reclutare [reklu'tare] VT (*Mil, fig*) to recruit.

recondito, a [re'kondito] AGG (*letter: luogo*) hidden, secluded; (*fig: significato*) secret, hidden.

record [′rɛkord] **1** SM INV (*Sport, Inform*) record; **a tempo di record** in record time; **detenere il record di** to hold the record for ▶ **record mondiale** world record.

2 AGG INV record *attr*; **in tempo record** in record time.

recriminare [rekrimi'nare] VI (*aus avere*): **recriminare (su qc)** to complain (about sth).

recriminatorio, ria, ri, rie [rekrimina'tɔrjo] AGG recriminatory.

recriminazione [rekriminat'tsjone] SF recrimination.

recrudescenza [rekrudeʃ'ʃentsa] SF (*di malattia*) fresh outbreak; (*fig: di violenza, scontri*) fresh wave.

recuperare [rekupe'rare] VT = **ricuperare**.

redarguire [redar'gwire] VT to rebuke, reproach.

redassi ecc [re'dassi] VB vedi **redigere**.

redatto, a [re'datto] PP di **redigere**.

redattore, trice [redat'tore] SM/F (*Stampa: chi cura*) editor; (: *chi scrive: articolo*) writer; (: *dizionario, enciclopedia*) compiler ▶ **redattore capo** chief editor.

redazionale [redattsjo'nale] AGG (*ufficio*) editorial; **articolo redazionale** *article signed by the entire staff.*

redazione [redat'tsjone] SF **a** (*Stampa: messa a punto*) editing; (: *stesura: di articolo*) writing; (: *di dizionario, enciclopedia*) compilation **b** (*personale*) editorial staff; (*ufficio*) editorial office(s) **b** (*versione di testo*) version.

redditività [redditivi'ta] SF profitability.

redditizio, zia, zi, zie [reddi'tittsjo] AGG profitable.

reddito ['rɛddito] SM (*privato*) income; (*statale*) revenue; (*di capitale*) yield ▶**reddito complessivo** gross income ▶**reddito fisso** fixed income ▶**reddito imponibile** taxable income ▶**reddito da lavoro** earned income ▶**reddito nazionale** national income ▶**reddito non imponibile** non-taxable income ▶**reddito pubblico** public revenue.

redditometro [reddi'tɔmetro] SM *system for assessing income.*

redensi *ecc* [re'dɛnsi] VB vedi **redimere.**

redento, a [re'dɛnto] [1] PP di **redimere.**
[2] SMPL: **i redenti** the redeemed.

redentore, trice [reden'tore] [1] AGG redeeming.
[2] SM: **il Redentore** the Redeemer.

redenzione [reden'tsjone] SF redemption.

redigere [re'didʒere] VT IRREG (*lettera, articolo*) to write; (*contratto, verbale*) to draft, draw up; (*dizionario*) to compile.

redimere [re'dimere] VB IRREG [1] VT to redeem.
[2] **redimersi** VR to redeem o.s.

redimibile [redi'mibile] AGG (*titoli, azioni*) redeemable.

redingote [rədɛ̃'gɔt] SF INV tailored coat, fitted coat.

redini ['rɛdini] SFPL (*anche fig*) reins; **tenere le redini** to hold the reins.

redivivo, a [redi'vivo] AGG: **sembri tua madre rediviva** you're the living image of your mother.

reduce ['rɛdutʃe] [1] AGG (*gen, Mil*): **reduce da** returning from, back from; **essere reduce da** (*esame, colloquio*) to have been through; (*malattia*) to be just over.
[2] SM/F (*sopravvissuto*) survivor; (*veterano*) veteran.

refe ['refe] SM (*filo*) thread; (: *più grosso*) yarn.

referendario, ria, ri, rie [referen'darjo] AGG referendary.

referendum [refe'rɛndum] SM INV referendum; **fare un referendum** to hold a referendum.

referente [refe'rɛnte] SM (*Ling*) referent.

referenza [refe'rɛntsa] SF reference; **avere buone referenze** (*impiegato ecc*) to have good references.

referenziare [referen'tsjare] VT: **referenziare qn** to give sb a reference.

referenziato, a [referen'tsjato] AGG (*in annunci economici*) with references.

referto [re'fɛrto] SM: **referto medico** medical report.

refettorio, ri [refet'tɔrjo] SM (*in convento*) refectory; (*Scol*) dining hall.

refezione [refet'tsjone] SF (*Scol*) school meal.

reflex ['rɛfleks] SF INV (*Fot*) reflex camera.

refrain [rə'frɛ̃] SM INV (*ritornello*) refrain.

refrattario, ria, ri, rie [refrat'tarjo] AGG (*materiale, Med*) refractory; (*fig scherz: persona*): **refrattario (a)** indifferent (to); **essere refrattario alla matematica** to have no aptitude for mathematics.

refrigerante [refridʒe'rante] [1] AGG (*Tecn*) cooling, refrigerating.
[2] SM (*Chim: fluido*) coolant; (*Tecn: apparecchio*) refrigerator.

refrigerare [refridʒe'rare] VT to refrigerate.

refrigeratore [refridʒera'tore] SM (*Tecn*) refrigerator.

refrigerazione [refridʒerat'tsjone] SF refrigeration; (*Tecn*) cooling.

refrigerio, ri [refri'dʒɛrjo] SM: **trovare refrigerio** to find somewhere cool.

refugium peccatorum [re'fudʒum pekka'tɔrum] SM INV (*scherz*) [a] (*persona*): **è il nostro refugium peccatorum** he's always ready to help us out [b] (*lavoro*) sinecure; **quella facoltà è un refugium peccatorum** that faculty is regarded as a cushy number.

refurtiva [refur'tiva] SF stolen goods *pl.*

refuso [re'fuzo] SM typographical error, literal (*Brit*).

Reg. ABBR [a] (= *reggimento*) Regt [b] (*Amm*) = **regolamento.**

regalare [rega'lare] VT: **regalare qc** to give sth (as a present), make a present of sth; (*fig: vendere a poco prezzo*) to give sth away; **cosa gli regali per il compleanno?** what are you giving him for his birthday?; **penso che mi regalerò una vacanza** I think I'll treat myself to a holiday.

regale [re'gale] AGG royal; (*fig: portamento*) regal.

regalia [rega'lia] SF (*Amm*) gratuity.

regalità [regali'ta] SF (*fig: di portamento*) regality.

regalmente [regal'mente] AVV regally.

regalo [re'galo] [1] SM present, gift; **"articoli da regalo"** "gifts"; **fare un regalo a qn** to give sb a present; **"con bagnoschiuma in regalo"** "with a free gift of bubble bath".
[2] AGG INV: **libro regalo** free book; **confezione regalo** gift pack.

regata [re'gata] SF regatta.

reggente [red'dʒɛnte] [1] AGG [a] (*sovrano*) reigning; **principe reggente** prince regent [b] (*Gramm: proposizione*) main.
[2] SM/F regent.
[3] SF (*Gramm*) main clause.

reggenza [red'dʒɛntsa] SF regency.

reggere ['rɛddʒere] VB IRREG [1] VT [a] (*tenere: persona*) to hold up, support; (: *pacco, valigia, timone*) to hold; **le gambe non lo reggevano più** his legs could carry him no longer
[b] (*sopportare: peso*) to bear, carry; (: *fig: situazione*) to stand, bear; **reggere l'alcol** to hold one's drink; **non lo reggo più** (*fig: persona*) I can't put up with him any more
[c] (*Gramm: sogg: proposizione*) to govern, take, be followed by; **reggere il dativo** to take the dative
[d] (*essere a capo di: Stato*) to govern, rule; (: *ditta*) to run, manage.
[2] VI (*aus avere*) [a] (*resistere*) to hold on; **reggere a** (*peso, pressione*) to bear; (*urto*) to stand up to; **reggere alla tentazione** to resist temptation; **non regge al paragone** it (*o he ecc*) doesn't stand comparison; **non ha retto a tali minacce** he was unable to hold out against such threats
[b] (*durare: bel tempo, situazione*) to last
[c] (*fig: stare in piedi: teoria*) to hold up, hold water; **è un discorso che non regge** the argument doesn't hold water.
[3] **reggersi** VR [a] (*stare dritto*) to stand; (*fig: dominarsi*) to control o.s.; (*tenersi*): **reggersi a** to hold on to; (*fig: ipotesi*): **reggersi su** to be based on; **reggersi sulle gambe o in piedi** to stand up; **non si reggeva in piedi** he could barely stand; **non mi reggo più dalla stanchezza** I'm so tired that I can barely stand; **reggiti a me** hold on to me; **reggiti forte** hold on tight
[b] (*uso reciproco*): **reggersi a vicenda** to support each another.

reggia, ge ['rɛddʒa] SF royal palace; (*fig*) palace.

reggiano, a [red'dʒano] [1] AGG of *o* from Reggio Emilia.
[2] SM/F inhabitant *o* native of Reggio Emilia.

reggicalze [reddʒi'kaltse] SM INV suspender (*Brit*) *o* garter

(*Am*) belt.
reggimentale [reddʒimen'tale] AGG regimental.
reggimento [reddʒi'mento] SM regiment; (*fig*) horde.
reggino, a [red'dʒino] **1** AGG of *o* from Reggio Calabria. **2** SM/F inhabitant *o* native of Reggio Calabria.
reggipetto [reddʒi'pɛtto], **reggiseno** [reddʒi'seno] SM bra.
regia, gie [re'dʒia] SF (*Teatro*) production; (*TV, Cine*) direction.
regicida, i, e [redʒi'tʃida] SM/F regicide (*person*).
regicidio, di [redʒi'tʃidjo] SM regicide (*crime*).
regime [re'dʒime] SM **a** (*Pol, anche pegg*) regime **b** (*sistema*) system ▸ **regime (monetario) aureo** (*Fin*) gold standard ▸ **regime tributario** tax system **c** (*regola*): **regime dietetico** diet; **essere a regime** to be on a diet ▸ **regime vegetariano** vegetarian diet **d** (*di fiume, torrente*) flow **e** (*Tecn*) (engine) speed; **funzionare a pieno regime** to run at top revs ▸ **regime di giri** (*di motore*) revs *pl* per minute.
regina [re'dʒina] SF (*Pol, Scacchi, Carte, fig*) queen; **la regina Elisabetta** Queen Elizabeth; **la regina madre** the Queen Mother; **la regina della festa** the belle of the ball.
reginetta [redʒi'netta] SF: **reginetta di bellezza** beauty queen.
regio, gia, gi, gie ['rɛdʒo] AGG royal.
regionale [redʒo'nale] **1** AGG regional. **2** SM (*treno*) slow local train.
regionalismo [redʒona'lizmo] SM regionalism.
regionalizzare [redʒonalid'dzare] VT to regionalize.
regionalmente [redʒonal'mente] AVV regionally.
regione [re'dʒone] SF **a** (*gen*) region; (*fig: zona*) area, region **b** (*autorità*) *there are 20 of these large administrative units, which have legislative power over the police, public health, schools, town planning and agriculture: a regione is run by a giunta regionale, headed by a presidente.*
regista, i, e [re'dʒista] SM/F (*Teatro*) producer; (*TV, Cine*) director.
registrare [redʒis'trare] VT **a** (*Amm: nascita, morte, veicolo*) to register; (*Comm: fattura, ordine*) to enter; **registrare i bagagli** (*Aer*) to check in one's luggage **b** (*notare, constatare*) to report, note; (*sogg: termometro, apparecchio*) to record, register; **è stato registrato un aumento della domanda** an increase in demand has been reported **c** (*su nastro*) to (tape-)record; (*su disco*) to record **d** (*Tecn: mettere a punto*) to adjust, regulate; **registrare i freni** to adjust the brakes.
registratore [redʒistra'tore] SM (*per incidere*) tape recorder; (*per misurare*) register, recorder ▸ **registratore di cassa** (*Comm*) till, cash register ▸ **registratore a cassette** cassette recorder ▸ **registratore di volo** (*Aer*) flight recorder.
registrazione [redʒistrat'tsjone] SF (*vedi vb*) registration; entry; check-in; reporting; recording; adjustment.
registro [re'dʒistro] SM **a** (*gen*) register ▸ **registro di bordo** log (*Brit*), logbook (*Am*) ▸ **registro di classe** class register ▸ **registro (di cassa)** (*Comm*) ledger **b** (*Amm, Dir*) registry; **ufficio del registro** registrar's office ▸ **(pubblico) registro automobilistico** motor registration office ▸ **registro immobiliare** land register **c** (*Tecn: di orologio*) regulator; (: *di treno*) adjuster

d (*Mus: di voce*) range, register; (: *di strumento*) register.
regnante [reɲ'ɲante] **1** AGG reigning, ruling. **2** SM/F ruler.
regnare [reɲ'ɲare] VI (*aus* avere) (*anche fig*) to reign; (*predominare*) to rule; **regnava il silenzio** silence reigned.
regno ['reɲɲo] SM **a** (*periodo*) reign; **durante il regno di** during the reign of **b** (*luogo*) kingdom; **il regno della fantasia** the realm of fantasy ▸ **il regno animale** the animal kingdom ▸ **il regno vegetale** the vegetable *o* plant kingdom.
Regno Unito ['reɲɲo u'nito] SM: **il Regno Unito** the United Kingdom.
regola ['rɛgola] SF **a** (*gen*) rule; **di regola** as a rule; **essere in regola** (*dipendente*) to be a registered employee; (*fig: essere pulito*) to be clean; (: *avere la coscienza a posto*) to have a clear conscience; **proporsi una regola di vita** to set o.s. rules to live by; **le regole del gioco** (*anche fig*) the rules of the game; **a regola d'arte** (*lavoro*) expert, professional; **per tua (norma e) regola** for your information; **avere le carte in regola** (*gen*) to have one's papers in order; (*fig: essere adatto*) to be the right person; **fare le cose in regola** to do things properly; **un'eccezione alla regola** an exception to the rule **b** (*Rel*) rule.
regolabile [rego'labile] AGG adjustable.
regolamentare [regolamen'tare] **1** AGG (*distanza, velocità*) regulation *attr*; (*disposizione*) statutory; **entro il tempo regolamentare** within the time allowed, within the prescribed time. **2** VT (*gen*) to control.
regolamento [regola'mento] SM **a** (*norme*) regulations *pl*; **regolamento scolastico** school rules *pl* **b** (*atto del regolare: di debito*) settlement; **un regolamento di conti** (*fig*) a settling of scores.
regolare¹ [rego'lare] AGG **a** (*senza variazioni: gen, Gramm, Mat*) regular; (: *velocità*) steady; (: *superficie*) even; (: *passo*) steady, even **b** (*in regola: documento, permesso*) in order; **presentare regolare domanda** to apply through the proper channels; **esercito regolare** regular army; **è tutto regolare!** everything is in order!; **tutto ciò non è regolare** that's entirely irregular.
regolare² [rego'lare] **1** VT (*gen*) to regulate, control; (*questione, debito, conto*) to settle; (*apparecchio*) to adjust, regulate; (*orologio*) to set; **regolare i conti** (*fig*) to settle old scores. **2 regolarsi** VR **a** (*moderarsi*): **regolarsi nel bere/nello spendere** to watch *o* control one's drinking/spending **b** (*comportarsi*) to behave, act; **non so come regolarmi** I don't know what to do; (*nell'usare ingredienti*) I don't know what quantities to add; **regolati come meglio credi** do as you think best.
regolarità [regolari'ta] SF **a** (*vedi agg a*) regularity; steadiness; evenness **b** (*nel pagare*) punctuality.
regolarizzare [regolarid'dzare] VT (*posizione*) to regularize; (*debito*) to settle.
regolarmente [regolar'mente] AVV **a** (*vedi agg a*) regularly; steadily; evenly; **arriva regolarmente in ritardo** he regularly arrives late **b** (*in modo debito, corretto*) duly; **ho presentato regolarmente domanda** I applied through the proper channels.
regolata [rego'lata] SF (*fig*): **darsi una regolata** to pull one's socks up, pull o.s. together.
regolatezza [regola'tettsa] SF (*ordine*) orderliness; (*mode-*

razione) moderation.

regolato, a [rego'lato] AGG (ordinato) orderly; (moderato) moderate.

regolatore, trice [regola'tore] [1] AGG (principio) controlling attr; **piano regolatore** (Amm) town-planning scheme.

[2] SM (Tecn) regulator ►**regolatore di frequenza** frequency control ►**regolatore di tensione** voltage regulator ►**regolatore di volume** volume control.

regolo[1] ['rɛgolo] SM ruler ►**regolo calcolatore** slide rule.

regolo[2] ['rɛgolo] SM (uccello) goldcrest.

regredire [regre'dire] VI (aus essere) to regress; **regredire negli studi** to fall behind in one's studies.

regressione [regres'sjone] SF regression.

regressivo, a [regres'sivo] AGG regressive.

regresso [re'grɛsso] SM (fig: declino) decline.

reidratare [reidra'tare] VT rehydrate.

reietto, a [re'jɛtto] SM/F outcast.

reimbarcare [reimbar'kare] VT, **reimbarcarsi** VR to re-embark.

reimpiegare [reimpje'gare] VT (riusare) to reuse; (assumere nuovamente) to re-employ; (Fin) to reinvest.

reimpiego [reim'pjɛgo] SM (vedi vt) reuse; re-employment; reinvestment.

reincarnare [reinkar'nare] [1] VT to reincarnate.

[2] **reincarnarsi** VIP to be reincarnated.

reincarnazione [reinkarnat'tsjone] SF reincarnation.

reinserimento [reinseri'mento] SM (dopo assenza) readjustment; (dopo carcere) rehabilitation, reintegration.

reinserire [reinse'rire] [1] VT (gen) to reinsert; (tossicodipendente, ex-detenuto) to rehabilitate, reintegrate.

[2] **reinserirsi** VR (dopo assenza) to readjust; (dopo carcere) to rehabilitate o.s.

reintegrare [reinte'grare] VT (produzione) to restore; (energie) to recover; (dipendente) to reinstate; **reintegrare qn in una carica** to reinstate sb in a post.

reintegrazione [reintegrat'tsjone] SF (di produzione) restoration; (di dipendente) reinstatement.

reinventare [reinven'tare] VT (gen) to reinvent; (Teatro) to reinterpret.

reiterare [reite'rare] VT to reiterate.

reiteratamente [reiterata'mente] AVV repeatedly.

reiterazione [reiterat'tsjone] SF reiteration.

relais [rə'lɛ] SM INV (Elettr) relay.

relativamente [relativa'mente] AVV relatively; **relativamente a** as regards.

relatività [relativi'ta] SF relativity.

relativo, a [rela'tivo] AGG (gen, Gramm, Mat) relative; (attinente) relevant; (rispettivo) respective; **relativo a** (che concerne) relating to, concerning; (proporzionato) in proportion to.

relatore, trice [rela'tore] SM/F (gen) spokesman/spokeswoman; (Univ: di tesi) supervisor.

relax [re'laks] SM relaxation.

relazione [relat'tsjone] SF **a** (legame, nesso) relationship; **non c'è relazione tra le due cose** there's no connection between the two things, the two things are in no way related; **essere in relazione** to be connected; **mettere in relazione** (fatti, elementi) to make the connection between; **in relazione a quanto detto prima** with regard to what has already been said

b (rapporto con persone) relationship; **essere in buone relazioni con qn** to be on good terms with sb; **relazione (sentimentale)** love affair; **relazione extraconiugale**

adulterous affair; **relazioni** SFPL (conoscenze) connections; **pubbliche relazioni** public relations ►**relazioni sindacali** labour relations

c (resoconto) report, account; **fare una relazione** to make a report, give an account.

relé [re'le] SM INV = **relais**.

relegare [rele'gare] VT (allontanare) to banish; (fig) to relegate.

religione [reli'dʒone] SF (gen, fig) religion; (fede) religious faith; **religione di Stato** state religion; **non c'è più religione!** (fig) what's the world coming to!

religioso, a [reli'dʒoso] [1] AGG (gen) religious; (arte) sacred; (scuola, matrimonio, musica) church attr; **in religioso silenzio** in reverent silence.

[2] SM/F monk/nun.

reliquia [re'likwja] SF (Rel, fig) relic; **tenere qc come una reliquia** (fig) to treasure sth.

reliquiario, ri [reli'kwjarjo] SM reliquary.

relitto [re'litto] SM (gen, fig) wreck; (persona) down-and-out.

rem [rɛm] SM INV (Fis) rem.

remainder [ri'meində] SM INV (libro) remainder.

remake ['ri:'meik] SM INV (Cine, Teatro) remake.

remare [re'mare] VI (aus avere) to row.

rematore, trice [rema'tore] SM/F oarsman/oarswoman.

reminiscenza [reminiʃ'ʃɛntsa] SF reminiscence.

remissione [remis'sjone] SF **a** (di peccato) remission ►**remissione del debito** (Dir) remission of debt ►**remissione di querela** (Dir) withdrawal of an action **b** (sottomissione) submissiveness, compliance.

remissivamente [remissiva'mente] AVV compliantly, submissively.

remissività [remissivi'ta] SF submissiveness.

remissivo, a [remis'sivo] AGG submissive, compliant.

Remo ['rɛmo] SM Remus.

remo ['rɛmo] SM oar; **barca a remi** rowing boat; **tirare i remi in barca** (anche fig) to rest on one's oars.

remora ['rɛmora] SF (letter: indugio) hesitation; **non avere remore!** don't hesitate!

remoto, a [re'mɔto] AGG **a** (lontano) remote **b** (Gramm): **passato remoto** past definite; **trapassato remoto** pluperfect.

remunerare ecc [remune'rare] = **rimunerare** ecc.

rena ['rena] SF sand.

renale [re'nale] AGG kidney attr.

renano, a [re'nano] AGG Rhine attr, of the Rhine.

rendere ['rɛndere] VB IRREG [1] VT **a** (ridare) to give back, return; **potresti rendermi la penna?** could you give me back my pen?; **gli sarà resa la libertà quanto prima** he will be released as soon as possible; **rendere la visita** to pay a return visit; "**vuoto a rendere**" (bottiglia) "please return empties"; **a buon rendere!** (anche iro) my turn next time!; **rendere l'anima a Dio** (euf) to breathe one's last

b (dare): **rendere grazie a qn** to thank sb; **rendere omaggio a qn** to honour sb; **rendere un servizio a qn** to do sb a service; **rendere una testimonianza** to give evidence; **rendersi conto di qc** to realize sth

c (fruttare) to yield, bring in; (uso assoluto: sogg: ditta) to be profitable; (: investimento, campo) to yield, be productive; **rendere il 10%** to yield 10%; **una ditta che non rende** an unprofitable firm

d (esprimere, tradurre) to render; **rendere l'idea** to give the idea; **non so se rendo l'idea!** I don't know if I'm

making myself clear!
e (+ *agg*: *far diventare*) to make; **il suo intervento ha reso possibile l'affare** his intervention made the whole affair possible; **l'hai resa felice** you made her happy; **rendere la vita impossibile a qn** to make life impossible for sb.
2 **rendersi** VR (+ *agg*: *apparire*) to make o.s. + *adj*; **rendersi antipatico/ridicolo/utile** to make o.s. unpleasant/ridiculous/useful.

rendez-vous [rɑ̃'de'vu] SM INV (*appuntamento*) rendez-vous; (: *galante*) date.

rendiconto [rendi'kɔnto] SM (*resoconto*) report, account; (*Amm, Comm*) statement (of accounts).

rendimento [rendi'mento] SM (*di manodopera, anche Fis*) efficiency; (*di industria*: *produttività*) productivity; (*di motore, studente*) performance; (*di podere*) yield; **avere un buon rendimento** (*atleta*) to perform well; (*studente*) to do well.

rendita ['rendita] SF (*di individuo*) private *o* unearned income; (*Comm*) revenue; **vivere di rendita** to have private means; (*fig*: *studente*) to survive on one's past results ▶**rendita annua** annuity ▶**rendita vitalizia** life annuity.

rene ['rɛne] SM kidney.

renetta [re'netta] SF (*frutto*) pippin.

reni ['reni] SFPL (*schiena*) back *sg*; **spezzare le reni a qn** (*fig*) to annihilate sb.

renitente [reni'tɛnte] AGG: **renitente (a)** unwilling (to), reluctant (to), loath (to); **renitente ai consigli di qn** unwilling to follow sb's advice; **essere renitente alla leva** (*Mil*) to fail to report for military service.

renna ['rɛnna] SF reindeer *inv*.

Reno ['reno] SM: **il Reno** the Rhine.

rentrée [rɑ̃'tre] SF INV comeback.

reo, a ['rɛo] 1 AGG: **reo (di)** guilty (of).
2 SM/F (*Dir*) offender; **reo confesso** confessed criminal.

reostato [re'ɔstato] SM rheostat.

reparto [re'parto] SM (*di ospedale*) ward; (*di ufficio, negozio*) department, section; (*Mil*: *di esercito*) unit, detachment ▶**reparti d'assalto** (*Mil*) assault troops ▶**reparto acquisti** purchasing office ▶**reparto d'attacco** (*Sport*) attack ▶**reparto uomo** (*in negozio*) men's department.

repellente [repel'lɛnte] AGG **a** (*che ripugna*) repulsive **b** (*Chim*: *insettifugo*): **liquido repellente** (liquid) repellent.

repentaglio [repen'taʎʎo] SM: **mettere a repentaglio** to put at risk, jeopardize, endanger.

repentinamente [repentina'mente] AVV suddenly, unexpectedly.

repentino, a [repen'tino] AGG (*gesto, decisione*) sudden, unexpected.

reperibile [repe'ribile] AGG (*articolo, prodotto*) available; **non è reperibile** (*persona*) he can't be reached.

reperire [repe'rire] VT to find, trace.

reperto [re'pɛrto] SM (*Archeol*) find; (*anche*: **reperto giudiziario**) exhibit; (*Med*) report.

repertorio, ri [reper'tɔrjo] SM (*Teatro*) repertoire, repertory; (: *di canzoni, fig*) repertoire; **immagini di repertorio** (*Cine, TV*) archive footage *sg*.

replay ['ri:'plei] SM INV (*TV*) (action) replay.

replica, che ['replika] SF **a** (*risposta*: *gen, Pol*) reply, answer; (: *obiezione*) objection **b** (*ripetizione*: *gen*) repetition; (: *Teatro, Cine*) repeat performance; **avere molte repliche** to have a long run **c** (*copia*) replica.

replicare [repli'kare] VT **a** (*rispondere*) to reply, answer **b**

(*Teatro, Cine*) to repeat.

reportage [rəpor'taʒ] SM INV (*Stampa*) report.

reporter [re'porter] SM/F INV reporter.

repressione [repres'sjone] SF repression.

repressivo, a [repres'sivo] AGG repressive.

represso, a [re'prɛsso] 1 PP di **reprimere**.
2 AGG repressed.
3 SM/F (*persona*) repressed person.

reprimere [re'primere] VT IRREG (*gen*) to suppress, repress; (*sommossa*) to put down, suppress; (*sentimenti*) to repress, hold back.

repubblica, che [re'pubblika] SF republic; **la Prima/ Seconda Repubblica** *terms used to refer to Italy before and after the political changes resulting from the 1994 elections*.

repubblicano, a [repubbli'kano] AGG, SM/F republican.

repulisti [repu'listi] SM INV (*scherz*): **fare (un) repulisti** to have a clean-out.

repulsione [repul'sjone] SF **a** (*Fis*) repulsion **b** (*fig*) = **ripulsione**.

reputare [repu'tare] 1 VT to consider, judge; **reputare qn intelligente** to consider *o* judge sb (to be) intelligent; **reputo che si possa fare** I think it can be done; **se lo reputerai opportuno** if you think it advisable.
2 **reputarsi** VR to consider o.s.

reputazione [reputat'tsjone] SF (*gen*) reputation; (*buon nome*) reputation, good name; **avere una buona/cattiva reputazione** to have a good/bad reputation; **farsi una cattiva reputazione** to get o.s. a bad name; **rovinarsi la reputazione** to ruin one's reputation.

requie ['rɛkwje] SF rest; **dare requie a qn** to give sb some peace; **non dare requie a qn** to give sb no quarter; **senza requie** unceasingly.

requiem ['rɛkwjem] 1 SM O F INV (*preghiera*) requiem, prayer for the dead.
2 SM INV (*Mus*) Requiem; (*fig*: *ufficio funebre*) requiem; **messa di requiem** Requiem (mass).

requisire [rekwi'zire] VT to requisition.

requisito [rekwi'zito] SM (*gen*) requirement; **avere i requisiti necessari per un lavoro** to have the necessary qualifications for a job.

requisitoria [rekwizi'tɔrja] SF (*Dir*) closing speech (for the prosecution).

requisizione [rekwizit'tsjone] SF requisition.

resa ['resa] SF **a** (*l'arrendersi*) surrender
b (*rendimento*: *di podere*) yield; (: *di operaio*) productivity
c : **resa dei conti** rendering of accounts; **è venuto il momento della resa dei conti** (*fig*) the day of reckoning has arrived
d (*Comm*: *restituzione*) repayment; (: *merce restituita*) unsold goods.

rescindere [reʃ'ʃindere] VT IRREG (*Dir*) to rescind, annul.

rescissione [reʃʃis'sjone] SF (*Dir*) rescission, annulment.

rescisso, a [reʃ'ʃisso] PP di **rescindere**.

resettare [reset'tare] VT (*Inform*: *macchina, computer*) to reset.

resi *ecc* ['resi] VB vedi **rendere**.

residence ['rezidəns] SM INV *hotel with suites of rooms complete with kitchen and bathroom rented for fairly long periods*.

residente [resi'dɛnte] AGG, SM/F resident.

residenza [resi'dɛntsa] SF **a** (*soggiorno*) stay **b** (*indirizzo, sede*) residence; **cambiare residenza** to change one's

address.

residenziale [residen'tsjale] AGG residential.
residuale [residu'ale] AGG residual.
residuo, a [re'siduo] [1] AGG (*rimanente*) remaining; (*Chim*) residual.
[2] SM (*gen*) remainder; (*Chim, fig*) residue ►**residui industriali** industrial waste *sg*.
resina ['rezina] SF resin.
resinoso, a [rezi'noso] AGG resinous.
resistente [resis'tɛnte] AGG (*persona, oggetto*) strong, tough; (*pianta*) hardy; (*tessuto*) strong, hard-wearing; (*colore*) fast; (*metallo*) strong, resistant; **resistente all'acqua** waterproof; **resistente al calore** heat-resistant; **resistente al fuoco** fireproof; **resistente al gelo** frost-resistant.
resistenza [resis'tɛntsa] SF **a** (*gen*) resistance; (*fisica*) stamina, endurance; (*mentale*) endurance, resistance; **opporre resistenza (a)** to offer *o* put up resistance (to); (*decisione, scelta*) to show opposition (to); **prova di resistenza** endurance test ►**resistenza passiva** passive resistance ►**resistenza a pubblico ufficiale** (*Dir*) use of force or threats against a public official **b** (*Elettr, Tecn, Fis*) resistance; (*Elettr: apparecchio*) resistor; **coefficiente di resistenza** drag coefficient ►**resistenza di attrito** frictional resistance **c** (*Pol*): **la Resistenza** the Resistance (*against Nazis and Fascists during the Second World War: it played a vital role in the Liberation and in the formation of the new democratic government*).
resistere [re'sistere] VI IRREG (*aus* **avere**): **resistere a** (*gen*) to resist; (*fatica, siccità*) to stand up to, withstand; (*peso*) to take; (*dolore*) to stand; (*tentazione*) to resist; (*tortura*) to endure; (*attacco*) to hold out against; **resistere al calore** to be heat-resistant; **resistere al fuoco** to be fireproof; **resistere alla prova del tempo** to stand the test of time; **resistere alla corrente di un fiume** to hold one's own against the current of a river; **colori che resistono al lavaggio** colours which are fast in the wash; **resistere al peso della responsabilità** to cope with the responsibility; **non ho resistito e gliel'ho detto** I couldn't contain myself any longer and I told him; **non resisterà molto in quell'ufficio** he won't last long in that office; **nessuno sa resistergli** no-one can resist him; **nessuno sa resistere al suo fascino** everybody succumbs to his charm.
resistito, a [resis'tito] PP di **resistere**.
reso, a ['reso] PP di **rendere**.
resoconto [reso'konto] SM (*gen*) account; (*di giornalista*) report, account; (*di seduta, assemblea*) minutes *pl*; **fare il resoconto di** to give an account of; to give a report of; to take the minutes of.
respingente [respin'dʒɛnte] SM (*Ferr*) buffer.
respingere [res'pindʒere] VT IRREG **a** (*attacco, nemico*) to drive back, repel; **respingere la palla** (*Calcio*) to kick the ball back; (*Pallavolo*) to return the ball **b** (*rifiutare: pacco, lettera*) to return; (: *invito*) to refuse; (: *proposta*) to reject, turn down; (: *persona*) to reject **c** (*Scol: studente*) to fail.
respinto, a [res'pinto] [1] PP di **respingere**.
[2] SM/F (*Scol*) failed candidate.
respirare [respi'rare] [1] VI (*aus* **avere**) (*gen*) to breathe; (*inspirare*) to breathe in, inhale; (*fig: distendersi*) to get one's breath (back); (: *rassicurarsi*) to breathe again; **non respiri!** (*dal medico*) hold your breath!.

[2] VT: **respirare un po' d'aria fresca** (*anche fig*) to get a breath of fresh air; **si respira un'aria di rinnovamento** there is a feeling of renewal in the air.
respiratore [respira'tore] SM (*Med*) respirator; (*di subacqueo*) breathing apparatus.
respiratorio, ria, ri, rie [respira'tɔrjo] AGG respiratory.
respirazione [respirat'tsjone] SF breathing ►**respirazione artificiale** artificial respiration ►**respirazione bocca a bocca** mouth-to-mouth resuscitation, kiss of life (*fam*).
respiro [res'piro] SM breathing *no pl*; (*singolo atto*) breath; (*fig*) respite, rest; **avere il respiro pesante** to breathe heavily; **trattenere il respiro** to hold one's breath; **esalare l'ultimo respiro** to breathe one's last; **godere di un momento di respiro** to enjoy a moment's rest; **lavorare senza respiro** to work non-stop; **dammi un attimo di respiro** give me a break; **di ampio respiro** (*opera, lavoro*) far-reaching.
responsabile [respon'sabile] [1] AGG **a** (*gen, fig*): **responsabile (di)** responsible (for); (*danni*) liable (for), responsible (for); **sentirsi responsabile di fronte a qn** (*moralmente*) to feel responsible to sb, hold o.s. accountable to sb **b** (*incaricato*): **responsabile (di)** responsible (for), in charge (of).
[2] SM/F **a**: **responsabile (di)** (*danni, delitto*) person responsible (for) **b**: **responsabile (di)** (*sezione, ufficio*) person in charge (of), manager (of).
responsabilità [responsabili'ta] SF INV: **responsabilità (di)** (*gen*) responsibility (for); (*Dir*) liability (for); **assumere la responsabilità di** to take on the responsibility for; **affidare a qn la responsabilità di qc** to make sb responsible for sth; **avere la responsabilità di** to be responsible for, have responsibility for; **fare qc sotto la propria responsabilità** to do sth on one's own responsibility ►**responsabilità civile** civil liability ►**responsabilità patrimoniale** debt liability ►**responsabilità penale** criminal liability.
responsabilizzare [responsabilid'dzare] [1] VT: **responsabilizzare qn** to make sb feel responsible.
[2] **responsabilizzarsi** VIP to become responsible.
responsabilmente [responsabil'mente] AVV responsibly.
responso [res'ponso] SM (*risposta*) answer, reply; (*Dir*) verdict.
ressa ['rɛssa] SF crowd, throng; **quanta ressa!** what a crush!; **far ressa intorno a qn** to throng round sb.
ressi ecc ['rɛssi] VB vedi **reggere**.
resta ['rɛsta] SF (*fig*): **partire con la lancia in resta** to be ready for battle.
restante [res'tante] [1] AGG (*rimanente*) remaining.
[2] SM (*resto*): **il restante** the remainder *no pl*, the rest *no pl*.
restare [res'tare] VI (*aus* **essere**) **a** (*in luogo*) to stay, remain; **restare a casa** to stay *o* remain at home; **restare a letto** to stay *o* remain in bed; **restare a cena** to stay for dinner; **restare a guardare la televisione** to stay and watch television; **che resti tra di noi** (*fig: segreto*) this is just between ourselves **b** (*in una condizione*) to stay, remain; **restare zitto** to remain *o* keep *o* stay silent; **restare sorpreso** to be surprised; **restare orfano** to become *o* be left an orphan; **restare cieco** to become blind; **restare in piedi** (*non sedersi*) to remain standing; (*non coricarsi*) to stay up; **restare amici** to remain friends; **restare in buoni**

rapporti to remain on good terms; **restare senza parole** to be left speechless

c (*sussistere*) to be left, remain; **non restano che poche pietre** there are only a few stones left; **è l'unico parente che le resta** he's her only remaining relative; **coi pochi soldi che mi restano** with what little money I have left; **restano da fare 15 km** there are still 15 km to go; **ne resta ancora un po'** there's still some left; **resta ancora molto da fare** there's still a lot to do; **non ti resta altro (da fare) che accettare** all you can do is accept; **mi resti solo tu** you're all I have left; **mi resta ben poco da dire se non...** I've little left to say except ...; **non resta più niente** there's nothing left.

restaurare [restau'rare] VT to restore.

restauratore, trice [restaura'tore] SM/F restorer.

restaurazione [restaurat'tsjone] SF (*Pol*) restoration.

restauro [res'tauro] SM (*Archit, Arte*) restoration; **in restauro** under repair; **sotto restauro** (*dipinto*) being restored; **chiuso per restauro** closed for repairs.

restio, tia, tii, tie [res'tio] AGG (*riluttante*): **restio a** reluctant to.

restituibile [restitu'ibile] AGG returnable.

restituire [restitu'ire] VT: **restituire qc (a)** (*gen*) to return sth (to), give sth back (to); (*colore, forma, forza*) to restore sth (to); **mi ha restituito i soldi oggi** he paid me back today; **restituire un favore** to return a favour.

restituzione [restitut'tsjone] SF (*gen*) return; (*di soldi*) repayment.

resto ['resto] SM **a** (*gen*) rest; (*di soldi*) change; (*Mat*) remainder; **tu porta il vino, al resto penso io** you bring the wine, and I'll see to the rest; **"il resto alla prossima puntata"** "to be continued"; **del resto** besides, moreover; **del resto, cos'altro potevo fare?** after all, what else could I do?

b : **resti** SMPL (*di cibo*) leftovers; (*di civiltà*) remains ►**resti mortali** (mortal) remains.

restringere [res'trindʒere] VB IRREG ① VT (*strada*) to narrow; (*abito, gonna*) to take in.

② **restringersi** VIP (*contrarsi*) to contract; (*farsi più stretto*: *strada, fiume*) to narrow; (: *tessuto*) to shrink; **il campo si restringe** (*fig*: *di ipotesi, possibilità*) the field is narrowing.

restrittivamente [restrittiva'mente] AVV restrictively.

restrittivo, a [restrit'tivo] AGG restrictive.

restrizione [restrit'tsjone] SF restriction.

resurrezione [resurret'tsjone] SF = **risurrezione**.

resuscitare [resuʃʃi'tare] VT, VI = **risuscitare**.

retaggio, gi [re'taddʒo] SM heritage.

retata [re'tata] SF **a** (*Pesca*) haul, catch **b** (*Polizia*): **fare una retata (di)** to round up.

rete ['rete] SF **a** (*tessuto, Pesca*) net; (*di equilibristi*) safety net; (*per bagagli*) (luggage) rack; (*di recinzione*) wire netting; (*maglia metallica, di plastica*) mesh; **finire nella rete** (*fig*: *trappola*) to be caught in the trap ►**rete del letto** (sprung) bed base ►**rete da pesca** fishing net

b (*sistema*) network ►**rete di distribuzione** distribution network ►**rete elettrica** (*nazionale*) (electricity) grid ►**rete ferroviaria** railway network ►**rete di spionaggio** spy network ►**rete stradale** road network ►**rete (televisiva)** (*sistema*) network; (*canale*) channel **c** (*Sport*) net; **segnare una rete** (*Calcio*) to score a goal; **tirare in rete** (*Calcio*) to take a shot at goal.

reticente [reti'tʃɛnte] AGG reticent.

reticenza [reti'tʃɛntsa] SF reticence; **parlare senza reticenze** to speak out.

reticolato [retiko'lato] SM (*gen*) grid; (*recinto*) wire netting; (*Mil*) barbed wire (fence).

reticolo [re'tikolo] SM network ►**reticolo cristallino** (*Chim*) crystal lattice ►**reticolo geografico** grid.

retina[1] ['retina] SF (*Anat*) retina.

retina[2] [re'tina] SF (*per capelli*) hairnet.

retino [re'tino] SM **a** (*Tip*) screen **b** (*da pesca*) landing net; (*per farfalle*) butterfly net.

retore ['retore] SM rhetorician.

retorica [re'tɔrika] SF (*anche fig*) rhetoric.

retoricamente [retorika'mente] AVV rhetorically.

retorico, a, ci, che [re'tɔriko] AGG rhetorical; **domanda retorica** rhetorical question; **figura retorica** rhetorical device.

retrattile [re'trattile] AGG (*Zool*: *unghie*) retractile; (*Aer*: *carrello*) retractable.

retribuire [retribu'ire] VT (*gen*) to pay; **retribuire il lavoro di qn** to pay sb for his (*o* her) work; **un lavoro mal retribuito** a poorly-paid job.

retributivo, a [retribu'tivo] AGG pay *attr*.

retribuzione [retribut'tsjone] SF (*stipendio*) pay, remuneration.

retrivo, a [re'trivo] AGG, SM/F reactionary.

retro[1] ['retro] ① SM (*gen*) back; (*di auto*) rear, back.

② AVV: **"vedi retro"** "see over(leaf)".

retro[2] [re'tro] AGG INV: **la moda retro** retro fashion.

retroattività [retroattivi'ta] SF (*Dir*) retroactivity.

retroattivo, a [retroat'tivo] AGG (*Dir*: *legge*) retroactive.

retrobottega, ghe [retrobot'tega] SF back shop.

retrocedere [retro'tʃɛdere] VB IRREG ① VT (*Mil*) to demote; (*Sport*) to relegate.

② VI (*aus* **essere**) (*gen*) to move back; (*esercito*) to retreat; (*fig*: *di fronte a minacce*) to back down; **retrocedere in serie B** (*Calcio*) to be relegated to the second division.

retrocessione [retrotʃes'sjone] SF (*Mil, di impiegato*) demotion; (*Sport*) relegation.

retrocesso, a [retro'tʃɛsso] PP di **retrocedere**.

retrodatare [retroda'tare] VT (*Amm*) to backdate.

retrodatazione [retrodatat'tsjone] SF backdating.

retrofit ['retrofit] SM INV (*Aut*: *catalizzatore*) catalytic converter (*fitted after manufacture*).

retrogrado, a [re'trɔgrado] ① AGG **a** (*retrivo*: *persona, idee*) reactionary, backward-looking **b** (*Astron*: *moto*) retrograde, backward.

② SM/F reactionary.

retroguardia [retro'gwardja] SF (*anche fig*) rearguard.

retromarcia [retro'martʃa] SF (*Aut*) reverse; (: *dispositivo*) reverse gear; **inserire la retromarcia** to select reverse gear; **andare in retromarcia** OR **fare retromarcia** to reverse.

retroscena [retroʃ'ʃɛna] ① SF INV (*Teatro*) backstage.

② SM INV (*fig*) behind-the-scenes activity.

retrospettivamente [retrospettiva'mente] AVV retrospectively.

retrospettivo, a [retrospet'tivo] ① AGG retrospective.

② SF (*Arte*) retrospective (exhibition).

retrostante [retros'tante] AGG: **retrostante (a)** at the back (of).

retroterra [retro'tɛrra] SM INV **a** (*zona*) hinterland **b** (*sfondo*): **retroterra culturale/storico** historical/cultural background.

retrovia [retro'via] SF (*Mil*) zone behind the front; **mandare nelle retrovie** to send to the rear.

retrovisore [retrovi'zore] SM (*Aut: anche:* **specchietto retrovisore**) rear-view mirror; (: *laterale*) wing (*Brit*) o side (*Am*) mirror.

retta ['rɛtta] SF a (*Geom*) straight line b (*di collegio, convitto*) fee, charge for bed and board c (*fig: ascolto*): **dare retta a** to pay attention to, listen to.

rettamente [retta'mente] AVV (*in modo onesto*) honestly; (*in modo esatto*) strictly.

rettangolare [rettango'lare] AGG rectangular.

rettangolo, a [ret'tangolo] 1 AGG right-angled. 2 SM rectangle.

rettifica, che [ret'tifika] SF correction, rectification; **pubblicare una rettifica** (*su giornale*) to publish a retraction; **rettifica delle valvole** (*Aut*) valve grinding.

rettificare [rettifi'kare] VT a (*gen*) to rectify, correct b (*Chim, Elettr, Mat*) to rectify.

rettificazione [rettifikat'tsjone] SF rectification.

rettifilo [retti'filo] SM (*di strada*) straight (stretch).

rettile ['rɛttile] SM reptile.

rettilineo, a [retti'lineo] 1 AGG (*gen, Mat*) rectilinear; (*strada*) straight. 2 SM (*di strada*) straight; **in rettilineo** on the straight; **rettilineo d'arrivo** (*Sport*) home straight.

rettitudine [retti'tudine] SF rectitude, uprightness.

retto, a ['rɛtto] 1 PP di **reggere**. 2 AGG a (*gen, linea*) straight; **angolo retto** right angle b (*fig: onesto*) honest, upright; **abbandonare la retta via** (*fig*) to stray from the straight and narrow; **seguire la retta via** (*fig*) to keep to the straight and narrow. 3 SM (*Anat*) rectum.

rettore [ret'tore] SM a (*Univ*) ≈ chancellor b (*Rel*) rector.

reumatico, a, ci, che [reu'matiko] AGG rheumatic.

reumatismo [reuma'tizmo] SM rheumatism.

Rev. ABBR (= *Reverendo*) Rev(d).

revanscismo [revan'ʃizmo] SM revanchism.

reverendo [reve'rɛndo] AGG, SM Reverend.

reverente [reve'rɛnte] AGG = **riverente**.

reverenza [reve'rɛntsa] SF = **riverenza**.

reverenziale [reveren'tsjale] AGG (*titolo*) reverential; **timore reverenziale** awe.

revers [rə'vɛr] SM INV lapel.

reversibile [rever'sibile] AGG (*gen*) reversible; (*Econ*) convertible, negotiable; (*Dir*) revertible.

reversibilità [reversibili'ta] SF (*vedi agg*) reversibility; convertibility, negotiability; revertibility.

revisionare [revizjo'nare] VT (*Aut*) to service, overhaul; (*Fin: conti*) to audit.

revisione [revi'zjone] SF (*di contratto, processo, sentenza*) review; (*di macchina*) servicing *no pl*, overhaul; (*di conti*) auditing *no pl*; (*di testo*) revision ▶ **revisione di bilancio** audit ▶ **revisione di bozze** proofreading ▶ **revisione contabile interna** internal audit ▶ **revisione dello stipendio** salary review.

revisionismo [revizjo'nizmo] SM (*Pol*) revisionism.

revisionista [revizjo'nista] AGG, SM/F (*Pol*) revisionist.

revisore [revi'zore] SM: **revisore di bozze** proofreader ▶ **revisore dei conti** auditor.

revival [ri'vaivəl] SM INV revival.

revivalismo [reviva'lizmo] SM revivalism.

revivalista, i, e [reviva'lista] SM/F revivalist.

reviviscenza [reviviʃ'ʃɛntsa] SF (*Bio, Med*) revivescence.

revoca, che ['rɛvoka] SF (*Dir*) repeal, revocation.

revocare [revo'kare] VT (*gen*) to revoke, repeal; (*licenza*) to revoke.

revocatorio, ria, ri, rie [revoka'tɔrjo] AGG revocatory, revocative.

revolver [re'vɔlver] SM INV revolver.

revolverata [revolve'rata] SF revolver shot.

Reykjavik ['reikjavik] SF Reykjavik.

RFT ['ɛrre'effe'ti] SIGLA F (= *Repubblica Federale Tedesca*) FRG.

Rh ['ɛrre'akka] SIGLA M (*Med*): **fattore Rh** rhesus factor; **Rh positivo/negativo** rhesus positive/negative.

riabbassare [riabbas'sare] 1 VT to lower again. 2 **riabbassarsi** VIP (*marea*) to ebb, recede.

riabbia *ecc* [ri'abbja] VB vedi **riavere**.

riabbottonare [riabbotto'nare] VT to button up again.

riabbracciare [riabbrat'tʃare] VT (*abbracciare di nuovo*) to embrace (o hug) again; (*rivedere*) to see (o meet) again; **spero di riabbracciarvi presto** (*nella corrispondenza*) hoping to see you again soon.

riabilitare [riabili'tare] 1 VT (*gen*) to rehabilitate; (*fig*) to restore to favour (*Brit*) o favor (*Am*); **quel gesto lo ha riabilitato ai miei occhi** his action restored my good opinion of him. 2 **riabilitarsi** VR to be rehabilitated; **riabilitarsi agli occhi di qn** to redeem o.s. in sb's eyes.

riabilitazione [riabilitat'tsjone] SF rehabilitation.

riabituare [riabitu'are] 1 VT to reaccustom. 2 **riabituarsi** VR: **riabituarsi a qc/a fare qc** to reaccustom o.s. to sth/to doing sth.

riaccendere [riat'tʃɛndere] VB IRREG 1 VT (*sigaretta, fuoco, gas*) to light again; (*luce, radio, TV*) to switch on again; (*fig: sentimenti, interesse*) to rekindle, revive. 2 **riaccendersi** VIP (*fuoco*) to catch again; (*luce*) to come back on again; (*fig: sentimenti, interesse*) to revive, be rekindled.

riacceso, a [riat'tʃeso] PP di **riaccendere**.

riacchiappare [riakkjap'pare] VT (*fam*) to nab again.

riacciuffare [riattʃuf'fare] VT = **riacchiappare**.

riacquistare [riakkwis'tare] VT (*gen*) to buy again; (*ciò che si era venduto*) to buy back; (*fig: buonumore, sangue freddo, libertà*) to regain; **riacquistare la salute** to recover (one's health); **riacquistare le forze** to regain one's strength.

riacutizzarsi [riakutid'dzarsi] VIP (*malattia*) to worsen again.

Riad [ri'ad] SF Riyadh.

riadattamento [riadatta'mento] SM (*a luogo, ambiente*) readjustment.

riadattare [riadat'tare] 1 VT (*abito*) to alter; (*locale*) to convert. 2 **riadattarsi** VR: **riadattarsi a qc/a fare qc** to readjust to sth/to doing sth.

riaddormentare [riaddormen'tare] 1 VT to put to sleep again. 2 **riaddormentarsi** VIP to fall asleep again.

riadoperare [riadope'rare] VT to reuse.

riaffacciarsi [riaffat'tʃarsi] 1 VR: **riaffacciarsi (a)** (*finestra*) to appear (at) again. 2 **riaffacciarsi** VIP: **l'idea gli si riaffacciò alla mente** the idea occurred to him again.

riaffondare [riaffon'dare] VI (*aus essere*) to sink again; **riaffondare nel fango** to sink back into the mud.

riaffrontare [riaffron'tare] VT (*questione*) to deal with again; (*discorso*) to take up again.

riagganciare [riaggan'tʃare] ① VT (*con un gancio*) to rehook; (*vagone*) to re-couple; (*Telec*): **riagganciare (il ricevitore)** to hang up.
② **riagganciarsi** VIP (*ricollegarsi*): **riagganciarsi a** (*fig*) to draw on, be connected with.
③ **riagganciarsi** VR: **per riagganciarmi a quanto hai detto prima**... in connection with what you were saying earlier ... .

riallacciare [riallat'tʃare] ① VT (*cintura, cavo ecc*) to refasten, to tie up *o* fasten again; (*cappotto*) to do up again; (*fig: rapporti, amicizia*) to resume, renew; **riallacciarsi il cappotto** to do one's coat up again.
② **riallacciarsi** VIP (*fig: ricollegarsi*): **riallacciarsi a** to draw on, to have links with.
③ **ricollegarsi** VR: **mi riallaccio a quello che ha detto il mio collega**... to go back to what my colleague was saying ... .

riallargare [riallar'gare] ① VT (*passaggio, strada*) to widen; (*vestiti*) to let out.
② **riallargarsi** VIP (*strada*) to get wider.

riallungare [riallun'gare] ① VT (*gen*) to lengthen again; (*vestiti*) to lengthen.
② **riallungarsi** VIP (*giornate*) to grow longer.

rialzare [rial'tsare] ① VT to raise, lift; (*fondo stradale, superficie*) to make higher, raise, heighten; (*prezzi*) to increase, put up, raise.
② VI (*aus essere*) (*prezzi, azioni, febbre*) to rise, go up.
③ **rialzarsi** VR (*persona*) to get up.

rialzato, a [rial'tsato] AGG: **piano rialzato** mezzanine, entresol.

rialzista, i, e [rial'tsista] SM/F (*Borsa*) bull.

rialzo [ri'altso] SM **a** (*Econ*): **rialzo (di)** rise (in), increase (in); **essere in rialzo** (*azioni, prezzi*) to be up; **giocare al rialzo** (*Borsa*) to bull; **tendenza al rialzo** (*Borsa*) upward trend, bullish tendency **b** (*rilievo: di terreno*) rise.

riamare [ria'mare] VT (*amare a propria volta*) to love in return; **amare senza essere riamati è doloroso** unrequited love is a painful experience.

riammalarsi [riamma'larsi] VIP to fall ill again.

riammettere [riam'mettere] VT (*alunno, socio*) to readmit.

riandare [rian'dare] VI IRREG (*aus essere*): **riandare (in)** *o* (**a**) to go back (to), return (to); **riandare con la memoria a qc** (*fig*) to reminisce about sth, think back to sth.

rianimare [riani'mare] ① VT (*Med*) to resuscitate; (*fig: rallegrare*) to cheer up; (*: dar coraggio*) to give heart to; **rianimare una festa** to liven up a party.
② **rianimarsi** VIP (*vedi vt*) to recover consciousness; to cheer up; to take heart; to liven up; **d'estate il paesino si rianima** the village comes to life in the summer.

rianimazione [rianimat'tsjone] SF (*Med*) resuscitation; **(centro di) rianimazione** intensive care (unit).

riannodare [rianno'dare] VT (*lacci*) to retie; (*cravatta*) to reknot; (*fig: amicizia*) to renew.

riaperto, a [ria'pɛrto] PP di **riaprire**.

riapertura [riaper'tura] SF reopening.

riapparire [riappa'rire] VI IRREG (*aus essere*) to reappear.

riapparizione [riapparit'tsjone] SF reappearance.

riapparso, a [riap'parso] PP di **riapparire**.

riappendere [riap'pɛndere] VT IRREG to hang up again, rehang; (*Telec*) to hang up.

riappeso, a [riap'pɛso] PP di **riappendere**.

riappisolarsi [riappizo'larsi] VIP to doze (*o* nod) off again.

riappropriarsi [riappro'prjarsi] VIP: **riappropriarsi di qc** to take sth back.

riaprire [ria'prire] (VB IRREG) VT, **riaprirsi** VIP to reopen, open again.

riarmare [riar'mare] VT, **riarmarsi** VR to rearm.

riarmo [ri'armo] SM (*Mil*) rearmament.

riarso, a [ri'arso] AGG (*terreno*) arid; (*gola*) parched; (*labbra*) dry.

riascoltare [riaskol'tare] VT: **riascoltare qn/qc** to listen to sb/sth again.

riassettare [riasset'tare] VT (*stanza*) to rearrange.

riassetto [rias'sɛtto] SM (*di sistema*) reorganization.

riassicurare [riassiku'rare] VT (*Assicurazioni*) to reinsure.

riassicurazione [riassikurat'tsjone] SF (*Assicurazioni*) re-insurance.

riassorbimento [riassorbi'mento] SM reabsorption.

riassumere [rias'sumere] VT IRREG **a** (*ricapitolare: storia, racconto*) to summarize **b** (*operaio, impiegato, domestico*) to re-employ **c** (*riprendere: attività, funzione*) to resume.

riassumibile [riassu'mibile] AGG (*conferenza, racconto*): **è riassumibile in poche parole** it can be summed up in a few words.

riassuntivo, a [riassun'tivo] AGG summarizing, recapitulatory.

riassunto, a [rias'sunto] ① PP di **riassumere**.
② SM summary.

riattaccare [riattak'kare] VT **a** (*attaccare di nuovo*): **riattaccare (a)** (*manifesto, francobollo*) to stick back (on); (*bottone*) to sew back (on); (*quadro*) to hang back up (on); **riattaccare (il telefono** *o* **il ricevitore)** to hang up (the receiver)
b (*riprendere*): **riattaccare discorso con qn** to begin talking to sb again; **riattaccare a fare qc** to begin doing sth again.

riattare [riat'tare] VT (*casa*) to do up, renovate.

riattivare [riatti'vare] VT **a** (*strada, linea ferroviaria*) to reopen **b** (*Med*) to stimulate; (*Cosmesi*) to reactivate; **riattivare la circolazione del sangue** to get the circulation going again **c** (*macchina, motore*) to start up again.

riattivazione [riattivat'tsjone] SF (*di strada, linea ferroviaria*) reopening; (*Med: della circolazione*) stimulation.

riavere [ria'vere] VB IRREG ① VT **a** (*gen*) to have again; **oggi ho riavuto la nausea** I felt sick again today **b** (*recuperare: soldi, libro ecc*) to get back; **far riavere qn** (*da svenimento*) to bring sb round.
② **riaversi** VIP (*da svenimento, stordimento*) to come round; **riaversi dallo stupore** to recover from one's surprise.

riavuto, a [ria'vuto] PP di **riavere**.

riavvicinamento [riavvitʃina'mento] SM (*di persone*) reconciliation; (*di paesi*) rapprochement.

riavvicinare [riavvitʃi'nare] ① VT: **riavvicinare qc a qc** to put sth near sth again; **riavvicinò la sedia al tavolo** he drew the chair up to the table again; **riavvicina i due quadri** put the two pictures next to one another again.
② **riavvicinarsi** VR: **riavvicinarsi a qc** to approach again; **riavvicinarsi a qn** (*riconciliarsi*) to make one's peace with sb, to make it up with sb.

ribadire [riba'dire] VT to reaffirm, confirm.

ribalta [ri'balta] SF **a** (*Teatro, proscenio*) front of the stage; (*: apparecchio d'illuminazione*) footlights pl; **essere/venire alla ribalta** (*fig*) to be in/come into the limelight; **tornare alla ribalta** (*personaggio*) to make a comeback;

(*problema*) to come up again **b** (*piano, sportello*) flap; (*mobile*) bureau (*Brit*).

ribaltabile [ribal'tabile] AGG (*sedile*) tip-up *attr*.

ribaltare [ribal'tare] **1** VT (*rovesciare*) to overturn, tip over; (*fig: situazione*) to reverse; (: *questione*) to turn round.
2 VI (*aus* essere), **ribaltarsi** VIP to overturn, tip over.

ribassare [ribas'sare] **1** VT (*prezzi*) to lower, bring down.
2 VI (*aus* essere) to fall, come down.

ribassista, i, e [ribas'sista] SM/F (*Borsa*) bear.

ribasso [ri'basso] SM (*Econ*): **ribasso (di)** fall *o* reduction (in); **essere in ribasso** (*azioni, prezzi*) to be down; (*fig: popolarità*) to be on the decline; **giocare al ribasso** (*Borsa*) to bear; **tendenza al ribasso** (*Borsa*) downtrend, bearish tendency.

ribattere [ri'battere] VT **a** (*controbattere a: accuse*) to refute; **ribattere che...** to retort that ... **b** (*battere di nuovo*) to beat again; (*con macchina da scrivere*) to type again; **ribattere (una palla)** to return a ball.

ribattezzare [ribatted'dzare] VT to rename.

ribellarsi [ribel'larsi] VIP: **ribellarsi (a** *o* **contro)** to rebel (against).

ribelle [ri'bɛlle] **1** AGG (*soldati, truppe*) rebel; (*carattere, ragazzo*) rebellious; (*capelli*) unruly.
2 SM/F rebel.

ribellione [ribel'ljone] SF: **ribellione (a** *o* **contro)** rebellion (against).

ribes ['ribes] SM INV (*Bot*) currant ►**ribes nero** blackcurrant ►**ribes rosso** redcurrant.

riboflavina [ribofla'vina] SF (*Chim*) riboflavin.

ribollire [ribol'lire] VI (*aus* avere) (*liquido*) to bubble, boil; (*mare*) to seethe; (*vino*) to ferment; **scene che fanno ribollire il sangue** (*fig*) scenes which make one's blood boil.

ribrezzo [ri'breddzo] SM disgust, repugnance, loathing; **avere ribrezzo di qc** OR **provare ribrezzo per qc** to be disgusted at *o* by sth; **far ribrezzo a qn** to disgust sb.

ributtante [ribut'tante] AGG disgusting, revolting.

ributtare [ribut'tare] **1** VT **a** (*buttare di nuovo*) to throw back **b** (*vomitare*) to bring up.
2 **ributtarsi** VR to throw o.s. back; **ributtarsi a letto** to jump back into bed.

ricacciare [rikat'tʃare] VT (*respingere*) to drive back; **ricacciare fuori qn** to throw sb out; **ricacciare un urlo in gola** to smother/stifle a cry.

ricadere [rika'dere] VI IRREG (*aus* essere) **a** (*cadere di nuovo*) to fall again; (*fig*): **ricadere nel vizio** to fall back into bad habits; **ricadere nell'errore** to lapse into error **b** (*riversarsi: responsabilità, colpa*): **ricadere su** to fall on **c** (*scendere*) to fall, drop; **i capelli le ricadevano sulle spalle** her hair hung down over her shoulders.

ricaduta [rika'duta] SF **a** (*Med, fig*) relapse **b** (*Fis*): **ricaduta radioattiva** fallout.

ricalcare [rikal'kare] VT (*Disegno*) to trace; (*fig: imitare*) to follow closely *o* faithfully; **ricalcare le orme di qn** (*fig*) to follow in sb's footsteps.

ricalcitrante [rikaltʃi'trante] AGG (*mulo*) kicking; (*fig: persona*) recalcitrant, refractory.

ricalcitrare [rikaltʃi'trare] VI (*aus* avere) (*cavallo, asino, mulo*) to kick; (*fig: persona*): **recalcitrare (di fronte a)** to be recalcitrant (to).

ricamare [rika'mare] VT (*anche fig*) to embroider; **ci ha ricamato su** (*fig*) he's exaggerated it.

ricambiare [rikam'bjare] VT (*contraccambiare*) to return.

ricambio, bi [ri'kambjo] SM **a** (*di biancheria, abiti*) change; **una camicia di ricambio** a spare shirt; **pezzi di ricambio** (*Tecn*) spare parts **b** (*Fisiologia*) metabolism **c** : **ricambio del lavoro** (labour (*Brit*) *o* labor (*Am*)) turnover ►**ricambio di magazzino** stock turnover.

ricamo [ri'kamo] SM embroidery; **da ricamo** embroidery *attr*; **senza ricami** (*fig*) without frills.

ricandidare [rikandi'dare] **1** VT (*Pol*) to present as a candidate again.
2 **ricandidarsi** VR to stand for election again.

ricapitolare [rikapito'lare] VT to recapitulate, sum up; **ricapitolando...** OR **per ricapitolare...** to sum up ... .

ricapitolazione [rikapitolat'tsjone] SF recapitulation, summary.

ricarica [ri'karika] SF (*di fucile*) reloading; (*di orologio*) rewinding; (*di penna*) refilling; (*di batteria*) recharging.

ricaricare [rikari'kare] VT (*arma, macchina fotografica*) to reload; (*orologio, giocattolo*) to rewind; (*penna*) to refill; (*batteria*) to recharge.

ricarico, chi [ri'kariko] SM (*Comm*) mark-up.

ricascare [rikas'kare] VI (*aus* essere) (*fam: in tranello, truffa*) to be had again.

ricattare [rikat'tare] VT to blackmail.

ricattatore, trice [rikatta'tore] SM/F blackmailer.

ricattatorio, ria, ri, rie [rikatta'tɔrjo] AGG (*lettera, telefonata*) blackmail *attr*; (*tono*) blackmailing.

ricatto [ri'katto] SM blackmail; **fare un ricatto a qn** to blackmail sb; **subire un ricatto** to be blackmailed ►**ricatto morale** emotional blackmail.

ricavare [rika'vare] VT **a** (*estrarre*): **ricavare (da)** to extract (from)
b (*ottenere*): **ricavare (da)** to get (from), obtain (from); **ricavare una gonna da un taglio di stoffa** to make a skirt out of a piece of material; **ricavare un profitto** to make a profit; **cosa ne ricavo io?** what do I get out of it?; **dalla vendita ha ricavato ben poco** he made very little on the sale.

ricavato [rika'vato] SM (*di vendite*) proceeds *pl*.

ricavo [ri'kavo] SM (*gen*) proceeds *pl*; (*Contabilità*) revenue.

riccamente [rikka'mente] AVV (*gen*) richly, sumptuously; **riccamente illustrato** lavishly illustrated.

ricchezza [rik'kettsa] SF **a** (*di persona, paese*) wealth; (*di terreno, colori*) richness; (*fig: abbondanza*) abundance; **con ricchezza di particolari** in great detail; **in questa zona c'è ricchezza di carbone** there's an abundance of coal in this area
b : **ricchezze** SFPL (*averi*) wealth *sg*, riches; (*tesori*) treasures; **ricchezze naturali** natural resources.

riccio¹, cia, ci, ce ['rittʃo] **1** AGG (*capelli*) curly; (*persona*) curly-haired, with curly hair.
2 SM **a** (*di capelli*) curl; **farsi i ricci** to curl one's hair **b** (*di legno, metallo*) shaving; (*di burro*) curl.

riccio², ci ['rittʃo] SM **a** (*Zool*) hedgehog; (: *anche*: **riccio di mare**) sea urchin **b** (*Bot*) chestnut husk.

ricciolo ['rittʃolo] SM curl.

ricciuto, a [rit'tʃuto] AGG (*testa*) curly; (*persona*) curly-haired.

ricco, a, chi, che ['rikko] **1** AGG **a** (*gen, fig*) rich; (*facoltoso*) rich, wealthy; (*fertile: terra*) rich, fertile; **è di famiglia ricca** he comes from a rich family; **essere ricco sfondato** to be rolling in money; **un piatto molto ricco** a very rich dish; **una ricca mancia** a large tip; **una ricca documentazione** a wealth of documentation

b : **ricco di** (*illustrazioni, idee*) full of; (*fauna, risorse, proteine, calorie*) rich in; **alimento ricco di vitamine** food rich in vitamins; **un ragazzo ricco di fantasia** a boy with a fertile imagination.

2 SM/F rich man/woman; **i ricchi** the rich, the wealthy.

ricerca, che [ri'tʃerka] SF **a** : **ricerca (di)** (*gen*) search (for); (*piacere, gloria*) pursuit (of); (*perfezione*) quest (for); **mettersi alla ricerca di** to go in search of, look *o* search *o* hunt for; **essere alla ricerca di** to be searching (*o* looking) for; **fare delle ricerche** (*inchiesta*) to make inquiries; **dopo anni di ricerche hanno ritrovato il bambino** after years of searching they found the child ▶**ricerca di mercato** market research ▶**ricerca operativa** operational research

b (*Univ*): **la ricerca** research; **lavoro di ricerca** piece of research; **fare delle ricerche su un argomento** to carry out *o* do research into a subject.

ricercare [ritʃer'kare] VT (*onore, gloria*) to seek; (*successo, piacere*) to pursue; (*motivi, cause*) to look for, try to determine; **è ricercato dalla polizia** he's wanted by the police.

ricercatamente [ritʃerkata'mente] AVV (*vestire*) elegantly, in a refined way; (*con affettazione*) affectedly.

ricercatezza [ritʃerka'tettsa] SF (*raffinatezza*) refinement; (: *pegg*) affectation.

ricercato, a [ritʃer'kato] 1 AGG **a** (*molto richiesto*) in great demand, much sought-after **b** (*raffinato: qualità, gusti, stile*) refined; (*pegg: affettato*) affected; (: *stile*) studied.

2 SM/F (*criminale*) wanted man/woman.

ricercatore, trice [ritʃerka'tore] SM/F (*Univ*) researcher.

ricetrasmettitore [ritʃetrazmetti'tore] SM, **ricetrasmittente** [ritʃetrazmit'tɛnte] SF transceiver, two-way radio.

ricetta [ri'tʃetta] SF **a** (*Med*) prescription; (*fig: antidoto*): **ricetta contro** remedy *o* cure *o* recipe for; **fare una ricetta a qn** to make out a prescription for sb **b** (*Culin*) recipe.

ricettacolo [ritʃet'takolo] SM (*luogo di raccolta*): **un ricettacolo per i microbi** a breeding-ground for germs; (*pegg: luogo malfamato*) den.

ricettario, ri [ritʃet'tarjo] SM **a** (*Med*) prescription pad **b** (*Culin*) recipe book.

ricettatore, trice [ritʃetta'tore] SM/F (*Dir*) receiver (of stolen goods).

ricettazione [ritʃettat'tsjone] SF (*Dir*) receiving (stolen goods).

ricettività [ritʃettivi'ta] SF receptiveness.

ricettivo, a [ritʃet'tivo] AGG receptive.

ricevente [ritʃe'vɛnte] 1 AGG (*Radio, TV*) receiving.

2 SM/F (*Comm*) receiver.

ricevere [ri'tʃevere] VT **a** (*gen*) to receive, get; (*voto*) to get; **ricevere uno schiaffo** to get *o* be given a slap; **ricevere un rifiuto** to meet with a refusal; **"confermiamo di aver ricevuto tale merce"** (*Comm*) "we acknowledge receipt of these goods"

b (*accogliere*) to welcome, receive; (*ammettere alla propria presenza*) to see, receive; **ricevere visite** to have visitors; **il dottore riceve il venerdì** the doctor has his surgery on Fridays; **il dottore la riceverà subito** the doctor will see you at once; **mi hanno ricevuto in salotto** they showed me into the living room

c (*TV, Radio*) to pick up, receive.

ricevimento [ritʃevi'mento] SM **a** (*festa*) reception; **ricevimento di nozze** wedding reception; **dare un ricevimento** to hold a reception *o* party **b** (*il ricevere*) receiving *no pl*,

receipt; **al ricevimento della merce** on receipt of the goods.

ricevitore [ritʃevi'tore] SM **a** (*Telec, Radio, Tecn*) receiver **b** : **ricevitore delle imposte** tax collector ▶**ricevitore del lotto** receiver for the State lottery ▶**ricevitore del totocalcio** football pools collector (*Brit*).

ricevitoria [ritʃevito'ria] SF: **ricevitoria delle imposte** ≈ Inland Revenue (*Brit*) *o* Internal Revenue (*Am*) Office ▶**ricevitoria del lotto** state lottery office ▶**ricevitoria del totocalcio** football pools office (*Brit*).

ricevuta [ritʃe'vuta] SF (*gen, Comm*) receipt; **accusare ricevuta di qc** to acknowledge receipt of sth ▶**ricevuta fiscale** official receipt (for tax purposes) ▶**ricevuta di ritorno** (*Posta*) advice of receipt ▶**ricevuta di versamento** receipt of payment.

ricezione [ritʃet'tsjone] SF (*Radio, TV*) reception.

richiamare [rikja'mare] 1 VT **a** (*gen, al telefono*) to call back; (*Mil, Inform*) to recall; **richiamare qn indietro** to call sb back; **richiamare le truppe** to withdraw the troops; **richiamare qn alla realtà** to bring sb back to earth; **richiamare qn in vita** to bring sb back to life

b (*attrarre: folla*) to attract, draw; **desidero richiamare la vostra attenzione su...** I should like to draw your attention to ...

c (*ricordare*): **richiamare qc alla memoria di qn** (*sogg: avvenimento*) to remind sb of sth; **è un colore che richiama il verde** it's a greenish colour

d (*rimproverare*) to reprimand; **richiamare qn all'ordine** to call sb to order.

2 **richiamarsi** VIP: **richiamarsi a** (*riferirsi a*) to refer to.

richiamato [rikja'mato] SM recalled serviceman.

richiamo [ri'kjamo] SM **a** (*di truppe*) recall

b (*voce, segno*) call; **il richiamo della foresta/della natura** the call of the wild/of nature; **uccello da richiamo** decoy; **servire da richiamo** (*fig: attrazione*) to act as a decoy

c (*ammonimento*) reprimand; **richiamo all'ordine** call to order

d (*Med: di vaccinazione*) booster

e (*rimando*) cross-reference.

richiedente [rikje'dɛnte] SM/F applicant.

richiedere [ri'kjɛdere] VT IRREG **a** (*chiedere: di nuovo*) to ask again; **richiedere qc** (*in restituzione*) to ask for sth back

b (*chiedere: prestito, aiuto*) to ask for; (: *passaporto, licenza*) to apply for; **hanno richiesto il suo intervento** they asked him to intervene; **tutto ciò non è richiesto** all that is not necessary; **il tuo intervento non era richiesto** no-one asked you to intervene; **essere molto richiesto** to be in great demand

c (*necessitare*) to need, require; **tutto ciò richiede tempo e pazienza** all this requires time and patience.

richiesta [ri'kjɛsta] SF **a** (*gen*): **richiesta (di)** request (for); (*impiego, documenti, congedo*) application (for); (*salario migliore, condizioni migliori*) demand (for); **su** *o* **a richiesta** on request; **a richiesta generale** by general request; **a grande richiesta** by popular demand; **programma a richiesta** (*Radio, TV*) request programme (*Brit*) *o* program (*Am*); **fermata a richiesta** request stop

b (*Comm, Econ*) demand.

richiesto, a [ri'kjɛsto] PP di **richiedere**.

richiudere [ri'kjudere] VB IRREG 1 VT (*porta, finestra, cassetto*) to close again, shut again; **aprì gli occhi e li richiuse subito** she opened her eyes and closed them again immediately.

2 richiudersi VIP (*porta*) to close again; (*ferita*) to close up, heal.

richiuso, a [ri'kjuso] PP di **richiudere**.

riciclaggio, gi [ritʃi'kladdʒo] SM (*di carta, vetro*) recycling; **riciclaggio di denaro sporco** money laundering.

riciclare [ritʃi'klare] VT (*carta, vetro*) to recycle; (*denaro sporco*) to launder.

ricino ['ritʃino] SM (*Bot*) castor-oil plant; **olio di ricino** castor oil.

ricognitore [rikoɲɲi'tore] SM (*Aer*) reconnaissance aircraft *pl inv.*

ricognizione [rikoɲɲit'tsjone] SF **a** (*Mil*) reconnaissance; **uscire in ricognizione** to reconnoitre **b** (*Dir*) recognition, acknowledgement.

ricollegare [rikolle'gare] **1** VT **a** (*collegare nuovamente*: *gen*) to join *o* link again **b** (*connettere*: *fatti*): **ricollegare (a, con)** to connect (with), associate (with).

2 ricollegarsi VIP: **ricollegarsi a** (*sogg*: *fatti*: *connettersi*) to be connected to, be associated with.

3 ricollegarsi VR (*persona*: *riferirsi*) to refer to.

ricolmare [rikol'mare] VT: **ricolmare qn di** (*fig*: *regali, gentilezze*) to shower sb with.

ricolmo, a [ri'kolmo] AGG: **ricolmo (di)** (*bicchiere*) full to the brim (with); (*stanza, armadio*) full (of); **ricolmo di gioia** overflowing with joy.

ricominciare [rikomin'tʃare] **1** VT to start again, begin again; **ricominciare a fare qc** to begin doing *o* to do sth again, start doing *o* to do sth again; **ha ricominciato a fumare** he's started smoking again; **ah, si ricomincia!** here we go again!; **ha ricominciato con la mania dei francobolli** he's off on his stamp craze again.

2 VI (*aus* **essere** *o* **avere**) (*spettacolo*) to start, begin; **è ricominciato l'inverno** winter is here again; **ricomincia a piovere** it's raining again.

ricomparire [rikompa'rire] VI IRREG (*aus* **essere**) (*riapparire*: *persona*) to reappear; (: *sole*) to come out again; (: *sorriso*) to return.

ricomparsa [rikom'parsa] SF reappearance.

ricomparso, a [rikom'parso] PP di **ricomparire**.

ricompensa [rikom'pensa] SF reward.

ricompensare [rikompen'sare] VT to reward.

ricomporre [rikom'porre] VB IRREG **1** VT **a** (*viso, lineamenti*) to recompose **b** (*Tip*) to reset.

2 ricomporsi VR to compose o.s., regain one's composure.

ricomposto, a [rikom'posto] PP di **ricomporre**.

riconciliare [rikontʃi'ljare] **1** VT to reconcile.

2 riconciliarsi VR **a**: **riconciliarsi con qn** to make it up with sb, make one's peace with sb **b** (*uso reciproco*) to be reconciled; (: *amici*) to make friends again, make it up again, make peace.

riconciliazione [rikontʃiliat'tsjone] SF reconciliation.

ricondotto, a [rikon'dotto] PP di **ricondurre**.

ricondurre [rikon'durre] VT IRREG (*gen*) to bring (*o* take) back.

riconferma [rikon'ferma] SF reconfirmation.

riconfermare [rikonfer'mare] VT to reconfirm.

ricongiungere [rikon'dʒundʒere] VB IRREG **1** VT to join together; (*persone*) to reunite.

2 ricongiungersi VR **a**: **ricongiungersi a** (*famiglia*) to be reunited with **b** (*uso reciproco*: *eserciti*) to reunite.

ricongiunto, a [rikon'dʒunto] PP di **ricongiungere**.

riconoscente [rikonoʃ'ʃente] AGG grateful.

riconoscenza [rikonoʃ'ʃɛntsa] SF gratitude.

riconoscere [riko'noʃʃere] VB IRREG **1** VT **a** (*identificare*) to recognize; (: *cadavere, salma*) to identify; **l'ho riconosciuto dalla voce** I recognized him by his voice; **per non farsi riconoscere** so as not to be recognized; **farsi riconoscere** (*esibendo documento*) to provide identification

b (*ammettere*: *gen*) to recognize; (: *errore, torto*) to admit, acknowledge; (: *superiorità*) to acknowledge; **devo riconoscere che hai ragione** I must admit you're right; **riconoscere i propri limiti** to recognize one's own limitations; **riconoscere a qn il diritto di fare qc** to acknowledge sb's right to do sth

c (*Dir*): **riconoscere un figlio** to acknowledge a child; **riconoscere qn colpevole** to find sb guilty.

2 riconoscersi VR **a** (*ammettere*): **riconoscersi colpevole** to admit one's guilt; **si riconobbe sconfitto** he admitted he was beaten

b (*uso reciproco*) to recognize each other.

riconoscibile [rikonoʃ'ʃibile] AGG recognizable.

riconoscimento [rikonoʃʃi'mento] SM (*gen, di diritti*) recognition; (*Dir*: *di figlio*) acknowledgement; (*di cadavere, salma*) identification; **documento di riconoscimento** means *pl* of identification; **come riconoscimento dei servizi resi** in recognition of services rendered; **segno di riconoscimento** distinguishing mark.

riconosciuto, a [rikonoʃ'ʃuto] **1** PP di **riconoscere**.

2 AGG recognized.

riconquista [rikon'kwista] SF (*Mil*) reconquest, recapture; (*di libertà*) recovery.

riconquistare [rikonkwis'tare] VT (*Mil*) to reconquer, recapture; (*libertà, stima*) to win back.

riconsegna [rikon'seɲɲa] SF (*restituzione*) handing back.

riconsegnare [rikonseɲ'ɲare] VT (*restituire*) to hand back, give back.

riconsiderare [rikonside'rare] VT to reconsider.

riconsiderazione [rikonsiderat'tsjone] SF reconsideration.

riconversione [rikonver'sjone] SF (*Econ*) reconversion.

ricoperto, a [riko'pɛrto] **1** PP di **ricoprire**.

2 SM (*gelato*): **un ricoperto (al cioccolato)** choc-ice (*Brit*) *o* ice cream bar (*Am*) on a stick.

ricopiare [riko'pjare] VT to copy; **ricopiare qc in bella (copia)** to make a fair copy of sth.

ricopiatura [rikopja'tura] SF copying.

ricopribile [riko'pribile] AGG (*divano, poltrona*) with loose covers.

ricoprire [riko'prire] VB IRREG **1** VT **a** (*gen*): **ricoprire (di)** to cover (with); (*divano, poltrona*) to re-cover (with); (*fig*: *persona*: *di gentilezze*) to shower (with); **ricoprire un dente** to cap a tooth

b (*carica*) to hold.

2 ricoprirsi VIP: **ricoprirsi di** (*polvere*) to become covered in; **il cielo si è ricoperto di nuvole** the sky clouded over; **il prato si è ricoperto di fiori** the field is covered with flowers.

ricordare [rikor'dare] **1** VT **a** (*nome, persona, fatto*) to remember, recall; **ricordare di fare qc** to remember to do sth; **ricordare di aver fatto qc** to remember having done *o* doing sth; **se ben ricordo** if I remember rightly; **ti ricordo con affetto** (*nella corrispondenza*) I often think of you

b (*far presente ad altri*): **ricordare a qn qc/di fare qc** to remind sb of sth/to do sth; **ti ricordo che c'ero prima io** I'd like to remind you that I was here first; **scene che**

ricordano il passato scenes which recall the past; **mi ricorda molto suo padre** he reminds me a lot of his father
  c (*menzionare*) to mention
  d (*commemorare*) to commemorate.
  [2] **ricordarsi** VIP: **ricordarsi (di)** to remember; **ricordarsi di fare qc** to remember to do sth; **ricordarsi di avere fatto qc** to remember having done *o* doing sth; **ti ricordi di me?** do you remember me?; **non si è più ricordato di darmi il libro** he forgot to give me the book; **non si ricorda dal naso alla bocca** (*fig fam*) he would forget his own name.

ricordino [rikor'dino] SM souvenir.

ricordo [ri'kɔrdo] [1] SM **a** (*memoria*) memory; **non ho che un vago ricordo di quella giornata** I have only a vague recollection of that day, I only remember that day vaguely; **vivere di ricordi** to live in the past
  b (*oggetto*) keepsake; (: *turistico*) souvenir; **prendere/dare qc per** *o* **in ricordo** to take/give sth as a keepsake; **un ricordo di famiglia** a family heirloom.
  [2] AGG INV (*foto*) souvenir *attr*.

ricorreggere [rikor'rɛddʒere] VT (*gen*) to correct again; (*esame*) to mark (*Brit*) *o* grade (*Am*) again.

ricorrente [rikor'rɛnte] [1] AGG recurring, recurrent.
  [2] SM/F (*Dir*) plaintiff.

ricorrenza [rikor'rɛntsa] SF **a** (*il ricorrere*) recurrence **b** (*anniversario*) anniversary.

ricorrere [ri'korrere] VI IRREG (*aus* **essere**) **a** (*ripetersi periodicamente*) to recur; **oggi ricorre il 5 anniversario di...** today is the 5th anniversary of ...; **è un elemento che ricorre in tutta la sua poesia** it's a recurring element in all his poetry
  b (*far ricorso a*): **ricorrere a** (*persona*) to turn to; (*forza, stratagemma*) to resort to; **ricorrere alle vie legali** to take legal action
  c (*Dir*): **ricorrere contro una sentenza** to appeal against a sentence; **ricorrere in appello** to lodge an appeal.

ricorso, a [ri'korso] [1] PP di **ricorrere**.
  [2] SM **a**: **fare ricorso a** (*persona*) to turn to; (*mezzo, cosa*) to resort to; **dovette far ricorso a tutto il suo coraggio** he had to summon up all his courage
  b (*Dir*) appeal; **fare ricorso (contro)** to appeal (against)
  c (*il ricorrere*) recurrence; **un tipico esempio dei corsi e ricorsi della storia** a typical example of history repeating itself.

ricostituente [rikostitu'ɛnte] [1] AGG (*Med*): **cura ricostituente** tonic treatment.
  [2] SM (*Med*) tonic.

ricostituire [rikostitu'ire] [1] VT (*società*) to build up again; (*governo, partito*) to re-form.
  [2] **ricostituirsi** VIP (*gruppo, partito*) to re-form.

ricostruire [rikostru'ire] VT (*edificio*) to rebuild, reconstruct; (*testo, fatti, delitto*) to reconstruct.

ricostruzione [rikostrut'tsjone] SF (*di edificio*) reconstruction, rebuilding *no pl*; (*di testo, fatti, delitto*) reconstruction.

ricotta [ri'kɔtta] SF ricotta, *soft white unsalted cheese made from sheep's milk*.

ricoverare [rikove'rare] VT (*Med*): **ricoverare qn in ospedale** to admit sb to hospital; **far ricoverare qn in ospedale** to have sb admitted to hospital; **è stato ricoverato d'urgenza (in ospedale)** he has been rushed to hospital.

ricoverato, a [rikove'rato] SM/F patient.

ricovero [ri'kovero] SM **a** (*rifugio*) shelter, refuge **b** (*Med*) admission (to hospital); **foglio di ricovero** admission sheet.

ricreare [rikre'are] [1] VT **a** (*creare di nuovo*) to recreate **b** (*fig: svagare*) to cheer, amuse; **ricreare lo spirito** to restore one's spirits.
  [2] **ricrearsi** VR (*fig: svagarsi, divertirsi*) to enjoy o.s.

ricreativo, a [rikrea'tivo] AGG recreational; **circolo ricreativo** (*per adulti*) social club; (*per giovani*) youth club.

ricreazione [rikreat'tsjone] SF **a** (*Scol*) break; (*alle elementari*) break, playtime **a** (*svago*) recreation, entertainment.

ricredersi [ri'kredersi] VR: **ricredersi (su qc/qn)** to change one's mind (about sth/sb).

ricrescere [ri'kreʃʃere] VI IRREG (*aus* **essere**): **farsi ricrescere la barba** to let one's beard grow again.

ricresciuto, a [rikreʃ'ʃuto] PP di **ricrescere**.

ricucire [riku'tʃire] VT (*vestito, colletto*) to stitch *o* sew again; (*strappo, buco*) to mend; (*Med: ferita*) to stitch *o* sew up; (*fam: paziente*) to stitch back up.

ricuperabile [rikupe'rabile] AGG (*gen*) recoverable; (*che si può usare di nuovo*) re-usable.

ricuperare [rikupe'rare] VT **a** (*gen*) to recover; (*soldi*) to get back; (*peso*) to put back on; **ricuperare il tempo perduto** to make up for lost time; **ricuperare la salute/le forze** to recover (one's health)/one's strength; **ricuperare lo svantaggio** (*anche Sport*) to close the gap
  b (*da naufragio, incendio: persone*) to rescue; (: *salme*) to recover; (: *oggetti, relitto*) to salvage
  c (*disadattato, ex detenuto*) to rehabilitate
  d (*usare di nuovo: cascami, rottami*) to re-use
  e (*Sport*): **ricuperare una partita** to play a match which had been postponed.

ricupero [ri'kupero] SM **a** (*di relitto*) salvaging; (*di disadattato, ex detenuto*) rehabilitation; **di ricupero** (*merce, materiali*) salvage *attr*; **capacità di ricupero** resilience; **partita di ricupero** (*Sport*) postponed match; **minuti di ricupero** (*Sport*) injury time ▸ **ricupero (di) crediti** (*Comm*) debt collection.

ricurvo, a [ri'kurvo] AGG (*linea*) curved; **avere le spalle ricurve** to be round-shouldered; **stava ricurvo sul proprio lavoro** he was bent over his work.

ricusare [riku'zare] VT **a** (*offerta, carica*) to decline, to refuse **b** (*Dir*): **ricusare un giudice** to challenge a judge.

ridacchiare [ridak'kjare] VI (*aus* **avere**) to snigger.

ridanciano, a [ridan'tʃano] AGG (*persona*) jolly, fun-loving; (*storiella*) funny, amusing.

ridare [ri'dare] VT IRREG (*oggetto*) to give back, return; (*salute, felicità*) to restore.

ridarella [rida'rɛlla] SF giggles *pl*.

ridda ['ridda] SF (*di pensieri*) jumble.

ridente [ri'dɛnte] AGG (*occhi, volto*) smiling; (*paesaggio*) delightful.

ridere ['ridere] VB IRREG [1] VI (*aus* **avere**) (*gen*) to laugh; (*deridere, beffare*): **ridere di** to laugh at, make fun of; **ridere alle spalle di qn** [ᴏʀ] **ridere dietro a qn** to laugh behind sb's back; **ridere in faccia a qn** to laugh in sb's face; **ridere sotto i baffi** to laugh up one's sleeve; **ridere a denti stretti** to give a forced laugh; **cerchiamo di riderci sopra** let's try and see the funny side of it; **ridendo e scherzando si è fatto tardi** (*fig*) what with one thing and another, it got late; **ridere di cuore** *o* **di gusto** to laugh heartily; **ridere fino alle lacrime** to laugh till one cries; **ma non farmi ridere!** don't be ridiculous!,

don't make me laugh!; **non c'è niente da ridere** OR **c'è poco da ridere** it's not a laughing matter; **lo ha detto per ridere** he was only joking, he said it in fun; **si fa così per ridere** we're just joking; **è roba da ridere** (*facile*) it's nothing, it's dead easy (*fam*); **che ridere!** what a laugh!; **c'è da morire dal ridere!** it's hilarious!, it's really funny!; **le ridevano gli occhi** her eyes sparkled; **ride bene chi ride ultimo** (*Proverbio*) he who laughs last laughs longest (*Brit*) o (*Am*) best.

[2] **ridersi** VIP: **ridersela (di qc)** to laugh (at sth); **se la rideva** he had a laugh to himself.

ridestare [rides'tare] [1] VT (*fig: ricordi, passioni*) to re-awaken.

[2] **ridestarsi** VIP (*fig: odio*) to be roused again; (*amore, speranza*) to be rekindled.

ridetto, a [ri'detto] PP di **ridire**.

ridicolaggine [ridiko'laddʒine] SF (*di situazione*) absurdity; (*cosa detta o fatta*) nonsense *no pl.*

ridicolizzare [ridikolid'dzare] VT to ridicule.

ridicolizzazione [ridikoliddzat'tsjone] SF ridiculing.

ridicolmente [ridikol'mente] AVV ridiculously.

ridicolo [ri'dikolo] [1] AGG (*gen*) ridiculous, absurd; **rendersi ridicolo** to make a fool of o.s.

[2] SM: **il ridicolo della situazione** the absurdity of the situation; **il ridicolo della storia era che...** the ridiculous o absurd thing about it was ...; **cadere nel ridicolo** to become ridiculous; **mettere in ridicolo** to ridicule; **coprirsi di ridicolo** to make a laughing stock of o.s.

ridimensionamento [ridimensjona'mento] SM reorganization; (*di fatto storico*) reappraisal.

ridimensionare [ridimensjo'nare] [1] VT (*ditta, industria*) to reorganize; (*fig: problema, autore, fatto storico*) to put in perspective, see in the right perspective.

[2] **ridimensionarsi** VIP (*sogni, ambizioni*) to become more realistic.

ridipingere [ridi'pindʒere] VT to repaint.

ridire [ri'dire] VT IRREG **a** (*ripetere, riferire*) to repeat; **te l'ho detto e ridetto mille volte** I've told you over and over again **b** (*criticare*): **trovare da ridire (su qc/qn)** to find fault (with sth/sb); **che c'è da ridire?** what's your objection?

ridiscendere [ridiʃ'ʃendere] VI (*aus essere*), VT to go (o come) down again.

ridistribuire [ridistribu'ire] VT to redistribute.

ridistribuzione [ridistribut'tsjone] SF redistribution.

ridiventare [ridiven'tare] VI (*aus essere*): **ridiventare serio** to grow serious again.

ridonare [rido'nare] VT (*salute, allegria*) to restore, give back.

ridondante [ridon'dante] AGG (*linguaggio, frase*) flowery; (*discorso*) bombastic; **uno stile ridondante** (*gonfio*) a pompous style.

ridosso [ri'dɔsso]: **a ridosso di** AVV (*dietro*) behind; (*contro*) against; **costruire una casa a ridosso di una montagna** to build a house in the shelter of a mountain.

ridotto, a [ri'dotto] [1] PP di **ridurre**.

[2] AGG (*misura, formato*) small; (*versione, edizione*) abridged; (*tariffa*) cheap; (*prezzo*) reduced, cut; **marcia ridotta** (*Aut*) low gear ratio.

[2] SM (*Teatro*) foyer.

riduco *ecc* [ri'duko] VB vedi **ridurre**.

ridurre [ri'durre] VB IRREG [1] VT **a** (*gen, Mat*) to reduce; (*prezzo*) to reduce, cut, bring down; (*pressione*) to lessen; (*produzione*) to cut (back), lower; (*spese*) to cut

down on, cut back on

b (*opera letteraria: per la radio, TV*) to adapt; (: *accorciare*) to abridge; (*brano musicale*) to arrange

c (*fraseologia*): **ridurre qc in cenere** to reduce sth to ashes; **ridurre qn in poltiglia** (*fig*) to make mincemeat of sb; **guarda come hai ridotto quella gonna!** look at the state of your skirt!; **è proprio ridotto male** o **mal ridotto** (*oggetto*) it's really in bad condition; (*persona*) he's really in a bad way.

[2]: **ridursi** VIP **a** (*quantità*): **ridursi (a)** to be reduced (to); (*fig: questione, problema*) to come down (to); **il livello si è ridotto di un decimo** the level dropped by a tenth

b (*persona*): **ridursi male** to be in a bad state o way; **ridursi pelle e ossa** to be reduced to skin and bone; **ridursi a uno straccio** to be washed out; **si è ridotto a mendicare** he was reduced to begging; **come ti sei ridotto!** what a state you're in!

ridussi *ecc* [ri'dussi] VB vedi **ridurre**.

riduttivo, a [ridut'tivo] AGG: **è un giudizio riduttivo** it's an oversimplification.

riduttore [ridut'tore] SM (*Tecn, Chim, Elettr*) reducer.

riduzione [ridut'tsjone] SF **a** (*diminuzione: di salario, personale*): **riduzione (di)** reduction (in), cut (in)

b (*sconto*) reduction, discount; **una riduzione del 10%** a 10% reduction o discount

c (*di opera letteraria: adattamento*) adaptation; (: *accorciamento*) abridgement; **riduzione televisiva a cura di...** adapted for television by ...

d (*Mat, Chim, Med*) reduction.

riebbi *ecc* [ri'ɛbbi] VB vedi **riavere**.

riecheggiare [rieked'dʒare] VI (*aus essere*) to re-echo; **in questi versi riecheggiano motivi leopardiani** in these lines we find echoes of Leopardi.

riedificare [riedifi'kare] VT to rebuild.

riedificazione [riedifikat'tsjone] SF rebuilding.

rieducare [riedu'kare] VT (*persona, arto*) to re-educate; (*malato*) to rehabilitate.

rieducazione [riedukat'tsjone] SF (*vedi vb*) re-education; rehabilitation; **centro di rieducazione** rehabilitation centre.

rieleggere [rie'leddʒere] VT IRREG to re-elect.

rieletto, a [rie'letto] PP di **rieleggere**.

rielezione [rielet'tsjone] SF re-election.

riemergere [rie'mɛrdʒere] VI IRREG (*aus essere*) (*sottomarino*) to re-emerge; (*fig: problema*) to re-emerge, come up again.

riemerso, a [rie'mɛrso] PP di **riemergere**.

riempimento [riempi'mento] SM filling (up); (*Edil*): **materiali di riempimento** filling *sg.*

riempire [riem'pire] VB IRREG [1] VT (*gen, fig*): **riempire (di)** to fill o fill up (with); (*Culin: farcire*) to stuff (with); **riempire un modulo** to fill in o out a form; **riempirsi le tasche di** to fill one's pockets with; **si è riempito la testa di sciocchezze** he has filled his head with nonsense.

[2] **riempirsi** VIP (*gen*): **riempirsi (di)** to fill o fill up (with); **quel quadro si è riempito di polvere** that painting is covered in dust.

[3] **riempirsi** VR: **riempirsi di** (*cibo*) to stuff o.s. with.

riempitivo [riempi'tivo] [1] AGG filling.

[2] SM (*anche fig*) filler.

rientrante [rien'trante] AGG (*Archit*) receding.

rientranza [rien'trantsa] SF (*di costruzione*) recess; (*di costa*) indentation.

rientrare [rien'trare] VI (*aus essere*) **a** (*entrare di nuovo*) to

come (*o* go) back in
b (*ritornare*) to return, get back; **rientrare (a casa)** to get back home; **rientrare alla base** (*Mil*) to return to base; **rientrare in possesso di qc** to regain possession of sth
c (*fig: far parte di, essere incluso*): **rientrare in** to be included among, form part of; **non rientra nei miei doveri** it isn't my duty; **non rientriamo nelle spese** we are not within our budget
d (*superficie, linea*) to curve inwards, go in; (*costa*) to be indented.

rientro [ri'ɛntro] SM (*gen, ritorno*) return; (*di astronave*) re-entry; **l'ora del rientro** (*dal lavoro*) the evening rush hour; **è cominciato il grande rientro (dalle vacanze)** everyone is coming back from holiday.

riepilogare [riepilo'gare] VT (*discorso, fatti*) to summarize; **dunque, riepilogando...** to sum up, then ... .

riepilogo, ghi [rie'pilogo] SM recapitulation; **fare un riepilogo di qc** to summarize sth.

riesame [rie'zame] SM re-examination.

riesaminare [riezami'nare] VT to re-examine.

riesco ecc [ri'ɛsko] VB vedi **riuscire**.

riessere [ri'ɛssere] VI (*aus* **essere**): **ci risiamo!** (*fam*) we're back to this again!, here we go again!

riesumare [riezu'mare] VT (*cadavere*) to exhume, disinter.

riesumazione [riezumat'tsjone] SF (*di cadavere*) exhumation, disinterment.

rievocare [rievo'kare] VT (*passato*) to recall; (*commemorare: figura, meriti*) to commemorate.

rievocativo, a [rievoka'tivo] AGG (*mostra, cerimonia*) commemorative, memorial *attr*.

rievocazione [rievokat'tsjone] SF (*vedi vb*) recalling; commemoration.

rifacimento [rifatʃi'mento] SM (*di film*) remake; (*di opera letteraria*) rehashing.

rifare [ri'fare] VB IRREG 1 VT (*ricominciare*) to redo, do again; (*ricostruire*) to make again; (*nodo*) to tie again, do up again; **è tutto da rifare!** it will have to be completely redone!; **rifarsi la bocca** (*anche fig*) to take away a bad taste; **rifarsi il naso** to have a nose job; **rifarsi gli occhi** to look at something pleasant for a change; **rifare il letto** to make the bed; **rifarsi il trucco** to touch up one's make-up; **rifarsi una vita** to make a new life for o.s.; **rifarsi una verginità** to try to clear one's name.
2 **rifarsi** VIP a : **rifarsi vivo** to re-appear, turn up again
b (*ricuperare*): **rifarsi di** (*perdita, spesa*) to recover from; **rifarsi del tempo perduto** to make up for lost time; **rifarsi di qc su qn** (*vendicarsi*) to get one's own back on sb for sth, get even with sb for sth
c (*riferirsi*): **rifarsi a** (*periodo, fenomeno storico*) to go back to; (*stile, autore*) to follow.

rifatto, a [ri'fatto] PP di **rifare**.

riferimento [riferi'mento] SM reference; **in** *o* **con riferimento a** [OR] **facendo riferimento a** with reference to; **far riferimento a** to refer to; **punto di riferimento** (*anche fig*) point of reference.

riferire [rife'rire] 1 VT a (*raccontare, riportare*) to report; **andare a riferire qc a qn** to go and tell sb sth; **riferirò** I'll pass on the message **b** (*attribuire*): **riferire qc a** to attribute sth to.
2 VI: (*aus* **avere**): **riferire (su qc)** to make *o* do a report (on sth).
3 **riferirsi** VIP: **riferirsi a** to refer to.

rifilare [rifi'lare] VT a (*fam: affibbiare*): **rifilare qc a qn** to palm sth off on sb; **gli ho rifilato un ceffone** I gave him a slap **b** (*tagliare a filo*) to trim.

rifinire [rifi'nire] VT (*lavoro*) to finish off; (*opera d'arte, vestito*) to put the finishing touches to.

rifinito, a [rifi'nito] AGG (*mobile, abito*) well-finished.

rifinitura [rifini'tura] SF (*gen*) finishing touch; (*di mobile, auto*) finish *no pl*.

rifiorire [rifjo'rire] VI (*aus* **essere**) (*anche fig: persona*) to bloom again; (*fig: studi, arti*) to flourish again, thrive again.

rifiutare [rifju'tare] 1 VT (*gen*) to refuse; (*invito, offerta*) to turn down, decline; (*pretendente*) to turn down; **rifiutare qc a qn** to deny sb sth; **rifiutare di fare qc** to refuse to do sth.
2 **rifiutarsi** VIP: **rifiutarsi di fare qc** to refuse to do sth.

rifiuto [ri'fjuto] SM a (*diniego*) refusal; **opporre un rifiuto** to refuse **b** (*scarto*) waste; **rifiuti** SMPL (*immondizie*) refuse *sg*, rubbish (*Brit*) *sg*, garbage (*Am*), trash (*Am*); **i rifiuti della società** (*fig*) the dregs of society ▶ **rifiuti solidi urbani** solid urban waste.

riflessione [rifles'sjone] SF a (*meditazione*) reflection, meditation, thought; (*osservazione*) observation, remark; **dopo matura riflessione** after due consideration; **ha fatto delle interessanti riflessioni** he made some interesting observations **b** (*Fis*) reflection.

riflessivo, a [rifles'sivo] AGG a (*persona*) thoughtful, reflective **b** (*Gramm*) reflexive.

riflesso, a [ri'flesso] 1 PP di **riflettere**.
2 AGG (*immagine*) reflected; (*atto*) reflex *attr*.
3 SM a (*di luce*) reflection; (*di capelli: naturale*) light; (: *artificiale*) highlight; (*fig: ripercussione*) effect, repercussion; **di riflesso** indirectly **b** (*Fisiologia*) reflex; **avere i riflessi pronti** to have quick reflexes ▶ **riflesso condizionato** conditioned reflex.

riflettente [riflet'tɛnte] AGG (*Fis*) reflective.

riflettere [ri'flɛttere] VB IRREG 1 VI (*aus* **avere**): **riflettere (su qc)** (*meditare*) to reflect (upon sth); (*pensare*) to think (over sth); **se ti fermi a riflettere** if you stop and think; **agire senza riflettere** to act without thinking; **riflettendoci su...** on reflection ....
2 VT (*Fis: fig*) to reflect.
3 **riflettersi** VR a (*rispecchiarsi, anche fig*) to be reflected
b (*ripercuotersi*): **riflettersi su** to have repercussions on.

riflettore [riflet'tore] SM a (*Fis, Elettr*) reflector; (*Teatro, TV*) spotlight; (*proiettore*) floodlight; (*Mil*) searchlight; **essere sotto i riflettori** (*fig*) to be in the limelight **b** (*telescopio*) reflecting telescope.

riflettuto, a [riflet'tuto] PP di **riflettere** (*vi*).

rifluire [riflu'ire] VI (*aus* **essere**) (*scorrere: nuovamente*) to flow again; (: *indietro*) to flow back; (*marea*) to go out.

riflusso [ri'flusso] SM (*gen*) flowing back; (*di sangue*) flow; (*di acqua, marea*) ebb; **flusso e riflusso** ebb and flow; **un'epoca di riflusso** an era of nostalgia.

rifocillarsi [rifotʃil'larsi] VR to take refreshment.

rifondazione [rifondat'tsjone] SF refounding ▶ **Rifondazione Comunista** *hard left party originating from former P.C.I.*

rifondere [ri'fondere] VT IRREG a (*rimborsare*) to refund, reimburse; **rifondere le spese a qn** to refund sb's expenses; **rifondere i danni a qn** to compensate sb for damages a (*metalli, cera*) to remelt, melt down again.

riforma [ri'forma] SF a (*gen*) reform; (*Rel*): **la Riforma** the

Reformation **b** (*Mil*: *di recluta*) declaration of unfitness for service; (: *di soldato*) discharge (*on health grounds*).

riformare [rifor'mare] **1** VT **a** (*formare di nuovo*) to form again, re-form **b** (*Rel*, *Pol*) to reform; (*Mil*: *recluta*) to declare unfit for military service; (: *soldato*) to discharge, invalid out.
2 **riformarsi** VIP (*formarsi di nuovo*) to form again, re-form.

riformato [rifor'mato] SM (*Rel*) Protestant; (*Mil*: *recluta*) recruit unfit for military service; (: *soldato*) discharged soldier.

riformatore, trice [riforma'tore] **1** AGG reforming.
2 SM/F reformer.

riformatorio, ri [riforma'tɔrjo] SM community home (*Brit*), reformatory (*Am*).

riformattare [riformat'tare] VT (*Inform*) to reformat.

riformista, i, e [rifor'mista] AGG, SM/F reformist.

rifornimento [riforni'mento] SM **a** (*operazione*) supplying, providing; (*di carburante*) refuelling; **fare rifornimento di** (*viveri*) to stock up with; (*benzina*) to fill up with; **stazione di rifornimento** filling *o* petrol (*Brit*) *o* gas (*Am*) station **b** : **rifornimenti** SMPL (*scorte*) stocks, supplies, provisions.

rifornire [rifor'nire] **1** VT: **rifornire di** to supply *o* provide with. **2** **rifornirsi** VR: **rifornirsi di** (*provviste*) to get in a supply of, stock up with; (*benzina*) to re-fuel (with), fill up (with).

rifrangere [ri'frandʒere] VB IRREG **1** VT (*Fis*) to refract.
2 **rifrangersi** VIP to be refracted.

rifratto, a [ri'fratto] PP di **rifrangere**.

rifrazione [rifrat'tsjone] SF (*Fis*) refraction.

rifuggire [rifud'dʒire] VI (*aus essere*): **rifuggire da qc** to be averse to sth, shun sth.

rifugiarsi [rifu'dʒarsi] VIP: **rifugiarsi in** (*gen*, *fig*) to take refuge in; (*da pioggia, freddo*) to (take) shelter in.

rifugiato, a [rifu'dʒato] SM/F refugee.

rifugio, gi [ri'fudʒo] SM (*gen*) shelter, refuge; (*in montagna*) shelter; (*fig*) refuge; **cercare rifugio in qc/presso qn** to seek refuge in sth/with sb ▶ **rifugio antiaereo** air-raid shelter ▶ **rifugio antiatomico** fallout shelter.

rifulgere [ri'fuldʒere] VI IRREG (*aus essere o avere*) (*anche fig*): **rifulgere (di)** to shine (with), glow (with).

rifulso, a [ri'fulso] PP di **rifulgere**.

rifusione [rifu'zjone] SF (*Tecn*) remelting.

rifuso, a [ri'fuzo] PP di **rifondere**.

riga, ghe [ˈriga] SF **a** (*linea*) line; (*striscia*) stripe; **a righe** (*foglio*) lined; (*tessuto*) striped
b (*scritta*) line; **buttare giù due righe** (*note*) to jot down a few notes; **mandami due righe appena arrivi** drop me a line as soon as you arrive
c (*Mil, Scol*: *fila*) line, row; (*Sport*) line; **rompete le righe!** break ranks!; **mettersi in riga** to line up; **mettere qn in riga** (*fig*) to make sb toe the line; **rimettersi in riga** (*fig*) to get back into line; **sopra le righe** (*fig*) over the top
d (*righello*) ruler
e (*scriminatura*) parting; **farsi la riga in mezzo/da una parte** to put one's hair in a middle parting/side parting.

rigaglie [ri'gaʎʎe] SFPL (*Culin*) giblets.

rigagnolo [ri'gaɲɲolo] SM rivulet.

rigare [ri'gare] **1** VT (*pagina, foglio*) to rule; (*superficie*: *sfregiare*) to score; **col volto rigato di lacrime** with a tear-stained face.
2 VI (*aus avere*) (*fig*): **rigare dritto** to toe the line.

rigatoni [riga'toni] SMPL (*Culin*) rigatoni, *short*, *ridged pasta shapes.*

rigattiere [rigat'tjɛre] SM junk dealer, secondhand dealer.

rigatura [riga'tura] SF (*di pagina, quaderno*) lining, ruling; (*di fucile*) rifling.

rigelo [ri'dʒɛlo] SM regelation.

rigenerare [ridʒene'rare] **1** VT (*gen*, *Tecn*) to regenerate; (*forze*) to restore; (*gomma*) to retread, remould (*Brit*), recap (*Am*); **gomma rigenerata** retread, remould, recap.
2 **rigenerarsi** VIP (*gen*) to regenerate; (*ramo, tumore*) to regenerate, grow again.

rigenerativo, a [ridʒenera'tivo] AGG (*processo*) regenerating.

rigeneratore, trice [ridʒenera'tore] AGG regenerative; **lozione rigeneratrice** (*per i capelli*) restorer; (*per la pelle*) rejuvenating lotion.

rigenerazione [ridʒenerat'tsjone] SF regeneration.

rigettare [ridʒet'tare] **1** VT **a** (*gettare*: *di nuovo*) to throw again; (: *indietro*) to throw back **b** (*respingere*: *proposta*) to reject, turn down; (: *Bio, Med*) to reject **c** (*vomitare*) to vomit, bring *o* throw up.
2 **rigettarsi** VR: **rigettarsi in acqua** to jump back into the water.

rigetto [ri'dʒetto] SM (*gen, Med*) rejection; **crisi di rigetto** (*Med*) rejection crisis; (*fig*) total rejection.

righello [ri'gɛllo] SM ruler.

righerò ecc [rige'rɔ] VB vedi **rigare**.

rigidamente [ridʒida'mente] AVV (*gen*) rigidly; (*giudicare*) severely.

rigidezza [ridʒi'dettsa], **rigidità** [ridʒidi'ta] SF (*gen*) rigidity; (*di membra*) stiffness; (*fig*: *di clima*) harshness, severity, rigours *pl* (*Brit*), rigors *pl* (*Am*); (: *severità*) strictness, sternness ▶ **rigidità cadaverica** rigor mortis.

rigido, a [ˈridʒido] AGG (*gen*) rigid; (*membra, berretto, colletto*) stiff; (*fig*: *clima, inverno*) harsh, severe; (: *disciplina, principi*) strict.

rigirare [ridʒi'rare] **1** VT (*gen*) to turn; **rigirare il discorso** to change the subject; **rigirare qc tra le mani** to turn sth over in one's hands.
2 **rigirarsi** VR (*voltarsi*: *di nuovo*) to turn round; (: *nel letto*) to turn over; **girarsi e rigirarsi nel letto** to toss and turn in bed.

rigo, ghi [ˈrigo] SM (*linea*) line; (*Mus*) staff, stave.

rigoglio, gli [ri'goʎʎo] SM (*di piante*) luxuriance; **essere in pieno rigoglio** (*fig*: *commercio, sviluppo*) to be thriving.

rigogliosamente [rigoʎʎosa'mente] AVV luxuriantly.

rigoglioso, a [rigoʎ'ʎoso] AGG (*pianta, giardino*) luxuriant; (*fig*: *commercio, sviluppo*) thriving.

rigonfiamento [rigonfja'mento] SM (*gonfiore*: *su parte del corpo*) swelling; (: *su legno, intonaco*) bulge.

rigonfiare [rigon'fjare] VT to blow up (again), reinflate.

rigonfio, fia, fi, fie [ri'gonfjo] AGG (*vela*) full; (*grembiule, sporta*): **rigonfio di** bulging with.

rigore [ri'gore] SM **a** (*di sentenza, legge*) severity; (*di disciplina*) strictness, severity; (*di clima*) severity, harshness, rigours *pl* (*Brit*), rigors *pl* (*Am*); **punire qn con rigore** to punish sb severely; **mettere qn in cella di rigore** (*Mil*) to put sb in solitary confinement; **essere di rigore** (*d'obbligo*) to be compulsory; "**è di rigore l'abito da sera**" "evening dress"; **a rigor di termini** *o* **di logica** strictly speaking; **i rigori dell'inverno** the rigo(u)rs of winter
b (*Calcio*: *anche*: **calcio di rigore**) penalty; **battere un**

rigore to take a penalty; **area di rigore** penalty area *o* box.

rigorosamente [rigorosa'mente] AVV (*vedi agg*) rigorously, exactly; severely, harshly; strictly; **seguì rigorosamente le istruzioni** he followed the instructions to the letter.

rigorosità [rigorosi'ta] SF (*precisione: di conclusioni*) rigour (*Brit*), rigor (*Am*); (*severità: di costumi*) strictness.

rigoroso, a [rigo'roso] AGG (*definizione, logica*) rigorous, exact; (*punizione*) severe, harsh; (*persona, ordine*) strict.

rigovernare [rigover'nare] VT (*piatti, stoviglie*) to wash (up); **non ho ancora rigovernato** I haven't done the washing-up yet.

riguadagnare [rigwadaɲ'ɲare] VT (*recuperare: velocità*) to make up, regain; (: *terreno*) to regain; (: *stima, affetto*) to win back; **riguadagnare il tempo perduto** to make up for lost time.

riguardare [rigwar'dare] 1 VT a (*concernere*) to concern, regard; **per quel che mi riguarda** as far as I'm concerned; **è un libro che riguarda la vita dei contadini** it's a book which deals with *o* looks at the life of country people; **sono affari che non ti riguardano** it's none of your business

c (*curare, tenere da conto*) to look after, take care of b (*guardare di nuovo*) to look at again, take another look at; (*controllare*) to check.

2 **riguardarsi** VR (*aver cura di sé*) to look after o.s., take care of o.s.; **ti devi riguardare dalle correnti d'aria** you should stay out of draughts.

riguardo [ri'gwardo] SM a (*rispetto*) respect; (*considerazione*) consideration, regard; **per riguardo a** out of respect for; **trattare qn col massimo riguardo** to treat sb with the greatest respect; **mancare di riguardo verso** *o* **a qn** to be disrespectful towards sb; **ospite/persona di riguardo** very important guest/person; **aver riguardo delle cose altrui** to respect other people's property; **agire/parlare senza (tanti) riguardi** to act/speak freely

b : **riguardo a** (*a proposito di*) regarding, concerning, as regards, with regard to; **riguardo a me** as far as I'm concerned.

riguardosamente [rigwardosa'mente] AVV respectfully.

riguardoso, a [rigwar'doso] AGG (*rispettoso*) respectful; (*premuroso*) considerate, thoughtful.

rigurgitare [rigurdʒi'tare] 1 VI (*aus* **essere**): **rigurgitare da** to gush out from.

2 VT (*vomitare*) to bring up.

rigurgito [ri'gurdʒito] SM (*Med*) regurgitation; (*fig: ritorno, risveglio*) revival.

rilanciare [rilan't ʃare] VT (*lanciare di nuovo: gen*) to throw again; (: *moda*) to bring back; (: *prodotto*) to re-launch; (*Carte*) to raise; **rilanciare un'offerta** (*asta*) to make a higher bid.

rilancio, ci [ri'lant ʃo] SM (*di prodotto*) re-launching; (*Carte, di offerta*) raising.

rilasciamento [rilaʃʃa'mento] SM (*di muscoli*) relaxation.

rilasciare [rilaʃ'ʃare] 1 VT a (*Amm: passaporto, certificato*) to issue; (*intervista*) to give; **rilasciare una dichiarazione** to make a statement b (*persona, prigioniero*) to release c (*muscoli, tensione, nervi*) to relax.

2 **rilasciarsi** VIP to relax.

rilascio, sci [ri'laʃʃo] SM (*di documento*) issue; (*di prigioniero*) release.

rilassamento [rilassa'mento] SM (*gen, Med*) relaxation.

rilassare [rilas'sare] 1 VT (*distendere: nervi, muscoli*) to

relax; (: *persona*) to help to relax.

2 **rilassarsi** VR (*gen*) to relax.

3 **rilassarsi** VIP (*fig: disciplina*) to become slack.

rilassatezza [rilassa'tettsa] SF (*fig: di costumi, disciplina*) laxity.

rilassato, a [rilas'sato] AGG (*persona, muscoli*) relaxed; (*disciplina, costumi*) lax.

rilegare [rile'gare] VT (*libro, volume*) to bind.

rilegato [rile'gato] AGG: **libro rilegato in pelle** leather-bound book.

rilegatore, trice [rilega'tore] SM/F bookbinder.

rilegatura [rilega'tura] SF binding.

rileggere [ri'leddʒere] VT IRREG (*leggere di nuovo*) to read again, reread; (: *per correggere*) to read over; **l'ho letto e riletto cento volte** I've read it over and over again.

rilento [ri'lento]: **a rilento** AVV slowly; **gli affari vanno a rilento** business is slow.

riletta [ri'letta] SF reread.

riletto, a [ri'letto] PP di **rileggere**.

rilettura [rilet'tura] SF (*vedi vt*) rereading; reading over; (*nuova interpretazione*) new interpretation.

rilevamento [rileva'mento] SM (*topografico, statistico, geologico*) survey; (*Naut*) bearing.

rilevante [rile'vante] AGG (*notevole*) remarkable, considerable; (*importante*) important.

rilevanza [rile'vantsa] SF importance.

rilevare [rile'vare] VT a (*notare*) to notice; **dai sintomi non si rileva alcun pericolo immediato** going by the symptoms, there is no immediate danger; **rilevo con soddisfazione che...** I note with satisfaction that ...; **far rilevare a qn che...** to point out to sb that ...

b (*raccogliere: dati*) to gather, collect; (*Topografia*) to survey; (*Naut: posizione*) to plot; **la polizia non ha potuto rilevare alcun indizio** the police have been unable to find any evidence

c (*Comm: negozio, ditta*) to take over

d (*Mil: sentinella*) to relieve

e (*levare di nuovo*) to take off again.

rilevazione [rilevat'tsjone] SF survey.

rilievo [ri'ljevo] SM a (*gen, Arte, Geog*) relief; **alto/basso rilievo** high/bas-relief; **i rilievi alpini** the Alps; **in rilievo** (*gen*) in relief; (*ricamo*) raised; **carta in rilievo** relief map

b (*importanza*) importance; **dar rilievo a** *o* **mettere in rilievo qc** (*fig*) to stress *o* highlight sth, bring sth out; **di poco/nessun rilievo** (*fig*) of little/no importance; **un personaggio di rilievo** an important person

c (*osservazione*) point, remark

c (*Topografia, Statistica*) survey.

riloga, ghe [ri'lɔga] SF curtain pole.

rilucente [rilu'tʃente] AGG bright, shining.

riluttante [rilut'tante] AGG reluctant; **essere riluttante a fare qc** to be reluctant to do sth.

riluttantemente [riluttante'mente] AVV reluctantly.

riluttanza [rilut'tantsa] SF (*gen*) reluctance; **con riluttanza** reluctantly.

riluttare [rilut'tare] VI (*aus* **avere**): **riluttare a fare qc** to be reluctant to do sth.

rima ['rima] SF (*gen*) rhyme; (*verso*) verse; **far rima con** to rhyme with; **mettere in rima** to put into rhyme; **rispondere a qn per le rime** (*fig*) to give as good as one gets ►**rima baciata** rhyming couplet ►**rime alternate** alternate rhymes.

rimandare [riman'dare] VT a (*mandare: di nuovo*) to send again; (: *indietro*) to send back, return; **rimandare qn a**

(*fig: far riferimento*) to refer sb to

b (*posporre: partenza, appuntamento*): **rimandare (a)** to postpone (till), put off (till); **non rimandare a domani quel che puoi fare oggi** (*Proverbio*) don't put off till tomorrow what you can do today

c (*Scol*): **rimandare qn (a settembre)** to make sb resit (in September); **essere rimandato** to have to resit one's exams; **è stato rimandato in matematica** he has a resit in Maths (*Brit*) *o* Math (*Am*).

rimando [ri'mando] SM (*in testo*) cross-reference; **di rimando** (*fig*) in return.

rimaneggiare [rimaned'dʒare] VT (*testo*) to reshape, recast; (*ministero*) to reshuffle.

rimanente [rima'nɛnte] **1** AGG remaining.

2 SM (*resto*): **il rimanente** the rest, the remainder; **i** (*o* **le**) **rimanenti** (*persone*) the rest *pl* (of them), the others.

rimanenza [rima'nɛntsa] SF (*gen*) rest, remainder ▶ **rimanenze di magazzino** (*Comm*) left-over stock *sg*, unsold stock *sg*.

rimanere [rima'nere] VI IRREG (*aus* **essere**) **a** (*in luogo*) to stay, remain; **rimanere a casa/a letto** to stay *o* remain at home/in bed; **rimanere a cena** to stay for dinner; **rimanere a guardare la televisione** to stay and watch television; **che rimanga tra noi** (*fig: segreto*) this is just between ourselves; **dove eravamo rimasti?** (*fig*) where were we?

b (*in una condizione*) to stay, remain; **rimanere in piedi** (*non sedersi*) to remain standing; (*non coricarsi*) to stay up; **rimanere senza benzina/pane** to run out of petrol (*Brit*) *o* gas (*Am*)/bread; **rimanere al buio/senz'acqua** to have one's electricity *o* water cut off; **rimanere indietro** to be left behind; **rimanere indietro col lavoro/con l'affitto** (*fig*) to fall behind with one's work/with the rent; **rimaniamo d'accordo così** that's agreed then, that's settled then; **rimanere amici** to remain friends; **rimanere in buoni rapporti** to remain on good terms; **rimanere senza parole** to be left speechless; **rimanere** *o* **rimanerci male** to be hurt *o* offended; **rimanere** *o* **rimanerci secco** (*fam: morire*) to drop dead; **rimanere sorpreso** to be surprised

c (*divenire*): **rimanere orfano** to become *o* be left an orphan; **rimanere vedovo** to be left a widower; **è rimasto ferito in un incidente d'auto** he was injured in a car accident; **rimanere incinta** to get pregnant

d (*sussistere*) to be left, remain; **è l'unico parente che le rimane** he's her only remaining relative; **coi pochi soldi che mi rimangono** with what little money I have left; **rimangono da fare 15 km** there are still 15 km to go; **ne rimane ancora un po'** there's still some left; **non rimane più niente** there's nothing left; **rimane ancora molto da fare** there's still a lot to do; **non ti rimane altro (da fare) che accettare** all you can do is accept; **mi rimani solo tu** you're all I have left; **mi rimane ben poco da dire se non...** I've little left to say except ...; **rimane da vedere se...** it remains to be seen whether ... .

rimangiare [riman'dʒare] VT to eat again; **rimangiarsi la parola/una promessa** (*fig*) to go back on one's word/ one's promise.

rimango *ecc* [ri'mango] VB *vedi* **rimanere**.

rimarcare [rimar'kare] VT to remark, observe.

rimarchevole [rimar'kevole] AGG (*notevole*) remarkable.

rimare [ri'mare] VT, VI (*aus* **avere**) to rhyme.

rimarginare [rimardʒi'nare] VT, VI (*aus* **essere**), **rimarginarsi** VIP to heal.

rimasto, a [ri'masto] PP di **rimanere**.

rimasuglio, gli [rima'suʎʎo] SM (*di stoffa*) remnant; (*di cibo*): **rimasugli** SMPL leftovers *pl*.

rimbalzare [rimbal'tsare] VI (*aus* **essere** *o* **avere**): **rimbalzare (su)** (*pavimento*) to bounce (off); (*muro*) to rebound (off), bounce back; (*sogg: proiettile*) to ricochet (off); **far rimbalzare una palla** to bounce a ball.

rimbalzo [rim'baltso] SM (*di palla*) bounce; (*di proiettile*) ricochet; **di rimbalzo** on the rebound; (*fig*) indirectly.

rimbambire [rimbam'bire] (*pegg*) VI (*aus* **essere**), **rimbambirsi** VIP to become stupid, grow foolish; **rimbambire** *o* **rimbambirsi con l'età** to become senile.

rimbambito, a [rimbam'bito] AGG (*pegg*) senile; **un vecchio rimbambito** a doddering old man.

rimbeccare [rimbek'kare] **1** VT (*persona*) to answer back; (*offesa*) to return.

2 **rimbeccarsi** VR (*uso reciproco: litigare*) to bicker.

rimbecillire [rimbetʃil'lire] VT, VI, VIP = **rincretinire**.

rimbecillito, a [rimbetʃil'lito] AGG (*rimbambito*) foolish, stupid; (*frastornato*) stunned, stupefied.

rimboccare [rimbok'kare] VT (*orlo*) to turn up; (*coperta*) to tuck in; (*pantaloni*) to turn *o* roll up; **rimboccarsi le maniche** (*anche fig*) to roll up one's sleeves.

rimbombante [rimbom'bante] AGG (*vedi vb*) resounding; roaring, rumbling; thundering; booming.

rimbombare [rimbom'bare] VI (*aus* **avere** *o* **essere**) (*suono, passi*) to resound; (*tuono*) to roar, rumble; (*cannonata*) to roar, thunder; (*voce*) boom.

rimbombo [rim'bombo] SM (*suono*) sound; (*di voce*) boom; (*di tuono*) roar, rumble; (*di cannonata*) roar, thunder.

rimborsare [rimbor'sare] VT (*persona*) to pay back, reimburse; (*spese, biglietto*) to refund, reimburse; **rimborsare qc a qn** to reimburse sb for sth.

rimborso [rim'borso] SM repayment, reimbursement; (*di spese, biglietto*) refund ▶ **rimborso d'imposta** tax rebate.

rimboschimento [rimboski'mento] SM re(af)forestation.

rimboschire [rimbos'kire] VT to re(af)forest.

rimbrottare [rimbrot'tare] VT to reproach.

rimbrotto [rim'brɔtto] SM reproach; **fare un rimbrotto a qn** to reproach sb.

rimediabile [rime'djabile] AGG (*errore*) remediable, which can be remedied.

rimediare [rime'djare] **1** VI (*gen*) to remedy; **rimediare a qc** to remedy sth; **e adesso come si rimedia?** what can we do about it now?; **ha cercato di rimediare al male fatto** he tried to make amends for the wrong he had done.

2 VT (*fam: procurarsi*) to scrape up *o* together.

rimedio, di [ri'mɛdjo] SM (*gen*) remedy; (*cura*) remedy, cure; **un rimedio per tutti i mali** a panacea, a cure-all; **porre rimedio a qc** to remedy sth; **non c'è rimedio** there's no way out, there's nothing to be done about it; **è una situazione senza rimedio** it's a situation which cannot be remedied.

rimescolare [rimesko'lare] VT to mix well, stir well; (*carte*) to shuffle; **sentirsi rimescolare il sangue** (*per paura*) to feel one's blood run cold; (*per rabbia*) to feel one's blood boil.

rimescolio, lii [rimesko'lio] SM (*turbamento*) shock; (*trambusto*) bustle.

rimessa [ri'messa] SF **a** (*per veicoli*) garage; (*per aerei*) hangar **b** (*Comm: di merce*) shipment, consignment;

(: di denaro) remittance **c** (*Tennis*) return **d** (*Sport*): **rimessa in gioco laterale** (*Calcio*) throw-in; (*Rugby*) line-out; **rimessa in gioco dal fondo** (*Calcio*) goal kick; (*Rugby*) drop-out.

rimesso, a [ri'messo] PP di **rimettere**.

rimestare [rimes'tare] VT (*mescolare*) to mix well, stir well; (*fig: passato*) to drag up again.

rimettere [ri'mettere] VB IRREG **1** VT **a** (*mettere: di nuovo*) to put back; (*indossare*) to put back on; **rimettere mano a qc** to take up sth again; **rimettere a nuovo** (*casa ecc*) to do up (*Brit*) o over (*Am*)

b (*affidare: decisione*): **rimettere a qn** to refer to sb, leave to sb; **rimettere l'anima a Dio** to entrust one's soul to God

c (*perdonare: peccato*) to forgive; (*condonare: pena*) to quash; (: *debito*) to remit

d (*inviare: merce*) to deliver; (: *somma*) to remit

e (*Sport: pallone*) to throw in; (*Tennis*) to return

f (*vomitare*) to bring up

g (*perdere*): **rimetterci** to lose; **rimetterci di tasca propria** to be out of pocket; **rimetterci la salute** to ruin one's health; **rimetterci la pelle** to lose one's life; **cosa ci rimetti?** what have you got to lose?.

2 rimettersi VIP **a** (*mettersi di nuovo*): **rimettersi a fare qc** to start doing sth again; **rimettersi in cammino** to set off again; **rimettersi al lavoro** to start working again; **rimettersi a dormire** to go back to sleep; **rimettersi con qn** to get back together with sb

b (*affidarsi*): **rimettersi a** to trust

c (*riprendersi*) to recover; **rimettersi in forze** to regain o recover one's strength; **rimettersi in salute** to get better, recover one's health; **rimettersi da uno shock** to recover from a shock; **il tempo si è rimesso al bello** the weather has cleared up.

3 rimettersi VR (*uso reciproco*): **rimettersi insieme** to get back together.

riminese [rimi'nese] **1** AGG of o from Rimini.

2 SM/F inhabitant o native of Rimini.

rimirare [rimi'rare] **1** VT to gaze at.

2 rimirarsi VR to gaze at o.s., admire o.s.

rimisi ecc [ri'mizi] VB vedi **rimettere**.

rimmel® ['rimmel] SM INV mascara.

rimodernamento [rimoderna'mento] SM modernization.

rimodernare [rimoder'nare] VT (*gen*) to modernize; (*vestito*) to remodel.

rimonta [ri'monta] SF (*Sport, gen*) recovery; **fare una rimonta in classifica** to climb back up the league.

rimontare [rimon'tare] **1** VT **a** (*montare di nuovo: meccanismo*) to reassemble, put back together again; (: *tenda*) to put up again

b (*risalire*): **rimontare la corrente** to go upstream.

2 VI (*aus essere*) **a** : **rimontare in** (*macchina, carrozza*) to get back into; **rimontare a cavallo** [OR] **rimontare in sella** to remount; **rimontare su una bici** to get back on a bike

b (*Sport*) to close the gap.

rimorchiare [rimor'kjare] VT (*veicolo*) to tow; (*nave*) to tug; **rimorchiare qn** (*fig fam*) to pick sb up.

rimorchiatore [rimorkja'tore] SM (*Naut*) tug(boat).

rimorchio, chi [ri'mɔrkjo] SM **a** (*operazione*) towing; **cavo da rimorchio** towrope; **andare a rimorchio** to be towed; **prendere a rimorchio** to tow **b** (*veicolo trainato*) trailer; **autocarro con rimorchio** articulated lorry (*Brit*), semi (trailer) (*Am*).

rimordere [ri'mɔrdere] VT IRREG (*fig*): **non ti rimorde la**

coscienza? isn't your conscience bothering you?

rimorso, a [ri'mɔrso] **1** PP di **rimordere**.

2 SM remorse; **essere preso dai rimorsi** to be stricken with remorse; **avere il rimorso di aver fatto qc** to deeply regret having done sth.

rimosso, a [ri'mɔsso] PP di **rimuovere**.

rimostranza [rimos'trantsa] SF protest, complaint; **fare le proprie rimostranze a qn** to remonstrate with sb.

rimovibile [rimo'vibile] AGG removable.

rimozione [rimot'tsjone] SF **a** (*gen*) removal; (*di veicolo*) towing away; **"rimozione forzata"** "illegally parked vehicles will be removed at owner's expense"; **"zona rimozione"** "vehicles will be towed away" **b** (*da incarico*) dismissal **c** (*Psic*) repression.

rimpaginare [rimpadʒi'nare] VT (*Tip*) to repaginate, make up again.

rimpallo [rim'pallo] SM (*Calcio*) bounce.

rimpastare [rimpas'tare] VT **a** (*pasta lievitata*) to knead again; (*cemento*) to mix again **b** (*Pol: governo*) to reshuffle.

rimpasto [rim'pasto] SM (*Pol*) reshuffle ▶ **rimpasto ministeriale** cabinet reshuffle.

rimpatriare [rimpa'trjare] **1** VT to repatriate.

2 VI (*aus essere*) to return to one's country.

rimpatriata [rimpa'trjata] SF (*fam*): **fare una rimpatriata** to have a get-together o reunion.

rimpatrio, tri [rim'patrjo] SM repatriation; **ottenere il rimpatrio** to be repatriated.

rimpiangere [rim'pjandʒere] VT IRREG (*gen*) to regret; (*passato, giovinezza*) to look back on with regret; **rimpiangere di (non) aver fatto qc** to regret (not) having done sth.

rimpianto, a [rim'pjanto] **1** PP di **rimpiangere**.

2 AGG (*persona, periodo*) sadly missed.

3 SM regret; **non aver rimpianti** to have no regrets.

rimpiattino [rimpjat'tino] SM (*gioco*) hide-and-seek, hide-and-go-seek (*Am*).

rimpiazzare [rimpjat'tsare] VT to replace.

rimpiazzo [rim'pjattso] SM (*persona, cosa*) replacement.

rimpicciolire [rimpittʃo'lire] **1** VT to make smaller.

2 VI (*aus essere*), **rimpicciolirsi** VIP to become smaller.

rimpinzare [rimpin'tsare] (*fam*) **1** VT: **rimpinzare (di)** to cram o stuff with.

2 rimpinzarsi VR: **rimpinzarsi (di)** to stuff o.s. (with).

rimpolpare [rimpol'pare] VT (*ingrassare*) to fatten (up); (*fig: articolo, discorso, finanze*) to pad out, fill out.

rimpossessarsi [rimposses'sarsi] VIP: **rimpossessarsi (di) qc** to take sth back.

rimproverare [rimprove'rare] VT (*figlio, scolaro*) to scold, tell off, rebuke; (*dipendente*) to reprimand; **rimproverare qc a qn** to reproach sb with sth; **non ho niente da rimproverarmi** I've nothing to reproach myself with.

rimprovero [rim'provero] SM reproach; **fare un rimprovero a qn** to reproach sb; (*bambino*) to tell sb off; **di rimprovero** (*tono, occhiata*) reproachful; (*parole*) of reproach.

rimuginare [rimudʒi'nare] VT: **rimuginare qc** to turn sth over in one's mind; **che starà rimuginando?** what can he be brooding over o about?

rimunerare [rimune'rare] VT (*retribuire*) to remunerate; **un lavoro ben rimunerato** a well-paid job.

rimunerativo, a [rimunera'tivo] AGG (*lavoro, attività*) remunerative, profitable.

rimunerazione [rimunerat'tsjone] SF (*retribuzione*) remu-

neration; (*ricompensa*) reward.

rimuovere [ri'mwɔvere] VT IRREG **a** (*gen, Med*) to remove; (*fig: dubbio*) to remove, eliminate; (: *sospetto*) to eliminate; (: *ostacolo*) to get rid of; **rimuovere qn da una carica** to dismiss sb; **rimuovere qn da un proposito** to deter sb from a purpose **b** (*Psic*) to repress.

rinascere [ri'naʃʃere] VI IRREG (*aus essere*) (*persona*) to be born again; (*pianta*) to sprout again; (*fig: speranza, interesse*) to be revived; **sentirsi rinascere** to feel a new man (*o woman*).

rinascimentale [rinaʃʃimen'tale] AGG Renaissance *attr*, of the Renaissance.

Rinascimento [rinaʃʃi'mento] SM: **il Rinascimento** the Renaissance.

rinascita [ri'naʃʃita] SF (*fig*) rebirth, revival.

rinato, a [ri'nato] PP di **rinascere**.

rincagnato, a [rinkaɲ'ɲato] AGG: **avere il muso rincagnato** to be pug-faced.

rincalzare [rinkal'tsare] VT (*coperte, lenzuola*) to tuck in; (*palo, albero*) to prop up, support.

rincalzo [rin'kaltso] SM **a** (*sostegno*) prop, support; (*Mil*): **truppe di rincalzo** reserves **b** (*Sport: giocatore*) reserve (player).

rincarare [rinka'rare] **1** VT (*prezzi*) to raise, put up; (*prodotto*) to raise *o* increase the price of; **rincarare la dose** (*fig*) to pile it on.

2 VI (*aus essere*) (*prezzo*) to go up, rise; (*prodotto*) to go up in price, become more expensive.

rincaro [rin'karo] SM: **rincaro (di)** (*prezzi, costo della vita*) increase (in); (*prodotto*) increase in the price (of).

rincartare [rinkar'tare] VT to rewrap.

rincasare [rinka'sare] VI (*aus essere*) to return home, go (*o come*) back home.

rinchiudere [rin'kjudere] VB IRREG **1** VT: **rinchiudere (in)** (*gen*) to shut up (in); (*persona: in prigione*) to shut *o* lock up (in); **far rinchiudere qn in prigione/manicomio** to have sb put away (in prison/in a madhouse).

2 rinchiudersi VR: **rinchiudersi in** (*stanza*) to shut o.s. up in; (: *a chiave*) to lock o.s. up in; **rinchiudersi in un convento/monastero** to withdraw into a convent/ monastery; **rinchiudersi in se stesso** to withdraw into o.s.; **si è rinchiuso in un mutismo assoluto** he maintained a stubborn silence.

rinchiuso, a [rin'kjuso] PP di **rinchiudere**.

rincitrullire [rintʃitrul'lire] VT, VI, VIP = **rincretinire**.

rincivilire [rintʃivi'lire] = **incivilire**.

rincoglionire [rinkoʎʎo'nire] (*fam*) VT, VI, VIP = **rincretinire**.

rincominciare [rinkomin'tʃare] = **ricominciare**.

rincontrare [rinkon'trare] **1** VT to meet again.

2 rincontrarsi VR (*uso reciproco*) to meet (each other) again.

rincorare [rinko'rare] **1** VT to cheer up.

2 rincorarsi VIP to cheer up.

rincorrere [rin'korrere] VB IRREG **1** VT to chase, run after; (*fig: sogno, chimere*) to pursue.

2 rincorrersi VR (*uso reciproco*) to run after each other; **giocare a rincorrersi** to play tag.

rincorsa [rin'korsa] SF (*Sport*) run-up; **prendere la rincorsa** (*atleta*) to take one's run-up; **prendi la rincorsa!** take a run at it!

rincorso, a [rin'korso] PP di **rincorrere**.

rincrescere [rin'kreʃʃere] VB IMPERS IRREG: **mi rincresce che...** I'm sorry that ..., I regret that ...; **mi rincresce di**

non poterlo fare I'm sorry I can't do it, I regret being unable to do it; **se non ti rincresce vorrei pensarci su** if you don't mind I'd like to think it over.

rincrescimento [rinkreʃʃi'mento] SM regret; **con mio grande rincrescimento** much to my regret.

rincresciuto, a [rinkreʃ'ʃuto] PP di **rincrescere**.

rincretinire [rinkreti'nire] **1** VT: **rincretinire qn** (*gen*) to make sb stupid; (*sogg: età*) to make sb feeble-minded; (: *televisione*) to addle sb's brain; (: *chiacchiere*) to make sb's head spin *o* go round; **tutto questo rumore mi rincretinisce** I can't think straight with all this noise.

2 VI (*aus essere*), **rincretinirsi** VIP (*gen*) to become stupid; (*per l'età*) to become senile.

rinculare [rinku'lare] VI (*aus avere*) (*arma*) to recoil.

rinculo [rin'kulo] SM (*di arma*) recoil.

rinfacciare [rinfat'tʃare] VT: **rinfacciare qc a qn** to cast sth up at sb, throw sth in sb's face.

rinfocolare [rinfoko'lare] VT (*fig: odio, passioni*) to rekindle; (: *risentimento, rabbia*) to stir up;.

rinforzare [rinfor'tsare] **1** VT (*muro, argomento, gruppo*) to reinforce; (*muscoli, posizione, prestigio*) to strengthen; (*presa, nodo*) to tighten.

2 VI (*aus essere*), **rinforzarsi** VIP (*persona*) to become *o* grow stronger; (*amicizia, legame*) to strengthen.

rinforzo [rin'fɔrtso] SM **a**: **mettere un rinforzo a** (*gen*) to strengthen; **di rinforzo** (*asse, sbarra*) strengthening; (*esercito*) supporting; (*personale*) extra, additional **b** (*Mil*): **rinforzi** SMPL reinforcements.

rinfrancare [rinfran'kare] **1** VT (*persona*) to encourage, reassure; (*spirito*) to cheer.

2 rinfrancarsi VIP to be reassured.

rinfrescante [rinfres'kante] AGG (*bibita*) refreshing.

rinfrescare [rinfres'kare] **1** VT (*gen*) to cool (down); (*aria*) to cool, freshen; (*fig: pareti, soffitto, abiti*) to freshen up; **rinfrescarsi la gola** to quench one's thirst; **rinfrescarsi il viso** to splash one's face; **rinfrescare la memoria a qn** to refresh sb's memory.

2 VI (*aus essere*) (*tempo*) to grow *o* get cooler.

3 rinfrescarsi VR (*persona: con bibita*) to have something to drink; (: *con bagno*) to freshen up.

rinfresco, schi [rin'fresko] SM **a** (*ricevimento*) reception; (*festa*) party **b**: **rinfreschi** SMPL (*cibi e bevande*) refreshments.

rinfusa [rin'fuza]: **alla rinfusa** AVV higgledy-piggledy, in confusion.

ringalluzzire [ringallut'tsire] (*scherz*) **1** VT to make cocky.

2 VI (*aus essere*), **ringalluzzirsi** VIP to get cocky.

ringhiare [rin'gjare] VI (*aus avere*) to growl, snarl.

ringhiera [rin'gjɛra] SF (*di balcone*) railing; (*di scale*) banisters *pl*.

ringhio, ghi ['ringjo] SM growl, snarl.

ringhioso, a [rin'gjoso] AGG growling, snarling.

ringiovanimento [rindʒovani'mento] SM rejuvenation.

ringiovanire [rindʒova'nire] **1** VT: **ringiovanire qn** (*sogg: vestito, acconciatura*) to make sb look younger; (: *vacanze*) to rejuvenate sb.

2 VI (*aus essere*), **ringiovanirsi** VIP to become (*o look*) younger; **sembra ringiovanita di dieci anni** she looks ten years younger.

ringraziamento [ringrattsja'mento] SM thanks *pl*; **gli ho mandato i miei ringraziamenti** I sent him my thanks; **lettera/biglietto di ringraziamento** thank-you letter/ card; **bel ringraziamento!** (*iro*) thanks for nothing!; **il giorno del Ringraziamento** (*negli USA*) Thanksgiving

(Day).

ringraziare [ringrat'tsjare] VT to thank; **ringraziare qn di qc/per aver fatto qc** to thank sb for sth/for doing sth; **ti ringrazio** thank you; **non so come ringraziarti** I don't know how to thank you; **se n'è andato senza neppure ringraziare** he left without even saying thank you *o* without as much as a thank you; **sia ringraziato il Cielo!** thank heavens!

rinnegare [rinne'gare] VT (*fede, idee, partito*) to renounce; (*famiglia, figlio, origini*) to disown, repudiate.

rinnegato, a [rinne'gato] AGG, SM/F renegade.

rinnovabile [rinno'vabile] AGG renewable.

rinnovamento [rinnova'mento] SM (*morale, civile*) renewal; (*economico*) revival.

rinnovare [rinno'vare] **1** VT (*gen, fig*) to renew; **rinnovare l'arredamento** to buy new furnishings; **l'intero personale è stato rinnovato** the entire staff has been replaced.
2 rinnovarsi VIP (*ripetersi: fenomeno, occasione*) to be repeated, recur.

rinnovatore, trice [rinnova'tore] AGG renewing.

rinnovo [rin'nɔvo] SM (*di contratto*) renewal; **"chiuso per rinnovo (dei) locali"** (*negozio*) "closed for alterations".

rinoceronte [rinotʃe'ronte] SM rhinoceros.

rinomato, a [rino'mato] AGG (*specialista, ristorante*) renowned, famous, celebrated; (*marca*) well-known.

rinsaldare [rinsal'dare] **1** VT (*fig: vincoli, amicizia*) to strengthen.
2 rinsaldarsi VIP to get stronger, be strengthened.

rinsanire [rinsa'nire] VI (*aus* **essere**) to become sane again.

rinsavire [rinsa'vire] VI (*aus* **essere**) (*anche fig*) to come to one's senses.

rinsecchire [rinsek'kire] VI (*aus* **essere**) (*ramo, pianta*) to shrivel up, wither; (*persona*) to grow gaunt, grow thin.

rinsecchito, a [rinsek'kito] AGG (*vecchio, albero*) thin, gaunt.

rinserrarsi [rinser'rarsi] VR: **rinserrarsi in casa** to lock o.s. up at home.

rintanarsi [rinta'narsi] VIP (*animale*) to go into its den; (*persona: nascondersi*) to hide; **rintanarsi in casa** to shut o.s. up in the house.

rintoccare [rintok'kare] VI (*aus* **avere**) (*campana*) to toll; (*ora, orologio*) to strike.

rintocco, chi [rin'tokko] SM toll; **i rintocchi della campana** the tolling of the bell.

rintontire [rinton'tire] **1** VT (*sogg: botta*) to stun, daze.
2 VI (*aus* **essere**), **rintontirsi** VIP to become dazed.

rintontito, a [rinton'tito] AGG (*stordito*) dazed, stunned.

rintracciare [rintrat'tʃare] VT (*selvaggina, ladro, persona assente*) to track down; (*persona scomparsa, documento*) to trace.

rintronare [rintro'nare] **1** VT (*fam: cervello*) to stun; (: *orecchi*) to deafen.
2 VI (*aus* **essere** *o* **avere**) (*tuono, cannone*) to boom, roar; **la casa rintronava sotto i colpi** the blows echoed round the house.

rintronato, a [rintro'nato] AGG dazed.

rintuzzare [rintut'tsare] VT (*ribattere*) to refute.

rinuncia, ce [ri'nuntʃa] SF (*gen, Rel*) renunciation; **rinuncia a** (*carica*) resignation from; (*eredità*) relinquishment of; **rinuncia agli atti del giudizio** (*Dir*) abandonment of a claim; **una vita di rinunce** a life of sacrifice.

rinunciare [rinun'tʃare] VI (*aus* **avere**): **rinunciare a** to give up, renounce; (*incarico*) to turn down; (*trono, eredità*) to renounce; **rinunciare a fare qc** to give up doing sth; **rinunciò a presentarsi come candidato** he decided not to stand as a candidate; **ci rinuncio!** I give up!

rinunciatario, ria, ri, rie [rinuntʃa'tarjo] AGG renunciatory, defeatist.

rinunzia *ecc* [ri'nuntsja] SF = **rinuncia** *ecc.*

rinvasare [rinva'zare] VT to re-pot.

rinvenimento [rinveni'mento] SM **a** (*ritrovamento*) recovery; (*scoperta*) discovery **b** (*dopo svenimento*) coming to, recovery.

rinvenire [rinve'nire] VB IRREG **1** VT (*trovare*) to discover, find out; (: *oggetto smarrito*) to recover, find.
2 VI (*aus* **essere**) (*persona*) to come round, regain consciousness; (*fiori*) to revive; **far rinvenire** (*funghi secchi*) to reconstitute.

rinvenuto, a [rinve'nuto] PP di **rinvenire**.

rinverdire [rinver'dire] VI (*aus* **essere**) (*bosco, ramo*) to become green again.

rinvestire [rinves'tire] VT (*Econ*) to reinvest.

rinviare [rinvi'are] VT **a** (*mandare indietro: pacco*) to send back, return; (: *persona*) to send away; (*Sport: pallone*) to return
b (*differire*): **rinviare (a/di)** (*partenza, manifestazione*) to put off (till/for), postpone (till/for); (*seduta*) to adjourn (till/for); **rinviare una riunione ad altra data** to put off *o* postpone a meeting till a later date
c (*in testo, regolamento*): **rinviare qn a** to refer sb to
d (*Dir*): **rinviare a giudizio** to indict.

rinvigorire [rinvigo'rire] **1** VT to reinvigorate, strengthen.
2 VI (*aus* **essere**), **rinvigorirsi** VIP to regain strength.

rinvio, vii [rin'vio] SM **a** (*gen*) postponement; (*restituzione*) return; (*Dir*) adjournment ▶ **rinvio a giudizio** (*Dir*) indictment **b** (*in testo: rimando*) cross-reference **c** (*Sport: di pallone*) clearance.

riò *ecc* [ri'ɔ] VB vedi **riavere**.

rioccupare [riokku'pare] VT to reoccupy.

Rio de Janeiro ['rio de dʒa'nɛiro] SF Rio de Janeiro.

rionale [rio'nale] AGG (*mercato, cinema*) local, district *attr.*

rione [ri'one] SM district, neighbourhood, quarter.

riordinamento [riordina'mento] SM (*di ente, azienda*) reorganization.

riordinare [riordi'nare] VT (*armadio, casa, scaffali*) to tidy up; (*finanze, amministrazione*) to reorganize.

riordino [ri'ordino] SM reorganization.

riorganizzare [riorganid'dzare] **1** VT to reorganize.
2 riorganizzarsi VR to reorganize o.s.

riorganizzazione [riorganiddzat'tsjone] SF reorganization.

riottoso, a [riot'toso] AGG (*letter: attaccabrighe*) quarrelsome; (*indocile*) unruly.

ripagare [ripa'gare] VT **a** (*ricompensare*) to repay; **ripagare qn di qc** to repay sb for sth; **ripagare qn con la stessa moneta** (*fig*) to pay sb back in his (*o* her) own coin, give sb tit for tat **b** (*pagare di nuovo*) to pay again.

riparare [ripa'rare] **1** VT **a** (*aggiustare*) to repair; **portare qc a riparare** to take sth to be repaired; **far riparare qc** to have sth repaired
b (*proteggere*): **riparare (da)** to protect (from); **ripararsi gli occhi dalla luce** to shield one's eyes from the light
c (*rimediare*): **riparare (a)** (*offesa, gaffe*) to make up (for); (*errore*) to put right

d (*Scol*): **riparare (una materia) a settembre** to resit an exam in September.

2 VI (*aus* **essere**), **ripararsi** VR (*rifugiarsi*) to take refuge *o* shelter; **ripararsi dalla pioggia** to shelter from the rain.

riparato, a [ripa'rato] AGG (*posto*) sheltered; **stare** *o* **tenersi riparato** to shelter.

riparatore, trice [ripara'tore] SM/F repairer.

riparazione [riparat'tsjone] SF **a** (*di guasto*) repairing *no pl*; (: *risultato*) repair **b** : **riparazione (di)** (*di torto, offesa*) reparation (for); (*di danno*) compensation (for) **c** (*Scol*): **esame di riparazione** resit (*Brit*), test retake (*Am*).

riparlare [ripar'lare] VI (*aus* **avere**): **riparlare di qc** to talk about sth again; **ne riparleremo!** (*in litigio*) you haven't heard the last of this!

riparo [ri'paro] SM (*gen*) shelter, protection; **al riparo da** (*sole, vento*) sheltered from; **ormai siamo al riparo** (*al sicuro*) we're safe now; **mettersi al riparo** to take shelter; **sparano, mettiti al riparo!** they're shooting, take cover!; **correre ai ripari** (*fig*) to take remedial action.

ripartire¹ [ripar'tire] VI (*aus* **essere**) (*partire di nuovo*: *persona*) to leave again; (: *motore, macchina*) to start again; **quando riparti?** when are you leaving?; **non riesco a far ripartire la macchina** I can't get the car to start.

ripartire² [ripar'tire] VT (*dividere*): **ripartire (in)** (*somma, lavoro*) to divide up (into); **ripartire (tra)** to share out (among), distribute (among); **ripartire la posta** to sort the mail; **si sono ripartiti il lavoro** they shared out the work.

ripartizione [ripartit'tsjone] SF **a** (*vedi vt*) division; sharing out, distribution **b** (*Amm*: *dipartimento*) department.

ripassare [ripas'sare] **1** VT **a** (*lezione*) to revise (*Brit*), review (*Am*) go over again

b (*varcare di nuovo*: *confine*) to cross again

c (*passare di nuovo*: *gen*) to pass again; **mi puoi ripassare Francesco?** (*al telefono*) can I speak to Francesco again?

d (*stirare*): **ripassare qc** to give sth a quick iron.

2 VI (*aus* **essere**) (*ritornare*) to call again; **ripasserò da lui più tardi** I'll call on him again later; **pensavo di ripassare in quel negozio** I was thinking of calling in at that shop again; **ripassiamo per Pisa?** are we passing through Pisa again?; **può ripassare più tardi?** can you call back later?

ripassata [ripas'sata] SF: **dare una ripassata a** (*pantaloni*) to give a quick iron to; (*lezione*) to have another look through; (*fig*: *sgridare*: *persona*) to give a telling-off to.

ripasso [ri'passo] SM (*di lezione*) revision (*Brit*), review (*Am*).

ripensamento [ripensa'mento] SM change of mind, second thoughts *pl*; **avere un ripensamento** to have second thoughts, change one's mind.

ripensare [ripen'sare] VI **a** (*riflettere*): **ripensare a qc** to think sth over; **ripensaci!** think it over!; **a ripensarci...** on thinking it over ...

b (*ricordare*): **ripensare a** to recall

c (*cambiare idea*): **ripensarci** to change one's mind; **però, ripensandoci...** on second thoughts (*Brit*) *o* thought (*Am*), however ....

ripercorrere [riper'korrere] VT IRREG (*itinerario*) to travel over again; (*strada*) to go along again; (*fig*: *ricordi, passato*) to go back over.

ripercorso, a [riper'korso] PP di **ripercorrere**.

ripercosso, a [riper'kɔsso] PP di **ripercuotersi**.

ripercuotersi [riper'kwɔtersi] VIP IRREG (*luce*) to be reflected; (*suono*) to reverberate; (*fig*: *avere effetto*): **ripercuotersi su** to have repercussions on.

ripercussione [riperkus'sjone] SF (*di luce*) reflection; (*di suono*) reverberation; (*fig*) repercussions *pl*; **avere una ripercussione** *o* **delle ripercussioni su** to have repercussions on.

ripescaggio, gi [ripes'kaddʒo] SM (*Sport*) repechage; (*Pol*) re-proposal.

ripescare [ripes'kare] VT **a** (*pesce*) to catch again; (*recuperare*: *persona, cosa*) to fish out; (*fig*) to dig out; **ripescare qn a fare qc** (*fig*: *sorprendere*) to catch sb doing sth again **b** (*riproporre*: *candidato, progetto*) to re-propose.

ripetente [ripe'tɛnte] SM/F student repeating the year, repeater (*Am*).

ripetere [ri'pɛtere] **1** VT (*parole, tentativo*) to repeat; **gliel'ho ripetuto cento volte!** I've told him dozens of times!; **non se l'è fatto ripetere due volte** he didn't have to be told twice; **dopo ripetuti tentativi** after repeated attempts; **scusi, può ripetere?** excuse me, could you repeat that?; **continua a ripetere le stesse cose** he keeps repeating the same things; **ripetere qc a memoria** to recite sth by heart; **ripetere una lezione** (*studiarla*) to go over a lesson; **ripetere l'anno (scolastico)** to repeat the (school) year.

2 ripetersi VR (*persona*) to repeat o.s.

3 ripetersi VIP (*avvenimento, fenomeno*) to recur; **che non si ripeta più!** don't let this happen again!

ripetitore [ripeti'tore] SM (*Radio, TV*) relay.

ripetizione [ripetit'tsjone] SF **a** (*gen*) repetition; **fucile a ripetizione** repeating rifle **b** (*Scol*: *ripasso*) revision (*Brit*), review (*Am*); (: *lezioni private*) private tutoring *o* coaching *sg*; **dare** *o* **fare ripetizioni a qn** to give sb private lessons; **andare a ripetizione da qn** to take private lessons from sb.

ripetutamente [ripetuta'mente] AVV repeatedly, again and again.

ripiano [ri'pjano] SM (*di mobile*) shelf; (*di terreno*) terrace.

ripicca [ri'pikka] SF: **per ripicca** out of spite.

ripidamente [ripida'mente] AVV steeply.

ripidezza [ripi'dettsa] SF steepness.

ripido, a ['ripido] AGG steep.

ripiegamento [ripjega'mento] SM (*Mil*) retreat.

ripiegare [ripje'gare] **1** VT **a** (*piegare*: *di nuovo*) to fold (again), refold; (: *più volte*) to fold up **b** (*reclinare*: *capo*) to lower.

2 VI (*aus* **avere**) (*Mil*) to retreat, fall back; **ripiegare su** (*fig*) to make do with, fall back on.

3 ripiegarsi VIP (*ramo ecc*) to bend.

ripiego, ghi [ri'pjɛgo] SM expedient; **una soluzione di ripiego** a makeshift solution.

ripieno, a [ri'pjɛno] **1** AGG: **ripieno (di)** full (of); (*panino*) filled (with); (*tacchino*) stuffed (with).

2 SM (*Culin*) stuffing.

ripigliare [ripiʎ'ʎare] VT (*pigliare*: *di nuovo*) to take again; (: *indietro*) to take back; (*fig*: *forza, vigore*) to recover, get back; **ripigliare fiato** to catch one's breath; (*fig*) to have a breather.

ripiombare [ripjom'bare] VI (*aus* **essere**) (*cadere*): **ripiombare per terra** to fall heavily to the ground; **ripiombare nella disperazione** (*fig*) to sink back into despair; **se ne è**

andato e poi è ripiombato qui mezz'ora più tardi he went away and then turned up here again half an hour later.

ripone [ri'pone], **ripongo** ecc [ri'pongo] VB vedi **riporre**.

ripopolare [ripopo'lare] ① VT (gen) to repopulate; **ripopolare un fiume di pesci** to restock a river with fish.

② **ripopolarsi** VIP (zona) to be repopulated.

riporre [ri'porre] VT IRREG a (mettere via) to put away; (: dov'era prima) to put back, replace; **riporre qc al suo posto** to put sth where it belongs b : **riporre qc in qn** (fiducia, speranza) to place o put sth in sb.

riportare [ripor'tare] ① VT a (portare di nuovo: gen) to take back; (: verso chi parla) to bring back; **mi ha riportato a casa** he took me back home; **riportalo in cucina** take it back to the kitchen; **la scena lo riportò col pensiero all'infanzia** the scene took him back to his childhood

b (ottenere) to receive, get; (: vittoria) to carry off, win; (: successo) to have; **ha riportato gravi ferite** he was seriously injured; (soldato) he was seriously wounded; **ha riportato una frattura al braccio** he received a fracture to his arm; **la casa ha riportato gravi danni** the house has suffered serious damage, the house has been seriously damaged

c (riferire: notizie) to report; (citare) to quote

d (Mat) to carry (forward); **scrivo 5 e riporto 3** put down 5 and carry 3.

② **riportarsi** VIP: **riportarsi a** (anche fig) to go back to; (riferirsi a) to refer to.

riporto [ri'porto] SM a (Mat) amount carried over; **col riporto di 1** carry 1 b (Calzoleria, Sartoria) appliqué; (fam: di capelli) comb-over c (Caccia): **cane da riporto** retriever.

riposante [ripo'sante] AGG (gen) restful; (musica, colore) soothing.

riposare [ripo'sare] ① VT a (dare sollievo a: occhi, membra) to rest; **per riposare un po' la mente** to give one's mind a rest

a (posare di nuovo) to put down again.

② VI (aus avere) a (gen) to rest; (dormire) to sleep; **è andato a riposare** he's having a rest; (a letto) he has gone to lie down; **riposi in pace** (defunto) may he rest in peace; **qui riposa...** (su tomba) here lies ...

b (Culin: pasta, liquido) to stand; (vino) to settle; (terra) to lie fallow.

③ **riposarsi** VIP to rest; (dormire) to sleep; **vado a riposarmi** I'm going to have a rest; (a letto) I'm going to lie down; **cerca di riposarti un po'** try to rest.

riposato, a [ripo'sato] AGG (viso, aspetto) rested; (mente) fresh.

riposi ecc [ri'posi] VB vedi **riporre**.

riposo [ri'poso] SM a rest; **eterno riposo** (morte) eternal rest; **casa di riposo** (per anziani) rest-home; **prendersi un giorno/un mese di riposo** (da lavoro) to take a day/a month off; **buon riposo!** sleep well!; **senza un attimo di riposo** without a moment's rest; **riposo!** (Mil, Sport) at ease!; **"oggi riposo"** (Cine, Teatro) "no performance today"; (ristorante) "closed today"

b (pensione): **andare a riposo** to go into retirement, retire; **generale a riposo** retired general

c (Mus) rest.

ripostiglio, gli [ripos'tiʎʎo] SM (stanzino) lumber room (Brit), storage room (Am).

riposto, a [ri'posto] ① PP di **riporre**.

② AGG (letter: nascosto: senso, significato) hidden.

riprendere [ri'prɛndere] VB IRREG ① VT a (prendere di nuovo: gen) to take again; (: prigioniero) to recapture; (: città) to retake; (: impiegato) to take on again, re-employ; (: raffreddore) to catch again; (: velocità) to pick up again; (: quota) to regain; **riprendere moglie/marito** to get married again; **riprendere i sensi** to recover consciousness, come to o round; **riprendere sonno** to go back to sleep; **fu ripreso dal desiderio di vederla** again he felt the desire to see her; **fu ripreso dai dubbi** he began to have doubts again

b (riavere) to get back; (ritirare: oggetto riparato) to collect; **riprenditi le tue cose** take your things; **passo a riprendere Francesco/l'impermeabile più tardi** I'll call by to pick up Francesco/the raincoat later; **si è ripreso le sue fotografie** he took his photos back

c (ricominciare: viaggio, lavoro) to resume, start again; **riprendere a fare qc** to start doing sth again; **riprendere il cammino** to set off again; **riprendere una conversazione** to continue a conversation; **riprendi tutta la storia dall'inizio** start your story all over again; **"dunque", riprese, "dove eravamo?"** "so", he continued, "where were we?"

d (Cine, TV) to shoot; **riprendere un attore in primo piano** to shoot a close-up of an actor; **questa foto li riprende in un atteggiamento affettuoso** this photo shows them in an affectionate pose

e (rimproverare) to reprimand

f (restringere: abito) to take in

g (Sport: raggiungere) to catch up with.

② **riprendersi** VIP a (riaversi) to recover; (: pianta) to revive; **era emozionato ma si è ripreso** he was nervous but he pulled himself together

b (correggersi) to correct o.s.

ripresa [ri'presa] SF a (di attività, trattative) resumption; (di opera teatrale) revival; **a più riprese** (a stadi) in stages; (più volte) on several occasions, several times

b (Calcio) second half; (Pugilato) round; (Equitazione) riding lesson

c (Cine, TV, Fot) shot; (: azione) shooting no pl; **in ripresa diretta** live

d (ricupero: di persona, paese) recovery; **essere in ripresa** to be on the road to recovery; **ripresa economica** economic recovery

e (Aut) acceleration; **quest'auto non ha ripresa** this car's got no acceleration.

ripresentare [riprezen'tare] ① VT (certificato) to submit again; (domanda) to put forward again; (persona) to introduce again.

② **ripresentarsi** VR (ritornare: persona) to come back; **ripresentarsi a** (esame) to sit (Brit) o take (Am) again; (concorso) to enter again; **ripresentarsi come candidato** (Pol) to stand (Brit) o run (Am) again (as a candidate).

③ **ripresentarsi** VIP (occasione) to arise again.

ripreso, a [ri'preso] PP di **riprendere**.

ripristinare [ripristi'nare] VT (gen) to restore; (Inform) to reset; (tradizione) to revive, bring back into use; (legge) to bring back into force.

ripristino [ri'pristino] SM (gen) restoration; (di tradizioni) revival.

riprodotto, a [ripro'dotto] PP di **riprodurre**.

riprodurre [ripro'durre] VB IRREG ① VT to reproduce.

② **riprodursi** VIP (moltiplicarsi) to reproduce; (ripetersi: situazione, fenomeno) to occur o happen again, recur.

riproduttivo, a [riprodut'tivo] AGG reproductive.

riproduttore, trice [riprodut'tore] [1] AGG (*organo*) reproductive. [2] SM: **riproduttore acustico** pick-up.

riproduzione [riprodut'tsjone] SF (*gen*) reproduction; "**riproduzione vietata**" "all rights reserved", "copyright".

ripromesso, a [ripro'messo] PP di **ripromettersi**.

ripromettersi [ripro'mettersi] VIP IRREG: **ripromettersi di fare qc** to intend to do sth.

riproporre [ripro'porre] VB IRREG [1] VT (*soluzione*) to put forward again; (*legge*) to propose again; **riproporre di fare qc** to suggest doing sth again.

[2] **riproporsi** VIP **a** (*intendere*): **riproporsi di fare qc** to intend to do sth; **si è riproposto una lunga vacanza** he's thinking of having a long holiday

b (*ripresentarsi: problema, situazione*) to come up again, arise again.

[3] **riproporsi** VR: **riproporsi come candidato** to propose oneself as candidate again.

riproposto, a [ripro'posto] PP di **riproporre**.

riprova [ri'prɔva] SF confirmation; **a riprova di** as confirmation of.

riprovare¹ [ripro'vare] [1] VT (*provare di nuovo: gen*) to try again; (: *vestito*) to try on again; (: *sensazione*) to experience again.

[2] VI (*aus* **avere**) (*tentare*): **riprovare (a fare qc)** to try (to do sth) again; **riproverò più tardi** I'll try again later; **guai a lui se ci riprova!** God help him if he tries that again!

riprovare² [ripro'vare] VT (*biasimare*) to disapprove of.

riprovazione [riprovat'tsjone] SF censure, disapproval.

riprovevole [ripro'vevole] AGG reprehensible.

riprovevolmente [riprovevol'mente] AVV reprehensibly.

ripubblicare [ripubbli'kare] VT to republish.

ripudiare [ripu'djare] VT (*moglie, marito*) to repudiate; (*famiglia, patria*) to disown; (*principi, idee*) to reject.

ripudio, di [ri'pudjo] SM (*vedi vb*) repudiation; disowning; rejection.

ripugnante [ripuɲ'ɲante] AGG repulsive, disgusting.

ripugnanza [ripuɲ'ɲantsa] SF repugnance, disgust; **provare ripugnanza per qc/qn** to loathe sth/sb; **avere ripugnanza a fare qc** to loathe doing sth.

ripugnare [ripuɲ'ɲare] VI (*aus* **avere**): **ripugnare a qn** to repel *o* disgust sb; **la sola idea mi ripugna** I find the very idea of it disgusting; **non ti ripugna fare una cosa del genere?** don't you loathe doing such a thing?

ripulire [ripu'lire] [1] VT **a** (*pulire: di nuovo*) to clean again; (: *a fondo*) to clean up; **ripulire il giardino dalle foglie secche** to clear the garden of dead leaves; **ha ripulito il frigorifero** (*fig*) he finished off *o* polished off everything in the refrigerator; **gli hanno ripulito le tasche** (*fig*) they cleaned him out

b (*perfezionare*) to polish, refine.

[2] **ripulirsi** VR to clean o.s. up.

ripulita [ripu'lita] SF clean-up; **dare una ripulita a qc** to clean sth up; **darsi una ripulita** to tidy o.s. up, spruce o.s. up.

ripulsione [ripul'sjone] SF repulsion.

riquadro [ri'kwadro] SM (*gen, spazio*) square; (*di parete, soffitto, mobile*) panel.

riqualificare [rikwalifi'kare] VT, **riqualificarsi** VR (*operaio*) to retrain.

risacca, che [ri'sakka] SF backwash.

risaia [ri'saja] SF paddy field.

risalire [risa'lire] [1] VT (*salire di nuovo: gen*) to go up again;

(*scale*) to climb again; **risalire la corrente** to go upstream.

[2] VI (*aus* **essere**) **a** (*gen, livello, prezzi*) to go up again, rise again; **risalire a cavallo** to remount; **risalire in macchina** to get back into the car; **risalire al piano di sopra** to go back upstairs; **risalire in cima alla classifica** to climb back (up) to the top of the league

b : **risalire a** (*data, periodo*) to date back to, go back to

c (*ritornare*): **risalire a** to go back to; **risalire alle fonti** to go back to source material.

risalita [risa'lita] SF: **impianti di risalita** (*Sci*) ski lifts.

risaltare [risal'tare] VI (*aus* **avere** *o* **essere**) (*anche fig*): **risaltare (su/fra)** to stand out (against/among); (*colore*) to show up (against/among).

risalto [ri'salto] SM (*rilievo*) prominence; (*enfasi*) emphasis; **dar risalto a qc** to give prominence to sth, lay emphasis on sth; **mettere** *o* **porre in risalto qc** to make sth stand out.

risanamento [risana'mento] SM **a** (*economico*) improvement ▶**risanamento del bilancio** reorganization of the budget **b** (*bonifica*) reclamation ▶**risanamento edilizio** urban redevelopment.

risanare [risa'nare] [1] VT **a** (*economia*) to improve; (*bilancio*) to reorganize **b** (*palude*) to reclaim; (*quartiere*) to redevelop **c** (*guarire*) to heal, cure.

[2] VI (*aus* **essere**), **risanarsi** VIP (*guarire, anche fig*) to heal.

risapere [risa'pere] VT to come to know of; **è risaputo che...** everyone knows that ..., it's common knowledge that ... .

risaputo, a [risa'puto] AGG: **sono cose risapute** it's common knowledge.

risarcibile [risar'tʃibile] AGG indemnifiable.

risarcimento [risartʃi'mento] SM: **risarcimento (di)** compensation (for); **chiedere il risarcimento** to claim compensation; **aver diritto al risarcimento dei danni** to be entitled to damages.

risarcire [risar'tʃire] VT (*compensare: cose*) to pay compensation for; (: *persona*): **risarcire qn di qc** to compensate sb for sth; **risarcire i danni a qn** to pay sb damages.

risata [ri'sata] SF laugh; **che risate!** what a laugh!, how we laughed!; **farsi una bella risata** to have a good laugh.

riscaldamento [riskalda'mento] SM heating ▶**riscaldamento autonomo** central heating (*for one home only*) ▶**riscaldamento centrale** central heating (*serving an entire block of flats*).

riscaldare [riskal'dare] [1] VT **a** (*scaldare: stanza, acqua*) to heat; (: *mani, persona*) to warm; **riscaldarsi le mani/i piedi** to warm one's hands/feet

b (*scaldare di nuovo*) to heat up, reheat.

[2] VI (*aus* **avere**) (*stufa*) to heat up; **il motore riscalda troppo** the engine overheats.

[3] **riscaldarsi** VIP (*persona*) to get warm, warm o.s. up; (*atleta*) to warm up; (*fig: infervorarsi*) to get worked up, get excited; (*adirarsi*) to get angry.

riscaldo [ris'kaldo] SM (*fam*) (slight) inflammation; **ha un po' di riscaldo** (*brufoletti*) he's got a bit of a rash.

riscattabile [riskat'tabile] AGG redeemable.

riscattare [riskat'tare] [1] VT (*Dir, fig*) to redeem; (*prigioniero*) to ransom, pay a ransom for.

[2] **riscattarsi** VR (*fig*) to redeem o.s.

riscatto [ris'katto] SM (*Dir, fig*) redemption; (*di rapimento*) ransom.

rischiarare [riskja'rare] [1] VT (*gen*) to light up; (*colore*) to

make lighter; **rischiararsi la voce** to clear one's throat. **2** VI (*aus* **essere**), **rischiararsi** VIP (*cielo*) to clear; (*fig: volto*) to brighten up; (*liquido*) to become clear; **si rischiarò in volto** his face lit up; **rischiara** OR **si sta rischiarando** (*tempo, cielo*) it's clearing up.

rischiare [ris'kjare] **1** VT to risk; **rischiare il tutto per tutto** to risk everything. **2** VI (*aus* **avere**): **rischiare di fare qc** to risk doing sth, run the risk of doing sth; **ha rischiato di cadere** he nearly fell.

rischio, chi ['riskjo] SM risk; **a rischio di fare qc** at the risk of doing sth; **a proprio rischio e pericolo** at one's own risk; **correre il rischio di fare qc** to run the risk of doing sth; **mettere a rischio qc** to put sth at risk; **un rischio calcolato** a calculated risk; **c'è il rischio che questo viaggio non si possa fare** there is a danger that we (*o* you *ecc*) won't be able to make this trip; **soggetto/ categoria a rischio** subject/group at risk; **capitale di rischio** (*Fin*) risk *o* venture capital ▶**rischio del mestiere** occupational hazard.

rischiosità [riskjosi'ta] SF riskiness.

rischioso, a [ris'kjoso] AGG risky, dangerous, hazardous.

risciacquare [riʃʃak'kware] VT (*panni, stoviglie*) to rinse; **risciaquarsi la bocca** to rinse one's mouth out.

risciacquatura [riʃʃakkwa'tura] SF **a** (*atto*) rinsing **b** (*dei piatti*) dishwater.

risciacquo [riʃ'ʃakkwo] SM rinse.

risciò [riʃ'ʃɔ] SM INV rickshaw.

riscontare [riskon'tare] VT (*Fin*) to rediscount.

riscontrare [riskon'trare] VT **a** (*rilevare*) to notice, find; **non ho riscontrato errori** I haven't found *o* noticed any mistakes **b** (*confrontare*) to compare; (*controllare: conti, motore*) to check, inspect; **riscontrare la copia con l'originale** to compare the copy with the original; (*Tip*) to read against copy.

riscontro [ris'kontro] SM **a** (*conferma*) confirmation; **le sue osservazioni non trovano riscontro nella realtà** his remarks are not borne out by the facts **b** (*confronto*) comparison; (*controllo*) check; **mettere a riscontro** to compare, check; **fare il riscontro della copia con l'originale** to compare the copy with the original; (*Tip*) to read against copy; **un avvenimento che non ha avuto riscontro in passato** an event which had no parallel in the past **c** (*Comm: risposta per iscritto*) reply; **in attesa di un vostro cortese riscontro** we look forward to your reply.

riscoperto, a [risko'pɛrto] PP di **riscoprire**.

riscoprire [risko'prire] VT IRREG to rediscover.

riscossa [ris'kɔssa] SF (*riconquista*) recovery, reconquest.

riscossione [riskos'sjone] SF collection.

riscosso, a [ris'kɔsso] PP di **riscuotere**.

riscritto, a [ris'kritto] PP di **riscrivere**.

riscrivere [ris'krivere] VT IRREG to rewrite; (*uso assoluto: scrivere in risposta*) to write back.

riscuotere [ris'kwɔtere] VB IRREG **1** VT (*stipendio, pensione*) to draw; (*tasse, affitto*) to collect; (*fig: applausi, approvazione, successo*) to win, earn; **riscuotere un assegno** to cash a cheque (*Brit*) *o* check (*Am*). **2** **riscuotersi** VIP: **riscuotersi (da)** (*fig*) to rouse o.s. (from), shake o.s. (out of).

rise *ecc* ['rise] VB vedi **ridere**.

risentimento [risenti'mento] SM resentment; **provare** *o* **avere del risentimento verso** *o* **contro qn** to feel resentful towards sb.

risentire [risen'tire] **1** VT (*sentire di nuovo*) to hear again; (*disco*) to listen to again. **2** VI: **risentire di** (*esperienza, trauma*) to feel the effects of; (: *portarne i segni*) to show the effects of; **risentire dell'influenza di** to show traces of the influence of; **le piante hanno risentito del freddo** the plants have felt the cold. **3** **risentirsi** VR (*offendersi*) to take offence (*Brit*) *o* offense (*Am*); **risentirsi di** *o* **per qc** to resent sth, take offence *o* offense at sth.

risentitamente [risentita'mente] AVV resentfully.

risentito, a [risen'tito] AGG resentful.

riserbo [ri'sɛrbo] SM reserve; **è una persona di grande riserbo** he's a very reserved person; **senza riserbo** unreservedly; **mantenere un assoluto riserbo (su qc)** to maintain a complete silence (about sth).

riserva [ri'sɛrva] SF **a** (*provvista, scorta*) reserve; **fare riserva di** (*acqua, cibo*) to get in a supply of, stock up on; **tenere di riserva** to keep in reserve; **entrare in riserva** OR **essere in riserva** (*Aut*) to be nearly out of petrol (*Brit*) *o* gas (*Am*); **di riserva** (*gen*) reserve *attr*; (*aereo, corriera*) back-up *attr* ▶**riserva aurea** gold reserves *pl* **b** (*Mil, Sport*) reserve; **(giocatore di) riserva** (player); **truppe della riserva** reserves **c** (*limitazione: anche: riserva mentale*) reservation; **con le dovute riserve** with certain reservations; **ha accettato con la riserva di potersi ritirare** he accepted with the proviso that he could pull out; **senza riserve** (*incondizionatamente*) unreservedly **d** (*territorio*): **riserva di caccia/pesca** hunting/fishing preserve ▶**riserva indiana** Indian reservation ▶**riserva naturale** nature reserve.

riservare [riser'vare] VT **a** (*tenere da parte*) to keep aside; (*mettere da parte*) to put aside; **riservare una sorpresa a qn** to have a surprise in store for sb; **cosa ci riserva il destino?** what has destiny in store for us?; **riservarsi di fare qc** to intend to do sth; **riservarsi il diritto di fare qc** to reserve the right to do sth **b** (*prenotare*) to book, reserve.

riservatamente [riservata'mente] AVV (*vedi agg a*) in confidence, confidentially; reservedly; discreetly.

riservatezza [riserva'tettsa] SF (*vedi agg a*) confidential nature; reserve; discretion.

riservato, a [riser'vato] AGG **a** (*lettera, informazione*) confidential; (*persona, carattere*) reserved; (: *discreto*) discreet **b** (*prenotato*) reserved, booked.

riservista, i [riser'vista] SM (*Mil*) reservist.

risguardo [riz'gwardo] SM (*di libro*) flyleaf.

risi *ecc* ['risi] VB vedi **ridere**.

risibile [ri'sibile] AGG laughable.

risicare [rizi'kare] VI: **chi non risica non rosica** (*Proverbio*) nothing ventured nothing gained.

risicato, a [rizi'kato] AGG (*maggioranza*) very narrow.

risicoltore, trice [risikol'tore] SM/F rice grower.

risicoltura [risikol'tura] SF rice growing.

risiedere [ri'sjɛdere] VI **a** (*vivere*): **risiedere in** *o* **a** to reside in **b** (*consistere, stare*): **risiedere in** to lie in; **il motivo del suo successo risiede nel suo senso dell'umorismo** the reason for his success is his sense of humour.

risma ['rizma] SF **a** (*di carta*) ream **b** (*fig: pegg: tipo*) kind, sort; **essere della stessa risma** to be all of a kind.

riso¹ ['riso] **1** PP di **ridere**. **2** SM (*pl f* **risa**) (*il ridere*) laughter; (*risata*) laugh; **uno scoppio di risa** a burst of laughter; **non riusciva a**

trattenere il riso he couldn't help laughing; **sbellicarsi** o **crepare dalle risa** (fam) to split one's sides laughing; **il riso fa buon sangue** laughter is the best medicine.

riso[2] ['riso] SM (Bot) rice; **riso in brodo** consommé with rice; **riso in bianco** rice with butter; **carta di riso** (Arte) rice paper.

risolare [riso'lare], **risuolare** [riswo'lare] VT (scarpe) to resole.

risolino [riso'lino] SM (di scherno, ironico) snigger.

risollevare [risolle'vare] ① VT (sollevare di nuovo: testa) to raise again, lift up again; (fig: questione) to raise again, bring up again; (: morale) to raise; **risollevare le sorti di qc** to improve the chances of sth.

② **risollevarsi** VR (da terra) to rise again; (fig: da malattia) to recover.

risolsi ecc [ri'sɔlsi] VB vedi **risolvere**.

risolto, a [ri'sɔlto] PP di **risolvere**.

risolubile [riso'lubile] AGG = risolvibile.

risolutamente [risoluta'mente] AVV resolutely.

risolutezza [risolu'tettsa] SF decisiveness, resolution, determination.

risolutivo, a [risolu'tivo] AGG (determinante) decisive; **arrivare ad una formula risolutiva** (che risolve) to come up with a formula to resolve a situation.

risoluto, a [riso'luto] AGG resolute, determined; **essere risoluto a fare qc** to be determined to do sth.

risoluzione [risolut'tsjone] SF **a** (soluzione, Mat) solution **b** (decisione) resolution **c** (Dir: di contratto) annulment, cancellation **d** (Chim) resolution.

risolvere [ri'sɔlvere] VB IRREG ① VT **a** (problema, Mat) to solve, work out; (mistero, indovinello) to solve; (difficoltà, faccenda, controversia) to resolve, sort out; **cosa risolvi facendo così?** what do you solve by doing that?

b (decidere) to decide, resolve; **abbiamo risolto di partire al più presto** we've decided to leave as soon as possible

c (Dir: contratto) to annul, cancel

d (Chim) to break down.

② **risolversi** VIP **a** (andare a finire): **risolversi in bene** to end well, turn out well; **risolversi in nulla** to come to nothing; **l'operazione si è risolta in un fiasco** the operation turned out to be a disaster

b (decidersi): **risolversi a fare qc** to make up one's mind to do sth

c (malattia) to clear up.

risolvibile [risol'vibile] AGG solvable.

risonante [riso'nante] AGG resonant.

risonanza [riso'nantsa] SF (Fis) resonance; (fig: eco) interest; **suscitare una grande risonanza** to arouse great interest; **aver vasta risonanza** (fatto, vicenda) to be known far and wide.

risonare [riso'nare] VT, VI = risuonare.

risorgere [ri'sɔrdʒere] VI IRREG (aus essere) (Rel, fig) to rise again; **risorgeva in lui la speranza** his hopes were revived.

risorgimentale [risordʒimen'tale] AGG of the Risorgimento.

risorgimento [risordʒi'mento] SM (di arte, cultura) revival; **il Risorgimento** movement which began in the early nineteenth century and led to the proclamation of the Kingdom of Italy (1861), and eventually unification (1871).

risorsa [ri'sorsa] SF (gen) resource; **è l'ultima risorsa** it's the last resort; **una persona piena di risorse** a resource-ful person.

risorsi ecc [ri'sorsi] VB vedi **risorgere**.

risorto, a [ri'sorto] PP di **risorgere**.

risotto [ri'sotto] SM (Culin) risotto.

risparmiare [rispar'mjare] ① VT **a** (denaro, cibo, tempo) to save; (gas, elettricità) to economize on, save on; **risparmiare fatica/fiato** to save one's energy/breath; **risparmiati il disturbo** o **la fatica** (anche iro) save yourself the trouble; **risparmiare qc a qn** (fig: evitare) to spare sb sth; **ti risparmio i particolari** I'll spare you the details **b** (non uccidere, non colpire) to spare; **risparmiare la vita a qn** to spare sb's life.

② VI (aus avere): **risparmiare su qc** to economize on sth, save on sth.

③ **risparmiarsi** VR to spare oneself.

risparmiatore, trice [risparmja'tore] SM/F saver.

risparmio, mi [ris'parmjo] SM **a** (azione) saving; **ci riuscimmo con un risparmio di tempo e denaro** we succeeded and saved time and money into the bargain; **senza risparmio di forze** sparing no effort **b** : **risparmi** SMPL (denaro risparmiato) savings pl.

rispecchiare [rispek'kjare] ① VT to reflect.

② **rispecchiarsi** VR to be reflected; **è così lucido che ti ci puoi rispecchiare** it's so shiny that you can see your face in it.

rispedire [rispe'dire] VT to send back; **rispedire qc a qn** to send sth back to sb.

rispettabile [rispet'tabile] AGG **a** (persona) respectable **b** (considerevole: somma) sizeable, considerable.

rispettabilità [rispettabili'ta] SF respectability.

rispettare [rispet'tare] ① VT (persona, idea) to respect, have respect for; (legge) to obey, comply with, abide by; (promessa) to keep; **farsi rispettare da qn** to command sb's respect; **far rispettare la legge** to enforce the law; **rispettare l'ordine alfabetico** to maintain alphabetical order; **rispettare i tempi (stabiliti)** to keep to schedule; **rispettare le distanze** to keep one's distance; **ogni medico che si rispetti** every self-respecting doctor.

② **rispettarsi** VR to respect o.s.

rispettivamente [rispettiva'mente] AVV respectively.

rispettivo, a [rispet'tivo] AGG respective.

rispetto [ris'petto] SM **a** : **rispetto (di** o **per)** (gen) respect (for); (norme, leggi) observance (of), compliance (with); **portare rispetto a qn/qc** to have o feel respect for sb/sth; **mancare di rispetto a qn** to be disrespectful to sb; **non ha alcun rispetto per le cose altrui** she has no respect for other people's property; **con rispetto** (nelle lettere) respectfully yours; **con rispetto parlando** if you will excuse my saying so, with respect

b : **rispetti** SMPL (frm: omaggi): **(porga) i miei rispetti alla signora** my regards to your wife

c (riguardo, relazione): **rispetto a** (in confronto) compared to, in comparison with; (riguardo a) as regards, with respect to, regarding, as for; **sotto questo rispetto** from this point of view; **sotto ogni rispetto** in every respect.

rispettosamente [rispettosa'mente] AVV respectfully.

rispettoso, a [rispet'toso] AGG respectful; **essere rispettoso verso qn** to be respectful to sb, show respect to sb; **essere rispettoso di qc** to have respect for sth.

risplendente [risplen'dɛnte] AGG (sole) bright, shining; (occhi) sparkling; **risplendente di gioia** (viso) shining with joy.

risplendere [ris'plɛndere] VI (gen) to shine; (luccicare) to

sparkle, glitter.

rispondente [rispon'dɛnte] AGG: **rispondente a** in accordance with, in keeping o conformity with.

rispondenza [rispon'dɛntsa] SF correspondence.

rispondere [ris'pondere] VB IRREG ⓵ VI (aus **avere**) **a** : **rispondere a** (domanda) to reply to, answer; (persona) to answer; (invito) to reply to; **rispondere al telefono** to answer the telephone; **rispondere di sì/di no** to say yes/no; **cosa vuoi che ti risponda?** what can I say?; **rispondere bene** to give the right o correct answer; **rispondere male** (sgarbatamente) to answer back, answer rudely; (in modo errato) to give the wrong answer; **rispondere al nome di** to answer to the name of **b** (rimbeccare): **rispondere (a qn)** to answer (sb) back; **rispondere per le rime** (fig) to give sb as good as one gets
c (reagire: veicolo, freni) to respond
d (corrispondere): **rispondere a** to correspond to; (: speranze, bisogno) to answer; **rispondere alle esigenze di** to meet the needs of
e (garantire): **rispondere di qn** to answer for sb, be responsible for sb, vouch for sb; (essere responsabile): **rispondere a qn di qc** to be answerable to sb for sth; **non rispondo più di me stesso** o **delle mie azioni** I can't answer for my actions
f (Carte) to follow, reply.
⓶ VT **a** : **rispondere che...** to answer that ..., reply that ...
b : **rispondere picche** (fig) to give a flat refusal, refuse flatly.

risposare [rispo'zare] ⓵ VT to marry again, remarry.
⓶ **risposarsi** VIP to get married again, remarry.

risposta [ris'posta] SF **a** (a domanda, lettera) answer, reply; **dare una risposta** to give an answer; **in risposta a** in reply to, in answer to; **diamo risposta alla vostra lettera del...** in reply to your letter of ...; **per tutta risposta mi ha sbattuto la porta in faccia** his only answer was to slam the door in my face
b (replica) reply, retort
c (Carte) reply
d (Tennis): **risposta al servizio** return of serve.

risposto [ris'posto] PP di **rispondere**.

rispuntare [rispun'tare] VI (aus **essere**) (sole) to come out again, reappear; (persona) to pop up again, reappear.

rissa ['rissa] SF fight, brawl.

rissoso, a [ris'soso] AGG quarrelsome.

rist. ABBR = **ristampa**.

ristabilire [ristabi'lire] ⓵ VT **a** (gen) to re-establish; (servizio) to put back in operation; (ordine, istituzione) to restore **b** (sogg: riposo ecc): **ristabilire qn** to restore sb to health.
⓶ **ristabilirsi** VIP (persona) to recover, get better; **ristabilirsi da** to recover from.

ristagnare [ristaɲ'ɲare] VI (aus **avere**) (acqua) to be stagnant; (sangue) to cease flowing; (fig: affari, industria) to stagnate.

ristagno [ris'taɲɲo] SM (anche fig) stagnation; **c'è un ristagno delle vendite** business is slack.

ristampa [ris'tampa] SF (il ristampare) reprinting no pl; (opera ristampata) reprint.

ristampare [ristam'pare] VT to reprint.

ristorante [risto'rante] ⓵ SM restaurant; **ristorante della stazione** station buffet.
⓶ AGG INV restaurant attr.

ristorare [risto'rare] ⓵ VT to revive, refresh; **ristorare le**

forze to restore one's strength.
⓶ **ristorarsi** VR (rifocillarsi) to have something to eat and drink; (riposarsi) to rest, have a rest.

ristoratore, trice [ristora'tore] ⓵ AGG refreshing, reviving.
⓶ SM/F restaurateur.

ristoro [ris'tɔro] SM (bevanda, cibo) refreshment; **posto di ristoro** refreshment bar, buffet, snack bar; **servizio di ristoro** (Ferr) refreshments pl.

ristrettezza [ristret'tettsa] SF **a** (scarsità) shortage, lack, scarcity; **ristrettezza di idee** narrow-mindedness **b** : **ristrettezze** SFPL poverty sg, straitened circumstances.

ristretto, a [ris'tretto] ⓵ PP di **restringere**.
⓶ AGG **a** (limitato) limited, restricted; (angusto) narrow; (racchiuso) enclosed, hemmed in; **ristretto a** restricted o limited to; **di idee ristrette** (fig) narrow-minded **b** (concentrato: brodo) thick; (: caffè) extra strong.

ristrutturante [ristruttu'rante] AGG (crema, balsamo) repair attr.

ristrutturare [ristruttu'rare] VT (appartamento) to do up; (: ridipingere ecc) to redecorate; (edificio) to restore; (azienda) to reorganize; (pelle, capelli) to repair.

ristrutturazione [ristrutturat'tsjone] SF (vedi vb) alteration; redecoration; restoration; reorganization; repair.

risucchiare [risuk'kjare] VT (sogg: vortice) to swallow up.

risucchio, chi [ri'sukkjo] SM (di acqua) undertow, pull; (di aria) suction.

risultante [risul'tante] ⓵ SM (Mat, Fis) resultant.
⓶ SF (fig) result, effect.

risultare [risul'tare] VI (aus **essere**) **a** (rivelarsi) to prove to be, turn out to be; (essere accertato) to be clear, emerge; (essere noto) to appear, seem; **le mie previsioni sono risultate errate** my forecasts proved to be wrong; **dalle analisi è risultato affetto da diabete** it is clear from the tests that he is suffering from diabetes; **risulta appartenere ad un determinato gruppo politico** he's known to belong to a specific political group; **è risultato vincitore** he emerged as the winner
b : **mi risulta che...** I understand that ..., as far as I know ...; **(ne) risulta che...** it follows that ...; **non mi risulta** not as far as I know; **ti risulta che sia ancora qui?** do you know whether he's still here?

risultato [risul'tato] SM (gen, Mat, Sport) result ► **risultati parziali** (Sport) half-time results.

risuonare [riswo'nare] ⓵ VI **a** (gen) to resound; **un grido risuonò nel silenzio** a scream pierced the silence; **mi risuonano nella mente le sue parole** his words still echo in my mind **b** (Fis) to resonate.
⓶ VT (suonare di nuovo: musica) to play again; (: campanello) to ring again.

risurrezione [risurret'tsjone] SF (Rel) resurrection.

risuscitare [risuʃʃi'tare] ⓵ VT to resuscitate, restore to life; (fig) to revive, bring back; **risuscitare qn dalla morte** to raise sb from the dead; **questo vino farebbe risuscitare un morto** (fig scherz) this wine would revive the dead.
⓶ VI (aus **essere**) to rise from the dead; (fig: riprendere vigore) to revive.

risvegliare [rizveʎ'ʎare] ⓵ VT (gen) to wake up, waken; (fig: dall'inerzia): **risvegliare qn (da)** to rouse sb (from); (fig: interesse) to stir up, arouse; (: curiosità) to arouse; **risvegliare l'appetito** to whet one's appetite; **risvegliare i ricordi** to bring back old memories.
⓶ **risvegliarsi** VIP to wake up, awaken; (fig: interesse,

curiosità) to be aroused; **il vulcano si è risvegliato** the volcano has become active again.

risveglio, gli [riz'veʎʎo] SM (*azione*) awakening, waking up; (*fig: di arte, cultura, interesse*) revival; **al risveglio** when he (*o* she *ecc*) woke up.

risvolto [riz'vɔlto] SM **a** (*di giacca*) lapel; (*di manica*) cuff; (*di pantaloni*) turn-up (*Brit*), cuff (*Am*); (*di tasca*) flap; (*di libro*) inside flap **b** (*fig: aspetto secondario*) implication.

ritagliare [ritaʎ'ʎare] VT (*tagliare via*): **ritagliare (da)** to cut out (of).

ritaglio, gli [ri'taʎʎo] SM (*di giornale*) cutting, clipping; (*di stoffa*) remnant, scrap; **nei ritagli di tempo** in one's spare time.

ritardare [ritar'dare] ① VT **a** (*differire*) to delay, hold up; **ritardare il pagamento** to defer payment

b (*rallentare: sviluppo, processo*) to slow down.

② VI (*aus con soggetto inanimato* **essere;** *con soggetto animato* **avere**) (*persona, treno*) to be late; (*orologio*) to be slow; **ritardare a fare qc** to be late in doing sth; **ritardare di un quarto d'ora** to be fifteen minutes late.

ritardatario, ria, ri, rie [ritarda'tarjo] SM/F latecomer.

ritardato, a [ritar'dato] AGG (*Psic*) retarded.

ritardo [ri'tardo] SM **a** (*di treno, posta*) delay; (*di persona*) lateness *no pl*; **essere in ritardo** to be late; **un ritardo di 2 ore** a 2-hour delay; **arrivò con 2 ore di ritardo** it (*o* he *ecc*) arrived 2 hours late; **scusa il ritardo** sorry I'm late **b** (*mentale*) backwardness, retardation; **un ritardo dello sviluppo mentale** a retarded mental development.

ritegno [ri'teɲɲo] SM restraint; **abbi un po' di ritegno!** restrain yourself!; **senza ritegno** unrestrained, without restraint.

ritemprare [ritem'prare] VT (*forze, spirito*) to restore.

ritenere [rite'nere] VB IRREG ① VT **a** (*considerare*) to think, believe, consider; **lo ritengo un ottimo insegnante** I think he's an excellent teacher; **ritenere opportuno fare qc** to think it opportune to do sth; **ho ritenuto che fosse opportuno fare così** I felt it opportune to do so; **ritengo di sì** I think so; **ritengo di no** I don't think so; **si ritiene che l'uomo sia fuggito in macchina** they think that the man escaped by car

b (*trattenere: denaro*) to withhold, deduct; (: *nozioni, concetti*) to retain; **gli hanno ritenuto due giorni di paga** they withheld 2 days' pay; **ho una memoria così labile che non riesco a ritenere nulla** my memory is so poor that I can't seem to retain anything

c (*umidità, liquidi*) to retain.

② **ritenersi** VR to consider o.s.; **si ritiene un genio** he thinks he's a genius.

ritengo [ri'tengo], **ritenni** [ri'tenni] *ecc* VB *vedi* **ritenere.**

ritentare [riten'tare] VT to try again, make another attempt at.

ritenuta [rite'nuta] SF deduction; **ritenuta sulla paga** deduction from one's pay ▶**ritenuta d'acconto** *advance tax deduction* ▶**ritenuta alla fonte** taxation at source.

ritenzione [riten'tsjone] SF (*Med*) retention ▶**ritenzione idrica** water retention.

riterrò *ecc* [riter'rɔ] VB *vedi* **ritenere.**

ritirare [riti'rare] ① VT **a** (*mano, braccio*) to pull back; (*soldi, candidatura*) to withdraw; (*certificato, bagaglio*) to collect, pick up; (*bucato*) to bring in; **appena ritiro (lo stipendio) ti restituisco i soldi** as soon as I draw my wages I'll pay you back; **ritirare il passaporto a qn** to

withdraw sb's passport; **gli hanno ritirato la patente** they disqualified him from driving (*Brit*), they took away his licence (*Brit*) *o* license (*Am*); **ritiro quello che ho detto** I take back what I said

b (*cambiale*) to retire

c (*tirare di nuovo*) to pull again; (*lanciare di nuovo*) to throw again.

② **ritirarsi** VR **a** (*Mil*) to retreat, withdraw; (*persona: da un'attività*) to retire; (: *appartarsi*) to withdraw, retire; **si ritirò nella sua stanza** he withdrew *o* retired to his room; **ritirarsi a vita privata** to withdraw from public life.

③ **ritirarsi** VIP **a** (*retrocedere: acque*) to recede, subside **b** (*tessuto*) to shrink.

ritirata [riti'rata] SF **a** (*Mil*) retreat, withdrawal; (: *in caserma*) tattoo; **suonare la ritirata** to sound the retreat (*o* the tattoo); **essere in ritirata** to be in retreat **b** (*latrina*) lavatory (*Brit*), toilet (*Brit*), bathroom (*Am*).

ritirato, a [riti'rato] AGG secluded; **fare vita ritirata** to live in seclusion.

ritiro [ri'tiro] SM **a** (*il ritirare: di truppe, candidatura, soldi*) withdrawal; (: *di biglietti, pacchi*) collection; (: *di passaporto*) confiscation; **ritiro bagagli** baggage reclaim; **la ricevuta vi verrà consegnata al momento del ritiro della merce** you will be given the receipt on collection of the goods; **"per il ritiro dei vaglia postali rivolgersi a..."** "postal orders are issued at ..."

b (*il ritirarsi: Mil*) withdrawal, retreat; (: *di acque*) subsidence; **dopo il suo ritiro dal mondo dello spettacolo** after retiring from show business; **dopo il suo ritiro dalla gara** after withdrawing from the competition

c (*luogo appartato: anche Rel*) retreat; **in ritiro** in retreat; **fare quindici giorni di ritiro** to go on a fortnight's retreat; **la squadra andrà in ritiro per una settimana** (*Sport*) the team will go away on a training session for a week.

ritmare [rit'mare] VT: **ritmare il passo** OR **ritmare la corsa** to keep the rhythm, keep in rhythm.

ritmato, a [rit'mato] AGG rhythmic(al).

ritmica ['ritmika] SF (*Mus*) rhythmics *sg*.

ritmicamente [ritmika'mente] AVV rhythmically.

ritmico, a, ci, che ['ritmiko] AGG rhythmic(al).

ritmo ['ritmo] SM **a** (*gen*) rhythm; **ballare al ritmo di valzer** to waltz **b** (*fig: velocità*) speed, rate; **al ritmo di** at a speed *o* rate of; **a questo ritmo** at this rate; **il ritmo frenetico della vita moderna** the frantic pace of life today.

rito ['rito] SM (*Rel*) rite; (*cerimonia*) ritual; **di rito** customary, usual.

ritoccare [ritok'kare] VT (*disegno, foto, trucco*) to touch up; (*testo, prezzi*) to alter.

ritocco, chi [ri'tokko] SM (*di disegno, trucco*) touching up *no pl*; (*di testo*) alteration; **dare un ritocco a qc** to touch sth up; alter sth.

ritorcere [ri'tɔrtʃere] VB IRREG ① VT (*filato*) to twist; (*fig: accusa, insulto*) to throw back.

② **ritorcersi** VIP (*tornare a danno di*): **ritorcersi contro** to turn against.

ritornare [ritor'nare] ① VI (*aus essere*) = **tornare.**

② VT (*restituire*): **ritornare qc a qn** to return sth to sb, give sth back to sb.

ritornello [ritor'nɛllo] SM (*Mus, Poesia*) refrain; (*fig: storia*) story; **è sempre il solito ritornello** it's always the same old story.

ritorno [ri'torno] SM **a** *(gen)* return; **essere di ritorno** to be back; **far ritorno** to return; **durante il (viaggio di) ritorno** on the return trip, on the way back; **al ritorno** *(tornando)* on the way back; **al mio/tuo ritorno** on my/your return; **girone di ritorno** *(Sport)* second half of the season; **avere un ritorno di fiamma** *(Aut)* to backfire; **hanno avuto un ritorno di fiamma** *(fig)* they're back in love again

  b *(in restituzione)*: **fammelo avere di ritorno entro la fine del mese** let me have it back by the end of the month.

ritorsione [ritor'sjone] SF *(rappresaglia)* retaliation.

ritorto, a [ri'torto] [1] PP di **ritorcere**.

  [2] AGG *(cotone, corda)* twisted.

ritradurre [ritra'durre] VT *(tradurre: di nuovo)* to re-translate; (: *nella lingua originale)* to back-translate.

ritrarre [ri'trarre] VB IRREG [1] VT **a** *(Pittura, fig)* to portray, depict **b** *(tirare indietro)* to withdraw.

  [2] **ritrarsi** VR to move back.

ritrasformare [ritrasfor'mare] [1] VT: **ritrasformare qc in** to turn sth back into.

  [2] **ritrasformarsi** VIP: **ritrasformarsi in** to turn back into.

ritrasmettere [ritraz'mettere] VT to re-broadcast.

ritrattabile [ritrat'tabile] AGG *(dichiarazione, accusa)* retractable.

ritrattare [ritrat'tare] VT **a** *(dichiarazione)* to retract, withdraw, take back **b** *(trattare nuovamente)* to deal with again, cover again.

ritrattazione [ritrattat'tsjone] SF withdrawal.

ritrattista, i, e [ritrat'tista] SM/F portrait painter.

ritrattistica [ritrat'tistika] SF *(Art)* portraiture.

ritratto, a [ri'tratto] [1] PP di **ritrarre**.

  [2] SM portrait; **essere il ritratto della salute** to be the picture of health; **è il ritratto di suo padre** he's his father's image.

ritrosamente [ritrosa'mente] AVV shyly.

ritrosia [ritro'sia] SF *(riluttanza)* reluctance, unwillingness; *(timidezza)* shyness.

ritroso, a [ri'troso] [1] AGG **a** *(timido)* shy, bashful **b** *(restio)*: **ritroso a fare qc** reluctant to do sth.

  [2]: **a ritroso** AVV *(indietro)* backwards.

ritrovamento [ritrova'mento] SM *(di cadavere, oggetto smarrito)* finding; *(oggetto ritrovato)* find.

ritrovare [ritro'vare] [1] VT **a** *(ricuperare: oggetto, persona)* to find; *(pace)* to find again; *(forza)* to find again, recover

  b *(rincontrare)* to meet again; (: *per caso)* to run into.

  [2] **ritrovarsi** VIP **a** *(finire)* to end up; **si ritrovò solo/a fare i lavori più umili** he ended up alone/doing the most menial tasks; **mi sono ritrovato con 5000 lire in più** I found myself with 5000 lire extra; **ci ritrovammo al punto di partenza** we ended up where we started

  b *(possedere: fam scherz)*: **con la fortuna che si ritrova...** with his luck ...

  b *(incontrarsi)*: **ritrovarsi con** *(amici)* to meet.

ritrovato [ritro'vato] SM discovery.

ritrovo [ri'trovo] SM *(punto d'incontro)* meeting place ▶**ritrovo notturno** night club.

ritto, a ['ritto] AGG *(in piedi: persona)* upright, on one's feet; **aveva i capelli ritti** his hair was standing on end.

rituale [ritu'ale] [1] AGG *(di rito)* ritual; *(fig: solito)* customary, usual.

  [2] SM *(Rel)* ritual.

ritualmente [ritual'mente] AVV ritually.

riunificare [riunifi'kare] VT to reunify.

riunificazione [riunifikat'tsjone] SF reunification.

riunione [riu'njone] SF *(adunanza)* meeting; *(riconciliazione)* reunion; **una riunione familiare** a family gathering; **il presidente è in riunione** the president is at a meeting.

riunire [riu'nire] [1] VT **a** *(mettere insieme: oggetti)* to gather together, collect; (: *persone)* to assemble, get together; (: *fig: riconciliare)* to bring together (again), reunite; **siamo qui riuniti per festeggiare...** we are gathered here to celebrate ...

  b *(ricongiungere)* to put together, join together.

  [2] **riunirsi** VIP *(radunarsi)* to meet; *(tornare insieme)* to come together again, be reunited.

riunito, a [riu'nito] AGG *(Comm)* associated; **cooperative riunite** associated cooperatives.

riusare [riu'zare] VT to reuse.

riuscire [riuʃ'ʃire] VI IRREG *(aus essere)* **a** *(aver successo)*: **riuscire (in qc/a fare qc)** to succeed (in sth/in doing sth), be successful (in sth/in doing sth); **il tentativo non è riuscito** the attempt was unsuccessful; **riuscire negli studi** to do well at school (o at university)

  b *(essere capace)* to be able, manage; **riuscire a fare qc** to manage o be able to do sth; **non riesco a farlo** I can't do it, I am unable to do it; **non mi riesce di farlo** I can't (manage to) do it; **non ci riesco** I can't

  c *(essere, risultare)* to be, prove (to be); **ti riuscirà più facile dopo un po' di pratica** it'll be easier o you'll find it easier after a bit of practice; **mi riesce antipatico** I don't like him; **mi riesce difficile** I find it difficult; **la festa è riuscita male** the party wasn't a success

  d *(uscire di nuovo)* to go out again, go back out.

riuscita [riuʃ'ʃita] SF *(esito)* result, outcome; *(buon esito)* success; **fare o avere una buona riuscita** to be a success, be successful.

riutilizzare [riutilid'dzare] VT to use again, reuse.

riutilizzazione [riutiliddzat'tsjone] SF reuse, reutilization.

riva ['riva] SF *(di mare, lago)* shore; *(di fiume)* bank; **in riva al mare** on the (sea) shore.

rivaccinare [rivattʃi'nare] VT to revaccinate.

rivale [ri'vale] [1] AGG rival attr.

  [2] SM/F rival; **non avere rivali** *(anche fig)* to be unrivalled.

rivaleggiare [rivaled'dʒare] VI *(aus avere)* to compete, vie; **rivaleggiare con qn per qc** to vie with sb for sth; **nessuno può rivaleggiare con lui** he is unrivalled.

rivalità [rivali'ta] SF INV rivalry.

rivalsa [ri'valsa] SF **a** *(risarcimento)* compensation **b** *(rivincita)* revenge; **prendersi una rivalsa su qn** to take revenge on sb.

rivalutare [rivalu'tare] VT *(Econ)* to revalue; *(fig)* to re-evaluate.

rivalutazione [rivalutat'tsjone] SF *(Econ)* revaluation; *(fig)* re-evaluation.

rivangare [rivan'gare] [1] VT *(ricordi)* to dig up (again).

  [2] VI *(aus avere)*: **rivangare nel passato** to dig up the past again.

rivedere [rive'dere] VB IRREG [1] VT **a** *(vedere di nuovo: film ecc)* to see again; (: *persona)* to see again, meet again; **guarda chi si rivede!** look who it is! **b** *(verificare, correggere)* to revise, check; **rivedere le bozze** to proofread.

  [2] **rivedersi** VR *(uso reciproco)* to see each other again, meet (again).

rivedibile [rive'dibile] AGG *(Mil)* *temporarily unfit for*

service.

rivedibilità [rivedibili'ta] SF (*Mil*) *temporary unfitness for service.*

rivedrò *ecc* [rive'drɔ] VB *vedi* **rivedere**.

rivelare [rive'lare] [1] VT (*svelare*) to reveal; (: *segreto*) to disclose, reveal; (*dimostrare: capacità*) to reveal, display, show; **quella commedia lo rivelò al grande pubblico** that play revealed him to the public at large.

[2] **rivelarsi** VIP (*tendenza, talento*) to be revealed, reveal itself.

[3] **rivelarsi** VR: **rivelarsi onesto** to prove to be honest.

rivelatore, trice [rivela'tore] [1] AGG revealing.

[2] SM (*Tecn*) detector; (*Fot*) developer.

rivelazione [rivelat'tsjone] SF (*gen*) revelation; (*di segreto, notizia*) disclosure; **quell'attore è stato la rivelazione dell'anno** that actor was the discovery of the year.

rivendere [ri'vendere] VT (*vendere: di nuovo*) to resell, sell again; (: *al dettaglio*) to retail, sell retail.

rivendicare [rivendi'kare] VT to claim, demand.

rivendicazione [rivendikat'tsjone] SF claim
▸ **rivendicazioni salariali** wage claims
▸ **rivendicazioni sindacali** union demands.

rivendita [ri'vendita] SF (*negozio*) retailer's (shop)
▸ **rivendita di tabacchi** tobacconist's (shop) (*Brit*), tobacco *o* smoke shop (*Am*).

rivenditore, trice [rivendi'tore] SM/F retailer
▸ **rivenditore autorizzato** authorized dealer.

riverberare [riverbe'rare] VT (*luce, calore*) to reflect; (*suono*) to reverberate.

riverbero [ri'vɛrbero] SM (*vedi vb*) reflection; reverberation.

riverente [rive'rɛnte] AGG reverent, respectful.

riverentemente [riverente'mente] AVV reverently, respectfully.

riverenza [rive'rɛntsa] SF **a** (*rispetto*) reverence, respect **b** (*inchino*) bow; (: *di donna*) curtsey; **fece una profonda riverenza** he bowed low.

riverire [rive'rire] VT (*rispettare*) to revere, respect; **la riverisco, professore** (*salutando*) my respects, professor.

riversare [river'sare] [1] VT **a** (*versare*) to pour; (: *di nuovo*) to pour again; (*fig: amore, affetto*): **riversare su** to shower on, lavish on; **ha riversato tutte le sue energie in quel lavoro** he threw himself into that job **b** (*Inform*) to dump.

[2] **riversarsi** VIP to pour (out); **la folla si riversò nelle strade** the crowd poured into the streets.

rivestimento [rivesti'mento] SM (*azione, materiale*) covering; (*strato: di vernice*) coating, veneer.

rivestire [rives'tire] [1] VT **a** (*ricoprire: gen*): **rivestire (di)** to cover (with); (: *con vernice*) to coat (with); **rivestire in stoffa l'interno di una scatola** to line a box with material; **rivestire di piastrelle** to tile
b (*carica*) to hold; **rivestire un grado elevato** to be high-ranking
c (*vestire di nuovo*) to dress again.

[2] **rivestirsi** VR to get dressed (again).

rivettatrice [rivetta'tritʃe] SF (*Tecn: macchina*) riveter.

rivetto [ri'vetto] SM (*Tecn*) rivet.

rividi *ecc* [ri'vidi] VB *vedi* **rivedere**.

riviera [ri'vjɛra] SF **a** COAST; **la Riviera Ligure** the Italian Riviera **b** (*Equitazione: ostacolo*) water jump.

rivincita [ri'vintʃita] SF (*Sport*) return match; (*Carte*) return game; (*fig*) revenge; **prendersi la rivincita (su qn)**

to take *o* get one's revenge (on sb).

rivissuto, a [rivis'suto] PP *di* **rivivere**.

rivista [ri'vista] SF **a** (*periodica*) magazine; (*letteraria*) review; (*Tecn, Med*) journal **b** (*Teatro, TV*) revue, variety show **c** (*Mil*) inspection; **passare in rivista** to review.

rivisto, a [ri'visto] PP *di* **rivedere**.

rivitalizzante [rivitalid'dzante] AGG (*prodotti cosmetici*) revitalizing.

rivitalizzare [rivitalid'dzare] VT to revitalize.

rivivere [ri'vivere] VB IRREG [1] VT: **rivivere qc** (*avventura, esperienza*) to live through sth again.

[2] VI (*aus essere*) (*vivere di nuovo*) to live again; (*prendere vigore*) to come to life again; (*tradizioni*) to be revived; **far rivivere** (*resuscitare*) to bring back to life; (*rinvigorire*) to revive, put new life into; (*epoca, moda*) to revive; **sentirsi rivivere** to feel a new man (*o* woman).

rivo ['rivo] SM (*di lava, lacrime*) stream.

rivolere [rivo'lere] VT (*volere: indietro*) to want back; (: *di nuovo*) to want again.

rivolgere [ri'vɔldʒere] VB IRREG [1] VT (*indirizzare: attenzione, sguardo, proiettore*) to turn, direct; (: *parole*) to address; **rivolgere un'arma contro qn** to point a weapon at sb; **rivolgere lo sguardo verso qn** to turn *o* direct one's gaze towards sb; **le rivolse uno sguardo di rimprovero** he gave her a disapproving look; **rivolgere un'accusa/una critica a qn** to accuse/criticize sb; **rivolgere la propria attenzione a un problema** to turn one's attention to a problem; **rivolgere la parola a qn** to talk to sb, address sb; **non si rivolgono più la parola** they are no longer on speaking terms; **rivolgere un saluto a qn** to greet sb.

[2] **rivolgersi** VR **a** : **rivolgersi a** (*per informazioni*) to go and see, go and speak to; **rivolgersi all'ufficio competente** to apply to the office concerned; **non mi rivolgevo a te** I wasn't talking to you; **si rivolse a lei dicendo...** he turned to her and said ...
b : **rivolgersi verso** (*girarsi*) to turn to.

rivolgimento [rivoldʒi'mento] SM upheaval.

rivolo ['rivolo] SM rivulet.

rivolsi *ecc* [ri'vɔlsi] VB *vedi* **rivolgere**.

rivolta [ri'vɔlta] SF revolt, rebellion; **in rivolta (contro)** in revolt (against).

rivoltante [rivol'tante] AGG revolting, disgusting.

rivoltare [rivol'tare] [1] VT **a** (*voltare: di nuovo*) to turn again; (: *pagine, carte*) to turn over again; (: *vestito*) to turn inside out; (: *bistecca, frittata*) to turn (over)
b (*disgustare*) to revolt, disgust; **una scena che fa rivoltare lo stomaco** a scene which turns one's stomach.

[2] **rivoltarsi** VR (*rigirarsi*) to turn; **rivoltarsi nel letto** to toss and turn (in bed).

[3] **rivoltarsi** VIP (*ribellarsi*): **rivoltarsi (a)** to revolt *o* rebel (against).

rivoltella [rivol'tɛlla] SF (*gen*) pistol; (: *a tamburo*) revolver.

rivoltellata [rivoltel'lata] SF (*vedi* **rivoltella**) (pistol) shot; (revolver) shot.

rivolto, a [ri'vɔlto] PP *di* **rivolgere**.

rivoltoso, a [rivol'toso] [1] AGG rebellious.

[2] SM/F rebel.

rivoluzionare [rivoluttsjo'nare] VT (*anche fig*) to revolutionize; (*fig: mettere sottosopra*) to turn upside down.

rivoluzionario, ria, ri, rie [rivoluttsjo'narjo] AGG, SM/F revolutionary.

rivoluzione [rivolut'tsjone] SF (*gen, Pol, Mat, Astron*) revolution; (*fig: scompiglio*) mess.

rizoma, i [rid'dzɔma] SM rhizome.
rizzare [rit'tsare] [1] VT (palo) to erect; (tenda) to pitch; (coda) to raise, lift; (orecchie) to prick up; **è roba da far rizzare i capelli** it's enough to make your hair stand on end.
[2] **rizzarsi** VR to stand up; **rizzarsi in piedi** to stand up, get to one's feet; **rizzarsi a sedere** to sit up.
[3] **rizzarsi** VIP: **gli si sono rizzati i capelli** his hair stood on end.
RN SIGLA = Rimini.
RNA [ɛrre ɛnne a] SIGLA M RNA (= ribonucleic acid).
RO SIGLA = Rovigo.
roano, a [ro'ano] AGG, SM (cavallo) roan.
roba ['rɔba] SF **a** (gen) things pl, stuff; (cose proprie) belongings pl, things pl, possessions pl; **roba da lavare** washing; **roba da mangiare** food, things to eat; **roba da stirare** ironing; **roba usata** secondhand goods; **roba di valore** valuables; **ho un sacco di roba da fare** I've got a lot to do; **ha ancora qui tutta la sua roba?** has he still got all his things here?; **che roba è questa?** what is this?; **e chiami whisky questa roba?** and you call this stuff whisky?
b (faccenda, affare) affair, matter; **non è roba che ti riguardi** this doesn't concern you
c (fraseologia): **bella roba!** (iro: che gran cosa!) so what!; (: che mascalzonata!) that's nice, isn't it!; **roba da matti** o **pazzi!** it's sheer madness o lunacy!, it's just incredible.
robinia [ro'binja] SF locust tree.
robivecchi [robi'vɛkki] SM/F INV junk dealer.
robot ['rɔbɔt] SM INV robot ▶**robot di** o **da cucina** food-processor.
robotica [ro'bɔtika] SF robotics sg.
robustezza [robus'tettsa] SF (di persona, pianta) robustness, sturdiness; (di edificio, ponte) soundness.
robusto, a [ro'busto] AGG (persona, pianta) robust, sturdy; (euf: persona: grasso) well-built; (edificio, ponte) sound, solid; (corda, catena) strong; (appetito) healthy; (vino) full-bodied; (voce) powerful.
rocambolesco, a, schi, sche [rokambo'lesko] AGG fantastic, incredible.
rocca, che ['rɔkka] SF fortress; **la Rocca di Gibilterra** the Rock of Gibraltar.
roccaforte [rokka'fɔrte] SF (pl **roccheforti**) (anche fig) stronghold.
rocchetto [rok'ketto] SM **a** (di filo) spool **b** (Cine) reel **c** (Elettr) coil.
roccia, ce ['rɔttʃa] SF (gen, Geol) rock; (sport) rock climbing; **fare roccia** to go rock climbing.
rocciatore, trice [rottʃa'tore] SM/F rock climber.
roccioso, a [rot'tʃoso] AGG rocky; **le Montagne Rocciose** the Rocky Mountains.
rock [rɔk] AGG, SM (Mus) rock ▶**rock acrobatico** (ballo) acrobatic rock.
roco, a, chi, che ['rɔko] AGG hoarse.
rodaggio, gi [ro'daddʒo] SM (Aut) running (Brit) o breaking (Am) in; **la macchina è ancora in rodaggio** the car is still being run o broken in; **periodo di rodaggio** (fig) period of adjustment.
Rodano ['rodano] SM: **il Rodano** the Rhone.
rodare [ro'dare] VT (Aut, Tecn) to run (Brit) o break (Am) in.
rodeo [ro'deo] SM rodeo.
rodere ['rodere] VB IRREG [1] VT (rosicchiare) to gnaw (at); (corrodere) to corrode; **rodersi il fegato** (fig) to torment o.s..

[2] **rodersi** VR: **rodersi dal rimorso/dall'invidia** to be consumed with remorse/with envy.
Rodi ['rɔdi] SF Rhodes sg.
roditore [rodi'tore] SM (Zool) rodent.
rododendro [rodo'dɛndro] SM (Bot) rhododendron.
rogito ['rɔdʒito] SM (Dir) (notary's) deed.
rogna ['rɔɲɲa] SF (Med) scabies sg; (di animale) mange; (fig: guaio) trouble, bother, nuisance; **cercar rogne** to be looking for trouble, to be asking for it; **ha avuto rogne con la polizia** he got into trouble with the police.
rognone [roɲ'ɲone] SM (Culin) kidney.
rognoso, a [roɲ'ɲoso] AGG (persona) scabby; (animale) mangy; (fig) troublesome.
rogo, ghi ['rɔgo] SM (funebre) funeral pyre; (supplizio): **il rogo** the stake; **mandare qn al rogo** to condemn sb to be burned at the stake; **la casa era ormai un rogo** the house was now a mass of flames.
rollare [rol'lare] [1] VI (aus avere) (Naut, Aer) to roll.
[2] VT (fam: sigaretta) to roll (up).
rollata [rol'lata] SF (Naut, Aer) (excessive) roll.
roll-bar ['roul ba:] SM INV (Aut) roll bar.
rollino [rol'lino] SM = **rullino**.
rollio, lii [rol'lio] SM (Naut, Aer) roll, rolling.
Roma ['roma] SF Rome.
romagnolo, a [romaɲ'ɲɔlo] [1] AGG of o from Romagna.
[2] SM/F inhabitant o native of Romagna.
romanesco, sca, schi, sche [roma'nesko] [1] AGG Roman.
[2] SM Roman dialect.
Romania [roma'nia] SF: **la Romania** Rumania, Romania.
romanico, a, ci, che [ro'maniko] AGG, SM (Arte) Romanesque.
romanità [romani'ta] SF (Storia): **la Romanità** the Roman world; (fig: spirito) the Roman spirit.
romano, a [ro'mano] [1] AGG Roman; **la Chiesa romana** the Roman Catholic Church; **fare** o **pagare alla romana** to go Dutch.
[2] SM/F Roman.
romanticamente [romantika'mente] AVV romantically.
romanticheria [romantike'ria] SF sentimentality.
romanticismo [romanti'tʃizmo] SM romanticism.
romantico, a, ci, che [ro'mantiko] AGG, SM/F romantic.
romanza [ro'mandza] SF (Mus, Letteratura) romance.
romanzare [roman'dzare] VT to romanticize.
romanzato, a [roman'dzato] AGG romanticized.
romanzescamente [romandzeska'mente] AVV fantastically, incredibly.
romanzesco, a, schi, sche [roman'dzesko] [1] AGG (stile, personaggi) fictional; (fig: amori, vicende) fantastic, storybook attr.
[2] SM: **avere del romanzesco** to sound like something out of a novel.
romanziere, a [roman'dzjɛre] SM/F novelist.
romanzo [ro'mandzo] [1] SM (gen) novel ▶**romanzo d'amore** love story ▶**romanzo d'appendice** serial novel, serial (story) ▶**romanzo d'avventure** adventure story ▶**romanzo cavalleresco** tale of chivalry ▶**romanzo di fantascienza** science-fiction novel o story ▶**romanzo fiume** saga ▶**romanzo giallo** detective story ▶**romanzo poliziesco** detective story ▶**romanzo rosa** romantic novel ▶**romanzo sceneggiato** novel adapted for television.
[2] AGG (lingua) Romance attr.
rombare [rom'bare] VI (aus avere) to roar, rumble, thun-

der.

rombo¹ ['rombo] SM (*rumore*) roar, rumble, thunder.

rombo² ['rombo] SM (*Geom*) rhombus.

rombo³ ['rombo] SM (*pesce*) turbot.

romeno, a [ro'mɛno], **rumeno, a** [ru'mɛno] [1] AGG, SM/F Rumanian, Romanian.

  [2] SM (*lingua*) Rumanian, Romanian.

Romolo ['rɔmolo] SM Romulus.

rompere ['rompere] VB IRREG [1] VT (*gen, fig*) to break; (*sfasciare*) to smash up; (*scarpe, calzoni*) to split; (*fidanzamento, negoziati*) to break off; **rompere qc in testa a qn** to break sth over sb's head; **il fiume ha rotto gli argini** the river burst its banks; **rompere un contratto** to break a contract; **rompere il silenzio/il ghiaccio** to break the silence/the ice; **rompere gli indugi** (*fig*) to take action; **rompere le scatole a qn** (*fam*) to get on sb's nerves; **hai proprio rotto (le scatole)!** (*fam*) knock it off!; **uffa quanto rompi!** (*fam*) what a pain the neck you are!; **rompere (i rapporti) con qn** to break off with sb; **un rumore che rompe i timpani** a deafening noise; **rompersi una gamba/l'osso del collo** to break a leg/one's neck; **rompersi la testa** (*fig*) to rack one's brains; **rompersi la schiena** (*fig*) to work hard.

  [2] **rompersi** VIP (*gen*) to break.

rompiballe [rompi'balle], **rompipalle** [rompi'palle] SM/F INV (*fam!*) pain in the arse (*Brit fam!*) o ass (*Am fam!*)

rompicapo [rompi'kapo] SM (*problema*) worry, headache; (*gioco enigmistico*) brain-teaser, puzzle.

rompicollo [rompi'kɔllo] SM daredevil.

rompighiaccio, ci [rompi'gjattʃo] SM icebreaker.

rompimento [rompi'mento] SM (*fig fam*) nuisance, bother, pain.

rompiscatole [rompis'katole] SM/F INV (*fam*) nuisance, pain in the neck, pest.

roncola ['ronkola] SF (*Agr*) bill hook.

ronda ['ronda] SF (*Mil*) rounds *pl*; (*Polizia*) beat, patrol, rounds *pl*; (*pattuglia*) patrol; **fare la ronda** to be on one's rounds (*o* on patrol); **essere di ronda** to be on patrol duty.

rondeau [rɔ̃'do], **rondò** [ron'dɔ] SM INV (*Aut*) roundabout (*Brit*), traffic circle (*Am*).

rondella [ron'dɛlla] SF (*Tecn*) washer.

rondine ['rondine] SF (*uccello*) swallow; **una rondine non fa primavera** (*Proverbio*) one swallow doesn't make a summer.

rondone [ron'done] SM (*uccello*) swift.

ronfare [ron'fare] VI (*aus* avere) (*persona: russare*) to snore; (*gatto: far le fusa*) to purr.

ronzare [ron'dzare] VI (*aus* avere) to buzz, hum; **ronzare intorno a qn** (*fig*) to hang about sb; **quell'idea continuava a ronzargli in testa** that idea was still buzzing around in his head; **mi ronzano le orecchie** my ears are buzzing.

ronzino [ron'dzino] SM (*pegg: cavallo*) nag.

ronzio, ii [ron'dzio] SM (*di insetti*) buzzing, humming; (*del motore*) humming; (*di orecchie*) buzzing, ringing ▶**ronzio auricolare** (*Med*) tinnitus *sg*.

R.O.S. [rɔs] SIGLA M (= *Reparto operativo speciale*) Special operations squad.

rosa ['rɔza] [1] AGG INV (*colore*) pink; (*sentimentale: letteratura, romanzo*) romantic; **vedere tutto rosa** to see everything through rose-coloured spectacles.

  [2] SF **a** (*Bot*) rose; **non sono tutte rose e fiori** (*fig*) it's not all a bed of roses; **se son rose fioriranno** (*fig*) the proof of the pudding is in the eating; **non c'è rosa senza spine** (*Proverbio*) there's no rose without a thorn ▶**rosa canina** dog rose ▶ **rosa di Natale** Christmas rose **b** (*fig: gruppo*): **rosa dei candidati** list of candidates **c** : **rosa dei venti** wind rose.

  [3] SM INV (*colore*) pink.

rosaio, ai [ro'zajo] SM (*pianta*) rosebush, rose tree; (*giardino*) rose garden; (*aiuola*) rosebed.

rosario, ri [ro'zarjo] SM (*Rel*) rosary; **dire** *o* **recitare il rosario** to say *o* recite the rosary.

rosatello [roza'tɛllo] SM rosè (wine).

rosato, a [ro'zato] [1] AGG (*colore*) pinkish, rosy; (*vino*) rosé.

  [2] SM INV (*vino*) rosé (wine).

rosbif ['rɔzbif] SM INV roast beef.

rosé [ro'ze] AGG INV, SM INV rosé.

roseo, a ['rɔzeo] AGG (*colorito*) pinkish, rosy; (*fig: ottimistico*) rosy, bright.

roseto [ro'zeto] SM rose garden.

rosetta [ro'zetta] SF **a** (*diamante*) rose-cut diamond **b** (*Tecn, rondella*) washer **c** (*pane*) kind of roll.

rosi ['rosi] *ecc* VB *vedi* rodere.

rosicchiare [rosik'kjare] VT (*rodere*) to gnaw (at); (*mangiucchiare*) to nibble (at); **rosicchiarsi le unghie** to bite one's nails.

rosicoltore, trice [rozikol'tore] SM/F rose grower.

rosmarino [rozma'rino] SM (*Bot*) rosemary.

roso, a ['roso] PP *di* rodere.

rosolare [rozo'lare] VT (*Culin*) to brown.

rosolatura [rozola'tura] SF (*Culin*) browning.

rosolia [rozo'lia] SF (*Med*) German measles *sg*, rubella (*termine tecn*).

rosone [ro'zone] SM (*finestra: su chiese*) rose window; **rosone da soffitto** ceiling rose.

rospo ['rɔspo] SM (*Zool*) toad; **è un rospo** (*pegg: persona*) she (*o* he) is hideous; **ingoiare un** *o* **il rospo** (*fig*) to swallow a bitter pill; **sputa il rospo!** out with it!

rosseggiare [rossed'dʒare] VI (*aus* essere) (*letter*) to redden, turn red.

rossetto [ros'setto] SM lipstick.

rossiccio, cia, ci, ce [ros'sittʃo] AGG reddish.

rosso, a ['rosso] [1] AGG **a** (*gen*) red; **diventare rosso (per la vergogna)** to blush *o* go red (with *o* for shame); **rosso come un gambero** *o* **un peperone** (*per la vergogna*) as red as a beetroot (*Brit*) *o* beet (*Am*); (*per il sole*) as red as a lobster; **l'Armata Rossa** the Red Army; **il mar Rosso** the Red Sea.

  [2] SM (*colore*) red; (*di roulette*) rouge, red; (*di semaforo*) red light; (*d'uovo*) yolk; (*vino*) red wine; **rosso di sera bel tempo si spera** (*Proverbio*) red sky at night shepherd's delight; **rosso di mattina maltempo s'avvicina** (*Proverbio*) red sky at dawning shepherd's warning; **essere in rosso** (*Banca*) to be in the red.

  [3] SM/F (*che ha i capelli rossi*) redhead; (*fig Pol*) Red; (*persona di sinistra*) red, left-winger.

rossore [ros'sore] SM (*per infiammazione*) redness; (*delle guance*) flush; (: *per vergogna*) blush; **sentirsi salire il rossore alle guance** (*per vergogna, pudore*) to begin to blush, feel one's cheeks go red.

rosticceria [rostittʃe'ria] SF *shop selling roast meat and other prepared food.*

rostro ['rɔstro] SM (*di rapace*) beak; (*sulle navi*) rostrum.

Rota ['rɔta] SF (*Rel: anche:* **Sacra Rota**) Rota.

rotabile [ro'tabile] AGG: **strada rotabile** carriageway,

roadway; materiale rotabile (*Ferr*) rolling stock.

rotaia [ro'taja] SF (*Ferr*) rail; (*guida metallica*) rut, track.

rotante [ro'tante] AGG rotating.

rotare [ro'tare] VT, VI (*aus avere*) to rotate.

rotativa [rota'tiva] SF rotary press.

rotativo, a [rota'tivo] AGG rotating, rotation *attr*.

rotatoria [rota'tɔrja] SF roundabout (*Brit*), traffic circle (*Am*); **segnale di rotatoria** "roundabout ahead" sign.

rotatorio, ria, ri, rie [rota'tɔrjo] AGG rotary.

rotazionale [rotattsjo'nale] AGG: **isola rotazionale** (*Aut*) roundabout (*Brit*), traffic circle (*Am*).

rotazione [rotat'tsjone] SF rotation; **rotazione delle colture** (*Agr*) crop rotation.

roteare [rote'are] ① VT (*spada, bastone*) to whirl; (*occhi*) to roll.
② VI (*aus essere*) (*uccello rapace*) to circle.

rotella [ro'tɛlla] SF (*gen*) small wheel; (*di pattini*) roller; (*di mobili*) castor; (*ingranaggio*) cog wheel; (*Culin: per la pasta*) pastry wheel; **gli manca una rotella** (*fig fam*) he's got a screw loose.

rotocalco, chi [roto'kalko] SM (*rivista*) illustrated magazine; (*Tip*) rotogravure.

rotolare [roto'lare] ① VT, VI (*aus essere*) to roll.
② **rotolarsi** VR to roll (about); **rotolarsi per terra** to roll about on the floor; **rotolarsi nell'erba** to roll (about) on the grass; **rotolarsi (per terra) dalle risate** to roll about laughing.

rotolio, lii [roto'lio] SM rolling.

rotolo ['rɔtolo] SM (*di carta, stoffa*) roll; (*di corda*) coil; (*di documenti*) scroll; **andare a rotoli** (*fig*) to go to rack and ruin; **mandare a rotoli** (*fig*) to ruin.

rotolone [roto'lone] SM tumble, fall; **fare un rotolone** to take a tumble; **fare un rotolone dalle scale** to tumble down the stairs.

rotoloni [roto'loni] AVV: **cadere rotoloni** to fall head over heels.

rotonda [ro'tonda] SF (*Archit*) rotunda; (*terrazza*) round terrace.

rotondeggiante [rotonded'dʒante] AGG roundish.

rotondità [rotondi'ta] SF INV roundness, rotundity; **le rotondità femminili** (*scherz*) feminine curves.

rotondo, a [ro'tondo] AGG (*circolare*) round; (*paffuto: viso*) round, full.

rotore [ro'tore] SM (*Tecn*) rotor.

rotta¹ ['rotta] SF (*Aer, Naut*) route, course; **essere in rotta per** to be en route for; **fare rotta su** *o* **per** *o* **verso** to head for *o* towards; **cambiare rotta** (*anche fig*) to change course; **in rotta di collisione** on a collision course; **ufficiale di rotta** navigator, navigating officer.

rotta² ['rotta] SF **a** (*fig: rottura*): **essere in rotta con qn** (*fig*) to be on bad terms with sb; **a rotta di collo** at breakneck speed **b** (*disfatta*): **mettere in rotta il nemico** to rout the enemy.

rottame [rot'tame] SM **a** (*pezzo di ferro*) piece of scrap iron; **rottami** SMPL (*di nave, auto, aereo*) wreckage *sg*; **rottami di ferro** scrap iron *sg* **b** (*fig pegg: persona, macchina*) wreck.

rotto, a ['rotto] ① PP di **rompere**.
② AGG (*gen*) broken; (*braccio, gamba*) broken, fractured; **avere le ossa rotte** (*fig*) to ache all over; **rotto a** (*persona: abituato*) accustomed *o* inured to; **è rotto ad ogni esperienza** (*fig*) he's seen it all, he's been through it all.
③ SM: **per il rotto della cuffia** by the skin of one's teeth.
④ SMPL: **30.000 lire e rotti** 30,000 odd lire.

rottura [rot'tura] SF (*azione*) breaking *no pl*; (*di rapporti*) breaking off *no pl*; (*fra amici*) split-up, break-up; (*di negoziati*) breakdown; (*di contratto*) breach; **è una tale rottura!** (*fam: persona*) he's such a pain (in the neck)!; (: *situazione*) it's such a drag *o* bore! ▶**rottura delle acque** (*Med*) breaking of the waters.

rotula ['rɔtula] SF kneecap.

roulette [ru'lɛt] SF INV roulette ▶**roulette russa** Russian roulette.

roulotte [ru'lɔt] SF INV caravan (*Brit*), trailer (*Am*).

round [raund] SM INV (*Sport*) round.

routine [ru'tin] SF INV routine; **di routine** routinely, as a routine.

rovente [ro'vɛnte] AGG (*ferro, carbone*) red-hot; (*fig: sabbia, sole*) burning.

rovere ['rovere] ① SM O F (*albero*) English oak.
② SM (*legno*) oak.

rovesciamento [roveʃʃa'mento] SM (*di macchina*) overturning; (*di barca*) capsizing; (*fig: di situazione*) reversal.

rovesciare [roveʃ'ʃare] ① VT (*far cadere: gen*) to knock over; (: *liquido: intenzionalmente*) to pour; (: *accidentalmente*) to spill; (*capovolgere: barca*) to capsize, turn upside down; (*fig: situazione*) to reverse; (: *governo*) to overthrow; **rovesciare qc addosso a qn** to pour sth over sb; **ha rovesciato tutto il latte per terra** she spilled all the milk on the floor; **rovesciare la testa all'indietro** to throw one's head back.
② **rovesciarsi** VIP (*sedia, macchina*) to overturn; (*barca*) to capsize; (*liquido*) to spill; (*fig: situazione*) to be reversed; **si è rovesciato tutto per terra** everything fell to the floor; (*liquido*) it all spilled on to the floor; **la folla si rovesciò nella piazza** the crowd poured into the square.

rovescio, scia, sci, sce [ro'veʃʃo] ① AGG (*Maglia*) purl *attr*.
② SM **a** (*lato: di stoffa, indumento*) wrong side, other side; (: *di medaglia*) reverse; **il rovescio della medaglia** (*fig*) the other side of the coin
b (*Meteor*) downpour, heavy shower
c (*fig*): **rovescio di fortuna** setback
d (*Maglia: anche: punto rovescio*) purl (stitch)
e (*Tennis*) backhand (stroke).
③: **a rovescio, alla rovescia** AVV (*con il davanti dietro*) back to front; (*sottosopra*) upside down; (*con l'esterno all'interno*) inside out; **oggi mi va tutto alla rovescia** everything is going wrong (for me) today; **capisce sempre tutto alla rovescia** he always gets things the wrong way round, he always gets the wrong end of the stick.

rovina [ro'vina] SF (*gen, fig*) ruin; **in rovina** (*palazzo*) in ruins; **rovina finanziaria** financial ruin; **mandare in rovina** to ruin; **andare in rovina** (*andare a pezzi*) to collapse; (*fig*) to go to rack and ruin; **sull'orlo della rovina** on the brink of ruin; **sarà la sua rovina** it (*o* she *ecc*) will be the ruination of him.

rovinare [rovi'nare] ① VT (*oggetto, persona, anche fig*) to ruin; (*fig: atmosfera, festa*) to ruin, spoil; **si è rovinata il vestito** she has ruined her dress.
② VI (*aus essere*) (*crollare*) to collapse, fall down; (*precipitare*) to fall.
③ **rovinarsi** VR (*persona*) to be ruined, ruin o.s.; **mi voglio rovinare!** (*fig: sogg: venditore*) I'm giving it away!.
④ **rovinarsi** VIP (*oggetto*) to get ruined.

rovinato, a [rovi'nato] AGG (*oggetto*) ruined, damaged;

(fig: persona) ruined.

rovinosamente [rovinosa'mente] AVV destructively; **è caduto rovinosamente giù dalle scale** he fell head over heels down the stairs.

rovinoso, a [rovi'noso] AGG ruinous.

rovistare [rovis'tare] VT (casa) to ransack; (tasche) to rummage in (o through), search thoroughly.

rovo ['rovo] SM (Bot) blackberry bush, bramble bush; (cespugli spinosi) briar.

royalty ['rɔiǝlti] SF INV (percentuale) royalty.

rozzezza [rod'dzettsa] SF (vedi agg) roughness; coarseness.

rozzo, a ['roddzo] AGG (gen) rough; (persona, modi) uncouth, coarse.

RP ['ɛrre'pi] SIGLA FPL (= relazioni pubbliche) PR.

RR ABBR (Posta) = **ricevuta di ritorno.**

Rrr ABBR = **raccomandata con ricevuta di ritorno.**

RSVP ABBR (= répondez s'il vous plaît) RSVP.

ruba ['ruba] SF: **andare a ruba** to sell like hot cakes.

rubacchiare [rubak'kjare] VT to pilfer.

rubacuori [ruba'kwɔri] SM/F INV heart-breaker, charmer.

rubare [ru'bare] VT: **rubare (qc a qn)** (gen) to steal (sth from sb); (fig: idea, affetti, posto) to steal (sth from sb), take (sth from sb); **gli hanno rubato tutto** they robbed him of everything; **rubare il mestiere a qn** to do sb out of a job; **posso rubarti un minuto?** can I steal a minute of your time?; **mi hai rubato le parole di bocca** you've taken the words right out of my mouth.

ruberia [rube'ria] SF (fig) theft; **è una (vera) ruberia** it's daylight robbery.

rubicondo, a [rubi'kondo] AGG ruddy.

rubinetto [rubi'netto] SM tap (Brit), faucet (Am).

rubino [ru'bino] SM ruby.

rubizzo, a [ru'bittso] AGG lively, sprightly.

rublo ['rublo] SM rouble.

rubrica, che [ru'brika] SF **a** (quaderno) index notebook; (: per indirizzi e numeri di telefono) address book **b** (di giornale: colonna) column; (: pagina) page; **rubrica sportiva** sports page **c** (Radio, TV: parte di un programma) spot, time; **"rubrica sportiva"** "sports time".

rucola ['rukola], **ruchetta** [ru'ketta] SF (Bot) rocket.

rude ['rude] AGG (duro, brusco) tough; (rozzo) rough, coarse.

rudemente [rude'mente] AVV (rispondere) bluntly, brusquely.

rudere ['rudere] SM (rovina) ruins pl; (fig: persona) wreck.

rudimentale [rudimen'tale] AGG rudimentary, basic.

rudimenti [rudi'menti] SMPL (di disciplina) rudiments; (di teoria) (basic) principles.

ruffiano, a [ruf'fjano] SM/F pander, pimp; (fig: leccapiedi) bootlicker.

ruga, ghe ['ruga] SF wrinkle.

rugby ['rugbi] SM INV rugby (football).

ruggente [rud'dʒɛnte] AGG roaring; **gli anni ruggenti** the Roaring Twenties.

ruggine ['ruddʒine] ① SF (Chim, Bot, colore) rust; (fig: rancore): **fra di loro c'è della vecchia ruggine** there's bad blood between them. ② AGG INV (colore) rust, rust-coloured.

rugginoso, a [ruddʒi'noso] AGG rusty.

ruggire [rud'dʒire] VI (aus avere) to roar.

ruggito [rud'dʒito] SM roar.

rugiada [ru'dʒada] SF dew.

rugoso, a [ru'goso] AGG (pieno di rughe) wrinkled; (scabro:

superficie) rough.

rullaggio, gi [rul'laddʒo] SM (Aer) taxiing.

rullare [rul'lare] ① VT (spianare con il rullo) to roll. ② VI (aus avere) **a** (tamburo) to roll **b** (Aer) to taxi.

rullino [rul'lino] SM (Fot) roll of film, spool.

rullio, lii [rul'lio] SM (di tamburi) roll.

rullo ['rullo] SM **a** (di tamburo) roll **b** (Tecn, Tip) roller; (di stampante, macchina da scrivere) platen; (Cine) reel ▶ **rullo compressore** steam-roller.

rum [rum] SM INV rum.

rumba ['rumba] SF rumba.

ruminante [rumi'nante] SM (Zool) ruminant.

ruminare [rumi'nare] VT (Zool) to ruminate; (fig) to ruminate on o over, chew over.

rumore [ru'more] SM (gen) noise; (di treno) rumble; (di motore) sound; (di piatti, stoviglie) clatter; **un rumore sordo** a thud; **un rumore stridente** a shrill noise; **un rumore di passi** the sound of footsteps; **rumore di sottofondo** background noise; **fare rumore** to make a noise; **senza far rumore** quietly; **non si sentiva alcun rumore** not a sound could be heard; **la notizia ha fatto molto rumore** (fig) the news aroused great interest.

rumoreggiare [rumored'dʒare] VI (aus avere) (tuono) to rumble; (fig: folla) to clamour (Brit), clamor (Am).

rumorosamente [rumorosa'mente] AVV noisily.

rumoroso, a [rumo'roso] AGG (gen) noisy; (voce, risata) loud, noisy.

ruolino [rwo'lino] SM: **ruolino di marcia** (Mil) marching orders pl; (fig) schedule, timetable.

ruolo ['rwɔlo] SM **a** (gen, Cine, Teatro) role, part; **avere un ruolo di primo piano in qc** (anche fig) to play a leading role o part in sth **b** (elenco) roll, register, list ▶ **ruolo d'imposta** (Fisco) tax-list, tax-roll **c**: **di ruolo** (personale, insegnante) permanent, on the permanent staff; **professore di ruolo** (Univ) ≈ lecturer with tenure; **fuori ruolo** (personale, insegnante) temporary.

ruota ['rwɔta] SF (gen) wheel; (di ingranaggio) cog (wheel); **fare la ruota** (Ginnastica) to do a cartwheel; **gonna a ruota** flared skirt; **a ruote** wheeled; **veicolo a due ruote** two-wheeled vehicle; **auto a 4 ruote motrici** 4-wheel-drive car; **ruote in lega leggera** light alloy wheel; **la ruota della fortuna** the wheel of fortune; **andare a ruota libera** to freewheel; **parlare a ruota libera** (fig) to speak freely; **essere l'ultima ruota del carro** (fig) to count for nothing ▶ **ruota anteriore** front wheel ▶ **ruota posteriore** back wheel ▶ **ruota di scorta** spare wheel ▶ **ruota di stampa** (su stampante) print wheel ▶ **ruota del timone** (Naut) (steering) wheel, helm.

rupe ['rupe] SF cliff, rock.

rupestre [ru'pɛstre] AGG rocky.

rupia [ru'pia] SF (moneta) rupee.

ruppi ecc ['ruppi] VB vedi **rompere.**

rurale [ru'rale] AGG rural, country attr.

ruscello [ruʃ'ʃɛllo] SM stream, brook.

ruspa ['ruspa] SF excavator.

ruspante [rus'pante] AGG (pollo) free-range.

russare [rus'sare] VI (aus avere) to snore.

Russia ['russja] SF: **la Russia** Russia.

russo, a ['russo] AGG, SM/F, SM Russian.

rustico, a, ci, che ['rustiko] ① AGG (gente) country attr, rural; (arredamento) rustic; (fig: modi) rough, unrefined. ② SM (Edil) shell, carcass; (deposito per attrezzi) shed;

(*alloggio di contadini*) farm labourer's (*Brit*) *o* farmhand's cottage.

ruta ['ruta] SF (*Bot*) rue.

ruttare [rut'tare] VI (*aus* **avere**) to belch.

ruttino [rut'tino] SM: **fare il ruttino** (*lattante*) to burp.

rutto ['rutto] SM belch; **fare un rutto** to belch.

ruttore [rut'tore] SM (*Elettr*) contact breaker.

ruvido, a ['ruvido] AGG (*gen, fig*) rough, coarse.

ruzzolare [ruttso'lare] VI (*aus* **essere**) to roll down, tumble down.

ruzzolone [ruttso'lone] SM tumble, fall; **un gran ruzzolone** a heavy fall; **ha fatto un ruzzolone per le scale** he tumbled down the stairs.

ruzzoloni [ruttso'loni] AVV: **venir giù ruzzoloni** to fall head over heels; **fare le scale ruzzoloni** to tumble down the stairs.

S

S, s ['ɛsse] SF O M INV (*lettera*) S, s; **S come Savona** ≈ S for Sugar.

S ABBR **a** (= *sud*) S **b** (= *santo*) St.

SA ⌐1¬ SIGLA = *Salerno*.

⌐2¬ ABBR = *società anonima*.

sa *ecc* [sa] VB vedi **sapere**.

sabato ['sabato] SM Saturday; (*Rel*) sabbath; **Sabato Santo** (*Rel*) Holy Saturday *per fraseologia vedi* **martedì**.

sabaudo, a [sa'baudo] AGG of (the House of) Savoy.

sabba ['sabba] SM witches' sabbath.

sabbatico, a, ci, che [sab'batiko] AGG sabbatical; **anno sabbatico** sabbatical (year).

sabbia ['sabbja] SF sand ▶ **sabbie mobili** quicksand *sg*, quicksands *pl*.

sabbiato, a [sab'bjato] AGG **a** (*superficie*) sandblasted **b** (*TV: immagine*) snowy.

sabbiatrice [sabbja'tritʃe] SF (*Tecn*) sandblaster.

sabbiatura [sabbja'tura] SF **a** (*Med*) sand bath; **fare le sabbiature** to take sand baths **b** (*Tecn*) sandblasting.

sabbioso, a [sab'bjoso] AGG sandy.

sabotaggio, gi [sabo'taddʒo] SM (*Mil, Pol, fig*) sabotage; (: *atto*) act of sabotage.

sabotare [sabo'tare] VT to sabotage.

sabotatore, trice [sabota'tore] SM/F saboteur.

sacca, che ['sakka] SF **a** (*borsa*) bag; **sacca portabiancheria** laundry bag; **sacca da viaggio** travelling bag **b** (*di fiume*) inlet **c** (*di pus*) pocket ▶ **sacca d'aria** air pocket.

saccarina [sakka'rina] SF saccharin(e).

saccaroide [sakka'rɔide] SM saccharoid.

saccarosio [sakka'rɔzjo] SM saccharose.

saccente [sat'tʃɛnte] ⌐1¬ AGG presumptuous, conceited. ⌐2¬ SM/F know-all (*Brit*), know-it-all (*Am*).

saccenteria [sattʃente'ria] SF presumption, conceit.

saccheggiare [sakked'dʒare] VT (*Mil*) to sack, plunder; (*fig*) to raid.

saccheggiatore [sakkeddʒa'tore] SM plunderer.

saccheggio, gi [sak'keddʒo] SM (*Mil*) plundering, sacking; (*fig*) plundering.

sacchetto [sak'ketto] SM **a** (*piccolo sacco*) (small) bag;

sacchetto di carta/di plastica paper/plastic bag **b** (*quantità*) bag(ful).

sacco, chi ['sakko] SM **a** (*contenitore*) sack, bag; (*quantità*) sack(ful); (*fig*) lots of, heaps of; **un sacco di** a lot of; **un sacco di gente** lots of people; **colazione al sacco** packed lunch; **sacco custodia** (*per vestiti*) clothes bag; **sacco da montagna** rucksack; **sacco per i rifiuti** bin bag (*Brit*), garbage bag (*Am*); **sacco postale** mailbag; **cogliere** *o* **prendere qn con le mani nel sacco** to catch sb redhanded; **vuotare il sacco** to confess, spill the beans (*fam*); **mettere qn nel sacco** to cheat sb ▶ **sacco a pelo** sleeping bag

b (*tessuto*) sacking

c (*Anat, Bio*) sac

d (*saccheggio*) plundering, sack(ing).

sacerdotale [satʃerdo'tale] AGG priestly.

sacerdote, essa [satʃer'dɔte] SM/F priest/priestess.

sacerdozio, zi [satʃer'dɔttsjo] SM priesthood.

Sacra Corona Unita ['sakra ko'rona u'nita] SF the Mafia in Puglia.

sacrale [sa'krale] AGG holy, sacred.

sacralità [sakrali'ta] SF sacredness.

sacramentale [sakramen'tale] AGG sacramental.

sacramentare [sakramen'tare] VT (*fam*) to blaspheme.

sacramento [sakra'mento] SM (*Rel*) sacrament.

sacrario, ri [sa'krarjo] SM memorial chapel.

sacrestano [sakres'tano] SM = **sagrestano**.

sacrestia [sakres'tia] SF = **sagrestia**.

sacrificare [sakrifi'kare] ⌐1¬ VT (*gen*) to sacrifice. ⌐2¬ **sacrificarsi** VR to sacrifice o.s.

sacrificato, a [sakrifi'kato] AGG (*gen, Rel*) sacrificed; (*fig: sprecato, sciupato*) wasted; **una vita sacrificata** a life of hardship.

sacrificio, ci [sakri'fitʃo] SM (*Rel, fig*) sacrifice; **fare un sacrificio** to make a sacrifice.

sacrilegio, gi [sakri'lɛdʒo] SM (*Rel, fig*) sacrilege; **fare sacrilegio** ⌐OR¬ **commettere un sacrilegio** to commit sacrilege.

sacrilego, a, ghi, ghe [sa'krilego] AGG (*Rel*) sacrilegious.

sacrista, i [sa'krista] SM = **sagrestano**.
sacro, a ['sakro] ①AGG **a** (*Rel*) holy, sacred; (: *arte, diritto*) sacred; **il Sacro Cuore (di Gesù)** the Sacred Heart (of Jesus); **musica sacra** church music **b** (*Anat*): **osso sacro** sacrum.
②SM the sacred.
sacrosanto, a [sakro'santo] AGG sacrosanct.
sadico, a, ci, che ['sadiko] ①AGG sadistic.
②SM/F sadist.
sadismo [sa'dizmo] SM sadism; **trattare qn con sadismo** to treat sb sadistically.
sadomasochismo [sadomazo'kizmo] SM sadomasochism.
sadomasochista, i, e [sadomazo'kista] SM/F sadomasochist.
sadomasochistico, a, ci, che [sadomazo'kistiko] AGG (*tendenza*) sadomasochistic.
saetta [sa'etta] SF (*fulmine*) thunderbolt; **essere (veloce come) una saetta** (*fig*) to be as quick as lightning.
safari [sa'fari] SM INV safari.
safena [sa'fɛna] SF (*Anat*) saphena.
saga, ghe ['saga] SF saga.
sagace [sa'gatʃe] AGG sagacious, shrewd.
sagacemente [sagatʃe'mente] AVV sagaciously, shrewdly.
sagacia [sa'gatʃa] SF sagacity, shrewdness.
saggezza [sad'dʒettsa] SF wisdom.
saggiamente [saddʒa'mente] AVV wisely.
saggiare [sad'dʒare] VT (*metalli preziosi*) to assay; (*fig: mettere alla prova*) to test.
saggina [sad'dʒina] SF (*Bot*) sorghum.
saggio¹, gia, gi, ge ['saddʒo] ①AGG wise.
②SM wise man; (*Antichità*) sage.
saggio², gi ['saddʒo] SM **a** (*prova: di abilità, forza*) proof; **dare saggio di** to give proof of; **saggio di ginnastica** gymnastics display; **saggio di musica** recital
b (*campione*) sample; (*di libro*) sample copy; **in saggio** as a sample
c (*scritto: letterario*) essay; (: *Scol*) written test
d (*di metalli preziosi*) assay.
saggista, i, e [sad'dʒista] SM/F essayist.
saggistica, che [sad'dʒistika] SF (*attività*) essay writing; (*produzione*) essays *pl*.
sagittaria [sadʒit'tarja] SF (*pianta*) arrowhead.
Sagittario, ri [sadʒit'tarjo] SM Sagittarius; **essere del Sagittario** to be Sagittarius.
sagola ['sagola] SF (*Naut*) line.
sagoma ['sagoma] SF (*profilo, linea*) outline, profile; (*forma*) shape, form; (*modello in cartone, legno*) template; (*nel tiro al bersaglio*) target; (*fig: persona*) character; **è una sagoma!** he's a scream!
sagomare [sago'mare] VT to shape, mould.
sagomato, a [sago'mato] AGG shaped, moulded; **ben sagomato** well-shaped.
sagra ['sagra] SF festival, feast.
sagrato [sa'grato] SM churchyard.
sagrestano [sagres'tano] SM sexton, sacristan.
sagrestia [sagres'tia], **sagristia** [sagris'tia] SF sacristy.
Sahara [sa'ara] SM: **il (deserto del) Sahara** the Sahara (Desert).
sahariana [saa'rjana] SF bush jacket.
sahariano, a [saa'rjano] AGG Saharan, Sahara *attr*.
Sahel [sa'ɛl] SM (*Geog*) Sahel.
sai *ecc*['sai] VB *vedi* **sapere**.
Saigon [sai'gon] SF Saigon.

saio, sai ['sajo] SM (*Rel*) habit; **prendere** *o* **vestire il saio** to take the habit.
sala ['sala] SF (*gen*) room; (*molto grande*) hall; (*salotto*) living room ▶**sala d'aspetto** *o* **d'attesa** waiting room ▶**sala da ballo** dance hall ▶**sala da biliardo** (*pubblica*) billiard hall; (*privata*) billiard room ▶**sala dei concerti** concert hall ▶**sala per conferenze** (*Univ*) lecture hall; (*in aziende*) conference room ▶**sala (dei) comandi** control room ▶**sala da gioco** gaming room ▶**sala macchine** (*Naut*) engine room ▶**sala operatoria** (*Med*) operating theatre (*Brit*) *o* room (*Am*) ▶**sala partenze** departure lounge ▶**sala da pranzo** dining room ▶**sala professori** staff room ▶**sala per ricevimenti** banqueting hall ▶**sala delle udienze** (*Dir*) courtroom.
salace [sa'latʃe] AGG (*spinto, piccante*) salacious, saucy; (*mordace*) cutting, biting.
salamandra [sala'mandra] SF (*Zool*) salamander.
salame [sa'lame] SM (*cibo*) salami *no pl*, salami sausage; (*fig: persona sciocca*) dope.
salamelecchi [salame'lɛkki] SMPL (*pegg*) bowing and scraping *no pl*; **fare salamelecchi** to bow and scrape; **senza tanti salamelecchi** without ceremony.
salamoia [sala'mɔja] SF (*Culin, Chim*) brine.
salare [sa'lare] VT **a** (*condire*) to salt, add salt to **b** (*mettere sotto sale: senza acqua*) to salt; (: *con acqua*) to brine.
salariale [sala'rjale] AGG wage *attr*, pay *attr*; **aumento salariale** wage *o* pay increase (*Brit*) *o* raise (*Am*).
salariato, a [sala'rjato] ①AGG wage-earning.
②SM/F wage-earner.
salario, ri [sa'larjo] SM pay, wage, wages *pl* ▶**salario base** basic wage ▶**salario minimo garantito** guaranteed minimum wage.
salassare [salas'sare] VT (*Med*) to bleed; (*fig*) to bleed dry *o* white.
salasso [sa'lasso] SM (*Med*) bleeding, bloodletting; (*fig: forte spesa*) drain.
salatino [sala'tino] SM cracker, salted biscuit.
salato, a [sa'lato] AGG (*sapore, cibo*) salty; (*acqua*) salt *attr*; (*burro*) salted; (*fig: costoso*) expensive, costly; (: *prezzo*) stiff, steep; (: *mordace: discorso*) sharp, cutting; **pagare qc salato** (*acquisto*) to pay through the nose for sth; **l'ha pagata salata** (*fig*) he paid dearly for it.
saldare [sal'dare] ①VT **a** (*Tecn, gen*) to join; (*con saldatore*) to solder; (*con saldatura autogena*) to weld **b** (*conto*) to settle, pay; (*fattura, debito*) to pay; **saldare un conto (con qn)** to settle an account (with sb); (*fig*) to settle a score (with sb).
②**saldarsi** VIP (*ferita*) to heal.
saldatore [salda'tore] SM **a** (*operaio*) (*vedi vt*) solderer; welder **b** (*utensile*) soldering iron.
saldatrice [salda'tritʃe] SF (*macchina*) welder, welding machine ▶**saldatrice ad arco** arc welder.
saldatura [salda'tura] SF (*vedi vt*) (*azione*) soldering; welding; (: *punto saldato*) soldered joint; weld ▶**saldatura ad arco** arc welding ▶**saldatura autogena** welding.
saldezza [sal'dettsa] SF firmness, strength.
saldo¹, a ['saldo] AGG (*gen*) steady, firm, stable; (*fig: rapporto*) steady; (: *principi*) sound.
saldo² ['saldo] SM **a** (*pagamento*) settlement, payment; (*somma residua da pagare*) balance; **pagare a saldo** to pay in full ▶**saldo attivo** credit ▶**saldo passivo** deficit

►**saldo riportato** balance brought forward **b** (*svendita*) sale.

sale ['sale] **1** SM **a** (*gen*) salt; **conservare sotto sale** to salt; **sotto sale** salted; **restare di sale** (*fig*) to be dumbfounded; **avere molto sale in zucca** to have a lot of good sense; **non ha molto sale in zucca** he doesn't have much sense

b : **sali** SMPL (*Med: da annusare*) smelling salts.

2 ►**sale da cucina** cooking salt ►**sale fino** table salt ►**sale grosso** cooking salt ►**sale da tavola** table salt ►**sali da bagno** bath salts ►**sali minerali** mineral salts ►**sali e tabacchi** tobacconist's (shop) *sg*.

salernitano, a [salerni'tano] **1** AGG of *o* from Salerno. **2** SM/F inhabitant *o* native of Salerno.

salesiano, a [sale'zjano] AGG, SM/F (*Rel*) Salesian.

salgemma [sal'dʒɛmma] SM rock salt.

salgo *ecc* ['salgo] VB *vedi* **salire**.

salice ['salitʃe] SM (*Bot*) willow ►**salice bianco** white willow ►**salice piangente** weeping willow.

saliente [sa'ljɛnte] AGG salient, main.

saliera [sa'ljɛra] SF (*Culin*) saltcellar.

salina [sa'lina] SF **a** (*serie di vasche*) saltworks *sg* **b** (*deposito naturale*) salt pan **c** (*miniera di salgemma*) salt mine.

salino, a [sa'lino] AGG saline.

salire [sa'lire] VB IRREG **1** VT (*scale, pendio*) to climb, go (*o* come) up.

2 VI (*aus* **essere**) **a** (*gen*) to go (*o* come) up; (*aereo*) to climb, go up; **sali tu** *o* **vengo giù io?** are you coming up or shall I come down?; **salimmo a piedi/con la bicicletta fino in cima** we walked/cycled up to the top; **la strada sale per 2 km** the road climbs for 2 km; **salì sull'albero** he climbed the tree; **salire in quota** (*Aer*) to gain altitude **b** : **salire in macchina** to get into the car; **salire sull'autobus/sul treno** to get on the bus/on the train; **salire a bordo di** to (get on) board; **salire a cavallo** to mount; **salire su una** *o* **in bicicletta** to get on a bicycle; **salire in sella** to get into the saddle **c** (*prezzo, temperatura*) to rise, go up; (*marea*) to come in; (*fumo*) to rise **d** (*fraseologia*): **salire in cielo** *o* **paradiso** to go to heaven; **salire al potere** to rise to power; **salire al trono** to ascend the throne; **salire alle stelle** (*prezzi*) to rocket; **salire nella stima di qn** to rise in sb's estimation.

saliscendi [saliʃ'ʃendi] SM INV latch.

salita [sa'lita] SF **a** (*azione*) climb, ascent; **salita a spina di pesce** (*Sci*) herringbone climb **b** (*strada*) hill, slope; **strada in salita** road going uphill.

saliva [sa'liva] SF saliva.

salivare[1] [sali'vare] AGG salivary.

salivare[2] [sali'vare] VI (*aus* **avere**) to salivate.

salma ['salma] SF body (*of dead person*).

salmastro, a [sal'mastro] **1** AGG (*acqua*) salt *attr*; (*sapore*) salty. **2** SM (*sapore*) salty taste; (*odore*) salty smell.

salmerie [salme'rie] SFPL (*Mil*) train *sg*.

salmì [sal'mi] SM INV (*Culin*) salmi; **lepre in salmì** salmi of hare.

salmista, i [sal'mista] SM (*Rel*) psalmist.

salmo ['salmo] SM (*Rel*) psalm.

salmodia [salmo'dia] SF psalmody.

salmone [sal'mone] SM salmon.

salmonella [salmo'nɛlla] SF salmonella.

salmonellosi [salmonel'lɔzi] SF INV salmonellosis.

salnitro [sal'nitro] SM (*Chim*) saltpetre.

Salomone[1] [salo'mone] SM Solomon.

Salomone[2] [salo'mone] SFPL: **le (isole) Salomone** the Solomon Islands.

salone [sa'lone] SM **a** (*stanza*) living room , sitting room (*Brit*), lounge (*Brit*); (*di ricevimento*) reception room; (*su nave*) lounge, saloon **b** (*mostra*) show, exhibition ►**salone dell'automobile** motor show **c** (*negozio: di parrucchiere*) hairdresser's (salon) ►**salone di bellezza** beauty salon.

saloon [sa'lu:n] SM INV saloon.

salopette [salo'pɛt] SF INV dungarees *pl*; (*Sci*) salopettes *pl*.

salottiero, a [salot'tjɛro] AGG mundane.

salotto [sa'lɔtto] SM **a** (*stanza*) living room , sitting room (*Brit*), lounge (*Brit*); (*mobilio*) lounge suite **b** (*circolo letterario*) salon; **chiacchiere da salotto** (*fig*) society gossip *sg*.

salpancora [sal'pankora] SM INV (*Naut*) windlass, anchor winch.

salpare [sal'pare] (*Naut*) **1** VT: **salpare l'ancora** to weigh anchor. **2** VI (*aus* **essere**) to set sail.

salsa ['salsa] SF sauce; **in tutte le salse** (*fig*) in all kinds of ways ►**salsa di pomodoro** tomato sauce ►**salsa verde** *savoury sauce made with parsley, anchovies, onion, olive oil and garlic*.

salsedine [sal'sedine] SF (*del mare, vento*) saltiness; (*incrostazione*) (dried) salt.

salsiccia, ce [sal'sittʃa] SF (pork) sausage.

salsiera [sal'sjɛra] SF gravy boat, sauceboat (*Brit*).

salso ['salso] SM (*salsedine*) saltiness.

saltare [sal'tare] **1** VT (*siepe, ostacolo*) to jump (over), leap (over); (*fig: capitolo, pasto*) to skip, miss (out); **saltare la corda** to skip.

2 VI (*aus* **essere** *o* **avere**) **a** (*gen*) to jump, leap; (*saltellare*) to skip; (: *su un piede solo*) to hop; **saltare su/sopra qc** to jump on/over sth; **saltare giù** to jump down; **saltare giù da qc** to jump off sth, jump down from sth; **saltare addosso a qn** (*aggredire*) to attack sb; **salta su!** (*in macchina*) jump in!; (*su moto, bici*) jump on!; **è saltato su e mi ha detto che...** he jumped up and told me that ...; **saltare a terra** to jump down; **saltare dal letto/dalla finestra** to jump out of bed/out of the window; **saltare al collo di qn** (*in segno di affetto*) to throw one's arms round sb's neck; (*per strangolarlo*) to grab sb by the neck; **saltare da un argomento all'altro** to jump from one subject to another; **saltare dalla gioia** to jump for joy; **salta agli occhi** it's obvious; **ma che ti salta in mente?** what are you thinking of?; **far saltare un bimbo sulle ginocchia** to bounce a child on one's knees **b** (*bottone*) to pop off; (*bomba*) to explode, blow up; (*ponte, ferrovia*) to blow up; (*valvola*) to blow; (*fig: impiegato*) to be fired; (: *corso*) to be cancelled; **saltare in aria** to blow up **c** : **far saltare** (*treno, ponte*) to blow up; (*fusibile*) to blow; (*mina*) to explode; (*serratura: forzare*) to break; (: *con esplosivo*) to blow; (*lezione, appuntamento*) to cancel; **far saltare il banco** (*Gioco*) to break the bank; **farsi saltare le cervella** to blow one's brains out **d** : **saltare fuori** (*apparire improvvisamente*) to jump out, leap out; (*venire trovato*) to turn up; **saltare fuori con** (*dire improvvisamente*) to come out with; **dall'auto sono saltati fuori due ladri** two thieves jumped *o* leapt out of the car; **quel libro è finalmente saltato fuori** that book

finally turned up; **da dove salti fuori?** where did you spring from?
e (*Culin*) to sauté.

saltatore, trice [salta'tore] SM/F (*Sport*: *persona*) jumper; (: *cavallo*) steeplechaser.

saltellare [saltel'lare] VI (*aus* **avere**) to skip; (*su un solo piede*) to hop.

saltello [sal'tɛllo] SM little jump; (*su un solo piede*) hop.

salterio, ri [sal'tɛrjo] SM (*Rel*) psalter.

saltimbanco, a, chi, che [saltim'banko] SM/F (*acrobata*) acrobat; (*pegg*) charlatan, fraud.

saltimbocca [saltim'bokka] SM INV (*Culin*) *rolled veal and ham.*

saltimpalo [saltim'palo] SM (*uccello*) stonechat.

salto ['salto] SM **a** (*gen*) jump, leap; **fare un salto** to jump, leap; (*per la paura*) to start; **fare un salto a Milano** to pop over to Milan; **fare un salto da qn** to pop over to sb's (place); **fare un salto da un amico** to drop in on a friend; **fare i salti dalla gioia** to jump for joy; **un salto nel buio** (*fig*) a leap in the dark
b (*Sport*) ► **salto in alto** high jump(*Sci*) ski jumping ►**salto con l'asta** pole vault ► **salto in lungo** long jump ►**salto mortale** somersault; **ho fatto i salti mortali per arrivare qui in tempo** (*fig*) I almost killed myself trying to get here on time ► **salto dal trampolino** ► **salto triplo** triple jump
c (*dislivello*, *anche Alpinismo*) drop; **un salto di qualità** a difference in quality; (*miglioramento*: *nel lavoro, in condizioni*) a step up the ladder.

saltuariamente [saltuarja'mente] AVV occasionally, from time to time.

saltuario, ria, ri, rie [saltu'arjo] AGG occasional.

salubre [sa'lubre] AGG healthy, salubrious (*frm*).

salubrità [salubri'ta] SF healthiness.

salume [sa'lume] SM (*Culin*) cured pork; **salumi** SMPL cured pork meats.

salumeria [salume'ria] SF ≈ delicatessen.

salumiere, a [salu'mjɛre] SM/F ≈ delicatessen owner.

salumificio, ci [salumi'fitʃo] SM cured pork meat factory.

salutare¹ [salu'tare] AGG healthy, salutary, beneficial.

salutare² [salu'tare] **1** VT **a** (*incontrandosi*) to greet; (*congedandosi*) to say goodbye to; (*trasmettere i saluti*) to give *o* send one's regards to; **mi saluti sua moglie** my regards to your wife; **salutami Lucia se la vedi** if you see Lucia say hello to her for me
b (*Mil*) to salute; **salutare la bandiera** to salute the flag.
2 **salutarsi** VR (*uso reciproco*: *incontrandosi*) to greet each other; (: *congedandosi*) to say goodbye (to each other).

salute [sa'lute] **1** SF health; **per motivi di salute** for health reasons; **godere di buona salute** to be healthy, enjoy good health; **avere una salute di ferro** to have an iron constitution; **bere alla salute di qn** to drink (to) sb's health.
2 ESCL (*a chi starnutisce*) bless you!; (*bevendo*) your health!, cheers!

salutista, i, e [salu'tista] SM/F **a** (*maniaco della salute*) health fanatic **b** (*dell'Esercito della Salvezza*) Salvationist.

saluto [sa'luto] SM **a** (*incontrandosi*) greeting; (*congedandosi*) goodbye, farewell; **rivolgere il saluto a qn** to greet sb; **gli ha tolto il saluto** he no longer says hello to him; **tanti saluti** [OR] **cari saluti** best regards; **cordiali saluti** [OR] **distinti saluti** yours truly, yours faithfully

b (*gesto*: *del capo*) nod; (: *con la mano*) wave; **mi fece un cenno di saluto** he nodded to me; he waved to me
c (*Mil*) salute.

salva ['salva] SF salvo; **sparare a salva** to fire a salute.

salvacondotto [salvakon'dotto] SM (*Mil*) pass, safe-conduct.

salvadanaio, ai [salvada'najo] SM moneybox, piggy bank.

salvadoregno, a [salvado'reɲɲo] AGG, SM/F Salvadorean.

salvagente [salva'dʒɛnte] SM **a** (*Naut*: *gen*) life buoy; (: *ciambella*) life belt; (: *giubbotto*) lifejacket (*Brit*), life preserver (*Am*) **b** (*stradale*: *pl inv*) traffic island.

salvagocce [salva'gottʃe] AGG INV: **tappo salvagocce** dripless pour spout.

salvaguardare [salvagwar'dare] VT to safeguard, protect.

salvaguardia [salva'gwardja] SF safeguard; **a salvaguardia di** for the safeguard of.

salvare [sal'vare] **1** VT (*gen*, *Inform*) to save; (*portare soccorso*) to rescue; **lo salvarono da morte sicura** they saved him from certain death; **hanno salvato poche persone dal naufragio** they rescued few people from the shipwreck; **salvare la vita a qn** to save sb's life; **mi hai salvato!** (*anche fig*) you saved me!; **hanno salvato poche cose dall'incendio** they salvaged very few items from the fire; **salvare la faccia** (*fam*) to save face; **salvare le apparenze** to keep up appearances; **salvare capra e cavoli** to have the best of both worlds; **Dio salvi la regina!** God save the Queen!.
2 **salvarsi** VR (*salvare la propria vita*) to save o.s.; **nessuno si è salvato dal disastro** nobody escaped the disaster; **si salvi chi può** every man for himself; **non si è salvato nulla** everything was destroyed.

salvataggio, gi [salva'taddʒo] SM rescue; **cintura di salvataggio** lifebelt.

salvatore, trice [salva'tore] SM/F rescuer, saviour (*Brit*), savior (*Am*); (*Rel*): **il Salvatore** the Saviour.

salvavita [salva'vita] SM INV (*Elettr*) circuit breaker; (*anche*: **farmaco salvavita**) life-saving drug.

salvazione [salvat'tsjone] SF (*Rel*) salvation.

salve¹ ['salve] ESCL (*ciao*) hello!, hi!

salve² ['salve] SF (*colpo*) = **salva**.

salveregina [salvere'dʒina] SF (*pl* **salveregina** *o* **salveregine**) (*preghiera*) Salve Regina.

salvezza [sal'vettsa] SF salvation; **cercare salvezza nella fuga** to seek safety in flight.

salvia ['salvja] SF (*Bot*) sage.

salvietta [sal'vjetta] SF napkin, serviette (*Brit*); (*di spugna*) hand towel.

salvo¹, a ['salvo] **1** AGG (*persona*) safe, unhurt, unharmed; (: *fuori pericolo*) safe, out of danger; **uscir salvo da qc** to come out of sth safely; **avere salva la vita** to have one's life spared.
2 SM: **essere in salvo** (*persona, cosa*) to be safe; **mettere qc in salvo** to put sth in a safe place; **mettersi in salvo** to reach safety; **portare qn in salvo** to lead sb to safety.

salvo² ['salvo] PREP **a** (*eccetto*) except (for); **è aperto tutti i giorni salvo il lunedì** it's open every day with the exception of *o* except Monday; **vennero tutti salvo lui** everybody came except him; **salvo errori, la somma ammonta a...** unless I am (*o* we are *ecc*) mistaken, it amounts to ...; **salvo imprevisti** barring accidents; **salvo errori e omissioni** errors and omissions excepted; **salvo contrordini** barring instructions to the contrary

b : **salvo che** (*eccetto che*) except (that); (*a meno che*) unless; **sono soddisfatto salvo che per una cosa** I'm quite satisfied except for one thing; **lo farò salvo che tu non voglia farlo** I'll do it unless you would rather do it.

Samaria [sa'marja] SF (*Bibbia*) Samaria.

samaritano, a [samari'tano] ① AGG Samaritan.

② SM/F Samaritan; **buon samaritano** (*anche fig*) Good Samaritan.

sambuca [sam'buka] SF (*liquore*) sambuca (*type of anisette*).

sambuco, chi [sam'buko] SM (*Bot*) elder (tree).

samurai [samu'rai] SM INV samurai.

san [san] AGG vedi **santo**.

sanamente [sana'mente] AVV (*in modo sano*) healthily; (*rettamente*) correctly, soundly.

sanare [sa'nare] VT (*malato*) to heal, cure; (*economia*) to cure, put right, restore.

sanatoria [sana'tɔrja] SF (*Dir*) act of indemnity.

sanatoriale [sanato'rjale] AGG sanatorium *attr* (*Brit*), sanitarium *attr* (*Am*).

sanatorio, ri [sana'tɔrjo] SM sanatorium (*Brit*), sanitarium (*Am*).

San Bernardo ['sam ber'nardo] SM INV (*cane*) Saint Bernard.

sancire [san'tʃire] VT (*sanzionare*) to sanction; (*ratificare*) to ratify.

sancta sanctorum ['sankta sank'tɔrum] SM INV (*fig*) holy of holies.

Sanctus ['sanktus] SM INV Sanctus.

sandalo ['sandalo] SM **a** (*calzatura*) sandal **b** (*Bot*) sandalwood.

sangallo [san'gallo] SM broderie anglaise.

sangria [san'gria] SF (*bibita*) sangria.

sangue ['sangwe] SM blood; **animale a sangue caldo/ freddo** warm-/cold-blooded animal; **uccidere a sangue freddo** to kill in cold blood; **all'ultimo sangue** (*duello, lotta*) to the death; **il sangue gli salì alla testa** the blood rushed to his head; **non corre buon sangue tra di loro** there's bad blood between them; **ha la musica nel sangue** music is in his blood; **sentirsi gelare il sangue nelle vene** to feel one's blood run cold; **farsi cattivo sangue per qc** to get worked up about sth; **buon sangue non mente!** blood will out!; **al sangue** (*Culin*) rare ▶ **sangue freddo** (*fig*) sang-froid, calm.

sanguigno, a [san'gwiɲɲo] AGG (*gruppo, pressione, vaso*) blood *attr*; (*fig: collerico*) bad-tempered; (*color rosso intenso*) blood-red.

sanguinaccio, ci [sangwi'nattʃo] SM (*Culin*) black pudding.

sanguinante [sangwi'nante] AGG bleeding.

sanguinare [sangwi'nare] VI (*aus avere*) (*anche fig*) to bleed.

sanguinario, ria, ri, rie [sangwi'narjo] AGG bloodthirsty.

sanguinolento, a [sangwino'lɛnto] AGG (*che sanguina*) bleeding; (*fig*) bloody.

sanguinoso, a [sangwi'noso] AGG bloody.

sanguisuga, ghe [sangwi'suga] SF (*Zool*) leech; (*fig*) leech, bloodsucker.

sanità [sani'ta] SF **a** (*gen*) health; **Ministero della Sanità** ≈ Department of Health (*Brit*), ≈ Department of Health and Human Services (*Am*) **b** (*Mil*) army medical corps *sg o pl*.

sanitario, ria, ri, rie [sani'tarjo] ① AGG (*servizio, misure*) health *attr*; (*condizioni*) sanitary; **Ufficiale Sanitario**

Health Officer; (**impianti**) **sanitari** bathroom *o* sanitary fittings.

② SM (*Amm: medico*) doctor.

San Marino [san ma'rino] SF: (**la Repubblica di**) **San Marino** (the Republic of) San Marino.

sanno *ecc* ['sanno] VB vedi **sapere**.

sano, a ['sano] AGG (*persona, fisico, denti*) healthy; (*alimento*) healthy, wholesome; (*frutto*) sound; (*fig: politica, ambiente*) good; **sano e salvo** safe and sound; **sano di mente** sane; **di sani principi** of sound principles; **una sana educazione** a good education; **essere sano come un pesce** to be (as) fit as a fiddle; **di sana pianta** completely, entirely.

sanscrito, a ['sanskrito] AGG, SM Sanskrit.

San Silvestro ['san sil'vɛstro] SM (*giorno*) New Year's Eve.

santamente [santa'mente] AVV devoutly; **vivere santamente** to lead a holy life.

Santiago [santi'ago] SF: **Santiago (del Cile)** Santiago (de Chile).

santificare [santifi'kare] VT (*dichiarare santo*) to sanctify, hallow; (*feste*) to observe.

santino [san'tino] SM holy picture.

santissimo, a [san'tissimo] ① AGG **a** : **il Santissimo Sacramento** the Blessed Sacrament; **il Padre Santissimo** (*papa*) the Holy Father **b** (*fig*): **fammi il santissimo piacere di star zitto!** do me a favour and keep quiet!.

② SM (*Rel*): **il Santissimo** the Blessed Sacrament.

santità [santi'ta] SF INV (*Rel*) sanctity, holiness; (*fig*) sanctity; **Sua/Vostra Santità** His/Your Holiness.

santo, a ['santo] ① AGG **a** (*sacro*) holy; **Venerdì Santo** Good Friday; **la Santa Sede** the Holy See; **santo cielo!** good heavens!; **Dio santo!** good God!

b (*seguito da sm*: **san** + *consonante*, **sant'** + *vocale*, **santo** + *s impura, gn, pn, ps, x, z*) (*seguito da sf*: **santa** + *consonante*, **sant'** + *vocale*) saint; **San Pietro** (*apostolo*) Saint Peter; (*chiesa*) Saint Peter's

c (*fig*) saint; **è una santa donna** she's a saint; **quel sant'uomo di tuo nonno** (*defunto*) your sainted grandfather; **parole sante!** very true!; **vuoi farmi il santo piacere di uscire?** would you do me a favour and get out?; **tutto il santo giorno** the whole blessed day, all day long.

② SM/F (*anche fig*) saint; **non sono una santa** I'm no saint; **qualche santo provvederà** something will turn up; **non c'è santo che tenga!** that's no excuse!; **quella santa di sua moglie** his wife, saint that she is.

③ : **santi** SMPL: **i Santi** (*Ognissanti*) All Saints' Day.

santone [san'tone] SM holy man.

Santo Stefano ['santo 'stefano] SM (*giorno*) Boxing Day (*Brit*).

santuario, ri [santu'arjo] SM sanctuary.

sanzionare [santsjo'nare] VT to sanction.

sanzione [san'tsjone] SF **a** (*approvazione*) sanction, approval **b** (*punizione*) sanction, penalty; **sanzioni economiche** economic sanctions.

sapere [sa'pere] VB IRREG ① VT **a** (*conoscere: lezione, nome*) to know; (*venire a sapere: notizia*) to hear; **sai dove abita?** do you know where he lives?; **sai se torna?** do you know if *o* whether he is coming back?; **lo so** I know; **non se so nulla** I don't know anything about it; **sa quattro lingue** he knows *o* can speak four languages; **non ne vuole più sapere di lei** he doesn't want to have anything more to do with her; **come l'ha saputo?** how did he find out *o* hear about it?; **ho saputo che ti sei sposato** I hear you

got married; **vuoi sapere la verità?** do you want to know *o* hear the truth?; **far sapere qc a qn** to let sb know (about) sth, inform sb about sth; **venire a sapere qc (da qn)** to find out *o* hear about sth (from sb)

b (*essere capace di*) to know how to; **non sa far niente** he can't do anything; **sai nuotare?** do you know how to swim?, can you swim?; **sa (come) cavarsela** he can manage

c (*rendersi conto*) to know; **non sa cosa dice** he doesn't know *o* realize what he's saying; **sa quello che fa** he knows what he's doing; **so com'è difficile parlargli** I know how difficult it is to talk to him; **senza saperlo** without realizing it, unwittingly

d (*fraseologia*): **è difficile, e io ne so qualcosa** it's difficult and don't I know it; **e chi lo sa?** who knows?; **si sa che...** it's well known that ..., everybody knows that ...; **non si sa mai** you never know; **non saprei** I don't *o* wouldn't know; **non saprei dire** I couldn't say; **mi dispiace, non so che farci** I'm sorry, I don't see what I can do about it; **averlo saputo!** had I (*o* we *ecc*) known!, if only I (*o* we *ecc*) had known!; **ci sa fare con le donne/macchine** he has a way with women/cars; **lui sì che ci sa fare** he's very good at it.

2 VI (*aus* **avere**) **a** : **sapere di** (*aver sapore*) to taste of; (*aver odore*) to smell of; (*fig*) to smack of, resemble; **è un film che non sa di niente** it's a very dull film

b : **mi sa che...** (*credo*) I think (that) ...; **mi sa che non viene** I don't think he's coming.

3 SM knowledge.

sapiente [sa'pjɛnte] **1** AGG (*dotto*) learned; (*che rivela abilità*) masterly; **con mano sapiente** with a skilful hand.

2 SM/F scholar.

sapientemente [sapjɛnte'mente] AVV (*con sapienza*) wisely; (*con capacità*) skilfully.

sapientone, a [sapjɛn'tone] SM/F (*pegg*) know-all (*Brit*), know-it-all (*Am*).

sapienza [sa'pjɛntsa] SF (*saggezza*) wisdom; (*conoscenza*) knowledge, learning.

saponaria [sapo'narja] SF (*Bot*) soapwort.

saponata [sapo'nata] SF (*acqua*) soapy water; (*schiuma*) (soap)suds *pl*.

sapone [sa'pone] SM soap ▶**sapone da barba** shaving soap ▶**sapone da bucato** washing soap ▶**sapone liquido** liquid soap ▶ **sapone in scaglie** soapflakes *pl*.

saponetta [sapo'netta] SF bar *o* cake of soap.

saponificazione [saponifikat'tsjone] SF saponification.

sapore [sa'pore] SM (*anche fig*) flavour (*Brit*), flavor (*Am*); **non ha alcun sapore** it hasn't any flavo(u)r, it doesn't taste of anything; **è ciò che dà sapore alla vita** this is what makes life worth living; **parole di sapore amaro** words with a bitter ring to them.

saporitamente [saporita'mente] AVV (*condito*) tastily; **dormire saporitamente** (*fig*) to sleep soundly.

saporito, a [sapo'rito] AGG (*cibo*) tasty; (*fig: battuta*) witty; **poco saporito** tasteless; **farsi una dormita saporita** (*fig*) to sleep soundly.

saporoso, a [sapo'roso] AGG tasty.

sappiamo *ecc*[sap'pjamo] VB vedi **sapere**.

saprò *ecc* [sa'prɔ] VB vedi **sapere**.

saprofita, i [sa'prɔfita] SM (*Bot*) saprophyte.

saputello, a [sapu'tɛllo] SM/F know-all (*Brit*), know-it-all (*Am*).

sarà *ecc* [sa'ra] VB vedi **essere**.

sarabanda [sara'banda] SF (*fig*) uproar.

saracinesca, sche [saratʃi'neska] SF rolling shutter.

sarcasmo [sar'kazmo] SM (*ironia*) sarcasm; (*commento*) sarcastic remark; **fare del sarcasmo** to be sarcastic, make sarcastic remarks.

sarcasticamente [sarkastika'mente] AVV sarcastically.

sarcastico, a, ci, che [sar'kastiko] AGG sarcastic.

sarchiare [sar'kjare] VT (*Agr*) to hoe.

sarchiatrice [sarkja'tritʃe] SF (*Agr*) hoeing machine.

sarcofago, gi *o* **ghi** [sar'kɔfago] SM sarcophagus.

sarda ['sarda] SF (*pesce*) = **sardina**.

Sardegna [sar'deɲɲa] SF: **la Sardegna** Sardinia.

sardina [sar'dina] SF sardine; **pigiati come sardine** (*fig*) packed like sardines.

sardo, a ['sardo] AGG, SM/F Sardinian.

sardonicamente [sardonika'mente] AVV sardonically.

sardonico, a, ci, che [sar'dɔniko] AGG sardonic.

sarei *ecc* [sa'rɛi] VB vedi **essere**.

sargasso [sar'gasso] SM sargasso, gulfweed; **il mar dei Sargassi** the Sargasso Sea.

sari ['sari] SM INV sari.

sarmento [sar'mento] SM (*Bot*) runner; (*di vite, edera*) shoot.

sarta ['sarta] SF dressmaker.

sartia ['sartja] SF (*Naut*) stay.

sartiame [sar'tjame] SM (*Naut*) stays *pl*.

sarto ['sarto] SM tailor; (*d'alta moda*) couturier; **sarto da donna** ladies' tailor.

sartoria [sarto'ria] SF **a** (*attività: di sarto*) tailoring; (: *di sarta*) dressmaking; **sartoria d'alta moda** haute couture

b (*laboratorio: di sarto*) tailor's (shop); (: *di sarta*) dressmaker's (shop); (: *d'alta moda*) couturier's, fashion house.

sassaia [sas'saja] SF (*terreno*) stony ground; (*lungo argini*) (stone) dyke.

sassaiola [sassa'jɔla] SF hail of stones.

sassata [sas'sata] SF blow with a stone; **infranse il vetro con una sassata** he broke the pane with a stone; **tirare una sassata contro** *o* **a qn/qc** to throw a stone at sb/sth.

sassifraga, ghe [sas'sifraga] SF (*pianta*) saxifrage.

sasso ['sasso] SM (*pietra*) stone; (*ciottolo*) pebble; (*roccia*) rock; **restare** *o* **rimanere di sasso** (*fig*) to be dumbfounded; **è una cosa che fa piangere i sassi** (*fig: penoso*) it's pitiful.

sassofonista, i, e [sassofo'nista] SM/F saxophonist.

sassofono [sas'sɔfono] SM saxophone.

sassola ['sassola] SF (*Naut*) bailer.

sassone ['sassone] AGG, SM/F Saxon.

sassoso, a [sas'soso] AGG (*vedi sm*) stony; pebbly; rocky.

Satana ['satana] SM Satan.

satanasso [sata'nasso] SM (*fig fam: persona*) devil.

satanico, a, ci, che [sa'taniko] AGG satanic; (*fig*) diabolical, devilish, fiendish.

satellite [sa'tɛllite] SM, AGG INV (*anche fig*) satellite.

satin [sa'tɛ̃] SM satin.

satinato, a [sati'nato] AGG with a satin finish.

satira ['satira] SF satire; **fare la satira di qn/qc** to satirize sb/sth.

satireggiare [satired'dʒare] **1** VT to satirize.

2 VI (*aus* **avere**) (*fare della satira*) to be satirical; (*scrivere satire*) to write satires.

satiricamente [satirika'mente] AVV satirically.

satirico, a, ci, che [sa'tiriko] AGG satiric(al).

satirione [sati'rjone] SM (*fungo*) stinkhorn.

satiro ['satiro] SM (*Mitol*) satyr; (*fig*) lecher, satyr.

satollarsi [satol'larsi] VIP to eat one's fill.

satollo, a [sa'tollo] AGG full, replete.

saturare [satu'rare] ① VT (*Fis, Chim*) to saturate; (*fig*: *riempire*) to fill, stuff.

② **saturarsi** VIP (*Fis, Chim*) to become saturated; (*fig*: *riempire*) to fill, stuff.

saturazione [saturat'tsjone] SF (*Fis, Chim*) saturation; **aver raggiunto il punto di saturazione** to have reached saturation point; (*fig*) to have had more than enough *o* as much as one can take.

satureia [satu'rɛja] SF (*Bot*) savory.

Saturno [sa'turno] SM (*Mitol, Astron*) Saturn; **gli anelli di Saturno** (*Astron*) the rings of Saturn.

saturo, a ['saturo] AGG (*gen*) saturated; **saturo (di)** (*fig*) full (of); **saturo d'acqua** (*terreno*) waterlogged.

saudita, i, e [sau'dita] ① AGG: **Arabia Saudita** Saudi Arabia.

② SM/F Saudi (Arabian).

sauna ['sauna] SF sauna; **fare la sauna** to have *o* take a sauna.

sauro, a ['sauro] AGG, SM/F (*cavallo*) sorrel.

savana [sa'vana] SF savannah.

savio, via, vi, vie ['savjo] ① AGG wise, sensible.

② SM wise man.

Savoia [sa'vojal] SF: **la Savoia** Savoy.

savoiardo, a [savo'jardo] ① AGG of Savoy, Savoyard.

② SM (*Culin*) sponge finger.

savoir-faire [sa'vwar'fɛr] SM INV savoir-faire.

sax [saks] SM INV (*sassofono*) sax.

saziare [sat'tsjare] ① VT (*anche fig*) to satisfy, satiate.

② **saziarsi** VIP: **saziarsi (di)** to eat one's fill (of); **non si sazia di guardarla** (*fig*) he never tires of looking at her.

sazietà [sattsje'ta] SF satiety, satiation; **mangiare a sazietà** to eat one's fill; **ce ne sono a sazietà** there are more than enough.

sazio, zia, zi, zie ['sattsjo] AGG: **sazio (di)** sated (with), full (of); **no, grazie, sono sazio** no thanks, I've had enough; **sono sazio di questi discorsi** (*fig*) I'm fed up with this talk.

sbaciucchiare [zbatʃuk'kjare] VT, **sbaciucchiarsi** VR (*uso reciproco*) to kiss and cuddle.

sbadataggine [zbada'taddʒine] SF (*sventatezza*) carelessness; (*azione*) oversight.

sbadatamente [zbadata'mente] AVV carelessly.

sbadato, a [zba'dato] AGG careless, inattentive.

sbadigliare [zbadiʎ'ʎare] VI (*aus avere*) to yawn.

sbadiglio, gli [zba'diʎʎo] SM yawn; **fare uno sbadiglio** to yawn.

sbafare [zba'fare] VT (*mangiare*) to devour, wolf (down); (*fig*: *scroccare*) to sponge, scrounge.

sbafo ['zbafo] SM: **a sbafo** at somebody else's expense.

sbagliare [zbaʎ'ʎare] ① VT (*gen*) to make a mistake in, get wrong; (*bersaglio*) to miss; **ha sbagliato tutto** he got everything wrong; **ha sbagliato tutto (nella vita)** he has made a mess of his life; **sbagliare strada** to take the wrong road; **sbagliare la mira** to miss one's aim; **sbagliare treno** to get *o* take the wrong train; **scusi, ho sbagliato numero** (*al telefono*) sorry, I've got the wrong number; **per me ha sbagliato mestiere** in my opinion he is in the wrong job; **sbagliò porta** he opened the wrong door; **sbagli tattica** you're going the wrong way about it; **sbagliare una mossa** (*al gioco*) to make a wrong move.

② VI (*aus avere*) to make a mistake; **hai sbagliato a dirle**

tutto it was a mistake to tell her everything; **ha sbagliato nel ricopiare il numero** he made a mistake in *o* when copying down the number; **potrei sbagliare ma...** I might be mistaken but ...; **ha sbagliato nei suoi confronti** he behaved badly towards her; **ho sbagliato di pochi centimetri** I miscalculated by a few centimetres, I was a few centimetres out (in my calculations).

③ **sbagliarsi** VIP (*fare errori*) to make a mistake (*o* mistakes); (*ingannarsi*) to be wrong, be mistaken; **si è sbagliato nel ricopiare** he made a mistake in *o* when copying; **non c'è da sbagliarsi** there can be no mistake.

sbagliato, a [zbaʎ'ʎato] AGG (*gen*) wrong; (*compito*) full of mistakes; (*conclusione*) erroneous.

sbaglio, gli ['zbaʎʎo] SM mistake, error; **fare uno sbaglio** to make a mistake; **ci deve essere uno sbaglio** there must be some mistake; **ha pagato per lo sbaglio commesso** he's paid for his mistake.

sbalestrare [zbales'trare] VT (*scagliare*) to fling, hurl.

sbalestrato, a [zbales'trato] AGG (*persona: scombussolato*) unsettled.

sballare [zbal'lare] ① VT (*merce*) to unpack.

② VI (*aus essere*) **a** (*nel fare un conto*) to overestimate **b** (*Carte*) to go out **b** (*fam*) to be high (on drugs).

sballato, a [zbal'lato] ① AGG (*calcolo*) wrong; (*fam*: *ragionamento, persona*) screwy.

② SM/F (*fam*: *spostato*) misfit; (: *drogato*) junkie.

sballo ['zballo] SM (*fam*) **a** (*droga*) trip **b** : **che sballo di macchina!** what a totally amazing car!; **un film da sballo** a knockout film.

sballottare [zballot'tare] VT to toss (about), throw (about).

sbalordire [zbalor'dire] ① VT to stun, amaze, astound.

② VI (*aus avere*) to be stunned, be amazed, be astounded.

sbalorditivamente [zbalorditiva'mente] AVV incredibly.

sbalorditivo, a [zbalordi'tivo] AGG (*abilità, memoria*) amazing, astounding; (*prezzo, affitto*) incredible, absurd.

sbalzare[1] [zbal'tsare] ① VT **a** (*scaraventare*) to throw, hurl; **è stato sbalzato a 10 metri di distanza** he was thrown 10 metres **b** (*rimuovere: da una carica, sede*) to remove, dismiss.

② VI (*aus essere*) (*temperatura: alzarsi burscamente*) to jump, rise; (: *abbassarsi bruscamente*) to fall, plummet.

sbalzare[2] [zbal'tsare] VT (*Arte*) to emboss.

sbalzo[1] ['zbaltso] SM (*sussulto*) start; **a sbalzi** jerkily; (*fig*) in fits and starts; **procedere a sbalzi** (*macchina*) to jolt along; **uno sbalzo di temperatura** a sudden change in temperature.

sbalzo[2] ['zbaltso] SM (*Arte*): **lavorare a sbalzo** to emboss.

sbancare[1] [zban'kare] VT (*nei giochi*) to break the bank at (*o* of); (*fig*) to ruin, bankrupt.

sbancare[2] [zban'kare] VT (*Edil*) to excavate.

sbandamento [zbanda'mento] SM (*di veicolo*) skid; (*Naut*) list; (*fig: di persona*) confusion; **ha avuto un periodo di sbandamento** he went off the rails for a bit.

sbandare [zban'dare] ① VI (*aus avere*) (*Aut*) to skid; (*Naut*) to list.

② **sbandarsi** VIP (*folla*) to disperse; (*truppe*) to scatter; (*fig: famiglia*) to break up.

sbandata [zban'data] SF (*Aut*) skid; (*Naut*) list; **prendere** *o* **prendersi una sbandata per qn** (*fig*) to fall for sb.

sbandato, a [zban'dato] SM/F mixed-up person.

sbandierare [zbandje'rare] VT (*bandiere*) to wave; (*fig*:

ostentare) to show off, flaunt, parade.

sbando ['zbando] SM: **essere allo sbando** (*fig*) to drift.

sbaraccare [zbarak'kare] VT (*fam: libri, piatti*) to clear (up); **sarà meglio sbaraccare** it's time we cleared out.

sbaragliare [zbaraʎ'ʎare] VT (*Mil*) to rout; (*in gare sportive*) to beat, defeat.

sbaraglio [zba'raʎʎo] SM: **andare** *o* **buttarsi allo sbaraglio** (*soldato*) to throw o.s. into the fray; (*fig: rischiare*) to risk everything.

sbarazzare [zbarat'tsare] ① VT to clear.
   ② **sbarazzarsi** VR: **sbarazzarsi di qn/qc** to get rid of sb/sth, rid o.s. of sb/sth.

sbarazzino, a [zbarat'tsino] ① AGG impish, cheeky.
   ② SM scamp, imp.

sbarbare [zbar'bare] VT, **sbarbarsi** VR to shave.

sbarbatello [zbarba'tɛllo] SM novice, greenhorn.

sbarcare [zbar'kare] ① VT (*merci*) to unload; (*passeggeri: da nave, aereo*) to disembark, land; (: *da autobus, macchina*) to put down; **sbarcare il lunario** (*fig*) to make ends meet.
   ② VI (*aus essere*): **sbarcare da** (*aereo, nave*) to get off, disembark; **sbarcare (da un treno)** to get off (a train), alight (from a train).

sbarco, chi ['zbarko] SM **a** (*vedi vb*) unloading; disembarkation, landing; putting down; **allo sbarco** on disembarking **b** (*Mil*): **forza da sbarco** landing party; **testa di sbarco** beachhead.

sbarra ['zbarra] SF **a** (*gen, Sport*) bar; (*di passaggio a livello*) barrier; (*di timone*) tiller; **dietro le sbarre** (*fig: in prigione*) behind bars; **presentarsi alla sbarra** (*Dir: in tribunale*) to appear in court; **mettere alla sbarra** (*fig*) to put on trial **b** (*lineetta*) stroke.

sbarramento [zbarra'mento] SM (*di strada, passaggio*) barrier; (*diga*) dam, barrage; (*Mil*) barrage; (*Pol*) cut-off point (*level of support below which a political party is excluded from representation in Parliament*).

sbarrare [zbar'rare] VT **a** (*bloccare*) to block, bar; **sbarrare la strada a qn** (*anche fig*) to bar sb's way **b** (*spalancare*): **sbarrare gli occhi** to open one's eyes wide **c** (*cancellare*) to cross out, strike out; **sbarrare un assegno** to cross a cheque (*Brit*), to endorse a check "for deposit only" (*Am*).

sbarrato, a [zbar'rato] AGG **a** (*porta*) barred; (*passaggio*) blocked, barred; (*strada*) blocked, obstructed **b** (*occhi*) staring **c** (*assegno*) crossed (*Brit*), endorsed "for deposit only" (*Am*).

sbatacchiare [zbatak'kjare] ① VT (*porta*) to slam, bang; (*ali*) to flap.
   ② VI (*aus avere*) to bang.

sbattere ['zbattere] ① VT **a** (*gen*) to beat; (*uova*) to beat, whisk; (*panna*) to whip; (*ali*) to beat, flap; (*porta*) to slam, bang; **sbattere un ginocchio contro qc** to knock one's knee against sth; **sbattere un pugno sul tavolo** to thump the table; **sbattere la porta in faccia a qn** (*anche fig*) to slam the door in sb's face; **non sapevo dove sbattere la testa** (*fig*) I didn't know which way to turn; **sbattere la testa contro un muro** (*fig*) to bang one's head against a brick wall; **finché non ci sbatte la testa contro non capirà** he'll find out the hard way **b** (*buttare*) to throw; **sbattere qc per terra** to throw sth to the ground; **sbattere qn fuori/in galera** to throw sb out/into prison; **sbattere via** to throw away *o* out; **sbattilo pure lì** just throw it over there; **sbattere una notizia in prima pagina** to splash a piece of news across

the front page
   c (*fam!: possedere sessualmente*) to fuck (*fam!*).
   ② VI (*aus avere*) **a** (*porta, finestra*) to bang; (*vele, ali*) to flap; **sbattere contro qc** to knock against sth
   b (*fam*): **sbattersene** not to give a damn; **me ne sbatto!** I don't give a damn!

sbattitore [zbatti'tore] SM (*Culin*) electric whisk.

sbattuto, a [zbat'tuto] AGG **a** (*uovo*) beaten **b** (*fig: persona*) worn out, dejected; (: *pallido*) peaky; **avere un'aria sbattuta** to look worn out.

sbavare [zba'vare] ① VI (*aus avere*) **a** (*gen*) to dribble **b** (*colore*) to run; (*rossetto, inchiostro*) to smudge, smear.
   ② VT: **sbavare qc** to dribble over sth.
   ③ **sbavarsi** VR to dribble down o.s.

sbavatura [zbava'tura] SF (*di persone*) dribbling; (*di lumache*) slime; (*di rossetto, vernice*) smear.

sbeccare [zbek'kare] VT to chip.

sbellicarsi [zbelli'karsi] VIP: **sbellicarsi dalle risa** to split one's sides laughing.

sbendare [zben'dare] VT (*togliere le bende*) to remove the bandage(s) from.

sberla ['zbɛrla] SF slap; **dare una sberla a qn** to slap *o* hit sb.

sberleffo [zber'lɛffo] SM: **fare uno sberleffo a qn** to make a face at sb; **fare gli sberleffi** to pull faces, grimace.

sbevazzare [zbevat'tsare] VI (*aus avere*) (*pegg*) to booze.

sbiadire [zbja'dire] ① VI (*aus essere*) to fade; **ricordi che sbiadiscono col tempo** memories which fade with time.
   ② VT to (cause to) fade.

sbiadito, a [zbja'dito] AGG (*scolorito*) faded; (*fig: stile*) colourless (*Brit*), colorless (*Am*), dull.

sbiancare [zbjan'kare] ① VI (*aus essere*), **sbiancarsi** VIP (*persona*): **sbiancare** *o* **sbiancarsi in viso** to pale, blanch, grow pale *o* white.
   ② VT to whiten.

sbieco, chi ['zbjɛko] ① AGG (*muro*) at an angle; (*pavimento*) sloping, slanting; **tagliare una stoffa di sbieco** to cut material on the bias; **guardare qn di sbieco** (*fig*) to look askance at sb.
   ② SM (*Cucito*) bias.

sbigottimento [zbigotti'mento] SM dismay, consternation.

sbigottire [zbigot'tire] ① VT to dismay, dumbfound.
   ② VI (*aus essere*), **sbigottirsi** VIP to be dismayed, be dumbfounded.

sbilanciamento [zbilantʃa'mento] SM (*di carico*) displacement.

sbilanciare [zbilan'tʃare] ① VT to throw off balance.
   ② **sbilanciarsi** VIP (*perdere l'equilibrio*) to lose one's balance, overbalance; (*fig: compromettersi*) to compromise o.s.

sbilancio, ci [zbi'lantʃo] SM (*Econ*) deficit.

sbilenco, a, chi, che [zbi'lɛnko] AGG (*sedia, tavolino*) rickety; (*persona*) crooked, misshapen; (*fig: idea, ragionamento*) twisted.

sbirciare [zbir'tʃare] VT to peep at, cast sidelong glances at, eye.

sbirciata [zbir'tʃata] SF: **dare una sbirciata a qc** to glance at sth, have a look at sth.

sbirro ['zbirro] SM (*pegg*) cop.

sbizzarrirsi [zbiddzar'rirsi] VIP (*sfogare i propri desideri*) to indulge one's whims; (*fare pazzie*) to go wild; **sbizzarrirsi a fare qc** to indulge o.s. in doing sth.

sbloccare [zblok'kare] ① VT (*gen*) to unblock, free;

(*passaggio*, *strada*) to clear, unblock; (*affitti*) to free from controls; (*freno*) to release; **sbloccare la situazione** to get things moving again.

2 **sbloccarsi** VIP (*gen*) to become unblocked; (*passaggio*, *strada*) to clear, become unblocked; (*Psic: persona*) to free o.s. from a psychological block; **la situazione si è sbloccata** things are moving again.

sblocco, chi ['zblɔkko] SM (*vedi vt*) unblocking; clearing; **dopo lo sblocco degli affitti** after the lifting of rent controls.

sbobba ['zbɔbba] SF (*fam pegg*) dishwater.

sboccare [zbok'kare] 1 VI (*aus essere*): **sboccare in** (*fiume*) to flow into; (*strada*) to lead (in)to; (*valle*) to open into; (*persona*) to emerge into, come (out) into; (*fig: concludersi*) to end (up) in.

2 VT (*rompere: vaso, brocca*) to chip.

sboccatamente [zbokkata'mente] AVV: **esprimersi sboccatamente** to use foul language.

sboccato, a [zbok'kato] AGG (*fig: persona*) foul-mouthed; (: *linguaggio*) coarse, foul.

sbocciare [zbot'tʃare] VI (*aus essere*) (*fiori*) to bloom, flower, open (out); (*fig: nascere*) to blossom.

sbocco, chi ['zbokko] SM a (*di fiume*) mouth; (*di tubazione*) outlet; (*di strada*) end; **una strada senza sbocco** a dead end; **siamo in una situazione senza sbocco** o **sbocchi** there's no way out of this for us b (*Comm*) outlet.

sbocconcellare [zbokkontʃel'lare] VT: **sbocconcellare (qc)** to nibble (at sth).

sbollentare [zbollen'tare] VT (*Culin*) to parboil.

sbollire [zbol'lire] VI (*aus essere*) (*fig: calmarsi*) to cool down.

sbolognare [zboloɲ'ɲare] VT (*fam*): **sbolognare qc/qn** to get rid of sth/sb.

sbornia ['zbɔrnja] SF (*fam*): **prendersi una sbornia** to get plastered.

sborsare [zbor'sare] VT to fork out, shell out.

sbottare [zbot'tare] VI (*aus essere*): **sbottare in una risata** to burst out laughing; **sono sbottato** I couldn't contain myself.

sbottonare [zbotto'nare] 1 VT to unbutton, undo.

2 **sbottonarsi** VR to undo one's buttons; (*fig fam: confidarsi*) to unburden o.s.

sbottonato, a [zbotto'nato] AGG undone, unbuttoned.

sbozzare [zbot'tsare] VT (*gen*) to sketch out; (*scultura*) to rough-hew; (*fig: progetto*) to draft.

sbracato, a [zbra'kato] AGG (*fam: sciatto*) dishevelled, slovenly.

sbracciarsi [zbrat'tʃarsi] VIP to wave (one's arms about).

sbracciato, a [zbrat'tʃato] AGG (*persona*) with bare arms, bare-armed; (*indumento: senza maniche*) sleeveless; (: *a maniche corte*) short-sleeved.

sbraitare [zbrai'tare] VI (*aus avere*) to shout, yell, bawl.

sbranare [zbra'nare] 1 VT to tear to pieces.

2 **sbranarsi** VR (*uso reciproco, anche fig*) to tear each other to pieces.

sbriciolare [zbritʃo'lare] VT, **sbriciolarsi** VIP to crumble.

sbriciolato, a [zbritʃo'lato] AGG crumbling.

sbrigare [zbri'gare] 1 VT (*lavoro, pratiche*) to deal with, get through; (*clienti*) to attend to, see to, deal with; **sbrigare le faccende domestiche** to do the housework; **se la sa sbrigare da solo** he can manage o do it by himself.

2 **sbrigarsi** VIP (*fare in fretta*) to hurry (up), get a move on.

sbrigativo, a [zbriga'tivo] AGG (*persona, modi*) quick, expeditious; (: *pegg*) abrupt, brusque; (*giudizio*) hasty; **è un piatto sbrigativo** it's a quick dish.

sbrigliare [zbriʎ'ʎare] VT (*fig: fantasia*) to give free rein to.

sbrinamento [zbrina'mento] SM defrosting.

sbrinare [zbri'nare] VT to defrost.

sbrinatore [zbrina'tore] SM defroster.

sbrindellato, a [zbrindel'lato] AGG tattered, in tatters.

sbrodolare [zbrodo'lare] 1 VT to stain, dirty.

2 **sbrodolarsi** VR to stain o.s., dirty o.s.; **ti sei tutto sbrodolato** you've spilt food all down yourself.

sbrodolato, a [zbrodo'lato] AGG stained.

sbrogliare [zbroʎ'ʎare] 1 VT (*filo, matassa*) to unravel; (*vele*) to unfurl; (*fig: problema*) to solve, find a solution to; **è riuscito a sbrogliarsela** he has managed to sort things out.

2 **sbrogliarsi** VR (*fig: persona*) to disentangle o.s., free o.s.

sbronza ['zbrontsa] SF (*fam*) = **sbornia**.

sbronzarsi [zbron'tsarsi] VR (*fam*) to get plastered.

sbronzo, a ['zbrontso] AGG (*fam*) plastered.

sbruffone, a [zbruf'fone] SM/F boaster, braggart.

sbucare [zbu'kare] VI (*aus essere*): **sbucare da** to pop out of o from; **sbucare fuori** to pop out; **da dove è sbucato quel libro?** where did that book spring from?

sbucciapatate [zbuttʃapa'tate] SM INV potato peeler.

sbucciare [zbut'tʃare] VT (*gen*) to peel; (*piselli*) to shell; **sbucciarsi un ginocchio** to graze one's knee.

sbucciatura [zbuttʃa'tura] SF graze.

sbucherò ecc [zbuke'rɔ] VB vedi **sbucare**.

sbudellare [zbudel'lare] 1 VT to disembowel.

2 **sbudellarsi** VR: **sbudellarsi dalle risate** (*fig*) to split one's sides laughing.

sbuffare [zbuf'fare] VI (*aus avere*) (*gen*) to puff; (: *con impazienza*) to snort, fume; (*ansimare*) to puff, pant; (*cavallo*) to snort; (*treno*) to puff.

sbuffo ['zbuffo] SM a (*di vento*) gust; (*di aria, fumo, vapore*) puff b : **maniche a sbuffo** puff(ed) sleeves.

sbullonare [zbullo'nare] VT to unbolt.

S.C. ABBR a = **stato civile** b = *Suprema Corte (di Cassazione)*.

sc. ABBR (*Teatro*: = *scena*) sc.

scabbia ['skabbja] SF (*Med*) scabies *sg*.

scabiosa [ska'bjosa] SF (*Bot*) field scabious.

scabro, a ['skabro] AGG (*superficie*) rough; (*fig: stile*) concise, terse.

scabrosamente [skabrosa'mente] AVV (*indecentemente*) indecently.

scabrosità [skabrosi'ta] SF (*vedi agg*) thorniness; embarrassing nature; indecency.

scabroso, a [ska'broso] AGG (*fig: difficile*) difficult, thorny; (: *imbarazzante*) embarrassing; (: *sconcio*) indecent.

scacchiera [skak'kjera] SF (*Scacchi*) chessboard; (*Dama*) draughtboard (*Brit*), checkerboard (*Am*).

scacchiere [skak'kjere] SM a (*Mil*) sector b (*Pol: in Gran Bretagna*): **Cancelliere dello Scacchiere** Chancellor of the Exchequer.

scacchista, i, e [skak'kista] SM/F chessplayer.

scacciacani [skattʃa'kani] SM O F INV pistol with blanks.

scacciapensieri [skattʃapen'sjɛri] SM INV (*Mus*) jew's-harp.

scacciare [skat'tʃare] VT (*mandar via*) to chase away o out, drive away o out; (*buttar fuori*) to throw out, turn out;

(*fig: malinconia, noia*) to overcome; (: *sospetto, dubbio*) to dispel; **scacciare qn di casa** to turn sb out of the house.

scacco, chi ['skakko] SM **a** (*pezzo del gioco*) chess piece, chessman; (*riquadro*) square; **scacchi** SMPL chess *sg*; **giocare a scacchi** to play chess; **dare scacco al re** to check the king; **subire uno scacco** (*fig: sconfitta*) to suffer a setback ▶ **scacco matto** checkmate; **dare scacco matto a qn** (*anche fig*) to checkmate sb
b (*quadretto*) square, check; **tessuto a scacchi** check(ed) material.

scaccolarsi [skakko'larsi] VR (*fam*) to pick one's nose.

scaddi *ecc* ['skaddi] VB vedi **scadere**.

scadente [ska'dɛnte] AGG (*qualità*) poor, shoddy; (*voto*) unsatisfactory; (*prodotto*) poor-quality *attr*; (*film, libro*) poor.

scadenza [ska'dɛntsa] SF (*di documento*) expiry; (*su prodotto*) sell-by date; (*di cambiale, contratto*) maturity; **data di scadenza** expiry date; (*su prodotto*) sell-by date; **con scadenza il 24 maggio** (*pagamento*) (which falls) due on the 24th of May; (*documento*) expiring on the 24th of May; **a breve/lunga scadenza** (*progetto, piano*) short-/long-term.

scadere [ska'dere] VI IRREG (*aus essere*) **a** (*perdere valore, stima*) to decline, go down; **scadere agli occhi di qn** OR **scadere nella stima di qn** to go down in sb's estimation **b** (*perdere validità: documento, contratto*) to expire; (: *cambiale, termine di pagamento*) to fall due.

scadimento [skadi'mento] SM decline.

scaduto, a [ska'duto] AGG (*passaporto*) out of date; **il biglietto è scaduto** the ticket is no longer valid; **il latte è scaduto** the milk is past its sell-by date.

scafandro [ska'fandro] SM (*di palombaro*) diving suit; (*di astronauta*) spacesuit.

scaffalatura [skaffala'tura] SF shelving, shelves *pl*.

scaffale [skaf'fale] SM (*ripiano*) shelf; (*mobile*) set of shelves.

scafo ['skafo] SM (*Naut*) hull.

scagionare [skadʒo'nare] **1** VT to exonerate, free from blame.
2 scagionarsi VR to exonerate o.s., free o.s. from blame.

scaglia ['skaʎʎa] SF (*squama*) scale; (*di metallo, pietra*) splinter, chip; (*di sapone*) flake.

scagliare [skaʎ'ʎare] **1** VT (*anche fig*) to throw, hurl, fling.
2 scagliarsi VR: **scagliarsi contro qn** OR **scagliarsi addosso a qn** to fling o.s. at sb, hurl o.s. at sb; (*fig: inveire*) to rail at sb.

scaglionamento [skaʎʎona'mento] SM (*Mil*) arrangement in echelons.

scaglionare [skaʎʎo'nare] VT (*truppe*) to echelon; (*pagamenti*) to space out, spread out.

scaglione [skaʎ'ʎone] SM (*Mil*) echelon; (*Geol*) terrace; **a scaglioni** (*fig*) in groups.

scagnozzo [skaɲ'ɲottso] SM (*pegg*) lackey, hanger-on.

scala ['skala] SF **a** (*gen*) stairs *pl*, staircase; **salire/scendere le scale** to go upstairs/downstairs, go up/down the stairs; **fece le scale in fretta** he hurried up (*o* down) the stairs; **una scala di corda** a rope ladder; **una scala di marmo** a marble staircase ▶ **scala a chiocciola** spiral staircase ▶ **scala a libretto** stepladder ▶ **scala mobile** escalator, moving staircase ▶ **scala a pioli** ladder ▶ **scala di servizio** backstairs *pl* ▶ **scala di sicurezza** (*antincendio*) fire escape
b (*Econ, Fis, Mat, Geog*) scale; **riproduzione in scala** reproduction to scale; **in scala di 1 a 100.000** on a scale of 1 cm to 1 km; **su larga/piccola scala** on a large/small scale; **su scala nazionale/mondiale** on a national/worldwide scale ▶ **scala Celsius/Fahrenheit** Celsius/Fahrenheit scale ▶ **scala di misure** system of weights and measures ▶ **scala mobile (dei salari)** index-linked pay scale ▶ **scala termometrica** scale of temperatures **d** (*Mus*) scale; **scala maggiore/minore** major/minor scale
e (*Carte*) straight ▶ **scala reale** straight flush.

scalare[1] [ska'lare] VT **a** (*Alpinismo, muro*) to climb, scale **b** (*ridurre*): **scalare un debito** to pay off a debt in instalments; **questa somma vi viene scalata dal prezzo originale** this sum is deducted from the original price **c** (*capelli*) to layer.

scalare[2] [ska'lare] AGG (*Mat, Fis*) scalar.

scalata [ska'lata] SF **a** (*azione*) scaling, climbing **b** (*arrampicata, fig*) climb; (*Alpinismo*) climb, ascent; **scalata al potere** climb to power.

scalatore, trice [skala'tore] SM/F climber.

scalcagnato, a [skalkaɲ'ɲato] AGG (*logoro*) worn; (*persona*) shabby.

scalciare [skal'tʃare] VI (*aus avere*) to kick.

scalcinato, a [skaltʃi'nato] AGG (*fig pegg*) shabby.

scaldaacqua [skalda'akkwa] SM INV (*per casa, Industria*) water heater.

scaldabagno [skalda'baɲɲo] SM (*per casa*) water heater.

scaldaletto [skalda'lɛtto] SM warming pan, bedwarmer.

scaldamuscoli [skalda'muskoli] SM INV legwarmer.

scaldare [skal'dare] **1** VT **a** (*latte, stanza*) to heat (up); **scaldare i muscoli** to warm up, do warming-up exercises; **scaldare il motore** to warm up the engine; **scaldare la sedia** (*fig*) to twiddle one's thumbs
b : **scaldarsi le mani/i piedi** to warm one's hands/feet.
2 scaldarsi VR to warm up; **scaldarsi al fuoco** to warm o.s. by the fire.
3 scaldarsi VIP (*stanza*) to heat up; (*fig: arrabbiarsi*) to get excited, get worked up.

scaldavivande [skaldavi'vande] SM INV dish warmer.

scaldino [skal'dino] SM (*per mani*) hand-warmer; (*per piedi*) foot-warmer; (*per letto*) bedwarmer.

scaletta [ska'letta] SF **a** (*gen*) short flight of steps; (*portatile*) small stepladder **b** (*di conferenza*) outline; (*Radio, TV*) summary **c** (*Sci*): **salita a scaletta** sidestepping.

scalfire [skal'fire] VT (*superficie*) to scratch; (*fig: sicurezza*) to undermine.

scalfittura [skalfit'tura] SF scratch.

scalinata [skali'nata] SF (*interna*) staircase, (flight of) stairs *pl*; (*esterna*) (flight of) steps *pl*.

scalino [ska'lino] SM (*gen, fig*) step; (*di scala a pioli*) rung.

scalmana [skal'mana] SF (*hot*) flush.

scalmanarsi [skalma'narsi] VIP (*affaticarsi*) to rush about, rush around; (*agitarsi, darsi da fare*) to get all hot and bothered; (*arrabbiarsi*) to get excited, get steamed up; **non scalmanarti a cercarlo** don't wear yourself out trying to find him.

scalmanato, a [skalma'nato] SM/F hothead.

scalmiera [skal'mjɛra] SF (*Naut*) rowlock (*Brit*), oarlock (*Am*).

scalo ['skalo] SM **a** (*per varo*) slipway, slips *pl*
b (*fermata: Naut, Aer*) stop; **fare scalo (a)** (*Naut*) to call (at), put in (at); (*Aer*) to make a stopover (at), land (at); **scalo tecnico** (*Aer*) technical stop *o* landing; **volo senza**

scalo non-stop flight
c (*luogo*: *Naut*) port of call; (: *Aer*) stopover
d (*Ferr*): **scalo merci** goods (*Brit*) o freight (*Am*) yard.

scalogna [ska'loɲɲa] SF (*fam*) bad luck.

scalognato, a [skaloɲ'ɲato] AGG (*fam*) unlucky.

scalogno [ska'loɲɲo] SM (*Bot*) shallot.

scaloppina [skalop'pina] SF (*Culin*) escalope.

scalpellare [skalpel'lare] VT to chisel.

scalpellino [skalpel'lino] SM stone-cutter.

scalpello [skal'pɛllo] SM (*gen*) chisel; (*Med*) scalpel; (*per pozzi petroliferi*) drill.

scalpiccio, cii [skalpit'tʃio] SM (*rumore*) shuffling (noise).

scalpitante [skalpi'tante] AGG (*cavallo*) pawing the ground; (*fig*: *persona*) champing at the bit.

scalpitare [skalpi'tare] VI (*aus* **avere**) (*cavallo*) to paw the ground; (*fig*: *persona*) to champ at the bit.

scalpitio, tii [skalpi'tio] SM (*di cavallo*) pawing of the ground.

scalpo ['skalpo] SM scalp.

scalpore [skal'pore] SM sensation; **fare** o **suscitare scalpore** to cause a sensation o a stir.

scaltramente [skaltra'mente] AVV (*vedi agg*) shrewdly, astutely; slyly, cunningly.

scaltrezza [skal'trettsa] SF (*vedi agg*) shrewdness, astuteness; slyness, cunning.

scaltrire [skal'trire] ▯1 VT: **scaltrire qn** to sharpen sb's wits.
▯2 **scaltrirsi** VIP to become shrewder.

scaltro, a ['skaltro] AGG shrewd, astute; (*pegg*) sly, cunning.

scalzacane [skaltsa'kane] SM/F (*incompetente*) bungler, blunderer.

scalzare [skal'tsare] VT (*pianta*) to bare the roots of; (*muro*, *fig*) to undermine.

scalzo, a ['skaltso] AGG barefoot(ed).

scambiare [skam'bjare] ▯1 VT **a** (*confondere*): **scambiare qn/qc per** to take o mistake sb/sth for; **scusa, l'ho scambiato per il mio** sorry, I thought it was mine
b (*barattare*): **scambiare qc per** to exchange sth for
c (*conversare*): **scambiare due parole** to exchange a few words.
▯2 **scambiarsi** VR (*uso reciproco*) to exchange; **scambiarsi gli auguri di Natale** to wish each other a Happy Christmas; **si scambiarono un'occhiata** they exchanged looks.

scambievole [skam'bjevole] AGG mutual, reciprocal.

scambievolmente [skambjevol'mente] AVV mutually, reciprocally; **aiutarsi scambievolmente** to help one another o each other.

scambio, bi ['skambjo] SM **a** (*di persone, cose*) exchange; **fare (uno) scambio** to make a swap **b** (*Comm*) trade; **libero scambio** free trade; **scambi con l'estero** foreign trade **c** (*Ferr*) points *pl* (*Brit*), switches (*Am*) **d** (*Calcio*) pass; (*Tennis*) shot and return **e** (*Chim*): **scambio ionico** ion exchange.

scambista, i [skam'bista] SM (*Ferr*) pointsman (*Brit*), switchman (*Am*); (*Comm*) trader.

scamiciato, a [skami'tʃato] ▯1 AGG in one's shirt sleeves.
▯2 SM pinafore (dress).

scamosciato, a [skamoʃ'ʃato] AGG suede.

scampagnata [skampaɲ'ɲata] SF trip to the country, outing to the country; **fare una scampagnata** to go on an outing o trip to the country.

scampanare [skampa'nare] ▯1 VI (*aus* **avere**) to peal.

▯2 VT (*gonna*) to flare.

scampanato, a [skampa'nato] AGG flared.

scampanellare [skampanel'lare] VI (*aus* **avere**) to ring loudly.

scampanellata [skampanel'lata] SF loud ringing.

scampanio, nii [skampa'nio] SM peal.

scampare [skam'pare] ▯1 VT (*pericolo*) to escape; **scampare la morte** to escape death; **scamparla bella** to have a lucky o narrow escape; **Dio ci scampi e liberi!** God forbid!.
▯2 VI (*aus* **essere**): **scampare (a qc)** (*pericolo, morte*) to survive (sth), escape (sth); **pochi scamparono alla strage** few escaped (from) the massacre; **pochi scamparono al disastro** few people were untouched o unaffected by the disaster.

scampo[1] ['skampo] SM (*salvezza*) escape, way out; **non c'è (via di) scampo** there's no way out; **cercare scampo nella fuga** to seek safety in flight.

scampo[2] ['skampo] SM (*Zool*) (Dublin Bay) prawn.

scampolo ['skampolo] SM remnant.

scanalatura [skanala'tura] SF (*azione*) grooving; (*incavo*) groove, channel; (*Archit*) fluting.

scandagliare [skandaʎ'ʎare] VT (*mare*) to sound, fathom; (*fig*: *indagare*) to sound out; (: *anima, sentimenti, intenzioni*) to probe.

scandaglio, gli [skan'daʎʎo] SM (*Naut*: *azione*) sounding, fathoming; (: *strumento*) sounding line.

scandalistico, a, ci, che [skanda'listiko] AGG (*settimanale*) sensational, sensationalist *attr*.

scandalizzare [skandalid'dzare] ▯1 VT to scandalize, to shock.
▯2 **scandalizzarsi** VIP to be scandalized, be shocked.

scandalizzato, a [skandalid'dzato] AGG scandalized, shocked.

scandalo ['skandalo] SM scandal; **il loro comportamento è motivo di scandalo** their behaviour is scandalous; **dare scandalo** to cause a scandal.

scandalosamente [skandalosa'mente] AVV scandalously, shockingly, outrageously.

scandaloso, a [skanda'loso] AGG scandalous, shocking, outrageous.

Scandinavia [skandi'navja] SF: **la Scandinavia** Scandinavia.

scandinavo, a [skandi'navo] AGG, SM/F Scandinavian.

scandire [skan'dire] VT (*versi*) to scan; (*parole*) to articulate, pronounce clearly o distinctly; **scandire il tempo** (*Mus*) to beat time.

scannare [skan'nare] VT (*animale*) to butcher, slaughter; (*persona*) to cut o slit the throat of.

scannatoio, oi [skanna'tojo] SM (*fig, fam*) bachelor pad.

scanno ['skanno] SM seat, bench.

scansafatiche [skansafa'tike] SM/F INV idler, loafer.

scansare [skan'sare] ▯1 VT **a** (*spostare*) to move (aside), shift **b** (*evitare*: *colpo*) to dodge; (: *pericolo*) to avoid.
▯2 **scansarsi** VR (*spostarsi*) to get out of the way, move out of the way; (: *per evitare un colpo*) to dodge.

scansia [skan'sia] SF (*ripiano*) shelf; (*mobile*) bookcase, shelves *pl*.

scansione [skan'sjone] SF **a** (*Poesia*) scansion **b** (*Tecn*, *Med*) scanning.

scanso ['skanso] SM: **a scanso di** in order to avoid, as a precaution against; **a scanso di equivoci** to avoid (any) misunderstanding.

scantinato [skanti'nato] SM basement.

scantonare [skanto'nare] vi (aus avere) **a** (per non essere visto) to duck round the corner **b** (fig) to become irrelevant.

scanzonato, a [skantso'nato] AGG easy-going.

scapaccione [skapat'tʃone] SM clout, slap; **dare uno scapaccione a qn** to clout sb; **prendere qn a scapaccioni** to slap sb about.

scapestrato, a [skapes'trato] ① AGG loose-living, dissolute.
② SM/F dissolute person.

scapigliare [skapiʎ'ʎare] VT: **scapigliare qn** to dishevel sb's hair.

scapigliato, a [skapiʎ'ʎato] AGG (spettinato) dishevelled; (fig: scapestrato) dissolute.

scapito ['skapito] SM: **a scapito di** to the detriment of.

scapola ['skapola] SF (Anat) shoulder blade.

scapolo ['skapolo] SM bachelor.

scappamento [skappa'mento] SM (Aut) exhaust; **tubo di scappamento** exhaust pipe.

scappare [skap'pare] vi (aus essere) **a** (gen): **scappare (da)** (città, stato, stanza) to escape (from); **scappare di casa** to run away from home; **far scappare qn** (mettere in fuga) to scare sb away; (aiutare a fuggire) to help sb to escape; **scappar via** to run away, escape; **scappare all'estero** to flee the country; **scusa, devo scappare** I'm sorry, but I must dash; **scappare a gambe levate** to take to one's heels
b (sfuggire): **mi è scappato di mano** it slipped out of my hands; **mi è scappato di mente** it has slipped my mind; **mi è scappato da ridere** I couldn't contain my laughter; **mi scappa la pipì** I'm bursting
c: **lasciarsi scappare** (occasione, affare) to miss, let go by; (dettaglio) to overlook; (parola) to let slip; (prigioniero) to let escape.

scappata [skap'pata] SF (breve visita): **fare una scappata da qn** to call o drop o in on sb; **farò una scappata a Parigi/a casa tua** I'll pop over to Paris/to your place; **faccio una scappata in centro** I'm just going to pop into town.

scappatella [skappa'tɛlla] SF escapade.

scappatoia [skappa'toja] SF (gen) way out; (nella burocrazia) loophole.

scappellotto [skappel'lotto] SM clout, slap; **dare uno scappellotto a qn** to clout sb.

scarabeo [skara'bɛo] SM (Zool) scarab (beetle).

scarabocchiare [skarabok'kjare] VT (fare scarabocchi) to scribble, doodle, scrawl; (scrivere svogliatamente) to scribble off.

scarabocchio, chi [skara'bokkjo] SM (sgorbio) scribble, scrawl; (disegno) doodle; (fig pegg: quadro) daub; (macchia d'inchiostro) blot.

scarafaggio, gi [skara'faddʒo] SM (Zool) cockroach.

scaramanzia [skaraman'tsia] SF: **per scaramanzia** for luck.

scaramuccia, ce [skara'muttʃa] SF skirmish.

scaraventare [skaraven'tare] ① VT to fling, hurl.
② **scaraventarsi** VR: **scaraventarsi contro qn/qc** to fling o.s. at sb/sth.

scarcerare [skartʃe'rare] VT to release (from prison).

scarcerazione [skartʃerat'tsjone] SF release (from prison).

scardinare [skardi'nare] VT to take off its hinges.

scarica, che ['skarika] SF **a** (di arma) shot; (fig: di insulti) flood; (: di sassi, pugni) hail, shower; **una scarica di mitra** a burst of machine-gun fire **b** (Elettr): **scarica (elettrica)** discharge (of electricity).

scaricabarili [skarikaba'rili] SM: **fare a scaricabarili** (fig) to blame each other.

scaricare [skari'kare] ① VT (merce, veicolo) to unload; (passeggeri) to set down; (batteria) to cause to run down, cause to go flat (Brit) o dead (Am); (fig: coscienza) to unburden, relieve; (: fam: fidanzata, amico) to drop; **scaricare qc in** (sogg: fabbrica) to discharge sth into; (: corso d'acqua) to empty sth into, pour sth into; **il canale scarica i rifiuti in mare** the canal deposits the rubbish in the sea; **scaricare un'arma** (togliendo la carica) to unload a gun; (sparando) to discharge a gun; **scaricare le proprie responsabilità su qn** to off-load one's responsibilities onto sb; **scaricare la colpa addosso a qn** to blame sb else; **scaricare la tensione** (fig: rilassarsi) to unwind; (: sfogarsi) to let off steam.
② **scaricarsi** VIP (molla, orologio) to run o wind down, stop; (batteria) to go flat (Brit) o dead (Am); **la batteria si è scaricata** the battery is flat; **il fulmine si scaricò su un albero** the lightning struck a tree.
③ **scaricarsi** VR (fig: persona) to unwind; (: sfogarsi) to let off steam; **scaricarsi di ogni responsabilità** to relieve o.s. of all responsibilities; **piangendo si è scaricata** she had a good cry and felt better for it.

scaricatore [skarika'tore] SM: **scaricatore di porto** docker.

scarico[1], a, chi, che ['skariko] AGG (fucile) unloaded, empty; (orologio) wound down; (batteria) run down, flat (Brit), dead (Am).

scarico[2], chi ['skariko] SM (di merci, materiali) unloading; (di immondizie) dumping, tipping (Brit); (: luogo) refuse o rubbish (Brit) o garbage (Am) dump; (Tecn: deflusso) draining; (: dispositivo) drain; (Aut) exhaust; **scarico del lavandino** waste outlet; **divieto di scarico** no dumping, no tipping (Brit).

scarlattina [skarlat'tina] SF scarlet fever.

scarlatto, a [skar'latto] AGG, SM scarlet.

scarmigliare [skarmiʎ'ʎare] ① VT to dishevel.
② **scarmigliarsi** VR to be dishevelled.

scarnificare [skarnifi'kare] VT to strip the flesh from.

scarno, a ['skarno] AGG (persona) lean, bony; (volto) gaunt; (mano) thin, bony; (fig: insufficiente) meagre (Brit), meager (Am); (: spoglio: stile) bare.

scarpa ['skarpa] SF shoe; **un paio di scarpe** a pair of shoes; **fare le scarpe a qn** (fig) to double-cross sb; **essere una scarpa** (fig fam) to be useless ▶**scarpe coi tacchi (alti)** high-heeled shoes ▶**scarpe col tacco basso** low-heeled shoes ▶**scarpe da ginnastica** gym shoes, plimsolls ▶**scarpe senza tacco** flat shoes ▶**scarpe sportive** trainers ▶**scarpe da tennis** tennis shoes.

scarpata [skar'pata] SF escarpment.

scarpiera [skar'pjera] SF shoe rack.

scarpinata [skarpi'nata] SF (fam) trek; **abbiamo fatto una scarpinata** it was some trek.

scarpone [skar'pone] SM boot ▶**scarponi da montagna** climbing boots ▶**scarponi da sci** ski boots.

scarrocciare [skarrot'tʃare] VI (aus avere) (Naut) to drift leeward.

scarroccio [skar'rottʃo] SM (Naut) leeway.

scarrozzare [skarrot'tsare] VT to drive around.

scarrucolare [skarruko'lare] VI (aus avere) to slip off a pulley.

scarsamente [skarsa'mente] AVV (preparato, organizzato)

poorly.

scarseggiare [skarsed'dʒare] VI (*aus* **avere**) (*viveri, risorse*) to be scarce, be lacking; **scarseggiare di qc** to lack sth, be short of sth.

scarsezza [skar'settsa] SF shortage, lack, scarcity.

scarsità [skarsi'ta] SF shortage.

scarso, a ['skarso] AGG (*raccolto*) poor, lean; (*risorse*) meagre (*Brit*), meager (*Am*); (*qualità*) poor; (*alunno, voto*) mediocre; **è un chilo/metro scarso** it's just under the kilo/metre; **ha dimostrato scarsa maturità/intelligenza** he showed little maturity/intelligence; **scarso di** lacking in.

scartabellare [skartabel'lare] VT to skim through, glance through.

scartafaccio, ci [skarta'fattʃo] SM notebook.

scartamento [skarta'mento] SM (*Ferr*) gauge; **a scartamento ridotto** narrow-gauge.

scartare[1] [skar'tare] VT (*regalo, caramella*) to unwrap.

scartare[2] [skar'tare] VT **a** (*Carte*) to discard **b** (*fig: possibilità, idea*) to reject **c** (*concorrente*) to reject, eliminate; (*Mil*) to declare unfit for military service.

scartare[3] [skar'tare] [1] VI (*aus* **avere**) (*deviare*) to swerve; **scartare a sinistra** to swerve to the left.

[2] VT (*Calcio*) to dodge (past); (*Equitazione*): **scartare (l'ostacolo)** to run out.

scarto[1] ['skarto] SM **a** (*prodotto, oggetto scartato*) reject **b** (*Carte*) discard.

scarto[2] ['skarto] SM **a** (*movimento brusco*) swerve; (*Equitazione*) run-out; **fare uno scarto** to swerve; to run out **b** (*differenza*) gap, difference; **scarto salariale** wage differential.

scartocciare [skartot'tʃare] VT (*gen*) to unwrap; (*mais*) to husk.

scartoffie [skar'tɔffje] SFPL (*pegg*) papers.

scassare [skas'sare] [1] VT **a** (*fam: rompere*) to wreck, smash **b** (*dissodare*) to plough up.

[2] **scassarsi** VIP (*rompersi*) to be wrecked.

scassinare [skassi'nare] VT to force, break open.

scassinatore, trice [skassina'tore] SM/F (*di case*) housebreaker, burglar; (*di banche*) bank robber; (*di casseforti*) safe-cracker.

scasso ['skasso] SM (*Dir*) breaking and entering; **furto con scasso** burglary.

scatenare [skate'nare] [1] VT (*reazione, rabbia*) to provoke; (*rivolta*) to spark off; (*guai*) to stir up.

[2] **scatenarsi** VIP (*temporale*) to break; (*rivolta*) to break out; (*persona*): **scatenarsi contro qn** to rage at sb.

scatenato, a [skate'nato] AGG wild.

scatola ['skatola] [1] SF (*gen*) box; (*di latta*) tin (*Brit*), can (*Am*); **cibo in scatola** tinned (*Brit*) *o* canned (*Am*) foods; **una scatola di sardine** a tin *o* can of sardines; **una scatola di cioccolatini** a box of chocolates; **comprare qc a scatola chiusa** to buy sth sight unseen; **accettare qc a scatola chiusa** (*fig*) to accept sth blindly; **avere le scatole piene (di qn/qc)** (*fam*) to be fed up to the back teeth (with sb/sth); **rompere le scatole a qn** (*fam*) to get on sb's nerves; **levati** *o* **togliti dalle scatole!** get out of the way!.

[2] ▶**scatola di cartone** cardboard box ▶**scatola cranica** cranium ▶**scatola del differenziale** (*Aut*) differential housing ▶**scatola di fiammiferi** (*vuota*) matchbox; (*piena*) box of matches ▶**scatola dei fusibili** fuse box ▶**scatola nera** (*Aer*) black box.

scatolame [skato'lame] SM tinned (*Brit*) *o* canned (*Am*)

food; (*insieme di scatole*) tins pl (*Brit*), cans pl (*Am*).

scatoletta [skato'letta] SF (*gen*) (small) box; (*di latta*) (small) tin (*Brit*), (small) can (*Am*).

scattante [skat'tante] AGG (*svelto*) quick off the mark; (*agile*) agile.

scattare [skat'tare] [1] VI (*aus* **essere**) (*molla*) to be released; (*grilletto, interruttore*) to spring back; (*serratura: aprirsi*) to click open; (*: chiudersi*) to click shut; (*iniziare: legge, provvedimento*) to come into effect; (*Sport*) to put on a spurt; **far scattare** to release; **scattare in piedi** to spring *o* leap to one's feet; **scattare sull'attenti** to spring *o* leap to attention; **scatta per niente** (*si arrabbia*) he flies off the handle at the slightest provocation; **domani scatta l'ora legale** tomorrow the clocks go forward (*o* back).

[2] VT (*Fot*): **scattare una foto** to take a photograph.

scattista, i, e [skat'tista] SM/F (*Sport*) sprinter.

scatto ['skatto] SM **a** (*congegno*) release; (*: di arma da fuoco*) trigger mechanism; (*rumore*) click; **serratura a scatto** spring lock; **ho sentito lo scatto della serratura** I heard the lock click ▶**scatto automatico** automatic release; (*Fot*) (automatic) timer

b (*Telec*) unit

c (*Sport*) spurt

d (*di persona*) jump, start; **muoversi a scatti** to move jerkily; **ha avuto uno scatto (d'ira)** he flew off the handle; **di scatto** suddenly; **si alzò di scatto** he sprang *o* leapt to his feet

e (*aumento*): **scatto d'anzianità** long service bonus ▶**scatto di stipendio** increment.

scaturire [skatu'rire] VI (*aus* **essere**) (*liquido*): **scaturire (da)** to spurt (from), gush (from); (*fig: avere origine*) to derive (from).

scavalcare [skaval'kare] VT (*ostacolo, anche fig*) to pass (*o* climb) over; (*fig: concorrenti*) to overtake, get ahead of; (*: collega*) to be promoted over (the head of).

scavare [ska'vare] VT (*gen, terreno*) to dig; (*trincea, Archeol*) to dig, excavate; (*pozzo, galleria*) to bore; (*tronco, pietra: renderlo cavo*) to hollow (out); **scavarsi la fossa** (*fig*) to dig one's own grave; **un volto scavato dalla stanchezza** a haggard face; **scavare nell'animo di qn** to search sb's soul; **scavare nel passato di qn** to dig into sb's past.

scavatore [skava'tore] SM (*macchina, persona*) digger.

scavatrice [skava'tritʃe] SF (*macchina*) excavator.

scavezzacollo, a [skavettsa'kɔllo] SM/F daredevil.

scavo ['skavo] SM (*luogo*) excavation; (*azione*) excavating *no pl*; **fare degli scavi in una zona** to excavate an area.

scazzarsi [skat'tsarsi] VIP (*fam!*) to be pissed off (*fam!*)

scazzato, a [skat'tsato] AGG (*fam!: stufo, annoiato*) pissed off (*fam!*)

scazzo ['skattso] SM (*fam!*): **hanno avuto uno scazzo ieri sera** they were knocking the shit out of each other last night (*fam!*)

scazzottare [skattsot'tare] (*fam*) [1] VT to beat up, give a thrashing to.

[2] **scazzottarsi** VR (*uso reciproco*) to beat each other up.

scazzottata [skattsot'tata] SF (*fam*) fight, punch-up.

scegliere ['ʃeʎʎere] VT IRREG (*gen*) to choose; (*prodotto, candidato*) to select, choose; **scegliere di fare qc** to choose to do sth; **scegliere il campo** (*Sport*) to toss for ends.

sceiccato [ʃeik'kato] SM (*titolo*) title of sheik; (*territorio*) sheikdom.

sceicco, chi [ʃe'ikko] SM sheik.

scekerare ecc [ʃekeˈrare] VT = **shakerare**.

scelgo ecc [ˈʃɛlgo] VB vedi **scegliere**.

scellerataggine [ʃelleraˈtaddʒine], **scelleratezza** [ʃelleraˈtettsa] SF (qualità) wickedness; (azione) wicked deed, crime.

scellerato, a [ʃelleˈrato] 1 AGG wicked, evil.
2 SM/F villain.

scellino [ʃelˈlino] SM (inglese, austriaco) schilling.

scelta [ˈʃelta] SF (gen) choice; (selezione) selection, choice; **fare una scelta** to make a choice, choose; **non avere scelta** to have no choice o option; **potete avere frutta o formaggio a scelta** you have the choice of fruit or cheese; **di prima scelta** top grade o quality; **c'è un'ampia scelta di prodotti** there's a wide selection o choice of products.

scelto, a [ˈʃelto] 1 PP di **scegliere**.
2 AGG (gruppo) carefully selected; (frutta, verdura) top-quality, choice; **brani scelti** selected passages; **una compagnia scelta** a distinguished company; **pubblico scelto** select audience; **tiratore scelto** crack shot, highly skilled marksman.

scemare [ʃeˈmare] VI (aus essere) (rumore, applausi, interesse) to lessen; (forze) to decline; (vento) to drop, abate.

scemata [ʃeˈmata] SF: **fare/dire una scemata** to do/say something foolish o silly; **il film era una scemata** it was a very stupid film.

scemenza [ʃeˈmentsa] SF stupidity no pl; **dire scemenze** to talk nonsense o rubbish; **ha fatto una scemenza** he behaved foolishly o stupidly; **è stata una scemenza** it was sheer stupidity.

scemo, a [ˈʃemo] 1 AGG stupid, foolish, silly.
2 SM/F idiot, fool; **fare lo scemo** to play the fool.

scempiaggine [ʃemˈpjaddʒine] SF (qualità) foolishness; (atto, discorso): **fare/dire una scempiaggine** to do/say something foolish o silly.

scempio, pi [ˈʃempjo] SM (strage) massacre, slaughter; (deturpazione) destruction; **fare scempio di qc** (fig) to destroy sth, wreak havoc with sth, ruin sth; **lo scempio dei centri storici** the destruction of historic town centres; **quel viadotto è uno scempio** that viaduct is an eyesore.

scena [ˈʃɛna] SF a (gen, Teatro, Cine) scene; **nella prima scena** in the first scene, in scene one; **la scena si svolge a Parigi** the action takes place in Paris, the scene is set in Paris; **cambiamento di scena** scene change; **una scena di caccia** a hunting scene; **sulla scena internazionale** on the international scene; **ho assistito a tutta la scena** I was present at o during the whole scene; **fare una scena** (fig) to make a scene; **fu una scena orribile** it was a horrible sight; **ha fatto scena muta** (fig) he didn't open his mouth
b (palcoscenico) stage; **entrare in scena** to come on stage; (fig) to come on the scene; **uscire di scena** to leave the stage; (fig) to leave the scene; **mettere in scena** (personaggio) to present on the stage; (commedia) to stage, direct.

scenario, ri [ʃeˈnarjo] SM (Teatro) scenery, set; (fig: sfondo) backdrop.

scenata [ʃeˈnata] SF row, scene; **fare una scenata (a qn)** to make a scene.

scendere [ˈʃendere] VB IRREG 1 VT (scale, sentiero) to go (o come) down, descend.
2 VI (aus essere) a (gen) to go (o come) down, descend; (fiume, torrente) to flow down; (strada) to slope down, descend; (aereo) to come down, descend; **scendere con l'ascensore** to go (o come) down in the lift (Brit) o elevator (Am); **scendere in città** to go into town; **scendere in strada** to go down into the street; **scendere in piazza** (folla, manifestanti) to take to the streets; **scendere in sciopero** to come out on strike; **scendere a piedi/correndo** to walk/run down; **scendo ad aprirgli il portone** I'll go down and open the door for him; **scendo subito!** I'm just coming!; **siamo scesi in mezz'ora** (da collina) we got down in half an hour; **quando i Longobardi scesero in Italia** when the Longobards descended on Italy; **i capelli le scendevano sulle spalle** her hair fell to her shoulders; **scendere a terra** (sbarcare) to go ashore; **scendere ad un albergo** to put up o stay at a hotel
b : **scendere da** (macchina, treno) to get out of; (nave) to disembark from, get off; (aereo, autobus, bici) to get off; **scendere da cavallo** to dismount, get off one's horse; **scendere dal letto** to get out of bed; **scendere dalle scale** to go (o come) down the stairs; **scendo alla prossima fermata** I'm getting off at the next stop; **scendi da quell'albero!** come down from that tree!
c (prezzi, temperatura) to fall, drop; (livello) to fall, drop, go down; (marea) to go out; (notte, oscurità) to fall; (sole, strada) to go down; (nebbia) to come down.

scendiletto [ʃendiˈletto] SM INV bedside rug.

sceneggiare [ʃenedˈdʒare] VT to dramatize.

sceneggiato [ʃenedˈdʒato] SM (TV) television drama.

sceneggiatore, trice [ʃeneddʒaˈtore] SM/F scriptwriter.

sceneggiatura [ʃeneddʒaˈtura] SF (Teatro) scenario; (Cine) screenplay, scenario.

scenico, a, ci, che [ˈʃɛniko] AGG stage attr.

scenografia [ʃenograˈfia] SF (Teatro) stage design; (Cine) set design; (elementi scenici) scenery.

scenografico, a, ci, che [ʃenoˈgrafiko] AGG stage attr, set attr.

scenografo, a [ʃeˈnografo] SM/F set designer.

sceriffo [ʃeˈriffo] SM sheriff.

scervellarsi [ʃervelˈlarsi] VIP: **scervellarsi (su qc)** to rack one's brains (over sth).

scervellato, a [ʃervelˈlato] 1 SM/F half-wit, idiot.
2 AGG feather-brained, scatterbrained.

sceso, a [ˈʃeso] PP di **scendere**.

scetticamente [ʃettikaˈmente] AVV sceptically (Brit), skeptically (Am).

scetticismo [ʃettiˈtʃizmo] SM scepticism (Brit), skepticism (Am).

scettico, a, ci, che [ˈʃettiko] 1 AGG sceptical (Brit), skeptical (Am).
2 SM/F sceptic (Brit), skeptic (Am).

scettro [ˈʃettro] SM sceptre (Brit), scepter (Am).

scevro, a [ˈʃevro] AGG (letter): **scevro di** free from, devoid of.

scheda [ˈskɛda] SF (di schedario) (index) card; (di elezioni) ballot paper; (in libro) inset; (servizio televisivo) brief report ► **scheda perforata** punch card ► **scheda telefonica** phonecard.

schedare [skeˈdare] VT (dati) to file; (registrare su scheda) to card-index; (: libri) to catalogue; (: della polizia) to put on record.

schedario, ri [skeˈdarjo] SM card index, file; (mobile) filing cabinet.

schedato, a [skeˈdato] 1 AGG with a (police) record.
2 SM/F person with a (police) record.

schedina [ske'dina] SF ≈ pools coupon (*Brit*).

scheggia, ge ['skeddʒa] SF (*gen*) splinter; (*di vetro*) splinter, sliver; (*di porcellana*) chip ▶ **scheggia impazzita** (*fig*) loose cannon.

scheggiare [sked'dʒare] VT, **scheggiarsi** (*gen*) VIP (*gen*) to splinter, chip; (*porcellana*) to chip.

scheggiatura [skeddʒa'tura] SF a (*azione: vedi vb*) splintering; chipping b (*punto scheggiato*) chip.

scheletrico, a, ci, che [ske'lɛtriko] AGG (*anche Anat*) skeletal; (*fig: essenziale*) skeleton *attr*.

scheletrito, a [skele'trito] AGG (*persona*) skeleton-like, all skin and bone; (*ramo, stile*) bare.

scheletro ['skɛletro] SM (*Anat*) skeleton; (*fig: struttura*) frame, framework; (: *di trama*) outline; **essere ridotto a uno scheletro** to be all skin and bone; **avere uno scheletro nell'armadio** (*fig*) to have a skeleton in the closet *o* cupboard (*Brit*).

schema, i ['skɛma] SM a (*gen*) outline; (*diagramma*) diagram, sketch; **schema riassuntivo** outline of the main points ▶ **schema di legge** bill b (*fig: modello*): **ribellarsi agli schemi** to rebel against traditional values; **secondo gli schemi tradizionali** in accordance with traditional values.

schematico, a, ci, che [ske'matiko] AGG schematic.

schematismo [skema'tizmo] SM (*di discorso, testo*) sketchiness.

schematizzare [skematid'dzare] VT to schematize.

scherma ['skerma] SF (*Sport*) fencing; **tirare di scherma** to fence.

schermaglia [sker'maʎʎa] SF (*fig*) skirmish.

schermare [sker'mare] VT to screen.

schermire [sker'mire] 1 VT to protect, shield.
2 **schermirsi** VR to defend o.s., protect o.s.

schermitore, trice [skermi'tore] SM/F (*Sport*) fencer.

schermo ['skermo] SM a (*gen*) screen; **farsi schermo con la mano** (*per proteggersi dalla luce*) to shield one's eyes with one's hand b (*TV, Cine*): **il piccolo/grande schermo** the small/big screen; **divo dello schermo** screen star.

schermografia [skermogra'fia] SF X-rays *pl*.

schermografico, a, ci, che [skermo'grafiko] AGG X-ray *attr*.

schernire [sker'nire] VT to mock, sneer at.

scherno ['skerno] SM scorn; **farsi scherno di** to sneer at; **essere oggetto di scherno** to be a laughing stock; **di scherno** (*parole*) scornful, sneering; (*gesto*) scornful; **grida di scherno** jeers.

scherzare [sker'tsare] VI (*aus* **avere**) (*gen*) to joke; **stavo scherzando** I was only joking *o* kidding; **è meglio non scherzare su queste cose** it's better not to joke about these things; **quello è un tipo che non scherza** he is not a man to be trifled with; **c'è poco da scherzare!** it's no laughing matter!, it's no joke!; **scherzare con i sentimenti altrui** to trifle with other people's feelings; **non scherzare col fuoco!** (*fig*) you shouldn't play with fire!

scherzo ['skertso] SM a (*gen*) joke; (*burla*) (practical) joke, prank; **fare uno scherzo a qn** to play a (practical) joke *o* prank *o* trick on sb; **per scherzo** as *o* for a joke, for a laugh, for fun; **fare un brutto scherzo a qn** to play a nasty trick on sb; **neppure per scherzo** not even in fun; **non sa stare allo scherzo** he can't take a joke; **scherzi a parte** seriously, joking apart; ... **e niente scherzi!** ...and no funny business!; **uno scherzo da prete** a dirty trick; **è uno scherzo!** (*facile*) it's child's play!, it's easy! ▶ **scherzi d'acqua** waterworks ▶ **scherzi di luce** effects of the light
b (*Mus*) scherzo.

scherzosamente [skertsosa'mente] AVV jokingly.

scherzoso, a [sker'tsoso] AGG (*tono, gesto*) playful; (*osservazione*) facetious; **è un tipo scherzoso** he likes *o* is fond of a joke.

schettinare [sketti'nare] VI (*aus* **avere**) to (roller) skate.

schettino ['skettino] SM (roller) skate.

schiaccianoci [skjattʃa'notʃi] SM INV nutcracker.

schiacciante [skjat'tʃante] AGG overwhelming.

schiacciapatate [skjattʃapa'tate] SM INV potato masher.

schiacciare [skjat'tʃare] 1 VT a (*gen*) to squash, crush; (*patate*) to mash; (*aglio*) to crush; (*noce*) to crack; (*mozzicone*) to stub out; **schiacciare la palla** (*Tennis, Pallavolo*) to smash the ball; **schiacciare un sonnellino** to take a nap; **schiacciarsi un dito nella porta** to shut one's finger in the door
b (*pulsante*) to press; (*pedale*) to press down
c (*fig: opposizione, nemico*) to crush; (: *squadra avversaria*) to hammer; **era schiacciato da un senso di colpa** he was weighed down by feelings of guilt.
2 **schiacciarsi** VIP to get squashed, get crushed.

schiacciasassi [skjattʃa'sassi] SM INV steamroller.

schiacciata [skjat'tʃata] SF (*Tennis, Pallavolo*) smash.

schiacciato, a [skjat'tʃato] AGG (*naso*) flat; **ha una forma schiacciata** it's flat.

schiaffare [skjaf'fare] 1 VT to throw, chuck; **lo hanno schiaffato dentro** (*fam: in prigione*) they threw him in the cooler, they put him away.
2 **schiaffarsi** VIP to throw o.s.

schiaffeggiare [skjaffed'dʒare] VT to smack, slap.

schiaffo ['skjaffo] SM slap (in the face); **dare uno schiaffo a qn** to slap sb; **prendere qn a schiaffi** to slap sb about *o* around; **uno schiaffo morale** a slap in the face, a rebuff; **avere una faccia da schiaffi** to look impudent.

schiamazzare [skjamat'tsare] VI (*aus* **avere**) (*galline, oche*) to squawk, cackle; (*fig: persone*) to make a din, make a racket.

schiamazzo [skja'mattso] SM (*fig: chiasso*) din, racket.

schiamazzatore, trice [skjamattsa'tore] SM/F rowdy.

schiantare [skjan'tare] 1 VT (*spezzare*) to break, tear apart; **il fulmine ha schiantato l'albero** the lightning split the tree.
2 **schiantarsi** VIP (*macchina*): **schiantarsi contro** to crash into; (*aereo*): **schiantarsi al suolo** to crash (to the ground).

schianto ['skjanto] SM (*rumore*) crash; **di schianto** (*improvvisamente*) all of a sudden; **quella macchina è uno schianto!** (*fam*) that car's great; **quella ragazza è uno schianto!** that girl's terrific!

schiappa ['skjappa] SF (*fig*): **essere una schiappa in qc** to be a washout at sth.

schiarimento [skjari'mento] SM (*del cielo*) clearing up, brightening; (*fig: delucidazione*) clarification, explanation.

schiarire [skja'rire] 1 VT (*gen*) to lighten, make lighter; (*Fot*) to make brighter; (*tende, tessuto: far sbiadire*) to fade; **schiarirsi la gola** *o* **la voce** to clear one's throat; **schiarire le idee a qn** (*fig*) to put sb straight.
2 VI (*aus* **essere**), **schiarirsi** VIP (*cielo, tempo*) to clear up; (*colore*) to become lighter; (: *sbiadire*) to fade.

schiarita [skja'rita] SF (*Meteor*) bright spell; (*fig*) improvement, turn for the better.

schiatta ['skjatta] SF (*poet*) lineage, descent.

schiattare [skjat'tare] VI (*aus* **essere**) (*fig*: *scoppiare*) to burst; **schiattare d'invidia** to be green with envy; **schiattare di rabbia** to be beside o.s. with rage.

schiavismo [skja'vizmo] SM slavery; (*Pol*) support of slavery, anti-abolitionism.

schiavista, i, e [skja'vista] ❶ AGG slave *attr.*
❷ SM/F (*trafficante*) slave trader, slaver; (*Pol*) supporter of slavery, anti-abolitionist; **il nostro capo è uno schiavista** (*fig*) our boss is a slave driver.

schiavistico, a, ci, che [skja'vistiko] AGG (*economia*) slave *attr.*

schiavitù [skjavi'tu] SF slavery; **ridurre in schiavitù** to subject, subjugate.

schiavizzare [skjavid'dzare] VT (*anche fig*) to reduce to slavery, enslave; (*dipendenti, figli*) to tyrannize over.

schiavo, a ['skjavo] ❶ AGG enslaved; **essere schiavo delle proprie abitudini** to be a slave to habit.
❷ SM/F slave.

schiena ['skjɛna] SF back; **soffrire di mal di schiena** to have a bad back; **avere mal di schiena** ⟨OR⟩ **avere la schiena a pezzi** to have backache, have a pain in one's back; **avere la schiena curva** (*con le spalle curve*) to be round-shouldered; (*con la spina dorsale curva*) to have a stoop; **voltare la schiena a qn** (*fig*) to turn one's back on sb; **rompersi la schiena** to break one's back; (*fig*: *lavorare sodo*) to work one's fingers to the bone; **visto di schiena** seen from behind *o* from the back; **a schiena di mulo** (*ponte*) humpback; (*strada*) steeply cambered.

schienale [skje'nale] SM **a** (*di poltrona, sedia*) back **b** (*di animale macellato*) saddle.

schiera ['skjɛra] SF (*Mil*: *linea*) rank; **le schiere dei nemici** the enemy forces; **una schiera di persone** a crowd of people; **arrivarono a schiere** they arrived in their hundreds; **villetta a schiera** ≈ terraced house.

schieramento [skjera'mento] SM (*Mil*) (rank) formation; (*Sport*) formation; (*fig*) alliance.

schierare [skje'rare] ❶ VT (*Mil*) to draw up, line up, marshal.
❷ **schierarsi** VR (*Mil*) to draw up; (*fig*): **schierarsi con** *o* **dalla parte di/contro qn** to side with/oppose sb.

schiettamente [skjetta'mente] AVV frankly.

schiettezza [skjet'tettsa] SF frankness, straightforwardness.

schietto, a ['skjɛtto] AGG frank, straightforward.

schifare [ski'fare] ❶ VT to disgust.
❷ **schifarsi** VIP to be disgusted.

schifezza [ski'fettsa] SF: **essere una schifezza** (*cibo, bibita*) to be disgusting; (*film, libro*) to be dreadful; **mangia un sacco di schifezze** he eats a lot of rubbish.

schifiltosamente [skifiltosa'mente] AVV fussily.

schifiltoso, a [skifil'toso] AGG fussy, difficult; **fare lo schifiltoso** to be fussy.

schifo ['skifo] SM (*sensazione*) disgust; **è uno schifo!** it's disgusting!; **fare schifo** (*cibo, insetto*) to be disgusting; (*libro, film*) to be dreadful *o* awful; **mi fai schifo** you make me sick; **la nostra squadra ha fatto schifo** our team was useless.

schifosamente [skifosa'mente] AVV (*vedi agg*) disgustingly, revoltingly; dreadfully, awfully; **sei schifosamente fortunato!** you're terribly lucky!

schifoso, a [ski'foso] AGG (*che fa ribrezzo*) disgusting, revolting; (*pessimo*) dreadful, awful; **hai avuto una fortuna schifosa** (*fam*) you've been terribly lucky.

schioccare [skjok'kare] VT (*frusta*) to crack; (*dita*) to snap,

click; (*lingua*) to click; (*labbra*) to smack; **le schioccò un bacio** he gave her a smacker (*fam*).

schiocco, chi ['skjɔkko] SM (*di frusta*) crack; (*di dita*) snap, click; (*di lingua*) click; (*di labbra*) smack.

schiodare [skjo'dare] VT to unnail; **non riesco a schiodarlo dal computer** (*fig fam*) I can't get him away from the computer.

schioppettata [skjoppet'tata] SF gunshot.

schioppo ['skjɔppo] SM rifle, gun; **essere a un tiro di schioppo da** to be a stone's throw from.

schiudere ['skjudere] VB IRREG ❶ VT to open.
❷ **schiudersi** VIP (*fiore*) to open, come out.

schiuma ['skjuma] SF (*gen*) foam; (*di bevande*) froth; (*di sapone*) lather; **avere la schiuma alla bocca** (*fig*: *arrabbiato*) to be foaming at the mouth.

schiumaiola [skjuma'jɔla] SF (*Culin*) skimmer.

schiumare [skju'mare] ❶ VT (*brodo*) to skim.
❷ VI (*aus* **avere**) to foam; **schiumare di rabbia** to foam at the mouth.

schiumoso, a [skju'moso] AGG foamy, frothy.

schiuso, a ['skjuso] PP di **schiudere**.

schivare [ski'vare] VT (*colpo, proiettile*) to dodge, avoid; (*persona, pericolo*) to avoid; (*domanda*) to evade.

schivo, a ['skivo] AGG (*ritroso*) reserved; (*timido*) shy.

schizofrenia [skiddzofre'nia] SF schizophrenia.

schizofrenico, a, ci, che [skiddzo'frɛniko] AGG, SM/F schizophrenic.

schizoide [skid'dzɔide] AGG, SM/F schizoid.

schizzare [skit'tsare] ❶ VT **a** (*gen*) to squirt; (*inzuppare*) to splash; (*macchiare*) to spatter; **mi ha schizzato d'acqua** he splashed water over me, he splashed me with water; **ha schizzato inchiostro sulla tovaglia** he spattered ink on the tablecloth, he spattered the tablecloth with ink **b** (*disegnare*) to sketch.
❷ VI (*aus* **essere**) (*liquido*) to squirt; (: *con violenza*) to gush, spurt; **schizzare via** (*animale, persona*) to dart away; (*macchina, moto*) to speed off; **schizzare fuori** (*persona*) to dash out; **schizzare fuori dal letto** to leap *o* jump out of bed; **gli occhi gli schizzarono dalle orbite** (*fig*) his eyes nearly popped out of his head.

schizzinosamente [skittsinosa'mente] AVV fussily.

schizzinoso, a [skittsi'noso] ❶ AGG fussy, difficult, finicky.
❷ SM/F fussy person, difficult person; **non fare lo schizzinoso!** don't be so fussy!

schizzo ['skittso] SM **a** (*di liquido*) squirt, splash; (*macchia*) stain, spot **b** (*abbozzo*) sketch.

schnauzer ['ʃnautsər] SM INV (*cane*) schnauzer.

schuss [ʃus] SM INV (*Sci*) schuss.

sci [ʃi] SM INV (*Sport*: *attività*) skiing; (: *attrezzo*) ski; **sci a monte** uphill ski; **un paio di sci** a pair of skis; **fare dello sci** to ski ▶**sci acrobatico** hot-dogging, free-styling ▶**sci alpinismo** *o* **d'alta quota** ski mountaineering ▶**sci alpino** alpine skiing ▶**sci di fondo** cross-country skiing, ski touring (*Am*) ▶**sci nautico** water-skiing.

scia ['ʃia] SF (*di imbarcazione*) wake; (*fig*: *di fumo, profumo*) trail.

scià [ʃa] SM INV shah.

sciabola ['ʃabola] SF sabre (*Brit*), saber (*Am*).

sciabolata [ʃabo'lata] SF sabre (*Brit*) *o* saber (*Am*) cut.

sciabordio, dii [ʃabor'dio] SF lapping.

sciacallo [ʃa'kallo] SM (*Zool*) jackal; (*fig pegg*: *profittatore*) shark, profiteer; (: *ladro*) looter.

sciacquadita [ʃakkwa'dita] SM INV fingerbowl.

sciacquare [ʃak'kware] VT (*mani, capelli*) to rinse; (*panni*) to rinse (out); **sciacquarsi la bocca** to rinse one's mouth.

sciacquata [ʃak'kwata] SF rinse; **dare una sciacquata a qc** to rinse sth, give sth a rinse.

sciacquatura [ʃakkwa'tura] SF (*azione*) rinsing; (*acqua*) rinsing water; (: *di piatti*) dishwater.

sciacquio, quii [ʃak'kwio] SM (*rumore*) swish.

sciacquo ['ʃakkwo] SM (*azione*) rinsing of the mouth; (*prodotto*) mouthwash; **fare degli sciacqui** to rinse one's mouth (with mouthwash).

sciacquone [ʃak'kwone] SM (*del water*) flush.

sciagura [ʃa'gura] SF disaster, calamity; **una sciagura aerea** an air disaster.

sciaguratamente [ʃagurata'mente] AVV (*malvagiamente*) wickedly; (*disgraziatamente*) unfortunately.

sciagurato, a [ʃagu'rato] [1] AGG (*disgraziato*) wretched, unfortunate; (*malvagio*) wicked.
[2] SM/F wretch.

scialacquare [ʃalak'kware] VT to squander.

scialacquatore, trice [ʃalakkwa'tore] SM/F squanderer.

scialare [ʃa'lare] VI (*aus avere*) throw one's money around; **c'è poco da scialare** there's little money to spare.

scialbo, a ['ʃalbo] AGG (*colore*) pale, dull; (*fig: persona*) dull, colourless (*Brit*), colorless (*Am*).

scialle ['ʃalle] SM shawl.

scialo ['ʃalo] SM squandering, waste; **fare scialo di qc** to squander sth (away).

scialuppa [ʃa'luppa] SF (*Naut*) sloop ▶**scialuppa di salvataggio** lifeboat.

sciamannato, a [ʃaman'nato] AGG, SM/F (*fig fam: disgraziato*) good-for-nothing.

sciamano [ʃa'mano] SM shaman.

sciamare [ʃa'mare] VI (*aus avere o essere*) to swarm.

sciame ['ʃame] SM swarm; (*fig: di persone*) crowd, swarm.

sciancato, a [ʃan'kato] AGG (*persona*) crippled, lame; (*fig: mobile*) rickety.

sciancrato, a [ʃan'krato] AGG (*abito*) waisted.

sciangai [ʃan'gai] SM (*gioco*) pick-up-sticks *sg*.

sciantosa [ʃan'tosa] SF cabaret singer.

sciantung ['ʃantung] SM shantung.

sciarada [ʃa'rada] SF charades *pl*.

sciare [ʃi'are] VI (*aus avere*) to ski; **andare a sciare** to go skiing.

sciarpa ['ʃarpa] SF scarf.

sciatica ['ʃatika] SF (*Med*) sciatica.

sciatico, a, ci, che ['ʃatiko] AGG (*Med*) sciatic.

sciatore, trice [ʃia'tore] SM/F skier.

sciattamente [ʃatta'mente] AVV in a slovenly manner.

sciattezza [ʃat'tettsa] SF slovenliness.

sciatto, a ['ʃatto] AGG (*persona*) slovenly, unkempt; (*lavoro*) sloppy, careless.

sciattone, a [ʃat'tone] SM/F sloven.

scibile ['ʃibile] SM knowledge.

sciccheria [ʃikke'ria] SF stylishness, chic; **che sciccheria!** how chic!; **questo vestito è una sciccheria** this dress is very chic.

sciccoso, a [ʃik'koso] AGG (*fam, elegante*) chic.

scientificamente [ʃentifika'mente] AVV scientifically.

scientifico, a, ci, che [ʃen'tifiko] AGG (*gen*) scientific; (*materia, insegnamento*) science *attr*; **la (polizia) scientifica** the forensic department.

scienza ['ʃɛntsa] SF a (*gen*) science; **scienze** SFPL (*Scol*)

science *sg* ▶**scienze naturali** natural sciences ▶**scienze occulte** occult sciences ▶**scienze politiche** political science *pl* b (*conoscenza*) knowledge, learning.

scienziato, a [ʃen'tsjato] SM/F scientist.

sciistico, a, ci, che [ʃi'istiko] AGG skiing *attr*.

Scilla ['ʃilla] SF Scylla.

Scilly ['ʃilli] SFPL: **le (isole) Scilly** the Scilly Isles.

scimmia ['ʃimmja] SF (*Zool*) monkey; (: *più grande*) ape; (*fig: persona brutta*) horror; **avere la scimmia** (*fam: dipendenza da droga*) to have a monkey on one's back (*Am*).

scimmiesco, a, schi, sche [ʃim'mjesko] AGG monkey-like, ape-like.

scimmiottare [ʃimmjot'tare] VT (*beffeggiare*) to mock, make fun of; (*imitare*) to mimic, ape.

scimpanzé [ʃimpan'tse] SM INV chimpanzee.

scimunito, a [ʃimu'nito] [1] AGG idiotic, stupid, silly.
[2] SM/F fool, idiot.

scindere ['ʃindere] VB IRREG [1] VT to split (up), divide.
[2] **scindersi** VIP to split (up), break up; **scindersi in** to split into.

scintilla [ʃin'tilla] SF (*anche fig*) spark; **fare scintille** to give off sparks, spark.

scintillante [ʃintil'lante] AGG (*occhi, diamante, acque*) sparkling; (*stelle*) twinkling; (*capelli*) shining, gleaming.

scintillare [ʃintil'lare] VI (*aus avere*) to give off sparks, spark; (*acqua, occhi*) to sparkle, glitter; **gli occhi le scintillavano di gioia** her eyes were sparkling with joy.

scintillio, lii [ʃintil'lio] SM sparkling, glittering.

scioccamente [ʃokka'mente] AVV foolishly.

scioccare [ʃok'kare] VT to shock.

sciocchezza [ʃok'kettsa] SF a (*qualità*) foolishness *no pl*, silliness *no pl*, stupidity *no pl*; **fare una sciocchezza** to do something silly; **è stata una sciocchezza** it was really foolish; **per me ha fatto una sciocchezza** I think it was very foolish o silly of him to do that; **ha detto un sacco di sciocchezze** he talked a load of nonsense; **sciocchezze!** nonsense!
b : **l'ho pagato una sciocchezza** I hardly paid anything for it; **è solo una sciocchezza** (*regalo*) it's only a trifle.

sciocco, a, chi, che ['ʃokko] [1] AGG silly, foolish, stupid.
[2] SM/F fool.

sciogliere ['ʃoʎʎere] VB IRREG [1] VT a (*liquefare*) to melt; (*nell'acqua: zucchero*) to dissolve; (*neve*) to melt, thaw; **sciogliere il ghiaccio** (*fig*) to break the ice
b (*disfare: nodo*) to undo, untie; (: *capelli*) to loosen
c (*slegare: persona, animale*) to set free, release, untie; (*fig: persona: da obbligo*) to absolve, release; (: *contratto*) to cancel, annul; (: *parlamento, matrimonio*) to dissolve; (: *riunione*) to break up, bring to an end; (: *società*) to dissolve, wind up; **sciogliere le vele** (*Naut*) to set sail; **sciogliere i muscoli** to limber up; (*far*) **sciogliere la lingua a qn** to loosen sb's tongue; **sciogliere un mistero** to solve o unravel a mystery.
[2] **sciogliersi** VIP a (*vedi vt a*) to melt; to dissolve; to thaw; **questa carne si scioglie in bocca** this meat melts in the mouth; **sciogliersi in lacrime** to burst into tears
b (*assemblea, corteo, duo*) to break up.
[3] **sciogliersi** VR (*liberarsi*) to free o.s., release o.s.; **sciogliersi dai legami** (*fig*) to free o.s. from all ties.

scioglilingua [ʃoʎʎi'lingwa] SM INV tongue-twister.

sciolgo ecc ['ʃolgo] VB vedi **sciogliere**.

sciolina [ʃio'lina] SF (ski) wax.

sciolinare [ʃioli'nare] VT to wax.

sciolinatura [ʃiolina'tura] SF waxing (of skis).

scioltezza [ʃol'tettsa] SF (*agilità*) agility, nimbleness, suppleness; (*disinvoltura*) ease, smoothness; (: *nel parlare*) fluency, ease.

sciolto, a ['ʃɔlto] [1] PP di **sciogliere**.
[2] AGG **a** (*persona: agile*) agile, nimble; (: *disinvolto*) easy-going, free and easy; **essere sciolto nei movimenti** to be supple; **avere la lingua sciolta** to have the gift of the gab **b** (*Comm: sfuso*) loose **c** (*in poesia*): **versi sciolti** blank verse.

scioperante [ʃope'rante] [1] AGG on strike.
[2] SM/F striker.

scioperare [ʃope'rare] VI (*aus* **avere**) (*fare sciopero*) to strike, go on strike; (*entrare in sciopero*) to go on strike.

scioperato, a [ʃope'rato] [1] AGG idle, lazy.
[2] SM/F idler, loafer.

sciopero ['ʃɔpero] SM strike; **essere in sciopero** [OR] **fare sciopero** to be on strike; **entrare in sciopero** to go on *o* come out on strike ►**sciopero bianco** work-to-rule (*Brit*), slowdown (*Am*) ►**sciopero della fame** hunger strike ►**sciopero selvaggio** wildcat strike ►**sciopero a singhiozzo** on-off strike ►**sciopero di solidarietà** sympathy strike.

sciorinare [ʃori'nare] VT **a** (*ostentare*) to show off, display **b** (*dire con disinvoltura: consigli, citazioni*) to rattle off; **sciorinare bugie** to tell one lie after another **c** (*bucato*) to hang out.

sciovia [ʃio'via] SF ski tow.

sciovinismo [ʃovi'nizmo] SM chauvinism.

sciovinista, i, e [ʃovi'nista] SM/F chauvinist.

sciovinistico, a, ci, che [ʃovi'nistiko] AGG chauvinistic.

scipito, a [ʃi'pito] AGG insipid.

scippare [ʃip'pare] VT: **scippare qn** to snatch sb's bag.

scippatore [ʃippa'tore] SM bag-snatcher.

scippo ['ʃippo] SM bag-snatching.

scirocco [ʃi'rɔkko] SM sirocco.

sciroppare [ʃirop'pare] VT (*frutta*) to put in syrup; **sciropparsi qn/qc** (*fig fam*) to put up with sb/sth.

sciroppato, a [ʃirop'pato] AGG in syrup.

sciroppo [ʃi'rɔppo] SM syrup ►**sciroppo per la tosse** cough syrup, cough mixture.

sciropposo, a [ʃirop'poso] AGG syrupy.

scisma, i ['ʃizma] SM (*Rel, Pol*) schism.

scismatico, a, ci, che [ʃiz'matiko] AGG, SM schismatic.

scissione [ʃis'sjone] SF (*Fis, Bio*) fission; (*di gruppo, partito*) splitting (up), division, split.

scisso, a ['ʃisso] PP di **scindere**.

sciupare [ʃu'pare] [1] VT **a** (*rovinare*) to ruin, spoil **b** (*sprecare: tempo, denaro*) to waste, throw away; (: *occasione*) to miss.
[2] **sciuparsi** VIP (*rovinarsi*) to get spoiled *o* ruined; **l'ho vista molto sciupata** she looked very run down when I saw her.

scivolamento [ʃivola'mento] SM (*gen*) slipping; (*Sci*) glide.

scivolare [ʃivo'lare] VI (*aus* **essere**) (*cadere*) to slip; **scivolare sul ghiaccio** (*persona*) to slip on the ice; (: *per gioco*) to slide on the ice; (*macchina*) to skid on the ice; **è scivolato giù dalle scale** he slipped and fell down the stairs; **attento, si scivola** be careful, it's slippery; **il vaso gli scivolò dalle mani** the vase slipped out of his hands; **scivolò via non visto** he slipped away unseen; **l'uomo scivolò silenziosamente nella stanza** the man slipped silently into the room; **gli fece scivolare il biglietto in tasca** he slipped the note into his pocket; **scivolare su una buccia di banana** (*anche fig*) to slip on a banana skin.

scivolata [ʃivo'lata] SF (*anche Aer*) slip; (*Sci*) glide; **fare una scivolata** to slip.

scivolo ['ʃivolo] SM (*gioco*) slide; (*Tecn*) chute.

scivolone [ʃivo'lone] SM tumble, fall; **fare uno scivolone** to take a tumble.

scivoloso, a [ʃivo'loso] AGG slippery.

sclera ['sklɛra] SF (*Anat*) sclerotic, sclera.

sclerosi [skle'rɔzi] SF INV (*Med*) sclerosis.

sclerotico, a, ci, che [skle'rɔtiko] [1] AGG sclerotic.
[2] SM/F sclerosis sufferer.

sclerotizzare [sklerotid'dzare] [1] VT (*fig*) to make inflexible.
[2] **sclerotizzarsi** VIP (*Med*) to become sclerotic; (*fig*) to become inflexible.

scocca, che ['skɔkka] SF (*Aut*) body.

scoccare [skok'kare] [1] VT **a** (*freccia*) to shoot **b** (*ore*) to strike; **l'orologio scoccò le 8** the clock struck 8 **c**: **scoccare un bacio a qn** to give sb a smacker.
[2] VI (*aus* **essere**) **a** (*freccia*) to shoot out; (*scintilla*) to fly up **b** (*ore*) to strike; **scoccavano le 11** it was striking 11.

scoccherò *ecc* [skokke'rɔ] VB vedi **scoccare**.

scocciare [skot't∫are] [1] VT to annoy, bother; **mi hai scocciato** (*stufato*) I'm fed up with you; (*seccato*) I'm annoyed with you; **se non ti scoccia** if it doesn't bother you; **ti scoccia se...?** do you mind if ...?; **e ancora faceva lo scocciato** and he still wasn't happy.
[2] **scocciarsi** VIP (*stufarsi*) to get fed up; (*seccarsi*) to get annoyed.

scocciato, a [skot't∫ato] AGG (*seccato*) annoyed; (*stufato*) fed up.

scocciatore, trice [skott∫a'tore] SM/F nuisance, pest (*fam*).

scocciatura [skott∫a'tura] SF nuisance, bore; **che scocciatura!** what a nuisance!

scodella [sko'dɛlla] SF (*ciotola*) bowl; (*piatto fondo*) soup plate.

scodellare [skodel'lare] VT to dish out, dish up.

scodinzolare [skodintso'lare] VI (*aus* **avere**) (*cane*) to wag its tail.

scogliera [skoʎ'ʎɛra] SF (*scogli*) rocks *pl*, reef; (*rupe*) cliff.

scoglio, gli ['skɔʎʎo] SM rock; (*fig: ostacolo*) difficulty, stumbling block.

scoglioso, a [skoʎ'ʎoso] AGG rocky.

scoiattolo [sko'jattolo] SM (*Zool*) squirrel; **agile come uno scoiattolo** (*fig*) agile as a monkey.

scolapasta [skola'pasta] SM INV colander.

scolapiatti [skola'pjatti] SM INV (*del lavandino*) draining board; (*rastrelliera*) plate rack.

scolaposate [skolapo'sate] SM INV cutlery drainer.

scolare¹ [sko'lare] [1] VT to drain; **si è scolato una bottiglia!** he's drained *o* downed a bottle!.
[2] VI (*aus* **essere**) to drip.

scolare² [sko'lare] AGG: **in età scolare** school-age *attr*.

scolaresca, sche [skola'reska] SF schoolchildren *pl*, pupils *pl*.

scolaro, a [sko'laro] SM/F pupil, schoolboy/schoolgirl; (*discepolo*) disciple, follower.

scolasticamente [skolastika'mente] AVV scholastically.

scolastico, a, ci, che [sko'lastiko] AGG (*gen*) scholastic; (*libro, anno, divisa*) school *attr*; (*pegg: cultura*) superficial.

scoliosi [sko'ljozi] SF INV (*Med*) scoliosis.

scollacciato, a [skollat'tʃato] AGG (*vestito*) low-cut, with a low neckline; (*donna*) in a low-necked dress (*o blouse ecc*).

scollare [skol'lare] ① VT to unstick, unglue.
② **scollarsi** VIP to come unstuck, come off *o* away.

scollato, a [skol'lato] AGG (*vestito*) low-cut, low-necked; (*donna*) wearing a low-cut dress (*o blouse ecc*).

scollatura [skolla'tura] SF, **scollo** ['skɔllo] SM neckline, neck; **scollo a barchetta** boat neck.

scolo ['skolo] SM **a** (*condotto*) drainage; (*sbocco*) drain; **canale di scolo** drain; **tubo di scolo** drainpipe **b** (*acqua*) waste water.

scolorare [skolo'rare], **scolorire** [skolo'rire] ① VT to discolour (*Brit*), discolor (*Am*); (*sbiadire*) to fade.
② **scolorarsi, scolorirsi** VIP (*vedi vt*) to become discolo(u)red; to fade, become faded; (*impallidire*) to turn pale.

scolorato, a [skolo'rato], **scolorito, a** [skolo'rito] AGG faded.

scolpare [skol'pare] ① VT to free from blame, exonerate.
② **scolparsi** VR to free o.s. from blame, exonerate o.s.

scolpire [skol'pire] VT (*pietra*) to sculpt, sculpture; (*legno*) to carve; (*metallo*) to engrave; **quelle parole rimasero scolpite nella sua memoria** (*fig*) those words were engraved on his memory.

scombinare [skombi'nare] VT (*scomporre*) to mess up, ruin, upset; (*mandare a monte*) to break off, cancel.

scombinato, a [skombi'nato] AGG confused, muddled.

scombussolare [skombusso'lare] VT (*persona*) to upset, disturb; (*piani*) to upset, mess up.

scommessa [skom'messa] SF (*azione*) bet; (*somma*) bet, stake; **fare una scommessa** to bet.

scommesso, a [skom'messo] PP di **scommettere**.

scommettere [skom'mettere] VT IRREG to bet; **scommettere 10.000 lire** to bet *o* wager 10,000 lire; **scommettere su un cavallo** to bet on a horse; **scommettiamo?** do you want to (take a) bet on it?; **non ci scommetterei** I wouldn't bet on it; **ci avrei scommesso!** I would have put money on it!; **puoi scommetterci** you can count on it; **quanto scommmettiamo che...?** what's the betting that ...?

scomodamente [skomoda'mente] AVV uncomfortably.

scomodare [skomo'dare] ① VT to disturb, bother, trouble; (*fig: nome famoso*) to involve, drag in.
② **scomodarsi** VR to bother, trouble (o.s.), put o.s. out.

scomodità [skomodi'ta] SF INV (*di sedia, letto*) discomfort; (*di orario, sistemazione*) inconvenience.

scomodo, a ['skɔmodo] AGG (*sedia, letto, posizione*) uncomfortable; (*orario, turno, sistemazione, posto*) inconvenient, awkward; **stare scomodo** to be uncomfortable; **mi è scomodo venire la sera** it's inconvenient for me to come in the evening; **è scomodo da portare** it's difficult to carry, it's cumbersome.

scompaginare [skompadʒi'nare] ① VT to upset, throw into disorder.
② **scompaginarsi** VIP to be thrown into disorder.

scompagnato, a [skompaɲ'nato] AGG (*scarpe, calzini*) odd.

scomparire [skompa'rire] VI IRREG (*aus essere*) (*sparire*) to disappear, vanish; (*fig: non risaltare*) to look (*o* be) insignificant.

scomparsa [skom'parsa] SF (*sparizione*) disappearance; (*euf*) passing away.

scomparso, a [skom'parso] PP di **scomparire**.

scompartimento [skomparti'mento] SM **a** (*sezione*) divi-sion **b** (*Ferr*) compartment.

scomparto [skom'parto] SM division, compartment.

scompenso [skom'pɛnso] SM imbalance, lack of balance; (*Med*) decompensation.

scompigliare [skompiʎ'ʎare] VT to mess up, muddle up; (*capelli*) to mess up, ruffle; (*fig: piani*) to upset; (: *idee*) to mess up, confuse.

scompigliato, a [skompiʎ'ʎato] AGG dishevelled.

scompiglio, gli [skom'piʎʎo] SM confusion, chaos; **portare lo scompiglio in** to cause confusion in.

scomporre [skom'porre] VB IRREG ① VT (*parola, numero*) to break up; (*Chim*) to decompose.
②: **scomporsi** VIP **a** (*Chim*) to decompose **b** (*fig: turbarsi*) to lose one's composure, get upset; **senza scomporsi** unperturbed.

scompostezza [skompos'tettsa] SF unseemliness.

scomposto, a [skom'posto] ① PP di **scomporre**.
② AGG **a** (*parola, numero*) broken up **b** (*persona: sguaiato*) unseemly **c** (*capelli, vestiti: in disordine*) dishevelled, in a mess.

scomunica, che [sko'munika] SF (*Rel*) excommunication.

scomunicare [skomuni'kare] VT (*Rel*) to excommunicate.

scomunicato, a [skomuni'kato] SM/F excommunicate.

sconcertante [skontʃer'tante] AGG disconcerting.

sconcertare [skontʃer'tare] ① VT to disconcert, bewilder.
② **sconcertarsi** VIP to be disconcerted.

sconcertato, a [skontʃer'tato] AGG disconcerted.

sconcezza [skon'tʃettsa] SF obscenity, indecency; **è una sconcezza!** it's a disgrace!

sconciamente [skontʃa'mente] AVV obscenely, indecently.

sconcio, cia, ci, ce ['skontʃo] ① AGG (*osceno*) obscene, indecent; (: *parole*) rude, dirty.
② SM (*cosa mal fatta*) disgrace.

sconclusionato, a [skonkluzjo'nato] AGG incoherent, illogical.

scondito, a [skon'dito] AGG (*minestra*) unseasoned; (*insalata*) without dressing.

sconfessare [skonfes'sare] VT (*ritrattare*) to renounce, retract; (*smentire*) to repudiate.

sconfiggere [skon'fiddʒere] VT IRREG (*gen, Pol, Sport*) to defeat, overcome.

sconfinamento [skonfina'mento] SM (*di frontiera*) border violation; (*di proprietà*) trespassing.

sconfinare [skonfi'nare] VI to cross the border; (*da proprietà*) to trespass; (: *involontariamente*) to stray; (*fig: uscire dai limiti fissati*): **sconfinare da** (*verità, sentiero*) to stray from; (*tema, argomento*) to digress from, stray from.

sconfinatamente [skonfinata'mente] AVV (*estendersi*) infinitely.

sconfinato, a [skonfi'nato] AGG (*spazio*) limitless, boundless; (*fig: conoscenza, pazienza*) unlimited.

sconfitta [skon'fitta] SF (*gen, Pol, Sport*) defeat; **subire** *o* **riportare una sconfitta** to be defeated.

sconfitto, a [skon'fitto] PP di **sconfiggere**.

sconfortante [skonfor'tante] AGG discouraging, disheartening.

sconfortare [skonfor'tare] ① VT to discourage, dishearten. ② **sconfortarsi** VIP to become discouraged, become disheartened, lose heart.

sconfortato, a [skonfor'tato] AGG dejected.

sconforto [skon'forto] SM dejection, despondency; **essere in preda allo sconforto** to be dejected.

scongelare [skondʒe'lare] vT to defrost.

scongiurare [skondʒu'rare] vT **a** (*supplicare*) to beg, implore, beseech **b** (*allontanare*) to avert, ward off.

scongiuro [skon'dʒuro] SM (*esorcismo*) exorcism; (*formula*) spell, charm; **fare gli scongiuri** to touch wood (*Brit*), knock on wood (*Am*).

sconnesso, a [skon'nɛsso] AGG (*staccato*) disconnected; (*fig: sconclusionato*) incoherent, disconnected, rambling.

sconosciuto, a [skonoʃ'ʃuto] 1 AGG unknown; **una gioia sconosciuta** a strange joy; **il suo viso mi è sconosciuto** his face is new to me.

2 SM/F unknown person, stranger.

sconquassare [skonkwas'sare] vT to shatter, smash.

sconquasso [skon'kwasso] SM (*danno*) damage; (*fig*) confusion.

sconsacrare [skonsa'krare] vT (*Rel*) to deconsecrate.

sconsacrato, a [skonsa'krato] AGG deconsecrated.

sconsideratezza [skonsidera'tettsa] SF lack of consideration, thoughtlessness.

sconsiderato, a [skonside'rato] 1 AGG thoughtless, inconsiderate, rash.

2 SM/F thoughtless person, inconsiderate person.

sconsigliare [skonsiʎ'ʎare] vT: **sconsigliare qc a qn** to advise sb against sth; **ti sconsiglio di provarci** I advise you against trying; **quel ristorante? te lo sconsiglio!** that restaurant? I wouldn't recommend it!; **volevo andare ma mi hanno sconsigliato** I wanted to go but they advised me not to.

sconsolatamente [skonsolata'mente] AVV disconsolately.

sconsolato, a [skonso'lato] AGG disconsolate.

scontare [skon'tare] vT **a** (*Comm: detrarre*) to deduct, discount; **scontare una cambiale** to discount a bill of exchange; **scontare un debito** to pay off a debt in instalments **b** (*peccato, colpa*) to pay for, suffer for; (*Dir: pena*) to serve; **scontare 5 anni di prigione** to serve 5 years in prison.

scontato, a [skon'tato] AGG **a** (*prezzo, merce*) discounted, at a discount **b** (*previsto*) foreseen, taken for granted; **era scontato che finisse così** it was bound to end that way; **dare qc per scontato** to take sth for granted.

scontentare [skonten'tare] vT to displease, dissatisfy.

scontentezza [skonten'tettsa] SF displeasure, dissatisfaction.

scontento, a [skon'tɛnto] 1 AGG dissatisfied, displeased; **essere scontento di qc** to be displeased o dissatisfied with sth.

2 SM discontent, dissatisfaction.

sconto ['skonto] SM (*Comm*) discount; **fare** o **concedere uno sconto** to give a discount; **uno sconto del 10%** a 10% discount; **sconto (sulla) quantità** quantity o volume discount.

scontrarsi [skon'trarsi] vR **a** (*veicolo, persona*): **scontrarsi con** to collide with **b** (*uso reciproco: veicoli, persone*) to collide, to crash; (*Mil, fig: opinioni*) to clash.

scontrino [skon'trino] SM (*biglietto*) ticket (*Brit*), check (*Am*); (*di cassa*) receipt.

scontro ['skontro] SM (*di veicoli*) collision, crash; (*Mil*) clash, engagement; (*fig: litigio*) disagreement; **ci sono stati scontri tra polizia e dimostranti** there were clashes between police and demonstrators, police and demonstrators clashed ▸ **scontro a fuoco** shoot-out.

scontrosità [skontrosi'ta] SF surliness.

scontroso, a [skon'troso] AGG (*poco socievole*) surly, sullen; (*permaloso*) touchy.

sconveniente [skonve'njɛnte] AGG **a** (*comportamento, modi*) unseemly; (*osservazione, proposta*) improper **b** (*prezzo, affare*) disadvantageous, unattractive.

sconvenientemente [skonvenjente'mente] AVV (*vedi agg*) in an unseemly manner; improperly; disadvantageously.

sconvenienza [skonve'njɛntsa] SF (*vedi agg*) unseemliness; impropriety; unattractiveness.

sconvolgente [skonvol'dʒɛnte] AGG (*notizia, brutta esperienza*) upsetting, disturbing; (*bellezza*) amazing; (*passione*) overwhelming.

sconvolgere [skon'voldʒere] VB IRREG 1 vT (*persona*) to upset, disturb; (*piani*) to upset; **sconvolgere l'opinione pubblica** to shock o shake public opinion; **la notizia ha sconvolto il mondo intero** the news shook the whole world; **la zona sconvolta dal terremoto** the area hit o affected by the earthquake; **le campagne sconvolte dall'alluvione** the flooded countryside, the countryside devastated by the floods.

2: **sconvolgersi** VIP to become upset.

sconvolgimento [skonvoldʒi'mento] SM (*scompiglio*) confusion; (*devastazione*) devastation.

sconvolto, a [skon'volto] 1 PP di **sconvolgere**.

2 AGG (*persona*) distraught, very upset; (*mente*) disturbed, deranged; **una faccia sconvolta** a ravaged face; **sconvolto dal dolore** beside o.s. with grief.

scopa[1] ['skopa] SF broom; **sembra un manico di scopa** (*fig*) he's as thin as a rake.

scopa[2] ['skopa] SF *Italian card game*.

scopare [sko'pare] 1 vT **a** (*spazzare*) to sweep **b** (*fam*) to bonk (*Brit*).

2 vI (*aus* **avere**) (*fam*) to bonk (*Brit*).

scopata [sko'pata] SF **a** sweep; **dare una scopata a qc** to give sth a sweep, sweep sth out; **dare una scopata a qn** to hit sb with a broom **b** (*fam*) bonk (*Brit fam*).

scoperchiare [skoper'kjare] vT (*pentola, vaso*) to take the lid off, uncover; (*casa*) to take the roof off.

scoperta [sko'pɛrta] SF discovery; **bella scoperta!** (*iro*) what a revelation!

scopertamente [skoperta'mente] AVV openly.

scoperto, a [sko'pɛrto] 1 PP di **scoprire**.

2 AGG **a** (*pentola*) uncovered, with the lid off; (*macchina*) open; (*spalle, braccia*) bare, uncovered; (*Mil*) exposed, without cover; **a capo scoperto** bare-headed; **dormire scoperto** to sleep uncovered; **giocare a carte scoperte** (*anche fig*) to put one's cards on the table **b** (*Banca*): **assegno scoperto** uncovered cheque (*Brit*) o check (*Am*); **conto scoperto** overdrawn account; **avere un conto scoperto** to be overdrawn.

3 SM **a**: **allo scoperto** (*dormire*) out in the open; **è uscito allo scoperto** (*fig*) he came out into the open **b** (*Banca*): **scoperto di conto** bank overdraft.

scopiazzare [skopjat'tsare] vT (*pegg*) to copy.

scopino [sko'pino] SM **a** (*spazzino*) roadsweeper (*Brit*), streetsweeper (*Am*) **b** (*del gabinetto*) lavatory brush (*Brit*).

scopo ['skɔpo] SM aim, purpose; **allo scopo di fare qc** in order to do sth; **cercare uno scopo nella vita** to look for an aim o a purpose in life; **senza scopo** (*fare, cercare*) pointlessly; **la sua vita è senza scopo** his life is pointless; **a scopo di lucro** for gain o money; **adatto allo scopo** fit for its purpose; **a che scopo?** what for?

scopone [sko'pone] SM *Italian card game*.

scoppiare [skop'pjare] VI (*aus* **essere**) **a** (*bomba, serbatoio*) to explode; (*pneumatico, palloncino*) to burst; (*fig: rivolta, guerra, epidemia*) to break out; **la notizia fece scoppiare uno scandalo** the news caused a scandal **b** (*fraseologia*): **scoppiare dal caldo** to be boiling; **scoppiare dall'invidia** to be dying of envy; **scoppiare a piangere** *o* **in lacrime** to burst into tears; **scoppiare a ridere** to burst out laughing; **scoppiare di salute** to be the picture of health; **scoppiare dalla voglia di fare qc** to be dying *o* longing to do sth; **a quel punto sono scoppiato** (*dalla rabbia, dal ridere*) at that point I couldn't contain myself any longer.

scoppiato, a [skop'pjato] AGG (*fig: pugile*) played out; (: *drogato*) strung out.

scoppiettante [skoppjet'tante] AGG (*fuoco*) crackling.

scoppiettare [skoppjet'tare] VI (*aus* **avere**) (*fuoco*) to crackle; (*motore*) to chug.

scoppiettio, tii [skoppjet'tio] SM crackling.

scoppio, pi ['skɔppjo] SM (*esplosione*) explosion; (*di pneumatico*) bang; (*di tuono, arma*) crash; (*fig: di rivolta, guerra, epidemia*) outbreak; **bomba a scoppio ritardato** delayed-action bomb; **reazione a scoppio ritardato** delayed *o* slow reaction; **uno scoppio di risa** a burst of laughter; **uno scoppio di collera** an explosion of anger.

scoprire [sko'prire] VB IRREG [1] VT **a** (*trovare*) to discover; (*causa, verità*) to discover, find out; **scoprire che.../come ...** to find out *o* discover that .../how ...; **ha scoperto di avere uno zio in India** he found out *o* discovered he has an uncle in India; **hai scoperto l'America!** (*iro*) you mean you've only just found out about it! **b** (*pentola*) to take the lid off; (*statua*) to unveil; (*rovine, cadaveri*) to uncover; (*spalle, braccia*) to bare, uncover; **una camicetta che scopre la schiena** a blouse with a low-cut back; **scoprirsi il capo** to take off one's hat, bare one's head; **scoprirsi il fianco** (*fig*) to leave one's flank exposed.

[2] **scoprirsi** VR (*esporsi: Sport, fig*) to expose o.s.; (*fig: rivelare le proprie idee*) to betray o.s., give o.s. away; **non scoprirti che fa freddo** keep well wrapped up because it's cold; **il bambino si è scoperto durante la notte** the child threw off the bedclothes during the night.

scopritore, trice [skopri'tore] SM/F discoverer.

scoraggiamento [skoraddʒa'mento] SM discouragement, dejection.

scoraggiante [skorad'dʒante] AGG discouraging.

scoraggiare [skorad'dʒare] [1] VT to discourage. [2] **scoraggiarsi** VIP to become discouraged, become disheartened, lose heart.

scorbutico, a, ci, che [skor'butiko] AGG (*fig*) peevish, cantankerous.

scorbuto [skor'buto] SM (*Med*) scurvy.

scorciare [skor'tʃare] VT = **accorciare**.

scorciatoia [skortʃa'toja] SF (*anche fig*) short cut.

scorcio, ci ['skortʃo] SM **a** (*Arte*) foreshortening **b** (*di paesaggio*) glimpse; (*fig: di secolo, periodo*) end, close.

scordare¹ [skor'dare] [1] VT (*gen*) to forget; (*appuntamento, preoccupazione*) to forget (about); **scordare di fare qc** to forget to do sth; **scordavo di avertelo già chiesto** I forgot that I had already asked you. [2] **scordarsi** VIP: **scordarsi di qc/di fare qc** to forget sth/to do sth.

scordare² [skor'dare] [1] VT (*Mus*) to put out of tune. [2] **scordarsi** VIP to go out of tune.

scoreggia, ge [sko'reddʒa], **scorreggia, ge** [skor'red-

dʒa] SF (*fam*) fart (*fam!*)

scoreggiare [skored'dʒare], **scorreggiare** [skorred'dʒare] VI (*aus* **avere**) (*fam*) to fart (*fam!*)

scorfano ['skɔrfano] SM (*Zool*) scorpion fish; (*fig: persona brutta*) fright.

scorgere ['skɔrdʒere] VT IRREG to see, catch sight of; (*fig: accorgersi di*) to become aware of, realize; **senza farsi scorgere** unnoticed, without being seen.

scoria ['skɔrja] SF (*di metalli*) slag; (*vulcanica*) scoria ▶ **scorie radioattive** (*Fis*) radioactive waste *sg*.

scornare [skor'nare] VT (*fig*) to humiliate.

scornato, a [skor'nato] AGG (*fig*) humiliated.

scorno ['skɔrno] SM humiliation, ignominy, disgrace.

scorpacciata [skorpat'tʃata] SF big feed; **farsi una scorpacciata (di qc)** to stuff o.s. (with sth).

scorpione [skor'pjone] SM **a** (*Zool*) scorpion **b** (*Astrol*): **Scorpione** Scorpio; **essere dello Scorpione** to be Scorpio.

scorporo [skɔrporo] SM (*Pol*) *transfer of votes aimed at increasing the chances of representation for minority parties.*

scorrazzare [skorrat'tsare] VI (*aus* **avere**) to run about, romp about.

scorrere ['skorrere] VB IRREG [1] VI (*aus* **essere**) (*liquido, fiume*) to run, flow; (*fune*) to run; (*cassetto, porta*) to slide easily; (*tempo*) to pass (by); (*traffico*) to flow; **lascia scorrere l'acqua** let the water run, leave the water running; **il tempo scorre lento** time passes slowly; **ha uno stile che scorre** he (*o* it *ecc*) has a flowing style. [2] VT (*leggere*) to glance through, run one's eye over.

scorreria [skorre'ria] SF raid, incursion.

scorrettamente [skorretta'mente] AVV (*vedi agg*) incorrectly; impolitely; unfairly.

scorrettezza [skorret'tettsa] SF (*vedi agg*) incorrectness; lack of politeness, rudeness; unfairness; **scorrettezza nel gioco** foul play *no pl*; **con scorrettezza** (*sgarbatamente*) rudely, impolitely; **è stata una scorrettezza da parte sua** it was rude of him, it was bad manners on his part; **commettere una scorrettezza** (*essere sleale*) to be unfair.

scorretto, a [skor'retto] AGG (*traduzione, uso*) incorrect; (*persona: sgarbato*) impolite, rude; (: *sleale*) unfair; (*gioco*) foul.

scorrevole [skor'revole] AGG (*porta*) sliding; (*nastro*) moving; (*fig: stile*) flowing, fluent.

scorrevolezza [skorrevo'lettsa] SF (*fig: di stile*) fluency.

scorribanda [skorri'banda] SF (*Mil*) raid, incursion; (*escursione*) trip, excursion.

scorsa ['skorsa] SF glance, quick look; **dare una scorsa a qc** to glance over *o* through sth.

scorsi *ecc* ['skorsi] VB vedi **scorgere**.

scorso, a ['skorso] [1] PP di **scorrere**. [2] AGG last; **lo scorso mese** last month.

scorsoio, oia, oi, oie [skor'sojo] AGG: **nodo scorsoio** slipknot, noose.

scorta ['skorta] SF **a** (*gen, di personalità, convoglio, Mil*) escort; **fare la scorta a qn** to escort sb; **sotto la scorta di due agenti** escorted by two policemen **b** (*provvista*) supply, stock; **fare scorta di** to stock up with, get in a supply of; **di scorta** (*materiali*) spare; **ruota di scorta** spare wheel.

scortare [skor'tare] VT to escort.

scortese [skor'tese] AGG impolite, discourteous, rude.

scortesemente [skortese'mente] AVV impolitely, discour-

teously, rudely.

scortesia [skorte'zia] SF (*qualità*) impoliteness, discourtesy, rudeness; (*azione*) discourtesy.

scorticare [skorti'kare] VT (*animali*) to skin, flay; **scorticarsi un gomito** to skin *o* graze one's elbow.

scorto, a ['skɔrto] PP di **scorgere**.

scorza ['skɔrdza] SF (*di albero*) bark; (*di agrumi*) peel, skin; **avere la scorza dura** (*fig: persona*) to be thick-skinned; **sotto la scorza c'è un animo gentile** he's kind-hearted beneath his crusty exterior.

scosceso, a [skoʃ'ʃeso] AGG steep.

scossa ['skɔssa] SF (*sobbalzo*) jolt, jerk; (*elettrica*) shock; **procedere a scosse** to jolt *o* jerk along; **dare una scossa a qn** (*fig*) to shake sb; **prendere la scossa** to get an electric shock ▶**scossa di terremoto** earth tremor.

scosso, a ['skɔsso] [1] PP di **scuotere**.

[2] AGG (*persona*) shaken, upset; **ho i nervi scossi** my nerves are shattered.

scossone [skos'sone] SM: **dare uno scossone a qn** to give sb a shake; **procedere a scossoni** (*auto*) to jolt *o* jerk along.

scostante [skos'tante] AGG (*persona, modi*) unpleasant, off-putting.

scostare [skos'tare] [1] VT to push aside, move aside; **far scostare qn** to push sb aside; **scosta la poltrona dal muro** move the armchair away from the wall.

[2] **scostarsi** VR to move aside; **scostati dal muro** move away from the wall.

scostumatamente [skostumata'mente] AVV (*vedi agg*) immorally, dissolutely; boorishly.

scostumato, a [skostu'mato] [1] AGG (*immorale*) immoral, dissolute; (*maleducato*) bad-mannered, boorish.

[2] SM (*vedi agg*) dissolute person; boor.

scotch¹ [skɔtʃ] SM INV (*whisky*) Scotch.

scotch²ᵉ [skɔtʃ] SM INV (*nastro adesivo*) Sellotape ® (*Brit*), Scotch tape ® (*Am*).

scotennare [skoten'nare] VT (*animale*) to skin; (*persona*) to scalp.

scotta ['skɔtta] SF (*Naut*) sheet.

scottante [skot'tante] AGG (*urgente*) pressing; (*delicato*) delicate.

scottare [skot'tare] [1] VT (*gen*) to burn; (*con liquido, vapore*) to scald, burn; (*Culin: in acqua*) to scald; (: *friggendo*) to sear; **scottarsi una mano** to burn one's hand; **sono già stato scottato una volta** (*fig*) I've already burnt my fingers once.

[2] VI (*aus avere*) (*gen*) to be very hot; (*sole, sabbia*) to be burning, be scorching; **è roba che scotta** (*fig: refurtiva*) it's hot; **sono argomenti che scottano** (*fig: delicati*) these are delicate issues; **gli scotta la terra sotto ai piedi** (*fig*) he's itching to be off.

[3] **scottarsi** VR (*gen*) to burn o.s.; (*con liquido, vapore*) to scald o.s., burn o.s.

scottata [skot'tata] SF (*Culin*): **dare una scottata a qc** (*in acqua*) to scald sth; (*friggendo*) to sear sth.

scottatura [skotta'tura] SF (*gen*) burn; (*con liquido, vapore*) scald, burn.

scotto¹, a ['skɔtto] AGG (*Culin*) overcooked, overdone.

scotto² ['skɔtto] SM (*fig: punizione*): **pagare lo scotto** to pay the consequences.

scovare [sko'vare] VT (*Caccia*) to drive out, flush out, put up; (*fig*) to unearth, find, discover.

Scozia ['skɔttsja] SF: **la Scozia** Scotland.

scozzese [skot'tsese] [1] AGG (*gen*) Scottish; (*whisky*)

Scotch; **tessuto scozzese** tartan; **gonna scozzese** kilt.

[2] SM/F Scot, Scotsman/Scotswoman; **gli scozzesi** the Scots.

screanzatamente [skreantsata'mente] AVV rudely, boorishly.

screanzato, a [skrean'tsato] [1] AGG ill-mannered.

[2] SM/F boor.

screditare [skredi'tare] [1] VT to discredit.

[2] **screditarsi** VIP to be discredited.

scremare [skre'mare] VT to skim.

scremato, a [skre'mato] AGG skimmed; **parzialmente scremato** semi-skimmed.

scrematrice [skrema'trice] SF skimmer.

screpolare [skrepo'lare] [1] VT (*pelle, labbra*) to chap, crack; (*mani*) to chap; (*intonaco*) to crack.

[2] **screpolarsi** VIP (*vedi vt*) to chap; to crack.

screpolato, a [skrepo'lato] AGG (*vedi vt*) chapped; cracked.

screpolatura [skrepola'tura] SF (*su pelle, labbra, mani*) chap; (*su intonaco*) crack, cracking *no pl*.

screziato, a [skret'tsjato] AGG (*striato*) streaked.

screzio, zi ['skrɛttsjo] SM friction, disagreement; **hanno avuto degli screzi** there was some friction between them.

scribacchiare [skribak'kjare] VT to scribble.

scribacchino [skribak'kino] SM (*pegg: impiegato*) penpusher; (: *scrittore*) hack.

scricchiolare [skrikkjo'lare] VI (*aus avere*) to creak, squeak.

scricchiolio, lii [skrikkjo'lio] SM creaking.

scricciolo ['skrittʃolo] SM (*uccello*) wren; **è uno scricciolo** (*fig: persona gracile*) she's like a little bird.

scrigno ['skriɲɲo] SM casket.

scriminatura [skrimina'tura] SF (*di capelli*) parting.

scripo ['skripo] SM (*Bot*) deer grass.

scrissi *ecc* ['skrissi] VB vedi **scrivere**.

scriteriato, a [skrite'rjato] [1] AGG scatterbrained.

[2] SM/F scatterbrain.

scritta ['skritta] SF (*iscrizione*) inscription; (*avviso*) notice; **cosa dice la scritta sul cartello?** what does the (writing on the) sign say?

scritto, a ['skritto] [1] PP di **scrivere**.

[2] AGG (*lingua, esame*) written.

[3] SM **a** (*lettera*) letter, note; **per** *o* **in scritto** in writing **b** (*opera*) work; **gli scritti di** the works *o* the writings of.

scrittoio, oi [skrit'tojo] SM (writing-)desk.

scrittore, trice [skrit'tore] SM/F writer, author.

scrittura [skrit'tura] SF **a** (*calligrafia*) (hand)writing; **avere una bella/brutta scrittura** to have good/bad handwriting

b (*Rel*): **la Sacra Scrittura** the Scriptures *pl*

c (*Cine, Teatro, TV: contratto*) contract

d (*Dir*) document ▶**scrittura privata** parol, contract

e (*Comm*): **scritture** SFPL accounts, books ▶**scritture contabili** (account) books.

scritturare [skrittu'rare] VT **a** (*Cine, Teatro, TV*) to engage, sign on *o* up **b** (*Comm*) to enter.

scrivania [skriva'nia] SF (writing-)desk.

scrivano [skri'vano] SM (*amanuense*) scribe; (*impiegato*) clerk.

scrivente [skri'vɛnte] SM/F writer.

scrivere ['skrivere] VT IRREG (*gen*) to write; **scrivere qc a qn** to write sth to sb; **scrivere qc a macchina** to type sth; **scrivere a penna/matita** to write in pen/pencil; **scrivere**

qc maiuscolo/minuscolo to write sth in capital/small letters; **scrivere alla lavagna** to write on the blackboard; **come si scrive questa parola?** how do you write *o* spell this word?; **era scritto che dovesse succedere** (*fig*) it was fated *o* bound to happen.

scroccare [skrok'kare] VT (*fam*) to scrounge, cadge.

scrocco[1] ['skrɔkko] SM: **vivere a scrocco** (*fam*) to be a sponger.

scrocco[2], **chi** ['skrɔkko] SM **a** (*rumore*) click **b** : **coltello a scrocco** jack-knife.

scroccone, a [skrok'kone] SM/F (*fam*) scrounger, sponger.

scrofa ['skrɔfa] SF (*Zool*) sow.

scrollare [skrol'lare] **1** VT **a** (*scuotere*) to shake; **scrollare la testa** to shake one's head; **scrollare le spalle** to shrug one's shoulders **b** : **scrollarsi qc di dosso** to shake sth off; (*fig: malinconia, stanchezza*) to shrug sth off.
2 scrollarsi VIP to shake o.s.; (*fig*) to stir o.s., give o.s. a shake.

scrollata [skrol'lata] SF shake; **dare una scrollata a qc** to give sth a shake; **scrollata di spalle** shrug (of one's shoulders).

scrosciante [skroʃ'ʃante] AGG (*pioggia*) pouring; (*fig: applausi*) thunderous.

scrosciare [skroʃ'ʃare] VI (*aus avere o essere*) (*pioggia*) to pelt down, pour down; (*torrente*) to thunder, roar; **gli applausi scrosciavano** there was thunderous applause.

scroscio, sci ['skrɔʃʃo] SM (*di torrente, cascata*) roar; (*di applausi*) thunder; **sentivamo lo scroscio della pioggia** we could hear the rain pelting down.

scrostare [skros'tare] **1** VT (*vernice, intonaco*) to scrape off, strip (off); (*tubo*) to descale; **scrostare una ferita** to remove the scab (from a wound).
2 scrostarsi VIP (*vernice, intonaco*) to peel off, flake off.

scroto ['skrɔto] SM (*Anat*) scrotum.

scrupolo ['skrupolo] SM (*morale*) scruple; (*diligenza*) care, conscientiousness; **scrupolo morale** OR **scrupolo di coscienza** scruple; **essere senza scrupoli** to be unscrupulous; **non farti tanti scrupoli con lui** I wouldn't have any scruples about him if I were you; **lavoro fatto con scrupolo** a conscientious piece of work; **è onesto fino allo scrupolo** he's scrupulously honest.

scrupolosamente [skrupolosa'mente] AVV scrupulously.

scrupolosità [skrupolosi'ta] SF (*vedi agg*) scrupulousness; conscientiousness.

scrupoloso, a [skrupo'loso] AGG (*onesto*) scrupulous; (*diligente*) conscientious.

scrutare [skru'tare] VT (*orizzonte, vallata*) to scan; (*cielo, volto*) to search; (*persona*) to scrutinize; (*intenzioni, causa*) to examine, scrutinize.

scrutatore, trice [skruta'tore] **1** AGG (*sguardo*) searching.
2 SM/F (*di votazione*) scrutineer.

scrutinare [skruti'nare] VT (*voti*) to scrutinize, count.

scrutinatore, trice [skrutina'tore] SM/F scrutineer.

scrutinio, ni [skru'tinjo] SM **a** (*votazione*) ballot; (*insieme delle operazioni*) poll; **scrutinio segreto** secret ballot **b** (*Scol*) (*meeting for*) *assignment of marks at end of a term or year.*

scucire [sku'tʃire] **1** VT (*abito, tasca*) to unstitch, unpick, undo; (*fam: soldi*) to fork out.
2 scucirsi VIP to come unstitched.

scucito, a [sku'tʃito] AGG unstitched.

scuderia [skude'ria] SF (*stalla*) stable; (*Aut*) team.

scudetto [sku'detto] SM (*Sport*) (championship) shield;

hanno vinto lo scudetto they won the national championship.

scudiero [sku'djɛro] SM squire.

scudiscio, sci [sku'diʃʃo] SM (riding) crop, (riding) whip.

scudo ['skudo] SM (*gen*) shield; **farsi scudo di *o* con qc** to shield o.s. with sth ▸ **scudo aereo** air defence (*Brit*) *o* defense (*Am*) ▸ **scudo missilistico** missile defence (*Brit*) *o* defense (*Am*) ▸ **scudo termico** heat shield.

scuffiare [skuf'fjare] VI (*aus avere*) (*barca*) to capsize.

scugnizzo [skuɲ'ɲittso] SM street urchin.

sculacciare [skulat'tʃare] VT to spank.

sculacciata [skulat'tʃata] SF, **sculaccione** [skulat'tʃone] SM spanking; **dare una sculacciata a qn** to spank sb, give sb a spanking.

sculettare [skulet'tare] VI (*aus avere*) to sway one's hips, wiggle one's hips.

scultore, trice [skul'tore] SM/F (*di pietra*) sculptor/sculptress; (*di legno*) woodcarver.

scultoreo, a [skul'tɔreo] AGG of sculpture, sculptural; **arte scultorea** sculpture.

scultura [skul'tura] SF (*di pietra*) sculpture; (*di legno*) woodcarving.

scuola ['skwɔla] **1** SF **a** (*istituzione, edificio*) school; **andare a scuola** to go to school; **non c'è scuola domani** there's no school tomorrow; **ci vediamo dopo la scuola** see you after school ▸ **scuola elementare** primary (*Brit*) *o* grade (*Am*) school (*attended by children aged 6 - 11*) ▸ **scuola guida** driving school ▸ **scuola materna** nursery school (*attended by children aged 3 - 6*) ▸ **scuola media inferiore** *school for pupils aged 11 - 14: education beyond this level is not compulsory* ▸ **scuola media superiore** secondary school, *schooling beyond age 14: pupils choose between a 5 year course at the liceo, 4 years at the istituto magistrale or 3 - 5 years at the istituto tecnico e professionale* ▸ **scuola dell'obbligo** compulsory education ▸ **scuola privata** private school ▸ **scuola pubblica** state school (*Brit*), public school (*Am*)
b (*Arte*) school; **un artista che ha fatto scuola** an artist who has developed a following.
2 AGG INV: **nave scuola** training ship.

scuolabus ['skwɔlabus] SM INV school bus.

scuotere ['skwɔtere] VB IRREG **1** VT **a** (*anche fig*) to shake; **scuotere la testa** to shake one's head; **scuotere le spalle** to shrug one's shoulders; **cercò di scuoterlo dalla sua apatia** he tried to shake him out of *o* rouse him from his apathy
b : **scuotersi di dosso qc** to shake sth off; (*fig: malinconia, stanchezza*) to shrug sth off.
2 scuotersi VIP to shake o.s.; (*fig*) to stir o.s.; **scuotersi dall'apatia** to rouse o.s. from one's apathy.

scure ['skure] SF axe (*Brit*), ax (*Am*).

scurire [sku'rire] **1** VT to darken, make darker.
2 VI (*aus essere*), **scurirsi** VIP to darken, become dark, grow dark.

scuro[1], **a** ['skuro] **1** AGG (*colore, vestito, capelli*) dark; **avere una faccia scura** to have a grim expression on one's face.
2 SM (*colore*) dark colour (*Brit*) *o* color (*Am*); **vestire di scuro** to wear dark colo(u)rs.

scuro[2] ['skuro] SM (*di finestra*) (window) shutter.

scurrile [skur'rile] AGG scurrilous.

scurrilità [skurrili'ta] SF INV (*qualità*) scurrility; (*parola*) obscenity.

scusa ['skuza] SF **a** *(gen)* apology; **vi prego di accettare le mie scuse** please accept my apologies; **chiedere scusa a qn per qc** to apologize to sb for sth; **chiedo** *o* **domando scusa** I apologize, I beg your pardon; **fare/presentare le proprie scuse** to make/give one's apologies

b *(pretesto)* excuse; **cercare una scusa/delle scuse** to look for an excuse/excuses; **questa è una scusa bella e buona!** that's some excuse!; **non c'è scusa che tenga!** there's no possible excuse!

scusare [sku'zare] **1** VT *(gen)* to excuse; *(perdonare)* to forgive; **scusare qn di** *o* **per qc** to forgive sb for sth; **scusami** OR **scusa** OR **mi scusi** (I'm) sorry; *(più formale)* I beg your pardon; **scusa il ritardo** I'm sorry I'm late; **tutto questo non ti scusa** this is no excuse; **scusi, sa dirmi dove...?** excuse me, can you tell me where ...?.

2 scusarsi VR: to apologize; **scusarsi con qn di** *o* **per qc** to apologize to sb for sth; **si è scusato del ritardo** he apologized for being late; **potresti almeno scusarti** you could at least say you're sorry; **non so come scusarmi** I don't know how to apologize; **non cercare di scusarti!** don't look for excuses!

S.C.V. SIGLA = *Stato della Città del Vaticano.*

sdaziare [zdat'tsjare] VT to pay customs duties on.

sdebitarsi [zdebi'tarsi] VR: **sdebitarsi (con qn di** *o* **per qc)** *(anche fig)* to repay (sb for sth).

sdegnare [zdeɲ'ɲare] **1** VT *(disprezzare)* to scorn, despise.

2 sdegnarsi VIP *(arrabbiarsi)*: **sdegnarsi (con)** to get angry (with).

sdegnato, a [zdeɲ'ɲato] AGG indignant, angry.

sdegno ['zdeɲɲo] SM *(disprezzo)* scorn, disdain; *(indignazione)* indignation.

sdegnosamente [zdeɲɲosa'mente] AVV scornfully, contemptuously, disdainfully.

sdegnosità [zdeɲɲosi'ta] SF scorn, disdain.

sdegnoso, a [zdeɲ'ɲoso] AGG scornful, contemptuous, disdainful.

sdentare [zden'tare] **1** VT *(sega)* to break the teeth of.

2 sdentarsi VIP to lose one's teeth.

sdentato, a [zden'tato] AGG *(senza denti: persona)* toothless; *(: sega)* without teeth.

sdilinquirsi [zdilin'kwirsi] VIP *(illanguidirsi)* to become sentimental.

sdoganare [zdoga'nare] VT *(Comm)* to clear through customs.

sdolcinatamente [zdoltʃinata'mente] AVV *(comportarsi, parlare)* in an affected way.

sdolcinato, a [zdoltʃi'nato] AGG *(persona)* gushing; *(parole)* sugary; *(modi)* affected; *(film, libro)* oversentimental, mawkish.

sdoppiamento [zdoppja'mento] SM *(Chim: di composto)* splitting; *(Psic)*: **sdoppiamento della personalità** split personality.

sdoppiare [zdop'pjare] VT, **sdoppiarsi** VIP to divide *o* split in two.

sdraiare [zdra'jare] **1** VT to lay down; **sdraiare qn a terra/sul letto** to lay sb down on the ground/on the bed.

2 sdraiarsi VR to lie down; **sdraiarsi a terra/sul letto** to lie down on the ground/on the bed; **sdraiarsi al sole** to stretch out in the sun.

sdraiato, a [zdra'jato] AGG lying down; **mettersi sdraiato** to lie down.

sdraio, ai ['zdrajo] SM *(anche:* **sedia a sdraio)** deckchair.

sdrammatizzare [zdrammatid'dzare] VT to play down, minimize.

sdrucciolare [zdruttʃo'lare] VI *(aus* **avere** *o* **essere)** *(persona)* to slip, slide.

sdrucciolevole [zdruttʃo'levole] AGG slippery.

sdrucciolo, a ['zdruttʃolo] **1** AGG *(Ling)* proparoxytone. **2** SM trisyllabic verse.

sdrucito, a [zdru'tʃito] AGG *(strappato)* torn; *(logoro)* threadbare.

---

se¹ [se]

1 CONG

a *(condizionale, concessiva)* if;

▷**se** *fosse* **più furbo verrebbe** if he were smarter he would come

▷**se** *fosse* **stato interessato sarebbe venuto** if he had been interested he would have come

▷**se** *fossi* **in te** if I were you

▷**deve essere così se** *lo dice* **lui** it must be so if he says so

▷**se** *nevica* **non vengo** OR **se** *nevicherà* **non verrò** I won't come if it snows

▷**se invece** *preferisci* **questo...** should you *o* if you prefer this one ...

b *(dubitativa, in domande indirette)* whether, if;

▷**mi** *chiedevo* **se avesse capito** I wondered whether he had understood

▷*guarda* **lì se c'è** look and see whether *o* if it's there

▷**non** *so* **se scrivere** *o* **telefonare** I don't known whether *o* if I should write or phone

▷**lo so io se mi manca** I know how much I miss him

c *(ottativa)* if only;

▷**se** *(solo)* **me l'avesse detto prima!** if only he had told me earlier!

▷**se** *ci fosse* **ancora lui!** if only he were still here!

d *(fraseologia)*

▷*come* **se** as if

▷*come* **se non lo sapesse!** as if he didn't know!

▷**e se andassimo in montagna?** how about going to the mountains?

▷**ma se l'ho visto io!** but I saw it myself!

▷**se** *mai* **passassi per di qua** should you ever *o* if ever you pass this way

▷**lascialo nell'atrio se** *mai* leave it in the hall if necessary

▷**siamo noi se** *mai* **che le siamo grati** it is we who should be grateful to you

▷**se** *no* *(altrimenti)* or (else), otherwise

▷**non fiatare, se** *no* **vedi!** don't breathe a word or else!

▷**mangia, se** *no* **non reggi fino a stasera** eat up, otherwise *o* or else you'll be starving by this evening

▷**scappo se** *no* **perdo l'autobus** I must dash or I'll miss the bus

▷**se** *non* *(anzi)* if not; *(tranne)* except

▷**costa lo stesso, se** *non* **meno** it costs the same, if not less

▷**non lo darò a nessuno se** *non* **a lui** I won't give it to anybody except *o* other than *o* but him

▷**se** *non altro* if nothing else, at least

▷**se** *non altro* **non disturba** at least he's no trouble

▷**se** *poi* **decidesse di restare** should he decide *o* were he to decide to stay

▷e se *poi* se ne accorge? and what if he notices?
▷se pure = seppure.
2 SM if;
▷c'è solo *un* grosso se there's just one big if.

se² [se]; vedi **si¹**.

sé [se] PRON RIFLESSIVO (*gen*) oneself; (*maschile*) himself; (*femminile*) herself; (*neutro*) itself; (*pl*) themselves; **l'ha fatto da sé** he did it (all) by himself; **lo portò con sé** he took it with him; **pensa solo a sé** *o* **se stesso** he thinks only of himself; **è piena di sé** she's full of herself; **di per sé non è un problema** it's no problem in itself; **parlare tra sé e sé** to talk to oneself; **tornare in sé** to come to (one's senses); **va da sé che...** it goes without saying that ..., it's obvious that ..., it stands to reason that ...; **è un caso a sé (stante)** it's a special case; **si chiude da sé** (*porta*) it closes automatically; **un uomo che s'è fatto da sé** a self-made man; **chi fa da sé fa per tre** (*Proverbio*) if you want something done well *o* properly do it yourself.

S.E. ABBR **a** (= *sud-est*) SE **b** (= *Sua Eccellenza*) HE.

S.E.A.T.O. [se'ato] SIGLA F SEATO (= *Southeast Asia Treaty Organization*).

sebaceo, a [se'batʃeo] AGG sebaceous.

sebbene [seb'bɛne] CONG (even) though, although; **sebbene non sia colpa sua...** although *o* (even) though it is not his fault ...; **lo farò, sebbene mi pesi molto** I'll do it, even though I'm not very happy about it.

sebo ['sɛbo] SM sebum.

sec. ABBR (= *secolo*) c. (= *century*).

SECAM ['sɛkam] SIGLA M (= *séquentiel couleur à mémoire*) SECAM.

secante [se'kante] SF (*Mat*) secant.

secca, che ['sekka] SF (*Naut*) bank, shallows *pl*; **andare in secca** to run aground.

seccamente [sekka'mente] AVV (*rispondere, rifiutare*) sharply, curtly.

seccante [sek'kante] AGG tiresome, annoying.

seccare [sek'kare] **1** VT **a** (*gen*) to dry; (*prosciugare*) to dry (up); (*fiori: far appassire*) to wither
b (*infastidire*) to annoy, bother; **questa volta mi hai proprio seccato** I've had enough of you this time; **ti secca se aspetto qui?** do you mind if I wait here?; **se ti secca chiederglielo lo faccio io** if you don't like to ask him I'll do it; **mi secca fare tutta questa fila** it annoys me having to queue like this.
2 VI (*aus* essere) to dry (up).
3 **seccarsi** VIP **a** (*diventar secco: gen*) to dry (up); (*pelle*) to become dry; (*fiori*) to wither
b (*infastidirsi*) to become annoyed, grow annoyed; **si è seccato molto** he got very annoyed.

seccato, a [sek'kato] AGG (*fig: infastidito*) bothered, annoyed; (: *stufo*) fed up.

seccatore, trice [sekka'tore] SM/F nuisance, bother.

seccatura [sekka'tura] SF nuisance, bother *no pl*, trouble *no pl*; **che seccatura!** what a nuisance!

seccherò *ecc* [sekke'rɔ] VB vedi **seccare**.

secchia ['sekkja] SF bucket, pail.

secchiata [sek'kjata] SF bucket(ful).

secchiello [sek'kjɛllo] SM (*per bambini*) bucket, pail ▶**secchiello del ghiaccio** ice bucket.

secchio, chi ['sekkjo] SM bucket, pail ▶**secchio della spazzatura** *o* **delle immondizie** dustbin (*Brit*), garbage

can (*Am*), trash can (*Am*).

secchione, a [sek'kjone] SM/F (*fam pegg*) swot (*Brit*), grind (*Am*).

secco, a, chi, che ['sekko] **1** AGG **a** (*gen*) dry; (*terreno*) arid, dry; (*uva, fichi, pesce*) dried; (*foglie, ramo*) withered; (*fig: risposta*) sharp; **avere la gola secca** to feel dry, be parched; **un no secco** a curt no; **un colpo secco** a sharp blow
b (*persona: magro*) thin, skinny; **secco come un chiodo** as thin as a rake
c (*fraseologia*): **fare secco qn** (*assassinare*) to knock sb off; **ci è rimasto secco** (*fig: morto*) it killed him.
2 SM **a** (*di clima*) dryness; (*siccità*) drought
b (*fraseologia*): **lavare a secco** to dry-clean; **tirare a secco** (*barca*) to beach; **essere a secco (di soldi)** to be broke; **rimanere a secco di benzina** to run out of petrol (*Brit*) *o* gas (*Am*).

secentesco, a, schi, sche [setʃen'tesko] AGG seventeenth-century.

secernere [se'tʃɛrnere] VT to secrete.

secessione [setʃes'sjone] SF (*Pol*) secession.

secolare [seko'lare] AGG **a** (*antico*) centuries-old, age-old
b (*laico*) secular, lay *attr*; **clero secolare** lay clergy.

secolarizzare [sekolarit'tsare] VT to secularize.

secolo ['sɛkolo] SM **a** century; (*epoca*) century, age; **nel terzo secolo a.C.** in the third century B.C.; **nel nostro secolo** this century; **l'avvenimento del secolo** the event of the century; **il secolo della Ragione** the Age of Reason; **per tutti i secoli dei secoli** (*Rel*) forever and ever; **Giovanni Paolo II, al secolo Carol Wojtyla** John Paul II, whose original name was Carol Wojtyla
b (*fig*): **è un secolo che non ti vedo** I haven't seen you in ages; **è un secolo che aspetto** I've been waiting for ages.

seconda [se'konda] **1** SF **a** (*Aut*) second (gear)
b (*Scol: elementare*) ≈ first year (at primary school) (*Brit*), ≈ second grade (*Am*); (: *media*) ≈ first year (at secondary school) (*Brit*), ≈ seventh grade (*Am*); (: *superiore*) ≈ fourth year (at secondary school) (*Brit*), ≈ tenth grade (*Am*)
c (*Ferr*) second class; **viaggiare in seconda** to travel second class; **un biglietto di seconda** a second-class ticket
d : **comandante in seconda** second-in-command.
2 : **a seconda di** PREP according to, in accordance with.

secondariamente [sekondarja'mente] AVV secondly.

secondario, ria, ri, rie [sekon'darjo] AGG secondary, minor; **di secondaria importanza** of secondary *o* minor importance; **scuola/istruzione secondaria** secondary school/education.

secondino [sekon'dino] SM prison officer, warder (*Brit*), prison guard (*Am*).

secondo¹, a [se'kondo] **1** AGG (*gen*) second; **in seconda fila** in the second row; **in secondo luogo** in the second place; **si è classificato al secondo posto** he came second; **figlio di seconde nozze** son by a second marriage; **passare a seconde nozze** to remarry, marry for a second time; **elevare alla seconda (potenza)** (*Mat*) to raise to the power of two; **Carlo secondo** Charles the Second; **è un secondo Picasso** he's another *o* a second Picasso; **un albergo di second'ordine** a second-class hotel; **di seconda mano** (*oggetto, informazione*) second-hand; **avere un secondo fine** to have an ulterior motive.
2 SM **a** (*tempo*) second; **aspetta un secondo!** wait a moment!

b (anche: **secondo piatto**) main course, second course. 3 SM/F second (person); **sei il secondo che me lo dice** you're the second person to tell me that per fraseologia vedi **quinto.**

secondo² [se'kondo] PREP **a** (in base a, nell'opinione di) according to; (nel modo prescritto da, stando a) in accordance with; **secondo lui** according to him, in his opinion; **secondo me** in my opinion; **secondo le mie possibilità** according to my means; **il Vangelo secondo Matteo** the Gospel according to St Matthew; **secondo la legge/quanto si era deciso** in accordance with the law/the decision taken; **agire secondo coscienza** to follow one's conscience

b (in direzione di: vento, corrente) with; (: linea) along.

secondogenito, a [sekondo'dʒɛnito] SM/F second-born.

secrêtaire [sokre'tɛr] SM INV secretaire, writing desk.

secrezione [sekret'tsjone] SF (Bio) secretion.

sedano ['sɛdano] SM celery ▶ **sedano rapa** celeriac.

sedare [se'dare] VT **a** (dolore) to soothe **b** (rivolta) to put down, suppress.

sedativo, a [seda'tivo] AGG, SM (Med) sedative.

sede ['sɛde] SF **a** (luogo di residenza) (place of) residence; **prendere sede** to take up residence; **cambiare sede** to change one's residence

b (di società: principale) head office; (: secondaria) branch (office); (di partito) headquarters pl; (di governo, parlamento) seat; (Rel) see; **la Santa Sede** the Holy See; **un'azienda con diverse sedi in città** a firm with several branches in the city; **il presidente è fuori sede** the chairman is not in the office ▶ **sede sociale** registered office

c (località) site; **Londra sarà sede di un'importante mostra** London will be the site of an important exhibition

d : **in sede di** (in occasione di) during; **in sede d'esame** during the exam; **in sede di discussione** during the discussion; **in sede legislativa** in legislative sitting; **in altra sede** on another occasion.

sedentario, ria, ri, rie [seden'tarjo] AGG sedentary.

sedere¹ [se'dere] VB IRREG 1 VI (aus essere) **a** (essere seduto) to be sitting, be seated; **sedeva a tavola** he was sitting at table; **posto a sedere** seat; **siede in Parlamento** he has a seat in Parliament

b (mettersi seduto) to sit (down); **siedi qui** sit here; **mettiti a sedere** sit down, take a seat; **sieda per cortesia** please sit down, please take a seat; **mettersi seduto** (da posizione orizzontale) to sit up.

2 **sedersi** VIP to sit (down); **siediti qui** sit down (here); **sedersi per terra** (in casa) to sit on the floor; (all'esterno) to sit on the ground.

sedere² [se'dere] SM (deretano) bottom; **lo ha spedito fuori a calci nel sedere** he kicked him out.

sedia ['sɛdja] SF chair ▶ **sedia elettrica** electric chair ▶ **sedia pieghevole** folding chair ▶ **sedia a rotelle** wheelchair.

sedicenne [sedi'tʃɛnne] AGG, SM/F sixteen-year-old per fraseologia vedi **cinquantenne.**

sedicente [sedi'tʃɛnte] AGG self-styled.

sedicesimo, a [sedi'tʃɛzimo] AGG, SM/F, SM **a** sixteenth **b** (Tip): **in sedicesimo** sexto decimo per fraseologia vedi **quinto.**

sedici ['seditʃi] AGG INV, SM INV sixteen per fraseologia vedi **cinque.**

sedile [se'dile] SM (in automezzi) seat.

sedimentare [sedimen'tare] VI (aus **essere** o **avere**) to leave o deposit a sediment.

sedimentario, ria, ri, rie [sedimen'tarjo] AGG sedimentary.

sedimento [sedi'mento] SM sediment.

sedizione [sedit'tsjone] SF uprising, insurrection.

sediziosamente [sedittsjosa'mente] AVV seditiously.

sedizioso, a [sedit'tsjoso] 1 AGG seditious.

2 SM/F insurrectionist.

sedotto, a [se'dotto] PP di **sedurre.**

seducente [sedu'tʃɛnte] AGG (donna) seductive; (proposta) very attractive.

sedurre [se'durre] VT IRREG **a** (abusare di) to seduce **b** (affascinare) to charm, captivate; (: sogg: idea) to appeal to.

seduta [se'duta] SF (gen) session, sitting; **essere in seduta** to be in session, be sitting; **seduta stante** (fig: immediatamente) straight away, immediately ▶ **seduta spiritica** seance.

seduttore, trice [sedut'tore] SM/F seducer/seductress.

seduzione [sedut'tsjone] SF (vedi vb) seduction; charm; appeal.

S.E.eO. ABBR (= salvo errori e omissioni) E and OE.

sega, ghe ['sega] SF **a** (Tecn) saw ▶ **sega circolare** circular saw ▶ **sega a mano** handsaw **b** : **farsi una sega** (fam!: masturbarsi) to have a wank (Brit fam!), to jerk off (Am fam!); **non capire una sega** (fam) to understand damn all.

segala ['segala], **segale** ['segale] SF (Bot) rye.

segare [se'gare] VT to saw; (in più parti) to saw up; **segare via** to saw off; **segare in due** to saw in two; **le corde le segavano i polsi** the ropes were cutting into her wrists.

segatrice [sega'tritʃe] SF: **segatrice a disco** circular saw ▶ **segatrice a nastro** band saw.

segatura [sega'tura] SF sawdust.

seggio, gi ['sɛddʒo] SM **a** (gen) seat **b** : **seggio elettorale** polling station.

seggiola ['sɛddʒola] SF chair.

seggiolino [sɛddʒo'lino] SM seat; (per bambini) child's chair ▶ **seggiolino di sicurezza** (su auto) child safety seat.

seggiolone [sɛddʒo'lone] SM (per bambini) highchair.

seggiovia [sɛddʒo'via] SF chair lift.

segheria [sege'ria] SF sawmill.

segherò ecc [sege'rɔ] VB vedi **segare.**

seghettare [seget'tare] VT to serrate.

seghettato, a [seget'tato] AGG serrated.

seghettatura [segetta'tura] SF serration.

seghetto [se'getto] SM hacksaw.

segmentare [segmen'tare] VT to segment.

segmentazione [segmentat'tsjone] SF segmentation.

segmento [seg'mento] SM segment.

segnalamento [seɲɲala'mento] SM signalling.

segnalare [seɲɲa'lare] 1 VT (essere segno di) to indicate, be a sign of; (avvertire) to signal; (menzionare) to indicate; (: fatto, risultato, aumento, guasto) to report; (: errore, dettaglio) to point out; **segnalare una svolta a sinistra** (Aut) to indicate o signal a left turn; **segnalare la posizione di una nave** to signal the position of a ship; **niente da segnalare** nothing to report; **segnalare qn a qn** (per lavoro) to bring sb to sb's attention.

2 **segnalarsi** VR (distinguersi) to distinguish o.s.

segnalazione [seɲɲalat'tsjone] SF **a** (azione) signalling; (segnale) signal ▶ **segnalazioni acustiche** acoustic o

sound signals

b (*annuncio*) report; (*raccomandazione*) recommendation.

segnale [sen'nale] SM (*gen*) signal; **ad un suo segnale tutti uscirono** when he gave the signal *o* sign everybody went out ▶ **segnale acustico** acoustic *o* sound signal ▶ **segnale d'allarme** alarm; (*sui treni*) communication cord (*Brit*) ▶ **segnale di linea libera** (*Telec*) dialling (*Brit*) *o* dial (*Am*) tone ▶ **segnale luminoso** light signal ▶ **segnale di occupato** (*Telec*) engaged tone (*Brit*), busy signal (*Am*) ▶ **segnale orario** (*Radio, TV*) time signal ▶ **segnale stradale** road sign.

segnaletica [senna'lɛtika] SF: **segnaletica (stradale)** road signs *pl*, traffic signs *pl*.

segnalibro [senna'libro] SM bookmark(er).

segnaposto [senna'posto] SM INV place card.

segnaprezzo [senna'prɛttso] SM INV (*anche:* **cartellino segnaprezzo**) price tag.

segnapunti [senna'punti] **1** SM/F INV scorer, scorekeeper. **2** SM INV scorecard.

segnare [sen'nare] **1** VT **a** (*fare un segno: gen*) to mark; (*scalfire*) to score, mark, cut into; (*graffiare*) to scratch; **segnare il passo** (*Mil, anche fig*) to mark time; **è molto segnato da quell'esperienza** that experience has left its mark on him; **aveva il volto segnato dalla stanchezza** his face was drawn and tired

b (*annotare*) to make a note of, jot down, note; **segna quanto ti devo** make a note of what I owe you

c (*indicare*) to show, indicate, mark; **quella lancetta serve a segnare le ore** that hand shows *o* indicates the hours; **il mio orologio segna le 5** my watch says 5 o'clock; **segnare a dito** to point at; **essere segnato a dito** (*fig*) to be talked about

d (*Sport*) to score.

2 segnarsi VR (*Rel*) to cross o.s., make the sign of the cross.

segnatura [senna'tura] SF (*in archivio, biblioteca*) shelf mark, pressmark (*Brit*).

segno ['senno] **1** SM **a** (*gen*) sign; (*traccia*) mark, sign; (*graffio*) scratch; (*indizio*) sign, indication; **lasciare un segno** (*anche fig*) to leave a mark; **non c'era segno di vita** there was no sign of life; **non ha dato segni di vita** he gave no sign of life; **è brutto segno** it's a bad sign; **in** *o* **come segno d'amicizia** as a mark *o* token of friendship; **diede segno di voler andare** he indicated that he wanted to leave; **perdere il segno** (*leggendo*) to lose one's place; **il segno dei suoi passi** his footprints *pl*; **fare segno di sì** to nod; **fare segno di no** to shake one's head; **fare segno con la mano** to make a sign with one's hand; **mi fece segno di spostarmi/avvicinarmi/fermarmi** he made a sign to me to move/come nearer/stop; **essere del segno dell'Acquario** *ecc* to be an Aquarian *ecc*

b (*bersaglio*) target; **tiro a segno** target shooting; **cogliere** *o* **colpire nel segno** to hit the target *o* mark; (*fig*) to hit the bullseye, hit the nail on the head.

2 ▶ **"segni particolari"** (*su documento*) "distinguishing marks" ▶ **il segno della croce** (*Rel*) the sign of the cross ▶ **segno meno** (*Mat*) minus sign ▶ **segno più** plus sign ▶ **segno zodiacale** sign of the zodiac.

segregare [segre'gare] **1** VT (*gen*) to segregate; (*pazzo*) to confine.

2 segregarsi VIP (*fig: isolarsi*): **segragarsi in casa** to shut o.s. up in the house.

segregazione [segregat'tsjone] SF segregation.

segregazionismo [segregattsjo'nizmo] SM segregationism.

segregazionista, i, e [segregattsjo'nista] AGG, SM/F segregationist.

segreta [se'greta] SF dungeon.

segretamente [segreta'mente] AVV secretly; **riunirsi segretamente** to meet secretly *o* in secret.

segretariato [segreta'rjato] SM secretariat.

segretario, ria, ri, rie [segre'tarjo] SM/F (*gen*) secretary ▶ **segretaria di direzione** personal assistant ▶ **segretario comunale** town clerk ▶ **segretario del partito** party leader.

segreteria [segrete'ria] SF **a** (*ufficio*) secretary's office; (*in enti*) secretarial offices *pl* **b** (*Pol: carica*) secretaryship, office of Secretary; (: *segretariato*) secretariat **c** : **segreteria telefonica** answering machine.

segretezza [segre'tettsa] SF secrecy; **notizie della massima segretezza** highly confidential information *sg*; **in tutta segretezza** in secret; (*confidenzialmente*) in confidence.

segreto, a [se'greto] **1** AGG (*gen*) secret; (*documenti*) confidential, secret; **tenere segreto qc** to keep sth secret; **passaggio segreto** secret passage.

2 SM (*gen*) secret; **in segreto** in secret, secretly; (*in confidenza*) in confidence; **mantenere** *o* **tenere un segreto** to keep a secret; **il segreto professionale** professional secrecy; **un segreto professionale** a professional secret; **il segreto di Pulcinella** an open secret; **il segreto del successo** the secret of *o* key to success; **nel segreto dell'animo** in the depths of one's soul, deep down.

seguace [se'gwatʃe] SM/F (*Rel, gen*) disciple, follower.

seguente [se'gwɛnte] AGG following, next; **il giorno seguente** the next *o* following day; **i seguenti candidati sono pregati di farsi avanti** would the following candidates please come forward; **nel modo seguente** as follows, in the following way.

segugio, gi [se'gudʒo] SM **a** (*Zool*) hound, hunting dog **b** (*fig*) private eye, sleuth.

seguire [se'gwire] **1** VT **a** (*gen*) to follow; **seguire qn come un'ombra** to follow sb about like a shadow; **segui quella macchina!** follow that car!; **ha fatto seguire la moglie** he had his wife followed; **mi segua, la prego** this way *o* follow me, please; **segui la statale per 15 km** follow *o* keep to the main road for 15 km; **seguire una cura** to follow a course of treatment; **seguire i consigli di qn** to follow *o* take sb's advice; **seguire una dieta** to be on a diet; **far seguire una dieta a qn** to put sb on a diet; **le cose seguono il loro corso** things are taking *o* running their course; **seguire un programma alla TV** to watch a programme on TV; **seguire un alunno** (*fig*) to follow the progress of a pupil; **seguire gli avvenimenti di attualità** to follow *o* keep up with current events

b (*capire: persona, argomento*) to follow; **scusa, non ti seguo** I'm sorry, I don't follow (you) *o* I'm not with you

c (*corso, lezione: gen*) to follow, take; (: *essere presente a*) to attend, go to; **seguire un corso per corrispondenza** to follow *o* take a correspondence course; **non è obbligatorio seguire le lezioni** attendance at lessons is not compulsory.

2 VI (*aus essere*) **a** (*venir dopo, fig: derivare*) to follow; **come segue** as follows; **a Pio XI seguì Pio XII** Pius XI was succeeded by Pius XII; **a ciò seguì un aumento dei prezzi** this was followed by a rise in prices

b (*continuare*) to continue; **"segue"** "to be continued".

seguitare [segwi'tare] ☐1 vt to continue, carry on with; **seguitare a fare qc** to continue doing sth.

☐2 vi (*aus* **avere** o **essere**) to continue, carry on.

seguito ['segwito] sm **a** (*di persone*) retinue, suite; (*discepoli, ammiratori*) followers *pl*; **essere al seguito di qn** to be among sb's suite, be one of sb's retinue

b (*continuazione*: *di film*) sequel; (: *nuovo episodio*) continuation; (*resto*) remainder, rest; **il seguito la settimana prossima** to be continued next week; **manca il seguito** the rest is missing

c (*conseguenze*): **non aver seguito** to have no repercussions

d : **in seguito** then, later on; **in seguito a** [OR] **a seguito di** following; **facciamo seguito alla lettera del...** further to o in answer to your letter of ...; **di seguito** at a stretch, on end; **è piovuto per tre settimane di seguito** it rained non-stop for three weeks.

sei[1] ['sɛi] agg inv, sm inv six *per fraseologia vedi* **cinque**.

sei[2] ['sɛi] vb *vedi* **essere**.

Seicelle [sei'tʃɛlle] sfpl: **le (isole) Seicelle** the Seychelles.

seicentesco, a, schi, sche [seitʃen'tesko] agg seventeenth-century.

seicento [sei'tʃɛnto] ☐1 agg inv six hundred.

☐2 sm inv six hundred; (*secolo*): **il Seicento** the seventeenth century.

seimila [sei'mila] agg inv, sm inv six thousand.

selce ['seltʃe] sf flint, flintstone.

selciato [sel'tʃato] sm cobbled surface; **si sentirono i suoi passi sul selciato** you could hear his footsteps on the cobbles.

selettività [selettivi'ta] sf selectivity.

selettivo, a [selet'tivo] agg selective.

selettore [selet'tore] sm (*Tecn*) selector ►**selettore dei canali** (*TV*) channel selector.

selezionare [selettsjo'nare] vt to select, choose.

selezionatore [selettsjona'tore] sm (*Sport*) selector.

selezione [selet'tsjone] sf selection, choice; **fare una selezione** to make a selection o choice ►**selezione naturale** (*Bio*) natural selection.

sella ['sɛlla] sf saddle; **montare in sella** to mount, get into the saddle.

sellaio, ai [sel'lajo] sm saddler.

sellare [sel'lare] vt to saddle, put a saddle on.

selleria [selle'ria] sf **a** (*equipaggiamento, negozio*) saddlery; (*di scuderia*) tack room **b** (*Aut*) (interior) trim.

sellino [sel'lino] sm saddle.

seltz [sɛlts] sm inv soda (water).

selva ['selva] sf (*letter: bosco*) wood; (: *foresta*) forest; (*fig: di gente, capelli*) mass.

selvaggina [selvad'dʒina] sf game.

selvaggio, gia, gi, ge [sel'vaddʒo] ☐1 agg (*gen*) wild; (*incontrollato: fenomeno, aumento*) uncontrolled; (*tribù*) savage, primitive, uncivilized; (*pegg: omicidio*) savage, ferocious; (: *torture*) brutal, cruel; **sciopero selvaggio** wildcat strike; **inflazione selvaggia** runaway inflation.

☐2 sm/f savage.

selvatico, a, ci, che [sel'vatiko] ☐1 agg (*animali, fiori*) wild; (*fig: persona, timido*) unsociable.

☐2 sm (*di selvaggina*): **sapere di selvatico** to taste gamy; **puzzare di selvatico** to smell high o gamy.

S.Em. abbr (= *Sua Eminenza*) HE.

semaforo [se'maforo] sm (*Aut*) traffic lights *pl*; (*Ferr*) signal.

semantica [se'mantika] sf semantics *sg*.

semantico, a, ci, che [se'mantiko] agg semantic.

semantista, i, e [seman'tista] sm/f semanticist.

sembiante [sem'bjante] sm (*poet: aspetto*) appearance; (: *volto*) countenance.

sembianza [sem'bjantsa] sf (*poet*) **a** (*aspetto*) appearance **b** : **sembianze** sfpl (*lineamenti*) features; (*fig: falsa apparenza*) semblance *sg*.

sembrare [sem'brare] (*aus* **essere**) ☐1 vi (*gen*) to seem; **sembra simpatico** he seems o appears (to be) nice; **sembrava più giovane** he seemed o looked younger; **sembra suo padre** he looks like his father; **sembra caffè** it tastes like coffee; **al tocco sembrava seta** it felt like silk; **sembra odore di bruciato** it smells as if something is burning.

☐2 vb impers: **sembra che** it seems that; **mi sembra che...** (*ho l'impressione*) it seems to me that ..., it looks to me as though ...; (*penso*) I think (that) ..., I have a feeling that ...; **ti sembra giusto?** do you think it's fair?; **non gli sembrava onesto farlo** he didn't think it was honest to do it; **le sembra di sapere tutto** she thinks she knows everything; **fai come ti sembra** do as you please o as you see fit; **non mi sembra vero!** I can't believe it!

seme ['seme] sm **a** (*gen*) seed; (*di agrumi, mela, pera*) pip; (*di ciliegia, pesca*) stone; **gettare il seme della discordia** to sow the seeds of discord **b** (*Anat: sperma*) semen **c** (*Carte*) suit.

semeiotica [seme'jɔtika] sf semiotics *sg*.

semente [se'mente] sf seed.

semestrale [semes'trale] agg (*che dura 6 mesi*) six-month *attr*; (*che avviene ogni 6 mesi*) six-monthly.

semestre [se'mɛstre] sm (*gen*) six months *pl*, six-month period, half-year; (*Scol*) semester; **nel primo semestre dell'anno** in the first half of the year.

semi... ['sɛmi] pref semi... .

semiaperto, a [semia'pɛrto] agg half-open.

semiasse [semi'asse] sm (*Aut*) drive shaft.

semiautomatico, a, ci, che [semiauto'matiko] agg semiautomatic.

semibreve [semi'brɛve] sf (*Mus*) semibreve (*Brit*), whole note (*Am*).

semicerchio, chi [semi'tʃɛrkjo] sm semicircle.

semichiuso, a [semi'kjuso] agg half shut; **lasciare la porta semichiusa** to leave the door ajar.

semicircolare [semitʃirko'lare] agg semicircular.

semiconduttore [semikondut'tore] sm semiconductor.

semicroma [semi'krɔma] sf (*Mus*) semiquaver (*Brit*), sixteenth note (*Am*).

semidetenzione [semideten'tsjone] sf *custodial sentence of a minimum 10 hours per day in prison*.

semidistrutto, a [semidis'trutto] agg partly destroyed.

semifinale [semifi'nale] sf (*Sport*) semifinal.

semifinalista, i, e [semifina'lista] sm/f semifinalist.

semifreddo [semi'freddo] sm (*Culin*) *chilled dessert made with ice cream*.

semilavorato, a [semilavo'rato] agg semifinished.

semilibertà [semiliber'ta] sf *custodial sentence allowing part-time study or work outside prison*.

semiminima [semi'minima] sf (*Mus*) crotchet (*Brit*), quarter note (*Am*).

semina ['semina] sf (*Agr*) sowing; **periodo della semina** sowing time.

seminale [semi'nale] agg (*Anat*) seminal, sperm *attr*.

seminare [semi'nare] vt **a** (*Agr*) to sow; (*fig: vestiti, libri*) to

scatter, leave lying around; **chi non semina non raccoglie** (*Proverbio*) as you sow, so shall you reap **b** (*inseguitore*) to lose, shake off.

seminario, ri [semi'narjo] SM **a** (*Rel*) seminary **b** (*Scol*) seminar.

seminativo, a [semina'tivo] AGG (*terreno*) arable.

seminato [semi'nato] SM: **uscire dal seminato** (*fig*) to wander off the point.

seminatore [semina'tore] SM sower.

seminatrice [semina'tritʃe] SF (*macchina*) seeder.

seminfermità [seminfermi'ta] SF (*Med*) partial infirmity.

seminterrato [seminter'rato] SM (*piano*) basement; (*appartamento*) basement flat (*Brit*) o apartment (*Am*).

seminudo, a [semi'nudo] AGG half-naked.

semiologia [semjolo'dʒia] SF semiology.

semiologico, a, ci, che [semio'lɔdʒiko] AGG semiological.

semiologo, a, gi, ghe [se'mjɔlogo] SM/F semiologist.

semioscurità [semioskuri'ta] SF half-light, semi-darkness.

semiotica [se'mjɔtika] SF semiotics *sg*.

semipermeabile [semiperme'abile] AGG (*terreno*) selectively permeable.

semireazione [semireat'tsjone] SF (*Chim*) half-reaction.

semisecco, a [semi'sekko] AGG (*vino*) medium-dry.

semiserio, ria, ri, rie [semi'sɛrjo] AGG half-serious.

semitico, a, ci, che [se'mitiko] AGG Semitic.

semitono [semi'tɔno] SM (*Mus*) semitone (*Brit*), half step (*Am*).

semivuoto, a [semi'vwɔto] AGG half empty.

semmai [sem'mai] **= se mai**; vedi **se¹**.

semola ['semola] SF bran ▶**semola di grano duro** durum wheat.

semolato [semo'lato] AGG: **zucchero semolato** caster sugar.

semolino [semo'lino] SM semolina.

semovente [semo'vɛnte] AGG self-propelled.

semplice ['semplitʃe] AGG **a** (*gen: non complicato*) simple; (*persona, modi: non affettato*) simple, unaffected; (: *ingenuo*) simple, ingenuous; **è semplice da capire** it's easy o simple to understand; **una visione della vita un po' semplice** a simplistic view of life; **è una semplice formalità** it's a mere formality; **è una semplice questione d'orgoglio** it's simply a matter of pride; **è pazzia pura e semplice** it's sheer madness; **acqua semplice** tap water
b (*Gramm*) simple
c (*Mil*): **marinaio semplice** ordinary seaman; **soldato semplice** private.

semplicemente [semplitʃe'mente] AVV **a** (*in maniera semplice*) simply, in a simple way; **parla semplicemente e lentamente** speak slowly and simply
b (*solamente*) only, merely, simply; **desidero semplicemente la verità** I merely want the truth; **è semplicemente ridicolo** it's simply ridiculous
c (*con modestia*) simply, modestly; **vive molto semplicemente** he lives very simply.

semplicione [sempli'tʃone] SM (*fam*) simpleton.

semplicistico, a, ci, che [sempli'tʃistiko] AGG simplistic.

semplicità [semplitʃi'ta] SF simplicity, simpleness.

semplificare [semplifi'kare] VT to simplify.

semplificativo, a [semplifika'tivo] AGG simplifying.

semplificazione [semplifikat'tsjone] SF simplification; **fare una semplificazione di** to simplify.

sempre ['sɛmpre] AVV **a** (*continuità*) always; (*eternamente*) always, forever; **viene sempre alle 5** he always comes at 5 o'clock; **crede di aver sempre ragione** she thinks she's always right; **ti amerò sempre** I'll always love you, I'll love you for ever; **è la persona di sempre** he's the same as ever, he's his usual self; **sei il cretino di sempre** [OR] **sei sempre il solito cretino** you are as stupid as ever; **per sempre** forever; **da sempre** always; **una volta per sempre** once and for all; **arriva sempre a disturbarmi** he's always o forever coming to disturb me; **è sempre nevicato** it snowed all the time; **è un abito che puoi indossare sempre** it's a dress you can wear any time o on any occasion; **è rimasto sempre lì fermo** he stayed there, immobile
b (*ancora, comunque*) still; **esci sempre con lui?** are you still going out with him?; **c'è sempre la possibilità che...** there's still a chance that ..., there's always the possibility that ...; **ha una certa età ma è sempre bella** she is getting on but is still very attractive; **è (pur) sempre tuo fratello** he is still your brother (however); **è sempre meglio che niente** it's better than nothing; **posso sempre tentare** I can always o still try
c: **sempre che** as long as, provided (that); **sempre che non piova** as long as o provided that it doesn't rain, unless it rains; **sempre che tu non cambi idea** as long as you don't change your mind, unless you change your mind
d (*rafforzativo*): **sempre più** more and more; **sempre meno** less and less; **va sempre meglio** things are getting better and better; **è sempre più giovane** she gets younger and younger.

sempreverde [sempre'verde] AGG, SM O F (*Bot*) evergreen.

sen. ABBR (= *senatore*) Sen.

senape ['sɛnape] **1** SF (*Bot, Culin*) mustard.
2 AGG INV (*colore*) mustard-coloured, mustard *attr*.

senapismo [sena'pizmo] SM mustard plaster.

senato [se'nato] SM **a** (*Storia*) senate **b**: **il Senato** *upper chamber of the Italian parliament: elections for the 315 senators are held every 5 years.*

senatore, trice [sena'tore] SM/F senator.

senatoriale [senato'rjale] AGG senatorial.

Seneca ['sɛneka] SM Seneca.

Senegal ['sɛnegal] SM: **il Senegal** Senegal.

senegalese [senega'lese] AGG, SM/F Senegalese *inv*.

senese [se'nese] **1** AGG Sienese, of o from Siena.
2 SM/F inhabitant o native of Siena.

senile [se'nile] AGG senile.

senilismo [seni'lizmo] SM premature old age.

senilità [senili'ta] SF senility.

Senna ['senna] SF: **la Senna** the Seine.

senno ['senno] SM judgment, good sense, (common) sense; **uscire di senno** to lose one's mind o wits; **col senno di poi** with hindsight; **del senno di poi son piene le fosse** (*Proverbio*) it's easy to be wise after the event.

sennò [sen'nɔ] AVV **= se no**; vedi **se¹**.

seno¹ ['seno] SM **a** (*Anat*) bosom; (: *mammella*) breast; (*grembo*) womb; **portare un figlio in seno** to carry a child (in one's womb); **in seno alla famiglia** in the bosom of the family; **in seno al partito/all'organizzazione** within the party/the organization **b** (*Anat, Zool: cavità*) sinus **c** (*Geog*) inlet, creek.

seno² ['seno] SM (*Mat*) sine.

Senofonte [seno'fonte] SM Xenophon.

sensale [sen'sale] SM (*Comm*) agent.

sensatamente [sensata'mente] AVV sensibly.

sensatezza [sensa'tettsa] SF good sense, good judgment.

sensato, a [sen'sato] AGG sensible.

sensazionale [sensattsjo'nale] AGG sensational, exciting.

sensazione [sensat'tsjone] SF feeling, sensation; **ho la sensazione di averlo già visto** I have a feeling I've seen him before; **fare sensazione** (*interesse, stupore*) to cause a sensation, create a stir; **essere a caccia di nuove sensazioni** to be after new thrills *o* experiences.

sensibile [sen'sibile] AGG **a** (*gen*) sensitive; **ha un animo sensibile** he's tender-hearted; **essere sensibile a** (*freddo, caldo*) to be sensitive to; (*complimenti, adulazioni, fascino*) to be susceptible to

b (*notevole: progresso, differenze*) appreciable, noticeable

c (*Fot: pellicola*) sensitive.

sensibilità [sensibili'ta] SF sensitivity, sensitiveness.

sensibilizzare [sensibilid'dzare] VT (*fig*) to make aware, awaken; **sensibilizzare le masse ai problemi del paese** to make the people aware of the country's problems.

sensibilmente [sensibil'mente] AVV (*notevolmente*) appreciably.

sensitività [sensitivi'ta] SF (*Med*) sensitivity.

sensitivo, a [sensi'tivo] 1 AGG **a** (*Anat*) sensory, sensorial; **percezioni sensitive** sensory perception *sg* **b** (*persona*) sensitive, susceptible.

2 SM/F sensitive person; (*medium*) medium.

senso ['sɛnso] SM **a** (*istinto, coscienza*) sense; **i 5 sensi** the 5 senses; **perdere/riprendere i sensi** to lose/regain consciousness; **senso d'orientamento** sense of direction; **avere senso pratico** to be practical; **senso del dovere/dell'umorismo** sense of duty/humour; **avere un sesto senso** to have a sixth sense; **i piaceri dei sensi** (*della sensualità*) sensual pleasures, the pleasures of the senses

b (*sensazione*) feeling, sense, sensation; **un senso di angoscia** a feeling *o* sense of anxiety; **provare un senso di inquietudine** to feel anxious; **fare senso (a qn)** (*ribrezzo*) to disgust (sb), repel (sb)

c (*significato*) meaning, sense; **nel senso letterale/figurato** in the literal/figurative sense; **senza** *o* **privo di senso** meaningless; **in un certo senso ha ragione lui** in a way *o* sense he's right; **nel senso che...** in the sense that ...; **che senso ha?** where's the sense in that?; **(per me) non ha senso** it doesn't make (any) sense (to me); **nel vero senso della parola** in the true sense of the word

d (*direzione*) direction; **in senso opposto** in the opposite direction; **nel senso della lunghezza** lengthwise, lengthways; **nel senso della larghezza** widthwise; **io venivo in senso contrario** I was coming from the opposite direction; **in senso orario** clockwise; **in senso antiorario** anticlockwise (*Brit*), counterclockwise (*Am*); **ho dato disposizioni in quel senso** I've given instructions to that end *o* effect

e (*Aut*): **a senso unico** (*strada*) one-way; **"senso vietato"** "no entry"

f (*Dir*): **ai sensi di legge** in compliance with the law.

sensoriale [senso'rjale] AGG sensory *attr*.

sensuale [sensu'ale] AGG (*persona, sguardo*) sensual; (*voce*) sensuous.

sensualità [sensuali'ta] SF (*vedi agg*) sensuality; sensuousness.

sensualmente [sensual'mente] AVV sensually.

sentenza [sen'tɛntsa] SF **a** (*Dir*) sentence; **pronunciare una sentenza di morte contro qn** to sentence sb to

death **b** (*massima*) maxim; **sputar sentenze** (*fig*) to moralize.

sentenziare [senten'tsjare] (*Dir*) 1 VT: **sentenziare che...** to rule that ...; **sentenziare la pena di morte** to pass the death sentence.

2 VI (*aus avere*) to pass judgment.

sentenzioso, a [senten'tsjoso] AGG sententious.

sentiero [sen'tjɛro] SM path.

sentimentale [sentimen'tale] 1 AGG (*gen*) sentimental; (*pegg*) soppy; **vita sentimentale** love life.

2 SM/F sentimentalist.

sentimentalmente [sentimental'mente] AVV (*vedi agg*) sentimentally; soppily.

sentimento [senti'mento] SM (*gen*) feeling; **una persona di nobili sentimenti** a person of noble sentiments; **urtare i sentimenti di qn** to hurt sb's feelings.

sentina [sen'tina] SF (*Naut*) bilge.

sentinella [senti'nɛlla] SF (*Mil*) sentry, guard; **essere di sentinella** to be on guard *o* sentry duty.

sentire [sen'tire] 1 VT **a** (*percepire: gen, al tatto*) to feel; **sentire freddo/caldo** to feel cold/hot; **sentire dolore** to feel pain; **sento un gran male qui** I've got a terrible pain here; **senti quanto pesa** feel how heavy it is; **non sento niente** I can't feel a thing; **il caldo si fa sentire** the heat is oppressive; **la sua assenza si fa sentire** his absence is noticeable

b (*emozione*) to feel; **sentire un profondo affetto per qn** to feel deep affection for sb; **non sento niente per lui** I don't feel anything for him; **sentire la mancanza di qn** to miss sb; **sento che succederà qualcosa** I sense that something is going to happen; **sento che mente** I can sense that he is lying; **sento che mi vuoi lasciare** I can sense that you want to leave me; **dice sempre quello che sente** he always says what he feels

c (*al gusto*) to taste; (*all'olfatto*) to smell; **senti se ti piace questa salsa** taste this sauce to see if you like it; **senti se ti piace questo profumo** smell this perfume to see if you like it; **ho il raffreddore e non sento gli odori/i sapori** I've got a cold and I can't smell/taste anything

d (*udire*) to hear; (*ascoltare*) to listen to; **sento dei passi** I can hear footsteps; **mi piace sentire la musica** I like listening to music; **stare a sentire** to listen; **hai sentito l'ultima?** have you heard the latest?; **senti, mi presti quel disco?** listen, will you lend me that record?; **ho sentito dire che...** I have heard that ...; **stammi bene a sentire!** just you listen to me!; **a sentir lui...** to hear him talk ...; **farsi sentire** to make o.s. heard; **fatti sentire** keep in touch; **non ci sente** (*sordo*) he's deaf, he can't hear; **non ci sente da quell'orecchio** (*fig*) he always turns a deaf ear to things like that; **senti quello che ti dice l'avvocato** go and ask your lawyer for advice; **intendo sentire il mio legale/il parere di un medico** I'm going to consult my lawyer/a doctor; **senti cosa vuole** see what he wants; **ma senti un po'!** just fancy that!; **senti questa!** just listen to this!; **si sente che è straniero** you can tell he's a foreigner; **per sentito dire** by hearsay.

2 **sentirsi** VR **a** (*gen*) to feel; **sentirsi bene/male** to feel well/unwell *o* ill; **come ti senti?** how are you?, how do you feel?; **sentirsi svenire** to feel faint

b (*essere disposto*): **sentirsi di fare qc** to feel like doing sth; **non me la sento** I don't feel like it; **proprio non se la sente di continuare** he doesn't feel like carrying on

c (*uso reciproco*) to hear from each other, be in touch; **si sono sentiti di recente** they were in touch (with each

other) recently.

sentitamente [sentita'mente] AVV sincerely; **ringraziare sentitamente** to thank sincerely.

sentito, a [sen'tito] AGG (*ringraziamenti, condoglianze*) sincere, deep.

sentore [sen'tore] SM talk, rumour (*Brit*), rumor (*Am*); **aver sentore di qc** to hear about sth.

senza ['sɛntsa] [1] PREP without; **uscì senza ombrello** he went out without an *o* his umbrella; **non so cosa farei senza il suo aiuto** I don't know what I'd do without his help; **non senza alcune riserve** not without some reservations; **non posso stare senza di te** I can't live without you; **siamo rimasti senza zucchero/tè** we've run out of sugar/tea, we have no sugar/tea left; **forza, senza tante chiacchiere** come on, stop the talking and let's get on with it; **senza casa** homeless; **senza padre** fatherless; **senza amici** friendless; **senza preoccupazioni** carefree; **senza scrupoli** unscrupulous; **senza impegno** without obligation; **un dettato senza errori** an error-free dictation; **un discorso senza senso** a meaningless speech; **i senza lavoro** the jobless, the unemployed; **senz'altro** of course, certainly; **senza dubbio** no doubt.

[2] CONG without; **senza batter ciglio** without batting an eyelid; **ho trascorso tutta la notte senza chiudere occhio** I didn't sleep a wink all night, I didn't get a wink of sleep all night; **senza dire niente** without saying a thing; **parlò senza riflettere** he spoke without thinking; **senza che tu lo sapessi** without your knowing about it; **senza dire che...** not to mention (the fact) that ...; **senza contare che...** without considering that ... .

senzatetto [sentsa'tetto] [1] SM/F INV homeless person; **i senzatetto** the homeless.

[2] AGG INV homeless.

sepalo ['sɛpalo] SM (*Bot*) sepal.

separare [sepa'rare] [1] VT (*gen*) to separate; (*litiganti*) to pull apart, part; (*aspetti, problemi*) to distinguish between; **le Alpi separano la Svizzera dall'Italia** the Alps divide *o* separate Italy from Switzerland; **separare il bene dal male** to distinguish between good and evil; **solo pochi chilometri lo separavano da casa** only a few kilometres separated him from home *o* stood between him and home.

[2] **separarsi** VR **a** (*lasciare*): **separarsi da** (*persona*) to leave; (*oggetto*) to part with; **gli dispiaceva separarsi dai propri cari/da quegli oggetti cari** he didn't want to leave his loved ones/to part with those dear objects; **si è separata dal marito** she has left her husband

b (*staccarsi*): **separarsi da** to split off from, separate off from

c (*uso reciproco*: *gen*) to part; (: *coniugi, soci*) to part, split up, separate; **dopo 2 ore di cammino si separarono** after 2 hours' walk they parted (company).

separatamente [separata'mente] AVV separately.

separatismo [separa'tizmo] SM separatism.

separatista, i, e [separa'tista] AGG, SM/F separatist.

separato, a [sepa'rato] AGG (*gen*) separate; **in separata sede** (*privatamente*) in private; **vivono separati** (*coniugi*) they have separated.

separazione [separat'tsjone] SF (*gen, Dir*) separation; **dopo la separazione** (*di coniugi*) after they parted; **separazione dei beni** (*Dir*) division of property.

séparé [sepa're] SM INV screen.

sepolcrale [sepol'krale] AGG sepulchral.

sepolcro [se'polkro] SM sepulchre (*Brit*), sepulcher (*Am*);

il Santo Sepolcro the Holy Sepulchre *o* Sepulcher.

sepolto, a [se'polto] [1] PP di **seppellire**.

[2] AGG (*gen, fig*) buried; **morto e sepolto** (*anche fig*) dead and buried; **sepolto nel profondo del cuore** buried deep in one's heart.

sepoltura [sepol'tura] SF burial; **dare sepoltura a qn** to bury sb.

seppellimento [seppelli'mento] SM burial.

seppellire [seppel'lire] VB IRREG [1] VT (*gen*) to bury; (*fig*: *passato, ricordi*) to bury, forget; **il villaggio era sepolto dalla neve** the village was buried under the snow; **seppellire antichi rancori** to bury the hatchet, let bygones be bygones.

[2] **seppellirsi** VR (*fig*: *isolarsi*) to shut o.s. off, cut o.s. off; **seppellirsi tra i libri** to bury o.s. in one's books.

seppi *ecc* ['sɛppi] VB vedi **sapere**.

seppia ['seppja] SF (*Zool*) cuttlefish; **nero di seppia** sepia.

seppure [sep'pure] CONG even if.

sequela [se'kwɛla] SF (*di avvenimenti*) series *inv*, sequence; (*di offese, ingiurie*) string.

sequenza [se'kwɛntsa] SF sequence.

sequenziale [sekwen'tsjale] AGG sequential.

sequestrare [sekwes'trare] VT **a** (*gen*) to confiscate; (*Dir, beni*) to sequestrate; (*film, libri*) to impound **b** (*rapire*) to kidnap.

sequestro [se'kwɛstro] SM **a** (*gen*) confiscation, seizure; (*Dir*) sequestration, impounding **b** (*anche*: **sequestro di persona**) kidnapping.

sequoia [se'kwɔja] SF sequoia ▶**sequoia gigante** giant sequoia ▶**sequoia sempreverde** redwood.

sera ['sera] SF evening; **si fa sera** it's getting dark, night is falling; **di sera** in the evening; **alle 6 di sera** at 6 o'clock in the evening, at 6 p.m.; **alle 11 di sera** at 11 o'clock at night, at 11 p.m.; **questa sera** this evening, tonight; **dalla mattina alla sera** from morning to night.

seracco [se'rakko] SM (*Alpinismo*) sérac.

serafico, a, ci, che [se'rafiko] AGG seraphic.

serafino [sera'fino] SM seraph.

serale [se'rale] AGG evening *attr*; **scuola serale** evening classes *pl*, night school.

serata [se'rata] SF **a** (*sera*) evening **b** (*ricevimento*) soirée, party ▶**serata danzante** dance **c** (*Teatro*) evening performance; **serata di gala/d'addio** gala/farewell performance.

serbare [ser'bare] VT (*tenere*) to keep; (*mettere da parte*) to put aside, keep; **serbare rancore a qn** to bear *o* harbour a grudge against sb.

serbatoio, oi [serba'tojo] SM (*gen*) tank; (*cisterna*) cistern; **serbatoio (della benzina)** (*Aut*) (petrol) (*Brit*) *o* (gas) (*Am*) tank.

serbo[1] ['sɛrbo] SM: **in serbo** (*sorpresa*) in store; **te lo tengo in serbo** I'll put it aside for you.

serbo[2]**, a** ['sɛrbo] [1] AGG Serbian.

[2] SM/F Serbian, Serb *attr*.

[3] SM (*lingua*) Serbian.

serbocroato, a [serbokro'ato] AGG, SM/F Serbo-Croat.

serenamente [serena'mente] AVV (*guardare*) serenely, calmly; (*giudicare*) dispassionately; (*vivere*) quietly.

serenata [sere'nata] SF serenade; **fare la serenata a qn** to serenade sb, sing sb a serenade, sing a serenade to sb.

serenità [sereni'ta] SF peace, tranquillity, serenity; **serenità d'animo** peace of mind.

sereno, a [se'reno] [1] AGG (*tempo, cielo*) clear, serene; (*volto, persona*) calm, serene; (*giudizio*) dispassionate;

(vita) quiet; **un fulmine a ciel sereno** *(fig)* a bolt from the blue.

2 SM *(tempo)* good weather.

serg. ABBR (= *sergente*) Sgt.

sergente [ser'dʒɛnte] SM *(Mil)* sergeant; **sergente maggiore** sergeant major.

seriale [se'rjale] AGG *(Inform)* serial.

seriamente [serja'mente] AVV *(gen)* **a** *(con serietà)* seriously, earnestly; **sto parlando seriamente!** I'm serious!; **lavorare seriamente** to take one's job seriously **b** *(gravemente)* seriously, gravely; **è seriamente malato** he's seriously ill.

sericoltura [serikol'tura] SF sericulture.

serie ['sɛrje] SF INV **a** *(gen)* series *inv*; *(di numeri)* series, sequence; *(di chiavi)* set; **tutta una serie di problemi** a whole string *o* series of problems **b** *(Sport)* division; **serie A/B** ≈ first/second division; *(Calcio)* ≈ Premier League *(England)*, ≈ Premier Division *(Scotland)*; *(fig)* first/second class **c** *(Comm)*: **produzione in serie** mass production; **produrre in serie** to mass-produce; **modello di serie/fuori serie** *(Aut)* standard/custom-built model.

serietà [serje'ta] SF *(vedi agg)* seriousness; earnestness; reliability.

serigrafia [serigra'fia] SF *(metodo)* serigraphy; *(stampa)* serigraph.

serio, ria, ri, rie ['sɛrjo] 1 AGG *(gen)* serious; *(persona, conversazione)* serious, earnest; *(persona, ditta: affidabile)* reliable, responsible, dependable; **restare serio** to keep a straight face; **sii serio!** be serious!; **aveva una faccia seria** he looked serious; **è una ragazza seria** *(per bene)* she's a respectable girl.

2 SM: **sul serio** seriously, in earnest; **sul serio ti ha invitato?** did he really invite you?; **non facevo sul serio** OR **non dicevo sul serio** I wasn't (being) serious; **faccio sul serio** I mean it; **prendere qn/qc sul serio** to take sb/sth seriously.

serioso, a [se'rjoso] AGG *(persona, modi)*: **un po' serioso** a bit too serious.

sermone [ser'mone] SM *(Rel)* sermon; *(fig)* lecture, sermon; **fare un sermone a qn** *(fig)* to give sb a lecture *o* sermon.

serpe ['sɛrpe] SF snake; *(fig pegg)* viper; **scaldare** *o* **allevare una serpe in seno** to nurse a viper in one's bosom.

serpeggiante [serped'dʒante] AGG winding, twisting.

serpeggiare [serped'dʒare] VI *(aus avere)* *(strada, fiume)* to wind, snake, twist; *(fig: malcontento, rivolta)* to spread (insidiously).

serpente [ser'pɛnte] SM **a** *(Zool)* snake, serpent ▸ **serpente a sonagli** rattlesnake **b** *(pelle)* snakeskin **c** *(Fin)*: **il serpente monetario** the (currency) snake.

serpentina [serpen'tina] SF **a**: **a serpentina** *(strada)* winding **b** *(Equitazione)* serpentine **c** *(Sci)* welden; **fare la serpentina** to welden.

serra[1] ['sɛrra] SF *(Agr)* greenhouse; (: *riscaldata*) hothouse.

serra[2] ['sɛrra] SF *(Geog)* sierra.

serraglio, gli [ser'raʎʎo] SM **a** *(di animali)* menagerie **b** *(di sultano)* harem.

serramanico [serra'maniko] SM: **coltello a serramanico** flick-knife, clasp knife.

serranda [ser'randa] SF *(rolling* o *roller)* shutter.

serrare [ser'rare] VT *(chiudere)* to close, shut; *(stringere)* to shut tightly; **serrare i pugni/i denti** to clench one's fists/teeth; **serrare le file** *(anche fig)* to close ranks; **serrare il nemico** to close in on the enemy.

serrata [ser'rata] SF *(Industria)* lockout.

serrato, a [ser'rato] AGG **a** *(porta, finestra)* closed, shut; *(pugni, denti)* clenched; *(occhi)* tightly closed **b** *(stringato)* logical, coherent **c** *(veloce)*: **a ritmo serrato** quickly, fast.

serratura [serra'tura] SF lock.

Serse ['sɛrse] SM Xerxes.

serva ['sɛrva] SF vedi **servo**.

servalo [ser'valo] SM *(animale)* serval.

servigio, gi [ser'vidʒo] SM favour *(Brit)*, favor *(Am)*, service.

servile [ser'vile] AGG **a** *(gen, fig)* servile **b** *(Gramm: verbo)* modal.

servilismo [servi'lizmo] SM servility.

servilmente [servil'mente] AVV servilely.

servire [ser'vire] 1 VT **a** *(essere al servizio di)* to serve; **servire qn** *(in negozio)* to attend to *o* serve sb; *(al ristorante)* to wait on *o* serve sb; **gli piace farsi servire** he likes to be waited on; **in cosa posso servirla?** *(negozio)* can I help you?; **adesso ti servo io!** *(iro)* now I'll show you!; **servire la Messa/la Patria** to serve Mass/one's country

b *(piatto)* to serve; **servire qc a qn** to serve sb with sth, help sb to sth; **"servire ghiacciato"** "serve chilled"; **servire a tavola** to wait on table; **servire da bere a qn** to serve a drink to sb; **il pranzo è servito** dinner is served

c *(Carte)* to deal

d *(Calcio: giocatore)* to pass the ball to.

2 VI **a** *(aus essere)*: **servire a (fare) qc** *(essere utile)* to be used for (doing) sth; **servire a qn** to be of use to sb; **a cosa serve questo aggeggio?** what is this gadget (used) for?; **serve a tagliare la frutta** it's for cutting fruit; **questa stanza serve da studio** this room is used as a study; **che ti serva da lezione** let that be a lesson to you; **ha insistito ma non è servito (a niente)** he insisted but to no purpose; **mi serve un paio di forbici** I need a pair of scissors; **non mi serve più** I don't need it any more; **te lo presto, se ti serve** I'll lend it to you, if you need it; **piangere non serve a niente** it's no use crying, crying doesn't help; **a che serve lamentarsi?** what would be the point of complaining?

b *(Tennis)* to serve.

3 **servirsi** VIP **a** *(fare uso)*: **servirsi di** to make use of, use

b *(a tavola)* to help o.s.

c : **servirsi da** *(negoziante)* to shop at, be a regular customer at, go to.

servitore, trice [servi'tore] SM/F servant.

servitù [servi'tu] SF INV **a** *(condizione)* slavery, bondage, servitude ▸ **servitù della gleba** *(Storia)* serfdom **b** *(domestici)* servants *pl*, domestic staff *sg o pl* **c** *(Dir)*: **servitù di passaggio** right of way.

servizievole [servit'tsjevole] AGG obliging, helpful, willing to help.

servizio, zi [ser'vittsjo] SM **a** *(lavoro)* duty; **essere di** *o* **in servizio** to be on duty; **non bevo in servizio** I don't drink on duty; **prendere servizio** to come on duty; **avere 20 anni di servizio** to have done *o* completed 20 years' service

b *(come domestico)* (domestic) service; **andare/essere a servizio** to go into/be in service; **entrata di servizio**

service *o* tradesman's (*Brit*) entrance

c : **servizio civile** community service (*chosen instead of military service, especially by conscientious objectors*) ▶ **il servizio militare** military service; **prestare servizio militare** to do one's military *o* national service ▶ **servizio d'ordine** (*Polizia*) police patrol; (*di manifestanti*) team of stewards (*for crowd control*) ▶ **servizio segreto** secret service ▶ **servizi di sicurezza** security forces

d (*istituzioni pubbliche*) service; ▶ **servizio postale/telefonico** postal/telephone service ▶ **servizio sanitario nazionale** ≈ National Health Service (*Brit*), ≈ Medicaid/Medicare (*Am*)

e (*funzionamento*) service; **fuori servizio** out of order; **rimettere in servizio** to put *o* bring back into service

f (*favore*) service, favour (*Brit*), favor (*Am*); (*prestazioni*): servizi services; **offrire i propri servizi a qn** to offer sb one's services, offer one's services to sb; **bel servizio mi hai fatto!** (*iro*) you've been a real help!; **sono al suo servizio** I am at your service

g (*al ristorante*) service; (*sul conto*) service (charge); **servizio a bordo** (*Aer*) in-flight service; **servizio compreso/escluso** service included/not included

h (*TV, Radio, Stampa*) report ▶ **servizio in diretta** live coverage ▶ **servizio fotografico** (*Stampa*) photo feature

I (*Rel*) service

j (*Tennis*) service ▶ **servizio vincente** ace; **al servizio Sampras** Sampras to serve

k (*insieme di oggetti*): **servizio all'americana** tablemat and napkin set; **servizio da tè** tea set; **servizio di cristallo** set of crystal glassware

l : **i servizi** SMPL (*di casa*) kitchen and bathroom; **casa con doppi servizi** house with two bathrooms

m (*Econ*): **servizi** SMPL services.

servo, a ['sɛrvo] SM/F servant, manservant/maidservant.

servofreno [servo'freno] SM (*Aut*) servo brake.

servomeccanismo [servomekka'nizmo] SM servomechanism.

servomotore [servomo'tore] SM servomotor.

servosterzo [servos'tɛrtso] SM (*Aut*) power steering.

sesamo ['sɛzamo] SM (*Bot*) sesame; **apriti sesamo!** open sesame!

sessanta [ses'santa] AGG INV, SM INV sixty *per fraseologia vedi* **cinquanta**.

sessantenne [sessan'tɛnne] AGG, SM/F sixty-year-old *per fraseologia vedi* **cinquantenne**.

sessantesimo, a [sessan'tɛzimo] AGG, SM/F, SM sixtieth *per fraseologia vedi* **quinto**.

sessantina [sessan'tina] SF: **una sessantina (di)** about sixty *per fraseologia vedi* **cinquantina**.

sessantottino, a [sessantot'tino] SM/F (*fam*) *a person who took part in the events of 1968 (sessantotto)*.

sessantotto [sessan'tɔtto] SM (*fam*): **il sessantotto** *student protest movement of 1968 which led to major political and social change*.

sessile ['sɛssile] AGG (*Bot, Bio*) sessile.

sessione [ses'sjone] SF session.

sesso ['sɛsso] SM sex; **il sesso debole/forte** the weaker/stronger sex; **sesso sicuro** safe sex.

sessuale [sessu'ale] AGG (*gen*) sexual; (*vita, organo, educazione*) sex *attr*, sexual.

sessualità [sessuali'ta] SF sexuality.

sessualmente [sessual'mente] AVV sexually.

sessuologia [sessuolo'dʒia] SF sexology.

sessuologo, a, gi, ghe [sessu'ɔlogo] SM/F sexologist, sex specialist.

sestante [ses'tante] SM (*Naut*) sextant.

sestetto [ses'tetto] SM (*Mus*) sextet(te).

sestina [ses'tina] SF (*Poesia: di sonetto*) sestet; (: *di canzone*) sestina, sextain.

sesto[1], a ['sɛsto] AGG, SM/F, SM (*numerale*) sixth *per fraseologia vedi* **quinto**.

sesto[2] ['sɛsto] SM (*Archit*): **arco a sesto acuto** pointed arch; **arco a tutto sesto** rounded arch.

sesto[3] ['sɛsto] SM: **rimettere in sesto** (*aggiustare*) to put back in order; (*fig: persona*) to put back on his (*o* her) feet; **rimettersi in sesto** (*riprendersi*) to recover, get well; (*riassettarsi*) to tidy o.s. up.

sestultimo, a [ses'tultimo] AGG, SM/F last but five, sixth from last.

set [set] SM INV set.

seta ['seta] SF silk.

setacciare [setat'tʃare] VT (*farina*) to sift, sieve; (*fig: zona*) to search, comb.

setaccio, ci [se'tattʃo] SM sieve; **passare al setaccio** (*fig*) to search, comb.

sete ['sete] SF (*anche fig*) thirst; **avere sete** to be thirsty; **soffrire la sete** to suffer from thirst; **morire di sete** to die of thirst; **sete di potere** thirst for power.

setificio, ci [seti'fitʃo] SM silk factory.

setola ['setola] SF bristle.

setoloso, a [seto'loso] AGG bristly.

setta ['sɛtta] SF (*Rel*) sect.

settanta [set'tanta] AGG INV, SM INV seventy *per fraseologia vedi* **cinquanta**.

settantenne [settan'tɛnne] AGG, SM/F seventy-year-old *per fraseologia vedi* **cinquantenne**.

settantesimo, a [settan'tɛzimo] AGG, SM/F, SM seventieth *per fraseologia vedi* **quinto**.

settantina [settan'tina] SF: **una settantina (di)** about seventy *per fraseologia vedi* **cinquantina**.

settario, ria, ri, rie [set'tarjo] AGG, SM sectarian.

settarismo [setta'rizmo] SM sectarianism.

sette ['sɛtte] AGG INV, SM INV seven *per fraseologia vedi* **cinque**.

settecentesco, a, schi, sche [settetʃen'tesko] AGG eighteenth-century.

settecento [sette'tʃɛnto] **1** AGG INV seven hundred.
2 SM INV seven hundred; **il Settecento** (*secolo*) the eighteenth century.

settembre [set'tɛmbre] SM September *per fraseologia vedi* **luglio**.

settentrionale [settentrjo'nale] **1** AGG northern; **Italia settentrionale** Northern Italy; **vento settentrionale** north *o* northerly wind.
2 SM/F northerner, person from the north.

settentrione [setten'trjone] SM north; **del settentrione** north(ern), of the north; (*vento*) north(erly).

setter ['sɛtter] SM INV (*cane*) setter.

setticemia [settitʃe'mia] SF blood poisoning, septicaemia (*Brit*), septicemia (*Am*).

settico, a, ci, che ['sɛttiko] AGG septic.

settimana [setti'mana] SF **a** week; **una volta/due volte alla settimana** once/twice a week; **questa settimana** this week; **la settimana scorsa/prossima** last/next week; **a metà settimana** in the middle of the week; **2 settimane fa** 2 weeks ago; **fra 2 settimane** in 2 weeks'

time; **prendere 3 settimane di ferie** to take 3 weeks' holiday; **settimana dopo settimana** week after week, week in, week out; **una settimana sì, una no** every other week; **settimana lavorativa** working week ▶ **settimana bianca** winter-sports holiday ▶ **settimana santa** Holy Week

b (*paga*) week's pay, wages *pl*; (*per bambini*) pocket money (*Brit*), allowance (*Am*).

settimanale [settima'nale] 1 AGG weekly.
2 SM (*rivista*) weekly (publication).

settimino, a [setti'mino] SM/F (*neonato*) *baby born two months premature.*

settimo, a ['sɛttimo] AGG, SM/F, SM seventh; **essere al settimo cielo** (*fig*) to be in seventh heaven *per fraseologia vedi* **quinto.**

setto ['sɛtto] SM (*Anat*) septum.

settore [set'tore] SM (*Econ, Geom, Mil*) sector; (*fig*) area; **settore primario/secondario/terziario** primary/secondary/tertiary sector; **settore privato/pubblico** private/public sector.

settoriale [setto'rjale] AGG sector-based.

Seul [se'ul] SF Seoul.

severamente [severa'mente] AVV (*vedi agg*) severely; strictly.

severità [severi'ta] SF (*vedi agg*) severity; strictness.

severo, a [se'vɛro] AGG (*gen*) severe; (*padre, insegnante, giudice*) strict.

seviziare [sevit'tsjare] VT (*torturare*) to torture; (*picchiare*) to beat up.

sevizie [se'vittsje] SFPL torture *sg.*

sexy ['sɛksi] AGG INV sexy.

sez. ABBR = *sezione.*

sezionare [settsjo'nare] VT (*gen*) to divide up, cut up; divide into sections; (*Med*) to dissect.

sezione [set'tsjone] SF (*gen, Geom, Archit, Tecn*) section; (*di ufficio*) department; (*a scuola*) ≈ class; (*Med*) dissection.

sfaccendato, a [sfattʃen'dato] 1 AGG lazy, idle.
2 SM/F idler, loafer.

sfaccettare [sfattʃet'tare] VT (*pietre preziose*) to cut, facet.

sfaccettatura [sfattʃetta'tura] SF (*azione*) faceting; (*parte sfaccettata, fig*) facet.

sfacchinare [sfakki'nare] VI (*aus* **avere**) (*fam*) to toil, drudge.

sfacchinata [sfakki'nata] SF (*fam*) toil *no pl*, chore, drudgery *no pl.*

sfacciataggine [sfattʃa'taddʒine] SF insolence, cheek; **ma che sfacciataggine!** what a cheek *o* nerve!; **avere la sfacciataggine di fare qc** to have the nerve *o* cheek to do sth.

sfacciatamente [sfattʃata'mente] AVV insolently, cheekily.

sfacciato, a [sfat'tʃato] AGG insolent, cheeky, impudent.

sfacelo [sfa'tʃɛlo] SM (*fig: di famiglia, organizzazione*) break-up; **andare in sfacelo** (*costruzione*) to fall to pieces; (*piani*) to be ruined.

sfaldarsi [sfal'darsi] VIP (*rocce*) to exfoliate.

sfalsare [sfal'sare] VT to stagger.

sfamare [sfa'mare] 1 VT (*nutrire*) to feed; (*soddisfare la fame*): **sfamare qn** to satisfy sb's hunger.
2 **sfamarsi** VR to satisfy one's hunger, fill o.s. up.

sfare ['sfare] VB IRREG 1 VT = **disfare.**
2 **sfarsi** VIP (*neve*) to melt.

sfarfallare [sfarfal'lare] VI (*aus* **avere**) **a** (*fig: persona*) to flutter about **b** (*Cine, TV*) to flicker.

sfarfallio, lii [sfarfal'lio] SM (*Cine, TV*) flickering.

sfarzo ['sfartso] SM pomp, splendour (*Brit*), splendor (*Am*), magnificence.

sfarzosamente [sfartsosa'mente] AVV splendidly, magnificently.

sfarzoso, a [sfar'tsoso] AGG splendid, magnificent.

sfasamento [sfaza'mento] SM (*Elettr*) phase displacement; (*fig*) confusion, bewilderment.

sfasato, a [sfa'zato] AGG (*Elettr, motore*) out of phase; (*fig: persona*) confused, bewildered.

sfasciare¹ [sfaʃ'ʃare] VT (*togliere una fascia*) to unbandage.

sfasciare² [sfaʃ'ʃare] 1 VT (*macchina*) to smash, wreck; (*vaso*) to smash, shatter; (*letto, sedia*) to wreck, break.
2 **sfasciarsi** VIP (*macchina*) to be smashed, be wrecked; (*vaso*) to shatter, smash; (*letto, sedia*) to fall to pieces.

sfatare [sfa'tare] VT (*leggenda, mito*) to explode.

sfaticato, a [sfati'kato] 1 AGG lazy, idle.
2 SM/F idler, loafer.

sfatto, a ['sfatto] 1 PP di **sfare.**
2 AGG (*letto*) unmade; (*orlo*) undone; (*gelato, neve*) melted; (*frutta*) overripe; (*riso, pasta*) overdone, overcooked; (*fam: persona, corpo*) flabby.

sfavillante [sfavil'lante] AGG (*vedi vb*) sparkling; flickering.

sfavillare [sfavil'lare] VI (*aus* **avere**) (*diamante, occhi*) to sparkle; (*fiamma*) to flicker, spark, send out sparks.

sfavillio, lii [sfavil'lio] SM (*vedi vb*) sparkling; flickering.

sfavore [sfa'vore] SM disfavour (*Brit*), disfavor (*Am*), disapproval.

sfavorevole [sfavo'revole] AGG unfavourable (*Brit*), unfavorable (*Am*).

sfavorevolmente [sfavorevol'mente] AVV unfavourably (*Brit*), unfavorably (*Am*).

sfebbrare [sfeb'brare] VI (*aus* **essere**): **entro qualche giorno sfebbrerà** his temperature will go down in a few days.

sfegatato, a [sfega'tato] AGG (*anche pegg*) fanatical.

sfera ['sfɛra] SF **a** (*anche fig*) sphere; **sfera d'influenza** sphere of influence **b** (*di macchina da scrivere*) golf ball.

sferico, a, ci, che [sfɛriko] AGG spherical.

sferragliare [sferraʎ'ʎare] VI (*aus* **avere**) to rattle, clatter.

sferrare [sfer'rare] 1 VT (*fig: attacco*) to launch; **sferrare un colpo a qn** to hit out at sb, lash out at sb (with one's fist); **sferrare un calcio a qn** to kick out at sb, lash out at sb (with one's foot).
2 **sferrarsi** VIP: **sferrarsi contro qn** (*lanciarsi*) to hurl *o* fling o.s. at sb.

sferruzzare [sferrut'tsare] VI (*aus* **avere**) to knit away.

sferza ['sfɛrtsa] SF whip, lash.

sferzante [sfer'tsante] AGG (*critiche, parole*) stinging.

sferzare [sfer'tsare] VT (*gen*) to whip; (*sogg: vento*) to lash; (: *onde*) to lash against, break on; (*fig*) to lash out at.

sferzata [sfer'tsata] SF (*frustata*) whipping; (*fig*) lashing.

sfiancare [sfjan'kare] 1 VT to wear out, exhaust.
2 **sfiancarsi** VIP to exhaust o.s., wear o.s. out.

sfiancato, a [sfjan'kato] AGG (*animale*) hollow-flanked; (*fig: persona*) exhausted, worn out.

sfiatare [sfja'tare] VI (*aus* **avere**) to allow air *o* gas to escape.

sfiatatoio, oi [sfjata'tojo] SM **a** (*Tecn*) vent **b** (*Zool*) blowhole.

sfibbiare [sfib'bjare] VT to undo, unbuckle.

sfibrante [sfi'brante] AGG exhausting, energy-sapping.

sfibrare [sfi'brare] VT (*indebolire*) to exhaust, enervate.

sfibrato, a [sfi'brato] AGG exhausted, worn out.

sfida ['sfida] SF challenge; **lanciare una sfida a qn** to challenge sb; **uno sguardo di sfida** (*fig*) a defiant look.

sfidante [sfi'dante] 1 AGG challenging.
2 SM/F challenger.

sfidare [sfi'dare] 1 VT a (*avversario*) to challenge; **sfidare qn a duello** to challenge sb to a duel; **sfidare qn a fare qc** to challenge sb to do sth
b (*fig: affrontare*) to defy, brave; **sfidare la morte** to defy death; **sfidare un pericolo** to brave a danger
c (*fraseologia*): **sfido io!** naturally!, of course!; **sfido che hai fame! - hai mangiato solo una mela** I should say you're hungry - you've only had an apple!.
2 **sfidarsi** VR (*uso reciproco*) to challenge each other.

sfiducia [sfi'dutʃa] SF distrust, mistrust; **avere sfiducia in qn/qc** to distrust sb/sth; **voto di sfiducia** (*Pol*) vote of no confidence.

sfiduciato, a [sfidu'tʃato] AGG discouraged, disheartened.

sfigurare [sfigu'rare] 1 VT (*persona*) to disfigure; (*quadro, statua*) to deface.
2 VI (*aus* **avere**) to make a bad impression, cut a poor figure.

sfilacciare [sfilat'tʃare] VT, VI (*aus* **essere**), **sfilacciarsi** VIP to fray.

sfilacciato, a [sfilat'tʃato] AGG (*tessuto*) frayed.

sfilare¹ [sfi'lare] 1 VT a (*orlo, tessuto*) to pull the threads out of (*perle*) to unstring; (*ago*) to unthread
b (*togliere: stivali, scarpe*) to take off, slip off; **gli sfilò il portafoglio** he pinched *o* lifted his wallet; **sfilarsi il vestito/le scarpe** to take one's dress/shoes off.
2 **sfilarsi** VIP (*orlo, tessuto*) to fray; (*calza*) to ladder, run; (*perle*) to come unstrung.

sfilare² [sfi'lare] VI (*aus* **avere** *o* **essere**) (*truppe*) to parade, march past; (*manifestanti*) to march; (*modelle*) to parade.

sfilata [sfi'lata] SF (*Mil*) parade; (*di manifestanti*) march; **sfilata (di moda)** fashion show.

sfilettare [sfilet'tare] VT (*Culin*) to fillet.

sfilza ['sfiltsa] SF (*di case*) row; (*di errori*) series *inv*.

sfinge ['sfindʒe] SF sphinx.

sfinimento [sfini'mento] SM exhaustion.

sfinire [sfi'nire] 1 VT to exhaust, wear out.
2 **sfinirsi** VIP to wear o.s. out, exhaust o.s.

sfinito, a [sfi'nito] AGG exhausted, worn out.

sfintere [sfin'tɛre] SM (*Anat*) sphincter.

sfiorare [sfjo'rare] VT (*acqua, cime di alberi*) to skim (over); (*volto, guancia*) to brush (against); **il proiettile l'ha solo sfiorato** the bullet only grazed him; **sfiorare un argomento** to touch on *o* upon a subject; **è un'idea che non mi sfiora nemmeno** it's an idea which hasn't even crossed my mind; **non ti ha mai sfiorato il dubbio che possa rifiutare?** has it never occurred to you *o* has it never crossed your mind that he might refuse?; **sfiorare la velocità di 150 km/h** to touch 150 km/h.

sfiorire [sfjo'rire] VI (*aus* **essere**) (*fiore, pianta*) to wither, fade; (*fig: bellezza*) to fade.

sfiorito, a [sfjo'rito] AGG (*fiore, bellezza*) faded.

sfitto, a ['sfitto] AGG vacant, empty.

sfizio, zi ['sfittsjo] SM whim, fancy; **togliersi lo sfizio di fare qc** to satisfy one's whim to do sth.

sfocare [sfo'kare] VT (*Fot*) to blur.

sfocato, a [sfo'kato] AGG (*Fot*) blurred, out of focus; (*fig: ricordo, immagine*) vague, dim.

sfociare [sfo'tʃare] VI (*aus* **essere**) (*fiume*): **sfociare in** to flow into; **il malcontento sfociò in una rivolta** (*fig*) the discontent developed into open rebellion.

sfoderare [sfode'rare] VT a (*spada, pugnale*) to draw, unsheathe; (*pistola*) to draw; (*fig: ostentare: cultura*) to display, parade, show off; **sfoderare un sorriso** to give a smile b (*togliere la fodera a*) to remove the lining from.

sfoderato, a [sfode'rato] AGG (*vestito*) unlined.

sfogare [sfo'gare] 1 VT (*gioia, tristezza*) to give vent to; (*energia*) to work off; **sfogare la propria rabbia su qn** to vent one's anger on sb.
2 VI (*aus* **essere**) (*liquido*) to flow out; (*gas*) to escape; (*malattia, febbre*) to run its course.
3 **sfogarsi** VR (*persona*) to give vent to one's feelings; (: *liberarsi di un peso*) to get a load off one's chest; **sfogarsi con qn** (*confidarsi*) to unburden o.s. *o* open one's heart to sb, pour out one's feelings to sb; **pianse e finalmente si sfogò** she had a good cry and finally let it all out; **non sfogarti su di me!** don't take it out on me!

sfoggiare [sfod'dʒare] VT to show off.

sfoggio, gi ['sfoddʒo] SM show, display; **fare sfoggio di** to show off, display.

sfoggherò ecc [sfoge'rɔ] VB vedi **sfogare**.

sfoglia ['sfoʎʎa] SF (*gen*) thin layer; (*Culin*) sheet of pasta dough; **pasta sfoglia** puff pastry.

sfogliare¹ [sfoʎ'ʎare] VT (*fiore*) to pluck the petals off.

sfogliare² [sfoʎ'ʎare] VT (*libro, rivista*) to leaf through.

sfogliata¹ [sfoʎ'ʎata] SF (*scorsa*) glance, look; **dare una sfogliata a** to leaf through.

sfogliata² [sfoʎ'ʎata] SF (*Culin*) puff.

sfogo, ghi ['sfogo] SM a (*di liquido, gas*) outlet; (*di aria*) vent; (*fig: di rabbia*) outburst; **dare sfogo a** (*fig*) to give vent to b (*eruzione cutanea*) rash.

sfolgorante [sfolgo'rante] AGG (*luce*) blazing; (*fig: vittoria*) brilliant.

sfolgorare [sfolgo'rare] VI (*aus* **avere**) to blaze.

sfolgorio, rii [sfolgo'rio] SM blaze, glare.

sfollagente [sfolla'dʒɛnte] SM INV truncheon (*Brit*), nightstick (*Am*), billy club (*Am*).

sfollamento [sfolla'mento] SM (*vedi vt*) clearing, emptying; evacuation.

sfollare [sfol'lare] 1 VT (*piazza, strada*) to clear, empty; (*edificio*) to evacuate, empty.
2 VI (*aus* **essere**) (*gente, dimostranti*) to disperse; **sfollare da una città** to evacuate a town.

sfollato, a [sfol'lato] 1 AGG evacuated.
2 SM/F evacuee.

sfoltire [sfol'tire] VT, **sfoltirsi** VIP to thin (out).

sfoltita [sfol'tita] SF thinning; **dare una sfoltita a qc** to thin sth.

sfondamento [sfonda'mento] SM (*di porta*) breaking down; (*di parete*) knocking down; (*Mil*) breaking through, breach.

sfondare [sfon'dare] 1 VT (*porta*) to break down; (*parete*) to break down, knock down; (*pavimento*) to break through; (*scarpe*) to wear through, wear a hole in; (*sedia, barca*) to knock the bottom out of; (*scatola*) to burst, knock the bottom out of; **sfondare le linee nemiche** (*Mil*) to break through the enemy lines; **sfondare il tetto di** (*fig*) to go beyond the limit of.
2 VI (*aus* **avere**) (*fig: attore, scrittore: avere successo*) to make a name for o.s..
3 **sfondarsi** VIP (*porta, sedia, pavimento*) to give way; (*parete*) to fall down; (*scarpe*) to wear out; (*scatola*) to

burst.

sfondato, a [sfon'dato] AGG (*scarpe*) worn out; (*scatola*) burst; (*sedia*) broken, damaged; **essere ricco sfondato** to be rolling in it.

sfondo ['sfondo] SM (*gen, Pittura, Fot*) background; (*di film, libro*) background, setting; **sullo sfondo** in the background.

sforare [sfo'rare] VI (*aus* **avere**) (*TV, Radio*) to overrun.

sforbiciata [sforbi'tʃata] SF **a** (*taglio*) snip, cut **b** (*Sport*) scissor kick.

sformare [sfor'mare] ① VT **a** to put out of shape, knock out of shape **b** (*dolce, budino*) to turn out.

② **sformarsi** VIP to lose shape, get out of shape.

sformato¹, a [sfor'mato] AGG (*che ha perso forma*) shapeless.

sformato² [sfor'mato] SM (*Culin*) type of soufflé.

sfornare [sfor'nare] VT (*Culin*) to take out of the oven; (*fig: libri, film*) to churn out.

sfornito, a [sfor'nito] AGG: **sfornito di** lacking in, without; (*negozio*) out of.

sfortuna [sfor'tuna] SF misfortune, bad *o* ill luck *no pl*; **avere sfortuna** to be unlucky; **per sfortuna!** unfortunately!; **che sfortuna!** how unfortunate!

sfortunatamente [sfortunata'mente] AVV unfortunately, unluckily.

sfortunato, a [sfortu'nato] AGG (*persona, numero*) unlucky; (*impresa, film*) unsuccessful.

sforzare [sfor'tsare] ① VT (*gen*) to force; (*voce, occhi*) to strain; **sforzare qn a fare qc** to force sb to do sth.

② **sforzarsi** VIP, **sforzarsi (a fare qc)** (*costringersi*) to force o.s. (to do sth); (*fare uno sforzo*) to make an effort (to do sth).

sforzo ['sfɔrtso] SM (*gen*) effort; (*Tecn*) stress, strain; **fare uno sforzo** to make an effort; **essere sotto sforzo** (*motore, macchina, fig: persona*) to be under stress; **che** *o* **bello sforzo!** (*iro*) that didn't take much effort!

sfottere ['sfottere] VT (*fam*) to tease.

sfracellare [sfratʃel'lare] ① VT to smash.

② **sfracellarsi** VIP to smash; **sfracellarsi al suolo** to crash to the ground.

sfrangiato, a [sfran'dʒato] AGG (*tessuto, orlo*) fringed.

sfrattare [sfrat'tare] VT to evict.

sfrattato, a [sfrat'tato] ① AGG evicted.

② SM/F evicted person.

sfratto ['sfratto] SM eviction; **dare lo sfratto a qn** to give sb notice to quit.

sfrecciare [sfret'tʃare] VI (*aus* **essere**) to shoot *o* flash past.

sfregamento [sfrega'mento] SM (*vedi vb*) rubbing; scratching.

sfregare [sfre'gare] VT (*strofinare*) to rub; (*graffiare*) to scratch; **sfregare un fiammifero** to strike a match; **sfregarsi le mani** to rub one's hands.

sfregiare [sfre'dʒare] ① VT to slash, gash; (*volto*) to disfigure, slash; (*quadro*) to deface, slash.

② **sfregiarsi** VIP to be disfigured.

sfregio, gi ['sfredʒo] SM **a** (*cicatrice*) scar; (*ferita*) gash; (*graffio*) scratch **b** (*fig: offesa*) affront, insult.

sfrenatamente [sfrenata'mente] AVV unrestrainedly, **vivere sfrenatamente** to lead a dissolute life.

sfrenato, a [sfre'nato] AGG (*persona*) wild, uncontrolled; (: *dissoluto*) dissolute; (*passioni*) unbridled, unrestrained; (*bambino*) unruly; **essere sfrenato nel bere/nel mangiare** to drink/eat excessively; **vivere in un lusso**

sfrenato to live in unrestrained luxury.

sfrigolare [sfrigo'lare] VI (*aus* **avere**) (*olio*) to sizzle; (*legno*) to crackle.

sfrondare [sfron'dare] VT (*albero*) to prune, thin out; (*fig: discorso, scritto*) to prune (down).

sfrontatamente [sfrontata'mente] AVV impudently, cheekily.

sfrontatezza [sfronta'tettsa] SF impudence, cheek; **avere la sfrontatezza di fare qc** to have the cheek to do sth.

sfrontato, a [sfron'tato] AGG impudent, cheeky.

sfruttamento [sfrutta'mento] SM exploitation.

sfruttare [sfrut'tare] VT (*terreno*) to overwork, exhaust; (*miniera*) to exploit, work; (*operaio*) to exploit; (*occasione, momento*) to make the most of, take advantage of.

sfruttato, a [sfrut'tato] AGG (*persona*) exploited; (*idea*) overworked.

sfruttatore, trice [sfrutta'tore] SM/F exploiter.

sfuggente [sfud'dʒɛnte] AGG (*fig: sguardo*) elusive; (*mento, fronte*) receding.

sfuggire [sfud'dʒire] VI (*aus* **essere**) (*gen*) to escape; **sfuggire alla polizia** to escape from the police; **sfuggire alla morte/alla cattura** to escape death/capture; **il sapone mi è sfuggito di mano** the soap slipped out of my hands; **mi sfugge il nome** his name escapes me; **mi è sfuggito di mente** it has slipped my memory; **si è lasciato sfuggire il nome** he let the name slip; **non ti sfugge niente** nothing escapes you, you don't miss a thing; **lasciarsi sfuggire un'occasione** to let an opportunity go by, miss an opportunity; **sfuggire al controllo** (*macchina*) to go out of control; (*situazione*) to get out of control.

sfuggita [sfud'dʒita] SF: **di sfuggita** (*notare, salutare*) in passing; **vedere di sfuggita** to catch a glimpse of.

sfumare [sfu'mare] ① VT (*colore: schiarire*) to soften, shade off; (*suono*) to fade out; (*capelli*) to taper.

② VI (*aus* **essere**) (*colore*): **sfumare in** to fade into, shade off into; (*fig: speranza*) to vanish, disappear, come to nothing.

sfumato, a [sfu'mato] AGG (*colore*) soft, mellow.

sfumatura [sfuma'tura] SF **a** (*azione: vedi vt*) softening, shading off; fading out; tapering **b** (*di colore*) shade, tone; **diverse sfumature di significato** different shades of meaning, different nuances; **una sfumatura d'ironia** a hint of irony.

sfuocato, a [sfwo'kato] AGG = **sfocato**.

sfuriata [sfu'rjata] SF outburst of rage, fit of rage *o* anger; **fare una sfuriata a qn** to give sb a good telling off.

sfuso, a ['sfuso] AGG (*caramelle*) loose, unpacked; (*vino*) unbottled; (*birra*) draught (*Brit*), draft (*Am*).

S.G. ABBR = *Sua Grazia*.

sg. ABBR = *seguente*.

sgabello [zga'bɛllo] SM stool.

sgabuzzino [zgabud'dzino] SM lumber room (*Brit*), storage room (*Am*).

sgambettare [zgambet'tare] VI (*aus* **avere**) to kick (one's legs) about; (*bambino*) to toddle.

sgambetto [zgam'betto] SM: **fare lo sgambetto a qn** to trip sb up; (*fig*) to oust sb.

sganasciarsi [zganaʃ'ʃarsi] VIP: **sganasciarsi dalle risate** *o* **dal ridere** to roar with laughter.

sganciamento [zgantʃa'mento] SM (*gen*) unhooking; (*treno*) uncoupling; (*di bombe*) dropping.

sganciare [zgan'tʃare] ① VT (*gen*) to unhook; (*chiusura*) to unfasten, undo; (*treno*) to uncouple; (*bombe*) to drop,

release; (*fig fam*: *soldi*) to fork out.

2 sganciarsi VIP (*gen*) to come unhooked; (*chiusura*) to come unfastened, come undone; (*treno*) to come uncoupled; **sganciarsi da** (*fig*: *persona*) to get away from.

sgangherare [zgange'rare] **1** VT (*porta*) to unhinge; (*cassa, baule*: *sfasciare*) to smash.

2 sgangherarsi VIP: **sgangherarsi dalle risate** to split one's sides laughing.

sgangherato, a [zgange'rato] AGG (*porta*) unhinged, off its hinges; (*auto*) ramshackle, rickety; (*risata*) wild, boisterous.

sgarbatamente [zgarbata'mente] AVV rudely, impolitely.

sgarbatezza [zgarba'tettsa] SF (*qualità*) rudeness, impoliteness, bad manners *pl*; **è stata una sgarbatezza arrivare tardi** it was rude to arrive late.

sgarbato, a [zgar'bato] AGG rude, ill-mannered, impolite.

sgarbo ['zgarbo] SM: **fare uno sgarbo a qn** to be rude to sb.

sgargiante [zgar'dʒante] AGG gaudy, showy.

sgarrare [zgar'rare] VI (*aus avere*) (*persona*) to step out of line; (*orologio*: *essere avanti*) to gain; (: *essere indietro*) to lose; **e guarda di non sgarrare!** watch your step!; **l'orologio sgarra di 2 minuti** the clock is 2 minutes fast (*o slow*).

sgarro ['zgarro] SM (*mancanza di correttezza*) mistake, inaccuracy; **non ammetto sgarri** I won't allow anyone to step out of line.

sgasare [zga'zare] VT (*bibita*) to make flat.

sgattaiolare [zgattajo'lare] VI (*aus essere*): **sgattaiolare fuori** to slip out, sneak out, **sgattaiolare via** to sneak away *o* off.

sgelare [zdʒe'lare] VT, VI (*aus essere*), **sgelarsi** VIP to melt, thaw.

sghembo, a ['zgembo] AGG (*storto*) crooked; **di sghembo** (*storto*) crookedly; (*obliquamente*) on the slant.

sghignazzare [zgiɲɲat'tsare] VI (*aus avere*) to laugh scornfully, sneer.

sghignazzata [zgiɲɲat'tsata] SF scornful laugh, sneer.

sghimbescio [zgim'beʃʃo] SM: **a** *o* **di sghimbescio** (*storto*) crookedly; (*obliquamente*) on the slant.

sghiribizzo [zgiri'biddzo] SM (*fam*: *capriccio*) whim, fancy; **avere lo sghiribizzo di (fare) qc** to fancy (doing) sth.

sgobbare [zgob'bare] VI (*aus avere*) (*fam*: *lavorare*) to slog, slave; (: *a scuola*) to swot (*Brit*), cram (*Am*); **sgobbare sui libri** to slog away at one's books.

sgobbata [zgob'bata] SF (*fam*: *lavoro*) slog, grind.

sgobbone [zgob'bone] SM (*fam*) slogger; (: *secchione*) swot (*Brit*), grind (*Am*).

sgocciolare [zgottʃo'lare] **1** VT (*acqua*) to drip; (*cosa immersa in un liquido*) to drain.

2 VI (*aus essere*) to drip.

sgocciolatura [zgottʃola'tura] SF **a** (*azione*) dripping **b** (*gocce*) drops *pl*; (*di pittura*) runs *pl*, streaks *pl*.

sgoccioli ['zgottʃoli] SMPL: **essere agli sgoccioli** (*lavoro, provviste*) to be nearly finished; (*periodo*) to be nearly over; **siamo agli sgoccioli** we've nearly finished, the end is in sight.

sgolarsi [zgo'larsi] VIP to become hoarse, talk (*o shout o sing*) o.s. hoarse; (*fig*: *parlare inutilmente*) to waste one's breath.

sgomberare [zgombe'rare] **1** VT (*stanza, aula, strada*) to clear; (*alloggio*) to move out of, vacate; (*zona*: *evacuare*) to evacuate.

2 VI (*aus avere*) (*traslocare*) to move.

sgombero ['zgombero] SM (*di strada, stanze*) clearing; (*di città*) evacuation; (*trasloco*) moving.

sgombrare [zgom'brare] VT = **sgomberare**.

sgombro[1], a ['zgombro] **1** AGG (*gen*) clear, empty.

2 SM = **sgombero**.

sgombro[2] ['zgombro] SM (*pesce*) mackerel.

sgomentare [zgomen'tare] **1** VT to dismay, alarm.

2 sgomentarsi VIP to be dismayed, be alarmed.

sgomento, a [zgo'mento] **1** AGG dismayed, alarmed.

2 SM dismay, alarm; **farsi prendere dallo sgomento** to be filled with dismay, be alarmed.

sgominare [zgomi'nare] VT (*nemico*) to rout; (*avversario*) to defeat; (*fig*: *epidemia*) to overcome.

sgonfiare [zgon'fjare] **1** VT (*gen*) to deflate, let the air out of, let down; (*fig*: *persona*) to bring down a peg or two.

2 sgonfiarsi VIP **a** (*gen*) to deflate; (*pneumatico*) to go flat; (*fig*: *persona*) to be deflated **b** (*Med*) to go down.

sgonfio, fia, fi, fie ['zgonfjo] AGG **a** (*pneumatico, pallone*) flat **b** (*Med*) no longer inflamed.

sgorbio, bi ['zgorbjo] SM (*macchia*) blot; (*scarabocchio*) scrawl, scribble; (*pegg*: *quadro*) daub; (*fam*: *persona brutta*) fright.

sgorgare [zgor'gare] VI (*aus essere*) (*gen*) to gush (out), spurt (out); (*lacrime*) to pour, flow; **il sangue sgorgava dalla ferita** the blood gushed *o* spurted from the wound.

sgottare [zgot'tare] VT (*barca, acqua*) to bale out.

sgozzare [zgot'tsare] VT to cut the throat of; (*macellare*: *anche fig*) to slaughter.

sgradevole [zgra'devole] AGG unpleasant; (*voce, odore*) unpleasant, disagreeable.

sgradevolmente [zgradevol'mente] AVV unpleasantly.

sgradito, a [zgra'dito] AGG unwelcome.

sgraffignare [zgraffiɲ'ɲare] VT (*fam*) to pinch, swipe.

sgrammaticato, a [zgrammati'kato] AGG ungrammatical.

sgranare [zgra'nare] VT (*fagioli*) to shell; (*pannocchia*) to remove the corn from; **sgranare gli occhi** (*fig*) to open one's eyes wide.

sgranchire [zgran'kire] VT to stretch; **sgranchirsi le gambe** to stretch one's legs.

sgranocchiare [zgranok'kjare] VT to munch, crunch.

sgrassare [zgras'sare] VT to remove the grease from.

sgravare [zgra'vare] **1** VT: **sgravare qn/qc (di)** (*peso, anche fig*) to relieve sb/sth (of).

2 sgravarsi VR (*partorire*) to give birth.

sgravio, vi ['zgravjo] SM: **sgravio fiscale** *o* **contributivo** tax relief.

sgraziato, a [zgrat'tsjato] AGG ungraceful, awkward, clumsy, ungainly.

sgretolamento [zgretola'mento] SM (*vedi vb*) splitting; flaking off; crumbling.

sgretolare [zgreto'lare] **1** VT (*roccia*) to split; (*intonaco*) to cause to flake off.

2 sgretolarsi VIP (*muro, creta, gesso*) to crumble; (*roccia*) to split.

sgretolato, a [zgreto'lato] AGG (*intonaco*) flaking, chipped; (*roccia, muro*) crumbling.

sgridare [zgri'dare] VT: **sgridare qn** to tell sb off, scold sb.

sgridata [zgri'data] SF telling off, scolding.

sgroppare [zgrop'pare] VI (*aus avere*) (*cavallo*) to buck.

sgroppata [zgrop'pata] SF (*di cavallo*) buck.

sgrossare [zgros'sare] VT (*marmo, legno*) to rough-hew; (*fig*: *modi*) to polish, refine.

sguaiataggine [zgwaja'taddʒine] SF coarseness.

sguaiato, a [zgwa'jato] AGG coarse, vulgar; **una risata sguaiata** a guffaw.

sguainare [zgwai'nare] VT to draw, unsheathe.

sgualcire [zgwal'tʃire] **1** VT to crumple (up), crease.
2 sgualcirsi VIP to become crumpled, become creased.

sgualcito, a [zgwal'tʃito] AGG crumpled, creased.

sgualdrina [zgwal'drina] SF trollop.

sguardo ['zgwardo] SM **a** (occhiata) glance, look; **dare uno sguardo a qc** to glance at sth, cast a glance o an eye over sth; **lanciare uno sguardo di rimprovero a qn** to give sb a reproachful look
b (espressione) expression, look (in one's eye); **avere lo sguardo fisso** to have a fixed expression; **ha uno sguardo intelligente** he has an intelligent expression
c (occhi): **alzare** o **sollevare lo sguardo** to raise one's eyes, look up; **abbassare lo sguardo** to lower one's eyes, look down; **cercare qn/qc con lo sguardo** to look (a)round for sb/sth; **distogliere lo sguardo da qn/qc** to take one's eyes off sb/sth; **fissare lo sguardo su qn/qc** to stare at sb/sth; **soffermarsi con lo sguardo su qn/qc** to let one's eyes rest on sb/sth; **volgere lo sguardo altrove** to look elsewhere; **attirare gli sguardi** (fig: attenzione) to attract (people's) attention.

sguarnire [zgwar'nire] VT **a** (togliere la guarnizione) to take the trimming off **b** (Mil: lasciare indifeso) to leave undefended.

sguarnito, a [zgwar'nito] AGG (vedi vb) untrimmed; undefended.

sguattero, a ['zgwattero] SM scullery boy/maid.

sguazzare [zgwat'tsare] VI (aus avere) (in acqua) to splash (about); (nel fango) to wallow; (fig: trovarsi a proprio agio) to be in one's element; **sguazzare nell'oro** to be rolling in money.

sguinzagliare [zgwintsaʎ'ʎare] VT (cane) to let off the leash; (fig: persona): **sguinzagliare qn dietro a qn** to set sb on sb.

sgusciare[1] [zguʃ'ʃare] VT (uovo, piselli) to shell.

sgusciare[2] [zguʃ'ʃare] VI (aus essere) to slip; **sgusciare di mano** to slip out of one's hand; **sgusciare via** (scappare) to escape, slip o slink away.

shaker ['ʃeikə] SM INV (cocktail) shaker.

shakerare [ʃeke'rare] VT (cocktail) to shake.

shakerato, a [ʃeke'rato] AGG (mescolato) shaken.

shampoo ['ʃampo] SM INV shampoo.

sherpa ['ʃɛrpa] SM INV sherpa.

sherry ['ʃɛri] SM INV sherry.

shoccare [ʃɔk'kare] VT = **scioccare**.

shock [ʃɔk] SM INV (gen, Med) shock; **sotto shock** in a state of shock.

shockare [ʃɔk'kare] VT = **scioccare**.

shorts [ʃɔ:ts] SMPL shorts.

SI SIGLA = Siena.

---

si[1] [si] PRON

davanti **la, li, le, ne** diventa **se**

a (in verbi riflessivi: impersonale) oneself; (: maschile) himself; (: femminile) herself; (: plurale) themselves; (in verbi intransitivi pronominali) itself;
▷**si crede** importante he (o she) thinks a lot of himself (o herself)
▷**se ne è dimenticata** she forgot about it
▷**si è dimenticato di me** he has forgotten me

▷**l'orologio si è fermato** the clock has stopped
▷**si guardava allo specchio** he was looking at himself in the mirror
▷**lavarsi** to wash (oneself)
▷**si nascosero** they hid
▷**pettinarsi** to comb one's hair
▷**si è rotto** it has broken
▷**digli di sbrigarsi** tell him to hurry up
▷**sporcarsi** to get dirty
▷**si è tagliato** he's cut himself
b (con complemento oggetto)
▷**si è tolto il cappello** he took off his hat
▷**lavarsi le mani** to wash one's hands
▷**si è sporcato i pantaloni** he got his trousers (Brit) o pants (Am) dirty
▷**se l'è ricordato** he remembered it
▷**si godette la vacanza** he (o she) enjoyed his (o her) holiday
c (uso reciproco) each other, one another;
▷**si baciarono** they kissed
▷**si incontrarono** alle 5 they met at 5 o'clock
▷**si odiano** they hate each other o one another
d (passivo)
▷**dove si parla russo** where Russian is spoken, where they speak Russian
▷**si ripara facilmente** it can easily be repaired
▷**si vende** al chilo it is sold by the kilo
e (impersonale)
▷**si dice** che... it is said that ..., people say that ...
▷**mi si dice** che... I am told that ...
▷**non si risponde così!** that's no way to answer somebody!
▷**non si sa mai** you never can tell, you never know
▷**si vede che è nuovo** one (o you) can tell it's new.

---

si[2] [si] SM INV (Mus) B; (: solfeggiando la scala) ti.

sì[1] [si] **1** AVV **a** yes; **hai finito? — sì** have you finished? — yes (I have); **sei sicuro? — sì, certo** are you sure? — yes, of course (I am); **ma sì!** yes, of course!, I should say so!; **sì e no** yes and no; **avrà sì e no 10 anni** he must be about 10 years old; **saranno stati sì e no in 20** there must have been about 20 of them; **uno sì e uno no** every other one; **un giorno sì e uno no** every other day; **sì, domani!** OR **sì, proprio!** (iro) you'll be lucky!, fat chance of that!
b (rafforzativo): **allora vieni, sì o no?** are you coming or not?; **questa sì che è bella!** that's a good one!
c : **dire di sì** to say yes; **spero/penso di sì** I hope/think so; **forse (che) sì, forse (che) no** maybe, maybe not; **fece di sì col capo** he nodded (his head); **vieni? se sì ci vediamo dopo** are you coming? if so I'll see you later; **e sì che...** and to think that ....
2 SM yes; **non mi aspettavo un sì** I didn't expect him (o her ecc) to say yes; **sono tra il sì e il no** I'm uncertain, I can't make up my mind; **per me è sì** I should think so, I expect so.

sì[2] [si] AVV = **così**.

sia[1] ['sia] CONG **a** : **sia... sia..., sia... che...** (tanto... quanto...) both ...and ...; **sia Franco sia Mario hanno accettato** OR **sia Franco che Mario hanno accettato** both Franco and Mario have accepted **b** : **sia che... sia che...** (o... o...) whether ...or ...; **sia che accetti sia che non accetti** whether he accepts or not.

sia[2] ['sia] VB vedi **essere**.

SIAE [si'ae] SIGLA F = *Società Italiana Autori ed Editori.*

sial ['sial] SM INV (*Geol*) sial.

Siam ['siam] SM: **il Siam** Siam.

siamese [sia'mese] 1 AGG Siamese; **gatto siamese** Siamese (cat); **fratelli siamesi** Siamese twins.
2 SM/F Siamese *inv.*
3 SM (*lingua*) Siamese.

siamo ['sjamo] VB vedi **essere.**

Siberia [si'bɛrja] SF: **la Siberia** Siberia.

siberiano, a [sibe'rjano] AGG, SM/F Siberian.

sibilante [sibi'lante] 1 AGG (*suono*) hissing; (*Fonetica*) sibilant.
2 SF (*Fonetica*) sibilant.

sibilare [sibi'lare] VI (*aus* avere) (*serpente*) to hiss; (*vento*) to whistle.

sibilla [si'billa] SF (*Mitol*) sibyl.

sibillino, a [sibil'lino] AGG (*anche fig*) sibylline; **parole sibilline** enigmatic words.

sibilo ['sibilo] SM (*di serpente*) hiss(ing); (*di vento*) whistling, whistle.

sicario, ri [si'karjo] SM hired assassin *o* killer.

sicché [sik'ke] CONG (*così che*) so (that), therefore; (*allora*) (and) so.

siccità [sittʃi'ta] SF drought.

siccome [sik'kome] CONG since, as.

Sicilia [si'tʃilja] SF: **la Sicilia** Sicily.

siciliano, a [sitʃi'ljano] AGG, SM/F Sicilian.

sicomoro [siko'mɔro] SM sycamore.

siculo, a ['sikulo] AGG, SM/F Sicilian.

sicura [si'kura] SF (*di arma, di spilla*) safety catch; (*di portiera*) safety lock.

sicuramente [sikura'mente] AVV (*con sicurezza, comportarsi, dichiarare*) confidently; (*certamente*) undoubtedly, certainly.

sicurezza [siku'rettsa] SF **a** (*immunità*) safety; **la sicurezza stradale** road safety; **di sicurezza** (*dispositivo, margine*) safety *attr*
b (*salvaguardia di diritti*) security; **per la sicurezza nazionale** for national security; **(forze di) Pubblica Sicurezza** police (force)
c (*certezza*) certainty; **avere la sicurezza di qc** to be sure *o* certain of sth; **lo so con sicurezza** I am quite certain
d (*fiducia, tranquillità*) confidence; **sicurezza (di sé)** self-confidence, self-assurance; **ha risposto con molta sicurezza** he answered very confidently.

sicuro, a [si'kuro] 1 AGG **a** (*senza pericolo*) safe; (*ben difeso*) safe, secure; **non è sicuro qui** it isn't safe here; **sentirsi sicuro** to feel safe *o* secure
b (*certo*) certain, sure; **la vittoria è sicura** victory is assured; **essere sicuro di qc/che...** to be sure of sth/that ...; **ne ero sicuro!** I knew it!; **ne sei proprio sicuro?** are you sure *o* certain?
c (*fiducioso, tranquillo*) (self-)confident, sure of o.s.; **essere sicuro di sé** to be self-confident, be sure of o.s.
d (*attendibile*) reliable, sure; (: *rimedio*) sure, safe; (*esperto*) skilled; **da fonte sicura** from reliable sources
e (*saldo*) firm, steady; **con mano sicura** with a steady hand.
2 AVV of course, certainly; **di sicuro** certainly.
3 SM **a** (*cosa certa*): **dare qc per sicuro** to be sure about sth; **dare per sicuro che...** to be sure that ...
b (*luogo sicuro*): **essere al sicuro** to be safe, be in a safe place; **mettersi al sicuro** to take cover; **mettere qc al sicuro** to put sth away (in a safe place)
c (*non rischiare*): **andare sul sicuro** to play safe.

siderurgia [siderur'dʒia] SF iron and steel industry.

siderurgico, a, ci, che [side'rurdʒiko] AGG iron and steel *attr.*

sidro ['sidro] SM cider.

siedo *ecc* ['sjɛdo] VB vedi **sedere.**

siepe ['sjɛpe] SF hedge; (*Sport*) hedge, hurdle.

siero ['sjɛro] SM serum; **siero del latte** whey ▶ **siero antivipera** snake bite serum ▶ **siero della verità** truth serum *o* drug.

sieronegatività [sjeronegativi'ta] SF HIV-negative status.

sieronegativo, a [sjeronega'tivo] 1 AGG HIV-negative.
2 SM/F HIV-negative (person).

sieropositività [sjeropozitivi'ta] SF HIV-positive status.

sieropositivo, a [sjeropozi'tivo] 1 AGG HIV positive.
2 SM/F HIV-positive (person).

sieroterapia [sjerotera'pia] SF serotherapy.

sierra ['sjɛrra] SF (*Geo*) sierra.

Sierra Leone ['sjɛrra le'one] SF: **la Sierra Leone** Sierra Leone.

siesta ['sjɛsta] SF siesta, (afternoon) nap; **fare la siesta** to have a nap *o* siesta.

siete ['sjɛte] VB vedi **essere.**

sifilide [si'filide] SF syphilis.

sifilitico, a, ci, che [sifi'litiko] AGG, SM/F syphilitic.

sifone [si'fone] SM (*Tecn*) siphon; (*per seltz*) (soda) siphon (*Brit*), soda-water siphon (*Am*).

Sig. ABBR (= *signore*) Mr.

sigaretta [siga'retta] SF cigarette.

sigaro ['sigaro] SM cigar.

Sigg. ABBR (= *signori*) Messrs.

sigillare [sidʒil'lare] VT to seal.

sigillo [si'dʒillo] SM seal; **mettere** *o* **porre i sigilli a qc** to seal sth, put seals on sth; **anello con sigillo** signet ring.

sigla ['sigla] SF **a** (*abbreviazione*) acronym, abbreviation; (*iniziali*) initials *pl*; (*monogramma*) monogram; **sigla automobilistica** *abbreviation of province on vehicle number plate* **b** : **sigla musicale** signature tune.

siglare [si'glare] VT to initial.

Sig.na ABBR (= *signorina*) Miss, Ms.

significare [siɲɲifi'kare] VT **a** (*aver senso*) to mean; **cosa significa?** what does this mean?; **cosa significa questa parola?** what does this word mean? **b** (*avere importanza*) to mean, matter; **tu significhi molto per me** you mean a lot to me.

significativamente [siɲɲifikativa'mente] AVV (*in modo significativo*) significantly; (*efficacemente*) effectively.

significativo, a [siɲɲifika'tivo] AGG significant.

significato [siɲɲifi'kato] SM meaning, sense; (*valore, importanza*) importance; **senza significato** meaningless; **non ha alcun significato per me** it doesn't mean anything to me.

signora [siɲ'ɲora] SF **a** (*donna*) lady; (*moglie*) wife; **ti cercava una signora** there was a lady looking for you; **è una vera signora** she's a real lady; **vive da signora** she leads a life of luxury; **le presento la mia signora** may I introduce my wife?; **il signor Rossi e signora** Mr Rossi and his wife; **Signore e Signori!** Ladies and Gentlemen!; **Nostra Signora** (*Rel*) Our Lady
b (*rivolgendosi a qualcuno*): **buon giorno signora** good morning; (*deferente*) good morning Madam; (*quando si conosce il nome*) good morning Mrs (*o* Ms) X; **signora maestra!** please Mrs (*o* Ms) X!, please Miss!
c (*parlando di qualcuno*): **la signora Rossi sta male** Mrs

(*o* Ms) Rossi is ill; **lo dirò alla signora** I'll let Mrs (*o* Ms) X know

d (*in lettere*): **Gentile Signora** Dear Madam; **Gentile** (*o* **Cara**) **Signora Rossi** Dear Mrs (*o* Ms) Rossi; **Gentile Signora Anna Rossi** (*sulle buste*) Mrs (*o* Ms) Anna Rossi.

signore [siɲˈɲore] SM **a** (*uomo*) gentleman; **c'è un signore che ti cerca** there's a gentleman looking for you; **è un vero signore** he's a real gentleman; **fa una vita da (gran) signore** he lives like a lord; **fanno una vita da signori** they lead a life of luxury; **il Signore** (*Rel*) the Lord; **oh Signore!** oh Lord!, oh God!

b (*rivolgendosi a qualcuno*): **buon giorno signore** good morning; (*deferente*) good morning Sir; (*quando si conosce il nome*) good morning Mr X; **signor maestro!** please Mr X!, please Sir!; **signor Presidente** Mr Chairman

c (*parlando di qualcuno*): **il signor Rossi sta male** Mr Rossi is ill; **lo dirò al signore** I'll let Mr X know; **i signori Bianchi** (*coniugi*) Mr and Mrs Bianchi

d (*in lettere*): **Gentile Signore** Dear Sir; **Gentile** (*o* **Caro**) **Signor Rossi** Dear Mr Rossi; **Gentile Signor Paolo Rossi** (*sulle buste*) Mr Paolo Rossi.

signoria [siɲɲoˈria] SF (*Storia*) seignory, signoria.

signorile [siɲɲoˈrile] AGG (*distinto*) refined, distinguished; (: *quartiere*) exclusive; (*da signore*) gentlemanly, gentlemanlike; (*da signora*) ladylike.

signorilità [siɲɲoriliˈta] SF (*raffinatezza*) refinement; (*eleganza*) elegance.

signorilmente [siɲɲorilˈmente] AVV (*comportarsi*) in a gentlemanly (*o* ladylike) manner.

signorina [siɲɲoˈrina] SF **a** (*giovane donna*) young woman; **ormai sei una signorina!** (*complimento*) how grown up you are!; (*rimprovero*) you're not a child any more!; **rimanere signorina** to remain a spinster

b (*rivolgendosi a qualcuno*): **buon giorno signorina** good morning; (*deferente*) good morning Madam; (*quando si conosce il nome*) good morning Miss (*o* Ms) X

c (*parlando di qualcuno*): **la signorina Rossi sta male** Miss (*o* Ms) Rossi is ill

d (*in lettere*): **Gentile signorina** Dear Madam; **Gentile** (*o* **Cara**) **Signorina Rossi** Dear Miss (*o* Ms) Rossi; **Gentile Signorina Anna Rossi** (*sulle buste*) Miss (*o* Ms) Anna Rossi.

signorino [siɲɲoˈrino] SM young master.

signorsì [siɲɲorˈsi] AVV (*anche scherz*) yes sir, aye aye sir.

Sig.ra ABBR (= *signora*) Mrs, Ms.

silenziatore [silentsjaˈtore] SM (*di arma, Tecn*) silencer.

silenzio, zi [siˈlɛntsjo] SM **a** (*gen*) silence; **fare silenzio** to be quiet, stop talking; **restare in silenzio** to keep quiet; **in silenzio** in silence; **far passare qc sotto silenzio** to keep quiet about sth, hush sth up ▶ **silenzio stampa** press blackout

b (*calma, pace*) silence, still(ness), quiet; **nel silenzio della notte** in the still of the night

c (*Mil*) lights out.

silenziosamente [silentsjosaˈmente] AVV silently, quietly.

silenzioso, a [silenˈtsjoso] AGG (*gen*) silent, quiet; (*motore*) quiet.

silhouette [siˈlwɛt] SF INV (*sagoma*) outline, silhouette; (*figura*) figure.

silice [ˈsilitʃe] SF silica.

silicio [siˈlitʃo] SM silicon.

silicone [siliˈkone] SM silicone.

silicosi [siliˈkɔzi] SF INV (*Med*) silicosis.

sillaba [ˈsillaba] SF syllable; **dividere in sillabe** to divide into syllables; **non ho capito una sillaba di quello che hai detto** I haven't understood a single word of what you've said; **senza cambiare una sillaba** word for word.

sillabare [sillaˈbare] VT to divide into syllables.

sillabario, ri [sillaˈbarjo] SM spelling book.

sillabico, a, ci, che [silˈlabiko] AGG syllabic.

sillogismo [silloˈdʒizmo] SM syllogism.

silo [ˈsilo] SM silo.

silografia [silograˈfia] SF wood engraving, xylography.

siluramento [siluraˈmento] SM (*Mil*) torpedoing; (*fig*: *progetto*) wrecking; (: *persona*) ousting, dismissal.

silurare [siluˈrare] VT (*Mil, fig*: *legge*) to torpedo; (: *progetto*) wreck; (: *persona di comando*) to remove from power, dismiss.

siluro [siˈluro] SM (*Mil*) torpedo.

silvestre [silˈvɛstre] AGG woodland *attr*.

Sim [sim] SIGLA F: **società di intermediazione mobiliare** brokerage company.

simbiosi [simbiˈɔzi] SF INV (*Bio, fig*) symbiosis.

simboleggiare [simboledˈdʒare] VT to symbolize, represent.

simbolicamente [simbolikaˈmente] AVV symbolically.

simbolico, a, ci, che [simˈbɔliko] AGG symbolic(al).

simbolismo [simboˈlizmo] SM symbolism.

simbolista, i, e [simboˈlista] ① AGG symbolist *attr*.

② SM/F symbolist.

simbolo [ˈsimbolo] SM (*gen, Mat, Chim*) symbol; **simbolo di successo** status symbol.

similare [simiˈlare] AGG similar.

simile [ˈsimile] ① AGG **a** (*gen, analogo*) similar; **simile a** like, similar to; **hai la gonna simile alla mia** you've got a skirt like mine; **avevo un vestito simile una volta** I had a dress like that once; **abbiamo gusti simili** we have similar tastes

b (*pegg*: *tale*) such; **una cosa simile** such a thing; **un uomo simile** such a man, a man like this

c : **di simile: non ho mai visto niente di simile** I've never seen anything of the sort *o* like that; **è insegnante** *o* **qualcosa di simile** he's a teacher or something like that.

② SM/F **a** (*spec al pl*: *persona*) fellow being; **i suoi simili** one's fellow men; (*pari*) one's peers

b (*oggetti*): **vendono vasi e simili** they sell vases and things like that.

similitudine [similiˈtudine] SF **a** (*Retorica*) simile **b** (*Mat*) similarity.

similmente [similˈmente] AVV similarly.

similpelle [similˈpɛlle] SF Leatherette ®.

simmetria [simmeˈtria] SF symmetry.

simmetrico, a, ci, che [simˈmɛtriko] AGG symmetric(al).

simpatia [simpaˈtia] SF (*qualità*) pleasantness; (*inclinazione*) liking; **è di una simpatia!** she's extremely nice *o* pleasant!; **con simpatia** (*su lettera*) with much affection; **avere** *o* **provare simpatia per qn** to like sb, have a liking for sb; **prendere qn in simpatia** to take (a liking) to sb; **guadagnarsi la simpatia di qn** to gain sb's affection; **avere una simpatia per qn** (*esserne attratto*) to feel attracted to sb.

simpaticamente [simpatikaˈmente] AVV (*sorridere, scherzare*) pleasantly, in a friendly fashion.

simpatico¹, a, ci, che [simˈpatiko] AGG **a** (*persona*) nice, pleasant, likeable; (*appartamento, albergo*) nice, pleasant; **mi è molto simpatico** I like him very much; **non è simpatico quando succedono queste cose** it's not

very nice when these things happen; **un modo di fare simpatico** a friendly manner

  b : **inchiostro simpatico** invisible ink.

simpatico², **a**, **ci che** [sim'patiko] [1] AGG (*nervo, sistema nervoso*) sympathetic.

  [2] (*Anat*) sympathetic nervous system.

simpatizzante [simpatid'dzante] SM/F sympathizer.

simpatizzare [simpatid'dzare] VI (*aus* **avere**): **simpatizzare con** to take a liking to.

simposio, **si** [sim'pozjo] SM symposium.

simulacro [simu'lakro] SM (*statua, immagine*) image, simulacrum; (*fig: traccia, parvenza*) semblance.

simulare [simu'lare] VT (*gen, Tecn*) to simulate; (*sentimento*) to fake, feign; **simulare uno svenimento** to pretend to faint; **simulare una malattia** to pretend to be ill, feign *o* fake illness.

simulatore [simula'tore] SM (*Tecn*) simulator ▸ **simulatore di volo** (*Aer*) flight simulator.

simulazione [simulat'tsjone] SF (*vedi vb*) simulation; faking, feigning; **fu tutta una simulazione** it was all a pretence.

simultaneamente [simultanea'mente] AVV simultaneously, at the same time.

simultaneità [simultanei'ta] SF simultaneity.

simultaneo, **a** [simul'taneo] AGG simultaneous.

sin. ABBR (= *sinistra*) L.

sinagoga [sina'gɔga] SF synagogue.

sinapsi [si'napsi] SF INV (*Bio*) synapse.

sinceramente [sintʃera'mente] AVV (*gen*) sincerely; (*francamente*) honestly, sincerely.

sincerarsi [sintʃe'rarsi] VIP: **sincerarsi (di qc)** to make sure (of sth).

sincerità [sintʃeri'ta] SF (*vedi agg*) sincerity; genuineness; **con tutta sincerità** in all sincerity, honestly.

sincero, **a** [sin'tʃɛro] AGG **a** (*onesto*) sincere, honest; **essere sincero con qn** to be honest with sb; **per essere sincero** to be honest, honestly **b** (*genuino*) real, genuine, true; **un amico sincero** a real friend.

sinclinale [sinkli'nale] SF, AGG (*Geol*) syncline.

sincopato, **a** [sinko'pato] AGG (*Mus*) syncopated.

sincope ['sinkope] SF (*Ling*) syncope; (*Med*) fainting fit, blackout; (*Mus*) syncopation.

sincronia [sinkro'nia] SF (*di movimento*) synchronism.

sincronico, **a**, **ci**, **che** [sin'krɔniko] AGG synchronic.

sincronizzare [sinkronid'dzare] VT to synchronize.

sincronizzato, **a** [sinkronid'dzato] AGG synchronized; **marce sincronizzate** (*Aut*) syncromesh (gears).

sincronizzatore [sinkroniddza'tore] SM synchronizer.

sincronizzazione [sinkroniddzat'tsjone] SF synchronization.

sindacale [sinda'kale] AGG (*legge, lotta, riunione*) (trade) union *attr*; (*dottrina*) unionist.

sindacalismo [sindaka'lizmo] SM (trade) unionism.

sindacalista, **i**, **e** [sindaka'lista] SM/F trade unionist.

sindacare [sinda'kare] VT **a** (*controllare*) to inspect **b** (*fig: criticare*) to criticize.

sindacato [sinda'kato] SM (*di lavoratori*) (trade) union; (*di datori di lavoro*) association.

sindaco, **ci** ['sindako] SM mayor.

sindone ['sindone] SF (*Rel*): **la Sacra Sindone** the Holy Shroud.

sindrome ['sindrome] SF (*Med*) syndrome.

sinedrio, **ri** [si'nɛdrjo] SM (*tribunale ebraico*) Sanhedrin.

sinergia, **gie** [siner'dʒia] SF (*anche: fig*) synergy.

sinfonia [sinfo'nia] SF symphony.

sinfonico, **a**, **ci**, **che** [sin'fɔniko] AGG symphonic; (*orchestra*) symphony *attr*.

singalese [singa'lese] AGG SM/F Sin(g)halese *inv*.

Singapore [singa'pore] SF Singapore.

singhiozzante [singjot'tsante] AGG sobbing.

singhiozzare [singjot'tsare] VI (*aus* **avere**) **a** (*piangere*) to sob **b** (*avere il singhiozzo*) to hiccup.

singhiozzo [sin'gjottso] SM **a** (*Med*) hiccup; **avere il singhiozzo** to have (the) hiccups; **a singhiozzo** *o* **singhiozzi** (*fig*) by fits and starts; **sciopero a singhiozzo** on-off strike; **la macchina andava a singhiozzi** the car jolted *o* jerked along

  b (*di pianto*) sob; **scoppiare in singhiozzi** to burst into tears; **addormentarsi tra i singhiozzi** to sob o.s. to sleep.

singolare [singo'lare] [1] AGG **a** (*Gramm*) singular; **1ª persona singolare** 1st person singular **b** (*insolito, particolare*) remarkable, singular; (*strano*) strange, peculiar, odd.

  [2] SM **a** (*Gramm*) singular; **al singolare** in the singular **b** (*Tennis*): **un singolare** a singles (match).

singolarmente [singolar'mente] AVV **a** (*separatamente*) individually, one at a time **b** (*in modo strano*) strangely, peculiarly, oddly.

singolo, **a** ['singolo] [1] AGG (*gen*) single, individual; **ogni singolo caso** every single case, each case; **ogni singolo individuo** each individual; **camera singola** single room.

  [2] SM **a** (*individuo*) individual **b** (*Tennis*): **un singolo** a singles (match).

sinistra [si'nistra] SF **a** (*mano*) left hand **b** (*parte*) left, left-hand side; **a sinistra** (*stato in luogo*) on the left; (*moto a luogo*) to the left; **a sinistra di** to the left of; **corsia di sinistra** left-hand lane; **guida a sinistra** left-hand drive; **tenere la sinistra** to keep to the left **c** (*Pol*): **la sinistra** the left; **di sinistra** left-wing.

sinistramente [sinistra'mente] AVV sinisterly, in a sinister way.

sinistrato, **a** [sinis'trato] [1] AGG damaged; **zona sinistrata** disaster area.

  [2] SM/F (*vittima di catastrofe*) disaster victim.

sinistro, **a** [si'nistro] [1] AGG **a** (*mano, piede*) left; (*parte, lato*) left(-hand) **b** (*bieco*) sinister.

  [2] SM **a** (*incidente*) accident **b** (*Pugilato*) left; (*Calcio*): **tirare di sinistro** to kick with one's left foot.

sinistroide [sinis'trɔide] AGG, SM/F (*pegg*) leftist.

sino ['sino] PREP = **fino**.

sino... ['sino] PREF sino... .

sinodo ['sinodo] SM (*Rel*) synod.

sinonimo [si'nɔnimo] [1] SM synonym.

  [2] AGG synonymous; **un nome che è sinonimo di qualità** a name which is synonymous with good quality.

sinoviale [sino'vjale] AGG (*Anat*) synovial.

sintagma, **i** [sin'tagma] SM syntagm.

sintassi [sin'tassi] SF INV syntax.

sintatticamente [sintattika'mente] AVV syntactically.

sintattico, **a**, **ci**, **che** [sin'tattiko] AGG syntactic.

sintesi ['sintezi] SF INV **a** (*Chim, Filosofia*) synthesis **b** (*riassunto*) summary, résumé; **fare la sintesi di qc** to make a summary of sth; **in sintesi** in brief, in short.

sinteticamente [sintetika'mente] AVV (*vedi agg*) briefly, concisely; synthetically.

sintetico, **a**, **ci**, **che** [sin'tɛtiko] AGG **a** (*conciso*) brief, concise **b** (*fibre, materiale*) synthetic.

sintetizzare [sintetid'dzare] VT (*Bio, Chim*) to synthesize;

(*riassumere*: *testo*) to summarize.

sintetizzatore [sintetiddza'tore] SM (*Mus*) synthesizer.

sintomatico, a, ci, che [sinto'matiko] AGG (*Med*, *fig*) symptomatic.

sintomo ['sintomo] SM (*Med*, *fig*) symptom; **presentare i sintomi di** to show symptoms of.

sintonia [sinto'nia] SF (*Radio*) tuning; **essere in sintonia con qn** (*fig*) to be on the same wavelength as sb.

sintonizzare [sintonid'dzare] [1] VT to tune (in).

[2] **sintonizzarsi** VIP: **sintonizzarsi su** to tune in to.

sintonizzatore [sintoniddza'tore] SM tuner.

sintonizzazione [sintoniddzat'tsjone] SF tuning.

sinuosamente [sinuosa'mente] AVV (*gen*) sinuously.

sinuosità [sinuosi'ta] SF INV (*di strada*, *fiume*) winding; (*di corpo*) curve.

sinuoso, a [sinu'oso] AGG (*gen*) sinuous; (*fiume*, *strada*) winding, sinuous.

sinusite [sinu'zite] SF (*Med*) sinusitis.

sinusoidale [sinuzoi'dale] AGG (*Mat*) sinusoidal.

sinusoide [sinu'zɔide] SF (*Mat*) sine curve, sinusoid.

sionismo [sio'nizmo] SM Zionism.

sionista, i, e [sio'nista] AGG, SM/F Zionist.

SIP [sip] SIGLA F (= *Società Italiana per l'esercizio telefonico*) *formerly*, *Italian telephone company*.

sipario, ri [si'parjo] SM (*Teatro*) curtain; **calare il sipario su qc** (*fig*: *concluderla*) to bring the curtain down over sth.

Siracusa [sira'kusa] SF Syracuse.

siracusano, a [siraku'zano] [1] AGG of *o* from Syracuse.

[2] SM/F inhabitant *o* native of Syracuse.

sire ['sire] SM (*al re*): **Sire** Sire.

sirena¹ [si'rɛna] SF (*Mitol*, *fig*) mermaid, siren.

sirena² [si'rɛna] SF (*segnale*: *di polizia*, *ambulanza*, *pompieri*) siren; (: *di fabbrica*) hooter; **sirena d'allarme** (*per incendio*) fire alarm; (*per furto*) burglar alarm.

Siria ['sirja] SF: **la Siria** Syria.

siriano, a [si'rjano] AGG, SM/F Syrian.

siringa, ghe [si'ringa] SF **a** (*Med*) syringe **b** (*Culin*) ≈ piping *o* forcing bag.

siringare [sirin'gare] VT (*Med*) to syringe.

SISDE ['sizde] SIGLA M (= *Servizio per l'informazione e la Sicurezza Democratica*) *security service*.

Sisifo ['sizifo] SM Sisyphus.

sisma, i ['sizma] SM earthquake.

SISMI ['sizmi] SIGLA M (= *Servizio per l'Informazione e la Sicurezza Militari*) *military security service*.

sismico, a, ci, che ['sizmiko] AGG (*gen*) seismic; (*zona*) earthquake *attr*.

sismografo [siz'mɔgrafo] SM seismograph.

sismologia [sizmolo'dʒia] SF seismology.

sismologo, a, gi, ghe [siz'mɔlogo] SM/F seismologist.

sissignore [sissiɲ'ɲore] AVV (*a un superiore*) yes, sir; (*enfatico*) yes indeed, of course.

sistema, i [sis'tɛma] SM **a** (*Anat*, *Mat*, *Filosofia*) system; **sistema decimale/nervoso/solare** decimal/nervous/solar system; **sistema di sicurezza** security system

b (*metodo*) method, way; (*procedimento*) process; **è meglio seguire questo sistema** it's better to follow this method; **il suo sistema di vita** his way of life; **trovare il sistema per fare qc** to find a way to do sth; **non è questo il sistema di lavorare!** this is no way to work!; **ti suggerisco di cambiare sistema** I suggest you go about things in a different way; **bel sistema di trovare la soluzione!** (*iro*) that's some solution!

c (*Totocalcio*) system.

sistemare [siste'mare] [1] VT **a** (*mettere a posto*: *stanza*) to tidy (up), put in order; (: *arredamento*) to arrange; **mi piace come hai sistemato la casa** I like the way you've got the house; **sistemarsi i capelli** to tidy one's hair; **sistemarsi i vestiti** to straighten one's clothes

b : **sistemare qn** (*trovargli lavoro*) to fix sb up with a job; (*trovargli marito o moglie*) to marry sb off; (*fare i conti con*) to fix sb; **sistemare qn in un albergo** to fix sb up with a hotel; **l'abbiamo sistemato da noi** we put him up; **sistemare qn per le feste** to beat sb up; **ti sistemo io!** I'll soon sort you out!

c (*questione*, *faccenda*) to settle, sort out; **sistemo tutto io** I'll see to everything.

[2] **sistemarsi** VR (*persona*: *trovare alloggio*) to find accommodation (*Brit*) *o* accommodations (*Am*); (: *trovarsi un lavoro*) to find a job, to get fixed up with a job; (: *sposarsi*) to get married; **è ora che ti sistemi** it's time you settled down; **si è sistemato in un albergo** he found a room in a hotel, he fixed himself up with a hotel; **si sistemò sul divano** he slept on the sofa.

[3] **sistemarsi** VIP (*problema*, *questione*) to be settled.

sistematicamente [sistematika'mente] AVV systematically.

sistematico, a, ci, che [siste'matiko] AGG systematic, methodical.

sistemazione [sistemat'tsjone] SF **a** (*di stanza*, *casa*: *assetto*) tidying up; (: *disposizione*) arrangement, layout, order

b : **cercare una sistemazione** (*alloggio*) to look for accommodation (*Brit*) *o* accommodations (*Am*); (*lavoro*) to look for work *o* employment

c (*di problema*, *questione*) settlement.

sistole ['sistole] SF systole.

sito, a ['sito] [1] AGG (*Amm*) situated.

[2] SM (*letter*) place.

situare [situ'are] VT (*casa*) to site, situate, locate; (*film*, *romanzo*) to set; **la casa è situata su una collina/in riva al mare** the house is situated on a hill/on the coast.

situazione [situat'tsjone] SF situation; **vista la tua situazione familiare** given your family situation *o* circumstances; **nella tua situazione** in your position *o* situation; **mi trovo in una situazione critica** I'm in a very difficult situation *o* position.

siviera [si'vjɛra] SF (*Metallurgia*) ladle.

skai® ['skai] SM Leatherette ®.

sketch [sketʃ] SM INV (*Teatro*) sketch.

ski-bob ['ski:bɔb] SM INV ski-bob.

ski-lift ['ski:lift] SM INV ski tow.

skinhead ['skin hed] SM/F skinhead.

skipass ['ski:pa:s] SM INV ski pass.

ski stopper ['ski:stɔpə'] SM INV ski stopper.

slabbrare [zlab'brare] VT (*ferita*) **slabbrarsi** VIP to open.

slabbrato, a [zlab'brato] AGG (*ferita*) open.

slacciare [zlat'tʃare] [1] VT (*nodo*) to untie, undo, unfasten; (*scarpa*) to unlace; (*bottoni*) to unfasten; (*abito*, *cravatta*, *cappotto*) to undo.

[2] **slacciarsi** VIP (*vedi vt*) to come untied, come undone; to come unlaced; to come unfastened.

slalom ['zlalom] SM INV (*Sci*) slalom; **fare lo slalom** to slalom ▶ **slalom gigante** giant slalom ▶ **slalom speciale** (special) slalom.

slalomista, i, e [zlalo'mista] SM/F slalom specialist, slalom racer.

slanciare [zlan'tʃare] [1] VT to hurl, fling, throw.

[2] **slanciarsi** VR to throw o.s., hurl o.s.; **slanciarsi contro qn** to throw o.s. on sb; **slanciarsi nella mischia** to throw o.s. into the fray.

slanciato, a [zlan'tʃato] AGG (*persona*) slender, slim; (*colonna*) slender.

slancio, ci ['zlantʃo] SM dash, leap; (*fig*) surge; **darsi o prendere lo slancio** (*da fermo*) to spring up; (*correndo*) to bound forward; **in uno slancio d'affetto** in a burst o rush of affection; **abbracciare qn con slancio** to hug sb enthusiastically; **agire di slancio** to act impetuously; **uno slancio di generosità** a fit of generosity.

slargo, ghi ['zlargo] SM widening.

slavato, a [zla'vato] AGG (*colore*) washed out, faded; (*persona*) mousy; (*viso*) pale, colourless (*Brit*), colorless (*Am*).

slavina [zla'vina] SF snowslide.

slavo, a ['zlavo] [1] AGG Slav(onic).
   [2] SM/F Slav.
   [3] SM (*lingua*) Slavonic.

sleale [zle'ale] AGG (*persona: non leale*) disloyal; (*concorrenza*) unfair; **essere sleale con** to be disloyal towards; **gioco sleale** (*Sport*) foul play; **essere sleale al gioco** to cheat.

slealmente [zleal'mente] AVV (*senza lealtà*) disloyally; (*senza correttezza*) unfairly.

slealtà [zleal'ta] SF (*vedi agg*) disloyalty; unfairness.

slegare [zle'gare] [1] VT (*gen*) to untie; (*liberare*) to free, release.
   [2] **slegarsi** VR (*vedi vt*) to untie o.s.; to free o.s.

slegato, a [zle'gato] AGG (*animale*) loose; (*fig: discorso, stile*) disconnected.

slip [zlip] SM INV (*mutandine*) briefs *pl*; (*da bagno: per uomo*) (swimming) trunks *pl*; (: *per donna*) bikini briefs *pl*.

slitta ['zlitta] SF (*gen*) sledge; (*trainata*) sleigh.

slittamento [zlitta'mento] SM (*vedi vb*) slipping; skidding; sliding; fall; postponement; **slittamento salariale** wage drift.

slittare [zlit'tare] VI (*gen*) to slip, slide; (*automobile*) to skid; (*fig: partito*) to slide; (: *valuta*) to fall; (: *incontro, conferenza*) to be put off, be postponed.

slittino [zlit'tino] SM toboggan; **andare in slittino** to toboggan.

s.l.m. ABBR (= *sul livello del mare*) a.s.l. (= *above see level*).

slogan ['zlɔgan] SM INV slogan.

slogare [zlo'gare] VT (*Med: caviglia, polso*) to sprain; (: *spalla*) to dislocate; **mi si è slogata la caviglia** I've sprained my ankle.

slogatura [zloga'tura] SF (*di spalla*) dislocation; (*di caviglia, polso*) sprain.

sloggiare [zlod'dʒare] [1] VT: **sloggiare (da)** (*nemico*) to dislodge (from), drive out (of); (*inquilino*) to turn out (of).
   [2] VI (*aus avere*): **sloggiare (da)** to move out (of); **sloggia!** (*fam*) shove off!, clear off!

slot machine ['slɔt məˈʃiːn] SF INV one-armed bandit, fruit machine (*Brit*), slot machine (*Am*).

Slovacchia [zlo'vakkja] SF: **la Slovacchia** Slovakia.

slovacco, a, ci, che [zlo'vakko] AGG, SM/F Slovak, Slovakian; **la Repubblica Slovacca** the Slovak Republic.

Slovenia [zlo'vɛnja] SF: **la Slovenia** Slovenia.

sloveno, a [zlo'vɛno] [1] AGG, SM/F Slovene, Slovenian.
   [2] SM (*lingua*) Slovene.

S.M. ABBR **a** (*Mil*) = **Stato Maggiore** **b** (= *Sua Maestà*) HM.

smaccato, a [zmak'kato] AGG (*fig*) excessive.

smacchiare [zmak'kjare] VT to remove stains from.

smacchiatore [zmakkja'tore] SM stain remover.

smacco, chi ['zmakko] SM humiliating defeat; **subire uno smacco** to be humiliated.

smagliante [zmaʎ'ʎante] AGG (*anche fig*) dazzling, brilliant.

smagliare [zmaʎ'ʎare] [1] VT (*catena, rete*) to break; (*calze*) to ladder (*Brit*), get a run in (*Am*).
   [2] **smagliarsi** VIP (*calze*) to ladder (*Brit*), run (*Am*).

smagliatura [zmaʎʎa'tura] SF **a** (*su calza*) ladder (*Brit*), run (*Am*) **b** (*sulla pelle*) stretch mark.

smagrire [zma'grire] [1] VT to make thin.
   [2] VI (*aus essere*), **smagrirsi** VIP to get o grow thin, lose weight.

smagrito, a [zma'grito] AGG: **essere smagrito** to have lost a lot of weight.

smaliziare [zmalit'tsjare] [1] VT: **smaliziare qn** to teach sb a thing or two.
   [2] **smaliziarsi** VIP to learn a thing or two.

smaliziato, a [zmalit'tsjato] AGG shrewd, cunning.

smaltare [zmal'tare] VT to enamel; (*ceramica*) to glaze; **smaltarsi le unghie** to put on nail polish o varnish (*Brit*).

smaltato, a [zmal'tato] AGG (*vedi vb*) enamelled; glazed; **aveva le unghie smaltate** she was wearing nail polish o varnish (*Brit*).

smaltimento [zmalti'mento] SM (*vedi vt*) digestion; loss; selling off; draining away o off; disposal ►**smaltimento dei rifiuti** waste disposal.

smaltire [zmal'tire] VT **a** (*cibo*) to digest; (*fig: peso*) to lose; (: *rabbia*) to get over; **smaltire la sbornia** to get over one's hangover; (*dormendo*) to sleep it off **b** (*merce*) to sell off **c** (*acque di scarico*) to drain away o off **d** (*rifiuti*) to dispose of.

smalto ['zmalto] SM **a** (*per metalli*) enamel; (*per ceramica*) glaze; **smalto per le unghie** nail polish, nail varnish (*Brit*); **mettersi lo smalto** to put on nail polish o varnish (*Brit*) **b** (*Anat: di denti*) enamel.

smammare [zmam'mare] VI (*fam*) to shove off, clear off.

smancerie [zmantʃe'rie] SFPL mawkishness *sg*.

smangiato, a [zman'dʒato] AGG (*corroso, consumato*) eaten away, corroded.

smania ['zmanja] SF (*agitazione*) agitation, restlessness; (*fig: di potere, ricchezze*): **smania di** craving for, thirst for; **ha una gran smania di andarsene** he's desperate to leave; **avere la smania addosso** to have the fidgets.

smaniare [zma'njare] VI (*aus avere*) to be agitated, be restless; **smaniare di fare qc** (*fig*) to long o yearn to do sth.

smanioso, a [zma'njoso] AGG eager; **essere smanioso di fare qc** to long o yearn to do sth; **sono smanioso di rivederla** I'm dying o longing to see her again.

smantellamento [zmantella'mento] SM (*anche fig*) dismantling.

smantellare [zmantel'lare] VT (*gen*) to dismantle; (*anche fig: demolire*) to demolish.

smarcante [zmar'kante] AGG (*Sport: passaggio*) well-placed.

smarcare [zmar'kare] (*Sport*) [1] VT: **smarcare qn** to help sb to get away from his (o her) marker.
   [2] **smarcarsi** VIP (*Sport*) to escape one's marker.

smargiasso [zmar'dʒasso] SM show-off; **fare lo smargiasso** to show off.

smarrimento [zmarri'mento] SM **a** (*perdita*) loss **b** (*fig*:

turbamento) confusion, bewilderment; (: *sgomento*) dismay; **avere un attimo di smarrimento** to be momentarily nonplussed *o* bewildered.

smarrire [zmar'rire] ☐1☐ VT (*perdere*) to lose, mislay; **smarrire la strada** to lose one's way.
☐2☐ **smarrirsi** VIP to get lost, lose one's way.

smarrito, a [zmar'rito] AGG **a** (*oggetto*) lost; **ufficio oggetti smarriti** lost property office (*Brit*), lost and found (*Am*) **b** (*fig: confuso: persona*) bewildered, nonplussed; (: *sguardo*) bewildered.

smascherare [zmaske'rare] ☐1☐ VT (*colpevole*) to unmask; (*intrigo, complotto*) to uncover.
☐2☐ **smascherarsi** VR to give o.s. away.

smaterializzarsi [zmaterjalid'dzarsi] VIP to dematerialize.

smazzata [zmat'tsata] SF (*Carte: mano*) hand.

SME [zmɛ] ☐1☐ ABBR = **Stato Maggiore Esercito**.
☐2☐ SIGLA M (= *Sistema Monetario Europeo*) EMS (= *European Monetary System*).

smembrare [zmem'brare] ☐1☐ VT (*gruppo, partito*) to split.
☐2☐ **smembrarsi** VIP to split up.

smemorataggine [zmemora'taddʒine] SF absent-mindedness.

smemorato, a [zmemo'rato] ☐1☐ AGG forgetful, absent-minded.
☐2☐ SM/F forgetful person, absent-minded person.

smentire [zmen'tire] ☐1☐ VT (*notizie*) to deny; (*testimonianza*) to refute; **smentisco quello che afferma il testimone** I refute what the witness is saying; **i fatti smentiscono le sue parole** the facts belie his words; **ha smentito la sua fama di dongiovanni** it gave the lie to his reputation of being a Don Juan.
☐2☐ **smentirsi** VR to be inconsistent; **non ti smentisci mai** you're always the same; **ancora una volta non si è smentita** once again she was true to herself.

smentita [zmen'tita] SF (*di notizie*) denial; (*di testimonianza*) refutation.

smeraldo [zme'raldo] SM, AGG INV emerald.

smerciare [zmer'tʃare] VT (*gen*) to sell; (*rimanenze*) to sell off.

smercio, ci ['zmɛrtʃo] SM sale; **avere poco/molto smercio** to have poor/good sales.

smergo, ghi ['zmɛrgo] SM (*anatra*) merganser ▶**smergo maggiore** goosander ▶**smergo minore** red-breasted merganser.

smerigliato, a [zmeriʎ'ʎato] AGG: **carta smerigliata** emery paper; **vetro smerigliato** frosted glass.

smerigliatrice [zmeriʎʎa'tritʃe] SF (*Tecn*) sander.

smeriglio, gli [zme'riʎʎo] SM emery.

smerlare [zmer'lare] VT to scallop.

smerlo ['zmɛrlo] SM: **punto (a) smerlo** scallop stitch.

smesso, a ['zmesso] ☐1☐ PP di **smettere**.
☐2☐ AGG: **abiti smessi** cast-offs.

smettere ['zmettere] VB IRREG ☐1☐ VT (*gen*) to stop; (*studi*) to give up; (*vestiti*) to stop wearing; **smettila!** stop it!; **smettila di urlare!** stop shouting!.
☐2☐ VI (*aus* avere) (*interrompersi*) to stop, cease; **smettere di fare qc** to stop doing sth; **smettere di fumare** to stop *o* give up smoking; **smise di piovere** it stopped raining; **a che ora smetti (di lavorare) stasera?** when do you finish (work) this evening?

smidollato, a [zmidol'lato] ☐1☐ AGG (*fig: persona*) spineless.
☐2☐ SM/F spineless person.

smilitarizzare [zmilitarid'dzare] VT to demilitarize.

smilitarizzazione [zmilitariddzat'tsjone] SF demilitarization.

smilzo, a ['zmiltso] AGG thin, lean.

sminuire [zminu'ire] ☐1☐ VT (*diminuire*) to diminish, lessen; (*fig*) to belittle, make light of, minimize; **sminuire l'importanza di qc** to play sth down.
☐2☐ **sminuirsi** VR (*fig*) to run o.s. down, belittle o.s.

sminuzzare [zminut'tsare] VT (*gen*) to break into small pieces; (*pane*) to crumble; (*carta*) to tear into small pieces.

smisi ecc ['zmizi] VB vedi **smettere**.

smistamento [zmista'mento] SM (*di posta*) sorting; (*Ferr*) shunting.

smistare [zmis'tare] VT (*posta*) to sort; (*Ferr*) to shunt; **hanno smistato gli alunni in varie classi** they sorted the pupils into different classes.

smisuratamente [zmizurata'mente] AVV (*crescere, allargarsi*) disproportionately, inordinately; (*mangiare*) excessively.

smisurato, a [zmizu'rato] AGG enormous, immense; (*eccessivo*) excessive; (*senza limiti*) boundless, immeasurable.

smitizzare [zmitid'dzare] VT to debunk.

smobilitare [zmobili'tare] VT to demobilize.

smobilitazione [zmobilitat'tsjone] SF demobilization.

smobilizzo [zmobi'liddzo] SM (*Comm*) disinvestment.

smoccolare [zmokko'lare] VI (*aus* avere) (*fam*) to swear.

smodato, a [zmo'dato] AGG excessive, unrestrained.

smoderatamente [zmoderata'mente] AVV immoderately.

smoderato, a [zmode'rato] AGG (*gen*) immoderate; **smoderato nel bere** intemperate.

smog [zmɔg] SM INV smog.

smoking ['smoukiŋ] SM INV dinner jacket (*Brit*), tuxedo (*Am*).

smontabile [zmon'tabile] AGG (*gen*) which can be dismantled.

smontare [zmon'tare] ☐1☐ VT (*gen*) to take to pieces; (*macchina, mobile*) to dismantle, take to pieces; (*motore*) to strip (down); (*fig: persona: scoraggiare*) to discourage, dishearten.
☐2☐ VI (*aus* essere): **smontare (da)** (*bicicletta, treno*) to get off; (*sedia*) to get down (from); (*macchina*) to get out (of); **smontare da cavallo** to dismount; **a che ora smonti?** (*fig: da lavoro*) when do you knock off?, when do you finish (work)?.
☐3☐ **smontarsi** VIP (*fig: persona: scoraggiarsi*) to lose heart, lose one's enthusiasm.

smorfia ['zmɔrfja] SF (*gen*) **a** grimace; **fare una smorfia di dolore** to grimace with pain; **fare smorfie** (*boccacce*) to make faces **b** (*atteggiamento lezioso*) simpering.

smorfioso, a [zmor'fjoso] ☐1☐ AGG simpering.
☐2☐ SM/F: **non fare lo smorfioso** stop simpering; **fare la smorfiosa con qn** (*ragazza: civettare*) to flirt with sb.

smorto, a ['zmɔrto] AGG (*viso*) pale, wan; (*colore, stile*) dull; (*voce, faccia*) expressionless, lifeless.

smorzare [zmor'tsare] ☐1☐ VT (*suoni*) to muffle, deaden; (*colori*) to tone down; (*luce*) to dim; (*sete*) to quench; (*entusiasmo*) to dampen.
☐2☐ **smorzarsi** VIP (*suoni*) to die down, fade; (*luce*) to fade; (*entusiasmo*) to dampen.

smorzata [zmor'tsata] SF (*Tennis*) drop shot.

smosso, a ['zmɔsso] PP di **smuovere**.

smottamento [zmotta'mento] SM landslide.

smottare [zmot'tare] VI (*aus* essere) to slide.

smunto, a ['zmunto] AGG haggard, pinched.

smuovere ['zmwɔvere] VB IRREG ① VT (*oggetto*) to move, shift; (*fig: persona: scuotere*) to rouse, stir; (: *dissuadere*): **smuovere qn da qc** to dissuade *o* deter sb from sth. ② **smuoversi** VIP (*fig: persona: scuotersi*) to rouse o.s.; (: *dissuadersi*): **smuoversi da qc** to change one's mind about sth.

smussare [zmus'sare] ① VT (*angolo*) to round off, smooth down; (*lama*) to blunt; (*fig: carattere*) to soften. ② **smussarsi** VIP (*lama*) to become blunt; (*fig: carattere*) to soften.

s.n. ABBR = *senza numero*.

snaturare [znatu'rare] VT (*intenzioni, idee*) to distort, misrepresent.

snaturato, a [znatu'rato] AGG cruel, heartless, inhuman.

snazionalizzare [znattsjonalid'dzare] VT to denationalize.

snellimento [znelli'mento] SM (*di traffico*) speeding up; (*di procedura*) streamlining.

snellire [znel'lire] ① VT (*persona*) to make slim; (*traffico*) to speed up; (*procedura*) to streamline. ② **snellirsi** VIP (*persona*) to (get) slim; (*traffico*) to speed up.

snello, a ['znɛllo] AGG (*slanciato*) slim, slender; (*fig: stile*) easy, flowing.

snervante [zner'vante] AGG (*attesa, lavoro*) exhausting.

snervare [zner'vare] VT to wear out, enervate.

snervato, a [zner'vato] AGG worn out.

snidare [zni'dare] VT (*selvaggina, anche fig*) to drive out, flush out; (*uccelli*) to flush (out).

sniffare [znif'fare] VT (*fam: cocaina*) to snort.

snob [znɔb] ① AGG snobbish *inv*. ② SM/F INV snob.

snobbare [znob'bare] VT to snub.

snobismo [zno'bizmo] SM snobbery.

snocciolare [znottʃo'lare] VT (*frutta*) to stone; (*fig: bugie, lamentele*) to rattle off; (: *verità*) to blab; (: *fam: soldi*) to shell out.

snocciolatoio, oi [znottʃola'tojo] SM stoner.

snodabile [zno'dabile] AGG (*lampada*) adjustable; (*tubo, braccio*) hinged; **rasoio con testina snodabile** swivel-head razor.

snodare [zno'dare] ① VT (*nodo*) to untie, undo; (*membra*) to loosen (up), limber up. ② **snodarsi** VIP (*tubatura*) to be hinged; (*fig: strada, fiume*) to wind.

SO SIGLA = *Sondrio*.

so [sɔ] VB vedi **sapere**.

S.O. ABBR (= *sud-ovest*) SW.

soave [so'ave] AGG (*voce, maniere*) gentle; (*volto*) delicate, sweet; (*musica*) soft, sweet; (*profumo*) delicate.

soavemente [soave'mente] AVV (*parlare*) gently; (*cantare*) sweetly; (*profumato*) delicately.

soavità [soavi'ta] SF (*vedi agg*) gentleness; delicacy, sweetness; softness.

sobbalzare [sobbal'tsare] VI (*aus avere*) (*veicolo*) to bump, jolt, jerk; (*persona: trasalire*) to jump, start.

sobbalzo [sob'baltso] SM (*vedi vb*) bump, jolt, jerk; jump, start.

sobbarcarsi [sobbar'karsi] VR: **sobbarcarsi a** to undertake, take on.

sobborgo, ghi [sob'borgo] SM suburb.

sobillare [sobil'lare] VT to stir up, incite.

sobillatore, trice [sobilla'tore] SM/F instigator.

sobriamente [sobrja'mente] AVV (*gen*) soberly; **vivere**

sobriamente to lead a simple life.

sobrietà [sobrje'ta] SF INV (*gen*) sobriety; (*nel mangiare, bere*) moderation; (*di colore, stile*) simplicity.

sobrio, ria, ri, rie ['sɔbrjo] AGG (*persona*) sober, moderate; (: *non ubriaco*) sober; (*colore, stile*) sober, simple; (*vita*) moderate, simple; **vestire in modo sobrio** to dress soberly.

Soc. ABBR (= *società*) Soc.

socchiudere [sok'kjudere] VT IRREG (*occhi*) to half-close; (*porta, finestra*) to leave ajar.

socchiuso, a [sok'kjuso] ① PP di **socchiudere**. ② AGG (*porta, finestra*) ajar; (*occhi*) half-closed.

soccida ['sɔttʃida] SF (*Dir*): **contratto di soccida** agistment contract.

soccombere [sok'kombere] VI DIF to succumb, give way.

soccorrere [sok'korrere] VT IRREG to help, assist.

soccorritore, trice [sokkorri'tore] SM/F rescuer.

soccorso, a [sok'korso] ① PP di **soccorrere**. ② SM (*gen*) help, assistance, aid; (*di vittime di terremoto ecc*) rescue; **organizzare soccorsi per i terremotati** to organize relief *o* aid for the earthquake victims; **prestare soccorso a qn** to help *o* assist sb; **venire in soccorso di qn** to help sb, come to sb's aid; **operazioni di soccorso** rescue operations; **omissione di soccorso** failure to offer assistance ▸ **soccorso stradale** breakdown service.

socialdemocratico, a, ci, che [sotʃaldemo'kratiko] ① AGG Social Democratic. ② SM/F Social Democrat.

socialdemocrazia [sotʃaldemokrat'tsia] SF Social Democracy.

sociale [so'tʃale] AGG **a** (*gen*) social; **la realtà sociale** the reality of life **b** (*di ditta, società*) company *attr* **c** (*di associazione*) club *attr*, association *attr*.

socialismo [sotʃa'lizmo] SM socialism.

socialista, i, e [sotʃa'lista] AGG, SM/F socialist.

socializzare [sotʃalid'dzare] VI (*aus* **avere**) to socialize.

socializzazione [sotʃaliddzat'tsjone] SF socialization.

socialmente [sotʃal'mente] AVV socially.

società [sotʃe'ta] SF INV **a** (*comunità*) society; **vivere in società** to live in society; **l'alta società** high society; **la buona società** polite society; **giochi di società** parlour games

b (*associazione*) association, club, society; **una società segreta** a secret society; **società sportiva** sports club **c** (*Comm*) company, firm; **in società con qn** in partnership with sb; **mettersi in società con qn** to go into business with sb ▸ **società per azioni** joint-stock company ▸ **società a responsabilità limitata** *type of limited liability company*.

socievole [so'tʃevole] AGG sociable.

socievolezza [sotʃevo'lettsa] SF sociability, sociableness.

socio, ci ['sɔtʃo] SM **a** (*Comm*) partner, associate (*Am*); **socio non attivo** silent partner; **"Bianchi e Soci"** "Bianchi & Co" **b** (*membro*) member; (*di società scientifiche*) fellow; **farsi socio di un circolo** to become a member of a club.

socioeconomico, a, ci, che [sotʃoeko'nɔmiko] AGG socioeconomic.

sociologia [sotʃolo'dʒia] SF sociology.

sociologico, a, ci, che [sotʃolo'lɔdʒiko] AGG sociological.

sociologo, a, gi, ghe [so'tʃɔlogo] SM/F sociologist.

sociopolitico, a, ci, che [sotʃopo'litiko] AGG sociopolitical.

Socrate ['sɔkrate] SM Socrates.

soda ['sɔda] SF **a** (*Chim*) soda ► **soda caustica** caustic soda **b** (*per bevande*) soda (water).

sodalizio, zi [soda'littsjo] SM association, society.

soddisfacente [soddisfa't ʃente] AGG satisfactory.

soddisfacentemente [soddisfat ʃente'mente] AVV satisfactorily.

soddisfare [soddis'fare] VB IRREG: VT, VI (*aus* **avere**): **soddisfare (a)** (*gen*) to satisfy; (*impegno*) to fulfil; (*richiesta*) to comply with, meet.

soddisfatto, a [soddis'fatto] **1** PP di **soddisfare**.

2 AGG satisfied, pleased; **essere soddisfatto di** to be satisfied *o* pleased with; **mostrarsi soddisfatto** to show one's satisfaction.

soddisfazione [soddisfat'tsjone] SF (*gen, di offesa*) satisfaction; **avere la soddisfazione di** to have the satisfaction of; **dare la soddisfazione a qn di** to give sb the satisfaction of; **la vita mi ha dato tante soddisfazioni!** life has given me so much satisfaction!

sodio ['sɔdjo] SM (*Chim*) sodium.

sodo, a ['sɔdo] **1** AGG (*terreno*) hard, firm; (*corpo*) firm; **uova sode** hard-boiled eggs.

2 SM: **venire al sodo** to come to the point.

3 AVV: **picchiare sodo** to hit hard; **dormire sodo** to sleep soundly; **lavorare sodo** to work hard.

sodomia [sodo'mia] SF sodomy.

sodomita, i [sodo'mita] SM sodomite.

sofà [so'fa] SM INV sofa.

sofferente [soffe'rɛnte] AGG suffering.

sofferenza [soffe'rɛntsa] SF **a** (*gen*) suffering; **dopo anni di sofferenze** (*povertà, stenti*) after years of hardship **b** (*Comm*): **in sofferenza** unpaid.

soffermare [soffer'mare] **1** VT: **soffermò lo sguardo su...** his eyes lingered on ....

2 soffermarsi VIP: **soffermarsi su** (*argomento, punto*) to dwell on.

sofferto, a [sof'fɛrto] **1** PP di **soffrire**.

2 AGG (*vittoria*) hard-fought; (*distacco*) painful; **ha un viso sofferto** she has the face of someone who has suffered.

soffiare [sof'fjare] **1** VT **a** (*gen*) to blow; **soffiarsi il naso** to blow one's nose; **soffiare il vetro** to blow glass **b** (*fig fam: rubare*): **soffiare qn/qc a qn** to pinch *o* steal sb/sth from sb.

2 VI (*aus* **avere**) (*gen*) to blow; (*sbuffare*) to puff (and blow); **soffiare sul fuoco** (*fig*) to fan the flames.

soffiata [sof'fjata] SF (*fam*) tip-off; **fare una soffiata alla polizia** to tip off the police.

soffice ['sɔffit ʃe] AGG soft.

sofficemente [soffit ʃe'mente] AVV softly.

soffietto [sof'fjetto] SM **a** (*Mus, per fuoco*) bellows *pl* **b** : **porta a soffietto** folding door.

soffio, fi ['sɔffjo] SM **a** (*di aria, vento*) breath; **in un soffio** (*fig*) in a flash; **per un soffio** (*fig*) by a hair's breadth **b** (*Med*) murmur ► **soffio cardiaco** heart murmur.

soffione¹ [sof'fjone] SM (*Geol*): **soffione boracifero** fumarole.

soffione² [sof'fjone] SM (*pianta*) dandelion.

soffitta [sof'fitta] SF (*solaio*) attic, loft; (*appartamento*) attic flat (*Brit*) *o* apartment (*Am*).

soffitto [sof'fitto] SM ceiling.

soffocamento [soffoka'mento] SM suffocation; **è morto per soffocamento** he died of suffocation.

soffocante [soffo'kante] AGG (*caldo, atmosfera*) suffocating, stifling; (*fig: persona*): **ma sei proprio soffocante!**

you're stifling me!

soffocare [soffo'kare] VT (*gen*) to suffocate; (*fiamme*) to smother, put out; (*fig: sommossa*) to suppress; (*sentimento*) to stifle, repress; (*sbadiglio*) to stifle; **qui dentro si soffoca** it's stifling in here; **soffocare qn di baci/d'affetto** to smother sb with kisses/with affection.

soffocato, a [soffo'kato] AGG (*gemito, grido*) stifled; **è morto soffocato** he was suffocated.

soffocazione [soffokat'tsjone] SF (*gen*) suffocation; (*di sommossa*) suppression.

soffriggere [sof'friddʒere] VB IRREG: VT, VI (*aus* **avere**) to fry lightly.

soffrire [sof'frire] VB IRREG **1** VT **a** (*patire*) to suffer; **soffrire la fame/sete** to suffer (from) hunger/thirst; **soffrire le pene dell'inferno** (*fig*) to go through *o* suffer hell **b** (*sopportare*) to stand, bear; **non lo posso soffrire** I can't stand him.

2 VI (*aus* **avere**) **a** to suffer, be in pain; **la tua vita privata ne soffrirà** your private life will suffer **b** (*Med*): **soffrire di qc** to suffer from sth.

soffritto, a [sof'fritto] **1** PP di **soffriggere**.

2 SM (*Culin*) *fried mixture of herbs, bacon and onions.*

soffuso, a [sof'fuzo] AGG (*luce*) suffused, diffused.

sofisticare [sofisti'kare] VT (*vino*) to adulterate.

sofisticato, a [sofisti'kato] AGG **a** (*vino*) adulterated **b** (*macchina, persona*) sophisticated.

sofisticazione [sofistikat'tsjone] SF (*di vino*) adulteration.

Sofocle ['sɔfokle] SM Sophocles.

software [sɔft'wɛə] SM INV: **software applicativo** applications package.

soggettista, i, e [soddʒet'tista] SM/F (*Cine, TV*) scriptwriter.

soggettivamente [soddʒettiva'mente] AVV subjectively.

soggettività [soddʒettivi'ta] SF subjectivity.

soggettivo, a [soddʒet'tivo] AGG subjective.

soggetto¹, a [sod'dʒɛtto] AGG: **soggetto a** (*a variazioni, danni*) subject *o* liable to; **soggetto a tassa** taxable; **andare** *o* **essere soggetto a frequenti mal di testa** to be prone to frequent headaches.

soggetto² [sod'dʒɛtto] SM **a** (*argomento*) subject, topic; **recitare a soggetto** (*Teatro*) to improvise **b** (*Gramm*) subject **c** (*persona: Med*) subject; (: *pegg*) sort; **è un cattivo soggetto** (*pegg*) he's a bad sort.

soggezione [soddʒet'tsjone] SF **a** (*imbarazzo, disagio*) uneasiness; **incutere soggezione a qn** [OR] **mettere qn in soggezione** to make sb feel uneasy; **avere soggezione di qn** to feel uneasy with sb, be ill at ease in sb's presence **b** (*sottomissione*) subjection.

sogghignare [soggiɲ'nare] VI (*aus* **avere**) to sneer.

sogghigno [sog'giɲɲo] SM sneer.

soggiacere [soddʒa't ʃere] VI IRREG (*aus* **essere**): **soggiacere a** (*leggi*) to be subject to; (*essere sottomesso a*) to be subjected to, submit to.

soggiogare [soddʒo'gare] VT to subdue, subjugate.

soggiornare [soddʒor'nare] VI (*aus* **avere**) to stay.

soggiorno [sod'dʒorno] SM **a** (*permanenza*) stay; **luogo di soggiorno** holiday (*Brit*) *o* vacation (*Am*) resort **b** (*stanza*) living room, sitting room (*Brit*), lounge (*Brit*) **c** (*mobili*) living-room suite.

soggiungere [sod'dʒundʒere] VT IRREG to add.

soggiunto, a [sod'dʒunto] PP di **soggiungere**.

soggolo [sog'golo] SM (*Rel*) wimple.

soglia ['sɔʎʎa] SF **a** (*di porta*) doorstep; (*fig*) threshold; **varcare la soglia** to cross the threshold; **essere sulla**

soglia della vecchiaia to be on the threshold of old age **b** (*Geol*) sill.

sogliola ['sɔʎʎola] SF (*pesce*) sole.

sognante [soɲ'ɲante] AGG dreamy.

sognare [soɲ'ɲare] **1** VT **a** : **sognare qc** to dream of *o* about sth; **ha sempre sognato una casa così/di avere una casa così** he has always dreamt of a house like that/of having a house like that

b (*fig fam*): **non me lo sogno nemmeno!** I wouldn't dream of it!; **te lo puoi sognare!** you can forget it!; **non me lo sono mica sognato!** I didn't dream it up!.

2 VI (*aus* avere) to dream; **sognare a occhi aperti** to daydream.

3 **sognarsi** VIP: **sognarsi di qn/qc** to dream of sb/sth.

sognatore, trice [soɲɲa'tore] SM/F dreamer.

sogno ['soɲɲo] SM dream; **fare un sogno** to have a dream; **un sogno ad occhi aperti** a daydream; **la donna dei suoi sogni** the woman of his dreams; **quella ragazza è un sogno** that girl is gorgeous; **una crociera/casa di sogno** a dream cruise/house; **nemmeno** *o* **neanche per sogno!** not on your life!

soia ['sɔja] SF (*Bot*) soya.

sol [sɔl] SM INV (*Mus*) G; (: *solfeggiando la scala*) so(h).

solaio, ai [so'lajo] SM (*soffitta*) attic, loft.

solamente [sola'mente] AVV only, just.

solanum [so'lanum] SM (*Bot*) solanum.

solare [so'lare] AGG **a** (*Astron*) solar; (*crema*) sun *attr*; **energia solare** solar energy; **luce solare** sunlight; **pannelli solari** solar panels; **plesso solare** (*Anat*) solar plexus **b** (*fig: ragionamento*) clear; **una persona solare** a sunny-natured person.

solarium [so'larjum] SM INV solarium.

solcare [sol'kare] VT (*terreno, fig: mari*) to plough (*Brit*), plow (*Am*).

solco, chi ['solko] SM (*di aratro*) furrow; (*di ruota*) track, rut; (*di nave*) wake; (*su disco*) groove; (*sulla fronte*) wrinkle, furrow.

solcometro [sol'kometro] SM (*Naut*) log (*device*).

soldatesca [solda'teska] SF (*pegg*) soldiers *pl*, troops *pl*.

soldatesco, a [solda'tesko] AGG (*pegg*) soldierlike, rough.

soldatino [solda'tino] SM toy soldier.

soldato [sol'dato] SM soldier; **fare il soldato** to serve in the army; **andare (a fare il) soldato** to enlist (in the army) ▶**soldato di leva** conscript ▶**soldato semplice** private.

soldo ['soldo] SM **a** (*quattrino, moneta*) penny, cent (*Am*); **non ho un soldo** I haven't got a penny; **non vale un soldo bucato** it isn't worth a penny; **per quattro soldi** for next to nothing; **è roba da pochi soldi** it's cheap stuff

b : **soldi** SMPL (*denaro*) money *sg*; **fare soldi** to make money; **essere pieno di soldi** to have lots of money; **buttare via i soldi** to throw one's money away; **avere un sacco di soldi** to be loaded, to be rolling in money.

sole ['sole] SM (*astro*) sun; (*luce*) sun(light); (*calore*) sun(shine); **c'è il sole** the sun is shining; **una giornata di sole** a sunny day; **prendere il sole** to sunbathe; **al calar del sole** at sunset ▶**il Sole che ride** (*Pol*) *symbol of the Italian Green Party*.

soleggiato, a [soled'dʒato] AGG sunny.

solenne [so'lɛnne] AGG (*giuramento, voto*) solemn; (*scherz: ceffone*) almighty, sound.

solennemente [solenne'mente] AVV solemnly.

solennità [solenni'ta] SF **a** (*di cerimonia*) solemnity **b** (*festività*) holiday, feast day.

solenoide [sole'nɔide] SM (*Elettr*) solenoid.

solere [so'lere] VB DIF **1** VT: **solere fare qc** to be in the habit of doing sth; **soleva raccontare lunghe storie della guerra** he used to tell long stories about the war.

2 VB IMPERS (*aus* essere): **come suole accadere** as is usually the case, as usually happens; **come si suol dire** as they say.

solerte [so'lɛrte] AGG diligent.

solertemente [solerte'mente] AVV diligently.

solerzia [so'lɛrtsja] SF diligence.

soletta [so'letta] SF **a** (*per scarpe*) insole **b** (*di sci*) running surface **c** (*Edil*) slab.

solfa ['sɔlfa] SF: **è sempre la solita solfa** it's always the same old story.

solfatara [solfa'tara] SF (*Geol*) solfatara.

solfato [sol'fato] SM (*Chim*) sulphate (*Brit*), sulfate (*Am*) ▶**solfato ferroso** iron sulphate *o* sulfate ▶**solfato di rame** copper sulphate *o* sulfate.

solfeggio, gi [sol'feddʒo] SM (*Mus*) solfeggio.

solfito [sol'fito] SM (*Chim*) sulphite.

solforico, a, ci, che [sol'fɔriko] AGG (*Chim*) sulphuric (*Brit*), sulfuric (*Am*); **acido solforico** sulphuric *o* sulfuric acid.

solfuro [sol'furo] SM (*Chim*) sulphur (*Brit*), sulfur (*Am*).

solidale [soli'dale] AGG in agreement; **essere solidale con qn** (*essere d'accordo*) to be in agreement with sb; (*appoggiare*) to be behind sb.

solidamente [solida'mente] AVV solidly.

solidarietà [solidarje'ta] SF solidarity.

solidarizzare [solidarid'dzare] VI (*aus* avere): **solidarizzare con** to express one's solidarity with.

solidificare [solidifi'kare] VT, VI (*aus* essere), **solidificarsi** VIP to solidify.

solidificazione [solidifikat'tsjone] SF solidification.

solidità [solidi'ta] SF (*vedi agg*) solidity; firmness; strength; soundness; reliability.

solido, a ['sɔlido] **1** AGG **a** (*non liquido*) solid **b** (*robusto: oggetto, muscoli, fede*) firm, strong; (*gambe, muri*) sturdy, sound; (*nervi, salute*) sound, strong; (*amicizia, matrimonio*) sound, solid; (*società*) reliable, sound.

2 SM (*Mat*) solid.

soliloquio, qui [soli'lɔkwjo] SM (*Teatro*) soliloquy; (*discorso tra sé e sé*) monologue.

solipsismo [solip'sizmo] SM (*Filosofia*) solipsism.

solista, i, e [so'lista] **1** AGG solo.

2 SM/F soloist.

solitamente [solita'mente] AVV usually, generally, as a rule.

solitaria [soli'tarja] SF (*Naut*): **in solitaria** single-handed.

solitariamente [solitarja'mente] AVV alone.

solitario, ria, ri, rie [soli'tarjo] **1** AGG (*gen*) solitary; (*passante, navigatore*) lone, solitary; (*luogo, strada*) lonely, deserted, secluded; (*vita*) lonely, secluded; **è un tipo solitario** he is a loner.

2 SM/F (*persona*) solitary person, loner.

3 SM **a** (*brillante*) solitaire **b** (*Carte*) patience.

solito, a ['sɔlito] **1** AGG usual; **essere solito fare qc** to be in the habit of doing sth; **è solito mangiare alle otto** he usually eats at eight o'clock, he is in the habit of eating at eight o'clock; **era solito passeggiare di notte** he used to go for walks during the night; **è sempre la solita storia!** it's always the same old story!; **siamo alle solite!** (*fam*) here we go again!.

2 SM: **di solito** usually, generally, as a rule; **(come) al**

solito as usual; **più tardi del solito** later than usual.

solitudine [soli'tudine] SF **a** (*tranquillità*) solitude; (*l'essere solo*) loneliness; (*di posto*) loneliness **b** (*luogo solitario*) solitude.

sollazzare [sollat'tsare] **1** VT to entertain.

2 sollazzarsi VIP to amuse o.s.

sollazzo [sol'lattso] SM amusement.

sollecitamente [solletʃita'mente] AVV promptly, quickly.

sollecitare [solletʃi'tare] VT **a** (*affrettare*: *pratica, lavoro, telefonata*) to speed up; (: *persona*) to urge on; (*chiedere con insistenza*) to press for, request urgently; **sollecitare qn perché faccia qc** to urge sb to do sth **b** (*stimolare*: *fantasia*) to stimulate, rouse **c** (*Tecn*) to stress.

sollecitazione [solletʃitat'tsjone] SF **a** (*richiesta*) request, entreaty; (*fig: stimolo*) stimulus, incentive; **lettera di sollecitazione** (*Comm*) reminder **b** (*Tecn*) stress.

sollecito, a [sol'letʃito] **1** AGG prompt, quick; **essere sollecito nel fare qc** to be prompt in doing sth.

2 SM (*Comm*) reminder ▸ **sollecito di pagamento** payment reminder.

sollecitudine [solletʃi'tudine] SF promptness, speed.

solleone [solle'one] SM (*periodo estivo*) dog days *pl*; (*gran caldo*) summer heat.

solleticare [solleti'kare] VT (*gen*) to tickle; (*fig: curiosità*) to arouse; (: *fantasia*) to excite; (: *appetito*) to whet.

solletico [sol'letiko] SM tickling; **fare il solletico a qn** to tickle sb; **soffrire il solletico** to be ticklish.

sollevamento [solleva'mento] SM **a** (*gen*) raising, lifting; **c'è stato un sollevamento del terreno** (*Geol*) the ground has risen ▸ **sollevamento pesi** (*Sport*) weightlifting **b** (*rivolta*) revolt, rebellion.

sollevare [solle'vare] **1** VT **a** (*peso, occhi, testa*) to lift, raise; (*polvere, sabbia*) to raise; (*con argani*) to hoist; **sollevare da terra** to lift up, lift off the ground; **il motoscafo sollevò delle onde** the motorboat made waves; **sollevare un'obiezione** (*fig*) to raise an objection **b** (*fig: dar conforto*) to comfort, cheer up; **sollevare il morale a qn** to raise sb's morale **c** (*rendere libero*): **sollevare qn da** (*incarico*) to dismiss sb from; (*fatica*) to relieve sb of; **sollevare qn da un peso** (*fig*) to take a load off sb's mind **d** (*fig: folla*) to rouse, stir up, stir (to revolt).

2 sollevarsi VIP **a** (*persona*) to get up; **sollevati un po'** (*dal letto*) sit up a little; (*da una sedia*) stand up a minute; **sollevarsi da terra** (*persona*) to get up from the ground; (*aereo*) to take off **b** (*vento, polvere*) to rise; (*nebbia*) to lift, clear; **si sollevarono onde enormi** the sea became very rough **c** (*fig: riprendersi*) to feel better, recover; **sollevarsi da qc** (*malattia, spavento*) to get over sth; **sentirsi sollevato** to feel relieved **d** (*fig: truppe, popolo*) to rise up, rebel.

sollievo [sol'ljevo] SM relief; (*conforto*) comfort; **con mio grande sollievo** to my great relief; **un sospiro di sollievo** a sigh of relief.

solluchero [sol'lukkero] SM: **andare in solluchero** (*fig*) to go into ecstasy.

solo, a ['solo] **1** AGG **a** (*senza compagnia*) alone, on one's (*o its ecc*) own, by oneself (*o itself ecc*); (*isolato*) lonely; **da solo** (*senza aiuti*) by oneself (*o himself ecc*); **entra pure, sono solo** please come in, I'm alone *o* there's no-one with me; **vive (da) solo** he lives on his own; **è tanto solo** he's very lonely; **riesci a farlo da solo?** can you do it by yourself?; **parlare da solo** to talk to oneself

b (*senza altri*): **finalmente soli!** alone at last!; **vogliono stare sole** they want to be alone; **possiamo vederci da soli?** can I see you in private? **c** (*seguito da sostantivo*) only; **il solo motivo** the only *o* sole reason; **c'è un solo libro** there is only one book; **ha un solo figlio** she has only one son; **è il solo proprietario** he's the sole proprietor; **essi sono una persona sola** they are as one; **non si vive di solo pane** man does not live by bread alone; **l'incontrò due sole volte** he only met him twice; **la sola idea mi fa tremare** the very *o* mere thought of it is enough to make me tremble; **la mia sola speranza è che...** my only hope is that ...; **non un solo istante ho creduto che...** I didn't believe for a single moment that ...

d (*con agg numerale*): **veniamo noi tre soli** just *o* only the three of us are coming.

2 AVV (*soltanto*) only, just; **resto solo un giorno** I'm only staying one day; **mancavi solo tu** only you were missing, you were the only one missing; **non solo ha negato, ma...** not only did he deny it, but ....

3: **solo che** CONG but; **l'ho visto, solo che non son riuscito a parlargli** I saw him, but I didn't get a chance to speak to him.

4 SM/F: **sono il solo a poter giudicare** I'm the only one who can judge; **è la sola che ha chiesto notizie** she was the only one to ask for news.

5: **a solo** SM (*Mus*) = **assolo**.

solstizio, zi [sol'stittsjo] SM solstice.

soltanto [sol'tanto] **1** AVV (*gen*) only; **c'era soltanto lui** there was only him; **restano qui soltanto 2 giorni** they are only staying 2 days; **sono arrivato soltanto ieri** I only arrived yesterday; **chiedo soltanto questo!** that's all I ask!.

2 CONG but, only; **vorrei, soltanto (che) non posso** I would like to, but I can't; **ha la macchina, soltanto temo che non funzioni** he has a car, only *o* but I don't think it's working.

solubile [so'lubile] AGG soluble; **caffè solubile** instant coffee.

solubilità [solubili'ta] SF (*Chim*) solubility.

soluto [so'luto] SM (*Chim*) solute.

soluzione [solut'tsjone] SF (*gen, Mat, Chim*) solution; (*di indovinello*) answer; **non c'è altra soluzione!** there's no alternative!; **senza soluzione di continuità** uninterruptedly.

solvente [sol'vɛnte] **1** AGG (*Chim*) solvent.

2 SM (*Chim*) solvent ▸ **solvente per unghie** nail polish *o* nail varnish (*Brit*) remover ▸ **solvente per vernici** paint remover.

solvenza [sol'vɛntsa] SF (*Comm*) solvency.

soma ['soma] SF burden, load; **bestia da soma** pack animal, beast of burden.

Somalia [so'malja] SF: **la Somalia** Somalia.

somalo, a ['somalo] **1** AGG, SM/F Somali, Somalian.

2 SM (*lingua*) Somali.

somaro [so'maro] SM (*Zool*) donkey, ass; (*fig*) dunce.

somatico, a, ci, che [so'matiko] AGG (*Bio*) somatic.

somatizzare [somatid'dzare] VT (*Psic*): **somatizzare le proprie ansie** to make o.s. physically ill with worry.

sombrero [som'brero] SM INV sombrero.

somigliante [somiʎ'ʎante] AGG similar; **essere somigliante a qc** to be similar to *o* like sth; **essere somigliante a qn** to look like sb; **sono molto somiglianti** they are very alike; **è un ritratto molto somigliante** it's a

somiglianza [somiʎ'ʎantsa] SF *(tra cose)* similarity; *(tra persone)* resemblance.

somigliare [somiʎ'ʎare] **1** VI *(aus avere)*: **somigliare a** to resemble, look like, be like; **somiglia a sua sorella** she looks like o resembles her sister; **somiglia al mio** it looks like mine.

2 somigliarsi VR *(uso reciproco)* to be alike, look alike, resemble each other; **non si somigliano affatto** they don't look at all like each other.

somma ['somma] SF **a** *(Mat)* addition; *(: risultato)* sum; *(fig: sostanza)* conclusion; **sai fare le somme?** can you add?; **tirare le somme** *(fig)* to sum up; **tirate le somme** *(fig)* all things considered **b** *(di denaro)* amount, sum (of money).

sommamente [somma'mente] AVV extremely, immensely.

sommare [som'mare] **1** VT *(Mat)* to add up, add together; *(aggiungere)* to add; **tutto sommato** *(fig)* all things considered.

2 VI *(aus avere o essere)* *(ammontare)*: **sommare a** to add up, amount to.

sommariamente [sommarja'mente] AVV *(analizzare, discutere)* in brief; **l'hanno giudicato sommariamente** *(Dir)* he was given a summary trial.

sommario, ria, ri, rie [som'marjo] **1** AGG **a** *(esame)* brief; *(lavoro)* rough; **racconto sommario** brief summary **b** *(Dir)* summary.

2 SM *(breve riassunto)* summary; *(compendio)* compendium; **sommario del telegiornale** *(TV)* news headlines *pl*.

sommelier [sɔmə'lje] SM INV wine waiter.

sommergere [som'mɛrdʒere] VT IRREG *(barca)* to submerge; **le onde hanno sommerso la barca** the waves swamped the boat; **sommergere qn di** *(doni, gentilezze)* to overwhelm sb with; *(baci)* to smother sb with.

sommergibile [sommer'dʒibile] **1** AGG submersible.

2 SM *(Naut)* submarine.

sommergibilista, i [sommerdʒibi'lista] SM submariner.

sommerso, a [som'mɛrso] **1** PP di **sommergere**.

2 AGG *(tesori, città)* sunken; **l'economia sommersa** the black economy.

3 SM: **il sommerso** *(economia)* the black economy.

sommesso, a [som'messo] AGG soft, low, subdued.

somministrare [somminis'trare] VT to give, administer.

somministrazione [somministrat'tsjone] SF giving, administration.

sommità [sommi'ta] SF INV summit, top; *(fig)* peak, height.

sommo, a ['sommo] **1** AGG *(grado, livello)* highest; *(rispetto)* highest, greatest; *(poeta, artista)* great, outstanding; **il Sommo Pontefice** the Supreme Pontiff; **per sommi capi** in short, in brief.

2 SM *(fig)* peak, height.

sommossa [som'mɔssa] SF uprising, revolt.

sommozzatore [sommottsa'tore] SM (deep-sea) diver; *(Mil)* frogman.

sonagliera [sonaʎ'ʎɛra] SF bell-collar.

sonaglio, gli [so'naʎʎo] SM *(di mucche)* bell; *(per bambini)* rattle.

sonante [so'nante] AGG: **denaro** o **moneta sonante** (ready) cash.

sonar ['sɔnar] SM INV *(Naut)* sonar, echo sounder.

sonare ecc [so'nare] = **suonare** ecc.

sonata [so'nata] SF *(Mus)* sonata.

sonda ['sonda] **1** SF *(Med, Meteor, Aer)* probe; *(Mineralogia)* drill.

2 AGG INV: **pallone sonda** weather balloon.

sondaggio, gi [son'daddʒo] SM *(vedi vb)* sounding; drilling, boring; probing; survey ▶ **sondaggio d'opinioni** opinion poll.

sondare [son'dare] VT *(Naut)* to sound; *(Mineralogia)* to drill, to bore; *(Meteor, Med)* to probe; *(fig: opinione)* to survey, poll.

sonetto [so'netto] SM sonnet.

sonnacchiosamente [sonnakkjosa'mente] AVV sleepily.

sonnacchioso, a [sonnak'kjoso] AGG sleepy.

sonnambulismo [sonnambu'lizmo] SM somnambulism, sleepwalking.

sonnambulo, a [son'nambulo] SM/F somnambulist, sleepwalker.

sonnecchiare [sonnek'kjare] VI *(aus avere)* to doze, drowse, nod.

sonnellino [sonnel'lino] SM nap.

sonnifero [son'nifero] SM *(pillola)* sleeping pill o drug; *(gocce)* sleeping draught *(Brit)* o draft *(Am)*.

sonno ['sonno] SM **a** *(il dormire)* sleep; **avere il sonno pesante/leggero** to be a heavy/light sleeper; **prendere sonno** to fall asleep; **ho perso 4 ore di sonno** I lost 4 hours' sleep; **il sonno eterno** *(euf)* eternal rest

b *(bisogno di dormire)* sleepiness, sleep; **avere sonno** to be sleepy; **cascare dal sonno** to be asleep on one's feet; **far venire sonno a qn** *(fig)* to send sb to sleep.

sonnolento, a [sonno'lɛnto] AGG *(persona)* sleepy, drowsy; *(movimenti)* sluggish.

sonnolenza [sonno'lɛntsa] SF sleepiness, drowsiness.

sono ['sono] VB vedi **essere**.

sonometro [so'nɔmetro] SM *(Fis)* sonometer.

sonoramente [sonora'mente] AVV: **schiaffeggiare qn sonoramente** to give sb a resounding slap.

sonorità [sonori'ta] SF sonority, resonance.

sonorizzare [sonorid'dzare] VT *(Ling)* to voice; *(Cine)* to add a soundtrack to.

sonorizzazione [sonoriddzat'tsjone] SF *(Cine)* addition of a soundtrack.

sonoro, a [so'nɔro] **1** AGG **a** *(ambiente)* resonant; *(voce)* sonorous; *(schiaffo, risata)* loud; *(fig: parole)* high-flown, high-sounding **b** *(Cine)* sound *attr*; **colonna sonora di un film** soundtrack of a film; **il cinema sonoro** the talkies *pl* **c** *(Ling)* voiced.

2 SM: **il sonoro** *(cinema)* the talkies *pl*; *(parte sonora)* soundtrack.

sontuosamente [sontuosa'mente] AVV sumptuously.

sontuosità [sontuosi'ta] SF INV sumptuousness.

sontuoso, a [sontu'oso] AGG sumptuous.

soperchieria [soperkje'ria] SF = **soverchieria**.

sopire [so'pire] VT *(dolore, tensione)* to soothe.

sopore [so'pore] SM drowsiness.

soporifero, a [sopo'rifero] AGG *(sostanza)* soporific; *(fig: discorso)* tedious, soporific.

sopperire [soppe'rire] VI *(aus avere)*: **sopperire a** to provide for; **sopperire alla mancanza di qc** to make up for the lack of sth.

soppesare [soppe'sare] VT to weigh in one's hand(s), feel the weight of; **soppesare i pro e i contro** to weigh up the pros and cons.

soppiantare [soppjan'tare] VT to supplant.

soppiatto [sop'pjatto] AVV: **di soppiatto** secretly, furtively; **se n'è andato di soppiatto** he stole off o away.

sopportabile [soppor'tabile] AGG tolerable, bearable.

sopportabilità [sopportabili'ta] SF: **è al limite della sopportabilità** it is scarcely tolerable.

sopportare [soppor'tare] VT **a** (*peso*) to support, bear **b** (*subire: perdita, spese*) to bear, sustain; (: *conseguenze, disagi*) to bear, suffer **c** (*tollerare: persona, comportamento*) to stand, put up with, bear, tolerate, endure; (: *temperatura, sforzo*) to take, stand, withstand; **non sopporto il pesce/il giallo** I can't stand fish/yellow; **non sopporto le persone disoneste!** I can't stand dishonest people!

sopportazione [sopportat'tsjone] SF patience; **avere spirito** *o* **capacità di sopportazione** to be long-suffering; **la mia sopportazione ha un limite** there is a limit to my patience; **ho raggiunto il limite della sopportazione** I am at the end of my tether.

soppressione [soppres'sjone] SF **a** (*di legge*) abolition; (*di linea ferroviaria*) closure; (*di servizio*) withdrawal **b** (*uccisione*) elimination, liquidation.

soppresso, a [sop'prɛsso] PP di **sopprimere**.

sopprimere [sop'primere] VT IRREG **a** (*privilegi, carica*) to do away with, abolish; (*servizio*) to withdraw; (*giornale*) to suppress; (*clausola, parola, frase*) to cut out, delete **b** (*uccidere*) to eliminate, liquidate.

sopra ['sopra] ① PREP **a** (*gen*) over; **c'era un lampadario sopra il tavolo** there was a chandelier over the table; **indossava un golf sopra la camicetta** she was wearing a sweater over her blouse; **mettiti il cappotto sopra le spalle** put your coat over your shoulders; **costruirono un ponte sopra il fiume** they built a bridge over the river; **guadagna sopra i 2 milioni al mese** he earns over 2 million lire a month; **pesa sopra il chilo** it weighs over *o* more than a kilo; **persone sopra i 30 anni** people over 30 (years of age); **passar sopra a qc** (*anche fig*) to pass over sth; **sopra pensiero** = **soprappensiero**
b (*più in su di*) above; **l'aereo volava sopra le nuvole** the plane was flying above the clouds; **100 metri sopra il livello del mare** 100 metres above sea level; **5 gradi sopra lo zero** 5 degrees above zero; **sopra l'orizzonte** above the horizon; **sopra l'equatore** north of *o* above the equator; **un paesino sopra Napoli** a village north of Naples; **abitano sopra di noi** they live above us; **ha un appartamento sopra il negozio** he has a flat (*Brit*) *o* apartment (*Am*) over the shop; **essere al di sopra di ogni sospetto** to be above suspicion; **amare qn sopra ogni cosa** to love sb above all else
c (*a contatto con*) on; (*moto*) on(to); (*in cima a*) on (top of); **il libro è sopra il tavolo** the book is on the table; **il gatto è salito sopra il tavolo** the cat climbed onto the table; **mettilo sopra l'armadio** put it on top of the wardrobe (*Brit*) *o* closet (*Am*); **si buttò sopra di lui** he threw himself on him
d (*intorno a, riguardo a*) about, on; **un dibattito sopra la riforma carceraria** a debate about *o* on prison reform; **chiedere un parere sopra qc** to ask for an opinion about *o* on sth.
② AVV **a** (*su*) up; (*in superficie*) on top; **metti tutto lì** *o* **là sopra** put everything up there; **sopra è un po' rovinato** (*libro, borsa*) it's a bit damaged on top; **una torta con sopra la panna** a cake topped with cream; **un disegno con sopra la firma** a signed drawing
b : (*al piano*) **di sopra** upstairs; **abitano di sopra** they live upstairs; **vado di sopra a chiudere le finestre** I'm just going upstairs to close the windows; **la tua è la stanza di sopra** yours is the upstairs room
c (*prima*) above; **per i motivi sopra illustrati** for the above-mentioned reasons, for the reasons shown above; **vedi/come sopra** see/as above; **mettilo nel cassetto sopra** put it in the drawer above
d : **pensaci sopra** think it over; **dormirci sopra** (*fig*) to sleep on it.
③ SM top; **il sopra del tavolo è in mogano** the top of the table is mahogany; **il di sopra** the top, the upper part.

soprabito [so'prabito] SM overcoat.

sopraccennato, a [soprattʃen'nato] AGG above-mentioned.

sopracciglio [soprat'tʃiʎʎo] SM (*pl m* **sopraccigli**, *pl f* **sopracciglia**) eyebrow.

sopracciliare [soprattʃi'ljare] AGG eyebrow *attr*.

sopraccoperta [soprakko'pɛrta] ① SF (*di letto*) bedspread; (*di libro*) jacket.
② AVV (*Naut*) on deck.

sopraddetto, a [soprad'detto] AGG aforesaid.

sopraffare [sopraf'fare] VT IRREG to overwhelm, overpower, overcome.

sopraffascia [sopraf'faʃʃa] SM INV (*Equitazione*) roller.

sopraffatto, a [sopraf'fatto] PP di **sopraffare**.

sopraffazione [sopraffat'tsjone] SF overwhelming, overpowering.

sopraffino, a [sopraf'fino] AGG (*olio*) extra fine; (*burro*) best-quality *attr*; (*pranzo, gusto*) excellent; (*fig: astuzia, mente*) masterly.

sopraggitto [soprad'dʒitto] SM (*Cucito*) whipstitch.

sopraggiungere [soprad'dʒundʒere] VI IRREG (*aus* essere) (*persone, rinforzi*) to arrive (unexpectedly); (*fig: difficoltà, complicazioni*) to arise *o* occur (unexpectedly).

sopraggiunto, a [soprad'dʒunto] PP di **sopraggiungere**.

sopralluogo, ghi [sopral'lwɔgo] SM (*di esperti*) inspection; (*di polizia*) on-the-spot investigation.

soprammobile [sopram'mɔbile] SM ornament.

soprannaturale [soprannatu'rale] AGG, SM supernatural.

soprannome [sopran'nome] SM nickname.

soprannominare [soprannomi'nare] VT to nickname.

soprannumero [sopran'numero] AVV: **in soprannumero** in excess; **in questa classe siamo in soprannumero** there are too many in this class.

soprano [so'prano] SM/F (*pl m* **soprani**, *pl f* **soprano**) (*Mus*) soprano.

soprappensiero [soprappen'sjɛro] AVV lost in thought.

soprappiù [soprap'pju] SM surplus, extra; **in soprappiù** (*in eccesso*) extra, surplus; (*per giunta*) besides, in addition; **l'offerta è in soprappiù rispetto alla domanda** there is more supply than demand.

soprassalto [sopras'salto] SM: **di soprassalto** with a jump, with a start.

soprassaturo, a [sopras'saturo] AGG supersaturated.

soprassedere [soprasse'dere] VI IRREG (*aus* avere): **soprassedere a** to put off, postpone, delay.

soprattassa [soprat'tassa] SF (*Fin*) surtax.

soprattutto [soprat'tutto] AVV **a** (*anzitutto*) above all **b** (*specialmente*) especially, particularly.

sopravvalutare [sopravvalu'tare] VT (*persona, capacità*) to overestimate, overrate.

sopravvalutazione [sopravvalutat'tsjone] SF overestimation, overevaluation.

sopravvenire [sopravve'nire] VI IRREG (*aus* essere) (*persone, macchine, rinforzi*) to arrive suddenly; (*difficoltà, complicazioni*) to arise, occur.

sopravvento [soprav'vɛnto] ⓵ SM: **avere/prendere il sopravvento su qn** to have/get the upper hand over sb. ⓶ AVV windward; **essere/mettersi sopravvento** to be/get on the windward side.

sopravvenuto, a [sopravve'nuto] PP di **sopravvenire**.

sopravvissuto, a [sopravvis'suto] ⓵ PP di **sopravvivere**. ⓶ SM/F survivor.

sopravvivenza [sopravvi'vɛntsa] SF survival.

sopravvivere [soprav'vivere] VI IRREG (*aus* **essere**) to survive; **sopravvivere a** (*incidente, guerra*) to survive; (*persona*) to outlive, survive.

soprelencato, a [soprelen'kato] AGG above-listed *attr*, listed above.

soprelevata [soprele'vata] SF (*di strada, ferrovia*) elevated section.

soprelevato, a [soprele'vato] AGG elevated, raised.

soprelevazione [soprelevat'tsjone] SF (*Edil*) raising; (*parte soprelevata*) raised part.

soprintendente [soprinten'dɛnte] SM/F (*gen*) superintendent, supervisor; (*funzionario: di museo*) director, head.

soprintendenza [soprinten'dɛntsa] SF **a** (*gen*) superintendence, supervision

b (*ente statale*): **Soprintendenza ai beni ambientali e architettonici** *government department responsible for the environment and historical buildings*; **Soprintendenza ai beni artistici e storici** *government department responsible for monuments and other treasures*.

soprintendere [soprin'tɛndere] VI IRREG: **soprintendere a** to superintend, supervise.

soprinteso, a [soprin'teso] PP di **soprintendere**.

sopruso [so'pruzo] SM abuse (of power); **subire un sopruso** to be abused; **questo è un sopruso!** this is an outrage!

soqquadro [sok'kwadro] SM: **mettere a soqquadro** to turn upside-down.

sorbettiera [sorbet'tjɛra] SF ice-cream churn.

sorbetto [sor'betto] SM sorbet, water ice (*Brit*).

sorbire [sor'bire] ⓵ VT to sip; **sorbirsi qn/qc** (*fig*) to put up with sb/sth.

sorbo ['sɔrbo] SM (*Bot*) service tree, sorb.

sorcio, ci ['sortʃo] SM mouse; **far vedere i sorci verdi a qn** (*fig*) to give sb a rough time.

sordidamente [sordida'mente] AVV (*vedi agg*) sordidly; meanly.

sordidezza [sordi'dettsa] SF (*vedi agg*) sordidness, squalor; meanness.

sordido, a ['sɔrdido] AGG (*locale, appartamento*) sordid, squalid; (*fig: affare, storia*) sordid; (: *gretto*) mean, stingy.

sordina [sor'dina] SF (*Mus*) mute; **mettere la sordina a qc** to mute sth; **cantare in sordina** to hum softly; **andarsene in sordina** (*fig*) to sneak off.

sordità [sordi'ta] SF deafness.

sordo, a ['sordo] ⓵ AGG **a** (*persona*) deaf; **essere sordo da un orecchio** to be deaf in one ear; **essere sordo come una campana** to be as deaf as a post; **sordo ai consigli** deaf to advice

b (*rumore, colpo*) muffled; (*dolore*) dull; (*odio, rancore*) veiled; (*lotta*) silent, hidden

c (*Fonetica*) voiceless.

⓶ SM/F deaf person; **i sordi** the deaf; **non fare il sordo!** don't pretend you didn't hear me!

sordomuto, a [sordo'muto] ⓵ AGG deaf-and-dumb. ⓶ SM/F deaf-mute.

sorella [so'rɛlla] ⓵ SF (*gen, Rel*) sister; **è come una sorella per me** she's like a sister to me. ⓶ AGG (*organizzazione, nave*) sister *attr*.

sorellanza [sorel'lantsa] SF sisterhood.

sorellastra [sorel'lastra] SF stepsister.

sorgente [sor'dʒɛnte] SF (*fonte*) spring; (*di fiume, fig, Fisica*) source; **acqua di sorgente** spring water ▶ **sorgente di calore** source of heat ▶ **sorgente luminosa** source of light, light source ▶ **sorgente termale** thermal spring.

sorgere ['sordʒere] VB IRREG ⓵ VI (*aus* **essere**) (*gen*) to rise; (*fig: difficoltà*) to arise; **mi sorge il dubbio che...** I am beginning to suspect that ...; **mi sorge un dubbio, forse ho lasciato il gas acceso** I wonder, did I leave the gas on?.

⓶ SM: **al sorgere del sole** at sunrise.

sorgo ['sorgo] SM (*Bot*) sorghum.

soriano, a [so'rjano] AGG, SM/F tabby.

sormontare [sormon'tare] VT (*fig: ostacoli, difficoltà*) to overcome, surmount.

sornione, a [sor'njone] ⓵ AGG sly, crafty. ⓶ SM/F sly one.

sorpassare [sorpas'sare] VT (*oltrepassare*) to go past; (*auto*) to overtake; (*fig*) to surpass; (*rivali*) to surpass, outdo; **sorpassare qn in intelligenza** to be more intelligent o brighter than sb; **l'ha sorpassato in altezza** she has grown taller than him.

sorpassato, a [sorpas'sato] AGG (*metodo, moda*) outmoded, old-fashioned; (*macchina*) obsolete.

sorpasso [sor'passo] SM overtaking; **fare un sorpasso** to overtake.

sorprendente [sorpren'dɛnte] AGG surprising; (*eccezionale, inaspettato*) astonishing, amazing.

sorprendentemente [sorprendente'mente] AVV surprisingly.

sorprendere [sor'prɛndere] VB IRREG ⓵ VT **a** (*cogliere di sorpresa*) to catch; (: *ladro*) to surprise, catch in the act; **l'ha sorpreso a fumare** she caught him smoking; **furono sorpresi dalla bufera** they were caught in the storm

b (*fig: stupire*) to surprise; **non mi sorprenderebbe affatto!** I wouldn't be at all surprised!.

⓶ **sorprendersi** VIP **a** (*meravigliarsi*): **sorprendersi di qc** to be surprised about o at sth

b (*trovarsi*): **sorprendersi a pensare a qn** to catch o find o.s. thinking of sb.

sorpresa [sor'presa] SF (*gen*) surprise; **fare una sorpresa a qn** to give sb a surprise; **attaccare di sorpresa** to make a surprise attack on; **prendere qn di sorpresa** to take sb by surprise o unawares; **risultato a sorpresa** surprise result.

sorpreso, a [sor'preso] PP di **sorprendere**.

sorreggere [sor'reddʒere] VT IRREG (*malato, bambino*) to support, hold up; (*fig: sogg: speranza*) to sustain.

sorretto, a [sor'rɛtto] PP di **sorreggere**.

sorridere [sor'ridere] VI IRREG (*aus* **avere**) to smile; **sorridere a qn** to smile at sb, give sb a smile; **la vita ti sorride** life smiles on you; **mi sorride l'idea di rivederlo** the idea of seeing him again appeals to me.

sorriso [sor'riso] ⓵ PP di **sorridere**. ⓶ SM smile; **mi ha fatto un sorriso** he gave me a smile, he smiled at me; **un accenno di sorriso** a faint smile.

sorsata [sor'sata] SF gulp; **bere a sorsate** to gulp.

sorseggiare [sorsed'dʒare] VT to sip.

sorsi *ecc* ['sorsi] VB *vedi* **sorgere**.

sorso ['sorso] SM sip; **ne ho bevuto solo un sorso** I only

had a sip; **d'un sorso** OR **in un sorso solo** at one gulp.

sorta ['sɔrta] SF sort, kind; **ogni sorta di** all sorts *pl* of; **di ogni sorta** of every kind; **non voglio regali di sorta** I want no presents whatsoever *o* of any kind *o* at all.

sorte ['sɔrte] SF (*fato*) fate, destiny; (*caso*) chance; **decidere della sorte di qn** to decide sb's fate; **tentare la sorte** to try one's luck; **tirare a sorte** to draw lots; **la sua sorte è segnata** his fate is sealed.

sorteggiare [sorted'dʒare] VT to draw for.

sorteggio, gi [sor'teddʒo] SM draw.

sortilegio, gi [sorti'lɛdʒo] SM spell, witchcraft *no pl*; **fare un sortilegio a qn** to cast *o* put a spell on sb.

sortire [sor'tire] VT (*ottenere*) to produce; **sortire l'effetto contrario** to have the opposite effect.

sortita [sor'tita] SF (*Mil*) sortie; (*fig*: *battuta*) witty remark.

sorto, a ['sorto] PP di **sorgere**.

sorvegliante [sorveʎ'ʎante] SM/F (*di carcere*) warder (*Brit*), guard (*Am*); (*di fabbrica*) supervisor; (*notturno*) night watchman.

sorveglianza [sorveʎ'ʎantsa] SF (*controllo*) supervision, watch; (: *Polizia, Mil*) surveillance; **fare sorveglianza agli esami** to invigilate (at) the exams.

sorvegliare [sorveʎ'ʎare] VT (*detenuto, bambino, bagaglio*) to watch, keep an eye on; (*casa*) to watch, keep watch on; (*operai, lavori*) to supervise, oversee.

sorvolare [sorvo'lare] VT, VI (*aus* avere), **sorvolare su** (*territorio*) to fly over; (*fig*: *argomento, dettagli*) to pass over, skim over; **sorvoliamo!** let's skip it!

S.O.S. ['ɛsse'o'ɛsse] SIGLA M SOS, mayday; **lanciare un S.O.S.** to send (out) an SOS.

sosia ['sɔzja] SM/F INV double.

sospendere [sos'pɛndere] VT IRREG **a** (*appendere*) to hang (up); **sospendere un quadro al muro/un lampadario al soffitto** to hang a picture on the wall / a chandelier from the ceiling

  b (*interrompere*: *gen*) to suspend; (: *vacanze, trasmissione*) to interrupt; (*seduta*) to adjourn

  c (*funzionario, alunno*) to suspend; **sospendere qn dal suo incarico** to suspend sb from office.

sospensione [sospen'sjone] SF (*gen, Aut, Chim*) suspension; (*rinvio*: *di processo*) adjournment; (: *di partita*) postponement.

sospeso, a [sos'peso] 1 PP di **sospendere**.

  2 AGG (*mano, braccio*) raised; (*vallata*) hanging; (*treno, autobus*) cancelled; **ponte sospeso** suspension bridge; **col fiato sospeso** with bated breath; **tenere qn col fiato sospeso** to keep sb in suspense; **in sospeso** (*pratica*) pending; (*discorso*) unfinished; (*conto*) outstanding.

sospettabile [sospet'tabile] AGG suspect.

sospettare [sospet'tare] 1 VT to suspect; **sospettare qn di qc** (*furto, omicidio*) to suspect sb of sth; **sospettare che...** to suspect (that) ...; **lo sospettavo!** I suspected as much!.

  2 VI (*aus* avere): **sospettare (di qn)** to suspect (sb); (*diffidare*) to be suspicious (of sb); **non sospetta di niente** he doesn't suspect a thing.

sospetto[1], a [sos'pɛtto] AGG (*individuo*) suspicious; (*affermazione*) suspect.

sospetto[2] [sos'pɛtto] SM suspicion; **destare i sospetti di qn** to arouse sb's suspicions; **destare sospetti** to give rise to suspicion, arouse suspicion; **avere dei sospetti** to have one's suspicions; **ho il sospetto che...** I suspect (that) ...; **guardare qn con sospetto** to look suspiciously at sb.

sospettosamente [sospettosa'mente] AVV suspiciously.

sospettoso, a [sospet'toso] AGG suspicious.

sospingere [sos'pindʒere] VT IRREG to push, to drive; (*fig*: *incitare*) to urge, impel; **il vento li sospinse al largo** the wind drove them out to sea.

sospinto, a [sos'pinto] PP di **sospingere**.

sospirare [sospi'rare] 1 VI (*aus* avere) to sigh.

  2 VT to yearn for, long for; **fare sospirare qc a qn** to keep sb waiting *o* hanging around for sth.

sospiro [sos'piro] SM sigh; **sospiro di sollievo** sigh of relief; **fare** *o* **trarre un sospiro** to sigh, heave a sigh.

sosta ['sɔsta] SF (*fermata*) stop, halt; (*pausa, interruzione*) pause, break; **"divieto di sosta"** (*Aut*) "no parking"; **senza sosta** without a break, non-stop; **avere un attimo di sosta** to have a moment's rest; **non dar sosta a qn** to give sb no peace, allow sb no respite.

sostantivare [sostanti'vare] VT (*Gramm*) to use as a noun.

sostantivato, a [sostanti'vato] AGG (*Gramm*): **aggettivo sostantivato** adjective used as a noun.

sostantivo [sostan'tivo] SM (*Gramm*) noun, substantive; **sostantivo in funzione di aggettivo** noun used as an adjective.

sostanza [sos'tantsa] SF **a** substance; **badare alla sostanza delle cose** to pay attention to essentials; **la sostanza del discorso** the essence of the speech; **in sostanza** in short, to sum up **b** : **sostanze** SFPL (*ricchezze*) wealth *sg*; (*beni*) property *sg*, possessions.

sostanziale [sostan'tsjale] AGG substantial.

sostanzialmente [sostantsjal'mente] AVV essentially, substantially.

sostanzioso, a [sostan'tsjoso] AGG (*cibo, pasto*) nourishing, substantial; (*fig*: *patrimonio, resoconto*) substantial; **un libro sostanzioso** a book of substance.

sostare [sos'tare] VI (*aus* avere) (*fermarsi*) to stop; (: *macchina*) to stop, park; (*fare una pausa*) to take a break; (*pernottare*: *in albergo*) to stay, stop (for a while); (: *in città*) to stop over; **sostare in preghiera/raccoglimento** to pause in prayer / in thought.

sostegno [sos'teɲɲo] SM support; **a sostegno di** in support of; **muro di sostegno** supporting wall.

sostenere [soste'nere] VB IRREG 1 VT **a** (*gen*: *tenere su*) to support, hold up; (*con medicina*) to sustain; **sostenere il peso di** (*anche fig*) to bear the weight of

  b (*candidato, partito*) to support, back; (*famiglia*) to support; **sostenere qn** (*moralmente*) to be a support to sb; (*difendere*) to stand up for sb, take sb's part

  c (*attacco, shock*) to stand up to, withstand; (*sguardo*) to bear, stand; (*sforzo*) to keep up, sustain; (*esame*) to take; **sostenere il confronto** to bear *o* stand comparison; **sostenere delle spese** to meet *o* incur expenses; **sostenere un'ingente spesa** to have a large outlay

  d (*teoria*) to maintain, uphold; (*diritti*) to assert; (*innocenza*) to maintain; **la tesi da lui sostenuta è che...** he maintains that ...

  e (*Teatro, Cine*): **sostenere una parte** to play a role; **sostenere la parte di** to play the part of.

  2 **sostenersi** VR **a** (*tenersi su*) to hold o.s. up, support o.s.; (*con medicine*) to keep o.s. going, keep one's strength up; **sostenersi al muro** (*appoggiarsi*) to hold on to the wall, lean on the wall

  b (*uso reciproco*) to hold each other up; (*fig*: *moralmente*) to stand by each other, support each other.

sostenibile [soste'nibile] AGG (*tesi*) tenable; (*spese*) bearable; **sviluppo sostenibile** sustainable development.

sostenitore, trice [sosteni'tore] SM/F (*di partito, candidato*) supporter, backer; (*di tesi*) upholder, supporter.

sostentamento [sostenta'mento] SM sustenance, maintenance, support; **mezzi di sostentamento** means of support.

sostenuto, a [soste'nuto] ①AGG (*stile*) elevated; (*prezzo, velocità*) high; **lavora a ritmo sostenuto** she works very fast.

② SM/F: **fare il sostenuto** to be standoffish, keep one's distance.

sostituibile [sostitu'ibile] AGG replaceable.

sostituire [sostitu'ire] ① VT **a** : **sostituire (a/con)** to substitute (for/with); **sostituire il rosso col verde** to replace red with green; **sostituire un pezzo difettoso** to replace a faulty part

b (*prendere il posto di: persona*) to replace, take the place of; (: *temporaneamente*) to stand in for; (: *cosa*) to take the place of.

② **sostituirsi** VR: **sostituirsi a qn** to replace sb, take the place of sb.

sostitutivo, a [sostitu'tivo] AGG (*Amm: documento, certificato*) equivalent.

sostituto, a [sosti'tuto] SM/F substitute, deputy ▶**sostituto procuratore della Repubblica** (*Dir*) ≈ deputy public prosecutor (*Brit*), assistant district attorney (*Am*).

sostituzione [sostitut'tsjone] SF substitution; **in sostituzione di** in place of, as a substitute for.

sostrato [sos'trato] SM (*Geol*) substratum; (*fig: essenza, fondamento*) basis, foundation.

sottaceto, sott'aceto [sotta't∫eto] (*Culin*) ① SM (*spec al pl*): **i sottaceti** pickles.

② AGG INV (*cetriolini, cipolline*) pickled.

③ AVV: **mettere sottaceto** to pickle.

sottana [sot'tana] SF (*gonna*) skirt; (*Rel*) cassock, soutane; **correre dietro alle sottane** (*fig*) to run after women; **stare sempre attaccato alla sottane della mamma** (*fig*) to be tied to one's mother's apron-strings.

sottecchi [sot'tekki] AVV: **guardare di sottecchi** to steal a glance at.

sotterfugio, gi [sotter'fudʒo] SM subterfuge.

sotterramento [sotterra'mento] SM burial, interment.

sotterranea [sotter'ranea] SF (*anche:* **ferrovia sotterranea**) underground, tube (*Brit*), subway (*Am*).

sotterraneo, a [sotter'raneo] ① AGG underground.

② SM (*spec al pl*) vault, cellar.

sotterrare [sotter'rare] VT (*oggetto*) to bury; (*morto*) to bury, inter; **mi sarei sotterrato per la vergogna!** (*fig fam*) I wished the ground would open up and swallow me!

sottigliezza [sottiʎ'ʎettsa] SF **a** (*di spessore*) thinness; (*fig: acutezza*) subtlety **b** : **sottigliezze** SFPL: **perdersi in sottigliezze** to get bogged down in details; **non bado a certe sottigliezze** I don't care about such niceties.

sottile [sot'tile] ① AGG **a** (*fetta, corda, viso*) thin; (*figura, caviglia*) slim, slender; (*capelli*) fine; (*profumo*) delicate

b (*fig: vista*) sharp, keen; (: *ragionamento, significato, ironia*) subtle; (: *mente*) subtle, shrewd; (*differenza*) slight.

② SM: **non andare troppo per il sottile** not to mince matters.

sottilizzare [sottilid'dzare] VI (*aus* avere) to split hairs.

sottilmente [sottil'mente] AVV (*tagliare*) finely; (*criticare*) subtly.

sottintendere [sottin'tɛndere] VT IRREG (*implicare*) to imply; **è sottinteso che...** it is understood that ..., it goes without saying that ...; **lasciare sottintendere che...** to let it be understood that ...; **il soggetto è sottinteso** (*Gramm*) the subject is understood.

sottinteso, a [sottin'teso] ① PP di **sottintendere**.

② SM insinuation, allusion; **smetti di parlare per sottintesi** or **parla senza sottintesi** speak plainly, speak your mind.

sotto ['sotto] ① PREP **a** (*posizione*) under, beneath, underneath; **dov'era? — sotto il giornale** where was it? — under *o* beneath *o* underneath the newspaper; **si riparò sotto un albero** he sheltered under *o* beneath *o* underneath a tree; **sotto la superficie** under *o* beneath the surface; **si nascose sotto il letto** he hid under *o* underneath the bed; **sotto il soprabito indossava un vestito verde** she was wearing a green dress under her coat; **portare qc sotto il braccio** to carry sth under one's arm; **vieni sotto l'ombrello** come under the umbrella; **dormire sotto la tenda** to sleep under canvas *o* in a tent; **camminare sotto la pioggia** to walk in the rain; **finire sotto un treno** to get run over by a train; **infilarsi sotto le lenzuola** to get in between the sheets; **c'incontriamo sotto casa** we'll meet outside my house; **sotto le mura** (*di città*) beneath the walls

b (*più in basso di*) below; (*a sud di*) south of, below; **sotto il livello del mare** below sea level; **sotto zero** below zero; **tutti quelli sotto i 18 anni** all those under 18 (years of age) (*Brit*) *o* under age 18 (*Am*); **quest'anno le gonne si portano sotto il ginocchio** this year skirts are being worn below the knee; **Palermo è sotto Napoli** Palermo is south of *o* below Naples; **sotto il chilo** under *o* less than a kilo; **abita sotto di noi** he lives below us

c (*durante il governo di*) under; **l'Italia sotto Vittorio Emanuele** Italy under Victor Emmanuel; **sotto il regno di** during the reign of

d (*soggetto a*) under; **ha 5 impiegati sotto di sé** he has 5 clerks under him; **sotto l'effetto dell'alcol** under the influence of alcohol; **sotto anestesia** under anaesthetic; **tenere qn sotto la propria protezione** to keep sb under one's wing; **tenere qn/qc sott'occhio** to keep an eye on sb/sth; **sotto l'alto patronato di** under the patronage of

e (*tempo: in prossimità di*) near; **siamo sotto Natale/Pasqua** it's nearly Christmas/Easter

f (*da*): **analizzare qc sotto un altro aspetto** to examine sth from another point of view; **sotto un certo punto di vista** in a sense

g (*fraseologia*): **sotto forma di** in the form of; **sotto falso nome** under a false name; **non c'è niente di nuovo sotto il sole** there is nothing new under the sun; **avere qc sotto il naso/gli occhi** to have sth under one's nose/before one's eyes.

② AVV **a** (*giù*) down; (*nella parte inferiore*) underneath, beneath; **qui/lì sotto** down here/there; **sotto c'è uno strato di cioccolato** underneath there's a layer of chocolate; **sotto, la scatola è rossa** underneath, the box is red; **sei sotto tu!** (*nei giochi*) you're it!

b : **(al piano) di sotto** downstairs; **ti aspetto (di) sotto** I'll wait for you downstairs; **quelli di sotto** the people who live downstairs

c (*oltre*) below; **vedi sotto** see below; **la riga sotto** the line below

d (*addosso*) underneath; **cos'hai sotto?** what have you got on underneath?.

3 SM INV bottom; **il sotto della pentola** the bottom of the pan.

sottoalimentato, a [sottoalimen'tato] AGG **a** (*denutrito*) undernourished, underfed **b** (*Elettr*, *Tecn*): **il circuito è sottoalimentato** not enough electricity is flowing through the circuit; **il motore è sottoalimentato** not enough fuel is reaching the engine.

sottoalimentazione [sottoalimentat'tsjone] SF undernourishment.

sottobanco [sotto'banko] AVV (*di nascosto*: *vendere, comprare*) under the counter; (*agire*) in an underhand way; **passare una notizia sottobanco** to hush up a piece of news.

sottobicchiere [sottobik'kjɛre] SM mat, coaster.

sottobosco, schi [sotto'bɔsko] SM undergrowth *no pl*.

sottobottiglia [sottobot'tiʎʎa] SM INV coaster.

sottobraccio [sotto'brattʃo] AVV by the arm; **prendere qn sottobraccio** to take sb by the arm; **camminare sottobraccio a qn** to walk arm in arm with sb.

sottocchio [sot'tɔkkjo] AVV in front of one, to hand; **non l'ho sottocchio** (*articolo, documento*) I haven't got it in front of me *o* to hand.

sottoccupazione [sottokkupat'tsjone] SF underemployment.

sottochiave [sotto'kjave] AVV under lock and key.

sottocoperta [sottoko'pɛrta] AVV (*Naut*) below deck.

sottocosto [sotto'kɔsto] AVV below cost (price).

sottocutaneo, a [sottoku'taneo] AGG subcutaneous.

sottoelencato, a [sottoelen'kato] AGG listed below, under-mentioned *attr*.

sottoesporre [sottoes'porre] VT IRREG (*Fot*) to underexpose.

sottoesposizione [sottoespozit'tsjone] SF (*Fot*) underexposure.

sottoesposto, a [sottoes'posto] **1** PP di **sottoesporre**. **2** AGG (*fotografia, pellicola*) underexposed.

sottofondo [sotto'fondo] SM background; **sottofondo musicale** background music.

sottogamba [sotto'gamba] AVV: **prendere qn/qc sottogamba** (*con leggerezza*) not to take sb/sth seriously; (*sottovalutare*) to underestimate sb/sth.

sottogonna [sotto'gonna] SF underskirt.

sottogoverno [sottogo'vɛrno] SM political patronage.

sottogruppo [sotto'gruppo] SM subgroup.

sottolineare [sottoline'are] VT to underline; (*fig*) to underline, emphasize, stress.

sottolineatura [sottolinea'tura] SF underlining.

sottolio, li, sott'olio [sot'tɔljo] **1** SM: **sottoli** SMPL vegetables pickled in oil. **2** AGG INV (*funghetti, melanzane, tonno*) in oil. **3** AVV: **conservare sottolio** to bottle in oil.

sottomano [sotto'mano] AVV **a** (*a portata di mano*) within reach, to *o* on *o* at hand **b** (*di nascosto*) secretly.

sottomarino, a [sottoma'rino] **1** AGG (*flora, paesaggio*) submarine; (*cavo, galleria, navigazione*) underwater *attr*. **2** SM (*Naut*) submarine.

sottomesso, a [sotto'messo] **1** PP di **sottomettere**. **2** AGG submissive.

sottomettere [sotto'mettere] VB IRREG **1** VT (*gen*) to subject; (*popolo, nemico*) to subjugate, subdue; **sottomettere qn alla propria volontà** to impose one's will on sb. **2** **sottomettersi** VR to submit; **sottomettersi alla volontà di qn** to bow to sb's will.

sottomissione [sottomis'sjone] SF submission.

sottopancia [sotto'pantʃa] SM INV (*Equitazione*) girth.

sottopassaggio, gi [sottopas'saddʒo] SM (*per auto*) underpass; (*pedonale*) subway (*Brit*), underpass (*Am*).

sottopentola [sotto'pentola] SM INV heat-resistant mat.

sottopiatto [sotto'pjatto] SM INV plate (*placed under another*).

sottoporre [sotto'porre] VB IRREG **1** VT **a** (*costringere*): **sottoporre qn/qc a** to subject sb/sth to; **sottoporre ad un esame** to subject to an examination **b** (*fig*: *presentare*): **sottoporre qc a qn** *o* **all'attenzione di qn** to submit sth to sb, put sth to sb. **2** **sottoporsi** VR: **sottoporsi a** (*volontà*) to submit to; (*operazione*) to undergo.

sottoposto, a [sotto'posto] PP di **sottoporre**.

sottoprodotto [sottopro'dotto] SM by-product.

sottoproduzione [sottoprodut'tsjone] SF underproduction.

sottoprogramma, i [sottopro'gramma] SM (*Inform*) subroutine.

sottoproletariato [sottoproleta'rjato] SM: **il sottoproletariato** the underclasses *pl*, the underprivileged classes *pl*.

sottoproletario, ria, ri, rie [sottoprole'tarjo] SM/F: **i sottoproletari** the underprivileged.

sottordine [sot'tordine] **1**: **in sottordine** AVV: **passare in sotordine** to become of minor importance. **2** SM (*Bot, Zool*) sub-order.

sottoscala [sottos'kala] SM INV (*ripostiglio*) cupboard (*Brit*) *o* closet (*Am*) under the stairs; (*stanza*) room under the stairs.

sottoscritto, a [sottos'kritto] **1** PP di **sottoscrivere**. **2** SM/F: **il(la) sottoscritto(a)** the undersigned.

sottoscrivere [sottos'krivere] VB IRREG **1** VT (*firmare*: *atto, petizione*) to sign; **sottoscrivere per diecimila lire** (*contribuire*) to contribute ten thousand lire. **2** VI (*aus* avere): **sottoscrivere a** (*programma*) to subscribe to.

sottoscrizione [sottoskrit'tsjone] SF **a** (*firma*) signing **b** (*raccolta di adesioni*) subscription; **è iniziata la sottoscrizione per il referendum** signatures in favour of a referendum are now being collected.

sottosegretario, ria, ri, rie [sottosegre'tarjo] SM/F (*Pol*) undersecretary ▶ **sottosegretario di stato** under-secretary of state (*Brit*), assistant secretary of state (*Am*).

sottosopra [sotto'sopra] AVV (*capovolto*) upside down, topsy-turvy; **mettere tutto sottosopra** to turn everything upside down; **sentirsi sottosopra** [OR] **avere lo stomaco sottosopra** to feel queasy; **sentirsi sottosopra** (*turbato*) to be in a whirl.

sottospecie [sottos'pɛtʃe] SF INV (*Bot, Zool*) subspecies *inv*; **è una sottospecie di musica** (*pegg*) it's hardly what you would call music.

sottostante [sottos'tante] AGG (*piani*) lower; (*zona*) underlying; **la valle sottostante** the valley below.

sottostare [sottos'tare] VI IRREG (*aus* essere): **sottostare a** (*assoggettarsi a*) to submit to; (: *richieste*) to give in to; (*subire*: *prova*) to undergo.

sottosterzante [sottoster'tsante] AGG (*Aut*): **essere sottosterzante** to understeer.

sottosuolo [sotto'swɔlo] SM subsoil.

sottosviluppato, a [sottozvilup'pato] AGG underdeveloped.

sottosviluppo [sottozvi'luppo] SM underdevelopment.

sottotenente [sottote'nɛnte] SM (Mil) second lieutenant.
sottoterra [sotto'tɛrra] AVV underground.
sottotetto [sotto'tetto] SM attic.
sottotitolo [sotto'titolo] SM subtitle.
sottovalutare [sottovalu'tare] ☐1 VT (persona, prova) to underestimate, underrate; (Econ) to undervalue.
☐2 **sottovalutarsi** VR to underrate o.s.
sottovalutazione [sottovalutat'tsjone] SF (gen) underestimation; (Econ) undervaluing.
sottovaso [sotto'vazo] SM flowerpot saucer.
sottovento [sotto'vɛnto] (Naut) ☐1 AVV leeward(s).
☐2 AGG INV (lato) leeward.
sottoveste [sotto'vɛste] SF petticoat, slip.
sottovoce [sotto'votʃe] AVV in a low voice, softly.
sottovuoto [sotto'vwɔto] ☐1 AVV: **confezionare sottovuoto** to vacuum-pack.
☐2 AGG INV: **confezione sottovuoto** vacuum pack.
sottrarre [sot'trarre] VB IRREG ☐1 VT **a** (Mat) to subtract, take away; (dedurre) to deduct; **sottratte le spese** once expenses have been deducted
b (portar via): **sottrarre a** to take away from; (liberare): **sottrarre a o da** to save from, rescue from; (rubare): **sottrarre da** to remove from, steal from; **gli hanno sottratto il portafoglio** they stole his wallet; **sottrarre qn/qc alla vista di qn** to remove sb/sth from sb's sight.
☐2 **sottrarsi** VR: **sottrarsi a** (sfuggire) to escape; (evitare) to avoid.
sottratto, a [sot'tratto] PP di **sottrarre**.
sottrazione [sottrat'tsjone] SF (Mat) subtraction; (furto) removal.
sottufficiale [sottuffi'tʃale] SM (Mil) non-commissioned officer; (Naut) petty officer.
soubrette [su'brɛt] SF INV showgirl.
soufflé [su'fle] SM INV (Culin) soufflé.
souvenir [suvə'nir] SM INV souvenir.
sovente [so'vɛnte] AVV (letter) frequently.
soverchiare [sover'kjare] VT to overpower, overwhelm.
soverchieria [soverkje'ria] SF (prepotenza) abuse (of power).
soverchio, chia, chi, chie [so'vɛrkjo] AGG (letter) excessive, immoderate.
soviet [so'vjɛt] SM INV soviet.
sovietico, a, ci, che [so'vjɛtiko] ☐1 AGG Soviet.
☐2 SM/F Soviet citizen.
sovrabbondante [sovrabbon'dante] AGG overabundant.
sovrabbondanza [sovrabbon'dantsa] SF overabundance; **in sovrabbondanza** in excess.
sovraccaricare [sovrakkari'kare] VT to overload; **sovraccaricare qn di lavoro** to overload sb with work.
sovraccarico, a, chi, che [sovrak'kariko] ☐1 AGG: **sovraccarico (di)** overloaded (with); **sovraccarico di lavoro** overworked.
☐2 SM excess load; **sovraccarico di lavoro** extra work.
sovraesporre [sovraes'porre] VT IRREG (Fot) to overexpose.
sovraesposizione [sovraespozit'tsjone] SF (Fot) overexposure.
sovraesposto, a [sovraes'posto] PP di **sovraesporre**.
sovraffollato, a [sovraffol'lato] AGG overcrowded.
sovralimentato, a [sovralimen'tato] AGG **a** (bambino) overfed **b** (Tecn: motore) supercharged; **circuito sovralimentato** (Elettr) overloaded circuit.
sovranità [sovrani'ta] SF (potere) sovereignty; (fig: superiorità) supremacy.
sovrannaturale [sovrannatu'rale] AGG = **soprannaturale**.

sovrano, a [so'vrano] ☐1 AGG (gen) sovereign attr; (fig: sommo) supreme. ☐2 SM/F sovereign.
sovraoccupazione [sovraokkupat'tsjone] SF overemployment.
sovrappopolare [sovrappopo'lare] VT to overpopulate.
sovrapporre [sovrap'porre] VB IRREG ☐1 VT (gen) to place on top of, put on top of; (Fot, Geom) to superimpose; **sovrapponili** place o put them one on top of the other.
☐2: **sovrapporsi** VIP (Fot) to be superimposed; (fig: aggiungersi): **sovrapporsi a** to arise in addition to.
sovrapposizione [sovrapposit'tsjone] SF superimposition.
sovrapposto, a [sovrap'posto] PP di **sovrapporre**.
sovrapproduzione [sovrapprodut'tsjone] SF overproduction.
sovrastante [sovras'tante] AGG (montagna) dominating; (pericolo) impending.
sovrastare [sovras'tare] VT IRREG **a** (sogg: montagna, fortezza) to dominate; (: nube) to hang over; **è così alto che sovrasta gli altri** he's so tall that he towers over the others; **il pericolo di un'epidemia sovrasta la città** the danger of an epidemic threatens the city **b** (fig: superare) to surpass.
sovrasterzante [sovraster'tsante] AGG (Aut): **essere sovrasterzante** to oversteer.
sovrastruttura [sovrastrut'tura] SF superstructure.
sovratensione [sovraten'sjone] SF (Elettr) overvoltage.
sovreccitabile [sovrettʃi'tabile] AGG overexcitable.
sovreccitabilità [sovrettʃitabili'ta] SF overexcitability.
sovreccitare [sovrettʃi'tare] VT to overexcite.
sovreccitazione [sovrettʃitat'tsjone] SF overexcitement.
sovrimpressione [sovrimpres'sjone] SF (Fot, Cine) superimposition; (: per errore) double exposure; **immagini in sovrimpressione** superimposed images.
sovrintendente [sovrinten'dɛnte] ecc = **soprintendente** ecc.
sovrumano, a [sovru'mano] AGG superhuman.
sovvenire [sovve'nire] VI IRREG (aus essere) (letter: venire in mente): **sovvenire a** to occur to; **mi sovvenne che...** it occurred to me that ... .
sovvenzionare [sovventsjo'nare] VT to subsidize; **sovvenzionato dallo Stato** state-subsidized.
sovvenzione [sovven'tsjone] SF subsidy, grant.
sovversione [sovver'sjone] SF subversion.
sovversivo, a [sovver'sivo] SM/F, AGG subversive.
sovvertimento [sovverti'mento] SM subverting, undermining.
sovvertire [sovver'tire] VT (Pol: ordine, stato) to subvert, undermine.
sovvertitore, trice [sovverti'tore] SM/F subverter.
sozzamente [sottsa'mente] AVV filthily.
sozzo, a ['sottso] AGG filthy, dirty.
sozzume [sot'tsume] SM filth.
sozzura [sot'tsura] SF filth.
SP SIGLA = La Spezia.
S.P. ABBR = **strada provinciale**; vedi **provinciale**.
S.p.A. ['ɛssepi'a] SIGLA F = **società per azioni**.
spaccalegna [spakka'leɲɲa] SM INV woodcutter.
spaccare [spak'kare] ☐1 VT (rompere) to break, split; (legna) to chop; (partito, maggioranza) to split; **ti spacco il muso!** I'll smash your face in!; **o la va o la spacca** it's all or nothing; **quest'orologio spacca il minuto** this watch keeps perfect time; **c'è un sole che spacca le pietre** it's hot enough to fry an egg; **una questione che ha spaccato**

l'opinione pubblica an issue which has split public opinion.

2 spaccarsi VIP (rompersi) to break, split; (fig: scindersi: partito) to split.

spaccata [spak'kata] SF (Ginnastica): fare una spaccata to do the splits.

spaccato, a [spak'kato] 1 AGG a (terreno, labbra) cracked b (fig): è sordo spaccato he is as deaf as a post; sei tuo padre spaccato you're the spitting image of your father.

2 SM (Archit) vertical section; (fig: descrizione) outline.

spaccatura [spakka'tura] SF (gen, fig) split; (in un muro) crack; (nel terreno) crack, fissure.

spaccherò ecc [spakke'rɔ] VB vedi spaccare.

spacciare [spat'tʃare] 1 VT (merce rubata) to traffic in; (droga) to sell, push; (denaro falso) to pass; spacciare per (far passare per) to pass off as; l'ha spacciata per sua moglie he passed her off as his wife.

2 spacciarsi VR (farsi credere): spacciarsi per to pass o.s. off as, pretend to be.

spacciato, a [spat'tʃato] AGG (fam: malato, fuggiasco): essere spacciato to be done for.

spacciatore, trice [spattʃa'tore] SM/F (di droga) pusher; (di denaro falso) dealer.

spaccio, ci ['spattʃo] SM a : spaccio (di) (merce rubata) trafficking (in); (denaro falso) passing (of); spaccio di droga drugpushing b (negozio) shop.

spacco, chi ['spakko] SM a (incrinatura) crack, split; (strappo) tear b (di gonna) slit; (di giacca) vent.

spacconata [spakko'nata] SF: non dire spacconate! stop boasting!; non fare spacconate! stop showing off!

spaccone, a [spak'kone] SM/F (fam) boaster, braggart.

spada ['spada] SF a sword b (Carte): spade SFPL suit in Neapolitan pack of cards.

spadaccino, a [spadat'tʃino] SM/F swordsman/woman.

spadino [spa'dino] SM dress sword.

spadroneggiare [spadroned'dʒare] VI (aus avere) to swagger; pensa di poter spadroneggiare he thinks he can boss everyone about; non ti permetto di spadroneggiare in casa mia I won't allow you to lord it in my house.

spaesato, a [spae'zato] AGG lost, disorientated; mi sentivo spaesato tra di loro I felt lost o out of my depth in their company.

spaghettata [spaget'tata] SF spaghetti meal.

spaghetteria [spagette'ria] SF spaghetti restaurant.

spaghetti [spa'getti] SMPL (Culin) spaghetti sg.

Spagna ['spaɲɲa] SF: la Spagna Spain.

spagnoletta [spaɲɲo'letta] SF spool.

spagnolo, a [spaɲ'nɔlo] 1 AGG Spanish.

2 SM/F (abitante) Spaniard; gli spagnoli the Spanish.

3 SM (lingua) Spanish.

spago, ghi ['spago] SM string, twine; un rotolo di spago a ball of string; dare spago a qn (fig) to let sb have his (o her) way.

spaiato, a [spa'jato] AGG (calza, guanto) odd.

spalancare [spalan'kare] 1 VT to open wide; spalancò la porta he flung the door open.

2 spalancarsi VIP to open wide.

spalancato, a [spalan'kato] AGG (porta, bocca) wide open; con gli occhi spalancati with eyes wide open; accogliere qn a braccia spalancate to welcome sb with open arms.

spalare [spa'lare] VT (terra, neve) to shovel.

spalatore [spala'tore] SM (lavoratore) shoveller.

spalatrice [spala'tritʃe] SF mechanical shovel.

spalla ['spalla] SF a (Anat, Geog, Alpinismo) shoulder; questa giacca mi sta grande di spalle this jacket is too big across the shoulders; avere le spalle curve to have round shoulders, be round-shouldered; avere le spalle larghe (anche fig) to have broad shoulders; portare qn/qc in o a spalle to carry sb/sth on one's shoulders; alzare le spalle to shrug one's shoulders; avere la famiglia sulle spalle to have a family to support; vivere alle spalle di qn to live off sb, live at sb's expense

b (schiena): spalle SFPL back; di spalle from behind; seduto alle mie spalle sitting behind me; voltare le spalle a qn/qc (fig) to turn one's back on sb/sth; ridere alle spalle di qn (fig) to laugh behind sb's back; prendere/colpire qn alle spalle to take/hit sb from behind; mettere qn con le spalle al muro (fig) to get sb with his (o her) back to the wall

c (Teatro) stooge; fare da spalla a qn to act as sb's stooge.

spallata [spal'lata] SF push (o shove) with the shoulder; dare una spallata a qc to give sth a push (o a shove) with one's shoulder.

spalleggiare [spalled'dʒare] VT to support, back up.

spalletta [spal'letta] SF parapet.

spalliera [spal'ljɛra] SF (di sedia, poltrona) back; (di letto: alla testa) head(board); (: ai piedi) foot(board); (Ginnastica) wall bars pl; (Agr) espalier.

spallina [spal'lina] SF a (di sottoveste, maglietta) strap; senza spalline strapless b (anche: spallina imbottita) shoulder pad c (Mil) epaulette.

spalluccia, ce [spal'luttʃa] SF: fare spallucce to shrug.

spalmare [spal'mare] 1 VT to spread; spalmare il burro sul pane OR spalmare il pane di burro to butter one's bread, spread butter on one's bread; spalmare una crema sulla pelle to rub a cream into one's skin.

2 spalmarsi VR: spalmarsi di to cover o.s. with.

spalti ['spalti] SMPL (di stadio) terraces (Brit), ≈ bleachers (Am).

spanare [spa'nare] VT (vite) to strip.

spanato, a [spa'nato] AGG (vite) stripped.

spanciarsi [span'tʃarsi] VIP (fig fam): spanciarsi dalle risate o dal ridere to split one's sides laughing.

spanciata [span'tʃata] SF belly flop.

spandere ['spandere] VB IRREG 1 VT a (stendere: cera, crema) to spread b (spargere: liquido) to pour (out); (: polvere) to scatter; (: calore, profumo) to give off; (: fig: notizie) to spread; spandere lacrime to shed tears.

2 spandersi VIP to spread.

spanna ['spanna] SF (lunghezza della mano) span; a spanne (approssimativamente) at a rough guess; è più alto di me di una spanna he's about half a head taller than me; essere alto una spanna (fig: persona) to be pint-sized.

spanto, a ['spanto] PP di spandere.

spappolare [spappo'lare] 1 VT (ossa, gamba) to crush; (fegato, milza) to rupture; non far spappolare le patate (cuocere troppo) don't reduce the potatoes to mush.

2 spappolarsi VIP (ossa, gamba) to be crushed; (fegato, milza) to rupture; (patate) to become mushy.

sparare [spa'rare] 1 VT (arma, colpo) to fire; sparare a bruciapelo to shoot at point-blank range; si è sparato un colpo alla tempia he shot himself in the head; sparare fandonie to talk nonsense; spararle grosse to exaggerate; ha sparato un prezzo assurdo he came out with a ridiculous price; sparare calci to kick out.

2 VI (*aus* **avere**) (*arma*) to fire; (*soldato, persona*) to shoot, fire; **sparare a qn/qc** (*colpire*) to shoot sb/sth; (*mirare*) to fire at sb/sth; **sparare a zero contro qn** (*fig*) to be ruthless with sb, to show sb no pity.

sparata [spa'rata] SF (*fig*) tall story (*Brit*) *o* tale (*Am*).

sparato [spa'rato] SM (*di camicia*) dicky.

sparatore, trice [spara'tore] SM/F gunman/ gun-woman.

sparatoria [spara'tɔrja] SF (*tra polizia e malviventi*) exchange of shots; (*tra malviventi*) shoot-out.

sparecchiare [sparek'kjare] VT: **sparecchiare (la tavola)** to clear the table.

spareggio, gi [spa'reddʒo] SM (*Sport*) play-off.

spargere ['spardʒere] VB IRREG **1** VT **a** (*sparpagliare*) to scatter **b** (*versare: vino*) to spill; (: *sangue, lacrime*) to shed **c** (*diffondere: notizia*) to spread; (: *luce*) to give off (*o* out).

2 **spargersi** VIP (*persone*) to scatter; (*voce, notizia*) to spread; **si è sparsa una voce sul suo conto** there is a rumour going round about him.

spargimento [spardʒi'mento] SM: **spargimento di sangue** bloodshed.

sparire [spa'rire] VI IRREG (*aus* **essere**) to disappear, vanish; **la nave sparì all'orizzonte** the ship disappeared over the horizon; **sparire dalla circolazione** (*fig fam*) to lie low, keep a low profile; **far sparire** (*fig: rubare*) to steal, pinch; (: *mangiare*) to go through, put away; **far sparire qn** (*uccidere*) to kill sb, bump sb off (*fam*); **chissà dove è sparito il mio passaporto!** I wonder where my passport has got to!; **sparisci!** (*fig fam*) scram!, beat it!

sparizione [sparit'tsjone] SF disappearance.

sparlare [spar'lare] VI (*aus* **avere**): **sparlare di qn/qc** run sb/sth down, bad-mouth sb/sth (*fam*).

sparo ['sparo] SM shot.

sparpagliare [sparpaʎ'ʎare] VT, **sparpagliarsi** VIP to scatter.

sparpagliato, a [sparpaʎ'ʎato] AGG scattered.

sparso, a ['sparso] **1** PP di **spargere**.

2 AGG (*fogli*) scattered; (*capelli*) loose; **in ordine sparso** (*Mil*) in open order.

Sparta ['sparta] SF Sparta.

spartano, a [spar'tano] **1** AGG (*Storia*) Spartan; (*fig*) spartan.

2 SM/F Spartan.

spartiacque [sparti'akkwe] SM INV (*Geog*) watershed; (*fig: divergenza*) basic difference.

spartineve [sparti'neve] SM INV snowplough (*Brit*), snowplow (*Am*).

spartire [spar'tire] VT **a** (*denaro, eredità*) to share out; **non ho nulla da spartire con lui** (*fig*) I have nothing in common with him; **ci siamo spartiti il bottino** we split up the loot **b** (*separare: avversari*) to separate.

spartito [spar'tito] SM (*Mus*) score.

spartitraffico [sparti'traffiko] **1** SM INV (*Aut: banchina: in città*) traffic island.

2 AGG INV: **aiuola spartitraffico** traffic island.

spartizione [spartit'tsjone] SF division; **la spartizione dell'eredità** the dividing up of the inheritance.

sparuto, a [spa'ruto] AGG (*scarno: viso*) gaunt, haggard; (*esiguo: gruppo*) small, thin.

sparviero [spar'vjɛro] SM (*Zool*) sparrowhawk.

spasimante [spazi'mante] SM (*corteggiatore*) suitor; (*scherz: innamorato*) sweetheart, lover.

spasimare [spazi'mare] VI (*aus* **avere**) to be in agony; **spasimare di fare** (*fig*) to long to do sth, be dying to do

sth, yearn to do sth; **spasimare per qn** to be madly in love with sb.

spasimo ['spazimo] SM pang; **morire tra atroci spasimi** to die in agony.

spasmo ['spazmo] SM (*Med*) spasm.

spasmodicamente [spazmodika'mente] AVV spasmodically.

spasmodico, a, ci, che [spaz'mɔdiko] AGG **a** (*affannoso: attesa, ricerca*) agonizing **b** (*Med*) spasmodic.

spassarsi [spas'sarsi] VIP (*aus* **essere**): **spassarsela** to enjoy o.s., have a good time.

spassionatamente [spassjonata'mente] AVV dispassionately.

spassionato, a [spassjo'nato] AGG (*parere, consiglio*) impartial, dispassionate.

spasso ['spasso] SM **a** (*divertimento*) amusement, enjoyment; **per spasso** for amusement; **che spasso!** what a laugh!; **sei uno spasso!** you're a scream!

b (*passeggiata*): **andare a spasso** to go out for a walk; **portare qn a spasso** to take sb out for a walk; **essere a spasso** (*fig*) to be unemployed *o* out of work; **mandare qn a spasso** (*fig fam: licenziare*) to give sb the sack.

spassoso, a [spas'soso] AGG amusing, entertaining.

spastico, a, ci, che ['spastiko] AGG, SM/F spastic.

spatola ['spatola] SF **a** (*Med*) spatula (*Brit*), tongue depressor (*Am*); (*di muratore*) trowel; (*di decoratore*) putty knife; (*di sci*) tip; (*Culin: di legno*) spatula; (: *di metallo*) palette knife **b** (*uccello*) spoonbill.

spauracchio, chi [spau'rakkjo] SM (*spaventapasseri*) scarecrow; (*fig*) bogey, bugbear.

spaurire [spau'rire] VT to frighten, terrify.

spaurito, a [spau'rito] AGG frightened, terrified.

spavaldamente [spavalda'mente] AVV cockily.

spavalderia [spavalde'ria] SF cockiness.

spavaldo, a [spa'valdo] AGG cocky.

spaventapasseri [spaventa'passeri] SM INV scarecrow.

spaventare [spaven'tare] **1** VT to frighten, scare.

2 **spaventarsi** VIP to become frightened, become scared.

spavento [spa'vento] SM fear, fright; **fare** *o* **mettere spavento a qn** to frighten *o* scare sb, give sb a fright; **morire di spavento** (*fig*) to be scared to death; **è uno spavento** OR **è brutto da far spavento** he is terribly ugly.

spaventosamente [spaventosa'mente] AVV (*in modo spaventoso*) frighteningly; (*fig fam: eccessivamente*) terribly, incredibly.

spaventoso, a [spaven'toso] AGG (*sogno, avventura*) frightening; (*incidente, delitto*) horrifying, terrible; (*fig fam: incredibile*) incredible; (: *tempesta*) terrible; (: *prezzi*) appalling; **ho una fame spaventosa** I'm ravenous; **ho fatto una figura spaventosa** I made an awful fool of myself.

spaziale [spat'tsjale] AGG **a** (*volo, nave, tuta*) space *attr* **b** (*Archit, Geom*) spatial.

spaziare [spat'tsjare] **1** VI (*aus* **avere**): **spaziare in** OR **spaziare per** to range over; **spaziare col pensiero** to let one's thoughts wander.

2 VT (*Tip: parole, lettere*) to space (out).

spaziatura [spattsja'tura] SF (*Tip*) spacing.

spazientirsi [spattsjen'tirsi] VIP to lose one's patience.

spazio, zi ['spattsjo] SM (*gen, Fis, Mus, Tip*) space; (*posto*) room, space; **fare spazio per qn/qc** to make room for sb/sth; **dare spazio a** (*fig*) to make room for; **ci manca lo spazio** we are short of room *o* space; **lo spazio tra le file**

the space o gap between the rows; **nello spazio di un'ora** within an hour, in the space of an hour ▶ **spazio aereo** airspace ▶ **spazio vitale** living space.

spazioso, a [spat'tsjoso] AGG (*casa, macchina*) spacious, roomy; (*strada*) wide.

spazzacamino [spattsaka'mino] SM chimney sweep.

spazzaneve [spattsa'neve] SM INV (*spartineve, Sci*) snowplough (*Brit*), snowplow (*Am*).

spazzare [spat'tsare] VT (*pavimento, strada*) to sweep; (*foglie, polvere*) to sweep up; **spazzare via** to sweep away; (*fig: cibo*) to put away.

spazzatura [spattsa'tura] [1] SF (*immondizia*) rubbish (*Brit*), garbage (*Am*), trash (*Am*); **camion della spazzatura** dustcart (*Brit*), garbage truck (*Am*).
[2] AGG INV (*giornale, romanzo*) trashy; **posta-spazzatura** junk mail *sg*.

spazzino, a [spat'tsino] SM/F roadsweeper (*Brit*), street sweeper (*Am*).

spazzola ['spattsola] SF brush; **capelli a spazzola** crew cut *sg* ▶ **spazzola per abiti** clothes brush ▶ **spazzola da bagno** back scrubber ▶ **spazzola per capelli** hairbrush ▶ **spazzola di ferro** wire brush ▶ **spazzola per le scarpe** shoebrush ▶ **spazzola rotante** (*Aut*) rotor arm.

spazzolare [spattso'lare] VT to brush.

spazzolata [spattso'lata] SF brush, brushing.

spazzolino [spattso'lino] SM (small) brush ▶ **spazzolino da denti** toothbrush ▶ **spazzolino per unghie** nailbrush.

spazzolone [spattso'lone] SM (*per pulire*) scrubbing brush; (*per lucidare*) floor polisher.

speaker ['spi:kə] SM/F INV announcer.

specchiarsi [spek'kjarsi] [1] VR to look at o.s. in a mirror; **si specchia in tutte le vetrine** she looks at herself in all the shop windows; **il pavimento è così pulito che ti ci puoi specchiare** the floor is so clean you can see your face in it.
[2] VIP: **le montagne si specchiano nel lago** the mountains are reflected in the lake.

specchiera [spek'kjɛra] SF **a** (*specchio*) large mirror **b** (*mobile*) dressing table.

specchietto[1]   [spek'kjetto]   SM   (small)   mirror ▶ **specchietto da borsetta** pocket mirror ▶ **specchietto di cortesia** (*Aut*) vanity mirror ▶ **specchietto per le allodole** (*Caccia*) lure; (*fig*) bait ▶ **specchietto retrovisore** (*Aut*) rear-view mirror.

specchietto[2] [spek'kjetto] SM (*tabella*) table, chart.

specchio, chi ['spɛkkjo] SM mirror; **la sua casa è uno specchio** her house is spotlessly clean; **il mare è uno specchio** the sea is as calm as a millpond; **uno specchio d'acqua** a sheet of water.

special ['spɛtʃal] SM INV (*TV*) special feature.

speciale [spe'tʃale] AGG (*gen*) special; (*specifico*) particular; (*singolare*) peculiar, singular; **hai qualche motivo speciale per sospettare di lui?** do you have any particular reason to suspect him?; **ha un modo tutto speciale di parlare** he has a highly individual way of speaking; **questo arrosto è speciale** this roast is delicious; **in special modo** especially; **inviato speciale** (*Radio, TV, Stampa*) special correspondent; **offerta speciale** special offer; **treno speciale** special o extra train; **poteri/leggi speciali** (*Pol*) emergency powers/legislation *sg*.

specialista, i, e [spetʃa'lista] SM/F (*gen*) expert, specialist; (*Med*) specialist.

specialistico, a, ci, che [spetʃa'listiko] AGG (*conoscenza,*

preparazione) specialized; **devo fare una visita specialista** (*Med*) I have to see a specialist.

specialità [spetʃali'ta] SF INV **a** (*prodotto tipico*) speciality (*Brit*), specialty (*Am*) **b** (*branca di studio*) specialism.

specializzare [spetʃalid'dzare] [1] VT (*industria*) to make more specialized.
[2] **specializzarsi** VR: **specializzarsi (in)** (*studio, professione*) to specialize (in); **mi sono specializzato nel fare torte** I'm a dab hand at baking cakes.

specializzato, a [spetʃalid'dzato] AGG (*manodopera*) skilled; (*elaboratore*) dedicated; **operaio non specializzato** unskilled worker; **essere specializzato in** to be a specialist in.

specializzazione [spetʃaliddzat'tsjone] SF specialization; **prendere la specializzazione in** to specialize in.

specialmente [spetʃal'mente] AVV especially, particularly.

specie ['spɛtʃe] [1] SF INV **a** (*Bio, Bot, Zool*) species *inv*; **la specie umana** mankind **b** (*tipo*) sort, kind, variety; **una specie di** a kind of; **gente di ogni specie** all kinds of people; **mi fa specie** it surprises me.
[2] AVV especially, particularly.

specifica, che [spe'tʃifika] SF specification.

specificamente [spetʃifika'mente] AVV specifically.

specificare [spetʃifi'kare] VT to specify, state (clearly).

specificatamente [spetʃifikata'mente] AVV in detail.

specificazione [spetʃifikat'tsjone] SF **a** (*gen*) specification **b** (*Gramm*): **complemento di specificazione** genitive case.

specificità [spetʃifitʃi'ta] SF specificity.

specifico, a, ci, che [spe'tʃifiko] AGG (*gen, Med*) specific; **mi ha rivolto accuse specifiche** his accusations were very specific; **nel caso specifico** in this particular case.

specioso, a [spe'tʃoso] AGG (*letter*) specious.

speck [ʃpɛk] SM INV *kind of smoked ham*.

speculare[1] [speku'lare] VI (*aus avere*) **a** (*Comm*) to speculate; (*fig: approfittare*): **speculare su** to take advantage of; **speculare in Borsa** to speculate on the Stock Exchange **b** (*Filosofia*): **speculare (su)** to speculate (on o about).

speculare[2] [speku'lare] AGG (*immagine, scrittura*) mirror *attr*.

speculativo, a [spekula'tivo] AGG (*Filosofia, Comm*) speculative.

speculatore, trice [spekula'tore] SM/F (*Comm*) speculator.

speculazione [spekulat'tsjone] SF speculation.

spedire [spe'dire] VT (*gen*) to send, dispatch; (*Comm*) to dispatch, forward; **spedire per posta** to post (*Brit*), mail (*Am*); **spedire per mare** to ship; **spedire qn all'altro mondo** to send sb to meet his (o her) maker.

speditamente [spedita'mente] AVV (*lavorare*) quickly; (*parlare: veloce*) quickly; (*: con sicurezza*) fluently; **camminare speditamente** to walk at a brisk pace.

spedito, a [spe'dito] [1] AGG (*gen*) quick; **con passo spedito** at a brisk pace; **ha una pronuncia spedita** he has a fluent manner of speaking.
[2] AVV = **speditamente**.

spedizione [spedit'tsjone] SF **a** (*atto*) sending, posting; (*Comm: gen*) forwarding; (*: via mare*) shipping; (*collo, merce*) consignment; (*: via mare*) shipment; **agenzia di spedizione** forwarding agency; **spese di spedizione** (*gen*) postal (*Brit*) o mail (*Am*) charges; (*Comm*) forwarding charges; **fare una spedizione** to send a consignment
b (*scientifica, Mil, Alpinismo*) expedition; **una spedizione**

punitiva a punitive raid.

spedizioniere [spedittsjo'njɛre] SM forwarding agent, shipping agent.

spegnere ['spɛɲɲere] VB IRREG 1 VT (*fuoco, sigaretta*) to put out, extinguish; (*apparecchio elettrico*) to switch o turn off; (*luce*) to switch o turn off; (*gas*) to turn off; (*fig: suoni, passioni*) to stifle; (: *debito*) to extinguish.

2 **spegnersi** VIP a (*fuoco, sigaretta*) to go out; (*apparecchio elettrico, luce*) to go off; (*fig: passioni, suoni*) to die down; (: *ricordo*) to fade

b (*euf: morire*) to pass away.

spegnimento [speɲɲi'mento] SM (*di debito*) extinguishing; (*di luce, apparecchio elettrico*) switching off; (*di incendio*) putting out.

spelacchiato, a [spelak'kjato] AGG (*gatto, cane*) mangy; (*coperta, tappeto*) threadbare, worn-out; (*pelliccia, animale di pezza*) shabby.

spelare [spe'lare] 1 VT (*Elettr: fili*) to strip.

2 **spelarsi** VIP (*animali*) to moult; (*pelliccia*) to lose hair.

speleologia [speleolo'dʒia] SF (*scienza*) speleology; (*pratica*) potholing (*Brit*), spelunking (*Am*).

speleologo, a, gi, ghe [spele'ɔlogo] SM/F (*vedi sf*) speleologist; potholer (*Brit*), spelunker (*Am*).

spellare [spel'lare] 1 VT a (*coniglio*) to skin; (*fam: scorticare*) to graze; **mi sono spellato il ginocchio** I grazed my knee b (*fig: cliente*) to fleece.

2 **spellarsi** VIP (*persona: per il troppo sole*) to peel; (: *scorticarsi*) to graze o.s.; (*rettile*) to shed its skin.

spelonca, che [spe'lonka] SF (*caverna*) cave, cavern; (*fig: casa squallida*) hovel.

spendaccione, a [spendat'tʃone] SM/F spendthrift.

spendere ['spɛndere] VT IRREG (*denaro, tempo*) to spend; **quanto ti hanno fatto spendere?** how much did they charge you?; **quanto hai speso?** how much did you spend?; **quanto hai speso per quel vestito?** how much did you spend on o pay for that dress?; **spendere un occhio della testa** to spend a fortune; **spendere una buona parola per qn** to put in a good word for sb; **spendere e spandere** to squander one's money; **spendere la vita sui libri** to spend one's life studying.

spengo ecc ['spɛngo] VB vedi **spegnere**.

spennacchiare [spennak'kjare] 1 VT (*gallina*) to pluck.

2 **spennacchiarsi** VIP to moult, lose its feathers.

spennacchiato, a [spennak'kjato] AGG (*con poche penne*) moulting.

spennare [spen'nare] 1 VT (*gallina*) to pluck; (*fig: cliente*) to fleece.

2 **spennarsi** VIP to moult, lose its feathers.

spennellare [spennel'lare] 1 VI (*aus avere*) to paint.

2 VT (*Med*): **spennellare una ferita con la tintura di iodio** to dab a wound with iodine; (*Culin*): **spennellare un dolce con l'uovo** to brush the cake with beaten egg.

spennellata [spennel'lata] SF brush-stroke.

spensi ecc ['spɛnsi] VB vedi **spegnere**.

spensieratamente [spensjerata'mente] AVV in a carefree manner, lightheartedly.

spensieratezza [spensjera'tettsa] SF carefreeness, lightheartedness.

spensierato, a [spensje'rato] AGG carefree, lighthearted.

spento, a ['spɛnto] 1 PP di **spegnere**.

2 AGG (*luce, fuoco, sigaretta*) out; (*colore*) dull, faded; (*vulcano, civiltà*) extinct; (*persona, sguardo, festa*) lifeless; (*suono*) muffled.

speranza [spe'rantsa] SF hope; **nella speranza di rivederti**

(*in lettera*) hoping to see o in the hope of seeing you again; **avere la speranza che...** to be hopeful that ...; **avere la speranza di qc/di fare qc** to be hopeful of sth/of doing sth; **hai qualche speranza di vincere?** have you any hope o chance of winning?; **pieno di speranze** hopeful; **senza speranza** (*situazione*) hopeless; (*amare*) without hope; **quel giovane è una speranza dell'atletica** that boy is a promising athlete.

speranzoso, a [speran'tsoso] AGG hopeful.

sperare [spe'rare] 1 VT: **sperare qc/di fare qc** to hope for sth/to do sth; **spero di sì** I hope so; **spero di no** I hope not; **speriamo bene!** let's hope so!; **lo spero** I hope so; **non speravo più di vederti** I'd given up hope of seeing you.

2 VI (*aus avere*): **sperare in** (*successo*) to hope for; **spero in Dio** to trust in God; **spero in te per risolvere la situazione** I'm counting on you to sort things out; **tutto fa sperare per il meglio** everything leads one to hope for the best.

sperduto, a [sper'duto] AGG (*isolato: casa, villaggio*) out-of-the-way; (*persona: smarrito*) lost; (: *a disagio*) ill at ease.

spergiurare [sperdʒu'rare] VI (*aus avere*) to commit perjury, perjure o.s.; **giurare e spergiurare** to swear blind.

spergiuro, a [sper'dʒuro] 1 AGG perjured.

2 SM/F perjurer.

3 SM perjury.

spericolato, a [speriko'lato] 1 AGG (*gen*) fearless, daring; (*guidatore*) reckless.

2 SM/F daredevil.

sperimentale [sperimen'tale] AGG experimental; **scuola sperimentale** pilot school; **fare qc in via sperimentale** to try sth out.

sperimentalmente [sperimental'mente] AVV experimentally.

sperimentare [sperimen'tare] VT a (*nuovo farmaco*) to experiment with, test; (*metodo*) to try out, test out; **sperimentare qc sugli animali** to test sth on animals b (*fig: tentare*) to try; (: *mettere alla prova*) to test, put to the test.

sperimentatore, trice [sperimenta'tore] SM/F experimenter.

sperimentazione [sperimentat'tsjone] SF experimentation.

sperma ['spɛrma] SM sperm, semen.

spermatozoo, i [spermatod'dzɔo] SM spermatozoon.

spermicida, i, e [spermi'tʃida] 1 AGG (*pomata, schiuma*) spermicidal.

2 SM spermicide.

speronamento [sperona'mento] SM ramming.

speronare [spero'nare] VT (*nave, auto*) to ram.

sperone [spe'rone] SM (*di stivali, Geog*) spur; (*Naut: rostro*) ram; (*Archit*) buttress; (*Zool*) dew claw.

sperperare [sperpe'rare] VT (*denaro*) to squander.

sperpero ['spɛrpero] SM (*di denaro*) squandering, waste; (*di cibo, materiali*) waste.

sperso, a ['spɛrso] AGG (*persona: smarrito*) lost; (: *a disagio*) ill at ease.

spersonalizzare [spersonalid'dzare] 1 VT (*persona*) to deprive of individuality; (*stile, narrazione*) to depersonalize.

2 **spersonalizzarsi** VIP (*persona*) to lose one's individuality.

spersonalizzazione [spersonaliddzat'tsjone] SF deper-

sonalization.

spesa ['spesa] ⟨1⟩SF **a** (*soldi spesi*) expense; (*uscita*) outlay, expenditure; (*costo*) cost; **la spesa è di 200.000 lire** it will cost 200,000 lire; **con la modica spesa di un milione di lire** for the modest sum *o* outlay of one million lire; **ridurre le spese** (*gen*) to cut down (on spending); (*Comm*) to reduce expenditure; **a spese della ditta** at the firm's expense; **a mie spese** (*fig*) at my expense; **fare le spese di qc** (*fig*) to pay the price for sth. **b** (*acquisto*) buy, purchase; (*fam: compere*) shopping *no pl*; **fare la spesa** to do the shopping; **fare delle spese** to go shopping ⟨2⟩ ▸**spesa pubblica** public expenditure ▸**spese in conto capitale** (*Comm*) capital expenditure *sg* ▸**spese generali** (*Comm*) overheads ▸**spese di gestione** operating expenses ▸**spese d'impianto** (*Comm*) initial outlay *sg* ▸**spese legali** legal costs ▸**spese di manutenzione** maintenance costs ▸**spese postali** postage *o* postal (*Brit*) *o* mail (*Am*) charges ▸**spese di trasporto** handling charges ▸**spese di viaggio** travelling (*Brit*) *o* traveling (*Am*) expenses.

spesare [spe'sare] VT: **sono spesato dalla società** the company pays my expenses; **un viaggio tutto spesato** an all-expenses-paid trip.

speso, a ['speso] PP di **spendere**.

spessimetro [spes'simetro] SM thickness gauge, feeler gauge.

spesso[1] ['spesso] AVV often; **andiamo spesso al cinema** we often go to the cinema; **anche troppo spesso** all too often; **spesso e volentieri** very often.

spesso[2]**, a** ['spesso] AGG (*nebbia, fumo*) thick, dense; (*stoffa*) heavy, heavyweight; (*carta*) thick, heavy; **spesso 40 mm** 40 mm thick.

spessore [spes'sore] SM **a** thickness; (*fig: importanza*: *di ricerca*) significance; (: *di personaggio*) stature; **ha uno spessore di 20 cm** it is 20 cm thick **b** (*Tecn*) gauge.

Spett. ABBR = **spettabile**.

spettabile [spet'tabile] AGG (*Comm*): **spettabile ditta X** (*sulla busta*) Messrs X and Co; (*inizio lettera*) Dear Sirs, ...; **avvertiamo la spettabile clientela...** we inform our customers ... .

spettacolare [spettako'lare] AGG spectacular.

spettacolarità [spettakolari'ta] SF spectacular nature.

spettacolo [spet'takolo] SM **a** (*Cine, TV, Teatro*) show, performance; **mettere su uno spettacolo** to put on a show; **gli spettacoli iniziano alle 20** performances begin at 8 pm; **primo/secondo spettacolo** (*Cine*) first/second showing **b** (*vista, scena*) sight; **dare spettacolo di sé** to make an exhibition *o* a spectacle of o.s.

spettacoloso, a [spettako'loso] AGG (*vista*) spectacular; (*fig*) amazing, incredible.

spettanza [spet'tantsa] SF **a** (*competenza*) concern; **non è di mia spettanza** it's no concern of mine **b** (*somma dovuta*): **spettanze** SFPL amount due; **non ho ancora avuto le mie spettanze** I haven't yet received what is owing to me.

spettare [spet'tare] VI (*aus* essere): **spettare a** (*decisione*) to be up to; (*stipendio*) to be due to; **spetta a te decidere** it's up to you to decide; **mi spetta una parte degli incassi** I'm due a share of the takings.

spettatore, trice [spetta'tore] SM/F (*Cine, Teatro*) member of the audience; (*TV*) viewer; (*Sport*) spectator; (*di avvenimento*) witness; **è stato spettatore di un incidente** he witnessed an accident.

spettegolare [spettego'lare] VI (*aus* avere) to gossip.

spettinare [spetti'nare] ⟨1⟩ VT: **spettinare qn** to ruffle sb's hair.
⟨2⟩ **spettinarsi** VR to get one's hair in a mess.

spettinato, a [spetti'nato] AGG dishevelled.

spettrale [spet'trale] AGG (*gen*) spectral, ghostly.

spettro ['spɛttro] SM **a** (*fantasma*) spectre (*Brit*), specter (*Am*), ghost **b** (*Fis*) spectrum.

spezie ['spɛttsje] SFPL (*Culin*) spices.

spezzare [spet'tsare] ⟨1⟩ VT (*rompere*) to break, snap; (*fig: interrompere*) to break up; **spezzare il cuore a qn** to break sb's heart; **spezzare il viaggio** to break one's journey; **mi spezza la giornata** it breaks up my day. ⟨2⟩ **spezzarsi** VIP to break, snap.

spezzatino [spettsa'tino] SM (*Culin*) stew.

spezzato, a [spet'tsato] ⟨1⟩ AGG (*unghia, ramo, braccio*) broken; **fare orario spezzato** to work a split shift. ⟨2⟩ SM (*abito maschile*) (coordinated) jacket and trousers (*Brit*) *o* pants (*Am*).

spezzettamento [spettsetta'mento] SM breaking up.

spezzettare [spettset'tare] VT to break up (*o* chop) into small pieces; **spezzettare il pane** to crumble bread.

spezzino, a [spet'tsino] ⟨1⟩ AGG of *o* from La Spezia. ⟨2⟩ SM/F inhabitant *o* native of La Spezia.

spezzone [spet'tsone] SM (*Cine*) clip.

spia ['spia] SF **a** (*gen*) spy; (*confidente della polizia*) informer; **non fare la spia** (*gen*) don't give me (*o* us *ecc*) away; (*di bambini*) don't be a telltale **b** (*Elettr*: *anche*: **spia luminosa**) warning light, indicating light; (*di porta*) spyhole, peephole; (*fig: sintomo*) sign, indication ▸**spia dell'olio** (*Aut*) oil warning light.

spiaccicare [spjattʃi'kare] VT (*fam: schiacciare*) to squash, crush; **ti spiaccico al muro** I'll flatten you.

spiacente [spja'tʃɛnte] AGG sorry; **siamo spiacenti di non poter accettare** we regret being unable to accept, we are sorry we cannot accept; **siamo spiacenti di quanto è successo** we regret what happened, we are sorry about what happened; **siamo spiacenti di dovervi annunciare che...** we regret to inform you that ...; **sono molto spiacente ma...** I am extremely sorry, but ... .

spiacere [spja'tʃere] = **dispiacere 2, 3**.

spiacevole [spja'tʃevole] AGG (*compito*) unpleasant; (*incidente, equivoco*) regrettable.

spiacevolmente [spjatʃevol'mente] AVV unpleasantly, disagreeably.

spiaggia, ge ['spjaddʒa] SF beach.

spianare [spja'nare] VT (*terreno*) to level, make level; (*palazzo, città*) to raze to the ground; (*pasta*) to roll out; **spianare il fucile** to level one's gun; **spianare la strada** (*fig*) to prepare *o* clear the ground.

spianata [spja'nata] SF (*radiura*) clearing.

spianatoia [spjana'toja] SF (*Culin*) pastry board.

spiano ['spjano]: **a tutto spiano** AVV (*lavorare*) flat out; (*spendere*) lavishly.

spiantato, a [spjan'tato] ⟨1⟩ AGG penniless. ⟨2⟩ SM penniless person.

spiare [spi'are] VT to spy on; **spiare le mosse di qn** to spy on sb's movements; **spiare l'occasione propizia** to wait for the right moment; **spiare da dietro la porta** to spy at the door; **spiare attraverso il buco della serratura** to spy through the keyhole.

spiata [spi'ata] SF tip-off.

spiattellare [spjattel'lare] VT (*fam: verità, segreto*) to blurt out; **spiattellare tutto** to spill the beans.

spiazzo ['spjattso] SM (*gen*) open space; (*radura*) clearing.

spiccare [spik'kare] 1 VT a : **spiccare un balzo** to jump, leap; **spiccare il volo** (*uccello*) to take wing; (*fig*) to spread one's wings b (*Dir, Comm: mandato, assegno*) to issue.
2 VI (*aus avere*) (*risaltare*) to stand out.

spiccatamente [spikkata'mente] AVV (*nettamente*) distinctly; **parla con un accento spiccatamente tedesco** he speaks with a strong German accent.

spiccato, a [spik'kato] AGG (*senso del dovere, dell'umorismo*) marked, strong; (*gusto*) definite, marked; (*accento*) broad; **ha una spiccata simpatia per lui** she is very fond of him.

spiccherò ecc [spikke'rɔ] VB vedi **spiccare**.

spicchio, chi ['spikkjo] SM (*di agrumi*) segment; (*di aglio*) clove; (*di formaggio*) piece; **fare** o **tagliare a spicchi** to divide into segments.

spicciare [spit't ʃare] 1 VT (*lavoro, faccenda*) to finish off; (*cliente*) to attend to.
2 **spicciarsi** VIP to hurry up, get a move on.

spicciativo, a [spitt ʃa'tivo] AGG quick.

spiccicare [spitt ʃi'kare] 1 VT (*adesivo, francobollo*) to unstick, detach; **non ha spiccicato parola** he didn't utter a word.
2 **spiccicarsi** VIP (*francobollo*) to come unstuck, come off.

spiccio, cia, ci, ce ['spitt ʃo] 1 AGG a (*faccenda*) quick; **andare per le spicce** not to waste time on niceties b : **denaro spiccio** (small) change.
2 SMPL (*moneta*): **spicci** (small) change *sg*.

spicciolata [spitt ʃo'lata] AVV: **alla spicciolata** in dribs and drabs, a few at a time.

spicciolo, a ['spitt ʃolo] 1 AGG: **denaro spicciolo** OR **moneta spicciola** (small) change.
2 SM: **non ho uno spicciolo** I'm penniless; **hai degli spiccioli?** have you got any (small) change?

spicco ['spikko] SM: **fare spicco** to stand out; **di spicco** (*personaggio*) prominent; (*tema*) main, principal.

spider ['spaidə] SM O F INV (*Aut*) two-seater convertible sports car.

spidocchiare [spidok'kjare] 1 VT to delouse.
2 **spidocchiarsi** VR to delouse o.s.

spiedino [spje'dino] SM a (*utensile*) skewer b (*Culin: di carne, pesce*) kebab.

spiedo ['spjɛdo] SM (*Culin*) spit; **allo spiedo** on a spit; **pollo allo spiedo** spit-roasted chicken.

spiegamento [spjega'mento] SM (*Mil*): **spiegamento di forze** deployment of forces.

spiegare [spje'gare] 1 VT a (*significato, mistero*) to explain; **spiegare qc a qn** to explain sth to sb; **farsi spiegare qc** to get o have sth explained
b (*tovaglia*) to unfold; (*vele*) to unfurl; **a voce spiegata** at the top of one's voice; **a sirene spiegate** with sirens wailing
c (*Mil*) to deploy.
2 **spiegarsi** VR (*farsi capire*) to explain o.s., make o.s. clear; (*capire*) to understand; **mi spiego?** do I make myself clear?; **non so se mi spiego!** need I say more!; **spieghiamoci una volta per tutte!** let's get things straight once and for all!; **non mi spiego come...** I can't understand how ...; **ora si spiega tutto!** now everything is clear!

spiegazione [spjegat'tsjone] SF explanation; **avere una spiegazione con qn** to have it out with sb.

spiegazzare [spjegat'tsare] VT to crease, crumple.

spiegazzato, a [spjegat'tsato] AGG creased, crumpled.

spiegherò ecc [spjege'rɔ] VB vedi **spiegare**.

spietatamente [spjetata'mente] AVV ruthlessly, without pity.

spietatezza [spjeta'tettsa] SF ruthlessness.

spietato, a [spje'tato] AGG (*persona*) ruthless, pitiless; (*guerra*) cruel, bitter; (*fig: concorrenza*) fierce; **fare una corte spietata a qn** to chase (after) sb.

spifferare [spiffe'rare] VT (*fam*) to blurt out, blab.

spiffero ['spiffero] SM (*fam: corrente d'aria*) draught (*Brit*), draft (*Am*).

spiga, ghe ['spiga] SF (*Bot: di grano*) ear.

spigato, a [spi'gato] AGG (*tessuto*) herringbone.

spigliatamente [spiʎʎata'mente] AVV confidently, with ease.

spigliatezza [spiʎʎa'tettsa] SF ease, self-confidence.

spigliato, a [spiʎ'ʎato] AGG (*persona*) self-confident, self-possessed; (*modi*) (free and) easy.

spignattare [spiɲɲat'tare] VI (*aus avere*) (*fam*) to slave over a hot stove.

spigola ['spigola] SF (*Zool*) bass.

spigolare [spigo'lare] VT (*anche fig*) to glean.

spigolatura [spigola'tura] SF (*anche fig*) gleaning.

spigolo ['spigolo] SM (*di mobile, muro*) corner, edge; (*Geom*) edge; **smussare gli spigoli** (*fig*) to knock off the rough edges.

spigoloso, a [spigo'loso] AGG (*mobile*) angular; (*persona, carattere*) difficult.

spilla ['spilla] SF (*gen*) brooch; (*da cravatta, cappello*) pin ▶ **spilla di sicurezza** o **da balia** safety pin.

spillare [spil'lare] VT a (*botte, vino, fig*) to tap; **spillare denaro/notizie a qn** to tap sb for money/information b (*fogli*) to clip together.

spillo ['spillo] SM (*gen*) pin; (*da cappello*) hatpin; (*da cravatta*) tiepin; **tacco a spillo** stiletto heel (*Brit*), spike heel (*Am*); **valvola a spillo** needle valve.

spillone [spil'lone] SM (*per cappello*) hatpin.

spilluzzicare [spilluttsi'kare] VT (*cibo*) to nibble, peck at.

spilorceria [spilort ʃe'ria] SF meanness, stinginess; **questa è una spilorceria!** that's really mean o stingy!

spilorciamente [spilort ʃa'mente] AVV meanly, stingily.

spilorcio, cia, ci, ce [spi'lort ʃo] 1 AGG mean, stingy, tight-fisted.
2 SM/F miser, stingy person.

spilungone, a [spilun'gone] SM/F beanpole.

spina ['spina] SF a (*Bot: di rosa*) thorn; **avere una spina nel cuore** to have a thorn in one's flesh o side; **stare sulle spine** (*fig*) to be on tenterhooks b (*Zool: di riccio, istrice*) spine, prickle; (: *di pesce*) bone ▶ **spina dorsale** (*Anat*) backbone c (*Elettr*) plug d (*di botte*) bunghole; **birra alla spina** draught (*Brit*) o draft (*Am*) beer.

spinacio, ci [spi'nat ʃo] SM (*Bot*) spinach; (*Culin*): **spinaci** SMPL spinach *sg*.

spinale [spi'nale] AGG (*Anat*) spinal.

spinare [spi'nare] VT (*pesce*) to bone.

spinato, a [spi'nato] AGG a : **filo spinato** barbed wire b (*tessuto*) herringbone *attr*.

spinello [spi'nɛllo] SM (*Droga*) joint.

spinetta [spi'netta] SF (*Mus*) spinet.

spingere ['spindʒere] VB IRREG 1 VT a (*gen*) to push; (*premere*) to press, push; **non spingete** don't push o shove; **"spingere" "push"; mi spingi?** (*sull'altalena*) can you give me a push?; **le onde ci hanno spinto contro gli scogli** the waves drove us onto the rocks; **spingere le**

cose all'eccesso to take *o* carry things too far *o* to extremes; **spingere lo sguardo lontano** to look into the distance

b (*fig: stimolare*): **spingere qn a fare qc** to urge *o* press sb to do sth; **spingere qn al delitto/suicidio** to drive sb to crime/suicide; **spinto dalla fame/disperazione** driven by hunger/despair; **che cosa ti spinge a continuare?** what drives you on?.

2 VI (*aus* avere) to push.

3 **spingersi** VIP: **spingersi troppo lontano** (*anche fig*) to go too far; **ci siamo spinti fino al faro** we ventured as far as the lighthouse.

spingidisco, schi [spindʒi'disko] SM (*Aut*) (clutch) pressure plate.

spinnaker ['spinəkə] SM INV (*Naut*) spinnaker.

spino ['spino] SM (*Bot*) thorn bush.

spinone [spi'none] SM (*cane*) griffon.

spinoso, a [spi'noso] AGG (*anche fig*) thorny, prickly.

spinsi *ecc* ['spinsi] VB *vedi* **spingere.**

spinta ['spinta] SF **a** (*gen*) push; (*urto*) push, shove; (*Fis*) thrust; **spinta verso l'alto** upthrust **b** (*fig: stimolo*) incentive, spur; (: *raccomandazione*): **ho bisogno di una spinta** I need someone to pull some strings for me.

spintarella [spinta'rɛlla] SF (*fig: raccomandazione*): **ha avuto una spintarella** someone pulled strings for him.

spinterogeno [spinte'rɔdʒeno] SM (*Aut*) ignition coil.

spinto, a ['spinto] **1** PP di **spingere.**

2 AGG (*film, barzelletta*) risqué.

spintonare [spinto'nare] VT (*spingere*) to shove, push.

spintone [spin'tone] SM shove, push.

spionaggio [spio'naddʒo] SM espionage, spying.

spioncino [spion'tʃino] SM peephole, spyhole.

spione, a [spi'one] SM/F (*fam*) telltale, sneak.

spionistico, a, ci, che [spio'nistiko] AGG (*organizzazione*) spy *attr*; **rete spionistica** spy ring.

spiovente [spjo'vɛnte] **1** AGG (*tetto*) sloping; **palla** *o* **tiro spiovente** (*Calcio*) arcing shot.

2 SM (*Calcio*) arcing shot.

spiovere[1] ['spjɔvere] VB IMPERS (*Meteor*) (*aus* essere *o* avere) to stop raining.

spiovere[2] ['spjɔvere] VI IRREG (*aus* essere) (*scorrere*) to flow down; (*ricadere: capelli*) to hang down, fall.

spira ['spira] SF (*gen*) coil; (*di fumo*) curl.

spiraglio, gli [spi'raʎʎo] SM (*fessura*) chink, narrow opening; (*raggio di luce, anche fig*) glimmer, gleam; **uno spiraglio di speranza** a glimmer of hope, a faint hope.

spirale [spi'rale] SF **a** spiral; **a spirale** spiral(-shaped); **molla a spirale** (*di orologio*) hairspring ▶ **spirale inflazionistica** inflationary spiral ▶ (*contraccettivo*) coil.

spirare[1] [spi'rare] VI (*aus* avere) (*vento*) to blow; (*odore: emanare*): **spirare da** to come from; **spira aria di burrasca** (*fig*) there's trouble brewing.

spirare[2] [spi'rare] VI (*aus* essere) (*morire*) to expire, pass away; (*scadere*) to expire.

spiritato, a [spiri'tato] **1** AGG (*occhi, espressione*) wild.

2 SM/F person possessed by a devil; **come uno spiritato** like one possessed.

spiritico, a, ci, che [spi'ritiko] AGG spiritualist; **seduta spiritica** séance.

spiritismo [spiri'tizmo] SM spiritualism.

spiritista, i, e [spiri'tista] SM/F spiritualist.

spirito ['spirito] SM **a** (*gen*) spirit; (*fantasma*) spirit, ghost; **lo Spirito Santo** the Holy Spirit *o* Ghost; **valori dello spirito** spiritual values; **aver paura degli spiriti** to be afraid of ghosts

b (*intelletto*) mind; **uno dei più grandi spiriti della storia** one of the greatest minds in history

c (*disposizione d'animo*) spirit, disposition; (*significato: di legge, epoca, testo*) spirit; **per sollevarti lo spirito** to raise your spirits; **in buone condizioni di spirito** in the right frame of mind; **non ha spirito di parte** he never takes sides; **spirito di squadra** team spirit; **ha detto di no per spirito di contraddizione** he said no just to be awkward

d (*arguzia*) wit; (*umorismo*) humour (*Brit*), humor (*Am*), wit; **battuta di spirito** joke; **è una persona di spirito** he has a sense of humo(u)r; **non fare dello spirito** don't try to be witty

e (*Chim*) spirit, alcohol; **sotto spirito** preserved in alcohol.

spiritosaggine [spirito'saddʒine] SF (*qualità*) wittiness; (*battuta*) witticism.

spiritosamente [spiritosa'mente] AVV wittily.

spiritoso, a [spiri'toso] **1** AGG witty.

2 SM/F wit, witty person; **non fare lo spiritoso!** don't try and be funny!

spirituale [spiritu'ale] AGG (*gen, Filosofia, Rel*) spiritual.

spiritualità [spirituali'ta] SF spirituality.

spiritualizzare [spiritualid'dzare] VT to spiritualize.

spiritualmente [spiritual'mente] AVV spiritually.

spizzicare [spittsi'kare] VT to nibble, peck at.

splendente [splen'dɛnte] AGG (*giornata*) bright, sunny; (*occhi*) shining; (*pavimento*) shining, gleaming.

splendere ['splɛndere] VI DIF to shine.

splendidamente [splendida'mente] AVV (*gen*) splendidly, magnificently; **l'esame è andato splendidamente** the exam went extremely well.

splendido, a ['splɛndido] AGG (*gen*) magnificent, splendid; (*carriera*) brilliant; **una giornata splendida** a glorious day.

splendore [splen'dore] SM splendour (*Brit*), splendor (*Am*); (*luce intensa*) brilliance, brightness; **gli splendori dell'antica Roma** the splendo(u)r of ancient Rome; **che splendore di ragazza!** what a beautiful girl!

spodestare [spodes'tare] VT (*sovrano*) to depose, dethrone; **spodestare da** to oust from.

spoetizzare [spoetid'dzare] VT (*momento, fatto*) to take the beauty out of.

spoglia ['spoʎʎa] SF **a** (*di rettile*) slough; **sotto mentite spoglie** (*fig*) in disguise **b** (*letter: salma*) remains *pl.*

spogliare [spoʎ'ʎare] **1** VT **a** (*svestire*) to undress; (: *con la forza*) to strip; (*fig: privare: di autorità*) to divest, strip; (: *di tesori*) to strip; **spogliare qn di qc** (*derubare*) to strip *o* rob sb of sth

b (*fare lo spoglio: di schede elettorali*) to count.

2 **spogliarsi** VR (*persona*) to undress, strip; (*serpente*) to slough (off) *o* shed its skin.

3 **spogliarsi** VIP (*albero*) to shed its leaves; (*persona*): **spogliarsi di** (*fig: ricchezze*) to strip o.s. of; (: *pregiudizi*) to get rid of, rid o.s. of.

spogliarellista, i, e [spoʎʎarel'lista] SM/F striptease artist, stripper.

spogliarello [spoʎʎa'rɛllo] SM striptease.

spogliatoio, oi [spoʎʎa'tojo] SM changing room.

spoglio[1]**, glia, gli, glie** ['spoʎʎo] AGG (*stanza*) empty, bare; (*terreno, albero*) bare; (*stile*) simple.

spoglio[2]**, gli** ['spoʎʎo] SM: **spoglio dei voti** counting of the votes.

spoiler ['spɔilə] SM INV (*Aut*) spoiler.

spola ['spola] SF (*Cucito: bobina*) spool; (: *navetta*) shuttle; **fare la spola (fra)** (*sogg: autobus, persona*) to go to and fro *o* shuttle (between).

spoletta [spo'letta] SF (*Cucito: bobina*) spool; (*di bomba*) fuse.

spoliticizzare [spolititʃid'dzare] [1] VT to make nonpolitical.

  [2] **spoliticizzarsi** VIP to become nonpolitical.

spoliticizzazione [spolititʃiddzat'tsjone] SF making nonpolitical.

spolmonarsi [spolmo'narsi] VIP to shout o.s. hoarse.

spolpare [spol'pare] VT (*pollo*) to strip the flesh off; (*fig fam: spennare*) to skin, fleece; **ci hanno spolpato con queste tasse** they have bled us white with these taxes.

spolverare[1] [spolve'rare] [1] VT (*mobile*) to dust; (*fig: mangiare*) to polish off.

  [2] VI (*aus avere*) to dust.

spolverare[2] [spolve'rare] VT (*Culin*): **spolverare (di)** to sprinkle (with), dust (with).

spolverata[1] [spolve'rata] SF (quick) dust(ing).

spolverata[2] [spolve'rata] SF (*di neve*) light fall; **dare una spolverata di zucchero a qc** to sprinkle sth with sugar.

spolverino [spolve'rino] SM (*soprabito*) dust coat, duster (*Am*).

spolverizzare [spolverid'dzare] VT (*Culin*): **spolverizzare qc di** to dust *o* sprinkle sth with.

spompato, a [spom'pato] AGG (*fam: sfinito*) worn out.

sponda ['sponda] SF a (*di fiume*) bank; (*di mare, lago*) shore b (*bordo: di letto, carro*) side, edge.

sponsor ['sponsə] SM/F INV sponsor.

sponsorizzare [sponsorid'dzare] VT to sponsor.

sponsorizzato, a [sponsorid'dzato] AGG sponsored.

sponsorizzazione [sponsoriddzat'tsjone] SF sponsorship.

spontaneamente [spontanea'mente] AVV (*agire*) naturally, spontaneously; (*reagire*) instinctively, spontaneously; (*pianta: crescere*) wild; **offrirsi spontaneamente di fare qc** to volunteer to do sth.

spontaneità [spontanei'ta] SF spontaneity.

spontaneo, a [spon'taneo] AGG (*gen*) spontaneous; (*affetto, persona*) natural, unaffected; (*vegetazione*) wild; **di sua spontanea volontà** of his own free will; **viene spontanea la domanda...** the question springs to mind ...; **sii spontanea quando ti fanno una foto!** try to be natural when you're having your photo taken!

spopolamento [spopola'mento] SM depopulation.

spopolare [spopo'lare] [1] VT to depopulate.

  [2] VI (*aus avere*) (*fam: aver successo: cantante, attore*) to draw the crowds.

  [3] **spopolarsi** VIP to become depopulated.

spora ['spora] SF spore.

sporadicamente [sporadika'mente] AVV sporadically.

sporadicità [sporaditʃi'ta] SF sporadic nature.

sporadico, a, ci, che [spo'radiko] AGG sporadic.

sporcaccione, a [sporkat'tʃone] [1] AGG filthy, disgusting; (*sessualmente*): **un vecchio sporcaccione** a dirty old man.

  [2] SM/F filthy person; (*sessualmente*) filthy beast, pig.

sporcare [spor'kare] [1] VT (*gen*) to dirty, make dirty; (*macchiare*) to stain; (*fig: reputazione*) to sully, soil; **sporcarsi le mani** (*anche fig*) to dirty one's hands; **sporcarsi la reputazione** to sully one's reputation; **sporcarsi la fedina penale** to get a police record.

  [2] **sporcarsi** VR to get dirty.

sporcizia [spor'tʃittsja] SF (*sudiciume*) filth, dirt; **c'era**

tanta di quella **sporcizia per le strade** the streets were really filthy *o* dirty; **vivere nella sporcizia** to live in squalor.

sporco, a, chi, che ['sporko] [1] AGG (*gen*) dirty, filthy; (*macchiato*) stained; (*fig: immorale*) dirty; (: *losco: politica, faccenda*) shady; (: *denaro*) dirty; **il fazzoletto è sporco di inchiostro/sangue** there is ink/blood on the handkerchief; **hai le scarpe sporche di fango** there is mud on your shoes, your shoes are muddy; **avere la coscienza sporca** to have a guilty conscience; **avere la fedina penale sporca** to have a police record; **sporco bastardo!** dirty bastard!; **farla sporca a qn** (*fig fam*) to do the dirty on sb.

  [2] SM dirt, filth.

sporgente [spor'dʒɛnte] AGG (*occhi*) protuberant, bulging; (*denti*) prominent, protruding; (*mento*) prominent; **ha le ossa sporgenti** his bones stick out.

sporgenza [spor'dʒɛntsa] SF (*su scogli, rocce*) projection; (*su parete*) bulge.

sporgere ['spordʒere] VB IRREG [1] VT a (*braccio, testa*): **sporgere da** to put out of, stretch out of b (*Dir*): **sporgere querela contro qn** to sue sb, take legal action against sb.

  [2] VI (*aus essere*) (*venire in fuori*) to stick out; (*protendersi: massi*) to jut out.

  [3] **sporgersi** VR: **sporgersi da** to lean out of (*Brit*).

sporsi *ecc* ['sporsi] VB vedi **sporgere**.

sport [sport] SM INV sport; **fare dello sport** to do sport; **che sport fai?** what sports do you play?; **fare qc per sport** to do sth for fun.

sporta ['sporta] SF (*borsa*) shopping bag; **dirne un sacco e una sporta a qn** (*insultare*) to give sb a mouthful.

sportello [spor'tɛllo] SM a (*di veicolo, mobile*) door b (*di banca, ufficio*) counter, window ▶ **sportello automatico** (*di banca*) cash dispenser (*Brit*), automated teller machine (*Am*).

sportivamente [sportiva'mente] AVV sportingly.

sportività [sportivi'ta] SF sportsmanship.

sportivo, a [spor'tivo] [1] AGG (*gara, giornale, auto*) sports *attr*; (*persona, spirito, atteggiamento*) sporting; (*abito*) casual; **giacca sportiva** sports (*Brit*) *o* sport (*Am*) jacket; **un atteggiamento molto poco sportivo** a very unsporting attitude; **campo sportivo** playing field.

  [2] SM/F sportsman/sportwoman.

sporto, a ['sporto] PP di **sporgere**.

sposa ['spoza] SF (*nel giorno delle nozze*) bride; (*moglie*) wife; **abito** *o* **vestito da sposa** wedding dress; **dare qn in sposa a** to give sb in marriage to.

sposalizio, zi [spoza'littsjo] SM wedding (ceremony).

sposare [spo'zare] [1] VT (*gen*) to marry; (*sogg: genitori*) to marry off; (*fig: idea, fede, causa*) to embrace, espouse.

  [2] **sposarsi** VR (*uso reciproco*) to get married, marry; **sposarsi con qn** to marry sb, get married to sb.

sposato, a [spo'zato] AGG married.

sposo ['spozo] SM (*nel giorno delle nozze*) (bride)groom; (*marito*) husband; **gli sposi** the newlyweds.

spossante [spos'sante] AGG exhausting.

spossare [spos'sare] VT to exhaust, wear out.

spossatezza [spossa'tettsa] SF exhaustion.

spossato, a [spos'sato] AGG exhausted, worn-out.

spostamento [sposta'mento] SM movement, change of position; **il mio lavoro mi costringe a continui spostamenti** I have to travel constantly for my work ▶ **spostamento d'aria** blast.

spostare [spos'tare] ☐1 VT **a** (*gen*) to move; (*mobile*) to move, shift **b** (*cambiare: orario, data*) to change; **hanno spostato la partenza di qualche giorno** they postponed *o* put off their departure for a few days.
☐2 **spostarsi** VR to move.
spostato, a [spos'tato] SM/F misfit.
spot [spot] SM INV **a** (*faretto*) spotlight, spot **b** (*TV*): **spot pubblicitario** advertisement, commercial.
spranga, ghe ['spranga] SF (*barra*) bar; (*catenaccio*) bolt.
sprangare [spran'gare] VT (*con barra*) to bar; (*con catenaccio*) to bolt.
spray ['sprai] ☐1 SM INV (*dispositivo, sostanza*) spray.
☐2 AGG INV (*bombola, confezione*) spray *attr*.
sprazzo ['sprattso] SM (*di luce, sole*) flash; (*fig: di gioia*) burst; (:*di intelligenza*) flash.
sprecare [spre'kare] ☐1 VT (*gen, fig*) to waste; (*denaro*) to waste, squander; **è fatica sprecata!** it's a waste of effort!; **è fiato sprecato!** it's a waste of breath!; **sei sprecato qui!** your talents are wasted here!.
☐2 **sprecarsi** VIP (*persona*) to waste one's energy; **non sprecarti!** (*iro: non affaticarti*) don't strain yourself!; **si sono sprecati!** (*iro*) they certainly didn't break the bank!
spreco, chi ['sprɛko] SM waste; **che spreco!** what a waste!
sprecone, a [spre'kone] SM/F waster.
spregevole [spre'dʒevole] AGG contemptible, despicable.
spregevolmente [spredʒevol'mente] AVV contemptibly, despicably.
spregiare [spre'dʒare] VT (*letter*) to despise, be contemptuous of.
spregiativo, a [spredʒa'tivo] ☐1 AGG pejorative, derogatory.
☐2 SM (*Gramm*) pejorative.
spregio, gi ['sprɛdʒo] SM (*disprezzo*) contempt, scorn, disdain.
spregiudicatezza [spredʒudika'tettsa] SF lack of scruples.
spregiudicato, a [spredʒudi'kato] AGG (*senza pregiudizi*) unprejudiced, unbiased; (*senza scrupoli*) unscrupulous.
spremere ['sprɛmere] VT (*agrumi*) to squeeze; (*olive*) to press; **spremere denaro a** *o* **da qn** to squeeze money out of sb; **spremersi le meningi** to rack one's brains.
spremiaglio, gli [spremi'aʎʎo] SM (*Culin*) garlic press.
spremiagrumi [spremia'grumi], **spremilimoni** [spremili'moni] SM INV lemon squeezer.
spremuta [spre'muta] SF fresh fruit juice ▶**spremuta d'arancia** fresh orange juice.
spretarsi [spre'tarsi] VIP to abandon the priesthood.
sprezzante [spret'tsante] AGG (*sguardo, modi, parole*) contemptuous, scornful, disdainful.
sprezzantemente [sprettsante'mente] AVV contemptuously, scornfully, disdainfully.
sprezzo ['sprɛttso] SM contempt, scorn, disdain; **con sprezzo del pericolo** without heeding the danger.
sprigionare [spridʒo'nare] ☐1 VT (*calore, odore*) to give off, emit; (*gas tossici*) to release; (*fig: energia*) to unleash.
☐2 **sprigionarsi** VIP: **sprigionarsi da** (*sogg: calore*) to emanate from, be given off by; (: *con impeto: gas*) to burst (out) from; (: *petrolio, acqua*) to gush out from.
sprimacciare [sprimat'tʃare] VT (*cuscino*) to plump up.
sprint [sprint] SM INV (*scatto*) sprint.
sprizzare [sprit'tsare] ☐1 VI (*aus essere*) to spurt.
☐2 VT (*scaturire*) to spurt; (*fig: gioia, vitalità*) to be bursting with; **sprizza salute da tutti i pori** he's bursting with health.
sprofondare [sprofon'dare] ☐1 VI (*aus essere*) (*casa, tetto*)

to collapse; (*pavimento, terreno*) to subside, give way; (*nave*) to sink; **i suoi piedi sprofondavano nella neve** his feet sank into the snow; **sprofondò nel dolore** he was overcome with grief.
☐2 **sprofondarsi** VR: **sprofondarsi in** (*poltrona*) to sink into; (*fig: studio, lavoro*) to become engrossed in.
sproloquiare [sprolo'kwjare] VI (*aus avere*) to ramble on.
sproloquio, qui [spro'lɔkwjo] SM rambling speech.
spronare [spro'nare] VT (*cavallo*) to spur (on); (*fig: persona*) to spur on, encourage; **spronare qn a fare qc** to encourage sb to do sth.
sprone ['sprone] SM (*sperone*) spur; (*fig*) spur, incentive; **fuggire a spron battuto** to take to one's heels.
sproporzionatamente [sproportsjonata'mente] AVV disproportionately.
sproporzionato, a [sproportsjo'nato] AGG (*gen*) disproportionate, out of all proportion; (*prezzo*) exorbitant; (*condanna*) excessive; **sproporzionato (rispetto) a** out of proportion to.
sproporzione [spropor'tsjone] SF disproportion.
spropositatamente [spropozitata'mente] AVV excessively.
spropositato, a [spropozi'tato] AGG (*costo*) excessive; (*lettera, discorso*) full of mistakes.
sproposito [spro'pɔzito] SM (*azione sconsiderata*) blunder; **ho fatto uno sproposito** (*pazzia*) I did something silly; **per quella donna farei uno sproposito** I'd do anything for that woman; **non dire spropositi** don't talk nonsense *o* rubbish (*Brit*); **non farmi dire uno sproposito** don't make me say something I'll regret; **costa uno sproposito!** it costs a fortune!; **arrivare a sproposito** to arrive at the wrong time; **parlare a sproposito** to talk out of turn.
sprovveduto, a [sprovve'duto] AGG inexperienced, naïve.
sprovvisto, a [sprov'visto] AGG **a** : **sprovvisto di** lacking in, without; **passeggeri sprovvisti di passaporto** passengers without a passport; **siamo sprovvisti di bicchieri** we haven't enough glasses; **ne siamo sprovvisti** (*negozio*) we are out of it (*o* them)
b : **prendere qn alla sprovvista** to catch sb unawares.
spruzzare [sprut'tsare] VT (*nebulizzare*) to spray; (*aspergere*) to sprinkle; (*inzaccherare*) to splash.
spruzzata [sprut'tsata] SF (*di acqua*) splash; (*di profumo*) spray; (*di neve*) light fall; **dare una spruzzata di zucchero a qc** to sprinkle sth with sugar.
spruzzatore [spruttsa'tore] SM (*per profumi*) spray, atomizer; (*per biancheria*) spray.
spruzzo ['spruttso] SM splash; **verniciatura a spruzzo** spray painting.
spudoratamente [spudorata'mente] AVV shamelessly.
spudoratezza [spudora'tettsa] SF shamelessness.
spudorato, a [spudo'rato] AGG shameless; **è stato così spudorato da venire a chiedermi aiuto** he had the cheek to come and ask me for help.
spugna ['spuɲɲa] SF (*Zool*) sponge; (*tessuto*) (terry) towelling, terrycloth; **bere come una spugna** to drink like a fish; **gettare la spugna** (*Pugilato, fig*) to throw in the sponge *o* towel.
spugnatura [spuɲɲa'tura] SF sponging, sponge down.
spugnoso, a [spuɲ'ɲoso] AGG spongy.
spulciare [spul'tʃare] VT (*animali*) to rid of fleas; (*fig: testo, compito*) to examine thoroughly.
spuma ['spuma] SF (*schiuma*) foam; (*bibita*) fizzy drink; (*Culin*) mousse.

spumante [spu'mante] SM sparkling wine.

spumeggiante [spumed'dʒante] AGG (*vino, fig*) sparkling; (*mare*) foaming.

spumeggiare [spumed'dʒare] VI (*aus avere*) (*vino*) to sparkle; (*mare*) to foam.

spumone [spu'mone] SM (*dolce*) *light, frothy dessert made with egg whites and cream*; (*gelato*) *soft ice cream made with whipped cream.*

spuntare¹ [spun'tare] ① VT (*lapis, coltello*) to break the point of; (*capelli, baffi*) to trim; **spuntarla** (*fig: vincere*) to succeed, win (through); (: *averla vinta*) to get one's own way.

② VI (*aus essere*) (*nascere: germogli*) to sprout; (: *capelli*) to begin to grow; (: *dente*) to come through; (*apparire: sole*) to rise; (: *giorno*) to dawn; **gli è spuntato un dente** he has cut a tooth; **è spuntato da chissà dove** (*fig*) he turned up from out of the blue.

③ **spuntarsi** VIP to lose its point, become blunt.

④ SM: **allo spuntare del sole** at sunrise; **allo spuntare del giorno** at daybreak.

spuntare² [spun'tare] VT (*elenco*) to tick off (*Brit*), check off (*Am*).

spuntino [spun'tino] SM snack; **fare uno spuntino** to have a snack.

spunto ['spunto] SM (*Mus, Teatro*) cue; (*fig: base*) starting point; (: *idea*) idea; **dare** *o* **fornire lo spunto a qc** (*polemiche*) to give rise to sth; **ciò mi ha dato lo spunto per iniziare a dipingere** it started me painting; **prendere spunto da qc** to take sth as one's starting point.

spuntone [spun'tone] SM (*Alpinismo*) (rocky) spike.

spupazzare [spupat'tsare] VT (*fam: portare in giro*) to cart around.

spurgare [spur'gare] VT (*fogna, canale*) to clear, clean; (*bronchi*) to clean; (*Aut: freni*) to bleed.

spurgo, **ghi** ['spurgo] SM (*di fogna, canale*) clearing, cleaning; (*di bronchi: azione*) cleaning; (: *materia espulsa*) discharge; (*di freni*) bleeding; **valvola di spurgo** bleeder.

spurio, **ria**, **ri**, **rie** ['spurjo] AGG (*non autentico: opera*) spurious, false.

sputacchiare [sputak'kjare] VT (*aus avere*) to spit.

sputacchiera [sputak'kjɛra] SF spittoon.

sputare [spu'tare] ① VT to spit (out); **mi ha fatto sputar sangue** (*fig*) he made me sweat blood; **sputare veleno** (*fig*) to talk spitefully; **sputa fuori!** (*anche fig*) spit it out!; **sputa l'osso!** (*fig*) out with it!; **è suo padre sputato** (*fam*) he's the spitting image of his father.

② VI (*aus avere*) to spit; **sputare in faccia a qn** (*fig*) to spit in sb's face; **sputare addosso a qn** (*fig*) to despise sb; **non ci sputerei sopra** (*fig*) I wouldn't turn my nose up at it; **non sputare nel piatto in cui mangi** don't bite the hand that feeds you.

sputasentenze [sputasen'tɛntse] SM/F INV know-all.

sputo ['sputo] SM spittle *no pl*, spit *no pl*; **questo libro deve essere appiccicato con lo sputo** this book just comes apart in your hands.

sputtanare [sputta'nare] ① VT (*sparlare*) to bad-mouth; (*sperperare*) to piss away (*fam!*).

② **sputtanarsi** VIP to make an arse of o.s. (*Brit fam!*).

sputtanato, **a** [sputta'nato] AGG (*fam*): **essere sputtanato** to be fucked (*fam!*).

squadra¹ ['skwadra] SF (*strumento*) (set) square; **a squadra** at right angles; **essere fuori squadra** (*gen*) to be crooked; (*fig: persona*) to be out of sorts.

squadra² ['skwadra] SF (*gruppo*) team, squad; (*di operai*) gang, squad; (*Sport*) team; (*Mil*) squad; (: *Aer, Naut*) squadron; **lavoro a squadre** teamwork ► **squadra del buon costume** (*Polizia*) vice squad ► **squadra mobile** flying squad (*Brit*) ► **squadra di soccorso** rescue party.

squadrare [skwa'drare] VT to square, make square; **squadrare qn da capo a piedi** to look sb up and down.

squadriglia [skwa'driʎʎa] SF (*Aer*) flight; (*Naut*) squadron.

squadrone [skwa'drone] SM (*Mil*) squadron.

squagliare [skwaʎ'ʎare] ① VT to melt.

② **squagliarsi** VIP to melt; **squagliarsi** OR **squagliarsela** (*fig fam*) to sneak off.

squalifica, **che** [skwa'lifika] SF disqualification.

squalificare [skwalifi'kare] ① VT (*gen, Sport*) to disqualify; (*fig: screditare*) to bring discredit on.

② **squalificarsi** VR to bring discredit on o.s.

squalificato, **a** [skwalifi'kato] AGG disqualified.

squallido, **a** ['skwallido] AGG (*luogo*) wretched, bleak; (*vita*) miserable; (*vicenda*) squalid, sordid.

squallore [skwal'lore] SM (*vedi agg*) wretchedness, bleakness; misery; squalor.

squalo ['skwalo] SM shark.

squama ['skwama] SF (*scaglia*) scale.

squamare [skwa'mare] ① VT to scale.

② **squamarsi** VIP (*pelle: gen*) to flake *o* peel (off); (: *per malattia*) to desquamate.

squarciagola [skwartʃa'gola]: **a squarciagola** AVV at the top of one's voice.

squarciare [skwar'tʃare] ① VT (*corpo*) to rip open; (*tessuto*) to rip; (*fig: tenebre, silenzio*) to split; (: *nuvole*) to pierce.

② **squarciarsi** VIP (*vedi vt*) to rip open; to rip; (*nuvole*) to part.

squarcio, **ci** ['skwartʃo] SM **a** (*ferita*) gash; (*in lenzuolo, abito*) rip; (*in nave*) hole; **uno squarcio di sole** a burst of sunlight **b** (*brano*) passage, excerpt.

squartare [skwar'tare] VT (*animale macellato*) to quarter, cut up; (*persona*) to dismember.

squattrinato, **a** [skwattri'nato] ① AGG penniless.

② SM/F (*gen*) penniless person.

squilibrare [skwili'brare] VT to unbalance; (*psicologicamente*) to derange, unbalance; **squilibrare qn finanziariamente** to upset sb's bank balance.

squilibrato, **a** [skwili'brato] ① AGG (*alimentazione*) unbalanced; (*mente*) deranged, unbalanced.

② SM/F (*anche*: **squilibrato mentale**) deranged person.

squilibrio, **ri** [skwi'librjo] SM **a** (*Psic: anche*: **squilibrio mentale**) derangement **b** (*Econ: differenza*) imbalance.

squillante [skwil'lante] AGG (*suono*) shrill, sharp; (*voce*) shrill; (*fig: colore*) loud.

squillare [skwil'lare] VI (*aus avere o essere*) (*campanello, telefono*) to ring (out); (*tromba*) to blare.

squillo ['skwillo] ① SM (*di campanello*) ring, ringing *no pl*; (*di tromba*) blast, blare; **ti avverto con tre squilli di telefono** I'll let the phone ring three times to warn you.

② SF INV (*anche*: **ragazza squillo**) call girl.

squinternato, **a** [skwinter'nato] ① AGG crazy.

② SM/F lunatic.

squisitamente [skwizita'mente] AVV exquisitely.

squisitezza [skwizi'tettsa] SF (*di sentimenti, gusto*) refinement; (*di modi*) considerateness; **questo pollo è una squisitezza** this chicken is delicious.

squisito, **a** [skwi'zito] AGG (*gen*) lovely, exquisite; (*gusto, gioiello*) exquisite; (*persona*) delightful; (*modi*) consid-

erate; (*cibo*) delicious.

squittire [skwit'tire] VI (*aus* **avere**) (*uccello*) to squawk; (*topo*) to squeak.

SR SIGLA = *Siracusa*.

sradicare [zradi'kare] VT (*albero*) to uproot; (*erba*) to root out; (*fig: vizio*) to eradicate; **sentirsi sradicato** to feel uprooted.

sragionare [zradʒo'nare] VI (*aus* **avere**) (*vaneggiare*) to rave; (*fare discorsi sconnessi*) to talk nonsense.

sregolatezza [zregola'tettsa] SF (*nel mangiare, bere*) lack of moderation; (*di vita*) dissoluteness, dissipation; **le sue sgregolatezze gli costeranno care** his excesses will cost him dear.

sregolato, a [zrego'lato] AGG (*vita: senza ordine*) disorderly; (: *dissoluta*) dissolute; **è sregolato nel mangiare** he has irregular eating habits.

Sri Lanka [sri'lanka] SM: **lo Sri Lanka** Sri Lanka.

srilankese, i [srilan'kese] AGG, SM/F Sri Lankan.

S.r.l ['ɛsse'ɛrre'ɛlle] SIGLA F = **società a responsabilità limitata.**

srotolare [zroto'lare] VT, **srotolarsi** VIP to unroll.

SS SIGLA = *Sassari*.

S.S. ABBR **a** (*Rel*)= *Sua Santità* **b** (*Rel*)= *Santa Sede* **c** (*Rel*)= *santi, santissimo* **d** (*Aut*) = **strada statale;** vedi **statale.**

S.S.N. ABBR (= *Servizio Sanitario Nazionale*) ≈ NHS (*Brit*), ≈ Medicaid (*Am*), ≈ Medicare (*Am*).

sta *ecc* [sta] VB vedi **stare.**

stabbio, bi ['stabbjo] SM **a** (*recinto*) pen, fold; (: *di maiali*) pigsty **b** (*letame*) manure.

stabile ['stabile] [1] AGG (*gen*) stable, steady; (*fondamenta*) solid; (*impiego*) steady, permanent; (*tempo*) settled; **la scala non è stabile** the ladder is shaky; **il ponte non è stabile** the bridge is unstable; **essere stabile nei propri propositi** to stick to one's decisions, keep to one's plans; **compagnia stabile** (*Teatro*) resident company; **teatro stabile** civic theatre.
　[2] SM (*edificio*) building.

stabilimento [stabili'mento] SM (*fabbrica*) plant, factory
▶**stabilimento balneare** bathing establishment
▶**stabilimento carcerario** prison ▶**stabilimento tessile** textile mill.

stabilire [stabi'lire] [1] VT (*gen*) to establish; (*fissare: prezzi, data*) to fix; (*decidere*) to decide; **hanno stabilito la chiusura di tutte le scuole** they decided to close all the schools; **stabilire un aumento dei prezzi** to decide on a price increase; **stabilire un collegamento** to establish contact; **resta stabilito che...** it is agreed that ....
　[2] **stabilirsi** VR (*prendere dimora*) to settle.

stabilità [stabili'ta] SF stability.

stabilizzare [stabilid'dzare] [1] VT to stabilize.
　[2] **stabilizzarsi** VIP (*situazione economica, malato*) to become stable; (*tempo*) to become settled.

stabilizzatore, trice [stabiliddza'tore] [1] AGG stabilizing.
　[2] SM (*Aer, Naut, Chim*) stabilizer; (*Elettr*): **stabilizzatore di tensione** voltage regulator.

stabilizzazione [stabiliddzat'tsjone] SF stabilization.

stabilmente [stabil'mente] AVV permanently; **l'hanno assunto stabilmente** they have employed him on a permanent basis.

stacanovista, i, e [stakano'vista] SM/F (*scherz*) eager beaver.

staccare [stak'kare] [1] VT **a** (*togliere*): **staccare (da)** to remove (from), take (from); (*quadro*) to take down (from); (*foglio, pagina*) to tear out (of), remove (from);

stacca quel tavolo dalla parete pull that table out from the wall; **staccare la televisione/il telefono** to disconnect the television/the phone; **staccare un assegno** to write a cheque; **non riusciva a staccare gli occhi da quella scena** he could not take his eyes off the scene before him
　b (*separare: anche fig*) to separate, divide; (: *buoi*) to unyoke; (: *cavalli*) to unharness; **staccare la locomotiva dal treno** to uncouple the locomotive from the train; **staccare le parole** to pronounce one's words clearly; **staccare le note** (*Mus*) to play staccato
　c (*Sport: distanziare*) to leave behind.
　[2] VI (*aus* **avere**) **a** (*risaltare*) to stand out
　b (*fam: finire di lavorare*) to knock off.
　[3] **staccarsi** VIP **a** (*venir via: bottone*) to come off; (: *foglio*) to come out; (*sganciarsi*) to break loose
　b (*persona*): **staccarsi da** (*allontanarsi*) to move away from; (: *dalla famiglia*) to leave; **non si stacca mai dalla televisione** he's always glued to the television.

staccato, a [stak'kato] [1] AGG (*foglio*) loose; (*fascicolo*) separate. [2] SM (*Mus*) staccato.

stacionata [stattʃo'nata] SF fence.

stacco, chi ['stakko] SM **a** (*intervallo*) gap; (: *tra due scene*) break; (*differenza*) difference; **fare uno stacco tra una parola e l'altra** to articulate one's words; **c'è troppo stacco tra i due colori** there's too much of a difference between the two colours; **fare stacco su** to stand out against **b** (*Sport: nel salto*) takeoff.

stadera [sta'dɛra] SF lever scales *pl.*

stadio, di ['stadjo] SM **a** (*Sport*) stadium **b** (*periodo, fase*) stage, phase; **a due/tre stadi** two-/three-stage *attr.*

staffa ['staffa] SF **a** (*gen, Tecn, Edil*) stirrup; (*Alpinismo*) étrier (*Brit*), stirrup (*Am*); **perdere le staffe** (*fig*) to fly off the handle; **tenere il piede in due staffe** (*fig*) to run with the hare and hunt with the hounds **b** (*Anat*) stirrup bone.

staffetta [staf'fetta] SF **a** (*messo*) courier, dispatch rider **b** (*Sport*) relay race.

staffile [staf'file] SM (*Equitazione*) stirrup leather; (: *sferza*) whip.

stafilococco, chi [stafilo'kɔkko] SM (*Bio*) staphylococcus.

stagflazione [stagflat'tsjone] SF (*Econ*) stagflation.

stagionale [stadʒo'nale] [1] AGG seasonal; **"apertura stagionale"** "open during the tourist season".
　[2] SM/F seasonal worker.

stagionare [stadʒo'nare] VT, VI (*aus* **essere**), **stagionarsi** VIP (*legno*) to season; (*formaggi*) to mature.

stagionato, a [stadʒo'nato] AGG (*vedi vb*) seasoned; matured; (*scherz: attempato*) getting on in years.

stagionatura [stadʒona'tura] SF (*vedi vb*) seasoning; maturing.

stagione [sta'dʒone] SF season; **la bella stagione** the summer months; **la stagione delle piogge** the rainy season; **in questa stagione** at this time of year; **frutta di stagione** seasonal fruit; **saldi di fine stagione** end-of-season sales; **vestiti di mezza stagione** clothes for spring and autumn; **alta/bassa stagione** (*Turismo*) high/low *o* off-season.

stagliarsi [staʎ'ʎarsi] VIP: **stagliarsi contro** *o* **su** to stand out against, be silhouetted against.

stagnante [stan'nante] AGG (*anche fig*) stagnant.

stagnare[1] [stan'nare] VT **a** (*ricoprire di stagno*) to tin-plate; (*saldare*) to solder **b** (*rendere ermetico*) to make watertight.

stagnare[2] [stan'ɲare] [1] VI (*aus* **avere**) (*acqua, Econ*) to stagnate; **l'aria stagnava nella stanza** the air in the room was stale.
[2] VT (*sangue*) to stop.

stagnatura [stanɲa'tura] SF tinning, tin-plating.

stagnino [stan'ɲino] SM tinsmith.

stagno[1] ['stanɲo] SM (*Chim*) tin; (*per saldare*) solder.

stagno[2] ['stanɲo] SM (*acquitrino*) pond.

stagno[3], **a** ['stanɲo] AGG (*a tenuta d'acqua*) watertight; (*a tenuta d'aria*) airtight.

stagnola [stan'ɲola] SF (*anche:* **carta stagnola**) tinfoil, aluminium foil (*Am*).

stalagmite [stalag'mite] SF stalagmite.

stalattite [stalat'tite] SF stalactite.

stalinismo [stali'nizmo] SM (*Pol*) Stalinism.

stalinista, i, e [stali'nista] AGG, SM/F Stalinist.

stalla ['stalla] SF (*per bovini*) cowshed; (*per cavalli*) stable; (*fig: casa sporca*) pigsty; **passare dalle stelle alle stalle** (*fig*) to come down in the world.

stallia [stal'lia] SF (*Comm*) lay days *pl*.

stalliere [stal'ljɛre] SM groom, stableboy.

stallo ['stallo] SM **a** stall, seat **b** (*Scacchi*) stalemate; (*Aer*) stall; **situazione di stallo** (*fig*) stalemate.

stallone [stal'lone] SM stallion.

stamani [sta'mani], **stamattina** [stamat'tina] AVV this morning.

stambecco, chi [stam'bekko] SM (*Zool*) ibex.

stamberga, ghe [stam'bɛrga] SF hovel.

stame ['stame] SM (*Bot*) stamen.

stampa ['stampa] SF **a** (*Tip, Fot: tecnica*) printing; (: *riproduzione, copia*) print; (*insieme dei quotidiani, giornalisti*): **la stampa** the press; **stampa a diffusione nazionale** national press; **andare in stampa** to go to press; **mandare in stampa** to pass for press; **il libro è in stampa** the book is being printed; **fuori stampa** out of print; **dare alle stampe un'opera** to have a work published; **errore di stampa** printing error; **prova di stampa** print sample; **libertà di stampa** freedom of the press; **"stampe"** "printed matter" *sg*
b (*Tecn: di plastica*) moulding (*Brit*), molding (*Am*); (: *di metallo*) pressing; (: *di tessuto*) printing.

stampabile [stam'pabile] AGG printable.

stampaggio, gi [stam'paddʒo] SM (*di plastica*) moulding (*Brit*), molding (*Am*); (*di metalli*) pressing.

stampante [stam'pante] SF (*Inform*) printer ▶**stampante ad aghi** dot-matrix printer ▶**stampante a getto d'inchiostro** bubble-jet printer ▶**stampante laser** laser printer ▶**stampante di linea** line printer ▶**stampante a margherita** daisy-wheel printer.

stampare [stam'pare] [1] VT **a** (*gen, Tip, Fot*) to print; (*denaro*) to strike, coin; (*pubblicare*) to publish; **ce l'ho stampato nella memoria** it's engraved in my memory; **stampatelo bene in testa!** get it into your head!; **gli ha stampato un bacio in fronte** she planted a kiss on his forehead; **non li stampo mica i soldi** I am not made of money
b (*Tecn: plastica*) to mould (*Brit*), to mold (*Am*); (: *metalli*) to press; (: *tessuti*) to print.
[2] **stamparsi** VIP: **stamparsi nella mente** *o* **nella memoria** to be imprinted in one's memory.

stampatello [stampa'tɛllo] SM block capitals *pl*, block letters *pl*; **scrivere in** *o* **a stampatello** to write in block capitals *o* letters.

stampato, a [stam'pato] [1] AGG printed.

[2] SM (*opuscolo*) leaflet; (*modulo*) form; (*Inform*) hard copy.

stampatore, trice [stampa'tore] [1] SM/F printer.
[2] SF (*Cine, Fot*) printing machine.

stampella [stam'pella] SF (*apparecchio ortopedico*) crutch.

stamperia [stampe'ria] SF (*di libri*) printing works *inv*, printing house; (*di tessuti*) printworks *inv*.

stampigliare [stampiʎ'ʎare] VT to stamp.

stampigliatura [stampiʎʎa'tura] SF (*atto*) stamping; (*marchio*) stamp.

stampinare [stampi'nare] VT (*disegno*) to stencil.

stampino [stam'pino] SM (*normografo*) stencil; (*punteruolo*) punch ▶**stampino per biscotti** (*Culin*) pastry cutter.

stampo ['stampo] SM (*gen, Culin*) mould (*Brit*), mold (*Am*); (*Tecn*) mo(u)ld, die; (*fig: indole*) type, kind, sort; **di stampo antico** old-fashioned; **essere fatto con lo stampo** (*fig*) to be all the same ▶**stampo a cerniera** (*Culin*) spring-release tin ▶**stampo per plum-cake** (*Culin*) loaf tin.

stanare [sta'nare] VT to drive out.

stanca ['stanka] SF (*negli affari*): **periodo di stanca** slack period.

stancamente [stanka'mente] AVV tiredly, wearily.

stancare [stan'kare] [1] VT (*spossare*) to tire, make tired; (*annoiare*) to bore; (*infastidire*) to annoy.
[2] **stancarsi** VIP to get tired, tire o.s. out; **stancarsi (di)** (*stufarsi*) to grow tired (of), get fed up (with), grow weary (of).

stanchezza [stan'kettsa] SF (*fisica*) fatigue, tiredness; (*mentale*) tiredness, weariness; (*fig: noia*) weariness, boredom; **dare segni di stanchezza** to show signs of tiredness; **che stanchezza!** [OR] **ho una stanchezza addosso!** I'm dead beat!

stanco, a, chi, che ['stanko] AGG tired; **stanco morto** dead tired; **con una voce stanca disse...** he said wearily ...; **stanco di** (*stufo*) tired of, fed up with; **stanco di vivere** tired of life; **nato stanco** (*scherz*) bone idle.

stand [stænd] SM INV (*in fiera*) stand.

standard ['standard] [1] AGG INV standard.
[2] SM INV standard ▶**standard di vita** standard of living.

standardizzare [standardid'dzare] VT to standardize.

standardizzato, a [standardid'dzato] AGG (*gen*) standardized; (*fig: teoria, idea*) unoriginal.

standardizzazione [standardiddzat'tsjone] SF standardization.

standista, i, e [stan'dista] SM/F (*in una fiera*) person responsible for a stand.

stanga, ghe ['stanga] SM (*gen*) bar; (*di carro*) shaft; (*fig fam: persona alta*) beanpole.

stangare [stan'gare] VT (*colpire*) to beat, thrash; (*fig: far pagare troppo*) to sting; (: *bocciare*) to fail.

stangata [stan'gata] SF (*gen, fig*) blow; (*Calcio*) shot; **prendere una stangata** (*fam: pagare troppo*) to get stung; (: *agli esami*) to fail miserably; **stangata fiscale** tax hike.

stanghetta [stan'getta] SF **a** (*di occhiali*) leg **b** (*Mus, di scrittura*) bar-line.

stanno ['stanno] VB *vedi* **stare**.

stanotte [sta'nɔtte] AVV (*nella notte in corso o che sta per venire*) tonight; (*nella notte appena passata*) last night.

stante ['stante] [1] AGG: **a sé stante** (*appartamento, casa*) independent, separate; **seduta stante** (*fig: subito*) on the spot.

[2] PREP owing to, because of.

stantio, tia, tii, tie [stan'tio] AGG (*anche fig*) stale; (*burro*) rancid; **sapere di stantio** to taste stale (*o* rancid); **idee stantie** old-fashioned ideas.

stantuffo [stan'tuffo] SM piston.

stanza ['stantsa] SF **a** (*vano*) room ▶**stanza da bagno** bathroom ▶**stanza dei bottoni** (*fig*) control room ▶**stanza da letto** bedroom **b** (*Poesia*) stanza **c** : **essere di stanza a** (*Mil*) to be stationed in.

stanziabile [stan'tsjabile] AGG allocatable.

stanziamento [stantsja'mento] SM allocation.

stanziare [stan'tsjare] [1] VT to allocate.

[2] **stanziarsi** VIP (*gen*) to settle; (*Mil*) to be stationed.

stanzino [stan'tsino] SM (*ripostiglio*) storeroom; (*spogliatoio*) changing room (*Brit*), locker room (*Am*).

stappare [stap'pare] VT (*bottiglia: con tappo di sughero*) to uncork; (: *con tappo a corona*) to uncap.

star [star] SF INV (*attore, attrice*) star.

stare ['stare] VI IRREG (*aus* **essere**) **a** (*rimanere*) to stay, be, remain; **stare in piedi** to stand; **stare fermo** to keep *o* stay still; **stare seduto** to sit, be sitting; **stare disteso** to lie; **stare zitto** to keep quiet; **stai dove sei!** stay where you are!; **starò a Roma per qualche giorno** I'll stay *o* be in Rome for a few days; **stare a casa** to be *o* stay at home; **è stato su tutta la notte** he stayed up *o* was up all night; **stare in equilibrio** to keep one's balance

b (*abitare: temporaneamente*) to stay; (: *permanentemente*) to live; **sta con i suoi** he lives with his parents; **sta da solo** he lives on his own; **sta in via Rossetti 5** he lives at No. 5 via Rossetti; **al momento sta con degli amici** he's staying with friends at the moment

c (*essere, trovarsi*) to be, be situated; **la casa sta in cima al colle** the house is at the top of the hill; **stando così le cose** given the situation; **le cose stanno così** this is the situation; **non voglio stare da solo** I don't want to be on my own; **sono stato dal dentista** I've been to the dentist; **come stai?** how are you?; **io sto bene/male** I'm very well/not very well; **sta bene!** (*d'accordo così*) that's fine!; **non sta bene ridacchiare mentre l'insegnante spiega** you really ought not to laugh when the teacher is explaining something; **quel vestito ti sta bene/male** that dress suits/doesn't suit you; **queste scarpe mi stanno strette** these shoes are too tight for me; **gli sta bene!** (*così impara*) it serves him right!; **stai sicuro che non la passerà liscia!** rest assured he won't get away with it!; **stare al banco** (*cameriere*) to serve at the bar; **stare alla cassa** to work at the till; **stare a dieta** to be on a diet

d (*seguito da gerundio*): **stavo andando a casa** I was going home; **cosa stai facendo?** what are you doing?; **stava piovendo** it was raining

e : **stare per fare qc** to be about to do sth, be on the point of doing sth; **stavo per dirgli tutto ma il telefono squillò** I was just about *o* going to tell him everything when the phone rang; **stavi per rovinare tutto** you nearly spoiled *o* ruined everything

f : **stare a sentire** to listen; **sta' a sentire** listen a minute; **stare ad insistere** to insist; **è inutile che stai a dirmi tutte queste cose** there's no good *o* use telling me all this; **sta a te decidere** it's up to you to decide; **stando a ciò che dice lui** according to him *o* to his version; **stando ai fatti, sembrerebbe che...** the facts would seem to indicate that ...; **stiamo a vedere cosa succede** let's wait and see (what happens); **stai a vedere che**

aveva ragione lei! she would have to be right!

g : **starci** (*essere contenuto*): **ci sta ancora qualcosa lì dentro?** is there room for anything else?; **nel baule non ci sta più niente** there's no more room in the boot (*Brit*) *o* trunk (*Am*); **non credo ci stia tutta quella pasta** I don't think there's room for all that pasta; **non ci stanno più di 4 persone in quella macchina** there is only room for 4 in that car; **il 5 nel 25 ci sta 5 volte** 5 goes into 25 5 times

h : **starci** (*essere d'accordo*): **ci stai se andiamo** *o* **ad andare fuori a cena?** do you want to go out for a meal?; **ha detto che non ci sta** he said he didn't agree, he said he was against the idea; **OK, ci sto** OK, that's fine

i : **starsene**: **se ne stava lì in un angolo** he was over in the corner; **se n'è stato zitto** he never opened his mouth; **non startene lì seduto, fa' qualcosa** don't just sit there, do something; **stasera me ne sto a casa** I'll be staying in tonight.

starna ['starna] SF (*Zool*) partridge.

starnazzare [starnat'tsare] VI (*aus* **avere**) to squawk; (*fig*: *far chiasso*) to make a din.

starnutire [starnu'tire] VI (*aus* **avere**) to sneeze.

starnuto [star'nuto] SM sneeze; **fare uno starnuto** to sneeze.

starter ['starter] SM INV (*Aut, Sport*) starter.

stasare [sta'sare] VT (*lavandino, condotto*) to unblock.

stasera [sta'sera] AVV this evening, tonight.

stasi ['stazi] SF (*Med, fig*) stasis.

statale [sta'tale] [1] AGG government *attr*, state *attr*; **bilancio statale** national budget; **impiegato statale** state employee, civil servant; **strada statale** ≈ main *o* trunk (*Brit*) road.

[2] SM/F (*impiegato*) state employee, ≈ civil servant.

[3] SF (*strada*) ≈ main *o* trunk (*Brit*) road.

statalizzare [statalid'dzare] VT to nationalize, put under state control.

statalizzazione [stataliddzat'tsjone] SF nationalization.

statica ['statika] SF statics *sg*.

staticità [statitʃi'ta] SF (*di situazione*) static nature.

statico, a, ci, che ['statiko] AGG (*Elettr, fig*) static.

statino [sta'tino] SM (*Univ*) *statement of examination results.*

statista, i [sta'tista] SM statesman.

statistica [sta'tistika] SF (*scienza*) statistics *sg*; (*raccolta di dati*) statistic; **fare una statistica** to carry out a statistical examination.

statisticamente [statistika'mente] AVV statistically.

statistico, a, ci, che [sta'tistiko] AGG statistical.

stato¹, a ['stato] PP di **essere, stare.**

stato² ['stato] [1] SM **a** (*condizione, gen*) state; (*di paziente*) condition; **stato d'animo** mood; **stato (di salute)** state of health; **guarda in che stato si è ridotto!** look at the state it (*o* he) is in!; **vivere allo stato selvaggio** to live in the wild

b (*fraseologia*): **essere in stato d'accusa** (*Dir*) to have been charged with an offence (*Brit*) *o* offense (*Am*), be committed for trial; **essere in stato d'arresto** (*Dir*) to be under arrest; **essere in stato d'assedio** to be under siege; **essere in stato d'emergenza** to be in a state of emergency; **essere in stato interessante** to be pregnant; **allo stato liquido/gassoso** in the liquid/gaseous state.

[2] ▶**stato civile** (*Amm*) marital status ▶**stato di famiglia** (*Amm*) *certificate giving details of a household and its dependents* ▶**Stato Maggiore** (*Mil*) general

staff *sg o pl* ▶**stato patrimoniale** statement of assets and liabilities.

stato³ ['stato] SM (*Pol*) state; **di stato** state *attr* ▶**gli Stati Uniti (d'America)** the United States (of America).

statua ['statua] SF statue.

statuario, ria, ri, rie [statu'arjo] AGG (*fig: bellezza, posa*) statuesque.

statunitense [statuni'tense] [1] AGG United States *attr*, of the United States.

[2] SM/F American citizen, citizen of the United States.

statura [sta'tura] SF (*gen*) height; (*fig*) stature; **essere alto/basso di statura** to be tall/short; **un uomo politico della sua statura** (*fig*) a politician of his stature.

status ['status] SM INV status.

statutario, ria, ri, rie [statu'tarjo] AGG statutory.

statuto [sta'tuto] SM statute; **regione a statuto speciale** *Italian region with political autonomy in certain matters* ▶**statuto della società** (*Comm*) articles *pl* of association.

stavolta [sta'vɔlta] AVV this time.

stazionamento [stattsjona'mento] SM (*Aut*) parking; (: *sosta*) waiting; **freno di stazionamento** handbrake.

stazionare [stattsjo'nare] VI (*aus avere*) (*veicolo*) to be parked.

stazionarietà [stattsjonarje'ta] SF: **stazionarietà (di)** lack of change (in).

stazionario, ria, ri, rie [stattsjo'narjo] AGG (*temperatura, condizioni di salute*) stable, unchanged.

stazione [stat'tsjone] SF [a] (*gen, Radio*) station ▶**stazione degli autobus** bus *o* coach (*Brit*) station ▶**stazione ferroviaria** railway (*Brit*) *o* railroad (*Am*) station ▶**stazione di lavoro** (*Inform*) work station ▶**stazione meteorologica** weather station ▶**stazione radio** radio station ▶**stazione di servizio** filling *o* petrol (*Brit*) *o* gas (*Am*) station ▶**stazione trasmittente** (*Radio, TV*) transmitting station

[b] (*località*): **stazione balneare** seaside resort ▶**stazione climatica** health resort ▶**stazione invernale** winter sports resort ▶**stazione termale** (thermal) spa

[c] (*Rel*): **stazione della Via Crucis** Station of the Cross.

stazza ['stattsa] SF (*gen*) tonnage; (*di regata*) rating.

st. civ. ABBR = **stato civile**.

stearina [stea'rina] SF (*Chim*) stearin(e).

stecca, che ['stekka] SF (*gen*) stick; (*di ombrello*) rib; (*da biliardo*) cue; (*Med*) splint; (*di sigarette*) carton; **prendere una stecca** (*fig: stonatura: cantando*) to sing a wrong note; (: *suonando*) to play a wrong note.

steccare [stek'kare] VT (*Med*) to splint.

steccato [stek'kato] SM fence.

stecchetto [stek'ketto] SM (*fam*): **tenere qn a stecchetto** to keep sb on short rations.

stecchino [stek'kino] SM toothpick.

stecchire [stek'kire] VT (*fam: ammazzare*) to kill (stone dead).

stecchito, a [stek'kito] AGG (*ramo*) dried up; (*persona*) skinny; **morto stecchito** stone dead; **lasciare qn stecchito** (*fig: sorpreso*) to leave sb flabbergasted.

stecco, chi ['stekko] SM (*ramo*) twig; (*bastoncino*) stick; (*fig: persona magra*) beanpole.

stechiometria [stekjome'tria] SF (*Chim*) stoichiometry.

stele ['stɛle] SF INV stele.

stella ['stella] SF star; **senza stelle** starless; **alla luce delle stelle** by starlight; **dormire sotto le stelle** to sleep out

under the stars; **vedere le stelle** (*per il dolore*) to see stars; **ringrazia la tua buona stella** thank your lucky stars; **nascere sotto una buona/cattiva stella** to be born under a lucky/an unlucky star; **i prezzi sono andati** *o* **saliti alle stelle** prices have gone sky-high; **portare alle stelle qn** to lavish praise on sb; **una stella del cinema** a cinema star; **la sua stella sta tramontando** his star is waning ▶**stella alpina** (*Bot*) edelweiss ▶**stella cadente** shooting star ▶**stella di mare** (*Zool*) starfish ▶**stella polare** pole *o* north star ▶**stelle filanti** (*per carnevale*) streamers.

stellare [stel'lare] AGG stellar; **luce stellare** starlight.

stellato, a [stel'lato] AGG (*cielo, notte*) starry.

stelletta [stel'letta] SF [a] (*Mil*) star; **guadagnarsi/rimetterci le stellette** to be promoted/demoted [b] (*Tip*) asterisk.

stelo ['stɛlo] SM (*Bot*) stem; (*asta*) rod; **lampada a stelo** standard lamp (*Brit*), floor lamp (*Am*).

stemma, i ['stemma] SM coat of arms.

stemmo *ecc* ['stemmo] VB vedi **stare**.

stemperare [stempe'rare] VT (*calce, colore*) to dissolve.

stempiarsi [stem'pjarsi] VIP to develop a receding hairline.

stempiato, a [stem'pjato] AGG with a receding hairline.

stempiatura [stempja'tura] SF receding hairline.

stendardo [sten'dardo] SM standard.

stendere ['stɛndere] VB IRREG [1] VT [a] (*braccia, gambe*) to stretch (out); (*tovaglia*) to spread (out); (*bucato*) to hang out; (*spalmare*) to spread; (*pasta*) to roll out

[b] (*persona: far giacere*) to lay (down); (: *gettare a terra, fig: vincere*) to floor; (: *uccidere*) to kill; **far stendere qn** to lay sb down

[c] (*lettera, verbale*) to draw up.

[2] **stendersi** VR (*persona*) to lie down; **stendersi a terra/sul letto** to lie down on the ground/on the bed.

[3] **stendersi** VIP (*pianura, vallata*) to extend, stretch.

stendibiancheria [stendibjanke'ria] SM INV clotheshorse.

stenditoio, oi [stendi'tojo] SM (*locale*) drying room; (*stendibiancheria*) clotheshorse.

stenodattilografia [stenodattilogra'fia] SF shorthand typing (*Brit*), stenography (*Am*).

stenodattilografo, a [stenodattil'lɔgrafo] SM/F shorthand typist (*Brit*), stenographer (*Am*).

stenografare [stenogra'fare] VT to take down in shorthand.

stenografia [stenogra'fia] SF shorthand, stenography (*Am*).

stenografico, a, ci, che [steno'grafiko] AGG shorthand *attr*, stenographic (*Am*).

stenografo, a [ste'nografo] SM/F shorthand typist (*Brit*), stenographer (*Am*).

stenosi [ste'nɔzi] SF (*Med*) stenosis.

stenotipia [stenoti'pia] SF stenotype.

stentare [sten'tare] VI (*aus avere*): **stentare a fare qc** to have difficulty in doing sth, find it hard to do sth; **stento a crederci** I find it hard to believe.

stentatamente [stentata'mente] AVV with difficulty.

stentato, a [sten'tato] AGG (*compito, stile*) laboured (*Brit*), labored (*Am*); (*sorriso*) forced.

stento ['stɛnto] SM [a]: **stenti** SMPL (*privazioni*) hardship *sg*, privation *sg*; **una vita di stenti** a life of hardship *o* privation; **vivere tra gli stenti** to live a life of hardship *o* privation [b]: **a stento** AVV with difficulty, barely; **capire qc a stento** to understand sth with difficulty.

stentoreo, a [sten'tɔreo] AGG stentorian.
steppa ['steppa] SF steppe.
sterco ['stɛrko] SM dung.
stereo ['stɛreo] AGG INV, SM INV stereo.
stereofonia [stereofo'nia] SF stereophony.
stereofonico, a, ci, che [stereo'fɔniko] AGG stereo (phonic).
stereoscopico, a, ci, che [stereos'kɔpiko] AGG stereoscopic.
stereoscopio, pi [stereos'kɔpjo] SM stereoscope.
stereotipato, a [stereoti'pato] AGG (anche fig) stereotyped.
stereotipia [stereoti'pia] SF (Tecn, Psic) stereotypy; (Tip) stereotype print.
stereotipo [stere'ɔtipo] SM stereotype; **pensare per stereotipi** to think in clichés.
sterile ['stɛrile] AGG (terreno) arid, barren; (persona) sterile; (fig: polemica) fruitless, futile.
sterilità [sterili'ta] SF (vedi agg) barrenness; sterility; fruitlessness.
sterilizzare [sterilid'dzare] VT to sterilize.
sterilizzazione [steriliddzat'tsjone] SF sterilization.
sterlina [ster'lina] SF pound (sterling).
sterminare [stermi'nare] VT to exterminate, wipe out.
sterminato, a [stermi'nato] AGG immense, endless.
sterminio, ni [ster'minjo] SM extermination, destruction; **campo di sterminio** death camp.
sterna ['stɛrna] SF (Zool) tern.
sterno ['stɛrno] SM (Anat) breastbone, sternum (termine tecn).
sterpaglia [ster'paʎʎa] SF brushwood.
sterpo ['stɛrpo] SM dry twig.
sterrare [ster'rare] VT to excavate.
sterratore [sterra'tore] SM labourer (Brit), laborer (Am), navvy (Brit).
sterzare [ster'tsare] VT, VI (aus avere) (Aut) to steer; (: bruscamente) to swerve; (Pol): **sterzare a destra/a sinistra** to veer to the right/the left.
sterzata [ster'tsata] SF (Aut) turn of the wheel; (: brusca) swerve; (fig) sudden shift; **fare o dare una sterzata** to steer; (bruscamente) to swerve.
sterzo ['stɛrtso] SM (volante) steering wheel.
steso, a ['steso] PP di **stendere**.
stessi ecc ['stessi] VB vedi **stare**.
stesso, a ['stesso] [1] AGG **a** (medesimo, identico) same; **aveva lo stesso vestito** she had the same dress; **abbiamo gli stessi gusti** we have the same tastes; **al tempo stesso** at the same time; **è sempre la stessa storia** it's always the same old thing **b** (esatto, preciso) very; **in quello stesso istante** at that very moment; **quello stesso giorno** the very same day; **oggi stesso** today **c** (rafforzativo: dopo sostantivo): **il medico stesso lo sconsiglia** even the doctor o the doctor himself advises against it; **è venuto il ministro stesso ad inaugurarlo** the minister himself came to inaugurate it **d** (rafforzativo: dopo pron pers sogg): **l'ho visto io stesso** I saw him myself; **voi stessi sapete bene che...** you (yourselves) know very well that ...; **lei stessa è venuta a dirmelo** she came and told me herself, she herself came and told me **e** (rafforzativo: dopo pron rifl): **me stesso** myself; **te stesso** yourself; **se stesso** himself; (neutro) itself; (indef) oneself; **se stessa** herself; **noi stessi** ourselves; **voi stessi**

yourselves; **loro stessi** themselves; **ama solo se stesso** he only loves himself; **di per sé stesso non ha un gran valore** it's not worth a lot in itself **f** (proprio) own; **l'ho visto con i miei stessi occhi** I saw it with my own eyes; **l'ha fatto con le sue stesse mani** he did it with his own hands. [2] PRON DIMOSTR: **lo(la) stesso(a)** the same (one); **è lo stesso di sempre** he (o it) is just the same as always; **chi canta? — lo stesso di prima** who's singing? — the same singer as before; **per me fa lo stesso** it's all the same to me; **per me è lo stesso** it doesn't matter to me. [3]: **lo stesso** AVV (comunque) all the same, even so; **parto lo stesso** I'm going all the same.
stesura [ste'sura] SF (azione) drafting no pl, drawing up no pl; (documento) draft.
stetoscopio, pi [stetos'kɔpjo] SM stethoscope.
stetti ecc ['stɛtti] VB vedi **stare**.
stia¹ ecc ['stia] VB vedi **stare**.
stia² ['stia] SF (chicken) coop.
Stige ['stidʒe] SM: **lo Stige** the Styx.
stigma, i ['stigma] SM (Bot, Zool, anche fig) stigma.
stigmate ['stigmate] SFPL (Rel) stigmata pl.
stigmatizzare [stigmatid'dzare] VT to stigmatize.
stilare [sti'lare] VT to draw up, draft.
stile ['stile] SM (gen) style; (classe) style, class; (Nuoto): **stile libero** freestyle, crawl; **mobili in stile** period furniture; **in grande stile** in great style; **è proprio nel suo stile** (fig) it's just like him; **non è nel suo stile** (fig) it's not like him.
stilettata [stilet'tata] SF (pugnalata) stab with a stiletto; (fig: dolore): **quelle parole furono una stilettata al cuore** those words cut him (o her ecc) to the quick; **fu ucciso con una stilettata** he was stabbed to death.
stiletto [sti'letto] SM stiletto.
stilista, i, e [sti'lista] SM/F (Moda) designer.
stilisticamente [stilistika'mente] AVV stylistically.
stilistico, a, ci, che [sti'listiko] AGG stylistic.
stilizzare [stilid'dzare] VT to stylize.
stilizzato, a [stilid'dzato] AGG stylized.
stillare [stil'lare] VT, VI (aus essere) (gocciolare) to drip; (trasudare) to ooze.
stillicidio, di [stilli't͡ʃidjo] SM (fig): **uno stillicidio di rivelazioni** a steady stream of revelations.
stilo ['stilo] SM (Bot) style.
stilografica, che [stilo'grafika] SF (anche: **penna stilografica**) fountain pen.
Stim. ABBR = **stimata**.
stima ['stima] SF **a** (buona opinione) respect, esteem; **avere stima di qn** to have respect for sb; **godere della stima di qn** to enjoy sb's respect **b** (Econ, Fin) estimate, valuation, assessment; **fare la stima di qc** to estimate the value of sth; **la stima dei danni** estimate of the damage; **stima approssimativa** guesstimate (fam).
stimabile [sti'mabile] AGG **a** (rispettabile) respectable, worthy of respect **b** (valutabile) assessable.
stimare [sti'mare] VT **a** (persona) to respect, esteem, hold in high regard **b** (Econ, Fin) to assess the value of, estimate the value of, value.
stimma, i ['stimma] SM = **stigma**.
stimolante [stimo'lante] [1] AGG stimulating. [2] SM stimulant.
stimolare [stimo'lare] VT (gen) to stimulate; **stimolare qn a fare qc** (incitare) to spur sb on to do sth.
stimolazione [stimolat'tsjone] SF stimulation.

stimolo ['stimolo] SM (*anche fig*) stimulus.

stinco, chi ['stinko] SM (*Anat: persona*) shinbone, shin; (: *di animale*) shank; **non essere uno stinco di santo** to be no saint.

stingere ['stindʒere] VB IRREG: VT, VI (*aus* **essere**), **stingersi** VIP to fade.

stinto, a ['stinto] 1 PP di **stingere**.
2 AGG faded.

stipare [sti'pare] 1 VT to cram, pack.
2 **stiparsi** VIP (*accalcarsi*): **stiparsi in** to crowd into, throng.

stipato, a [sti'pato] AGG (*merce, gente*) packed, crammed.

stipendiare [stipen'djare] VT (*pagare*) to pay (a salary to).

stipendiato, a [stipen'djato] 1 AGG salaried.
2 SM/F salaried worker.

stipendio, di [sti'pɛndjo] SM salary.

stipetto [sti'petto] SM (*armadietto*) locker.

stipite ['stipite] SM (*di porta, finestra*) jamb.

stipulare [stipu'lare] VT (*accordo, contratto*) to draw up.

stipulazione [stipulat'tsjone] SF (*di contratto, stesura*) drafting; (: *firma*) signing.

stiracalzoni [stirakal'tsoni] SM INV trouser press.

stiracchiare [stirak'kjare] 1 VT (*fig: significato di una parola*) to stretch, force.
2 **stiracchiarsi** VR (*persona*) to stretch.

stiracchiato, a [stirak'kjato] AGG (*sforzato*) forced.

stiramaniche [stira'manike] SM INV sleeve board.

stiramento [stira'mento] SM (*Med*) sprain.

stirare [sti'rare] 1 VT a (*con ferro da stiro*) to iron b (*distendere*) to stretch; (*Med*): **stirarsi un legamento** to pull a ligament.
2 **stirarsi** VR to stretch (o.s.).

stiratoio, oi [stira'tojo] SM (*Tecn*) drawing frame.

stiratrice [stira'tritʃe] SF (*donna*) laundry worker; (*macchina*) laundry press.

stiratura [stira'tura] SF a (*con ferro da stiro*) ironing b (*Med*) sprain.

stiro ['stiro] SM: **ferro da stiro** iron; **asse** o **tavolo da stiro** ironing board.

stirpe ['stirpe] SF a (*schiatta*) birth, stock; **di nobile stirpe** of noble descent b (*discendenti*) descendants *pl*.

stitichezza [stiti'kettsa] SF constipation.

stitico, a, ci, che ['stitiko] AGG constipated.

stiva ['stiva] SF (*di nave, aereo*) hold.

stivale [sti'vale] SM boot; **quel medico dei miei stivali!** (*pegg*) that apology for a doctor! ▶ **stivale da birra** boot-shaped beer glass.

stivaletto [stiva'letto] SM ankle boot.

stivare [sti'vare] VT to stow, load.

stizza ['stittsa] SF anger, vexation.

stizzire [stit'tsire] 1 VT to irritate.
2 **stizzirsi** VIP to become irritated, become vexed.

stizzosamente [stittsosa'mente] AVV angrily.

stizzoso, a [stit'tsoso] AGG (*persona*) irascible, quick-tempered; (*risposta*) angry.

stoccafisso [stokka'fisso] SM stockfish, dried cod.

stoccaggio [stok'kaddʒo] SM (*Comm*) warehousing.

Stoccarda [stok'karda] SF Stuttgart.

stoccata [stok'kata] SF (*Scherma*) thrust, stab; (*Calcio*) shot; (*fig: allusione*) gibe, cutting remark.

Stoccolma [stok'kolma] SF Stockholm.

stock [stɔk] SM INV (*Comm*) stock.

stoffa ['stɔffa] SF material, fabric; **avere della stoffa** (*fig*) to have what it takes; **avere la stoffa per diventare qc** to have the makings of sth.

stoicamente [stoika'mente] AVV stoically.

stoicismo [stoi'tʃizmo] SM stoicism.

stoico, a, ci, che ['stɔiko] AGG, SM/F (*anche fig*) stoic(al).

stoino [sto'ino] SM doormat.

stola ['stɔla] SF (*gen, Rel*) stole.

stolidità [stolidi'ta] SF INV stolidity.

stolido, a ['stɔlido] AGG stolid.

stolone [sto'lone] SM (*Bot*) stolon.

stoltezza [stol'tettsa] SF (*qualità*) stupidity; (*azione*) foolish action.

stolto, a ['stolto] 1 AGG stupid, foolish.
2 SM/F fool.

stoma, i ['stɔma] SM (*Bot*) stoma.

stomacare [stoma'kare] 1 VT (*nauseare*) to nauseate.
2 **stomacarsi** VIP: **stomacarsi di qc** to become nauseated by sth.

stomachevole [stoma'kevole] AGG disgusting.

stomaco, chi ['stɔmako] SM stomach; **dare di stomaco** to be sick; **avere qc sullo stomaco** to have sth lying on one's stomach; **quel tipo mi sta sullo stomaco** I can't stand that guy; **mi fa rivoltare lo stomaco** (*anche fig*) it makes me sick; **bisogna avere dello stomaco per fare quel lavoro** you need a strong stomach to do that kind of work.

stomatite [stoma'tite] SF (*Med*) stomatitis.

stomatologico, a, ci, che [stomato'lɔdʒiko] AGG (*Med*) stomatological; **reparto stomatologico** department of oral medicine.

stonare [sto'nare] 1 VT (*cantando*) to sing out of tune; (*suonando*) to play out of tune.
2 VI (*aus* **avere**) to be out of tune, to sing o play out of tune; (*fig: colori*) to clash.

stonato, a [sto'nato] AGG (*persona, strumento*) off-key, out of tune; **c'era una nota stonata** (*fig*) something didn't ring true.

stonatura [stona'tura] SF (*suono*) false note.

stop [stɔp] SM INV a (*Aut: fanalino*) brake-light; (: *segnale stradale*) stop sign b (*Telegrafia*) stop.

stoppa ['stoppa] SF tow; **come stoppa** (*capelli*) tow-coloured (*Brit*), tow-colored (*Am*); **essere come un pulcino nella stoppa** to look lost and helpless.

stoppare [stop'pare] VT (*Calcio*) to stop; **stoppare la palla** to trap the ball.

stoppata [stop'pata] SF (*Calcio*) action of stopping the ball.

stoppia ['stoppja] SF stubble.

stoppino [stop'pino] SM (*di candela*) wick; (*miccia*) fuse.

stoppione [stop'pjone] SM (*Bot*) thistle.

stopposo, a [stop'poso] AGG tow-coloured (*Brit*), tow-colored (*Am*).

storcere ['stɔrtʃere] VB IRREG 1 VT (*gen*) to twist; **storcere il naso** (*fig*) to turn up one's nose; **storcersi la caviglia** to twist one's ankle.
2 **storcersi** VIP to writhe, twist.

stordimento [stordi'mento] SM (*gen*) daze; (*da droga*) stupefaction.

stordire [stor'dire] 1 VT (*sogg: colpo, notizia, droga*) to stun, daze.
2 **stordirsi** VR (*fig*): **stordirsi col bere** to dull one's senses with drink, drink o.s. stupid.

stordito, a [stor'dito] AGG (*intonito*) dazed, stunned; (*sventato*) scatterbrained, heedless.

storia ['stɔrja] SF a (*scienza, materia, opera*) history; **libro**

di storia history book; **passare alla storia** to go down in history

b (*racconto, bugia*) story; (*pretesto*) excuse, pretext; **mi ha raccontato un sacco di storie** he told me a lot of nonsense *o* rubbish (*Brit*); **sono tutte storie!** it's all lies!

c (*faccenda*) business; **non voglio saperne più di questa storia** I don't want to hear any more about this business; **è sempre la solita storia** it's always the same old story

d : **storie** SFPL (*smorfie*) fuss *sg*; **non ha fatto storie** he didn't make a fuss; **senza tante storie!** don't make such a fuss!

e (*relazione amorosa*) affair.

storicamente [storika'mente] AVV historically.

storicità [storitʃi'ta] SF historical authenticity.

storico, a, ci, che ['stɔriko] ① AGG (*gen*) historical; (*memorabile*) historic.
② SM/F historian.

storiella [sto'rjɛlla] SF (*storia divertente*) funny story; (*frottola*) story.

storiografia [storjogra'fia] SF historiography.

storiografo, a [sto'rjɔgrafo] SM/F historiographer.

storione [sto'rjone] SM (*Zool*) sturgeon.

stormire [stor'mire] VI (*aus avere*) to rustle.

stormo ['stormo] SM (*di uccelli*) flock.

stornare [stor'nare] VT **a** (*Comm*) to transfer **b** (*fig*: *evitare*: *pericolo*) to avert.

stornello [stor'nɛllo] SM *kind of folk song*.

storno ['storno] SM **a** (*Zool*) starling **b** (*Comm*) transfer.

storpiare [stor'pjare] ① VT (*persona*) to cripple, maim; (*fig*: *parole*) to mangle.
② **storpiarsi** VIP to become crippled.

storpiatura [storpja'tura] SF (*fig*: *di significato*) mangling.

storpio, pia, pi, pie ['stɔrpjo] ① AGG crippled, maimed.
② SM/F cripple.

storsi *ecc* ['stɔrsi] VB *vedi* **storcere**.

storta¹ ['stɔrta] SF (*distorsione*) sprain, twist; **prendere una storta al piede** to sprain one's foot.

storta² ['stɔrta] SF (*alambicco*) retort.

storto, a ['stɔrto] ① PP *di* **storcere**.
② AGG (*tubo, chiodo*) twisted, bent; (*ruota*) buckled, warped; (*manubrio, quadro*) crooked; (*fig*: *ragionamento*) false, wrong; **avere le gambe storte** to have crooked legs; **avere gli occhi storti** to have a squint, be cross-eyed; **mi va tutto storto** [OR] **mi vanno tutte storte** (*fam*) everything's going wrong.
③ AVV: **guardare storto qn** (*fig*) to look askance at sb.

stoviglie [sto'viʎʎe] SFPL dishes.

str ABBR (*Geog*) = **stretto**.

strabico, a, ci, che ['strabiko] AGG (*occhi*) squint; (*persona*): **essere strabico** to have a squint.

strabiliante [strabi'ljante] AGG astonishing, amazing.

strabiliare [strabi'ljare] VI (*aus avere*) to astonish, amaze.

strabismo [stra'bizmo] SM squinting.

strabuzzare [strabud'dzare] VT: **strabuzzare gli occhi** to open one's eyes wide.

stracarico, a, chi, che [stra'kariko] AGG overloaded.

straccare [strak'kare] VT (*sfinire*) to tire out.

stracchino [strak'kino] SM *type of soft cheese*.

stracciare [strat'tʃare] ① VT to tear up, rip up; **stracciare gli avversari** to wipe the floor with one's opponents.
② **stracciarsi** VIP to tear, rip.

stracciatella [strattʃa'tɛlla] SF (*minestra*) *broth made with beaten eggs, semolina and parmesan cheese*; (*gelato*) *vanilla-flavoured ice-cream with chocolate chips.*

straccio, cia, ci, ce ['strattʃo] ① AGG: **carta straccia** wastepaper.
② SM (*gen*) rag; (*per pulire*) cloth, duster; (*fig*: *persona*) wretch; **non ho uno straccio di vestito** I haven't got a thing to wear; **non ha nemmeno uno straccio di marito** she hasn't got a husband of any description.

straccione, a [strat'tʃone] SM/F ragamuffin.

straccivendolo [strattʃi'vendolo] SM ragman.

stracco, a, chi, che ['strakko] AGG: **stracco (morto)** exhausted, dead tired.

stracotto, a [stra'kɔtto] ① PP *di* **stracuocere**.
② AGG overcooked.
③ SM (*Culin*) beef stew.

stracuocere [stra'kwɔtʃere] VT IRREG to overdo, overcook.

strada ['strada] SF **a** (*gen*) road; (*di città*) street; **andare fuori strada** (*Aut*) to go off the road; **tagliare la strada a qn** to cut across in front of sb; **l'uomo della strada** (*fig*) the man in the street; **donna di strada** (*fig pegg*) streetwalker; **ragazzo di strada** (*fig pegg*) street urchin ▶ **strada ferrata** railway (*Brit*), railroad (*Am*) ▶ **strada principale** main road ▶ **strada a senso unico** one-way street ▶ **strada senza uscita** dead end, cul-de-sac

b (*percorso*) way; **qual è la strada per andare al cinema?** which is the way to the cinema?, how does one get to the cinema?; **mostrare la strada a qn** to show sb the way; **c'è tanta strada da fare?** is it a long way?; **tre ore di strada (a piedi)/(in macchina)** three hours' walk/drive; **non è sulla mia strada** it's not on my way; **facciamo la strada insieme?** shall we go along together?; **strada facendo** on the way

c (*fig*) path, way, road; **essere sulla buona strada** (*nella vita*) to be on the right road *o* path; (*Polizia, ricerca*) to be on the right track; **essere fuori strada** (*Polizia*) to be on the wrong track; **portare qn sulla cattiva strada** to lead sb astray

d (*fraseologia*): **fare** *o* **farsi strada** (*fig*: *persona*) to get on in life; **farsi strada tra la folla** to make one's way through the crowd; **trovarsi in mezzo ad una strada** to find o.s. out on the streets; **fare strada a qn** to show sb the way.

stradale [stra'dale] ① AGG (*gen*) road *attr*; (*polizia, regolamento*) traffic *attr*.
② SF (*polizia*) traffic police.

stradario, ri [stra'darjo] SM street guide.

stradino [stra'dino] SM road worker.

stradista, i [stra'dista] SM (*Ciclismo*) road rider, road racer.

stradivario, ri [stradi'varjo] SM Stradivarius.

stradone [stra'done] SM wide road.

strafalcione [strafal'tʃone] SM (*errore*) howler, blunder.

strafare [stra'fare] VI IRREG (*aus avere*) to overdo it.

strafatto, a [stra'fatto] PP *di* **strafare**.

straforo [stra'foro]: **di straforo** AVV (*di nascosto*) on the sly.

strafottente [strafot'tɛnte] ① AGG arrogant.
② SM/F arrogant person.

strafottenza [strafot'tɛntsa] SF arrogance.

strage ['stradʒe] SF massacre, slaughter; **fare una strage** to carry out a massacre *o* slaughter; **fare strage di** (*animali*) to slaughter; **fare strage di cuori** to be a heartbreaker.

stragismo [stra'dʒizmo] SM campaign of violence.

stragista [stra'dʒista] SM/F terrorist killer.

stragrande [stra'grande] AGG: **la stragrande maggioranza**

the overwhelming majority.

stralciare [stral'tʃare] VT to remove.

stralcio, ci ['straltʃo] **1** SM (*Comm*): **vendere a stralcio** to sell off (at bargain prices), clear.

2 AGG INV: **legge stralcio** *abridged version of an act.*

strale ['strale] SM (*fig letter: freccia*) arrow, dart.

strallo ['strallo] SM (*Naut*): **strallo di prua** forestay ▶ **strallo di poppa** backstay.

stralunato, a [stralu'nato] AGG (*occhi*) staring; (*persona*) dazed, thunderstruck.

stramaledetto, a [stramale'detto] **1** PP di **stramaledire**.

2 AGG (*fam*) damned.

stramaledire [stramale'dire] VT IRREG (*fam*) to curse.

stramazzare [stramat'tsare] VI (*aus essere*) to collapse, fall heavily; **stramazzare al suolo** to crash to the floor.

strambamente [stramba'mente] AVV oddly, strangely.

strambare [stram'bare] VI (*aus avere*) (*Naut*) to gybe.

stramberia [strambe'ria] SF eccentricity.

strambo, a ['strambo] AGG strange, queer.

strame ['strame] SM hay, straw.

strampalato, a [strampa'lato] AGG odd, eccentric.

stranamente [strana'mente] AVV (*comportarsi, vestirsi*) oddly, strangely; **e lui, stranamente, ha accettato** and, surprisingly, he agreed.

stranezza [stra'nettsa] SF (*qualità*) strangeness; (*atto*): **le sue stranezze mi preoccupano** his strange behaviour (*Brit*) *o* behavior (*Am*) worries me.

strangolamento [strangola'mento] SM (*atto*) strangling; (*effetto*) strangulation.

strangolare [strango'lare] **1** VT to strangle.

2 VIP to choke.

straniero, a [stra'njɛro] **1** AGG (*gen*) foreign; (*Amm*) alien.

2 SM/F (*gen*) foreigner; (*Amm*) alien; **cacciare lo straniero** to drive out foreigners.

stranito, a [stra'nito] AGG (*sguardo, aria*) dazed.

strano, a ['strano] AGG (*gen*) strange; (*bizzarro*) strange, odd, queer; **è strano che...** it is odd that ...; **e cosa strana...** strangely enough ... .

straordinariamente [straordinarja'mente] AVV extraordinarily.

straordinario, ria, ri, rie [straordi'narjo] **1** AGG (*gen*) extraordinary; (*treno, imposta*) special; (*impiegato*) temporary; **lavoro straordinario** overtime.

2 SM (*impiegato*) temporary employee; (*lavoro*) overtime; **ho fatto tre ore di straordinario** I did three hours overtime.

straorzare [straor'tsare] VI (*aus avere*) (*Naut*) to broach.

strapagare [strapa'gare] VT (*persona*) to overpay; (*merce*) to pay too much for.

strapazzare [strapat'tsare] **1** VT (*maltrattare: persona, oggetto*) to handle roughly, ill-treat; (*affaticare*) to tire out.

2 **strapazzarsi** VR to tire o.s. out, overdo things.

strapazzata [strapat'tsata] SF **a** (*gran fatica*) strain **b** (*rimprovero*) telling-off; **dare una strapazzata a qn** to give sb a telling-off, tear sb off a strip (*Brit*).

strapazzato, a [strapat'tsato] AGG (*persona: affaticato*) worn out; **uova strapazzate** scrambled eggs.

strapazzo [stra'pattso] SM **a** strain, fatigue **b**: **da strapazzo** (*fig pegg: persona*) third-rate.

strapieno, a [stra'pjɛno] AGG overflowing, full to overflowing; **essere** *o* **sentirsi strapieno** to be *o* feel full up.

strapiombo [stra'pjombo] SM (*roccia*) overhanging rock; **a strapiombo** overhanging.

strapotere [strapo'tere] SM excessive power.

strappalacrime [strappa'lakrime] AGG INV (*fam*): **romanzo** (*o film*) **strappalacrime** tear-jerker.

strappare [strap'pare] **1** VT (*gen*) to tear, rip; (*pagina*) to tear off, tear out; (*erbacce*) to pull up; (*bottone*) to pull off; **strappare qc di mano a qn** to snatch sth out of sb's hand; **si strappò la gonna** she tore *o* ripped her skirt; **strapparsi i vestiti di dosso** to rip one's clothes off; **strapparsi i capelli** to tear one's hair; **strapparsi un muscolo** to tear a muscle; **strappare una promessa a qn** to extract a promise from sb; **strappare un segreto a qn** to wring a secret from sb; **strappare gli applausi del pubblico** to win the audience's applause; **strappare qn dal suo ambiente** to take sb away from his (*o* her) own environment; **una scena che strappa il cuore** a heart-rending scene.

2 **strapparsi** VIP (*lacerarsi*) to tear, rip.

strappato, a [strap'pato] AGG (*lacerato*) torn, ripped.

strappo ['strappo] SM **a** (*lacerazione*) tear, rip ▶ **strappo muscolare** (*Med*) strain, tear, torn muscle **b** (*strattone*) tug, pull; **dare uno strappo a qc** to give sth a tug; **fare uno strappo alla regola** to make an exception to the rule **c** (*fig fam: passaggio*) lift (*Brit*), ride (*Am*); **puoi darmi uno strappo (fino) in centro?** can you give me a lift *o* ride into town?

strapuntino [strapun'tino] SM (*sedile*) foldaway seat, jump seat.

straricco, a, chi, che [stra'rikko] AGG extremely rich.

straripamento [straripa'mento] SM overflowing.

straripare [strari'pare] VI (*aus essere o avere*) (*fiume*) to overflow, burst its banks.

Strasburgo [straz'burgo] SF Strasbourg.

strascicare [straʃʃi'kare] **1** VT (*trascinare*): **strascicare qc per terra** to drag sth along the ground, trail sth along the ground; **strascicare i piedi** to drag one's feet; **strascicare le parole** to drawl; **strascicare un lavoro** to drag out *o* draw out a piece of work; **strascicare una malattia** to be unable to shake off an illness.

2 VI (*aus avere*) to trail.

3 **strascicarsi** VR (*trascinarsi*) to drag o.s. (along).

strascico, chi ['straʃʃiko] SM **a** (*di abito*) train; **reggere lo strascico a qn** to carry sb's train; (*fig*) to lick sb's boots **b**: **rete a strascico** trawl (net); **pesca a strascico** trawling **c** (*fig: conseguenza*) after-effect.

strascinare [straʃʃi'nare] **1** VT to drag.

2 **strascinarsi** VIP to drag o.s. (along); (*fig: lavoro*) to drag on.

strass [stras] SM INV paste, strass.

stratagemma, i [strata'dʒɛmma] SM (*Mil, fig*) stratagem.

stratega, ghi [stra'tɛga] SM strategist.

strategia, gie [strate'dʒia] SF (*Mil, fig*) strategy.

strategicamente [stratedʒika'mente] AVV (*gen*) strategically; (*astutamente*) cunningly.

strategico, a, ci, che [stra'tɛdʒiko] AGG (*Mil, fig*) strategic.

stratificare [stratifi'kare] **1** VT to stratify.

2 **stratificarsi** VIP to become stratified.

stratificato, a [stratifi'kato] AGG (*roccia*) stratified; (*parabrezza, vetro*) laminated.

stratificazione [stratifikat'tsjone] SF stratification.

stratiforme [strati'forme] AGG stratiform.

strato ['strato] SM (*gen*) layer; (*di vernice*) coat, coating; (*Meteor*) stratus; (*Geol*) stratum; **i vari strati della società** the various strata of society ▶ **strato sociale**

social stratum.

stratosfera [stratos'fɛra] SF stratosphere.

strattone [strat'tone] SM tug, jerk; **dare uno strattone a qc** to tug *o* jerk sth, give sth a tug *o* jerk.

stravaccarsi [stravak'karsi] VR: **stravaccarsi su** to flop down on, sprawl out on.

stravaccato, a [stravak'kato] AGG sprawling.

stravagante [strava'gante] AGG eccentric, odd.

stravaganza [strava'gantsa] SF eccentricity.

stravecchio, chia, chi, chie [stra'vɛkkjo] AGG (*gen*) very old; (*vino*) mellow; (*formaggio*) very mature.

stravedere [strave'dere] VI IRREG (*aus* **avere**): **stravedere per qn** to dote on sb.

stravincere [stra'vintʃere] VT IRREG to win easily; **stravincere qn** to beat sb hollow.

stravinto, a [stra'vinto] PP di **stravincere**.

stravisto, a [stra'visto] PP di **stravedere**.

stravizio, zi [stra'vittsjo] SM excess; **darsi agli stravizi** to lead a dissolute life.

stravolgere [stra'vɔldʒere] VT IRREG (*persona*) to upset; (*volto*) to contort; (*organizzazione, sistema*) to shake, rock; (*significato*) to twist, distort.

stravolto, a [stra'vɔlto] **1** PP di **stravolgere**.

2 AGG (*persona: per stanchezza*) in a terrible state; (: *per sofferenza*) distraught; **aveva la faccia stravolta** he looked terrible.

straziante [strat'tsjante] AGG (*scena*) harrowing; (*urlo*) bloodcurdling; (*dolore*) excruciating.

straziare [strat'tsjare] VT (*carni, corpo*) to torment, torture; **straziare il cuore a qn** to break sb's heart; **una musica che strazia le orecchie** an excruciating piece of music.

strazio, zi ['strattsjo] SM (*di torture*) torment; **fare strazio di** (*corpo, vittima*) to mutilate; **la scena era uno strazio** it was a harrowing scene; **questo libro è uno strazio!** this book is appalling!; **che strazio!** (*compito*) what a mess!; (*spettacolo*) what a disaster!

strega, ghe ['strega] SF (*anche fig: donna malvagia*) witch; (*pegg: donna brutta*) old hag, old witch.

stregare [stre'gare] VT (*anche fig*) to bewitch.

stregato, a [stre'gato] AGG (*castello, anello*) enchanted; (*persona*) bewitched.

stregone [stre'gone] SM (*in tribù*) witch doctor; (*mago*) sorcerer, wizard.

stregoneria [stregone'ria] SF (*pratica*) witchcraft; (*incantesimo*) spell; **fare una stregoneria** to cast a spell.

stregua ['stregwa] SF: **alla (stessa) stregua di** on a par with; **trattare tutti alla stessa stregua** to treat everybody in the same manner.

stremare [stre'mare] VT to exhaust.

stremato, a [stre'mato] AGG exhausted, worn out.

stremo ['strɛmo] SM: **essere allo stremo (delle forze)** to be at the end of one's tether.

strenna ['strɛnna] SF: **strenna natalizia** (*regalo*) Christmas present; (*libro*) *book published for the Christmas market*.

strenuo, a ['strɛnuo] AGG (*valoroso*) brave, courageous; (*infaticabile*) tireless.

strepitare [strepi'tare] VI (*aus* **avere**) to yell and shout.

strepito ['strɛpito] SM (*di voci, folla*) clamour (*Brit*), clamor (*Am*); (*di catene*) clanking, rattling; **fare strepito** (*notizia, scandalo*) to cause an uproar.

strepitosamente [strepitosa'mente] AVV: **vincere strepitosamente** to win a resounding victory.

strepitoso, a [strepi'toso] AGG (*successo*) resounding;

(*applauso*) clamorous, deafening.

streptococco, chi [strepto'kɔkko] SM streptococcus.

stress [strɛs] SM INV stress.

stressante [stres'sante] AGG stressful.

stressare [stres'sare] VT to put under stress.

stressato, a [stres'sato] AGG under stress.

stretta ['stretta] SF (*gen*) grip, firm hold; **una stretta di mano** a handshake; **dare una stretta di mano a qn** to shake hands with sb, shake sb's hand; **una stretta di spalle** a shrug (of one's shoulders); **una stretta al cuore** a sudden sadness; **essere alle strette** to be in a tight corner, have one's back to the wall; **mettere qn alle strette** to put sb in a tight corner, get sb with his (*o* her) back to the wall ▶**stretta creditizia** (*Econ*) credit squeeze.

strettamente [stretta'mente] AVV **a** (*in modo stretto*) tightly **b** (*fig: rigorosamente*) strictly, closely; **attenersi strettamente alle regole** to keep strictly to the rules, stick closely to the rules.

strettezza [stret'tettsa] SF **a** (*gen*) narrowness **b** : **strettezze** SFPL poverty *sg*, straitened circumstances.

stretto, a ['stretto] **1** PP di **stringere**.

2 AGG **a** (*corridoio, stanza, limiti*) narrow; (*gonna, scarpe, nodo*) tight; (*curva*) tight, sharp; **questa gonna mi è stretta** this skirt is tight on me; **stavamo stretti in macchina** we were packed tight in the car; **tieni stretto!** hold on tight!; **tenere stretto qn/qc** to hold sb/sth tight; **a denti stretti** with clenched teeth

b (*parente, amico*) close

c (*preciso, esatto: significato*) strict, exact; (*rigoroso: osservanza*) strict

d (*soltanto*): **lo stretto necessario** the bare minimum.

3 SM (*di mare*) strait.

strettoia [stret'toja] SF (*di strada*) bottleneck; (*fig*) tricky situation.

stria ['stria] SF streak.

striare [stri'are] VT to streak.

striato, a [stri'ato] AGG streaked.

striatura [stria'tura] SF (*atto*) streaking; (*effetto*) streaks *pl*.

stricnina [strik'nina] SF strychnine.

stridente [stri'dɛnte] AGG (*rumore*) strident; (*colori*) clashing.

stridere ['stridere] VI DIF (*porta*) to squeak; (*animale*) to screech, shriek; (*colori*) to clash.

stridio, dii [stri'dio] SM screeching.

strido ['strido] SM (*fpl* **strida**) (*di animale*) screech, shriek; (*urlo*) scream.

stridore [stri'dore] SM screeching, shrieking.

stridulo, a ['stridulo] AGG (*voce*) shrill.

striglia ['striʎʎa] SF currycomb.

strigliare [striʎ'ʎare] VT (*cavallo*) to curry.

strigliata [striʎ'ʎata] SF (*di cavallo*) currying; (*fig*): **dare una strigliata a qn** to give sb a dressing-down.

strillare [stril'lare] **1** VI (*aus* **avere**) (*gridare*) to scream, shriek; **non strillare!** (*parla piano*) don't shout!.

2 VT: **strillare aiuto** to cry for help; **strillò arrivederci** he shouted goodbye.

strillo ['strillo] SM scream, shriek; **fare uno strillo** to let out a scream.

strillone [stril'lone] SM news vendor, newspaper seller.

striminzito, a [strimin'tsito] AGG (*misero*) shabby; (*molto magro*) skinny.

strimpellare [strimpel'lare] VT (*chitarra*) to strum away on; (*pianoforte*) to plonk away on.

stringa, ghe ['stringa] SF (*cordoncino*) lace; (*Inform, Ling*) string.

stringare [strin'gare] VT (*fig*: *discorso*) to condense.

stringatamente [stringata'mente] AVV concisely.

stringatezza [stringa'tettsa] SF concision, terseness.

stringato, a [strin'gato] AGG (*fig*) concise.

stringere ['strindʒere] VB IRREG **1** VT **a** (*con la mano*) to grip, hold tight; **stringere il braccio di qn** to clasp sb's arm; **stringere la mano a qn** (*afferrarla*) to squeeze *o* press sb's hand; (*salutando*) to shake sb's hand, shake hands with sb; **si strinsero la mano** they shook hands; **stringere qn alla gola** to grab sb by the throat

b (*pugno, mascella*) to clench; (*labbra*) to compress; **una scena che stringe il cuore** a scene which brings a lump to one's throat; **stringere i denti** to clench one's teeth; (*fig*) to grit one's teeth

c (*gonna*) to take in

d (*vite*) to tighten; (*rubinetto*) to turn tight; (*cintura, nodo*) to tighten, pull tight

e (*avvicinare*: *oggetti*) to close up, put close together; (: *persone*) squeeze together

f (*fraseologia*): **stringere qn tra le braccia** to clasp sb in one's arms; **stringere amicizia con qn** to make friends with sb; **stringere un patto** to conclude a treaty; **stringere un'alleanza** to form an alliance; **stringi stringi** in conclusion; **stringi!** get to the point!; **stringere qn in curva** (*Aut*) to cut in on sb on a bend.

2 VI (*aus* avere) (*essere stretto*) to be tight; (*scarpe*) to pinch, be tight; (*fig*: *arrivare al dunque*) to come to the point; **il tempo stringe** time is short.

3 **stringersi** VR (*persona*): **stringersi a** (*muro, parete*) to press o.s. up against; **si strinse a lui** she drew close to him.

strinsi *ecc* ['strinsi] VB *vedi* **stringere**.

striptease ['strip ti:z] SM INV striptease; **fare lo striptease** to do a striptease.

striscia, sce ['striʃʃa] SF (*di tessuto, carta, fumetto*) strip; (*riga*) stripe; **a strisce** striped ▸ **strisce pedonali** zebra crossing *sg* (*Brit*), crosswalk *sg* (*Am*).

strisciante [striʃ'ʃante] AGG **a** (*fig pegg*) unctuous **b** (*Econ*: *inflazione*) creeping.

strisciare [striʃ'ʃare] **1** VT (*piedi*) to drag; (*muro, macchina*) to scrape, graze.

2 VI (*aus* avere) (*gen*) to crawl, creep; **strisciare contro un muro** to sidle along a wall; **strisciare con la macchina contro il muro** to scrape one's car against the wall; **lo farò strisciare ai miei piedi** I'll make him crawl at my feet.

strisciata [striʃ'ʃata] SF (*segno*) scratch.

striscio, sci ['striʃʃo] SM **a** (*segno*) scratch; **colpire di striscio** to graze **b** (*Med*: *esame*) smear (test), pap smear (*Am*).

striscione [striʃ'ʃone] SM banner.

stritolamento [stritola'mento] SM crushing.

stritolare [strito'lare] VT (*anche fig*) to crush, grind.

strizzare [strit'tsare] VT (*panni*) to wring (out); **strizzare l'occhio (a qn)** to wink (at sb).

strizzata [strit'tsata] SF: **dare una strizzata a qc** to give sth a wring; **una strizzata d'occhio** a wink.

strofa ['strɔfa] SF, **strofe** ['strɔfe] SF INV strophe.

strofinaccio, ci [strofi'nattʃo] SM (*gen*) duster, cloth; (*per piatti*) dishcloth; (*per pavimenti*) floorcloth.

strofinare [strofi'nare] **1** VT (*gen*) to rub; (*lucidare*) to polish; (*pavimento*) to wipe; **strofinarsi gli occhi/le mani** to rub one's eyes/one's hands.

2 **strofinarsi** VR: **strofinarsi (contro)** to rub o.s. (against).

strofinio, nii [strofi'nio] SM (*continual*) rubbing.

strombazzare [strombat'tsare] **1** VT (*divulgare*) to proclaim; **strombazzare i propri meriti** to blow one's own trumpet; **strombazzare qc ai quattro venti** to proclaim sth to the four winds.

2 VI (*aus* avere) (*fam*: *suonare il clacson*) to hoot.

strombettare [strombet'tare] VI (*aus* avere) (*con tromba*) to blare away; (*con clacson*) to hoot.

stroncare [stron'kare] VT (*ramo*) to break off; (*fig*: *rivolta*) to put down, suppress; (: *libro, film*) to pan, tear to pieces; **fu stroncato da un infarto** he was carried off by a heart attack.

stronzata [stron'tsata] SF (*fam!*) damned stupid thing to do (*o* say); **non puoi credere a queste stronzate!** surely you don't believe such bullshit! (*fam!*) *o* crap (*fam!*); **come si possono fare certe stronzate?** how can people do such damned stupid things?

stronzio ['strɔntsjo] SM (*Chim*) strontium.

stronzo ['strontso] SM (*fig fam!*: *persona*) shit (*fam!*), turd (*fam!*); (*sterco*) turd.

stropicciare [stropit'tʃare] VT **a** (*strofinare*) to rub; **stropicciarsi gli occhi** to rub one's eyes **b** (*spiegazzare*) to crease.

strozzare [strot'tsare] **1** VT (*persona*) to choke, strangle; (*sogg*: *cibo*) to choke; (*conduttura*) to narrow.

2 **strozzarsi** VIP to choke.

strozzascotte [strottsa'skɔtte] SM INV (*Naut*) clam cleat.

strozzatura [strottsa'tura] SF (*di conduttura*) narrowing; (*di strada, fig*) bottleneck.

strozzinaggio, gi [strottsi'naddʒo] SM usury.

strozzino, a [strot'tsino] SM/F (*usuraio*) usurer; (*fig*) shark.

struccare [struk'kare] **1** VT to remove make-up from.

2 **struccarsi** VR to remove one's make-up.

struccatore [strukka'tore] SM make-up remover.

strudel ['strudel] SM INV (*Culin*) strudel.

struggere ['struddʒere] VB IRREG (*letter*) **1** VT (*sogg*: *amore*) to consume.

2 **struggersi** VIP: **struggersi d'amore per qn** to be consumed with love for sb; **struggersi dal dolore** to be consumed with grief.

struggimento [struddʒi'mento] SM (*desiderio*) yearning.

strumentale [strumen'tale] AGG (*gen, Mus*) instrumental; (*Aer*: *volo*) instrument *attr*; **fare uso strumentale di qc** to make (instrumental) use of sth.

strumentalizzare [strumentalid'dzare] VT to exploit, use for one's own ends.

strumentalizzazione [strumentaliddzat'tsjone] SF exploitation, use for one's own ends.

strumentare [strumen'tare] VT (*Mus*) to orchestrate.

strumentazione [strumentat'tsjone] SF **a** (*Mus*) orchestration **b** (*Tecn*) instrumentation.

strumentista, i, e [strumen'tista] SM/F (*Mus*) instrumentalist.

strumento [stru'mento] SM **a** (*arnese*) tool; **essere lo strumento di qn** (*fig*: *persona*) to be sb's tool ▸ **strumenti di bordo** (*Aer*) flight instruments; (*Naut*) ship instruments ▸ **strumenti di precisione** precision instruments

b (*Mus*) instrument ▸ **strumento ad arco** string(ed) instrument ▸ **strumento a corda** string(ed) instrument ▸ **strumento a fiato** wind instrument.

strusciare [struʃ'ʃare] ① VT (*piedi*) to shuffle; (*gomiti*) to rub.

② **strusciarsi** VR: **strusciarsi contro qc** to rub o.s. against sth; **gli si strusciava addosso** she was all over him.

strussi ecc ['strussi] VB vedi **struggere**.

strutto¹, a ['strutto] PP di **struggere**.

strutto² ['strutto] SM (*Culin*) lard.

struttura [strut'tura] SF (*tutti i sensi*) structure ▶**struttura portante** (*Edil*) supporting structure ▶**struttura sociale** social structure.

strutturale [struttu'rale] AGG (*gen, Gramm*) structural.

strutturalismo [struttura'lizmo] SM structuralism.

strutturalista, i, e [struttura'lista] SM/F structuralist.

strutturalistico, a, ci, che [struttura'listiko] AGG structuralist.

strutturalmente [struttural'mente] AVV structurally.

strutturare [struttu'rare] VT to structure.

struzzo ['struttso] SM (*Zool*) ostrich; **piume di struzzo** ostrich feathers; **fare lo struzzo** [OR] **fare la politica dello struzzo** to bury one's head in the sand; **avere uno stomaco di struzzo** to have a cast-iron stomach.

stuccare [stuk'kare] VT (*muro*) to plaster; (*vetro*) to putty; (*decorare con stucchi*) to stucco.

stuccatore, trice [stukka'tore] SM/F (*operaio*) plasterer; (*artista*) stucco worker.

stuccatura [stukka'tura] SF (*vedi vb*) plastering; puttying; stuccoing.

stucchevole [stuk'kevole] AGG (*cibo*) nauseating; (*scena, spettacolo*) tedious, boring.

stucco, chi ['stukko] SM (*per muro*) plaster; (*per vetri*) putty; (*ornamentale*) stucco; **rimanere di stucco** to be dumbfounded, be left speechless.

studente, essa [stu'dɛnte] SM/F (*gen*) student; (*scolaro*) pupil, schoolboy/schoolgirl; (*Univ*) student, undergraduate.

studentesco, a, schi, sche [studen'tesko] AGG student *attr.*

studiacchiare [studjak'kjare] VT, VI (*aus* **avere**) to study halfheartedly.

studiare [stu'djare] ① VT (*gen*) to study; (*lezione*) to learn; **studiare un sistema per fare qc** to try to find a way of doing sth; **una persona che studia i gesti/le parole** a person of studied manners/speech.

② VI (*aus* **avere**) to study.

③ **studiarsi** VR a (*osservarsi*) to examine o.s. b (*uso reciproco*) to eye *o* weigh one another up.

studiato, a [stu'djato] AGG (*modi, sorriso*) affected.

studio, di ['studjo] SM a (*gen: azione*) studying, study; **una giornata di studio** a day's studying; **mantenersi agli studi** to pay one's way through college (*o* university); **fare studi letterari/scientifici** to study arts/science; **alla fine degli studi** at the end of one's course (of studies) b (*lavoro, ricerca, disegno*) study; **fare uno studio o degli studi su qn/qc** to do research on sb/sth, make a study of sb/sth; **secondo recenti studi, appare che ...** recent research indicates that ...; **uno studio critico** a critical study; **uno studio dal vero** a life study c (*progettazione*) project; **la proposta è allo studio** the proposal is under consideration d (*stanza*) study; (*di professionista*) office; (*di medico*) surgery (*Brit*), office (*Am*) ▶**studio fotografico** photographer's studio ▶**studio legale** lawyer's office e (*TV, Cine*) studio; **trasmettiamo dagli studi di Roma**

we are broadcasting from our Rome studios.

studiosamente [studjosa'mente] AVV (*con diligenza*) diligently; (*a bella posta*) carefully.

studioso, a [stu'djoso] ① AGG studious, hardworking.

② SM/F scholar.

stufa ['stufa] SF (*gen*) stove; (*elettrica*) electric fire *o* heater; **stufa a legna/carbone** wood-burning/coal stove.

stufare [stu'fare] ① VT a (*Culin*) to stew b (*fig fam*) to bore, weary; **mi avete proprio stufato con le vostre lamentele** I am really fed up with your moaning; **mi hai proprio stufato** I am really fed up with you.

② **stufarsi** VIP: **stufarsi (di)** to grow weary (of); **si è stufato di ascoltarlo** he got fed up listening to him.

stufato [stu'fato] SM (*Culin*) stew.

stufo, a ['stufo] AGG (*fam*): **essere stufo (di)** to be fed up (with), be sick and tired (of).

stuoia ['stwɔja] SF (*tappeto*) mat; (*tessuto*) rush matting.

stuolo ['stwɔlo] SM crowd, host.

stupefacente [stupefa'tʃɛnte] ① AGG amazing, astounding.

② SM drug, narcotic.

stupefare [stupe'fare] VT IRREG to stun, astound.

stupefatto, a [stupe'fatto] PP di **stupefare**.

stupefazione [stupefat'tsjone] SF astonishment.

stupendo, a [stu'pɛndo] AGG marvellous, wonderful.

stupidaggine [stupi'daddʒine] SF (*qualità*) stupidity, foolishness; (*atto, discorso*): **dire una stupidaggine** to say something stupid; **dire stupidaggini** to talk nonsense; **fare una stupidaggine** to do something stupid; **ti ho preso una stupidaggine** (*regalino*) I bought you a little something.

stupidamente [stupida'mente] AVV stupidly; **ho sbagliato stupidamente** I made a stupid mistake.

stupidità [stupidi'ta] SF (*qualità*) stupidity.

stupido, a ['stupido] ① AGG stupid.

② SM/F fool, idiot.

stupire [stu'pire] ① VT to amaze, stun.

② VI (*aus* **essere**), **stupirsi** VIP to be amazed (at), be stunned (by); **non c'è da stupirsi** it's not surprising.

stupito, a [stu'pito] AGG amazed.

stupore [stu'pore] SM amazement, astonishment.

stuprare [stu'prare] VT to rape.

stupratore [stupra'tore] SM rapist.

stupro ['stupro] SM rape.

sturare [stu'rare] VT (*lavandino*) to unblock; (*bottiglia*) to uncork; **sturati le orecchie!** (*fig*) clean your ears out!

stuzzicadenti [stuttsika'dɛnti] SM INV toothpick; (*fig: persona magra*) beanpole.

stuzzicante [stuttsi'kante] AGG (*gen*) stimulating; (*appetitoso*) appetizing; **che idea stuzzicante** what a nice idea.

stuzzicare [stuttsi'kare] VT (*ferita*) to poke (at), prod (at); (*fig: persona*) to tease; (: *appetito*) to whet; (: *curiosità*) to stimulate; **stuzzicarsi i denti** to pick one's teeth.

stuzzichino [stuttsi'kino] SM (*Culin*) appetizer.

---

su [su]
① PREP

| su + il=**sul**, su + lo=**sullo**, su + l'=**sull'**, su + la=**sulla**, su + i=**sui**, su + gli=**sugli**, su + le=**sulle** |

a (*gen*) on; (*moto*) on(to); (*in cima a*) on (top of); ▷**non è mai stato su un** *aereo* he's never been in a plane

▷**puntare una somma su un** *cavallo* to bet a sum on a horse
▷**è sulla** *destra* it's on the right
▷**conto su** *di te* I'm counting on you
▷**fa errori su** *errori* he makes one mistake after another
▷**fece fuoco sulla** *folla* he fired on the crowd
▷**la finestra dà sul** *giardino* the window looks onto the garden
▷**l'ho visto sul** *giornale* I saw it in the paper
▷**fecero rotta su** *Palermo* they set out towards Palermo
▷**gettarsi sulla** *preda* to throw o.s. on one's prey
▷**la marcia su** *Roma* the march on Rome
▷**mettilo sulla** *scrivania* put it on the desk
▷**ricamo su** *seta* embroidery on silk
▷**procedi sulla** *sinistra* keep on o to the left
▷**sta sulle** *sue* he keeps to himself
▷**è salito sul** *tavolo* he got up on(to) the table
▷**olio su** *tela* oil on canvas
▷**basare un argomento su** to base an argument on
▷**il libro è sul** *tavolo* the book is on the table
b (*addosso*) over;
▷**buttati uno scialle sulle** *spalle* throw a shawl over o round your shoulders
▷**sul** *vestito* **indossava un golf rosso** she was wearing a red sweater over her dress
c (*da una parte all'altra*) over;
▷**un ponte sul** *fiume* a bridge over the river
▷**un aereo passò sulle nostre** *teste* an aeroplane flew over our heads
d (*autorità, dominio*) over;
▷**non ha alcun potere su** *di lui* he has no power over him
e (*più in alto di*) above;
▷**100 metri sul** *livello* **del mare** 100 metres above sea level
f (*argomento*) about, on;
▷**discutere su un** *argomento* to discuss a subject
▷**un articolo sulla prima** *guerra* **mondiale** an article on o about the First World War
▷**una conferenza sulla** *pace* **nel mondo** a conference on o about world peace
g (*circa*) about, around;
▷**è costato sui trenta** *milioni* it cost about thirty million lire
▷**c'erano sulle 100** *persone* there were about 100 people
▷**sarà sulla** *sessantina* he must be about sixty
h (*proporzione*) out of, in;
▷**50 su 100 hanno votato contro** 50 out of 100 voted against (it)
▷**2 giorni su 3** 2 days out of 3, 2 days in 3
▷**uno su tre** one in three
▷**5 su 10** (*voto*) 5 out of 10
i (*modo*)
▷**scarpe su** *misura* handmade shoes
▷**spedire qc su** *richiesta* to send sth on request.
2 AVV
a (*in alto, verso l'alto*) up; (*al piano superiore*) upstairs;
▷*guarda* **su** look up
▷*lì* **su** up there
▷**su le** *mani*! hands up!
▷*qui* **su** up here

▷**era su che ci aspettava** he was waiting for us upstairs
b (*in poi*) onwards;
▷**dal numero 39** *in* **su** from number 39 onwards
▷**dai 20 anni** *in* **su** from the age of 20 onwards
▷**prezzi dalle diecimila lire** *in* **su** prices from ten thousand lire (upwards)
c (*addosso*) on;
▷**cos'***hai* **su?** what have you got on?
▷**aveva su una strana tunica** she had a strange tunic on
▷**posso** *metterlo* **su?** can I put it on?
d (*fraseologia*)
▷**su** *coraggio*! come on, cheer up!
▷**andare su** *e giù* to go up and down
▷**andava su** *e giù* **per il corridoio** he paced up and down the corridor
▷**su** *per giù* **= suppergiù**
▷**su** *smettila*! come on, that's enough of that!
▷**su** *su* **non fare così!** now, now, don't behave like that!
▷**su** *svelto*! come on, hurry up!
▷*venir* **su dal niente** to rise from nothing.

sua ['sua] vedi **suo**.
suadente [sua'dɛnte] AGG persuasive.
sub [sub] **1** SM/F INV skin-diver. **2** SM (*sport*) skin diving.
subacqueo, a [su'bakkweo] **1** AGG underwater *attr.* **2** SM skin-diver.
subaffittare [subaffit'tare] VT to sublet.
subaffitto [subaf'fitto] SM (*contratto*) sublet.
subalterno, a [subal'tɛrno] AGG, SM (*gen*) subordinate; (*Mil*) subaltern.
subappaltare [subappal'tare] VT to subcontract.
subappalto [subap'palto] SM subcontract.
subatomico, a, ci, che [suba'tɔmiko] AGG subatomic.
subbuglio [sub'buʎʎo] SM confusion, turmoil; **essere/mettere in subbuglio** to be in/throw into a turmoil.
subconscio, scia, sci, scie [sub'kɔnʃo], **subcosciente** [subkoʃ'ʃɛnte] AGG, SM subconscious.
subdolamente [subdola'mente] AVV in an underhand manner.
subdolo, a ['subdolo] AGG sneaky, underhand.
subentrare [suben'trare] VI (*aus* **essere**): **è subentrato a suo padre nella direzione della ditta** he took over from his father as director of the firm; **alla sorpresa subentrò la paura** surprise gave way to fear; **sono subentrati altri problemi** other problems have arisen.
subequatoriale [subekwato'rjale] AGG subequatorial.
subire [su'bire] VT (*gen*) to suffer, endure; (*operazione*) to undergo; **subire un interrogatorio** to undergo an interrogation, be interrogated; **subire una tortura** to be tortured; **ha dovuto subire e tacere** he had to suffer in silence; **per quanto ancora dobbiamo subire questo despota?** for how long must we put up with this despot?
subissare [subis'sare] VT: **subissare qn di** (*domande, richieste*) to overwhelm with; (*doni, lodi*) to shower sb with.
subitamente [subita'mente] AVV suddenly.
subitaneo, a [subi'taneo] AGG sudden.
subito ['subito] AVV immediately, at once, straight away; **torno subito** I'll be right back; **è subito fatto** it's easily done.

sublimare [subli'mare] VT (*Rel, fig*) to exalt; (*Psic*) to sublimate; (*Chim*) to sublime.

sublimazione [sublimat'tsjone] SF (*Rel, fig*) exaltation; (*Psic, Chim*) sublimation.

sublime [su'blime] AGG, SM sublime.

sublimemente [sublime'mente] AVV sublimely.

sublocare [sublo'kare] VT to sublease.

sublocazione [sublokat'tsjone] SF sublease.

subnormale [subnor'male] ⬜1 AGG subnormal.

⬜2 SM/F mentally handicapped person.

subodorare [subodo'rare] VT (*insidia*) to smell, suspect.

subordinare [subordi'nare] VT to subordinate.

subordinata [subordi'nata] SF (*Gramm*) subordinate clause.

subordinato, a [subordi'nato] AGG (*gen, Gramm*) subordinate; (*dipendente*): **subordinato a** dependent on, subject to.

subordinazione [subordinat'tsjone] SF subordination.

subordine [su'bordine] SM: **in subordine** secondarily.

subsonico, a, ci, che [sub'soniko] AGG subsonic.

substrato [sub'strato] SM (*gen*) substrate, substratum; (*Bio, Chim: di enzima*) substrate.

subtropicale [subtropi'kale] AGG subtropical.

suburbano, a [subur'bano] AGG suburban.

succedaneo, a [suttʃe'daneo] ⬜1 AGG substitute *attr*

⬜2 SM substitute.

succedere [sut'tʃedere] VB IRREG ⬜1 VI (*aus* **essere**) **a** (*accadere*) to happen; **sapessi cosa mi è successo!** wait till you hear what happened to me!; **cosa ti succede?** what's the matter with you?; **sono cose che succedono** these things happen

b: **succedere a** (*seguire: persona*) to succeed; (*venire dopo*) to follow; **succedere al trono** to succeed to the throne.

⬜2 **succedersi** VIP to follow each other; **i mesi si succedevano lenti** the months dragged on.

successione [suttʃes'sjone] SF succession; **imposta di successione** death duty (*Brit*), inheritance tax (*Am*).

successivamente [suttʃessiva'mente] AVV (*in seguito*) later, subsequently.

successivo, a [suttʃes'sivo] AGG (*continuo*) successive; (*che segue*) following; **il giorno successivo** the following *o* next day; **in un momento successivo** subsequently.

successo, a [sut'tʃɛsso] ⬜1 PP di **succedere**.

⬜2 SM (*gen*) success; (*disco*) hit; (*libro*) bestseller; (*film*) box-office success, hit; **arrivare al successo** to become a success; **avere successo** (*persona*) to be successful; (*idea*) to be well received; **non ho avuto successo** I was unsuccessful; **ho provato, ma senza successo** I tried, but without success, I tried in vain; **di successo** (*attore, cantante*) successful; **canzone di successo** hit (song).

successore [suttʃes'sore] ⬜1 AGG successive.

⬜2 SM successor.

succhiare [suk'kjare] VT (*gen*) to suck (up); **succhiare il sangue a qn** (*fig*) to bleed sb dry.

succhiello [suk'kjɛllo] SM gimlet.

succhiotto [suk'kjɔtto] SM (*tettarella*) dummy (*Brit*), pacifier (*Am*), comforter (*Am*); (*fam: segno sul collo*) lovebite, hickey (*Am*).

succintamente [suttʃinta'mente] AVV (*parlare*) succinctly; (*vestito*) scantily.

succinto, a [sut'tʃinto] AGG (*discorso*) succinct; (*abito*) scanty.

succo, chi ['sukko] SM (*Anat, di frutto*) juice; (*fig: della conferenza*) gist; **il succo del discorso** (*fig*) the essence of the speech ▸ **succo di frutta** fruit juice ▸ **succo di pomodoro** tomato juice.

succosità [sukkosi'ta] SF juiciness; (*fig*) pithiness.

succoso, a [suk'koso] AGG juicy; (*fig*) pithy.

succube ['sukkube] SM/F victim; **essere succube di qn** to be dominated by sb, be under sb's thumb.

succulento, a [sukku'lɛnto] AGG (*sugoso*) succulent; (*gustoso: pranzo, cibo*) tasty.

succulenza [sukku'lɛntsa] SF (*vedi agg*) succulence; tastiness.

succursale [sukkur'sale] SF branch (office).

sud [sud] ⬜1 SM south; **a sud (di)** south (of); **esposto a sud** facing south; **verso sud** south, southwards; **i mari del Sud** the South Seas; **l'Italia del Sud** Southern Italy; **l'America del Sud** South America.

⬜2 AGG INV (*gen*) south; (*regione*) southern; **partirono in direzione sud** they set off southwards *o* in a southerly direction, they headed south.

Sudafrica [su'dafrika] SM: **il Sudafrica** South Africa.

sudafricano, a [sudafri'kano] AGG, SM/F South African.

Sudamerica [suda'merika] SM: **il Sudamerica** South America.

sudamericano, a [sudameri'kano] AGG, SM/F South American.

Sudan [su'dan] SM: **il Sudan** (the) Sudan.

sudanese [suda'nese] AGG, SM/F Sudanese *inv*.

sudare [su'dare] ⬜1 VI (*aus* **avere**) to perspire, sweat; **ho dovuto sudare per finire quella traduzione** (*fig*) I had to work hard to finish that translation; **mi ha fatto sudare** (*fig*) he made me work hard; **sudare freddo** (*anche fig*) to come out in a cold sweat.

⬜2 VT to work hard for; **sudarsi il pane** to earn one's bread by the sweat of one's brow.

sudario, ri [su'darjo] SM shroud.

sudata [su'data] SF (*anche fig*) sweat; **ho fatto una bella sudata per finire in tempo** (*fig*) it was a real sweat to finish in time.

sudaticcio, cia, ci, ce [suda'tittʃo] AGG sweaty, damp.

sudato, a [su'dato] AGG (*persona, mani*) sweaty; (*fig: denaro*) hard-earned; **una vittoria sudata** a hard-won victory.

suddetto, a [sud'detto] AGG above-mentioned *attr*.

suddiaconato [suddiako'nato] SM subdiaconate.

suddiacono [suddi'akono] SM subdeacon.

sudditanza [suddi'tantsa] SF subjection.

suddito, a ['suddito] SM/F subject.

suddividere [suddi'videre] VT IRREG to subdivide.

suddivisione [suddivi'zjone] SF subdivision.

suddiviso, a [suddi'vizo] PP di **suddividere**.

sud-est [su'dest] SM south-east; **vento di sud-est** south-easterly wind ▸ **il sud-est asiatico** South-East Asia.

sudiceria [suditʃe'ria] SF (*qualità*) filthiness, dirtiness; (*cosa sporca*) dirty thing; **libro pieno di sudicerie** filthy *o* obscene book.

sudicio, cia, ci, ce ['suditʃo] ⬜1 AGG dirty, filthy; (*fig: indecente*) dirty, filthy, indecent; (: *disonesto*) dirty.

⬜2 SM (*anche fig*) dirt, filth.

sudicione, a [sudi'tʃone] SM/F (*anche fig*) filthy person, pig (*fam*).

sudiciume [sudi'tʃume] SM (*anche fig*) dirt, filth.

sudore [su'dore] SM perspiration, sweat; **essere in un bagno di sudore** to be bathed in sweat; **col sudore della propria fronte** (*fig*) with the sweat of one's brow.

sudoriparo, a [sudo'riparo] AGG: **ghiandola sudoripara** sweat gland.

sud-ovest [su'dɔvest] SM south-west; **vento di sud-ovest** south-westerly wind.

sue ['sue] vedi **suo.**

Suez ['suez] SF: **il canale di Suez** the Suez Canal.

sufficiente [suffi'tʃɛnte] ① AGG **a** (adeguato) sufficient, enough; (abbastanza) enough; (voto) satisfactory; **questo fu sufficiente a farlo tacere** that was enough to shut him up; **non c'è spazio sufficiente per tutti** there is not enough room for everyone; **credi sia sufficiente?** do you think that will do?; **è più che sufficiente** it is more than enough

b (borioso) self-important.

② SM: **avere il sufficiente per vivere** to have enough to live on.

sufficientemente [suffitʃɛnte'mente] AVV (guadagnare, darsi da fare) enough; **sufficientemente bene** well enough, sufficiently well.

sufficienza [suffi'tʃɛntsa] SF **a** : **ne ho a sufficienza** I have got plenty; **ne ho avuto a sufficienza!** (sono stufo) I've had enough of this!; **ce ne sono a sufficienza** there are enough **b** : **con un'aria di sufficienza** (fig) with a condescending air **c** (Scol) pass mark.

suffisso [suf'fisso] SM (Gramm) suffix.

suffragare [suffra'gare] VT (fig: affermazioni) to support.

suffragetta [suffra'dʒetta] SF suffragette.

suffragio, gi [suf'fradʒo] SM **a** (Pol: voto) vote ▶ **suffragio universale** universal suffrage **b** (Rel) intercession; **messa di suffragio** mass for somebody's soul.

suggellare [suddʒel'lare] VT (anche fig) to seal.

suggello [sud'dʒello] SM (anche fig) seal.

suggerimento [suddʒeri'mento] SM suggestion, hint; **dietro suo suggerimento** on his advice.

suggerire [suddʒe'rire] VT (gen) to suggest; (soluzione) to suggest, put forward; (Teatro) to prompt; **suggerirei di trovarci lì** I'd suggest that we meet there, I'd suggest meeting there; **suggerire a qn di fare qc** to suggest to sb that he (o she) do (o should do) sth; **mi ha suggerito un periodo di riposo** he advised me to take some time off; **non suggerire!** (in classe) don't whisper the answer!

suggeritore, trice [suddʒeri'tore] SM/F (Teatro) prompter.

suggestionare [suddʒestjo'nare] ① VT to influence; **non lasciarti suggestionare da quello che dice** don't let yourself be influenced by what he says.

② **suggestionarsi** VIP to be influenced.

suggestione [suddʒes'tjone] SF (Psic) suggestion; (fascino) fascination.

suggestivamente [suddʒestiva'mente] AVV evocatively.

suggestivo, a [suddʒes'tivo] AGG (paesaggio) evocative; (veduta) enchanting; (teoria) interesting, attractive.

sughero ['sugero] SM (gen) cork; (albero) cork oak; **tappo di sughero** cork.

sugli ['suʎʎi] PREP + ART vedi **su.**

sugna ['suɲɲa] SF lard.

sugo, ghi ['sugo] SM (succo) juice; (di carne) gravy; (per pastasciutta) sauce; (fig: del discorso) essence; **senza sugo** (fig: persona) insipid, wishy-washy; (discorso) pointless, senseless.

sugoso, a [su'goso] AGG (frutto) juicy; (fig: articolo) pithy.

sui ['sui] PREP + ART vedi **su.**

suicida, i, e [sui'tʃida] ① AGG suicidal.

② SM/F suicide (person).

suicidarsi [suitʃi'darsi] VR to commit suicide.

suicidio, di [sui'tʃidjo] SM suicide (action).

suino, a [su'ino] ① AGG: **carne suina** pork.

② SM pig; **i suini** swine pl.

sul [sul] PREP + ART vedi **su.**

sulfamidico, a, ci, che [sulfa'midiko] AGG, SM sulphonamide attr.

sulfureo, a [sul'fureo] AGG sulphur attr (Brit), sulfur attr (Am).

sulky ['sʌlki] SM INV (Ippica) sulky.

sull' [sull], **sulla** ['sulla], **sulle** ['sulle], **sullo** ['sullo] PREP + ART vedi **su.**

sultanina [sulta'nina] SF: (uva) **sultanina** sultana.

sultano, a [sul'tano] SM/F sultan/sultana.

Sumatra [su'matra] SF Sumatra.

summa ['summa] SF (Rel, Filosofia) summa.

summit ['summit] SM INV summit.

S.U.N.I.A. [su'nia] SIGLA M (= sindacato unitario nazionale inquilini e assegnatari) national association of tenants.

sunnominato, a [sunnomi'nato] AGG aforesaid attr.

sunto ['sunto] SM summary; **fare il sunto di qc** to summarize sth.

suo¹, a ['suo] (pl suoi, sue) ① AGG POSS: **il(la) suo(a)** (maschile) his; (femminile) her; (neutro) its; **il suo giardino** his (o her) garden; **sua madre** his (o her) mother; **suo padre** his (o her) father; **un suo amico** a friend of his (o hers); **è colpa sua** it's his (o her) fault; **è casa sua** OR **è la sua casa** it's his (o her) house; **per amor suo** for love of him (o her); **Sua Altezza** His (o Her) Highness.

② PRON POSS: **il(la) suo(a)** (maschile) his, his own; (femminile) hers, her own; (neutro) its, its own; **la mia barca è più lunga della sua** my boat is longer than his (o hers); **il suo è stato solo un errore** it was simply an error on his (o her) part.

③ PRON POSS M **a** : **ha speso del suo** he (o she) spent his (o her) own money; **vive del suo** he (o she) lives on his (o her) own income

b : **i suoi** SMPL (genitori, famiglia) his (o her) family; (amici) his (o her) own people, his (o her) side; **lui è dei suoi** he is on his (o her) side.

④ PRON POSS F: **la sua** (opinione) his (o her) view; **è dalla sua** (parte) he's on his (o her) side; **anche lui ha avuto le sue** (disavventure) he's had his problems too; **sta sulle sue** he keeps himself to himself.

suo², a ['suo] (pl suoi, sue) (forma di cortesia: anche: Suo) ① AGG POSS: **il(la) suo(a)** your; **il suo ombrello, signore!** your umbrella, sir!; **Sua Altezza** Your Highness; **suo devotissimo** (in lettere) your devoted servant.

② PRON POSS: **il(la) suo(a)** yours, your own; **la sua è pura scortesia** that's sheer discourtesy on your part.

③ PRON POSS M: **ha speso del suo?** did you spend your own money?.

④ PRON POSS F: **la sua** (opinione) your view; **è dalla sua** he's on your side; **alla sua!** your very good health!

suocera ['swɔtʃera] SF mother-in-law.

suocero ['swɔtʃero] SM father-in-law; **i suoceri** father-and mother-in-law.

suoi ['swɔi] vedi **suo.**

suola ['swɔla] SF (di scarpa) sole; **rifare le suole alle scarpe** to have one's shoes resoled.

suolo ['swɔlo] SM (terreno) ground; (terra) soil; **cadde al suolo** he fell to the ground; **in suolo italiano** on Italian soil.

suonare [swo'nare] ① VT (strumento, pezzo musicale) to

play; (*campana, campanello*) to ring; (*clacson, allarme, ritirata*) to sound; **l'orologio ha suonato le cinque** the clock struck five; **ha suonato il clacson** he sounded the horn; **gliele ho suonate** (*fam*) I gave him a thrashing.

2 VI (*aus* **avere**) (*musicista*) to play; (*campane, campanello, telefono*) to ring; (*ore*) to strike; (*fig: discorso*) to sound, ring; **le campane suonano a morto** the bells are sounding a death knell; **mi suona strano** (*fig*) it sounds strange to me.

suonato, a [swo'nato] AGG **a** (*compiuto*): **ha cinquant'anni suonati** he is well over fifty **b** (*Pugilato*) punch-drunk; (*fig fam*: *rimbambito*) soft in the head.

suonatore, trice [swona'tore] SM/F player ▶ **suonatore ambulante** street musician.

suoneria [swone'ria] SF alarm.

suono ['swɔno] SM (*gen*) sound; (*di campane*) sound, ringing; **ballare al suono di un'orchestra** to dance to the music of an orchestra; **lo accolsero a suon di fischi** they booed and jeered him as he arrived.

suora ['swɔra] SF (*Rel*) nun; **Suor Maria** Sister Maria.

super ['super] 1 AGG INV: **(benzina) super** four-star (petrol) (*Brit*), premium (*Am*).

2 PREF super..., over... .

superaffollamento [superaffolla'mento] SM overcrowding.

superaffollato, a [superaffol'lato] AGG overcrowded.

superalcolico, a, ci, che [superal'kɔliko] 1 AGG alcoholic (*of drink made with distilled alcohol*).

2 SM: **i superalcolici** spirits, liquors.

superalimentazione [superalimentat'tsjone] SF overfeeding.

superamento [supera'mento] SM (*di ostacolo*) overcoming; (*di montagna*) crossing; **arrivare al superamento di** (*idee, dottrine*) to move on from.

superare [supe'rare] VT (*limite, aspettative*) to exceed; (*traguardo, montagne*) to cross; (*esame*) to pass; (*muro*) to get over; (*fig: ostacolo, malattia, paura*) to overcome; (: *rivale*) to beat, surpass, outdo; (*Aut: sorpassare*) to overtake; **superare i limiti di velocità** to exceed the speed limit; **superare qn in altezza/peso** to be taller/ heavier than sb; **ha superato la cinquantina** he's over fifty (years of age); **stavolta ha superato se stesso** this time he has surpassed himself.

superato, a [supe'rato] AGG outmoded.

superattico, ci [supe'rattiko] SM penthouse.

superbamente [superba'mente] AVV **a** (*vantarsi*) proudly; (*comportarsi, rispondere*) haughtily **b** (*magnificamente*) superbly, magnificently.

superbia [su'pɛrbja] SF pride.

superbo, a [su'pɛrbo] 1 AGG **a** (*persona*) proud, haughty **b** (*fig: grandioso, splendido*) superb, magnificent.

2 SM/F haughty person.

supercarcere [super'kartʃere] SM maximum security prison.

superconduttività [superkonduttivi'ta] SF superconductivity.

superconduttore [superkondut'tore] SM superconductor.

superdonna [super'dɔnna] SF (*iro*) superwoman.

superdotato, a [superdo'tato] 1 AGG highly gifted.

2 SM/F highly gifted person.

Super-Ego [super'ɛgo] SM INV (*Psic*) superego.

superficiale [superfi'tʃale] 1 AGG (*gen*) superficial; **acque superficiali** surface water *sg*.

2 SM/F superficial person.

superficialità [superfitʃali'ta] SF superficiality.

superficialmente [superfitʃal'mente] AVV superficially.

superficie [super'fitʃe] SF **a** (*di muro, specchio*) surface; **superficie terrestre** surface of the earth; **tornare in superficie** (*a galla*) to return to the surface; (*fig: problemi*) to resurface; **non va mai oltre la superficie delle cose** he has a superficial approach

b (*area*) surface area ▶ **superficie alare** (*Aer*) wing area ▶ **superficie velica** (*Naut*) sail area.

superfluità [superflui'ta] SF INV (*vedi agg*) superfluity; unnecessariness; **le superfluità** the extras.

superfluo, a [su'pɛrfluo] 1 AGG (*gen*) superfluous; (*spese*) unnecessary; **peli superflui** unwanted hair *sg*.

2 SM surplus.

Super-Io [super'io] SM INV (*Psic*) superego.

superiora [supe'rjora] SF (*Rel*: *anche*: **madre superiora**) mother superior.

superiore [supe'rjore] 1 AGG **a** (*intelligenza, qualità*) superior; (*numero*) greater; (*quantità, somma*) larger; **intelligenza superiore alla media** above-average intelligence; **è superiore alle mie forze** it's beyond me; **sono superiore a queste cose** I'm above such things

b (*che sta più in alto: rami, classe*) upper; (*livello*) higher; **il corso superiore di un fiume** the upper reaches *pl* of a river; **al piano superiore** on the upper floor; (*di edificio a più piani*) on the floor above; **scuola superiore** OR **scuole superiori** ≈ secondary school (*Brit*), senior high (school) (*Am*); **istruzione superiore** higher education; **per ordine superiore** on orders from above.

2 SM superior.

3 SFPL (*Scol*): **le superiori** ≈ secondary school (*Brit*), ≈ senior high (school) (*Am*).

superiorità [superjori'ta] SF INV superiority; **ha dimostrato una netta superiorità sull'avversario** he was clearly superior to his opponent; **aria di superiorità** air of superiority.

superiormente [superjor'mente] AVV on the upper part.

superlativo, a [superla'tivo] AGG, SM (*gen, Gramm*) superlative.

superlavoro [superla'voro] SM overwork.

supermercato [supermer'kato] SM, **supermarket** [super'market] SM INV supermarket.

supernova, ae [super'nɔva] SF (*Astron*) supernova.

superpotenza [superpo'tentsa] SF (*Pol*) superpower.

supersonico, a, ci, che [super'sɔniko] AGG supersonic.

superstite [su'pɛrstite] 1 AGG surviving.

2 SM/F survivor.

superstizione [superstit'tsjone] SF superstition.

superstizioso, a [superstit'tsjoso] 1 AGG superstitious.

2 SM/F superstitious person.

superstrada [super'strada] SF ≈ motorway (*Brit*), ≈ expressway (*Am*).

supertestimone [supertesti'mone] SM/F star witness.

superuomo [supe'rwɔmo] SM (*pl* **-uomini**) superman.

supervisione [supervi'zjone] SF supervision.

supervisore [supervi'zore] SM supervisor.

supino, a [su'pino] AGG supine; **dormire supino** to sleep on one's back; **accettazione supina** (*fig*) blind acceptance.

suppellettile [suppel'lɛttile] SF (*gen*) ornaments *pl*; (*arredo*) furnishings *pl*; (*Archeol*) grave goods.

suppergiù [supper'dʒu] AVV roughly, more or less, approximately.

suppl. ABBR (= *supplemento*) supp(l).

supplementare [supplemen'tare] AGG **1** (*gen*) extra; (*entrate*) additional; (*treno*) relief *attr*; **tempi supplementari** (*Sport*) extra time *sg* **b** (*Geom*) supplementary.

supplemento [supple'mento] SM supplement.

supplente [sup'plɛnte] **1** AGG (*insegnante*) supply *attr* (*Brit*), substitute *attr* (*Am*).
2 SM/F supply *o* substitute teacher.

supplenza [sup'plɛntsa] SF (*Scol*): **fare supplenza** to do supply (*Brit*) *o* substitute (*Am*) teaching; **ha avuto una supplenza di un anno** he's been asked to do a year's supply *o* substitute teaching.

suppletivo, a [supple'tivo] AGG (*gen*) supplementary; (*sessione d'esami*) extra.

supplì [sup'pli] SM INV (*Culin*) rice croquette.

supplica, che ['supplika] SF (*Rel, fig*) supplication, plea; **con un tono di supplica** in an imploring voice.

supplicare [suppli'kare] VT to implore, beseech; **ti supplico, non andartene** don't go, I beg you.

supplichevole [suppli'kevole] AGG imploring.

supplichevolmente [supplikevol'mente] AVV imploringly.

supplire [sup'plire] **1** VT to stand in for, replace temporarily.
2 VI (*aus avere*): **supplire a** (*difetto, mancanza*) to make up for, compensate for.

supplizio, zi [sup'plittsjo] SM (*tortura*) torture; (*fig*) torment; **fu condotto al supplizio** (*a morte*) he was led to execution.

suppongo [sup'pongo], **supponi** ecc [sup'poni] VB vedi **supporre**.

supporre [sup'porre] VT IRREG (*gen*) to suppose; **supponiamo che...** let's *o* just suppose that ...; **suppongo che sia lo stesso** I imagine it's the same; **suppongo di sì/di no** I suppose so/not.

supporto [sup'porto] SM (*sostegno*) support; (*struttura*) stand, holder.

supposizione [suppozit'tsjone] SF supposition; **le mie sono solo supposizioni** I'm only guessing; **è una supposizione infondata** it's a groundless assumption.

supposta [sup'posta] SF (*Med*) suppository.

supposto [sup'posto] **1** PP di **supporre**.
2: **supposto che...** CONG supposing that ... .

suppurare [suppu'rare] VI (*aus avere*) to suppurate.

suppurazione [suppurat'tsjone] SF suppuration.

supremazia [supremat'tsia] SF supremacy.

supremo, a [su'prɛmo] AGG (*gen*) supreme; **con supremo disprezzo** with the utmost contempt; **l'ora suprema** (*fig*) one's last hour; **il giudizio supremo** (*Rel*) the Last Judgement.

surclassare [surklas'sare] VT to outclass.

surgelamento [surdʒela'mento] SM (deep-)freezing.

surgelare [surdʒe'lare] VT to (deep-)freeze.

surgelato, a [surdʒe'lato] **1** AGG (deep-)frozen.
2 SMPL: **i surgelati** frozen food *sg*.

surmenage [syrmə'naʒ] SM INV (*fisico*) overwork; (*mentale*) mental strain; (*Sport*) overtraining.

surplus [syr'ply] SM INV (*Econ*) surplus ▶ **surplus di manodopera** overmanning.

surreale [surre'ale] AGG surrealistic.

surrenale [surre'nale] SF (*Anat: anche*: **ghiandola surrenale**) adrenal gland.

surriscaldamento [surriskalda'mento] SM (*gen, Tecn*) overheating.

surriscaldare [surriskal'dare] VT, VIP, **surriscaldarsi** (*gen,*

Tecn) to overheat.

surriscaldato, a [surriskal'dato] AGG overheated.

surrogato, a [surro'gato] AGG, SM substitute *attr*.

suscettibile [suʃʃet'tibile] AGG **a** (*permaloso*) touchy, sensitive **b**: **suscettibile di** (*cambiamento*) subject to; **suscettibile di miglioramento** open to improvement.

suscettibilità [suʃʃettibili'ta] SF touchiness; **urtare la suscettibilità di qn** to hurt sb's feelings.

suscitare [suʃʃi'tare] VT (*provocare*) to cause, provoke; (*destare: ira*) to arouse; **suscitare uno scroscio di applausi** to provoke thunderous applause.

susina [su'sina] SF plum.

susino [su'sino] SM plum (tree).

suspense [səs'pens] SF INV suspense.

susseguire [susse'gwire] **1** VT, VI (*aus essere*) to follow; **da ciò sussegue che...** it follows that ....
2 **susseguirsi** VR (*uso reciproco*) to succeed each other, follow each other; **le sorprese continuavano a susseguirsi** there was a continual succession of surprises.

sussidiario, ria, ri, rie [sussi'djarjo] AGG (*gen*) subsidiary; (*fermata*) request, (*nave*) supply *attr*.

sussidio, di [sus'sidjo] SM **a** (*aiuto*) aid ▶ **sussidi audiovisiv** audiovisual aids ▶ **sussidi didattici** teaching aids **b** (*sovvenzione*) subsidy ▶ **sussidio di disoccupazione** unemployment benefit (*Brit*) *o* benefits *pl* (*Am*) ▶ **sussidio per malattia** sickness benefit.

sussiego [sus'sjɛgo] SM haughtiness; **con aria di sussiego** haughtily.

sussistenza [sussis'tɛntsa] SF **a** (*esistenza*) existence **b** (*sostentamento*) subsistence; **mezzi di sussistenza** means of substinence **c** (*Mil*) provisioning.

sussistere [sus'sistere] VI (*aus essere*) (*esistere*) to exist; (*essere fondato: motivi*) to be valid *o* sound.

sussultare [sussul'tare] VI (*aus avere*) (*per spavento*) to start.

sussulto [sus'sulto] SM start; **dare** *o* **avere un sussulto** to give a start, start.

sussurrare [sussur'rare] **1** VT to whisper; **gli sussurrò qualcosa all'orecchio** he whispered something in his ear; **si sussurra che...** it's rumoured (*Brit*) *o* rumored (*Am*) that ....
2 VI (*aus avere*) (*fronde*) to rustle; (*acque*) to murmur.

sussurro [sus'surro] SM (*vedi vb*) whisper; rustle; murmur.

sutura [su'tura] SF (*Med*) suture.

suturare [sutu'rare] VT (*Med*) to stitch up, suture.

suvvia [suv'via] ESCL come on!

suzione [sut'tsjone] SF sucking.

SV SIGLA = *Savona*.

S.V. ABBR = **Signoria Vostra**.

svagare [zva'gare] **1** VT (*divertire*) to amuse; (*distrarre*): **svagare qn** to take sb's mind off things.
2 **svagarsi** VR (*divertirsi*) to amuse o.s.; (*distrarsi*) to take one's mind off things.

svagato, a [zva'gato] AGG (*persona*) absent-minded; (*scolaro*) inattentive.

svago, ghi ['zvago] SM (*riposo*) relaxation; (*passatempo*) pastime, amusement; **l'ho fatto per svago** I did it just to pass the time.

svaligiare [zvali'dʒare] VT (*banca*) to rob; (*casa*) burgle (*Brit*), burglarize (*Am*).

svaligiatore, trice [zvalidʒa'tore] SM/F (*di banca*) robber; (*di casa*) burglar.

svalutare [zvalu'tare] **1** VT (*Econ*) to devalue; (*fig*) to belittle.

2 **svalutarsi** VIP (*Econ*) to be devalued.

svalutazione [zvalutat'tsjone] SF (*Econ*) devaluation.

svampito, a [zvam'pito] 1 AGG absent-minded.

2 SM/F absent-minded person.

svanire [zva'nire] VI (*aus* **essere**) (*anche fig*) to disappear, vanish; (*rumore*) to fade; **svanire nel nulla** to disappear *o* vanish completely.

svanito, a [zva'nito] 1 AGG (*fig: persona*) absent-minded.

2 SM/F absent-minded person.

svantaggiato, a [zvantad'dʒato] AGG at a disadvantage.

svantaggio, gi [zvan'taddʒo] SM disadvantage; (*inconveniente*) drawback, disadvantage; **tornerà a suo svantaggio** it will work against you; **sono in svantaggio rispetto a te** you have an advantage over me; **essere in svantaggio di due gol** (*Calcio*) to be two goals down; **essere in svantaggio di due minuti** (*Sport*) to be two minutes behind.

svantaggiosamente [zvantaddʒosa'mente] AVV disadvantageously.

svantaggioso, a [zvantad'dʒoso] AGG disadvantageous; **è un'offerta svantaggiosa per me** it is not in my interest to accept this offer; **è un prezzo svantaggioso** it is not an attractive price.

svaporare [zvapo'rare] VI (*aus* **essere**) to evaporate.

svaporato, a [zvapo'rato] AGG (*bibita*) flat.

svariatamente [zvarjata'mente] AVV: **un tessuto svariatamente colorato** a multicoloured fabric.

svariato, a [zva'rjato] AGG (*numeroso*) various; (*vario, diverso*) varied; **di questa macchina esistono svariati modelli** this car comes in a variety of models.

svasare [zva'zare] VT **a** (*pianta*) to repot **b** (*Cucito: gonna*) to flare.

svasato, a [zva'zato] AGG (*gonna*) flared.

svastica, che ['zvastika] SF swastika.

svedese [zve'dese] 1 AGG **a** (*della Svezia*) Swedish **b**: **(fiammiferi) svedesi** safety matches.

2 SM/F Swede.

3 SM (*lingua*) Swedish.

sveglia ['zveʎʎa] SF **a** (*azione*) waking up; (*Mil*) reveille; **la sveglia è alle 7** we have to get up at 7; **mi può dare la sveglia alle 9?** would you wake me up at 9?; **suonare la sveglia** (*Mil*) to sound the reveille **b** (*orologio*) alarm (clock) ▶ **sveglia telefonica** alarm call.

svegliare [zveʎ'ʎare] 1 VT (*persona*) to wake (up), waken; (*fig: sentimenti*) to awaken, arouse; **la camminata ha svegliato il suo appetito** the walk gave him an appetite.

2 **svegliarsi** VR to wake up; (*fig*) to waken o.s. up.

sveglio, glia, gli, glie ['zveʎʎo] AGG (*gen*) awake; (*fig: attento, pronto*) quick-witted, alert; (: *furbo*) smart; **sei sveglio?** are you awake?; **non è molto sveglio** (*fig*) he's not very bright.

svelare [zve'lare] 1 VT (*segreto*) to reveal; (*mistero*) to uncover.

2 **svelarsi** VR to show o.s.; **con quell'azione si è svelato per quello che è** that action has shown him up for what he is.

svellere ['zvɛllere] VT to uproot.

sveltamente [zvelta'mente] AVV (*vedi agg*) quickly; briskly; quick-wittedly.

sveltezza [zvel'tettsa] SF (*gen*) speed; (*mentale*) quick-wittedness.

sveltire [zvel'tire] 1 VT (*gen*) to speed up; (*procedura*) to streamline; **sveltire il traffico** to speed up the flow of traffic; **sveltire il passo** to quicken one's pace.

2 **sveltirsi** VR (*fig: persona*) to waken o.s. up.

svelto, a ['zvelto] AGG (*gen*) quick; (*passo*) brisk; (*fig: persona: sveglio*) quick-witted, alert; (*linea*) slim, slender; **essere svelto di mano** (*rubare*) to be light-fingered; (*picchiare*) to be free with one's hands *o* fists; **alla svelta** quickly; **facciamo alla svelta** let's get a move on.

svenare [zve'nare] 1 VT to slash the veins of; (*fig: privare di tutto*) to bleed dry.

2 **svenarsi** VR to slash one's wrists; (*fig*) to reduce o.s. to poverty.

svendere ['zvendere] VT to sell off, clear.

svendita ['zvendita] SF (*Comm*) (clearance) sale.

svenevole [zve'nevole] AGG mawkish.

svengo *ecc* ['zvɛngo] VB vedi **svenire**.

svenimento [zveni'mento] SM fainting fit, faint; **avere uno svenimento** to faint.

svenire [zve'nire] VI IRREG (*aus* **essere**) to faint, pass out.

sventare [zven'tare] VT to foil, thwart.

sventatezza [zventa'tettsa] SF (*qualità: distrazione*) absent-mindedness; (: *mancanza di prudenza*) rashness; **è stata una sventatezza da parte sua accettare...** it was rash of him to accept ... .

sventato, a [zven'tato] 1 AGG (*distratto*) scatterbrained; (*imprudente*) rash.

2 SM/F scatterbrain.

sventola ['zventola] SF **a** (*fig: sberla*) slap; **mollare una sventola a qn** to slap sb **b** : **orecchie a sventola** sticking-out ears.

sventolare [zvento'lare] 1 VT (*bandiera*) to wave.

2 VI (*aus* **avere**) to flutter.

sventrare [zven'trare] VT (*animale*) to disembowel; (*persona*) to rip open; **hanno completamente sventrato il centro medievale** they have demolished the medieval town centre.

sventura [zven'tura] SF (*sorte avversa*) misfortune; (*disgrazia*) mishap; **per colmo di sventura** to crown it all; **è stata una sventura** it was a piece of bad luck; **compagno di sventura** (*scherz*) fellow sufferer.

sventuratamente [zventurata'mente] AVV unluckily, unfortunately.

sventurato, a [zventu'rato] 1 AGG unlucky, unfortunate.

2 SM/F (*sfortunato*) unlucky person; (*scherz*) poor unfortunate.

svenuto, a [sve'nuto] PP di **svenire**.

sverginare [zverdʒi'nare] VT to deflower.

svergognare [zvergoɲ'ɲare] VT to shame.

svergognatamente [zvergoɲɲata'mente] AVV shamelessly.

svergognato, a [zvergoɲ'ɲato] 1 AGG (*privo di: pudore*) shameless, brazen; (: *ritegno*) impudent.

2 SM/F (*vedi agg*) shameless person; impudent person.

svernare [zver'nare] VI (*aus* **avere**) to winter, spend the winter.

sverrò *ecc* [zver'rɔ] VB vedi **svenire**.

svestire [zves'tire] 1 VT to undress.

2 **svestirsi** VR to get undressed.

svettare [zvet'tare] VI (*aus* **avere**) (*montagna*): **svettare nel cielo** to stand out against the sky.

Svezia ['zvetsja] SF: **la Svezia** Sweden.

svezzamento [zvettsa'mento] SM (*anche fig*) weaning.

svezzare [zvet'tsare] VT to wean.

sviare [zvi'are] VT (*sospetti*) to divert; (*attenzione*) to distract; (*colpo*) to ward off; (*traviare*) to lead astray; **sviare le indagini della polizia** to put the police off the

track; **sviare il discorso** to change the subject.

svicolare [zviko'lare] VI (*aus* **essere** *o* **avere**) (*scantonare*) to slip down an alley; (*fig*) to sneak off.

svignarsela [zviɲ'narsela] VIP to slip away, sneak off.

svilimento [zvili'mento] SM debasement.

svilire [zvi'lire] VT to debase.

sviluppare [zvilup'pare] ☐1 VT (*gen*, *Fot*, *Mat*) to develop; (*commercio*) to expand; (*incendio*) to cause; (*gas*) to emit.

☐2 **svilupparsi** VIP (*gen*) to develop; (*città*) to expand, grow; (*commercio*) to develop, expand; **si sviluppano dei gas** there is a build-up of gas.

sviluppatrice [zviluppa'tritʃe] SF (*Fot*, *Chim*) developer.

sviluppo [zvi'luppo] SM (*gen*, *Fot*, *Mat*, *Econ*) development; (*di città*) development, growth; (*di concetto*, *tema*) development, treatment; (*di industria*) expansion; **gli sviluppi della situazione** the developments in the situation; **in via di sviluppo** in the process of development; **paesi in via di sviluppo** developing countries ► **sviluppo economico** economic growth ► **sviluppo sostenibile** sustainable development.

svincolare [zvinko'lare] ☐1 VT (*da vincolo*) to free, release; (*Comm*: *merce*) to clear.

☐2 **svincolarsi** VR to free o.s.

svincolo ['zvinkolo] SM **a** (*Aut*) motorway (*Brit*) *o* expressway (*Am*) intersection **b** (*Comm*) clearance.

sviolinata [zvioli'nata] SF (*fam*) fawning.

svisare [zvi'zare] VT (*fig*: *fatti*) to twist.

sviscerare [zviʃʃe'rare] VT (*fig*: *argomento*) to examine *o* analyse in depth.

svisceratamente [zviʃʃerata'mente] AVV passionately.

sviscerato, a [zviʃʃe'rato] AGG (*amore*, *odio*) passionate.

svista ['zvista] SF oversight, slip.

svitare [zvi'tare] VT to unscrew.

svitato, a [zvi'tato] (*fam*) ☐1 AGG (*persona*) unhinged, nutty.

☐2 SM/F screwball.

Svizzera ['zvittsera] SF: **la Svizzera** Switzerland.

svizzero, a ['zvittsero] AGG, SM/F Swiss *inv*.

svogliatamente [zvoʎʎata'mente] AVV (*vedi agg*) listlessly; indolently.

svogliatezza [zvoʎʎa'tettsa] SF (*vedi agg*) listlessness; indolence.

svogliato, a [zvoʎ'ʎato] ☐1 AGG (*senza entusiasmo*) listless; (*pigro*) lazy, indolent.

☐2 SM/F lazybones *sg*.

svolazzare [zvolat'tsare] VI (*aus* **avere**) to flutter (about).

svolazzo [zvo'lattso] SM (*fig*: *di calligrafia*) flourish.

svolgere ['zvɔldʒere] VB IRREG ☐1 VT (*rotolo*) to unroll; (*gomitolo*) to unwind; (*fig*: *argomento*, *tema*) to discuss, develop; (: *piano*, *programma*) to carry out; **quale professione svolge?** what is your occupation?.

☐2 **svolgersi** VIP (*filo*) to unwind; (*rotolo*) to unroll; (*fig*: *vita*, *eventi*: *procedere*) to go on; (: *aver luogo*: *scena*, *film*) to be set, take place; **ecco come si sono svolti i fatti** this was the sequence of events; **tutto si è svolto secondo i piani** everything went according to plan.

svolgimento [zvoldʒi'mento] SM (*di tema*) discussion; (*di programma*) carrying out; **lo svolgimento dei fatti** the sequence of events.

svolsi *ecc* ['zvɔlsi] VB vedi **svolgere**.

svolta ['zvɔlta] SF (*curva*) turn, bend; (*fig*: *mutamento*) turning point; **divieto di svolta a sinistra** no left turn; **prendi la prima svolta a destra** take the first turning on your right; **svolta a destra/a sinistra** (*Pol*) swing to the right/to the left; **essere ad una svolta nella propria vita** to be at a crossroads in one's life.

svoltare [zvol'tare] VI (*aus* **avere**) to turn.

svolto, a ['zvɔlto] PP di **svolgere**.

svuotamento [zvwota'mento] SM emptying.

svuotare [zvwo'tare] VT (*vuotare*) to empty (out); (: *fig*): **svuotare di** to deprive of.

Swaziland ['swadziland] SM: **lo Swaziland** Swaziland.

Sydney ['sidnei] SF Sydney.

T

T, t [ti] SF O M INV (*lettera*) T, t; **T come Taranto** ≈ T for Tommy.

T [ti] ABBR = **tabaccheria**.

t [ti] ABBR **a** = **tara b** = **tonnellata**.

TA SIGLA = *Taranto*.

tabaccaio, aia, ai, aie [tabak'kajo] SM/F tobacconist (*Brit*), tobacco dealer (*Am*).

tabaccheria [tabakke'ria] SF tobacconist's (shop) (*Brit*), tobacco *o* smoke shop (*Am*).

tabacchiera [tabak'kjɛra] SF snuffbox.

tabacco, chi [ta'bakko] SM tobacco.

tabagismo [tabe'dʒizmo] SM nicotine *o* smoking addiction.

tabagista [taba'dʒista] SM/F (*Med*) nicotine addict; (*fumatore incallito*) heavy smoker.

tabella [ta'bɛlla] SF (*prospetto*) table, list; (*cartellone*) board; (*Inform*) array ▶**tabella di marcia** schedule ▶**tabella dei prezzi** price list.

tabellina [tabel'lina] SF (*Scol*) (multiplication) table; **studiare la tabellina del 3** to learn one's 3 times table.

tabellone [tabel'lone] SM (*per pubblicità*) billboard; (*per informazioni*) notice board (*Brit*), bulletin board (*Am*); (: *in stazione*) timetable board.

tabernacolo [taber'nakolo] SM tabernacle.

tabù [ta'bu] AGG INV, SM INV taboo.

tabula rasa ['tabula 'raza] SF tabula rasa; **fare tabula rasa** (*fig*) to make a clean sweep; **ha fatto tabula rasa di tutti i dolci** he polished off all the cakes.

tabulare [tabu'lare] VT (*compilare una tabella*) to tabulate.

tabulato [tabu'lato] SM (*Inform*) printout.

tabulatore [tabula'tore] SM (*anche:* **tasto tabulatore**) tabulator.

tabulatrice [tabula'tritʃe] SF (*Inform*) printer.

tabulazione [tabulat'tsjone] SF tabulation.

TAC [tak] SIGLA F (*Med*)= *tomografia assiale computerizzata* **a** (*esame*) CT *o* CAT scan **b** (*apparecchiatura*) CT *o* CAT scanner.

tacca, che ['takka] SF (*gen*) notch; (*meno profondo*) nick; **di mezza tacca** (*fig pegg*) mediocre.

taccagneria [takkaɲɲe'ria] SF meanness, stinginess.

taccagno, a [tak'kaɲɲo] ① AGG mean, stingy.
② SM/F miser, mean *o* stingy person.

taccheggiare [takked'dʒare] VT to shoplift.

taccheggiatore, trice [takkeddʒa'tore] SM/F shoplifter.

taccheggio, gi [tak'keddʒo] SM (*furto*) shoplifting.

tacchetto [tak'ketto] SM (*di scarpa*) low heel; (: *Sport*) stud.

tacchino [tak'kino] SM turkey.

taccia, ce ['tattʃa] SF bad reputation.

tacciare [tat'tʃare] VT: **tacciare qn di** (*vigliaccheria ecc*) to accuse sb of.

taccio *ecc* ['tattʃo] VB vedi **tacere**.

tacco, chi ['takko] SM **a** (*di scarpe*) heel; **coi tacchi bassi/alti** low-/high-heeled ▶**tacco a spillo** stiletto (heel) (*Brit*), spike heel (*Am*) **b** (*cuneo per fermare le ruote*) chock.

taccuino [takku'ino] SM notebook.

tacere [ta'tʃere] VB IRREG ① VI (*aus* avere) (*stare in silenzio*) to be silent *o* quiet; (*smettere di parlare*) to fall silent; **continuava a tacere** he remained silent; **taci!** keep quiet!; **fatelo tacere** make him be quiet; **tutto taceva** all was silent *o* quiet; **i cannoni tacquero** the cannons fell silent; **mettere a tacere qc** to hush sth up.
② VT (*particolare, accaduto*) to keep silent about, keep to oneself, say nothing about; **tacere la verità** to hold back the truth.

tachicardia [takikar'dia] SF (*Med*) tachycardia.

tachimetro [ta'kimetro] SM speedometer.

tacitamente [tatʃita'mente] AVV (*vedi agg*) tacitly; silently.

tacitare [tatʃi'tare] VT (*creditore*) to pay off; (*scandalo*) to hush up.

Tacito ['tatʃito] SM Tacitus.

tacito, a ['tatʃito] AGG (*sottinteso*) tacit, unspoken; (*silenzioso*) silent.

taciturno, a [tatʃi'turno] AGG taciturn.

taciuto, a [ta'tʃuto] PP di **tacere**.

tacqui *ecc* ['takkwi] VB vedi **tacere**.

tafano [ta'fano] SM horsefly.

tafferuglio, gli [taffe'ruʎʎo] SM brawl, scuffle.

taffettà [taffet'ta] SF INV taffeta.

taglia ['taʎʎa] SF **a** (*misura: di abito*) size; **che taglia porti?** what size do you wear *o* take? ▶**taglia forte** outsize ▶**taglia unica** one size **b** (*misura: di animali*) size **c** (*su criminale*) reward; **c'è una taglia sulla sua testa** there is a price on his head.

tagliaboschi [taʎʎa'bɔski] SM INV woodcutter.

tagliacarte [taʎʎa'karte] SM INV paperknife.

tagliaerba [taʎʎa'ɛrba] SM INV lawn-mower.

taglialegna [taʎʎa'leɲɲa] SM INV woodcutter, lumberjack (*Am*).

tagliando [taʎ'ʎando] SM **a** (*cedola*) coupon, voucher ▶**tagliando controllo bagaglio** (*Aer*) luggage (*Brit*) *o* baggage (*Am*) identification tag **b** (*Aut*): **fare il tagliando** to have one's car serviced.

tagliapietre [taʎʎa'pjɛtre] SM INV stonecutter.

tagliare [taʎ'ʎare] **1** VT **a** (*gen*) to cut; (*torta, salame*) to cut, slice; (*arrosto*) to carve; (*siepe*) to trim; (*fieno, prato*) to mow; (*grano*) to reap; (*albero*) to fell, cut down; **tagliare qc in due/in più parti** to cut sth in two/into several pieces; **tagliare la gola a qn** to cut *o* slit sb's throat; **tagliare il capo** *o* **la testa a qn** to behead sb, cut sb's head off; **mi tagli una fetta di torta?** would you cut me a slice of cake?; **tagliarsi le unghie** to cut one's nails; **farsi tagliare i capelli** to have one's hair cut; **una lama che taglia** a sharp blade

b (*articolo, scritto, scena*) to cut; (*acqua, telefono, gas*) to cut off; **mio padre mi ha tagliato i viveri** my father is refusing to support me any more

c (*intersecare: sogg: strada*) to cut across; **tagliare la strada a qn** to cut across in front of sb

d (*curva*) to cut; (*traguardo*) to cross; (*palla*) to put a spin on

e (*carte*) to cut

f (*vini*) to blend; (*droga*) to cut

g (*fraseologia*): **tagliare la testa al toro** to settle things once and for all; **tagliare corto** to cut short; **tagliare le gambe a qn** (*fig*) to make it impossible for sb to act, tie sb's hands; **un vino che taglia le gambe** a very strong wine; **tagliare i panni addosso a qn** (*sparlare*) to tear sb to pieces.

2 VI (*aus* **avere**) (*prendere una scorciatoia*) to take a short-cut; **tagliare per i campi** to cut across the fields; **tagliamo per di là** let's cut across that way.

tagliatelle [taʎʎa'tɛlle] SFPL tagliatelle *sg.*

tagliato, a [taʎ'ʎato] AGG: **essere tagliato per qc** (*fig*) to be cut out for sth.

tagliatrice [taʎʎa'tritʃe] SF (*Tecn*) cutter.

tagliaunghie [taʎʎa'ungje] SM INV nail clippers *pl.*

taglieggiare [taʎʎed'dʒare] VT to exact a tribute from.

tagliente [taʎ'ʎɛnte] AGG (*lama*) sharp; (*fig: tono, parole*) cutting, sharp.

tagliere [taʎ'ʎɛre] SM (*gen*) chopping board; (*per il pane*) bread board.

taglierina [taʎʎe'rina] SF (*Tecn: per metalli, tessuti*) cutter; (: *per carta*) guillotine; (: *per fotografie*) trimmer.

taglierini [taʎʎe'rini] SMPL (*Culin*) thin soup noodles.

taglio, gli ['taʎʎo] SM **a** (*gen: atto*) cutting, cut; (*di capelli*) (hair)cut; (*di fieno, erba*) mowing; (*di vini*) blending; **vino da taglio** blending wine; **dare un taglio netto a qc** (*fig*) to make a clean break with sth ▶**taglio cesareo** (*Med*) Caesarean section **b** (*effetto*) cut; **farsi un taglio al dito** to cut one's finger; **taglio netto** clean cut; **c'erano dei tagli nel film/nel libro** cuts were made in the film (*Brit*) *o* movie (*Am*)/in the book; **un taglio alla spesa pubblica** a cut in public spending **c** (*pezzo: di carne*) piece; (: *di stoffa*) length; **pizza al taglio** pizza by the slice; **banconote di piccolo/grosso taglio** small-/large-denomination notes **d** (*stile: di abito*) cut, style; (: *di capelli*) (hair)style; (: *di pietra preziosa*) cut; **di taglio classico** with a classic cut; **scuola di taglio** dressmaking school **e** (*di lama*) cutting edge, edge; **colpire qc di taglio** to hit sth on edge *o* edgeways **f** (*Sport*) spin; **dare il taglio alla palla** to put a spin on the ball.

tagliola [taʎ'ʎɔla] SF trap, snare.

taglione [taʎ'ʎone] SM: **la legge del taglione** the concept of an eye for an eye (and a tooth for a tooth).

tagliuzzare [taʎʎut'tsare] VT to cut into small pieces.

Tahiti [ta'iti] SF Tahiti.

tailandese [tailan'dese] **1** AGG, SM/F Thai. **2** SM (*lingua*) Thai.

Tailandia [tai'landja] SF: **la Tailandia** Thailand.

tailleur [ta'jœr] SM INV (lady's) suit.

talamo ['talamo] SM (*letter*) bridal bed.

talare [ta'lare] AGG: **abito** *o* **veste talare** priest's cassock; **indossare l'abito talare** to become a priest.

talassemia [talasse'mia] SF (*Med*) thalassaemia (*Brit*), thalassemia (*Am*).

talco, chi ['talko] SM talcum powder.

---

tale ['tale]

1 AGG DIMOSTR

a (*simile, così grande*) such (a);

▷**è di una tale *arroganza*** he is so arrogant

▷**tale *articolo* è in vendita presso tutte le nostre filiali** the above-mentioned article is on sale at all our branches

▷**tali *discorsi* sono inaccettabili** such talk is not acceptable

▷**non avevo mai visto un tale *disordine*** I had never seen such a mess

▷**e con tali *scuse* è riuscito ad evitare la punizione** and with excuses like those he managed to escape punishment

▷**cosa ti fa credere che nutra tali *sentimenti*?** what makes you think he feels like that?

b (*nelle similitudini*): **tale... tale...** like ...like ...

▷**tale *padre* tale *figlio*** like father like son

▷**è tale** *quale* **suo nonno** he's the spitting image of *o* exactly like his grandfather

▷**il tuo vestito è tale** *quale* **il mio** your dress is just *o* exactly like mine

▷**hanno riportato una vittoria tale,** *quale* **non avevano sperato** they won an even greater victory than they had expected

2 AGG INDEF

a (*certo*)

▷*quella* **tale persona desidera parlarti** that man (*o* woman) wants to see you

▷**ti cercava** *una* **tale Giovanna** somebody called Giovanna was looking for you

▷**ha detto che vedeva un amico,** *un* **tal Rossi** he said he was meeting a friend, a certain Rossi

b (*persona o cosa indeterminata*) such-and-such;

> ▷ il tale *giorno* alla tale *ora* on such and such a day at such and such a time.
> **3** PRON INDEF
> **a**: *un(una)* tale (*una certa persona*) someone; (*quella persona già menzionata*) the one, the person, that person, that man/woman
> ▷ è fidanzata con *un* tale dell'ufficio contabilità she's engaged to someone in accounts
> ▷ hai più visto *quel* tale di cui mi dicevi? did you ever see that person *o* man you were telling me about again?
> ▷ ha telefonato di nuovo *quella* tale that woman phoned again
> **b**: il *tal dei tali* whatshisname
> ▷ la *tal dei tali* whatshername
> ▷ diciamo che l'ho saputo dal *tal dei tali* let's just say I had *o* heard it from you know who.

talea [ta'lɛa] SF (*Giardinaggio*) cutting.

taleggio [ta'leddʒo] SM *type of soft cheese.*

talento [ta'lɛnto] SM (*capacità*) talent; (*persona*) talented person; **essere privo/pieno di talento** to be untalented/very talented.

Talete [ta'lɛte] SM Thales.

talismano [taliz'mano] SM talisman.

talk-show ['tɔːkʃou] SM INV chat (*Brit*) *o* talk (*Am*) show.

tallonaggio, gi [tallo'naddʒo] SM (*Rugby*) close marking.

tallonamento [tallona'mento] SM (*di giocatore*) close marking.

tallonare [tallo'nare] VT (*inseguire*) to follow (hot) on the heels of, to pursue; (*Sport*) to pursue; **tallonare il pallone** (*Rugby*) to heel the ball; (*Calcio*) to back-heel the ball.

tallonata [tallo'nata] SF (*Rugby*) heel; (*Calcio*) back-heel.

talloncino [tallon'tʃino] SM stub, counterfoil (*Brit*) ► **talloncino del prezzo** (*di medicinali*) tear-off tag.

tallone [tal'lone] SM heel ► **tallone di Achille** Achilles' heel.

talmente [tal'mente] AVV (*così tanto*) so; **sono talmente contento!** I'm so happy!; **ero talmente emozionato che...** I was so excited that ...; **è stato talmente ingenuo da cascarci** he was naïve enough to fall for it.

Talmud [tal'mud] SM: **il Talmud** the Talmud.

talora [ta'lora] AVV = **talvolta**.

talpa ['talpa] SF (*Zool*, *fig*) mole; **cieco come una talpa** as blind as a bat.

talvolta [tal'vɔlta] AVV sometimes, at times.

tamarindo [tama'rindo] SM tamarind.

tamburellare [tamburel'lare] VI (*aus* **avere**) (*pioggia*) to drum; **tamburellare con le dita** to drum one's fingers.

tamburello [tambu'rɛllo] SM (*Mus*) tambourine; (*gioco*) *ball game played with tambourine-shaped bats.*

tamburino [tambu'rino] SM drummer boy.

tamburo [tam'buro] SM **a** (*Mus*: *strumento*) drum; (: *suonatore*) drummer; **a tamburo battente** (*fig*) immediately, at once **b** (*Tecn*, *Aut*) drum; (*di armi*) cylinder; (*di orologio*) barrel; **freni a tamburo** drum brakes; **pistola a tamburo** revolver.

tamerice [tame'ritʃe] SF tamarisk.

tamia ['tamja] SM INV: **tamia striato** chipmunk.

Tamigi [ta'midʒi] SM: **il Tamigi** the Thames.

tamponamento [tampona'mento] SM (*Aut*) collision ► **tamponamento a catena** pile-up.

tamponare [tampo'nare] VT **a** (*urtare*: *macchina*) to ram into **a** (*otturare*) to plug.

tampone [tam'pone] **1** SM **a** (*assorbente interno*) tampon **b** (*Med*: *gen*) plug; (: *di cotone*) wad; (: *per pulire una ferita*) swab; (: *per stendere un liquido*) pad **c** (*cuscinetto*: *per timbri*) ink-pad; (: *di carta assorbente*) blotter.
2 AGG INV: **provvedimento tampone** stopgap measure.

tamtam, tam-tam [tam'tam] SM INV (*Mus*) tomtom; (*fig*): **il tamtam dei carcerati** the prison grapevine.

tana ['tana] SF (*gen*) lair, den; (*di coniglio*) burrow; (*fig*: *nascondiglio*) den, hideout.

tandem ['tandem] SM INV (*bicicletta*) tandem; (*fig*: *coppia*) duo.

tanfo ['tanfo] SM stench.

tanga ['tanga] SM INV tanga.

tangente [tan'dʒɛnte] **1** AGG (*Geom*): **tangente (a)** tangential (to).
2 SF **a** (*Geom*) tangent; **filare per la tangente** (*fig*: *svignarsela*) to make one's getaway; **partire per la tangente** (*fig*: *divagare*) to go off at a tangent **b** (*pizzo*) protection money *sg*; (*bustarella*) kickback; **lo scandalo delle tangenti** the kickback scandal.

tangentizio, zia, zi, zie [tandʒen'tittsjo] AGG (*relativo alle tangenti*) corrupt.

tangentopoli [tandʒen'tɔpoli] SF *corruption scandal involving government ministers, industrialists and businessmen: it began in 1992, in Milan, which was consequently dubbed Tangentopoli (Bribesville).*

tangenza [tan'dʒɛntsa] SF (*Geom*) tangency; (*Aer*) ceiling.

tangenziale [tandʒen'tsjale] **1** AGG (*Geom*) tangential; **retta tangenziale** tangent.
2 SF (*anche*: **strada tangenziale**) bypass.

Tangeri ['tandʒeri] SF Tangier(s).

tanghero ['tangero] SM (*pegg*) bumpkin.

tangibile [tan'dʒibile] AGG tangible.

tangibilità [tandʒibili'ta] SF tangibleness.

tangibilmente [tandʒibil'mente] AVV tangibly.

tango, ghi ['tango] SM tango.

tanica, che ['tanika] SF (*contenitore*) jerry can; (*Naut*: *serbatoio*) tank.

tannino [tan'nino] SM tannin.

tantino [tan'tino] **1**: **un tantino** AVV (*un po'*) a little, a bit; (*alquanto*) rather.
2 SM: **un tantino di** a little bit of.

> **tanto , a** ['tanto]
> **1** AGG INDEF
> **a** (*molto*: *quantità*) a lot of, much; (: *numero*) a lot of, many; (*così tanto*: *quantità*) so much, such a lot of; (: *numero*) so many, such a lot of;
> ▷ **ogni tanti** *chilometri/giorni* every so many kilometres/days
> ▷ **tante** *persone*, **tante** *opinioni* **diverse** there are as many different opinions as there are people
> ▷ **c'è ancora tanta** *strada* **da fare!** there's still a long way to go!
> ▷ **tante** *volte* so many times, so often
> **b** (*rafforzativo*) such;
> ▷ **l'ha detto con tanta** *gentilezza* he said it with such kindness *o* so kindly
> ▷ **ho aspettato per tanto** *tempo* I waited so long *o* for such a long time
> **c**: **tanto...** *quanto...* (*quantità*) as much ...as ...

(*numero*) as many ...as ...;

▷ho tanta pazienza *quanta* ne hai tu I am as patient as you are, I have as much patience as you (have)

▷ha tanti amici *quanti* nemici he has as many friends as he has enemies

▷ho tanti libri *quanti* ne ha lui I have as many books as him *o* as he has.

2 PRON INDEF

a (*molto*) much, a lot; (*così tanto*) so much, such a lot; (*plurale*): tanti(e) (*molti*) many, a lot; (*così tanti*) so many, such a lot

▷è una ragazza *come* tante she's like any other girl

▷è solo *uno dei* tanti che... he's just one of the many who ...

▷credevo ce ne fosse tanto I thought there was (such) a lot, I thought there was plenty

▷se cerchi un bicchiere, lassù ce ne sono tanti if you are looking for a glass there are a lot *o* lots up there

▷tanti credono sia semplice farlo many people believe it is easy to do

b (*altrettanto*): tanto *quanto* as much as; (*plurale*): tanti *quanti* as many as

▷tempo? ne ho tanto *quanto* basta time? I have as much as I need

c (*con valore indeterminato*)

▷riceve *un* tanto al mese he receives so much a month

▷costa *un* tanto al metro it costs so much per *o* a metre

▷della somma che ho a disposizione tanto andrà per il vitto, tanto per l'alloggio of the money I've got so much will go on food and so much on accommodation

▷nell'anno millecinquecento e tanti in the year fifteen hundred and something

d (*fraseologia*)

▷me ne ha *dette* tante! he gave me a real mouthful!

▷*di* tanto *in* tanto every so often, (every) now and again

▷è rimasto con tanto *di naso* he was left feeling disappointed

▷tanto di *guadagnato*! so much the better!

▷tanto *meglio* così! so much the better!

▷se tanto *mi dà* tanto oh well, if that's the case ...

▷guardare qc con tanto *d'occhi* to gaze wide-eyed at sth

▷ogni tanto every so often, (every) now and then

▷ascoltava con tanto *d'orecchi* he was all ears

▷tanto *vale* che... you may *o* might as well ... .

3 AVV

a (*così, in questo modo*: con verbo) so much, such a lot; (: con avverbio, aggettivo) so; (*così a lungo*) so long;

▷tanto... *che*... so ...(that) ...

▷è tanto bello *che* sembra finto it's so beautiful (that) it seems unreal

▷tanto... *da*... so ...as ...

▷saresti tanto gentile *da* prendermi una tazza? would you be so kind as to get me a cup?

▷è stato tanto idiota *da* crederci he was stupid enough to believe it

▷non lavorare tanto! don't work so hard!

▷perché piangeva tanto? why was she crying so (much)?

▷stanno tanto bene insieme! they go so well together!

b (*nei comparativi*): tanto... *quanto*... as ...as ...

▷è tanto gentile *quanto* discreto he is as kind as he is discreet

▷non è poi tanto difficile *quanto* sembra it is not as difficult as it seems after all

▷mi piace non tanto per l'aspetto *quanto* per il suo carattere I like her not so much for her looks as for her personality

▷conosco tanto Carlo *quanto* suo padre I know both Carlo and his father

c (*molto*) very;

▷un'ora *a dir* tanto an hour at the most

▷non *ci vuole* tanto a capirlo it doesn't take much to understand it

▷non è poi tanto *giovane* he is not all that young after all

▷l'ho visto tanto *giù* he seemed *o* looked very down to me

▷*scusami* tanto I'm very sorry, do excuse me

▷sono *tanto* tanto contento di vederti I'm so very happy to see you

▷vengo tanto *volentieri* I'd love to come

d (*a lungo*) (for) long;

▷starai via tanto? will you be away (for) long?

▷non stare fuori tanto don't stay out for long

e (*solamente*) just;

▷tanto *per cambiare* (*anche iro*) just for a change

▷parla tanto *per parlare* he talks just for the sake of talking

▷tanto *per ridere* just for a laugh

▷una *volta* tanto just for once

f (*con valore moltiplicativo*)

▷due *volte* tanto twice as much

▷tre *volte* tanto three times as much

g

▷tanto *più* insisti tanto *più* non mollerà the more you insist the more stubborn he'll be

▷tanto *più* lo vedo tanto *meno* mi piace the more I see him the less I like him.

4 CONG after all;

▷lo farò, tanto non mi costa niente I'll do it, after all it won't cost me anything

▷fanne a meno, tanto a me non importa do without then, I don't care

▷tanto è inutile in any case it's useless.

Tanzania [tanˈdzanja] SF: **la Tanzania** Tanzania.

tapioca [taˈpjɔka] SF tapioca.

tapiro [taˈpiro] SM tapir.

tapis roulant [taˈpi ruˈlã] SM INV travolator (*Brit*), moving sidewalk (*Am*).

tappa [ˈtappa] SF **a** (*luogo di sosta, fermata*) stop, halt; **fare tappa** to stop off **b** (*Sport: parte di percorso*) stage, leg; (*fig: stadio*) stage; **a tappe** in stages; **bruciare le tappe** (*fig*) to get there fast.

tappabuchi [tappaˈbuki] SM/F INV stopgap; **fare da tappabuchi** to act as a stopgap.

tappare [tapˈpare] **1** VT (*otturare*) to plug, stop up; (: *bottiglia*) to cork; **tappare un buco** (*fig*) to provide a short-term remedy; **tappare la bocca a qn** (*fig*) to shut sb up; **tapparsi il naso** to hold one's nose; **tapparsi le orecchie/gli occhi** to turn a deaf ear/a blind eye. **2** **tapparsi** VR: **tapparsi in casa** to shut o.s. up at home.

tapparella [tappa'rɛlla] SF rolling shutter.

tappatrice [tappa'tritʃe] SF (bottle-)corking machine.

tappetino [tappe'tino] SM (per auto) car mat ▶ **tappetino antiscivolo** (da bagno) non-slip mat.

tappeto [tap'peto] SM (gen) carpet; (piccolo) rug; (stuoia) mat; (per tavolo) cloth; **bombardamento a tappeto** carpet bombing; **andare al tappeto** (Pugilato) to go down for the count; (fig) to be floored; **mandare qn al tappeto** (fig) to floor sb; **mettere sul tappeto** (fig: questione) to table ▶ **tappeto erboso** lawn ▶ **tappeto verde** (panno) green baize (cloth); (tavolo da gioco) gaming table.

tappezzare [tappet'tsare] VT (pareti) to paper; (divano, sedia) to cover; **tappezzare una stanza di manifesti** to cover a room with posters.

tappezzeria [tappettse'ria] SF (arredamento) soft furnishings pl; (carta da parati) wallpaper; (tessuto) wall covering; (di automobile) upholstery; **fare da tappezzeria** (fig) to be a wallflower.

tappezziere, a [tappet'tsjɛre] SM/F upholsterer.

tappo ['tappo] SM (di bottiglia: in sughero) cork; (: in vetro, plastica) stopper; (di barattolo, serbatoio, radiatore) cap; (di penna) top; (di vasca, lavandino) plug; (scherz: persona bassa) shorty ▶ **tappo a corona** bottle top ▶ **tappo salvagocce** dripless pour spout ▶ **tappo di scarico della coppa** (Aut) drain plug ▶ **tappo con serratura** (Aut) locking petrol cap ▶ **tappo a vite** screw top.

T.A.R. [tar] SIGLA M = Tribunale Amministrativo Regionale.

tara ['tara] SF **a** (peso) tare **b** (Med) hereditary defect; (difetto) flaw.

tarantella [taran'tɛlla] SF (danza) tarantella.

tarantino, a [taran'tino] [1] AGG of o from Taranto.
[2] SM/F inhabitant o native of Taranto.

tarantola [ta'rantola] SF tarantula.

tarare [ta'rare] VT (Comm) to tare; (Tecn) to calibrate.

tarato, a [ta'rato] AGG **a** (Comm) tared; (Tecn) calibrated **b** (Med) with a hereditary defect; **ma tu sei tarato** (scherz) you're nuts.

taratura [tara'tura] SF (Comm) taring; (Tecn) calibration.

tarchiato, a [tar'kjato] AGG stocky, thickset.

tardare [tar'dare] [1] VI (aus avere) to be late; **ha tardato molto** he was very late; **tardare a fare qc** (involontariamente) to be late in doing sth; (apposta) to delay doing sth.
[2] VT (consegna) to delay.

tardi ['tardi] AVV late; **svegliarsi tardi** to wake up late, oversleep; **arrivare tardi** to arrive late; **lavorare fino a tardi** to work late; **far tardi** (essere in ritardo) to be late; (restare alzato) to stay up late; **meglio tardi che mai** better late than never; **più tardi** later (on); **a più tardi!** see you later!; **al più tardi** at the latest; **presto o tardi** sooner or later; **si è fatto tardi** it is late; **sul tardi** (verso sera) late in the day; **ci siamo incontrati sul tardi** we met quite late.

tardivamente [tardiva'mente] AVV late.

tardivo, a [tar'divo] AGG (primavera, fioritura, sviluppo) late; (rimedio, pentimento) belated.

tardo, a ['tardo] AGG (lento, ottuso) slow; (avanzato: mattinata, primavera) late; (tardivo: pentimento) belated.

tardona [tar'dona] SF (pegg): **essere una tardona** to be mutton dressed as lamb (Brit).

targa, ghe ['targa] SF (gen) plate; (su una porta) nameplate; (Aut) numberplate (Brit), license plate (Am); (placca) plaque; **circolazione a targhe alterne** (Aut) anti-pollution measure whereby, on days with an even date, only cars whose numberplate ends in an even number may be on the road, while on days with an odd date, only cars whose numberplate ends in an odd number may be on the road.

targare [tar'gare] VT (Aut) to register.

targato, a [tar'gato] AGG (Aut): **una macchina targata BO** a car with a Bologna numberplate (Brit) o license plate (Am); (fig): **una vacanza targata Soletur** a Soletur holiday; **un attentato targato IRA** a bombing bearing all the hallmarks of the IRA.

targhetta [tar'getta] SF (con nome) nameplate (on door); (su bagaglio) name tag.

tariffa [ta'riffa] SF (gen) rate, tariff; (di trasporti) fare; **la tariffa in vigore** the going rate ▶ **tariffa inserzioni per pagina** (Stampa) page rate ▶ **tariffa normale** (gen) standard rate; (su mezzi di trasporto) full fare ▶ **tariffa professionale** fee ▶ **tariffa ridotta** (gen) reduced rate; (su mezzi di trasporto) concessionary fare ▶ **tariffa salariale** wage rate ▶ **tariffa unica** flat rate ▶ **tariffe doganali** customs rates o tariff sg ▶ **tariffe postali** postal charges ▶ **tariffe telefoniche** telephone charges.

tariffare [tarif'fare] VT (beni, servizi pubblici) to fix the charges o rates for.

tariffario, ria, ri, rie [tarif'farjo] [1] AGG: **aumento tariffario** increase in charges o rates.
[2] SM tariff, table of charges.

tarlare [tar'lare] VI (aus essere), **tarlarsi** VIP (legno) to have woodworm; (tessuto) to be moth-eaten.

tarlato, a [tar'lato] AGG (legno) worm-eaten; (tessuto) moth-eaten.

tarlo ['tarlo] SM **a** (insetto) woodworm **b**: **il tarlo della gelosia** the pangs pl of jealousy; **il tarlo del dubbio lo assillava** doubts ate away at him.

tarma ['tarma] SF moth.

tarmare [tar'mare] VI (aus essere), **tarmarsi** VIP to be moth-eaten.

tarmicida, i [tarmi'tʃida] AGG, SM moth-killer.

tarocco, chi [ta'rɔkko] SM tarot card; **il gioco dei tarocchi** tarot.

tarpare [tar'pare] VT (fig): **tarpare le ali a qn** to clip sb's wings.

tarso ['tarso] SM (Anat) tarsus.

tartagliare [tartaʎ'ʎare] [1] VI (aus avere) to stutter, stammer.
[2] VT to mutter.

tartan[1] ['tartan] SM INV (tessuto) tartan.

tartan[2®] ['tartan] SM INV Tartan®.

tartaro, a ['tartaro] [1] AGG (Storia) Tartar; (Culin) tartar(e); **bistecca alla tartara** steak tartare.
[2] SM/F Tartar.

tartaruga, ghe [tarta'ruga] SF (testuggine) tortoise; (: di mare) turtle; (materiale) tortoiseshell; **zuppa di tartaruga** turtle soup; **essere lento come una tartaruga** to be a slowcoach (Brit) o slowpoke (Am).

tartassare [tartas'sare] VT (fam): **tartassare qn** to give sb the works; **tartassare qn a un esame** to give sb a grilling at an exam; **smettila di tartassare quel piano!** stop thumping on that piano!; **essere tartassato dal fisco** to be hard hit by the taxman.

tartina [tar'tina] SF canapé.

tartufo [tar'tufo] SM **a** (fungo) truffle; (semifreddo) individual filled chocolate ice-cream cake **b**: **tartufo di**

mare (*Zool*) Venus clam **c** (*naso di cane*) nose.

tasca, **sche** ['taska] SF (*gen*) pocket; (*scomparto: di valigia*) compartment; (*Zool, Anat*) pouch; **tasca dei pantaloni** trouser (*Brit*) *o* pants (*Am*) pocket; **da tasca** pocket *attr*; **non ho un soldo in tasca** (*al momento*) I haven't any money *o* a penny on me; (*essere al verde*) I'm broke; **riempirsi le tasche di qc** to fill one's pockets with sth; **non startene con le mani in tasca** (*fig*) don't just stand there with your hands in your pockets; **non me ne viene niente in tasca** I get nothing out of it; **che cosa me ne viene in tasca?** what's in it for me?; **fare i conti in tasca a qn** to meddle in sb's affairs; **conosco Roma come le mie tasche** I know Rome like the back of my hand; **averne le tasche piene di** to be fed up with ▶**tasca da pasticciere** piping bag.

tascabile [tas'kabile] [1] AGG (*libro*) pocket *attr*.
[2] SM ≈ paperback.

tascapane [taska'pane] SM haversack.

taschina [tas'kina] SF (*Filatelia*) stamp envelope.

taschino [tas'kino] SM breast pocket.

Tasmania [taz'manja] SF: **la Tasmania** Tasmania.

tassa ['tassa] SF (*imposta*) tax; (*doganale*) duty; (*Scol, Univ*) fee; **soggetto a tasse** taxable ▶**tassa di circolazione** road tax (*Brit*) ▶**tassa di soggiorno** tourist tax.

tassabile [tas'sabile] AGG taxable.

tassametro [tas'sametro] SM taximeter.

tassare [tas'sare] [1] VT (*gen*) to tax; (*sogg: dogana*) to levy a duty on.
[2] **tassarsi** VR: **tassarsi per** to chip in, contribute.

tassativamente [tassativa'mente] AVV (*dire, ordinare*) peremptorily; **è tassativamente vietato** it is strictly forbidden.

tassativo, **a** [tassa'tivo] AGG peremptory.

tassazione [tassat'tsjone] SF taxation; **soggetto a tassazione** taxable.

tassello [tas'sɛllo] SM **a** (*anche:* **tassello a espansione**) Rawlplug ® **b** (*pezzetto: di legno, pietra*) plug; (*per vestiti*) gusset; (*assaggio: di formaggio, cocomero*) wedge.

tassì [tas'si] SM INV = **taxi**.

tassidermia [tassider'mia] SF taxidermy.

tassidermista, **i**, **e** [tassider'mista] SM/F taxidermist.

tassista, **i**, **e** [tas'sista] SM/F taxi driver, cab driver.

tasso[1] ['tasso] SM (*di natalità, mortalità*) rate ▶**tasso agevolato** (*Banca*) special rate ▶**tasso di cambio** rate of exchange ▶**tasso di crescita** growth rate ▶**tasso glicemico** (*Med*) blood sugar level ▶**tasso d'inquinamento** pollution level ▶**tasso di interesse** rate of interest ▶**tasso ufficiale di sconto** (*Econ*) official discount rate.

tasso[2] ['tasso] SM (*Bot*) yew.

tasso[3] ['tasso] SM (*Zool*) badger.

tassonomia [tassono'mia] SF taxonomy.

tastare [tas'tare] VT to feel; **tastare il polso a qn** to feel sb's pulse; **tastare il terreno** to test the ground; (*fig*) to see how the land lies.

tastiera [tas'tjera] SF (*gen, Mus, Inform*) keyboard; (*di strumenti a corda*) fingerboard; **apparecchio (telefonico) a tastiera** push-button phone.

tastierino [tastje'rino] SM: **tastierino numerico** numeric keypad.

tastierista [tastje'rista] SM/F (*gen*) keyboard operator, keyboarder; (*Mus*) keyboard(s) player, keyboardist.

tasto ['tasto] SM (*gen, Tecn, Mus*) key; (*tatto*) touch, feel; (*fig: argomento*) topic, subject; **toccare un tasto delicato** to touch on a delicate subject; **toccare il tasto giusto** (*fig*) to strike the right note ▶**tasto di controllo** (*Inform*) control key ▶**tasto funzione** (*Inform*) function key ▶**tasto delle maiuscole** (*su macchina da scrivere*) shift key ▶**tasto di ritorno a margine** (*Inform*) return key ▶**tasto tabulatore** (*su macchina da scrivere*) tab (key).

tastoni [tas'toni] AVV: **procedere (a) tastoni** to grope one's way forward.

tata ['tata] SF (*linguaggio infantile*) nanny.

tattica ['tattika] SF tactics *pl*.

tatticamente [tattika'mente] AVV tactically.

tatticismo [tatti'tʃizmo] SM use of tactics.

tattico, **a**, **ci**, **che** ['tattiko] [1] AGG tactical.
[2] SM (*Mil, fig*) tactician.

tattile ['tattile] AGG tactile.

tatto ['tatto] SM **a** (*senso*) touch; **duro al tatto** hard to the touch **b** (*diplomazia*) tact; **aver tatto** to be tactful, have tact; **essere privo di tatto** [OR] **non avere tatto** to be tactless.

tatuaggio, **gi** [tatu'addʒo] SM (*operazione*) tattooing; (*disegno*) tattoo.

tatuare [tatu'are] [1] VT to tattoo.
[2] **tatuarsi** VR to have o.s. tattooed.

taumaturgico, **a**, **ci**, **che** [tauma'turdʒiko] AGG (*fig*) miraculous.

taumaturgo, **ghi** [tauma'turgo] SM miracle worker.

taurino, **a** [tau'rino] AGG bull-like; **ha un collo taurino** he is bull-necked.

tauromachia [tauroma'kia] SF (*arte*) bullfighting, tauromachy (*termine tecn*); (*corrida*) bullfight.

tautologia, **gie** [tautolo'dʒia] SF tautology.

taverna [ta'vɛrna] SF (*osteria*) tavern.

tavola ['tavola] [1] SF **a** (*mobile*) table; **a tavola!** come and eat!; **essere a tavola** to be having a meal, be at table; **preparare la tavola** to lay *o* set the table; **sedersi a tavola** to sit down to eat, sit down at the table; **ama i piaceri della tavola** he enjoys his food; **la buona tavola** good food
b (*asse*) plank, board; **il mare è una tavola** the sea is like a millpond
c (*tabella*) table; (*illustrazione*) plate; (*quadro su legno*) panel (painting).
[2] ▶**tavola calda** snack bar ▶**tavola periodica degli elementi** (*Chim*) periodic table ▶**tavola pitagorica** multiplication table ▶**tavola reale** (*gioco*) backgammon ▶**tavola rotonda** (*anche fig*) round table.

tavolata [tavo'lata] SF (*commensali*) table.

tavolato [tavo'lato] SM **a** (*gen*) planking, boarding; (*di palco*) boards *pl* **b** (*Geog*) plateau.

tavoletta [tavo'letta] SF (*di cioccolata*) bar; **andare a tavoletta** (*Aut*) to go flat out.

tavoliere [tavo'ljɛre] SM (*Geog*) tableland, plateau.

tavolino [tavo'lino] SM (*gen*) small table; (*scrittoio, banco*) desk; **mettersi a tavolino** to get down to work; **decidere qc a tavolino** (*fig*) to decide sth on a theoretical level *o* in theory; **il risultato della partita è stato deciso a tavolino** the result of the match was decided by the referee ▶**tavolino da gioco** card table ▶**tavolino da tè** coffee table.

tavolo ['tavolo] SM (*gen*) table; (*scrittoio*) desk; **da tavolo** table *attr* ▶**tavolo anatomico** mortuary slab ▶**tavolo da disegno** drawing board ▶**tavolo da lavoro** (*gen*) desk; (*Tecn*) workbench ▶**tavolo operatorio** operating table ▶**tavolo pieghevole** folding table ▶**tavolo da**

ping-pong table-tennis table ▶**tavolo a ribalta** drop-leaf table.

tavolozza [tavo'lɔttsa] SF (*Arte*) palette.

taxi ['taksi] SM INV taxi.

tazza ['tattsa] SF (*recipiente*) cup; (*contenuto*) cupful; (*fam: di gabinetto*) bowl, pan (*Brit*); **una tazza di caffè/tè** a cup of coffee/tea ▶**tazza da caffè** coffee cup ▶**tazza da tè** teacup.

tazzina [tat'tsina] SF coffee cup.

TBC [tibi'tʃi] SIGLA F (= *tubercolosi*) TB.

T.C.I. [titʃi'i] SIGLA M = *Touring Club Italiano*.

TE SIGLA = *Teramo*.

te [te] PRON PERS **a** (*dopo prep, accentato*) you; **lo ha dato a te, non a me** he gave it to you *o* YOU, not to me; **parlavamo di te** we were talking about you; **vengo con te** I'm coming with you; **dietro di te** behind you; **verrò da te** I'll come round to your place, I'll drop in and see you; **fallo da te** do it yourself; **se fossi in te** if I were you; **povero te!** poor you!

b (*nelle comparazioni*) you; **è alto come te** he's as tall as you (are); **parla come te** she speaks like you (do); **è più giovane di te** he's younger than you (are)

c vedi **ti**.

tè [te] SM INV (*bevanda*) tea; (*pianta*) tea plant; (*trattenimento*) tea party; **da tè** tea *attr*; **vuoi un tè?** would you like a cup of tea?

teatrale [tea'trale] AGG (*spettacolo*) theatrical, stage *attr*; (*stagione, compagnia, attore*) theatre *attr* (*Brit*), theater *attr* (*Am*); (*fig: gesto, atteggiamento*) theatrical; **siamo andati a vedere uno spettacolo teatrale** we went to the theatre *o* theater.

teatralità [teatrali'ta] SF (*anche fig*) theatricality.

teatralmente [teatral'mente] AVV (*rappresentare*) on the (the) stage; (*fig: comportarsi*) theatrically.

teatro [te'atro] SM **a** (*edificio*) theatre (*Brit*), theater (*Am*); (*pubblico*) house, audience; (*fig: luogo*) scene; **andare a teatro** to go to the theatre *o* theater; **il teatro era pieno** there was a full house; **il teatro delle operazioni** (*Mil*) the theatre *o* theater of operations; **la sua casa è stata teatro di un orrendo delitto** his house was the scene of a hideous crime ▶**teatro all'aperto** open-air theatre *o* theater ▶**teatro di posa** film studio ▶**teatro tenda** marquee (*used for pop concerts ecc*)

b (*genere*) theatre (*Brit*), theater (*Am*); (*professione*) theatre (*Brit*), theater (*Am*), stage; **il teatro classico** classical theatre *o* theater *o* drama; **il teatro di Pirandello** Pirandello's plays *o* dramatic works, the theatre *o* theater of Pirandello; **interessarsi di teatro** to be interested in drama *o* the theatre *o* theater; **è un uomo di teatro** he's in the theatre *o* theater ▶**teatro comico** comedy ▶**teatro lirico** opera.

Tebe ['tebe] SF Thebes *sg*.

teca, che ['tɛka] SF (*Rel*) reliquary.

technicolor® [tekni'kɔlor] SM Technicolor ®.

tecnica, che ['tɛknika] SF (*scienza*) technology; (*metodo*) technique.

tecnicamente [teknika'mente] AVV technically.

tecnicismo [tekni'tʃizmo] SM **a** (*predominio dell'aspetto tecnico*) excessive attention to technical details **b** (*termine tecnico*) technical term.

tecnico, a, ci, che ['tɛkniko] ① AGG technical. ② SM/F (*gen*) technician; (*esperto*) expert ▶**tecnico del suono** sound engineer ▶**tecnico della televisione** television engineer.

tecnigrafo [tek'nigrafo] SM (*squadra*) draughtsman's (*Brit*) *o* draftsman's rule (*Am*) (*tavolo*) drawing table.

tecnocrate [tek'nɔkrate] SM/F technocrat.

tecnocrazia [teknokrat'tsia] SF technocracy.

tecnologia, gie [teknolo'dʒia] SF (*scienza*) technology; (*tecnica*) technique; **alta tecnologia** high technology, hi-tech.

tecnologico, a, ci, che [tekno'lɔdʒiko] AGG technological.

tecnologo, a, gi, ghe [tek'nɔlogo] SM/F technologist.

tedesco, a, schi, sche [te'desko] ① AGG, SM/F German. ② SM (*lingua*) German.

tediare [te'djare] VT (*infastidire*) to bother, annoy; (*annoiare*) to bore.

tedio ['tɛdjo] SM tedium, boredom.

tediosità [tedjosi'ta] SF tediousness.

tedioso, a [te'djoso] AGG tedious, boring.

Teflon® ['tɛflon] SM Teflon ®.

tegame [te'game] SM (*Culin*) (frying) pan, skillet (*Am*); (*contenuto*) panful; **al tegame** fried.

teglia ['teʎʎa] SF (*Culin: per dolci*) (baking) tin (*Brit*), cake pan (*Am*); (*: per arrosti*) (roasting) tin *o* pan.

tegola ['tegola] SF (roofing) tile.

tegumento [tegu'mento] SM (*Bio*) integument.

Teheran [te'ran] SF Teh(e)ran.

teiera [te'jɛra] SF teapot.

teina [te'ina] SF (*Chim*) theine.

tek ['tɛk] SM INV teak.

tel. [tel] ABBR (= *telefono*) tel.

tela ['tela] ① SF **a** (*tessuto*) cloth; **di tela** (*lenzuolo*) linen; (*pantaloni*) (heavy) cotton *attr*; (*scarpe, borsa*) canvas *attr*; **rilegato in tela** clothbound **b** (*Pittura: supporto*) canvas; (*: dipinto*) canvas, painting. ② ▶**tela cerata** oilcloth ▶**tela (da) vela** sailcloth ▶**tela di ragno** spider's web, cobweb ▶**tela di sacco** sackcloth, sacking.

telaio, ai [te'lajo] SM (*per tessere*) loom; (*struttura*) frame; (*Aut*) chassis ▶**telaio da ricamo** embroidery frame.

Tel Aviv [tela'viv] SF Tel Aviv.

tele ['tɛle] SF INV (*fam*) telly (*Brit*), TV (*Am*).

tele... ['tɛle] PREF tele... .

teleabbonato, a [teleabbo'nato] SM/F television *o* TV licence holder (*Brit*).

telecabina [teleka'bina] SF (*Sci*) cablecar.

telecamera [tele'kamera] SF television *o* TV camera.

telecomandare [telekoman'dare] VT to operate by remote control.

telecomandato, a [telekoman'dato] AGG operated by remote control.

telecomando [teleko'mando] SM remote control.

telecomunicazioni [telekomunikat'tsjoni] SFPL telecommunications.

teleconferenza [telekonfe'rentsa] SF teleconference.

telecronaca, che [tele'krɔnaka] SF television *o* TV report ▶**telecronaca differita** (pre-)recorded (TV) report ▶**telecronaca diretta** live (TV) report.

telecronista, i, e [telekro'nista] SM/F (television) commentator.

teleferica, che [tele'fɛrika] SF cableway.

telefilm [tele'film] SM INV television *o* TV film (*Brit*) *o* movie (*Am*).

telefonare [telefo'nare] ① VI (*aus* **avere**) (*gen*) to (tele)phone, ring; (*fare una chiamata*) to make a phone call; **telefonare a qn** to telephone sb, phone *o* ring *o* call sb (up); **sta telefonando** he is on the phone.

[2] VT to (tele)phone.

telefonata [telefo'nata] SF (telephone) o (phone) call ▶**telefonata a carico del destinatario** reverse charge (*Brit*) o collect (*Am*) call ▶**telefonata interurbana** long-distance call ▶**telefonata in teleselezione** STD (*Brit*) o direct-dialing (*Am*) call ▶**telefonata urbana** local call.

telefonia [telefo'nia] SF telephony.

telefonicamente [telefonika'mente] AVV by (tele)phone.

telefonico, a, ci, che [tele'fɔniko] AGG (tele)phone *attr*.

telefonino [telefo'nino] SM mobile phone.

telefonista, i, e [telefo'nista] SM/F (*gen*) telephonist; (*di centralino*) switchboard operator.

telefono [te'lɛfono] SM (*sistema*) telephone; (*apparecchio*) (tele)phone; **avere il telefono** to be on the (tele)phone; **un colpo di telefono** a call, a ring ▶**telefono amico** ≈ the Samaritans *pl* ▶**telefono azzurro** ≈ Childline ▶**telefono a disco** dial (tele)phone ▶**telefono a gettoni** ≈ pay phone ▶**telefono interno** internal phone ▶**telefono pubblico** public (tele)phone ▶**telefono rosa** rape crisis line ▶**telefono a scheda (magnetica)** cardphone (*Brit*) ▶**telefono a tastiera** push-button phone.

telegenico, a, ci, che [tele'dʒɛniko] AGG telegenic.

telegiornale [teledʒor'nale] SM (*notiziario*) television news *sg*.

telegrafare [telegra'fare] VT, VI (*aus* avere) to telegraph, cable.

telegrafia [telegra'fia] SF telegraphy.

telegraficamente [telegrafika'mente] AVV (*anche fig*) telegraphically; (*trasmettere*) by telegraph.

telegrafico, a, ci, che [tele'grafiko] AGG telegraph *attr*; (*fig*: *stile*) telegraphic.

telegrafista, i, e [telegra'fista] SM/F telegraphist, telegraph operator.

telegrafo [te'lɛgrafo] SM (*apparecchio*) telegraph; (*ufficio*) telegraph office.

telegramma, i [tele'gramma] SM telegram.

teleguidare [telegwi'dare] VT (*telecomandare*) to radio-control, operate by remote control.

telelibera [tele'libera] SF (local) independent television station.

Telemaco [te'lɛmako] SM Telemachus.

telematica [tele'matika] SF (*servizio*) data transmission; (*disciplina*) telematics *sg*.

telemetro [te'lɛmetro] SM telemeter.

telenovela [teleno'vɛla] SF soap opera.

teleobiettivo [teleobjet'tivo] SM telephoto lens *sg*.

teleologia [teleolo'dʒia] SF teleology.

telepatia [telepa'tia] SF telepathy.

telepatico, a, ci, che [tele'patiko] AGG telepathic.

telequiz [tele'kwits] SM INV (TV) game show.

teleromanzo [telero'mandzo] SM television o TV serial.

teleschermo [teles'kermo] SM television o TV screen.

telescopico, a, ci, che [teles'kɔpiko] AGG telescopic.

telescopio, pi [teles'kɔpjo] SM telescope; **a telescopio** telescopic.

telescrivente [teleskri'vɛnte] [1] AGG teleprinting. [2] SF teleprinter (*Brit*), teletypewriter (*Am*).

teleselettivo, a [teleselet'tivo] AGG: **prefisso teleselettivo** STD code (*Brit*), dialling code (*Brit*), dial code (*Am*).

teleselezione [teleselet'tsjone] SF ≈ subscriber trunk dialling (*Brit*), ≈ direct dialing (*Am*); **telefonata in teleselezione** STD (*Brit*) o direct-dialing (*Am*) call.

telespettatore, trice [telespetta'tore] SM/F (television) viewer.

teletext [tele'tɛkst] SM INV Teletext ®.

teletrasmesso, a [teletraz'messo] PP di **teletrasmettere**.

teletrasmettere [teletraz'mettere] VT IRREG to televise.

teleutente [teleu'tɛnte] SM/F television subscriber.

televideo [tele'video] SM ≈ Teletext ®.

televisione [televi'zjone] SF (*gen*) television (*in Italy there are 3 state-owned channels, RAI 1, 2 and 3, and many private channels: all compete for advertising*); (*televisore*) television (set); **alla televisione** on television.

televisivo, a [televi'zivo] AGG television *attr*.

televisore [televi'zore] SM television set.

telex ['tɛleks] [1] AGG INV telex *attr*. [2] SM INV telex.

tellurico, a, ci, che [tel'luriko] AGG (*Geol*) telluric.

telo ['telo] SM length of cloth ▶**telo da bagno** bath towel.

telone [te'lone] SM **a** (*per copertura*) tarpaulin **b** (*sipario*) drop curtain.

tema, i ['tɛma] SM **a** (*argomento*) theme; (: *di conversazione*) subject, topic; (*Mus*) theme, motif; (*Scol*) essay, composition; **tema libero** (*Scol*) free composition; **andare fuori tema** to go off the subject **b** (*Ling*) theme, stem.

tematica [te'matika] SF basic themes *pl*.

tematico, a, ci, che [te'matiko] AGG (*tutti i sensi*) thematic.

temerariamente [temerarja'mente] AVV recklessly, rashly.

temerarietà [temerarje'ta] SF recklessness, rashness.

temerario, ria, ri, rie [teme'rarjo] [1] AGG reckless, rash. [2] SM/F reckless person.

temere [te'mere] [1] VT to be afraid of, to fear; **temo il pericolo** I am afraid of danger; **temo che non venga** I am afraid he won't come; **temo di non farcela** I am afraid I won't make it; **temere il peggio** to fear the worst; **temere una brutta sorpresa** to expect a nasty surprise; **mi hai fatto temere che...** you had me worried that ...; **temere il freddo** (*pianta*) to be sensitive to cold. [2] VI (*aus* avere) to be afraid; **temere per** (*preoccuparsi*) to worry about; **non temere!** (*non aver paura*) don't be afraid!; (*non preoccuparti*) don't worry!

tempaccio [tem'pattʃo] SM bad weather.

tempera ['tɛmpera] SF **a** (*Arte*: *colore, tecnica*) tempera; (: *dipinto*) painting in tempera; **colori a tempera** tempera *sg*; **dipingere a tempera** to paint in tempera **b** (*Tecn*) = **tempra**.

temperalapis [tempera'lapis], **temperamatite** [temperama'tite] SM INV pencil sharpener.

temperamento [tempera'mento] SM (*carattere*) temperament, character; **è nervoso di temperamento** he has a nervous temperament o disposition o character; **avere del temperamento** to have a strong personality; **manca di temperamento** he's weak-willed.

temperante [tempe'rante] AGG moderate.

temperare [tempe'rare] VT **a** (*matita*) to sharpen **b** (*metalli*) to temper.

temperato, a [tempe'rato] AGG **a** (*moderato*) moderate, temperate; (*clima*) temperate **b** (*acciaio*) tempered.

temperatura [tempera'tura] SF temperature ▶**temperatura ambiente** room temperature.

temperino [tempe'rino] SM penknife.

tempesta [tem'pɛsta] SF **a** (*Meteor*) storm; **il mare era in tempesta** the sea was stormy; **una tempesta in un**

bicchier d'acqua a storm in a teacup (*Brit*), a tempest in a teapot (*Am*); **c'è aria di tempesta** (*fig*) there is a storm brewing ▶ **tempesta magnetica** magnetic storm ▶ **tempesta di neve** snowstorm ▶ **tempesta di sabbia** sandstorm

b (*fitta serie*): **una tempesta di pugni** a hail of blows; **una tempesta di domande** a barrage of questions.

tempestare [tempes'tare] VT **a** : **tempestare qn di colpi** to rain blows on sb; **tempestare qn di domande/telefonate** to bombard sb with questions/(phone)calls **b** (*ornare*) to stud.

tempestivamente [tempestiva'mente] AVV opportunely, at the right time.

tempestività [tempestivi'ta] SF timeliness.

tempestivo, a [tempes'tivo] AGG timely, well-timed.

tempestoso, a [tempes'toso] AGG stormy.

tempia ['tɛmpja] SF (*Anat*) temple.

tempio, pi ['tɛmpjo] SM (*Rel, anche fig*) temple.

tempismo [tem'pizmo] SM sense of timing.

tempista, i, e [tem'pista] SM/F person with a good sense of timing.

templare [tem'plare] SM (*Rel, Storia*) (Knight) Templar.

tempo ['tɛmpo] SM **a** (*gen*) time; **il tempo e lo spazio** time and space; **il tempo vola!** time flies!; **il tempo stringe** time is short; **ci vuole tempo** it takes time; **abbiamo tempo 3 giorni** we have 3 days; **c'è o abbiamo tempo** there is plenty of time; **c'è sempre tempo** there is still time; **non c'è tempo da perdere** there is no time to lose; **perdere tempo** (*sprecare tempo*) to waste time; (*far tardi*) to lose time; **trovare il tempo di fare qc** to find the time to do sth; **con l'andare del tempo** with the passing of time; **a tempo di record** in record time; **un impiego a tempo pieno** a full-time job; **nei ritagli di tempo** [OR] **a tempo perso** in one's spare moments; **tempo libero** free *o* spare time

b (*periodo*) time; **da tempo** for a long time now; **da quanto tempo?** since when?; **tempo fa** some time ago; **poco tempo dopo** not long after; **per qualche tempo** for a while; **dove sei stato tutto questo tempo?** where have you been all this time?; **a tempo e luogo** at the right time and place; **a suo tempo** in due course, at the appropriate time; **ogni cosa a suo tempo** we'll (*o* you'll *ecc*) deal with it in due course; **in tempo utile** in due time *o* course; **al tempo stesso** [OR] **a un tempo** at the same time; **fare in tempo a fare qc** to manage to do sth; **farai in tempo a prendere il treno?** will you be in time for the train?; **arrivare/essere in tempo** to arrive/be in time; **per tempo** in good time, early; **un tempo** once

c (*durata di un'operazione*) time; (*fase*) stage; **rispettare i tempi** to keep to the schedule *o* timetable; **stringere i tempi** to speed things up ▶ **tempi di esecuzione** (*Comm*) time scale *sg* ▶ **tempi di lavorazione** (*Industria*) throughput time *sg* ▶ **tempi morti** (*Comm*) downtime *sg*, idle time *sg* ▶ **tempo di accesso** (*Inform*) access time ▶ **tempo di cottura** cooking time ▶ **tempo reale** (*Inform, Comm*) real time

d (*stagione*) season; **quando arriva il tempo delle ciliege** when the cherries ripen

e (*epoca*) time, times *pl*; **al tempo della Rivoluzione Culturale** at the time of *o* in the days of the Cultural Revolution; **tempi duri** hard times; **altri tempi!** those were the days!; **con i tempi che corrono** these days; **andare al passo con i tempi** to keep pace *o* keep up with the times; **nella notte dei tempi** in the dim and distant past; **in tempo di pace** in peace time; **in questi ultimi tempi** of late; **ai miei tempi** in my day; **aver fatto il proprio tempo** to have had its (*o* his *ecc*) day

f (*Meteor*) weather; **che tempo fa?** what's the weather like?; **fa bel/brutto tempo** the weather's fine/bad; **con questo tempo!** in this weather!; **tempo da lupi** *o* **da cani** foul weather; **condizioni del tempo** weather conditions; **previsioni del tempo** weather forecast *sg*

g (*Mus*) time; (: *battuta*) beat; (: *grado di velocità*) tempo; (: *movimento*) movement; **andare a tempo** to keep time; **essere fuori tempo** to be out of time; **battere** *o* **segnare il tempo** to mark time; **in tre tempi** in triple time

h (*Gramm*) tense; **tempo presente** present tense

i : **primo/secondo tempo** (*Teatro, Cine*) first/second part; (*Sport*) first/second half ▶ **tempi supplementari** (*Sport*) extra time *sg*

j (*di motore a scoppio*) stroke; **motore a due tempi** two-stroke engine

k (*fraseologia*): **dare tempo al tempo** to let matters take their course; **chi ha tempo non aspetti tempo** there's no time like the present; **fare il bello e il cattivo tempo** to rule the roost; **il tempo è denaro** time is money; **è un provvedimento che lascia il tempo che trova** it's a measure that doesn't really change anything; **cerchiamo di guadagnare tempo** (*indugiare*) let's play for time; (*finire in anticipo*) let's try to gain some time; **senza tempo** timeless.

temporale[1] [tempo'rale] SM (*Meteor*) (thunder)storm.

temporale[2] [tempo'rale] **1** AGG (*gen*) temporal; **avverbi temporali** adverbs of time.

2 SF (*Gramm*) temporal *o* time clause.

temporalesco, a, schi, sche [tempora'lesko] AGG stormy.

temporaneamente [temporanea'mente] AVV temporarily.

temporaneità [temporanei'ta] SF temporariness, provisional nature.

temporaneo, a [tempo'raneo] AGG temporary.

temporeggiamento [temporedʤa'mento] SM playing for time, temporizing.

temporeggiare [tempored'ʤare] VI (*aus* **avere**) to play for time, temporize.

temporeggiatore, trice [temporedʤa'tore] SM/F temporizer.

temporizzatore [temporiddza'tore] SM (*Elettr*) timer.

tempra ['tɛmpra] SF **a** (*Tecn*: *atto*) tempering, hardening; (: *effetto*) temper **b** (*fig*: *costituzione fisica*) constitution; (: *intellettuale*) temperament.

temprare [tem'prare] **1** VT (*gen, Tecn*) to temper; (*fig*) to strengthen, toughen.

2 temprarsi VR, VIP (*anche fig*) to become stronger *o* tougher.

tenace [te'natʃe] AGG (*odio*) lasting; (*volontà*) strong, firm; (*persona*) tenacious.

tenacemente [tenatʃe'mente] AVV tenaciously.

tenacia [te'natʃa] SF tenacity.

tenacità [tenatʃi'ta] SF (*di metallo*) toughness.

tenaglie [te'naʎʎe] SFPL (*arnese, chele*) pincers *pl*; (*del dentista*) forceps *pl*.

tenda ['tɛnda] SF **a** (*di finestra*) curtain; (*riparo: di negozio, terrazza*) awning; **tirare le tende** to draw the curtains *o* drapes (*Am*) ▶ **tenda per doccia** shower curtain

b (*Mil, da campeggio*) tent; **piantare le tende** to pitch one's tent; (*fig*) to settle down; **è ora di levar le tende** (*fig*) it's time to hit the trail *o* pack up and go

c : **tenda a ossigeno** oxygen tent.

tendaggio [tenˈdaddʒo] SM curtaining, curtains *pl*, drapes *pl* (*Am*).

tendenza [tenˈdɛntsa] SF (*gen*) tendency; (*inclinazione*) inclination; (*orientamento*: *Pol, Econ*) trend; **ha tendenza a ingrassare** he tends to put on weight; **avere tendenza a** *o* **per qc** to have a bent for sth; **con tendenza al bello** (*Meteor*) tending to fair ▶**tendenza al rialzo** (*Borsa*) upward trend ▶**tendenza al ribasso** (*Borsa*) downward trend.

tendenzialmente [tendentsjalˈmente] AVV: **è tendenzialmente sincero** he tends to be frank with people.

tendenziosamente [tendentsjosaˈmente] AVV tendentiously.

tendenziosità [tendentsjosiˈta] SF tendentiousness.

tendenzioso, a [tendenˈtsjoso] AGG tendentious, bias(s)ed.

tendere [ˈtɛndere] VB IRREG ① VT **a** (*mettere in tensione*: *corda*) to tighten, pull tight; (: *elastico, muscoli*) to stretch; (: *tessuto*) to stretch, pull *o* draw tight; **tendere una trappola a qn** to set a trap for sb

b (*sporgere*: *collo*) to crane; (: *mano*) to hold out; (: *braccio*) to stretch out; **tendere la mano** to hold out one's hand; (*fig*: *chiedere l'elemosina*) to beg; (: *aiutare*) to lend a helping hand; **tendere gli orecchi** (*fig*) to prick up one's ears.

② VI (*aus avere*): **tendere a qc/a fare qc** (*aver la tendenza*) to tend towards sth/to do sth; (*mirare a*) to aim at sth/to do sth; **tutti i nostri sforzi sono tesi a...** all our efforts are geared towards ...; **tende al pessimismo** he tends to be pessimistic; **tendere a sinistra** (*Pol*) to have left-wing tendencies; **la situazione tende a migliorare** the situation is improving; **il tempo tende al bello** the weather is improving; **un blu che tende al verde** a greenish blue.

tendina [tenˈdina] SF curtain.

tendine [ˈtɛndine] SM tendon, sinew.

tendiracchetta [tendirakˈketta] SM INV racket press.

tendiscarpe [tendisˈkarpe] SM INV shoetree.

tendone [tenˈdone] SM (*da circo*) big top.

tendopoli [tenˈdɔpoli] SF INV (*large*) camp.

tenebre [ˈtɛnebre] SFPL darkness *sg*, gloom *sg*.

tenebrosamente [tenebrosaˈmente] AVV (*misteriosamente*) mysteriously.

tenebroso, a [teneˈbroso] ① AGG (*gen*) dark, gloomy; (*fig*) mysterious.

② SM/F: **un bel tenebroso** a tall, dark and handsome man.

tenente [teˈnɛnte] SM lieutenant.

teneramente [teneraˈmente] AVV tenderly.

tenere [teˈnere] VB IRREG ① VT **a** (*reggere*: *in mano*) to hold; (: *in posizione*) to hold, to keep; (: *in una condizione*) to keep; **tieni!** (*prendilo*) here, take it!; **tenere qn per mano** to hold sb by the hand; **tenere una pentola per il manico** to hold a pan by the handle; **tieni la porta aperta** hold the door open; **tengono sempre la porta aperta** they always keep their door open; **tiene sempre la camicia sbottonata** he always has his shirt unbuttoned; **tenere le mani in tasca** to keep one's hands in one's pockets; **tieni gli occhi chiusi** keep your eyes shut *o* closed; **un cappotto che tiene caldo** a warm coat; **tiene la casa molto bene** her house is always tidy; **tenere presente qc** to bear sth in mind; **tenere la rotta** (*Naut*) to keep *o* stay on course; **il nemico teneva la città** the enemy had the city under its control *o* held the city; **tenere la destra/la sinistra** (*Aut*) to keep to the right/the left

b (*dare*: *conferenza, lezione*) to give; (*organizzare*: *riunione, assemblea*) to hold

c (*occupare*: *spazio*) to take up, occupy; **tenere il posto a qn** to keep sb's seat

d (*contenere*: *sogg*: *recipiente*) to hold

e (*resistere a*): **tenere il mare** (*Naut*) to be seaworthy; **tenere la strada** (*Aut*) to hold the road

f (*considerare*): **tenere conto di qn/qc** to take sb/sth into account *o* consideration; **tenere in gran conto** *o* **considerazione qn** to have a high regard for sb, think highly of sb.

② VI (*aus avere*) **a** (*resistere*) to hold out, last; (: *chiusura, nodo*) to hold; **tiene quella scatola?** is that box strong enough?; **questa vite non tiene** this screw is loose; **non ci sono scuse che tengano** I'll take no excuses; **tenere duro** (*resistere*) to stand firm, hold out

b (*parteggiare*): **tenere per qn/qc** to support sb/sth; **io tengo per lui** I am on his side

c : **tenere a** (*reputazione, persona, vestiario*) to attach great importance to; **tiene molto all'educazione** he is a great believer in education

d (*dare importanza*): **tenere a, tenerci a** to care about, attach great importance to; **tenere a fare** to want to do, be keen to do; **ci tengo ad ottenere la presidenza** it's important for me to become chairman; **ci tenevo ad andare** I was keen on going; **ci tiene che lo sappia** he wants him to know; **non ci tengo** I don't care about it, it's not that important to me; **se ci tieni proprio!** if you really want!.

③ **tenersi** VR **a** (*reggersi*): **tenersi a qn/qc** to hold onto sb/sth; **tenersi per mano** (*uso reciproco*) to hold hands; **tenersi in piedi** to stay on one's feet; **non si teneva più dal ridere** (*fig*) he couldn't help laughing, he couldn't keep from laughing

b (*mantenersi*) to keep, be; **tenersi pronto (a fare qc)** to be ready (to do sth); **tenersi vicino al/lontano dal muro** to keep close to/away from the wall; **tenersi sulla corsia di destra** to stay in the right-hand lane; **tenersi a destra/sinistra** to keep right/left

c (*attenersi*): **tenersi a** to comply with, stick to.

tenerezza [teneˈrettsa] SF tenderness; **che tenerezza che mi fa questo piccolino!** what a lovely little baby!; **non sono abituato a tutte queste tenerezze** I am not used to all this attention.

tenero, a [ˈtɛnero] ① AGG **a** (*carne, verdura*) tender; (*pietra, cera, colore*) soft; **grano tenero** soft wheat; **erba tenera** young grass; **è morto in tenera età** he died young; **alla sua tenera età** (*scherz*) at his tender age

b (*indulgente*) soft, tender; (*che esprime tenerezza*) tender, loving; **un tenero padre** a loving father; **avere il cuore tenero** to be tender-hearted; **che tenero!** how lovely!.

② SM **a** (*parte tenera*) tender part

b (*affetto*): **tra quei due c'è del tenero** there's a romance budding between those two.

tengo *ecc* [ˈtɛngo] VB vedi **tenere**.

tenia [ˈtɛnja] SF tapeworm.

tenni *ecc* [ˈtɛnni] VB vedi **tenere**.

tennis [ˈtɛnnis] SM INV tennis; **giocare a tennis** to play tennis; **da tennis** tennis *attr* ▶**tennis da tavolo** table tennis.

tennista, i, e [tenˈnista] SM/F tennis player.

tennistico, a, ci, che [tenˈnistiko] AGG tennis *attr*.

tenore [te'nore] SM **a** (*tono*) tone; **il tenore della sua lettera** the tone of his letter ▶**tenore di vita** (*modo di vivere*) way of life; (*livello*) standard of living **b** (*Mus*) tenor.

tensiometro [ten'sjɔmetro] SM (*Tecn*) tensiometer.

tensione [ten'sjone] SF (*gen*) tension; (*Elettr*) tension, voltage; **ad alta tensione** (*Elettr*) high-voltage *attr*, high-tension *attr*; **c'è un po' di tensione** (*fig*) things are a bit tense.

tensivo, a [ten'sivo] AGG: **cefalea tensiva** tension headache.

tentabile [ten'tabile] **1** AGG worth attempting, worth a try; **è una strada tentabile per risolvere il problema** it's a possible way of solving the problem.
2 SM: **tentare il tentabile** to try everything possible.

tentacolare [tentako'lare] AGG (*appendice, protuberanza*) tentacular; (*fig: città*) magnet-like.

tentacolo [ten'takolo] SM (*anche fig*) tentacle.

tentare [ten'tare] VT **a** (*provare*): **tentare qc/di fare qc** to attempt *o* try sth/to do sth; **ho tentato l'esame, ma non l'ho passato** I attempted the exam but I didn't pass it; **tentare il suicidio** to attempt suicide, try to commit suicide; **tentato suicidio** attempted suicide; **tentare un nuovo metodo** (*sperimentare*) to try out a new method; **le ho tentate tutte** (*per convincere qn*) I have tried every way; **tentare la sorte** to try one's luck; **tentar non nuoce** there's no harm in trying
b (*cercare di corrompere, allettare*) to tempt; (*mettere alla prova*) to test.

tentativo [tenta'tivo] SM attempt; **fa' ancora un tentativo** try again.

tentatore, trice [tenta'tore] **1** AGG tempting.
2 SM/F tempter/temptress.

tentazione [tentat'tsjone] SF temptation; **aver la tentazione di fare qc** to be tempted to do sth.

tentennamento [tentenna'mento] SM (*fig*) hesitation, wavering; **dopo molti tentennamenti** after much hesitation.

tentennare [tenten'nare] **1** VI (*aus* avere) (*persona*) to totter, stagger; (*fig*) to hesitate, waver; **gli tentenna un dente** he's got a wobbly *o* loose tooth; **il vecchio uscì tentennando** the old man staggered out.
2 VT: **tentennare il capo** to shake one's head.

tentoni [ten'toni] AVV (*anche fig*): **a tentoni** gropingly; **andare (a) tentoni** to grope one's way.

tenue ['tɛnue] AGG **a** (*colore*) soft; (*voce*) feeble; (*luce*) faint; (*fig: speranza*) slender, slight **b** (*Anat*): **intestino tenue** small intestine.

tenuemente [tenue'mente] AVV (*colorato*) softly; (*illuminato*) dimly.

tenuta [te'nuta] SF **a** (*capacità*) capacity; **a tenuta d'aria** airtight ▶**tenuta di strada** (*Aut*) roadholding **b** (*divisa*) uniform; **in tenuta da lavoro** in one's work(ing) clothes; **in tenuta da sci** in a skiing outfit; **in tenuta da calciatore** in a football strip (*Brit*) **c** (*podere*) estate.

tenutario, ria, ri, rie [tenu'tarjo] SM/F brothel-keeper.

tenzone [ten'tsone] SF (*letter: combattimento*) strife; (: *disputa letteraria*) literary dispute.

teocentrico, a, ci, che [teo'tʃɛntriko] AGG theocentric.

teologale [teolo'gale] AGG theological; **virtù teologali** theological virtues.

teologia [teolo'dʒia] SF theology ▶**la teologia della liberazione** the liberation theology.

teologico, a, ci, che [teo'lɔdʒiko] AGG theological.

teologo, a, gi, ghe [te'ɔlogo] SM/F theologian.

teorema, i [teo'rɛma] SM (*Mat*) theorem.

teoreticamente [teoretika'mente] AVV theoretically.

teoretico, a, ci, che [teo'rɛtiko] AGG theoretical.

teoria [teo'ria] SF theory; **in teoria** in theory, theoretically.

teoricamente [teorika'mente] AVV in theory.

teorico, a, ci, che [te'ɔriko] **1** AGG theoretic(al); **a livello teorico** [OR] **in linea teorica** theoretically, in theory.
2 SM/F theorist, theoretician.

teorizzare [teorid'dzare] VT to theorize.

tepido, a ['tɛpido] AGG = tiepido.

tepore [te'pore] SM warmth.

teppa ['teppa] SF mob, hooligans *pl*.

teppaglia [tep'paʎʎa] SF hooligans *pl*.

teppismo [tep'pizmo] SM hooliganism.

teppista, i, e [tep'pista] SM/F hooligan.

tequila [te'kila] SF INV tequila.

terapeutica [tera'pɛutika] SF therapeutics *sg*.

terapeutico, a, ci, che [tera'pɛutiko] AGG therapeutic.

terapia [tera'pia] SF (*Med*) therapeutics *sg*, therapy; (: *cura*) therapy, treatment ▶**terapia di gruppo** group therapy ▶**terapia intensiva** intensive care ▶**terapia d'urto** massive-dose treatment; (*fig*) shock treatment *o* therapy.

terapista, i, e [tera'pista] SM/F therapist.

tergere ['tɛrdʒere] VT IRREG (*sudore, pianto*) to wipe.

tergicristallo [terdʒikris'tallo] SM windscreen (*Brit*) *o* windshield (*Am*) wiper ▶**tergicristallo (a funzionamento) intermittente** intermittent wiper.

tergilunotto [terdʒilu'nɔtto] SM (*Aut*) rear wiper.

tergiversare [terdʒiver'sare] VI (*aus* avere) to beat about the bush, shilly-shally.

tergo, ghi ['tɛrgo] SM back; (*di moneta*) reverse; **a tergo** behind; **vedi a tergo** please turn over, see overleaf.

terital® ['tɛrital] SM INV Terylene ®.

termale [ter'male] AGG thermal; **sorgente termale** hot spring; **stazione termale** spa resort.

terme ['tɛrme] SFPL (thermal) baths.

termico, a, ci, che ['tɛrmiko] AGG (*Fis*) thermic, thermal; **borsa termica** cool bag *o* box (*Brit*), cooler (*Am*); **centrale termica** thermal power station.

terminal ['tɜːminl] SM INV (*gen*) terminal; (*Aer*) air terminal.

terminale [termi'nale] **1** AGG (*fase, parte*) final; (*Med*) terminal; **i malati terminali** the terminally ill *pl*; **tratto terminale** (*di fiume*) lower reaches *pl*.
2 SM terminal.

terminalista, i, e [termina'lista] SM/F computer operator, VDU operator.

terminare [termi'nare] **1** VT (*gen*) to end; (*lavoro*) to finish; **dopo aver terminato l'università** after finishing university.
2 VI (*aus* essere) to end; **terminare a punta** to end in a point; **terminare in consonante** to end in *o* with a consonant; **dove termina la valle c'è un lago** there is a lake at the end of the valley.

terminazione [terminat'tsjone] SF (*fine*) end; (*Gramm*) ending ▶**terminazioni nervose** (*Anat*) nerve endings.

termine ['tɛrmine] SM **a** (*confine*) boundary, limit; (*punto estremo*) end; **al termine della strada** at the end of the road; **porre termine a qc** to put an end to sth; **avere termine** to end; **portare a termine qc** to bring sth to a conclusion
b (*spazio di tempo*) stipulated period; (*scadenza*) dead-

line; **entro un termine di tre ore** within three hours; **fissare un termine** to set a deadline; **entro il termine convenuto** within the stipulated period; **qual è il termine per la presentazione delle domande?** what is the deadline for applications?; **a breve/lungo termine** short-/long-term; **contratto a termine** (*Dir*) fixed-term contract; (*Comm*) forward contract

c : **termini** (*condizioni*) terms; (*limiti*) limits; **ai termini di legge** by law; **questo contratto non è valido ai termini di legge** this contract is not valid under law; **fissare i termini della questione** to define the problem; **la questione sta in questi termini** this is how the matter stands; **essere in buoni/cattivi termini con qn** to be on good/bad terms with sb

d (*Gramm, Mat*) term; **un termine tecnico/scientifico** a technical/scientific term; **ridurre ai minimi termini** (*Mat*) to reduce to the lowest terms; **termini di paragone** terms of comparison; **in altri termini** in other words; **modera i termini!** moderate your language!; **parlare senza mezzi termini** not to mince one's words.

terminologia [terminolo'dʒia] SF terminology.

termite ['tεrmite] SF termite.

termo... ['tεrmo] PREF thermo....

termoconvettore [termokonvet'tore] SM convector heater.

termocoperta [termoko'pεrta] SF electric blanket.

termodinamica [termodi'namika] SF thermodynamics *sg*.

termodinamico, a, ci, che [termodi'namiko] AGG thermodynamic.

termoelettrico, a, ci, che [termoe'lεttriko] AGG thermoelectric(al).

termoindurente [termoindu'rεnte] AGG thermosetting.

termometro [ter'mɔmetro] SM (*anche fig*) thermometer.

termonucleare [termonukle'are] AGG thermonuclear.

termoplastico, a, ci, che [termo'plastiko] AGG thermoplastic.

termoregolazione [termoregolat'tsjone] SF thermostatic temperature control.

termos ['tεrmos] SM INV = thermos.

termosaldare [termosal'dare] VT (*materie plastiche*) to heat-seal.

termosifone [termosi'fone] SM (*radiatore*) radiator; (*sistema di riscaldamento*) central heating.

termostato [ter'mɔstato] SM thermostat.

termoterapia [termotera'pia] SF heat treatment.

terna ['tεrna] SF (*gen*) set of three; (*lista di tre nomi*) list of three candidates ▶**terna arbitrale** (*Calcio*) referee and linesmen.

ternario, ria, ri, rie [ter'narjo] AGG (*Poesia: verso*) three-syllable *attr*; (*Chim*) ternary.

terno ['tεrno] SM (*al lotto*) (set of) three winning numbers; **vincere un terno al lotto** (*fig*) to hit the jackpot.

terra ['tεrra] ☐1 SF **a** : **la Terra** (*pianeta*) the earth; (*fig: mondo*) the world; **sulla faccia della terra** on the face of the earth; **i piaceri di questa terra** the pleasures of this world

b (*terreno, suolo*) ground; (*sostanza*) soil, earth; (*argilla*) clay; **per terra** (*appoggiare, sedersi*) on the ground; (*cadere*) to the ground; **il tesoro è sotto terra** the treasure is buried; **il fiume passa sotto terra** the stream runs underground; **strada in terra battuta** dirt track

c (*distesa, campagna*) land *no pl*; **un pezzo di terra** (*gen*) a piece of land; (*fabbricabile, per orto*) a plot of land; **una lingua di terra** a strip of land; **le sue terre** (*possedimento*)

his estate

d (*terraferma*) land *no pl*; **scendere a terra** to go ashore; **via terra** (*viaggiare*) by land, overland

e (*paese, regione*) land, country; **in terra straniera** in foreign parts; **è della mia terra** he is a fellow countryman; **tattica della terra bruciata** (*Mil*) scorched earth policy

f (*Elettr*) earth (*Brit*), ground (*Am*); **mettere a terra** to earth *o* ground

g (*fraseologia*): **avere una gomma a terra** to have a flat tyre; **essere a terra** (*fig: depresso*) to be at rock bottom; **terra terra** (*fig: persona, argomento*) prosaic, pedestrian; **cercare qn/qc per mare e per terra** to look high and low for sb/sth; **non sta né in cielo né in terra** it is quite unheard of; **stare con i piedi per terra** (*fig*) to have both feet on the ground.

☐2 ▶**terra di nessuno** no-man's-land ▶**la terra promessa** the Promised Land ▶**la Terra Santa** the Holy Land ▶**terra di Siena** sienna.

terra-aria ['tεrra 'arja] AGG INV (*Mil*) ground-to-air, surface-to-air.

terracotta [terra'kɔtta] SF (*pl* **terrecotte**) terracotta *no pl*; **di terracotta** terracotta *attr*; **vasellame di terracotta** earthenware; **terracotta smaltata** glazed earthenware.

terracqueo, a [ter'rakkweo] AGG: **il globo terracqueo** the globe.

terraferma [terra'ferma] SF (*terra emersa*) dry land, terra firma; (*continente*) mainland; **avvistare la terraferma** to sight land.

terraglia [ter'raʎʎa] SF **a** pottery *sg* **b** : **terraglie** SFPL (*oggetti*) crockery *sg*, earthenware *sg*.

Terranova [terra'nɔva] SF Newfoundland.

terrapieno [terra'pjɛno] SM embankment, bank.

terra-terra ['tεrra 'tεrra] AGG INV (*Mil*) ground-to-ground, surface-to-surface.

terrazza [ter'rattsa] SF (*gen, Agr*) terrace.

terrazzamento [terrattsa'mento] SM (*Agr*) terracing.

terrazzare [terrat'tsare] VT (*gen, Agr*) to terrace.

terrazzato, a [terrat'tsato] AGG (*gen, Agr*) terraced.

terrazzino [terrat'tsino] SM (*small*) balcony.

terrazzo [ter'rattso] SM (*gen, Agr, Geog*) terrace; (*balcone*) balcony.

terremotato, a [terremo'tato] ☐1 AGG (*zona*) devastated by an earthquake. ☐2 SM/F earthquake victim.

terremoto [terre'mɔto] SM earthquake; (*fig scherz: bambino*) terror; (: *sconvolgimento*) havoc.

terreno, a [ter'reno] ☐1 SM **a** (*gen*) ground; (*suolo*) soil, ground; **un terreno montuoso** a mountainous terrain; **dissodare il terreno** to till the soil; **preparare il terreno** (*fig*) to prepare the ground; **tastare il terreno** (*fig*) to see how the land lies ▶**terreno alluvionale** (*Geol*) alluvial soil

b (*area coltivabile, edificabile*) land *no pl*, plot (of land); **ho comprato un terreno** I bought a piece *o* a plot of land; **una casa con 500 ettari di terreno** a house with 500 hectares of land

c (*Mil: teatro di operazioni*) field; (: *guadagnato, perduto*) ground; **perdere terreno** (*anche fig*) to lose ground

d (*Sport*): **terreno di gioco** field; **una partita sospesa a causa del terreno pesante** a match postponed because of ground waterlogged.

☐2 AGG **a** (*vita, beni*) earthly

b (*a livello della strada*): **piano terreno** ground floor (*Brit*), first floor (*Am*).

terreo, a ['tɛrreo] AGG (*viso, colorito*) wan.

terrestre [ter'rɛstre] [1] AGG (*della terra: superficie*) of the earth, earth's *attr*; (: *magnetismo*) terrestrial; (*di terra: battaglia, animale*) land *attr*; **il globo terrestre** the globe. [2] SM/F earthling.

terribile [ter'ribile] AGG (*orribile*) terrible, dreadful; (: *nemico*) terrible; (: *visione*) fearful; (: *forza*) tremendous; (*fam: formidabile*) terrific, tremendous; **ho una fame terribile** I am terribly hungry.

terribilmente [terribil'mente] AVV terribly.

terriccio, ci [ter'rittʃo] SM soil.

terrier [tɛ'rje] SM INV (*cane*) terrier.

terriero, a [ter'rjɛro] AGG: **proprietà terriera** landed property; **proprietario terriero** landowner.

terrificante [terrifi'kante] AGG terrifying.

terrina [ter'rina] SF (*zuppiera*) tureen; (*ciotola*) terracotta bowl; (*per patè*) terrine.

territoriale [territo'rjale] AGG territorial.

territorialistico, a, ci, che [territorja'listiko] AGG territorial.

territorio, ri [terri'tɔrjo] SM (*gen*) territory; (*di comune*) precinct; (*di giudice*) jurisdiction.

terrone, a [ter'rone] SM/F *derogatory term used by Northern Italians to describe Southern Italians.*

terrore [ter'rore] SM (*anche fig*) terror; **il Terrore** (*Storia*) the Reign of Terror; **incutere terrore a qn** to strike terror into sb's heart; **avere (il) terrore di qc** to be terrified of sth; **con terrore** in terror; **del terrore** (*film, racconto*) horror *attr*.

terrorismo [terro'rizmo] SM terrorism.

terrorista, i, e [terro'rista] SM/F terrorist.

terroristico, a, ci, che [terro'ristiko] AGG terrorist *attr*.

terrorizzare [terrorid'dzare] VT (*gen*) to terrify; (*popolazione*) to terrorize; **l'idea di viaggiare in aereo lo terrorizza** he is terrified of flying.

terroso, a [ter'roso] AGG (*acqua*) muddy; (*sporco di terra*) covered with earth; (*Chim: metallo*) earth *attr*.

terso, a ['tɛrso] [1] PP di **tergere**. [2] AGG clear.

terza ['tɛrtsa] SF (*gen*) third; (*Aut*) third gear; (*Scol: elementare*) ≈ third year (at primary school) (*Brit*), ≈ third grade (*Am*); (: *media*) ≈ second year (at secondary school) (*Brit*), ≈ eighth grade (*Am*); (: *superiore*) ≈ fifth year (at secondary school) (*Brit*), ≈ eleventh grade (*Am*).

terzetto [ter'tsetto] SM (*Mus*) trio, terzetto; (*di persone*) trio.

terziario, ria, ri, rie [ter'tsjarjo] [1] AGG (*Geol, Econ*) tertiary. [2] SM [a] (*Geol*) tertiary period [b] (*Econ*) tertiary *o* service sector ▶ **terziario avanzato** high-tech service sector. [3] SM/F (*Rel*) tertiary.

terzina [ter'tsina] SF (*Letteratura*) tercet; (*Mus*) triplet.

terzino [ter'tsino] SM (*Calcio*) fullback, back; **terzino destro/sinistro** right/left back.

terzo, a ['tɛrtso] [1] AGG third; **terzo** [OR] **in terzo luogo** thirdly, in the third place; **di terz'ordine** third-rate; **il terzo mondo** the Third World; **la terza pagina** (*Stampa*) the Arts page; **la terza età** old age. [2] SM/F [a] third [b]: **terzi** SMPL (*altri*) others, other people *pl*; (*Dir*) third party *sg*; **agire per conto terzi** to act on behalf of a third party; **assicurazione contro terzi** third-party insurance (*Brit*), liability insurance (*Am*). [3] SM (*frazione*) third *per fraseologia vedi* **quinto**.

terzogenito, a [tertso'dʒenito] AGG, SM/F third-born, third eldest.

terzultimo, a [ter'tsultimo] AGG, SM/F third from last, last but two.

tesa ['tesa] SF (*di cappello*) brim; **a larghe tese** wide-brimmed.

teschio, chi ['tɛskjo] SM skull.

Teseo [te'zeo] SM Theseus.

tesi ['tɛsi] SF INV (*gen*) thesis; (*Univ: anche:* **tesi di laurea**) (degree) thesis; **sostenere una tesi** to uphold a theory.

tesi *ecc* ['tesi] VB *vedi* **tendere**.

teso, a ['teso] [1] PP di **tendere**. [2] AGG (*corda*) taut, tight; (*nervi, volto*) tense; (*rapporti*) strained; (*braccia*) outstretched; **è molto teso in questi giorni** he's very tense these days; **con la mano tesa** with outstretched hand; **stava lì con le orecchie tese** he was all ears; **essere teso come una corda di violino** to be very tense.

tesoreria [tezore'ria] SF treasury.

tesoriere, a [tezo'rjɛre] SM/F treasurer.

tesoro [te'zɔro] SM [a] (*gen, fig*) treasure; **far tesoro dei consigli di qn** to take sb's advice to heart; **sei un tesoro!** how nice of you!; **che tesoro di ragazza** what a nice girl; **grazie tesoro!** thank you darling! [b] (*Fin*): **il Tesoro** the Exchequer (*Brit*); **il ministero del Tesoro** the Treasury; **buono del Tesoro** Treasury Bond.

tessera ['tɛssera] SF [a] (*di socio*) (membership) card; (*di abbonato*) season ticket; (*di giornalista*) pass, press card; **ha la tessera del partito** he's a party member ▶ **tessera magnetica** magnetic-strip card ▶ **tessera di riduzione ferroviaria** ≈ Railcard (*Brit*) [b] (*di mosaico*) tessera.

tesseramento [tessera'mento] SM: **campagna di tesseramento (di un partito)** (party) membership drive.

tesserare [tesse'rare] [1] VT (*iscrivere*) to give a membership card to. [2] **tesserarsi** VIP to get one's membership card.

tesserato, a [tesse'rato] SM/F (*di società sportiva*) (fully paid-up) member; (*Pol*) (card-carrying) member.

tessere ['tɛssere] VT (*gen*) to weave; (*fig: inganni, tradimenti*) to plan, plot; **tessere le lodi di qn** to sing sb's praises.

tessile ['tɛssile] [1] AGG textile. [2] SM/F textile worker.

tessitore, trice [tessi'tore] SM/F weaver.

tessitura [tessi'tura] SF (*operazione*) weaving; (*impianto*) weaving mill *o* factory.

tessuto [tes'suto] SM [a] material, fabric; (*di lana*) cloth, material; **tessuti** SMPL textiles [b] (*Bio*) tissue.

test ['tɛst] SM INV test.

testa ['tɛsta] SF [a] (*gen, Anat*) head; **a testa alta** with one's head held high; **a testa bassa** (*correre*) headlong; (*con aria dimessa*) with head bowed; **gettarsi in qc a testa bassa** to rush headlong into sth; **cadere a testa in giù** to fall head first; **dalla testa ai piedi** from head to foot; **15.000 lire a testa** 15.000 lire apiece *o* a head *o* per person; **vincere di mezza testa** (*Ippica*) to win by half a head; **testa della racchetta** (*Tennis*) racket head; **una testa d'aglio** a bulb of garlic [b] (*fig: cervello*) head, brain(s); **testa di rapa** blockhead; **che testa di cavolo!** what a moron!; **essere una testa calda** to be hot headed; **avere la testa dura** to be stubborn; **avere la testa vuota** to be empty-headed; **avere la testa tra le nuvole** to have one's head in the

clouds; **non avere testa** to be scatterbrained; **usare la testa** to use one's head *o* brains; **ma dove hai la testa?** what on earth are you thinking of?; **ha poca testa per la matematica** he hasn't got much of a head for maths (*Brit*) *o* math (*Am*); **fare di testa propria** to do as one pleases; **far entrare qc in testa a qn** to din sth into sb's head; **mettersi in testa di fare qc** to take it into one's head to do sth; **che cosa gli hai messo in testa?** what ideas have you been putting into his head?; **non so che cosa gli sia passato per la testa** I don't know what's come over him

c (*parte anteriore*: *di treno, processione*) front, head; (: *di colonna militare*) head; (: *di pagina, lista*) top, head; **le carrozze di testa** (*Ferr*) the front of the train; **essere in testa** (*pilota, ciclista*) to be in the lead, be the leader; **essere in testa alla classifica** (*pilota, ciclista*) to be number one; (*squadra*) to be top of the league; (*disco*) to be top of the charts, be number one; **essere alla testa di qc** (*società*) to be the head of; (*esercito*) to be at the head of ▶**testa di serie** (*Sport*: *giocatore*) seed, seeded player; (: *squadra*) top of the league

d (*fraseologia*): **avere la testa sulle spalle** to have one's head screwed on; **dare alla testa** to go to one's head; **montarsi la testa** to become big-headed; **mettere la testa a posto** *o* **a partito** to settle down; **essere fuori** *o* **via di testa** to be off one's head; **perdere la testa per qn** to lose one's head over sb; **perdere la testa** (*per ira*) to lose one's head; **ci scommetterei la testa** I'd bet my boots; **tener testa a qn** (*nemico, avversario*) to stand up to sb; **lavata di testa** telling-off, ticking-off (*Brit*); **testa o croce?** heads or tails?; **fare a testa o croce** to toss up.

testa-coda ['tɛsta 'koda] SM INV (*Aut*) spin.

testamentario, ria, ri, rie [testamen'tarjo] AGG (*Dir*) testamentary; **le sue disposizioni testamentarie** the provisions of his will.

testamento [testa'mento] SM **a** (*Dir*) will, testament; **fare testamento** to make one's will; **testamento spirituale** (*fig*) spiritual testament **b** (*Rel*): **l'Antico/il Nuovo Testamento** the Old/New Testament.

testardaggine [testar'daddʒine] SF stubbornness, obstinacy.

testardamente [testarda'mente] AVV obstinately, stubbornly.

testardo, a [tes'tardo] **1** AGG stubborn, obstinate. **2** SM/F stubborn *o* obstinate person.

testare [tes'tare] VT to test.

testata [tes'tata] SF **a** (*di letto*) headboard **b** (*di giornale*) heading; (*il giornale stesso*) paper; **concentrazione delle testate** concentration of press ownership **c** (*Aut*) (cylinder) head; (*Aer*: *di missile*) head; **missile a testata nucleare** nuclear missile **d** (*colpo*: *accidentale*) bang on the head; (: *intenzionale*) head butt; **dare una testata contro qc** to bang one's head on sth; **dare una testata a qn** to head-butt sb.

teste ['tɛste] SM/F (*Dir*) witness.

testicolo [tes'tikolo] SM testicle.

testiera [tes'tjɛra] SF **a** (*del letto*) headboard **b** (*di cavallo*) headpiece.

testimone [testi'mone] **1** SM/F witness; **fare da testimone alle nozze di qn** to be a witness at sb's wedding; **queste rovine sono testimoni della grandezza di Roma** these ruins bear witness to the former greatness of Rome ▶**testimone di Geova** (*Rel*) Jehovah's Witness

▶**testimone oculare** eye witness. **2** SM (*Sport*) baton.

testimonial [testi'mounjəl] SM/F INV *celebrity who advertises a particular product*.

testimoniale [testimo'njale] AGG: **prova testimoniale** testimonial evidence.

testimonianza [testimo'njantsa] SF (*atto*) deposition; (*effetto*) evidence; (*fig*: *prova*) proof; **accusare qn di falsa testimonianza** to accuse sb of perjury; **rilasciare una testimonianza** to give evidence; **ne fanno testimonianza altri autori contemporanei** (*fig*) other contemporary authors testify to it; **ha dato testimonianza di grande fedeltà** he proved his great loyalty.

testimoniare [testimo'njare] **1** VT: **testimoniare che...** to testify that ...; **testimoniare il vero** to tell the truth; **testimoniare il falso** to perjure o.s.; **le impronte testimoniano la sua colpevolezza** the fingerprints are proof of his guilt; **testimoniare a favore di/contro qn** to testify for/against sb; **è stato chiamato a testimoniare** he was called upon to give evidence. **2** VI (*aus* avere) to testify, to give evidence; **non ha voluto testimoniare sull'accaduto** he didn't want to give evidence on *o* about what happened.

testina [tes'tina] SF (*di registratore, rasoio*) head ▶**testina rotante** (*di macchina da scrivere*) golf ball ▶**testina di stampa** (*Inform*) print head.

testo ['tɛsto] SM (*gen*) text; (*originale di traduzione*) original text; **libro di testo** (*Scol*) textbook; **fare testo** (*autore*) to be authoritative; (*opera*) be a standard work; **questo libro non fa testo** this book is not essential reading; **le sue parole fanno testo** his words carry weight.

testone, a [tes'tone] SM/F (*ostinato*) pig-headed person; (*stupido*) blockhead, dunderhead.

testosterone [testoste'rone] SM testosterone.

testuale [testu'ale] AGG textual; **le sue testuali parole furono...** his (o her) actual *o* exact words were ... .

testuggine [tes'tuddʒine] SF (*Zool*) tortoise; (: *marina*) turtle.

tetano ['tɛtano] SM (*Med*) tetanus.

tête-à-tête ['tɛta'tɛt] SM INV tête-à-tête.

tetramente [tetra'mente] AVV gloomily.

tetravalente [tetrava'lɛnte] AGG tetravalent.

tetro, a ['tɛtro] AGG (*anche fig*) gloomy; **era di umore tetro** he was gloomy *o* glum.

tetta ['tɛtta] SF (*fam*) boob, tit.

tettarella [tetta'rɛlla] SF teat.

tetto ['tɛtto] SM **a** (*gen*) roof; (*di veicolo*) roof, top; (*fig*) house, home; **restare senza tetto** to be homeless *o* without a roof over one's head; **abbandonare il tetto coniugale** to desert one's family ▶**tetto apribile** (*Aut*) sun roof ▶**tetto a cupola** dome ▶**tetto a terrazza** roof terrace **b** (*limite massimo*: *Econ*) (maximum) limit, ceiling; **porre un tetto alla spesa pubblica** to impose a limit on public spending.

tettoia [tet'toja] SF (*gen*) canopy; (*di stazione*) roof.

tettonica [tet'tɔnika] SF tectonics *sg*.

teutonico, a, ci, che [teu'tɔniko] AGG Teutonic.

Tevere ['tevere] SM: **il Tevere** the Tiber.

TG, Tg [ti'dʒi] SIGLA M INV (= *telegiornale*) TV news *sg*.

thermos® ['tɛrmos] SM INV Thermos ® (flask).

thriller ['θrilə] SM INV (*libro, film*) thriller.

ti [ti] PRON PERS (dav **lo, la, li, le, ne** diventa **te**) **a** (*ogg diretto*) you; **non ti ascolta mai** he never listens to you;

non ti ho visto stamattina I didn't see you this morning **b** (*complemento di termine*) (to) you; **ti dirò tutto** I'll tell you everything; **te lo ha dato?** did he give it to you? **c** (*riflessivo e medio*) yourself; **ti sei lavata?** have you washed (yourself)?; **ti sei pettinato?** have you combed your hair?; **quando ti prendi una vacanza?** when are you going to have yourself a holiday?

tiara ['tjara] SF tiara.

Tibet ['tibet] SM: **il Tibet** Tibet.

tibetano, a [tibe'tano] AGG, SM/F Tibetan.

tibia ['tibja] SF (*Anat*) tibia, shinbone.

tiburio, ri [ti'burjo] SM (*Archit*) lantern.

tic [tik] SM INV **a** (*gen*) click; (*di orologio*) tick **b** (*Med*: anche: **tic nervoso**) tic; (*fig*) mannerism.

ticchettio, tii [tikket'tio] SM (*di macchina da scrivere*) clatter; (*di orologio*) ticking; (*di pioggia*) pattering, patter.

ticchio, chi ['tikkjo] SM (*tic*) tic; (*fig: capriccio*) whim; **mi è preso il ticchio di andare in Africa** I've taken a notion to visit Africa.

ticket ['tikit] SM INV (*sui farmaci*) prescription charge (*Brit*); (*per prestazioni mediche*) medical charge.

tictac [tik'tak] SM INV tick-tock.

tiene ecc ['tjɛne] VB vedi **tenere**.

tiepidamente [tjepida'mente] AVV (*fig*) in a lukewarm way, half-heartedly; **accogliere qn/qc tiepidamente** to give sb/sth a lukewarm reception.

tiepidezza [tjepi'dettsa] SF (*di clima*) warmth; (*di accoglienza*) lukewarmness.

tiepido, a ['tjɛpido] AGG (*gen*) lukewarm, tepid; (*fig: accoglienza*) lukewarm; (: *entusiasmo*) half-hearted.

tifare [ti'fare] VI (*aus avere*): **tifare per** (*squadra*) to be a fan of, support; (*parteggiare*) to side with.

tifo ['tifo] SM **a** (*Med*) typhus **b** (*Sport*): **fare il tifo per** to be a fan of, support.

tifone [ti'fone] SM (*Meteor*) typhoon.

tifoseria [tifose'ria] SF fans *pl*, supporters *pl*.

tifoso, a [ti'foso] **1** AGG: **essere tifoso di** to be a fan of; **sono tifoso del Milan** I'm a Milan supporter. **2** SM/F (*Sport*) supporter, fan.

tight ['tait] SM INV morning suit.

tiglio, gli ['tiʎʎo] SM lime (tree), linden (tree).

tigna ['tiɲɲa] SF (*Med*) ringworm.

tignola [tiɲ'ɲola] SF (*Zool*) moth.

tignosa [tiɲ'ɲosa] SF (*Bot*) amanita (*mushroom*).

tigrato, a [ti'grato] AGG striped.

tigre ['tigre] SF tiger; (*femmina*) tigress; **cavalcare la tigre** (*fig*) to have a tiger by the tail; **occhio di tigre** (*Mineralogia*) tiger's eye, tigereye ▶ **tigre di carta** (*fig*) paper tiger.

tigrotto [ti'grɔtto] SM tiger cub.

tilde ['tilde] SM o F tilde.

tilt [tilt] SM INV: **andare** o **essere in tilt** (*macchina*) to go/be on the blink; (*fig*) to go/be haywire.

timballo [tim'ballo] SM (*Culin*) timbale.

timbrare [tim'brare] VT (*gen*) to stamp; (*annullare: francobolli*) to postmark; **timbrare il cartellino** to clock in.

timbratura [timbra'tura] SF (*vedi vb*) stamping; postmarking.

timbro ['timbro] SM **a** (*strumento*) (rubber) stamp; (*su documento*) stamp; (*su francobollo*) postmark; **mettere il timbro su qc** to stamp sth **b** (*Mus*) tone, timbre.

timidamente [timida'mente] AVV (*vedi agg*) shyly, timidly; bashfully.

timidezza [timi'dettsa] SF shyness, timidity.

timido, a ['timido] **1** AGG (*persona, animale*) shy, timid; (*tentativo*) bashful. **2** SM/F shy person.

timo¹ ['timo] SM (*Bot*) thyme.

timo² ['timo] SM (*Anat*) thymus.

timone [ti'mone] SM (*Naut*) helm; (: *parte sommersa*) rudder; (*Aer*) rudder; (*di carro*) shaft; **barra del timone** (*Naut*) tiller; **ruota del timone** (*Naut*) wheel; **essere al timone** (*anche fig*) to be at the helm; **prendere il timone** (*anche fig*) to take the helm ▶ **timone di direzione** (*Aer*) rudder ▶ **timone di profondità** (*Aer*) tail flap.

timoneria [timone'ria] SF (*Naut: apparecchiature*) steering gear.

timoniera [timo'njɛra] SF pilot house, wheelhouse.

timoniere [timo'njɛre] SM (*Naut*) helmsman; (*Canottaggio*) cox.

timorato, a [timo'rato] AGG conscientious; **timorato di Dio** God-fearing.

timore [ti'more] SM (*paura*) fear, dread; (*preoccupazione*) fear; (*rispetto*) awe; **avere timore di qn/qc** (*paura*) to be afraid of sb/sth; **ho il timore che non ci arriveremo** I fear we won't make it; **i miei timori si sono rivelati infondati** my fears proved to be unfounded; **ha un timore reverenziale di suo padre** he stands in awe of his father.

timorosamente [timorosa'mente] AVV fearfully.

timoroso, a [timo'roso] AGG (*diffidente*) timid, timorous; (*pauroso*) frightened, afraid; (*preoccupato*) worried, afraid.

timpano ['timpano] SM **a** (*Anat*) tympanum, eardrum; **rompere i timpani a qn** to burst sb's eardrums **b** (*Mus*) kettledrum; **i timpani** the timpani.

tinca, che ['tinka] SF tench.

tinello [ti'nɛllo] SM small dining room.

tingere ['tindʒere] VB IRREG **1** VT (*stoffa, capelli*) to dye; **il tramonto tingeva il cielo di rosso** the sunset was reddening the sky o was turning the sky red. **2** **tingersi** VIP: **il cielo si è tinto di rosso** the sky turned red.

tino ['tino] SM vat.

tinozza [ti'nɔttsa] SF tub.

tinsi ecc ['tinsi] VB vedi **tingere**.

tinta ['tinta] SF **a** (*colore*) shade, colour (*Brit*), color (*Am*); **una stoffa di tinta scura** a dark material; **una borsetta in tinta con le scarpe** a bag and matching shoes; **un vestito (in** o **a) tinta unita** a plain suit **b** (*per muri*) paint; (*per capelli*) dye; **dare una mano di tinta a qc** to give sth a coat of paint; **dipingere qc a tinte fosche** (*fig*) to paint a gloomy picture of sth; **un racconto a forti tinte** a dramatic story.

tintarella [tinta'rɛlla] SF (*fam*) (sun)tan; **prendere la tintarella** to get a tan.

tinteggiare [tinted'dʒare] VT to paint.

tintinnare [tintin'nare] VI (*aus avere*) (*campanelle*) to tinkle; (*bicchieri*) to clink, tinkle.

tintinnio, nii [tintin'nio] SM tinkling.

tinto, a ['tinto] PP di **tingere**.

tintore [tin'tore] SM (*di tessuti*) dyer.

tintoria [tinto'ria] SF (*lavasecco*) dry cleaner's (shop); (*officina*) dyeworks *inv*.

tintura [tin'tura] SF **a** (*operazione*) dyeing; (*soluzione colorante*) dye ▶ **tintura per capelli** hair dye **b** (*Med*) tincture ▶ **tintura di iodio** tincture of iodine.

tipicamente [tipika'mente] AVV typically.

tipicità [tipitʃi'ta] SF typicalness.

tipico, a, ci, che ['tipiko] AGG typical.

tipo, a ['tipo] [1] SM [a] (*genere*) kind, sort, type; **vestiti di tutti i tipi** all kinds of clothes; **sul tipo di questo** of this sort; **non è il mio tipo** he is not my type; **non è bella ma è un tipo** she might not be beautiful but she's got something
[b] (*modello*) type, model.
[2] SM/F (*fam: individuo*) character; **sei un bel tipo!** you're a fine one!; **chi era quel tipo?** who was that guy?; **è una tipa molto sicura di sé** she's very self-confident.
[3] AGG INV average, typical.

tipografia [tipogra'fia] SF typography.

tipografico, a, ci, che [tipo'grafiko] AGG typographic(al).

tipografo, a [ti'pografo] SM/F typographer.

tipologia [tipolo'dʒia] SF typology.

tip tap [tip tap] SM INV tap dancing.

T.I.R. [tir] SIGLA M (= *Transports Internationaux Routiers*) International Heavy Goods Vehicle.

tira e molla [tirae'mɔlla] SM INV = **tiremmolla**.

tiraggio, gi [ti'raddʒo] SM (*di camino*) draught (*Brit*), draft (*Am*).

tiralinee [tira'linee] SM INV drawing pen.

tiramisù [tirami'su] SM INV tiramisu, *dessert with a sponge base soaked in coffee and topped with a cream cheese dredged with chocolate.*

Tirana [ti'rana] SF Tirana.

tiranneggiare [tiranned'dʒare] VT to tyrannize.

tirannia [tiran'nia] SF tyranny.

tirannicamente [tirannika'mente] AVV tyrannically.

tirannico, a, ci, che [ti'ranniko] AGG tyrannical.

tirannide [ti'rannide] SF tyranny.

tiranno, a [ti'ranno] [1] SM tyrant.
[2] AGG tyrannical.

tirannosauro [tiranno'sauro] SM tyrannosaurus.

tirante [ti'rante] SM (*Naut, di tenda*) guy; (*Edil*) brace.

tirapiedi [tira'pjɛdi] SM/F INV hanger-on.

tirapugni [tira'puɲɲi] SM INV knuckle-duster (*Brit*), brass knuckles *pl* (*Am*).

tirare [ti'rare] [1] VT [a] (*gen*) to pull; (*slitta*) to pull, drag; (*rimorchio*) to tow; (*Culin: pasta*) to stretch; **tirare qn per la manica** to tug at sb's sleeve; **tirare qn da parte** to take *o* draw sb aside; **tirare gli orecchi a qn** to tweak sb's ears; **tirare qn per i capelli** to pull sb's hair; (*fig*) to force sb; **tirare qc per le lunghe** to drag sth out; **tirare le somme** (*fig*) to draw a conclusion; **tirare un sospiro di sollievo** to heave a sigh of relief; **una cosa tira l'altra** one thing leads to another; **tirare fuori** to pull out, take out; **il vigile mi fece tirare fuori i documenti** the policeman made me produce my identification papers; **alla fine ha tirato fuori tutta la verità** in the end he came out with the whole truth; **tirare giù** to pull down; **tirare su qn/qc** to pull sb/sth up; **tirare su qn** (*fig: rallegrare*) to cheer sb up; (*: allevare*) to bring sb up; **tirarsi dietro qn** to bring *o* drag sb along; **tirarsi su i capelli** to put one's hair up; **tirarsi addosso qc** to pull sth down on top of o.s.; (*fig*) to bring sth upon o.s.
[b] (*chiudere: tende*) to draw, close, pull; **tirare la porta** to close the door, pull the door to
[c] (*tracciare, disegnare*) to draw, trace; (*stampare*) to print
[d] (*lanciare: sasso, palla*) to throw, fling; (*: colpo, freccia*) to fire; (*: fig: bestemmie, imprecazioni*) to hurl, let fly; **gli ho tirato un pugno** I punched him; **gli ho tirato uno schiaffo** I slapped him; **tirare calci** to kick; **tirare il**

pallone (*Calcio*) to kick the ball.
[2] VI (*aus avere*) (*sogg: pipa, camino*) to draw; (*: vestito, indumento*) to be tight; **tirare avanti** (*fig: vivere*) to get by; (*: proseguire*) to struggle on; **tirare diritto** to keep right on going; **tirare tardi/mattina** to stay up late/till the early hours *o* dawn; **tirare col fucile/con l'arco** to shoot with a rifle/with a bow and arrow; **tirava un forte vento** a strong wind was blowing; **che aria tira?** (*fig*) what are things like?, what's the situation like?; **tirare a campare** to keep going as best one can; **tirare a indovinare** to take a guess; **tirare sul prezzo** to bargain; **tirare di scherma** to fence; **tirare in porta** (*Calcio*) to shoot (at goal); **la fantascienza è un genere che tira molto** science fiction is very popular; **il mercato/l'economia tira** the market/the economy is thriving.
[3] **tirarsi** VR: **tirarsi indietro** to draw *o* move back; (*fig*) to back out; **tirarsi su** to pull o.s. up; (*fig*) to cheer o.s. up.

tirata [ti'rata] SF [a] (*strattone*) pull, tug; **tirata d'orecchi** (*fig*) telling-off, ticking-off (*Brit*) [b] (*di sigaretta*) drag, puff [c] (*svolgimento ininterrotto*): **abbiamo fatto tutta una tirata** we did it all in one go; **l'ho letto in una tirata** I read it at one go [d] (*discorso polemico*) tirade.

tirato, a [ti'rato] AGG (*teso*) taut; (*stanco: viso, espressione*) drawn; (*avaro: persona*) stingy.

tiratore, trice [tira'tore] SM/F shot; **franco tiratore** (*Mil*) irregular; (*: cecchino*) sniper; (*Pol*) ≈ rebel (*who votes against his/her own party in a secret ballot*) ▶ **tiratore scelto** marksman.

tiratura [tira'tura] SF (*di giornali*) circulation; (*di libri*) printing, (print) run.

tirchieria [tirkje'ria] SF meanness, stinginess.

tirchio, chia, chi, chie ['tirkjo] [1] AGG mean, stingy.
[2] SM/F miser.

tiremmolla [tirem'mɔlla] SM INV hesitation, shilly-shallying *no pl*.

tiritera [tiri'tɛra] SF (*fam*) drivel, hot air.

tiro ['tiro] [1] SM [a] (*di cavalli, buoi*) team; **tiro a quattro** coach and four; **cavallo da tiro** draught (*Brit*) *o* draft (*Am*) horse
[b] (*di pistola, freccia, Calcio*) shooting *no pl*; (*: colpo*) shot; **è stato un buon tiro** that was a good shot; **essere a tiro** to be in range; (*fig*) to be within reach; **se mi capita *o* viene a tiro!** if I get my hands on him (*o her*)!; **a un tiro di schioppo** a stone's throw away
[c] (*lancio*) throwing *no pl*; (*: effetto*) throw
[d] (*fig*): **giocare un brutto tiro *o* un tiro mancino a qn** to play a dirty trick on sb.
[2] ▶ **tiro al bersaglio** target shooting ▶ **tiro alla fune** tug-of-war ▶ **tiro con l'arco** archery ▶ **tiro al piattello** clay pigeon shooting, skeet shooting (*Am*) ▶ **tiro al piccione** pigeon shooting ▶ **tiro a segno** (*esercitazione*) target shooting; (*luogo*) shooting range.

tirocinante [tirotʃi'nante] [1] AGG apprentice *attr*, trainee *attr*.
[2] SM/F apprentice, trainee.

tirocinio, ni [tiro'tʃinjo] SM: **tirocinio (in)** (*di mestiere*) apprenticeship (in); (*di professione*) training (in); **fare il proprio tirocinio** to serve one's apprenticeship; to do one's training.

tiroide [ti'rɔide] SF (*Anat*) thyroid (gland).

tirolese [tiro'lese] AGG, SM/F Tyrolean, Tyrolese *inv*.

Tirolo [ti'rɔlo] SM: **il Tirolo** the Tyrol.

tirrenico, a, ci, che [tir'rɛniko] AGG Tyrrhenian.

Tirreno [tir'rɛno] SM: **il (mar) Tirreno** the Tyrrhenian Sea.

tirso ['tirso] SM (*Mitol*) thyrsus.

tisana [ti'zana] SF herb tea, tisane.

tisi ['tizi] SF (*Med*) consumption.

tisico, a, ci, che ['tiziko] ⬛1 AGG (*Med*) consumptive; (*fig*: *gracile*) frail.
⬛2 SM/F (*Med*) consumptive (person).

tisiologo, gi [ti'zjɔlogo] SM phthisiologist.

titanico, a, ci, che [ti'taniko] AGG gigantic, enormous; **un'impresa titanica** an operation of titanic proportions.

titanio [ti'tanjo] SM (*Chim*) titanium.

titano [ti'tano] SM (*Mitol, fig*) titan.

titillare [titil'lare] VT (*solleticare*) to tickle; (*fig*) to titillate.

titolare [tito'lare] ⬛1 AGG (*gen*) appointed; (*Univ*) with a full-time appointment; (*sovrano, vescovo*) titular.
⬛2 SM/F (*gen*) holder, incumbent; (*proprietario*) owner, proprietor; (*Sport*: *in squadra*) regular first-team player; (: *a livello nazionale*) regular member of the national team ▶ **titolare di cattedra** (*Univ*) full professor.

titolato, a [tito'lato] AGG (*persona*) titled.

titolazione [titolat'tsjone] SF (*Chim*) titration.

Tito Livio ['tito 'livjo] SM (Titus) Livy.

titolo ['titolo] SM ⬛a (*di libro*) title; (*di giornale*) headline ▶ **titoli di coda** (*Cine, TV*) closing credits ▶ **titoli di testa** (*Cine, TV*) opening credits
⬛b (*Fin*: *gen*) security; (: *azione*) share, stock ▶ **titoli esteri** foreign securities ▶ **titoli di stato** government securities o bonds ▶ **titolo di credito** document of credit ▶ **titolo obbligazionario** bond, share certificate ▶ **titolo al portatore** bearer bond ▶ **titolo di proprietà** title deed
⬛c (*qualifica*: *nobiliare, Sport*) title; (: *di studio*) qualification ▶ **titolo mondiale** (*Sport*) world title
⬛d (*fig*: *motivo*): **a che titolo sei venuto?** why o for what reason have you come?; **a titolo di amicizia** for o out of friendship; **a titolo di curiosità** out of curiosity; **a titolo di prestito/favore** as a loan/favour (*Brit*) o favor (*Am*); a **titolo di cronaca** for your information.

titubante [titu'bante] AGG hesitant, undecided, irresolute; **è titubante per natura** he is a born ditherer.

titubanza [titu'bantsa] SF hesitation, indecision.

titubare [titu'bare] VI (*aus* **avere**) to hesitate; **titubare nel fare qc** to hesitate to do sth.

tivù [ti'vu] SF INV (*fam*) TV, telly (*Brit*).

tizio, zia, zi, zie ['tittsjo] SM/F character, individual; **chi era quel tizio?** who was that guy?; **chi era quella tizia?** who was that girl?; **Tizio, Caio e Sempronio** Tom, Dick and Harry.

tizzone [tit'tsone] SM (*di legno*) (fire)brand; (*di carbone*) live coal.

T.M.G. ['ti'ɛmme'dʒi] SIGLA M (= *tempo medio di Greenwich*) GMT.

TN SIGLA = *Trento*.

TNT [tienne'ti] SIGLA M (*Chim*: = *trinitrotoluene*) TNT.

TO SIGLA = *Torino*.

to' [tɔ] ESCL ⬛a (*dando qualcosa*) here you are!; **to', tieni!** here, take this! ⬛b (*guarda un po'*): **to'!** **chi si vede** look who's here!; **to'!** **questa è bella** (*iro*) well, that's very nice!

toast ['toust] SM INV toasted sandwich.

toccante [tok'kante] AGG (*commovente*) touching, moving.

toccare [tok'kare] ⬛1 VT ⬛a (*gen*) to touch; (*tastare*) to feel; (*fig*: *sfiorare*: *argomento, tema*) to touch on; **non toccare**

la mia roba don't touch my things; **non ha toccato cibo** he hasn't touched his food; **non voglio toccare i miei risparmi** I don't want to touch my savings; **toccare un tasto delicato** to touch a sore point; **hai toccato il mio punto debole** you have hit on my weak point; **toccare con mano** (*fig*) to find out for o.s.
⬛b (*raggiungere*) to touch, reach; **si tocca?** (*in acqua*) can you touch the bottom?; **toccare il fondo** to touch the bottom; (*fig*) to touch rock bottom; **toccare terra** (*Naut*) to reach land; (*Aer*) to touch down; **abbiamo toccato diverse città** we stopped at a number of towns; **abbiamo toccato diversi porti** we put in at various ports; **ha appena toccato la cinquantina** he has just turned fifty
⬛c (*commuovere*) to touch, move; (*ferire*) to hurt, wound; **le tue allusioni non mi toccano** your remarks don't bother me; **toccare qn sul vivo** to cut sb to the quick; **la vicenda ci tocca da vicino** the matter concerns o affects us closely.
⬛2 VI (*aus* **essere**) ⬛a (*capitare*): **mi è toccata una bella fortuna** I've had great good fortune; **perché toccano sempre a me queste cose?** why is it always me who has to do these things?; **a chi tocca, tocca** that's life
⬛b (*essere costretto*): **mi tocca andare** I have to go; **che cosa mi tocca sentire!** what's this I hear?; **sai che cosa mi è toccato fare?** do you know what I had to do?
⬛c (*spettare*): **toccare a** to be the turn of; **a chi tocca?** whose turn o go is it?; **tocca a me** it's my turn o go; **non tocca a me giudicare** it is not for me to judge; **tocca a te difenderci** it's up to you to defend us.
⬛3 **toccarsi** VR ⬛a (*masturbarsi*) to play with o.s.
⬛b (*uso reciproco*): **gli estremi si toccano** (*anche fig*) extremes meet.

toccasana [tokka'sana] SM INV miracle cure.

toccata [tok'kata] SF (*gen*) touch; (*Mus*) toccata.

toccato, a [tok'kato] AGG ⬛a (*come escl*: *Scherma, anche fig*) touché ⬛b (*svitato*) mad, touched.

toccherò ecc [tokke'rɔ] VB vedi **toccare**.

tocco¹, a, chi, che ['tɔkko] AGG mad, touched.

tocco², chi ['tɔkko] SM ⬛a (*gen, Mus*) touch; **gli ultimi tocchi** the finishing touches ⬛b (*colpo*: *di campana, orologio, pennello*) stroke.

tocco³, chi ['tɔkko] SM (*di pane, formaggio*) piece, chunk.

toc toc [tɔk tɔk] ESCL knock knock.

toeletta [toe'letta] SF = **toilette**.

toga, ghe ['tɔga] SF (*di magistrato*) gown, robe; (*Storia*) toga.

togato, a [to'gato] AGG: **giudice togato** magistrate.

togliere ['tɔʎʎere] VB IRREG ⬛1 VT ⬛a (*gen*) to remove, take away o off; **togli il quadro dal muro** take the picture off the wall; **togliere le mani di tasca** to take one's hands out of one's pockets; **togliere qn di mezzo** (*allontanare*) to get rid of sb; (*uccidere*) to bump sb off; **togliere qc a qn** to take sth (away) from sb; **togliere la parola a qn** to interrupt sb; **togliere la parola di bocca a qn** to take the words out of sb's mouth; **togliere il saluto a qn** to ignore sb, snub sb; **mi hai tolto un peso** you've taken a weight off my mind; **volevo togliermi un peso (dalla coscienza)** I wanted to get it off my chest; **togliersi la vita** to take one's (own) life; **togliersi i guanti/il vestito/il trucco** to take off one's gloves/suit/make-up; **togliersi una voglia** to satisfy an urge o a whim; **togliersi la soddisfazione di** to have the satisfaction of; **ciò non toglie che...** that doesn't alter the fact that ..., nevertheless ..., be that as

it may ...

  b (*Mat*) to take away, subtract; **togliere 3 da 7** to take 3 away from 7.

  2 **togliersi** VR: **togliersi di mezzo** to get out of the way; **togliti dai piedi!** get out of the way!

Togo ['tɔgo] SM: **il Togo** Togo.

toilette [twa'lɛt] SF INV, **toletta** [to'letta] SF **a** (*gabinetto*) toilet (*Brit*), bathroom (*Am*) **b** (*abbigliamento*) gown, dress **c** (*mobile*) dressing table **d** : **fare toilette** to make o.s. beautiful.

Tokyo ['tɔkjo] SF Tokyo.

tolgo *ecc* ['tɔlgo] VB *vedi* **togliere**.

tollerante [tolle'rante] AGG tolerant.

tolleranza [tolle'rantsa] SF (*gen*) tolerance; (*Rel*) toleration; **non ha un minimo di tolleranza** he is completely intolerant; **casa di tolleranza** brothel.

tollerare [tolle'rare] VT **a** (*sopportare: ingiustizia, offese*) to tolerate, put up with; (: *alcolici*) to take; (: *persona*) to put up with, bear, stand; **tollerare il freddo/caldo** to stand *o* take the cold/the heat **b** (*ammettere*) to tolerate, allow; **non tollero repliche** I won't stand for objections; **non sono tollerati ritardi** lateness will not be tolerated.

Tolosa [to'loza] SF Toulouse.

tolsi *ecc* ['tɔlsi] VB *vedi* **togliere**.

tolto,a ['tɔlto] 1 PP di **togliere**.

  2 PREP (*eccetto*) except for.

  3 SM: **mal tolto = maltolto**.

tomaia [to'maja] SF (*di scarpa*) upper.

tomba ['tomba] SF (*gen*) grave; (*cappella sotterranea*) tomb; **è una tomba** (*fig: persona*) he won't give anything away; **non temere, sarò una tomba** don't worry, my lips are sealed; **nelle strade c'era un silenzio di tomba** it was as silent as the grave in the streets; **lo accolsero con un silenzio di tomba** he was greeted with a deathly hush; **avere un piede nella tomba** to have one foot in the grave.

tombale [tom'bale] AGG: **pietra tombale** tombstone, gravestone.

tombarolo [tomba'rɔlo] SM (*fam*) grave robber.

tombino [tom'bino] SM (*pozzetto*) manhole; (*coperchio*) manhole cover.

tombola¹ ['tombola] SF (*gioco*) tombola, bingo.

tombola² ['tombola] SF (*fam: caduta*) tumble; **tombola!** upsy-daisy!

tombolo ['tombolo] SM **a** (*per ricamo*) lace pillow; **merletto a tombolo** bobbin lace **b** (*fam scherz: persona grassoccia*) podge.

tomo ['tɔmo] SM **a** (*volume*) volume, tome **b** (*persona*) queer fish.

tomografia [tomogra'fia] SF (*Med*) tomography ▶**tomografia assiale computerizzata** computerised axial tomography.

tonaca, che ['tɔnaka] SF (*Rel*) habit; **indossare la tonaca** (*frate*) to take the habit; (*monaca*) to take the veil.

tonale [to'nale] AGG (*Mus*) tonal, tone *attr*; (*Pittura*) tonal.

tonalità [tonali'ta] SF INV **a** (*di colore*) shade **b** (*Mus*) tonality.

tonante [to'nante] AGG (*voce*) loud, booming.

tonare [to'nare] VI = **tuonare**.

tondeggiante [tonded'dʒante] AGG roundish.

tondino [ton'dino] SM (*Edil*) reinforcing rod.

tondo, a ['tondo] 1 AGG (*circolare*) round; **fare cifra tonda** to round up (*o* down); **tre mesi tondi** exactly three months; **gli ho detto chiaro e tondo** I told him very

clearly *o* bluntly; **parentesi tonde** round brackets.

  2 SM (*cerchio*) circle; **scultura a tutto tondo** full-relief sculpture.

tonfo ['tonfo] SM (*rumore sordo*) thud, thump; (*nell'acqua*) plop; **fare un tonfo** (*cadere*) to take a tumble.

Tonga ['tɔnga] SM: **il Tonga** Tonga.

tonico, a, ci, che ['tɔniko] 1 AGG tonic.

  2 SM **a** (*cosmetico*) toner **b** (*Med*) tonic.

tonificante [tonifi'kante] AGG invigorating, bracing.

tonificare [tonifi'kare] VT (*gen*) to invigorate; (*muscoli, pelle*) to tone up.

tonnara [ton'nara] SF tuna-fishing nets *pl*.

tonnato, a [ton'nato] AGG (*Culin*): **salsa tonnata** tuna fish sauce; **vitello tonnato** veal with tuna fish sauce.

tonneau [tɔ'no] SM INV (*Aer*) (acrobatic) roll.

tonnellaggio [tonnel'laddʒo] SM (*Naut*) tonnage.

tonnellata [tonnel'lata] SF ton.

tonno ['tonno] SM tuna (fish).

tono ['tɔno] SM (*gen, Mus*) tone; (*di colore*) tone, shade; **parlare con tono minaccioso** to speak in a threatening tone *o* threateningly; **abbassa il tono (della voce)!** lower your tone (of voice)!; **il tono della lettera/del discorso** the tone of the letter/speech; **se la metti su questo tono...** if that's the way you want to put it ...; **rispondere a tono** (*a proposito*) to answer to the point; (*nello stesso modo*) to answer in kind; (*per le rime*) to answer back; **essere giù di tono** to be unwell *o* off-colour (*Brit*); **cercava di darsi un tono** she tried to act in a more refined way.

tonsilla [ton'silla] SF (*Med*) tonsil; **operarsi di tonsille** to have one's tonsils out.

tonsillare [tonsil'lare] AGG tonsillar, of the tonsils.

tonsillectomia [tonsillekto'mia] SF tonsillectomy.

tonsillite [tonsil'lite] SF (*Med*) tonsillitis.

tonsura [ton'sura] SF tonsure.

tonto, a ['tonto] 1 AGG stupid, silly, dumb.

  2 SM/F blockhead, dunce; **fare il finto tonto** to play dumb.

top [tɔp] SM INV (*vertice, Abbigliamento*) top.

topaia [to'paja] SF (*casa*) hovel, dump; (*tana: di topo*) mousehole; (: *di ratto*) rat's nest.

topazio, zi [to'pattsjo] SM topaz.

topicida, i [topi'tʃida] SM rat poison.

topinambur [topinam'bur] SM INV Jerusalem artichoke.

topino [to'pino] SM (*uccello*) sand martin.

topless ['tɔplis] SM INV topless bathing costume.

top model SF INV supermodel.

topo ['tɔpo] SM **a** (*Zool*) mouse; (*ratto*) rat; **veleno per topi** rat poison; **color grigio topo** mousey grey ▶**topo campagnolo comune** fieldmouse ▶**topo delle chiaviche** brown rat ▶**topo domestico** house mouse ▶**topo muschiato** muskrat

  b (*persona*): **topo d'albergo** hotel thief ▶**topo d'auto** car thief ▶**topo di biblioteca** bookworm.

topografia [topogra'fia] SF topography.

topografico, a, ci, che [topo'grafiko] AGG topographic(al).

topografo [to'pɔgrafo] SM topographer.

topolino [topo'lino] SM (*piccolo topo*) baby mouse; (*scherz: bambino*) scamp ▶**topolino delle risaie** harvest mouse.

toponimo [to'pɔnimo] SM place name.

toponomastica [topono'mastika] SF toponymy.

toporagno [topo'raɲɲo] SM shrewmouse.

toppa ['tɔppa] SF **a** (*di stoffa*) patch; **mettere una toppa** (*fig*) to find a stopgap *o* short term solution **b** (*serratura*) keyhole.

torà [to'ra] SM INV Torah.

torace [to'ratʃe] SM (*Anat*) thorax, chest; (*Zool*) thorax.

toracico, a, ci, che [to'ratʃiko] AGG thoracic, chest *attr*; **gabbia** *o* **cassa toracica** rib cage.

torba ['tɔrba] SF peat.

torbidamente [torbida'mente] AVV (*fig*) sinisterly.

torbidezza [torbi'dettsa] SF (*vedi agg*) cloudiness; muddiness; darkness.

torbido, a ['tɔrbido] **1** AGG (*liquido*) cloudy; (: *fiume*) muddy; (*fig: pensieri*) dark, sinister.
2 SM: **qui c'è del torbido** there is something fishy going on here; **pescare nel torbido** to fish in troubled waters.

torbiera [tor'bjɛra] SF peat bog.

torcere ['tɔrtʃere] VB IRREG **1** VT **a** (*gen*) to twist; (*biancheria*) to wring (out); **torcere un braccio a qn** to twist sb's arm; **torcere il naso** (*per disgusto*) to wrinkle (up) one's nose; **avrei voluto torcergli il collo** I felt like wringing his neck; **non torcere un capello a qn** not to hurt a hair of sb's head; **dare del filo da torcere a qn** to make life *o* things difficult for sb
b (*piegare*) to bend.
2 torcersi VR: **torcersi dal dolore** to writhe in pain; **torcersi dalle risa** to double up laughing.

torchiare [tor'kjare] VT (*olive*) to press; (*fig fam: persona*) to grill.

torchiatura [torkja'tura] SF (*di olive*) pressing.

torchio, chi ['tɔrkjo] SM press; **mettere** *o* **tenere qn sotto il torchio** (*fig fam: interrogare*) to grill sb.

torcia, ce ['tɔrtʃa] SF (*fiaccola*) torch ►**torcia elettrica** torch (*Brit*), flashlight (*Am*) ►**torcia umana** (*fig*) human torch.

torcicollo [tortʃi'kɔllo] SM: **avere il torcicollo** to have a stiff neck.

tordo ['tɔrdo] SM thrush; **grasso come un tordo** fat as a pig ►**tordo comune** song thrush.

torero [to'rɛro] SM bullfighter, toreador.

torinese [tori'nese] **1** AGG of *o* from Turin.
2 SM/F inhabitant *o* native of Turin.

Torino [to'rino] SF Turin.

torma ['tɔrma] SF crowd, throng.

tormalina [torma'lina] SF tourmaline.

tormenta [tor'menta] SF snowstorm, blizzard.

tormentare [tormen'tare] **1** VT (*gen*) to torment; (*fig: infastidire*) to bother, pester.
2 tormentarsi VR to worry, torture o.s., fret.

tormentato, a [tormen'tato] AGG (*gen*) tormented; **tormentato dal dolore/dal rimorso** racked by pain/remorse; **un'anima tormentata** a tormented soul.

tormento [tor'mento] SM **a** (*dolore fisico, morale*) torment, agony; **morire fra atroci tormenti** to die in terrible agony **b** (*fastidio: di zanzare, caldo*) torment; (: *fam: persona*) pest.

tormentosamente [tormentosa'mente] AVV tormentingly.

tormentoso, a [tormen'toso] AGG (*angoscia*) tormenting; (*dubbio, pena*) tormenting, nagging; (*esistenza*) tormented.

tornaconto [torna'konto] SM advantage, benefit; **pensa solo al proprio tornaconto** he thinks only of his own interest.

tornado [tor'nado] SM tornado.

tornante [tor'nante] SM hairpin bend (*Brit*) *o* curve (*Am*).

tornare [tor'nare] **1** VI (*aus* essere) **a** to return, go (*o* come) back; **tornare a casa** to go (*o* come) home; **tornare da scuola** to come home from school; **un'occasione così non torna più** such an opportunity won't repeat itself, you won't get another chance like this; **non torniamo più sull'argomento** let's drop the subject; **continua a tornare sull'argomento** he harps on about it; **è tornato alla carica con la sua idea di...** he's gone back to the old idea of ...; **è tornato a dire/a fare...** he's back to saying/doing ...; **mi è tornato alla mente** I've just remembered; **tornare al punto di partenza** to start again; **siamo tornati al punto di partenza** we are back where we started; **tornare in sé** (*dopo svenimento*) to regain consciousness, come to one's senses, come round; (*rinsavire*) to be back to one's old self; **tornare su** to come up; **la cipolla mi torna su** onions repeat on me
b (*ridiventare*) to become again; **tornare di moda** to become *o* be fashionable again, be back in fashion (again); **il cielo è tornato sereno** it's cleared up again
c (*quadrare*) to be right, be correct; **i conti tornano** the accounts balance; (*fig*) it all falls into place; **qualcosa non torna in questa storia** there's something not quite right about this business
d (*essere, risultare*) to turn out (to be), prove (to be); **tornare utile** to prove *o* turn out (to be) useful; **tornerà a tuo danno** it will come home to roost; **tornare a onore di qn** to be a credit to sb, do sb credit.
2 VT (*fam*): **tornare qc a qn** to return sth to sb, give sth back to sb.

tornasole [torna'sole] SM INV litmus.

tornata [tor'nata] SF: **tornata elettorale** election.

torneo [tor'nɛo] SM (*Sport*) tournament, competition; (*Storia*) tournament.

tornio, ni ['tɔrnjo] SM lathe ►**tornio da vasaio** potter's wheel.

tornire [tor'nire] VT (*Tecn*) to turn (on a lathe); (*fig*) to shape, polish.

tornito, a [tor'nito] AGG: **ben tornito** (*gambe, braccia*) well-shaped.

tornitore, trice [torni'tore] SM/F (*Tecn*) (lathe-)turner.

tornitura [torni'tura] SF **a** (*Tecn*) turning; (*di legno*) wood turning **b** (*trucioli: di legno, metallo*) shavings *pl*.

torno ['tɔrno] SM: **levarsi** *o* **togliersi qn di torno** to get rid of sb; **levati di torno!** clear off!

toro ['tɔro] SM **a** (*Zool, fig*) bull; **essere forte come un toro** to be as strong as an ox; **prendere il toro per le corna** (*fig*) to take the bull by the horns **b** (*Astron, Astrol*): **Toro** Taurus; **essere del Toro** to be Taurus **c** (*Borsa*) bull.

torpedine [tor'pɛdine] SF **a** (*Zool*) stingray **b** (*Mil: mina*) torpedo.

torpediniera [torpedi'njɛra] SF (*Naut*) torpedo boat.

torpedo [tor'pɛdo] SF INV (*Aut*) tourer (*Brit*), touring car (*Am*).

torpedone [torpe'done] SM (*tourist*) coach (*Brit*) *o* bus (*Am*).

torpidamente [torpida'mente] AVV sluggishly.

torpido, a ['tɔrpido] AGG torpid.

torpore [tor'pore] SM torpor.

torre ['torre] SF **a** (*di città, castello*) tower ►**torre d'avorio** (*fig*) ivory tower ►**torre di controllo** (*Aer*) control tower ►**torre di osservazione** lookout tower **b** (*Scacchi*) rook, castle.

torrefare [torre'fare] VT IRREG (*caffè*) to roast.

torrefatto, a [torre'fatto] PP di **torrefare**.

torrefazione [torrefat'tsjone] SF (*del caffè*) roasting.

torreggiare [torred'dʒare] VI (*aus avere*): **torreggiare (su)** to tower (over).

torrente [tor'rɛnte] SM torrent; (*fig*) flood, stream.

torrentizio, zia, zi, zie [torren'tittsjo] AGG (*di torrente*) torrential.

torrenziale [torren'tsjale] AGG (*pioggia*) torrential.

torretta [tor'retta] SF (*gen, Mil*) turret; (*Naut*) tower ▶ **torretta di comando** (*Naut*) conning tower.

torrido, a ['tɔrrido] AGG scorching, torrid; **zona torrida** (*Geog*) Torrid Zone.

torrione [tor'rjone] SM (*torre*) keep, tower; (*Naut*) conning tower.

torrone [tor'rone] SM (*Culin*) *kind of nougat*.

torsi ecc ['tɔrsi] VB vedi **torcere**.

torsione [tor'sjone] SF (*gen*) twisting; (*Tecn*) torsion; (*Ginnastica*) twist.

torso ['tɔrso] SM (*Anat, Arte*) torso; (*di frutta*) core; **a torso nudo** bare-chested.

torsolo ['tɔrsolo] SM (*di cavolo*) stump; (*di mela*) core.

torta ['tɔrta] SF (*Culin*) cake; **spartirsi la torta** (*fig*) to split the loot ▶ **torta di mele** apple pie; (*tipo crostata*) apple tart (*Brit*) o pie (*Am*) ▶ **torta salata** savoury flan.

tortellino [tortel'lino] SM (*Culin*) tortellino (*single piece of pasta*); **tortellini** SMPL (*piatto*) tortellini.

tortelloni [tortel'loni] SMPL (*Culin*): **tortelloni di magro** *ravioli-like pasta filled with cheese, eggs and spinach*.

tortiera [tor'tjɛra] SF cake tin (*Brit*), cake pan (*Am*).

tortino [tor'tino] SM (*Culin*) savoury pie.

torto[1], a ['tɔrto] PP di **torcere**.

torto[2] ['tɔrto] SM (*ingiustizia*) wrong; (*colpa*) fault; **fare un torto a qn** to wrong sb; **ricevere un torto** to be wronged; **avere torto** to be wrong; **hai torto marcio** you're dead wrong; **a torto** wrongly, unjustly; **a torto o a ragione** rightly or wrongly; **ho avuto l'unico torto di dissentire da lui** the only thing I did wrong was to disagree with him; **quest'azione ti fa torto** this action is unworthy of you; **gli ho dato torto** I said he was wrong; **i fatti gli hanno dato torto** the facts proved him wrong; **passare/essere dalla parte del torto** to put o.s./be in the wrong; **non ha tutti i torti** there's something in what he says.

tortora ['tɔrtora] [1] SF (*Zool*) turtledove. [2] AGG INV: **grigio tortora** dove-grey.

tortuosamente [tortuosa'mente] AVV (*esprimersi, pensare*) in a convoluted way.

tortuosità [tortuosi'ta] SF INV (*qualità: di strada*) winding nature; (*: di ragionamento*) convoluted nature; (*curva*): **le tortuosità del fiume** the twists and turns of the river.

tortuoso, a [tortu'oso] AGG (*strada*) winding; (*fig: discorso, ragionamento*) convoluted; (*: politica*) tortuous; **esprimersi in modo tortuoso** to express o.s. in a convoluted way.

tortura [tor'tura] SF (*sevizia*) torture; (*fig*) torment, torture; **sottoporre qn alla tortura** to torture sb.

torturare [tortu'rare] [1] VT to torture; (*fig*) to torment, torture; **torturarsi il cervello** to rack one's brains. [2] **torturarsi** VR to torment o.s.

torvamente [torva'mente] AVV: **guardare qn torvamente** to give sb a surly look.

torvo, a ['tɔrvo] AGG (*occhi, sguardo*) surly, menacing, grim; **era torvo in viso** he looked grim; **guardare qn con occhi torvi** to give sb a surly look.

tosaerba [toza'ɛrba] SM INV (lawn)mower.

tosare [to'zare] VT (*pecore*) to shear; (*cani*) to clip; (*siepi*) to trim, clip; **ti hanno tosato** (*scherz*) you've been scalped.

tosasiepi [toza'sjɛpi] SM INV hedge clippers *pl*.

tosatrice [toza'tritʃe] SF (*per pecore*) electric shears *pl*; (*per capelli*) clippers *pl*.

tosatura [toza'tura] SF (*di pecore*) shearing; (*di cani*) clipping; (*di siepi*) trimming, clipping.

Toscana [tos'kana] SF: **la Toscana** Tuscany.

toscano, a [tos'kano] [1] AGG, SM/F Tuscan. [2] SM (*anche*: **sigaro toscano**) *strong Italian cigar*.

tosse ['tosse] SF cough; **colpo di tosse** fit of coughing; **avere la tosse** to have a cough ▶ **tosse asinina** o **canina** whooping cough.

tossicchiare [tossik'kjare] VI (*aus avere*) to cough.

tossicità [tossitʃi'ta] SF toxicity.

tossico, a, ci, che ['tossiko] [1] AGG toxic. [2] SM/F (*fam: drogato*) junkie, druggie.

tossicodipendente [tossikodipen'dɛnte] SM/F drug addict.

tossicodipendenza [tossikodipen'dɛntsa] SF drug addiction.

tossicologia [tossikolo'dʒia] SF toxicology.

tossicologo, a, gi, ghe [tossi'kɔlogo] SM/F toxicologist.

tossicomane [tossi'komane] SM/F drug addict.

tossicomania [tossikoma'nia] SF drug addiction.

tossiemia [tossie'mia] SF toxaemia (*Brit*), toxemia (*Am*).

tossina [tos'sina] SF toxin.

tossire [tos'sire] VI (*aus avere*) to cough.

tostapane [tosta'pane] SM INV toaster.

tostare [tos'tare] VT (*pane*) to toast; (*caffè, mandorle*) to roast.

tostatura [tosta'tura] SF (*di pane*) toasting; (*di caffè*) roasting.

tosto[1] ['tɔsto] AVV (*letter*) forthwith, immediately; **tosto che** as soon as.

tosto[2], a ['tɔsto] AGG **a**: **che faccia tosta!** what cheek!; **hai una bella faccia tosta!** you've got a real cheek! **b** (*fam: eccezionale*) ace.

tot [tɔt] [1] AGG INDEF so many, X; **il giorno tot all'ora tot** on such and such a day at such and such a time; **diciamo che costa tot milioni** let's say it costs so many o X million. [2] SM: **un tot** so much; **mi dà un tot al mese** he gives me so much a month.

totale [to'tale] [1] AGG (*gen*) total; **anestesia totale** general anaesthetic (*Brit*) o anesthetic (*Am*). [2] SM total.

totalità [totali'ta] SF totality, entirety; **nella totalità dei casi** in all cases; **la totalità dei presenti** all of those present.

totalitario, ria, ri, rie [totali'tarjo] AGG (*Pol*) totalitarian.

totalitarismo [totalita'rizmo] SM (*Pol*) totalitarianism.

totalizzare [totalid'dzare] VT to total, make a total of; (*Sport: punti*) to score.

totalizzatore [totaliddza'tore] SM (*Tecn*) totalizator; (*Ippica*) totalizator, tote.

totalmente [total'mente] AVV (*gen*) totally, completely.

totem ['tɔtem] SM INV totem (pole).

totip [to'tip] SM *gambling pool based on horse racing*.

totocalcio [toto'kaltʃo] SM ≈ (football) pools *pl* (*Brit*); **giocare al totocalcio** to do the pools.

touche [tuʃ] SF INV (*Rugby*) line-out.

toupet [tu'pɛ] SM INV toupee.

tour [tur] SM INV (*giro*) tour; (*Ciclismo: anche*: **tour de**

France) tour de France.

tourbillon [turbi'jõ] SM INV (*di luci, colori*) whirl; (*di notizie*) flurry.

tour de force [turdɛ'fɔrs] SM INV (*Sport, anche fig*) tremendous effort.

tournée [tur'ne] SF INV tour; **essere in tournée** to be on tour.

tout court [tu'kur] AVV (*rispondere, domandare*) bluntly.

tovaglia [to'vaʎʎa] SF tablecloth.

tovaglietta [tovaʎ'ʎetta] SF: **tovaglietta all'americana** place mat.

tovagliolo [tovaʎ'ʎɔlo] SM napkin, serviette (*Brit*) ▶**tovagliolo di carta** paper napkin.

tozzo[1]**, a** ['tɔttso] AGG (*persona*) stocky, thickset; (*cosa*) squat.

tozzo[2] ['tɔttso] SM piece, morsel; **tozzo di pane** crust of bread; **per un tozzo di pane** (*fig*) for a song.

TP SIGLA = *Trapani*.

TR SIGLA = *Terni*.

Tr. ABBR (*Comm*) = *tratta*.

tra [tra] PREP a (*fra due*) between; (*fra più di due*) among(st); **c'è un giardino tra le due case** there's a garden between the two houses; **era tra gente sconosciuta** he was among strangers; **tra i presenti c'era anche il sindaco** the mayor was also among those present; **esitare tra il sì e il no** to hesitate between yes and no; **avrà tra i 15 e i 20 anni** he must be between 15 and 20 years old; **costerà tra le venti e le venticinquemila lire** it'll cost between twenty and twenty-five thousand lire; **(sia) detto tra noi...** between you and me ...; **mi raccomando, che resti tra noi** remember, that's between you and me; **tra sé e sé** (*parlare, riflettere*) to oneself; **scomparire tra la folla/gli alberi** to disappear into the crowd/among the trees; **tra una cosa e l'altra** what with one thing and another; **tra vitto e alloggio fanno 850.000 lire** food and accommodation together come to 850.000 lire; **tra casa mia e casa loro ci sono 10 minuti di strada** it's 10 minutes from my house to theirs b (*attraverso*) through; **il sole filtrava tra le persiane** the sun filtered through the shutters; **una strada tra i campi** a road through the fields; **farsi strada tra la folla** to make one's way through the crowd c (*in*) in; **prendere qn tra le braccia** to take sb in one's arms; **tra venti chilometri c'è un'area di servizio** there's a service area in twenty kilometres d (*tempo*) in, within; **torno tra un'ora** I'll be back in an hour; **tra qualche giorno** in a few days; **tra 5 giorni** in 5 days' time; **sarà qui tra poco** he'll be here soon *o* shortly; **tra breve** soon, shortly e : **tra l'altro** (*inoltre*) besides which, what is more; **tra tutti non saranno più di venti** there won't be more than twenty in all.

traballante [trabal'lante] AGG (*mobile*) shaky.

traballare [trabal'lare] VI (*aus avere*) (*persona*) to stagger, totter; (*mobile, fig: governo*) to be shaky.

trabeazione [trabeat'tsjone] SF (*Archit*) trabeation.

trabiccolo [tra'bikkolo] SM (*scherz: vecchia auto*) jalopy, old banger (*Brit*).

traboccare [trabok'kare] VI a (*aus essere*) (*liquido*): **traboccare (da)** to overflow (from) b (*aus avere*) (*contenitore*): **traboccare (di)** to overflow (with); **il teatro traboccava di gente** the theatre was full to bursting; **il suo cuore traboccava di felicità** his heart was bursting with happiness.

trabocchetto [trabok'ketto] [1] SM (*botola*) trap door; (*fig*) trap; **tendere un trabocchetto a qn** to set a trap for sb. [2] AGG INV trap *attr*; **domanda trabocchetto** trick question.

tracagnotto, a [trakaɲ'ɲɔtto] [1] AGG dumpy. [2] SM/F dumpy person.

tracannare [trakan'nare] VT to down, gulp down.

traccia, ce ['trattʃa] SF a (*gen, fig: segno*) mark; (*di lumaca*) trace; (*di ruota*) track, trail; (*di animale*) tracks *pl*; (*di persona*) footprints *pl*; **essere sulle tracce di qn** to be on sb's trail; **perdere le tracce di qn** to lose track of *o* lose the trail of sb; **seguire le tracce di qn** to follow sb's footprints *o* tracks; (*fig*) to follow in sb's footsteps; **la polizia sta chiaramente seguendo una falsa traccia** the police are clearly on the wrong track; **è sparito senza lasciare tracce** he vanished without trace b (*residuo, vestigia di civiltà*) trace; (*indizio*) sign; **nella sua voce non c'è traccia di accento straniero** he speaks without a trace of a foreign accent; **hanno fatto sparire ogni traccia della loro presenza** they removed all sign of their presence c (*schema*) outline.

tracciare [trat'tʃare] VT a (*percorso, strada*) to mark out, trace; (*confini*) to map out; (*rotta*) to plot b (*disegnare*) to sketch, draw; **tracciare una linea** to draw a line; **tracciare un arco** to describe a curve c (*fig*) to sketch out, outline; **tracciare un quadro della situazione** to outline the situation.

tracciato [trat'tʃato] SM (*grafico*) layout, plan; **strada dal tracciato irregolare** winding road ▶**tracciato di gara** (*Sport*) (race) route.

tracciatore [trattʃa'tore] SM (*Inform*): **tracciatore di grafici** plotter.

trachea [tra'kɛa] SF windpipe, trachea.

tracheale [trake'ale] AGG tracheal.

tracheite [trake'ite] SF tracheitis.

tracimare [tratʃi'mare] VI (*aus avere*) (*fiume*) to burst its banks, overflow.

tracolla [tra'kɔlla] SF shoulder strap; **portare qc a tracolla** to carry sth over one's shoulder; **borsa a tracolla** shoulder bag.

tracollo [tra'kɔllo] SM (*fig*) collapse, ruin; **avere un tracollo** (*Med*) to have a setback; (*Fin*) to slip, fall; (*Comm*) to collapse ▶**tracollo finanziario** crash.

tracotante [trako'tante] [1] AGG arrogant, overbearing. [2] SM/F arrogant person.

tracotanza [trako'tantsa] SF arrogance.

trad. ABBR = *traduzione*.

tradimento [tradi'mento] SM (*gen*) betrayal; (*Dir, Mil*) treason; **alto tradimento** high treason; **a tradimento** by surprise; **mangiare (il) pane a tradimento** to live off other people.

tradire [tra'dire] [1] VT a (*gen*) to betray; (*coniuge*) to cheat on, be unfaithful to; **tradire la fiducia di qn** to betray sb's trust; **ha tradito le attese di tutti** he let everyone down; **se la memoria non mi tradisce** if my memory serves me well b (*rivelare: segreto*) to reveal, let out, give away. [2] **tradirsi** VR to give o.s. away.

traditore, trice [tradi'tore] [1] SM/F traitor. [2] AGG treacherous.

tradizionale [tradittsjo'nale] AGG traditional.

tradizionalismo [tradittsjona'lizmo] SM traditionalism.

tradizionalista [tradittsjona'lista] SM/F traditionalist,

conservative.

tradizionalistico, a, ci, che [tradittsjona'listiko] AGG traditionalist.

tradizionalmente [tradittsjonal'mente] AVV traditionally.

tradizione [tradit'tsjone] SF tradition; **secondo la tradizione** traditionally, according to tradition.

tradotta [tra'dotta] SF (*Mil*) troop train.

tradotto, a [tra'dotto] PP di **tradurre**.

tradurre [tra'durre] VT IRREG a (*testo: scritto, orale*) to translate; **tradurre dall'inglese in italiano** to translate from English into Italian; **tradurre alla lettera** to translate literally; **tradurre parola per parola** to translate word for word
b (*esprimere*) to render, convey; **tradurre in parole povere** to explain simply; **tradurre in cifre** to put into figures; **tradurre in atto** (*fig*) to put into effect
c (*Dir*): **tradurre qn in carcere/tribunale** to take sb to prison/court; **tradurre qn davanti al giudice** to bring sb before the court.

traduttore, trice [tradut'tore] SM/F translator ▶**traduttore elettronico** hand-held electronic translator ▶**traduttore simultaneo** simultaneous interpreter.

traduzione [tradut'tsjone] SF a (*di lingue*) translation ▶**traduzione simultanea** simultaneous interpreting b (*Dir*) transfer.

trae ['trae] VB vedi **trarre**.

traente [tra'ɛnte] SM/F (*di assegno*) drawer.

trafelato, a [trafe'lato] AGG breathless, out of breath.

trafficante [traffi'kante] SM/F (*di droga*) trafficker.

trafficare [traffi'kare] 1 VI (*aus avere*) a (*commerciare*): **trafficare (in)** to traffic (in), deal o trade illicitly (in) b (*affaccendarsi*) to busy o.s.. 2 VT (*droga*) to traffic in.

trafficato, a [traffi'kato] AGG (*strada, zona*) busy.

traffico ['traffiko] SM a (*stradale*) traffic; **regolare il traffico** to control o regulate the traffic; **chiudere una strada al traffico** to close a road to traffic b (*movimento*) traffic ▶**traffico aereo** air traffic ▶**traffico ferroviario** rail traffic c (*commercio illecito*) traffic ▶**traffico di droga** drug trafficking.

trafficone, a [traffi'kone] SM/F wheeler-dealer.

trafiggere [tra'fiddʒere] VT IRREG (*ferire*) to run through, stab; (*: fig*) to pierce.

trafila [tra'fila] SF procedure; **bisognerà seguire la solita trafila** we'll have to go through the usual routine o rigmarole.

trafiletto [trafi'letto] SM (*di giornale*) short article.

trafitto, a [tra'fitto] PP di **trafiggere**.

traforare [trafo'rare] VT (*gen*) to pierce; (*montagna*) to tunnel through, make a tunnel through; (*legno, metallo*) to drill, bore; **il proiettile gli ha traforato il cuore** the bullet pierced his heart.

traforato, a [trafo'rato] AGG (*calze, orlo*) openwork.

traforo [tra'foro] SM a (*operazione: vedi vb*) piercing; tunnelling; drilling, boring b (*galleria*) tunnel c: **lavoro di traforo** (*su metallo, legno*) fretwork.

trafugamento [trafuga'mento] SM purloining ▶**trafugamento di opere d'arte** purloining of works of art ▶**trafugamento di salme** body snatching.

trafugare [trafu'gare] VT to purloin.

tragedia [tra'dʒɛdja] SF (*Teatro, fig: disastro*) tragedy; **tragedia greca/latina** Greek/Roman tragedy; **non farne una tragedia** don't make a fuss about it.

traggo *ecc* ['traggo] VB vedi **trarre**.

traghettare [traget'tare] VT (*persone*) to ferry; (*fiume*) to cross by ferry.

traghettatore, trice [tragetta'tore] SM/F ferryman/ferrywoman.

traghetto [tra'getto] 1 SM (*trasporto*) ferrying, crossing; (*luogo*) ferry; (*mezzo*) ferry(boat). 2 AGG INV ferry *attr*.

tragicamente [tradʒika'mente] AVV tragically.

tragicità [tradʒitʃi'ta] SF tragedy.

tragico, a, ci, che ['tradʒiko] 1 AGG tragic. 2 SM/F (*tragediografo*) tragedian; **non fare il tragico** (*fig*) don't make a song and dance over it. 3 SM: **il tragico della faccenda è che...** the worst thing about it is ... .

tragicomico, a, ci, che [tradʒi'komiko] AGG tragicomic.

tragicommedia [tradʒikom'mɛdja] SF tragicomedy.

tragitto [tra'dʒitto] SM a (*viaggio*) journey; **durante il tragitto** on the journey b (*tratto di strada*) way; **durante il tragitto** on the way.

traguardo [tra'gwardo] SM (*Sport*) finish, finishing post; (*: linea*) finishing line; (*fig*) aim, goal; **tagliare il traguardo** to cross the line; **raggiungere il traguardo** (*in gara*) to reach the finish; (*fig*) to reach one's goal.

trai *ecc* ['trai] VB vedi **trarre**.

traiettoria [trajet'tɔrja] SF trajectory.

trainante [trai'nante] AGG (*cavo, fune*) towing; (*Econ: settore*) driving; (*: paese*) leading.

trainare [trai'nare] VT (*carro*) to draw, pull, drag, haul; (*auto*) to tow; **farsi trainare** (*fig*) to follow blindly.

training ['treiniŋ] SM INV (*di personale*) training.

traino ['traino] SM a (*operazione*) drawing, pulling; (*: di auto*) towing; **al traino** on tow; **fare da traino** (*Econ*) to be a driving force b (*cosa trainata*) trailer load.

trait d'union ['trɛ dy'njɔ̃] SM INV: **fare da trait d'union** to liaise.

tralasciare [tralaʃ'ʃare] VT a (*omettere: dettagli*) to leave out, omit; **tralasciamo i particolari** let's skip the details b (*trascurare: studi*) to neglect.

tralcio, ci ['traltʃo] SM shoot (*of a plant*).

traliccio, ci [tra'littʃo] SM (*pilone*) pylon; (*struttura*) trellis.

tralice [tra'litʃe]: **in tralice** AVV: **guardare qn in tralice** to look askance at sb.

trallallà [tralal'la] ESCL tra-la-la!

tram [tram] SM INV tram (*Brit*), streetcar (*Am*).

trama ['trama] SF a (*filo*) weft b (*di opera*) plot; (*inganno*) plot, conspiracy; **ordire una trama ai danni di qn** to hatch a plot against sb.

tramandare [traman'dare] VT to hand down, pass on.

tramare [tra'mare] VT to plot, scheme; **tramare un complotto** to plot.

trambusto [tram'busto] SM (*rumore*) racket; (*disordine*) turmoil.

tramestio, tii [trames'tio] SM bustle, bustling.

tramezzare [tramed'dzare] VT (*Edil*) to partition (off).

tramezzino [tramed'dzino] SM sandwich.

tramezzo [tra'mɛddzo] SM partition, dividing wall.

tramite ['tramite] 1 SM means *pl*; **agire/fare da tramite** to act as/be a go-between. 2 PREP (*per mezzo di: cosa*) by means of; (*: persona*) through.

tramontana [tramon'tana] SF (*Meteor*) north wind; **perdere la tramontana** (*fig*) to lose one's bearings.

tramontare [tramon'tare] VI (*aus essere*) (*astri*) to go

down, set; (*fig*: *bellezza*, *gloria*) to fade.

tramonto [traˈmonto] SM (*del sole*) sunset; (*di astri*) setting; **è sul viale del tramonto** (*attore*) he has passed his peak.

tramortire [tramorˈtire] [1] VT to knock out, knock unconscious, stun.

[2] VI (*aus* **essere**) to pass out, faint, lose consciousness.

trampolino [trampoˈlino] SM (*Sport*: *per tuffi*) springboard; (: *in muratura*) diving board; (: *per lo sci*) ski jump; **servire da trampolino** (*fig*) to serve as a springboard.

trampolo [ˈtrampolo] SM stilt.

tramutare [tramuˈtare] [1] VT: **tramutare in** to change *o* turn into.

[2] **tramutarsi** VR: **tramutarsi in** to change *o* turn into.

trance [ˈtraːns] SF INV trance; **in (stato di) trance** in a (state of) trance; **cadere in trance** to fall into a trance.

tranche de vie [trɑ̃ʃ də vi] SF INV slice of life.

trancia, ce [ˈtrantʃa] SF **a** (*Tecn*) shears *pl*, shearing machine **b** (*fetta*) slice; **trancia di salmone** (*Culin*) salmon steak; **a trance** in slices.

tranciare [tranˈtʃare] VT (*Tecn*) to shear.

trancio, ci [ˈtrantʃo] SM = trancia b.

tranello [traˈnɛllo] SM trap; **tendere un tranello a qn** to set a trap for sb; **cadere in un tranello** to fall into a trap.

trangugiare [tranguˈdʒare] VT to gulp down; (*fig*: *amarezze*) to swallow.

tranne [ˈtranne] [1] PREP (*eccetto*) except (for), but (for); **c'erano tutti tranne lui** they were all there except *o* but him; **tutti i giorni tranne il venerdì** every day except *o* with the exception of Friday; **va d'accordo con tutti tranne che con me** he gets on with everybody except *o* but me.

[2] : **tranne che** CONG unless.

tranquillamente [trankwillaˈmente] AVV (*vivere*, *dormire*) peacefully; (*rispondere*, *spiegare*) calmly.

tranquillante [trankwilˈlante] SM (*Med*) tranquillizer.

tranquillità [trankwilliˈta] SF (*stabilità*) tranquillity; (*immobilità*) calm, stillness; (*calma*) quietness; (*di animo*) peace of mind; **è ritornata la tranquillità** the situation has returned to normal; **per mia tranquillità** to set my mind at ease.

tranquillizzare [trankwillidˈdzare] [1] VT to reassure.

[2] **tranquillizzarsi** VIP to calm down.

tranquillo, a [tranˈkwillo] AGG **a** (*luogo*) calm, peaceful, quiet; **il mare è tranquillo** the sea is calm **b** (*persona*) calm; (: *sicuro*) sure, confident; **dormire sonni tranquilli** to sleep easy *o* peacefully; **avere la coscienza tranquilla** to have a clear conscience; **stai tranquillo che ce la fa!** don't worry - he'll do it all right!

transalpino, a [transalˈpino] AGG transalpine.

transatlantico, a, ci, che [transatˈlantiko] [1] AGG transatlantic.

[2] SM **a** (*Naut*) transatlantic liner **b** (*Pol*) *corridor used as a meeting place by members of the lower chamber of the Italian Parliament*.

transatto, a [tranˈsatto] PP di **transigere**.

transazione [transatˈtsjone] SF (*Dir*) settlement; (*Comm*) transaction, deal.

transcodificazione [transkodifikatˈtsjone] SF (*Inform*) data conversion.

transenna [tranˈsenna] SF (*cavalletto*) barrier.

transessuale [transessuˈale] SM/F transsexual.

transetto [tranˈsɛtto] SM (*Archit*) transept.

transfert [ˈtransfert] SM INV (*Psic*) transference.

transiberiano, a [transibeˈrjano] AGG trans-Siberian.

transigere [tranˈsidʒere] VI IRREG (*aus* **avere**) to compromise; **è uno che non transige** he is intransigent; **in fatto di sincerità io non transigo** I won't put up with insincerity.

transistor [tranˈsistor] SM INV (*Elettr*) transistor; (*Radio*) transistor (radio).

transitabile [transiˈtabile] AGG passable; **"strada transitabile solo con catene"** "road passable only with snow chains".

transitabilità [transitabiliˈta] SF INV: **transitabilità delle strade** road *o* driving conditions *pl*.

transitare [transiˈtare] VI (*aus* **essere**) to pass.

transitivo, a [transiˈtivo] AGG transitive.

transito [ˈtransito] SM transit; **"divieto di transito"** "no entry"; **"transito interrotto"** "road closed"; **stazione di transito** transit station.

transitorio, ria, ri, rie [transiˈtɔrjo] AGG (*temporaneo*: *provvedimenti*, *disposizioni*) temporary, provisional; (: *gloria*) transitory, fleeting, transient.

transizione [transitˈtsjone] SF transition; **età/periodo di transizione** age/period of transition.

transoceanico, a, ci, che [transotʃeˈaniko] AGG transoceanic.

transumanza [transuˈmantsa] SF transhumance.

transustanziarsi [transustanˈtsjarsi] VR (*Rel*) to transubstantiate.

transustanziazione [transustantsjatˈtsjone] SF (*Rel*) transubstantiation.

tran tran [tran ˈtran] SM INV routine; **il solito tran tran** the same old routine.

tranvia [tranˈvia] SF tramway (*Brit*), streetcar line (*Am*).

tranviario, ria, ri, rie [tranˈvjarjo] AGG tram *attr* (*Brit*); streetcar *attr* (*Am*); **linea tranviaria** tramline, streetcar line.

tranviere [tranˈvjɛre] SM (*conducente*) tram driver (*Brit*), streetcar driver (*Am*); (*bigliettaio*) tram *o* streetcar conductor.

trapanare [trapaˈnare] VT to drill.

trapanazione [trapanatˈtsjone] SF drilling ▶**trapanazione del cranio** trepanation, trephination.

trapano [ˈtrapano] SM drill ▶**trapano da dentista** dentist's drill ▶**trapano elettrico** electric drill ▶**trapano a mano** hand drill.

trapassare [trapasˈsare] [1] VT to go through, pierce.

[2] VI (*aus* **essere**) (*fig letter*: *morire*) to pass away.

trapassato, a [trapasˈsato] SM (*Gramm*) past perfect.

trapasso [traˈpasso] SM **a** (*Dir*: *passaggio*): **trapasso di proprietà** (*di case*) conveyancing; (*di auto*) legal transfer **b** : **l'ora del trapasso** (*letter*) one's final hour.

trapelare [trapeˈlare] VI (*aus* **essere**) (*luce*) to filter through; (*fig*: *segreto*, *indiscrezione*) to leak (out); **dal suo viso trapelava tutta la sua gioia** his face shone with joy.

trapezio, zi [traˈpɛttsjo] SM **a** (*Mat*) trapezium **b** (*Sport*) trapeze **c** (*Anat*) trapezius.

trapezista, i, e [trapetˈtsista] SM/F trapeze artist.

trapiantare [trapjanˈtare] [1] VT (*Bot*, *Med*) to transplant; (*fig*: *moda*, *usanza*) to introduce.

[2] **trapiantarsi** VIP to move; **ormai si sono trapiantati in Kenia** they have now settled in Kenya.

trapianto [traˈpjanto] SM (*Med*) transplant; (*Bot*) transplanting.

trappista, i [trapˈpista] SM Trappist (monk).

trappola [ˈtrappola] SF **a** (*anche fig*) trap; **prendere qn/qc**

in trappola (*anche fig*) to catch sb/sth in a trap; **cadere in trappola** (*anche fig*) to fall into a trap; **tendere una trappola a qn** to set a trap for sb **b** (*pegg*: *auto*) old wreck.

trapunta [tra'punta] SF quilt.

trarre ['trarre] VB IRREG [1] VT **a** to draw, pull; **la sua aria innocente trae in inganno** his innocent appearance is misleading *o* deceptive; **sono stato tratto in inganno dal suo modo di fare** I was misled *o* deceived by his manner; **trarre qn d'impaccio** to get sb out of an awkward situation; **trarre in salvo** to rescue **b** (*estrarre*) to pull out, draw **c** (*derivare*) to obtain, get; **trarre guadagno** to make a profit; **trarre beneficio** *o* **profitto da qc** to benefit from sth; **trarre origine da qc** to have its origins *o* originate in sth; **trarre esempio da qn** to follow sb's example; **trarre un film da un libro** to make a film (*Brit*) *o* movie (*Am*) from a book; **trarre le conclusioni** to draw one's own conclusions.
[2]: **trarsi** VR: **trarsi da** to get (o.s.) out of; **stai tranquillo che sa trarsi d'impaccio da solo** don't worry, he knows how to look after himself.

trasalire [trasa'lire] VI (*aus* avere *o* essere) to jump, (give a) start; **fare trasalire qn** to make sb jump *o* start.

trasandato, a [trazan'dato] AGG (*persona, abito*) scruffy, shabby; **è trasandato nel vestire** he is a sloppy dresser.

trasbordare [trazbor'dare] [1] VT (*gen*) to transfer; (*Naut*) to tran(s)ship.
[2] VI (*aus* avere) (*Naut*) to change ship; (*Aer*) to change plane; (*Ferr*) to change trains.

trasbordo [traz'bordo] SM transfer.

trascendentale [traʃʃenden'tale] AGG (*Filosofia*) transcendental; (*fig*): **non è niente di trascendentale** it (*o* he *ecc*) is nothing exceptional.

trascendentalità [traʃʃendentali'ta] SF transcendental nature.

trascendente [traʃʃen'dɛnte] AGG (*Filosofia*) transcendent(al); (*Mat*) transcendental.

trascendere [traʃ'ʃendere] VT IRREG (*Filosofia, Rel*) to transcend; (*fig*: *superare*) to surpass, go beyond.

trasceso, a [traʃ'ʃeso] PP di **trascendere**.

trascinante [traʃʃi'nante] AGG (*musica, spettacolo*) enthralling.

trascinare [traʃʃi'nare] [1] VT (*gen*) to drag; **trascinare i piedi** to drag one's feet; **trascina una gamba** he has a stiff leg; **trascinare qn in tribunale** to take sb to court; **sa trascinare la folla** he knows how to carry the crowd; **la sua musica ti trascina** his music is enthralling; **trascinare qn sulla via del male** to lead sb astray.
[2] **trascinarsi** VR (*strisciare*) to drag o.s. (along).
[3] **trascinarsi** VIP (*controversia*) to drag on.

trascinatore [traʃʃina'tore] SM: **trascinatore fogli a modulo continuo** paper feed.

trascolorare [traskolo'rare] VI (*aus* essere): **trascolorò in volto** his face changed colour.

trascorrere [tras'korrere] VB IRREG [1] VT (*vacanze, giorni*) to spend, pass.
[2] VI (*aus* essere) (*passare*: *ore, mesi, giorni*) to pass; **le ore trascorrevano lente** the hours dragged by; **sono trascorsi sei giorni da allora** six days have passed since then; **hai lasciato trascorrere troppo tempo** you've allowed too much time to pass.

trascorso, a [tras'korso] [1] PP di **trascorrere**.
[2] AGG past.

[3] SM mistake; **non voglio conoscere i suoi trascorsi** I don't want to know about his past.

trascritto, a [tras'kritto] PP di **trascrivere**.

trascrivere [tras'krivere] VT IRREG **a** (*citazioni, frasi, idee*) to write down, copy down **b** (*traslitterare*) to transliterate; (: *sistema fonetico e delle note musicali*) to transcribe.

trascrizione [traskrit'tsjone] SF (*gen*) writing down, copying down; (*di discorso*) transcript; (*traslitterazione*) transliteration; (: *nel sistema fonetico e delle note musicali*) transcription.

trascurabile [trasku'rabile] AGG negligible.

trascurare [trasku'rare] [1] VT **a** (*studio, lavoro, famiglia*) to neglect **b** (*omettere*) to omit, skip, leave out **c** (*non tener conto di*) to ignore, overlook; (*non considerare*) to disregard. [2] **trascurarsi** VR to neglect o.s.

trascuratamente [traskurata'mente] AVV carelessly.

trascuratezza [traskura'tettsa] SF (*negligenza*) carelessness, negligence; (*disordine*) untidiness.

trascurato, a [trasku'rato] AGG **a** (*sciatto*) slovenly **b** (*negligente*) careless, negligent **c** (*non curato*) neglected; **sentirsi trascurato** to feel neglected; **un'influenza trascurata può portare alla polmonite** if you neglect a bout of flu it can develop into pneumonia.

trasduttore [trazdut'tore] SM (*Fis*) transducer.

trasecolare [traseko'lare] VI (*aus* avere *o* essere) to be dumbfounded.

trasecolato, a [traseko'lato] AGG astounded, amazed, dumbfounded.

trasferibile [trasfe'ribile] AGG transferable; **"non trasferibile"** (*su assegno*) "account payee only".

trasferimento [trasferi'mento] SM **a** (*cambiamento di sede*) transfer; **ha chiesto il trasferimento** he requested a transfer **b** (*Dir*: *di titoli*) transfer; (: *di proprietà*) conveyancing.

trasferire [trasfe'rire] [1] VT **a** (*sede, potere*) to transfer **b** (*Dir*: *titoli*) to transfer; (: *proprietà*) to transfer, convey.
[2] **trasferirsi** VIP to move.

trasferta [tras'fɛrta] SF **a** (*di funzionario*) temporary transfer; **essere in trasferta** to be on temporary transfer **b** (*anche*: **indennità di trasferta**) travel allowance, travel expenses *pl* **c** (*Sport*) away game; **giocare in trasferta** to play away (from home).

trasfigurare [trasfigu'rare] [1] VT to transfigure.
[2] **trasfigurarsi** VIP to be transfigured.

trasfigurazione [trasfigurat'tsjone] SF transfiguration.

trasfondere [tras'fondere] VT (*fig*) to instil.

trasformabile [trasfor'mabile] AGG (*divano*) convertible.

trasformare [trasfor'mare] [1] VT **a** (*gen*) to change, alter; (*radicalmente*) to transform; **hanno trasformato la stalla in un ristorante** they converted the stable into a restaurant; **la strega trasformò il principe in un albero** the witch turned the prince into a tree; **quel vestito ti trasforma** that dress completely transforms you **b** (*Rugby*) to convert; **trasformare un rigore** (*Calcio*) to score from a penalty.
[2] **trasformarsi** VIP (*embrione, larva*) to be transformed, transform itself; (*energia*) to be converted; (*persona, paese*) to change, alter; (: *radicalmente*) to be transformed.

trasformatore [trasforma'tore] SM (*Elettr*) transformer.

trasformazionale [trasformattsjo'nale] AGG transformational.

trasformazione [trasformat'tsjone] SF (*vedi vb*) change,

alteration; transformation; conversion.

trasformismo [trasfor'mizmo] SM (*Pol*) *system whereby a government attempts to hold on to power by forming coalitions to prevent the formation of any credible opposition.*

trasformista, i, e [trasfor'mista] SM/F a (*Pol*) transformist (*politician who attempts to hold on to power by forming coalitions to prevent the formation of any credible opposition*); (*fig*) opportunist; (*pegg*) timeserver b (*artista*) quick-change artist.

trasfusione [trasfu'zjone] SF (*Med*) transfusion.

trasgredire [trazgre'dire] VT, VI (*aus* avere): **trasgredire a** (*legge, regola*) to break, infringe; (*ordini*) to disobey.

trasgressione [trazgres'sjone] SF a (*vedi vb*) breaking, infringement; disobeying b (*anticonformismo*) transgression, rule-breaking.

trasgressivo, a [trazgres'sivo] AGG (*personaggio, atteggiamento*) rule-breaking *attr*.

trasgressore, trasgreditrice [trazgres'sore, trazgredi'tritʃe] SM/F (*Dir*) transgressor.

traslare [traz'lare] VT (*salma*) to transfer.

traslato, a [traz'lato] 1 AGG metaphorical, figurative. 2 SM metaphor.

traslazione [trazlat'tsjone] SF a (*gen, Fin*) transfer b (*Fis*) translation.

traslitterare [trazlitte'rare] VT to transliterate.

traslitterazione [trazlitterat'tsjone] SF transliteration.

traslocare [trazlo'kare] VT, VI (*aus* avere) to move.

trasloco, chi [traz'lɔko] SM removal.

traslucido, a [traz'lutʃido] AGG translucent.

trasmesso, a [traz'messo] PP di **trasmettere**.

trasmettere [traz'mettere] VB IRREG 1 VT a (*Telec*) to transmit; (*Radio, TV*) to broadcast; **trasmettere una partita in diretta** to broadcast a match live; **trasmettono un western** (*TV*) they're showing a western b (*usanza, diritto, titolo*) to pass on; (*lettera, telegramma, notizia*) to send; **trasmettere una malattia a qn** to pass a disease on to sb. 2 **trasmettersi** VIP (*usanza*) to be passed on; (*Med*) to be spread, be transmitted.

trasmettitore, trice [trazmetti'tore] 1 AGG transmitting. 2 SM transmitter.

trasmigrazione [trazmigrat'tsjone] SF (*di anime*) transmigration.

trasmissione [trazmis'sjone] SF a (*gen*) transmission; (*di titolo, eredità*) passing on, handing down; **albero di trasmissione** (*Aut*) transmission shaft ▶**trasmissione (dei) dati** (*Inform*) data transmission ▶**trasmissione del pensiero** thought trasference b (*Radio, TV: programma*) transmission, broadcast, programme (*Brit*), program (*Am*); **le trasmissioni riprenderanno domani** program(me)s will resume tomorrow.

trasmittente [trazmit'tente] 1 AGG transmitting. 2 SF transmitter, transmitting *o* broadcasting station.

trasognato, a [trason'nato] AGG dreamy.

trasparente [traspa'rɛnte] 1 AGG (*anche fig*) transparent; (*sottile*) wafer-thin. 2 SM transparency.

trasparenza [traspa'rɛntsa] SF (*anche fig*) transparency; **guardare qc in trasparenza** to look at sth against the light.

trasparire [traspa'rire] VI IRREG (*aus* essere) a to shine through; **lasciare trasparire la luce** to let the light shine through

b (*vedersi*) to be visible, show (through); **sotto il vestito traspare la sottoveste** her slip shows *o* can be seen through her dress; **dal suo volto traspariva la gioia** his face shone with joy; **la sua espressione non lasciava trasparire nulla** his face gave nothing away.

trasparso, a [tras'parso] PP di **trasparire**.

traspirare [traspi'rare] VI (*aus* essere) (*sudare*) to perspire; (*fig: trapelare*) to leak out.

traspirazione [traspirat'tsjone] SF (*sudorazione*) perspiration; (*Bot*) transpiration.

trasporre [tras'porre] VT IRREG to transpose.

trasportare [traspor'tare] VT a (*gen, fig*) to carry; (*con veicolo*) to carry, transport, convey; **lo hanno trasportato d'urgenza in ospedale** they rushed him to hospital; **questo libro ci trasporta al Rinascimento** this book takes us back to the Renaissance b : **lasciarsi trasportare (da qc)** (*gioia, entusiasmo*) to let o.s. be carried away (by sth); **lasciarsi trasportare dall'ira** to lose one's temper c (*trascinare*) to carry off; **l'hanno trasportato in questura** they took him off to the police station.

trasportatore, trice [trasporta'tore] 1 AGG transport *attr*. 2 SM/F (*persona*) transporter, carrier; (: *per strada*) haulier (*Brit*), hauler (*Am*). 3 SM (*macchina*) conveyor.

trasporto [tras'pɔrto] SM a (*gen*) transport; **danneggiato durante il trasporto** damaged in transit; **mezzi di trasporto** means of transport; **nave/aereo da trasporto** transport ship/aircraft *inv*; **compagnia di trasporto** carrier; (*per strada*) hauliers *pl* (*Brit*), haulers *pl* (*Am*); **i trasporti** transport *sg*; **il ministero dei trasporti** ≈ the Department of Transport (*Brit*), ≈ the Department of Transportation (*Am*) ▶**trasporti pubblici** public transport *sg* ▶**trasporto aereo** air transport ▶**trasporto marittimo** sea transport ▶**trasporto stradale** (road) haulage b (*fig*) rapture, passion; **con trasporto** passionately; **un trasporto d'ira** a fit of anger.

trasposizione [traspozit'tsjone] SF (*Ling*) transposition.

trasposto, a [tras'posto] PP di **trasporre**.

trassato [tras'sato] SM (*di assegno*) drawee.

trassi *ecc* ['trassi] VB vedi **trarre**.

trastullare [trastul'lare] 1 VT (*bambino*) to play with, amuse. 2 **trastullarsi** VR (*divertirsi*): **trastullarsi con qc** to amuse o.s. with sth; (*gingillarsi*) to fritter away one's time.

trastullo [tras'tullo] SM game.

trasudare [trasu'dare] 1 VT to ooze with. 2 VI (*aus* essere) to ooze (out).

trasversale [trazver'sale] AGG (*taglio, sbarra*) cross *attr*; (*retta*) transverse; **via trasversale** side street; **motore trasversale** (*Aut*) transverse engine; **una camicia a righe trasversali** a shirt with horizontal stripes; **partito trasversale** (*fig*) *unofficial grouping of diverse political interests.*

trasversalmente [trazversal'mente] AVV (*di traverso*) horizontally; (*indirettamente*) indirectly.

trasvolare [trazvo'lare] VT to fly across *o* over.

trasvolata [trazvo'lata] SF non-stop long-haul flight.

tratta ['tratta] SF a (*traffico*): **la tratta delle bianche** the white slave trade b (*Comm*) draft ▶**tratta documentaria** documentary bill of exchange.

trattamento [tratta'mento] SM a (*gen*) treatment; (*servi-*

zio *in ristorante*) service; **trattamento di riguardo** special treatment; **ricevere un buon trattamento** (*cliente*) to get good service; **fare un trattamento di favore** to give special treatment

b (*Tecn, Med*) treatment ►**trattamento di bellezza** beauty treatment

c (*Econ*) payment ►**trattamento di fine rapporto** severance pay

d (*Inform*): **trattamento testi** word processing.

trattare [trat'tare] **1** VT **a** (*discutere: tema, argomento*) to deal with, discuss; (*negoziare: pace, resa*) to negotiate; **trattare un affare** to negotiate a deal

b (*comportarsi con*) to treat; **trattare bene/male qn** to treat sb well/badly; **trattare qn con i guanti** to handle *o* treat sb with kid gloves

c (*Comm: vendere*) to deal in, handle

d (*Tecn, Med*) to treat.

2 VI (*aus* **avere**) **a** (*libro, film*): **trattare di** to deal with, be about

b (*avere relazioni*): **trattare con** to deal with; **con lui non si può trattare** he's impossible to deal with

c (*forma impers*): **si tratta di sua moglie** it's about his wife; **si tratta di pochi minuti** it will only take a few minutes; **si tratterebbe solo di poche ore** it would just be a matter of a few hours; **di che si tratta?** what's it about?; **si tratta di vita o di morte** it's a matter of life or death.

3 VR: **trattarsi bene** to look after o.s. (well).

trattativa [tratta'tiva] SF negotiation; **trattative** SFPL (*tra Stati, governi*) talks; **essere in trattativa con qn** to be in negotiation with sb.

trattato [trat'tato] SM **a** (*accordo*) treaty; **firmare/ratificare un trattato** to sign/ratify a treaty ►**trattato commerciale** trade agreement ►**trattato di pace** peace treaty **b** (*opera*) treatise.

trattazione [trattat'tsjone] SF treatment.

tratteggiare [tratted'dʒare] VT (*ombreggiare*) to hatch; (*abbozzare*) to sketch; (*fig: descrivere*) to outline; **linea tratteggiata** dotted line.

tratteggio, gi [trat'teddʒo] SM (*Disegno*) hatching.

trattenere [tratte'nere] VB IRREG **1** VT **a** (*fermare*) to keep back; (: *in ospedale*) to keep; (: *in carcere*) to detain; **trattenere qn dal fare qc** to restrain sb *o* hold sb back from doing sth; **trattenere in osservazione** (*in ospedale*) to keep in for observation; **ho cercato di trattenerlo** I tried to hold him back; **sono stato trattenuto in ufficio** I was delayed at the office; **mi hanno trattenuto a pranzo** they had me stay for lunch

b (*lacrime, riso*) to hold back, keep back, restrain; (*respiro*) to hold

c (*detrarre*) to withhold, keep back, deduct.

2 trattenersi VIP (*fermarsi*) to stay, remain; **mi sono trattenuto in ufficio** I stayed on at the office; **mi sono trattenuto a cena** I stayed for dinner.

3 trattenersi VR (*astenersi*) to restrain o.s., stop o.s.; **trattenersi dal fare qc** to keep *o* stop o.s. from doing sth; **non sono più riuscito a trattenermi** I just couldn't stop myself.

trattenimento [tratteni'mento] SM (*festa*) party ►**trattenimento danzante** dance.

trattenuta [tratte'nuta] SF (*anche*: **trattenuta sullo stipendio**) deduction.

trattino [trat'tino] SM (*nelle parole composte*) hyphen; (*per iniziare il discorso diretto*) dash.

tratto¹, a ['tratto] PP di **trarre**.

tratto² ['tratto] SM **a** (*di penna, matita*) stroke; **disegnare a grandi tratti** to sketch; **descrivere qc a grandi tratti** to give an outline of sth

b : **tratti** SMPL (*caratteristiche*) features; **ha i tratti molto marcati** he has very prominent features; **i tratti essenziali del periodo/del suo carattere** the essential features of the period/his character

c (*segmento*) part, section; (: *di mare*) stretch, expanse; (: *di strada*) stretch; **dobbiamo fare ancora un bel tratto a piedi** we still have quite a long way to walk; **alcuni tratti del suo romanzo** some parts of his novel

d (*spazio di tempo*) time, period (of time); **a tratti** at times; **(tutto) ad un tratto** OR **d'un tratto** (*all'improvviso*) suddenly.

trattore [trat'tore] SM tractor.

trattoria [tratto'ria] SF trattoria, small restaurant.

trauma, i ['trauma] SM (*Med: anche:* **trauma psichico**) trauma; **la morte di suo padre è stata un trauma** his father's death was a traumatic experience for him ►**trauma cranico** concussion.

traumatico, a, ci, che [trau'matiko] AGG traumatic.

traumatizzante [traumatid'dzante] AGG traumatizing, traumatic.

traumatizzare [traumatid'dzare] VT (*Med*) to traumatize; (*fig: impressionare*) to shock.

traumatizzato, a [traumatid'dzato] AGG (*vedi vb*) traumatized; shocked.

traumatologia [traumatolo'dʒia] SF traumatology.

traumatologico, a, ci, che [traumato'lɔdʒiko] AGG traumatological; **centro traumatologico** accident and emergency unit *o* hospital.

traumatologo, a, gi, ghe [trauma'tɔlogo] SM/F trauma specialist, accident and emergency specialist.

travagliare [travaʎ'ʎare] **1** VT (*affliggere*) to trouble, afflict; (*fig: tormentare*) to torment; **ha avuto un'esistenza travagliata** he has had a difficult life.

2 VI (*aus* **avere**) (*letter*) to suffer.

travaglio, gli [tra'vaʎʎo] SM **a** (*sofferenza: mentale*) anguish, distress; (: *fisica*) pain, suffering **b** (*Med: anche:* **travaglio di parto**) labour (*Brit*) *o* labor (*Am*) pains pl.

travasare [trava'zare] VT (*liquidi*) to pour; (: *vino*) to decant.

travaso [tra'vazo] SM (*vedi vb*) pouring; decanting.

travatura [trava'tura] SF beams pl.

trave ['trave] SF beam.

traveggole [tra'veggole] SFPL: **avere le traveggole** to be seeing things.

traversa [tra'versa] SF **a** (*trave trasversale*) crossbeam, crosspiece; (*Ferr*) sleeper (*Brit*), (railroad) tie (*Am*); (*Calcio, Rugby*) crossbar **b** (*lenzuolo*) draw-sheet **c** (*via*) sideroad, sidestreet; **prendi la seconda traversa a destra** take the second right.

traversare [traver'sare] VT (*attraversare*) to cross; **traversare un fiume a nuoto** to swim across a river.

traversata [traver'sata] SF (*gen, Naut*) crossing; (*Aer*) flight, trip.

traversie [traver'sie] SFPL hardships.

traversina [traver'sina] SF (*Ferr*) sleeper (*Brit*), (railroad) tie (*Am*).

traverso, a [tra'vɛrso] **1** AGG cross *attr*, transverse; **flauto traverso** (transverse) flute; **via traversa** sideroad; **ottenere qc per vie traverse** to obtain sth in an underhand way.

2 : **di traverso** AVV: **camminare di traverso** to walk

sideways (on); **andare di traverso** (*cibo*) to go down the wrong way; **guardare qn di traverso** to give sb a nasty look; **avere la luna di traverso** to be in a bad mood; **messo di traverso** sideways on.

travertino [traver'tino] SM travertine.

travestimento [travesti'mento] SM (*gen*) disguise; (*per carnevale*) costume.

travestire [traves'tire] ① VT (*camuffare*) to disguise; (*in costume*) to dress up.

② **travestirsi** VR (*vedi vt*) to disguise o.s.; to dress up; **travestirsi da donna** to dress up as a woman.

travestitismo [travesti'tizmo] SM transvestism, cross-dressing.

travestito [traves'tito] SM transvestite, cross-dresser.

traviare [travi'are] ① VT to lead astray.

② **traviarsi** VIP to go off the straight and narrow.

traviato, a [travi'ato] AGG corrupt.

travisare [travi'zare] VT to distort, misrepresent.

travolgente [travol'dʒɛnte] AGG (*entusiasmo*) overwhelming; (*bellezza, fascino*) captivating; (*comicità, umorismo*) side-splitting; (*passione*) uncontrollable; (*amore*) passionate.

travolgere [tra'vɔldʒere] VT IRREG (*sogg: piena, valanga*) to sweep away; (*fig*) to overwhelm; **è stato travolto da un'auto** he was run over by a car; **si è lasciato travolgere dalla passione** he was overwhelmed by passion.

travolto, a [tra'vɔlto] PP di **travolgere**.

trazione [trat'tsjone] SF (*Med, Tecn*) traction; (*Aut*) drive ▶ **trazione anteriore** (*Aut*) front-wheel drive ▶ **trazione posteriore** (*Aut*) rear-wheel drive.

tre [tre] ① AGG INV three; **tre volte** three times.

② SM INV three; **non c'è due senza tre** it never rains but it pours *per fraseologia vedi* **cinque**.

trealberi [tre'alberi] SM INV (*Naut*) three-master.

trebbia ['trebbja] SF (*Agr: operazione*) threshing; (: *stagione*) threshing season.

trebbiare [treb'bjare] VT (*Agr*) to thresh.

trebbiatrice [trebbja'tritʃe] SF (*Agr*) threshing machine.

trebbiatura [trebbja'tura] SF threshing.

trebisonda [trebi'zonda] SF: **perdere la trebisonda** to lose one's head.

treccia, ce ['trettʃa] SF (*di capelli*) plait, braid; (*di tessuti, fili*) braid; **lavorato a trecce** (*pullover*) cable-knit.

trecentesco, a, schi, sche [tretʃen'tesko] AGG fourteenth-century.

trecento [tre'tʃɛnto] ① AGG INV three hundred.

② SM INV three hundred; (*secolo*): **il Trecento** the fourteenth century.

tredicenne [tredi'tʃɛnne] AGG, SM/F thirteen-year-old *per fraseologia vedi* **cinquantenne**.

tredicesima [tredi'tʃɛzima] SF *Christmas bonus of a month's pay.*

tredicesimo, a [tredi'tʃɛzimo] AGG, SM/F, SM thirteenth *per fraseologia vedi* **quinto**.

tredici ['treditʃi] ① AGG INV thirteen.

② SM INV thirteen; **fare tredici** (*Totocalcio*) to win the pools (*Brit*) *per fraseologia vedi* **cinque**.

tregenda [tre'dʒɛnda] SF: **notte di tregenda** stormy night.

tregua ['tregwa] SF (*Mil, Pol*) truce; (*fig*) rest, respite; **il dolore non gli dà tregua** the pain gives him no peace, he is in constant pain; **senza tregua** non-stop, without stopping, uninterruptedly.

tremante [tre'mante] AGG trembling, shaking.

tremare [tre'mare] VI (*aus* **avere**) ⓐ (*gen*) to tremble,

shake; (*fig: temere*) to be afraid; **tremare di** (*freddo*) to shiver *o* tremble with; (*paura, rabbia*) to shake *o* tremble with; **tremare come una foglia** to shake like a leaf; **mi tremano le gambe** my legs are shaking; **tremare per la sorte di qn** to fear for sb; **faceva tremare gli studenti** he made the students tremble with fear

ⓑ (*oscillare: vetri*) to vibrate; (: *terra*) to shake; (: *voce*) to shake, tremble; (: *luce, candela*) to flicker; **mi trema la vista** I can't see straight.

tremarella [trema'rɛlla] SF shivers *pl*; **ho la tremarella** I have got the shivers; **mi ha fatto venire la tremarella** it gave me the shivers.

tremendamente [tremenda'mente] AVV (*divertente, imbarazzato*) terribly, awfully.

tremendo, a [tre'mɛndo] AGG (*in tutti i sensi*) terrible, awful, dreadful; **avere una fame tremenda** to be awfully *o* terribly hungry, be famished; **faceva un caldo tremendo** it was dreadfully *o* terribly hot.

trementina [tremen'tina] SF turpentine.

tremila [tre'mila] AGG INV, SM INV three thousand.

tremito ['tremito] SM trembling *no pl*; **mi è venuto un tremito** I started to tremble.

tremolante [tremo'lante] AGG (*vedi vb*) trembling, shaking; flickering; twinkling; quivering.

tremolare [tremo'lare] VI (*aus* **avere**) (*gen*) to tremble, shake; (*luci, candele*) to flicker; (*stelle*) to twinkle; (*foglie*) to quiver.

tremolio, lii [tremo'lio] SM (*gen*) trembling, shaking; (*di luci*) flickering.

tremolo ['tremolo] SM (*Mus*) tremolo.

tremore [tre'more] SM tremor.

tremulo, a ['tremulo] AGG ⓐ (*gen*) trembling, shaking; (*stelle*) twinkling; (*luci*) flickering ⓑ (*Bot*): **pioppo tremulo** trembling poplar.

trend [trend] SM INV (*Econ*) trend.

trenette [tre'nette] SFPL (*Culin*) *long, flat noodles.*

trenino [tre'nino] SM (*giocattolo*) toy train.

treno ['trɛno] SM ⓐ (*Ferr*) train; **prendere/perdere il treno** to catch/miss the train; **salire in/scendere dal treno** to get on/get off the train; **andare/viaggiare in treno** to go/travel by train ▶ **treno diretto** fast train ▶ **treno espresso** express train ▶ **treno interregionale** slow long-distance train ▶ **treno locale** stopping (*Brit*) *o* local (*Am*) train ▶ **treno merci** goods (*Brit*) *o* freight (*Am*) train ▶ **treno rapido** express (train) (*for which supplement must be paid*) ▶ **treno regionale** stopping *o* local train ▶ **treno straordinario** special train ▶ **treno viaggiatori** passenger train

ⓑ (*Aut*): **treno di gomme** set of tyres (*Brit*) *o* tires (*Am*).

trenta ['trenta] ① AGG INV thirty.

② SM INV ⓐ thirty ⓑ (*Univ*): **trenta su trenta** full marks; **trenta e lode** full marks plus distinction *o* cum laude *per fraseologia vedi* **cinquanta**.

trentenne [tren'tɛnne] AGG, SM/F thirty-year-old *per fraseologia vedi* **cinquantenne**.

trentennio, ni [tren'tɛnnjo] SM period of thirty years.

trentesimo, a [tren'tɛzimo] AGG, SM/F, SM thirtieth *per fraseologia vedi* **quinto**.

trentina [tren'tina] SF about thirty, thirty or so *per fraseologia vedi* **cinquantina**.

trentino, a [tren'tino] ① AGG of *o* from Trento.

② SM/F inhabitant *o* native of Trento.

trepidante [trepi'dante] AGG anxious.

trepidare [trepi'dare] VI (*aus* **avere**) to be anxious; **trepi-**

dare per qn to be anxious about sb; **trepidava nell'attesa** she waited in trepidation.

trepido, a ['trɛpido] AGG (*letter*) anxious.

treppiede [trep'pjede] SM (*per fotografia*) tripod; (*per cucina*) trivet.

trequarti [tre'kwarti] SM INV **a** (*indumento*) three-quarter-length coat **b** (*Rugby*) three-quarter.

tresca, sche ['treska] SF (*relazione amorosa*) affair; (*intrigo*) intrigue, plot.

trespolo ['trespolo] SM (*sostegno*) trestle; (: *per uccelli*) perch.

trevigiano, a [trevi'dʒano], **trevisano, a** [trevi'sano] [1] AGG of *o* from Treviso.
[2] SM/F inhabitant *o* native of Treviso.

triade ['triade] SF (*gen, Mus*) triad.

triangolare [triango'lare] AGG triangular.

triangolo [tri'angolo] SM (*gen, fig, Mat, Mus*) triangle; (*Aut*) warning triangle; **il solito** *o* **classico triangolo** (*fig*) the eternal triangle ▶**triangolo ottusangolo** obtuse-angled triangle ▶**triangolo rettangolo** right-angled triangle.

tribalismo [triba'lizmo] SM tribalism.

tribolare [tribo'lare] VI (*aus avere*) (*patire*) to suffer; (*fare fatica*) to have a lot of trouble; **ha finito di tribolare** (*euf*: *è morto*) death has put an end to his suffering; **ha tribolato parecchio per ottenerlo** he went to a lot of trouble to get it.

tribolazione [tribolat'tsjone] SF tribulation, suffering; **quel figlio è la mia tribolazione** that son of mine brings me nothing but suffering; **una vita di tribolazioni** a life of trials and tribulations.

tribordo [tri'bordo] SM (*Naut*) starboard.

tribù [tri'bu] SF INV tribe.

tribuna [tri'buna] SF **a** (*per oratore*) platform **b** (*per il pubblico*) gallery; (: *di stadio*) stand; (: *di ippodromo*) grandstand; **tribuna della stampa/riservata al pubblico** press/public gallery **c** (*TV, Radio*): **tribuna politica** ≈ party political broadcast (*Brit*), ≈ paid political broadcast (*Am*).

tribunale [tribu'nale] SM (*Dir*) court; **chiamare in tribunale** to take to court; **presentarsi** *o* **comparire in tribunale** to appear in court ▶**tribunale amministrativo regionale** regional administrative court ▶**tribunale militare** military tribunal.

tribuno [tri'buno] SM (*Storia*) tribune.

tributare [tribu'tare] VT to bestow; **tributare gli onori dovuti a qn** to pay tribute to sb.

tributario, ria, ri, rie [tribu'tarjo] AGG **a** (*Fisco*) tax *attr*, fiscal **b** (*Geog*): **fiume tributario** tributary.

tributo [tri'buto] SM (*imposta*) tax; (*Storia*: *fig*) tribute.

tricheco, chi [tri'kɛko] SM walrus.

triciclo [tri'tʃiklo] SM tricycle.

triclinio, ni [tri'klinjo] SM (*Storia*) triclinium.

tricolore [triko'lore] [1] AGG three-coloured (*Brit*), three-colored (*Am*).
[2] SM (*bandiera*) tricolo(u)r; **il tricolore** the Italian flag.

tridente [tri'dɛnte] SM (*gen*) trident; (*per fieno*) pitchfork.

tridimensionale [tridimensjo'nale] AGG three-dimensional.

triennale [trien'nale] AGG (*che dura 3 anni*) three-year *attr*; (*che avviene ogni 3 anni*) three-yearly.

triennio, ni [tri'ɛnnjo] SM (period of) three years.

triestino, a [tries'tino] [1] AGG of *o* from Trieste.
[2] SM/F inhabitant *o* native of Trieste.

trifase [tri'faze] AGG INV (*Elettr*) three-phase.

trifoglio, gli [tri'fɔʎʎo] SM clover ▶**trifoglio bianco** white clover ▶**trifoglio pratense** *o* **rosso** red clover.

trifolato, a [trifo'lato] AGG (*Culin*) *cooked in oil, garlic and parsley.*

trigemino, a [tri'dʒemino] [1] AGG **a** (*Med*): **avere un parto trigemino** to give birth to triplets **b** (*Anat*) trigeminal.
[2] SM (*Anat*) trigeminal (nerve).

triglia ['triʎʎa] SF mullet; **fare gli occhi di triglia a qn** to make sheep's eyes at sb ▶**triglia di scoglio** red mullet.

trigonometria [trigonome'tria] SF trigonometry.

trigonometrico, a, ci, che [trigono'metriko] AGG trigonometric.

trilaterale [trilate'rale] AGG (*accordo, patto, alleanza*) trilateral.

trilione [tri'ljone] SM trillion.

trillare [tril'lare] VI (*aus avere*) (*Mus*) to trill; (*campanello*) to ring.

trillo ['trillo] SM (*Mus*) trill; (*di campanello*) ring.

trimarano [trima'rano] SM trimaran.

trimestrale [trimes'trale] AGG (*periodo, abbonamento*) three-month *attr*; (*scadenza, pubblicazione*) quarterly.

trimestralmente [trimestral'mente] AVV every three months, quarterly.

trimestre [tri'mɛstre] SM **a** (*periodo*) three months, period of three months, quarter; (: *Scol*) term, quarter (*Am*) **b** (*rata*) quarterly payment.

trimotore [trimo'tore] SM (*Aer*) three-engined plane.

trina ['trina] SF lace.

trincare [trin'kare] VT (*fam*: *bere alcolici*) to knock back; **trinca come una spugna** he drinks like a fish.

trincea [trin'tʃea] SF (*Mil*) trench; **guerra di trincea** trench warfare.

trinceramento [trintʃera'mento] SM (*Mil*) entrenchment.

trincerare [trintʃe'rare] [1] VT (*Mil*) to entrench.
[2] **trincerarsi** VIP (*Mil*) to entrench o.s.; **trincerarsi nel silenzio più assoluto** to take refuge in silence; **trincerarsi dietro un pretesto** to hide behind an excuse.

trincetto [trin'tʃetto] SM cobbler's knife.

trinchetto [trin'ketto] SM (*Naut*: *albero*) foremast; (: *vela*) foresail.

trinciapollo [trintʃa'pollo] SM INV poultry shears *pl*.

trinciare [trin'tʃare] VT **a** to cut up **b** (*fig*): **trinciare giudizi (su qn/qc)** to make rash judgments (about sb/sth).

Trinidad ['trinidad] SM: **Trinidad e Tobago** Trinidad and Tobago.

trinità [trini'ta] SF trinity; **la (santissima) Trinità** the (Holy) Trinity.

trinomio, mi [tri'nɔmjo] SM (*Mat*) trinomial.

trio, trii ['trio] SM (*Mus, fig*) trio.

trionfale [trion'fale] AGG (*arco, entrata*) triumphal; (*successo*) triumphant.

trionfalismo [trionfa'lizmo] SM triumphalism.

trionfalista [trionfa'lista] SM/F triumphant winner.

trionfalistico, a [trionfa'listiko] AGG triumphalist.

trionfalmente [trionfal'mente] AVV triumphantly.

trionfante [trion'fante] AGG triumphant.

trionfare [trion'fare] VI (*aus avere*) **a** (*gen, Mil*) to triumph; (*commedia, film*) to be a great success; **la verità alla fine trionfa sempre** truth will out; **trionfare su** to triumph over, overcome; **trionfare sui nemici** to triumph over one's enemies **b** (*esultare*) to rejoice; **trionfare per qc** to rejoice at *o* over sth.

trionfatore, trice [trionfa'tore] ☐1 AGG (*truppe*) triumphant, victorious.
☐2 SM/F victor.

trionfo [tri'onfo] SM (*gen*) triumph; (*morale*) (moral) victory; **in trionfo** in triumph.

tripartitico, a, ci, che [tripar'titiko], **tripartito**, [tripar'tito] AGG (*Pol*) tripartite, three-party *attr*.

tripletta [tri'pletta] SF (*Calcio*) hat trick (*Brit*); **realizzare una tripletta** to score a hat trick.

triplicare [tripli'kare] VT, VI (*aus* essere), **triplicarsi** VIP to treble, triple.

triplice ['triplitʃe] AGG triple; **in triplice copia** in triplicate; **la Triplice Alleanza** the Triple Alliance.

triplo, a ['triplo] ☐1 AGG triple, treble; **salto triplo** (*Sport*) triple jump; **la spesa è tripla** it costs three times as much.
☐2 SM: **il triplo (di)** three times as much (as); **mi occorre il triplo** I need three times as much; **lavorare il triplo** to work three times as hard.

tripode ['tripode] SM tripod.

tripolare [tripo'lare] AGG (*Elettr*) triple-pole *attr*.

Tripoli ['tripoli] SF Tripoli.

trippa ['trippa] SF (*Culin*) tripe; (*fig: pancia*) paunch.

tripsina [trip'sina] SF (*Bio*) trypsin.

tripudiare [tripu'djare] VI (*aus* avere) to exult, rejoice.

tripudio, di [tri'pudjo] SM (*esultanza*) triumph, jubilation; (*fig: di colori*) galaxy.

trireattore [trireat'tore] SM three-engine jet.

tris [tris] SM INV (*Carte*): **tris d'assi/di re** three aces/kings *pl*.

trisavolo, a [tri'zavolo] SM/F great-great-grandfather/grandmother; (*antenato*) forebear, ancestor.

trisillabo, a [tri'sillabo] ☐1 AGG trisyllabic.
☐2 SM trisyllable.

triste ['triste] AGG (*gen*) sad; (*persona, destino*) unhappy, sad; (*sguardo*) sorrowful, sad; (*spettacolo, condizioni*) miserable; (*luogo*) gloomy, dismal, dreary; (*esperienza*) painful.

tristemente [triste'mente] AVV (*gen*) sadly; **finire tristemente** to come to a sorry end; **tristemente famoso per** notorious for.

tristezza [tris'tettsa] SF (*gen*) sadness; (*dolore*) sorrow; (*di paesaggio*) bleakness, dreariness; **che tristezza!** how sad!

tristo, a ['tristo] AGG (*letter: cattivo*) wicked, evil; (: *meschino*) poor, mean, sorry.

tritacarne [trita'karne] SM INV mincer, grinder (*Am*).

tritaghiaccio [trita'gjattʃo] SM INV ice crusher.

tritaprezzemolo [tritapret'tsemolo] SM INV parsley chopper.

tritare [tri'tare] VT (*carne*) to mince, grind (*Am*); (*verdura, cipolla*) to chop.

tritarifiuti [tritari'fjuti] SM INV waste (*Brit*) o garbage (*Am*) disposal unit.

tritatutto [trita'tutto] SM INV mincer, grinder (*Am*).

trito, a ['trito] ☐1 AGG (*carne*) minced, ground (*Am*); **trito e ritrito** (*idee, argomenti, frasi*) trite, hackneyed.
☐2 SM: **fare un trito di cipolla** to chop an onion finely.

tritolo [tri'tolo] SM trinitrotoluene.

tritone [tri'tone] SM a (*Zool*) newt b (*Mitol*): **Tritone** Triton.

trittico, ci ['trittiko] SM triptych.

trittongo, ghi [trit'tongo] SM triphthong.

triturare [tritu'rare] VT to grind.

triunvirato [triunvi'rato] SM triumvirate.

trivella [tri'vɛlla] SF (*Falegnameria*) auger; (*per miniera, pozzi*) drill.

trivellare [trivel'lare] VT to drill.

trivellazione [trivellat'tsjone] SF drilling; **torre di trivellazione** derrick.

triviale [tri'vjale] AGG (*volgare*) coarse, crude, vulgar.

trivialità [trivjali'ta] SF INV (*volgarità*) coarseness, crudeness; (: *osservazione*) coarse o crude remark.

trivialmente [trivjal'mente] AVV coarsely, crudely.

trofeo [tro'fɛo] SM trophy.

troglodita, i, e [troglo'dita] SM/F troglodyte, cave dweller; (*fig*) barbarian.

trogolo ['trɔgolo] SM trough.

Troia ['trɔja] SF Troy.

troia ['trɔja] SF (*fam: scrofa*) sow; (*fam! pegg*) whore.

troiaio, ai [tro'jajo] SM (*fam: luogo sporco*) pigsty.

troiano, a [tro'jano] AGG, SM/F Trojan.

troika ['trɔika] SF INV (*anche fig*) troika.

tromba ['tromba] ☐1 SF a (*Mus*) trumpet; (*Aut*) horn; **partire in tromba** (*fig*) to be off like a shot
b (*suonatore*) trumpeter; (: *Mil*) bugler.
☐2 ▶**tromba d'aria** (*Meteor*) whirlwind ▶**tromba d'Eustachio** (*Anat*) Eustachian tube ▶**tromba di Falloppio** (*Anat*) Fallopian tube ▶**tromba marina** (*Meteor*) waterspout ▶**tromba delle scale** (*Archit*) stairwell.

trombare [trom'bare] VT a (*fam!: avere rapporti sessuali*) to fuck (*fam!*), screw (*fam!*) b (*fig: bocciare: candidato*) to reject.

trombetta [trom'betta] SF toy trumpet.

trombettiere [trombet'tjɛre] SM (*Mil*) bugler.

trombettista, i, e [trombet'tista] SM/F trumpeter, trumpet (player).

trombone [trom'bone] SM a (*Mus: strumento*) trombone; (: *suonatore*) trombonist, trombone (player) b (*fig: persona*) windbag c (*Bot*) daffodil.

trombosi [trom'bɔzi] SF INV thrombosis.

troncamento [tronka'mento] SM (*Ling*) apocope.

troncare [tron'kare] VT a (*spezzare*) to break off; (*con cesoie, ascia*) to cut off b (*Ling*) to apocopate c (*amicizia, relazione*) to break off; (*carriera*) to ruin, cut short; **una salita che tronca le gambe** a tiring climb.

tronchese [tron'kese] SM O F clippers *pl*.

tronchesina [tronke'sina] SM (*per unghie*) nail clippers *pl*.

tronco¹, a, chi, che ['tronko] AGG (*colonna, parola*) truncated; **licenziare qn in tronco** to fire sb on the spot.

tronco², chi ['tronko] SM (*Bot, Anat*) trunk; (*d'albero tagliato*) log; (*fig: tratto: di strada, ferrovia*) section ▶**tronco di cono** (*Geom*) truncated cone.

troneggiare [troned'dʒare] VI (*aus* avere) a (*sovrastare*): **troneggiare su qn/qc** to tower over o dominate sb/sth b (*imporsi all'attenzione*): **troneggiare in mezzo a qc** to dominate sth; **un grosso brillante troneggiava al centro della vetrina** a large diamond dominated the window display.

tronfio, fia, fi, fie ['tronfjo] AGG conceited, pompous.

trono ['trɔno] SM throne; **salire** o **ascendere al trono** to come to o ascend the throne.

tropicale [tropi'kale] AGG tropical.

tropico, ci ['trɔpiko] SM tropic; **i tropici** the tropics ▶**tropico del Cancro** Tropic of Cancer ▶**tropico del Capricorno** Tropic of Capricorn.

tropismo [tro'pizmo] SM (*Bot, Bio*) tropism.

troppo, **a** ['trɔppo]

1 AGG INDEF (*quantità*: *tempo*, *acqua*) too much; (*numero*: *persone*, *promesse*) too many;

▷**non vorrei causarvi troppo** *disturbo* I wouldn't like to put you to too much trouble

▷**c'era troppa** *gente* there were too many people.

2 PRON INDEF (*quantità eccessiva*) too much; (*numero eccessivo*) too many;

▷**ha detto** *anche* **troppo** he's said far too much *o* quite enough

▷**non ne prendo più, ne ho** *fin* **troppi** I won't take any more, I've got far too many

▷**eravamo** *in* **troppi** there were too many of us

▷**ne vorrei ancora un po', ma** *non* **troppo** I'd like a little more, but not too much though

▷**troppi la pensano come lui** too many (people) think like him.

3 AVV

a (*con aggettivo, avverbio*) too; (*con verbo*: *gen*) too much; (: *aspettare, durare*) too long;

▷**ho** *aspettato* **troppo** I've waited too long

▷**è troppo** *bello* **per essere vero** it's too good to be true

▷**fa troppo** *caldo* it's too hot

▷**fidarsi troppo di qn** to trust sb too much

▷**è fin troppo** *furbo*! he's too clever by half!

▷**troppo** *poco* too little

▷**sei arrivato troppo** *tardi* you arrived too late

b (*rafforzativo*) too, so (very);

▷**troppo** *buono* **da parte tua!** (*anche iro*) you're too kind!

▷**non ci sarebbe troppo** *da stupirsi* **se rifiutasse** I wouldn't be surprised if he refused

▷**non esserne troppo** *sicuro*! don't be too *o* so sure of that!

▷**non troppo** *volentieri* none too willingly

c: *di* **troppo** too much

▷**3.000 lire** *di* **troppo** 3,000 lire too much

▷**essere** *di* **troppo** to be in the way

▷**ha bevuto qualche bicchiere** *di* **troppo** he's had a few too many.

trota ['trɔta] SF trout ▶**trota arcobaleno** *o* **iridea** rainbow trout ▶**trota di mare** sea trout ▶**trota salmonata** salmon trout.

trottare [trot'tare] VI (*aus* avere) (*cavallo, cavaliere*) to trot; (*bambino, cucciolo*) to trot along.

trottata [trot'tata] SF trot.

trottatore, **trice** [trotta'tore] SM/F (*cavallo*) trotter.

trotterellare [trotterel'lare] VI (*aus* avere) (*cavallo*) to jog along; (*cucciolo*) to trot along; (*bambino*) to trot along, toddle.

trotto ['trɔtto] SM trot; **andare al trotto** to trot; **corse al trotto** trotting races.

trottola ['trɔttola] SF (spinning) top.

troupe [trup] SF INV troupe, company.

trousse [trus] SF INV (*di cosmetici*) make-up set; (*borsetta da sera*) evening bag.

trovare [tro'vare] **1** VT **a** (*gen*) to find; (*per caso*) to find, come upon *o* across; (*difficoltà*) to come up against, meet with; **trovare lavoro/casa** to find work *o* a job/a house; **far trovare qc a qn** to help sb find sth; **non trovo**

le scarpe I can't find my shoes; **andare/venire a trovare qn** to go/come and see sb; **trovare la morte** to meet one's death

b : **trovare da ridire (su tutto)** to find sth to criticize (in everything); **trovare da dormire** to find somewhere to sleep

c (*giudicare*): **trovare che...** to find *o* think that ...; **lo trovo un po' invecchiato** I think he has aged a bit; **ti trovo dimagrito** you look thinner; **trovi?** do you think so?; **trovo giusto/sbagliato che...** I think/don't think it's right that ...; **lo trovo bello** *o* **buono** I like it; **trovare qn colpevole** to find sb guilty

d (*cogliere*) to find, catch; **la notizia ci trovò impreparati** the news caught us unawares.

2 **trovarsi** VIP **a** (*essere situato*) to be; **dove si trova la stazione?** where is the station?

b (*capitare*) to find o.s.; **ci siamo trovati a Napoli** we found ourselves in Naples

c (*essere*) to be; **trovarsi bene/male** to get on well/badly; **trovarsi in pericolo/smarrito** to be in danger/lost; **trovarsi nell'impossibilità di rispondere** to be unable to answer; **trovarsi d'accordo con qn** to be in agreement with sb; **trovarsi a disagio** to feel ill at ease; **trovarsi solo** to find o.s. alone; **trovarsi nei pasticci** to find o.s. in trouble; **trovarsi con un pugno di mosche in mano** to be left empty-handed.

3 **trovarsi** VR (*uso reciproco*: *incontrarsi*) to meet; **si sono trovati in piazza** they met (each other) in the square.

trovata [tro'vata] SF (*idea*) brainwave, stroke of genius ▶**trovata pubblicitaria** publicity stunt, (advertising) gimmick.

trovatello, **a** [trova'tɛllo] SM/F foundling.

truccare [truk'kare] **1** VT **a** (*Sport*: *partita, incontro*) to fix, rig; (*carte da gioco*) to mark; (*dadi*) to load; (*Aut*: *motore*) to soup up **b** (*attore, viso, occhi*) to make up; **truccarsi il viso** to make up one's face; **truccarsi gli occhi** to put on eye make-up.

2 **truccarsi** VR (*gen, Teatro, Cine*) to make o.s. up; **truccarsi da** to make o.s. up as.

truccato, **a** [truk'kato] AGG **a** (*partita, incontro*) rigged; (*carte*) marked; (*dadi*) loaded; (*motore*) souped-up **b** (*occhi, viso*) made up; **non ti ho mai vista truccata** I've never seen you with make-up on.

truccatore, **trice** [trukka'tore] SM/F make-up artist.

trucco, chi ['trukko] SM **a** (*cosmesi*) make-up **b** (*artificio*) trick; (*Cine*) effect, trick; **i trucchi del mestiere** the tricks of the trade.

truce ['trutʃe] AGG (*viso, sguardo*) grim, cruel; (*tiranno*) cruel.

trucidare [trutʃi'dare] VT to slay, massacre, slaughter.

truciolato [trutʃo'lato] SM chipboard.

truciolo ['trutʃolo] SM (*di legno, metallo*) shaving; **trucioli di paglia/carta** straw/paper packing material *sg*.

truculento, **a** [truku'lɛnto] AGG (*persona, espressione*) truculent, grim; (*film, romanzo*) gory.

truffa ['truffa] SF (*Dir*) fraud; (*imbroglio*) swindle.

truffare [truf'fare] VT to swindle, cheat.

truffatore, **trice** [truffa'tore] SM/F swindler, cheat.

trullo ['trullo] SM (*nelle Puglie*) *cylindrical house with conical roof*.

truppa ['truppa] SF **a** (*Mil*) troop; (*soldati semplici*) troops *pl*; **truppe d'assalto** assault troops, shock troops **b** (*fig*: *di amici*) group, band, troop.

trust [trʌst] SM INV (*Econ*) trust ▶**trust di cervelli** brains

trust.

TS SIGLA = *Trieste*.

tse-tse [tsɛt'tsɛ] AGG INV: **mosca tse-tse** tsetse fly.

tu [tu] 1 PRON PERS you; **tu faresti meglio a tacere!** you'd do better to keep quiet!; **questo lo dici tu!** that's what you say!; **proprio tu lo dici!** you're a right one to talk!; **sei tu quello che fa sempre storie** you're the one who always causes a fuss.

2 SM: **dare del tu a qn** to address sb as "tu", ≈ be on first-name terms with sb; **trovarsi a tu per tu con qn** to find o.s. face to face with sb; **perché non gli parli a tu per tu?** why don't you have a word with him in private?

tua ['tua] vedi **tuo**.

tuba ['tuba] SF **a** (*Mus*) tuba **b** (*Anat*) tube **c** (*cappello*) top hat.

tubare [tu'bare] VI (*aus* **avere**) (*colombi*) to coo; (*fig: innamorati*) to bill and coo.

tubatura [tuba'tura], **tubazione** [tubat'tsjone] SF pipes *pl*, piping *no pl*.

tubercolare [tuberko'lare] AGG tubercular.

tubercolina [tuberko'lina] SF tuberculin.

tubercolo [tu'bɛrkolo] SM tubercle.

tubercolosi [tuberko'lɔzi] SF tuberculosis.

tubero ['tubero] SM (*Bot*) tuber.

tuberosa [tube'rosa] SF tuberose.

tubetto [tu'betto] SM (*di dentifricio*) tube.

tubino [tu'bino] SM **a** (*abito da donna*) sheath dress **b** (*cappello*) bowler (hat) (*Brit*), derby (*Am*).

tubo ['tubo] 1 SM (*gen*) tube; (*per condutture*) pipe; **non capisce/non sa un tubo** (*fam*) he doesn't understand/know a thing; **non me ne importa un tubo** (*fam*) I couldn't care less, I don't give a damn.

2 ▶**tubo catodico** *o* **a raggi catodici** (*Fis*) cathode-ray tube ▶**tubo digerente** (*Anat*) digestive tract, alimentary canal ▶**tubo elettronico** (*Tecn*) electron tube ▶**tubo di scappamento** (*Aut*) exhaust (pipe) ▶**tubo di scarico** waste pipe.

tubolare [tubo'lare] 1 AGG tubular; **elastico tubolare** elastic thread.

2 SM tubeless tyre (*Brit*) *o* tire (*Am*).

tucano [tu'kano] SM toucan.

Tucidide [tu'tʃidide] SM Thucydides.

tue ['tue] vedi **tuo**.

tuffare [tuf'fare] 1 VT (*immergere*) to plunge; (*intingere*) to dip.

2 **tuffarsi** VR (*gen*) to dive; **tuffarsi in mare** to dive *o* plunge into the sea; **tuffarsi nella mischia** to rush *o* dive into the fray; **tuffarsi nello studio** to bury *o* immerse o.s. in one's studies; **tuffarsi a capofitto in qc** to throw o.s. into sth.

tuffatore, trice [tuffa'tore] SM/F (*Sport*) diver.

tuffo ['tuffo] SM (*gen*) dive; (*breve bagno*) dip; (*Sport*): **tuffi** diving *no pl*; **fare un tuffo** to dive; **fare un tuffo nel passato** to jump back into the past; **ho provato un tuffo al cuore** my heart skipped *o* missed a beat.

tufo ['tufo] SM tuff.

tuga ['tuga] SF (*Naut*) deckhouse.

tugurio, ri [tu'gurjo] SM hovel.

tulipano [tuli'pano] SM tulip.

tulle ['tulle] SM INV (*tessuto*) tulle.

tumefare [tume'fare] 1 VT to cause to swell.

2 **tumefarsi** VIP to swell.

tumefatto, a [tume'fatto] 1 PP di **tumefare**.

2 AGG swollen.

tumefazione [tumefat'tsjone] SF swelling.

tumido, a ['tumido] AGG (*gonfio*) swollen; (*carnoso: labbra*) thick.

tumore [tu'more] SM tumour (*Brit*), tumor (*Am*) ▶**tumore benigno** benignant tumo(u)r ▶**tumore maligno** malignant tumo(u)r.

tumulazione [tumulat'tsjone] SF burial.

tumulo ['tumulo] SM (*Archeol*) tumulus.

tumulto [tu'multo] SM **a** (*di folla: rumore*) commotion, uproar; (: *agitazione*) turmoil, tumult; (*sommossa*) riot **b** (*fig: di pensieri, desideri*) turmoil; **avere l'animo in tumulto** to be in a turmoil.

tumultuosamente [tumultuosa'mente] AVV turbulently.

tumultuoso, a [tumultu'oso] AGG (*folla*) turbulent, rowdy, unruly; (*assemblea*) stormy, turbulent; (*fiume*) turbulent; (*passione*) tumultuous, turbulent.

tundra ['tundra] SF tundra.

tungsteno [tung'stɛno] SM tungsten.

tunica, che ['tunika] SF tunic.

Tunisi ['tunizi] SF Tunis.

Tunisia [tuni'zia] SF: **la Tunisia** Tunisia.

tunisino, a [tuni'zino] AGG, SM/F Tunisian.

tunnel ['tunnel] SM INV tunnel.

tuo, a ['tuo] (*pl f* **tue**, *pl m* **tuoi**) 1 AGG POSS: **il(la) tuo(a)** ecc your; **il tuo cane** your dog; **tuo padre** your father; **una tua amica** a friend of yours; **è colpa tua** it's your fault; **è casa tua** OR **è la tua casa** it's your house; **per amor tuo** for love of you.

2 PRON POSS: **il(la) tuo(a)** ecc yours, your own; **la nostra barca è più lunga della tua** our boat is longer than yours; **è questo il tuo?** is this yours?; **il tuo è stato solo un errore** it was simply an error on your part.

3 PRON POSS M **a**: **hai speso del tuo?** did you spend your own money?; **vivi del tuo?** do you live on your own income?

b: **i tuoi** (*genitori, famiglia*) your family; (*amici*) your (own) people, your side; **è dei tuoi** he is on your side.

4 PRON POSS F: **la tua** (*opinione*) your view; **è dalla tua** he is on your side; **ne hai fatta una delle tue!** (*sciocchezze*) you've done it again!; **anche tu hai avuto le tue** (*disavventure*) you've had your problems too; **alla tua!** (*brindisi*) your health!

tuoi ['twɔi] vedi **tuo**.

tuonare [two'nare] 1 VI (*aus* **avere**) (*fig: armi, voce*) to thunder, boom; **tuonare contro qn/qc** (*inveire*) to rage against sb/sth.

2 VB IMPERS (*aus* **avere** *o* **essere**): **sta tuonando** there is thunder, it is thundering.

tuono ['twɔno] SM (*anche fig*) thunder.

tuorlo ['twɔrlo] SM yolk.

turacciolo [tu'rattʃolo] SM (*tappo*) stopper; (*di sughero*) cork.

turare [tu'rare] VT (*buco, falla*) to stop, plug; (*bottiglia*) to cork; **turarsi il naso** to hold one's nose; **ho il naso turato** my nose is blocked; **turarsi le orecchie** to stop one's ears.

turba ['turba] SF **a** (*folla*) crowd, throng; (: *pegg*) mob **b** (*Med*) disorder; **soffrire di turbe psichiche** to suffer from a mental disorder.

turbamento [turba'mento] SM (*di animo*) anxiety, agitation; (*della pace, quiete*) disturbance; **provò un profondo turbamento** he was extremely upset.

turbante [tur'bante] SM turban.

turbare [tur'bare] 1 VT to disturb, trouble; **turbare la**

quiete pubblica (*Dir*) to disturb the peace; **turbare l'opinione pubblica** to upset public opinion.

[2] **turbarsi** VIP to get upset.

turbina [tur'bina] SF turbine.

turbinare [turbi'nare] VI (*aus* **avere**) (*anche fig*) to whirl.

turbine ['turbine] SM whirlwind; **il turbine della danza** the whirl of the dance; **il turbine della passione** the turmoil of passion ▶**turbine di neve** gust *o* swirl of snow ▶**turbine di polvere** dust storm ▶**turbine di sabbia** sandstorm.

turbinosamente [turbinosa'mente] AVV: **volteggiare turbinosamente** to whirl round and round.

turbinoso, a [turbi'noso] AGG (*vento, danza*) whirling.

turbo... ['turbo] PREF turbo... .

turboelica, ché [turbo'ɛlika] [1] SF (*motore*) turbojet (engine).

[2] SM INV (*velivolo*) turbojet.

turbolento, a [turbo'lɛnto] AGG (*ragazzo*) boisterous, unruly; (*tempi, anni*) turbulent.

turbolenza [turbo'lɛntsa] SF (*vedi agg*) boisterousness; turbulence.

turboreattore [turboreat'tore] SM turbojet engine.

turchese [tur'kese] [1] AGG, SM (*colore*) turquoise.

[2] SF (*minerale*) turquoise.

Turchia [tur'kia] SF: **la Turchia** Turkey.

turchino, a [tur'kino] AGG, SM deep blue.

turco, a, chi, che ['turko] [1] AGG Turkish; **bagno turco** Turkish bath; **ho fatto un bagno turco** (*fig*) I sweated like a pig (*fam*); **caffè alla turca** Turkish coffee.

[2] SM/F (*persona*) Turk; **fumare come un turco** (*fig*) to smoke like a chimney; **bestemmiare come un turco** (*fig*) to swear like a trooper.

[3] SM (*lingua*) Turkish; **parlare turco** (*fig*) to talk double Dutch.

turgido, a ['turdʒido] AGG swollen.

turgore [tur'gore] SM swelling.

turibolo [tu'ribolo] SM (*Rel*) thurible, censer.

turismo [tu'rizmo] SM tourism.

turista, i, e [tu'rista] SM/F tourist.

turisticamente [turistika'mente] AVV: **una zona turisticamente rinomata** a well-known tourist area; **turisticamente parlando** from the tourist point of view.

turisticizzare [turistitʃid'dzare] VT to open to tourism.

turistico, a, ci, che [tu'ristiko] AGG tourist *attr*.

turlupinare [turlupi'nare] VT to cheat.

turnista, i, e [tur'nista] SM/F shift worker.

turno ['turno] SM (*volta*) turn; (*di lavoro*) shift; **è il tuo turno** it's your turn; **essere di turno** (*soldato, medico, custode*) to be on duty; **qual è la farmacia di turno domenica?** which chemist (*Brit*) *o* drugstore (*Am*) will be open on Sunday?; **rispondere a turno** to answer in turn; **aspettare il proprio turno** to await one's turn; **fare a turno a fare qc** to take (it in) turns to do sth ▶**turni articolati** split shifts ▶**turno di guardia** (*Mil*) sentry *o* guard duty ▶**turno di notte** nightshift.

turpe ['turpe] AGG (*voglia*) filthy; (*accusa*) foul, vile; (*persona*) vile, repugnant.

turpemente [turpe'mente] AVV (*comportarsi*) vilely.

turpiloquio, qui [turpi'lɔkwjo] SM obscene *o* foul language.

turrito, a [tur'rito] AGG turreted.

T.U.S. SIGLA M (*Econ*) ≈ **Tasso ufficiale di sconto**.

T.U.T. SIGLA F (*Telec*: = *Tariffa urbana a tempo*) local rate.

tuta ['tuta] SF overalls *pl*; (*Sport*) tracksuit; (*Sci*) ski suit ▶**tuta mimetica** (*Mil*) camouflage clothing ▶**tuta spaziale** spacesuit ▶**tuta subacquea** wetsuit ▶**le tute blu** (*gli operai*) blue collar workers.

tutela [tu'tɛla] SF **a** (*Dir*) guardianship; **essere sotto la tutela di qn** to be sb's ward; **tutela di un minore** guardianship of a minor

b (*protezione*) protection; **fare qc a tutela dei propri interessi** to do sth to protect one's interests ▶**tutela dell'ambiente** environmental protection ▶**tutela del consumatore** consumer protection.

tutelare[1] [tute'lare] [1] VT to protect, defend.

[2] **tutelarsi** VR to protect o.s.

tutelare[2] [tute'lare] AGG (*Dir*): **giudice tutelare** *judge with responsibility for guardianship cases*.

tutina [tu'tina] SF (*per neonato*) Babygro ®; (*per ginnastica*) leotard.

tutore, trice [tu'tore] SM/F (*Dir*) guardian; (*protettore*) protector, defender; **i tutori dell'ordine pubblico** the police *pl*.

tuttavia [tutta'via] CONG nevertheless, yet.

---

tutto, a ['tutto]

[1] AGG

a (*intero*) all (of), the whole (of);
▷**ha letto tutto Dante** he has read all of Dante
▷**tutta l'Europa** the whole of *o* all Europe
▷**ho tutta la sua fiducia** I have his complete confidence
▷**ha studiato tutto il giorno** he studied the whole day *o* all day long
▷**famoso in tutto il mondo** world-famous, famous the world over
▷**rimanere sveglio tutta la notte** to stay awake all night (long)
▷**a tutt'oggi** so far, up till now
▷**si diffuse in tutto il paese** it spread through the whole country
▷**sarò qui tutta la settimana** I'll be here all week *o* the whole week
▷**tutta una bottiglia** a whole bottle
▷**tutta la verità** the whole truth

b (*proprio*)
▷**è tutt'altra cosa** [OR] **è tutta un'altra cosa** (*è ben diverso*) that's quite another thing
▷**viaggiare in aereo è tutt'altra cosa** (*è meglio*) travelling by plane is altogether different
▷**è tutta sua madre** she's just *o* exactly like her mother
▷**è tutto l'opposto di...** it's the exact opposite of ...

c (*completamente*)
▷**era tutta contenta** she was overjoyed
▷**è tutta gambe e braccia** she's all arms and legs
▷**è tutto naso** he's got a big nose
▷**essere tutt'occhi** to be all eyes
▷**essere tutt'orecchi** to be all ears
▷**è tutta presa dal suo lavoro** she's completely *o* entirely taken up by her work
▷**era tutta sorrisi e sorrisetti** she was all smiles
▷**tremava tutto** he was trembling all over
▷**era tutta vestita di nero** she was dressed all in black

d (*plurale, collettivo*) all;

▷**tutti gli** *animali* all animals
▷**tutte queste** *cose* all these things
▷**in tutte le** *direzioni* in all directions, in every direction
▷**tutti e** *cinque* all five of us (*o* them)
▷**tutti e** *due* both *o* each of us (*o* them)
▷**con tutti i** *pensieri* **che ho** worried as I am, with all my worries
▷**tutti i** *posti* **erano occupati** all the seats were *o* every seat was occupied
▷**tutti i** *ragazzi* all the boys
▷**tutti gli** *uomini* all men
▷**una** *volta* **per tutte** once and for all
[e] (*qualsiasi*) all;
▷**a tutti i** *costi* at all costs;
▷**in tutti i** *modi* (*a qualsiasi costo*) at all costs; (*comunque*) anyway
▷**telefona a tutte le** *ore* she phones at all hours
[f] (*ogni*)
▷**tutti gli** *anni* every year
▷**tutti i** *santi giorni* every blessed day
▷**tutti i** *venerdì* every Friday
▷**tutte le** *volte* **che** every time (that)
[g] (*fraseologia*)
▷**con tutta l'***anima* wholeheartedly
▷**con tutto il** *cuore* wholeheartedly
▷**la sua fedeltà è a tutta** *prova* his loyalty is unshakeable *o* will stand any test
▷**per me è tutt'***uno* it's all one and the same to me
▷**a tutta** *velocità* at full *o* top speed
▷**con tutta la mia buona** *volontà*, **non posso aiutarti** however much I may want to, I can't help you.
[2] PRON
[a] (*ogni cosa*) everything, all; (*qualunque cosa*) anything;
▷**ha fatto (un po')** *di* **tutto** he's done (a bit of) everything
▷**essere capace** *di* **tutto** to be capable of anything
▷**mangia** *di* **tutto** he eats anything
▷**farebbe** *di* **tutto per ferirti** he would do anything to hurt you
▷*dimmi* **tutto** tell me everything
▷**tutto** *dipende* **da lui** everything *o* it all depends on him
▷**tutto è** *in ordine* everything's in order
▷**questo è** *quello* **che ho** this is all I have
▷**tutto** *sta* **a vedere se...** it all depends on whether or not ...
▷**tutto** *sta* **nel cominciare** the essential *o* important thing is to get started
[b]: **tutti(e)** SM/FPL (*tutte le persone*) all (of them); (*ognuno*) everybody
▷**erano tutti presenti** everybody was *o* they were all present
▷**vengono tutti** they are all coming, everybody's coming
▷**tutti** *quanti* all and sundry

[c] (*fraseologia*)
▷**tutto** *compreso* inclusive, all-in (*Brit*)
▷**questo è tutto** that's all (I have to say)
▷*con* **tutto che** (*malgrado*) although
▷**tutto** *considerato* all things considered
▷**... che è tutto** *dire* ...and that's saying a lot
▷*ecco* **tutto** that's all (I have to say)
▷**in tutto** (*complessivamente*) in all
▷*in* **tutto sono 18.000 lire** that's 18,000 lire in all
▷*in* **tutto e** *per* **tutto** (*completamente*) entirely, completely
▷**dipende** *in* **tutto e** *per* **tutto dai suoi** he is entirely *o* completely dependent on his parents
▷*innanzi* **tutto** first of all
▷**e** *non* **è tutto** and that's not all
▷*prima di* **tutto** first of all
▷**tutto** *sommato* all things considered.
[3] AVV
[a] (*completamente*) entirely, quite, completely;
▷**è tutto il** *contrario* it's quite *o* exactly the opposite
▷**è tutto il** *contrario* **di ciò che credi** it's not what you think at all
▷**fa tutto il** *contrario* **di quello che gli dico** he does the exact opposite of what I tell him to do
▷*del* **tutto** completely
▷**non sono** *del* **tutto convinto/sicuro** I'm not entirely convinced/sure
▷**è tutto l'***opposto* it's quite *o* exactly the opposite
[b] (*fraseologia*)
▷**saranno stati tutt'***al più* **una cinquantina** there were about fifty of them at (the very) most
▷**tutt'***al più* **possiamo prendere un treno** if the worst comes to the worst we can catch a train
▷**tutt'***altro* (*al contrario*) on the contrary; (*affatto*) not at all
▷**tutt'***altro* **che felice** anything but happy
▷**tutt'***intorno* all around
▷**tutto a un** *tratto* all of a sudden, suddenly.
[4] SM (*l'insieme*): **il tutto** the whole lot, all of it
▷*il* **tutto costa 300.000 lire** the whole thing *o* lot costs 300,000 lire
▷**vi manderemo** *il* **tutto nel corso della settimana** we'll send you the (whole) lot during the course of the week
▷*il* **tutto si è risolto in bene** everything turned out for the best
▷**rischiare** *il* **tutto** *per tutto* to risk everything.

tuttofare [tutto'fare] [1] AGG INV: **domestica tuttofare** general maid; **ragazzo tuttofare** office boy.
[2] SM/F INV handyman/woman.
tuttora [tut'tora] AVV still.
tutù [tu'tu] SM INV tutu.
TV [ti'vu] [1] SF INV TV.
[2] SIGLA = *Treviso*.

U

U, u [u] SF O M INV (*lettera*) U, u; **U come Udine** ≈ U for Uncle; **inversione ad U** U-turn.

uadi ['wadi] SM INV wadi.

ubbia [ub'bia] SF (*letter*) irrational fear.

ubbidiente [ubbi'djɛnte] AGG obedient.

ubbidientemente [ubbidjente'mente] AVV obediently.

ubbidienza [ubbi'djɛntsa] SF obedience.

ubbidire [ubbi'dire] VI (*aus* **avere**): **ubbidire a** to obey; (*sogg: veicolo, macchina*) to respond to; **farsi ubbidire** to enforce *o* compel obedience.

ubertoso, a [uber'toso] AGG (*letter*) fertile.

ubicato, a [ubi'kato] AGG situated, located.

ubicazione [ubikat'tsjone] SF site, location.

ubiquità [ubikwi'ta] SF ubiquity; **non ho il dono dell'ubiquità!** I can't be everywhere at once!

ubriacare [ubria'kare] 1 VT: **ubriacare qn** (*sogg: persona*) to get sb drunk; (: *bevanda*) to make sb drunk, intoxicate sb; (*con discorsi, promesse*) to intoxicate sb, make sb's head spin *o* reel.
2 **ubriacarsi** VIP to get drunk.

ubriacatura [ubriaka'tura] SF: **prendersi una solenne ubriacatura** to get blind *o* roaring drunk (*fam*).

ubriachezza [ubria'kettsa] SF drunkenness; **essere arrestato per ubriachezza molesta** to be arrested for being drunk and disorderly; **guidare in stato di ubriachezza** to drive under the influence of alcohol.

ubriaco, a, chi, che [ubri'ako] 1 AGG drunk; **essere ubriaco fradicio** to be blind *o* roaring drunk (*fam*); **ubriaco di stanchezza** reeling from tiredness; **ubriaco di gelosia** beside o.s. with jealousy.
2 SM/F drunkard, drunk.

ubriacone, a [ubria'kone] SM/F drunkard.

uccellagione [uttʃella'dʒone] SF bird catching.

uccellatore, trice [uttʃella'tore] SM/F bird catcher.

uccelliera [uttʃel'ljɛra] SF aviary.

uccellino [uttʃel'lino] SM baby bird, chick.

uccello [ut'tʃello] SM **a** (*Zool*) bird; **uccello del malaugurio** (*fig*) bird of ill omen; **essere uccel di bosco** (*latitante*) to be nowhere to be found, have flown the coop **b** (*fam!*: *pene*) dick (*fam!*)

uccidere [ut'tʃidere] VB IRREG 1 VT (*gen*) to kill; (*assassinare*) to murder, kill; (*sogg: malattia*) to carry off, kill; **uccidere a colpi d'arma da fuoco** to shoot dead; **uccidere a coltellate** to stab to death; **è rimasto ucciso in un incidente** he was killed in an accident; **il fumo uccide** smoking kills; **uccidere un uomo morto** (*fig*) to kick a man when he's down.
2 **uccidersi** VR **a** (*uso reciproco*) to kill each other **b** (*suicidarsi*) to kill o.s.; **uccidersi col gas** to gas o.s.
3 **uccidersi** VIP (*perdere la vita*) to be killed.

uccisione [uttʃi'zjone] SF (*gen*) killing; (*assassinio*) murder.

ucciso, a [ut'tʃizo] 1 PP di **uccidere**.
2 SM/F person killed, victim; **gli uccisi** the dead.

uccisore [uttʃi'zore] SM killer.

Ucraina [u'kraina] SF Ukraine.

ucraino, a [u'kraino] AGG, SM/F Ukranian.

UD SIGLA = *Udine*.

udente [u'dɛnte] SM/F: **i non udenti** the hard of hearing.

udibile [u'dibile] AGG audible.

udienza [u'djɛntsa] SF (*gen*) audience; (*Dir*) hearing; **dare udienza a** to grant an audience to ▶ **udienza a porte chiuse** hearing in camera.

udire [u'dire] VT IRREG (*gen*) to hear; **l'abbiamo udita piangere** we heard her crying.

uditivo, a [udi'tivo] AGG auditory.

udito [u'dito] SM (sense of) hearing.

uditore, trice [udi'tore] SM/F (*Univ*) unregistered student (*who is allowed to attend lectures (Brit)*), auditor (*Am*) ▶ **uditore giudiziario** (*Dir*) auditor.

uditorio, ri [udi'tɔrjo] SM audience.

U.E. [u'e] 1 SIGLA F (= *Unione Europea*) EU.
2 ABBR = **uso esterno**.

U.E.F.A. [u'efa] SIGLA F UEFA (= *Union of European Football Associations*).

uffa ['uffa], **uff** [uff] ESCL (*con insofferenza*) oh!; **uff! che caldo!** phew! it's hot!

ufficiale [uffi'tʃale] 1 AGG (*gen*) official.

2 SM **a** (*Mil, Naut*) officer; **primo ufficiale** (*Naut*) first mate ▶**ufficiale di marina** naval officer

b (*Amm*) official, officer; **pubblico ufficiale** public official ▶**ufficiale giudiziario** (*Dir*) clerk of the court ▶**ufficiale sanitario** health inspector ▶**ufficiale di stato civile** registrar.

ufficializzare [uffitʃalid'dzare] VT to make official.

ufficialmente [uffitʃal'mente] AVV officially.

ufficio, ci [uf'fitʃo] SM **a** (*luogo: gen*) office; (*organo*) office, bureau, agency; (*reparto*) department; **andare in ufficio** to go to the office ▶**ufficio brevetti** patent office ▶**ufficio di collocamento** employment office ▶**ufficio informazioni** information bureau ▶**ufficio oggetti smarriti** lost property office (*Brit*), lost and found (*Am*) ▶**ufficio del personale** personnel department ▶**ufficio postale** post office ▶**ufficio vendite** sales department

b (*incarico*) office; (*dovere*) duty; (*mansione*) function, task, job; **l'ufficio di direttore generale** the office *o* position of general manager; **coprire/accettare un ufficio** to hold/accept a position; **provvedere d'ufficio** to act officially

c (*Dir*): **difensore** *o* **avvocato d'ufficio** court-appointed counsel for the defence (*Brit*) *o* defense (*Am*); **convocare d'ufficio** to summons

d (*intervento*): **grazie ai suoi buoni uffici** thanks to his good offices

e (*Rel*) office, service.

ufficiosamente [uffitʃosa'mente] AVV unofficially, off the record.

ufficioso, a [uffi'tʃoso] AGG unofficial.

UFO, ufo ['ufo] SM INV UFO (= *unidentified flying object*).

ufo ['ufo]: **a ufo** AVV free, for nothing; **mangiare a ufo** to sponge a meal.

ufologia [ufolo'dʒia] SF ufology.

Uganda [u'ganda] SF: **l'Uganda** Uganda.

ugandese [ugan'dese] AGG, SM/F Ugandan.

ugello [u'dʒello] SM nozzle.

uggia, ge ['uddʒa] SF (*noia*) boredom; (*fastidio*) bore; **avere/prendere qn in uggia** to dislike/take a dislike to sb.

uggiolare [uddʒo'lare] VI (*aus* **avere**) to whine.

uggiolio, lii [uddʒo'lio] SM whine.

uggioso, a [ud'dʒoso] AGG (*gen*) tiresome; (*tempo*) dull, dreary.

ugola ['ugola] SF (*Anat*) uvula.

uguaglianza [ugwaʎ'ʎantsa] SF (*gen*) equality; (*Mat*) identity; **su una base di uguaglianza** on an equal footing, on equal terms; **segno di uguaglianza** (*Mat*) equals sign.

uguagliare [ugwaʎ'ʎare] **1** VT **a** (*livellare: persone, stipendi*) to make equal; (: *siepe*) to straighten

b (*raggiungere, essere uguale a*) to equal, be equal to; **uguagliare qn in bellezza/bravura** to equal sb *o* be equal to sb in beauty/skill; **uguagliare un record** (*Sport*) to equal a record; **in lui l'intelligenza uguaglia la bontà** he is as intelligent as he is good.

2 uguagliarsi VR (*paragonarsi*): **uguagliarsi a** *o* **con qn** to compare o.s. to sb.

3 uguagliarsi VIP to be equal.

uguale [u'gwale] **1** AGG **a** (*avente il medesimo valore*) equal; (*identico*) identical, tl.e same; **di peso/valore uguale** of equal weight/value; **a uguale distanza da** equidistant from; **abbiamo stipendi uguali** our salaries are the same; **il tuo maglione è uguale al mio** your

sweater is the same as mine; **per me è uguale** (*lo stesso*) it's all the same to me

b (*uniforme: superficie*) even, level; (: *andatura*) even; (: *voce*) steady.

2 AVV: **costano uguale** they cost the same; **siamo alti uguale** we are the same height; **sono bravi uguale** they're equally good.

3 SM/F equal; **non ha uguali per ostinazione** when it comes to stubbornness there's no-one like him.

ugualmente [ugwal'mente] AVV **a** (*allo stesso modo*) equally **b** (*lo stesso*) all the same, just the same; **lo farò ugualmente** I'm going to do it anyway.

U.I. ABBR = **uso interno**.

UIL [wil] SIGLA F (= *Unione Italiana del Lavoro*) *trade union federation*.

ulcera ['ultʃera] SF ulcer; **avere l'ulcera** to have an ulcer.

ulcerazione [ultʃerat'tsjone] SF ulceration.

Ulisse [u'lisse] SM Ulysses.

uliva *ecc* [u'liva] = **oliva** *ecc*.

ulna ['ulna] SF ulna.

ulteriore [ulte'rjore] AGG further.

ulteriormente [ulterjor'mente] AVV further.

ultimamente [ultima'mente] AVV lately, of late.

ultimare [ulti'mare] VT to finish, complete.

ultimatum [ulti'matum] SM INV ultimatum.

ultimissime [ulti'missime] SFPL latest news *sg*; (*in corso di stampa*) stop press *sg*.

ultimo, a ['ultimo] **1** AGG **a** (*di serie: gen*) last; (: *piano*) top; (: *fila*) back; (: *mano di vernice*) last, final; **l'ultimo scalino** (*in basso*) the bottom step; (*in alto*) the top step; **abitare all'ultimo piano** to live on the top floor; **le ultime 20 pagine** the last 20 pages; **in ultima pagina** (*di giornale*) on the back page; **per ultimo** (*entrare, arrivare*) last

b (*tempo: gen*) last; (: *più recente*) latest; (: *finale*) final; **negli ultimi tempi** recently; **gli ultimi giorni prima di partire** the last days before leaving; **l'ultima volta che l'ho visto** the last time I saw him; **all'ultimo momento** at the last minute; **il termine ultimo** the deadline; **le ultime notizie** the latest news; **all'ultima moda** in the latest fashion; **... la vostra lettera del 7 aprile ultimo scorso** ...your letter of April 7th last

c (*estremo: speranza, risorsa*) last, final; (: *più lontano*) farthest, utmost; **l'ultimo lembo di terra italiana** the farthest tip of Italy; **spendere fino all'ultimo centesimo** to spend every last penny; **dare un'ultima occhiata a qc** to have one last look at sth

d (*per importanza*) last; **è l'ultimo film che vorrei andare a vedere** that's the last film I would want to go and see; **qual è l'ultimo prezzo (che mi può fare)?** what's the lowest you'll go?

e (*Filosofia*) ultimate

f (*fraseologia*): **in ultima analisi** in the final *o* last analysis; **in ultimo luogo** finally; **avere** *o* **dire l'ultima parola** to have the last word; **le ultime parole famose!** famous last words!; **esalare** *o* **rendere l'ultimo respiro** to breathe one's last.

2 SM/F last (one); **l'ultimo nato** youngest (child); **gli ultimi ad entrare** the last (person) to come in; **gli ultimi arrivati** the last ones to arrive; **è l'ultima della classe** she's (at the) bottom of the class; **questa è l'ultima delle mie preoccupazioni** that's the least of my worries; **è l'ultimo degli ultimi** he's the lowest of the low; **quest'ultimo** (*tra due*) the latter; (*tra più di due*) this last, the last-mentioned.

3 SM: **l'ultimo del mese/dell'anno** the last day of the month/year; **all'ultimo ho deciso di restare** in the end I decided to stay; **fino all'ultimo** to the last, till the end, until the end; **in ultimo** OR **da ultimo** in the end, finally; **essere all'ultimo** o **agli ultimi** to be at death's door.

4 SF (*notizia, barzelletta*): **hai sentito l'ultima?** have you heard the latest?; **questa è l'ultima (che mi combini)** that's the last time you'll play that trick on me.

ultimogenito, a [ultimo'dʒɛnito] **1** AGG (*figlio*) last-born.

2 SM/F last-born child, youngest child.

ultrà, ultra [ul'tra] SM/F INV (*Pol*) extremist; (*Sport*): **gli ultrà della Juve** fanatical Juventus supporters.

ultramoderno, a [ultramo'dɛrno] AGG ultramodern.

ultrapiatto, a [ultra'pjatto] AGG (*orologio*) ultra-thin.

ultrarapido, a [ultra'rapido] AGG (*Fot*) high-speed.

ultrasensibile [ultrasen'sibile] AGG ultrasensitive.

ultrasonico, a, ci, che [ultra'sɔniko] AGG ultrasonic.

ultrasuono [ultra'swɔno] SM ultrasound.

ultraterreno, a [ultrater'reno] AGG: **la vita ultraterrena** the afterlife.

ultravioletto, a [ultravio'letto] AGG, SM ultraviolet.

ululare [ulu'lare] VI (*aus avere*) to howl.

ululato [ulu'lato] SM (*urlo*) howl; (*l'ululare*) howling *no pl*.

umanamente [umana'mente] AVV (*con umanità*) humanely; (*nei limiti delle capacità umane*) humanly; **è umanamente impossibile** it's not humanly possible.

umanesimo [uma'nezimo] SM humanism.

umanità [umani'ta] SF (*gen*) humanity; **l'umanità** humanity, mankind.

umanitario, ria, ri, rie [umani'tarjo] AGG humanitarian.

umanitarismo [umanita'rizmo] SM humanitarianism.

umanizzare [umanid'dzare] VT to humanize.

umano, a [u'mano] **1** AGG (*gen*) human; (*comprensivo*) humane; **essere** o **mostrarsi umano (con qn)** to show humanity (towards sb), act humanely (towards sb); **errare è umano** to err is human; **un essere umano** a human being; **è umano che si comporti così** it's quite normal to behave like that.

2 SM human.

umbro, a ['umbro] AGG, SM/F Umbrian.

umettare [umet'tare] VT (*labbra*) to moisten.

umidiccio, cia, ci, ce [umi'dittʃo] AGG (*terreno*) damp; (*mano*) moist, clammy.

umidificare [umidifi'kare] VT to humidify.

umidificatore [umidifika'tore] SM humidifier.

umidità [umidi'ta] SF (*vedi agg*) dampness; moistness, clamminess; humidity; **proteggere qc dall'umidità** to protect sth from damp; **"teme l'umidità"** (*su etichetta*) "to be kept dry".

umido, a ['umido] **1** AGG (*gen*) damp; (*mano*) moist, clammy; (*clima: caldo*) humid; (: *freddo*) damp; **aveva gli occhi umidi di pianto** her eyes were moist with tears.

2 SM **a** (*umidità*) dampness, damp **b** (*Culin*): **carne in umido** stew.

umile ['umile] **1** AGG (*gen*) humble; **di umili origini** of humble origin; **i lavori più umili** the most menial tasks.

umiliante [umi'ljante] AGG humiliating.

umiliare [umi'ljare] **1** VT (*gen*) to humiliate; **umiliare la carne** to mortify the flesh.

2 **umiliarsi** VR: **umiliarsi (davanti a)** to humiliate o humble o.s. (before).

umiliazione [umiljat'tsjone] SF humiliation.

umilmente [umil'mente] AVV (*con umiltà*) humbly; (*in modo modesto*) unpretentiously.

umiltà [umil'ta] SF humility, humbleness; **con umiltà** humbly.

umore [u'more] SM **a** (*indole*) temper, temperament; (*disposizione d'animo*) mood, humour (*Brit*), humor (*Am*); **un vecchio d'umore irascibile** an irascible o bad-tempered old man; **di buon/cattivo umore** in a good/bad mood o humo(u)r **b** (*Bio*) humo(u)r.

umorismo [umo'rizmo] SM humour (*Brit*), humor (*Am*); **senso dell'umorismo** sense of humo(u)r; **ti sembra il momento di fare dell'umorismo?** this is no time to be funny!

umorista, i, e [umo'rista] SM/F humorist.

umoristicamente [umoristika'mente] AVV humorously.

umoristico, a, ci, che [umo'ristiko] AGG (*battuta, racconto*) humorous, funny.

un [un], **un'** [un], **una** [una]; vedi **uno.**

unanimamente [unanima'mente] AVV unanimously.

unanime [u'nanime] AGG unanimous.

unanimità [unanimi'ta] SF unanimity; **all'unanimità** unanimously.

una tantum ['una 'tantum] **1** AGG one-off *attr.*

2 SF INV (*imposta*) one-off tax.

uncinare [untʃi'nare] VT to hook.

uncinato, a [untʃi'nato] AGG (*amo*) barbed; (*ferro*) hooked; **croce uncinata** swastika.

uncinetto [untʃi'netto] SM crochet hook; **lavorare all'uncinetto** to crochet; **lavoro all'uncinetto** crochet work.

uncino [un'tʃino] SM hook.

undicenne [undi'tʃɛnne] AGG, SM/F eleven-year-old *per fraseologia vedi* **cinquantenne.**

undicesimo, a [undi'tʃɛzimo] AGG, SM/F, SM eleventh *per fraseologia vedi* **quinto.**

undici ['unditʃi] AGG INV, SM INV eleven *per fraseologia vedi* **cinque.**

U.N.E.S.C.O. [u'nɛsko] SIGLA F UNESCO (= *United Nations Educational, Scientific and Cultural Organization*).

ungere ['undʒere] VB IRREG **1** VT (*macchina*) to oil, lubricate; (*teglia*) to grease; (*Rel*) to anoint; (*fig*) to flatter; **ungere le ruote a qn** (*fig: corrompere*) to grease sb's palm.

2 **ungersi** VR: **ungersi con la crema** to put cream on.

3 **ungersi** VIP (*macchiarsi*) to get covered in grease.

ungherese [unge'rese] **1** AGG, SM/F Hungarian.

2 SM (*lingua*) Hungarian.

Ungheria [unge'ria] SF: **l'Ungheria** Hungary.

unghia ['ungja] SF **a** (*Anat*) nail; (*di animale*) claw; (*di rapace*) talon; (*di cavallo, bue*) hoof; **le unghie delle mani** the fingernails; **le unghie dei piedi** the toenails; **difendersi con le unghie e con i denti** to defend o.s. tooth and nail; **tirar fuori le unghie** (*anche fig*) to show one's claws; **pagare sull'unghia** to pay on the nail ▶**unghia incarnita** ingrown nail

b (*di temperino*) groove

c (*quantità*): **ce ne vuole un'unghia di più/di meno** a fraction more/less is needed.

unghiata [un'gjata] SF (*graffio*) scratch.

unguento [un'gwɛnto] SM ointment.

unicamente [unika'mente] AVV only.

unicamerale [unikame'rale] AGG (*Pol*) unicameral.

U.N.I.C.E.F. ['unitʃef] SIGLA M UNICEF (= *United Nations Children's Fund*).

unicellulare [unitʃellu'lare] AGG unicellular.

unicità [unitʃi'ta] SF uniqueness.

unico, a, ci, che ['uniko] **1** AGG **a** (*solo*) only; (*esclusivo*) sole; **è la mia unica speranza** it's my only hope; **la mia**

unica speranza è che... my one *o* only hope is that ...; **è figlio unico** he's an only child; **è l'unico esemplare in Italia** it's the only one of its kind in Italy; **due aspetti di un unico problema** two aspects of one and the same problem; **atto unico** (*Teatro*) one-act play; **agente unico** (*Comm*) sole agent; **binario unico** (*Ferr*) single track; **numero unico** (*di giornale*) special issue; **senso unico** (*Aut*) one way

b (*eccezionale*) unique; **unico nel suo genere** unique of its kind; **unico al mondo** absolutely unique, the only one of its kind in the world; **sei unico!** you're priceless!; **è un tipo più unico che raro** he's one of a kind.

2 SM/F the only one; **fu l'unico a capire** he was the only one who understood *o* to understand.

3 SF only thing to do; **l'unica è aspettare** the only thing to do is to wait, all we can do is wait.

unicorno [uni'kɔrno] SM unicorn.

unidirezionale [unidirettsjo'nale] AGG unidirectional.

unifamiliare [unifami'ljare] AGG (*villetta*) one-family *attr*.

unificare [unifi'kare] VT (*stato, leggi*) to unify, unite; (*standardizzare: prodotti*) to standardize.

unificazione [unifikat'tsjone] SF (*vedi vb*) unification; standardization.

uniformare [unifor'mare] **1** VT (*terreno, superficie*) to level; **uniformare qc a** to adjust *o* relate sth to.

2 uniformarsi VR: **uniformarsi a** to conform to.

uniforme[1] [uni'forme] AGG (*gen*) uniform; (*superficie*) even.

uniforme[2] [uni'forme] SF (*divisa*) uniform; **in uniforme** in uniform; **alta uniforme** dress uniform.

uniformemente [uniforme'mente] AVV (*vedi agg*) uniformly; evenly.

uniformità [uniformi'ta] SF (*vedi agg*) uniformity; evenness.

unigenito [uni'dʒenito] AGG (*Rel*): **figlio unigenito di Dio** God's only-begotten son.

unilaterale [unilate'rale] AGG (*Dir, Pol*) unilateral; (*fig*) one-sided.

unilateralità [unilaterali'ta] SF (*arbitrarietà*) one-sidedness.

unilateralmente [unilateral'mente] AVV (*vedi agg*) unilaterally; one-sidedly.

uninominale [uninomi'nale] AGG (*Pol*): **collegio uninominale** single-member constituency.

unione [u'njone] SF (*alleanza, matrimonio*) union; (*di colori*) combination, blending; (*di elementi*) cohesion; (*fig: concordia*) unity, harmony; **l'unione fa la forza** strength through unity ▶**l'Unione Sovietica** the Soviet Union ▶**unione sindacale** trade union (*Brit*), labor union (*Am*).

unionista, i, e [unjo'nista] SM/F unionist.

unire [u'nire] **1** VT **a** (*associare*): **unire (a)** to unite (with); **unire in matrimonio** to unite *o* join in matrimony; **il sentimento che li unisce** the feeling which binds them together *o* unites them

b (*congiungere: città, linee*) to join, link, connect; (*mescolare: ingredienti*) to mix

c (*colori, suoni*) to combine.

2 unirsi VR: **unirsi contro/a** to unite against/with; **unirsi in matrimonio** to be joined (together) in marriage.

3 unirsi VIP: **unirsi a** to join; **unirsi a un gruppo** to join a group.

unisex ['uniseks] AGG INV unisex.

unisono [u'nisono]: **all'unisono** AVV (*Mus, fig*) in unison.

unità [uni'ta] SF INV **a** (*unione*) unity

b (*Mat, Comm, elemento*) unit ▶**unità di misura** unit of measure ▶**unità monetaria** monetary unit

c (*Mil*) unit; (*Naut*) (war)ship; (*Aer*) aeroplane

d (*Inform*): **unità centrale (di elaborazione)** central processing unit ▶**unità disco** disk drive ▶**unità periferica** peripheral unit ▶**unità video** visual display unit.

unitamente [unita'mente] AVV (*d'accordo*) unitedly, together; (*insieme*): **unitamente a** *o* **con** (together) with.

unitariamente [unitarja'mente] AVV (*lavorare, votare, decidere*) together, as a unit.

unitario, ria, ri, rie [uni'tarjo] AGG (*gen*) unitary; (*Pol, Rel*) unitarian; **prezzo** *o* **costo unitario** unit price, price per unit.

unito, a [u'nito] AGG **a** (*gen*) united; (*amici, coppia*) close; (*famiglia*) close(-knit), united **b** (*colore*) plain; **in tinta unita** plain, self-coloured (*Brit*), self-colored (*Am*).

universale [univer'sale] AGG (*gen*) universal; (*plauso, consenso*) general; (*mente, genio*) wide-ranging; **il giudizio universale** (*Rel*) the Last Judgment; **suffragio universale** (*Pol*) universal suffrage; **erede universale** sole heir; **donatore universale** universal donor.

universalità [universali'ta] SF universality.

universalizzare [universalid'dzare] VT to make universal.

universalmente [universal'mente] AVV universally.

università [universi'ta] SF INV university.

universitario, ria, ri, rie [universi'tarjo] **1** AGG (*gen*) university *attr*; (*studi*) university, academic.

2 SM/F (*studente*) university student; (*docente*) academic, university lecturer.

universo [uni'vɛrso] SM universe.

univoco, a, ci, che [u'nivoko] AGG unambiguous.

Unno ['unno] SM Hun.

---

uno , a ['uno]

> davanti a sm **un** + consonante, vocale, **uno** + s impura, gn, pn, ps, x, z; davanti a sf **un'** + vocale, **una** + consonante

1 AGG one;
▷**non ha una** *lira* he hasn't a penny, he's penniless
▷**ho comprato una** *mela* **e due pere** I bought one apple and two pears
▷**ho passato un** *mese* **in Italia** I spent one month in Italy.

2 ART INDET
a a, an (+ *vocale*);
▷**era una** *giornata* **splendida** it was a beautiful day
▷**un** *giorno* **gli ho telefonato** one day I called him
▷**uno** *gnomo* a gnome
▷**dammene un** *po'* give me some
▷**è uno** *sciocco* he's a fool
▷**ho visto un** *uomo* I saw a man
▷**uno** *zingaro* a gypsy
b (*intensivo*)
▷**una** *noia*! such a bore!
▷**ho una** *paura*! I'm terrified!
▷**ma questo è un** *porcile*! it's an absolute pigsty in here!
c (*circa*)
▷**disterà un 10** *km* it's round about 10 km away
▷**costerà un 500.000** *lire* it'll cost round about

500,000 lire.

3 PRON

a one;

▷**me ne dai uno?** will you give me one (of them)?

▷**ne ho comprato uno stamattina** I bought one this morning

▷**a uno** *a* **uno** one by one

▷**è uno** *dei* **più veloci** it's one of the fastest

▷**uno** *dei* **tanti** one of the many

▷**uno** *di* **noi** one of us

▷**facciamo metà** *per* **uno** let's go halves

b (*un tale*) somebody, someone;

▷**ho incontrato uno che ti conosce** I met someone who knows you

▷**c'era una al telefono** there was a woman on the phone

▷**è una del mio paese** she's from the same village as I am

c (*in costruzione impersonale*) one, you;

▷*se* **uno vuole** if one wants, if you want

▷*se* **uno ha i soldi** if one has the money

d (*con articolo determinativo*): *l'*uno one

▷**non confondere** *gli* **uni** *con* **gli altri** don't confuse one lot with the other

▷**abbiamo visto** *l'*uno e *l'*altro we've seen both of them

▷**sono entrati** *l'*uno dopo *l'*altro they came in one after the other

▷**si amano** *l'*un *l'*altro they love each other.

e: **ne ha** *detta* **una!** you should have heard what he said!

▷**ne hai** *combinata* **una delle tue!** you've done it again, haven't you!

▷**ne vuoi** *sentire* **una?** do you want to hear a good one?

▷**non me ne** *va* **mai bene una** nothing ever goes right for me.

4 SM one;

▷**uno** *più* **uno fa due** one plus one equals two.

5 SF (*ora*) one o'clock;

▷**è l'una** it's one (o'clock)

unsi *ecc* ['unsi] VB vedi **ungere**.

unto, a ['unto] **1** PP di **ungere**. **2** AGG greasy, oily; **unto e bisunto** filthy dirty. **3** SM grease.

untuosità [untuosi'ta] SF greasiness; (*fig: servilismo*) unctuousness.

untuoso, a [untu'oso] AGG (*pelle*) greasy, oily; (*cibo*) oily; (*fig: persona*) unctuous, smooth.

unzione [un'tsjone] SF: **l'Estrema Unzione** (*Rel*) Extreme Unction.

uomo ['wɔmo] (*pl* **uomini**) **1** SM (*gen*) man; (*specie umana*): **l'uomo** mankind, humanity; **da** *o* **per uomo** (*abito, scarpe*) men's, for men; **parlare da uomo a uomo** to have a man-to-man talk, talk man to man; **a memoria d'uomo** since the world began; **a passo d'uomo** at walking pace; **è un uomo finito** he's finished; **l'uomo della strada** the man in the street; **uomo avvisato mezzo salvato** (*Proverbio*) forewarned is forearmed. **2** ▶**uomo d'affari** businessman ▶**uomo d'azione**

man of action ▶**uomo delle caverne** caveman ▶**uomo d'equipaggio:una nave con 30 uomini d'equipaggio** a ship with a crew of 30 men ▶**uomo di fatica** workhand ▶**uomo di fiducia** right-hand man ▶**uomo del gas** gasman ▶**uomo di mondo** man of the world ▶**uomo di paglia** stooge ▶**uomo rana** frogman.

uopo ['wɔpo] SM: **all'uopo** if necessary, in case of need; **è d'uopo far così** it is necessary to do this.

uovo ['wɔvo] SM (*pl f* **uova**) **a** egg; **uovo fresco** new-laid *o* fresh egg ▶**uova strapazzate** scrambled eggs ▶**uovo affogato** *o* **in camicia** poached egg ▶**uovo bazzotto** soft-boiled egg ▶**uovo in cocotte** baked egg ▶**uovo alla coque** (soft-)boiled egg ▶**uovo all'ostrica** prairie oyster ▶**uovo di Pasqua** Easter egg ▶**uovo sodo** hard-boiled egg ▶**uovo al tegame** *o* **all'occhio di bue** *o* **fritto** fried egg

b (*fraseologia*): **è l'uovo di Colombo!** it's as plain as the nose on your face!; **essere pieno come un uovo** to be full (up); **cercare il pelo nell'uovo** to split hairs; **rompere le uova nel paniere a qn** to upset sb's plans; **meglio un uovo oggi che una gallina domani** (*Proverbio*) a bird in the hand is worth two in the bush.

upupa ['upupa] SF hoopoe.

uragano [ura'gano] SM hurricane; (*fig: di applausi, proteste*) storm.

Urali [u'rali] SMPL: **gli Urali** the Urals; **i monti Urali** the Ural Mountains.

uranio [u'ranjo] SM uranium.

Urano [u'rano] SM (*Mitol, Astron*) Uranus.

urbanamente [urbana'mente] AVV courteously, politely.

urbanesimo [urba'nezimo] SM urbanization.

urbanista, i, e [urba'nista] SM/F town planner.

urbanistica [urba'nistika] SF town planning.

urbanistico, a, ci, che [urba'nistiko] AGG urban, town *attr*.

urbanità [urbani'ta] SF urbanity.

urbanizzare [urbanid'dzare] VT to urbanize.

urbanizzazione [urbaniddzat'tsjone] SF urbanization.

urbano, a [ur'bano] AGG **a** (*gen: sviluppo ecc*) urban, city *attr*, town *attr*; (*telefonata*) local **b** (*cortese: modi, risposta*) urbane.

urea [u'rɛa] SF urea.

uretere [ure'tɛre] SM ureter.

uretra [u'retra] SF urethra.

urgente [ur'dʒɛnte] AGG urgent.

urgentemente [urdʒente'mente] AVV urgently.

urgenza [ur'dʒɛntsa] SF (*di decisione, situazione*) urgency; **non c'è urgenza** there's no hurry; **fare qc d'urgenza** to do sth as a matter of urgency; **trasportare qn d'urgenza all'ospedale** to rush sb to hospital; **il direttore l'ha convocato d'urgenza** the director requested to see him urgently *o* immediately; **questo lavoro va fatto con urgenza** this work is urgent; **chiamata/provvedimento d'urgenza** emergency call/measure; **diritto d'urgenza** (*Amm*) surtax paid for faster handling.

urgere ['urdʒere] VI DIF: **urge aiuto** help is needed urgently; **urge provvedere** something needs to be done urgently.

uria ['urja] SF (*Zool*) guillemot.

urina [u'rina] SF urine.

urinare [uri'nare] VI (*aus avere*) to urinate.

urlante [ur'lante] AGG (*vedi vb*) screaming, yelling; howling.

urlare [ur'lare] **1** VI (*aus avere*) (*persona*) to scream, yell; (*animale, vento*) to howl; **non urlare, ti sento benissimo**

there's no need to shout, I can hear you perfectly well; **urlare di dolore** to scream with pain.

[2] VT: **urlare qc (a qn)** to scream *o* yell sth (at sb); **urlare a qn di fare qc** to scream at sb to do sth; **gliene ho urlate dietro di tutti i colori** I hurled abuse at him.

urlatore, trice [urla'tore] AGG howling, shrieking.

urlo ['urlo] SM (*pl m* **urli**, *pl f* **urla**) (*di persona*) scream, yell; (*di animale, vento*) howl; (*di sirena*) wail; **lanciare un urlo (di)** to scream (with).

urna ['urna] SF **a** (*vaso*) urn **b** (*Pol*): **urna (elettorale)** ballot box; **andare alle urne** to vote, to go to the polls.

urogenitale [urodʒeni'tale] AGG urogenital.

urrà [ur'ra] ESCL hurrah!

U.R.S.S. [urs] SIGLA F = *Unione delle Repubbliche Socialiste Sovietiche*: **l'U.R.S.S.** the USSR.

urtante [ur'tante] AGG (*comportamento*) irritating, annoying.

urtare [ur'tare] [1] VT **a** (*persona, ostacolo*) to bump into, knock against; (*gomito, testa*) to knock, bump **b** (*irritare*) to annoy, irritate; **urtare i nervi a qn** to get on sb's nerves.

[2] VI (*aus* avere): **urtare contro** (*auto, barca*) to bump into; (*persona*) to bump into, knock against.

[3] **urtarsi** VR (*uso reciproco: scontrarsi*) to collide; (: *fig*) to clash.

[4] **urtarsi** VIP (*irritarsi*) to get annoyed, get irritated.

urto ['urto] SM (*collisione*) crash, collision; (*colpo*) knock, bump; (*fig: contrasto*) clash; (*Mil*) attack; **nell'urto si è rotto il vetro** the impact of the crash broke the glass; **essere in urto con qn per qc** (*fig*) to clash with sb over sth; **terapia d'urto** (*Med*) massive-dose treatment; (*fig*) shock treatment *o* therapy; **dose d'urto** (*Med*) massive dose; **contingente d'urto** (*Mil*) shock troops *pl*.

uruguaiano, a [urugwa'jano] AGG, SM/F Uruguayan.

Uruguay [uru'gwai] SM: **l'Uruguay** Uruguay.

u.s. ABBR = ultimo scorso.

U.S.A. ['uza] SIGLA MPL: **gli U.S.A.** the USA.

usa e getta [uzae'dʒetta] AGG INV (*rasoio, siringa*) disposable, throwaway.

usanza [u'zantsa] SF (*costume*) custom; **è l'usanza** it's the custom, it's what's done; **secondo l'usanza** according to custom, as is customary.

usare [u'zare] [1] VT **a** (*adoperare*) to use; **posso usare la tua macchina?** may I use your car?; **me lo fai usare?** will you let me use it?; **grazie per il tavolo, l'ho usato molto** thank you for the table, I got a lot of use out of it; **sai usare** *o* **come si usa la lavatrice?** do you know how to use the washing machine?; **non usare tutta l'acqua** (*consumare*) don't use (up) all the water; **cerca di usare il cervello!** try to use your head!; **usa gli occhi/le orecchie!** use your eyes/ears!; **usare la forza** to use force; **usare violenza a qn** (*violentare*) to rape sb; **usare le mani** (*picchiare*) to use one's fists; **usare la massima cura nel fare qc** to exercise great care when doing sth; **dovresti usare un po' di comprensione** you should show a little understanding; **potresti usarmi la cortesia di spegnere la radio?** would you be so kind as to switch off the radio?

b (*aver l'abitudine*): **usare fare qc** to be in the habit of doing sth, be accustomed to doing sth; **a casa nostra si usa fare così** this is how we do things at home.

[2] VI (*aus* avere) **a** (*essere di moda*) to be fashionable; **usano di nuovo i tacchi alti** high heels are fashionable again *o* are back in fashion

b: **usare di** (*servirsi di*) to use; (: *diritto*) to exercise.

[3] VB IMPERS to be customary; **da queste parti usa così** it's the custom round here, this is customary round here.

usato, a [u'zato] [1] AGG **a** (*logoro*) worn (out) **b** (*di seconda mano*) used, second-hand.

[2] SM (*gen*) second-hand goods *pl*; **il mercato dell'usato** the second-hand market.

uscente [uʃ'ʃɛnte] AGG (*Amm*) outgoing.

usciere [uʃ'ʃɛre] SM usher.

uscio, sci [u'ʃʃo] SM door; **sull'uscio** on the doorstep.

uscire [uʃ'ʃire] VI IRREG (*aus* essere) **a** (*persona: andare fuori*) to go out, leave; (: *venire fuori*) to come out, leave; (: *a piedi*) to walk out; (: *a spasso, la sera*) to go out; **uscire in automobile** to go out in the car, go for a drive; **uscire a prendere il giornale** to go for the paper; **lasciatemi** *o* **fatemi uscire!** let me out!; **uscite!** get out!; **uscire da** (*posto*) to go (*o* come) out of, leave; (: *carcere*) to get out of; **uscire da** *o* **di casa** to go out; **è uscito dalla porta di servizio/per la finestra** he left by the tradesman's entrance/got out through the window; **da dove sei uscito?** where did you spring from?; **uscire dall'acqua/dal letto** to get out of the water/of bed

b (*oggetto: gen*) to come out; **la merce che esce dal paese dev'essere dichiarata** goods leaving *o* going out of the country must be declared

c (*giornale, libro*) to come out; (*disco, film*) to be released; (*numero alla lotteria*) to come up

d (*andar fuori, sconfinare*): **uscire dagli argini** (*fiume*) to overflow its banks; **uscire dai binari** (*treno*) to leave the rails; **uscire di strada** (*auto*) to go off *o* leave the road; **l'acqua sta uscendo dalla vasca** the bath is overflowing; **uscire dall'ordinario** to be out of the ordinary

e (*passare da una condizione a un'altra*): **uscire dall'adolescenza** to leave adolescence behind; **uscire da una brutta malattia** to recover from *o* get over a bad illness; **è uscito bene da quella storia** he came out of that business well; **è uscito illeso dall'incidente** he emerged from the accident unscathed

f (*fraseologia*): **chissà cosa uscirà da tutta questa storia?** who knows what will come of all this?; **se ne uscì con una delle sue** he came out with one of his typical remarks; **uscire dai gangheri** to fly off the handle; **uscire di senno** *o* **di sé** to fly into a rage; **mi è uscito di mente** it slipped my mind.

uscita [uʃ'ʃita] SF **a** (*azione: di persona*) leaving, exit; **è l'ora dell'uscita degli scolari** school's over for the day, the children are coming out of school; **un'uscita veloce** a quick exit; **sono in libera uscita** (*Mil*) I'm off duty

b (*porta, passaggio*) exit, way out; (*Aer*) gate; **"vietata l'uscita"** "no exit" ▶ **uscita di sicurezza** emergency exit

c (*passeggiata*) outing; (*Mil*) foray; **è la sua prima uscita dopo la malattia** it's his first day out since his illness

d (*fig: battuta*) witty remark; **ha di quelle uscite** he comes out with some odd remarks

e (*Comm*) outlay; **entrate ed uscite** income and expenditure *sg*

f (*Elettr*) output.

usignolo [uziɲ'ɲɔlo] SM nightingale.

U.S.L. [uzl] SIGLA F (= *unità sanitaria locale*) (*distretto*) local health authority; (*ospedale*) local health centre.

uso[1] ['uzo] SM **a** (*gen*) use; (*di parola*) usage; (*Dir*) exercise; **a uso di** for (the use of); **testo a uso delle elementari** book for use in primary (*Brit*) *o* elementary (*Am*) schools; **per uso esterno** (*Med*) for external use only;

per uso personale for personal use; **fare buon/cattivo uso di qc** to make good/bad use of sth; **istruzioni per l'uso** instructions; **fuori uso** out of use; **fare uso di qc** to use sth; **perdere l'uso della ragione** to go out of one's mind

b (*esercizio*) practice; **con l'uso** with practice

c (*abitudine*) usage, custom; **d'uso** (*corrente*) in use; **essere in uso** to be in common *o* current use; **gli usi e costumi dei Romani** Roman customs.

uso², **a** ['uzo] AGG (*letter*): **uso a qc/a fare qc** accustomed to sth/to doing sth.

ustionare [ustjo'nare] ① VT to burn.

② **ustionarsi** VR to burn o.s.

ustionato, **a** [ustjo'nato] ① AGG burnt.

② SM/F: **centro (grandi) ustionati** burns unit.

ustione [us'tjone] SF burn ▶ **ustioni di terzo grado** third-degree burns.

ustorio, **ria**, **ri**, **rie** [us'tɔrjo] AGG: **specchio ustorio** burning glass.

usuale [uzu'ale] AGG (*frase*) everyday *attr*; (*oggetto*) everyday, ordinary, common.

usualmente [uzual'mente] AVV usually, as a rule.

usucapione [uzuka'pjone] SF (*Dir*) usucaption.

usufruire [uzufru'ire] VI (*aus avere*): **usufruire di** (*valersi di*) to take advantage of, make use of.

usufrutto [uzu'frutto] SM (*Dir*) usufruct.

usufruttuario, **ri** [uzufruttu'arjo] SM (*Dir*) usufructuary.

usura¹ [u'zura] SF usury; **prestare a usura** to lend at exorbitant interest.

usura² [u'zura] SF (*logoramento*) wear (and tear); **usura dei freni** wear on the brakes.

usuraio, **aia**, **ai**, **aie** [uzu'rajo] SM/F usurer.

usurpare [uzur'pare] VT (*trono, potere*) to usurp.

usurpatore, **trice** [uzurpa'tore] SM/F usurper.

usurpazione [uzurpat'tsjone] SF usurpation.

utensile [uten'sile] ① AGG: **macchina utensile** machine tool.

② SM tool, implement ▶ **utensili da cucina** kitchen utensils.

utensileria [utensile'ria] SF **a** (*utensili*) tools *pl* **b** (*reparto*) tool room.

utente [u'tɛnte] SM/F (*gen*) user; (*di gas*) consumer; (*del telefono*) subscriber ▶ **utente finale** end user ▶ **utente della strada** road user.

utenza [u'tɛntsa] SF **a** (*uso*) use **b** (*utenti*) users *pl*; (: *di gas*) consumers *pl*; (: *del telefono*) subscribers *pl*.

uterino, **a** [ute'rino] AGG uterine.

utero ['utero] SM uterus, womb ▶ **utero in affitto** host womb.

utile ['utile] ① AGG (*gen*) useful; (*consiglio, persona*) helpful; **mi è stato molto utile** (*oggetto*) it came in very handy, it was very useful; **questo ti sarà utile** this will be of use to you; **posso esserle utile?** can I help you?, can I be of help?; **posso esserti utile?** can I do anything for you?; **in tempo utile per** in time for; **rendersi utile** to be helpful.

② SM **a**: **badare solo all'utile** to think only of what is useful; **unire l'utile al dilettevole** to combine business with pleasure

b (*vantaggio*) advantage, benefit; (*Econ*) profit; **partecipare agli utili** to share in the profits; **non ha saputo trarne alcun utile** (*fig*) he couldn't get anything out of it.

utilità [utili'ta] SF usefulness; (*vantaggio*) benefit; **senza utilità pratica** without practical application, of no real use; **essere di grande utilità** to be very useful.

utilitaria [utili'tarja] SF (*Aut*) runabout, economy car.

utilitario, **ria**, **ri**, **rie** [utili'tarjo] AGG utilitarian.

utilitarista, **i**, **e** [utilita'rista] SM/F utilitarian.

utilitaristico, **a**, **ci**, **che** [utilita'ristiko] AGG utilitarian.

utilizzare [utilid'dzare] VT to use, make use of, utilize.

utilizzazione [utiliddzat'tsjone] SF use, utilization.

utilizzo [uti'liddzo] SM (*Amm*) utilization; (*Banca: di credito*) availment.

utilmente [util'mente] AVV usefully, profitably.

utopia [uto'pia] SF utopia; **è pura utopia** that's sheer utopianism.

utopistico, **a**, **ci**, **che** [uto'pistiko] AGG utopian.

UVA [uvi'a] SIGLA M (= *ultravioletto A*) UVA.

uva ['uva] SF grapes *pl* ▶ **uva passa** raisins *pl* ▶ **uva spina** gooseberry ▶ **uva sultanina** sultanas *pl*.

UVB [uvi'bi] SIGLA M (= *ultravioletto B*) UVB.

uvetta [u'vetta] SF raisins *pl*.

uxoricida, **i**, **e** [uksori'tʃida] SM/F: **essere uxoricida** to have killed one's own husband (*o* wife).

V

V, v [vu, vi] SF O M INV (lettera) V, v; **V come Venezia** ≈ V for Victor.

V ABBR (= volt) V.

v. ABBR **a** (= vedi) v. (= vide: see) **b** (= verso) v. (= verse).

VA SIGLA = Varese.

va, va' [va] VB vedi **andare**.

vacante [va'kante] AGG vacant.

vacanza [va'kantsa] SF **a** (riposo, ferie) holiday(s pl) (Brit), vacation (Am); (giorno di permesso) day off; **essere/ andare in vacanza** to be/go on holiday o vacation; **prendersi una vacanza** to take a holiday o vacation; **un giorno/mese di vacanza** a day's/month's holiday o vacation; **far vacanza** to have a holiday o vacation; **vacanze** SFPL (periodo di ferie) holidays, vacation sg; **le vacanze di Pasqua** the Easter holidays ▶ **vacanze estive** summer holiday(s) o vacation

b (l'essere vacante: di cattedra) vacancy.

vacanziere [vakan'tsjɛre] SM holiday-maker (Brit), vacationer (Am), vacationist (Am).

vacanziero, a [vakan'tsjɛro] AGG (folla) holiday (Brit) attr, vacationing (Am) attr.

vacca, che ['vakka] SF **a** (mucca) cow; **tempo delle vacche grasse/magre** fat/lean years **b** (pegg: sgualdrina) slut.

vaccinare [vattʃi'nare] VT (Med): **vaccinare qn contro qc** to vaccinate sb against sth; **farsi vaccinare** to have a vaccination, get vaccinated; **ormai sono vaccinato contro le delusioni amorose** I am immune to disappointments in love now; **essere grande e vaccinato (per fare qc)** to be big enough and ugly enough (to do sth).

vaccinazione [vattʃinat'tsjone] SF vaccination.

vaccino, a [vat'tʃino] **1** AGG: **latte vaccino** cow's milk.

2 SM vaccine; **fare un vaccino** to have a vaccination; **fare un vaccino a qn** to vaccinate sb.

vacillante [vatʃil'lante] AGG (edificio, vecchio) shaky, unsteady; (salute, memoria) shaky, failing; (fiamma) flickering; **camminava con passo vacillante** he was walking shakily o unsteadily.

vacillare [vatʃil'lare] VI (aus avere) **a** (edificio, muro, ubriaco) to sway (to and fro); **camminare vacillando** (vecchio) to totter along; (ubriaco, persona stanca) to stagger along; **il pugno lo fece vacillare** the punch made him reel

b (salute, memoria) to be shaky, be failing; (fiamma) to flicker; (trono, governo) to be unstable; (fede) to waver, be shaky; (coraggio) to falter, waver, be failing.

vacuità [vakui'ta] SF vacuity, vacuousness.

vacuo, a ['vakuo] AGG vacuous, empty.

vacuometro [vaku'ɔmetro] SM vacuum gauge.

vademecum [vade'mɛkum] SM INV vademecum.

vado ecc ['vado] VB vedi **andare**.

va e vieni [va e 'vjɛni] SM INV (di persone) coming and going.

vaffanculo [vaffan'kulo] ESCL (fam!) fuck off! (fam!)

vagabondaggio, gi [vagabon'daddʒo] SM wandering, roaming; (Dir) vagrancy.

vagabondare [vagabon'dare] VI (aus avere) to roam, wander; **vagabondare per le strade** to roam o wander (about) the streets.

vagabondo, a [vaga'bondo] **1** AGG (gente, vita) wandering attr; (fig: fannullone) idle.

2 SM/F (gen) vagrant, tramp, vagabond; (fig: fannullone) layabout, loafer, idler.

vagamente [vaga'mente] AVV vaguely.

vagante [va'gante] AGG (gen) wandering; **"animali vaganti"** (segnale stradale) wandering o stray animals; **proiettile vagante** stray bullet; **mina vagante** (fig: pericolo) time bomb.

vagare [va'gare] VI (aus avere): **vagare per** (persona) to wander about, roam about; (animale) to roam; **vagare con la mente** to let one's mind wander; **vagare con la fantasia** to give free rein to one's imagination, let one's imagination run away with one.

vagheggiare [vaged'dʒare] VT (letter: desiderare) to long for, yearn for.

vagherò ecc [vage'rɔ] VB vedi **vagare**.

vaghezza [va'gettsa] SF vagueness.

vagina [va'dʒina] SF vagina.

vaginale [vadʒi'nale] AGG vaginal.

vagire [va'dʒire] VI (aus avere) (neonato) to cry, wail.

vagito [va'dʒito] SM (*di neonato*) crying, wailing.

vaglia ['vaʎʎa] SM INV (*Comm*) money order ▶**vaglia bancario** bank draft ▶**vaglia cambiario** promissory note ▶**vaglia postale** postal order.

vagliare [vaʎ'ʎare] VT (*sabbia*) to riddle, sift; (*grano*) to sift; (*fig: proposta, problema*) to weigh up.

vaglio, gli ['vaʎʎo] SM sieve; **passare al vaglio** (*fig*) to examine closely.

vago, a, ghi, ghe ['vago] ① AGG (*gen*) vague.
② SM **a** vagueness; **tenersi nel vago** to keep it all rather vague, stick to generalities **b** (*Anat*) vagus (nerve).

vagone [va'gone] SM (*Ferr: per merci*) truck (*Brit*), wagon (*Brit*), freight car (*Am*); (: *per passeggeri*) carriage (*Brit*), car (*Am*) ▶**vagone letto** sleeping car, sleeper ▶**vagone ristorante** restaurant o dining car.

vai ecc ['vai] VB vedi **andare**.

vaiolo [va'jɔlo] SM smallpox.

val. ABBR = **valuta**.

valanga, ghe [va'langa] SF avalanche; (*fig: grande quantità: di lettere, regali*) flood; **arrivare/riversarsi a valanghe** (*fig: turisti*) to flood in/pour out.

valchiria [val'kirja] SF (*Mitol*) Valkyrie.

valdese [val'dese] AGG, SM/F (*Rel*) Waldensian.

valente [va'lɛnte] AGG able, talented.

valenza [va'lɛntsa] SF (*fig: significato*) content; (*Chim*) valency (*Brit*), valence (*Am*).

valere [va'lere] VB IRREG ① VI (*aus* **essere**) **a** (*persona: contare*) to be worth; **come medico non vale molto** he's not much of a doctor; **vale tanto oro quanto pesa** she's worth her weight in gold; **far valere le proprie ragioni** to make o.s. heard; **far valere la propria autorità** to assert one's authority; **farsi valere** to make o.s. appreciated o respected
b (*avere efficacia: documento*) to be valid; (*avere vigore*) to hold, apply; **questo vale anche per te** that applies to you, too
c (*essere regolamentare: partita*) to be valid, count; **non vale!** that's not fair!
d (*giovare*) to be of use; **i suoi sforzi non sono valsi a niente** his efforts came to nought; **i tuoi consigli sono valsi a fargli cambiare idea** your advice convinced him to change his mind; **prima o poi lo saprà, tanto vale dirglielo subito** he'll find out sooner or later, so we (o you ecc) might as well tell him now
e (*equivalere*) to be equal to; (*essere comparabile a*) to be worth; (*significare*) to amount to; **l'uno vale l'altro** the one is as good as the other, they amount to the same thing; **valere la pena** to be worth the effort o worth it; **vale a dire** that is to say
f (*cosa: avere pregio*) to be worth; **vale 2 milioni (di lire)** it's worth 2 million lire; **non vale niente** it's worthless.
② VT (*procurare*): **gli ha valso il primo premio** it earned him first prize; **ciò gli ha valso un esaurimento** that was what brought on o caused his nervous breakdown.
③ **valersi** VIP: **valersi di** to take advantage of; **valersi dei consigli di qn** to take o act upon sb's advice.

valeriana [vale'rjana] SF (*Bot, Med*) valerian.

valevole [va'levole] AGG valid.

valgo[1], a, ghi, ghe ['valgo] AGG (*Med*) valgus.

valgo[2] ecc ['valgo] VB vedi **valere**.

valicare [vali'kare] VT (*catena montuosa*) to cross.

valico, chi ['valiko] SM pass.

validamente [valida'mente] AVV (*intervenire, contribuire*) effectively.

validità [validi'ta] SF validity; **ha una validità di tre mesi** it is valid for three months.

valido, a ['valido] AGG **a** (*gen*) valid; **l'incontro non è valido per la finale** the match doesn't count for the final; **non è valido!** (*in giochi*) that doesn't count!
b (*efficace: resistenza, rimedio*) effective; (: *aiuto*) real; (: *contributo*) substantial; (: *scusa, argomento*) valid; **essere di valido aiuto a qn** to be a great help to sb
c (*persona: bravo*) worthy; (: *vigoroso*) healthy, strong; **uno dei registi più validi degli ultimi anni** one of the best directors of recent years.

valigeria [validʒe'ria] SF (*assortimento*) leather goods *pl*; (*negozio*) leather goods shop; (*fabbrica*) leather goods factory.

valigia, gie o **ge** [va'lidʒa] SF (suit)case; **fare le valigie** to pack (one's bags); (*fig*) to pack (up); **disfare le valigie** to unpack (one's bags) ▶**valigia diplomatica** (*Pol*) diplomatic bag.

vallata [val'lata] SF valley.

valle ['valle] SF **a** valley; **a valle** (*di fiume*) downstream; **scendere a valle** to go downhill **b**: **valli** SFPL (*tipo di laguna*) marshes.

valletta [val'letta] SF (*TV*) assistant.

valletto [val'letto] SM **a** (*domestico*) valet **b** (*TV*) assistant.

valligiano, a [valli'dʒano] SM/F inhabitant of a valley.

vallo ['vallo] SM (*fortificazione*) wall; **il vallo Adriano** Hadrian's Wall.

vallone[1] [val'lone] SM **a** (*valle: grande*) deep valley; (: *stretto*) narrow valley; (*burrone*) ravine **b** (*canale marino*) deep inlet.

vallone[2], a [val'lone] AGG, SM/F Walloon.

valore [va'lore] SM **a** (*pregio: di merce*) value, worth; (*Fin: di moneta, titolo*) value, price; **il valore della merce** the value of the goods; **crescere/diminuire di valore** to go up/down in value, gain/lose in value; **è di gran valore** it's worth a lot, it's very valuable; **privo di valore** worthless
b: **valori** SMPL (*titoli*) securities; (*oggetti preziosi*) valuables; **Borsa Valori** Stock Exchange
c (*di persona*) worth, merit; (*di opera*) merit, value; (*di vita, amicizia*) value; **artista di valore** artist of considerable merit; **valori morali/estetici** moral/aesthetic values; **scala dei valori** scale of values; **per te l'amicizia non ha alcun valore** friendship means nothing to you
d (*significato*) meaning; (*funzione*) value; **le sue parole hanno (il) valore di una promessa** what he said amounts to o is tantamount to a promise; **il valore di un vocabolo** the exact meaning of a word; **qui il participio ha valore di aggettivo** the participle acts as o is used as an adjective here
e (*coraggio*) courage, valour (*Brit*), valor (*Am*); **difendersi/combattere con gran valore** to defend o.s./fight with great courage; **medaglia al valor militare** medal for gallantry; **atti di valore** acts of bravery o gallantry
f (*Dir: validità*): **questo documento non ha valore legale** this document has no value in law ▶**valore contabile** book value ▶**valore effettivo** real value ▶**valore facciale** nominal value ▶**valore nominale** nominal value ▶**valore di realizzo** break-up value ▶**valore di riscatto** surrender value ▶**valori bollati** (revenue) stamps ▶**valori mobiliari** transferable securities.

valorizzare [valorid'dzare] VT **a** (*prodotto*) to enhance the value of **b** (*mettere in risalto*) to set off, make the most

of; **quel trucco valorizza i suoi occhi** that make-up makes the most of her eyes *o* accentuates her eyes.

valorizzazione [valoriddzat'tsjone] SF increase in value.

valorosamente [valorosa'mente] AVV courageously, bravely.

valoroso, a [valo'roso] AGG courageous, valorous.

valso, a ['valso] PP di **valere**.

valuta [va'luta] SF **a** (*Fin*: *moneta*) currency, money ▶**valuta estera** foreign currency **b** (*Banca*): **con valuta 15 gennaio** interest to run from January 15th.

valutare [valu'tare] VT **a** (*Econ*: *stimare*: *casa, gioiello*) to value; (: *danni, costo*) to assess, evaluate; (: *approssimativamente*) to estimate; (*fig*: *capacità*) to appreciate **b** (*vagliare*) to weigh (up); **valutare il pro e il contro** to weigh up the pros and cons.

valutario, ria, ri, rie [valu'tarjo] AGG (*Fin*: *norme*) currency *attr*.

valutativo, a [valuta'tivo] AGG (*criterio*) assessment *attr*.

valutazione [valutat'tsjone] SF (*vedi vb a*) valuation; assessment, evaluation; estimate; **stando alle prime valutazioni,...** going by initial estimates, ...

valva ['valva] SF (*Zool, Bot*) valve.

valvola ['valvola] SF (*gen, Anat*) valve; (*Elettr*: *fusibile*) fuse ▶**valvola a farfalla** (*Aut*) throttle ▶**valvola di sicurezza** (*anche fig*) safety valve ▶**valvola in testa** (*Aut*) overhead valve.

valzer ['valtser] SM INV waltz.

vamp [vamp] SF INV vamp.

vampa ['vampa] SF (*del sole*) burning heat; (*fiamma*) flame; (*fig*: *rossore*: *per calore, ira*) flush; (: *per vergogna*) blush.

vampata [vam'pata] SF (*fiammata*) blaze; (*di calore*) blast; (*fig*: *al viso*) flush.

vampiro [vam'piro] SM (*gen*) vampire; (*Zool*) vampire bat.

vanadio [va'nadjo] SM vanadium.

vanagloria [vana'glɔrja] SF boastfulness.

vanaglorioso, a [vanaglo'rjoso] AGG boastful.

vanamente [vana'mente] AVV (*inutilmente*) in vain, pointlessly; (*con vanità*) vainly, conceitedly.

vandalicamente [vandalika'mente] AVV (*comportarsi*) like a vandal.

vandalico, a, ci, che [van'daliko] AGG vandal *attr*; **atto vandalico** act of vandalism.

vandalismo [vanda'lizmo] SM vandalism.

vandalo, a ['vandalo] SM/F vandal.

vaneggiamento [vaneddʒa'mento] SM raving, delirium.

vaneggiare [vaned'dʒare] VI (*aus* **avere**) to rave, be delirious; **ma tu vaneggi!** you must be mad!

vanesio, sia, si, sie [va'nɛzjo] AGG vain, conceited.

vanga, ghe ['vanga] SF spade.

vangare [van'gare] VT to dig.

vangata [van'gata] SF (*colpo*) blow with a spade; (*quantità di terra*) spadeful.

vangelo [van'dʒɛlo] SM (*Rel, fig*) gospel; **per me è vangelo** (*fig*) it's gospel as far as I'm concerned.

vanificare [vanifi'kare] VT to nullify.

vaniglia [va'niʎʎa] SF vanilla.

vanigliato, a [vaniʎ'ʎato] AGG: **zucchero vanigliato** (*Culin*) vanilla sugar.

vanillina [vanil'lina] SF vanillin.

vaniloquio, qui [vani'lɔkwjo] SM (*discorso futile*) nonsense.

vanità [vani'ta] SF **a** (*vanagloria*) vanity, pride, conceit **b** (*futilità*: *di promessa*) emptiness, vanity; (: *di sforzo*) futility, fruitlessness.

vanitosamente [vanitosa'mente] AVV vainly.

vanitoso, a [vani'toso] **1** AGG vain, conceited. **2** SM/F vain person.

vanno ['vanno] VB vedi **andare**.

vano, a ['vano] **1** AGG **a** (*illusione, promessa*) vain, empty; (*fatiche*) vain, futile, fruitless; (*proteste, minacce*) idle; **riuscire vano** to come to nothing **b** (*vanitoso*) vain, conceited. **2** SM **a** (*spazio vuoto*) space; **il vano della porta** the doorway ▶**vano portabagagli** (*Aut*) boot (*Brit*), trunk (*Am*) **b** (*stanza*) room; **un appartamento di quattro vani** a four-roomed flat (*Brit*) *o* apartment (*Am*).

vantaggio, gi [van'taddʒo] SM **a** (*gen*) advantage; **avere il vantaggio (di)** to have the advantage (of) **b** (*profitto*) benefit, advantage; **tornerà a tuo vantaggio** it will be to your advantage; **trarre vantaggio da qc** to benefit from sth; **non trarre alcun vantaggio da qc** to get nothing out of sth **c** (*distacco*) start; (: *Sport*) lead; (: *Tennis*) advantage; **hanno un vantaggio di 3 ore su di noi** they have a 3-hour start on us; (*Sport*) they have a 3-hour lead over us; **essere/portarsi in vantaggio** (*Sport*) to be in/take the lead; **ha 2 punti di vantaggio sull'avversario** he has a 2-point lead over his opponent.

vantaggiosamente [vantaddʒosa'mente] AVV advantageously, favourably (*Brit*), favorably (*Am*).

vantaggioso, a [vantad'dʒoso] AGG advantageous, favourable (*Brit*), favorable (*Am*).

vantare [van'tare] **1** VT **a** (*lodare*: *persona, cosa, prodotto*) to speak highly of, praise; (*avere*: *qualità*) to boast, have **b** (*andare fiero di*) to boast of *o* about, vaunt. **2 vantarsi** VR: **vantarsi di qc/di aver fatto qc** to boast *o* brag about sth/about having done sth; **non faccio per vantarmi** without false modesty, without wishing to boast *o* brag.

vanteria [vante'ria] SF (*qualità*) boasting; (*atto, detto*) boast.

vanto ['vanto] SM **a** : **menar vanto di** to boast *o* brag about **b** (*merito*) merit, virtue **c** (*orgoglio*) pride; **è il vanto di sua madre** he's his mother's pride and joy.

vanvera ['vanvera]: **a vanvera** AVV haphazardly; **parlare a vanvera** to talk nonsense.

vapore [va'pore] SM **a** (*Chim, Fis*) vapour (*Brit*), vapor (*Am*); **vapori** SMPL fumes; **vapore acqueo** steam, (water) vapour; **a vapore** (*ferro, locomotiva, turbina*) steam *attr*; **al vapore** (*Culin*) steamed; **andare a tutto vapore** (*fig*: *persona, macchina*) to go at full speed **b** (*nave*) steamer.

vaporetto [vapo'retto] SM steamer.

vaporiera [vapo'rjɛra] SF steam engine.

vaporizzare [vaporid'dzare] VT to vaporize; (*Cosmesi*) to steam.

vaporizzatore [vaporiddza'tore] SM spray.

vaporizzazione [vaporiddzat'tsjone] SF vaporization.

vaporosità [vaporosi'ta] SF (*vedi agg*) filminess; fullness.

vaporoso, a [vapo'roso] AGG (*tessuto*) filmy; (*capelli*) soft and full.

varano [va'rano] SM (*Zool*) monitor.

varare [va'rare] VT (*Naut, fig*) to launch; (*legge*) to pass.

varcare [var'kare] VT to cross; **varcare i limiti** to overstep *o* exceed the limits; **ha varcato l'ottantina** he's just over eighty.

varco, chi ['varko] SM passage; **aprirsi un varco tra la folla**

to push one's way through the crowd; **aspettare qn al varco** (*fig*) to lie in wait for sb.

varechina [vare'kina] SF bleach.

variabile [va'rjabile] ⒈ AGG (*gen*) variable; (*tempo*) changeable, unsettled, variable; (*umore*) changeable.
⒉ SF (*Mat, Econ*) variable.

variabilità [varjabili'ta] SF INV (*gen, Bio*) variability; (*di tempo, umore*) changeableness.

variamente [varja'mente] AVV (*distribuiti, colorati*) variously.

variante [va'rjante] SF (*gen*) variation, change; (*di percorso*) alternative route; (*di piano, progetto*) modification; (*Ling*) variant.

variare [va'rjare] ⒈ VT to vary.
⒉ VI (*aus sogg: persona* **essere**; *sogg: cosa* **avere**) (*sogg: persona, cosa*) to vary; (*prezzi*) to range.

variato, a [va'rjato] AGG varied.

variazione [varjat'tsjone] SF (*gen*) variation, change; (*Mat, Mus*) variation; **una variazione di programma** a change of plan; **variazioni sul tema** (*Mus, fig*) variations on a theme.

varice [va'ritʃe] SF varicose vein.

varicella [vari'tʃɛlla] SF chickenpox.

varicoso, a [vari'koso] AGG: **vena varicosa** varicose vein.

variegato, a [varje'gato] AGG variegated.

varietà [varje'ta] ⒈ SF (*gen*) variety.
⒉ SM INV: **(spettacolo di) varietà** variety show.

vario, ria, ri, rie ['varjo] ⒈ AGG **a** (*diversificato: stile, paesaggio*) varied
b : **vari(e)** (*parecchi: oggetti, argomenti*) various; **avere varie cose da fare** to have quite a few things to do; **varie volte** several times
c (*instabile: tempo*) unsettled; (: *umore*) changeable, uncertain.
⒉ PRON PL: **vari** several people.
⒊ SFPL: **varie ed eventuali** (*nell'ordine del giorno*) any other business.

variopinto, a [varjo'pinto] AGG multicoloured (*Brit*), multicolored (*Am*).

varo ['varo] SM (*Naut, fig*) launch, launching; (*di leggi*) passing.

varrò ecc [var'rɔ] VB vedi **valere**.

Varsavia [var'savja] SF Warsaw.

vasaio, aia, ai, aie [va'zajo] SM/F potter.

vasca, sche ['vaska] SF **a** (*gen*) tub; (*per pesci*) tank; (*cisterna*) water butt; (*da bucato*) basin; (*anche*: **vasca da bagno**) bath(tub) **b** (*piscina*) (swimming) pool; (: *lunghezza della vasca*) length; **fare una vasca** to swim a length.

vascello [vaʃ'ʃɛllo] SM (*Naut*) vessel, ship; **capitano di vascello** captain; **tenente di vascello** lieutenant.

vaschetta [vas'ketta] SF (*per gelato*) tub; (*per sviluppare fotografie*) basin, dish; **vaschetta per il ghiaccio** ice tray.

vascolare [vasko'lare] AGG vascular.

vasectomia [vazekto'mia] SF vasectomy.

vasectomizzare [vazektomid'dzare] VT to give a vasectomy to; **farsi vasectomizzare** to have a vasectomy.

vaselina [vaze'lina] SF vaseline, petroleum jelly.

vasellame [vazel'lame] SM (*stoviglie*) crockery; (: *di porcellana*) china; (: *d'oro, argento*) plate.

vaso ['vazo] SM **a** (*recipiente: per fiori*) vase; (: *per piante*) flowerpot; (: *ornamentale*) vase, pot; (: *per conserve*) jar, pot ►**vaso da notte** chamber pot ►**vaso di Pandora** (*also fig*) Pandora's box

b (*Anat, Bot, Fis*) vessel ►**vasi comunicanti** (*Fis*) communicating vessels ►**vasi sanguigni** (*Anat*) blood vessels.

vasocostrittore, trice [vazokostrit'tore] AGG, SM vasoconstrictor.

vasodilatatore, trice [vazodilata'tore] AGG, SM vasodilator.

vassallo [vas'sallo] SM vassal.

vassoio, oi [vas'sojo] SM tray.

vastamente [vasta'mente] AVV vastly.

vastità [vasti'ta] SF vastness.

vasto, a ['vasto] AGG (*gen*) vast, huge, immense; **di vasta cultura** widely read; **di vaste proporzioni** (*incendio*) huge; (*fenomeno, rivolta*) widespread; **su vasta scala** on a vast *o* huge scale.

vaticano, a [vati'kano] ⒈ AGG Vatican *attr*.
⒉ SM: **il Vaticano** the Vatican; **la Città del Vaticano** the Vatican City.

vaticinare [vatitʃi'nare] VT (*letter*) to foretell, prophesy.

vaticinio, ni [vati'tʃinjo] SM (*profezia*) prophecy.

vattelappesca [vattelap'peska] ESCL (*fam*): **come si chiama? — vattelappesca!** what's his name? — who knows?

VB SIGLA = *Vibo Valenza*.

VC SIGLA = *Vercelli*.

VE ⒈ SIGLA = *Venezia*.
⒉ ABBR = *Vostra Eccellenza*.

ve [ve] PRON, AVV vedi **vi**.

vecchiaia [vek'kjaja] SF old age; **sarai il bastone della mia vecchiaia** you'll support me in my old age.

vecchio, chia, chi, chie ['vekkjo] ⒈ AGG **a** (*gen*) old; **è più vecchio di me** he is older than me; **è una vecchia storia** it's an old story; **è un mio vecchio amico** he's an old friend of mine; **è un uomo vecchio stile** *o* **stampo** he's an old-fashioned man; **è vecchio del mestiere** he's an old hand at the job; **vecchia volpe** (*fig*) cunning *o* wily old fox; **vecchio come il mondo** as old as the hills
b (*precedente*) old, former; **il vecchio sindaco** the old *o* former mayor; **la sua macchina vecchia** his old car
c (*stagionato: vino, formaggio*) mature; (: *legno*) weathered; (*stantio: pane*) stale.
⒉ SM old; **il contrasto tra il vecchio e il nuovo** the contrast between old and new.
⒊ SM/F (*persona*) old man/woman; **i vecchi** SMPL the old *o* aged, old *o* elderly people, old folk; **come stanno i tuoi vecchi?** (*fam: genitori*) how are your folks?; **il mio vecchio** (*padre*) the *o* my old man; **la mia vecchia** (*madre*) the *o* my old woman; **vecchio mio!** old man!, old chap!

vecchiume [vek'kjume] SM (*pegg: cose*) old junk, old rubbish (*Brit*); **il vecchiume delle sue idee** his old-fashioned ideas.

veccia, ce ['vettʃa] SF (*Bot*) vetch.

vece ['vetʃe] SF (*funzione*) place, stead; **firma del padre o di chi ne fa le veci** signature of the father or guardian; **in vece mia/tua** in my/your place *o* stead.

vedente [ve'dɛnte] SM/F: **non vedente** visually handicapped.

vedere [ve'dere] VB IRREG ⒈ VT **a** to see; **senza occhiali, non ci vedo** I can't see without my glasses; **non si vede niente** [OR] **non (ci) si vede** (*è buio*) you can't see a thing; **non si vede** (*non è visibile*) it doesn't show, you can't see it; **vedere qn fare qc** to see sb do sth; **è una partita da vedere** it'll be a match worth seeing; **l'ho visto nascere** (*fig*) I've known him since he was born; **ho visto**

costruire questa casa I saw this house being built **b** (*raffigurarsi*) to see; **vedere tutto nero** to take a bleak view of things; **non vedo una via d'uscita** I can see no way out; **modo di vedere** outlook, view of things; **vorrei vedere te al posto suo!** I would like to see you in his place!; **lo vedo male questo progetto** I can't see this project working

c (*esaminare: libro, prodotto*) to see, look at; (: *conti*) to go over, check; **vedi pagina 8** see page 8; **mi fai vedere il vestito nuovo?** let me see *o* have a look at the new dress **d** (*scoprire*) to see, find out; **vai a vedere cos'è successo** go and see *o* find out what has happened; **voglio vedere come vanno le cose/che possibilità ci sono** I want to see *o* find out how things are going/what opportunities there are; **vediamo se funziona** let's see if it works; **è da vedere se...** it remains to be seen whether ...

e (*incontrare*) to see, meet; **guarda chi si vede!** look who it is!; **fatti vedere ogni tanto** come and see us (*o me ecc*) from time to time; **non farsi più vedere in giro** to disappear from the scene; **non si è più fatto vedere** he hasn't shown his face since; **non la posso proprio vedere** (*fig*) I can't stand her

f (*visitare: museo, mostra*) to visit; (*consultare: medico, avvocato*) to see, consult; **farsi vedere da un medico** to go and see a doctor

g (*capire*) to see, grasp; **ho visto subito che...** I immediately realized that ...; **si vede!** that's obvious!; **non vedo la ragione di farlo** I can't see any reason to do it *o* for doing it; **è triste ma non lo dà a vedere** he is sad but he isn't letting it show *o* he is hiding it; **ci vedo poco chiaro in questa faccenda** I can't quite understand this business

h (*fare in modo*): **vedere di fare qc** to see (to it) that sth is done, make sure that sth is done; **vedi di non arrivare in ritardo** see *o* make sure you don't arrive late; **vedi tu se ci riesci** see if you can do it; **vedi tu** (*decidi tu*) it's up to you

i (*fraseologia*): **vedetevela voi** you see to it; **se l'è vista brutta** he thought his last hour had come; **essere ben/mal visto da qn** to be/not to be well thought of by sb; **visto che...** seeing that ...; **non vedere qn di buon occhio** to disapprove of sb; **non avere niente a che vedere con qn/qc** to have nothing to do with sb/sth; **vedere la luce** (*nascere*) to come into being, see the light of the day; **vedere le stelle** (*dal dolore*) to see stars; **vederci doppio** to see double; **vedere lontano** (*fig*) to be farsighted; **non vedere più lontano del proprio naso** to be unable to see beyond the end of one's nose; **chi s'è visto s'è visto!** and that's that!; **non vederci più dalla rabbia** to be beside o.s. with rage; **non vederci più dalla fame** to be ravenous *o* starving; **non vedere l'ora di fare qc** to look forward to doing sth; **non vedo l'ora che arrivino** I can't wait for them to arrive; **a vederlo si direbbe che...** by the look of him you'd think that ...; **in vita mia ne ho viste di tutti i colori** I've been through a lot in my time; **ti faccio vedere io!** I'll show you!.

2 vedersi VR **a** (*specchiarsi, raffigurarsi*) to see o.s.

b : **si vide perduto** he realized (that) he was lost; **si vide negare l'ingresso** he was refused admission; **si vide costretto a...** he found himself forced to ...

c (*uso reciproco*) to see each other, meet; **ci vedremo da mio cugino** I'll see you at my cousin's; **ci vediamo domani!** see you tomorrow!

vedetta [ve'detta] SF **a** (*Mil: luogo, guardia*) lookout;

essere *o* **stare di vedetta** to be on lookout duty **b** (*Naut*) patrol ship *o* boat.

vedette [və'dɛt] SF INV (*attore, attrice*) star.

vedova ['vedova] SF widow ▶**vedova nera** (*Zool*) black widow spider.

vedovanza [vedo'vantsa] SF widowhood.

vedovo, a ['vedovo] **1** AGG widowed; **rimaner vedovo** to be widowed.

2 SM widower.

vedrò ecc [ve'drɔ] VB vedi **vedere**.

veduta [ve'duta] SF **a** (*panorama, rappresentazione di paesaggio*) view **b** : **vedute** SFPL (*fig*) views, opinions; **di larghe** *o* **ampie vedute** broad-minded; **di vedute ristrette** *o* **limitate** narrow-minded.

veemente [vee'mɛnte] AGG (*discorso, azione*) vehement; (*assalto*) vigorous; (*passione, desiderio*) overwhelming.

veementemente [veemente'mente] AVV vehemently.

veemenza [vee'mɛntsa] SF vehemence; **con veemenza** vehemently; **la veemenza dell'attacco** the force of the attack.

vegetale [vedʒe'tale] **1** AGG (*gen*) vegetable *attr*; (*organismo*) plant *attr*; **regno vegetale** plant *o* vegetable kingdom.

2 SM plant.

vegetaliano, a [vedʒeta'ljano] AGG, SM/F vegan.

vegetare [vedʒe'tare] VI (*aus avere*) **a** (*piante*) to grow **b** (*fig: persona*) to vegetate.

vegetarianismo [vedʒetarja'nizmo] SM vegetarianism.

vegetariano, a [vedʒeta'rjano] AGG, SM/F vegetarian.

vegetativo, a [vedʒeta'tivo] AGG vegetative.

vegetazione [vedʒetat'tsjone] SF vegetation.

vegeto, a ['vɛdʒeto] AGG (*pianta*) thriving; (*persona*) strong, robust, vigorous; **vivo e vegeto** (*persona*) hale and hearty.

veggente [ved'dʒɛnte] SM/F (*indovino*) clairvoyant.

veglia ['veʎʎa] SF **a** (*atto*) vigil, watch; **fare la veglia a un malato** to watch over a sick person ▶**veglia funebre** wake **b** : **ha passato ore di veglia sui libri** he stayed up late working away at his books; **tra la veglia e il sonno** half awake.

vegliardo, a [veʎ'ʎardo] SM/F venerable old man/woman, elder.

vegliare [veʎ'ʎare] **1** VT (*malato, morto*) to watch over, sit up with.

2 VI (*aus avere*) **a** (*stare sveglio*) to stay up, sit up; **vegliare al capezzale di qn** to sit up with sb, watch by sb's bedside; **vegliare pregando** to pass the night in prayer **b** (*prendersi cura*): **vegliare su qn** to watch over sb.

veglione [veʎ'ʎone] SM ball, dance ▶**veglione di Capodanno** New Year's Eve dance ▶**veglione danzante** all-night dance.

veicolare[1] [veiko'lare] AGG vehicular, of vehicles; **traffico veicolare** vehicular traffic.

veicolare[2] [veiko'lare] VT (*malattia*) to carry.

veicolo [ve'ikolo] SM **a** (*Tecn*) vehicle ▶**veicolo industriale** industrial vehicle ▶**veicolo a motore** motor vehicle ▶**veicolo spaziale** spacecraft *inv* **b** (*mezzo di diffusione: di idee, suoni*) vehicle, medium; (: *di malattia*) carrier; **veicolo pubblicitario** advertising medium.

vela ['vela] SF **a** (*Naut*) sail; **issare/spiegare/ammainare le vele** to hoist/unfurl/strike the sails; **far vela per** (*salpare*) to set sail for; **tutto va a gonfie vele** (*fig*) everything is going perfectly **b** (*Sport*) sailing; **andare a**

vela to go sailing.

velare[1] [ve'lare] [1] VT (*anche fig*) to veil, cover; **velarsi il volto** to cover one's face (with a veil); **le lacrime gli velarono gli occhi** his eyes were clouded with tears.

[2] **velarsi** VIP (*occhi, luna*) to mist over; (*voce*) to become husky; **gli occhi le si velarono di pianto** *o* **lacrime** her eyes clouded with tears; **lo sguardo le si velò** her eyes grew dim; **l'acqua si velò di ghiaccio** ice formed on the water.

velare[2] [ve'lare] AGG (*Ling*) velar.

velatamente [velata'mente] AVV (*alludere, accennare*) covertly.

velato, a [ve'lato] AGG (*anche fig: accenno*) veiled; **occhi velati di lacrime** eyes clouded with tears; **sorriso velato di tristezza** smile tinged with sadness; **con la voce velata per l'emozione** in a voice thick with emotion; **calze velate** sheer stockings.

velatura [vela'tura] SF (*Naut*) sails *pl.*

velcro® ['vɛlkro] SM INV velcro ®.

veleggiare [veled'dʒare] VI (*aus* **avere**) **a** (*Naut*) to sail **b** (*aliante, deltaplano*) to soar, glide.

veleggiatore [veleddʒa'tore] SM (*Aer*) sailplane.

veleno [ve'leno] SM (*sostanza tossica*) poison; (*di serpente*) venom; **gli alcolici sono un veleno per il fegato** alcohol poisons your liver; **parole piene di veleno** venomous words; **sputa sempre veleno su tutti** he is always making spiteful remarks about everybody.

velenosamente [velenosa'mente] AVV maliciously, venomously.

velenoso, a [vele'noso] AGG (*sostanza, fungo, animale*) poisonous; (*persona, lingua, risposta*) venomous.

veleria [vele'ria] SF sailmaker's (shop).

veletta [ve'letta] SF (*di cappello*) veil.

velico, a, ci, che ['vɛliko] AGG (*regata*) sailing *attr*; **superficie velica** sail area.

veliero [ve'ljero] SM (*Naut*) sailing ship.

velina [ve'lina] SF (*anche:* **carta velina**: *per impacchettare*) tissue paper; (: *per copie*) flimsy paper; (: *copia*) carbon (copy).

velista, i, e [ve'lista] SM/F yachtsman/yachtswoman.

velivolo [ve'livolo] SM aircraft.

velleità [vellei'ta] SF INV vain ambition, vain desire.

velleitario, ria, ri, rie [vellei'tarjo] AGG (*aspirazione*) fanciful, unrealistic; (*politica, tentativo*) unrealistic.

vello ['vɛllo] SM (*di pecora, montone*) fleece.

vellutato, a [vellu'tato] AGG (*stoffa, petalo, pesca, colore*) velvety; (*voce*) mellow.

velluto [vel'luto] SM (*stoffa*) velvet; **velluto di cotone/seta** cotton/silk velvet; **di velluto** (*fig: pelle, guance*) velvety ▶**velluto a coste** corduroy, cord.

velo ['velo] SM **a** (*gen*) veil; (*strato sottile*) film, layer; (: *di nebbia*) layer, veil; **prendere il velo** (*Rel*) to take the veil; **un velo di ghiaccio** a film of ice; **nel suo sorriso c'era un velo di tristezza** there was a hint *o* touch of sadness in his smile; **senza veli** (*nudo*) without a stitch on; (*fig: esplicito*) explicit; **stendere un velo (pietoso) su qc** (*fig*) to draw a veil over sth ▶**velo nuziale** *o* **da sposa** bridal veil

b (*tessuto*) voile

c (*Anat*): **velo palatino** soft palate.

veloce [ve'lotʃe] [1] AGG (*gen*) quick, rapid; (*veicolo, cavallo, corridore*) fast; **il veloce scorrere del tempo** the swift passage of time; **veloce come un lampo** as quick as lightning; **più veloce della luce** (*fig*) as quick as a flash.

[2] AVV fast, quickly.

velocemente [velotʃe'mente] AVV quickly.

velocipede [velo'tʃipede] SM velocipede.

velocista, i, e [velo'tʃista] SM/F (*Sport*) sprinter.

velocità [velotʃi'ta] SF INV **a** (*gen, Fis*) speed, velocity; **la sua velocità nel reagire** the swiftness of his reaction; **a grande velocità** very quickly *o* fast; **a forte velocità** at high speed; **a tutta velocità** at full speed; **aumentare la velocità** to accelerate; **diminuire** *o* **ridurre la velocità** to reduce speed; **prendere velocità** to gain speed; **viaggiava alla velocità di 130 chilometri all'ora** it (*o* he) was travelling at a speed of 130 kilometres an hour; **a una velocità costante di 90 km/h** at a constant 90 kilometres per hour; **alta velocità** (*Ferr: servizio ferroviario*) high-speed rail service ▶**velocità di crociera** cruising speed ▶**velocità di fuga** (*Fis*) escape velocity ▶**velocità di reazione** (*Chim*) rate of reaction

b (*Sport*): **gara** *o* **corsa di velocità** sprint, dash.

velocizzare [velotʃid'dzare] [1] VT to speed up, make faster.

[2] **velocizzarsi** VIP to speed up.

velodromo [ve'lɔdromo] SM velodrome.

vena ['vena] SF **a** (*Anat*) vein; (*aurifera, di piombo*) vein, lode; (*di carbone*) seam; (*d'acqua*) spring; (*venatura: di marmo*) vein, streak; (: *di legno*) grain; **tagliarsi le vene** to slash one's wrists; **una vena di tristezza** (*fig*) a hint of sadness

b (*estro*) inspiration; (*disposizione*) mood; **essere/sentirsi in vena di fare qc** to be/feel in the mood to do sth; **non sono in vena di scherzi** I'm not in the mood for jokes, I'm not in a joking mood.

venale [ve'nale] AGG **a** (*Comm: valore*) market *attr*; (: *prezzo*) selling, market *attr*; **cose venali** (*fig*) material things **b** (*fig: persona*) venal; **ma come sei venale!** how mercenary you are!

venalità [venali'ta] SF venality.

venalmente [venal'mente] AVV venally.

venato, a [ve'nato] AGG (*marmo*) veined, streaked; (*legno*) grained.

venatorio, ria, ri, rie [vena'tɔrjo] AGG hunting *attr*; **la stagione venatoria** the hunting season.

venatura [vena'tura] SF (*di marmo*) vein, streak; (*di legno*) grain *no pl*; **le venature del legno** the grain of the wood.

vendemmia [ven'demmja] SF (*attività*) grape harvest, vintage; (*quantità d'uva*) grape crop, grapes *pl*; **fare la vendemmia** to pick *o* harvest the grapes.

vendemmiare [vendem'mjare] [1] VI (*aus* **avere**) to pick *o* harvest the grapes.

[2] VT (*uva*) to pick, harvest.

vendemmiatore, trice [vendemmja'tore] SM/F grape-picker.

vendere ['vɛndere] [1] VT (*anche fig*) to sell; **vendere qc a qn** to sell sb sth, sell sth to sb; **vendere qc a** *o* **per 20 sterline** to sell sth for £20; **vendere all'ingrosso/al dettaglio** *o* **minuto** to sell wholesale/retail; **vendere a rate** to sell on hire purchase (*Brit*) *o* the instalment plan (*Am*); **una pubblicità che fa vendere** an advertisement which increases sales; **"vendesi"** "for sale"; **vendere all'asta** to auction, sell by auction; **vendere a buon mercato** to sell cheaply *o* at a good price; **questi articoli si vendono bene/male** these articles sell well/don't sell well; **vendere cara la pelle** (*fig*) to sell one's life dearly; **vendere l'anima al diavolo** to sell one's soul to the devil; **vendere il proprio corpo** (*prostituirsi*) to sell one's body;

vendere fumo to talk hot air; **averne da vendere** (*fig*) to have enough and to spare; **vendere la pelle dell'orso prima di averlo ucciso** to count one's chickens before they're hatched.

[2] **vendersi** VR **a** (*tradire*): **vendersi al nemico** to sell out to the enemy

b (*prostituirsi*) to prostitute o.s., sell o.s.

vendetta [ven'detta] SF revenge, vengeance; **prendersi una vendetta** to take one's revenge, wreak vengeance; **essere assetato di vendetta** to thirst for revenge ▶**vendetta trasversale** (*della mafia*) *revenge against somebody by attacking his family or friends.*

vendicare [vendi'kare] [1] VT to avenge, revenge.

[2] **vendicarsi** VR: **vendicarsi (di qc)** to avenge *o* revenge o.s. (for sth); (*per rancore*) to take one's revenge (for sth); **vendicarsi su qn** to avenge *o* revenge o.s. on sb.

vendicativamente [vendikativa'mente] AVV vindictively.

vendicativo, a [vendika'tivo] AGG (*persona, carattere*) vindictive.

vendicatore, trice [vendika'tore] [1] AGG (*furia*) avenging. [2] SM/F avenger.

vendita ['vendita] SF sale; **la vendita** (*attività*) selling; (*smercio*) sales *pl*; **contratto di vendita** sales agreement; **reparto vendite** sales department; **mettere in vendita** to put on sale; **in vendita presso** on sale at; **punto (di) vendita** retail outlet ▶**vendita all'asta** auction (sale), sale by auction ▶**vendita per corrispondenza** mail order ▶**vendita al dettaglio** retail ▶**vendita a domicilio** door-to-door selling ▶**vendita all'ingrosso** wholesale ▶**vendita al minuto** retail ▶**vendita porta a porta** door-to-door selling.

venditore, trice [vendi'tore] SM/F seller, vendor, salesman/saleswoman ▶**venditore ambulante** hawker, pedlar ▶**venditore al dettaglio** retailer ▶**venditore all'ingrosso** wholesaler ▶**venditore al minuto** retailer.

venduto, a [ven'duto] [1] AGG (*merce*) sold; (*fig: corrotto*) corrupt. [2] SM (*Comm*) goods *pl* sold.

venefico, a, ci, che [ve'nɛfiko] AGG poisonous; (*fig: insinuazione*) poisonous, venomous.

venerabile [vene'rabile], **venerando, a** [vene'rando] AGG venerable.

venerare [vene'rare] VT to venerate, revere.

venerazione [venerat'tsjone] SF veneration, reverence.

venerdì [vener'di] SM INV Friday; **venerdì santo** Good Friday; **gli manca qualche venerdì** (*fig*) he's got a screw loose *per fraseologia vedi* **martedì.**

Venere ['vɛnere] SF (*Astron, Mitol*) Venus; **monte di Venere** (*Anat*) mons veneris.

venereo, a [ve'nɛreo] AGG venereal; **malattia venerea** venereal disease.

veneto, a ['vɛneto] [1] AGG of *o* from the Veneto. [2] SM/F inhabitant *o* native of the Veneto.

Venezia [ve'nettsja] SF Venice.

veneziana [venet'tsjana] SF (*tenda*) venetian blind.

veneziano, a [venet'tsjano] AGG, SM/F Venetian.

Venezuela [venet'tswɛla] SM: **il Venezuela** Venezuela.

venezuelano, a [venettsue'lano] AGG, SM/F Venezuelan.

vengo *ecc* ['vɛngo] VB *vedi* **venire.**

venia ['vɛnja] SF: **chiedere venia** to beg pardon, apologize.

veniale [ve'njale] AGG (*Rel: peccato*) venial.

venire [ve'nire] VB IRREG [1] VI (*aus essere*) **a** to come;

verremo a salutarti/trovarti we'll come and say good-bye/see you; **è venuto in macchina/treno** he came by car/train; **sono venuto a piedi** I came on foot; **vieni di corsa** come quickly; **vengo!** I'm coming!, just coming!

b (*giungere*) to come, arrive; **non è ancora venuto** he hasn't come *o* arrived yet; **prendere le cose come vengono** to take things as they come; **fallo come viene viene** do it any old how; **venire al mondo** *o* **alla luce** to come into the world; **venire a patti/alle mani** to come to an agreement/to blows; **venire a capo di qc** to unravel sth, sort sth out; **venire a sapere qc** to learn sth; **venire al dunque** *o* **nocciolo** *o* **fatto** *o* **sodo** to come to the point; **questo lavoro/quel tipo mi è venuto a noia** I'm fed up with this work/with that guy; **è venuto il momento di...** the time has come to ...; **negli anni a venire** in the years to come, in future; **sono cose di là da venire** these things are still a long way off; **mi è venuta un'idea** I've had an idea; **ma che ti viene in mente?** whatever are you thinking of?; **gli era venuto il dubbio** *o* **sospetto che...** he began to suspect that ...; **mi è venuto un dubbio** I began to have doubts; **mi è venuto il raffreddore** I've got a cold; **mi viene da vomitare/ridere** I feel sick/like laughing; **ti venisse un colpo/accidente!** (*fam*) drop dead!

c (*provenire*): **venire da** to come from

d (*riuscire: lavoro*) to turn out; **venire bene/male** to turn out well/badly; **il maglione viene troppo lungo/stretto** the sweater is going to end up too long/tight; **non mi viene** (*problema, operazione, calcolo*) I can't get it to come out right

e (*fam: raggiungere l'orgasmo*) to come

f (*costare*) to cost; **quanto viene?** how much is it *o* does it cost?

g (*essere sorteggiato*) to come up

h (*con avv*): **venire fuori** to come out; **venire fuori con** (*battuta*) to come out with; **venire giù** to come down; **venire meno** (*svenire*) to faint; **venire meno a** (*promessa*) to break; (*impegno, dovere*) not to fulfil (*Brit*) *o* fulfill (*Am*); **venire su** (*crescere: persona*) to grow (up); (*: pianta*) to come up; **il bambino sta venendo su molto robusto** the baby's growing very strong; **venire via** to come away; (*macchia*) to come out

i : **far venire** (*medico*) to call, send for; **mi hai fatto venire per niente** you got me to come *o* you made me come for nothing; **mi fa venire il vomito** (*anche fig*) it (*o* he *ecc*) makes me sick; **mi fa venire i brividi** (*anche fig*) it (*o* he *ecc*) gives me creeps

l (*come ausiliare: essere*): **viene ammirato da tutti** he is admired by everyone; **venire stimato da tutti** to be respected by everybody; **verrà giudicato in base al suo punteggio** he will be judged on his marks (*Brit*) *o* grades (*Am*).

[2] **venirsene** VIP: **venirsene via** to come away; **venirsene verso casa** to come home.

[3] SM: **tutto quell'andare e venire mi rendeva nervoso** all that coming and going made me irritable.

venni *ecc* ['venni] VB *vedi* **venire.**

venoso, a [ve'noso] AGG venous.

ventaglio, gli [ven'taʎʎo] SM fan; **a ventaglio** fan-shaped; **disporsi a ventaglio** to fan out.

ventata [ven'tata] SF (*folata*) gust (of wind); **come una ventata d'aria fresca** (*fig*) like a breath of fresh air; **una ventata di nazionalismo** a wave of nationalism.

ventennale [venten'nale] AGG (*che dura 20 anni*) twenty-

year *attr*; (*che ricorre ogni 20 anni*) which takes place every twenty years.

ventenne [ven'tɛnne] AGG, SM/F twenty-year-old *per fraseologia vedi* **cinquantenne**.

ventennio, ni [ven'tɛnnjo] SM period of twenty years; **il ventennio fascista** the Fascist period.

ventesimo, a [ven'tɛzimo] AGG, SM/F, SM twentieth *per fraseologia vedi* **quinto**.

venti ['venti] AGG INV, SM INV twenty *per fraseologia vedi* **cinquanta**.

ventilare [venti'lare] VT **a** (*stanza*) to air, ventilate; (*fig*: *idea, proposta*) to air **b** (*Agr*) to winnow.

ventilato, a [venti'lato] AGG (*camera, zona*) airy; **poco ventilato** airless; **una zona troppo ventilata** a windy area.

ventilatore [ventila'tore] SM (*per ambienti*) fan; (*Med*) ventilator.

ventilazione [ventilat'tsjone] SF ventilation.

ventina [ven'tina] SF: **una ventina (di)** around twenty, twenty or so, about twenty *per fraseologia vedi* **cinquantina**.

ventiquattro [venti'kwattro] [1] AGG INV twenty-four; **ventiquattr'ore su ventiquattro** around the clock, 24 hours a day.

[2] SM INV twenty-four *per fraseologia vedi* **cinque**.

ventiquattr'ore [ventikwat'trore] [1] SFPL (*periodo*) twenty-four hours.

[2] SF INV **a** (*valigetta*) overnight case **b** (*Sport*) twenty-four-hour race.

ventisette [venti'sɛtte] [1] AGG INV twenty-seven.

[2] SM INV: **il ventisette** (*giorno di paga*) ≈ (monthly) pay day *per fraseologia vedi* **cinque**.

ventitré [venti'tre] [1] AGG INV, SM INV twenty-three *per fraseologia vedi* **cinque**.

[2] SFPL: **portava il cappello sulle ventitré** he wore his hat at a jaunty angle.

vento ['vɛnto] SM wind; **un vento caldo** a warm wind; **c'è vento** it's windy; **un colpo di vento** a gust of wind; **a prova di vento** windproof; **contro vento** against the wind; **c'è una barca sopra/sotto vento** (*Naut*) there is a boat to windward/leeward of us; **con i capelli al vento** with windswept hair; **fatica buttata al vento** wasted effort; **parlare al vento** to waste one's breath; **non andare a dirlo ai quattro venti** don't go spreading it around; **un vento di rivolta** a wind of revolt; **qual buon vento ti porta?** to what do I (*o* we) owe the pleasure of seeing you? ►**vento contrario** (*Naut*) headwind.

ventola ['vɛntola] SF (*Aut, Tecn*) fan.

ventosa [ven'tosa] SF (*di gomma*) suction cap *o* pad; (*Zool*) sucker; **funziona a ventosa** it works by suction.

ventoso, a [ven'toso] AGG windy.

ventotto [ven'tɔtto] AGG INV, SM INV twenty-eight *per fraseologia vedi* **cinque**.

ventrale [ven'trale] AGG (*gen*) abdominal; (*pinna, diaframma*) ventral.

ventre ['vɛntre] SM (*addome*) stomach; (*grembo*) womb; **avere dolori al ventre** to have (a) stomach ache; **sdraiato sul ventre** lying on one's stomach *o* front; **il ventre della terra** (*fig*) the depths of the earth; **il basso ventre** lower abdomen; **colpire qn al basso ventre** to hit sb in the groin.

ventricolare [ventriko'lare] AGG (*Anat*) ventricular.

ventricolo [ven'trikolo] SM ventricle.

ventriglio, gli [ven'triʎʎo] SM (*Zool*) gizzard.

ventriloquo, a [ven'trilokwo] SM/F ventriloquist.

ventuno [ven'tuno] AGG INV, SM INV twenty-one *per fraseologia vedi* **cinque**.

ventura [ven'tura] SF fortune, chance; **andare alla ventura** to trust to luck; **soldato di ventura** mercenary; **compagnia di ventura** company of mercenaries.

venturo, a [ven'turo] AGG next, coming.

venuta [ve'nuta] SF coming, arrival; **per la venuta della regina hanno organizzato un ricevimento** they have organized a reception for the queen's visit.

venuto, a [ve'nuto] [1] PP di **venire**.

[2] SM/F: **il primo venuto, la prima venuta** the first person who comes along.

ver. ABBR = **versamento**.

vera ['vera] SF wedding ring.

verace [ve'ratʃe] AGG (*testimone*) truthful; (*testimonianza*) accurate, veracious; (*cibi*) real, genuine.

veracità [veratʃi'ta] SF (*vedi agg*) truthfulness; accuracy, veracity; genuineness.

veramente [vera'mente] AVV (*realmente*) really; **veramente? really?**; **è veramente cretino** he's a real idiot; **io, veramente, al posto tuo...** frankly, in your place, I ...; **veramente, non ne sapevo niente** actually, I didn't know anything about it.

veranda [ve'randa] SF veranda(h).

verbale [ver'bale] [1] AGG **a** (*orale*) verbal, spoken; **accordo verbale** verbal agreement **b** (*Gramm*) verbal.

[2] SM (*di riunione*) minutes *pl*; (*Dir*) record; **le faccio il verbale** (*Polizia*) I'll have to report this; **mettere a verbale** to place in the minutes *o* on record.

verbalmente [verbal'mente] AVV verbally.

verbena [ver'bɛna] SF (*Bot*) vervain, verbena.

verbo ['vɛrbo] SM **a** (*Gramm*) verb **b** (*parola*) word; **il Verbo** (*Rel*) the Word.

verbosamente [verbosa'mente] AVV verbosely.

verbosità [verbosi'ta] SF wordiness, verbosity.

verboso, a [ver'boso] AGG wordy, verbose.

verdastro, a [ver'dastro] AGG greenish.

verdazzurro, a [verdad'dzurro] AGG bluish green.

verde ['verde] [1] AGG **a** (*colore*) green; **verde dalla bile** livid *o* white with rage; **verde d'invidia** green with envy **b** (*acerbo: frutta*) green, unripe; (*legna*) green; **gli anni verdi** youth **c** (*Telec*): **numero verde** freefone (line) **d** (*ecologista: associazione, gruppo*) green; (*ecologico*) ecological, green; **benzina verde** lead-free *o* unleaded petrol.

[2] SM **a** (*colore*) green; **essere al verde** to be broke ►**verde bottiglia** bottle green ►**verde oliva** olive green ►**verde pisello** pea green **b** (*vegetazione*) greenery; **c'è molto verde in questa città** this city is very green; **una casa immersa nel verde** a house surrounded by greenery; **ho bisogno di un po' di verde** I feel in need of country air **c** (*semaforo*) green (light).

[3]: **i Verdi** SMPL (*Pol*) the Greens.

verdeggiante [verded'dʒante] AGG green, verdant.

verdeggiare [verded'dʒare] VI (*aus avere*): **una distesa di prati verdeggiava davanti a noi** green fields spread out before us; **qualcosa verdeggiava in lontananza** there was something green in the distance.

verdemare [verde'mare] AGG INV, SM INV sea-green.

verderame [verde'rame] SM (*Chim*) verdigris.

verdetto [ver'detto] SM (*Dir, gen*) verdict.

verdognolo, a [ver'doɲɲolo] AGG greenish.
verdone [ver'done] SM (Zool) greenfinch.
verdura [ver'dura] SF (Culin) vegetables pl; **minestra di verdura** vegetable soup; **negozio di frutta e verdura** fruit and vegetable shop, greengrocer's (Brit).
verecondia [vere'kondja] SF modesty.
verecondo, a [vere'kondo] AGG modest.
verga, ghe ['verga] SF (bastone) cane, rod; (di pastore) crook; **percuotere qn con la verga** to cane sb ▶**verga d'oro** (lingotto) gold bar; (pianta) goldenrod.
vergare [ver'gare] VT **a** (scrivere) to write **b** (percuotere) to cane, beat.
vergatina [verga'tina] SF (anche: **carta vergatina**: per macchina da scrivere) flimsy.
vergato, a [ver'gato] AGG: **carta vergata** laid paper.
verginale [verdʒi'nale] AGG virginal, virgin attr.
vergine ['verdʒine] **1** SF **a** (gen) virgin; **la Vergine** the Virgin Mary o Mother **b** (Astrol): **Vergine** Virgo; **essere della Vergine** to be Virgo.
2 AGG (persona, terra) virgin attr; **foresta vergine** virgin forest; **pura lana vergine** pure new wool; **olio vergine d'oliva** virgin olive oil; **cassetta vergine** blank cassette.
verginità [verdʒini'ta] SF virginity; **rifarsi una verginità** (fig) to regain one's reputation, clear one's name.
vergogna [ver'goɲɲa] SF **a** (gen) shame; (timidezza) shyness; (imbarazzo) embarrassment; **provava vergogna per ciò che era successo** he felt ashamed about what had happened; **provo vergogna davanti a lui** he makes me feel shy; **vincere la propria vergogna** to overcome one's shyness; **non avere vergogna di nessuno** to be shameless; **sprofondare per la vergogna** to be overcome by embarrassment **b** (onta, disonore) disgrace; **è una vergogna che non abbiano fatto niente** the fact that they haven't done anything is a disgrace; **è la vergogna della famiglia** he is a disgrace to his family.
vergognarsi [vergoɲ'narsi] VIP (vedi sf a): **vergognarsi (di)** to be o feel ashamed (of); to be o feel shy (about); be o feel embarrassed (about); **vergognati!** you should be ashamed of yourself!, shame on you!
vergognosamente [vergoɲɲosa'mente] AVV (vedi agg) timidly, shyly; shamefully; disgracefully.
vergognoso, a [vergoɲ'ɲoso] AGG (timido) timid, shy; (pieno di vergogna) ashamed, embarrassed; (che causa vergogna) shameful; (che causa disonore) disgraceful.
veridicità [veridit'ʃi'ta] SF truthfulness; **nessuno mette in dubbio la veridicità delle sue parole** nobody doubts the truth of what he said.
veridico, a, ci, che [ve'ridiko] AGG truthful.
verifica, che [ve'rifika] SF **a** checking no pl; **fare una verifica di** (freni, testimonianza, firma) to check; **questo lavoro è una continua verifica delle proprie capacità** (fig) this work is a continual test of one's abilities **b** (Fin): **verifica contabile** audit.
verificabile [verifi'kabile] AGG verifiable.
verificabilità [verifikabili'ta] SF verifiability.
verificare [verifi'kare] **1** VT **a** (controllare: verità) to check, verify **b** (Fin) to audit **c** (Mat: teoria, postulato) to prove.
2 verificarsi VIP (accadere) to happen, occur, take place; (avverarsi) to prove (to be).
verità [veri'ta] SF INV **a** (gen) truth; **la pura verità** the absolute truth; **la verità nuda e cruda** the plain unvarnished truth; **è una verità sacrosanta** it's gospel; travi-

sare la verità to distort the truth; **a dire la verità** OR **per la verità** to tell the truth, actually; **macchina della verità** lie-detector; **siero della verità** truth serum **b** (assioma) truth; **le verità scientifiche** scientific truths.
veritiero, a [veri'tjɛro] AGG (conforme a verità) true, accurate; (che dice la verità) truthful.
verme ['vɛrme] SM (gen, fig) worm; (di frutto, formaggio) maggot; **nudo come un verme** stark naked; **mi sento un verme!** (fig) I could die!, I feel awful! ▶**verme solitario** tapeworm.
vermicelli [vermi'tʃelli] SMPL (pasta) vermicelli sg.
vermifugo, a [ver'mifugo] AGG, SM vermifuge.
vermiglio, glia, gli, glie [ver'miʎʎo] AGG, SM vermilion, scarlet.
vermouth, vermut ['vɛrmut] SM INV vermouth.
vernacolo, a [ver'nakolo] AGG, SM vernacular.
vernice [ver'nitʃe] SF **a** (trasparente) varnish; (pittura: lucida) gloss (paint); (: opaca) matt (paint); **"vernice fresca"** "wet paint" **b** (pelle) patent leather; **scarpe/borsa di vernice** patent leather shoes/bag.
verniciare [verni'tʃare] VT (con vernice trasparente) to varnish; (pitturare) to paint.
verniciatore [vernitʃa'tore] SM **a** (operaio) varnisher **b** (dispositivo): **verniciatore a spruzzo** spray gun.
verniciatura [vernitʃa'tura] SF (con vernice trasparente) varnishing; (con vernice colorata) painting.
verniero [ver'njɛro] SM (calibro) vernier.
vernissage [vɛrni'saʒ] SM INV (Arte) preview.
vero, a ['vero] **1** AGG (gen) true; (reale) real; (autentico) genuine; **è una storia vera** it is a true story; **incredibile ma vero** incredible but true; **un vero e proprio delinquente** a real criminal, an out and out criminal; **il suo vero nome è Giovanni** his real o true name is Giovanni; **ma è vero questo Modigliani?** is this a genuine o real Modigliani?; **perle vere** genuine pearls; **quei fiori sembrano veri** those flowers look real; **il vero problema è...** the real problem is ...; **fosse vero!** if only it were true!; **nulla di più vero!** you've said it!, how true!; **non mi pare vero!** it doesn't seem possible!; **come è vero Dio** I swear to God; **tant'è vero che...** so much so that ...; **vero?** isn't that right?; **hai tu il mio libro, vero?** you've got my book, haven't you?; **sei italiano, vero?** you're Italian, aren't you?; **è andata stamattina, vero?** she went this morning, didn't she?; **vorresti andare, vero?** you'd like to go, wouldn't you?
2 SM (verità) truth; **c'è del vero in ciò che dice** there is some truth in what he says; **sto dicendo il vero** I am telling the truth; **a onor del vero** OR **a dire il vero** to tell the truth; **è una copia dal vero** (disegno) it's a copy from life.
Verona [ve'rona] SF Verona.
veronese [vero'nese] AGG, SM/F Veronese inv.
veronica¹ [ve'ronika] SF (Bot) veronica.
veronica² [ve'ronika] SF (in corrida) veronica.
verosimiglianza [verosimiʎ'ʎantsa] SF (vedi agg) likelihood, probability; plausibility.
verosimile [vero'simile] AGG (racconto, ipotesi) likely, probable; (trama) plausible, convincing; **poco verosimile** (racconto) improbable, unlikely; (trama) implausible.
verosimilmente [verosimil'mente] AVV realistically.
verro ['vɛrro] SM (Zool) boar.
verrò ecc [ver'rɔ] VB vedi venire.
verruca, che [ver'ruka] SF (Med, Bot) verruca, wart.

versaccio, ci [ver'sattʃo] SM: **fare i versacci (a qn)** (*smorfie*) to make faces (at sb); (*grida di scherno*) to jeer (at sb).

versamento [versa'mento] SM **a** (*gen*) payment; (*deposito in banca*) deposit; **modulo** *o* **distinta di versamento** (*Banca*) pay-in slip **b** (*Med*) effusion.

versante [ver'sante] SM (*Geog*) side, slopes *pl*; **sul versante del lavoro non ci sono novità** there's no news on the work front.

versare¹ [ver'sare] ① VT **a** (*liquido, polvere*) to pour; (*servire: caffè*) to pour (out); **versare da bere a qn** to pour sb a drink; **versare la minestra** to serve (up) the soup; **versare a filo** (*olio*) to drizzle

  b (*spargere: liquidi, polvere*) to spill; (: *lacrime, sangue*) to shed; **mi sono versato il caffè addosso** I've spilt coffee over myself; **versare acqua sul fuoco** (*fig*) to pour oil on troubled waters

  c: **il Po versa le proprie acque nell'Adriatico** the Po flows into the Adriatic

  d (*Econ: pagare*) to pay; (: *depositare*) to deposit, pay in; **ho versato la somma sul mio conto** I paid the sum into my account, I deposited the sum in my account; **versare una cauzione** to pay a deposit.

  ② **versarsi** VIP **a** (*rovesciarsi*) to spill; **il latte si è versato sul fuoco** the milk has boiled over

  b: **versarsi in** (*sogg: fiume*) to flow into; (: *folla*) to pour into.

versare² [ver'sare] VI (*aus avere*): **versare in fin di vita** to be dying; **versare in gravi difficoltà** to find o.s. with serious problems.

versatile [ver'satile] AGG versatile.

versatilità [versatili'ta] SF versatility.

versato, a [ver'sato] AGG: **essere versato in** to be (well-) versed in.

verseggiare [versed'dʒare] ① VT to put into verse.

  ② VI (*aus avere*) to write verse, write poetry.

  ③ SM verse, poetry.

versetto [ver'setto] SM (*di poesia*) line; (*Rel*) verse.

versione [ver'sjone] SF **a** (*gen*) version; **in versione originale** (*libro*) in the original (version); (*film*) in the original language *o* version; **la versione cinematografica del suo ultimo libro** the film of his latest book; **versione lusso** (*Aut*) luxury model; **versione 4 porte** (*Aut*) 4-door model **b** (*traduzione*) translation.

verso¹ ['vɛrso] SM INV (*di pagina*) verso; (*di moneta*) reverse.

verso² ['vɛrso] SM **a** (*di animale, uccello*) call, cry; **qual è il verso del gatto?** what noise *o* sound does a cat make?; **verso di richiamo** call; **ha fatto un verso di dolore** she cried out in pain *o* gave a cry of pain; **smettila di fare tutti quei versi** stop making those noises; **rifare il verso a qn** (*imitare*) to take sb off, mimic sb

  b (*riga: di poesia*) line, verse; **versi** SMPL (*poesia*) verse *sg*; **in versi** in verse ▶ **versi sciolti** blank verse *sg*

  c (*direzione, Mat*) direction; (*di legno, stoffa*) grain; **prendere qn/qc per il verso giusto** to approach sb/sth the right way; **non c'è verso di convincerlo** it is impossible to persuade him, there's no way of persuading him, he can't be persuaded; **per un verso o per l'altro** one way or another; **per un verso sono d'accordo, per l'altro...** on the one hand I agree (with you), but on the other ...; **chi per un verso, chi per un altro tutti decisero di partire** for one reason or another they all decided to leave.

verso³ ['vɛrso] PREP **a** (*in direzione di*) toward(s), to; **andando verso la stazione** going towards the station;

veniva verso di me he was coming towards me; **verso l'alto** upwards; **verso il basso** downwards; **guardare verso il cielo** to look heavenwards *o* skywards; **navigare verso sud** to sail south(wards)

  b (*nei pressi di*) near, around (about); **abito verso il centro** I live near the centre (*Brit*) *o* center (*Am*)

  c (*in senso temporale*) about, around; **arrivi verso che ora?** around *o* about what time will you arrive?; **verso sera** towards evening; **verso la fine dell'anno** towards the end of the year

  d (*nei confronti di*) for, towards; **dimostrare rispetto verso gli anziani** to show respect for *o* towards the elderly.

vertebra ['vɛrtebra] SF vertebra.

vertebrale [verte'brale] AGG vertebral; **colonna vertebrale** spinal column, spine.

vertebrato, a [verte'brato] AGG, SM vertebrate.

vertenza [ver'tɛntsa] SF (*lite*) lawsuit, case; (*sindacale*) dispute.

vertere ['vɛrtere] VI DIF: **vertere su** to deal with, be about.

verticale [verti'kale] ① AGG vertical.

  ② SF **a** (*linea*) vertical **b** (*Ginnastica*: *sulle mani*) handstand; (: *sulla testa*) headstand; **fare la verticale** to do a handstand (*o* headstand) **c** (*nei cruciverba*) clue (*o* word) down.

verticalmente [vertikal'mente] AVV vertically.

vertice ['vɛrtitʃe] SM **a** (*Geom*) vertex **b** (*vetta*) summit, peak, top; (*fig: punto più alto*) peak, height; **il vertice della carriera** the peak of one's career **c** (*Pol*) summit; **incontro/conferenza al vertice** summit meeting/conference.

vertigine [ver'tidʒine] SF giddiness *no pl*, dizziness *no pl*, dizzy spell; (*Med*) vertigo; **soffrire di vertigini** to be afraid of heights, to have vertigo (*termine tecn*); **mi fa venire le vertigini** it makes my head spin; **avere le vertigini** to feel dizzy.

vertiginosamente [vertidʒinosa'mente] AVV (*girare*) dizzily; **aumentare/diminuire vertiginosamente** (*prezzi*) to rise/fall steeply.

vertiginoso, a [vertidʒi'noso] AGG (*altezza*) dizzy; (*velocità*) breakneck *attr*; (*danza*) breathless; (*cifra*) exorbitant; (*scollatura*) plunging; **il ritmo vertiginoso della vita moderna** the frenetic pace of modern life.

verve [vɛrv] SF INV verve.

verza ['verdza] SF Savoy cabbage.

vescia, sce ['veʃʃa] SF (*fungo*) puffball.

vescica, che [veʃ'ʃika] SF **a** (*Anat*) bladder **b** (*Med*: *bolla*) blister.

vescovado [vesko'vado] SM (*Rel*: *diocesi*) bishopric; (: *sede*) bishop's palace.

vescovile [vesko'vile] AGG episcopal.

vescovo ['veskovo] SM bishop.

vespa¹ ['vɛspa] SF (*Zool*) wasp; **ha un vitino di vespa** she's wasp-waisted.

vespa²® ['vɛspa] SF (motor) scooter, Vespa ®.

vespaio, ai [ves'pajo] SM wasps' nest; **suscitare un vespaio** (*fig*) to stir up a hornets' nest.

Vespasiano [vespa'zjano] SM (*Storia*) Vespasian.

vespasiano [vespa'zjano] SM urinal.

vespro ['vɛspro] SM (*letter: sera*) evening; (*Rel*) vespers *pl*.

vessare [ves'sare] VT (*letter*) to oppress.

vessazione [vessat'tsjone] SF (*letter*) oppression.

vessillo [ves'sillo] SM (*Mil*) standard; (*bandiera*) flag; (*fig*) banner, ensign; **il vessillo della libertà** the banner of

freedom.

vestaglia [ves'taʎʎa] SF dressing gown (*Brit*), bathrobe (*Am*).

vestale [ves'tale] SF vestal virgin.

veste ['vɛste] SF **a** (*gen*) garment; (*da donna*) dress; (*di monaco, suora*) habit; **vesti** SFPL clothes, clothing *sg* ▶**veste da camera** dressing gown (*Brit*), bathrobe (*Am*)
b (*fig: di libro*): **veste editoriale** layout
c (*funzione*) capacity; (*fig: apparenza*) appearance; **in veste di** (in one's capacity) as; **in veste ufficiale** in an official capacity; **si è presentato in veste di amico** he passed himself off as a friend.

vestiario, ri [ves'tjarjo] SM wardrobe, clothes *pl*; **capo di vestiario** article of clothing, garment.

vestibolo [ves'tibolo] SM **a** (*ingresso*) (entrance) hall; (*Archeol*) vestibule **b** (*Anat*) vestibule.

vestigia [ves'tidʒa] SFPL **a** (*tracce*) vestiges, traces **b** (*rovine*) ruins, remains.

vestire [ves'tire] **1** VT **a** (*gen*): **vestire (di)** to dress (in); (*mascherare*): **vestire da** to dress up as
b (*provvedere degli indumenti necessari*) to clothe; **Valentino veste le attrici più famose** Valentino makes *o* designs clothes for all the most famous actresses
c (*indossare: stato*) to wear, have on; (: *atto*) to put on. **2** VI (*aus* essere) (*indossare*) to wear; (*abbigliarsi*) to dress; **vestire di bianco/a lutto** to wear white/mourning; **vestire con eleganza** to dress smartly; **questa giacca veste bene** this is a well-cut jacket.
3 **vestirsi** VR (*gen*) to dress, get dressed; (*abbigliarsi*) to dress; **vestirsi da** (*negozio*) to buy *o* get one's clothes at; (*sarto*) to have one's clothes made at; **vestirsi da pirata/Peter Pan** to dress up as a pirate/Peter Pan; **vestirsi a festa** to wear one's Sunday best *o* one's best clothes; **vestirsi a lutto** to wear mourning; **vestirsi bene/con gusto** to dress well/tastefully; **come mi devo vestire stasera?** what should I wear this evening?

vestito¹, a [ves'tito] AGG dressed; **vestito di bianco** dressed in white; **vestito da** (*in maschera*) dressed up as; **vestito di tutto punto** all dressed up; **dormire vestito** to sleep in one's clothes.

vestito² [ves'tito] SM (*gen*) garment; (*abito: da donna*) dress; (: *da uomo*) suit; **vestiti** SMPL clothes; **cambiare vestiti** to change one's clothes; **farsi fare un vestito** to have a dress (*o* suit) made.

Vesuvio [ve'zuvjo] SM: **il Vesuvio** Vesuvius.

veterano, a [vete'rano] **1** SM (*Mil*) veteran.
2 SM/F (*fig*) veteran, old hand.

veterinaria [veteri'narja] SF veterinary medicine.

veterinario, ria, ri, rie [veteri'narjo] **1** AGG veterinary.
2 SM vet (*Brit*), veterinary surgeon (*Brit*), veterinarian (*Am*).

veto ['vɛto] SM (*Dir, fig*) veto; **diritto di veto** right of veto; **porre il veto a qc** to veto sth.

vetraio, ai [ve'trajo] SM (*gen*) glazier, glass-worker; (*chi soffia il vetro*) glass-blower, glassmaker.

vetrata [ve'trata] SF glass door (*o* window); (*di chiesa*) stained-glass window.

vetrato, a [ve'trato] AGG glass *attr*; (*porta, finestra*) glazed; **carta vetrata** sandpaper.

vetreria [vetre'ria] SF (*fabbrica*) glassworks *inv*; (*oggetti di vetro*) glassware *no pl*.

vetrificante [vetrifi'kante] AGG vitrescent.

vetrificare [vetrifi'kare] **1** VT to vitrify; (*ceramica*) to

glaze.
2 **vetrificarsi** VIP to vitrify.

vetrificazione [vetrifikat'tsjone] SF vitrification.

vetrina [ve'trina] SF **a** (*di negozio*) (shop) window; **in vetrina** in the window; **allestire una vetrina** to dress a window; **andare a guardare le vetrine** to go window-shopping; **mettersi in vetrina** (*fig*) to show off **b** (*rassegna*) showcase **c** (*mobile: di museo*) showcase, display cabinet; (: *di negozio*) display cabinet.

vetrinista, i, e [vetri'nista] SM/F window dresser.

vetrinistica [vetri'nistika] SF window dressing.

vetrino [ve'trino] SM (*di microscopio*) slide.

vetriolo [vetri'ɔlo] SM vitriol; **al vetriolo** (*fig: critica, risposta*) vitriolic.

vetro ['vetro] **1** SM **a** (*materiale*) glass; (*frammento*) piece of glass; (*scheggia*) splinter of glass; **lana di vetro** glass fibre (*Brit*) *o* fiber (*Am*); **fibra di vetro** fibreglass (*Brit*) *o* fiberglass (*Am*); **mettere qc sotto vetro** to put sth under glass
b (*di finestra, porta*) (window) pane; (*di orologio*) watch glass; **devo pulire i vetri** I have to clean the windows; **porta a vetri** glass door
c (*oggetto*): **i vetri di Murano** Murano glassware *sg*.
2 ▶**vetro blindato** bulletproof glass ▶**vetro infrangibile** shatterproof glass ▶**vetro di sicurezza** safety glass ▶**vetro smerigliato** frosted glass.

vetroresina [vetro'rɛzina] SF fibreglass (*Brit*) *o* fiberglass (*Am*).

vetroso, a [ve'troso] AGG vitreous.

vetta ['vetta] SF (*di montagna*) top, summit, peak; (*di albero*) top; **toccare le più alte vette del successo** to reach the top of the ladder; **essere in vetta alla classifica** (*squadra*) to be at the top of the league; (*canzone*) to be at the top of the charts.

vettore [vet'tore] **1** SM **a** (*Mat, Fis*) vector **b** (*trasportatore*) carrier.
2 AGG: **razzo vettore** booster rocket.

vettoriale [vetto'rjale] AGG (*Mat*) vectorial; **calcolo vettoriale** vector analysis.

vettovagliamento [vettovaʎʎa'mento] SM provisioning.

vettovagliare [vettovaʎ'ʎare] VT to supply with provisions, provision.

vettovaglie [vetto'vaʎʎe] SFPL provisions, supplies.

vettura [vet'tura] SF **a** (*carrozza*) coach, carriage ▶**vettura di piazza** hackney carriage **b** (*Ferr*) coach, carriage (*Brit*), car (*Am*); **in vettura!** all aboard! **c** (*auto*) car, automobile (*Am*); **vettura da noleggio senza autista** car for self-drive hire (*Brit*) *o* rent (*Am*).

vetturino [vettu'rino] SM coach driver, coachman.

vezzeggiamento [vettseddʒa'mento] SM caressing.

vezzeggiare [vettsed'dʒare] VT to make a fuss of.

vezzeggiativo, a [vettseddʒa'tivo] **1** AGG of endearment.
2 SM term of endearment.

vezzo ['vettso] SM **a** (*abitudine*) (affected) habit; **avere il vezzo di fare qc** to have the habit of doing sth **b** (*gesto affettuoso*) caress **c**: **vezzi** SMPL (*moine*) affected ways; (*grazia*) charm *sg*, charms.

vezzosamente [vettsosa'mente] AVV (*vedi agg*) charmingly; affectedly.

vezzosità [vettsosi'ta] SF INV (*grazia*) charm; (*leziosità*) affected ways *pl*, affectation.

vezzoso, a [vet'tsoso] **1** AGG **a** (*grazioso*) pretty, charming **b** (*lezioso*) affected.
2 SM/F: **fare il(la) vezzoso(a)** to turn on the charm.

V.F. ABBR = **vigili del fuoco**.
V.G. ABBR = *Vostra Grazia*.
VI SIGLA = *Vicenza*.
vi [vi] (dav **lo, la, li, le, ne** diventa **ve**) [1] PRON PERS **a** (*ogg diretto*) you; **vi stavo cercando** I was looking for you; **vorrei aiutarvi** I'd like to help you
  b (*complemento di termine*) (to) you; **ve l'hanno dato** they gave it to you; **vi darò un consiglio** I'll give you some advice
  c (*riflessivo*) yourselves; (*reciproco*) each other; **vestitevi** get dressed; **divertitevi** enjoy yourselves; **ve ne pentirete** you'll regret it; **vi conoscete?** do you know each other?.
  [2] PRON DIMOSTR = **ci**.
  [3] AVV (*in questo luogo*) here; (*in quel luogo*) there; **non vi erano che pochi turisti** there were only a few tourists there; **vi sono molti modi di farlo** there are many ways of doing it.
via¹ ['via] SF **a** (*strada*) road; (: *di città*) street, road; (*cammino*) way; (*percorso*) route; (*sentiero, pista*) path, track; **abito in via Cairoli 14** I live at number 14 Via Cairoli; **la via dell'oppio** the opium trail; **vie di comunicazione** communication routes; **che via fai di solito?** what route do you usually take?; **sulla via di casa** on one's way home; **hai via libera** (*a un incrocio*) the road is clear; **dare via libera a qc** (*fig*) to give the green light o the go-ahead; **allontanarsi dalla retta via** (*fig*) to stray from the straight and narrow; **in via di guarigione** on the road to recovery; **paese in via di sviluppo** developing country; **la sua laurea gli apre molte vie** his degree offers him many possibilities
  b (*mezzo*) way, means; (*procedimento*) channels *pl*; (*fig: modo*) way; **tentare tutte le vie** to try everything possible; **per vie traverse** by underhand means; **non avevo altra via** I had no alternative; **non c'è via di scampo** o **d'uscita** there's no way out; **non c'è via di mezzo** there's no middle ground; **scegliere la via di mezzo** to compromise; **te lo dico in via privata** o **confidenziale** I'm telling you in confidence; (*ufficiosamente*) I'm telling you unofficially; **in via eccezionale** as an exception; **in via provvisoria** provisionally; **in via amichevole** in a friendly manner; **comporre una disputa in via amichevole** (*Dir*) to settle a dispute out of court; **adire le vie legali** to take legal proceedings; **le vie del Signore** the ways of the Lord; **passare alle vie di fatto** to resort to violence; **per via aerea** by air; (*lettere*) by airmail; **via satellite** by satellite; **via Dover** via Dover; **per via di** because of, on account of
  c (*Anat*) tract; **le vie respiratorie** the respiratory tracts; **per via orale** (*Med*) orally
  d (*Astron*): **la Via Lattea** the Milky Way.
via² ['via] [1] AVV **a** (*allontanamento*) away; (: *temporaneo*) out; **buttare** o **gettare via qc** to throw sth away; **tagliare via** to cut off o away; **dare via qc** to give sth away; **è andato via** (*per poco tempo*) he has gone out; (*per molto tempo*) he has gone away; **sono stato via per 3 settimane** I was away for three weeks; **vai via!** go away!, clear off! (*fam*); **questa macchia non va via** this mark won't come out
  b (*eccetera*): **e così via** and so on; **e via dicendo** OR **e via di questo passo** and so on (and so forth)
  c : **via via** (*pian piano*) gradually; **via via che** (*man mano*) as.
  [2] : **via da** PREP away from; **non andare via da me** don't

leave me.
  [3] ESCL (*suvvia*) come on!; (*allontanati*) go away!; (: *a un animale*) shoo!; **pronti, via!** ready, steady, go!.
  [4] SM (*Sport*) (signal to) start, starting signal; **dare il via** to start the race, give the starting signal; **dare il via a un progetto** to give the green light to a project; **hanno dato il via ai lavori** they've begun o started work.
V.I.A. ['via] SIGLA F (= *Valutazione d'impatto ambientale*) environmental (impact) study.
viabilità [viabili'ta] SF (*percorribilità*) practicability; (*rete stradale*) roads *pl*, road network; **per migliorare la viabilità del centro** in order to improve traffic circulation in the centre (*Brit*) o center (*Am*).
Viacard® [via'kard] SF INV *credit card used to pay motorway tolls.*
via crucis [via'krutʃis] SF (*Rel*): **la Via Crucis** the Way of the Cross; **la sua vita da emigrato è stata una via crucis** his life as an emigrant has been purgatory o a real trial.
viado [vi'ado] SM INV *Brazilian transsexual prostitute.*
viadotto [via'dotto] SM viaduct.
viaggiare [viad'dʒare] VI (*aus* **avere**) **a** (*gen*) to travel; **a me piace viaggiare** I like travelling (*Brit*) o traveling (*Am*); **viaggiare in treno/aereo** to travel by train/plane; **è uno che ha viaggiato molto** he's well-travel(l)ed, he has travel(l)ed a lot; **la macchina viaggiava a 50 chilometri all'ora** the car was travel(l)ing at (a speed of) 50 kilometres per hour; **il treno viaggia con 50 minuti di ritardo** the train is running 50 minutes late; **le merci viaggiano via mare** the goods go o are sent by sea
  b (*fare il commesso viaggiatore*): **viaggiare per una ditta** to be a travel(l)ing salesman o a sales representative for a company; **viaggio in tessuti** I travel in textiles.
viaggiatore, trice [viaddʒa'tore] [1] AGG travelling (*Brit*), traveling (*Am*); **piccione viaggiatore** carrier pigeon; **commesso viaggiatore** travel(l)ing salesman.
  [2] SM/F (*gen*) traveller (*Brit*), traveler (*Am*); (*passeggero*) passenger.
viaggio, gi [vi'addʒo] SM (*gen*) travel, travelling (*Brit*), traveling (*Am*); (*tragitto*) journey, trip; (*in aereo*) flight; (*via mare*) voyage; **è in viaggio** he's away; **agenzia di viaggi** travel agency; **spese di viaggio** travel(l)ing expenses; **ho dovuto fare due viaggi per portar su i libri** I had to make two trips to bring the books up; **fare un viaggio a vuoto** to make a wasted journey; **mi hanno rimborsato il viaggio** they gave me my travel(l)ing expenses; **buon viaggio!** have a good trip! ▶ **viaggio d'affari** business trip ▶ **viaggio di nozze** honeymoon ▶ **viaggio organizzato** package tour o holiday ▶ **viaggio di piacere** pleasure trip.
viale [vi'ale] SM **a** (*in città*) avenue **b** (*in parco*) path, walk **c** : **è sul viale del tramonto** his star is on the wane.
viandante [vian'dante] SM/F wayfarer.
viario, ria, ri, rie [vi'arjo] AGG (*Aut*): **rete viaria** road network; (*in città*) street network.
viatico, ci [vi'atiko] SM (*Rel*) viaticum.
viavai [via'vai] SM INV coming and going, bustle.
vibrafono [vi'brafono] SM vibraphone.
vibrante [vi'brante] AGG (*membrana*) vibrating; (*voce, suono*) vibrant, resonant; **vibrante di** vibrant with.
vibrare [vi'brare] [1] VT (*dare con forza*): **vibrare un colpo a qn** to strike sb; **vibrare una coltellata a qn** to stab sb.
  [2] VI (*aus* **avere**) **a** (*gen, Fis*) to vibrate; **vibrare (di)** (*voce*) to quiver (with), be vibrant (with); **il suo cuore vibrava di emozione** her heart throbbed with emotion **b**

(*risuonare*) to resound, ring.

vibrato [vi'brato] SM (*Mus*) vibrato.

vibratore, trice [vibra'tore] [1] AGG vibrating.
[2] SM vibrator.

vibratorio, ria, ri, rie [vibra'tɔrjo] AGG vibratory.

vibrazione [vibrat'tsjone] SF vibration.

vibrissa [vi'brissa] SF (*Zool*) vibrissa.

vibromassaggiatore [vibromassaddʒa'tore] SM: **vibromassaggiatore (elettrico)** vibrator.

viburno [vi'burno] SM (*Bot*) viburnum.

vicario, ri [vi'karjo] SM (*Rel*) vicar.

vice ['vitʃe] SM/F deputy.

vice- ['vitʃe] PREF vice-; **viceammiraglio** vice-admiral.

viceconsole [vitʃe'kɔnsole] SM vice-consul.

vicedirettore, trice [vitʃediret'tore] SM/F (*gen*) deputy manager/manageress, assistant manager/manageress; (*di giornale*) deputy editor; (*di scuola*) deputy headmaster/headmistress (*Brit*), vice-principal (*Am*).

vicenda [vi'tʃɛnda] [1] SF **a** (*episodio*) event **b** : **vicende** SFPL (*sorte*) fortunes; **con alterne vicende** with mixed fortunes.
[2] : **a vicenda** AVV **a** (*reciprocamente*) each other, one another **b** (*alternativamente*) in turn(s).

vicendevole [vitʃen'devole] AGG mutual, reciprocal.

vicendevolmente [vitʃendevol'mente] AVV each other, one another, mutually; **si rimproverano vicendevolmente** they blame each other.

vicentino, a [vitʃen'tino] [1] AGG of o from Vicenza.
[2] SM/F inhabitant o native of Vicenza.

vicepreside [vitʃe'prɛside] SM/F deputy headmaster/headmistress (*Brit*), vice-principal (*Am*).

vicepresidente [vitʃepresi'dɛnte] SM (*di stato*) vice-president; (*di società*) vice-chairman.

vicepresidenza [vitʃepresi'dɛntsa] SF (*di stato*) vice-presidency; (*di società*) vice-chairmanship.

viceré [vitʃe're] SM INV viceroy.

vicesegretario, ri [vitʃesegre'tarjo] SM vice-secretary, deputy secretary.

viceversa [vitʃe'vɛrsa] AVV vice versa; **da Roma a Pisa e viceversa** from Rome to Pisa and back.

vichingo, a, ghi, ghe [vi'kingo] AGG, SM/F Viking.

vicinanza [vitʃi'nantsa] SF **a** (*prossimità*) proximity, closeness, nearness **b** : **vicinanze** SFPL (*paraggi*) vicinity *sg*; **nelle vicinanze ci sono due panettieri** there are two bakers in the vicinity o in the area.

vicinato [vitʃi'nato] SM (*zona*) neighbourhood (*Brit*), neighborhood (*Am*); (*vicini*) neighbo(u)rs *pl*; **avere rapporti di buon vicinato** to get on well with one's neighbo(u)rs.

vicino, a [vi'tʃino] [1] AGG **a** (*a poca distanza*) near, nearby; (: *paese*) neighbouring (*Brit*), neighboring (*Am*), nearby; **vicino a** near, close to; **la stazione è vicina** the station is near, the station is close (by); **dov'è il ristorante più vicino?** where is the nearest restaurant?; **quei quadri sono troppo vicini** those pictures are too close (together o to each other); **mi sono stati molto vicini** (*fig*) they were very supportive towards me **b** (*accanto*) next; **la mia stanza è vicina alla tua** my room is next to yours **c** (*nel tempo*) near, close at hand; **la fine è vicina** the end is near o imminent; **siamo vicini alla fine** we've almost o nearly finished; **le vacanze sono vicine** the holidays are (*Brit*) o the vacation is (*Am*) approaching; **è vicina ai trent'anni** she's almost thirty.

[2] AVV **a** (*a poca distanza*) near, nearby, close (by); (: *nel tempo*) near, close; **vieni più vicino come closer; abitiamo qui vicino** we live near here; **stai vicino!** stay close to me!
b : **da vicino** close to; (*esaminare, seguire*) closely; (*sparare*) at close quarters; (*guardare*) close up; **da vicino è più bella** she's much prettier when you see her close up; **fai la fotografia da vicino** take the photograph close up
c : **vicino a** close to, near (to); (*accanto a*) beside, next to; **vivono vicino al mare** they live close to o near the sea; **era seduto vicino a me** he was sitting near me; (*accanto a*) he was sitting next to o beside me; **state vicino a vostro padre** (*anche fig*) stay close to your father; **ci sono andato vicino** (*fig: quasi indovinato*) I almost got it.
[3] SM/F neighbour (*Brit*), neighbor (*Am*); **i nostri vicini di casa** our next-door neighbo(u)rs; **il mio vicino di banco** the person at the desk next to mine, my neighbo(u)r.

vicissitudini [vitʃissi'tudini] SFPL trials and tribulations; **le vicissitudini della vita** the ups and downs of life.

vicolo ['vikolo] SM alley ▸ **vicolo cieco** blind alley.

video ['video] SM INV **a** (*TV: schermo*) screen; **ci sono dei disturbi al video** the picture is not very good **b** (*Inform: schermo*) screen; (: *videoterminale*) visual display unit **c** (*video musicale*) video.

videocamera [video'kamera] SF camcorder.

videocassetta [videokas'setta] SF videocassette.

videocitofono [videotʃi'tɔfono] SM video entryphone.

videogioco, chi [video'dʒɔko] SM video game.

videoleso, a [video'lezo] AGG, SM/F visually handicapped.

videoregistratore [videoredʒistra'tore] SM video (recorder).

videoscrittura [videoskrit'tura] SF computer printing.

videoteca, che [video'tɛka] SF video shop.

videotel® [video'tɛl] SM INV ≈ Videotex®.

videoterminale [videotermi'nale] SM visual display unit.

vidi ecc ['vidi] VB vedi **vedere**.

vidimare [vidi'mare] VT (*Amm*) to authenticate.

vidimazione [vidimat'tsjone] SF (*Amm*) authentication.

Vienna ['vjenna] SF Vienna.

viennese [vjen'nese] AGG, SM/F Viennese *inv*.

vietare [vje'tare] VT (*proibire*) to forbid; (*Amm: importazione, sosta*) to prohibit, ban; (: *sciopero, manifestazione*) to ban, prohibit; **vietare a qn di fare qc** to forbid sb to do sth, prohibit sb from doing sth; **il dottore mi ha vietato gli alcolici** the doctor has forbidden me to take alcohol; **hanno vietato il passaggio dei camion in centro** lorries have been banned from o prohibited in the centre; **nulla ti vieta di farlo** there is nothing to prevent o stop you doing it; **nulla vieta che io lo faccia** there is nothing to stop me; **e chi te lo vieta?** who's stopping you?

vietato, a [vje'tato] AGG (*vedi vb*) forbidden; prohibited; banned; **"vietato calpestare le aiuole"** "keep off the grass"; **"vietato fumare"** "no smoking"; **"vietato sporgersi dal finestrino"** "do not lean out of the window"; **"senso vietato"** (*Aut*) "no entry"; **"sosta vietata"** (*Aut*) "no parking"; **"vietata l'affissione"** "post o stick no bills", "bill stickers will be prosecuted"; **"vietato ai minori di 14/18 anni"** "prohibited to children under 14/18".

Vietnam [vjet'nam] SM: **il Vietnam** Vietnam.

vietnamita, i, e [vjetna'mita] AGG, SM/F, SM Vietnamese *inv*.

vieto, a ['vjɛto] AGG (*antiquato*) antiquated.

vigente [vi'dʒɛnte] AGG (*Dir: legge*) in force; (*fig*) current, in

use.

vigere ['vidʒere] VI DIF (*si usa solo alla terza persona*) to be in force; **in Italia vige ancora l'obbligo del servizio militare** in Italy national service is still compulsory; **in casa mia vige l'abitudine di**... at home we are in the habit of ... .

vigilante [vidʒi'lante] 1 AGG vigilant, watchful.
2 SM/F security guard.

vigilanza [vidʒi'lantsa] SF (*sorveglianza*: *di operai, alunni*) supervision; (: *di sospetti, criminali*) surveillance ▶**vigilanza notturna** night-watchman service.

vigilare [vidʒi'lare] 1 VT (*sorvegliare*: *bambini*) to watch over, keep an eye on; (: *operai, studenti, lavori*) to supervise; (: *sospetti, criminali*) to keep under surveillance.
2 VI (*aus* avere) (*provvedere a*): **vigilare che**... to make sure that ..., see to it that ... .

vigilato, a [vidʒi'lato] 1 AGG (*Dir*): **essere in libertà vigilata** to be on probation.
2 SM/F (*Dir*) person under police surveillance.

vigilatrice [vidʒila'tritʃe] SF: **vigilatrice d'infanzia** nursery assistant, nursery nurse (*Brit*).

vigile ['vidʒile] 1 AGG (*persona, occhio*) vigilant, watchful; (*cura*) vigilant.
2 SM/F (*anche:* **vigile urbano**) (traffic) policeman/policewoman; **i vigili urbani** *municipal police: their duties include enforcement of laws relating to traffic, commerce and public works and services.*
3 SM: **vigile del fuoco** fireman; **chiamare i vigili del fuoco** to call the fire brigade (*Brit*) *o* department (*Am*).

vigilia [vi'dʒilja] SF a (*giorno antecedente*) eve; **alla vigilia degli esami** on the eve of the exams ▶**vigilia di Capodanno** New Year's Eve ▶**vigilia di Natale** Christmas Eve b (*Rel*: *digiuno*) vigil c (*letter*: *veglia*) vigil.

vigliaccamente [viʎʎakka'mente] AVV in a cowardly way.

vigliaccheria [viʎʎakke'ria] SF (*qualità*) cowardice; (*azione*) act of cowardice, cowardly action; **è stata una vigliaccheria da parte sua** it was contemptible of him.

vigliacco, a, chi, che [viʎ'ʎakko] 1 AGG (*persona, azione*) cowardly; (: *spregevole*) contemptible.
2 SM/F a (*codardo*) coward b (*profittatore*) rogue, scoundrel.

vigna ['viɲɲa] SF vineyard.

vigneto [viɲ'ɲeto] SM (large) vineyard.

vignetta [viɲ'ɲetta] SF (*disegno*) illustration; (*umoristica*) cartoon.

vignettista, i, e [viɲɲet'tista] SM/F illustrator; (*di vignette umoristiche*) cartoonist.

vigogna [vi'goɲɲa] SF vicuña.

vigore [vi'gore] SM a (*gen*) vigour (*Brit*), vigor (*Am*), strength; (*fig: forza*) vigo(u)r, force; **nel suo pieno vigore** in his prime, in the prime of life; **perdere vigore** (*persona*) to lose strength; (*campagna elettorale*) to lose impetus; (*discorso, stile*) to become less vigorous *o* energetic; **riacquistare vigore** (*persona*) to regain one's strength
b (*Dir*): **essere in vigore** to be in force; **entrare in vigore** to come into force *o* effect; **non è più in vigore** it is no longer in force, it no longer applies.

vigoria [vigo'ria] SF vigour (*Brit*), vigor (*Am*), strength.

vigorosamente [vigorosa'mente] AVV (*opporsi, protestare*) strongly; (*remare*) vigorously.

vigoroso, a [vigo'roso] AGG (*gen*) vigorous; (*membra*) strong, powerful; (*stile*) vigorous, energetic; (*resistenza*) vigorous, strenuous; **una vigorosa stretta di mano** a firm handshake.

vile ['vile] 1 AGG (*vigliacco*) cowardly; (*spregevole*) contemptible, base, low, mean; **una vile menzogna** a wicked lie; **il vile denaro** filthy lucre. 2 SM/F coward.

vilipendere [vili'pɛndere] VT IRREG to despise, scorn.

vilipendio, di [vili'pɛndjo] SM (*Dir*) contempt, scorn; **vilipendio alla bandiera** contempt for the national flag.

vilipeso, a [vili'peso] PP di **vilipendere**.

villa ['villa] SF (*in città*) detached house; (*in campagna*) country house; (*al mare*) villa.

villaggio, gi [vil'laddʒo] SM village ▶**villaggio globale** global village ▶**villaggio olimpico** Olympic village ▶**villaggio residenziale** commuter town ▶**villaggio turistico** holiday village (*Brit*).

villanamente [villana'mente] AVV rudely.

villanata [villa'nata] SF (*azione*) rude act, impolite act; (*parola*) piece of rudeness.

villania [villa'nia] SF (*sgarbataggine*) rudeness, bad manners *pl*, lack of manners; **è stata una villania da parte sua** it was very rude of him; **fare** (*o* **dire**) **una villania a qn** to be rude to sb.

villano, a [vil'lano] 1 AGG rude, ill-mannered; **modi villani** bad manners.
2 SM/F a (*maleducato*) lout, boor b (*letter*: *contadino*) peasant; **un villano rifatto** (*pegg*) a nouveau riche, an upstart.

villanzone, a [villan'tsone] SM/F ill-bred person, boor.

villeggiante [villed'dʒante] SM/F holiday-maker (*Brit*), vacationer (*Am*), vacationist (*Am*).

villeggiare [villed'dʒare] VI (*aus* avere) to holiday (*Brit*), spend one's holidays (*Brit*), vacation (*Am*).

villeggiatura [villeddʒa'tura] SF holiday(s *pl*) (*Brit*), vacation (*Am*); **andare/essere in villeggiatura** to go/be on holiday *o* vacation; **luogo di villeggiatura** (holiday *o* vacation) resort.

villetta [vil'letta] SF, **villino** [vil'lino] SM (*in città*) small (detached) house (*with a garden*); (*in campagna*) cottage.

villoso, a [vil'loso] AGG hairy.

vilmente [vil'mente] AVV (*vigliaccamente*) like a coward, in a cowardly way; (*spregevolmente*) contemptibly.

viltà [vil'ta] SF INV cowardice *no pl*; **atto di viltà** act of cowardice, cowardly act.

viluppo [vi'luppo] SM tangle.

Viminale [vimi'nale] SM *the Ministry of the Interior, located on one of the Seven Hills of Rome, from which it takes its name.*

vimine ['vimine] SM (*Bot*) osier; **di vimini** (*sedia*) wicker *attr*, wickerwork *attr*.

vinaio, ai [vi'najo] SM wine merchant.

vincente [vin'tʃente] AGG winning; **carta vincente** winning card; (*fig*) trump card.

vincenzina [vintʃen'tsina] SF Sister of Charity.

vincere ['vintʃere] VB IRREG 1 VT a (*gen*) to win; **vincere una causa** (*Dir*) to win a case *o* suit; **vincere un premio** to win a prize
b (*sconfiggere: nemico*) to defeat, vanquish; (: *avversario*) to beat; **vincere qn a tennis** to beat sb at tennis
c (*superare: sentimenti*) to overcome; (*avere ragione di*) to get the better of, outdo; **fu vinto dalla stanchezza** tiredness overcame him; **lasciarsi vincere dalla tentazione** to succumb *o* yield to temptation; **vincere qn in** (*abilità*) to outdo *o* surpass sb in; (*bellezza*) to surpass sb in; **vuole sempre averla vinta** he always wants to have the upper hand.

2 VI (aus avere) a (in gioco, battaglia) to win; **vinca il migliore** may the best man win b (prevalere) to win, prevail. 3 **vincersi** VR to control o.s.

vincita ['vintʃita] SF (il vincere) win, victory; (cosa vinta) winnings pl.

vincitore, trice [vintʃi'tore] 1 AGG winning, victorious. 2 SM/F (in gara) winner; (in battaglia) victor, winner.

vincolante [vinko'lante] AGG binding.

vincolare [vinko'lare] VT a (Dir) to bind; (fig: sogg: famiglia, lavoro) to tie down b (Fin): **vincolare una somma in banca** to place a sum on fixed deposit.

vincolato, a [vinko'lato] AGG (vedi vt) bound; tied; **deposito vincolato** fixed deposit.

vincolo ['vinkolo] SM (gen) bond, tie; (di sangue) tie; (Dir) encumbrance, obligation; **libero da ogni vincolo** free from all ties; (Dir) unencumbered.

vinicolo, a [vi'nikolo] AGG wine attr; **regione vinicola** wine-producing area.

vinificatore [vinifika'tore] SM wine-maker, wine-producer.

vinificazione [vinifikat'tsjone] SF wine-making.

vinile [vi'nile] SM vinyl.

vinilpelle® [vinil'pɛlle] SF Leatherette ®.

vino ['vino] SM wine; **lista o carta dei vini** wine list; **vino bianco/rosso/rosato** white/red/rosé wine; **buon vino fa buon sangue** (Proverbio) good wine makes good cheer ►**vin brûlé** mulled wine.

vinsanto [vin'santo] SM type of sweet white wine.

vinsi ecc ['vinsi] VB vedi **vincere**.

vinto, a ['vinto] 1 PP di **vincere**. 2 AGG a (sconfitto) defeated, beaten b (oggetto): **i soldi vinti al gioco** money won gambling; **darla vinta a qn** to let sb have his (o her) way; **darsi per vinto** to give up, give in; **vuol sempre avere partita vinta** he always wants to have the upper hand. 3 SM/F (gen) loser; (Mil): **i vinti** SMPL the defeated (side), the vanquished.

viola¹ ['vi'ɔla] 1 SF (Bot) violet ►**viola del pensiero** pansy. 2 SM INV (colore) violet, purple.

viola² [vi'ɔla] SF (Mus) viola.

violacciocca, che [violat'tʃɔkka] SF (Bot) stock.

violaceo, a [vio'latʃeo] AGG mauvish.

violare [vio'lare] VT (gen) to violate; (legge) to violate, infringe, break; (promessa) to break; (domicilio) to break into; (tempio) to desecrate; (donna) to rape; **violare la privacy di qn** to invade sb's privacy.

violazione [violat'tsjone] SF (vedi vb) violation; infringement, breach; breaking; breaking into; desecration ►**violazione di domicilio** (Dir) unlawful entry.

violentare [violen'tare] VT to use violence on; (sessualmente) to rape; (fig: coscienza) to outrage; **in questo modo violenti la sua volontà** you are forcing him to do it against his will.

violentemente [violente'mente] AVV violently.

violento, a [vio'lento] 1 AGG (gen) violent; (suono) loud; (luce) blinding; (colore) loud, garish; (incendio) raging; **usare un tono violento** to express o.s. with violence; **usare modi violenti** to use violence; **morire di morte violenta** to die a violent death. 2 SM/F violent person.

violenza [vio'lɛntsa] SF (gen) violence; (di vento, temporale) violence, force; **ricorrere alla/far uso della violenza** to resort to/use violence; **ottenere qc con la violenza** to obtain sth by violent means o by the use of violence ►**violenza carnale** (Dir) rape.

violetta [vio'letta] SF (Bot) violet.

violetto, a [vio'letto] AGG, SM (colore) violet.

violinista, i, e [violi'nista] SM/F violinist.

violino [vio'lino] SM violin; **essere teso come una corda di violino** (fig) to be very tense; **primo violino** first violin; **chiave di violino** treble clef.

violoncellista, i, e [violontʃel'lista] SM/F cellist, cello player.

violoncello [violon'tʃɛllo] SM violoncello, cello.

viottolo [vi'ɔttolo] SM path, track.

VIP [vip] SM/F INV (= Very Important Person) VIP.

vipera ['vipera] SF (Zool) viper, adder; (fig) catty person; **ha una lingua di vipera** she has a vicious tongue.

viperino, a [vipe'rino] AGG (Zool) viper attr, viper's attr; (fig) venomous.

viraggio, gi [vi'raddʒo] SM a (Naut) coming about; (Aer) turn b (Fot) toning.

virago [vi'rago] SF virago.

virale [vi'rale] AGG viral.

virare [vi'rare] VI (aus avere) a (Naut) to come about; (Aer) to turn; **virare di bordo** to change course b (Fot) to tone.

virata [vi'rata] SF (vedi vb a) coming about; turning; change of course; (Sport: nuoto) turn; **la virata del governo in materia fiscale** the government's U-turn on fiscal policy.

Virgilio [vir'dʒiljo] SM Virgil.

virgola ['virgola] SF (nella punteggiatura) comma; (Mat) (decimal) point; **non c'è una virgola fuori posto** (fig: in uno scritto) it's an excellent piece of work; **non cambiare una virgola** (fig) don't change a thing; **punto e virgola** semicolon.

virgolette [virgo'lette] SFPL quotation marks, inverted commas (Brit); **tra virgolette** in quotation marks o inverted commas.

virgulto [vir'gulto] SM (Bot) shoot; (letter fig: discendente) scion.

virile [vi'rile] AGG (aspetto, voce) masculine; (atteggiamento, lineamenti) manly, virile; (bellezza) male attr; (stile) vigorous, virile; (linguaggio) firm; **età virile** manhood.

virilità [virili'ta] SF (vedi agg) masculinity; manliness; virility; vigour (Brit), vigor (Am); firmness.

virilmente [viril'mente] AVV in a manly way.

virologia [virolo'dʒia] SF virology.

virtù [vir'tu] SF INV a (Rel) virtue; (pregio, qualità) virtue, quality; (virtuosità, castità) virtuousness; **un modello di virtù** a paragon of virtue; **fare di necessità virtù** to make a virtue of necessity b (capacità: di persona) ability; (proprietà: di erbe, sostanze) property; **in virtù di questa legge** by virtue of this law; **in virtù della nostra amicizia** for friendship's sake.

virtuale [virtu'ale] AGG (gen) potential; (Fis) virtual; **realtà virtuale** virtual reality.

virtualmente [virtual'mente] AVV potentially.

virtuosamente [virtuosa'mente] AVV virtuously.

virtuosismo [virtuo'sizmo] SM (abilità) virtuosity; **esibirsi in inutili virtuosismi** to show off.

virtuoso, a [virtu'oso] 1 AGG virtuous. 2 SM/F (del violino, pennello) virtuoso, master/mistress.

virulento, a [viru'lɛnto] AGG virulent.

virulenza [viru'lɛntsa] SF virulence.

virus ['virus] SM INV (Med, Inform) virus.

visagista, i, e [viza'dʒista] SM/F beautician.

vis-à-vis [viz a 'vi] AVV: eravamo seduti vis-à-vis we were sitting opposite each other.

viscerale [viʃʃe'rale] AGG (Med) visceral; (fig) profound, deep-rooted.

viscere ['viʃʃere] [1] SM (Anat) internal organ.
[2] SFPL (di animale) entrails pl; (fig) depths pl, bowels pl; nelle viscere della terra in the bowels of the earth.

vischio ['viskjo] SM a (Bot) mistletoe b (pania) birdlime.

vischiosità [viskjosi'ta] SF (collosità) stickiness; (Fis, Chim) viscosity.

vischioso, a [vis'kjoso] AGG (colloso) sticky; (viscoso) viscous.

viscidamente [viʃʃida'mente] AVV (vedi agg) slimily; smarmily.

viscidità [viʃʃidi'ta] SF (vedi agg) sliminess; smarminess.

viscido, a ['viʃʃido] AGG (lumaca, pelle) slimy; (fig: persona) smarmy.

visciola ['viʃʃola] SF sour cherry.

visconte, essa [vis'konte] SM/F viscount/viscountess.

viscosa [vis'kosa] SF viscose.

viscosità [viskosi'ta] SF viscosity.

viscoso, a [vis'koso] AGG viscous.

visibile [vi'zibile] AGG (gen) visible; (imbarazzo) obvious, evident, visible; (progresso) clear, perceptible.

visibilio [vizi'biljo] SM: andare in visibilio (per qc) to go into ecstasies o raptures (over sth).

visibilità [vizibili'ta] SF visibility.

visibilmente [vizibil'mente] AVV visibly.

visiera [vi'zjɛra] SF (di cappello) peak; (di elmo, casco) visor.

Visigoto [vizi'gɔto] SM Visigoth.

visionare [vizjo'nare] VT (gen) to look at, examine; (Cine) to screen.

visionario, ria, ri, rie [vizjo'narjo] AGG, SM/F visionary.

visione [vi'zjone] SF a (gen, Rel) vision; (scena) sight; (idea, concetto) view; ma tu hai le visioni! you must be seeing things!; avere una visione limitata della realtà to have a narrow view of reality
b (atto del vedere) vision, sight; prendere visione di qc to have a look at sth, examine sth, look sth over; mandare qc in visione (Comm) to send sth on approval; prima/seconda visione (Cine) first/second showing, first run/rerun; trasmettiamo in prima visione il film... we're showing the first screening of the film ...; cinema di prima visione cinema where films are shown on first release.

visir [vi'zir] SM INV (Storia) vizier.

visita ['vizita] SF a (gen) visit; (di amico, rappresentante) visit, call; far visita a qn [OR] andare in visita da qn to visit sb, pay sb a visit; in visita ufficiale in Italia on an official visit to Italy; biglietto da visita (visiting) card; abbiamo visite we have visitors o guests
b (turistica: di città) tour; (: di museo) tour, visit; la visita del castello dura 2 ore the tour of the castle takes 2 hours, it takes 2 hours to go round the castle ▶visita guidata guided tour
c (Med: esame) examination; il medico sta facendo il giro delle visite the doctor is doing his rounds; orario di visite (ospedale) visiting hours; (ambulatorio) consulting o surgery (Brit) hours; marcare visita (Mil) to report sick ▶visita di controllo checkup ▶visita domiciliare

house call ▶visita fiscale house call made on state employee by doctor to verify condition of patient ▶visita di leva (Mil) medical (Brit) o physical (Am) examination.

visitare [vizi'tare] VT a (andare in visita) to visit, call on, go and see; (rappresentante) to call on; andare a visitare qn to go and see o visit sb
b (museo) to visit, go round; ci ha fatto visitare la casa/il castello he showed us round the house/castle
c (Med) to examine; visitare i pazienti a casa to see patients at home; il medico sta visitando the doctor is seeing o receiving patients now; il medico visita solo il giovedì the doctor only sees patients on Thursdays; bisogna che mi faccia visitare I must go and have a medical examination o a checkup.

visitatore, trice [vizita'tore] SM/F a (ospite) visitor, guest
b (turista) visitor, tourist.

visivamente [viziva'mente] AVV visually.

visivo, a [vi'zivo] AGG visual; memoria visiva visual memory; gli organi visivi the eyes.

viso ['vizo] SM face; crema per il viso face cream; guardare in viso qn to look sb in the face, look straight at sb; fare buon viso a cattivo gioco to make the best of things; a viso aperto openly ▶viso pallido (uomo bianco) paleface.

visone [vi'zone] SM (Zool) mink; (pelliccia) mink (coat).

visore [vi'zore] SM (Fot) viewer.

vispo, a ['vispo] AGG (bambino) lively; (vecchietto) sprightly; (occhi) bright.

vissi ecc ['vissi] VB vedi vivere.

vissuto, a [vis'suto] [1] PP di vivere.
[2] AGG a : storia di vita vissuta story from real life b (persona) experienced, who has had many experiences.

vista ['vista] SF a (gen) sight; (capacità visiva) eyesight, sight; avere la vista buona to have good eyesight; avere la vista corta/lunga to be short-/long-sighted; (fig) to be short-/far-sighted; ho avuto un improvviso abbassamento della vista my eyesight suddenly got worse; difetti della vista eye problems; esame della vista eye test; occhiali da vista glasses; sottrarsi alla vista di qn to disappear from sb's sight; mettersi in vista to draw attention to o.s.; (pegg) to show off; essere in vista (persona) to be in the public eye; terra in vista! land ahoy!; è in vista una ripresa economica economic recovery is in sight; a prima vista at first sight; conoscere qn di vista to know sb by sight; in vista di qc in view of sth; sparare a vista to shoot on sight; pagabile a vista payable on demand; avere in vista qc to have sth in view; a vista d'occhio as far as the eye can see; (fig) before one's very eyes; perdere qn di vista (anche fig) to lose sight of sb
b (veduta) view; con vista sul lago with a view over the lake.

vistare [vis'tare] VT to approve; (Amm: passaporto) to visa.

visto, a ['visto] [1] PP di vedere.
[2] SM a (segno) tick (Brit), check (Am); (Amm: approvazione) approval b (Amm) visa ▶visto d'ingresso entry visa ▶visto permanente permanent visa ▶visto di soggiorno ▶ visto di transito transit visa.

vistosamente [vistosa'mente] AVV (vestirsi) gaudily, showily, garishly.

vistosità [vistosi'ta] SF gaudiness, showiness, garishness.

vistoso, a [vis'toso] AGG (colore) garish; (bellezza) flashy; (scritta, insegna) showy; (aumento) enormous, huge.

visuale [vizu'ale] ① AGG visual.
② SF (gen) view; (Ottica) line of vision; (nel tiro) line of sight; **togliere la visuale a qn** to block sb's view.
visualizzare [vizualid'dzare] VT to visualize.
visualizzatore [vizualiddza'tore] SM (Inform) display, visual display unit, VDU; **visualizzatore a cristalli liquidi** liquid crystal display.
visualizzazione [vizualiddzat'tsjone] SF (Inform) display.
vita[1] ['vita] SF **a** (gen) life; **essere in vita** to be alive; **perdere la vita** to lose one's life; **far ritornare in vita qn** to bring sb back to life; **dare la vita per qn/qc** to give one's life for sb/sth; **pieno di vita** full of life; **ha dato un po' di vita alla festa** he livened up the party a bit
b (modo di vivere) life, lifestyle; **nella vita quotidiana** o **di ogni giorno** in everyday life; **la vita da studente** life as a student; **la vita in Scozia** life in Scotland; **la vita degli animali** animal life; **condurre una vita attiva** to lead an active life; **avere una doppia vita** to lead a double life; **cambiare vita** to change one's way of life o one's lifestyle
c (mezzi di sussistenza) living; **guadagnarsi la vita** to earn one's living; **il costo della vita** the cost of living; **la vita è cara a Parigi** it's expensive to live in Paris
d (durata) life, lifetime; **ti amerò per tutta la vita** I'll love you for ever o all my life; **ho lavorato per tutta la vita** I've worked all my life; **capita una volta sola nella vita** it only happens once in a lifetime; **membro a vita** life member; **carcere a vita** life imprisonment; **avere sette vite** to have nine lives; **non basterebbe una vita per spiegartelo** it would take a lifetime to explain it to you; **vita media** average life expectancy
e (biografia) life (story); **mi ha raccontato tutta la sua vita** she told me her life story o the story of her life
f (fraseologia): **l'altra vita** the hereafter; **o la borsa o la vita!** your money or your life!; **ci metti una vita!** you are taking ages!; **è la vita!** that's life!; **che vita da cani!** what a dog's life!; **fare la vita** (euf) to be on the game (Brit); **fare la bella vita** to lead the good life o a life of pleasure; **finché c'è vita c'è speranza** while there's life there's hope; **pena la vita** on pain of death; **rendere la vita difficile a qn** to make life difficult for sb; **sapere vita, morte e miracoli di qn** to know all the ins and outs of sb's life, know all there is to know about sb.
vita[2] ['vita] SF (Anat) waist; **abito a vita alta/bassa** dress with a high/low waist; **punto (di) vita** (Sartoria) waist; **su con la vita!** (fig) cheer up.
vitale [vi'tale] AGG **a** (gen) vital; (vivace: persona) lively, vital; **spazio vitale** living space **b** (che può vivere) viable.
vitalità [vitali'ta] SF vitality, vigour (Brit), vigor (Am).
vitalizio, zia, zi, zie [vita'littsjo] ① AGG life attr.
② SM (Dir) life annuity.
vitamina [vita'mina] SF vitamin.
vitaminico, a, ci, che [vita'miniko] AGG vitamin attr.
vitaminizzare [vitaminid'dzare] VT to enrich with vitamins.
vitaminizzato, a [vitaminid'dzato] AGG with added vitamins, vitamin-enriched.
vite[1] ['vite] SF (Bot) (grape)vine ▶**vite del Canada** Virginia creeper.
vite[2] ['vite] SF **a** (Tecn) screw; **giro di vite** (anche fig) turn of the screw; **tappo a vite** screw(-on) cap o top ▶**vite senza fine** endless screw **b** (Aer) (tail)spin.
vitella [vi'tɛlla] SF **a** (Zool) calf **b** (Culin) veal.
vitello [vi'tɛllo] SM **a** (Zool) calf **b** (Culin) veal; **vitello**

tonnato veal in tuna fish sauce **c** (pelle) calf(skin).
vitellone [vitel'lone] SM **a** (Zool) bullock **b** (Culin) tender young beef **c** (fig) loafer.
viticcio, ci [vi'tittʃo] SM (Bot) tendril.
viticoltore [vitikol'tore] SM vine grower.
viticoltura [vitikol'tura] SF vine growing.
vitreo, a ['vitreo] AGG (sostanza) vitreous; (occhio, sguardo) glassy.
vittima ['vittima] SF (gen) victim; (di incidente) casualty, victim; **fare la vittima** to play the martyr.
vittimismo [vitti'mizmo] SM self-pity.
vittimista, i, e [vitti'mista] SM/F self-pitying person.
vittimistico, a, ci, che [vitti'mistiko] AGG self-pitying.
vitto ['vitto] SM (cibo) food; (in pensioni) board ▶**vitto e alloggio** room and board, board and lodging.
vittoria [vit'tɔrja] SF victory; **cantar vittoria** to crow (over one's victory).
vittoriano, a [vitto'rjano] AGG, SM/F Victorian.
vittoriosamente [vittorjosa'mente] AVV victoriously, triumphantly.
vittorioso, a [vitto'rjoso] AGG victorious, triumphant.
vituperare [vitupe'rare] VT (letter) to berate, rail at o against.
vituperio, ri [vitu'pɛrjo] (letter) SM insult.
viuzza [vi'uttsa] SF (in città) alley.
viva ['viva] ESCL long live; **viva il re!** long live the king!; **viva il Milan!** three cheers for Milan!
vivacchiare [vivak'kjare] VI (aus avere) to scrape a living.
vivace [vi'vatʃe] AGG **a** (gen) lively; (intelligenza) lively, keen; (colore) vivid, brilliant, bright **b** (Mus) vivace.
vivacemente [vivatʃe'mente] AVV (discutere, giocare) in a lively way; (contrastare: colori) vividly.
vivacità [vivatʃi'ta] SF (vedi agg) liveliness; keenness; vividness, brilliance, brightness.
vivacizzare [vivatʃid'dzare] VT to liven up.
vivaio, ai [vi'vajo] SM (di piante) nursery; (di pesci) fish farm, hatchery; (fig) breeding ground.
vivamente [viva'mente] AVV (commuoversi) deeply, profoundly; (ringraziare) sincerely, warmly.
vivanda [vi'vanda] SF (cibo) food no pl; (piatto) dish.
vivente [vi'vɛnte] ① AGG living, alive; **è il ritratto vivente del nonno** he is the spitting image of his grandfather; **l'autore è ancora vivente** the author is still alive; **è il massimo poeta vivente** he is the greatest living poet.
② SMPL: **i viventi** the living.
vivere ['vivere] VB IRREG ① VI (aus essere) **a** (gen) to live; (essere vivo) to live, be alive; **vivere fino a 100 anni** to live to be 100; **non gli resta molto da vivere** he hasn't long to live; **ha cessato di vivere** he is dead; **finché vivrò** as long as I live; **chi vivrà vedrà** only time will tell; **vivi e lascia vivere** live and let live; **vivere fuori dalla realtà** to live in another world, be out of touch with reality
b (abitare) to live; **vivo in campagna** I live in the country; **viviamo insieme** we live together
c (sostentarsi): **vivere (di)** to live (on); (cibarsi): **vivere di** to live on, feed on; **io vivo di poco o niente** I live on little or nothing; **ho giusto di che vivere** I have just enough to live on; **guadagnarsi da vivere dando lezioni di piano** to earn one's living by giving piano lessons; **vivere d'aria e d'amore** to live on love alone; **vivere alla giornata** to live from day to day; **vivere nell'indigenza** to live in utter poverty; **vivere da signore** to live like a lord; **vivere nel lusso** to live a life of luxury
d (comportarsi) to live; **devi ancora imparare a vivere**

you've still got a lot to learn about life **e** (*Tip*): **vive stet.**

2 VT (*vita*) to live; (*avvenimento, esperienza*) to live through, go through; **vivere una vita tranquilla** to lead a quiet life; **vivere giorni di dolore** to live through a sad period; **ha vissuto la scuola come una punizione** he hated his school days.

3 SM life; **lo faccio per il quieto vivere!** anything for a quiet life!

viveri ['viveri] SMPL food *sg*, provisions, supplies.

viveur [vi'vœr] SM INV pleasure-seeker.

vivido, a ['vivido] AGG (*ricordo*) vivid, very clear; (*luce*) bright, brilliant; (*colore*) bright, vivid; **di vivido ingegno** quick-witted, bright.

vivificare [vivifi'kare] VT (*materia*) to give life to, enliven; (*ravvivare: piante*) to revive, refresh; (*fig: racconto*) to bring to life.

viviparo, a [vi'viparo] AGG viviparous.

vivisezionare [vivisettsjo'nare] VT to vivisect.

vivisezione [vviset'tsjone] SF vivisection.

vivo, a ['vivo] **1** AGG **a** (*in vita*) alive, living; (*in uso: espressione, tradizione*) living; **è ancora vivo** he is still alive *o* living; **esperimenti su animali vivi** experiments on live *o* living animals; **lingua viva** living language; **non c'era anima viva** there wasn't a (living) soul there; **me lo mangerei vivo!** (*fig*) I could eat him alive!, I could murder him!; **essere più morto che vivo** to be more dead than alive

b (*intenso: ricordo*) vivid, very clear; (: *emozione*) intense; (: *luce*) brilliant, bright; (: *colore*) bright, vivid; **sguardo vivo** bright eyes; **viva commozione** intense emotion; **con vivo rammarico** with deep regret; **congratulazioni vivissime** sincerest *o* heartiest congratulations; **con i più vivi ringraziamenti** with deepest *o* warmest thanks; **cuocere a fuoco vivo** to cook on a high flame *o* heat

c (*vivace: persona*) lively, vivacious; (: *città, strada, discussione*) lively, animated; **ha un'intelligenza molto viva** he has a very lively mind

d (*fraseologia*): **farsi vivo** to show one's face; **fatti vivo!** get in touch!; **è tanto che non si fa vivo** he hasn't been in touch for ages; **spese vive** immediate *o* out-of-pocket expenses; **spigolo vivo** sharp edge; **l'ho sentito dalla sua viva voce** I heard it from the horse's mouth *o* from his own lips.

2 SM **a** (*essere*) living being; **i vivi** SMPL the living

b : **entrare nel vivo di una questione** to get to the heart of a matter; **registrazione dal vivo** live recording; **ritrarre dal vivo** to paint from life; **pungere** *o* **colpire qn nel vivo** to cut sb to the quick.

vivrò *ecc* [viv'rɔ] VB *vedi* **vivere.**

viziare [vit'tsjare] VT **a** (*persona*) to spoil **b** (*Dir*) to invalidate; (*rovinare: rapporti, ragionamento*) to ruin, spoil.

viziato, a [vit'tsjato] AGG **a** (*persona*) spoilt **b** (*Dir*) invalid, invalidated; (*rapporti, ragionamento*) ruined, spoiled **c** (*aria*) stale, foul.

vizio, zi ['vittsjo] SM **a** (*morale*) vice; (*cattiva abitudine*) bad habit; **vivere nel vizio** to live a life of vice **b** (*Dir*) flaw, defect ►**vizio di forma** legal flaw *o* irregularity ►**vizio procedurale** procedural error **c** (*Med*): **vizio cardiaco** heart defect.

viziosamente [vittsjosa'mente] AVV (*vivere*) in a depraved way.

vizioso, a [vit'tsjoso] **1** AGG **a** (*corrotto*) depraved; **vita viziosa** life of vice **b** (*difettoso*) incorrect, wrong; **circolo vizioso** vicious circle.

2 SM/F depraved person.

vizzo, a ['vittso] AGG (*Bot*) withered; (*fig: pelle, guance*) withered, wrinkled.

V.le ABBR (= *viale*) Ave. (= *Avenue*).

v.o. ABBR (*Cine*: = *versione originale*) original version.

vocabolario, ri [vokabo'larjo] SM (*dizionario*) dictionary; (*lessico personale*) vocabulary.

vocabolo [vo'kabolo] SM word.

vocale[1] [vo'kale] AGG (*Anat, Mus*) vocal.

vocale[2] [vo'kale] SF vowel.

vocalico, a, ci, che [vo'kaliko] AGG vowel *attr*, vocalic.

vocalizzare [vokalid'dzare] VI, VT to vocalize.

vocativo, a [voka'tivo] AGG, SM vocative.

vocazione [vokat'tsjone] SF (*anche Rel*) vocation; (*inclinazione naturale*) (natural) bent; **non ho vocazione per la matematica** I'm not cut out to study Maths (*Brit*) *o* Math (*Am*), I have no gift for Math(s).

voce ['votʃe] SF **a** (*gen*) voice; **ho avuto un abbassamento di voce** I lost my voice; **la voce della coscienza** the voice of conscience; **parlare a alta/bassa voce** to speak in a loud/low *o* soft voice; **con un fil di voce** in a weak voice; **dar voce a qc** to voice *o* give voice to sth; **dare una voce a qn** to call sb, give sb a call; **fare la voce grossa** to raise one's voice; **a gran voce** in a loud voice, loudly; **l'hanno acclamato a gran voce** they greeted him with thunderous applause; **me l'ha detto a voce** he told me himself *o* in person; **te lo dico a voce** I'll tell you when I see you; **a una voce** unanimously

b (*opinione*) opinion; (*diceria*) rumour (*Brit*), rumor (*Am*); **aver voce in capitolo** to have a say in the matter; **circolano delle voci secondo cui il governo si dimetterà** it is rumo(u)red *o* rumo(u)r has it that the government will resign; **voci di corridoio** rumo(u)rs

c (*Mus*) voice; **cantare a due voci** to sing in two parts

d (*Gramm*) voice

e (*vocabolo*) word; (*di elenco, bilancio*) item; (*di dizionario*) entry; **è una voce antiquata** it is an obsolete term *o* word.

vociare [vo'tʃare] **1** VI (*aus avere*) to shout, yell.

2 SM shouting.

vociferare [votʃife'rare] VI (*aus avere*): **si vocifera che...** it's rumoured (*Brit*) *o* rumored (*Am*) that ....

vocio [vo'tʃio] SM shouting.

vodka ['vɔdka] SF INV vodka.

voga[1] ['voga] SF (*Naut*) rowing.

voga[2] ['voga] SF: **essere in voga** (*abito*) to be fashionable, be in fashion *o* in vogue; (*canzone*) to be popular.

vogare [vo'gare] VI (*aus avere*) to row.

vogata [vo'gata] SF (*colpo di remi*) stroke; **fare una vogata** to go for a row, go rowing.

vogatore, trice [voga'tore] **1** SM/F oarsman/oarswoman.

2 SM rowing machine.

vogherò *ecc* [voge'rɔ] VB *vedi* **vogare.**

voglia ['vɔʎʎa] SF **a** (*desiderio*) wish, desire; (*di donna incinta*) craving; **aver voglia di qc/di fare qc** to feel like sth/like doing sth; (*più forte*) to want sth/to do sth; **morire dalla voglia di fare qc/di qc** to be dying *o* longing to do sth/for sth; **e chi ne ha voglia?** I don't feel like it at the moment; **hai voglia di gridare, tanto non ti sente!** (*fam*) he can't hear you however much you shout

b (*disposizione*) will; **di buona voglia** willingly; **contro voglia** ⟨OR⟩ **di mala voglia** unwillingly **c** (*desiderio sessuale*) desire, lust **d** (*macchia della pelle*) birthmark.

voglio *ecc* ['vɔʎʎo] VB *vedi* **volere**.

vogliosamente [voʎʎosa'mente] AVV longingly, yearningly.

voglioso, a [voʎ'ʎoso] AGG (*sguardo*) longing; (*sessualmente*) full of desire.

voi ['voi] PRON PERS **a** (*soggetto*) you; **voi tutti lo sapete** all of you know, you all know; **voi che ne dite?** what do you think?; **voi italiani** you Italians; **voi stessi(e)** you yourselves; **siete stati voi a dirglielo** it was you who told him, you were the ones to tell him

b (*oggetto: per dare rilievo, con preposizione*) you; **vuol vedere proprio voi** it's you he wants to see; **parlo a voi, non a lui** I'm talking to YOU, not to him; **tocca a voi** it's your turn; **da voi** (*nel vostro paese*) where you come from, in your country; (*a casa vostra*) at your house

c (*comparazioni*) you; **sono alti come voi** they are as tall as you (are); **faremo come voi** we'll do as you do, we'll do the same as you; **siamo più giovani di voi** we are younger than you.

voialtri, e ['vojaltri] PRON PERS you.

voilà [vwa'la] ESCL: **e voilà!** hey presto!

voile [vwal] SM INV voile.

vol. ABBR (= *volume*) vol.

volano [vo'lano] SM **a** (*palla*) shuttlecock; (*gioco*) badminton **b** (*Tecn*) flywheel.

volant [vɔ'lã] SM INV frill.

volante[1] [vo'lante] [1] AGG (*gen*) flying; (*foglio*) loose; (*indossatrice*) freelance.

[2] SF (*Polizia: anche*: **squadra volante**) flying squad.

volante[2] [vo'lante] SM (*Aut*) (steering) wheel; **essere al volante** to drive, be at the wheel; **un asso del volante** ace driver.

volantinaggio [volanti'naddʒo] SM leafleting.

volantinare [volanti'nare] VI (*aus* **avere**) to leaflet.

volantino [volan'tino] SM (*foglietto*) leaflet, pamphlet.

volare [vo'lare] VI (*aus* **avere** *o* **essere**) **a** (*aereo, uccello, passeggero*) to fly; **far volare un aquilone** to fly a kite

b (*fig: tempo*) to fly, go by very quickly; (: *notizie*) to spread quickly; (: *pugni, insulti*) to fly; **quando ho sentito la notizia sono volato da lei** when I heard the news I rushed round to her place; **il pallone è volato fuori dal campo** the ball flew off the pitch; **volare in cielo** *o* **paradiso** (*euf: morire*) to go to heaven

c (*allontanarsi*): **volare via** (*cappello, fogli*) to blow away, fly away *o* off; (*fig: tempo*) to fly; (*cadere*): **volare giù** (*vaso, persona*) to fall.

volata [vo'lata] SF **a** (*fig: corsa*) rush; **faccio una volata a casa** I am just going to pop home; **passare da volata da qn** to drop in on sb briefly **b** (*Ciclismo*) final sprint; **vincere in volata** to sprint home to win **c**: **volata di uccelli** (*stormo*) flock *o* flight of birds.

volatile [vo'latile] [1] AGG (*Chim*) volatile.

[2] SM (*uccello*) bird, winged creature.

volatilizzare [volatilid'dzare] [1] VT (*Chim*) to volatilize.

[2] **volatilizzarsi** VIP (*Chim*) to volatilize; (*fig*) to vanish, disappear.

vol-au-vent ['vɔlovã] SM INV (*Culin*) vol-au-vent.

volée [vɔle] SF INV (*Tennis*) volley; **volée smorzata** drop volley.

volente [vo'lɛnte] AGG: **verrai volente o nolente** you'll

come whether you like it or not, you'll come willy-nilly.

volenterosamente [volenterosa'mente] AVV willingly.

volenteroso, a [volente'roso] AGG willing, keen.

volentieri [volen'tjɛri] AVV willingly, gladly; **spesso e volentieri** frequently, very often; **volentieri!** with pleasure!, I'd be glad to!

volere [vo'lere] VB IRREG [1] VT (*nei tempi composti prende l'ausiliare del verbo che accompagna*) **a** (*gen*) to want; **voglio una risposta da voi** I want an answer from you; **voglio che ti lavi le mani** I want you to wash your hands; **che tu lo voglia o no** whether you like it or not; **vuol venire a tutti i costi** he wants to come at all costs; **quanto vuole per quel quadro?** how much does he want for that painting?

b (*desiderare*): **vorrei del pane** I would like some bread; **vorrei farlo/che tu lo facessi** I would like to do it/you to do it; **mi vorrebbero vedere sposato** they would like to see me married, they would like me to marry; **se volete, possiamo partire subito** if you like *o* want, we can leave right away; **come vuoi** as you like; **volevo parlartene** I meant to talk to you about it; **se volesse potrebbe farcela** he could do it if he wanted to

c (*con funzione di richiesta o offerta*): **vuole** *o* **vorrebbe essere così gentile da...?** would you be so kind as to ...?; **vuoi chiudere la finestra?** would you mind closing the window?; **non vuole accomodarsi?** won't you sit down?; **vogliamo sederci?** shall we sit down?; **prendine quanto vuoi** help yourself, take as many (*o* much) as you like; **ne vuoi ancora?** would you like some more?; **vuoi che io faccia qualcosa?** would you like me to do something?, shall I do something?; **ma vuoi star zitto!** oh, do be quiet!

d (*consentire*): **se la padrona di casa vuole, ti posso ospitare** if my landlady agrees I can put you up; **ho chiesto di parlargli, ma non ha voluto ricevermi** I asked to have a word with him but he wouldn't see me; **la macchina non vuole partire** the car won't start; **parla bene l'inglese quando vuole** he can speak English well when he has a mind to *o* when he feels like it

e (*aspettarsi*) to want, expect; (*richiedere*) to want, require, demand; **vuole** *troppo* **dai suoi studenti** he expects too much of his students; **che** *cosa* **vuoi da me?** what do you want from me?, what do you expect of me?; **la** *tradizione* **vuole che...** custom requires that ...; **il** *verbo* **transitivo vuole il complemento oggetto** transitive verbs require a direct object

f: **volerne a qn** to have sth against sb, have a grudge against sb, bear sb a grudge; **me ne vuole ancora per quello che gli ho fatto** he still bears me a grudge for what I did to him; **non me ne volere** don't hold it against me

g: **voler dire (che)...** (*significare*) to mean (that) ...; **se non puoi oggi vorrà dire che ci vediamo domani** if you can't make it today, I'll see you tomorrow; **vuoi dire che non parti più?** do you mean that you're not leaving after all?; **voglio dire...** (*per correggersi*) I mean ...; **volevo ben dire!** I thought as much!

h (*ritenere*) to think; **la leggenda vuole che...** legend has it that ...; **si vuole che anche lui sia coinvolto nella faccenda** he is also thought to be involved in the matter

i: **volerci** (*essere necessario: materiale, attenzione*) to need; (: *tempo*) to take; *quanto* **ci vuole per andare da Roma a Firenze?** to how long does it take to go from Rome to Florence?; **quanta farina ci vuole per questa**

torta? how much flour do you need to make this cake?; **ci vorrebbe un bel caffè** a nice cup of coffee is just what's needed; **è *quel* che ci vuole** it's just what is needed; **ce ne vuole per farglielo entrare nella zucca** it's not easy to get it into his thick skull; **ci vuol ben *altro* per farmi arrabbiare** it'll take a lot more than that to make me angry

j (*fraseologia*); **voler *bene* a qn** (*amore*) to love sb; (*affetto*) to be fond of sb, like sb very much; **voler *male* a qn** to dislike sb; **chi *troppo* vuole nulla stringe** (*Proverbio*) don't ask for too much or you may come away empty-handed; ***qui* ti voglio** that's the problem; ***senza* volere** unwittingly, without meaning to, unintentionally; **te la sei voluta** you asked for it; **volere è *potere*** where there's a will there's a way; **se *Dio* vuole** God willing; **volesse il *cielo* che...** God grant that ...; **non vorrei sbagliarmi, ma...** I may be wrong, but ...; **voglio *vedere* se rifiuta** I bet she doesn't refuse; **vorrei proprio vedere!** I'm not at all surprised!, that doesn't surprise me in the slightest!; **sembra che voglia *piovere*** it looks like rain; **sembra che voglia mettersi al bello** the weather seems to be clearing up; ***vuoi*... vuoi...** either ... or ....

2 **volersi** VR (*uso reciproco*): **volersi bene** (*amore*) to love each other; (*affetto*) to be fond of o like each other.

3 SM will, wish(es); ***contro* il volere di** against the wishes of; ***per* volere del padre** in obedience to his father's will o wishes.

volgare [vol'gare] 1 AGG **a** (*grossolano*) vulgar, coarse **b** (*comune*) common, popular.

2 SM vernacular.

volgarità [volgari'ta] SF INV vulgarity.

volgarizzare [volgarid'dzare] VT **a** (*divulgare*) to popularize **b** (*tradurre*) to translate into the vernacular.

volgarmente [volgar'mente] AVV **a** (*in modo volgare*) vulgarly, coarsely **b** (*comunemente*) commonly, popularly.

volgere ['voldʒere] VB IRREG 1 VI (*aus* avere) **a** : **volgere a** (*piegare verso*) to turn to o towards, bend round to o towards; **la strada volge a destra** the road bends round to the right

b (*avvicinarsi a*): **volgere al peggio** to take a turn for the worse; **volgere al termine** to draw to an end; **le vacanze volgono al termine** the holidays are coming to an end; **il giorno volge al termine** the day is drawing to its close; **il tempo volge al brutto/al bello** the weather is breaking/is setting fair; **la situazione volge al peggio** the situation is deteriorating; **un rosso che volge al viola** a red verging on purple.

2 VT **a** (*voltare*) to turn; **volgere le spalle a qn** (*anche fig*) to turn one's back on sb

b (*trasformare*) to turn; **volge sempre tutto in tragedia** he always turns everything into a tragedy.

3 **volgersi** VR to turn; **si volse e mi guardò** he turned round and looked at me; **si volse verso di lui** he turned to o towards him; **la sua ira si volse contro di noi** he turned his anger on us.

volgo, ghi ['volgo] SM (*anche pegg*) common people *pl.*

voliera [vo'ljera] SF aviary.

volitivo, a [voli'tivo] 1 AGG wilful (*Brit*), willful (*Am*); (*persona*) wil(l)ful, strong-willed.

2 SM/F strong-willed person.

volli *ecc* ['vɔlli] VB vedi **volere**.

volo ['volo] SM **a** (*gen*) flight; **il tuo volo è alle tre** your flight leaves at three o'clock; **ci sono due ore di volo da Londra a Milano** it is a two-hour flight between London and Milan; **velocità/condizioni di volo** flying speed/conditions; **essere in volo** (*uccello*) to be in flight; (*Aer*) to be flying; **colpire un uccello in volo** to shoot a bird on the wing o in flight; "**volo cancellato**" "flight cancelled"; "**volo in chiusura**" "flight closing" ►**volo di addestramento** training flight ►**volo di andata** outward flight ►**volo di linea** scheduled flight ►**volo di ritorno** return flight ►**volo a vela** gliding

b (*fraseologia*): **capire al volo** to understand straight away; **prendere al volo** (*autobus, treno*) to catch at the last possible moment; (*palla*) to catch as it flies past; (*fig: occasione*) to seize; **prendere il volo** (*aereo*) to take off; (*uccello*) to fly away; (*fig: giovane*) to leave home; (: *cosa: sparire*) to vanish; **ha fatto un volo dalle scale** (*cadere*) he went flying down the stairs; **veduta a volo d'uccello** bird's-eye view.

volontà [volon'ta] SF INV **a** (*capacità di volere*) will; **ha molta volontà** he has a very strong will; **non ha volontà** he is weak-willed; **contro la sua volontà** against his will; **di sua spontanea volontà** of his own free will; **riuscire a forza di volontà** to succeed through sheer willpower o determination

b (*disposizione*): **manifestare la volontà di fare qc** to show one's desire to do sth; **buona/cattiva volontà** goodwill/lack of goodwill; **ci ho messo tutta la mia buona volontà** I did it to the best of my ability; **a volontà** (*mangiare, bere*) as much as one likes; **ce ne sono a volontà** there are more than enough of them; **prendine a volontà** help yourself, take as much (o many) as you like; "**zuccherare a volontà**" "sugar to taste"

c : **le sue ultime volontà** (*testamento*) his last will and testament *sg*; **quali sono le sue ultime volontà?** what are his last wishes?

volontariamente [volontarja'mente] AVV voluntarily.

volontariato [volonta'rjato] SM **a** (*Mil*) voluntary service **b** (*attività gratuita*) voluntary work.

volontario, ria, ri, rie [volon'tarjo] 1 AGG (*gen*) voluntary; (*Mil*) volunteer *attr*; **esilio volontario** voluntary exile.

2 SM/F (*gen, Mil*) volunteer; (*di organizzazione*) voluntary worker.

volpe ['volpe] SF (*Zool*) fox; (: *femmina*) vixen; (*pelliccia*) fox; (*fig*) sly fox, crafty person; (: *ironico*) clever person, bright spark ►**volpe della sabbia** o **del deserto** fennec.

volpino, a [vol'pino] 1 AGG (*pelo, coda*) fox's *attr*; (*aspetto, astuzia*) fox-like.

2 SM (*cane*) Pomeranian.

volpoca, che [vol'pɔka] SF (*Zool*) shelduck; (*maschio*) sheldrake.

volpone, a [vol'pone] SM/F (*fig*): **un vecchio volpone** a crafty old fox.

volsi *ecc* ['vɔlsi] VB vedi **volgere**.

volt [vɔlt] SM INV (*Elettr*) volt.

volta¹ ['vɔlta] SF **a** (*gen*) time; **una volta** once; **due volte** twice; **tre volte** three times; **una volta ogni due settimane** once every two weeks; **9 volte su 10** 9 times out of 10; **la prima/l'ultima volta che l'ho visto** the first/last time I saw him; **per questa volta passi** I'll let you off this time; **ci ho pensato due volte prima di decidere** I thought twice about it before making a decision; **tutto in una volta** all at once; **deciditi una buona volta** make

up your mind once and for all; **una volta tanto** just for once; **una volta sola** only once; **una volta per tutte** once and for all; **di volta in volta** from time to time; **delle** o **alle** o **certe volte** OR a volte sometimes, at times; **una volta** o **l'altra** one of these days; **una cosa per volta** one thing at a time; **te le darò volta per volta** (*istruzioni*) I'll give them to you a few at a time

b (*tempo, occasione*): **c'era una volta...** once upon a time there was ...; **una volta** (*un tempo*) once, in the past; **le cose di una volta** the things of the past; **una volta che sei partito** once o when you have left; **ti ricordi quella volta che...** do you remember (the time) when ...; **pensa a tutte le volte che...** think of all the occasions on which ...; **lo facciamo un'altra volta** we'll do it another time o some other time

c (*Mat*): **3 volte 2** 3 times 2; **4 volte di più** 4 times as much

d (*fraseologia*): **a sua volta** (*turno*) in (his o her *ecc*) turn; **partire alla volta di** to set off for; **ti ha dato di volta il cervello?** have you gone out of your mind?

volta² ['vɔlta] SF (*Archit, Anat*) vault; **la volta celeste** the vault of heaven.

voltafaccia [volta'fattʃa] SM INV about-turn, volte-face.

voltagabbana [voltagab'bana] SM/F INV turncoat.

voltaggio [vol'taddʒo] SM voltage.

voltare [vol'tare] ① VT (*girare*) to turn; (: *moneta*) to turn over; (*rigirare*) to turn round; **voltare pagina** (*fig*) to turn over a new leaf; **voltare le spalle a qn** (*anche fig*) to turn one's back on sb.

② VI (*aus* avere) to turn; **voltare a destra/sinistra** to turn (to the) left/right.

③ **voltarsi** VR to turn; **voltarsi da un lato** to turn to one side; **voltarsi indietro** to turn back; **voltarsi dall'altra parte** to turn the other way; **non sapere da che parte voltarsi** (*fig*) not to know which way to turn.

voltastomaco [voltas'tɔmako] SM nausea; **la sua ipocrisia mi dà il voltastomaco** his hypocrisy makes me sick.

volteggiare [volted'dʒare] VI **a** (*volare girando*: *uccello, piuma*) to circle; **la ballerina volteggiava sul palco** the dancer twirled o spun across the stage **b** (*Ginnastica*) to vault; (*sul cavallo*) to do trick riding.

voltmetro ['vɔltmetro] SM voltmeter.

volto¹, a ['vɔlto] ① PP di **volgere**.

② AGG: **volto a a** (*rivolto verso*: *casa*) facing **b** (*inteso a*): **il mio discorso è volto a spiegare...** in my speech I intend to explain ...; **il corso è volto a introdurre gli studenti all'analisi matematica** the course is intended to introduce students to calculus.

volto² ['volto] SM (*faccia*) face; (*fig*) face, nature.

voltolarsi [volto'larsi] VR: **voltolarsi in** to wallow in, roll about in.

voltura [vol'tura] SF (*Dir: trascrizione*) registration; **voltura di contratto** (*di telefono, gas*) transfer of contract.

volubile [vo'lubile] AGG (*persona*) changeable, fickle; (*tempo*) changeable, variable.

volubilità [volubili'ta] SF (*di persona*) fickleness, inconstancy; (*di tempo*) variability.

volubilmente [volubil'mente] AVV (*comportarsi*) in a fickle way.

volume [vo'lume] SM (*gen*) volume; **fa volume** (*oggetto*) it takes up a lot of space, it is very bulky; **volume delle vendite** (*Comm*) sales volume.

volumetrico, a, ci, che [volu'metriko] AGG volumetric.

voluminoso, a [volumi'noso] AGG bulky, voluminous.

voluta [vo'luta] SF (*gen*) spiral; (*Archit*) volute.

volutamente [voluta'mente] AVV deliberately, intentionally.

voluto, a [vo'luto] AGG **a** (*intenzionale*) deliberate, intentional; **era voluto** it was intentional; **un errore voluto** a deliberate mistake **b** (*desiderato*: *bambino*) wanted; (: *somma*) desired.

voluttà [volut'ta] SF INV sensual pleasure o delight.

voluttuario, ria, ri, rie [voluttu'arjo] AGG (*spese*) unnecessary, non-essential.

voluttuosamente [voluttuosa'mente] AVV voluptuously.

voluttuosità [voluttuosi'ta] SF INV voluptuousness.

voluttuoso, a [voluttu'oso] AGG voluptuous, sensual.

volvente [vol'vɛnte] AGG (*Fis*): **attrito volvente** rolling friction.

vombato [vom'bato] SM (*Zool*) wombat.

vomere ['vɔmere] SM (*Agr*) ploughshare (*Brit*), plowshare (*Am*).

vomico, a, ci, che ['vɔmiko] AGG: **noce vomica** nux vomica.

vomitare [vomi'tare] ① VT to vomit, throw up; **vomitare ingiurie** (*fig*) to spew out insults; **questo quadro mi fa vomitare** this painting makes me sick.

② VI (*aus* avere) to be sick, vomit, throw up.

vomitevole [vomi'tevole] AGG (*anche fig*) nauseating.

vomito ['vomito] SM vomit; **ho il vomito** I feel sick; **mi fa venire il vomito** (*anche fig*) it makes me sick.

vongola ['vongola] SF (*Zool*) clam.

vorace [vo'ratʃe] AGG (*appetito*) voracious, greedy; **è un bambino vorace** this child has a voracious appetite.

voracemente [voratʃe'mente] AVV voraciously.

voracità [voratʃi'ta] SF voracity, voraciousness.

voragine [vo'radʒine] SF chasm, abyss.

vorrò *ecc* [vor'rɔ] VB vedi **volere**.

vorticare [vorti'kare] VI (*aus* avere) to whirl, swirl.

vortice ['vɔrtitʃe] SM whirl, vortex; (*fig*) vortex; **un vortice di vento** a whirlwind.

vorticosamente [vortikosa'mente] AVV: **ruotare** o **girare vorticosamente** to whirl round and round.

vorticoso, a [vorti'koso] AGG whirling.

vostro, a ['vɔstro] ① AGG POSS: **il(la) vostro(a)** your; **il vostro cane** your dog; **un vostro conoscente** an acquaintance of yours; **vostra zia** your aunt; **è colpa vostra** it's your fault; **a casa vostra** at your house.

② PRON POSS: **il(la) vostro(a)** yours, your own; **la nostra casa è più lontana della vostra** our house is further away than yours; **la vostra è stata una brutta storia** your story is an unpleasant one.

③ PRON POSS M **a** : **avete speso del vostro?** did you spend your own money?; **ci potreste rimettere del vostro in quell'affare** you could well lose money in that business **b** : **i vostri** SMPL (*famiglia*) your family; **è dei vostri** he's on your side.

④ PRON POSS F: **la vostra** (*opinione*) your view; **l'ultima vostra** (*Comm*: *lettera*) your most recent letter; **alla vostra!** (*brindisi*) here's to you!, your health!; **è dalla vostra** he's on your side.

votante [vo'tante] SM/F voter.

votare [vo'tare] ① VI (*aus* avere) to vote.

② VT **a** (*gen*) to vote for; (*sottoporre a votazione*) to take a vote on; (*approvare*) to pass **b** : **votare a** (*vita*) to devote to, dedicate to.

③ **votarsi** VR: **votarsi a** to devote o.s. to.

votazione [votat'tsjone] SF **a** (*gen, Pol*: *atto*) voting, vote;

alle votazioni at the elections **b** (Scol) mark (Brit), grade (Am); **votazione finale** results pl.

votivo, a [vo'tivo] AGG votive.

voto ['voto] SM **a** (Scol) mark (Brit), grade (Am); **laurearsi a pieni voti** ≈ to graduate with a first class degree (Brit) o summa cum laude (Am) **b** (Pol) vote ▶**voto di fiducia** vote of confidence ▶**voto di scambio** vote-buying **c** (Rel) vow; (: offerta) votive offering; **prendere i voti** to take one's vows.

voyeur [vwa'jœr] SM INV voyeur.

voyeurismo [voje'rizmo] SM voyeurism.

V.P. ABBR (= vicepresidente) VP.

VR SIGLA = Verona.

v.r. ABBR (= vedi retro) PTO (= please turn over).

V.S. ABBR **a** = Vostra Santità **b** = Vostra Signoria.

v.s. ABBR = vedi sopra.

vs. ABBR (= vostro) yr (= your).

VT SIGLA = Viterbo.

V.U. ABBR = vigile urbano.

vu' cumprà [vucum'pra] SM/F INV street pedlar, usually of African origin.

vudù [vu'du] SM INV, AGG INV voodoo attr.

vuduismo [vudu'izmo] SM voodooism.

vulcanico, a, ci, che [vul'kaniko] AGG volcanic; **ha una fantasia vulcanica** he has a fertile imagination.

vulcanismo [vulka'nizmo] SM volcanism.

vulcanizzare [vulkanid'dzare] VT (Tecn) to vulcanize.

vulcanizzazione [vulkaniddzat'tsjone] SF (Tecn) vulcanization.

Vulcano [vul'kano] SM (Mitol) Vulcan.

vulcano [vul'kano] SM volcano; **quel ragazzo è un vulcano di idee** that boy is bursting with ideas.

vulnerabile [vulne'rabile] AGG vulnerable.

vulnerabilità [vulnerabili'ta] SF vulnerability.

vulva ['vulva] SF (Anat) vulva.

vuoi ['vwɔi], **vuole** ['vwɔle] VB vedi volere.

vuotare [vwo'tare] **1** VT (bicchiere, stanza) to empty; (vasca, piscina) to drain, empty; **vuotare il sacco** (fig) to confess, spill the beans (fam); **i ladri mi hanno vuotato la casa** the burglars cleaned out my house.
2 vuotarsi VIP to empty.

vuoto, a ['vwɔto] **1** AGG **a** (gen) empty; **a stomaco vuoto** on an empty stomach; **a mani vuote** empty-handed
b (non occupato: posto) vacant, free; (: spazio) empty
c (fig: discorso, persona) shallow, superficial; **è una testa vuota** he's an empty headed person; **mi sento la testa vuota** my mind feels a complete blank.
2 SM **a** (spazio) void, empty space, gap; (: in bianco) blank; (fig: mancanza) gap, void; (Fis) vacuum; **è rimasto sospeso nel vuoto** (alpinista) he was left hanging in mid-air; **aver paura del vuoto** to be afraid of heights; **guardare nel vuoto** to gaze into space; **fare il vuoto intorno a sé** to alienate o.s. from everybody; **ha lasciato un vuoto fra di noi** he has left a real gap; **ho un vuoto allo stomaco** my stomach feels empty; **sotto vuoto** = sottovuoto ▶**vuoto d'aria** (Aer) air pocket
b (bottiglia) empty ▶**"vuoto a perdere"** "no deposit" ▶**"vuoto a rendere"** "returnable (bottle)".
3 : **a vuoto** AVV (inutilmente) vainly, in vain; (senza effetto) to no purpose; **parlare a vuoto** to waste one's breath; **ho fatto un viaggio a vuoto** I have had a wasted journey; **andare a vuoto** to come to nothing, fail; **assegno a vuoto** dud cheque (Brit), bad check (Am); **girare a vuoto** (Aut) to idle.

V.V. ABBR (= vostro) yr (= your).

W

W, w ['dɔppjo vu] SF O M INV (*lettera*) W, w; **W come Washington** ≈ W for William.
W ['dɔppjo vu] ABBR = **evviva**.
wafer ['vafer] SM INV (*Culin, Elettr*) wafer.
wagon-lit [vagɔ̃'li] SM INV (*Ferr*) sleeping car.
walkie-talkie ['wɔːkiˈtɔːki] SM INV walkie-talkie.
walkman® ['wɔːkmən] SM INV Walkman®, personal stereo.
Washington ['wɔʃiŋtən] SF Washington.
wassermann ['vasərman] SF INV (*Med*) Wassermann test, Wassermann reaction.
water ['vater] SM INV toilet (bowl).
water closet ['wɔːtə 'klɔzit] SM INV toilet (*Brit*), lavatory (*Brit*), bathroom (*Am*).

watt [vat] SM INV (*Elettr*) watt.
wattora [vat'tora] SM INV (*Elettr*) watt-hour.
WC [viˈtʃi] SM INV WC (*Brit*), bathroom (*Am*).
weekend [wiˈkɛnd] SM INV weekend.
Wellington ['wɛllinŋtən] SF (*Geog*) Wellington.
western ['wɛstern] ☐1 AGG (*Cine*) cowboy *attr.*
☐2 SM INV (*Cine*) western, cowboy film (*Brit*) o movie (*Am*)
▶ **western all'italiana** spaghetti western.
whisky ['wiski] SM INV whisky.
windsurf [wind'sɛrf] SM INV (*tavola*) windsurfer, windsurfing board, sailboard; (*sport*) windsurfing; **andare in windsurf** to windsurf.
würstel ['vyrstəl] SM INV frankfurter.

X

X, x [iks] SF O M INV (*lettera*) X, x; **X come Xeres** ≈ X for Xmas.

xeno ['ksɛno] SM (*Chim*) xenon.

xenofobia [ksenofo'bia] SF xenophobia.

xenofobo, a [kse'nofobo] [1] AGG xenophobic. [2] SM/F xenophobe.

xeres ['ksɛres] SM INV sherry.

xerocopia [ksero'kɔpja] SF photocopy, xerox®.

xerocopiare [kseroko'pjare] VT to photocopy, xerox®.

xerografia [kserogra'fia] SF xerography.

xilema, i [ksi'lɛma] SM (*Bot*) xylem.

xilofono [ksi'lɔfono] SM xylophone.

Y

Y, y ['ipsilon] SF O M INV (*lettera*) Y, y; **Y come Yacht** ≈ Y for Yellow (*Brit*), ≈ Y for Yoke (*Am*).

yacht [jɔt] SM INV yacht.

yak [jak] SM INV (*animale*) yak.

yankee ['jænki] SM/F INV Yank, Yankee.

Y.C.I. ['itʃi] SIGLA M = *Yacht Club d'Italia*.

Yemen ['jɛmen] SM: **lo Yemen** Yemen.

yemenita, i, e [jeme'nita] AGG, SM/F Yemeni.

yen [jen] SM INV (*moneta*) yen.

yiddish ['jidiʃ] AGG INV, SM INV Yiddish.

yoga ['jɔga] AGG INV, SM INV yoga *(attr)*.

yogurt ['jɔgurt] SM INV yog(h)urt.

yogurtiera [jogur'tjɛra] SF yog(h)urt-maker.

yuppie ['jʌppi] SM/F yuppie.

Z

Z, z ['dzɛta] SF O M INV (*lettera*) Z, z; **Z come Zara** ≈ Z for Zebra.

zabaione [dzaba'jone], **zabaglione** [dzabaʎ'ʎone] SM zabaglione, *dessert made of egg yolks, sugar and marsala*.

zaffata [tsaf'fata] SF (*di odore*) stench, stink.

zafferano [dzaffe'rano] SM saffron.

zaffiro [dzaf'firo] SM sapphire.

zagara ['dzagara] SF orange blossom.

zainetto [dzai'netto] SM (small) rucksack.

zaino ['dzaino] SM rucksack (*Brit*), backpack (*Am*).

Zaire [dza'ire] SM: **lo Zaire** Zaire.

zairese [dzai'rese] AGG, SM/F Zairian.

Zambia ['dzambja] SM: **lo Zambia** Zambia.

zambiano, a [dzam'bjano] AGG, SM/F Zambian.

zampa ['tsampa] SF (*di animale*) leg; (: *con artigli*) paw; (*di elefante, uccello*) foot; **calzoni a zampa d'elefante** bell-bottom trousers, bell-bottoms; **camminare a quattro zampe** to go on all fours; **giù le zampe!** (*fam*) paws off! ▶ **zampe di gallina** (*rughe*) crow's feet; (*calligrafia*) scrawl *sg*.

zampata [tsam'pata] SF (*di cane, gatto*) blow with a paw.

zampettare [tsampet'tare] VI (*aus* **avere**) to scamper.

zampillante [tsampil'lante] AGG gushing, spurting.

zampillare [tsampil'lare] VI (*aus* **avere**) to gush, spurt.

zampillo [tsam'pillo] SM gush, spurt.

zampino [tsam'pino] SM paw; **ci ha messo lo zampino lui** (*fig*) he's had a hand in this ▶ **zampino di coniglio** (*portafortuna*) lucky rabbit's foot.

zampirone [dzampi'rone] SM mosquito repellent.

zampogna [tsam'poɲɲa] SF Italian bagpipes *pl*.

zampognaro [tsampoɲ'ɲaro] SM Italian bagpipes player.

zampone [tsam'pone] SM (*Culin*) *stuffed pig's trotter*.

zangola ['tsangola] SF churn.

zanna ['tsanna] SF (*di elefante, cinghiale*) tusk; (*di cane, lupo*) fang.

zanzara [dzan'dzara] SF mosquito.

zanzariera [dzandza'rjɛra] SF mosquito net.

zappa ['tsappa] SF (*Agr*) hoe; **darsi la zappa sui piedi** (*fig*)

to shoot o.s. in the foot.

zappare [tsap'pare] VT (*Agr*) to hoe.

zappatore [tsappa'tore] SM (*Agr*) hoer; (*Mil*) sapper (*Brit*).

zappatrice [tsappa'tritʃe] SF (*Agr: macchina*) mechanical hoe.

zappatura [tsappa'tura] SF (*Agr*) hoeing.

zar [tsar] SM INV tsar.

zarina [tsa'rina] SF tsarina.

zattera ['tsattera] SF raft ▶ **zattera di salvataggio** life raft.

zavorra [dza'vɔrra] SF (*Naut, Aer*) ballast; (*fig*) junk; **gettare la zavorra** to dump ballast.

zazzera ['tsattsera] SF shock of hair, mop.

zebra ['dzɛbra] SF **a** (*Zool*) zebra **b** : **le zebre** SFPL (*Aut*) zebra crossing *sg* (*Brit*), crosswalk *sg* (*Am*).

zebrato, a [dze'brato] AGG with black and white stripes; **passaggio** *o* **attraversamento zebrato** (*Aut*) zebra crossing (*Brit*), crosswalk (*Am*).

zebù [dze'bu] SM INV (*animale*) zebu.

zecca[1], **che** ['tsekka] SF (*insetto*) tick.

zecca[2] ['tsekka] SF (*di monete*) mint; **nuovo di zecca** brand-new.

zecchino [tsek'kino] SM gold coin; **oro zecchino** pure gold.

zefiro ['dzɛfiro] SM (*vento*) zephyr.

zelante [dze'lante] AGG zealous.

zelantemente [dzelante'mente] AVV zealously.

zelo ['dzelo] SM zeal; **mostrare troppo zelo** to be over-zealous.

zenit ['dzɛnit] SM (*Astron*) zenith.

zenzero ['dzendzero] SM ginger.

zeppa ['tseppa] SF (*di mobili*) wedge; (*di scarpe*) platform.

zeppelin ['tsɛpəli:n] SM INV zeppelin, airship.

zeppo, a ['tseppo] AGG: **zeppo** *o* **pieno zeppo (di)** jam-packed (with), crammed (with).

zerbino [dzer'bino] SM (door)mat.

zerbinotto [dzerbi'nɔtto] SM dandy, fop.

zero ['dzɛro] [1] SM **a** (*gen, Scol, Mat*) zero, nought (*Brit*); (*in un numero di telefono*) O; **zero virgola cinque** (zero *o* nought) point five; **2 gradi sopra zero** 2 degrees above